W9-DCL-003

MIDDLE AND JUNIOR HIGH CORE COLLECTION

FOURTEENTH EDITION

CORE COLLECTION SERIES

FORMERLY
STANDARD CATALOG SERIES

SHAUNA GRIFFIN, MLS, GENERAL EDITOR

CHILDREN'S CORE COLLECTION
FICTION CORE COLLECTION
GRAPHIC NOVELS CORE COLLECTION
MIDDLE AND JUNIOR HIGH CORE COLLECTION
PUBLIC LIBRARY NONFICTION CORE COLLECTION
SENIOR HIGH CORE COLLECTION
YOUNG ADULT FICTION CORE COLLECTION

MIDDLE AND JUNIOR HIGH CORE COLLECTION

FOURTEENTH EDITION

EDITED BY

JULIE CORSARO, MLIS

KENDAL SPIRES, MLIS

H. W. Wilson
A Division of EBSCO Information Service, Inc.
Ipswich, Massachusetts
2019

GREY HOUSE PUBLISHING

Cover: © iStock/Grandfailure

ISBN 978-1-64265-259-8

Middle and Junior High Core Collection, 2019, published by Grey House Publishing, Inc., Amenia, NY, under exclusive license from EBSCO Information Services, Inc.

A catalog record for this title is available from the Library of Congress.

PRINTED IN CANADA

TABLE OF CONTENTS

PREFACE

MIDDLE AND JUNIOR HIGH CORE COLLECTION is a curated list of books recommended for young people in grades five through nine, together with professional aids for librarians and library media specialists. This list is available in full as an EBSCO*host* database, updated weekly.

What's in this Edition?

A star (★) at the start of an entry indicates that a book is a "Most Highly Recommended" title. These titles constitute a short list of the essential books in a given category or on a given subject. There are often a number of recommended titles on a single subject, and the stars help a user who wants only one or two. Other titles included represent "Core Collection" titles, a longer list of core books. MIDDLE AND JUNIOR HIGH CORE COLLECTION, Fourteenth Edition, contains over 9,000 titles at the "Most Highly Recommended" and "Core Collection" levels, the best of the best books for young people.

History

JUNIOR HIGH SCHOOL LIBRARY CATALOG, first published in 1965, was developed to address the unique needs of younger adolescents. It developed from the STANDARD CATALOG FOR HIGH SCHOOL LIBRARIES, which was subsequently modified in scope and renamed SENIOR HIGH SCHOOL LIBRARY CATALOG. With the seventh edition in 1995, the title of the Catalog was changed from JUNIOR HIGH SCHOOL LIBRARY CATALOG to MIDDLE AND JUNIOR HIGH SCHOOL CATALOG to reflect the prevalence of middle school programs and the extension of coverage to grades five and six. With the ninth edition in 2009, the title was changed to MIDDLE AND JUNIOR HIGH CORE COLLECTION. The collection subsequently evolved, along with the other Core Collections, into an online resource called WilsonWeb. EBSCO Information Services acquired H. W. Wilson in July 2011, and the collections became EBSCO*host* databases in January 2012. The eleventh edition in 2014 contained broad revisions in the areas of computers, math, and the sciences. In addition, it offered an expanded list of works for librarians and media specialists including bibliographies and other resources for the selection and evaluation of materials for the age range. Despite many changes over the last 100 years, the Core Collections remain premier collection development tools.

Scope

All books listed are published in the United States, or published in Canada or the United Kingdom and distributed in the United States.

MIDDLE AND JUNIOR HIGH CORE COLLECTION is intended to serve the needs of any library serving readers of children's literature regardless of library or patron type. School, public, and even academic libraries, such as those with teacher education and library science degree programs, use the MIDDLE AND JUNIOR HIGH CORE COLLECTION to identify the highest quality books. Recommendations contained herein stand as a basic or "opening day" collection, with "Most Highly Recommended" and "Core Collection" titles. The newer titles help in identifying areas in a collection that can be updated or strengthened. Retention of useful material from the previous edition enables the librarian to make informed decisions about weeding a collection.

The librarians of Core Collections are committed to creating and maintaining collections that reflect the diversity of the human experience. We consider a multitude of factors when choosing a title for the Core Collections, such as the book's critical consensus and its contribution to the breadth and depth of viewpoints present in the database. We mitigate biases to the best of our ability by seeking out multiple opinions on books and actively staying educated on issues of diversity and representation in publishing. We are always seeking to improve the Core Collections and welcome feedback and suggestions regarding potential prejudices or blind spots. Email us at corecollections@ebsco.com.

The MIDDLE AND JUNIOR HIGH CORE COLLECTION excludes the following: non-English-language materials, with the exception of bilingual materials, dictionaries, and similar items; works of adult fiction other than books originally written for adults but read by young people or books widely used in the curriculum; textbooks; and books about individual computer programs or versions of programs, and other topics that quickly become outdated. This volume includes a generous selection of graphic novels, even though a more comprehensive collection of recommended graphic novels can be found in the GRAPHIC NOVELS CORE COLLECTION database on EBSCO*host*. This collection also excludes most works widely known as "classic literature." This was done as an effort to both save space and to concentrate on recommending titles that are perhaps less well known. Additionally, extensive conversations with high school librarians indicated that additions of classics to the collection were primarily based on local curricula, not on recommendations from the Core Collection. While some classics remain in the collection, the removed titles can still be found on EBSCO*host*.

Database

Additional metadata for the titles in this volume, plus full-text book reviews, full-color cover art, Lexile® measures, and all of the Supplementary and Archival book recommendations appear only in the MIDDLE AND JUNIOR HIGH CORE COLLECTION database available from EBSCO. For more information or for a free trial, contact your EBSCO sales rep or visit https://www.ebsco.com/products/research-databases/core-collections.

Preparation

Books included in this edition were selected by experienced librarians representing public library systems, school libraries, and academic libraries across the United States and Canada who also act as a committee of advisors on library policy and trends. The names of participating librarians and their affiliations are listed in the Acknowledgments.

Additional Products

For additional recommendations of children's books, librarians are encouraged to investigate these other databases and their print versions:

CHILDREN'S CORE COLLECTION

GRAPHIC NOVELS CORE COLLECTION

SENIOR HIGH CORE COLLECTION

PURPOSE AND ORGANIZATION

PURPOSE

MIDDLE AND JUNIOR HIGH CORE COLLECTION is designed to serve a number of purposes:

As an aid in purchasing. The Core Collection is designed to assist in the selection and ordering of titles. Annotations are provided for each title along with information concerning the publisher, ISBN, price, and availability. Since Part 1, Classified Collection, is arranged according to the Dewey Decimal Classification, the Core Collection may be used to identify parts of the library collection that should be updated or strengthened. In evaluating the suitability of a work each library will want to consider the special character of the school and community it serves.

As an aid to the reader's advisor. The work of the reader's advisor is furthered by the information about sequels and companion volumes and the descriptive and critical annotations in the Classified Collection, and by the subject access in the Index.

As an aid in verification of information. For this purpose full bibliographical data are provided in the Classified Collection. Entries also include recommended subject headings based upon *Sears List of Subject Headings* and a suggested classification derived from the *Abridged Dewey Decimal Classification and Relative Index.* Notes describe editions available, awards, publication history, and other titles in the series.

As an aid in curriculum support. The classified approach, subject indexing, and annotations are helpful in identifying materials appropriate for classroom use.

As an aid in collection maintenance. Information about titles available on a subject facilitates decisions to rebind, replace, or discard items. If a book has been deleted from the Core Collection in this edition because it is no longer in print, that deletion is not intended as a sign that the book is no longer valuable or that it should necessarily be weeded from the collection.

As an instructional aid. The Core Collection is useful in courses that deal with literature and book selection for young people.

ORGANIZATION

The Core Collection is organized into two parts: a Classified Collection, and an Author, Title, and Subject Index.

As in previous editions, the MIDDLE AND JUNIOR HIGH CORE COLLECTION contains a generous selection of graphic novels. Most fiction graphic novels are in 741.5 with nonfiction either in biography, 92, or under specific Dewey headings by subject. For the comprehensive list of recommended graphic novels, refer to the GRAPHIC NOVELS CORE COLLECTION database on EBSCO*host*.

Part 1. Classified Collection

The Classified Collection is arranged with nonfiction books first, classified according to the Dewey Decimal Classification in numerical order from 000 to 999. Individual biographies are classed at 92 and precede the 920s (collective biography). Fiction books (Fic) follow the nonfiction. Short story collections (S C) follow fiction. The information supplied for each book includes bibliographic description, suggested subject headings, an annotation, and frequently, an evaluation from a quote source.

An Outline of Classification, which serves as a table of contents for the Classified Collection, is reproduced below. It should be noted that many topics can be classified in more than one discipline. If a particular title is not found where it might be expected, the Index should be consulted to determine if it is classified elsewhere.

Within classes, works are arranged alphabetically under main entry, usually the author. Works of individual biography are arranged alphabetically under the biography's subject.

Each listing consists of a full bibliographical description. Prices, which are always subject to change, have been obtained from the publisher, when available, and are as current as possible. Entries include recommended subject headings derived from the *Sears List of Subject Headings,* a suggested classification number from the *Abridged Dewey Decimal Classification and Relative Index,* a brief description of the contents, and, whenever possible, an evaluation from a quoted source. The following is an example of a typical entry and a description of its components:

Fleming, Candace

★ The **family** Romanov; murder, rebellion, and the fall of imperial Russia. Candace Fleming. Schwartz & Wade Books 2014 304 p. il, maps, genealogical table $18.99
Grades 7 8 9 10 11 12 **947.08**

1. Russia -- History -- 1917-1921, Revolution 2. Russia -- History -- Nicholas II, 1894-1917 3. Soviet Union -- History -- Revolution, 1917-1921

ISBN 0375867821; 9780375867828; 9780375967825

LC 2013037904

YALSA Award for Excellence in Nonfiction for Young Adults: Finalist (2015)

Boston Globe-Horn Book Award: Nonfiction (2015)

Robert F. Sibert Honor Book (2015)

This book, by Candace Fleming, describes how "when Russia's last tsar, Nicholas II, inherited the throne in 1894, he was unprepared to do so. With their four daughters (including Anastasia) and only son, a hemophiliac, Nicholas and his reclusive wife, Alexandra, buried their heads in the sand, living a life of opulence as World War I raged outside their door and political unrest grew into the Russian Revolution." (Publisher's note)

"Fleming crafts an exciting narrative from this complicated history and its intriguing personalities. It is full of rich details about the Romanovs, insights into figures such as Vladimir Lenin and firsthand accounts from ordinary Russians affected by the tumultuous events. A variety of photographs adds a solid visual dimension." Kirkus

Includes bibliographical references and index

The star at the start of the entry indicates that this is a "most highly recommended" title. The name of the author, Candace Fleming, is given in conformity with *Anglo-American Cataloguing Rules, 2nd edition,* 2002 revision. The title of the book is *The family Romanov; murder, rebellion, and the fall of imperial Russia.* The book was published by Schwartz & Wade Books in 2014.

The book has 304 pages and contains illustrations, maps, and a genealogy table. It sells for $18.99. (Prices given were current when the Collection went to press.) The book is recommended for any of the following grade levels: 7 8 9 10 11 12.

At the end of the last line of type in the body entry is the figure 947.08 in boldface type. This is the classification number derived from the fifteenth edition of the *Abridged Dewey Decimal Classification.* The number 947.08 is the classification number for "Russia since 1855".

The numbered terms "1. Russia -- History -- 1917-1921, Revolution," "2. Russia -- History -- Nicholas II, 1894-1917," and "3. Soviet Union -- History -- Revolution, 1917-1921" are recommended subject headings for this book based on *Sears List of Subject Headings.*

The ISBN (International Standard Book Number) is included to facilitate ordering. The Library of Congress control number is provided when available.

Following are four notes supplying additional information about the book. The first is a listing of three awards the book won or was shortlisted for. The second is a description of the book's content, in this case a summary from the publisher. The third is a critical note from *Kirkus Reviews.* Such annotations are useful in evaluating books for selection and in determining which of several books on the same subject is best suited for the individual reader. The final note describes special features, in this case a bibliography and an index. Notes are also made to describe sequels and companion volumes, editions available, and publication history.

Part 2. Author, Title, and Subject Index

The Index is a single alphabetical list of all the books entered in the Core Collection. Each book is entered under author; title (if distinctive); and subject. The classification number, displayed in boldface type, is the key to the location of the main entry for the book in the Classified Collection.

Appropriate added entries are made for joint authors and editors. "See" references are made from forms of names or subjects that are not used as headings. "See also" references are made to related or more specific headings.

The following are examples of Index entries for the book cited above:

Author	**Fleming, Candace**	
	The family Romanov	**947.08**
Title	The **family** Romanov. Fleming, C.	**947.08**
Subject	**RUSSIA -- HISTORY -- 1917-1921, REVOLUTION**	
	Fleming, C. The family Romanov	**947.08**

Standards Used

Anglo-American Cataloguing Rules, 2nd ed., 2002 revision, 2005 update. Chicago: American Library Association, 2005.

Dewey, Melvil. *Abridged Dewey Decimal Classification and Relative Index.* 15th ed. Edited by Joan S. Mitchell, et al. Dublin, Ohio: OCLC, 2012.

Bristow, Barbara and Christi Showman Farrar, eds. *Sears List of Subject Headings.* 21st ed. Ipswich, MA: H. W. Wilson, 2014.

OUTLINE OF CLASSIFICATION

Reproduced below is the Second Summary of the Dewey Decimal Classification. * As Part 1 of this Core Collection is arranged according to this classification, the outline will serve as a table of contents for it. Please note, however, that the inclusion of this outline is not to be considered a substitute for consulting the Dewey Decimal Classification itself.

000 Computer science, knowledge & systems
010 Bibliographies
020 Library & information sciences
030 Encyclopedias & books of facts
040 [Unassigned]
050 Magazines, journals & serials
060 Associations, organizations & museums
070 News media, journalism & publishing
080 Quotations
090 Manuscripts & rare books

100 Philosophy
110 Metaphysics
120 Epistemology
130 Parapsychology & occultism
140 Philosophical schools of thought
150 Psychology
160 Logic
170 Ethics
180 Ancient, medieval & eastern philosophy
190 Modern western philosophy

200 Religion
210 Philosophy & theory of religion
220 The Bible
230 Christianity & Christian theology
240 Christian practice & observance
250 Christian pastoral practice & religious orders
260 Christian organization, social work & worship
270 History of Christianity
280 Christian denominations
290 Other religions

300 Social sciences, sociology & anthropology
310 Statistics
320 Political science
330 Economics
340 Law
350 Public administration & military science
360 Social problems & social services
370 Education
380 Commerce, communications & transportation
390 Customs, etiquette & folklore

400 Language
410 Linguistics
420 English & Old English languages
430 German & related languages
440 French & related languages
450 Italian, Romanian & related languages
460 Spanish & Portuguese languages
470 Latin & Italic languages
480 Classical & modern Greek languages
490 Other languages

500 Science
510 Mathematics
520 Astronomy
530 Physics
540 Chemistry
550 Earth sciences & geology
560 Fossils & prehistoric life
570 Life sciences; biology
580 Plants (Botany)
590 Animals (Zoology)

600 Technology
610 Medicine & health
620 Engineering
630 Agriculture
640 Home & family management
650 Management & public relations
660 Chemical engineering
670 Manufacturing
680 Manufacture for specific uses
690 Building & construction

700 Arts
710 Landscaping & area planning
720 Architecture
730 Sculpture, ceramics & metalwork
740 Drawing & decorative arts
750 Painting
760 Graphic arts
770 Photography & computer art
780 Music
790 Sports, games & entertainment

800 Literature, rhetoric & criticism
810 American literature in English
820 English & Old English literatures
830 German & related literatures
840 French & related literatures
850 Italian, Romanian & related literatures
860 Spanish & Portuguese literatures
870 Latin & Italian literatures
880 Classical & modern Greek literatures
890 Other literatures

900 History
910 Geography & travel
920 Biography & genealogy
930 History of ancient world (to ca. 499)
940 History of Europe
950 History of Asia
960 History of Africa
970 History of North America
980 History of South America
990 History of other areas

* Reproduced from Edition 15 of the Abridged Dewey Decimal Classification and Relative Index, published in 2012, by permission of OCLC Online Computer Library Center, Inc., owner of copyright.

ACKNOWLEDGMENTS

EBSCO Information Services and NoveList expresses special gratitude to the following librarians who assisted in the selection and weeding of titles for this Core Collection:

Advisory Board

Gail de Vos
Adjunct Associate Professor, SLIS
University of Alberta
Edmonton, Alberta

Francisca Goldsmith
Consulting Librarian
Worcester, Massachusetts

Joquetta Johnson
Library Media Specialist
Randallstown High School
Randallstown, Maryland

Angela Leeper
Director, Curriculum Materials Center
University of Richmond
Richmond, Virginia

Marcela Peres
Library Director
Lewiston Public Library
Lewiston, Maine

Linda Ward-Callaghan
Manager, Youth Services
Joliet Public Library
Joliet, Illinois

The editors would like to thank NoveList librarians Isabel Crevasse, Rebecca Honeycutt, and Suzanne Temple, whose help was instrumental in the weeding of this collection.

MIDDLE AND JUNIOR HIGH CORE COLLECTION

FOURTEENTH EDITION

CLASSIFIED COLLECTION

000 COMPUTER SCIENCE, KNOWLEDGE & SYSTEMS

001.9 Controversial knowledge

Allen, Judy

Unexplained. Kingfisher 2006 144p il $19.95

Grades: 5 6 7 8 **001.9**

1. Parapsychology 2. Curiosities and wonders

ISBN 978-0-7534-5950-8; 0-7534-5950-7

This addresses such topics as ghosts, psychic phenomena, superstitions, mysterious natural phenomena, alleged monsters, disappearances, secrets and mysteries of ancient history, and possible extraterrestrials.

"A seamless combination of absorbing fact-filled text and stunning visuals in an investigation of mysteries that continue to baffle, tantalize, and spark endless debate." SLJ

Includes glossary

Barton, Chris

Can I see your I.D.? true stories of false identities. illustrated by Paul Hoppe. Dial Books for Young Readers 2011 121p il $16.99

Grades: 6 7 8 9 **001.9**

1. Identity (Psychology) 2. Impostors and imposture 3. Impersonation

ISBN 978-0-8037-3310-7; 0-8037-3310-0

LC 2010-11878

"In 10 impeccably crafted profiles, Barton . . . shares the stories of individuals—many just teenagers—who adopted false identities for amusement, profit, or survival. . . . Barton reveals the motivations behind and the consequences of each deception. The use of second-person narration is very effective, allowing readers to assume the identities of each individual. Barton's prose captures the daring, ingenuity, and quick thinking required of each imposter. . . . Hoppe contributes dynamic comic book style panel art." Publ Wkly

Includes bibliographical references

Gee, Joshua

Encyclopedia horrifica; the terrifying truth! about vampires, ghosts, monsters, and more. Scholastic Inc. 2007 129p il $14.99

Grades: 4 5 6 7 **001.9**

1. Ghosts 2. Monsters 3. Vampires

ISBN 978-0-439-92255-5; 0-439-92255-0

LC 2007061733

A visual reference contains true stories of such creatures as vampires, aliens, werewolves, and ghosts, accompanied by photographic evidence, eyewitness accounts, and original interviews.

"Each topic is replete with color illustrations and photos and is accompanied by a light, readable text that tries to separate fact from fiction." Voice Youth Advocates

Includes bibliographical references

Halls, Kelly Milner

★ **Tales** of the cryptids; mysterious creatures that may or may not exist. by Kelly Milner Halls, Rick Spears, Roxyanne Young; [illustrated by Rick Spears] Darby Creek 2006 72p il map $18.95

Grades: 4 5 6 7 **001.9**

1. Monsters

ISBN 1-58196-049-2

This considers the existance of creatures such as Bigfoot, the Loch Ness Monster, Marozi of Kenya, the Orang-pendek of Sumatra, and the Thylacine of Tasmania.

"The conversational text makes for fun reading, and a plethora of pictures . . . will prove enticing." SLJ

Karst, Ken

Area 51; Ken Karst. Creative Education 2014 48 p. color illustrations, map (Enduring mysteries) (hardcover : alk. paper) $35.65

Grades: 5 6 7 8 **001.9**

1. Nevada 2. Air bases 3. Unidentified flying objects 4. Area 51 (Nev.) 5. Air bases -- Nevada 6. Research aircraft -- United States 7. Unidentified flying objects -- Sightings and encounters -- Nevada

ISBN 1608183998; 9781608183999

LC 2013036073

This book, by Ken Karst, part of the "Enduring Mysteries" series, "takes an investigative approach to the curious phenomena and mysterious circumstances surrounding Area 51, from conspiracy theories to claims of extraterrestrial sightings to hard facts." (Publisher's note)

"With only the barest dashes of skepticism, these handsomely produced surveys present budding cryptozoologists and conspiracy theorists with rich arrays of historical anecdotes and encounters, supposed evidence, 'scientific' explanations of varying plausibility, and tantalizing speculations." SLJ

Includes bibliographical references and index

Other titles in the series are:

Atlantis (2014)

Bigfoot (2014)

Loch Ness Monster (2014)

Bermuda Triangle (2015)

Matthews, Rupert

Strange animals. QEB Pub. 2011 30p il (Unexplained) lib bdg $28.50

Grades: 4 5 6 7 **001.9**

1. Monsters

ISBN 978-1-59566-856-1; 1-59566-856-X

LC 2010017915

This discusses the possible existance of cryptids such as Bigfoot, the Loch Ness monster, the Bunyip, sea monsters, the Orang Pendek, and the Marozi.

"This well-written and thoughtfully designed [book] features [an] engrossing [topic]. . . . Though the pages are profusely illustrated with large, well-reproduced photographs and drawings, the layout is not cluttered. This [book] just might inspire kids to seek out more in-depth materials." SLJ

Includes glossary and bibliographical references

Stewart, Gail

UFOs; by Gail B. Stewart. ReferencePoint Press 2007 96p il (The mysterious & unknown) lib bdg $24.95

Grades: 6 7 8 9 **001.9**

1. Unidentified flying objects

ISBN 978-1-60152-030-2; 1-60152-030-1

This book "combines numerous stories of [UFO] sightings with historical and scientific details about investigations, providing a balanced view of a controversial topic. . . . Colorful illustrations and appealing design will encourage readers." SLJ

Includes bibliographical references

001.94 Mysteries

Hawkins, John

Atlantis and other lost worlds; by John Hawkins. PowerKids Press 2012 32 p. col. ill. (Mystery hunters) (library) $25.25; (paperback) $10.60

Grades: 4 5 6 7 **001.94**

1. Extinct cities 2. Cities and towns 3. Atlantis (Legendary place)

ISBN 1448864291; 9781448864294; 9781448864416; 9781448864423

LC 2011021292

This book by John Hawkins is part of the Mystery Hunters series and focuses on lost and legendary cities. "The sunken city of Atlantis is a popular myth, and is just one of the many myths of lost worlds featured in this . . . volume. This book explores the history behind these . . . stories. It presents readers with evidence that lost worlds are real and evidence that they are all made up, so that they can gather the information and make up their own minds." (Publisher's note)

001.942 Unidentified flying objects (UFOs)

Karst, Ken

Alien abductions; Ken Karst. Creative Education 2018 48 p. (hardcover : alk. paper) $96.99

Grades: 5 6 7 8 **001.942**

1. Alien abduction 2. Human-alien encounters 3. Unidentified flying objects -- Sightings and encounters

ISBN 1640260056; 9781628325560; 9781640260054

LC 2017060031

This children's mystery book in the Enduring Mysteries series, by Ken Karst, presents "an investigative approach to the curious phenomena and mysterious circumstances surrounding alien abductions, from abductees' hypnotic recollections to conspiracy theories to hard facts." (Publisher's note)

Includes bibliographical references and index

004 Computer science; computer programming, programs, data; special computer methods

Lohr, Steve

Digital revolutionaries; the men and women who brought computing to life. Flash Point 2009 165p il pa $11.99

Grades: 5 6 7 8 **004**

1. Computer industry 2. Computers -- History

ISBN 978-1-59643-532-2 pa; 1-59643-532-1 pa

"This text will be a fascinating read for students who are curious about the development of the technology present in every aspect of their lives and the many people behind it. The five chapters are written in a lively, conversational voice. Lohr describes how many independent and creative thinkers helped to develop computers as we know them today. His history includes topics from software programs to animation, from FORTRAN to BASIC, and from Bill Gates to Steve Jobs, bringing technology to life along the way. . . . A positive, upbeat, and enlightening read." SLJ

Includes bibliographical references

004.6 Interfacing and communications

Mooney, Carla

Online predators; Melissa Abramovitz. ReferencePoint Press 2016 80 p il (Issues in the digital age) hardcover $30.95

Grades: 7 8 9 10 11 12 **004.6**

1. Cyberbullying 2. Computer crimes 3. Child sexual abuse 4. Internet -- Safety measures

ISBN 9781682820926; 978-1-60152-193-4

LC 2016021581

"Packed with frightening cases of online attacks by sexual predators, financial predators, and bullies, this detailed, up-to-date, highly readable guide is a warning to young people—and adults—about Internet-based crime and identity theft. . . . Computer-savvy teens will especially welcome the coverage of emerging careers in cybersecurity and forensics. . . . A clean design with color photos and extensive back matter . . . further add to this title's appeal." Booklist

Includes bibliographical references

005.1 Computer programming and programs

Bedell, Jane

So, you want to be a coder? The Ultimate Guide to a Career in Programming, Video Game Creation, Robotics, and More! Jane (J. M.) Bedell. Aladdin 2016 247 p. illustrations (hardcover) $19.99

Grades: 4 5 6 7 **005.1**

1. Robotics 2. Video games 3. Computer programming 4. Programming languages 5. Computer programming -- Vocational guidance 6. Programming languages (Electronic computers)

ISBN 1582705798; 1582705801; 9781582705798; 9781582705804

LC 2015040640

This book by Jane (J. M.) Bedell, part of the "Be What You Want" series, presents a "comprehensive guide that reveals a whole host of careers working with code. . . . Covering everything from navigating the maze of computer languages to writing code for games to cyber security and artificial intelligence, . . . [the book] debugs the secrets behind a career in the diverse and state-of-the-art industry." (Publisher's note)

"Quizzes, tech timelines, resource lists, and sidebars on related topics further round out the career advice. While it's a solid resource for any reader, the focus on female coders and innovators make it an especially apt choice for girls interested in STEM fields." Pub Wkly

Includes bibliographical references (pages 227-247)

McManus, Sean

How to Code in 10 Easy Lessons; Sean McManus. Walter Foster 2015 64 p. color illustrations $12.95

Grades: 4 5 6 7 8 **005.1**

1. Computer games 2. Computer programming

ISBN 1633220508; 9781633220508

In this book from author Sean McManus "from writing simple coding instructions using Scratch software, to learning the coding skills to create your own computer game and even design your own website, this book leads the way. By breaking this daunting subject down into the 10 'super skills' needed, young readers can get familiar with computer coding and build on their skills." (Publisher's note)

"The book is made more accessible with plenty of colorful graphics as visual references, information divided into manageable chunks, and a concluding list of useful web links. Kids will bite at this first taste of coding." Booklist

Redding, Anna Crowley

Google it; a history of Google. Anna Crowley Redding. Feiwel & Friends 2018 240 p. (hardcover) $19.99

Grades: 7 8 9 10 **005.1**

1. Businesspeople -- United States -- Biography 2. Computer programmers -- United States -- Biography 3. Google 4. Google (Firm) 5. Webmasters -- United States -- Biography 6. Telecommunications engineers -- United States -- Biography

ISBN 9781250148223

LC 2017041741

In this book, author Anna Crowley Redding, shares "the true history of Google--from its humble beginnings as a thesis project made out of 'borrowed' hardware and discount toys through its revolution of the world's relationship with technology to a brief glimpse of where they might take us next. . . . Redding shares an inspiring story of innovation, personal and intellectual bravery, and most importantly, of shooting for the moon in order to change the world." (Publisher's note)

Includes bibliographical references

Young Rewired State (Organization)

Get coding! learn HTML, CSS, and JavaScript and build a website, app, and game. Young Rewired State. Candlewick Press 2017 207 p. color illustrations (paperback) $12.99

Grades: 4 5 6 7 8 **005.1**

1. Computer programming 2. Programming languages

ISBN 9780763692766; 076369276X

This book is an essential guide to computer programming for kids. "Open this book and set off on several fun missions--while simultaneously learning the basics of writing code. . . . Presented by Young Rewired State--an international collective of tech-savvy kids--in easy-to-follow, bite-size chunks, the real-life coding skills taught in this engaging, comprehensive guide may just set young readers on the path to becoming technology stars of the future." (Publisher's note)

"There's been considerable demand for resources on kids and coding, and this new entry deserves center stage." Booklist

005.13 Programming languages

Payne, Bryson

Teach your kids to code; a parent-friendly guide to Python programming. by Bryson Payne. No Starch Press 2015 xxvi, 308 p.p color illustraitons (paperback) $29.95

Grades: 6 7 8 9 10 11 12 Adult Professional **005.13**

1. Python (Computer language) 2. Computer programming 3. Computer programming -- Study and teaching (Elementary) 4. Computer programming -- Study and teaching (Middle school) 5. Python (Computer program language) -- Study and teaching (Elementary) 6. Python (Computer program language) -- Study and teaching (Middle school)

ISBN 9781593276140; 1593276141

LC 2015006794

This book, by Bryson Payne, "is a parent's and teacher's guide to teaching kids basic programming and problem solving using Python, the powerful language used in college courses and by tech companies like Google and IBM. Step-by-step explanations will have kids learning computational thinking right away, while visual and game-oriented examples hold their attention." (Publisher's note)

"The full-color printing includes charming spot illustrations, code-output screenshots, and example codes in a layout and color scheme identical to the Python editor. Sophisticated concepts and serious programming make for an easy, enjoyable game for families." Kirkus

Ziter, Rachel

Coding from Scratch; Rachel Ziter. Capstone Press, a Capstone imprint 2018 160 p. $14.95

Grades: 4 5 6 7 8 **005.13**

1. Computer programming 2. Programming languages

ISBN 1543535895; 9781543535891

This book in the Code It Yourself series, by Rachel Ziter, presents instructions for creating "your own games, animation, presentations, and musical projects in no time at all. . . . Whether you're just learning to code or need a refresher, this visual guide to coding will cover all the basics--coding tools, where to find them, and how to use them--with hands-on, step-by-step instructions designed to make 'Coding from Scratch' second nature." (Publisher's note)

005.35 Mobile apps

Gregory, Josh

Apps; from concept to consumer. by Josh Gregory. Children's Press, an imprint of Scholastic Inc. 2015 64 p. illustrations (color) (library binding : alk. paper) $30

Grades: 6 7 8 9 10 **005.35**

1. Computer applications 2. Mobile computing 3. Application software 4. Application software -- Development -- Vocational guidance

ISBN 0531205398; 053121236X; 9780531205396; 9780531212363

LC 2014030460

With this book, by Josh Gregory, part of the "Calling all innovators: A career for you?" series, "[r]eaders will learn how the first mobile apps were created and find out which apps are making the biggest splash today. They will also see how easy it is to get started creating their own apps and what it takes to score the next big hit on the app stores." (Publisher's note)

"Despite a few flaws, [the titles in this series] are recommended for their in-depth descriptions of the histories of different careers." SLJ

Includes bibliographical references and index

005.7 Data in computer systems

Mooney, Carla

Big data; information in the digital world with science activities for kids. Carla Mooney ; illustrated by Alexis Cornell. Nomad Press 2018 122 p. $22.95

Grades: 5 6 7 8 **005.7**

1. Big data 2. Internet 3. Computers

ISBN 1619306794; 9781619306790

In this book in the Build It Yourself series, by Carla Mooney, illustrated by Alexis Cornell, "kids ages 10 to 15 explore the definition of data and learn about the relationship between data, computers, and people. They learn about the history of data, the transition from paper to computers, and the role that search engines such as Google play in handling data." (Publisher's note)

006.3 Artificial intelligence

Henderson, Harry

Artificial intelligence; mirrors for the mind. Chelsea House 2007 190p il (Milestones in discovery and invention) $35

Grades: 7 8 9 10 11 12 **006.3**

1. Artificial intelligence

ISBN 0-8160-5749-4; 978-0-8160-5749-8

LC 2006-16639

This book includes "portraits of the men and women in the vanguard of this innovative field. Subjects include Alan Turing, who made the connection between mathematical reasoning and computer operations; Allen Newell and Herbert Simon, who created a program that could reason like a human being; Pattie Maes, who developed computerized agents to help people with research and shopping; and Ray Kurzweil, who, besides inventing the flatbed scanner and a reading machine for the blind, has explored relationships between people and computers that may exceed human intelligence." Publisher's note

Includes glossary and bibliographical references

006.7 Multimedia systems

Cooper, Nate

Build your own website; a comic guide to HTML, CSS, and WordPress. Nate Cooper. No Starch Press 2014 250 p. illustrations $19.95

Grades: 7 8 9 10 11 12 **006.7**

1. Websites -- Design 2. HTML (Document markup language) 3. Web sites -- Design -- Humor 4. Web site development -- Humor

ISBN 1593275226; 9781593275228

LC 2014019597

Author Nate Cooper and illustrator Kim Gee present this "illustrated introduction to the basics of creating a website. Join Kim and her little dog Tofu as she learns HTML, the language of web pages, and CSS, the language used to style web pages, from the Web Guru and Glinda, the Good Witch of CSS." (Publisher's note)

"The comic art engages the readers and gives the broad picture of what the reader will learn from Cooper's text which follows. Best suited for beginning self-learning, it is one of the few books on the topic which entertains as well as educates."

Rowell, Rebecca

YouTube; the company and its founders. ABDO Pub. Co. 2011 112p il (Technology pioneers) lib bdg $32.44

Grades: 5 6 7 8 **006.7**

1. Internet 2. YouTube, Inc.

ISBN 978-1-61714-813-2 lib bdg; 1-61714-813-X lib bdg; 978-1-61758-971-3 e-book

LC 2010043379

This is an introduction to YouTube and its founders.

"Written in a clear, linear fashion, this series offers vivid, well-researched details about the development of technological advancements considered essential in today's society. . . . Readers who are interested in technology and inventions will be thoroughly engrossed." SLJ

Includes glossary and bibliographical references

Truesdell, Ann

Wonderful wikis; by Ann Truesdell. Cherry Lake Publishing 2013 32 p. (Information explorer) (library) $28.50; (paperback) $14.21

Grades: 4 5 6 7 **006.7**

1. Wikis (Computer science)

ISBN 1610804805; 9781610804806; 9781610806541

LC 2012001758

This juvenile nonfiction book, by Ann Truesdell, as part of the publisher's "Explorer Library" series, presents a profile and guidelines for school children to make use of wikis online for educational purposes. Topics addressed include definitions of what a wiki is, how to contribute to them properly, and what ways they are most useful.

Includes bibliographical references and index

011.6 General bibliographies and catalogs of works for young people and people with disabilities; for specific types of libraries

Barnhouse, Rebecca

The **Middle** Ages in literature for youth; a guide and resource book. Scarecrow Press 2004 183p (Literature for youth) pa $30

Grades: Adult Professional **011.6**

1. Reference books 2. Middle Ages -- Bibliography 3. Children's literature -- Bibliography 4. Young adult literature -- Bibliography

ISBN 0-8108-4916-X

LC 2004-74

"Searchable by subject, title, location, or author, this is a comprehensive guide to books about the period. Each chapter presents a topic, such as Vikings or Crusades, and then gives annotated lists of both fiction and nonfiction titles. Added features include classroom activities such as creative-writing prompts, medieval measurements using tools from the time period, and math involving computations using Roman numerals. . . . Professional sources for educators round out this useful bibliography." SLJ

Meese, Ruth Lyn

Family matters; adoption and foster care in children's literature. Libraries Unlimited 2010 147p pa $35

Grades: Adult Professional **011.6**

1. Adoption -- Bibliography 2. Foster home care -- Bibliography 3. Children's literature -- Bibliography

ISBN 978-1-59158-782-8 pa; 1-59158-782-4 pa

LC 2009040750

"Meese's goal is to help adults, particularly educators, select high-quality children's books about adoption and foster care and to raise awareness about the unique issues that adoptees often face. . . . Charts, Venn diagrams, and extensive annotations supplement the annotated list of books for children in kindergarten through grade eight. Meese explains her rationale for choosing these books so that readers have the tools to evaluate other selections." SLJ

Includes bibliographical references

Reid, Rob

Reid's read-alouds 2; modern day classics from C.S. Lewis to Lemony Snicket. American Library Association 2011 160p

Grades: Adult Professional **011.6**

1. Books and reading 2. Children's literature 3. Young adult literature 4. Children's literature -- Bibliography 5. Young adult literature -- Bibliography

ISBN 0-8389-1072-6; 978-0-8389-1072-6

LC 2010028985

"The very successful first edition of Reid's Read-Alouds (ALA, 2009) profiled children's and young adult books published between the years 2000 and 2008. This companion volume showcases 200 strong titles that were published from 1950 to 1999. Reid offers a variety of genres and age levels, and a good balance between male and female protagonists. . . . The focus is on books that are great to read to groups of young people. Each entry includes a brief plot summary, suggested grade level, and Reid's signature '10 Minute Selections,' which are engaging episodes from the books that can be read in one sitting. These alone make the book a valuable resource." SLJ

Includes bibliographical references

016 Bibliographies and catalogs of works on specific subjects

Fichtelberg, Susan

Encountering enchantment; a guide to speculative fiction for teens. Susan Fichtelberg. 2nd edition Libraries Unlimited 2015 393 p. (hardback) $55

Grades: Adult Professional **016**

1. Fantasy fiction -- Bibliography 2. Science fiction -- Bibliography 3. Young adult literature -- Bibliography 4. Speculative fiction -- Bibliography

ISBN 9781610691130; 161069113X

LC 2015015833

"The second edition of this useful guide to teen speculative fiction, first published in 2006, includes 1,700 titles from a broad range of genres and subgenres, organized within fourteen chapters. Fantasy, science fiction, and horror are broken down into categories, such as 'steampunk,' 'fairy tale fantasy,' and 'romance fantasy.' Within each chapter, there are sections to further distinguish the myriad types, creatures, and time periods within speculative fiction. Books are annotated, including grade level recommendation, and symbols are used to indicate whether they have won awards." (VOYA)

Includes bibliographical references and indexes

Scales, Pat R.

★ **Books** under fire; a hit list of banned and challenged children's books. Pat Scales. ALA Editions, an imprint of the American Library Association 2015 xvi, 208 p.p illustrations (pbk.) $47

Grades: Adult Professional **016**

1. Books -- Censorship 2. Children -- Books and reading -- United States 3. School libraries -- Censorship -- United States 4. Challenged books -- United States -- Bibliography 5. Prohibited books -- United States -- Bibliography 6. Children's literature -- Censorship -- United States

ISBN 0838911099; 9780838911099

LC 2014023945

This book on banned and challenged books, by Pat R. Scales, "covers both children's and young adult books. The main section profiles 34 books (and series such as 'Harry Potter' and 'Captain Underpants') that have recently been challenged for library or curriculum suitability in the US. . . . Each entry includes a . . . synopsis, quotations from some reviews, details of known challenges, awards/accolades, and a 'Further Reading' section." (Choice)

Includes bibliographical references and index

Wee, Patricia Hachten

World War II in literature for youth; a guide and resource book. [by] Patricia Hachten Wee, Robert James Wee. Scarecrow Press 2004 391p (Literature for youth) pa $48

Grades: Adult Professional **016**

1. Reference books 2. World War, 1939-1945 -- Bibliography 3. Children's literature -- Bibliography 4. Young adult literature -- Bibliography

ISBN 0-8108-5301-9

LC 2004-11087

This "offers more than 3,000 annotated bibliographies for resources on the Second World War. Entries are arranged according to well-thought-out subjects and cover multiple genres (biographies, memoirs, fiction, eyewitness accounts, technical reports, etc.) and formats (monographs, reference sets, periodicals, Web sites, CDs, videos, DVDs). Annotations are succinct but informative and include both positive and negative comments." Booklist

Includes bibliographical references

025.04 Information storage and retrieval systems

Barnett, Diana

Putting it all together; teaching the research process. Upstart 2009 74p pa $17.95

Grades: Adult Professional **025.04**

1. Research 2. Information literacy

ISBN 978-1-932146-99-8 pa; 1-932146-99-7 pa

"This well-organized and to-the-point title focuses on practical application of the AASL standards of information literacy for student learning in middle and high schools. The research process is broken down into eight integrated steps, with teacher modeling ideas and printable student exercises for each one. . . . An excellent starting point for teaching research." SLJ

025.1 Administration

Johnson, Doug

The **indispensable** librarian; surviving and thriving in school libraries in the information age. Doug Johnson ; illustrations by Brady Johnson. Linworth, an imprint of ABC-CLIO, LLC 2013 xix, 207 p.p illustrations (pbk.) $40

Grades: Adult Professional **025.1**

1. Librarians 2. School libraries 3. School librarians -- United States 4. School libraries -- United States -- Administration

ISBN 161069239X; 9781610692397

LC 2012051394

This book, by Doug A. Johnson, "defines and clarifies the role of the school library media specialist in a technologically enhanced school, providing relevant examples and useful advice on a variety of topics; and underscores the importance of strong management skills, especially regarding collaborative planning and communications. The book is written especially for K-12 school librarians, both new and experienced, and is also suitable for pre-service librarians as a textbook." (Publisher's note)

"Johnson offers both theory and practical suggestions on ways to embed [librarians] and [their] jobs into the fabric of a school's culture and curriculum." Lib Med Con

Includes bibliographical references and index

MacDonell, Colleen

Essential documents for school libraries; 2nd ed.; Linworth 2010 xxiv, 156p il $50

Grades: Adult Professional **025.1**

1. Libraries -- Administration

ISBN 978-1-58683-400-5

LC 2010-21241

First published 2004

"Each chapter begins with why the documents are needed, followed by practical advice for writing the documents, and examples of how the documents make an effective change in the library media program." Libr Media Connect [review of 2004 edition]

Includes bibliographical references

Marek, Kate

Organizational storytelling for librarians; using stories for effective leadership. American Library Association 2011 105p pa $50

Grades: Adult Professional **025.1**

1. Leadership 2. Storytelling 3. Communication

ISBN 978-0-8389-1079-5; 0-8389-1079-3

LC 2010033485

"This professional offering teaches librarians to use storyteling as an effective leadership tool. . . . Marek has written a clear and thorough introduction to organizational storytelling for librarians. Carefully researched, the book includes notes at the end of each chapter. A comprehensive resource list encourages further study. Controlling own's own story and the story of one's library is a useful skill, especially during times of budgetary turbulence. Individual librarians and library leaders need to be able to convey personal and shared values effectively; this title provides a wealth of information on the topic." Voice Youth Advoactes

Includes bibliographical references

Martin, Barbara Stein

Fundamentals of school library media management; a how-to-do-it manual. [by] Barbara Stein Martin and Marco Zannier. Neal-Schuman Publishers 2009 172p il (How-to-do-it manuals for librarians) pa $59.95

Grades: Adult Professional **025.1**

1. School libraries 2. Instructional materials centers

ISBN 978-1-55570-656-2; 1-55570-656-8

LC 2009-7930

This book "contains useful information to help school librarians manage a myriad of tasks and roles. . . . [The authors] have created a book that is helpful, accessible, and full of down-to-earth, concrete examples." Booklist

Includes bibliographical references

★ **School** library management; Judi Repman and Gail K. Dickinson, editors. Seventh edition Linworth 2015 xvii, 335 p.p illustrations

Grades: Adult Professional **025.1**

1. School libraries 2. School libraries -- United States -- Administration

ISBN 9781610691406

LC 2014037465

"Librarians working with children, any school library serving children, and any school with or without a library can benefit from the useful information that can be gleaned from these articles." VOYA

Includes bibliographical references and index.

The **whole** library handbook; teen services. edited by Heather Booth and Karen Jensen. ALA Editions, an imprint of the American Library Association 2014 xi, 204 p.p illustrations (alk. paper) $60

Grades: Adult Professional **025.1**

1. Teenagers -- Books and reading 2. Library services to young adults 3. Libraries and teenagers 4. Young adult services librarians 5. Young adults' libraries -- Administration 6. Young adults' libraries -- United States -- Administration

ISBN 0838912249; 9780838912249

LC 2014004303

This book, edited by Heather Booth and Karen Jensen, part of the Whole Library Handbook series from the American Library Association, is "specifically geared towards those who serve young adults, gathering . . . articles and commentary from . . . innovative and successful teen services librarians. Sections focusing on practice, theory, and the philosophical underpinnings of the profession are supported by current research and historical perspectives." (Publisher's note)

"This guide to providing teen services in public libraries is quite comprehensive, earning its place as part of The Whole Library Handbook series." VOYA

Includes bibliographical references and index

Woolls, Blanche

The **School** Library Manager; Surviving and Thriving. Blanche Woolls, Ann C. Week, and Sharon Coatney. 6th edition Libraries Unlimited, an Imprint of ABC-CLIO, LLC 2017 paperback $60

Grades: Professional **025.1**

1. School libraries 2. Instructional materials centers

ISBN 9781440852565; 1440852561

LC 2017024832

Originally published in 1994

"This sixth edition of Library Unlimited's classic school library management text describes new approaches to management and addresses the realities that school librarians face in today's quickly evolving information-based world.This sixth edition of Library Unlimited's classic school library management text describes new approaches to management and addresses the realities that school librarians face in today's quickly evolving information-based world." (Publisher's note)

025.2 Acquisitions and collection development

Franklin, Patricia

School library collection development; just the basics. Claire Gatrell Stephens and Patricia Franklin. Libraries Unlimited 2012 x, 71 p.p ill. (Just the basics) (paperback) $35

Grades: Adult Professional **025.2**

1. School libraries 2. Libraries -- Collection development 3. Collection management (Libraries) -- United States 4. School libraries -- Collection development -- United States

ISBN 1598849433; 9781598849431

LC 2012016990

This book, by Claire Gatrell Stephens and Patricia Franklin, discusses collection development for school librarians. This volume offers a "manual that explains the fundamentals of purchasing, developing, and managing a collection. Containing information useful to anyone from a paraprofessional working under the guidance of a certified school librarian to a newcomer to the field to a certified media specialist, this book covers all of the basics through best practices." (Publisher's note)

Goldsmith, Francisca

The **readers'** advisory guide to graphic novels; Francisca Goldsmith. Second edition ALA Editions, an imprint of the American Library Association 2017 xvi, 215 p.p (paperback) $54

Grades: Adult Professional **025.2**

1. Readers' advisory services 2. Graphic novels -- Bibliography 3. Readers' advisory services -- United States 4. Libraries -- Special collections -- Graphic novels

ISBN 0838915094; 9780838915097

LC 2016042034

Goldsmith "presents a readers' advisory guide to graphic novels. She discusses the key qualities of graphic novels and the characteristics of its readers; basic readers' advisory methods, with reference to the graphic novel format; tips for working with adults and teens experienced or not experienced with the format; working with teens who are becoming self-aware; reading development, interests, and advisory methods for children; materials by interest, topic, and age group; multimedia aspects; and professional tools." (Publisher's note)

"This is a book to spend time with, not flip through, although a strong index and table of contents make it easily consultable for patron interactions as well." VOYA

Includes bibliographical references and index

★ **Intellectual** Freedom Manual; compiled by the Office for Intellectual Freedom of the American Library Association ; Trina Magi, editor ; Martin Garnar, assistant editor. 9th ed. ALA Editions, An imprint of the American Library Association 2015 434 p. $70

Grades: Adult Professional **025.2**

1. Censorship 2. Library science 3. Intellectual freedom 4. Freedom of information -- United States -- Handbooks, manuals, etc. 5. Libraries -- Censorship -- United States -- Handbooks, manuals, etc.

ISBN 0838912923; 9780838912928

LC 2014037437

First published 1974

This newest edition "is more than just an invaluable compendium of guiding principles and policies. It's also an indispensable resource for day-to-day guidance on maintaining free and equal access to information for all people. Fortifying and emboldening professionals and students from across the library spectrum, this manual includes . . . 34 ALA policy statements and documents [and] explanations of legal points." (Publisher's note)

"All libraries should have a copy of this book to use when writing or revising policies; indispensable." Libr J

Includes bibliographical references and index

Mayer, Brian

Libraries got game; aligned learning through modern board games. [by] Brian Mayer and Christopher Harris. American Library Association 2010 134p il pa $45

Grades: Adult Professional **025.2**

1. Board games 2. Libraries -- Special collections

ISBN 978-0-8389-1009-2; 0-8389-1009-2

LC 2009-26839

"This is a valuable resource for K-12 librarians interested in building curriculum-aligned 'designer' game collections. The authors . . . explain how specific games enhance language-arts, social-studies, and math units, and build literacy skills. The two chapters devoted to promoting and justifying the inclusion of games in the library are well documented and a wonderful source to have to convince skeptical administrators. Suggestions for building a core collection, which highlights top recommended games for elementary school, middle school, and high school; a list of game publishers; a list of games discussed; and a glossary of terminology are included." SLJ

Includes bibliographical references

Scales, Pat R.

★ **Protecting** intellectual freedom in your school library; scenarios from the front lines. [by] Pat R. Scales for the Office for Intellectual Freedom. American Library Association 2009 148p (Intellectual freedom front lines) pa $55

Grades: Adult Professional **025.2**

1. School libraries 2. Intellectual freedom

ISBN 978-0-8389-3581-1; 0-8389-3581-8

LC 2008-39893

"Scales uses court opinions, federal and state laws, and ALA documents to offer solutions for responding to infringements. A broad range of potential scenarios—from challenges to materials in both the library and the classroom, the legality of film rating systems, using computerized reading programs as selection tools and labeling books by reading levels, policies for interlibrary loans and reserves to confidentiality of children's and teens' circulation records—are covered. . . . This resource should be in every school library's professional collection." Voice Youth Advocates

Includes bibliographical references

025.3 Bibliographic analysis and control

★ **Cataloging** correctly for kids; an introduction to the tools and practices. edited by Michele Zwierski, Joanna F. Fountain, and Marilyn McCroskey. 6th edition Association for Library Collections and Technical Services, American Library Association 2019 192 p paperback $59.99

Grades: Adult Professional **025.3**

1. Cataloging 2. Reference books 3. Children's literature --

Cataloging

ISBN 9780838918715 paperback; 978-0-8389-3589-7

First published 1989 by the Cataloging for Children's Materials Committee

Among the topics discussed are: guidelines for standardized cataloging for children; how children search; using AACR2 and MARC 21; copy cataloging; using RDA; Sears List of Subject Headings; LC Children's headings; sources for Dewey numbers; cataloging nonbook materials; authority control; how the CIP program helps children; cataloging for kids in the academic library; cataloging for non-English-speaking children and preliterate children; automating the children's catalog; vendors of cataloging for children's materials.

Includes bibliographical references

025.4 Subject analysis and control

★ **Sears** List of Subject Headings; Barbara A. Bristow, editor; Christi Showman Farrar, associate editor. 21st edition Grey House Publishing/H.W. Wilson 2014 946 pp. (hardcover) $165.00

Grades: Adult Professional **025.4**

1. Cataloging 2. Library science 3. Subject headings

ISBN 9781619251908

LC 2013498263

This book, edited by Barbara A. Bristow and Christi Showman Farrar, presents the frameworks for the Sears List of Subject Headings cataloging system. "This resource lists subject headings used by small and medium-sized libraries, with patterns, examples, and notes on usage. The subject headings are listed alphabetically and aligned with the Dewey Decimal Classification system and include a list of canceled and replacement headings, as well as a discussion of the theoretical foundations of the list and the general principles of subject cataloging." (Book News)

025.5 Services for users

American Association of School Librarians

Standards for the 21st-century learner in action. American Association of School Librarians 2009 120p pa $39

Grades: Adult Professional **025.5**

1. Information literacy 2. Libraries -- Standards

ISBN 978-0-8389-8507-6 pa; 0-8389-8507-6 pa

"Standards in Action attempts to expand upon AASL's Standards for the 21st Century Learner by providing benchmarks and action examples. The original document was a nine-page brochure that outlined nine common beliefs, four learning standards, four strands, and indicators under each strand. It was an excellent starting point, but the addition of benchmarks at grades two, five, eight, ten, and twelve helps flesh out the original vision. . . . School libraries should own a copy of this professional, which has a role within any program." Voice Youth Advocates

Includes glossary and bibliographical references

027.6 Libraries for special groups and organizations

Klipper, Barbara

Programming for children and teens with autism spectrum disorder; Barbara Klipper. ALA Editions 2014 168 p. illustrations (pbk) $45

Grades: Adult Professional **027.6**

1. Autism 2. Autistic children 3. Libraries and people with disabilities 4. Children's libraries -- Activity programs 5. Youth with autism spectrum disorders -- Services for 6. Children with autism spectrum disorders -- Services for

ISBN 9780838912065; 0838912060

LC 2013044207

This book, by Barbara Klipper, is "[f]or librarians who offer or are thinking about offering programming to children and/or teens with autism spectrum disorders (ASD). . . . There are storytime models; programming for school-age children, teens, and families; and program plans for school libraries. Helpful side boxes include tips on ways to supplement or adapt existing programs and library spaces. . . . The appendixes include valuable resources such as vendors, websites, and publishers." (School Library Journal)

Includes bibliographical references and index

027.62 Libraries for specific age groups

Alessio, Amy J.

A **year** of programs for teens. American Library Association 2007 159p il pa $35

Grades: Adult Professional **027.62**

1. Library services to young adults 2. Young adults' libraries 3. Teenagers -- Books and reading 4. Young adults' library services -- Activity projects

ISBN 0-8389-0903-5; 978-0-8389-0903-4

LC 2006-13758

"Following an overview of the planning component of successful teen programming, this guide is presented as a calendar of ideas for each month of the year. Each month offers three to four programs with the preparation time, the length of the program, the recommended number of teen participants, age range, a shopping list, the setup required, variations or extra activities, and resources. . . . Librarians working with teens will find plenty of fresh ideas here." Booklist

Includes bibliographical references

Burek Pierce, Jennifer

Sex, brains, and video games; information and inspiration for youth services librarians. Jennifer Burek Pierce. Second edition ALA Editions, an imprint of the American Library Association 2017 240 p. (pbk. : alk. paper) $57

Grades: Adult Professional **027.62**

1. Teenagers -- United States 2. Adolescence -- United States 3. Libraries and teenagers -- United States 4. Young adults' libraries -- United States

ISBN 9780838915486

LC 2017001197

"How do we break through and truly reach our young adult patrons? It begins with understanding them. Librarians who work with teens need information and a big-picture perspective on adolescence that reflects the latest knowledge of cognate fields and the contemporary realities of young people's lives. In this greatly revised and updated edition of her popular guide Burek Pierce provides exactly that, selecting and synthesizing emerging information from multiple fields of research to effectively support librarians' work with teens. Far-reaching but pragmatic, this book discusses such important topics as identity and community, sex and sexualities, what experts can tell us about the adolescent brain, and how teens use technology to mediate the world; replaces outdated developmental theories that have been discarded in their home fields but are still sometimes used in the LIS world; looks at how to blend what research tells us about teens with day-to-day work in libraries; reflects new norms of professional practice, such as the increased importance of community engagement and partnerships, offering librarians a path towards cooperation and collaboration with peers outside the library world; and includes a bibliography of essential reading for YA librarians." (Publisher's note)

"A new chapter takes on diversity and the changing and multiple identities of teens. . . This is not a guidebook with step-by-step instructions for updating teen services; rather, it presents information for librarians to use as they come to their own conclusions about what today's teens need and want from their library." SLJ

Includes bibliographical references and index

Colston, Valerie

Teens go green! tips, techniques, tools, and themes for YA programming. Valerie Colston. Libraries Unlimited 2012 xiii, 142 p.p ill. (acid-free paper) $40

Grades: Adult Professional **027.62**

1. School libraries -- Activity projects 2. Environmental education -- Activity projects 3. Libraries and teenagers -- United States 4. Environmental education -- Activity programs -- United States 5. Young adults' libraries -- Activity programs -- United States

ISBN 1591589290; 1591589304; 9781591589297; 9781591589303

LC 2011029006

This book is a reference resource "for librarians or high school teachers looking for low-cost, environmentally themed art projects and programs that teens will relate to and find fun. In Part 1, the author explains the needs for these programs, offers tips for teaching them, and suggests ways to expand teen involvement in the library. Part 2 provides dozens of . . . art project ideas that demonstrate how simple teaching green teen art projects can be." (Publisher's note)

"A nice resource to have on hand for librarians whose community is ecominded or for those who want affordable programming options to consult." Booklist

Includes bibliographical references and index

Flowers, Sarah

Young adults deserve the best; YALSA's competencies in action. [by] Sarah Flowers for the Young Adult Library Services Association. American Library Association 2011 126p pa $45

Grades: Adult Professional **027.62**

1. Librarians 2. Library services to young adults 3. Young adults' libraries

ISBN 978-0-8389-3587-3; 0-8389-3587-7

LC 2010-14148

This "guide to the professional competencies developed by the Young Adult Library Services Association of ALA aims to 'outline the skills, the knowledge, and the philosophy that should be a part of the makeup of every librarian who serves teens.' Flowers begins by elaborating on and demonstrating how to execute the YALSA competencies. From there she discusses how to advocate for a teen-services department when none exists. The final section is a compilation of various resources, including the Library Bill of Rights and ALA interpretations of them with regard to labels and rating systems, Internet activity, ethics, and nonprint materials.. . . The information is presented in a clear, concise, and conversational manner, making this resource both easy to navigate and a pleasure to read." SLJ

Includes bibliographical references

Hardesty, Constance

The **teen** -centered writing club; bringing teens and words together. Libraries Unlimited 2008 174p il (Libraries Unlimited professional guides for young adult librarians) pa $40

Grades: Adult Professional **027.62**

1. Creative writing 2. Library services to young adults 3. Young adults' libraries 4. English language -- Composition and exercises

ISBN 978-1-59158-548-0; 1-59158-548-1

LC 2008-11519

"Hardesty encourages librarians to listen to teens and assist them in their search for identity through the written word. . . . From starting a club and the writing activities to share, to grand finales and how to evaluate the program's effectiveness, the author details all the information needed to create such a club. Particularly useful are chapters on the four roles of facilitators, creating a nonfiction writing club, and how to take your efforts online. Many handouts are included, a boon to any busy librarian. An appendix includes resources for publishing. All this information is laid out in a straightforward, positive manner. An essential resource for planning or presenting writing clubs." SLJ

Includes bibliographical references

Ludwig, Sarah

Starting from scratch; building a teen library program. Libraries Unlimited 2011 xiv, 202p pa $40; ebook $40

Grades: Adult Professional **027.62**

1. Library services to young adults 2. Young adults' libraries

ISBN 978-1-59884-607-2 pa; 1-59884-607-8 pa; 978-1-59884-608-9 ebook; 1-59884-608-6 ebook

LC 2011020103

This book offers a practical, comprehensive guide to creating a successful, vibrant, and youth-centered teen services program with limited resources.

"Ludwig provides plenty of real-world advice and ideas. . . . This well-written and helpful book will be invaluable to both new and seasoned teen librarians as well as those thinking about pursuing a career working with teens." SLJ

Includes bibliographical references

Miller, Donna P.

Crash course in teen services. Libraries Unlimited 2008 128p (Crash course) pa $30

Grades: Adult Professional **027.62**

1. Library services to young adults 2. Young adults' libraries

ISBN 978-1-59158-565-7; 1-59158-565-1

LC 2007-32758

"Designed for public librarians new to teen service, the book offers advice on relating to teens and creating teen-friendly space as well as tips on teen-centered reference, collection development, readers' advisory, programming, and 'the three Ps': professional resources, professional development, and public relations." Booklist

Includes bibliographical references

Sima, Judy

Raising voices; creating youth storytelling groups and troupes. [by] Judy Sima, Kevin Cordi. Libraries Unlimited 2003 xxviii, 241p pa $32.50

Grades: Adult Professional **027.62**

1. Storytelling

ISBN 1-56308-919-X

LC 2003-47631

This offers a "blueprint for beginning and sustaining a successful group or troupe of storytellers from grades 4 to 12. . . . The book includes reproducible forms that will save a lot of work and lists of valuable resources. . . . Raising Voices is the complete, and essential, handbook for this special group of storytellers." SLJ

Includes bibliographical references

027.8 School libraries

Donham, Jean

Enhancing Teaching and Learning; A Leadership Guide for School Libraries. third edition Neal Schuman 2013 382 p. paperback $72

Grades: Professional **027.8**

1. School libraries 2. Instructional materials centers

ISBN 9781555708870; 1555708870

LC 2013006365

This book attempts to show "how to develop and implement an effective library media program by integrating it into the total education environment. Part One covers all aspects of the school environment: students, curriculum and instruction, principals, school district administrators, and the community. Part Two shows you how to use interaction and collaboration to make the school library media program integral to all of these communities." Publisher's note

Franklin, Patricia

Library 101; A Handbook for the School Librarian. Claire Gatrell Stephens and Patricia Franklin. Second edition Libraries Unlimited Inc 2015 233 p. illustrations paperback $45

Grades: Adult Professional **027.8**

1. School libraries 2. Instructional materials centers 3. Libraries -- Handbooks, manuals, etc.

ISBN 1610694511; 9781610694513

LC 2015012914

"This handbook provides information for brand-new and inexperienced librarians preparing for a first job in a school library media center. Articles are divided into four subcategories covering day-to-day operations (library organization, circulation policies, media management, scheduling, staffing, and media center arrangement); collaboration with teachers; collection development and management; and equipment. Current issues in the field are discussed, and sidebars offer perspectives from experts in the field as well as practicing school librarians at all levels. This is a very beginning-level introduction that would be of use to those who do not have the opportunity to intern in a school library or to discuss library media center basics with other librarians in their communities or school districts." Booklist

"This manual will be seen on many new media specialists' bookshelves, with plenty of colored pieces of paper marking oft-referenced pages. Experienced professionals will also find ideas and suggestions to improve or enhance their established programs." VOYA

Mardis, Marcia A.

The **collection** program in schools; concepts and practices. Marcia A. Mardis. 6th edition Libraries Unlimited 2016 330 p illustrations paperback $65

Grades: Adult Professional **027.8**

1. Children's literature 2. Libraries -- Collection development

ISBN 1610698231; 9781610698238; 9781610698245

First published 1988 under the authorship of Phyllis J. Van Orden

"This thorough treatment of collection development will serve school library educators and students as well as practicing school librarians, providing quick access to information that is both immediately useful and helpful as unforeseen situations arise." (Publisher's note)

"The latest edition of this well-known textbook incorporates discussions of how the adoption of the Common Core State Standards and the Next Generation Science Standards impact collection development and management; revises and updates bibliographic references and resources; and adds information on digital resources and new technologies." VOYA

Morris, Betty J.

Administering the school library media center; 5th ed.; Libraries Unlimited 2010 580p il $75; pa $60

Grades: Adult Professional **027.8**

1. School libraries 2. Instructional materials centers

ISBN 978-1-59158-685-2; 1-59158-685-2; 978-1-59158-689-0 pa; 1-59158-689-5 pa

LC 2010015939

First published 1973 under the authorship of John T. Gillespie and Diana L. Spirt with title: Creating a school media program

"This updated edition provides a comprehensive and current examination of the multiple and varied jobs media specialists do to manage today's school library media centers. . . . Sample job description statements, media center budgets, and budget justification tools are thorough and valuable references. Morris addresses the proactive and visible leadership role that today's media specialists must take on to remain viable and support student learning. . . . The title supports concepts on current standards. It is a forward thinking text for new or future library media specialists and a realistic, functional reference for practitioners." Libr Media Connect

Includes bibliographical references

Sykes, Judith A.

Conducting action research to evaluate your school library; Judith Anne Sykes. Libraries Unlimited, an imprint of ABC-CLIO, LLC 2013 118 p. illustrations (hard copy) $40

Grades: Adult Professional **027.8**

1. School libraries 2. Librarians -- Rating 3. Educational evaluation 4. School librarians 5. Teacher-librarians 6. Action research in education 7. School libraries -- Evaluation

ISBN 161069077X; 9781610690775

LC 2012051277

In this book, author Judith Anne Sykes "coalesces current expert opinions on the topic of action research in the school library environment and highlighting what other teacher librarians in the field have identified as the pros and cons of using the process. Readers are directed to focus on mitigating the 'cons' through the use of specific working pages and templates and by initially exploring 'five favorite' links." (Publisher's note)

"When budget issues hit, school librarianship can be in danger, and this text provides tools for professionals to evaluate their programs and make necessary changes to stay a vital part of their schools. . . This purchase would be worthwhile for any teacher-librarian interested in evaluating his or her program and taking advantage of Sykes' extensive research and expertise." Booklist

Includes bibliographical references and index

028.1 Reviews

Baxter, Kathleen A.

From cover to cover; evaluating and reviewing children's books. rev ed.; Collins 2010 229p $14.99

Grades: Adult Professional **028.1**

1. Books -- Reviews 2. Children's literature -- History and criticism

ISBN 978-0-06-077757-9; 0-06-077757-5

First published 1997

The author addresses the distinctions between evaluation and review, and what makes a good children's book. She discusses categories of children's books including nonfiction; traditional literature (folktales, myths, legends, etc.); poetry, verse, rhymes, and songs; picture books; easy readers and transitional books; and fiction. She then describes the process of writing a review.

This is a "very complete resource that will continue to be the venerable reference tool and required reading for education and library-science students, youth librarians, teachers, and anyone else interested in kids, reading, and children's literature." SLJ

028.5 Reading and use of other information media by young people

Bartel, Julie

Annotated book lists for every teen reader; the best from the experts at YALSA-BK. [by] Julie Bartel and Pam Spencer Holley for the Young Adult Library Services Association. Neal-Schuman Publishers 2011 270p pa $65

Grades: Adult Professional **028.5**

1. Best books 2. Young adult literature 3. Teenagers -- Books and reading 4. Young adult literature -- Bibliography 5. Young adult literature -- Stories, plots, etc.

ISBN 1-55570-658-4; 978-1-55570-658-6

LC 2010-33312

"Bartel and Holley have scoured the YALSA-BK archives to find more than 1100 books with broad teen readership. While the book's primary purpose is for readers' advisory, the authors also suggest it will be useful in creating displays as well as igniting creativity. . . . The scope is wide ranging with a good mix of standards, classics, and newer titles. With a highly appropriate title, this volume hits the mark." SLJ

Includes bibliographical references

Cart, Michael

★ **Young** adult literature; from romance to realism. Michael Cart. 3rd edition American Library Association 2016 pbk $68

Grades: Adult Professional **028.5**

1. Teenagers -- Books and reading 2. Young adult literature -- History and criticism

ISBN 9780838914625; 0838914624

LC 2016014835

"Thoroughly updated to make it even more relevant and comprehensive, Cart's survey sketches in the origins of literature targeted at young adults and shows how the best of the genre continues evolving to deal with subjects every bit as complex as its audience. He includes updated treatment of best-selling authors like John Green, Suzanne Collins, and Veronica Roth, plus new and expanded coverage of perennially popular genre fiction, including horror, sci fi, and dystopian fiction." (Publisher's note)

★ **Dear** author; letters of hope. edited by Joan F. Kaywell; with an introduction by Catherine Ryan Hyde. Philomel Books 2007 222p $14.99

Grades: 8 9 10 11 12 **028.5**

1. Authors, American 2. Teenagers -- Books and reading

ISBN 978-0-399-23705-8; 0-399-23705-4

LC 2006-21050

"Chris Lynch, Nancy Garden, and Christopher Paul Curtis and are just a few of the well-known authors who respond to real teens' letters in this powerful compilation. Not mere fan mail, the selections speak about teens' gravest concerns—bullying, derailed friendships, racism, date rape, incest, illness, divorce, and more—and they describe how the authors' books helped them face the heartaches. . . . For some readers, this dialogue between writers and readers will be inspiring; for those harboring their own wounding secrets, it may be lifesaving." Booklist

Includes bibliographical references

Embracing, evaluating, and examining African American children's and young adult literature; edited by Wanda M. Brooks, Jonda C. McNair; foreword by Rudine Sims Bishop. Scarecrow Press 2008 251p pa $45

Grades: Adult Professional **028.5**

1. African Americans in literature 2. Children -- Books and reading 3. Children's literature -- History and criticism 4. Young adult literature -- History and criticism 5. American literature -- African American authors -- History and criticism

ISBN 978-0-8108-6027-8 pa; 0-8108-6027-9 pa

LC 2007025703

"Brooks and McNair have compiled 12 scholarly studies about the use of books by and about African-American children and young adults in classrooms across the United States. Selections include a detailed textual analysis of the work of Arna Bontemps and Langston Hughes; a sociolinguistic perspective on readers' response to books containing African-American Vernacular English; and a detailed study of the books used as classroom read-alouds by teachers in rural schools, which found that only three percent were about African Americans. While each study is complete in and of itself, the text as a whole gives a broad picture of what is currently being done in this field, both in K-12 classrooms and college classes that emphasize children's literature." SLJ

Includes bibliographical references

Handbook of research on children's and young adult literature; edited by Shelby A. Wolf . . . [et al.] Routledge 2010 555p $295; pa $119.95

Grades: Adult Professional **028.5**

1. Children's literature -- History and criticism 2. Young adult literature -- History and criticism

ISBN 978-0-415-96505-7; 0-415-96505-5; 978-0-415-96506-4 pa; 0-415-96506-3 pa; 978-0-203-84354-3 e-book

LC 2010-16339

"The book examines readers, texts, and cultural contexts of children's literature and across the three intersecting disciplines of Education, English, and Library and Information Science, in an effort to model a multidisciplinary approach to children's literature research. Thirty-seven scholarly articles, by figures such as Eliza Dresang, Rudine Sims Bishop, and Roderick McGillis . . . are counterpointed by responses that often provide more personal perspectives, including insights from noted authors such as Lois Lowry, M. T. Anderson, and Markus Zusak." Bull Cent Child Books

Harlan, Mary Ann

★ The **girl** -positive library; inspiring confidence, creativity, and curiosity in young women. Mary Ann Harlan. Libraries Unlimited 2019 161 p. hardcover $45

Grades: Adult Professional **028.5**

1. Girls in literature 2. Feminism and literature 3. Libraries and teenagers 4. Libraries -- Special collections -- Girls 5. Girls -- Books and reading -- United States 6. Young adult literature -- History and criticism 7. Teenage girls -- Books and reading -- United States 8. Libraries -- Special collections -- Young adult literature 9. Young adults' libraries -- Activity programs -- United States

ISBN 9781440860638

LC 2018037626

"This well-researched, straightforward work offers librarians guidance in reading, critiquing, and recommending YA books that advance positive and accurate representation of girls and young women. Harlan discusses complex issues: character archetypes that define norms of adolescent behavior, bodily autonomy and sex positivity, and the importance of reading YA fiction through a lens of intersectional feminism. Less of a programming handbook and more of a social critique, the text provides an accessible and thorough foundation for meaningful conversations surrounding representations of girlhood in media." (School Library Journal)

Includes bibliographical references and index

Keane, Nancy J.

101 great, ready-to-use book lists for teens; Nancy J. Keane. Libraries Unlimited, an imprint of ABC-CLIO, LLC 2012 xiv, 263 p.p (paperback) $40; (ebook) $40

Grades: Adult Professional **028.5**

1. Book selection 2. Books and reading 3. Young adult literature -- Bibliography 4. High school libraries -- Book lists 5. Young adults' libraries -- Book lists 6. Teenagers -- Books and reading -- United States

ISBN 1610691342; 9781610691345; 9781610691352

LC 2011051428

This book offers a "compilation of YA [Young Adult] materials . . . published prior to August 2011. The book is divided . . . into themed lists such as 'Genres,' 'Readalikes,' and 'Teaching Literary Elements.' The themes . . . include . . . topics such as 'Romance,' 'Autism & Asperger's Syndrome,' 'Different Belief Systems,' and 'Crossing the Border.' Each entry includes the title, author, publisher, publication date, page numbers, an annotation, Lexile level when available, and interest level by grade or age range." (School Library Journal)

"This is a useful resource for new librarians and may also be helpful to seasoned librarians. The emphasis is on books published within the last ten years, but some older titles are included." Lib Med Con

Includes bibliographical references and index

Khailova, Ladislava N.

The **stories** we share; a guide to Pre-K-12 books on the experience of immigrant children and teens in the United States. Ladislava N. Khailova. ALA Editions 2018 248 p. (print : alk. paper) $55

Grades: Adult Professional **028.5**

1. Immigrants 2. Books and reading 3. Children of immigrants 4. Libraries and immigrants -- United States 5. Immigrant children -- Books and reading -- United States 6. Children of immigrants -- Books and reading -- United States

ISBN 0838916511; 9780838916513

LC 2017052427

This book, by Ladislava N. Khailova, "spotlights dozens of award-winning titles that primarily feature a first- or second-generation immigrant child or teen as a narrator or main character. . . . Khailova identifies both fiction and non-fiction titles published in the United States and Canada between 1990 and 2015 that focus on the twentieth or twenty-first century immigrant experience." (Publisher's note)

Includes bibliographical references and index

Krashen, Stephen D.

The **power** of reading; insights from the research. by Stephen D. Krashen. 2nd ed; Libraries Unlimited 2004 199p bibl diag tab $25

Grades: Adult Professional **028.5**

1. Reading 2. Literacy

ISBN 1-59158-169-9 pa

LC 2004-44207

First published 1993

The author presents research for "the argument that free voluntary reading (FVR) is the most effective tool available for increasing literacy. . . . Some of the topics he explores include the research surrounding second language acquisition, reading rewards and incentives programs, and some of today's popular 'electronic reading products.'" Publisher's note

Includes bibliographical references

Saccardi, Marianne

Books that teach kids to write; [by] Marianne C. Saccardi. Libraries Unlimited 2011 150p pa $30; e-book $30

Grades: Adult Professional **028.5**

1. Creative writing 2. Books and reading 3. Literature -- Study and teaching

ISBN 978-1-59884-451-1 pa; 978-1-59884-452-8 e-book

LC 2011001866

"Divided into sections such as 'Making Stories Unique,' 'Creating Memorable Characters,' and 'Putting Passion and Voice into Nonfiction Writing,' this book gives countless recommendations for teaching various skills. Saccardi offers short, annotated summaries of mentor texts and describes how they can be used to model good writing techniques. . . . After reading this resource, educators will have a long wish list of materials to purchase." SLJ

Includes bibliographical references

030 General encyclopedic works

★ The **World** Almanac and Book of Facts. World Almanac Education

Grades: 5 6 7 8 9 10 11 12 Adult **030**

1. Almanacs 2. Geography 3. Popular culture

Originally published in 1868

"The World Almanac® and Book of Facts is America's top-selling reference book of all time, with more than 82 million copies sold. Since 1868, this compendium of information has been the authoritative source for all your entertainment, reference, and learning needs." (Publisher's note)

031 General encyclopedic works in specific languages and language families

Children's illustrated encyclopedia; senior editor, Ann Kramer ; senior art editor, Miranda Kennedy. 2nd rev ed; DK Publishing 2016 600 p. illustrations (chiefly color) (hardcover) $29.99

Grades: 4 5 6 7 8 **031**

1. Illustrated books 2. Encyclopedias and dictionaries 3. Children's encyclopedias and dictionaries

ISBN 9781465451699; 9781465456649; 1465451692

LC 2016462729

"Covering more than 380 topics from dinosaurs to digital technology, this highly visual guide engages young readers with photographic spreads and illustrations annotated with amazing trivia. Featuring full-color photographs, maps, cutaway diagrams, charts, and more, [it] is written in a clear and child-friendly style with updates that include recent space missions, scientific breakthroughs, and the latest significant events." (Publisher's note)

"DK's strength has always been its famous scannable and illustration-laden pages; this one is no different, containing more than 3,000 photos and illustrations, maps, graphs, lists, and charts." SLJ

Knowledge Encyclopedia. Dk Pub 2013 360 p. $29.99

Grades: 4 5 6 7 8 **031**

1. Encyclopedias and dictionaries

ISBN 1465414177; 9781465414175

This book, by the Smithsonian Institution, is a "family reference using 3-D rendered images to explore the wonders of the world . . . Divided into six chapters . . . a wide range of topics come to life. Illustrated with fascinating facts, maps, timelines, and graphics, the Knowledge Encyclopedia makes complex subjects easy to understand and is the perfect resource for kids, whether to help with homework or to pique their curiosity." (Publisher's note)

Turner, Tracey

World of the weird. Firefly Books 2009 144p il $14.95

Grades: 5 6 7 8 **031**

1. Curiosities and wonders

ISBN 978-1-55407-481-5; 1-55407-481-9

"A first-rate browsing item, from the bicycle-riding frog on the front cover to the recipe for chocolate-covered crickets at the end. . . . Turner presents barrages of snippets on extreme sports ('chessboxing'), uncommon maladies ('exploding head syndrome'), oddball festivals, bizarre beliefs ('Eating stolen bacon is a cure for constipation.' Do tell!), strange creatures real or otherwise, supernatural phenomena and . . . more. . . . Illustrated with photos that are often startling but never gory or gross, this compact page-turner will light up the imaginations of motivated young readers and jaded nonreaders alike." Kirkus

The World Book Encyclopedia. World Book, Inc 22 v col ill, col maps

Grades: 4 5 6 7 8 9 10 11 12 Adult **031**

1. Reference books 2. Encyclopedias and dictionaries

New editions published yearly; revised frequently

"A 22-volume, highly illustrated, A-Z general encyclopedia for all ages, featuring sections on how to use World Book, other research aids, pronunciation key, a student guide to better writing, speaking, and research skills, and comprehensive index." (Publisher's note)

031.02 Books of miscellaneous facts

Boyer, Crispin

Why not? Crispin Boyer. National Geographic 2018 223 p. color illustrations (hardcover) $19.99

Grades: 3 4 5 6 7 **031.02**

1. Questions and answers 2. Curiosities and wonders 3. Children's questions and answers

ISBN 1426331916; 1426331924; 9781426331916; 9781426331923

LC 2018288866

"From the absurd (vampires and coffins) to the serious (vertigo and phobias), this book takes a scientific approach to relevant questions that will elicit laughs, 'awws,' and 'ewws!' With the publisher's trademark stock photos and readable layouts, this title offers valuable information, and even the goofiest of questions receive respectful, accurate responses." (School Library Journal)

Farndon, John

Do not open; written by John Farndon. DK Publishing 2007 256p il $24.99

Grades: 4 5 6 7 **031.02**

1. Curiosities and wonders

ISBN 978-0-7566-3205-2; 0-7566-3205-6

LC 2007300131

This encyclopedic tome catalogues "the mysterious and unusual. . . . Flaps, foldout pages and varied styles of illustration—from photomontage to digital cartoons and more conventional line art—keep the book visually fresh and ably complement the subject matter. . . . Taking in everything from weird weather like St. Elmo's fire and raining frogs to possible locations of Atlantis, the book incites curiosity—and expansively rewards it." Publ Wkly

Mills, Andrea

Strange but true! DK Publishing. DK Publishing 2015 192 p. illustrations, map $19.99

Grades: 4 5 6 7 **031.02**

1. Animals 2. Curiosities and wonders

ISBN 1465439110; 9781465439116

LC 2015487476

This book from DK Publishing is a "collection of extreme, unusual, and cryptic animals, places, and phenomena. 'Fast facts' panels on each spread provide background to the main subject or details of related cases in a stripped-down and engaging style, while the infographic spreads in each section offer even more weird facts and stories while debunking popular strange-but-untrue myths." (Publisher's note)

"Full-bleed photographs dominate the layout: up-close images provide intimate views of unusual creatures like the Satanic leaf-tailed gecko, which camouflages itself as a rotting leaf, while small sidebars augment the 70+ entries with information about the greenhouse effect, the reflexes of carnivorous plants, and more." Pub Wkly

National Geographic kids almanac. National Geographic il map

Grades: 3 4 5 6 **031.02**

1. Almanacs

Annual. First published 2009.

"Kids can have fun keeping up with our quickly changing world with the New York Times best-selling Almanac, packed with incredible photos, tons of fun facts, crafts, activities, and fascinating features about animals, science, nature, technology, and more." (Publisher's note)

Terry, Paul

Top 10 of everything 2017; Paul Terry. Portable Press 2016 304 p. (pbk.) $19.99

Grades: 6 7 8 9 10 11 **031.02**

1. Curiosities and wonders 2. Handbooks, vade-mecums, etc
ISBN 1626868468; 9781626868465

LC 2016017945

This book, by Paul Terry, "includes just about everything you didn't know you wanted to know. Get ready to learn about the fattest herbivores, canyons much deeper than the Grand Canyon, the hugest creepy crawlers (eek!), a record-breaking hot air balloon ride, and which animals you never want to race…because you will lose." (Publisher's note)

Winterbottom, Julie

Frightlopedia; An Encyclopedia of Everything Scary, Creepy, and Spine-Chilling, from Arachnids to Zombies. by Julie Winterbottom, illustrated by Stefano Tambellini. Workman Pub Co 2016 224 p. illustrations (ebook) $9.95; (paperback) $9.95

Grades: 4 5 6 **031.02**

1. Fear -- Encyclopedias 2. Ghost stories 3. Curiosities and wonders
ISBN 9780761189640; 9780761183792; 0761183795

This children's book by Julie Winterbottom, illustrated by Stefano Tambellini "is an illustrated A-Z collection of some of the world's most frightening places, scariest stories, and gruesomest creatures, both real and imagined. Discover Borneo's Gomantong Cave, where literally millions of bats, cockroaches, spiders, and rats coexist. . . . Learn about mythical creatures like the Mongolian Death Worm--and scarily real ones like killer bees." (Publisher's note)

"A prime source of thrills and chills, equally suitable for casual browsing or quick reference." Booklist

Wonders of the world. Barron's 2016 32 p. illustrations (chiefly color) $6.99

Grades: 4 5 6 7 **031.02**

1. Seven Wonders of the World 2. Curiosities and wonders
ISBN 1438008309; 9781438008301

LC 2015956070

In this children's book, "learn about the biggest, oldest and most spectacular natural and man-made wonders of our world, including the Great Wall of China, Taj Mahal, Great Barrier Reef, and more. Engaging text, detailed facts, and impressive statistics give children exciting scientific insight into the many wonders of the world." (Publisher's note)

"Inexpensive and relatively sturdy, these large-format paperbacks make for a visually enticing series." Booklist

032 General encyclopedic works in English

Guinness world records 2018; Guinness world records. Guinness World Records, Ltd. 2017 255 p. illustrations (hardcover) $28.95

Grades: 6 7 8 9 10 11 12 Adult **032**

1. World records 2. World records -- Periodicals 3. Curiosities and wonders -- Periodicals
ISBN 191056172X; 9781910561720

"The record-breaking records annual is back and packed with more incredible accomplishments, stunts, cutting-edge science and amazing sporting achievements than ever before. With more than 3,000 new and updated records and 1,000 eye-popping photos, it has thousands of new stats and facts and dazzling new features." (Publisher's note)

070.4 Journalism

Bausum, Ann

★ **Muckrakers**; how Ida Tarbell, Upton Sinclair, and Lincoln Steffens helped expose scandal, inspire reform, and invent investigative journalism. by Ann Bausum; foreword by Daniel Schorr. National Geographic 2007 111p il $21.95; lib bdg $32.90

Grades: 6 7 8 9 **070.4**

1. Authors 2. Novelists 3. Historians 4. Journalism 5. Journalists 6. Essayists 7. Biographers 8. Social reformers 9. Socialist leaders 10. Writers on politics
ISBN 978-1-4263-0137-7; 1-4263-0137-5; 978-1-4263-0138-4 lib bdg; 1-4263-0138-3 lib bdg

LC 2007-11391

This describes "muckrakers, 20th-century journalists who investigated corruption and called for reform. . . . The well-captioned, black-and-white illustrations, mainly photos, are sometimes reproduced with a sepia tone. . . . Clearly written, this offers a very readable and informative introduction to American muckrakers." Booklist

Includes bibliographical references

Currie, Stephen

Sharing posts; the spread of fake news. Stephen Currie. ReferencePoint Press, Inc. 2017 80 p. $29.95

Grades: 7 8 9 10 11 12 **070.4**

1. Blogs 2. Journalism 3. Online journalism
ISBN 1682822974; 9781682822975

LC 2017025487

This book, by Stephen Currie, "helps readers to critically think about how technology has helped in exacerbating the spread of misinformation. Currie is thorough in defining what fake news is and contrasting it against propaganda and satire. He explores types of bipartisan news from both America and other countries to emphasize how the spread of misinformation has invaded not only blogs and websites but also social media sites as well." (Booklist)

Jarrow, Gail

★ **Spooked!** how a radio broadcast and the war of the worlds sparked the 1938 invasion of America. Gail Jarrow. Calkins Creek 2018 144 p. $18.95

Grades: 5 6 7 8 **070.4**

1. Radio broadcasting 2. Science fiction radio programs
ISBN 9781629797762

LC 2018933314

Sibert Honor Book (2019)

"In this nonfiction title for young readers, acclaimed author Gail Jarrow explores in riveting detail the famous 'War of the Worlds' radio broadcast from 1938, highlighting the artists behind the broadcast, the broadcast itself, the aftermath, and the repercussions of 'fake news' today." (Publisher's note)

"Jarrow effectively uses full-page spreads with excerpts of letters written to the Federal Communications Commission and Orson Welles that communicate the divided reactions to the broadcast. A discussion of the show's legacy, journalism, and noted hoaxes allows readers to evaluate current events in light of this notorious event. Jarrow concludes with a well-organized list of online resources." SLJ

Miller, Michael

Fake news; separating truth from fiction. Michael Miller. Twenty-First Century Books 2018 112 p. (lb : alk. paper) $37.32

Grades: 8 9 10 11 12 **070.4**

1. Journalism 2. Truthfulness and falsehood 3. Fake news 4. Journalism -- History -- 21st century

ISBN 9781541528147

LC 2018010572

This book, by Michael Miller, "explores journalistic and fact-checking standards, Constitutional protections, and real-world case studies, helping readers identify the mechanics, perpetrators, motives, and psychology of fake news. A final chapter explores methods for assessing and avoiding the spread of fake news." (Publisher's note)

Includes bibliographical references and index

081 General collections in specific languages and language families

Hudson, Wade

Powerful words; more than 200 years of extraordinary writing by African Americans. illustrated by Sean Qualls; foreword by Marian Wright Edelman. Scholastic Nonfiction 2004 178p il $19.95

Grades: 5 6 7 8 **081**

1. African Americans -- History 2. African Americans -- Biography 3. American literature -- African American authors

ISBN 0-439-40969-1

LC 2003-42792

A collection of speeches and writings by African Americans, with commentary about the time period in which each person lived, information about the speaker/writer, and public response to the words.

"Short enough to hold attention, the selections . . . are also long enough to show the writers' tone and style. Many sensitive full-page portraits are included. . . . This well-designed volume will be an excellent addition to many library collections." Booklist

Includes bibliographical references

100 PHILOSOPHY, PARAPSYCHOLOGY AND OCCULTISM, PSYCHOLOGY

Law, Stephen

Really, really big questions; about the weird, the wonderful, and everything else. illustrated by Nishant Choksi. Kingfisher 2009 62p il $16.99

Grades: 5 6 7 8 **100**

1. Philosophy

ISBN 978-0-7534-6309-3; 0-7534-6309-1

An introduction to philosophy which uses clear analogies to explore some of life's biggest moral and scientific questions, including the origins of the universe and the meaning of life

"Through a combination of vibrant colors; hip, retro illustrations; and interesting quotes, Law has produced a stimulating work for young minds that is sure to spark conversation and, of course, more questions." SLJ

130 Parapsychology and occultism

Steiger, Brad

Gale encyclopedia of the unusual and unexplained; [by] Brad E. Steiger and Sherry Hansen Steiger. Thomson/Gale 2003 3v il map set $205

Grades: 7 8 9 10 11 **130**

1. Reference books 2. Occultism -- Encyclopedias 3. Supernatural -- Encyclopedias

ISBN 0-7876-5382-9

LC 2003-3995

"These volumes cover broad concepts from 'Afterlife Mysteries' to 'Invaders from Outer Space.'. . . [This is] an encyclopedia for believers. The volumes are meant to 'explore and describe the research of those who take such phenomena seriously.'. . . The work covers material of interest to a large segment of the public in a way that is clear and readable." Booklist

Includes bibliographical references

133.1 Apparitions

Hawes, Jason

Ghost hunt; chilling tales of the unknown. [by] Jason Hawes & Grant Wilson; with Cameron Dokey. Little Brown & Co. 2010 218p il $16.99

Grades: 4 5 6 7 8 9 **133.1**

1. Ghosts

ISBN 978-0-316-09959-2; 0-316-09959-7

"This collection of stories is based on case files from The [Atlantic] Paranormal Society, TAPS, founded by Hawes and Wilson. Each of the eight selections describes the sightings and paranormal activity from the perspective of the observer, then describes how members of TAPS researched, set up equipment, and discovered explanations for what happened. . . . The stories have enough elements of the unknown to make them spine-tingling, but they are more mystery than horror. . . . The easy-to-read format and subject matter will keep even the most reluctant of readers interested." SLJ

Followed by: Ghost hunt 2: more chilling tales of the unknown (2011)

Ghost hunt 2; more chilling tales of the unknown. by Jason Hawes and Grant Wilson; with Cameron Dokey. Little Brown & Co. 2011 297p il $16.99

Grades: 4 5 6 7 8 **133.1**

1. Ghosts

ISBN 978-0-316-09958-5; 0-316-09958-9

"From ghostly spirits roaming Alcatraz to glowing red eyes in the woods, The Atlantic Paranormal Society (aka the popular reality television series Ghost Hunters) is back with a compilation of even more chilling and terrifying tales. Selections include a restless spirit terrorizing a house-sitting victim through her dreams, ghosts reappearing in the O.K. Corral in Tombstone, AZ, and a saddened ghost revisiting a lighthouse where her family was eradicated long ago." SLJ

133.4 Demonology and witchcraft

Hirschmann, Kris

Demons. ReferencePoint Press 2011 80p il (Monsters and mythical creatures) $26.95

Grades: 5 6 7 8 **133.4**

1. Demonology

ISBN 978-1-60152-147-7; 1-60152-147-2

LC 2010029905

"Beginning with an introduction that explains the origins of the devilish creatures, the book discusses demon-like entities throughout cultures and religions. . . . The book's visuals, which include contemporary photos of ceremonies and artists' rendering of demons, can be quite startling. Excellent sidebars . . . cover topics such as the number of exorcists in the Catholic Church." Booklist

Includes bibliographical references

Kerns, Ann

Wizards and witches. Lerner Publications 2010 48p il (Fantasy chronicles) lib bdg $27.93

Grades: 4 5 6 7 **133.4**

1. Witches

ISBN 978-0-8225-9983-8 lib bdg; 0-8225-9983-X lib bdg

LC 2008050757

"The explanations and history behind . . . witches [and wizards] . . . will provide satisfaction for readers who want to know more about these familiar characters from myth, fantasy, and folk and fairy tales. Brief and concise." SLJ

Includes bibliographical references

Schanzer, Rosalyn

★ **Witches!** the absolutely true tale of disaster in Salem. National Geographic Society 2011 144p il $16.95; lib bdg $27.99

Grades: 6 7 8 9 **133.4**

1. Witchcraft 2. Salem (Mass.) -- History

ISBN 978-1-4263-0869-7; 1-4263-0869-8; 978-1-4263-0870-3 lib bdg; 1-4263-0870-1 lib bdg; 978-1-4263-0888-8 e-book

LC 2011012989

"With text that flows like a dramatic novel, Schanzer brings readers into the famous Salem trials, asking them to ponder the motivations of the accusers and the tribulations of the accused. Black-and-white ink prints and red accents are wonderfully evocative and set an appropriately horrific tone." SLJ

152.1 Sensory perception

Jackson, Donna M.

Phenomena; secrets of the senses. Little, Brown and Company 2008 174p il $16.99

Grades: 6 7 8 9 **152.1**

1. Senses and sensation 2. Extrasensory perception

ISBN 978-0-316-16649-2; 0-316-16649-9

LC 2008-31215

"Students with an interest in the weird and unusual will find this book fascinating. It begins with an introduction to human senses and continues with chapters devoted to phenomena such as the 'sixth sense,' synethesia, and intuition. One of the most interesting sections discusses animals that use their senses in unusual ways. . . . The black-and-white illustrations and photographs are plentiful enough to make the text accessible to reluctant readers. Accurate, entertaining nonfiction." SLJ

Includes glossary and bibliographical references

152.14 Visual Perception

Brown, Jordan D.

Fooled ya! how your brain gets tricked by optical illusions, magicians, hoaxes & more. Jordan D. Brown, illustrated by Emily Bornoff. Quarto Pub Group USA 2017 80 p. $14.95

Grades: 5 6 7 8 **152.14**

1. Magic tricks 2. Optical illusions 3. Visual perception

ISBN 163322158X; 9781633221581

This book, by Jordan D. Brown, illustrated by Emily Bornoff, "is a kid's guide to the mind bending world of illusions, perception, and why we can be tricked. Don't be fooled again, learn the tricks! Discover the variety of ways our brains can trick us, from the visual trickery of optical illusions, to magicians' masterful use of misdirection, to strategies used by con artists." (Publisher's note)

Vry, Silke

Trick of the eye; art and illusion. Prestel 2010 89p il $14.95

Grades: 4 5 6 **152.14**

1. Art appreciation 2. Optical illusions

ISBN 978-3-7913-7026-2; 3-7913-7026-X

"From the Parthenon to the Mona Lisa to the Op-Art of the 1960s, images and text reveal the many ways our eyes play tricks on us. Perception of size and color is discussed using standard optical illusions, but this book includes much more. Anecdotes, such as the story of dueling Greek painters Zeuxis and Parrhasius, and unique reproductions, like portraits with altered facial features, lend excitement. The author has taken an interactive approach, filling the pages with questions, puzzles, and project ideas. . . . Text explains the images, which are large and clear. The broad range of styles represented and the fun of the interactive approach will no doubt appeal to young art lovers and curious kids alike." SLJ

Wick, Walter

★ **Walter** Wick's optical tricks; by Walter Wick. 10th anniversary edition; Cartwheel Books 2008 43p il $14.99

Grades: 4 5 6 7 **152.14**

1. Optical illusions

ISBN 978-0-439-85520-4; 0-439-85520-9

First published 1998

Presents a series of optical illusions and explains what is seen.

The author "has produced a stunning picture book of optical illusions. With crystal-clear photographs, he creates a series of scenes that fool the eye and the brain." Booklist [review of 1998 ed.]

152.4 Emotions

DiConsiglio, John

Out of control; how to handle anger--yours and everyone else's. Franklin Watts 2008 112p il (Scholastic choices) lib bdg $22.50

Grades: 7 8 9 10 **152.4**

1. Anger

ISBN 978-0-531-18846-0 lib bdg; 0-531-1-8846-9 lib bdg

LC 2007008648

This book has "a magazine-like feel to [it], with glossy pages, lots of photos and graphics, an eye-catching layout with sidebars and boxes, and even tests and quizzes. There is solid content behind the slick facade, though. [The book] delves into the physical and emotional roots of anger, exploring the differences between healthy and unhealthy reactions, and discussing anger-management techniques." Voice Youth Advocates

Includes glossary and bibliographical references

Guarino, Robert

Me and my feelings; what emotions are and how we can manage them. written by Robert Guarino; illustrated by Jeff

Jackson; foreword by Robert Ornstein. Hoopoe Books 2011 162p il pa $15.99

Grades: 7 8 9 10 **152.4**

1. Emotions

ISBN 978-1-933779-71-3; 1-933779-71-3

This "title devotes a chapter each to the 'primary' emotions—fear, anger, sadness, happiness, surprise, and disgust—and how to handle them, along with an easy-to-understand discussion. . . . 'Secondary' emotions like pride, jealousy, and love are briefly explored in a separate section. With cartoonlike illustrations throughout, interesting situations, and concise scientific explanations, the book offers a wealth of information in an accessible format." SLJ

153.1 Memory and learning

Hudmon, Andrew

★ **Learning** and memory. Chelsea House Publishers 2005 136p il (Gray matter) $32.95

Grades: 8 9 10 11 12 **153.1**

1. Brain 2. Memory 3. Psychology of learning

ISBN 0-7910-8638-0

LC 2005-11699

This "volume provides fascinating insights into various processes involved in how we learn different things in different ways. Particularly enlightening is the section differentiating explicit memory (learning facts) and implicit memory (learning processes) . . . The [book features] colorful historical photos and illustrations, process models, and shaded insets." SLJ

Includes bibliographical references

153.4 Thought, thinking, reasoning, intuition, value, judgment

Watanabe, Ken

No problem! an easy guide to getting what you want. illustrated by Elwood H. Smith; adapted by Sarah L. Thomson. Viking 2010 70p il $16.99; pa $9.99

Grades: 4 5 6 **153.4**

1. Problem solving

ISBN 978-0-670-01203-9; 0-670-01203-3; 978-0-670-01254-1 pa; 0-670-01254-8 pa

Adaptation of: Problem solving 101, published 2009 for adults

"This little gem explains how to approach intimidating goals or jobs by breaking them down into simple tasks. Realistic scenarios such as finding money for a big purchase or choosing a high school are approached with data-driven evaluation tools. The author defines the steps involved along with terms such as hypotheses, logic trees, matrixes, and evaluation charts." SLJ

153.6 Communication

Jackson, Donna M.

★ **Every** body's talking; what we say without words. by Donna M. Jackson. Twenty-First Century Books 2014 64 p. illustrations (lib. bdg. : alk. paper) $30.60

Grades: 5 6 7 8 9 **153.6**

1. Body language 2. Nonverbal communication 3. Body language

ISBN 1467708585; 9781467708586

LC 2013019674

This book, by Donna M. Jackson, "explores the complexities of body language. Discover what is really being expressed when people stand, sit, or move in certain ways and learn how you can use your body and facial expressions to communicate more effectively in a variety of situations." (Publisher's note)

"Nonverbal clues including stance, facial expression, posture, eye contact, and others add meaning to our words, or sometimes contradict them. Using second-person narration to engage readers, suggestions for interpreting body language is followed by a chapter explaining how cultural differences affect interpretations. A final chapter encourages readers to practice physical positions to increase confidence. Plentiful full-color pictures illustrate concepts." Horn Book

Includes bibliographical references and index

153.8 Will (Volition)

Sobel, David

What's the catch? how to avoid getting hooked and manipulated. illustrated by Jeff Jackson; foreword by Robert Ornstein. Hoopoe Books 2011 138p il pa $15.99

Grades: 7 8 9 10 **153.8**

1. Mass media 2. Advertising 3. Persuasion (Psychology)

ISBN 978-1-933779-78-2; 1-933779-78-2

This "is a guide for teens to understand how they are influenced by parents, peers, and the media, often without knowing it. Chapters explain advertising methods and their effect on consumers, and a discussion of Internet safety is included. . . . Although [this] clearly written, well-organized [book] could be read independently, [it includes] questions for discussion and classroom activities, making [it an] excellent [resource] for group discussions." SLJ

153.9 Intelligence and aptitudes

Armstrong, Thomas

You're smarter than you think; a kid's guide to multiple intelligences. edited by Jennifer Brannen. Free Spirit 2003 186p il pa $15.95

Grades: 7 8 9 10 11 12 **153.9**

1. Intellect

ISBN 1-57542-113-5

LC 2002-2687

"A self-help book that's clear, concise, and fun to peruse." SLJ

Includes bibliographical references

155.3 Sex psychology; psychology of people by gender or sex, by sexual orientation

Rosen, Michael J.

Girls vs. guys; surprising differences between the sexes. by Michael J. Rosen. Twenty-First Century Books 2015 72 p. color illustrations (lib. bdg. : alk. paper) $33.27

Grades: 6 7 8 9 10 **155.3**

1. Gender role 2. Sex differences (Psychology) 3. Gender identity

4. Sex differences
ISBN 1467716103; 9781467716109

LC 2013021833

In this book "author Michael J. Rosen explores the ways in which environment and experience, as well as neurology, physiology, and genetics come together to shape personality and gender behavior - in both expected and unexpected ways." (Publisher's note)

"Approachable format, attractive design, and breezy writing make this look at the science of sex differences both appealing and informative. Rosen highlights current research around varied intriguing topics such as what makes each gender laugh, which is more likely to be struck by lightning, and which sex is more attractive to mosquitoes." Horn Book

Includes bibliographical references and index

155.4 Psychology of specific ages

Mone, Gregory

Quiet power; the secret strengths of introverts. Susan Cain with Gregory Mone and Erica Moroz ; illustrated by Grant Snider. Dial Books 2016 288 p. illustrations (hardback) $17.99

Grades: 6 7 8 9 **155.4**

1. Interpersonal relations 2. Self-esteem 3. Families 4. Introverts
ISBN 9781101629802; 9780803740600

LC 2015040911

This book, by Susan Cain, with Gregory Mone and Erica Moroz, illustrated by Grant Snider, "is all about kids' world—school, extracurriculars, family life, and friendship. You'll read about actual kids who have tackled the challenges of not being extroverted and who have made a mark in their own quiet way. You'll hear Susan Cain's own story, and you'll be able to make use of the tips at the end of each chapter. There's even a guide at the end of the book for parents and teachers." (Publisher's note)

"Many will find value in this title that emphasizes that being an introvert is not a blemish on one's personality but a benefit. An excellent addition." SLJ

Includes bibliographical references and index.

155.45 Exceptional children; children by social and economic levels, by ethnic or national group

Fonseca, Christine

101 success secrets for gifted kids; the ultimate guide. Prufrock Press 2011 xi, 191p pa $14.95

Grades: 4 5 6 7 8 **155.45**

1. Gifted children
ISBN 978-1-59363-544-2; 1-59363-544-3

LC 2011004912

"Fonseca explains what it means to be labeled 'gifted,' how to cope in school, and how to interact with friends and family. Information is delivered in a friendly, conversational manner with firsthand advice from gifted kids and their parents. The myriad tips include how to deal with stress, how to complete homework assignments effectively, how to be respectful of others, how to accept oneself, and even how to deal with bullies. All are incredibly useful." SLJ

Includes bibliographical references

155.5 Psychology of young people twelve to twenty

Andrus, Aubre

Project you; more than 50 ways to calm down, de-stress, and feel great. by Aubre Andrus, with Karen Bluth, Ph.D. Switch Press, a Capstone imprint 2017 157 p. color illustrations (pbk.) $14.95

Grades: 8 9 10 11 12 **155.5**

1. Stress management 2. Stress (Psychology) 4. Stress in adolescence 5. Stress management for teenagers
ISBN 1630790915; 9781630790912

LC 2017003996

This book, by Aubre Andrus, with Karen Bluth, Ph.D, helps you "find your balance. Make a protein-packed smoothie to energize for a busy day. Center yourself after a stressful week by taking five minutes to write in your journal. Strengthen your body and calm your mind with simple yoga poses and breathing techniques. Craft a vision board to help you achieve your goals." (Publisher's note)

"The authors have designed a self-help book for students interested in ways to combat the everyday stresses of school, family, and friends." SLJ

Hugel, Bob

I did it without thinking; true stories about impulsive decisions that changed lives. Franklin Watts 2008 112p il (Scholastic choices) lib bdg $27; pa $8.95

Grades: 6 7 8 9 10 **155.5**

1. Decision making 2. Adolescent psychology 3. Risk-taking (Psychology)
ISBN 978-0-531-13868-7 lib bdg; 0-531-13868-2 lib bdg; 978-0-531-20526-6 pa; 0-531-20526-6 pa

LC 2008-690

Teenagers give their stories of impulsive decisions, their reasons for making them, and the consequences—whether good or bad.

This book is "colorful and compact, with . . . an appealing layout. . . . The stories, while not overly preachy, are brief and generally upbeat. . . . [The] book has excellent black-and-white photographs of a diverse array of teens." SLJ

Includes glossary and bibliographical references

Saval, Malina

The **secret** lives of boys; inside the raw emotional world of male teens. Basic Books 2009 257p $25.95

Grades: Adult Professional **155.5**

1. Boys -- Psychology
ISBN 978-0-465-00254-2; 0-465-00254-4

LC 2008-49703

The author "sought to find out if teen boys really were seriously at risk, and to offer, if possible, a more nuanced portrayal of young males. On both counts, she has succeeded. Through in-depth interviews and research, she portrays the lives of 10 young males. . . . It is a fascinating take on the subject, written in a clear and lively style with a useful index and interesting endnotes that can lead to further exploration." SLJ

Includes bibliographical references

Van Wagenen, Maya

★ **Popular**; Vintage wisdom for a modern geek. Maya Van Wagenen. Dutton Juvenile 2014 272 p. illustrations (hardback) $18.99

Grades: 7 8 9 10 **155.5**

1. Popularity 2. Middle schools 3. Autobiographies 4. Teenage

girls 5. Self-confidence 6. Life skills -- Humor
ISBN 0525426817; 9780525426813
LC 2014000236

YALSA Award for Excellence in Nonfiction for Young Adults (2015)

This memoir by Maya Van Wagenen tells how "stuck near the bottom of the social ladder at 'pretty much the lowest level of people at school who aren't paid to be here,' Maya has never been popular. But before starting eighth grade, she decides to begin a unique social experiment: spend the school year following a 1950s popularity guide, written by former teen model Betty Cornell." (Publisher's note)

"The clash of eras and cultures is funny—the author wears a girdle, hat, and pearls to class; learns how to apply makeup; improves her posture and poise; and tries a diet. But the best lessons she learns . . . are about how to talk to and understand the people around her." SLJ

155.9 Environmental psychology

De la Bedoyere, Camilla

Balancing work and play. Amicus 2010 46p il (Healthy lifestyles) lib bdg $32.80

Grades: 7 8 9 10 11 12 **155.9**

1. Stress (Psychology)
ISBN 978-1-60753-083-1; 1-60753-083-X

This book is "well-written and satisfyingly informative. . . . [The] magazine-like format includes numerous sidebars, color photos, and charts." SLJ

Includes glossary

Gootman, Marilyn E.

★ **When** a friend dies; a book for teens about grieving & healing. edited by Pamela Espeland. Rev. and updated ed.; Free Spirit Pub. 2005 118p pa $9.95

Grades: 7 8 9 10 **155.9**

1. Death 2. Bereavement
ISBN 1-57542-170-4
LC 2005-447

First published 1994

This offers "information on subjects including: How can I stand the pain? How should I be acting? What is 'normal'? What if I can't handle my grief on my own? and How can I find a counselor or a therapist? Interspersed throughout the book . . . are quotes by teenagers who have experienced grief. . . . Quotes from well-known writers and philosophers give insight into the grieving process and healing." SLJ

Harmon, Dan

Frequently asked questions about overscheduling and stress; [by] Daniel E. Harmon. Rosen Pub. 2010 64p il (FAQ: teen life) lib bdg $29.25

Grades: 7 8 9 10 **155.9**

1. Stress (Psychology)
ISBN 978-1-4358-3514-6; 1-4358-3514-X
LC 2009-17825

"Common stressors such as multi-tasking and over-filling one's schedule are discussed, along with how too much stress can cause damage to one's body. Suggestions are made on how to rethink scheduling and de-stress one's life. . . . This is a good resource for teens struggling to understand what is happening to themselves or to their friends." Voice Youth Advocates

Includes glossary and bibliographical references

Myers, Edward

★ **When** will I stop hurting? teens, loss, and grief. illustrations by Kelly Adams. Scarecrow Press 2004 159p il (It happened to me) $34.50

Grades: 7 8 9 10 **155.9**

1. Bereavement 2. Loss (Psychology)
ISBN 0-8108-4921-6
LC 2003-23698

This book "will be extremely helpful for teens struggling to understand their emotions following the loss of a loved one. Grieving is well explained and the individual nature of grief is stressed." Libr Media Connect

Includes bibliographical references

Phillips, Tracy A.

Losing someone you love; dealing with death and dying. Enslow Publishers 2009 104p il (Issues in focus today) lib bdg $31.93

Grades: 7 8 9 10 **155.9**

1. Death 2. Bereavement
ISBN 978-0-7660-3067-1 lib bdg; 0-7660-3067-9 lib bdg
LC 2008042872

"The final chapters are most helpful, detailing typical responses and reactions to grief as well as how to find support and to be supportive. . . . Bold subheads, interior color photos, and pull quotes break up the text. . . . Keep this title on the assignment shelf." SLJ

Includes glossary and bibliographical references

Simons, Rae

Survival skills; how to handle life's catastrophes. Mason Crest Publishers 2009 128p il (Survivors: ordinary people, extraordinary circumstances) lib bdg $24.95

Grades: 5 6 7 8 **155.9**

1. Life skills 2. Survival skills
ISBN 978-1-4222-0456-6 lib bdg; 1-4222-0456-1 lib bdg
LC 2008-50320

"Begins with a brief and accessible discussion of the psychology of stress and its role in adolescence, and offers twelve pieces of advice for overcoming difficult experiences and catastrophes. . . . [This book features] important, and sometimes complex, information in an easy-to-read format, offering high gloss photographs, marginal glossary notes, concept definitions, a bibliography, and further reading reccommendations." Voice Youth Advocates

Includes glossary and bibliographical references

158 Applied psychology

Amblard, Odile

Friends forever? why your friendships are so important. by Odile Amblard; illustrated by Andree Prigent; edited by Andrea Bussell. Amulet Books 2008 112p il (Sunscreen) $9.95

Grades: 5 6 7 8 **158**

1. Friendship 2. Interpersonal relations
ISBN 978-0-8109-9480-5; 0-8109-9480-1
LC 2007-43138

"The importance of friendship is stressed in the opening of Friends Forever?, followed by brief discussions on the types of friendships and how they are formed and maintained. . . . The tone of the [book] is breezy and light without being flippant. The [author] never [talks] down to the teen reader." Voice Youth Advocates

Auderset, Marie-Josee

Walking tall; how to build confidence and be the best you can be. by Marie-Jose Auderset; illustrated by Gaetan de Seguin; edited by N.B. Grace. Amulet Books 2008 112p il (Sunscreen) $9.95

Grades: 5 6 7 8 **158**

1. Self-confidence

ISBN 978-0-8109-9479-9; 0-8109-9479-8

LC 2007-43416

This "addresses issues of self-confidence and section one deals with feelings of high and low self-esteem, acceptance of oneself, and body image issues. It includes an exercise to help the reader realize her strengths and use that realization to build self-confidence. . . . The tone of the [book] is breezy and light without being flippant. The [author] never [talks] down to the teen reader." Voice Youth Advocates

Includes bibliographical references

Bezdecheck, Bethany

Relationships; 21st-century roles. Rosen Pub. 2010 112p il (A young woman's guide to contemporary issues) lib bdg $31.95

Grades: 7 8 9 10 **158**

1. Family 2. Friendship 3. Interpersonal relations

ISBN 978-1-4358-3540-5; 1-4358-3540-9

LC 2009-12065

"Facts are shared in a conversational tone, creating the sense of a chat with a big sister. . . . [Though] designed for personal reading and browsing, the data provided are accurate and also lend themselves to use in reports. This . . . will be of great interest." SLJ

Includes glossary and bibliographical references

Canfield, Jack

Chicken soup for the teenage soul [I-IV] [by] Jack Canfield, Mark Victor Hansen, Kimberly Kirberger. Health Communications 1997 4v il hardcover o.p. v1 pa $14.95; v2 pa $9.99; v3 pa $14.95; v4 pa $14.95

Grades: 7 8 9 10 11 12 **158**

1. Emotions 2. Interpersonal relations

ISBN 1-55874-468-1 [I]; 1-55874-463-0 [I pa]; 1-55874-615-3 [II]; 1-55874-616-1 [II pa]; 1-55874-761-3 [III]; 0-7573-0233-5 [IV]

These books cover "teenage subjects running the gamut from love, family ties, and self-esteem to developing values and life crises, such as a death in the family. . . . Teenagers not only helped select the poems, stories, and accounts that have been included but also have written some of them . . . with a few contributions by well-known people, including Sandra Cisneros, Helen Keller, and Robert Fulghum. . . . This isn't a religious book, but it is an inspirational and motivational one, sometimes funny, sometimes poignant." Booklist [review of 1997 volume]

Includes bibliographical references

Chicken soup for the teenage soul's the real deal; school: cliques, classes, clubs, and more. [compiled by] Jack Canfield, Mark Victor Hansen, Deborah Reber. Health Communications 2005 292p pa $12.95

Grades: 7 8 9 10 **158**

1. Emotions 2. Interpersonal relations

ISBN 0-7573-0255-6

LC 2005046051

"The stories included here were submitted by students and are based on their own experiences. Almost every page includes a fun fact, a statistic, or a quiz." SLJ

Crist, James J.

What to do when you're sad & lonely; a guide for kids. [by] James J. Crist. Free Spirit Pub. 2006 124p il pa $9.95

Grades: 4 5 6 7 **158**

1. Solitude 2. Depression (Psychology)

ISBN 978-1-57542-189-6 pa; 1-57542-189-5 pa

LC 2005021794

"Advising his audience to read this book and work through negative feelings with an adult, Crist describes sad and lonely feelings, distinguishes them from more serious conditions such as depression, and then suggests 'Blues Busters' and ways to ask for help. . . . Crist's clear explanations and simple techniques . . . are relevant for both children and adults." Voice Youth Advocates

Includes bibliographical references

★ **What** to do when you're scared & worried; a guide for kids. [by] James Crist. Free Spirit Pub. 2004 128p il pa $9.95

Grades: 4 5 6 7 **158**

1. Fear 2. Worry

ISBN 1-57542-153-4

"Part one deals with normal anxiety, offering detailed steps for developing 10 coping mechanisms. Expert help is needed to deal with the more serious problems discussed in Part two (e.g., phobias, separation anxiety, obsessive-compulsive disorder). Throughout, the author provides information, case histories, and coping skills in a manner that is both reassuring and encouraging. . . . Illustrations lighten the tone of the subject matter." SLJ

Includes bibliographical references

Fox, Annie

Be confident in who you are; [by] Annie Fox. Free Spirit Pub. 2008 92p il (Middle school confidential) pa $9.95

Grades: 5 6 7 8 **158**

1. Self-confidence

ISBN 978-1-57542-302-9; 1-57542-302-2

LC 2008-4754

"The book contains quizzes, is chock-full of helpful hints, and lists other resources to help readers increase their self-esteem. Kindt's cartoons include several great panels that move the teens' story forward. The graphic-novel-like design will make this self-help tool stand out and appeal to fans of that format." SLJ

Real friends vs. the other kind. Free Spirit Pub. 2009 90p il

Grades: 5 6 7 8 **158**

1. Friendship 2. Interpersonal relations

ISBN 1-57542-319-7 pa; 978-1-57542-319-7 pa

LC 2008031368

"Jack, Abby, Mateo, Jen, Chris, and Michelle are the middle school students of various ethnicities who take readers through this slim, interactive guide. Chapters cover such topics as friendship dilemmas, so-called friends, when friendships aren't working, crushes, and making new friends. Each chapter opens with a scene played out by the students in cartoon panels. Next, bits of text, along with a multitude of side boxes, address the topic at hand. . . . Lists of questions are offered, along with the answers. There's a lot packed into this colorful title that falls somewhere between self-help and peer advice." SLJ

★ **Too** stressed to think? a teen guide to staying sane when life makes you crazy. by Annie Fox and Ruth Kirschner; edited by Elizabeth Verdick. Free Spirit Pub. 2005 163p il pa $14.95
Grades: 7 8 9 10 **158**

1. Stress (Psychology)
ISBN 1-57542-173-9

LC 2005018484

"This well-organized, upbeat book discusses what stress is and how it affects the body and brain, talks about tools to reduce and control it, and gives suggestions for recognizing the myriad situations that can trigger stress at home and at school and seeking help when necessary. Best of all, each one of these scenarios includes information on how the situation might be addressed." SLJ

Includes bibliographical references

Hantman, Clea

30 days to getting over the dork you used to call your boyfriend; a heartbreak handbook. by Clea Hantman. Delacorte Press 2008 161p il pa $7.99
Grades: 8 9 10 11 12 **158**

1. Loss (Psychology)
ISBN 978-0-385-73549-0 pa; 0-385-73549-9 pa

LC 2007005945

"Hautman outlines a thirty-day process to help teens get through the five stages of a break-up—denial, anger, bargaining, depression, and acceptance. . . . Each day involves exercises to help put events, one's ex, and oneself in perspective. Each day also has a song of the day, which highlights the day's theme, and a bonus inspirational haiku. . . . The process and activities are helpful and even fun." Voice Youth Advocates

Harris, Ashley Rae

★ **Cliques,** crushes & true friends; developing healthy relationships. ABDO Pub. Co. 2009 112p il (Essential health: strong, beautiful girls) lib bdg $22.95
Grades: 6 7 8 9 **158**

1. Friendship 2. Interpersonal relations 3. Girls -- Psychology
ISBN 978-1-60453-099-5; 1-60453-099-5

LC 2008-12103

This guide to healthy relationships covers the social world of adolescent girls.

"Each chapter tells a personal narrative, with a consulting doctor giving insight and making suggestions. The topics are well selected, the design is attractive, and the stories feature girls from a variety of cultures." Booklist

Includes glossary and bibliographical references

★ **Girl** in the mirror; understanding physical changes. ABDO Pub. 2009 112p il (Essential health: strong, beautiful girls) lib bdg $22.95
Grades: 6 7 8 9 **158**

1. Puberty 2. Self-esteem
ISBN 978-1-60453-100-8; 1-60453-100-2

LC 2008-11903

This features fictional narratives paired with firsthand advice from a licensed psychologist to help preteen and teen girls feel comfortable with their changing bodies and know that they are not alone. Situations include developing early and "late-bloomers".

Includes glossary and bibliographical references

Jones, Jami Biles

Bouncing back; dealing with the stuff life throws at you. [by] Jami L. Jones. Franklin Watts 2007 112p il (Choices) lib bdg $22.50; pa $8.95
Grades: 6 7 8 9 10 11 12 **158**

1. Personality 2. Problem solving
ISBN 0-531-12404-5 lib bdg; 978-0-531-12404-8 lib bdg; 0-531-17730-0 pa; 978-0-531-17730-3 pa

LC 2004018426

"The image of a bouncing ball is used effectively throughout this book to discuss the concept of resiliency in the context of adjusting to life's problems. Each chapter begins with a short vignette of a teen facing a stressful situation and ends by reminding readers of the story and hypothesizing solutions. . . . The advice given is psychologically sound, the writing is clear and easy to read, the pages are visually appealing, and photos show teens of both genders and various racial backgrounds." SLJ

Includes glossary and bibliographical references

McIntyre, Thomas

★ The **behavior** survival guide for kids; how to make good choices and stay out of trouble. [by] Thomas McIntyre. Free Spirit Pub. 2003 167p pa $14.95
Grades: 5 6 7 8 **158**

1. Conduct of life 2. Interpersonal relations
ISBN 1-57542-132-1

LC 2003-4565

"The author provides skills and activities to learn and practice so that new behaviors can replace those that have resulted in getting students into trouble. . . . Those motivated to make better choices for how they behave in school or with friends and family will find much to help them." Voice Youth Advocates

Moss, Wendy

Being me; a kid's guide to boosting confidence and self-esteem. by Wendy L. Moss. Magination Press 2010 112p il $14.95; pa $9.95
Grades: 5 6 7 8 **158**

1. Self-esteem 2. Self-confidence
ISBN 978-1-4338-0883-8; 1-4338-0883-8; 978-1-4338-0884-5 pa; 1-4338-0884-6 pa

LC 2010014384

"Moss encourages her young audience to concentrate on two areas: focusing on inner self-esteem and building social confidence. Through procedure and practice . . . Moss reminds kids that real confidence doesn't come from being the smartest, prettiest, or the most popular one in the room but from the comfort one has with him- or herself. . . . Moss' offering gives great tips for the truly interested." Booklist

Orr, Tamra

★ **Beautiful** me; finding personal strength & self acceptance. ABDO Pub. 2009 112p il (Essential health: Strong, beautiful girls) lib bdg $22.95
Grades: 6 7 8 9 **158**

1. Self-esteem 2. Depression (Psychology)
ISBN 978-1-60453-098-8; 1-60453-098-7

LC 2008-11902

"The topics are well selected, the design is attractive, and the stories feature girls from a variety of cultures." Booklist

Includes glossary and bibliographical references

Owens, L. L.

★ **Frenemies**; dealing with friend drama. content consultant, Robyn J. A. Silverman. ABDO Pub. 2010 112p il (Essential health: strong, beautiful girls) lib bdg $32.79

Grades: 6 7 8 9 **158**

1. Friendship 2. Interpersonal relations 3. Girls -- Psychology

ISBN 978-1-60453-750-5; 1-60453-750-7

LC 2009-2132

In this book about friendships "each chapter tells a personal narrative, with a consulting doctor giving insight and making suggestions. The topics are well selected, the design is attractive, and the stories feature girls from a variety of cultures." Booklist

Perrier, Pascale

Flying solo; how to soar above your lonely feelings, make friends, and find the happiest you. by Pascale Perrier with Erin Zimring; illustrated by Klaas Verplancke. Amulet Books 2007 112p il pa $9.95

Grades: 5 6 7 8 **158**

1. Solitude 2. Friendship

ISBN 978-0-8109-9281-8 pa; 0-8109-9281-7 pa

LC 2006023609

"A self-help book with solid, practical advice. The text is divided into three sections or, as they are called here, phases: 'Why do I feel alone?,' 'How to stop feeling lonely,' and 'Finding solitude.' Each section has a series of subsections with quick discussions of mini-topics designed to hold readers' attention while imparting the necessary information. For the most part, the presentation is clear, understandable, and immediate. . . . The cartoon drawings are colorfully bright and match the text in its attempt to keep the tone light." SLJ

Piquemal, Michel

When life stinks; how to deal with your bad moods, blues, and depression. [by] Michel Piquemal with Melissa Daly; illustrated by Olivier Tossan ; [translated by Jane Moseley] Amulet Books 2004 112p il pa $9.95

Grades: 7 8 9 10 **158**

1. Depression (Psychology)

ISBN 0-8109-4932-6

LC 2004-13001

"The pleasing use of blocks of color and cartoon illustrations enhances the text. . . . Using the common-sense suggestions provided, readers will more successfully navigate the turmoil of adolescence." SLJ

Includes bibliographical references

Romain, Trevor

★ **Cliques,** phonies & other baloney; Trevor Romain & Elizabeth Verdick ; illustrated by Steve Mark. Revised and updated edition Free Spirit 2018 129p il paperback $9.99

Grades: 7 8 9 10 **158**

1. Friendship 2. Social groups 3. Interpersonal relations

ISBN 9781631982422 paperback; 1-57542-045-7

LC 2017041579

Discusses cliques, what they are and their negative aspects, and gives advice on forming healthier relationships and friendships

"With a sense of ease and lighthearted humor . . . the author serves up solid advice in friendly, reassuring prose." SLJ

Includes bibliographical references

Webber, Diane

Your space; dealing with friends and peers. F. Watts 2008 112p il (Scholastic choices) lib bdg $27; pa $8.95

Grades: 6 7 8 9 **158**

1. Friendship 2. Peer pressure

ISBN 978-0-531-18849-1 lib bdg; 0-531-18849-3 lib bdg; 978-0-531-14774-0 pa; 0-531-14774-6 pa

LC 2007006579

Provides advice and tips for teenagers on making and maintaining worthwhile friendships, evaluating friendships and clique behavior, handling peer pressure, bullying, and staying safe on the Internet.

Includes bibliographical references

158.1 Personal improvement and analysis

Weeks, Marcus

Heads up psychology; Marcus Weeks. First American edition Dk Pub 2014 160 p. illustrations (some color) hbk $15.99

Grades: 7 8 9 10 **158.1**

1. Psychology 2. Psychologists 3. Human behavior

ISBN 1465419934; 9781465419934

In this book by Marcus Weeks, "psychological theories are explained with the help of cleverly conceived graphic illustrations and diagrams to show how they relate to everyday life. Biography spreads give interesting insights into the lives and work of Freud, Pavlov, and more, while other psychologists and their big ideas are profiled in a comprehensive directory, and case study panels describe groundbreaking experiments in the field." (Publisher's note)

"By interspersing explanations of topics and research studies with biographies of great thinkers, psychological pioneers, and researchers, Weeks helps readers connect fields of psychological study with names they may have heard or read. In true DK fashion, format, graphics, text boxes, pixelated portraits of scientists, bubbles, and balloons all contribute to making this a busy but appealing companion for high-school psychology textbooks." Booklist

170 Ethics (Moral philosophy)

Nevertheless, we persisted; 43 voices of defiance, strength, and courage. Alfred A. Knopf 2018 320 p. $18.99

Grades: 8 9 10 11 12 **170**

1. Courage 2. Anthologies 3. Persistence 4. Conduct of life

ISBN 9781524771966; 9781524771973

LC 2017043558

This anthology features various voices, including "actress Alia Shawkat [who] reflects on all the parts she was told she was too 'ethnic' to play. Former NFL player Wade Davis recalls his bullying of gay classmates in an attempt to hide his own sexuality. Teen Gavin Grimm shares the story that led to the infamous 'bathroom bill.' . . . Holocaust survivor Fanny Starr tells of her harrowing time in Aushwitz, where she watched her family disappear, one by one." (Publisher's note)

Weinstein, Bruce D.

★ **Is** it still cheating if I don't get caught? [by] Bruce Weinstein; illustrations by Harriet Russell. Roaring Brook 2009 160p il pa $12.95

Grades: 8 9 10 11 12 **170**

1. Ethics

ISBN 978-1-59643-306-9; 1-59643-306-X

"This appealing guide speaks to the ethical dilemmas that all young people experience in their daily lives, and it should prompt considerable conversation and reflection." Kirkus

174 Occupational ethics

★ **Ethics** in school librarianship; a reader. edited by Carol Simpson. Linworth Pub. 2003 164p pa $44.95
Grades: Adult Professional **174**
1. School libraries 2. Librarians -- Ethics
ISBN 1-58683-084-8
LC 2003-7956

This is a compilation of "articles dealing with the ethical aspects of collection development, access, confidentiality, technology, intellectual freedom, intellectual property, administration, Internet use, and professional relationships. . . . School librarians and administrators would do well to have this thought and discussion-provoking book on hand." SLJ

Includes bibliographical references

174.2 Medical and health professions

Schafer, Susan

Cloning. M.E. Sharpe 2009 88p il (Genetics: the science of life) $38.95
Grades: 6 7 8 9 **174.2**
1. Cloning
ISBN 978-0-7656-8138-6; 0-7656-8138-2
LC 2008-8115

This discusses what cloning is, how it works, its ethics and future.

"Chock-full of information. . . . Interest is maintained through countless fascinating examples. . . . Illustrations and color photographs enhance [the text]." SLJ

Includes bibliographical references

Uschan, Michael V., 1948-

Forty years of medical racism; the Tuskegee experiments. Lucent Books 2005 112p il map (Lucent library of Black history) lib bdg $28.70
Grades: 8 9 10 11 12 **174.2**
1. Syphilis 2. Human experimentation in medicine 3. African Americans -- Health and hygiene
ISBN 1-59018-486-6

This is an account of "the Tuskegee Study of Untreated Syphilis in the Negro Male. . . . Halftone photographs of participants and of the persons who designed, conducted, or criticized the project supplement the text. Informational sidebars provide additional descriptions and photographs of some of the damage done by untreated syphilis." SLJ

Includes bibliographical references

Wittenstein, Vicki Oransky

For the good of mankind? the shameful history of human medical experimentation. Vicki Oransky Wittenstein. Twenty-First Century Books 2014 96 p. (lib. bdg. : alk. paper) $35.93
Grades: 7 8 9 10 11 12 **174.2**
1. Medical ethics 2. Science -- Experiments 3. Human experimentation in medicine -- History 4. Medical sciences -- Research -- Methodology -- History
ISBN 1467706590; 9781467706599
LC 2012043413

In this book, Vicki Oransky Wittenstein "describes many cringe-inducing examples of the ways doctors have exploited the marginalized, powerless and voiceless of society as human guinea pigs over the centuries. . . . Some experiments did lead to important discoveries and breakthroughs, but readers are challenged to consider the costs of violating individual rights for the cause of advancing medical knowledge." (Kirkus Reviews)

Includes bibliographical references (page 89) and index

176 Ethics of sex and reproduction

★ **Cloning;** Louise I. Gerdes, book editor. Greenhaven Press 2006 141p il (Introducing issues with opposing viewpoints) $32.45
Grades: 7 8 9 10 11 12 **176**
1. Cloning
ISBN 0-7377-3220-2
LC 2005-46292

"In this compilation, authors debate some of the controversies surrounding the cloning of people and animals." Publisher's note

Includes bibliographical references

177 Ethics of social relations

Vermond, Kira

Half -truths and Brazen Lies; An Honest Look at Lying. by Kira Vermond ; illustrated by Clayton Hanmer. Owlkids Books 2016 48 p. color illustrations (hardcover) $16.95
Grades: 5 6 7 8 **177**
1. Truthfulness and falsehood
ISBN 9781771471466; 1771471468

This juvenile book, by Kira Vermond, illustrated by Clayton Hanmer, "answers questions like: Why do we lie? What types of lies are there? What are the consequences of lying? What methods are used to detect lies? And when is it okay or even good to lie? From forgeries and hoaxes to plagiarism and placebos, . . . [it] offers historical anecdotes, scientific studies, and sociocultural analyses to help unpack the complex world of untruths." (Publisher's note)

"Rich with evidence, explanation, and food for thought, this well-documented approach to an issue not often covered in-depth for this age group will be enjoyed for curiosity's sake as well as a resource for study." Booklist

Includes bibliographical references (page 47) and index.

178 Ethics of consumption

Kerr, Jim

★ **Food**; ethical debates on what we eat. Smart Apple Media 2009 46p il map (Dilemmas in modern science) lib bdg $34.25
Grades: 7 8 9 10 **178**
1. Food industry 2. Genetic engineering
ISBN 978-1-59920-094-1; 1-59920-094-5
LC 2007-39651

This title is "easy to navigate as evocative photographs, charts, and sidebars help break down complicated arguments into manageable parts for easy digestion." SLJ

Includes glossary and bibliographical references

179 Other ethical norms

Belanger, Jeff

What it's like; to climb Mount Everest, blast off into space, survive a tornado, and other extraordinary stories. Sterling Pub. Co. 2010 136p il pa $9.95

Grades: 5 6 7 8 **179**

1. Courage 2. Anecdotes 3. Adventure and adventurers

ISBN 978-1-4027-6711-1; 1-4027-6711-0

LC 2009040875

"This illustrated collection presents short, first-person accounts of high-octane adventures—and, in some cases, personal disasters—by the people who actually experienced them. . . . The stories are told in present-tense, straightforward language, filled in with many pertinent and fascinating details. . . . The exciting action and the entries' short length will draw reluctant readers, as will the many color photographs, which are imaginatively laid out. This attractive package will be an easy sell." Booklist

Cheating; Stefan Kiesbye, book editor. Greenhaven Press 2010 107p (Social issues firsthand) $31.80

Grades: 7 8 9 10 **179**

1. Ethics 2. Honesty 3. Cheating (Education)

ISBN 978-0-7377-5009-6; 0-7377-5009-X

LC 2010000920

"The 13 entries in this book were written from the perspective of those who have cheated, for example, an 'economic hit man,' and those who have observed cheating, such as college professors. The selections are organized in several sections, including the school setting, the work-place, and sports. A list of organizations is included. This collection is particularly interesting because of the use of the personal narrative, and it is a good addition for libraries." SLJ

Includes bibliographical references

Factory farming; Debra A. Miller, book editor. Greenhaven Press 2010 183p (Current controversies) lib bdg $38.50; pa $26.75

Grades: 8 9 10 11 12 **179**

1. Livestock industry

ISBN 0-7377-4909-1 lib bdg; 0-7377-4910-5 pa; 978-0-7377-4909-0 lib bdg; 978-0-7377-4910-6 pa

LC 2009053380

"This solid volume looks at the economics, ethics, environmental impact, and future of factory farming. The issues are explored through diverse pro and con articles that have been edited for brevity, highlighting various points in the discussion surrounding the large-scale production and slaughter of animals for food. . . . This is a valuable addition to collections needing information on the state of modern food production." SLJ

Includes bibliographical references

Ravilious, Kate

Power; ethical debates about resources and the environment. Black Rabbit Books 2009 46p il map (Dilemmas in modern science) lib bdg $29.25

Grades: 7 8 9 10 **179**

1. Conservation of natural resources 2. Natural resources -- Management

ISBN 978-1-59920-096-5; 1-59920-096-1

LC 2007-35691

This title is "easy to navigate as evocative photographs, charts, and sidebars help break down complicated arguments into manageable parts for easy digestion." SLJ

Includes glossary and bibliographical references

Sepahban, Lois

Animal testing; life-saving research vs. animal welfare. by Lois Sepahban. First edition Compass Point Books 2015 30 p. (hardcover : alk. paper) $33.32

Grades: 6 7 8 9 10 **179**

1. Animal rights 2. Animal experimentation

ISBN 0756549965; 9780756549961; 9780756550455; 9780756550493

LC 2014026544

This book, by Lois Sepahban, is "like two books in one: Start from one end and learn why some people argue animal testing is needed. Then flip it over and discover why others argue it should be banned. Critical thinking questions help you analyze both perspectives and form your own opinions about the issue." (Publisher's note)

"There's tons of text here, but it's clear and engaging, featuring charts, real-life examples, color photos, and text boxes that supplement the narrative . . . [a] pertinent series for personal or academic use." SLJ

Includes bibliographical references

179.3 Treatment of animals

Abramovitz, Melissa

Thinking critically; animal rights. by Melissa Abramovitz. ReferencePoint Press, Inc. 2018 80 p. (Thinking critically) (hardback) $29.95

Grades: 7 8 9 10 11 12 **179.3**

1. Animal rights 2. Animal welfare

ISBN 9781682822630; 9781682822647

LC 2016047506

In this book, by Melissa Abramovitz, "debates about animal rights affect industries as diverse as entertainment, biomedical research, and food. Through a narrative-driven pro/con format supported by facts, quotes, anecdotes, and full-color illustrations, this title examines issues related to animal rights debates.Topics include: Should Animals Have Similar Rights As Humans? . . . Should Animals Be Used for Entertainment? Is It Ethical To Experiment On Animals?" (Publisher's note)

"Rather than face unwieldy results from an Internet search, students can use this series to frame their research coherently." Booklist

Includes bibliographical references and index

179.7 Respect and disrespect for human life

Death and dying; Jane Langwith, book editor. Greenhaven Press 2008 128p il (Introducing issues with opposing viewpoints) lib bdg $33.70

Grades: 7 8 9 10 **179.7**

1. Death 2. Bereavement 3. Future life 4. Right to die 5. Terminal care -- Ethical aspects

ISBN 978-0-7377-3974-9; 0-7377-3974-6

Presents essays covering different viewpoints on death, including the role of religion in death, the possibility of the afterlife, and whether physicians should assist in the process of dying.

Includes bibliographical references

Stefoff, Rebecca

The **right** to die. Marshall Cavendish Benchmark 2009 126p il (Open for debate) lib bdg $29.95

Grades: 7 8 9 10 **179.7**

1. Suicide 2. Euthanasia 3. Right to die 4. Medical ethics

ISBN 978-0-7614-2948-7 lib bdg; 0-7614-2948-4 lib bdg

LC 2008000361

This presents arguments for and against euthanasia and assisted suicide in ancient and modern times

Includes bibliographical references

181 Eastern philosophy

Whitfield, Susan

Philosophy and writing. Sharpe Focus 2009 80p il map (Inside ancient China) $34.95

Grades: 7 8 9 10 **181**

1. Chinese literature 2. Chinese philosophy 3. China -- Civilization

ISBN 978-0-7656-8168-3; 0-7656-8168-4

LC 2008-31167

"Whitfield covers religion and philosophy [of ancient China] and how they have been passed down using various precursors to books and printing. . . . [This is illustrated with] fine and frequent color photographs and reproductions. Readers will be rewarded . . . with clear, accessible writing, peppered liberally with entertaining stories from history." SLJ

Includes glossary and bibliographical references

183 Sophistic, Socratic, related Greek philosophies

Jun Lim

Socrates; the public conscience of Golden Age Athens. by Jun Lim. 1st ed. Rosen Pub. 2006 112 p. col. ill., col. map (library) $34.60

Grades: 5 6 7 8 **183**

1. Philosophers

ISBN 1404205640; 9781404205642

LC 2005012259

This book by Jun Lim is part of the Library of Greek Philosophers series and looks at Socrates. "This series introduces students to the great philosophers and mathematicians who helped shape the intellectual world in modern times." Examples are given "of the kinds of knowledge these men taught to their students. The early years, travels, and education of each man are told, and the contributions to society are detailed in the context of the times." (Library Media Connection)

Includes bibliographical references (p. 107-108) and index.

200 RELIGION

Bowker, John

World Religions; The Great Faiths Explored & Explained. Dorling Kindersley 2006 216 p. ill. (chiefly col.) $27.95

Grades: 8 9 10 11 12 Adult **200**

1. Religion 2. Religions 3. Religions -- Handbooks, manuals, etc.

ISBN 9780756617721; 0756617723

LC bl2006011130

This book, by John Bowker, takes a "new approach to understanding different faiths. . . . [It] looks at the beliefs and practices of many different religions, including Christianity, Judaism, Hinduism, Buddhism, Jainism, Sikhism and Islam." (Publisher's note)

"This book is a bold attempt to meld religious information with expressive art and to use the art as a tool for pedagogy. . . . World Religions has generous discussions of the ancient Egyptian, Greek, Roman, Norse, and Celtic religions, topics not even included in the Oxford Dictionary. . . . Ultimately, World Religions is the more commendable publication, though both books are recommended for most libraries." LJ

Breuilly, Elizabeth

★ **Religions** of the world; the illustrated guide to origins, beliefs, traditions & festivals. [by] Elizabeth Breuilly, Joanne O'Brien, Martin Palmer; consultant editor, Martin E. Marty. rev ed; Facts on File 2005 160p il map $29.95

Grades: 7 8 9 10 **200**

1. Religions

ISBN 0-8160-6258-7

LC 2005051101

First published 1997

This "is a valuable resource, covering the beliefs and practices of 10 major religions and lavishly illustrated with color photos, maps, diagrams, and charts." SLJ

Includes bibliographical references

The **encyclopedia** of world religions; Robert S. Ellwood, general editor; Gregory D. Alles, associate editor. Rev. ed.; Facts on File 2006 514p il map (Facts on File library of religion and mythology) $50

Grades: 7 8 9 10 11 12 **200**

1. Reference books 2. Religions -- Encyclopedias

ISBN 978-0-8160-6141-9; 0-8160-6141-6

LC 2005-56750

First published 1998

This encyclopedia "covers all the major and minor religions of the world, including the religions of the ancient world; the major religions practiced around the world today; religions of contemporary indigenous peoples; definitions of religious symbols and ideas; key leaders and thinkers; and terms and definitions." Publisher's note

Includes bibliographical references

Hackney Blackwell, Amy

Lent, Yom Kippur, and other Atonement days. Chelsea House 2009 112p il (Holidays and celebrations) $40

Grades: 6 7 8 9 **200**

1. Lent 2. Yom Kippur 3. Religious holidays

ISBN 978-1-60413-100-0; 1-60413-100-4

LC 2009010109

This "presents a welcome worldview of various atonement days, headlined by Lent, Yom Kippur, and the Buddhist holiday Rains Retreat. . . . Each gets an introduction to its associated religion, a brief history of the holiday, and a rundown of the significant days, rituals, and practices of observation. Then, readers are treated to a trip around the world . . . to investigate the unique ways in which different cultures observe similar holidays. The layout is text-dominated but dotted with colorful quality photos and a few informational insets. A good choice to help explain the significance behind holidays, . . . illuminating the many similarities lurking behind cultural and religious differences." Booklist

Includes glossary and bibliographical references

Langley, Myrtle

Religion; written by Myrtle Langely; special photography by Ellen Howden . . . [et al.] Rev. ed.; DK Pub. 2005 72p il (DK eyewitness books) $15.99; lib bdg $19.99

Grades: 4 5 6 7 **200**

1. Religion

ISBN 978-0-7566-1087-6; 0-7566-1087-7; 978-0-7566-1088-3 lib bdg; 0-7566-1088-5 lib bdg

LC 2005-278287

First published 1996 by Knopf

Introduces the history, philosophies, and rituals of various world religions including Hinduism, Buddhism, Shintoism, Zoroastrianism, and Christianity.

"Text consists of comprehensive, elucidative captions for the eye-catching, full-color photographs, drawings, and reproductions of paintings clustered on the pages. . . . This is a superb, succinct overview of the founders, tenets, and ways of worship of the world's major religions." SLJ

Mooney, Carla

Comparative religion; investigate the world through religious tradition. by Carla Mooney. Nomad Press 2015 120 p. col. ill., col. maps $22.95

Grades: 5 6 7 8 **200**

1. Religion

ISBN 1619303019; 9781619303010

In this book, by Carla Mooney, "readers seek answers . . . by comparing and contrasting the cultural, spiritual, and geographical underpinnings of five different religions. By developing a better understanding of the similarities and differences among religions of the world, readers gain a strong foothold in a dialogue that has continued for thousands of years." (Publisher's note)

"By examining complex beliefs and doctrine in an accessible and reader-friendly format, Mooney effectively teases out the commonalities among major world religions." Booklist

Includes bibliographical references (pages 116-117) and index.

Murphy, Larry

★ **African** -American faith in America; [by] Larry G. Murphy. Facts on File 2003 128p il (Faith in America) $30

Grades: 7 8 9 10 **200**

1. African Americans -- Religion

ISBN 0-8160-4990-4

LC 2002-28593

"In-depth coverage of diverse religious worship practiced among African Americans is presented. Murphy examines popular Christian religions, but also explores Judaism, Islam, Buddhism, and more. The well-written account begins with the religious experiences of the first Africans in America, moves to the establishment of pioneer religious institutions, and culminates with a chapter on the current status of diverse congregations. . . . Students will find ample material on well-known historical figures and current leaders" SLJ

Includes bibliographical references

National Geographic concise history of world religions; an illustrated time line. edited by Tim Cooke. National Geographic 2011 352 p. col. ill. (hardcover) $40.00

Grades: 8 9 10 11 12 Adult **200**

1. Ethics 2. World history 3. Religious institutions 4. Religions -- Encyclopedias 5. Religion -- History -- Chronology 6. Religions 7. Religion and ethics 8. Religions -- History

ISBN 1426206984; 9781426206986

LC 2011276808

This book "continues the 'Concise History' series with [a] . . . take on major religions and lesser-known faiths of all times and nations." It offers a "global perspective on the history of faith in the Americas, Europe, Asia and Oceania, and Africa and the Middle East. . . . 50 feature essays explore in detail the origins, development and influence of faith." (Publisher's Note)

Includes bibliographical references (p. 343-344) and index

Osborne, Mary Pope

★ **One** world, many religions; the ways we worship. Knopf 1996 86p il map $19.95

Grades: 4 5 6 7 **200**

1. Islam 2. Taoism 3. Judaism 4. Buddhism 5. Hinduism 6. Religions 7. Christianity 8. Confucianism

ISBN 0-679-83930-5

LC 96-836

"The presentation is notable for its respect to each group, succinctness, and clarity. . . . The artful, full-page, color and black-and-white photographs tell much of the story." SLJ

Includes glossary and bibliographical references

What do you believe? religion and faith in the world today. DK Pub. 2011 96p il map $16.99

Grades: 4 5 6 7 **200**

1. Religions 2. Philosophy

ISBN 978-0-7566-7228-7; 0-7566-7228-7

"This extensive guidebook covers the beliefs and history of the world's major religions. Focusing in particular on Buddhism, Christianity, Hinduism, Islam, Judaism, and Sikhism, the book also explores atheism and agnosticism, indigenous belief systems, East Asian religions, philosophy, and morality. . . . The graphically bold format—which mixes photographs, cartoons, and sidebars—will keep kids' attention, whether they are seeking truth, knowledge, or more to ponder." Publ Wkly

200.9 History, geographic treatment, biography

Cappacio, George

Religion in colonial America; George Capaccio. Cavendish Square Publishing 2014 80 p. (library binding) $35.64

Grades: 6 7 8 **200.9**

1. United States -- Religion 2. United States -- History -- 1600-1775, Colonial period 3. United States -- Religion -- To 1800

ISBN 1627128883; 9781627128889; 9781627128896

LC 2013050650

In this book on religion in Colonial America, author George Capaccio "launches his narrative with a description of the state of religious affairs in both the Old and New Worlds. He explores the failure of John Winthrop's goal to achieve Puritan perfection, the controversy over Anne Hutchinson's tenacious faith, the evangelizing stamina of ex-slave and Methodist preacher Absalom Jones, and the spiritual resilience of the Catawba Indians." (Publisher's note)

"Thoroughly researched and expertly executed, this series describes in rich detail the lives of Native Americans, African Americans, and white settlers, including children, women, and criminals. The introductory material that prefaces each title is of particular value, as it demonstrates that the colonists were part of a larger world picture. For instance, Religion takes readers back to Jerusalem to chronicle the expansion of

Protestantism and Catholicism there and abroad. . . . Strong, attractive titles for those looking for more coverage of Colonial America." SLJ

★ Religion in America: opposing viewpoints; David Haugen and Susan Musser, book editors. Greenhaven Press 2011 237p il (Opposing viewpoints series) $39.70; pa $27.50
Grades: 8 9 10 11 12 **200.9**
1. United States -- Religion
ISBN 978-0-7377-4988-5; 0-7377-4988-1; 978-0-7377-4989-2 pa; 0-7377-4989-X pa
LC 2010016975

This volume explores the topics relating to religion in the United States by presenting varied expert opinions that examine many of the different aspects that comprise these issues.

Includes bibliographical references

201 Specific aspects of religion

Hamilton, Virginia

★ **In** the beginning; creation stories from around the world; told by Virginia Hamilton; illustrated by Barry Moser. Harcourt Brace Jovanovich 1988 161p il hardcover o.p. pa $20
Grades: 5 6 7 8 **201**
1. Creation 2. Mythology
ISBN 0-15-238740-4; 0-15-238742-0 pa
LC 88-6211

A Newbery Medal honor book, 1989

"Hamilton has gathered 25 creation myths from various cultures and retold them in language true to the original. Images from the tales are captured in Moser's 42 full-page illustrations, tantalizing oil paintings that are rich with somber colors and striking compositions. Included in the collection are the familiar stories (biblical creation stories, Greek and Roman myths), and some that are not so familiar (tales from the Australian aborigines, various African and native American tribes, as well as from countries like Russia, China, and Iceland). At the end of each tale, Hamilton provides a brief commentary on the story's origin and originators." Booklist

Includes bibliographical references

Leeming, David A.

The **handy** mythology answer book; by David A. Leeming Ph.D. Visible Ink Press 2015 xiii, 402 p.p (paperback) $21.95
Grades: 7 8 9 10 11 12 Adult **201**
1. Mythology 2. Mythology -- Miscellanea
ISBN 1578594758; 9781578594757
LC 2014013298

This book, by David A. Leeming, addresses myths "from the ancient Greek and Roman to Egypt and Babylon, from Native North American Indian to Celtic, Middle Eastern, Indian, Asian, African, and the lesser known myths from around the world. . . . This helpful resource demystifies the myth, looks at different archetypes and motifs, and even shows how myths help explain our existence and institutions." (Publisher's note)

Includes bibliographical references (pages 377-384) and index

World mythology; the illustrated guide. Roy Willis, general editor. Oxford University Press 2006 311p il map pa $22.50
Grades: 8 9 10 11 12 **201**
1. Mythology
ISBN 0-19-530752-6; 978-0-19-530752-8
LC 2005-30779

First published 1993 by Holt & Co.

This book describes "the myths of Egypt, the Middle East, India, China, Tibet, Mongolia, Japan, Greece, Rome, the Celtic lands, Northern and Eastern Europe, the Arctic, North and South America, Mesoamerica, Africa, Australia, Oceania, and Southeast Asia." Libr J [review of 1993 edition]

Includes bibliographical references

204 Religious experience, life, practice

Philip, Neil

★ **In** the house of happiness; a book of prayers and praise. selected by Neil Philip; illustrated by Isabelle Brent. Clarion Bks. 2003 un il $17
Grades: 6 7 8 9 **204**
1. Prayers
ISBN 0-618-23481-0
LC 2002-10269

A collection of short prayers from major religions—Christianity, Judaism, Hinduism, Buddhism, and Islam—along with tribal chants, folk rhymes, and poems of praise and devotion

"The beautiful art encourages readers to pick up the book. Brent, who was inspired by the Book of Hours, lavishly employs illumination to highlight her pictures of nature. . . . This book offers the opportunity for quiet moments of reflection in a lovely setting." Booklist

209 Sects and reform movements

Stein, Stephen J.

Alternative American religions. Oxford Univ. Press 1999 156p il (Religion in American life) lib bdg $28
Grades: 7 8 9 10 **209**
1. Cults 2. Sects 3. United States -- Religion
ISBN 0-19-511196-6
LC 99-42370

Examines various alternative religions, or New Religious Movements, that have existed in the United States from colonial times through the twentieth century and from the perspectives of both insiders and outsiders

"The tone throughout is nonjudgmental and the emphasis is on people and their ideas. Black-and-white photos and reproductions add information and perspective to the presentation." SLJ

220 Bible

Atkinson, Peter

The **Lion** encyclopedia of the Bible; illustrated by Peter Dennis. Lion 2009 127p il map $19.99
Grades: 7 8 9 10 11 12 **220**
1. Reference books 2. Bible -- Encyclopedias
ISBN 978-0-7459-6010-4; 0-7459-6010-3

Taking a chronological approach to the story line of the Bible, this resource integrates and explores the Bible's historical, geographical, and social origins. It also overviews the different types of writing found within the texts and shows how they relate to Christian beliefs.

This is "thematically immense but skillfully distilled in presentation. . . . Complex and potentially confusing material is explained succintly. . . . Maps and colorful and dramatic drawings, paintings, and photographs appear throughout. . . . With its inviting format and unaffected writing, this is a welcome resource." SLJ

220.3 Encyclopedias and topical dictionaries

Oxford University Press

The **Oxford** companion to the Bible; edited by Bruce M. Metzger, Michael D. Coogan. Oxford Univ. Press 1993 xxi, 874p il map $70

Grades: 8 9 10 11 12 Adult **220.3**

1. Reference books 2. Bible (as subject) -- Dictionaries

ISBN 0-19-504645-5

LC 93-19315

This volume "contains more than 700 signed entries treating the formation, transmission, circulation, sociohistorical situation, interpretation, theology, uses, and influence of the Bible." Libr J

220.5 Modern versions and translations

The **Bible**: Authorized King James Version; with an introduction and notes by Robert Carroll and Stephen Prickett. Oxford University Press 2008 lxxiv, 1039, 248, 445p il map (Oxford world's classics) pa $18.95

Grades: 5 6 7 8 9 10 11 12 Adult **220.5**

ISBN 978-0-19-953594-1

LC 2008-273825

This Oxford World's Classics version first published 1997

The authorized or King James Version originally published 1611.

Includes bibliographical references

Good news Bible; today's English version. American Bible Soc. 2006 $10.99

Grades: 8 9 10 11 12 Adult **220.5**

ISBN 978-1-58516-154-6; 1-58516-154-3

"Begun in 1964 with the Gospel of Mark, The New Testament was completed in 1966, with rev. eds. in 1971 and 1976. The whole Bible was published in 1976. An extremely popular, inexpensive translation using contemporary American English. . . . Especially useful for youth or lay Bible study as well as for private reading." Bollier. Lit of Theology

The **Holy** Bible; containing the Old and New Testaments with the Apocryphal/Deuterocanonical books: New Revised Standard Version. Oxford University Press 1989 xxi, 996, 298, 284p map $29.99

Grades: 5 6 7 8 9 10 11 12 Adult **220.5**

ISBN 0-19-528330-9; 978-0-19-528330-3

LC 90-222105

"Intended for public reading, congregational worship, private study, instruction, and meditation, it attempts to be as literal as possible while following standard American English usage, avoids colloquialism, and prefers simple, direct terms and phrases." Sheehy. Guide to Ref Books. 10th edition. suppl

The **New** American Bible; translated from the original languages with critical use of all the ancient sources including the revised Psalms and the revised New Testament. authorized by the Board of Trustees of the Confraternity of Christian Doctrine and approved by the Administrative Committee Board of the National Conference of Catholic Bishops and the United States Catholic Conference. Oxford University Press 2006 xxiii, 1514p $39.99

Grades: 8 9 10 11 12 Adult **220.5**

ISBN 978-0-19-528904-6; 0-19-528904-8

First published 1970 by Kenedy

"Roman Catholic version based on modern English translations; replaces the Douay edition." N Y Public Libr Book of How & Where to Look It Up

The **new** Jerusalem Bible; [general editor: Henry Wansbrough] Doubleday 1985 2108p map $45; pa $29.95

Grades: 7 8 9 10 11 12 Adult **220.5**

ISBN 0-385-14264-1; 978-0-385-14264-9; 0-385-24833-4 pa; 978-0-385-24833-4 pa

LC 85-16070

First published in this format 1966 with title: The Jerusalem Bible

"Derives from the French version edited at the Dominican Ecole Biblique de Jerusalem and known as 'La Bible de Jerusalem.' The introductions and notes are 'a direct translation from the French, though revised and brought up to date in some places' but translation of the Biblical text goes back to the original languages." Guide to Ref Books. 11th edition

220.9 Geography, history, chronology, persons of Bible lands in Bible times

Lottridge, Celia Barker

Stories from Adam and Eve to Ezekiel; retold from the Bible. by Celia Barker Lottridge; illustrated by Gary Clement. Douglas & McIntyre/Groundwood 2004 192p il $24.95

Grades: 4 5 6 7 **220.9**

1. Bible stories

ISBN 0-88899-490-7

"Lottridge uses her storyteller's ear to bring ancient stories from the Hebrew Bible to a young audience, tailoring them to make them more age appropriate. . . . The numerous, well-drawn ink-and-watercolor illustrations are reminiscent of Warwick Hutton's work. Some pictures . . . are quite spectacular." Booklist

Murphy, Claire Rudolf

★ **Daughters** of the desert; stories of remarkable women from Christian, Jewish, and Muslim traditions. [by] Claire Rudolf Murphy . . . [et al.] SkyLight Paths Pub. 2003 178p $19.95

Grades: 7 8 9 10 **220.9**

1. Bible 2. Bible stories 3. Women in the Bible 4. Women in the Qur'an 5. Women in the Koran

ISBN 1-89336-172-1

LC 2002-153821

"Using sacred writings as their basis, the five women authors have reshaped the stories of such individuals as Sarah, Mary Magdalene, Eve, and Khadiji, the wife of Mohammed. . . . The stories are short and simply told, but they are intriguing and invite discussion." Booklist

Includes bibliographical references

221.9 Geography, history, chronology, persons of Old Testament lands in Old Testament times

Ward, Elaine M.

Old Testament women; [by] Elaine Ward. Enchanted Lion 2004 32p il (Art revelations) $18.95

Grades: 5 6 7 8 **221.9**

1. Bible stories 2. Women in the Bible

ISBN 1-59270-011-X

These Old Testament stories about women include "explanatory paragraphs, sidebars, and captions by the author. Art masterpieces . . . illustrate each story. . . . The captions provide background on the artist and the significance of each painting or mosaic. . . . The 18 women . . . include Rachel, Leah, Ruth, and Bathsheba. . . . Bosch, Botticelli, and Poussin are among the painters whose work appears here. . . . Visually stunning." SLJ

Yolen, Jane, 1939-

Meet me at the well; the girls and women of the Bible. Jane Yolen and Barbara Diamond Goldin ; illustrated by Vali Mintzi. Charlesbridge 2017 112 p. (reinforced for library use) $18.99

Grades: 5 6 7 8 **221.9**

1. Women in the Bible 2. Bible. Old Testament 3. Bible. Old Testament -- Criticism, interpretation, etc

ISBN 9781580893749

LC 2016053962

This book, by Jane Yolen and Barbara Diamond Goldin, illustrated by Vali Mintzi, tells the stories of girls and women of the Bible. "From first woman, Eve, to Deborah the judge, to Queen Esther, . . . females in the Hebrew bible are resourceful and courageous. Each chapter is devoted to a single story with text complemented by sidebars, known in Jewish tradition as 'midrashim,' that pose questions, provide more information, and include nondenominational interpretations." (Publisher's note)

222 Historical books of Old Testament

The **contemporary** Torah; a gender-sensitive adaptation of the JPS translation. revising editor, David E.S. Stein; consulting editors, Adele Berlin, Ellen Frankel, and Carol L. Meyers. Jewish Publication Society 2006 xlii, 412p $28

Grades: 8 9 10 11 12 Adult **222**

ISBN 0-8276-0796-2; 978-0-8276-0796-5

LC 2006-40608

A modern adaptation of the Jewish Publication Society's translation of the Torah. "In places where the ancient audience probably would not have construed gender as pertinent to the text's plain sense, the editors changed words into gender-neutral terms; where gender was probably understood to be at stake, they left the text as originally translated, or even introduced gendered language where none existed before. They made these changes regardless of whether words referred to God, angels, or human beings." Publisher's note

Ehrlich, Amy, 1942-

With a mighty hand; the story of the Torah. Amy Ehrlich, Daniel Nevins. Candlewick Press 2013 224 p. $29.99

Grades: 2 3 4 5 6 7 8 **222**

1. Bible 2. Bible stories 3. Picture books for children

ISBN 0763643955; 9780763643959

LC 2012947723

This book is an interpretation of the Torah for children. Amy Ehrlich has "changed the traditional phrasing" of the Bible's first five books. She "describes Moses' basket as "a little ark of papyrus," reminding readers of how much danger the baby was in, floating in the middle of the Nile. . . . Not every word of the Bible has been included, the text having been pared down to a series of interconnected stories." (Kirkus Reviews)

Feiler, Bruce S.

★ **Walking** the Bible; an illustrated journey for kids through the greatest stories ever told. by Bruce Feiler; illustrated by Sasha Meret. HarperCollinsPublishers 2004 108p il map $16.99; lib bdg $17.89

Grades: 5 6 7 8 **222**

1. Bible (as subject) 2. Middle East

ISBN 0-06-051117-6; 0-06-051118-4 lib bdg

LC 2003-15861

The author describes his journey through places mentioned in the Old Testament

"In this version of his adult book with the same title (Morrow, 2001), Feiler largely succeeds in slimming rather than dumbing down his account of his trip across the 10,000-mile setting of the earliest Bible stories. The author's unpretentious . . . tone and astute pacing help make the volume accessible, and his sincerity is palpable." SLJ

The **Torah**: the five books of Moses; a new translation of the Holy Scriptures according to the Masoretic text; first section. Jewish Publication Society 1963 393p $20; pa $15

Grades: 8 9 10 11 12 Adult **222**

ISBN 0-8276-0015-1; 0-8276-0680-X pa

This "translation of Genesis, Exodus, Leviticus, Numbers, and Deuteronomy was prepared . . . to present a version of the Bible that takes into account modern insights and knowledge of ancient times. . . . Of chief value to persons of the Jewish religion but of interest to Bible scholars of any religion." Booklist

223 Poetic books of Old Testament

Dillon, Leo

★ **To** every thing there is a season; verses from Ecclesiastes. illustrations by Leo and Diane Dillon. Blue Sky Press (NY) 1998 un il $16.95

Grades: 4 5 6 7 8 **223**

1. Bible -- O.T -- Ecclesiastes

ISBN 0-590-47887-7

LC 97-35124

"The words of Ecclesiastes I:4 and III:1-8, adapted from the King James Version of the Bible, are . . . {illustrated here in} 16 full- and double-page paintings. . . . Kindergarten and up." (SLJ)

"The Dillons compellingly convey the relevance of the Ecclesiastes verse throughout history, via a stunning array of artwork that embraces motifs from cultures the world over." Publ Wkly

226 Gospels and Acts

Connolly, Sean

New Testament miracles; 1st American ed; Enchanted Lion Books 2004 32p il (Art revelations) $18.95

Grades: 7 8 9 10 **226**

1. Christian art 2. Miracles -- Christianity

ISBN 1-59270-012-8

LC 2003-49414

"The 12 miracles discussed . . . include Jesus healing the man born blind, Jesus raising Lazarus from the dead, and the conversion of Paul. Each one is told from verses in the four Gospels or the Book of Acts, with explanatory paragraphs, sidebars, and captions by the author. Art masterpieces . . . illustrate each story. Works by El Greco, Rembrandt, Tintoretto, and Witz, among others, are featured. . . . Visually stunning." SLJ

230 Christianity

Hale, Rosemary Drage

Christianity. Rosen Pub. 2010 112p il (Understanding religions) lib bdg $31.95

Grades: 7 8 9 10 **230**

1. Christianity

ISBN 978-1-4358-5621-9; 1-4358-5621-X

LC 2009-10295

This book about Christianity "discusses origins and historical development; aspects of the divine; sacred texts, persons, space, and time; ethical principles; death and the afterlife; and society and religion." SLJ

Includes glossary and bibliographical references

Nardo, Don

Christianity. Compass Point Books 2010 48p il map (World religions) lib bdg $27.99

Grades: 5 6 7 8 **230**

1. Christianity

ISBN 978-0-7565-4237-5 lib bdg; 0-7565-4237-5 lib bdg

LC 2009-15811

"The colorful, attractive layout includes high-quality reproductions of photographs, maps, and paintings. Students who are new to religious studies, as well as those doing reports, will find that this . . . meets their needs." SLJ

Includes glossary and bibliographical references

Self, David

★ **Christianity**; [by] David Self. World Almanac Library 2005 48p il map (Religions of the world) lib bdg $30

Grades: 5 6 7 8 **230**

1. Christianity

ISBN 0-8368-5866-2

LC 2005041712

This is a summary of the Christian religion including history, beliefs, worship, festivals, practice, and current disagreements.

"Wonderfully colorful in images, language, and fact. . . . [This is] enumerated with full-color photographs on every page, charts, maps, and tables." SLJ

Includes bibliographical references

232.9 Family and life of Jesus

Lottridge, Celia Barker

Stories from the life of Jesus; retold from the Bible by Celia Barker Lottridge; illustrated by Linda Wolfsgruber. Doulgas & McIntyre 2004 140p il $24.95

Grades: 4 5 6 7 **232.9**

1. Bible stories

ISBN 0-88899-497-4

A retelling of selected events from the life of Christ based on biblical accounts

This is an "exceptional collection. . . . Each story is retold in three or four pages of clear, concise prose that is meant to be read aloud. . . . Each selection is enhanced by dramatic and atmospheric, mixed-media illustrations that are executed in warm earth tones." SLJ

Spirin, Gennady

★ **Jesus**; his life in verses from the King James Holy Bible. art by Gennady Spirin. Marshall Cavendish Children 2010 un il $21

Grades: 5 6 7 8 **232.9**

ISBN 978-0-7614-5630-8; 0-7614-5630-9

LC 2009005956

"In an unusual project, a tempera painting by Spirin has been digitally dissected to create individual images for this picture book that portrays 13 events from the life of Jesus. . . . Details from the larger work illustrate key moments—including the Annunciation, Jesus' baptism, and the raising of Lazarus, among others—beside passages from the King James Bible (Jesus' words are printed in red). The result is an elegant, large-format volume that offers a reverent and arresting visual interpretation of biblical events." Publ Wkly

248.4 Christian life and practice

Tebow, Tim, 1987-

Shaken; fighting to stand strong no matter what comes your way. Tim Tebow, with AJ Gregory. WaterBrook 2017 194 p. color illustrations (hardcover : alk. paper) $17.99

Grades: 5 6 7 8 9 10 **248.4**

1. Success 2. Christian life 3. Identity (Psychology) 4. Students -- Religious life 5. Success -- Religious aspects -- Christianity 6. Identity (Psychology) -- Religious aspects -- Christianity

ISBN 9780735289963; 9780735289871

LC 2017016085

In this book, "Heisman Trophy winner Tim Tebow passionately shares glimpses of his journey staying grounded in the face of disappointment, criticism, and intense media scrutiny. Following an exceptional college football career with the Florida Gators and a promising playoff run with the Denver Broncos, Tebow was traded to the New York Jets. He was released after one season." (Publisher's note)

"While this resource will largely appeal to the young football fan, the inspirational stories will resonate with anyone willing to approach it with an open mind. A Christian perspective with a wider appeal." Kirkus

Includes bibliographical references and index

270 History, geographic treatment, biography of Christianity; Church history; Christian denominations and sects

Nardo, Don

The **birth** of Christianity. Morgan Reynolds Pub. 2011 112p il (World religions and beliefs) lib bdg $28.95

Grades: 7 8 9 10 **270**
1. Christianity 2. Church history
ISBN 978-1-59935-145-2; 1-59935-145-5
LC 2010038443

This covers the beginnings of Christianity "in an impartial way. The [context] in which the [religion] developed [is] explained, offering insight into how [Christianity] came to be and introducing major concepts from the [religion]." SLJ

Includes glossary and bibliographical references

274 Christianity by specific continents, countries, localities in modern world

Schomp, Virginia

The **church**. Marshall Cavendish Benchmark 2010 80p il (Life in Victorian England) lib bdg $34.21
Grades: 6 7 8 9 **274**
1. Church of England 2. Great Britain -- Religion 3. Great Britain -- History -- 19th century
ISBN 978-1-60870-031-8 lib bdg; 1-60870-031-3 lib bdg
LC 2010006901

Describes the role of religion in the lives of Victorians, including how it influenced the way they lived, how they observed special occasions, and how they coped with the many changes and challenges of their times

This "is clearly written, thorough, and informative. The visually rich layout includes photographs and paintings from the time period, full-page illustrations, and attention-grabbing sidebars. Most appealing are the primary source quotations, which are plentiful and relevant." Libr Media Connect

Includes glossary and bibliographical references

280 Denominations and sects of Christian church

Brown, Stephen F.

Catholicism & Orthodox Christianity; by Stephen F. Brown and Khaled Anatolios. 3rd ed.; Chelsea House 2009 144p il (World religions) $40
Grades: 7 8 9 10 11 12 **280**
1. Catholic Church 2. Orthodox Eastern Church
ISBN 978-1-60413-106-2; 1-60413-106-3
LC 2008-43046

First published 2002 by Facts and File

This "traces the roots of [Catholicism and Orthodox Christianity] from the early Christian churches to today. The historical passage of the Catholic and Orthodox faiths is recounted, from the original teachings of Jesus Christ to the separation of the Eastern and Western Churches to recent attempts at reconciliation." Publisher's note

Includes glossary and bibliographical references

Protestantism; 3rd ed.; Chelsea House 2009 144p il map (World religions) $40
Grades: 7 8 9 10 11 12 **280**
1. Protestantism
ISBN 978-1-60413-112-3; 1-60413-112-8
LC 2008-29659

First published 1991 by Facts on File

This "explores the origins, customs, and history of Protestantism, from its beginnings in the Middle Ages to its role in today's world. Current issues, such as the development of new religious denominations, its stance on abortion, the ordination of gays and women, and the relationship between religion and politics, are explored within the framework of the fundamental moral tenets of the faith." Publisher's note

Includes glossary and bibliographical references

Noll, Mark A.

★ **Protestants** in America; general editors, Jon Butler and Harry S. Stout. Oxford University Press 2000 155p il (Religion in American life) lib bdg $28
Grades: 7 8 9 10 **280**
1. Protestantism 2. Protestant churches
ISBN 0-19-511034-X
LC 00-27271

Discusses the origins of Protestantism, the diversity of Protestant churches in the United States, and the role of Protestants in American life from colonial times to the present

"This volume is especially valuable for its discussion of the church in the African-American community and its coverage of smaller sects, like the Shakers. The many black-and-white photographs and reproduction add immensely to the text." SLJ

Includes bibliographical references

289.3 Latter-Day Saints (Mormons)

Bial, Raymond

Nauvoo; Mormon city on the Mississippi River. [by] Raymond Bial. Houghton Mifflin Co. 2006 44p il map $17
Grades: 5 6 7 8 **289.3**
1. Mormons 2. Church of Jesus Christ of Latter-day Saints 3. Illinois -- History
ISBN 978-0-618-39685-6; 0-618-39685-3
LC 2005027528

"Bial introduces readers to a city that was established by the Church of Jesus Christ of Latter Day Saints in 1839. . . . This effectively written account provides a sympathetic but balanced introduction to Mormon beliefs. . . . Excellent color photographs grace almost every page." SLJ

Book of Mormon

★ The **Book** of Mormon; another testament of Jesus Christ. [translated by Joseph Smith, Jr.] Doubleday 2004 586p $24.95
Grades: 8 9 10 11 12 Adult **289.3**
1. Mormons 2. Church of Jesus Christ of Latter-day Saints
ISBN 0-385-51316-X
LC 2004-51982

First published 1830

"Based on golden plates which Joseph Smith claimed were revealed to him, and which he unearthed from Cumorah Hill, New York, this book is roughly similar in structure to the Bible. . . . Emphasized are the doctrines of pre-existence, perfection, the afterlife, and Christ's second coming." Haydn. Thesaurus of Book Dig

Bushman, Claudia L.

★ **Mormons** in America; [by] Claudia Lauper Bushman and Richard Lyman Bushman. Oxford Univ. Press 1998 142p il (Religion in American life) $28
Grades: 7 8 9 10 **289.3**
1. Mormons 2. Church of Jesus Christ of Latter-day Saints
ISBN 0-19-510677-6
LC 98-18605

Chronicles the history of the Church of Jesus Christ of Latter-Day Saints beginning in America in the early 1800s and continuing to the present day throughout the world

"A solid resource for libraries. Illustrated with historical material and black-and-white photos. Time line and bibliography appended." Booklist

Includes bibliographical references

292 Classical religion (Greek and Roman religion)

Bryant, Megan E.

Oh my gods! a look-it-up guide to the gods of mythology. Franklin Watts 2009 128p il map (Mythlopedia) lib bdg $39; pa $13.95

Grades: 4 5 6 7 **292**

1. Gods and goddesses 2. Classical mythology

ISBN 978-1-60631-026-7 lib bdg; 1-60631-026-7 lib bdg; 978-1-60631-058-8 pa; 1-60631-058-5 pa

LC 2009-17169

Presents a guide to Greek mythology, providing profiles of gods and goddesses along with information on monsters, heroes, and the underworld.

"The book is organized around entries on major gods and titans, each with vital stats and a Top 10 Things to Know about Me, followed by a few highlights from their lore and sidebars that delve into their cultural relevance. Illustrations abound, from embellished stock images to original cartoons, and the pastel-heavy color scheme may entice readers otherwise resistant to the grays and ivories that tend to dominate classicism." Booklist

Includes glossary and bibliographical references

She's all that! a look-it-up guide to the goddesses of mythology. Franklin Watts 2009 128p il map (Mythlopedia) lib bdg $39; pa $13.95

Grades: 4 5 6 7 **292**

1. Gods and goddesses 2. Classical mythology

ISBN 978-1-60631-027-4 lib bdg; 1-60631-027-5 lib bdg; 978-1-60631-059-5 pa; 1-60631-059-3 pa

LC 2009-17168

Presents a guide to Greek mythology, providing profiles of goddesses and the myths surrounding them.

This "spices things up with sassy artwork, a pastel color scheme, and an OMG sensibility. . . . Aside from the heaps of information coming from all angles on just about every page, . . . [this] book also contains a decent family tree, a rudimentary star chart, and lists of further reading. . . . For kids unconvinced that anything so old and gray could have any bearing on their lives, . . . [this provides] a feisty . . . guide to the many cultural references lingering from antiquity." Booklist

Includes glossary and bibliographical references

D'Aulaire, Ingri

D'Aulaire's Book of Greek myths. Doubleday 1962 192 p. il col il

Grades: 4 5 6 7 8 **292**

ISBN 9780385071086; 0385071086

LC 62015877

This illustrated collection of Greek myths "includes mighty Zeus with his fistful of thunderbolts; mischievous little Hermes; gray-eyed Athena, goddess of wisdom; Asclepius, the first physician; Orpheus and his beloved Euridice; [and] Helios the sun, crossing the heavens in his fiery chariot." (Publisher's note)

Daly, Kathleen N.

Greek and Roman mythology, A to Z; [by] Kathleen N. Daly; revised by Marian Rengel. 3rd ed.; Chelsea House Publishers 2009 162p il (Mythology A to Z) lib bdg $45

Grades: 8 9 10 11 12 **292**

1. Classical mythology

ISBN 978-1-60413-412-4; 1-60413-412-7

LC 2009-8243

First published 1992 by Facts on File

Alphabetically listed entries identify and explain the characters, events, important places, and other aspects of Greek and Roman mythology

"The format is accessible, making the book useful for school assignments, as well as enjoyable for general reading. Each entry provides a clear definition, and retells the stories associated with the character or place. The broad coverage, ample cross-references, and extensive index enable readers to recognize the many connections and interrelationships between characters and myths." SLJ [review of 1992 edition]

Includes bibliographical references

Fleischman, Paul

★ **Dateline** : Troy; [by] Paul Fleischman; collages by Gwen Frankfeldt & Glenn Morrow. new updated ed.; Candlewick Press 2006 80p il $18.99

Grades: 7 8 9 10 **292**

1. Trojan War

ISBN 978-0-7636-3083-6; 0-7636-3083-7

First published 1996

A retelling of the story of the Trojan War illustrated with collages featuring newspaper clippings of modern events from World War I through the Iraq War

Hamilton, Edith

Mythology; illustrated by Steele Savage. Little, Brown 1942 497p il $27.95; pa $13.95

Grades: 8 9 10 11 12 Adult **292**

1. Trojan War 2. Norse mythology 3. Gods and goddesses 4. Classical mythology 5. Perseus (Greek mythology) 6. Theseus (Greek mythology) 7. Odysseus (Greek mythology) 8. Argonauts (Greek mythology) 9. Aeneas (Legendary character) 10. Hercules (Legendary character)

ISBN 0-316-34114-2; 0-316-34151-7 pa

A retelling of Greek, Roman and Norse myths

McCaughrean, Geraldine

★ **Hercules**; retold by Geraldine McCaughrean. Cricket Books 2005 142p il (Heroes) $16.95

Grades: 5 6 7 8 **292**

1. Classical mythology 2. Hercules (Legendary character)

ISBN 978-0-8126-2737-4; 0-8126-2737-7

LC 2005004524

First published 2003 by Oxford University Press

This is a retelling of the twelve labors of Hercules including his battles with the Cretan Bull, the many-headed Hydra, the Nemean Lion, and the three-headed guardian of hell, Cerberus.

"This volume does a creditable job of making Hercules a dimensional character whose struggles against fate and the vindictiveness of the gods arouse readers' sympathy. . . . McCaughrean enlivens the familiar story with arresting imagery." SLJ

★ **Odysseus**; retold by Geraldine McCaughrean. Cricket Books 2004 148p il (Heroes) $16.95

Grades: 5 6 7 8 292

1. Classical mythology 2. Odysseus (Greek mythology)
ISBN 978-0-8126-2721-3; 0-8126-2721-0

LC 2004-10734

"With mounting suspense, wild action, and simple, rhythmic prose, this dramatic retelling of Homer's classic makes a gripping read-aloud as well as an exciting introduction to the story." Booklist

★ **Perseus**; retold by Geraldine McCaughrean. Cricket Books 2005 118p il (Heroes) $16.95
Grades: 5 6 7 8 292

1. Classical mythology 2. Perseus (Greek mythology)
ISBN 978-0-8126-2735-0; 0-8126-2735-0

This "makes a thrilling read-aloud. . . . McCaughrean blends the colloquial and contemporary into the heroic quest." Booklist

Nardo, Don

The **Greenhaven** encyclopedia of Greek and Roman mythology; Don Nardo, author; Barbette Spaeth, consulting editor. Greenhaven Press 2002 304p il (Greenhaven encyclopedia of) lib bdg $76.20
Grades: 7 8 9 10 292

1. Classical mythology
ISBN 0-7377-0719-4

LC 2001-40864

This is an overview of classical mythology, its heroes, and its influence on the history of Western civilization

Includes bibliographical references

Otfinoski, Steven

All in the family; a look-it-up guide to the in-laws, outlaws, and offspring of mythology. F. Watts 2009 128p il (Mythlopedia) lib bdg $39; pa $13.95
Grades: 4 5 6 7 292

1. Classical mythology
ISBN 978-1-60631-025-0 lib bdg; 1-60631-025-9 lib bdg; 978-1-60631-057-1 pa; 1-60631-057-7 pa

LC 2009-20999

"Jam-packed with trivia, brief profiles, god and goddess relationships, stories, 'Top 10 Things to Know About Me' facts, and entertaining illustrations, this title explores 20 heroes and mortals of classic Greek mythology. The selections include the well-known Achilles, Heracles, Odysseus, and Pandora and the more obscure Meleager, Orion, Atalanta, and Bellerophon; each one is given lively treatment. . . . The lighthearted style and humorous collage and cartoon illustrations may draw even the most reluctant of readers. " SLJ

Includes glossary and bibliographical references

Rylant, Cynthia

The **beautiful** stories of life; six Greek myths, retold. illustrated by Carson Ellis. Harcourt 2009 71p il $16
Grades: 5 6 7 8 292

1. Classical mythology
ISBN 978-0-15-206184-5; 0-15-206184-3

LC 2007-34808

"Rylant retells the stories of Pandora, Persephone, Orpheus, Pygmalion, Narcissus, and Psyche in this trim, handsome book. Written in a modern style with an old-fashioned feel, the selections sit well with other titles in the genre. . . . Accompanied by full-page black-and-white illustrations and sprinkled with decorations, the whole package is nicely done." SLJ

Schomp, Virginia

The **ancient** Greeks; [by] Virginia Schomp. Marshall Cavendish Benchmark 2007 96p il map (Myths of the world) lib bdg $22.95
Grades: 6 7 8 9 292

1. Classical mythology 2. Greece -- Civilization
ISBN 978-0-7614-2547-2

LC 2006028375

"With [its] beautiful illustrations, high-quality production, and focus on source material, the [book] should whet the interest of readers." SLJ

Includes glossary and bibliographical references

Steer, Dugald

The **mythology** handbook; a course in ancient Greek myths. by Hestia Evans; edited by Dugald A. Steer and Clint Twist. Candlewick Press 2009 71p il map $12.99
Grades: 4 5 6 7 292

1. Classical mythology
ISBN 978-0-7636-4291-4

"This follow-up to Mythology (Candlewick, 2007) again uses the voice of a fictional 19th-century scholar. Here, Lady Hestia Evans offers a guide to elements of Greek myth for her two children, providing information in 'lessons' . . . with exercises based on each topic. Some of the activities encourage students to do further research . . . while others suggest that they draw new monsters, write hymns with the Muses' help, or design a new pentathlon for the Olympics. Mazes and a word search (using Greek letters) are also included. . . . The activities are engaging, and the illustrations of creatures and maps of the ancient world will add to the knowledge of even more experienced myth fans." SLJ

Turnbull, Ann

★ **Greek** myths; retold by Ann Turnbull; illustrated by Sarah Young. Candlewick Press 2011 165p il
Grades: 5 6 7 8 9 10 292

1. Classical mythology
ISBN 0-7636-5111-7; 978-0-7636-5111-4

LC 2010-39178

Turnbull divides sixteen Greek myths "under three headings: Earth, the Heavens, and the Underworld; Monsters and Heroes; Gods and Mortals. . . . Grades five to ten." (Bull Cent Child Books)

"Sixteen Greek myths . . . are retold here with stylistic grace well matched to beautiful visual presentation. . . . Turnbull narrates with . . . vibrancy. . . . Sarah Young's mixed-media artwork—regal, yet sensuous compositions in richly textured earthtones touch[ed] with gold—is sufficiently representational to assist younger readers with context clues, and sufficiently elegant and sophisticated to satisfy seasoned readers." Bull Cent Child Books

293 Germanic religion

Daly, Kathleen N.

Norse mythology A to Z; [by] Kathleen N. Daly; revised by Marian Rengel. 3rd ed.; Chelsea House 2009 128p il map (Mythology A to Z) lib bdg $45
Grades: 8 9 10 11 12 293

1. Reference books 2. Norse mythology -- Dictionaries
ISBN 978-1-60413-411-7; 1-60413-411-9

LC 2009-13338

First published 1991

Alphabetically listed entries identify and explain the characters, events, and important places of Norse mythology

Includes bibliographical references

294 Religions of Indic origin

Mann, Gurinder Singh

Buddhists, Hindus, and Sikhs in America; [by] Gurinder Singh Mann, Paul David Numrich & Raymond B. Williams. Oxford University Press 2001 158p il (Religion in American life) hardcover o.p. pa $12.95

Grades: 7 8 9 10 **294**

1. Sikhism 2. Buddhism 3. Hinduism 4. Asian Americans -- Religion

ISBN 0-19-512442-1; 0-19-533311-X pa

LC 2001-45151

Presents the basic tenets of these three Asian religions and discusses the religious history and experience of their practitioners after immigration to the United States

"Solid information, a large selection of historical and contemporary photographs, interesting readings from primary sources, and accounts from school-age Buddhists, Hindus, and Sikhs combine to make this is a valuable resource." Booklist

Includes bibliographical references

Ollhoff, Jim

Indian mythology. ABDO Pub. 2012 32 p. il map lib bdg $27.07

Grades: 5 6 7 8 **294**

1. Hinduism 2. Indic mythology 3. India -- Religion

ISBN 978-1-61714-722-7; 1-61714-722-2

LC 2010041628

'This book offers information about Indian mythology, answering questions such as "Who is Devi? What is Ganesha? Why are myths so important in our lives? Myths are a rich source of history. People use them to make sense of our world. Even before myths were written down, people told and retold the stories of the gods and goddesses of their homeland. Readers of Indian Mythology will learn the history of myths, as well as their deeper meaning." (Publisher's note) The book "introduces Brahma, Vishnu, Shiva, Kali, and other Hindu gods and goddesses while also discussing how the deities often took on different forms called avatars." (Booklist)

"Ollhoff writes in a clear and engaging fashion, presenting complex issues in a way that will be easy for youngsters to grasp. . . . The photographs and reproductions of art tie directly to the [text]." SLJ

294.3 Buddhism

Demi

★ **Buddha**. Holt & Co. 1996 un il $21.95

Grades: 4 5 6 **294.3**

1. Philosophers 2. Buddhist leaders

ISBN 0-8050-4203-2

LC 95-16906

Demi "uses clear, uncomplicated storytelling to present complex philosophical concepts. . . . The gilded illustrations (based, according to the jacket, on 'Indian, Chinese, Japanese, Burmese, and Indonesian paintings, sculptures, and sutra illustrations') are delicate, yet the colors and composition are bold, with central figures and action cascading beyond the careful borders." Bull Cent Child Books

★ The **Dalai** Lama; a biography of the Tibetan spiritual and political leader. Henry Holt & Co. 1998 un il $18.95

Grades: 4 5 6 7 **294.3**

1. Buddhism 2. Tibet (China) 3. Buddhist leaders 4. Political leaders 5. Nobel laureates for peace

ISBN 0-8050-5443-X

LC 97-30654

In this biography of the Buddhist spiritual leader, Demi "uses straightforward prose and fluid, eastern-influenced art—small pen-and-ink and watercolor images with fine, intricate detail. . . . Told with respect and devotion, this is an inspirational picture-book biography." Horn Book

Eckel, Malcolm David

Buddhism. Rosen Pub. 2010 112p il (Understanding religions) lib bdg $31.95

Grades: 7 8 9 10 **294.3**

1. Buddhism

ISBN 978-1-4358-5619-6; 1-4358-5619-8

LC 2009-10083

Subjects covered in this book include "buddhas and boddhisattvas, Zen meditation, Tantric scriptures, pilgrimage, temples, and festivals and rites." Publisher's note

Includes glossary and bibliographical references

Ganeri, Anita

★ **Buddhism**; [by] Anita Ganeri. World Almanac Library 2006 48p il map (Religions of the world) lib bdg $30.60

Grades: 5 6 7 8 **294.3**

1. Buddhism

ISBN 0-8368-5865-4

LC 2005041708

The author "presents a survey of Buddhist history, beliefs, sacred texts, festivals, and lifecycle events. . . . There is discussion of the art and folk literature associated with the religious tradition. Colorful photographs, illustrations, and art reproductions appear throughout." SLJ

Includes bibliographical references

Lee, Jeanne M.

I once was a monkey; stories Buddha told. Farrar, Straus & Giroux 1999 un il $16

Grades: 4 5 6 7 **294.3**

1. Jataka stories

ISBN 0-374-33548-6

LC 98-17651

A retelling of six Jatakas, or birth stories, which illustrate some of the central tenets of Buddha's teachings, such as compassion, honesty, and thinking clearly before acting

"The appealing character of the monkey will pull children into the tales, which convey lessons in a direct yet gentle way that is never preachy. The accompanying linocut illustrations are lovely." Booklist

Wangu, Madhu Bazaz

Buddhism; 4th ed.; Chelsea House 2009 144p il (World religions) $40

Grades: 7 8 9 10 11 12 **294.3**

1. Buddhism

ISBN 978-1-60413-105-5; 1-60413-105-5

LC 2008-51265

First published 1993 by Facts on File

This "tells the story of Buddhism's origins and its development into three major schools of thought—and presents the particular beliefs and practices of those schools of Buddhism. . . . [This] title explores the concept of the 'socially engaged Buddhist,' the growth and practice of Buddhism in America, and the recent revival of Buddhism in Asia." Publisher's note

Includes glossary and bibliographical references

Winston, Diana

★ **Wide** awake: a Buddhist guide for teens. Perigee Bk. 2003 290p pa $13.95

Grades: 7 8 9 10 11 12 **294.3**

1. Buddhism

ISBN 0-399-52897-0

LC 2002-192666

"Switching between anecdotes of her own journey in Buddhism and advice on how teens can apply the Buddha's teachings to their lives, Winston offers a personal and thoughtful introduction to Buddhist thought and practice." Booklist

294.5 Hinduism

Narayanan, Vasudha

Hinduism. Rosen Pub. 2010 112p il (Understanding religions) lib bdg $31.95

Grades: 7 8 9 10 **294.5**

1. Hinduism

ISBN 978-1-4358-5620-2; 1-4358-5620-1

LC 2009-11026

This book about Hinduism "discusses origins and historical development; aspects of the divine; sacred texts, persons, space, and time; ethical principles; death and the afterlife; and society and religion." SLJ

Includes glossary and bibliographical references

Nardo, Don

Understanding hinduism; By Don Nardo. ReferencePoint Press 2019 80 p. (hardback) $29.95

Grades: 8 9 10 11 12 **294.5**

1. Hinduism 2. Religions 3. Interfaith relations 4. Hinduism -- Rituals 5. Hinduism -- Doctrines 6. Hinduism -- Relations 7. Hinduism -- Customs and practices

ISBN 9781682824634

LC 2018017161

This book in the Understanding World Religions series, by Don Nardo, "reveals Hinduism's origins, beliefs, common practices, and the challenges its adherents face. Hindus worship many deities, including the sacred trinity (Brahma, Vishnu, and Shiva), but all are considered different sides of Brahman, the one god. Described also are the Four Aims of Hindu life, and beliefs in reincarnation and karma." (Booklist)

"This entry in the Understanding World Religions series reveals Hinduism's origins, beliefs, common practices, and the challenges its adherents face." (Booklist)

Includes bibliographical references and index

Plum-Ucci, Carol

Celebrate Diwali; [by] Carol Plum-Ucci. Enslow Publishers 2008 128p il map (Celebrate holidays) $31.93

Grades: 5 6 7 8 **294.5**

1. Divali

ISBN 978-0-7660-2778-7; 0-7660-2778-3

LC 2006028106

This describes the history, cultural significance, customs, symbols and celebrations around the world of the Hindu holiday of Diwali.

"Captioned photographs, maps, drawings, and sidebars combine with accessible text to present a thorough discussion of [Diwali]. . . . This . . . is a useful resource." Horn Book Guide

Includes glossary and bibliographical references

Rasamandala Das

★ **Hinduism**. World Almanac Library 2006 48p il map (Religions of the world) $30.60

Grades: 5 6 7 8 **294.5**

1. Hinduism

ISBN 0-8368-5867-0

Hinduism is "explored in an accessible introductory manner, including information on [its] history, teachings, religious practices, culture and lifestyle, and the [faith's role] in today's global society. Vibrant full-color photographs are appropriately placed within the [text]. Ideal for . . . school reports or for general interest." SLJ

Includes bibliographical references

Singh, Rina

Diwali; festival of lights. Rina Singh. Orca Book Publishers 2016 96 p. illustrations (chiefly color) (hardcover) $24.95

Grades: 5 6 7 8 **294.5**

1. Divali 2. Festivals

ISBN 1459810074; 9781459810075; 9781459810082; 9781459810099; 9781459815124

LC 2016931882

In this second book in the Orca Origins series, author Rina Singh "explores her Indian roots as she tells the Diwali stories, which remind us that eventually light will prevail over darkness. Enriched by personal stories and spiced with festive recipes, including two by acclaimed chef, Vikram Vij, 'Diwali' brings to life the holiday's traditions, food and rituals and takes you on a journey to see how this festival is celebrated around the world!" (Publisher's note)

"An exceptionally valuable resource." Kirkus

Includes bibliographical references and index.

294.6 Sikhism

Singh, Nikky-Guninder Kaur

Sikhism; 3rd ed.; Chelsea House 2009 144p il (World religions) $40

Grades: 7 8 9 10 11 12 **294.6**

1. Sikhism

ISBN 978-1-60413-114-7; 1-60413-114-4

LC 2008-29662

First published 1993 by Facts on File

This "describes the basic tenets of Sikhism, examines the recent move toward greater political independence within the Indian nation, and covers issues of cultural adaptation, persecution, and subsequent education now taking place in the West." Publisher's note

Includes glossary and bibliographical references

295 Zoroastrianism (Mazdaism, Parseeism)

Hartz, Paula

Zoroastrianism; by Paula R. Hartz. 3rd ed.; Chelsea House 2009 144p il (World religions) $40

Grades: 7 8 9 10 11 12 **295**

1. Zoroastrianism

ISBN 978-1-60413-116-1; 1-60413-116-0

LC 2008-35811

First published 1999 by Facts on File

This "analyzes how [Zoroastrianism] has a crucial place in religious history and continues to maintain a devoted following today." Publisher's note

Includes glossary and bibliographical references

296 Judaism

Buxbaum, Shelley M.

Jewish faith in America; {by} Shelley M. Buxbaum, Sara E. Karesh. Facts on File 2003 128p il (Faith in America) $30

Grades: 7 8 9 10 **296**

1. Judaism 2. Jews -- United States 3. United States -- Ethnic relations

ISBN 0-8160-4986-6

LC 2002-29392

"Thoroughly researched and heavily illustrated." Libr Media Connect

Includes glossary and bibliographical references

Ehrlich, Carl S.

Judaism. Rosen Pub. 2010 112p il (Understanding religions) lib bdg $31.95

Grades: 7 8 9 10 **296**

1. Judaism

ISBN 978-1-4358-5622-6; 1-4358-5622-8

LC 2009-10055

This "book provides students with an overview of the great religious tradition of Judaism. Readers learn about the covenant with God, the Bible, the Mishnah, and the Talmud. They also read about sects, messianic movements, mysticism, and the Kabbalah. Rabbinical systems of law and custom are covered as are various principles and practices, holy days, and contemporary movements in Judaism." Publisher's note

Includes glossary and bibliographical references

Morrison, M. A.

Judaism; by Martha A. Morrison and Stephen F. Brown. 4th ed.; Chelsea House 2009 144p il (World religions) $40

Grades: 7 8 9 10 11 12 **296**

1. Judaism

ISBN 978-1-60413-110-9; 1-60413-110-1

LC 2008-29657

First published 1991 by Facts on File under the authorship of Fay Carol Gates

This "presents the basic beliefs of the Jewish religious heritage and highlights the different manners in which these traditions can be upheld. Both Orthodox Judaism and the religious practices and movements within Reformed Judaism, including Reform Judaism, Conservative Judaism, and Reconstructionist Judaism, are explored." Publisher's note

Includes glossary and bibliographical references

The **Oxford** dictionary of the Jewish religion; editor in chief, Adele Berlin. 2nd ed. Oxford University Press 2011 xxiv, 934 p.p (hardcover) $195

Grades: 8 9 10 11 12 Adult **296**

1. Judaism -- Dictionaries 2. Judaism -- Encyclopedias

ISBN 0199730040; 9780199730049; 9780199759279

LC 2010035774

This book, by Maxine Grossman, edited by Adele Berlin, presents an updated, second edition of its original 1997 publication. It "focuses on recent and changing rituals in the Jewish community. . . . Nearly 200 internationally renowned scholars have created a new edition that incorporates updated bibliographies, biographies of 20th-century individuals who have shaped the recent thought and history of Judaism, and an index with alternate spellings of Hebrew terms." (Publisher's note)

Includes bibliographical references and index.

Rosinsky, Natalie M.

Judaism. Compass Point Books 2009 48p il map (World religions) lib bdg $27.99

Grades: 5 6 7 8 **296**

1. Judaism

ISBN 978-0-7565-4240-5 lib bdg; 0-7565-4240-5 lib bdg

LC 2009-15813

"The colorful, attractive layout includes high-quality reproductions of photographs, maps, and paintings. Students who are new to religious studies, as well as those doing reports, will find that this . . . meets their needs." SLJ

Includes glossary and bibliographical references

296.4 Traditions, rites, public services

Kimmel, Eric A.

★ **Wonders** and miracles; a Passover companion. illustrated with art spanning three thousand years; written and compiled by Eric A. Kimmel. Scholastic Press 2004 136p il $18.95

Grades: 4 5 6 7 **296.4**

1. Passover

ISBN 0-439-07175-5

LC 2002-4732

Presents the steps performed in a traditional Passover Seder, plus stories, songs, poetry, and pictures that celebrate the historical significance of this holiday to Jews all over the world.

"The marvelous selection of art—paintings, photographs, artifacts, and illustrations from historical Haggadahs—illuminates each step in the service. . . . Both the presentation of information and the overall design attest to the careful and loving attention given to every detail. This inviting, handsome, and informative compendium should find a place of honor in every library." SLJ

Includes bibliographical references

Metter, Bert

Bar mitzvah, bat mitzvah; the ceremony, the party, and how the day came to be. by Bert Metter; illustrated by Joan Reilly. Clarion Books 2007 un il $16; pa $5.95

Grades: 4 5 6 7 **296.4**

1. Bar mitzvah 2. Bat mitzvah

ISBN 978-0-618-76772-4; 0-618-76772-X; 978-0-618-76773-1 pa; 0-618-76773-8 pa

LC 2006032942

The author "describes a typical ceremony and explains how this custom began for boys during the Middle Ages and how it was adapted for girls beginning in 1922. He also discusses the recent custom of adult bar and bat mitzvahs and celebratory parties. The writing is clear and concise; ink illustrations . . . help break up the text." Booklist

Includes bibliographical references

297 Islam, Babism, Bahai Faith

Ashkar, Michael

Islam; Michael Ashkar. Mason Crest 2017 112 p. (hc) $25.95

Grades: 5 6 7 8 **297**

1. Islam 2. Religions 3. Islam -- Essence, genius, nature

ISBN 9781422238196

LC 2016048088

This book in the Major World Religions series, by Michael Ashkar, "discusses the origins of Islam, the major sects that follow the faith, important religious centers such as Mecca and Medina, and the elemental religious practices that unite all members of the umma, or Islamic community." (Publisher's note)

Includes bibliographical references (pages 105-106) and index

Aslan, Reza, 1972-

No god but God; the origins and evolution of Islam. Delacorte Press 2011 166p $16.99; lib bdg $19.99

Grades: 7 8 9 10 **297**

1. Islam -- History

ISBN 0-385-73975-3; 0-385-90805-9 lib bdg; 978-0-385-73975-7; 978-0-385-90805-4 lib bdg

LC 2010020408

Adaptation of: No god but God: the origins, evolution, and future of Islam, published 2006 by Random House for adults

"Packing in a formidable amount of research, legend, and critical analysis, Aslan condenses his adult book of the same name to create a concise introduction to Islam. By breaking up chapters with clear subheadings, maintaining a conversational tone, and incorporating numerous anecdotes that both inform and entertain, Aslan makes 15 centuries of religious history digestible without oversimplifying complex material. . . . This welcome addition to Islamic studies provides a valuable context for reflection about the origins of issues facing Muslims and their neighbors today." Publ Wkly

Barnard, Bryn

★ The **genius** of Islam; how Muslims made the modern world. Alfred A. Knopf 2011 37p il map $17.99; lib bdg $20.99

Grades: 4 5 6 7 **297**

1. Islamic civilization 2. Islam -- History

ISBN 978-0-375-84072-2; 0-375-84072-9; 978-0-375-94072-9 lib bdg; 0-375-94072-3 lib bdg

LC 2010-12777

This is a "concise and eloquent exploration of the far-reaching influence of Islam over the centuries. Each spread is devoted to a different subject (writing, Arabic numerals, architecture, astronomy, agriculture), while captioned spot art homes in on specific inventions and innovations (the zither, the astrolabe, advanced medical knowledge)." Publ Wkly

Includes bibliographical references

Demi

★ **Muhammad**; written and illustrated by Demi. Margaret K. McElderry Bks. 2003 un il $19.95

Grades: 4 5 6 7 **297**

1. Islam 2. Prophets 3. Islamic leaders 4. Writers on religion

ISBN 0-689-85264-9

LC 2002-2985

"With dramatic scenes extending past the borders of the intricately patterned frames, the art will be a continual source of interest for young people. . . . [An] excellent retelling of the Prophet's life that combines beauty and scholarship." Booklist

Includes bibliographical references

Gordon, Matthew

Islam; by Matthew S. Gordon. 4th ed. Chelsea House 2009 144 p. col. ill., map (World religions) (library) $40.00

Grades: 7 8 9 10 11 12 **297**

1. Islam

ISBN 978-1-60413-109-3; 1-60413-109-8

LC 2008035810

First published 1991 by Facts on File

This describes the founding of Islam and its spread, The Koran, Hadith, and Islamic law, branches of Islam and their basic beliefs, Muslim customs and rituals, the pattern of Islamic life, and the place of Islam in the modern world.

Includes bibliographical references (p. 138-139) and index.

Hafiz, Dilara

★ The **American** Muslim teenager's handbook; by Dilara Hafiz, Imran Hafiz, and Yasmine Hafiz. [new ed.]; Atheneum Books for Young Readers 2009 168p il pa $11.99

Grades: 7 8 9 10 11 12 **297**

1. Islam 2. Conduct of life 3. Muslims -- United States 4. Teenagers -- Religious life

ISBN 978-1-4169-8578-5; 1-4169-8578-6

A revised edition of the title first published 2007 by Acacia Pub.

"Casual, colloquial, joking, contemporary, and passionate, this interactive handbook by two Arizona teens and their mom talks about their faith, about what it is like to be both proud Americans and proud Muslims, and about misunderstandings and stereotypes. . . . There are also step-by-step guides on how to pray, how to read the Qur'an, and how to fast at Ramadan. Muslim and non-Muslim teens alike will be caught by the candor, the humor, and the call for interfaith dialogue and tolerance." Booklist

Includes bibliographical references

Illustrated dictionary of the Muslim world; [editor, Felicity Crowe and others] Marshall Cavendish Reference 2010 192p il (Muslim world) $85.64

Grades: 7 8 9 10 **297**

1. Reference books 2. Islam -- Dictionaries 3. Islamic civilization -- Dictionaries

ISBN 978-0-7614-7929-1; 0-7614-7929-5

LC 2010008613

Contains hundreds of short entries on Islamic concepts, religious practices, historical events and personalities, geographical places, and fact files of nations with large Muslim populations.

"Attractive trim on the pages, colorful fonts, quality illustrations, and framed (often illustrated) sideboxes create a pleasing layout. Excellent for assignments." SLJ

Includes glossary and bibliographical references

Islam in America; Laura K. Egendorf, book editor. Greenhaven Press 2006 112p (At issue) lib bdg $28.70; pa $19.95
Grades: 7 8 9 10 11 12 **297**
1. Islam 2. Muslims -- United States
ISBN 0-7377-2727-6 lib bdg; 0-7377-2728-4 pa
LC 2005046317

The selections in this collection "treat such subjects as whether American Muslims support terrorist groups and whether or not they experience discrimination. The pieces on African-American Muslims and the growing popularity of Islam among Hispanic Americans are particularly interesting." SLJ

Includes bibliographical references

Islamic beliefs, practices, and cultures. Marshall Cavendish Reference 2010 352p il (Muslim world) lib bdg $114.21
Grades: 7 8 9 10 **297**
1. Islamic civilization 2. Islam -- Customs and practices
ISBN 978-0-7614-7926-0; 0-7614-7926-0
LC 2010008611

"Attractive trim on the pages, colorful fonts, quality illustrations, and framed (often illustrated) sideboxes create a pleasing layout. Excellent for assignments." SLJ

Luxenberg, Alan

Radical Islam. Mason Crest 2009 64p il (World of Islam) lib bdg $22.95
Grades: 7 8 9 10 11 12 **297**
1. Islam 2. Radicalism
ISBN 978-1-4222-0536-5 lib bdg; 1-4222-0536-3 lib bdg

Luxenberg "describes Islam's historical background, its rise to world prominence, its decline, the factions that have arisen, and the move of some toward radicalism. . . . In examing specific radical arms (and their leaders), the book suggests ways for U.S. leaders to interpret intentions and future implications. . . . The book . . . would be a good addition for world-religion collections." Booklist

Includes glossary and bibliographical references

Modern Muslim societies. Marshall Cavendish Reference 2010 416p il (Muslim world) lib bdg $114.21
Grades: 7 8 9 10 **297**
1. Islam -- Customs and practices
ISBN 978-0-7614-7927-7; 0-7614-7927-9
LC 2010008612

"Attractive trim on the pages, colorful fonts, quality illustrations, and framed (often illustrated) sideboxes create a pleasing layout. Excellent for assignments." SLJ

Nardo, Don

The **birth** of Islam. Morgan Reynolds Pub. 2011 112p (World religions and beliefs) lib bdg $28.95
Grades: 7 8 9 10 **297**
1. Islamic civilization 2. Islam -- History
ISBN 978-1-59935-146-9; 1-59935-146-3
LC 2010038442

This covers the beginnings of Islam "in an impartial way. The [context] in which the [religion] developed [is] explained, offering insight into how [Islam] came to be and introducing major concepts the [religion]." SLJ

Includes glossary and bibliographical references

297.09 History, geographic treatment, biography

Allman, Toney

The **rise** of Islam; Toney Allman. ReferencePoint Press, Inc. 2015 96 p. (Understanding world history series) (hardback) $28.95
Grades: 7 8 9 10 11 12 **297.09**
1. Islam -- History 2. Islamic civilization 3. Islam -- Origin
ISBN 1601527446; 9781601527448
LC 2014006453

This book, by Toney Allman, part of the "Understanding World History" series, describes how "Islam, as a faith and as a political power, rose to world dominance in an astoundingly brief timespan--little more than one hundred years. From the fascinating events of Muhammad's life to the founding of a vast empire, the rise of Islam is the story of a people, a vibrant culture, and the growth of a civilization." (Publisher's note)

"This latest addition to the Understanding World History series gives a thorough, well-researched background of Islam, from the birth and youth of Muhammad and his call from God to the religion's golden age (750–1258 CE). The introductory time line of important events during the rise of Islam sets the stage for events discussed in the text. . . . Detailed chapter source notes and an extensive list of additional books and websites give young researchers alternate access points to complete their projects on Muhammad or Islam—hot topics that show no signs of cooling down." Booklist

Includes bibliographical references and index

297.1 Islam

The **meaning** of the glorious Koran; an explanatory translation by Marmaduke Pickthall; with an introduction by William Montgomery Watt. A.A. Knopf 1992 xxiv, 693p il $22
Grades: 7 8 9 10 11 12 Adult **297.1**
1. Qur'an
ISBN 0-679-41736-2; 978-0-679-41736-1
LC 92-52928

This translation first published 1930

"The sacred scripture of Islam, regarded by Muslims as the Word of God, and except in sura I.—which is a prayer to God—and some few passages in which Muhammad or the angels speak in the first person, the speaker throughout is God." Ency Britannica

The **Qur'an;** English translation and parallel Arabic text. translated, with an introduction and notes, by M.A.S. Abdel Haleem. Oxford University Press 2010 xxxix, 624 p.p maps (hardcover) $45
Grades: 7 8 9 10 11 12 Adult **297.1**
1. Qur'an
ISBN 019957071X; 9780199570713
LC 2010281328

This book, by M. A. S. Abdel Haleem, offers an English translation of the Qur'an with Arab text presented in parallel. "This translation is written in contemporary language . . . , set page-for-page against the most widespread traditional calligraphic Arabic text. . . . Furthermore, Haleem includes notes that explain geographical, historical, and personal allusions as well as an index in which Qur'anic material is arranged into topics for easy reference." (Publisher's note)

"Because the Koran stresses its Arabic nature, devout Muslims believe that only an Arabic version is the actual Koran and insist that its translation cannot be more than an approximate interpretation. . . Yet anyone wishing to understand Islamic civilization and global affairs may find this Koran very useful. . . . Highly recommended." LJ

Includes bibliographical references and index

297.3 Islamic worship

Jeffrey, Laura S.

Celebrate Ramadan; [by] Laura S. Jeffrey. Enslow Publishers 2007 112p il (Celebrate holidays) lib bdg $31.93

Grades: 5 6 7 8 **297.3**

1. Islam 2. Ramadan 3. Id al-Adha

ISBN 978-0-7660-2774-9 lib bdg; 0-7660-2774-0 lib bdg

LC 2006028107

"This book opens by introducing a contemporary Muslim, Bushra, who celebrated Ramadan as a girl growing up in England [and] later immigrated to the United States. . . . An informative chapter surveys the history, beliefs, and practices of Islam. . . . The remainder of the book offers a detailed discussion of Ramadan, prayer, and spiritual awareness, and of I'Id al Fitr. . . . Punctuated by sidebars and illustrated with color photos, this clearly written book offers a good overview of how the holidays of Islam are celebrated." Booklist

Includes glossary and bibliographical references

297.9 Babism and Bahai Faith

Hartz, Paula

Baha'i Faith; 3rd ed.; Chelsea House 2009 144p il (World religions) $40

Grades: 7 8 9 10 11 12 **297.9**

1. Bahai Faith

ISBN 978-1-60413-104-8; 1-60413-104-7

LC 2008043045

First published 2002 by Facts on File

This "explores all aspects of the Baha'i faith, from the original teachings of its founder, Baha'u'llah, to the modern-day communities that exist in 236 countries and territories throughout the world." Publisher's note

Includes glossary and bibliographical references

299 Religions not provided for elsewhere

Harpur, James

Celtic myth; a treasury of legends, art, and history. [by] James Harpur. M.E. Sharpe 2008 96p il (The world of mythology) $35.95

Grades: 8 9 10 11 12 **299**

1. Celtic mythology 2. Celtic civilization

ISBN 978-0-7656-8102-7

LC 2007006015

"With lots of heroic adventures and exciting, sometimes gruesome detail, Harpur retells stories of the Irish and Welsh Celts and weaves in facts about their culture and the history of their struggle for dominence. The dense text is broken up with beautiful, color images on every page, including paintings and photos of the settings, sculptures, weapons, and other artifacts." Booklist

Includes glossary and bibliographical references

Matson, Gienna

Celtic mythology A to Z; [by] Gienna Matson. Facts on File 2004 114p il map (Mythology A to Z) $40

Grades: 8 9 10 11 12 Adult **299**

1. Celtic mythology

ISBN 0-8160-4890-8

LC 2004-47111

"This title is an excellent introduction to the mythology of Celtic cultures and should be in most public and school libraries." Booklist

Includes bibliographical references

299.31 Ancient Egyptian Religion

Napoli, Donna Jo, 1948-

★ **Treasury** of Egyptian Mythology; Classic Stories of Gods, Goddesses, Monsters & Mortals. by Donna Jo Napoli and illustrated by Christina Balit. National Geographic Children's books 2013 192 p. $24.95

Grades: 3 4 5 6 **299.31**

1. Egyptian mythology 2. Gods and goddesses

ISBN 1426313802; 9781426313806

Author Donna Jo Napoli presents a "tableau of Egyptian myths, including those of pharaohs, queens, the boisterous Sun God Ra, and legendary creatures like the Sphinx. The stories are embellished with sidebars that provide historical, cultural, and geographic context and a mapping feature that adds to the fun and fascination. Resource notes and ample back matter direct readers to discover more about ancient Egypt." (Publisher's note)

299.5 Religions of East and Southeast Asian origin

Demi

★ The **legend** of Lao Tzu and the Tao te ching. Margaret K. McElderry Books 2007 un il $21.99

Grades: 4 5 6 7 **299.5**

1. Taoism 2. Philosophers

ISBN 1-4169-1206-1; 978-1-4169-1206-4

LC 2005029695

"This is the legend of Lao Tzu . . . who may or may not have founded Taoism, one of the greatest religions of the world. Demi's elegant picture-book introduction to the legendary Chinese philosopher . . . combines nuggets of his purported life with 20 verses from the Tao Te Ching. . . . The narrative and graceful paintings are contained in a gold circular frame on each parchment shaded page." SLJ

Hartz, Paula

Daoism; by Paula R. Hartz. 3rd ed.; Chelsea House 2009 144p il (World religions) $40

Grades: 7 8 9 10 11 12 **299.5**

1. Taoism

ISBN 978-1-60413-115-4; 1-60413-115-2

LC 2008-35809

First published 1993 by Facts on File with title: Taoism

This "traces the history of Daoism and explains its basic thoughts, traditions, and practices. It also details the Daoist movement worldwide and how the limitations of consumerism are leading a younger generation to search for their own spiritual harmony." Publisher's note

Includes glossary and bibliographical references

Shinto; by Paula R. Hartz. 3rd ed.; Chelsea House 2009 144p il (World religions) $40
Grades: 7 8 9 10 11 12 **299.5**
1. Shinto
ISBN 978-1-60413-113-0; 1-60413-113-6
LC 2008-29661
First published 1997 by Facts on File
This "examines the basic tenets of Shinto, its evolution in response to other religious influences, and how the original Shinto religion—rooted in an agrarian society—survives in contemporary Japan." Publisher's note
Includes glossary and bibliographical references

Kallen, Stuart A.
Shinto. Lucent Bks. 2002 128p il map (Religions of the world) lib bdg $27.45
Grades: 6 7 8 9 **299.5**
1. Shinto
ISBN 1-56006-988-0
LC 2001-6120
Discusses historical origins, the teachings, practices, and the spread of Shinto into modern times
Includes glossary and bibliographical references

Levin, Judith
Japanese mythology; [by] Judith Levin. The Rosen Pub. Group 2008 64p il map (Mythology around the world) $29.95
Grades: 5 6 7 8 **299.5**
1. Shinto 2. Buddhism 3. Japanese mythology 4. Japan -- Civilization
ISBN 978-1-4042-0736-3; 1-4042-0736-8
LC 2005035279
This "presents not only an introduction to Shinto and Buddhist beliefs, but also Japanese history and mythology in general. . . . The most remarkable part of [this book] . . . is the respect [it shows] for the mythological customs, treating them throughout with the same care that writers of books on major religions might offer. The illustrations show both ancient and modern incarnations of the deities and heroes." SLJ
Includes glossary and bibliographical references

Roberts, Jeremy
Chinese mythology A to Z; 2nd ed.; Chelsea House 2009 172p il (Mythology A to Z) lib bdg $45
Grades: 8 9 10 11 12 **299.5**
1. Chinese mythology 2. China -- Religion
ISBN 978-1-60413-436-0; 1-60413-436-4
LC 2009-10176
First published 2004
"Coverage includes: Buddhist deities and legendary characters; animal stories, such as the fox legends; important locations, such as shrines and sacred places; [and] allegorical figures, such as the Jade Emperor, the Rain Master, and the Lord of the Granary." Publisher's note
Includes bibliographical references

299.6 Religions originating among Black Africans and people of Black African descent

Lugira, Aloysius Muzzanganda
African traditional religion; by Aloysius M. Lugira. 3rd ed.; Chelsea House 2009 144p il map (World religions) $40
Grades: 7 8 9 10 11 12 **299.6**
1. Africa -- Religion
ISBN 978-1-60413-103-1; 1-60413-103-9
LC 2008-51188
First published 1999 by Facts on File with title: African religion
"The African continent is home to more than 6,000 different ethnic and cultural groups, each with its own religious traditions. Yet these many traditions have much in common. . . . [This book] offers a . . . perspective on the beliefs that are a permanent part of Africa's history and future." Publisher's note
Includes glossary and bibliographical references

Lynch, Patricia Ann
African mythology, A to Z; revised by Jeremy Roberts. 2nd ed.; Chelsea House 2010 xxiv, 149p il map (Mythology A to Z) lib bdg $45
Grades: 8 9 10 11 12 **299.6**
1. African mythology 2. Africa -- Religion
ISBN 978-1-60413-415-5; 1-60413-415-1
LC 2009-33612
First published 2004
This is a "reference to the deities, places, events, animals, beliefs, and other subjects that appear in the myths of various African peoples." Publisher's note
Includes bibliographical references

299.7 Religions of North American native origin

Hartz, Paula
Native American religions; [by] Paula R. Hartz. 3rd ed.; Chelsea House 2009 144p il (World religions) $40
Grades: 7 8 9 10 11 12 **299.7**
1. Native Americans -- Religion
ISBN 978-1-60413-111-6; 1-60413-111-X
LC 2008051197
First published 1997 by Facts on File
This "presents the history of the Native American religions, starting from their roots as tribal religions, and then details the detrimental effects of European colonization, the annihilation of the Native Americans that threatened the religions, and their sudden restoration in the 20th century." Publisher's note
Includes glossary and bibliographical references

Martin, Joel
★ **Native** American religion. Oxford University Press 1999 157p il (Religion in American life) $28
Grades: 7 8 9 10 **299.7**
1. Native Americans -- Religion
ISBN 0-19-511035-8
LC 98-50155
An "examination of religious life and practices from ancient times through the Colonial period and the Western Expansion, and into the 20th century. Martin acknowledges the importance of religion in all aspects of Native American daily life and explores some of the differences among the various cultures. He also addresses the impact of the arrival of Europeans on spiritual life." SLJ
Includes bibliographical references

300 SOCIAL SCIENCES

ProQuest Statistical Abstract of the United States; The National Data Book. ProQuest. Rowman & Littlefield $199
Grades: 8 9 10 11 12 Adult **300**
1. United States -- Statistics
"The Statistical Abstract of the United States has provided a statistical portrait of social, political, demographic and economic conditions of America since 1878. " (Publisher's note)

302.14 Social Participation

Marcovitz, Hal
Teens and volunteerism; Hal Marcovitz. 2nd edition Mason Crest Publishers 2014 112 p. color illustrations (hc) $24.95
Grades: 7 8 9 10 11 **302.14**
1. Volunteer work 2. Teenagers -- United States 3. Teenage volunteers in social service -- United States
ISBN 1422229602; 9781422229606
LC 2013007185
In this book, by Hal Marcovitz, a "recent report showed that each year an estimated 13 million teenagers donate more than 2.4 billion hours of their time to charitable causes, and the Gallup Youth Survey has found that roughly one-third of all teens participate in volunteer work. This volume examines the opportunities young people have for volunteering, and explores the issue of school-mandated community service." (Publisher's note)
"All of the books are well documented. This attention to detail makes them solid additions to libraries, particularly those with active debate or speech units in their curriculum." SLJ
Includes bibliographical references and index

302.23 Media (Means of communication)

Mass media; Margaret Haerens and Lynn M. Zott, book editors. Greenhaven Press 2014 208 p. ill. (chiefly col.) (Opposing viewpoints)
Grades: 8 9 10 11 12 **302.23**
1. Mass media
ISBN 0737766603; 9780737766608
LC 2013032063
Replaces 2010 edition
This book "addresses the role of the news media, examines the issue of media bias, explores the impact of media on society, and speculates on the future of mass media." (Publisher's note)

Media bias; Ebonie Ledbetter, book editor. Greenhaven Press 2015 153 p. color illustrations (Introducing issues with opposing viewpoints) (hardcover) $42
Grades: 6 7 8 9 10 **302.23**
1. Mass media 2. Prejudices 3. Journalism -- Objectivity 4. Mass media -- Objectivity -- United States
ISBN 0737772360; 9780737772364
LC 2014035143
This book, edited by Ebonie Ledbetter, part of the "Introducing Issues with Opposing Viewpoints" series, "examines the facets of media bias: is it real; does it matter; is it polarized into liberal and conservative issues; does big business play a part; and how does it affect society as a whole?" (Publisher's note)
Includes bibliographical references and index

Rojas, Meridith Valiando
Selfie made; your ultimate guide to social media stardom. Meridith Valiando Rojas. Wednesday Books 2018 260 p. (hardback) $19.99
Grades: 8 9 10 11 12 **302.23**
1. Social media 2. Internet industry 3. New business enterprises
ISBN 9781250196750; 9781250196743
LC 2018018517
This book, by Meridith Valiando Rojas, "is a one-of-a-kind guide to creating a digital identity, finding an audience, and building a powerful brand--your own!--on the Internet. Whether you want to be in front of or behind the camera, produce click-worthy content or start your own business, this book is the place to begin. . . . This collection of . . . professional advice . . . and behind-the-screen secrets, will give you everything you need for your social media toolkit." (Publisher's note)

Rowell, Rebecca
Social media; like it or leave it. Rebecca Rowell. Compass Point Books, a Capstone imprint 2015 30 p. (Perspectives flip books: issues) (hardcover : alk. paper) $33.32
Grades: 6 7 8 9 10 **302.23**
1. Internet -- Social aspects 2. Social media
ISBN 0756549949; 9780756549947; 9780756550240; 9780756550479
LC 2014026596
This book, by Rebecca Rowell, is an entry of the "Perspectives flip books: issues" series exploring social media. "Perspectives Flip Books are like two books in one: Start from one end and learn why people are logging off. Then flip it over and discover why others believe responsible social media use can be beneficial. Critical thinking questions help you analyze both perspectives and form your own opinions about the issue." (Publisher's note)
"This cleverly designed Perspectives Flip Book shows the pros and cons of social media . . . students will likely find this book a helpful guide to understanding and safely using this exciting technology." Booklist
Includes bibliographical references

302.3 Social interaction within groups

Bullying; Beth Rosenthal, book editor. Greenhaven Press 2008 120p il (Introducing issues with opposing viewpoints) lib bdg $33.70
Grades: 7 8 9 10 **302.3**
1. Bullies
ISBN 978-0-7377-3801-8; 0-7377-3801-4
LC 2007-32382
"Topics covered in this book range from the causes of bullying, what role society plays in encouraging bullying, the roles of TV and/or video games in violence and bullying, the responsibility of parents, the value of anti-bullying programs, and the ways that the behavior can be reduced. . . . Articles are presented in a pro/con format; 'active reading' questions preface each viewpoint and are designed to help students focus on the main points and to read carefully. Full-color photos and other graphics appear throughout." SLJ
Includes bibliographical references

Dear bully; seventy authors tell their stories. edited by Carrie Jones and Megan Kelley Hall. HarperTeen 2011 369p
Grades: 7 8 9 10 11 12 **302.3**
1. Bullies
ISBN 9780062060983; 9780062060976
LC 2011010166

In this book, edited Megan Kelley Hall and Carrie Jones, "top authors for teens and young people come together to share their stories about bullying--as bystanders, as victims, and as the bullies themselves. . . . For those working to support social and emotional learning and anti-bullying programs, 'Dear Bully' can help foster reflection and empathy. " (Publisher's note)

"In brief, true stories about bullying victims, perpetrators, and bystanders, 70 children's authors look back at what was often the hell of growing up, especially in junior high. . . . This timely collection is an excellent resource, especially for group discussion." Booklist

DiPiazza, Francesca Davis

Friend me! six hundred years of social networking in America. by Francesca Davis DiPiazza. Twenty-First Century Books 2012 112 p.
Grades: 6 7 8 9 **302.3**
1. Social networking -- History 2. Social groups -- United States -- History 3. Community life -- United States -- History 4. United States -- Social life and customs -- History
ISBN 0761358692; 9780761358695
LC 2011021268

This book's title "makes [it] appear to be about the recent phenomena of electronic social networks. However, the subtitle is a clue that the scope includes so much more. The whole of the American history of socializing is covered, beginning with the Iroquois and their method of weaving beads into wampum belts. Early religious groups, colonial coffeehouses, broadsides, secret gatherings of slaves, circuit riders, telegraphs, mail orders, and groups such as the YMCA and NAACP are profiled as examples of social networking. Today's online communities (Facebook, Twitter, blogs, e-mail, etc.) are touched upon with the supposition that face-to-face socializing is still important." (Booklist)

Includes bibliographical references and index

Ellis, Deborah

★ **We** want you to know; kids talk about bullying. Coteau Books 2010 120p il $19.95; pa $15.95
Grades: 5 6 7 8 9 10 **302.3**
1. Bullies
ISBN 978-1-55050-417-0; 1-55050-417-7; 978-1-55050-463-7 pa; 1-55050-463-0

"As part of her work with an anti-bullying campaign in her local Canadian community, Ellis interviewed young people between the ages of 9 and 19 about their experiences. In honest, straightforward prose, she shares their stories, many as targets and some as perpetrators or bystanders. . . . Each story is written from the first-person point of view, some with real names and photos, providing an intimacy and immediacy that are critical with these kinds of issues. Readers will find at least one or two stories they can relate to, and educators should be able to use many of the narratives to jumpstart conversation." SLJ

Includes bibliographical references

Hillstrom, Laurie Collier

Online social networks. Lucent Books 2010 96p il (Technology 360) $32.45
Grades: 8 9 10 11 12 **302.3**
1. Online social networks
ISBN 978-1-4205-0167-4; 1-4205-0167-4
LC 2009045044

This book explores "the early development and advances of [online social network] technology, its impact on society both positive and negative, and the importance it plays in our lives. . . . [It] begins with the history of the Internet. It explains the early purpose of the ARPANET, its expansion, the changes from text-based to the graphic interface of the World Wide Web, email communication, the features of some of the first social sites, and the differentiating characteristics of MySpace, Facebook, and Twitter. . . . Numerous color photos, diagrams, 'Bits & Bytes' boxes as well as many other additional text boxes create appeal and provide beneficial informative and complementary material to aid in understanding the technical details of the [text]." SLJ

Includes glossary and bibliographical references

Kevorkian, Meline

101 facts about bullying; what everyone should know. [by] Meline Kevorkian and Robin D'Antona. Rowman & Littlefield Pub. 2008 148p $32.95
Grades: Adult Professional **302.3**
1. Bullies
ISBN 9781578868964; 978-1-57886-849-0; 1-57886-849-1

"A user-friendly, accessible, and well-organized resource. . . . The format will lend itself well to group discussions and give teachers and others who work with young people a solid basis upon which to explore the issues surrounding this prevalent problem." SLJ

Leavitt, Amie Jane

Combatting Toxic Online Communities; Amie Jane Leavitt. Rosen Publishing 2016 48 p. (Combatting shaming and toxic communities)
Grades: 6 7 8 9 10 **302.3**
1. Bullies 2. Internet 3. Social networking 4. Internet and children 5. Internet and teenagers
ISBN 9781508171171

"The emergence of the Internet and social media has made it easier than ever to be part of a community. But what happens when those communities turn toxic? The anonymity and viral nature of modern technology can sometimes turn individuals into a target, a single comment or photo can now draw the judgment or ire of thousands within the Internet community." (Publisher's note)

Lusted, Marcia Amidon

Social networking: MySpace, Facebook, & Twitter. ABDO Pub. Co. 2011 112p il (Technology pioneers) lib bdg $34.22
Grades: 5 6 7 8 **302.3**
1. Online social networks 2. Facebook Inc. 3. MySpace, Inc. 4. Twitter, Inc.
ISBN 978-1-61714-811-8 lib bdg; 1-61714-811-3 lib bdg; 978-1-61758-969-0 e-book
LC 2010037885

This is an introduction to social networking sites, MySpace, Facebook, and Twitter.

"Written in a clear, linear fashion, this series offers vivid, well-researched details about the development of technological advancements considered essential in today's society. . . . Readers who are interested in technology and inventions will be thoroughly engrossed." SLJ

Includes glossary and bibliographical references

Schwartz, Heather E.

Safe social networking; by Heather E. Schwartz. Capstone Press 2013 32 p. col. ill. (Fact finders. Tech safety smarts) (library) $26.65

Grades: 4 5 6 7 **302.3**

1. Internet security 2. Online social networks 3. Social networking 4. Social networks 5. Internet -- Security measures 6. Online social networks -- Security measures

ISBN 1429699434; 9781429699433; 9781620658024

LC 2012026027

This children's resource book, by Heather E. Schwartz, is part of the publisher's "Fact Finders" series, providing guidance for young children to safely use and navigate online social media. "If a strange person asks to be your online friend, do you know what to do? . . . This book is here to help! Learn tech-savvy ways to keep your social networking sites safe sites without taking away all the fun!" (Publisher's note)

Includes bibliographical references (p. 31) and index.

Shapiro, Ouisie

Bullying and me; schoolyard stories. illustrated by Steven Vote. Albert Whitman & Company 2010 un il $16.99

Grades: 4 5 6 7 **302.3**

1. Bullies

ISBN 978-0-8075-0921-0; 0-8075-0921-3

LC 2010000754

"Thirteen individuals, including some adults, who have been bullied at school share their painful experiences. . . . Vote's full-color portraits sensitively depict the faces at the receiving end of abuse. . . . An educational psychologist specifically addresses each individual's dilemma, but the book's strength lies in the honestly conveyed through the personal stories." Publ Wkly

Solomon, Laura

Doing social media so it matters; a librarian's guide. American Library Association 2011 65p pa $37

Grades: Adult Professional **302.3**

1. Online social networks 2. Libraries and community

ISBN 978-0-8389-1067-2; 0-8389-1067-X

LC 2010034319

"This slim manual is packed with useful advice. Solomon, a library services manager for the Ohio Public Information Network, sprinkles her account with real-world examples of the power of libraries leveraging social media. She makes a strong case for establishing social-media accounts. . . . Discussions about branding, social capital, and other strategies for success are especially important. Wrapping up with chapters on statistics and whether the investment of time and effort is worthwhile, Solomon gives libraries the knowledge they need to proceed on their own." SLJ

Includes bibliographical references

302.34 Social interaction in primary groups

Bazelon, Emily, 1971-

★ **Sticks** and stones; defeating the culture of bullying and rediscovering the power of character and empathy. by Emily Bazelon. Random House 2013 viii, 386 p.p ill. (hardcover) $27

Grades: Adult Professional **302.34**

1. Bullies 2. Adolescence 3. Social media 4. Bullying 5. Bullying in schools 6. Bullying -- Prevention 7. Bullying in schools -- Prevention

ISBN 0812992806; 9780679644002; 9780812992809

LC 2012022773

This book, by Emily Bazelon, discusses teen culture in the U.S., focusing on bullying. "Being a teenager has never been easy, but in recent years, with the rise of the Internet and social media, it has become exponentially more challenging. . . . Bazelon defines what bullying is and, just as important, what it is not. She explores when intervention is essential and when kids should be given the freedom to fend for themselves. She also dispels persistent myths." (Publisher's note)

"While less prescriptive than other books on the topic, very useful FAQs are included, as are resource lists for readers. Masterfully written, Bazelon's book will increase understanding, awareness, and action." Pub Wkly

Includes bibliographical references and index

Strauss, Susan L.

★ **Sexual** harassment and bullying; a guide to keeping kids safe and holding schools accountable. Susan L. Strauss. Rowman & Littlefield Publishers 2012 290 p. (cloth : alk. paper) $34.95

Grades: Adult Professional **302.34**

1. Bullies 2. Social media 3. Sexual harassment 4. Bullying 5. Bullying -- Prevention 6. Sexual harassment in education 7. Sexual harassment -- Prevention

ISBN 1442201622; 9781442201620

LC 2011031731

In this book, "[Susan L.] Strauss draws on her experiences as consultant, former high-school teacher, and parent of a child who was sexually harassed to advise parents, teachers, and other adults on how to protect children" from bullying and harassment. She gives definitions of bullying and harassment, "offers a particular focus on the kind of harassment of gay, bisexual, and transgendered students," and examines "how social media . . . have ramped up bullying and harassment." (Booklist)

Includes bibliographical references and index.

Vicious; true stories by teens about bullying. edited by Hope Vanderberg. Free Spirit Pub. Inc. 2012 167 p. (Real teen voices) (paperback) $11.99

Grades: 6 7 8 **302.34**

1. Bullies 2. Teenagers' writings 3. Bullying -- Case studies 4. Self-esteem in adolescence -- Case studies 5. Aggressiveness in adolescence -- Case studies 6. Interpersonal conflict in adolescence -- Case studies

ISBN 1575424134; 9781575424132

LC 2012015908

This book is a collection of "autobiographical essays" from teenagers involved with the New York-based organization Youth Communication in which they detail "their struggles with bullies, anger about bad home situations and unfair treatment, and pressure to conform or be successful." (School Library Journal)

Includes bibliographical references and index

302.343 Bullying

Cyberbullying; Lauri Scherer, book editor. Greenhaven Press 2015 137 p. ills. (chiefly col.), col. map (Introducing issues with opposing viewpoints) (hardcover) $42

Grades: 6 7 8 9 10 **302.343**

1. Bullies 2. Bullying 3. Cyberbullying 4. Internet and

teenagers
ISBN 9780737772340; 0737772344
LC 2014030230

This book on bullying, by Lauri S. Scherer, part of the "Introducing issues with opposing viewpoints" series, "promotes issue awareness as well as critical thinking. . . . It offers a wealth of information at a lower reading level, in a bright, engaging package. This appealing combination helps more students grasp the controversies of our increasingly complex world." (Publisher's note)

Includes bibliographical references (pages 121-129) and index

Subramanian, Mathangi

Bullying; the ultimate teen guide. Mathangi Subramanian. Rowman & Littlefield 2014 213 p. illustrations (It happened to me) (cloth : alk. paper) $50

Grades: 8 9 10 11 12 **302.343**

1. Bullies 2. Bullying 3. Cyberbullying
ISBN 9780810890541
LC 2013044839

In this book, by Mathangi Subramanian, "Bullying is a widespread problem that affects thousands of teens across the United States and around the world. Victims of bullying battle depression, anxiety, insecurity, and fear. Sadly, some victims internalize their frustration by harming themselves or become bullies as well. But if young people agree that bullying is so devastating, why does it continue? Most importantly, how can it be stopped?" (Publisher's note)

Includes bibliographical references and index

303.3 Coordination and control

Tarshis, Thomas Paul

Living with peer pressure and bullying. Facts on File 2010 167p (Teen's guides) $34.95; pa $14.95

Grades: 6 7 8 9 **303.3**

1. Bullies 2. Peer pressure 3. Adolescent psychology
ISBN 978-0-8160-7914-8; 0-8160-7914-5; 978-0-8160-7915-5 pa; 0-8160-7915-3 pa
LC 2009024521

"Tarshis examines topics such as peer pressure, managing difficult situations, the risks and rewards of telling the truth, mental-health problems, cyberbullying, and finding and paying for medical care. Each chapter begins with a personal account about a teen facing the chapter topic; includes explanations presented in clear language, at times accompanied by questionnaires and explanatory charts; and ends with 'What You Need to Know,' which summarizes the main ideas. [This book is an] important [addition] for most libraries." SLJ

Includes glossary and bibliographical references

Webber, Diane

Totally tolerant; spotting and stopping prejudice. [by] Diane Webber and Laurie Mandel. Franklin Watts 2008 112p il (Scholastic choices) lib bdg $27; pa $8.95

Grades: 5 6 7 8 **303.3**

1. Prejudices 2. Toleration
ISBN 978-0-531-13867-0 lib bdg; 0-531-13867-4 lib bdg; 978-0-531-20525-9 pa; 0-531-20525-8 pa
LC 2007-51873

This book about tolerance contains "vignettes and quotes from teens. . . . Statistics, quizzes, historical photos that illustrate prejudice in the 1950s and even recent news stories such as the Jena Six are peppered throughout for a professional perspective. The young reader is also motivated to think critically and use other tools such as journaling or volunteering to create change in their own lives. . . . Plenty of photos accompany . . . [this] book, and words are defined not only in a glossary but used clearly in context as well, providing a great introduction to the topic for the beginning reader." Voice Youth Advocates

Includes glossary and bibliographical references

303.4 Social change

Harris, Ashley Rae

★ **Txt** me l8r; using technology responsibly. content consultant, Robyn J. A. Silverman. ABDO Pub. Co. 2010 112p il (Essential health: strong, beautiful girls) $34.22

Grades: 6 7 8 9 **303.4**

1. Technology 2. Information technology 3. Technological innovations 4. Internet -- Social aspects
ISBN 978-1-60453-754-3; 1-60453-754-X
LC 2009-2138

Using personal narratives, with a consulting doctor giving insight and making suggestions, this discusses the responsible use of technology and the dangers of overuse of cell phones, social websites, texting, and other online communication.

"The topics are well selected, the design is attractive, and the stories feature girls from a variety of cultures." Booklist

Includes bibliographical references

Hill, Laban Carrick

★ **America** dreaming; how youth changed America in the sixties. Little, Brown & Company 2007 165p il pa $12.99

Grades: 6 7 8 9 10 **303.4**

1. Social change 2. Youth movement 3. Baby boom generation 4. United States -- History -- 1961-1974
ISBN 978-0-316-00904-1; 0-316-00904-0; 978-0-316-07148-2 pa; 0-316-07148-X pa
LC 2006-27898

"An excellent textbook for the children and, probably, grandchildren of baby boomers who want to know what the youth culture of the time as all about." NY Times Book Rev

Includes bibliographical references

Solway, Andrew

Communication; the impact of science and technology. Gareth Stevens Pub. 2010 64p il (Pros and cons) lib bdg $35

Grades: 5 6 7 8 **303.4**

1. Communication 2. Telecommunication 3. Information technology
ISBN 978-1-4339-1986-2 lib bdg; 1-4339-1986-9 lib bdg
LC 2009-12435

An "active layout that features color photographs, maps, graphs or charts on every spread, this . . . [book] has much to offer. . . . It conveniently outlines the range of views . . . helping students to learn how to view both sides of [the] issue[s]." SLJ

Includes glossary and bibliographical references

★ **We** rise, we resist, we raise our voices; edited by Wade Hudson and Cheryl Wells Hudson ; foreword by Ashley Bryan. Random House Childrens Books 2018 96 p. $18.99

Grades: 3 4 5 6 7 **303.4**

1. Racism 2. Prejudices
ISBN 0525580425; 9780525580423

In this book, edited by Wade Hudson and Cheryl Wells Hudson, "fifty of the foremost diverse children's authors and illustrators--including Jason Reynolds, Jacqueline Woodson, and Kwame Alexander--share answers to the question, 'In this divisive world, what shall we tell our children?' . . . Featuring poems, letters, personal essays, art, and other works . . . , this anthology empowers the nation's youth to listen, learn, and build a better tomorrow." (Publisher's note)

"When it seems like all around us there is bad news, tension, injustice, and racism, children now have an additional source of inspiration in their search for peace, strength, equality, and hope in this vibrant and heartfelt anthology."

303.48 Causes of change

Braun, Eric

★ **Protest** movements; then and now. by Eric Braun. Capstone Press 2018 64 p. (hardcover) $33.99

Grades: 5 6 7 8 **303.48**

1. United States -- Social conditions -- 1960-1980 2. Protest movements -- United States -- History -- 20th century 3. Political participation -- United States -- History -- 20th century 4. United States -- History -- 1961-1969

ISBN 9781543503852; 9781543503890

LC 2017038578

This children's book in the America: 50 Years of Change series, by Eric Braun, "discusses the main concerns of the protest movements of the 1960s [in the United States], and how those have evolved since; what's changed for the better, what might be worse, and where do we go from here." (Publisher's note)

Includes bibliographical references and index

Chambers, Veronica

Resist; 35 profiles of ordinary people who rose up against tyranny and injustice. Veronica Chambers ; illustrated by Paul Ryding. HarperCollins 2018 224 p. (hardback) $16.99

Grades: 5 6 7 8 9 **303.48**

1. Social change 2. Political activists -- Biography 3. Social change -- History 4. Revolutionaries -- Biography 5. Social reformers -- Biography

ISBN 0062796259; 9780062796257

LC 2017057335

This book, by Veronica Chambers, illustrated by Paul Ryding, "profiles men and women who resisted tyranny, fought the odds, and stood up to bullies that threatened to harm their communities. Along with their portraits and most memorable quotes, their stories will inspire you to speak out and rise up--every single day." (Publisher's note)

Changemakers; rebels and radicals who changed US history. edited by Michele Bollinger and Dao X. Tran. Haymarket Books 2012 210 p. (alk. paper) $19.95

Grades: 6 7 8 **303.48**

1. Change 2. Radicalism 3. Social justice 4. United States -- Biography 5. Social movements -- United States 6. Social reformers -- United States -- Biography

ISBN 1608461564; 9781608461561

LC 2012034044

This book, edited by Michele Bollinger and Dao X Tran, "offers a 'people's history' version of the individuals who have shaped [the U.S.] for middle school students. In the place of founding fathers, presidents, and titans of industry, are profiles of those who . . . fought for social justice in America: Tecumseh, Harriet Tubman, Mark Twain, César Chávez, Rachel Carson, Harvey Milk, Henry Wallace, and many more." (Publisher's note)

Johnson, Steven, 1968-

How we got to now; six innovations that made the modern world. by Steven Johnson. Viking, Published by Penguin Group 2018 160 p. (hardcover) $19.99

Grades: 6 7 8 9 **303.48**

1. Inventions -- History 2. Technological innovations 3. Technology and civilization 4. Inventions -- Social aspects 5. Technology -- Social aspects

ISBN 0425287785; 9780425287781; 9780425287798

LC 2017060707

This book, by Steven Johnson, "explores the fascinating and interconnected stories of innovations--like clean drinking water and electricity--that changed the way people live. . . . Johnson looks at how accidental genius, brilliant mistakes, and unintended consequences shape the way we live in the modern world. . . . His fascinating account is organized into six topics: glass, cold, sound, clean, time, light." (Publisher's note)

Scandiffio, Laura

People who said no; courage against oppression. Laura Scandiffio. Annick Press 2012 168 p. $24.95

Grades: 5 6 7 **303.48**

1. Demonstrations 2. Protest movements 3. Civil disobedience 4. Resistance to government

ISBN 1554513839; 9781554513833

This book, by Laura Scandiffio, profiles activists who broke the law to protest injustices. "Sometimes it's okay to ignore the rules or break the law. . . . This . . . book features people who did just that: Sophie and Hans Scholl . . . and Andrei Sakharov. . . . Also included are Helen Suzman, . . . Aung San Suu Kyi, . . . and the people of Egypt, who recently brought down the repressive government of Hosni Mubarak." (Publisher's note)

303.49 Social forecasts

Schutten, Jan Paul

Hello from 2030; the science of the future and you. Jan Paul Schutten. Beyond Words Publishing Company 2014 224 p. color illustrations (hardcover : alk. paper) $15.99

Grades: 4 5 6 7 **303.49**

1. Forecasting 2. World history -- 21st century 3. Social prediction 4. Science -- Forecasting 5. Technological forecasting

ISBN 1582704740; 9781582704746

LC 2013044906

In this book on the science of the future, Jan Paul Schutten "asserts that the future is nothing to fear and that while 2030 might present some daunting challenges, what happens is largely within our control in the present. He highlights the potential for longer and healthier lives, faster technology, and smarter homes. Yet the book retains a cautionary tone regarding environmental issues like water usage and energy consumption." (Booklist)

"Extremely detailed source notes for each chapter draw on current research and news articles and include links to further reading. The engaging text is supported by plenty of full-color visuals presented in a dynamic format. Presenting an overwhelmingly optimistic outlook on the future, the book reminds us that we might as well welcome change with open arms." Booklist

Includes bibliographical references and index

303.6 Conflict and conflict resolution

Dawson, Eric David

★ **Putting** peace first; seven commitments to change the world. Eric David Dawson. Viking 2018 160 p. (trade pbk.) $9.99

Grades: 5 6 7 8 9 **303.6**

1. Peace 2. Toleration 3. Peace-building 4. Children and peace
ISBN 9781101997338

LC 2017033431

This book, by Eric David Dawson, empowers "young people [who] are hungry to change the world, but often aren't given the chance. . . . Using the inspiring stories of real life peacemakers, each chapter highlights a different aspect of peacemaking, from Opening Your Heart to Taking a Stand. With clear, step-by-step explanations of how each peacemaker achieved their goals, this book is a guide for anyone who wants to make a difference." (Publisher's note)

"Issues of cyberbullying, gun violence, and attacks on immigrant students are ones that are faced in these pages and also every day in schools around the world. By internalizing the seven commitments, standing up, and taking action—choosing to put peace first—Dawson argues, the world could change, one student at a time. These anecdotes are inspirational, but Dawson also includes a practical starting guide for any readers who need concrete steps on how to begin to think and plan for change. Dawson is careful to point out (the seventh commitment is "Keep Trying," and the epilogue is aptly named "Pending Disasters") that nothing is perfect. Change is difficult, especially if you are trying to right an injustice, but this manual helps readers past excuses." Kirkus

Ellis, Deborah

★ **Off** to war; voices of soldiers' children. Groundwood Books/House of Anansi Press 2008 175p il $15.95; pa $9.95

Grades: 5 6 7 8 **303.6**

1. Children and war 2. Iraq War, 2003-2011 3. Afghanistan
ISBN 978-0-88899-894-1; 0-88899-894-5; 978-0-88899-895-8 pa; 0-88899-895-3 pa

The wars in Iraq and Afghanistan have impacted the children of soldiers—men and women who have been called away from their families to fight in a faraway war. In their own words, some of these children describe how their experience has marked and shaped their lives

"Accessible and utterly readable. . . . The book is an excellent resource for opening discussions about the current events." SLJ

Includes glossary and bibliographical references

Gottfried, Ted

The **fight** for peace; a history of antiwar movements in America. 21st Century Bks. 2006 136p il (People's history) $26.60

Grades: 7 8 9 10 **303.6**

1. War 2. Peace 3. Pacifism
ISBN 0-7613-2932-3

"Gottfried starts out by explaining that a group in Connecticut rallied together in 2003 to peacefully protest the war against Iraq. . . . Then the author discusses the antiwar movement during the Civil War and proceeds through history, beginning with the ancient Greek play Lysistrata. . . . The pictures, political cartoons, and quotes are an excellent addition. . . . This is a book that can be read for general interest as well as for reports." SLJ

Includes bibliographical references

Judson, Karen

Resolving conflicts; how to get along when you don't get along. Enslow Pubs. 2005 112p il (Issues in focus today) $31.93

Grades: 7 8 9 10 11 12 **303.6**

1. Conflict management
ISBN 0-7660-2359-1

LC 2004-28119

The author "describes different kinds of conflicts and how they can be resolved, with a special focus on teens and building their conflict-resolution skills and understanding." Publisher's note

Includes bibliographical references

O'Brien, Anne Sibley

After Gandhi; one hundred years of nonviolent resistance. [by] Anne Sibley O'Brien and Perry Edmond O'Brien. Charlesbridge 2009 181p il map $15.95

Grades: 7 8 9 10 **303.6**

1. Nonviolence 2. Passive resistance
ISBN 978-1-58089-129-5; 1-58089-129-2

LC 2008-10660

"Using Gandhi as its starting point, this large-format book traces the history of nonviolent resistance by looking at significant adherents from 1908 to 2003 including Martin Luther King, Jr., Nelson Mandela, Charles Perkins, César Chávez, Aung San Suu Kyi, Vaclav Havel, and Wangari Maathi and groups such as the student activists of Tiananmen Square and the Madres de Plaza de Mayo (Mothers of the Disappeared) in Argentina. . . . The handsome design and striking black-and-white illustrations are strong visuals that complement the story of nonviolent resistance in action." Booklist

Includes bibliographical references

Walker, Niki

Why do we fight? conflict, war, and peace. Niki Walker. Owlkids Books 2013 80 p. $16.95

Grades: 5 6 7 8 **303.6**

1. War 2. Culture conflict 3. Conflict management
ISBN 1926973860; 9781926973869

LC 2013930981

In this book, Niki Walker explains "different types of conflict and then contemplat[es] ways conflict can escalate." (Kirkus Reviews) "Using real-world examples, such as the 1979 peace deal between Egypt and Israel or the history of Afghanistan over multiple centuries, Walker offers . . . explanations of power and resource inequities, cultural divisions, the global role of the United Nations, bias, prejudice, and more." (Publishers Weekly)

Weinberg, Leonard

★ **What** is terrorism? [by] Leonard Weinberg and William Eubank. Chelsea House Publishers 2006 104p il (The roots of terrorism) lib bdg $35

Grades: 7 8 9 10 **303.6**

1. Terrorism
ISBN 0-7910-8305-5

LC 2005027569

This "gives a history of terrorism from its early beginnings through current events. This volume describes the actions and goals of numerous terrorist groups. . . . This . . . has a great deal of information. . . . The glossy pages show off an eye-pleasing color format with neat sections and well-placed pictures." Voice Youth Advocates

Includes bibliographical references

304.2 Human ecology

Carson, Mary Kay

Inside Biosphere 2; earth science under glass. by Mary Kay Carson ; with photographs by Tom Uhlman. Houghton Mifflin Harcourt 2015 80 p. color illustrations $18.99

Grades: 7 8 9 10 **304.2**

1. Biosphere 2. Earth sciences 3. Science 4. Human ecology 5. Ecology -- Research 6. Biosphere 2 (Project) 7. Closed ecological systems (Space environment)

ISBN 0544416643; 9780544416642

LC 2014047046

This book by Mary Kay Carson looks at how "in the Arizona desert, scientists conduct studies and experiments aimed to help us better understand our environment and what sort of things are happening to it due to climate change. The location is Biosphere 2, an immense structure that contains a replica ocean, savannah, and rainforest, among other Earth biomes." (Publisher's note)

"Well-chosen, clearly captioned photographs support the text, while flashback boxes inform readers of what came before. For middle and high school readers, an encouraging example of earth scientists working to understand and deal with climate change in new and amazing ways." Kirkus

304.6 Population

Altman, Linda Jacobs

Genocide; the systematic killing of a people. rev. and expanded; Enslow Publishers 2009 128p il map (Issues in focus today) lib bdg $31.93

Grades: 6 7 8 9 **304.6**

1. Genocide

ISBN 978-0-7660-3358-0 lib bdg; 0-7660-3358-9 lib bdg

LC 2007050697

First published 1995

This is written in "short accessible chapters." Horn Book Guide

Includes glossary and bibliographical references

Barber, Nicola

Coping with population growth; Nicola Barber. Raintree 2011 48 p. col. ill. paperback $9.49

Grades: 4 5 6 7 **304.6**

1. Population 2. Population -- Environmental aspects

ISBN 9781410942968; 9781410943033; 9781410943248

LC 2010052702

"Barber examines the pressures exerted on the environment and global resources due to population growth... Color photographs add interest, and helpful diagrams effectively convey statistical concepts." Horn Book

Includes bibliographical references (p. 46-47) and index

304.8 Movement of people

Lawlor, Veronica

I was dreaming to come to America; memories from the Ellis Island Oral History Project. selected and illustrated by Veronica Lawlor; foreword by Rudolph W. Giuliani. Viking 1995 38p il hardcover o.p. pa $6.99

Grades: 4 5 6 7 **304.8**

1. Ellis Island Immigration Station 2. United States -- Immigration and emigration

ISBN 0-670-86164-2; 0-14-055622-2 pa

LC 95-1281

"Begun in 1975, the Ellis Island Oral History Project is . . . {a} collection of interviews with individuals who immigrated to the U.S. through Ellis Island. Short selections—each 1 or 2 paragraphs long—from 15 of those interviews are reprinted here. The subjects were for the most part children when they arrived in the period 1900-1925. . . . Grades four to six." (SLJ)

"There is a flavor of Chagall in the peasant figures dancing above the ship or hopping ashore near the turreted towers of the huge building on Ellis Island. The elegant rendering offers a timeless view of this significant journey that is at once personal and universal." Horn Book

Osborne, Linda Barrett

This land is our land; the history of American immigration. by Linda Barrett Osborne. Abrams Books for Young Readers 2016 124 p. color illustrations $24.95

Grades: 5 6 7 8 9 10 **304.8**

1. Immigrants -- United States 2. United States -- Emigration and immigration 3. Immigrants -- United States -- History 4. United States -- Emigration and immigration -- History

ISBN 9781419716607; 1419716603

LC 2015017877

YALSA Award for Excellence in Nonfiction for Young Adults: Finalist (2017)

This book, by Linda Barrett Osborne, "explores the history of American immigration from the early colonization of the continent to the contemporary discussions involving undocumented aliens. The so-called American melting pot has a history of exclusion, discrimination, and strife that has resulted in anti-immigration laws, segregation, and, in the case of the Japanese during World War II, unjustified internment." (School Library Journal)

"Well researched, clearly written, and informative, the discussion is particularly useful in offering the broad look at immigration over time, showing how similar arguments and legal restrictions have been used against different groups in different periods. Throughout the book, the perspectives of individual immigrants emerge in paragraphs detailing their personal stories and including quotes. Handsomely designed, the book offers many captioned period illustrations, especially photos. A strong introduction to American immigration." Booklist

Includes bibliographical references and index

305.23 Young people

America, border, culture, dreamer; the young immigrant experience from A to Z. Wendy Ewald [editor and photographer] Little, Brown & Co. 2018 64 p. (hardcover) $18.99

Grades: 5 6 7 8 9 **305.23**

1. Immigrants 2. Children of immigrants 3. Immigrant children -- United States -- Biography 4. Immigrant children -- United States -- Portraits 5. Children of immigrants -- United States -- Biography 6. Children of immigrants -- United States -- Portraits 7. Immigrants -- Cultural assimilation -- United States

ISBN 9780316484954

LC 2018010742

In this book, "first- and second-generation immigrants to the US from all around the world collaborate with renowned photographer Wendy Ewald to create a stunning, surprising catalog of their experiences from A to Z. . . . [E]ighteen immigrant teenagers create an alphabet defining their experiences in pictures and words. Wendy helped the teenagers pose for and design the photographs, interviewing them along the way about their own journeys and perspectives." (Publisher's note)

"This unique alphabet book is the result of collaboration between Ewald and 18 high school teenagers who attend Al-Bustan Seeds of Culture, an arts and education organization in Philadelphia." (School Library Journal)

Burton, Bonnie

Girls against girls; why we are mean to each other and how we can change. Zest Books 2009 128p il pa $12.95

Grades: 7 8 9 10 **305.23**

1. Bullies 2. Girls -- Psychology

ISBN 0-9790173-6-X; 978-0-9790173-6-0

This guide for teenage girls explains why girls can sometimes be mean to each other, what to do if you are a victim of bullying, and the importance of treating other girls with respect.

This offers "excellent coping techniques. . . . Burton never talks down to her readers, nor does she pull her punches. Readers will respond to the author's clear respect for the painful nature of the problem." Booklist

★ The **Courage** to be yourself; true stories by teens about cliques, conflicts, and overcoming peer pressure. edited by Al Desetta with Educators for Social Responsibility. Free Spirit Pub. 2005 145p pa $13.95

Grades: 7 8 9 10 11 12 **305.23**

1. Teenagers 2. Conduct of life

ISBN 1-57542-185-2

LC 2005-5173

"There is certainly some value in hearing teens of many ethnicities and orientations speaking plainly about being fat, or being from India in a school full of blond, blue-eyed folk, or being Arab after 9/11." Booklist

Includes bibliographical references

Dias, Marley

Marley Dias gets it done; and so can you! Marley Dias, with Siobhan McGowan. Scholastic Press 2018 208 p. (pbk. : alk. paper) $14.99

Grades: 5 6 7 8 9 **305.23**

1. Social action 2. African American girls 3. Equality -- United States 4. Social action -- United States 5. Literacy programs -- United States 6. African American girls -- Social conditions

ISBN 1338136895; 9781338136890

LC 2017016415

In this book for children, author "Marley Dias explores activism, social justice, volunteerism, equity and inclusion, and using social media for good. Drawing from her experience, Marley shows kids how they can galvanize their strengths to make positive changes in their communities. . . . Focusing on the importance of literacy and diversity, Marley offers suggestions on book selection, and delivers hands-on strategies for becoming a lifelong reader." (Publisher's note)

Freedman, Russell

Children of the Great Depression. Clarion Books 2005 118p il lib bdg $20

Grades: 4 5 6 7 **305.23**

1. Great Depression, 1929-1939 2. Children -- United States 3. United States -- Social conditions

ISBN 0-618-44630-3

LC 2005-06506

"This stirring photo-essay combines . . . unforgettable personal details with a clear historical overview of the period and black-and-white photos by Dorothea Lange, Walker Evans, and many others." Booklist

Mangan, Tricia

How to feel good; 20 things teens can do. by Tricia Mangan. Magination Press 2012 125 p. (pbk. : alk. paper) $12.95

Grades: 8 9 10 11 12 **305.23**

1. Teenagers 2. Life skills 3. Adolescent psychology 4. Teenagers -- Conduct of life 5. Teenagers -- Life skills guides

ISBN 1433810409; 9781433810404

LC 2011020623

This book offers advice to teenagers in areas of psychological health in order "to feel good about . . . [themselves] and . . . [their] abilities. For teens, new relationships and experiences are happening all around them, and can make them feel overwhelmed and stressed. Being confident and secure can seem miles away. . . . [This book] provides interactive exercises and questions to help teens recognize and understand why they feel the way they do and to change hurtful thought patterns and habits. With these 20 . . . steps, teens can use this book to learn how to be confident and happy with themselves." (Publisher's note)

"With a gentle, firm but never condescending tone . . . clinical psychologist Mangan leads anxious teens through the A's (activating events), B's (beliefs), and C's (consequences) of taking control of spiraling and self-defeating moods." Booklist

Smith, David J.

This child, every child; a book about the world's children. written by David J. Smith; illustrated by Shelagh Armstrong. Kids Can Press 2011 36p il (CitizenKid) $18.95

Grades: 4 5 6 7 **305.23**

1. Children

ISBN 978-1-55453-466-1; 1-55453-466-6

This title "takes a global look at the lives of contemporary children. Balancing statistics with fictional profiles of kids, Smith's concise narrative focuses on such topics as families, homes, health, work, war, and play. Each spread contains accessible summaries of articles from 1989's United Nations Convention on the Rights of the Child, underscoring the disparity between many children's lives and that document's vision and goals. . . . Rendered in acrylics with digital textures, Armstrong's gauzy paintings sometimes span multiple cultures in a single illustration . . . reinforcing the universal nature of children's needs." Publ Wkly

Wilson, Janet

One peace; true stories of young activists. written and illustrated by Janet Wilson. Orca Book Publishers 2008 43p il $19.95

Grades: 4 5 6 7 **305.23**

1. Peace 2. Children and war

ISBN 978-1-55143-892-4; 1-55143-892-5

"The stories of young people who have been refugees from war, injured by land mines, or learned about the consequences of violence through other means are interspersed with children's poems, quotes, artwork, and photographs. The brief, powerful accounts document how these children ages 8 to 15 worked for or became symbols of peace." SLJ

Yousafzai, Malala, 1997-

We are displaced; my journey and stories from refugee girls around the world. Malala Yousafzai. Little, Brown & Co. 2019 224 p. (hardcover) $18.99

Grades: 8 9 10 11 12 **305.23**

1. Refugees 2. Forced migration 3. Immigration and emigration
ISBN 9780316523646; 9780316529488

LC 2018043763

In this book, "author Malala Yousafzai introduces some of the people behind the statistics and news stories about the millions of people displaced worldwide. . . . Part memoir [and] part communal storytelling, Malala not only explores her own story, but she also shares the personal stories of some of the incredible girls she has met on her journeys--girls who have lost their community, relatives, and often the only world they've ever known." (Publisher's note)

"In this uplifting work Yousafzai shares the survival stories of female refugees from around the world." (Kirkus Reviews)

305.235 Young people twelve to twenty

Alifirenka, Caitlin

I will always write back; how one letter changed two lives. by Caitlin Alifirenka and Martin Ganda ; with Liz Welch. Little, Brown & Co. 2015 400 p. (hardcover) $18

Grades: 6 7 8 9 10 11 12 Adult **305.235**

1. Africans 2. Letter writing 3. Teenagers' writings 4. Friendship 5. Pen pals -- Zimbabwe 6. Pen pals -- United States 7. Teenagers -- Zimbabwe -- Social conditions 8. Teenagers -- United States -- Social conditions
ISBN 0316241318; 9780316241311

LC 2014030355

This memoir by Martin Ganda and Caitlin Alifirenka, with Liz Welch, "true story of an all-American girl and a boy from Zimbabwe and the letter that changed both of their lives forever. Everyone in Caitlin's class wrote to an unknown student somewhere in a distant place. Martin was lucky to even receive a pen-pal letter. There were only ten letters, and fifty kids in his class. But he was the top student, so he got the first one. That letter was the beginning of a correspondence that spanned six years and changed two lives." (Publisher's note)

Bialik, Mayim, 1975-

Girling up; how to be strong, smart and spectacular. Mayim Bialik, PhD. Philomel Books 2017 177 p. illustrations (hardcover) $18.99

Grades: 7 8 9 **305.235**

1. Adolescence 2. Teenage girls 3. Teenage girls -- Psychology
ISBN 9780399548628; 9780399548604

LC 2016044334

In this book, author Mayim Bialik, "talks to teens about the science of growing up and getting ahead. . . . Using scientific facts, personal anecdotes, and wisdom gained from the world around us, . . . [she] shares what she has learned from her life and her many years studying neuroscience to tell you how you grow from a girl to a woman biologically, psychologically and sociologically." (Publisher's note)

Ellis, Deborah

Kids of Kabul; living bravely through a never-ending war. Deborah Ellis. Groundwood Books 2012 143 p. $15.95

Grades: 6 7 8 9 10 11 12 **305.235**

1. Taliban 2. Interviews 3. Children -- Afghanistan
ISBN 1554981816; 9781554981816

This book is a collection of interviews with Afghani children who "mostly don't remember the Taliban's fall more than a decade ago, but they can't help but be shaped by the damage the Taliban did to their country. . . . One girl is imprisoned for fleeing a forced child marriage, while another's mother is a member of Parliament; one boy's damaged by a landmine, and another's proud to be a Scout. . . . [I]ntroductions to each young person provide historical, legal and social context." (Kirkus Reviews)

Shandler, Sara

Ophelia speaks; adolescent girls write about their search for self. HarperPerennial 1999 285p pa $12.95

Grades: 7 8 9 10 **305.235**

1. Girls 2. Adolescence
ISBN 0-06-095297-0

LC 99-13534

"Shandler collected writings from adolescent girls all over the country on topics that include sexuality, eating disorders, feminism, family dynamics, and friendship; their words, framed by Shandler's own reflections, are riveting and revealing." Libr J

305.3 People by gender or sex

Bornstein, Kate

My new gender workbook; a step-by-step guide to achieving world peace through gender anarchy and sex positivity. Kate Bornstein. Routledge 2013 xiii, 293 p.p ill. (paperback) $39.95

Grades: 7 8 9 10 11 12 **305.3**

1. Sex 2. Gender role 3. Sex education 4. Sex -- Psychological aspects 5. Gender identity 6. Sex (Psychology)
ISBN 0415538653; 9780203109038; 9780415538640; 9780415538657

LC 2012033355

"Since its first publication in 1997, My Gender Workbook has been challenging, encouraging, questioning, and helping those trying to figure out how to become a 'real man,' a 'real woman,' or 'something else entirely.' In this exciting new edition of her classic text, Bornstein re-examines gender in light of issues like race, class, sexuality, and language. With new quizzes, new puzzles, new exercises, and plenty of Kate's playful and provocative style, My New Gender Workbook promises to help a new generation create their own unique place on the gender spectrum." (Publisher's note)

"It makes a sometimes-intimidating set of theories accessible and friendly for any reader, not just those already working on their gender. Bornstein dismantles some of the social mores we take the most for granted, and we are all the better for it. " LJ

305.4 Women

Bausum, Ann

★ **With** courage and cloth; winning the fight for a woman's right to vote. by Ann Bausum. National Geographic 2004 111 p. ill. (some col.), maps $32.90

Grades: 5 6 7 8 9 **305.4**

1. Women -- Suffrage 2. Women's rights -- History 3. Women -- United States -- History 4. Women -- Suffrage -- United States
ISBN 0792269969; 0792276477; 9780792269960

LC 2004001191

Jane Addams Award Book (2005)

This book, by Ann Bausum, is a history of the movement for women's suffrage in the United States. "After covering the importance of familiar issues, she devotes the bulk of the book to the events of 1906 to 1920, when a new group of young women emerged who were willing to truly suffer for suffrage. The movement split into two camps-Carrie Chapman Catt's larger National American Woman Suffrage Association, . . . and a smaller . . . National Woman's Party led by Alice Paul." (School Library Journal)

"Bausum's lucid and nuanced study focuses on 1913-20, the last years of the more than seven decades when women in the US fought for the right to vote. She summarizes what went before and she teases out, remarkably clearly, how hard it was. . . . Bausum focuses on Alice Paul and some other lesser-known lights of the movement, and all the while she makes the history live as she explains, exhorts, and lets nothing drop by the wayside. The entire volume is put together wonderfully, using some never-before-published photos and a lively layout. . . . Excellent." Kirkus

Because I was a girl; true stories for girls of all ages. edited by Melissa de la Cruz. Henry Holt & Co. 2017 241 p. illustrations, portraits (hardcover) $18.99

Grades: 7 8 9 10 11 **305.4**

1. Women 2. Anecdotes 3. Teenage girls 4. Women -- Anecdotes

ISBN 9781250154460; 9781250154477

LC 2017934604

This book, edited by Melissa de la Cruz, "is an inspiring collection of true stories by women and girls about the obstacles, challenges, and opportunities they've faced...because of their gender. The collection includes writings from an impressive array of girls and women who are trailblazers in their fields." (Publisher's note)

"Thoughtful, encouraging, and honest, this compilation should inspire readers looking for guidance in charting the directions their own lives take." Pub Wkly

Bingham, Jane

Women at war; the progressive era, World War I and women's suffrage, 1900-1920. Chelsea House 2011 il (A cultural history of women in America) $35

Grades: 5 6 7 8 **305.4**

1. World War, 1914-1918 2. Women -- Employment 3. Women -- Social conditions 4. Women -- United States -- History

ISBN 978-1-6041-3932-7; 1-6041-3932-3

LC 2010044828

An "eye-catching [layout] with good use of color, photographs, and informative sidebars, many of which use primary-source quotations, are the highlights of [this] appealing [volume]. . . . After a succinct overview of contemporary events, the chapters describe women's lives at home, at work, in education, in politics, in the arts, and their role in the general culture. . . . [This book] explores the changing role of women during the Progressive Era, the impact of World War I on their lives, and the struggle for voting rights." SLJ

Includes glossary and bibliographical references

Gelletly, LeeAnne

A **woman's** place in early America; LeeAnne Gelletly. Mason Crest Publishers 2013 64 p. (Finding a voice : women's fight for equality in U.S. society) (hc) $22.95

Grades: 4 5 6 7 8 **305.4**

1. Women -- United States -- History 2. United States -- Social conditions 3. United States -- Politics and government 4. Women's rights -- United States 5. United States -- Social life and customs 8. Women -- United States -- Social conditions

ISBN 1422223558; 9781422223550; 9781422223659

LC 2011043480

Author LeeAnne Gelletly's book focuses on women in Early America. "In early America, married women had no rights under law. They belonged to their husbands. Their voices were not heard in public. But with the War of Independence, women found a voice as patriots. They supported the rebellion with boycotts. During wartime, women spied on the enemy. They served as messengers. They tended the wounded. Some even served as soldiers. Women performed daring feats of bravery. And they proved they were capable of doing much more than 18-century society allowed them." (Publisher's note)

Includes bibliographical references and index

Gorman, Jacqueline Laks

The **modern** feminist movement; sisters under the skin, 1961-1979. Chelsea House 2011 il (A cultural history of women in America) $35

Grades: 5 6 7 8 **305.4**

1. Feminism 2. Women -- Social conditions 3. Women -- United States -- History

ISBN 978-1-6041-3935-8; 1-6041-3935-8

LC 2010045990

An "eye-catching [layout] with good use of color, photographs, and informative sidebars, many of which use primary-source quotations, are the highlights of [this] appealing [volume]. . . . After a succinct overview of contemporary events, the chapters describe women's lives at home, at work, in education, in politics, in the arts, and their role in the general culture. . . . [This book] delves into the years of protest and quest for equal rights." SLJ

Includes glossary and bibliographical references

Senker, Cath

Strength in numbers; industrialization and political activism, 1861-1899. Chelsea House 2011 il (A cultural history of women in America) $35

Grades: 7 8 9 10 **305.4**

1. Feminism 2. Women's rights 3. Women -- United States -- History 4. United States -- Social conditions

ISBN 978-1-60413-931-0; 1-60413-931-5

LC 2010045964

This is a history of American women from 1861-1899.

This book offers a "comprehensive, vivid, and thought-provoking [look] at the struggles and triumphs of . . . the women who [participated] in shaping our nation. Through succinct, informative text, [this] heavily illustrated volume incorporates the history of three major groups of people: the Natives, European settlers, and African slaves. Featured quotes from books, articles, letters, and speeches bring the history to life." SLJ

Includes glossary and bibliographical references

Stearman, Kaye

Women of today; contemporary issues and conflicts, 1980-present. [by] Kaye Stearman and Patience Coster. Chelsea House 2011 il (A cultural history of women in America) $35

Grades: 5 6 7 8 **305.4**

1. Feminism 2. Women -- United States 3. Women -- Social conditions

ISBN 978-1-6041-3936-5; 1-6041-3936-6

LC 2010046014

An "eye-catching [layout] with good use of color, photographs, and informative sidebars, many of which use primary-source quotations, are the highlights of [this] appealing [volume]. . . . After a succinct overview of contemporary events, the chapters describe women's lives at home, at work, in education, in politics, in the arts, and their role in the general culture. . . . [This book] highlights women's achievements, including

U.S. Supreme Court justices, Speaker of the U.S. House of Representatives, and presidential candidates." SLJ

Includes glossary and bibliographical references

Taschek, Karen

Daughters of liberty; the American Revolution and the Early Republic, 1775-1827. Chelsea House 2011 64p il (A cultural history of women in America) $35

Grades: 7 8 9 10 **305.4**

1. Women -- United States -- History 2. United States -- Social conditions 3. United States -- History -- 1775-1783, Revolution

ISBN 978-1-60413-928-0; 1-60413-928-5

LC 2010033717

This is a history of women in America from 1775-1827.

This book offers a "comprehensive, vivid, and thought-provoking [look] at the struggles and triumphs of . . . the women who [participated] in shaping our nation. Through succinct, informative text, [this] heavily illustrated volume incorporates the history of three major groups of people: the Natives, European settlers, and African slaves. Featured quotes from books, articles, letters, and speeches bring the history to life." SLJ

Includes glossary and bibliographical references

Woolf, Alex, 1964-

Finding an identity; early America and the Colonial Period, 1492-1774. Chelsea House 2011 64p il (A cultural history of women in America) $35

Grades: 7 8 9 10 **305.4**

1. Women -- United States -- History 2. United States -- History -- 1600-1775, Colonial period

ISBN 978-1-6041-3927-3; 1-6041-3927-7

LC 2010029225

This is a history of women in America from 1492-1774.

This book offers a "comprehensive, vivid, and thought-provoking [look] at the struggles and triumphs of . . . the women who [participated] in shaping our nation. Through succinct, informative text, [this] heavily illustrated volume incorporates the history of three major groups of people: the Natives, European settlers, and African slaves. Featured quotes from books, articles, letters, and speeches bring the history to life." SLJ

Includes glossary and bibliographical references

305.42 Social role and status of women

★ **Here** we are; feminism for the real world. edited by Kelly Jensen. Algonquin Young Readers 2017 218 p. illustrations (paperback) $16.95

Grades: 7 8 9 10 11 12 **305.42**

1. Feminism 2. Women -- Social conditions

ISBN 9781616205867; 9781616207106

LC 2016032054

In this book, edited by Kelly Jensen, "44 writers, dancers, actors, and artists contribute essays, lists, poems, comics, and illustrations about everything from body positivity to romance to gender identity to intersectionality to the greatest girl friendships in fiction. Together, they share diverse perspectives on and insights into what feminism means and what it looks like." (Publisher's note)

"The ever-evolving concept of feminism is approached through a variety of mediums, from essays and drawings to comics and poems, in this fantastic collected work." SLJ

Includes bibliographical references.

Higgins, Nadia Abushanab

Feminism; reinventing the F word. by Nadia Abushanab Higgins. Twenty-First Century Books 2016 160 p. (lb : alk. paper) $35.99

Grades: 6 7 8 9 10 **305.42**

1. Women's movement 2. Feminism

ISBN 9781467761475

LC 2015000898

In this juvenile book, by Nadia Abushanab Higgins, "explore the history of US feminism. . . . Meet modern leaders . . . who are striving to empower women at work, in government, at home—and in cultural and personal arenas. Learn from interviews with movement leaders, scholars, pop stars, and average women, what it means to be a feminist—or to reject it altogether." (Publisher's note)

"This informative, impeccably researched investigation of the history of feminism will do more than fill a collection gap—it firmly emphasizes that feminism and feminist are not dirty words." SLJ

Includes bibliographical references and index

Nardo, Don

★ The **women's** rights movement; by Don Nardo. ReferencePoint Press, Inc. 2018 80 p. illustrations (hardback) $29.95

Grades: 7 8 9 10 11 12 **305.42**

1. Feminism 2. Women's rights -- United States 3. Feminism -- History 4. Women's rights -- United States -- History

ISBN 168282425X; 9781682824252

LC 2018001350

In this book in the Push for Social Change series, by Don Nardo, "beginning in the nineteenth century, women in the United States and some other Western countries began to demand equal rights with men. Through public demonstrations, complaints to newspapers and congressmen, and other means, women eventually gained the right to vote and hold public office. This book examines how and why social change occurs and the lasting influence of the women's movement." (Publisher's note)

"The images throughout are well chosen, and visually accented time lines helpfully open each volume." Booklist

Includes bibliographical references and index

Sarkeesian, Anita, ca. 1983-

History vs women; the defiant lives that they don't want you to know. Anita Sarkeesian & Ebony Aster with illustrations by T.S. Abe. Feiwel and Friends 2018 138 p. (hardcover) $19.99

Grades: 7 8 9 10 **305.42**

1. Culture 2. Feminism 3. Women -- History

ISBN 9781250146731

LC 2018002811

"Looking through the ages and across the globe, Anita Sarkeesian, founder of Feminist Frequency, along with Ebony Adams PHD, have reclaimed the stories of twenty-five remarkable women who dared to defy history and change the world around them. From Mongolian wrestlers to Chinese pirates, Native American ballerinas to Egyptian scientists, Japanese novelists to British Prime Ministers, History vs Women will reframe the history that you thought you knew." (Publisher's note)

Includes bibliographical references (pages 137-138)

305.48 Specific groups of women

★ **#notyourprincess;** voices of Native American women. edited by Lisa Charleyboy and Mary Beth Leatherdale. Annick Press 2017 116 p. illustrations (chiefly color) $19.95
Grades: 7 8 9 10 11 12 **305.48**

1. Native American women 2. Women -- Social conditions
ISBN 1554519586; 9781554519583

YALSA Honor Book for Excellence in Nonfiction for Young Adult (2018)

This book, edited by Lisa Charleyboy and Mary Beth Leatherdale, "presents an eclectic collection of poems, essays, interviews, and art that combine to express the experience of being a Native woman. Stories of abuse, humiliation, and stereotyping are countered by the voices of passionate women making themselves heard and demanding change." (Publisher's note)

"The vital message that it offers is that Indigenous women continue to shatter stereotypes through their personal successes and creative expression. Both testament to the complexity of Indigenous women's identities and ferocious statement that these women fully inhabit the modern world." (Kirkus)

Arce, Julissa

Someone like me; how one undocumented girl fought for her American dream. Julissa Arce. Little, Brown & Co. 2018 240 p. $16.99
Grades: 6 7 8 9 **305.48**

1. Immigrants 2. Mexican American women 3. Mexican Americans -- Biography 4. Immigrants -- Texas -- Biography 5. Illegal aliens -- Texas -- Biography 6. Mexican American women -- Texas -- Biography
ISBN 9780316481748

LC 2018007526

"A remarkable true story from social justice advocate and national bestselling author Julissa Arce about her journey to belong in America while growing up undocumented in Texas. . . . This moving, at times heartbreaking, but always inspiring story will show young readers that anything is possible. Julissa's story provides a deep look into the little-understood world of a new generation of undocumented immigrants in the United States today." (Publisher's note)

"Offering young people a clear autobiographical viewpoint of a controversial issue, this is a must for all collections." (Booklist)

305.5 People by social and economic levels

Miller, Michael

Exposing hate; prejudice, hatred, and violence in action. Michael Miller. Twenty-First Century Books 2019 144 p. (library binding) $37.32
Grades: 8 9 10 11 12 **305.5**

1. Violence 2. Prejudices 3. Hate crimes 4. Hate 5. Hate groups 6. Hate speech 7. Right-wing extremists
ISBN 9781541539259; 9781541552449

LC 2018021233

"Experts have documented an explosive rise in the number of hate groups since the turn of the century, driven by anger over immigration and demographic projections showing that whites will no longer hold majority status in the United States by 2040. . . . What is a hate group and how does it operate? How do we legally define hate speech and hate crimes? . . . These are [some of] the salient issues readers will investigate in this . . . [book by Michael Miller.]" (Publisher's note)

"The book does not sensationalize; it just gives solid facts on how injustices are committed due to ignorance, fear, and misinformation. Stories of how people have reformed after interacting with those they have learned to hate give the factual text emotional heft. A necessary book on a hot-button social issue that can help students develop critical thinking skills while they learn more about heinous organizations." Booklist.

Includes bibliographical references and index

305.8 Ethnic and national groups

The **African** American almanac; Christopher A. Brooks, editor; foreword by Benjamin Jealous. 11th ed; Gale Cengage Learning 2011 1601p il map $297
Grades: 8 9 10 11 12 Adult **305.8**

1. Reference books 2. African Americans
ISBN 978-1-4144-4547-2

First edition under the editorship of Harry A. Ploski published 1967 by Bellwether with title: The Negro almanac. Periodically revised. Editors vary

"Reference covering the cultural and political history of Black Americans. Includes generous amount of statistical information and biographies of Black Americans, both historical and contemporary." N Y Public Libr. Book of How & Where to Look It Up

Bolden, Tonya

★ **Tell** all the children our story; memories and mementos of being young and Black in America. Abrams 2001 128p il $24.95
Grades: 5 6 7 8 **305.8**

1. African American children 2. United States -- Race relations
ISBN 0-8109-4496-0

LC 2001-1353

"This compilation of the African American experience, from colonial times through the twentieth century, reads and looks like a family scrapbook. . . . Photographs, excerpts from diaries and memoirs, and reproductions of artwork by black artists such as Charles Altson beautifully bring the story of each generation to life. Bolden vibrantly delivers her historical message through a contemporary perspective." Booklist

Includes bibliographical references

It's not all black and white; multiracial youth speak out. St. Stephen's Community House. Annick Press 2012 109 p. $12.95
Grades: 8 9 10 11 12 **305.8**

1. Prejudices 2. Minority youth 3. Identity (Psychology) 4. Racially mixed people
ISBN 1554513804; 9781554513802

In this collection of "poems, interviews, and short essays, a group of young people describe being biracial, multiracial, or of mixed race. . . . Themes include navigating mixed-race relationships, dealing with prejudice and the assumptions people make based on appearances, and working through identity confusion to arrive at a strong and positive sense of self." (Publisher's note)

Katz, William Loren

Black Indians; a hidden heritage. Updated edition Atheneum 2012 254 p il paperback $13.99
Grades: 8 9 10 11 12 **305.8**

1. Native Americans 2. African Americans
ISBN 0-689-31196-6; 0-689-80901-8; 9781442446373 paperback
Originally published 1986

Traces the history of relations between blacks and American Indians, and the existence of black Indians, from the earliest foreign landings through pioneer days.

The author "has provided a valuable addition to titles on American Indians. Excellent for assignments, it contains important information many history instructors may be unaware of. His sections on black Indians and the Seminoles of Florida and their views about living together are particularly good." Child Book Rev Serv

Includes bibliographical references

Marsico, Katie

The **Trail** of Tears; the tragedy of the American Indians. Marshall Cavendish Benchmark 2010 128p il (Perspectives on) lib bdg $27.95

Grades: 7 8 9 10 **305.8**

1. Cherokee Indians 2. Native Americans -- Relocation

ISBN 978-0-7614-4029-1; 0-7614-4029-1

LC 2008-41217

"Marsico uses primary sources to show 'conflicting vantage points' to provide an objective, reasoned account that places the Cherokee relocation and the Trail of Tears into the context of American history. She opens with well-written background about the 'principal people,' as the Cherokee called themselves, and then discusses how the post-American Revolution expansion created conflict between the Cherokee and white settlers, the divisions that assimilation efforts and resistance to relocation caused within the tribe and its leadership, and the disastrous removal to Oklahoma. . . . Marsico's book will help students better understand the tragic events and their place in history." SLJ

Includes bibliographical references

Petrillo, Valerie

A **kid's** guide to Latino history; more than 70 activities. Chicago Review Press 2009 214p il pa $14.95

Grades: 4 5 6 7 **305.8**

1. Hispanic Americans -- History

ISBN 978-1-55652-771-5 pa; 1-55652-771-3 pa

LC 2008040433

"This big, lively overview examines the history of Latinos in the U.S. . . . The chatty, informative text, presented in readable, spacious layouts, will draw kids with lots of fun, illustrated instructions for related activities. . . . The accessible facts and the individual portraits of notable authors, athletes, entertainers, and politicians portray Latinos' rich contribution to U.S. heritage, and kids will want to talk about the well-presented issues." Booklist

Includes bibliographical references

Rea, Amy C.

Muslim immigrants; in their shoes. Amy C. Rea. Childs World 2019 32 p. library $28.50

Grades: 4 5 6 7 **305.8**

1. Muslims -- United States 2. Immigrants -- United States 3. United States -- Immigration and emigration

ISBN 9781503828001 library

LC 2018944222

This book in the Immigrant Experiences series, by Amy C. Rea, "offers readers a compelling look into the lives, challenges, and successes of Muslim immigrants. Additional features include a Fast Facts page, a timeline, informative photo captions, critical-thinking questions, primary source quotes and accompanying source notes, a phonetic glossary, additional resources for further study, and an index." (Publisher's note)

"Muslim Immigrants traces the first immigrants from the ottoman empire to today, emphasizing their need for religious spaces, jobs, and acceptance." (Booklist)

Rodger, Marguerite

Racism and prejudice; [by] Marguerite Rodger and Jessie Rodger. Crabtree Pub. Co. 2010 48p il (Straight talk about. . .) lib bdg $29.27; pa $9.95

Grades: 7 8 9 10 **305.8**

1. Racism 2. Prejudices

ISBN 978-0-7787-2129-1 lib bdg; 0-7787-2129-9 lib bdg; 978-0-7787-2136-9 pa; 0-7787-2136-1 pa

LC 2010019132

The authors "cover topics ranging from overt racism to homophobia to the treatment of people with mental and physical disabilities. They discuss the history of hate and include personal accounts from those who've dealt with being stereotyped. The book is well laid out and easy to read. . . . Readers will appreciate the relevant photos of teens, the quotes, and the honest writing style." SLJ

Includes glossary

Wright, Simeon

Simeon's story; an eyewitness account of the kidnapping of Emmett Till. [by] Simeon Wright; with Herb Boyd. Lawrence Hill Books 2010 144p il map paperback $12.95

Grades: 6 7 8 9 10 **305.8**

1. Racism 2. Children 3. Lynching 4. Trials (Homicide) 5. Murder victims 6. Mississippi -- Race relations 7. African Americans -- Mississippi

ISBN 9781569768198 paperback; 978-1-55652-783-8

LC 2009-33631

"Simeon Wright was 12 years old when his cousin Emmett 'Bobo' Till came from Chicago to visit relatives in Mississippi. . . . One hot August night in 1955, Till whistled at a white female store clerk, setting off a chain of events that left an indelible mark not only on our nation's history, but also on the cousin who witnessed Till's gaffe and eventual kidnapping. Wright's story is chilling, and his honest account will hook readers from the beginning." SLJ

305.868 Spanish Americans

Hutchison, Patricia

Central American immigrants; in their shoes. Patricia Hutchison. Child's World 2019 32 p. color illustrations (Immigrant experiences) library $28.50

Grades: 4 5 6 7 **305.868**

1. Immigrants -- United States 2. United States -- Emigration and immigration

ISBN 9781503827950

LC 2018944110

This book in the Immigrant Experiences series, by Patricia Hutchison, "offers readers a compelling look into the lives, challenges, and successes of Central American immigrants. Additional features include a Fast Facts page, a timeline, informative photo captions, critical-thinking questions, primary source quotes and accompanying source notes, a phonetic glossary, additional resources for further study, and an index." (Publisher's note)

Includes bibliographical references (pages 31-32) and index

305.891 East Slavs

Krasner, Barbara

Russian immigrants; in their shoes. by Barbara Krasner. Child's World 2019 32 p. (library reinforced : alk. paper) $28.50

Grades: 4 5 6 7 **305.891**

1. Russians 2. United States -- Ethnic relations 3. United States -- Emigration and immigration

ISBN 1503828018; 9781503828018

LC 2018944223

This book, by Barbara Krasner, "offers readers a compelling look into the lives, challenges, and successes of Russian immigrants. Additional features include a fast facts page, a timeline, informative photo captions, critical-thinking questions, primary source quotes and accompanying source notes, a phonetic glossary, additional resources for further study, and an index." (Publisher's note)

Includes bibliographical references (page 32) and index.

305.896 Africans and people of African descent

Hartfield, Claire

★ A **few** red drops; the Chicago Race Riot of 1919. Claire Hartfield. Clarion Books, Houghton Mifflin Harcourt 2018 198 p. illustrations (hardcover) $18.99

Grades: 7 8 9 10 **305.896**

1. Race relations 2. Riots -- United States 3. Chicago (Ill.) -- History -- 20th century 4. Chicago (Ill.) -- History -- 1875- 5. Chicago Race Riot, Chicago, Ill., 1919 6. Chicago (Ill.) -- Race relations -- History -- 20th century 7. African Americans -- Illinois -- Chicago -- Social conditions

ISBN 0544785134; 9780544785137

LC 2016026969

Coretta Scott King (Author) Book Award (2019)

In this book, by Claire Hartfield, "on a hot day in July 1919, five black youths went swimming in Lake Michigan, unintentionally floating close to the 'white' beach. An angry white man began throwing stones at the boys, striking and killing one. Racial conflict on the beach erupted into days of urban violence that shook the city of Chicago. . . . This . . . narrative draws on contemporary accounts as it traces the roots of the explosion that had been building for decades." (Publisher's note)

"This readable, compelling history explores the longstanding and deeply rooted causes of the 1919 Chicago Race Riot, which left thirty-eight people dead and 537 wounded." Horn Book Magazine

Includes bibliographical references and index

Osborne, Linda Barrett

★ **Miles** to go for freedom; segregation and civil rights in the Jim Crow years. by Linda Barrett Osborne. Abrams Books for Young Readers 2011 118 p.

Grades: 6 7 8 **305.896**

1. United States -- History 2. United States -- Race relations 3. African Americans -- Segregation 4. African Americans -- Civil rights 5. African Americans -- Segregation -- History -- 20th century 6. African Americans -- Civil rights -- History -- 20th century 7. Civil rights movements -- United States -- History -- 20th century

ISBN 9781419700200

LC 2011022854

In this book, the "companion volume to 'Traveling the Freedom Road' (2009), Osborne . . . offers a[n] . . . overview of African American history, focusing here on both the South and the North during the late nineteenth-century through the mid-twentieth century. . . . Period images, including photos of public events, such as lynchings; magazine illustrations; and prints fill every double-page spread. After the first section on the South, the following section about the North focuses on the Great Migration, exploring not only the reasons why African Americans left but also the often chilly reception they received when they arrived. The final short section about the nation as a whole ends with the triumph of Brown v. Board of Education." (Booklist)

Includes bibliographical references and index

305.897 North American native peoples

Urban Tribes; Native Americans in the City. Edited by Lisa Charleyboy and Mary Beth Leatherdale. Firefly Books Ltd 2015 136 p. illustrations, color, b/w $21.95

Grades: 7 8 9 10 11 12 **305.897**

1. Native Americans

ISBN 1554517516; 9781554517510

This book, edited by Lisa Charleyboy and Mary Beth Leatherdale, "profiles young urban Natives from across North America, exploring how they connect with Native culture and values in their contemporary lives. Their stories are as diverse as they are. From a young Dene woman pursuing a MBA at Stanford to a Pima photographer in Phoenix to a Mohawk actress in New York, these urban Natives share their unique perspectives to bridge the divide between their past and their future." (Publisher's note)

"A refreshingly authentic, edgy, and captivating work that will appeal to young people." SLJ

Companion to Dreaming in Indian

305.9 People by occupation and miscellaneous social statuses; people with disabilities and illnesses, gifted people

Leatherdale, Mary Beth

Stormy seas; stories of young boat refugees. Mary Beth Leatherdale and [illustrated by] Eleanor Shakespeare. Annick Press 2017 56 p. ills (chiefly col.), col. maps (hardcover) $24.95

Grades: 5 6 7 8 9 **305.9**

1. Refugees 2. Immigration and emigration

ISBN 9781554518968; 1554518962

This book, by Mary Beth Leatherdale, illustrated by Eleanor Shakespeare, "presents five true stories about young people who lived through the harrowing experience of setting sail in search of asylum: Ruth and her family board the St. Louis to escape Nazism; Phu sets out alone from war-torn Vietnam; José tries to reach the U.S. from Cuba; Najeeba flees Afghanistan and the Taliban; Mohamed, an orphan, runs from his village on the Ivory Coast." (Publisher's note)

"Together, the words and images offer an affecting perspective on the plight of refugees and emphasizes that this human-rights crisis is an ongoing, urgent issue." Booklist

Includes bibliographical references (page 54).

306 Culture and institutions

Bales, Kevin

Slavery today; [by] Kevin Bales and Becky Cornell. Groundwood Books 2008 141p il (Groundwork guides) $18.95; pa $10

Grades: 7 8 9 10 **306**

1. Slavery

ISBN 978-0-88899-772-2; 0-88899-772-8; 978-0-88899-773-9 pa; 0-88899-773-6 pa

"Easy to read and extremely engaging, the work traces the existence and occurrence of slavery in modern factories, jungles, and farms around the world, and discusses prostitution and strategies for ending slavery in the global market. . . . Students will find this book of great use for research papers, but it is also highly readable for personal enrichment. The language used is not complicated, the prose is understandable, and the personal narratives are passionate, even when describing awful, inhumane acts." Libr Media Connect

Includes bibliographical references

Paul, Caroline

You are mighty; a guide to changing the world. by Caroline Paul ; illustrated by Lauren Tamaki. Bloomsbury 2018 128 p. (hardcover) $17.99

Grades: 5 6 7 8 9 **306**

1. Social action 2. Social change 3. Social problems

ISBN 9781681198224

LC 2017034366

This book, by Caroline Paul, illustrated by Lauren Tamaki, "features change-maker tips, tons of DIY activities, and stories about the kids who have paved the way before, from famous activists like Malala Yousafzai and Claudette Colvin to the everyday young people whose habit changes triggered huge ripple effects. So make a sign, write a letter, volunteer, sit-in, or march! There are lots of tactics to choose from, and you're never too young to change the world." (Publisher's note)

306.3 Economic institutions

Behnke, Alison Marie

Up for sale; by Alison Marie Behnke. Twenty-First Century Books 2015 72 p. illustrations (lib. bdg. : alk. paper) $34.60

Grades: 7 8 9 10 11 12 **306.3**

1. Slavery 2. Human trafficking 3. Prostitution

ISBN 1467716111; 9781467716116

LC 2013022607

This book by Alison Marie Behnke describes how "Victims of human traffickers include workers in restaurants and in garment factories, maids and nannies in the homes of wealthy families, child sex workers, beggars on the street, boy soldiers, even infants kidnapped for foreign adoptions. Women and children are more likely to be coerced or seized than men and boys, especially if they are poor and uneducated." (Publisher's note)

Includes bibliographical references and index

Huey, Lois Miner

Forgotten bones; uncovering a slave cemetery. by Lois Miner Huey. Millbrook Press 2016 112 p. illustrations (library binding : alkaline paper) $30.65

Grades: 4 5 6 7 **306.3**

1. Slavery 2. Cemeteries 3. Human remains (Archeology) 4. Northeastern States -- Antiquities 5. Slaves -- Tombs -- Northeastern States 6. Slave cemeteries -- Northeastern States 7. Slaves -- Northeastern States -- History 8. African American cemeteries -- Northeastern States 9. Human remains (Archaeology) -- Northeastern States 10. African Americans -- Northeastern States -- History

ISBN 1467733938; 9781467733939

LC 2014009379

This children's book by Lois Miner Huey tells how "when a skeleton's head rolled off a dirt pile, all work came to a halt at a construction project in upstate New York. Archaeologists began excavating and found thirteen skeletons. Further investigation revealed that the bones were those of eighteenth-century African American slaves who had worked at the nearby Schuyler farm. Find out what these skeletons tell us about slavery and daily life long ago." (Publisher's note)

"Together with chronicles of two other noted northern slave cemeteries and full-color photos of the excavation in process, this account provides a vivid description of both the eighteenth-century slave experience and the field of archaeology." Booklist

Includes bibliographical references and index

McClafferty, Carla Killough

Buried lives; the enslaved people of George Washington's Mount Vernon. by Carla Killough McClafferty. Holiday House 2018 168 p. (hardcover) $24.99

Grades: 6 7 8 9 **306.3**

1. Slaves 2. Slavery -- United States -- History 3. Slaves -- Virginia -- Mount Vernon (Estate) 4. Mount Vernon (Va. : Estate) -- Race relations

ISBN 9780823436972

LC 2016058471

This book, by Carla Killough McClafferty, "look[s] at the complex relationships between George Washington and the enslaved people of Mount Vernon, and the history still being uncovered there. . . . McClafferty sheds light on the lives of several people George Washington owned; the property laws of the day that complicated his decision to free them; and the Cemetery Survey, an archeological dig . . . that is shaping our understanding of Mount Vernon's Slave Cemetery." (Publisher's note)

306.362 Slavery

Conkling, Winifred

Passenger on the Pearl; the true story of Emily Edmonson's flight from slavery. Winifred Conkling. First edition Algonquin Young Readers 2015 176 p. illustrations, maps $17.95

Grades: 7 8 9 10 **306.362**

1. Fugitive slaves 2. Pearl (Schooner) 3. Underground Railroad -- Washington Region 4. Fugitive slaves -- Washington Region -- History -- 19th century 5. Antislavery movements -- United States -- History -- 19th century

ISBN 1616201967; 9781616201968

LC 2014029246

This book presents a "historical narrative concerning several people involved in an attempted slave escape in 1848. The Pearl was to ferry 13-year-old Emily Edmonson and scores of other runaway slaves from Washington DC down the Potomac River and up the Chesapeake Bay. However, the ship was captured before reaching free soil. [Winifred] Conkling narrates the tumultuous stories of Edmonson, her family, and the others involved." (School Library Journal)

"By examining the intersecting experiences of enslaved people, abolitionists, free people of color, slave owners, and slave traders, this book provides an effective antidote to the oversimplified picture of slavery in America painted by some outdated textbooks." Booklist

Includes bibliographical references

306.4 Specific aspects of culture

Palad, Thea

★ **Mixed** messages; interpreting body image & social norms. ABDO Pub. Co. 2009 112p il (Essential health: strong, beautiful girls) lib bdg $22.95

Grades: 6 7 8 9 **306.4**

1. Self-esteem 2. Self-acceptance 3. Girls -- Psychology

ISBN 978-1-60453-102-2 lib bdg; 1-60453-102-9 lib bdg

LC 2008-19351

This features fictional narratives paired with firsthand advice from a licensed psychologist to help preteen and teen readers better understand the countless media messages that are presented to them daily. Topics include body image, stereotypes, and feeling comfortable in one's own skin.

"The topics are well selected, the design is attractive, and the stories feature girls from a variety of cultures." Booklist

Includes glossary and bibliographical references

306.7 Sexual relations

Feinstein, Stephen

Sexuality and teens; what you should know about sex, abstinence, birth control, pregnancy, and stds. Enslow Publishers 2010 104p il (Issues in focus today) lib bdg $31.93

Grades: 7 8 9 10 **306.7**

1. Youth -- Sexual behavior

ISBN 978-0-7660-3312-2; 0-7660-3312-0

LC 2009-1373

"This text provides a well-balanced look at sexual attitudes and behaviors as they relate to today's youth. . . . The book could be useful for basic report and debate information or as a jumping-off point for class discussions." SLJ

Includes glossary and bibliographical references

Wallis, Pete

★ **What** does consent really mean? written by Pete Wallis and Thalia Wallis ; illustrated by Joseph Wilkins. Singing Dragon 2017 62 p. color illustrations (hardcover) $19.95

Grades: 8 9 10 11 12 **306.7**

1. Rape 2. Sexual harassment 3. Teenagers -- Sexual behavior

ISBN 1848193300; 9780857012852; 9781848193307

LC 2017030844

In this book, by Pete Wallis and Thalia Wallis, illustrated by Joseph Wilkins, "following the sexual assault of a classmate, a group of teenage girls find themselves discussing the term consent, what it actually means for them in their current relationships, and how they act and make decisions with peer influence. . . . This rich graphic novel uncovers the need for more informed conversations with young people around consent and healthy relationships." (Publisher's note)

"Content that could be heavy with pedagogy is instead lightened by informal, occasionally profane language and friendly teasing." SLJ

Includes bibliographical references.

306.76 Sexual orientation, transgenderism, intersexuality

Bausum, Ann

★ **Stonewall**; breaking out in the fight for gay rights. Ann Bausum. Viking Books for Young Readers 2015 128 p. illustrations (hardback) $16.99

Grades: 8 9 10 11 12 **306.76**

1. Gay rights 2. Civil rights 3. Stonewall Riots, New York, N.Y., 1969 4. Gay men -- United States -- History -- 20th century 5. Lesbians -- United States -- History -- 20th century 6. Greenwich Village (New York, N.Y.) -- History -- 20th century 7. Gay liberation movement -- United States -- History -- 20th century

ISBN 0670016799; 9780670016792

LC 2014039812

Author Ann Bausum presents this "exploration of the Stonewall Riots and the national Gay Rights movement that followed. In 1969 being gay in the United States was a criminal offense. It meant living a closeted life or surviving on the fringes of society. The Stonewall Inn, a Mafia-run, filthy, overpriced bar in New York City's Greenwich Village, was one of them." (Publisher's note)

"Bausum begins her history of the gay rights movement with a careful, detailed exposition of the June 1969 Stonewall riots, laying out the events leading up to the clash between the Greenwich Village gay community and the police and putting those events in the context of time and place. She dedicates the first half of the book to the riots themselves, drawing on reports, interviews, and other first-person accounts to put together a candid linear narrative that takes into consideration the perspectives of both sides of the conflict. . . . Bausum writes with the precision of a journalist; there is never any doubt as to what she wonders, what she conjectures, and what she knows." Horn Book

Includes filmography and bibliographical references (pages 111-115) and index

Hurt, Avery Elizabeth

Confronting LGBTQ+ discrimination; Avery Elizabeth Hurt. Rosen Publishing 2018 64 p. (library bound) $34.45

Grades: 7 8 9 10 **306.76**

1. Homophobia 2. Prejudices 3. Discrimination 4. Homophobia -- United States 5. Discrimination -- United States 6. Sexual minorities -- Civil rights -- United States

ISBN 9781538381724; 9781538381731; 9781538381748

LC 2017017641

This book in the Speak Up! Confronting Discrimination in Your Daily Life series, by Avery Elizabeth Hurt, "empowers readers to confront discrimination and offers practical guidance on navigating a sometimes hostile world where not everyone believes that LGBTQ+ people should have the same rights as everyone else. Readers who define as LGBTQ+ will find themselves encouraged, and those who do not will learn how to be supportive allies of their LGBTQ+ friends and classmates." (Publisher's note)

Includes bibliographical references and index

It gets better; coming out, overcoming bullying, and creating a life worth living. [edited by] Dan Savage [and] Terry Miller. Penguin 2012 352p pbk $16.00

Grades: 6 7 8 9 10 11 12 **306.76**

1. Bullies 2. Happiness 3. Gay teenagers 4. Bullying 5. Coming out (Sexual orientation)

ISBN 9780452297616

"It Gets Better is a collection of original essays and expanded testimonials written to teens from celebrities, political leaders, and everyday people, because while many LGBT teens can't see a positive future for themselves, we can." (Publisher's note)

""I wish I could have told you things get better." The words that became a call to action were born in the comments section on a blog post written by Savage about 15-year-old Billy Lucas. Savage, an author (The Kid, 1999), gay activist, and sex-advice columnist, together with his partner, Miller, launched the It Gets Better project on YouTube as a reaction to Lucas' and two other suicides precipitated by gay bullying during the summer of 2010. . . . It Gets Better—the book—expands on a selection of those videos, capturing stories from people of every background, including a startling collection of famous writers, entertainers, and politicians. Particularly noteworthy are essays from President Obama and David Sedaris and a bilingual entry from a Mexican student now living in Canada. This a resource every library should have on hand." Booklist

Jennings, Jazz

Being Jazz; my life as a (transgender) teen. Jazz Jennings. Crown 2016 265 p. illustrations (some color) (hbk) $17.99
Grades: 6 7 8 9 **306.76**

1. Transgender people 2. Transgender teenagers 3. Transgender people -- Identity 4. Transgender youth -- United States -- Biography 5. Transgender people -- United States -- Biography
ISBN 9780399554643; 9780399554650
LC 2016009206

Rainbow List 2017

In this memoir, Jazz Jennings reflects on her "very public experiences and how they have helped shape the mainstream attitude toward the transgender community. . . . Jazz has faced . . . bullying, discrimination, and rejection, yet she perseveres as she educates others about her life as a transgender teen. Through it all, her family has been beside her on this journey, standing together against those who don't understand the true meaning of tolerance and unconditional love." (Publisher's note)

"A great introduction to trans life for middle schoolers and a balancing addition to the more harrowing stories available." SLJ

Kuklin, Susan

★ **Beyond** magenta; transgender teens speak out. Susan Kuklin. Candlewick Press 2014 192 p. ill. (some col.) $22.99
Grades: 7 8 9 10 11 12 **306.76**

1. Teenagers 2. Transgender people
ISBN 0763656119; 9780763656119
LC 2013943071

Stonewall Honor Book: Children's & Young Adult Literature (2015)

For this book, author Susan Kuklin "met and interviewed six transgender or gender-neutral young adults . . . to represent them thoughtfully and respectfully before, during, and after their personal acknowledgment of gender preference. Portraits, family photographs, and candid images grace the pages, augmenting the emotional and physical journey each youth has taken." (Publisher's note)

"The level of detail about their lives, and the diversity of their identities--including gender, sexuality, ethnicity, religion, and geography--provide a powerful antidote to the isolation and stigma that some transgender youth experience." SLJ

Includes bibliographical references

Madrone, Kelly Huegel

★ **LGBTQ**; the survival guide for lesbian, gay, bisexual, transgender, and questioning teens. Kelly Huegel Madrone. 3rd edition Free Spirit Publishing 2018 viii, 263 p.p illustrations
Grades: 7 8 9 10 11 12 **306.76**

1. Bisexuals -- United States 2. Gay teenagers -- United States 3. Homosexuality -- United States 4. Lesbian teenagers -- United States 5. Transgender people -- United States 6. Coming out (Sexual orientation) -- United States
ISBN 1631983024; 9781631983023
LC 2018002137

"This affirming guide covers a wide range of topics, educating readers and helping them become better advocates for themselves. Using the acronym LGBTQ and the word queer, this updated and revised third edition includes updated data and emphasizes evolving concepts and understandings of gender and sexuality, advances in LGBTQ rights, cultural shifts and changing attitudes, and a look at a wider range of experience and identity. With information from experts, advice from advocacy groups, and stories from teenagers, chapters tackle accepting and questioning identity, trans and nonbinary teens, what to consider when coming out, harassment and bullying, finding community, dating (including a look at relationship violence), sex and sexually transmitted infections, mental health, and religious life." (School Library Journal)

Includes bibliographical references (pages 250-253) and index

Seba, Jaime

Gallup guides for youth facing persistent prejudice; The LGBT community. by Jaime Seba. Mason Crest Publishers 2013 64 p. col. ill., photographs (library) $22.95
Grades: 5 6 7 8 **306.76**

1. LGBT people -- Civil rights 2. Homophobia 3. Gay youth -- United States 4. Homophobia -- United States 5. Sexual minorities -- Civil rights -- United States
ISBN 1422224678; 9781422224670
LC 2012017108

This book by Jaime Seba on the LGBT community "discusses the history of prejudice toward this group, the laws that protect people against discrimination-and what you can do to fight the prejudice you find in the world." (Publisher's note) As part of the "Gallup Guides for Youth Facing Persistent Prejudice" series, it "emphasiz[es] recent violence and other problems, such as bullying and depression, which are, unfortunately, still routine for many LGBT youth." (Booklist)

Includes bibliographical references (p. 62) and index.

Testa, Rylan Jay

The **gender** quest workbook; a guide for teens and young adults exploring gender identity. Rylan Jay Testa, PhD, Deborah Coolhart, PhD, Jayme Peta, MA, MS ; foreword by Ryan K. Sallans, M.A. ; afterword by Arlene Istar Lev, LCSW-R, CASAC. New Harbinger Publications, Inc. 2015 168 p. illustrations (pbk. : alk. paper) $16.95
Grades: 7 8 9 10 11 12 Professional **306.76**

1. Gender role 2. Transgender teenagers 3. Sex differences (Psychology) 4. Transgenderism 5. Gender identity 6. Sex differences (Psychology)
ISBN 9781626252974
LC 2015032696

This guidebook "incorporates skills, exercises, and activities from evidence-based therapies—such as cognitive behavioral therapy (CBT)—to help you address the broad range of struggles you may encounter related to gender identity, such as anxiety, isolation, fear, and even depression." (Publisher's note)

"From inconspicuous activities such as people watching to more task-oriented ideas for encouraging young people to broach their concerns to family members, this volume serves as a valuable resource. While this isn't the best acquisition for libraries (it is truly a workbook), librarians would do well to be informed of its availability." LJ

McGrody, Ellen

Coping with gender dysphoria; Ellen McGrody. Rosen Publishing 2018 112 p. color illustrations (Coping) (library binding) $37.00

Grades: 7 8 9 10 **306.76**

1. Mental health 2. Gender identity 3. Depression (Psychology) 4. Gender identity disorders

ISBN 9781508173915

LC 2017005822

This book in the Coping series, by Ellen McGrody, "describes the various types of gender dysphoria--including but not limited to being transgender--and discusses ways of presentation, medical care, dealing with prejudice, mental health situations, and relationships." (Publisher's note)

"This entry in the Coping series expertly addresses the issue of gender dysphoria . . ." Booklist

Includes bibliographical references and index

306.8 Marriage and family

Lynette, Rachel

★ **What** makes us a family? living in a nontraditional family. content consultant, Robyn J. A. Silverman. ABDO Pub. Co. 2009 112p il (Essential health: strong beautiful girls) lib bdg $32.79

Grades: 6 7 8 9 **306.8**

1. Family

ISBN 978-1-60453-756-7 lib bdg; 1-60453-756-6 lib bdg

LC 2009004416

"The topics are well selected, the design is attractive, and the stories feature girls from a variety of cultures." Booklist

Shantz-Hilkes, Chloe

My Girlfriend's Pregnant! A Teen's Guide to Becoming a Dad. Chloe Shantz-Hilkes. Firefly Books Ltd 2015 128 p. (hardcover) $19.95

Grades: 7 8 9 10 11 12 **306.8**

1. Teenage fathers 2. Teenage pregnancy 3. Pregnancy -- Psychological aspects 4. Parenthood -- Psychological aspects 5. Teenage fathers -- Life skills guides

ISBN 9781554517428; 9781554517435; 1554517435

This book, by Chloe Shantz-Hilkes, seeks to help "teens faced with an unplanned pregnancy. . . . Teenage fathers also face a future filled with fear, doubt, and guilt. . . . With an extensive list of further readings and resources to help with issues ranging from child support to bonding with your child, this book illustrates to young dads that they are not alone and that there are positive ways of dealing with the difficult choices that lie ahead." (Publisher's note)

"Intended to provide teen fathers-to-be some support and guidance, this book sheds light on a variety of topics: pregnancy, childbirth, and parenting; the different options ahead (keeping the baby, adoption, abortion), how to deal with the relationship with the mother, and how to manage stress. Interspersed throughout are firsthand accounts from men who became fathers in their teens or early twenties." SLJ

306.84 Types of marriage and relationships

Sheen, Barbara

Multiracial families; by Barbara Sheen. ReferencePoint Press, Inc. 2018 64 p. (hardback) $29.95

Grades: 7 8 9 10 11 12 **306.84**

1. Interracial marriage 2. Racially mixed people 3. Interracial marriage -- United States 4. Racially mixed families -- United States

ISBN 168282361X; 9781682823613

LC 2018013485

In this book in the Changing Families series, by Barbara Sheen, "multiracial families are becoming more and more common. In fact, multiracial youngsters are the fastest growing segment of the population. Their numbers are predicted to triple by 2060. This book presents a real-world look at how American families are changing and helps teen rea7ders gain an understanding of what it is like to be part of a multiracial family." (Publisher's note)

"This volume in the Changing Families series (five titles) thoughtfully inspects multiracial or multiethnic families and kicks off with the eye-opening statistic that 'multiracial kids and teens are the fastest growing segment of the population.'" (Booklist)

Includes bibliographical references and index

306.87 Intrafamily relationships

Apelqvist, Eva

LGBTQ families; the ultimate teen guide. Eva Apelqvist. Scarecrow Press, Inc. 2013 208 p. (It happened to me) (cloth : alk. paper) $50

Grades: 7 8 9 10 11 12 **306.87**

1. LGBT people 2. Families 3. Children of gay parents 4. Gays -- Family relationships 5. Sexual minorities -- Family relationships

ISBN 0810885360; 9780810885363

LC 2013015488

This book by Eva Apelqvist is part of the It Happened to Me series. This entry "begins with an overview of each letter of the iconic acronym and progresses into a more thorough look at LGBTQ adolescents, LGBTQ parents, and how trans individuals may affect family dynamics. Other chapters investigate same-sex marriage, other issues (e.g., rights of sperm donors), LGBTQ rights around the world, bullying, . . . and the ongoing debate between the LGBTQ community and various religious, political, and business groups." (Booklist)

Includes bibliographical references and index

306.874 Parent-child relationship

Buscemi, Karen

Split in two; keeping it together when your parents live apart. Karen Buscemi. Zest 2009 120 p. ill. (paperback) $12.95

Grades: 7 8 9 10 11 12 **306.874**

1. Children of divorced parents

ISBN 0980073219; 9780980073218

LC 2008936059

"Provides advice to children of divorced parents on living in two homes simultaneously, including how to organize during moves, managing different lifestyles, and coping with the emotional stress of separation." Publisher's note

"Written in a casual, genuine tone, the substantive chapters begin with valuable questions that help kids assess whether their basic needs for privacy and comfort are met in each household. . . . Like the text, Mucha's quirky cartoon illustrations find humor in the complicated situations and feelings, adding further appeal to this hip, reassuring guide filled with straightforward, honest advice." Booklist

306.9 Institutions pertaining to death

Noyes, Deborah

★ **Encyclopedia** of the end; mysterious death in fact, fancy, folklore, and more. Houghton Mifflin Co. 2008 143p il $25

Grades: 7 8 9 10 11 12 **306.9**

1. Death 2. Reference books 3. Funeral rites and ceremonies

ISBN 978-0-618-82362-8; 0-618-82362-X

LC 2008-1872

"This stylish A-to-Z encounter with all things related to death and dying shows Noyes . . . at her liveliest. . . . The author offers a broad illumination of spiritual, historical and biological aspects of death. Photos, paintings and engravings in homage to 'the end' make the book dynamic visually, too." Publ Wkly

Thornhill, Jan

I found a dead bird; the kids' guide to the cycle of life & death. Maple Tree Press 2006 64p il $21.95; pa $9.95

Grades: 4 5 6 **306.9**

1. Death 2. Bereavement

ISBN 1-897066-70-8; 1-897066-71-6 pa

Explores the cycle of life and death, and how the process is necessary in nature, while also commenting on how death effects people personally, and the skills they use to cope with such a trauma when it occurs.

"This straightforward, no holds barred approach to the subject will captivate children. Chock-full of color photographs, the well-designed book contains boxes with tidbits of information on a wide variety of topics, such as death of a species, human destruction, plant decomposition, trapped in time, and learning from death." SLJ

307 Communities

Hopkinson, Deborah

Shutting out the sky; life in the tenements of New York, 1880-1924. Orchard Bks. 2003 134p il $17.95

Grades: 5 6 7 8 9 10 **307**

1. Poor 2. Immigrants -- United States 3. Lower East Side (New York, N.Y.)

ISBN 0-439-37590-8

LC 2002-44781

Photographs and text document the experiences of five individuals who came to live in the Lower East Side of New York City as children or young adults from Belarus, Italy, Lithuania, and Romania at the turn of the twentieth century.

"The text is supported by numerous tinted archival photos of living and working conditions. Although this book will appeal to students looking for material for projects, the writing lends immediacy and vivid images make it simply a fascinating read." SLJ

Includes bibliographical references

307.2 Movement of people to, from, within communities

Harris, Laurie Lanzen

The **great** migration north, 1910-1970; by Laurie Lanzen Harris. Omnigraphics, Inc. 2012 xvi, 241 p.p

Grades: 7 8 9 10 11 12 **307.2**

1. Internal migration 2. African Americans -- History 3. United States -- History -- 20th century 4. African Americans -- Migrations -- History -- 20th century 5. Rural-urban migration -- United States -- History -- 20th century

ISBN 0780811860; 9780780811867

LC 2011033540

This historical survey by Laurie Lanzen Harris "explains the social and economic factors that drove the African-American exodus out of the rural South to the industrial cities of the North during the first half of the twentieth century. The book also details the transformative impact of this migration on U.S. industry, culture, and race relations, as well as the daily experiences of the men, women, and children who built new lives for themselves in New York, Chicago, Philadelphia, Detroit, and other cities of the North. Finally, it explains how this multi-generational flight from oppression to opportunity changed the internal dynamics of African-American families and communities across America." (Publisher's note)

Includes bibliographical references and index.

307.7 Specific kinds of communities

Lorinc, John

Cities. Groundwood Books/House of Anansi Press 2008 144p (Groundwork guides) $18.95; pa $10

Grades: 7 8 9 10 11 12 **307.7**

1. Urbanization 2. Cities and towns

ISBN 978-0-88899-820-0; 0-88899-820-1; 978-0-88899-819-4 pa; 0-88899-819-8 pa

"This packed, highly readable [title] . . . does an excellent job of tracing urban history worldwide, raising the big social, political, and economic issues of poverty, migration, conservation, public health, crime, transportation, and much more, always rooted in specific examples of the problems and riches of city life." Booklist

Includes bibliographical references

307.76 Urban communities

Reilly, Kathleen M.

Cities; Discover How They Work. by Kathleen M. Reilly, illustrated by Tom Casteel. Pgw 2014 128 p. $16.95

Grades: 4 5 6 **307.76**

1. Urban ecology 2. Cities and towns 3. City planning 4. Civil engineering

ISBN 1619302136; 1619302179; 9781619302136; 9781619302174

This book, by Kathleen M. Reilly and illustrated by Tom Casteel, "will give kids a view into the inner functioning of . . . urban areas. They'll learn about all the parts that come together to make cities work and how they've grown and changed since the very first riverside settlements. . . . Sidebars, unique illustrations, . . . and fun . . . facts combine with age-appropriate hands-on activities to make learning about complex urban environments fun and reinforce learning." (Publisher's note)

"According to the 2010 Census, 80% of Americans live in urban areas." But do they know what it takes to make a city run? From this well-organized and engaging text, readers will learn how cities developed and grew...The simple black-and-white illustrations are helpful, but young readers accustomed to photos might pass on it when leafing through the book. Even so, this is a worthy title for any library collection." SLJ

Spilsbury, Richard

Towns and cities; by Richard Spilsbury. Heinemann Library 2012 64 p. (The impact of environmentalism) (library) $35.00; (paperback) $9.99

Grades: 6 7 8 **307.76**

1. Cities and towns 2. Environmental protection 3. City planning 4. Urban ecology (Sociology)

ISBN 1432965190; 9781432965198; 9781432965259

LC 2012001039

This book by Richard Spilsbury is part of the Impact of Environmentalism series and looks at cities and towns. The series provides "a global overview of environmentalism from different, often overlapping, perspectives." This entry "supplies insights into sustainable urbanization, including information about solar-energy efforts in cities worldwide." (School Library Journal)

Includes bibliographical references and index.

320 Political science (Politics and government)

Cooper, Ilene

A **woman** in the House and Senate; how women came to washington and changed the nation. by Ilene Cooper ; illustrations by Elizabeth Baddeley. Revised and updated edition Abrams Books for Young Readers 2020 160 p. illustrations hardcover $19.99

Grades: 5 6 7 8 **320**

1. Women in politics -- United States 2. United States. Congress -- History 3. Women legislators -- United States -- History 4. Women -- Political activity -- United States -- History

ISBN 9781419742668 hardcover; 9781419710360

Originally published 2014

"From the women's suffrage movement to the 2018 election, Ilene Cooper highlights influential and diverse female leaders who opened doors for women in politics. Women featured include Nancy Pelosi (the first woman Speaker of the House), Margaret Chase Smith (the first woman elected to the Senate), Patsy Mink (the first woman of color to serve in the House), and newcomers like Representatives Alexandria Ocasio-Cortez and Ilhan Omar. This updated book includes archival photographs and lively illustrations from Elizabeth Baddeley, as well as a chart of all the women who have served in Congress." (Publisher's note)

Includes bibliographical references and index

320.01 Philosophy and theory

McCulloch, Amanda

Building consensus; respecting different points of view. Amanda McCulloch. PowerKids Press 2018 32 p. (library bound book) $26.25

Grades: 5 6 7 8 **320.01**

1. Decision making 2. Social sciences 3. Political science 4. Civics 5. Consensus (Social sciences)

ISBN 9781508163930; 9781538327869; 9781538327982

LC 2017019867

In this book in the Spotlight on Civic Action series, by Amanda McCulloch, "it can be difficult to take each person's ideas into consideration when trying to make a decision. However, respecting different points of view is essential to coming to a consensus. . . . [This book will help] students . . . understand how reaching a consensus can help reach a decision by making each person involved in a decision feel as though their point of view has value." (Publisher's note)

The **politics** book; Big ideas simply explained. edited by Rebecca Warren and Kate Johnsen ; illustrated by James Graham. 1st American ed. DK Pub. 2013 352 p. ill. (some col.) (Big ideas simply explained) (hardcover) $25.00

Grades: 8 9 10 11 12 Adult **320.01**

1. Political philosophy

ISBN 1465402144; 9781465402141

LC 2012533724

This book, part of the Big Ideas Simply Explained series, looks at political philosophy. "More than 100 political philosophers, among them Confucius, Plato, Machiavelli, Mary Wollstonecraft, Karl Marx, Ito Hirobumi, Emiliano Zapata, Jomo Kenyatta, and Mao Zedong, are covered in seven chronological sections ranging from 'Ancient Political Thought' to 'Postwar Politics.'" (Library Journal)

320.082 Women in Politics

Ross, Michael Elsohn, 1952-

She takes a stand; 16 fearless activists who have changed the world. Michael Elsohn Ross. Chicago Review Press 2015 208 p. illustrations (hardback) $19.95

Grades: 6 7 8 9 10 **320.082**

1. Women political activists 2. Women -- Political activity 3. Women's rights 4. Women social reformers

ISBN 9781613730263

LC 2015001401

This book, by Michael Elsohn Ross, "offers a realistic look at the . . . bold actions of women and girls around the world working to improve their personal situations and the lives of others. This . . . collection of short biographies features the stories of extraordinary figures past and present who have dedicated their lives to fighting for human rights, civil rights, workers' rights, reproductive rights, and world peace." (Publisher's note)

"Ross portrays his subjects with honesty, highlighting both their missteps and accomplishments, while emphasizing how anyone can become an activist with enough passion and will." Pub Wkly

Includes bibliographical references and index

320.083 Politics -- Youth

How I resist; activism and hope for a new generation. edited by Maureen Johnson. Wednesday Books 2018 xiv, 201 p.p illustrations (trade pbk.) $18.99

Grades: 8 9 10 11 12 **320.083**

1. Youth -- Political activity 2. Political participation -- United States 3. Youth -- Political activity -- United States

ISBN 9781250168375; 9781250168368

LC 2018001590

This book, edited by Maureen Johnson, is "an all-star collection of essays about activism and hope. . . . Now, more than ever, young people are motivated to make a difference in a world they're bound to inherit. They're ready to stand up and be heard--but with much to shout about, where they do they begin? . . . [This book] is the response, and a way to start the conversation. To show readers that they are not helpless, and that anyone can be the change." (Publisher's note)

"A useful classroom tool that will generate discussion around topics that matter to many young people today." Kirkus

Styron, Alexandra

Steal this country; a handbook for resistance, persistence, and fixing almost anything. Alexandra Styron. Viking 2018 212 p. (hardback) $19.99

Grades: 7 8 9 10 11 12 **320.083**

1. Youth -- Political activity 2. Social action -- United States 3. Community organization -- United States 4. Youth -- Political activity -- United States

ISBN 9780451479372

LC 2017060705

In this book author Alexandra Styron's "call for resistance and citizen activism will be clearly heard by young people who don't accept 'it is what it is,' who want to make sure everybody gets an equal piece of the American pie. . . . Styron's . . . informative primer on how to make a difference is organized into three sections: The Why, The What, and The How. The book opens with a personal essay and a historic look at civil disobedience and teenage activism in America." (Publisher's note)

320.4 Structure and functions of government

Han, Lori Cox

Handbook to American democracy; Lori Cox Han and Tomislav Han. Facts On File 2011 224 p.

Grades: 8 9 10 11 12 Adult **320.4**

1. United States -- History 2. Democracy -- United States -- History 3. United States -- Politics and government 4. United States -- Politics and government -- Handbooks, manuals, etc

ISBN 0816078548; 9780816078547

LC 2011005185

The authors "address the foundations of American democracy and the three branches of American government. The books introduce offices, history, and issues in eight chapters each (e.g., 'The Founding Fathers and the American Revolution,' 'How Congress Is Organized,' and 'Vice Presidents, Presidential Advisers, and America's First Ladies'). The material is complemented by black-and-white photos and sidebars on legal cases, laws and legislation, statistics, maps, biographies of major figures such as Henry VIII, and other primary materials, and chapters close with a summary. . . . [The volumes] each include an individual glossary, index, selected bibliography, and table of contents." (Libr J)

Includes bibliographical references and index

320.973 United States -- Politics

Khan, Khizr, 1950-

This is our Constitution; discover America with a Gold Star father. Khizr Khan. Random House Childrens Books 2017 224 p. $19.99

Grades: 6 7 8 9 **320.973**

1. United States -- History 2. United States -- Politics and government

ISBN 1524770914; 1524770922; 9781524770914; 9781524770921

This book "is a personal journey that [author] Khizr Khan is taking with our nation's young people. The book includes: A highly personal introduction and conclusion; Notes throughout that share Khizr Khan's reflections on and connections to the U.S. Constitution; The fascinating history of why and how the Constitution was written; Article by article and section by section, an easy-to-follow explanation of what the Constitution means; . . . [and] why the Constitution matters." (Publisher's note)

321 Systems of governments and states

Davidson, Tish

★ **Theocracy**; Tish Davidson. Mason Crest 2013 64 p. col. ill. (Major forms of world government) (library) $22.95; (ebook) $28.95

Grades: 6 7 8 9 10 **321**

1. Theocracy 2. Political science

ISBN 1422221431; 9781422221433; 9781422294604

LC 2012027863

This book, by Tish Davidson, as part of the publisher's "Major Forms of World Government" series, "examines theocratic governments, from ancient Egypt to present-day Iran. It explores how different theocracies arose, how their leaders maintained authority, and what it was like for ordinary people living under religious rule." (Publisher's note)

Includes bibliographical references and index.

321.5 Elitist systems

Gelletly, LeeAnne

Oligarchy; LeeAnne Gelletly. Mason Crest 2013 64 p. illustrations (Major forms of world government) (hc) $22.95

Grades: 6 7 8 9 10 **321.5**

1. Oligarchy

ISBN 1422221423; 9781422221426; 9781422294598

LC 2012027858

In this book, by LeeAnne Gelletly, part of the "Major Forms of World Government" series, "Oligarchs may exercise power directly or indirectly, but they often act out of selfish or corrupt motives. This book examines the history of oligarchy, which was first described by the ancient Greeks more than 2,300 years ago. The book also asks whether today's superrich constitute a new oligarchy that threatens to undermine American democracy." (Publisher's note)

Includes bibliographical references (p. 60) and index

321.6 Absolute monarchy

Gelletly, LeeAnne

Monarchy; LeeAnne Gelletly. Mason Crest 2013 64 p. illustrations (Major forms of world government) (hc) $22.95

Grades: 6 7 8 9 10 **321.6**

1. Monarchy 2. Kings and rulers

ISBN 1422221415; 9781422221419; 9781422294581

LC 2012027846

In this book, by LeeAnne Gelletly, part of the "Major Forms of World Government" series, "Monarchies have existed since the dawn of human civilization. But while the kings and queens, emperors and empresses of the past wielded broad (and often absolute) power, many of today's monarchs perform ceremonial functions only. This book examines the various forms that monarchy has taken. Students of government and history will find it a valuable and fascinating resource." (Publisher's note)

Includes bibliographical references (p. 61) and index

321.8 Democratic government

Laxer, James

Democracy. Groundwood Books 2009 143p (Groundwork guides) $18.95; pa $10

Grades: 8 9 10 11 12 **321.8**

1. Democracy

ISBN 978-0-88899-912-2; 0-88899-912-7; 978-0-88899-913-9 pa; 0-88899-913-5 pa

This title "stands out for its accessible introduction to historical and contemporary democracy across the globe. Laxer skillfully supports his arguments with examples and avoids pat definitions." Booklist

Includes bibliographical references

Meersman, Erika

Majority rule vs. individual rights; Erika Meersman. PowerKids Press 2018 32 p. (library bound) $26.25

Grades: 5 6 7 8 **321.8**

1. Civil rights -- United States 2. United States -- Politics and government 3. Majorities 4. Political rights -- United States

ISBN 1508163944; 9781508163947; 9781538327920; 9781538328040

LC 2017027522

"Majority rule refers to a democracy being governed by decisions upon which a greater portion of people has agreed. However, U.S. citizens have basic and inalienable rights that can't be violated by the government. This book[, by Erika Meersman,] explores these basic and inalienable rights in relation to majority rule, and provides insight to how these concepts are laid out in the U.S. Constitution." (Publisher's note)

321.9 Authoritarian government

Bailey, Diane

Dictatorship; Diane Bailey. Mason Crest 2013 64 p. color illustrations (Major forms of world government) (hc) $22.95

Grades: 6 7 8 9 10 **321.9**

1. Dictators 2. Dictatorship

ISBN 1422221385; 9781422221389; 9781422294550

LC 2012027899

This book, by Diane Bailey, part of the "Major Forms of World Government" series, focuses on dictatorship. "The books in this series will focus on the major types of government found in the world today. They will explain, in terms that are clear and understandable to young adults, not only how the major forms of government function but also their philosophical underpinnings. The books will illustrate how ideas about good governance have evolved over the course of history." (Publisher's note)

Includes bibliographical references and index

322.4 Political action groups

Bartoletti, Susan Campbell

★ **They** called themselves the K.K.K. the birth of an American terrorist group. Houghton Mifflin 2010 172p il map $19

Grades: 7 8 9 10 **322.4**

1. Racism 2. Ku Klux Klan 3. White supremacy movements 4. Reconstruction (1865-1876) 5. United States -- Race relations 6. Racism -- United States 7. Hate groups -- United States

ISBN 0-618-44033-X; 978-0-618-44033-7

LC 2009-45247

This is a history of the Ku Klux Klan. Bibliography. Index. "Middle school, high school." (Horn Book)

"In this comprehensive, accessible account, . . . [the author] draws from documentary histories, slave narratives, newspapers, congressional testimony, and other sources to chronicle the origins and proliferation of the Ku Klux Klan against the charged backdrop of Reconstruction politics and legislation. . . . The author lives up to her introductory promise to avoid censoring racist language and images, and includes some horrifying descriptions of lynchings and murders perpetuated during KKK raids. . . . Her account of attending a Klan meeting while researching the book is chilling to the core." Publ Wkly

Includes bibliographical references

323 Civil and political rights

Brimner, Larry Dane, 1949-

★ **Blacklisted!** Hollywood, the Cold War, and the First Amendment. Larry Dane Brimner. Calkins Creek 2018 176 p. $17.95

Grades: 7 8 9 10 11 12 **323**

1. United States. Congress 2. Blacklisting of entertainers 3. Motion picture industry -- History

ISBN 9781620916032; 9781684371440

LC 2018931176

In this book, author Larry Dane Brimner "follows in vivid detail the story of 19 men from the film industry who were investigated for suspected communist ties during the Cold War, and the 10--known as the Hollywood Ten--who were blacklisted for standing up for their First Amendment rights and refusing to cooperate." (Publisher's note)

"Brimner (Twelve Days in May) provides a cinematic recounting of the 1947 investigation into the motion picture industry by the House Un-American Activities Committee."

Civil liberties; Lauri S. Friedman, book editor. Greenhaven Press 2010 144p il map (Introducing issues with opposing viewpoints) lib bdg $34.70

Grades: 7 8 9 10 11 12 **323**

1. Terrorism 2. Civil rights 3. National security

ISBN 978-0-7377-4732-4; 0-7377-4732-3

LC 2009-51887

This book "of pro/con essays . . . [is] intended to stimulate discussion of critical social issues and to open readers' minds to divergent opinions. Civil Liberties includes discussions of the Patriot Act, the rights of Muslims and Arab Americans, and racial profiling. . . . Active-reading questions preface the essays, which are followed by directions for evaluating the arguments presented. Color photos and other graphics throughout enliven the reading experience." SLJ

Includes bibliographical references

Kimmel, Allison Crotzer

The **Montgomery** Bus Boycott; a primary source exploration of the protest for equal treatment. Allison Crotzer Kimmel. Capstone Press 2015 32 p. illustrations (Fact finders. We shall overcome) (library binding) $27.32

Grades: 6 7 8 9 10 **323**

1. Montgomery (Ala.) 2. African Americans -- Civil rights 3. Montgomery (Ala.) -- Race relations 4. Montgomery Bus Boycott, Montgomery, Ala., 1955-1956 5. Civil rights movements -- Alabama -- Montgomery -- History -- 20th century 6. African Americans -- Civil rights -- Alabama -- Montgomery -- History --

20th century
ISBN 149142043X; 9781491420430; 9781491422182
LC 2014019815

In this book, by Allison Crotzer Kimmel, "the Montgomery Bus Boycott began when Rosa Parks was arrested for refusing to give up her seat on the bus. The campaign that followed was one of the most important protests against racial segregation in the United States. The boycotters endured violence and vicious words. But they stood up for their beliefs. Explore the points of view of the boycotters and the people who opposed them through powerful primary sources and historical photos." (Publisher's note)

Includes bibliographical references (page 30) and index

National Geographic Society (U.S.)

★ **Every** human has rights; a photographic declaration for kids. based on the United Nations Universal Declaration of Human Rights; with poetry from the ePals community; foreword by Mary Robinson. National Geographic 2009 30p il $26.90
Grades: 4 5 6 7 8 **323**

1. Human rights
ISBN 978-1-4263-0511-5; 1-4263-0511-7

"On the sixtieth anniversary of the Universal Declaration of Human Rights, this full-color photo-essay combines prize-winning poems by young people with beautiful photographs from all over the world. . . . The stirring pictures will stimulate classroom discussion about the declaration, which is quoted in full at the back." Booklist

Smith-Llera, Danielle

Lunch counter sit-ins; how photographs helped foster peaceful civil rights protests. by Danielle Smith-Llera. Compass Point Books 2019 64 p. (pbk.) $8.95
Grades: 5 6 7 8 **323**

1. African Americans -- Civil rights -- History -- Pictorial works 2. Photography -- Social aspects -- United States -- History -- 20th century 3. Civil rights movements -- United States -- History -- 20th century -- Pictorial works 4. Greensboro Four (Greensboro, N.C.) 5. Greensboro (N.C.) -- Race relations 6. Greensboro (N.C.) -- History -- 20th century 7. F.W. Woolworth Company -- History -- Social aspects 8. Civil rights workers -- North Carolina -- Greensboro 9. African Americans -- Civil rights -- North Carolina -- Greensboro
ISBN 9780756558789; 9780756558802
LC 2018018483

In this book in the Captured History series, by Danielle Smith-Llera, "on point historical photographs combined with strong narration bring the saga of the Woolworth lunch counter sit-ins in the early 1960s to life. Readers will learn about the four brave college students who started it all, as well as the many who came after. These events changed the world." (Publisher's note)

Includes bibliographical references (pages 63) and index

323.092 Civil rights leaders

Bodden, Valerie

The **assassination** of Martin Luther King Jr. Valerie Bodden. Creative Education 2016 48 p. illustrations (some color) (Turning Points)
Grades: 5 6 7 8 **323.092**

1. Assassination
ISBN 9781608187478
LC 2016000993

This book by Valerie Bodden is "a historical account of Martin Luther King's assassination, including the events leading up to it, the people involved, the conditions of racial tension, and the lingering aftermath."

"Large glossy photographs are included throughout, along with sidebars providing background or expanding on information." Horn Book

Includes bibliographical references and index

323.1 Civil and political rights of nondominant groups

Archer, Jules

★ **They** had a dream; the civil rights struggle from Frederick Douglass to Marcus Garvey to Martin Luther King and Malcolm X. Viking 1993 258p il (Epoch biographies) hardcover o.p. pa $7.99
Grades: 6 7 8 9 **323.1**

1. Clergy 2. Slaves 3. Authors 4. Abolitionists 5. Memoirists 6. Nonfiction writers 7. Writers on politics 8. Black Muslim leaders 9. Civil rights activists 10. Nobel laureates for peace 11. African Americans -- Biography 12. African Americans -- Civil rights
ISBN 0-14-034954-5 pa
LC 92-40071

Traces the progression of the civil rights movement and its effect on history through biographical sketches of four prominent and influential African Americans: Frederick Douglass, Marcus Garvey, Martin Luther King, Jr., and Malcolm X

"This discussion of the contributions of four pivotal civil rights activists is balanced and substantive." Publ Wkly

Includes bibliographical references

Aretha, David

Freedom Summer. Morgan Reynolds Pub. 2007 128p (The civil rights movement) lib bdg $27.95
Grades: 7 8 9 10 11 12 **323.1**

1. Mississippi Freedom Project 2. Mississippi -- Race relations 3. African Americans -- Civil rights
ISBN 978-1-59935-059-2; 1-59935-059-9
LC 2007-23815

This "discusses the collaborative strategies black and white Americans . . . devised to dismantle the restrictive, often violent measures used in the South to prevent most African Americans from voting. . . . [This title is] visually appealing with generous white space around the [text]. Throughout, mostly black-and-white historical photos . . . enhance the [narrative]. Also adding impact are numerous dramatic accounts by participants in the struggle." SLJ

Includes bibliographical references

Montgomery bus boycott. Morgan Reynolds Pub. 2009 128p il (The civil rights movement) $28.95
Grades: 7 8 9 10 **323.1**

1. African Americans -- Civil rights 2. Montgomery (Ala.) -- Race relations
ISBN 978-1-59935-020-2; 1-59935-020-3
LC 2008-18679

"The wrenching consequences of Rosa Parks's decision that sparked the Civil Rights Movement are depicted in this well-written book. Descriptions of civil rights activism dating back to 1865 . . . provide historical context and a sense of the fervor surrounding discrimination and segregation. The facts of the boycott are documented with supportive news articles, relevant quotations, moving individual stories, and significant court cases. . . . [Photographs] depict significant figures and document incidents such as meetings and carpooling to avoid buses." SLJ

Includes bibliographical references

Sit -ins and freedom rides. Morgan Reynolds Pub. 2009 128p il lib bdg $28.95

Grades: 5 6 7 8 **323.1**

1. African Americans -- Civil rights 2. Southern States -- Race relations

ISBN 978-1-59935-098-1 lib bdg; 1-59935-098-X lib bdg

LC 2008039600

"Aretha opens with an introduction to the four college students who orchestrated the famous sit-in at Woolworth's in Greensboro, NC, in 1960. He follows that with chapters that describe slavery, Reconstruction, and Jim Crow in terms of how they set the stage for the resistance efforts. . . . [The book] offers insight into to workings of the protests at the grassroots level. Individual anecdotes interspersed thoughout the detailed narrative provide personal and effective accounts that go beyond mere facts. Black-and-white and some color photographs appear on almost every page." SLJ

Includes bibliographical references

Bausum, Ann

★ **Freedom** Riders; John Lewis and Jim Zwerg on the front lines of the civil rights movement. by Ann Bausum; forewords by Freedom Riders Congressman John Lewis and Jim Zwerg. National Geographic 2006 79p il por $18.95; lib bdg $28.90

Grades: 5 6 7 8 **323.1**

1. Members of Congress 2. Civil rights activists 3. African Americans -- Civil rights 4. Southern States -- Race relations

ISBN 0-7922-4173-8; 0-7922-4174-6 lib bdg

LC 2005012947

"Bausum's narrative style, fresh, engrossing, and at times heart-stopping, brings the story of the turbulent and often violent dismantling of segregated travel alive in vivid detail. The language, presentation of material, and pacing will draw readers in and keep them captivated." SLJ

Includes bibliographical references

★ **Marching** to the mountaintop; how poverty, labor fights, and civil rights set the stage for Martin Luther King, Jr.'s final hours. by Ann Bausum. National Geographic 2012 104 p.

Grades: 7 8 9 10 **323.1**

1. Memphis (Tenn.) -- History 2. African Americans -- Civil rights 3. Strikes -- United States -- History 4. African Americans -- Economic conditions 5. Sanitation Workers Strike, Memphis, Tenn., 1968 6. Memphis (Tenn.) -- Race relations -- History -- 20th century 7. Labor movement -- Tennessee -- Memphis -- History -- 20th century 8. African Americans -- Tennessee -- Memphis -- Social conditions -- 20th century

ISBN 1426309392; 1426309406; 9781426309397; 9781426309403

LC 2011024661

"In early 1968 the grisly on-the-job deaths of two African-American sanitation workers in Memphis, Tennessee, prompted an extended strike by that city's segregated force of trash collectors. Workers sought union protection, higher wages, improved safety, and the integration of their work force. Their work stoppage became a part of the larger civil rights movement and drew an impressive array of national movement leaders to Memphis, including, on more than one occasion, Dr. Martin Luther King, Jr. . . . Marching to the Mountaintop explores how the media, politics, the Civil Rights Movement, and labor protests all converged to set the scene for one of King's greatest speeches and for his tragic death." (Publisher's note)

Includes bibliographical references (p. 100-102) and index

Bowers, Rick

★ The **spies** of Mississippi; the true story of the spy network that tried to destroy the Civil Rights Movement. National Geographic 2010 120p il $16.95; lib bdg $26.90

Grades: 7 8 9 10 **323.1**

1. Mississippi -- Race relations 2. African Americans -- Civil rights 3. Mississippi State Sovereignty Commission

ISBN 978-1-4263-0595-5; 1-4263-0595-8; 978-1-4263-0596-2 lib bdg; 1-4263-0596-6 lib bdg

LC 2009-18944

"Bowers draws upon archival material, supplemented with his own extensive research, to document the activities of the Mississippi State Sovereignty Commission, a Civil Rights-era state agency that disseminated segregationist propaganda and used Soviet-style methods to spy upon, harass, and harm those who challenged white supremacy. . . . This book's unique perspective will help students understand the previously unknown history of the despicable actions of Mississippi leaders who opposed civil rights and the silent citizens who supported their activities." SLJ

Includes bibliographical references

Brimner, Larry Dane

Birmingham Sunday. Calkins Creek 2010 48p il

Grades: 5 6 7 8 **323.1**

1. Bombings 2. Hate crimes 3. Racism 3. African Americans -- Civil rights 4. Birmingham (Ala.) -- Race relations 5. Sixteenth Street Baptist Church (Birmingham, Ala.) 6. Hate crimes -- Birmingham (Ala.) 7. Bombings -- Alabama -- Birmingham 8. Sixteenth Street Baptist Church (Birmingham, Ala.)

ISBN 1590786130; 9781590786130

LC 2009035716

This book describes the bombing of the Sixteenth Street Church in 1963 by Ku Klux Klan members, which killed four girls, and discusses how the event contributed to the civil rights movement. "Grades five to eight." (Bull Cent Child Books)

"This moving photo-essay covers much more than just an account of the Birmingham, Alabama, Baptist Church bombing that killed four young girls in 1963. The detailed text, illustrated with black-and-white photos on every spacious double-page spread, sets the shocking assassination of the children within a general overview of both the racist segregation of the times and the struggle against it." Booklist

★ **Black** & white; the confrontation of Reverend Fred L. Shuttlesworth and Eugene Bull O'Connor. Calkins Creek 2011 109p il

Grades: 7 8 9 10 11 12 **323.1**

1. Clergy 2. Police officials 3. Civil rights activists 4. Organization officials 5. African Americans -- Civil rights 6. Birmingham (Ala.) -- Race relations

ISBN 1-59078-766-8; 978-1-59078-766-3

"Reverend Fred L. Shuttlesworth led the civil rights struggle for equality in Birmingham, Alabama. . . . Eugene 'Bull' Connor, backed by the Ku Klux Klan, became a symbol of racist hatred and violence against Shuttlesworth. With a spacious design that includes archival pictures and primary-source documents on almost every page, this accessible photo-essay recounts the events in three sections, which focus first on the preacher, then on the commisioner, and finally, on their confrontation. . . . Never simplistic in his depictions, Brimner shows the viewpoints from all sides. . . . A penetrating look at elemental national history." Booklist

Includes bibliographical references

Civil rights; Jill Karson, book editor. Greenhaven Press 2003 238p il map (Great speeches in history series) lib bdg $33.70; pa $22.45

Grades: 7 8 9 10 **323.1**

1. Speeches 2. United States -- Race relations 3. African Americans -- Civil rights

ISBN 0-7377-1593-6 lib bdg; 0-7377-1594-4 pa

LC 2002-32209

"A collection of the speeches of well-known individuals who participated in or supported the American Civil Rights Movement from early pioneers through the 1960s up until today. Selections from Frederick Douglass, Malcolm X, Fannie Lou Hamer, Jesse Jackson, and Nelson Mandela emphasize the power of oratory to inform, persuade, and make an impact." SLJ

Includes bibliographical references

Cooper, John

Season of rage; Hugh Burnett and the struggle for civil rights. [by] John Cooper. Tundra Books 2005 71p il pa $9.95

Grades: 7 8 9 10 **323.1**

1. Race discrimination 2. Carpenters 3. Civil rights activists 4. Canada -- Race relations

ISBN 0-88776-700-1

"Cooper has chosen the small town of Dresden, Ontario, to paint a picture of what life was like for black Canadians in the middle of the last century. One Sunday in the early 1930s, when 12-year-old Hugh Burnett and his younger brother had a hankering for ice cream, they entered a restaurant. The boys were told that they would have to eat in the kitchen. . . . The event in the restaurant sparked a lifelong crusade for Burnett, who spearheaded the formation of the National Unity Association. . . . A number of archival photos enhance the text. . . . An eye-opening story." SLJ

Des Chenes, Betz

American civil rights: primary sources; [compiled by] Phillis Engelbert; edited by Betz Des Chenes. U.X.L 1999 xl, 200p il $58

Grades: 8 9 10 11 12 **323.1**

1. Civil rights

ISBN 0-7876-3170-1

LC 99-27167

Presents fifteen documents, including speeches, autobiographical texts, and proclamations, related to the civil rights movement and arranged by category under economic rights, desegregation, and human rights

"The uniqueness of this set lies in the range of people covered. Students will find it an excellent resource for reports and interesting reading." Booklist

Includes bibliographical references

Freedman, Russell

★ **Freedom** walkers; the story of the Montgomery bus boycott. Holiday House 2006 114p il $18.95

Grades: 4 5 6 7 **323.1**

1. Clergy 2. Historians 3. College teachers 4. Nonfiction writers 5. Civil rights activists 6. Nobel laureates for peace 7. African Americans -- Civil rights 8. Montgomery (Ala.) -- Race relations

ISBN 978-0-8234-2031-5; 0-8234-2031-0

LC 2006-41148

This account of the Montgomery bus boycott of 1955 focuses on Jo Ann Robinson, Claudette Colvin, Rosa Parks, Martin Luther King, and other participants.

This offers "expertly paced text, balanced but impassioned. . . . The narrative arc is compelling; well-captioned black-and-white photographs enhance the impact." Horn Book

Includes bibliographical references

Kasher, Steven

The **civil** rights movement: a photographic history, 1954-68; [by] Steven Kasher; foreword by Myrlie Evers-Williams. Abbeville Press 1996 255p il $45; pa $29.95

Grades: 8 9 10 11 12 Adult **323.1**

1. African Americans -- Civil rights

ISBN 0-7892-0123-2; 0-7892-0656-0 pa

LC 96-4337

"This book contains images by more than 50 photographers, whose images were borrowed from photo agencies, galleries, and private collections. Ten accompanying essays break the Civil Rights movement into chronological periods. Kasher's research, writing, and photo selection are impeccable and engaging." Libr J

Includes bibliographical references

King, Martin Luther, Jr.

The **words** of Martin Luther King, Jr. selected by Coretta Scott King. Newmarket Press 1983 112p il $15.95; pa $11.95

Grades: 8 9 10 11 12 Adult **323.1**

1. United States -- Race relations 2. African Americans -- Civil rights

ISBN 0-937858-28-5; 1-55704-483-X pa

LC 83-17306

This "volume of selections from Dr. King's speeches and writings . . . focuses on seven areas of his concerns: 'The Community of Man, Racism, Civil Rights, Justice and Freedom, Faith and Religion, Nonviolence, and Peace'" Publisher's note

Includes bibliographical references

Levinson, Cynthia Y.

We've got a job; the 1963 Birmingham Children's March. written by Cynthia Levinson. Peachtree Publishers 2012 176 p.

Grades: 6 7 8 9 **323.1**

1. Political activists 2. African American youth 3. African Americans -- Civil rights 4. Birmingham (Ala.) -- Race relations 5. Civil rights demonstrations -- Alabama 6. African American youth -- Alabama -- Birmingham -- History -- 20th century 7. Civil rights movements -- Alabama -- Birmingham -- History -- 20th century

ISBN 9781561456277

LC 2011031738

YALSA Award for Excellence in Nonfiction for Young Adults Finalist (2013)

In this book, "[c]overing the history of the Birmingham Children's March from inception to full impact, [author Cynthia Y.] Levinson traces the stories of four young people between the ages of 9 and 15 in 1963. Audrey Hendricks, Washington Booker III, Arnetta Streeter, and James Stewart came from very different segments of the city's black community, but all risked their lives and spent time in jail to fight for their freedom." (School Library Journal)

Mayer, Robert H.

When the children marched; the Birmingham civil rights movement. Enslow Publishers 2008 176p il map (Prime) $34.60

Grades: 7 8 9 10 **323.1**

1. African American children 2. African Americans -- Civil rights 3. Birmingham (Ala.) -- Race relations

ISBN 978-0-7660-2930-9; 0-7660-2930-1

LC 2007-25590

"Children played a significant role in Birmingham's crucial civil rights struggle, and this stirring history of the movement, with many photos, news reports, and quotes from all sides, emphasizes the connections between the young people's power and that of the big leaders. . . . From the cover picture of police escorting African American children to jail, the numerous photos of youth in nonviolent confrontation—marching, attacked by dogs and fire hoses, crammed in prisons—will draw readers with their gripping drama." Booklist

Includes glossary and bibliographical references

McWhorter, Diane

A **dream** of freedom; the Civil Rights Movement from 1954 to 1968. foreword by Reverend Fred Shuttlesworth. Scholastic Nonfiction 2004 160p il $19.95

Grades: 5 6 7 8 **323.1**

1. United States -- Race relations 2. African Americans -- Civil rights

ISBN 0-439-57678-4

The author discusses "the national civil rights movement from Brown v. the Board of Education to the assassination of Martin Luther King Jr. . . . This account is both factual and personal. She discusses her feelings as a white child in the South, and she focuses in on the many ways in which both white and black children were involved in the movement. . . . The breadth and depth of McWhorter's book is exemplary." Booklist

Mitchell, Don

The **Freedom** Summer Murders; Don Mitchell. Scholastic 2014 256 p. $18.99

Grades: 7 8 9 10 **323.1**

1. Homicide 2. African Americans -- Civil rights 3. Mississippi Freedom Project 4. Civil rights workers -- Mississippi -- Biography 5. Mississippi -- Race relations -- History -- 20th century 6. Murder -- Mississippi -- Neshoba County -- History -- 20th century

ISBN 0545477255; 9780545477253

This young adult book by Don Mitchell tells how "In June of 1964, three idealistic young men . . . were lynched by the Ku Klux Klan in Mississippi. They were trying to register African Americans to vote as part of the Freedom Summer effort to bring democracy to the South. Their disappearance and murder caused a national uproar and was one of the most significant incidents of the Civil Rights Movement, and contributed to the passage of the Civil Rights Act of 1964." (Publisher's note)

"The murders of three young civil rights workers--James Chaney, Andrew Goodman, and Michael Schwerner--are the focus of Mitchell's absorbing book. He conducted interviews with friends and family members of the men, and provides a fascinating biographical sketch of each, along with a thorough account of the police investigation. This compelling book will grab you from its opening paragraphs and won't let go. Bib., ind." Horn Book

Nardo, Don

Birmingham 1963; how a photograph rallied Civil Rights support. Compass Point 2011 64p il (Captured history) lib bdg $33.99

Grades: 6 7 8 9 **323.1**

1. Documentary photography 2. Photojournalists 3. African Americans -- Civil rights 4. Birmingham (Ala.) -- Race relations

ISBN 978-0-7565-4398-3; 0-7565-4398-3

This book about Charles Moore's 1963 photograph of young African American civil rights protesters being blasted with a fire hose places the photo "in historical context, profiles the photographer, describes the conditions under which it was taken, and analyzes both its immediate and its continuing impact. The [text includes] ample background information and details and [is] enhanced by large photos and sidebars." SLJ

Includes glossary and bibliographical references

Partridge, Elizabeth

★ **Marching** for freedom; walk together, children, and don't you grow weary. Viking 2009 72p il $19.99

Grades: 6 7 8 9 10 11 12 **323.1**

1. Selma (Ala.) -- Race relations 2. African Americans -- Civil rights 3. Civil rights movements 4. African American children

ISBN 978-0-670-01189-6; 0-670-01189-4

LC 2009-9696

Boston Globe-Horn Book Award: Nonfiction (2010)

An examination of the march from Selma to Montgomery in 1965 led by Dr. Martin Luther King, Jr., this book focuses on the children who faced terrifying violence in order to walk alongside him in their fight for freedom and the right to vote.

This is a "stirring photo-essay. . . . The vivid text is filled with quotes collected from Partridge's personal interviews with adults who remember their youthful experiences. . . . Filled with large black-and-white photos, every spread brings readers up close to the dramatic, often violent action." Booklist

Includes bibliographical references

Turck, Mary

★ **Freedom** song; young voices and the struggle for civil rights. [by] Mary C. Turck. Chicago Review Press 2009 146p il pa $18.95

Grades: 7 8 9 10 **323.1**

1. African American music 2. Chicago Children's Choir 3. Freedom Singers (Musical group) 4. African Americans -- Civil rights

ISBN 978-1-55652-773-9; 1-55652-773-X

LC 2008-29673

"The book is divided into chapters that represent the history of the Civil Rights Movement. 'Sunday of Song,' 'Singing in the Churches,' and 'South Africa,' for example, contain information about the factual events while including how the evolution of the music captured the mood and sentiment of the time. The importance of music in the lives of African Americans is described in depth. . . . The accompanying CD allows students to internalize the words and their emotional impact as they listen. Overall, this informative and well-written book is an excellent addition to any collection." SLJ

Includes bibliographical references

Wexler, Sanford

The **civil** rights movement; an eyewitness history. introduction by Julian Bond. Facts on File 1993 356p il maps (Eyewitness history series) $75

Grades: 7 8 9 10 **323.1**

1. United States -- Race relations 2. African Americans -- Civil rights

ISBN 0-8160-2748-X

LC 92-28674

Uses speeches, articles, and other writings of those involved to trace the history of the civil rights movement in the United States, primarily from 1954 to 1965

"This very readable source deserves a place in every public and middle and high school library, though it may fit better in the circulating collection." Booklist

Includes bibliographical references

Williams, Juan

Eyes on the prize: America's civil rights years, 1954-1965; [by] Juan Williams with the Eyes on the prize production team; introduction by Julian Bond. Viking 1987 300p il hardcover o.p. pa $20

Grades: 7 8 9 10 **323.1**

1. United States -- Race relations 2. African Americans -- Civil rights

ISBN 0-670-81412-1; 0-14-009653-1 pa

LC 86-40271

"Highly recommended both as a socio-historical document and as a heartfelt, poignant remembrance of a movement and its activists." Booklist

Includes bibliographical references

Williams, Mary E.

Civil rights; edited by Mary E. Williams. Greenhaven Press 2002 94p il (Examining issues through political cartoons) lib bdg $24.95; pa $16.20

Grades: 7 8 9 10 **323.1**

1. Affirmative action programs 2. African Americans -- Civil rights -- Cartoons and caricatures

ISBN 0-7377-1100-0 lib bdg; 0-7377-1099-3 pa

LC 2001-55743

The author provides "readers with an overview of African Americans' struggle for those rights enjoyed by other citizens and of the historical role of the political cartoon. . . . Four chapters ('The Struggle for Justice,' 'Has the Civil Rights Movement Benefited Minorities?' 'How Has Affirmative Action Affected Civil Rights?' and 'What Is the Legacy of the Civil Rights Movement?') examine three to six cartoons each. All are reproduced in the book, and information about the artist is provided." SLJ

Includes bibliographical references

323.11 Ethnic and national groups

Bausum, Ann

★ The **March** against Fear; the last great walk of the civil rights movement and the emergence of Black power. by Ann Bausum. National Geographic Partners 2017 144 p. illustrations (library binding : alk. paper) $28.90; (ebook) $28.90

Grades: 7 8 9 10 11 12 **323.11**

1. Black power 2. Civil rights demonstrations 3. Civil rights workers -- Mississippi -- Biography 4. Racism -- Mississippi -- History -- 20th century 5. Black power -- Mississippi -- History -- 20th century 6. Mississippi -- Race relations -- History -- 20th century 7. African American college students -- Mississippi -- Biography 8. African American civil rights workers -- Mississippi -- Biography 9. Civil rights demonstrations -- Mississippi -- History -- 20th century 10. African Americans -- Civil rights -- Mississippi -- History -- 20th century

ISBN 9781426326653; 9781426326660; 9781426326684

LC 2016027880

This book, by Ann Bausum, retells "James Meredith's 1966 march in Mississippi [that] began as one man's peaceful protest for voter registration and became one of the South's most important demonstrations of the civil rights movement. It brought together leaders like Martin Luther King Jr. and Stokely Carmichael, who formed an unlikely alliance that resulted in the Black Power movement, which ushered in a new era in the fight for equality." (Publisher's note)

"This compelling account will be equally engaging for classroom resource material or individual research." Booklist

Includes bibliographical references and index

Blohm, Craig E.

The **civil** rights movement; Craig E. Blohm. ReferencePoint Press, Inc. 2019 80 p. (hardback) $29.95

Grades: 7 8 9 10 11 12 **323.11**

1. United States -- Race relations 2. African Americans -- Civil rights -- History 3. United States -- Race relations 4. Civil rights movements -- United States -- History -- 20th century

ISBN 1682824195; 9781682824191

LC 2018017166

"America is a nation founded on the idea that all men are created equal, but it took African Americans years of hard-fought struggles to even approach equality in jobs, education, and the right to vote. And in the twenty-first century, the struggle goes on. This book, [by author Craig Blohm,] examines how and why social change occurs and the lasting influence of the Civil Rights Movement." (Publisher's note)

"Despite the fact each book has a different author, the series' hallmark is the clarity of the writing and a deep dig into the history, often highlighting personal stories or pieces of history that are lesser known." (Booklist)

Includes bibliographical references and index

Brimner, Larry Dane, 1949-

★ **Twelve** days in May; freedom ride 1961. Larry Dane Brimner. Calkins Creek 2017 112 p. illustrations $18.95

Grades: 5 6 7 8 9 10 **323.11**

1. Civil rights demonstrations 2. Southern States -- Race relations 3. African Americans -- Civil rights -- History

ISBN 9781629795867; 9781629799179

LC 2017937780

Robert F. Sibert Information Book Award (2018)

In this book, by Larry Dane Brimner, "on May 4, 1961, a group of thirteen black and white civil rights activists launched the Freedom Ride, aiming to challenge the practice of segregation on buses and at bus terminal facilities in the South. The Ride would last twelve days. . . . As the Riders traveled deeper into the South, they encountered increasing violence and opposition." Publisher's note)

"While the introductory and concluding sections offer helpful summaries of four major Supreme Court rulings on segregation from 1896 to 1960 and short biographies of the 13 Freedom Riders, the heart of the book is its straightforward, concise, day-by-day reporting of the journey. A memorable presentation of inherently dramatic and historically significant events." (Booklist)

Freedman, Russell, 1929-2018

★ **Because** they marched; the people's campaign for voting rights that changed America. Russell Freedman. Holiday House 2014 83 p. (hardcover) $20

Grades: 6 7 8 9 10 **323.11**

1. Selma (Ala.) 2. African Americans -- Civil rights 3. Civil rights demonstrations -- Alabama 4. Selma (Ala.) -- Race relations 5. Civil rights movements -- Alabama -- Selma -- History -- 20th century 6. African Americans -- Suffrage -- Alabama -- Selma -- History -- 20th century 7. African Americans -- Civil rights -- Alabama -- Selma -- History -- 20th century

ISBN 0823429210; 9780823429219

LC 2013038991

This book, by Russell Freedman, celebrates "the 50th anniversary of the 1965 march for voting rights from Selma to Montgomery, Alabama. . . . [The author] has written a riveting account of this pivotal event in the history of civil rights. . . . In the early 1960s, tensions in the segregated South intensified. Tired of reprisals for attempting to register to vote, Selma's black community began to protest." (Publisher's note)

"With characteristically clear prose sprinkled liberally with primary source quotes and carefully selected photographs, Freedman documents the historic 1965 Selma-to-Montgomery march that sparked the passing of the Voting Rights Act, "the crowning achievement of the civil rights movement." Freedman's opening chapter is particularly effective because it focuses on the teachers' march to the courthouse to register as a major trigger for the movement."

Includes bibliographical references and index

Lowery, Lynda Blackmon

Turning 15 on the road to freedom; my story of the 1965 Selma to Montgomery March. by Lynda Blackmon Lowery ; as told to Elspeth Leacock and Susan Buckley. Dial Books, an imprint of Penguin Group (USA) LLC 2015 128 p. (hardcover) $19.99

Grades: 7 8 9 10 11 12 **323.11**

1. African Americans -- Civil rights 2. Selma (Ala.) -- Race relations 3. Civil rights movements -- Alabama -- Selma -- History -- 20th century 4. African Americans -- Suffrage -- Alabama -- Selma -- History -- 20th century

ISBN 0803741235; 9780803741232

LC 2013047316

Robert F. Sibert Honor Book (2016)

This book, by Lynda Blackmon Lowery, is "a memoir of the Civil Rights Movement from one of its youngest heroes. As the youngest marcher in the 1965 voting rights march from Selma to Montgomery, Albama, Lynda Blackmon Lowery proved that young adults can be heroes. Jailed eleven times before her fifteenth birthday, Lowery fought alongside Martin Luther King, Jr. for the rights of African-Americans." (Publisher's note)

"The illustrations are a mix of photographs and cartoonish drawings, which bring a graphic novel-like feel to this memoir. A concluding chapter explains the fight for voting rights and contains short biographies of those who died for the cause. This is an honest, powerful historical work, straight from the source." SLJ

Parks, Peggy J., 1951-

The **Black** lives matter movement; by Peggy J. Parks. ReferencePoint Press 2017 80 p. illustrations (hardback : alk. paper) $29.95

Grades: 8 9 10 11 12 **323.11**

1. United States -- Race relations 2. African Americans -- Civil rights 3. Racial profiling in law enforcement 4. Racism -- United States 5. Black lives matter movement 6. Racial profiling in law enforcement -- United States 7. African Americans -- Social conditions -- 21st century

ISBN 9781682822852; 9781682822869

LC 2017023860

This book on the Black Lives Matter movement, by Peggy J. Parks, "discusses the origins of the movement in the uneasy relationships that often exist between African Americans and law enforcement, the events that triggered its formation, reactions, efforts to hold police accountable, and police reform." (Publisher's note)

"Using recent news stories, anecdotal accounts, social media, and the Justice Department's investigative reports, this book, one of the first to be published on the topic, takes an impressively no-nonsense approach." Booklist

Includes bibliographical references (pages 65-70) and index

Rubin, Susan Goldman

Freedom Summer; the 1964 Struggle for Civil Rights in Mississippi. by Susan Rubin. Holiday House 2014 120 p. illustrations (hardcover) $18.95

Grades: 5 6 7 8 9 10 **323.11**

1. African Americans -- Civil rights 2. Mississippi Freedom Project 3. African Americans -- Suffrage 4. Civil rights workers -- Mississippi 5. Civil rights movements -- Mississippi

ISBN 0823429202; 9780823429202

LC 2013020208

"Rubin has created a narrative retelling of the events and occurrences from the summer of 1964. Chock-full of primary sources, such as photographs, memos sent to applicants regarding the growing tensions in Mississippi, and pencil drawings depicting various settings from Neshoba County, Mississippi, Freedom Summer is organized in a time-line fashion, from June 1964 until late August 1964." (VOYA)

"This work gives a real sense of the time and place, the issues and the opposing sides, and the impact on the nation. Including myriad period photos and drawings, facsimiles of reports and records, meticulous source notes, an extensive bibliography, picture credits, and an extensive index, this title is the epitome of excellent historical reporting, with the human element never forgotten." SLJ

Includes bibliographical references and index

323.3 Civil and political rights of other social groups

Hayes, Amy

Disability rights movement; Amy Hayes. PowerKids Press 2017 32 p. illustrations (some color)

Grades: 4 5 6 7 **323.3**

1. United States. Americans with Disabilities Act of 1990 2. People with disabilities -- Civil rights -- United States 3. People with disabilities -- Legal status, laws, etc. -- United States 4. Discrimination against people with disabilities -- Law and legislation -- United States

ISBN 9781499426793; 9781499426809; 9781499428506

LC 2016037017

This book by Amy Hayes "explores the ways in which people with disabilities have fought for their right to equal access, equal opportunities, and equal treatment. Key figures and events are highlighted to give readers a well-rounded sense of the movement. Photographs and primary sources bring the movement to life. Readers are challenged to think about what could be changed in the future to help people with disabilities live a full, fair life." (Publisher's note)

"A fine introductory survey of civil rights issues that prompts reader involvement. Consider for report writers." SLJ

Rarus, Pat

★ The **LGBT** rights movement; by Pat Rarus. ReferencePoint Press, Inc. 2019 80 p. illustrations (hardback) $29.95

Grades: 7 8 9 10 11 12 **323.3**

1. Gay rights -- United States 2. Civil rights -- United States 3. Sexual minorities -- United States

ISBN 9781682824214

LC 2018006110

This book in the Push for Social Change series, by Pat Rarus, describes how "LGBT rights have advanced greatly since the homophobic days of the 1960s. Still, challenges remain, including passage of a federal law mandating job equality nationwide. This book examines how and why social change occurs and the lasting influence of the LGBT movement on mainstream society." (Publisher's note)

"Despite the fact each book has a different author, the series' hallmark is the clarity of the writing and a deep dig into the history, often highlighting personal stories or pieces of history that are lesser known." Booklist

Includes bibliographical references and index

Serres, Alain

I have the right to be a child; author, Alain Serres ; illustrator, Aurélia Fronty ; translator, Helen Mixter. Groundwood Books 2012 48 p.

Grades: 3 4 5 6 7 **323.3**

1. Treaties 2. Human rights 3. Children -- Civil rights

ISBN 1554981492; 9781554981496

In this children's book, "a young narrator describes what it means to be a child with rights -- from the right to food, water and shelter, to the right to go to school, to the right to be free from violence, to the right to breathe clean air, and much more. The book emphasizes that these rights belong to every child on the planet. . . . A brief afterword explains that the rights outlined in the book come from the Convention on the Rights of the Child." (Publisher's note)

Transgender rights; Martin Gitlin, book editor. Greenhaven Publishing 2017 112 p. (paperback) $28.30

Grades: 7 8 9 10 **323.3**

1. Transgender people 2. Sexual minorities -- United States 3. LGBT people -- Legal status, laws, etc. 4. Transgender people -- Legal status, laws, etc. 5. Sexual minorities -- Legal status, laws, etc. -- United States 6. Transgender people -- Legal status, laws, etc. -- United States

ISBN 153450222X; 9781534502222; 9781534502833

LC 2017031275

In this book in the Issues That Concern You series, edited by Martin Gitlin, "transgender rights are not just limited to bathroom bills, though the controversial issue has dominated news headlines for the past few years. . . . The viewpoints in this resource lay out the issues in a concise and informative way, offering measured arguments as to why trans Americans are a protected class, as well as arguments for why they don't need special treatment." (Publisher's note)

Includes bibliographical references and index

323.44 Freedom of action (Liberty)

January, Brendan

Information Insecurity; privacy under siege. Brendan January. Twenty-First Century Books 2016 96 p. (lib. bdg. : alk. paper) $34.65

Grades: 7 8 9 10 **323.44**

1. Privacy 2. Right of privacy 3. Internet security

ISBN 9781467725170

LC 2014018682

This young adult nonfiction book, by Brendan January, explores how "the Internet gives us information, communication options, shopping opportunities, entertainment, and much more--all at the touch of a fingertip and much of it for free. But in exchange for these benefits, we may be losing a basic right: the right to privacy." (Publisher's note)

"With an engaging, direct tone and plenty of further reading suggestions, this informative title will provide valuable, accessible insight into an up-to-the-minute topic." Booklist

Includes bibliographical references and index

Kyi, Tanya Lloyd, 1973-

Eyes and spies; how you're tracked and why you should know. Tanya Lloyd Kyi ; art by Belle Wuthrich. Annick Press 2017 140 p. (paperback) $22.95

Grades: 6 7 8 **323.44**

1. Right of privacy 2. Electronic surveillance

ISBN 9781554519118; 9781554519125; 9781554519101

LC 2017279846

This book, by Tanya Lloyd Kyi, illustrated by Belle Wuthrich, "looks at the way information and data about us is collected and used by individuals, governments, companies, and organizations. Each chapter covers one aspect of the subject, from data collection to computer surveillance to personal privacy. Arguments for both increased security and increased privacy are offered, which encourages readers to think critically about issues and decide for themselves." (Publisher's note)

Senker, Cath

Privacy and surveillance; Cath Senker. Rosen Central 2012 48 p. (Ethical debates)

Grades: 7 8 9 10 **323.44**

1. Right of privacy 2. Electronic surveillance 3. Electronic surveillance -- Case studies

ISBN 1448870119; 9781448860227; 9781448870110; 9781448870127

LC 2011028565

This book by Cath Senker, part of the Ethical Debates series, "[d]iscusses the controversies regarding privacy and surveillance, including the ethical aspects of electronic surveillance of citizens by the government, security of identity over the Internet, and students under surveillance at schools." (WorldCat)

Includes bibliographical references and index

323.6 Citizenship and related topics

Maury, Rob

Citizenship; rights and responsibilities. Mason Crest Publishers 2009 64p il (Major American immigration) lib bdg $22.95; pa $9.95

Grades: 6 7 8 9 **323.6**

1. Citizenship 2. United States -- Immigration and emigration

ISBN 978-1-4222-0618-8 lib bdg; 1-4222-0618-1 lib bdg; 978-1-4222-0685-0 pa; 1-4222-0685-8 pa

LC 2008-28223

Presents the rights and responsibilities held by United States citizens, and describes the U.S. naturalization process.

"The chapters are short and easy to read, the sidebars are informative, and the chronology is helpful." Voice Youth Advocates

Includes glossary and bibliographical references

Raatma, Lucia

Citizenship; by Lucia Raatma. Children's Press 2012 64 p. ill. (chiefly col.), col. map (Cornerstones of freedom) (library) $30; (paperback) $8.95

Grades: 4 5 6 **323.6**

1. Citizenship -- United States

ISBN 0329917374; 0531230643; 0531281647; 9780329917371; 9780531230640; 9780531281642

LC 2011031340

This book on citizenship by Lucia Raatma "covers everything from basic facts about naturalization to debates over hot issues such as gun control." It is part of the "Cornerstones of Freedom" series for students in grades 4 to 6. Included are "a two-page map of 'What Happened Where?'; a two-page epilogue; glossary-style identifications of significant people; a page of primary sources; a bibliography of books; a glossary; and an index plus author bio." (Booklist)

Includes bibliographical references (p. 61) and index.

324.6 Election systems and procedures; suffrage

Aretha, David

Selma and the Voting Rights Act. Morgan Reynolds Pub. 2007 128p il (The civil rights movement) lib bdg $27.95

Grades: 7 8 9 10 11 12 **324.6**

1. Voting Rights Act of 1965 2. African Americans -- Suffrage 3. Selma (Ala.) -- Race relations 4. African Americans -- Civil rights

ISBN 978-1-59935-056-1; 1-59935-056-4

LC 2007-24655

The author discusses "mid-1960s Alabama and the black struggle to exercise the constitutional right to vote. Even those who know the story of the famous protest marches will be interested in the details here. . . . There are quotes from and photos of the famous as well as the unknown, as well as excerpts from speeches and news photos." Booklist

Includes bibliographical references

Fleischer, Jeff

Votes of Confidence; A Young Person's Guide to American Elections. by Jeff Fleischer. Turtleback Books 2016 240 p. $13.99

Grades: 6 7 8 9 10 11 12 **324.6**

1. Elections -- United States

ISBN 0606379827; 1936976900; 9780606379823; 9781936976904

In this book, author Jeff Fleischer "attempts to make Civics 101 a little more interesting. He breaks down many terms and aspects of the election process to bring some clarity to what seems to be a long, convoluted method of choosing our nation's leaders. The author provides many historical examples to illustrate his discussions of how and why elections work the way they do." (School Library Journal)

"Fleischer's well-contextualized, nonpartisan approach results in a valuable resource for readers looking to understand and become involved in a complicated system while avoiding spin." Pub Wkly

Includes bibliographical references (pages 221-224).

Hollihan, Kerrie Logan

Rightfully ours; how women won the vote : 21 activities. Kerrie Logan Hollihan. 1st ed. Chicago Review Press 2012 xiii, 130 p.p ill. (some col.) (paperback) $16.95

Grades: 4 5 6 7 8 **324.6**

1. Women -- Suffrage 2. Women -- United States -- History 3. Suffragists -- United States -- History 4. Women's rights -- United States -- History 5. Women -- Suffrage -- United States -- History 6. Women's rights -- Study and teaching -- Activity programs -- United States 7. Women -- Suffrage -- Study and teaching -- Activity programs -- United States

ISBN 1883052890; 9781883052898

LC 2012006044

This book is an "account of the struggle for women's suffrage. The first three chapters focus on notable activists Lucy Stone, Elizabeth Cady Stanton, and Susan B. Anthony. [Kerrie Logan] Hollihan recounts how this battle was inexorably tied to the antislavery movement and the role played by women of color in both movements, including Harriett Tubman, Sojourner Truth, and Ida Wells-Barnett." (School Library Journal)

Includes bibliographical references (p. 121-124) and index

Senker, Cath

Women claim the vote; the rise of the women's suffrage movement, 1828-1860. Chelsea House 2011 64p il (A cultural history of women in America) $35

Grades: 7 8 9 10 **324.6**

1. Feminism 2. Women -- Suffrage 3. Women -- United States -- History 4. United States -- Social conditions

ISBN 978-1-60413-930-3; 1-60413-930-7

LC 2010045960

This is a history of the women's suffrage movement in America from 1828-1860 .

This book offers a "comprehensive, vivid, and thought-provoking [look] at the struggles and triumphs of . . . the women who [participated] in shaping our nation. Through succinct, informative text, [this] heavily illustrated volume incorporates the history of three major groups of people: the Natives, European settlers, and African slaves. Featured quotes from books, articles, letters, and speeches bring the history to life." SLJ

Includes glossary and bibliographical references

324.973 Elections – United States

Burgan, Michael

TV shapes presidential politics in the Kennedy-Nixon debates; 4D an augmented reading experience. by Michael Burgan. Compass Point Books 2019 64 p. (pbk.) $8.99

Grades: 5 6 7 **324.973**

1. Television and politics 2. United States -- Politics and government -- 20th century 3. Political campaigns -- United States -- History 4. Campaign debates -- United States -- History -- Pictorial works 5. Presidents -- United States -- Election -- 1960 -- Pictorial works 6. Television in politics -- United States -- History -- Pictorial works

ISBN 9780756558239; 9780756558277

LC 2018006449

This book in the Captured Television History 4D series, by Michael Burgan, shows how television (TV) influenced U.S. politics during the presidential campaign of John F. Kennedy and Richard Nixon. "Readers will learn just how much effect seeing the debates had on the results of the election and how they changed presidential campaigning forevermore." (Publisher's note)

325 International migration and colonization

Anderson, Dale

Arriving at Ellis Island. World Almanac Library 2002 48p il map (Landmark events in American history) lib bdg $26.60; pa $11.95

Grades: 5 6 7 8 **325**

1. Ellis Island Immigration Station 2. United States -- Immigration and emigration

ISBN 0-8368-5337-7 lib bdg; 0-8368-5351-2 pa

LC 2002-24627

Discusses immigration to the United States during the nineteenth and early twentieth centuries and describes the small island in New York harbor that served as the point of entry for millions of immigrants from 1892 to 1954

The "design is attractive, with drawings, maps, paintings, and photos; primary sources, such as excerpts from diaries, letters, and newspapers, support and enhance the [text]. . . . Informative, competently written." Booklist

Includes glossary and bibliographical references

Bausum, Ann

★ **Denied,** detained, deported; stories from the dark side of American immigration. National Geographic 2009 111p il $21.95; lib bdg $32.90

Grades: 6 7 8 9 10 11 12 **325**

1. Essayists 2. Anarchists 3. Memoirists 4. Writers on politics 5. Family planning advocates 6. Immigrants -- United States 7. United States -- Immigration and emigration

ISBN 978-1-4263-0332-6; 1-4263-0332-7; 978-1-4263-0333-3 lib bdg; 1-4263-0333-5 lib bdg

"This volume deals frankly with the more troubling aspects of United States immigration policy. The author chose the stories of three immigrants. . . . Twelve-year-old German-Jew Herb Karliner was denied entry to the United States at the border when he attempted to escape Nazi Germany. Sixteen-year-old Japanese-American Mary Matsuda was detained with the rest of her family during World War II. Labor-activist Emma Goldman was deported for her 'un-American' views. . . . The themes of the three stories are unified by the introduction and conclusion, which deal with Chinese immigration during the late 19th century and the history of immigration across the southern border of the United States, respectively. Photographs throughout will help students relate to the narrative. . . . This is an interesting and readable book." SLJ

Includes bibliographical references

Bial, Raymond

Ellis Island; coming to the land of liberty. Houghton Mifflin Books for Children 2009 56p il $18

Grades: 4 5 6 7 **325**

1. Ellis Island Immigration Station 2. United States -- Immigration and emigration

ISBN 978-0-618-99943-9; 0-618-99943-4

LC 2008-36794

"Bial examines the history of the famed immigration station. . . . He looks at the socio-historical roots of the mass exodus to America and provides a detailed look at the immigrant experience from ship to shore, with Ellis Island in between. Primary-source quotes and period photos pair eloquently with the modern narrative voice and color photographs of the museum exhibits. . . . The generously sized period photos and Bial's museum shots tell a vivid and poignant tale." SLJ

Includes bibliographical references

Fields, Julianna

First -generation immigrant families. Mason Crest 2009 64p il map (The changing face of modern families) $22.95

Grades: 6 7 8 9 **325**

1. Family 2. Immigrants -- United States

ISBN 978-1-4222-1499-2; 1-4222-1499-0

This describes the unique set of challenges facing first-generation immigrant families as they live with two cultures and, often, two languages.

"Colorful photographs and sidebars appear throughout. [This book is a] good [introduction] to the study of sociology and interpretation of data." SLJ

326 Slavery and emancipation

Bial, Raymond

The **Underground** Railroad. Houghton Mifflin 1995 48p il map hardcover o.p. pa $6.95

Grades: 4 5 6 7 **326**

1. Underground railroad 2. Slavery -- United States

ISBN 0-395-69937-1; 0-395-97915-3 pa

LC 94-19614

"Although the text covers ground often trodden by other works on this popular subject, Bial's shots of places and things which now appear tidy and innocent conjure spirits of desperate freedom-seekers as handily as do more detailed narratives." Bull Cent Child Books

Includes bibliographical references

Fradin, Judith Bloom

★ **5,000** miles to freedom; Ellen and William Craft's flight from slavery. [by] Judith Bloom Fradin and Dennis Brindell Fradin. National Geographic 2006 96p il $19.95; lib bdg $29.90

Grades: 5 6 7 8 9 10 **326**

1. Slaves 2. Memoirists 3. Slavery -- United States

ISBN 0-7922-7885-2; 0-7922-7886-0 lib bdg

"In 1848, light-skinned Ellen Craft, dressed in the clothing of a rich, white man, assumed the identity of Mr. William Johnson and, escorted by his black slave, William, traveled by railroad and boat to reach the North. With the passage of a more stringent Fugitive Slave Law in 1850, the couple . . . decided to travel to England. . . . In 1869, they returned to the United States, opening a school and operating a farm in Georgia. . . . This lively, well-written volume presents the events in their lives in an exciting, page-turner style that's sure to hold readers attention. Black-and-white photographs, illustrations, and reproductions enhance the text." SLJ

Includes bibliographical references

Gann, Marjorie

★ **Five** thousand years of slavery; [by] Marjorie Gann and Janet Willen. Tundra Books 2011 168p il map $27.95; paperback $15.99

Grades: 7 8 9 10 **326**

1. Slavery 2. Slavery -- History

ISBN 978-0-88776-914-6; 0-88776-914-4; 9781101917923 paperback

"This well-researched global survey introduces readers to slavery practices, customs, suffering, uprisings, and revolts as well as antislavery efforts from ancient Greece and Rome to today's world. . . . Informative documentary photos and factually rich sidebars enhance the text. . . . [This is a] groundbreaking title." SLJ

Includes bibliographical references

Speak a word for freedom; women against slavery. Janet Willen, Marjorie Gann. Tundra Books of Northern New York 2015 216 p. illustrations, portraits (hardcover) $21.99

Grades: 7 8 9 10 **326**

1. Abolitionists 2. Women political activists

ISBN 9781770496514; 9781770496538

LC 2014939465

This book, by Janet Willen and Marjorie Gann, profiles women antislavery activism. "From the early days of the antislavery movement, when political action by women was frowned upon, British and American women were tireless and uncompromising campaigners. . . . And the commitment of today's women . . . descends directly from that of the early female activists. . . . [This volume] tells the story of fourteen of these women." (Publisher's note)

"With the exceptions of Harriet Tubman and Harriet Beecher Stowe, most of the women featured will be new to most readers. The powerful message, that the fight to end slavery is ongoing and depends on a wide variety of actions and individuals, will both educate teens on this important issue and inspire them to take active roles in civic life." Booklist

Grayson, Robert

The **Amistad**. ABDO Pub. 2011 112p il (Essential events) lib bdg $23.95

Grades: 7 8 9 10 11 12 **326**

1. Slave trade 2. Amistad (Schooner)

ISBN 978-1-61714-761-6; 1-61714-761-3

LC 2010044662

This "is dramatic history, focusing on the 1839-40 trial of the kidnapped Africans who rebelled on the slave ship from Cuba and were captured and tried in the U.S. on charges of piracy. Were the Afticans property? . . . The spacious . . . design is inviting, with many color illustrations and screens, and the extensive back matter includes a detailed time line, glossary, bibliography and source notes." Booklist

Includes glossary and bibliographical references

327 International relations

Renehan, Edward J.

The **Monroe** doctrine; the cornerstone of American foreign policy. [by] Edward J. Renehan Jr. Chelsea House 2007 122p il map (Milestones in American history) lib bdg $35

Grades: 7 8 9 10 **327**

1. Monroe Doctrine 2. United States -- Foreign relations

ISBN 0-7910-9353-0 lib bdg; 978-0-7910-9353-5 lib bdg

LC 2006034126

This description of the Monroe Doctrine is "accessible, lively. . . . Many quotations, sidebars, art reproductions, and maps support the [text]. Excerpts from primary source materials also help give readers a sense of time and place." Horn Book Guide

Includes bibliographical references

327.12 Espionage and subversion

Earnest, Peter

The **real** spy's guide to becoming a spy; by Peter Earnest and Suzanne Harper, in association with the Spy Museum. Abrams Books for Young Readers 2009 144p il $16.95

Grades: 4 5 6 7 **327.12**

1. Spies 2. Espionage 3. Intelligence service

ISBN 978-0-8109-8329-8; 0-8109-8329-X

LC 2009-00518

"This guide, written by the executive director of the International Spy Museum, gives readers a glimpse at how spies work. Along with descriptions of the different types of intelligence officers and agencies and the tasks they perform, the text includes brief stories of spies in action." Horn Book Guide

Goodman, Michael E.

The **CIA** and other American spies; Michael E. Goodman. Creative Eduation 2012 48 p. ill. (Spies around the world) (library) $35.65

Grades: 6 7 8 9 **327.12**

1. Intelligence service -- United States 2. United States. Central Intelligence Agency 3. Espionage, American 4. Spies -- United States

ISBN 1608182266; 9781608182268

LC 2011035789

This book is part of the Spies Around the World series. "Focused more on the histories of spying organizations, each title looks at a different agency, making references to popular culture (e.g., the work of the CIA is compared to the 'Bourne' trilogy) and showing the difference between reality and movies. While not adding career how-to's, the volumes showcase famous spies from history, going back to the origins of each agency, as well as 'Tools of the Trade' and major cases." (School Library Journal)

Includes bibliographical references and index

The **KGB** and other Russian spies; Michael E. Goodman. Creative Education 2012 48 p. col. ill. (Spies around the world) (library) $35.65

Grades: 6 7 8 9 **327.12**

1. Spies 2. Russia 3. Espionage, Soviet 4. Spies -- Soviet Union 5. Intelligence service -- Soviet Union

ISBN 1608182274; 9781608182275

LC 2011035790

This book is part of the Spies Around the World series and focuses on Russian spies. "Each title contains an introduction to that particular country's spying apparatus plus chapters covering origins and famous individuals, and an explanation of this shadowy occupation. Each table of contents lists eight special features under the 'Evolution of Espionage' heading, where a particular event or spy-related item is highlighted." (Library Media Connection)

Includes bibliographical references (p. 47) and index

The **SIS** and other British spies; Michael E. Goodman. Creative Education 2012 48 p. ill. (library) $35.65

Grades: 6 7 8 9 **327.12**

1. Intelligence service 2. Spies 3. Espionage, British 4. Great Britain. MI6 5. Spies -- Great Britain 6. Intelligence service -- Great Britain

ISBN 1608182290; 9781608182299

LC 2011035791

This book is part of the Spies Around the World series and focuses on the British SIS and other British spies. "Each title contains an introduction to that particular country's spying apparatus plus chapters covering origins and famous individuals, and an explanation of this shadowy occupation. Each table of contents lists eight special features under the 'Evolution of Espionage' heading, where a particular event or spy-related item is highlighted." (Library Media Connection)

Includes bibliographical references (p. 47) and index

Janeczko, Paul B.

The **dark** game; true spy stories. Candlewick Press 2010 248p il $16.99

Grades: 5 6 7 8 **327.12**

1. Espionage

ISBN 978-0-7636-2915-1; 0-7636-2915-4

"From Benedict Arnold and Mata Hari to the lesser-known Elizabeth Van Lew and Juan Pujol, Janeczko delves into [spies'] stories with delicious detail, drawing readers into a world of intrigue and danger. Did you ever wonder why invisible ink works? How a code breaker deciphers a message? Or whether dentistry could affect a secret agent's success? The answers to these questions and more can be found here. Each chapter covers a historical era and chronicles the maturation of spying, while primary-source photographs are interspersed throughout, lending an authentic feel to each section." SLJ

Lassieur, Allison

Spies! the history of secret agents and double-crossers. Rebecca Langston-George and Allison Lassieur. Capstone Young Readers 2017 240 p. (pbk.) $14.95

Grades: 6 7 8 **327.12**

1. Espionage 2. Intelligence service 3. Spies 4. Spies -- Biography 5. Espionage -- History 6. Intelligence service -- History

ISBN 1623709113; 9781623709112

LC 2017015907

In this book, by Rebecca Langston-George and Allison Lassieur, "explore the dangerous, daring world of real-life spies! From World War I to the Cold War and beyond, experience the most notorious, ingenious spies of the 20th century through present day. With vivid, full-color photographs, detailed maps, and thoroughly researched time lines, get to know the unknowables, including cyber spies, secret agents, deep-cover spies, and no-good double-crossers." (Publisher's note)

Includes bibliographical references and index

Mitchell, Susan K.

Spy gizmos and gadgets. Enslow Publishers 2011 48p il (The secret world of spies) lib bdg $23.93

Grades: 4 5 6 **327.12**

1. Espionage 2. Electronic surveillance

ISBN 978-0-7660-3710-6

LC 2010006177

Discusses different gadgets used by spies, such as invisible ink, hidden cameras, small guns made to look like ordinary objects, and bugs, and includes career information.

Includes glossary and bibliographical references

328 The legislative process

Bow, James

What is the legislative branch? by James Bow. Crabtree Publishing Company 2013 32 p. (Your guide to government) (reinforced library binding) $26.60

Grades: 4 5 6 7 **328**

1. Legislative bodies 2. United States. Congress 3. United States -- Politics and government

ISBN 0778708799; 9780778708797; 9780778709053

LC 2013001277

This book, by James Bow "provide[s] solid introductory material about the U.S. government. [The] book discusses the purpose of [the legislative] branch; the different positions, . . . the work done; and the strengths and the challenges of each branch and how they interact." (School Library Journal)

330 Economics

Hlinka, Michael

Follow Your Money; Who Gets It, Who Spends It, Where Does It Go? by Kevin Sylvester and Michael Hlinka ; illustrated by Kevin Sylvester. Annick Press 2013 56 p. col. ill. (paperback) $14.95; (hardcover) $24.95

Grades: 5 6 7 8 **330**

1. Pricing 2. Money

ISBN 1554514800; 1554514819; 9781554514809; 9781554514816

This book by Kevin Sylvester and Michael Hlinka answers the questions "what happens to your money after you hand it to the cashier? Who actually pockets it or puts it into the bank? Was the price you paid fair? Why do things cost what they do? Kids will also discover the trail their money takes through advertising, banks [and] charitable giving. [It is an] introduction to the . . .people and companies that we influence and are influenced by when we pay for a product or service." (Publisher's note)

Hollander, Barbara

Money matters; an introduction to economics. [by] Barbara Gottfried Hollander. Heinemann Library 2010 56p il map (The global marketplace) $33.50

Grades: 6 7 8 9 **330**

1. Money 2. Economics

ISBN 978-1-4329-3929-8; 1-4329-3929-7

LC 2010003996

This introduction to economics covers "a wealth of material in concise paragraphs with pertinent sub-headings. . . . [It includes] excellent photos, charts, maps, and tables that help with the understanding of some sophisticated concepts." SLJ

Includes glossary and bibliographical references

Outman, James L.

Industrial Revolution: biographies; [by] James L. Outman, Elisabeth M. Outman. U.X.L 2003 218p il (Industrial revolution reference library) $55

Grades: 8 9 10 11 12 **330**

1. Industrial revolution

ISBN 0-7876-6514-2

LC 2002-155421

"The 25 essays in [this volume] provide biographical information with an emphasis on each person's contribution or impact on the Industrial Revolution. . . . More than 50 black-and-white photographs complement the text. . . . This is an excellent adjunct to American and world history units and classes on economics and labor movements." Booklist

Includes bibliographical references

330.9 Economic situation and conditions

Bair, Sheila, 1954-

The **Bullies** of Wall Street; this is how greedy adults messed up our economy. Sheila Bair. Simon & Schuster Books for Young Readers 2015 272 p. illustrations (hardcover) $17.99

Grades: 8 9 10 11 12 **330.9**

1. Working class 2. Financial crises 3. Global Financial Crisis, 2008-2009 4. United States -- Economic conditions 5. United States -- Economic conditions -- 2001-2009 6. Global Financial Crisis, 2008-2009 -- Social aspects 7. Working class -- United States -- Economic conditions 8. Financial crises -- United States -- History -- 21st century

ISBN 1481400851; 9781481400855; 9781481400862

LC 2014005948

In this book, author Sheila Bair "explains how the Great Recession impacted families on a personal level using language that everyone can understand. . . . [S]he describes the many ways in which a broken system led families into financial trouble, and also explains the decisions being made at the time by the most powerful people in the country-- from CEOs of multinational banks, to heads of government regulatory committees-- that led to the recession." (Publisher's note)

"The case studies themselves are interesting and clear, but the explanatory, bolded inserts are difficult to follow. Bair's personal story is interesting, but it contains information beyond the scope of youth understanding. A list of government agencies and their acronyms would be helpful throughout the book. Best used as supplemental reading for advanced finance classes." Booklist

Mooney, Carla

The **Industrial** Revolution; investigate how science and technology changed the world with 25 projects. illustrated by Jen Vaughn. Nomad Press 2011 120p il (Build it yourself) $21.95; pa $15.95

Grades: 4 5 6 7 **330.9**

1. Industrial revolution

ISBN 978-1-936313-81-5; 1-936313-81-2; 978-1936313-80-8; 1-936313-80-4 pa

This "gives on overview of the era known as the Industrial Revolution as well as the consequences, good and bad, of each new development upon the average citizen. Topics covered include the transformation of textiles from homespun to manufactured, the birth of labor unions, advances in transportation and communication, the inventions of Thomas Edison, and brief profiles of 'Captains of Industry,' such as Carnegie, Vanderbilt, and Rockefeller. Each chapter ends with enticing projects related to the topic. . . . The crisp, clear format, featuring ample black-and-white sketches and diagrams and pleasingly arranged type in a large font, is in sync with the straightforward text." Booklist

Outman, James L.

Industrial Revolution: almanac; [by] James L. Outman, Elisabeth M. Outman. U.X.L 2003 242p il (Industrial revolution reference library) $55

Grades: 8 9 10 11 12 **330.9**

1. Reference books 2. Industrial revolution

ISBN 0-7876-6513-4

LC 2002-155422

"This is an excellent adjunct to American and world history units and classes on economics and labor movements." Booklist

Includes bibliographical references

330.973 Economic conditions – United States

Riggs, Kate

★ The **Great** Recession; Kate Riggs. Creative Eduation 2017 48 p. illustrations (some color) (Turning Points) $12.00

Grades: 5 6 7 8 **330.973**

1. Recessions 2. Economic policy -- United States 3. Global Financial Crisis, 2008-2009 4. United States -- Economic conditions

ISBN 9781628323450

LC 2016002552

This book by Kate Riggs is "a historical account of the Great Recession, including the causes of the economic downturn, the role played by the Federal Reserve and other government offices, and the lingering aftermath." Publisher's note

"Despite the complicated nature of the subject matter, this account stays engaging thanks to clear writing, glossy photographs, and helpful sidebars throughout." Horn Book

331.3 Labor force by personal attributes

Bartoletti, Susan Campbell

★ **Growing** up in coal country. Houghton Mifflin 1996 127p il $17; pa $7.95

Grades: 5 6 7 8 **331.3**

1. Child labor 2. Coal mines and mining 3. Immigrants 4. Coal miners 5. Pennsylvania -- History 6. Children -- Employment -- United States

ISBN 0-395-77847-6; 0-395-97914-5 pa

LC 96-3142

This is an "account of working and living conditions in Pennsylvania coal towns. The first half of the volume . . . {describes} various duties in the mines, from jobs performed by the youngest boys to the tasks of adult miners, while the second half describes the company village, common customs and recreational activities, and the accidents and diseases that frequently beset the workers. Preceding each chapter and within the text {are} quotes from personal interviews with miners, as well as taped interviews and transcripts." (Horn Book) Bibliography. "Grade five and up." (Booklist)

"With compelling black-and-white photographs of children at work in the coal mines of northeastern Pennsylvania about 100 years ago, this handsome, spacious photo-essay will draw browsers as well as students doing research on labor and immigrant history." Booklist

Includes bibliographical references

Burgan, Michael

Breaker boys; how a photograph helped end child labor. Compass Point Books 2011 64p il (Captured history) lib bdg $33.99; pa $8.95

Grades: 6 7 8 9 **331.3**

1. Photographers 2. Coal mines and mining 3. Documentary photography 4. Child labor -- United States

ISBN 978-0-7565-4439-3 lib bdg; 0-7565-4439-4; 978-0-7565-4510-9 pa; 0-7565-4510-2 pa

LC 2011003316

This book explains how Lewis Hine's photographs of children who worked in coal mines in Pennsylvania helped lead to the passage of child labor laws.

This "is model nonfiction. . . . The design is fresh and inviting, the writing clear, and the back matter . . . is useful and extensive. An all-around winner." Booklist

Includes glossary and bibliographical references

Freedman, Russell

★ **Kids** at work; Lewis Hine and the crusade against child labor. with photographs by Lewis Hine. Clarion Bks. 1994 104p il $20; pa $9.95

Grades: 5 6 7 8 **331.3**

1. Child labor 2. Photographers

ISBN 0-395-58703-4; 0-395-79726-8 pa

LC 93-5989

Freedman "does an outstanding job of integrating historical photographs with meticulously researched and highly readable prose." Publ Wkly

Includes bibliographical references

Gifford, Clive

Child labor. Smart Apple Media 2010 46p il (Voices) lib bdg $34.25

Grades: 7 8 9 10 11 12 **331.3**

1. Child labor

ISBN 978-1-59920-279-2 lib bdg; 1-59920-279-4 lib bdg

LC 2008-50429

The "text offers statistics, graphs, quotations (from politicians and scientists to children and laborers), and many photographs to make clear how . . . [child labor affects] the world today. An eye to how the issue affects young people—and how young people can help—is also a priority. . . . [This] book is quick to read and stocked with quotations and statistics that will assist in research as well as general interest." Voice Youth Advocates

Includes glossary and bibliographical references

331.4 Women workers

Colman, Penny

★ **Rosie** the riveter; women working on the home front in World War II. Crown 1995 120p il hardcover o.p. pa $10.99

Grades: 5 6 7 8 **331.4**

1. Women -- Employment 2. World War, 1939-1945 -- United States

ISBN 0-517-59790-X; 0-517-88567-0 pa

LC 94-3614

"A thoughtfully prepared look at women's history and wartime society, this dynamic book is characterized by extensive research." Horn Book

Includes bibliographical references

331.7 Labor by industry and occupation

Farrell, Courtney

Green jobs. ABDO Pub. 2011 112p il (Inside the industry) lib bdg $34.22

Grades: 8 9 10 11 12 **331.7**

1. Occupations 2. Vocational guidance 3. Environmental protection

ISBN 978-1-61714-801-9; 1-61714-801-6

LC 2010039122

"This book contains an interesting overview of jobs that fall beneath the 'green' umbrella. Farrell writes in clear prose about the wide range of career opportunities that students with environmental interests can pursue. She focuses on four fields: green architect, organic farmer, professional conservationist, and alternative-energy expert." SLJ

Includes glossary and bibliographical references

Hopkinson, Deborah

★ **Up** before daybreak; cotton and people in America. Scholastic Nonfiction 2005 120p il $18.99

Grades: 5 6 7 8 **331.7**

1. Cotton 2. Working class 3. Textile industry -- History

ISBN 0-439-63901-8

LC 2005-8128

"From the industrial revolution to the 1950s demise of the Lowell cotton mills, Hopkinson discusses the history and sociology of king cotton, frequently emphasizing the children who labored under slave masters, endured dead-end mill jobs, or helped sharecropping parents claw out a living. . . . Stories of real people . . . sharply focus the dramatic history, as do arresting archival photos of stern youngsters manipulating hoes, cotton sags, or bobbins." Booklist

J.G. Ferguson Publishing Company

Encyclopedia of careers and vocational guidance; 17th edition Ferguson 2017 5v il set $299.95

Grades: 8 9 10 11 12 Adult **331.7**

1. Reference books 2. Occupations -- Encyclopedias 3. Vocational guidance -- Encyclopedias

ISBN 978-0-8160-8313-8; 978-0-8160-8514-9

First published 1967

"These five volumes contain more than 700 . . . [articles] on careers in nearly 100 industries. Each three to five-page entry provides a concise and engaging profile of fields like accounting, animal care, computers, the environment, publishing, sales, and the visual arts. Included in each job entry are an overview, a history, a description, requirements, employers, advancement, earnings, work environment, outlook, and more." Libr J [review of 2008 edition]

Includes bibliographical references

331.702 Choice of vocation

Careers; the graphic guide to finding the perfect job for you. consultant and principal author, Sarah Pawlewski. DK Publishing 2015 320 p. color illustrations (softcover) $19.99

Grades: 6 7 8 9 10 11 12 **331.702**

1. Vocational guidance 2. Occupations 3. Professions

ISBN 1465429735; 9781465429735

LC 2015303113

"Covering more than 400 jobs, [this book on careers] is organized . . . [to] guide teen and tween readers. Check at-a-glance summary panels for chosen careers to learn about salary, working hours, training, and career paths. Cross-referenced job matrix tables offer another way to learn about all the options. Tweens and teens with no idea of what kind of job to look for can start with their favorite school subjects or hobbies and find relevant careers from there." (Publisher's note)

"A typical library's collection of career books can quickly become dated or out of touch. Enter this manual. With simple graphics, bright colors, and a vast compendium of information, this guide will engage teens who are wondering, "What now?" . . . This strong addition will be fun for browsers as well as for those selecting college majors and making job decisions." SLJ

331.8 Labor unions, labor-management bargaining and disputes

Baker, Julie

The **Bread** and Roses strike of 1912. Morgan Reynolds Pub. 2007 160p il (American workers) $27.95

Grades: 6 7 8 9 10 **331.8**

1. Strikes 2. Lawrence (Mass.) -- History 3. Textile industry -- History

ISBN 978-1-59935-044-8; 1-59935-044-0

LC 2006101826

A history of the 1912 strike of textile workers in Lawrence, Massachusetts.

"Baker's style is readable, and the well-chosen, well-reproduced photos make the subject all the more real." SLJ

Includes bibliographical references

Bartoletti, Susan Campbell

★ **Kids** on strike! Houghton Mifflin 1999 208p il $20; pa $8.95

Grades: 5 6 7 8 **331.8**

1. Strikes 2. Child labor 3. Centenarians 4. Labor leaders

ISBN 0-395-88892-1; 0-618-36923-6 pa

LC 98-50575

Describes the conditions and treatment that drove workers, including many children, to various strikes, from the mill workers strikes in 1828 and 1836 and the coal strikes at the turn of the century to the work of Mother Jones on behalf of child workers

"This well-researched and well-illustrated account creates a vivid portrait of the working conditions of many American children in the 19th and early 20th centuries." SLJ

Includes bibliographical references

Brimner, Larry Dane, 1949-

Strike! the farm workers' fight for their rights. Larry Dane Brimner. Calkins Creek 2014 172 p. ill. (some col.), maps hbk $16.95

Grades: 6 7 8 9 **331.8**

1. Agricultural industry 2. Strikes -- United States -- History

ISBN 1590789970; 9781590789971

LC 2014935299

"Author Larry Dane Brimner follows the five-year-long strike through the rise of César Chávez and the United Farm Workers. . . . In the 1960s, while the United States was at war and racial tensions were boiling over, Filipino American workers were demanding fair wages and decent living conditions in California's vineyards. When the workers walked out of the fields in September 1965, the great Delano grape strike began." (Publisher's note)

"Brimner's inclusion of information about the Filipino workers who began the movement, quotes and balanced discussion of Chavez's strengths and weaknesses provides a fresh perspective on the movement, making this book a first-purchase choice for middle-level researchers." SLJ

Includes bibliographical references and index

Laughlin, Rosemary

The **Ludlow** massacre of 1913-14; [by] Rosemary Laughlin. 1st ed.; Morgan Reynolds Pub. 2006 144p il (American workers) lib bdg $27.95

Grades: 6 7 8 9 **331.8**

1. Strikes 2. Coal mines and mining 3. Labor movement -- History

ISBN 978-1-931798-86-0; 1-931798-86-9

LC 2005030050

"In the autumn of 1913, coal miners working for the Colorado Fuel and Iron Company walked off the job, demanding recognition of their union. This . . . chronicles the long strike that frequently erupted into armed combat between the Colorado state militia and the miners. Vivid portraits are presented of the protagonists in the struggle. . . . Laughlin presents the facts with a storyteller's flair, supplemented by frequent quotes, period photographs, and engravings that show what life was like for the miners." Booklist

Includes bibliographical references

The **Pullman** strike of 1894; [by] Rosemary Laughlin. Morgan Reynolds Pub. 2006 144p il (American workers) lib bdg $27.95

Grades: 6 7 8 9 **331.8**

1. Strikes 2. Railroads -- History 3. Labor movement -- History

ISBN 978-1-931798-89-1; 1-931798-89-3

LC 2005028637

First published 2000 in the series Great events

This "tells the story of the strike and explains its long-term effects on the labor movement and the nation. The author examines the arguments made by labor and management and explains how the strike affected all of those involved. . . . [This is] a good choice for report material on industrialization, labor history, or the Gilded Age." SLJ

Includes bibliographical references

Skurzynski, Gloria

Sweat and blood; a history of U.S. labor unions. Twenty-First Century Books 2008 112p il (People's history) lib bdg $31.93

Grades: 7 8 9 10 **331.8**

1. Labor unions 2. Working class

ISBN 978-0-8225-7594-8; 0-8225-7594-9

LC 2007-50270

This "begins with the roots of unionization in colonial America, cruises through the frenzy of industrialization in the twentieth century, and ends in the present day. . . . The period prints and photographs are well chosen to highlight and comment on the text. Classes studying any part of the industrial or social history of this country will be well served by this valuable resource." Booklist

Includes bibliographical references

Whitelaw, Nancy

The **Homestead** Steel Strike of 1892; [by] Nancy Whitelaw. 1st ed.; Morgan Reynolds Pub. 2006 144p il (American workers) lib bdg $27.95

Grades: 6 7 8 9 **331.8**

1. Strikes 2. Steel industry 3. Philanthropists 4. Homestead Strike, 1892 5. Art collectors 6. Labor movement -- History 7. Metal industry executives

ISBN 978-1-931798-88-4; 1-931798-88-5

LC 2005027113

This is the story of the 1892 strike against the Homestead Steel company owned by Andrew Carnegie and Henry Clay Frick which led to bloodshed and a breaking of the union.

"This is a riveting story told in 11 well-written, lively chapters, with well-placed, good-quality reproductions and drawings throughout the text." SLJ

Includes bibliographical references

332 Financial economics

Bostick, Nan

Managing Money. Saddleback Educational Pub. 2012 120 p. ill.

Grades: 8 9 10 11 12 **332**

1. Life skills 2. Banks and banking 3. Household budgets 4. Teenagers -- Personal finance 5. Economics -- Handbooks, manuals, etc. 6. Adult education 7. Finance, Personal 8. Life skills--Handbooks, manuals, etc.

ISBN 1616516593; 9781616516598

This book is a part of the "Life Skills Handbooks" series. "With the text split into four main topics—controlling your spending, banking basics, buying now and paying later, and improving your budgeting skills—young adults get a comprehensive look at the world of personal finance. . . . When it comes to sticking to a budget, teens are encouraged to keep their needs and wants in sharp focus. There's even a chapter devoted to unexpected purchases and variable spending. . . . There are also helpful hints for paying those expenses without credit cards. Credit-card debt, loans, and spending more than one earns are issues that are addressed . . . . Basic advice, such as how to write out a check and read a bank statement, is included." (Booklist) Index.

"Young adults get a comprehensive look at the world of personal finance in digestible doses." Booklist

Sylvester, Kevin

Follow your stuff; who makes it, where does it come from, how does it get to you? Kevin Sylvester and Michael Hlinka. Annick Press 2019 96 p. (hardback) $24.95

Grades: 5 6 7 8 9 **332**

1. Consumers 2. Consumer goods 3. Consumption (Economics)

ISBN 9781773212531; 9781773212562; 9781773212548

LC 2019300313

This book, by Kevin Sylvester and Michael Hlinka, "tackle the complex dynamics of the global economy, examining the often-complex journey of ordinary goods from production right to our doorsteps. . . . Using familiar examples, easy-to-follow charts and graphs, and a big helping of humor, Hlinka and Sylvester introduce young readers to concepts such as relative value and fair wages and how to think critically about our purchasing decisions." (Publisher's note)

332.024 Personal finance

Bochner, Rose

The **new** totally awesome money book for kids (and their parents) [by] Arthur Bochner & Rose Bochner; foreword by Adriane G. Berg. 3rd ed., rev & updated.; Newmarket Press 2007 189p il pa $9.95

Grades: 4 5 6 7 **332.024**

1. Personal finance

ISBN 978-1-55704-738-0

LC 2006038930

First published 1993 with title: The totally awesome money book for kids (and their parents)

An introduction to money for kids including the basics of saving, investing, working, and taxes.

"Using an easy and comfortable style that young people will find unthreatening, the book presents a wealth of information. . . . The cute illustrations are also fun." Voice Youth Advocates

Includes bibliographical references

Chatzky, Jean

Not your parents' money book; making, saving, and spending your own money. [by Jean Sherman Chatzky]; illustrated by Erwin Haya. Simon & Schuster Books for Young Readers 2010 162p il pa $12.99

Grades: 5 6 7 8 **332.024**

1. Money 2. Personal finance

ISBN 978-1-4169-9472-5 pa; 1-4169-9472-6 pa

LC 2010008840

"Written in a light, somewhat jocular tone and sprinkled with amusing but eye-opening and conversation-starting quotes from 12, 13, and 14-year-olds, this book is sure to hold readers' attention. The content includes how you get money, via allowances and jobs, and notes the difference between cash-only and paychecks. Tracking typical teen expenditures, both long-term and short, is juxtaposed against keeping money in checking, savings, and money-market accounts. . . . Chatzky's presentation is engaging. . . . Cartoons appear on almost every page, adding humor and some additional material." SLJ

Includes bibliographical references

Hall, Alvin

★ **Show** me the money; [by] Alvin Hall. Updated edition DK 2016 96p il

Grades: 4 5 6 **332.024**

1. Money 2. Personal finance

ISBN 978-0-7566-3762-0; 9781465440006

"Four main sections cover the history of money, expenses/income, the basics of economics, and the world of work and business. Brief profiles of eight wealthy entrepreneurs and their paths to prosperity and eight significant economists and their theories are included. The lively writing features real-life examples that will be meaningful to students and is presented in a balanced, nonjudgmental style that encourages them to decide for themselves among the various ideas concerning economic policies. . . . Color photos and graphics excel at conveying the concepts presented and represent diversity well." SLJ

Includes glossary

Holyoke, Nancy

Money; how to make it, save it, and spend it. by Nancy Holyoke ; illustrated by Brigette Barrager. American Girl Publishing 2014 94 p. color illustrations (A smart girl's guide) (pbk.) $12.99

Grades: 4 5 6 7 **332.024**

1. Women -- Personal finance 2. Money 3. Finance, Personal 4. Money-making projects for children 5. Teenage girls -- Finance, Personal

ISBN 1609584074; 9781609584078

LC 2013025896

In this book, by Nancy Holyoke, illustrated by Brigette Barrager, "learn how to not only spend that cash, but also how to earn it. The quizzes, tips, and helpful quotes from other girls will make learning about money management easy and fun." (Publisher's note)

Roderick, Stacey

Centsibility; the Planet Girl guide to money. [by] Stacey Roderick and Ellen Warwick; illustrated by Monika Melnychuk. Kids Can Press 2008 80p il (Planet girl) $12.95

Grades: 5 6 7 8 **332.024**

1. Personal finance

ISBN 978-1-55453-208-7

"This book presents handy methods for managing money. . . . Chapters are broken down into subsections . . . which are peppered with quizzes and craft projects to keep readers engaged. . . . The book's sound advice is both practical and approachable." Horn Book Guide

Scott, Elaine

Dollars and sense; A Kid's Guide to Using--Not Losing--Money. by Elaine Scott ; illustrated by David Clark. Charlesbridge 2015 112 p. illustrations (reinforced for library use) $16.95

Grades: 4 5 6 7 **332.024**

1. Money 2. Personal finance 3. Money -- United States 4. Finance, Personal -- United States

ISBN 9781580893961; 9781607345404; 9781607346241

LC 2013022069

This book by Elaine Scott, illustrated by David Clark, "is a basic operating instruction manual for money that will teach readers about the history of money, the way our American economy works, and how to make important decisions about personal finance. . . . An engaging and approachable guide for kids tackling how to responsibly manage their money. Included are sidebars, time lines, . . . as well as information on related topics such as the Great Recession and sequestration." (Publisher's note)

"An informative primer on how money functions that doesn't trigger the dismal science's snooze button." Kirkus

Includes bibliographical references and index.

Wiseman, Blaine

Budgeting. Weigl Publishers 2009 32p il (Everyday economics) lib bdg $26; pa $9.95

Grades: 5 6 7 **332.024**

1. Budget

ISBN 978-1-60596-643-4 lib bdg; 1-60596-643-6 lib bdg; 978-1-60596-644-1 pa; 1-60596-644-4 pa

LC 2009018439

This "informative [book introduces budgeting in] U.S. economic theory and practices using everyday language and real-life examples. [It] includes history, a brief annotated chronology, sidebar and intext explanations of terminology, and helpful diagrams. . . . With brief paragraphs; large, captioned photographs; ample margins; and well-organized graphics, the [book's] design makes economics accessible without sacrificing content. . . . [This is] easy to navigate and full of solid information and interesting facts." SLJ

Includes glossary

332.4 Money

Brezina, Corona

How deflation works. Rosen Pub. 2011 80p il (Real world economics) lib bdg $30.60

Grades: 7 8 9 10 **332.4**

1. Deflation (Finance)

ISBN 978-1-4358-9465-5; 1-4358-9465-0

LC 2009045292

This "discusses the possible correlations between a recession and deflation, expanding at length about why deflation, expanding at length about why deflation is ultimately unhealthy for the economy." SLJ

Includes bibliographical references

Cribb, Joe

★ **Eyewitness** money; written by Joe Cribb. 3rd edition DK Publishing 2016 72 p illustrations (DK Eyewitness) paperback $9.99; library $19.99

Grades: 4 5 6 7 **332.4**

1. Money

ISBN 9781465451781; 9781465451798; 146545179X; 1465451781

"From the earliest forms of money to the intricate banking systems we have today, currency has been around for millennia, whether made from stones and shells to the coins and paper we see today. This guide details various types of currency from both the past and present, from the sea salt money of Ethiopia to the modern Euro. Discover where the term piggy bank came from, why Ancient Greeks put coins in the mouths of dead people, and how coins and banknotes are made today. . . . [The revised edition] retains the stunning artwork and photography from the groundbreaking original series, but the text has been reduced and reworked to speak more clearly to younger readers." (Publisher's note)

Jenkins, Martin

The **history** of money; from bartering to banking. Martin Jenkins, illustrated by Satoshi Kitamura. First U.S. Edition Candlewick Press 2014 64 p. color illustrations $16.99

Grades: 4 5 6 7 8 **332.4**

1. Money -- History

ISBN 0763667633; 9780763667634

LC 2013952840

"Martin Jenkins and Satoshi Kitamura take readers on a . . . tour of the history of money. What can take the form of a stone with a hole in the middle, a string of shells, a piece of paper, or a plastic card? The answer is money, of course. But when did we start using it? And why? What does money have to do with writing? And how do taxes and interest work?" (Publisher's note)

"This cleverly designed picture book uses just the right balance of information and explanation to guide students through both the global history of currency and the application of market pressures on exchange methods." Booklist

Includes bibliographical references and index

332.6 Investment

Furgang, Kathy

How the stock market works. Rosen Pub. 2011 80p il (Real world economics) lib bdg $30.60

Grades: 7 8 9 10 **332.6**

1. Stocks 2. Stock exchanges

ISBN 978-1-4358-9466-2; 1-4358-9466-9

LC 2009045687

This "includes a history of Wall Street and discusses the ups and downs of the stock market and its impact on people's everyday lives in a general and accessible manner for students." SLJ

Includes glossary and bibliographical references

Healey, Aaron

Making the trade; stocks, bonds, and other investments. Heinemann Library 2011 56p il (The global marketplace) lib bdg $33.50

Grades: 6 7 8 9 **332.6**

1. Investments 2. Stock exchanges 3. Saving and investment

ISBN 978-1-4329-3931-1; 1-4329-3931-9

LC 2010004094

This title covers "a wealth of material in concise paragraphs with pertinent subheadings. . . . [The book] reinforces the concept of balancing stock investments with an umbrella-versus-suntan-lotion example that has the great subtext of suggesting stock investment can be as risky as the weather." SLJ

Includes glossary and bibliographical references

Thompson, Helen

Understanding the stock market. Mason Crest Publishers 2010 64p il (Junior library of money) $22.95; pa $9.95

Grades: 6 7 8 9 **332.6**

1. Investments 2. Stock exchanges

ISBN 978-1-4222-1773-3; 1-4222-1773-6; 978-1-4222-1892-1 pa; 1-4222-1892-9 pa

LC 2010028431

This is an introduction to how the stock market works, including concepts such as shares, investing, The Dow Jones Industrial Average, bull markets and bear markets, and the stock market's effect on the economy.

This title presents "solid information and [has] eye-catching and relevant illustrations. . . . [It is] clearly written, making understandable connections between daily life and financial concepts." SLJ

Includes glossary and bibliographical references

332.64 Exchange of securities and commodities; speculation

Blumenthal, Karen

Six days in October; the stock market crash of 1929. Atheneum Bks. for Young Readers 2002 156p il $17.95

Grades: 7 8 9 10 **332.64**

1. Great Depression, 1929-1939 2. New York Stock Exchange, Inc. 3. United States -- Economic conditions -- 1919-1933

ISBN 0-689-84276-7

LC 2001-46360

A comprehensive review of the events, personalities, and mistakes behind the Stock Market Crash of 1929, featuring photographs, newspaper articles, and cartoons of the day

"This fast-paced, gripping . . . account of the market crash of October 1929 puts a human face on the crisis." Publ Wkly

Includes bibliographical references

332.7 Credit

Byers, Ann

First credit cards and credit smarts. Rosen Pub. 2010 64p il (Get smart with your money) lib bdg $29.95; pa $12.95

Grades: 7 8 9 10 11 12 **332.7**

1. Credit cards 2. Consumer credit

ISBN 978-1-4358-5271-6 lib bdg; 1-4358-5271-0 lib bdg; 978-1-4358-5548-9 pa; 1-4358-5548-5 pa

LC 2008-54969

This offers advice on managing credit, including topics such as credit scores, interest, and money management.

This offers "practical information and advice. The writing is accessible. . . . [The book is] heavily illsutrated with large, clear, up-to-date photographs of teens." SLJ

Includes glossary and bibliographical references

Tomljanovic, Tatiana

Borrowing. Weigl Pubs. 2009 32p il (Everyday economics) lib bdg $26; pa $9.95

Grades: 5 6 7 **332.7**

1. Credit

ISBN 978-1-60596-645-8 lib bdg; 1-60596-645-2 lib bdg; 978-1-60596-646-5 pa; 1-60596-646-0 pa

LC 2009018444

This "informative [book introduces borrowing in] U.S. economic theory and practices using everyday language and real-life examples. [It] includes history, a brief annotated chronology, sidebar and intext explanations of terminology, and helpful diagrams. . . . With brief paragraphs; large, captioned photographs; ample margins; and well-organized graphics, the [book's] design makes economics accessible without sacrificing content. . . . [This is] easy to navigate and full of solid information and interesting facts." SLJ

Includes glossary

333.7 Natural resources and energy

Gazlay, Suzy

Managing green spaces; careers in wilderness and wildlife management. Crabtree 2010 64p il (Green-collar careers) lib bdg $30.60; pa $10.95

Grades: 4 5 6 7 **333.7**

1. Wildlife 2. Wilderness areas 3. Vocational guidance

ISBN 978-0-7787-4855-7 lib bdg; 0-7787-4855-3 lib bdg; 978-0-7787-4866-3 pa; 0-7787-4866-9 pa

LC 2009-28145

"Passions often lead to professions, as this upbeat title . . . shows. . . . There is inevitable overlap among the categories: government-run parks and forestry, outdoor adventure, science, and wildlife sanctuaries. The browsable format, combining many crisp color photos with blocks of narrative texts and sidebars featuring specific ecoprofessionals, will easily lead students through the survey of nature-focused careers." Booklist

Howell, Izzi

Earth's resources geo facts; Izzi Howell. Crabtree Publishing Co. 2018 32 p. (reinforced library binding) $27.60

Grades: 4 5 6 7 **333.7**

1. Earth sciences 2. Natural resources 3. Conservation of natural resources

ISBN 9780778743835; 9780778743989

LC 2017050653

This book in the Geo Facts series, by Izzi Howell, presents the "kind[s] of resources Earth holds, and how they are extracted and used. Discover the problems and challenges posed by human consumption of these resources, from overfishing to dwindling supplies of fossil fuels. Read about the efforts being made to protect Earth's resources, including finding sustainable energy solutions and making our cities eco-friendly." (Publisher's note)

333.72 Conservation and protection

Kriesberg, Daniel A.

Think green, take action; books and activities for kids. illustrated by Kathleen A. Price. Libraries Unlimited 2010 136p il pa $30; e-book $30

Grades: Adult Professional **333.72**

1. Environmental sciences -- Study and teaching

ISBN 978-1-59884-378-1 pa; 1-59884-378-8 pa; 978-1-59884-379-8 e-book

LC 2010014409

"A resource for teaching environmental understanding and activism through stewardship, this book outlines teaching strategies for ages 6-10, provides resources for understanding environmental concerns for ages 10-13, and promotes action and growth for ages 13+. Chapters focus on local ecology, endangered species, resource depletion, and pollution. Extensive annotated bibliographies of both recent and older fiction and nonfiction selections . . . supplement the activities." SLJ

Includes bibliographical references

McKay, Kim

True green kids; 100 things you can do to save the planet. [by] Kim McKay and Jenny Bonnin. National Geographic 2008 143p il $15.95

Grades: 4 5 6 7 **333.72**

1. Environmental protection

ISBN 978-1-4263-0442-2; 1-4263-0442-0

Presents an overview of global warming and describes 100 simple ways to be more environmentally friendly in the bedroom, in the house, at school, and on vacation.

"Accompanied by attractive, up-to-date pictures in a lively design, the one hundred suggestions are direct . . . and generally practical." Horn Book Guide

Includes glossary

Nagle, Jeanne

Living green; [by] Jeanne Nagle. Rosen Pub. 2009 64p il (In the news) lib bdg $21.95

Grades: 7 8 9 10 **333.72**

1. Environmental protection

ISBN 978-1-43585037-8; 1-435-85037-8

"Accessible and up-to-date. . . . Living Green presents theories of climate change and short biographies of green pioneers before examining the role of government and NGOs in environmental protection, as well as basic, earth-friendly lifestyle changes that individuals can make. Throughout, Nagle addresses the controversies that surround issues, encouraging readers to take a wide, nuanced view." Booklist

Petronis, Lexi

47 things you can do for the environment. Zest 2011 il pa $10.99

Grades: 6 7 8 9 **333.72**

1. Environmental protection

ISBN 978-0-9827322-1-2; 0-9827322-1-X

"Divided into categories revolving around habits at home, school, in the community, or on the road, [this book] offers such suggestions as shopping at vintage or secondhand stores, eating less meat, donating old cellphones, and carpooling. Each green venture is followed by concrete ideas . . . that encourage direct action. Cheerful cartoon spot art underscores the positive tone." Publ Wkly

Recycle this book; 100 top children's book authors tell you how to go green. edited by Dan Gutman. Yearling 2009 267p pa $5.99

Grades: 5 6 7 8 **333.72**

1. Authors 2. Recycling 3. Environmental protection

ISBN 978-0-385-73721-0 pa; 0-385-73721-1 pa

LC 2008-10800

"This lively collection of brief essays (and a poem) by 100 outstanding children's and young adult authors teaches through example. Each selection highlights a small step (or steps) taken by the writer toward a greener Earth. . . . The essays also provide insight into the lives and thoughts of many familiar and beloved authors such as Laurie Halse Anderson, Ralph Fletcher, Gary Schmidt, Lois Lowry, Susan Patron, and Rick Riordan. Several pages of Web sites offer a starting point for action and information. Highly useful for classroom and family discussions and science-project ideas." SLJ

Reilly, Kathleen M.

Planet Earth; 25 environmental projects you can build yourself. Nomad Press 2008 122p il (Projects you can build yourself) $21.95; pa $14.95

Grades: 4 5 6 7 **333.72**

1. Science projects 2. Environmental sciences

ISBN 978-1-934670-05-7; 1-934670-05-7; 978-1-934670-04-0 pa; 1-934670-04-9 pa

"Both comprehensive and approachable, this title . . . combines explanations of science concepts and environmental issues with hands-on projects. . . . Elementary- and middle-school students will find the succinct overview of the facts very useful, and they'll welcome the clearly presented projects." Booklist

Rohmer, Harriet

★ **Heroes** of the environment; true stories of people who are helping to protect our planet. illustrated by Julie McLaughlin. Chronicle Books 2009 109p il map $16.99

Grades: 4 5 6 **333.72**

1. Environmentalists

ISBN 0-8118-6779-X; 978-0-8118-6779-5

LC 2009004366

"Engaging graphics and clear writing combine to provide a compelling reading experience." Sci Books Films

Sivertsen, Linda

Generation green; the ultimate teen guide to living an eco-friendly life. written by Linda Sivertsen and Tosh Sivertsen. Simon Pulse 2008 248p pa $10.99

Grades: 5 6 7 8 **333.72**

1. Environmental movement

ISBN 978-1-4169-6122-2; 1-4169-6122-4

"A thorough yet accessible manual on green living. . . . The book's incisive voice, using teen idioms, is accessible to those who have little or no background in environmental issues, yet the standards within will likewise engage readers already committed to being green. . . . [This book is] unique, for its central focus is not to explain the science behind current environmental challenges, but rather to reveal how young people can work to solve those problems in their everyday lives." SLJ

Includes bibliographical references

Smalley, Carol Parenzan

Green changes you can make around your home. Mitchell Lane Publishers 2010 47p il (Tell your parents) lib bdg $21.50

Grades: 4 5 6 7 **333.72**

1. Environmental movement 2. Environmental protection

ISBN 978-1-58415-764-9 lib bdg; 1-58415-764-X lib bdg

LC 2009-4527

This book that explains how to be environmentally friendly "offers numerous facts and statistics, all of which are cited. . . . Chapters cover present-day issues and . . . are interspersed with full-color photographs and short 'Did You Know' trivia boxes. . . . Back matter includes detailed resource lists and 'Try This!' experiments." SLJ

Includes glossary and bibliographical references

Try this at home; planet-friendly projects for kids. Jackie Farquhar, D.I.Y. editor. Owlkids 2009 93p il pa $10.95

Grades: 5 6 7 8 **333.72**

1. Environmental protection

ISBN 978-2-89579-192-8 pa; 2-89579-192-9 pa

"Many of these projects are unique or innovative, featuring ideas like growing your own pizza ingredients and making a foosball game out of recycled corks, clothespins, and plastic fruit baskets. One of the best projects provides tips on making sure a bike is road ready, offering advice on checking the cables, gears, and oiling the chain. The book also includes sections designed to increase environmental awareness, including information on carbon footprint and 'eco all-stars.' Interactive elements, like a game board, should appeal to children. Illustrations are hip collages of full-color photographs and cartoons." SLJ

Includes bibliographical references

333.736 Arid lands

Maccarald, Clara

Bringing back our deserts; Clara MacCarald. Abdo Pub. 2018 112 p. $37.07

Grades: 7 8 9 10 **333.736**

1. Deserts 2. Environmental protection 3. Conservation of natural resources

ISBN 9781532113130; 9781532152016

LC 2017946749

This book in the Conservation Success Stories series, by Clara MacCarald, "explains why deserts are at risk and how people are combating invasive species, restoring damaged areas, and preserving deserts for future generations. This title also explores the science behind nitrogen pollution and the life in desert soil. Features include a cause-and-effect flow chart, a glossary, references, websites, source notes, and an index." (Publisher's note)

333.75 Forest lands

Littlewood, Antonia

Rain forest destruction; Peter and Antonia Littlewood. Smart Apple Media 2012 46 p. col. ill., col. maps (Mapping global issues) (library) $35.65

Grades: 6 7 8 **333.75**

1. Rain forests 2. Forest conservation 3. Deforestation 4. Rain forest ecology 5. Rain forest conservation

ISBN 1599205122; 9781599205120

LC 2011017067

This book is part of the Mapping Global Issues series and it focuses on rainforest destruction. "Colorful layouts with numerous maps and graphs dominate this series, which provides an international perspective on important issues. Brief chapters frame problems, discuss their causes, and suggest possible solutions, using maps to illustrate the locations and extent of threats." (School Library Journal)

Includes bibliographical references (p. 45) and index

Stenstrup, Allen

Forests. Morgan Reynolds Pub. 2009 112p il (Diminishing resources) lib bdg $28.95

Grades: 8 9 10 11 12 **333.75**

1. Forest conservation 2. Forests and forestry

ISBN 978-1-59935-116-2; 1-59935-116-1

LC 2009-31025

"This highly readable [book] provides a unique viewpoint on the utilization of natural resources, as scientific and environmental concerns are discussed from a historical perspective. . . . [It contains] beautiful, full-page photographs, as well as a helpful time line." SLJ

Includes bibliographical references

333.76 Rural lands

Morris, Neil

The **landscape**; Neil Morris. Heinemann Library 2012 64 p. (The impact of environmentalism) (library) $35.00; (paperback) $9.99

Grades: 6 7 8 **333.76**

1. Landscape protection 2. Environmental movement 3. Landscape changes 4. Landscape assessment 5. Landscapes -- Environmental aspects

ISBN 1432965247; 9781432965181; 9781432965242

LC 2012001036

This book by Neil Morris is part of the "Impact of Environmentalism" series. It "looks at the way changing ideas about the environment and sustainability have affected our attitudes to the landscape, and will do so in the future." (Publisher's note) "Visual evidence shows how lands have been changed by human activities." The "book also discusses . . . efforts by humankind to protect the environment and create sustainable smaller environments." (School Library Journal)

Includes bibliographical references and index

333.78 Recreational and wilderness areas

Carson, Mary Kay

The **park** scientists; Mary Kay Carson ; with photographs by Tom Uhlman. Houghton Mifflin Harcourt 2014 80 p. (Scientists in the field) $18.99

Grades: 4 5 6 7 8 9 **333.78**

1. Science 2. National parks and reserves -- United States 3. Park rangers -- United States 4. Interpretation of cultural and natural resources -- United States

ISBN 0547792689; 9780547792682

LC 2013039895

Written by Mary Kay Carson and illustrated by Tom Uhlman, this children's book describes how "America's National Parks are protected places and have become living museums for as many as 270 million visitors per year! In addition, researchers are able to perform long term studies of a wide number of subjects from salamanders the size of thumbnails to gigantic geothermal geysers. These parks are natural laboratories for scientists." (Publisher's note)

"The National Park System is often known as the nation's own backyard due to the possibilities it provides for leisure, recreation, and scientific study. This entry into the long-running Scientists in the Field series celebrates this by focusing on three specific parks: Yellowstone, Saguaro, and the Great Smoky Mountains... With a conservationist bent, Carson describes just how accessible these real-life "natural laboratories and living museums" are and how each individual can act with the same spirit of inquiry as the scientist-explorers detailed here." Booklist

McHugh, Erin

National Parks; A Kid's Guide to America's Parks, Monuments and Landmarks. Erin McHugh ; Art by Neal Aspinall, Doug Leen, and Brian Maebius. Black Dog & Leventhal Publishers 2012 128 p. col. ill., col. map (hbk.) $19.95; (hbk.) $19.95

Grades: 4 5 6 **333.78**

1. National parks and reserves -- United States

ISBN 157912884X; 9781579128845

This book, "arranged alphabetically by state . . . tours more than 75 U.S. parks, monuments, and landmarks, from the rocky shores of Maine's Acadia National Park to the ancient redwood groves of Northern California. Also included is a removable, fold-out collector map to house" the commemorative quarters from the America the Beautiful series. (Publisher's note)

333.79 Energy

Brezina, Corona

Jobs in sustainable energy. Rosen Pub. 2010 80p il (Green careers) lib bdg $30

Grades: 5 6 7 8 **333.79**

1. Vocational guidance 2. Renewable energy resources

ISBN 978-1-4358-3569-6 lib bdg; 1-4358-3569-7 lib bdg

LC 2009021855

This "well-conceived [introduction focuses] on various jobs in [sustainable energy], the education and experience required, and expected earnings. The [book is] well organized, making it easy to gain an overview of the major aspects of the work. . . . [This book] will make [a] good [addition] to career collections. Photographs from the field and website and contact information for professional organizations add value." SLJ

Includes glossary and bibliographical references

Energy Alternatives; Sylvia Engdahl, book editor. Greenhaven Press 2015 220 pages illustrations (Opposing Viewpoints) pbk $33.80; library binding $48.80

Grades: 8 9 10 11 12 **333.79**

1. Renewable energy resources

ISBN 0737772581; 9780737772593; 9780737772586

LC 2014036031

Replaces 2010 edition

Articles in this anthology address such topics as whether alternative energy sources are necessary, different types of alternative energy, and the government's role in advocating the use of alternative sources.

Includes bibliographical references and index

Friedman, Lauri S.

Energy alternatives; Lauri S. Friedman, book editor. Greenhaven Press 2011 154p il map (Introducing issues with opposing viewpoints) $36.82

Grades: 7 8 9 10 **333.79**

1. Renewable energy resources

ISBN 978-0-7377-5198-7; 0-7377-5198-3

LC 2011000872

Essays examine both sides of the questions raised about energy alternatives.

This is is an "excellent [resource] both for student research and for personal interest." Booklist

Includes bibliographical references

Gardner, Robert

Energy; green science projects about solar, wind, and water power. Enslow Publishers 2011 128p il (Team Green science projects) lib bdg $31.93

Grades: 6 7 8 9 10 **333.79**

1. Energy resources 2. Science projects 3. Science -- Experiments

ISBN 978-0-7660-3643-7; 0-7660-3643-X

This book offers science experiments about energy resources and energy conservation.

"Gardner provides plenty of information, well-designed experiments, and demonstrations, and then shares brief science-fair ideas. . . . Experiments and demonstrations are presented with clear step-by-step instructions and occasional illustrations and represent a wide range of complexity." SLJ

Includes glossary and bibliographical references

Laidlaw, Jill A.

Energy; by Jill Laidlaw. Amicus 2011 44p il map (Sustaining our environment) lib bdg $31.35

Grades: 6 7 8 9 **333.79**

1. Energy resources 2. Renewable energy resources

ISBN 978-1-60753-136-4 lib bdg; 1-60753-136-4 lib bdg

LC 2009-29985

"The tone is refreshingly optimistic with its examples of specific steps being taken to reduce harm to the environment. Sidebars highlight case studies and campaigns from around the world and from the individual to the national levels. Clear, informative captions accompany the excellent selection of color photographs, charts and graphs." SLJ

Includes glossary

McPherson, Stephanie Sammartino

★ **Arctic** thaw; climate change and the global race for energy resources. Stephanie Sammartino McPherson. Twenty-First Century Books 2015 64 p. color illustrations, color map (library binding : alkaline paper) $34.60

Grades: 6 7 8 9 10 **333.79**

1. Global warming 2. International relations 3. Arctic regions -- Exploration 4. Climate change -- Arctic regions 5. Power resources -- Arctic regions 6. Natural resources -- Arctic regions 7. Economic development -- Arctic regions

ISBN 1467720437; 9781467720434

LC 2013025164

In this book on climate change, author Stephanie Sammartino McPherson "describe[s] the changes in polar ice cover that are encouraging exploration and allowing access to previously inaccessible energy resources. Subsequent chapters describe new, shorter ocean passages, the jockeying for territory as nearby nations lay claim and others look for ways to get involved, and the likely difficulties of development." (Kirkus Reviews)

"Succinct and clearly written, the text offers up-to-date information, illustrated with clear color photos and useful maps. An articulate introduction to the Arctic in a time of profound, striking changes." Booklist

Includes bibliographical references (pages 59-60) and index

Miller, Debra A.

Energy production and alternative energy; Michael E. Miller consulting editor. Greenhaven Press 2011 123p il map (Confronting global warming) lib bdg $37.10

Grades: 7 8 9 10 11 12 **333.79**

1. Electric power 2. Renewable energy resources

ISBN 978-0-7377-5106-2; 0-7377-5106-1

LC 2010024976

Discusses the world's history of energy production and consumption, and explains how alternative energy sources may help with the coming fossil fuel energy crisis and protecting the worldwide environment.

"Presented in a scholarly design that will appeal to older readers. . . . The illustrations and pictures support the text, and the graphics and sidebars are well placed." Libr Media Connect

Includes glossary and bibliographical references

Rigsby, Mike

Doable renewables; 16 alternative energy projects for young scientists. Chicago Review Press 2010 196p il pa $16.95

Grades: 6 7 8 9 10 **333.79**

1. Renewable energy resources 2. Science -- Experiments

ISBN 978-1-56976-343-8 pa; 1-56976-343-7 pa

LC 2010019520

This is a "collection of science-oriented projects, focused . . . on renewable energy sources. From a windmill . . . to a human-powered LED light that relies on a hand-cranked generator, this activities range in complexity and skill, but all use simple technology to show basic and fascinating processes." Booklist

Sneideman, Joshua

Renewable Energy; Discover the Fuel of the Future With 20 Projects. by Joshua Sneideman and Erin Twamley ; illustrated by Heather Jane Brinesh. Nomad Press 2016 128 p. color illustrations $22.95

Grades: 4 5 6 7 **333.79**

1. Renewable energy resources

ISBN 1619303566; 9781619303560

In this book, by Joshua Sneideman and Erin Twamley, illustrated by Heather Jane Brinesh, "readers ages 9 to 12 learn about . . . renewable energy sources and discover how sunshine can be used to power light bulbs and how the earth's natural heat can be used to warm our houses. Young readers weigh the pros and cons of different energy sources and make their own informed opinions about which resources are the best choices for different uses." (Publisher's note)

"Links to online sources couple with essential questions and writing prompts about a range of interdisciplinary topics to make this book a quality choice for both the classroom and pleasure reading." Booklist

Includes bibliographical references (pages 117-118) and index.

Sobey, Ed

Solar cell and renewable energy experiments. Enslow Publishers 2011 128p il (Cool science projects with technology) lib bdg $31.93

Grades: 6 7 8 9 **333.79**

1. Renewable energy resources 2. Science -- Experiments

ISBN 978-0-7660-3305-4; 0-7660-3305-8

LC 2010027430

This explains what solar cells do and how they work, how wind and water power electronics, and offers experiments in renewable energy.

Includes glossary and bibliographical references

Thaddeus, Eva

Powering the future; new energy technologies. with illustrations by Catherine Paplin. University of New Mexico Press 2010 125p il map (Worlds of wonder) $24.95

Grades: 6 7 8 9 10 **333.79**

1. Renewable energy resources

ISBN 978-0-8263-4901-9; 0-8263-4901-3

LC 2009044300

The author tackles "environmental issues with depth and rigor, attuned to both current events and the concerns of today's teens. . . . The excellent [text is] enhanced by color photographs and diagrams that further explain scientific ideas." Horn Book Guide

Includes glossary

333.8 Subsurface resources

Mooney, Carla

Oil spills and offshore drilling. ReferencePoint Press 2011 96p il map (Compact research: energy and the environment) lib bdg $26.95

Grades: 7 8 9 10 11 12 **333.8**

1. Oil spills 2. Offshore oil well drilling

ISBN 978-1-60152-141-5; 1-60152-141-3

LC 2010037325

This volume has "up-to-date information with frequent references to . . . the Deepwater Horizon disaster in the Gulf of Mexico. . . . [It] asks if the U.S. needs to drill offshore, if it's an environmental risk, if regulations are adequate, and discusses the future of offshore drilling. . . . Each chapter is followed by a section of primary-source quotes espousing pro and con views. . . . [This is a] first-rate ready-reference [book] and excellent to use in teaching research with primary documents." SLJ

Includes bibliographical references

333.9 Other natural resources

Conley, Kate A.

Biofuels; by Kate Conley. Core Library 2016 48 p. illustrations (chiefly color) (Alternative Energy) $32.79

Grades: 4 5 6 7 **333.9**

1. Biomass energy 2. Biomass energy industries 3. Renewable energy resources

ISBN 9781680784534

This book by Kate Conley "explains what biofuels are, the history of the technology, how they generate electricity, and their future uses." (Publisher's note)

"Text-heavy yet comprehensible, each book delves into the specific energy source's origins, current applications, and outlook; addresses its benefits and drawbacks; and encourages readers to come to their own conclusions." SLJ

Dobson, Clive

Wind power; 20 projects to make with paper. Firefly Books 2010 96p il $24.95; pa $12.95

Grades: 5 6 7 8 **333.9**

1. Wind power 2. Paper crafts

ISBN 978-1-55407-659-8; 1-55407-659-5; 978-1-55407-749-6 pa; 1-55407-749-4 pa

"In this informative craft book, a celebration of wind and of innovative efforts to harness its energy, Dobson describes the geometric and aerodynamic principles behind windmills, sails, and wind turbines, then implements these concepts via 20 paper projects, ranging from a two-blade pinwheel to a dramatic 'Squirrel Cage' turbine. . . . Readers should gain a more palpable understanding of the subject matter by building and watching the graceful compositions function." Publ Wkly

Woll, Kris

Wind Energy; by Kris Woll. Core Library 2017 48 p. illustrations (chiefly color) (Alternative Energy) $32.79

Grades: 4 5 6 7 **333.9**

1. Wind power 2. Renewable energy resources

ISBN 9781680784602

This book by Kris Woll "explains what wind power is, the history of the technology, how it generates electricity, and its future uses." (Publisher's note)

"With its impeccable content, this dynamic series is a must for school and public libraries." SLJ

333.91 Water and lands adjoining bodies of water

Kallen, Stuart A.

Running dry; the global water crisis. by Stuart A. Kallen. Twenty-First Century Books 2015 64 p. illustrations (chiefly color) (lib. bdg. : alk. paper) $33.32

Grades: 4 5 6 7 8 **333.91**

1. Water supply 2. Water conservation 3. Water consumption 4. Water -- Pollution

ISBN 146772646X; 9781467726467; 9781467763080

LC 2014003223

This book, by Stuart A. Kallen "provides information on the growing water crisis. Looking at the subject globally, the discussion includes matters such as the dwindling supply of fresh water, its pollution by agriculture and industry, the dramatic effects of climate change, and the increasing competition for water. . . . Sidebars and full-page features spotlight pertinent topics such as the desalination of sea water." (Booklist)

"This title provides a clear and concise look at the importance of fresh water in sustaining life on earth . . . the book will appeal to those with little or no background on the subject. An excellent source for student research." SLJ

Includes bibliographical references and index

Kaye, Cathryn Berger

★ **Going** blue; a teen guide to saving our oceans & waterways. by Cathryn Berger Kaye; with Philippe Cousteau and Earth Echo International. Free Spirit Pub. 2010 151p il map pa $14.95

Grades: 6 7 8 9 10 **333.91**

1. Marine ecology 2. Marine pollution 3. Environmental protection

ISBN 978-1-57542-348-7; 1-57542-348-0

LC 2010-16589

Teaches young people about the Earth's water crisis and provides practical suggestions on how readers can identify water-related needs in the community and transform their ideas into action.

"This valuable how-to manual is suitable for an individual student, a family, a youth group, or a school wishing to protect our precious resource of water. This upbeat treasure will challenge anyone interested in environmental activism, whether water related or not. It is a must for any library serving youth." Voice Youth Advocates

Includes bibliographical references

Mulder, Michelle, 1976-

★ **Every** last drop; bringing clean water home. Michelle Mulder. Orca Book Pub 2014 48 p. illustrations (some color) (Orca footprints) (hardcover) $19.95

Grades: 4 5 6 7 **333.91**

1. Water conservation 2. Water resources development 3. Water quality management

ISBN 9781459802247; 9781459807129; 1459802233; 9781459802230

LC 2013951377

This book, by Michelle Mulder, "looks at why the world's water resources are at risk and how communities around the world are finding innovative ways to quench their thirst and water their crops. Maybe you're not ready to drink fog, as they do in Chile, or use water made from treated sewage, but you can get a low-flush toilet, plant a tree, protect a wetland or just take shorter showers." (Publisher's note)

"Divided into four chapters, this book explores the history of water use by humans; the natural cycle of water on earth; how people access, clean, and desalinate water; and ways in which we can conserve and preserve our water resources. Plenty of well-captioned photos, including some from the author's own travels, illustrate and personalize the accessible text." Horn Book

333.95 Biological resources

Castaldo, Nancy F.

Back from the brink; saving animals from extinction. by Nancy F. Castaldo. Houghton Mifflin Harcourt 2018 176 p. $17.99

Grades: 6 7 8 9 **333.95**

1. Endangered species 2. Wildlife conservation 3. Wildlife recovery -- United States 4. Endangered species -- United States 5. Wildlife conservation -- United States

ISBN 9780544953437

LC 2017015664

In this book, author Nancy F. Castaldo, "details the successful efforts of scientists to bring threatened animals back from the brink of extinction, perfect for animal lovers and reluctant nonfiction readers. . . . This rich, informational look at the problem of extinction has a hopeful tone: all of these animals' numbers are now on the rise." (Publisher's note)

Includes bibliographical references

Kurlansky, Mark, 1948-

The **world** without fish; how could we let this happen? illustrations by Frank Stockton. Workman Pub. 2011 183p il paperback $14.95

Grades: 5 6 7 8 9 10 **333.95**

1. Water pollution 2. Commercial fishing

ISBN 9780761185000; 978-0-7611-5607-9

LC 2011-15516

It was the author's intent to communicate that "our 'enduring misconception' about nature's bounty may lead to the extinction of many of the fish we eat (such as cod, salmon, swordfish, and tuna) and the subsequent collapse of marine ecosystems . . . . To avoid the dystopia he fears, Kurlansky stresses the importance of supporting sustainable fishing and hopes to enlist his readers to act to help 'change the way we do things!'" (Science)

"Brief sections in graphic-novel format follow a young girl, Ailat, and her father over a couple of decades as the condition of the ocean grows increasingly dire, eventually an orange, slimy mess mostly occupied by jellyfish and leatherback turtles. At the end, Ailat's young daughter doesn't even know what the word fish means. This is juxtaposed against nonfiction chapters with topics including types of fishing equipment and the damage each causes, a history of the destruction of the cod and its consequences, the international politics of the fishing industry and the effects of pollution and global warming. . . . Depressing and scary yet grimly entertaining." Kirkus

Laidlaw, Rob

★ **Saving** lives & changing hearts; animal sanctuaries and rescue centres. Fitzhenry & Whiteside 2012 62 p. $19.95

Grades: 4 5 6 7 8 **333.95**

1. Wildlife refuges 2. Wildlife rehabilitation

ISBN 1554552125; 9781554552122

This book "profiles a variety of sanctuaries throughout the world and the people who work to safeguard the wildlife. . . . The author offers the . . . stories behind the founding of many of these sanctuaries and presents . . . conclusions to the many . . . stories of rescued animals. A section showing the difference between true sanctuaries and those neither meeting the needs of animals in their care nor preparing them for rehabilitation into the wild is" included. (School Library Journal)

Salmansohn, Pete, 1947-

Saving birds; heroes around the world. [by] Pete Salmansohn and Stephen W. Kress. Tilbury House 2003 39p il $16.95; pa $7.95

Grades: 5 6 7 8 **333.95**

1. Endangered species 2. Wildlife conservation 3. Birds -- Protection

ISBN 0-88448-237-5; 0-88448-276-6 pa

LC 2002-6710

Profiles adults and children working in six habitats around the world to save wild birds, some of which are on the brink of extinction.

"As a teaching aid, this volume is an exceptional supplement. The six articles relating the heroic rescue of the endangered birds are accurate and enhanced by appropriate color photographs." Sci Books Films

Walker, Niki

Biomass; fueling change. [by] Niki Walker. Crabtree Pub. 2007 32p il (Energy revolution) lib bdg $19.95; pa $8.95

Grades: 5 6 7 8 **333.95**

1. Biomass energy

ISBN 978-0-7787-2914-3 lib bdg; 0-7787-2914-1 lib bdg; 978-0-7787-2928-0 pa; 0-7787-2928-1 pa

LC 2006016035

This "book presents a range of historical uses of the various forms of biomass, from charcoal smelters in ancient Egypt to ethanol-fueled lanterns in the 19th century and gasifiers during World War II. Vivid color photographs with informative captions extend the [text]." SLJ

Includes glossary

336.2 Taxes

La Bella, Laura

How taxation works. Rosen Pub. 2011 80p il (Real world economics) lib bdg $30.60

Grades: 7 8 9 10 **336.2**

1. Taxation -- United States

ISBN 978-1-4358-9463-1; 1-4358-9463-4

LC 2009047165

This describes how taxation works.

Includes glossary and bibliographical references

338 Production

Rankin, Kenrya

Start it up; the complete guide to turning your passions into pay. [illustrated by Eriko Takada and Marissa Fiend] Zest Books 2011 155p il pa $14.95

Grades: 7 8 9 10 11 12 **338**

1. Entrepreneurship 2. Business enterprises

ISBN 978-0-9819733-5-7; 0-9819733-5-3

"Combining a conversational style with a systematic approach, [this book] walks teens through starting their own business. . . . Rankin gives a good overview of such difficult concepts as start-up and operating costs and asks readers to consider potentially overlooked topics like the pros and cons of publicizing prices and things to consider when working with family and friends." Booklist

338.1 Specific kinds of industries

Goldstein, Margaret J.

Fuel Under Fire; Petroleum and Its Perils. by Margaret J. Goldstein. Twenty-First Century Books 2016 104 p. illustrations (some color) (lib. bdg. : alk. paper) $34.65; (ebook) $34.65

Grades: 7 8 9 10 11 12 **338.1**

1. Petroleum 2. Petroleum industry

ISBN 9781467738316; 9781467788021

LC 2014020890

This book on petroleum, by Margaret J. Goldstein, focuses on how, "alongside its benefits, petroleum has serious drawbacks. It is not a renewable resource, and many of Earth's most easily accessed petroleum deposits have been used up. Companies have begun to search for oil in more difficult-to-reach places, using controversial methods. Extracting, processing, and refining oil is often environmentally destructive." (Publisher's note)

"Though concise, a solid purchase for schools and public libraries." Booklist

Includes bibliographical references and index

Green, Jen

Food and farming; Jen Green. 1st ed. Heinemann Library 2012 64 p. (The impact of environmentalism) (hardcover) $35

Grades: 6 7 8 9 10 **338.1**

1. Environmental movement 2. Agriculture -- Environmental aspects 3. Food supply 4. Environmentalism

ISBN 1432965174; 9781432965174; 9781432965235

LC 2012001033

This book by Jen Green is part of the Impact on Environmentalism series. In "discussing the impact of the environmental movement on food and farming, Green also explores controversies surrounding modern agriculture and its distribution practices. A brief history of farming . . . leads to a discussion of more recent trends, including high-yield varieties of crops, monoculture, genetically modified foods, pesticides, water management, factory farming, organic farming, [and] fair trade." (Booklist)

Pollan, Michael, 1955-

★ The **omnivore's** dilemma; the secrets behind what you eat. adapted by Richie Chevat. Young readers ed.; Dial Books 2009 298p il $17.99

Grades: 5 6 7 8 9 10 **338.1**

1. Food supply 2. Food chains (Ecology) 3. Food habits 4. Food preferences 5. Sustainable agriculture

ISBN 0803734158; 9780803734159

LC 2009-9283

Adapted from: The omnivore's dilemma: a natural history of four meals, published 2006 by Penguin Press

This volume is adapted from Pollan's 2006 work for adults, The Omnivore's Dilemma: A Natural History of Four Meals. It presents information about food production in the United States and "encourages kids to consider the personal and global health implications of their food choices." (Publisher's note) Bibliography. Index. "Grades seven to ten." (Bull Cent Child Books)

"Adopting the role of food detective, the author 'peers behind the curtain' of the modern food industry and finds that the industrial approach to the food chain imperils our health and planet. The four sections of the volume describe differing types of meals: industrial; industrial organic; local sustainable; and hunted, gathered and found. Clear organization and lively writing rooted in fascinating examples make this accessible and interesting." Kirkus

Includes bibliographical references

338.6 Organization of production

Bezdecheck, Bethany

Bailout! government intervention in business. Rosen Pub. 2011 64p il (In the news) lib bdg $29.95; pa $12.95

Grades: 7 8 9 10 **338.6**

1. Bankruptcy 2. Corporations 3. Industrial policy -- United States

ISBN 978-1-4358-9449-5 lib bdg; 1-4358-9449-9 lib bdg; 978-1-4488-1681-1 pa; 1-4488-1681-5 pa

LC 2009052247

This " succinctly and objectively covers corporate bailouts and includes a history of government intervention in business dating back to 1970, when the government provided the Penn Central Transportation Company with $700 million to pay its creditors. . . . With numerous photos, concise and manageable chapters, and a glossary, . . . [this provides] an excellent background for students with an interest in social sciences or a jumping off point for school assignments." Voice Youth Advocates

Includes glossary and bibliographical references

338.7 Business enterprises

Buckley, A. M.

Pixar; the company and its founders. ABDO Pub. Co. 2011 112p il (Technology pioneers) lib bdg $34.22

Grades: 5 6 7 8 **338.7**

1. Animated films 2. Computer animation 3. Pixar Animation Studios

ISBN 978-1-61714-810-1 lib bdg; 1-61714-810-5 lib bdg; 978-1-61758-968-3 e-book

LC 2010044831

An introduction to Pixar Animation Studios and its founders.

"Written in a clear, linear fashion, this series offers vivid, well-researched details about the development of technological advancements considered essential in today's society. . . . Readers who are interested in technology and inventions will be thoroughly engrossed." SLJ

Includes glossary and bibliographical references

Other titles in the series include:

Apple (2012)
Craigslist (2011)
eBay (2011)
Facebook (2013)
Google (2011)
Microsoft (2013)
Netflix (2013)
Nintendo (2011)
Sony (2013)
Tivo (2013)
Twitter (2013)

Firestone, Mary

Nintendo; the company and its founders. ABDO Pub. Co. 2011 112p il (Technology pioneers) lib bdg $34.22

Grades: 5 6 7 8 **338.7**

1. Video games 2. Nintendo of America Inc.

ISBN 978-1-61714-809-5 lib bdg; 1-61714-809-1 lib bdg; 978-1-61758-967-6 e-book

LC 2010044664

This is an introduction to the Nintendo video game company and its founders.

"Written in a clear, linear fashion, this series offers vivid, well-researched details about the development of technological advancements considered essential in today's society. . . . Readers who are interested in technology and inventions will be thoroughly engrossed." SLJ

Includes glossary and bibliographical references

Frydenborg, Kay

Chocolate; sweet science and dark secrets of the world's favorite treat. Kay Frydenborg. Houghton Mifflin Harcourt 2015 272 p. 16 plates; color illustrations $18.99

Grades: 7 8 9 10 **338.7**

1. Cocoa 2. Science 3. Chocolate 4. Chocolate -- History 5. Cocoa trade 6. Chocolate industry 7. Cocoa trade -- History 8. Chocolate industry -- History

ISBN 9780544175662; 0544175662

LC 2014015885

In author Kay Frydenborg's book on the history of chocolate, "cutting-edge genetic science whisked in with a strong social conscience, history, and culture yield one thought-provoking look into one of the world's most popular foods." (Publisher's note)

"Covering controversy over labor laws, the chemical makeup of chocolate, and recent attempts to map the cacao genome, Frydenborg offers a wealth of information that will likely encourage students to think critically about the ecological and human cost of their favorite candies and maybe even prompt them to choose sustainable alternatives." Booklist

Includes bibliographical references

Gitlin, Marty

EBay; the company and its founder. ABDO Pub. Co. 2011 112p il (Technology pioneers) lib bdg $34.22

Grades: 5 6 7 8 **338.7**

1. Auctions 2. Executives 3. Businesspeople 4. Internet marketing 5. eBay Inc. 6. Software engineers 7. Internet executives

ISBN 978-1-61714-807-1 lib bdg; 1-61714-807-5 lib bdg; 978-1-61758-965-2 e-book

LC 2010044663

This is an introduction to eBay internet auction site and its founder, Pierre Omidyar.

"Written in a clear, linear fashion, this series offers vivid, well-researched details about the development of technological advancements considered essential in today's society. . . . Readers who are interested in technology and inventions will be thoroughly engrossed." SLJ

Includes glossary and bibliographical references

Hamen, Susan E.

Google; the company and its founders. ABDO Pub. Co. 2011 112p il (Technology pioneers) lib bdg $34.22

Grades: 5 6 7 8 **338.7**

1. Computer industry 2. Web search engines 3. Computer scientists 4. Google, Inc. 5. Internet executives 6. Information technology executives

ISBN 978-1-61714-808-8; 1-61714-808-3

LC 2010037884

This book about Google and its founders "provides a compact, direct, well-researched, and relevant explanation of how Sergey Brin, Larry Page, and their brand have changed the world. . . . This title presents just the right amount of background on the two men . . . before it moves into more thorough explorations of how the founders' creation has grown far beyond providing basic Web searching. . . . Dynamically designed with clear and colorful photographs, sidebars, and wide margins, this is at once a dual biography, Internet history, and business primer." Booklist

Includes bibliographical references

339.2 Distribution of income and wealth

Frazer, Coral Celeste

★ **Economic** inequality; the American dream under siege. Coral Celeste Frazer. Twenty-First Century Books 2018 128 p. color illustrations (library binding) $37.32

Grades: 7 8 9 10 **339.2**

1. Income gap -- United States 2. United States -- Economic Policy -- 2009- 3. United States -- Economic conditions -- 2009- 4. United States -- Economic policy 5. Income distribution -- United States 6. United States -- Economic conditions

ISBN 9781512498868; 9781512431070; 9781541521926

LC 2017032058

This book, by Coral Celeste Frazer, is about the economic inequality in the U.S. "Millions of Americans don't earn enough money to pay for decent housing, food, health care, and education. . . . [In this book] readers will learn how state and local governments, businesses, and ordinary citizens, including young people, are fighting to close the gap between rich and poor, to preserve the promises of American democracy, and to give everyone a fair shot at the American Dream." (Publisher's note)

"This remarkably evenhanded, lucid volume confidently leads readers through the murky world of wealth and economics in America." Booklist

Includes bibliographical references and index

339.4 Factors affecting income and wealth

Thompson, Helen

Cost of living. Mason Crest Publishers 2010 63p il (Junior library of money) $22.95; pa $9.95

Grades: 6 7 8 9 **339.4**

1. Prices 2. Personal finance 3. Cost and standard of living

ISBN 978-1-4222-1762-7; 1-4222-1762-0; 978-1-4222-1866-2 pa; 1-4222-1866-X pa

LC 2010029402

This defines the cost of living as the amount of money a person needs to spend on housing, food, transportation, clothing, and other items that people need to live and explains how it can go up and down based on the conditions in the economy, and depending on where you live.

This title presents "solid information and [has] eye-catching and relevant illustrations. . . . [The book is] clearly written, making understandable connections between daily life and financial concepts." SLJ

Includes glossary and bibliographical references

340.092 Biography

Stevenson, Bryan, 1959-

Just mercy; adapted for young adults: a true story of the fight for justice. Bryan Stevenson. Delacorte Press 2018 277 p. (hardback) $18.99

Grades: 7 8 9 10 11 12 **340.092**

1. Lawyers -- Biography 2. Equality -- United States 3. Discrimination in criminal justice administration -- United States 4. Equal Justice Initiative 5. Lawyers -- United States -- Biography 6. Equality before the law -- United States 7. Social reformers -- United States -- Biography 8. Sentences (Criminal procedure) -- United States 9. Criminal justice, Administration of -- United States

ISBN 9780525580058; 9780525580034; 9780525580041

LC 2018015248

In this book, "Bryan Stevenson recounts many and varied stories of his work as a lawyer in the U.S. criminal justice system on behalf of those in society who have experienced some type of discrimination and/or have been wrongly accused of a crime and who deserve a powerful advocate and due justice under the law. Through the Equal Justice Initiative (EJI), an organization Stevenson founded as a young lawyer . . . , this important work continues." (Publisher's note)

Includes bibliographical references (pages 264-272) and index

341.6 Law of war

Kenney, Karen Latchana

Korematsu v. the United States; World War II Japanese-American internment camps. by Karen Latchana Kenney ; content consultant Richard D. Friedman. ABDO Pub. Co. 2013 160 p. ill. (some col.) (library) $35.64

Grades: 8 9 10 11 12 **341.6**

1. Korematsu v. United States (Supreme Court case) 2. Japanese Americans -- Evacuation and relocation, 1942-1945 3. United States -- Trials, litigation, etc.

ISBN 1617834734; 9781617834738

LC 2012001277

This book by Karen Latchana Kenney is part of the Landmark Supreme Court Cases series and focuses on the case of Korematsu v. the United States. It "looks at the historical impact of World War II and the internment of Japanese American citizens out of fear and hysteria following the bombing of Pearl Harbor." (School Library Journal)

Includes bibliographical references (p. 146-154) and index.

342 Branches of law; laws, regulations, cases; law of specific jurisdictions, areas, socioeconomic regions

The **Constitutional** Convention; Richard Haesly, book editor. Greenhaven Press 2002 240p il maps (History firsthand) lib bdg $34.95; pa $23.70

Grades: 7 8 9 10 **342**

1. Constitutional history -- United States

ISBN 0-7377-1072-1 lib bdg; 0-7377-1071-3 pa

LC 2001-23832

This is a "study of the historical and political events that led up to the ratification of the U.S. Constitution. Using accounts and opinions by actual delegates and other prominent figures such as Patrick Henry and Thomas Jefferson, Haesly outlines the concepts of the Declaration of Independence, the Articles of Confederation, and the Constitution/Bill of Rights. The volume is enlivened by personal stories of those who lived through and influenced the events depicted, and includes discussions on slavery and the nature of the presidency. . . . Well suited for reports." SLJ

Includes bibliographical references

Feinberg, Barbara Silberdick

The **Articles** of Confederation; the first constitution of the United States. 21st Cent. Bks. (Brookfield) 2002 110p il maps lib bdg $24.90

Grades: 7 8 9 10 **342**

1. Constitutional history -- United States 2. United States -- Articles of Confederation 3. United States -- Politics and government -- 1775-1783, Revolution

ISBN 0-7613-2114-4

LC 2001-27441

"Feinberg introduces the history and text of 'The Articles of Confederation and Perpetual Union,' the constitution that guided the U.S. government from 1776 to 1787. . . . Attractively laid out, this solid choice includes many black-and-white illustrations, including portrait paintings, engravings, and maps." Booklist

Includes bibliographical references

Furgang, Kathy

The **Ninth** Amendment; rights retained by the people. Rosen Central 2011 64p il (Amendments to the United States Constitution: The Bill of Rights) $29.25; pa $12.95

Grades: 5 6 7 8 **342**

1. Civil rights 2. Constitutional law -- United States 3. United States -- Constitution -- 1st-10th amendments

ISBN 978-1-4488-1264-6; 1-4488-1264-X; 978-1-4488-2310-9 pa; 1-4488-2310-2 pa

LC 2010020091

This book about the Ninth Amendment to the U.S. Constitution is "well-written, objective and informative. . . . [It discusses] the historical reasons for [the] amendment, its basis in British and American common law, and the statutory and case law that shaped its implementation and development. . . . While primarily useful for reports, [this book] will also give students perspective on current events." SLJ

Includes glossary and bibliographical references

Gold, Susan Dudley

Roberts v. Jaycees; women's rights. Marshall Cavendish Benchmark 2009 144p il (Supreme Court milestones) $29.95

Grades: 7 8 9 10 **342**

1. Sex discrimination

ISBN 978-0-7614-2952-4; 0-7614-2952-2

LC 2007043021

First published 1984 by Twenty-First Century Books with title: Roberts v. U.S. Jaycees

This examines the Supreme Court case regarding sex discrimination against women members of the the Jaycees organization.

Includes bibliographical references

Haynes, Charles C.

First freedoms; a documentary history of the First Amendment Rights in America. [by] Charles C. Haynes, Sam Chaltain, Susan M. Glisson. Oxford University Press 2005 255p il $40

Grades: 8 9 10 11 12 **342**

1. Freedom of speech 2. Freedom of religion 3. Freedom of the press 4. Constitutional history -- United States 5. United States -- Constitution -- 1st-10th amendments

ISBN 978-0-19-515750-5; 0-19-515750-8

LC 2005-31880

This is "an excellent resource for all libraries, as well as enjoyable reading for history buffs." SLJ

Jones, Molly

The **First** Amendment; freedom of speech, the press, and religion. Rosen Central 2011 64p il (Amendments to the United States Constitution: The Bill of Rights) lib bdg $29.25; pa $12.95

Grades: 5 6 7 8 **342**

1. Freedom of speech 2. Freedom of religion 3. Freedom of the press 4. United States -- Constitution -- 1st-10th amendments

ISBN 978-1-4488-1252-3 lib bdg; 1-4488-1252-6 lib bdg; 978-1-4488-2302-4 pa; 1-4488-2302-1 pa

LC 2010023234

This book about the First Amendment to the U.S. Constitution is "well-written, objective and informative. . . . [It discusses] the historical reasons for [the] amendment, its basis in British and American common law, and the statutory and case law that shaped its implementation and development. . . . While primarily useful for reports, [this book] will also give students perspective on current events." SLJ

Includes glossary and bibliographical references

Orr, Tamra

The **Tenth** Amendment; limiting federal powers. Rosen Central 2011 64p il (Amendments to the United States Constitution: The Bill of Rights) lib bdg $29.25; pa $12.95

Grades: 5 6 7 8 **342**

1. Federal government 2. State rights 3. United States -- Constitution -- 1st-10th amendments

ISBN 978-1-4488-1265-3 lib bdg; 1-4488-1265-8 lib bdg; 978-1-4488-2311-6 pa; 1-4488-2311-0 pa

LC 2010021852

This book about the Tenth Amendment to the U.S. Constitution is "well-written, objective and informative. . . . [It discusses] the historical reasons for [the] amendment, its basis in British and American common law, and the statutory and case law that shaped its implementation and development. . . . While primarily useful for reports, [this book] will also give students perspective on current events." SLJ

Includes glossary and bibliographical references

Patrick, John J.

The **Bill** of Rights; a history in documents. Oxford Univ. Press 2003 205p il map (Pages from history) lib bdg $32.95

Grades: 7 8 9 10 **342**

1. Civil rights 2. United States -- Constitution -- 1st-10th amendments

ISBN 0-19-510354-8

LC 2002-6294

Uses contemporary documents to explore the history of the first ten amendments to the U.S. Constitution, the British traditions on which they were based, and their impact on American society

"This attractive and informative volume will be a valuable resource for most collections." SLJ

Includes bibliographical references

Pendergast, Tom

Constitutional amendments: from freedom of speech to flag burning; [by] Tom Pendergast, Sara Pendergast, and John Sousanis; Elizabeth Shaw Grunow, editor. U.X.L 2001 3v set $165

Grades: 7 8 9 10 **342**

1. Civil rights 2. Constitutional law -- United States 3. United States -- Constitution -- 1st-10th amendments

ISBN 0-7876-4865-5

LC 00-67236

"Presentation is very clear. . . . This is definitely a set that belongs in school and public libraries." Booklist

Includes glossary and bibliographical references

Porterfield, Jason

The **Third** Amendment; the right to privacy in the home. Rosen Central 2011 64p il (Amendments to the United States Constitution: The Bill of Rights) lib bdg $29.25; pa $12.95

Grades: 5 6 7 8 **342**

1. Right of privacy 2. United States -- Constitution -- 1st-10th amendments

ISBN 978-1-4488-1256-1 lib bdg; 1-4488-1256-9 lib bdg; 978-1-4488-2304-8 pa; 1-4488-2304-8 pa

LC 2010015855

This book about the Third Amendment to the U.S. Constitution is "well-written, objective and informative. . . . [It discusses] the historical reasons for [the] amendment, its basis in British and American common law, and the statutory and case law that shaped its implementation and development. . . . While primarily useful for reports, [this book] will also give students perspective on current events." SLJ

Includes glossary and bibliographical references

Ritchie, Donald A.

Our Constitution. Oxford University Press 2006 255p il map $40

Grades: 7 8 9 10 **342**

1. United States -- Constitution 2. Constitutional history -- United States

ISBN 978-0-19-522385-9; 0-19-522385-3

LC 2005031885

This "volume begins with five chapters of background (Why have a constitution? How has it changed?) and then goes on to discuss the preamble, articles, and amendments, using a What It Says (word for word) and What It Means format. Every spread contains photos, reproductions, and sidebars, all of which invite students to read and understand this living document. . . . This is an excellent, well-documented addition for most libraries." SLJ

Includes glossary and bibliographical references

Stefoff, Rebecca

U.S. v. Nixon; the limits of presidential privilege. Marshall Cavendish Benchmark 2009 127p il (Supreme Court milestones) lib bdg $29.95

Grades: 7 8 9 10 **342**

1. Presidents 2. Vice-presidents 3. Watergate Affair, 1972-1974 4. Senators 5. Nonfiction writers 6. Members of Congress

ISBN 978-0-7614-2955-5 lib bdg; 0-7614-2955-7 lib bdg

LC 2007031607

This examines the Supreme Court regarding the Watergate scandal.

Includes bibliographical references

Van Zee, Amy

Dred Scott v. Sandford; slavery and freedom before the American civil war. by Amy Van Zee ; content consultant, Earl Maltz. ABDO Pub. Co. 2013 160 p. ill. (some col.) (Landmark Supreme Court cases) (hbk. : alk. paper) $35.64

Grades: 8 9 10 11 12 **342**

1. Slavery -- United States 2. United States. Supreme Court 3. Slavery -- Law and legislation -- United States -- History -- 19th century

ISBN 1617834726; 9781617834721

LC 2012001276

This book is part of the Landmark Supreme Court Cases Series. This title focuses on Dred Scott v. Sandford and explains how "the origins of slavery in the United States in regard to societal acceptance and black inferiority, deeply ingrained throughout the growth and development of the country, played a major role in every aspect of the developing nation with the continuing struggle between both sides of the issue." (School Library Journal)

Includes bibliographical references (p. 146-153) and index

342.73 Constitutional law – United States

Baxter, Roberta

The **Bill** of Rights; by Roberta Baxter. Heinemann Library 2012 48 p.

Grades: 4 5 6 7 **342.73**

1. Legislation 2. United States -- Politics and government 3. Constitutional history -- United States 4. Civil rights -- United States -- History 5. United States. Constitution. 1st-10th Amendments

ISBN 9781432967512; 9781432967604

LC 2011037780

In this book, Roberta Baxter, readers can "learn about the Bill of Rights, one of the most significant documents in U.S. history. [They can] find out about those who were involved in its creation and why studying this primary source is [considered] so important." (Publisher's note)

Includes bibliographical references (p. 47) and index

Cates, David

Plessy v. Ferguson; segregation and the separate but equal policy. David Cates ; content consultant, Margalynne Armstrong. ABDO Pub. 2013 160 p. illustrations (some color) (Landmark Supreme Court cases) $37.07

Grades: 8 9 10 11 12 **342.73**

1. Segregation -- History 2. Race discrimination -- Law and legislation -- United States 3. Segregation in transportation -- Law and legislation -- Louisiana -- History -- 19th century

ISBN 1617834750; 9781617834752

LC 2012001279

This book in the Landmark Supreme Court Cases series, by David Cates, edited by Melissa York, focuses on the case "Plessy v. Ferguson, which decided the constitutionality of separate but equal policies in 1896. . . . Major players and key events are discussed, including Homer Plessy and the Citizens' Committee, and their fight against Louisiana's separate train cars law." (Publisher's note)

Includes bibliographical references (p. 146-153) and index

Heppermann, Christine

Bush v. Gore; the Florida recounts of the 2000 presidential election. Christine Heppermann ; content consultant Richard D. Friedman. ABDO Pub. 2013 160 p. illustrations (chiefly color) (Landmark Supreme Court cases) (hbk. : alk. paper) $37.07

Grades: 8 9 10 11 12 **342.73**

1. United States. Supreme Court 2. Presidents -- United States -- Election -- 2000 3. Contested elections -- Florida 4. Contested

elections -- United States
ISBN 1617834718; 9781617834714

LC 2012001274

In this book, by Christine Heppermann, focuses on the U.S. Supreme Court case Bush v. Gore. "Readers will follow this case from beginning to end, including the social and political climates that led up to it and the effects it had after the court made its ruling. Major players and key events are discussed, including George W. Bush, Albert Gore Junior, Dick Cheney, Joseph Lieberman, Karl Rove, William Daley, Katherine Harris, and William H. Rehnquist." (Publisher's note)

Includes bibliographical references (p. 146-156) and index

Jacobs, Tom

Every vote matters; the power of your voice, from student elections to the Supreme Court. by Tom Jacobs and Natalie Jacobs. Free Spirit Pub. Inc. 2016 208 p. (Teens & the Law) (soft cover) $15.99

Grades: 7 8 9 10 11 12 **342.73**

1. Political science 2. Political participation 3. United States. Supreme Court 4. Law -- United States
ISBN 1631980696; 9781631980695

LC 2015032349

Author Tom Jacobs and Natalie Jacobs present this "book focused on Supreme Court decisions that came down to a single vote. Chapters examine key Supreme Court rulings and explore how these cases have affected the lives and rights of U.S. citizens--especially teens. Using a straightforward, impartial tone, the authors take a close look at often controversial cases and at the history of voting in the United States." (Publisher's note)

Includes bibliographical references and index

Krull, Kathleen

A **kids'** guide to America's Bill of Rights; Kathleen Krull ; illustrated by Anna DiVito. 2nd edition Harper 2015 230 p illustrations hardcover $16.99; paperback $6.99

Grades: 4 5 6 7 8 **342.73**

1. Constitutional amendments -- United States 2. Civil rights -- United States 3. United States. Constitution. 1st-10th Amendments
ISBN 9780062352316; 9780062352309

LC 2015506104

"Beginning with the text of the Bill of Rights and an overview of its history and importance, the book is divided into chapters focusing on each amendment. Legal cases (often involving children's rights) are well explained. Final chapters discuss later amendments and constitutional controversies. The casual prose and amusing illustrations make this updated edition a kid-friendly introduction." (Horn Book)

Includes bibliographical references (pages 219-221) and index

Levinson, Sanford, 1941-

★ **Fault** lines in the constitution; the framers, their fights, and the flaws that affect us today. by Cynthia Levinson and Sanford Levinson. Peachtree Publishers 2017 235 p. illustrations, maps (hardcover) $19.95

Grades: 6 7 8 9 10 11 12 **342.73**

1. Political science literature 2. Constitutional law -- United States 3. Civics 4. United States -- Constitution 5. United States -- Politics and government
ISBN 9781561459452

LC 2017011413

This book, by Cynthia Levinson and Sanford Levinson, "takes readers back to the creation of . . . [the United States Constitution] and discuss how contemporary problems were first introduced--then they offer possible solutions. Think Electoral College, gerrymandering, even the Senate. Many of us take these features in our system for granted. But they came about through haggling in an overheated room in 1787, and we're still experiencing the ramifications." (Publisher's note)

"A fascinating, thoughtful, and provocative look at what in the Constitution keeps the United States from being 'a more perfect union.'" Kirkus

Includes bibliographical references and index

Lüsted, Marcia Amidon

Tinker vs. Des Moines; the right to protest in schools. by Marcia Amidon Lusted ; content consultant: Gerald Thain. ABDO Pub. 2013 160 p. illustrations (some color) (Landmark Supreme Court cases) (hbk. : alk. paper) $37.07

Grades: 8 9 10 11 12 **342.73**

1. High school students 2. Freedom of speech -- United States 3. Vietnam War, 1961-1975 -- Protest movements -- United States 4. High school students -- Civil rights -- United States 5. Vietnam War, 1961-1975 -- Protest movements -- Iowa -- Des Moines 6. Des Moines Independent Community School District -- Trials, litigation, etc.
ISBN 1617834777; 9781617834776

LC 2012001280

This book, by Marcia Amidon Lusted, "introduces readers to The United States v. Nixon, a landmark case that addressed the Watergate Scandal and limits to US presidential power. Chapters investigate the courts ruling, including its compelling backstory and appeals process, as well as the political climate at the time due to the Vietnam War and Nixons reelection campaign. The aftermath of this important decision, including Nixons impeachment trial and resignation from office are also detailed." (Publisher's note)

Includes bibliographical references (p. 146-154) and index

Vile, John R.

The **United** States Constitution; questions and answers. John R. Vile. Second edition ABC-CLIO 2014 xii, 308 p.p illustrations (hbk. : alk. paper) $68

Grades: 8 9 10 11 12 **342.73**

1. Constitutional law -- United States
ISBN 1610695712; 9781610695718

LC 2013029941

"An up-to-date, all-encompassing, and nonpartisan presentation of questions and answers about the U.S. Constitution and its amendments--an invaluable tool for readers regardless of their political orientation." (Publisher's note)

Includes bibliographical references and index

344 Labor, social service, education, cultural law

Anderson, Wayne

Brown v. Board of Education; the case against school segregation. Rosen Pub. Group 2004 64p il (Supreme Court cases through primary sources) lib bdg $29.95

Grades: 6 7 8 9 **344**

1. Clergy 2. Segregation in education 3. Welders 4. Railroad workers 5. Civil rights activists 6. Topeka (Kan.) -- Board of Education
ISBN 0-8239-4009-8

LC 2003-219

This is a discussion of the Supreme Court decision which ended racial segregation in public schools.

This "deserves a place in every library. . . . Copious and well-chosen primary source documents give extra value to this [book]. . . . Each document adds human drama to the already engaging text." Lib Media Connect

Includes glossary and bibliographical references

Mountjoy, Shane

Engel v. Vitale; school prayer and the establishment clause. Chelsea House 2007 128p il (Great Supreme Court decisions) lib bdg $30

Grades: 7 8 9 10 **344**

1. Church and state 2. Religion in the public schools

ISBN 0-7910-9241-0; 978-0-7910-9241-5

LC 2006-7328

This describes the 1962 Supreme Court case which ruled that official prayers in public schools were unconstitutional.

"Excellent period photos, magazine covers, and portraits of historical figures are closely cued to the [text]. . . . Handsomely packaged, accessible." SLJ

Includes glossary and bibliographical references

Perl, Lila

Cruzan v. Missouri; the right to die? Marshall Cavendish Benchmark 2007 143p il (Supreme Court milestones) $27.95

Grades: 7 8 9 10 **344**

1. Metalworkers 2. Accident victims 3. Right to die -- Law and legislation

ISBN 978-0-7614-2581-6; 0-7614-258-0

LC 2006-25740

"Perl discusses Nancy Cruzan's parents quest for her right to die following an auto accident and her resulting vegetative state. Highlights include the discussion of religious arguments, physician-assisted suicide, and the cases of Karen Ann Quinlan and Terry Schiavo. . . . Additional information is presented in sidebars. Occasional black-and-white photos add interest." SLJ

Includes bibliographical references

344.73 Labor, social service, education, cultural law – United States

Louis, David

The **right** to bear arms; a look at the Second Amendment. David Louis. PowerKids Press 2019 32 p.

Grades: 5 6 7 8 **344.73**

1. Gun control -- United States 2. United States. Constitution. 2nd Amendment 3. Firearms -- Law and legislation -- United States

ISBN 9781538342923; 9781538342947

LC 2018020444

"In 1791, the U.S. Congress ratified the first 10 amendments to the Constitution, known as the Bill of Rights. The Second Amendment states, 'the right of the people to keep and bear arms shall not be infringed.'. . . With this book [by David Louis], readers go beyond the sensational headlines to explore the origins of the Second Amendment, both in a historical and contemporary context." (Publisher's note)

Rubin, Susan Goldman

★ **Brown** v. Board of Education; a fight for simple justice. Susan Goldman Rubin. Holiday House 2016 160 p. illustrations (ebook) $18.95; (hardcover) $18.95

Grades: 5 6 7 8 **344.73**

1. Segregation in education 2. Topeka (Kan.). Board of Education -- Trials, litigation, etc. 3. African Americans -- Civil rights 4. Segregation in education -- Law and legislation -- United States

ISBN 9780823437085; 9780823436460

LC 2016004631

This book, by Susan Goldman Rubin, focuses on the Supreme Court decision that "aimed to end school segregation in the United States. Although known as Brown v. Board of Education, the ruling applied not just to the case of Linda Carol Brown, an African American third grader refused entry to an all-white Topeka, Kansas school, but to cases involving children in South Carolina, Delaware, Virginia, and Washington, DC." (Publisher's note)

"A rich, compelling story of the many people who stood up to racial inequality, risking significant danger and hardship for the cause of justice." Kirkus

Includes bibliographical references (pages 118-120) and index.

345 Criminal law

Aretha, David

The **trial** of the Scottsboro boys. Morgan Reynolds Pub. 2007 128p il (The civil rights movement) lib bdg $27.95

Grades: 7 8 9 10 11 12 **345**

1. Trials 2. Scottsboro case 3. African Americans -- Civil rights

ISBN 978-1-59935-058-5; 1-59935-058-0

LC 2007-23818

This describes the case of nine young black men between the ages of 13 and 20 who were accused of rape in the 1930s in Alabama by two white women and were sentenced to death.

"Aretha writes clearly, with objectivity and compassion." SLJ

Includes bibliographical references

Brezina, Corona

The **Fifth** Amendment; double jeopardy, self-incrimination, and due process of law. Rosen Central 2011 64p il (Amendments to the United States Constitution: The Bill of Rights) lib bdg $29.25; pa $12.95

Grades: 5 6 7 8 **345**

1. Criminal procedure 2. United States -- Constitution -- 1-10th amendments

ISBN 978-1-4488-1260-8 lib bdg; 1-4488-1260-7 lib bdg; 978-1-4488-2306-2 pa; 1-4488-2306-4 pa

LC 2010018820

This book about the Fifth Amendment to the U.S. Constitution is "well-written, objective and informative. . . . [It discusses] the historical reasons for [the] amendment, its basis in British and American common law, and the statutory and case law that shaped its implementation and development. . . . While primarily useful for reports, [this book] will also give students perspective on current events." SLJ

Includes glossary and bibliographical references

Burgan, Michael

The **Scopes** trial; faith, science, and American education. Marshall Cavendish Benchmark 2010 112p il (Perspectives on) $39.93

Grades: 7 8 9 10 **345**

1. Geologists 2. Science teachers 3. Evolution -- Study and teaching

ISBN 978-0-7614-4981-2; 0-7614-4981-7

An account of the trial of John T. Scopes, prosecuted in 1925 for teaching evolution.

This "well-written [book begins] with [an overview] and some historical background, and then [proceeds] chronologically to the current decade. . . . Burgan presents both sides with respect and objectivity. . . . It is evident that . . . the author [has] done [his] research. [The book contains] information that is perhaps less well-known to student researchers, including the preliminary events leading up to the Scopes trial. . . . Black-and-white and color photographs along with some period cartoons place readers in the time period, and sidebars interspersed throughout present issues that aren't easily covered within the main [text]." SLJ

Cates, David

The **Scottsboro** boys; by David Cates. ABDO Pub. Co. 2012 112 p. ill. $34.22

Grades: 6 7 8 9 **345**

1. Scottsboro case 2. Civil rights -- United States -- History 3. Trials (Rape) -- Alabama -- Scottsboro 4. Scottsboro Trial, Scottsboro, Ala., 1931 5. African Americans -- Civil rights -- History

ISBN 161783310X; 9781617833106

LC 2011036128

This book "tells the story of the nine African American teenagers accused of raping two white women on a train in Scottsboro, Alabama in 1931, covering the arrests and . . . legal proceedings." The book "explores the history of America at the time of the trials, the accounts of the nine men on trial regarding their train ride from Tennessee to Alabama, their sentences, and the effects of this event on society." (Publisher's notes)

"These titles are excellent introductions to these important topics, particularly for developing an analytical framework for debate." SLJ

Includes bibliographical references (p. 104-109) and index

Coleman, Wim

Racism on trial; From the Medgar Evers murder case to 'Ghosts of Mississippi' [by] Wim Coleman and Pat Perrin. Enslow Publishers 2009 112p il (Famous court cases that became movies) lib bdg $31.93

Grades: 5 6 7 8 **345**

1. Lynching 2. Trials (Homicide) 3. Murderers 4. White supremacists 5. Civil rights activists 6. Mississippi -- Race relations

ISBN 978-0-7660-3059-6; 0-7660-3059-8

LC 2008-21483

"Examines the Byron De La Beckwith murder trials, including the mistrials and his eventual conviction, key figures in the case, and the inspiration for the movie Ghosts of Mississippi." Publisher's note

Includes glossary and bibliographical references

Galiano, Dean

The **Fourth** Amendment; unreasonable search and seizure. Rosen Central 2011 64p il (Amendments to the United States Constitution: The Bill of Rights) lib bdg $29.25; pa $12.95

Grades: 5 6 7 8 **345**

1. Searches and seizures 2. United States -- Constitution -- 1st-10th amendments

ISBN 978-1-4488-1259-2 lib bdg; 1-4488-1259-3 lib bdg; 978-1-4488-2305-5 pa; 1-4488-2305-6 pa

LC 2010017394

This book about the Fourth Amendment to the U.S. Constitution is "well-written, objective and informative. . . . [It discusses] the historical reasons for [the] amendment, its basis in British and American common law, and the statutory and case law that shaped its implementation and development. . . . While primarily useful for reports, [this book] will also give students perspective on current events." SLJ

Includes glossary and bibliographical references

Higgins, Melissa

Roe v. Wade; abortion and a woman's right to privacy. Melissa Higgins ; content consultant Joseph Dellapenna. ABDO Pub. 2013 160 p. illustrations (chiefly color) (Landmark Supreme Court cases) (hbk.) $37.07

Grades: 8 9 10 11 12 **345**

1. Pro-choice movement 2. Abortion -- Law and legislation 3. Trials (Abortion) -- United States 4. Abortion -- Law and legislation -- United States

ISBN 1617834769; 9781617834769

LC 2012001275

In this book on Roe v. Wade in the Landmark Supreme Court Cases series, by Melissa Higgins, "readers will follow this case from beginning to end, including the social and political climates that led up to it and the effects it had after the court made its ruling. Major players and key ideas and events are discussed, including Jane Roe, aka Norma McCorvey, Linda Coffee, Sarah Weddington, women's rights, [and] feminism." (Publisher's note)

Includes bibliographical references (p. 146-154) and index

Jacobs, Thomas A.

★ **They** broke the law, you be the judge; true cases of teen crime. edited by Al Desetta. Free Spirit Pub. 2003 213p il pa $15.95

Grades: 7 8 9 10 **345**

1. Juvenile courts 2. Administration of criminal justice

ISBN 1-57542-134-8

LC 2003-4814

"An excellent introduction to how juvenile justice works, this will be a great resource for classroom and group discussions." Booklist

Includes bibliographical references

Miller, Sarah

The **Borden** murders; Lizzie Borden and the trial of the century. Sarah Miller. Schwartz & Wade Books 2016 304 p. 16 plates; illustrations $17.99

Grades: 6 7 8 9 10 **345**

1. True crime stories 2. Fall River (Mass.) -- History 3. Murder -- Massachusetts -- Fall River 4. Trials (Murder) -- Massachusetts -- New Beford 5. Murder -- Investigation -- Massachusetts -- Fall River

ISBN 9780553498080; 9780553498097; 9780553498103

LC 2015005371

This book, by Sarah Miller, presents a true crime narrative of the "August 4, 1892 murders of . . . Andrew and Abby Borden. The accused? Mild-mannered and highly respected Lizzie Borden. . . . Most of what is known about Lizzie's arrest and subsequent trial (and acquittal) comes from sensationalized newspaper reports; as Miller sorts fact from fiction, and as a legal battle gets under way, a gripping portrait of a woman and a town emerges." (Publisher's note)

"Photos, diagrams, and Miller's thoughtful note on researching the book combine with the energetic text to engage readers in their own debate as to Lizzie Borden's guilt or innocence." Pub Wkly

Includes bibliographical references and index

Rosaler, Maxine

★ The **devil** on trial; witches, anarchists, atheists, communists, and terrorists in America's courtrooms. by Phillip Marguiles and Maxine Rosaler. Houghton Mifflin Co. 2008 218 p. ill., ports $22

Grades: 7 8 9 10 11 12 **345**

1. Lawyers 2. Trials -- History 3. Administration of criminal justice -- United States 4. Diplomats 5. Trials -- United States 6. Criminal justice, Administration of -- Social aspects -- United States 7. Discrimination in criminal justice administration -- United States -- History

ISBN 061871717X; 9780618717170

LC 2008001870

The authors examine cases such as the Scopes 'monkey' trial, the two trials of Alger Hiss trials, and the witch trials in Salem, Mass. Glossary. Bibliography. Index. "Grades seven to ten." (Bull Cent Child Books)

The authors "examine five highly emotional court cases, each of which served as a litmus test for the health of America's justice system at the time it occurred. . . . Each chapter gives historical context of the court proceeding, describes its progression in some detail, and comments on the political and intellectual aftermath. . . . [This is] a highly relevant and riveting book." SLJ

Includes bibliographical references (p. [203] - 207) and index

Roza, Greg

The **Eighth** Amendment; preventing cruel and unusual punishment. Rosen Central 2011 64p il (Amendments to the United States Constitution: The Bill of Rights) lib bdg $29.25; pa $12.95

Grades: 5 6 7 8 **345**

1. Punishment 2. United States -- Constitution -- 1st-10th amendments

ISBN 978-1-4488-1263-9 lib bdg; 1-4488-1263-1 lib bdg; 978-1-4488-2309-3 pa; 1-4488-2309-9 pa

LC 2010015857

This book about the Eighth Amendment to the U.S. Constitution is "well-written, objective and informative. . . . [It discusses] the historical reasons for [the] amendment, its basis in British and American common law, and the statutory and case law that shaped its implementation and development. . . . While primarily useful for reports, [this book] will also give students perspective on current events." SLJ

Includes glossary and bibliographical references

Shea, Therese

The **Sixth** Amendment; the rights of the accused in criminal cases. Rosen Central 2011 64p il (Amendments to the United States Constitution: The Bill of Rights) lib bdg $29.25; pa $12.95

Grades: 5 6 7 8 **345**

1. Criminal procedure 2. United States -- Constitution -- 1st-10th amendments

ISBN 978-1-4488-1261-5 lib bdg; 1-4488-1261-5 lib bdg; 978-1-4488-2307-9 pa; 1-4488-2307-2 pa

LC 2010021318

This book about the Sixth Amendment to the U.S. Constitution is "well-written, objective and informative. . . . [It discusses] the historical reasons for [the] amendment, its basis in British and American common law, and the statutory and case law that shaped its implementation and development. . . . While primarily useful for reports, [this book] will also give students perspective on current events." SLJ

Includes glossary and bibliographical references

345.73 Criminal justice law – United States

Goldstein, Margaret J.

Legalizing marijuana; promises and pitfalls. Margaret J. Goldstein. Twenty-First Century Books 2016 104 p. illustrations (chiefly color) (lb : alk. paper) $35.99

Grades: 7 8 9 10 11 12 **345.73**

1. Marijuana 2. Drug legalization 3. Marijuana -- Law and legislation -- United States 4. Drug legalization -- United States

ISBN 9781512411447; 9781467792431

LC 2016008283

This book, by Margaret J. Goldstein, examines the "issues including the history of the movement toward legalization [of marijuana] in the United States, efforts toward legalization around the globe, the risks/benefits of marijuana use, how it works in the body, safety regulations, economic impact of legalization, problems surrounding patchwork legalization across the nation, and the dark side of marijuana: addiction." (Publisher's note)

"A well-tempered examination of the current standing of marijuana in the United States, with important forays into its medicinal use." Kirkus

Includes bibliographical references (pages 96-99) and index.

346 Private law

Butler, Rebecca P.

★ **Copyright** for teachers & librarians in the 21st century. Neal-Schuman Publishers 2011 274p il pa $70

Grades: Adult Professional **346**

1. Copyright 2. Fair use (Copyright)

ISBN 978-1-55570-738-5

LC 2011012600

First published 2004 with title: Copyright for teachers and librarians

"Library educator Rebecca Butler explains fair use, public domain, documentation and licenses, permissions, violations and penalties, policies and ethics codes, citations, creation and ownership, how to register copyrights, and gives tips for staying out of trouble." Publisher's note

Includes bibliographical references

Harris, Lesley Ellen

Licensing digital content; a practical guide for librarians. Lesley Ellen Harris. 3rd edition American Library Association 2018 181p paperback $65

Grades: Adult Professional **346**

1. Copyright 2. Electronic publishing 3. Information resources

ISBN 9780838916308

LC 2017044800

First published 2002

"As with the previous edition (2009), this single volume is a good first resource for librarians who want to gain a better understanding of how to license digital content. Copyright lawyer and educator Harris (Digital Property, 1997) offers readers firsthand advice and knowledge that is helpful in license-agreement negotiations." (Booklist)

Includes bibliographical references

Popek, Emily

Copyright and digital ethics. Rosen Central 2011 48p il (Digital and information literacy) lib bdg $26.50; pa $11.75

Grades: 5 6 7 8 **346**

1. Ethics 2. Internet 3. Copyright

ISBN 978-1-4488-1323-0 lib bdg; 1-4488-1323-9; 978-1-4488-2294-2 pa; 1-4488-2294-7 pa

LC 2010027018

Though this "title is a broad overview of a sometimes-complex subject, the detail is significant. . . . Touches of blue enhance the clean design. . . . [This] explains concepts like fair use and tries to persuade readers of the damage done by digital piracy and plagiarism." Booklist

Includes bibliographical references

346.04 Property

Crews, Kenneth D.

★ **Copyright** law for librarians and educators; creative strategies and practical solutions. with contributions from Dwayne K. Buttler . . . [et al.] 4th edition American Library Association 2019 304 p ill. paperback $68

Grades: Adult Professional **346.04**

1. Copyright 2. Sound recordings 3. Fair use (Copyright) 4. Copyright -- United States 5. Fair use (Copyright) -- United States 6. Teachers -- United States -- Handbooks, manuals, etc 7. Librarians -- United States -- Handbooks, manuals, etc

ISBN 9780838916292

First published 2000 with title: Copyright essentials for librarians and educators

Author Kenneth D. Crews' book "allows readers to get up to speed on current interpretations of the Digital Millennium Copyright Act from a librarian-educator viewpoint." It also "draws on cutting-edge case law in 18 discrete areas of copyright, including specialized and controversial music and sound recording issues. [This guide offers] information professionals . . . the tools they need to take control of their rights and responsibilities as copyright owners and users." (Publisher's note)

The author "addresses 18 areas of copyright in 5 parts. He begins with the scope of protectable works as well as works without copyright protection. Next, he discusses the rights of ownership, including duration and exceptions. He then explains fair use and its related guidelines. Part 4 focuses on the TEACH Act, Section 108, and responsibilities and liabilities. Lastly, Crews examines special issues such as the Digital Millennium Copyright Act." Booklist

Includes bibliographical references and index.

Russell, Carrie

Complete copyright for K-12 librarians and educators; Carrie Russell. American Library Association 2012 xi, 173 p.p ill. (chiefly col.) (alk. paper) $50

Grades: Professional **346.04**

1. Copyright 2. Fair use (Copyright) 3. Segregation -- Law and legislation 4. Copyright -- United States 5. Fair use (Copyright) -- United States 6. Librarians -- Legal status, laws, etc. -- United States 7. School libraries -- Law and legislation -- United States

ISBN 0838910831; 9780838910832

LC 2012016674

This book by Carrie Russell "is designed as a resource for educators, offering guidance for providing material to students while carefully observing copyright law. The book offers detailed advice on distinctive issues of intellectual property in the school setting; explores scenarios often encountered by educators . . . and precisely defines 'fair use,' by showing readers exactly what's possible within the law." (Education Digest)

Includes bibliographical references and index

347 Procedure and courts

Panchyk, Richard

Our Supreme Court; a history with 14 activities. Chicago Review Press 2006 195p il $16.95

Grades: 7 8 9 10 **347**

1. United States -- Supreme Court 2. Constitutional law -- United States

ISBN 978-1-55652-607-7; 1-55652-607-5

LC 2006009018

"The history and evolution of the court and how it works are discussed in the first chapter. Thematic sections follow, covering such topics as free speech, privacy, and civil rights, with significant decisions included. . . . This a solid work that makes a complex and important subject accessible to students." SLJ

Includes bibliographical references

347.73 Civil procedure and courts of the United States

Rodger, Ellen

What is the judicial branch? by Ellen Rodger. Crabtree Publishing Company 2013 32 p. (Your guide to government) (reinforced library binding) $26.60

Grades: 4 5 6 7 **347.73**

1. Law -- United States 2. Courts -- United States 3. Procedure (Law) -- United States

ISBN 0778708802; 9780778708803; 9780778709060

LC 2013001275

This book, by Ellen Rodger "provide[s] solid introductory material about the U.S. government. [The] book discusses the purpose of [the judicial] branch; the different positions, . . . the work done; and the strengths and the challenges of each branch and how they interact." (School Library Journal)

Valentine, Rebecca

Supreme Court drama; Daniel E. Brannen, Richard Clay Hanes, & Rebecca Valentine. 2nd edition UXL 2011 5v $481

Grades: 7 8 9 10 **347.73**

1. United States. Supreme Court 2. Constitutional law -- United States

ISBN 9781414486567; 1414486561

LC 2011001495

"This five-volume resource provides exciting details on key events, people and outcomes of approximately 200 major Supreme Court decisions that had a significant impact on American society. Cases are arranged by topic, introduced with an overview essay. Entries are three to five pages in length, and describe the events leading up to the case, key moments in the proceedings and the Supreme Court's decision, including its contemporary relevance. Also featured are helpful callout boxes providing significant court details and sidebars highlighting court justices, key court figures or important facts about the amendment or part of the Constitution being argued." (Publisher's note)

351 Public administration

Bow, James

What is the executive branch? by James Bow. Crabtree Publishing Company 2013 32 p. (Your guide to government) (reinforced library binding) $26.60

Grades: 4 5 6 7 351

1. Presidents -- United States 2. Executive power -- United States 3. Executive departments -- United States

ISBN 0778709027; 9780778709022; 9780778709077

LC 2013001276

This book, by James Bow "provide[s] solid introductory material about the U.S. government. [The] book discusses the purpose of [the executive] branch; the different positions, . . . the work done; and the strengths and the challenges of each branch and how they interact." (School Library Journal)

355 Military science

Holmes, Richard, 1946-2011

Battle; written by Richard Holmes; photographed by Geoff Dann & Geoff Brightling. Revised edition DK Publishing 2009 72 p. color illustrations $16.99

Grades: 4 5 6 7 8 355

1. War 2. Battles 3. Military history 4. Battles -- Encyclopedias

ISBN 9780756650278

LC 2010485660

This book by Richard Holmes "is DK's classic look at the history of military science and warfare, now reissued with a CD and wall chart." (Publisher's note)

Humphreys, Jessica Dee

Child Soldier; When Boys and Girls Are Used in War. Michel Chikwanine, Jessica Dee Humphreys ; illustrated by Claudia Davila. Kids Can Press 2015 48 p. color illustrations $17.95

Grades: 5 6 7 8 355

1. Child soldiers

ISBN 1771381264; 9781771381260

Eisner Nominee: Best Publication for Kids (2016)

This children's book, written by Michel Chikwanine and Jessica Dee Humphreys, and illustrated by Claudia Davila, describes the experience of a child solder. "Michel Chikwanine was five years old when he was abducted from his schoolyard soccer game in the Democratic Republic of Congo and forced to become a soldier for a brutal rebel militia. Against the odds, Michel managed to escape . . . , but he was never the same again." (Publisher's note)

"Chikwanine's narration is matter of fact but never didactic, emphasizing less the gruesome details and more young Michel's emotional response and attempts to make sense of the world around him. Earthy hued and gentle, the images make a potentially disturbing topic accessible." SLJ

Solway, Andrew

Graphing war and conflict. Raintree 2010 32p il (Real world data) $28.21; pa $7.99

Grades: 4 5 6 7 355

1. Graphic methods 2. Military history

ISBN 978-1-4329-2620-5; 1-4329-2620-9; 978-1-4329-2629-8 pa; 1-4329-2629-2 pa

LC 2009001188

This "uses graphs and charts to talk about global conflicts between 1990 and 2005, from guerilla warfare and civil war to nuclear attacks, with a special section on terrorism, including 9/11 and suicide bombers. . . . The clear design, with lots of full-color photos and sidebars, will encourage browsers as much as the up-to-date examples and the clear directions for remaining 'chart smart.'" Booklist

Includes glossary and bibliographical references

355.009 History, geographic treatment, biography

Goldsmith, Connie

Women in the military; from drill sergeants to fighter pilots. by Connie Goldsmith. Twenty-First Century Books 2019 120 p. (lb : alk. paper) $37.32

Grades: 7 8 9 10 11 12 355.009

1. Sex discrimination 2. Women in the military 3. United States -- Armed forces 4. Women soldiers -- Biography 5. Women in combat -- United States 6. United States -- Armed Forces -- Women 7. Women and the military -- United States 8. Women soldiers -- Crimes against -- United States 9. Sexual harassment in the military -- United States 10. United States -- Armed Forces -- Women -- Biography 11. Women soldiers -- United States -- Social conditions 12. United States -- Armed Forces -- Women -- Social conditions

ISBN 9781541528123

LC 2018026893

This book, by Connie Goldsmith, is about women soldiers in the U.S. "In December 2015, the Pentagon changed a rule to allow American women to serve for the first time ever in front-line ground combat troops. . . . Yet no matter their official title, they have faced devastating discrimination--from lack of advancement, . . . to sexual harassment and rape. Meet the women who have served their country courageously and who are standing up for fairness in the US military." (Publisher's note)

Includes bibliographical references and index

355.02 War and warfare

Benoit, Peter

The **nuclear** age; by Peter Benoit. Children's Press 2012 64 p. ill. (chiefly col.), col. map (Cornerstones of freedom) (library) $30.00; (paperback) $8.95

Grades: 4 5 6 355.02

1. Nuclear energy -- History 2. Nuclear weapons -- History

ISBN 0531230627; 0531281620; 9780531230626; 9780531281628

LC 2011031341

This book by Peter Benoit, part of the "Cornerstones of Freedom" series, "offers comprehensive coverage of all concepts related to the nuclear age beginning in the late 1800s through current times. . . . Four chapters highlight issues that emerge--birth of the new age, cold war, atom's legacy and human dilemma." Topics include "the atomic bomb, [Adolf] Hitler versus allies, international competitions, precautions, peaceful pursuits and cleaner sources of energy." (Children's Literature)

Includes bibliographical references (p. 61) and index.

War; David Haugen, book editor. Greenhaven Press 2014 261 p. illustrations (some color) (Opposing viewpoints series) (hardcover) $48.80

Grades: 8 9 10 11 12 355.02

1. War 2. Military policy -- United States 3. War -- Causes 4. War (Philosophy) 5. United States -- Military policy 6. War -- Moral

and ethical aspects
ISBN 0737769718; 0737769726; 9780737769715; 9780737769722
LC 2013008078

This book, by David Haugen, part of the "Opposing Viewpoints" series, "examines whether warfare can be justified, the likely causes of future wars, how the United States is faring in the War on Terror, and the principles that should guide US conduct during war." (Publisher's note)

Includes bibliographical references (pages 239-242) and index

355.1 Military life and customs

Hart, Joyce

Frequently asked questions about being part of a military family. Rosen Pub. 2009 64p il (FAQ: teen life) lib bdg $29.25

Grades: 6 7 8 9 **355.1**

1. Family life 2. Military personnel 3. United States -- Armed forces

ISBN 978-1-4358-5328-7 lib bdg; 1-4358-5328-8 lib bdg
LC 2008055612

"While conversational, [this volume is] surprisingly helpful—and even emotive. [This] starts big: who's in the military, what are the branches, etc. Mostly, though, this is mentor-to-friend reassurance." Booklist

Includes glossary and bibliographical references

Military families; Sylvia Engdahl, book editor. Greenhaven Press, a part of Gale, Cengage Learning 2014 213 p. (Current controversies) (hardcover) $46.40

Grades: 8 9 10 11 12 **355.1**

1. Military spouses 2. Military personnel -- Family relationships 3. Soldiers -- United States -- Social conditions 4. Soldiers -- United States -- Pay, allowances, etc 5. Soldiers -- Services for -- United States -- Evaluation 6. Families of military personnel -- United States -- Social conditions 7. Families of military personnel -- Services for -- United States -- Evaluation

ISBN 0737768789; 9780737768787; 9780737768794
LC 2013041402

This book, by Sylvia Engdahl, "explores issues related to military families, including: do rising costs justify reducing benefits; personal and social problems facing military families; is being part of a military family detrimental to children; and what the government is do; Each anthology is composed of a wide spectrum of sources written by many of the foremost authorities in their respective fields." (Publisher's note)

Includes bibliographical references (198-204) and index

355.4 Military operations

Grayson, Robert

Military. Marshall Cavendish Benchmark 2010 62p il (Working animals) lib bdg $28.50

Grades: 4 5 6 7 **355.4**

1. Animals -- War use

ISBN 978-1-60870-164-3 lib bdg; 1-60870-164-6 lib bdg

"Attractively designed and packed with information. . . . The composition of each page is attractively set up with well-selected and reproduced stock and historical photos." SLJ

Includes glossary and bibliographical references

355.8 Military equipment and supplies (Materiel)

Byam, Michèle

Arms & armor; written by Michèle Byam ; [special photography, Dave King] Revised edition DK Publishing 2011 72 p ill. (chiefly col.) hardcover $16.99

Grades: 4 5 6 7 **355.8**

1. Armor 2. Weapons

ISBN 9780756689513; 9780756673192; 0756673194

First published 1988 by Knopf

A photo essay examining the design, construction, and uses of hand weapons and armor from a Stone Age axe to the revolvers and rifles of the Wild West

Perritano, John

Bomb squad technician; by John Perritano. Mason Crest 2016 48 p. color illustrations (Other titles in series include: FBI Agent; Dogs on Patrol; Firefighter; SWAT Team; Paramedic; Undercover Police Officer; Search and Rescue Team; Secret Service Agent.) (hardback : alk. paper) $20.95

Grades: 4 5 6 7 **355.8**

1. Ordnance disposal units 2. Explosives -- Safety measures 3. Bombs -- Safety measures 4. Explosive ordnance disposal

ISBN 9781422233917; 9781422233924
LC 2015004820

This book, by John Perritano, "demonstrates the bravery and courage Bomb Squad Technicians show every time they go to work. It tells how they train their minds and bodies to handle the stress of disarming explosive devices and stay ahead of bombers." (Publisher's note)

"Excitement never flags in this book, as every chapter is accompanied by explosive stories, such as Guy Fawkes and the Boston Marathon bombing." Booklist

Sullivan, Edward T.

The **ultimate** weapon; the race to develop the atomic bomb. Holiday House 2007 182p il $24.95

Grades: 6 7 8 9 **355.8**

1. Atomic bomb 2. Manhattan Project

ISBN 978-0-8234-1855-8; 0-8234-1855-3
LC 2005-50330

This history of the Manhattan Project "effectively distills the science behind the development of the atomic bomb into understandable terms that turns the human story behind the project into compelling drama." Booklist

Includes bibliographical references

Vander Hook, Sue

The **Manhattan** Project. ABDO Pub. 2011 112p il map (Essential events) lib bdg $23.95

Grades: 7 8 9 10 11 12 **355.8**

1. Atomic bomb 2. Manhattan Project

ISBN 978-1-61714-767-8; 1-61714-767-2
LC 2010041429

This describes the project that developed the first atomic bomb, and discusses the political, social, and technical issues pertaining to it.

Includes glossary and bibliographical references

356 Specific kinds of military forces and warfare

Earl, C. F.

Army Rangers; by Gabrielle Vanderhoof and C.F. Earl. Mason Crest Publishers 2011 96p il (Special forces: protecting, building, teaching and fighting) lib bdg $22.95

Grades: 6 7 8 9 **356**

1. United States -- Army -- Rangers

ISBN 978-1-4222-1838-9; 1-4222-1838-4

LC 2010023795

This describes the Army Rangers unit and its history, training, weapons, modern missions.

"The well-chosen color photographs help make this series a fun armchair experience for military enthusiasts as well as a good resource for reports and for males considering military careers." Booklist

Includes bibliographical references

Green Berets. Mason Crest Publishers 2011 64p il (Special forces: protecting, building, teaching and fighting) lib bdg $22.95

Grades: 6 7 8 9 **356**

1. United States -- Army -- Special Forces

ISBN 978-1-4222-1841-9; 1-4222-1841-4

LC 2010025293

This is an overview of the training, duties, and characteristics of Green Beret personnel.

"The well-chosen color photographs help make this series a fun armchair experience for military enthusiasts as well as a good resource for reports and for males considering military careers." Booklist

Includes bibliographical references

Haney, Eric L.

Inside Delta Force; the story of America's elite counterterrorist unit. Delacorte Press 2006 246p il hardcover o.p. pa $17

Grades: 8 9 10 11 12 **356**

1. United States -- Army -- Delta Force

ISBN 0-385-73251-1; 0-385-33936-4 pa

LC 2004-30945

"In this adaptation of an adult book, Retired Command Sergeant Major Haney relates a . . . story of the 1977 founding of the ultrasecret counterterrorist unit of the U.S. Army known as Delta Force. . . . Better stock up on copies; you won't want to ration this one." Booklist

358 Air and other specialized forces and warfare; engineering and related services

Marcovitz, Hal

Biological & chemical warfare. ABDO Pub. Co. 2010 112p il (Essential issues) lib bdg $22.95

Grades: 7 8 9 10 **358**

1. Chemical warfare 2. Biological warfare

ISBN 978-1-60453-951-6; 1-60453-951-8

LC 2009-29947

The text is "well-written, providing examples that put a human face to each problem. Quotes and facts are clearly attributed, and their sources are noted in the extensive back matter. . . . Sidebars provide further information, or, more compellingly, offer stories about those touched by the topic. . . . [This] will be of great assistance to students writing reports." SLJ

Includes glossary and bibliographical references

359.9 Specialized combat forces; engineering and related services

McIntosh, J. S.

Marines; by Jack Montana. Mason Crest Publishers 2011 64p il (Special forces: protecting, building, teaching and fighting) lib bdg $22.95

Grades: 6 7 8 9 **359.9**

1. United States -- Marine Corps

ISBN 978-1-4222-1842-6; 1-4222-1842-2

LC 2010020681

Briefly describes the history, training, and missions of the United States Marine Corps.

"The well-chosen color photographs help make this series a fun armchair experience for military enthusiasts as well as a good resource for reports and for males considering military careers." Booklist

Includes bibliographical references

Montana, Jack

Navy SEALs; by Jack Montana. Mason Crest Publishers 2011 96p il (Special forces: protecting, building, teaching and fighting) lib bdg $22.95

Grades: 6 7 8 9 **359.9**

1. United States -- Navy -- Sea Air Land Team

ISBN 978-1-4222-1843-3; 1-4222-1843-0

LC 2010021842

This describes the history of the Navy SEALs, their training and selection, their survival tactics and modern missions around the world.

"The well-chosen color photographs help make this series a fun armchair experience for military enthusiasts as well as a good resource for reports and for males considering military careers." Booklist

Includes bibliographical references

Ritland, Mike

Navy seal dogs; my tale of training canines for combat. Mike Ritland. St. Martin's Griffin 2013 208 p. (hardback) $17.99

Grades: 7 8 9 **359.9**

1. Dogs -- War use 2. Dogs -- War use -- Iraq 3. Afghan War, 2001- -- Dogs 4. Iraq War, 2003-2011 -- Dogs 5. Dogs -- War use -- Afghanistan 6. Dogs -- War use -- United States

ISBN 1250041821; 9781250041821

LC 2013026244

This book is a special retelling for young readers of Michael Ritland's book "Trident K9 Warriors," which details his experiences training and handling U.S. Navy SEAL dogs. The story brings readers "through the training process; these are dogs schooled to the nth degree in nonlethal force. They also spend a good amount of time with Brett (a 12-year Navy SEAL veteran—last names are rarely used in SEAL literature) and dog Chopper in Ritland's current work with the nonprofit Warrior Dog Foundation." (Kirkus Reviews)

361.2 Social action

Drake, Jane

Yes you can! your guide to becoming an activist. [by] Jane Drake & Ann Love. Tundra Books 2010 136p pa $12.95

Grades: 7 8 9 10 **361.2**

1. Social action

ISBN 978-0-88776-942-9; 0-88776-942-X pa

"Young people who want to effect change are guided by a sequence of nine steps and inspirational examples of grassroots activism. . . . Each step, or chapter, includes a story, strategies, skills, and a time line of milestones and setbacks. . . . The style is conversational and the tone offers realistic encouragement to teens looking to solve problems. . . . This title will primarily serve as a how-to, although the time lines, an accessible index, and factual information about anti-smoking campaigns, recycling, and children's rights make it a useful historical perspective of activism." SLJ

Halpin, Mikki

★ **It's** your world--if you don't like it, change it; activism for teenagers. Simon Pulse 2004 305p pa $8.99

Grades: 7 8 9 10 **361.2**

1. Social action

ISBN 0-689-87448-0

"Animal rights, racism, war protest, AIDS, school violence and bullying, women's rights, and promoting tolerance are among the topics covered here. Halpin provides basic information about each one and then makes myriad suggestions for action at home, in the community, the 'five-minute activist,' etc. The ideas are easy to implement. . . .This is an important book that will empower any young adult who would like to make a difference." SLJ

Includes bibliographical references

361.7 Private action

Cerone, Lulu

Philanthroparties! a party-planning guide for kids who want to give back. Lulu Cerone. Aladdin 2017 xiv, 194 p.p (hardcover) $17.99

Grades: 5 6 7 8 9 10 11 12 **361.7**

1. Charities 2. Volunteer work 3. Special events -- Planning 4. Young volunteers in social service 5. Young volunteers in community development

ISBN 9781582705873

LC 2016037987

"Seventeen-year-old Lulu Cerone shows teens how to bring social activism into their daily lives--and have fun while doing it--with this colorful DIY party planning guide perfect for every socially conscious kid! . . . [This book] gives readers what they need to know . . . to incorporate philanthropy into one's social life. It includes party ideas and plans, event checklists, recipes, crafts, personal stories, and brief profiles of causes readers should know about." (Publisher's note)

Includes bibliographical references (pages 193-194).

Reusser, Kayleen

Celebrities giving back. Mitchell Lane Publishers 2011 47p (How to help: a guide to giving back) lib bdg $29.95

Grades: 4 5 6 **361.7**

1. Charities 2. Celebrities 3. Philanthropists

ISBN 978-1-58415-922-3 lib bdg; 1-58415-922-7 lib bdg

LC 2010014904

"Reusser writes about 17 people, including Bono and his interest in eliminating world hunger and poverty, President Carter's dreams of building homes for the homeless, and charitable works by Rihanna, Shakira, Tony Hawk, and others." SLJ

Includes bibliographical references

361.9 History, geographic treatment, biography

Slavicek, Louise Chipley, 1956-

Jane Addams. Chelsea House 2011 126 p. ill (some col.) (Women of achievement) lib bdg $35

Grades: 6 7 8 9 **361.9**

1. Authors 2. Philanthropists 3. Hull House (Chicago, Ill.) 4. Essayists 5. Pacifists 6. Social welfare leaders 7. Nobel laureates for peace 8. Chicago (Ill.) -- Social conditions

ISBN 978-1-60413-907-5; 1-60413-907-2

LC 2011000038

This book "traces [Jane] Addams' life and considerable accomplishments in social welfare, labor reform, and women's suffrage . . . [and] portrays Addams' difficult path to good education and her determination to use her life well." It is "supplemented with sidebars and illustrations . . . [and] includes a chronology, notes for the many quotes, a source bibliography, and lists of recommended books and websites." (Booklist) Details on her role in "found[ing] the pioneering settlement house, Hull House, where she and a dedicated staff of volunteers, most of them college-educated women like herself, lived and worked among some of Chicago's most destitute residents" are also presented. (Publisher's note)

This "traces Addams' life and considerable accomplishments in social welfare, labor reform, and women's suffrage. Slavicek vividly portrays Addams' difficult path to good education and her determination to use her life well. . . . Solid fare for the biography collection." Booklist

Includes bibliographical references and index.

362 Specific social problems and services

Clayborne, Leigh

The **benefits** of medical marijuana; from cancer to PTSD. Leigh Clayborne. Mason Crest 2018 80 p. $24.95

Grades: 8 9 10 11 12 **362**

1. Marijuana -- Therapeutic use

ISBN 1422241084; 9781422241080

In this book in the Marijuana Today series, by Leigh Clayborne, "you'll learn how various countries treat medical marijuana, studies that support its benefits for a wide variety of condition (and some that don't), potential side effects of marijuana, and much more. As you learn more, you'll have a better understanding of the issues facing patients, government officials, and the public. You'll have the facts to decide what you believe and the facts to discuss it with others." (Publisher's note)

"With much talk surrounding marijuana legalization in the United States, this informative series comes at just the right time. Instead of providing answers to the debate, the authors present current, credible information from numerous studies and reputable research, allowing readers to draw their own conclusions." (School Library Journal)

362.1 People with illnesses and disabilities

Dreyer, ZoAnn

Living with cancer; ZoAnn Dreyer. Facts On File 2008 202p $34.95

Grades: 8 9 10 11 12 **362.1**
1. Cancer
ISBN 978-0-8160-6484-7
LC 2007-10675

"Although written for teens with these conditions, these titles will have more general appeal... Material in both titles is presented in a straightforward manner. "SLJ

Includes bibliographical references (p. 192-194) and index.

Fast food; Lauri S. Friedman, book editor. Greenhaven Press 2010 122p il map (Introducing issues with opposing viewpoints) $34.70
Grades: 7 8 9 10 11 12 **362.1**
1. Obesity 2. Restaurants 3. Convenience foods
ISBN 978-0-7377-4733-1; 0-7377-4733-1
LC 2009-51963

This is a collection of essays arguing various viewpoints about fast foods and their effects on health, and whether or not fast food restaurants should be banned, taxed, or regulated.

This "contains some fascinating arguments, including the central question of whether or not fast food makes people fat and sick. Active-reading questions preface the essays, which are followed by directions for evaluating the arguments presented. Color photos and other graphics throughout enliven the reading experience." SLJ

Includes bibliographical references

Fleischman, John

★ **Phineas** Gage: a gruesome but true story about brain science. Houghton Mifflin 2002 86p il $16; pa $8.95
Grades: 5 6 7 8 9 **362.1**
1. Railroad workers 2. Brain -- Wounds and injuries
ISBN 0-618-05252-6; 0-618-49478-2 pa
LC 2001-39253

"The author deftly introduces readers to a diverse range of relevant scientific history as well as more specific beliefs that influenced the medical establishment's understanding of Gage, then goes on to examine subsequent neurological discoveries that have changed and enhanced our understanding of Gage's fate. The book's present-tense narrative is inviting and intimate, and the text is crisp and lucid." Bull Cent Child Books

Includes glossary and bibliographical references

Jones, Molly

Health care for everyone. Rosen Pub. 2011 64p il (Headlines!) lib bdg $29.95
Grades: 7 8 9 10 **362.1**
1. Medical care 2. Health insurance
ISBN 978-1-4488-1290-5; 1-4488-1290-9
LC 2010024137

This book "begins with President Obama's 2010 [health care] legislation then discusses problems within the industry. . . . Good organization, clear writing, captioned photos, and sidebars deliver the information cleanly." Horn Book Guide

Includes glossary and bibliographical references

Naden, Corinne J.

Patients' rights; [by] Corinne Naden. Marshall Cavendish Benchmark 2008 144p il (Open for debate) lib bdg $27.95
Grades: 7 8 9 10 **362.1**
1. Medical care
ISBN 978-0-7614-2576-2; 0-7614-2576-4
LC 2006-21786

This book maintains a "balanced tone while providing an abundance of examples and factual information. Many captioned color photos enhance the text." SLJ

Includes bibliographical references

Pruessen, Linda

Saving Eyesight; Adventures of Seva Around the World. Linda Pruessen. Firefly Books Ltd 2015 64 p. color ill., color portraits $19.95
Grades: 4 5 6 7 **362.1**
1. Vision 2. Medical charities
ISBN 1770856161; 9781770856165
LC 2015458723

This book, by Linda Pruessen, is a " travelogue chronicling the efforts of Seva, an international development agency. Readers will learn about how the eye works and how eye problems are corrected. Illustrations reveal how the eyes work to transmit images to the brain." (Publisher's note)

"A good choice for youth community service groups looking for a worthy cause, this offering might even inspire a career in ophthalmology." SLJ

What can I do now?: Health care. Ferguson 2007 222p $29.95
Grades: 8 9 10 11 12 **362.1**
1. Medicine 2. Vocational guidance
ISBN 0-8160-6031-2; 978-0-8160-603-1
LC 2006030410

"This volume offers an overview of the health-care industry, a look at different careers, ideas for getting experience, and additional resources. . . . The layout is attractive, the font a good size, and the information accessible. . . . An excellent addition." SLJ

Winick, Judd

Pedro & me; friendship, loss, & what I learned. Henry Holt and Co. 2009 187p il pa $16.99
Grades: 7 8 9 10 11 12 **362.1**
1. Graphic novels 2. Television personalities 3. Biographical graphic novels 4. AIDS patients 5. AIDS activists 6. Friendship -- Graphic novels 7. AIDS (Disease) -- Graphic novels 8. Real world (Television program) -- Graphic novels
ISBN 978-0-8050-8964-6
First published 2000
2001 Robert F. Sibert Honor Book for informational books for youth

In this "volume—part graphic novel, part memoir—professional cartoonist Winick pays tribute to his Real World housemate and friend Pedro Zamora, an AIDS activist who died of the disease in 1994." Publ Wkly

362.19 Services to patients with specific conditions

Stevenson, Robin

★ **My** body my choice; the fight for abortion rights. Robin Stevenson. Orca Book Publishers 2019 176 p. (pbk.) $19.95
Grades: 7 8 9 10 11 12 **362.19**
1. Abortion 2. Pro-choice movement
ISBN 9781459817128
LC 2018954165

This book, by Robin Stevenson, talks about abortion being "one of the most common of all medical procedures. . . . Making abortion illegal or hard to access doesn't make it any less common; it just makes it dangerous. . . . People who support abortion rights have been fighting hard to create a world in which the right to access safe and legal abortion services is guaranteed. . . . This book is about the history, and the future, of that fight." (Publisher's note)

"Reproductive rights have a long history of conflict and controversy around the globe, and this exceptional installment in the orca issues series (2 titles) provides an in-depth look at abortion rights and services, both historically and as they exist today." (Booklist)

Wilcox, Christine

Abortion; by Christine Wilcox. ReferencePoint Press, Inc. 2018 80 p. (hardback) $29.95

Grades: 8 9 10 11 12 **362.19**

1. Abortion 2. Pregnancy
ISBN 9781682822616

LC 2016052613

In this book, by Christine Wilcox, "there are few issues as divisive and emotionally charged as abortion. Through a narrative-driven pro/con formatsupported by relevant facts, quotes, anecdotes, and full-color illustrations[,] this title examines issues related to abortion. Topics include: Is a Fetus a Person with a Right to Life? Is Abortion Harmful to Women? Is Abortion Harmful to Society? Are Laws Regulating Abortion Adequate?" (Publisher's note)

Includes bibliographical references and index

362.2 People with mental illness and disabilities

Flath, Camden

21st -century counselors; new approaches to mental health & substance abuse. Mason Crest Publishers 2011 64p il (New careers for the 21st century: finding your role in the global renewal) lib bdg $22.95

Grades: 7 8 9 10 **362.2**

1. Counseling 2. Vocational guidance 3. Drug abuse counseling
ISBN 978-1-4222-1825-9 lib bdg; 1-4222-1825-2 lib bdg

LC 2010021812

"Chapters identify and emphasize specific careers—important strengths, necessary aptitudes and interests, education and training, projected earnings, closely related occupations, type of work environment, and predictions for the future of the field. . . . Color photos have a small role amid the many statistics, figures, graphs and charts that support and supplement the . . . [text]." SLJ

Includes bibliographical references

362.28 Suicide

Galas, Judith C.

The **power** to prevent suicide; a guide for teens helping teens. [by] Richard E. Nelson, Judith C. Galas; foreword by Bev Cobain; edited by Pamela Espeland. Updated ed; Free Spirit 2006 115p pa $13.95

Grades: 7 8 9 10 11 12 **362.28**

1. Suicide
ISBN 1-57542-206-9; 978-1-57542-206-0
First published 1994

"The authors' premise is that, as trusted and caring friends, YAs have a special role in the prevention of suicide among their peers, and discuss what to do if they observe the danger signals. . . . This book provides clear, practical information and advice." SLJ

362.29 Substance abuse

Berne, Emma Carlson

Methamphetamine. ReferencePoint Press 2007 102p il map (Compact research) $24.95

Grades: 8 9 10 11 12 **362.29**

1. Drug abuse 2. Methamphetamine
ISBN 978-1-60152-004-3; 1-60152-004-2

LC 2006032206

"Berne explores whether methamphetamine usage in the U.S. has reached epidemic proportions, its dangers, the link between addiction and crime, and abuse prevention." SLJ

Includes bibliographical references

Bjornlund, Lydia

Marijuana; by Lydia Bjornlund. ReferencePoint Press 2012 136 p. (Compact research series) (hardcover) $27.95

Grades: 7 8 9 10 11 12 **362.29**

1. Marijuana 2. Drug education 3. Medical botany 4. Drugs -- Physiological effect 5. Drugs -- Law and legislation -- United States 6. Marijuana -- United States 7. Marijuana -- Law and legislation -- United States
ISBN 160152160X; 9781601521606

LC 2011007743

This book on marijuana is a part of the Compact Research: Drugs series and "focus[es] on three types of information: "objective single-author narratives, opinion-based primary source quotations, and facts and statistics." What this translates to on the page is an overview of the topic and an in-depth chapter-by chapter discussion of the points raised in the overview." Lydia Bjornlund "looks at questions such as whether marijuana is a dangerous drug, whether it should be legalized, and the most pressing dilemma: Should the drug be readily available for medical use?" (Booklist)

Includes bibliographical references and index.

Bjornlund, Lydia D.

Teen smoking. Reference Point Press 2010 104p il (Compact research. Current issues) $25.95

Grades: 8 9 10 11 12 **362.29**

1. Smoking
ISBN 978-1-60152-098-2; 1-60152-098-0

LC 2009-28008

This addresses the following questions: How serious a problem is teen smoking?; Who is to blame for teen smoking?; How should teen smoking be regulated?; How can we prevent teen smoking?

"The straightforward presentation of serious subject matter, graphics, and easy access to facts . . . [make this book] excellent . . . for reports and debates." SLJ

Breguet, Amy

Vicodin, OxyContin, and other pain relievers; [by] Amy E. Breguet. Chelsea House 2008 112p il (Junior drug awareness) $30

Grades: 6 7 8 9 **362.29**

1. Narcotics 2. Analgesics 3. Drug abuse
ISBN 978-0-7910-9700-7; 0-7910-9700-5

LC 2007032350

This describes the effects of Vicodin and OxyContin and other pain relievers, how they are used and abused, and how to get help for addiction.

Includes glossary and bibliographical references

Drugs, alcohol, and tobacco; learning about addictive behavior. Rosalyn Carson-DeWitt, editor in chief. Macmillan Ref. USA 2003 3v set $295

Grades: 7 8 9 10 **362.29**

1. Reference books 2. Drug abuse -- Encyclopedias

ISBN 0-02-865756-X

LC 2002-9270

Based on the Encyclopedia of drugs, alcohol & addictive behavior, 2nd edition, published 2001

"The 190 alphabetically arranged articles range from one to six pages in length and yield a comprehensive look at the nature of, treatments for, and social issues surrounding addictive substances and behaviors. Topics include specific drugs, diagnoses, treatments, legal and social implications, drug trafficking, cultural pressures, and related compulsive behaviors." SLJ

Includes bibliographical references

Egendorf, Laura K.

Performance -enhancing drugs. Reference point 2007 96p il (Compact research) lib bdg $24.95

Grades: 8 9 10 11 12 **362.29**

1. Drugs 2. Athletes -- Drug use

ISBN 978-1-60152-003-6 lib bdg; 1-60152-003-4 lib bdg

This "well-organized [volume presens] general information that report writers, particularly reluctant readers, will find useful. Brightly colored illustrated facts and statistics charts invite perusal. Thought-provoking questions introduce most of the chapters. . . . [This book] covers ethical issues and dangers in usage, effectiveness of testing, and prevention. . . . Primary-source quotes are well documented." SLJ

Gottfried, Ted

Marijuana; by Ted Gottfried with Lisa Harkrader. Marshall Cavendish Benchmark 2010 32p il (Drug facts) $19.95

Grades: 4 5 6 7 **362.29**

1. Marijuana

ISBN 978-0-7614-4351-3; 0-7614-4351-7

LC 2008-52761

"Provides clear explanations about effects, followed by diagrams of the body to clarify the specific organs/body systems that suffer the most damage. . . . An excellent starting point." SLJ

Includes glossary

Harris, Duchess

The **opioid** crisis; by Duchess Harris, JD, PHD with John L. Hakala. Essential Library, an imprint of Abdo Publishing 2019 112 p. $37.07

Grades: 7 8 9 10 **362.29**

1. Drug abuse 2. Medication abuse 3. Opioid abuse 4. Drug abuse -- Social aspects -- United States

ISBN 1532116799; 9781532116797

LC 2018948307

This book in the Special Reports series, by Duchess Harris and John L. Hakala, "examines the reasons behind the opioid epidemic in the United States and its far-reaching effect on people's everyday lives. The brain science behind opioid addiction is also explored, and the book encourages readers to form their own opinions. Features include a glossary, references, websites, source notes, and an index." (Publisher's note)

"The Opioid Crisis is a probing examination of this problem, featuring a wide-ranging discussion that looks at everything from pain management to poverty, race, and class issues to Big Pharma." Booklist

Includes bibliographical references (pages 104-109) and index

Koellhoffer, Tara

Inhalants and solvents; [by] Tara Koellhoffer. Chelsea House 2008 112p il (Junior drug awareness) lib bdg $30

Grades: 6 7 8 9 **362.29**

1. Inhalant abuse

ISBN 978-0-7910-9698-7 lib bdg; 0-7910-9698-X lib bdg

LC 2007024824

This "provides useful, balanced, and comprehensive information." Horn Book Guide

Includes glossary and bibliographical references

LeVert, Suzanne

Ecstasy; by Suzanne LeVert with Jeff Hendricks. Marshall Cavendish Benchmark 2010 32p il (Drug facts) $19.95

Grades: 4 5 6 7 **362.29**

1. Drug abuse 2. Designer drugs 3. Ecstasy (Drug)

ISBN 978-0-7614-4349-0; 0-7614-4349-5

LC 2008-52753

"Provides clear explanations about effects, followed by diagrams of the body to clarify the specific organs/body systems that suffer the most damage. . . . An excellent starting point." SLJ

Includes glossary

Menhard, Francha Roffe

The **facts** about inhalants; by Francha Roffe Menhard with Laura Purdie Salas. Marshall Cavendish Benchmark 2010 32p il (Drug facts) $19.95

Grades: 4 5 6 7 **362.29**

1. Inhalant abuse

ISBN 978-0-7614-4350-6; 0-7614-4350-9

LC 2008-52739

"Provides clear explanations about effects, followed by diagrams of the body to clarify the specific organs/body systems that suffer the most damage. . . . An excellent starting point." SLJ

Includes glossary

Olive, M. Foster

Ecstasy; consulting editor, David J. Triggle. Chelsea House Publishers 2010 109p il (Understanding drugs) lib bdg $34.95

Grades: 8 9 10 11 12 **362.29**

1. Ecstasy (Drug)

ISBN 978-1-60413-538-1; 1-60413-538-7

LC 2010-5458

This book "book delves into the effects of using Ecstasy, from the initial pleasure to the dangerous aftereffects." Publisher's note

Includes glossary and bibliographical references

Parks, Peggy J., 1951-

Bath salts and other synthetic drugs; by Peggy J. Parks. ReferencePoint Press, Inc. 2014 96 p. (Compact research series) (hardback) $28.95

Grades: 8 9 10 11 12 **362.29**

1. Drugs 2. Designer drugs 3. Drugs of abuse 4. Synthetic drugs

ISBN 1601525168; 9781601525161

LC 2013015820

This book, by Peggy J. Parks, "describes the rise in use of these newer and perhaps lesser known but potentially deadly drugs, as well as problems associated with elusive marketing and hard-to-track Internet sales. Additional back matter comprises lists of key people, advocacy groups, and related organizations." (Booklist)

"Backed by current facts, statistics, and first-person experiences, every chapter includes further documentation with concluding "Primary Source Quotes," from former addicts and law enforcement to health care workers and government officials. In this visual, by-the-numbers era, the series responds with end-of-chapter charts and graphs that display drug-related information." (Booklist)

Includes bibliographical references and index

Methamphetamine; by Peggy J. Parks. ReferencePoint Press, Inc. 2013 96 p. (Compact research series) (hardback) $28.95

Grades: 8 9 10 11 12 **362.29**

1. Drug abuse 2. Methamphetamine 3. Methamphetamine abuse

ISBN 1601525206; 9781601525208

LC 2013009272

This book, by Peggy J. Parks, "looks at the serious dangers of meth production and abuse and the difficulties in treating meth addiction and passing laws to regulate the drug. Backed by current facts, statistics, and first-person experiences, every chapter includes further documentation with concluding 'Primary Source Quotes,' from former addicts and law enforcement to health care workers and government officials." (Booklist)

"In this visual, by-the-numbers era, the series responds with end-of-chapter charts and graphs that display drug-related information. Additional back matter comprises lists of key people, advocacy groups, and related organizations; a bibliography; and a chronology. This series is the next go-to resource for drug-abuse research." (Booklist)

Includes bibliographical references and index

Quinones, Sam

Dreamland; the true tale of America's opiate epidemic. by Sam Quinones. Bloomsbury Childrens Books 2019 216 p. (hardcover) $18.99

Grades: 8 9 10 11 12 **362.29**

1. Narcotics 2. Drug abuse 3. Heroin abuse 4. American Dream 5. Drug traffic -- Mexico 6. Narcotics -- United States 7. Oxycodone -- United States 8. Heroin abuse -- United States 9. Drug addiction -- United States

ISBN 9781547601318

LC 2018045397

In this book, author Sam Quinones, "explains how the rise of the prescription drug OxyContin, a miraculous and extremely addictive painkiller pushed by pharmaceutical companies, paralleled the massive influx of black tar heroin--cheap, potent, and originating from one small county on Mexico's west coast, independent of any drug cartel. . . . "Dreamland" is a revelatory account of the massive threat facing America and its heartland." (Publisher's note)

"A scrupulously researched, well-crafted tale that sheds light on a timely topic." --Kirkus

Includes bibliographical references and index

Scott, Celicia

Caffeine; energy drinks, coffee, soda, & pills. Celicia Scott. Mason Crest 2015 48 p. (Downside of drugs) $20.95

Grades: 6 7 8 **362.29**

1. Caffeine 2. Drugs -- Physiological effect 3. Drug abuse 4. Caffeine habit

ISBN 142223018X; 9781422230183

LC 2014466074

This juvenile book, by Celicia Scott, part of the "Downside of Drugs" series, explores how "people around the world consume . . . drinks . . . and pills that contain caffeine, without a thought for the consequences the caffeine may have on their lives. . . . With a vast industry targeting its marketing at young people, educating yourself is the essential first step to counter caffeine's possible effects on your life, from sleep problems to addiction." (Publisher's note)

"Written with a Harvard Medical School consultant, this series discusses drugs in a tone that is appropriately sober yet not alarmist or condescending." SLJ

Sommers, Annie Leah

College athletics; steroids and supplement abuse. Rosen Pub. Group 2010 48p il (Disgraced! the dirty history of performance-enhancing drugs in sports) lib bdg $26.50

Grades: 5 6 7 8 **362.29**

1. Steroids 2. College sports 3. Athletes -- Drug use 4. Sports -- Corrupt practices

ISBN 978-1-4358-5303-4 lib bdg; 1-4358-5303-2 lib bdg

LC 2008-55408

Discusses efforts to enhance performance in sports, the use of steroids and supplements by college athletes, including the case of football player Tommy Chaikin, college players as role models, and the influence of the NCAA

"Amazing statements from athletes giving reasons why they took illegal drugs are good for discussion topics. . . . Concludes with thoughts regarding future additional legislation. Useful updates." SLJ

Includes glossary and bibliographical references

Sommers, Michael A.

The **NFL**; steroids and human growth hormone. Rosen Central 2010 48p il (Disgraced! the dirty history of performance-enhancing drugs in sports) lib bdg $26.50

Grades: 5 6 7 8 **362.29**

1. Football 2. Steroids 3. Athletes -- Drug use 4. National Football League

ISBN 978-1-4358-5304-1 lib bdg; 1-4358-5304-0 lib bdg

LC 2008-56131

Discusses the uses of performance enhancing drugs, particularly anabolic steroids, by professional football players, their effects on the players and the sport, and the successes and failures of efforts to control their use

"Amazing statements from athletes giving reasons why they took illegal drugs are good for discussion topics. . . . Concludes with thoughts regarding future additional legislation. [A] useful [update]." SLJ

Includes glossary and bibliographical references

Sterngass, Jon

Steroids. Marshall Cavendish Benchmark 2011 112p il (Controversy!) lib bdg $25.95

Grades: 8 9 10 11 12 **362.29**

1. Steroids

ISBN 9780761449034; 0761449035

Discusses what steroids are, how they are used in sports, how they can be used in other areas, and the debate surrounding them.

This is "written in clear, sophisticated language and will serve well . . . for research papers or debates." Voice Youth Advocates

Includes bibliographical references

Tobacco and Smoking; Roman Espejo, book editor. Greenhaven Press 2015 242 p. illustrations (Opposing viewpoints) (hardcover) $48.80; (pbk.) $33.80

Grades: 8 9 10 11 12 **362.29**

1. Smoking 2. Tobacco industry 3. Smoking -- United States 4. Tobacco use -- United States 5. Teenagers -- Tobacco use -- United

States 6. Smoking -- Health aspects -- United States
ISBN 0737772956; 0737772948 ; 9780737772944 ; 9780737772951

LC 2014026089

This book "explores the questions of whether or not smoking is a serious problem, how tobacco use can be reduced, how smoking alternatives should be regulated, and how the media affects the choice to smoke or not to smoke." (Publisher's note)

Includes bibliographical references and index

Walker, Ida

Addiction treatment; escaping the trap. Ida Walker ; series consultant Jack E. Henningfield, Ph.D. Mason Crest 2013 128 p

Grades: 7 8 9 10 **362.29**

1. Drug addiction -- Treatment
ISBN 9781422224274; 9781422292914

Provides information on the history of addiction treatment and treatment options along with information on ways to avoid a relapse.

Recreational Ritalin; the not-so-smart drug. by Ida Walker. Mason Crest 2013 128 p

Grades: 7 8 9 10 **362.29**

1. Methylphenidate 2. Medication abuse 3. Children -- Drug use 4. Teenagers -- Drug use. 5. Attention-deficit hyperactivity disorder -- Chemotherapy
ISBN 9781422224397; 9781422293034

Looks at aspects of the ADHD drug, ritalin, including how it is used to treat the disorder, the ways it can be abused, and how to help those addicted to it.

Sedatives and hypnotics; deadly downers. Ida Walker. Mason Crest 2013 128 p

Grades: 7 8 9 10 **362.29**

1. Hypnotics 2. Sedatives
ISBN 9781422293041; 9781422224403

Looks at some of the more common sedatives and hypnotics, discussing how they work, how they are abused and misused, and what can be done for those addicted to them.

West, Krista

Cocaine and crack; [by] Krista West. Chelsea House Publishers 2008 119p il map (Junior drug awareness) lib bdg $30

Grades: 6 7 8 9 **362.29**

1. Cocaine 2. Drug abuse 3. Crack (Drug)
ISBN 978-0-7910-9704-5 lib bdg; 0-7910-9704-8 lib bdg

LC 2007024971

This "provides useful, balanced, and comprehensive information." Horn Book Guide

Includes glossary and bibliographical references

362.292 Alcohol

Bjornlund, Lydia D.

Alcohol; [by] Lydia Bjornlund. Cherry Lake Pub. 2009 32p il (Health at risk) lib bdg $27.07

Grades: 4 5 6 7 **362.292**

1. Alcohol 2. Alcoholism
ISBN 978-1-60279-280-7 lib bdg; 1-60279-280-1 lib bdg

LC 2008017495

This describes the effects of alcohol, the dangers of driving drunk, how to get help, and how to make good choices.

"Great for reports or reluctant readers." Booklist

Includes bibliographical references

Gottfried, Ted

Alcohol; by Ted Gottfried with Katherine Follett. Marshall Cavendish Benchmark 2010 32p il (Drug facts) $19.95

Grades: 4 5 6 7 **362.292**

1. Alcoholism 2. Drinking of alcoholic beverages 3. Alcohol -- Physiological effect
ISBN 978-0-7614-4348-3; 0-7614-4348-7

LC 2008-52751

"Provides clear explanations about effects, followed by diagrams of the body to clarify the specific organs/body systems that suffer the most damage. . . . An excellent starting point." SLJ

Includes glossary

Walker, Ida

Alcohol addiction; not worth the buzz. by Ida Walker. Mason Crest 2013 128 p

Grades: 7 8 9 10 **362.292**

1. Alcoholism -- Treatment -- United States -- History.
ISBN 9781422292921; 9781422224281

Looks at the issue of alcohol abuse, including its history, how it affects the body, and what can be done for alcoholics.

Youngerman, Barry

The **truth** about alcohol; Robert N. Golden, general editor; Fred L. Peterson, general editor; Barry Youngerman, principal author; Heath Dingwell, contributing author; Richelle Rennegarbe, adviser. 2nd ed.; Facts on File 2010 230p (Truth about series) $35

Grades: 8 9 10 11 12 **362.292**

1. Alcoholism 2. Teenagers -- Alcohol use
ISBN 978-0-8160-7639-0; 0-8160-7639-1

LC 2009-53476

First published 2004

This discusses such topics as binge drinking, underage drinking, the prevalence of drinking on college campuses, drunken driving, dealing with alcohol abuse in the family, alcohol advertising and counter-advertising, and seeking help for an alcohol problem.

Includes glossary and bibliographical references

362.293 Narcotics

Marcovitz, Hal

★ The **opioid** epidemic; by Hal Marcovitz. ReferencePoint Press, Inc. 2018 80 p. illustrations (hardback) $29.95

Grades: 7 8 9 10 11 12 **362.293**

1. Drug abuse 2. Opioid abuse
ISBN 9781682823002; 9781682822999

LC 2017017982

In this book, by Hal Marcovitz, "when synthetic opioids were developed a quarter-century ago, many physicians believed the drugs would help alleviate the pain caused by severe injuries and debilitating diseases. But while the drugs do deaden pain, they can lead to devastating addiction as well as death through overdose. Meanwhile, the natural opioid heroin continues to be a much-abused illegal drug that threatens the lives of its users." (Publisher's note)

"Marcovitz offers a timely exploration of the issue. . . . Both reasoned and impassioned." Kirkus

Includes bibliographical references and index

362.4 People with physical disabilities

Lambert, Joseph

The **Center** for Cartoon Studies presents Annie Sullivan and the trials of Helen Keller; by Joseph Lambert. Disney Hyperion Books 2012 92 p. chiefly col. ill.

Grades: 5 6 7 **362.4**

1. Women authors -- Biography 2. Female friendship -- Graphic novels 3. People with disabilities -- Graphic novels 4. Graphic novels 5. Women -- United States -- History 6. Women -- United States -- Biography 7. Female friendship -- United States -- History

ISBN 1423113365; 9781423113362

LC 2011036324

This nonfiction graphic novel about Annie Sullivan and Helen Keller "focuses on the trials both Annie and Helen struggle with in their lives," particularly the incident when Helen was accused of plagiarism in her story 'The Frost King' and interrogated at the Perkins Institution. "Helen's perspective is . . . communicated in dialogue-free black panels in which she is represented as only a gray silhouette" by author/illustrator Joseph Lambert. (Kirkus Reviews)

Martin, Claudia

Helpers. Marshall Cavendish Benchmark 2010 64p il (Working animals) lib bdg $28.50

Grades: 4 5 6 7 **362.4**

1. Animals and people with disabilities

ISBN 978-1-60870-163-6 lib bdg; 1-60870-163-8 lib bdg

"Attractively designed and packed with information. . . . The composition of each page is attractively set up with well-selected and reproduced stock and historical photos." SLJ

Thornton, Denise

Physical disabilities; the ultimate teen guide. Scarecrow Press 2007 162p il (It happened to me) $42

Grades: 7 8 9 10 11 12 **362.4**

1. People with physical disabilities 2. People with disabilities

ISBN 978-0-8108-5300-3; 0-8108-5300-0

LC 2006-29235

"Thornton interviewed hundreds of young people to help readers understand disabilities from a personal viewpoint. She divides this very broad subject into eight areas—school, technologies and tools, getting around, sports, the arts, relationships, independence, and advocacy. In each section, she includes personal stories plus essential information helpful to the disabled. . . . Well-organized and helpful." SLJ

Includes bibliographical references

362.5 Poor people

Senker, Cath

Poverty; [by] Cath Senker. World Almanac Library 2007 48p il (What if we do nothing?) lib bdg $30.60; pa $11.95

Grades: 5 6 7 8 **362.5**

1. Poor 2. Poverty

ISBN 978-0-8368-7757-1 lib bdg; 978-0-8368-8157-8 pa

LC 2006030447

"After discussing patterns of poverty, each chapter raises specific 'What would you do?' questions, with brief suggested answers at the back of the book. Whether the issue is increased taxation of the wealthy, cancellation of unpayable debts, improving primary health care, or more, student activists will want to talk about it, and social-studies teachers will find this a strong curriculum title." Booklist

Includes bibliographical references

Poverty and hunger; Cath Senker. Smart Apple Media 2012 46 p. col. ill., col. maps (Mapping global issues) (library) $35.65

Grades: 6 7 8 **362.5**

1. Hunger 2. Poverty 3. Poor 4. Food security

ISBN 1599205114; 9781599205113

LC 2011017066

This book is part of the Mapping Global Issues series and it focuses on poverty and hunger. "Colorful layouts with numerous maps and graphs dominate this series, which provides an international perspective on important issues. Brief chapters frame problems, discuss their causes, and suggest possible solutions, using maps to illustrate the locations and extent of threats." (School Library Journal)

Includes bibliographical references (p. 45) and index.

362.7 Young people

Gordon, Sherri Mabry

Beyond bruises; the truth about teens and abuse. Enslow 2009 128p il (Issues in focus today) lib bdg $31.93

Grades: 7 8 9 10 **362.7**

1. Date rape 2. Invective 3. Child abuse 4. Domestic violence

ISBN 978-0-7660-3064-0; 0-7660-3064-4

LC 2008-12273

"Discusses the various types of abuse teenagers face, including both domestic and dating abuse, the impact abuse has on teens, and several ways to help teens who suffer from some form of abuse." Publisher's note

Includes glossary and bibliographical references

Jocelyn, Marthe

A **home** for foundlings. Tundra Books 2005 128p il pa $15.95

Grades: 7 8 9 10 **362.7**

1. Abandoned children 2. Foundling Hospital (London, England)

ISBN 0-88776-709-5

"Black-and-white reproductions of early admission documents and ledgers as well as period photographs and engravings appear throughout. This is a useful resource." SLJ

Langwith, Jacqueline

Adoption; Jacqueline Langwith, book editor. Greenhaven Press 2014 130 p (Introducing issues with opposing viewpoints) $38.45

Grades: 7 8 9 10 **362.7**

1. Adoption

ISBN 9780737769180

LC 2013033191

This book about adoption is part of the "Opposing Viewpoints series, which explores important issues, placing expert opinions from a wide range of sources in a unique pro/con format. . . . [It] features useful charts, graphs and cartoons, engaging fact boxes that provide at-a-glance information and questions that focus on vocabulary and reading comprehension." (Publisher's note)

This book "features useful charts, graphs and cartoons, engaging fact boxes that provide at-a-glance information and questions that focus on vocabulary and reading comprehension." Publisher's note

Includes bibliographical references and index

Saul, Laya

Ways to help disadvantaged youth. Mitchell Lane Publishers 2011 47p (How to help: a guide to giving back) lib bdg $29.95

Grades: 4 5 6 **362.7**

1. Poor 2. Social action

ISBN 978-1-58415-918-6; 1-58415-918-9

LC 2010006536

This "well-organized [book] will encourage children to contribute to the world around them. [This] title is filled with examples of volunteer opportunities that can be accomplished with some adult involvement and supervision to guide, steer, and maintain focus so that youngsters will have varied and successful experiences. . . . [The book] suggests tutoring, having a toy or food drive, etc." SLJ

Includes bibliographical references

Simons, Rae

Adoptive parents. Mason Crest Publishers 2009 64p il map (The changing face of modern families) $22.95

Grades: 6 7 8 9 **362.7**

1. Adoption

ISBN 978-1-4222-1502-9; 1-4222-1502-4

LC 2009026372

This discusses some the questions facing adoptive parents such as 'What role do birth families play? Are they going to be a part of the child's life?' and 'What do you tell the child about his birth and adoption?'

"Colorful photographs and sidebars appear throughout. These books are good introductions to the study of sociology and interpretation of data." SLJ

Includes bibliographical references

Stewart, Sheila

A **house** between homes; kids in the foster care system. by Sheila Stewart and Camden Flath. Mason Crest Publishers 2010 48p il lib bdg $19.95; pa $7.95

Grades: 3 4 5 6 **362.7**

1. Foster home care

ISBN 978-1-4222-1692-7 lib bdg; 1-4222-1692-6 lib bdg; 978-1-4222-1905-8 pa; 1-4222-1905-4 pa

LC 2010012756

Discusses the foster care system, including the reasons why children enter the system, what happens in foster care, the types of children, foster parents, and what happens next, and provides a story about siblings who are placed in foster care.

"The prose is respectable in its dialogue, character development, and pacing. . . . This series will be well placed in a school media center, as well as in any institution that serves high-risk children." SLJ

Warren, Andrea

Orphan train rider; one boy's true story. Houghton Mifflin 1996 80p il hardcover o.p. pa $7.95

Grades: 4 5 6 7 **362.7**

1. Orphans 2. Adoption 3. Abandoned children

ISBN 0-395-69822-7; 0-395-91362-4 pa

LC 94-43688

"Between 1854 and 1930, more than 200,000 orphaned and abandoned children from the cities of the eastern seaboard were 'placed out' to new homes and families in the midwest and western states. . . . {This is an} account of the 'orphan-train' phenomena, and of one man's story of how it affected his life. . . . The chapters alternate information about the largest agency, the Children's Aid Society, and its history, with the story of Lee Nailling, from whom the author has gathered the facts of his own childhood journey to Texas and his eventual reunion, late in life, with some of his long-lost siblings. {Bibliography. Index.} Grades four to eight." (SLJ)

"An excellent introduction to researching or discussing children-at-risk in an earlier generation. The book is clearly written and illustrated with numerous black-and-white photographs and reproductions." SLJ

Includes bibliographical references

362.73 Institutional and related services

Warren, Andrea

We rode the orphan trains. Houghton Mifflin 2001 132p il $18; pa $8.95

Grades: 4 5 6 7 **362.73**

1. Orphans

ISBN 0-618-11712-1; 0-618-11712-1 pa

LC 00-47279

"This is powerful nonfiction for classroom and personal reading and for discussion." Booklist

Includes bibliographical references

362.76 Abused and neglected young people

Abuse and violence information for teens; health tips about the causes and consequences of abusive and violent behavior. edited by Keith Jones. Omnigraphics 2017 xi, 325 p.p (Teen health series) (hardcover) $69

Grades: 8 9 10 11 12 **362.76**

1. Youth and violence -- United States 2. Youth and violence -- United States -- Prevention

ISBN 9780780814561

LC 2016049906

"This updated handbook from Jones . . . covers definitions and risk factors for varying types of abuse, including sections such as 'Recognizing and Treating the Consequences' and 'Prevention,' along with resources for further research." (Library Journal)

Includes bibliographical references and index

362.82 Families

Domestic violence; Louise I. Gerdes, book editor. Greenhaven Press 2012 238 p (Opposing viewpoints) paperback $33.80; library $48.80

Grades: 8 9 10 11 12 **362.82**

1. Family violence

ISBN 9780737757200; 9780737757194

Articles in this anthology discuss domestic violence, including its causes and possible remedies.

Zehr, Howard

What will happen to me? by Howard Zehr and Lorraine Stutzman Amstutz; portraits by Howard Zehr. Good Books 2010 94p il pa $14.95

Grades: 7 8 9 10 **362.82**

1. Children of prisoners

ISBN 978-1-56148-689-2

LC 2010-12419

This discusses issues facing "children of incarcerated parents. . . . In part one, the statements from the children interviewed are accompanied by full-color photo portraits. What comes through is that they all love their parents unequivocally, but here it is tangible and poignant both in their words and faces. . . . Part two offers advice for caregivers and includes 10 questions often asked by children whose parents are in jail." SLJ

Includes bibliographical references

362.87 Displaced persons

Nelson, Sheila

In defense of our country; survivors of military conflict. by Sheila Stewart with Joyce Zoldak. Mason Crest Publishers 2009 128p il map (Survivors: ordinary people, extraordinary circumstances) lib bdg $24.95

Grades: 7 8 9 10 **362.87**

1. War 2. Soldiers 3. Ethnic relations 4. Military history

ISBN 978-1-4222-0452-8 lib bdg; 1-4222-0452-9 lib bdg

LC 2008-50556

The title "looks at wars in Africa, Southeast Asia, Eastern Europe, and the Middle East, though plenty of inset boxes cover other topics such as trench warfare in World War I, the Red Cross, and the American Civil War. . . . [This book] will be valued for . . . [its] ability to generate empathy for survivors and their strengths and resilience in difficult situations." SLJ

Includes bibliographical references

362.88 Victims of war

Bickerstaff, Linda

Violence against women; public health and human rights. Rosen Pub. 2010 112p il (A young woman's guide to contemporary issues) lib bdg $31.95

Grades: 7 8 9 10 **362.88**

1. Violence 2. Abused women

ISBN 978-1-4358-3539-9; 1-4358-3539-5

LC 2009-12062

"Facts are shared in a conversational tone, creating the sense of a chat with a big sister. . . . [Though] designed for personal reading and browsing, the data provided are accurate and also lend themselves to use in reports." SLJ

Includes glossary and bibliographical references

362.883 Rape

Conley, Kate

Date rape drugs; by Kate Conley ; Content Consultant R.E. Gaensslen, PhD, Professor Emeritus, Forensic Science, University of Illinois at Chicago. Essential Library, an imprint of Abdo Publishing 2019 112 p. $35.95

Grades: 8 9 10 11 **362.883**

1. Drugs 2. Date rape 3. Rape 4. Drug control 5. Date rape drugs 6. Dating violence

ISBN 153211415X; 9781532114151

LC 2017961351

This book in the Drugs in Real Life series, by Kate Conley, explores how Date Rape Drugs (DFSA) "affect the body, the laws and policies surrounding them, and how potential victims can protect themselves from DFSA. Features include a glossary, references, websites, source notes, and an index. Aligned to Common Core Standards and correlated to state standards." (Publisher's note)

Includes bibliographical references (pages 104-109) and index

Ghafoerkhan, Olivia

★ **Sexual** assault; the ultimate teen guide. Olivia Ghafoerkhan. Rowman & Littlefield 2017 xv, 197 p.p illustrations (It happened to me) (hardback : alk. paper) $45

Grades: 7 8 9 10 11 12 **362.883**

1. Rape 2. Sex crimes 3. Sexual abuse victims -- Services for 4. Sexually abused teenagers -- Services for

ISBN 9781442252479; 9781442252486

LC 2016020501

In this book in the It Happened to Me series, author Olivia Ghafoerkhan "describes the various ways sexual violence can be perpetrated, discusses myths many teens believe about the subject, and outlines how young adults can get the help they need to begin the healing process. Topics covered include date rape, abusive relationships, incest, breaking the silence, victim blaming, support, [and] healing." (Publisher's note)

"A wealth of deeply moving first-person accounts brings home the repercussions of unwanted sexual contact. While mustering a staggering array of statistics, the author keeps the focus personal (the prevailing voice is second person) and restorative as well as preventative." Booklist

Includes bibliographical references and index

Things we haven't said; sexual violence survivors speak out. edited by Erin Moulton. Zest Books 2018 224 p. (paperback) $16.99

Grades: 8 9 10 11 12 **362.883**

1. Incest 2. Rape victims 3. Adult child sexual abuse victims 4. Sexual abuse victims 5. Incest victims 6. Sexually abused children 7. Incest victims -- Family relationships -- Personal narratives 8. Sexually abused children -- Family relationships -- Personal narratives

ISBN 9781942186342; 1942186347

This book, edited by Erin Moulton, "is a powerful collection of poems, essays, letters, vignettes and interviews written by a diverse group of impressive adults who survived sexual violence as children and adolescents. . . . [T]his anthology is a valuable resource of hope, grit and honest conversation that will help teens tackle the topic of sexual violence, upend stigma and maintain hope for a better future." (Publisher's note)

"Moulton has does an impressive job pulling together a collection of works to provide empowerment, empathy, and compassion to all who are willing to listen." Booklist

Includes bibliographical references (pages 204-207).

363 Other social problems and services

Eriksson, Ann

Dive in! exploring our connection with the ocean. Ann Eriksson. Orca Book Publishers 2018 48 p. (hardcover) $19.95
Grades: 4 5 6 7 8 **363**

1. Ocean 2. Oceanography 3. Environmental sciences
ISBN 9781459815865

LC 2018933740

This book in the Orca Footprints series, by Ann Eriksson, "explores our intimate connection with the ocean and provides every reader with an achievable set of actions that can help improve ocean health for our sake and the sake of the millions of marine plants and animals that share the planet with us. Filled with colorful photos and positive stories, 'Dive In!' is as informative as it is inspirational." (Publisher's note)

363.1 Public safety programs

Aronson, Marc, 1950-

★ **Trapped**; how the world rescued 33 miners from 2,000 feet below the Chilean desert. Atheneum 2011 144p il
Grades: 4 5 6 7 **363.1**

1. Rescue work 2. Gold mines and mining 3. Copper mines and mining 4. Mine accidents -- Chile
ISBN 1-4169-1397-1; 978-1-4169-1397-9

LC 2011000777

This title is about thirty-three miners trapped in a copper-gold mine in San Jose, Chile and how experts from around the world, from drillers, to astronauts, to submarine specialists, came together to make their remarkable rescue possible.

This is "a riveting, in-depth recounting of the events that held the world rapt. . . . Twelve short chapters with photos and diagrams keep the story well-paced." Publ Wkly

Includes bibliographical references

Ballard, Carol

Food safety. Gareth Stevens Pub. 2010 48p il (What if we do nothing?) lib bdg $31
Grades: 7 8 9 10 **363.1**

1. Food poisoning 2. Food contamination
ISBN 978-1-4339-1982-4 lib bdg; 1-4339-1982-6 lib bdg

LC 2008-52284

This describes the precautions taken by food producers, retailers, and food safety organizations to guard against food-borne illnesses from such causes as pesticides, microbes, pollution, and chemical additives.

"Meaningful illustrations include color photos and text-enhancing charts. . . . [This is] well written and useful for reports." SLJ

Includes glossary and bibliographical references

Bennie, Paul

The **great** Chicago fire of 1871; [by] Paul Bennie. Chelsea House 2008 128p il (Great historic disasters) $35
Grades: 7 8 9 10 **363.1**

1. Fires -- Chicago (Ill.)
ISBN 978-0-7910-9638-3; 0-7910-9638-6

LC 2007-36550

"On October 8, 1871, a fire started in the O'Learys' barn in Chicago. . . . [This occurence] brought about lasting changes in fire prevention and building codes. . . . [This book], which [describes] the [disaster] and [its] aftermath in detail, [is] well written and informative. . . . [This is] first-rate for reports and general browsing." SLJ

Includes bibliographical references

Chernobyl; David Erik Nelson, book editor. Greenhaven Press 2010 220p il map (Perspectives on modern world history) $38.50
Grades: 8 9 10 11 12 **363.1**

1. Chernobyl Nuclear Accident, Chernobyl, Ukraine, 1986
ISBN 978-0-7377-4555-9; 0-7377-4555-X

LC 2009-27203

"This volume contains a wealth of relevant information representing many viewpoints of the current discussions surrounding the 1986 disaster at the Chernobyl nuclear power plant in Ukraine, which led to an official death toll of 56 people. Each article, skillfully drawn from multinational secondary sources, provides researchers with an admirable base for reports." SLJ

Includes glossary and bibliographical references

Lace, William W.

The **Hindenburg** disaster of 1937. Chelsea House Publishers 2008 120p il (Great historic disasters) lib bdg $35
Grades: 6 7 8 9 10 **363.1**

1. Aircraft accidents 2. Hindenburg (Airship)
ISBN 978-0-7910-9739-7; 0-7910-9739-0

LC 2008004890

On May 6, 1937, the celebrated airship Hindenburg caught fire during its landing in Lakehurst, New Jersey, killing 36 people. This describes the disaster and its aftermath.

The book covers its topic "thoroughly and [includes] high-quality photographs and occasional sidebars. Lace's account of the airship has a good deal of intrigue and drama and could be useful for reports or recreational reading." SLJ

Includes glossary and bibliographical references

Lusted, Marcia Amidon

The **Chernobyl** Disaster. ABDO Pub. 2011 112p il (Essential events) lib bdg $23.95
Grades: 7 8 9 10 11 12 **363.1**

1. Nuclear power plants 2. Chernobyl Nuclear Accident, Chernobyl, Ukraine, 1986
ISBN 978-1-6171-4763-0; 1-6171-4763-X

LC 2010045019

This describes "the technology and engineering detail of how a nuclear power plant generates electricity and why it is dangerous, as well as the politics of why the disaster happened. . . . The spacious . . . design is inviting, with many color illustrations and screens, and the extensive back matter includes a detailed time line, glossary, bibliography and source notes." Booklist

Includes glossary and bibliographical references

The **Three** Mile Island nuclear disaster; by Marcia Amidon Lusted. ABDO Pub. Company 2012 112 p. il (Essential events)
Grades: 6 7 8 **363.1**

1. Nuclear energy 2. Nuclear power plants 3. Nuclear power plants -- Accidents 4. Three Mile Island Nuclear Power Plant (Pa.)
ISBN 1617833118; 9781617833113

LC 2011036182

This children's educational book by Marcia Amidon Lusted "examines an important historic event — the Three Mile Island nuclear disaster near Middletown, Pennsylvania. . . . [It] explores the history of nuclear power in the United States, how a nuclear plant works, details of the emergency at Metropolitan Edison Company's nuclear power plant, handling of the disaster by the Nuclear Regulatory Commission, President Jimmy Carter's visit to Three Mile Island, the investigation into the disaster, and the effects of this event on society. Features include a table of contents, glossary, selected bibliography, Web links, source notes, and an index, plus a timeline and essential facts." (Publisher's note)

Includes glossary and bibliographical references.

Mara, Wil

The **Chernobyl** disaster; legacy and impact on the future of nuclear energy. Marshall Cavendish Benchmark 2010 112p il (Perspectives on) $39.93

Grades: 7 8 9 10 **363.1**

1. Chernobyl Nuclear Accident, Chernobyl, Ukraine, 1986

ISBN 978-0-7614-4984-3; 0-7614-4984-1

"Briefly outlines the nuclear disaster in an easy-to-read format. It examines the nuclear crisis from the moment it occurred to the fallout afterwards. The volume begins with a moment-by-moment account of the disaster itself. Color illustrations of the reactor provide a detailed explanation of the process behind its failure. . . . This is a recommended addition to any school or public library." Voice Youth Advocates

Parks, Peggy J., 1951-

Drunk driving. ReferencePoint Press 2009 96p il (Compact research. Current issues) lib bdg $25.95

Grades: 7 8 9 10 **363.1**

1. Drunk driving

ISBN 978-1-60152-072-2; 1-60152-072-7

LC 2008-48499

This "title has an overview of [drunk driving] as well as topic-specific chapters such as 'Who Drives Drunk?' and 'How Should Drunk Drivers Be Punished?' It offers differing ideas on questions that have more than one answer. The colorful graphs and charts contain current information." SLJ

Includes bibliographical references

Sherman, Jill

The **Hindenburg** disaster. ABDO Pub. Co. 2010 112p il (Essential events) lib bdg $34.22

Grades: 6 7 8 9 **363.1**

1. Airships 2. Aircraft accidents 3. Hindenburg (Airship)

ISBN 978-1-60453-944-8; 1-60453-944-5

LC 2009-30427

This book offers "vivid detail as well as historical and political context. . . . Recounting the [Hindenburg] crash, Sherman captures readers' attention with an opening chapter devoted to the actual crash. She then paints a full picture of the invention of the zeppelin and its uses and development. The author then works her way back to a full description of the crash and a discussion of the theories around its cause. [This title has] pertinent sidebars with primary source material. Archival photos add to the dramatic [narrative]." SLJ

Includes bibliographical references

363.11 Occupational and industrial hazards

Bodden, Valerie

The **Deepwater** Horizon oil spill; Valerie Bodden. Creative Education 2018 48 p.

Grades: 4 5 6 7 8 **363.11**

1. Oil spills -- Mexico, Gulf of 2. BP Deepwater Horizon Explosion and Oil Spill, 2010

ISBN 9781628325485; 9781640260030

LC 2017051378

"The 2010 BP oil spill in the Gulf of Mexico—the worst spill in a body of water—is examined here within the context of the oil industry's development (moving from land to offshore drilling), previous spills, and industry safety procedures. Illustrations dominate the volume—high-quality photos fill full and partial pages, along with infographics and pertinent quotes—thus keeping the text to roughly two paragraphs per spread." (Booklist)

Includes bibliographical references and index

Scott, Elaine

★ **Buried** alive! how 33 miners survived 69 days deep under the Chilean desert. Elaine Scott. Houghton Mifflin Harcourt 2012 80 p. col. ill., col. maps (hardcover) $17.99; (ebook) $17.99

Grades: 4 5 6 7 8 **363.11**

1. Miners 2. Disasters 3. Industrial accidents 4. San José Mine Accident, Chile, 2010 5. Mine rescue work -- Chile -- Copiapó Region 6. Gold mines and mining -- Accidents -- Chile -- Copiapó Region 7. Copper mines and mining -- Accidents -- Chile -- Copiapó Region 8. Mine rescue work -- Chile -- Copiapó Region

ISBN 0547707789; 9780547707785; 9780547691787

LC 2011025945

Author Elaine Scott chronicles the events that took place "[o]n August 5, 2010, [when] a copper mine in Chile collapsed, trapping 33 miners nearly half a mile underground . . . [The author] describes the choices the miners' strong leader advised that prolonged their survival long enough to be rescued and the creative solutions that effected that rescue. They drilled through over 2,000 feet of especially hard rock, delivered supplies to the trapped men through a tiny bore hole and then invented a way to carry the men, one at a time, to the surface in a very small capsule." (Kirkus)

Includes bibliographical references (p. 78) and index.

363.12 Transportation hazards

Burgan, Michael

The **Hindenburg** in flames; by Michael Burgan. Compass Point Books, an imprint of Capstone Press 2017 64 p. (pbk.) $8.95; (ebook) $34.65

Grades: 5 6 7 8 **363.12**

1. Hindenburg (Airship) 2. Airships -- Germany -- History 3. Documentary photography -- United States -- History 4. Aircraft accidents -- New Jersey -- History -- 20th century 5. Airships -- History

ISBN 9780756554415; 9780756554439; 9780756554453

LC 2016008220

This book by Michael Burgan describes how "when it went down in flames, the Hindenburg went down in history. The era of airship travel ended with a disastrous explosion May 6, 1937. Sam Shere's photo of the Hindenburg in flames has been called the most famous news photograph ever taken." (Publisher's note)

"The fact-filled texts are inviting but never talk down to the audience. Mark this series as a great way to discuss history, photography, and the way both shape public perception." Booklist

Includes bibliographical references (pages 61-63) and Index

363.17 Hazardous materials

Kops, Deborah

The **Great** Molasses Flood; Boston, 1919. Deborah Kops. Charlesbridge 2012 102 p.

Grades: 6 7 8 9 **363.17**

1. Molasses 2. Industrial accidents 3. Boston (Mass.) -- History 4. Floods -- Massachusetts -- Boston -- History -- 20th century 5. Industrial accidents -- Massachusetts -- Boston -- History -- 20th century 6. Alcohol industry -- Accidents -- Massachusetts -- Boston -- History -- 20th century 7. Molasses industry -- Accidents -- Massachusetts -- Boston -- History -- 20th century

ISBN 1580893481; 9781580893480; 9781580893497

LC 2011000655

This historical survey by Deborah Kops follows the events of "January 15, 1919 . . . an unseasonable warm day in Boston, Massachusetts, and a day that would go down in history. One minute it was business as usual on the waterfront and the next - KABOOM! A large tank holding molasses exploded, sending shards of metal hundreds of feet away, collapsing buildings, and coating the harborfront community with a thick layer of sticky-sweet sludge." (Publisher's note)

"The combination of the sepia-toned photographs, the use of brown to highlight the chapter headings, and the choice of cream-colored paper gives this book a rich, elegant quality while staying consistent with the subject matter." Booklist

363.2 Police services

Ballard, Carol

Crimebusting! identifying criminals and victims. Enslow Publishers 2010 48p il lib bdg $23.93

Grades: 5 6 7 8 **363.2**

1. Criminals -- Identification

ISBN 978-0-7660-3375-7 lib bdg; 0-7660-3375-9 lib bdg

LC 2008-34803

This "title boasts in-depth information, sidebars detailing events of true crime, and activities that will increase understanding. . . . Photographs are colorful, well-captioned, and related to the text." SLJ

Behnke, Alison Marie

★ **Racial** profiling; everyday inequality. Alison Marie Behnke. Twenty-First Century Books 2017 160 p. illustrations (lb : alk. paper) $35.99

Grades: 8 9 10 11 12 **363.2**

1. Racial profiling in law enforcement 2. Racial profiling in law enforcement -- United States

ISBN 9781512439212; 9781512402681

LC 2016009454

In this book, by Alison Marie Behnke, "in the United States, racial profiling affects thousands of Americans every day. . . . The high-profile deaths of unarmed people of color at the hands of police officers have brought renewed national attention to racial profiling and have inspired grassroots activism from groups such as Black Lives Matter." (Publisher's note)

"A courageous historical examination of one of the most critical civil rights issues of our time." Kirkus

Includes bibliographical references and index

Bell, Suzanne

Encyclopedia of forensic science; foreword by Barry A.J. Fisher; preface by Robert C. Shaler. rev ed; Facts on File 2008 402p il (Facts on File science library) $85

Grades: 8 9 10 11 12 Adult **363.2**

1. Reference books 2. Forensic sciences -- Encyclopedias

ISBN 978-0-8160-6799-2; 0-8160-6799-6

LC 2008-5862

First published 2003

"In addition to explaining the science of forensics, Bell . . . reviews various disciplines related to forensic science, among them entomology, odontology, and psychology. Other entries cover professional organizations, government agencies, famous names in the field of forensics, evidence, and legal issues. . . . With its clear language and brief entries [this] volume will provide readers with a nuts-and-bolts understanding of the real world of forensic science." Booklist [review of 2003 edition]

Includes bibliographical references

Denega, Danielle

Skulls and skeletons; true life stories of bone detectives. Franklin Watts 2007 64p il map (24/7: Science behind the scenes) lib bdg $26; pa $7.95

Grades: 6 7 8 9 **363.2**

1. Forensic sciences 2. Forensic anthropology

ISBN 978-0-531-12064-4 lib bdg; 0-531-12064-3 lib bdg; 978-0-531-17527-9 pa; 0-531-17527-8 pa

LC 2006-21229

Explains how forensic anthropologists figure out a victim's profile and examines three case studies in which forensic anthropologists help identify the victims.

Includes glossary and bibliographical references

Evans, Colin

★ **Crime** lab. Chelsea House 2011 134p il (Law enforcement agencies) lib bdg $35

Grades: 6 7 8 9 **363.2**

1. Forensic sciences 2. Criminal investigation

ISBN 978-1-60413-612-8; 1-60413-612-X

LC 2010043271

This describes the work of crime labs from the 19th century to the present, including the technology used such as ballistics, toxicology, atomic evidence, radio carbon dating, DNA, and fingerprints.

"The Law Enforcement Agencies series is as formidable as the various groups it introduces. Solidly and comprehensively researched. . . . An attractive design, plenty of photos, and solid back matter complete each package. Extremely useful for students and appealing for browsers." Booklist

Includes bibliographical references

Evidence. Chelsea House 2010 132p il (Criminal justice) lib bdg $35

Grades: 6 7 8 9 **363.2**

1. Forensic sciences 2. Criminal investigation

ISBN 978-1-60413-615-9 lib bdg; 1-60413-615-4 lib bdg

The author "describes with authority how varieties of direct and circumstantial evidence . . . are gathered and analyzed. . . . He explains how crime-scene reconstructions, autopsies, and careful observation—as well as traces of blood, skin, poison, carpet fiber, and other substances—played central roles in obtaining convictions. . . . This makes a compelling introduction to a perennially popular topic." Booklist

★ **Interpol**. Chelsea House Publishers 2011 112p il (Law enforcement agencies) lib bdg $35
Grades: 6 7 8 9 **363.2**

1. Law enforcement 2. Criminal investigation 3. International Criminal Police Organization

ISBN 978-1-60413-613-5; 1-60413-613-8

LC 2010048099

This is a history of Interpol from 1914 to the present, covering some of its international cases.

Includes bibliographical references

★ **New** York Police Department. Chelsea House Publishers 2011 120p il (Law enforcement agencies) lib bdg $35
Grades: 6 7 8 9 **363.2**

1. Law enforcement 2. Police -- New York (N.Y.) 3. New York (N.Y.) -- Police Dept.

ISBN 978-1-60413-614-2; 1-60413-614-6

LC 2010049866

This is a history of the New York City Police Department from 1800 to the present, covering such topics as The Mafia, fingerprints, The Son of Sam, police corruption, John Gotti, and the attacks of September 11, 2001.

Includes bibliographical references

Gardner, Robert

Forensic science projects with a crime lab you can build; [by] Robert Gardner. Enslow Publishers 2007 128p il (Build-a-lab! science experiments) $23.95
Grades: 6 7 8 9 **363.2**

1. Science projects 2. Forensic sciences 3. Criminal investigation

ISBN 978-0-7660-2806-7; 0-7660-2806-2

LC 2006039026

Describes how to build a crime lab out of everyday materials so that things like fingerprints and handwriting can be analyzed.

"Gardner creatively handles the challenging task of assembling activities that connect strongly with his often grisly theme. . . . While the forensics information will draw students' interest, the potential dangers may lead some recommenders to set this aside for use in classrooms, where adult supervision can be ensured." Booklist

Includes bibliographical references

Graham, Ian

Forensic technology. Smart Apple Media 2011 il (New technology) lib bdg $34.25
Grades: 4 5 6 7 **363.2**

1. Forensic sciences 2. Criminal investigation

ISBN 978-1-599-20532-8; 1-599-20532-7

LC 2010044238

Describes the technology used by forensic scientists to gather and analyze evidence from crime scenes.

This "offers a fine overview for reports, and its attractive design may also entice middle-grade readers to learn more." Booklist

Gray, Leon

Virtual crime! solving cybercrime. Enslow Publishers 2009 48p il (Solve that crime!) lib bdg $23.93
Grades: 5 6 7 8 **363.2**

1. Computer crimes

ISBN 978-0-7660-3376-4 lib bdg; 0-7660-3376-7 lib bdg

LC 2008-33308

This "title boasts in-depth information, sidebars detailing events of true crime, and activities that will increase understanding. . . . Photographs are colorful, well-captioned, and related to the text." SLJ

Includes glossary and bibliographical references

Harris, Elizabeth Snoke

★ **Crime** scene science fair projects. Lark Books 2006 112p il $25.95
Grades: 6 7 8 9 10 **363.2**

1. Science projects 2. Forensic sciences 3. Criminal investigation

ISBN 1-57990-765-2

LC 2006-16803

"Harris begins with an explanation of forensic science and how it's applied in the everyday world, followed by a discussion of how to plan for a successful project. The projects involve lie detection, lifting fingerprints, recovering data from burned documents, and so on. . . . The author's concise, lively style will even engage students who aren't fond of reading nonfiction." SLJ

Harris, Nathaniel

Crime fighting; the impact of science and technology. Gareth Stevens Pub. 2010 64p il (Pros and cons) lib bdg $35
Grades: 5 6 7 8 **363.2**

1. Criminal investigation

ISBN 978-1-4339-1985-5 lib bdg; 1-4339-1985-0 lib bdg

LC 2009-12433

An "active layout that features color photographs, maps, graphs or charts on every spread, this . . . [book] has much to offer. . . . It conveniently outlines the range of views . . . helping students to learn how to view both sides of [the] issue[s]." SLJ

Includes glossary and bibliographical references

Lane, Brian

Crime and detection; written by Brian Lane. Dorling Kindersley 2005 61p il (DK eyewitness books) $15.99
Grades: 4 5 6 7 **363.2**

1. Crime 2. Forensic sciences 3. Criminal investigation

ISBN 0-7566-1386-8

First published 1998 by Knopf

Explores the many different methods used to solve crimes, covering such topics as criminal, detectives, and forensics

MacLeod, Elizabeth

Bones Never Lie; How Forensics Helps Solve History's Mysteries. Elizabeth MacLeod. Firefly Books Ltd 2013 iv, 156 p.p (hardcover) $24.95
Grades: 4 5 6 7 8 **363.2**

1. Forensic sciences -- Encyclopedias

ISBN 1554514835; 9781554514830

This children's book, by Elizabeth MacLeod, explores how through "forensics--the scientific way of examining physical evidence--we now know what killed Napoleon and whether Anastasia survived the massacre of the Russian royal family. Seven intriguing stories about historical royal figures whose demise was suspicious, and hard scientific facts about crime-solving techniques make each event seem like an episode of CSI rather than a history lesson." (Publisher's note)

"In real life, forensics can be slow and tedious, but MacLeod invests these high-profile deaths with considerable vim and drama. A good selection of staged and archival photographs and artwork accompany the stories. A fully fleshed and crisply told story of forensics at its romantic best." Kirkus

Mezzanotte, Jim

Police. Marshall Cavendish Benchmark 2010 64p il (Working animals) lib bdg $28.50

Grades: 4 5 6 7 **363.2**

1. Animals in police work

ISBN 978-1-60870-166-7 lib bdg; 1-60870-166-2 lib bdg

LC 2010007006

Describes animals, such as dogs and horses, which work with police in such areas as search-and-rescue, tracking criminals, and sniffing out explosives

"Attractively designed and packed with information. . . . The composition of each page is attractively set up with well-selected and reproduced stock and historical photos." SLJ

Newton, Michael

Bomb squad. Chelsea House Publishers 2010 127p il (Law enforcement agencies) lib bdg $35

Grades: 6 7 8 9 **363.2**

1. Bombs 2. Police

ISBN 978-1-60413-624-1; 1-60413-624-3

LC 2010022102

"Solidly and comprehensively researched. . . . Bomb Squad shows that explosives have always been a means of striking terror throughout history. The volume covers the making and defusing of bombs, nuclear devices, and headline-making acts of terror. . . . An attractive design, plenty of photos, and solid back matter complete [the] package. Extremely useful for students and appealing for browsers." Booklist

Includes bibliographical references

Drug Enforcement Administration. Chelsea House Publishers 2011 128p il (Law enforcement agencies) lib bdg $35

Grades: 6 7 8 9 **363.2**

1. Drug traffic 2. Drugs -- Law and legislation 3. United States -- Drug Enforcement Administration

ISBN 978-1-60413-641-8; 1-60413-641-3

LC 2010036940

This describes the work of the Drug Enforcement Administration, including some of its cases concerning marijuana, cocaine, heroin, and methamphetamine.

"The Law Enforcement Agencies series is as formidable as the various groups it introduces. Solidly and comprehensively researched. . . . An attractive design, plenty of photos, and solid back matter complete each package. Extremely useful for students and appealing for browsers." Booklist

Includes bibliographical references

★ **SWAT** teams. Chelsea House Publishers 2010 127p il (Law enforcement agencies) lib bdg $35

Grades: 6 7 8 9 **363.2**

1. Police 2. Law enforcement

ISBN 978-1-60413-625-8; 1-60413-625-1

LC 2010026511

This describes the work of SWAT (Special Weapons and Tactics) teams in law enforcement, including missions ranging from hostage rescue and apprehension of violent felons to drug raids and natural-disaster relief. The book traces the history of special police teams worldwide, examining their techniques, tools, successes, and failures.

Includes bibliographical references

U.S. marshals. Chelsea House Publishers 2011 128p il (Law enforcement agencies) lib bdg $35

Grades: 6 7 8 9 **363.2**

1. Law enforcement 2. United States -- Marshals Service

ISBN 978-1-60413-627-2; 1-60413-627-8

LC 2010038195

This describes the U. S. Marshals Service, its history, and its work in fighting counterfeiting, in court security, the Witness Security Program, and fugitive investigations.

"The Law Enforcement Agencies series is as formidable as the various groups it introduces. Solidly and comprehensively researched. . . . An attractive design, plenty of photos, and solid back matter complete each package. Extremely useful for students and appealing for browsers." Booklist

Includes bibliographical references

Orr, Tamra

Racial profiling. ABDO Pub. Co. 2010 112p il (Essential viewpoints) lib bdg $32.79

Grades: 7 8 9 10 **363.2**

1. Racial profiling in law enforcement 2. Racial profiling

ISBN 978-1-60453-535-8; 1-60453-535-0

LC 2008-34915

"This timely book covers racial profiling as practiced in the United States since the terrorist attacks of 9/11, when it has come to center on young men of Middle Eastern extraction. . . . Orr presents arguments for and against the practice in focused, clearly written essays that will help students become informed. . . . There are plenty of color photographs. This book will enhance most collections." SLJ

Includes bibliographical references

Perritano, John

Science beats crime. Marshall Cavendish Benchmark 2010 48p il (Cool science) lib bdg $28.50

Grades: 5 6 7 8 **363.2**

1. Forensic sciences 2. Criminal investigation

ISBN 978-1-60870-078-3 lib bdg; 1-60870-078-X lib bdg

LC 2009053774

"Perritano briefly traces the history of forensic science, . . . discusses different subspecialities, such as toxicology and forensic anthropology, and then gets into the good stuff—fingerprinting, DNA profiling, ballistics, splatter patterns, even a gross-out spread of how studying maggots can determine time of death. Interspersed throughout are real-life case studies. . . . This solid, amply illustrated, and easy-reading introduction to forensic science ends with a look at the future of the field." Booklist

Includes glossary and bibliographical references

Rainis, Kenneth G.

★ **Blood** & DNA evidence; crime-solving science experiments. science consultant, Brian Gestring. Enslow Publishers 2006 104p il (Forensic science projects) lib bdg $31.93

Grades: 7 8 9 10 **363.2**

1. Forensic sciences 2. DNA fingerprinting

ISBN 0-7660-1958-6

LC 2005029214

This "invites readers to complete scientific experiments that emulate the solution to actual murders. . . . Following each real-life scenario, the book provides a checklist of materials and a step-by-step experiment to get the same results as the detectives. . . . The format is easy to follow, the scenarios intriguing, and the experiments complex enough for real science buffs to feel challenged." Booklist

Includes glossary and bibliographical references

Ricciuti, Edward R.

★ **Federal** Bureau of Investigation. Chelsea House Publishers 2010 144p il (Law enforcement agencies) lib bdg $35

Grades: 6 7 8 9 **363.2**

1. Criminal investigation 2. United States -- Federal Bureau of Investigation

ISBN 978-1-60413-636-4; 1-60413-636-7

"Solidly and comprehensively researched. . . . Federal Bureau of Investigation is a broad and deep look at the agency from its inception. Many of its most famous cases, including the Rosenbergs' arrest, terror cases, and the fight against organized crime, are discussed. Common criticisms, such as the overreach of the agency (J. Edgar Hoover in particular) are included. . . . An attractive design, plenty of photos, and solid back matter complete [the] package. Extremely useful for students and appealing for browsers." Booklist

Includes bibliographical references

Ryan, Bernard

★ The **Secret** Service. Chelsea House Publishers 2010 128p il (Law enforcement agencies) lib bdg $35

Grades: 6 7 8 9 **363.2**

1. United States -- Secret Service

ISBN 978-1-60413-623-4; 1-60413-623-5

This describes the work of The Secret Service including protecting the president, other key government figures, and visiting foreign leaders, investigating financial fraud and protecting crowds, buildings, and locations from potential threats.

"The Law Enforcement Agencies series is as formidable as the various groups it introduces. Solidly and comprehensively researched. . . . An attractive design, plenty of photos, and solid back matter complete each package. Extremely useful for students and appealing for browsers." Booklist

Includes bibliographical references

Schindler, Howard

Science sleuths; solving mysteries using scientific inquiry. [by] Howard Schindler and Dennis Mucenski. Prufrock Press Inc. 2010 vii, 195p il pa $19.95

Grades: Adult Professional **363.2**

1. Forensic sciences 2. Science -- Methodology

ISBN 978-1-59363-397-4 pa; 1-59363-397-1 pa

LC 2009042622

"This professional resource uses [the] field [of forensics] to develop skills in scientific inquiry. The book features three activities in which students, working in groups or individually, analyze the evidence presented to them to solve a case. The activities are keyed to national standards for scientific inquiry. The tasks for 3-4 days of activities, culminating in a final essay, assist the teacher in planning the solution. . . . This is a most valuable resource for the science teacher of grades 6-9." Voice Youth Advocates

Includes bibliographical references

Stefoff, Rebecca

Crime labs. Marshall Cavendish Benchmark 2010 95p il (Forensic science investigated) $23.95

Grades: 6 7 8 9 10 **363.2**

1. Forensic sciences 2. Graphologists 3. Criminologists

ISBN 978-0-7614-4140-3; 0-7614-4140-9

LC 2010-10536

The "titles in the Forensic Science Investigated series stand out not only for their thorough overviews of how forensic science is practiced today but also for their fascinating historical perspectives. . . . Crime labs introduces nineteenth-century Frenchman Edmond Locard, creator of the world's first forensic lab." Booklist

Includes bibliographical references

Criminal profiling. Marshall Cavendish Benchmark 2010 93p il (Forensic science investigated) $23.95

Grades: 6 7 8 9 **363.2**

1. Physicians 2. Criminal investigation 3. Criminologists 4. Writers on medicine

ISBN 978-0-7614-4141-0; 0-7614-4141-7

LC 2010010535

The "titles in the Forensic Science Investigated series stand out not only for their thorough overviews of how forensic science is practiced today but also for their fascinating historical perspectives. . . . Criminal Profiling spotlights early criminologists, such as Cesare Lombroso, who believed that criminal instincts manifested in physical features." Booklist

Includes bibliographical references

Forensic anthropology. Marshall Cavendish Benchmark 2010 95p il (Forensic science investigated) $19.95

Grades: 6 7 8 9 **363.2**

1. Forensic anthropology 2. Criminal investigation

ISBN 978-0-7614-4142-7; 0-7614-4142-5

LC 2010010534

The "titles in the Forensic Science Investigated series stand out not only for their thorough overviews of how forensic science is practiced today but also for their fascinating historical perspectives. . . . Forensic Anthropology starts off with a riveting account of scientists who cracked an 1849 Harvard murder case by finding clues among the victim's remains." Booklist

Includes bibliographical references

Stewart, Gail

K -9 police units; by Gail B. Stewart. Lucent Books 2010 104p il (Crime scene investigations) lib bdg $32.45

Grades: 7 8 9 10 **363.2**

1. Working dogs 2. Animals in police work

ISBN 978-1-4205-0137-7 lib bdg; 1-4205-0137-2 lib bdg

LC 2009-27456

This describes "the rigorous selection and training process of both dog and handler. Also discussed are the many different types of applications for these brave animals, as well as the bond of mutual trust that is required between the police officer and his canine companion while working in true life-and-death situations. . . . [This] should not only be a popular addition to any collection but will also go a long way in setting the record straight regarding who does what within a criminal investigation." Voice Youth Advocates

Includes bibliographical references

Townsend, John

Famous forensic cases. Amicus 2011 il (Amazing crime scene science) $19.95

Grades: 4 5 6 7 **363.2**

1. Forensic sciences 2. Criminal investigation

ISBN 978-1-60753-169-2; 1-60753-169-0

In this book "readers will find a straight presentation of fascinating information. Loosely organized by era, the book opens with a history of fingerprinting . . . which focuses on the 1920s and 1930s. Other topics include hair science in the 1950s, voiceprints in the 1970s, and recent advancements in DNA forensics. Scatter throughout are case studies. . . .

This entry features an eye-catching layout, plenty of sidebars, and well-chosen photos. . . . Kids will go for this one." Booklist

Walker, Pamela

Forensic science experiments; [by] Pamela Walker, Elaine Wood. Facts on File 2009 150p il (Facts on File science experiments) $35

Grades: 7 8 9 10 **363.2**

1. Forensic sciences 2. Science -- Experiments

ISBN 978-0-8160-7804-2; 0-8160-7804-1

LC 2008-39900

This "contains 20 experiments that allow students to actively engage in scientific inquiry. Projects are presented in a uniform format, with an introduction to the topic, time requirements (35 minutes to 2 weeks), a materials list, numbered procedures, and several analysis questions. . . . The experiments themselves are timely and fascinating. . . . In [this book], a banana autopsy, blood-spatter inquiry, and 'Glitter as Trace Evidence' will hook CSI fans. Despite detailed instructions, close teacher supervision is a must." SLJ

Includes glossary and bibliographical references

Webber, Diane

Do you read me? famous cases solved by handwriting analysis! [by] Diane Webber. Franklin Watts 2007 64p il map (24/7, science behind the scenes) lib bdg $27; pa $7.95

Grades: 5 6 7 8 **363.2**

1. Graphology 2. Forensic sciences

ISBN 978-0-531-12066-8 lib bdg; 0-531-12066-X lib bdg; 978-0-531-15456-4 pa; 0-531-15456-4 pa

LC 2006006797

"Cases such as the infamous Lindbergh kidnapping and the discovery of Hitler's lost diaries are used to explore how handwriting can be used to solve a mystery. Subsequent sections tackle questions such as the validity of handwriting analysis as well as explore some of the nuances of the science." Voice Youth Advocates

Includes glossary and bibliographical references

Weir, William

★ **Border** patrol. Chelsea House 2010 125p il (Law enforcement agencies) lib bdg $35

Grades: 6 7 8 9 **363.2**

1. Smuggling 2. Unauthorized immigrants 3. Illegal aliens 4. United States -- Border Patrol 5. United States -- Immigration and emigration

ISBN 978-1-60413-635-7; 1-60413-635-9

LC 2010030051

"Solidly and comprehensively researched. . . . Border Patrol takes on a topic much in the news. The hottest issues of border control are all examined: drugs, bandits, and smuggling of goods and people. There is also great information on the technology used, as well as a levelheaded discussion on the terror threat presented by illegal immigrants. . . . An attractive design, plenty of photos, and solid back matter complete [the] package. Extremely useful for students and appealing for browsers." Booklist

Includes glossary and bibliographical references

Young, Karen Romano

Crime scene science; 20 projects and experiments about clues, crimes, criminals, and other mysterious things. illustrations by David Goldin. National Geographic 2009 80p il (Science fair winners) $12.95; lib bdg $24.90

Grades: 6 7 8 9 **363.2**

1. Science projects 2. Forensic sciences 3. Criminal investigation

ISBN 978-1-4263-0521-4; 1-4263-0521-4; 978-1-4263-0522-1 lib bdg; 1-4263-0522-2 lib bdg

LC 2009-20387

This is a "collection of 20 science fair show-stoppers. . . . Significantly deeper than most science-fair tutorials. . . . High-interest topics abound: footprint casting, crime scene mapping, lie detection, and even compelling tricks like decoding those weird little bars the postal service stamps onto letters." Booklist

Includes bibliographical references

363.28 Services of special kinds of security and law enforcement agencies

Martin, Claudia

Drug wars; Claudia Martin. Cavendish Square Publishing 2018 48 p. $31.36

Grades: 6 7 8 9 **363.28**

1. Crime -- United States 2. Drug abuse -- United States 3. Drug traffic -- United States

ISBN 1502632586; 9781502632586

"The violence that surrounds drug dealing and drug trafficking has decimated whole communities, and, in some cases, reshaped daily life in entire countries. This volume [in the I Witness War series, by Claudia Martin,] takes a closer look at the people affected by the drug trade and the efforts being made to combat it. The book includes firsthand stories, critical thinking questions, and a summative activity, all with the aim of showing the human toll of the drug economy." (Publisher's note)

363.3 Other aspects of public safety

Cunningham, Kevin

Wildfires. Morgan Reynolds Pub. 2009 112p il (Extreme threats) lib bdg $28.95

Grades: 7 8 9 10 **363.3**

1. Wildfires

ISBN 978-1-59935-120-9; 1-59935-120-X

LC 2009-25709

This book about wildfires has "black-and-white and color photographs on almost every page. . . . Frequent sidebars, covering as much as a spread, discuss peripheral and often unusual information. The conclusion . . . explains what scientists are doing, or what they anticipate doing, to ameliorate the threat." SLJ

Includes glossary and bibliographical references

Media violence; Noah Berlatsky, book editor. Greenhaven Press 2012 206 p illustrations (Opposing viewpoints)

Grades: 8 9 10 11 12 **363.3**

1. Mass media and children 2. Violence in mass media

ISBN 9780737763294; 9780737763287

This anthology "begins with articles that probe the scope and severity of the phenomenon and then moves on to sections about how violence in the media should be regulated, the effects of violence in the news, and cyberbullying." Booklist (review of 2009 edition)

363.31 Censorship

Gottfried, Ted

★ **Censorship**. Benchmark Books 2005 143p il (Open for debate) $37.07

Grades: 7 8 9 10 **363.31**

1. Censorship

ISBN 0-7614-1883-0

This discusses censorship issues in regard to such topics as pornography, the internet, motion pictures, politics, and literature.

Includes bibliographical references

363.32 Social conflict

Bedell, J. M.

Combating terrorism. Compass Point Books 2010 48p il (Terrorism) lib bdg $27.99

Grades: 6 7 8 9 **363.32**

1. Terrorism

ISBN 978-0-7565-4309-9 lib bdg; 0-7565-4309-6 lib bdg

LC 2009-38908

"The style stays consistently clear and strightforward throughout , and the tone remains objective. A well-designed layout, with plenty of white space and well-placed sidebars, adds to the acessibility. . . . A great choice." SLJ

Includes glossary and bibliographical references

Burgan, Michael

Terrorist groups. Compass Point Books 2010 48p il (Terrorism) lib bdg $27.99

Grades: 6 7 8 9 **363.32**

1. Terrorism 2. Terrorists

ISBN 978-0-7565-4311-2 lib bdg; 0-7565-4311-8 lib bdg

Discusses terrorist groups such as al-Qaida, the Colombian FARC, and the Palestinian PFLP.

"The style stays consisently clear and straightforward throughout, and the tone remains objective. A well-designed layout, with plenty of white space and well-placed sidebars, adds to the accessibility. . . . A great choice." SLJ

Includes glossary and bibliographical references

Fremont-Barnes, Gregory

Rescue at the Iranian Embassy; the most daring SAS raid. Rosen Pub. 2011 64p il map (The most daring raids in history) lib bdg $29.25

Grades: 7 8 9 10 **363.32**

1. Iran -- History -- 1979- 2. Great Britain -- Army -- Special Air Service Regiment

ISBN 978-1-4488-1869-3; 1-4488-1869-9

LC 2010029625

First published 2009 in the United Kingdom with title: Who dares wins

On May 5, 1980, the world watched as the SAS performed a daring raid on the Iranian Embassy in London. The raid was a huge success for the SAS, rescuing nineteen hostages with near-perfect military execution, although two were killed by the terrorists.

This book is "packed with facts, covering the details of the action, the people involved, and the tools used, in engaging prose. The authors cite their sources thoroughly. . . . Diagrams, photos, . . . and maps make the action easy to follow and provide visual context for the raids. . . . This . . . is sure to find a large readership." SLJ

Includes glossary and bibliographical references

Friedman, Lauri S.

Terrorist attacks. ReferencePoint Press 2008 128p il map (Compact research. Current issues) lib bdg $24.95

Grades: 7 8 9 10 11 12 **363.32**

1. Terrorism

ISBN 978-1-60152-022-7; 1-60152-022-0

LC 2007-9907

This "introduces theories as to why people carry out terrorist attacks, how they are executed, and how the attacks might be prevented. . . . [The] volume includes people and groups associated with the issue, a chronology of events, related organizations, and suggestions for further research. Chapters open and end with an array of quotes that argue for or against a particular argument or aspect of the issue, complete with full citation." SLJ

Includes glossary and bibliographical references

Gupta, Dipak K.

★ **Who** are the terrorists? Chelsea House 2006 116p il map (The roots of terrorism) lib bdg $35

Grades: 7 8 9 10 **363.32**

1. Islam 2. Terrorism

ISBN 0-7910-8306-3

LC 2005021627

This "volume discusses the world history as well as the groups and individuals behind today's headlines. . . . Gupta emphasizes that equating Islam with the barbaric acts of a few terrorists is like making the burning crosses of the Ku Klux Klan the essence of Christianity. He also points out the role of the American invasion of Iraq and the images from Abu Ghraib. . . . This is sure to spark vehement group discussion." Booklist

Includes bibliographical references

Nardo, Don

The **history** of terrorism. Compass Point Books 2010 48p il (Terrorism) lib bdg $27.99

Grades: 6 7 8 9 **363.32**

1. Terrorism

ISBN 978-0-7565-4310-5 lib bdg; 0-7565-4310-X lib bdg

Discusses the use of terrorism throughout history, and examines the individuals and groups who have resorted to violent actions in order to generate fear

"The style stays consisently clear and straightforward throughout, and the tone remains objective. A well-designed layout, with plenty of white space and well-placed sidebars, adds to the accessibility. . . . A great choice." SLJ

Includes glossary and bibliographical references

Terrorism; an opposing viewpoints guide. Stephen Currie, book editor. Greenhaven Press 2006 111 p. ill. (chiefly col.) (Opposing viewpoints series) (library) $33.75

Grades: 8 9 10 11 12 **363.32**

1. Terrorism 2. Authorship

ISBN 9780737732061; 0737732067

LC 2005049314

This title "makes use of the . . . Opposing Viewpoints format (with selections that argue crucial issues from many sides), adding exercises, suggestions, and models for students' writing. More than half the book is published articles from alternative viewpoints, and the vital contemporary questions (Are terrorist attacks inevitable? Is the threat of terrorism exaggerated? etc.) will spark debate and discussion." Booklist

Includes bibliographical references (p. 104-106) and index.

Tougas, Shelley

What makes a terrorist? Compass Point Books 2010 48p il (Terrorism) lib bdg $27.99

Grades: 6 7 8 9 **363.32**

1. Terrorism 2. Terrorists

ISBN 978-0-7565-4312-9 lib bdg; 0-7565-4312-6 lib bdg

Discusses terrorism and the traits of terrorists.

"The style stays consistently clear and straightforward throughout, and the tone remains objective. A well-designed layout, with plenty of white space and well-placed sidebars, adds to the accessibility. . . . A great choice." SLJ

Includes glossary and bibliographical references

363.33 Control of firearms

Allen, John, 1957-

Gun control; by John Allen. Referencepoint Press 2018 80 p illustrations (Thinking critically)

Grades: 8 9 10 11 12 **363.33**

1. Gun control

ISBN 9781682823378

Examines the issue of gun control, asking if control laws reduce deaths, if background checks should be expanded, if military-style assault weapons should be banned, and if concealed handguns should be permitted.

Atkin, S. Beth

★ **Gunstories**; life-changing experiences with guns. interviews and photographs by S. Beth Atkin. HarperCollins Publishers 2006 245p il $16.99; lib bdg $17.89

Grades: 7 8 9 10 11 12 **363.33**

1. Guns 2. Firearms

ISBN 0-06-052659-9; 0-06-052660-2 lib bdg

LC 2005-2076

"This book should be useful for students involved in the debate about guns in our culture as well as for those with a general interest in the subject." SLJ

363.34 Disasters

Bailey, Gerry

Fragile planet. Gareth Stevens Pub. 2011 48p il map (Planet SOS) lib bdg $31.95; pa $14.05

Grades: 4 5 6 **363.34**

1. Natural disasters

ISBN 978-1-4339-4974-6 lib bdg; 1-4339-4974-1 lib bdg; 978-1-4339-4975-3 pa; 1-4339-4975-X pa

LC 2010032886

This "well-designed [book]. . . . discusses natural events and disasters, such as avalanches, earthquakes, floods, hurricanes, lightning, volcanoes, and windstorms. . . . The many large, colorful photos will engage readers and assist them in understanding the important concepts introduced." SLJ

Includes glossary

Brown, Don, 1949-

★ **Drowned** City; Hurricane Katrina and New Orleans. by Don Brown. Houghton Mifflin Harcourt 2015 96 p. chiefly color illustrations $18.99; $18.99

Grades: 7 8 9 10 **363.34**

1. Hurricane Katrina, 2005 2. New Orleans (La.) -- History

ISBN 054415777X; 9780544157774

LC 2015458266

Eisner Nominee: Best Publication for Teens (2016)

Robert F. Sibert Honor Book (2016)

In this work of graphic nonfiction by Don Brown, "when the calamitous category five Katrina's gusty winds hurl into the city of New Orleans, most people have evacuated the city. The rest of the scared, stubborn, and simply stranded must face the dangers of what is to come--broken levees quickly swelling the city with water. Many families seek safety on their roofs or via floatation devices as a way to row to safety. However, some are not as fortunate." (Children's Literature)

"Brown's narrative is clear and precise, relying exclusively on data and statistics interspersed with quotes from residents, rescue crews, journalists, and news reports. Alone, the text might lack impact, but combined with the haunting imagery, it hits readers like a punch in the gut." Booklist

Includes bibliographical references

Butts, Edward

SOS : stories of survival; true tales of disaster, tragedy, and courage. by Ed Butts. Tundra Books 2007 119p il pa $12.95

Grades: 6 7 8 9 **363.34**

1. Disasters

ISBN 978-0-88776-786-9 pa

"Butts writes with taut excitement about 13 devastating events—floods, fires, explosions, mountain slides, and more—from the 1891 Canadian Springhill Mine Disaster and the Triangle Shirtwaist Fire to Chernobyl, the Tsunami of 2004, and Hurricaine Katrina. . . . The personal eyewitness accounts and occasional archival photos dramatize the cataclysmic events." Booklist

Includes bibliographical references

Fradin, Judith Bloom

★ **Droughts**; [by] Judy & Dennis Fradin. National Geographic 2008 48p il map (Witness to disaster) $16.95; lib bdg $20.90

Grades: 4 5 6 7 **363.34**

1. Droughts

ISBN 978-1-4263-0339-5; 1-4263-0339-4; 978-1-4263-0340-1 lib bdg; 1-4263-0340-8 lib bdg

LC 2008020424

"This book examines the lessons from the Dust Bowl droughts for farmers, including the importance of topsoil. The history of droughts around the world compares impacts on a wide variety of societies. The final chapter looks at the latest tools and technologies developed to help us survive future droughts." Publisher's note

Includes glossary and bibliographical references

Garbe, Suzanne

The **Worst** wildfires of all time; by Suzanne Garbe. Capstone Press 2013 32 p. ill. (chiefly col.), col. maps (library) $27.32

Grades: 4 5 6 7 **363.34**

1. Wildfires 2. Natural disasters

ISBN 1429684186; 9781429684187

LC 2011053150

This book by Suzanne Garbe is part of the Epic Disasters series and looks at the worst wildfires of all time. "These uncontrolled fires can strike in the blink of an eye and spread just as quickly. Put out the flames and read about the worst wildfires in history." The series allows readers to "witness the destructive power of hurricanes, earthquakes, and more." (Publisher's note)

Includes bibliographical references and index.

Langley, Andrew

Hurricanes, tsunamis, and other natural disasters; [by] Andrew Langley. Kingfisher 2006 63p il map (Kingfisher knowledge) $12.95

Grades: 5 6 7 8 **363.34**

1. Natural disasters

ISBN 978-0-7534-5975-1; 0-7534-5975-2

LC 2005027200

This briefly describes such natural disasters as hurricanes, tsunamis, avalanches, brush fires, earthquakes, floods, tornadoes, drought and famine, pandemics, with many color illustrations and maps

"This book presents a high-interest topic in an attractively designed format that features colorful, eye-catching graphics and a solidly written text." Booklist

Includes glossary and bibliographical references

Markle, Sandra

Rescues! Millbrook Press 2006 88p il map lib bdg $25.26; paperback $11.99

Grades: 4 5 6 7 **363.34**

1. Rescue work 2. Survival after airplane accidents, shipwrecks, etc.

ISBN 978-0-8225-3413-6 lib bdg; 0-8225-3413-4 lib bdg; 9781512433432

LC 2005-09707

"From the collapse of a Pennsylvania coal mine in 2002 to the tsunami that struck 11 countries in 2004 to Hurricane Katrina in 2005, the 11 disasters Markle describes are straight from news headlines. In this full-color photo-essay, she uses individual experiences of rescue and survival to bring each drama close." Booklist

Includes bibliographical references

Miller, Mara

Hurricane Katrina strikes the Gulf Coast; disaster & survival. [by] Mara Miller. Enslow Publishers 2006 48p il map (Deadly disasters) $23.93

Grades: 4 5 6 7 **363.34**

1. Hurricanes 2. Rescue work 3. Hurricane Katrina, 2005

ISBN 0-7660-2803-8

LC 2005030989

"Miller begins with an account of the development of Hurricane Katrina as it struck Florida and then threatened the Gulf Coast. She discusses the subsequent flooding of New Orleans, the damage it caused, rescue and recovery attempts, and planning for the aftermath of future hurricanes. The author includes a clear scientific description of hurricanes, defining key terms. Color photos and graphics help explain concepts such as the structure of a hurricane, Katrina's path, and the conditions endured by the victims." SLJ

Includes glossary and bibliographical references

Mooney, Carla

Surviving in cold places; by Carla Mooney. Lerner Publications Company 2014 32 p. (Shockzone--True survival stories) (lib. bdg. : alk. paper) $26.60

Grades: 5 6 7 8 **363.34**

1. Survival skills 2. Wilderness survival 3. Cold -- Physiological effect 4. Survival -- Polar regions 5. Polar regions -- Environmental conditions

ISBN 1467714348; 9781467714341

LC 2013019868

This book on survival in cold climates, by Carla Mooney, is part of the "Shock Zone: True Survival Stories" series. It presents "historic accounts of incidents in the Andes, Antarctic, and Alaska." The book provides "survival tips . . . an extended bibliography, and gateways to more information." (Voice of Youth Advocates)

"Each thin volume shares six to eight (mostly) contemporary stories of extreme survival, including a 2005 grizzly bear attack on a father and daughter and a boy's eight-day ordeal buried in rubble in the 2010 Haiti earthquake. Readers will be grabbed by a mix of harrowing details and eye-catching color photographs. The stories and appended safety tips are superficially presented but are nonetheless fascinating.' Horn Book

Includes bibliographical references (pages 30, 32) and index

Other titles in the series include:

Surviving in the Wilderness (2014)

Surviving Natural Disasters (2014)

Pietras, Jamie

Hurricane Katrina; [by] Jamie Pietras. Chelsea House 2008 128p il map (Great historic disasters) $35

Grades: 7 8 9 10 **363.34**

1. Hurricane Katrina, 2005

ISBN 978-0-7910-9639-0; 0-7910-9639-4

LC 2007036551

"This book details the meteorological, political, and social circumstances that came together so fatally during 2005's Hurricane Katrina. Mostly objective, the writing is occasionally peppered with commentary on the local and federal governments' missteps and inaction following the storm and ensuing floods. Gripping photographs support the text." Horn Book Guide

Includes glossary and bibliographical references

Reilly, Kathleen M.

Natural disasters; investigate Earth's most destructive forces. by Kathleen M. Reilly ; illustrated by Tom Casteel. Nomad Press 2012 121 p. (paperback) $15.95

Grades: 4 5 6 7 **363.34**

1. Weather 2. Natural disasters

ISBN 1619301466; 9781619301467

In this book, "spiraling winds, surging waters, eruptions, blazing forests, and chilling snows are discussed." Topics include "the MMS Scale and the Enhanced Fujita Scale." In addition to an "explanation of each type of phenomenon, safety tips, historical incidences, pen-and-ink line drawings, and correlative projects using simple materials are included." (School Library Journal)

Rusch, Elizabeth

★ **Eruption!** volcanoes and the science of saving lives. text by Elizabeth Rusch ; illustrated by Tom Uhlman. Houghton Mifflin Harcourt 2013 76 p. col. ill. (hardcover) $18.99

Grades: 5 6 7 8 **363.34**

1. Disaster response and recovery 2. Volcanoes 3. Natural disasters 4. Volcanic eruptions

ISBN 0547503504; 9780547503509

LC 2012034055

This book by Elizabeth Rusch contains "photographs and sidebars [which] reveals the perilous . . . life-saving work of an international volcano crisis team (VDAP) and the sleeping giants they study, from Colombia to the Philippines, from Chile to Indonesia. [It presents an] stunning account of volcanologists Andy Lockhart, John Pallister, and their group of scientists who risk their lives, investigating deadly volcanoes that remain constant threats to people around the world." (Publisher's note)

Includes bibliographical references (pages 74-75) and index.

Sanna, Ellyn

Nature's wrath; surviving natural disasters. Mason Crest Publishers 2009 128p il map (Survivors: ordinary people, extraordinary circumstances) lib bdg $24.95

Grades: 7 8 9 10 **363.34**

1. Natural disasters 2. Hurricane Katrina, 2005 3. Indian Ocean earthquake and tsunami, 2004

ISBN 978-1-4222-0454-2 lib bdg; 1-4222-0454-5 lib bdg

LC 2008-33334

Describes how natural disasters have decimated areas and lives, and how people have worked to reclaim their lives in the aftermath

"Supplemented by fact boxes, large color photos, and color-blocked vocabulary, . . . [this book is] . . . visually appealing as well as informational." SLJ

Includes bibliographical references

Stefoff, Rebecca

Forensics and modern disasters. Marshall Cavendish Benchmark 2010 95p il (Forensic science investigated) $23.95

Grades: 6 7 8 9 10 **363.34**

1. Disasters 2. Forensic sciences 3. Criminal investigation

ISBN 978-0-7614-4144-1; 0-7614-4144-1

LC 2010-10533

The "titles in the Forensic Science Investigated series stand out not only for their thorough overviews of how forensic science is practiced today but also for their fascinating historical perspectives. . . . Forensics and Modern Disasters dives directly into contemporary practices and shows how techniques . . . have helped identify victims of large-scale tragedies, including 9/11." Booklist

Includes bibliographical references

363.37 Fire hazards

Cooper, Michael L., 1950-

Fighting fire! ten of the deadliest fires in American history and how we fought them. Michael L. Cooper. Henry Holt and Co. 2014 224 p. illustrations, maps (hardback) $19.99

Grades: 5 6 7 8 **363.37**

1. Fires 2. Fire fighting 3. Fire extinction -- United States -- History

ISBN 0805097147; 9780805097146

LC 2013043580

This book, by Michael L. Cooper, "brings to life ten of the deadliest infernos . . . [the United States] has ever endured: the great fires of Boston, New York, Chicago, Baltimore, and San Francisco, the disasters of the Triangle Shirtwaist Factory, the General Slocum, and the Cocoanut Grove nightclub, the wildfire of Witch Creek in San Diego County, and the catastrophe of 9/11." (Publisher's note)

"Throughout history, fires have wreaked destruction but have also sparked innovation and reform. The Great Chicago Fire (1871) destroyed a third of the city but brought about a new architecture style; the Triangle Shirtwaist Factory Fire (1911) killed 146 people but led to the passage of laws protecting workers. Entries are lively, with dramatic illustrations to match." Horn Book

Includes bibliographical references and index

363.4 Controversies related to public morals and customs

Blumenthal, Karen

★ **Bootleg**; murder, moonshine, and the lawless years of Prohibition. Roaring Brook Press 2011 154p il $18.99

Grades: 8 9 10 11 12 **363.4**

1. Temperance 2. Prohibition 3. United States -- History -- 1919-1933 4. Alcoholic beverage industry 5. Prohibition -- United States

ISBN 978-1-59643-449-3; 1-59643-449-X

LC 2010032687

The author "offers a highly readable, well-shaped look at the Eighteenth Amendment. . . . She provides concise, clearly written insights into the seeds of temperance movements in the late eighteenth century. . . . The section on Al Capone will satisfy readers hungry for the gangster-warfare side of Prohibition. A closing chapter makes an argument that despite the mostly disastrous results, there were bright points to Prohibition. . . . Plenty of archival images lend to the book's pleasant design, and an ample bibliography and source notes close out this top-notch resource." Booklist

Includes bibliographical references

Hill, Jeff

Prohibition. Omnigraphics 2004 xxv, 201p il (Defining moments) $38

Grades: 7 8 9 10 **363.4**

1. Prohibition

ISBN 0-7808-0768-5

LC 2004-22643

This book provides an "historical analysis of the Prohibition era (1920-33), including the politics of the Eighteenth Amendment; the Mob wars; the roles played by important public figures, from mobster Al Capone to Prohibition activist Carry Nation to President Warren Harding; and much more. . . . With a detailed glossary, a chronology, and an annotated bibliography, this is an important curriculum resource on the social and political history of an era." Booklist

Includes glossary and bibliographical references

Worth, Richard

Teetotalers and saloon smashers; the temperance movement and prohibition. Enslow Publishers 2009 128p il map (America's living history) lib bdg $31.93

Grades: 5 6 7 8 **363.4**

1. Temperance 2. Prohibition

ISBN 978-0-7660-2908-8 lib bdg; 0-7660-2908-5 lib bdg

LC 2008-13905

"Discusses the temperance movement in American history, including important figures in the movement, the history of temperance, and the period of Prohibition in the United States." Publisher's note

Includes glossary and bibliographical references

363.45 Drug traffic

Drug legalization; Noël Merino, book editor. Greenhaven Press 2015 185 p (Current controversies)

Grades: 8 9 10 11 12 **363.45**

1. Drug control -- United States 2. Drug legalization -- United

States
ISBN 9780737772166; 9780737772159
Discusses the issues surrounding drug legalization, including asking why drug policies have failed in the past, if drug use is dangerous to society, and how drug policy should be reformed.

Harris, Nathaniel
Drug trafficking. Gareth Stevens Pub. 2010 48p il (What if we do nothing?) lib bdg $31
Grades: 7 8 9 10 **363.45**
1. Drug abuse 2. Drug traffic
ISBN 978-1-4339-1981-7 lib bdg; 1-4339-1981-8 lib bdg
LC 2008-52495
This "explains how drugs are grown, created, and distributed, and the problems individuals face when they become addicted. Meaningful illustrations include color photos and text-enhancing charts. . . . [This title is] well written and useful for reports." SLJ
Includes glossary and bibliographical references

Sherman, Jill
Drug trafficking. ABDO Pub. Co. 2010 112p il (Essential issues) lib bdg $22.95
Grades: 7 8 9 10 **363.45**
1. Drug abuse 2. Drug traffic
ISBN 978-1-60453-953-0; 1-60453-953-4
LC 2009-29935
This is "well-written, providing examples that put a human face to each problem. Quotes and facts are clearly attributed, and their sources are noted in the extensive back matter. . . . [This] will be of great assistance to students writing reports." SLJ
Includes glossary and bibliographical references

363.46 Abortion

★ **Abortion;** Noel Merino, book editor. Greenhaven Press 2014 188 p illustrations (Opposing viewpoints)
Grades: 8 9 10 11 12 **363.46**
1. Abortion
ISBN 9780737769401; 9780737769395
Provides opposing viewpoints on the topic of abortion.

363.5 Housing

Rubel, David
If I had a hammer; building homes and hope with Habitat for Humanity. with a foreword by Jimmy Carter. Candlewick Press 2009 148p il $19.99
Grades: 6 7 8 9 10 **363.5**
1. Housing 2. Social action 3. Habitat for Humanity International Inc.
ISBN 978-0-7636-4701-8; 0-7636-4701-2
LC 2009025691
"Technology and faith are the subjects in this hands-on account of Habitat for Humanity, the organization that helps create safe, decent housing for those in need in the U.S. and across the globe. . . . The book's open design, with clear type on thick, quality paper, includes many color photos. . . . The text's details about the essentials of providing shelter, fresh water, electricity, and effective sewage systems for all combine into a powerful message that will inspire many readers." Booklist

363.6 Public utilities and related services

Brown, Cynthia Light
Discover National Monuments, National Parks; natural wonders. illustrated by Blair Shedd. Nomad Press 2009 106p il (Discover your world) pa $19.95
Grades: 5 6 7 8 **363.6**
1. National parks and reserves
ISBN 978-1-9346702-8-6 pa; 1-9346702-8-6 pa
"With an inviting, browsable design and a chatty style, this large-sized volume . . . covers 15 national monuments and parks in the U.S. that celebrate and protect natural phenomena . . . The science will excite readers, with detailed explanations of tectonic plates, radiometric dating, and dendrochronology." Booklist

Burgan, Michael
Not a drop to drink; water for a thirsty world. Peter H. Gleick, consultant. National Geographic 2008 64p il map (National Geographic investigates) $17.95
Grades: 4 5 6 7 **363.6**
1. Water 2. Water supply
ISBN 978-1-4263-0360-9; 1-4263-0360-2
Explores the important connections between human activity and the water cycle and shows how researchers are working to understand such issues as how climate change affects water supplies and how the oceans can help solve the water crisis.

Workman, James G.
Water. Morgan Reynolds Pub. 2009 111p il (Diminishing resources) lib bdg $28.95
Grades: 8 9 10 11 12 **363.6**
1. Water supply 2. Water conservation
ISBN 978-1-59935-115-5; 1-59935-115-3
LC 2009-28708
This discussion of world water supply and conservation "will draw activists, but even readers who do not think they care that much will find the facts devastating. Quotes from authoritative sources—environmentalists, scientists, and survivors—about both the historic overview and the contemporary crisis accompany full-color double-page photos that show what is happening now. . . . The discussion ranges from the pros and cons of dams to the price of bottled water." Booklist
Includes bibliographical references

363.7 Environmental problems

Albee, Sarah
Poop happened! a history of the world from the bottom up. illustrated by Robert Leighton. Walker 2010 170p il lib bdg $20.89; pa $15.99; paperback $18.99
Grades: 4 5 6 7 **363.7**
1. Feces 2. Toilets 3. Sanitation 4. Refuse and refuse disposal
ISBN 978-0-8027-9825-1 lib bdg; 978-0-8027-2077-1 pa; 9780802720771 paperback
"Albee deposits a heaping history of human sanitation—or rather lack thereof— and its effects. . . . She pumps out a steady stream of comments on the miasmic effects of urbanization, waste disposal, and the roles of (not) bathing in ancient Greece, Rome, medieval Europe, . . . and the 'Reeking Renaissance.' She then digs into the gradual adoption of better practices in the nineteenth century. . . . The cartoon illustrations feature sludgy green highlights." Booklist

Bellamy, Rufus

Waste and pollution. Amicus 2010 44p il map (Sustaining our environment) lib bdg $31.35

Grades: 6 7 8 9 **363.7**

1. Pollution 2. Waste products 3. Industrial waste 4. Refuse and refuse disposal

ISBN 978-1-60753-139-5 lib bdg; 1-60753-139-9 lib bdg

LC 2009-40709

Introduces problems associated with pollution and waste disposal and how we may be able to ease the bad effects on the environment.

"The tone is refreshingly optimistic with its examples of specific steps being taken to reduce harm to the environment. Sidebars highlight case studies and campaigns from around the world and from the individual to the national levels. Clear, informative captions accompany the excellent selection of color photographs, charts and graphs." SLJ

Includes glossary

Berne, Emma Carlson

Global warming and climate change. ReferencePoint Press 2008 112p il (Compact research) $24.95

Grades: 8 9 10 11 12 **363.7**

1. Greenhouse effect 2. Climate -- Environmental aspects

ISBN 978-1-60152-019-7; 1-60152-019-0

LC 2007-8371

This discusses global warming and climate change, its consequences and controversies and possible solutions.

"Useful for reports. . . . [This] presents pertinent questions with appropriate and well-documented quotations from a variety of viewpoints and basic facts and diagrams." SLJ

Includes bibliographical references

Bryan, Nichol

Love Canal; pollution crisis. World Almanac Library 2004 48p il map (Environmental disasters) hardcover o.p. lib bdg $29.27

Grades: 5 6 7 8 **363.7**

1. Pollution 2. Love Canal Chemical Waste Landfill (Niagara Falls, N.Y.)

ISBN 0-8368-5508-6 lib bdg; 0-8368-5515-9 pa

LC 2003-57162

Traces the history and eventual cleanup of the ecological disaster known as Love Canal, which resulted from building a neighborhood over a chemical dumpsite that poisoned the environment and endangered the health of residents.

This is "well-illustrated. . . . [It does] a fine job of placing [the] disaster within a larger context by including detailed background about America's industrial and environmental history; quotes from eyewitnesses, politicians, and journalists; and clear explanations of the changes in policy that [the] disaster instigated." Booklist

Includes glossary and bibliographical references

Byrnes, Patricia

Environmental pioneers. Oliver Press (Minneapolis) 1998 160p il (Profiles) lib bdg $19.95

Grades: 7 8 9 10 **363.7**

1. Authors 2. Governors 3. Cartoonists 4. Naturalists 5. Conservationists 6. Environmentalists 7. Senators 8. Feminists 9. Centenarians 10. College teachers 11. Marine biologists 12. State legislators 13. Writers on nature 14. Writers on science 15. Organization officials

ISBN 1-881508-45-5

LC 97-30233

Profiles people who have been influential in the environmental movement: John Muir, Jay Norwood "Ding" Darling, Rosalie Edge, Aldo Leopold, Olaus and Margaret Murie, Rachel Carson, David Brower, and Gaylord Nelson

"Unlike most authors of books on this topic for a young audience, Byrnes is an experienced environmental writer, and takes an affectionate tone in describing her subjects." SLJ

Includes bibliographical references

Cherry, Lynne

★ **How** we know what we know about our changing climate; scientists and kids explore global warming. by Lynne Cherry and Gary Braasch; with a foreword by David Sobel. Dawn Publications 2008 66p il $18.95; pa $11.95

Grades: 4 5 6 7 **363.7**

1. Greenhouse effect 2. Climate -- Environmental aspects

ISBN 978-1-58469-103-7; 0-1-58469-103-4; 978-1-58469-130-3 pa; 1-58469-130-1 pa

LC 2007-37255

"The can-do emphasis helps to make the topic less depressing, and the intriguing color photographs are thoughtful and upbeat." Booklist

Collard, Sneed

Global warming; a personal guide to causes and solutions. Lifelong Learning 2011 il $18

Grades: 6 7 8 9 **363.7**

1. Greenhouse effect 2. Climate -- Environmental aspects

ISBN 978-0-97853677-0

"After a quick introduction and opening discussion of the basics and impacts of global warming, Collard identifies the causes, challenges, and related issues and examines the complex issue of what needs to be done. He suggests various solutions and gives global examples to support his arguments. His knowledgeable and persuasive tone convinces readers that change is necessary and achievable. . . . The informative text is broken into columns, making the extra-wide-page format easy to read. More than eight pages of references give students many further-research options. . . . An excellent resource for reports and debates." SLJ

David, Laurie

The **down** -to-earth guide to global warming; [by] Laurie David and Cambria Gordon. Orchard Books 2007 112p il map pa $15.99

Grades: 4 5 6 7 **363.7**

1. Greenhouse effect 2. Climate -- Environmental aspects

ISBN 978-0-439-02494-5 pa; 0-439-02494-3 pa

LC 2006-35705

The authors "put forth the basics on global warming, climate change, and how readers can green up the environment. They temper the book's often troubling subject matter with kid-friendly humor, some celebrity shout-outs, and explanations of the scientific underpinnings. An amply illustrated layout, featuring attention-grabbing sidebars, dramatic photos, and diagrams, will sustain reader interest." Booklist

Includes bibliographical references

Davies, Nicola, 1958-

Gaia warriors; urgent; the fight is on! with an afterword by James Lovelock. Candlewick Press 2011 192p il $14.99

Grades: 5 6 7 8 **363.7**

1. Gaia hypothesis 2. Environmental protection 3. Greenhouse effect 4. Climate -- Environmental aspects 5. Climatic changes

ISBN 978-0-7636-4808-4; 0-7636-4808-6

LC 2010-40126

This "offers a dynamic overview of global warming's causes and concerns. Davies . . . devotes half the book to exciting profiles of individuals . . . who are working to slow climate change. . . . They include scientists, rock musicians, food distributors, architects, and youth organizers, and their broad variety reinforces the sense that every creative individual effort matters. Highly browsable layouts combine color photos and quotes printed in varied, eye-catching fonts. . . . [This has a] humorous, conversational tone." Booklist

Includes glossary

Delano, Marfe Ferguson

Earth in the hot seat; bulletins from a warming world. National Geographic 2009 63p il (Preserve our planet) $19.95; lib bdg $28.90

Grades: 5 6 7 8 **363.7**

1. Greenhouse effect 2. Climate -- Environmental aspects

ISBN 978-1-4263-0434-7; 1-4263-0434-X; 978-1-4263-0435-4 lib bdg; 1-4263-0435-8 lib bdg

LC 2008029317

"This book lays out . . . the evidence for global warming and the part that human activity plays in it. Five chapters lay out the signs and evidences of a warming world. . . . Subsequent chapters of the book are devoted to what humankind can expect in a warming world and steps that must be taken to avert catastrophe for humans and the planet. . . . The illustrative photos are fully up to National Geographic high standards. This [is a] fine book, reasonably priced and carefully researched." Voice Youth Advocates

Includes bibliographical references

Dorion, Christiane

Pollution. Gareth Stevens Pub. 2010 48p il (What if we do nothing?) lib bdg $31

Grades: 7 8 9 10 **363.7**

1. Pollution 2. Environmental protection

ISBN 978-1-4339-1984-8 lib bdg; 1-4339-1984-2 lib bdg

LC 2008-52494

This "title covers the main sources of air, water, and ground pollution and offers some suggestions for reducing it. . . . Meaningful illustrations include color photos and text-enhancing charts. . . . [This title is] well written and useful for reports." SLJ

Includes glossary and bibliographical references

The **environment;** Lynn M. Zott, book editor. Greenhaven Press 2014 224 p illustrations (Opposing viewpoints)

Grades: 8 9 10 11 12 **363.7**

1. Environmental policy 2. Environmental quality 3. Environmental protection 4. Environmental degradation

ISBN 9780737766547; 9780737766554

This collection of essays offers varying viewpoints on environmental pollution and protection.

Farrell, Courtney

The **Gulf** of Mexico oil spill. ABDO Pub. 2011 112p il (Essential events) lib bdg $23.95

Grades: 7 8 9 10 11 12 **363.7**

1. BP Deepwater Horizon Explosion & Oil Spill, 2010 2. Gulf of Mexico oil spill, 2010

ISBN 978-1-61714-765-4; 1-61714-765-6

LC 2010044976

This describes the political, social, and technical issues concerning the 2010 oil spill in the Gulf of Mexico.

Includes glossary and bibliographical references

Fleischman, Paul

★ **Eyes** wide open; what's behind the environmental headlines. Paul Fleischman. Candlewick Press 2014 208 p. illustrations hbk $17.99; pbk $9.99

Grades: 8 9 10 11 12 **363.7**

1. Environmental sciences 2. Environmental degradation 3. Environmental quality 4. Environmental protection

ISBN 0763671029; 0763675458 ; 9780763671020; 9780763675455

LC 2013953458

This book by Paul Fleischman describes how "we're living in an Ah-Ha moment. Take 250 years of human ingenuity. Add abundant fossil fuels. The result: a population and lifestyle never before seen. The downsides weren't visible for centuries, but now they are. Suddenly everything needs rethinking--suburbs, cars, fast food, cheap prices. It's a changed world. This book explains it." (Publisher's note)

"With simple, matter-of-fact language, an attractive layout and an abundance of references, this compact guide to addressing climate change is a must-read for millennials and for all who seek solutions to global warming. . . . Readers are offered advice on how to analyze and interpret what they hear in person and discover through the media." Kirkus

Includes bibliographical references, filmography and index

Fridell, Ron

Protecting Earth's water supply; by Ron Fridell. Lerner Publications Co. 2009 72p il (Saving our living Earth) lib bdg $30.60

Grades: 5 6 7 8 **363.7**

1. Water pollution 2. Water conservation

ISBN 9781580138550; 978-0-8225-7557-3 lib bdg; 0-8225-7557-4 lib bdg

LC 2007-35924

"Provides a thorough, interesting discussion of multiple aspects of [water supply protection], including historical origins, the current situation, and potential solutions. . . . Photos from around the world accompany discussions. . . . [This is a] solid choice to replace outdated books." SLJ

Includes glossary and bibliographical references

Geiger, Beth

Clean water. Roaring Brook Press 2009 40p il (Sally Ride science) pa $7.99

Grades: 5 6 7 8 **363.7**

1. Water supply 2. Water pollution

ISBN 978-1-59643-577-3 pa; 1-59643-577-1 pa

This is a "well-written, engaging book. . . . The [book']s best feature is the conversational tone that simply and clearly conveys important, and sometimes complicated, scientific concepts. Illustrations and layout are well done, and include colorful photographs and charts. Excellent." SLJ

Gore, Al

★ An **inconvenient** truth; the crisis of global warming. adapted for young readers by Jane O'Connor. rev ed.; Viking 2007 191p il map $23; pa $16

Grades: 5 6 7 8 **363.7**

1. Greenhouse effect 2. Climate -- Environmental aspects

ISBN 978-0-670-06271-3; 978-0-670-06272-0 pa

Adapted from the title for adults published 2006 by Rodale Press

This explains what global warming is, what causes it, and explains how to take action to stop this crisis.

This is illustrated with "easy-to-grasp graphics and revealing before-and-after photos. . . . O'Connor rephrases Gore's arguments in briefer, simpler language without compromising their flow." SLJ

Our choice; how we can solve the climate crisis. [text adapted by Richie Chevat] Young readers ed.; Puffin Books 2009 207p il map $24.99; pa $16.99

Grades: 6 7 8 9 10 **363.7**

1. Human ecology 2. Environmental policy 3. Environmental protection 4. Greenhouse effect

ISBN 978-0-670-01248-0; 0-670-01248-3; 978-0-14-240981-7 pa; 0-14-240981-2 pa

LC 2010-455157

"This colorful, well-designed volume presents the climate crisis in an easy-to-understand format. Covering many aspects of this complex problem, it addresses the effects of pollution on the environment, the search for alternative energy sources, and offers suggestions for conserving power and reducing the impact of human habitation on the planet. . . . Although the urgency of the current global situation is stressed, the chapters are also laced with hope. Suggestions for change offer positive steps that anyone can take to reduce his carbon footprint, and extend a call to unite globally to save the planet for future generations." Voice Youth Advocates

Gunderson, Jessica

Global warming. Creative Education 2011 48p il (Earth issues) lib bdg $23.95

Grades: 6 7 8 9 10 **363.7**

1. Climate 2. Greenhouse effect

ISBN 978-1-58341-982-3; 1-58341-982-9

"An examination of the causes and potential effects of increasing global temperatures, exploring how humans and natural phenomena are involved, as well as how people can contribute to a healthier planet." Publisher's note

Includes glossary and bibliographical references

Henningfeld, Diane Andrews

Health and disease; Michael E. Mann, consulting editor. Greenhaven Press 2011 136p il map (Confronting global warming) lib bdg $37.10

Grades: 7 8 9 10 11 **363.7**

1. Weather 2. Environmentally induced diseases 3. Greenhouse effect

ISBN 978-0-7377-4858-1; 0-7377-4858-3

LC 2010014227

"Presented in a scholarly design that will appeal to older readers. . . . The illustrations and pictures support the text, and the graphics and sidebars are well placed." Libr Media Connect

Includes glossary and bibliographical references

Hirschmann, Kris

Pollution. Kidhaven Press 2004 48p il (Our environment) lib bdg $23.70

Grades: 5 6 7 8 **363.7**

1. Pollution

ISBN 0-7377-1563-4

This briefly describes the sources and effects of air and water pollution and refuse disposal and suggests possible solutions

Includes glossary and bibliographical references

Hodge, Susie

Global warming. New Forest Press 2010 64p il map (Cutting-edge science) lib bdg $34.25

Grades: 7 8 9 10 **363.7**

1. Greenhouse effect 2. Climate -- Environmental aspects

ISBN 978-1-84898-320-5; 1-84898-320-4

This book covers "the topical science [issue] of climate change. . . . [It] includes contemporary scientific findings, the more stable science underlying the [issue], and the social [context]. The color photographs throughout are mainly stock images. Sidebars profile scientists in action or delve deeper into the research methods and studies producting this information." Horn Book Guide

Includes bibliographical references

Jankeliowitch, Anne

Kids who are changing the world; photographs by Yann Arthus-Bertrand ; text by Anne Jankéliowitch. Sourcebooks Jabberwocky 2014 144 p. illustrations (tp : alk. paper) $14.99

Grades: 4 5 6 7 **363.7**

1. Child environmentalists 2. Environmental protection -- Fiction 3. Nature conservation -- Citizen participation 4. Environmental protection -- Citizen participation

ISBN 9781402295324; 9781492608462; 1402295324

LC 2014011237

This book, by by Anne Jankéliowitch, photographs by Yann Arthus-Bertrand, offers "inspiring stories of 45 young heroes who have made an impact on our planet. . . . With skills ranging from singing, drawing, and painting to fund-raising, public demonstrations, and events, they have fought climate change and pollution, and worked to protect animals and their natural habitats." (Publisher's note)

"Each story is styled as an interview with direct quotes from the kids involved. Photographs are dynamic and stunning, and background information and statistics on environmental issues are included in the margins." - Booklist

Includes bibliographical references and index

Kallen, Stuart A.

The **environmental** movement; Stuart A. Kallen. ReferencePoint Press, Inc. 2019 80 p. (hardback) $29.95

Grades: 7 8 9 10 11 12 **363.7**

1. Environmental policy -- United States 2. Environmental movement -- United States 3. Environmental protection -- United States 4. Environmentalism -- United States -- History 5. Environmental policy -- United States -- History 6. Environmental protection -- United States -- History

ISBN 9781682824238

LC 2017058278

"When Rachel Carson described the dangers of DDT in the late 1950s she launched a movement that continues to influence society. The Environmental Movement provides a fascinating eco-tour from Carson through Earth Day, the environmental decade of the 1970s, and the challenges facing a new generation of twenty-first century environmentalists. This book, [by Stuart A. Kallen,] examines how and why social change occurs and the lasting influence of the environmental movement." (Publisher's note)

"Environmental Movement begins with the Cuyahoga River catching fire in 1969, due to waste, and extends into twenty-first-century concerns, such as climate change. The images throughout are well chosen, and visually accented time lines helpfully open each volume." (Booklist)

Includes bibliographical references and index

Macgillivray, Alex

Understanding Rachel Carson's Silent Spring. Rosen Pub. 2011 128p il (Words that changed the world) lib bdg $31.95
Grades: 7 8 9 10 **363.7**

1. Authors 2. Insect pests 3. Conservationists 4. Pesticides and wildlife 5. College teachers 6. Marine biologists 7. Writers on nature 8. Writers on science 9. Pesticides -- Environmental aspects
ISBN 978-1-4488-1670-5; 1-4488-1670-X
LC 2010-9260

"This focused title examines Rachel Carson's Silent Spring, zeroing in on the content and enduring impact of the watershed 1962 work. . . . The text begins with a brief introduction to Carson and her times before moving into an analysis of the text and its indictment of pesticide use, . . . the immediate postpublication response, and its hugely influential legacy today. . . . A useful supplement to environmental-science units, this will easily support student research." Booklist

Includes glossary and bibliographical references

Marcovitz, Hal

How serious a threat is climate change? ReferencePoint Press 2011 96p il (In controversy) lib bdg $26.95
Grades: 7 8 9 10 **363.7**

1. Environmental protection 2. Greenhouse effect
ISBN 978-1-60152-142-2; 1-60152-142-1
LC 2010033916

Discusses the scientific evidence for climate change, what countries around the world are doing to combat it, and why some people are skeptical.

"The author presents substantial amounts of information in a readable, student-friendly manner. Useful for reports." SLJ

Includes bibliographical references

Is offshore oil drilling worth the risks? ReferencePoint Press 2011 96p il (In controversy) lib bdg $26.95
Grades: 7 8 9 10 **363.7**

1. Oil spills 2. Offshore oil well drilling
ISBN 978-1-60152-143-9; 1-60152-143-X
LC 2010037854

Discusses the issues surrounding offshore oil drilling.

"The author presents substantial amounts of information in a readable, student-friendly manner. Useful for reports." SLJ

Includes bibliographical references

McCutcheon, Chuck

What are global warming and climate change? answers for young readers. University of New Mexico Press 2010 103p il map (Worlds of wonder) $24.95
Grades: 6 7 8 9 10 **363.7**

1. Greenhouse effect 2. Climate -- Environmental aspects
ISBN 978-0-8263-4745-9; 0-8263-4745-2

The author tackles "environmental issues with depth and rigor, attuned to both current events and the concerns of today's teens. . . . The excellent [text is] enhanced by color photographs and diagrams that further explain scientific ideas." Horn Book Guide

Mileham, Rebecca

Global pollution. New Forest Press 2010 64p il map (Cutting-edge science) lib bdg $34.25
Grades: 7 8 9 10 **363.7**

1. Pollution
ISBN 978-1-84898-322-9; 1-84898-322-0

This book covers "the topical science [issue] of . . . pollution. . . . [It] includes contemporary scientific findings, the more stable science underlying the [issue], and the social [context]. The color photographs throughout are mainly stock images. Sidebars profile scientists in action or delve deeper into the research methods and studies producing this information." Horn Book Guide

Inlcudes bibliographical references

Morris, Neil

★ **Global** warming. World Almanac Library 2007 48p il (What if we do nothing?) lib bdg $22.95; pa $11.95
Grades: 5 6 7 8 **363.7**

1. Greenhouse effect 2. Climate -- Environmental aspects
ISBN 978-0-8368-7755-7 lib bdg; 0-8368-7755-1 lib bdg; 978-0-8368-155-4 pa; 0-8368-8155-9 pa
LC 2006-30444

This "boasts an attractive format, with large pages that allow room for pictures, excellent charts and graphs, as well as a thoughtful, clear discussion of the topic." Booklist

Includes bibliographical references

Oil spill; disaster. Scholastic Press 2010 31p il pa $5.99
Grades: 4 5 6 7 8 **363.7**

1. Oil spills 2. BP Deepwater Horizon Explosion & Oil Spill, 2010 3. Gulf of Mexico oil spill, 2010
ISBN 978-0-545-31776-4; 0-545-31776-2

Explores the immediate and future consequences of the Gulf of Mexico oil spill in April 2010, when the offshore oil rig Deepwater Horizon exploded, causing major environmental and economical damage along the Gulf coast of the United States.

"While text and color photographs convey the extent of the devastation to the Gulf, the book also highlights some innovative attempts to clean up oil spills and profiles two middle school students, who researched cleaning up oil in their own neighborhood." Publ Wkly

Oxlade, Chris

Climate change. Smart Apple Media 2010 44p il map (Science in the news) lib bdg $34.25
Grades: 6 7 8 9 **363.7**

1. Greenhouse effect
ISBN 978-1-59920-319-5 lib bdg; 1-59920-319-7 lib bdg
LC 2008-41437

The narrative "move[s] smoothly, occasionally pausing for the definition of a term. [The title] boast[s] plenty of attractive photos, and a clean layout allows the information to be easily consumed. . . . Provides the information that younger teens need." SLJ

Includes glossary

Parker, Steve

Population. QEB Pub. 2010 32p il (QEB changes in . . .) lib bdg $28.50
Grades: 3 4 5 6 **363.7**

1. Human ecology 2. Human influence on nature
ISBN 978-1-59566-774-8 lib bdg; 1-59566-774-1 lib bdg
LC 2008-56070

"The information is presented in brief paragraphs and sidebars. Suggestions for kids to help improve the planet are sprinkled throughout. . . . Students will enjoy this appealing layout and the information can spark further research on the topic[s]. . . . Either digitally or on paper, students could make fantastic presentations using a similar design." Libr Media Connect

Includes glossary

Pollution: opposing viewpoints; Louise I. Gerdes, book editor. Greenhaven Press 2011 262p il (Opposing viewpoints series) lib bdg $39.70; pa $26.50
Grades: 8 9 10 11 12 **363.7**
1. Pollution
ISBN 978-0-7377-5231-1 lib bdg; 0-7377-5231-9 lib bdg; 978-0-7377-5232-8 pa; 978-0-7377-5232-7 pa
LC 2010-51681

"The authors in this . . . anthology debate several controversial questions, including whether various forms of pollution continue to be a serious problem, whether pollution poses a public health threat, and what policies and programs will best reduce pollution." Publisher's note

Includes bibliographical references

Robinson, Matthew

America debates global warming; crisis or myth? Rosen Central 2008 64p il (America debates) lib bdg $29.25
Grades: 5 6 7 8 9 10 11 12 **363.7**
1. Greenhouse effect 2. Climate -- Environmental aspects
ISBN 978-1-4042-1925-0 lib bdg; 1-4042-1925-0 lib bdg
LC 2007-10931

This "is especially effective in laying out the information in a simple, logical format." SLJ

Includes glossary and bibliographical references

Silverstein, Alvin

Global warming; by Alvin Silverstein, Virginia Silverstein, Laura Silverstein Nunn. rev. ed.; Twenty-First Century Books 2009 112p il (Science concepts, second series) $31.93
Grades: 5 6 7 8 **363.7**
1. Greenhouse effect 2. Climate -- Environmental aspects
ISBN 978-0-7613-3935-9; 0-7613-3935-3
First published 2003

The authors "explain how human activity and the greenhouse effect have changed the climate on Earth and the effect this has on people and animals. The authors also explore ways that everyone can 'go green' to help fight global warming." (Publisher's note)

Includes bibliographical references

363.72 Sanitation

Fyvie, Erica

Trash revolution; breaking the waste cycle. by Erica Fyvie ; illustrated by Bill Slavin. Kids Can Press 2018 64 p. $18.99
Grades: 4 5 6 7 8 **363.72**
1. Recycling 2. Environmental protection 3. Refuse and refuse disposal
ISBN 1771380780; 9781771380782

In this book, by Erica Fyvie, illustrated by Bill Slavin, "all the stuff that surrounds us has a life cycle: materials are harvested, the stuff is made and distributed, it's consumed and then it gets trashed or recycled. . . . [T]his book explores those stages in detail, including lots of ways to reduce, reuse or recycle waste along the way. Children will gain new insight into the routine decisions they make about their own consuming and trashing or recycling practices." (Publisher's note)

Goldstein, Margaret J.

Garbage in space; a space discovery guide. Margaret J. Goldstein. Lerner Publications 2017 48 p. color illustrations (Space discovery guides) (lb : alk. paper) $31.99
Grades: 5 6 7 8 **363.72**
1. Space debris 2. Space pollution
ISBN 9781512425901
LC 2016018175

"Did you know that companies and governments send more than one hundred satellites into space every year? And that most of those satellites continue to orbit Earth—even after they have stopped working? More than 500,000 old satellites, pieces of metal, and other bits of junk currently pollute Earth's orbit. And that number is growing. Astronomers, engineers, and politicians all agree that the future of space exploration is in danger if this debris isn't taken care of." (Publisher's note)

"A thoroughly researched and authoritative addition to science collections." School Library Journal.

Includes bibliographical references and index

Kallen, Stuart A.

Trashing the planet; examining our global garbage glut. Stuart A. Kallen. Twenty-First Century Books 2017 104 p. color illustrations (lb : alk. paper) $37.32
Grades: 7 8 9 10 11 12 **363.72**
1. Marine pollution 2. Environmental policy 3. Refuse and refuse disposal
ISBN 9781512467970; 9781512413144
LC 2016033032

Green Earth Book Award (2018)

In this book, by Stuart A. Kallen, "humans create around 2.6 trillion pounds of waste every year. . . . What can we do to keep garbage from swallowing up Earth? Reducing, reusing, recycling, and upcycling are some of the answers. Learn more about the work of the US Environmental Protection Agency, the Ocean Cleanup Array, the zero waste movement, and the many other government, business, research, and youth efforts working to solve . . . [the] garbage crisis." (Publisher's note)

"Soundly researched and carefully sourced, the text speaks to the complexity of the issue, while offering suggestions for action in readers' own backyards." Booklist

Includes bibliographical references (99-102) and index.

363.728 Wastes

Eamer, Claire

What a waste! where does garbage go? Claire Eamer ; illustrated by Bambi Edlund. Annick Press 2017 89 p. color illustrations $12.95; $22.95
Grades: 4 5 6 7 **363.728**
1. Recycling (Waste, etc.) 2. Refuse and refuse disposal
ISBN 9781554519187; 1554519187; 1554519195; 9781554519194

This book, by Claire Eamer, illustrated by Bambi Edlund, "answers the question: when we throw something away, where is 'away'? Ever since cave people cracked open seafood shells for dinner, humans have produced garbage, and we've had to figure out what to do with it. . . . [It] explores the history of garbage from earliest times to today, covering subjects including dumps, human waste, water pollution, 'problem' garbage, and modern 'throwaway' culture." (Publisher's note)

"This selection will be useful for environmentally minded upper elementary and middle school readers as well as those needing a resource for science and classroom projects." School Library Journal

Includes bibliographical references (pages 79-83) and index.

363.73 Pollution

Solway, Andrew

Transportation; by Andrew Solway. Heinemann Library 2013 64 p. (The impact of environmentalism) (library) $35.00; (paperback) $9.99

Grades: 6 7 8 **363.73**

1. Environmental movement 2. Transportation -- Environmental aspects 3. Pollution 4. Environmentalism

ISBN 1432965204; 9781432965204; 9781432965266

LC 2012001043

This book Andrew Solway is part of the "Impact of Environmentalism" series. It "discusses global warming, climate change, and energy alternatives such as biofuels and renewable energies." It "also discusses the history of human activities and its environmental impact, and efforts by humankind to protect the environment and create sustainable smaller environments. Sidebars and full-color photos appear throughout." (School Library Journal)

Includes bibliographical references and index.

363.738 Pollutants

Bow, James

Earth's climate change; carbon dioxide overload. James Bow. Crabtree Publishing Company 2016 32 p. illustrations paperback $8.95; library $27.60

Grades: 5 6 7 8 **363.738**

1. Climate change 2. Global warming 3. Carbon dioxide

ISBN 9780778720010; 9780778719786

LC 2015020964

Humans "live in an energy-rich age, in which we can turn on a light with the flick of a switch or drive anywhere by turning a key. But, our vehicles, factories, and power stations, which create the electricity needed to light and heat our buildings, pump carbon dioxide into Earth's atmosphere. Carbon dioxide overload from these human activities is making our planet hotter and hotter--and is causing the Earth's climate to change." (Publisher's note)

Includes bibliographical references and index

Dalton, Anna

Examining oil spills; by Anna Dalton. Clara House Books 2015 48 p. (Examining disasters)

Grades: 4 5 6 7 8 **363.738**

1. Oil spills -- Cleanup 2. Oil spills -- Prevention 3. Oil spills -- Environmental aspects 4. Petroleum industry and trade -- Safety measures

ISBN 9781934545812; 9781934545652

LC 2014044474

"Did you know that more than 100 countries produce crude oil? If workers are not careful, transporting this oil can cause spills. Oil spills can have long-lasting effects, such as the 2013 Lac-Mégantic derailment in Quebec. More than 1.6 million gallons (6 million L) of crude oil spilled into the land and water there, where it will remain for years. In this book, you'll examine oil spills and explore what they are, how they happen, and how to prevent them in the future" (Back cover)

Includes bibliographical references (page 47) and index

Global warming; Mary E. Williams, book editor. Greenhaven Press 2006 96 p. ill. (chiefly col.) (Writing the critical essay) (library) $26.20

Grades: 8 9 10 11 12 **363.738**

1. Essays 2. Authorship 3. Greenhouse effect

ISBN 0737732105; 9780737732108

LC 2005055066

"Section one presents five opposing excerpts from recent periodicals, each one beginning with a short summary and questions for readers to consider and including relevant illustrations, political cartoons, and color photographs. Section two offers information on essay writing and includes annotated examples. . . . This volume provides a useful way for English composition, science, and social science teachers to integrate library research into their classrooms." SLJ

Includes bibliographical references (p. 92-93) and index.

Heos, Bridget

It's getting hot in here; the past, the present, and the future of global warming. Bridget Heos. HMH Books for Young Readers 2016 224 p. color illustrations (hardback) $17.99

Grades: 7 8 9 10 **363.738**

1. Climate change 2. Global warming

ISBN 9780544303478

LC 2014035584

This book, by Bridget Heos, "tackles the past, present, and future of global warming, examining the effects it's having across the world, the politics behind denial, and the ways in which we can all work to lessen the harsh effects of our warming world. Perfect for young environmentalists looking to learn about the ways in which we can take action against global warming." (Publisher's note)

Newman, Patricia

Plastic, ahoy! investigating the great Pacific garbage patch. Patricia Newman ; photographs by Annie Crawley. Millbrook Press 2014 48 p. (lib. bdg. : alk. paper) $30.60

Grades: 5 6 7 8 9 10 **363.738**

1. Plastics 2. Marine pollution 3. Refuse and refuse disposal 4. Waste disposal in the ocean 5. Marine pollution -- Pacific Ocean 6. Marine pollution 7. Plastic scrap -- Environmental aspects 8. Plastic marine debris -- Environmental aspects

ISBN 1467712833; 9781467712835

LC 2013017773

This book, by Patricia Newman, focuses on "what happens when [plastic] ends up where it doesn't belong--like in the Pacific Ocean? How does it affect ocean life? Is it dangerous? And exactly how much is out there? A team of researchers went on a scientific expedition to find out. They explored the Great Pacific Garbage Patch, where millions of pieces of plastic have collected. The plastic has drifted there from rivers, beaches, and ocean traffic all over the world." (Publisher's note)

"Here readers travel to the Pacific Garbage Patch with three graduate-student scientists as they try to determine the effect of plastics on the sea. There's solid explanation of their hypotheses and research, and emphasis on the researchers' experiences lends a personal feel. Questions of how plastic may harm the oceans, its inhabitants, and even humans encourage further inquiry." Horn Book

Sneideman, Joshua

Climate Change; Discover How It Impacts Spaceship Earth. by Joshua Sneideman and Erin Twamley ; illustrated by Mike Crosier. Nomad Press 2015 128 p. color illustrations, color map $22.95

Grades: 4 5 6 7 **363.738**

1. Climate change 2. Earth sciences 3. Science projects

ISBN 1619302691; 9781619302693

In this book on climate change, by Joshua Sneideman and Erin Twamley, illustrated by Mike Crosier, "young readers examine real studies concerning planetary science, Arctic ice bubbles, and migratory patterns. Kids explore the history of human impact from the Industrial Revolution to our modern-day technology, as well as the innovations underway around the world to address global climate change." (Publisher's note)

"This installment of the well-known series encourages students to examine the timely subject of climate change. The volume is full of questions, words to know, primary sources, and fun-filled learning activities. The introductory chapter reminds readers of the importance of taking care of the planet. . . . The text and activities work together to remind students that the future is in their hands and they can be a part of the solution." SLJ

363.8 Food supply

Barker, Geoff P.

Hunger; by Geoff Barker. Smart Apple Media 2010 46p il (Voices) lib bdg $34.25

Grades: 7 8 9 10 11 12 **363.8**

1. Famines 2. Food relief

ISBN 978-1-59920-281-5 lib bdg; 1-59920-281-6 lib bdg

LC 2008-50430

This book about hunger "addresses the causes, the possible solutions, and outlooks, both good and bad, of . . . [the] issue. Each brief chapter covers basic questions, answered with a simple definition or explanation, then supported by pertinent quotes and statistics from well-known experts and organizations. Color photographs, sidebars, graphs and charts pull the content together in a busy but cohesive presentation. . . . Students . . . will appreciate the quotes and statistics plus commentary that addresses the . . . [issue] from several angles." Libr Media Connect

Includes glossary

363.9 Population problems

Birth control; Jack Lasky, book editor. Greenhaven Press 2016 203 p illustrations (Opposing viewpoints)

Grades: 7 8 9 10 11 12 **363.9**

1. Birth control

ISBN 9780737775068; 9780737775068

Collects articles on topics related to birth control that represent diverse viewpoints on issues relating to it, including access to birth control, the Affordable Care Act in relation to it, concerns related to it, and its social consequences.

Wittenstein, Vicki Oransky

Reproductive rights; who decides? Vicki Oransky Wittenstein. Twenty-First-Century Books 2014 160 p. color illustrations $38.65

Grades: 8 9 10 11 12 **363.9**

1. Reproduction 2. Birth control 3. Birth control -- History 4. Family planning -- History 5. Reproductive rights -- History

ISBN 9781467741873; 1467741876

LC 2014040830

This book, by Vicki Oransky Wittenstein, examines how "as society changes--and as new reproductive technologies expand the possibilities for controlling and initiating pregnancy--Americans will continue to debate reproductive rights for all. Throughout history, men and women have always found ways to control reproduction. Others turned to methods that are still used in the twenty-first century, such as abstinence, condoms, and abortions." (Publisher's note)

"Well written and impeccably researched, this volume will appeal to budding activists and feminists and to those concerned about human rights." SLJ

Includes bibliographical references and index

364.1 Criminal offenses

Hanel, Rachael

Identity theft. Marshall Cavendish Benchmark 2011 143p il (Controversy!) lib bdg $25.95

Grades: 8 9 10 11 12 **364.1**

1. Identity theft

ISBN 978-0-7614-4901-0; 0-7614-4901-9

"Hanel explores types of identity theft, common scams, and prevention, which is a contentious point. Many argue that governmental proposals to secure data are invading people's privacy and civil liberties. . . . With rapid changes in technology and legislation, [this book is] recommended for all libraries seeking quality and current materials on [this topic]." SLJ

Marcovitz, Hal

Gangs. ABDO Pub. Co. 2010 112p il (Essential issues) lib bdg $22.95

Grades: 7 8 9 10 **364.1**

1. Gangs

ISBN 978-1-60453-954-7; 1-60453-954-2

LC 2009-29862

The text is "well-written, providing examples that put a human face to each problem. . . . [This] will be of great assistance to students writing reports." SLJ

Includes glossary and bibliographical references

Swift, Richard

★ **Gangs**; Richard Swift. Groundwood 2011 144 p. (Groundwork guides)

Grades: 7 8 9 10 11 12 **364.1**

1. Gangs 2. Ethnic groups 3. Urban sociology 4. Crime -- History

ISBN 088899978X pa; 0888999798; 9780888999788 pa; 9780888999795

In this book, "[a] short history, definition, and insight into the romantic idea of gangs as opposed to the actual reality of gang life, provide an overview of the book's focus. The role of poverty, family and home environment, communities and schools is explained. An explanation of the hierarchy that governs their world, code of conduct, gang locations throughout the world, differences in ethnic gangs, and an explanation for institutionalized groups . . . [is provided]. Supplementary information, such as gray pages and sidebars within chapters, provide additional material. A page of unique gang vocabulary and a timeline, complete chapter notes, further reading, viewing, and web lists, and a detailed index complete this . . . book." (Library Media Connection)

"This riveting volume, which is both comprehensive and concise, explores a complex and potentially controversial issue. Swift frames the issue against the gross social inequities that create gangs and discusses the factors that contribute to their existence, such as racism, poverty, drug use and trafficking, lack of jobs, crumbling global economies, etc. . . . Despite its conveniently compact size, the book is packed with information. . . . This interesting and accessible volume is an essential purchase." SLJ

364.15 Offenses against the person

Bascomb, Neal

★ The **Nazi** hunters; How a Team of Spies and Survivors Captured the World's Most Notorious Nazi. Neal Bascomb. Arthur A. Levine Books, an imprint of Scholastic Inc. 2013 256 p. (hardcover : alk. paper) $16.99

Grades: 6 7 8 9 10 **364.15**

1. War crimes 2. War criminals 3. Nazi hunters 4. Nazis -- Biography 5. Secret service -- Israel 6. Holocaust, Jewish (1939-1945) 7. World War, 1939-1945 -- Atrocities 8. War criminals -- Germany -- Biography 9. Fugitives from justice -- Argentina -- Biography

ISBN 0545430992; 9780545430999; 9780545431002; 9780545562393

LC 2012041757

YALSA Award for Excellence in Nonfiction for Young Adults (2014)

In this book, by Neal Bascomb, "Adolf Eichmann was among the Gestapo war criminals who managed to escape from Europe and establish new lives in Argentina. The search for him involved an international group of Nazi hunters who left no stone unturned to determine where and how he had fled, find him and bring him to justice." (Kirkus Reviews)

"This is a splendid example of fascinating storytelling blended with significant historical events." Booklist

Blumenthal, Karen

Bonnie and Clyde; the making of a legend. by Karen Blumenthal. Viking Childrens Books 2018 256 p. illustrations (hardcover) $19.99

Grades: 7 8 9 10 **364.15**

1. Criminals -- United States -- Biography

ISBN 9780147513830; 9780451471222

LC 2017033414

This biography, by Karen Blumenthal, tells the story of the celebrated outlaw couple Bonnie and Clyde. "Blumenthal devoted months to tracing the footsteps of Bonnie and Clyde, unearthing new information and debunking many persistent myths. The result is an impeccably researched, breathtaking nonfiction tale of love, car chases, kidnappings, and murder set against the backdrop of the Great Depression." (Publisher's note)

"That Bonnie and Clyde were young people, close to their families, often kind, and placed in extraordinarily difficult circumstances is not disputed, but neither is the extent of their crimes; in sidebars, Blumenthal profiles each of the people that the Barrow Gang killed. Additional sidebars investigate some of the legends surrounding the duo, and the circumstances that led to their popularity. An extraordinarily successful resource about a painful time in history and a complicated, infamous pair." Booklist

Draper, Allison Stark

The **assassination** of Malcolm X. Rosen Pub. Group 2002 64p il (Library of political assassinations) lib bdg $26.50

Grades: 5 6 7 8 **364.15**

1. Black Muslims 2. Black Muslim leaders 3. Civil rights activists 4. African Americans -- Biography

ISBN 0-8239-3542-6

LC 2001-3323

"Draper confronts the important issues with exceptional candor and clarity, including the ongoing controversy of who ordered the murder." Booklist

Includes glossary and bibliographical references

Marcovitz, Hal

★ **Hate** crimes; Hal Marcovitz. ReferencePoint Press 2018 80 p. (hardback) $29.95

Grades: 8 9 10 11 12 **364.15**

1. Prejudices 2. Hate crimes 3. Offenses against the person

ISBN 9781682824726; 9781682824719

LC 2018021023

This book, by Hal Marcovitz, discusses hate crimes. "Crimes committed against people because of their race, ethnicity, or religion have become common in the United States and other countries in 2016. [T]he FBI said [that] more than six thousand such crimes were committed in America. Hate crimes can range from small acts of vandalism to horrific mass shootings, such as the 2015 murders of nine African Americans attending church services in Charleston, South Carolina." (Publisher's note)

Includes bibliographical references and index

364.151 Genocide

Friedman, Mark

Genocide; Mark Friedman. Heinemann Library 2012 64 p. ill. (some col.), col. maps (Hot topics) (pb) $9.99

Grades: 7 8 9 10 **364.151**

1. Genocide 2. Genocide -- History

ISBN 1432960423; 9781432960346; 9781432960421

LC 2011017831

This book, by Mark Friedman, "explains what genocide is and gives several examples of it. It also explains the reasons why it happened. It takes an in-depth look at the topic and asks difficult questions such as, if genocide is happening, whose responsibility is it to stop it?" (Publisher's note)

Includes bibliographical references (p. 62-63) and index.

364.152 Homicide

Aretha, David

The **murder** of Emmett Till. Morgan Reynolds Pub. 2007 160p il (The civil rights movement) lib bdg $27.95

Grades: 7 8 9 10 11 12 **364.152**

1. Children 2. Lynching 3. Murder victims 4. Mississippi -- Race relations 5. African Americans -- Civil rights

ISBN 978-1-59935-057-8; 1-59935-057-2

LC 2007-26250

"The heinous murder of Emmett Till galvanized the civil rights movement and raised the nation's awareness of the extreme racism in the South. . . . This title . . . details the events surrounding Till's murder, the trial and acquittal of his killers, and the nation's racial climate before and after this milestone in civil rights history." Booklist

Includes bibliographical references

Crowe, Chris

★ **Getting** away with murder: the true story of the Emmett Till case. Phyllis Fogelman Bks. 2003 128p il map $18.99

Grades: 7 8 9 10 **364.152**

1. Racism 2. Children 3. Lynching 4. Trials (Homicide) 5.

Murder victims 6. Mississippi -- Race relations
ISBN 0-8037-2804-2

LC 2002-5736

This is the story of "the black 14-year-old from Chicago who was brutally murdered while visiting relatives in the Mississippi Delta in 1954. . . . The gruesome, racially motivated crime and the court's failure to convict the white murderers was a powerful national catalyst for the civil rights movement. . . . Crowe's powerful, terrifying account does justice to its subject in bold, direct telling, supported by numerous archival photos and quotes from those who remember." Booklist

Includes bibliographical references

Denson, Bryan

The **Unabomber**; Agent Kathy Puckett and the hunt for a serial bomber. Bryan Denson. Roaring Brook Press 2019 xi, 162 p.p (hardcover) $15.99

Grades: 4 5 6 7 **364.152**

1. Serial killers -- Fiction 2. Terrorism -- United States
ISBN 9781250199133; 9781250199140; 9781250199157

LC 2018955824

This book, by Bryan Denson, is "a new true-crime series that follows FBI agents behind the scenes as they work to keep Americans safe. The Unabomber was a lone-wolf terrorist who carried out fourteen bombings that left three people dead and another twenty-three injured. A cunning genius, he dodged his FBI pursuers for nearly two decades . . . Denson presents the story of the FBI's investigation of the Unabomber and the agent who helped bring him to justice." (Publisher's note)

"An enthralling, well-researched introduction to true crime for upper elementary/middle school readers." --School Library Journal 06/19

Includes bibliographical references (pages [143]-149) and index

Faryon, Cynthia J.

Guilty of being weird; the story of Guy Paul Morin. Cynthia J. Faryon. James Lorimer & Co. 2013 144 p. (Lorimer Real Justice) (hardcover) $18.95

Grades: 7 8 9 10 11 12 **364.152**

1. False accusation
ISBN 1459400933; 9781459400931

"At twenty-four, Guy Paul Morin was considered a bit strange. . . . So when the nine-year-old girl next door went missing, the police were convinced that Morin was responsible. . . . This book tells his story, showing how the justice system not only failed to help an innocent young man, but conspired to convict him." (Publisher's note)

"Structured like a data log, each chapter covers a specific date. . . . Teens interested in CSI can turn a critical eye to badly executed procedures and biased criminal investigation." SLJ

Harris, Duchess

Mass shootings in America; Duchess Harris, Jennifer Simms. Abdo Pub. 2019 112 p. (lib. bdg.) $37.07

Grades: 7 8 9 10 **364.152**

ISBN 9781532116780; 9781532159626

LC 2018948306

This book in the Special Reports series, by Duchess Harris and Jennifer Simms, "looks at the history of mass shootings, from the 1966 mass shooting at the University of Texas, Austin, to the 2018 MSD High School shooting. The debates surrounding gun rights are also explored. The book encourages readers to form their own opinions. Features include a glossary, references, websites, source notes, and an index." (Publisher's note)

"Attractively designed with well-chosen stock photos, these excellent books will certainly be useful for reports; but, perhaps more important, they may well be picked up by readers who want to be better informed about current events—and they will be." (Booklist)

Houser, Aimee

Tragedy in Tucson; the Arizona shooting rampage. by Aimee Houser. ABDO Pub. Co. 2012 112 p. col. ill., col. map (hc) $34.22

Grades: 6 7 8 9 10 **364.152**

1. Gun control 2. Schizophrenia 3. Murder -- Arizona -- Tucson 4. Mental health laws -- United States 5. Firearms and crime -- Arizona -- Tucson 6. Firearms -- Social aspects -- United States
ISBN 1617833126; 9781617833120

LC 2011038452

This book "examines . . . the shooting of Representative Gabrielle Giffords and 18 others in Tucson, Arizona." It "explores the man behind the shooting, Jared Loughner, and his history of mental illness, the disease schizophrenia, Giffords's rise in politics, [and] the political climate in America, including the hot button issue of health-care reform, Giffords's fight for her life, and the effects of this event on society. Also discussed are the gun laws in America." (Publisher's note)

"These titles are excellent introductions to these important topics, particularly for developing an analytical framework for debate." SLJ

Includes bibliographical references (p. 104-109, 112) and index

Marsico, Katie

The **Columbine** High School massacre; murder in the classroom. Marshall Cavendish Benchmark 2010 128p il (Perspectives on) lib bdg $39.93

Grades: 7 8 9 10 **364.152**

1. School shootings 2. Columbine High School (Littleton, Colo.)
ISBN 978-0-7614-4985-0; 0-7614-4985-X

LC 2009020590

This "is a well-written examination of this violent school shooting and the controversies it inspired. The roles of society and the controversial effect s of violent video games are discussed, as well as the evolution of school security. . . . The title provides a complete and concise examination of the issue at hand, from its occurrence to the impact on society. It also contains a timeline of events and well-chosen illustrations. This is a recommended addition to any school or public library." Voice Youth Advocates

Includes bibliographical references

Uschan, Michael V., 1948-

Lynching and murder in the deep South; [by] Michael V. Uschan. Lucent Books 2007 104p il map (Lucent library of Black history) $32.45

Grades: 8 9 10 11 12 **364.152**

1. Lynching 2. African Americans -- Civil rights 3. Southern States -- Race relations
ISBN 1-59018-845-4

LC 2005037807

"Uschan deals honestly with this important historical topic . . . that occurred from the end of Reconstruction through the 1920s, '30s, and into the '40s and '50s. Writing in clear and telling prose, the author chronicles the horrific history of this practice in the South, why it was so pervasive, and how it was eventually brought to an end. This is a book that fills a gap. . . . Black-and-white photos and reproductions appear throughout." SLJ

Includes bibliographical references

364.16 Offenses against property

Guillain, Charlotte

Great art thefts; by Charlotte Guillain. Capstone Raintree 2013 48 p. col. ill. (Treasure hunters) (library) $29.33; (paperback) $8.99

Grades: 5 6 7 8 **364.16**

1. Theft -- History 2. Art thefts

ISBN 1410949583; 9781410949516; 9781410949585

LC 2012012759

This book by Charlotte Guillain, part of the Treasure Hunters series, looks at art thefts. "After . . . introductions that lay foundations so children will understand why thieves might want to steal art or treasure hunters take such risks, each volume contains chapters that follow the discovery and/or quests for objects such as 'Roman Riches' or locations such as the legendary city of Troy." (School Library Journal)

Includes bibliographical references and index.

Hynson, Colin

Cyber crime; by Colin Hynson. Smart Apple Media 2012 44 p. col. ill. (Inside crime) (library) $35.65

Grades: 7 8 9 10 **364.16**

1. Computer crimes 2. Computer crimes -- Prevention

ISBN 1599203960; 9781599203966

LC 2010043232

This book, part of the Crime and Detection Series, focuses on cyber crime. "These titles examine the diversity of crimes committed around the world. Each . . . illustrated, oversized volume has a photograph or reproduction on every spread, many times taking up a full page." Andrew Grant-Adamson "looks at hackers, viruses, and computer crimes that have come to light in the age of the Internet." (School Library Journal)

Includes bibliographical references (p. 43) and index

Juettner, Bonnie

Blackmail and bribery; by Bonnie Juettner. Lucent Books 2009 104 p. col. ill. (Crime scene investigations) (hardcover) $35.45

Grades: 7 8 9 10 **364.16**

1. Bribery 2. Forensic sciences 3. Extortion 4. White collar crimes

ISBN 1420500686; 9781420500684

LC 2008025864

This book, part of the Crime Scene Investigations series, focuses on blackmail and bribery. This series "unveils the tools and techniques used by today's (and yesterday's) professionals. . . . Each title focuses on a particular type of crime, and includes features like crime stats, facts versus fiction sections, full-color photos and more." (Publisher's note)

Includes bibliographical references (p. 92-95) and index.

364.3 Offenders

Scandiffio, Laura

Outlaws, spies, and gangsters; chasing notorious criminals. Firefly Books Ltd 2014 146 p. col. ill., col. portraits $24.95; paperback $14.95

Grades: 4 5 6 7 **364.3**

1. Manhunts 2. Criminals 3. Fugitives from justice

ISBN 1554516218; 9781554516216; 9781554516209

"In 'Outlaws, Spies, and Gangsters,' Laura Scandiffio chronicles eight of history's most famous manhunts, from searches for drug dealers to dictators, hackers to henchmen. Discover the danger and intrigue behind these riveting stories of daring and perseverance." (Publisher's note)

Stemple, Heidi E. Y.

Bad girls; sirens, Jezebels, murderesses, thieves, and other female villains. Jane Yolen and Heidi E. Y. Stemple ; illustrated by Rebecca Guay. Charlesbridge 2012 176 p. (reinforced for library use) $18.95

Grades: 6 7 8 9 10 11 12 **364.3**

1. Women criminals 2. Criminals -- Biography 3. Femmes fatales -- Biography 4. Women murderers -- Biography 5. Female offenders -- Biography

ISBN 1580891853; 9781580891851

LC 2012000783

This book, by Jane Yolen and Heidi E. Stemple, illustrated by Rebecca Guay, examines the history of "twenty-six . . . notorious women. Each bad girl has a rotten reputation, but there are two sides to every tale. Decide whether Tituba was really a conspiring witch or just a humble housemaid. Analyze the evidence stacked for and against Lizzie Borden. And what made the brazen Cleopatra so dishonorable . . . or honorable?" (Publisher's note)

Includes bibliographical references and index

364.41 Identification of potential offenders

Doeden, Matt

Whistle -blowers; exposing crime and corruption. Matt Doeden. Twenty-First Century Books 2015 96 p. illustrations (chiefly color) (lib. bdg.) $33.32

Grades: 5 6 7 8 9 **364.41**

1. Business ethics 2. Whistle blowing 3. Political corruption 4. Ethics 5. Crime prevention 6. Corruption -- Prevention

ISBN 1467742090; 9781467742092; 9781467763127

LC 2014011850

Author Matt Doeden "looks at the most famous cases of whistleblowing in the recent past. Doeden starts off by examining what kinds of protections have been put in place over time to help protect whistleblowers from potential threats. Each chapter includes a different whistle-blower, such as W. Mark Felt, aka Deep Throat; Jeffrey Wigand, who exposed the risks of tobacco and nicotine; . . . and Edward Snowden, who exposed the extensive surveillance by the National Security Agency." (School Library Journal)

"In addition to telling what happened in each case, Doeden reflects on matters such as the complex motivations of individual whistle-blowers and the degrees of risk that they were willing to take. This thought-provoking volume will fill a gap in many library collections." Booklist

Includes bibliographical references and index

364.6 Penology

Gerber, Larry

Torture. Rosen Pub. 2011 64p il (Headlines!) lib bdg $29.95

Grades: 7 8 9 10 **364.6**

1. Torture

ISBN 978-1-4488-1291-2; 1-4488-1291-7

LC 2010018898

This book "looks at the history and modern practice of torture, ending with discussion of Abu Ghraib and Guantanamo. Good organization, clear writing, captioned photos, and sidebars deliver the information cleanly." Horn Book Guide

Includes glossary and bibliographical references

Small, Cathleen

Deportation; Cathleen Small. Greenhaven Press 2018 64 p. $33.45

Grades: 6 7 8 **364.6**

1. Deportation 2. Immigration law 3. Unauthorized immigrants

ISBN 1534562257; 9781534562257

In this book in the Crossing the Border series, by Cathleen Small, "deportation can be a frightening concept, especially for immigrants or people whose friends or relatives are from another country. Why do people get deported, and what happens to them after the deportation decision is made? The answers to these questions and more are found in this thorough examination of a topic that is often in the news." (Publisher's note)

Torture; Lauri S. Friedman, book editor. Greenhaven Press 2011 147p il (Introducing issues with opposing viewpoints) $36.75

Grades: 7 8 9 10 **364.6**

1. Torture

ISBN 978-0-7377-5203-8; 0-7377-5203-3

LC 2011005638

This is an "excellent [resource] both for student research and for personal interest. . . . Torture discusses the ethics of state-approved torture, particularly of terrorism suspects, and covers the Geneva Conventions, the death penalty, and whether torture produces good information." Booklist

Includes bibliographical references

364.66 Capital punishment

Kuklin, Susan

★ **No** choirboy; murder, violence, and teenagers on death row. Henry Holt and Co. 2008 212p il $17.95

Grades: 8 9 10 11 12 **364.66**

1. Capital punishment 2. Juvenile delinquency

ISBN 978-0-8050-7950-0; 0-8050-7950-5

LC 2007-46940

"The book opens with candid interviews that introduce three inmates, all of them teenagers when they committed their crimes. . . . This eye-opening account will likely open minds. . . . The book concludes with solid back matter—notes, glossary, bibliography, and index." Horn Book

Includes glossary and bibliographical references

Watson, Stephanie

The **death** penalty; by Stephanie Watson. ReferencePoint Press, Inc. 2018 80 p. (Thinking critically) (hardback) $29.95

Grades: 8 9 10 11 12 **364.66**

1. Crime prevention 2. Capital punishment -- United States 3. Crime prevention -- United States 4. Punishment in crime deterrence -- United States

ISBN 9781682822654; 9781682822661

LC 2017007978

"The death penalty has existed in Western civilization for thousands of years, and its use has remained controversial throughout that time. Through a narrative-driven pro/con format--supported by facts, quotes, anecdotes, and full-color illustrations--this . . . [book, by Stephanie Watson] examines issues related to the death penalty." (Publisher's note)

"Rather than face unwieldy results from an Internet search, students can use this series to frame their research coherently." Booklist

Includes bibliographical references and index

365 Penal and related institutions

America's prisons; Jack Lasky, book editor. Greenhaven Press 2016 202 p illustrations (Opposing viewpoints)

Grades: 8 9 10 11 12 **365**

1. Prisons -- United States 2. Imprisonment -- United States 3. Criminals -- Rehabilitation -- United States 4. Alternatives to imprisonment -- United States 5. Criminal justice, Administration of -- United States

ISBN 9780737775372; 9780737775365

Collects articles on issues related to the American prison system that represent diverse viewpoints on the issues relating to it, including the problems that prisons pose, who is imprisoned, humane treatment, and alternatives to imprisonment.

370.15 Educational psychology

LaGarde, Jennifer

Fact vs. fiction; teaching critical thinking skills in the age of fake news. Jennifer LaGarde and Darren Hudgins. International Society for Technology in Education 2018 160 p. (pbk.) $29.95

Grades: Adult Professional **370.15**

1. Fake news -- Study and teaching 2. Mass media -- Study and teaching 3. Critical thinking -- Study and teaching 4. Information literacy -- Study and teaching

ISBN 9781564847041

LC 2018051063

"The advent of the 24-hour news cycle, citizen journalism and an increased reliance on social media as a trusted news source . . . coupled with the 'fake news' industry . . . [have left] educators . . . facing a . . . challenging landscape. . . . [This book by Jennifer LaGarde and Darren Hudgins] provides educators with tools and resources to help students discern fact from fiction in the information they access not only at school, but on the [electronic] devices they carry." (Publisher's note)

Includes bibliographical references

370.71 Education

Growing schools; librarians as professional developers. Debbie Abilock, Kristin Fontichiaro, and Violet H. Harada, editors. Libraries Unlimited 2012 390 p. (pbk.) $45

Grades: Professional **370.71**

1. Teachers -- Training 2. Educational technology 3. Academic libraries 4. Information technology 5. Technological literacy 6. Libraries and teachers -- United States 7. School libraries -- Information technology

ISBN 1610690419; 9781610690416

LC 2012016191

In this book, "editors [Debbie] Abilock, [Kristin] Fontichiaro, and [Violet H.] Harada examine ways school librarians can act as professional developers within their pedagogical communities. Thirty-two articles in sixteen thematic chapters offer real-world examples of how teacher librarians have leveraged their skills and expertise to provide learning experiences for other teachers, community members, and students." (Voice of Youth Advocates)

"This book promotes the role of the school librarian as a leader in school, district, and online professional development in 16 essays written by school librarians, school district personnel, and professors...A rich smorgasbord of ideas, this book would be invaluable for an individual librarian looking to become a professional development leader, and for district librarians to use in planning and implementing meaningful district-wide professional development." (Library Media Connection)

Includes bibliographical references and index

McKeown, Rosalyn

Into the classroom; a practical guide for starting student teaching. Rosalyn McKeown. University of Tennessee Press 2011 xv, 165 p.p (pbk.) $14.95

Grades: Adult Professional **370.71**

1. Teaching 2. Student teaching 3. Student teaching -- United States

ISBN 1572338164; 9781572338166

LC 2011011282

This book offers suggestions to those "just starting out in a secondary school classroom. . . . After exploring the pitfalls of inexperience and providing . . . guidance on maintaining order in the classroom, [Rosalyn] McKeown focuses on teaching skills. She advises readers on writing objectives and lesson plans, creating interesting ways to start and end class, introducing variety into the classroom, lecturing, asking meaningful questions, and using visual aids." (Amazon.com)

Includes bibliographical references and index.

370.973 Education - United States

Cappacio, George

Schools in Colonial America; George Capaccio. Cavendish Square Publishing 2015 80 p. (library binding) $35.64

Grades: 6 7 8 **370.973**

1. Schools -- United States -- History 2. United States -- History -- 1600-1775, Colonial period 3. Schools -- United States -- History -- Colonial period, ca. 1600-1775

ISBN 1627128948; 9781627128940; 9781627128957

LC 2014003452

This book on schools in Colonial America, by George Cappacio, "describes in rich detail the lives of Native Americans, African Americans, and white settlers, including children, women, and criminals." (School Library Journal)

"Thoroughly researched and expertly executed, this series describes in rich detail the lives of Native Americans, African Americans, and white settlers, including children, women, and criminals. The introductory material that prefaces each title is of particular value, as it demonstrates that the colonists were part of a larger world picture...Content in each title incorporates quotes from period letters and journals as well as a plethora of well-chosen, colorful illustrations. Strong, attractive titles for those looking for more coverage of Colonial America." SLJ

371.1 Schools and their activities

Harada, Violet H.

Inquiry learning through librarian-teacher partnerships; [by] Violet H. Harada and Joan M. Yoshina. Linworth Pub. 2004 172p il pa $39.95

Grades: Adult Professional **371.1**

1. Teaching teams 2. School libraries

ISBN 1-58683-134-8

LC 2004-662

"The authors describe what happens in an inquiry-based classroom and library media center and show teachers/librarians how to develop a curriculum that incorporates essential questions and important habits of mind, all aligned with content standards. . . . The volume contains everything a teacher-librarian team would need to create, teach, research, and assess major interdisciplinary units." SLJ

Includes bibliographical references

371.2 School administration; administration of student academic activities

Odden, Allan R.

Improving student learning when budgets are tight; Allan R. Odden. Corwin 2012 xxi, 184 p.p

Grades: Adult Professional **371.2**

1. Schools -- Finance 2. Academic achievement 3. Schools -- Administration 4. School budgets -- United States 5. School improvement programs -- United States

ISBN 1452217084; 9781452217086

LC 2011045908

This book by Allan R. Odden "offers a comprehensive framework to enhance student achievement in good times and in bad. . . . Odden outlines a school improvement action plan focused sharply on student learning and then shows how to target resources to implement each strategy in that plan. . . . Educators will find a wide range of real-life examples of schools and districts that have implemented these strategies and significantly improved student learning." (Publisher's note)

Includes bibliographical references and index

371.3 Methods of instruction and study

Fox, Janet S.

★ **Get** organized without losing it; Janet S. Fox ; illustrated by Steve Mark. Revised & updated edition Free Spirit Pub. 2017 112p il (Laugh & learn) paperback $9.99

Grades: 5 6 7 8 **371.3**

1. Life skills 2. Study skills 3. Time management

ISBN 978-1-63198-173-9 paperback; 978-1-57542-193-3

First published 2006

"In this handbook for students, Fox uses humor to provide practical, easy-to-follow ideas for organizing desks, backpacks, and lockers; managing time for homework and after school activities; planning long-term projects; and taking better notes. . . . Fox writes in a conversational style. . . . Humorous illustrations complement the text." Voice Youth Advocates

Includes bibliographical references

Green, Julie

Write it down. Cherry Lake Pub. 2010 32p il (Super smart information strategies) lib bdg $27.07

Grades: 3 4 5 6 **371.3**

1. Note-taking

ISBN 978-1-60279-645-4 lib bdg; 1-60279-645-9 lib bdg

LC 2009024741

"The appealing layout includes manageable paragraphs, a variety of engaging illustrations, and examples that clearly guide readers through each topic. . . . Effective note taking and highlighting are the focus of [this book], but the book also suggests using sticky notes and creating diagrams and charts." SLJ

Includes glossary and bibliographical references

Greenberg, Michael

Painless study techniques; illustrations by Michele Earle-Bridges. Barron's Educational Series 2009 234p il pa $9.99

Grades: 6 7 8 9 10 **371.3**

1. Study skills

ISBN 978-0-7641-4059-4 pa; 0-7641-4059-0 pa

LC 2008-42609

"This book provides helpful information on topics such as time management, homework organization, note taking, creating outlines, studying for tests and quizzes, grammar, and writing a research paper. Greenberg breaks down each main topic into smaller, more manageable subtopics, giving examples to help illustrate his ideas. . . . Greenberg's writing style is clear and interesting. . . . A solid resource for most libraries." SLJ

Includes bibliographical references

Johnson, Steve

Digital tools for teaching; 30 e-tools for collaborating, creating, and publishing across the curriculum. Maupin House Pub. 2011 $23.95

Grades: Adult Professional **371.3**

1. Internet in education 2. Computer-assisted instruction

ISBN 978-1-934338-84-1; 1-934338-84-2

LC 2010037430

"Considering the vast number of e-tools now available, . . . Johnson does an excellent job of sorting through them, listing his top choices, and even including ideas for using them. The book is divided into two parts. Part one provides information on today's tech-driven student, the importance of utilizing new technology, ways to start using the technology, and how to assess student products. Part two describes the e-tools, giving the following for each: a brief overview, how to get started, ways to use the tool in the classroom, and any other issues that need to be considered. . . . [This] provides a wealth of information in a user-friendly, practical format that would benefit all educators regardless of grade level or content area." Voice Youth Advocates

Includes bibliographical references

Superbrain; the insider's guide to getting smart. Toronto Public Library ; art by Dave Whamond. Firefly Books Ltd 2015 72 p. color illustrations $19.95

Grades: 4 5 6 7 **371.3**

1. Study skills

ISBN 1554517354; 9781554517350

This book presents "a guide to research practices and intellectual property for students in the middle-grade set. Continuing the superhero theme evinced in the title, the book presents many of the explanations and tips about the appropriate use of print and Internet sources. . . . Sidebars offer portraits of diverse young people who used good research practices to change their own and others' lives." (Booklist)

371.33 Teaching aids, equipment, materials

Baule, Steven M.

Social networking for schools; by Steven M. Baule and Julie E. Lewis. Linworth 2012 220 p. (hardcopy : alk. paper) $45

Grades: Professional **371.33**

1. Schools 2. Social media 3. Educational technology 4. Students -- Social networks 5. Educational technology -- Social aspects 6. Education -- Effect of technological innovations on

ISBN 1586835378; 9781586835378; 9781586835385

LC 2012014933

This book by Steven M. Baule and Julie E. Lewis "take[s] a comprehensive look at the topic of social media use in schools. Starting with the numerous justifications for integrating social media into schools, it provides real-world examples of how to seamlessly integrate social media within your classroom or library, examines the methodologies for crafting the necessary policies and procedures to ensure that staff members." (Publisher's note)

"This detailed book will help schools incorporate social media tools into communication, curriculum, and professional development...This is an excellent resource that provides a blueprint for utilizing social media to facilitate teaching and learning." (Library Media Connection)

Includes bibliographical references and index

371.5 School discipline and related activities

Beaudoin, Marie-Nathalie

Responding to the culture of bullying and disrespect; new perspectives on collaboration, compassion, and responsibility. [by] Marie-Nathalie Beaudoin, Maureen Taylor. rev 2nd ed.; Corwin Press 2009 281p il $76.95; pa $36.95

Grades: Adult Professional **371.5**

1. Bullies 2. School discipline

ISBN 978-1-4129-6853-9; 1-4129-6853-4; 978-1-4129-6854-6 pa; 1-4129-6854-2 pa

LC 2008-55933

First published 2004 with title: Breaking the culture of bullying and disrespect

"This profound resource explores the behaviors that cultivate a culture of bullying and disrespect. . . . Concrete solutions to issues are offered, and the authors make sure to load this title with practical suggestions for affecting change. They delve into ways to work directly with young people to better address their concerns. . . . This purchase is essential for any educator, counselor, or parent. It should be a staple of the school library reference collection because the information provided should be used daily. It will be a title that can be referenced for years to come and will help with adults struggling to overcome bullying." Voice Youth Advocates

Includes glossary and bibliographical references

★ **Bully;** an action plan for teachers and parents to combat the bullying crisis. edited by Lee Hirsch and Cynthia Lowen ; with Dina Santorelli. Perseus Books Group 2012 viii, 295 p.p ill. $15.99

Grades: Adult Professional **371.5**

1. Bullies 2. Bullying 3. Bullying -- Prevention 4. Cyberbullying -- Prevention 5. Bullying in schools -- Prevention

ISBN 1602861846; 1602861854; 9781602861848; 9781602861855

LC 2012289039

"This companion book to the documentary film Bully was edited by filmmaker [Lee]Hirsch and writer/producer [Cynthia] Lowen, with contributing chapters by a number of celebrities, authors, experts, government officials, and educators. Part homage to the film, part resource, the book interweaves the stories of children who have been bullied with practical information and advice for parents and other readers." (Publishers Weekly)

Includes bibliographical references (p. 281-289) and index

Myers, Jill J.

Responding to cyber bullying; an action tool for school leaders. [by] Jill J. Myers, Donna S. McCaw, Leaunda S. Hemphill. Corwin Press 2011 195p pa $33.95

Grades: Adult Professional **371.5**

1. Bullies 2. Cyberbullying 3. School violence

ISBN 978-1-4129-9484-2; 1-4129-9484-5

LC 2010040679

"The book's introduction addresses the nature of 'digital generation' students. The problem of cyberbullying is introduced in light of the generational reality. The book covers decisions made to resolve real-life situations, practical principles about censorship, and the capacity and limitations of school authority, Included is a matrix that serves as a decision-making tool for administration. This resource is a healthy blend of the theoretical and practical." Libr Media Connect

Includes bibliographical references

371.7 Student welfare

Lily, Henrietta M.

School violence and conflict resolution; Marilyn E. Smith, Matthew Monteverde, Henrietta M. Lily. Rosen Pub. 2013 48 p.

Grades: 9 10 11 12 **371.7**

1. School violence 2. Conflict management 3. Conflict management -- United States 4. School violence -- United States -- Prevention

ISBN 9781448868919

LC 2012003027

"These newest additions to the Teen Mental Health series tackle topics that are at once timely and timeless in adolescents' lives. Filled with statistics on the recent history of violence in schools, School Violence and Conflict Resolution explains potential warning signs of violent offenders and how schools are combating violence, particularly through peer mediation. All of these easy-to-read books emphasize seeking support from friends, family, and counselors and even suggest "10 Great Questions to Ask a Guidance Counselor." Other features include "Myths and Facts" (such as the myth that only females worry about their bodies and self-image), a glossary, and a list of related organizations. These titles are good beginning resources for both health reports and personal research." (Booklist)

Includes bibliographical references and index

March for Our Lives (Organization)

Glimmer of hope; how tragedy sparked a movement. by the founders of March for Our Lives. Razorbill 2018 208 p. (hardback) $18

Grades: 8 9 10 11 12 **371.7**

1. Teenagers 2. Protest movements 3. Social movements -- United States 4. Student movements -- United States 5. March for Our Lives (2018 : Washington, D.C.) 6. Marjory Stoneman Douglas High School Massacre, Parkland, Fla., 2018

ISBN 1984836099; 9781984836090

LC 2018044805

This book "tells the story of how a group of teenagers raced to channel their rage and sorrow into action, and went on to create one of the largest youth-led movements in global history. March For Our Lives Action Fund is a nonprofit 501c4 organization dedicated to furthering the work of March For Our Lives students to end gun violence across the . . . [United States]." (Publisher's note)

McPherson, Stephanie Sammartino

Stressed out in school? learning to deal with academic pressure. Enslow Publishers 2009 112p il (Issues in focus today) lib bdg $31.93

Grades: 7 8 9 10 **371.7**

1. Students 2. Stress (Psychology)

ISBN 978-0-7660-3069-5 lib bdg; 0-7660-3069-5 lib bdg

LC 2008-40339

"Examines the stress and academic pressure students of all ages encounter, including early education, homework, standardized tests, college applications, peer pressure, and alternative learning styles." Publisher's note

Includes glossary and bibliographical references

Parkland speaks; survivors from Marjory Stoneman Douglas share their stories. edited by Sarah Lerner. Crown Books for Young Readers 2019 192 p. $20.99

Grades: 8 9 10 11 12 **371.7**

1. Autobiography 2. School shootings 3. High school students 4. Teenagers' art -- Florida -- Parkland 5. High school students' writings, American -- Florida -- Parkland 6. Marjory Stoneman Douglas High School (Parkland, Fla.) -- Students 7. Marjory Stoneman Douglas High School Massacre, Parkland, Fla., 2018

ISBN 1984849999; 1984850008; 9781984849991; 9781984850003

LC 2018050403

This book, edited by Sarah Lerner, is a "raw look at the events of [the] February 14 [Marjory Stoneman Douglas High School shooting], and a poignant representation of grief, healing, and hope. The students . . . share their emotional journeys that began on February 14, 2018, and continue today. . . . The intimate collection includes poetry, eyewitness accounts, letters, speeches, journal entries, drawings, and photographs from the . . . [incident] and its aftermath." (Publisher's note)

Includes bibliographical references and index

Schier, Helga

The **causes** of school violence; by Helga Schier. ABDO Publishing 2008 112 p. ill. (chiefly col.) (library) $34.22

Grades: 7 8 9 10 **371.7**

1. School violence 2. School violence -- United States

ISBN 160453060X; 9781604530605

LC 2007031920

This book is part of the Essential Viewpoints series and looks at the causes of school violence. The series "examines critical debates occurring today, including the legislation that has shaped the issue as well as the numerous sides of each argument. Color photos, detailed maps, and informative sidebars accompany" the text. (Publisher's note)

Includes bibliographical references (p. 102-103) and index.

We say #neverAgain; reporting by the Parkland student journalists. edited by MSD teachers, Melissa Falkowski and Eric Garner. Crown Books for Young Readers 2019 272 p. (glb : alk. paper) $20.99

Grades: 7 8 9 10 11 12 **371.7**

1. School shootings 2. High school students 3. Gun control -- United States 4. School shootings -- Florida -- Parkland 5. Journalism, School -- Florida -- Parkland 6. Marjory Stoneman Douglas High School Massacre, Parkland, Fla., 2018 7. Marjory Stoneman Douglas High School Massacre, Parkland, Fla., 2018 --

Press coverage
ISBN 1984849972; 9781984849960; 9781984849977
LC 2018050328

This book, edited by Melissa Falkowski and Eric Garner, "look[s] at the shooting at Marjory Stoneman Douglas High School in Parkland and the fight for gun control--as told by the student reporters for the school's newspaper and TV station. . . . It showcases how the teens have become media savvy and the skills they have learned and honed--harnessing social media, speaking to the press, and writing effective op-eds." (Publisher's note)

"Throughout, the students express appreciation for peers and faculty who exhibited courage during the shootings, and they stress the importance of journalistic integrity. An impressive roundup of eloquent, well-reasoned, and inspiring writing." PW

Includes bibliographical references and index

371.8 Students

Kallen, Stuart A.

★ **Teen** guide to student activism; Stuart A. Kallen. ReferencePoint Press 2018 80 p. (hbk.) $29.95

Grades: 7 8 9 10 11 12 **371.8**

1. Youth movement 2. Students -- Political activity 3. Student movements
ISBN 9781682825419; 1682825418
LC 2018031466

This book, by Stuart A. Kallen, "features stories about teens who are making a difference and shows other teens how they can do the same. The book discusses organizing, reaching out, and student rights. It also features insights from student activists about the challenges of balancing school and activism and the many lessons learned from their own activities and from earlier activists. The book includes many fully documented quotes from teens" (Publisher's note)

Includes bibliographical references and index

Tym, Kate

School survival; a guide to taking control of your life. [by] Kate Tym and Penny Worms. Raintree 2005 48p il (Get real) $29.93

Grades: 7 8 9 10 **371.8**

1. Schools 2. Peer pressure 3. Socialization
ISBN 1-4109-0577-2
LC 2004-8070

"Chapters consist of a spread presenting an overview of a topic such as . . . peer pressure, followed by three case studies about teens dealing with the problem. On the same page, three 'experts' . . . offer advice. . . . The advice of professionals lends credibility to the information presented. . . . [This volume is] sure to appeal to readers looking for advice." SLJ

371.82 Specific groups of students; schools for specific groups of students

Cahill, Sean

LGBT youth in America's schools; Jason Cianciotto and Sean Cahill. The University of Michigan Press 2012 236 p. (pbk. : alk. paper) $30

Grades: Adult Professional **371.82**

1. Bullies 2. Gay youth 3. LGBT people 4. Discrimination 5. Schools -- Administration 6. Gay students -- United States 7. Sexual minorities -- Education 8. Lesbian students -- United States 9. Bisexual students -- United States 10. Homosexuality and education -- United States 11. Transgender youth -- Education -- United States
ISBN 0472031406; 9780472028320; 9780472031405; 9780472118229
LC 2011045478

In this book, "[Jason] Cianciotto and [Sean] Cahill use statistics and real-life anecdotes to show the pervasiveness of gender- and sexual orientation-based harassment in American schools, and argue for institutional reform and policy changes. . . . [R]esearch shows that . . . more young people are coming out . . . while still technically a minor, and thus subject to the rules of their educational institutions, and increasingly the abuse of their peers, teachers, and school administrators." (Publishers Weekly)

Includes bibliographical references and index.

Finkelstein, Norman H.

Schools of hope; the Rosenwald Schools of the American South. Norman H. Finkelstein. Calkins Creek 2014 80 p. illustrations $16.95

Grades: 5 6 7 8 **371.82**

1. African Americans -- History 2. African Americans -- Education
ISBN 1590788419; 9781590788417
LC 2013951346

"When Booker T. Washington, the famed African American educator, asked Julius Rosenwald, the wealthy president of Sears, Roebuck and Company and noted philanthropist, to help him build well-designed and fully equipped schools for black children, the face of education in the South changed for the better. . . . In this inspiring story, noted nonfiction writer Norman H. Finkelstein spotlights one man's legacy and the power of community action." (Publisher's note)

"This straightforward narrative is substantially supported with many photographs of the period, especially of the schools and the students. Source notes, a bibliography (which could have used a few more titles for the target readership), a list of websites, an index and picture credits add to its authenticity. Clean layout and design augment a quality introduction to an important chapter in the history of American education." -Kirkus

371.822 Women students

Stone, Tanya Lee

★ **Girl** rising; changing the world one girl at a time. Tanya Lee Stone in association with Girl Rising. Wendy Lamb Books 2017 193 p. color illustrations, map (trade : alk. paper) $22.99

Grades: 7 8 9 10 11 12 **371.822**

1. Girls -- Education 2. Teenage girls -- Conduct of life 3. Social change 4. Girls -- Conduct of life 5. Girls -- Education -- Cross-cultural studies
ISBN 9780553511468; 9780553511475; 9780553511499; 9780553511482
LC 2015026152

This book, by Tanya Lee Stone, is "a global campaign for girls' education, created a film that chronicled the stories of nine girls in the developing world, allowing viewers the opportunity to witness how education can break the cycle of poverty. . . . [It] examines barriers to education in depth--early child marriage, . . . slavery, sexual trafficking, . . . and poverty--and shows how removing these barriers means . . . [a] safer, healthier, and more prosperous communities." (Publisher's note)

"This visually stunning companion piece to the 2013 film of the same name seeks to explain why 62 million girls worldwide do not go to school." SLJ

Includes bibliographical references (pages [169]-174) and index.

371.9 Special education

Kent, Deborah

Athletes with disabilities. Watts 2003 63p il (Watts library) hardcover o.p. lib bdg $24

Grades: 4 5 6 7 **371.9**

1. Sports for people with disabilities

ISBN 0-531-12019-8 lib bdg; 0-531-16664-3 pa

LC 2002-8883

Explores the people and events involved in sports competitions for people with disabilities and discusses people with disabilities who play professional sports

"Information is effectively conveyed through clear, straightforward prose and accounts of individual athletes. . . . [This is] informative, often inspirational and thought-provoking." Booklist

Includes bibliographical references

Stanley, Jerry

Children of the Dust Bowl; the true story of the school at Weedpatch Camp. Crown 1992 85p il map hardcover o.p. pa $9.95

Grades: 5 6 7 8 **371.9**

1. Migrant labor 2. Great Depression, 1929-1939 3. Education -- Social aspects

ISBN 0-517-88094-6; 0-517-58782-3 pa

LC 92-393

Describes the plight of the migrant workers who traveled from the Dust Bowl to California during the Depression and were forced to live in a federal labor camp and discusses the school that was built for their children

"Stanley's text is a compelling document. . . . The story is inspiring and disturbing, and Stanley has recorded the details with passion and dignity." Booklist

Includes bibliographical references

371.91 Students with physical disabilities

Hauser, Peter C.

★ **How** deaf children learn; what parents and teachers need to know. Marc Marschark Peter C. Hauser. Oxford University Press 2012 156 p. $26.50

Grades: Adult Professional **371.91**

1. Teaching 2. Deaf children 3. Elementary education 4. Deaf -- Education 5. Deaf -- Means of communication

ISBN 0195389751; 9780195389753

LC 2011012553

This book is "about teaching deaf children. Written primarily for parents and teachers of deaf or hard-of-hearing children, this work covers general information about their education, gives insights into their cognitive development, and provides steps to their school success. The authors also discuss issues such as the value of cochlear implants and the debate over signing vs. speaking." (Library Journal)

Includes bibliographical references.

372 Specific levels of education

Alexander, Kwame, 1968-

The **write** thing; Kwame Alexander engages students in writing workshop (and you can too!) Kwame Alexander ; foreward by Kylene Beers. Shell Education 2018 208 p. illustrations $29.99

Grades: Adult Professional **372**

1. Authorship 2. Creative writing 3. Poetry -- Study and teaching

ISBN 1493888420; 9781493888429

This book, by Kwame Alexander, "teaches you how to move students step-by-step from ideas, to drafts, to finished works. Not only will you successfully motivate your students to write, you'll take that motivation one step further by providing guidance on how to create student-driven publications of their work. The confidence students will attain when they see their writing authentically published will be off the charts!" (Publisher's note)

Includes bibliographical references (pages 197-200) and index

Brooks-Young, Susan

Teaching with the tools kids really use; learning with Web and mobile technologies. Corwin 2010 137p pa $26.95

Grades: Adult Professional **372**

1. Web 2.0 2. Teachers -- Training

ISBN 978-1-4129-7275-8 pa; 1-4129-7275-2 pa

LC 2009-43856

"In this book, we see how technology can be used, but we also see the reponsibility of the educator to make sure it is done appropriately, so 21st-century skills are addressed. The author addresses technologies and applications, and also discusses their ethical uses and how to think ahead to make adjustments for the future. . . . This book will be incredibly useful for those who are unsure about Web 2.0 tools, want to explore their possibilities, and would like to educate themselves further about usage in their own schools." Libr Media Connect

Includes bibliographical references

Gates, Pamela

Cultural Journeys; Multicultural Literature for Elementary and Middle School Students. Rowman & Littlefield Pub Inc 2010 258 p. (paperback) $29.95

Grades: Adult Professional **372**

1. Best books 2. Multicultural literature

ISBN 144220687X; 9781442206878

This book looks at multicultural literature for elementary and middle school students. The first chapter asks "the question of 'why.' Why use multicultural literature? . . . The 'why' is further developed as the chapter continues with a definition of multicultural literature." The seventh chapter looks at "works that challenge stereotypes and go beyond the common one-dimensional diversity theme." (Alberta Journal of Educational Research)

Mackey, Bonnie

A **librarian's** guide to cultivating an elementary school garden; [by] Bonnie Mackey and Jennifer Mackey Stewart. Linworth Pub. 2009 124p il pa $39.95

Grades: Adult Professional **372**

1. Gardening 2. School libraries -- Activity projects

ISBN 978-1-58683-328-2 pa; 1-58683-328-6 pa

LC 2008-34963

"Its unusual topic makes this book a standout." Libr Media Connect

Includes bibliographical references

Mary Elizabeth (Mary Elizabeth Miller)

Painless spelling; Mary Elizabeth. 3rd edition Barrons Educational Series, Inc. 2011 284 p. ill. pbk $9.99

Grades: 7 8 9 10 **372**

1. Spelling 2. English language -- Spelling

ISBN 0764147137; 9780764147135

LC 2010941464

First published 1998

Provides guidelines for spelling American English words; explains visual and sound patterns, letter combinations, syllables, compound words, and hyphenation; and includes practical exercises.

372.4 Reading

Bernadowski, Carianne

Research -based reading strategies in the library for adolescent learners; [by] Carianne Bernadowski and Patricia Liotta Kolencik. Libraries Unlimited 2010 108p il pa $40

Grades: Adult Professional **372.4**

1. Reading 2. School libraries

ISBN 978-1-58683-347-3; 1-58683-347-2

LC 2009-21198

"This book explains six proven strategies—question/answer, think-alouds, reciprocal teaching, anticipation guides, questioning the author, and SQR3 (survey, question, read, recite, and review)—for reading comprehension and three strategies (Semantic Feature Analysis, word maps/journals, and Frayer Models/word sorts) for vocabulary building. . . . Although the strategies are standard approaches, weaving in librarian roles makes this book useful for librarians who serve teens." Booklist

Includes bibliographical references

Teaching literacy skills to adolescents using Coretta Scott King Award winners. Libraries Unlimited 2009 136p il pa $35

Grades: Adult Professional **372.4**

1. Coretta Scott King Award 2. African Americans in literature 3. Teenagers -- Books and reading

ISBN 978-1-58683-337-4; 1-58683-337-5

LC 2009-15279

"The book includes award-winning book selections and Coretta Scott King Honor Books. It is a showcase for African-American authors' works, and helps educators working with adolescent students and their reading needs. . . . Each chapter covers one title and contains an annotation, grade level discussion starters, writing prompts, pre-reading activities, literary strategies for reading, post-reading activities, additional information about the author, and additional resources. This book would be a great professional resource, and a must have for those educators that teach adolescents." Libr Media Connect

Includes bibliographical references

Fuhrken, Charles

What every middle school teacher needs to know about reading tests (from someone who has written them) Charles Fuhrken. Stenhouse Publishers 2012 vii, 237 p.p ill. (pbk. : alk. paper) $24

Grades: Professional **372.4**

1. Achievement tests 2. Examinations -- Study guides 3. Educational tests and measurements 4. Reading (Middle school) -- Ability testing

ISBN 1571108858; 1571109455; 9781571108852; 9781571109453

LC 2011037287

This book's author, "Charles Furhrken, has spent years working with several major testing companies and contributing to the reading assessments of various testing programs." He "offers . . . strategies to help students perform well on test day." Particular focus is given to "information about reading tests, including . . . preparation materials, samples of the most frequently assessed reading standards, and . . . core-reading activities." (Publisher's note)

Includes bibliographical references and index.

Grover, Sharon

Listening to learn; audiobooks supporting literacy. by Sharon Grover and Lizette D. Hannegan. American Library Association 2011 xi, 188 p.p (alk. paper) $45

Grades: Adult Professional **372.4**

1. Literacy 2. Audiobooks 3. Educational technology 4. Reading -- United States 5. Children -- Books and reading 6. Libraries -- Special collections -- Audiobooks 7. Literacy -- Study and teaching -- United States 8. School librarian participation in curriculum planning

ISBN 0838911072; 9780838911075

LC 2011041814

Authors Sharon Grover and Lizette D. Hannegan "make the case that audiobooks not only present excellent opportunities to engage the attention of young people but also advance literacy. 'Listening to Learn' connects audiobooks with K-12 curricula and demonstrates how the format can support national learning standards and literacy skills." (Publisher's note)

"This informative resource establishes the literacy benefits of audiobooks as an alternate reading delivery method...Discussions of audiobook formats and recommended sources for building an audiobook collection are also included. The authors provide a collaborative resource that would benefit a classroom, library, or home setting." (Library Media Connection)

Includes bibliographical references (p. 175-178) and index

Moreillon, Judi

Collaborative strategies for teaching reading comprehension; maximizing your impact. [by] Judi Moreillon. American Library Association 2007 170p il $38

Grades: Adult Professional **372.4**

1. Reading comprehension

ISBN 978-0-8389-0929-4; 0-8389-0929-9

LC 2006036132

This "begins by emphasizing the importance of collaboration between classroom teachers and teacher-librarians. . . . The bulk of the book focuses on seven reading comprehension strategies and how to teach them. . . . Overall this book is a cut above other 'how-to' books with its plethora of suggestions and resources for teachers and librarians." Voice Youth Advocates

Includes glossary and bibliographical references

372.6 Language arts (Communication skills)

Chatton, Barbara

Using poetry across the curriculum; learning to love language. 2nd ed; Libraries Unlimited 2010 241p pa $40

Grades: Adult Professional **372.6**

1. Poetry -- Study and teaching

ISBN 978-1-59158-697-5; 1-59158-697-6

LC 2009-36711

First published 1993

"With the emphasis in most schools on improving literacy, fluency, and reading and writing test scores, this book is extremely valuable. Sections are divided into various curricula areas. Each section begins with the national standards for that discipline, then a few paragraphs explain how the poetry in the extensive listing can be used. . . . Because all teachers must incorporate writing into their teaching, having relevant poetry for their curriculum and ideas on how to use it, will make this book popular." Libr Media Connect

Includes bibliographical references

Hamilton, Martha

Children tell stories; teaching and using storytelling in the classroom. [by] Martha Hamilton and Mitch Weiss. 2nd ed.; Richard C. Owen Publishers 2005 xx, 264p il pa $29.95

Grades: Adult Professional **372.6**

1. Storytelling

ISBN 978-1-57274-663-3 pa; 1-57274-663-7 pa

LC 2005021667

First published 1990

"Combining enthusiasm and inspiration with practical tips, handouts, and resources, Hamilton and Weiss offer a comprehensive second edition that will be useful to both novice and experienced tellers. . . . The accompanying high-quality DVD shows children and adults telling stories, gives Web links, and includes 25 stories to download and print." SLJ

Includes bibliographical references

Hopkins, Lee Bennett

★ **Pass** the poetry, please! 3rd ed; HarperCollins Pubs. 1998 277p $25; pa $5.99

Grades: Adult Professional **372.6**

1. Poetry -- Study and teaching

ISBN 0-06-027746-7; 0-06-446199-8 pa

LC 98-19617

First published 1972

"This a must-purchase." SLJ

Includes bibliographical references

Hostmeyer, Phyllis

Storytelling and QAR strategies; [by] Phyllis Hostmeyer and Marilyn Adele Kinsella. Libraries Unlimited 2010 123p pa $30

Grades: Adult Professional **372.6**

1. Storytelling

ISBN 978-1-59884-494-8 pa; 1-59884-494-6 pa; 978-1-59884-495-5 e-book

LC 2010036576

"The authors, both storytellers with backgrounds in education and library work, present 18 stories based on six aspects of character development. These selections, which include folktales, fables, and myths, are just right for youngsters in third through eighth grades. Each one is followed by telling tips, a story path, and questions using the QAR (Question-Answer Relationships) model." SLJ

Includes bibliographical references

Literacy development in the storytelling classroom; Sherry Norfolk, Jane Stenson, and Diane Williams, editors. Libraries Unlimited 2009 342p il $40

Grades: Adult Professional **372.6**

1. Storytelling 2. Language arts

ISBN 978-1-59158-694-4; 1-59158-694-1

LC 2009-11550

"This excellent essay collection connects storytelling to music, poetry, art, social studies, math, science, and physical education and provides sample stories and hands-on lesson plans for preschool through middle school-plus classrooms. Opening articles use research and anecdotal experience to tell why a multiple sensory activity like storytelling trumps teach-to-the-test exercises. Chapters two through five present the 'how-to' and for each lesson, include the appropriate national standards met, objectives, materials, instructional plans, some adaptations, assessments, and bibliography. The extensive suggested resource section includes book, non-book, professional, and student materials. . . . It is a fascinating collection with useful, creative surprises for classrooms and library programs." Voice Youth Advocates

Includes bibliographical references

Miller, Donalyn

★ The **book** whisperer; awakening the inner reader in every child. [by] Donalyn Miller; foreword by Jeff Anderson. Jossey-Bass 2009 227p

Grades: Adult Professional **372.6**

1. Books and reading

ISBN 0-4703-7227-3; 978-0-4703-7227-2

LC 2008055666

Donalyn Miller's approach to reading promotion "is simple yet provocative: affirm the reader in every student, allow students to choose their own books, carve out extra reading time, model authentic reading behaviors, discard time-worn reading assignments such as book reports and comprehension worksheets, and develop a classroom library filled with high-interest books. . . . Miller provides many tips for teachers and parents and includes a useful list of ultimate reading suggestions picked by her students. This outstanding contribution to the literature is highly recommended." Libr J

Includes bibliographical references

Roth, Rita

The **story** road to literacy; [by] Rita Roth. Teacher Ideas Press 2006 176p il pa $30

Grades: Adult Professional **372.6**

1. Language arts 2. Children of immigrants 3. English language -- Study and teaching

ISBN 1-59158-323-3

LC 2005030835

"Roth advances the idea that using traditional literature with students who are learning English will help them acquire critical communication skills while tying unfamiliar new places to familiar elements of their own heritages. The author provides practical, ready-to-use lesson plans, story samples, and suggested activities." SLJ

Includes bibliographical references

372.62 Written and spoken expression

★ **Breakfast** on Mars and 37 Other Delectable Essays; Edited by Rebecca Stern and Brad Wolfe. Roaring Brook Press 2013 xii, 211p.p ill. (hardcover) $16.99
Grades: 6 7 8 9 10 11 12 **372.62**

1. American essays 2. Authorship -- Handbooks, manuals, etc. 3. Essay -- Authorship 4. English language -- Composition and exercises -- Study and teaching (Elementary) 5. English language -- Composition and exercises -- Study and teaching (Middle school)
ISBN 1596437375; 9781596437371

LC 2012040918

This book, edited by Rebecca Stern and Brad Wolfe, is a collection of essays meant for middle- and high-school students. "Thirty-eight short essays . . . come from Sloane Crosley, Sarah Prineas, Ned Vizzini, Scott Westerfeld, Rita Williams-Garcia, and more. Assigned a genre . . . and topic . . . , the contributors [wrote essays meant to] inspire and entertain." (Publishers Weekly)

"This handy volume fills a gap. Thirty-eight essays for young readers by contemporary writers demonstrate that 'essays can be just as enjoyable to read as fiction" . . . An important collection that ought to become a staple in writing classes." Kirkus

372.63 Spelling and handwriting

Cunha, Stephen F.

How to ace the National Geographic Bee; official study guide. by Stephen F. Cunha. 5th edition National Geographic 2017 173 p. ill., maps library $23.90; paperback $13.99
Grades: 4 5 6 7 8 **372.63**

1. Maps 2. Geography 3. Examinations -- Study guides 4. Contests 5. Geography -- Competitions 6. School contests -- United States
ISBN 9781426330810; 9781426330803

LC 2017297008

This book "is a study guide to prepare the reader for test questions in geographic trivia. . . . The book then separates into six distinct chapters. It begins with defining geography and giving the reader an overall understanding of how the bee is conducted. Chapter 3 . . . defines the various types of maps and how they should be interpreted and also explains map features and landforms." (Voice of Youth Advocates)

Includes bibliographical references (p. 109-117).

372.64 Literature appreciation

Pellowski, Anne

The **storytelling** handbook; a young people's collection of unusual tales and helpful hints on how to tell them. illustrated by Martha Stoberock. Simon & Schuster Bks. for Young Readers 1995 129p il hardcover o.p. pa $7.99
Grades: Adult Professional **372.64**

1. Storytelling
ISBN 0-689-80311-7; 978-1-4169-7598-4 pa; 1-4169-7598-5 pa

LC 95-2991

This work "addresses the young person who wants to tell stories in a public setting. It is similar in format to many adult books on storytelling how-tos, with sections on getting started and selecting and preparing stories, as well as a selection of sample tales. Pellowski's notes are extensive and will be very useful to novices looking for ways to research stories." Booklist

Includes bibliographical references

373.1 Organization and activities in secondary education

Glasser, Debbie

New kid, new scene; a guide to moving and switching schools. by Debbie Glasser and Emily Schenck. Magination Press 2012 112p il $14.95; pa 9.95
Grades: 5 6 7 8 **373.1**

1. Moving 2. Students
ISBN 978-1-4338-1039-8; 1-4338-1039-5; 978-1-4338-1038-1 pa; 1-4338-1038-7 pa

LC 2011013608

"Students making the transition to new schools, new communities, or new homes will always experience a bit of anxiety, and this self-help book offers practical advice on how to make those changes smoother. The ideas and suggestions are sound and practical. . . . The eye-catching layout will keep students flipping through the pages." SLJ

Serritella, Judy

Look again! appealing bulletin board ideas for secondary students. Linworth Pub. 2002 160p pa $36.95
Grades: Adult Professional **373.1**

1. Bulletin boards 2. Teenagers -- Books and reading
ISBN 1-58683-053-8

LC 2002-16181

"Basic practical tips suggest ways to liven up board displays, for example, by using three-dimensional materials such as corrugated cardboard or wallpaper. Ideas focus on providing students with information they need, as well as on promoting reading and library services." Book Rep

Includes bibliographical references

375 Curricula

Bishop, Kay

Connecting libraries with classrooms; the curricular roles of the media specialist. 2nd. ed.; Linworth 2011 122p pa $45
Grades: Adult Professional **375**

1. Librarians 2. School libraries 3. Instructional materials centers
ISBN 978-1-59884-599-0; 1-59884-599-3

LC 2010051623

This book provides an . . . exploration of the topics that are currently relevant in K-12 curricula, including the school librarian's role in dealing with these issues, collaborating with teachers, and connecting to classrooms.

"Kay Bishop's book covers a wide range of topics and issues within the school library field. . . . Collaborative planning between classroom teacher, principal, students, and the community is also addressed. This material will be a welcome addition to the Library Media Specialist's arsenal of resources to stay current and involved." Libr Media Connect

Includes bibliographical references

379 Public policy issues in education

Magoon, Kekla

Today the world is watching you; the Little Rock Nine and the fight for school integration, 1957. Twenty-First Century Books 2011 160p il map lib bdg $38.60
Grades: 6 7 8 9 **379**

1. School integration 2. Segregation in education 3. Arkansas --

Race relations 4. African Americans -- Education 5. Central High School (Little Rock, Ark.)
ISBN 978-0-7613-5767-4; 0-7613-5767-X
LC 2010028443

On September 4, 1957, nine African American teenagers made their way toward Central High School in Little Rock, Arkansas. Armed soldiers of the Arkansas National Guard blocked most of them at the edge of campus. The three students who did make it onto campus faced an angry mob. But the U.S. Supreme Court had ruled in 1955 that school segregation—that is, separate schools for black children and white children—was unconstitutional.

"Well-paced and engaging, the book is broken up into manageable chapters and gives background information on racial tensions in America starting with slavery. The information is carefully documented. . . . Black-and-white photographs and text boxes give additional information and context. . . . An ideal purchase for research purposes." SLJ

Includes glossary and bibliographical references

Sharp, Anne Wallace

Separate but equal; the desegregation of America's schools. [by] Anne Wallace Sharp. Lucent Books 2007 104p il (Lucent library of black history) $28.70

Grades: 7 8 9 10 **379**

1. School integration 2. Segregation in education 3. African Americans -- Education
ISBN 1-59018-953-1; 978-1-59018-953-5
LC 2006008269

"This simple and direct overview begins with the ban against educating slaves and the efforts of Prudence Crandall to provide black girls with schooling in Connecticut in 1832. Following a history of segregation, the major battles to desegregate public schools in the North and in the South, as well as those to desegregate universities and colleges, are highlighted. The violent white backlash that occurred in both Southern and Northern states in the 1960s and '70s is also covered." SLJ

Includes bibliographical references

Stokes, John

★ **Students** on strike; Jim Crow, civil rights, Brown, and me; a memoir. by John A. Stokes with Lois Wolfe, and Herman J. Viola. National Geographic 2008 127p il $15.95; lib bdg $23.90

Grades: 4 5 6 7 **379**

1. Segregation in education 2. African Americans -- Education
ISBN 978-1-4263-0153-7; 1-4263-0153-7; 978-1-4263-0154-4 lib bdg; 1-4263-0154-5 lib bdg

"In 1951, a group of African-American high school students in Prince Edward County, VA, went on strike to protest the substandard conditions in their segregated schools. They eventually became plaintiffs in a lawsuit that was one of the five that were part of the 1954 Brown decision . . . Fear of retribution and lingering bitterness has kept the strike leaders silent, but Stokes, who was among them, has decided that the story of the strike and its aftermath need to be told. . . . Stoke's inspiring story reveals an almost completely unreported part of one of the most important court cases of the 20th century." SLJ

Tougas, Shelley

★ **Little** Rock girl 1957; how a photograph changed the fight for integration. Compass Point Books 2011 64p il (Captured history) lib bdg $33.99; pa $8.95

Grades: 6 7 8 9 **379**

1. Students 2. School integration 3. Documentary photography 4. Segregation in education 5. Photojournalists 6. Arkansas -- Race relations 7. African Americans -- Education 8. Central High School (Little Rock, Ark.)
ISBN 978-0-7565-4440-9 lib bdg; 0-7565-4440-8; 978-0-7565-4512-3 pa; 0-7565-4512-9 pa
LC 2010054303

This explains how Will Counts' 1957 photograph of an African American student, Elizabeth Eckford, attempting to enter the all-white Central High School in Little Rock, Arkansas while surrounded by an angry mob, helped focus national attention on racial segregation.

This "is model nonfiction. . . . The design is fresh and inviting, the writing clear, and the back matter . . . is useful and extensive. An all-around winner." Booklist

Includes glossary and bibliographical references

Walker, Paul Robert

★ **Remember** Little Rock; the time, the people, the stories. by Paul Robert Walker. National Geographic 2008 61p il map $17.95; lib bdg $27.90

Grades: 5 6 7 8 9 **379**

1. School integration 2. Segregation in education 3. Arkansas -- Race relations 4. African Americans -- Education 5. Central High School (Little Rock, Ark.)
ISBN 978-1-4263-0402-6; 1-4263-0402-1; 978-1-4263-0403-3 lib bdg; 1-4263-0403-X lib bdg
LC 2008-24959

"The story of the battle to integrate Central High School in 1957 Little Rock, Arkansas, is presented through photographs and firsthand accounts from those who were there. . . . The multitude of eyewitness accounts, the poignant photographs, and the contextual background make this text a must-have addition to any classroom or library." Voice Youth Advocates

Includes bibliographical references

379.2 Specific policy issues in public education

Aretha, David

With all deliberate speed; court-ordered busing and American schools. David Aretha. Morgan Reynolds Pub. 2012 128 p. ill. (some col.) (The civil rights movement) (lib. bdg.) $28.95

Grades: 7 8 9 10 **379.2**

1. School integration 2. Busing (School integration) 3. Boston (Mass.) -- Race relations 4. Busing for school integration 5. School integration -- History 6. Busing for school integration -- History 7. School integration -- United States -- History 8. Busing for school integration -- United States -- History
ISBN 1599351811; 1599352176; 9781599351810; 9781599352176
LC 2011019530

This book, part of the "Civil Rights Movement" series, "details the slow, painful, unpopular, and often ineffective process of integrating public schools by busing students outside their neighborhoods in the decades following the 1954 landmark Brown v. Board of Education decision. In addition to a detailed account of experiences in Boston, [David] Aretha includes specific information on busing in numerous large and small metropolitan areas around the country." (Booklist)

"The latest books from the Civil Rights Movement series offer well-researched and clearly-written discussions of events and issues that helped define their times." Booklist

Includes bibliographical references (p. 122-124) and index

Levy, Debbie

★ **This** promise of change; one girl's story in the fight for school equality. by Jo Ann Allen Boyce and Debbie Levy. Bloomsbury Children's Books 2019 320 p. (hardcover) $17.99
Grades: 5 6 7 8 9 **379.2**

1. School integration -- Tennessee -- Clinton 2. African American students -- Tennessee -- Clinton -- Biography 3. Clinton (Tenn.) -- Race relations 4. African American teenage girls -- Tennessee -- Clinton -- Biography
ISBN 9781681198521

LC 2018026349

This book, by Jo Ann Allen Boyce and Debbie Levy, presents the story of " Jo Ann Allen [who] was one of twelve African-American students who broke the color barrier and integrated Clinton High School in Tennessee [in 1956.] . . . Jo Ann . . . found herself called on as the spokesperson of the group. But what about just being a regular teen? This is the heartbreaking and relatable story of her four months thrust into the national spotlight and as a trailblazer in history." (Publisher's note)

"Engrossing, informative, and important for middle-grade collections." Booklist

381 Commerce (Trade)

Freese, Susan M.

Craigslist; the company and its founder. ABDO Pub. Co. 2011 112p il (Technology pioneers) lib bdg $34.22
Grades: 5 6 7 8 **381**

1. Advertising 2. Businessmen 3. Internet marketing 4. Online social networks 5. Webmasters 6. Craigslist Inc. 7. Software engineers
ISBN 978-1-61714-806-4 lib bdg; 1-61714-806-7 lib bdg; 978-1-61758-964-5 e-book

LC 2010042448

This is an introduction to Craigslist and its founder, Craig Newmark.

"Written in a clear, linear fashion, this series offers vivid, well-researched details about the development of technological advancements considered essential in today's society. . . . Readers who are interested in technology and inventions will be thoroughly engrossed." SLJ

Includes glossary and bibliographical references

Gilbert, Sara

★ The **story** of eBay. Creative Education 2011 il (Built for success) $23.95
Grades: 6 7 8 9 **381**

1. eBay Inc.
ISBN 978-1-60818-062-2; 1-60818-062-X

LC 2010031226

A look at the origins, leaders, growth, and holdings of eBay, the online auction and shopping company that was founded in 1995 and today sells a multitude of collectibles and other consumer products.

This book is "written in a lively style, yet with a minimum of fuss. . . . The slim, gleaming format, well-chosen photos, and the effort to explore what makes a company successful today [makes this title] unique." Booklist

Includes bibliographical references

382 International commerce (Foreign trade)

Cottman, Michael H.

Shackles from the deep; tracing the path of a sunken slave ship, a bitter past, and a rich legacy. by Michael Cottman. National Geographic Partners 2016 128 p. (hardcover : alk. paper) $17.99
Grades: 6 7 8 9 **382**

1. Shipwrecks 2. Slave ships 3. Slave trade -- History 4. Henrietta Marie (Ship) 5. Underwater archaeology 6. Excavations (Archaeology)
ISBN 9781426326639; 9781426326646

LC 2016016708

This book describes how "a pile of lime-encrusted shackles, discovered on the seafloor in the remains of a ship called the Henrietta Marie, lands [journalist] Michael Cottman . . . in the middle of an amazing journey that stretches across three continents. . . . Told from the author's perspective, this book introduces young readers to the wonders of diving, detective work, and discovery, while shedding light on the history of slavery." (Publisher's note)

"Cottman wrote a well-received version of this story for adults... and this retelling for young readers is just as intriguing." Kirkus

Includes bibliographical references and index

Gifford, Clive

The **arms** trade. Chrysalis Education 2004 61p il (World issues) $29.95
Grades: 7 8 9 10 **382**

1. Defense industry 2. Firearms industry
ISBN 1-59389-154-7

"This book packs in copious information from a well-rounded perspective. . . . Very effective color photos . . . add a startling and engrossing element." Booklist

Includes glossary and bibliographical references

Major, John S.

The **Silk** Route; 7,000 miles of history. illustrated by Stephen Fieser. HarperCollins Pubs. 1995 32p il maps hardcover o.p. pa $6.99
Grades: 4 5 6 7 **382**

1. Trade routes 2. China -- History
ISBN 0-06-443468-0

LC 92-38169

"The pictures and short segments make the book a teaching tool as well as a resource when learning about China and its silk industry." Child Book Rev Serv

385 Railroad transportation

Gimpel, Diane

The **transcontinental** railroad. ABDO Pub. Co. 2011 112p il (Essential events) lib bdg $23.95
Grades: 7 8 9 10 11 12 **385**

1. Railroads -- History 2. West (U.S.) -- History
ISBN 978-1-61714-768-5; 1-61714-768-0

LC 2010044830

Describes how and why the Transcontinental Railroad was built and tells how it affected the westward expansion of settlers.

Includes glossary and bibliographical references

Landau, Elaine

The **transcontinental** railroad; [by] Elaine Landau. Franklin Watts 2005 63p il (Watts library) $25.50

Grades: 5 6 7 8 **385**

1. Frontier and pioneer life 2. Railroads -- History 3. Central Pacific Railroad 4. Union Pacific Railroad Company

ISBN 0-531-12326-X

LC 2005000914

"Landau describes how people traveled prior to the building of the railroads and how the concept of Manifest Destiny influenced the development of the railroads. . . . Black-and-white and color illustrations, maps, sidebars, and time lines enhance the well-organized [text]." SLJ

Includes bibliographical references

McMahon, Peter

Ultimate trains. Kids Can Press 2010 40p il (Machines of the future) $16.95

Grades: 4 5 6 7 **385**

1. Railroads 2. Science -- Experiments

ISBN 978-1-55453-366-4; 1-55453-366-X

"In simple engaging text and illustrations, McMahon and Mora present a brief history of [railroads]. Integral to the book are five experiments children can create. . . . Each experiment ties in well with a particular type of train, features clear instructions, and offers safety precautions." Booklist

Includes glossary

Murphy, Jim

★ **Across** America on an emigrant train. Clarion Bks. 1993 150p il hardcover o.p. pa $10.95

Grades: 5 6 7 8 **385**

1. Poets 2. Authors 3. Novelists 4. Authors, Scottish 5. Essayists 6. Travel writers 7. Short story writers 8. Railroads -- History 9. United States -- Description and travel

ISBN 0-395-63390-7; 0-395-76483-1 pa

LC 92-38650

"Murphy presents a forthright and thoroughly engrossing history of the transcontinental railway, with entries from Robert Louis Stevenson's 1879 journal as he rode cross country. It's also an inviting introduction to Stevenson, with a romance in the bargain." SLJ

Includes bibliographical references

Sandler, Martin W.

Iron rails, iron men, and the race to link the nation; the story of the transcontinental railroad. Martin S. Sandler. Candlewick Press 2015 224 p. illustrations, maps $22.99

Grades: 6 7 8 **385**

1. Railroads 2. United States -- History -- 19th century

ISBN 9780763665272; 0763665274

LC 2014954533

In this book author Martin W. Sandler "chronicles the development of the transcontinental railroad, from its genesis through its legacy. Alternating chapters describe the progress made by the two companies--the Central Pacific and the Union Pacific--and the author incorporates maps and images, appropriately placed along the way, to further convey the magnitude of the railroad." (School Library Journal)

"A fascinating epilogue relates what later happened to each of the key players introduced in the narrative, and a thorough timeline serves as a summary of important events. A dramatic story related in dramatic fashion." Kirkus

Includes bibliographical references (pages 201-204) and index.

Spilsbury, Louise

Maglev trains; Louise Spilsbury, Richard Spilsbury. Gareth Stevens Publishing 2016 48 p. (library binding) $31.95

Grades: 5 6 7 8 **385**

1. High speed trains 2. Technological innovations

ISBN 148245159X; 9781482451597; 9781482451658

LC 2016056795

This juvenile book, by Louise Spilsbury and Richard Spilsbury, part of the "Cutting-Edge Technology" series, profiles "maglev trains . . . , yet another scientific marvel that engineers have made a reality. These superfast trains float above their rails, darting from place to place at remarkable speeds. This book explores how maglev trains work, the science behind the magnets at work, and the history of maglev technology." (Publisher's note)

"Rock-solid choices that will update and deepen science and technology collections." SLJ

Zimmermann, Karl R.

All aboard! passenger trains around the world. [by] Karl Zimmermann; photography by the author. Boyds Mills Press 2006 48p il $19.95

Grades: 5 6 7 8 **385**

1. Railroads

ISBN 1-59078-325-5

LC 2005-24990

Zimmermann "has traveled by train across six continents, and his beautiful, big color photos appear on every double-page spread of this enthusiastic account, which blends history, geography, business, and engineering with his personal focus." Booklist

★ **Steam** locomotives; whistling, chugging, smoking iron horses of the past. Boyds Mills Press 2004 48p il $19.95

Grades: 4 5 6 7 **385**

1. Locomotives 2. Steam engines

ISBN 1-59078-165-1

"In this photo-essay, Zimmermann shares his excitement for steam locomotives with young readers, tracing the development of the early engines and their impact on the history of the U.S. He includes a clear explanation . . . of how a steam engine works. The photographs, some archival and some from the present day, are excellent. . . . The engaging text clearly imparts the author's enthusiasm and love for the subject." SLJ

Includes glossary

386 Inland waterway and ferry transportation

Bial, Raymond

The **canals**. Benchmark Bks. 2002 56p il map (Building America) lib bdg $27.07

Grades: 6 7 8 9 **386**

1. Canals

ISBN 0-7614-1336-7

LC 00-65078

This describes the history of canals in America from colonial times to the 19th century

This book is "marked by strong research, clear writing, good organization, and very handsome color photographs." Booklist

Includes glossary and bibliographical references

Coleman, Wim

The amazing Erie Canal and how a big ditch opened up the West; [by] Wim Coleman & Pat Perrin. MyReportLinks.com Books 2006 128p il map (The wild history of the American West) lib bdg $33.27

Grades: 6 7 8 9 **386**

1. Erie Canal (N.Y.)

ISBN 1-59845-017-4

LC 2005029389

This book "shares a brief, informative history of canals; the geographic need for the Erie Canal; and an explanation of how its creation impacted American commerce and history. . . . Throughout the text, illustrations of Web pages invite readers to search online for more detailed information. The book's text is clear, and the format is attractive, with excellent black-and-white photos and color illustrations on nearly every page." Booklist

Includes bibliographical references

Roop, Peter

River roads west; America's first highways. [by] Peter and Connie Roop. Calkins Creek 2007 64p il map $19.95

Grades: 6 7 8 9 **386**

1. Canals 2. Rivers 3. United States -- History 4. Transportation -- History

ISBN 1-59078-430-8; 978-1-59078-430-3

"The role of transportation in national history has seldom been more clearly delineated than in this meticulous treatment. Spanning prehistory to the 19th century, the sparkling text, inflected with wry humor, focuses sequentially on the Hudson River and Erie Canal, the Ohio, Mississippi, Missouri, Rio Grande, and the Colorado Rivers, and the Columbia River." SLJ

Includes bibliographical references

387.1 Ports

House, Katherine L.

Lighthouses for kids; history, science, and lore with 21 activities. [by] Katherine L. House. Chicago Review Press 2008 118p il pa $14.95

Grades: 4 5 6 7 8 **387.1**

1. Lighthouses

ISBN 978-1-55652-720-3 pa; 1-55652-720-9 pa

LC 2007-27093

"This book is noteworthy for the way in which the activities are related to the information in the text. . . . Readers learn about the challenges of building . . . [lighthouses], inventions to make them more reliable, and how lighthouses function as historical relics today." SLJ

Includes glossary and bibliographical references

387.2 Ships

Zimmermann, Karl R.

Ocean liners; crossing and cruising the seven seas. photographs by the author. Boyds Mills Press 2008 48p il $17.95

Grades: 5 6 7 8 **387.2**

1. Ocean liners 2. Ocean travel

ISBN 978-1-59078-552-2; 1-59078-552-5

LC 2007049323

This is "a comprehensive overview of ships from sail to steam to diesel, from the important modes of transportation to the modern resorts at sea. The information is organized in chapters about the history and development of the ships, the star ships of the Atlantic crossings and the conversion to modern cruising. . . . All is accompanied by photographs taken over the years by the author and supplemented by historic drawings, photos and documents. . . . A fascinating voyage." Kirkus

Includes glossary

387.7 Air transportation

Parker, Steve

By air. Marshall Cavendish Benchmark 2011 il (Future transport)

Grades: 4 5 6 **387.7**

1. Aeronautics 2. Forecasting

ISBN 1608707776; 9781608707775

LC 2011000998

"Beginning with a speculative illustration featuring people of the future traveling through the air in carlike personal jets, this title . . . offers a fascinating look at prototypes for all sorts of aircraft, from small planes to passenger airliners to lighter-than-air vehicles. . . . The various possibilities for future aircraft are covered in double-page spreads that are well laid out and easy to digest. Illustrated with plenty of striking, digitally enhanced color pictures, this will probably be of equal interest to those doing reports and browsers." Booklist

Includes bibliographical references

388 Transportation

Diaz, Julio

Tesla model s; Julio Diaz ; [edited by] Keli Sipperley. Rourke Educational Media 2016 32 p. $32.79

Grades: 4 5 6 7 8 **388**

1. Automobiles

ISBN 1681917491; 9781681917498; 9781681918501

LC 2016932712

In this middle grades book, by Julio Diaz, part of the "Vroom! Hot Cars" series, "the ground-breaking Tesla is featured in this title with information on how it is changing the automobile world." (Publisher's note)

"Some of the hottest sports car available today are highlighted in this sleek series, which delivers strong content, impressive details, and eye-popping images to young car fanatics." SLJ

Mulder, Michelle, 1976-

Pedal it! how bicycles are changing the world. Michelle Mulder. Orca Book Publishers 2013 48 p. (Footprints) (hardcover) $19.95

Grades: 3 4 5 6 7 8 **388**

1. Cycling 2. Bicycles

ISBN 1459802195; 9781459802193

LC 2012953464

This book, by Michelle Mulder, "celebrates the humble bicycle--from the very first boneshakers to the sleek racing bikes of today, from handlebars to spokes to gear sprockets--and shows you why and how bikes can make the world a better place. Not only can bikes be used to power computers and generators, they can also reduce pollution, promote wellness and get a package across a crowded city--fast!" (Publisher's note)

388.03 Transportation -- Encyclopedias

Graham, Ian

Firefly encyclopedia of transportation; a comprehensive look at the world of transportation. Oliver Green, Ian Graham, Philip Wilkinson, & Andrew Nahum. Firefly Books Ltd 2017 160 p. $14.95

Grades: 4 5 6 7 **388.03**

1. Transportation -- Encyclopedias 2. Motor vehicles 3. Transportation

ISBN 1770859314; 9781770859319

This book, by Oliver Green, Ian Graham, Philip Wilkinson and Andrew Nahum, "transports readers through the amazing history of how we get around today, how we got around in the past, and how we might be getting around in the future. Packed with more than 1000 accurate illustrations, this encyclopedic reference is divided into six easy-to-follow sections. . . . The double-page spreads are organized according to modes of transportation and purpose or method." (Publisher's note)

388.3 Vehicular transportation

Bjornlund, Lydia

What is the future of alternative energy cars? by Lydia Bjornlund. ReferencePoint Press, Inc. 2014 80 p. color illustrations (Future of renewable energy series) (hardback) $28.95

Grades: 6 7 8 9 **388.3**

1. Alternative fuel vehicles 2. Automobiles -- Fuel consumption 3. Automobiles -- Technological innovations

ISBN 1601526105; 9781601526106

LC 2013036244

This book on alternative energy cars, by Lydia Bjornlund, is "organized around a narrative-driven, pro-con [design]. . . . [It] examine[s] . . . cost, environmental impact, practicality when measured against fossil fuels, and the role of government in renewable energy's future. Important ideas are supported throughout each book by current and relevant facts, quotes, full-color statistical illustrations, and anecdotes." (Publisher's note)

"Well written and understandable, the authors use a wide variety of source material to present each side fairly and completely. The question/answer format of the chapters breaks the topics into simplified arguments that can easily be absorbed." VOYA

Includes bibliographical references and index

388.4 Local transportation

Reis, Ronald A.

The **New** York City subway system. Chelsea House 2009 136p il (Building America: then and now) lib bdg $35

Grades: 6 7 8 9 **388.4**

1. Subways 2. New York (N.Y.) 3. Transportation -- History

ISBN 978-1-60413-046-1 lib bdg; 1-60413-046-6 lib bdg

LC 2008-25550

This is a history of New York City's subway system

Includes glossary and bibliographical references

Sandler, Martin W.

★ **Secret** subway; the fascinating tale of an amazing feat of engineering. National Geographic 2009 96p il map $17.95; lib bdg $26.90

Grades: 5 6 7 8 **388.4**

1. Subways 2. New York (N.Y.) -- History

ISBN 978-1-4263-0462-0; 1-4263-0462-5; 978-1-4263-0463-7 lib bdg; 1-4263-0463-3 lib bdg

LC 2008-39831

"Sandler takes an in-depth look at the building of New York's first subway. . . . [He] writes about the subway in a well-put-together book with interesting information, great pictures, and a compelling true story." Voice Youth Advocates

Includes bibliographical references

391 Customs

Albee, Sarah

Why'd They Wear That? Fashion As the Mirror of History. by Sarah Albee ; foreword by Tim Gunn. Natl Geographic Soc Childrens books 2015 192 p. $19.99

Grades: 5 6 7 8 9 **391**

1. Fashion -- History 2. Clothing and dress -- History

ISBN 1426319193; 9781426319198

In this book, by Sarah Albee, "kids will learn about outrageous, politically-perilous, funky, disgusting, regrettable, and life-threatening creations people have worn throughout the course of human history, all the way up to the present day. From spats and togas to hoop skirts and hair shirts, why people wore what they did is an illuminating way to look at the social, economic, political, and moral climates throughout history." (Publisher's note)

"As the subtitle says, this hefty, extensively illustrated book uses fashion to discuss the ways and whys people dress and how it reflects what's happening in their civilization. . . . The many photographs are well chosen and reproduced, and Albee writes in a conversational style that, though occasionally repetitive, is instantly appealing to readers. Tim Gunn writes the foreword, and a timeline and bibliography conclude." Booklist

Bailey, Diane

Tattoo art around the world. Rosen Pub. 2011 64p il (Tattooing) lib bdg $30.60; pa $12.95

Grades: 7 8 9 10 **391**

1. Tattooing

ISBN 978-1-4488-4618-4 lib bdg; 1-4488-4618-8 lib bdg; 978-1-4488-4622-1 pa; 1-4488-4622-6 pa

LC 2010048428

This book "discusses how different cultures have used tattoos. . . . The design and the reading level are accessible without talking down to the audience, so this is a good choice for enticing reluctant readers with an interest in body art." Booklist

Includes bibliographical references

Baker, Patricia

Fashions of a decade, The 1940s. Chelsea House Publishers 2006 64p il $35

Grades: 7 8 9 10 11 12 **391**

1. Costume

ISBN 0-8160-6720-1; 978-0-8160-6720-6

LC 2006-49934

First published 1992

Chronicles clothing trends of the 1940s and the influence of World War II on styles of dress, availability of many fabrics, and the new ideas of "designers at war"

Includes glossary and bibliographical references

Fashions of a decade, The 1950s. Chelsea House Publishers 2006 64p il $35

Grades: 7 8 9 10 11 12 **391**

1. Costume

ISBN 0-8160-6721-X; 978-0-8160-6721-3

LC 2006-50142

First published 1992

Surveys the fads, fashions, trends, and cultural and intellectual preoccupations of the 1950s

Includes glossary and bibliographical references

Bix, Cynthia Overbeck

Petticoats and frock coats; revolution and Victorian Age fashions from the 1770s to the 1860s. Twenty-First Century Books 2011 64p il (Dressing a nation: the history of U.S. fashion) lib bdg $31.93

Grades: 7 8 9 10 **391**

1. Fashion 2. American national characteristics 3. Clothing and dress -- History 4. United States -- Social life and customs 5. United States -- History -- 1600-1775, Colonial period

ISBN 978-0-7613-5888-6; 0-7613-5888-9

LC 2010053384

This is a history of fashion in the U.S. from the 1770s to the 1860s.

Includes bibliographical references

Bliss, John

Preening, painting, and piercing; body art. Raintree 2010 32p il (Culture in action) lib bdg $29

Grades: 5 6 7 8 **391**

1. Body art 2. Cosmetics 3. Tattooing 4. Theatrical makeup

ISBN 978-1-4109-3924-1; 1-4109-3924-1

LC 2009051182

"This book covers different looks achieved through makeup, body painting, tattoos, and piercing. Photographs, advertisements, paintings, and artifacts show a variety of cultures and time periods and help readers see the huge changes in the fashion of physical appearance. . . . The author does a good job of explaining that some cultures have negative stereotypes of tattooed people being criminals and some piercing can be dangerous to people with allergies. Fun activities are included. . . . This book . . . is well written and has few biases." SLJ

Includes glossary and bibliographical references

Carnegy, Vicky

Fashions of a decade, The 1980s. Chelsea House Publishers 2006 64p il $35

Grades: 7 8 9 10 11 12 **391**

1. Costume

ISBN 978-0-8160-6724-4; 0-8160-6724-4

LC 2006-49458

First published 1992

A pictorial survey chronicling the international clothing fashions of the 1980s

This "provides an accessible overview of the decade, placing fashion trends within their appropriate political and historical contexts. . . . Browsers and fashion design students alike will be intrigued." Booklist

Includes glossary and bibliographical references

Clancy Steer, Deirdre

The **1980s** and 1990s. Chelsea House 2009 64p il (Costume & fashion source books) $35

Grades: 6 7 8 9 **391**

1. Costume -- History 2. Fashion -- History 3. Clothing and dress -- History 4. United States -- Social life and customs

ISBN 978-1-60413-386-8; 1-60413-386-4

LC 2009-6700

This describes how gender, occasion, class, and social clime affected fashion during the 1980s and 1990s.

This is written "in a clear, engaging style. . . . [The] volume is profusely and gorgeously illustrated with period paintings and photographs, movie and TV stills, design sketches, and photographs from period reenactments. Each illustration is captioned with intriguing, relevant facts that enhance the text." SLJ

Includes glossary and bibliographical references

Colonial America; [by] Deirdre Clancy Steer and Amela Baksic. Chelsea House 2009 64p il (Costume & fashion source books) $35

Grades: 6 7 8 9 **391**

1. Costume -- History 2. Fashion -- History 3. Clothing and dress -- History 4. United States -- Social life and customs -- 1600-1775, Colonial period

ISBN 978-1-60413-380-6; 1-60413-380-5

A look at what kinds of clothing people in colonial America wore.

This is written "in a clear, engaging style. . . . [The] volume is profusely and gorgeously illustrated with period paintings and photographs, movie and TV stills, design sketches, and photographs from period reenactments. Each illustration is captioned with intriguing, relevant facts that enhance the text." SLJ

Connikie, Yvonne

Fashions of a decade, The 1960s. Chelsea House Publishers 2006 64p il $35

Grades: 7 8 9 10 11 12 **391**

1. Costume

ISBN 0-8160-6722-8; 978-0-8160-6722-0

First published 1992

A pictorial survey chronicling the international fashions of the 1960s

This is "not for serious students of fashion, but will be fun for browsers and those interested in an introduction to the concept of clothing design in the context of contemporary events." SLJ

Includes glossary and bibliographical references

Costantino, Maria

Fashions of a decade, The 1930s. Chelsea House Publishers 2006 64p il $35

Grades: 7 8 9 10 11 12 **391**

1. Costume

ISBN 0-8160-6719-8; 978-0-8160-6719-0

LC 2006-49933

First published 1992

Chronicles trends in 1930s styles such as lower hemlines and broader shoulders; the introduction of synthetic fabrics; and new views of fitness, health, and personal beauty

Includes glossary and bibliographical references

Croll, Jennifer

Bad boys of fashion; style rebels and renegades through the ages. Jennifer Croll, illustrated by Aneta Pacholska. Annick Press 2019 184 p. $24.95

Grades: 6 7 8 9 10 11 12 **391**

1. Men's clothing 2. Fashion -- History

ISBN 1773212435; 9781773212432

LC 2019300024

This book, by Jennifer Croll, illustrated by Aneta Pacholska, "shows us the power of clothes and the links between fashion and politics, art, social movements, and more. Croll's lively and engaging prose draws in the reader, providing enough information to satisfy both budding fashionistas and pop-culture junkies alike. . . . Pacholska's illustrations are modern and fun, perfectly complementing the text and making the book as exciting to look at as it is to read." (Publisher's note)

Elgin, Kathy

Elizabethan England. Chelsea House 2009 64p il (Costume & fashion source books) $35

Grades: 6 7 8 9 **391**

1. Costume -- History 2. Fashion -- History 3. Clothing and dress -- History 4. Great Britain -- History -- 1485-1603, Tudors

ISBN 978-1-60413-379-0; 1-60413-379-1

LC 2008-47258

This describes how gender, occasion, class, and social clime affected fashion in Elizabethan England.

This is written "in a clear, engaging style. . . . [The] volume is profusely and gorgeously illustrated with period paintings and photographs, movie and TV stills, design sketches, and photographs from period reenactments. Each illustration is captioned with intriguing, relevant facts that enhance the text." SLJ

Includes glossary and bibliographical references

The **medieval** world. Chelsea House 2009 64p il (Costume & fashion source books) $35

Grades: 6 7 8 9 **391**

1. Medieval civilization 2. Costume -- History 3. Fashion -- History 4. Clothing and dress -- History

ISBN 978-1-60413-378-3; 1-60413-378-3

LC 2008-47259

This describes how gender, occasion, class, and social clime affected clothing and dress during the Middle Ages.

This is written "in a clear, engaging style. . . . [The] volume is profusely and gorgeously illustrated with period paintings and photographs, movie and TV stills, design sketches, and photographs from period reenactments. Each illustration is captioned with intriguing, relevant facts that enhance the text." SLJ

Includes glossary and bibliographical references

★ Fashions of a decade [series] Chelsea House Publishers 2006 8v il set $280

Grades: 7 8 9 10 11 12 **391**

1. Costume

ISBN 0-8160-7059-8; 978-0-8160-7059-6

First published 1991-1992

This set describes clothing styles of the 20th century in the context of world events, social movements, and cultural movements of each decade.

"These titles provide colorful and fascinating information. . . . Attractive black-and-white illustrations, color photos, reproductions, sketches from magazines and newspapers, and fact boxes enhance and bring to life these lively and accessible texts." SLJ

Gerber, Larry

Getting inked; what to expect when you get a tattoo. Rosen Pub. 2011 64p il (Tattooing) lib bdg $30.60; pa $12.95

Grades: 7 8 9 10 **391**

1. Tattooing

ISBN 978-1-4488-4616-0 lib bdg; 978-1-4488-4621-4 pa

LC 2010045970

This book "details how to find a competent tattoo artist, what the inking process is like, and how to care for the tattoo afterward. . . . Illustrations . . . are of high quality. . . . The design and the reading level are accessible without talking down to the audience, so this is a good choice for enticing reluctant readers with an interest in body art." Booklist

Includes bibliographical references

Graydon, Shari

In your face; the culture of beauty and you. Annick 2004 176p il hardcover o.p. pa $14.95

Grades: 7 8 9 10 **391**

1. Body image 2. Personal appearance

ISBN 1-55037-857-0; 1-55037-856-2 pa

The author "looks at fashion across time and cultures, and analyzes the underlying messages in today's focus . . . on thinness, long nails, and high heels. Along the way, she warns both young men and women of the very real dangers of eating disorders, plastic surgery, liposuction, and other body-image 'solutions.' . . . Graydon will make readers laugh as well as think about the issues." Booklist

Includes bibliographical references

Herald, Jacqueline

Fashions of a decade, The 1920s. Chelsea House Publishers 2006 64p il $35

Grades: 7 8 9 10 11 12 **391**

1. Costume

ISBN 0-8160-6718-X; 978-0-8160-6718-3

LC 2006-49932

First published 1992

Surveys the fads, fashions, trends, and cultural and intellectual preoccupations of the 1920s

"Students interested in fashion and societal changes, as well as those in need of a good outline reference, will find this volume . . . helpful." Booklist

Includes glossary and bibliographical references

Fashions of a decade, The 1970s. Chelsea House Publishers 2006 64p il $35

Grades: 7 8 9 10 11 12 **391**

1. Costume

ISBN 0-8160-6723-6; 978-0-8160-6723-7

LC 2006-46807

First published 1992

This volume in the series looks at how the fashions of the 1970s reflected the social, historical and cultural events of that decade

This "includes chapters on 'Black is Beautiful,' 'Dressed to Clash,' 'Trash Culture,' etc. . . . An abundance of full-color and black-and-white illustrations and photographs amplify the text with generally appropriate placement and captions." SLJ

Includes glossary and bibliographical references

Kyi, Tanya Lloyd

The **blue** jean book; the story behind the seams. Annick Press 2005 79p il $24.95; pa $12.95 **391**

1. Jeans (Clothing)

ISBN 1-55037-917-8; 1-55037-916-X pa

"Kyi traces the history of these pants from the early life of Levi Strauss and the patented riveted pocket to the stiff competition and controversy of production in our modern world. . . . History and social issues are intertwined to show how activities, jobs, and the economy influence the development and production of clothing. . . . This is an enjoyable read for anyone wishing to know more about this fashion item and an excellent resource for an introduction to product development and economy." SLJ

McEvoy, Anne

The **1920s** and 1930s. Chelsea House 2009 64p il (Costume & fashion source books) $35

Grades: 6 7 8 9 **391**

1. Fashion -- History 2. Clothing and dress -- History 3. United States -- Social life and customs

ISBN 978-1-60413-383-7; 1-60413-383-X

LC 2009-1236

This describes how gender, occasion, class, and social clime affected fashion during the 1920s and 1930s.

This is written "in a clear, engaging style. . . . [The] volume is profusely and gorgeously illustrated with period paintings and photographs, movie and TV stills, design sketches, and photographs from period reenactments. Each illustration is captioned with intriguing, relevant facts that enhance the text." SLJ

Includes glossary and bibliographical references

The **American** West. Chelsea House 2009 64p il (Costume & fashion source books) $35

Grades: 6 7 8 9 **391**

1. Native American costume 2. Frontier and pioneer life 3. Costume -- History 4. Fashion -- History 5. Clothing and dress -- History 6. West (U.S.) -- Social life and customs

ISBN 978-1-60413-382-0; 1-60413-382-1

LC 2008-47261

A look at what was worn by pioneers and settlers as well as Native Americans as the West opened up.

This is written "in a clear, engaging style. . . . [The] volume is profusely and gorgeously illustrated with period paintings and photographs, movie and TV stills, design sketches, and photographs from period reenactments. Each illustration is captioned with intriguing, relevant facts that enhance the text." SLJ

Includes glossary and bibliographical references

Fashions of a decade, The 1990s. Chelsea House Publishers 2006 64p il $35

Grades: 7 8 9 10 11 12 **391**

1. Costume

ISBN 0-8160-6725-2; 978-0-8160-6725-1

LC 2006-41268

First published 1992

A pictorial survey of the 1990s fashion trends

"The major flaw is that the book understandably includes only two years' worth of information; certainly the years 1992-1999 deserve treatment before a volume may purport to be about the entire decade." SLJ

Includes glossary and bibliographical references

Nagle, Jeanne

Why people get tattoos and other body art. Rosen 2011 64p il (Tattooing) lib bdg $30.60; pa $12.95

Grades: 7 8 9 10 **391**

1. Tattooing

ISBN 978-1-4488-4617-7 lib bdg; 978-1-4488-4620-7 pa

LC 2011000276

This book "explains the appeal of tattoos for a wide variety of people as a way of expressing themselves aesthetically, religiously, or for other reasons. Illustrations . . . are of high quality. . . . The design and the reading level are accessible without talking down to the audience, so this is a good choice for enticing reluctant readers with an interest in body art." Booklist

Includes bibliographical references

Pendergast, Sara

Fashion, costume, and culture; clothing, headwear, body decoration, and footwear through the ages. [by] Sara Pendergast and Tom Pendergast. U.X.L 2004 5v il set $275

Grades: 6 7 8 9 **391**

1. Fashion 2. Clothing and dress 3. Costume -- History

ISBN 0-7876-5417-5

This set "surveys how people have covered and adorned themselves through the ages and around the world. . . . There are 430 entries in all, ranging from a paragraph or two to a page. . . . The work is notable for its organization, breadth of coverage, and attractive design. Strongly recommended for school and public libraries." Booklist

Platt, Richard

They wore what?! the weird history of fashion and beauty. [by] Richard Platt. Two-Can 2007 48p il $16.95; pa $9.95

Grades: 4 5 6 **391**

1. Personal appearance 2. Fashion -- History

ISBN 978-1-58728-582-0; 1-58728-582-7; 978-1-58728-584-4 pa; 1-58728-584-3 pa

LC 2006039159

Published in the United Kingdom with title: Would you believe in 1500, platform shoes were outlawed?

"Busy, colorful pages recount the historical, social, and political sides of clothing, hair, hats, and shoes, from legal and moral issues such as wearing fur to dangerous practices like cinched waists and bound feet. . . . Ever-fluctuating ideas of beauty and body image are also explored." Horn Book Guide

Includes glossary and bibliographical references

Rooney, Anne

The **1950s** and 1960s. Chelsea House 2009 64p il (Costume & fashion source books) $35

Grades: 6 7 8 9 **391**

1. Costume -- History 2. Fashion -- History 3. Clothing and dress -- History 4. United States -- Social life and customs

ISBN 978-1-60413-385-1; 1-60413-385-6

LC 2008-47260

This describes how gender, occasion, class, and social clime affected fashion during the 1950s and 1960s

This is written "in a clear, engaging style. . . . [The] volume is profusely and gorgeously illustrated with period paintings and photographs, movie and TV stills, design sketches, and photographs from period reenactments. Each illustration is captioned with intriguing, relevant facts that enhance the text." SLJ

Includes glossary and bibliographical references

Spalding, Frank

Erasing the ink; getting rid of your tattoo. Rosen Pub. 2011 64p il (Tattooing) lib bdg $30.60; pa $12.95

Grades: 7 8 9 10 **391**

1. Skin 2. Tattooing

ISBN 978-1-4488-4615-3 lib bdg; 978-1-4488-4619-1 pa

LC 2010045920

This book "focuses . . . on the negatives of getting a tattoo and the difficulties of removing them. . . . Illustrations . . . are of high quality. . . . The design and the reading level are accessible without talking down to the audience, so this is a good choice for enticing reluctant readers with an interest in body art." Booklist

Includes bibliographical references

Taschek, Karen

The **Civil** War. Chelsea House 2009 64p il (Costume & fashion source books) $35

Grades: 6 7 8 9 **391**

1. Costume -- History 2. Fashion -- History 3. Clothing and dress -- History 4. United States -- History -- 1861-1865, Civil War

ISBN 978-1-60413-381-3; 1-60413-381-3

LC 2008-47262

A look at the clothing and styles on both sides of the Civil War.

This is written "in a clear, engaging style. . . . [The] volume is profusely and gorgeously illustrated with period paintings and photographs, movie and TV stills, design sketches, and photographs from period reenactments. Each illustration is captioned with intriguing, relevant facts that enhance the text." SLJ

Includes glossary and bibliographical references

391.009 History, geographic treatment, biography

Croll, Jennifer

Fashion that changed the world; Jennifer Croll. Prestel Verlag 2014 192 p. ill. (chiefly color), portrait $19.95

Grades: 6 7 8 9 10 11 12 **391.009**

1. Fashion -- History

ISBN 3791347896; 9783791347899

LC 2014940422

This book, by Jennifer Croll, is an "exploration of the most influential fashion icons, ideas, designers, pieces, and trends from throughout history. What did Vogue's first cover look like? When did film stars become part of the fashion industry? What led to the development of ready-to-wear clothing? How did the paintings of Mondrian, Dalí and Warhol end up on the runway?" (Publisher's note)

Includes bibliographical references (page 192) and index.

391.4 Kinds of garments; accessories; buttons

Kyi, Tanya Lloyd, 1973-

50 underwear questions; a bare-all history. by Tanya Kyi and illustrated by Ross Kinnaird. Annick Press 2011 116 p. $21.95

Grades: 4 5 6 7 **391.4**

1. Underwear 2. Clothing and dress -- History

ISBN 1554513537; 9781554513536

This book, by Tanya Kyi and illustrated by Ross Kinnaird, examines the history of underwear. "The format, as the title indicates, is question-and-answer. Beginning with 'ancient undies,' the questions cover everything from what's worn under certain kinds of dress to how the modern bra came into being, and reasons for wearing underclothes in the first place." (Booklist)

392 Customs of life cycle and domestic life

Hepplewhite, Peter

Loos, poos, and number twos; a disgusting journey through the bowels of history! Peter Hepplewhite. Gareth Stevens Publishing 2016 32 p. color illustrations $26.60

Grades: 4 5 6 7 8 **392**

1. Sewage disposal

ISBN 9781482431186

LC 2015458295

This children's book, by Peter Hepplewhite, explores the history of the toilet "from the sewage system of ancient Athens to the muckrakers of the Middle Ages. . . . Unique information reframes common social studies topics and time periods including ancient China, Victorian times, and more." (Publisher's note)

"A lively, surprisingly informative, high-interest volume that manages to both entertain and educate." Booklist

Includes bibliographical references and index

393 Death customs

Colman, Penny

★ **Corpses,** coffins, and crypts; a history of burial. Holt & Co. 1997 212p il $17.95

Grades: 7 8 9 10 **393**

1. Death 2. Burial 3. Funeral rites and ceremonies

ISBN 0-8050-5066-3

LC 97-7842

Documents the burial process throughout the centuries and in different cultures.

The author "is both candid and detailed in her handling of the gruesome nitty-gritty. . . . Many of the photographs in the liberally illustrated text are from her own explorations, and all are captioned, some in great detail. . . . She's filled her sensitive, solid book with answers to questions people often need and want to know but are too reluctant to ask." Booklist

Includes glossary and bibliographical references

Deem, James M.

★ **Bodies** from the ice; melting glaciers and the recovery of the past. Houghton Mifflin 2008 58p il map $17

Grades: 5 6 7 8 9 10 **393**

1. Mummies 2. Glaciers

ISBN 978-0-618-80045-2; 0-618-80045-X

LC 2008-01868

A Sibert Medal honor book, 2009

This describes the discovery of human remains preserved in glaciers in the Alps, the Andes, The Himalayas, and other places around the world and what can be learned from them

"Full-color photographs, reproductions, and maps are clearly captioned; grand images of glaciated mountain peaks span entire pages, and detailed pictures of recovered objects . . . are presented. . . . [This] is a fantastic resource. Deem superbly weaves diverse geographical settings, time periods, and climate issues into a readable work that reveals the increasing interdisciplinary dimensions of the sciences." SLJ

Includes bibliographical references

Greene, Meg

Rest in peace; a history of American cemeteries. Twenty-First Century Books 2008 112p il map (People's history) lib bdg $30.60

Grades: 8 9 10 11 12 **393**

1. Burial 2. Cemeteries 3. United States -- Social life and customs
ISBN 978-0-8225-3414-3 lib bdg; 0-8225-3414-2 lib bdg
LC 2007022093

"This account of cemeteries in the U.S. offers a sweeping history . . . as well as plenty of noteworthy details, illustrated thoughout with black-and-white photos shaded in sepia tones. . . . This book . . . presents many aspects of an unusual topic." Booklist

Includes bibliographical references

Halls, Kelly Milner

Mysteries of the mummy kids. Darby Creek Pub. 2007 72p il map $18.95

Grades: 4 5 6 7 **393**

1. Mummies
ISBN 978-1-58196-059-4; 1-58196-059-X

"Halls presents an eerily fascinating exploration of mummified children and teens found in South and North America, Europe, and Asia. . . . The writing style is plain yet absorbing, presenting scientific and historical information in simple terms." Voice Youth Advocates

Includes bibliographical references

Hollihan, Kerrie Logan

★ **Mummies** exposed! by Kerrie Logan Hollihan. Abrams Books for Young Readers 2019 208 p. (hardcover) $16.99

Grades: 5 6 7 8 9 **393**

1. Archeology 2. Mummies 3. Mummification
ISBN 9781419731679
LC 2018014310

This book about mummies, in the Creepy and True series, by Kerrie Logan Hollihan, "goes beyond what you expect and uncovers both old favorites and recent discoveries; among them a Moche princess in Peru, the bog people of England and Ireland, and a Buddhist monk discovered within a sculpture! Featuring the most contemporary research, a touch of humor, and full-color illustrations, this exciting read is perfect for curious young minds." (Publisher's note)

"This wide-ranging and well-researched survey of mummies from around the world is a highly recommended purchase for school and public libraries." (School Library Journal)

Includes bibliographical references and index

Knapp, Ron

Mummy secrets uncovered. Enslow Publishers 2011 48p il (Bizarre science) lib bdg $23.93

Grades: 5 6 7 8 **393**

1. Mummies
ISBN 978-0-7660-3670-3; 0-7660-3670-7
LC 2010000976

First published 1996 with title: Mummies

This describes mummies such as the Iceman found in the Italian Alps in 1991, King Tut of Egypt, the people of Pompeii killed by the eruption of Mount Vesuvius, Tollund Man found in Denmark in 1950, and the Ice Maiden found in the Siberian Steppes.

"Aimed at reluctant readers, [this title is] sure to disgust and delight in equal measure. . . . [The title] will pique interest and get kids lining up at the reference desk looking for more. The text is complemented by illustrations and magnified photos of things that you would hope never to see." SLJ

Includes glossary and bibliographical references

Malam, John

Mummies; foreword by Ron Beckett and Gerald Conlogue. Kingfisher 2003 63p il (Kingfisher knowledge) $11.95

Grades: 5 6 7 8 **393**

1. Mummies
ISBN 0-7534-5623-0
LC 2003-44630

"Malam covers Egyptian mummies; the discovery of a variety of preserved bodies throughout history and the world in bogs, deserts, and ice; animal mummies; and mummies today. [The title includes] stunning, captioned photos and illustrations that emphasize the many intriguing factual details in the text." SLJ

Includes glossary and bibliographical references

Markle, Sandra

★ **Outside** and inside mummies. Walker & Co. 2005 40p il $17.95; lib bdg $18.85

Grades: 4 5 6 7 **393**

1. Mummies
ISBN 0-8027-8966-8; 0-8027-8967-6 lib bdg
LC 2004-66128

"Markle explores a global smorgasbord of mummy varieties, both those created by human procedures and those caused by nature. Crisp (if gruesome) color photos accompany the readable, informative text, which discusses not only the mummification process, but also the cutting-edge technologies used by forensic anthropologists and others to study the mummies themselves." SLJ

Includes glossary

Perl, Lila

Mummies, tombs, and treasure; secrets of ancient Egypt. drawings by Erika Weihs. Clarion Bks. 1987 120p il lib bdg $16; pa $8.95

Grades: 4 5 6 7 **393**

1. Mummies 2. Funeral rites and ceremonies 3. Egypt -- Antiquities
ISBN 0-89919-407-9 lib bdg; 0-395-54796-2 pa
LC 86-17646

This "book is attractive, readable, plentifully illustrated with drawings and black-and-white photographs. . . . Phonetic pronunciations throughout make this easily accessible." Appraisal

Includes bibliographical references

Robson, David

The **mummy**. ReferencePoint Press 2011 il (Monsters and mythical creatures) $27.95

Grades: 6 7 8 9 **393**

1. Mummies
ISBN 978-1-60152-182-8; 1-60152-182-0
LC 2011022437

This is "an ideal starting point for young researchers interested in the weird, mysterious, and paranormal. Using fleet, descriptive prose to communicate the impressively researched (and sourced) information, [this] medium-length [work manages] to rope in just about everything, from folklore to history to pop culture. . . . TheMummy begins with the seminal 1932 Boris Karloff film before backtracking into the worldwide 'mummy lust' that began with the 1922 discovery of King Tut's tomb and and the subsequent curses and legends. . . . The illustrations are fine and varied, the sidebars always illuminating, and the back matter robust." Booklist

Includes bibliographical references

Sloan, Christopher

Mummies. National Geographic 2010 48p il (National Geographic Kids) $17.95; lib bdg $26.90

Grades: 4 5 6 7 **393**

1. Mummies

ISBN 978-1-4263-0695-2; 1-4263-0695-4; 978-1-4263-0696-9 lib bdg; 1-4263-0696-2 lib bdg

LC 2010-08498

"A gratifyingly grisly album of choice photos accompanies Sloan's lucid, informative text as he describes not only the mummification processes but also individual mummies produced whether by intent or by chance. From the dried Beauty of Kroràn in China to the bundled Lady of Cao in a Peruvian pyramid or the familiar Boy King Tut in Egypt, a global variety is offered to fascinated readers. . . . [This is a] well-written, heavily illustrated glimpse into the world of after-death preservation, either by accident or design." SLJ

Includes glossary and bibliographical references

394.1 Eating, drinking; using drugs

Augustin, Byron

The **food** of Mexico. Marshall Cavendish Benchmark 2011 il (Flavors of the world) $21.95

Grades: 4 5 6 7 **394.1**

1. Mexican cooking 2. Festivals -- Mexico 3. Mexico -- Social life and customs

ISBN 978-1-6087-0237-4

LC 2010013830

"Explores the culture of Mexico through its food." (Publisher's note)

Includes bibliographical references

Kras, Sara Louise

The **food** of Italy. Marshall Cavendish Benchmark 2011 il (Flavors of the world) $21.95

Grades: 4 5 6 7 **394.1**

1. Italian cooking 2. Festivals -- Italy 3. Italy -- Social life and customs

ISBN 978-1-6087-0236-7

LC 2010021542

This explores the culture, traditions, and festivals of Italy through its food.

Includes bibliographical references

Kummer, Patricia K.

The **food** of Thailand. Marshall Cavendish Benchmark 2011 il (Flavors of the world) $21.95

Grades: 4 5 6 7 **394.1**

1. Thai cooking 2. Festivals -- Thailand 3. Thailand -- Social life and customs

ISBN 978-1-6087-0238-1

LC 2010023508

This explores the culture, traditions, and festivals of Thailand through its food.

Includes bibliographical references

Orr, Tamra

The **food** of China; [by] Tamra B. Orr. Marshall Cavendish Benchmark 2011 il (Flavors of the world)

Grades: 4 5 6 7 **394.1**

1. Chinese cooking 2. Festivals -- China 3. China -- Social life and customs

ISBN 1-608-70234-0; 978-1-608-70234-3; 978-1-608-70687-7 e-book

LC 2010039293

This explores the culture, traditions, and festivals of China through its food.

"Numerous high-quality, close-up color photos of outdoor vegetable markets, food in various stages of preparation, and families gathering around the table will keep readers engaged (and hungry) throughout the accessible and enlightening food tour." Booklist

Includes bibliographical references

The **food** of Greece; [by] Tamra B. Orr. Marshall Cavendish Benchmark 2011 il (Flavors of the world) $21.95

Grades: 4 5 6 7 **394.1**

1. Greek cooking 2. Festivals -- Greece 3. Greece -- Social life and customs

ISBN 978-1-6087-0235-0; 978-1-6087-0688-4 e-book

LC 2010035820

This explores the culture, traditions, and festivals of Greece through its food.

Includes bibliographical references

Schlosser, Eric

★ **Chew** on this; everything you don't want to know about fast food. by Eric Schlosser and Charles Wilson. Houghton Mifflin Co. 2006 304p il $16; pa $9.99

Grades: 6 7 8 9 10 **394.1**

1. Eating habits 2. Food industry 3. Convenience foods

ISBN 0-618-71031-0; 0-618-59394-2 pa

LC 2005-27527

"An adaptation of Schlosser's Fast Food Nation (Houghton, 2001), Chew on This covers the history of the fast-food industry and delves into the agribusiness and animal husbandry methods that support it. . . . Equally disturbing is his revelation of the way that the fast-food giants have studied childhood behavior and geared their commercials and free toy inclusions to hook the youngest consumers. The text is written in a lively, layout-the-facts manner. Occasional photographs add bits of visual interest." SLJ

Silverstein, Alvin

Chocolate ants, maggot cheese, and more; the yucky food book. by Alvin and Virginia Silverstein and Laura Silverstein Nunn; illustrated by Gerald Kelley. Enslow Publishers 2010 48p il (Yucky science) lib bdg $23.93

Grades: 4 5 6 7 **394.1**

1. Eating customs

ISBN 978-0-7660-3315-3 lib bdg; 0-7660-3315-5 lib bdg

LC 2009012283

"Written in an engaging and conversational style and full of revolting descriptions and entertaining cartoon illustrations . . . [this is] sure to turn even the strongest stomach. An introduction . . . puts 'yucky' in perspective, reminding kids that our world is diverse and that everyone has a different definition of repulsive." SLJ

Includes glossary and bibliographical references

Whitman, Sylvia

What's cooking? the history of American food. Lerner Publs. 2001 88p il (People's history) lib bdg $22.60

Grades: 5 6 7 8 **394.1**

1. Food -- History 2. United States -- Social life and customs

ISBN 0-8225-1732-9

LC 00-9168

A look at food in the United States from colonial times to the present, describing what we have eaten, where it came from, and how it reflected events in American history

"The text is very accessible, and there are many interesting black-and-white photographs. . . . Intriguing as well as informative." Booklist

Includes bibliographical references

Zimmern, Andrew

Andrew Zimmern's field guide to exceptionally weird, wild, & wonderful foods; an intrepid eater's digest. by Andrew Zimmern. 1st ed. Feiwel & Friends 2012 197 p. ill. (paperback) $14.99; (hardcover) $19.99

Grades: 5 6 7 **394.1**

1. Food 2. Cooking

ISBN 0312606613; 125001929X; 9780312606619; 9781250019295

LC 2012289475

This book is a "guide to world cuisine." The authors Andrew Zimmern and Molly Mogren "focus on 40 unusual foodstuffs including cockroaches, guinea pigs, headcheese, lutefisk, turducken, and Twinkies. Recipes, interviews, and a great many facts . . . lead to . . . digressions, including suggestions on how to survive a zombie outbreak . . . and a time line of popular dances, following a discussion of eating 'dancing' (live) shrimp." (Publishers Weekly)

394.2 Special occasions

Heath, Alan

Windows on the world; multicultural festivals for schools and libraries. Scarecrow Press 1995 392p il hardcover o.p. pa $47.95

Grades: Adult Professional **394.2**

1. Festivals 2. Multiculturalism

ISBN 0-8108-2880-4; 0-8108-3958-X pa

LC 94-10032

This guide "promotes reading through thematic festive activities centered around diverse cultural celebrations. Students explore varied art forms, from sculpture, print-making, batik, and puppetry to drama, music, dancing, cooking, and writing. . . . The book is profusely illustrated with photographs, diagrams, activity sheets, maps, bulletin board ideas, and . . . instructions for arts and crafts projects." Publisher's note

Includes bibliographical references

394.26 Holidays

Bowler, Gerald

The **world** encyclopedia of Christmas; [by] Gerry Bowler. McClelland & Stewart 2000 257p il hardcover o.p. pa $12.95

Grades: 8 9 10 11 12 **394.26**

1. Reference books 2. Christmas -- Encyclopedias

ISBN 0-7710-1531-3; 0-7710-1535-6 pa

This "provides more than 1,000 entries on worldwide secular and religious Christmas practices expressed in song, literature, events, film, arts, and trivia and is aimed at young adult and adult readers as well as researchers. Entries are primarily descriptive, but a number of them, especially those on films, contain critical commentary. . . . The book is enticing reading with its many descriptions of exotic customs and its blend of the ancient and the modern. It is written well and concisely." Booklist

Breuilly, Elizabeth

Festivals of the world; the illustrated guide to celebrations, customs, events, and holidays. [by] Elizabeth Breuilly, Joanne O'Brien, Martin Palmer. Checkmark Bks. 2002 160p il maps $29.95

Grades: 6 7 8 9 **394.26**

1. Festivals 2. Reference books 3. Religious holidays

ISBN 0-8160-4481-3

LC 2001-59876

The religions featured include Judaism, Christianity, Islam, Hinduism, Buddhism, Sikhism, Taoism, and Zoroastrianism

"A unique approach to holidays, organized by religion rather than alphabet, marks this thoughtful reference book. The introduction relates world festivals to the universal human search for meaning, and offers thematic relationships between seemingly disparate events. . . . Beautiful full-color photographs, diagrams, and maps bring the celebrations to life, and informative text boxes offer additional facts. . . . This book deserves to be in every reference collection." SLJ

Includes glossary and bibliographical references

Colman, Penny

Thanksgiving; the true story. [by] Penny Colman. Henry Holt 2008 149p il $18.95

Grades: 5 6 7 8 **394.26**

1. Thanksgiving Day 2. United States -- Social life and customs

ISBN 978-0-8050-8229-6; 0-8050-8229-8

LC 2007046943

"Drawing on historical research and the results of a written questionaire, Colman first retraces the growth of Thanksgiving as a national holiday and then surveys the wide range of customs and mouthwatering comestibles associated with the celebration. Both tracks are illuminating. . . . A selection of old photos and prints illustrate this engagingly presented [title]." Booklist

Includes bibliographical references

★ **Giving** thanks; poems, prayers, and praise songs of thanksgiving. edited and with reflections by Katherine Paterson ; illustrated by Pamela Dalton. Chronicle Books LLC 2013 56 p. $18.99

Grades: 3 4 5 6 7 8 **394.26**

1. Thanksgiving Day 2. Picture books for children 3. Gratitude 4. Children's poetry 5. Children -- Prayers and devotions 6. Religious poetry 7. Gratitude -- Religious aspects

ISBN 1452113394; 9781452113395

LC 2013009517

Katherine Paterson presents a collection of speeches, songs, and prayers related to giving thanks. She "offers an essay before each section: 'Gather Around the Table,' 'A Celebration of Life,' 'The Spirit Within' and 'Circle of Community.'" (Kirkus Reviews)

Henderson, Helene

Patriotic holidays of the United States; an introduction to the history, symbols, and traditions behind the major holidays and days of observance. by Helene Henderson; foreword by Matthew Dennis. Omnigraphics 2006 408p il map $63

Grades: 7 8 9 10 11 12 **394.26**

1. Holidays 2. Patriotism 3. United States -- Social life and

customs
ISBN 0-7808-0733-2
LC 2005024870

"Henderson defines patriotic holidays as those dealing with aspects of democratic civic rights, responsibilities, and values consistent with the ideals laid out in the nation's founding documents. . . . The book begins with a fascinating look at patriotism. Along with several definitions and views on it, the author explores different symbols of the U.S., including those of political parties, the cornucopia, the eagle, and the flag. She then considers each holiday in alphabetical order, describing any customs, songs, and foods associated with it; the history behind the observance; and a sampling of activities and observances around the country. . . . The volume also contains almost 100 pages of useful primary documents related to holidays, including The Mayflower Compact; The Declaration of Independence; flag laws; and excerpts from diaries, letters, and speeches." SLJ

Includes bibliographical references

★ **Holidays,** festivals, and celebrations of the world dictionary; detailing more than 3,000 observances from all 50 states and more than 100 nations: a compendious reference guide to popular, ethnic, religious, national, and ancient holidays. . . edited by Cherie D. Abbey. 4th ed.; Omnigraphics 2010 1323p $144

Grades: 8 9 10 11 12 Adult **394.26**

1. Reference books 2. Holidays -- Dictionaries 3. Festivals -- Dictionaries
ISBN 978-0-7808-0994-9
LC 2009-41138

First edition published 1994 compiled by Sue Ellen Thompson and Barbara W. Carlson

"A comprehensive dictionary that describes more than 3,000 holidays and festivals celebrated around the world. Features both secular and religious events from many different cultures, countries, and ethnic groups. Includes contact information for events; multiple appendices with background information on world holidays; extensive bibliography; multiple indexes." Publisher's note

Jeffrey, Laura S.

Celebrate Martin Luther King, Jr., Day; [by] Laura S. Jeffrey. Enslow 2006 104p il (Celebrate holidays) lib bdg $31.93

Grades: 5 6 7 8 **394.26**

1. Clergy 2. Martin Luther King Day 3. Nonfiction writers 4. Civil rights activists 5. Nobel laureates for peace 6. African Americans -- Civil rights
ISBN 0-7660-2492-X
LC 2005028110

This offers a brief introduction to the life of Martin Luther King and the Civil Rights movement in the United States and how Martin Luther King Day became a holiday and is celebrated.

Includes glossary and bibliographical references

Celebrate Tet; [by] Laura S. Jeffrey. Enslow Publishers 2008 104p il map (Celebrate holidays) lib bdg $31.93

Grades: 5 6 7 8 **394.26**

1. Vietnamese New Year
ISBN 978-0-7660-2775-6 lib bdg; 0-7660-2775-9 lib bdg
LC 2006031922

"Captioned photographs, maps, drawings, and sidebars combine with an accessible text to present a thorough discussion of the Vietnamese New Year celebration. Jeffrey discusses the holiday's legendary origins and ancient traditions along with people's modern-day observances." Horn Book Guide

Includes glossary and bibliographical references

Marks, Diana F.

Let's celebrate today; calendars, events, and holidays. illustrated by Donna L. Farrell. 2nd ed; Libraries Unlimited 2003 340p il pa $38.95

Grades: Adult Professional **394.26**

1. Holidays 2. Calendars 3. Festivals
ISBN 1-59158-060-9
LC 2003-47723

First published 1998

This is a "day-by-day calendar . . . for planning . . . activities and classroom units based on national and international holidays, multicultural and historic events, famous firsts, inventions, birthdays of important individuals (including authors), and more. The entries are annotated and include contact information and Web site addresses to facilitate further research and learning. In addition, three suggested learning activities are provided for each day of the year." Publisher's note

Includes bibliographical references

Mattern, Joanne

Celebrate Christmas; [by] Joanne Mattern. Enslow Publishers 2007 112p il (Celebrate holidays) lib bdg $31.93

Grades: 5 6 7 8 **394.26**

1. Christmas
ISBN 978-0-7660-2776-3 lib bdg; 0-7660-2776-7 lib bdg
LC 2006025258

The author "devotes several pages to the origins of Christmas, first as a pagan holiday, then as a celebration of Jesus' birth, and its evolution into the holiday as it is observed today. Symbols of Christmas, important people, and traditions from around the world are explored, and there is a fair amount of discussion about the commercialization of the holiday. . . . Full-color photos and reproductions appear throughout. There is plenty here for reports." SLJ

Includes glossary and bibliographical references

Celebrate Cinco de Mayo; [by] Joanne Mattern. Enslow Pub. 2006 104p il map (Celebrate holidays) lib bdg $31.93

Grades: 5 6 7 8 **394.26**

1. Cinco de Mayo 2. Mexico -- History 3. Mexico -- Social life and customs
ISBN 0-7660-2579-9
LC 2005028107

This describes the history of Cinco de Mayo and how it is celebrated.

Includes glossary and bibliographical references

Rajtar, Steve

United States holidays and observances; by date, jurisdiction, and subject, fully indexed. McFarland & Co. 2003 165p $45

Grades: 11 12 Adult **394.26**

1. Holidays 2. Festivals
ISBN 0-7864-1446-4
LC 2002-154293

This "concentrates on observances and holidays established by statute in the U.S. and American Samoa, District of Columbia, Guam, the Northern Mariana Islands, Puerto Rico, and the U.S. Virgin Islands. In addition, UN-designated holidays are included. . . . The text is arranged by month, and chapters for each month are divided into 'Observances with Variable Dates' and 'Observances with Fixed Dates.' Each entry identifies the observance as federal or specific to a state and offers a description that ranges in length from three or four lines to a quarter page. . . . [This] would be a good addition to ready-reference desks in public libraries and information centers in schools." Booklist

395 Etiquette (Manners)

Aboukhair, Rachel

The **grumpy** girl's guide to good manners. New Chapter Pub. 2011 93p il pa $14.95

Grades: 6 7 8 9 395

1. Etiquette

ISBN 978-0-9827918-4-4; 0-9827918-4-4

"In this hilarious and satirical memoir, written when the author was 16, readers meet Rachel, a uncooperative teen whose mother decreed a week of etiquette lessons in the middle of the Texas desert. What follows is an account of the 15-year-old's trials: a cousin who never stops talking about her ex-boyfriend and instructions on how to hold silverware, apply makeup, dress properly, walk in high heels, and dance with a boy. . . . Occasional bullet point tips are offered on such topics as manicuring nails and a proper handshake. Readers will enjoy the author's conversational style and sympathize with her plight, and, who knows, they just might learn a few manners along the way." SLJ

Packer, Alex J.

★ **How** rude! the teen guide to good manners, proper behavior, and not grossing people out. Alex J. Packer, Ph.D. Rev. and updated ed. Free Spirit Publishing Inc. 2014 xiv, 489 p.p illustrations $23.99

Grades: 7 8 9 10 395

1. Etiquette 2. Teenagers -- Conduct of life 3. Etiquette for children and teenagers

ISBN 1575424541; 9781575424545

LC 2014001602

"It is difficult to make a topic like etiquette seem relevant and appealing to teenagers, but that is exactly what Packer accomplishes. Drawing heavily on surveys of teens, parents, and teachers to target which situations were most pertinent, the opening chapters successfully sell the importance of manners to both the individual and society. . . . The text acknowledges social mores for other cultures and discusses the changeable nature of etiquette depending on context." Booklist

Includes bibliographical references and index

Post, Peggy

Emily Post's table manners for kids. Collins 2009 96p $15.99

Grades: 4 5 6 7 395

1. Etiquette

ISBN 978-0-06-111709-1; 0-06-111709-9

LC 2008010655

"This deceptively slim guide teems with advice about everything from meal courses to table settings, from the art of conversation to dining out. The tone is measured and mildly proscriptive, offset by Bjorkman's amusing cartoons. . . . A strength: the excellent troubleshooting for specific concerns, such as eating fondue and using chopsticks." Kirkus

Emily Post's The guide to good manners for kids; by Peggy Post & Cindy Post Senning. HarperCollins 2004 144p il $15.99; lib bdg $16.89

Grades: 4 5 6 7 395

1. Etiquette

ISBN 0-06-057196-9; 0-06-057197-7 lib bdg

LC 2003-26426

This offers advice on etiquette at home, at school, and other places, including letter writing and on-line communication, table manners, phone answering, and behavior at social gatherings, and public places.

"The writing is clear, friendly, and sometimes clever. . . . The advice is consistently practical and simple." SLJ

Senning, Cindy Post

Emily Post prom and party etiquette. Collins 2010 134p il $15.99

Grades: 7 8 9 10 11 12 395

1. Parties 2. Etiquette

ISBN 978-0-06-111713-8; 0-06-111713-7

LC 2009-2795

"Covering parties and special occasions like prom, homecoming, quinceañera, and graduation, the authors have developed a modern set of rules for navigating today's more relaxed social customs with finesse and confidence. Myriad issues are tackled, from how to rent a tuxedo and who pays for what on prom night to table settings and crafting the perfect thank-you note, with important points highlighted. The comprehensive guide gives proper respect to religious occasions and thoughtfully explains how to determine from an invitation whether bringing a date is acceptable or not. Witty line drawings complement the text." SLJ

Teen manners; from malls to meals to messaging and beyond. by Cindy Post Senning and Peggy Post. 1st ed.; Collins 2007 134p il $15.99; lib bdg $16.89

Grades: 7 8 9 10 395

1. Etiquette

ISBN 978-0-06-088198-6; 0-06-088198-4; 978-0-06-088199-3 lib bdg; 0-06-088199-2 lib bdg

LC 2007010991

This offers advice on etiquette in personal relationships, in communication, dining, school, getting a job or getting into college, parties and dating, and other social situations.

398 Folklore

Allen, Judy

Fantasy encyclopedia; 1st ed.; Kingfisher 2005 144p il $19.95

Grades: 4 5 6 7 398

1. Fairies 2. Mythical animals

ISBN 0-7534-5847-0

LC 2004-29475

"This highly visual presentation introduces readers to fantasy characters within their habitats and genres. . . . More than 50 types of characters are arranged in nine chapters covering topics such as 'The Little People,' 'Mysterious Animals,' and 'Ghosts and Spirits.' . . . Student fans of the fantasy genre will find this tool exceedingly browsable, and school and public libraries will want to purchase reference and circulating copies." Booklist

Includes glossary

Curran, Robert

The **zombie** handbook; an essential guide to zombies and more importantly, how to avoid them. Barron's 2011 il $14.99

Grades: 6 7 8 9 **398**

1. Zombies

ISBN 978-0-7641-6409-5; 0-7641-6409-0

"This compact book does a good job of introducing zombies: what they are, how they look, where you find them. . . . The text is highly readable, the interspersed artwork is creepy and plentiful." Booklist

Etingoff, Kim

Howling at the moon; vampires & werewolves in the New World. Mason Crest Publishers 2011 63p il (The making of a monster: vampires & werewolves) lib bdg $22.95; pa $9.95

Grades: 7 8 9 10 **398**

1. Vampires 2. Werewolves

ISBN 978-1-4222-1805-1 lib bdg; 1-4222-1805-8 lib bdg; 978-1-4222-1958-4 pa; 1-4222-1958-5 pa

LC 2010022670

Explores New World variants of myths and folklore about werewolves and vampires.

"The writing is engaging and accessible, and peppered easily with teen vernacular. . . . Large, clear photographs and period and contemporary drawings appear on every other page or so. . . . First-rate entertainment." SLJ

Includes glossary and bibliographical references

The **science** of the beast; the facts behind the fangs. Mason Crest Publishers 2011 63p il (The making of a monster: vampires & werewolves) lib bdg $22.95; pa $9.95

Grades: 7 8 9 10 **398**

1. Vampires 2. Werewolves

ISBN 978-1-4222-1808-2 lib bdg; 1-4222-1808-2 lib bdg; 978-1-4222-1961-4 pa; 1-4222-1961-5 pa

LC 2010023660

Describes medical conditions and other observable phenomena that may have influenced early belief in vampires and werewolves.

"The writing is engaging and accessible, and peppered easily with teen vernacular. . . . Large, clear photographs and period and contemporary drawings appear on every other page or so. . . . First-rate entertainment." SLJ

Includes glossary and bibliographical references

Indovino, Shaina Carmel

Transylvania and beyond; vampires & werewolves in old Europe. Mason Crest Publishers 2011 63p il (The making of a monster: vampires & werewolves) lib bdg $22.95; pa $9.95

Grades: 7 8 9 10 **398**

1. Vampires 2. Werewolves

ISBN 978-1-4222-1809-9 lib bdg; 1-4222-1809-0 lib bdg; 978-1-4222-1962-1 pa; 1-4222-1962-3 pa

LC 2010021831

Explores European variants of myths and folklore about werewolves and vampires.

"The writing is engaging and accessible, and peppered easily with teen vernacular. . . . Large, clear photographs and period and contemporary drawings appear on every other page or so. . . . First-rate entertainment." SLJ

Includes glossary and bibliographical references

Kallen, Stuart A.

The **sphinx**; part of the Monsters and mythical creatures series. by Stuart A. Kallen. ReferencePoint Press 2012 80 p. ill. (chiefly col.) (Monsters and mythical creatures series) (hardback) $27.95

Grades: 4 5 6 7 8 **398**

1. Sphinxes (Mythology)

ISBN 1601522223; 9781601522221

LC 2011026636

This book, part of the "Monsters and Mythical Creatures" series, looks at the "history . . . [and] associated mythology" of the Sphinx. (School Library Journal). It "reveals the significant symbolic role this creature has played in human civilization from ancient Egypt through classical Greece and the Renaissance into the twenty-first century. . . . The ancient mythical creature has been an inspiration for artists, writers, architects, scholars, and theologians for millennia." (Publisher's note)

"Children will get a well-rounded look at the featured subjects and how they have evolved into the creatures that still fascinate many today." SLJ

Includes bibliographical references and index

Vampire history and lore. ReferencePoint Press 2010 80p il (The vampire library) lib bdg $26.95

Grades: 7 8 9 10 **398**

1. Vampires

ISBN 978-1-60152-132-3; 1-60152-132-4

LC 2010005866

Explores vampire beliefs from the blood sucking beasts of ancient times to the immortal teen heartthrobs of the twenty first century.

"Energetic and surprisingly educational, this lively [book] seizes upon a zeitgeist topic and takes it as far as possible." Booklist

Werewolves. Reference Point Press 2010 104p il (The mysterious & unknown) $25.95

Grades: 4 5 6 7 **398**

1. Werewolves

ISBN 978-1-60152-097-5; 1-60152-097-2

Describes the history and lore surrounding the topic of werewolves, examining how the shape-shifting beast has been feared by various cultures around the world, and its continuing influence on popular culture

This is "surprisingly exhaustive. . . . Breakout summaries and quotes enliven the layout. . . . There is . . . plenty of creepy stuff to scrutinize." Booklist

Includes bibliographical references

Kelly, Sophia

What a beast! a look-it-up guide to the monsters and mutants of mythology. Scholastic 2010 128p il map (Mythlopedia) lib bdg o.p.; pa $13.95

Grades: 4 5 6 7 **398**

1. Monsters 2. Classical mythology

ISBN 978-1-60631-028-1 lib bdg; 978-1-60631-060-1 pa

LC 2009-20998

Describes some of the creatures and monsters in Greek mythology.

This "spices things up with sassy artwork, a pastel color scheme, and an OMG sensibility. . . . [This title is] loaded with information on the inspired methods with which various nasty creatures could put an end to bothersome heroes. Aside from the heaps of information coming from all angles on just about every page, . . . [the] book also contains a decent family tree, a rudimentary star chart, and lists of further reading. . . . For kids unconvinced that anything so old and gray could have any bearing on their lives, . . . [this book provides] a feisty . . . guide to the many cultural references lingering from antiquity." Booklist

Includes glossary and bibliographical references

Knudsen, Shannon

Fairies and elves. Lerner 2010 48p il (Fantasy chronicles) lib bdg $27.93

Grades: 4 5 6 7 **398**

1. Fairies

ISBN 978-0-8225-9979-1 lib bdg; 0-8225-9979-1 lib bdg

LC 2008050207

"The explanations and history behind . . . fairies [and elves] . . . will provide satisfaction for readers who want to know more about these familiar characters from myth, fantasy, and folk and fairy tales. Brief and concise." SLJ

Includes bibliographical references

Losure, Mary

The **Fairy** Ring, or, Elsie and Frances Fool the World; Mary Losure. Candlewick Press 2012 184 p. ill.

Grades: 5 6 7 8 **398**

1. Deception 2. Fairies 3. Fairies -- England

ISBN 9780763656706; 0763656704

LC 2011046081

This book offers explores an event that occurred "[t]owards the end of World War I, [when] two girls in Yorkshire took photographs that purported to capture the fairies they regularly saw, and these pictures . . . became a national sensation when . . . Sir Arthur Conan Doyle . . . championed them as authentic. . . . [The] book . . . conveys the widening of the ripples from the event and . . . the impulses behind the creation of the photographs." (Bulletin of the Center for Children's Books)

Martin, Nicholas

Fighting the fangs; a guide to vampires and werewolves. Mason Crest Publishers 2011 63p il (The making of a monster: vampires & werewolves) lib bdg $22.95; pa $9.95

Grades: 7 8 9 10 **398**

1. Vampires 2. Werewolves

ISBN 978-1-4222-1804-4 lib bdg; 1-4222-1804-X lib bdg; 978-1-4222-1957-7 pa; 1-4222-1957-7 pa

LC 2010025187

A guide to identifying and defeating vampires and werewolves.

"The writing is engaging and accessible, and peppered easily with teen vernacular. . . . Large, clear photographs and period and contemporary drawings appear on every other page or so. . . . First-rate entertainment." SLJ

Includes glossary and bibliographical references

Myths and legends. Macmillan Lib. Ref. USA 2000 436p (Macmillan profiles) $95

Grades: 7 8 9 10 **398**

1. Reference books 2. Folklore -- Dictionaries 3. Mythology -- Dictionaries

ISBN 0-02-865376-9

LC 99-51558

This volume "contains informative, accurate, and detailed information." SLJ

Nelson, Sheila

The **psychology** of our dark side; humans' love affair with vampires & werewolves. by Sheila Stewart. Mason Crest Publishers 2011 63p il (The making of a monster: vampires & werewolves) lib bdg $22.95; pa $9.95

Grades: 7 8 9 10 **398**

1. Vampires 2. Werewolves 3. Superstition

ISBN 978-1-4222-1807-5 lib bdg; 1-4222-1807-4 lib bdg; 978-1-4222-1960-7 pa; 1-4222-1960-7 pa

LC 2010025294

Explores some of the reasons that many people, both past and present, are fascinated by vampires and werewolves.

"The writing is engaging and accessible, and peppered easily with teen vernacular. . . . Large, clear photographs and period and contemporary drawings appear on every other page or so. . . . First-rate entertainment." SLJ

Includes glossary and bibliographical references

Regan, Sally

The **vampire** book. DK Pub. 2009 93p il $19.99

Grades: 5 6 7 8 **398**

1. Vampires

ISBN 978-0-7566-5551-8; 0-7566-5551-X

"This guide covers the origins and evolution of vampires throughout history, giving a worldwide perspective on legends, mythology, and lore, from African tales of terror to blood-drinking witches of Southeast Asia. It also covers vampires in literature, film, and television. . . . The vivid colors in the often full-page art leap from the pages, and the bold font demands attention." SLJ

Robson, David

Encounters with vampires. ReferencePoint Press 2010 80p il (Vampire library) lib bdg $26.95

Grades: 7 8 9 10 **398**

1. Vampires

ISBN 978-1-6015-2133-0; 1-6015-2133-2

LC 2010-10100

The author "lays out both folklore and real-world reports of blood-sucking beings. Expanding beyond familiar Transylvanian tales and stories of vampires in strictly human form, the author's survey is global, from the Malaysian langsuyar, believed to be responsible for many newborn deaths, to the red-eyed, monstrous Latin American chupacabra, notorious for preying on livestock. . . . Young vampire-fiction fans will find much to ponder here, while the accounts of contemporary murders with purported vampire links may emerge as the most chilling and grisly." Booklist

Includes bibliographical references

Sanna, Emily

Pop monsters; the modern-day craze for vampires and werewolves. Mason Crest Publishers 2011 63p il (The making of a monster: vampires & werewolves) lib bdg $22.95; pa $9.95

Grades: 7 8 9 10 **398**

1. Vampires 2. Werewolves

ISBN 978-1-4222-1806-8 lib bdg; 1-4222-1806-6 lib bdg; 978-1-4222-1959-1 pa; 1-4222-1959-3 pa

LC 2010025186

Describes the current phenomenon of vampires and werewolves in popular culture, from books, television, and movies, to computer games.

"The writing is engaging and accessible, and peppered easily with teen vernacular. . . . Large, clear photographs and period and contemporary drawings appear on every other page or so. . . . First-rate entertainment." SLJ

Includes glossary and bibliographical references

Stewart, Gail

Vampires : do they exist? [by] Gail B. Stewart. ReferencePoint Press 2010 80p il (The vampire library) $26.95

Grades: 7 8 9 10 **398**

1. Vampires

ISBN 978-1-60152-110-1; 1-60152-110-3

Examines the legends about the forms vampires can take, how they feed on the living, and the dangers of encountering them.

"Energetic and surprisingly educational, this lively [book] seizes upon a zeitgeist topic and takes it as far as possible." Booklist

Vande Velde, Vivian

Tales from the Brothers Grimm and the Sisters Weird. Harcourt Brace & Co. 1995 128p il hardcover o.p. pa $5.95

Grades: 7 8 9 10 **398**

1. Fairy tales 2. Short stories

ISBN 0-15-200220-0; 0-15-205572-X pa

LC 94-26341

This collection presents alternative versions of such familiar fairy tales as Rumpelstiltskin, Hansel and Gretel, and The Princess and the Pea

"Vande Velde challenges readers' notions of good, bad, and ugly. . . . Modern references and sensibilities . . . add to the humor (often the gallows variety). Entertaining and provocative, these selections make good read-alouds and can be used to spark discussion or creative writing exercises." SLJ

398.2 Folk literature

Abrahams, Roger D.

African folktales; traditional stories of the black world. selected and retold by Roger D. Abrahams. Pantheon Bks. 1983 354p il (Pantheon fairy tale & folklore library) hardcover o.p. pa $18

Grades: 8 9 10 11 12 Adult **398.2**

1. Folklore -- Africa

ISBN 0-394-72117-9 pa

LC 83-2474

These stories are arranged in five groupings. "The first section, by way of introduction, is given over to a few wonder tales of the kind that Europeans and Americans are most accustomed to, but that are found here in typically African renderings. The sections that then follow are: shorter stories used to introduce a subject for moral discussions; moral stories specific to the problems of keeping family and community together (and which, therefore, might be called domestic dramas); tales told in praise of great deeds; and finally, a large section of outrageous stories, told primarily to entertain, about the antisocial doings of one or another trickster figure." (Preface) Bibliography. Index of tales.

Includes bibliographical references

American Indian myths and legends; selected and edited by Richard Erdoes and Alfonso Ortiz. Pantheon Bks. 1984 527p il hardcover o.p. pa $18

Grades: 8 9 10 11 12 Adult **398.2**

1. Native Americans -- Folklore 2. Native Americans -- Religion

ISBN 0-394-74018-1

LC 84-42669

"This volume comprises 160 tales of native folklore and myth ranging from one geographical end of our continent to the other. The book is organized according to type of myth. . . . Erdoes and Ortiz seek to keep Indian myth intact and pure through their retellings, using, as often as possible, primary sources." Booklist

Includes bibliographical references

The **August** House book of scary stories; spooky tales for telling out loud. edited by Liz Parkhurst. August House 2009 144p $15.95

Grades: 4 5 6 7 8 **398.2**

1. Folklore 2. Storytelling 3. Short stories 4. Horror fiction

ISBN 978-0-87483-915-9; 0-87483-915-7

LC 2009008711

An anthology of spooky stories drawn from folklore, local history, and the storytellers' imaginations, and divided into the categories "Just Desserts and Lessons Learned," "Ghostly Guardians," "Dark Humor," "Urban Legends and Jump Tales," and "Fearless Females."

"Each of these 20 chilling tales is meant to be told out loud and includes author notes about how to maximize the spooky effect. Middle schoolers will relish reading and sharing these tales, hoping to creep each other out." SLJ

Baynes, Pauline

Questionable creatures; a bestiary. [by] Pauline Baynes. Eerdmans Books for Young Readers 2006 47p il $18

Grades: 4 5 6 7 **398.2**

1. Bestiaries 2. Mythical animals

ISBN 978-0-8028-5284-7; 0-8028-5284-X

LC 2005033658

"Baynes introduces readers to the creatures and myths found in medieval bestiaries and explains how the books were made and how they were viewed by the general public. The rest of the volume details the commonly held beliefs that both peasants and scholars embraced about specific animals. . . . Baynes's detailed gouache and colored-pencil illustrations . . . are done in the style of medieval illuminations. . . . The artist shows great respect for the early bestiary creators while also giving the stories relevance for modern readers." SLJ

Includes bibliographical references

Bedard, Michael

The **painted** wall and other strange tales; selected and adapted from the Liao-chai of Pu Sung-ling by Michael Bedard. Tundra Books 2003 109p $16.95

Grades: 7 8 9 10 **398.2**

1. Folklore -- China

ISBN 0-88776-652-8

"Known as the Liao-chai, these . . . stories were first collected by a scholar named Pu Sung-ling. . . . Wildly popular in China but little known in the West, they draw on the supernatural or unusual to cast their spell. . . . The stories are short and accessible to reluctant readers." SLJ

Bennett, Adelaide

Ancient werewolves and vampires; the roots of the teeth. Mason Crest Publishers 2011 63p il (The making of a monster: vampires & werewolves) lib bdg $22.95; pa $9.95

Grades: 7 8 9 10 **398.2**

1. Vampires 2. Werewolves

ISBN 978-1-4222-1802-0 lib bdg; 1-4222-1802-3 lib bdg; 978-1-4222-1955-3 pa; 1-4222-1955-0 pa

LC 2010023796

Explores the earliest tales and folklore about werewolves and vampires.

"The writing is engaging and accessible, and peppered easily with teen vernacular. . . . Large, clear photographs and period and contemporary drawings appear on every other page or so. . . . First-rate entertainment." SLJ

Includes glossary and bibliographical references

Global legends and lore; vampires and werewolves around the world. Mason Crest Publishers 2011 63p il (The making of a monster: vampires & werewolves) lib bdg $22.95; pa $9.95

Grades: 7 8 9 10 **398.2**

1. Vampires 2. Werewolves

ISBN 978-1-4222-1810-5 lib bdg; 1-4222-1810-4 lib bdg; 978-1-4222-1963-8 pa; 1-4222-1963-1 pa

LC 2010025778

Presents legends about vampires and werewolves from around the world.

"The writing is engaging and accessible, and peppered easily with teen vernacular. . . . Large, clear photographs and period and contemporary drawings appear on every other page or so. . . . First-rate entertainment." SLJ

Includes glossary and bibliographical references

Blackwood, Gary L.

Legends or lies? Marshall Cavendish Benchmark 2006 72p il (Unsolved history) lib bdg $34.21

Grades: 4 5 6 7 **398.2**

1. Legends

ISBN 978-0-7614-1891-7 lib bdg; 0-7614-1891-1 lib bdg

Describes several legends that have intrigued people for centuries: the lost civilization of Atlantis, the Amazons, King Arthur, St Brendon, Pope Joan, and El Dorado

This collection "of tidbits about lingering mysteries of the past . . . [offers] more substance than most. . . . [It offers] a full-page illustration opening each chapter; reproductions, many in color; and a generously spaced format." SLJ

Includes glossary and bibliographical references

Boughn, Michael

Into the world of the dead; astonishing adventures in the underworld. Annick Press 2006 56p il lib bdg $24.95; pa $12.95

Grades: 5 6 7 8 **398.2**

1. Death -- Folklore 2. Future life -- Folklore

ISBN 1-55037-959-3 lib bdg; 1-55037-958-5 pa

"Boughn retells stories from many cultures on every continent except South America, including quite a few from Mesoamerica, Asia, Africa, and Oceania. Readers will find heroes who have traveled to and returned from the underworld as well as the gods and monsters who dwell there. Full-color and black-and-white illustrations, including reproductions, photos, and plenty of graphics of skulls, appear on every page. . . . This is a book that many young people may find appealing." SLJ

Brown, Dee Alexander

Dee Brown's folktales of the Native American; retold for our times. Holt & Co. 1993 174p pa $12

Grades: 7 8 9 10 **398.2**

1. Native Americans -- Folklore

ISBN 0-8050-2607-X

LC 93-12449

First published 1979 by Holt, Rinehart & Winston with title: Teepee tales of the American Indian

This is a collection of 36 folktales from Native American tribes, including the Seneca, Hopi, Navaho, Creek, Cheyenne, Cherokee, and Blackfoot, grouped by themes such as tricksters and magicians, heroes and heroines, and ghost stories

Includes bibliographical references

Bryan, Ashley

★ **Ashley** Bryan's African tales, uh-huh. Atheneum Bks. for Young Readers 1998 198p $22

Grades: 4 5 6 **398.2**

1. Folklore -- Africa

ISBN 0-689-82076-3

LC 97-77743

This volume combines three previously published titles: The ox of the wonderful horns and other African folktales (1971), Beat the story-drum, pum-pum (1980), Lion and the ostrich chicks and other African folktales (1986)

This collection of African folktales is "told with Bryan's distinctive rhythmic word patterns and filled with humor, life lessons, and the antics of trickster Ananse. . . . Quality reproductions of the original woodcuts enrich this handsome volume." Horn Book Guide

Burns, Batt

★ The **king** with horse's ears and other Irish folktales; [by] Batt Burns; illustrated by Igor Oleynikov. Sterling Pub. Co. 2009 96p il (Folktales of the world) $14.95

Grades: 4 5 6 7 **398.2**

1. Fairy tales 2. Folklore -- Ireland

ISBN 978-1-4027-3772-5; 1-4027-3772-6

LC 2007035258

"These 13 Irish tales retold by storyteller Burns follow fairies and warriors, heroes and clever thieves. . . . The stories are cleanly retold in contemporary, accessible language, and each is introduced with a short paragraph providing cultural or other information. . . . Oleynikov's paintings have a rough texture that suits the energy of the retellings and adds to the lively tone. This is a hearty collection, handsomely produced with Celtic-knot borders and gouache full-page and spot illustrations." Booklist

Includes glossary

Chase, Richard

The **Jack** tales; told by R.M. Ward and his kindred in the Beech Mountain section of western North Carolina and by other descendants of Council Harmon (1803-1896) elsewhere in the southern mountains; with three tales from Wise County, Virginia; set down from these sources and edited by Richard Chase; with an appendix compiled by Herbert Halpert; and illustrated by Berkeley Williams, Jr. Houghton Mifflin 2003 216p il pa $7.95

Grades: 5 6 7 8 Adult Professional **398.2**

1. Folklore -- Southern States

ISBN 978-0-618-34692-9 pa; 0-618-34692-9 pa

LC 2003276676

First published 1943

A collection of folk tales from the southern Appalachians that center on a single character, the irrepressible Jack

"Humor, freshness, colorful American background, and the use of one character as a central figure in the cycle mark these 18 folk tales, told here in the dialect of the mountain country of North Carolina. A scholarly appendix by Herbert Halpert, giving sources and parallels, increases the book's value as a contribution to American folklore. Black-and-white illustrations in the spirit of the text." Booklist

Includes bibliographical references

Currie, Stephen

African American folklore. Lucent Books 2008 104p il (Lucent Library of Black History) $32.45
Grades: 7 8 9 10 **398.2**

1. African Americans -- Folklore
ISBN 978-1-4205-0082-0; 1-4205-0082-1
LC 2008020201

Examines African American folklore in context so that readers will understand the connection between black history and the broad sweep of America's story.

The book is "highly accessible and [provides] cultural context to help readers understand [the] topic. . . . [The] book includes captioned color and black-and-white photographs and reproductions on every spread. Well-organized and clearly written." SLJ

Includes bibliographical references

Delacre, Lulu

Golden tales; myths, legends, and folktales from Latin America. [retold by] Lulu Delacre. Scholastic 1996 73p hardcover o.p. pa $5.99
Grades: 5 6 7 8 **398.2**

1. Folklore -- Latin America 2. Native Americans -- Folklore
ISBN 0-439-24398-X pa
LC 94-36724

This includes 12 "stories from four native cultures (Taino, Zapotec, Muisca, and Quechua), including pourquoi tales, legends of the conquistadores, and folktales from before and after the age of Columbus. . . . [The author's] . . . retellings are done in a clear and confident voice and are accompanied by her robust, colorful oil paintings. . . . This impressively presented and referenced collection will inspire readers and tellers alike." Booklist

Includes bibliographical references

Dembicki, Matt

★ **Trickster** : Native American tales; a graphic collection. edited by Matt Dembicki. Fulcrum 2010 231p il pa $22.95
Grades: 5 6 7 8 **398.2**

1. Graphic novels 2. Folklore -- Graphic novels 3. Native Americans -- Folklore
ISBN 978-1-55591-724-1 pa; 1-55591-724-0 pa
LC 2009-49668

"More than 40 storytellers and cartoonists have contributed to this original and provocative compendium of traditional folklore presented in authentic, colorful, and engaging sequential art. The stories are drawn from a variety of Native peoples across North America, and so the trickster character appears variously as Rabbit, a raccoon, Coyote, and in other guises; landscapes, clothing and rhythms of speech and action also vary in keeping with distinct traditions. Realistic, impressionistic, painterly, and cartoon styles of art are employed to echo and announce the tone of each tale and telling style, making this a rich visual treasure as well as cultural trove." SLJ

DiPrimio, Pete

The **sphinx**. Mitchell Lane Publishers 2010 48p il map (Monsters in myth) lib bdg $29.95
Grades: 4 5 6 7 **398.2**

1. Sphinxes (Mythology)
ISBN 978-1-58415-931-5; 1-58415-931-6
LC 2010006560

This describes the mythic Sphinx that has appeared in both Egyptian and Greek myth.

This book is "thorough and respectful of a number of ancient and modern sources and [bends] over backward to navigate often contradictory, interlinked legends. . . . A number of paintings and photos break up the otherwise text-heavy pages, and copious chapter notes and reading suggestions conclude. This is by no means entry-level stuff, but for kids handy with the basics and ready to delve deeper, [this book] will be of great use." Booklist

Includes glossary and bibliographical references

English folktales; edited by Dan Keding and Amy Douglas. Libraries Unlimited 2005 231p il map (World folklore series) $35
Grades: Adult Professional **398.2**

1. Folklore -- Great Britain
ISBN 1-59158-260-1
LC 2005016075

"This collection of more than 50 English folktales contains a variety of stories arranged by common themes: The Fool in All His Glory, Wily Wagers and Tall Tales, Dragons and Devils, etc. The work of 22 storytellers is represented and their tellings are lively and inflected with the rhythms and speech of the regions from which their stories emanate. It is a delightful compendium for storytellers." SLJ

Forest, Heather

Wisdom tales from around the world; retold by Heather Forest. August House 1996 156p $28; pa $17.95
Grades: 7 8 9 10 **398.2**

1. Folklore
ISBN 0-87483-478-3; 0-87483-479-1 pa
LC 96-31141

A collection of traditional stories from around the world, reflecting the cumulative wisdom of Sufi, Zen, Taoist, Buddhist, Jewish, Christian, African, and Native American cultures

"Forest retells folktales, proverbs, and parables in a thoughtful and satisfying style that amuses as it deftly imparts lessons for living." SLJ

Includes bibliographical references

Gavin, Jamila

Tales from India; illustrated by Amanda Hall. Candlewick Press 2011 il
Grades: 5 6 7 8 **398.2**

1. Hindu mythology 2. Folklore -- India
ISBN 0-7636-5564-3; 978-0-7636-5564-8
LC 2010047651

"Gavin, . . . presents 10 classic Hindu stories, accompanied by Hall's lush and elegant gouache illustrations. . . . . Readers should be drawn toward the valor, action, and dramatic transformations in these powerful tales." Publ Wkly

Grimm, Wilhelm, 1786-1859

Tales from the Brothers Grimm; selected & illustrated by Lisbeth Zwerger. Lisbeth Zwerger. Minedition 2013 96 p. (hbk.) $29.99
Grades: 4 5 6 7 8 **398.2**

1. Fairy tales 2. Fairy tales -- Germany
ISBN 9789888240531; 9888240536

In this book, Lisbeth Zwerger selects and illustrates stories "from the well-known collection of fairy tales by the Brothers Grimm. Old favorites such as 'Hansel and Gretel' and 'The Bremen Town Musicians' are included as are some lesser-known stories such as 'The Seven Ravens' and 'Hans My Hedgehog.'" (Publisher's note)

"High production values give this mix of new and recycled translations and illustrations a suitably sumptuous air. . . . Like Zwerger's figures, which are nearly all small on the page and tend to look off into the distance, Bell's translations are more often lyrical than intimate or earthy." Kirkus

Hamilton, Virginia

★ The **people** could fly: American Black folktales; told by Virginia Hamilton; illustrated by Leo and Diane Dillon. 2009 178p il $24.99; pa $13

Grades: 5 6 7 8 **398.2**

1. African Americans -- Folklore

ISBN 978-0-394-86925-4; 0-394-86925-7; 978-0-679-84336-8 pa; 0-679-84336-1 pa

A reissue of the title first published 1985

Coretta Scott King honor book for illustration, 1986

The author "has been successful in her efforts to write these tales in the Black English of the slave storytellers. Her scholarship is unobtrusive and intelligible. She has provided a glossary and notes concerning the origins of the tales and the different versions in other cultures. Handsomely illustrated." NY Times Book Rev

Includes bibliographical references

Hausman, Gerald

Horses of myth; [by] Gerald and Loretta Hausman; pictures by Robert Florczak. Dutton Children's Books 2004 100p il $12

Grades: 4 5 6 7 **398.2**

1. Folklore 2. Horses -- Folklore

ISBN 0-525-46964-8

LC 2002-40809

"These five tales each feature a different type of horse, remarkable for both its individuality and the qualities representative of its breed. . . . Florczak's illustrations adapt characteristics appropriate to the locations and time periods of each selection's origins. . . . This is an attractive volume, useful to teachers and librarians for read-alouds and of interest to horse-loving youngsters." SLJ

Hayes, Joe

Dance, Nana, dance; Cuban folktales in English and Spanish. retold by Joe Hayes; illustrated by Mauricio Trenard Sayago. Cinco Puntos Press 2008 128p il $20.95

Grades: 5 6 7 8 9 **398.2**

1. Folklore -- Cuba 2. Bilingual books -- English-Spanish

ISBN 978-1-933693-17-0; 1-933693-17-7

LC 2007-38295

A collection of stories from Cuban folklore, representing the cultures of Spain, Africa, and the Caribbean.

"Each tale is accompanied by a full-page illustration that is colorful and contributes to the text. This book is a great addition to folktale and Spanish language collections. Students will enjoy these stories that could easily be incorporated into the curriculum." Libr Media Connect

Helbig, Alethea

Myths and hero tales; a cross-cultural guide to literature for children and young adults. [by] Alethea K. Helbig and Agnes Regan Perkins. Greenwood Press 1997 288p $49.95

Grades: 8 9 10 11 12 Adult **398.2**

1. Reference books 2. Mythology -- Bibliography

ISBN 0-313-29935-8

LC 97-8778

"Brief, incisive critical reviews of 189 books, published between 1985 and 1996, that contain 1455 myths and hero tales form the heart of this . . . sourcebook. Scholarly accuracy and literary quality are the authors' chief criteria for inclusion, but they also comment trenchantly on illustrations. Indexes list stories by writer, tale type, culture, character and place name, grade level, title, or illustrator." SLJ

Hirschmann, Kris

Medusa. ReferencePoint Press 2011 il (Monsters and mythical creatures) $27.95

Grades: 6 7 8 9 **398.2**

1. Medusa (Greek mythology)

ISBN 978-1-60152-181-1; 1-60152-180-4

LC 2011020993

This is "an ideal starting point for young researchers interested in the weird, mysterious, and paranormal. Using fleet, descriptive prose to communicate the impressively researched (and sourced) information, [this] medium-length [work manages] to rope in just about everything, from folklore to history to pop culture. . . . Medusa goes into the monster's roots in Greek storytelling before delving more deeply into Homer's Iliad, the story of Perseus, and the Gorgan's appearance in art, theater, opera, and more. . . . The illustrations are fine and varied, the sidebars always illuminating, and the back matter robust." Booklist

Includes bibliographical references

Horowitz, Anthony

Death and the underworld; illustrated by Thomas Yeates. Kingfisher 2011 133p il (Legends) $9.99

Grades: 6 7 8 **398.2**

1. Folklore 2. Death -- Folklore 3. Future life -- Folklore

ISBN 978-07534-6542-4; 0-7534-6542-6

This retells classic myths and legends of afterlife.

"Balancing the heroic and the macabre, these dryly humorous, sometimes gory retellings hold particular appeal for reluctant readers. The conversational language also lends itself well to reading aloud. Black-and-white illustrations provide occasional breaks in the text while adding visual interest." Horn Book Guide

Heroes and villains; illustrated by Thomas Yeates. Kingfisher 2011 165p il (Legends) $9.99

Grades: 6 7 8 **398.2**

1. Folklore

ISBN 978-0-7534-6546-2; 0-7534-6546-9

This retells classic myths and legends of heroes and villains.

"Balancing the heroic and the macabre, these dryly humorous, sometimes gory retellings hold particular appeal for reluctant readers. The conversational language also lends itself well to reading aloud. Black-and-white illustrations provide occasional breaks in the text while adding visual interest." Horn Book Guide

Houston, James A.

James Houston's Treasury of Inuit legends. Harcourt 2006 268p $18; pa $8.95

Grades: 5 6 7 8 **398.2**

1. Inuit -- Folklore

ISBN 978-0-15-205924-8; 978-0-15-205930-9 pa

LC 2006043577

"This collection includes four previously published stories: 'Tiktaliktak' (1965), 'The White Archer' (1967), 'Akavak' (1968), and 'Wolf Run' (1971). Noted artist Houston lived among the Inuit people for fourteen years and brought their culture to life through his books and artwork." Horn Book Guide

Jaffe, Nina

The **cow** of no color: riddle stories and justice tales from around the world; [by] Nina Jaffe and Steve Zeitlin; pictures by Whitney Sherman. Holt & Co. 1998 159p il $17

Grades: 4 5 6 7 **398.2**

1. Folklore

ISBN 0-8050-3736-5

LC 98-14167

In each of these stories, collected from around the world, a character faces a problem situation which requires that he make a decision about what is fair or just

"Sherman's black-and-white line drawings have a stark gracefulness that complements the tales' form and structure; the tales themselves are simply told with little embellishment." Bull Cent Child Books

Includes bibliographical references

Krasno, Rena

Cloud weavers; ancient Chinese legends. [by] Rena Krasno and Yeng-Fong Chiang; illustrations from the collection of Yeng-Fong Chiang. Pacific View Press 2003 96p il $22.95

Grades: 5 6 7 8 **398.2**

1. Folklore -- China

ISBN 1-881896-26-9

LC 2002-35911

Presents legends and tales from China, including ancient folktales, stories that reflect Chinese traditions and virtues, historical tales, and selections from literature

This collection "provides a showcase for some remarkable pieces of Chinese calendar art and advertising posters from the 1920s and 1930s. . . . Prefaces provide cultural insight for some stories, and the brisk retellings weave important background unobtrusively into the narrative." Booklist

Lester, Julius

★ **Uncle** Remus, the complete tales; with a new introduction. as told by Julius Lester; illustrated by Jerry Pinkney. 1999 xxi, 686p il lib bdg $35

Grades: 4 5 6 7 **398.2**

1. Animals -- Folklore 2. African Americans -- Folklore

ISBN 0-8037-2451-9

LC 99-17121

Reprint in one volume of works originally published separately, 1987-1994

Lester retells stories of the trickster rabbit from African American folklore collected by Joel Chandler Harris

"This is a landmark collection. . . . Lester's retellings are sharp and flavorful and grounded in the here and now." [review of book 1] Booklist

Livo, Norma J.

Folk stories of the Hmong; peoples of Laos, Thailand, and Vietnam. [by] Norma J. Livo and Dia Cha. Libraries Unlimited 1991 135p il $26

Grades: 8 9 10 11 12 Adult **398.2**

1. Hmong Americans

ISBN 0-87287-854-6

LC 91-370

This is a collection of folktales of the Hmong people of Asia which also includes a description of Hmong history and culture, with 16 pages of color photographs of Hmong dress and needlework

Includes bibliographical references

Marshall, James Vance

Stories from the Billabong; retold by James Vance Marshall; illustrated by Francis Firebrace. Frances Lincoln Children's Books 2009 61p il $19.95

Grades: 3 4 5 6 **398.2**

1. Aboriginal Australians -- Folklore

ISBN 978-1-84507-704-4; 1-84507-704-0

"With the help of Aboriginal storytellers who have collected the tales and myths of their people, Marshall has assembled 10 fascinating stories of the Dreamtime. . . . Each selection is beautifully told and is illustrated by a traditional artist who uses the distinctive symbols and colors of the Aboriginal people. . . . This is an engaging, colorful book that belongs in most libraries." SLJ

Martin, Rafe

★ The **world** before this one; a novel told in legend. with paper sculpture by Calvin Nicholls. Levine Bks. 2002 195p il hardcover o.p. pa $5.99

Grades: 4 5 6 7 **398.2**

1. Seneca Indians -- Folklore

ISBN 0-590-37976-3; 978-0-590-37980-9 pa; 0-590-37980-1 pa

LC 2001-23403

"Written in the style of a novel, this collection of 14 Seneca tales is presented through the retelling of one central story into which all of the others are artfully woven. . . . Martin offers sources for the tales along with an introductory note by Seneca Elder Peter Jemison. Each chapter includes a painstakingly detailed white paper sculpture of a character (often an animal) from one of the stories." SLJ

McCaughrean, Geraldine

★ The **epic** of Gilgamesh; retold by Geraldine McCaughrean; illustrated by David Parkins. Eerdmans Bks. for Young Readers 2003 95p il $18

Grades: 5 6 7 8 **398.2**

1. Gilgamesh 2. Folklore -- Iraq

ISBN 0-8028-5262-9

LC 2003-1086

A retelling, based on seventh-century B.C. Assyrian clay tablets, of the wanderings and adventures of the god king, Gilgamesh, who ruled in ancient Mesopotamia (now Iraq) in about 2700 B.C., and of his faithful companion, Enkidu

This is "clearly a telling for our time, but one that honors its source. Parkins captures the epic's primitive power and universal emotions in rough, broadly rendered portraits." Horn Book

McKinley, Robin

★ The **outlaws** of Sherwood. Greenwillow Bks. 1988 282p hardcover o.p. pa $14

Grades: 8 9 10 11 12 **398.2**

1. Robin Hood (Legendary character)

ISBN 0-688-07178-3; 0-441-01325-2 pa

LC 88-45227

"McKinley takes a fresh look at a classic, changing some of the events or deviating from standard characterization to gain new dimensions. Her afterword explains her artistic compromise with myth and history, her wish to write a version that is 'historically unembarrassing.' With a few exceptions, she has done that admirably, creating a story that has pace and substance and style, and that is given nuance and depth by the characterization." Bull Cent Child Books

Menchu, Rigoberta

The **secret** legacy; [by] Rigoberta Menchu with Dante Liano; pictures by Domi; translated by David Unger. Groundwood Books/House of Anansi Press 2008 64p il $19.95

Grades: 4 5 6 7 8 **398.2**

1. Mayas -- Folklore 2. Folklore -- Guatemala

ISBN 978-0-88899-896-5; 0-88899-896-1

"On her first day watching over her Mayan grandfather's cornfields, young Ixkem is invited by the b'e'n , spirits in the form of small humans, to visit them underground. They feed her generously and she tells them stories that explain Mayan customs and include bits of folklore. . . . The Mexican artist Domi has provided bright paintings in a naturalistic, folk-art style. The lyrical translation preserves the storyteller's voice." SLJ

Mhlophe, Gcina

African tales; a Barefoot collection. written by Gcina Mhlophe; illustrated by Rachel Griffin. Barefoot Books 2009 95p il map

Grades: 5 6 7 8 **398.2**

1. Folklore -- Africa

ISBN 1-84686-118-7; 978-1-84686-118-5

LC 2008028042

"Each of these eight tales is preceded by information and interesting facts about the country from which it originated. A basic map of Africa helps orient readers to the location of the various countries represented. Extensive source notes are appended. . . . There are many choices that could be read aloud or told using a call-and-response format. The book design . . . is a feast for the eyes. Griffin employs a collage technique using colored beads, sewn fabric, and textured papers, and incorporates them into shapes and faces of animals and humans. . . . This compilation contains a wealth of information and will enhance folklore collections." SLJ

Includes bibliographical references

Monte, Richard

The **mermaid** of Warsaw; and other tales from Poland. illustrated by Paul Hess. Frances Lincoln 2011 il pa $8.95

Grades: 4 5 6 7 **398.2**

1. Folklore -- Poland

ISBN 978-1-84780-164-7; 1-84780-164-1

"A gratifying and unusual collection of folktales from Poland. There are a number of good stock characters in these pages: beautiful princesses who get themselves into trouble, warty-nosed ogres, . . . buffoons who overstep themselves or commit one-too-many deadly sins. There are also talking trees, dark forests, miraculous springs and . . . monsters. . . . The tales are told . . . in an unwavering voice, with portent enough to keep an audience listening close, and Hess' artwork has the right spidery look and sinister atmosphere. . . . That the locales are ancient and real gives the whole collection added wallop." Kirkus

Morpurgo, Michael

★ **Beowulf**; illustrated by Michael Foreman. Candlewick Press 2006 92p il $17.99

Grades: 5 6 7 8 **398.2**

1. Beowulf 2. Folklore -- Europe 3. Monsters -- Folklore

ISBN 978-0-7636-3206-9; 0-7636-3206-6

"Morpurgo retells the classic story of the courageous young warrior . . . who used his brute strength to save the neighboring Danes, then his own kinsmen, by slaying two horrible monsters, a sea serpent, and a massive dragon. . . . Many attractive full-page watercolor and pastel paintings illustrate important action-filled scenes. . . . This is a fine retelling." SLJ

Sir Gawain and the Green Knight; as told by Michael Morpurgo; illustrated by Michael Foreman. Candlewick Press 2004 114p il $18.99

Grades: 5 6 7 8 **398.2**

1. Arthurian romances 2. Gawain (Legendary character)

ISBN 0-7636-2519-1

LC 2003-65527

The quest of Sir Gawain for the Green Knight teaches him a lesson in pride, humility, and honor

"Morpurgo's sprightly writing brings out all the humor as well as the horror of the original tale, and Foreman's profuse, evocative watercolor-and-pastel illustrations highlight the drama in each scene." SLJ

Napoli, Donna Jo, 1948-

★ **Tales** from the Arabian nights; Stories of Adventure, Magic, Love, and Betrayal. by Donna Jo Napoli ; illustrated by Christina Balit. National Geographic Partners 2016 208 p. color ill., color map (ebook) $34.90; (hardcover : alk. paper) $24.99

Grades: 5 6 7 8 **398.2**

1. Fairy tales 2. Arabs -- Folklore 3. Folklore -- Arab countries

ISBN 9781426326387; 9781426325403; 9781426325410

LC 2016016718

In this book, by Donna Jo Napoli, illustrated by Christina Balit, "classic stories and dazzling illustrations of princesses, kings, sailors, and genies come to life in a stunning retelling of the Arabian folk tales from One Thousand and One Nights and other collections, including those of Aladdin, Sinbad the Sailor, and Al Baba and the Forty Thieves." (Publisher's note)

"A brilliant tapestry woven not of yarn but of stories, both fresh and faithful to its historical roots." Kirkus

★ **Treasury** of Greek mythology; classic stories of gods, goddesses, heroes & monsters. National Geographic Society 2011 191p il map $24.95; lib bdg $33.90

Grades: 5 6 7 8 **398.2**

1. Greek mythology

ISBN 978-1-4263-0844-4; 1-4263-0844-2; 978-1-4263-0845-1 lib bdg; 1-4263-0845-0 lib bdg

LC 2011024327

"Napoli presents 25 tales introducing the major players of the Greek pantheon along with an assortment of celebrated heroes and mortals. . . . At once eloquent and elemental, these lyrically written portraits deftly detail each character's origins, realm of power, and legendary story lines. Filled with sensual imagery, the language is poetic, yet balanced by amusing asides and wry observations that add a contemporary, almost conversational accessibility. . . . Stunning stylized paintings featuring luminous colors, rich patterns, and star-infused motifs add depth and drama to the text. . . . Interesting sidebars appear throughout, providing historical, scientific, and cultural information." SLJ

Norman, Howard

★ **Between** heaven and earth; bird tales from around the world. illustrated by Leo & Diane Dillon. Harcourt 2004 78p il lib bdg $22

Grades: 4 5 6 7 **398.2**

1. Folklore 2. Birds -- Folklore

ISBN 0-15-201982-0

LC 2003-7874

A collection of folktales from around the world, all of which have a bird as a main character

This is "a collection of stories that are rich in cultural references from the lands of their origins. . . . The Dillons' luminous watercolor-and-pencil illustrations, detailed with patterns drawn from each tale's culture of origin, will draw readers and listeners back to the stories." Booklist

Oberman, Sheldon

★ **Solomon** and the ant; and other Jewish folktales. retold by Sheldon Oberman; introduction and commentary by Peninnah Schram. Boyds Mills Press 2006 165p $19.95

Grades: 5 6 7 8 **398.2**

1. Jews -- Folklore

ISBN 1-59078-307-7

LC 2005020115

"This collection of 43 traditional Jewish stories is authoritative as well as immensely entertaining. . . . The stories, from both Ashkenazi and Sephardic traditions, are arranged more or less chronologically—from biblical days through the talmudic period to more contemporary times. There are legends, medieval fables, trickster tales, and more. . . . The stories, wonderful for storytelling and sharing, are accessible even to listeners younger than the target audience, and the notes and commentary will provide older children with context and history." Booklist

Includes bibliographical references

Ollhoff, Jim

Japanese mythology. ABDO Pub. 2011 32p il (The world of mythology) lib bdg $27.07

Grades: 5 6 7 8 **398.2**

1. Japanese mythology

ISBN 978-1-61714-723-4

LC 2010042019

'This book offers information about Japanese mythology, answering questions such as "Who is Hachiman? What is the Seven Gods of Fortune? Why are myths so important in our lives? Myths are a rich source of history. People use them to make sense of our world. Even before myths were written down, people told and retold the stories of the gods and goddesses of their homeland. Readers of Japanese Mythology will learn the history of myths, as well as their deeper meaning." (Publisher's note) "A Shinto creation story forms the backbone of [this book], which also introduces the sun goddess Amaterasu; the fabled first emperor of Japan, Jimmu; and the impish Oni." (Booklist)

"Ollhoff writes in a clear and engaging fashion, presenting complex issues in a way that will be easy for youngsters to grasp. . . . The photographs and reproductions of art tie directly to the [text]." SLJ

Olson, Arielle North

Ask the bones: scary stories from around the world; selected and retold by Arielle North Olson and Howard Schwartz; illustrated by David Linn. Viking 1999 145p il hardcover o.p. pa $5.99

Grades: 4 5 6 7 **398.2**

1. Folklore

ISBN 0-670-87581-3; 0-14-230140-X pa

LC 98-19108

A collection of scary folktales from countries around the world including China, Russia, Spain, and the United States

"David Linn's bone-chilling black-and-white illustrations . . . will stay with the reader long after the book is closed. Excellent for reading aloud, this collection will satisfy even jaded genre fans." Booklist

Includes bibliographical references

More bones; scary stories from around the world. selected and retold by Arielle North Olson and Howard Schwartz; illustrated by E.M. Gist. Viking 2008 162p il $15.99

Grades: 4 5 6 7 **398.2**

1. Folklore

ISBN 978-0-670-06339-0; 0-670-06339-8

"This tour of the world's shadowy corners is full of dark wizards, unkind witches, and other untrustworthy creatures. . . . The 22 tales, as retold by Olson and Schwartz, give a vivid glimpse into unfamiliar, unnerving territory. . . . The atmospheric illustrations, while not intricately detailed, are somewhat startling in their imagery." Booklist

Orr, Tamra

The **monsters** of Hercules. Mitchell Lane Publishers 2011 48p il map (Monsters in myth) lib bdg $29.95

Grades: 4 5 6 7 **398.2**

1. Monsters 2. Hercules (Legendary character)

ISBN 978-1-58415-927-8; 1-58415-927-8

LC 2010028764

This book about the monsters of Hercules is "thorough and respectful of a number of ancient and modern sources and [bends] over backward to navigate often contradictory, interlinked legends. . . . A number of paintings and photos break up the otherwise text-heavy pages, and copious chapter notes and reading suggestions conclude. This is by no means entry-level stuff, but for kids handy with the basics and ready to delve deeper, [this book] will be of great use." Booklist

Includes glossary and bibliographical references

The **sirens**. Mitchell Lane Publishers 2011 48p il map (Monsters in myth) lib bdg $29.95

Grades: 4 5 6 7 **398.2**

1. Sirens (Mythology)

ISBN 978-1-58415-930-8; 1-58415-930-8

LC 2010026965

This book examines the various stories that surround the myths of the Sirens.

This book is "thorough and respectful of a number of ancient and modern sources and [bends] over backward to navigate often contradictory, interlinked legends. . . . A number of paintings and photos break up the otherwise text-heavy pages, and copious chapter notes and reading suggestions conclude. This is by no means entry-level stuff, but for kids handy with the basics and ready to delve deeper, [this book] will be of great use." Booklist

Includes glossary and bibliographical references

Philip, Neil

★ **Celtic** fairy tales; retold with an introduction by Neil Philip; illustrated by Isabelle Brent. Viking 1999 137p il $21.99

Grades: 4 5 6 7 **398.2**

1. Fairy tales 2. Celts -- Folklore 3. Folklore -- Great Britain

ISBN 0-670-88387-5

LC 98-50081

An illustrated collection of twenty stories from many Celtic regions, including "The Battle of the Birds," "Finn MacCool and the Scotch Giant," and "The Ship that Went to America."

"There's a mix of the almost familiar and nicely exotic in this collection, which is lavishly illustrated with a glowing full-page painting for each tale and Celtic motifs on every page." Booklist

Pyle, Howard

The **merry** adventures of Robin Hood; [by] Howard Pyle; illustrated by Scott McKowen. Sterling Pub. 2004 335p il (Sterling unabridged classics) $9.95

Grades: 8 9 10 11 12 **398.2**

1. Folklore -- Great Britain 2. Robin Hood (Legendary character)
ISBN 978-1-4027-1456-6; 1-4027-1456-4

LC 2004016213

Recounts the legend of Robin Hood, who plundered the king's purse and poached his deer and whose generosity endeared him to the poor.

The **story** of King Arthur and his knights; written and illustrated by Howard Pyle. Scribner 1984 312p il $22.95

Grades: 1 2 8 9 10 11 **398.2**

1. Arthurian romances 2. Kings
ISBN 0-684-14814-5

LC 84-50167

A reissue of the title first published 1903

This is an account of the times "when Arthur, son of Uther-Pendragon, was Overlord of Britain and Merlin was a powerful enchanter, when the sword Excalibur was forged and won, when the Round Table came into being." Publisher's note

The **story** of Sir Launcelot and his companions. Dover Publications 1991 340p il pa $13.95

Grades: 8 9 10 11 12 **398.2**

1. Arthurian romances 2. Lancelot (Legendary character)
ISBN 0-486-26701-6

LC 90-22326

A reissue of the title first published 1907 by Scribner

This third book of the series follows "Sir Launcelot's adventures as he rescues Queen Guinevere from the clutches of Sir Mellegrans, does battle with the Worm of Corbin, wanders as a madman in the forest and is finally returned to health by the Lady Elaine." Best Sellers

The **story** of the champions of the Round Table; written and illustrated by Howard Pyle. Dover Publications 1968 328p il pa $11.95

Grades: 8 9 10 11 12 **398.2**

1. Arthurian romances
ISBN 0-486-21883-X

A reissue of the title first published 1905 by Scribner

"Pyle's second volume of Arthurian legends will be of interest to motivated students of literature and history, as well as useful in professional collections for comparisons and source work. In spite of the archaic language . . . the narrative depth and graphic force . . . will draw in readers." Booklist

The **story** of the Grail and the passing of Arthur. Dover Publications 1992 258p il pa $12.95

Grades: 8 9 10 11 12 **398.2**

1. Arthurian romances 2. Kings 3. Grail -- Fiction
ISBN 0-486-27361-X

LC 92-29058

A reissue of the title first published 1910 by Scribner

This fourth volume of the series follows the adventures of Sir Geraint, Galahad's quest for the holy Grail, the battle between Launcelot and Gawaine, and the slaying of Mordred

Rapunzel and other magic fairy tales; selected and illustrated by Henriette Sauvant; translated by Anthea Bell. Trafalgar Square 2008 157p il $15.95

Grades: 5 6 7 8 **398.2**

1. Folklore 2. Fairy tales
ISBN 1-4052-2702-8

"Sauvant has selected 14 tales of German, English, and French origin, many of them written down by the Grimm brothers. While most of them are familiar . . . others will be unknown to most readers. . . . The illustrations, which range in size from tiny fillers to full-page and double-page pictures, appear to be painted in watercolor or acrylic on a textured surface. While some are painted in classic fairy-tale style, others are best described as surreal. . . . The sophistication of both stories and artwork makes this collection most suitable for older readers." SLJ

Raven, Nicky

★ **Beowulf**; a tale of blood, heat, and ashes. retold by Nicky Raven; illustrated by John Howe. 1st U.S. ed.; Candlewick Press 2007 72p il $18.99

Grades: 7 8 9 10 11 12 **398.2**

1. Beowulf 2. Folklore -- Europe 3. Monsters -- Folklore
ISBN 978-0-7636-3647-0; 0-7636-3647-9

LC 2007027094

A modern, illustrated retelling of the Anglo-Saxon epic about the heroic efforts of Beowulf, son of Ecgtheow, to save the people of Heorot Hall from the terrible monster, Grendel.

This is "a gripping rendition of the Anglo-Saxon epic. . . . Raven takes some liberties that add welcome nuance to the story. . . . Howe's artwork . . . is . . . spectacular, easily capturing the heroic grandeur and horrific gruesomeness of the tale." Booklist

Rumford, James

★ **Beowulf**; a hero's tale retold. Houghton Mifflin Company 2007 un il $17

Grades: 4 5 6 7 **398.2**

1. Beowulf 2. Folklore -- Europe 3. Monsters -- Folklore
ISBN 0-618-75637-X; 978-0-618-75637-7

A simplified and illustrated retelling of the exploits of the Anglo-Saxon warrior, Beowulf, and how he came to defeat the monster Grendel, Grendel's mother, and a dragon that threatened the kingdom.

"Superb on all counts—from the elegant bookmaking to the vigorous, evocative prose . . . to the pen-and-ink and watercolor illustrations that strikingly recall the work of Edmund Dulac." Horn Book

San Souci, Robert

★ **Cut** from the same cloth; American women of myth, legend, and tall tale. collected and told by Robert D. San Souci; illustrated by Brian Pinkney; introduction by Jane Yolen. Philomel Bks. 1993 140p il hardcover o.p. pa $6.99

Grades: 4 5 6 7 **398.2**

1. Tall tales 2. Women -- Folklore 3. Folklore -- United States
ISBN 0-399-21987-0; 0-698-11811-1 pa

LC 92-5233

A collection of fifteen stories about legendary American women from Anglo-American, African American, and Native American folklore

"San Souci's language is vigorous and action verbs abound; Pinkney's black-and-white block prints match the strength of the telling. The inclusion of notes on the sources and a general bibliography make this an academic resource as well as a good collection of rollicking stories." Child Book Rev Serv

★ A **terrifying** taste of short & shivery; thirty creepy tales. retold by Robert D. San Souci; illustrated by Lenny Wooden. Delacorte Press 1998 159p il $14.95; pa $10.95
Grades: 4 5 6 7 **398.2**

1. Folklore 2. Ghost stories
ISBN 0-385-32635-1; 0-385-32255-0 pa

LC 98-5551

"Drawing on urban legends, myths, folktales, and ghost stories from around the world and across time, the reteller serves up 30 tales of the supernatural that range from eerie to downright scary. . . . Suspenseful, accessible, and energetic, the tales are uniformly brief and gripping." SLJ

Includes bibliographical references

Sanna, Ellyn

★ **Latino** folklore and culture; stories of family, traditions of pride. [by] Ellyn Sanna. Mason Crest Publishers 2005 112p il (Hispanic heritage) $22.95
Grades: 7 8 9 10 **398.2**

1. Folklore -- Latin America 2. Latin Americans -- Social life and customs
ISBN 1-59084-932-9

LC 2004024248

This "book begins with a description of the place of folklore in culture and the differences between the terms Latino and Hispanic. Specific folktales, such as the many versions of 'La Llorona,' and dominant themes, such as machismo, strong women, and religion, are described in subsequent chapters. . . . [This is] an excellent resource both for students researching Latino arts for reports and for general readers." SLJ

Includes bibliographical references

Schwartz, Howard

The **day** the Rabbi disappeared: Jewish holiday tales of magic; retold by Howard Schwartz; illustrated by Monique Passicot. Viking 2000 80p il hardcover o.p. pa $9.95
Grades: 4 5 6 7 **398.2**

1. Jews -- Folklore 2. Jewish holidays -- Fiction
ISBN 0-670-88733-1; 0-8276-0757-1 pa

LC 99-42061

Retellings of twelve traditional tales from Jewish folklore featuring elements of magic and relating to holidays, including Rosh Hodesh, Sukkot, Tu bi-Shevat, and Shabbat

"Schwartz follows these brief, clear, and simply told tales with rich and highly readable notes about the history of the holiday, the importance of the rabbi, and the sources of the story." Horn Book

Shelby, Anne

The **adventures** of Molly Whuppie and other Appalachian folktales; [by] Anne Shelby; illustrations by Paula McArdle. The University of North Carolina Press 2007 88p il $14.95
Grades: 4 5 6 7 **398.2**

1. Folklore -- Appalachian Mountains
ISBN 978-0-8078-3163-2

LC 2007013789

A collection of Appalachian folktales featuring Molly Whuppie and her adventures.

"Shelby has captured the language of Appalachia. . . . Her adaptations are true to the traditional folktales. . . . Young readers and listeners will make these stories their own and enjoy retelling them." SLJ

Includes bibliographical references

Stewart, Gail

Trolls. ReferencePoint Press 2011 il (Monsters and mythical creatures) $27.95
Grades: 6 7 8 9 **398.2**

1. Trolls
ISBN 978-1-60152-183-5; 1-60152-183-9

LC 2011016391

This is "an ideal starting point for young researchers interested in the weird, mysterious, and paranormal. Using fleet, descriptive prose to communicate the impressively researched (and sourced) information, [this] medium-length [work manages] to rope in just about everything, from folklore to history to pop culture. . . . Trolls [twines] together the various strands of Norse legends into a coherent, readable, eye-opening narrative that begins in the ninth century and ends with Harry Potter. . . . The illustrations are fine and varied, the sidebars always illuminating, and the back matter robust." Booklist

Includes bibliographical references

Talk that talk: an anthology of African-American storytelling; edited by Linda Goss & Marian E. Barnes. Simon & Schuster 1989 521p hardcover o.p. pa $32.95
Grades: 8 9 10 11 12 Adult **398.2**

1. African Americans -- Folklore
ISBN 0-671-67167-7; 0-671-67168-5 pa

LC 89-10582

The selections included range "from slave stories and the animal legends of Brer Rabbit and Brer Fox to the comedy monologues of Dick Gregory and rap routines. . . . Interspersed throughout are brief sections of commentary and analysis." Booklist

Includes bibliographical references

Tarnowska, Wafa'

★ **Arabian** nights; written by Wafa' Tarnowska; illustrated by Carole Hénaff. Barefoot Books 2010 125p il $24.99
Grades: 5 6 7 8 **398.2**

1. Fairy tales 2. Arabs -- Folklore
ISBN 978-1-84686-122-2; 1-84686-122-5

LC 2008028159

"With bright, lush, stylized acrylic illustrations, this collection of eight stories from A Thousand and One Nights is designed for reading aloud. . . . Throughout, the spacious paintings capture the sense of the supernatural in daily life, including magical images of people taking flight above city, trees, and desert." Booklist

Taylor, C. J.

Peace walker; the legend of Hiawatha and Tekanawita. Tundra Books 2004 45p il $15.95
Grades: 6 7 8 9 **398.2**

1. Indian leaders 2. Iroquois Indians -- Folklore
ISBN 0-88776-547-5

Using sources from her own Mohawk oral tradition, Taylor relates a historical legend about "the Iroquois Confederacy and its Great Law of Peace . . . (which still guides the Grand Council of the People of the Longhouse today). Nine chapters portray a period of internal warring that led to domination by Atotarho, a cruel Onondaga sorcerer chief. The narrative concludes with the successful efforts of Hiawatha, [an] . . . Onondaga chief, and Tekanawita, a . . . Huron, who converted a culture of accusation, suspicion, and revenge to one of virtue, honesty, and patience. . . . Age eight and up." (Quill Quire)

"The events surrounding the collaboration of two chiefs, the Onandaga Hiawatha and Tekanawita of the Mohawk, to upset the tyrant Atotarho are related simply and abound with graphic details of Native life. . . . Each chapter includes one full-page illustration done in acrylic on canvas in a slightly naive style. . . . The writing is eloquent and poetically rhythmic." SLJ

Tchana, Katrin Hyman

★ **Changing** Woman and her sisters; stories of goddesses from around the world. retold by Katrin Hyman Tchana; illustrated by Trina Schart Hyman. Holiday House 2006 80p il $18.95

Grades: 5 6 7 8 **398.2**

1. Folklore 2. Gods and goddesses

ISBN 978-0-8234-1999-9; 0-8234-1999-1

LC 2005-52504

An illustrated collection of traditional tales which feature goddesses from different cultures, including Navajo, Mayan, and Fon. Notes explain each goddess's place in her culture, the reason for the book, and how the illustrations were developed

"This large, handsome volume assembles well-chosen, well-told stories. . . . Hyman . . . contributed distinctive portrayals of the goddesses using a technique that melded photographs and found materials into full-page ink and acrylic paintings." Booklist

Includes bibliographical references

Thomas, Joyce Carol

★ The **skull** talks back and other haunting tales; collected by Zora Neale Hurston; adapted by Joyce Carol Thomas; illustrated by Leonard Jenkins. HarperCollins 2004 56p $15.99; lib bdg $16.89

Grades: 4 5 6 7 **398.2**

1. Authors 2. Novelists 3. Dramatists 4. Horror fiction 5. Memoirists 6. Folklorists 7. Short story writers 8. African Americans -- Folklore

ISBN 0-06-000631-5; 0-06-000634-X lib bdg

LC 2003-22215

"Using a direct style that loses none of the colloquial immediacy of the original voices, Thomas has done a great job of retelling six of Hurston's supernatural tales, and Jenkins' monochromatic collages and silhouettes capture the delicious, shivery glow of skeletons and graveyards." Booklist

Tingle, Tim

Spirits dark and light; supernatural tales from the five civilized tribes. [by] Tim Tingle. August House 2006 192p $15.95

Grades: 6 7 8 9 **398.2**

1. Supernatural -- Fiction 2. Native Americans -- Folklore

ISBN 0-87483-778-2

LC 2006042709

"Choctaw storyteller Tingle tells 25 deliciously scary tales collected from the five major Native American tribes of the southeastern U.S.the Cherokee, Chickasaw, Choctaw, Creek, and Seminole. . . . For each tribe, Tingle begins with background on history, culture, and folklore. The language is clear and informal, and the dialogue is immediate." Booklist

Walking the Choctaw road. Cinco Puntos Press 2003 142p il $24.95; pa $10.95

Grades: 7 8 9 10 **398.2**

1. Choctaw Indians -- Folklore 2. Folklore -- Southern States

ISBN 0-938317-74-1; 0-938317-73-3 pa

LC 2003-1069

A collection of stories of the Choctaw people, including traditional lore arising from beliefs and myths, historical tales passed down through generations, and personal stories of contemporary life

"Sophisticated narrative devices and some subtle character nuances give these stories a literary cast, but the author's evocative language, expert pacing, and absorbing subject matter will rivet readers and listeners both." Booklist

Tracy, Kathleen

Cerberus. Mitchell Lane Publishers 2011 48p il map (Monsters in myth) lib bdg $29.95

Grades: 4 5 6 7 **398.2**

1. Classical mythology

ISBN 978-1-58415-924-7; 1-58415-924-3

LC 2010026968

This describes myths of Cerberus, Hades three-headed watchdog who guarded the gates of the Greek Underworld.

This book is "thorough and respectful of a number of ancient and modern sources and [bends] over backward to navigate often contradictory, interlinked legends. . . . A number of paintings and photos break up the otherwise text-heavy pages, and copious chapter notes and reading suggestions conclude. This is by no means entry-level stuff, but for kids handy with the basics and ready to delve deeper, [this book] will be of great use." Booklist

Includes glossary and bibliographical references

Valentino, Serena

How to be a werewolf; the claws-on guide for the modern lycanthrope. Candlewick Press 2011 144p il $14.99

Grades: 7 8 9 10 **398.2**

1. Werewolves

ISBN 978-0-7636-5387-3; 0-7636-5387-X

LC 2010039173

"This handbook is divided into three distinct segments: 'Unleashing Your Wild Side,' 'The Stylish Lycanthrope,' and 'Moonlight Mystery.' Each chapter quizzes readers or is full of helpful tips to advise them on their path toward lycanthropy. The guide sheds light on understanding your werewolf self, hunting strategies and lunar charts, living quarters, party recipes, and music to howl by. The volume . . . includes research on werewolf legends and lore as well as movies, TV shows, comics, games, books, and further study. An entertaining read full of color photos and illustrations that add to the book's charm." SLJ

Yep, Laurence, 1948-

★ The **rainbow** people; [retold by] Laurence Yep; illustrated by David Wiesner. Harper & Row 1989 194p il hardcover o.p. pa $6.99

Grades: 4 5 6 7 **398.2**

1. Folklore -- China

ISBN 0-06-026760-7; 0-06-026761-5; 0-06-440441-2 pa

LC 88-21203

"Twenty Chinese folktales, selected and retold by Yep from those collected in the 1930s in the Oakland Chinatown as part of a WPA project. . . . The tales, while drawn from the depicting Chinese culture, present a variety of familiar motifs and types: wizards and saints, shape changing and magical objects, pourquoi tales and lessons. An 'Afterword' provides suggestions for further reading on Chinese folktales. This is an excellent introduction to Chinese and Chinese-American folklore." SLJ

Includes bibliographical references

Yolen, Jane

★ **Mightier** than the sword; world folktales for strong boys. collected and told by Jane Yolen; with illustrations by Raul Colón. Silver Whistle/Harcourt 2003 112p il $19

Grades: 4 5 6 7 **398.2**

1. Folklore

ISBN 0-15-216391-3

LC 2002-9886

A collection of folktales from around the world which demonstrate the triumph of brains over brawn

Yolen's "versions of these stories are lively, expressively written, ready for reading aloud or telling, and illustrative of her point." SLJ

Includes bibliographical references

398.209 History, geographic treatment, biography

Lupton, Hugh

The **adventures** of Achilles; retold by Hugh Lupton and Daniel Morden ; illustrated by Carole Henaff. Barefoot Books 2012 94 p. color illustrations $23.99

Grades: 5 6 7 8 **398.209**

1. Trojan War 2. Greek mythology 3. Legendary characters 4. Achilles (Greek mythology)

ISBN 1846864208; 9781846864209

LC 2011044731

This book in the Advanced Placement (AP) Crash Course series, by Hugh Lupton and Daniel Morden, illustrated by Carole Henaff, focuses on Achilles, "the son of a king and a goddess and also the best warrior in Greece. So when Prince Paris claims Helen from a Greek king and Troy declares war, everyone knows that Achilles will be vital to the Greek cause. With the help of the gods, can young Achilles lead his fellow countrymen to victory against the Trojans?" (Publisher's note)

"This retelling of the Iliad will rivet both readers and listening audiences." Kirkus.

Includes bibliographical references.

Napoli, Donna Jo, 1948-

Treasury of Norse mythology; stories of intrigue, trickery, love, and revenge. by Donna Jo Napoli ; illustrated by Christina Balit. National Geographic 2015 191 p. color illustrations, map (hardcover : alk. paper) $24.99

Grades: 5 6 7 8 **398.209**

1. Norse legends 2. Norse mythology 3. Tales -- Scandinavia 4. Gods, Norse 5. Mythology, Norse

ISBN 9781426320989; 9781426320996

LC 2015013321

This book, by Donna Jo Napoli, illustrated by Christina Balit, is "a new look at Asgard and the timeless tales of ancient Scandinavia. Classic stories and dazzling illustrations of gods, goddesses, heroes and monsters come to life in a stunning tableau of Norse myths, including those of the thunder god Thor, the one-eyed god and Allfather Odin, and the trickster god Loki." (Publisher's note)

"Buy it, and if space is an issue, weed to make it fit." SLJ

Includes bibliographical references and index

Ollhoff, Jim

Middle Eastern Mythology; by Jim Ollhoff. ABDO Publishing Company 2011 32p il (The world of mythology) lib bdg $27.07

Grades: 5 6 7 8 **398.209**

1. Mythology 2. Middle East 3. Children -- Books and reading 4. Mythology -- Middle East

ISBN 1617147257; 9781617147258; 1-61714-725-7; 978-1-61714-725-8

LC 2010042977

This describes the history of myths of the Middle East, their meaning, and their gods and goddesses including Mithra, Mot, the Mesopotamian goddess Ishtar, and the Canaanite thunder god, Baal.

"Ollhoff writes in a clear and engaging fashion, presenting complex issues in a way that will be easy for youngsters to grasp. . . . The photographs and reproductions of art tie directly to the [text]." SLJ

Smith, Charles R., Jr., 1969-

The **mighty** 12; superheroes of Greek myth. by Charles R. Smith, Jr. ; illustrated by P. Craig Russell. 1st ed. Little, Brown 2008 48 p. col. ill. (hardcover) $16.99; (paperback) $7.99

Grades: 5 6 7 8 **398.209**

1. Gods and goddesses 2. Classical mythology

ISBN 031601043X; 9780316010436 out of print; 9780316073660; 0316073660

LC 2007048729

"Future students of Homer get a handy checklist of musclebound Greek gods in this combo of mythology, comics and loose rhyme. . . . Smith and Russell make the pairing of classical material and a comics-like format look completely natural, with a gee-why-didn't-we-think-of-that simplicity." Publ Wkly

Includes bibliographical references (p. 48).

398.21 Tales and lore on a specific topic

Hearne, Betsy Gould

Beauties and beasts; by Betsy Hearne; illustrated by Joanne Caroselli. Oryx Press 1993 179p il (Oryx multicultural folktale series) pa $33.95

Grades: 8 9 10 11 12 Adult **398.21**

1. Folklore 2. Mythology 3. Fairy tales

ISBN 0-89774-729-1

LC 93-16

"Professionals will be very grateful for this sensitively written, thoughtful, and accessible interpretive collection." J Youth Serv Libr

Includes bibliographical references

Tan, Shaun

★ The **singing** bones; inspired by Grimms' fairy tales. Shaun Tan ; foreword by Neil Gaiman ; introduced by Jack Zipes. Arthur A. Levine Books, an imprint of Scholastic Inc. 2016 192 p. color illustrations (hardcover : alk. paper) $24.99

Grades: 5 6 7 8 9 **398.21**

1. Legends -- Germany 2. Folklore -- Germany 3. Fairy tales -- Adaptations 4. Fairy tales 5. Fairy tales -- Germany

ISBN 9780545946124

LC 2016014031

This book, by Shaun Tan, includes "wicked stepmothers, traitorous brothers, cunning foxes, lonely princesses: There is no mistaking the world of the Brothers Grimm and the beloved fairy tales that have captured generations of readers. Now internationally acclaimed artist Shaun Tan shows us the beautiful, terrifying, amusing, and downright peculiar heart of these tales as never before seen." (Publisher's note)

"A unique addition to special and robust folktale and fairy-tale and/or art collections." SLJ

Includes bibliographical references and index

398.24 Tales and lore of plants and animals

Drake, Ernest

Drake's comprehensive compendium of dragonology; by Ernest Drake and edited by Dugald A. Steer. Candlewick Press 2009 182 p. $19.99

Grades: 4 5 6 7 **398.24**

1. Dragons

ISBN 0763646237; 9780763646233

LC 2009016525

This book, by Ernest Drake and edited by Dugald A. Steer, presents an encyclopedia of dragonology. It features "a guide to dragon species, with entries on everything from the well-known European dragon to the lesser-known hydra — as well as pseudo-species such as the phoenix and the incognito, insight into dragon biology, from flight to reproduction [and] an in-depth look at dragons' habits, including migration, communication, camouflage, and notorious hoarding practices." (Publisher's note)

Hirschmann, Kris

The **werewolf**; by Kris Hirschmann. ReferencePoint Press 2012 80 p. (hardback) $27.95

Grades: 4 5 6 7 8 **398.24**

1. Werewolves

ISBN 160152238X; 9781601522382

LC 2011036347

This book on werewolves "examines these legendary creatures . . . describing their bodies, their behavior, and their monstrous transformations. It also goes snout to snout with some of history's most infamous real-life werewolves and discusses the many books and films these encounters have inspired." (Publisher's note)

"Children will get a well-rounded look at the featured subjects and how they have evolved into the creatures that still fascinate many today.—" SLJ

Includes bibliographical references and index

Mayor, Adrienne, 1946-

The **Griffin** and the Dinosaur; How Adrienne Mayor Discovered a Fascinating Link Between Myth and Science. Natl Geographic Soc Childrens books 2014 48 p. col. ill. $18.99

Grades: 5 6 7 8 **398.24**

1. Griffins 2. Dinosaurs

ISBN 1426311087; 9781426311086

"Could Griffins have been real? When [author] Adrienne Mayor carefully read the ancient Greek and Roman descriptions, this mythic hybrid of a lion and an eagle sounded like something people had actually seen." Co-written by Mayor and Marc Aronson, with illustrations by Chris Muller, "Here is the story of one insightful, curious, and determined woman who solved the mystery of the Griffin, and invented a new science. Now she and others travel the world matching myths and fossils." (Publisher's note)

"With the suspense of a detective story, the narrative details Mayor's research process as she consults with experts, conducts fieldwork, and seeks out ancient documents, artifacts, and stories." - PM reviews

Nigg, Joe

Wonder beasts; tales and lore of the phoenix, the griffin, the unicorn, and the dragon. Libraries Unlimited 1995 160p il $27.50

Grades: 7 8 9 10 **398.24**

1. Dragons 2. Unicorns 3. Animals -- Folklore

ISBN 1-56308-242-X

LC 94-46797

The author "has compiled material ranging from Herodotus, Ovid, Pliny the Elder, to Chinese and Native American folk tales, and fantasies by Edith Nesbit. Each entry is carefully documented and a reference list at the end provides dozens of full citations for those who'd like to delve deeper. Wonder Beasts will be useful to students who are researching myth and folklore, and to librarians and scholars who are looking for a comprehensive source list on the topic." Voice Youth Advocates

398.25 Ghost stories

Schwartz, Alvin, 1927-1992

★ **More** scary stories to tell in the dark; collected by Alvin Schwartz ; drawings by Stephen Gammell. Harpercollins Childrens Books 2017 99 p illustrations paperback $6.99

Grades: 4 5 6 7 **398.25**

1. Ghost stories 2. Horror fiction 3. Folklore -- United States

ISBN 0062682857; 9780062682857

Originally published 1984. Also available with illustrations by Brett Helquist.

This volume contains stories of ghosts, murders, graveyards and other horrors.

★ **Scary** stories 3; more tales to chill your bones. collected by Alvin Schwartz ; drawings by Stephen Gammell. Harpercollins Childrens Books 2017 115 p illustrations paperback $6.99

Grades: 4 5 6 7 **398.25**

1. Ghost stories 2. Horror fiction 3. Folklore -- United States

ISBN 9780062682871; 0062682873

Originally published 1991. Also available with illustrations by Brett Helquist.

Traditional and modern-day stories of ghosts, haunts, superstitions, monsters, and horrible scary things.

★ **Scary** stories to tell in the dark; collected by Alvin Schwartz ; drawings by Stephen Gammell. Harpercollins Children's Books 2017 111 p. illustrations paperback $6.99

Grades: 4 5 6 7 **398.25**

1. Ghost stories 2. Horror fiction 3. Folklore -- United States

ISBN 9780062682826; 0062682822

Originally published 1981. Also available with illustrations by Brett Helquist.

Stories of ghosts and witches, 'jump' stories, scary songs, and modern-day scary stories.

398.8 Rhymes and rhyming games

Bodden, Valerie

Nursery rhymes. Creative Education 2010 32p il (Poetry basics) $28.50

Grades: 5 6 7 8 **398.8**

1. Nursery rhymes

ISBN 978-1-58341-778-2; 1-58341-778-8

LC 2008009157

This book describes nursery rhymes' "history, characteristics, and variations. Many examples are provided as well as ideas for how children can write their own pieces. The information is accessible, and the writing is sufficiently lively to engage readers. The well-designed pages feature a variety of art reproductions from different literary eras and some photographs." Horn Book Guide

Includes glossary and bibliographical references

400 LANGUAGE

401 Philosophy and theory

Lunge-Larsen, Lise

★ **Gifts** from the gods; written by Lise Lunge-Larsen; illustrated by Gareth Hinds. Houghton Mifflin Harcourt/Childrens 2011 90p. $18.99

Grades: 4 5 6 7 401

1. Vocabulary 2. Classical mythology

ISBN 978-0-547-15229-5; 0-547-15229-9

LC 2010031635

In this book "[Lise] Lunge-Larsen and [Gareth] Hinds explain what words like echo, grace, hypnotize, and janitor have in common, tracing the origins of common words and expressions to Greek and Roman myths. Readers may know that 'arachnid' derives from the story of Arachne and that modern-day 'sirens' have mythical antecedents, but this collection . . . [also explains] the roots of 'nemesis' (the goddess of justice) or 'tantalize,' after doomed Tantalus. Lunge-Larsen provides additional context, including dictionary definitions, and quotes from children's literature. Hinds incorporates graphic novel–style elements into his . . . illustrations, including dialogue balloons and filmic perspectives." (Publishers Weekly)

411 Writing systems of standard forms of languages

Donoughue, Carol

The **story** of writing; [by] Carol Donoughue. Firefly Books 2007 48p il map $19.95

Grades: 4 5 6 7 411

1. Writing -- History 2. Alphabet -- History

ISBN 978-1-55407-306-1; 1-55407-306-5

This is an "introduction to the history of the Roman alphabet. . . . Beginning sections about early civilizations' alphabets, starting with Sumerian cuniforms, include a you-are-there narrative. . . . Later spreads cover European illuminated manuscripts and the development of printing technology. A final section [covers] Chinese characters. . . . Numerous carefully chosen color photos of artifacts . . . greatly enhance the book's appeal." Booklist

Includes bibliographical references

Robb, Don

★ **Ox,** house, stick; the history of our alphabet. illustrated by Anne Smith. Charlesbridge 2007 48p il $16.95; pa $7.95

Grades: 4 5 6 7 411

1. Writing -- History 2. Alphabet -- History

ISBN 978-1-57091-609-0; 978-1-57091-610-6 pa

LC 2005-06015

"Robb traces the history of each letter from its origin to its modern appearance in the Roman alphabet. He explains the birth of writing in pictogram form and the eventual transition to written symbols that stand for sounds. . . . Smith's whimsical paintings are a fitting companion to Robb's lighthearted text." SLJ

418 Standard usage (Prescriptive linguistics)

Ostenson, Jonathan W.

Integrating young adult literature through the common core standards; Rachel L. Wadham and Jonathan W. Ostenson. Libraries Unlimited, an imprint of ABC-CLIO, LLC 2013 x, 260 p.p (paperback) $45

Grades: Adult Professional 418

1. Reading 2. Young adult literature 3. Reading (Secondary) 4. Reading comprehension 5. Teenagers -- Books and reading -- United States 6. Language arts (Secondary) -- Standards -- United States 7. Young adult literature -- Study and teaching (Secondary)

ISBN 1610691180; 9781610691185

LC 2012036269

This text "examines the various components to be considered when determining the complexity of YA texts. The book is divided into two sections with the first part dealing with the various elements that make texts complex and the second section providing specific instructional suggestions for integrating the CCSS [common core standards] with YAL [young adult literature]." (New England Reading Association Journal)

Includes bibliographical references and indexes

419 Sign languages

Butterworth, Rod R.

The **Perigee** visual dictionary of signing; an A-to-Z guide to over 1,350 signs of American Sign Language. [by] Rod R. Butterworth and Mickey Flodin. rev & expanded 3rd ed; Berkley Pub. Group 1995 478p il pa $15.95

Grades: 8 9 10 11 12 Adult 419

1. Reference books 2. Sign language -- Dictionaries

ISBN 0-399-51952-1

LC 95-1380

First published 1983

This guide to American Sign Language features more than 1,350 alphabetically arranged signs with directions on how to form them. Illustrations show precise hand positions and movements. Includes memory aids

Costello, Elaine

Random House Webster's American Sign Language dictionary: unabridged. Random House Reference 2008 xxxii, 1200p $55

Grades: 8 9 10 11 12 Adult 419

1. Reference books 2. Sign language -- Dictionaries

ISBN 978-0-375-42616-2; 0-375-42616-7

First published 1994 with title: Random House American Sign Language dictionary

This dictionary includes "over 5,600 signs for the novice and experienced user alike. It includes complete descriptions of each sign, plus full-torso illustrations. There is also a subject index for easy reference as well as alternate signs for the same meaning." Publisher's note

★ The **Gallaudet** dictionary of American Sign Language; Clayton Valli, editor in chief; illustrated by Peggy Swartzel

Lott, Daniel Renner, and Rob Hills. Gallaudet University Press 2005 xli, 558p il $49.95
Grades: 8 9 10 11 12 Adult 419
1. Reference books 2. Sign language -- Dictionaries
ISBN 1-56368-282-6; 978-1-56368-282-7
LC 2005-51129

"This is a very valuable language resource for parents, students, and teachers learning ASL as a first language and as a second language." Choice

Includes bibliographical references

Sternberg, Martin L. A.

★ **American** Sign Language; a comprehensive dictionary. illustrated by Herbert Rogoff. Unabridged; HarperCollins Pubs. 1998 xxi, 983p il $60; pa $24
Grades: 8 9 10 11 12 Adult 419
1. Reference books 2. Sign language -- Dictionaries
ISBN 0-06-271608-5; 0-06-273634-5 pa
LC 98-26649

First published 1981

Arranged alphabetically, this dictionary features 7,000 sign entries, with cross-references and more than 12,000 illustrations

Includes bibliographical references

Warner, Penny

Signing fun; American sign language vocabulary, phrases, games & activities. illustrated by Paula Gray. Gallaudet Univ. Press 2006 225p il pa $19.95
Grades: 4 5 6 7 8 419
1. Sign language
ISBN 1-56368-292-3

"This book is a great resource for readers who want to learn more signs, or for teachers and librarians looking for fun ways to share them with kids." SLJ

420 Specific languages

Dubosarsky, Ursula

The **word** snoop; illustrated by Tohby Riddle. Dial Books 2009 246p il $16.99
Grades: 5 6 7 8 420
1. English language -- History
ISBN 978-0-8037-3406-7; 0-8037-3406-9
LC 2009-8306

First published 2008 in Australia with title: The word spy

A tour of the English language from the beginning of the alphabet in 4000 BC to modern text messaging and emoticons

"Short chapters, clear explanations, and humorous examples bring the subject to life, while word puzzles and coded messages at the end of each section invite reader participation. The attractive design adds to the appeal." Booklist

421 Writing system, phonology, phonetics of standard English

Truss, Lynne

Eats, shoots & leaves; the zero tolerance approach to punctuation. Gotham Books 2004 xxvii, 209p $19.95; pa $12
Grades: 8 9 10 11 12 Adult 421
1. Punctuation
ISBN 1-59240-087-6; 1-59240-203-8 pa
LC 2004-40646

First published 2003 in the United Kingdom

The author "dissects common errors that grammar mavens have long deplored (often, as she readily points out, in isolation) and makes . . . arguments for increased attention to punctuation correctness. . . . Truss serves up delightful, unabashedly strict and sometimes snobby little book, with cheery Britishisms ('Lawks-a-mussy!') dotting pages that express a more international righteous indignation." Publ Wkly

Includes bibliographical references

422 Etymology of standard English

Baker, Rosalie F.

In a word; 750 words and their fascinating stories and origins. by Rosalie Baker; illustrated by Tom Lopes. Cobblestone Pub. 2003 221p il $17.95
Grades: 5 6 7 8 422
1. English language -- Etymology
ISBN 0-8126-2710-5
LC 2003-25582

"The entries in this book discuss the meanings and derivations of 750 words and phrases. . . . While exploring word origins, Baker also touches on interesting facets of European history and Greek mythology. The jaunty illustrations are reproduced in black and shades of gray. . . . This informative book fosters an appreciation for the richness of the English language." Booklist

Gorrell, Gena K.

Say what? the weird and mysterious journey of the English language. Tundra Books 2009 146p il pa $10.95
Grades: 7 8 9 10 11 12 422
1. English language -- Etymology
ISBN 978-0-88776-878-1; 0-88776-878-4

"Gorrell takes readers on a quick and amusing historical tour of the English language, looking at how it has been influenced by Latin, Old English, French, and German. . . . This clever and funny book also integrates explanations for tricky grammar and spelling problems as part of the historical explanation for our changing language. Readers are not only given examples of malapropisms but also a list of several words that are often confused. . . . Supplementary materials including a time line and a large number of illustrations will make this book a valuable addition to both public and school libraries." Voice Youth Advocates

Hitchings, Henry

The **secret** life of words; how English became English. Farrar, Straus and Giroux 2008 440p $27
Grades: 8 9 10 11 12 Adult 422
1. English language -- Etymology
ISBN 978-0-374-25410-0; 0-374-25410-9
LC 2008-26055

"Hitchings here provides a colorful, thematic history of the English language. Treating borrowings and coinages as psychological windows to history, the author takes the reader on a tour of the lexicon from Anglo-Saxon to the present day and shows how new words answer linguistic needs. . . . Hitchings treats the reader to some 3,000 word histories. . . . With 90-plus pages of notes, sources, and useful indexes, this is a fine choice for libraries and a 'smorgasbord' for language aficionados." Choice

Includes bibliographical references

423 Dictionaries of standard English

★ The **American** Heritage student dictionary; Updated ed.; Houghton Mifflin 2007 xx, 1068p il $19.95

Grades: 6 7 8 9 423

1. Reference books 2. English language -- Dictionaries

ISBN 978-0-618-70149-0; 0-618-70149-4

LC 2006277388

First published 1977 with title: The American Heritage school dictionary

Contains more than 65,000 entries, including hundreds of notes on usage, word histories, accompanied by 2000 color photo and illustrations.

Bartlett's Roget's thesaurus. Little, Brown 1996 xxxii, 1415p $21.95; pa $16.95

Grades: 8 9 10 11 12 Adult 423

1. Americanisms 2. Reference books 3. English language -- Synonyms and antonyms

ISBN 0-316-10138-9; 0-316-73587-6 pa

LC 96-18343

This thesaurus "reflects the current state of American English, including terminology from the worlds of composers and television, with such sub-categories as 'Living Things,' 'The Arts,' 'Feelings.' But what really makes the book a joy to use is the tremendously useful lists—everything from phobias to styles and periods of furniture." Am Libr

The **Merriam**-Webster dictionary of synonyms and antonyms. Merriam-Webster 1992 443p pa $4.99

Grades: 8 9 10 11 12 Adult 423

1. Reference books 2. English language -- Synonyms and antonyms

ISBN 0-87779-906-7

LC 93-119503

First published 1942 with title: Webster's dictionary of synonyms

"This synonym dictionary is an outstanding work. . . . Synonyms and similar words, alphabetically arranged, are carefully defined, discriminated, and illustrated with thousands of quotations. The entries also include antonyms and analogous words." Nichols. Guide to Ref Books for Sch Media Cent. 4th edition

★ **Merriam**-Webster's intermediate dictionary; Revised and updated edition Merriam Webster 2016 1008 p illustrations hardcover $19.95

Grades: 5 6 7 8 423

1. Vocabulary 2. Encyclopedias and dictionaries 3. English language -- Dictionaries

ISBN 9780877796978; 0877796971

LC 2016299963

"Includes 200 newly added words and meanings across a variety of fields including technology, social media, science, health, and popular culture." (Publisher's note)

Merriam-Webster's school thesaurus; revised edition Merriam Webster 2017 704 p $19.95

Grades: 8 9 10 11 423

1. English language -- Synonyms and antonyms

ISBN 0877793654; 9780877793656

LC 2016043885

First published 1978 with title: Webster's student thesaurus

This new edition offers over 154,000 word choices and 37,000 usage examples.

★ **Merriam**-Webster's visual dictionary. Merriam-Webster, Inc. 2012 1112 p. (hbk.) $39.95

Grades: 6 7 8 9 10 11 12 Adult 423

1. English language -- Dictionaries

ISBN 0877791511; 9780877791515

This visual dictionary, edited by Jean-Claude Corbeil, has "more than 8,000 highly detailed, full-color illustrations, organized by subject in specialized fields from all aspects of life, . . . [and] nearly 25,000 . . . technical and everyday terms with clear, concise definitions. . . . Themes include a wide variety of fields: astronomy, the earth, human beings, the animal kingdom, plants and gardening, . . . food, arts and architecture, . . . sports and games" and more. (Publisher's note)

Roget's 21st century thesaurus in dictionary form; the essential reference for home, school, or office. edited by the Princeton Language Institute; Barbara Ann Kipfer, head lexicographer. 3rd ed; Bantam Dell 2005 962p $15; pa $5.99

Grades: 8 9 10 11 12 Adult 423

1. Reference books 2. English language -- Synonyms and antonyms

ISBN 0-385-33895-3; 0-440-24269-X pa

First published 1992

This thesaurus, cross referencing each word with the same concept, provides 500,000 synonyms and antonyms in a dictionary format and includes recently coined and common slang terms and commonly used foreign terms.

Roget's international thesaurus; edited by Barbara Ann Kipfer. 7th edition HarperReference 2011 1282 p paperback $19.99; hardcover $24.99

Grades: 8 9 10 11 12 Adult 423

1. English language -- Synonyms and antonyms

ISBN 9780061715211; 0061715212; 9780061715228; 0061715239; 9780061715235

LC 2008055359

First copyright edition published 1911 with title: The standard thesaurus of English words and phrases classified and arranged so as to facilitate the expression of ideas and assist in literary composition

"The most comprehensive, user-friendly thesaurus available, Roget's features more than 325,000 words and phrases, including more than 2,000 all-new entries that reflect the very latest in culture and technology, from "alpha male" to"zero tolerance." The seventh edition has reduced archaic terminology and added 50 new word lists." (Publisher's note)

Terban, Marvin

★ **Scholastic** dictionary of idioms; new & updated; Scholastic 2006 298p il pa $19.85

Grades: 4 5 6 7 423

1. Reference books 2. English language -- Idioms

ISBN 978-0-439-77083-5 pa; 0-439-77083-1 pa

First published 1996

This "introduction to American slang and phrase origins identifies and defines more than six hundred commonly used idioms, complementing the entries with . . . sample sentences and . . . illustrations." Publisher's note

425.55 English language – Pronouns

Bongiovanni, Archie

A **quick** and easy guide to they/them pronouns; Archie Bongiovanni, Tristan Jimerson ; [edited by] Ari Yarwood. Limerence Press 2018 64 p. illustrations $7.99

Grades: 7 8 9 10 11 12 Adult **425.55**

1. Gender identity 2. Pronouns (Grammar) 3. Interpersonal communication

ISBN 1620104997; 9781620104996

LC 2017959095

"Archie [Bongiovanni], a snarky genderqueer artist, is tired of people not understanding gender neutral pronouns. Tristan [Jimerson], a cisgender dude, is looking for an easy way to introduce gender neutral pronouns to his increasingly diverse workplace. The longtime best friends team up in this short and fun comic guide that explains what pronouns are, why they matter, and how to use them." (Publisher's note)

"In addition to supplying best practices for allies, situational examples illustrate what it's like to be misgendered and how that feels to someone who identifies as nonbinary." LJ

428 Standard English usage (Prescriptive linguistics)

★ The **American** Heritage student thesaurus; updated edition Houghton Mifflin Harcourt 2015 378 p hardcover $18.95

Grades: 6 7 8 9 10 **428**

1. Vocabulary 2. English language -- Synonyms and antonyms

ISBN 054433664X; 9780544336643

"A refreshed version of the award-winning thesaurus . . ., providing burgeoning writers with 70,000 synonyms shown in contexts students can relate to, as well as clear sample sentences showing typical usage." (Publisher's note)

Budzik, Mary

Punctuation : the write stuff! [created by Basher; written by Mary Budzik] Kingfisher 2010 64p il (Basher basics) pa $7.99

Grades: 4 5 6 7 **428**

1. Punctuation

ISBN 978-0-7534-6420-5 pa; 0-7534-6420-9 pa

"This slim volume uses catchy graphic design and an informal narrative to spark interest in the subject. In a presentation reminiscent of manga and Saturday-morning cartoons, each punctuation mark is introduced as a unique character who conveys his job through chatty dialogue. . . . The book explains the various uses of each mark and some basics of sentence structure." SLJ

Includes glossary

Farwell, Sybil M.

Supporting reading in grades 6-12; a guide. by Sybil M. Farwell and Nancy L. Teger. Libraries Unlimited 2012 xiii, 358 p.p

Grades: Professional **428**

1. Motivation (Psychology) 2. Children -- Books and reading 3. Reading (Secondary) 4. Motivation in education 5. School librarian participation in curriculum planning

ISBN 9781598848038; 9781598848045

LC 2012010826

This book, by Sybil M. Farwell and Nancy L. Teger, "addresses head-on the disturbing trend of declining leisure reading among students and demonstrates how school librarians can contribute to the development of lifelong reading habits as well as improve students' motivation and test scores. The book provides a comprehensive framework for achieving this: the READS curriculum, which stands for Read as a personal activity." (Publisher's note)

Includes bibliographical references and index

Fogarty, Mignon

Grammar girl presents the ultimate writing guide for students; with illustrations by Erwin Haya. Henry Holt and Co. 2010 294p il $19.99; pa $12.99

Grades: 6 7 8 9 10 **428**

1. Rhetoric 2. Report writing 3. English language -- Grammar

ISBN 978-0-8050-8943-1; 0-8050-8943-8; 978-0-8050-8944-8 pa; 0-8050-8944-6 pa

LC 2010011699

"This text is evenly divided into five sections: parts of speech, sentence structure, punctuation, usage, and a final segment on how readers can improve their writing. Fogarty's style mimics her podcasts with pithy but helpful rules and advice laced with examples. Pop quizzes and cartoon illustrations are also included. Libraries should purchase this book for reference use if nothing else, but budding writers will find it invaluable." SLJ

Includes bibliographical references

O'Conner, Patricia T.

Woe is I Jr; the junior grammarphobes' guide to better English in plain English. [by] Patricia O'Conner; drawings by Tom Stiglich. G.P. Putnam's Sons 2007 152p il $16.99; paperback $9.99

Grades: 4 5 6 7 8 **428**

1. English language -- Usage 2. English language -- Grammar

ISBN 978-0-399-24331-8; 9780147519160

LC 2006020575

An adaptation of Woe is I, published 2003 for adults by Riverhead Books

The author "covers pronouns, plurals, possessives, verb usage, subject-verb agreement, capitalization, and punctuation with jargon-free explanations and entertaining examples. . . . She knows her subject, can convey her message with wit and ease, and does it all in a compact, easy-to-read format." SLJ

Terban, Marvin

★ **Scholastic** dictionary of spelling; rev ed; Scholastic Reference 2006 272p il pa $9.99

Grades: 4 5 6 **428**

1. Spellers 2. Reference books

ISBN 978-0-439-76421-6; 0-439-76421-1

First published 1998

This spelling dictionary gives instructions for looking up a word the reader does not know how to spell, offers more than 150 memory tricks to correct commonly misspelled words, explains general spelling rules and their exceptions, and includes sections such as "The Four Longest Words in the English Language" and "The Spelling Words That Made Kids Champions." To aid pronunciation, each word is divided into syllables with the accented syllable in boldface.

433 Dictionaries of standard German

Betteridge, Harold T.

Cassell's German-English, English-German dictionary; completely revised by Harold T. Betteridge. Websters New World 1978 1580p 2v in 1 $27

Grades: 8 9 10 11 12 Adult **433**

1. Reference books 2. German language -- Dictionaries
ISBN 9780025229303

First compiled 1888 by Elizabeth Weir and published by Heath. Periodically revised. Previous American editions published by Funk & Wagnalls with title: The New Cassell's German dictionary

This dictionary incorporates "many new words and usages. Gives phonetic transcriptions of headwords. One of the most useful bilingual dictionaries." Guide to Ref Books. 11th edition

443 Dictionaries of standard French

Girard, Denis

Cassell's French dictionary; French-English, English-French. completely revised by Denis Girard with the assistance of Gaston Dulong, Oliver Van Oss, and Charles Guinness. Wiley 2002 762, 655p thumb-indexed $24.95

Grades: 8 9 10 11 12 Adult **443**

1. Reference books 2. French language -- Dictionaries
ISBN 0-02-522620-7

First published 1920 with title: Cassell's French-English, English-French dictionary. Previous American editions published by Funk & Wagnalls with title: The New Cassell's French dictionary

"New words including colloquialisms, slang, American English and French-Canadian terms [are included]. . . . There are also sections on French verbs and French and English abbreviations. Reliable, standard dictionary. A first choice." N Y Public Libr. Ref Books for Child Collect. 2d edition

453 Dictionaries of standard Italian

Cassell's Italian dictionary; Italian-English, English-Italian. compiled by Piero Rebora, with the assistance of Francis M. Guercio and Arthur L. Hayward. Wiley 2002 xxi, 1128p thumb-indexed $24.95

Grades: 8 9 10 11 12 Adult **453**

1. Reference books 2. Italian language -- Dictionaries
ISBN 0-02-522540-5

First published 1958 in the United Kingdom with title: Cassell's Italian-English, English-Italian dictionary. Previous United States editions published by Funk & Wagnalls

"A general dictionary of the Italian language as currently written and spoken." Ref Sources for Small & Medium-sized Libr. 5th edition

463 Dictionaries of standard Spanish

Gooch, Anthony

Cassell's Spanish-English, English-Spanish dictionary; completely revised by Anthony Gooch, Angel Garcia de Paredes. Wiley 2002 xxv, 1109p $22.95

Grades: 8 9 10 11 12 Adult **463**

1. Reference books 2. Spanish language -- Dictionaries
ISBN 0-02-522910-9

Previously published in 1978 by Macmillan

This dictionary emphasizes the Spanish of Latin America, and includes both classical and literary Spanish as well as the language of the modern Spanish-speaking world.

473 Dictionaries of classical Latin

Simpson, D. P.

Cassell's Latin dictionary; Latin-English, English-Latin. by D. P. Simpson. Macmillan 1977 883p thumb-indexed $24.95

Grades: 8 9 10 11 12 Adult **473**

1. Reference books 2. Latin language -- Dictionaries
ISBN 0-02-522580-4

LC 77-7670

First published 1854. This edition first published 1959. Previous United States editions published by Funk & Wagnalls with title: Cassell's New Latin dictionary

"Cassell's incorporates current English idiom and Latin spelling into the traditional presentation of classical Latin. The 30,000 entries include generic terms, geographical and proper nouns. Etymological notes and illustrative quotations are provided within entries." Wynar. Guide to Ref Books for Sch Media Cent. 3d edition

493 Non-Semitic Afro-Asiatic languages

Giblin, James

The **riddle** of the Rosetta Stone; key to ancient Egypt. [by] James Cross Giblin. Crowell 1990 85p il hardcover o.p. pa $7.99

Grades: 5 6 7 8 **493**

1. Hieroglyphics 2. Rosetta stone 3. Egyptian language
ISBN 0-06-446137-8 pa

LC 89-29289

Describes how the discovery and deciphering of the Rosetta Stone unlocked the secret of Egyptian hieroglyphics

"Suspense keeps the reader glued to this fine piece of nonfiction as the mystery of hieroglyphs is slowly unraveled. . . . The author has done a masterful job of distilling information, citing the highlights, and fitting it all together in an interesting and enlightening look at a puzzling subject." Horn Book

Includes bibliographical references

500 NATURAL SCIENCES AND MATHEMATICS

★ The **big** idea science book; incredible concepts that show how science works in the real world. editor, Matilda Gollon; consultant, Lisa Burke. DK Pub. 2010 304p il $29.99

Grades: 4 5 6 7 **500**

1. Science
ISBN 978-0-7566-6287-5; 0-7566-6287-7

LC 2010-281143

"Aimed at grabbing readers' general interest in science, this lively overview is split into sections on life, earth, and physical science; within each category, specific subjects are plainly labeled for easy reference.

. . . Full-color photographs, drawings, and diagrams further inform, and readers can visit an interactive Web site for more exploration. For breadth of material and clarity, it's hard to beat." Publ Wkly

Bryson, Bill

A **really** short history of nearly everything. Delacorte Press 2009 169p il $19.99

Grades: 4 5 6 7 **500**

1. Science

ISBN 978-0-385-73810-1; 0-385-73810-2

A newly illustrated, abridged and adapted edition of A short history of nearly everything, published 2003 by Broadway Books for adults; this edition first published in the United Kingdom 2008

Bryson "whirls through mind-numbing notions such as the creation of the universe and the life span of an atom with good cheer and accessible, even exciting, writing. The two-page speads meander their way through the various recesses of science with a combination of explanatory prose, historical anecdotes, wry asides, and illustrations that range from helpful to comical." Booklist

Isabella, Jude

Hoaxed! fakes & mistakes in the world of science. by the editors of YES mag; illustrated by Howie Woo. Kids Can Press 2009 48p il lib bdg $16.95; pa $8.95

Grades: 5 6 7 8 **500**

1. Fraud 2. Science

ISBN 978-1-55453-206-3 lib bdg; 1-55453-206-X lib bdg; 978-1-55453-207-0 pa; 1-55453-207-8 pa

This title examines hoaxes, fakes and mistakes from the world of science, including crop circles, Bigfoot and the Loch Ness monster, and UFOs reported at Roswell, New Mexico. Index. "Ages nine to twelve." (Quill Quire)

"Piltdown man, Richard Meinertzhagen the light-fingered bird collector, 'Stone Age' Tasaday in the Philippines, crop circles in England, cold fusion energy and UFOs in Roswell, N.M., are the fakes and mistakes described in this lively introduction to fraud in science. The breezy text opens with a clear description of the scientific process of hypothesis, experiment, publication in professional magazines and replication of results before proceeding to the many colorful fakes exposed." Kirkus

Includes index.

Murphy, Glenn

Why is snot green; and other extremely important questions (and answers) Roaring Brook Press 2009 236p il pa $9.95

Grades: 4 5 6 7 **500**

1. Science 2. Technology

ISBN 978-1-59643-500-1 pa; 1-59643-500-3 pa

"Conservation, evolution, technology, animal life, space travel, physics, and much more are discussed in this lively science book. . . . [This offers] chatty questions and answers . . . with text that is compelling, never intimidating, and sometimes deliberately outrageous. . . . Children will have fun browsing the spacious pages and sharing what they read with adults." Booklist

O'Meara, Stephen James

Are you afraid yet? the science behind scary stuff; written by Stephen James O'Meara; illustrated by Jeremy Kaposy. Kids Can Press 2009 78p il $17.95; pa $9.95

Grades: 5 6 7 8 **500**

1. Science 2. Supernatural

ISBN 978-1-55453-294-0; 1-55453-294-9; 978-1-55453-295-7 pa; 1-55453-295-7 pa

"This book cleverly weaves together the supernatural and the scientific in an entertaining read that answers questions about ghosts, UFOs, vampires, werewolves, and how long a decapitated head can remain conscious. Examples depicting such things in classical fiction and popular movies are seamlessly interjected between the factual explanations. Each page is filled with detailed black-and-white illustrations, emphasizing the sometimes-humorous, yet often-macabre descriptions." SLJ

Rice, Dona

★ **What** a scientist sees; Dona Herweck Rice. Teacher Created Materials 2016 32 p. (pbk.) $8.99

Grades: 4 5 6 **500**

1. Scientists 2. Observation (Scientific method) 3. Science -- Methodology

ISBN 1480746916; 9781480746916

LC 2014045214

This children's book by Dona Rice shows how "scientists see things much differently than the average person. They observe and research, create hypotheses, make predictions, and much more when conducting experiments. A Think Like a Scientist lab activity that supports STEM instruction is included at the end of the book for students to use what they learned in the text and apply that knowledge to the activity." (Publisher's note)

"Smartly written, these innovative and imaginative volumes make learning fun... First-rate nonfiction." SLJ

Richardson, Gillian

Kaboom! explosions of all kinds. Annick Press 2009 83p il $22.95; pa $12.95

Grades: 4 5 6 7 **500**

1. Science 2. Explosions

ISBN 978-1-55451-204-1; 1-55451-204-2; 978-1-55451-203-4 pa; 1-55451-203-4 pa

"With comic-style sound-effect headings and fact boxes galore, Kaboom! highlights the supercharged of the natural and manmade worlds, from astronomy, geology, biology, herbology, and entomology to chemistry, mechanics, pyrotechnics, and art. Text is broken into asymmetrical panels for bite-size explanations. Some explosions are captured in sequence and detail with historical and high-speed photography and illustrations in comic-style panel frames. . . . Kaboom! is an engrossing attention-getter, effectively tapping the sensationalism of all types of blasts." SLJ

Wood, Matthew Brenden

The **science** of science fiction; by Matthew Brenden Wood ; illustrated by Tom Casteel. Nomad Press 2017 120 p. illustrations (some color) (Inquire and investigate) (hardcover) $22.95

Grades: 6 7 8 9 **500**

1. Science fiction 2. Science -- Miscellanea 3. Technology

ISBN 161930466X; 9781619304680; 9781619304666

This book, by Matthew Brenden Wood, illustrated by Tom Casteel, "explore[s] the science behind classic and modern science fiction stories, including artificial intelligence, androids, and the search for alien life. . . . [The book] promotes critical thinking skills through inquiry, discovery, research, analysis, and reflection of key scientific ideas and concepts made popular by many titles in science fiction." (Publisher's note)

"This latest addition to the award-winning Inquire and Investigate series will be a welcome acquisition for librarians wanting to spice up their STEAM collections." Booklist

Includes bibliographical references (page 116) and index.

500.5 Space sciences

Perritano, John

Space science; John Perritano. Mason Crest 2017 64 p. color illustrations (hardback) $23.95

Grades: 6 7 8 9 10 **500.5**

1. Space sciences 2. Technological innovations

ISBN 1422235955; 9781422235959

LC 2016004810

This juvenile book, by John Perritano, part of the "STEM in Current Events" series, explores how "just about every part of our lives is touched by one or more of those fields. In this book, check out many stories from the world of Space Science. . . . [like] the exploration of space, on the missions humans attempt, the discoveries we make, and more." (Publisher's note)

"A great fit for classroom or school libraries and a strong consideration for public libraries interested in the integration of STEM into everyday life." SLJ

502 Miscellany

Murphy, Glenn

How loud can you burp? more extremely important questions (and answers!) Roaring Book Press 2009 284p il pa $10.99

Grades: 4 5 6 7 **502**

1. Science 2. Questions and answers

ISBN 978-1-59643-506-3 pa; 1-59643-506-2 pa

"'Why does pollen give you hay fever?' 'Why don't big metal ships just sink?' These are but a couple of the questions that Murphy received on the Web site he set up to solicit inquiries from kids. Written in an informal, question-and-answer format, he delivers serious scientific information in an easygoing, humorous manner, with several pages dedicated to each topic. . . . A few line drawings break up the text and sidebars highlight interesting facts or are, at times, simply funny. . . . This is an entertaining, accessible approach to science that's sure to appeal to science buffs and general browsers alike." SLJ

502.8 Auxiliary techniques and procedures; apparatus, equipment, materials

Kramer, Stephen

★ **Hidden** worlds: looking through a scientist's microscope; photographs by Dennis Kunkel. Houghton Mifflin 2001 57p il (Scientists in the field) $16; pa $5.95

Grades: 4 5 6 7 **502.8**

1. Microscopes 2. Microscopists

ISBN 0-618-05546-0; 0-618-35405-0 pa

LC 00-58083

This book takes a "look at the work of a microscopist. Kunkel works with microscopes to explore science. . . . This book contains many of his photos, most taken with electron microscopes. . . . Several opening pages, along with the front and back endpapers, are visually dazzling. The heart of the book, though, is what readers learn about how Kunkel produces these images, and to what uses scientists put them. . . . This title offers a wealth of scientific information along with an insightful look at the world of an individual scientist." SLJ

Includes bibliographical references

Levine, Shar

★ The **ultimate** guide to your microscope; [by] Shar Levine & Leslie Johnstone. Sterling Pub. 2008 143p il pa $9.95

Grades: 5 6 7 8 9 **502.8**

1. Microscopes

ISBN 978-1-4027-4329-0 pa; 1-4027-4329-7 pa

LC 2006-100967

"Through this fun and inviting book, readers can begin to explore the world using a microscope. Students are encouraged to learn the basics in the two first chapters and then undertake the 41 hands-on activities in the next eight chapters. Activities are presented in manageable one or two-page uniformly formatted modules." SLJ

503 Dictionaries, encyclopedias, concordances

The **Kingfisher** science encyclopedia; 4th edition Kingfisher 2017 488 p. ill. (some col.) hardcover $34.99

Grades: 5 6 7 8 **503**

1. Science -- Encyclopedias 2. Science

ISBN 9780753466889; 9780753473849

This book is a science encyclopedia, arranged thematically and "most topics are presented on . . . two-page spreads, with relevant charts, timelines, and other illustrations surrounding the text. In the bottom right corner of the spread is a 'See Also Pages' box that directs readers to related topics with their page numbers." (Voice of Youth Advocates)

Topical chapters present "basic surveys of physics, geology, chemistry, biology, anatomy, the environment, and space. . . . Articles are generally, though not rigidly, confined to a spread each, and all have see-also references. . . . The illustrations are a plus; they are crisply reproduced, finely detailed, and labeled, enhancing the text rather than competing with it." SLJ

507.2 Research

Swanson, Diane, 1944-

Nibbling on Einstein's brain; the good, the bad & the bogus in science. by Diane Swanson ; illustrated by Francis Blake. 2nd edition Annick Press 2009 151 p. il (pbk.) $12.95; (hbk.) $24.95

Grades: 5 6 7 8 **507.2**

1. Science -- Methodology

ISBN 1554511860; 1554511879; 9781554511860; 9781554511877

This book, by Diane Swanson, illustrated by Francis Blake, presents "strategies for sorting the good from the misleading in science. Through playful scenarios and fascinating real-world examples, each chapter encourages critical thinking. You'll find tips for spotting bad science, ideas for identifying reports that misrepresent facts and ways to keep your own brain from muddling the science news you receive." (Publisher's note)

The author "discusses topics such as the difference between correlation and cause-and-effect relationships, the importance of asking the right questions about advertisers' claims, and the links between superstition, coincidence, and probability. With a highly readable text and jaunty line illustrations, the book encourages critical thinking and skepticism when evaluating science reporting and media hype." Booklist

507.8 Use of apparatus and equipment in study and teaching

Austin, John

Labcraft wizards; Magical Projects and Experiments. John Austin. Chicago Review Press 2016 256 p. illustrations (chiefly color) (paperback) $16.99; (ebook) $16.99

Grades: 4 5 6 7 **507.8**

1. Magic 2. Handicraft 3. Science -- Experiments 4. Physics -- Experiments

ISBN 9781613736210; 9781613736227

LC 2016027300

This book, by John Austin, "provides dozens of step-by-step projects to transform everyday objects into instruments of magic, such as a sculpted magic wand, gooey ogre snot, bouncy dragon eggs, edible brewed slugs, an enchanted hourglass, and more! Through its creative activities, [it] encourages scientific observation and helps eager minds explore basic concepts in chemistry and physics through experimentation." (Publisher's note)

"Keep this one close at hand—it's screaming to be used for a Harry Potter–themed program or party and would fit well in the classroom or in a public library." Booklist

Banqueri, Eduardo

Everyday science; 66 Experiments that explain the small and big things all around us. by Eduardo Banqueri, Joseph M. Barras and Octavi López Coronado ; illustrations by Roger Zanni. Barrons Educational Series, Inc. 2016 144 p. color illustrations (paperback) $14.99

Grades: 3 4 5 6 **507.8**

1. Science -- Experiments

ISBN 9781438008622

LC 2015951730

In this book by Eduardo Banqueri, Joseph M. Barras and Octavi López Coronado, with illustrations by Roger Zanni, "kids can learn how to find the science that exists in everyday activities. Four main chapters offer experiments in physics, chemistry, geology, and biology. Budding scientists will gain practical knowledge while learning how to: build a time machine, guess tomorrow's weather, generate salty stalactites, [and] make a rainbow disappear, [among others]." (Publisher's note)

"Lively cartoons, photographs of kids, and clear step-by-step directions make each project easy to follow, and sidebars dive into the hard science behind the complex subjects explored." Pub Wkly

Bonnet, Robert L.

46 science fair projects for the evil genius. McGraw-Hill 2009 194p il (Evil genius series) pa $19.95

Grades: 6 7 8 9 **507.8**

1. Science projects 2. Science -- Experiments

ISBN 978-0-07-160027-9; 0-07-160027-2

LC 2008008078

Provides instructions and plans for science projects across various disciplines, including physics, astronomy, energy, environmental science and economics.

Challoner, Jack

★ **Maker** Lab; 28 Super Cool Projects: Build * Invent * Create * Discover. Jack Challoner ; foreword by Jack Andraka. DK Publishing 2016 160 p. color illustrations hardcover $19.99

Grades: 3 4 5 6 7 8 **507.8**

1. Science projects 2. Science -- Experiments

ISBN 9781465451354; 9781465458728; 1465451358

LC 2016427641

This book by Jack Challoner, with foreword by Jack Andraka, "includes 28 kid-safe projects and crafts that will get young inventors' wheels turning and make science pure fun. Each step-by-step activity is appropriate for kids ages 8–12 and ranked easy, medium, or hard, with an estimated time frame for completion. Requiring only household materials, young makers can build an exploding volcano, race balloon rocket cars, construct a solar system, make a lemon battery, and more." (Publisher's note)

"Though not all projects are innovative, what sets this book apart is that each experiment is accompanied by real-world applications that tie new observations to kids' existing understanding and offer endless opportunities for STEM-related discussions. Not only are young scientists encouraged to experiment, they are challenged to apply the information gleaned to real-world problem-solving." Booklist

Churchill, E. Richard

365 more simple science experiments with everyday materials; by E. Richard Churchill, Louis V. Loeschnig, and Muriel Mandell ; illustrated by Frances Zweifel. Black Dog & Leventhal Pub 2014 320 p. ill. $12.95

Grades: 4 5 6 7 **507.8**

1. Science -- Experiments 2. Experiments 3. Science -- Experiments 4. Scientific recreations

ISBN 1579129676; 9781579129675

LC 96053239

In this book "kids ages 9 through 12 get a year's worth of fun and educational hands-on experiments while gaining knowledge of the fundamentals of science. . . . The hundreds of experiments are divided into 32 chapters, . . . which focus on . . . basic principles of physics, . . . science using common foods, . . . concepts having to do with time and space, and . . . some puzzling ideas about nature. The final chapters explore the science of outer space." (Publisher's note)

"The projects are diverse, considering that some experiments take just minutes to complete, while others are more involved and even require days to see complete results. However, all of the included experiments are inquiry-based and dynamic, making the book perfect for formal instructional settings or entertaining curious minds with scientific fundamentals." Booklist

Cobb, Vicki

See for yourself; more than 100 amazing experiments for science fairs and school projects. illustrated by Dave Klug. 2nd ed; Skyhorse Pub. 2010 192p il pa $14.95

Grades: 4 5 6 7 **507.8**

1. Science -- Experiments

ISBN 978-1-61608-083-9; 1-61608-083-3

LC 2010020800

First published 2001 by Scholastic

This is an "accessible and often intriguing collection of activities and experiments. . . . The experiments are grouped by their source of inspiration: humans, the supermarket, the toy store, drugstore, and hardware and stationery stores. . . . Cartoon-style illustrations are . . . in full color." SLJ

★ **We** dare you! hundreds of science bets, challenges, and experiments you can do at home. Vicki Cobb. Revised edition Skyhorse Pub. 2015 321p il hardcover o.p. paperback $12.95

Grades: 4 5 6 7 **507.8**

1. Science -- Experiments

ISBN 978-1-60239-225-0; 978-1-60239-775-0; 9781629146317 paperback

First published 2007

"Divided into chapters with titles such as 'The Human Wonder,' 'Fluid Feats,' 'Energy Entrapments,' and 'Mathematical Duplicity,' this volume has more than 200 experiments with clear how-to instructions. All of the projects are doable and the science behind them is explained in a kid-accessible manner. . . . Black-and-white line drawings add humor and clarify instructions. This is a great resource for teachers, parents, and budding scientists—and for any youngster who can't resist a challenge." SLJ

Includes bibliographical references

Connolly, Sean

The **book** of potentially catastrophic science; 50 experiments for daring young scientists. Workman Pub. 2010 305p il

Grades: 5 6 7 8 **507.8**

1. Science -- Experiments

ISBN 0-7611-5687-9; 978-0-7611-5687-1

LC 2010-07044

This book presents thirty-four experiments. "Each chapter starts with a brief outline of the scientific advances of the time, followed by a clarification of the science and then one or more hands-on experiments to illustrate the object or concept presented. . . . Grades five to eight." (Sci Books Films)

"This volume approaches science historically, spotlighting certain periods, processes, individuals, discoveries, and inventions. Each of the 34 chapters includes a discussion and one or two related activities, such as making a Stone Age tool, creating an earthquake in Jell-O, building a parachute for an egg drop, and extracting a banana's DNA. Safety concerns are addressed for each project, and adult help will be necessary to complete some of the experiments successfully. . . . Connolly's writing is engaging, and the historical approach works well, offering kids a quick introduction to science history and the opportunity to explore certain ideas along the way." Booklist

Gardner, Robert

Light, sound, and waves science fair projects; revised and expanded using the scientific method. Enslow Publishers 2010 160p il (Physics science projects using the scientific method) lib bdg $34.60

Grades: 7 8 9 10 **507.8**

1. Light 2. Sound 3. Waves 4. Science projects 5. Science -- Experiments

ISBN 978-0-7660-3416-7 lib bdg; 0-7660-3416-X lib bdg

LC 2009006493

First published 2004 with title: Light, sound, and waves science fair projects using sunglasses, guitars, CDs, and other stuff

"Explains how to use the scientific method to conduct several science experiments about light, sound, and waves. Includes ideas for science fair projects." Publisher's note

Includes bibliographical references

Goodstein, Madeline

Ace your sports science project; great science fair ideas. [by] Madeline Goodstein, Robert Gardner, and Barbara Gardner Conklin. Enslow Publishers 2009 128p il (Ace your physics science project) lib bdg $31.93

Grades: 5 6 7 8 **507.8**

1. Sports 2. Physics 3. Science projects 4. Science -- Experiments

ISBN 978-0-7660-3229-3 lib bdg; 0-7660-3229-9 lib bdg

LC 2008-4689

"Presents several science experiments and project ideas dealing with the physics of sports." Publisher's note

Includes bibliographical references

Goal! science projects with soccer. Enslow Publishers 2009 104p il (Score! Sports science projects) lib bdg $31.93

Grades: 5 6 7 8 **507.8**

1. Motion 2. Soccer 3. Force and energy 4. Science projects 5. Science -- Experiments

ISBN 978-0-7660-3106-7 lib bdg; 0-7660-3106-3 lib bdg

LC 2008-2999

"Introductions include information about the history of the sport, safety steps to follow, and the scientific method. . . . Detailed diagrams help clarify many of the directions." SLJ

Includes glossary and bibliographical references

Graham, Ian

Science rocks! written by Ian Graham; additional text by Dr. Mike Goldsmith; step illustrations by Dan Wright. DK Pub. 2011 144p il $19.99

Grades: 6 7 8 9 **507.8**

1. Science -- Experiments

ISBN 978-0-7566-7198-3; 0-7566-7198-1

"Physics, chemistry, biology, and human physiology are the subjects covered in this huge, lavishly illustrated volume, packed with detailed suggestions for experiments to perform at home, at school, and for science-fair projects. The tone is relaxed but never cute, and the browsable design blends how-to with explanations of the forces at play." Booklist

Leavitt, Loralee

Candy experiments; Loralee Leavitt. Andrews McMeel Pub., LLC 2012 146 p. $14.99

Grades: 4 5 6 **507.8**

1. Candy 2. Science -- Experiments

ISBN 1449418368; 9781449418366

LC 2011944678

This book presents science activities for children involving candy. "Grouped by physical properties that include 'Color,' 'Secret Ingredients,' and 'Sticky' or processes like 'Blow It Up,' 'Squash It,' and 'Dissolve This,' the activities begin with an introductory question and tend to flow incrementally. Each one includes the time required, a list of ingredients . . . step-by-step directions, and a discussion, including a cursory scientific explanation." (School Library Journal)

Margles, Samantha

Mythbusters science fair book. Scholastic 2011 128p il pa $9.99

Grades: 4 5 6 7 **507.8**

1. Science projects 2. Science -- Experiments

ISBN 978-0-545-23745-1; 0-545-23745-9

This offers "50 original ideas for science fair projects or long, boredom-riddled summer days. Much like the popular television program on which it's based, the book stays true to the scientific method. . . . Divided into chapters on chemical reactions, temperature, energy and force, and more, the two- to three-page experiments on busily designed pages feature easy step-by-step procedures." Booklist

McCallum, Ann

Eat your science homework; recipes for inquiring minds. Ann McCallum ; illustrated by Leeza Hernandez. Charlesbridge 2014 48 p. colored illustrations (reinforced for library use) $16.95

Grades: 5 6 7 8 **507.8**

1. Science -- Experiments 2. Cooking 3. Food -- Composition 4. Food -- Experiments 5. Cooking -- Experiments 6. Science -- Experiments

ISBN 157091298X; 9781570912986; 9781570912993

LC 2013022070

This book, by Ann McCallum, illustrated by Leeza Hernandez, helps "readers discover delicious and distinct recipes. . . . A main text explains upper-elementary science concepts, including subatomic particles, acids and bases, black holes, and more. Alongside simple recipes, side-bars encourage readers to also experiment and explore outside of the kitchen. A review, glossary, and index make the entire book easy to digest." (Publisher's note)

"Scientific terms are explained in each chapter, and recipes are given and reinforced with a glossary. Bright illustrations and clear instructions will appeal to younger readers, while older readers will find the concepts and vocabulary educational; the recipes will appeal to a wide range of ages." SLJ

VanCleave, Janice Pratt

Janice VanCleave's engineering for every kid; easy activities that make learning science fun. Jossey-Bass 2007 205p il (Science for every kid series) pa $14.95

Grades: 4 5 6 7 **507.8**

1. Engineering 2. Science projects 3. Science -- Experiments

ISBN 978-0-471-47182-0 pa; 0-471-47182-8 pa

LC 2006-10540

Explains some of the basic physical principles of engineering, accompanied by activities that illustrate those principles

Vickers, Tanya M.

Teen science fair sourcebook; winning school science fairs and national competitions. Enslow Publishers 2009 160p il lib bdg $34.60

Grades: 7 8 9 10 **507.8**

1. Science projects 2. Science -- Exhibitions 3. Science -- Experiments

ISBN 978-0-7660-2711-4; 0-7660-2711-2

LC 2008-30779

"The book is clearly written, and its page design, which includes the occasional photo, is colorful. . . . A useful resource for highly motivated students." Booklist

Includes glossary and bibliographical references

Walker, Pamela

Environmental science experiments; [by] Pamela Walker, Elaine Wood. Facts on File 2010 153p il (Facts on File science experiments) $35

Grades: 7 8 9 10 **507.8**

1. Environmental science 2. Science -- Experiments

ISBN 978-0-8160-7805-9; 0-8160-7805-X

LC 2008-53715

This "contains 20 experiments that allow students to actively engage in scientific inquiry. Projects are presented in a uniform format, with an introduction to the topic, time requirements (35 minutes to 2 weeks), a materials list, numbered procedures, and several analysis questions. . . . Line drawings, colorful images, and data tables enhance instructions. . . . The experiments themselves are timely and fascinating. [The book] includes high-interest investigations into what people throw away, the safety of reusing water bottles, and a 'bottled versus tap water' taste test." SLJ

Includes glossary and bibliographical references

Williams, Jennifer

★ **Oobleck,** slime, & dancing spaghetti; twenty terrific at-home science experiments inspired by favorite children's books. by Jennifer Williams. Bright Sky Press 2009 192 p. ill. (paperback) $14.95

Grades: 4 5 6 **507.8**

1. Science -- Experiments

ISBN 1933979348; 9781933979342

LC 2009000876

This book "provides a series of science experiments designed to explore concepts and ideas that spring from various stories. At the beginning of each chapter, a children's book is . . . summarized. The author then explains a related science concept, suggests discussion questions that connect the experiment to the story, and offers ideas for taking the project further. . . . The experiments cover concepts including polymers, chemical reactions, and non-Newtonian fluids." (School Library Journal)

"Using children's literature as a springboard, this title provides a series of science experiments designed to explore concepts and ideas that spring from various stories. At the beginning of each chapter, a children's book is nicely summarized. The author then explains a related science concept, suggests discussion questions that connect the experiment to the story, and offers ideas for taking the project further. This is serious science. . . . The experiments do a really wonderful job of emphasizing the importance of observation and data collection. The writing is relatively clear. . . . This book is great choice for home use and science units." SLJ

Includes bibliographical references.

Young, Karen Romano

Junkyard science; 20 projects and experiments about junk, garbage, waste, things we don't need anymore, and ways to recycle or reuse it--or lose it. illustrations by David Goldin. National Geographic 2010 80p il (Science fair winners) $24.90; pa $12.95

Grades: 3 4 5 6 **507.8**

1. Recycling 2. Environmental sciences 3. Science -- Experiments

ISBN 978-1-4263-0690-7; 1-4263-0690-3; 978-1-4263-0689-1 pa; 1-4263-0689-X pa

This volume provides "outlines for science fair projects in the . . . environmental . . . sciences. The procedures include just enough structure to help novice experimenters get started. . . . Well-placed questions encourage creativity and further thinking. [The] volume includes humorous cartoon spot illustrations and a section on preparing presentations." Horn Book Guide

Try this! extreme 50 fun and safe experiments for the mad scientist in you. by Karen Romano Young ; photographs by Mattew Rakola. National Geographic Kids 2017 160 p. (hardcover : alk. paper) $26.90

Grades: 4 5 6 7 8 **507.8**

1. Science projects 2. Science -- Experiments

ISBN 9781426328633; 9781426328640

LC 2017010397

This book, by Karen Romano Young, with photographs by Mattew Rakola, presents "hands-on science experiments [for children] that takes interactivity to a whole new level. Weird, wacky science facts and basic principles are explained as a first step to launching these creative (and safe) science projects. Dynamic photos and art clearly highlight each step so kids can conduct experiments with confidence and accuracy." (Publisher's note)

508 Natural history

Art, Henry Warren

Woodswalk; peepers, pikas, and exploding puff balls. [by] Henry W. Art and Michael W. Robbins. Storey Books 2003 122p il map $21.95; pa $14.95

Grades: 4 5 6 **508**

1. Seasons 2. Nature study 3. Forest plants 4. Forest animals

ISBN 1-58017-477-9; 1-58017-452-3 pa

"This inviting introduction to forests describes the sights, sounds, and smells that await young explorers. The accessible text details the wonders of each season in both eastern and western locales, while full-color photos depict the flora and fauna that inhabit these intriguing environments." SLJ

Beer, Amy-Jane

Cool nature; Filled with facts & projects for kids of all ages. Amy-Jane Beer. Trafalgar Square Books 2016 111 p. color illustrations $14.99

Grades: 4 5 6 7 **508**

1. Nature 2. Natural history

ISBN 1910232254; 9781910232255

This children's book in the My Cool series by Amy-Jane Beer "contains everything . . . [a] naturalist needs to know. Meet nature's most fearsome predators, explore the wonders of the ocean, and marvel at the ability of animals to survive in the harshest environments. . . . Learn about why we should all care about endangered species, who would win in a fight between a shark and a honey badger, and where to go to see whales in the wild." (Publisher's note)

"Nature enthusiasts who enjoy learning about the life cycle of the guinea worm or understanding basic scientific principles such as photosynthesis will enjoy this colorful and informative book." SLJ

Chin, Jason

★ **Island**; a story of the Galapagos. Jason Chin. 1st ed. Roaring Brook Press 2012 40 p. (alk. paper) $16.99

Grades: 3 4 5 6 **508**

1. Birds 2. Droughts 3. Reptiles 4. Natural history -- Galapagos Islands 5. Galapagos Islands

ISBN 1596437162; 9781596437166

LC 2011033797

The author, Jason Chin, explains "how species of reptiles and birds on the Galapagos have evolved. He begins with the birth of the islands themselves, a process in which volcanic eruptions punch successive holes in the Earth's surface as tectonic plates move over them, [and] the adaptations of the islands' animals. . . . [Chin also provides information on the] droughts [that] become more common [due to the] climate and geology." (Publishers Weekly)

Includes bibliographical references and index.

Hamilton, Neil A.

Scientific exploration and expeditions; from the age of discovery to the twenty-first century. [by] Neil Hamilton. M.E. Sharpe 2011 2v il map set $165

Grades: 7 8 9 10 11 12 **508**

1. Reference books 2. Scientific expeditions

ISBN 978-0-7656-8076-1; 0-7656-8076-9

LC 2010-12118

"Hamilton's 115 entries in this set describe the courses and discoveries of significant scientific expeditions from the early 15th century to mid 2009. . . . The presentations are systematic, carefully detailed, not exclusively Eurocentric, and when appropriate, skeptical. The currency of information and focus on science will make this work particularly useful." SLJ

Includes bibliographical references

Hile, Lori

Rachel Carson; environmental pioneer. Lori Hile. Heinemann Library 2015 48 p. illustrations (some color) (Women in conservation) (hardcover) $32.65

Grades: 5 6 7 8 **508**

1. Conservationists 2. Carson, Rachel, 1907-1964 3. Pesticides -- Environmental aspects 4. Naturalists -- United States -- Biography 6. Science writers -- United States -- Biography 7. Environmentalists -- United States -- Biography

ISBN 1484604717; 1484604768; 9781484604717; 9781484604762

LC 2013040529

This book by Lori Hile "takes an engaging look at the work of ground-breaking conservationist, Rachel Carson, and her work to uncover the dangers of pesticides. It covers Carson's inspiration, her methods, findings, and the impact of her work on the environment movement." (Publisher's note)

"Students will appreciate her dedication—2000 hours of observing gorillas. The graphics present a time line of primate development and maps that are as excellent and informative as the rest of this must-have series." SLJ

Includes bibliographical references (pages 46-47) and index

Lloyd, Christopher

The **nature** timeline wallbook; unfold the story of nature--from the dawn of life to the present day! by Christopher Lloyd and Patrick Skipworth ; illustrated by Andy Forshaw ; designed by Will Webb. What on Earth Publishing 2017 24 p. illustrations (What on Earth? Timeline) $19.95

Grades: 5 6 7 8 **508**

1. Animals 2. Natural history

ISBN 0993284736; 9780993284731

This book in the What on Earth? Timeline series, by Christopher Lloyd and Patrick Skipworth, illustrated by Andy Forshaw, presents a timeline that "stretches back 4 billion years to the first signs of life. . . . The emergence of multi-cellular life, the colonization of the land, the reign of dinosaurs, mass extinctions, the migration of mammals, and . . . the story of humanity from the first two-legged hominids to a world populated by more than 7 billion people today." (Publisher's note)

"This utterly browsable and very engaging large-format title is chock-full of scientific facts and stories." SLJ

Lynch, Wayne

The **Everglades**; text and photographs by Wayne Lynch. NorthWord Books for Young Readers 2007 64p il (Our wild world: ecosystems) $16.95; pa $8.95

Grades: 4 5 6 7 **508**

1. Everglades (Fla.) 2. Natural history -- Florida

ISBN 978-1-55971-970-4; 1-55971-970-2; 978-1-55971-971-1 pa; 1-55971-971-0 pa

LC 2006-101497

This "provides an up-close look at the fascinating flora and fauna of the world-famous Everglades. . . . Lynch . . . smoothly pairs engaging prose with numerous color photographs that capture the beauty of the region in both sweeping panorama and close-up detail." Booklist

Paquette, Ammi-Joan

Two truths and a lie; it's alive! Ammi-Joan Paquette and Laurie Ann Thompson. Walden Pond Press 2017 x, 166 p.p illustrations (chiefly color) (hardcover) $17.99

Grades: 4 5 6 7 **508**

1. Natural history -- Miscellanea 2. Natural history 3. Questions and answers -- Fiction

ISBN 9780062418791; 9780062418821

LC 2016950349

This book, by Ammi-Joan Paquette, Laurie Ann Thompson, "presents some of the most crazy-but-true stories about the living world as well as a handful of stories that are too crazy to be true--and asks readers to separate facts from the fakes! . . . Just like the old game in this book's title, two out of every three stories are completely true and one is an outright lie. . . . Some false stories are based on truth, and some of the true stories are just plain unbelievable." (Publisher's note)

"The authors' casual tone should easily draw readers in, and activities at the end of each chapter underscore a key goal underneath all the fun: developing critical thinking skills." Pub Wkly

Includes bibliographical references (pages 136-153) and index.

Wood, A. J.

Charles Darwin and the Beagle adventure; countries visited during the voyage round the world of HMS Beagle under the command of Captain Fitzroy, Royal Navy, including extracts from the works of Charles Darwin. written by A.J. Wood & Clint Twist. Candlewick Press 2009 un il map $19.99

Grades: 4 5 6 7 8 **508**

1. Evolution 2. Naturalists 3. Travel writers 4. Writers on science 5. Beagle Expedition (1831-1836)

ISBN 978-0-7636-4538-0; 0-7636-4538-9

LC 2009-921214

"This beautifully illustrated large-format book immediately appeals to both the eye and the mind. Imitating a 19th-century scrapbook to a certain extent, including various pullouts . . . the book draws the young reader in. . . . Included are copious quotes from Darwin's journals and other writings, as well as reproductions . . . of numerous 19th-century engravings, drawings, and watercolors, some from the Beagle voyage itself. . . . Integrated into the 19th-century material are modern illustrations and well-written narratives relating background information, the story of the Beagle's voyage . . . and notes on Darwin's life and work. . . . This volume provides an excellent introduction to Darwin and his accomplishments." Sci Books Films

Woods, Michael

Seven natural wonders of Africa; by Michael Woods and Mary B. Woods. Twenty-First Century Books 2009 80p il map (Seven natural wonders) lib bdg $33.26

Grades: 5 6 7 8 **508**

1. Curiosities and wonders 2. Africa 3. Natural history -- Africa

ISBN 978-0-8225-9071-2; 0-8225-9071-9

LC 2008-21867

This book "takes seven noteworthy wonders in [Africa] and spotlights them in separate chapters. The text introduces each one from a historical perspective, and beautiful color photographs offer inviting views, while maps, sidebars, and featured quotes add variety to the pages. [This book] looks at mountain gorillas, the Nile, Victoria Falls, the Sahara Desert, Mount Kilimanjaro, the Seychelles Islands and the Serengeti Plain." Booklist

Includes bibliographical references

Seven natural wonders of Asia and the Middle East; by Michael Woods and Mary B. Woods. Twenty-First Century Books 2009 80p il (Seven natural wonders) lib bdg $33.26

Grades: 5 6 7 8 **508**

1. Curiosities and wonders 2. Asia 3. Middle East 4. Natural history -- Asia 5. Natural history -- Middle East

ISBN 978-0-8225-9073-6; 0-8225-9073-5

LC 2008027605

Chapters in this book describe Mount Everest, the Gobi Desert, Mount Fuji, Sumatra rain forests, the Dead Sea, Cappadocia, and the Chocolate Hills, including historical perspectives and color photographs.

Includes bibliographical references

Seven natural wonders of Australia and Oceania; by Michael Woods and Mary B. Woods. Twenty-First Century Books 2009 80p il (Seven natural wonders) lib bdg $33.26

Grades: 5 6 7 8 **508**

1. Curiosities and wonders 2. Australia 3. Natural history -- Australia

ISBN 978-0-8225-9074-3 lib bdg; 0-8225-9074-3 lib bdg

LC 2008014003

Chapters in this book describe the Australian outback, Aoraki/Mount Cook, Mount Kilauea, the Bungle Bungles, the Tasmanian wilderness, Bora Bora, and New Caledonia, including historical perspectives and color photographs.

Includes bibliographical references

Seven natural wonders of Europe; by Michael Woods and Mary B. Woods. Twenty-First Century Books 2009 80p il (Seven natural wonders) lib bdg $33.26

Grades: 5 6 7 8 **508**

1. Curiosities and wonders 2. Natural history -- Europe 3. Europe -- Description and travel

ISBN 978-0-8225-9072-9 lib bdg; 0-8225-9072-7 lib bdg

LC 2008027604

Chapters in this book describe Loch Ness, Westmann Islands, Lake Baikal, Black Forest, Mons Klint, Fjords of Norway, and The Alps, including historical perspectives and color photographs.

Includes bibliographical references

Seven natural wonders of North America; by Michael Woods and Mary B. Woods. Twenty-First Century Books 2009 80p il map (Seven natural wonders) lib bdg $33.26

Grades: 5 6 7 8 **508**

1. Curiosities and wonders 2. North America 3. Natural history -- North America

ISBN 978-0-8225-9069-9; 0-8225-9069-7

LC 2008021864

This book "takes seven noteworthy wonders in [North America] . . . and spotlights them in separate chapters. The text introduces each one from a historical perspective, and beautiful color photographs offer inviting views, while maps, sidebars, and featured quotes add variety to the pages. . . . [This book] takes readers to Dinosaur Provincial

Park, Pacific Rim National Park, the redwood forests, Niagara Falls, the Grand Canyon, Yellowstone National Park, and the Paricutin Volcano." Booklist

Includes glossary and bibliographical references

509 History, geographic treatment, biography

Blanchard, Anne

★ **Arab** science and invention in the golden age; [illustrated by Emmanuel Cerisier; translated by R.M. Brent] Enchanted Lion Books 2008 65p il map $19.95

Grades: 6 7 8 9 **509**

1. Arab civilization 2. Science -- History 3. Islamic countries -- History

ISBN 978-1-59270-080-6; 1-59270-080-2

LC 2008-26431

"The Muslim world led an amazing scientific revolution for hundreds of years with breakthroughs in math, geography, physics, astronomy, and medicine. This large-size, attractive volume packs in a wealth of information about the rise and fall of the immense empire. . . . The open format, with lots of boxed inserts and detailed illustrations on each double-page spread, is dense with information." Booklist

Includes glossary and bibliographical references

Currie, Stephen

African American inventors; Stephen Currie. Lucent Books 2010 104 p. ill. (some col.) (hardcover) $36.10

Grades: 6 7 8 9 10 **509**

1. Inventions 2. African American inventors 3. Inventions -- United States -- History 4. African American inventors -- Biography

ISBN 1420501216; 9781420501216

LC 2009038456

This book is part of the Lucent Library of Black History and focuses on African-American Inventors and Inventions. "Each volume in the Lucent Library of Black History examines an event or time period of particular significance in African American history. . . . Each chapter contains sidebars that highlight relevant personalities and events. Numerous photos and illustrations" are included. (Publisher's note)

"Particular attention is given to historical, social, and political contexts and challenges faced by the inventors (e.g., institutionalized racism; difficulties with the patent system). The text is dense but informative." Horn Book

Includes bibliographical references (p. 93-98) and index.

Eamer, Claire

Before the World Was Ready; Stories of Daring Genius in Science. by Claire Eamer. Firefly Books Ltd 2013 125 p. (paperback) $14.95; $24.95

Grades: 5 6 7 8 **509**

1. Inventions 2. Scientists

ISBN 1554515351; 9781554515356; 9781554515363

This book looks at eight scientists and inventors. "Alfred Wegener struggled to convince geologists that the ground beneath our feet is moving. . . . Nikola Tesla's futuristic ideas about electricity were dismissed. Charles Darwin delayed publishing his controversial theory of evolution for decades." Also included are Charles Babbage, Ada Lovelace, Rachel Carson, and George Cayley. (Publisher's note)

Hakim, Joy

★ The **story** of science: Aristotle leads the way. Smithsonian Books 2004 282p (Story of science) $24.95

Grades: 8 9 10 11 12 **509**

1. Ancient civilization 2. Science -- History

ISBN 1-58834-160-7

"Hakim has interwoven creation myths, history, physics, and mathematics to present a seamless, multifaceted view of the foundation of modern science. . . . The entire volume is beautifully organized." SLJ

Includes bibliographical references

★ The **story** of science: Einstein adds a new dimension. Smithsonian Books 2007 468p il (Story of science) $27.95

Grades: 8 9 10 11 12 **509**

1. Cosmology 2. Quantum theory 3. Science -- History

ISBN 978-1-58834-162-4; 1-58834-162-3

LC 2007-14096

Hakim delivers a "brisk, intellectually challenging account of the development of quantum theory and modern cosmology. . . . She introduces a teeming cast of deep thinkers who . . . delivered a series of brilliant experiments and insights. . . . Supplemented by a digestible resource list and a generous assortment of illustrations." Booklist

Includes bibliographical references

★ The **story** of science: Newton at the center. Smithsonian Books 2005 463p (Story of science) $24.95

Grades: 8 9 10 11 12 **509**

1. Physics 2. Astronomy 3. Science -- History

ISBN 1-58834-161-5

LC 2004-58465

This "is an account of the history of astronomy and physics from c.1500 to 1900."

"Teachers will find anecdotal information to enliven their lessons; browsers will be fascinated by the sidebars and captioned illustrations that enhance the text or show related information." SLJ

Includes bibliographical references

Jackson, Donna M.

★ **Extreme** scientists; exploring nature's mysteries from perilous places. Houghton Mifflin Harcourt 2009 63p il (Scientists in the field) $18

Grades: 5 6 7 8 **509**

1. Botanists 2. Explorers 3. Scientists 4. Spelunkers 5. Meteorologists 6. Microbiologists 7. College teachers

ISBN 978-0-618-77706-8; 0-618-77706-7

LC 2008-36796

This volume "profiles three scientists working far out in the field. Hurricane hunter Paul Flaherty, . . . Hazel Barton, a microbiologist specializing in single-cell organisms living in extreme conditions, . . . [and] ecologist and college professor Steve Sillett, who . . . climbs into the canopies to study redwoods. While the clearly written text includes vivid passages about the dangers these scientists face, it goes on to discuss what drives them to pursue their subjects and what they have discovered along the way. . . . The many excellent color photos portray these adventures as scientists intently focused on their work." Booklist

Includes glossary and bibliographical references

Nardo, Don

The **scientific** revolution; by Don Nardo. Lucent Books 2011 104 p. ill. (World history series) (library) $34.95

Grades: 6 7 8 9 **509**

1. Science -- History 2. Discoveries in science -- Europe

ISBN 1420506137; 9781420506136

LC 2011006556

This book by Don Nardo is part of the World History series and looks at the Scientific Revolution. The series entries offer an "overview of an important historical event or period. The series is designed both to acquaint readers with the basics of history and to make them aware that their lives and their own historical era are an intimate part of the ongoing human saga." (Publisher's note)

Includes bibliographical references (p. 96-98) and index.

Stefoff, Rebecca, 1951-

Flat Earth and Round Earth; Rebecca Stefoff. Cavendish Square 2014 48 p. color illustrations (It Is Science) $29.93

Grades: 6 7 8 **509**

1. Pseudoscience 2. Literature and science 3. Science -- Popular works

ISBN 1627125124; 9781627125123

This middle grade book by Rebecca Stefoff "explores the historical relationships between science and pseudoscience. Though she explains the scientific method in detail and injects healthy doses of skepticism . . . she shows how . . . alchemy split into . . . practical and spiritual approaches before the former evolved into modern chemistry. In contrast, . . . astrology and astronomy continue to coexist as active pursuits, and so do conventional and alternative medicine." (School Library Journal)

"What sets this series apart is its comparative approach to 'hard' and 'soft' science. Each title contains a chapter covering pseudoscience and how the scientific method works. Illustrations are practical, often images of scientists or scientific instruments. The writing is clear, concise, and matter-of-fact. Content is occasionally recycled throughout the series." Lib Med Con

509.2 Scientists

Allman, Toney

Women scientists and inventors; by Toney Allman. ReferencePoint Press, Inc. 2017 80 p. (hardback) $29.95

Grades: 6 7 8 9 **509.2**

1. Women scientists -- Biography

ISBN 9781682820322

LC 2015050839

In this book, by Toney Allman, "women have made more significant and important contributions to science than most people realize. Profiled in this book are six admirable women scientists and inventors: Lise Meitner, Pearl Kendrick, Virginia Apgar, Jane Goodall, Shirley Ann Jackson, and Rosalind W. Picard." (Publisher's note)

"Clearly written and well-documented short narratives suitable for formal research." SLJ

Includes bibliographical references and index

Davidson, Tish

African American scientists and inventors; by Tish Davidson. Mason Crest Publishers 2013 64 p. ill. (some col.) (Major Black contributions from Emancipation to civil rights) (library) $22.95

Grades: 4 5 6 **509.2**

1. African American inventors 2. African American scientists 3. African American inventors -- Biography 4. African American scientists -- Biography

ISBN 1422223752; 9781422223758

LC 2011051942

This book by Tish Davidson profiles African American scientists and inventors. "Some of them were elementary school dropouts. Others became medical doctors or college professors. Some were famous, while some toiled in obscurity. . . . Lewis Latimer devised a manufacturing process that made electric lights affordable for ordinary people. Charles Drew did pioneering work in blood storage, helping save countless lives. Garrett Woods figured out how to send messages from moving trains." (Publisher's note)

Includes bibliographical references (pages 60-61) and index.

Di Domenico, Kelly

Women scientists who changed the world; by Kelly Di Domenico. Rosen Pub. 2012 106 p. col. ill. (library) $34.60

Grades: 5 6 7 8 **509.2**

1. Women scientists -- Biography 2. Women in science -- Biography

ISBN 1448859999; 9781448859993

LC 2011032120

In this collective biography by Kelly Di Domenico, "readers meet eleven women scientists, whose research and discoveries are outstanding in their fields. . . . Readers are introduced to each scientist's life and work, including the obstacles each woman had to overcome to achieve success. Profiles include biologist Rachel Carson, orangutan researcher Birute Galdikas, and Nobel Prize-winning biochemist Ada Yonath." (Publisher's note)

Includes bibliographical references (p. 101) and index.

Grant, John

Eureka! 50 scientists who shaped human history. by John Grant. Houghton Mifflin Harcourt 2016 221 p. illustrations (paperback) $14.99

Grades: 7 8 9 10 **509.2**

1. Scientists -- Biography

ISBN 1942186177; 9781942186175

This juvenile book, by John Grant, "offers fifty vivid portraits of groundbreaking scientists. From lutes and owls to astronomy and evolution, [it] explains how these scientific geniuses have shaped our understanding – and how they spent their free time as well." (Publisher's note)

"More for pleasure reading than reports. Put this in the hands of students with an interest in STEM and history." SLJ

Includes bibliographical references and index.

Krull, Kathleen

Lives of the scientists; experiments, explosions (and what the neighbors thought) Kathleen Krull, Illustrated by Kathryn Hewitt. Houghton Mifflin Harcourt 2013 96 p. $20.99

Grades: 4 5 6 7 **509.2**

1. Science -- History 2. Scientists -- Biography

ISBN 0152059091; 9780152059095

LC 2012953333

The author Kathleen Krull's book focuses on the history of science. "This latest in the Lives of . . . series is summed up by the subtitle's 'What the Neighbors Thought.' The authors delve into intriguing, obscure, and peculiar facts about 20 famous scientists from all fields of study, regions of the globe, and eras of history." Topics include James D. Watson, Francis Crick, Marie Curie, Edwin Hubble, Barbara McClintock, and Grace Murray Hopper." (Booklist)

Miles, Liz

Louis Pasteur; by Liz Miles. Raintree 2009 48 p. ill. (chiefly col.) (Great scientists) (library) $32.00

Grades: 4 5 6 **509.2**

1. Science -- History -- 19th century 2. Scientists -- France --

Biography 3. Microbiologists -- France -- Biography
ISBN 141093229X; 9781410932297
LC 2007050125

This book by Liz Miles is part of the Leveled Biographies series and looks at Louis Pasteur. "What is Pasteurization? How has Pasteur's work helped treat many diseases? The 'Leveled Biographies' series offers leveled, high-interest nonfiction in a range of text genres. Each title tells the story of one memorable life, using pictures, maps, sidebars, and engaging text to make each person's story come alive." (Publisher's note)

Includes bibliographical references (p. 46) and index.

Swaby, Rachel

Trailblazers; 33 Women in Science Who Changed the World. Rachel Swaby. Delacorte Press 2016 208 p. (hardcover) $15.99; (ebook) $47.97

Grades: 5 6 7 8 **509.2**

1. Women scientists 2. Women inventors -- Biography 3. Women scientists -- Biography
ISBN 9780399553967; 9780399554162; 9780399554179
LC 2016003806

This book, by Rachel Swaby, is a "collection of profiles of some of the world's most influential women in science. . . . These women have made strides in fields including biology, medicine, astronomy, and technology. In addition, Swaby emphasizes the fact that people aren't born brilliant scientists. They observe and experiment as kids and as adults, testing ideas again and again, each time learning something new." (Publisher's note)

"Readers with scientific ambitions of their own will find much to admire in these accomplished and unconventional women." Pub Wkly

Includes bibliographical references (pages [171]-189) and index.

509.56 History of science – Middle East

Romanek, Trudee

Science, medicine, and math in the early Islamic world; Trudee Romanek. Crabtree Pub. Company 2012 48 p. (reinforced library binding : alk. paper) $30.60

Grades: 4 5 6 7 **509.56**

1. Science -- History 2. Medicine -- History 3. Mathematics -- History 4. Islamic civilization 5. Science -- Islamic Empire -- History
ISBN 0778721701; 9780778721703; 9780778721772; 9781427195630; 9781427198402
LC 2012000077

This children's educational book, by Trudee Romanek, describes "the scientific contributions of the early Islamic empires to science, medicine, and mathematics. . . . This . . . book explores their public hospitals, libraries, and universities; their achievements in mathematics and astronomy, and the pursuit of alchemy; Arabic numbers; optics; music and musical instruments; poetry; and education." (Publisher's note)

510 Mathematics

Ball, Johnny

Go figure! Johnny Ball. Revised edition DK Publishing 2016 96p color illustrations $9.99

Grades: 3 4 5 6 7 **510**

1. Numbers 2. Mathematics
ISBN 9781465443854; 1465443851

"Discover why there are 60 minutes in an hour, why daisies have to have 34, 55, or 89 petals, and why finding a prime number could make you a millionaire." (Publisher's note)

McKellar, Danica, 1975-

★ **Math** doesn't suck; how to survive middle school math without losing your mind or breaking a nail. [by] Danica McKellar. Hudson Street Press 2007 297p il $23.95

Grades: 5 6 7 8 **510**

1. Mathematics
ISBN 1-59463-039-9; 978-1-59463-039-2
LC 2007017091

This "covers some of the most basic ideas of middle-grade math, including concepts relating to fractions, decimals, and ratios, making each comprehensible, interesting, and fun. Using real-world constructions, such as tangled necklaces, boyfriends, and pizza, concepts are thoroughly explained." Voice Youth Advocates

O'Reilly, Gillian

The **Great** Number Rumble; a story of math in surprising places. Cora Lee & Gillian O'Reilly ; illustrations by Lil Crump. 2nd edition Annick Press 2016 104 p. chiefly color illustrations pbk $12.95; hbk $19.95

Grades: 3 4 5 6 **510**

1. Mathematics
ISBN 9781554518494; 9781554518500; 1554518504

"Math can show up in the most unlikely places! When the schools in Jeremy's town ban math, all the kids cheer, all except his friend Sam, a self-proclaimed mathnik, who sets out to prove that math is not only important, but fun. Running parallel to the fictional narrative are informative sidebars that discuss the weird, puzzling, and amusing aspects of mathematics. Some topics covered are math in nature, art, music, magic and tricks, crime solving, and sports." (Publisher's note)

"This is a fun romp with lots of unexpected bits about geometry, consonance in music, geographic profiling, virtual reality, and a whole lot of other neat stuff, carefully packaged to entice readers." SLJ

Includes bibliographical references (pages 92-94) and index

Salvadori, Mario George

★ **Math** games for middle school; challenges and skill-builders for students at every level. [by] Mario Salvadori and Joseph P. Wright. Chicago Review Press 1998 168p il pa $16.95

Grades: 6 7 8 9 **510**

1. Mathematics -- Study and teaching
ISBN 1-55652-288-6
LC 97-51422

Uses explanations, word problems, and games to cover some mathematical topics that middle school students need to know, including the invention of numerical notations, basic arithmatical operations, measurements, geometry, graphs, and probability

510.23 Math -- Careers

Hynson, Colin

Dream jobs in math; Colin Hynson. Crabtree Publishing Co. 2017 32 p. color illustrations (Cutting-Edge Careers in STEM) (hardcover : alk. paper) $27.60

Grades: 5 6 7 8 **510.23**

1. Mathematics 2. Vocational guidance 3. Mathematics --

Vocational guidance
ISBN 9780778729631; 9780778729716

LC 2016045933

This book, by Colin Hynson, "explores some of the amazing careers available in the field of mathematics and they're not just limited to the classroom! From helping athletes gain a competitive edge to helping eradicate hunger around the world, readers may be surprised to learn what exciting careers math can lead to." (Publisher's note)

"The book's information is light but grounded, making it a useful preliminary resource to get mathematically inclined readers thinking about their futures." Booklist

510.92 Mathematicians

McCully, Emily Arnold, 1939-

★ **Dreaming** in code; Ada Byron Lovelace, computer pioneer. Emily Arnold McCully. Candlewick Press 2019 176 p. $19.99

Grades: 5 6 7 8 9 10 **510.92**

1. Computers -- History 2. Women mathematicians -- Biography
ISBN 9780763693565

LC 2018961266

"This illuminating biography [by Emily Arnold McCully] reveals how [Ada Byron Lovelace], the daughter of Lord Byron, Britain's most infamous Romantic poet, became the world's first computer programmer. . . . At seventeen, Ada met eccentric inventor Charles Babbage. . . . Their ensuing collaborations resulted in ideas and concepts that presaged computer programming by almost two hundred years, and Ada Lovelace is now recognized as a pioneer and prophet of the information age." (Publisher's note)

"Interest in Ada Byron Lovelace and other female pioneers of science has soared of late. This young adult biography is a particularly exemplary example of the burgeoning genre and should find a home in all libraries." (Booklist)

512 Algebra

Gonick, Larry

The **cartoon** guide to algebra; by Larry Gonick. HarperCollins 2015 233 p. illustrations $18.99

Grades: 6 7 8 9 10 **512**

1. Algebra
ISBN 0062202693; 9780062202697

LC 2015458390

This book, by Larry Gonick, "offers a complete and up-to-date illustrated course to help students understand [algebra]. Using engaging graphics and lively humor, Gonick covers all of the algebra essentials, including linear equations, polynomials, quadratic equations, and graphing techniques. He also offers a concise overview of algebra's history and its many practical applications in modern life." (Publisher's note)

"A valuable choice for visual learners or students in need of additional instruction." SLJ

Schwartz, Richard Evan

You can count on monsters; the first 100 numbers and their characters. A.K. Peters 2010 un il pa $24.95

Grades: 5 6 7 8 **512**

1. Counting 2. Prime numbers 3. Factoring (Mathematics)
ISBN 978-1-56881-578-7 pa; 1-56881-578-6 pa

LC 2009-38661

"This hybrid math/art book is both ambitious and imaginative. An introductory section explains the colored-dot configurations and factor trees for numbers 1 to 100, which appear on the verso of each spread. These factor trees are 'all the way grown out' to the lowest common factors, or prime numbers. On the opposite page is a monster scene that represents the number. Schwartz has created a creature for each prime number. . . . Thus, the monster for 5 is a five-featured, five-pointed star, and the 13 monster sports a pink-and-white eye-patch with 13 segments. . . . Readers will need patience and an open, undaunted mind to deconstruct the monster scenes. This is a book for math lovers who want to have some fun. Challenge these students to create their own prime monsters and combinations." SLJ

513 Arithmetic

Caron, Lucille

Fraction and decimal smarts! [by] Lucille Caron, Philip M. St. Jacques. Enslow Publishers 2011 64p il (Math smarts!) lib bdg $27.93

Grades: 5 6 7 8 **513**

1. Fractions 2. Decimal fractions
ISBN 978-0-7660-3936-0

LC 2011008382

"This clearly written series provides definitions and examples of many concepts... examples are realistic and appropriate for the target age group." SLJ

Includes bibliographical references

Percent and ratio smarts! [by] Lucille Caron, Philip M. St. Jacques. Enslow Publishers 2011 64p il (Math smarts!) lib bdg $27.93

Grades: 5 6 7 8 **513**

1. Fractions 2. Ratios (Statistics)
ISBN 978-0-7660-3940-7

LC 2011008164

This helps re-inforce classroom learning of important percent and ratio skills including reducing ratios, the golden rectangle, and the meaning of percents

Includes bibliographical references

Julius, Edward H.

Arithmetricks; 50 easy ways to add, subtract, multiply, and divide without a calculator. illustrations by Dale M. Gladstone. Wiley 1995 142p il pa $12.95

Grades: 7 8 9 10 **513**

1. Arithmetic
ISBN 0-471-10639-9

LC 94-41836

This book "offers fifty ways to do simple arithmetic calculations in one's head. . . . Each trick is covered on two facing pages. The first page presents the problem and gives two examples of how to use the trick. The facing page has a black and white cartoon and extra exercises to practice. The correct answers are given at the end of the book. This would be a fun book for mathematically inclined Middle-Schoolers and up. Math teachers will enjoy using this book for extra-curricular activities." Appraisal

516 Geometry

Caron, Lucille

Geometry smarts! [by] Lucille Caron, Philip M. St. Jacques. Enslow Publishers 2011 64p il (Math smarts!) lib bdg $27.93

Grades: 5 6 7 8 **516**

1. Geometry

ISBN 978-0-7660-3935-3

LC 2011008384

This helps re-inforce classroom learning of geometry skills such as points, lines, planes, triangles, circles, quadrilaterals, perimeter, area, and circumference

Includes bibliographical references

Other titles in this series are:

Fraction and decimal smarts

Percent and ratio smarts

516.2 Euclidean geometry

Blatner, David

Joy of [pi] Walker and Co. 1997 129p il hardcover o.p. pa $12

Grades: 8 9 10 11 12 **516.2**

1. Numbers 2. Geometry

ISBN 0-8027-1332-7; 0-8027-7562-4 pa

"Why does an irrational number impel rational people to do irrational things—like calculating pi to several billion digits? That's what's happening with a pair of characters in Blatner's delightful excursion through the history of pi. . . . Even numerically challenged readers will find Blatner's tale immensely appealing, both for the graphic layout, in day-glo colors, no less, and for the amusing and informative anecdotes Blatner relates." Booklist

Green, Dan

Algebra & geometry; anything but square. illustrated by Simon Basher. Kingfisher 2011 il (Basher science) $14.99; pa $8.99

Grades: 4 5 6 **516.2**

1. Algebra 2. Geometry

ISBN 978-0-7534-6627-8; 978-0-7534-6597-4 pa

"This creative team introduces the components of algebra and geometry as cartoon-style characters. The book begins with a brief introduction to the subject of mathematics and Pythagoras. . . . Each chapter begins with an introduction and then the concepts are presented on a spread. One page features a drawing of the concept's character, while the opposing page provides a brief introduction to its characteristics and personality." (School Library Journal)

Wingard-Nelson, Rebecca

Trigonometry smarts! Enslow Publishers 2012 64p il (Math smarts!) lib bdg $27.93

Grades: 5 6 7 8 **516.2**

1. Trigonometry

ISBN 978-0-7660-3944-5

LC 2011006492

This helps re-inforce classroom learning of important trigonometry topics such as square roots, the Pythagorean Theorem, tangents, radians, and degrees.

Includes bibliographical references

519.2 Probabilities

Wingard-Nelson, Rebecca

Graphing and probability word problems; no problem! Enslow Publishers 2010 64p il (Math busters word problems) lib bdg $27.93

Grades: 6 7 8 9 **519.2**

1. Mathematics 2. Problem solving

ISBN 978-0-7660-3372-6; 0-7660-3372-4

LC 2010003281

This offers ways to tackle word math problems with graphing and probability using real world examples.

520 Astronomy and allied sciences

Aguilar, David A.

Cosmic catastrophes; Seven Ways to Destroy a Planet Like Earth. David A. Aguilar. Viking 2016 79 p. color illustrations (hardcover) $18.99

Grades: 5 6 7 8 **520**

1. Planets 2. Earth (Planet) 3. Natural disasters 4. Catastrophes (Geology) 5. Astronomy

ISBN 9780425288047; 9780451476845

LC 2015044536

This book, in the Smithsonian series by David Aguilar, speculates on seven scientific "extreme events that could impact Earth. . . . [Aguilar] tells an exciting nonfiction story about how and why these space catastrophes could happen and then creates beautiful, original art to show just how devastatingly spectacular it will be when any one of these seven 'big ones' hit!" (Publisher's note)

"A wild and thought-provoking look at what potential calamities await our planet. A good addition for collections in need of browsables titles on space." SLJ

Includes bibliographical references and index.

Carson, Mary Kay

★ **Beyond** the solar system; exploring galaxies, black holes, alien planets, and more : a history with 21 activities. by Mary Kay Carson. Chicago Review Press 2013 vii, 127 p.p col. ill. (paperback) $18.95

Grades: 5 6 7 8 **520**

1. Creative activities 2. Astronomy -- History

ISBN 1613745443; 9781613745441

LC 2012046330

In this book, "Mary Kay Carson traces the evolution of humankind's astronomical knowledge, from the realization that we are not at the center of the universe to recent telescopic proof of planets orbiting stars outside our solar system. . . . This book contains 21 hands-on projects to further explore the subjects discussed" as well as "minibiographies of famous astronomers, a time line of major scientific discoveries . . .[and] a glossary of technical terms." (Publisher's note)

Includes bibliographical references (p. 121) and index.

Dickinson, Terence

★ **NightWatch** : a practical guide to viewing the universe; foreword by Timothy Ferris; illustrations by Adolf Schaller, Victor Costanzo, Roberta Cooke, Glenn LeDrew; principal photography by Terence Dickinson. 4th ed.; Firefly Books 2006 192p il $35

Grades: 8 9 10 11 12 Adult **520**

1. Astronomy

ISBN 978-1-55407-147-0; 1-55407-147-X

LC 2006-491527

First published 1983

This "handbook for amateur astronomers combines a text both meaty and hard to put down with a great array of charts, boxes, tables, and dazzling full-color photos of the sky." SLJ [review of 1998 edition]

Includes bibliographical references

The **Facts** on File dictionary of astronomy; edited by John Daintith, William Gould. 5th ed.; Facts on File 2006 550p il (Facts on File science library) $59.50

Grades: 7 8 9 10 11 12 **520**

1. Reference books 2. Astronomy -- Dictionaries

ISBN 0-8160-5998-5; 978-0-8160-5998-0

LC 2006-40860

First published 1979 under the editorship of Valerie Illingworth

This dictionary includes "more than 3,700 entries . . . that reflect all aspects of astronomy, together with associated terms in spectroscopy, photometry, and particle physics." Publisher's note

Includes bibliographical references

Garlick, Mark A.

Atlas of the universe. Simon & Schuster Books for Young Readers 2008 128p il map (Insiders) $19.99

Grades: 5 6 7 8 **520**

1. Astronomy 2. Cosmology

ISBN 978-1-4169-5558-0; 1-4169-5558-5

"Seamlessly commingling luscious, color space photographs and dramatic, sharply detailed digital imagery, this tour of the universe earns high marks for visual impact. It's not too shabby in breadth of coverage either." SLJ

Gilliland, Ben

Rocket science for the rest of us; cutting-edge concepts made simple. written by Ben Gilliand ; consultant, Jack Challoner. Dk Pub 2015 192 p. color illustrations (paperback) $15.99

Grades: 7 8 9 10 **520**

1. Science -- Popular works 2. Astrophysics

ISBN 9781465433657; 1465433651

LC 2015297118

In this book, by Ben Gilliand, readers will "get a grip on even the most mysterious and complex sciences with . . . [this] guide to dark matter, exo-planets, Planck time, earth sciences, and more. . . . [The author] breaks it all down so science and physics are easy to understand." (Publisher's note)

Green, Dan

Astronomy; out of this world! illustrated by Simon Basher. Kingfisher 2009 128p il pa $8.95

Grades: 5 6 7 8 **520**

1. Astronomy

ISBN 978-0-7534-6290-4 pa; 0-7534-6290-7 pa

"Basher has created a portrait gallery of personified planets, comets, space probes, galaxies, several kinds of stars, and an array of other celestial bodies in a hyper-cute, pastel cartoon style. . . . Along with short bulleted lists of additional information, each figure offers a fact-based self-description. . . . Green's astro-narrative is both accurate and spiced with seldom-mentioned details." SLJ

Includes glossary

Jenkins, Martin

Exploring Space; From Galileo to the Mars Rover and Beyond. by Martin Jenkins, illustrated by Stephen Biesty. Candlewick Press 2017 64 p. color illustrations $17.99

Grades: 5 6 7 8 **520**

1. Outer space -- Exploration 2. Outer space

ISBN 0763689319; 9780763689315

LC 2017942646

This book, by Martin Jenkins, illustrated by Stephen Biesty, is an "examination of the past, present, and future of humans in space. . . . Find out what life is like on the International Space Station, what the chances are that we will ever settle on Mars, where in the solar system we might find alien life, and why visiting other stars will almost certainly remain a dream." (Publisher's note)

"In exceptionally clear prose, Jenkins surveys the history and possible future of SPACE EXPLORATION ... The subject matter is thrilling on its own, but this expert portrayal of the facts makes it all the more captivating." Booklist.

Includes bibliographical references and index

Mitchell, Chris

How Do Astronauts Wee in Space? Chris Mitchell. Trafalgar Square Books 2016 192 p. illustrations (Dr Dino's Learnatorium) $8.99

Grades: 4 5 6 7 8 **520**

1. Outer space 2. Space sciences

ISBN 1784186538; 9781784186531

LC 2016023616

In this book in Dr Dino's Learnatorium series, by Chris Mitchell, "amaze your friends with facts about planets made from diamonds, stars that could destroy our solar system, and how long humans could survive in space! This book is packed with the wildest, weirdest, funniest, filthiest, foulest, wisest, grossest, brainiest, biggest, and best facts about space and the universe." (Publisher's note)

"Frequent comic spot art keeps things light, and as for that title question? The answer is more involved than you might think." Booklist

Saucier, C. A. P.

Explore the cosmos like Neil DeGrasse Tyson; a space science journey. by C.A.P. Saucier. Prometheus Books 2015 177 p. color illustrations (pbk.) $14.99

Grades: 4 5 6 **520**

1. Astronomy 2. Cosmology 3. Astronomy -- Popular works 4. Astronomers -- United States -- Biography 5. Astrophysicists -- United States -- Biography

ISBN 1633880141; 9781633880146

LC 2014039219

In this book author "CAP Saucier interweaves up-to-date information about the universe and the science of astrophysics with a biographical portrait of the famous astrophysicist. Quotes from [Neil deGrasse] Tyson appear throughout each chapter, personalizing the science." (Publisher's note)

"Perhaps a bit overly ambitious, this guide is nonetheless an excellent jumping-off point for those pursuing a deeper interest in space, while its level of detail may deter others. Its focus is brought back to Earth in Tyson's belief that knowledge and curiosity are of the utmost importance, challenging readers to grab some binoculars, go outside, and start asking questions." Booklist

Includes bibliographical references and index

Space: a visual encyclopedia. DK Pub. 2010 254p il $24.99

Grades: 5 6 7 8 **520**

1. Astronomy 2. Astronautics 3. Space sciences

ISBN 978-0-7566-6277-6; 0-7566-6277-X; 9781465454720

"Any reader wishing to gain a fair introductory understanding of astronomy in one concise book will find much satisfaction in this work. An abundance of fascinating information is contained within these pages, and the format is such that excellent and attractive related photographs and diagrams directly accompany the text. . . . The book is very well organized and very well written." Sci Books & Films

Stefoff, Rebecca, 1951-

Astrology and Astronomy; Rebecca Stefoff. Cavendish Square 2014 48 p. color illustrations (Is it Science?) $29.93

Grades: 6 7 8 **520**

1. Astrology 2. Astronomy 3. Science -- Popular works

ISBN 162712506X; 9781627125062

LC 2015015837

This middle grades book by Rebecca Stefoff, part of the Is It Science? series, "explores the historical relationships between science and pseudoscience." It discusses how, "along with similarly shared ancient origins, astrology and astronomy continue to coexist as active pursuits. . . . There are even still a few geocentrists around, Stefoff notes." (Publisher's note)

"Each volume is heavily illustrated with period images and modern photographs, and each closes with particularly generous lists of further resources."

Trefil, James

Space atlas; mapping the universe and beyond. James Trefil ; includes "The moon fifty years later" by Buzz Aldrin. 2nd edition National Geographic 2018 352 p. illustrations hardcover $50

Grades: 7 8 9 10 11 12 Adult **520**

1. Stars -- Atlases 2. Galaxies -- Atlases 3. Solar system -- Atlases 4. Astronomy -- Charts, diagrams, etc

ISBN 9781426219696

"In this guided tour of our planetary neighborhood, the Milky Way and other galaxies, and beyond, detailed maps and fascinating imagery from recent space missions partner with clear, authoritative scientific information. Starting with the sun and moving outward into space, acclaimed science writer and physicist James Trefil illuminates each planet, the most important moons, significant asteroids, and other objects in our solar system. Looking beyond, he explains what we know about the Milky Way and other galaxies--and how we know it, with clear explanations of the basics of astrophysics, including dark matter and gravitational waves. For this new edition, and to celebrate the 50th anniversary of his moonwalk, astronaut and American hero Buzz Aldrin offers a new special section on Earth's moon and its essential role in space exploration past and future." (Publisher's note)

Vamplew, Anton

The **practical** astronomer; [by] Will Gater and Anton Vamplew; consultant Jacqueline Mitton. 2nd edition, revised & updated Dk Pub 2017 264 p illustrations $19.95

Grades: 7 8 9 10 11 12 **520**

1. Astronomy 2. Astronomy -- Observers' manuals

ISBN 9781465445131

"Informative and easy-to-use with illustrated, step-by-step instructions and star charts with constellations visible all over the globe, the book offers practical advice with naked-eye observation, while illustrated instructions show readers how to setup and use binoculars and telescopes, and take pictures. A solar system chapter contains advice on finding and observing planets and objects such as moons, comets, and asteroids. This updated edition also includes an almanac section to identify significant events such as eclipses, plus the newest equipment and latest images of the universe to guide readers from beginner level to accomplished amateur astronomer." (Publisher's note)

VanCleave, Janice Pratt, 1942-

Step -by-step science experiments in astronomy; by Janice VanCleave. Rosen Pub. 2013 80 p. col. ill. (Janice Vancleave's first-place science fair projects) (library) $33.25; (paperback) $14.15

Grades: 5 6 7 8 **520**

1. Astronomy 2. Science -- Experiments 3. Science projects 4. Astronomy -- Experiments

ISBN 1448869781; 9781448869787; 9781448884612

LC 2012000715

This book by Janice VanCleave presents 22 science experiments in astronomy for children. "Van Cleave states the basic goal of the experiments, followed by a list of necessary materials. . . . Step-by-step instructions are . . . accompanied by diagrams where needed. The results section states exactly what is expected to happen and the 'Why?' section explains in accessible terms why those specific results were achieved." (School Library Journal)

Includes bibliographical references (p. 77-78) and index

Walker, Pamela

★ **Space** and astronomy experiments; [by] Pamela Walker, Elaine Wood. Facts on File 2010 xx, 152p il (Facts on File science experiments) $35

Grades: 7 8 9 10 11 12 **520**

1. Astronomy 2. Space sciences 3. Science -- Experiments

ISBN 978-0-8160-7809-7; 0-8160-7809-2

LC 2009-32825

This book "presents experiments designed to foster understanding of space science and astronomy. Geared to middle and high-school students and their teachers, the 20 experiments convey basic astronomy principles, draw from historic experiments, or explore new technologies. . . . Schools and libraries where students and teachers are looking for science experiments on space and astronomy will find this volume a useful addition to the collection." Booklist

Includes glossary and bibliographical references

Ward, D. J.

Seven wonders of space phenomena; by D.J. Ward. Twenty-First Century Books 2011 80 p. ill. (chiefly col.) (library) $33.26

Grades: 5 6 7 8 **520**

1. Universe 2. Astronomy 3. Astronomy -- Miscellanea

ISBN 0761354522; 9780761354529

LC 2010028447

This book by D.J. Ward looks at "space phenomena, such as dark matter, dark energy, and the beginning of the universe. Read what astronomers and space scientists have discovered about these amazing wonders—and what they have yet to learn." (Publisher's note)

Includes bibliographical references (p. 76-78) and index.

Yount, Lisa

Edward Pickering and his women "computers" analyzing the stars. Lisa Yount. Chelsea House 2011 130 p. (Trailblazers in science and technology) (library) $35

Grades: 7 8 9 10 11 12 **520**

1. Women astronomers 2. Pickering, Edward C. (Edward Charles), 1846-1919 3. Physicists -- United States -- Biography 4. Astronomers -- United States -- Biography

ISBN 1604136642; 9781604136647

LC 2011002792

This book, by Lisa Yount, is part of the "Trailblazers in Science and Technology" series. "In the 42 years that Edward Pickering directed the Harvard College Observatory, he and his team of women 'computers' made strides in promoting the new field of astrophotography. . . . The advances these women made under Pickering's direction broadened the window of professional opportunity for women as well as our greater understanding of the universe." (Publisher's note)

Includes bibliographical references and index

522 Techniques, procedures, apparatus, equipment, materials

Cole, Michael D.

Eye on the universe; the incredible hubble space telescope. Michael D. Cole. Enslow Publishers 2013 48 p. $23.93

Grades: 4 5 6 7 8 **522**

1. Hubble Space Telescope 2. Outer space -- Exploration 3. Picture books for children 4. Astronomy -- Research 5. Astronautics in astronomy

ISBN 0766040771; 9780766040779

LC 2011047074

This book looks at the Hubble Space Telescope. "Orbiting high above Earth, the Hubble Telescope captures . . . wonders of space. . . . Photographs are relayed back to Earth, allowing scientists and astronomers to study parts of space that were once completely unknown. Michael D. Cole explores the . . . journey of launching this telescope into space and how it has unlocked many of the . . . mysteries in the universe." (Publisher's note)

Includes bibliographical references and index

Galat, Joan Marie

Dark matters; nature's reaction to light pollution. Joan Marie Galat. Red Deer Press 2017 70 p. color illustrations (hardcover) $19.95

Grades: 3 4 5 6 7 8 **522**

1. Light 2. Ecology 3. Light pollution

ISBN 9780889955158; 0889955158

This book, by Joan Marie Galat, "introduces young readers to the fragile wonders that thrive below our increasingly threatened night-time skies. This book is packed with fascinating and unexpected facts and illustrations about how plants and animals react to light pollution, and comes up with tips and suggestions on how young people can help protect our important night-time environments. Because - dark really matters." (Publisher's note)

"Combining science with storytelling, the author presents the case for less light and more darkness." SLJ

Mooney, Carla

Telescopes; Carla Mooney. Rourke Pub Group 2017 48 p. $10.95

Grades: 4 5 6 7 **522**

1. Telescopes 2. Astronomical instruments 3. Scientific apparatus and instruments

ISBN 1683424603; 9781683424604

This children's book in the Engineering Wonders series, by Carla Mooney, presents "an in-depth look at the design and engineering of massive scientific telescopes. Addresses the obstacles of construction, the impact on society, and the science of engineering such superstructures." (Publisher's note)

Scott, Elaine

★ **Space,** stars, and the beginning of time; what the Hubble telescope saw. Clarion Books 2011 66p il $17.99

Grades: 5 6 7 8 **522**

1. Astronomy 2. Hubble Space Telescope 3. Outer space -- Exploration

ISBN 0-547-24189-5; 978-0-547-24189-0

LC 2010-08040

This book examines data collected from the Hubble Space Telescope. Index. "Grades four to eight." (Bull Cent Child Books)

This examines "some of the data that has been collected over the two decades of the Hubble Telescope's operation. Opening chapters discuss the satellite's instrumentation and its 2009 repairs, and then the real fun begins with sections on calculating the age of the universe and its speed of expansion; the nature of dark matter, dark energy, and black holes; star formation; and planet formation, particularly outside our solar system. . . . Gasp-worthy photographs should fire up the most sluggish imaginations." Bull Cent Child Books

523 Specific celestial bodies and phenomena

Pasachoff, Jay M.

A **field** guide to the stars and planets; 4th ed; Houghton Mifflin 2000 578p il map (Peterson field guide series) $30; pa $19

Grades: 8 9 10 11 12 Adult **523**

1. Stars 2. Astronomy

ISBN 0-395-93432-X; 0-395-93431-1 pa

LC 99-27354

First published 1964 under the authorship of Donald H. Menzel and Jay M. Pasachoff

This guide contains 24 monthly sky maps, 54 atlas charts, information and numerous color photographs from NASA and other sources, and time-sensitive material through 2010

Includes bibliographical references

523.1 The universe, galaxies, quasars

Aguilar, David A.

Space encyclopedia; a tour of our solar system and beyond. written & illustrated by David A. Aguilar ; contributing writers Christine Pulliam & Patricia Daniels. National Geographic 2013 191 p. color illustrations (National Geographic kids) (reinforced library binding) $24.95

Grades: 7 8 9 10 11 12 **523.1**

1. Planets 2. Astronomy 3. Cosmology 4. Outer space 5. Solar system

ISBN 1426309481; 1426315600; 1426316291; 9781426309489; 9781426315602; 9781426316296

LC 2013444119

This book on outer space by David A. Aguilar is "broken up into five sections. . . . Aguilar moves from the origins of the universe, to the planets and bodies of our Solar System, and then to the impressive phenomena from all corners of the universe. Everything from black holes to dark matter and theories about multiple universes is touched upon." (Children's Literature)

"This attractive compendium of information about space is encyclopedic in the sense that its scope is broad. The facts are presented in two- to eight-page highly illustrated articles within five thematic sections. . . . The articles are clearly written and informative, but the visuals steal the show." Booklist

Includes bibliographical references (page 191) and index

Dunbar, James Lu

The **Universe** Verse; James Lu Dunbar. James & Kenneth Pub 2014 112 p. color illustrations $24.95

Grades: 5 6 7 8 9 10 **523.1**

1. Science -- Popular works 2. Universe -- Comic books strips, etc. 3. Science 4. Cosmology 5. Human beings 6. Life -- Origin 7. Comic books, strips, etc.

ISBN 1888047259; 9781888047257

This comic book, by James Lu Dunbar, "is a scientifically-accurate rhyming comic book about the origins of the universe, life on Earth and the human race. It introduces and illuminates the most fundamental features of our existence in a way that is engaging and accessible to a wide audience. . . . This book contains most major scientific milestones known to humanity." (Publisher's note)

"The images slowly transition from black and white in the first section to unobtrusive color in last section....Young students will revel in the artwork, while older kids could use the text as an introduction to advanced high school science." SLJ

Goldsmith, Mike

Universe; journey into deep space. Mike Goldsmith ; illustrated by Mark A. Garlick. Kingfisher 2012 48 p. (hardcover) $17.99

Grades: 4 5 6 7 **523.1**

1. Universe 2. Astronomy 3. Outer space

ISBN 075346876X; 9780753468760

This book, by Mike Goldsmith, illustrated by Mark A. Garlick, profiles "some of the Universe's most intriguing places, and along the way . . . [describes] the amazing history of the Cosmos. A series of . . . spreads give . . . snapshots of distant galactic locations as the reader journeys . . . from red cold Mars (3 light minutes away) to a massive Supernova (10,000 light years away) and beyond." (Publisher's note)

523.2 Planetary systems

Benson, Michael

★ **Beyond**; a solar system voyage. Abrams Books for Young Readers 2009 121p il $19.95

Grades: 5 6 7 8 9 10 **523.2**

1. Astronomy 2. Solar system

ISBN 0-8109-8322-2; 978-0-8109-8322-9

LC 2008-22297

This book presents the solar system from the perspective of the space probes sent there. Glossary. Index. "Ages nine to twelve." (Sci Books Films)

"The book's focus is the exploration of the solar system by space probes, with many full-page photos. . . . The author skillfully blends lively narrative with the photos to contribute to the excitement of the explorations. . . . It is an inexpensive but valuable addition for any library." Voice Youth Advocates

Includes glossary and bibliographical references

Carson, Mary Kay

Exploring the solar system; a history with 22 activities. by Mary Kay Carson. Chicago Review Press 2008 vii, 168 p.p ill. (paperback) $17.95

Grades: 4 5 6 7 **523.2**

1. Astronomy 2. Solar system

ISBN 1556527152; 9781556527159

This book by Mary Kay Carson is a "mix of facts, history, and hands-on activities [about the solar system]. Beginning with a two-page table of contents with chapters arranged as planets in our solar system and an introductory time line, the author takes readers on a historical journey of what was known and/or discovered in each of eight time periods." (School Library Journal)

Kenney, Karen Latchana

Exoplanets; worlds beyond our solar system. by Karen Latchana Kenney. Twenty-First Century Books 2017 88 p. color illustrations (ebook) $35.99; (lb : alk. paper) $35.99

Grades: 8 9 10 11 **523.2**

1. Planets 2. Milky Way 3. Extrasolar planets

ISBN 9781512428490; 9781512400861

LC 2016010442

This book, by Karen Latchana Kenney, provides information about the planets that exist outside of our solar system. "Until the mid-1990s, scientists only guessed that the universe held exoplanets, or planets beyond our solar system. But using advanced physics and powerful telescopes, scientists have since identified more than three thousand exoplanets. This work has revealed fascinating worlds, including a planet that oozes lavalike fluids and a planet that glows bright pink." (Publisher's note)

"Perfect for outer space enthusiasts and out of this world for report writers." SLJ

Includes bibliographical references and index

Stefoff, Rebecca, 1951-

The **Sun** and the Earth; Rebecca Stefoff. Cavendish Square 2014 48 p. color illustrations (Is It Science?) $29.93

Grades: 6 7 8 **523.2**

1. Sun 2. Earth 3. Astronomy -- History

ISBN 1627125213; 9781627125215

LC 2015015844

This book, by Rebecca Stefoff, explores the astronomical relationship between the Earth and the Sun. Topics addressed include the history and politics surrounding various scientific models throughout history, the science behind the rising and setting of the sun as seen from the Earth, and the unique features of the Earth's solar orbit compared to other planets.

"Each volume is heavily illustrated with period images and modern photographs, and each closes with particularly generous lists of further resources." SLJ

Tourville, Amanda Doering

Exploring the solar system. Rourke Pub. 2010 48p il (Let's explore science) $32.79; pa $9.95

Grades: 4 5 6 7 **523.2**

1. Solar system

ISBN 978-1-61590-323-8; 1-61590-323-2; 1-61590-562-6 pa; 9781615905621 pa

LC 2010009910

This "moves from basic definitions . . . to more technical information, such as the formula for calculating the speed of light. Also included is up-to-date coverage of Pluto's demotion from planet to plutoid, as well as a section on dwarf planets. . . . In [this] title, well-chosen boxed examples, abundant color photos, diagrams, and an appended glossary add interest and support the engaging [text].” Booklist

Includes glossary and bibliographical references

Wittenstein, Vicki Oransky

Planet hunter; Goeff Marcy and the search for other earths. Boyds Mills Press 2010 48p il $17.95

Grades: 5 6 7 8 **523.2**

1. Extrasolar planets 2. Life on other planets 3. Astrophysicists 4. College teachers

ISBN 978-1-59078-592-8; 1-59078-592-4

“The profound thrill of searching for (and finding!) planets orbiting stars other than our own is deftly captured in this profile of Geoff Marcy, one of the great hunt’s most successful practitioners. Matched to big, sharp color photos of scientists (mostly) at work and compelling speculative views of exotic suns and landscapes, Wittenstein’s matter-of-fact narrative first introduces readers to Marcy and his team on the night shift . . . at the W. M. Keck Observatory atop Hawaii’s Mauna Kea. . . . This handsomely packaged introduction is just the ticket for turning earthbound (for now) children into budding skywatchers.” SLJ

Includes glossary and bibliographical references

523.3 Specific parts of solar system

Scott, Elaine

Our moon; new discoveries about Earth’s closest companion. Elaine Scott. Clarion Books 2015 72 p. chiefly color illustrations (hardcover) $18.99

Grades: 4 5 6 7 **523.3**

1. Moon 2. Astronomy 3. Earth (Planet) 4. Moon -- Exploration 5. Space flight to the moon

ISBN 9780547483948

LC 2015006855

This children’s book, by Elaine Scott, “presents a wealth of captivating, kid-friendly information, covering everything from the newest theories on how the moon formed, to the recent, startling discovery of water on its surface and the very real possibility of future moon colonies.” (Publisher’s note)

“Broader in focus, more detailed, and more up-to-date than most children’s books on the subject, this well-designed volume will be a useful addition to astronomy collections.” Booklist

Includes bibliographical references and index

Simon, Seymour

★ The **moon**; rev ed.; Simon & Schuster Bks. for Young Readers 2003 un il $17.95

Grades: 4 5 6 7 **523.3**

1. Moon 2. Moon -- Exploration

ISBN 0-689-83563-9

LC 2001-31303

First published 1984 by Four Winds Press

A basic introduction to Earth’s closest neighbor, its composition, and man’s missions to it

“The digitally remastered color photographs in this update are incredible. . . . The text has undergone minimal change. . . . The facts remain true and relevant, and the writing reflects the graphics: beautiful. This is a must-have for astronomy sections.” SLJ

523.4 Planets, asteroids, trans-Neptunian objects of solar system

Capaccio, George

Jupiter. Marshall Cavendish Benchmark 2009 64p il (Space!) lib bdg $22.95

Grades: 4 5 6 7 **523.4**

1. Jupiter (Planet)

ISBN 978-0-7614-4244-8 lib bdg; 0-7614-4244-8 lib bdg; 9780761445555

LC 2008037276

“Describes Jupiter, including its history, its composition, and its role in the solar system.” Publisher’s note

Includes glossary and bibliographical references

Mars. Marshall Cavendish Benchmark 2010 64p il (Space!) lib bdg $22.95

Grades: 4 5 6 7 **523.4**

1. Mars (Planet)

ISBN 978-0-7614-4247-9 lib bdg; 0-7614-4247-2 lib bdg; 9780761445579

LC 2008037280

Describes Mars, including its history, its composition, and its role in the solar system

Includes glossary and bibliographical references

Colligan, L. H.

Mercury. Marshall Cavendish Benchmark 2009 64p il (Space!) lib bdg $22.95

Grades: 4 5 6 7 **523.4**

1. Mercury (Planet)

ISBN 0-7614-4239-1 lib bdg; 9780761442394 lib bdg; 9780761445517

LC 2008037278

“Describes Mercury, including its history, its composition, and its role in the solar system.” Publisher’s note

Includes glossary and bibliographical references

Hicks, Terry Allan

Saturn. Marshall Cavendish Benchmark 2010 64p il (Space!) lib bdg $22.95

Grades: 4 5 6 7 **523.4**

1. Saturn (Planet)

ISBN 978-0-7614-4249-3 lib bdg; 0-7614-4249-9 lib bdg; 9780761445593

LC 2008037453

“Describes Saturn, including its history, its composition, and its role in the solar system.” Publisher’s note

Includes glossary and bibliographical references

Jones, Thomas D.

★ **Planetology**; unlocking the secrets of the solar system. [by] Tom Jones and Ellen Stofan. National Geographic 2008 217p il $35

Grades: 7 8 9 10 11 12 **523.4**

1. Planets 2. Astrogeology

ISBN 978-1-4262-0121-9; 1-4262-0121-4

LC 2008-10726

“This beautifully produced book provides an introduction to comparative planetology for a general audience. The large-format volume focuses on comparing and contrasting different processes that shape and form the primary planets in the solar system. . . . The writing is crisp and clear, and the choice of imagery and examples is very strong." Choice

Includes bibliographical references

Miller, Ron

Seven wonders of the gas giants and their moons. Twenty-First Century Books 2011 80p il (Seven wonders) lib bdg $33.26

Grades: 5 6 7 8 **523.4**

1. Planets

ISBN 978-0-7613-5449-9 lib bdg; 0-7613-5449-2 lib bdg; 9780761372813

LC 2010-15558

This book describes seven phenomena about the outer planets of the solar system and their moons, including the great red spot of Jupiter and the underground sea of Europa. Index. "Grades five to eight." (Sci Books Films)

This "celebrates the most unique features of Jupiter, Saturn, Uranus and Neptune, including companion moons and Saturn's mysterious rings. . . . [This] volume makes basic concepts clear in lively, energetic language that, along with the mesmerizing color photos and artists' renderings of space, will easily captivate a young audience, while up-to-date examples, including discoveries made in the last five years, will only increase the sense of immediacy and excitement." Booklist

Includes glossary and bibliographical references

Seven wonders of the rocky planets and their moons. Twenty-First Century Books 2011 80p il (Seven wonders) lib bdg $33.26

Grades: 4 5 6 **523.4**

1. Planets

ISBN 978-0-7613-5448-2 lib bdg; 0-7613-5448-4 lib bdg; 9780761372837

LC 2010-15553

This book shows "views of features on Mercury, Venus, Earth (and its moon), and Mars. [Glossary. Index.] Grades five to eight." (Sci Books Films)

This "compares the fascinating diversity of Earth's land masses with those on Mars, Venus and Mercury. . . . [This] volume makes basic concepts clear in lively, energetic language that, along with the mesmerizing color photos and artists' renderings of space, will easily captivate a young audience, while up-to-date examples, including discoveries made in the last five years, will only increase the sense of immediacy and excitement." Booklist

Includes glossary and bibliographical references

Nardo, Don

Asteroids and comets. Morgan Reynolds Pub. 2009 112p il (Extreme threats) lib bdg $28.95

Grades: 7 8 9 10 **523.4**

1. Comets 2. Asteroids

ISBN 978-1-59935-121-6; 1-59935-121-8

LC 2009-26295

This book covers "evidence of impacts, types of impactors, giant impacts and mass extinctions, recent impacts and near misses, the current and future danger of near-earth-objects (NEOs), and scientific research on how to address the threat. . . . Features high-gloss pages in mottled green, full-color pictures, and informative sidebars. . . . [It is] well written, nicely designed, and interesting." Voice Youth Advocates

Includes glossary and bibliographical references

Sherman, Josepha

Neptune. Marshall Cavendish Benchmark 2009 63p il (Space!) lib bdg $22.95

Grades: 4 5 6 7 **523.4**

1. Neptune (Planet)

ISBN 978-0-7614-4246-2 lib bdg; 0-7614-4246-4 lib bdg; 9780761445562

LC 2008037279

"Describes Neptune, including its history, its composition, and its role in the solar system." Publisher's note

Includes glossary and bibliographical references

Siy, Alexandra

Voyager's greatest hits; the epic trek to interstellar space. by Alexandra Siy. Charlesbridge 2017 74 p. illustrations (chiefly color) (reinforced for library use) $18.99

Grades: 6 7 8 **523.4**

1. Project Voyager 2. Outer space -- Exploration 3. Voyager Project 4. Planets -- Exploration

ISBN 9781580897280

LC 2016013223

This book, by Alexandra Siy, focuses on "the Voyager mission as the twin space probes that traveled to Jupiter, Saturn, Uranus, and Neptune, now journey beyond our solar system into interstellar space, where no probe has ventured before. Learn the fascinating story of the scientists, how the Voyager probes work, where the probes have been and what they've seen, and what they carry on board—including the Golden Record, a recording of sounds and images about life on Earth." (Publisher's note)

"Writing in a conversational style, Siy presents a good deal of information in an accessible way. She creates a sense of discovery as scientists interpret data, and images are sent back by the probes." Booklist

Sparrow, Giles

Destination Uranus, Neptune, and Pluto. PowerKids Press 2010 32p il lib bdg $23.95; pa $10

Grades: 3 4 5 6 **523.4**

1. Uranus (Planet) 2. Neptune (Planet) 3. Pluto (Dwarf planet) 4. Pluto (Planet)

ISBN 978-1-4358-3446-0 lib bdg; 978-1-4358-3463-7 pa

LC 2009-2985

Examines the outer planets, and discusses their moons, interiors, atmospheres, locations, and exploration.

Tyson, Neil deGrasse

The **Pluto** files; the rise and fall of America's favorite planet. Neil deGrasse Tyson. Reissue W.W. Norton 2014 194p il paperback $15.95

Grades: 8 9 10 11 12 Adult **523.4**

1. Pluto (Dwarf planet) 2. Pluto (Planet)

ISBN 978-0-393-06520-6; 9780393350364 paperback; 0-393-33732-4; 978-0-393-33732-7

The author, who is the director of the Hayden Planetarium and the Rose Center for Earth and Space at the American Museum of Natural History in New York City, discusses the "history of Pluto and the debate over its planethood. . . [Tyson cites Pluto's] entrenchment in America's cultural and patriotic view of the cosmos to explain its considerable popularity and the reasons why so many people campaigned for the preservation of its status." (Publisher's note)

Tyson "uses an engaging mix of facts, photographs, cartoons, illustrations, songs, e-mails, and humor to explain what's up (and down) with Pluto." Christ Sci Monit

Includes bibliographical references

523.43 Mars

Aldrin, Buzz, 1930-

Welcome to Mars; making a home on the Red Planet. Buzz Aldrin, with Marianne J. Dyson. National Geographic 2015 96 p. color illustrations (hardcover : alk. paper) $18.99

Grades: 4 5 6 7 8 **523.43**

1. Space flight to Mars 2. Mars (Planet) -- Exploration 3. Space colonies

ISBN 9781426322068; 9781426322075

LC 2014038088

This children's book, by Buzz Aldrin, with Marianne J. Dyson, "challenges curious kids to think about Mars as not just a faraway red planet but as a possible future home for Earthlings! What will your new home be like? How will you get there? What will you eat for breakfast? Find out what life might be like far, far from Earth." (Publisher's note)

"Colorful images, a time line, and a map of Mars enhance the text. . . . A solid option for readers doing school reports or those curious about exploring a new frontier." SLJ

Includes bibliographical references and index

Miller, Ron

Curiosity's mission on Mars; exploring the red planet. by Ron Miller. TFCB, Twenty-First Century Books 2014 64 p. color illustrations (lib. bdg. : alk. paper) $33.26

Grades: 7 8 9 10 11 12 **523.43**

1. Mars (Planet) -- Exploration

ISBN 1467710873; 9781467710879

LC 2013009290

"This clearly written book provides a solid, basic introduction to the Curiosity rover, which NASA launched into space on November 26, 2011. It landed on Mars in August 2012, began drilling into rocks, and has found many key ingredients necessary for life. . . . Sidebars provide additional information on related topics, such as the naming of Curiosity by Kansas sixth-grader Clara Ma, the likelihood of ice beneath the surface of Mars, and the layers of the planet's atmosphere." (Booklist)

Includes bibliographical references (pages 55-56) and index

Rusch, Elizabeth

★ The **mighty** Mars rovers; the incredible adventures of Spirit and Opportunity. by Elizabeth Rusch. Houghton Mifflin Books for Children 2012 79 p. ill. (chiefly col.) (hardcover) $18.99; (hardcover) $18.99

Grades: 4 5 6 **523.43**

1. Mars probes 2. Mars (Planet) -- Exploration 3. Astronautics 4. Mars probes 5. Mars (Planet) -- Exploration 6. Roving vehicles (Astronautics)

ISBN 054747881X; 9780547478814

LC 2011012159

In this book, "[Elizabeth] Rusch covers not only the scientific aspects of Mars exploration but also the personalities of the people who made it happen, and profiles the rovers themselves, Spirit and Opportunity." She looks at "the behind-the-scenes efforts of launching a scientific mission." Also included are "[f]ull-color photographs," a glossary, and a list of further resources. (School Library Journal)

Includes bibliographical references (p. 76), discography (p. 78), filmography (p. 78), and index.

523.8 Stars

Abramson, Andra Serlin

Inside stars; by Andra Serlin Abramson and Mordecai-Mark Mac Low. Sterling Children's Books 2011 48p il (Inside . . .) $16.95; pa $9.95

Grades: 5 6 7 8 **523.8**

1. Stars

ISBN 978-1-4027-7709-7; 1-4027-7709-4; 978-1-4027-8162-9 pa; 1-4027-8162-8 pa

LC 2011283564

Presents an illustrated overview of stars, including information on how they affect the Earth, how scientists study them, how they are classified, how they form and die, and specific information about our star, the Sun.

"On full but not crowded-looking pages, the captions, vocabulary words and digestible blocks of text are set into and around an engagingly diverse mix of cutaway views, digital paintings and eye-widening deep-space photographs. . . . There's plenty here to stimulate both random browsers and confirmed young sky watchers." Kirkus

Includes bibliographical references

Aguilar, David A.

Super stars; the biggest, hottest, brightest, and most explosive stars in the Milky Way. National Geographic 2010 48p il $16.95; lib bdg $27.90

Grades: 4 5 6 7 **523.8**

1. Stars

ISBN 978-1-4263-0601-3; 1-4263-0601-6; 978-1-4263-0602-0 lib bdg; 1-4263-0602-4 lib bdg

LC 2009-37124

"Pairing dramatic space art with souped-up prose, Aguilar introduces more than a dozen types of stars and stellar phenomena. . . . Aside from the occasional alien or interstellar spacecraft set against glowing star fields, the information in both pictures and texts sticks to the facts, accurately reflecting current knowledge without ever coming close to turning into a dry recitation of data. . . . [This is an] unusually exuberant ticket to ride for young sky watchers and armchair space travelers." SLJ

Includes glossary and bibliographical references

Croswell, Ken

The **lives** of stars. Boyds Mills Press 2009 72p il $19.95

Grades: 5 6 7 8 **523.8**

1. Stars 2. Astronomy

ISBN 978-1-59078-582-9; 1-59078-582-7

LC 2008033913

"Extensive, detailed information about stars is coupled with amazing colorful photographs, many from the Hubble Space Telescope, in this stunning book. Packed with facts about the stars and their life cycle, the text often relates them to situations or objects familiar to readers." SLJ

Includes glossary

DeCristofano, Carolyn Cinami

★ A **black** hole is not a hole; Carolyn Cinami DeCristofano ; Illustrated by Michael Carroll. Charlesbridge 2012 v, 74 p.p col ill. (reinforced for library use) $18.95

Grades: 4 5 6 7 **523.8**

1. Stars 2. Universe 3. Black holes (Astronomy)
ISBN 9781570917837; 9781570917844
LC 2010022764

In this non-fiction children's book, Carolyn Cinami DeCristofano discusses black holes. "Covering the life cycles of stars; the formation of black holes and weird optical and physical effects associated with them; more recent revelations of super-sized black holes at the centers of galaxies; and the general effects of mass on space, light, and matter, she presents a . . . picture of the strange structure and stranger physics of black holes." (Booklist)

Jackson, Ellen B.

★ The **mysterious** universe; supernovae, dark energy, and black holes. text by Ellen Jackson; photographs and illustrations by Nic Bishop. Houghton Mifflin 2008 60p il (Scientists in the field) $18

Grades: 5 6 7 8 9 **523.8**

1. Supernovas 2. Black holes (Astronomy)
ISBN 978-0-618-56325-8; 0-618-56325-3
LC 2007-41165

"Splitting its attention evenly between the scientist and his field, this handsomely designed volume displays the joys of being fascinated by one's work in a way that will encourage students to seek similar professional satisfaction for themselves." Booklist

Includes glossary and bibliographical references

Latta, Sara

Black holes; the weird science of the most mysterious objects in the universe. by Sara Latta. Twenty-First Century Books 2017 120 p. (lb : alk. paper) $37.32

Grades: 6 7 8 9 **523.8**

1. Astronomy 2. Black holes (Astronomy)
ISBN 9781512415681
LC 2016038386

This book, by Sara Latta, presents information on black holes. "Meet the scientists who first thought of black holes hundreds of years ago, and learn about contemporary astrophysicists whose work is radically shaping how we understand black holes, our universe, and how it originated." (Publisher's note)

Includes bibliographical references and index

Mack, Gail

The **stars**. Marshall Cavendish Benchmark 2009 64p il (Space!) lib bdg $32.79

Grades: 4 5 6 7 **523.8**

1. Stars 2. Galaxies
ISBN 978-0-7614-4250-9 lib bdg; 0-7614-4250-2 lib bdg
LC 2009014655

This stands out for its "clear, accurate [presentation] of basic facts punctuated by lively turns of phrase and, sometimes, details not commonly found in the plethora of similar tours of the solar system and beyond." SLJ

Includes glossary and bibliographical references

Miller, Ron

Seven wonders beyond the solar system. Twenty-First Century Books 2011 80p il (Seven wonders) lib bdg $33.26

Grades: 5 6 7 8 **523.8**

1. Extrasolar planets 2. Solar system
ISBN 978-0-7613-5454-3; 0-7613-5454-9
LC 2010028446

This "discusses how stars and galaxies form and how scientists search for 'the most Earthlike planet,' as well as the noteworthy nebulae, pulsars, and superclusters. . . . [This] volume makes basic concepts clear in lively, energetic language that, along with the mesmerizing color photos and artists' renderings of space, will easily captivate a young audience, while up-to-date examples, including discoveries made in the last five years, will only increase the sense of immediacy and excitement." Booklist

Includes glossary and bibliographical references

525 Earth (Astronomical geography)

Nardo, Don

The **Blue** marble; how a photograph revealed Earth's fragile beauty. by Don Nardo. Compass Point Books 2014 64 p. (Compass point books. Captured history) (library binding) $33.99

Grades: 5 6 7 8 9 **525**

1. Earth 2. Photographs 3. Apollo project 4. Apollo 17 (Spacecraft) 5. Photographs -- History 6. Earth (Planet) -- Photographs from space
ISBN 0756547326; 9780756547325; 9780756547882
LC 2013031184

"The astronauts headed to the moon in December 1972 thought they knew what to expect. . . . But what they didn't expect came as a huge bonus. The astronauts of Apollo 17 would produce an amazing photograph of planet Earth--a lonely globe floating in inky black space. Their stunning Blue Marble image was destined to become one of the most reproduced and recognizable photos in history." (Publisher's note)

"This outstanding follow-up to Capstone's 'Captured History' series continues the same format, focusing on a single, emblematic photograph that defines an era or event. . . . This set will show students how a single image can 'capture' history and influence the perceptions and actions of those who see it. The books will certainly draw a large readership and are must-buys for all middle-level and secondary collections." SLJ

Includes bibliographical references (page 63) and index

Ride, Sally K.

Mission : planet Earth; our world and its climate--and how humans are changing them. [by] Sally Ride & Tam O'Shaughnessy. Roaring Brook Press 2009 80p il map (Sally Ride science) $19.95

Grades: 5 6 7 8 **525**

1. Earth 2. Climate -- Environmental aspects
ISBN 978-1-59643-310-6; 1-59643-310-8
LC 2009-29253

"This environmental-science primer introduces a range of important concepts necessary to understand climate change and global warming. Topics include the carbon cycle, water cycle, long-range carbon emissions data, biological evidence of climate change, and much more. The authors have an extensive background in science education, and their text exhibits an excellent balance of concept thoroughness with ease of comprehension. Attractive photographs and colorful graphics, including many charts and diagrams, are incorporated throughout." SLJ

Simon, Seymour

★ **Earth** : our planet in space; rev ed; Simon & Schuster Bks. for Young Readers 2003 un il $17.95

Grades: 4 5 6 7 **525**
1. Earth
ISBN 0-689-83562-0
LC 2001-31304

First published 1984 by Four Winds Press

This describes the relationship between the Earth, the sun, and the moon and explains the seasons, day and night, the atmosphere, and changes in the planet's surface. Illustrated with photographs taken from space

529 Chronology

Formichelli, Linda

Timekeeping; Explore the History and Science of Telling Time With 15 Projects. by Linda Formichelli, W. Eric Martin ; illustrated by Sam Carbaugh. Independent Pub Group 2012 128 p. (hardcover) $21.95
Grades: 4 5 6 7 8 **529**
1. Time 2. Science -- Experiments
ISBN 1619301369; 9781619301368

This juvenile activity book, by Linda Formichelli, W. Eric Martin, with illustrations by Sam Carbaugh, is part of the "Build It Yourself" series. It teaches "the cultural history of time" through providing several activities and projects such as "making a shadow clock, tracking time like an ancient Egyptian, using a protractor to create a sundial, measuring time with water, and making a candle clock." (Publisher's note)

Kagayame, Johnny

Discovering the construct of time; [by] Johnny Kagayame, Josepha Sherman. Rosen Pub. 2011 112p il (The scientist's guide to physics)
Grades: 7 8 9 10 **529**
1. Time 2. Calendars 3. Space and time 4. Clocks and watches
ISBN 1448847036; 9781448847037
LC 2010042035

"Beginning with a brief discussion of the concept of time and its meaning in different cultures, this book presents the history of time measurement. . . . A section of the chapter 'Time in Modern Times' introduces Einstein's theories of relativity. . . . Illustrated chiefly with clearly reproduced color photos, this volume provides an accessible, basic introduction to its subject." Booklist

Includes glossary and bibliographical references

530 Physics

Bonnet, Robert L.

Home run! science projects with baseball and softball. [by] Robert L. Bonnet and Dan Keen. Enslow Publishers 2009 104p il (Score! Sports science projects) lib bdg $31.93
Grades: 5 6 7 8 **530**
1. Motion 2. Baseball 3. Force and energy 4. Science projects 5. Science -- Experiments
ISBN 978-0-7660-3365-8 lib bdg; 0-7660-3365-1 lib bdg
LC 2008-3005

"In addition to colorful, digital drawings illustrating the projects, a few photos and period prints also brighten the pages. . . . [This] will appeal to those looking for fresh science-project ideas." Booklist

Includes glossary and bibliographical references

Brown, Jordan D.

Science stunts; fun feats of physics. by Jordan D. Brown. Charlesbridge Publishing, an Imagine Book 2016 80 p. illustrations (some color) (reinforced for library use) $16.95
Grades: 4 5 6 7 **530**
1. Physics 2. Science -- Experiments 3. Physics -- Experiments
ISBN 9781607349419; 9781607349426; 9781623540647
LC 2014045661

In this book, by Jordan D. Brown, "readers will be amazed and delighted as they try magic tricks that are based in important physics concepts such as gravity, inertia, magnetism, sound vibrations, and more. Narrated by a humorous science showman, Dr. Dazzleberry . . . , readers go on a journey through many amazing scientific discoveries. Amusing, edifying commentary from cartoon versions of Newton, Galileo, and Einstein inspire student scientist to experiment with glee." (Publisher's note)

"Magical science that's amazing, astounding, and sure to appeal to middle-grade and middle school readers." Kirkus

Gardner, Robert

Ace your physical science project; great science fair ideas. [by] Robert Gardner, Madeline Goodstein, and Thomas R. Rybolt. Enslow Publishers 2009 128p il (Ace your physics science project) lib bdg $31.93
Grades: 5 6 7 8 **530**
1. Physics 2. Science projects 3. Science -- Experiments
ISBN 978-0-7660-3225-5 lib bdg; 0-7660-3225-6 lib bdg
LC 2008-29637

"Dozens of . . . science activities are presented with background information, step-by-step instructions, and suggestions for extending to the science fair level. . . . Color illustrations and important safety information are included." Horn Book Guide

Includes bibliographical references

Science fair projects about the properties of matter; revised and expanded using the scientific method. Enslow Publishers 2010 160p il (Physics science projects using the scientific method) lib bdg $34.60
Grades: 7 8 9 10 **530**
1. Matter 2. Science projects 3. Science -- Experiments
ISBN 978-0-7660-3417-4 lib bdg; 0-7660-3417-8 lib bdg
LC 2009014804

First published 2004 with title: Science fair projects about the properties of matter using marbles, water, balloons, and more

"Explains how to use the scientific method to conduct several science experiments about the properties of matter. Includes ideas for science fair projects." Publisher's note

Includes bibliographical references

Slam dunk! science projects with basketball; [by] Robert Gardner and Dennis Shortelle. Enslow Publishers 2009 104p il (Score! sports science projects) lib bdg $31.93
Grades: 5 6 7 8 **530**
1. Physics 2. Basketball 3. Science projects 4. Science -- Experiments
ISBN 978-0-7660-3366-5 lib bdg; 0-7660-3366-X lib bdg
LC 2008-24879

"Introductions include information about the history of the sport, safety steps to follow, and the scientific method. . . . Detailed diagrams help clarify many of the directions." SLJ

Includes glossary and bibliographical references

Green, Dan

Physics; why matter matters! [by] Dan Green; Simon Basher, illustrator. Kingfisher 2008 128p il pa $8.95

Grades: 5 6 7 8 **530**

1. Physics

ISBN 978-0-7534-6214-0 pa; 0-7534-6214-1 pa

LC 2007-31805

This "introduces the elements of physics as anthropomorphic, cartoon-style characters. . . . Each of the groupings begins with an introduction and each concept is given its own spread that shows the cartoon figure and describes its 'personality.' The information is presented in a chatty and conversational tone. . . . Along with the narrative, which is written in the first person from the concept's point of view, other key facts are presented. This book would be handy as a supplement to a physics curriculum." SLJ

Includes glossary

Hartman, Eve

Light and sound; [by] Eve Hartman and Wendy Meshbesher. Revised edition Raintree 2016 48p il (Sci-hi: physical science) paperback $8.99

Grades: 5 6 7 8 **530**

1. Light 2. Sound

ISBN 978-1-4109-3378-2; 9781410985361 paperback; 978-1-4109-3383-6

First published 2008

A "compelling read for both browsers and science buffs. . . . Information is clearly presented and flows smoothly. . . . A treasure trove of information." SLJ

Includes glossary and bibliographical references

Lee, Cora

The **great** motion mission; a surprising story of physics in everyday life. illustrated by Steve Rolston. Annick Press 2009 114p il $24.95; pa $14.95

Grades: 4 5 6 **530**

1. Physics

ISBN 978-1-55451-185-3; 1-55451-185-2; 978-1-55451-184-6 pa; 1-55451-184-4 pa

"This book is a combination of narrative and concepts about physics. . . . Jeremy and his friends are distraught when the local summer fair is canceled in order to host a physics conference. While Jeremy helps his uncle campaign to save the fair, his new neighbor, Aubrey, sets out to prove that physics isn't only necessary, but also fun. The text is chatty and accessible to students. Topics include 'Physics and Sight,' 'Physics and Sound,' and 'Physics in Motion.' Each chapter profiles a featured physicist, from Albert Einstein to Richard Feynman. . . . Cartoon illustrations help to explain concepts such as the water cycle and wave patterns. Photographs are scattered throughout, and boxed areas highlight specific topics. This title would be especially useful for students wanting a good introduction to physics." SLJ

Includes glossary and bibliographical references

Matter; edited by Andrea R. Field. 1st ed. Britannica Educational Pub. in association with Rosen Educational Services 2013 77 p. ill. (some col.) (Introduction to physics) (library) $31.70

Grades: 7 8 9 10 **530**

1. Matter 2. Physics

ISBN 1615308393; 9781615308392

LC 2011052216

This book by Andrea R. Field is part of the Introduction to Physics series and focuses on Matter. The entry "covers the basic properties and states of matter; its relationship to energy, including Einstein's theory of special relativity; and physicists' quandaries with dark matter and antimatter." (Booklist)

Includes bibliographical references (p. 73) and index.

Mercer, Bobby

Junk drawer physics; 50 awesome experiments that don't cost a thing. Bobby Mercer. First edition Chicago Review Press, Inc. 2014 208 p. (trade paper) $14.95

Grades: 5 6 7 8 **530**

1. Physics 2. Science -- Experiments 3. Physics -- Experiments

ISBN 1613749201; 9781613749203

LC 2013046726

In this book, Bobby Mercer "provides readers with more than 50 . . . hands-on experiments. . . . Turn a plastic cup into a pinhole camera using waxed paper, a rubber band, and a thumbtack. Build a swinging wave machine using a series of washers suspended on strings from a yardstick. . . . Each project has a materials list, detailed step-by-step instructions with illustrations, and a brief explanation of the scientific principle being demonstrated." (Publisher's note)

"This book is filled with practical and easy experiments that demonstrate many different principles of physics. Though it joins a crowded market of similar at-home science books, this title offers experiments that are fresh and different." SLJ

Pohlen, Jerome

Albert Einstein and relativity for kids; his life and ideas with 21 activities and thought experiments. Jerome Pohlen. Chicago Review Press 2012 xv, 126 p.p (pbk.) $16.95

Grades: 5 6 7 **530**

1. Physicists 2. Relativity (Physics) 3. Physicists -- Biography 4. Relativity (Physics) -- Experiments

ISBN 161374028X; 9781613740286

LC 2012021342

This biography of physicist Albert Einstein "includes the science, politics, and people that surrounded the" scientist. "Einstein's role in the development of the atomic bomb is included along with an explanation of how nuclear fission works. His humanitarian efforts, including his regret at being the instigator behind the bomb are described along with his marriages, his relationships with his children, his eccentricities, and his scientific shortcomings." (School Library Journal)

Includes bibliographical references (page 117) and index

The **science** of physics; edited by Andrea Field. Britannica Educational Pub. 2012 80 p. (Introduction to physics) (library binding) $31.70

Grades: 7 8 9 10 **530**

1. Physics

ISBN 1615306765; 9781615306763

LC 2011026548

This book, edited by Andrea R. Field, is part of the Introduction to Physics series. It "surveys some of the major branches of physics, the laws, and theories significant to each. Also chronicled are some of the historical milestones in the field by such great minds as Galileo and Isaac Newton." (Publisher's note)

Includes bibliographical references and index

530.078 Physics experiments

Gardner, Robert

Solids, liquids, and gases experiments using water, air, marbles, and more; one hour or less science experiments. Robert Gardner. Enslow Publishers 2013 48 p. color illustrations (Last minute science projects) (hbk.) $25.27

Grades: 4 5 6 7 **530.078**

1. Science -- Experiments 2. Change of state (Physics) -- Experiments

ISBN 0766039625; 9780766039629

LC 2011019957

In this book, author "Robert Gardner comes to the rescue of busy students everywhere. Each experiment . . . follows the scientific method, and is designed to be completed in under an hour. Discover how to weigh air, estimate the volume of matter, and the science of why water holds together. There are also ideas for more science experiments if you have extra time." (Publisher's note)

Includes bibliographical references (p. 46-47) and index

530.092 Physicists

Bailey, Diane

Physics; Diane Bailey. Mason Crest, an imprint of National Highlights, Inc. 2017 64 p. color illustrations (Black achievement in science) $23.95

Grades: 7 8 9 10 11 12 **530.092**

1. African American physicists -- Biography 2. African American scientists -- Biography

ISBN 1422235548; 1422235629; 9781422235546; 9781422235621

LC 2016002447

In this tenth book in the Black Achievement in Science series, by Diane Bailey, in "the last century, discoveries in physics have happened at a rapid pace, and scientists of African heritage from around the world have been in the middle of the action. Inside, read inspiring stories of men and women who changed our ideas about how the universe was made, who examined the Earth and how it moves, and many more." (Publisher's note)

"This book is well suited to reports, with a list of text-dependent questions, suggested research projects, a bibliography of websites and books, a series glossary of key terms, and QR codes that link to videos about the scientists." Booklist

Includes bibliographical references and index

Baxter, Roberta

Ernest Rutherford and the birth of the atomic age; by Roberta Baxter. Morgan Reynolds Pub. 2011 ill. (Profiles in science) (library) $28.95

Grades: 7 8 9 10 11 12 **530.092**

1. Nuclear physics 2. Nuclear physics -- History 3. Physicists -- New Zealand -- Biography

ISBN 1599351714; 9781599351711; 9781599352756

LC 2010049096

This book profiles the nuclear physicist Ernest Rutherford. Topics include a profile of his life as a child growing up in New Zealand, his work researching physics in Canada, his Nobel Prize, and the legacy of his work after his death.

"This is a well-rounded portrait of the 20th century's greatest experimental scientists. Baxter not only explains Rutherford's major accomplishments . . . in lucid but not oversimplified terms, but she also paints a vivid picture of an ambitious but not egotistical man with a big personality and close family ties. Enlightening diagrams and plenty of photographs . . . add solid visual elements." SLJ

Includes bibliographical references and index

Kenney, Karen Latchana

Stephen Hawking; extraordinary theoretical physicist. Karen Latchana Kenney. Core Library 2015 48 p. color illustrations (hbk) $32.79

Grades: 4 5 6 **530.092**

1. Physicists 2. People with disabilities 3. Amyotrophic lateral sclerosis -- Patients 4. Physicists -- Great Britain -- Biography 5. People with disabilities -- Great Britain -- Biography 6. Amyotrophic lateral sclerosis -- Patients -- Great Britain -- Biography

ISBN 1624033814; 9781624033810

LC 2014932696

This children's book by Karen Latchan Kenney, part of the Great Minds of Science book series, "chronicles the life and career of the theoretical physicist, from his battle with ALS to his work on black holes." (Publisher's note)

"Students will learn about the different accomplishments of each scientist while joining them on the often tumultuous journey to success. A staple for libraries." SLJ

Includes bibliographical references (page 47) and index

Mooney, Carla

Isaac Newton; genius mathematician and physicist. Carla Mooney. Core Library 2015 48 p. illustrations (some color) $32.79

Grades: 4 5 6 **530.092**

1. Physicists 2. Mathematicians 3. Physicists -- Great Britain -- Biography 4. Mathematicians -- Great Britain -- Biography

ISBN 1624033822; 9781624033827

LC 2014932619

This children's book by Carla Mooney, part of the Great Minds of Science book series, "chronicles the life and career of the genius physicist [Isaac Newton], from his time at Cambridge to his landmark book, known as the 'Principia.'" (Publisher's note)

"Students will learn about the different accomplishments of each scientist while joining them on the often tumultuous journey to success. A staple for libraries." SLJ

Includes bibliographical references (page 47) and index

530.11 Relativity theory

Hunter, Nick

Is time travel possible? Nick Hunter. Heinemann Raintree, a Capstone imprint 2016 48 p. color illustrations (library binding) $33.32; (ebook) $33.32

Grades: 5 6 7 8 **530.11**

1. Physics 2. Time travel

ISBN 9781410981622; 9781410981707

LC 2015024556

In this book, in the Top secret! series, by Nick Hunter, "a mysterious figure called the Mystery Master sets you the challenge of investigating all the scientific theories surrounding time travel and encourages you to analyse the information that you have gathered. Once you have read the information in this book, you can figure out for yourselves: Is time travel possible?" (Publisher's note)

"The discourse is, unsurprisingly, only ankle deep, but readers will be swept off their feet by the flood of big ideas, cosmic theories, silly speculations, and tantalizing hints of awesome scientific discoveries waiting just around the corner." Booklist

Includes bibliographical references and index

Whiting, Jim

Space and time; Jim Whiting ; photographs by Getty Images ; folio illustration, Alex Ryan. 1st ed. Creative Education 2013 48 p. col. ill., col. maps (library) $35.65

Grades: 4 5 6 7 **530.11**

1. Physics 2. Space and time 3. Relativity (Physics)

ISBN 1608181928; 9781608181926

LC 2011040146

This book, by Jim Whiting, explores the concepts of space and time as part of the "Mysteries of the Universe" series. It appeals "to report writers and serious astronomy students. Each book carefully examines the history behind attempts to unravel explanations for the subjects, going back to Anaxagoras's work on energy in 450 B.C. all the way up to the contemporary findings of Stephen Hawking." (School Library Journal)

Includes bibliographical references (p. 46-47) and index.

530.4 States of matter

Claybourne, Anna

The **nature** of matter; [by] Anna Claybourne. Gareth Stevens Pub. 2007 48p il (Gareth Stevens vital science: physical science) lib bdg $26.60; pa $11.95

Grades: 4 5 6 7 **530.4**

1. Matter

ISBN 978-0-8368-8088-5 lib bdg; 978-0-8368-8097-7 pa

LC 2006033732

This describes uses for matter and what happens when it changes from one form to another, the basic physical laws and properties of matter, and the various ways in which we control how matter behaves.

This is "straightforward and clear. . . . The layout is bright and colorful, with photographs and illustrations on almost every page." SLJ

Includes glossary and bibliographical references

Meyer, Susan

Gases and their properties. Rosen Central 2011 64p il (Science made simple) lib bdg $29.25; pa $12.95

Grades: 5 6 7 8 **530.4**

1. Gases

ISBN 978-1-4488-1233-2 lib bdg; 1-4488-1233-X lib bdg; 978-1-4488-2243-0 pa; 1-4488-2243-2 pa

LC 2010015858

This introduction to gases and their properties includes "a lot of detailed information, making [it] useful as [a] resource . . . for science projects and reports. . . . The [book] also [includes a] brief discussion of scientists important in the field, the history of the topic, and current and future applications. . . . The straightforward, no-nonsense [narrative] and simple design make this . . . a nice package for basic science." SLJ

Includes glossary and bibliographical references

Reilly, Kathleen M.

Explore solids and liquids! With 25 Great Projects. by Kathleen M. Reilly ; illustrated by Bryan Stone. Nomad Press 2014 92 p. color illustrations $14.95

Grades: 4 5 6 **530.4**

1. Solids 2. Liquids 3. Science projects 4. Matter -- Properties -- Experiments

ISBN 1619301717; 1619302373; 9781619301719; 9781619302372

In this book, by Kathleen M. Reilly and illustrated by Bryan Stone, "kids experience the wonder of different states of matter. They'll learn what matter is made of, how it can change, and how these interactions really work in our universe. With plenty of activities and projects, young readers gain a solid understanding of the matter they touch, see, feel, and experience every single day." (Publisher's note)

"This is an attractive presentation, easy to navigate, that encourages young readers to learn through text and experimentation." Library Media Connection Reviews

530.8 Measurement

Ball, Johnny

Why pi; how math applies to everyday life. DK Pub. 2009 93p il map $16.99

Grades: 4 5 6 7 **530.8**

1. Pi 2. Mathematics 3. Measurement

ISBN 978-0-7566-5164-0; 0-7566-5164-6

"Author Johnny Ball focuses on how people have used numbers to measure things through the ages, from the ways the ancient Egyptians measured the pyramids to how modern scientists measure time and space." Publisher's note

Gardner, Robert

Ace your math and measuring science project; great science fair ideas. Enslow Publishers 2009 128p il (Ace your physics science project) lib bdg $31.93

Grades: 5 6 7 8 **530.8**

1. Measurement 2. Science projects 3. Weights and measures 4. Science -- Experiments

ISBN 978-0-7660-3224-8 lib bdg; 0-7660-3224-8 lib bdg

LC 2008-23926

"Dozens of . . . science activities are presented with background information, step-by-step instructions, and suggestions for extending to the science fair level. . . . Color illustrations and important safety information are included." Horn Book Guide

Includes bibliographical references

531 Classical mechanics

Claybourne, Anna

Forms of energy; Revised edition Raintree 2016 48p il (Sci-hi: physical science) paperback $8.99

Grades: 5 6 7 8 **531**

1. Force and energy

ISBN 9781410985323 paperback; 978-1-4109-3377-5; 978-1-4109-3382-9

First published 2008

A "compelling read for both browsers and science buffs. . . . Information is clearly presented and flows smoothly. . . . A treasure trove of information." SLJ

Includes glossary and bibliographical references

Gut -wrenching gravity and other fatal forces; Anna Claybourne. Crabtree Publishing Company 2013 32 p. (Disgusting & dreadful science) (pbk. : alk. paper) $9.95

Grades: 4 5 6 **531**

1. Gravity 2. Physics 3. Force and energy

ISBN 0778709574; 9780778709503; 9780778709572

LC 2012043529

This book by Anna Claybourne is part of the Disgusting & Dreadful Science series and focuses on gravity and other physical forces. It shares facts including that "a mouse can survive a 328-foot fall, black holes have superstrong gravity that causes 'spaghettification,' and" more. Illustrations are included. (Booklist)

Includes bibliographical references and index

Energy; edited by Andrea R. Field. Britannica Educational Pub. in association with Rosen Educational Services 2012 79 p. ill. (some col.) (Introduction to physics)

Grades: 7 8 9 10 **531**

1. Force and energy -- Study and teaching (Middle school)

ISBN 9781615306732

LC 2011021493

"This series fills a gap in the high school library by truly being an introduction to physics, electronics, and energy. It introduces readers to the major figures who discovered the laws of physics, and gives definitions of terms while providing common examples of such things as electrostatic induction, applications of magnetism, or conductivity and resistance in a circuit." (Library Media Connection)

"With attractive, lively graphics, [this] will make a good supplement in libraries needing lots of science-experiment background information." Booklist

Includes bibliographical references (p. 72-75) and index

Gardner, Robert

Forces and motion science fair projects; revised and expanded using the scientific method. Enslow Publishers 2010 160p il (Physics science projects using the scientific method) lib bdg $34.60

Grades: 7 8 9 10 **531**

1. Force and energy 2. Science projects 3. Science -- Experiments

ISBN 978-0-7660-3415-0 lib bdg; 0-7660-3415-1 lib bdg

LC 2008050066

First published 2004 with title: Forces and motion science fair projects using water balloons, pulleys, and other stuff

"Explains how to use the scientific method to conduct several physics experiments with forces and motion. Includes ideas for science fair projects." Publisher's note

Includes bibliographical references

O'Leary, Denyse

What are Newton's laws of motion? Crabtree Pub. Co. 2011 64p il (Shaping modern science) lib bdg $30.60; pa $10.95

Grades: 5 6 7 8 **531**

1. Motion 2. Physicists 3. Mathematicians 4. Writers on science

ISBN 978-0-7787-7200-2 lib bdg; 0-7787-7200-4 lib bdg; 978-0-7787-7207-1 pa; 0-7787-7207-1 pa

LC 2010-52629

This book examines how Sir Isaac Newton developed three basic laws that govern the way in which objects move. It explains how Newton expanded on the work of other scientists, including Galileo and Copernicus, to make his discovery. The book also explains how Newton's laws have influenced modern science and technology in areas such as sports and transportation.

This title is "not only written and organized well, but [it is] also gorgeous in design. Full-color photographs and illustrations are set over colorful backgrounds that add depth but not distraction. [The title] includes thought-provoking quotes from famous authors and scientists and some eyebrow-raising 'Quick Facts' throughout." SLJ

Includes glossary and bibliographical references

Orr, Tamra

Motion and forces. Rosen Central 2011 64p il (Science made simple) lib bdg $29.25; pa $12.95

Grades: 5 6 7 8 **531**

1. Motion 2. Force and energy

ISBN 978-1-4488-1232-5 lib bdg; 1-4488-1232-1 lib bdg; 978-1-4488-2240-9 pa; 1-4488-2240-8 pa

LC 2010020535

This introduction to motion and forces includes "a lot of detailed information, making [it] useful as [a] resource . . . for science projects and reports. . . . The [book] also [includes a] brief discussion of scientists important in the field, the history of the topic, and current and future applications. . . . The straightforward, no-nonsense [narrative] and simple design make this . . . a nice package for basic science." SLJ

Includes glossary and bibliographical references

Rooney, Anne

You wouldn't want to live without gravity! written by Anne Rooney ; illustrated by Mark Bergin ; series created by David Salariya. Franklin Watts, an imprint of Scholastic Inc. 2016 32 p. color illustrations (library binding : alkaline paper) $29.00

Grades: 3 4 5 6 **531**

1. Gravity 2. Weightlessness

ISBN 9780531214879; 9780531224373

LC 2015036599

In this book, by Anne Rooney, illustrated by Mark Bergin, "you don't really get a choice about gravity. If you live on Earth, you're going to have to live with it. . . . But gravity does a lot of useful things - such as keeping us on the Earth and holding the entire universe together! Learn how gravity was discovered and why it helps us to understand everything from how toothpaste comes out of the tube to the movements of the planets." (Publisher's note)

"The books feature a time line and numerous ancillaries, but the myriad entertaining facts are the real hit. Who wouldn't want to read them? " Booklist

Includes bibliographical references and index

VanCleave, Janice Pratt, 1942-

Step -by-step science experiments in energy; by Janice VanCleave. Rosen Pub. 2013 80 p. col. ill. (Janice VanCleeve's first-place science fair projects) (library) $33.25; (paperback) $14.15

Grades: 5 6 7 8 **531**

1. Energy 2. Science -- Experiments 3. Science projects 4. Force and energy -- Experiments

ISBN 144886979X; 9781448869794; 9781448884711

LC 2012006835

This book by Janice VanCleave is part of the First-Place Science Fair Projects series. The books have an introduction to the subject—here, energy, followed by 22 simple . . . experiments. Van Cleave states the basic goal of the experiments, followed by a list of necessary materials, most of which can be found around the house or easily acquired with minimal cost. Step-by-step instructions are clearly detailed and accompanied by diagrams where needed." (School Library Journal)

Includes bibliographical references and index.

533 Pneumatics (Gas mechanics)

Gardner, Robert

Air; green science projects for a sustainable planet. Enslow Publishers 2011 128p il (Team Green science projects) lib bdg $31.93

Grades: 6 7 8 9 10 **533**

1. Air 2. Air pollution 3. Science projects 4. Science -- Experiments

ISBN 978-0-7660-3646-8; 0-7660-3646-4

LC 2010-1120

This book offers science experiments that explain the properties of air, how to conserve energy while heating and cooling air, and how to reduce air pollution.

"Gardner provides plenty of information, well-designed experiments, and demonstrations, and then shares brief science-fair ideas. . . . Experiments and demonstrations are presented with clear step-by-step instructions and occasional illustrations and represent a wide range of complexity." SLJ

Includes glossary and bibliographical references

534 Specific forms of energy

Sound; edited by Sherman Hollar. Britannica Educational Pub. in association with Rosen Educational Services 2013 79 p. ill. (Introduction to physics) (library) $31.70

Grades: 7 8 9 10 **534**

1. Sound

ISBN 1615308415; 9781615308415

LC 2012010563

This book on sound, edited by Sherman Hollar, is part of the "Introduction to Physics" series. It "describes how sound is produced, carried, and processed and features a chapter on acoustical engineers' applications in the life sciences, earth sciences, architecture, and the arts." (Booklist) "Also covered are functions and diseases of the human ear." (Publisher's note)

Includes bibliographical references and index.

535 Light and related radiation

Caes, Charles J.

★ **Discovering** the speed of light; by Charles J. Caes. 1st ed. Rosen Pub. 2012 112 p. ill. (chiefly col.) (Scientist's guide to physics) (library) $34.60

Grades: 5 6 7 8 **535**

1. Light -- Speed 2. Light -- Study and teaching -- History 3. Light -- Speed -- Measurement

ISBN 1448846994; 9781448846993

LC 2010048426

This book by Charles J. Caes is part of the "Scientist's Guide to Physics" series. It "uncovers the earliest study of the speed of light, around 550 BCE in classical Greece. From classical Greece to Galileo and later Albert Einstein, this title also details the history of the discovery of light speed measurement and theories." (VOYA)

Includes bibliographical references (p. 107-108) and index.

Light; edited by Michael Anderson. Britannica Educational Pub. in association with Rosen Educational Services 2013 77 p. ill. (some col.) (Introduction to physics) (library) $31.70

Grades: 7 8 9 10 **535**

1. Light 2. Light -- Speed

ISBN 1615308407; 9781615308408

LC 2012010241

This book "teaches the reader about light's many properties. It illuminates the path between light and matter, focusing in on reflection. refraction/dispersion, and light speed." Some chapters "explain light as a wave and as a particle. This book connects the past and present theories of light" and "explains in no-nonsense terms and real life applications the hows, the whats, and the whys of light theory." (NSTA Recommends)

Includes bibliographical references (p. 74) and index.

Winterberg, Jenna

★ **Light** and its effects; Jenna Winterberg. Teacher Created Materials 2016 32 p. (pbk.) $8.99

Grades: 4 5 6 **535**

1. Light 2. Wave theory of light

ISBN 9781480746855

LC 2014045208

This children's book, by Jenna Winterberg, part of the "Content and Literacy in Science Grade 4" series, describes the characteristics and effects of light for elementary school students. It includes "high-interest text and vibrant images and photographs . . . [and a] lab activity that supports STEM instruction. . . . A helpful glossary, table of contents, and index are also included for additional support." (Publisher's note)

"Smartly written, these innovative and imaginative volumes make learning fun... First-rate nonfiction." SLJ

536 Heat

Gardner, Robert

Easy genius science projects with temperature and heat; great experiments and ideas. by Robert Gardner and Eric Kemer. Enslow Publishers 2009 128p il (Easy genius science projects) lib bdg $31.93

Grades: 5 6 7 8 **536**

1. Heat 2. Temperature 3. Science projects 4. Science -- Experiments

ISBN 978-0-7660-2939-2 lib bdg; 0-7660-2939-5 lib bdg

LC 2008-4675

"Presents several science experiments and science project ideas dealing with temperature and heat." Publisher's note

Includes glossary and bibliographical references

Heat; edited by Andrea R. Field. Britannica Educational Pub. 2013 76 p. ill. (some col.) (library) $31.70

Grades: 7 8 9 10 **536**

1. Heat 2. Physics

ISBN 1615308385; 9781615308385

LC 2011053232

This book looks at heat, or "the energy that is transferred from one object to another because of a difference in temperature," as well as "the related concepts of temperature, thermal energy, and thermodynamics and introduces readers to some of the great minds that furthered our understanding of this . . . area of physics." (Publisher's note)

Includes bibliographical references (p. 73) and index.

537 Electricity and electronics

Claybourne, Anna

Electric shocks and other energy evils; Anna Claybourne. Crabtree Publishing Company 2013 32 p. (Disgusting & dreadful science) (reinforced library binding) $27.60

Grades: 4 5 6 **537**

1. Electricity 2. Electricity 3. Electric shock

ISBN 0778709264; 9780778709268; 9780778709534; 9781427191731; 9781427192493

LC 2012043527

This book, by Anna Claybourne, is part of the Disgusting and Dreadful Science series. It "features a look at the weird, revolting and shocking aspects of science for children. . . From electricity to sound and from light to forces, the books offer . . . fascinating facts, fun examples and true-life stories to provide ways in to understanding solid scientific principles." (Publisher's note)

"These brief and lively introductions provide a plethora of fun and gross facts. Sounds explains the science behind sound, how ears work, ultrasound, and more. It also includes a scientific explanation of how whoopee cushions work. Shocks covers electrical current, circuits, lightning, etc. In both volumes, each subject is presented on a spread with a brief introduction. The explanations are clear and concise..." SLJ

Includes index

Other titles in the series include:

Ear-splitting sounds and other vile noises (2013)

Glaring light and other eye-burning rays (2013)

Gut-wrenching gravity and other fatal forces (2013)

Electricity; edited by Michael Anderson. Britannica Educational Pub. in association with Rosen Educational Services 2012 79 p. ill. (some col.) (Introduction to physics)

Grades: 7 8 9 10 **537**

1. Electricity

ISBN 161530665X; 9781615306657

LC 2011017090

"...Features clear diagrams and is a narrow enough topic to be well covered, with chapters on circuits, magnetic fields, and generators." Booklist

Includes bibliographical references (p. 76) and index

Galiano, Dean

Electric and magnetic phenomena. Rosen Central 2011 64p il (Science made simple) lib bdg $29.25; pa $12.95

Grades: 5 6 7 8 **537**

1. Magnetism 2. Electricity

ISBN 978-1-4488-1231-8 lib bdg; 1-4488-1231-3 lib bdg; 978-1-4488-2239-3 pa; 1-4488-2239-4 pa

LC 2010014546

This introduction to electric and magnetic phenomena includes "a lot of detailed information, making [it] useful as [a] resource . . . for science projects and reports. . . . The [book] also [includes a] brief discussion of scientists important in the field, the history of the topic, and current and future applications. . . . The straightforward, no-nonsense [narrative] and simple design make this . . . a nice package for basic science." SLJ

Includes glossary and bibliographical references

Gardner, Robert

Easy genius science projects with electricity and magnetism; great experiments and ideas. Enslow Publishers 2009 128p il (Easy genius science projects) lib bdg $31.93

Grades: 5 6 7 8 **537**

1. Magnetism 2. Electricity 3. Science projects 4. Science -- Experiments

ISBN 978-0-7660-2923-1 lib bdg; 0-7660-2923-9 lib bdg

LC 2007-38470

"Science projects and experiments about electricity and magnetism." Publisher's note

Includes glossary and bibliographical references

Easy genius science projects with light; great experiments and ideas. [by] Robert Gardner. Enslow Publishers 2008 128p il (Easy genius science projects) lib bdg $31.93

Grades: 6 7 8 9 **537**

1. Light 2. Science projects 3. Science -- Experiments

ISBN 978-0-7660-2926-2; 0-7660-2926-3

LC 2007-38468

This includes science projects and experiments about such light-related topics as colors, lenses, mirages, reflections, refraction, particle theory, polarization, and after images.

"The physics involved are . . . fascinating and will grab curious readers. . . . The inviting and chatty text for each project includes a boxed list of 'things you will need,' all of them commonly available, followed by detailed step-by-step instructions with clear diagrams." Booklist

Includes glossary and bibliographical references

Electricity and magnetism science fair projects; revised and expanded using the scientific method. Enslow Publishers 2010 160p il (Physics science projects using the scientific method) lib bdg $34.60

Grades: 7 8 9 10 **537**

1. Magnetism 2. Electricity 3. Science projects 4. Science -- Experiments

ISBN 978-0-7660-3418-1 lib bdg; 0-7660-3418-6 lib bdg

First published 2004 with title: Electricity and magnetism science fair projects: using batteries, balloons, and other hair-raising stuff

"This describes experiments on such topics as static electricity, moving charges, magnets and magnetic fields, and electricity and chemistry. Includes suggestions for science projects." Publisher's note

Includes bibliographical references

Woodford, Chris

Experiments with electricity and magnetism. Gareth Stevens Pub. 2010 32p il (Cool science) lib bdg $28; pa $10.50

Grades: 4 5 6 7 **537**

1. Magnetism 2. Electricity 3. Science -- Experiments

ISBN 9781433934445 lib bdg; 1433934442 lib bdg; 9781433934452 pa; 1433934450 pa

LC 2009037141

"The book [is] written in an easy-to-understand, straightforward style with helpful real-life photographs... Students who need simple experiments or those who need more advanced projects will find [it] helpful." Library Media Connection

Includes bibliographical references

539 Modern physics

Claybourne, Anna

Who split the atom? Arcturus Pub. 2010 46p il (Breakthroughs in science and technology) lib bdg $32.80

Grades: 5 6 7 8 **539**

1. Atoms 2. Matter

ISBN 978-1-84837-683-0 lib bdg; 1-84837-683-9 lib bdg

LC 2010-11015

This book explores the ways in which scientists uncovered the atom. The book is "divided into easy to read short chapters with large, colorful photographs and graphics on every page. . . . The added inserts provide additional information to engage readers and help them connect with the scientific details." Libr Media Connect

Includes glossary and bibliographical references

539.7 Atomic and nuclear physics

Campbell, Margaret Christine

★ **Discovering** atoms; Margaret Christine Campbell, Natalie Goldstein. 1st ed. Rosen Pub. 2012 112 p. ill. (The scientist's guide to physics) (library) $34.60

Grades: 5 6 7 8 9 **539.7**

1. Atoms 2. Atomic theory -- History 3. Atomic structure 4. Matter -- Constitution

ISBN 1448847001; 9781448847006

LC 2010048416

This book by Margaret Christine Campbell is part of the "Scientist's Guide to Physics" series. It "presents the . . . story of the atom's discovery, which is full of bizarre theories, false starts, dead ends, and . . . intellectual insight." (Publisher's note) "Campbell includes a . . . chronological foundation upon which the discovery of elements and the creation of the periodic table build up to the discovery of the atom, atomic rays, particles, models . . . and subatomic particles." (VOYA)

Includes bibliographical references and index.

Chaffee, Joel

Atomic and molecular structure. Rosen Central 2011 64p il (Science made simple) lib bdg $29.25; pa $12.95

Grades: 5 6 7 8 **539.7**

1. Atoms 2. Molecules

ISBN 978-1-4488-1230-1 lib bdg; 1-4488-1230-5 lib bdg; 978-1-4488-2238-6 pa; 1-4488-2238-6 pa

LC 2010015454

This introduction to atomic and molecular structure includes "a lot of detailed information, making [it] useful as [a] resource . . . for science projects and reports. . . . The [book] also [includes a] brief discussion of scientists important in the field, the history of the topic, and current and future applications. . . . The straightforward, no-nonsense [narrative] and simple design make this . . . a nice package for basic science." SLJ

Includes glossary and bibliographical references

Conkling, Winifred

Radioactive! how Irene Curie and Lise Meitner revolutionized science and changed the world. Winifred Conkling. Algonquin Young Readers 2016 240 p. illustrated $17.95

Grades: 7 8 9 10 **539.7**

1. Physicists 2. Radioactivity 3. Nuclear fission 4. Women scientists -- France -- Biography 5. Women scientists -- Germany -- Biography

ISBN 9781616204150; 161620415X

LC 2015017256

This book, by Winifred Conkling, "presents the story of [Irène Curie and Lise Meitner,] two women breaking ground in a male-dominated field, scientists still largely unknown despite their crucial contributions to cutting-edge research, in a nonfiction narrative that reads with the suspense of a thriller. Photographs and sidebars illuminate and clarify the science in the book." (Publisher's note)

"Black-and-white period photos, scientific asides and diagrams, and a time line enhance the well-cited text." Booklist

Includes bibliographical references and index

Cregan, Elizabeth R.

The **atom**. Compass Point Books 2009 40p il (Mission: science) lib bdg $26.60

Grades: 4 5 6 **539.7**

1. Atoms 2. Atomic theory 3. Nuclear energy

ISBN 978-0-7565-3953-5 lib bdg; 0-7565-3953-6 lib bdg

LC 2008007724

"Cregan discusses the structure of the atom, key scientists, cathode rays and electrons, radioactivity, and atom smashers. . . . The [book has an] open [layout] and large, easy-to-read type. . . . Large eye-catching and colorful photographs and illustrations appear on every page. The [book] includes a simple activity." SLJ

Includes glossary and bibliographical references

Henderson, Harry

The **Curie** family; exploring radioactivity. Harry Henderson. Chelsea House 2012 117 p. (Trailblazers in science and technology) $35

Grades: 7 8 9 10 11 12 **539.7**

1. Radioactivity 2. Curie, Marie, 1867-1934 3. Curie, Pierre, 1859-1906 4. Radioactivity -- History 5. Physicists -- France -- Biography 6. Physicists -- Poland -- Biography

ISBN 1604136758; 9781604136753

LC 2011011800

This book, by Harry Henderson, is part of the "Trailblazers in Science and Technology" series. "Marie and Pierre Curie, their daughter Irène Joliot-Curie, and her husband Frédéric Joliot-Curie were one of science's most remarkable and influential families. Their painstaking research into the mysteries of radioactivity allowed scientists to reach a new understanding about the structure of atoms and opened a new field of medical treatment." (Publisher's note)

Includes bibliographical references and index

Jerome, Kate Boehm

Atomic universe; the quest to discover radioactivity. by Kate Boehm Jerome. National Geographic 2006 59p il (Science quest) $17.95; lib bdg $25.90

Grades: 5 6 7 8 **539.7**

1. Radioactivity 2. Nuclear physics

ISBN 0-7922-5543-7; 0-7922-5544-5 lib bdg

LC 2006001316

The text offers "key concepts in a pleasing and readable format that would appeal to reluctant readers." SLJ

Includes glossary and bibliographical references

Latta, Sara

SMASH! exploring the mysteries of the universe with the Large Hadron Collider. written by Sara Latta ; illustrated by Jeff Weigel. Graphic Universe, a division of Lerner Publishing Group, Inc. 2017 72 p. illustrations (paperback) $11.99

Grades: 6 7 8 9 **539.7**

1. Science -- Graphic novels 2. Large Hadron Collider (France and Switzerland) 3. Particles (Nuclear physics) 4. Higgs bosons 5.

European Organization for Nuclear Research
ISBN 9781467785518; 1467785512; 1512430706; 9781512430707; 9781512427011
LC 2016017321

In this graphic novel, by Sara Latta, illustrated by Jeff Weigel, "Nick and Sophie, two cousins, are about to visit CERN for a tour of the mysteries of the cosmos. Sophie's a physics wiz. Nick, not so much. But by the time they're through, Nick and Sophie will both feel the power of hidden particles, fundamental forces, dark matter, and more." (Publisher's note)

"An accessible look at the Large Hadron Collider (LHC) and particle physics." SLJ

Includes bibliographical references.

Lepora, Nathan

Atoms and molecules. Marshall Cavendish Benchmark 2010 48p il (Invisible worlds) lib bdg $28.50
Grades: 4 5 6 7 **539.7**

1. Atoms 2. Molecules 3. Nanotechnology
ISBN 978-0-7614-4192-2 lib bdg; 0-7614-4192-1 lib bdg
LC 2008037237

This describes the details and characteristics of atoms and molecules that are too small for the unaided eye to see.

The narrative is "clear, well written, broken down into manageable pieces, and peppered with eye-opening facts. The numerous photographs are so phenomenal that they will inspire kids to read the text . . . so that they can wrap their minds around what they see." SLJ

Includes glossary and bibliographical references

Manning, Phillip

Atoms, molecules, and compounds. Chelsea House 2008 137p il (Essential chemistry) $35
Grades: 7 8 9 10 **539.7**

1. Atoms 2. Matter 3. Molecules 4. Chemical reactions
ISBN 978-0-7910-9534-8; 0-7910-9534-7
LC 2007-11403

"In relatively few pages, and with lots of colorful, clear illustrations, Manning takes us from Thompson's plum-pudding model of the atom to Rutherford's model to the quantum model, and through the discovery of atomic particles and the teasing out of atomic forces, in a very clear, compelling path. . . . The clear linkages he makes between the different types of chemical bonds and the nature of various materials will remain with the reader." Sci Books Films

Includes glossary and bibliographical references

McLean, Adam

What is atomic theory? Crabtree Pub. Co. 2011 64p il (Shaping modern science) lib bdg $30.60; pa $10.95
Grades: 5 6 7 8 **539.7**

1. Atoms 2. Chemists 3. Physicists 4. Atomic theory 5. Nuclear energy 6. Writers on science
ISBN 978-0-7787-7197-5 lib bdg; 0-7787-7197-0 lib bdg; 978-0-7787-7204-0 pa; 0-7787-7204-7 pa

This title is "not only written and organized well, but [it is] also gorgeous in design. Full-color photographs and illustrations are set over colorful backgrounds that add depth but not distraction. [The title] includes thought-provoking quotes from famous authors and scientists and some eyebrow-raising 'Quick Facts' throughout." SLJ

Includes glossary and bibliographical references

540 Chemistry and allied sciences

Coelho, Alexa

Why Is Milk White? & 200 Other Curious Chemistry Questions. Alexa Coelho and Simon Quellen Field. Independent Pub Group 2013 288 p. ill. (paperback) $14.95
Grades: 4 5 6 7 8 **540**

1. Chemistry -- Miscellanea 2. Chemistry
ISBN 1613744528; 9781613744529
LC 2012040205

This juvenile chemistry book, by Alexa Coelho and Simon Quellen Field, is a "question-and-answer primer [that] provides straightforward, easy-to-understand explanations for inquisitive young scientists' questions. . . . From lifting latent fingerprints from a 'crime scene' using super glue (for smooth surfaces) or iodine (for paper) to hollowing out the zinc interior of a penny using muriatic acid . . . , this handy guide is [a] . . . resource for the budding chemist." (Publisher's note)

Farndon, John

Experimenting with chemistry. Marshall Cavendish Benchmark 2009 104p il (Experimenting with science) $35.64
Grades: 7 8 9 10 **540**

1. Chemistry 2. Science -- Experiments
ISBN 978-0-7614-3928-8; 0-7614-3928-5
LC 2008017570

"Explores and explains chemistry concepts and provides experiments to aid in understanding chemistry." Publisher's note

Gardner, Robert

Chemistry science fair projects using inorganic stuff; revised and expanded using the scientific method. Enslow Publishers 2010 160p il (Chemistry science projects using the scientific method) lib bdg $34.60
Grades: 7 8 9 10 **540**

1. Chemistry 2. Science projects 3. Science -- Experiments
ISBN 978-0-7660-3413-6 lib bdg; 0-7660-3413-5 lib bdg
LC 2008046505

First published 2004 with title: Chemistry Science Fair Projects Using Acids, Bases, Metals,Salts, and Inorganic Stuff

"Colorful drawings complement the material and illustrations of chemical structures help to convey chemical processes. . . . Useful." SLJ

Includes bibliographical references

Green, Dan

Chemistry; getting a big reaction. created by Basher; written by Dan Green. Kingfisher 2010 128p il $14.99; pa $8.99
Grades: 4 5 6 7 **540**

1. Chemistry
ISBN 978-0-7534-6615-5; 0-7534-6615-5; 978-0-7534-6413-7 pa; 0-7534-6413-6 pa

This "begins with a short overview of [chemistry] and information on Antoine Lavoisier's 18th-century scientific findings. Concepts are grouped by associations: 'Basic States' (solid, liquid, etc.), 'Nuts and Bolts' (atom, ion, etc.), 'Nasty Boys' (acid, base, etc.), and more. The individual concepts are each introduced over a spread that features a computer-generated cartoon of a character representing the idea and a brief introduction to its characteristics and personality. . . . The information is presented in a chatty, first-person voice." SLJ

Hardyman, Robyn

Pierre and Marie Curie; Robyn Hardyman. Gareth Stevens Publishing 2014 48 p. illustrations (some color) $31.95

Grades: 4 5 6 **540**

1. Chemists 2. Curie, Marie, 1867-1934 3. Curie, Pierre, 1859-1906

ISBN 1482414740; 9781482414745

This children's book by Robyn Hardyman on scientists Pierre Curie and Marie Curie is part of a series known for its "graphics and ability to make complex concepts accessible. The authors have . . . select[ed] key quotes from the scientists' writings that young readers can understand (provided in sidebars titled 'In Their Own Words')." (School Library Journal)

"Readers learn that Alfred Russel Wallace and Darwin, rivals as well as supporters, shared much of the same information, making similar discoveries. Reading their parallel stories will let children see how different people solve the same problems. Original takes on science biographies." SLJ

Mooney, Carla

Chemistry; Investigate the Matter That Makes Up Your World. Carla Mooney, illustrated by Samuel Carbaugh. Nomad Press 2016 128 p. color illustrations $22.95; (ebook) $12.99

Grades: 6 7 8 9 10 **540**

1. Chemistry

ISBN 1619303612; 9781619303614; 9781619303621

LC 2016499313

This book in the Inquire and Investigate series, by Carla Mooney, illustrated by Samuel Carbaugh, "introduces readers 12 through 15 to the fascinating world of protons, neutrons, and electrons. Learn how these molecules combine to form ordinary objects such as the chair you're sitting on, the water in your glass, even you!" (Publisher's note)

"Those with a science bent will find the information easily accessible and concise, while those with little interest will be drawn to the colorful graphic illustrations and highlighted sidebars. The experiments provided will inspire and encourage further discovery of the world of science." SLJ

Includes bibliographical references (pages 115-116) and index.

Newmark, Ann

Chemistry; written by Ann Newmark. rev ed; DK Pub. 2005 72p il (DK eyewitness books) $15.99

Grades: 4 5 6 7 **540**

1. Chemistry

ISBN 0-7566-1385-X

First published 1993

Explores the world of chemical reactions and shows the role that chemistry plays in our world.

Stefoff, Rebecca, 1951-

Alchemy and Chemistry; Rebecca Stefoff. Cavendish Square 2014 48 p. ill. (Is it Science?) $29.93

Grades: 6 7 8 **540**

1. Alchemy 2. Chemistry 3. Science -- Popular works

ISBN 1627125094; 9781627125093

LC 2014054653

This middle grade book by Rebecca Stefoff, part of the Is It Science? series, "explores the historical relationships between science and pseudoscience. Though she explains the scientific method in detail and injects healthy doses of skepticism into her accounts, rather than just denigrate pseudosciences as superstition, she shows how . . . alchemy split into equally serious practical and spiritual approaches before the former evolved into modern chemistry." (Publisher's note)

"Each volume is heavily illustrated with period images and modern photographs, and each closes with particularly generous lists of further resources." SLJ

540.7 Education, research, related topics

Gardner, Robert

Ace your chemistry science project; great science fair ideas. [by] Robert Gardner, Salvatore Tocci, and Kenneth G. Rainis. Enslow Publishers 2009 112p il (Ace your science project) lib bdg $31.93

Grades: 5 6 7 8 **540.7**

1. Chemistry 2. Science projects 3. Science -- Experiments

ISBN 978-0-7660-3227-9 lib bdg; 0-7660-3227-2 lib bdg

LC 2008-30800

"Presents several science projects and science project ideas about chemistry." Publisher's note

Includes bibliographical references

Ace your science project using chemistry magic and toys; great science fair ideas. Enslow Publishers 2009 128p il (Ace your science project) lib bdg $31.93

Grades: 5 6 7 8 **540.7**

1. Toys 2. Chemistry 3. Science projects 4. Science -- Experiments

ISBN 978-0-7660-3226-2 lib bdg; 0-7660-3226-4 lib bdg

LC 2008-4685

"Dozens of . . . science activities are presented with background information, step-by-step instructions, and suggestions for extending to the science fair level. . . . Color illustrations and important safety information are included." Horn Book Guide

Includes bibliographical references

★ **Easy** genius science projects with chemistry; great experiments and ideas. Enslow Publishers 2009 112p il (Easy genius science projects) lib bdg $31.93

Grades: 5 6 7 8 **540.7**

1. Chemistry 2. Science projects 3. Science -- Experiments

ISBN 978-0-7660-2925-5 lib bdg; 0-7660-2925-5 lib bdg

LC 2007-38469

This book offers science projects and experiments about chemistry divided into the following chapters: atoms, molecules, elements, and compounds; chemical reactions; oxygen and oxidation; separating and testing substances

"Illustrations are bright and useful in explaining the techniques presented. . . . An excellent resource." Sci Books Films

Includes glossary and bibliographical references

Goodstein, Madeline

Plastics and polymers science fair projects; revised and expanded using the scientific method. Enslow Publishers 2010 160p il (Chemistry science projects using the scientific method) lib bdg $34.60

Grades: 7 8 9 10 **540.7**

1. Plastics 2. Polymers 3. Science projects 4. Science -- Experiments

ISBN 978-0-7660-3412-9 lib bdg; 0-7660-3412-7 lib bdg

LC 2008046504

"Explains how to use the scientific method to conduct several science experiments with plastics and polymers. Includes ideas for science fair projects." Publisher's note

Includes bibliographical references

541 Chemistry

Ballard, Carol

Mixtures and solutions. Raintree 2010 48p il (Sci-hi: physical science) lib bdg $22; pa $8.99

Grades: 5 6 7 8 541

1. Chemistry 2. Molecules

ISBN 978-1-4109-3376-8 lib bdg; 1-4109-3376-8 lib bdg; 978-1-4109-3381-2 pa; 1-4109-3381-4 pa

LC 2009-13452

A "compelling read for both browsers and science buffs. . . . Information is clearly presented and flows smoothly. . . . A treasure trove of information." SLJ

Includes glossary and bibliographical references

Manning, Phillip

Chemical bonds. Chelsea House 2009 134p il (Essential chemistry) lib bdg $35

Grades: 7 8 9 10 541

1. Chemistry

ISBN 978-0-7910-9740-3; 0-7910-9740-4

LC 2008-1981

Examines the nature of the chemical bonds, answering questions about how they form, how they are broken, and how they help define life as we know it

Includes glossary and bibliographical references

Wolny, Philip

Chemical reactions. Rosen Central 2011 64p il (Science made simple) lib bdg $29.25; pa $12.95

Grades: 5 6 7 8 541

1. Chemistry 2. Chemical reactions

ISBN 978-1-4488-1235-6 lib bdg; 1-4488-1235-6 lib bdg; 978-1-4488-2242-3 pa; 1-4488-2242-4 pa

LC 2010018818

This introduction to chemical reactions includes "a lot of detailed information, making [it] useful as [a] resource . . . for science projects and reports. . . . The [book] also [includes a] brief discussion of scientists important in the field, the history of the topic, and current and future applications. . . . The straightforward, no-nonsense [narrative] and simple design make this . . . a nice package for basic science." SLJ

Includes glossary and bibliographical references

542 Techniques, procedures, apparatus, equipment, materials

Connolly, Sean

The **book** of ingeniously daring chemistry; 24 experiments for young scientists. Sean Connolly. Workman Pub Co 2018 256 p. $14.95

Grades: 4 5 6 7 8 542

1. Chemistry 2. Science -- Experiments

ISBN 0761180109; 9780761180104

This book in the Irresponsible Science series, by Sean Connolly, presents "a collection of more than 20 hands-on experiments that are like an interactive journey through the periodic table of elements. . . . [E]ach chapter of . . . [the book] focuses on a single element--its properties, how it was discovered, and even its potential danger level. Easy-to-follow experiments help readers put their newfound knowledge into action." (Publisher's note)

546 Inorganic chemistry

Angliss, Sarah

Gold; [by] Sarah Angliss. Benchmark Bks. 2000 32p il (The elements) lib bdg $28.50

Grades: 5 6 7 8 546

1. Gold

ISBN 978-0-7614-0887-1; 0-7614-0887-8

LC 98-46800

Explores the history of the precious metal gold and explains its chemistry, how it reacts, its uses, and its importance in our lives.

Includes glossary

Beatty, Richard

Boron; [by] Richard Beatty. Marshall Cavendish Benchmark 2005 32p il (The elements) lib bdg $28.50

Grades: 5 6 7 8 546

1. Boron

ISBN 978-0-7614-1921-1; 0-7614-1921-7

LC 2005-42159

"Included in the discussion are the uses of boron in pottery, in the nuclear industry, in living organisms, and in glassmaking. A review of the periodic table and boron's place in it, including the element's relationship to other elements, is provided." Sci Books Films

Includes glossary

The **lanthanides**; [by] Richard Beatty. Marshall Cavendish Benchmark 2008 32p il (The elements) lib bdg $28.50

Grades: 5 6 7 8 546

1. Lanthanides

ISBN 978-0-7614-2687-5; 0-7614-2687-6

LC 2006-53053

Introduces the lanthanide elements, also known as the rare earth metals, discussing their physical and chemical properties, where they are found, and how they are used.

"Provides a comprehensive, yet easy-to-read overview. . . . The explanations are succinct and clear, without being oversimplified, and the layout is attractive. Diagrams and photographs complement the text on every page." SLJ

Includes glossary

Phosphorus; by Richard Beatty. Benchmark Books 2001 32p il (The elements) lib bdg $28.50

Grades: 5 6 7 8 546

1. Phosphorus

ISBN 978-0-7614-0946-5; 0-7614-0946-7

LC 99-88821

Explores the history of the nonmetallic element phosphorus and explains its chemistry, its reactions with other substances, its uses, and its importance in our lives

Offers "clear, basic information, without oversimplification, in an appealing format." SLJ

Includes glossary

Sulfur; [by] Richard Beatty. Benchmark Books 2000 32p il (The elements) lib bdg $28.50

Grades: 5 6 7 8 **546**

1. Sulphur

ISBN 978-0-7614-0948-9; 0-7614-0948-3

LC 99-86992

Explores the history of the element sulfur and explains its chemistry, its reactions with other substances, its uses, and its importance in our lives

Offers "clear, basic information, without oversimplification, in an appealing format." SLJ

Includes glossary

Dingle, Adrian

★ The **periodic** table; elements with style! [created by Simon Basher; written by Adrian Dingle] Kingfisher 2007 128p il pa $8.95

Grades: 4 5 6 7 **546**

1. Chemical elements

ISBN 978-0-7534-6085-6 pa; 0-7534-6085-8 pa

LC 2006022515

"After a brief introduction to Mendeleev's famous table and a spread on the chart-topping loner, hydrogen, Dingle presents the elements by group. . . . Data on featured elements includes symbol, atomic number and weight, color, standard state, classification, density, boiling and melting points, . . . a diagram of the position in the periodic table, a full-page original anime-styled icon, . . . and descriptive paragraphs that rise from informative all the way to entertaining." Bull Cent Child Books

Farndon, John

Aluminum; [by] John Farndon. Benchmark Books 2001 32p il (The elements) lib bdg $28.50

Grades: 5 6 7 8 **546**

1. Aluminum

ISBN 978-0-7614-0947-2; 0-7614-0947-5

Describes the discovery, versatility and other special characteristics, various uses, and affect on the human body of this most common metal in the world.

Includes glossary

Oxygen; [by] John Farndon. Benchmark Bks. 1999 32p il (The elements) lib bdg $28.50

Grades: 5 6 7 8 **546**

1. Oxygen

ISBN 978-0-7614-0879-6; 0-7614-0879-7

LC 97-52236

Explores the history of the chemical element oxygen and explains its chemistry, how it works in the body, and its importance in our lives.

"The captioned, full-color drawings, photographs, and diagrams clarify the text. . . . [This] will be of interest for both general reading and report writing." SLJ

Includes glossary

Furgang, Adam

The **noble** gases; helium, neon, argon, krypton, xenon, radon. Rosen Central 2010 48p il (Understanding the elements of the periodic table) lib bdg $26.50

Grades: 7 8 9 10 **546**

1. Gases 2. Periodic law 3. Chemical elements

ISBN 978-1-4358-3558-0 lib bdg; 1-4358-3558-1 lib bdg

LC 2009014409

This overview discusses "the history of each element, where it can be found, and how it is used in everyday life. . . . Charts show each element's chemical symbol, atomic number, atomic weight, melting point, and boiling point. Colorful photographs and illustrations are included on most pages. Lengthy sidebars highlight key information—some . . . present boxed information on helium versus hydrogen and on the Hindenburg disaster." SLJ

Includes bibliographical references

Goodstein, Madeline

Water science fair projects; revised and expanded using the scientific method. Enslow Publishers 2010 160p il (Chemistry science projects using the scientific method) lib bdg $34.60

Grades: 7 8 9 10 **546**

1. Water 2. Science projects 3. Science -- Experiments

ISBN 978-0-7660-3411-2 lib bdg; 0-7660-3411-9 lib bdg

LC 2008026265

First published 2004 with title: Water science fair projects using ice cubes, super soakers, and other wet stuff

"Explains how to use the scientific method to conduct several science experiments with water. Includes ideas for science fair projects." Publisher's note

Includes bibliographical references

Gray, Leon

Iodine; [by] Leon Gray. Benchmark Books 2005 32p il (The elements) lib bdg $28.50

Grades: 5 6 7 8 **546**

1. Iodine

ISBN 978-0-7614-1812-2; 0-7614-1812-1

LC 2004-47644

"After discussing the structure of the iodine atom and its place on the periodic table, Gray considers its special characteristics, the history of its discovery, and its production and uses, particularly in the medical field. . . . The color illustrations include well-designed, clearly labeled diagrams and many excellent photographs. A solid choice for science collections." Booklist

Includes glossary

Tin; [by] Leon Gray. Benchmark Books 2003 32p il (The elements) lib bdg $28.50

Grades: 5 6 7 8 **546**

1. Tin

ISBN 978-0-7614-1551-0; 0-7614-1551-3

LC 2003-52083

Examines the characteristics, sources, and uses of the element tin, as well as tin's importance in our lives

"Numerous captioned color photos and sidebars augment the accurate and well-organized but information-dense text." Horn Book GUide

Includes glossary

Zinc; [by] Leon Gray. Marshall Cavendish Benchmark 2006 32p il (The elements) lib bdg $28.50

Grades: 5 6 7 8 **546**

1. Zinc

ISBN 978-0-7614-1922-8; 0-7614-1922-5

LC 2005-42163

Discusses zinc and where it can be found, how it was discovered, its special characteristics, and their importance.

"Numerous captioned photos and sidebars augment the accurate and well-organized text." Horn Book Guide

Includes glossary

Green, Dan

The **elements**; Dan Green. Scholastic 2012 105 p. col. ill. (pbk.) $15.99

Grades: 7 8 9 10 11 12 **546**

1. Chemical elements

ISBN 054533019X; 9780545330190

LC 2011278730

This book on the elements, part of the "Discover More" series, is "arranged in single-topic spreads grouped in five chapters based on sections of the Periodic Table." It "highlights either selected single elements or related groups. The layout includes color photos, digital diagrams and images, fact boxes, explanatory captions, and other text in a variety of sizes and weights. . . . A downloadable ebook supplement . . . extends the overall topic." (School Library Journal)

"...This broad introduction is current enough to include mention of Element #117 (probably observed in 2010) and chock-full of basic information cranked up with a generous admixture of "gosh-wow" facts about our universe's building blocks.—" SLJ

Hall, Linley Erin

The **transactinides**; rutherfordium, dubnium, seaborgium, bohrium, hassium, meitnerium, darmstadtium, roentgenium. Rosen Central 2010 48p il (Understanding the elements of the periodic table) lib bdg $26.50

Grades: 5 6 7 8 **546**

1. Periodic law 2. Chemical elements

ISBN 978-1-4358-3559-7 lib bdg; 1-4358-3559-X lib bdg

LC 2009014943

This overview discusses "the history of each element, where it can be found, and how it is used in everyday life. . . . Charts show each element's chemical symbol, atomic number, atomic weight, melting point, and boiling point. Colorful photographs and illustrations are included on most pages. Lengthy sidebars highlight key information. . . . [The book] devotes a chapter to the controversies surrounding naming its elements." SLJ

Includes bibliographical references

Hasan, Heather

Iron; by Heather Hasan. Rosen Pub. Group 2004 48p il (Understanding the elements of the periodic table) lib bdg $26.50

Grades: 5 6 7 8 **546**

1. Iron 2. Periodic law

ISBN 978-1-4042-0157-6; 1-4042-0157-2

LC 2003-22262

Explains the characteristics of iron, where it is found, how it is used by humans, and its relationship to other elements found in the periodic table

Includes bibliographical references

★ **Just** add water; science projects you can sink, squirt, splash & sail. Children's Press 2008 32p il (Experiment with science) lib bdg $25; pa $7.95

Grades: 5 6 7 8 **546**

1. Water 2. Science -- Experiments

ISBN 978-0-531-18545-2 lib bdg; 0-531-18545-1 lib bdg; 978-0-531-18762-3 pa; 0-531-18762-4 pa

LC 2007-21682

"The book consists of nine hands-on activities that target physical science concepts inherent in water (e.g. density, buoyancy, and hardness.) . . . Students . . . will likely find the age-appropriate activities engaging and purposeful. . . . The colorful photos augment the narrative and the science is sound." Sci Books Films

Includes glossary and bibliographical references

La Bella, Laura

The **oxygen** elements; oxygen, sulfur, selenium, tellurium, polonium. Rosen Central 2010 48p il (Understanding the elements of the periodic table) lib bdg $26.50

Grades: 7 8 9 10 **546**

1. Periodic law 2. Chemical elements

ISBN 978-1-4358-3555-9 lib bdg; 1-4358-3555-7 lib bdg

LC 2009012541

This overview discusses "the history of each element, where it can be found, and how it is used in everyday life. . . . Charts show each element's chemical symbol, atomic number, atomic weight, melting point, and boiling point. Colorful photographs and illustrations are included on most pages. Lengthy sidebars highlight key information. . . . [The book] details the use of sulfur in rubber and gunpowder for example." SLJ

Includes bibliographical references

Lepora, Nathan

Chromium; [by] Nathan Lepora. Marshall Cavendish Benchmark 2005 32p il (The elements) lib bdg $28.50

Grades: 5 6 7 8 **546**

1. Chromium

ISBN 978-0-7614-1920-4; 0-7614-1920-9

LC 2005-42160

Discusses chromium and where it can be found, how it was discovered, its special characteristics, and its importance to the human body.

"Numerous captioned photos and sidebars augment the accurate and well-organized text." Horn Book Guide

Includes glossary

Molybdenum; [by] Nathan Lepora. Marshall Cavendish Benchmark 2007 32p il (The elements) lib bdg $28.50

Grades: 5 6 7 8 **546**

1. Molybdenum

ISBN 978-0-7614-2201-3; 0-7614-2201-3

LC 2005-57096

Introduces the element of molybdenum, discussing its physical and chemical properties, where it is found, and what processes or objects it is used in.

"Provides a comprehensive, yet easy-to-read overview in large, bold print. Explanations are concise and clear without being oversimplified, and the arrangement is attractive." SLJ

Includes glossary

Lew, Kristi

The **15** lanthanides and the 15 actinides. Rosen Central 2010 48p il (Understanding the elements of the periodic table) lib bdg $26.50

Grades: 7 8 9 10 **546**

1. Periodic law 2. Chemical elements

ISBN 978-1-4358-3557-3; 1-4358-3557-3

LC 2009014416

This overview discusses "the history of each element, where it can be found, and how it is used in everyday life. . . . Charts show each element's chemical symbol, atomic number, atomic weight, melting point, and boiling point. Colorful photographs and illustrations are included on most pages. Lengthy sidebars highlight key information." SLJ

Includes bibliographical references

Acids and bases. Chelsea House 2008 124p il (Essential chemistry) $35

Grades: 7 8 9 10 **546**

1. Acids 2. Bases (Chemistry)

ISBN 978-0-7910-9783-0; 0-7910-9783-8

LC 2008-24015

"Annotated, colorful photographs and illustrations appear on most spreads, and boxed areas and sidebars highlight specific subjects and areas. The explanations are clear and detailed." SLJ

Includes glossary and bibliographical references

Miller, Ron

★ The **elements**. Twenty-First Century Books 2006 135p il lib bdg $28.90

Grades: 8 9 10 11 12 **546**

1. Chemical elements

ISBN 0-7613-2794-0

LC 2003-20874

Discusses the history of the periodic table of the elements, includes biographies of major figures in the field of chemistry, and provides information on each element.

"A useful overview." SLJ

Includes bibliographical references

O'Daly, Anne

Sodium; [by] Anne O'Daly. Benchmark Books 2001 32p il (The elements) lib bdg $28.50

Grades: 5 6 7 8 **546**

1. Sodium

ISBN 978-0-7614-1271-7; 0-7614-1271-9

LC 2001-25253

Discusses the characteristics, sources, and uses of sodium.

Includes glossary

Oxlade, Chris

Metals; [by] Chris Oxlade. rev. and updated; Heinemann Library 2007 48p il (Chemicals in action) lib bdg $31.43; pa $8.99

Grades: 6 7 8 9 **546**

1. Metals

ISBN 978-1-4329-0054-0 lib bdg; 978-1-4329-0061-8 pa

First published 2002

"This title explores what metals are like, how they are mixed with each other to form alloys, and how they are used to make everything from paper clips to skyscrapers. [It also includes] several experiments that can be done at home." Publisher's note

Includes glossary and bibliographical references

Roza, Greg

The **halogen** elements; fluorine, chlorine, bromine, iodine, astatine. Rosen Central 2010 48p il (Understanding the elements of the periodic table) lib bdg $26.50

Grades: 7 8 9 10 **546**

1. Periodic law 2. Chemical elements

ISBN 978-1-4358-3556-6 lib bdg; 1-4358-3556-5 lib bdg

LC 2009012539

This overview discusses "the history of each element, where it can be found, and how it is used in everyday life. . . . Charts show each element's chemical symbol, atomic number, atomic weight, melting point, and boiling point. Colorful photographs and illustrations are included on most pages. Lengthy sidebars highlight key information." SLJ

Includes bibliographical references

Saunders, N.

Who invented the periodic table? [by] Nigel Saunders. Arcturus Pub. 2010 46p il (Breakthroughs in science and technology) lib bdg $32.80

Grades: 5 6 7 8 **546**

1. Chemists 2. Periodic law

ISBN 978-1-84837-680-9; 1-84837-680-4

LC 2010011016

"After a very brief presentation of atoms and elements, and a short, but comprehensive, view of the modern periodic table, the author presents a series of vignettes, starting with alchemy. Through these vignettes, the reader gets an appreciation of the personalities of, and challenges faced by, key contributors. . . . [This] presents an engaging story behind the story of the discovery of the periodic table." Sci Books & Films

Includes glossary

Sparrow, Giles

Iron; [by] Giles Sparrow. Benchmark Bks. 1999 32p il (The elements) lib bdg $28.50

Grades: 5 6 7 8 **546**

1. Iron

ISBN 978-0-7614-0880-2; 0-7614-0880-0

LC 97-48524

Discusses the origin, discovery, special characteristics, and uses of iron.

Includes glossary

Uttley, Colin

Magnesium; [by] Colin Uttley. Benchmark Bks. 2000 32p il (The elements) lib bdg $28.50

Grades: 5 6 7 8 **546**

1. Magnesium

ISBN 978-0-7614-0889-5; 0-7614-0889-4

LC 98-53200

Explores the history of the bright-colored metal magnesium and explains its chemistry, how it reacts, its uses, and its importance in our lives.

Includes glossary

Watt, Susan

Zirconium; [by] Susan Watt. Marshall Cavendish Benchmark 2008 32p il (The elements) lib bdg $28.50

Grades: 5 6 7 8 **546**

1. Zirconium

ISBN 978-0-7614-2688-2; 0-7614-2688-4

LC 2007-60885

Introduces the element of zirconium, discussing its physical and chemical properties, where it is found, and how it is used.

"Provides a comprehensive, yet easy-to-read overview. . . . The explanations are succinct and clear, without being oversimplified, and the layout is attractive." SLJ

Includes glossary

West, Krista

Bromine; [by] Krista West. Marshall Cavendish Benchmark 2008 32p il (The elements) lib bdg $28.50

Grades: 5 6 7 8 **546**

1. Bromine

ISBN 978-0-7614-2685-1; 0-7614-2685-X

LC 2006-51812

Introduces the element of bromine and its compoinds, discussing its physical and chemical properties, where it is found, and how it is used.

"Provides a comprehensive, yet easy-to-read overview. . . . The explanations are succinct and clear, without being oversimplified, and the layout is attractive. Diagrams and photographs complement the text on every page." SLJ

Includes glossary

Carbon chemistry. Chelsea House 2008 117p il (Essential chemistry) lib bdg $35

Grades: 7 8 9 10 **546**

1. Carbon

ISBN 978-0-7910-9708-3; 0-7910-9708-0

LC 2007-51318

Explains how carbon is integrated into all facets of life as we know it and discusses the unique properties of this essential element.

"Annotated, colorful photographs and illustrations appear on most spreads, and boxed areas and sidebars highlight specific subjects and areas. The explanations are clear and detailed." SLJ

Includes glossary and bibliographical references

Woodford, Chris

Titanium; [by] Chris Woodford. Benchmark Books 2003 32p il (The elements) lib bdg $28.50

Grades: 5 6 7 8 **546**

1. Titanium

ISBN 978-0-7614-1461-2; 0-7614-1461-4

LC 2001-8743

Discusses the characteristics, sources, and uses of the element titanium.

"The well-selected photographs and diagrams are appropriate to the text." Horn Book Guide

Includes glossary

547 Organic chemistry

Gardner, Robert

Organic chemistry science fair projects; revised and expanded using the scientific method. [by] Robert Gardner and Barbara Gardner Conklin. Enslow Publishers 2010 160p il (Chemistry science projects using the scientific method) lib bdg $34.60

Grades: 7 8 9 10 **547**

1. Science projects 2. Organic chemistry 3. Science -- Experiments

ISBN 978-0-7660-3414-3 lib bdg; 0-7660-3414-3 lib bdg

LC 2008050078

First published 2004 with title: Chemistry science fair projects using french fries, gumdrops, soap, and other organic stuff

"Colorful drawings complement the material and illustrations of chemical structures help to convey chemical processes. . . . Useful." SLJ

Includes bibliographical references

549 Mineralogy

Chesterman, Charles W.

The **Audubon** Society field guide to North American rocks and minerals; scientific consultant, Kurt E. Lowe. Knopf 1979 850p il $19.95

Grades: 8 9 10 11 12 Adult **549**

1. Rocks 2. Minerals

ISBN 0-394-50269-8

LC 78-54893

"Pocket guide providing color photos and descriptions of some 232 mineral species and forty types of rocks. Includes guide to mineral environments, glossary, bibliography, and indexes by name and locality." Ref Sources for Small & Medium-sized Libr. 5th edition

Hirsch, Rebecca E., 1969-

Crystals; Rebecca E. Hirsch. Core Library 2015 48 p. color illustrations $32.79

Grades: 5 6 7 **549**

1. Crystals 2. Minerals 3. Mineralogy

ISBN 1624033849; 9781624033841

LC 2014932342

This children's book by Hirsch Rebecca Eileen, part of the Rock and Minerals series, "provides a definition of crystals and describes the six basic categories of crystalline shapes, along with a discussion of how crystals grow, how they break up, and their many everyday uses." (Publisher's note)

"Aligned to Common Core and state standards, the series provides ample opportunity for additional research ("Stop and Think"), hands-on experimentation ("In the Field"), and critical thinking ("Changing Minds") that will have readers looking at the world around them with a better understanding of just what exactly they're seeing. Despite a few issues, these are solid choices." SLJ

Includes bibliographical references (page 47) and index

Pellant, Chris

Rocks and minerals; Helen Pellant, editorial consultant; photography by Harry Taylor. 2nd American ed; Dorling Kindersley 2002 256p il (Smithsonian handbooks) pa $20

Grades: 11 12 Adult **549**

1. Rocks 2. Minerals

ISBN 0-7894-9106-0; 978-0-7894-9106-0

First published 1992 as part of the Eyewitness handbooks series

This field guide to identification of rocks and minerals includes techniques for collection and classification, and facts about physical and chemical composition and formation.

Simon and Schuster's guide to rocks and minerals; edited by Martin Prinz, George Harlow, and Joseph Peters. Simon & Schuster 1978 607p il hardcover o.p. pa $17

Grades: 8 9 10 11 12 Adult **549**

1. Rocks 2. Minerals

ISBN 0-671-24417-5 pa

LC 78-8610

Original Italian edition, 1977

"Half of this book consists of color plates; the other half is an authoritative text which describes the elements of mineralogy and petrology. Crystal system or family, physical and chemical properties, occurrence, uses, and rarity are included for each species." Libr J

550 Earth sciences

Allaby, Michael

Visual encyclopedia of earth. National Geographic 2008 256p il map $24.95; lib bdg $32.90

Grades: 7 8 9 10 **550**

1. Reference books 2. Earth sciences -- Encyclopedias

ISBN 978-1-4263-0366-1; 1-4263-0366-1; 978-1-4263-0367-8 lib bdg; 1-4263-0367-X lib bdg

LC 2008-301484

"This overview of the earth . . . cover[s] all aspects of earth science. . . . [This] is a feast for the eyes and an exceptional introduction to earth science. It will be a useful resource for science teachers who want to engage their students in this subject matter." Libr Media Connect

Bow, James

Earth's secrets. Marshall Cavendish Benchmark 2010 48p il (Invisible worlds) lib bdg $28.50

Grades: 4 5 6 7 **550**

1. Earth sciences

ISBN 978-0-7614-4196-0 lib bdg; 0-7614-4196-4 lib bdg

The narrative is "clear, well written, broken down into manageable pieces, and peppered with eye-opening facts. The numerous photographs are so phenomenal that they will inspire kids to read the text . . . so that they can wrap their minds around what they see." SLJ

Includes glossary and bibliographical references

Calhoun, Yael

Earth science fair projects; revised and expanded using the scientific method. Enslow Publishers 2010 160p il (Earth science projects using the scientific method) lib bdg $34.60

Grades: 7 8 9 10 **550**

1. Earth sciences 2. Science projects 3. Science -- Experiments

ISBN 978-0-7660-3425-9 lib bdg; 0-7660-3425-9 lib bdg

First published 2005 with title: Earth science fair projects using rocks, minerals, magnets, mud, and more

"Each volume begins with an overview of the scientific method and safety, then presents a collection of activities encouraging readers to explore central concepts in the featured fields. The activities include step-by-step instructions and helpful color diagrams, interspersed with extended coverage of scientific ideas. The "Results" sections ask questions rather than giving away the answers. Reading list, websites." (Horn Book)

Includes glossary and bibliographical references

Earth; the definitive visual guide. editors-in-chief, James F. Luhr and Jeffrey E. Post. Revised and updated ed. DK Publishing 2013 528 p. ill. (chiefly col.) (hbk.) $50

Grades: 8 9 10 11 12 Adult **550**

1. Earth 2. Earth (Planet) 3. Earth (Planet) -- Pictorial works

ISBN 1465414371; 9781465414373

LC 2013444093

First published 2003

This book, edited by James F. Luhr, presents "insight into the forces and processes that formed our environment and which continue to influence its evolution. With thousands of . . . photographs and unique visual catalogues of the features and phenomena that take place on Earth -- such as rocks, minerals, and mountains to tropical rain forests and the different types of clouds -- [it] contains the most up-to-date ideas on how our world works." (Publisher's note)

"Specially commissioned new 3-D digital artwork provides a striking, informative guide to the features of our planet, explains the scientific processes that govern our world, and looks at the complex relationship between humans and the natural environment." Publisher's note

Gilpin, Daniel

Planet Earth; what planet are you on? created by Basher; written by Dan Gilpin. Kingfisher 2010 128p il $14.99; pa $8.99

Grades: 5 6 7 8 **550**

1. Earth sciences

ISBN 978-0-7534-6616-2; 0-7534-6616-3; 978-0-7534-6412-0 pa; 0-7534-6412-8 pa

LC 2010015976

Presents concepts in earth sciences using lively descriptions and cartoon illustrations personifying each concept.

"The authors blend a surprising wealth of facts into the chatty, humorous text, which is filled with analogies kids can relate to. . . . The highly approachable language, animated cast of characters, awe-inspiring facts, and conservation messages make this an appealing starting point for students seeking basic earth-science information." Booklist

550.78 Earth science experiments

VanCleave, Janice Pratt, 1942-

Step -by-step science experiments in earth science; by Janice VanCleave. Rosen Pub. 2013 80 p. col. ill. (library) $33.25; (paperback) $14.15

Grades: 5 6 7 8 **550.78**

1. Earth sciences 2. Science -- Experiments 3. Earth sciences -- Experiments

ISBN 1448869838; 9781448869831; 9781448884674

LC 2012007944

This book by Janice VanCleave is part of the First-Place Science Fair Projects series. The books have an introduction to the subject—here, earth science, followed by 22 simple . . . experiments. Van Cleave states the basic goal of the experiments, followed by a list of necessary materials, most of which can be found around the house or easily acquired with minimal cost. Step-by-step instructions are clearly detailed and accompanied by diagrams where needed." (School Library Journal)

Includes bibliographical references (p. 78) and index.

551 Geology, hydrology, meteorology

Kelly, Erica

★ **Evolving** planet; [by] Erica Kelly & Richard Kissel. Harry N. Abrams 2008 136p il map $19.95

Grades: 5 6 7 8 **551**

1. Evolution 2. Earth 3. Field Museum of Natural History

ISBN 978-0-8109-9486-7; 0-8109-9486-0

LC 2007-36342

"Based on a exhibit at Chicago's Field Museum, this big spacious volume packs in a wealth of information about evolution over four billion years. . . . There are detailed, beautiful photographs and glorious paintings on every double-page spread and the chatty text is accessible for grade-schoolers." Booklist

Includes glossary and bibliographical references

551.1 Gross structure and properties of the earth

Reilly, Kathleen M.

Fault lines & tectonic plates; discover what happens when the Earth's crust moves. by Kathleen M. Reilly, illustrated by Chad Thompson. Nomad Press 2017 122 p. color ill., color maps $22.95; (ebook) $12.99

Grades: 4 5 6 7 **551.1**

1. Earth -- Surface 2. Volcanoes 3. Earthquakes

ISBN 1619304619; 9781619304611; 9781619304628

LC 2017000861

In this book, by Kathleen M. Reilly, illustrated by Chad Thompson, "readers ages 9 through 12 learn what exactly is going on under the dirt. When slowly drifting continents bump up against each other along fault lines we experience earthquakes, volcanoes, and tidal waves! Mountains and trenches are visible results of the slow movement of the earth's crust, as tectonic plates create the landscape of our world over time." (Publisher's note)

Includes bibliographical references (pages 118-119) and index.

Saunders, Craig

What is the theory of plate tectonics? Crabtree Pub. Co. 2011 64p il (Shaping modern science) lib bdg $30.60; pa $10.95

Grades: 5 6 7 8 **551.1**

1. Plate tectonics 2. Geophysicists 3. Meteorologists 4. College teachers

ISBN 978-0-7787-7202-6 lib bdg; 0-7787-7202-0 lib bdg; 978-0-7787-7209-5 pa; 0-7787-7209-8 pa

LC 2010-52622

This title is "not only written and organized well, but [it is] also gorgeous in design. Full-color photographs and illustrations are set over colorful backgrounds that add depth but not distraction. [The title] includes thought-provoking quotes from famous authors and scientists and some eyebrow-raising 'Quick Facts' throughout." SLJ

Includes glossary and bibliographical references

551.2 Volcanoes, earthquakes, thermal waters and gases

Fradin, Judith Bloom

Earthquakes; witness to disaster. by Judy and Dennis Fradin. National Geographic 2008 48p map (Witness to disaster) $16.95; lib bdg $26.90

Grades: 4 5 6 7 **551.2**

1. Earthquakes

ISBN 978-1-4263-0211-4; 1-4263-0211-8; 978-1-4263-0212-1 lib bdg; 1-4263-0212-6 lib bdg

LC 2007044164

"The combination of good writing and excellent graphics paired with archival and personal perspectives makes this book a valuable addition." SLJ

Includes glossary and bibliographical references

Volcanoes; by Judy and Dennis Fradin. National Geographic 2007 48p il map (Witness to disaster) $16.95; lib bdg $26.90

Grades: 4 5 6 7 **551.2**

1. Volcanoes

ISBN 978-0-7922-5376-1; 0-7922-5376-0; 978-0-7922-5377-8 lib bdg; 0-7922-5377-9 lib bdg

LC 2006-102817

This "introduces readers to these violent eruptions, using eyewitness accounts to explain the history and science involved. They begin with a report of the 1943 birth of a volcano in Paricutín, Mexico. . . . Subsequent chapters describe other celebrated volcanoes, explain their causes and types, note the benefits of these eruptions, and clarify how they are currently predicted. . . . Numerous clear, well-chosen photographs and diagrams help to convey the great power of volcanic activity and the consequences to humans. . . . This will be useful for report writers, and a fascinating pick for browsers." Booklist

Includes bibliographical references

Hague, Bradley

Alien deep; Revealing the Mysterious Living World at the Bottom of the Ocean. by Bradley Hague. National Geographic 2012 48 p. col. ill. (hardcover : alk. paper) $17.95

Grades: 5 6 7 8 **551.2**

1. Oceanography -- Research 2. Hydrothermal vent ecology 3. Natural history -- Galapagos Islands 4. Hydrothermal vents 5. Hydrothermal vent animals

ISBN 1426310676; 9781426310676; 9781426310683

LC 2012012939

This book by Bradley Hague "depicts adventurous and thrilling elements in oceanographic fieldwork in conjunction with a National Geographic television show." (Publisher's note) "The book takes readers along on the 2011 exploration of vents in the Galapagos Reef area of the Pacific Ocean. . . . Future scientists will be hooked by the excitement of finding newly developing vents and the disappointment of finding older vents that once disappeared under layers of magma." (Booklist)

Includes bibliographical references and index.

Nargi, Lela

★ **Absolute** expert volcanoes; Lela Nargi, with National Geographic explorer Arianna Soldati. National Geographic 2018 112 p. color illustrations, color map (Absolute expert) $14.99

Grades: 4 5 6 7 8 **551.2**

1. Geology 2. Volcanoes 3. Science 4. National Geographic Society (U.S) -- Photograph collections

ISBN 1426331428; 1426331436; 9781426331428; 9781426331435

LC 2018289128

"Plunge deep beneath Earth's crust to find out how volcanoes form. Get up close to clouds of ash and molten lava. Learn about the biggest, most extreme volcanic eruptions to date. On the hunt for incredible volcanoes, you'll travel around the globe, dive into the depths of the oceans, journey into space...and so much more!" (Publisher's note)

"The books' attractive design and tone will appeal to casual readers, but even those with serious interests will unearth scads of new information." Booklist

Includes bibliographical references (page 108) and index

Silverstein, Alvin

Earthquakes; the science behind seismic shocks and tsunamis. [by] Alvin Silverstein, Virginia Silverstein, and Laura

Silverstein Nunn. Enslow Publishers 2010 48p il map (The science behind natural disasters) lib bdg $23.93

Grades: 4 5 6 **551.2**

1. Tsunamis 2. Earthquakes

ISBN 978-0-7660-2975-0 lib bdg; 0-7660-2975-1 lib bdg

LC 2008-38589

"Scientific explanations are accompanied by plentiful color diagrams that will help students to grasp causes and effects. . . . Photos . . . are effective, and are sometimes turned into helpful, lively diagrams by the addition of such features as wind-direction arrows." SLJ

Includes glossary and bibliographical references

Stewart, Melissa

Inside Earthquakes. Sterling Publishing Co., Inc. 2011 48p il map (Inside . . .) $16.95; pa $9.95

Grades: 5 6 7 8 **551.2**

1. Earthquakes

ISBN 978-1-4027-5877-5; 978-1-4027-8163-6 pa

LC 2010046452

This book about earthquakes "explores its topic in an engaging way, and the many illustrations work well with adjacent text and captions. . . . The [book's] varied page layouts and attractive and the quality of photos, computer-generated images, original illustrations, and charts is . . . excellent. . . . [The book] looks at the geology of the earth's crust as well as the effects of quakes on people and cities, landforms and coastlines." Booklist

Includes bibliographical references

Inside Volcanoes. Sterling Publishing Co. 2011 48p il map (Inside) $16.95; pa $9.95

Grades: 5 6 7 8 **551.2**

1. Volcanoes

ISBN 978-1-4027-5876-8; 1-4027-5876-6; 978-1-4027-8164-3 pa; 1-4027-8164-4 pa

LC 2010046451

Examines the nature of volcanoes, how they are formed, what they look like, and how they are measured, in a text with ten foldout pages.

"With pages that fold out or flip up, well-reproduced photographs of volcanoes at rest and in action, diagrams, maps, charts, timelines and short explanations, there is much to look at and to learn. . . . Appropriately for a book that is clearly designed to stimulate interest, there are solid suggestions for both books and websites for further exploration. A good starting-place for volcano explorations." Kirkus

Winchester, Simon

★ **When** the earth shakes; earthquakes, volcanoes, and tsunamis. Simon Winchester. Viking 2015 71 p. color ill., color maps (hardcover) $18.99

Grades: 5 6 7 8 **551.2**

1. Earthquakes 2. Tsunamis 3. Volcanoes 4. Earthquakes -- Psychological aspects

ISBN 9780670785360

LC 2014039743

In this book, by Simon Winchester,"Earthquakes, volcanoes, tsunamis making natural disasters with devastating consequences for millions of people.The author who's been shaken by earthquakes in New Zealand . . .looks at the science, technology, and societal impact of these interconnected natural phenomena. . . .And the earthquake that flattened San Francisco, to the 21st-century tsunamis that devastated Indonesia and Japan." (Publisher's note)

"A must-buy for libraries serving middle school, this title works both as a basic overview of earth science and as a fine example of how to incorporate personal narrative into nonfiction" SLJ

Includes bibliographical references (page 66) and index.

551.3 Surface and exogenous processes and their agents

Rusch, Elizabeth

Impact! asteroids and the science of saving the world. by Elizabeth Rusch ; photos by Karin Anderson. Houghton Mifflin Harcourt 2017 80 p. (hardcover) $18.99

Grades: 6 7 8 9 10 **551.3**

1. Asteroids 2. Meteorites 3. Extinction (Biology) 4. Asteroids -- Collisions with Earth

ISBN 9780544671591

LC 2016030626

School Library Journal Best Books (2017)

In this book in the Scientists in the Field Series, "follow the award-winning author Elizabeth Rusch, [with photographer Karin Anderson,] into the field with scientists as they search for dangerous asteroids in space, study asteroids that have smashed into the ground, and make plans to prevent an asteroid strike if one ever threatens our planet." (Publisher's note)

"Accompanied by photographs of scientists in action and requisite space shots, the book concludes with citizen science connections and resources and is sure to have an impact on young astronomers." Booklist

551.4 Geomorphology and hydrosphere

Berlatsky, Noah

Water and ice; Michael E. Mann, consulting editor. Greenhaven Press 2011 120p il map (Confronting global warming) lib bdg $37.10

Grades: 7 8 9 10 11 **551.4**

1. Ice 2. Glaciers 3. Greenhouse effect

ISBN 978-0-7377-4861-1; 0-7377-4861-3

LC 2010011348

"After useful introductions to climate change science and background information on related atmospheric and oceanic sciences, the volumes examine the rise of average global and ocean temperatures. Evidence for and against causal relationships between these increases and extreme weather events such as hurricanes, droughts, and heat waves are then thoughtfully discussed. Some color photographs and diagrams are included." (Horn Book)

Includes glossary and bibliographical references

551.45 Plane and coastal regions

Thomas, Keltie

Rising seas; flooding, climate change and our new world. Keltie Thomas, illustrated by Belle Wuthrich, Kathy Boake. Firefly Books Ltd 2018 64 p. (hardcover : alk. paper) $19.95

Grades: 4 5 6 7 **551.45**

1. Floods 2. Climate change 3. Sea level -- Forecasting

ISBN 9780228100218; 9780228100225

LC 2017954639

This book, by Keltie Thomas, illustrated by Belle Wuthrich and Kathy Boake, "gives youth an eye-popping view of what the Earth might look like under the rising and falling water levels of climate change. Photographs juxtapose the present-day with that same area's projected future. The shocking images will help them understand the urgency for action." (Publisher's note)

551.46 Oceanography and submarine geology

Aronin, Miriam

Slammed by a tsunami! Bearport Pub. 2010 32p il map (Disaster survivors) lib bdg $25.27

Grades: 4 5 6 7 **551.46**

1. Tsunamis

ISBN 978-1-936087-48-8 lib bdg; 1-936087-48-0 lib bdg

LC 2009-34574

"Captivating photos and illustrations and sidebars present interesting facts or brief anecdotes. . . . [This] should be purchased for all school and public libraries as . . . [it gives] a new perspective on the topic." Libr Media Connect

Includes glossary and bibliographical references

Bodden, Valerie

To the ocean deep; by Valerie Bodden. Creative Education 2011 48 p. col. ill. (Great expeditions) (library) $34.25

Grades: 5 6 7 8 **551.46**

1. Ocean 2. Underwater exploration 3. Explorers -- Biography 4. Trieste (Bathyscaphe) -- History 5. Bathyscaphe -- History -- 20th century 6. Underwater exploration -- History -- 20th century

ISBN 1608180670; 9781608180677

LC 2010033416

This book by Valerie Bodden is part of the Great Expeditions series and looks at oceanic exploration expeditions. "Bodden includes brief biographies of major people involved in each expedition, interspersed with the text. There are also numerous photographs or reproductions of paintings and woodcuts from the time of the expeditions." (Library Media Connection)

Includes bibliographical references (p. 46-47) and index.

Burns, Loree Griffin

★ **Tracking** trash; flotsam, jetsam, and the science of ocean motion. Houghton Mifflin 2007 56p il map (Scientists in the field) $18

Grades: 5 6 7 8 **551.46**

1. Pollution 2. Ocean currents 3. Oceanographers 4. Marine debris

ISBN 0-618-58131-6; 978-0-618-58131-3

LC 2006-11534

Boston Globe-Horn Book Honor: Nonfiction (2007)

This book describes "Curt Ebbesmeyer's ongoing work. . . . The oceanographer has been tracing the surface currents of the seas via the movement of plastic rubbish that has escaped from broken cargo containers. [Index.] Grades five to nine." (Bull Cent Child Books)

"The book profiles two oceanographers who devised experiments using computer-modeling programs of ocean surface current movement to predict the landfall of . . . drifting objects. . . . Spacious layout, exceptionally fine color photos, and handsome maps give this book an inviting look. . . . A unique and often fascinating book." Booklist

Includes glossary and bibliographical references

Fradin, Judith Bloom

Tsunamis; witness to disaster. [by] Judy & Dennis Fradin. National Geographic 2008 48p il map (Witness to disaster) $16.95; lib bdg $20.90

Grades: 4 5 6 7 **551.46**

1. Tsunamis

ISBN 978-0-7922-5380-8; 0-7922-5380-9; 978-0-7922-5381-5 lib bdg; 0-7922-5381-7 lib bdg

LC 2008010536

This "explores the science, history, and personal experience of tsunamis and shows kids what scientists are doing to develop early warning systems so we can survive such disasters in the future." Publisher's note

Includes glossary and bibliographical references

Friedman, Lauri S.

Oceans; Lauri S. Friedman, book editor. Greenhaven Press 2011 (Introducing issues with opposing viewpoints) $36.82

Grades: 7 8 9 10 **551.46**

1. Ocean 2. Marine pollution

ISBN 978-0-7377-5200-7; 0-7377-5200-9

LC 2011005910

"These volumes present previously published articles and essays from journals, magazines, and websites to provide opposing viewpoints about alternative energy sources and environmental threats to Earth's oceans. Though the many photographs, sidebars, and charts make the books visually approachable, the lack of contextual information about primary sources makes for texts that are more inflammatory than useful." (Horn Book)

Includes bibliographical references

Kusky, Timothy M.

Tsunamis; giant waves from the sea. [by] Timothy Kusky. Facts on File 2008 134p il (The hazardous Earth) $39.50

Grades: 8 9 10 11 12 **551.46**

1. Tsunamis

ISBN 978-0-8160-6464-9; 0-8160-6464-4

LC 2007-23477

"This detailed study of the causes and physics of massive waves covers not only the oceanic sort but also similar phenomena, 'seiches,' that occur in closed bodies of water. . . . After analyzing tsunamis' various forms and behaviors, Kusky delivers harrowing accounts of over a dozen disasters, from those centuries past to the devastating Indian Ocean tsunami in 2004. He then closes with a discussion of early-warning systems. Occasional photos capture the devastation of which these waves are capable." Booklist

Includes bibliographical references

MacQuitty, Miranda

Eyewitness ocean; written by Miranda MacQuitty ; photographed by Frank Greenaway. DK Publishing 2008 72 p. illustrations (chiefly color) $9.99

Grades: 4 5 6 7 **551.46**

1. Ocean 2. Marine animals 3. Marine biology 4. Marine ecology 5. Ocean

ISBN 1465420541; 1465420967; 9780756637767; 9781465420541

LC 2008276032

In this book, by Miranda MacQuitty, "dive in and discover the watery world covering most of our earth and the amazing wildlife in its depths. . . . Through images, maps and informative text learn about life on the shore to the darkest depths of the ocean floor, including predators and prey, gas and oil exploration, products of the ocean, brave explorers and what the human race can do to help preserve one of the earth's most valuable resources." (Publisher's note)

Mallory, Kenneth

Adventure beneath the sea; living in an underwater science station. [photographs by Brian Skerry] Boyds Mills Press 2010 48p il map $18.95

Grades: 4 5 6 7 **551.46**

1. Underwater exploration

ISBN 978-1-59078-607-9; 1-59078-607-6

The author "invites readers to squeeze into Aquarius, a venerable science-station habitat resting on the sea floor at a depth of 60 feet in the Florida Keys. The readable text explains the complexities of training for a weeklong stay, the aims of the scientists on the team, and what it is like to spend 24/7 in squashed companionship in a 43' × 9' cylinder as part of a crew of seven. . . . Sidebars contain interesting information. . . . Full-color photos abound." SLJ

Includes glossary and bibliographical references

Oceans; Lauri S. Friedman, book editor. Greenhaven Press 2011 144 p. (Introducing issues with opposing viewpoints) (hardcover) $36.82 **551.46**

1. Ocean 2. Marine pollution 3. Marine resources conservation

ISBN 9780737752007; 0737752009

LC 2011005910

"These volumes present previously published articles and essays from journals, magazines, and websites to provide opposing viewpoints about alternative energy sources and environmental threats to Earth's oceans. Though the many photographs, sidebars, and charts make the books visually approachable, the lack of contextual information about primary sources makes for texts that are more inflammatory than useful." (Horn Book)

Includes bibliographical references and index

551.48 Hydrology

Amstutz, Lisa J.

Bringing back our freshwater lakes; Lisa J. Amstutz. Abdo Pub. 2018 112 p. $37.07

Grades: 7 8 9 10 **551.48**

1. Lakes 2. Environmental protection 3. Conservation of natural resources

ISBN 9781532113147; 9781532152023

LC 2017946774

This book in the Conservation Success Stories series, by Lisa J. Amstutz, "explains why freshwater lakes are at risk and how people are combating overfishing, cleaning up polluted waters, and preserving our freshwater lakes for future generations. This title also explores the science behind watersheds and the water cycle. Features include a cause-and-effect flow chart, a glossary, references, websites, source notes, and an index." (Publisher's note)

Gardner, Robert

Water; green science projects for a sustainable planet. Enslow Publishers 2011 128p il (Team Green science projects) lib bdg $31.93

Grades: 6 7 8 9 10 **551.48**

1. Water 2. Science projects 3. Science -- Experiments

ISBN 978-0-7660-3645-1; 0-7660-3645-6

LC 2009-37902

This book offers science experiments that explain the properties of water, the water cycle, and how you can conserve water.

"Gardner takes familiar experiments geared toward motivated science learners and gives them an eco-twist. Some are straightforward demonstrations of basic science while others explore aspects of alternative and sustainable science and technologies. Sections of background information further expand the green science coverage. Photographs and diagrams help illustrate the necessary equipment and setups.' (Horn Book)

Includes glossary and bibliographical references

Peters, Marilee

10 rivers that shaped the world; by Marilee Peters ; illustrated by Kim Rosen. Firefly Books Ltd 2015 135 p. $24.95

Grades: 4 5 6 7 **551.48**

1. Rivers 2. Nile River 3. Rhine River 4. Amazon River 5. Tigris River 6. Yangtze River 7. Euphrates River 8. Mississippi River 9. Thames River (England) 10. Ganges River (India and Bangladesh) 11. Rivers -- History 12. Rivers -- Social aspects -- History

ISBN 1554517397; 9781554517398

This book, by Marilee Peters, illustrated by Kim Rosen, presents "10 surprising stories about the power of rivers through the ages." (Publisher's note)

"Each of the 10 rivers detailed in this book has its own chapter, which includes chronological narratives about the groups of people who have called the river home. Full-color maps show each river's headwaters and terminus, and photographs detail major cultural attractions, wildlife, and artifacts. . . . The book is intent on helping young readers make the connection between physical and human geography and on understanding the myriad of forces that shape a people's culture. With a colorful, engaging layout and a unique approach to its topic, this title is a solid entry point to both geography and world history." Booklist

551.5 Meteorology

Cosgrove, Brian

Weather; written by Brian Cosgrove. Relaunch edition DK Publishing 2016 72p il map (DK eyewitness books) library $19.99

Grades: 4 5 6 7 **551.5**

1. Climate 2. Weather 3. Atmosphere

ISBN 9781465451811

First published 1991 by Knopf

"Discover the world's weather—from heat waves and droughts to blizzards and floods"—Cover. Includes discussion of why the climate may change in the future.

"Accompanying the book are a poster, additional images on CD-ROM, and a useful glossary. Altogether, this book and its supplements are well crafted to motivate young learners about the importance of weather, to deepen their conceptual understanding of it, and to pique their interest in participating in its study." Sci Books Films

Includes glossary

DeLallo, Laura

Hammered by a heat wave! consultants, Daphne Thompson, Keith C. Heidorn. Bearport Pub. 2010 32p il map (Disaster survivors) lib bdg $25.27

Grades: 4 5 6 7 **551.5**

1. Meteorology

ISBN 978-1-936087-51-8 lib bdg; 1-936087-51-0 lib bdg

"Captivating photos and illustrations and sidebars present interesting facts or brief anecdotes. . . . [This] should be purchased for all school and public libraries as . . . [it gives] a new perspective on the topic." Libr Media Connect

Includes glossary and bibliographical references

Roker, Al, 1954-

Al Roker's Extreme Weather; Tornadoes, Typhoons, and Other Weather Phenomena. Al Roker. Harper 2017 48 p. ill., photographs, maps

Grades: 3 4 5 6 **551.5**

1. Storms 2. Climate 3. Weather 4. Extreme weather

ISBN 9780062484994

This book by Al Roker provides a look at weather phenomena both common place and extraordinary. "Readers will learn about the conditions that generate unique weather occurrences like red sprites, thundersnow, and fogsicles. Surprising facts, colorful spreads, and captivating pictures will hook children and adults alike as they uncover the mysteries of extreme weather—some they never even knew existed!" (Publisher's note)

Streissguth, Thomas

Extreme weather; [by] Tom Streissguth; Michael E. Mann, consulting editor. Greenhaven Press/Gale, Cengage Learning 2011 116p il map (Confronting global warming) lib bdg $37.10

Grades: 7 8 9 10 11 12 **551.5**

1. Weather 2. Climate -- Environmental aspects

ISBN 978-0-7377-4859-8; 0-7377-4859-1

LC 2010-24973

"Presented in a scholarly design that will appeal to older readers. . . . The illustrations and pictures support the text, and the graphics and sidebars are well placed." Libr Media Connect

Includes glossary and bibliographical references

U-X-L encyclopedia of weather and natural disasters; Amy Hackney Blackwell, editor ; Elizabeth Manar, project editor. Second edition U-X-L, a part of Gale Cengage Learning 2016 1200 p. color illustrations (set : alk. paper) $458.00

Grades: 9 10 11 12 Adult **551.5**

1. Meteorology 2. Natural disasters 3. Meteorology -- Encyclopedias, Juvenile 4. Natural disasters -- Encyclopedias, Juvenile

ISBN 141033290X; 9781410332905

LC 2015032053

This book, edited by Amy Hackney Blackwell, "is a revision and update of the 2008 edition that presents comprehensive, up-to-date information on weather and climate basics, weather conditions and phenomena, natural disasters, forecasting, and human influences on weather and climate. Approximately 300 entries, arranged alphabetically across a five volume set, introduce students to the science behind the topics in clear, nontechnical language." (Publisher's note)

"Each of the five volumes concludes with a comprehensive list of books, periodicals, and websites for further information, and a general index. This set would be a welcome addition to public or middle-school libraries." Booklist

Includes bibliographical references and index

551.55 Atmospheric disturbances and formations

Aronin, Miriam

Mangled by a hurricane! consultant, James L. Franklin. Bearport Pub. 2010 32p il map (Disaster survivors) lib bdg $25.27

Grades: 4 5 6 7 **551.55**

1. Hurricanes 2. Hurricane Katrina, 2005

ISBN 978-1-936087-49-5 lib bdg; 1-936087-49-9 lib bdg

"Captivating photos and illustrations and sidebars present interesting facts or brief anecdotes. . . . [This] should be purchased for all school and public libraries as . . . [it gives] a new perspective on the topic." Libr Media Connect

Includes glossary and bibliographical references

Carson, Mary Kay

★ **Inside** hurricanes. Sterling 2010 48p il map (Inside) $16.95; pa $9.95

Grades: 5 6 7 8 **551.55**

1. Hurricanes

ISBN 978-1-4027-5880-5; 1-4027-5880-4; 978-1-4027-7780-6 pa; 1-4027-7780-9 pa

"This trip into the eye of the storm is enveloping in more ways than one. . . . The pages fold up, or down, or left, or right, with every turn guided by an icon familiar to anyone who lives in a storm zone: a circular blue 'Hurricane Evacuation Route' road sign. This constant motion can't help but engage. . . . The design and layout is well above par, featuring excellent cutaways of storm systems, meteorological maps, thrilling photography, and a spectacular foldout Saffir-Simpson Hurricane Scale. The text is packed with info, data, and case studies broken into digestible chunks, and boxes and sidebars . . . make this . . . very appealing." Booklist

★ **Inside** tornadoes. Sterling 2010 48p il map (Inside) $16.95; pa $9.95

Grades: 5 6 7 8 **551.55**

1. Tornadoes

ISBN 978-1-4027-5879-9; 1-4027-5879-0; 978-1-4027-7781-3 pa; 1-4027-7781-7 pa

"This visually tempting title defines and explains the storms people call twisters, gives examples of four particularly devastating ones in this country, describes tornado watchers at work, offers hands-on activity and suggests precautions for tornado safety. . . . It includes step-by-step explanatory text, striking images and helpful graphics." Kirkus

Includes glossary and bibliographical references

Fleisher, Paul

Lightning, hurricanes, and blizzards; the science of storms. Lerner Publications 2011 48p il (Weatherwise) lib bdg $29.27

Grades: 4 5 6 7 **551.55**

1. Blizzards 2. Lightning 3. Hurricanes

ISBN 978-0-8225-7536-8; 0-8225-7536-1

LC 2009044918

This describes how storms form, where they strike, and what makes them so powerful.

"Chapters are well-organized and contain clear explanations. The crisp layout contains plenty of captioned photos and diagrams, as well as sidebars that feature interesting facts and suggestions for observations readers can record in their backyards." Horn Book Guide

Includes glossary and bibliographical references

Fradin, Dennis Brindell

Tornado! the story behind these twisting, turning, spinning, and spiraling storms. by Judith Bloom Fradin & Dennis Brindell Fradin. National Geographic 2011 63p il map (National Geographic kids) $16.95; lib bdg $26.90

Grades: 4 5 6 7 **551.55**

1. Tornadoes

ISBN 978-1-4263-0779-9; 1-4263-0779-9; 978-1-4263-0780-5 lib bdg; 1-4263-0780-2 lib bdg

LC 2010042813

"Two of the four chapters describe deadly twisters in the U.S., while the others discuss the science and predictability of tornadoes. Throughout, there are first-person accounts. . . . Excellent color photos make this book a magnet for browsers, while the informative text and diagrams bring meaning to the images and provide content that students will find helpful for reports." Booklist

Includes glossary and bibliographical references

Fradin, Judith Bloom

Hurricanes; by Judy and Dennis Fradin. National Geographic 2007 48p il (Witness to disaster) $16.95; lib bdg $26.90

Grades: 4 5 6 7 **551.55**

1. Hurricanes

ISBN 978-1-4262-0111-0; 1-4262-0111-7; 978-1-4262-0112-7 lib bdg; 1-4262-0112-5 lib bdg

LC 2006-103003

This describes Hurricane Katrina, the science of hurricanes, some hurricanes of the past, and the prediction of hurricanes.

This offers "dramatic first-person quotes and an array of impressive photographs." Horn Book Guide

Includes glossary and bibliographical references

Markovics, Joyce L.

Blitzed by a blizzard! by Joyce Markovics; consultant, Daphne Thompson. Bearport Pub. 2010 32p il map (Disaster survivors) lib bdg $25.27

Grades: 4 5 6 7 **551.55**

1. Blizzards

ISBN 978-1-936087-54-9 lib bdg; 1-936087-54-5 lib bdg

LC 2009-36960

"Captivating photos and illustrations and sidebars present interesting facts or brief anecdotes. . . . [This] should be purchased for all school and public libraries as . . . [it gives] a new perspective on the topic." Libr Media Connect

Includes glossary and bibliographical references

Miller, Ron

Chasing the storm; tornadoes, meteorology, and weather watching. by Ron Miller. Twenty-First Century Books 2014 64 p. color illustrations (lib. bdg. : alk. paper) $33.26

Grades: 6 7 8 **551.55**

1. Storm chasers 2. Tornadoes

ISBN 1467712841; 9781467712842

LC 2013009291

This book "offers a window into the world of scientists and lay enthusiasts who follow violent storms, particularly tornadoes." Author Ron Miller "explains how tornadoes are formed, discusses climate change and its probable connection to the increase in extreme weather events, describes the work of meteorologists and others who watch the weather . . . and concludes by suggesting ways readers can prepare to become storm chasers themselves." (Kirkus Reviews)

"This pleasing book on storm chasers is packed with information. Supported by colorful visuals and succinct explanations, the book takes a multimedia approach to presenting the phenomena of storms and the people who chase them. Hurricanes, tornadoes, and weather in general, are some of the topics covered, as well as tips on meteorology as a career. Included is a hands-on experience to build a weather station. The reading level is rigorous but not inaccessible to struggling readers, as comprehension is aided by the graphs and illustrations." Lib Med Con

Includes bibliographical references and index

Prokos, Anna

Tornadoes; by Anna Prokos. Gareth Stevens Pub. 2009 48p il map (The ultimate 10. Natural disasters) lib bdg $31

Grades: 5 6 7 8 **551.55**

1. Tornadoes

ISBN 978-0-8368-9153-9 lib bdg; 0-8368-9153-8 lib bdg

LC 2008-18949

Tornadoes "are described, while color photos illustrate the resulting damage, conveying a significant part of the information through their captions. . . . Explanations of weather terms . . . are included; additional facts are boxed off from the text; and preparation/safety tips are appended. . . . An especially useful book." SLJ

Includes glossary and bibliographical references

Royston, Angela

Hurricanes! Marshall Cavendish Benchmark 2010 32p il map (Eyewitness disaster) lib bdg $28.50

Grades: 4 5 6 **551.55**

1. Hurricanes

ISBN 978-1-60870-003-5; 1-60870-003-8

LC 2010001800

Provides information about hurricanes through eyewitness accounts from survivors and rescue workers.

"Bold subheadings and color captions break information into readable chunks for the younger learner. Important vocabulary is in bold print. . . . An excellent addition to your science collection." Libr Media Connect

Includes glossary and bibliographical references

Storms! Marshall Cavendish Benchmark 2010 32p il map (Eyewitness disaster) lib bdg $28.50

Grades: 4 5 6 **551.55**

1. Storms

ISBN 978-1-60870-004-2; 1-60870-004-6

LC 2009041697

Provides information about storms through eyewitness accounts from survivors and rescue workers.

"Bold subheadings and color captions break information into readable chunks for the younger learner. Important vocabulary is in bold print. . . . An excellent addition to your science collection." Libr Media Connect

Includes glossary and bibliographical references

Rudolph, Jessica

Erased by a tornado! Bearport Pub. 2010 32p il map (Disaster survivors) lib bdg $25.27

Grades: 4 5 6 7 **551.55**

1. Tornadoes

ISBN 978-1-936087-52-5 lib bdg; 1-936087-52-9 lib bdg

LC 2009-34363

"Captivating photos and illustrations and sidebars present interesting facts or brief anecdotes. . . . [This] should be purchased for all school and public libraries as . . . [it gives] a new perspective on the topic." Libr Media Connect

Includes glossary and bibliographical references

Ryback, Carol

Hurricanes; by Carol Ryback and Jayne Keedle. Gareth Stevens Pub. 2009 48p il map (The ultimate 10. Natural disasters) lib bdg $31

Grades: 5 6 7 8 **551.55**

1. Hurricanes

ISBN 978-0-8368-9152-2 lib bdg; 0-8368-9152-X lib bdg

LC 2008-24628

Hurricanes "are described, while color photos illustrate the resulting damage, conveying a significant part of the information through their captions. . . . Explanations of weather terms . . . are included; additional facts are boxed off from the text; and preparation/safety tips are appended. . . . An especially useful book." SLJ

Includes glossary and bibliographical references

Simon, Seymour

Tornadoes; Seymour Simon. Updated edition HarperCollins 2017 un il map hardcover $17.99

Grades: 4 5 6 7 **551.55**

1. Tornadoes

ISBN 9780062470331

Describes the location, nature, development, measurement, and destructive effects of tornadoes, as well as how to stay out of danger from them

"Incredible full-color photographs and diagrams, clearly portraying the different formations and devastating power of the windstorms, complement the text perfectly." Booklist

Stewart, Mark

Blizzards and winter storms. Gareth Stevens Pub. 2009 48p il map (The ultimate 10. Natural disasters) lib bdg $31

Grades: 5 6 7 8 **551.55**

1. Storms 2. Blizzards

ISBN 978-0-8368-9150-8 lib bdg; 0-8368-9150-3 lib bdg

LC 2008-28230

Blizzards and winter storms "are described, while color photos illustrate the resulting damage, conveying a significant part of the information through their captions. . . . An especially useful book." SLJ

Includes glossary and bibliographical references

551.56 Atmospheric electricity and optics

Person, Stephen

Struck by lightning! Bearport Pub. 2010 32p il map (Disaster survivors) lib bdg $25.27

Grades: 4 5 6 7 **551.56**

1. Lightning

ISBN 978-1-936087-47-1 lib bdg; 1-936087-47-2 lib bdg

"Introduces lightning, discussing how it is formed and where it tends to strike, and describing some of the experiences of survivors who have been hit by lightning." Publisher's note

Includes glossary and bibliographical references

Stewart, Melissa

★ **Inside** lightning; illustrations by Cynthia Shaw. Sterling 2011 48p il (Inside . . .) $16.95

Grades: 5 6 7 8 **551.56**

1. Lightning

ISBN 978-1-4027-5878-2; 1-4027-5878-2

This book about lightning "explores its topic in an engaging way, and the many illustrations work well with adjacent text and captions. . . . The [book's] varied page layouts and attractive and the quality of photos, computer-generated images, original illustrations, and charts is . . . excellent. . . . Featuring a step-by-step, illustrated explanation of lightning formation as well as comments from people who have had close encounters with the phenomenon, Inside Lightning provides a vivid and unusually informative introduction to the subject." Booklist

Includes bibliographical references

551.6 Climatology and weather

Aitken, Stephen

Ecosystems at risk; Stephen Aitken. Marshall Cavendish Benchmark 2013 63 p. (Climate crisis) (print) $31.36

Grades: 4 5 6 7 **551.6**

1. Ecology 2. Climate change 3. Biodiversity conservation 4. Climatic changes 5. Climatic changes -- Environmental aspects

ISBN 1608704637; 9781608704637; 9781608706341

LC 2011025243

In this book, by Stephen Aitken, "readers are introduced to topics relating to climatology, thermal expansion, and biodiversity. . . . The case studies . . . provide a global perspective on the ecological concepts being presented. In addition, teachers may find the book helpful in meeting several Common Core literacy standards. . . .The book concludes with . . . ways that individuals can take action to prevent species extinctions, followed by a glossary of conservation-related terms." (Science & Children)

"These sobering overviews present current observable results of climate change and offer scientific predictions about its future effects on the Earth's ecosystems and inhabitants...Suggested websites from educational and action-oriented organizations offer more options. These books should be considered to update collections on this important topic." SLJ

Includes bibliographical references and index

Other titles include:

Animal Life

People

Ocean Life

Plants and Insects

Bailey, Gerry

Changing climate. Gareth Stevens Pub. 2011 48p il map (Planet SOS) lib bdg $31.95; pa $14.05

Grades: 4 5 6 **551.6**

1. Climate -- Environmental aspects

ISBN 978-1-4339-4962-3 lib bdg; 1-4339-4962-8 lib bdg; 978-1-4339-4963-0 pa; 1-4339-4963-6 pa

LC 2010032885

This "well-designed [book presents changing climate] . . . and how [it affects] human beings. With information about water supplies and melting ice and their impact on ecosystems, the discussion . . . of global water levels is especially enlightening. . . . The many large, colorful photos will engage readers and assist them in understanding the important concepts introduced." SLJ

Includes glossary

Christie, Peter

50 climate questions; a blizzard of blistering facts. Peter Christie ; illustrated by Ross Kinnaird. Annick Press 2012 117 p. ill. (50 Questions) (paperback) $14.95; (hardcover) $22.95; (ebook) $10.99

Grades: 4 5 6 7 **551.6**

1. Climate 2. Climate change 3. Climate -- History

ISBN 155451374X; 9781554513741; 9781554513758; 9781554515165

This book by Peter Christie presents a "survey of the effects of climate through history and prehistory." (Kirkus Reviews) "Topics include global warming's effect on the Arctic . . . and how a cooling climate 2.5 million years ago forced early humans to diversify their diets. Christie also provides insight into weather events throughout history -- for example, how weather change contributed to civil unrest that spawned the French Revolution." (Publishers Weekly)

Flannery, Tim F.

We are the weather makers; the history of climate change. [by] Tim Flannery; adapted by Sally M. Walker. Candlewick Press 2009 303p il map $17.99

Grades: 7 8 9 10 **551.6**

1. Greenhouse effect 2. Climate -- Environmental aspects

ISBN 978-0-7636-3656-2; 0-7636-3656-8

LC 2008-939840

An adaptation of The weather makers, published 2005 for adults by Atlantic Monthly Press

"Arguing that climate change and global warming affect us all and that we can be part of the solution, this comprehensive look at the issue includes a clear explanation of the mechanism of the carbon cycle, the role of greenhouse gases on Earth, historical instances of climate change and their causes, descriptions of effects on a variety of habitats, future scenarios and suggestions—both personal and global—about what might be done. . . . A copy belongs in every middle and high-school library." Kirkus

Includes bibliographical references

551.68 Artificial modification and control of weather

Swanson, Jennifer

Geoengineering Earth's climate; resetting the thermostat. Jennifer Swanson. Twenty-First Century Books 2018 96 p. color illustrations (lb : alk. paper) $35.99

Grades: 7 8 9 10 **551.68**

1. Climate change 2. Global warming 3. Climatic changes 4. Carbon sequestration 5. Climate change mitigation 6. Environmental engineering

ISBN 9781512467888; 9781512415698

LC 2016059722

This book, by Jennifer Swanson, deals with the proposal by some scientists on the use of geoengineering as a way to prevent global warming. "Ideas include thickening clouds with chemicals to reduce the amount of sunlight and pulling carbon dioxide from the air with machines. However, critics say that geoengineering could backfire and create even worse weather." (Publisher's note)

"This book succinctly introduces ideas proposed by geoengineers to counteract climate change, and addresses each idea's benefits and risks." Booklist

Includes bibliographical references and index

551.7 Historical geology

Brown, Don, 1949-

Older than dirt; a wild but true history of Earth. by Don Brown & Mike Perfit. Houghton Mifflin Harcourt 2017 112 p. chiefly color illustrations (hardcover) $18.99

Grades: 4 5 6 7 8 **551.7**

1. Earth sciences 2. Historical geology 3. Earth (Planet) 4. Earth (Planet) -- Origin

ISBN 9781328468277; 9780544805033; 0544805038

LC 2016018643

This book, by Don Brown and Mike Perfit, describes how, "almost 14.5 billion years ago, it all started with a BIG BANG and what began as a cloud of gas, dust, and rock eventually took shape and bloomed into a molten sphere. Battered by asteroid collisions, ice ages, and shifting tectonic plates, our fledgling planet finally pushed forth continents. . . . Geological activity continues to sculpt the earth's landscape, sometimes with terrible consequences for its inhabitants." (Publisher's note)

"In 100 fact-crammed but surprisingly zippy pages, nonfiction graphic novelist extraordinaire Brown covers 14 billion years of Earth's development. From the big bang to our planet's origin to landmass formation to the appearance of life, Brown and scientific consultant Perfit provide an astonishingly comprehensive overview and manage to humanize it with witty asides from the woodchuck and worm who serve as surrogate teacher and student, as well as quick visits with important historical scientists." Booklist

Includes bibliographical references (pages 98-101)

552 Petrology

Calver, Paul

Rocks, crystals, and gems. Barron's Educational Series, Inc. 2016 32 p. color illustrations $6.99

Grades: 4 5 6 7 **552**

1. Gems 2. Rocks 3. Crystals

ISBN 1438008287; 9781438008288

LC 2015956071

In this children's book by Toby Reynolds and illustrated by Paul Calver, part of the Visual Explorers series, "engaging text, detailed facts, and impressive statistics give children exciting scientific insight into the rocks, crystals, and gems...and the world around them. A glossary at the end of the book helps reinforce the information. Parents, teachers, and librarians will want to collect all of the books in this series to create a very cool first encyclopedia to build early research skills." (Publisher's note)

"Inexpensive and relatively sturdy, these large-format paperbacks make for a visually enticing series." Booklist

Davis, Barbara J.

Minerals, rocks, and soil. Raintree 2010 48p il map (Sci-hi: Earth and space science) lib bdg $31.43; pa $8.99

Grades: 4 5 6 7 **552**

1. Rocks 2. Minerals 3. Petrology

ISBN 978-1-4109-3347-8 lib bdg; 1-4109-3347-4 lib bdg; 978-1-4109-3357-7 pa; 1-4109-3357-1 pa

LC 2009-13459

"Multiple colorful sidebars and large and small diagrams and photographs will help students to grasp the fundamentals being discussed, and the easy but interesting science experiments will act as further reinforcements." SLJ

Includes glossary and bibliographical references

Farndon, John

Rocks, minerals and gems; John Farndon. Firefly Books 2016 120 p. color illustrations (hardcover) $24.95

Grades: 7 8 9 10 11 12 **552**

1. Gems 2. Rocks 3. Minerals 4. Gems -- Identification 5. Rocks -- Identification 6. Minerals -- Identification

ISBN 1770857400; 1770858687; 9781770858688; 9781770857407

LC 2016440110

This book, by John Farndon, "shows how to read the landscape for clues and identify different rock types -- from dazzling diamonds to grainy sandstone. It describes fascinating facts and data boxes provide short facts to help with quick identification. Earth's most precious rocks, minerals and gems can be anywhere and everywhere in the world -- from riverbeds to beaches, cliff faces to fields." (Publisher's note)

"Highly detailed and methodologically sound, the book is a quality introduction to geology and to applying scientific principles in practical settings." Booklist

Green, Dan

★ The **rock** & gem book; and other treasures of the natural world. written by Dan Green. DK Publishing 2016 208 p. color illustrations $22.99; (ebook) $65

Grades: 7 8 9 10 11 12 **552**

1. Gems 2. Geology 3. Precious stones 4. Rocks 5. Minerals 6. Fossils 7. Gems -- Identification 8. Rocks -- Identification -- 9. Minerals -- Identification 10. Precious stones -- Identification

ISBN 146545070X; 9781465450708; 9781465455321

LC 2016427656

This children's reference book, by Dan Green, "is the perfect encyclopedia for young geologists to consult. Chapters are organized according to scientific classifications with straightforward explanations that bring each specimen to life. From the quartz in watches to the limestone in the Great Pyramids, the earth's natural treasures are used in architecture, art, and science." (Publisher's note)

"The perfect book for the rock hound, public or school library browser, or the at-risk student who shuns science, this compendium speaks to the eyes." VOYA

Hirsch, Rebecca E., 1969-

The **rock** cycle; Rebecca E. Hirsch. Core Library 2015 48 p. color illustrations $32.79

Grades: 5 6 7 **552**

1. Rocks 2. Geology 3. Petrology 4. Geochemical cycles

ISBN 162403389X; 9781624033896

LC 2014932350

This children's book by Rebecca Hirsh, part of the Rocks and Minerals series, "identifies the three types of rock present on Earth--sedimentary, metamorphic, and igneous--discussing their properties, where they can be found, and how they are formed." (Publisher's note)

"Aligned to Common Core and state standards, the series provides ample opportunity for additional research ("Stop and Think"), hands-on experimentation ("In the Field"), and critical thinking ("Changing Minds") that will have readers looking at the world around them with a better understanding of just what exactly they're seeing." SLJ

Includes bibliographical references (page 47) and index

Sedimentary rocks; Rebecca E. Hirsch. Core Library 2015 48 p. color illustrations (hbk.) $32.79

Grades: 5 6 7 **552**

1. Rocks 2. Geology 3. Sedimentary rocks

ISBN 1624033903; 9781624033902

LC 2014932344

This children's book by Rebecca E. Hirsch, part of the Rocks and Minerals series, "introduces sedimentary rocks, discussing their characteristics; types; the rock cycle; how and where they are formed; how they are classified, identified, and used; and landforms that are composed of them." (Publisher's note)

Includes bibliographical references (page 47) and index

Honovich, Nancy

Rocks & minerals; Nancy Honovich. National Geographic 2016 160 p. color illustrations $22.90

Grades: 4 5 6 7 8 **552**

1. Rocks 2. Minerals

ISBN 1426323018; 1426323026; 9781426323010; 9781426323027

LC 2016304812

This book, by Nancy Honovich, is a "fact-packed guide to rocks and minerals. . . . Created for the ultimate explorer, this book gives kids the knowledge and skills they need to identify just about anything they dig up and become true rock hounds. With tons of info and interactivity prompts, it's the perfect companion for backyard or field trip, camping and vacation. Durable and portable, it's just right for pocket or backpack." (Publisher's note)

"A useful supplement for elementary and middle-school science curricula, the book includes a well-considered glossary and further resources." Booklist

Includes bibliographical references (page 157) and index

Hynes, Margaret

Rocks & fossils; foreword by Jack Horner. Kingfisher 2006 63p il (Kingfisher knowledge) $12.95

Grades: 5 6 7 8 **552**

1. Rocks 2. Fossils

ISBN 978-0-7534-5974-4; 0-7534-5974-4

LC 2005-23897

This is a "lavishly illustrated book. . . . The well-written text is pithy and comprehensible." Voice Youth Advocates

Includes glossary and bibliographical references

Owings, Lisa

Igneous rocks; Lisa Owings. Core Library 2015 48 p. color illustrations (hbk.) $32.79

Grades: 5 6 7 **552**

1. Rocks 2. Geology 3. Igneous rocks

ISBN 1624033873; 9781624033872

LC 2014932348

This children's book by Lisa Owings, part of the Rocks and Minerals book series, "introduces igneous rocks, discussing their characteristics; types; the rock cycle; how they are formed, classified, identified, and used; and landforms that are composed of them." (Publisher's note)

"Aligned to Common Core and state standards, the series provides ample opportunity for additional research ('Stop and Think'), hands-on experimentation ('In the Field'), and critical thinking ('Changing Minds') that will have readers looking at the world around them with a better understanding of just what exactly they're seeing. Despite a few issues, these are solid choices." SLJ

Includes bibliographical references (page 47) and index

Smith, Miranda

Rocks, minerals & gems; by Sean Callery and Miranda Smith, with photos by Gary Ombler. Scholastic 2016 224 p. illustrations (chiefly color) $19.99

Grades: 6 7 8 9 10 **552**

1. Gems 2. Rocks 3. Minerals

ISBN 0545947197; 9780545947190

In this book, by Sean Callery and Miranda Smith, with photos by Gary Ombler, "readers will learn about hundreds of rocks, minerals, crystals, and gems that were forged by the most powerful events in prehistory. Explore what specimens look like and how they're used today--readers can use the information to identify rocks and minerals themselves and open up a spectacular new world." (Publisher's note)

"A browser's delight but less useful for reference, this hefty album features hundreds of sharply reproduced close-up photos of geological specimens—including fossils, meteorites, China's terra-cotta army, and amber with small animals inside." SLJ

Swanson, Jennifer

Metamorphic rocks; Jennifer Swanson. Core Library 2015 48 p. color illustrations, color map $32.79

Grades: 5 6 7 **552**

1. Rocks 2. Geology 3. Metamorphic rocks

ISBN 1624033881; 9781624033889

LC 2014932346

This children's book by Jennifer Swanson, from the Rocks and Minerals book series, "introduces metamorphic rocks, discussing their characteristics and types, how they are formed, and what they can be used for." (Publisher's note)

"Despite a few issues, these are solid choices." SLJ

Includes bibliographical references (page 47) and index

Symes, R. F. (Robert Frederick), 1939-2016

Rocks & minerals; written by R.F. Symes and the staff of the Natural History Museum, London ; special photography by Colin Keates and Andreas Einsiedel. Revised ed. DK Pub. 2008 72 p. ill. (some col.) (hardcover: boxed; package) $29.99; (hardcover) $16.99

Grades: 5 6 7 8 **552**

1. Gems 2. Rocks 3. Geology

ISBN 9780756631321 out of print; 0756637775; 9780756637774

LC 2009499083

This book is a guide to "rocks, fossils, minerals, precious metals, crystals, jewels and gemstones." Readers "see rocks that have come from outer space, stalactites as old as dinosaurs, the strange and beautiful shapes of natural crystals and priceless nuggets of gold, silver and platinum. Learn what the Earth is made of and how its rocks were formed, how early humans made the first flint tools and how diamonds and precious stones are cut, polished, and made into jewelry." (Publisher's note)

553.2 Carbonaceous materials

Belton, Blair

How coal is formed; Blair Belton. Gareth Stevens Publishing 2017 32 p. color illustrations (library bound) $26.60

Grades: 5 6 7 **553.2**

1. Coal 2. Coal mines and mining 3. Carbon cycle (Biogeochemistry)

ISBN 9781482447033; 9781482447064; 9781482447071; 9781482447088

LC 2016000747

In this book in the From the Earth: How Resources Are Made series, by Blair Belton, "the processes that transform organic remains into coal, coal mines, and the carbon cycle are important topics covered. . . . Readers will learn about the pollution attributed to the burning of coal as well as about coal alternatives. Graphic organizers, instructive photographs, and thoughtful sidebars help present a well-balanced look at this relevant and timely subject." (Publisher's note)

"This series would be a great addition to school or public libraries, as it makes an often dull topic really shine." SLJ

Includes bibliographical references and index

Marcovitz, Hal

What is the future of fossil fuels? by Hal Marcovitz. ReferencePoint Press, Inc. 2013 80 p. color illustrations, maps (Future of renewable energy series) (hardback) $28.95

Grades: 6 7 8 9 **553.2**

1. Fossil fuels

ISBN 1601526121; 9781601526120

LC 2013029017

This book, by Hal Marcovitz, "examines the future of fossil fuels. Topics include: Are Fossil Fuels Affordable? Can Fossil Fuels Be Compatible with the Environment? Can Alternative Energy Take the Place of Fossil Fuels? Should the Government Continue to Support Fossil Fuels as an Energy?" (Publisher's note)

"Well written and understandable, the authors use a wide variety of source material to present each side fairly and completely. The question/answer format of the chapters breaks the topics into simplified arguments that can easily be absorbed. The author's style is rather dispassionate which elevates the quality of the works by allowing reader to come to their own conclusions." VOYA

Includes bibliographical references and index

Nagelhout, Ryan

How natural gas is formed; Ryan Nagelhout. Gareth Stevens Publishing 2017 32 p. color illustrations (library bound) $26.60; (ebook) $26.60

Grades: 5 6 7 **553.2**

1. Natural gas 2. Energy resources 3. Gas industry 4. Natural gas -- Geology

ISBN 1482447185; 9781482447163; 9781482447170; 9781482447187; 9781482447194

LC 2016012598

This book "focuses on how . . . [natural] gas is formed as well as examines how its mined and used today. The text highlights the most relevant and engrossing information, while graphic organizers help readers identify the most important concepts." (Publisher's note)

"This series would be a great addition to school or public libraries, as it makes an often dull topic really shine." SLJ

Includes bibliographical references and index

Nelson, Kristen Rajczak

How oil is formed; Kristen Rajczak Nelson. Gareth Stevens Publishing 2017 32 p. (library bound) $26.60

Grades: 5 6 7 **553.2**

1. Petroleum 2. Petroleum industry 3. Petroleum -- Geology

ISBN 148244724X; 9781482447217; 9781482447231; 9781482447248

LC 2016011773

This book focuses on how "oil, also known as petroleum, is one of the most significant sources of energy in an energy-hungry world. . . . This . . . book covers the important processes of this fossil fuel, from its origins and formation to its extraction and refining, aided by perfectly selected photographs." (Publisher's note)

"This series would be a great addition to school or public libraries, as it makes an often dull topic really shine." SLJ

Includes bibliographical references and index

553.3 Iron

Kennon, Caroline

How iron ore forms; Caroline Kennon. Gareth Stevens Publishing 2017 32 p. illustrations (chiefly color) (library bound) $26.60

Grades: 5 6 7 **553.3**

1. Iron 2. Iron ores

ISBN 9781482447132; 9781482447149; 9781482447156

LC 2016006959

In this book in the From the Earth: How Resources Are Made series, by Caroline Kennon, "future architects and engineers will discover how the mineral substance iron ore forms, where it's found, and how its transformed through smelting into a useful industrial metal. Charts, diagrams, and photographs present more beneficial information, while sidebars help readers understand why iron ore is significant to their lives." (Publisher's note)

"This series would be a great addition to school or public libraries, as it makes an often dull topic really shine." SLJ

Includes bibliographical references (page 31) and index.

553.8 Gems

Fretland VanVoorst, Jenny, 1972-

Gems; Jenny Fretland VanVoorst. Core Library 2015 48 p. illustrations (chiefly color) $32.79

Grades: 5 6 7 **553.8**

1. Gems 2. Minerals 3. Precious stones

ISBN 1624033865; 9781624033865

LC 2014932347

This children's book by Jennifer Fretland VanVoorst, part of the Rocks and Minerals book series, "introduces gemstones, discussing how they are formed, their shapes, and how they are used." (Publisher's note)

"Aligned to Common Core and state standards, the series provides ample opportunity for additional research ('Stop and Think'), hands-on experimentation ('In the Field'), and critical thinking ('Changing Minds') that will have readers looking at the world around them with a better understanding of just what exactly they're seeing. Despite a few issues, these are solid choices." SLJ

Includes bibliographical references (p. 47) and index

Keppeler, Jill

How gems are formed; Jill Keppeler. Gareth Stevens Publishing 2017 32 p. color illustrations (library bound) $26.60

Grades: 5 6 7 **553.8**

1. Gems 2. Geology 3. Precious stones

ISBN 9781482447095; 9781482447101; 9781482447118; 9781482447125

LC 2015046972

This book "informs readers about the remarkable processes that take place under the surface of Earth to form different kinds of gems. They'll also learn how some gems are mined, while others are replicated in laboratories. Future lapidaries will also find out how they might find and polish gems for themselves." (Publisher's note)

"This series would be a great addition to school or public libraries, as it makes an often dull topic really shine." SLJ

Includes bibliographical references and index

557 Earth sciences of North America

Chin, Jason

Grand Canyon; Jason Chin. Roaring Brook Press 2017 56 p. color illustrations (hardcover) $19.99

Grades: 1 2 3 4 5 6 **557**

1. Grand Canyon (Ariz.) 2. Geology 3. Natural history 4. Geology -- Arizona -- Grand Canyon 5. Natural history -- Arizona -- Grand Canyon

ISBN 1596439505; 9781596439504

LC 2016025024

Caldecott Honor Book (2018)

Robert F. Sibert Informational Book Award Honor Book (2018)

This book, by Jason Chin, focuses on "the Grand Canyon. Home to an astonishing variety of plants and animals that have lived and evolved within its walls for millennia, the Grand Canyon is much more than just a hole in the ground. Follow a father and daughter as they make their way through the cavernous wonder, discovering life both present and past." (Publisher's note)

"With vivid imagination, a crystal-clear grasp of the facts, and brilliant artwork, this illuminating look at one of the planet's most fascinating features will entrance young readers." Booklist

Includes bibliographical references

Collier, Michael

★ **Over** the mountains; an aerial view of geology. foreword by John S. Shelton. Mikaya Press 2007 un il map (An aerial view of geology) $29.95

Grades: 8 9 10 11 12 **557**

1. Mountains 2. Aerial photography 3. Geology -- North America

ISBN 1-931414-18-1; 978-1-931414-18-0

LC 2006-47151

The author "expresses his passion for geology through awe-inspiring aerial photographs that reveal how mountains were formed and modified across the eons of time. . . . The four sections of this book explore what mountains are, why some are peaked and others rounded, and why they are often strung together in ranges. . . . Collier's love for the land is contagious, and his flying field trips over the mountains are thrilling." Voice Youth Advocates

Includes bibliographical references

560 Paleontology

Bradley, Timothy J.

Paleo bugs; survival of the creepiest. written and illustrated by Timothy J. Bradley. Chronicle Books 2008 44p il $15.99

Grades: 4 5 6 7 **560**

1. Fossils 2. Insects 3. Prehistoric animals

ISBN 978-0-8118-6022-2; 0-8118-6022-1

LC 2007-18174

This offers an "eye-widening gallery of extinct arthropods, from the mayfly-like heptagenia to a seven-foot-long arthropleura. . . . Bradley decks out each of his painted figures in bright hues, poses them in natural settings . . . and sets them aside a human hand or body in silhouette to suggest scale. . . . Readers will . . . pore over the pictures and come away knowing more about both these extinct animals and their modern descendants." Booklist

Includes glossary and bibliographical references

Fretland VanVoorst, Jenny, 1972-

Fossils; Jenny Fretland VanVoorst. Core Library 2015 48 p. color illustrations $32.79

Grades: 5 6 7 **560**

1. Fossils 2. Geology 3. Paleontology

ISBN 1624033857; 9781624033858

LC 2014932345

This children's book by Jennifer Fretland VanVoorst "presents general information about fossils, explaining how they are formed, how they are extracted from the sites where they are discovered, and how scientists use them to gain an understanding of Earth's past." (Publisher's note)

"Aligned to Common Core and state standards, the series provides ample opportunity for additional research ("Stop and Think"), hands-on experimentation ('In the Field'), and critical thinking ('Changing Minds') that will have readers looking at the world around them with a better understanding of just what exactly they're seeing. Despite a few issues, these are solid choices." SLJ

Includes bibliographical references (page 47) and index

Holmes, Thom

Dinosaur scientist; careers digging up the past. Enslow Publishers 2009 128p il (Wild science careers) lib bdg $31.93

Grades: 5 6 7 8 **560**

1. Fossils 2. Vocational guidance

ISBN 978-0-7660-3053-4 lib bdg; 0-7660-3053-9 lib bdg

LC 2008-19634

"A great read for middle school students, the book provides vocational guidance while introducing the reader to a challenging, but very exciting, career as a paleontologist." Sci Books Films

Includes glossary and bibliographical references

Johnson, Rebecca L.

Battle of the dinosaur bones; Othniel Charles Marsh vs. Edward Drinker Cope. by Rebecca L. Johnson. Twenty-First Century Books 2013 64 p. ill., plates, charts (Scientific rivalries and scandals) (library) $33.27

Grades: 5 6 7 8 **560**

1. Paleontology -- History 2. Paleontologists -- United States -- Biography 3. Paleontology -- United States -- History -- 19th century

ISBN 0761354883; 9780761354888

LC 2011045648

"This entry in the Scientific Rivalries and Scandals series focuses on the bitter antagonism between two pioneering nineteenth-century paleontologists. Marsh and Cope. Their contentious rivalry to discover the largest and most unusual dinosaur fossils of the American West became know as the Bone Wars and was at the forefront of American science for decades. The moral of the story is clear, revealing how rivalry can be positive and detrimental." (Booklist)

Includes bibliographical references (p. 58 - 60) and index.

Taylor, Paul D.

★ **Fossil**; written by Dr. Paul D. Taylor. Relaunch edition DK Pub. 2017 72p il map (DK eyewitness books) paperback $9.99; hardcover $19.99

Grades: 4 5 6 7 **560**

1. Fossils

ISBN 9781465462473 paperback; 9781465462558 hardcover

First published 1990 by Knopf

This book describes different types of fossils, from algae to birds and mammals

567.9 Reptiles

Bacchin, Matteo

Giant vs. giant; Argentinosaurus and Giganotosaurus. drawings and story, Matteo Bacchin; essays, Marco Signore; translated from the Italian by Marguerite Shore. Abbeville Kids 2010 61p il (Dinosaurs) $15.95

Grades: 4 5 6 7 **567.9**

1. Fossils 2. Dinosaurs

ISBN 978-0-7892-1013-5; 0-7892-1013-4

LC 2010-21120

This "book is split into two sections: the first contains parts . . . of a serial graphic novel about dinosaur survival, complete with dramatic narrative and grisly, to-the-death battles. The second half is a higher-level traditional nonfiction text with color photographs and diagrams, focusing on the science behind the comics. The unique format is generally engaging and effective." Horn Book Guide

T. rex and the great extinction; drawings and story, Matteo Bacchin; essays, Marco Signore; translated from the Italian by Marguerite Shore. Abbeville Kids 2010 il (Dinosaurs) $15.95

Grades: 4 5 6 7 **567.9**

1. Fossils 2. Dinosaurs

ISBN 9780789210142; 0789210142

LC 2010021123

This "book is split into two sections: the first contains parts . . . of a serial graphic novel about dinosaur survival, complete with dramatic narrative and grisly, to-the-death battles. The second half is a higher-level traditional nonfiction text with color photographs and diagrams, focusing on the science behind the comics. The unique format is generally engaging and effective." Horn Book Guide

Berkowitz, Jacob

Jurassic poop; what dinosaurs (and others) left behind. written by Jacob Berkowitz; illustrated by Steve Mack. Kids Can Press 2006 40p il $14.95; pa $7.95

Grades: 4 5 6 7 **567.9**

1. Feces 2. Fossils 3. Dinosaurs

ISBN 978-1-55337-860-0; 1-55337-860-1; 978-1-55337-867-9 pa; 1-55337-867-9 pa

This describes fossilized feces, or coprolites, and what we can learn from them

"Berkowitz' style is goofy and lighthearted, but there's plenty of real information. . . . The browsable format combines cartoony digital art, photographs . . . and design elements such a spiky borders and background shading." Bull Cent Child Books

Includes glossary

Bonner, Hannah

When dinos dawned, mammals got munched, and Pterosaurs took flight; a cartoon pre-history of life in the Triassic. Hannah Bonner. National Geographic Children's Books 2012 44 p. col. ill., col. maps (hardback) $25.90

Grades: 3 4 5 6 7 **567.9**

1. Dinosaurs 2. Triassic Period 3. Graphic novels 4. Paleontology -- Triassic -- Comic books, strips, etc.

ISBN 9781426308628; 9781426308635

LC 2011029212

In this book Hannah Bonner "chronicles developments in the Triassic Period, during which life got a fresh lease on the planet in the wake of the massive Permian extinction. She tracks an explosion of biological diversity as the oceans were repopulated, lush forests grew and the dominant kinds of land animals went from clumsy-looking therapsids to sleek archosaurian dinosaurs and proto-crocodiles. Early mammals are already waiting in the wings." (Kirkus Reviews)

Includes bibliographical references and index

Dixon, Dougal

Meat -eating dinosaurs; by Dougal Dixon. North American ed. New Forest Press 2010 47 p. col. ill., col. maps (Dinosaur files) (library) $28.50

Grades: 4 5 6 7 **567.9**

1. Fossils 2. Dinosaurs 3. Carnivorous animals

ISBN 9781848983342; 1848983344

LC 2010925204

This volume "contains detailed information about dinosaurs and other prehistoric life, covering species development in chronological order. Careful links to the fossil finds that helped scientists with their explanations are found throughout. Additional text boxes cover topics from structure-function to footprints, and interpretive color illustrations and photographs further enhance the [text]." Horn Book Guide

Includes bibliographical references (p. 44-45) and index.

Plant -eating dinosaurs; by Dougal Dixon. North American ed. New Forest Press 2010 48 p. col. ill., col. maps (library) $28.50

Grades: 4 5 6 7 **567.9**

1. Fossils 2. Dinosaurs 3. Herbivores

ISBN 1848983336; 9781848983335

LC 2010925201

This volume "contains detailed information about dinosaurs and other prehistoric life, covering species development in chronological order. Careful links to the fossil finds that helped scientists with their explanations are found throughout. Additional text boxes cover topics from structure-function to footprints, and interpretive color illustrations and photographs further enhance the [text]." Horn Book Guide

Includes bibliographical references (p. 44-45) and index.

Guiberson, Brenda Z., 1946-

Feathered dinosaurs; Brenda Z. Guiberson ; illustrated by William Low. Henry Holt & Co. 2016 40 p. color illustrations (hardcover) $17.99

Grades: 2 3 4 5 **567.9**

1. Feathers 2. Dinosaurs 3. Birds -- Origin

ISBN 9780805098280

LC 2015003535

This juvenile book, by Brenda Z. Guiberson and illustrated by William Low, describes how "millions of years ago, before there were red-breasted robins and busy blue jays . . . there were feathered dinosaurs. Scientists have found evidence that Anchiornis, Caudipteryx, Confuciusornis, and many more dinosaurs all had feathers." (Publisher's note)

"An intriguing introduction to the evolutionary connection between dinosaurs and birds, as well as the process of ongoing scientific discovery." Booklist

Kelsey, Elin

Canadian dinosaurs; Elin Kelsey. Reprint Maple Tree Press 2009 96 p. ill. (prebind) $28.95

Grades: 4 5 6 **567.9**

1. Fossils 2. Dinosaurs

ISBN 1442060409; 9781442060401

This book offers a "history of fossil hunting north of the border, including bio-material on dino-hunters past and present, followed by a compendium of carnivores and herbivores. . . . Illustrations, mainly in color, appear on every page. . . . The whole is rounded out with a list of dino locations, a time line, and a listing of institutions where these splendid fossils may be examined at leisure." (School Library Journal)

Lessem, Don

The **ultimate** dinopedia; the most complete dinosaur reference ever. illustrated by Franco Tempesta; with a foreword by Rodolfo Coria. National Geographic 2010 272p il map $24.95; lib bdg $34.90

Grades: 3 4 5 6 **567.9**

1. Dinosaurs

ISBN 978-1-4263-0164-3; 1-4263-0164-2; 978-1-4263-0165-0 lib bdg; 1-4263-0165-0 lib bdg

LC 2010-07146

In the opening chapter, Lessem "presents broad basics on [dinosaur] behavior and habitats as well as a look at major discoveries in paleontology. However, it's the later chapters, which devote two pages each to specific dinosaurs, that will hook hard-core dino lovers. . . . Tempesta's full-page illustrations appear on every spread and jump off the page, and the dynamic layout . . . is immensely appealing. . . . Lessem's comprehensive overview will satisfy the interested browser as much as the ardent dinosaur enthusiast." Booklist

Includes bibliographical references

Long, John A.

Feathered dinosaurs; the origin of birds. foreword by Luis M. Chiappe. Oxford University Press 2008 193p il $39.95

Grades: 7 8 9 10 **567.9**

1. Birds 2. Fossils 3. Dinosaurs

ISBN 978-0-19-537266-3; 0-19-537266-2

LC 2008-1232

A "record of feathered dinosaurs illuminates the evolutionary march from these . . . prehistoric creatures through to the first true flying birds and includes . . . text that places these feathered dinosaurs within the larger family of dinosaurs." Publisher's note

Includes bibliographical references

Malam, John

Dinosaur atlas; authors, John Malam and John Woodward; consultant Michael Benton. Dorling Kindersley 2006 96p il map $19.99

Grades: 5 6 7 8 **567.9**

1. Dinosaurs

ISBN 978-0-7566-2235-0; 0-7566-2235-2

LC 2006-285529

"The atlas is organized by continent. Each section is prefaced with a large map showing where various species are found, with a picture and a brief synopsis of each species on the facing page. . . . Each introductory map is followed by several regional maps, surveying important local fossil sites and formations. Each section provides attractive diorama snapshots for a wide range of periods and locations." Sci Books Films

Includes glossary

Manning, Phillip Lars

Dinomummy; the life, death, and discovery of Dakota, a dinosaur from Hell Creek. foreword by Tyler Lyson. Kingfisher 2007 64p il map $18.95

Grades: 4 5 6 7 **567.9**

1. Dinosaurs 2. North Dakota

ISBN 978-0-7534-6047-4; 0-7534-6047-5

LC 2007-02878

Tells about the discovery of the fossil remains of a hadrosaur in the hills of the Hell Creek Formation in North Dakota.

"The color photographs and simple text offer a detailed account of carefully unearthing the fossil and transporting it safely to the laboratory, where many tests were performed. Dinosaurs buffs and young scientists will love this book. It is a thrilling story that is part narrative, part mystery, and part science lesson." Voice Youth Advocates

McGowan, Chris

Dinosaur discovery; everything you need to be a paleontologist. illustrated by Erica Lyn Schmidt. Simon & Schuster Books for Young Readers 2011 48p il $17.99

Grades: 4 5 6 7 **567.9**

1. Fossils 2. Dinosaurs

ISBN 978-1-4169-4764-6; 1-4169-4764-7; 1416947647; 9781416947646

LC 2009044604

"In-depth facts about 13 dinosaurs are interspersed with activities that teach readers about anatomy and how paleontologists understand body structure. . . . The 27 activities and experiments illustrate the concepts presented and focus on the featured dinosaurs. By following the well-written directions as well as the picture steps, budding paleontologists will explore how a tail affects balance, discover binocular vision and learn how the two parts of a bone make them both stiff and elastic. . . . Schmidt's acrylic illustrations give life to the dinosaurs, and her scientific renderings of bones could have come straight out of an anatomy textbook. . . . A thinking, active alternative for readers who fall between adult nonfiction and all the rhyming dino fare meant for the younger set." Kirkus

Nardo, Don

Deadliest dinosaurs; by Don Nardo. ReferencePoint Press, Inc. 2017 80 p. (hardback) $29.95; (ebook) $29.95

Grades: 6 7 8 9 10 **567.9**

1. Dinosaurs 2. Predatory animals

ISBN 9781682820483; 9781682820490

LC 2016004075

This book in the Deadliest Predators series, by Don Nardo, reveals that "many of the creatures that populated the so-called age of dinosaurs were highly lethal, and for diverse reasons. Some were fast and powerful, while others swam, glided through the air, or cooperated by hunting in packs. Six deadly dinosaurs, including Tyrannosaurus rex and Troodon, are profiled." (Publisher's note)

"First-rate nonfiction on a high-interest topic." SLJ

Includes bibliographical references and index

Nargi, Lela

★ **Absolute** expert dinosaurs; Lela Nargi with National Geographic explorer Steve Brusatte. National Geographic 2018 112 p. color illustrations (Absolute expert) $14.99

Grades: 4 5 6 7 8 **567.9**

1. Dinosaurs 2. Paleontology

ISBN 1426331401; 142633141X; 9781426331404; 9781426331411

LC 2018289127

"Have you met Pinocchio rex? Meet this fascinating dino along with favorites, such as Tyrannosaurus, Stegosaurus, Triceratops, Velociraptor, Apatosaurus, Ankylosaurus, and Giganotosaurus. Plus, check out some weird or newly discovered dinos you may not know about. See how fossils are formed. Learn about the epic, earth-shaking extinctions that paved the way for life today." (Publisher's note)

"The books' attractive design and tone will appeal to casual readers, but even those with serious interests will unearth scads of new information." Booklist

Peterson, Sheryl

Pterodactyl. Creative Education 2010 48p il (Age of dinosaurs) lib bdg $34.25

Grades: 5 6 7 8 **567.9**

1. Dinosaurs

ISBN 978-1-58341-975-5 lib bdg; 1-58341-975-6 lib bdg

LC 2009025175

"Peterson nicely balances the known with conjecture. . . . The inviting design, on glossy pages, elegantly detours from the main text into details tantalizing . . .; informative . . .; and incredible. . . . The illustrations, from sharp diagrams to dramatic paintings to B-movie-worthy recreation scenes, add some nice flair to this solid entry." Booklist

Reed, M. K.

Dinosaurs; fossils and feathers. by MK Reed, illustrated by Joe Flood. First Second 2016 117 p. chiefly color illustrations ebook $60; hardcover $19.99; $9.99

Grades: 4 5 6 7 8 **567.9**

1. Dinosaurs 2. Paleontology

ISBN 9781626727281; 9781626721449; 1626721432; 9781626721432; 1626721440

LC 2016012765

In this graphic novel by MK Reed, illustrated by Joe Flood, published as part of the Science Comics series, "learn all about the history of paleontology! This fascinating look at dinosaur science covers the last 150 years of dinosaur hunting, and illuminates how our ideas about dinosaurs have changed--and continue to change." (Publisher's note)

"There's some humor along with a solid presentation of facts, and the clean design helps makes the information accessible; the somewhat advanced content makes the book most appropriate for upper-elementary-age readers." Horn Book

Includes bibliographical references.

Thimmesh, Catherine

★ **Scaly** spotted feathered frilled; how do we know what dinosaurs really looked like? by Catherine Thimmesh. Houghton Mifflin Books for Children, Houghton Mifflin Harcourt 2013 64 p. $17.99

Grades: 4 5 6 7 **567.9**

1. Dinosaurs 2. Paleontology 3. Paleoart

ISBN 0547991347; 9780547991344

LC 2012048466

Author Catherine Thimmesh "explores the border between science and speculation in this [book about] how paleontologists . . . reconstruct prehistoric creatures from fossil evidence. . . . [She] explains how surviving evidence—including fossilized bone fragments, plant matter, bits of skin and, recently, feathers, prehistoric 'trackways' (preserved pathways of dino footprints) and similar physical features in modern animals—is assembled and interpreted by scientists." (Kirkus Reviews)

Includes bibliographical references (page 55) and index

Woodward, John

3 -D dinosaur; by John Woodward ; consultant, Darren Naish. 1st American ed. DK 2011 71 p. ill. (chiefly col.), col. maps (hardcover: interactive) $17.99

Grades: 6 7 8 **567.9**

1. Fossils 2. Dinosaurs 3. Paleontology

ISBN 0756672155; 9780756672157

LC 2011282389

This children's book on dinosaurs by John Woodward includes "special activating boxes that indicate the presence of digital pop outs that when held up to a webcam attached to your PC, feature . . . 3D digital animation." It explores "the anatomy, diet, and behavior of dinosaurs and how paleontologists piece together the past." (Publisher's note)

Includes bibliographical references (p. [72]) and index.

Dinosaur! dinosaurs and other amazing prehistoric creatures as you've never seen them before. written by John Woodward ; consultant, Darren Naish ; illustrators, Peter Minister, Arran Lewis, Andrew Kerr, Peter Bull, Vlad Konstantinov. First American edition DK Publishing 2014 208 p. color illustraions, color maps (hardcover) $24.99

Grades: 5 6 7 8 **567.9**

1. Dinosaurs 2. Dinosaurs -- Pictorial works

ISBN 1465420479; 9781465420473

LC 2012287452

This book, by John Woodward, "[p]rofiles a range of dinosaur and prehistoric animal species from the Triassic, Jurassic, and Cretaceous Eras, featuring such animals as allosaurus, diplodocus, and mosasaurus." (Publisher's note)

"For those budding paleontologists and dinosaur fans willing to dig a little, there's a wealth of material on this ever-evolving subject." Booklist

567.91 Specific dinosaurs and other archosaurs

Sloan, Christopher

Tracking Tyrannosaurs; meet T. rex's fascinating family, from tiny terrors to feathered giants. by Christopher Sloan. National Geographic 2013 48 p. (trade hard cover) $18.95

Grades: 5 6 7 8 **567.91**

1. Tyrannosaurus rex 2. Dinosaurs

ISBN 1426313748; 9781426313745; 9781426313752

LC 2013004988

This book, by Christopher Sloan, "highlights a newly discovered T. rex relative in China with a coat of downy feathers! This one-ton predator is the largest known animal to ever have walked the Earth. [Readers] meet 19 kinds of tyrannosaurs--including seven new species discovered in the last two years--that came before T. rex." (Publisher's note)

569 Fossil mammals

Bardoe, Cheryl

Mammoths and mastodons; titans of the Ice Age. Abrams Books for Young Readers 2010 43p il map

Grades: 4 5 6 7 **569**

1. Fossils 2. Mammoths 3. Mastodon

ISBN 0-8109-8413-X lib bdg; 978-0-8109-8413-4 lib bdg

LC 2009-22006

The author presents a "case study in how paleontologists examine both ancient and modern clues for insights into the diets, physical development and behavior of extinct animals. Cousins to modern elephants, mammoths and mastodons once roamed large portions of the Earth, but for reasons that are not completely understood . . . vanished relatively suddenly. Focusing particularly on . . . remnants like the 55 fossilized skeletons found near one sinkhole in South Dakota and 'Lyuba,' the well preserved 'prehistoric popsicle' discovered in 2007 in Siberia, the author presents both facts and educated guesses--while leaving it clear that there is much still to be learned." (Kirkus)

"This well-designed book opens with two boys finding a strange animal dead on the arctic tundra. Their father hikes four days to a village where the news can be spread; then scientists take away the frozen baby mammoth, the first example found intact, and study it intensively. The book intersperses accounts of the scientists' research and deductions with general information about mammoths and mastodons as well as imagined scenes taking place when they walked the earth. . . . A handsome introduction." Booklist

Includes glossary and bibliographical references

Turner, Alan

★ **National** Geographic prehistoric mammals; illustrated by Mauricio Antón. National Geographic 2004 192p il map $29.95; lib bdg $49.90

Grades: 5 6 7 8 **569**

1. Fossil mammals

ISBN 0-7922-7134-3; 0-7922-6997-7 lib bdg

LC 2004-1189

This describes the Age of Mammals and profiles over 100 prehistoric mammals, including time lines, fact boxes, distribution maps, photos of fossils, and illustrations

"Dramatic full-color pictures . . . and captions enhance the brief, informative text." SLJ

569.9 Humans and related genera

Aronson, Marc, 1950-

★ The **skull** in the rock; how a scientist, a boy, and Google Earth opened a new window on human origins. by Marc Aronson and Lee Berger. National Geographic 2012 64 p. (hardcover : alk. paper) $18.95

Grades: 5 6 7 8 9 10 **569.9**

1. Human origins 2. Fossil hominids 3. Paleoanthropology 4. Excavations (Archeology) 5. Paleoanthropology 6. Human beings -- Origin 7. Fossil hominids -- South Africa -- Witwatersrand Region 8. Human evolution -- South Africa -- Witwatersrand Region 9. Excavations (Archaeology) -- South Africa -- Witwatersrand Region

ISBN 1426310102; 9781426310102; 9781426310539

LC 2012012943

This book by Marc Aronson and Lee R. Berger tells the story of how "in 2008 [Berger]--with the help of his curious 9-year-old son--discovered two remarkably well preserved, two-million-year-old fossils . . . known as 'Australopithecus sediba'; a previously unknown species of ape-like creatures that may have been a direct ancestor of modern humans." (Publisher's note)

Includes bibliographical references and index.

Deem, James M.

Bodies from the bog. Houghton Mifflin 1998 42p il hardcover o.p. pa $5.95

Grades: 4 5 6 7 **569.9**

1. Mummies 2. Archeology 3. Prehistoric peoples
ISBN 0-395-85784-8; 0-618-35402-6 pa
LC 97-12010

Describes the discovery of bog bodies in northern Europe and the evidence which their remains reveal about themselves and the civilizations in which they lived

"The text is engaging and accessible, and the starkly dramatic photos are given dignity by the spacious and understated page design." Horn Book Guide

Includes bibliographical references

570 Biology

Green, Dan

Extreme biology; from superbugs to clones... get to the edge of science. written and illustrated by Simon Basher. Kingfisher 2013 64 p. col. ill. (hardcover) $12.99

Grades: 4 5 6 7 **570**

1. Biology
ISBN 0753470519; 9780753470510

This book written and illustrated by Simon Basher is designed to help readers "learn about the amazing research that is revolutionizing biology, from advances in medicine to genetic engineering. [Readers will] meet the world's toughest bacterium and a biologically immortal flatworm whilst learning about epigenetics, superbugs, nanomedicine and cloning. 'Extreme Biology' is a compelling guide to developments at the very forefront of science." (Publisher's note)

Latham, Donna

★ **Backyard** Biology; Investigate Habitats Outside Your Door With 25 Projects. by Donna Latham ; illustrated by Beth Hetland. Nomad Press 2013 128 p. ill. (Build it yourself) (paperback) $15.95

Grades: 4 5 6 7 **570**

1. Biology 2. Front yards and backyards
ISBN 1619301512; 9781619301511

This book, part of the Built It Yourself series, "incorporates 25 projects for kids to try as they explore the 'ecosystems that are outside your door.' The book's eight chapters cover biology (and microbiology), cells, and the life cycles of both plants and animals, among other topics; definitions of key terms appear throughout, as do [illustrator Beth] Hetland's cartoons and diagrams." (Publishers Weekly)

McManus, Lori

Cell systems. Heinemann Library 2011 48p il (Investigating cells) lib bdg $32

Grades: 5 6 7 8 **570**

1. Cells 2. Life (Biology)
ISBN 978-1-4329-3879-6; 1-4329-3879-7
LC 2009049974

This book looks at cell systems, including the cell, tissues, organ, and organ system hierarchy.

"The abundant graphic matter—photographs, diagrams, charts and graphs—work together with the text to create visually appealing pages. . . . [This] would be very useful in any kind of formal investigation of the topic and yet attractive enough to encourage browsing. . . . [This] . . . is exceptionally well done." Libr Media Connect

Includes glossary and bibliographical references

VanCleave, Janice Pratt, 1942-

Step -by-step science experiments in biology; by Janice VanCleave. Rosen 2013 80 p. col. ill. (Janice Vancleave's first-place science fair projects) (library) $33.25; (paperback) $14.15

Grades: 5 6 7 8 **570**

1. Biology 2. Science -- Experiments 3. Biology -- Experiments
ISBN 144886982X; 9781448869824; 9781448884636
LC 2012007943

This book by Janice VanCleave presents 22 science experiments in biology for children. "Van Cleave states the basic goal of the experiments, followed by a list of necessary materials. . . . Step-by-step instructions are . . . accompanied by diagrams where needed. The results section states exactly what is expected to happen and the 'Why?' section explains in accessible terms why those specific results were achieved." (School Library Journal)

Includes bibliographical references and index.

Winston, Robert

Life as we know it; Robert Winston. 1st American ed. DK Publishing 2012 96 p. col. ill. (hardcover) $16.99

Grades: 4 5 6 **570**

1. Ecology 2. Zoology 3. Food chains (Ecology) 4. Life (Biology)
ISBN 0756691699; 9780756691691
LC 2011277462

Author Robert Winston "begins with Earth's formation billions of years ago and continues to the present day, exploring cells, the animal kingdom, ecosystems, food chains, and creatures that tolerate extreme conditions (including bacteria that thrive in volcanic pools and coffinfish that live under high pressure on the sea floor). The book's . . . design incorporates numerous photographs, sidebars, . . . digital art, and light humor, usually in the form of speech-bubble captions for the animals." (Publishers Weekly)

570.7 Education, research, related topics

Calhoun, Yael

Plant and animal science fair projects; revised and expanded using the scientific method. Enslow Publishers 2010 160p il (Biology science projects using the scientific method) lib bdg $34.60

Grades: 7 8 9 10 **570.7**

1. Natural history 2. Science projects 3. Science -- Experiments
ISBN 978-0-7660-3421-1 lib bdg; 0-7660-3421-6 lib bdg
LC 2009-14805

First published 2005 with title: Plant and animal science fair projects using beetles, weeds, seeds, and more

"Each volume begins with an overview of the scientific method and safety, then presents a collection of activities encouraging readers to explore central concepts in the featured fields. The activities include step-by-step instructions and helpful color diagrams, interspersed with extended coverage of scientific ideas. The "Results" sections ask questions rather than giving away the answers." (Horn Book)

Includes bibliographical references

571 Internal biological processes and structures

Green, Jen

Inside animals. Marshall Cavendish Benchmark 2010 48p il (Invisible worlds) $28.50

Grades: 4 5 6 7 **571**

1. Cells 2. Anatomy 3. Physiology 4. Microorganisms

ISBN 978-0-7614-4195-3; 0-7614-4195-6

LC 2008037241

This describes the animal details that are too small for the unaided eye to see, and how these microscopic systems work to keep the animal alive and healthy.

The narrative is "clear, well written, broken down into manageable pieces, and peppered with eye-opening facts. The numerous photographs are so phenomenal that they will inspire kids to read the text . . . so that they can wrap their minds around what they see." SLJ

Includes glossary and bibliographical references

571.4 Biophysics

Amstutz, Lisa J.

Discover cryobiology; Lisa J. Amstutz. Lerner Publications 2017 40 p. color illustrations (ebook) $30.65; (ebook) $30.65; (lb : alk. paper) $30.65

Grades: 3 4 5 **571.4**

1. Cryobiology 2. Cold -- Physiological effect 3. Cryopreservation of organs, tissues, etc

ISBN 9781512423082; 9781512410631; 9781512408072; 9781512412840

LC 2015047375

This book, by Lisa J. Amstutz, part of the Searchlight Books What's Cool about Science? series, explores the theories behind cryobiology. "Cryobiologists study how cold affects living things. This research has many amazing uses, but what do icy temperatures have to do with organ transplants? And how can researchers use a freezer to save endangered species? Learn about the work cryobiologists are doing today and the breakthroughs they hope to achieve in the future." (Publisher's note)

"In four clear, concise chapters, accompanied by glossy close-up photos of technological gear and frozen organs, this explains the effects, both preservative and damaging, of cold on bodies and examines the natural reactions of animals (i.e., hibernation), before more thoroughly discussing the potential for freezing—and perhaps one day reanimating—human bodies." Booklist

Includes bibliographical references and index

571.6 Cell biology

Ballard, Carol

Cells and cell function. Rosen Central 2010 46p il (Living processes) lib bdg $26.50; pa $11.75

Grades: 5 6 7 **571.6**

1. Cells

ISBN 978-1-61532-342-5 lib bdg; 1-61532-342-2 lib bdg; 978-1-61532-349-4 pa; 1-61532-349-X pa

Describes what cells are and how they work.

"With colorful, quality photography, the well-organized content is divided into short chapters with bold subheadings making information easy to find. Clear and interesting writing distinguishes this . . . from older titles. The captions for pictures are used to provide identification and additional explanation for topics not included in the text." Libr Media Connect

Includes glossary and bibliographical references

Cohen, Marina

What is cell theory? Crabtree Pub. Co. 2011 64p il (Shaping modern science) lib bdg $30.60; pa $10.95

Grades: 5 6 7 8 **571.6**

1. Cells

ISBN 978-0-7787-7199-9 lib bdg; 0-7787-7199-9 lib bdg; 978-0-7787-7206-4 pa; 0-7787-7206-3 pa

LC 2010052633

This title is "not only written and organized well, but [it is] also gorgeous in design. Full-color photographs and illustrations are set over colorful backgrounds that add depth but not distraction. [The title] includes thought-provoking quotes from famous authors and scientists and some eyebrow-raising 'Quick Facts' throughout." SLJ

Includes glossary and bibliographical references

Rainis, Kenneth G.

Cell and microbe science fair projects; revised and expanded using the scientific method. Enslow Publishers 2010 160p il (Biology science projects using the scientific method) lib bdg $34.60

Grades: 7 8 9 10 **571.6**

1. Cells 2. Biology 3. Microbiology 4. Science projects 5. Science -- Experiments

ISBN 978-0-7660-3420-4 lib bdg; 0-7660-3420-8 lib bdg

LC 2009019374

First published 2005 with title: Cell and microbe science fair projects using microscopes, mold, and more

"Each book focusing on biology will be helpful to middle school students and contains a section about the scientific method as well as experiments that are outlined to cover the experimental question, hypothesis, materials, procedures, results and conclusions." (Publisher's Note)

Includes bibliographical references

Somervill, Barbara A.

Animal cells and life processes. Heinemann Library 2011 48p il (Investigating cells) lib bdg $32

Grades: 5 6 7 8 **571.6**

1. Cells 2. Life (Biology)

ISBN 978-1-4329-3877-2; 1-4329-3877-0

LC 2009049971

Overview of animal cells and how they function.

"The abundant graphic matter—photographs, diagrams, charts and graphs—work together with the text to create visually appealing pages. . . . [This] would be very useful in any kind of formal investigation of the topic and yet attractive enough to encourage browsing. . . . [This] . . . is exceptionally well done." Libr Media Connect

Includes glossary and bibliographical references

Plant cells and life processes. Heinemann Library 2010 48p il (Investigating cells) lib bdg $32

Grades: 5 6 7 8 **571.6**

1. Cells 2. Plant physiology

ISBN 978-1-4329-3878-9; 1-4329-3878-9

LC 2009049973

This book explores the features of the plant cell and their life processes.

"The abundant graphic matter—photographs, diagrams, charts and graphs—work together with the text to create visually appealing pages. .

. . [This] would be very useful in any kind of formal investigation of the topic and yet attractive enough to encourage browsing. . . . [This] . . . is exceptionally well done." Libr Media Connect

Includes glossary and bibliographical references

Stewart, Melissa

Cell biology; by Melissa Stewart. Revised ed. Twenty-First Century Books 2013 80 p. col. ill. (chiefly col.) ebook $31.95

Grades: 5 6 7 8 **571.6**

1. Cells 2. Science -- History 3. Cytology

ISBN 9781467703666; 1467703664

LC 2006028542

This book looks at cells. "From the nucleus, the cell's control center, to the tiny ribosomes, which help manufacture proteins, each part of a cell plays an essential role. This book tells the story of how biologists unlocked the secrets of cells and revolutionized the way we look at living things." (Publisher's note)

Includes bibliographical references (p. 76-77) and index

Stimola, Aubrey

Cell biology. Rosen Pubs. 2011 64p il (Science made simple) lib bdg $29.25; pa $12.95

Grades: 5 6 7 8 **571.6**

1. Cells

ISBN 978-1-4488-1234-9 lib bdg; 1-4488-1234-8 lib bdg; 978-1-4488-2241-6 pa; 1-4488-2241-6 pa

LC 2010021319

This introduction to cell biology includes "a lot of detailed information, making [it] useful as [a] resource . . . for science projects and reports. . . . The [book] also [includes a] brief discussion of scientists important in the field, the history of the topic, and current and future applications. . . . The straightforward, no-nonsense [narrative] and simple design make this . . . a nice package for basic science." SLJ

Includes glossary and bibliographical references

571.8 Reproduction, development, growth

Spilsbury, Richard

Plant growth; [by] Richard & Louise Spilsbury. Revised edition Heinemann Library 2016 48p il (The life of plants) paperback $7.99

Grades: 5 6 7 8 **571.8**

1. Plants -- Growth

ISBN 9781484636947 paperback; 978-1-4329-1507-0; 978-1-4329-1500-1

First published 2003

Describes plant growth and development.

This book "contains many bright and colorful photographs and diagrams to support the text, boldface vocabulary terms, a series of experiments and activities to provide further investigation, a complete glossary, an index, and a list of sources for additional information. . . . [This] volume is a complete and well-rounded unit." Sci Books Films

Includes glossary and bibliographical references

571.9 Diseases

Somervill, Barbara A.

Cells and disease. Heinemann Library 2011 48p il (Investigating cells) lib bdg $32

Grades: 5 6 7 8 **571.9**

1. Cells 2. Bacteria 3. Diseases

ISBN 978-1-4329-3881-9; 1-4329-3881-9

LC 2009-49981

This book describes cells and diseases.

"The abundant graphic matter—photographs, diagrams, charts and graphs—work together with the text to create visually appealing pages. . . . [This] would be very useful in any kind of formal investigation of the topic and yet attractive enough to encourage browsing. . . . [This] . . . is exceptionally well done." Libr Media Connect

Includes glossary and bibliographical references

572 Biochemistry

Haelle, Tara

Edible Sunlight; by Tara Haelle. Rosen Publishing 2016 48 p. color illustrations $10.95; (ebook) $24.95

Grades: 5 6 7 8 **572**

1. Sun 2. Food 3. Agriculture

ISBN 1681913992; 1681914417; 9781681913995; 9781681914411; 9781681914800

LC 2015951566

This children's nonfiction book, by Tara Haelle, part of the "Let's Explore Science" series, presents "a taste of sunshine! [It] discusses the fascinating ways the Sun is involved in food production." (Publisher's note)

Includes bibliographical references (page 47) and index.

Sitarski, Anita

★ **Cold** light; creatures, discoveries, and inventions that glow. Boyds Mills Press 2007 48p il $16.95

Grades: 5 6 7 8 **572**

1. Light 2. Bioluminescence

ISBN 1-59078-468-5; 978-1-59078-468-6

"A clearly written, chatty text not only discusses the expected bioluminescent critters (think fireflies), but delves into the realms of chemiluminescence, photoluminescence, and LEDs (light-emitting diodes) as well. . . . The text lays out the historical hows and whys of cold light, its success in the natural world, and its application in medicine and domestic/industrial illumination. Clear color photos and information boxes abound." SLJ

Zimmer, Marc

Bioluminescence; Nature and Science at Work. by Marc Zimmer. Twenty-First Century Books 2016 72 p. color illustrations $34.65

Grades: 6 7 8 9 10 **572**

1. Bioluminescence 2. Green fluorescent protein

ISBN 1467757845; 9781467757843

LC 2014025675

This book, by Marc Zimmer, "takes readers into the world of bioluminescence, or the production and emission of light by living creatures. After providing a brief explanation of how 19th-century physiologist Raphaël Dubois discovered that bioluminescence is a product of the enzyme luciferase and the molecule luciferin, Zimmer presents many fascinating examples of animals making use of this ability." (School Library Journal)

"Featuring top-notch photos, this succinct presentation of a complex topic will make a stimulating addition to most science collections." SLJ

Includes bibliographical references and index

572.8 Biochemical genetics

Anders, Mason

DNA, genes, and chromosomes; by Mason Anders. Capstone Press 2018 32 p. color illustrations

Grades: 3 4 5 6 **572.8**

1. DNA 2. Genes 3. Heredity 4. Genetic disorders

ISBN 151577256X; 1515772608; 9781515772569; 9781515772606

LC 2016055790

"Did you know that most of our bodies' cells contain about 6 feet (2 meters) of DNA? Learn how DNA and genes determine each unique trait of plants and animals by taking a close look at the make up and structure of DNA." (Publisher's note)

Includes bibliographical references (page 31) and index

Anniss, Matt

James Watson and Francis Crick; Matt Anniss. Gareth Stevens Publishing 2014 48 p. illustrations (chiefly color) $31.95

Grades: 4 5 6 **572.8**

1. Genetics

ISBN 1482414716; 9781482414714

This children's book by Matt Anniss on physicists James Watson and Francis Crick is part of a series known for its "graphics and ability to make complex concepts accessible. The authors have . . . select[ed] key quotes from the scientists' writings that young readers can understand (provided in sidebars titled 'In Their Own Words')." (Publisher's note)

"Reading their parallel stories will let children see how different people solve the same problems. Original takes on science biographies." SLJ

Arbuthnott, Gill

What makes you you? Gill Arbuthnott ; illustrated by Marc Mones. Crabtree Publishing Company 2016 64 p. color illustrations (reinforced library binding : alk. paper) $31.93

Grades: 5 6 7 8 **572.8**

1. DNA 2. Heredity 3. Genetics

ISBN 9780778722397; 9780778722472

LC 2015042097

This book, by Gill Arbuthnott, illustrated by Marc Mones, "is a mind-blowing introduction to the building blocks of life DNA! Amazing 3D-style illustrations and diagrams help explain what it is, how it works, and what we can do with it. Breaking down complex scientific concepts and processes into bite-sized chunks, this fascinating book explains everything from the basics of evolution to the incredible achievements of modern-day genetic research and what's in store for the future!" (Publisher's note)

"While this is a lot to tackle, the book is extremely well organized and always supplies readers with page references so they can refresh on previously covered topics." Booklist

Includes index

Helfand, Lewis

They Changed the World; Bell, Edison and Tesla. writer, Lewis Helfand ; illustrator, Naresh Kumar. Random House Inc 2014 96 p. color illustrations $12.99

Grades: 7 8 9 10 **572.8**

1. Inventors -- Biography 2. Graphic novels 3. Inventors -- United States -- Biography -- Comic books, strips, etc.

ISBN 9380741871; 9789380741871

"Find out how Alexander Graham Bell, Thomas Edison and Nicola Tesla changed the world we live in forever! Three men, three great minds and three completely different approaches to science." (Publisher's note)

"Kumar shows not only the fundamental intelligence but also the hard work and productive attitudes these three geniuses brought to their work. Helfand's solid research is a great jumping-off point for student researchers, and the inclusion of a DIY project--building a rudimentary phone--adds to the appeal." Booklist

Rand, Casey

DNA and heredity. Heinemann Library 2011 48p il (Investigating cells) lib bdg $32

Grades: 5 6 7 8 **572.8**

1. DNA 2. Cells 3. Heredity

ISBN 978-1-4329-3880-2; 1-4329-3880-0

LC 2009049978

Learn about cells, DNA and scientists who made an impact in cell research.

"The abundant graphic matter—photographs, diagrams, charts and graphs—work together with the text to create visually appealing pages. . . . [This] would be very useful in any kind of formal investigation of the topic and yet attractive enough to encourage browsing. . . . [This] . . . is exceptionally well done." Libr Media Connect

Includes glossary and bibliographical references

Vaughan, Jenny

Who discovered DNA? Arcturus Pub. 2010 46p il (Breakthroughs in science and technology) lib bdg $32.80

Grades: 5 6 7 8 **572.8**

1. DNA

ISBN 978-1-84837-679-3; 1-84837-679-0

LC 2010011021

"This brief well-done book presents accurate information in an interesting way, using appropriate and appealing graphics. . . . The book not only tells us that Frederick Miesche discovered DNA in 1869, but presents many relevant discoveries before that time and, especially, after it. Applications of the discoveries are also presented, as are controversies related to the genetic knowledge of our day. . . . [This] would be useful as reference and should be available to all interested students." Sci Books & Films

Includes glossary and bibliographical references

Yount, Lisa

Rosalind Franklin; photographing biomolecules. by Lisa Yount. Chelsea House 2011 xix, 125 p.p col. ill. (Trailblazers in science and technology) (library) $35.00

Grades: 7 8 9 10 11 12 **572.8**

1. Women scientists 2. DNA -- History 3. Molecular biologists -- Great Britain -- Biography 4. Women molecular biologists -- Great Britain -- Biography

ISBN 160413660X; 9781604136609

LC 2010048229

This book by Lisa Yount is part of the Trailblazers in Science and Technology series and looks at Rosalind Franklin. "Tracing her life from her birth in Great Britain to her education at Cambridge, to her groundbreaking research [in X-ray crystallography], and to her tragic and untimely death," this book offers an "overview of the life and career of one of the most influential scientific figures of the 20th century." (Publisher's note)

Includes bibliographical references and index.

573.8 Nervous and sensory systems

Buchanan, Shelly C.

★ **Animal** senses; by Shelly C. Buchanan. Teacher Created Materials 2016 32 p. (pbk. : alk. paper) $8.99

Grades: 4 5 6 **573.8**

1. Animals 2. Senses and sensation in animals 3. Physiology 4. Senses and sensation

ISBN 9781480746787

LC 2014045243

This book, by Shelly C. Buchanan, focuses on "the unique ways in which animals use their senses. . . . High-interest text paired with colorful images and graphics fill the pages of this book to engage students from cover to cover. Encourage students to apply what they've learned in the text by completing the Think Like a Scientist activity, that supports STEM instruction, included at the end of the book." (Publisher's note)

"First-rate nonfiction." SLJ

575.6 Reproductive organs

Buchanan, Shelly C.

★ **Plant** reproduction; Shelly C. Buchanan, M.S. Teacher Created Materials 2016 32 p. (pbk.) $8.99

Grades: 4 5 6 **575.6**

1. Plants 2. Reproduction 3. Seeds 4. Pollination 5. Plants -- Reproduction

ISBN 1480746762; 9781480746763

LC 2014045201

In this juvenile reference book, by Shelly C. Buchanan, part of the publisher's "Content and Literacy in Science Grade 4" series, "filled with engaging diagrams and interesting facts, students will get an in-depth look at how plant reproduction works and why each plant is quite different. High-interest text and vibrant images and photographs fill the pages of this book to make learning about plant reproduction fun and interesting." (Publisher's note)

"The latest additions to this ongoing series deliver the same authoritative, comprehensive, and relevant information that educators have come to expect from the publisher. The high-interest subjects support inquiry-based learning and encourage readers to think critically about science, and they do so in an engaging way that holds students' attention. . . . First-rate nonfiction." SLJ

576 General and external biological phenomena

Schutten, Jan Paul

The **mystery** of life; how nothing became everything. Jan Paul Schutten ; illustrated by Floor Rieder ; translated by Laura Watkinson. Aladdin 2015 240 p. color illustrations (hardcover) $15.99

Grades: 7 8 9 10 **576**

1. Evolution 2. Life (Biology) 3. Life -- Origin 4. Discoveries in science

ISBN 9781582705255

LC 2014039916

In this book, originally published in the Netherlands, author Jan Paul Schutten "looks into the miracle of life, whether the specimen in question is a microscopic bacterium or an invented sample human, 'Joe Schmo from Buffalo,' exploring the age of the planet, natural selection, and the development of life on Earth along the way." (Publishers Weekly)

"Though his discussion of hiccups is blurred by fuzzy logic, and virus es and extinction events rate barely a mention, his overall account of life's origins and tenure is as rich in detail as it is entertaining. Rieder likewise supplies a flood of line drawings that provide humorous visual commentary as well as additional information.A glib and occasionally spotty picture but eminently readable and generally on target." Kirkus

Includes bibliographical references and index

576.5 Genetics

Day, Trevor

Genetics; investigating the function of genes and the science of heredity. Trevor Day. 1st ed. Rosen Central 2013 48 p. ill. (chiefly col.) (Scientific pathways) (library) $29.25

Grades: 6 7 8 9 **576.5**

1. Genetics 2. Scientists 3. Heredity

ISBN 1448871999; 9781448871995

LC 2011047887

This book by Trevor Day is part of the Scientific Pathways series and looks at genetics. The series authors "look at science as a process of discovery and explain how each discipline developed in different cultures over time. Significant names and important terms are printed in bold . . . . Brief biographies of thinkers, inventors, and scientists are provided along with important experiments and the conclusions that were made in relation to them." (School Library Journal)

Includes bibliographical references and index.

Duke, Shirley Smith

You can't wear these genes. Rourke Pub. LLC 2010 48p il (Let's explore science) $32.79

Grades: 4 5 6 7 **576.5**

1. Genetics

ISBN 978-1-61590-324-5; 1-61590-324-0

LC 2010009911

This "offers a clear introduction to the complexities of genetics while inviting students to think about how their own DNA shaped who they are. In [this] title, well chosen boxed examples, abundant color photos, diagrams, and an appended glossary add interest and support the engaging [text]." Booklist

Includes glossary and bibliographical references

Hand, Carol

Introduction to genetics. Rosen Pub. 2010 80p il lib bdg $30.60

Grades: 6 7 8 9 10 11 12 **576.5**

1. Genetics 2. Heredity

ISBN 978-1-4358-9531-7

LC 2009-40364

"The moderately technical language in the other titles discusses significant discoveries, current directions in research and–superficially–ethical and other issues. Illustrations include helpful charts, microphotos, portraits of scientists, and color photos; extensive back matter provides plenty of support for further research." SLJ

Mooney, Carla

Genetics; Breaking the Code of Your DNA. by Carla Mooney ; illustrated by Samuel Carbaugh. Nomad Press 2014 128 p. illustrations (Inquire and Investigate) $21.95

Grades: 6 7 8 9 10 11 **576.5**

1. Genetics 2. DNA 3. Genes

ISBN 161930208X; 9781619302082

This book on genetics, by Carla Mooney, illustrated by Samuel Carbaugh, "presents the main concepts of the science, including what a chromosome does, how DNA is structured, and how genetic inheritance works. Students learn about new discoveries in the field of genetics and how those discoveries have helped to cure or even prevent certain diseases, as well as examine controversial issues in genetics such as genetically modified foods and stem cell research." (Publisher's note)

"Although the book can be used independently, it will be better appreciated with some background knowledge. A solid resource that shows life science and biology students the practicalities and marvels of genetics." Booklist

Schafer, Susan

Heredity. M.E. Sharpe 2009 96p il (Genetics: the science of life) $38.95

Grades: 6 7 8 9 **576.5**

1. Genetics 2. Heredity

ISBN 978-0-7656-8136-2; 0-7656-8136-6

LC 2008-8105

This discusses the history of genetics, genetic dominance, hybrid animals, and the role of heredity in disease.

"Chock-full of information. . . . The material is well organized and accessible. . . . Interest is maintained through countless fascinating examples. . . . Illustrations and color photographs enhance [the text]." SLJ

Includes bibliographical references

Simpson, Kathleen

★ **Genetics**; from DNA to designer dogs. Sarah Tishkoff, consultant. National Geographic 2008 64p il map (National Geographic investigates) $27.90

Grades: 4 5 6 7 **576.5**

1. Genetics

ISBN 978-1-4263-0361-6; 1-4263-0361-0; 978-1-4263-0327-2 lib bdg; 1-4263-0327-0 lib bdg

This discusses topics in genetics such as the identification of an Egyptian mummy by DNA testing, the genetics of pea plants studied by Gregor Mendel, cloning, the Human Genome Project, and stem cell research.

"The content is fairly exciting and should grab the attention of its target audience. . . . The photographs throughout are of high quality. . . . An engaging look at a complex topic." Booklist

576.8 Evolution

Berkowitz, Jacob

Out of this world; the amazing search for an alien earth. Kids Can Press 2009 48p il $16.95; pa $8.95

Grades: 4 5 6 7 **576.8**

1. Life on other planets 2. Outer space -- Exploration

ISBN 978-1-55453-197-4; 1-55453-197-7; 978-1-55453-198-1 pa; 1-55453-198-5 pa

The author "has written a miniencyclopedic, profusely illustrated, picture book that describes, in much detail, what we all know about the universe in which we live and about the conditions that must be present on any planet in our solar system, or on an exoplanet . . . for life as we know it to exist." Sci Books Films

Claybourne, Anna

Who discovered natural selection? Arcturus Pub. 2010 46p il (Breakthroughs in science and technology) lib bdg $32.80

Grades: 5 6 7 8 **576.8**

1. Heredity 2. Naturalists 3. Natural selection 4. Travel writers 5. Writers on science

ISBN 978-1-84837-682-3; 1-84837-682-0

LC 2010011020

"Earning high marks for clarity, organization, and visual appeal, this introduction to evolution and natural selection takes a historical approach, beginning with the philosophies of the ancients and tracing the development of evolution theory through the 19th century naturalists who set the stage for the conceptualization of natural selection. . . . Short narrative sections are interspersed with high-interest sidebars to keep the pace lively. The book ends with examples of rapid natural selection in viral strains and in antibiotic-resistant bacteria, and it raises the question of how mutually supportive behaviors evolve among social species. Colorful photographs and illustrations, each carefully chosen and placed, support the book's central theme. . . . Claybourne has made evolution theory accessible to young learners in a fresh and accurate way. This is a must buy for school libraries." Sci Books & Films

Includes glossary and bibliographical references

Colson, Mary

Charles Darwin and Alfred Russel Wallace; Mary Colson. Gareth Stevens Publishing 2014 48 p. color illustrations $31.95

Grades: 4 5 6 **576.8**

1. Scientists

ISBN 1482414694; 9781482414691

This book by Mary Colson focuses on scientists Charles Darwin and Alfred Russel Wallace and is part of a series known for "graphics and [the] ability to make complex concepts accessible. The authors have [selected] key quotes from the scientists' writings that young readers can understand (provided in sidebars titled 'In Their Own Words')." (School Library Journal)

★ **Evolution;** Clay Farris Naff, book editor. Greenhaven Press 2005 222 p. (Exploring science and medical discoveries) lib bdg $34.95

Grades: 8 9 10 11 12 **576.8**

1. Evolution

ISBN 9780737728231

LC 2004-60590

In this anthology, "nineteen selections are arranged in roughly chronological order, beginning with ancient Greek philosophers whose ideas about nature hinted at evolutionary theories to come. . . . This solid survey provides a good overview with manageable amounts of primary-source materials that would be dauntingly difficult to comprehend in their entirety." SLJ

Includes bibliographical references

Gamlin, Linda

Evolution; written by Linda Gamlin. rev ed.; DK Pub. 2009 72p il (DK eyewitness books) $16.99

Grades: 4 5 6 7 576.8

1. Evolution

ISBN 978-0-7566-5028-5; 0-7566-5028-3

First published 1993

Text about and photography of experiments, animals, plants, bones, and fossils reveal the ideas and discoveries that have changed our understanding of the natural world and how life began. Includes a CD and wall chart.

Holmes, Thom

Evolution. Chelsea House 2010 109p il (Science foundations) lib bdg $35

Grades: 7 8 9 10 576.8

1. Evolution

ISBN 978-1-60413-338-7; 1-60413-338-4

LC 2010015738

"A solid, competent history of the evolution of ideas and the theory of evolution itself. . . . Certainly not for browsing or easy light reading, but definitely of use to teachers or serious researchers." (School Library Journal)

Includes glossary and bibliographical references

Johnson, Sylvia A.

★ **Shaking** the foundation; Charles Darwin and the theory of evolution. by Sylvia A. Johnson. Twenty-First Century Books 2013 88 p. (library) $33.27

Grades: 6 7 8 9 576.8

1. Evolution 2. Evolution (Biology)

ISBN 0761354867; 9780761354864

LC 2012018075

This book offers an "overview of how [Charles] Darwin's theories of natural selection and evolution shook the foundations of religious beliefs and long-held scientific views. . . .[Sylvia A.] Johnson devotes the first half of her book to discussing the intellectual, philosophical and societal changes brought by the Enlightenment and Industrial Revolution that would make people receptive to Darwin's ideas. . . . The second half chronicles how Darwin formulated his theories." (Kirkus Reviews)

"In this thoughtful history of both Darwin and his theories of evolution, Johnson explains how the scientist lived and worked, religious and scientific challenges to his theories, and American legal challenges to evolution that continue in contemporary times. Numerous historical photographs and scientific illustrations, many from scientists of his time, greatly enhance the text." (Horn Book)

Includes bibliographical references and index

Newland, Sonya

Extinction! by Jim Pipe. Crabtree Publishing Company 2013 48 p. col. ill. (Crabtree chrome) (library) $30.60; (paperback) $9.95

Grades: 4 5 6 576.8

1. Extinct animals 2. End of the world 3. Mass extinctions 4. Extinction (Biology)

ISBN 0778779254; 9780778779254; 9780778779346

LC 2012032046

This book by Sonya Newland "explores both the history of extinction--dating back to the mass extinction of the Ordovician period 450 million years ago and the extinction of the dinosaurs 65 million years ago--as well as the possibility of the extinction of species in existence today. . . . In addition . . . Newland considers possible scenarios that might end life on Earth: an asteroid colliding with our planet . . . or an exploding nuclear bomb that blocks out the sun." (School Library Journal)

Includes bibliographical references and index

Pringle, Laurence, 1935-

★ **Billions** of years, amazing changes; the story of evolution. Boyds Mills Press 2011 102p il $17.95

Grades: 4 5 6 7 576.8

1. Evolution

ISBN 978-1-59078-723-6; 1-59078-723-4

"Pringle provides an accessible introduction to complex concepts such as natural selection and genetics, paired with Jenkins's characteristically elegant collages. . . . Compelling photographs of fossils and living creatures, as well as Jenkins's paper collages, augment the substantial text. The presentation should help children gain a confident grasp on the fundamentals of evolution." Publ Wkly

Solway, Andrew

Why is there life on Earth? Raintree 2012 48p il (Earth, space, and beyond) $32; pa $8.99

Grades: 5 6 7 8 576.8

1. Life on other planets 2. Earth 3. Life -- Origin

ISBN 978-1-4109-4160-2; 978-1-4109-4166-4 pa

LC 2010040160

"Delivering compact but broad summations about...life on Earth, [this] survey [is] well suited for review or reinforcement reading." SLJ

Includes glossary and bibliographical references

Turner, Pamela S.

Life on earth--and beyond; an astrobiologist's quest. Charlesbridge 2008 109p il map lib bdg $19.95; pa $11.95

Grades: 5 6 7 8 576.8

1. Space biology 2. Life on other planets 3. Astrophysicists

ISBN 978-1-58089-133-2 lib bdg; 1-58089-133-0 lib bdg; 978-1-58089-134-9 pa; 1-58089-134-9 pa

LC 2007-01475

"Astrobiologists look outward from the Earth seeking evidence of life elsewhere in the universe. But, as this fascinating book shows, they also travel to places on Earth where extreme conditions may be similar to those on distant worlds. Turner follows astrobiologist Chris McKay as he looks for life in apparently hostile environments. . . . Illustrated with many excellent color photos and other images." Booklist

Includes bibliographical references

Walker, Robert

What is the theory of evolution? Crabtree Pub. Co. 2011 64p il (Shaping modern science) lib bdg $30.60; pa $10.95

Grades: 5 6 7 8 576.8

1. Evolution 2. Naturalists 3. Travel writers 4. Writers on science

ISBN 978-0-7787-7198-2 lib bdg; 0-7787-7198-9 lib bdg; 978-0-7787-7205-7 pa; 0-7787-7205-5 pa

LC 2010052628

This title is "not only written and organized well, but [it is] also gorgeous in design. Full-color photographs and illustrations are set over colorful backgrounds that add depth but not distraction. [The title] includes thought-provoking quotes from famous authors and scientists and some eyebrow-raising 'Quick Facts' throughout." SLJ

Includes glossary and bibliographical references

Winston, Robert M. L.

Evolution revolution; [by] Robert Wilson. DK Pub. 2009 96p il hardcover $16.99; paperback $9.99

Grades: 5 6 7 8 576.8

1. Evolution

ISBN 9780756645243; 9781465451378

"The first two thirds of the book are devoted to the history of thought and research on evolution, from stories of Creation, through Darwin, to genetics. The last third looks at 'Evolution in Action.' Information on the fetuses of related species rubs shoulders with variations within species and a time line of the Earth. Visually, the book snaps with colored backgrounds, cool graphics, topflight photos, and clever word balloons coming from vintage black-and-white reproductions." SLJ

577 Ecology

Ballard, Carol

Food webs. Rosen Central 2010 46p il (Living processes) lib bdg $26.50; pa $11.75 **577**

1. Food chains (Ecology)

ISBN 978-1-61532-340-1 lib bdg; 1-61532-340-6 lib bdg; 978-1-61532-351-7 pa; 1-61532-351-1 pa

LC 2009-28379

"With colorful, quality photography, the well-organized content is divided into short chapters with bold subheadings making information easy to find. Clear and interesting writing distinguishes this . . . from older titles. The captions for pictures are used to provide identification and additional explanation for topics not included in the text." Libr Media Connect

Includes glossary and bibliographical references

Ecology; the delicate balance of life on earth. edited by Sherman Hollar. Rosen Educational Services, LLC 2012 87 p. col. ill. (library) $31.70

Grades: 5 6 7 8 **577**

1. Ecology 2. Environmentalism

ISBN 1615305076; 9781615305070

LC 2010052490

This book on ecology, edited by Sherman Hollar, "explores the formation of ecological communities and examines the biological diversity that forms the backbone of life on the planet. . . . By parsing the natural world into various ecosystems and biomes" it looks at "interaction among species and between organisms and their natural habitats". (Publisher's note)

Includes bibliographical references (p. 84) and index.

Latham, Donna

Amazing biome projects you can build yourself; illustrated by Farah Rizvi. Nomad Press 2009 122p il map (Build it yourself) pa $15.95

Grades: 4 5 6 7 **577**

1. Ecology 2. Handicraft 3. Earth sciences 4. Science -- Experiments

ISBN 978-1-934670-40-8; 1-934670-40-5

"Although the text addresses young 'eco explorers' directly, this book will likely be used as much by teachers, parents, and organization leaders in planning group activities. Offering an overview of eight terrestrial biomes as well as the ocean, Latham crams a lot of information about climate, plants, animals, soil, and other characteristics onto every page. . . . Instructions for hands-on activities related to different biomes include craft projects such as pictographs and a cornhusk doll. Students can learn how to make a glacier, an erupting volcano, and a tornado in a bottle." SLJ

Includes glossary and bibliographical references

Montgomery, Sy

Amazon adventure; how tiny fish are saving the world's largest rainforest. written by Sy Montgomery ; photographs by Keith Ellenbogen. Houghton Mifflin Harcourt 2017 65 p. color illustrations, color map (Scientists in the field series) (hardcover) $18.99

Grades: 5 6 7 8 9 **577**

1. Amazon River 2. Rain forests 3. Amazon River valley 4. Fishes -- Amazon River 5. Rio Negro (Amazonas, Brazil) 6. Ecology -- Amazon River Region 7. Fishes -- Brazil -- Rio Negro (Amazonas) 8. Biotic communities -- Amazon River Region 9. Ecology -- Brazil -- Rio Negro (Amazonas)

ISBN 9781328694980; 9780544352995

LC 2016014693

In this book, "join the award-winning author Sy Montgomery and the photographer Keith Ellenbogen as they traverse the river and rainforest to discover how tiny fish, called piabas, can help preserve the Amazon, its animals, and the rich legacy of its people." (Publisher's note)

"An expansive and engaging story of biological interconnectedness and beauty." Pub Wkly

Includes bibliographical references and index.

Shaw, Daniel

Eco -tracking; on the trail of habitat change. with photographs by Melanie Keithley, Jon Livingston MacLake, and the author. University of New Mexico Press 2010 85p il (Worlds of wonder) $19.95

Grades: 6 7 8 9 10 **577**

1. Ecology 2. Environmental protection

ISBN 978-0-8263-4531-8; 0-8263-4531-X

LC 2010010319

"The authors tackle environmental issues with depth and rigor, attuned to both current events and the concerns of today's teens. Global Warming and Powering look at the science and human impact of climate change and alternative energies, while Eco-tracking encourages citizen-science investigation for young environmentalists. The excellent texts are enhanced by color photographs and diagrams that further explain scientific ideas. " (Horn Book)

Includes glossary

Stille, Darlene R.

Nature interrupted; the science of environmental chain reactions. Compass Point Books 2009 48p il map (Headline science) lib bdg $27.93

Grades: 5 6 7 8 **577**

1. Ecology 2. Food chains (Ecology) 3. Environmental degradation

ISBN 978-0-7565-3949-8 lib bdg; 0-7565-3949-8 lib bdg

LC 2008007282

This "reviews the importance of subtle links in the environmental chain and the far-reaching consequences of its disruption. The possible harm to the food chain caused by the use of antibacterial soap is one case study. The flow of energy from one organism to the next in the food web and the unexpected results when this relationship is disrupted are shown in examinations of monarch butterflies, zebra mussels, and algal blooms. The color illustrations and charts . . . are clear and helpful, and the text, although information rich, is not overly difficult." SLJ

Includes glossary and bibliographical references

Suzuki, David T., 1936-

★ **You** are the Earth; know your world so you can make it better. [by] David Suzuki and Kathy Vanderlinden; art by

Wallace Edwards; diagrams by Talent Pun. rev ed; Greystone Books 2010 159p il $16.95
Grades: 4 5 6 7 **577**

1. Ecology 2. Human ecology
ISBN 1-55365-476-5; 978-1-55365-476-6

First published 1999 with title: You are the Earth: from dinosaur breath to pizza from dirt

"After devoting a chapter to each of life's necessities—air, water, soil (earth), energy (fire), love, and a spiritual connection with the universe—the authors close with a look at three social and environmental initiatives by young people; a set of review questions (with answers); and 10 consciousness-raising activities, from science projects to storytelling. Sourced, briefly told versions of folktales from several traditions are interspersed throughout, and the plentiful illustrations include color diagrams, comics, and crisply reproduced photos. . . . [The authors'] eloquent plea to see ourselves and the Earth as interdependent will inspire readers to sit up, look around, and take a little less for granted." SLJ

Includes glossary

VanCleave, Janice Pratt, 1942-

Step -by-step science experiments in ecology; by Janice VanCleave. Rosen Pub. 2013 80 p. col. ill. (Janice VanCleave's first-place science fair projects) (library) $33.25; (paperback) $14.15
Grades: 5 6 7 8 **577**

1. Ecology 2. Science -- Experiments 3. Ecology -- Experiments
ISBN 1448869803; 9781448869800; 9781448884698

This book by Janice VanCleave is part of the First-Place Science Fair Projects series. The books have an introduction to the subject—here, ecology, followed by 22 simple . . . experiments. Van Cleave states the basic goal of the experiments, followed by a list of necessary materials, most of which can be found around the house or easily acquired with minimal cost. Step-by-step instructions are clearly detailed and accompanied by diagrams where needed." (School Library Journal)

Includes bibliographical references (p. 76-78) and index.

Walker, Pamela

Ecosystem science fair projects; revised and expanded using the scientific method. [by] Pam Walker and Elaine Wood. Enslow Publishers 2010 160p il (Biology science projects using the scientific method) lib bdg $34.60
Grades: 7 8 9 10 **577**

1. Ecology 2. Science projects 3. Science -- Experiments
ISBN 978-0-7660-3419-8 lib bdg; 0-7660-3419-4 lib bdg

LC 2009019375

First published 2005 with title: Ecosystem science fair projects using worms, leaves, crickets, and other stuff

"Explains how to use the scientific method to conduct several science experiments about ecosystems. Includes ideas for science fair projects." Publisher's note

Includes bibliographical references

Woodford, Chris

Arctic tundra and polar deserts; Revised ed. Raintree 2011 64p il map (Biomes atlases) $34
Grades: 5 6 7 8 9 **577**

1. Tundra ecology 2. Polar regions
ISBN 978-1-4329-4172-7; 1-4329-4172-0

LC 2010012428

Information about the animals and plants that typically make polar regions and tundra environments their homes.

"Provides detailed information suitable for middle school research projects, and browsing potential is high due to the colorful, graphic nature." Library Media Connection

Includes bibliographical references

577.2 Specific factors affecting ecology

Simon, Seymour

★ **Wildfires**; Seymour Simon. 2nd edition Collins 2016 32 p illustrations hardcover $17.99; paperback $6.99
Grades: 4 5 6 7 **577.2**

1. Forest fires 2. Forest ecology
ISBN 9780062345035; 9780062345028; 9780062345066; 0062345028

"Simon lays out the evidence for the important role fires play in forest ecosystems. Featuring the 1988 Yellowstone fire, he explains its progress, the impact on plants and animals (many of which have evolved interdependence on fire events), and the use of controlled fires. In this updated edition, per usual, excellent photographs are well linked to the text." Horn Book

577.3 Ecology of specific environments

Allaby, Michael

Temperate forests; illustrations by Richard Garratt. rev ed; Facts on File 2008 336p il map (Ecosystem) $70
Grades: 7 8 9 10 **577.3**

1. Forest ecology 2. Forests and forestry
ISBN 0-8160-5930-6; 978-0-8160-5930-0

LC 2006-28859

First published 1999

"Those who are curious about or who are studying the environment and ecosystems . . . will find this book both fascinating and enlightening." Sci Books Films

Includes glossary and bibliographical references

Bulion, Leslie

Leaf litter critters; Leslie Bulion ; illustrated by Robert Meganck. Peachtree Publishers 2018 48 p. $14.95
Grades: 4 5 6 7 **577.3**

1. Forest plants 2. Forest animals 3. Forest ecology 4. Leaves 5. Forest litter
ISBN 9781561459506

LC 2017015586

This book, by Leslie Bulion, illustrated by Robert Megan, presents "nineteen poems in a variety of verse forms with accompanying science notes [that] take readers on a decomposer safari through the 'brown food web,' from bacteria through tardigrades and on to rove beetle predators with other busy recyclers in-between. Glossary, hands-on investigations, and resources are included in the back matter." (Publisher's note)

Includes bibliographical references

Burnie, David

Shrublands; David Burnie. Raintree 2011 64 p. col. ill., col. maps (Biomes atlases) (library) $34
Grades: 6 7 8 **577.3**

1. Biomes 2. Habitat (Ecology) 3. Shrublands 4. Shrubland ecology
ISBN 143294178X; 9781432941789

LC 2010013019

This book is from the Biomes Atlases Series and focuses on shrublands. Each book offers an introduction to a different biome. "Brief notes for 10 to 12 highlights appear on each one, commenting on the diversity of flora, fauna, and landforms that occurs. Longer overviews of climate, plants, animals, people, and future prospects for the biome alternate with the regional close-ups." (School Library Journal)

Includes bibliographical references (p. 63) and index

Quinlan, Susan E.

The **case** of the monkeys that fell from the trees; and other mysteries in tropical nature. Boyds Mills Press 2003 171p il map paperback $11.95

Grades: 6 7 8 9 **577.3**

1. Natural history 2. Rain forest ecology

ISBN 1-56397-902-0; 9781590787755 paperback

LC 2002-108914

"Quinlan's book is well organized and clearly written. . . . Besides presenting some fascinating case studies in a style that conveys the thrill of the scientific chase, it also provides information on the different kinds of tropical forests and how they function." SLJ

Includes bibliographical references

Vogt, Richard Carl

Rain forests. Simon & Schuster Books for Young Readers 2009 64p il (Insiders) $16.99

Grades: 4 5 6 7 **577.3**

1. Rain forests

ISBN 978-1-4169-3866-8; 1-4169-3866-4

LC 2008061111

"The layers of a rain forest are drawn with exacting detail in every imaginable shade of green, while circular inserts zoom in on flora with accompanying stats. Running down the length of the spread are markers delineating the cutoff points for each layer—emergent, canopy, and so on. The rest of the book is similarly fine, bringing animals, reptiles, and insects into the mix. . . . Some photographs join the mostly hand-illustrated affair. . . . What will grab browsers are the 3D cover and vivid drawings on thick, oversize pages, but what will keep them reading is a cumulative sense of the rain forest as a verdant universe nearly festering with life." Booklist

Warhol, Tom

Chaparral and scrub; [by] Tom Warhol. Marshall Cavendish Benchmark 2006 80p il (Earth's biomes) lib bdg $32.79

Grades: 6 7 8 9 **577.3**

1. Chaparral ecology 2. Forests and forestry

ISBN 978-0-7614-2195-5 lib bdg; 0-7614-2195-5 lib bdg

LC 2006015824

"Explores chaparral and scrub biomes and covers where they are located as well as the plants and animals that inhabit them." Publisher's note

Includes glossary and bibliographical references

577.34 Rain forest ecology

Hand, Carol

★ **Bringing** back our tropical forests; Carol Hand ; content consultant, Bénédicte Bachelot. Abdo Pub. 2018 112 p. color illustrations, color map (Conservation success stories) $37.07

Grades: 7 8 9 10 **577.34**

1. Rain forests 2. Forest conservation 3. Rain forest ecology

ISBN 1532113161; 9781532113161; 9781532152047

LC 2017946791

This book "explains why tropical forests are at risk and how people are combating deforestation, encouraging sustainable agricultural practices, and preserving tropical forests. This title also explores the science behind tropical peatland forests and the layers of a rain forest. Features include a cause-and-effect flow chart, a glossary, references, websites, source notes, and an index." (Publisher's note)

"The design of these books is roomy and attractive, featuring many high-quality photos, 'Science Connection' spreads, and relevant fact boxes--often highlighting indigenous peoples' rights and plights within vulnerable areas." Booklist

Includes bibliographical references (pages 104-109) and index

Johnson, Robin

Rain forests inside out; Robin Johnson. Crabtree Publishing 2015 32 p. color illustrations (reinforced library binding) $27.60

Grades: 4 5 6 **577.34**

1. Ecology 2. Rain forests 3. Rain forest ecology

ISBN 0778706370; 9780778706373; 9780778714583

LC 2014020968

This children's book on the rain forests by Robin Johnson is part of a series that "takes readers on a tour of Earth's six major biomes, exploring their distinctive characteristics as well as the unique creatures who have made each habitat their home. Key words are highlighted via bold font and are defined in the extensive glossary while sidebars . . . provides students with a greater understanding of each environment's interdependent relationship between living and nonliving organisms." (School Library Journal)

"The lush photos of locations worldwide may inspire further investigation of the topic. Great selections." SLJ

Includes bibliographical references and index

Welsbacher, Anne

Protecting Earth's rain forests; by Anne Welsbacher. Lerner Publications 2009 72p il map (Saving our living Earth) lib bdg $30.60

Grades: 5 6 7 8 **577.34**

1. Rain forests 2. Environmental protection

ISBN 978-0-8225-7562-7 lib bdg; 0-8225-7562-0 lib bdg

LC 2007-38859

"Provides a thorough, interesting discussion of multiple aspects of [rain forest protection], including historical origins, the current situation, and potential solutions. . . . Photos from around the world accompany discussions. . . . Solid choice to replace outdated books." SLJ

Includes glossary and bibliographical references

577.4 Grassland ecology

Bow, James

Grasslands inside out; James Bow. Crabtree Publishing 2015 32 p. color illustrations; maps (reinforced library binding) $27.60

Grades: 4 5 6 **577.4**

1. Ecology 2. Grasslands 3. Grassland ecology

ISBN 0778706338; 9780778706335; 9780778707066

LC 2014020967

This children's book by James Bow "discusses the landscape and climate of grasslands and savannas, explores the types of grasslands found around the world, describes the plant and animal life, and explains the factors currently threatening grassland ecosystems." (Publisher's note)

"The lush photos of locations worldwide may inspire further investigation of the topic. Great selections." SLJ

Hoare, Ben

Temperate grasslands; Ben Hoare. Raintree 2011 64 p. col. ill., col. maps (Biomes atlases) (library) $34.00

Grades: 6 7 8 9 **577.4**

1. Prairies 2. Grasslands 3. Prairie animals 4. Prairie ecology 5. Grassland ecology

ISBN 143294181X; 9781432941819

LC 2010013034

This book, by Ben Hoare, is part of the publisher's "Biomes Atlases" nonfiction series. "Untouched temperate grasslands can be hard to find, since the fertile soil is often converted to farmland." This book presents a profile of the wild flora and fauna which does exist in these areas. (Publisher's note)

"Each volume opens with a colorful world map featuring the eleven biomes of the world; individual books then diverge into a specific biome. Five topics are covered in each book: climate, plants, animals, people, and future of the biome. Each of these main sections is separated by a two-page layout featuring a specific example of the region...While the majority of the information is available online, students will enjoy learning with these books much more than an electronic search." (Library Media Connection)

Includes bibliographical references (p. 63) and index.

577.5 Ecology of miscellaneous environments

Allaby, Michael

Deserts; illustrations by Richard Garratt. rev ed; Facts on File 2008 320p il map (Ecosystem) $70

Grades: 7 8 9 10 **577.5**

1. Deserts 2. Desert ecology

ISBN 0-8160-5929-2; 978-0-8160-5929-4

LC 2007-00477

First published 2001

"This book is a good mix of text, excellent maps, photographs, and scientific information." Sci Books Films

Includes glossary and bibliographical references

Banting, Erinn

Caves; Erinn Banting. AV2 by Weigl 2012 32 p. col. ill., col. map (Ecosystems) (hardcover) $28.55; (paperback) $13.95

Grades: 4 5 6 **577.5**

1. Caves 2. Cave ecology 3. Ecology

ISBN 1616906391; 1616906456; 9781616906399; 9781616906450

LC 2010050985

This book by Erinn Banting is part of the "Biomes" series. "Caves are unique ecosystems that are found on all seven continents. This book explores the plants and animals that have adapted to life in this unique environment." (Publisher's note) "Explanations of climate and physical characteristics are accompanied by appropriate diagrams and illustrations." (School Library Journal)

Bow, James

Tundras inside out; James Bow. Crabtree Publishing 2015 32 p. color illustrations (reinforced library binding) $27.60

Grades: 4 5 6 **577.5**

1. Environment 2. Tundra ecology 3. Tundras

ISBN 0778706397; 9780778706397; 9780778707240

LC 2014020249

Author James Bow's children's book on tundras is part of a series which "takes readers on a tour of Earth's six major biomes, exploring their distinctive characteristics as well as the unique creatures who have made each habitat their home. Key words are highlighted via bold font and are defined in the extensive glossary." (School Library Journal)

"The lush photos of locations worldwide may inspire further investigation of the topic. Great selections." SLJ

Includes bibliographical references and index

Burns, Loree Griffin

★ **Life** on Surtsey; Iceland's upstart island. by Loree Griffin Burns. Houghton Mifflin Harcourt 2017 73 p. illustrations (chiefly color) (Scientists in the field) (hardcover) $18.99

Grades: 4 5 6 7 8 9 **577.5**

1. Scientists 2. Island ecology 3. Surtsey (Iceland) 4. Scientists -- Iceland -- Surtsey

ISBN 9781328828835; 9780544687233

LC 2016042892

In this book in the Scientists in the Field Series, author "Loree Griffin Burns follows entomologist Erling Ólafsson on a five-day trip to Surtsey, where since 1970 he has studied the arrival and survival of insects and other species. Readers see how demanding conditions on Surtsey can be, what it's like to eat and work while making the smallest impact possible, and the passion driving [this] remarkable [scientist] in one of the world's most unique fields ever!" (Publisher's note)

"An amazing science adventure well worth the trip." Kirkus

Includes bibliographical references and index

Cohen, Marina

Deserts inside out; by Marina Cohen. Crabtree Publishing Company 2015 32 p. color illustrations, color map (reinforced library binding) $27.60

Grades: 4 5 6 **577.5**

1. Deserts 2. Desert ecology

ISBN 9780778706274; 9780778706731

LC 2014020252

This book, by Marina Cohen, part of the "Ecosystems Inside Out" series, "[d]iscusses the landscape and climate of deserts, explores the types of deserts found around the world, describes the plant and animal life, and explains how to protect and conserve desert ecosystems." (Publisher's note)

"The even-handed tone, dynamic page layouts, extensive glossary, and concise writing make this an engaging and informative resource." Booklist

Lynch, Wayne

Sonoran Desert; text and photographs by Wayne Lynch; assisted by Aubrey Lang. NorthWord Books 2009 64p il (Our wild world ecosystems) $16.95

Grades: 5 6 7 8 **577.5**

1. Desert ecology 2. Sonoran Desert 3. Natural history -- Sonoran Desert

ISBN 978-1-58979-389-7; 1-58979-389-7

LC 2008036635

"An in-depth look at a vibrant ecosystem. Spilling over the Mexican border into Arizona and New Mexico, the Sonoran Desert is especially rich in varied plants, animals, insects, and other critters that call it home. Lynch shares his expertise and experiences in a clearly written, conversational text, lavishly illustrated with his own crisp color photos." SLJ

577.6 Aquatic ecology

Lynette, Rachel

River food chains. Heinemann Library 2011 48p il map (Protecting food chains) lib bdg $32; pa $8.99

Grades: 4 5 6 7 **577.6**

1. River ecology 2. Food chains (Ecology)

ISBN 978-1-4329-3861-1 lib bdg; 1-4329-3861-4 lib bdg; 978-1-4329-3868-0 pa; 1-4329-3868-1 pa

LC 2009049552

This book explores the species found in river food chains and webs, and discusses why these food chains and webs need to be protected.

"Featuring colorful, glossy images and accessible prose, this . . . offers a good introduction to the web of life in rivers. . . . Conservation issues are highlighted throughout, with specific suggestions for youth to get involved. . . . An informative, thought-provoking resource that conveys the fragile, interconnected web that holds ecosystems together." Booklist

Includes glossary and bibliographical references

577.68 Wetland ecology

Bow, James

Wetlands inside out; James Bow. Crabtree Publishing 2015 32 p. color illustrations (Ecosystems inside out) (reinforced library binding) $27.60

Grades: 4 5 6 **577.68**

1. Wetlands 2. Ecology 3. Wetland ecology

ISBN 0778706419; 9780778706410; 9780778707264

LC 2014020969

This book by James Bow on wetlands is part of a "series [that] takes readers on a tour of Earth's six major biomes, exploring their distinctive characteristics as well as the unique creatures who have made each habitat their home. Key words are highlighted via bold font and are defined in the extensive glossary while sidebars . . . provides students with a greater understanding of each environment's interdependent relationship between living and nonliving organisms. Activities and activism also play a part in the volumes." (School Library Journal)

"Each spread includes a few paragraphs discussing the particular wetland and one species living there. A large color photo shows the site, while a smaller close-up illustrates the featured plant or animal." Booklist

Includes bibliographical references and index.

577.7 Marine ecology

Carson, Rachel

The **edge** of the sea; with illustrations by Bob Hines. Houghton Mifflin 1955 276p il hardcover o.p. pa $14

Grades: 7 8 9 10 11 12 Adult **577.7**

1. Seashore 2. Marine biology

ISBN 0-395-92496-0 pa

"The seashores of the world may be divided into three basic types: the rugged shores of rock, the sand beaches, and the coral reefs and all their associated features. Each has its typical community of plants and animals. The Atlantic coast of the United States [provides] clear examples of each of these types. I have chosen it as the setting for my pictures of shore life." Preface

Cousteau, Philippe, 1980-

Make a splash! a kid's guide to protecting our oceans, lakes, rivers & wetlands. by Cathryn Berger Kaye ; with Philippe Cousteau and EarthEcho International. Free Spirit Pub. Inc. 2013 125 p. ill. (chiefly col.) (paperback) $13.99

Grades: 3 4 5 6 **577.7**

1. Environmentalists 2. Water conservation 3. Marine ecology 4. Environmentalism 5. Marine pollution -- Prevention

ISBN 1575424177; 9781575424170

LC 2012032120

This book for elementary-age readers has "colorful photos and digital drawings [that] illustrate many aspects of water on Earth, while the text provides information and tells stories of children in elementary schools around the world who have translated their own environmental concerns into action." (Booklist)

Johnson, Robin

Oceans inside out; Robin Johnson. Crabtree Publishing 2015 32 p. color illustrations (reinforced library binding) $27.60

Grades: 4 5 6 **577.7**

1. Ocean 2. Ecology 3. Oceanography 4. Marine ecology

ISBN 0778706354; 9780778706359; 9780778714576

LC 2014020250

This children's book by Robin Johnson "discusses ocean temperatures and zones, explores the different types of marine ecosystems found around the world, describes the plant and animal life, and explains how to protect and conserve marine ecosystems." (Publisher's note)

"The lush photos of locations worldwide may inspire further investigation of the topic. Great selections." SLJ

Includes index

O'Neill, Michael Patrick

Wild waters photo journal. Batfish Books 2010 106p il $29.95

Grades: 6 7 8 9 10 **577.7**

1. Marine animals 2. Marine ecology

ISBN 978-0-9728653-6-4; 0-9728653-6-5

"This personal collection of stunning, full-color photographs highlights unique underwater habitats and the life found in select natural communities around the world. Full spreads provide either an overview of an ecosystem, e.g., Komodo National Park or Bali in Indonesia, or a signature animal, e.g., the great white shark at Guadalupe Island, Mexico, or a dwarf caiman in Brazil. . . . The photographs are compelling by themselves and beautiful to browse. This book informs readers and gives them a deeper understanding of the ever-present threats to the ecological diversity and beauty of the planet." SLJ

Parker, Steve

Seashore; written by Steve Parker. rev ed; DK Pub. 2004 72p il (DK eyewitness books) $15.99

Grades: 4 5 6 7 **577.7**

1. Seashore 2. Marine plants 3. Marine animals

ISBN 0-7566-0721-3; 0-7566-0720-5 lib bdg

First published 1989 by Knopf

Brief text and photos introduce the animal inhabitants of the seashore, including fish, crustaceans, snails, and shorebirds

Pyers, Greg

The **biodiversity** of coral reefs. Marshall Cavendish 2010 32p il map lib bdg $28.50

Grades: 4 5 6 7 **577.7**

1. Coral reefs and islands

ISBN 978-1-60870-070-7 lib bdg; 1-60870-070-4 lib bdg

"Discusses the variety of living things in a coral reef's ecosystem." Publisher's note

Wicks, Maris

Coral reefs; Cities of the Ocean. by Maris Wicks. First Second 2016 119 p. color illustrations $9.99; $19.99

Grades: 4 5 6 7 8 **577.7**

1. Marine biology 2. Ocean 3. Marine ecology 4. Coral reef ecology

ISBN 9781626727250; 1626721459; 1626721467; 9781626721456; 9781626721463

In this graphic novel by Maris Wicks, published as part of the Science Comics series, "learn all about these tiny, adorable sea animals! This absorbing look at ocean science covers the biology of coral reefs as well as their ecological importance. . . . Wicks brings to bear her signature combination of hardcore cuteness and in-depth science." (Publisher's note)

"The jokes, puns, and humorous commentary will draw sea-life fans to this informative, tropical-hued introduction to coral reefs." Booklist

Includes bibliographical references (page 118).

578 Natural history of organisms and related subjects

Kelsey, Elin

Strange new species; astonishing discoveries of life on earth. Maple Tree Press 2005 96p il $24.95; pa $16.95

Grades: 5 6 7 8 **578**

1. Biology 2. Scientists 3. Natural history

ISBN 1-897066-31-7; 1-897066-32-5 pa

"This large-format book showcases new species . . . and the scientists who have discovered them. . . . The discussion ends with information on cloning, genetically modified food, and the future of life. . . . With many excellent photos, this introductory book on new species will be an intriguing addition to classroom units on classification or biology." Booklist

578.4 Adaptation

Davies, Monika

★ **Adaptations**; Monika Davies. Teacher Created Materials 2016 32 p. (pbk.) $8.99

Grades: 4 5 6 **578.4**

1. Adaptation (Biology) 2. Animals 3. Animals -- Adaptation 4. Competition (Biology)

ISBN 1480746797; 9781480746794

LC 2014045202

This children's book by Monika Davies explains "how adaptation has helped animals survive and change over time. High-interest, age appropriate text paired with colorful images and graphics fill the pages of this book to make learning about adaptation fun and interesting! A Think Like a Scientist activity that supports STEM instruction is included at the end of the book for students to apply what they've learned." (Publisher's note)

Schafer, Susan

Adaptations. M.E. Sharpe 2009 96p il (Genetics: the science of life) $38.95 **578.4**

1. Adaptation (Biology)

ISBN 978-0-7656-8137-9; 0-7656-8137-4

LC 2008-8106

This discusses genetic adaptations in regard to defenses, feeding, and reproduction.

"Chock-full of information. . . . The material is well organized and accessible. . . . Interest is maintained through countless fascinating examples. . . . Illustrations and color photographs enhance [the text]." SLJ

Includes bibliographical references

Spilsbury, Richard

Adaptation and survival. Rosen Central 2010 46p il map (Living processes) lib bdg $26.50; pa $11.75

Grades: 5 6 7 **578.4**

1. Ecology 2. Adaptation (Biology)

ISBN 978-1-61532-343-2 lib bdg; 1-61532-343-0 lib bdg; 978-1-61532-348-7 pa; 1-61532-348-1 pa

LC 2009-30418

"With colorful, quality photography, the well-organized content is divided into short chapters with bold subheadings making information easy to find. Clear and interesting writing distinguishes this . . . from older titles. The captions for pictures are used to provide identification and additional explanation for topics not included in the text." Libr Media Connect

Includes glossary and bibliographical references

578.6 Miscellaneous nontaxonomic kinds of organisms

Fleisher, Paul

Parasites; latching on to a free lunch. Twenty-First Century Books 2006 112p il (Discovery!) lib bdg $29.27

Grades: 7 8 9 10 **578.6**

1. Parasites

ISBN 978-0-8225-3415-0; 0-8225-3415-0

LC 2005-10521

This is "well organized and quite up to date. The photos . . . are plentiful, colorful, and excellent. . . . Clear, concise, and interesting." Voice Youth Advocates

Includes bibliographical references

578.68 Rare and endangered species

Endangered species: opposing viewpoints; Viqi Wagner, book editor. Greenhaven Press 2008 230p map (Opposing viewpoints series) lib bdg $38.50; pa $26.75

Grades: 8 9 10 11 12 **578.68**

1. Endangered species 2. Nature conservation

ISBN 978-0-7377-2931-3 lib bdg; 978-0-7377-2932-0 pa

LC 2007-38314

This collection of articles offers varying viewpoints on extinction, preservation, property rights, and international cooperation.

Includes bibliographical references

Pobst, Sandy

Animals on the edge; science races to save species threatened with extinction. by Sandra Pobst; Todd K. Fuller, consultant. National Geographic 2008 64p il (National Geographic investigates) $17.95; lib bdg $27.90

Grades: 4 5 6 7 **578.68**

1. Endangered species 2. Wildlife conservation

ISBN 978-1-4263-0358-6; 1-4263-0358-0; 978-1-4263-0265-7 lib bdg; 1-4263-0265-7 lib bdg

This "eye-catching [title features] full-color photographs. . . . The approach is to understand the challenges to protecting endangered animals, including global warming, destruction of habitat, tagging and tracking, poaching, captive breeding, and cloning." Voice Youth Advocates

Includes glossary and bibliographical references

578.7 Organisms characteristic of specific kinds of environments

Fertig, Dennis

Sylvia Earle; ocean explorer. Dennis Fertig. Heinemann Library 2015 48 p. color illustrations; map (Women in conservation) (hardcover) $32.65

Grades: 5 6 7 8 **578.7**

1. Underwater exploration 2. Women explorers -- United States -- Biography 3. Marine biologists -- United States -- Biography 4. Women marine biologists -- United States -- Biography

ISBN 1484604709; 148460475X; 9781484604700; 9781484604755; 9781484604854

LC 2013040527

This biography, by Dennis Fertig, "takes an engaging look at the work of ground-breaking conservationist, Sylvia Earle, and her work to protect oceans and ocean life. It covers Earle's inspiration, her methods, findings, and the impact of her work." (Publisher's note)

"With helpful back matter, eye-catching layouts, and many pictures (all of which have informative labels), these titles offer easy-to-read, in-depth introductions to pioneering women in science." Booklist

Includes bibliographical references (pages 46-47) and index

Hirsch, Rebecca E., 1969-

Birds vs. blades? Offshore Wind Power and the Race to Protect Seabirds. Rebecca E. Hirsch. lvl Millbrook Press 2017 48 p. color illustrations (hardback) $33.32

Grades: 4 5 6 7 8 **578.7**

1. Sea birds 2. Coastal ecology 3. Wind power -- Environmental aspects 4. Offshore wind power plants -- Environmental aspects

ISBN 9781467795203

LC 2015044328

"Politicians and engineers are looking for places to construct offshore wind farms, similar to those already providing clean energy around the country. [Rebecca E.] Hirsch's timely text explains this energy source, touches on why we need wind farms and how they work, and describes a four-year scientific study of gannets, scoters, and red-throated loons. . . . She concludes with a more nuanced explanation of the hazards facing gannets and other seabirds." (Kirkus Reviews)

"The many illustrations include helpful, digital maps and diagrams as well as many color photos that are clearly reproduced, pertinent to the topic, and often eye-catching." Booklist

Includes bibliographical references (page 46) and index

Kirby, Richard R.

Ocean drifters; a secret world beneath the waves. Firefly Books 2011 192p il $29.95

Grades: 5 6 7 8 9 10 11 12 Adult **578.7**

1. Marine plankton

ISBN 978-1-55407-982-7; 1-55407-982-9

LC 2011284690

"Kirby (Marine Inst. Research Fellow, Plymouth Univ., UK), who has published widely in scientific journals, combines in this book his area of expertise-plankton-with magnificent color photography of each species. He details the importance of the ocean's plankton layer to the health of the globe and its effects on sea and human life in the photos' descriptions...Recommended for readers interested in the smaller denizens of the natural world, the ocean, or microphotography." (Library Journal)

Includes bibliographical references

Montgomery, Sy

The **Great** White shark scientist; written by Sy Montgomery. Houghton Mifflin Harcourt 2016 80 p. color illustrations (hardcover) $18.99

Grades: 5 6 7 8 9 **578.7**

1. Marine biologists 2. White shark 3. Wildlife conservation 4. Marine resources conservation 5. Marine biologists -- United States -- Biography

ISBN 9780544352988

LC 2015003494

This juvenile book, by Sy Montgomery with photographs by Keith Ellenbogen, part of the "Scientists in the Field" series, follows "Dr. Greg Skomal, biologist and head of the Massachusetts Shark Research Program, [who] is investigating a controversial possibility: Might Cape Cod's waters serve as a breeding ground for the great white shark, the largest and most feared predatory fish on Earth?" (Publisher's note)

"This appreciative introduction to a much-maligned species will thrill readers while it encourages them to see great white sharks in a new way." Kirkus

Includes bibliographical references

Somervill, Barbara A.

Marine biologist. Cherry Lake Pub. 2009 32p il (Cool science careers) lib bdg $27.07

Grades: 3 4 5 6 **578.7**

1. Marine biology 2. Vocational guidance

ISBN 978-1-60279-504-4 lib bdg; 1-60279-504-5 lib bdg

LC 2008045234

This describes the career of marine biologist, including ways to become involved in the profession, the interests and skills required, and activities for learning more

This is "highly readable. . . . Colorful photographs illustrate [the] book." SLJ

Includes glossary and bibliographical references

Thomas, William David

Marine biologist. Gareth Stevens Pub. 2010 32p il (Cool careers: cutting edge) lib bdg $26; pa $8.95

Grades: 4 5 6 **578.7**

1. Marine biology 2. Vocational guidance

ISBN 978-1-4339-1957-2 lib bdg; 1-4339-1957-5 lib bdg; 978-1-4339-2156-8 pa; 1-4339-2156-1 pa

LC 2009000239

Describes the work of a marine biologist.

This title offers "clear, solid information in a large font. . . . [This] short [book is] packed with relevant, current material." SLJ

Includes glossary and bibliographical references

Wallace, Marianne D.

America's forests; guide to plants and animals. Fulcrum Pub. 2009 47p il (America's ecosystems) pa $11.95

Grades: 5 6 7 8 **578.7**

1. Forest plants 2. Forest animals 3. Forest ecology 4. Forests and forestry

ISBN 978-1-55591-595-7 pa; 1-55591-595-7 pa

LC 2008041005

This "is a guide to plants and animals within the context of forest communities. Marianne Wallace . . . expertly crafts this introduction to forests. . . . The book contains abundant illustrations." Sci Books Films

Includes glossary

Wechsler, Doug

Marvels in the muck; life in the salt marshes. Boyds Mills Press 2008 48p il $17.95

Grades: 4 5 6 7 **578.7**

1. Salt marshes 2. Marsh ecology

ISBN 978-1-59078-588-1

LC 2007052583

"A season-by-season look at the ecology of an oft-overlooked habitat. Wechsler's lucid text introduces the insects, birds, reptiles, crustaceans, and other critters that claim this salty expanse as home. . . . Clear color photos present species mentioned in the text." SLJ

Includes glossary and bibliographical references

579 Natural history of microorganisms, fungi, algae

Arato, Rona

Protists; algae, amoebas, plankton, and other protists. Crabtree Pub. Co. 2010 48p il (A class of their own) lib bdg $29.27; pa $9.95

Grades: 5 6 7 8 **579**

1. Algae 2. Protists 3. Protozoa

ISBN 978-0-7787-5377-3 lib bdg; 0-7787-5377-8 lib bdg; 978-0-7787-5391-9 pa; 0-7787-5391-3 pa

LC 2009-51386

Looks at the protist kingdom, providing information and examples of species from the major phyla, as well as information about the role of protists in the food chain and in various diseases.

"Lively section headings . . . and notes on uncommon achievements, . . . lighten the substantial load of biological terminology. Illustrated with a plethora of closeup color photos and microphotos, and closing with annotated lists of recommended Web sites, . . . [this captures] the remarkable diversity of life." SLJ

Includes glossary and bibliographical references

Bardhan-Quallen, Sudipta

Kitchen science experiments; how does your mold garden grow? illustrated by Edward Miller. Sterling 2010 64p il (Mad science) $12.95

Grades: 4 5 6 **579**

1. Biology 2. Microbiology 3. Science -- Experiments

ISBN 978-1-4027-2413-8; 1-4027-2413-6

LC 2010003749

"The language is as much fun as the science, including wordplay warnings . . . and the design is inviting, with colorful diagrams on each spacious, double-page spread. . . . Many students will be hooked by the fascinating revelations about the world around them." Booklist

Includes bibliographical references

Brown, Jordan

Micro mania; a really close-up look at bacteria, bedbugs & the zillions of other gross little creatures that live in, on & all around you! [by] Jordan D. Brown. Imagine! 2010 80p il $19.95

Grades: 4 5 6 **579**

1. Microorganisms

ISBN 978-0-9823064-2-0; 0-9823064-2-3

"This engrossing book goes into squirm-inducing detail about the bacteria, microbes, and other assorted mini-organisms that dwell in our bodies and our homes. Each spread is well laid out with plenty of white space, large text, and colorful photos of these little critters . . . and the havoc they wreak. The writing is vivid without being breathless." SLJ

Eamer, Claire

Inside your insides; A Guide to the Microbes That Call You Home. by Claire Eamer ; illustrated by Marie-Eve Tremblay. Kids Can Press 2016 36 p. color illustrations $17.95

Grades: 3 4 5 6 **579**

1. Bacteria 2. Microorganisms 3. Human body

ISBN 1771383321; 9781771383325

AAAS/Subaru SB&F Prize Finalist (2018)

In this book, by Claire Eamer, illustrated by Marie-Eve Tremblay, "six of the most common critters that live in and on our bodies are introduced: . . . bacteria, archaea, viruses, fungi, protists and mites. Each one has its own preferred environment, and readers will be startled (and likely a little grossed out!) by the many places they live, including the hair follicles on our faces, the folds of our tongues and the lengths of our guts." (Publisher's note)

"The jazzy design and plentiful, brightly colored illustrations add appeal. Solid information presented in a sprightly manner that's sure to appeal." Kirkus

Micro monsters. Kingfisher 2010 47p il (Kingdom) $14.99; pa $8.99

Grades: 3 4 5 6 **579**

1. Insects 2. Microorganisms

ISBN 978-0-7534-3014-9; 0-7534-3014-2; 978-0-7534-6455-7 pa; 0-7534-6455-1 pa

This book illustrates the unseen world of microscopic monsters and shows the reader how they survive and triumph. Some pages have movable flaps to show different pictures.

"Hyper-close-up photos detail all manner of stingers, stabbers, pincers, and chompers poking out from plated exoskeletons and hairy abdomens. This . . . is a great way to sneak in some basic science learning amid the din of death and destruction." Booklist

Wearing, Judy

Fungi; mushrooms, toadstools, molds, yeasts, and other fungi. Crabtree 2010 48p il (A class of their own) lib bdg $29.27; pa $9.95

Grades: 5 6 7 8 **579**

1. Fungi

ISBN 978-0-7787-5375-9 lib bdg; 0-7787-5375-1 lib bdg; 978-0-7787-5389-6 pa; 0-7787-5389-1 pa

Features an examination of the four major groups of fungi: yeasts, toadstools, chytrids, and bread molds.

"Lively section headings . . . and notes on uncommon achievements, . . . lighten the substantial load of biological terminology. Illustrated with a plethora of closeup color photos and microphotos, and closing with annotated lists of recommended Web sites, . . . [thi scaptures] the remarkable diversity of life." SLJ

Includes glossary and bibliographical references

Zamosky, Lisa

Simple organisms. Compass Point Books 2009 40p il (Mission: science) lib bdg $26.60

Grades: 4 5 6 **579**

1. Microorganisms

ISBN 978-0-7565-3955-9 lib bdg; 0-7565-3955-2 lib bdg

LC 2008-7723

An introduction to microscopic organisms, including germs

Includes glossary and bibliographical references

579.3 Prokaryotes (Bacteria)

Barker, David M.

Archaea; salt-lovers, methane-makers, thermophiles, and other archaeans. by David Barker. Crabtree Pub. 2010 48p il (A class of their own) lib bdg $29.27; pa $9.95

Grades: 5 6 7 8 **579.3**

1. Bacteria

ISBN 978-0-7787-5373-5 lib bdg; 0-7787-5373-5 lib bdg; 978-0-7787-5387-2 pa; 0-7787-5387-5 pa

LC 2009-51393

Looks at the archaea domain, providing information and examples of species from the three major phyla, as well as information about why so little is known about this diverse domain.

"Lively section headings . . . and notes on uncommon achievements, . . . lighten the substantial load of biological terminology. Illustrated with a plethora of closeup color photos and microphotos, and closing with annotated lists of recommended Web sites, . . . [this captures] the remarkable diversity of life." SLJ

Includes glossary and bibliographical references

Gardy, Jennifer

It's catching; the infectious world of germs and microbes. Jennifer Gardy, PhD, Josh Holinaty. Owlkids Books, Inc. 2014 63 p. $18.95

Grades: 5 6 7 **579.3**

1. Viruses 2. Bacteria 3. Germ theory of disease 4. Microorganisms

ISBN 1771470011; 9781771470018; 9781771470537

LC 2013949230

In this book, author Jennifer Gardy "picks up her microscope to bring expert insight to the microbes that are all around us but are too small to see. [She] discusses a range of germs and the diseases they cause, from the common cold to food poisoning to the Ebola virus." (Publisher's note)

"An amusing but information-packed look at all things infectious. The cartoon illustrations and chatty text with terms like "tummy" and "cooties" and phrases such as "a quick pit stop in the liver" might lead some to assume this is a lightweight read, but there's plenty to offer in this complex but comprehensible work...This readable, slender introduction to the world of microbial life is an entertaining and informative eye-opener." SLJ

Wearing, Judy

Bacteria; staph, strep, clostridium, and other bacteria. Crabtree 2010 48p il (A class of their own) lib bdg $29.27; pa $9.95

Grades: 5 6 7 8 **579.3**

1. Bacteria

ISBN 978-0-7787-5374-2 lib bdg; 0-7787-5374-3 lib bdg; 978-0-7787-5388-9 pa; 0-7787-5388-3 pa

Examines bacteria that are found in virtually every environment-including those that are characterized by extreme heat, cold, and depth-and, of course, bacteria that are found inside our bodies.

"Lively section headings . . . and notes on uncommon achievements, . . . lighten the substantial load of biological terminology. Illustrated with a plethora of closeup color photos and microphotos, and closing with annotated lists of recommended Web sites, . . . [this captures] the remarkable diversity of life." SLJ

Includes glossary and bibliographical references

579.6 Mushrooms

Lincoff, Gary

★ The **Audubon** Society field guide to North American mushrooms; [by] Gary H. Lincoff; visual key by Carol Nehring. Knopf 1981 926p il $19.95

Grades: 7 8 9 10 11 12 Adult **579.6**

1. Mushrooms

ISBN 0-394-51992-2

LC 81-80827

This guide to 703 species of common mushrooms provides 762 color photographs and descriptions as keys to identifying these plants.

"The author is an expert on mushroom toxins and instills responsible cautions. The photos are uncommonly beautiful." SLJ

580 Natural history of plants and animals

Ballard, Carol

Plant variation and classification. Rosen Central 2010 46p il (Living processes) lib bdg $26.50; pa $11.75

Grades: 5 6 7 **580**

1. Plants 2. Variation (Biology) 3. Biology -- Classification

ISBN 978-1-61532-345-6 lib bdg; 1-61532-345-7 lib bdg; 978-1-61532-346-3 pa; 1-61532-346-5 pa

Explains how our plant classification system works and looks at how scientists use it to identify and group plant species. The book also examines the variation between and within plants species and discusses how and why such variations have occurred.

"With colorful, quality photography, the well-organized content is divided into short chapters with bold subheadings making information easy to find. Clear and interesting writing distinguishes this . . . from older titles. The captions for pictures are used to provide identification and additional explanation for topics not included in the text." Libr Media Connect

Includes glossary and bibliographical references

Levine, Shar

Plants; flowering plants, ferns, mosses, and other plants. by Shar Levine and Leslie Johnstone. Crabtree Pub. 2010 48p il (A class of their own) lib bdg $29.27; pa $9.95

Grades: 5 6 7 8 **580**

1. Plants

ISBN 978-0-7787-5376-6 lib bdg; 0-7787-5376-X lib bdg; 978-0-7787-5390-2 pa; 0-7787-5390-5 pa

LC 2009-51342

Describes the main groups of plants, including mosses, ferns, conifers, and flowering plants.

"Lively section headings . . . and notes on uncommon achievements, . . . lighten the substantial load of biological terminology. Illustrated with a plethora of closeup color photos and microphotos, and closing with annotated lists of recommended Web sites, . . . [this captures] the remarkable diversity of life." SLJ

Includes glossary and bibliographical references

Taylor, Barbara

Inside plants. Marshall Cavendish Benchmark 2010 48p il (Invisible worlds) lib bdg $28.50

Grades: 4 5 6 7 **580**

1. Plants

ISBN 978-0-7614-4189-2 lib bdg; 0-7614-4189-1 lib bdg

LC 2008037247

This describes the plant details that are too small for the unaided eye to see, and how these microscopic systems work to keep the plant alive and healthy.

The narrative is "clear, well written, broken down into manageable pieces, and peppered with eye-opening facts. The numerous photographs are so phenomenal that they will inspire kids to read the text . . . so that they can wrap their minds around what they see." SLJ

Includes glossary and bibliographical references

Willis, Kathy

★ **Botanicum**; illustrated by Katie Scott ; written by Kathy Willis. Big Picture Press 2017 95 p. color illustrations (Welcome to the museum) (hardcover) $35

Grades: 6 7 8 9 **580**

1. Botany 2. Plants

ISBN 9780763689230

LC 2017930910

This book, by Kathy Willis, is a "curated guide to plant life. With artwork from Katie Scott of Animalium fame, Botanicum gives readers the experience of a fascinating exhibition from the pages of a beautiful book. From perennials to bulbs to tropical exotica, Botanicum is a wonderful feast of botanical knowledge complete with superb cross sections of how plants work." (Publisher's note)

"Visually stunning, it's an engrossing overview of Earth's remarkable and diverse plant life that provides opportunities for ongoing discovery on every page." Pub Wkly

580.7 Education, research, related topics

Gardner, Robert

Ace your plant science project; great science fair ideas. [by] Robert Gardner and Phyllis J. Perry. Enslow Publishers 2009 104p il (Ace your biology science project) lib bdg $31.93

Grades: 5 6 7 8 **580.7**

1. Plants 2. Science projects 3. Science -- Experiments

ISBN 978-0-7660-3221-7 lib bdg; 0-7660-3221-3 lib bdg

LC 2008-4687

"Presents several science experiments and project ideas using plants." Publisher's note

Includes bibliographical references

580.75 Museum activities and services

Silvey, Anita

The **plant** hunters; true stories of their daring adventures to the far corners of the Earth. Anita Silvey. Farrar Straus Giroux 2012 88 p. col. ill. $19.99

Grades: 6 7 8 9 10 **580.75**

1. Botanists 2. Collectors and collecting 3. Plants -- Collection and preservation 4. Plant collecting -- History 5. Plant collectors -- Biography

ISBN 0374309086; 9780374309084

LC 2011005161

This book "introduces European and North American plant hunters, primarily from the nineteenth and twentieth centuries. Driven by curiosity, commerce, and 'botonomania,' they sought to collect valuable plant specimens around the world. Likening Baron Alexander von Humboldt to Indiana Jones and calling the plant hunters' experiences 'amazing escapades,' [Anita] Silvey . . . recount[s] horrific experiences reported by various plant hunters." (Booklist)

"The slim, engaging narrative paints vivid portraits of these botanic adventurers. It is smoothly written, smartly paced and filled with exciting tales of risk taking and derring-do." Kirkus

581.4 Adaptation

Castaldo, Nancy F.

The **Story** of Seeds; From Mendel's Garden to Your Plate, and How There's More of Less to Eat Around the World. Nancy Castaldo. Houghton Mifflin Harcourt 2016 144 p. color illustrations (hardcover) $17.99

Grades: 6 7 8 9 **581.4**

1. Seeds 2. Agriculture

ISBN 9780544320239; 0544320239

This book, by Nancy Castaldo, "speaks to the current ways we think about our food, the more thoughtful and philosophical questions about regulating which crops farmers are allowed to grow, and what consumers are able to eat. Readers will discover just how important seeds are to the functioning of our global economy--and how much power we as a world-wide community have to keep seeds around, because once a seed disappears, it's gone forever." (Publisher's note)

This stellar interdisciplinary resource may need hand-selling to get readers beyond its plain packaging, but be prepared to satisfy readers' thirst for more information about, for instance, protecting Russia's international seed vaults during WWII, finding Glass Gem corn, and fighting biopiracy. A terrific, engrossing resource." Booklist

581.6 Miscellaneous nontaxonomic kinds of plants

Farrell, Courtney

Plants out of place. Rourke Pub. 2010 48p il (Let's explore science) $32.79

Grades: 4 5 6 7 **581.6**

1. Plants 2. Biological invasions 3. Food chains (Ecology)

ISBN 978-1-61590-322-1; 1-61590-322-4

LC 2010009909

This "takes a lively look at invasive plants . . . and shows both the destruction that non-native plants cause and what can be done about it. . . . In [this] title, well-chosen boxed examples, abundant color photos, diagrams, and an appended glossary add interest and support the engaging [text]." Booklist

Includes glossary and bibliographical references

581.7 Plant ecology, plants characteristic of specific environments

Bodden, Valerie

Critical plant life. Creative Education 2010 48p il (Earth issues) $23.95

Grades: 7 8 9 10 **581.7**

1. Plant ecology

ISBN 978-1-58341-984-7; 1-58341-984-5

"The scientific information is up to date, well written for a lay audience, and presented in a highly engaging and visually appealing format." Sci Books Films

Includes glossary and bibliographical references

Koch, Melissa

Forest talk; how trees communicate. Melissa Koch. Twenty-First Century Books 2019 96 p. (lb : alk. paper) $37.32

Grades: 5 6 7 8 9 **581.7**

1. Trees 2. Botany 3. Forest ecology 4. Plant ecophysiology 5. Plant chemical ecology 6. Human-plant relationships 7. Plant cellular signal transduction

ISBN 9781541519770

LC 2018010569

This book, by Melissa Koch, focuses on the discovery by "researchers and citizen scientists . . . that trees communicate with each other through an underground system of soil fungi and other methods. Complex social networks help trees survive and thrive by transferring resources to each other, sending defense signals, communicating with their kin, and more. Meet the tree scientists and learn more of their fascinating discoveries." (Publisher's note)

"An intriguing volume that describes the surprising hidden lives of trees and underscores their key role in our world." Booklist

Includes bibliographical references

582.13 Plants noted for their flowers

Spellenberg, Richard

★ **National** Audubon Society field guide to North American wildflowers, western region; 2nd ed rev; Knopf 2001 862p il map $19.95

Grades: 7 8 9 10 11 12 Adult **582.13**

1. Wild flowers

ISBN 0-375-40233-0

LC 2001-269242

First published 1979

"More than 940 . . . full-color images show the wildflowers of western North America close-up and in their natural habitats. . . . Images are grouped by flower color and shape and keyed to . . . descriptions that reflect current taxonomy." Publisher's note

Thieret, John W.

★ **National** Audubon Society field guide to North American wildflowers: eastern region; revising author, John W. Thieret; original authors, William A. Niering and Nancy C. Olmstead. Knopf 2001 879p il map (National Audubon Society field guide series) $19.95

Grades: 7 8 9 10 11 12 Adult **582.13**

1. Wild flowers

ISBN 0-375-40232-2

LC 2001-269241

First published 1979 under the authorship of William A. Niering and Nancy C. Olmstead

"Covers the area east of the Rockies and east of the Big Bend area of Texas to the Atlantic. Color photographs together with family and species descriptions make this a most useful field guide." Sci News {review of 1979 edition}

582.16 Trees

Brockman, C. Frank

Trees of North America; a field guide to the major native and introduced species north of Mexico. by C. Frank Brockman; illustrated by Rebecca Merrilees; revised by Jonathan P. Latimer and Karen Stray Nolting with David Challinor. rev and updated ed.; St. Martin's Press 2001 280p il map (Golden field guides) pa $14.95

Grades: 8 9 10 11 12 Adult **582.16**

1. Trees -- North America

ISBN 978-1-58238-092-6 pa; 1-58238-092-9 pa

LC 2001272405

First published 1968 by Golden Press

This "field guide features . . . characteristics—tree shape, bark, leaf, flower, fruit and twig—for quick identification. . . . [It includes] over 730 species in 76 families and 160 range maps." Publisher's note

Includes bibliographical references

Galat, Joan Marie

Branching out; How Trees Are Part of Our World. Joan Marie Galat. Owlkids Books, Inc. 2014 64 p. color illustrations (hardcover) $18.95

Grades: 4 5 6 7 **582.16**

1. Trees

ISBN 1771470496; 9781771470490; 9781771470827

LC 2014932714

This book, by Joan Marie Galat, " takes an in-depth look at [trees], introducing the basics of tree biology and profiling 11 different trees from around the world, including familiar ones such as the Red Maple and lesser-known trees like the Tall-Stilted Mangrove. Showcasing the inextricable ways in which trees are part of our society, culture, and economy, this illustrated volume also outlines how animals need trees and how, sometimes, they even help trees survive through symbiosis." (Publisher's note)

"This short, lively introduction to the subject focuses on 11 trees from all over the world...This title is truly worldwide in its coverage; only one tree, the Red Maple, is a native of North America. Appended glossary and index are extensive and complete. A solid overview." SLJ

Hirsch, Andy

Trees; kings of the forest. Andy Hirsch. First Second 2018 128 p. chiefly color illustrations (Science comics) (hardback) $19.99

Grades: 4 5 6 7 8 **582.16**

1. Trees 2. Plants 3. Forests and forestry

ISBN 9781250143105; 9781250143112

LC 2017946156

In this volume in the Science Comics series, by Andy Hirsch, "we follow an acorn as it learns about its future as Earth's largest, longest-living plant. Starting with the seed's germination, we learn about each stage until the tree's maturation, different types of trees, and the roles trees take on in our ecosystem." (Publisher's note)

"It's hard not to see the wonder in this dense, pithy comic, and kids who are under the misapprehension that trees are boring will quickly learn otherwise." Booklist

Includes bibliographical references (page 120)

Petrides, George A.

A **field** guide to western trees; eastern [i.e. western] United States and Canada. illustrated by Olivia Petrides. 1st ed., expanded.; Houghton Mifflin 1998 428p il map (The Peterson field guide) pa $20

Grades: 7 8 9 10 11 12 Adult **582.16**

1. Trees -- North America

ISBN 978-0-395-90454-1 pa; 0-395-90454-4 pa

LC 98013624

First published 1992

This "guide features detailed descriptions of 387 species, arranged in six major groups by visual similarity." Publisher's note

Includes bibliographical references

Russo, Monica

★ **Treecology**; 30 activities and observations for exploring the world of trees and forests. Monica Russo ; photographs by Kevin Byron. Chicago Review Press Incorporated 2016 144 p. (trade paper) $15.99; (ebook) $15.99

Grades: 3 4 5 6 7 8 9 **582.16**

1. Trees 2. Trees -- Study and teaching (Elementary) -- Activity programs 3. Forest ecology -- Study and teaching (Elementary) -- Activity programs

ISBN 1613733968; 9781613733967; 9781613733998

LC 2015050678

In this book in the Young Naturalists series by Monica Russo with photographs by Kevin Byron, "young nature enthusiasts will learn . . . fascinating facts about the wonderful world of trees. . . . [This] resource includes plentiful full-color photos and drawings and clear, kid-friendly discussions of tree structures, families, and foods; the interaction between trees and the wildlife that depend on them; tree and forest–related jobs and preservation, and much more." (Publisher's note)

"A labor of love reflecting years of experience in the field as well as in writing for young readers, this offers a path to interesting explorations of the natural world." Kirkus

Includes bibliographical references and index

Tate, Nikki

Deep Roots; How Trees Sustain Our Planet. Orca Book Publishers 2016 48 p. color illustrations (ebook) $19.99; $19.95

Grades: 4 5 6 7 **582.16**

1. Trees 2. Ecology 3. Forest ecology

ISBN 9781459805835; 1459805828; 9781459805828

LC 2015944487

Written by Nikki Tate, "'Deep Roots' celebrates the central role trees play in our lives, no matter where we live. Each chapter in 'Deep Roots' focuses on a basic element--water, air, fire and earth--and explores the many ways in which we need trees to keep our planet healthy and livable. From making rain to producing fruit to feeding fish, trees play an integral role in maintaining vibrant ecosystems all over the world." (Publisher's note)

"Color photographs, activity suggestions, trivia bursts, sidebars, and Tate's own arboreal anecdotes create an accessible and involving layout, while supplying a broad take on the global diversity and varying roles of trees." Pub Wkly

Includes bibliographical references (page 43-44) and index.

583 Dicotyledons

Aaseng, Nathan

Weird meat-eating plants. Enslow Publishers 2011 48p il (Bizarre science) lib bdg $23.93

Grades: 5 6 7 8 **583**

1. Carnivorous plants

ISBN 978-0-7660-3672-7; 0-7660-3672-3

LC 2010016602

First published 1996 with title: Meat-eating plants

This describes meat-eating plants such as butterworts, sundews, byblis, pitcher plants, cobra lilies, venus flytraps, and bladderworts.

"Aimed at reluctant readers, [this title is] sure to disgust and delight in equal measure. . . . [The title] will pique interest and get kids lining up at the reference desk looking for more. The text is complemented by illustrations and magnified photos of things that you would hope never to see." SLJ

Includes glossary and bibliographical references

590 Animals

BishopRoby, Joshua

Animal kingdom. Compass Point Books 2009 40p il (Mission: science) lib bdg $26.60

Grades: 4 5 6 **590**

1. Animals -- Classification

ISBN 978-0-7565-4057-9 lib bdg; 0-7565-4057-7 lib bdg

LC 2008-37574

An introduction to the animal kingdom, which is made up of a variety of animals that are organized into categories based on physical attributes or ancestors

Includes glossary

Broom, Jenny

Animalium; Jenny Broom, illustrated by Katie Scott. Candlewick Press 2014 112 p. color illustrations (reinforced) $35

Grades: 3 4 5 6 7 **590**

1. Animals 2. Museums

ISBN 9780763675080; 0763675083

LC 2013952848

"Open 365 days a year and unrestricted by the constraints of physical space, each title in this series is organized into galleries that display more than 200 full-color specimens accompanied by lively, informative text. Offering hours of learning, this first title within the series--[Jenny Broom's book] Animalium--presents the animal kingdom in glorious detail with illustrations from Katie Scott." (Publisher's note)

"Each basic group includes several spreads offering examples from subgroups within the class as well as a spread with a connected habitat: coastal waters, coral reefs, rain forest, deserts, woodlands and tundra.

No information sources are given, but there are good suggestions for general websites for further learning." Kirkus

Buckley, James

Animals; a visual encylopedia. James Buckley, Beth Landis Hester, Catherine Nichols, Carl Jackson, Anita Ganeri, and Lori Stein. Time Home Entertainment Inc 2015 303 p. color illustrations (hardcover) $24.95

Grades: 3 4 5 6 7 **590**

1. Animals 2. Encyclopedias and dictionaries

ISBN 1618931539; 9781618931535

LC 2015940344

This book, by James Buckley, Beth Landis Hester, Catherine Nichols, Carl Jackson, Anita Ganeri, and Lori Stein, "profiles the seven major animal classes--mammals, birds, reptiles, amphibians, fish, arthropods, and other invertebrates--and features more than 1,000 stunning color photographs of animals in action." (Publisher's note)

"Gorgeous photographs of a panoply of animals are surrounded with various interesting factoids." Booklist

Campbell, Jeff

Daisy to the Rescue; True Stories of Daring Dogs, Paramedic Parrots, and Other Animal Heroes. by Jeff Campbell, illustrated by Ramsey Beyer. Houghton Mifflin Harcourt 2014 336 p. illustrations $17.99

Grades: 6 7 8 9 10 **590**

1. Human-animal relationship 2. Animal behavior 3. Cognition in animals 4. Animal heroes -- Anecdotes

ISBN 1936976625; 9781936976621

This book, by Jeff Campbell, illustrated by Ramsey Beyer, "celebrates over fifty . . . heroic animals with stunning illustrated portraits and detailed accounts of their exploits. The book asks important questions about why these animals act the way they do . . . often putting themselves in harm's way in the process." (Publisher's note)

"Inherent animal abilities are discussed alongside the accounts, as are animal traits and scientific theories in layman's terms. Individual stories of animal derring-do, illustrated with pencil portraits, make for quick, compelling reads that prompt the reader to wonder what really goes on in an animal's head and heart." Booklist

Davies, Nicola, 1958-

Extreme animals; the toughest creatures on Earth. illustrated by Neal Layton. Candlewick Press 2006 61p il $12.99; pa $7.99

Grades: 3 4 5 6 **590**

1. Animals 2. Adaptation (Biology)

ISBN 978-0-7636-3067-6; 0-7636-3067-5; 978-0-7636-4127-6 pa; 0-7636-4127-8 pa

LC 2005-43544

"There is life everywhere on Earth . . . and much of that life thrives in conditions that humans could not endure for five minutes or less. This funny and appealing little book describes who these amazing life-forms are and how they manage to survive. Simple and inviting cartoon drawings enliven the text and convey the types of extremes in an easy-to-understand manner." SLJ

Includes glossary

Green, Jen

Barron's totally wild fact-packed fold-out animal atlas; Jen Green. Barrons Educational Series, Inc. 2015 56 p. color ill., color maps (hardcover) $18.99

Grades: 4 5 6 7 **590**

1. Atlases 2. Animals

ISBN 9780764168086

LC 2015932861

In this children's book, by Jen Green and illustrated by Christiane Engel, "all of the weird and wonderful animals that inhabit our extraordinary earth are here to delight and enchant young readers (Mom and Dad, too!). . . . Youngsters love learning about animals, natural history and world geography, and this book teaches them all about each topic in fun, engaging ways." (Publisher's note)

"Green and Engel follow their 2014 atlas with an animal-themed tour of the world, and a large foldout map greets readers when they open the book." Pub Wkly

Hestermann, Josh

Zoology for kids; understanding and working with animals : with 21 activities. Josh and Bethanie Hestermann. Chicago Review Press, Incorporated 2015 144 p. color illustrations $18.95

Grades: 5 6 7 8 9 **590**

1. Zoology 2. Vocational guidance 3. Zoology -- Vocational guidance 4. Zoology -- Study and teaching -- Activity programs

ISBN 1613749619; 9781613749616

LC 2014042745

This book, by Josh and Bethanie Hestermann, "invites the next generation of zoologists to discover the animal kingdom through clear, entertaining information and anecdotes, lush color photos, hands-on activities, and peer-reviewed research. Young minds are introduced to zoology as a science by discussing animals' forms, functions, and behaviors as well as the history behind zoos and aquariums." (Publisher's note)

"Studded with fun activities and attractive animal photos, this comprehensive resource will excite those not already smitten with the animal world to enthusiastically join in the delightful exploration of what it means to study and care for animals in today's world. . . . Charming photos, hand-drawn graphics, highlighted words, and a correlative glossary enhance the clear-cut writing style." SLJ

Includes bibliographical references and index

Johnson, Jinny

Animal tracks & signs. National Geographic Society 2008 192p il $24.95; lib bdg $32.90

Grades: 5 6 7 8 **590**

1. Animals 2. Animal tracks 3. Tracking and trailing

ISBN 978-1-4263-0253-4; 1-4263-0253-3; 978-1-4263-0254-1 lib bdg; 1-4263-0254-1 lib bdg

"This attractive book describes the tracks (paw prints, bird claw prints, slimy trails) and signs (molted skin, food remains, scat, tree markings) that animals leave in their wake. . . . A typical two-page layout includes a photo and short paragraph about the animal category, three or four colored boxes containing a photo or drawing of a specific animal (serval, bobcat), and a description of its size, geographic range, habitat, food, tracks and signs, and comments. . . . The beautiful photos vary from action . . . to informational. . . . The language is simple and readable." Voice Youth Advocates

Includes glossary and bibliographical references

Montgomery, Heather L.

★ **Wild** discoveries; wacky new animals. by Heather L. Montgomery. Scholastic, Inc. 2013 62 p. (pbk.) $6.99

Grades: 3 4 5 6 7 **590**

1. Discoveries in science 2. Animals

ISBN 0545477670; 9780545477673

LC 2012285070

This book by Heather Montgomery features "newly discovered species from around the world--such as the Shocking Pink Dragon and the Green Bomber. These . . . species are organized by region with . . . facts about each one's . . . abilities and traits. The book . . . has a special section featuring new species discovered by kids." (Publisher's note)

Silverstein, Alvin

Dung beetles, slugs, leeches, and more; the yucky animal book. by Alvin and Virginia Silverstein, and Laura Silverstein Nunn; illustrated by Gerald Kelley. Enslow Publishers 2010 48p il (Yucky science) lib bdg $23.93

Grades: 4 5 6 7 **590**

1. Insects 2. Invertebrates 3. Animal behavior

ISBN 978-0-7660-3317-7 lib bdg; 0-7660-3317-1 lib bdg

LC 2009012281

"Explores 'yucky' things animals do, including slime-producing animals, blood-ingesting animals, and more." Publisher's note

Includes glossary and bibliographical references

Siwanowicz, Igor

Animals up close; zoom in on the world's most incredible creatures. DK Pub. 2009 96p il $19.99

Grades: 4 5 6 **590**

1. Animals

ISBN 978-0-7566-4513-7; 0-7566-4513-1

"An eye-catching cover will attract readers to this amazing look at some of the world's insects, fish, mammals, reptiles, amphibians, and birds. The focus is on animals small enough to fit in a child's hand. Siwanowicz showcases each creature with a spread containing a full-color, high-quality, close-up photo surrounded by multiple factual asides. . . . The book is packed with interesting material that captures the author's fascination for small creatures." SLJ

Includes glossary

Spelman, Lucy

Animal encyclopedia; 2,500 animals with photos, maps, and more! National Geographic 2012 303 p. col. ill., col. maps (hardcover) $24.95; (library) $33.90

Grades: 5 6 7 **590**

1. Animals -- Encyclopedias 2. Animals

ISBN 1426310226; 9781426310225; 9781426310232

LC 2012023783

This encyclopedia about animals "is separated into vertebrate and invertebrate animals and then further subdivided by phylum. Each species gets its own page with dynamic color photos of creatures in their natural habitat, while . . . information on variations within the species celebrates the diversity of animals across the globe." (Booklist)

Includes bibliographical references (p. 295) and index.

Spilsbury, Richard

Animal variation and classification. Rosen Central 2010 46p il (Living processes) lib bdg $26.50; pa $11.75

Grades: 5 6 7 **590**

1. Variation (Biology) 2. Animals -- Classification

ISBN 978-1-61532-344-9 lib bdg; 1-61532-344-9 lib bdg; 978-1-61532-347-0 pa; 1-61532-347-3 pa

LC 2009-30564

Explains how our animal classification system works and looks at how scientists use it to identify and group animal species, explores the variation between and within animal species and discusses how and why such variations have occurred.

"With colorful, quality photography, the well-organized content is divided into short chapters with bold subheadings making information easy to find. Clear and interesting writing distinguishes this . . . from older titles. The captions for pictures are used to provide identification and additional explanation for topics not included in the text." Libr Media Connect

Includes glossary and bibliographical references

590.72 Research

Burns, Loree Griffin

Citizen scientists; be a part of scientific discovery from your own backyard. Loree Griffin Burns ; photographs by Ellen Harasimowicz. H. Holt 2012 80 p. col. ill., col. maps

Grades: 3 4 5 6 7 8 **590.72**

1. Suburbs 2. Animals -- Classification 3. Research -- Citizen participation 4. Wildlife -- Geographical distribution 5. Suburban animals -- Research -- Citizen participation 6. Suburban animals -- Monitoring -- Citizen participation

ISBN 0805090622; 9780805090628; 9780805095173

LC 2011021673

AAAS/Subaru SB&F Prize for Excellence in Science Books: Hands On Science Book (2013)

In this children's book, Loree Griffin Burns "brings . . . attention to four . . . scientific projects that enlist regular people in data collection. . . . The projects include . . . the Monarch Watch butterfly tagging project, . . . the Audubon Christmas Bird Count," and a "project documenting ladybug species . . . . For each project, Burns gives detailed accounts of the procedures employed by citizen scientists." (Horn Book Magazine)

Includes bibliographical references and index

Jenkins, Steve, 1952-

★ **Animals** by the Numbers; A Book of Animal Infographics. Steve Jenkins. Houghton Mifflin Harcourt 2016 48 p. color illustrations (ebook) $16.99; $17.99

Grades: 3 4 5 6 **590.72**

1. Animals -- Miscellanea 2. Animals 3. Graphic methods 4. Charts, diagrams, etc.

ISBN 9781328664129; 0544630920; 9780544630925

LC 2016288289

In this children's book, Steve Jenkins answers various questions about animals "with numbers, images, innovation, and authoritative science. . . . Jenkins layers his signature cut-paper illustrations alongside computer graphics and a text that is teeming with fresh, unexpected, and accurate zoological information ready for readers to easily devour." (Publisher's note)

"A brilliantly executed take on a perennially high-interest topic." Booklist

Includes bibliographical references (page 48).

590.9 History, geographic treatment, biography

Coste, Marion

Hawaii's animals do the most amazing things! Marion Coste ; illustrated by Rena Ekmanis. University of Hawaii Press 2015 47 p. color illustrations (cloth : alk. paper) $14.99

Grades: 5 6 7 8 **590.9**

1. Hawaii 2. Animals -- Habitations 3. Animals -- Hawaii

ISBN 0824839625; 9780824839628

LC 2014014460

This book on the animals of Hawaii, by Marion Coste and illustrated by Rena Ekmanis, "includes 12 endemic and indigenous animals, covering both rare and more well known creatures, such as the great frigate bird, fisher bird, fairy tern, pacific golden plover, Hawaiian green sea turtle, spinner dolphin, humpback whale, and mountain shrimp." (School Library Journal)

"Middle school students will find useful material to extract for report writing, but the text is complex enough to entice older readers, too. A well-written overview of Hawaiian animals." SLJ

Includes bibliographical references (page 47)

Johnson, Rebecca L.

Chernobyl's wild kingdom; life in the dead zone. Rebecca L. Johnson. Twenty-First Century Books 2015 64 p. illustrations (some color) (lib. bdg. : alk. paper) $34.60

Grades: 7 8 9 10 11 12 **590.9**

1. Chernobyl Nuclear Accident, Chernobyl, Ukraine, 1986 2. Radioecology -- Ukraine -- Chornobyl

ISBN 1467711543; 9781467711548

LC 2013039471

This book, by Rebecca L. Johnston, describes how "some wildlife flourishes in Chernobyl, Ukraine, more than 25 years after the explosion at the nuclear power plant there. After opening with a background chapter describing the 1986 disaster, evacuation and cleanup efforts, Johnson goes on to describe scientific studies on the wildlife in the area from which humans have been excluded." (Kirkus Reviews) "This clear presentation is supplemented with captioned photographs, explanatory boxes and a helpful map. The appropriate background and clear, easy-to-understand explanations make this one-of-a-kind title both accessible and interesting. An important story clearly and engagingly told by an experienced science writer." Kirkus

Includes bibliographical references (pages 59-61) and index

Kainen, Dan

Polar; a photicular book. Dan Kainen and Carol Kaufmann. Workman Publishing 2015 24 p. color illustrations (alk. paper) $25.95

Grades: 4 5 6 7 8 **590.9**

1. Animals 2. Polar regions 3. Photicular books 4. Animals -- Polar regions 5. Polar regions -- Pictorial works 6. Animals -- Polar regions -- Pictorial works

ISBN 9780761185697; 0761185690

LC 2015026789

This book by Dan Kainen and Carol Kaufmann "brings the reader along on a voyage to the North and South Poles, and writes a lively and informative essay for each image, including vital statistics for each animal, such as their size, range, habitat, and more. Photicular technology uses sliding lenses and video imagery to display realistic living motion in the pages of a book." (Publisher's note)

"Perhaps no place on earth is more extreme than the poles, and the environmental changes occurring there take center stage in the future of all of the animals included in this intriguing," Booklist

Moberg, Julia

Historical animals; the dogs, cats, horses, snakes, goats, rats, dragons, bears, elephants, rabbits, and other creatures that changed the world. by Julia Moberg ; illustrated by Jeff Albrecht Studios. Charlesbridge Publishing 2015 91 p. color illustrations $15.95

Grades: 4 5 6 **590.9**

1. Animals and civilization 2. Animals and history 3. Animals and civilization -- History

ISBN 1623540488; 9781623540487

LC 2014018171

This book, by Julia Moberg abd illustrated by Jeff Albrecht Studios, is an "inside look at history's most famous animals. . . . Meet Alexander the Great's horse Bucephalus, who was his battle companion for nearly 30 years. Learn about Mozart's starling bird that helped him write music by singing along as he composed. Read about the Ethiopian goats that discovered the coffee bean, Marco Polo seeing dragons in China, and a dog named Boatswain that saved Napoleon's life." (Publisher's note)

"While adults might groan at the sometimes forced humor and poetry, the intended audience will eat this one up. Historical fluff? Maybe, but if nothing else, this silly yet persuasive effort will coax readers into enjoying history." SLJ

591 Specific topics in natural history of animals

Wildlife of the world; contributors Jamie Ambrose [and nine others] DK Publishing 2015 480 p. illustrations, color maps $50

Grades: K 1 2 3 4 5 6 7 8 9 10 11 12 Adult **591**

1. Animals 2. Animals -- Pictorial works

ISBN 1465438041; 9781465438041

LC 2015458474

This book, by DK Publishing, foreword by Don E. Wilson and produced in association with the Smithsonian Institution,"takes you on a journey through some of the most scenic and rich animal habitats--from the Amazon rain forests to the Himalayas, the Sahara to the South Pole--meeting the most important animals in each ecosystem along the way. . . . An additional eighty-page illustrated reference section on the animal kingdom explains the animal groups and profiles additional species." (Publisher's note)

"A chart at the beginning of each section indicates the number of species in each order, class, or phylum. . . . [T]his is an important, gorgeous, accessible introduction to hundreds of species and their habitats throughout the world at a very small price." Booklist

Yolen, Jane, 1939-

National Geographic animal stories; heartwarming true tales from the animal kingdom. by Jane Yolen, Heidi E.Y. Stemple, Adam Stemple, and Jason Stemple; illustrated by Jui Ishida. National Geographic 2014 160 p. illustrations hardcover $24.99

Grades: 5 6 7 8 **591**

1. Animals in literature 2. Animals -- Anecdotes

ISBN 1426317255; 9781426317255; 9781426317262

LC 2014015729

This children's book, by Jane Yolen, shares "animal stories that span the centuries. . . . Some are sweet, some funny, some surprising, but all are emotionally powerful -- the Capitolene geese who saved the Roman empire, Balto the Alaskan sled dog, Smoky the Bear, the passenger pigeon of WWI Cher Ami, and the latest internet sensation Christian the lion." (Publisher's note)

"In nineteen engaging short stories, Yolen and her children explore extraordinary animals from history and the connections they made with other creatures and people. Some stories will likely be familiar to readers (e.g., sled dog Balto), while others will be new discoveries. Ishida's colorful illustrations enliven the tales, and sidebars give further information." Horn Book

Includes bibliographical references and index

591.3 Genetics, evolution, age characteristics

Collard III, Sneed B.

One iguana, two iguanas; a story of accident, natural selection, and evolution. Sneed B. Collard III. Tilbury House Publishers 2018 48 p. (hardcover) $17.95

Grades: 8 **591.3**

1. Iguanas 2. Animals -- Galapagos Islands 3. Natural selection

ISBN 9780884486497; 9780884486510

LC 2018956504

In this book in the How Nature Works series, by Sneed B. Collard III, "natural selection and speciation are all but ignored in children's nonfiction. To help address this glaring deficiency, . . . Collard traveled to the Galapagos Islands to see for himself . . . how new species form. The result is this fascinating story of two species of iguana, one land-based and one marine, both of which developed from a single ancestor that reached the islands millions of years ago." (Publisher's note)

"The evolution of iguanas in the Galápagos provides a striking example of the workings of natural selection. This entry in the How Nature Works series explains how scientists have determined that two surprisingly different species evolved from a single ancestor" (Kirkus Reviews).

Ridley, Kimberly

Extreme survivors; animals that time forgot. Kimberly Ridley. Tilbury House Publishers 2017 48 p. (hardcover) $17.95

Grades: 6 7 8 9 **591.3**

1. Zoology 2. Living fossils 3. Natural selection

ISBN 9780884485001; 9780884485780

LC 2017950556

This book, by Kimberly Ridley, "provides detailed life histories and strange 'survival secrets' of ten ancient animals and explains evolution and natural selection. Extensive back matter includes glossary, additional facts and geographic range for each organism and a geologic timeline of Earth." (Publisher's note)

591.47 Protective and locomotor adaptations, color

Johnson, Rebecca L.

★ **When** lunch fights back; wickedly clever animal defenses. by Rebecca L. Johnson. Millbrook Press 2015 48 p. (lib. bdg. : alk. paper) $29.27

Grades: 4 5 6 7 **591.47**

1. Animal defenses 2. Animals

ISBN 1467721093; 9781467721097

LC 2013046646

This book, by Rebecca L. Johnson, explains that "in nature, good defenses can mean the difference between surviving a predator's attack and becoming its lunch. Some animals rely on sharp teeth and claws or camouflage. But that's only the beginning. Meet creatures with some of the strangest defenses known to science." (Publisher's note)

"Along with the ever popular hagfish (aka "snot eel") and the horned lizard—which can indeed squirt blood from one or both eyes—Johnson... profiles 10 animals with particularly noxious defense mechanisms... This is an outstanding way for readers to meet scientists at work in both field and lab, as well as to learn that, for instance, fulmar chicks can project vomit up to 6 feet and, creepily, that a school of the Amazonian two-spot astyanax will attack and eject one of its own to distract an approaching predator.Thrilling reading for budding biologists." Kirkus

Includes bibliographical references and index

Wilsdon, Christina

Animal defenses. Chelsea House 2009 136p il (Animal behavior) lib bdg $32.95

Grades: 6 7 8 9 **591.47**

1. Animal defenses

ISBN 978-1-60413-089-8 lib bdg; 1-60413-089-X lib bdg

LC 2008-40116

"The detailed information is well organized. . . . Color photographs appear throughout." SLJ

Includes glossary and bibliographical references

591.5 Behavior

Castaldo, Nancy F.

Beastly brains; exploring how animals think, talk, and feel. Nancy F. Castaldo. Houghton Mifflin Harcourt 2017 152 p. illustrations (chiefly color) (hardcover) $16.99

Grades: 7 8 9 10 **591.5**

1. Animal behavior 2. Animal intelligence 3. Cognition in animals

ISBN 9780544633353; 9780544999152

LC 2015045421

This book, by Nancy Castaldo, "delves into the minds of animals and explores animal empathy, communication, tool use, and social societies through interviews and historical anecdotes. Researchers from Charles Darwin to Jane Goodall have spent years analyzing the minds of animals, and today's science is revolutionizing old theories and uncovering surprising similarities to our own minds." (Publisher's note)

"This eye-opening, cogent, and well-structured volume will enlighten students to both the richness of the animal kingdom and the nature of intelligence." Booklist

Includes bibliographical references and index.

Cusick, Dawn

Get the Scoop on Animal Puke; From Zombie Ants to Vampire Bats, 251 Cool Facts About Vomit, Regurgitation & More. Dawn Cusick. Random House Distribution childrens 2014 80 p. color illustrations $14.95

Grades: 3 4 5 **591.5**

1. Animals 2. Vomiting 3. Animal behavior

ISBN 1623540453; 9781623540456

This children's book, by Dawn Cusick, describes how "animal puke serves many purposes in the natural world: it can scare and distract predators, feed family and neighbors, protect animals from poisoning (they can't call 911), aid with digestion, and so much more." (Publisher's note)

"What do hyenas, proboscis monkeys, and vampire bats have in common? Vomit. This companion to Cusick's Get the Scoop on Animal Poop! examines how and why various animals regurgitate their food... Cusick presents the material in a (very) immediate manner, providing readers with plenty of science, humor, and animal behavior facts to chew over—and even regurgitate." PW

De la Bédoyère, Camilla

Creatures of the Night; Camilla Bedoyere. Firefly Books Ltd 2014 80 p. color illustrations $9.95

Grades: 4 5 6 **591.5**

1. Animal behavior 2. Nocturnal animals 3. Picture books for children

ISBN 1770854592; 9781770854598

This book by Camilla Bedoyere "features more than a dozen extraordinary animals that live in the dark. These are mammals, birds, insects and spiders whose unique physical features help them to survive in the pitch-black darkness of jungles, fields and in the air. Intricately drawn artworks give accurate details of each animal's anatomy and behavior, and stunning photographs show how each animal hunts." (Publisher's note)

"This detailed look at creatures that go bump in the night is a reminder of just how amazing animal adaptations are." Booklist

Goldstein, Natalie

Animal hunting and feeding. Chelsea House 2009 110p il (Animal behavior) lib bdg $32.95

Grades: 6 7 8 9 **591.5**

1. Animals -- Food

ISBN 978-1-60413-143-7 lib bdg; 1-60413-143-8 lib bdg

LC 2008-40124

"All animals have to eat, but feeding behavior goes far beyond predators and prey. Animals have a variety of ways to find food. Some sit and wait for food to come to them. Others chase or trap their food. Other animals are scavengers and decomposers, breaking down the leftovers of other animals' meals. [This book] explains these various techniques as well as the importance of food chains and food webs." Publisher's note

Includes glossary and bibliographical references

Holland, Jennifer S.

Unlikely heroes; 37 inspiring stories of courage and heart from the animal kingdom. by Jennifer S. Holland. Workman Publishing 2014 246 p. illustrations (chiefly color) (pbk.) $13.95

Grades: 5 6 7 8 **591.5**

1. Altruism 2. Animal behavior 3. Animal behavior -- Anecdotes 4. Altruistic behavior in animals -- Anecdotes

ISBN 0761174419; 9780761174417

LC 2014033713

In this book, author Jennifer S. Holland "uncovers and celebrates . . . [a] side of animals that we often think belongs primarily to people—heroism, that indefinable quality of going above and beyond, often for altruistic reasons, often at great personal risk. These 37 inspiring true tales show animals whose quick acts have saved lives." (Publisher's note)

"In this heartwarming follow-up to Unlikely Friendships: 47 Remarkable Stories from the Animal Kingdom (2011) and Unlikely Loves: 43 Heartwarming True Stories from the Animal Kingdom (2013, both Workman), Holland whips up enthusiasm for the selfless acts of different animals . . . A sweet look at the animal kingdom." SLJ

Includes bibliographical references (pages 241-244) and index

Knapp, Ron

Bloodsucking creatures. Enslow Publishers 2011 48p il (Bizarre science) lib bdg $23.93

Grades: 5 6 7 8 **591.5**

1. Bloodsucking animals

ISBN 978-0-7660-3671-0; 0-7660-3671-5

LC 2010009761

First published 1996 with title: Bloodsuckers

This describes bloodsucking animals such as mosquitoes, vampire bats, and fleas.

"Aimed at reluctant readers, [this title is] sure to disgust and delight in equal measure. . . . [The title] will pique interest and get kids lining up at the reference desk looking for more. The text is complemented by illustrations and magnified photos of things that you would hope never to see." SLJ

Includes glossary and bibliographical references

591.518 Nocturnal behavior

Scott, Traer

★ **Nocturne**; creatures of the night. Traer Scott. Princeton Architectural Press 2014 128 p. color illustrations $19.95

Grades: 7 8 9 10 11 12 Adult **591.518**

1. Animal behavior 2. Photography of animals 3. Nocturnal animals

ISBN 1616892889; 9781616892883

LC 2014006210

In this book "photographer Traer Scott takes the viewer on a journey through nighttime in the animal kingdom, revealing some of nature's most elusive creatures. Bats, big cats, flying squirrels, tarantula, owls, kangaroo mice, giant moths, sloth, several species of snakes, and a Madagascar hissing cockroach are only a few of the animals illuminated in these . . . portraits." (Publisher's note)

"In this exquisite collection of portraits of 42 nocturnal animals, photographer Scott sets her subjects against dark backgrounds that give the images quiet dignity and power, while making the animals' fur, feathers, quills, and skin all the more luminous. . . . The brilliance of the photographs is in their minimalism, allowing the animals to dictate the mood of the compositions." Pub Wkly

591.56 Behavior relating to life cycle

Allman, Toney

Animal life in groups. Chelsea House 2009 124p il (Animal behavior) lib bdg $32.95

Grades: 6 7 8 9 **591.56**

1. Animal behavior

ISBN 978-1-60413-142-0 lib bdg; 1-60413-142-X lib bdg

LC 2008-40120

This "explores the social lives of bees, meerkats, monkeys, and others, with a special emphasis on how different packs compare to one another and how living in groups benefits individual members." Publisher's note

Includes glossary and bibliographical references

Downer, Ann

The **animal** mating game; The Wacky, Weird World of Sex in the Animal Kingdom. by Ann Downer. Twenty-First Century Books 2016 104 p. (lb : alk. paper) $35.99

Grades: 7 8 9 10 11 12 **591.56**

1. Animal courtship 2. Sexual behavior in animals 3. Courtship in animals 4. Sexual selection in animals

ISBN 9781467785716

LC 2015035704

In this book, by Ann Downer, "birds do it, bees do it, penguins do it, and orangutans do it. By having sex and giving birth to offspring, animals ensure that their species will survive into the next generation. And in this quest for survival, animals go to great lengths." (Publisher's note)

"Downer's investigation of the myriad ways different species produce offspring is sure to enthrall researchers and browsers." SLJ

Includes bibliographical references and index

O'Sullivan, Joanne

Migration Nation; Animals on the Go from Coast to Coast. Joanne O'Sullivan. Imagine Publishing Incorporated 2015 96 p. col. illustrations, col. maps $15.95

Grades: 4 5 6 7 8 **591.56**

1. Animals 2. Animals -- Migration 3. Animal migrations

ISBN 162354050X; 9781623540500

This children's book, by Joanne O'Sullivan, part of the "Ranger Rick" series, "introduces the migratory habits of a dozen (mostly) North American animals. O'Sullivan explores migration by land (examining snakes, pronghorns, bison, and polar bears), by sea (salmon, manatees, and gray whales), and by sky (cranes and monarch butterflies)." (School Library Journal)

Safina, Carl

Beyond words; what elephants and whales think and feel. Carl Safina (author and photographer) Roaring Brook Press 2019 176 p. (hardcover) $17.99

Grades: 4 5 6 7 8 9 **591.56**

1. Animals 2. Elephants 3. Animal behavior

ISBN 9781250144638; 9781250144645

LC 2018944871

In this book, "follow researcher Carl Safina as he treks with a herd of elephants across the Kenyan landscape, then travel with him to the Pacific Northwest to track and monitor whales in their ocean home. Along the way, find out more about the interior lives of these giants of land and sea--how they play, how they fight, and how they communicate with one another, and sometimes with us, too." (Publisher's note)

"A profound, scientifically based appeal for recognition of the kinship of all living things." Kirkus

Schueller, Gretel H.

Animal migration; [by] Gretel H. Schueller and Sheila K. Schueller. Chelsea House 2009 120p il (Animal behavior) lib bdg $32.95

Grades: 6 7 8 9 **591.56**

1. Animals -- Migration

ISBN 978-1-60413-127-7 lib bdg; 1-60413-127-6 lib bdg

LC 2008-40125

This describes "why animals are compelled to migrate, as well as the various patterns and cycles of their migrations." Publisher's note

Includes glossary and bibliographical references

Spilsbury, Richard

Life cycles. Rosen Central 2010 46p il (Life processes) lib bdg $26.50; pa $11.75

Grades: 5 6 7 **591.56**

1. Life cycles (Biology)

ISBN 978-1-61532-341-8 lib bdg; 1-61532-341-4 lib bdg; 978-1-61532-350-0 pa; 1-61532-350-3 pa

LC 2009-30414

"With colorful, quality photography, the well-organized content is divided into short chapters with bold subheadings making information easy to find. Clear and interesting writing distinguishes this . . . from older titles. The captions for pictures are used to provide identification and additional explanation for topics not included in the text." Libr Media Connect

Includes glossary and bibliographical references

West, Krista

Animal courtship. Chelsea House 2009 120p il (Animal behavior) lib bdg $32.95

Grades: 6 7 8 9 **591.56**

1. Animal courtship

ISBN 978-1-60413-090-4 lib bdg; 1-60413-090-3 lib bdg

LC 2008-40121

This describes "the various ways species attract mates, including by singing, dancing, glowing, and even attacking." Publisher's note

Includes glossary and bibliographical references

591.59 Communication

Tomecek, Steve

Animal communication; [by] Stephen M. Tomecek. Chelsea House 2009 104p il (Animal behavior) lib bdg $32.95

Grades: 6 7 8 9 **591.59**

1. Animal communication

ISBN 978-1-60413-091-1 lib bdg; 1-60413-091-1 lib bdg

LC 2008-40115

This explains "the many different ways in which animals and insects express themselves and examines some of the latest scientific discoveries involving animal intelligence." Publisher's note

Includes glossary and bibliographical references

591.6 Miscellaneous nontaxonomic kinds of animals

Hammond, Paula

The **atlas** of the world's most dangerous animals; mapping nature's born killers. Marshall Cavendish 2010 224p il map lib bdg $99.93

Grades: 7 8 9 10 11 12 **591.6**

1. Dangerous animals

ISBN 978-0-7614-7870-6 lib bdg; 0-7614-7870-1 lib bdg

LC 2008-44960

First published 2004 in the United Kingdom

Explores each of the world's continents, featuring deadly species of animals.

"Each of these beautifully illustrated books features an appealing layout; logical organization; and plenty of full-color drawings, maps, and photographs. The volumes are organized by continent, with an additional chapter covering animals in the world's oceans...These volumes are ideal for reports, but animal lovers will enjoy perusing them as well." (School Library Journal)

591.68 Rare and endangered animals

Cotton, Katie

★ **Counting** lions; Portraits from the Wild. Katie Cotton ; illustrated by Stephen Walton ; with a foreword by Virginia McKenna. Candlewick Press 2015 40 p. illustrations $22

Grades: 5 6 7 8 **591.68**

1. Animals 2. Counting

ISBN 9780763682071

LC 2014957760

This book, by Katie Cotton, illustrated by Steven Walton, is a "spectacular, visually stunning celebration of wildlife—and gentle counting book—that can be enjoyed by the entire family. Exquisite charcoal drawings of ten endangered creatures—lions, elephants, giraffes, pandas, tigers, chimpanzees, penguins, turtles, macaws, and zebras—startle the viewer with their size and astonishing detail." (Publisher's note)

Hammond, Paula

The **atlas** of endangered animals; wildlife under threat around the world. Marshall Cavendish 2010 224p il map lib bdg $99.93

Grades: 7 8 9 10 11 12 **591.68**

1. Atlases 2. Reference books 3. Endangered species

ISBN 978-0-7614-7872-0; 0-7614-7872-8

LC 2008-44956

First published 2006 in the United Kingdom

This "beautifully illustrated . . . [book] features an appealing layout; logical organization; and plenty of full-color drawings, maps, and photographs. . . . Ideal for reports, but animal lovers will enjoy perusing them as well." SLJ

Hirsch, Rebecca E., 1969-

De -extinction; the science of bringing lost species back to life. by Rebecca E. Hirsch. Twenty-First Century Books 2017 120 p. color ills., color maps (lb : alk. paper) $35.99

Grades: 5 6 7 **591.68**

1. Extinct animals 2. Extinction (Biology) 3. DNA, Fossil 4. Rare animals -- Cloning 5. Extinct animals -- Cloning 6. Extinct animals -- Genetics

ISBN 9781512428483; 9781467794909

LC 2016019335

In this book, by Rebecca E. Hirsch, "because of climate change and other human activities, many animal species have become extinct, and many others are at risk of extinction. Once they are gone, we cannot bring them back or can we? With techniques such as cloning, scientists want to reverse extinction and return lost species to the wild. Some scientists want to create clones of recently extinct animals, while others want to make new hybrid animals." (Publisher's note)

"A staid but intellectually stimulating excursion across one of modern biology's most promising, and controversial, frontiers." Kirkus

Includes bibliographical references (pages 107-112) and index.

591.7 Animal ecology, animals characteristic of specific environments

Dawes, John

★ **Exploring** the world of aquatic life; [consultant editor, John P. Friel; authors, John Dawes and Andrew Campbell] Chelsea House Publishers 2009 6v il set $210

Grades: 5 6 7 8 **591.7**

1. Reference books 2. Marine animals -- Encyclopedias

ISBN 978-1-60413-255-7 set; 1-60413-255-8 set

LC 2008-30416

This set "offers an introduction to the diversity of animals that inhabit oceans, rivers, and lakes. . . . Entries are arranged alphabetically. . . . [The set includes] more than 100 articles. . . . Large photographs and illustrations appear on every two-page spread. . . . With its large typeface, clear explanations, and open layout, this set will appeal to younger students and would be a useful addition to school and public libraries." Booklist

Includes bibliographical references

Downer, Ann

Wild animal neighbors; sharing our urban world. Ann Downer. Twenty-First Century Books 2014 64 p. (library binding : alkaline paper) $33.27

Grades: 5 6 7 8 **591.7**

1. Wildlife 2. Urban ecology 3. Suburban life 4. Urban animals 5. City and town life 6. Human-animal relationships 7. Nature -- Effect of human beings on

ISBN 0761390219; 9780761390213

LC 2012043817

This book, by Ann Downer, explains that "as the human population tops seven billion, animals are running out of space. Their natural habitats are surrounded and sometimes even replaced by highways, shopping centers, office parks, and subdivisions. The result? A wildlife invasion of our urban neighborhoods. What kinds of animals are making cities their new home? How can they survive in our ecosystem of concrete, steel, and glass? And what does their presence there mean for their future and ours?" (Publisher's note)

"Although this book's editorial stance advocates for wild animals in city habitats, it's candid about problems such animals cause humans--from messy raccoons that may carry rabies to potentially dangerous mountain lions in Los Angeles. Accurate information unhampered by a rigid template and supported by good documentation is presented in readable, balanced prose; compelling photographs illustrate the text." (Horn Book)

Includes bibliographical references (page 62) and index

Johnson, Jinny

Simon & Schuster children's guide to sea creatures. Simon & Schuster Bks. for Young Readers 1998 80p il $21.95

Grades: 4 5 6 7 **591.7**

1. Marine animals

ISBN 0-689-81534-4

LC 97-8227

Describes the major groups of marine animals, including fish, birds, mammals, and crustaceans

"A beautifully illustrated guide, with a full-color drawing of each animal. . . . The book has enough information to be a useful research tool in the library. The organization, by habitat, is outstanding." Book Rep

Includes glossary

Johnson, Rebecca L.

★ **Journey** into the deep; discovering new ocean creatures. with a foreword by Sylvia A. Earle. Millbrook Press 2010 64p il lib bdg $31.93

Grades: 4 5 6 7 **591.7**

1. Ocean bottom 2. Marine animals 3. Scientific expeditions

ISBN 978-0-7613-4148-2 lib bdg; 0-7613-4148-X lib bdg

LC 2009049603

"This strikingly illustrated book takes its readers on a series of research voyages exploring the ocean from its shallow edges to unfathomable depths during the recently completed ten-year International Census of Marine Life. Clearly organized text and pictures combine to introduce newly discovered marine creatures of all kinds. . . . The excitement and challenge of discovery in tangible. Scientific photographs printed on blue-to-black background . . . illustrate animals mentioned in a nicely legible text. . . . Rich, revealing and rewarding." Kirkus

Includes glossary and bibliographical references

Miller, Sara Swan

Secret lives of burrowing beasts. Marshall Cavendish Benchmark 2010 48p il (Secret lives) lib bdg $29.93

Grades: 3 4 5 6 **591.7**

1. Burrowing animals

ISBN 978-0-7614-4221-9 lib bdg; 0-7614-4221-9 lib bdg

"The bright, sharp color photos . . . enhance, but take second fiddle to Miller's lively, well-knit [narrative]. . . . [This] volume closes with a generous selection of print and web resources." SLJ

Includes glossary

Secret lives of cave creatures. Marshall Cavendish Benchmark 2010 48p il (Secret lives) lib bdg $29.93

Grades: 3 4 5 6 **591.7**

1. Animals 2. Cave dwellers

ISBN 978-0-7614-4224-0 lib bdg; 0-7614-4224-3 lib bdg

"The bright, sharp color photos . . . enhance, but take second fiddle to Miller's lively, well-knit [narrative]. . . . [This] volume closes with a generous selection of print and web resources." SLJ

Includes glossary

Secret lives of deep-sea creatures. Marshall Cavendish Benchmark 2010 48p il (Secret lives) lib bdg $29.93

Grades: 3 4 5 6 **591.7**

1. Marine animals

ISBN 978-0-7614-4226-4 lib bdg; 0-7614-4226-X lib bdg

LC 2010000376

"The bright, sharp color photos . . . enhance, but take second fiddle to Miller's lively, well-knit [narrative]. . . . [This] volume closes with a generous selection of print and web resources." SLJ

Includes glossary

Secret lives of soil creatures. Marshall Cavendish Benchmark 2010 48p il (Secret lives) lib bdg $29.93

Grades: 3 4 5 6 **591.7**

1. Animals 2. Soil ecology

ISBN 978-0-7614-4229-5 lib bdg; 0-7614-4229-4 lib bdg

"The bright, sharp color photos . . . enhance, but take second fiddle to Miller's lively, well-knit [narrative]. . . . [This] volume closes with a generous selection of print and web resources." SLJ

Includes glossary

Montgomery, Heather L.

Something rotten; a fresh look at roadkill. by Heather Montgomery ; illustrated by Kevin O'Malley. Bloomsbury 2018 176 p. (hardcover) $16.99

Grades: 4 5 6 7 8 **591.7**

1. Roadkill 2. Animal carcasses

ISBN 9781547601875; 9781681199009

LC 2017056223

In this children's book, by Heather Montgomery, illustrated by Kevin O'Malley, Heather's "fascination with roadkill sets her off on a journey from her own backyard and the roadways of the American South to scientists and kids in labs and homes across the globe. . . . [This] narrative nonfiction is an eye-opening and irreverent look at the dead and dying animals that we pass by without a second thought--as well as a fascinating insight to the scientific research process." (Publisher's note)

Read, Nicholas

City critters; wildlife in the urban jungle. Nicholas Read. Orca Book Publishers 2012 134 p. (pbk.) $19.95

Grades: 6 7 8 **591.7**

1. Urban ecology 2. Birds 3. Animals 4. Mammals 5. Urban animals

ISBN 1554693942; 9781554693948

LC 2011942577

This book, by Nicholas Read, offers "a closer look [that] . . . reveals . . . we share our urban environment with a great many untamed creatures. . . . [The book] examines how and why so many wild animals choose to live in places that, on first glance at least, seem contrary to their needs. How do those . . . [animals] manage to survive in the big city? . . . And what are our responsibilities in ensuring that these animals can continue to share our city lives?" (Publisher's note)

Includes bibliographical references and index.

Turner, Pamela S.

Prowling the seas; exploring the hidden world of ocean predators. Walker & Co. 2009 39p il map $17.99; lib bdg $18.89

Grades: 4 5 6 **591.7**

1. Ocean 2. Marine animals 3. Predatory animals

ISBN 978-0-8027-9748-3; 0-8027-9748-2; 978-0-8027-9749-0 lib bdg; 0-8027-9749-0 lib bdg

"In each chapter, a clearly delineated map makes it easy to follow the animals' routes, and many clear color photos show the animals and the scientists who study them. . . . A clearly written presentation of an unusual topic." Booklist

Webb, Sophie

Far from shore; a naturalist explores the deep ocean. written and illustrated by Sophie Webb. Houghton Mifflin Books for Children 2011 80p il $17.99

Grades: 4 5 6 7 **591.7**

1. Dolphins 2. Water birds 3. Marine animals

ISBN 978-0-618-59729-1; 0-618-59729-8

LC 2010025121

Webb "returns with another richly detailed journal of her travels as a naturalist, combining scientific information, field guide-like illustrations, and a thorough account of the day-to-day experiments of a field scientist. The setting is a four-month-long research cruise on a National Ocean and Atmospheric Administration ship to study the impact of fishing on two dolphin populations that reside in the Eastern Tropical Pacific." Horn Book

Includes glossary

591.77 Marine animals

De la Bédoyère, Camilla

Monsters of the deep; by Camilla Bedoyere. Firefly Books Ltd. 2014 80 p. color illustrations (bound) $9.95

Grades: 4 5 6 **591.77**

1. Marine animals 2. Deep-sea animals

ISBN 1770854657; 9781770854659

LC 2014497405

In this book, by Camilla Bedoyere, "readers get a look into the watery deep and find 14 of nature's strangest creatures. Intricately drawn artworks and 200 stunning photographs highlight the extraordinary features of each animal's anatomy and survival tactics, such as bioluminescence to ward off predators and jet propulsion (in one case, jet vomit) to escape quickly." (Publisher's note)

"These attractive volumes cover a wide variety of unusual animals . . . [t]he layouts are dramatic, featuring fascinating, sometimes stunning, photos and drawings set against black backgrounds . . . [c]harming looks at some odd creatures." SLJ

Hoyt, Erich

★ **Weird** sea creatures; Erich Hoyt. Firefly Books 2013 63 p. (pbk.) $9.95; (bound) $19.95

Grades: 5 6 7 8 9 10 **591.77**

1. Marine biology 2. Abyssal zone 3. Deep-sea animals -- Pictorial works

ISBN 9781770851917; 1770851917; 1770851976; 9781770851979

LC 2012554415

This book celebrates "odd and recently discovered [undersea] species. Through 50 . . . photos, readers are introduced to a yeti crab; a spined pigmy shark; Dumbo, the octopod; and many other deep-sea dwellers." The introduction "presents the physical characteristics of the abyssal ocean—its cold darkness, its cruel pressure—and of the difficulties in finding, collecting, and photographing the creatures that call it home." (School Library Journal)

"Eerie, riveting eye candy for budding biologists and casual browsers alike." Kirkus

Rake, Matthew

Creatures of the deep; Matthew Rake; illustrated by Simon Mendez. Hungry Tomato 2016 32 p. color illustrations (pb : alk. paper) $7.99

Grades: 3 4 5 6 **591.77**

1. Marine biology 2. Aquatic animals 3. Marine animals 4. Dangerous marine animals

ISBN 1467776432; 9781467763608; 9781467776431

LC 2015014282

In this children's book by Matthew Rake, illustrated by Simon Mendez, readers will "encounter the ten strangest creatures living in the oceans, seas, and rivers. You'll discover a fish with an angling light, a snail that harpoons its prey, a squid with eyes bigger than a human head, and more. Come face to face with these extreme animals and learn their secrets!" (Publisher's note)

Woodward, John

Ocean; an amazing window on our world. written by John Woodward ; illustrations by Gary Hanna. DK Pub. 2012 59 p. col. ill. (Look closer) (hardcover) $10.99

Grades: 4 5 6 **591.77**

1. Picture books for children 2. Ocean 3. Marine biology 4. Marine animals

ISBN 0756692377; 9780756692377

LC 2011277622

This book is part of DK Publishing's Look Closer series and allows readers to "explore different perspectives of . . . underwater scenes as they zoom in, zoom out, and go sideways, forward, and backward. . . . Specially commissioned computer-generated imagery" is included. (Publisher's note)

592 Specific taxonomic groups of animals

Downer, Ann

Smart and spineless; brainy without a backbone. by Ann Downer. Twenty-First Century Books 2016 88 p. color illustrations (lib. bdg.) $33.32

Grades: 6 7 8 9 10 **592**

1. Invertebrates 2. Invertebrates -- Psychology

ISBN 1467737399; 9781467737395

LC 2014025658

Downer explains that "invertebrates can be astonishingly intelligent. These animals exhibit surprising feats of learning, memory, and problem-solving using their relatively simple, tiny brains some the size of a sesame seed or even smaller. In fact, some intelligent invertebrates have no brain at all! Scientists around the world are putting invertebrate intelligence to use in mind-boggling ways." (Publisher's note)

"Lucid and well organized, the writing grips readers with a combination of facts and related narrative accounts of scientists at work. Clear color photos illustrate the main text and the many sidebars, which often highlight related research projects." Booklist

Includes bibliographical references and index

Marsico, Katie

Leeches; by Katie Marsico. Children's Press, an imprint of Scholastic Inc. 2016 48 p. color illustrations library $28

Grades: 3 4 5 6 **592**

1. Leeches

ISBN 0531213943; 0531214974; 9780531214978; 9780531213940

LC 2014046960

This children's book, by Katie Marsico, part of the "Nature's Children" series, profiles leeches. "These additions to this ongoing series follow a tried-and-true format: text on one page facing a full-page photo. An opening 'Fact File' breaks down info such as taxonomy, habits, habitats, and diets and provides a preview for the information that will be covered. . . . [And] the first chapter depicts an encounter with the animal and describes a typical behavior." (School Library Journal)

"With more than 700 species, readers will learn about blood-sucking and nonparasitic varieties and their role in human medicine." Booklist

Includes bibliographical references (page 46) and index

Meinkoth, Norman August

★ The **Audubon** Society field guide to North American seashore creatures; [by] Norman A. Meinkoth. Knopf 1981 799p il maps flexible bdg $19.95

Grades: 7 8 9 10 11 12 Adult **592**

1. Invertebrates 2. Marine biology

ISBN 0-394-51993-0

LC 81-80828

This "unique field guide covers some 850 marine invertebrate animals living in or around the shallow waters of the temperate seacoasts of the United States and Canada. Excellent color photographs are grouped at the beginning of the book, followed by text that gives, for each animal, a short description, common and scientific names, habitat, range, and comments." Malinowsky. Best Sci & Technol Ref Books for Young People

594 Mollusks and molluscoids

Arthur, Alex

Shell; written by Alex Arthur; special photography by Andreas von Einsiedel, Dave King and Colin Keates. Dk Pub 2013 72 p. (Eyewitness books) (library) $19.99

Grades: 6 7 8 **594**

1. Shells 2. Conchology

ISBN 1465409041; 9781465409041

This book is part of the DK Eyewitness Books series and focuses on shells. The titles in this series "focus on subjects that complement students' personal interests and areas of study to make learning simple and fun." Wall charts, clip art CDs, and photographs and illustrations are included. (Publisher's note)

Cerullo, Mary M.

Giant squid; searching for a sea monster. by Mary M. Cerullo with Clyde F.E. Roper. Capstone Press 2012 48 p. ill. (chiefly col.) (Smithsonian) (library) $26.86; (paperback) $8.95

Grades: 4 5 6 **594**

1. Giant squids

ISBN 1429680237; 9781429675413; 9781429680233

LC 2011029181

This book "recounts some of the legends and historical clues that led to the giant squid's identification in the 19th century before focusing on Dr. Clyde Roper, a renowned specialist on cephalopods. . . . The text describes how Roper gathered facts by autopsying the carcasses of giant squids and sperm whales (its chief predator), examining other squid species, etc.; it also outlines several expeditions he led in search of a live specimen." (School Library Journal)

Douglass, Jackie Leatherbury

Peterson first guide to shells of North America; illustrations by John Douglass. Houghton Mifflin 1989 128p il pa $5.95

Grades: 7 8 9 10 11 12 Adult **594**

1. Shells

ISBN 0-395-91182-6

LC 88-32884

"Shell collectors will enjoy the basic descriptions of shell types. Douglass has included the 'most colorful, not necessarily the most common, shells.' . . . Filled with precise color drawings and concise identification information." Booklist

Miller, Sara Swan

Secret lives of seashell dwellers. Marshall Cavendish Benchmark 2010 48p il (Secret lives) lib bdg $29.93

Grades: 3 4 5 6 **594**

1. Mollusks

ISBN 978-0-7614-4228-8 lib bdg; 0-7614-4228-6 lib bdg

LC 2010000377

"The bright, sharp color photos . . . enhance, but take second fiddle to Miller's lively, well-knit [narrative]. . . . [This] volume closes with a generous selection of print and web resources." SLJ

Includes glossary

Montgomery, Sy

★ The **Octopus** Scientists; exploring the mind of a mollusk. written by Sy Montgomery; photographs by Keith Ellenbogen. Houghton Mifflin Harcourt 2015 80 p. illustrations (chiefly color) $18.99

Grades: 5 6 7 8 9 **594**

1. Octopuses 2. Marine biology 3. Octopuses -- Research -- French Polynesia -- Morea

ISBN 0544232704; 9780544232709

This book by Sy Montogomery and illustrated by Keith Ellenborgen, "an inquiry into the mind of an intelligent invertebrate, is also a foray into our own unexplored planet. With three hearts and blue blood, its gelatinous body unconstrained by jointed limbs or gravity, the octopus seems to be an alien, an inhabitant of another world. But most intriguing of all, octopuses--classed as mollusks, like clams--are remarkably intelligent with quirky personalities." (Publisher's note)

"Amazing photographs reveal the octopuses' remarkable shape-changing abilities and help readers visualize this experience. Science in the field at its best." Kirkus

Newquist, H. P.

Here there be monsters; the legendary kraken and the giant squid. Houghton Mifflin Harcourt 2010 73p il map $18

Grades: 4 5 6 7 **594**

1. Squids

ISBN 978-0-547-07678-2; 0-547-07678-9

"This intriguing book offers a chronological account of giant squids, beginning with sailors' tales about krakens and leading up to the groundbreaking discoveries of the past few decades. . . . The many illustrations, in color when available, include photos, engravings, and maps. . . . An attractive, informative book on an underrepresented topic." Booklist

Rand, Casey

Glass squid and other spectacular squid. Raintree 2011 32p il lib bdg $29; pa $7.99

Grades: 3 4 5 6 **594**

1. Squids

ISBN 978-1-4109-4194-7 lib bdg; 978-1-4109-4201-2 pa

LC 2010038186

"This informative and colorful series will engage younger children to learn more about the sea and its creatures." Library Media Connection

Rehder, Harald Alfred

The **Audubon** Society field guide to North American seashells; {by} Harald A. Rehder; with photographs by James H. Carmichael, Jr.; visual key by Carol Nehring and Mary Beth Brewer. Knopf 1981 894p il flexible bdg $19.95

Grades: 7 8 9 10 11 12 Adult **594**

1. Shells 2. Mollusks

ISBN 0-394-51913-2

LC 80-84239

"[T]his guide explores more than 705 seashells, living mollusks, abalone, periwinkles, conchs, limpets, oysters, clams, mussels, and cockles found on the Atlantic, Pacific, and Gulf coasts of North America and the West Indies. The photographs are arranged by shape and color, making identification quick and easy." Publisher's note

"The more than 700 color plates are arranged according to shape and color rather than family or genus, making identification very simple for even the rankest amateur. . . . The text gives the common name, scientific name, description, habitat, range, and comments for each species. This is the most comprehensive field guide to North American seashells." Libr J

595 Arthropods

Reynolds, Toby

Insects and spiders. Barron's Educational Series 2016 32 p. color illustrations (paperback) $6.99

Grades: 4 5 6 7 **595**

1. Insects 2. Spiders

ISBN 1438008279; 9781438008271

LC 2015956068

In this children's book by Toby Reynolds and illustrated by Paul Calver, part of the Visual Explorers series, "engaging text, detailed facts, and impressive statistics give children exciting scientific insight into the world of insects and spiders. A glossary at the end of the book helps reinforce the information. Parents, teachers, and librarians will want to collect all of the books in this series to create a very cool first encyclopedia to build early research skills." *(Publisher's note)

"Inexpensive and relatively sturdy, these large-format paperbacks make for a visually enticing series." Booklist

595.4 Chelicerates

Heos, Bridget

Stronger Than Steel; Spider Silk DNA and the Quest for Better Bulletproof Vests, Sutures, and Parachute Rope. Bridget Heos ; [illustrated by] Andy Comins. Houghton Mifflin Books for Children 2013 79 p. col. ill. (hardcover) $18.99

Grades: 5 6 7 8 **595.4**

1. Silk 2. Spiders 3. Inventions 4. Scientists 5. Spider webs 6. Nephila maculata 7. Spider webs -- Therapeutic use

ISBN 0547681267; 9780547681269

LC 2012010992

This children's book, by Bridget Heos, illustrated by Andy Comis, is part of the "Scientists in the Field" series. In it "readers enter Randy Lewis' lab where they come face to face with golden orb weaver spiders, and transgenic alfalfa, silkworm silk, and goats, whose milk contains the proteins to spin spider silk--and to weave a nearly indestructible fiber." (Publisher's note)

Hirschmann, Kris

Deadliest spiders; by Kris Hirschmann. ReferencePoint Press 2017 80 p. (hardback) $29.95

Grades: 6 7 8 9 10 **595.4**

1. Spiders 2. Predation (Biology) 3. Poisonous spiders

ISBN 1682820580; 9781682820582

LC 2016020674

This children's book, by Kris Hirschmann, part of the "Deadliest Predators" series, describes how "spiders are small but fierce hunters with all the tools and skills they need to capture and kill their prey. Some species have venom that is lethal to humans as well as their normal prey. Six deadly spiders, including the black widow and the Chilean recluse, are profiled." (Publisher's note)

"First-rate nonfiction on a high-interest topic." SLJ

Includes bibliographical references and index

Lasky, Kathryn

Silk & venom; searching for a dangerous spider. photographs by Christopher G. Knight. Candlewick Press 2011 57p il map

Grades: 4 5 6 7 **595.4**

1. Spiders 2. Biologists 3. Arachnologists 4. College teachers

ISBN 0-7636-4222-3; 978-0-7636-4222-8

LC 2010-41888

This book focuses on the the field work of arachnologist Greta Binford. "Binford's effort to trace the migration of Loxosceles from South American to North America . . . [led] her to field exploration in the Dominican Republic. [Glossary. Index.] Grades four to seven." (Bull Cent Child Books)

"Biology professor Greta Binford studies spiders in an Oregon lab and in the field in the Dominican Republic, where she searches for L. Taino, a Caribbean relative of the venomous brown recluse that might provide clues to how and when the recluse genus arrived in North America. . . . In leisurely, literary prose, Lasky presents the ancient class of arachnids before introducing the scientist and explaining her quest. . . . On most spreads, a full-bleed photograph is opposed by substantial text and one or two smaller pictures." Kirkus

Markle, Sandra

Black widows; deadly biters. Lerner Publications 2011 48p il (Arachnid world) lib bdg $29.27

Grades: 5 6 7 8 **595.4**

1. Spiders

ISBN 978-0-7613-5038-5; 0-7613-5038-1

This describes how black widows are similar to and different from other arachnids. Close-up photographs and diagrams reveal details about the black widow's body both inside and out. A hands-on activity compares the black widow's web to a human hair.

Markle "presents a mix of common and less-common facts . . . and her commentary accompanies a particularly strong suite of illustrations featuring large, clear, labeled outside and inside views that display body parts. Photos go beyond the standard portraits. . . . First rate." SLJ

Includes glossary and bibliographical references

Crab spiders; phantom hunters. Sandra Markle. Lerner Pub. Company 2012 48 p. col. ill. (Arachnid world)

Grades: 4 5 6 7 **595.4**

1. Spiders 2. Zoology 3. Predatory animals 4. Arachnids 5. Crab spiders

ISBN 0761350454; 9780761350453

LC 2011020443

This book is part of Sandra Markle's "Arachnid World" series. "In this book, you will learn how crab spiders are similar to and different from other arachnids. Close-up photographs and diagrams reveal extraordinary details about the crab spider's body both inside and out. A hands-on activity illustrates how a crab spider can quickly ambush a flying insect. . . . Enter the . . . world of the arachnid family with award-winning science author Sandra Markle! Too often lumped together with insects, these fascinating animals have distinctive characteristics and habits that are all their own." (Publisher's note)

Includes bibliographical references (p. 44-45) and index

Fishing spiders; water ninjas. Sandra Markle. Lerner Publications Company 2012 48 p. col. ill. (Arachnid world)

Grades: 4 5 6 7 **595.4**

1. Spiders 2. Aquatic animals 3. Predatory animals 4. Zoology -- Encyclopedias 5. Arachnids 6. Dolomedes

ISBN 9780761350446

LC 2011020442

This book is part of Sandra Markle's "Arachnid World" series. "In this book, you will learn how fishing spiders are similar to and different from other arachnids. Close-up photographs and diagrams reveal extraordinary details about the fishing spider's body both inside and out. A hands-on activity shows how the fishing spider's hairy coat helps it walk on water. . . . Enter the . . . world of the arachnid family with award-winning science author Sandra Markle! Too often lumped together with insects, these fascinating animals have distinctive characteristics and habits that are all their own." (Publisher's note)

Includes bibliographical references and index

Harvestmen; secret operatives. Lerner Publications 2011 48p il (Arachnid world) lib bdg $29.27

Grades: 5 6 7 8 **595.4**

1. Spiders

ISBN 978-0-7613-5042-2; 0-7613-5042-X

LC 2010023491

This describes how harvestmen are similar to and different from other arachnids. Close-up photographs and diagrams reveal details about the harvestmen's bodies, both inside and out. A hands-on activity reveals how harvestmen walk on long legs using only their sense of touch to get around.

Markle "presents a mix of common and less-common facts . . . and her commentary accompanies a particularly strong suite of illustrations featuring large, clear, labeled outside and inside views that display body parts. Photos go beyond the standard portraits. . . . First rate." SLJ

Includes glossary and bibliographical references

Jumping spiders; gold-medal stalkers. by Sandra Markle. Lerner Publications 2012 48 p. col. ill.

Grades: 4 5 6 7 **595.4**

1. Spiders 2. Animal behavior 3. Zoology -- Encyclopedias 4. Arachnids 5. Jumping spiders

ISBN 0761350470; 9780761350477

LC 2011021598

This book is part of Sandra Markle's "Arachnid World" series. "In this book, you will learn how jumping spiders are similar to and different from other arachnids. Close-up photographs and diagrams reveal extraordinary details about the jumping spider's body both inside and out. A hands-on activity compares the reader's jumping ability with that of a jumping spider. . . . Enter the . . . world of the arachnid family with award-winning science author Sandra Markle! Too often lumped together with insects, these fascinating animals have distinctive characteristics and habits that are all their own." (Publisher's note)

Includes bibliographical references (p. 44-45) and index

Mites; master sneaks. by Sandra Markle. Lerner Publications 2012 48 p. (Arachnid world)

Grades: 4 5 6 7 **595.4**

1. Mites 2. Animals -- Anatomy 3. Arachnids

ISBN 9780761350460

LC 2011021462

In this book, a volume of the Arachnid World series, readers "will learn how mites are similar to and different from other arachnids. Close-up photographs, micrographs, and diagrams reveal . . . details about a mite's body both inside and out. A hands-on activity shows how quickly a few mites can multiply into hundreds." (Publisher's note) The book "discuss[es] . . . [their] physical structure, life cycle, and characteristic behaviors. . . . In "Mites," [author Sandra] Markle discusses a variety of these . . . creatures." (Booklist)

Includes bibliographical references and index

Orb weavers; hungry spinners. Lerner Publications 2011 48p il (Arachnid world) lib bdg $29.27

Grades: 5 6 7 8 **595.4**

1. Spiders

ISBN 978-0-7613-5039-2; 0-7613-5039-X

LC 2010023490

This describes how orb weavers are similar to and different from other arachnids. Close-up photographs and diagrams reveal details about the spider's body both inside and out. And a hands-on activity will give you an idea of how the orb weaver can detect prey caught in its web.

Markle "presents a mix of common and less-common facts . . . and her commentary accompanies a particularly strong suite of illustrations featuring large, clear, labeled outside and inside views that display body parts. Photos go beyond the standard portraits. . . . First rate." SLJ

Includes glossary and bibliographical references

Scorpions; armed stingers. Lerner Publications 2011 48p il (Arachnid world) lib bdg $29.27

Grades: 5 6 7 8 **595.4**

1. Scorpions

ISBN 978-0-7613-5037-8; 0-7613-5037-3

LC 2010004275

This describes how scorpions are similar to and different from other arachnids. Close-up photographs and diagrams reveal details about the scorpion's body both inside and out. And a hands-on activity reveals how a scorpion's senses help it find its prey.

Markle "presents a mix of common and less-common facts . . . and her commentary accompanies a particularly strong suite of illustrations featuring large, clear, labeled outside and inside views that display body parts. Photos go beyond the standard portraits. . . . First rate." SLJ

Includes glossary and bibliographical references

Ticks; dangerous hitchhikers. Lerner Publications 2011 48p il (Arachnid world) lib bdg $29.27

Grades: 4 5 6 7 **595.4**

1. Ticks

ISBN 978-0-7613-5041-5; 0-7613-5041-1

LC 2010023484

This book about ticks offers "a clear, conversational text that will draw young people into the zoological facts with gripping, even gruesome examples that are well matched with unsparingly detailed photos. . . . The handsome design, featuring crisply magnified photos, and the approachable text from an experienced writer combine into a strong offering for both personal and classroom reading." Booklist

Includes bibliographical references

Tarantulas; supersized predators. by Sandra Markle. Lerner Publications Company 2012 48 p. (Arachnid world)

Grades: 4 5 6 7 **595.4**

1. Tarantulas 2. Predatory animals 3. Arachnids

ISBN 9780761350439

LC 2011020437

In this book, a volume of the Arachnid World series, readers "will learn how tarantulas are similar to and different from other arachnids. Close-up photographs and diagrams reveal extraordinary details about the tarantula's body both inside and out. A hands-on activity illustrates how a tarantula grows bigger and bigger by molting." (Publisher's note) The book "discuss[es] . . . [their] physical structure, life cycle, and characteristic behaviors. . . . "Tarantulas" looks at the lives of these large, hairy spiders and points out that they help control insect populations." (Booklist)

Includes bibliographical references and index

Wind scorpions; killer jaws. Sandra Markle. Lerner Publications 2012 48 p. (Arachnid world) (lib. bdg. : alk. paper) $30.60

Grades: 4 5 6 7 **595.4**

1. Scorpions 2. Animals -- Anatomy 3. Arachnids 4. Solpugida

ISBN 0761350489; 9780761350484

LC 2011021599

In this book, a volume of the Arachnid World series, readers "will learn how wind scorpions are similar to and very different from other arachnids. Close-up photographs and diagrams reveal extraordinary details about the wind scorpion's body both inside and out. A hands-on activity demonstrates how wind scorpions are able to pick up prey to eat it." (Publisher's note) The book "discuss[es] . . . [their] physical structure, life cycle, and characteristic behaviors. . . . 'Wind Scorpions' introduces a group of arachnids that use supersize jaws to defend themselves and to attack their prey." (Booklist)

Includes bibliographical references and index

Wolf spiders; mothers on guard. Lerner Publications 2010 48p il (Arachnid world) lib bdg $29.27

Grades: 5 6 7 8 **595.4**

1. Spiders

ISBN 978-0-7613-5040-8; 0-7613-5040-3

LC 2010004273

This describes how wolf spider mothers carry their young on their backs and how wolf spiders are similar to and different from other arachnids. Close-up photographs and diagrams reveal details about the spider's body both inside and out. And hands-on activities will let you experience how a wolf spider female keeps her eggs and young safe.

Markle "presents a mix of common and less-common facts . . . and her commentary accompanies a particularly strong suite of illustrations featuring large, clear, labeled outside and inside views that display body parts. Photos go beyond the standard portraits. . . . First rate." SLJ

Includes glossary and bibliographical references

Montgomery, Sy

★ The **tarantula** scientist. Houghton Mifflin Co. 2004 80p il map (Scientists in the field) $18; pa $7.95

Grades: 4 5 6 7 **595.4**

1. Tarantulas

ISBN 0-618-14799-3; 0-618-91577-X pa

LC 2003-20125

Describes the research that Samuel Marshall and his students are doing on tarantulas, including the largest spider on earth, the Goliath birdeating tarantula

"Enthusiasm for the subject and respect for both Marshall and his eight-legged subjects come through on every page of the clear, informative, and even occasionally humorous text. Bishop's full-color photos . . . are amazing." Booklist

Includes glossary and bibliographical references

595.7 Insects

Albee, Sarah

Bugged; How Insects Changed History. by Sarah Albee. Bloomsbury/Walker 2014 176 p. illustrations (some color) (pbk.) $17.99; (library edition) $23.89

Grades: 4 5 6 7 **595.7**

1. Insects 2. Human-animal relationship 3. Insects -- History 4. Human-animal relationships -- History

ISBN 0802734227; 0802734235; 9780802734228; 9780802734235

LC 2013025968

This book, by Sarah Albee, illustrated by Robert Leighton, focuses on the impact of insects on the world throughout history. According to the book, "beneficial bugs have built empires. Bad bugs have toppled them." The book is a "combination of world history, social history, natural science, epidemiology, public health, conservation, and microbiology." (Publisher's note)

"Overall, this title is astonishing, disgusting, revolting, and ultimately fascinating, making it perfect for emerging entomologists, budding historians, reluctant readers, and gross-out junkies alike." SLJ

Anderson, Margaret Jean

Bugged -out insects; [by] Margaret J. Anderson. Enslow Publishers 2011 48p il (Bizarre science) lib bdg $23.93

Grades: 4 5 6 7 **595.7**

1. Insects

ISBN 978-0-7660-3674-1; 0-7660-3674-X

LC 2010006474

First published 1996 with title: Bizarre insects

This describes insects such as cicadas, butterflies, praying mantises, walkingsticks, beetles, stinkbugs, botflies, mayflies, mosquitoes, bees, ants, and locusts.

"Aimed at reluctant readers, [this title is] sure to disgust and delight in equal measure. . . . [The title] will pique interest and get kids lining up at the reference desk looking for more. The text is complemented by illustrations and magnified photos of things that you would hope never to see." SLJ

Includes glossary and bibliographical references

Beccaloni, George

Biggest bugs life-size. Firefly Books 2010 84p il $19.95

Grades: 4 5 6 7 **595.7**

1. Insects

ISBN 978-1-55407-699-4; 1-55407-699-4

"This book presents 35 of the world's biggest, longest, and heaviest bugs. . . . Double-page spreads feature each bug's statistics, a map with its area of distribution, and straightforward text that explains its living conditions, eating habits, and life cycle. . . . The highlights, of course, are the numerous life-size and up-close full-color photographs of the bugs. . . . The visual appeal alone will entice even the most reluctant readers." Booklist

Evans, Arthur V.

National Wildlife Federation field guide to insects and spiders & related species of North America; written by Arthur Evans; foreword by Craig Tufts. Sterling Pub. 2007 496p il map pa $19.95

Grades: 7 8 9 10 11 12 Adult **595.7**

1. Insects 2. Spiders

ISBN 978-1-4027-4153-1; 1-4027-4153-7

LC 2006-19491

"This guide presents a glimpse of the incredible array of colors, shapes, and forms found within the phylum Arthropoda. . . . Over 380 pages of color photographs follow, most showing two or three different species. . . . This is a very good guide that will find a wide audience." Choice

Includes bibliographical references

Hamilton, Sue L.

Swarmed by bees; [by] Sue Hamilton. ABDO Pub. Co. 2010 32p il (Close encounters of the wild kind) lib bdg $27.07

Grades: 4 5 6 7 **595.7**

1. Bees 2. Animal attacks

ISBN 978-1-60453-933-2 lib bdg; 1-60453-933-X lib bdg

LC 2009-45598

Readers learn of actual human-bee encounters, information about bees, survival strategies, and attack statistics.

"Students will be drawn to the realistic full-color photographs, the realistic diagrams of the creatures' bodies, the real-life stories told by victims, and the interesting, attractive formatting that includes text, diagrams, photographs, and graphics on each page. . . . [This is] exciting and attractive in a 'gross' sort of way and will appeal particularly to boys for both leisure reading and research." Libr Media Connect

Includes glossary

Latimer, Jonathan P.

Caterpillars; [by] Jonathan P. Latimer, Karen Stray Nolting; illustrations by Amy Bartlett Wright; foreword by Virginia Marie Peterson. Houghton Mifflin 2000 48p il (Peterson field guides for young naturalists) pbk. $5.95

Grades: 4 5 6 7 **595.7**
1. Caterpillars
ISBN 9780395979457
LC 99-38944

Describes the physical characteristics, behavior, and habitat of a variety of caterpillars, arranged by the categories "Smooth," "Bumpy," "Sluglike," "Horned," "Hairy," "Bristly," and "Spiny".

Marshall, Stephen A.

Insects A to Z. Firefly 2009 32p il lib bdg $19.95; pa $7.95
Grades: 4 5 6 **595.7**
1. Insects
ISBN 978-1-55407-555-3 lib bdg; 1-55407-555-6 lib bdg; 978-1-55407-503-4 pa; 1-55407-503-3 pa

This is an illustrated dictionary of 26 insects which includes the Latin and common names of the order, family, genus and species, as well as information on geographic distribution. Fact boxes for each entry provide information detailing each insect's scientific name, diet, average size and the location at which each was photographed.

"The photography . . . is well composed and sharply focused, with a nicely varied layout from page to page. . . . The [text is] clearly written." SLJ

Milne, Lorus Johnson

★ The **Audubon** Society field guide to North American insects and spiders; [by] Lorus and Margery Milne; visual key by Susan Rayfield. Knopf 1980 989p il $19.95
Grades: 7 8 9 10 11 12 Adult **595.7**
1. Insects 2. Spiders
ISBN 0-394-50763-0
LC 80-7620

The authors "have based their field guide on 702 excellent color photographs (75 of which are of spiders and other arachnids). In addition to some general information, the text (two thirds of the book) is made up of brief comments on each kind of arthropod pictured." Choice

Includes glossary

Stewart, Amy

Wicked bugs; the meanest, deadliest, grossest bugs on earth. Amy Stewart ; illustrated by Briony Morrow Cribbs. Algonquin Young Readers 2017 xi, 177 p.p color illustrations (hardcover) $19.95
Grades: 4 5 6 7 8 **595.7**
1. Arachnids 2. Insect pests
ISBN 9781616207700; 9781616206994; 9781616207557
LC 2017013260

This book, by Amy Stewart, "provides information on insects, arachnids and arthropods. "Organized into thematic categories . . . and featuring full-color illustrations by Briony Morrow-Cribbs, 'Wicked Bugs' is an educational and creepy-cool guide to the worst of the worst of insects, arachnids, and other arthropods. This is the young readers adaptation of Amy Stewart's bestselling book for adult readers." (Publisher's note)

Includes bibliographical references and index

Woodward, John

Super bug encyclopedia; DK Publishing. DK Publishing 2016 207 p. color illustrations (ebook) $65; $24.99
Grades: 4 5 6 7 8 **595.7**
1. Insects
ISBN 9781465455000; 1465446001; 9781465446008
LC 2016427602

This book takes "a look at the 100 most amazing insects on the planet! . . . With incredible facts and stats for every bug, [it] showcases the superstars of the insect world. Find out which insect can snap a pencil in half, how a tiny moth can fly up to 70 miles an hour, and meet a dung beetle that can pull over 1,100 times its own body weight." (Publisher's note)

"This selection has high appeal for browsers and will be useful for report writers." SLJ

Young, Karen Romano

Bug science; 20 projects and experiments about arthropods: insects, arachnids, algae, worms, and other small creatures. illustrations by David Goldin. National Geographic 2009 80p il (Science fair winners) lib bdg $24.90; pa $12.95
Grades: 6 7 8 9 **595.7**
1. Insects 2. Arthropoda 3. Science projects 4. Science -- Experiments
ISBN 978-1-4263-0520-7 lib bdg; 1-4263-0520-6 lib bdg; 978-1-4263-0519-1 pa; 1-4263-0519-2 pa
LC 2009-12734

Twenty projects and experiments about arthropods: insects, arachnids, algae, worms, and other small creatures.

This book is "engaging, visually stimulating, and very student friendly. . . . Includes an introduction to the topic, suggestions for how to present the findings, and an index making the information really accessible. . . . The planning steps, guidance, and tips along the way for implementing projects are very sound." Libr Media Connect

Includes bibliographical references

595.76 Beetles

Burns, Loree Griffin

★ **Beetle** busters; a rogue insect and the people who track it. Loree Griffin Burns ; photographs by Ellen Harasimowicz. Houghton Mifflin Harcourt 2014 64 p. color illustrations, color map (Scientists in the field) $18.99
Grades: 5 6 7 8 **595.76**
1. Beetles 2. Insects 3. Nonindigenous pests 4. Beetles 5. Asian longhorned beetle
ISBN 0547792670; 9780547792675
LC 2013050160

This book, by Loree Griffin Burns, focuses on the "Asian longhorned beetle (ALB). . . . These beetles came to America from China, living in wood turned into shipping material. At first the beetles invaded urban areas, where hardwood trees were in limited supply. . . . But . . . now . . . infestations have erupted in . . . hardwood forests, and these beetles, while bad at flying, are very good at killing trees. Clint McFarland's job? Stop the ALB at any cost." (Publisher's note)

"The author lives within the quarantined area in Massachusetts and has seen firsthand areas where swatches of infested (and other) trees have been cut down. Her questions about the method employed will leave readers asking some of their own--as they should. A timely, well-told story and a call to action." SLJ

Jenkins, Steve, 1952-

★ The **beetle** book; Steve Jenkins. Houghton Mifflin Books for Children 2011 31 p. $16.99
Grades: 4 5 6 7 **595.76**
1. Beetles 2. Ecology -- Encyclopedias 3. Insects -- Encyclopedias
ISBN 9780547680842
LC 2011027129

This nonfiction natural history book presents pictures and information about an "array of beetles." Author/illustrator Steve Jenkins describes "the colors and patterns of this ubiquitous insect . . . [and] the details about the various adaptations that beetles have made over millennia in response to their environment, diet, and predators." Jenkins claims that "one out of four creatures on the planet is a beetle." (Kirkus Reviews)

595.78 Moths and butterflies

Hirsch, Rebecca E., 1969-

The **monarchs** are missing; a butterfly mystery. by Rebecca E. Hirsch. Millbrook Press 2018 56 p. (lb : alk. paper) $31.99

Grades: 3 4 5 6 7 **595.78**

1. Butterflies 2. Monarch butterflies 3. Butterflies -- Losses 4. Butterflies -- Conservation 5. Monarch butterfly -- Migration

ISBN 9781512452501

LC 2017010743

In this book, author Rebecca E. Hirsch "introduces the mysteries of monarch butterfly migration while encouraging readers to get involved to halt the butterfly's population decline. The author recounts how scientists developed tagging methods to track the path of eastern monarchs and to identify their wintering grounds in Mexico . . . [and explains] the generational life cycles required to complete the yearly migratory journey." (Publisher's note)

Includes bibliographical references and index

Pasternak, Carol

How to raise monarch butterflies; a step-by-step guide for kids. Carol Pasternak. Firefly Books 2012 48 p. col. ill. (bound) $19.95

Grades: 3 4 5 6 7 **595.78**

1. Caterpillars 2. Insects -- Care 3. Monarch butterflies 4. Monarch butterfly -- Life cycles

ISBN 1770850015; 1770850023; 9781770850019; 9781770850026

LC 2012419489

This book by Carol Pasternak presents a "detailed guide to locating and hatching. . . Monarch butterflies. . . . [R]eaders will learn about the life cycle of the Monarch and how to encourage populations in their own backyards, with tips on which plants to grow, as well as the care and feeding of their pet caterpillars. 'How to Raise Monarch Butterflies' explains what threats face Monarchs and how readers can help conserve the Monarch's feeding grounds from encroachment." (Publisher's note)

Includes bibliographical references and index.

Pyle, Robert Michael

★ The **Audubon** Society field guide to North American butterflies; visual key by Carol Nehring and Jane Opper. Knopf 1981 916p il $19.95

Grades: 7 8 9 10 11 12 Adult **595.78**

1. Butterflies

ISBN 0-394-51914-0

LC 80-84240

This guide "introduces more than 600 species of North American butterfly, including those native to the Hawaiian Islands. A section of brilliant color plates (more than 1,000 of them) featuring butterflies in their natural habitats, follows a general introduction and notes on text organization and use." Booklist

Whalley, Paul

Butterfly & moth; written by Paul Whalley. Revised ed. DK Pub. 2012 72 p. ill. (chiefly col.), col. map (Eyewitness books) (hardcover) $16.99; (library) $19.99

Grades: 4 5 6 7 **595.78**

1. Moths 2. Butterflies

ISBN 0756692989; 0756692997; 9780756692988; 9780756692995

LC 2012418030

This book is part of the DK Eyewitness Books series and focuses on butterflies and moths. The titles in this series "focus on subjects that complement students' personal interests and areas of study to make learning simple and fun." Wall charts, clip art CDs, and photographs and illustrations are included. (Publisher's note)

595.79 Hymenoptera

Blobaum, Cindy

Explore Honey Bees! With 25 Great Projects. by Cindy Blobaum ; illustrated by Bryan Stone. Nomad Press 2015 96 p. color illustrations $19.95

Grades: 3 4 5 6 **595.79**

1. Bees

ISBN 1619302861; 9781619302860

In this book, by Cindy Blobaum, illustrated by Bryan Stone, "young readers learn about honey bee colonies, why honey bees live in hives, how honey bees communicate with each other, and why they are so important to human lives. . . . Activities include designing a hive and making a model of a flower's reproductive system, reinforcing the math and science skills readers gain from the text." (Publisher's note)

"A solid text that lends itself well to classroom use as well as to individual research," SLJ

Markle, Sandra

The **case** of the vanishing honey bees; a scientific mystery. by Sandra Markle. Lerner Pub Group 2013 48 p. (lib. bdg. : alk. paper) $29.27

Grades: 4 5 6 7 8 **595.79**

1. Bees 2. Honey 3. Insects -- Behavior 4. Honeybee 5. Honeybee -- Health

ISBN 1467705926; 9781467705929

LC 2012046913

This book, by Sandra Markle, "explores the world of honeybees and the mysterious malady that threatens them. After an opening in which a beekeeper discovers that most of the bees in his 400 hives are gone due to colony collapse disorder (CCD), the book describes how healthy honeybees pollinate flowering plants, gather nectar, and raise their young." (Booklist)

597 Cold-blooded vertebrates

Gilbert, Carter Rowell

National Audubon Society field guide to fishes, North America; [by] Carter R. Gilbert, James D. Williams. rev ed, 2nd ed, fully rev; Alfred A. Knopf 2002 607p il maps pa $19.95

Grades: 7 8 9 10 11 12 Adult **597**

1. Fishes -- North America

ISBN 0-375-41224-7

LC 2002-20773

First published 1983 with title: The Audubon Society field guide to North American fishes, whales, and dolphins

This guide covers over 600 freshwater and saltwater species in detail, with notes on 771 more species.

Hamilton, Sue L.

Eaten by a shark; [by] Sue Hamilton. ABDO Pub. 2010 32p il (Close encounters of the wild kind) lib bdg $22.61

Grades: 4 5 6 7 **597**

1. Sharks 2. Animal attacks

ISBN 978-1-60453-931-8 lib bdg; 1-60453-931-3 lib bdg

LC 2009-37230

In this volume, readers learn of actual human-wildlife encounters, creature information, survival strategies, and attack statistics.

"Students will be drawn to the realistic full-color photographs, the realistic diagrams of the creatures' bodies, the real-life stories told by victims, and the interesting, attractive formatting that includes text, diagrams, photographs, and graphics on each page. . . . [This is] exciting and attractive in a 'gross' sort of way and will appeal particularly to boys for both leisure reading and research." Libr Media Connect

Includes glossary

Page, Lawrence M.

★ **Peterson** field guide to freshwater fishes of North America north of Mexico; [by] Lawrence M. Page, Brooks M. Burr; illustrations by Eugene C. Beckham III . . . [et al.]; maps by Griffin E. Sheehy. 2nd ed.; Houghton Mifflin Harcourt 2011 663p il map pa $21

Grades: 7 8 9 10 11 12 Adult **597**

1. Fishes -- North America

ISBN 978-0-547-24206-4; 0-547-24206-9

LC 2010-49219

First published 1991 with title: A field guide to freshwater fishes: North America north of Mexico

This guide to identifying different species of freshwater fish in North America includes "maps and information showing where to locate each species of fish—whether that species can be found in miles-long stretches of river or small pools that cover only dozens of square feet." Publisher's note

Includes glossary and bibliographical references

Swinney, Geoff

Fish facts; illustrated by Janeen Mason. Pelican Pub. Co. 2011 48p il $17.99

Grades: 5 6 7 8 **597**

1. Fishes

ISBN 978-1-58980-908-6; 1-58980-908-4

LC 2010046220

"This comprehensive collection of facts about fish is sure to educate as well as fascinate. . . . From fish that produce light and fish that are capable of powered flight, to fish that can change sex and fish that carry their offspring in their mouths, this is chock full of both the amazing and the weird. . . . While the rather advanced vocabulary and biology that Swinney delves into mark this as a book for older readers, younger ones can certainly enjoy both the illustrations and the occasional factoid. Mason's artwork is both painstakingly detailed and realistically colored, even down to the muting effect that water has on colors. Few books come close to this one's inclusiveness." Kirkus

Turner, Pamela S.

★ **Project** Seahorse; [photographs by Scott Tuason] Houghton Mifflin Harcourt 2010 56p il (Scientists in the field) $18

Grades: 4 5 6 7 **597**

1. Sea horses

ISBN 978-0-547-20713-1; 0-547-20713-1

LC 2009-49707

"With striking images of coral-reef inhabitants, this photo-essay introduces Project Seahorse, an international effort to protect and rehabilitate the Danajon Bank, a double reef off a Philippine Island where seahorses once flourished . . . Tuason, a noted Asian marine photographer whose specialty is the Philippines, seems equally adept at photographing the land and people and the underwater world. This is another splendid demonstration of the work of Scientists in the Field." Kirkus

597.3 Selachii, Holocephali, fleshy-finned fishes

Abramovitz, Melissa

Deadliest sharks; by Melissa Abramovitz. ReferencePoint Press, Inc. 2017 80 p. (hardback) $29.95

Grades: 6 7 8 9 10 **597.3**

1. Sharks 2. Predatory animals

ISBN 9781682820544

LC 2015050838

This book in the Deadliest Predators series, by Melissa Abramovitz, focuses on sharks. "Their fearsome teeth, speed, acute senses of sight, smell, and hearing, and sensitivity to underwater vibrations help them efficiently locate and kill their prey. Six deadly sharks, including the great white and bull shark, are profiled." (Publisher's note)

"First-rate nonfiction on a high-interest topic." SLJ

Includes bibliographical references and index

Cerullo, Mary M.

Journey to shark island; a shark photographer's close encounters. by Mary M. Cerullo ; photographs by Jeffrey L. Rotman. Compass Point Books, a Capstone imprint 2015 40 p. color illustrations, color map (library binding) $31.32

Grades: 5 6 7 **597.3**

1. Deep diving 2. Wildlife photography 3. Sharks 4. Underwater photography 5. Sharks -- Pacific Ocean 6. Cocos Island (Costa Rica)

ISBN 075654887X; 9780756548872; 9780756549107

LC 2014008678

This book, by Mary M. Cerullo, part of the "Shark Expedition" series, follows "photographer Jeff Rotmans diving team into the shark-infested waters of Cocos Island to discover sharks secrets, and perhaps to save their lives." (Publisher's note)

"With their focus on more spectacular species, Seeking Giant Sharks and Great White Shark have the highest appeal, but all four books are fresh looks at an always popular subject." SLJ

Includes bibliographical references

Searching for Great white sharks; a shark diver's quest for Mr. Big. by Mary M. Cerullo. Compass Point Books, a Capstone imprint 2015 40 p. col. illustrations, col. map (Compass point books. Shark expedition) (library binding : alk. paper) $31.32

Grades: 5 6 7 **597.3**

1. Sharks 2. Underwater photography 3. Deep diving 4. White

shark 5. Wildlife photographers

ISBN 0756548845; 9780756548841; 9780756549077

LC 2014006007

This juvenile book, by Mary M. Cerullo, illustrated by Jeffrey L. Rotman, profiles how "diver and photographer Jeff Rotman goes to extremes to find and photograph great whites in their natural habitats. It takes a shark cage, a blood and fish recipe, patience, and courage to get up close photos of these powerful hunters." (Publisher's note)

"Well-reproduced, close-up photos of sharks (and, trigger warning, one shark-attack victim) fill every dynamic, eye-catching page, and Cerullo's concise paragraphs present shark facts in a clear, engaging, and often suspenseful tone. With a high-interest topic and a graphics-heavy layout, this would be a hit with reluctant readers, as well as researchers." Booklist

Includes bibliographical references and index

Seeking giant sharks; a shark diver's quest for whale sharks, basking sharks, and manta rays. by Mary M. Cerullo ; photographs by Jeffrey L. Rotman. Compass Point Books, a Capstone imprint 2015 40 p. illustration (color) (library binding) $31.32

Grades: 5 6 7 **597.3**

1. Deep diving 2. Wildlife photography 3. Sharks 4. Underwater photography 5. Manta rays 6. Whale shark 7. Basking shark 8. Manta birostris

ISBN 0756548853; 9780756548858; 9780756549084

LC 2014008991

This book, by Mary M. Cerullo, part of the "Shark Expedition" series, follows "photographer Jeff Rotmans . . . on his quest to reveal the quiet mysteries of filter feeders such as the whale shark and basking sharks, and why these giant creatures need our help." (Publisher's note)

"Centered on the experiences photographer and diver Jeff Rotman, this set offers exciting insight into the world of sharks . . . With their focus on more spectacular species, Seeking Giant Sharks and Great White Shark have the highest appeal, but all four books are fresh looks at an always popular subject." SLJ

Includes bibliographical references"||"Includes bibliographical references and index

Sharks of the deep; a shark photographer's search for sharks at the bottom of the sea. by Mary M. Cerullo ; photographs by Jeffrey L. Rotman. Compass Point Books, a Capstone imprint 2015 40 p. col. illustrations, col. map (library binding) $31.32

Grades: 5 6 7 **597.3**

1. Deep diving 2. Wildlife photography 3. Sharks 4. Underwater photography 5. Ocean bottom

ISBN 0756548861; 9780756548865; 9780756549091

LC 2014009112

This book, by Mary M. Cerullo, part of the "Shark Expedition" series, follows "photographer Jeff Rotmans . . . to the ocean floor to see the sharks and other creatures he calls living sculptures, from stingrays to the unusual wobbegong shark and other fascinating species. Look beyond the headlines and get to know the real story of sharks, their surprising beauty, and the important roles they play in their underwater world." (Publisher's note)

"Centered on the experiences photographer and diver Jeff Rotman, this set offers exciting insight into the world of sharks . . . all four books are fresh looks at an always popular subject." SLJ

Includes bibliographical references and index

MacQuitty, Miranda

Shark; written by Miranda MacQuitty. Updated edition DK Pub. 2014 72 p. col. ill (Eyewitness books) hardcover o.p.; library $19.99; paperback $9.99

Grades: 4 5 6 7 **597.3**

1. Sharks 2. Marine biology

ISBN 9780756637781; 9781465426192; 9781465426154

This book is part of the DK Eyewitness Books series and focuses on sharks. The titles in this series "focus on subjects that complement students' personal interests and areas of study to make learning simple and fun." Wall charts, clip art CDs, and photographs and illustrations are included. (Publisher's note)

Mallory, Kenneth

Swimming with hammerhead sharks. Houghton Mifflin 2001 48p il (Scientists in the field) pbk. $7.99

Grades: 4 5 6 7 **597.3**

1. Sharks

ISBN 9780618250790

LC 00-61401

"Mallory, editor-in-chief of publishing programs at the New England Aquarium, uses the context of an IMAX film production on hammerhead sharks to explain how scientists—in particular, marine biologist Pete Klimley—are studying these {animals. Index.} Intermediate." (Horn Book)

This book follows "marine biologist Pete Klimley and an IMAX film team to seamounts off Cocos Island in the Pacific Ocean to observe and film schooling hammerhead sharks. . . . A fascinating record of research and investigation, this inviting book is larded with numerous dramatic color photos." SLJ

Includes bibliographical references

Sharks; facts at your fingertips. DK Pub. 2012 156 p. col. ill., map (Pocket genius) (hc) $7.99

Grades: 5 6 7 8 **597.3**

1. Sharks 2. Rays (Fishes)

ISBN 0756692865; 9780756692865

LC 2011277726

This book, part of the "Pocket Genius" encyclopedia series, "profiles more that 150 sharks and rays -- from the great white to the tiny dwarf lantern -- and tells what they eat, where they live and how fast they swim." It "offers a . . . catalog-style presentation, which clearly lays out individual subcategories." (Publisher's note)

Walker, Sally M.

★ **Fossil** fish found alive; discovering the coelacanth. Carolrhoda Bks. 2002 72p il map lib bdg $17.95

Grades: 5 6 7 8 **597.3**

1. Coelacanth

ISBN 1-57505-536-8

LC 2001-3815

Describes the 1938 discovery of the coelacanth, a fish previously believed to be extinct, and subsequent research about it

"Walker writes well, making this relatively unknown area of science history an exciting story of exploration and discovery. Excellent, full-color photos illustrate the text." Booklist

Includes bibliographical references

597.8 Amphibians

Crump, Marty

★ The **mystery** of Darwin's frog; by Marty Crump ; illustrated by Steve Jenkins and Edel Rodriquez. Boyds Mills Press 2013 40 p. ill. (reinforced) $16.95

Grades: 3 4 5 6 7 **597.8**

1. Picture books for children 2. Frogs

ISBN 1590788648; 9781590788646

LC 2012947844

In this book, Marty Crump, a researcher who has investigated the Rhinoderma darwinii, an inch-long frog discovered by Charles Darwin in Chile in 1834, "describes the earlier investigations of this intriguing frog and records her own efforts to document how it lives in the wild. She discusses her findings and goes on to present the problems facing not only Darwin's frogs, but also frogs in general-loss of habitat, pollution, and the assault of the lethal Bd fungus." (School Library Journal)

Markle, Sandra

★ The **case** of the vanishing golden frogs. Milbrook Press 2011 48p il

Grades: 4 5 6 **597.8**

1. Frogs 2. Endangered species 3. Wildlife conservation

ISBN 0761351086; 9780761351085

LC 2010042642

"The golden frog, a Panamanian national symbol, began vanishing from its high mountain forests in the late 1990s, prompting a scientific investigation and rescue process that continues today. . . . Markle . . . describes a mission that has involved scientists from around the world." Kirkus

Includes glossary and bibliographical references

Pringle, Laurence, 1935-

Frogs! strange and wonderful. Laurence Pringle ; illustrated by Meryl Henderson. Boyds Mills Press 2012 30 p. col. ill (reinf. trade ed.) $16.95

Grades: 3 4 5 **597.8**

1. Frogs 2. Poisonous animals 3. Camouflage (Biology) 4. Picture books for children 5. Amphibians

ISBN 1590783719; 9781590783719

LC 2011928834

In this book, author Laurence P. Pringle offers a "look at the similarities and differences among the many and varied species of frogs . . . The Reinwardt's flying frog glides between trees, the mantella and poison frogs come in all the colors of the rainbow and one can guess what makes the marsupial frog stand out. Camouflage, mating, development, coloring, size, locomotion, how and what they eat and how and why they make sounds are just some of the topics." (Kirkus)

Includes bibliographical references

Stefoff, Rebecca

★ The **amphibian** class; [by] Rebecca Stefoff. Marshall Cavendish Benchmark 2008 96p il (Family trees) lib bdg $22.95

Grades: 6 7 8 9 **597.8**

1. Amphibians

ISBN 978-0-7614-2692-9 lib bdg; 0-7614-2692-2

LC 2007003487

This is "meticulously detailed. . . . Sharp color photographs appear on about every other page. Other illustrations consist of classification charts and anatomical diagrams. . . . [This is] well-organized and clearly written." SLJ

Includes glossary and bibliographical references

Turner, Pamela S.

★ The **frog** scientist; photographs by Andy Comins. Houghton Mifflin Books for Children 2009 58p il (Scientists in the field) lib bdg $18

Grades: 5 6 7 8 **597.8**

1. Frogs 2. Biologists 3. College teachers

ISBN 978-0-618-71716-3 lib bdg; 0-618-71716-1 lib bdg

LC 2008-39770

This volume "opens with biologist Tyrone Hayes and his team collecting frogs at a pond in Wyoming. After a short chapter on Hayes' background, the discussion returns to his work: he addresses the general question of why amphibian populations world-wide are declining by studying the effects of atrizine, an agricultural pesticide, on the reproductive organs of leopard frogs from a particular pond. Well organized and clearly written. . . . Excellent color photos offer clear pictures of frogs and of this scientific team at work in the field and in the lab. . . . A vivid, realistic view of one scientist at work." Booklist

Includes glossary and bibliographical references

597.9 Reptiles

Hirschmann, Kris

Deadliest reptiles; Kris Hirschmann. ReferencePoint Press, Inc. 2016 80 p. (hardback) $29.95

Grades: 6 7 8 9 10 **597.9**

1. Reptiles 2. Dangerous animals 3. Dangerous reptiles

ISBN 1682820521; 9781682820520

LC 2016004758

This children's book, by Kris Hirschmann, part of the "Deadliest predators" series, explores how, "while most reptiles are not dangerous to people, some have habits or traits that make them deadly. They may use size, strength, venom, speed, stealth, or other abilities to capture and kill their prey. Six deadly reptiles, including the saltwater crocodile and the Komodo dragon, are profiled." (Publisher's note)

"First-rate nonfiction on a high-interest topic." SLJ

Includes bibliographical references and index

Hutchinson, Mark

Reptiles. Simon & Schuster Books for Young Readers 2011 64p il (Insiders) $16.99

Grades: 4 5 6 7 **597.9**

1. Reptiles

ISBN 978-1-4424-3276-5; 1-4424-3276-4

"Arranged around the digitally rendered, sharply focused central images . . . smaller inset pictures and blocks of text systematically present distinctive physical features, typical behaviors, habitats, ranges, diets, and other information about each type of reptile. . . . This book will wow casual browsers and budding herpetologists alike." Booklist

McCarthy, Colin

Reptile; written by Colin McCarthy. Revised edition DK Publishing 2012 72 p color illustrations (DK Eyewitness) library $19.99

Grades: 4 5 6 7 **597.9**

1. Reptiles

ISBN 0756693055; 9780756693053

Photographs and text depict the many different kinds of reptiles, their similarities and differences, habitats, and behavior.

Powell, Robert

Peterson field guide to reptiles and amphibians of eastern and central North America; Robert Powell, Roger Conant, and Joseph T. Collins ; illustrated by Isabelle Hunt Conant, Tom R. Johnson, and Errol D. Hooper Jr. ; maps by Travis W. Taggart. 4th edition Houghton Mifflin Harcourt 2016 494 p illustrations $21.99

Grades: 7 8 9 10 11 12 Adult **597.9**

1. Reptiles -- Canada -- Identification 2. Amphibians -- Canada -- Identification 3. Reptiles -- United States -- Identification 4. Amphibians -- United States -- Identification

ISBN 9780544129979

4th edition

"The new edition of this definitive guide reflects 25 years' worth of changes in our knowledge of reptiles and amphibians. It includes descriptions of 122 newly recognized or recently established non-native species, updated maps, and new figures and photos. Color illustrations and drawings show key details for accurate identification. More than 100 color photographs and 322 color distribution maps accompany the species descriptions. Clear and concise species accounts provide key characteristics, similar species, habitats, and ranges, as well as subspecies, voice descriptions, and conservation status." (Publisher's note)

Includes bibliographical references (pages 456-457) and index

Stebbins, Robert C.

★ **Peterson** field guide to Western reptiles & amphibians; Samuel M. McGinnis & Robert C. Stebbins. 4th edition Houghton Mifflin 2018 533p il map (Peterson field guide series) paperback $24.99

Grades: 7 8 9 10 11 12 Adult **597.9**

1. Reptiles 2. Amphibians

ISBN 9781328715500 paperback; 0-395-98272-3

First published 1966

This "covers all the species of reptiles and amphibians found in western North America. More than 650 full-color paintings and photographs show key details for making accurate identifications. . . . Color range maps give species' distributions. . . . [Includes] information on conservation efforts and survival status." Publisher's note

Includes bibliographical references

Zabludoff, Marc

★ The **reptile** class. Benchmark Books 2005 95p il (Family trees) lib bdg $29.92

Grades: 6 7 8 9 **597.9**

1. Reptiles

ISBN 0-7614-1820-2

LC 2004-21820

This examines physical traits, adaptations, diets, habitats, and life cycles of reptiles.

"Fact-filled, yet surprisingly readable. . . . [This] title contains a wide variety of excellent-quality, full-color photos; interesting sidebars; and diagrams." SLJ

597.92 Turtles

Swinburne, Stephen R.

★ **Sea** turtle scientist; by Stephen R. Swinburne. Houghton Mifflin Harcourt 2013 65 p. ill. (chiefly col.), col. map (Scientists in the field) $18.99

Grades: 5 6 7 8 9 **597.92**

1. Biologists 2. Sea turtles

ISBN 0547367554; 9780547367552

LC 2012034045

"Dr. Kimberly Stewart, also known as the Turtle Lady of St. Kitts, is already waiting at midnight when an 800-pound leatherback sea turtle crawls out of the Caribbean surf and onto the sandy beach. The mother turtle has a vital job to do: dig a nest in which she will lay eggs that will hatch into part of the next generation of leatherbacks." (Publisher's note)

"This refreshing journey with a dedicated woman hard at work in her chosen field will resonate with readers." SLJ

Includes bibliographical references and index

597.95 Lizards

Collard III, Sneed B.

Sneed B. Collard III's most fun book ever about lizards; Sneed B. Collard III. Charlesbridge 2012 47 p. (reinforced for library use) $16.95

Grades: 3 4 5 6 7 **597.95**

1. Lizards 2. Lizards as pets 3. Wildlife photography 4. Lizards -- Miscellanea

ISBN 9781580893244; 9781580893251

LC 2011000809

This book offers an "introduction to the world of lizards [which] describes their . . . variety and life in the wild and offers cautions from a long-time reptile fan for those who want to keep lizards as pets. [Author Sneed B.] Collard . . . turns his attention . . . to modern-day lizards. After presenting an exemplar, 'Joe Lizard,' a western fence lizard, he goes on to describe other well-known species, including Komodo dragons, Gila monsters, chameleons and iguanas, as well as some with unusual talents, including 'religious lizards' that can walk on water. He covers eating and being eaten, the ways saurians keep warm and reproduce, and threats to their survival. . . . [Photographs] show lizard characteristics. . . . Captions and sidebars add further information." (Kirkus)

Gish, Melissa

Komodo dragons. Creative Education 2011 48p il (Living wild) lib bdg $23.95; pa $8.99

Grades: 5 6 7 8 **597.95**

1. Komodo dragon

ISBN 978-1-60818-080-6 lib bdg; 1-60818-080-8 lib bdg; 978-0-89812-672-3 pa; 0-89812-672-X pa

LC 2010028307

A look at Komodo dragons, including their habitats, physical characteristics such as their sawlike teeth, behaviors, relationships with humans, and threatened status in the world today.

"Stunning, full-page photographs create immediate visual interest. A brief narrative introduction sets the scene for the richer, more scientific information in the rest of the text." Booklist

Includes glossary and bibliographical references

Somervill, Barbara A.

Monitor lizard. Cherry Lake 2010 32p il (Animal invaders) lib bdg $27.07

Grades: 5 6 7 8 **597.95**

1. Lizards 2. Biological invasions

ISBN 978-1-60279-627-0 lib bdg; 1-60279-627-0 lib bdg

This offers "an introduction to the problems caused by [the monitor lizard], a discussion of its physical characteristics and habits, a history of how it arrived in its new habitat, and an analysis of challenges encountered by those trying to limit its spread. . . . [It] describes the threat posed by these aggressive 7-foot reptiles, sold as babies by pet vendors and now loose in Florida. . . . [This] well-focused [book is] clearly written. The uncluttered page design features at least one color photo on each page." Booklist

Includes glossary and bibliographical references

597.96 Snakes

Franchino, Vicky

Black mambas; by Vicky Franchino. Children's Press, an imprint of Scholastic Inc. 2015 48 p. color ill., color map (pbk. : alk. paper) $6.95

Grades: 3 4 5 6 **597.96**

1. Snakes 2. Black mamba

ISBN 9780531213926; 9780531214954

LC 2014043960

This children's book, by Vicky Franchino, part of the "Nature's Children" series, profiles Black Mamba snakes. "An opening 'Fact File' breaks down info such as taxonomy, habits, habitats, and diets. . . . Five chapters are broken down into several single-page sections. The first chapter depicts an encounter with the animal and describes a typical behavior. The rest of the book delves further into the topics brought up in the 'Fact File.'" (School Library Journal)

"Sophisticated scientific terms such as bilateral symmetry or anticoagulant are often defined in-text. "Fun Fact" boxes are scattered throughout." SLJ

Includes bibliographical references and index

Hamilton, Sue L.

Bitten by a rattlesnake; [by] Sue Hamilton. ABDO Pub. 2010 32p il (Close encounters of the wild kind) lib bdg $27.07

Grades: 4 5 6 7 **597.96**

1. Rattlesnakes 2. Animal attacks

ISBN 978-1-60453-930-1 lib bdg; 1-60453-930-5 lib bdg

LC 2009-45423

Readers learn of actual human-rattlesnake encounters, information about rattlesnakes, survival strategies, and attack statistics.

"Students will be drawn to the realistic full-color photographs, the realistic diagrams of the creatures' bodies, the real-life stories told by victims, and the interesting, attractive formatting that includes text, diagrams, photographs, and graphics on each page. . . . [This is] exciting and attractive in a 'gross' sort of way and will appeal particularly to boys for both leisure reading and research." Libr Media Connect

Includes glossary

Hirschmann, Kris

Deadliest snakes; by Kris Hirschmann. ReferencePoint Press, Inc. 2017 80 p. (hardback) $29.95

Grades: 6 7 8 9 10 **597.96**

1. Poisonous snakes 2. Predatory animals

ISBN 9781682820568

LC 2015046499

This book in the Deadliest Predators series, by Kris Hirschmann, focuses on poisonous snakes. "Deadly snakes abound in the world. They rely on sight, sound, speed, and venom to capture and kill their prey. Six deadly snakes, including the black mamba and king cobra, are profiled." (Publisher's note)

"First-rate nonfiction on a high-interest topic." SLJ

Includes bibliographical references and index

Hofer, Charles C.

Snakebite! antivenom and a global health crisis. Charles C. Hofer. Twenty-First Century Books 2019 104 p. (library binding : alk. paper) $37.32

Grades: 7 8 9 10 11 12 **597.96**

1. Medical care 2. Snakes 3. Poisonous animals 4. Antivenins 5. Snakebites 6. Poisonous snakes

ISBN 1512483737; 9781512483734

LC 2017046976

This book, by Charles Hofer, examines "the biology of venomous snakes, the pharmacology and biochemistry of antivenom, its use in treating disease, and the politics of bringing life-saving antivenom drugs to market. Meet the doctors, herpetologists, medical researchers, conservationists, and patients working together to address an international crisis." (Publisher's note)

"Readers will gain an understanding of the complexity of this issue and meet several scientists and researchers at the vanguard of antivenin program development. This thoroughly sourced text is a fascinating resource that can be used across many disciplines." Booklist

Includes bibliographical references (pages 99-101) and index

Montgomery, Sy

★ The **snake** scientist; photographs by Nic Bishop. Houghton Mifflin 1999 48p il map $16; pa $5.95

Grades: 4 5 6 7 **597.96**

1. Snakes

ISBN 0-395-87169-7; 0-618-11119-0 pa

LC 98-6124

Discusses the work of Bob Mason and his efforts to study and protect snakes, particularly red-sided garter snakes

"The lively text communicates both the meticulous measurements required in this kind of work and the thrill of new discoveries. Large, full-color photos of the zoologist and young students at work, and lots of wriggly snakes, pull readers into the presentation." SLJ

Includes bibliographical references

Somervill, Barbara A.

Python. Cherry Lake Pub. 2010 32p il map (Animal invaders) lib bdg $27.07

Grades: 5 6 7 8 **597.96**

1. Pythons 2. Biological invasions

ISBN 978-1-60279-629-4 lib bdg; 1-60279-629-7 lib bdg

LC 2009026013

This describes "the 19-foot nocturnal snake that has infiltrated the Florida Everglades, having no natural predators above it in the food chain. . . . [This] well-focused [book is] clearly written. The uncluttered page design features at least one color photo on each spread." Booklist

Includes glossary and bibliographical references

597.98 Crocodilians

Gish, Melissa

Alligators. Creative Education 2010 46p il (Living wild) $23.95; pa $9.95

Grades: 5 6 7 8 **597.98**

1. Alligators

ISBN 978-1-58341-967-0; 1-58341-967-5; 978-0-89812-550-4 pa; 0-89812-550-2 pa

LC 2010017372

The "book lucidly discusses conservation and the animals' often tenuous relationships with humans. The layout is uniformly simple but effective, constructed with a nice balance of main text for the report writers, smaller chunks of esoterica for browsers, and . . . killer photos." Booklist

Hamilton, Sue L.

Attacked by a crocodile; [by] Sue Hamilton. ABDO Pub. 2010 32p il (Close encounters of the wild kind) lib bdg $27.07

Grades: 4 5 6 7 **597.98**

1. Crocodiles 2. Animal attacks

ISBN 978-1-60453-929-5; 1-60453-929-1

LC 2009-45514

Readers learn of actual human-crocodile encounters, information about crocodiles, survival strategies, and attack statistics.

"Students will be drawn to the realistic full-color photographs, the realistic diagrams of the creatures' bodies, the real-life stories told by victims, and the interesting, attractive formatting that includes text, diagrams, photographs, and graphics on each page. . . . [This is] exciting and attractive in a 'gross' sort of way and will appeal particularly to boys for both leisure reading and research." Libr Media Connect

Includes glossary

598 Birds

Alderfer, Jonathan

National Geographic kids bird guide of North America; the best birding book for kids from National Geographic's bird experts. by Jonathan Alderfer. National Geographic 2013 176 p. (paperback) $15.95; (library) $23.90

Grades: 4 5 6 7 8 **598**

1. Birds -- North America 2. Birds -- Identification 3. Birds -- North America -- Identification

ISBN 1426310943; 9781426310942; 9781426310959

LC 2012028615

Author "[Jonathan] Alderfer offers in-depth studies of 60 birds native to North America (plus 'mini-profiles' of another 60 specimens) in a guide for nascent birders. . . . The book is organized by region, and each bird's spread offers . . . color photographs, 'vital statistics' (including its call, diet, and habitat), maps of where it can be found, and other background." (Publishers Weekly)

Includes bibliographical references and index

Bull, John L.

★ The **National** Audubon Society field guide to North American birds, Eastern region; [by] John Bull and John Farrand, Jr.; revised by John Farrand, Jr.; visual key by Amanda Wilson and Lori Hogan. rev ed; Knopf 1994 797p il maps pa $19.95

Grades: 7 8 9 10 11 12 Adult **598**

1. Birds -- North America

ISBN 0-679-42852-6

LC 94-7768

Companion volume to National Audubon Society field guide to North American birds, Western region, by Miklos D. F. Udvardy

First published 1977

This pictorial guide to 508 eastern species arranges birds by color and shape to simplify identification. It also includes information on bird-watching and conservation status

Includes bibliographical references

Burnie, David

Bird; written by David Burnie. rev ed.; DK Pub. 2008 72p il (DK eyewitness books) $15.99

Grades: 4 5 6 7 **598**

1. Birds

ISBN 978-0-7566-3768-2; 0-7566-3768-6

First published 1988 by Knopf

A photo essay on the world of birds examining such topics as body construction, feathers and flight, the adaptation of beaks and feet, feeding habits, courtship, nests and eggs, and bird watching.

Includes glossary

Gish, Melissa

★ **Eagles**. Creative Education 2010 46p il (Living wild) lib bdg $23.95; pa $9.95

Grades: 5 6 7 8 **598**

1. Eagles

ISBN 978-1-58341-968-7 lib bdg; 1-58341-968-3 lib bdg; 978-0-89812-551-1 pa; 0-89812-551-0 pa

LC 2010-17373

This "book lucidly discusses conservation and the animals' often tenuous relationship with humans. The layout is uniformly simple but effective, constructed with a nice balance of main text for the report writers, smaller chunks of esoterica for browsers, and . . . killer photos." Booklist

Hummingbirds. Creative Education 2011 46p il map (Living wild) lib bdg $23.95; pa $8.95

Grades: 5 6 7 8 **598**

1. Hummingbirds

ISBN 978-1-60818-078-3; 1-60818-078-6; 978-0-89812-670-9 pa; 0-89812-670-3 pa

LC 2010028314

A look at hummingbirds, including their habitats, physical characteristics such as their ability to hover, behaviors, relationships with humans, and admired status in the world today.

"Stunning, full-page photographs create immediate visual interest. A brief narrative introduction sets the scene for the richer, more scientific information in the rest of the text." Booklist

Includes glossary and bibliographical references

Owls. Creative Education 2011 46p il map (Living wild) lib bdg $23.95

Grades: 5 6 7 8 **598**

1. Owls

ISBN 978-1-60818-081-3; 1-60818-081-6

LC 2010028308

A look at owls, including their habitats, physical characteristics such as their large and observant eyes, behaviors, relationships with humans, and protected status in the world today.

"Stunning, full-page photographs create immediate visual interest. A brief narrative introduction sets the scene for the richer, more scientific information in the rest of the text." Booklist

Includes glossary and bibliographical references

Hanel, Rachael

Penguins. Smart Apple Media 2009 46p il (Living wild) lib bdg $32.80
Grades: 4 5 6 7 **598**

1. Penguins

ISBN 978-1-58341-658-7 lib bdg; 1-58341-658-7 lib bdg
LC 2007008503

"The 17 species of penguins . . . fill [this] slim, informative [volume]. [The] overview is divided into several chapters . . . describing the shared and distinct physical characteristics of the various species, the location of their particular habitats, life cycle, social behavior, and the history of human awareness of and impact on these animals. Fine color photographs face pages of text with smaller views placed in colored sidebars or insets. The [book concludes] with current environmental threats and conservation efforts. . . . Handsome and appealing." SLJ

Helget, Nicole Lea

Swans; by Nicole Helget. Smart Apple Media 2009 46p il (Living wild) lib bdg $32.80
Grades: 4 5 6 7 **598**

1. Swans

ISBN 978-1-58341-659-4 lib bdg; 1-58341-659-5 lib bdg
LC 2007015242

The "7 [species] of swans fill [this] slim, informative [volume]. [The] overview is divided into several chapters . . . describing the shared and distinct physical characteristics of the various species, the location of their particular habitats, life cycle, social behavior, and the history of human awareness of and impact on these animals. Fine color photographs face pages of text with smaller views placed in colored sidebars or insets. The [book concludes] with current environmental threats and conservation efforts. . . . Handsome and appealing." SLJ

Includes bibliographical references

Hoose, Phillip M., 1947-

★ **Moonbird**; a year on the wind with the great survivor B95. Phillip Hoose. Farrar Straus Giroux 2012 148 p. col. ill. (hardcover) $21.99
Grades: 5 6 7 8 **598**

1. Endangered species 2. Birds -- Protection 3. Wildlife conservation 4. Red knot 5. Bird watching 6. Red knot -- Migration

ISBN 0374304688; 9780374304683
LC 2011035612

Robert F. Sibert Honor Book (2013)

YALSA Award for Excellence in Nonfiction for Young Adults Finalist (2013)

In this book, Phillip Hoose "explores the tragedy of extinction through a single bird species, but there is hope for survival in this story, and that hope is pinned on understanding the remarkable longevity of a single bird. . . . Hoose takes readers around the hemisphere, showing them the obstacles rufa red knots face, introducing a global team of scientists and conservationists, and offering insights about what can be done to save them before it's too late." (Kirkus Reviews)

The **race** to save the Lord God Bird; [by] Phillip Hoose. Farrar, Straus and Giroux 2004 196p il map $20
Grades: 7 8 9 10 **598**

1. Woodpeckers 2. Endangered species

ISBN 0-374-36173-8

Boston Globe-Horn Book Award: Nonfiction (2005)

Tells the story of the ivory-billed woodpecker's extinction in the United States, describing the encounters between this species and humans, and discussing what these encounters have taught us about preserving endangered creatures

"Sharp, clear, black-and-white archival photos and reproductions appear throughout. The author's passion for his subject and high standards for excellence result in readable, compelling nonfiction." SLJ

Includes glossary and bibliographical references

Larson, Jeanette C.

Hummingbirds; facts and folklore from the Americas. written by Jeanette Larson and Adrienne Yorinks; illustrated by Adrienne Yorinks. Charlesbridge 2011 64p il $16.95; pa $8.95
Grades: 5 6 7 8 **598**

1. Hummingbirds 2. Birds -- Folklore 3. Native Americans -- Folklore

ISBN 978-1-58089-332-9; 1-58089-332-5; 978-1-58089-333-6 pa; 1-58089-333-3 pa
LC 2010-07578

"In a narrative that flows easily between fact and lore, hummingbird behavior is thoroughly described and interwoven with the folktales it generated among Native American peoples. . . . All the stories show how ancient people answered the 'how and why' questions of the behaviors they observed, and these stories beautifully echo modern-day scientific observations. The full-color photos of quilts and embroidery by Yorinks invite readers to stop and savor each one." SLJ

Includes glossary and bibliographical references

Latimer, Jonathan P.

Backyard birds; [by] Jonathan P. Latimer, Karen Stray Nolting; illustrations by Roger Tory Peterson; foreword by Virginia Marie Peterson. Houghton Mifflin 1999 48p il (Peterson field guides for young naturalists) hardcover o.p. pa $5.95
Grades: 4 5 6 7 **598**

1. Birds

ISBN 0-395-92276-3
LC 98-35509

This is an identification guide to birds "'you are likely to see where you live.' . . . [It] includes a . . . selection of about 20 creatures . . . grouped by color. . . . Bright, full-color photographs and drawings clearly indicate distinguishing features. Useful, accessible." SLJ

Songbirds; [by] Jonathan P. Latimer, Karen Stray Nolting; illustrations by Roger Tory Peterson; foreword by Virginia Marie Peterson. Houghton Mifflin 2000 48p il (Peterson field guides for young naturalists) $15; pa $5.95
Grades: 4 5 6 7 **598**

1. Birds 2. Birdsongs

ISBN 0-395-97941-2; 0-395-97946-3 pa
LC 99-38293

Describes the physical characteristics, habitats, feeding habits, and voices of a variety of songbirds, arranged under the categories "Simple Songs," "Complex Songs," "Whistling Songs," "Warbling Songs," "Trilling Songs," "Name-sayers," and "Mimics"

Peterson, Roger Tory, 1908-1996

Peterson field guide to birds of Eastern and Central North America; [by] Roger Tory Peterson, with contributions from Michael DiGiorgio [et al.] 6th ed; Houghton Mifflin Harcourt 2010 445p il map (Peterson field guide series) $19.95

Grades: 5 6 7 8 9 10 11 12 Adult **598**

1. Birds -- North America

ISBN 978-0-547-15246-2; 0-547-15246-9

LC 2009-37681

First published 1934 with title: A field guide to the birds

This guide to birds found east of the Rocky Mountains contains colored illustrations painted by the author, with a description of each species on the facing page. Views of young birds and seasonal variations in plumage are included.

★ **Peterson** field guide to birds of North America; with contributions from Michael DiGiorgio . . . [et al.] Houghton Mifflin Co. 2008 527p il map (Peterson field guide series) $26

Grades: 5 6 7 8 9 10 11 12 Adult **598**

1. Birds -- North America

ISBN 0-618-96614-5; 978-0-618-96614-1

LC 2007-39803

First published 1934 with title: A field guide to the birds. Previously published in two separate parts as A field guide to western birds (1990) and A field guide to the birds of eastern and central North America (2002)

This guide to birds found in North America contains colored illustrations painted by the author, with a description of each species on the facing page. Views of young birds and seasonal variations in plumage are included. The book also includes a URL to video podcasts.

"This field guide is of high quality and should be in millions of birders' and other nature lovers' backpacks." Sci Books Films

Peterson field guide to birds of Western North America; with contributions from Michael DiGiorgio [et al.] 4th ed; Houghton Mifflin Harcourt 2010 493p il map (Peterson field guide series) pa $19.95

Grades: 5 6 7 8 9 10 11 12 Adult **598**

1. Birds -- North America

ISBN 978-0-547-15270-7; 0-547-15270-1

LC 2009-39158

First published 1941 with title: A field guide to western birds

This guide illustrates over 600 species of birds on 176 color plates. In addition, over 588 range maps are included.

Stefoff, Rebecca

★ The **bird** class; [by] Rebecca Stefoff. 1st ed.; Marshall Cavendish Benchmark 2008 96p il (Family trees) $22.95

Grades: 6 7 8 9 **598**

1. Birds

ISBN 978-0-7614-2693-6; 0-7614-2693-0

LC 2007007706

"Skillful weaving of engaging text and superb illustrations will incite interest." Voice Youth Advocates

Includes glossary and bibliographical references

Thornhill, Jan

★ The **tragic** tale of the great auk; Jan Thornhill. Groundwood Books 2016 44 p. color ill., color map (hardcover) $18.95; (ebook) $14.95

Grades: 2 3 4 5 **598**

1. Auks 2. Extinct animals

ISBN 9781554988655; 1554988659; 9781554988662

LC 2016043874

In this illustrated book, author "Jan Thornhill tells the tragic story of [auk birds.] . . . Their demise came about in part because of their anatomy. They could swim swiftly underwater, but their small wings meant they couldn't fly and their feet were so far back on their bodies, they couldn't walk very well. Still the birds managed to escape their predators much of the time . . . until humans became seafarers." (Publisher's note)

"A sobering, beautifully presented extinction story." Kirkus

Includes bibliographical references.

Udvardy, Miklos D. F.

★ **National** Audubon Society field guide to North American birds, Western region; revised by John Farrand, Jr.; visual key by Amanda Wilson and Lori Hogan. rev ed; Knopf 1994 822p il maps pa $19.95

Grades: 6 7 8 9 10 11 12 Adult **598**

1. Birds -- North America

ISBN 0-679-42851-8

LC 94-7415

Companion volume to National Aududon Society field guide to North American birds, Eastern region by John L. Bull

First published 1977

In this guide, "virtually every bird found in North America is brought to life in a full-color photograph and with textual information on the bird's voice, nesting habits, habitat, range, and interesting behaviors. Accompanying range maps; overhead flight silhouettes; sections on bird-watching, accidental species, and endangered birds" are also included. (Publisher's note)

Includes bibliographical references

Vogel, Carole Garbuny

The **man** who flies with birds; [by] Carole G. Vogel and Yossi Leshem. Kar-Ben Pub. 2009 64p il map lib bdg $18.95

Grades: 5 6 7 8 **598**

1. Aircraft accidents 2. Birds -- Migration

ISBN 978-0-8225-7643-3 lib bdg; 0-8225-7643-0 lib bdg

LC 2008-31198

Discusses the work of the bird expert whose lifelong study of the patterns of bird migration in Israel has led to a significant reduction in the number of collisions between aircraft and bird flocks.

"The book is heavily illustrated with good-quality color photos, maps, and diagrams, many of them captioned with incredible facts about wildlife and migration. This inspiring title on a most timely topic will appeal to those who are fascinated with wildlife, Earth science, and technology." SLJ

Includes bibliographical references

Warhol, Tom

Owls; [by] Tom Warhol. Marshall Cavendish Benchmark 2007 111p il (Animalways) lib bdg $34.21

Grades: 6 7 8 9 **598**

1. Owls

ISBN 978-0-7614-2537-3

LC 2006019708

This describes the place of owls in the animal kingdom, owl lore and legend, owls' evolution, diversity, anatomy and behavior, life cycle, and endangered status.

This "will pique readers' curiosity, and the content will keep them hooked. Vivid color photographs and illustrations and a clear font make [this work] stand out." SLJ

Includes glossary and bibliographical references

Wolf, Sallie

★ The **robin** makes a laughing sound; a birder's journal. designed by Micah Bornstein. Charlesbridge 2010 43p il $11.95

Grades: 5 6 7 8 **598**

1. Birds 2. Bird watching

ISBN 978-1-58089-318-3; 1-58089-318-X

LC 2008-7248

Presents observations made through every season of the year of different birds and their behavior, from robins taking a bath, to cardinals searching for food in the snow, to an owl perched on a tree at night.

"The charming, eye-catching format includes short dated nature notes written in script, some of them on glued or taped-in torn paper pieces; other paper scraps contain short typeset poems and small, labeled watercolors. . . . Pen-and-ink sketches capture a baby house sparrow, a V-formation of geese, a downy woodpecker at a suet feeder, and more. . . . This small, instructional guide may provide the inspiration for young authors with even a bit of artistic talent to begin keeping nature journals of their own." SLJ

598.3 Water birds

Gish, Melissa

Flamingos; Melissa Gish. Creative Education 2014 46 p. color illustrations (hardcover : alk. paper) $37.10

Grades: 5 6 7 8 **598.3**

1. Animals 2. Flamingos

ISBN 1608184161; 9781608184163

LC 2013031813

This book, by Melissa Gish, is a "scientific look at flamingos, including their habitats, physical characteristics such as their coloration, behaviors, relationships with humans, and numbers of the tropical birds in the world today." (Publisher's note)

"Stewart continues with a topic near and dear to devotees of the 590s, once more providing both fascinating and well-written facts and some truly arresting images. Scientific material on each species is offered, along with pop cultural and historical information. . . . Thorough in scope and elegant in design, these stellar titles will attract the browser and the report writer alike." SLJ

Includes bibliographical references and index

Part of recommended series "Living Wild," which includes 62 titles, each with details on different animals.

598.6 Galliformes and Columbiformes

Gish, Melissa

Peacocks; Melissa Gish. Creative Education 2016 46 p. ill. (chiefly color), map (hardcover : alk. paper) $39.95

Grades: 5 6 7 8 **598.6**

1. Peacocks 2. Peafowl

ISBN 9781608187072

LC 2015026823

This children's book in the Living Wild series, by Melissa Gish, offers "a look at peacocks, including their habitats, physical characteristics such as the males colorful plumage, behaviors, relationships with humans, and the protected status of Congo and green peacocks in the world today." (Publisher's note)

"Whether weird, beautiful, or simply adorable, this series has its animals covered." Booklist

Includes bibliographical references and index.

Hutto, Joe

When I was a turkey; based on the Emmy award-winning PBS documentary my life as a turkey. Joe Hutto with Brenda Z. Guiberson ; illustrations by Joe Hutto. Henry Holt & Co. 2017 ix, 178 p.p illustrations (some color) (hardcover) $19.99

Grades: 4 5 6 7 8 **598.6**

1. Turkeys 2. Animal behavior 3. Birds -- Behavior 4. Human-animal relationships 5. Imprinting (Psychology) 6. Wild turkey -- Behavior

ISBN 9781627793865; 9781627793858

LC 2017007364

This book, by Joe Hutto and Brenda Z. Guiberson, is an "adaptation of the . . . true story of a naturalist who raised a flock of wild turkeys using imprinting. After a local farmer left a bowl of wild turkey eggs on . . . Hutto's front porch, his life was forever changed. Hutto incubated the eggs and waited for them to hatch. . . . Hutto dutifully cared for his family . . . immersing himself in their world. In return, they taught him how to see the world through their eyes." (Publisher's note)

"An unusual, engaging choice for animal-lovers." Booklist

Includes bibliographical references and index.

598.8 Perching birds (Passeriformes)

Turner, Pamela S.

Crow smarts; inside the brain of the world's brightest bird. by Pamela S. Turner; photographs by Andy Comins. Houghton Mifflin Harcourt 2016 80 p. color illustrations (ebook) $18.99; $18.99

Grades: 4 5 6 7 8 **598.8**

1. Crows 2. Animal behavior 3. Animal intelligence 4. Crows -- Behavior

ISBN 9780544829336; 9780544416192

LC 2015013903

This book in the Scientists in the Field Series, by Pamela S. Turner, with photographs by Andy Comins, "describes New Caledonian crows [that] seem to possess the intelligence to understand [the] 'causal' concept [of 'If I do X, Y might happen.'] Why do crows have this ability? What does the crow know and what does it tell us about brain size, the evolution of intelligence, and just who is the smartest creature on the planet?" (Publisher's note)

"With an approachable writing style and photos of crows festooning almost every page, this engaging volume will attract budding scientists, and the lively descriptions not only of the crows but of the scientists at work will give students plenty to ponder." Booklist

Includes bibliographical references (page 71) and index.

598.9 Falconiformes, Caprimulgiformes, owls

Hoena, Blake

Everything birds of prey; Blake Hoena ; with National Geographic explorer Hillary S. Young. National Geographic 2015 64 p. color ill., color maps (pbk.) $12.99

Grades: 2 3 4 5 **598.9**

1. Birds of prey

ISBN 1426318898; 1426318901; 9781426318894; 9781426318900

LC 2015304787

This book, by Blake Hoena, "introduces readers to the world's most ferocious fliers. With stunning visuals and energetic, impactful design, readers won't stop until they've learned everything there is to know about birds of prey." (Publisher's note)

"The bold and brassy, factoid-filled text is broken into chapters that flow logically from the birds' characteristics and behavior to geography and interactions with humans." Booklist

Includes bibliographical references (page 62) and index

Latimer, Jonathan P.

Birds of prey; [by] Jonathan P. Latimer, Karen Stray Nolting; illustrations by Roger Tory Peterson; foreword by Virginia Marie Peterson. Houghton Mifflin 1999 48p il (Peterson field guides for young naturalists) $15; pa $5.95

Grades: 4 5 6 7 **598.9**

1. Birds of prey

ISBN 0-395-95211-5; 0-395-92277-1 pa

LC 98-35516

This illustrated volume introduces the physical characteristics, behavior, and habitats of such birds of prey as eagles, hawks, falcons, and owls.

599 Mammals

Mammals of the Northern Hemisphere; edited by Tim Harris. Brown Bear Books 2011 64 p. col. ill., col. maps (Facts at Your Fingertips: endangered animals) (library binding) $35.65

Grades: 7 8 9 **599**

1. Mammals 2. Endangered species 3. Wildlife conservation 4. Rare mammals -- Northern Hemisphere

ISBN 1936333341; 9781936333349

LC 2010053969

This book is part of the "Facts at Your Fingertips: Endangered Animals" series. "Each page has all benefits of a picture book with large, colorful photographs that accompany the encyclopedia-style text. Each new animal is accompanied by a 'data panel,' which summarizes . . . information such as location, size, habitat, population and diet. This series focuses on animals facing extinction all over the world. Factors contributing to the animal's endangered status as well as preservation techniques are also discussed." The book "talks about well-known animals like the Polar Bear and Giant Panda as well as lesser-known mammals such as the Ryukyu Flying Fox." (Children's Literature)

Includes bibliographical references (p. 63) and index.

Whitaker, John O.

★ **National** Audubon Society field guide to North American mammals; rev ed; Knopf 1996 937p il maps pa $19.95

Grades: 6 7 8 9 10 11 12 Adult **599**

1. Mammals

ISBN 0-679-44631-1

LC 95-81456

First published 1980

This field guide describes 390 species of mammals of North America and includes keys for identification, range maps, information on tracks and anatomy, and 375 color photos

599.2 Marsupials and monotremes

Gish, Melissa

Kangaroos. Creative Education 2010 46p il (Living wild) $23.95; pa $9.95

Grades: 5 6 7 8 **599.2**

1. Kangaroos

ISBN 978-1-58341-970-0; 1-58341-970-5; 978-0-89812-553-5 pa; 0-89812-553-7 pa

LC 2010017375

"A look at kangaroos, including their habitats, physical characteristics such as the females' pouches, behaviors, relationships with humans, and valued status in the world today." Publisher's note

Montgomery, Sy

★ **Quest** for the tree kangaroo; an expedition to the cloud forest of New Guinea. text by Sy Montgomery; photographs by Nic Bishop. Houghton Mifflin 2006 79p il map (Scientists in the field) $18

Grades: 5 6 7 8 **599.2**

1. Zoologists 2. Tree kangaroos 3. New Guinea

ISBN 0-618-49641-6

LC 2005-34849

"The writer and photographer of this exemplary description of science field work accompanied researcher Lisa Dabek on an expedition high in New Guinea's mountains to study tree kangaroos and promote the conservation of this elusive and endangered species. . . . Montgomery . . . paces her narrative well . . . keeping the reader engaged and concerned. . . . Bishop's photographs . . . are beautifully reproduced." Publ Wkly

599.3 Miscellaneous orders of placental mammals

Gregory, Josh

Hedgehogs; by Josh Gregory. Children's Press, an imprint of Scholastic Inc. 2016 48 p. color illustrations, map (library binding : alk. paper) $28

Grades: 3 4 5 6 **599.3**

1. Hedgehogs

ISBN 0531213900; 0531214931; 9780531213902; 9780531214930

LC 2014043978

This children's book, by Josh Gregory, part of the "Nature's children" series, profiles hedgehogs. "An opening 'Fact File' breaks down info such as taxonomy, habits, habitats, and diets and provides a preview for the information that will be covered. . . . The first chapter depicts an encounter with the animal and describes a typical behavior. The rest of the book delves further into the topics brought up in the 'Fact File.'" (Publisher's note)

"Sophisticated scientific terms such as bilateral symmetry or anticoagulant are often defined in-text." SLJ

Includes bibliographical references (page 46) and index

Sloths; by Josh Gregory. Children's Press, an imprint of Scholastic Inc. 2016 48 p. color illustrations (library binding : alk. paper) $28

Grades: 3 4 5 6 599.3

1. Sloths

ISBN 0531213919; 053121494X; 9780531213919; 9780531214947

LC 2014044037

This children's book, by Josh Gregory, part of the "Nature's Children" series, explores sloths. "These additions to this ongoing series follow a tried-and-true format: text on one page facing a full-page photo. An opening 'Fact File' breaks down info such as taxonomy, habits, habitats, and diets and provides a preview for the information that will be covered. . . . [And] the first chapter depicts an encounter with the animal and describes a typical behavior." (School Library Journal)

"Sophisticated scientific terms such as bilateral symmetry or anticoagulant are often defined in-text. "Fun Fact" boxes are scattered throughout." SLJ

Includes bibliographical references (page 46) and index

599.312 Armadillos

Gish, Melissa

Armadillos; Melissa Gish. Creative Education 2016 46 p. color ill., color map (hardcover : alk. paper) $39.95

Grades: 5 6 7 8 **599.312**

1. Mammals 2. Zoology 3. Armadillos

ISBN 9781608187034

LC 2015026813

In this book in the Living Wild series, by Melissa Gish, "vivid photographs help take readers on a virtual field study to observe the life cycle and behaviors of each featured mammal, bird, or reptile. . . . [This book] looks at armadillos, including their habitats, physical characteristics such as their armored bodies, behaviors, relationships with humans, and threatened status of some species in the world today." (Publisher's note)

"Whether weird, beautiful, or simply adorable, this series has its animals covered." Booklist

Includes bibliographical references and index.

599.313 Sloths

Gish, Melissa

Sloths; Melissa Gish. Creative Education 2016 46 p. color ill., color map (hardcover : alk. paper) $39.95

Grades: 5 6 7 8 **599.313**

1. Sloths

ISBN 1608187098; 9781608187096

LC 2015026882

In this book, by Melissa Gish, part of the Living Wild series, "vivid photographs help take readers on a virtual field study to observe the life cycle and behaviors of [sloths]. . . . [It] also looks at past and present scientific research and includes a unique storytelling element in the form of an animal tale drawn from mythology or folklore. Progressively complex text draws readers into this interdisciplinary life science series." (Publisher's note)

"Whether weird, beautiful, or simply adorable, this series has its animals covered." Booklist

Includes bibliographical references and index.

599.32 Lagomorphs

Collard, Sneed B.

Hopping Ahead of Climate Change; snowshoe hares, science, and survival. Sneed B. Collard III. Bucking Horse Books 2016 64 p. color ill., color maps $18.00

Grades: 4 5 6 7 **599.32**

1. Rabbits 2. Climate change 3. Snowshoe rabbit 4. Adaptation (Biology)

ISBN 0984446087; 9780984446087

LC 2016907272

This book, by Sneed B. Collard III, "describes one of the most intriguing and important studies of our time: the work of biologist Scott Mills, who is trying to answer the critical question: Can animals that change their coat colors with the seasons survive shorter winters caused by climate change? Working with an international team of colleagues and students, Professor Mills has been conducting a range of studies that explore the impacts of a hotter world on animals." (Publisher's note)

Includes bibliographical references (pages 60), filmography (page 61), webliography (page 61), and index.

599.35 Rodents

Marrin, Albert

Oh, rats! the story of rats and people. illustrated by C.B. Mordan. Dutton Children's Books 2006 48p il $16.99

Grades: 3 4 5 6 **599.35**

1. Rats

ISBN 0-525-47762-4

LC 2004-24512

This is "lively and informative. . . . The nine short chapters are set in a handsome slim book with striking black-and-white scratchboard illustrations and muted red framing on many pages." SLJ

Includes bibliographical references

Stefoff, Rebecca

The **rodent** order; by Rebecca Stefoff. Marshall Cavendish Benchmark 2008 96p il (Family trees) $23.95

Grades: 6 7 8 9 **599.35**

1. Rodents

ISBN 978-0-7614-3073-5; 0-7614-3073-3

LC 2008-17555

"Explores the habitats, life cycles, and other characteristics of rodents." Publisher's note

Includes glossary and bibliographical references

599.37 Beavers

Gish, Melissa

★ **Beavers**; Melissa Gish. Creative Education 2014 46 p. (Living Wild) (hardcover : alk. paper) $37.10

Grades: 5 6 7 8 **599.37**

1. Animals 2. Beavers

ISBN 1608184145; 9781608184149

LC 2013031814

This book, by Melissa Gish, focuses on beavers. It provides "both fascinating and well-written facts and some truly arresting images. Scientific material . . . is offered, along with pop cultural and historical information." (School Library Journal)

" Fans of previous books in this series, such as Sea Lions and Piranhas (both of which SLJ called "remarkable for their clear information and exceptional photography") and Bats, Crocodiles, and Killer Whales will flock to these new entries. Thorough in scope and elegant in design, these stellar titles will attract the browser and the report writer alike." SLJ

Includes bibliographical references and index

599.4 Bats

Carson, Mary Kay

★ The **bat** scientists; with photographs by Tom Uhlman. Houghton Mifflin Books for Children 2010 79p il (Scientists in the field) $18

Grades: 4 5 6 7 **599.4**

1. Bats 2. Bat Conservation International 3. Conservation biology -- Research

ISBN 0-547-19956-2; 978-0-547-19956-6

LC 2010006767

This title in the Scientists in the Field series looks at the work of Dr. Merlin Tuttle and his colleagues at Bat Conservation International. It explores the bat's role in the natural world while seeking to "raise awareness about the problems threatening bat populations, including white-nose syndrome." (Publisher's note) Glossary. Index. "Intermediate, middle school." (Horn Book)

This describes "patient field work, rescue and conservation efforts to save bats. . . . Woven into particular researchers' stories is an enormous amount of information about bat biology and behavior. Uhlman's photographs are clearly identified in context and the backmatter supports further research." Kirkus

Includes glossary and bibliographical references

Gish, Melissa

Bats. Creative Paperbacks 2010 46p il (Living wild) $23.95; pa $9.95

Grades: 5 6 7 8 **599.4**

1. Bats

ISBN 978-1-58341-966-3; 1-58341-966-7; 978-0-89812-549-8 pa; 0-89812-549-9 pa

LC 2010017371

The "book lucidly discusses conservation and the animals' often tenuous relationship with humans. The layout is uniformly simple but effective, constructed with a nice balance of main text for the report writers, smaller chunks of esoterica for browsers, and . . . killer photos." Booklist

Koch, Falynn

Science comics; bats: learning to fly. Falynn Koch. First Second 2017 128 p. color illustrations (hardcover) $19.99

Grades: 3 4 5 6 **599.4**

1. Bats 2. Animal flight 3. Animal rescue

ISBN 9781626724082; 9781626724099

LC 2016938728

This graphic novel in the Science Comics series, by Falynn Koch, follows "a little brown bat whose wing is injured by humans on a nature hike. He is taken to a bat rehabilitation center where he meets many different species of bats. They teach him how they fly, what they eat, and where they like to live." (Publisher's note)

"With plenty of informative back matter, this inviting, engaging nonfiction comic is perfect for kids hungry for science." Booklist

Markle, Sandra, 1946-

The **case** of the vanishing little brown bats; a scientific mystery. Sandra Markle. Millbrook Press 2014 48 p. illustrations, maps (lib. bdg. : alk. paper) $29.27

Grades: 4 5 6 **599.4**

1. Bats 2. Animals -- Diseases 3. Little brown bat

ISBN 1467714631; 9781467714631

LC 2013030953

"This informative title sheds light on a mystery of nature: how little brown bats, nature's insect eaters, are mysteriously dying in their caves during hibernation. Each chapter takes readers into the problems that plague this endangered member of our ecosystem, describing how teams of scientists examined how 'white-nose syndrome,' caused by a fungus called Pd, is infecting the brown bat population." (School Library Journal)

"With plentiful details about the scientific work, photographs showing scientists and their tiny subjects, clear explanations, and an organization that is both topical and chronological, this title brings science to life." Kirkus

Includes bibliographical references and index

Taschek, Karen

Hanging with bats; ecobats, vampires, and movie stars. University of New Mexico Press 2008 94p il (Worlds of wonder) $16.95

Grades: 6 7 8 9 **599.4**

1. Bats

ISBN 978-0-8263-4403-8; 0-8263-4403-8

LC 2008-2076

"This book provides an all-inclusive look at the flying mammal many people do not understand well enough to appreciate. From the scientific discussion of where bats are found on the evolutionary tree to the whys and hows of building a bat house, there is little that cannot be learned from within these pages. . . . The text is written in a friendly style, with unusual words further defined or explained as needed, nicely allowing generous amounts of information to be absorbed without it feeling like work. The photographs and illustrations are fascinating, helping to lure in a reluctant reader. It should be noted that the photos of bats in action are particularly eye-catching. . . . It is a good choice for any library." Voice Youth Advocates

Includes glossary

599.5 Cetaceans and sea cows

Baker, Molly

The **secret** world of whales; illustrated by Molly Baker. Chronicle Books 2011 108p il $16.99

Grades: 4 5 6 7 **599.5**

1. Whales

ISBN 978-0-8118-7641-4; 0-8118-7641-1

LC 2010-27355

"In this small-format volume, Siebert creates a concise introduction to whales, addressing myths and stories, the history of the whaling industry, communication and intelligence, and encounters between whales and humans. With playful, anthropomorphic cartoons, striking photographs, and a discussion of the dangers facing whales—noise pollution from boats, potentially lethal sonar—readers should gain a vivid impression of their behavior in the wild, as well as an appreciation for their majesty." Publ Wkly

Gish, Melissa

Killer whales. Creative Paperbacks 2010 46p il map (Living wild) $23.95; pa $9.95

Grades: 5 6 7 8 **599.5**

1. Whales

ISBN 978-1-58341-971-7; 1-58341-971-3; 978-0-89812-554-2 pa; 0-89812-554-5 pa

LC 2010017376

"A look at killer whales, including their habitats, physical characteristics such as their unique coloration, behaviors, relationships with humans, and protected status in the world today." Publisher's note

Whales. Creative Education 2011 46p il map (Living wild) lib bdg $23.95

Grades: 5 6 7 8 **599.5**

1. Whales

ISBN 978-1-60818-084-4

LC 2010028414

A look at whales, including their habitats, physical characteristics such as their streamlined bodies, behaviors, relationships with humans, and threatened status in the world today.

Includes glossary and bibliographical references

Greenberg, Daniel A.

Whales; [by] Dan Greenberg, with Nina Hess. Cavendish Square Publishing 2010 24p il map lib bdg $16.95

Grades: 3 4 5 6 **599.5**

1. Whales

ISBN 978-0-7614-4346-9; 0-7614-4346-0

LC 2008-52110

"Describes the physical characteristics, habitat, behavior, diet, life cycle, and conservation status of whales." Publisher's note

Hodgkins, Fran

★ The **whale** scientists; solving the mystery of whale strandings. Houghton Mifflin Co. 2007 63p il map (Scientists in the field) $18

Grades: 5 6 7 8 **599.5**

1. Whales

ISBN 978-0-618-55673-1; 0-618-55673-7

LC 2006-34634

This describes the evolution of whales and their relationship to humans and offers various scientific theories about their strandings.

"Hodgkins packs her text with an impressive amount of information. . . . Well-chosen color photographs amply illustrate the well-organized discussion." SLJ

Includes glossary and bibliographical references

Hoyt, Erich

Encyclopedia of whales, dolphins and porpoises; Erich Hoyt ; principal photography by Brandon Cole ; illustrations by Uko Gorter. Firefly Books Ltd 2017 300 p. illustrations (some color) (hardcover) $49.95

Grades: 5 6 7 8 9 10 11 12 Adult **599.5**

1. Whales 2. Dolphins 3. Marine mammals 4. Marine mammals -- Encyclopedias

ISBN 9781770859418; 1770859411

LC 2017300268

In this book, "author and whale researcher Erich Hoyt takes readers into the field for an intimate encounter with some 90 species of cetaceans that make their homes in the world's oceans. Drawing on decades of firsthand experience and a comprehensive familiarity with the current revolution in cetacean studies, Hoyt provides unique insights into the life histories of these compelling marine mammals." (Publisher's note)

Includes bibliographical references (page 297) and index.

Lockwood, Sophie

Whales; by Sophie Lockwood. Child's World 2008 40p il map (World of mammals) lib bdg $29.93

Grades: 4 5 6 **599.5**

1. Whales

ISBN 978-1-59296-930-2 lib bdg; 1-59296-930-5 lib bdg

LC 2007020890

This book about whales presents "all the basics for reports: an introduction to the creatures' challenges, the role humans play, physical traits and behaviors, habitats, and struggles for survival. Every part of their life [cycle], including sexual maturity, birth, and family relationships, is explained. . . . Clear bright photographs pump up the content. . . . The detail that Lockwood imparts is startlingly high. The [text is] written in a dynamic and engaging style." SLJ

Includes glossary and bibliographical references

Lourie, Peter

★ The **manatee** scientists; saving vulnerable species. Houghton Mifflin Books for Children 2011 80p il map (Scientists in the field) $18.99

Grades: 4 5 6 7 **599.5**

1. Manatees 2. Scientists 3. Marine biology 4. Endangered species 5. Wildlife conservation

ISBN 978-0-547-15254-7; 0-547-15254-X

This book highlights the work scientists are doing to protect the manatee, including John Reynolds, who does an aerial count of manatees from the Florida sky; Lucy Keith who spends a weekend rescuing manatees trapped in a dam in Senegal; and Fernando Rosas who takes the author on an Amazonian boat trip, looking for a young manatee he released back into the wild.

"The manatees photographed by Lourie and others add plenty of visual appeal. . . . A sturdy addition to a standard-setting nonfiction series." Booklist

★ **Whaling** season; a year in the life of an arctic whale scientist. Houghton Mifflin Books for Children 2009 80p il map (Scientists in the field) $18

Grades: 4 5 6 7 **599.5**

1. Inuit 2. Whales 3. Biologists 4. Alaska

ISBN 978-0-618-77709-9; 0-618-77709-1

LC 2009-18596

Profiles the work of John Craighead George, an Arctic whale scientist, as he studies the bowhead whale and works with the indigenous people of Alaska to better understand the history of the animal.

"Combining exemplary color photos and simple, vivid language, the chapters detail not only George's day-today methodology but also his motivation." Booklist

Includes glossary and bibliographical references

O'Connell, Jennifer

The **eye** of the whale; a rescue story. Jennifer O'Connell. 1st hardcover ed. Tilbury House, Publishers 2012 32 p. col. ill. (hardcover) $16.95

Grades: 5 6 7 8 **599.5**

1. Whales 2. Animal rescue 3. Humpback whale -- California

-- San Francisco 4. Wildlife rescue -- California -- San Francisco
ISBN 0884483355; 9780884483359

LC 2012031165

This true children's story, by Jennifer O'Connell, begins when, "near San Francisco, a distress call was radioed to shore by a local fisherman. He had discovered a humpback whale tangled in hundreds of yards of crab-trap lines. . . . A team of volunteers answered the call, and four divers risked their lives to rescue the enormous animal." (Publisher's note)

599.53 Dolphins and porpoises

Turner, Pamela S.

The **dolphins** of Shark Bay; by Pamela S. Turner. Houghton Mifflin Harcourt 2013 76 p. $18.99

Grades: 5 6 7 8 **599.53**

1. Dolphins 2. Bottlenose dolphin -- Behavior -- Australia -- Shark Bay (W.A.)
ISBN 0547716389; 9780547716381

LC 2012048463

In this book, "ride alongside the author Pamela S. Turner and her scientific team . . . as they seek to answer the question: just why are dolphins so smart? And what does their behavior tell us about human intelligence, captive animals, and the future of the ocean?" (Publisher's note)

599.55 Sea cows

Gish, Melissa

Manatees; Melissa Gish. Creative Education 2016 46 p. color illustrations, map (hardcover : alk. paper) $39.95

Grades: 5 6 7 8 **599.55**

1. Manatees
ISBN 9781608187058

LC 2015026824

This children's book in the Living Wild series, by Melissa Gish, offers "a look at manatees, including their habitats, physical characteristics such as their unique respiratory system, behaviors, relationships with humans, and the protected status of these intelligent creatures in the world today." (Publisher's note)

"Whether weird, beautiful, or simply adorable, this series has its animals covered." Booklist

Includes bibliographical references (page 46) and index.

599.64 Bovids

Gish, Melissa

Bison. Creative Education 2011 46p il map (Living wild) $23.95

Grades: 5 6 7 8 **599.64**

1. Bison
ISBN 978-1-60818-077-6; 1-60818-077-8

LC 2010028305

A look at bison, including their habitats, physical characteristics such as their shaggy coats, behaviors, relationships with humans, and threatened status in the world today.

This offers "an array of interesting facts. Photography is large and beautiful—a real draw." SLJ

Includes bibliographical references

599.65 Deer

Gish, Melissa

Moose. Creative Education 2010 46p il map (Living wild) $23.95; pa $9.95

Grades: 5 6 7 8 **599.65**

1. Moose
ISBN 978-1-58341-973-1; 1-58341-973-X; 978-0-89812-556-6 pa; 0-89812-556-1 pa

LC 2010017378

"A look at moose, including their habitats, physical characteristics such as their imposing antlers, behaviors, relationships with humans, and secure status in the world today." Publisher's note

599.66 Odd-toed ungulates

Carson, Mary Kay

★ **Emi** and the rhino scientist; [by] Mary Kay Carson; with photographs by Tom Uhlman. Houghton Mifflin Company 2007 57p il (Scientists in the field) $18

Grades: 5 6 7 8 **599.66**

1. Rhinoceros 2. Zoo employees 3. Animal scientists
ISBN 978-0-618-64639-5; 0-618-64639-6

LC 2006-34517

This describes "how Terri Roth, an expert in endangered-species reproduction at the Cincinnati Zoo, helped Emi to give birth to the first Sumatran rhino born in captivity in more than 100 years. . . . The text is full of important details, and the photographs are unfailingly crisp, bright, and full of variety." SLJ

Farley, Terri

★ **Wild** at Heart; mustangs and the young people fighting to save them. by Terri Farley ; photographs by Melissa Farlow. Houghton Mifflin Harcourt 2015 208 p. $19.99

Grades: 5 6 7 8 **599.66**

1. Horses 2. Mustang -- Conservation -- West (U.S.) 3. Mustang 4. Wild horses -- West (U.S.) 5. Wild horses -- Conservation
ISBN 9780544392946

LC 2014041975

This book, by Terri Farley, with photographs by Melissa Farlow, "focuses on the plight of feral horses in this country. . . . In appeals to the emotions that are underscored by Farlow's lyrical photos of mustangs running free or posing in graceful stances, Farley also describes the social behavior of wild horses, their history on this continent, . . . and the achievements of rescue workers from early champion Velma Johnston to nine young current activists." (School Library Journal)

"Beginning with 'Wild Horse Annie,' the 1950s activist who secured protections for America's wild horses, this wide-ranging volume explores horses' prehistoric ancestors, herd dynamics, the horrors of government roundups, and today's young activists fighting to make a difference. Emotional language and first-person sidebars try to recruit readers to the cause, while crisp color photos depict beautiful horses in their natural habitats." Horn Book

Frydenborg, Kay

The **wild** horse scientists; written by Kay Frydenborg. Houghton Mifflin Harcourt 2013 80 p. (Scientists in the field) $18.99

Grades: 7 8 9 10 **599.66**

1. Horses 2. Scientists 3. Conservationists 4. Assateague Island

National Seashore (Md. and Va.) 5. Wild horses -- Assateague Island National Seashore (Md. and Va.) 6. Wildlife conservationists -- Assateague Island National Seashore (Md. and Va.)

ISBN 0547518315; 9780547518312

LC 2011039912

This book by Kay Frydenbourg, part of the "Scientists in the Field" series, "focuses on research leading to the use of porcine zona pellucida vaccine on wild horses for reliable, reversible birth control. Frydenborg introduces her readers to several scientists involved in this work. . . . Along the way are chapters on horse ancestry and the history of wild horses in this country, as well as information about color and size and other research and researchers." (Kirkus Reviews)

Includes bibliographical references.

Gish, Melissa

Rhinoceroses. Creative Education 2011 46p il map (Living wild) lib bdg $23.95

Grades: 5 6 7 8 **599.66**

1. Rhinoceros

ISBN 978-1-60818-083-7; 1-60818-083-2

LC 2010028316

A look at rhinoceroses, including their habitats, physical characteristics such as their horned noses, behaviors, relationships with humans, and protected status in the world today.

Includes glossary and bibliographical references

Markle, Sandra, 1946-

The **great** rhino rescue; saving the southern white rhinos. Sandra Markle. Millbrook Press 2019 48 p. (library binding : alk. paper) $33.32

Grades: 3 4 5 6 7 **599.66**

1. Animal rescue -- South Africa 2. White rhinoceros -- Conservation -- Southern Africa 3. White rhinoceros -- Southern Africa -- Conservation

ISBN 1512444367; 9781512444360

LC 2017040488

In this book in the Sandra Markle's Science Discoveries series, by Sandra Markle, "Southern white rhinos are in trouble. For years, a rumor has been spreading that their horns can be used to cure cancer, and poachers have been targeting these gentle creatures. . . . Markle takes readers behind the scenes to see how civilians, volunteer organizations, and African governments are working together to protect rhinos." (Publisher's note)

Includes bibliographical references (page 47) and index

Montgomery, Sy

★ The **tapir** scientist; written by Sy Montgomery ; photographed by Nic Bishop. Houghton Mifflin Harcourt 2013 80 p. $18.99

Grades: 5 6 7 8 **599.66**

1. Brazil 2. Tapirs 3. Tapirs -- Brazil 4. Tapirs -- Research -- Brazil

ISBN 0547815484; 9780547815480

LC 2012018678

In this book, author Sy Montgomery and photographer Nic Bishop "experience long, hot days, cramped conditions, nervous waiting and itchy tick bites while searching for [tapirs]. . . . In less than a week, they see tapirs in the wild, find their tracks, take photographs, locate them through radio telemetry, collect 'samples of tapir poop, skin, fur, and blood,' and capture and collar two new tapirs, with more to come. This research matters, and the author . . . explains why." (Kirkus Reviews)

599.67 Elephants

Downer, Ann

Elephant talk; the surprising science of elephant communication. Twenty-First Century Books 2011 112p il map lib bdg $33.26

Grades: 4 5 6 7 8 **599.67**

1. Elephants 2. Animal communication

ISBN 978-0-7613-5766-7 lib bdg; 0-7613-5766-1 lib bdg

LC 2010-24880

"The complex behavior of wild elephants is introduced in a flowing narrative accompanied by full-color photographs, diagrams and maps. Downer provides an overview of elephant evolution, places the creatures in their African and Asian contexts, and describes the lives of these intelligent social animals. Her narrative then focuses on the elephants' inticate verbal and nonverbal communication techniques. . . . The illustrations and clearly labeled diagrams and maps are well placed to amplify the text. . . . Throughout this highly readable, informative title are profiles of individuals . . . who work with these animals." SLJ

Includes glossary and bibliographical references

O'Connell, Caitlin

★ The **elephant** scientist; by Caitlin O'Connell and Donna M. Jackson; photographs by Caitlin O'Connell and Timothy Rodwell. Houghton Mifflin Books for Children 2011 70p il map $17.99

Grades: 4 5 6 7 **599.67**

1. Elephants 2. Biologists 3. Ecologists

ISBN 9780547053448; 0547053444

LC 2010014134

Boston Globe-Horn Book Honor: Nonfiction (2012)

In this book, "O'Connell traveled to Africa in 1992 to observe wild animals; the trip turned into a job offer to study elephants at Etosha National Park; the text focuses on the scientists' work, findings, and problems encountered. The authors offer [a] . . . look at new discoveries about elephant communication and how this knowledge can be used to slow the animal's slump into extinction. Combined with . . . full-color photographs by the scientists, the elephants' world is brought to the forefront. Readers enter the researchers' camp to see their setup, fieldwork, and takedown in action. They will learn how elephant anatomy and hierarchy work together to aid in communication." (School Library Journal)

O'Connell "worked with other scientists to [identify] the vibration-sensitive cells in elephants' feet and trunks that enabled to them to 'hear' sounds transmitted through the ground. Illustrated with many well-captioned, color photos, this eye-catching book provides a sometimes fascinating look at O'Connell's work with elephants in America and in Namibia." Booklist

599.7 Carnivores

Allman, Toney

Deadliest mammals; Toney Allman. ReferencePoint Press, Inc. 2016 80 p. (hardback) $29.95; (ebook) $29.95

Grades: 6 7 8 9 10 **599.7**

1. Mammals 2. Carnivorous animals 3. Carnivora

ISBN 1682820505; 9781682820506; 9781682820513

LC 2016023812

This children's book, by Toney Allman, part of the "Deadliest predators" series, describes how in order "to hunt and kill their prey, the worlds deadliest mammals rely on a variety of traits including teeth, claws, size, strength, speed, and stealth. Six deadly mammals, including the wolverine, are profiled." (Publisher's note)

"First-rate nonfiction on a high-interest topic." SLJ

Includes bibliographical references and index

599.74 Land carnivores

Montgomery, Sy

The hyena scientist; written by Sy Montgomery ; photographs by Nic Bishop. Houghton Mifflin Harcourt 2018 80 p. $18.99

Grades: 5 6 7 8 **599.74**

1. Hyenas 2. Mammalogists 3. Hyenas -- Research

ISBN 9780544635111

LC 2017015658

This book about hyenas in the Scientists in the Field series, by Sy Montgomery, with photographs by Nic Bishop, "sets the record straight about one of history's most hated and misunderstood mammals, while featuring the groundbreaking, pioneering research of a female scientist in a predominately male field. . . . As a scientist studying one of the only mammalian societies led entirely by females, zoologist Kay Holecamp has made it her life's work to understand hyenas." (Publisher's note)

Includes bibliographical references

Read, Tracy C.

Exploring the world of raccoons. Firefly Books 2010 24p il (Exploring the world . . .) lib bdg $16.95; pa $6.95

Grades: 6 7 8 9 **599.74**

1. Raccoons

ISBN 978-1-55407-626-0 lib bdg; 1-55407-626-9 lib bdg; 978-1-55407-617-8 pa; 1-55407-617-X pa

"This slender book from the Exploring the World of . . . series introduces the raccoon. The discussion begins with its gradual migration, over the past 100 years, from disappearing North American forests into suburbs and cities. In illustrated two-page and four-page spreads, the book presents information on aspects of raccoon anatomy, habitat, food, seasonal cycle, care of young, and predators...The text is clearly written and informative, though its vocabulary would suit a high-school reader better than the elementary-school students who might be drawn to such a short, highly illustrated book. Still, capable middle-school readers looking for a succinct, informative introduction to raccoons will find it here." (Booklist)

Somervill, Barbara A.

Small Indian Mongoose. Cherry Lake Pub. 2010 32p il map (Animal invaders) lib bdg $27.07

Grades: 5 6 7 8 **599.74**

1. Mongooses 2. Biological invasions

ISBN 978-1-60279-630-0 lib bdg; 1-60279-630-0 lib bdg

LC 2009028179

This offers "an introduction to the problems caused by [the Small Indian Mongoose], a discussion of its physical characteristics and habits, a history of how it arrived in its new habitat, and an analysis of challenges encountered by those trying to limit its spread. . . . [This] considers the destructive effects of these mammals on islands (including several in Hawaii), where they were initially introduced to prey on rats. . . . [This] well-focused [book is] clearly written. The uncluttered page design features at least one color photo on each spread." Booklist

Includes glossary and bibliographical references

599.75 Cat family

Becker, John E.

Wild cats: past & present; illustrations by Mark Hallett. Darby Creek 2008 80p il $18.95

Grades: 5 6 7 8 **599.75**

1. Wild cats 2. Felidae

ISBN 1-58196-052-2; 978-1-58196-052-5

This is an account of the various species of wild cats and their ancestors. Bibliography. Index. "Age eleven and up." (Publisher's note)

"Becker provides an informative introduction to wild cats, including an account of their ancient ancestors, an overview of the family Felidae and its subdivisions, accounts of wild cats alive in the world today, and woven throughout, discussions of the endangered status of many species. . . . Clearly written and well organized, the text is enhanced by many side-bars, maps, photos, and paintings." Booklist

Clutton-Brock, Juliet

Cat; by Juliet Clutton-Brock. DK Publishing 2014 72 p color illustrations (DK Eyewitness) library $19.99

Grades: 4 5 6 7 **599.75**

1. Cats 2. Wild cats

ISBN 1465420924; 9781465420923

First published 1991

Text and photographs present the anatomy, behavior, habitats, and other aspects of wild and domestic cats.

Gish, Melissa

Jaguars. Creative Education 2011 46p il map (Living wild) lib bdg $23.95

Grades: 5 6 7 **599.75**

1. Jaguars

ISBN 978-1-60818-079-0; 1-60818-079-4

LC 2010028315

A look at jaguars, including their habitats, physical characteristics such as their powerful jaws, behaviors, relationships with humans, and threatened status in the world today.

This offers "an array of interesting facts. Photography is large and beautiful–a real draw." SLJ

Includes glossary and bibliographical references

Leopards. Creative Education 2010 46p il (Living wild) lib bdg $34.25; pa $8.99

Grades: 5 6 7 8 **599.75**

1. Leopards

ISBN 978-1-58341-972-4 lib bdg; 1-58341-972-1 lib bdg; 978-0-89812-555-9 pa; 0-89812-555-3 pa

LC 2010017377

"A look at leopards, including their habitats, physical characteristics such as their spotted fur, behaviors, relationships with humans, and threatened status in the world today." Publisher's note

Hamilton, Sue L.

Ambushed by a cougar; [by] Sue Hamilton. ABDO Pub. Co. 2010 32p il (Close encounters of the wild kind) lib bdg $27.07

Grades: 4 5 6 7 **599.75**

1. Pumas 2. Animal attacks

ISBN 978-1-60453-928-8 lib bdg; 1-60453-928-3 lib bdg

LC 2009-45521

Readers learn of actual human-cougar encounters, information about cougars, survival strategies, and attack statistics.

"Students will be drawn to the realistic full-color photographs, the realistic diagrams of the creatures' bodies, the real-life stories told by victims, and the interesting, attractive formatting that includes text, diagrams, photographs, and graphics on each page. . . . [This is] exciting and attractive in a 'gross' sort of way and will appeal particularly to boys for both leisure reading and research." Libr Media Connect

Includes glossary

Markle, Sandra, 1946-

The **great** leopard rescue; Saving the Amur Leopards. Sandra Markle. Millbrook Press 2017 48 p. color ill., color maps (ebook) $30.65; (ebook) $30.65; (lb : alk. paper) $30.65

Grades: 3 4 5 6 **599.75**

1. Leopard -- Amur River Valley (China and Russia) 2. Animal rescue -- Amur River Valley (China and Russia) 3. Wildlife conservation -- Amur River Valley (China and Russia) 4. Wildlife rescue -- Amur River Valley (China and Russia)

ISBN 9781512420494; 9781467797559; 9781467792479

LC 2015044387

This book, by Sandra Markle, focuses on saving Amur leopards. " In 2007 only thirty Amur leopards remained in the wild. . . . With the help of new technology and the cooperation of scientists and governments around the world, people have learned more than ever before about these rare cats. An innovative plan is under way to give Amur leopards a more secure future. Can these cats rebound from the brink before it's too late?" (Publisher's note)

"An informative presentation showing what is being done to save this beautiful but critically endangered species." Booklist

Includes bibliographical references and index

Montgomery, Sy

★ **Chasing** cheetahs; the race to save Africa's fastest cats. written by Sy Montgomery ; photographs by Nic Bishop. Houghton Mifflin Harcourt 2014 80 p. illustrations (Scientists in the field) $18.99

Grades: 5 6 7 8 **599.75**

1. Cheetahs 2. Cheetah -- Africa 3. Cheetah Conservation Fund

ISBN 0547815492; 9780547815497

LC 2013017611

This book, by Sy Montgomery, focuses on cheetahs. "At the Cheetah Conservation Fund's (CCF) African headquarters in Namibia, Laurie Marker and her team save these . . . creatures from extinction. Since the organization's start in 1990, they've rescued more than 900 cheetahs. . . . But this arduous challenge continues. For most African livestock farmers, cheetahs are the last thing they want to see on their properties. In the 1980s, as many as 19 cheetahs per farmer died each year." (Publisher's note)

"Montgomery introduces readers to Laurie Marker and her team at the Cheetah Conservation Fund's site in Namibia. Scientific information about the cheetahs and profiles of the people who study them are interspersed with in-the-moment, journal-style accounts of activities at the site. Striking photographs capture the dedication of the scientists and the awesome power of the cheetahs." Horn Book

Includes bibliographical references and index.

★ **Saving** the ghost of the mountain; an expedition among snow leopards in Mongolia. text by Sy Montgomery; photographs by Nic Bishop. Houghton Mifflin Books for Children 2009 48p il map (Scientists in the field) $18

Grades: 5 6 7 8 **599.75**

1. Biologists 2. Snow leopard 3. Conservationists 4. Mongolia

ISBN 978-0-618-91645-0; 0-618-91645-8

LC 2008-36762

Author Sy Montgomery and photographer Nic Bishop accompany conservationist Tom McCarthy and his team as they travel to Mongolia's Altai Mountains to gather data about snow leopard populations in an attempt to save this endangered species

"Montgomery's enthusiasm translates well to the page and will have readers cheering for the entourage as they attempt to spot a snow leopard. This slender book abounds with information. Bishop's trademark stunning photography fills out the book with breathtaking views of the extreme environs of Central Asia and warm portraits of the charming people who live there." SLJ

599.756 Tiger

Montgomery, Sy

★ The **man** -eating tigers of Sundarbans; with photographs by Eleanor Briggs. Houghton Mifflin 2001 57p il map hardcover o.p. pa $6.95

Grades: 4 5 6 7 **599.756**

1. Tigers

ISBN 0-618-07704-9; 0-618-49490-1 pa

LC 00-32031

"To draw readers into this scientific puzzle, Montgomery integrates science, storytelling, anthropology, and adventure in a unique treatment, illustrated with excellent color photos and diagrams." Horn Book Guide

Includes bibliographical references

599.757 Lion

Hague, Bradley

Rise of the lioness; Restoring a Habitat and its Pride on the Liuwa Plains. by Bradley Hague. National Geographic 2016 56 p. hardcover $18.99

Grades: 4 5 6 7 **599.757**

1. Lions 2. Wildlife refuges -- Zambia 3. Wildlife conservation -- Zambia 4. Lion -- Zambia

ISBN 9781426325335; 9781426325328

LC 2015024883

In this children's book by Bradley Hague, "poaching and war damaged an isolated wilderness in West Zambia, reducing its lion population to just one: Lady, the last lioness. Witness Lady's fight for survival in this evocative narrative on the decline, fall, and rebirth of the Liuwa Plains. Follow Lady as she grapples with a landscape altered by human hands and discover how both Lady and humankind restore balance to the environment." (Publisher's note)

"Full color photographs document the journey of Lady and her pride. This enlightening work offers in-depth information on the diverse needs of an ecosystem and offers hope for its restoration." SLJ

Includes bibliographical references and index

599.769 Otters

Newman, Patricia

Sea otter heroes; the predators that saved an ecosystem. Patricia Newman. Millbrook Press 2017 56 p. ill. (chiefly col.), col. maps (lb : alk. paper) $31.99

Grades: 6 7 8 9 10 **599.769**

1. Sea otter 2. Marine ecology 3. Marine habitats 4. Seagrasses -- Ecology 5. Elkhorn Slough (Calif.) -- Ecology

ISBN 9781512426311

LC 2016020573

Robert F. Sibert Information Book Award Honor Book (2018)

This book, by Patricia Newman, "follows marine biologist Brent Hughes and his study of Elkhorn Slough, which grew healthy seagrass while other inlets in similar conditions suffered. Eventually, careful research revealed that it was the presence of sea otters, the local apex predator, that allowed the slough to flourish. In four chapters, Newman details Hughes' research processes and examines the workings of ecosystems in general and how its inhabitants affect it at every level." (Booklist)

"A very informative selection for environmental studies." School Library Journal.

Includes bibliographical references and index

599.77 Dog family

Lockwood, Sophie

Foxes. Child's World 2008 40p il map (World of mammals) lib bdg $29.93

Grades: 4 5 6 **599.77**

1. Foxes

ISBN 978-1-59296-932-6; 1-59296-932-1

LC 2007-21943

Explores the physical and behavioral characteristics of foxes.

Includes glossary and bibliographical references

McAllister, Ian

The **sea** wolves; living wild in the Great Bear Rainforest. written by Ian McAllister and Nicholas Read; photographs by Ian McAllister. Orca Book Publishers 2010 121p il $19.95

Grades: 5 6 7 8 **599.77**

1. Wolves 2. Rain forest ecology

ISBN 978-1-55469-206-4; 1-55469-206-7

The coastal wolf, a genetically distinct strain that swims and fishes, inhabits the Great Bear Rainforest on British Columbia's rugged west coast.

"This extensive, informative text is illustrated with remarkable photographs taken by McAllister, who has lived in and studied the area for years. They show the lush, old-growth forest and rocky shoreline and a variety of animals that share this habitat, but the wolves are the stars: at rest, at play, on the prowl and catching fish. . . . Fascinating and useful." Kirkus

599.78 Bears

Cherrix, Amy

Backyard bears; conservation, habitat changes, and the rise of urban wildlife. by Amy Cherrix. Houghton Mifflin Harcourt 2018 80 p. (hardcover) $18.99

Grades: 4 5 6 7 8 9 **599.78**

1. Bears 2. Wildlife conservation 3. Human-animal relationships 4. Human-bear encounters 5. Black bear -- Behavior 6. Black bear -- Conservation 7. Black bear -- North Carolina

ISBN 9781328858689

LC 2017060898

This book in the Scientists in the Field Series, by Amy Cherrix, "looks at black bears--and other animals around the globe--who are rapidly becoming our neighbors in urban and suburban areas. North Carolina's black bears were once a threatened species, but now their numbers are rising. . . . Can humans and bears live compatibly? What are the long-term effects for the bears? . . . Cherrix follows the scientists who . . . are trying to answer . . . these questions and more." (Publisher's note)

Includes bibliographical references and index

Gish, Melissa

Brown bears; Melissa Gish. Creative Education 2014 46 p. (Living wild) (hardcover : alk. paper) $37.10

Grades: 5 6 7 8 **599.78**

1. Brown bear

ISBN 1608184153; 9781608184156

LC 2013031808

In this book, by Melissa Gish, "[v]ivid photographs help take readers on a virtual field study to observe the life cycle and behaviors of [brown bears]. . . . [It] also looks at past and present scientific research and includes a unique storytelling element in the form of an animal tale drawn from mythology or folklore." (Publisher's note)

"Thorough in scope and elegant in design, these stellar titles will attract the browser and the report writer alike." SLJ

Includes bibliographical references and index

Pandas. Creative Education 2011 48p il (Living wild) lib bdg $23.95; pa $8.95

Grades: 5 6 7 8 **599.78**

1. Giant panda

ISBN 978-1-60818-082-0 lib bdg; 1-60818-082-4 lib bdg; 978-1-60818-082-0 pa; 1-60818-082-4 pa

LC 2010028311

A look at pandas, including their habitats, physical characteristics such as their black-and-white fur, behaviors, relationships with humans, and threatened status in the world today.

Includes glossary and bibliographical references

Hamilton, Sue L.

Mauled by a bear; [by] Sue Hamilton. ABDO Pub. Co. 2010 32p il (Close encounters of the wild kind) lib bdg $27.07

Grades: 4 5 6 7 **599.78**

1. Bears 2. Animal attacks

ISBN 978-1-60453-932-5 lib bdg; 1-60453-932-1 lib bdg

LC 2009-35078

Readers learn of actual human-bear encounters, information about bears, survival strategies, and attack statistics.

"Students will be drawn to the realistic full-color photographs, the realistic diagrams of the creatures' bodies, the real-life stories told by victims, and the interesting, attractive formatting that includes text, diagrams, photographs, and graphics on each page. . . . [This is] exciting and attractive in a 'gross' sort of way and will appeal particularly to boys for both leisure reading and research." Libr Media Connect

Includes glossary

McAllister, Ian

★ **Salmon** bears; giants of the Great Bear Rainforest. [by] Ian McAllister & Nicholas Read; photographs by Ian McAllister. Orca Book Publishers 2010 89p il map pa $18.95

Grades: 5 6 7 8 **599.78**

1. Bears 2. Salmon 3. Rain forest ecology

ISBN 978-1-55469-205-7 pa; 1-55469-205-9 pa

"Read's conversational text and McAllister's excellent photos provide a perfect framework for this evocative look at the big bears of the Great Bear Rainforest of British Columbia, and an intriguing investigation of its ecological pattern of dependency. The authors present a round of seasons from one winter to the next, touching upon such topics as the effects of fish farms on wild salmon populations, what happens during a salmon run, and what the future may hold for the fish, the bears, and the Great Bear Rainforest itself. . . . Superbly readable, informative, and attractive." SLJ

Includes bibliographical references

Montgomery, Sy

★ **Search** for the golden moon bear; science and adventure in the Asian tropics. Houghton Mifflin 2004 80p il $17

Grades: 5 6 7 8 **599.78**

1. Bears

ISBN 0-618-35650-9

LC 2004-5236

The author reports on an expedition into Laos and Thailand in search of a rare species of bear

"The exciting narrative is complemented by an array of full-color photos. . . . This attractive and informative offering is an intelligent reportage of science as it happens." SLJ

Includes bibliographical references

599.786 Polar bear

Castaldo, Nancy F.

Mission : polar bear rescue; all about polar bears and how to save them. Nancy F. Castaldo and Karen de Seve with Daniel Raven-Ellison. Natl Geographic Soc Childrens books 2014 112 p. illustrations (chiefly color) $21.9

Grades: 4 5 6 **599.786**

1. Polar bear 2. Wildlife conservation

ISBN 1426317328; 9781426317323

LC 2014048265

This book on polar bears, by Nancy F. Costaldo and Karen de Seve, with Daniel Raven-Ellison, is part of the "Mission: Animal Rescue" series, which "shine[s] a spotlight on endangered animals and what can be done to help them." The book "emphasizes how climate change is drastically reducing the bears' habitat and what young people can do to curtail its effects." (Booklist)

"These attractive books offer a good deal of information about endangered animals as well as encouragement for kids who want to help." Booklist

Includes bibliographical references (pages 108-109) and index.

599.789 Giant panda

Thimmesh, Catherine

Camp panda; helping cubs to survive in the wild. by Catherine Thimmesh. Houghton Mifflin Harcourt 2018 64 p. $17.99

Grades: 5 6 7 **599.789**

1. Giant panda 2. Environmental literature 3. Wildlife conservation 4. Giant panda -- Conservation

ISBN 9780544818910

LC 2017024801

Sibert Honor Book (2019)

This book, by Catherine Thimmesh, presents "a riveting, timely account of panda conservation efforts in China, perfect for budding environmentalists and activists. Roughly a thousand years ago, an estimated 23,000 pandas roamed wild and free through their native China. But within the past forty years, more than fifty percent of the panda's already shrinking habitat has been destroyed by humans, leaving the beautiful and beloved giant panda vulnerable to extinction." (Publisher's note)

599.79 Marine carnivores

Snyder, Eleanor

Alarming leopard seals; Eleanor Snyder. Gareth Stevens Publishing 2017 24 p. color ill., color map (ebook) $22.60; (library bound) $22.60

Grades: 3 4 5 **599.79**

1. Leopard seal 2. Marine animals

ISBN 9781482449037; 9781482448979; 9781482449099; 9781482449150

LC 2015046971

In this children's book in the Cutest Animals...That Could Kill You! series by Eleanor Snyder, "leopard seals look so cute, but even their name gives us a clue about their true nature: they're carnivores with a taste for penguin meat. The marine mammals' size, sometimes exceeding 12 feet (3.7 m), makes them dangerous, even to people. This absorbing volume combines attention-grabbing text with exciting photographs of leopard seals in their native habitats." (Publisher's note)

"An informative, highly readable, and high-interest series." Booklist

Includes bibliographical references and index

599.8 Primates

Doak, Robin S.

Jane Goodall; chimpanzee protector. Robin S. Doak. Heinemann Library 2015 48 p. illustrations; color map (hardcover) $32.65

Grades: 5 6 7 8 **599.8**

1. Conservationists 2. Wildlife conservation 3. Women primatologists -- England -- Biography 4. Chimpanzees -- Tanzania -- Gombe National Park

ISBN 1484604695; 1484604741; 9781484604694; 9781484604748

LC 2013040526

This book by Robin S. Doak " takes an engaging look at the work of ground-breaking conservationist, Jane Goodall, and her work with chimpanzees. It covers Goodall's inspiration, her methods, findings, and the impact of her work in Africa." (Publisher's note)

"Students will appreciate her dedication—2000 hours of observing gorillas. The graphics present a time line of primate development and maps that are as excellent and informative as the rest of this must-have series." SLJ

Includes bibliographical references (pages 46-47) and index

Gish, Melissa

Gorillas. Creative Education 2010 46p il (Living wild) $23.95; pa $9.95

Grades: 5 6 7 8 **599.8**

1. Gorillas

ISBN 978-1-58341-969-4; 1-58341-969-1; 978-0-89812-552-8 pa; 0-89812-552-9 pa

LC 2010017374

This "book lucidly discusses conservation and the animals' often tenuous relationship with humans. The layout is uniformly simple but effective, constructed with a nice balance of main text for the report writers, smaller chunks of esoterica for browsers, and . . . killer photos." Booklist

Lockwood, Sophie

Baboons. Child's World 2006 40p il map (World of mammals) lib bdg $29.93

Grades: 4 5 6 **599.8**

1. Baboons

ISBN 978-1-59296-497-0; 1-59296-497-4

LC 2005-533

Explores the physical and behavioral characteristics of baboons, examines their habitat and natural history, and discusses the role of humans in ensuring the continued survival of the species.

"Lockwood's dynamic and engaging style and intriguing insight . . . [make the] book shine. . . . Will give children solid information for reports." SLJ

Includes glossary and bibliographical references

Sobol, Richard

Breakfast in the rainforest; a visit with mountain gorillas. with an afterword by Leonardo DiCaprio. Candlewick 2008 40p il map $18.99

Grades: 3 4 5 6 **599.8**

1. Gorillas 2. Rain forest ecology 3. Uganda

ISBN 978-0-7636-2281-7; 0-7636-2281-8

"Wildlife photographer Sobol recounts his travels to Uganda to observe gorillas living in the Virunga Mountains. In his personable text, he also touches on the creatures' habits, diet, and threats. Closeup photographs of the gorillas in addition to many pictures of the surrounding countryside and villagers help round out an understanding of the endangered animals' homeland." Horn Book Guide

599.9 Humans

Deem, James M.

Faces from the past; forgotten people of North America. by James M. Deem. Houghton Mifflin Harcourt 2012 154 p. $18.99

Grades: 6 7 8 9 10 **599.9**

1. Skeleton 2. Human body 3. Physical anthropology 4. North America -- Population 5. Radiocarbon dating -- North America 6. Forensic anthropology -- North America 7. Human remains (Archaeology) -- North America 8. Facial reconstruction (Anthropology) -- North America

ISBN 0547370245; 9780547370248

LC 2012006819

This book by James M. Deem looks at "nine cases in which" facial "reconstructions help interpret a specific moment in American history. . . . This title brings to life such diverse figures as paleoamerican Spirit Cave Man; 'Pearl,' a slave from eighteenth-century upstate New York; a buffalo soldier whose corpse was reassembled and given an honorable burial; [and] nine persons among the 1,271 bodies found in pauper's graves in an almshouse cemetery." (Bulletin of the Center for Children's Books)

Szpirglas, Jeff

You just can't help it! your guide to the wild and wacky world of human behavior. Josh Holinaty, illustrator. Owlkids Books 2011 64p il $22.95; pa $10.95

Grades: 4 5 6 7 **599.9**

1. Human behavior 2. Human biology

ISBN 1-926818-07-5; 1-926818-08-3 pa; 978-1-926818-07-8; 978-1-926818-08-5 pa

"How many times have you been frightened and felt the hairs on the back of your neck stand up? Or been unable to hold back a laugh? Or flinched when an object whizzed by, too close for comfort? . . . [This] book provides a cultural, historical, and sociobiological perspective on human behavior. . . . [It is an] exploration of the basic human biology that determines our reactions, social interactions, and the ways we communicate with one another." (Publisher's note) Index. "Ages nine to twelve." (Quill Quire)

This is a "collection of curious facts and intriguing studies about human behavior. With a breezy text supported by a lively design, the author . . . presents science in a way certain to attract middle-grade and middle-school readers. Chapters on the senses, emotions, communication, and interactions with other human beings cover a variety of topics. . . . The digital art includes bits of photographs, line drawings, the use of color and shapes to help organize the print and plenty of symbols." Kirkus

Includes index

599.909 Physical anthropologists

Henderson, Harry, 1951-

The **Leakey** family; unearthing human ancestors. Harry Henderson. Chelsea House 2011 127 p. (Trailblazers in science and technology) (library) $35

Grades: 7 8 9 10 11 12 **599.909**

1. Olduvai Gorge (Tanzania) -- Antiquities 2. Fossil hominids -- Tanzania -- Olduvai Gorge 3. Excavations (Archaeology) -- Tanzania -- Olduvai Gorge 4. Paleoanthropolgists -- Tanzania -- Olduvai Gorge -- Biography 5. Physical anthropologists -- Tanzania -- Olduvai Gorge -- Biography

ISBN 160413674X; 9781604136746

LC 2011001972

This book, by Harry Henderson, profiles the Leakey family as part of the "Trailblazers in Science and Technology" series. "In the 20th century, the family name . . . became synonymous with paleoanthropology. . . . Louis S.B. Leakey explored East Africa and what is now Tanzania, finding skulls of human ancestors to fill in the evolutionary roadmap to modern man. Leakey worked alongside his wife, Mary, herself an experienced archaeologist and anthropologist." (Publisher's note)

Includes bibliographical references and index

599.93 Genetics, sex and age characteristics, evolution

Stefoff, Rebecca

★ **First** humans. Marshall Cavendish Benchmark 2009 112p il map (Humans: an evolutionary history) lib bdg $37.07

Grades: 7 8 9 10 **599.93**

1. Human origins 2. Fossil hominids
ISBN 978-0-7614-4184-7; 0-7614-4184-0

LC 2008-34330

"Stefoff provides an enlightening and entertaining history of the evolution of Homo sapiens, their ancestors, and cousins, from primitive origins to today. The clear, insightful [text is] accented by intriguing sidebars and colorful photos, maps, and graphs." SLJ

Includes glossary and bibliographical references

★ **Modern** humans. Marshall Cavendish Benchmark 2009 112p il map (Humans: an evolutionary history) lib bdg $37.07

Grades: 7 8 9 10 **599.93**

1. Genetics 2. Evolution 3. Human origins 4. Fossil hominids
ISBN 978-0-7614-4187-8; 0-7614-4187-5

LC 2009-12364

"Stefoff provides an enlightening and entertaining history of the evolution of Homo sapiens, their ancestors, and cousins, from primitive origins to today. The clear, insightful [text is] accented by intriguing sidebars and colorful photos, maps, and graphs." SLJ

Includes glossary and bibliographical references

Thimmesh, Catherine

★ **Lucy** long ago; uncovering the mystery of where we came from. Houghton Mifflin Harcourt 2009 63p il $18

Grades: 4 5 6 7 **599.93**

1. Human origins 2. Fossil hominids
ISBN 978-0-547-05199-4; 0-547-05199-9

LC 2008-36761

"The 1974 discovery of the fossilized partial skeleton of a small-brained primate who apparently walked upright 3.2 million years ago in what is now Ethiopia significantly changed accepted theories about human origins. Step by step, Thimmesh presents the questions the newly discovered bones raised and how they were answered.... Extensive research, clear organization and writing, appropriate pacing for new ideas and intriguing graphics all contribute to this exceptionally accessible introduction to the mystery of human origins." Kirkus

600 TECHNOLOGY (APPLIED SCIENCES)

Macaulay, David

The **Way** Things Work Now; From Levers to Lasers, Windmills to Wi-fi, a Visual Guide to the World of Machines. [by] David Macaulay with Neil Ardley. Houghton Mifflin Harcourt 2016 400 p. illustrations hbk $35

Grades: 4 5 6 7 8 9 10 11 12 Adult **600**

1. Machinery 2. Inventions 3. Technology
ISBN 9780544824386; 0544824385

Originally published 1988 and 1998 as The Way Things Work and The New Way Things Work

"Famously packed with information on the inner workings of everything from windmills to Wi-Fi, this extraordinary and humorous book both guides readers through the fundamental principles of machines, and shows how the developments of the past are building the world of tomorrow. This sweepingly revised edition embraces all of the latest developments, from touchscreens to 3D printer." (Publisher's note)

"Macaulay's brilliantly designed, engagingly informal diagrams and cutaways bring within the grasp of even casual viewers a greater understanding of the technological wonders of both past and present." Kirkus

608 Patents

Lee, Dora

Biomimicry; Inventions inspired by nature. written by Dora Lee ; illustrated by Margot Thompson. Kids Can Press 2011 40 p. $18.95

Grades: 4 5 6 **608**

1. Inventions 2. Nature study 3. Human ecology 4. Technological innovations
ISBN 9781554534678

This book explores "modern innovations [that] have sprung from observation and imitation of the natural world. In topically organized double-page spreads, [Dora] Lee describes shapes and structures, materials and designs, as well as systems for exploration, communication, rescue and delivery. . . . Three or four specific examples, each with illustrative vignettes, follow or sometimes precede the general explanation. These topics range widely and include medical marvels, new power sources, [and] biological computers and robots. . . . [The book] includes a strong ecological message: The most important natural model is the sustainable ecosystem. Through biomimicry, humans can learn to live in balance on the Earth as well." (Kirkus)

609 History, geographic treatment, biography

125 cool inventions; contributing writers, Crispin Boyer, Laura Daily, Michelle Harris, Cathy Lu, Sean McCollum, Douglas E. Richards, Sarah Wassner Flynn. National Geographic Kids 2015 112 p. color illustrations $12.99

Grades: 5 6 7 8 **609**

1. Inventions
ISBN 1426318855; 1426318863; 9781426318856; 9781426318863

LC 2015288146

This book, by National Geographic Kids, "gives curious kids the inside scoop on 125 amazing real inventions. It's sure to get gadget gurus, techies, and computer geeks thinking about the world of infinite possibilities." (Publisher's note)

"Even the most madcap of these inventions will engage readers and leave them wondering, 'Why didn't someone think of that sooner?' Browsers who love weird stuff will be tickled by the contents of this book." Booklist

Bender, Lionel

Invention; by Lionel Bender. 3rd edition DK Publishing 2013 72 p ill. (chiefly col.) (DK Eyewitness) library $16.99; hardcover $16.99

Grades: 4 5 6 7 **609**

1. Inventions 2. Technology
ISBN 9781465409027; 9781465409010

"A fascinating look at the world's earliest simple machines--wheels, gears, pulleys, and levers--to today's complicated telephones and plastics." (Publisher's note)

Cole, D. J.

Encyclopedia of modern everyday inventions; [by] David J. Cole, Eve Browning, and Fred E.H. Schroeder. Greenwood Press 2003 285p il $57.95

Grades: 7 8 9 10 11 12 Adult **609**

1. Reference books 2. Inventions -- History

ISBN 0-313-31345-8

LC 2002-69620

"The analysis of each invention is thorough and lively. . . . This book . . . would make an excellent addition to any school or public library needing books on technology and inventions in the modern world." Voice Youth Advocates

Includes bibliographical references

Ferris, Julie

Ideas that changed the world; authors, Julie Ferris [et al.] DK Pub. 2010 256p il map $24.99

Grades: 6 7 8 9 10 **609**

1. Inventions -- History 2. Technology -- History

ISBN 978-0-7566-6531-9; 0-7566-6531-0

LC 2010282281

A guide to technological developments that changed the world describes each invention and explores its place in history and how it influenced civilization, discussing inventions from the wheel to computers.

"Brightly colored and packed with information, this reference volume delivers. . . . This book could be used in multiple subject areas. English classes might use it for general research or units on the decades, social studies for the major changes over time, and science due to the technological advancements." Libr Media Connect

Horne, Richard

101 things you wish you'd invented--and some you wish no one had; designed and illustrated by Richard Horne; written by Tracey Turner and Richard Horne. Walker & Co. 2008 un il pa $11.99

Grades: 6 7 8 9 **609**

1. Inventions

ISBN 978-0-80279-788-9; 0-80279-788-1

LC 2008-4990

"The authors have chosen interesting subjects and written concise and engaging histories and trivia. The quality of the book is quite impressive. With an appearance much like a field guide, this well-bound book is made with quality paper and has a very eye-catching layout." Voice Youth Advocates

Lee, Richard B.

Africans thought of it! amazing innovations. [by] Bathseba Opini [and] Richard B. Lee. Annick Press 2011 48p il (We thought of it) $21.95; pa $11.95

Grades: 3 4 5 6 **609**

1. Inventions 2. Africa -- Civilization

ISBN 978-1-55451-277-5; 1-55451-277-8; 978-1-55451-276-8 pa; 1-55451-276-X pa

Describes the inventions created by the peoples of Africa in hunting, agriculture, architecture, metalwork, medicine, the arts, and other fields, and how they have spread through the world and continue to fit into modern African civilization.

"Vivid photographs feature authentic objects used . . . while people engaged in activities capture an enthusiastic look at the reliance on community. Colored backgrounds and borders present a busy, though uncluttered, dynamic portrayal of nuanced cultures. . . . Succinct definitions and compact descriptions provide a brief and interesting blend of the contemporary with the traditional." SLJ

Rossi, Ann

Bright ideas; the age of invention in America, 1870-1910. [by] Ann Rossi. National Geographic 2005 40p il (Crossroads America) $12.95

Grades: 4 5 6 **609**

1. Inventions -- History

ISBN 0-7922-8276-0

LC 2003-19834

This describes the history of late 19th and early 20th century inventions such as the light bulb, the telegraph, the telephone, and the automobile.

This "solid [title] for report writers may even pull in a few curious browsers because of [its] plentiful, full-color photos and reproductions. The [layout is] inviting, and the [text is] clear, informative, and readable." SLJ

Includes glossary

Tomecek, Steve

★ **What** a great idea! inventions that changed the world. [by] Stephen M. Tomecek; illustrated by Dan Stuckenschneider. Scholastic Ref. 2003 112p il $22.99

Grades: 4 5 6 7 **609**

1. Inventions -- History

ISBN 0-590-68144-3

LC 2001-20937

"Tomecek puts significant inventions and discoveries in a historical context. Dividing the text into five broad time periods, he offers a series of essays on important advances that occurred in each 'age'. . . . What emerges is a sense of interconnectedness that other books often lack. . . . Full-color diagrams and illustrations are well integrated into each spread." SLJ

Includes bibliographical references

Ye, Ting-xing

The **Chinese** thought of it; amazing inventions and innovations. Annick Press 2009 48p il map (We thought of it) $19.95; pa $9.95

Grades: 5 6 7 8 **609**

1. China -- Civilization 2. Inventions -- History 3. Technology -- History

ISBN 978-1-55451-196-9; 1-55451-196-8; 978-1-55451-195-2 pa; 1-55451-195-X pa

In this survey of Chinese inventions "at least one double-page spread is devoted to each of the eleven topics: farming, working with metal, transportation and exploration, canals and bridges, weapons and warfare, paper and printing, silk, and everyday innovations. . . . The layout of the book is appealing and just right for quick reading or browsing. . . . The author's personal story about her childhood in Shanghai effectively draws the reader in." Voice Youth Advocates

Includes bibliographical references

609.2 Biography

MacLeod, Elizabeth

How to become an accidental genius; Elizabeth MacLeod, Frieda Wishinsky, illustrated by Jenn Playford. Orca Book Publishers 2019 128 p. (hardcover) $24.95

Grades: 4 5 6 7 **609.2**

1. Inventions -- History 2. Inventors -- Biography
ISBN 9781459816763

LC 2018954163

This book, by Elizabeth MacLeod, Frieda Wishinsky, illustrated by Jenn Playford, "is full of inspiring tales of famous and lesser-known inventors who have changed the world, from George Washington Carver, Mary Anderson (inventor of the windshield wiper) and inventor and actress Hedy Lamarr to Frank Epperson (of Popsicle fame) and Mary Sherman Morgan (The Woman Who Saved the U.S. Space Race). Readers will be amazed at the inventiveness of these geniuses." (Publisher's note)

610 Medicine and health

Dawson, Ian

Renaissance medicine. Enchanted Lion Books 2005 64p il (History of medicine) lib bdg $19.95

Grades: 6 7 8 9 **610**

1. Renaissance 2. Medicine -- History
ISBN 1-59270-038-1

This "offers a concise overview of the fascinating advancements in European medicine between 1450 and 1750. . . . Dawson carefully shows how inventions such as the printing press and microscope and the work of artists such as da Vinci influenced medical knowledge. Quotes from primary sources enhance the plainspoken language, and numerous reproductions of paintings and engravings vividly evoke the realities of surgery, leech treatments, and the horrors of the plague." Booklist

Includes glossary and bibliographical references

Kelly, Kate

Early civilizations; prehistoric times to 500 C.E. Facts on File 2010 174p il map (The history of medicine) $40

Grades: 6 7 8 9 10 **610**

1. Ancient civilization 2. Medicine -- History
ISBN 978-0-8160-7205-7; 0-8160-7205-1

LC 2008-43441

"This eye-opening and information-rich [volume] . . . shows that ancient human beings were quite knowledgeable about health and well-being. This book discusses medical advances from prehistoric times through the Roman Empire. . . . Coverage is global. . . . Readers will gain a deepened appreciation of and insights into modern medicine by examining this book. Because of its inclusion of new research, it is recommended as a first purchase for most libraries." SLJ

Includes bibliographical references

Morley, David

Healing our world. Fitzhenry & Whiteside 2007 121p il map $18.95

Grades: 6 7 8 9 **610**

1. War relief 2. Disaster relief 3. Medical assistance 4. Médecins Sans Frontières (Organization)
ISBN 978-1-55041-565-0

The author was the executive director of MSF Canada from 1998 to 2005. "When children are caught in civil wars, when earthquakes destroy homes and villages, when AIDS and other diseases shatter families and communities—the volunteers of Doctors Without Borders are there. . . . Médecins Sans Frontières, known in English as Doctors Without Borders and by its volunteers as MSF, is the world's largest independent medical humanitarian relief organization. . . . In Healing Our World, David Morley presents his own story and the stories of other MSFers who have volunteered in . . . [places like] the Congo, El Salvador, Chechnya, Bangladesh, Mozambique, Afghanistan, [and] southern Africa." (Publisher's note) "Age twelve and up." (Quill Quire)

"Morley is a former executive director of the Canadian section of Doctors Without Borders, a humanitarian organization known throughout most of world as Medecins Sans Frontieres (MSF). With clarity and passion, he introduces the organization's history, charter, and current efforts to provide health care where it is needed most." Booklist

Newquist, H. P.

The **human** body; HP Newquist. Viking, published by the Penguin Group 2015 112 p. illustrations (some color) (ebook) $56.97; (hardcover) $18.99

Grades: 4 5 6 7 **610**

1. Human body 2. Medicine -- History 3. Human physiology 4. Medical technology 5. Medical innovations
ISBN 9781101997147; 9780451476432

LC 2015011670

A book written by H. P. Newquist and part of the Invention and Impact series, "From artificial eyeballs to aspirin to 3-D printed body parts, 'The Human Body' profiles the objects that scientists and tinkerers throughout history have invented (or cobbled together) to protect, repair, or improve our physical selves." (Publisher's note)

"The open page design and ample full-color photos and historical diagrams will easily draw in middle-grade readers, especially those looking for a more macabre look at history and science. A list of resources, including abundant websites, closes out this handsome volume." Booklist

Includes bibliographical references and index.

Stefoff, Rebecca, 1951-

Magic and Medicine; Rebecca Stefoff. Cavendish Square 2014 48 p. illustrations (Is It Science?) $29.93

Grades: 6 7 8 **610**

1. Magic 2. Medicine -- History 3. Science -- Methodology
ISBN 1627125159; 9781627125154

LC 2014054661

This book, edited by Rebecca Stefoff, is part of the "Is It Science?" series. The volume and the series explore the history and methodology of science in various disciplines, contrasting them with the older ideas and frameworks that were proved wrong over time. This volume explores the history of medicine and the development from earlier magical thinking to the contemporary scientific to the discipline.

"Each volume is heavily illustrated with period images and modern photographs, and each closes with particularly generous lists of further resources." SLJ

Woolf, Alex, 1964-

Death and disease; [by] Alex Woolf. Lucent Books 2004 48p il map (Medieval realms) $29.95

Grades: 5 6 7 8 **610**

1. Medieval civilization 2. Medicine -- History
ISBN 1-59018-533-1

LC 2003-61797

"Clear, well-organized [text] along with full-color reproductions of art and artifacts and photos of period structures immerse readers in . . . medieval life and offer sufficient information for reports." SLJ

Includes glossary and bibliographical references

610.28 Auxiliary techniques and procedures; apparatus, equipment, materials

Strange, Cordelia

Medical technicians; health-care support for the 21st century. Mason Crest Publishers 2011 64p il (New careers for the 21st century: finding your role in the global renewal) lib bdg $22.95

Grades: 7 8 9 10 **610.28**

1. Medical personnel 2. Vocational guidance

ISBN 978-1-4222-1817-4 lib bdg; 1-4222-1817-1 lib bdg

LC 2010014934

"Chapters identify and emphasize specific careers-important strengths, necessary aptitudes and interests, education and training, projected earnings, closely related occupations, type of work environment, and predictions for the future of the field. . . . Color photos have a small role amid the many statistics, figures, graphs and charts that support and supplement the . . . [text]." SLJ

Includes bibliographical references

610.73 Nursing and services of allied health personnel

Glasscock, Sarah

How nurses use math; math curriculum consultant: Rhea A. Stewart. Chelsea Clubhouse 2010 32p il (Math in the real world) lib bdg $28

Grades: 4 5 6 **610.73**

1. Nurses 2. Mathematics 3. Vocational guidance

ISBN 978-1-60413-607-4 lib bdg; 1-60413-607-3 lib bdg

LC 2009-20199

This describes how nurses use math in such tasks as giving eye tests, keeping records, taking the pulse, and measuring medicine and includes relevant math problems and information about how to become a nurse

Includes glossary and bibliographical references

Strange, Cordelia

Physicians assistants & nurses; new opportunities in the 21st-century health system. Mason Crest Publishers 2011 64p il (New careers for the 21st century: finding your role in the global renewal) lib bdg $22.95

Grades: 7 8 9 10 **610.73**

1. Nurses 2. Vocational guidance

ISBN 978-1-4222-1820-4 lib bdg; 1-4222-1820-1 lib bdg

LC 2010017919

"Chapters identify and emphasize specific careers-important strengths, necessary aptitudes and interests, education and training, projected earnings, closely related occupations, type of work environment, and predictions for the future of the field. . . . Color photos have a small role amid the many statistics, figures, graphs and charts that support and supplement the . . . [text]." SLJ

Includes bibliographical references

610.9 Medicine--history

Rooney, Anne

The **history** of medicine; Anne Rooney. Rosen Pub. Group 2013 208 p. (The history of science) (library) $42.60

Grades: 7 8 9 10 11 12 **610.9**

1. Medicine -- History 2. Medical innovations -- History

ISBN 1448872286; 9781448872282

LC 2012009971

This book, by Anne Rooney, is part of "The History of Science" series. "Organized thematically, this . . . entry . . . delves into the history of disease, diagnosis, treatment and surgery. Because of its broad scope, the book is able to make comparisons across eras, transforming . . . history into something relevant to today's teens. . . . Insets offer medical milestones, biographical sketches, and primary resources." (Booklist)

"Organized thematically, this enlightening entry into the History of Science series delves into the history of disease, diagnosis, treatment, and surgery... Rooney has crafted a highly readable tome about a dense topic." Booklist

Includes bibliographical references (p. 205) and index

Younker, J. Marin

Bleed, Blister, Puke, and Purge; The Dirty Secrets Behind Early American Medicine. J. Marin Younker. Houghton Mifflin Harcourt 2016 112 p. illustrations (hardcover) $13.99; (ebook) $9.99

Grades: 9 10 11 12 **610.9**

1. Medicine -- United States -- History

ISBN 9781942186328; 1942186320; 9781942186335

This children's book by J. Marin Younker "exposes the extraordinary practices and major players of American medical history, from the colonial era to the late 1800s. It's hard to believe that today's cutting-edge medicine originated from such crude beginnings, but this book reminds us to be grateful for today's medical care, while also raising the question: what current medical practices will be the horrors of tomorrow?" (Publisher's note)

"An engrossing, entertaining history of medicine for those who enjoy it told with a heavy dose of blood and guts." Kirkus

Includes bibliographical references and index.

Zuchora-Walske, Christine, 1968-

Your head shape reveals your personality! science's biggest mistakes about the human body. by Christine Zuchora-Walske. Lerner Publishing Group 2015 32 p. color illustrations (lib. bdg. : alk. paper) $26.60

Grades: 4 5 6 7 **610.9**

1. Human body 2. Science -- History 3. Medicine -- History

ISBN 1467736619; 9781467736619

LC 2013041696

In this book, by Christine Zuchora-Walske, part of the "Science Gets It Wrong" series, "[d]iscover science's biggest mistakes and oddest assumptions about the human body, and see how scientific thought changed over time." (Publisher's note)

"Although each volume [in the Science Gets It Wrong series] has its merits, Your ead Shape Reveals Your Personality! stands out due in large part to the subject matter—the human body—and its gross-out potential." SLJ

Includes bibliographical references and index

611 Human anatomy, cytology, histology

Hall, Linley Erin

DNA and RNA. Rosen Pub. 2010 80p il lib bdg $30.60

Grades: 7 8 9 10 11 12 **611**

1. DNA 2. RNA

ISBN 978-1-4358-9532-4

LC 2009-46612

"Introduces DNA and RNA, discussing how heredity works, what can happen when the code goes wrong, replication, and new advances in science and technology." (Publisher's note)

"These hi/lo resources, with the liberal use of color illustrations, color sidebars, subsections labeled in bold color fonts, and patterns of chemical bonds as backgrounds, will appeal to less able and reluctant readers." Libr Media Connect

Haywood, Karen Diane

Skeletal system; [by] Karen Haywood. Marshall Cavendish Benchmark 2009 80p il (The amazing human body) lib bdg $34.21

Grades: 6 7 8 9 **611**

1. Skeleton

ISBN 978-0-7614-3056-8; 0-7614-3056-3

LC 2008-17574

"A good choice for students beginning to research the topic." Libr Media Connect

Includes glossary and bibliographical references

612 Human physiology

Basher, Simon

Human body; a book with guts! by Simon Basher and Dan Green; illustrated by Simon Basher. Kingfisher 2011 128p il $14.95; pa $8.99

Grades: 5 6 7 8 **612**

1. Human body

ISBN 978-0-7534-6628-5; 0-7534-6628-7; 978-0-7534-6501-1 pa; 0-7534-6501-9 pa

"Basher brings his signature informative irreverence and smiley little cartoon icons to the world of human biology. Not a comprehensive resource, but supplemental science reading doesn't come much more fun." Booklist

Buller, Laura

Open me up; written by Laura Buller . . . [et al.]; editorial consultant: Richard Walker. Dorling Kindersley 2009 256p il $24.99

Grades: 7 8 9 10 11 12 **612**

1. Human body

ISBN 978-0-7566-5532-7; 0-7566-5532-3

Provides details about the human body, from human cells and senses to brain structure and body systems.

"The juxtaposition of photographs, humor, . . . historical narratives and a variety of artwork should generate hours of gratifying discovery." Publ Wkly

★ The **complete** human body; the definitive visual guide. Alice Roberts. 2nd edition DK Publishing 2016 512p il hardcover $50

Grades: 8 9 10 11 12 Adult **612**

1. Diseases 2. Human body

ISBN 9781465449184 hardcover; 978-0-7566-6733-7

This incorporates "hundreds of stunning images and clearly written text. . . . The extraordinary detail of these pictures will give students an excellent understanding of the body's structure and organization." SLJ

Farndon, John

Stuff you need to know about the human body; John Farndon ; illustrated by Tim Hutchinson. Firefly Books 2017 80 p. $14.95

Grades: 3 4 5 **612**

1. Human body 2. Human anatomy 3. Human biology 4. Human physiology

ISBN 1770859810; 9781770859814

LC 2017446453

This book, by John Farndon, illustrated by Tim Hutchinson, "follows teams of tiny people as they run around performing the actions explained in the text. Stops are made at all of the body's organs, processes, and systems, from the hippocampus to blood to DNA and ear wax. Readers will discover answers to the questions they didn't know they had, like: what exactly happened when I broke my leg? why did my Dad have a heart attack? why do I feel so awful when I get the flu?" (Publisher's note)

Gardner, Robert

Ace your human biology science project; great science fair ideas. [by] Robert Gardner and Barbara Gardner Conklin. Enslow Publishers 2009 128p il (Ace your biology science project) lib bdg $31.93

Grades: 5 6 7 8 **612**

1. Biology 2. Science projects 3. Science -- Experiments

ISBN 978-0-7660-3219-4 lib bdg; 0-7660-3219-1 lib bdg

LC 2008-30799

"Dozens of . . . science activities are presented with background information, step-by-step instructions, and suggestions for extending to the science fair level. . . . Color illustrations and important safety information are included." Horn Book Guide

Includes bibliographical references

Easy genius science projects with the human body; great experiments and ideas. Enslow Publishers 2009 112p il (Easy genius science projects) lib bdg $31.93

Grades: 7 8 9 10 **612**

1. Human body 2. Science -- Experiments

ISBN 978-0-7660-2927-9 lib bdg; 0-7660-2927-1 lib bdg

LC 2007-32315

"Both simple and complex science experiments involving the human body are included in this guide for young scientists. An introduction reviews the issues of safety and adult supervision, plus a quick review of the scientific method is included. . . . The high level vocabulary indicates that this is a book for more advanced science students. This would be a great book to put in the hands of a highly motivated student needing fresh ideas for a science fair." Libr Media Connect

Goddard, Jolyon

Inside the human body. Marshall Cavendish Benchmark 2010 48p il (Invisible worlds) lib bdg $28.50

Grades: 4 5 6 7 **612**

1. Human body 2. Physiology

ISBN 978-0-7614-4190-8 lib bdg; 0-7614-4190-5 lib bdg

LC 2008037254

This describes the details of the human body that are too small for the unaided eye to see, and how these microscopic systems work to keep the body alive and healthy.

The narrative is "clear, well written, broken down into manageable pieces, and peppered with eye-opening facts. The numerous photographs are so phenomenal that they will inspire kids to read the text . . . so that they can wrap their minds around what they see." SLJ

Includes glossary and bibliographical references

Hirsch, Rebecca E., 1969-

The **Human** Microbiome; The Germs That Keep You Healthy. Rebecca E. Hirsch. Twenty-First Century Books, a division of Lerner Publishing Group, Inc. 2016 112 p. illustrations (some color) (lb : alk. paper) $34.65

Grades: 7 8 9 10 **612**

1. Medical microbiology 2. Human body -- Microbiology 3. Drug resistance in microorganisms

ISBN 9781467785686

LC 2015014264

This book, by Rebecca E. Hirsch, focuses on the "trillions and trillions of microbial cells [that] live on and inside your body. A small number of these microbes are unhealthy germs. But most belong on your body and perform essential jobs. Microbes help digest your food, protect you from dangerous germs, and help your body fight disease." (Publisher's note)

"Unexpectedly informative and up-to-the-minute in research, this is a nifty look through a clear window at our unsuspected personal passengers. Consider this in-depth resource for reports and students who are not easily made squeamish" SLJ

Includes bibliographical references and index

Macaulay, David

★ The **way** we work; getting to know the amazing human body. [by] David Macaulay, with Richard Walker. Houghton Mifflin 2008 336p il $35

Grades: 6 7 8 9 10 **612**

1. Human body

ISBN 978-0-618-23378-6; 0-618-23378-4

LC 2008-25109

Boston Globe-Horn Book Award honor book: Nonfiction (2009)

"The opening chapter introduces basic concepts of biology and chemistry at the cellular level while subsequent chapters take us through the various systems of the body. . . . [Humor] occasionally leavens the information, which, though often complex and technical, is clearly and succintly presented in double-page spreads, accompanied by an illuminating array of illustrations." Horn Book

Reilly, Kathleen M.

The **human** body; 25 fantastic projects illuminate how the body works. illustrated by Shawn Braley. Nomad Press 2008 120p il $21.95; pa $15.95

Grades: 5 6 7 8 **612**

1. Human body

ISBN 978-1-934670-25-5; 1-934670-25-1; 978-1-934670-24-8 pa; 1-934670-24-3 pa

"The workings of the human body are expertly summarized in 11 tidy chapters, which include experiments that explain how the body works by creating models that either imitate or test its functions. . . . Many of the activities require adult supervision due to the materials required. . . . Simple drawings and cartoons enliven and illuminate the text. . . . The scientific explanations are superb." SLJ

Somervill, Barbara A.

The **human** body. Gareth Stevens Pub. 2008 48p il (Gareth Stevens vital science: life science) lib bdg $26.60; pa $11.95

Grades: 5 6 7 8 **612**

1. Human body

ISBN 978-0-8368-8441-8 lib bdg; 978-0-8368-8450-0 pa

LC 2007-16175

First published 2006 in the United Kingdom

This describes "human anatomy and physiology. . . . Factoids are scattered throughout the text in a fashion that captures the reader's attention and interest. . . . [The book offers] excellent graphics, namely photos and diagrams. The artwork complements and enhances the written content." Sci Books Films Includes glossary and bibliographical references

Walker, Richard, 1951-

Dr. Frankenstein's human body book; the monstrous truth about how your body works. [author, Richard Walker; artist, Nick Abadzis] DK Pub. 2008 93p il $24.99

Grades: 4 5 6 7 **612**

1. Human body

ISBN 978-0-7566-4091-0; 0-7566-4091-1

"This anatomy book is as engrossing as any science fiction. Dr. Frankenstein, shown in a sepia photograph standing in a laboratory, gazing at a skull he holds in one hand, invites readers to join him as he creates a human being. . . . The story line is sustained with brief, pun-happy journal entries. . . . Gothic fonts and engraved illustrations and vignettes (in red and black and also hand-colored) blend with state-of-the-art images from MEG scans, gamma scans and other advanced technology. Clear explanations broken into easily assimilable captions and text blocks encourage the reader." Publ Wkly

Includes glossary

Human body; written by Richard Walker. DK Pub. 2009 72 p. ill. (chiefly col.) (DK eyewitness books) (hardcover) $16.99

Grades: 4 5 6 7 **612**

1. Human body

ISBN 9780756645458; 075664545X

LC 2009419529

In this book, text and illustrations present information on the parts of the body and how they work

Includes glossary and bibliographical references

Ouch! how your body makes it through a very bad day. written by Richard Walker. DK Pub. 2007 71p il $16.99

Grades: 4 5 6 7 **612**

1. Human body

ISBN 978-0-7566-2536-8; 0-7566-2536-X

"Tag along on a rotten day as a body copes with sneezing, getting cut, being stung by a bee, and vomiting, as well as performing more mundane actions such as urinating, tapping into its melanin supply, acting reflexively, and sweating. . . . Dramatic color graphics, both large and small, are accompanied by a multitude of informative captions. Researchers who find the information on the busy pages hard to grasp can pop in the accompanying CD-ROM and catch a ride up the esophagus on a wave of vomit. . . . Eye-catching, highly pictorial, informative, and with a megadose of ick! factor." SLJ

Includes glossary

Wicks, Maris

★ **Human** body theater; a nonfiction revue. Maris Wicks. First Second 2015 240 p. chiefly color illustrations (hardcover) $19.99

Grades: 4 5 6 7 8 **612**

1. Human anatomy

ISBN 1626722773; 9781626722774; 9781596439290

This book by, Maris Wicks explores human anatomy on a performing stage. In it, "your master of ceremonies is going to lead you through a theatrical revue of each and every biological system of the human body! Starting out as a skeleton, the MC puts on a new layer of her costume (her body) with each 'act.'" (Publisher's note)

"Wicks' playful cartoon artwork in saturated colors makes the potentially daunting and embarrassing subject of anatomy approachable and fun, but never at the expense of accuracy or clarity. This informative, frank exploration of the body perfectly balances science and silliness." Booklist

Includes bibliographical references

612.1 Specific functions, systems, organs

Bjorklund, Ruth

Circulatory system. Marshall Cavendish Benchmark 2009 80p il (The amazing human body) lib bdg $34.21

Grades: 6 7 8 9 **612.1**

1. Cardiovascular system

ISBN 978-0-7614-3053-7; 0-7614-3053-9

LC 2007-50436

"A good choice for students beginning to research the topic." Libr Media Connect

Includes glossary and bibliographical references

Gold, John Coopersmith

Learning about the circulatory and lymphatic systems; by John C. Gold. Enslow Publishers 2013 48 p. (library) $23.93

Grades: 5 6 7 8 **612.1**

1. Picture books for children 2. Lymphatic system 3. Lymphatics 4. Cardiovascular system

ISBN 0766041565; 9780766041561

LC 2012011099

This book by John Coopersmith Gold is part of the Learning About the Human Body Systems series and looks at the circulatory and lymphatic systems. "The circulatory system runs through the body carrying oxygen and nutrients to our cells and removes waste. It's driven by the never-resting heart, which pumps blood through more than 60,000 miles of arteries and veins. The lymphatic system regulates the amount of liquid in the body among other tasks." (Publisher's note)

Includes bibliographical references and index.

Markle, Sandra

Faulty hearts; true survival stories. Lerner Pub. 2010 48p il (Powerful medicine) lib bdg $27.93

Grades: 5 6 7 8 **612.1**

1. Heart 2. Heart diseases 3. Cardiovascular system

ISBN 978-0-8225-8699-9 lib bdg; 0-8225-8699-1 lib bdg

LC 2009-33980

This book "is extremely well done, with a number of great examples of survival stories. The examples exemplify different and important heart diseases, symptoms, and treatments. . . . That the author is a former science teacher enables her to write clearly for the intended audience. The illustrations and photographs are perfect, adding to a full understanding of the diseases described." Sci Books & Films

Includes glossary and bibliographical references

Newquist, H. P.

The **book** of blood; from legends and leeches to vampires and veins. HP Newquist. Houghton Mifflin Books for Children 2012 160 p. ill. (chiefly col.) (hardback) $17.99

Grades: 4 5 6 **612.1**

1. Blood

ISBN 0547315848; 9780547315843

LC 2011025134

In this book, "[H.P.] Newquist . . . demystifies one of the most elemental and (literally) vital components of life as we know it. After an overview of the complex makeup of blood, Newquist dives into humankind's history with, beliefs about, and study of blood, including missteps and misconceptions along the way . . . . Newquist goes into detail to explain how blood moves through the human body and the critical role it plays in keeping us alive." (Publishers Weekly)

Simon, Seymour

★ The **heart**; our circulatory system. [by] Seymour Simon. rev ed.; Collins 2006 30p il hardcover o.p. pa $6.99

Grades: 4 5 6 7 **612.1**

1. Heart 2. Cardiovascular system

ISBN 978-0-06-087720-0; 0-06-087720-0; 978-0-06-087721-7 pa; 0-06-087721-9 pa

LC 2006-279215

First published 1996

Describes the heart, blood, and other parts of the body's circulatory system and explains how each component functions

"The text is succinct and direct, making the details understandable without losing the sense that the whole process of circulation is 'strange and wonderful.' . . . The often striking pictures include many computer-enhanced photographs as well as diagrams and highly enlarged images made possible by electron microscopes. Handsome and well-conceived in every way." Booklist [review of 1996 edition]

612.2 Respiratory system

Siy, Alexandra

★ **Sneeze!** [by] Alexandra Siy and Dennis Kunkel. Charlesbridge 2007 45p il lib bdg $16.95; pa $6.95

Grades: 4 5 6 7 **612.2**

1. Allergy 2. Sneezing

ISBN 978-1-57091-653-3 lib bdg; 978-1-57091-654-0 pa

LC 2005-27567

"Kunkel's big, clear, beautiful color electron micrographs on every double-page spead show everything from dust mites, mildew, and pollen to the influenza A virus." Booklist

Includes glossary and bibliographical references

612.3 Digestive system

Allman, Toney

Nutrition and disease prevention. Chelsea House 2010 191p il map (Healthy eating: a guide to nutrition) lib bdg $35

Grades: 7 8 9 10 11 12 **612.3**

1. Nutrition 2. Preventive medicine

ISBN 978-1-60413-777-4; 1-60413-777-0

LC 2009-41337

This "volume uses boldface type to introduce important and unknown words to the reader and explains them in an easy to understand manner so the reader can grasp the concept being discussed. . . . [For] classes needing information about the importance of good nutrition . . . [this] would be valuable." Libr Media Connect

Includes glossary and bibliographical references

Donovan, Sandra, 1967-

Hawk & Drool; gross stuff in your mouth. by Sandy Donovan; illustrated by Michael Slack. Millbrook Press 2010 48p il (Gross body science) lib bdg $29.27

Grades: 4 5 6 **612.3**

1. Saliva 2. Mouth -- Diseases

ISBN 978-0-8225-8966-2 lib bdg; 0-8225-8966-4 lib bdg

LC 2008-50699

Presents disgusting facts about the human mouth, how it works to aid in digestion, the organisms that live there, and ways to keep it clean and healthy

"Solid information layered between sarcastic comments and kid-friendly terminology like fart, poop, barf, and puke will keep readers engaged. . . . Labeled, captioned (and graphic) photographs, cartoon-style illustrations, and micrographs add information." SLJ

Includes glossary and bibliographical references

Rumble & spew; gross stuff in your stomach and intestines. by Sandy Donovan; illustrated by Michael Slack. Millbrook Press 2010 48p il (Gross body science) lib bdg $29.27

Grades: 4 5 6 **612.3**

1. Intestines

ISBN 978-0-8225-8899-3 lib bdg; 0-8225-8899-4 lib bdg

LC 2008-37713

Presents disgusting facts about the human digestive system and its functions

"Solid information layered between sarcastic comments and kid-friendly terminology like fart, poop, barf, and puke will keep readers engaged. . . . Labeled, captioned (and graphic) photographs, cartoon-style illustrations, and micrographs add information." SLJ

Includes glossary and bibliographical references

Gold, Susan Dudley

Learning about the digestive and excretory systems; by Susan Dudley Gold. Enslow Publishers 2013 48 p. (Learning about the human body systems) (library) $23.93

Grades: 5 6 7 8 **612.3**

1. Picture books for children 2. Digestive system 3. Urinary organs 4. Digestive organs

ISBN 0766041573; 9780766041578

LC 2012011100

This book by Susan Dudley Gold is part of the Learning About the Human Body Systems series and looks at the digestive and excretory systems. She "explains why these systems are discussed together, how they work, and ways to keep healthy." Illustrations and color photographs are included. (Publisher's note)

Includes bibliographical references and index.

Hoffmann, Gretchen

Digestive system. Marshall Cavendish Benchmark 2009 80p il (The amazing human body) lib bdg $34.21

Grades: 6 7 8 9 **612.3**

1. Digestion

ISBN 978-0-7614-3058-2; 0-7614-3058-X

LC 2008-17573

"A good choice for students beginning to research the topic." Libr Media Connect

Includes glossary and bibliographical references

Simon, Seymour

★ **Guts**; our digestive system. [by] Seymour Simon. Revised and updated edition HarperCollins 2019 un il hardcover $17.99; paperback $6.99

Grades: 4 5 6 7 **612.3**

1. Digestion

ISBN 9780062470423; 9780062470416

"Simon's specialty of drawing in readers through large, detailed, breathtaking photos and then entertaining them with facts is again in evidence. . . . The text is enhanced with detailed colored X rays, computer-generated pictures, and microscopic photos." SLJ

Woolf, Alex

You wouldn't want to live without poop! written by Alex Woolf ; illustrated by David Antram ; series created by David Salariya. Franklin Watts, an imprint of Scholastic Inc. 2016 32 p. color illustrations (library binding) $29.00

Grades: 3 4 5 6 **612.3**

1. Feces 2. Digestion 3. Defecation 4. Animal droppings

ISBN 9780531214893; 9780531224397

LC 2015031490

This book, by Alex Woolf, illustrated by David Antram, explains that "going to the toilet is a natural and necessary part of our lives. We couldn't live without poop because there are some parts of our food that contain no nutrients that can be used by our bodies . . . and those parts have to be ejected. But poop can also be used to power our cars, heat our homes and help grow our crops. Learn why and how animals and people produce poop, and about [its] many marvelous uses." (Publisher's note)

"The books feature a time line and numerous ancillaries, but the myriad entertaining facts are the real hit. Who wouldn't want to read them?" Booklist

612.4 Hematopoietic, lymphatic, glandular, urinary systems

Kim, Melissa

Learning about the endocrine and reproductive systems; by Melissa L. Kim. Enslow Publishers 2013 48 p. (Learning about the human body systems) (library) $23.93

Grades: 5 6 7 8 **612.4**

1. Picture books for children 2. Endocrine glands 3. Reproductive system 4. Generative organs

ISBN 0766041581; 9780766041585

LC 2012011101

This book by Melissa L. Kim is part of the Learning About the Human Body Systems series and looks at the endocrine and reproductive systems. "The endocrine system is essential to human life. It enables a person to grow, respond to change and stress, and helps turn food into energy. The reproductive system has one crucial task: that of making the next generation of people." (Publisher's note)

Includes bibliographical references and index.

Klosterman, Lorrie

Endocrine system. Marshall Cavendish Benchmark 2009 79p il (The amazing human body) lib bdg $34.21

Grades: 6 7 8 9 **612.4**

1. Endocrine glands

ISBN 978-0-7614-3055-1; 0-7614-3055-5

LC 2007-50444

"A good choice for students beginning to research the topic." Libr Media Connect

Includes glossary and bibliographical references

Excretory system. Marshall Cavendish Benchmark 2010 77p il (The amazing human body) lib bdg $23.95

Grades: 6 7 8 9 **612.4**

1. Feces 2. Urine 3. Excretion

ISBN 978-0-7614-4037-6 lib bdg; 0-7614-4037-2 lib bdg

LC 2008037261

"Discusses the parts that make up the human excretory system, what can go wrong, how to treat those illnesses and diseases, and how to stay healthy." Publisher's note

Includes glossary and bibliographical references

612.6 Reproduction, development, maturation

Bailey, Jacqui

Sex, puberty and all that stuff; a guide to growing up. by Jacqui Bailey. 2nd edition Barron's 2016 112 p illustrations paperback $13.99

Grades: 5 6 7 8 **612.6**

1. Puberty 2. Adolescence 3. Sex education

ISBN 9781438008578; 1438008570

This book "talks to teens in their own language, with emphasis on the subject that is first and foremost in the minds of adolescent boys and girls: Sex. Separate chapters titled Boy Stuff and Girl Stuff describe body changes that occur during puberty, with frank and open discussions about male and female genitals, how they feel, and how they function. Chapters that follow discuss typical teen problems, as well as those entirely new feelings that come with sexual development, and offer tips on making it through those sometimes exciting, sometimes crazy teen years." (Publisher's note)

Brynie, Faith Hickman

101 questions about reproduction; or how 1 + 1. Twenty-First Century Books 2006 176p il (101 questions) lib bdg $27.90

Grades: 7 8 9 **612.6**

1. Pregnancy 2. Childbirth 3. Sex education

ISBN 0-7613-2311-2

LC 2003-16350

Uses a question-and-answer format to present information about physical, medical, and social issues surrounding human reproduction, including birth control, pregnancy, and childbirth.

"This is a splendid companion to Brynie's 101 Questions about Sex and Sexuality (21st Century Bks, 2003); together the books present informative, complementary coverage for browsers and researchers." SLJ

Includes bibliographical references

Gravelle, Karen

The **period** book; a girl's guide to growing up. Karen Gravelle ; illustrated by Debbie Palen. 3rd edition Bloomsbury USA 2017 136 p illustrations paperback $13.99

Grades: 4 5 6 7 **612.6**

1. Menstruation

ISBN 9781619636620; 161963662X

First published 1996

"Written in consultation with preteen girls, this guide offers a supportive, practical approach, providing clear and sensitive answers to common questions on periods, as well as advice dealing with pimples and mood swings." (Publisher's note)

Holmes, Melisa

Girlology's there's something new about you; a girl's guide to growing up. [by] Melisa Holmes & Trish Hutchison. Health Communications 2010 122p il pa $12.95

Grades: 6 7 8 9 **612.6**

1. Girls 2. Puberty

ISBN 978-0-7573-1526-8; 0-7573-1526-7

LC 2010021169

Written by physicians who are mothers of preteen and teen girls, this guide explains the changes girls will be facing as they grow up.

"The graphics are informative without being offensive, pictures of the friends are cute and appealing, giving a fresh lightheartedness to the book. This is a must-have book for all homes and libraries." Voice Youth Advocates

Katz, Anne

Girl in the know; your inside-and-out guide to growing up. written by Anne Katz; illustrated by Monika Melnychuk. Kids Can Press 2010 111p il $18.95

Grades: 4 5 6 7 **612.6**

1. Puberty 2. Girls -- Health and hygiene 3. Life skills guides 4. Girls -- Psychology

ISBN 978-1-55453-303-9; 1-55453-303-1

"This reassuring title is aimed at girls who want clear facts about puberty but who may not be ready to read in-depth specifics of sex and birth-control. The author . . . offers a holistic guide that covers the body changes puberty brings as well as tips about maintaining physical and emotional health. . . . The warm, straightforward, useful advice on a broad range of topics . . . will captivate both middle graders and middle-schoolers, and the frequent color drawings of stylish, diverse girls . . . reinforce the book's appeal to a wide age group." Booklist

Madaras, Lynda

The **what's** happening to my body? book for boys; [by] Lynda Madaras with Area Madaras; drawings by Simon Sullivan. 3rd rev ed.; Newmarket Press 2007 xx, 233p il $24.95; pa $12.95

Grades: 4 5 6 7 **612.6**

1. Puberty 2. Adolescence 3. Sex education 4. Boys -- Health and hygiene

ISBN 978-1-55704-769-4; 1-55704-769-3; 978-1-55704-765-6 pa; 1-55704-765-0 pa

LC 2007009874

First published 1984

Discusses the changes that take place in a boy's body during puberty, including information on the body's changing size and shape, the growth spurt, reproductive organs, pubic hair, beards, pimples, voice changes, wet dreams, and puberty in girls

Includes bibliographical references

The **what's** happening to my body? book for girls; [by] Lynda Madaras with Area Madaras; drawings by Simon Sullivan. 3rd rev ed.; Newmarket Press 2007 xxvi, 259p il $24.95; pa $12.95

Grades: 4 5 6 7 **612.6**

1. Puberty 2. Adolescence 3. Sex education 4. Girls -- Health and hygiene

ISBN 978-1-55704-768-7; 1-55704-768-5; 978-1-55704-764-9 pa; 1-55704-764-2 pa

LC 2007009862

Discusses the changes that take place in a girl's body during puberty, including information on the body's changing size and shape, pubic hair, breasts, reproductive organs, the menstrual cycle, and puberty in boys

Includes bibliographical references

Mar, Jonathan

The **body** book for boys; by Jonathan Mar and Grace Norwich. Scholastic 2010 128p il pa $8.99

Grades: 4 5 6 **612.6**

1. Boys 2. Puberty 3. Adolescence

ISBN 978-0-545-23751-2 pa; 0-545-23751-3 pa

"In this reassuring title aimed at boys just entering adolescence, the authors present frank information on such topics as hygiene, the changes brought on by puberty, exercise, and dealing with girls. The tone is kept light, and the many bright illustrations also have a fun, jokey quality." Booklist

Nuchi, Adah

Bunk 9's guide to growing up; secrets, tips, and expert advice on the good, the bad & the awkward. as told to Adah Nuchi ; illustrated by Meg Hunt ; Dr. Meryl Newman - Cedar, Medical Consultant. Workman Pub Co 2017 189 p. color illustrations (paperback) $12.95

Grades: 4 5 6 7 **612.6**

1. Girls 2. Puberty 3. Physiology 4. Adolescence

ISBN 9781523501991; 9780761193593; 0761193596

This book, by Adah Nuchi, illustrated by Meg Hunt, is a "supportive guide that covers the head-to-toe changes that young girls go through as they grow up. Since it is written in the voices of different girls, reading it is like listening to your best friend or older sister giving no-nonsense information, advice, and tips on menstruation, breasts, hygiene, health and nutrition, boys, and all the complicated feelings that go along with these changes." (Publisher's note)

"With an engaging premise, lively design, and comprehensive, inclusive content, this has sure-fire appeal—especially to girls who have been to summer camp or dreamed of going. A fresh approach to a subject of perennial interest." Kirkus

Plaisted, Caroline

Boy talk; a survival guide to growing up. illustrated by Chris Dickason. QEB Pub. 2011 il (Growing up)

Grades: 4 5 6 7 **612.6**

1. Boys 2. Puberty

ISBN 1-60992-085-6; 978-1-60992-085-2

LC 2011009206

Discusses body changes that happen to boys during puberty, such as acne, body hair, body odor, mood swings, crushes, and more, and gives suggestions to teen boys for taking care of their hygiene and keeping good relationships.

"Using a colorful design featuring Dickason's wacky, mugging cartoon characters, this is about as appealing as a book on these topics can get, and it maintains a mildly funny, usually frank, and always healthy tone." Booklist

Rand, Casey

Human reproduction. Raintree 2009 48p il (Sci-hi: life science) lib bdg $31.43; pa $8.99

Grades: 5 6 7 8 **612.6**

1. Reproduction 2. Sex education

ISBN 978-1-4109-3327-0 lib bdg; 1-4109-3327-X lib bdg; 978-1-4109-3335-5 pa; 1-4109-3335-0 pa

LC 2009003464

In this introduction to human reproduction "clear language, embedded definitions, and interesting examples illustrate abstract concepts through both text and well-chosen photographs. . . . [It] includes suggested activities to test ideas as well as a thorough glossary and a Webliography." SLJ

Includes glossary and bibliographical references

Waters, Sophie

The **female** reproductive system. Rosen Central 2008 48p il (Girls' health) lib bdg $26.50

Grades: 5 6 7 8 **612.6**

1. Pregnancy 2. Birth control 3. Reproductive system

ISBN 9781435844018; 978-1-4042-1950-2; 1-4042-1950-1

LC 2006101218

Describes the parts of the female reproductive system, explains how pregnancy occurs and the steps in embryo development, and discusses various forms of birth control

"Generously interspersed with color photographs and diagrams . . . [this book will] offer girls a safe, comfortable place to get straight, honest answers about their personal health issues." Libr Media Connect

Includes glossary and bibliographical references

612.7 Musculoskeletal system, integument

Brynie, Faith Hickman

★ **101** questions about muscles to stretch your mind and flex your brain; by Faith Hickman Brynie. Twenty-First Century Books 2008 176p il (101 questions) lib bdg $30.60

Grades: 8 9 10 11 12 **612.7**

1. Muscles

ISBN 978-0-8225-6380-8; 0-8225-6380-0

LC 2006-37041

This answers such questions as "What do tendons do? What causes muscle cramps? . . . [This book] makes human physiology accessible, with questions everyone has always wondered about and up-to-date, detailed answers that discuss the complex science in chatty but never condescending style. Like the text, the clear diagrams and photographs deal with everything from basic information . . . to the more advanced." Booklist

Includes glossary and bibliographical references

Colligan, L. H.

Muscles. Marshall Cavendish Benchmark 2010 78p il (The amazing human body) lib bdg $34.21

Grades: 6 7 8 9 **612.7**

1. Muscles

ISBN 978-0-7614-4038-3 lib bdg; 0-7614-4038-0 lib bdg

LC 2008037257

Discusses human musculature, what can go wrong, how to treat those diseases and injuries, and how to stay health

Includes glossary and bibliographical references

Gold, Susan Dudley

Learning about the musculoskeletal system and the skin; Susan Dudley Gold. Enslow Publishers 2013 48 p. (Learning about the human body systems) (library) $23.93

Grades: 5 6 7 8 **612.7**

1. Picture books for children 2. Musculoskeletal system 3. Skin

ISBN 076604159X; 9780766041592

LC 2012011102

This book by Susan Dudley Gold is part of the Learning About the Human Body Systems series and looks at the musculoskeletal system. "Bone and muscles join forces to move us from one place to another. The musculoskeletal system controls our breathing, allows our eyes to focus, and shapes our smiles. It enables us to talk and to eat. Our strong bones support our weight. Skin wraps our body in a tough layer of tissue that keeps moisture in and germs out." (Publisher's note)

Includes bibliographical references and index..

Hall, Margaret

Skin deep. Raintree 2007 32p il (Raintree fusion) lib bdg $28.21; pa $7.99

Grades: 5 6 7 8 **612.7**

1. Skin

ISBN 978-1-4109-2582-4 lib bdg; 1-4109-2582-X lib bdg; 978-1-4109-2611-1 pa; 1-4109-2611-7 pa

LC 2006-8771

Explains what skin is and why it is important, including protecting the body from germs, helping cool down the body when it gets too hot, and absorbing Vitamin D from sunlight.

Includes glossary and bibliographical references

Klosterman, Lorrie

Skin. Marshall Cavendish Benchmark 2009 79p il (The amazing human body) lib bdg $34.21

Grades: 6 7 8 9 **612.7**

1. Skin

ISBN 978-0-7614-3057-5; 0-7614-3057-1

LC 2008-17580

"A good choice for students beginning to research the topic." Libr Media Connect

Includes glossary and bibliographical references

Mooney, Carla

Human movement; how the body walks, runs, jumps, and kicks. Carla Mooney ; illustrated by Samuel Carbaugh. Nomad Press 2017 vii, 120 p.p illustrations (some color) (Inquire and investigate) (paperback) $17.95

Grades: 6 7 8 9 **612.7**

1. Anatomy 2. Human locomotion 3. Biomechanics 4. Human anatomy

ISBN 9781619304857; 9781619304826; 1619304856

In this book in the Inquire and Investigate series, by Carla Mooney, illustrated by Samuel Carbaugh, "readers ages 12 to 15 learn the basic anatomy and physiology of the human body and discover how bones, muscles, tendons, organs, and nerves work together to make movement possible. 'Human Movement' takes a look at all of the components of the human body and examines how they allow you to move and interact with the world around you." (Publisher's note)

Includes bibliographical references (page 116) and index.

612.8 Nervous system

Brynie, Faith Hickman

★ **101** questions about sleep and dreams that kept you awake nights . . . until now. Twenty-First Century Books 2006 176p il (101 questions) lib bdg $27.93

Grades: 7 8 9 10 11 12 **612.8**

1. Sleep 2. Dreams

ISBN 978-0-7613-2312-9; 0-7613-2312-0

LC 2005-17276

This book describes the physical and psychological aspects of sleep and dreams. Glossary. Index. "Grades nine to twelve." (Sci Books Films)

The author "presents sometimes rather complicated scientific material in a way that is not only easily understood, but also thoroughly enjoyable." Sci Books Films

Includes bibliographical references

Chudler, Eric H.

Brain lab for kids; 52 mind-blowing experiments, models, and activities to explore neuroscience. Eric H. Chudler. Quarry Books, an imprint of The Quarto Group 2018 144 p. (flexibind) $22.99

Grades: 4 5 6 7 8 **612.8**

1. Brain 2. Neurosciences 3. Science projects 4. Brain -- Experiments 5. Neurosciences -- Experiments 6. Senses and sensation -- Experiments

ISBN 9781631593963

LC 2017054801

This book in the Lab Series, by Eric H. Chudler, "offers 52 family-friendly activities, science experiments, and models to help us understand how the brain accomplishes all that it does. Each lab in this book is divided into several sections. After the title of each lab, the approximate time it will take to do the experiment is listed. The 'Methods' section provides a step-by-step guide of the procedures and materials you will need to complete the lab." (Publisher's note)

Gardner, Robert

Ace your science project about the senses; great science fair ideas. [by] Robert Gardner . . . [et al.] Enslow Publishers 2009 112p il (Ace your biology science project) lib bdg $31.93

Grades: 5 6 7 8 **612.8**

1. Science projects 2. Senses and sensation 3. Science -- Experiments

ISBN 978-0-7660-3217-0 lib bdg; 0-7660-3217-5 lib bdg

LC 2008-30797

"Presents several science projects and science project ideas about the senses." Publisher's note

Includes glossary and bibliographical references

Gold, Martha V.

Learning about the nervous system; by Martha V. Gold. Enslow Publishers 2013 48 p. (Learning about the human body systems) (library) $23.93

Grades: 5 6 7 8 **612.8**

1. Picture books for children 2. Nervous system

ISBN 0766041603; 9780766041608

LC 2012011103

This book by Martha V. Gold is part of the Learning About the Human Body Systems series and looks at the nervous system. "The nervous system is made up of the brain, the spinal cord and nerves. It is responsible for telling the heart to beat, the lungs to breathe, and the muscles to move. The brain—the central command center—processes everything from understanding a teacher's instructions to enjoying a piece of chocolate cake." (Publisher's note)

Includes bibliographical references and index.

Larsen, C. S.

Crust and spray; gross stuff in your eyes, ears, nose, and throat. illustrated by Michael Slack. Millbrook Press 2010 48p il (Gross body science) lib bdg $29.27

Grades: 4 5 6 **612.8**

1. Ear 2. Eye 3. Nose 4. Throat

ISBN 978-0-8225-8964-8 lib bdg; 0-8225-8964-8 lib bdg

LC 2008-33777

"Solid information layered between sarcastic comments and kid-friendly terminology like fart, poop, barf, and puke will keep readers engaged. . . . Labeled, captioned (and graphic) photographs, cartoon-style illustrations, and micrographs add information." SLJ

Includes glossary and bibliographical references

Mooney, Carla

The **Brain**; Journey Through the Universe Inside Your Head. by Carla Mooney ; illustrated by Tom Casteel. Nomad Press 2015 119 p. color illustrations $17.95

Grades: 5 6 7 8 **612.8**

1. Brain

ISBN 1619302780; 9781619302785

This book, by Carla Mooney, illustrated by Tom Casteel, "introduces students to the fascinating world of the human brain and its effect on behavior. Readers learn about the main anatomy and functions of the brain while discovering the brain's role in learning, memory, communication, and emotions. Kids also read about new technologies being used to research the brain in its various states of performance while being introduced to the effects of sleep, alcohol, and exercise." (Publisher's note)

"Sidebars offer descriptions of jobs that involve the brain, links to online resources, and questions for discussion; ideas for experiments and activities appear throughout. It's an extensive introduction to the brain's capability and function, with just enough humor and interactivity to keep readers engaged." Pub Wkly

Includes bibliographical references (page 116) and index.

Rau, Dana Meachen

Freaking out! the science of the teenage brain. Compass Point Books 2011 64p il (Everyday science) lib bdg $33.32; pa $8.95

Grades: 7 8 9 10 **612.8**

1. Brain

ISBN 978-0-7565-4486-7 lib bdg; 0-7565-4486-6; 978-0-7565-4500-0 pa; 0-7565-4500-5 pa

LC 2010054302

This "offers a solid overview of the brain. The book begins with an explanation of what the brain does, how it looks, and its various components. It then goes on to discuss more specialized topics, such as mood changes, developmental skills, and memory. The attractive format, with easy-to-read print, features bright photographs . . . and plenty of sidebars on a variety of topics." Booklist

Includes glossary and bibliographical references

Scott, Elaine

All about sleep from A to ZZZZ; by Elaine Scott; illustrated by John O'Brien. Viking 2008 58p il $17.99

Grades: 5 6 7 8 9 10 **612.8**

1. Sleep

ISBN 978-0-670-06188-4; 0-670-06188-3

LC 2008-6074

"The book covers a range of topics, including circadian rhythms, dreams, and the functions and stages of sleep." Booklist

Simon, Seymour

The **brain**; our nervous system. [by] Seymour Simon. rev ed.; Collins 2006 30p il $17.99; pa $6.99

Grades: 4 5 6 7 **612.8**

1. Brain 2. Nervous system

ISBN 978-0-06-087718-7; 0-06-087718-9; 978-0-06-087719-4 pa; 0-06-087719-7 pa

LC 2007-272349

First published 1997

Describes the various parts of the brain and the nervous system and how they function to enable us to think, feel, move, and remember.

Simon's "clear, concise writing style is complemented by stunning color images taken with radiological scanners, such as CAT scans, MRIs, and SEMs (scanning electron microscopes.)" SLJ [review of 1997 edition]

Includes bibliographical references

Eyes and ears. HarperCollins Pubs. 2003 un il hardcover o.p. pa $6.99

Grades: 4 5 6 7 **612.8**

1. Ear 2. Eye 3. Vision 4. Hearing

ISBN 0-688-15303-8; 978-0-06-073302-5 pa; 0-06-073302-0 pa

LC 2002-19060

Describes the anatomy of the eye and ear, how those organs function and some ways in which they may malfunction, and how the brain is also involved in our seeing and hearing

"Simon is at his very best here. . . . The large, exquisitely reproduced photographs from a number of sources look like fiery planets, galaxies, and monster creatures. . . . The anatomy and physiology are detailed and accurate, with clear diagrams." Booklist

Simpson, Kathleen

The **human** brain; inside your body's control room. National Geographic 2009 64p il (National Geographic investigates) hardcover $17.95; lib bdg $27.90

Grades: 5 6 7 8 **612.8**

1. Brain

ISBN 9781426304200 hardcover; 978-1-4263-0421-7 lib bdg

"Readers will learn about . . . new brain research in this title, which includes a basic discussion of the parts of the brain, their functions, and how neurons send messages throughout the body. Information is also included about the role of the brain during sleep, dreaming, and various emotional states, as well as explanations of the various technologies available to measure brain activity. This is a well-organized, compelling introduction, sure to pique the curiosity of many children. Full-color photographs and illustrations enliven the text." SLJ

Includes bibliographical references

Wilson, M. R.

Frequently asked questions about how the teen brain works; [by] Michael R. Wilson. Rosen Pub. 2009 64p il (FAQ: teen life) lib bdg $29.25

Grades: 6 7 8 9 **612.8**

1. Brain 2. Teenagers -- Health and hygiene

ISBN 978-1-4358-5324-9 lib bdg; 1-4358-5324-5 lib bdg

LC 2008049322

Describes how the brains of adolescents differ from those of infants or adults, the structure and development of the human brain, the implications of recent discoveries for teen life and behavior, and possible future developments

"A conversational tone keeps the [book] readable, and specific topics have information relevant to teens' lives. . . . Illustrated throughout with captioned color photos." SLJ

Includes glossary and bibliographical references

Woollcott, Tory

The **brain**; the ultimate thinking machine. written by Tory Woolcott ; illustrated by Alex Graudins. First Second 2018 128 p. chiefly color illustrations (Science comics) (pbk.) $12.99

Grades: 4 5 6 7 **612.8**

1. Brain -- Fiction 2. Anatomy -- Fiction

ISBN 9781626728004; 9781626728011

LC 2017957416

In this book in the Science Comics series, by Tory Woollcott, illustrated by Alex Graudins, "Fahama has been kidnapped by a mad scientist and his zombie assistant, and they are intent on stealing her brain! She'll need to learn about the brain as fast as possible in order to plan her escape! How did the brain evolve? How do our senses work in relation to the brain? How do we remember things? What makes you, YOU?" (Publisher's note)

"Colorful illustrations illuminate the text. The combination of an entertaining story line (note: Fahama does escape), engaging and clear language, and bold, crisp panels makes for a highly effective introduction to the workings of the human brain." SLJ

613 Personal health and safety

Complementary and alternative medicine information for teens; health tips about diverse medical and wellness systems. 3rd edition Omnigraphics, Inc. 2018 399 p hardcover $69

Grades: 7 8 9 10 11 12 **613**

1. Alternative medicine 2. Teenagers -- Health and hygiene 3. Alternative medicine -- Popular works 4. Teenagers -- Health and hygiene -- Popular works

ISBN 9780780816176 hardcover; 9780780813113

LC 2017057394

This book offers information about alternative medicine for teenagers. The "volume is divided into 60 chapters, each focusing on a specific natural medicine or therapy that can be used in combination with or in place of conventional drugs to enhance health . . . . The nine parts address major categories, such as whole-medicine systems, manipulative and body-based practices, dietary and herbal remedies, and energy medicines, as well as sensory and emotional-based therapies." (School Library Journal)

Includes bibliographical references and index.

Couwenhoven, Terri

The **boys'** guide to growing up; choices & changes during puberty. Terri Couwenhoven. Woodbine House 2012 viii, 64 p.p $16.95

Grades: 6 7 8 **613**

1. Puberty 2. Teenagers -- Sexual behavior 3. People with mental disabilities 4. Teenage boys -- Physiology 5. Sex instruction for children with mental disabilities

ISBN 1606130897; 9781606130896

LC 2012025776

This book on puberty by Terri Couwenhoven "is geared to boys with "developmental disabilities." It explains basic information that includes body changes in growth, hair, skin, voice, and feelings. It is not a sex guide though it does not shy away from emerging sexuality." (School Library Journal) Topics include "how to know when flirting is reciprocated (or not!) . . . what information is okay to share with others versus what should remain private, and how to stay safe." (Publisher's note)

De la Bedoyere, Camilla

Personal hygiene and sexual health. Amicus 2010 46p il (Healthy lifestyles) lib bdg $32.80

Grades: 7 8 9 10 **613**

1. Puberty 2. Teenagers -- Health and hygiene

ISBN 978-1-60753-087-9; 1-60753-087-2

LC 2009-47571

This book is "well-written and satisfyingly informative. . . . [The] magazine-like format includes numerous sidebars, color photos, and charts." SLJ

Includes glossary

Dunham, Kelli

The **boy's** body book; everything you need to know for a happy, healthy YOU! by Kelli Dunham, R.N. ; illustrated by Steve Bjorkman. 5th edition Applesauce Press 2019 147 p color illustrations paperback $12.95

Grades: 4 5 6 7 **613**

1. Puberty 2. Adolescence 3. Boys -- Health and hygiene

ISBN 9781604338324

This new edition "has been fully updated and expanded to include everything you need to know about your changing body, texting and social media, friendship and peer pressure, leadership, and so much more!" (Publisher's note)

The **girl's** body book; by Kelli Dunham, R.N. ; illustrated by Laura Tallardy. 5th edition Applesauce Press 2019 147 p color illustrations paperback $12.95

Grades: 4 5 6 7 **613**

1. Puberty 2. Adolescence 3. Girls -- Health and hygiene

ISBN 9781604338331

This new edition "has been fully updated and expanded to include everything you need to know about your changing body, texting and social media, friendship and peer pressure, leadership, and so much more!" (Publisher's note)

Gardner, Robert

Ace your exercise and nutrition science project: great science fair ideas; [by] Robert Gardner, Barbara Gardner Conklin, and Salvatore Tocci. Enslow Publishers 2009 128p il (Ace your biology science project) lib bdg $31.93

Grades: 5 6 7 8 **613**

1. Exercise 2. Nutrition 3. Science projects 4. Science --

Experiments
ISBN 978-0-7660-3218-7 lib bdg; 0-7660-3218-3 lib bdg
LC 2008-30798

"Presents several science projects and science project ideas about exercise and nutrition." Publisher's note

Includes bibliographical references

Lehman, Robert

★ **Will** puberty last my whole life? real answers to real questions from preteens about body changes, sex, and other growing-up stuff. Julie Metzger and Robert Lehman ; illustrated by Lia Cerizo. Revised edition Little Bigfoot 2018 206 p illustrations $18.99

Grades: 4 5 6 7 8 **613**

1. Puberty 2. Boys -- Health and hygiene 3. Girls -- Health and hygiene
ISBN 9781632171795

"A medical doctor and a registered nurse answer questions about puberty collected over years of experience conducting classes for young people and their parents or trusted adults. Questions about body changes; feelings; friendships and relationships; sex, sexuality, and gender identity; and babies reflect preteen concerns, are loosely organized by subject, and are answered honestly and informatively. The dos-à-dos format (girls' queries on one side, boys' on the other) has the advantage of allowing readers to concentrate on their own issues but also to explore the ways others think. . . . This revision of a 2012 title includes many of the original questions and sensible answers but has been expanded to reflect today's changing attitudes and understandings about gender fluidity." (Kirkus)

McCoy, Kathleen

The **teenage** body book; Kathy McCoy, Ph.D., & Charles Wibbelsman, M.D. ; illustrations by Bob Stover and Kelly Grady Callarman. revised and updated edition Hatherleigh 2016 300 p illustrations paperback $19.95

Grades: 7 8 9 10 11 12 **613**

1. Adolescence 2. Sex education 3. Teenagers -- Health and hygiene
ISBN 1578266432; 9781578266432; 9781578266449

A handbook for teenagers discussing nutrition, health, fitness, emotions, and sexuality, including such topics as body image, drugs, STDs, fad diets, and hazards and benefits of the Internet.

McMahon, Serah-Marie

★ **Killer** style; how fashion has injured, maimed, and murdered through history. by Alison Matthews David and Serah-Marie McMahon, illustrated by Gillian Wilson. Owlkids Books, Inc. 2019 48 p. (hardcover) $17.95

Grades: 4 5 6 7 8 **613**

1. Fashion -- History 2. Clothing and dress -- History
ISBN 9781771472531
LC 2018946401

This book, by Serah-Marie McMahon and Alison Matthews David, illustrated by Gillian Wilson, reveals that "history is full of fashions that have harmed or even killed people. From silhouette-cinching corsets and combustible combs to lethal hair dyes and flammable flannel, this nonfiction book looks back at the times people have suffered pain, injury, and worse, all in the name of style." (Publisher's note)

"From lead-based cosmetics to radioactive wristwatches; from arsenic-green gowns to sandblasted denims: fashion's victims are sometimes the wearers and sometimes the creators." (Kirkus Reviews)

Natterson, Cara

The **care** & keeping of you 2; the body book for older girls. Dr. Cara Natterson ; illustrated by Josee Masse. American Girl 2013 96 p. (paperback) $12.99

Grades: 5 6 7 8 **613**

1. Puberty 2. Life skills -- Handbooks, manuals, etc. 3. Teenage girls -- Health and hygiene 4. Girls -- Life skills guides
ISBN 1609580427; 9781609580421
LC 2012045813

This book, by Cara Natterson, illustrated by Josee Masse, is a body image and physiology guide written for girls going through puberty.

"The friendly illustrations support the overall tone and style. . . . Its neutral, matter-of-fact approach will help show readers . . . that all the changes they may be feeling are perfectly normal." SLJ

Orr, Tamra

★ **Playing** safe, eating right; making healthy choices. ABDO Pub. 2009 112p il (Essential health: strong beautiful girls) lib bdg $22.95

Grades: 6 7 8 9 **613**

1. Health 2. Nutrition 3. Teenagers -- Health and hygiene
ISBN 978-1-60453-103-9 lib bdg; 1-60453-103-7 lib bdg
LC 2008-17015

This features fictional narratives paired with firsthand advice from a licensed psychologist to help preteen and teen girls evaluate options and choose healthy ways of living. Topics include diet and exercise, sleep, drugs and alcohol.

"The topics are well selected, the design is attractive, and the stories features girls from a variety of cultures." Booklist

Includes glossary and bibliographical references

Pfeifer, Kate Gruenwald

★ **American** Medical Assocation boy's guide to becoming a teen. Jossey-Bass 2006 128p il pa $12.95

Grades: 4 5 6 7 **613**

1. Puberty 2. Adolescence 3. Boys -- Health and hygiene
ISBN 0-7879-8343-8

"This guide addresses puberty's changes clearly. . . . The text's approach is straightforward, accessible, and nonjudgmental, whether the topic is same-sex attraction or divorcing parents. The volume closes with an extensive resource section, including hotlines." Booklist

Includes bibliographical references

★ **American** Medical Association girl's guide to becoming a teen. Jossey-Bass 2006 128p pa $12.95

Grades: 4 5 6 7 **613**

1. Puberty 2. Adolescence 3. Girls -- Health and hygiene
ISBN 0-7879-8344-6

This "covers the physical and emotional changes that puberty brings, along with solid tips about grooming, diet, exercise, and other health issues, such as eating disorders. . . . The clear text communicates concepts clearly . . . and girls will find plenty of useful information." Booklist

Includes bibliographical references

613.2 Dietetics

Are you what you eat? Discovery Kids. DK Publishing 2015 94 p. color illustrations $16.99
Grades: 3 4 5 6 **613.2**
1. Nutrition 2. Eating customs 3. Food habits
ISBN 1465429441; 9781465429445
LC 2015295275

This children's book "uses color and fun presentation to communicate nutritional information in a fun and eye-catching way. Kids learn to see their food as more than just taste, learning things like which foods will make you sleepy, how to tell if you're hungry or full, and why our bodies need nutrition." (Publisher's note)

Can diets be harmful? edited by Christine Watkins. Greenhaven Press 2012 101 p. (At issue) (library) $34.45; (paperback) $25.45
Grades: 8 9 10 11 12 **613.2**
1. Diet 2. Eating habits 3. Diet in disease 4. Reducing diets -- Heath aspects 5. Reducing diets -- Health aspects
ISBN 0737755563; 0737755571 pa; 9780737755565 lib bdg; 9780737755572
LC 2011020813

This book, edited by Christine Watkins, is part of the At Issue series and looks at diets. The series "provides a wide range of opinions on individual social issues. Each volume focuses on a specific issue and offers a variety of perspectives—eyewitness accounts, governmental views, scientific analysis, newspaper and magazine accounts, and many more—to illuminate the issue." (Publisher's note)

Includes bibliographical references (p. 93-97) and index.

★ **Diabetes** information for teens; health tips about managing diabetes and preventing related complications, including facts about insulin, glucose control, healthy eating, physical activity, and learning to live with diabetes. edited by Angela L. Williams. 3rd edition Omnigraphics 2019 341 p. ill. hardcover $69
Grades: 7 8 9 10 11 12 **613.2**
1. Diabetes 2. Teenagers -- Health and hygiene 3. Diabetes in adolescence
ISBN 9780780817371 hardcover; 9780780812185

This book for teenagers on the topic of diabetes "examines the alarming trends in diabetes prevalence, and it provides information about positive steps that can be taken. The book provides facts about the different types of diabetes, its medical management, and the roles of nutrition and physical activity in averting its consequences. Suggestions are included for handling problematic situations, such as caring for diabetes at school." (Publisher's note)

Includes bibliographical references and index

★ **Diet** information for teens; health tips about nutrition fundamentals and eating plans including facts about vitamins, minerals, food additives, and weight-related concerns. 5th edition Omnigraphics, Inc. 2019 400 p ill. (Teen health series) (hardcover : alk. paper) $69
Grades: 8 9 10 11 12 **613.2**
1. Diet 2. Health 3. Teenagers -- Health and hygiene 4. Teenagers -- Nutrition
ISBN 0780811569; 9780780811560
LC 2011031595

This book is a "compendium of diet and nutrition" for teenagers comprising "articles on all facets of nutrition, drawn mainly from FDA documents. . . . Chapters of specialized appeal include 'Special Dietary Guidelines for Teenage Mothers' and 'Assessing School Lunches,' as well as coverage of teen snacking." (School Library Journal)

Includes bibliographical references and index

Etingoff, Kim

Building a healthy diet with the 5 food groups; Kim Etingoff. Mason Crest, an imprint of National Highlights 2015 48 p. (On my plate : building a healthy diet with the 5 food groups) (hardback) $20.95
Grades: 5 6 7 **613.2**
1. Diet 2. Health 3. Eating customs 4. Health 5. Food habits
ISBN 1422230953; 9781422230954
LC 2014010544

This book, by Kim Etingoff, "provides a thorough overview of different food groups: where they come from and what role they play in our overall health. Suggested research projects are strong and engaging. Students can do research to find out the closest place where beans, nuts, and seeds are grown." (School Library Journal)

"The sidebars and illustrations supplement the text well and the research project suggestions are especially useful for students and teachers." VOYA

Furgang, Adam

Carbonated beverages; the incredibly disgusting story. Rosen Central 2011 48p il (Incredibly disgusting food) lib bdg $26.50; pa $11.75
Grades: 4 5 6 7 **613.2**
1. Carbonated beverages
ISBN 978-1-4488-1266-0 lib bdg; 1-4488-1266-6 lib bdg; 978-1-4488-2282-9 pa; 1-4488-2282-3 pa
LC 2010023227

This presents "straightforward information about why [carbonated beverages] are unhealthy without resorting to extreme gross-out factors. The [book contains] a breakdown of the foods' components . . . insight into how they are processed, and both short- and long-term effects of consumption. . . . Readers may or may not be disgusted, but they will definitely learn a thing or two about smart eating habits." SLJ

Includes glossary and bibliographical references

Salty and sugary snacks; the incredibly disgusting story. Rosen Central 2011 48p il (Incredibly disgusting food) lib bdg $26.50; pa $11.75
Grades: 4 5 6 7 **613.2**
1. Salt 2. Sugar 3. Nutrition 4. Snack foods
ISBN 978-1-4488-1267-7 lib bdg; 1-4488-1267-4 lib bdg; 978-1-4488-2283-6 pa; 1-4488-2283-1 pa
LC 2010025751

This book describes how salty and sugary snacks put dangerous amounts of sugar and salt into our bodies and how these unnecessary calories can have terrible effects on the body.

"Readers may or may not be disgusted, but they will definitely learn a thing or two about smart eating habits." SLJ

Includes glossary and bibliographical references

Gay, Kathlyn

The **scoop** on what to eat; what you should know about diet and nutrition. Enslow Publishers 2009 112p il (Issues in focus today) lib bdg $31.93

Grades: 7 8 9 10 **613.2**

1. Nutrition

ISBN 978-0-7660-3066-4; 0-7660-3066-0

LC 2008-40382

"Bolstered with well-integrated quotes and relevant statistics, [this book offers] an excellent starting point for students seeking [a] broad, thoroughly researched [introduction] to [diet and nutrition]. . . . Illuminating case studies, enhanced with multiple viewpoints, personalize the facts and place them in boarder context." Booklist

Includes glossary and bibliographical references

Johanson, Paula

Fake foods; fried, fast, and processed: the incredibly disgusting story. Rosen Central 2011 48p il (Incredibly disgusting food) lib bdg $26.50; pa $11.75

Grades: 4 5 6 7 **613.2**

1. Nutrition 2. Natural foods 3. Convenience foods

ISBN 978-1-4488-1269-1 lib bdg; 1-4488-1269-0 lib bdg; 978-1-4488-2285-0 pa; 1-4488-2285-8 pa

LC 2010020534

This presents "straightforward information about why various junk foods are unhealthy without resorting to extreme gross-out factors. The [book contains] a breakdown of the foods' components . . . insight into how they are processed, and both short- and long-term effects of consumption. . . . Readers may or may not be disgusted, but they will definitely learn a thing or two about smart eating habits." SLJ

Includes glossary and bibliographical references

Juettner, Bonnie

Diet and disease. Lucent Books 2011 104p il (Nutrition & health) $30.85

Grades: 6 7 8 9 **613.2**

1. Nutrition 2. Preventive medicine

ISBN 978-1-4205-0269-5; 1-4205-0269-7

LC 2010035236

This "discusses the food choices that lead to the 'big four' diseases of cancer, heart disease, stroke, and type 2 diabetes and shows how good nutrition can help prevent deadly disease. . . . [This] volume is clearly written, addressing real-life concerns with solid information and perspective, and includes color photographs, notes, and [a list] of further resources." Booklist

Includes bibliographical references

Mihaly, Christy

Diet for a changing climate; food for thought. Christy Mihaly and Sue Heavenrich. Twenty-First Century Books 2019 128 p. (library bound : alk. paper) $37.32

Grades: 7 8 9 10 11 12 **613.2**

1. Diet 2. Local foods 3. Insect pests 4. Pests 5. Food habits -- Environmental aspects

ISBN 9781512481211

LC 2017043702

This book, by Christy Mihaly and Sue Heavenrich, "explore[s] the vast world of unexpected foods that may help solve the global hunger crisis. Weeds, wild plants, invasive and feral species, and bugs are all food for thought. Learn about the nutritional value of various plant and animal species . . . and discover more about climate change, sustainability, green agriculture, indigenous foods, farm-to-table restaurants, and how to be an eco-friendly producer, consumer, and chef." (Publisher's note)

Includes bibliographical references and index

Mooney, Carla

Junk food junkies. Lucent Books 2010 104p il (Nutrition & health) $30.85

Grades: 6 7 8 9 **613.2**

1. Nutrition

ISBN 978-1-4205-0271-8; 1-4205-0271-9

LC 2010016858

"A solid, detailed overview of the negative effects of a poor diet on health. Mooney livens up the dry subject matter with interesting nutrition facts, photographs, charts, tables, and anecdotes. She discusses health risks such as obesity and diabetes. The last chapter is particularly useful because it offers healthy alternatives for snacks and meals. It also explains how to read a nutrition label and tells readers what to avoid in terms of amounts of fat and calories. This book is useful for research and reports and as a teaching aid." SLJ

Includes glossary and bibliographical references

Rau, Dana Meachen, 1971-

Going vegetarian; a healthy guide to making the switch. by Dana Meachen Rau. Compass Point Books 2012 64 p. (hardcover) $33.99

Grades: 5 6 7 8 9 **613.2**

1. Nutrition 2. Vegetarianism 3. Vegetarian cooking

ISBN 0756545226; 9780756545222; 9780756545307

LC 2011040836

Author Dana Meachen Rau presents a guide to becoming a vegetarian. "Learn about the benefits and challenges of a diet that does not include red meat, poultry, or fish. Helpful tips, delicious vegetarian recipes, and how tos will make the switch so much easier." The book also offers various organic, meatless, and vegan recipes and meal ideas. (Publisher"s note)

"Whether looking to go organic, ovo-lacto vegetarian, or vegan, kids will find the information necessary to make the switch in these titles. . . . Serve these up to budding health foodies." SLJ

Includes bibliographical references (p. 62) and index

Going organic; a healthy guide to making the switch. by Dana Meachen Rau. Compass Point Books 2012 64 p. col. ill. (paperback) $8.95; (hardcover) $33.99

Grades: 6 7 8 9 **613.2**

1. Diet 2. Nutrition 3. Natural foods 4. Organic farming 5. Health

ISBN 0756545234; 0756545285; 9780756545239; 9780756545284

LC 2011040704

"[Rau] outlines the perils of factory farms and industrial food lots, both on an environmental and personal scale; distinguishes the often interrelated terms organic, sustainable, and local; offers a rundown of potentially misleading marketing terms; and even tosses in a few recipes, charts, and other helpful sidebars. Readers who find their interest piqued by this informative and concise treatment..." Booklist

Includes bibliographical references (p. 62) and index.

Waters, Rosa

My daily diet; dairy. Rosa Waters. Mason Crest, an imprint of National Highlights 2015 48 p. (hardback) $20.95

Grades: 5 6 7 **613.2**

1. Dairy products 2. Dairy products 3. Dairy products in human nutrition

ISBN 1422230961; 9781422230947; 9781422230961

LC 2014010564

This book on dairy, by Rosa Waters, "gives young readers the health information and practical tools they need to make better food decisions and eat a balanced diet that includes all five food groups. . . . [It] give[s] young readers the tools they need to choose nutritious foods and begin a life-long commitment to health." (Publisher's note)

"Created with help from a consultant who is a pediatrician and professor at Harvard Medical School, this series provides a thorough overview of different food groups: where they come from and what role they play in our overall health. Suggested research projects are strong and engaging." SLJ

Includes bibliographical references and index

Other titles in the series include:

My Daily Diet: Fruits (2014)

My Daily Diet: Grains (2014)

My Daily Diet: Proteins (2014)

My Daily Diet: Vegetables (2014)

Watson, Stephanie

Mystery meat; hot dogs, sausages, and lunch meats: the incredibly disgusting story. Rosen Pub. Group 2011 48p il (Incredibly disgusting food) lib bdg $26.50; pa $11.75

Grades: 4 5 6 7 **613.2**

1. Meat 2. Sausages 3. Nutrition 4. Frankfurters

ISBN 978-1-4488-1268-4 lib bdg; 1-4488-1268-2 lib bdg; 978-1-4488-2284-3 pa; 1-4488-2284-X pa

LC 2010013649

"The short but substantive chapters begin with a look at typical hot-dog ingredients and manufacturing practices, followed by discussions of how 'mystery meats,' including common, highly processed sandwich fillers, affect the body. A closing chapter about the components of a healthy diet widens the book into an opportunity for adults and kids to discuss general nutrition and includes useful tips on reading food labels. . . . Young readers will find plenty of browsing and report fodder in these pages." Booklist

Includes bibliographical references

613.262 Vegetarian diet

Traugh, Susan M.

Vegetarianism. Lucent Books 2011 96p il (Nutrition & health) lib bdg $30.85

Grades: 6 7 8 9 **613.262**

1. Vegetarianism

ISBN 978-1-4205-0272-5; 1-4205-0272-7

LC 2010014015

"The attractively designed title in the Nutrition & Health series will help middle-grade and high-school students make good decisions about the food they eat. Unlike some nutrition books, the tone remains mostly positive, informing readers about the negative effects of poor choices such as obesity and disease while also encouraging them to take control of their own decisions by reading nutrition labels. Although it uses the nutrition pyramid, recently put aside for the newer 'plate' model, the information remains very current, and each book highlights recent scientific studies." Booklist

Includes bibliographical references

613.4 Personal cleanliness

Ashenburg, Katherine

All the Dirt; A History of Getting Clean. by Katherine Ashenburg. Annick Press 2016 108 p. illustrations (chiefly color) $12.95

Grades: 5 6 7 8 **613.4**

1. Hygiene 2. Cleanliness

ISBN 1554517893; 1554517907; 9781554517893; 9781554517909

This book, by Katherine Ashenburg, "is a lively, informative exploration of the evolution of keeping clean. Starting with a number of myths about cleanliness, the author quickly establishes how our ideas have changed drastically over time, and how the definition of cleanliness in one part of the world may differ radically from another." (Publisher's note)

"With its lively writing and presentation, this informative book makes the history of cleanliness unexpectedly fun." Booklist

613.6 Personal safety and special topics of health

Champion, Neil

Finding food and water. Amicus 2010 32p il (Survive alive) lib bdg $28.50

Grades: 4 5 6 7 **613.6**

1. Wilderness survival

ISBN 978-1-60753-037-4 lib bdg; 1-60753-037-6 lib bdg

LC 2009030889

This offers survival tips for finding food and water in the wild, including how to know what is safe to eat or drink from land, plant, and animal sources.

This "colorful [book contains] numerous photos and illustrations that effectively break the [text] into small, readable chunks. There's lots of practical, everyday information here. . . . Brief yet gripping real-life survival stories are interspersed throughout the [book]." SLJ

Includes glossary

Finding your way. Amicus 2011 32p il (Survive alive) lib bdg $28.50

Grades: 4 5 6 7 **613.6**

1. Orienteering 2. Wilderness survival

ISBN 978-1-60753-038-1 lib bdg; 1-60753-038-4 lib bdg

LC 2009030888

"With eye-catching photographs, clear explanations, a survival skills quiz, a glossary, Web sites, and 'True Survival' stories . . . this engaging text encourages readers to figure out where they are and where they want to go." Booklist

Includes glossary

In an emergency. Amicus 2010 32p il (Survive alive) lib bdg $28.50

Grades: 4 5 6 7 **613.6**

1. Survival skills

ISBN 978-1-60753-040-4; 1-60753-040-6

LC 2010002517

This offers survival tips on what to do in emergency situations. Includes scenarios about fire, bad weather, accidents, injuries, extreme conditions, and more.'

This "colorful [book contains] numerous photos and illustrations that effectively break the [text] into small, readable chunks. There's lots of practical, everyday information here. . . . Brief yet gripping real-life survival stories are interspersed throughout the [book]." SLJ

Includes glossary

Making shelter. Amicus 2010 32p il (Survive alive) lib bdg $28.50

Grades: 4 5 6 7 **613.6**

1. Wilderness survival

ISBN 978-1-60753-041-1 lib bdg; 1-60753-041-4 lib bdg

LC 2010001378

This offers survival tips for building shelter in the wild, including using natural means in different regions such as the desert, forest, jungle, and cold areas. Also includes information on what to bring for aid when building shelters.

Long, David

Survivors; extraordinary tales from the wild and beyond. David Long, illustrated by Kerry Hyndman. Faber & Faber 2017 192 p. $19.95

Grades: 4 5 6 7 **613.6**

1. Creative nonfiction 2. Survival at sea 3. Wilderness survival

ISBN 0571316018; 9780571316014

This book, David Long, illustrated by Kerry Hyndman, presents true stories of adventure and survival. "Combining classic tales such as Ernest Shackleton's Antarctic voyage, as well as more modern exploits such as the adventurer who inspired the movie 127 Hours, these astonishing stories will be retold by young readers to all of their friends." (Publisher's note)

"Thrilling accounts of peril that are sure to draw in casual readers." (SLJ)

Long, Denise

Survivor kid; a practical guide to wilderness survival. Chicago Review Press 2011 222p il $12.95

Grades: 4 5 6 7 **613.6**

1. Wilderness survival

ISBN 978-1-56976-708-5; 1-56976-708-4

LC 2011004952

"Long offers lessons on how to stay healthy and out of trouble while awaiting rescue. Her matter-of-fact, no-nonsense tone will play well with young readers, and the clear writing style is appropriate to the content. The engaging guide covers everything from building shelters to avoiding pigs and javelinas. . . . The volume invites browsing as much as studying. . . . An excellent bibliography will lead young readers to a host of fascinating websites, and 150 clipart-style line drawings complement the text." Kirkus

Includes bibliographical references

613.7 Physical fitness

Aikman, Louise

Pilates step-by-step; [by] Louise Aikman and Matthew Harvey. Rosen Central 2011 93p il (Skills in motion) lib bdg $31.95

Grades: 5 6 7 8 **613.7**

1. Pilates method

ISBN 978-1-4488-1549-4; 1-4488-1549-5

LC 2010007510

Presents a general guide to the Pilates exercise system using a sequence of stop-action images and text instructions to illustrate some of the most common movements.

Includes bibliographical references

Bellenir, Elizabeth

Fitness Information for Teens; Health Tips About Exercise & Active Lifestyles. edited by Elizabeth Bellenir. 3rd ed. Omnigraphics 2012 xiii, 387 p.p ill. (Teen health series) (hardcover : alk. paper) $69.00

Grades: 7 8 9 10 11 12 **613.7**

1. Physical fitness 2. Teenagers -- Health and hygiene 3. Physical fitness for youth

ISBN 9780780812673; 0780812670

LC 2012024737

This book is "earmarked to provide the tools and information needed for teens to engage in a healthier lifestyle before entering adulthood. . . . Seven main sections cover information on the human body, personal fitness plans, exercise fundamentals, team activities, sports safety, obstacles to finding fitness, and resources." (Booklist)

"In this thorough, easy-to-follow single volume, seven main sections cover information on the human body, personal fitness plans, exercise fundamentals, team activities, sports safety, obstacles to finding fitness, and resources... Highly recommended." Booklist

Includes bibliographical references and index

Birkemoe, Karen

Strike a pose; the Planet Girl guide to yoga. written by Karen Birkemoe; illustrated by Heather Collett. Kids Can Press 2007 96p il (Planet girl) spiral $12.95

Grades: 5 6 7 8 **613.7**

1. Yoga 2. Girls -- Health and hygiene

ISBN 978-1-55337-004-8

"This compact book offers a well-rounded overview of Hatha yoga. Using an easy conversational tone, Birkemoe relates the general practice and specific poses to reader's lives. The simple line drawings and color illustrations partner effectively with text to explain each move." SLJ

Includes glossary

Dicker, Katie

Exercise. Amicus 2010 46p il (Healthy lifestyles) lib bdg $32.80

Grades: 7 8 9 10 **613.7**

1. Exercise 2. Physical fitness

ISBN 978-1-60753-086-2; 1-60753-086-4

LC 2009-47566

This book is "well-written and satisfyingly informative. . . . [The] magazine-like format includes numerous sidebars, color photos, and charts." SLJ

Includes glossary

Gates, Mariam

★ **This** moment is your life (and so is this one) a fun and easy guide to mindfulness, meditation, and yoga for teens and tweens. Mariam Gates ; illustrated by Libby VanderPloeg. Dial Books 2018 248 p. (hardcover) $18.99

Grades: 6 7 8 9 10 11 **613.7**

1. Hatha yoga 2. Meditation 3. Mindfulness (Psychology) 4. Hatha yoga for teenagers

ISBN 9780399186622

LC 2017043500

This guide to happiness, by Mariam Gates, illustrated by Libby VanderPloeg, is "packed with simple exercises and endearing full-color artwork, [and] provides a handy starting point for bringing mindfulness into your daily life. Chapters on meditation, yoga, and mindful breathing explain the benefits of these practices, and you are free to pick and choose what to try. There are quick exercises throughout, and a more extensive tool kit at the end of each chapter." (Publisher's note)

Jennings, Madeleine

Tai chi step-by-step; [by] Madeleine Jennings and James Drewe. Rosen Central 2011 93p il (Skills in motion) lib bdg $31.95

Grades: 5 6 7 8 **613.7**

1. Tai chi

ISBN 978-1-4488-1551-7; 1-4488-1551-7

LC 2010008411

This book introduces both basic and higher level techniques of tai chi, with step-by-step instructions, illustrated by stop-motion sequential photography.

Includes bibliographical references

Kuskowski, Alex

Cool relaxing; healthy & fun ways to chill out! Alex Kuskowski. ABDO Pub. Co. 2012 32 p. col. ill. (Cool health and fitness) (library) $28.50

Grades: 4 5 6 **613.7**

1. Creative activities 2. Rest 3. Relaxation

ISBN 1617834289; 9781617834288

LC 2012010345

This nonfiction children's book by Alex Kuskowski presents a "hodgepodge of activities and techniques to achieve zen calm. The suggestions in this 'Cool Health and Fitness' title are all over the place--cooking, running, reading, baths, even cleaning--but that's the unspoken truth: whatever pleasantly distracts you does the trick. Eight activities are given step-by-step attention, including yoga, stretching, making a lavender pillow, and meditation." (Booklist)

Mason, Paul, 1967-

Improving endurance. PowerKids Press 2011 32p il (Training for sports) lib bdg $25.25

Grades: 5 6 7 8 **613.7**

1. Sports 2. Exercise

ISBN 978-1-4488-3300-9; 1-4488-3300-0

LC 2010024356

This offers "detailed tips on improving . . . endurance. All-around athletes will love this and so will kids who just want to work on getting fit." Booklist

Improving flexibility. PowerKids Press 2011 32p il (Training for sports) lib bdg $25.25

Grades: 5 6 7 8 **613.7**

1. Sports 2. Exercise

ISBN 978-1-4488-3299-6; 1-4488-3299-3

LC 2010024359

This offers tips on improving flexibility for sports.

"All-around athletes will love this and so will kids who just want to work on getting fit." Booklist

Improving speed. PowerKids Press 2011 32p il (Training for sports) lib bdg $25.25

Grades: 5 6 7 8 **613.7**

1. Speed 2. Sports 3. Exercise

ISBN 978-1-4488-3302-3; 1-4488-3302-3

LC 2010024354

This offers "detailed tips on improving speed. . . . All-around athletes will love this and so will kids who just want to work on getting fit." Booklist

Improving strength & power. PowerKids Press 2011 32p il (Training for sports) lib bdg $25.25

Grades: 5 6 7 8 **613.7**

1. Exercise 2. Physical fitness

ISBN 978-1-4488-3301-6; 1-4488-3301-6

LC 2010024425

This offers tips on improving strength and power for sports.

"All-around athletes will love this and so will kids who just want to work on getting fit." Booklist

Purperhart, Helen

Yoga exercises for teens; developing a calmer mind and a stronger body. Hunter House Publishers 2008 160p il pa $14.95

Grades: 7 8 9 10 **613.7**

1. Yoga 2. Physical fitness 3. Teenagers -- Health and hygiene

ISBN 978-0-8979-3503-6; 0-8979-3503-9

LC 2008-24262

This book about yoga "includes the eight yoga rules for life, the five precepts, and the five yoga abstinences." Publisher's note

Includes bibliographical references

Rissman, Rebecca

Yoga for your mind and body; a teenage practice for a healthy, balanced life. by Rebecca Rissman. Capstone Press 2015 208 p. color illustrations (library binding : alk. paper) $14.95

Grades: 8 9 10 11 **613.7**

1. Yoga 2. Hatha yoga 3. Hatha yoga for teenagers 4. Teenage girls -- Mental health 5. Teenage girls -- Health and hygiene

ISBN 9781630790134

LC 2014048583

With this book, by Rebecca Rissman, "release your inner guru and unleash yoga's healing power. Relieve stress. Focus your mind. Build strength. Clear step-by-step instructions and photos guide you through more than 80 specific yoga poses. Study the perfect yoga poses and unlock the key to a healthy, fit, and calmer you." (Publisher's note)

"Newbies and experienced yogis alike will benefit from this easy-to-follow guide." Booklist

Includes bibliographical references and index

613.8 Substance abuse (Drug abuse)

Cashin, John

The **heroin** crisis; John Cashin. Mason Crest 2018 64 p. illustrations (chiefly color) (Opioids and opiates: the silent epidemic) (library binding) $23.95

Grades: 7 8 9 10 11 12 **613.8**

1. Heroin 2. Narcotics 3. Heroin abuse

ISBN 9781422279656; 9781422238257; 1422238253

LC 2017301511

This book in the Opioids and Opiates: The Silent Epidemic series, by John Cashin, "examines the facts about the ongoing heroin crisis. It provides information about the drug cartels and their role in supplying this deadly drug, how heroin is distributed in American communities large and small, and the dangerous effects of the drug on its users." (Publisher's note)

Includes bibliographical references (page 59-61) and index

★ **Drug** information for teens; health tips about the physical and mental effects of substance abuse. 4th edition Omnigraphics 2016 339 p illustrations hardcover $69

Grades: 7 8 9 10 11 12 **613.8**

1. Drugs 2. Drug abuse 3. Teenagers -- Drug use

ISBN 9780780813588; 0780813588

LC 2015038887

Provides basic consumer health information for teens on drug use, abuse, and addiction, along with facts about related health concerns, treatment, and recovery.

Includes bibliographical references and index

Redmond, Jodee

★ The **dangers** of drug abuse; Jodee Redmond. Mason Crest 2018 64 p. illustrations (chiefly color) (Opioids and opiates: the silent epidemic) (library binding) $23.95

Grades: 7 8 9 10 11 12 **613.8**

1. Heroin 2. Narcotics 3. Drug abuse 4. Heroin abuse

ISBN 9781422238240; 9781422279649; 1422238245

LC 2017301510

This book in the Opioids and Opiates: The Silent Epidemic series, by Jodee Redmond, "provides the facts about the current opioid epidemic that is sweeping the United States today. It examines the most dangerous drugs including two new deadly new opioids that are on the street. The book also focuses on the problems and issues that result from drug abuse and addiction." (Publisher's note)

"A good starting point for research and substance-abuse units." Booklist

Includes bibliographical references (page 59-61) and index

613.81 Alcohol

★ **Alcohol** information for teens; health tips about alcohol use, abuse & dependence including facts about alcohol's effects on mental and physical health, the consequences of underage drinking & understanding alcoholic family members. edited by Karen Bellenir. 3rd ed. Omnigraphics, Inc. 2013 371 p. ill (Teen health series) (hardcover) $69

Grades: 7 8 9 10 11 12 **613.81**

1. Alcoholism 2. Teenagers -- Alcohol use 3. Drinking of alcoholic beverages

ISBN 0780813138; 9780780813137

LC 2013000216

This book "provides updated information about the use and misuse of alcohol. It describes ways alcohol can affect mental and physical health. It discusses the special vulnerabilities of the teen brain and the changes in brain functioning that lead to dependency. A section on treatment and recovery discusses achieving and maintaining sobriety, and a section on alcohol abuse in the family addresses the special concerns of teens who live with an alcoholic relative." (Publisher's note)

Includes bibliographical references and index

613.85 Tobacco

Tobacco Information for Teens; edited by Keith Jones. 3rd edition Omnigraphics Inc 2016 400 p. $69

Grades: 8 9 10 11 12 **613.85**

1. Tobacco 2. Tobacco habit

ISBN 0780813871; 9780780813878

This book "offers updated information about the health consequences associated with smoking and other forms of tobacco use. It explains some of the cultural influences that can make tobacco use seem attractive and how teen curiosity can lead to nicotine-related problems. The various methods by which nicotine is consumed, including different types of cigarettes, cigars, hookah pipes, smokeless products, and even secondhand smoke, are explained. A section on cancers associated with tobacco describes the organs most commonly affected. A section on other health concerns related to tobacco use discusses some of the most common smoking-related diseases." (Publisher's note)

613.9 Birth control, reproductive technology, sex hygiene, sexual techniques

Bell, Ruth

★ **Changing** bodies, changing lives; a book for teens on sex and relationships. [by] Ruth Bell and other co-authors of Our bodies, ourselves and Ourselves and our children, together with members of the Teen Book Project. expanded 3rd ed; Times Bks. 1998 411p il pa $24.95

Grades: 7 8 9 10 11 12 **613.9**

1. Sex education

ISBN 0-8129-2990-X

LC 97-29249

First published 1980

This is a "book on sex, physical and emotional health, and personal relationships. . . . Readers . . . will find emotional support as well as specific answers to most of their questions in this nonjudgmental resource." Booklist

Cole, Joanna

Asking about sex & growing up; a question-and-answer book for kids. illustrated by Bill Thomas. rev ed.; Collins 2009 89p il $15.99; pa $6.99

Grades: 4 5 6 **613.9**

1. Sex education

ISBN 978-0-06-142987-3; 0-06-142987-2; 978-0-06-142986-6 pa; 0-06-142986-4 pa

LC 2008022710

First published 1988 by Morrow Junior Books

This book "offers straightforward information about topics such as physical changes in puberty, masturbation, birth control, pregnancy, homosexuality, and STDs. . . . Libraries . . . should consider adding it as a source of basic information for curious preteens." SLJ

Harris, Robie H., 1940-

★ **It's** perfectly normal; changing bodies, growing up, sex and sexual health. Robie H. Harris ; illustrated by Michael Emberley. 20th anniversary edition Candlewick Press 2014 98 p. color illustrations (reinforced) $22.99; (pbk) $12.99

Grades: 4 5 6 7 **613.9**

1. Puberty 2. Sex education

ISBN 0763668710; 0763668729; 9780763668716; 9780763668723

This provides information about sex, puberty, family relationships and reproduction, sexual decision-making and birth control, abortion laws, sexual abuse, sexual health, sexually transmitted diseases, and internet safety.

"This edition has been revised for a new generation, including updates in scientific and medical information about reproduction, birth control, abortion, sexual abuse, and sexually transmitted diseases." SLJ

Murray, Craig

Sexpectations; Sex Stuff Straight Up. Allen & Unwin 2012 111 p. $19.95

Grades: 7 8 9 10 11 12 **613.9**

1. Sex education 2. Sexual hygiene 3. Teenagers -- Sexual behavior

ISBN 1741751438; 9781741751437

Includes bibliographical references.

This book, by Craig Murray and Leissa Pitts, offers a "teenage-friendly sex education and sexual health guide book, for both boys and girls, in one . . . volume. Designed to help teens make healthy, positive choices, . . . It takes teens through knowing themselves and their bodies, keeping safe, protecting themselves, thinking through pregnancy, knowing about relationships, and tapping into their personal power to make positive choices." (Publisher's note)

Pardes, Bronwen

Doing it right; making smart, safe, and satisfying choices about sex. by Bronwen Pardes. Simon Pulse 2013 146 p. il $17.99

Grades: 7 8 9 10 11 12 **613.9**

1. Sex education

ISBN 1442483709; 9781442483705

LC 2006-928450

This book, by Bronwen Pardes, presents sex education for teenagers. "Chapters, which often use a question-and-answer format based on teens' actual queries, delve into sexual anatomy, questions to consider before sex, contraception, safe-sex practices, homosexuality, masturbation, and sexual violence. Throughout, Pardes avoids a heterosexual bias, and her discussion of sexual activity is explicit and inclusive." (Publisher's note)

The author "tackles the tough questions about sexual orientation, size, abuse, orgasm, pregnancy, STDs, and masturbation among others." Voice Youth Advocates

Includes bibliographical references

★ **Sexual** health information for teens; health tips about sexual development, reproduction, contraception, and sexually transmitted infections. 5th edition Omnigraphics 2018 355 p hardcover $69

Grades: 7 8 9 10 11 12 **613.9**

1. Sex education 2. Teenagers -- Health and hygiene

ISBN 9780780816442 hardcover; 9780780813854

LC 2018029168

Provides basic consumer health information for teens about puberty, development, and sexuality, maintaining sexual health, and preventing pregnancy and sexually transmitted diseases.

Includes bibliographical references and index

614 Forensic medicine; incidence of injuries, wounds, disease; public preventive medicine

Spilsbury, Richard

Bones speak! solving crimes from the past. Enslow Publishers 2009 48p il (Solve that crime!) lib bdg $23.93

Grades: 5 6 7 8 **614**

1. Forensic sciences 2. Forensic anthropology

ISBN 978-0-7660-3377-1 lib bdg; 0-7660-3377-5 lib bdg

LC 2008-33309

This "title boasts in-depth information, sidebars detailing events of true crime, and activities that will increase understanding. . . . Photographs are colorful, well-captioned, and related to the text." SLJ

Includes glossary and bibliographical references

Stefoff, Rebecca

Forensics and medicine. Marshall Cavendish Benchmark 2011 95p il (Forensic science investigated) $23.95

Grades: 6 7 8 9 **614**

1. Forensic sciences 2. Medical jurisprudence

ISBN 978-0-7614-4143-4; 0-7614-4143-3

LC 2010010526

"Numerous color photos and digital illustrations . . . add further interest." Booklist

Includes bibliographical references

Walker, Sally M.

★ **Written** in bone; buried lives of Jamestown and Colonial Maryland. Carolrhoda Books 2009 144p il map $22.95

Grades: 6 7 8 9 10 **614**

1. Forensic sciences 2. Maryland -- History 3. Jamestown (Va.) -- History 4. Excavations (Archeology) -- United States 5. United States -- History -- 1600-1775, Colonial period

ISBN 978-0-8225-7135-3; 0-8225-7135-8

LC 2007-10768

"Walker takes readers on an archaeological investigation of human and material remains from 17th- and 18th-century Jamestown and colonial Maryland, while addressing relevant topics in forensic anthropology, history, and archaeology. . . . The text succinctly explains complex forensic concepts. . . . Captioned, full-color photographs of skeletal, dental, and artifactual remains shed light on colonial life. Historical documents, illustrated maps, and anatomical drawings complement images of various specialists at work in the field. Photographs of reenactors performing period tasks . . . provide insight into the daily life of the recovered individuals." SLJ

Includes bibliographical references

614.4 Incidence of and public measures to prevent disease

Barnard, Bryn

★ **Outbreak**; plagues that changed history. written and illustrated by Bryn Barnard. Crown Publishers 2005 47p il maps $17.95

Grades: 5 6 7 8 **614.4**

1. Diseases 2. Epidemics 3. Diseases and history 4. Communicable diseases

ISBN 0-375-82986-5

LC 2005-15086

This "assessment of the historical role of diseases examines plague, smallpox, yellow fever, cholera, tuberculosis, and influenza. [Glossary.] Grades six to nine." (Bull Cent Child Books)

This "volume explores specific plagues that have impacted society. Barnard begins with an introduction to microbes and the positive and negative effects that they can have on humans. A history of the study of microorganisms follows. The bulk of the book then focuses on specific plagues with a chapter devoted to each, including the Black Death, smallpox, yellow fever, cholera, tuberculosis, and influenza. The final chapter discusses the modern struggle against disease. . . . The evocative paintings help to clarify the text. Browsers and report writers alike will find this to be a fascinating and informative resource." SLJ

Brownlee, Christen

Cute, furry, and deadly; diseases you can catch from your pet! [by] Christen Brownlee. Franklin Watts 2008 64p il map (24/7, science behind the scenes) lib bdg $26

Grades: 6 7 8 9 10 **614.4**

1. Communicable diseases 2. Pets -- Health and hygiene

ISBN 0-531-12072-4 lib bdg; 978-0-531-12072-9 lib bdg

LC 2006-21230

Hopefully, the worst thing your pet ever comes home with is bad breath. But some furry friends can carry nasty germs, and that's where zoonotic disease researchers come in and investigate and stop animal diseases before they get you!

"This series is a great pick for reluctant readers, busy teens, and anyone looking for a fun (if somewhat frightening) nonfiction read." Voice Youth Advocates

Includes glossary and bibliographical references

Gleason, Carrie

Feasting bedbugs, mites, and ticks. Crabtree Pub. Co. 2010 32p il (Creepy crawlies) lib bdg $26.60; pa $8.95

Grades: 4 5 6 7 **614.4**

1. Mites 2. Ticks 3. Bedbugs

ISBN 978-0-7787-2500-8 lib bdg; 0-7787-2500-6 lib bdg; 978-0-7787-2507-7 pa; 0-7787-2507-3 pa

LC 2010009552

"The informational yet easy-to-read text in double-page spreads explains the classification, anatomy, life cycles, and ideal feeding and living conditions for mites, ticks, and bedbugs as well as the differences among them. . . . Children will be most interested in the long history, myths, and lore associated with these pests as well as the eye-catching layout, with numerous color photographs. . . . [This is an] equally repulsive and fascinating book." Booklist

Includes glossary and bibliographical references

Goldsmith, Connie

Pandemic; how climate, the environment, and superbugs increase the risk. by Connie Goldsmith. Twenty-First Century Books, a division of Lerner Publishing Group, Inc. 2018 136 p. (lb : alk. paper) $42.65

Grades: 5 6 7 8 9 **614.4**

1. Epidemics 2. Communicable diseases 3. Human influence on nature 4. Nature -- Effect of human beings on 5. Communicable diseases -- Climatic factors

ISBN 9781512452150

LC 2017043693

In this book, by Connie Goldsmith, "learn about factors that contribute to the spread of disease by examining past pandemics and epidemics. Examine case studies of potential pandemic diseases, and discover how scientists strive to contain and control the spread of disease both locally and globally. See how human activities such as global air travel and the disruption of animal habitats contribute to the risk of a new pandemic." (Publisher's note)

Includes bibliographical references and index

Hand, Carol

Epidemiology; the fight against ebola & other diseases. Carol Hand. Abdo Pub. 2015 112 p. color ill., color map (ebook) $35.64; $35.64

Grades: 6 7 8 9 **614.4**

1. Epidemics 2. Epidemiology 3. Communicable diseases

ISBN 9781629691299; 9781624035593

LC 2014943869

In this book in the History of Science series, by Carol Hand, "vivid text details how early studies of the spread of disease led to vaccines and medications that can halt pandemics. It also puts a spotlight on the brilliant scientists who made these advances possible. A case study on the current Ebola outbreak is also included."(Publisher's note)

"Complex scientific principles are made accessible through meaningful, straightforward language, and in-text citations and source notes provide greater credibility and authority." SLJ

Includes bibliographical references and index.

Miller, Debra A.

Pandemics; [by] Debra A. Miller. Lucent Books 2006 un (Hot topics) $32.45

Grades: 7 8 9 10 **614.4**

1. Epidemics 2. Communicable diseases

ISBN 9781420502589; 1-59018-965-5; 978-1-59018-965-8

LC 2006007057

"This comprehensive and well-organized book covers potential threats; the control and prevention of pandemics; and factors that may facilitate the outbreak and transmission of diseases, such as pollution, poverty, overpopulation, and globalization. Teens will appreciate the interesting sidebars, quotations, diagrams, and full-color photos that are integrated throughout the text and will find the annotated lists of organizations and further-reading suggestions useful." SLJ

Includes bibliographical references

Tilden, Thomasine E. Lewis

Help! What's eating my flesh? runaway staph and strep infections! [by] Thomasine E. Lewis Tilden. Franklin Watts 2008 64p il map (24/7, science behind the scenes) lib bdg $26

Grades: 6 7 8 9 10 **614.4**

1. Communicable diseases

ISBN 0-531-12073-2; 978-0-531-12073-6

LC 2006-5871

"A splashy tabloid-style presentation, including gross and disgusting photographs, will attract curious young teens who will be unable to resist. . . . [This] book also includes career information, resources (including Web sites and books), a historical section with key dates, and an author's note." Voice Youth Advoctaes

Includes glossary and bibliographical references

614.5 Incidence of and public measures to prevent specific diseases and kinds of diseases

Cunningham, Kevin

Flu. Morgan Reynolds Pub. 2009 176p il (Diseases in history) lib bdg $28.95

Grades: 8 9 10 11 12 **614.5**
1. Influenza
ISBN 978-1-59935-105-6; 1-59935-105-6
LC 2008-51620

"This informative title reveals the continued concerns surrounding this killer disease and the possibility of a future pandemic. The text, though somewhat scientific, will help students to better understand the history of the virus, how it has mutated and jumped from animals to humans, and new concerns regarding more dangerous forms. . . . Color and black-and-white archival photos, as well as reproduction of a three-dimensional rendering of the flu virus, enhance the text." SLJ

Includes glossary and bibliographical references

Malaria. Morgan Reynolds Pub. 2009 144p il (Diseases in history) lib bdg $28.95
Grades: 8 9 10 11 12 **614.5**
1. Malaria
ISBN 978-1-59935-103-2; 1-59935-103-X
LC 2008-51619

"Provides fascinating information about an ongoing scourge. . . . Here readers have an accessible, well presented account of the continuing struggle against a deadly disease." Voice Youth Advocates

Includes glossary and bibliographical references

Plague. Morgan Reynolds Pub. 2009 144p il (Diseases in history) lib bdg $28.95
Grades: 8 9 10 11 12 **614.5**
1. Plague
ISBN 978-1-59935-102-5; 1-59935-102-1
LC 2008-51618

"Chapters based upon plagues include one on Justinian's Plague, the Black Death, The Dreadful Pestilence, the Great Plague of London, and the current H1N1 swine flu pandemic. This detailed overview . . . will appeal to more advanced students. The research is thorough and the writing is insightful, thought provoking, and accessible." Voice Youth Advocates

Includes glossary and bibliographical references

Currie, Stephen

★ The **black** death; by Stephen Currie. ReferencePoint Press, Inc. 2013 94 p. (Understanding world history series) (hardcover) $27.95
Grades: 7 8 9 10 **614.5**
1. Plague -- History 2. Black Death -- History
ISBN 1601524803; 9781601524805
LC 2012021114

This book on the Black Death by Stephen Currie is part of the "Understanding World History" series. "Readers learn the surprising benefits of depopulation and how technology, medicine, and even religion changed as a result of this tragic epidemic. . . . While it briefly covers the beginnings of the plague in Asia and the many people killed there, the bulk of the book is about the impact of the disease on Europe." (School Library Journal)

Includes bibliographical references and index.

Currie-McGhee, L. K.

Sexually transmitted diseases; [by] Leanne Currie-McGhee. ReferencePoint Press 2009 104p il map (Compact research. Diseases and disorders) lib bdg $25.95
Grades: 8 9 10 **614.5**
1. Sexually transmitted diseases
ISBN 978-1-60152-045-6; 1-60152-045-X
LC 2008-12554

Presents information on sexually transmitted diseases through essays, quotations, statistics, and suggestions for further research.

"Sobering, enlightening, and up-to-date, this title . . . uses an effective blend of primary sources, diagrams, and thorough text to bring the latest facts about STDs to young readers. . . . A time line and lists of key advocacy groups and further reading close this valuable resource for teens." Booklist

Includes bibliographical references

Hartman, Ashley Strehle

Teens and STDs; Ashley Strehle Hartman. ReferencePoint Press, Inc. 2019 80 p. (hardcover : alk. paper) $29.95
Grades: 7 8 9 10 11 12 **614.5**
1. Teenagers -- Health and hygiene 2. Sexually transmitted diseases -- Prevention 3. Sexual health 4. Sexually transmitted diseases -- Treatment
ISBN 9781682825136
LC 2018011553

"Many teens are hesitant to talk about sexually transmitted diseases (STDs), but it is important to discuss these health issues openly in order to treat them and improve the lives of people affected by them. . . . [In this book, author Ashley Strehle Hartman] explores the causes of this health issue, how it affects teens, and the ways in which teens can protect themselves and get help." (Publisher's note)

"Hartman delivers a matter-of-fact, if somewhat clinical, appraisal of STDs and teen sexual health in this entry in the Teen Health and Safety series." (Booklist)

Includes bibliographical references and index

Jarrow, Gail

Bubonic panic; when plague invaded America. Gail Jarrow. Calkins Creek 2016 200 p. illustrations (some color) (hardcover) $18.95
Grades: 5 6 7 8 9 **614.5**
1. Plague 2. Public health -- United States
ISBN 9781620917381; 9781629795621
LC 2015953543

This book, by Gail Jarrow, "tells the true story of America's first plague epidemic—the public health doctors who desperately fought to end it, the political leaders who tried to keep it hidden, and the brave scientists who uncovered the plague's secrets. Jarrow brings the history of a medical mystery to life in vivid and exciting detail for young readers. This title includes photographs and drawings, a glossary, a timeline, further resources, an author's note, and source notes." (Publisher's note)

"In her third book in this trilogy (Red Madness; Fatal Fever), Jarrow focuses on the nineteenth century, when the bubonic plague reared its ugly head in places like Hong Kong, Honolulu, and San Francisco. The thorough, fascinating treatment is complemented by a handsome design that includes numerous primary source artifacts. An exemplary contribution to the history of science and medicine." Horn Book

Includes bibliographical references (p. 188-192) and index.

Fatal fever; tracking down Typhoid Mary. Gail Jarrow. Calkins Creek 2015 192 p. illustrations (some color) $16.95
Grades: 6 7 8 9 10 **614.5**
1. Typhoid fever
ISBN 1620915979; 9781620915974
LC 2014948476

This children's book by Gail Jarrow "tells the true story of [Typhoid Mary,] the woman who unwittingly spread deadly bacteria, the epidemiologist who discovered her trail of infection, and the health department that decided her fate. This gripping story follows this tragic disease as it shatters lives from the early twentieth century to today." (Publisher's note)

"Jarrow has written a suspenseful medical mystery for inquisitive readers. Timeline, glossary, author's note, source notes, bibliography, and index are included among the extensive back matter." Horn Book

Jurmain, Suzanne

★ The **secret** of the yellow death; a true story of medical sleuthing. Houghton Mifflin Books for Children 2009 104p il $19

Grades: 6 7 8 9 10 **614.5**

1. Epidemics 2. Physicians 3. Yellow fever 4. Army officers 5. Cuba -- History 6. Microbiologists 7. Writers on medicine 8. Medicine -- Research

ISBN 978-0-618-96581-6; 0-618-96581-5

LC 2009-22499

"This medical mystery is extremely interesting, easy to read, and well illustrated with period photos." SLJ

Includes glossary and bibliographical references

Koch, Falynn

Plagues; the microscopic battlefield. Falynn Christine Koch. First Second 2017 128 p. chiefly color illustrations (Science comics) (hardback) $19.99

Grades: 4 5 6 7 8 **614.5**

1. Plague 2. Epidemics 3. Microorganisms

ISBN 9781626727533; 9781626727526

LC 2016945566

In this book in the Science Comics series, by Falynn Christine Koch, "we get to know the critters behind history's worst diseases. We delve into the biology and mechanisms of infections, diseases, and immunity, and also the incredible effect that technology and medical science have had on humanity's ability to contain and treat disease." (Publisher's note)

"A reassuring picture of ever more stout defenses ranged against a scary, invisible world." Kirkus

Includes bibliographical references (page 122)

Kupperberg, Paul

The **influenza** pandemic of 1918-1919. Chelsea House 2008 120p il map (Great historic disasters) $35

Grades: 7 8 9 10 **614.5**

1. Epidemics 2. Influenza

ISBN 978-0-7910-9640-6; 0-7910-9640-8

This is "well written and informative. . . . The inclusion of black-and-white and color photographs and drawings and sidebars help to make [this book] first-rate for reports and general browsing." SLJ

Marrin, Albert, 1936-

Very, very, very dreadful; the influenza pandemic of 1918. Albert Marrin. Alfred A. Knopf 2018 198 p. illustrations, maps (library binding) $24.99

Grades: 7 8 9 10 11 12 **614.5**

1. Influenza 2. Epidemics -- History 3. Influenza -- History 4. Influenza Epidemic, 1918-1919 5. Diseases 6. Epidemics

ISBN 1101931469; 1101931477; 9781101931462; 9781101931486; 9781101931479

This book, by Albert Marrin, focuses on the 1918 flu pandemic. "Of all diseases, the 1918 flu was by far the worst that has ever afflicted humankind. . . [From] 1918-1919, about 500 million people . . . came down with influenza. The exact total of lives lost will never be known, but the best estimate is between 50 and 100 million. . . . Marrin examines the history, science, and impact of this great scourge--and the possibility for another worldwide pandemic today." (Publisher's note)

"Fusing hard science and 'jump-rope rhymes,' first-person accounts and crystalline prose, cold reason and breathtaking sensitivity, Marrin crafts an impeccably researched, masterfully told, and downright infectious account—complete with lurid black-and-white photos throughout." Booklist

Includes bibliographic notes, references (pages 183-190) and index.

Murphy, Jim

★ An **American** plague; the true and terrifying story of the yellow fever epidemic of 1793. Clarion Bks. 2003 165p il map $18

Grades: 5 6 7 8 **614.5**

1. Yellow fever 2. Philadelphia (Pa.) -- History

ISBN 0-395-77608-2

LC 2002-151355

Boston Globe-Horn Book Award: Nonfiction (2004)

National Book Award Finalist: Young People's Literature (2003)

"Murphy culls from a number of historical records the story of the yellow fever epidemic that swept Philadelphia in 1793, skillfully drawing out from these sources the fear and drama of the time and making them immediate to modern readers. . . . Thoroughly documented, with an annotated source list, the work is both rigorous and inviting." Horn Book

Person, Stephen

Bubonic plague; the Black Death! Bearport Pub. 2010 32p il map (Nightmare plagues) lib bdg $25.27

Grades: 4 5 6 7 **614.5**

1. Plague

ISBN 978-1-936088-03-4; 1-936088-03-7

This describes what causes bubonic plague and how it affects the body.

"The writing is accessible and interspersed with interesting photographs and fact boxes. . . . [The book relies] on an honest discussion of [bubonic plague and is an] . . . effective, easily navigated [introduction]." SLJ

Includes glossary and bibliographical references

Malaria; super killer! Bearport Pub. 2011 32p il map (Nightmare plagues) lib bdg $25.27

Grades: 4 5 6 7 **614.5**

1. Malaria

ISBN 978-1-936088-07-2 lib bdg; 1-936088-07-X lib bdg

LC 2010012018

Discover what causes malaria and how it affects the body.

"The writing is accessible and interspersed with interesting photographs and fact boxes. . . . [The book relies] on an honest discussion of [malaria and is an] . . . effective, easily navigated [introduction]." SLJ

Includes glossary and bibliographical references

Peters, Stephanie True

Smallpox in the new world. Benchmark Books 2004 69p il (Epidemic!) lib bdg $32.79

Grades: 4 5 6 7 8 **614.5**

1. Smallpox

ISBN 0-7614-1637-4; 9780761416371

LC 2003-2646

Describes the history of smallpox in the Americas, covering the arrival of the Spanish as carriers, its spread throughout the New World, the development of the smallpox vaccine, the elimination of the disease, and its potential use as a terrorist weapon.

Includes glossary and bibliographical references

Reingold, Adam

Smallpox; is it over? Bearport Pub. 2010 32p il map (Nightmare plagues) lib bdg $25.27

Grades: 4 5 6 7 **614.5**

1. Smallpox

ISBN 978-1-936088-02-7; 1-936088-02-9

LC 2010009371

Discover what causes smallpox and how it affects the body.

"The writing is accessible and interspersed with interesting photographs and fact boxes. . . . [The book relies] on an honest discussion of [smallpox and is an] . . . effective, easily navigated [introduction]." SLJ

Includes glossary and bibliographical references

Rudolph, Jessica

The **flu** of 1918; millions dead worldwide! Bearport Pub. 2011 32p il map (Nightmare plagues) lib bdg $25.27

Grades: 4 5 6 7 **614.5**

1. Influenza

ISBN 978-1-936088-05-8 lib bdg; 1-936088-05-3 lib bdg

LC 2010004684

Discover what caused the Influenza epidemic of 1918 and how it affected the body.

"The writing is accessible and interspersed with interesting photographs and fact boxes. . . . [The book relies] on an honest discussion of [Influenza epidemic of 1918 and is an] . . . effective, easily navigated [introduction]." SLJ

Includes glossary and bibliographical references

615 Pharmacology and therapeutics

Allman, Toney

Vaccine research. ReferencePoint Press 2010 96p il (Inside science) lib bdg $26.95

Grades: 7 8 9 10 **615**

1. Vaccination 2. Medicine -- Research

ISBN 978-1-60152-131-6; 1-60152-131-6

LC 2010-20635

This book "offers the necessary information for stellar reports. Politics, debates, and ethical concerns are briefly and fairly mentioned, but the . . . [book concentrates] on consistent, documented, and well-balanced scientific coverage. The human stories sprinkled throughout will help kids identify with both scientists and patients." SLJ

Includes bibliographical references

Bjornlund, Lydia

Oxycodone; by Lydia Bjornlund. ReferencePoint Press 2012 96 p. (Compact research series)

Grades: 7 8 9 10 11 12 **615**

1. Narcotics 2. Analgesics 3. Drug abuse 4. Drug education 5. Drugs -- Law and legislation -- United States 6. Oxycodone 7. Oxycodone abuse

ISBN 1601521618; 9781601521613

LC 2011020202

This book on oxycodone is a part of the Compact Research: Drugs series and "focus[es] on three types of information: "objective single-author narratives, opinion-based primary source quotations, and facts and statistics." What this translates to on the page is an overview of the topic and an in-depth chapter-by chapter discussion of the points raised in the overview." Lydia Bjornlund "discuss[es] . . . the health dangers of the drug and its legitimacy in medical use, government regulation of the drug, and how oxycodone abuse can be prevented." (Booklist)

Includes bibliographical references and index

Hyde, Natalie

What is germ theory? Crabtree Pub. Co. 2011 64p il (Shaping modern science) lib bdg $30.60; pa $10.95

Grades: 5 6 7 8 **615**

1. Chemists 2. Germ theory of disease 3. Microbiologists 4. Writers on science

ISBN 978-0-7787-7201-9 lib bdg; 0-7787-7201-9 lib bdg; 978-0-7787-7208-8 pa; 0-7787-7208-X pa

LC 2010052631

This title is "not only written and organized well, but [it is] also gorgeous in design. Full-color photographs and illustrations are set over colorful backgrounds that add depth but not distraction. [The title] includes thought-provoking quotes from famous authors and scientists and some eyebrow-raising 'Quick Facts' throughout." SLJ

Includes glossary and bibliographical references

Kidd, J. S.

Potent natural medicines; Mother Nature's pharmacy. [by] J.S. Kidd and Renee A. Kidd. rev ed.; Chelsea House 2006 212p il (Science and society) lib bdg $35

Grades: 7 8 9 10 **615**

1. Pharmacology 2. Medical botany

ISBN 9781438122946; 0-8160-5607-2

LC 2005041741

This introduces "plants' medicinal properties, pioneers who hunted for sources of and applications for botanical treatments, and the ways phytochemical nutrients prevent disease. . . . [Also included] are chapters about recent research, including investigation into animal sources for medicine; the impact of field research on native peoples; and the federal regulation of herb and plant supplements. . . . This [is] a good choice to support research and debate projects." Booklist

Includes bibliographical references

Klosterman, Lorrie

The **facts** about depressants; [by] Lorrie Klosterman. Marshall Cavendish Benchmark 2005 96p il (Drugs) lib bdg $42.79; pa $6.99

Grades: 7 8 9 10 **615**

1. Drug abuse 2. Tranquilizing drugs

ISBN 0-7614-1976-4 lib bdg; 0-7614-1976-4 lib bdg; 978-0-7614-3594-5 pa; 0-7614-3594-8 pa

LC 2005001729

This "useful [volume is] attractively packaged and will be of interest to report writers and general readers. [Text] and photos do an excellent job of showing how [this] group of drugs affects the body." SLJ

Includes glossary and bibliographical references

Knowles, Jo

Over -the-counter drugs. Chelsea House 2008 106p il (Junior drug awareness) lib bdg $30

Grades: 6 7 8 9 **615**

1. Drug abuse 2. Nonprescription drugs

ISBN 978-0-7910-9759-5 lib bdg; 0-7910-9759-5 lib bdg; 9781438118253

LC 2007-43665

This describes the uses and abuses of such over-the-counter drugs as cough medicines, diet pills, sleep aids, bodybuilding supplements, motion sickness medications, and caffeine

"The content is reliable and comprehensive." Horn Book Guide

Includes glossary and bibliographical references

Koellhoffer, Tara

Prozac and other antidepressants. Chelsea House 2008 120p il (Junior drug awareness) lib bdg $30

Grades: 6 7 8 9 **615**

1. Antidepressants 2. Depression (Psychology)

ISBN 978-0-7910-9747-2 lib bdg; 0-7910-9747-1 lib bdg; 9781438118260

LC 2007-43663

This "examines antidepressant therapies available today and explains how they affect the bodies and minds of people who are treated with them." Publisher's note

Includes glossary and bibliographical references

Peterson, Judy Monroe

Frequently asked questions about antidepressants. Rosen Pub. 2010 64p il (FAQ: teen life) lib bdg $29.95

Grades: 7 8 9 10 **615**

1. Antidepressants 2. Depression (Psychology)

ISBN 978-1-4358-3547-4 lib bdg; 1-4358-3547-6 lib bdg

LC 2009-18962

"Defines 'antidepressants' and 'depression' in an easy-to-understand language, using words and illustrations to show the science of how these drugs work and the warning signs of different types of depression. . . . This is a good resource for teens struggling to understand what is happening to themselves or to their friends." Voice Youth Advocates

Includes glossary and bibliographical references

Winner, Cherie

★ **Circulating** life; blood transfusion from ancient superstition to modern medicine. Twenty-First Century Books 2007 112p il (Discovery!) $30.60

Grades: 6 7 8 9 10 **615**

1. Blood -- Transfusion

ISBN 978-0-8225-6606-9; 0-8225-6606-0

LC 2006-29921

This is a study of how bloodletting was replaced by blood transfusion as a medical therapy. Index. "Grades seven to twelve." (Sci Books Films)

This "compendium is both a history of the art of transfusions and a scientific discourse on the chemistry of blood. From early 'bleeding treatments' to the discovery of the circulatory system; from the earliest attempts at transfusions to Charles Drew's heroic work with plasma in World War II, Winner's clear text takes readers on an epic trip." SLJ

Includes bibliographical references

615.1 Drugs (Materia medica)

Goldsmith, Connie

Dietary supplements; Harmless, Helpful, or Hurtful? by Connie Goldsmith. Twenty-First Century Books 2016 96 p. color illustrations (lib. bdg. : alk. paper) $34.65

Grades: 6 7 8 9 **615.1**

1. Dietary supplements

ISBN 9781467738484

LC 2014024851

This book, by Connie Goldsmith, "explores the value vs. the potential danger of [dietary supplements]. . . . Goldsmith devotes considerable detail to such hot-button topics as: vitamin and mineral supplements; herbal products, both those proven moderately effective and those that are dangerous; and weight-loss and sports supplements, legal and banned." (Kirkus Reviews)

"Excellent, detailed endmatter rounds out a balanced exploration of a timely topic. Equally apt for research projects and as a single go-to source of information." Kirkus

Includes bibliographical references and index

615.3 Organic drugs

Haelle, Tara

★ **Vaccination** investigation; the history and science of vaccines. by Tara Haelle. Twenty-First Century Books 2018 120 p. illustrations (chiefly color) (lb : alk. paper) $37.32

Grades: 7 8 9 10 11 12 **615.3**

1. Public health 2. Vaccines -- History 3. Vaccination -- History

ISBN 9781541522107; 9781512425307

LC 2017005193

"Vaccines are biological substances that cause the human immune system to build up its defenses against specific diseases. . . . The effort to wipe out diseases using vaccines continues. . . . [This book, by Tara Haelle,] recounts the fascinating history of vaccines, their important role in protecting community health, and the excitement of cutting-edge research." (Publisher's note)

"This is an organized, documented, and accessible account of the history of vaccinations." Booklist

Includes bibliographical references and index

615.7 Pharmacokinetics

Esherick, Joan

The **FDA** & psychiatric drugs; how a drug is approved. Joan Esherick. revised edition Mason Crest Publishers, Inc. 2014 128 p. (hardcover) $24.95

Grades: 7 8 9 10 **615.7**

1. Drugs 2. Psychotropic drugs 3. Drug approval -- United States 4. Mental illness -- Chemotherapy 5. United States. Food and Drug Administration 6. Psychotropic drugs -- Testing -- Law and legislation -- United States

ISBN 1422228266; 9781422228265

LC 2013008197

Revision of: The FDA and psychiatric drugs, 2004

Details the FDA's approval process for psychiatric drugs and explains how the drugs work, where they come from, and adverse reactions people experience from taking them.

Rooney, Anne

You wouldn't want to live without antibiotics! written by Anne Rooney ; illustrated by David Antram. Franklin Watts, an imprint of Scholastic Inc. 2015 32 p. color illustrations (library binding : alk. paper) $29

Grades: 5 6 7 8 **615.7**

1. Antibiotics 2. Drug resistance in microorganisms

ISBN 0531212181; 9780531212189; 9780531213094

LC 2014039629

This children's book by Anne Rooney on antibiotics "takes us on a historical journey to see how people coped in the past, and how they developed ingenious ways to make life safer and more pleasant." (School Library Journal)

"Time lines chart the inventions' major developments and discoveries, providing a solid background for each subject, while brief yet interesting historical examples will appeal to even the most reluctant reader." SLJ

Includes bibliographical references and index

615.9 Toxicology

Albee, Sarah

Poison; deadly deeds, perilous professions, and murderous medicines. Sarah Albee. Crown Books for Young Readers 2017 x, 182 p.p illustrations (paperback) $17.99

Grades: 5 6 7 8 **615.9**

1. Poisons and poisoning 2. Poisons 3. Poisoning 4. Toxicology 5. Poisons -- History 6. Hazardous substances

ISBN 9781101932247; 9781101932230; 9781101932254

LC 2016009205

This book, by Sarah Albee, is a "humorous account of the role poisons have played in human history. . . . From spurned spouses and rivals, to condemned prisoners like Socrates, to endangered emperors like Alexander the Great, to modern-day leaders like Joseph Stalin and Yasser Arafat, poison has played a starring role in the demise of countless individuals." (Publisher's note)

"Albee's approach to the subject is lively, accessible, and likely to inspire many readers to delve deeper. A compelling, entertaining, and informative introduction to a sinister aspect of human history." Kirkus

Includes bibliographical references (pages 169-175) and index.

Landau, Elaine

Food poisoning and foodborne diseases. Twenty-First Century Books 2010 128p il (USA Today health reports: diseases and disorders) lib bdg $34.60

Grades: 7 8 9 10 11 12 **615.9**

1. Food poisoning 2. Communicable diseases

ISBN 978-0-8225-7290-9; 0-8225-7290-7

LC 2009-20325

This book "will drawn an audience with its everyday examples of food risks as well as instructions about how to buy, prepare, cook, and store food. . . . Also included are warnings about how to keep hands and kitchen surfaces clean and what to watch out for in cafeteria and fast-food outlets. . . . [The] accessible design extends the impressive educational data." Booklist

Includes bibliographical references

616 Diseases

Barber, Nicola

Cloning and genetic engineering; Nicola Barber. Rosen Pub.'s Rosen Central 2013 48 p. (Both sides of the story) (library binding) $29.25

Grades: 5 6 7 8 **616**

1. Cloning 2. Genetic engineering

ISBN 1448871875; 9781448871872

LC 2012013797

Author Nicola Barber's book focuses on cloning and genetic engineering. The book "offers arguments for both sides of the cloning and genetic engineering debate. Among the subjects examined are the human genome, transgenics, reproductive cloning, research cloning, stem cell therapy, genetic disease and testing, gene therapy, plant and animal pharming, genetically modified animals and crops, and gene doping." (Publisher's note)

Includes bibliographical references (p. 46) and index

Calamandrei, Camilla

Fever. Marshall Cavendish Benchmark 2009 64p il (Health alert) $22.95

Grades: 4 5 6 7 **616**

1. Fever

ISBN 978-0-7614-2915-9; 0-7614-2915-8

LC 2007-26002

This "title features a handsome format, with well-chosen illustrations, a substantial amount of information, and some practical insights." Booklist

Includes glossary

Dendy, Leslie A.

★ **Guinea** pig scientists; bold self-experimenters in science and medicine. [by] Leslie Dendy and Mel Boring; with illustrations by C. B. Mordan. Henry Holt & Co. 2005 213p il paperback $13.99

Grades: 5 6 7 8 **616**

1. Scientists 2. Medicine -- Research

ISBN 9781250050656 paperback; 9780805073164

LC 2004-52364

This is a collection of "stories of human 'guinea pigs' who have tested the limits of the human body for the sake of science. Starting with Sir Charles Blagden, M.D., and his heat experiments, the stories are chronologically ordered from the 1770s to 1989. Included are descriptions of experiments dealing with digestion, laughing gas, vaccinations, mosquitoes as vectors of yellow fever, radioactivity, [and] G-forces." (Sci Books Films) Index.

"The accounts are lively, compelling, and not always for the squeamish. . . . The authors cogently discuss each experiment's significance in advancing our understanding of science and medicine. Illustrated with a mix of period black-and-white photos and Mordan's nineteenth-century-style portraits." Booklist

Includes bibliographical references

Evans, Michael

The **adventures** of Medical Man; kids' illnesses and injuries explained. by Michael Evans & David Wichman; illustrated by Gareth Williams. Annick 2010 72p il $21.95; pa $12.95

Grades: 5 6 7 8 **616**

1. Diseases 2. Wounds and injuries

ISBN 978-1-55451-263-8; 1-55451-263-8; 978-1-55451-262-1 pa; 1-55451-262-X pa

"Using tangible experiences that kids can relate to, this book does a fantastic job of explaining common medical issues in an accessible way. A variety of heroic characters explain otherwise complicated and seemingly scary conditions and occurrences. Through the use of science fiction, adventure, and comics, the book covers nut allergies, concussions, broken bones, strep throat, ear infections, and asthma. . . . The extensive glossary is straightforward and user-friendly. The pumped-up graphic illustrations are extremely engaging and further bring these otherwise abstract concepts to life." SLJ

Skloot, Rebecca

The **immortal** life of Henrietta Lacks; by Rebecca Skloot. 1st paperback ed. Crown Publishers 2010 369 p ill. (some col.) (hardcover) $26.00; (paperback) $16.00

Grades: 8 9 10 11 12 Adult **616**

1. Cancer 2. Homemakers 3. Medical ethics 4. Human experimentation in medicine 5. African American women -- Biography

ISBN 1400052173; 9781400052172; 9781400052189

LC 200931785

Here, Rebecca Skloot tells the story of Henrietta Lacks, an African American Virginia tobacco farmer who died of cervical cancer in 1951. Unbeknownst to Mrs. Lacks and her family, scientists harvested her cells to create a human cell line known as HeLa, from the first two letters of her first and last names, "that has been kept alive indefinitely, enabling discoveries in such areas as cancer research, in vitro fertilization and gene mapping." (Publisher's note)

Includes bibliographical references and index.

Stoyles, Pennie

The **A** -Z of health. Black Rabbit/Smart Apple 2010 6v il set $119.70

Grades: 5 6 7 8 **616**

1. Health 2. Reference books 3. Medicine -- Encyclopedias

ISBN 978-1-59920-654-7; 1-59920-654-4

"This reference set provides a simple, brief, and easy-to-read introduction to key aspects of physical and mental health, including various body processes and diseases as well as information on treatments and preventative measures. . . . The explanations are concise, clear, and easy to understand. In addition to the abundance of images, the large type and white space that is prevalent on every page will make this set accessible to a broad array of young readers." Booklist

616.07 Pathology

Murray, Elizabeth A.

Death; corpses, cadavers, and other grave matters. Twenty-First Century Books 2010 112p il (Discovery!) lib bdg $31.93

Grades: 7 8 9 10 **616.07**

1. Death 2. Forensic sciences

ISBN 978-0-7613-3851-2; 0-7613-3851-9

LC 2009-17436

The author "has written a book that deals with the scientific aspect of life and death. Her experience as a teacher of anatomy and physiology comes through as she explains the living body, what happens when systems shut down, and how postmortem remains can give evidence to solve crimes and the mysteries of diseases. . . . First-person accounts of terminally ill patients and those working in the fields of pathology, hospice, and anatomy clarify subjects presented in the chapters. Color photographs are included throughout, some of which are potentially disturbing. The glossary and bibliography are extensive and helpful. This book provides information for those who are curious about a subject that is not easy to discuss." SLJ

Includes glossary and bibliographical references

Sherrow, Victoria

Medical imaging; [by] Victoria Sherrow. Marshall Cavendish Benchmark 2007 127p il (Great inventions) lib bdg $39.93

Grades: 7 8 9 10 **616.07**

1. Diagnostic imaging

ISBN 978-0-7614-2231-0; 0-7614-2231-5

LC 2006003229

"An examination of the origins, history, development, and societal impact of various medical-imaging devices, from X-rays to the MRI" Publisher's note

Includes glossary and bibliographical references

616.2 Diseases of respiratory system

Asthma information for teens; health tips about managing asthma and related concerns including facts about asthma causes, triggers and symptoms, diagnosis, and treatment. edited by Kim Wohlenhaus. 2nd ed.; Omnigraphics 2010 427p il (Teen health series) $69

Grades: 7 8 9 10 11 12 **616.2**

1. Asthma

ISBN 978-0-7808-1086-0; 0-7808-1086-4

LC 2009048694

First published 2005 under the editorship of Karen Bellenir

"Provides basic consumer health information for teens about asthma causes and treatments, controlling triggers, and coping with asthma at home and school. Includes index, resource information and recommendations for further reading." Publisher's note

Includes bibliographical references

Goldsmith, Connie

Influenza. Twenty-First Century Books 2010 128p il (USA Today health reports: diseases and disorders) lib bdg $34.60

Grades: 7 8 9 10 11 12 **616.2**

1. Influenza

ISBN 9780761363767; 978-0-7613-5881-7; 0-7613-5881-1

LC 2010-01030

"This book provides information about flu, how it spreads, and how it is prevented and treated." (Introduction) Glossary. Bibliography. Index. "Grades seven to twelve." (Sci Books Films)

This book "talks about the science behind the highly contagious disease, how it has spread to millions, and how to prevent and treat it. . . . [The] accessible design extends the impressive educational data." Booklist

Includes bibliographical references

Kelly, Evelyn B.

Investigating influenza and bird flu; real facts for real lives. [by] Evelyn B. Kelly and Claire Wilson. Enslow Publishers 2010 160p il (Investigating diseases) lib bdg $34.60

Grades: 6 7 8 9 10 **616.2**

1. Influenza 2. Avian influenza

ISBN 978-0-7660-3341-2; 0-7660-3341-4

LC 2009-14802

"The authors have explained the difficult problems in a clear, readable manner with lots of added pictures. . . . [Recommended] . . . for junior and senior high school students and for the general public." Sci Books Films

Includes glossary and bibliographical references

Marcovitz, Hal

★ **Asthma**. ReferencePoint Press 2010 96p il (Compact research: diseases and disorders) lib bdg $25.95

Grades: 7 8 9 10 **616.2**

1. Asthma

ISBN 978-1-60152-104-0 lib bdg; 1-60152-104-9 lib bdg

LC 2009036844

This "title begins with an overview of [asthma], followed by chapters that define the condition, explain its causes, and discuss possible treatments. . . . The last chapter . . . is about how to live with the condition. Chapters present material in accessible language, provide report-ready, primary-source quotes from experts, and end with a Facts and Illustrations section in which information is summarized in bullet points and accompanied by colorful graphs and charts that will appeal to visual learners." SLJ

Includes bibliographical references

Parks, Peggy J., 1951-

Influenza. ReferencePoint Press 2011 96p il map (Compact research: diseases and disorders) lib bdg $26.95

Grades: 7 8 9 10 11 12 **616.2**

1. Influenza 2. Swine influenza

ISBN 978-1-60152-118-7; 1-60152-118-9

LC 2010-26063

This book about influenza "begins with a general overview followed by a focus on statistics, causes, symptoms, treatments, and prevention. [The book] discusses the virus that causes the disease; presents information on prevention through proper hygiene as well as vaccination, especially during epidemics; and warns against public apathy. . . . The readable page design features pull quotes and subtitles, with occasional photos throughout." Booklist

Includes bibliographical references

Royston, Angela

Explaining asthma. Smart Apple Media 2010 45p il (Explaining) lib bdg $34.25

Grades: 5 6 7 8 **616.2**

1. Asthma

ISBN 978-1-59920-315-7 lib bdg; 1-59920-315-4 lib bdg

LC 2008-49284

Describes what living with asthma is like, discussing symptoms, triggers, treatments, and lifestyle changes that may be necessary to prevent asthma attacks

The book provides a "basic [overview] of the health concerns related to the disease; information on diagnosis and treatment; and a discussion of the challenges or complications experienced by the affected person and their family/friends, and how to manage those problems. . . . The incorporation of quotes and personal accounts in 'Case Notes' sidebars adds to the sensitive tone found throughout [the title]." SLJ

Includes glossary

Smith, Terry L.

Asthma; [by] Terry L. Smith. Chelsea House 2008 128p il (Genes & disease) lib bdg $35

Grades: 7 8 9 10 **616.2**

1. Asthma

ISBN 978-0-7910-9663-5 lib bdg; 0-7910-9663-7 lib bdg

LC 2008-44774

This book opens "with accounts of people who have [asthma] . . . followed by information on history, symptoms, variations, diagnosis, treatments, and research. . . . Chapters devoted to current genetic research and therapies can become dense as they introduce complex topics but photos, diagrams and charts help to clarify the details. . . . Controversial issues . . . are introduced fairly." SLJ

Includes glossary and bibliographical references

Yancey, Diane

Tuberculosis; rev ed; Twenty-First Century Books 2008 128p il (Twenty-first century medical library) lib bdg $30.60

Grades: 8 9 10 11 12 **616.2**

1. Tuberculosis

ISBN 978-0-8225-9190-0 lib bdg; 0-8225-9190-1 lib bdg

LC 2007-30486

The author begins this book with a history of tuberculosis, "tracing evidence of it back to the Neolithic Age and then explores the variety of treatments used to combat it. . . . The three personal cases related are from three different socioeconomic situations. Good-quality, black-and-white photos appear throughout." SLJ [review of 2001 edition]

Includes bibliographical references

616.3 Diseases of digestive system

Bjorklund, Ruth

Cystic fibrosis. Marshall Cavendish Benchmark 2009 64p il (Health alert) $22.95

Grades: 4 5 6 7 **616.3**

1. Cystic fibrosis

ISBN 978-0-7614-2912-8; 0-7614-2912-3

LC 2007-46674

This "title features a handsome format, with well-chosen illustrations, a substantial amount of information, and some practical insights." Booklist

Currie-McGhee, Leanne K.

Childhood obesity; by Leanne K. Currie-McGhee. Lucent Books 2012 104 p. ill. (some col.) (Nutrition and health) (hardcover) $30.95

Grades: 7 8 9 10 11 12 **616.3**

1. Obesity in children

ISBN 1420507230; 9781420507232

LC 2012002939

This book by Leanne K. Currie-McGhee, part of the "Nutrition & Health" series, "explores global issue of childhood obesity. Causes of and proposed solutions to this public health issue are explored, and the findings of current studies are detailed. The text features comments from scientists and researchers, but also includes first-hand accounts from children and teens who have struggled with obesity." (Publisher's note)

Includes bibliographical references (p. 90-93) and index.

Giddings, Sharon

Cystic fibrosis. Chelsea House 2009 128p il (Genes & disease) lib bdg $35

Grades: 7 8 9 10 **616.3**

1. Cystic fibrosis

ISBN 978-0-7910-9694-9; 0-7910-9694-7

LC 2008-44771

"Cystic fibrosis is one of the most widespread fatal genetic diseases in the United States. . . . [This book] discusses this genetic disease, its history, current treatments, and how scientists are searching for a cure." Publisher's note

Includes glossary and bibliographical references

Goldsmith, Connie

Hepatitis. Twenty-First Century Books 2010 128p il (USA Today health reports: diseases and disorders) lib bdg $34.60

Grades: 7 8 9 10 11 12 **616.3**

1. Liver -- Diseases

ISBN 978-0-8225-6787-5; 0-8225-6787-3

LC 2009-20720

This "reveals that an estimated five million Americans have viral Hepatitis A, B, and C, making it a major public health problem. . . . The detailed information is combined with photos and diagrams portraying transmission, vaccines, and effective treatment. . . . [The] accessible design extends the impressive educational data." Booklist

Includes bibliographical references

Hicks, Terry Allan

Obesity. Marshall Cavendish Benchmark 2009 63p il (Health alert) $22.95

Grades: 4 5 6 7 **616.3**

1. Obesity

ISBN 978-0-7614-2911-1; 0-7614-2911-5

LC 2007-31246

This "title features a handsome format, with well-chosen illustrations, a substantial amount of information, and some practical insights." Booklist

Includes glossary

Jarrow, Gail

Red madness; how a medical mystery changed what we eat. Gail Jarrow. Calkins Creek 2014 192 p. $16.95

Grades: 5 6 7 8 9 **616.3**

1. Diseases 2. Malnutrition 3. Pellagra -- History 4. Epidemics -- United States -- History 5. United States. Public Health Service -- History

ISBN 1590787323; 9781590787328

LC 2008049497

In this book, author Gail Jarrow "tracks [a] disease, commonly known as pellagra, and highlights how doctors, scientists, and public health officials finally defeated it. Illustrated with 100 archival photographs, [it] includes stories about real-life pellagra victims and accounts of scientific investigations. It concludes with a glossary, timeline, further resources, author's note, bibliography, and index." (Publisher's note)

"In 1902, a young man in Georgia displayed symptoms of a disease believed to be nonexistent in the U.S.: pellagra, a deficiency disease. Jarrow unfolds the suspenseful search for a cause of the South's epidemic, as corn fungus, insect- and bird-born parasites, and more were all blamed and rejected." Horn Book

Marcovitz, Hal

Hepatitis. ReferencePoint Press 2009 112p il (Compact research. Diseases and disorders) lib bdg $25.95

Grades: 8 9 10 11 12 **616.3**

1. Liver -- Diseases

ISBN 978-1-60152-039-5 lib bdg; 1-60152-039-5 lib bdg

LC 2007-38874

Presents information on hepatitis through essays, quotations, statistics, and suggestions for further research

"The coverage is succinct . . . [and] includes colorful illustrations and figures, chronologies, related organizations, advocacy groups and sources for additional research." Libr Media Connect

Includes bibliographical references

Powell, Jillian

Explaining cystic fibrosis. Smart Apple Media 2010 45p il (Explaining) lib bdg $34.25

Grades: 5 6 7 8 **616.3**

1. Cystic fibrosis

ISBN 978-1-59920-312-6 lib bdg; 1-59920-312-X lib bdg

LC 2008-49288

Describes the illness, including its causes, how it is diagnosed, current treatments for the illness, and how those with cystic fibrosis lead everyday lives

The book provides a "basic [overview] of the health concerns related to the disease; information on diagnosis and treatment; and a discussion of the challenges or complications experienced by the affected person and their family/friends, and how to manage those problems. . . . The incorporation of quotes and personal accounts in 'Case Notes' sidebars adds to the sensitive tone found throughout [the title]." SLJ

Includes glossary and bibliographical references

616.4 Diseases of endocrine, hematopoietic, lymphatic, glandular systems; diseases of male breast

Allman, Toney

Diabetes. Chelsea House 2008 136p il (Genes & disease) lib bdg $35

Grades: 7 8 9 10 **616.4**

1. Diabetes

ISBN 978-0-7910-9585-0; 0-7910-9585-1

LC 2008-1195

This "well-written book . . . [discusses] diabetes, its treatments, genetic variations contributing to the disease, and the prospects for a cure. The narrative starts with the diagnosis of diabetes and follows with seven chapters." Sci Books Films

Includes glossary and bibliographical references

Ambrose, Marylou

Investigating diabetes; real facts for real lives. Enslow Publishers 2010 160p il (Investigating diseases) lib bdg $34.60

Grades: 6 7 8 9 10 **616.4**

1. Diabetes

ISBN 978-0-7660-3338-2; 0-7660-3338-4

LC 2008-30778

"The book is a comprehensive primer that can well serve patients with newly diagnosed diabetes and their families with its detailed account of diabetes, the causes of the disease, and its potential consequences." Sci Books Films

Includes glossary and bibliographical references

Brill, Marlene Targ, 1945-

Diabetes. Twenty-First Century Books 2011 128p il (USA Today health reports: diseases and disorders) lib bdg $34.60

Grades: 7 8 9 10 11 12 **616.4**

1. Diabetes

ISBN 978-0-7613-6085-8; 0-7613-6085-9

LC 2010049454

This volume explores the history of diabetes, and explains the various treatments that are available today.

"This is an important endeavor from the author [that] will be very helpful for patients and others who are looking for basic information about diabetes. The author has done a good job of helping readers understand how their bodies function and the underlying mechanism of diabetes." Sci Books Films

Includes glossary and bibliographical references

Yuwiler, Janice

Diabetes. ReferencePoint Press 2009 96p il (Compact research. Diseases and disorders) lib bdg $25.95

Grades: 7 8 9 10 **616.4**

1. Diabetes

ISBN 978-1-60152-076-0; 1-60152-076-X

LC 2009-6173

"Yuwiler discusses type 1 diabetes and its management, type 2 diabetes and its prevention, metabolic syndrome, and medical advances. . . . Subtopics are delineated by brightly colored burgundy headings; blocks of orange-colored sidebars with bright-red print and relevant color photos and illustrations appear throughout. Each chapter ends with several pages of primary-source quotes and facts and illustrations that offer greater clarity to the text." SLJ

Includes bibliographical references

616.5 Diseases of integument

Faulk, Michelle

The **case** of the flesh-eating bacteria; Annie Biotica solves skin disease crimes. by Michelle Faulk. Lake Book Manufacturing, Inc. 2013 48 p. (Body system disease investigations) (library) $23.93

Grades: 5 6 7 8 **616.5**

1. Picture books for children 2. Skin -- Diseases 3. Virus diseases 4. Skin -- Infections

ISBN 0766039455; 9780766039452

LC 2011023985

This book by Michelle Faulk "from the Body System Disease Investigations series introduces Agent Annie Biotica, a 'Disease Scene Investigator with the Major Health Crimes Unit'. This cartoon-style heroine is called in to solve a series of skin-related medical cases . . . caused by flesh-eating bacteria, pinkeye, ringworm, chicken pox, [and] measles." (Booklist)

Includes bibliographical references (p. 47) and index

Skin health information for teens; health tips about dermatological disorders and activities that affect the skin, hair, and nails. edited by Siva Ganesh Maharaja. 4th edition Omnigraphics, Inc. 2017 424 p. hardcover $69

Grades: 7 8 9 10 **616.5**

1. Skin -- Care 2. Skin -- Diseases 3. Teenagers -- Health and hygiene 4. Beauty, Personal 5. Skin -- Care and hygiene

ISBN 9780780815797 hardcover; 9780780813175

LC 2017033342

This book "provides updated information about the skin, hair, and nails. It explains how the skin and its related structures grow and how to keep them healthy. Common ailments, including acne, eczema, impetigo, psoriasis, vitiligo, and warts are explained, and a section on skin cancer provides information about cancer risks, prevention strategies, warning signs, and treatments. The care of skin injuries, including cuts, scrapes, burns, bites, and stings, is also discussed." (Publisher's note)

Includes bibliographical references and index.

616.6 Diseases of urogenital system

★ The **kidneys** and the renal system; edited by Kara Rogers. Britannica Educational Pub. in association with Rosen Educational Services 2012 xvii, 174 p.p col. ill.

Grades: 7 8 9 10 11 12 **616.6**

1. Kidneys 2. Human anatomy 3. Urinary organs 4. Kidneys -- Diseases

ISBN 161530679X; 9781615306794

LC 2011026615

This biology reference work, edited by Kara Rogers, describes the Human waste system. "Responsible for managing the body's waste and regulating the balance of water and electrolytes, the kidneys and renal system, in a sense, make up the body's plumbing network. . . . This volume examines the various components of the renal, or urinary, system, and the consequences of dysfunction and disease." (Publisher's note)

Includes bibliographical references and index

616.8 Diseases of nervous system and mental disorders

Bender, Lionel

Explaining epilepsy. Smart Apple Media 2010 45p il (Explaining) lib bdg $34.25

Grades: 5 6 7 8 **616.8**

1. Epilepsy

ISBN 978-1-59920-309-6 lib bdg; 1-59920-309-X lib bdg

LC 2008-49292

Describes the nature, symptoms, and possible causes of epilepsy, gives a history of its study, and discusses its treatment

The book provides a "basic [overview] of the health concerns related to the disease; information on diagnosis and treatment; and a discussion of the challenges or complications experienced by the affected person and their family/friends, and how to manage those problems. . . . The incorporation of quotes and personal accounts in 'Case Notes' sidebars adds to the sensitive tone found throughout [the title]." SLJ

Includes glossary and bibliographical references

Colligan, L. H.

★ **Sleep** disorders. Marshall Cavendish Benchmark 2009 64p il (Health alert) $22.95

Grades: 4 5 6 7 **616.8**

1. Sleep disorders

ISBN 978-0-7614-2913-5; 0-7614-2913-1

This "title features a handsome format, with well-chosen illustrations, a substantial amount of information, and some practical insights." Booklist

Includes glossary

Dittmer, Lori

Parkinson's disease. Creative Education 2011 il (Living with disease) $23.95

Grades: 6 7 8 9 **616.8**

1. Parkinson's disease

ISBN 978-1-60818-076-9; 1-60818-076-X

LC 2010030366

A look at Parkinson's disease, examining the ways in which it develops, its symptoms and diagnosis, the effects it has on a person's daily life, and research toward finding better treatments.

"The text is clearly written. . . . The book's design is simple and bold. . . . A brief but informative introduction to Parkinson's disease." Booklist

Includes glossary and bibliographical references

Dougherty, Terri

Epilepsy. Lucent Books 2010 104p il (Diseases and disorders series) lib bdg $33.45

Grades: 7 8 9 10 11 12 **616.8**

1. Epilepsy

ISBN 978-1-4205-0218-3; 1-4205-0218-2

LC 2009-33344

This "offers a thorough explanation of [epilepsy], giving a basic definition; a discussion of the causes, symptoms, and treatments; a description of living with the disease; and ideas of future treatment and diagnoses. The color photographs and sidebars help to make the information in the dense text more easily understood, and personal stories provide insight into how individuals deal with their disease. . . . Different types of seizures and the varied triggers are explained." Voice Youth Advocates

Includes bibliographical references

Freedman, Jeri

Tay -Sachs disease. Chelsea House 2009 128p il (Genes & disease) lib bdg $35

Grades: 7 8 9 10 **616.8**

1. Tay-Sachs disease

ISBN 978-0-7910-9634-5; 0-7910-9634-3

LC 2008-44770

This book "discusses the nature of the disease, why it affects certain groups of people more often than others, how genetic screening can help detect carriers of the Tay-Sachs gene, and what options genetic testing and counseling provide for having children." Publisher's note

Includes glossary and bibliographical references

Klosterman, Lorrie

Meningitis. Marshall Cavendish Benchmark 2007 64p il (Health alert) lib bdg $31.36

Grades: 4 5 6 7 **616.8**

1. Meningitis

ISBN 978-0-7614-2211-2; 0-7614-2211-0

LC 2006015819

This "title features a handsome format, with well-chosen illustrations, a substantial amount of information, and some practical insights." Booklist

Includes glossary and bibliographical references

Levete, Sarah

Explaining cerebral palsy. Smart Apple Media 2010 45p il (Explaining) lib bdg $34.25

Grades: 5 6 7 8 **616.8**

1. Cerebral palsy

ISBN 978-1-59920-311-9 lib bdg; 1-59920-311-1 lib bdg

LC 2008-49287

Describes the illness, including its causes, how it is diagnosed, current treatment methods, and how those with cerebral palsy live everyday lives

The book provides a "basic [overview] of the health concerns related to the disease; information on diagnosis and treatment; and a discussion of the challenges or complications experienced by the affected person and their family/friends, and how to manage those problems. . . . The incorporation of quotes and personal accounts in 'Case Notes' sidebars adds to the sensitive tone found throughout [the title]." SLJ

Includes glossary and bibliographical references

Marcovitz, Hal

Meningitis. ReferencePoint Press 2009 112p il (Compact research. Diseases and disorders) lib bdg $25.95

Grades: 7 8 9 10 **616.8**

1. Meningitis

ISBN 978-1-60152-043-2 lib bdg; 1-60152-043-3 lib bdg

LC 2007-45213

Presents an overview of meningitis and discusses symptoms, disease contraction, social impacts, and prevention

"The coverage is succinct . . . [and] includes colorful illustrations and figures, chronologies, related organizations, advocacy groups, and sources for additional research." Libr Media Connect

Includes bibliographical references

★ **Sleep** disorders. ReferencePoint Press 2009 104p il (Compact research. Diseases and disorders) lib bdg $25.95

Grades: 7 8 9 10 11 12 **616.8**

1. Sleep disorders

ISBN 978-1-60152-071-5; 1-60152-071-9

LC 2008-46115

"Marcovitz's coverage ranges from insomnia to potential medical conditions that can lead to death, such as sleep apnea and narcolepsy. This book is a comprehensive overview of an often misunderstood subject." SLJ

Includes bibliographical references

616.85 Miscellaneous diseases of nervous system and mental disorders

Ambrose, Marylou

Investigating eating disorders (anorexia, bulimia, and binge eating) real facts for real lives. [by] Marylou Ambrose and Veronica Deisler. Enslow Publishers 2011 160p il (Investigating diseases) lib bdg $34.60

Grades: 6 7 8 9 10 **616.85**

1. Eating disorders

ISBN 978-0-7660-3339-9; 0-7660-3339-2

LC 2009-6492

"This book is a well-organized, clear, succinct, and attractive presentation on anorexia, bulimia, and binge eating. In it, the authors have gathered helpful definitions, early religious history, international viewpoints, statistics, family issues, medical and psychological assessments, treatments, medications, and legislation to present information on the future outlook of, and research into, these eating disorders." Sci Books Films

Includes glossary and bibliographical references

Baish, Vanessa

Self -image and eating disorders; by Rita Smith ... [et al.] 1st ed. Rosen Pub. 2013 48 p. col. ill. (Teen mental health) (library) $29.25

Grades: 6 7 8 9 **616.85**

1. Body image 2. Eating disorders 3. Body image in adolescence 4. Eating disorders in adolescence -- Treatment 5. Eating disorders in adolescence -- Psychological aspects

ISBN 1448868947; 9781448868940

LC 2012003030

This book on self-image and eating disorders by Rita Smith is part of the "Teen Mental Health" series. It "addresses self-esteem and negative body image. Eating disorders include anorexia nervosa, bulimia nervosa, binge eating, orthorexia nervosa, and compulsive exercise, along with related health and emotional problems. The books discuss techniques for coping and encourage teens to seek out available resources such as professional help, support groups, or school programs." (School Library Journal)

Includes bibliographical references (p. 43-46) and index.

Barbour, Scott

Post -traumatic stress disorder. ReferencePoint Press 2009 104p (Compact research: diseases and disorders) lib bdg $25.95

Grades: 7 8 9 10 **616.85**

1. Post-traumatic stress disorder

ISBN 978-1-60152-101-9 lib bdg; 1-60152-101-4 lib bdg

LC 2009033216

This "title begins with an overview of [post-traumatic stress disorder], followed by chapters that define the condition, explain its causes, and discuss possible treatments. . . . The final chapter discusses how society should help soldiers with the problem. . . . Chapters present material in accessible language, provide report-ready, primary-source quotes from experts, and end with a Facts and Illustrations section in which information is summarized in bullet points and accompanied by colorful graphs and charts that will appeal to visual learners." SLJ

Includes bibliographical references

Barton, Michael

It's raining cats and dogs; an autism spectrum guide to the confusing world of idioms, metaphors, and everyday expressions. Michael Barton ; foreword, Delia Barton ; illustrator, Michael Barton. Jessica Kingsley Publishers 2012 95 p. (alk. paper) $15.95

Grades: 3 4 5 6 **616.85**

1. Autism 2. Metaphor 3. Figures of speech 4. English language -- Idioms 5. Autistic people -- Language 6. Autism spectrum disorders -- Patients -- Language

ISBN 1849052832; 9781849052832

LC 2011039514

This book offers "insight into the mind of someone with an ASD [autism spectrum disorder]. It . . . illustrates why people with ASDs have problems understanding common phrases and idioms that others accept unquestioningly as part of everyday speech. The . . . drawings" are meant to "entertain and inspire those on the spectrum, giving them the confidence to recognise figures of speech, feel less alienated and even use idioms themselves. The drawings" are designed to "form instantly memorable references for those with ASDs to recall whenever they need to and" should "be helpful for anyone curious to understand the ASD way of thinking." (Publisher's note)

Bingham, Jane

Stress and depression; [by] Jane Bingham. Gareth Stevens 2009 48p il (Emotional health issues) lib bdg $31

Grades: 6 7 8 9 **616.85**

1. Stress (Psychology) 2. Depression (Psychology)

ISBN 978-0-8368-9203-1 lib bdg; 0-8368-9203-8 lib bdg

LC 2008-5237

First published 2008 in the United Kingdom

This book about stress and depression has "clear language and explanations. . . . [It is] suitable for fact-finding missions, but the abundant graphics and case studies are likely to draw in browsers as well. Throughout, unfamiliar vocabulary is highlighted in bold and explained in context and in the glossary. . . . Fact boxes and case study sidebars add information." SLJ

Includes glossary and bibliographical references

Bjornlund, Lydia D.

Personality disorders; by Lydia Bjornlund. ReferencePoint Press 2011 96p il (Compact research: diseases and disorders) lib bdg $26.95

Grades: 7 8 9 10 **616.85**

1. Personality disorders

ISBN 978-1-60152-139-2; 1-60152-139-1

LC 2010031384

This title provides "a systematic and focused look at [personality disorders]. . . . [It] covers 10 types, including paranoid and schizoid disorders. . . . [It explores] causes and the ways these conditions impact patients' lives and ultimately [addresses] whether sufferers can overcome them. Short sections containing primary-source quotes and bulleted facts and charts that highlight important information are appended to each chapter." SLJ

Includes bibliographical references

Cobain, Bev

When nothing matters anymore; a survival guide for depressed teens. edited by Elizabeth Verdick. rev and updated ed.; Free Spirit Pub. 2007 146p il pa $14.95

Grades: 7 8 9 10 **616.85**

1. Depression (Psychology)

ISBN 978-1-57542-235-0; 1-57542-235-2

LC 2006-36325

First published 1998

This book written for teens defines depression, describes the symptoms, and explains that depression is treatable

"This practical, reassuring book should be made available to all teens." Voice Youth Advocates

Includes bibliographical references

Currie-McGhee, L. K.

Exercise addiction; by Leanne Currie-McGhee. Lucent Books 2011 96p il (Diseases & disorders) lib bdg $33.45

Grades: 7 8 9 10 **616.85**

1. Exercise addiction

ISBN 978-1-4205-0551-1; 1-4205-0551-3

LC 2010039535

"Extremely readable, with helpful illustrations and sidebars, this book includes a definition of exercise addiction (with symptoms), describes how it may be related to other psychological disorders, profiles the types of people most at risk for developing it, discusses psychological and physiological dangers, and offers treatment options. . . . Personal stories appear throughout, and there is a helpful list of questions for readers to ask themselves. This volume is interesting enough to read even if not required for an assignment." SLJ

Includes bibliographical references

Denkmire, Heather

★ The **truth** about anxiety and depression; Heather Denkmire, principal author; John Perritano, contributing author; Robert N. Golden, general editor, Fred L. Peterson, general editor. 2nd ed.; Facts on File 2010 199p il (Truth about series) $35

Grades: 7 8 9 10 **616.85**

1. Anxiety 2. Depression (Psychology)

ISBN 978-0-8160-7643-7; 0-8160-7643-X

LC 2010005461

First published 2004 with title: The truth about fear and depression

Presents information on anxiety and depression, including the genetics of mood and anxiety disorders, gender and depression, types of treatments available, related disorders, and more.

Includes glossary and bibliographical references

Depression; Emma Carlson Berne, book editor. Greenhaven 2007 184p (Contemporary issues companion) $36.20; pa $24.95

Grades: 8 9 10 11 12 **616.85**

1. Depression (Psychology)

ISBN 978-0-7377-3645-8; 0-7377-3645-3; 978-0-7377-2451-6 pa; 0-7377-2451-X pa

LC 2007-19643

First published 1999 under the editorship of Henny H. Kim

"Eighteen field specialists have each contributed an essay on topics as diverse as deep brain stimulation and alternative therapies. A chapter on antidepressants and their heavily debated effects concludes the book. Thoughtfully composed, this excellent introduction to a widely recognized condition contains an extensive bibliography and support organization contact list." Libr J

Includes bibliographical references

Donovan, Sandra, 1967-

Keep your cool! what you should know about stress. illustrations by Jack Desrocher. Lerner Publications Co. 2009 64p il (Health zone) lib bdg $30.60

Grades: 4 5 6 7 **616.85**

1. Stress (Psychology)

ISBN 978-0-8225-7555-9; 0-8225-7555-8

LC 2007038858

This describes what causes stress and what you can do to relieve it.

"The format is beyond lively, with lots of color, cartoons, and an informal writing style, but it manages to present sometimes frightening material in a non-threatening and browsable way." Booklist

Includes glossary and bibliographical references

★ **Eating** disorders information for teens; health tips about anorexia, bulimia, binge eating, and body image disorders, including information about risk factors, prevention, diagnosis, treatment, health consequences, and other related issues. 4th edition Omnigraphics, Inc. 2013 xiii, 380 p.p ill. hardcover $69

Grades: 7 8 9 10 11 12 **616.85**

1. Eating disorders 2. Teenagers -- Health and hygiene 3. Eating disorders in adolescence

ISBN 9780780812697; 9780780815599 hardcover

LC 2017010041

This book "provides information about a wide range of eating and body image disorders. The volume is broken into six parts covering general information about eating disorders; specific disorders such as anorexia nervosa, bulimia nervosa, and others; the heath consequences of eating disorders; prevention, diagnosis, and treatment; healthy eating and exercise; and additional reading, research studies, and organizations." (Voice of Youth Advocates)

Includes bibliographical references and index.

Evans-Martin, Fay

Down syndrome; [by] F. Fay Evans-Martin. Chelsea House 2008 128p il (Genes & disease) lib bdg $35

Grades: 7 8 9 10 **616.85**

1. Down syndrome

ISBN 978-0-7910-9644-4; 0-7910-9644-0

LC 2008-44773

"Down syndrome is a developmental disorder caused by the presence of an extra copy of chromosome 21. . . . [This book] explains this genetic disease, its history and characteristics, and what scientists are doing to study it." Publisher's note

Includes glossary and bibliographical references

Farrar, Amy

ADHD. Twenty-First Century Books 2010 112p il (USA Today health reports: diseases and disorders) lib bdg $34.60

Grades: 7 8 9 10 11 12 **616.85**

1. Attention deficit disorder

ISBN 978-0-7613-5455-0; 0-7613-5455-7

LC 2010-870

This book describes attention deficit-hyperactivity disorder, its causes and treatments.

This is "liberally sprinkled with relevant articles and 'snapshots' (graphs showing statistical breakdowns of the topic at hand) from the newspaper, providing a competent introduction to primary-source material." SLJ

Includes glossary and bibliographical references

Ford, Emily

★ **What** you must think of me; a firsthand account of one teenager's experience with social anxiety disorder. by Emily Ford with Michael R. Liebowitz and Linda Wasmer Andrews. Oxford University Press 2007 xxi, 152p (Annenberg Foundation Trust at Sunnylands' adolescent mental health initiative) $30; pa $9.95

Grades: 7 8 9 10 11 12 **616.85**

1. Social phobia

ISBN 978-0-19-531302-4; 0-19-531302-X; 978-0-19-531303-1 pa; 0-19-531303-8 pa

LC 2006102285

"A professor of clinical psychiatry and a woman whose life has been adversely impacted by social anxiety disorder provide a unique view of the condition and its treatment in this slim volume. . . . Readers will find helpful charts throughout the book and an appendix loaded with further reading and contact information for advocacy groups. Thanks to its informative guide to diagnosis, suggestions for treatment and tips on dealing with the health care system, this is a must read for anyone who suffers from the disorder." Publ Wkly

Includes bibliographical references

Honos-Webb, Lara

The **ADHD** workbook for teens; activities to help you gain motivation and confidence. Lara Honos-Webb. Instant Help Books 2010 vi, 132 p.p (pbk. : alk. paper) $15.95

Grades: 7 8 9 10 11 12 **616.85**

1. Adolescent psychology 2. Attention deficit disorder 3. Attention-deficit disorder in adolescence -- Popular works

ISBN 1572248653; 9781572248656

LC 2010040282

According to this workbook by Lara Honos-Webb, "Symptoms of attention deficit/hyperactivity disorder, or ADHD, can strike at any time-during class, when you're listening to a friend's story, while doing homework, and did we mention during class? You might find it difficult to pay attention and sit still when your impulses are constantly tempting you to do the opposite." (Publisher's note)

This book helps ADHD-affected teens "learn simple skills [they] can use to confidently handle school, make and keep friends, and organize and finish every project [they] start." Publisher's note

Jones, Viola

Conquering negative body image; Viola Jones and Edward Willett. Rosen Publishing 2016 64 p. illustrations (chiefly color) (ebook) $34.45; (library bound) $34.45

Grades: 6 7 8 9 **616.85**

1. Body image 2. Self-acceptance 3. Eating disorders -- Psychological aspects 4. Body image in adolescence 5. Self-acceptance in adolescence 6. Body image -- Social aspects -- United States

ISBN 9781499462067; 9781499462050

LC 2015019516

This book in the Conquering eating disorders series, by Viola Jones and Edward Willett, "helps readers determine whether they have a negative body image, understand the roots and potential dangers of such thinking, and learn to overcome the problem and accept and celebrate their bodies." (Publisher's note)

"Young readers will find it a useful and engaging starting point for discussions on a difficult topic." Booklist

Includes bibliographical references and index

Levy, Joel

Phobiapedia; all the things we fear the most! Scholastic 2011 80p il pa $8.99

Grades: 4 5 6 7 **616.85**

1. Phobias

ISBN 978-0-545-34929-1; 0-545-34929-X

This briefly describes over 50 phobias.

"With an appealing layout, plenty of color, and enough germs, snakes, and bats to get the heart racing, this title has kid written all over it." Booklist

Marcovitz, Hal

Phobias. ReferencePoint Press 2009 112p il (Compact research. Diseases and disorders) lib bdg $25.95

Grades: 7 8 9 10 **616.85**

1. Phobias

ISBN 978-1-60152-044-9 lib bdg; 1-60152-044-1 lib bdg

LC 2008-10894

Through overviews, primary sources, and full color illustrations this title examines phobias

"The coverage is succinct . . . [and] includes colorful illustrations and figures, chronologies, related organizations, advocacy groups, and sources for additional research." Libr Media Connect

Includes bibliographical references

Mooney, Carla

Mood disorders. ReferencePoint Press 2010 96p il (Compact research: diseases and disorders) lib bdg $26.95

Grades: 8 9 10 11 12 **616.85**

1. Depression (Psychology) 2. Manic-depressive illness

ISBN 978-1-60152-119-4; 1-60152-119-7

LC 2010-5868

This book about mood disorders "begins with a general overview followed by focus on statistics, causes, symptoms, treatments, and prevention. . . . [The book] discusses the two main categories [of mood disorders]: unipolar (if untreated the number-one risk for suicide) and bipolar (which swings between depression and mania.) . . . The readable page design features pull quotes and subtitles, with occasional photos throughout." Booklist

Includes bibliographical references

What is anxiety disorder? by Carla Mooney. ReferencePoint Press, Inc. 2016 80 p. (hardback) $28.95

Grades: 8 9 10 11 12 **616.85**

1. Anxiety -- Treatment 2. Anxiety 3. Anxiety disorders 4. Anxiety disorders -- Treatment

ISBN 1601529201; 9781601529206

LC 2015016548

This juvenile book, by Carla Mooney, part of the publisher's "Understanding mental disorders" series, presents an overview of clinical anxiety. "Experts estimate that as many as 40 million American adults experience anxiety disorder in a given year, making it the most common mental illness in the United States. . . . [The volume] examines what this disorder is, what causes it, what it is like to live with it, and how or whether it can be treated or cured." (Publisher's note)

"This explores what it is like to live with the illness as well as its causes and treatments, and the well-organized, jargon-free information allows readers not already familiar with the topic to easily understand. Graphs, color photos, and side boxes containing supplemental facts break up the text, but this volume, unlike many of its contemporaries, is ultimately more invested in providing substantive information than in creating an engaging reading experience. A list of chapter notes, organizations, and sources round up the reference credentials of the book, which will be of value to student researchers." Booklist

Includes bibliographical references and index

Moragne, Wendy

Depression. Twenty-First Century Books 2011 128p (USA Today health reports: diseases and disorders) lib bdg $34.60

Grades: 8 9 10 11 12 **616.85**

1. Depression (Psychology)

ISBN 978-0-7613-5882-4; 0-7613-5882-X

LC 2010034122

This book about depression will serve as "solid report fodder. . . . [The] volume has an introduction, a description of the condition, chapters on what it is like to live with it, and material on research and treatments. A healthy smattering of statistics and personal stories appear throughout." SLJ

Includes bibliographical references

Parks, Peggy J., 1951-

Anorexia. ReferencePoint Press 2009 104p il (Compact research. Diseases and disorders) lib bdg $25.95
Grades: 7 8 9 10 **616.85**

1. Anorexia nervosa
ISBN 978-1-60152-042-5; 1-60152-042-5

LC 2008-4238

Presents information on anorexia, including its causes, its effect on health, and the possiblity of curing it, through essays, quotations, statistics, and suggestions for further research.

"[This] quality [source] could be used in a variety of different ways–: straight reporting for speech or debate ideas, or as a springboard for further research." SLJ

Includes bibliographical references

Anxiety disorders. ReferencePoint Press 2011 96p il (Compact research: diseases and disorders) lib bdg $26.95
Grades: 7 8 9 10 **616.85**

1. Anxiety 2. Panic disorders 3. Obsessive-compulsive disorder
ISBN 978-1-60152-137-8; 1-60152-137-5

LC 2010031813

This title provides "a systematic and focused look at [anxiety disorders]. . . . [It] covers six main types, including panic and obsessive-compulsive disorder. . . . [This title is] useful for reports as well as general interest." SLJ

Includes bibliographical references

Obsessive -compulsive disorder. ReferencePoint Press 2010 96p il (Compact research: diseases and disorders) lib bdg $26.95
Grades: 8 9 10 11 12 **616.85**

1. Obsessive-compulsive disorder
ISBN 978-1-60152-120-0; 1-60152-120-0

LC 2010-5872

This book about obsessive-compulsive disorder is written "with objectivity and depth. . . . [It] begins with a general overview followed by a focus on statistics, treatments, and prevention. . . . [The book] shows that the irrational fears of OCD affect males and females across race and class. . . . The readable page design features pull quotes and subtitles, with occasional photos throughout." Booklist

Includes bibliographical references

Online addiction; by Peggy J. Parks. ReferencePoint Press, Inc. 2013 96 p. (hardcover) $27.95
Grades: 7 8 9 10 11 12 **616.85**

1. Internet 2. Internet gambling 3. Addiction 4. Internet addiction -- Popular works
ISBN 1601522703; 9781601522702

LC 2012014191

In this book about online addiction, Peggy J. Parks "addresses four basic questions: Is online addiction real? Can people get addicted to social networking? How serious of a problem is compulsive online gaming and gambling? Can people recover from online addiction? . . . Parks addresses each of her four questions in separate sections of her book." (Booklist)

Includes bibliographical references and index.

Self -injury disorder. ReferencePoint Press 2011 96p il (Compact research: diseases and disorders) lib bdg $26.95
Grades: 8 9 10 11 12 **616.85**

1. Self-mutilation
ISBN 978-1-60152-112-5; 1-60152-112-X

LC 2009-50483

This book about self-injury disorder "begins with a general overview followed by a focus on statistics, causes, symptoms, treatments, and prevention. . . . [The book] states that the main cause of self-inflicted injury is to gain relief from unbearable emotional pain, and it also covers methods of treatment and prevention. The readable page design features pull quotes and subtitles, with occasional photos throughout." Booklist

Includes bibliographical references

Petro-Roy, Jen

★ **You** are enough; Jen Petro-Roy. Feiwel & Friends 2019 283 p. (hardcover) $19.99
Grades: 5 6 7 8 9 **616.85**

1. Body image in adolescence 2. Eating disorders in adolescence 3. Eating disorders in adolescence -- Treatment 4. Eating disorders in adolescence -- Psychological aspects
ISBN 9781250151025

LC 2018019396

In "this nonfiction self-help book for young readers with disordered eating and body image problems[, author Jen Petro-Roy,] delivers real talk about eating disorders and body image, tools and information for recovery, and suggestions for dealing with the media messages that contribute so much to disordered eating." (Publisher's note)

"Resources on eating disorders for the middle-grade set are few and far between, but Petro-Roy writes for this age group with knowledge, compassion, empathy, and inclusivity." Booklist.

Includes bibliographical references

Powell, Jillian

Self -harm and suicide; by Jillian Powell. Gareth Stevens 2009 48p il (Emotional health issues) lib bdg $31
Grades: 6 7 8 9 **616.85**

1. Suicide 2. Self-mutilation
ISBN 978-0-8368-9202-4; 0-8368-9202-X

LC 2008-4276

First published 2008 in the United Kingdom

This book about self-destructive behavior has "clear language and explanations. . . . [It is] suitable for fact-finding missions, but the abundant graphics and case studies are likely to draw in browsers as well. Throughout, unfamiliar vocabulary is highlighted in bold and explained in context and in the glossary. . . . Fact boxes and case study sidebars add information." SLJ

Includes glossary and bibliographical references

Price, Janet

Take control of Asperger's syndrome; the official strategy guide for teens with Asperger's syndrome and nonverbal learning disorder. [by] Janet Price and Jennifer Engel Fisher. Prufrock Press 2010 168p pa $16.95
Grades: 6 7 8 9 10 **616.85**

1. Asperger's syndrome
ISBN 978-1-59363-405-6; 1-59363-405-6

LC 2009-50852

"Directly addressing teens diagnosed with Asperger's Syndrome or Nonverbal Learning Disorder, two educational consultants experienced in special-needs issues lay out feasible strategies for success in school and in social interactions." Booklist

Includes bibliographical references

Quinn, Patricia O.

Attention, girls! a guide to learn all about your AD/HD. illustrated by Carl Pearce. Magination Press 2009 119p il $16.95; pa $12.95

Grades: 4 5 6 7 **616.85**

1. Attention deficit disorder

ISBN 978-1-4338-0447-2; 1-4338-0447-6; 978-1-4338-0448-9 pa; 1-4338-0448-4 pa

LC 2008054524

"Quinn has attention deficit hyperactivity disorder and is a medical doctor; she addresses the types of AD/HD; who can help; differences between girls and boys with AD/HD; making friends; talking with adults about the condition; relaxation techniques; and medication. Her aim is to give girls a variety of ways to manage their disorders. . . . The book is attractive and inviting with colorful cartoon illustrations, sidebars, and highlighted reminders." SLJ

Rea, Amy C.

Living with learning disabilities; by Amy C. Rea. ReferencePoint Press, Inc. 2019 80 p. (hardcover : alk. paper) $29.95

Grades: 6 7 8 9 **616.85**

1. Learning disabilities 2. Slow learning children 3. Learning disabled children

ISBN 9781682824818

LC 2018011537

In this book in the Living With Disorders and Disabilities series, by Amy C. Rea, "people with learning disabilities may have trouble reading, writing, or doing math. They face challenges in school, work, and daily life. . . . [This book] examines the causes and symptoms of this condition, looks at the everyday realities of people with learning disabilities, and explores the management and treatment options available today." (Publisher's note)

"Discussions on mental health still have much stigma attached to them, yet are quite often a reality for young people. Six conditions are explored in depth, striving to alleviate some of that stigma." (School Library Journal)

Includes bibliographical references and index

Rodriguez, Ana Maria

Autism spectrum disorders; the complete guide to understanding autism, Asperger's syndrome, pervasive developmental disorder, and other ASDs. Ana Maria Rodriguez. Twenty-First Century Books 2011 128 p (USA Today health reports: diseases and disorders) library $34.65

Grades: 8 9 10 11 12 **616.85**

1. Autism 2. Autistic children 3. Asperger's syndrome

ISBN 9780761372882; 0761358838; 9780761358831

LC 2010034236

Introduces autism spectrum disorders, discusses the causes, describes treatment options, and provides information on support groups and other organizations.

"Back matter includes a glossary, annotated lists of resource organizations and websites, selected bibliographies, very brief lists of source notes, and recommended reading lists." Booklist

Includes bibliographical references (p. [337]-350) and index

Royston, Angela

★ **Explaining** down syndrome. Smart Apple Media 2010 45p il (Explaining) lib bdg $34.25

Grades: 5 6 7 8 **616.85**

1. Down syndrome

ISBN 978-1-59920-308-9 lib bdg; 1-59920-308-1 lib bdg

LC 2008-49291

This book about down syndrome provides a "basic [overview] of the health concerns related to the disease; information on diagnosis and treatment; and a discussion of the challenges or complications experienced by the affected person and their family/friends, and how to manage those problems. . . . The incorporation of quotes and personal accounts in 'Case Notes' sidebars adds to the sensitive tone found throughout [the title]." SLJ

Includes glossary

Scarlet, Janina

Superhero therapy; mindfulness skills to help teens & young adults deal with anxiety, depression & trauma. Janina Scarlet, PhD ; illustrated by Wellinton Alves. Instant Help Books, New Harbinger Publications, Inc. 2017 107 p. color illustrations (pbk. : alk. paper) $17.95

Grades: 7 8 9 10 11 12 **616.85**

1. Teenagers 2. Mental health 3. Anxiety 4. Psychic trauma -- Treatment -- Handbooks, manuals, etc. 5. Teenagers -- Mental health 6. Depression in adolescence 7. Psychic trauma in adolescence 8. Acceptance and commitment therapy

ISBN 9781684030354; 9781684030347; 1684030331; 9781684030330

LC 2017020706

This book, by Janina Scarlet, illustrated by Wellinton Alves, "provides everything you need to begin your very own superhero training using evidence-based ACT and mindfulness skills. Within these colorful pages, you'll team up with a group of troubled heroes—inspired by both fictional characters and real-life people—enlisted at the Superhero Training Academy. By learning to face up to their inner villains and monsters, these characters will inspire you to overcome your problems as well." (Publisher's note)

"The conceit, along with some eye-catching art and a focus on setting simple, achievable daily goals, makes this a promising alternative to more conventional self-help programs." Booklist

Scowen, Kate

My kind of sad; what it's like to be young and depressed. [by] Kate Scowen; art by Jeff Szuc. Annick Press 2006 168p il $19.95; pa $10.95

Grades: 7 8 9 10 **616.85**

1. Depression (Psychology)

ISBN 1-55037-941-0; 1-55037-940-2 pa

"The book discusses the history of depression, adolescence and depression, and treatment options. Scowen's focus is on understanding the difference between simply being sad and suffering from depression. Topics such as bipolar disorder, self-mutilation, anorexia, and suicide are also discussed. . . . Scowen's book is well-written, easy to read and use, and quite informative." Voice Youth Advocates

Includes bibliographical references

Skotko, Brian

Fasten your seatbelt; a crash course on Down syndrome for brothers and sisters. [by] Brian G. Skotko and Susan P. Levine. Woodbine House 2009 191p il pa $18.95

Grades: 4 5 6 7 **616.85**

1. Siblings 2. Down syndrome

ISBN 978-1-890627-86-7 pa; 1-890627-86-0 pa

LC 2008049753

"Skotko and Levine address preteens and teenagers who have a sibling with Down syndrome, answering questions that have been generated through their work with this population. . . . With a wealth of information, numerous resources, and the reassurance that all siblings of people with disabilities sometimes go through periods of contradictory feelings, this is an excellent guide for young people who are trying to figure out how to negotiate an often-confusing relationship." SLJ

Includes bibliographical references

Snedden, Robert

Explaining autism. Smart Apple Media 2010 45p il (Explaining) lib bdg $34.25

Grades: 5 6 7 8 **616.85**

1. Autism 2. Asperger's syndrome

ISBN 978-1-59920-307-2 lib bdg; 1-59920-307-3 lib bdg

LC 2008-49285

Describes the illness, including its symptoms, how it affects physical and mental health, current treatments, and how people with autism live everyday lives

"The incorporation of quotes and personal accounts in 'Case Notes' sidebars adds to the sensitive tone found throughout [the title]." SLJ

Includes glossary and bibliographical references

Sonenklar, Carol

Anorexia and bulimia. Twenty-First Century Books 2010 128p il (USA Today health reports: diseases and disorders) lib bdg $34.60

Grades: 7 8 9 10 11 12 **616.85**

1. Bulimia 2. Anorexia nervosa

ISBN 978-0-8225-6786-8; 0-8225-6786-5

This describes the symptoms and treatment of anorexia and bulimia.

This book "stands out for the substantial amount of information conveyed in a lively writing style. . . . Graphs, sidebars, diagrams, and other illustrations [are] used judiciously." Booklist

Stefanski, Daniel, 1997-

★ **How** to talk to an autistic kid; illustrated by Hazel Mitchell. Free Spirit 2011 43p il $12.99

Grades: 3 4 5 6 **616.85**

1. Autism

ISBN 978-1-57542-365-4; 1-57542-365-0

"Stefanski provides clear, sometimes blunt, often humorous advice for readers on how to interact with autistic classmates. An authority on this topic—he is a 14-year-old boy with autism—he begins by describing autism. . . . He describes, using a brief paragraph or two per page, some of the traits many autistic people share. . . . For each trait, he offers down-to-earth suggestions for resolving problems. . . . His insightful, matter-of-fact presentation demystifies behaviors that might confuse or disturb non-autistic classmates. Simple cartoon illustrations in black, gray and two shades of turquoise accompany the text. . . . A thought-provoking introduction to autism . . . and an essential purchase for every primary and middle-school classroom." Kirkus

Stewart, Gail

Anorexia; [by] Gail B. Stewart. Cherry Lake Pub. 2009 32p il (Health at risk) lib bdg $27.07

Grades: 4 5 6 7 **616.85**

1. Anorexia nervosa

ISBN 978-1-60279-281-4 lib bdg; 1-60279-281-X lib bdg

LC 2008017496

This explains why anorexics feel the need to keep losing weight, what can happen to them as a result of their desperate struggle to be thin, and how they can get help.

"Great for reports or reluctant readers." Booklist

Includes bibliographical references

Bulimia; [by] Gail B. Stewart. Cherry Lake Pub. 2009 32p il (Health at risk) lib bdg $27.07

Grades: 4 5 6 7 **616.85**

1. Bulimia

ISBN 978-1-60279-282-1 lib bdg; 1-60279-282-8 lib bdg

LC 2008-17497

This describes the health risks of bulimia and what can be done to help people fight this disease.

"Great for reports or reluctant readers." Booklist

Includes bibliographical references

Tabone, Francis

Autism spectrum disorder; The Ultimate Teen Guide. Francis Tabone. Rowman & Littlefield 2016 232 p. illustrations (ebook) $56; (hardback : alk. paper) $45

Grades: 8 9 10 11 **616.85**

1. Autism 2. Teenagers -- Life skills guides 3. Autism spectrum disorders -- Popular works

ISBN 9781442262423; 9781442262416

LC 2016000780

This book, by Francis Tabone, part of the It Happened To Me series, "provides a comprehensive look at autism spectrum disorder. Designed to help teens and their families gain a social, medical, and historical understanding of ASD, this book addresses the factors that have influenced the treatment of this condition. Featuring stories and quotes from teens and young adults who live with ASD." (Publisher's note)

"A useful research tool and an essential resource for secondary school libraries." SLJ

Includes bibliographical references and index

Tompkins, Michael A.

My anxious mind; a teen's guide to managing anxiety and panic. by Michael A. Tompkins and Katherine A. Martinez; illustrated by Michael Sloan. Magination Press 2009 196p il pa $14.95

Grades: 7 8 9 10 11 12 **616.85**

1. Anxiety 2. Panic disorders

ISBN 978-1-4338-0450-2 pa; 1-4338-0450-6 pa

LC 2009011442

"Tompkins and Martinez directly address their readers: 'If you have an anxious mind,' giving teens the sense of a caring adult speaking to them. . . . Following the first chapters on definitions and how to seek help, there are several chapters with increasingly more complicated aids that teens can implement. . . . The final chapters stress the importance of proper nutrition, exercise, and sleep, and the possible need for medication. Throughout the book, first-person vignettes describe specific anxieties or phobias and how they were dealt with using the strategies outlined in the middle chapters. . . . They serve the purpose, along with the appealing line drawings, of catching readers' interest and enlivening the text." SLJ

Zucker, Bonnie

Take control of OCD; the ultimate guide for kids with OCD. Prufrock Press 2010 179p il pa $16.95

Grades: 6 7 8 9 10 **616.85**

1. Obsessive-compulsive disorder

ISBN 978-1-59363-429-2; 1-59363-429-3

LC 2010-34863

The author "addresses affected young readers directly and offers a structured set of self-help strategies for coping with diagnosed obsessive-compulsive behavior. Suggesting that the chapters be read in order for best results, she opens with a nontechnical explanation of the disorder's genetic and neurological roots, then goes on to discuss creating written behavioral 'ladders,' using relaxation techniques effectively, building self-awareness, handling uncertainty, and managing stress." Booklist

Includes bibliographical references

616.86 Substance abuse (Drug abuse)

Allman, Toney

Drugs. Cherry Lake Pub. 2009 32p il (Health at risk) lib bdg $27.07

Grades: 4 5 6 7 **616.86**

1. Drug abuse

ISBN 978-1-60279-283-8 lib bdg; 1-60279-283-6 lib bdg

LC 2008017503

This describes the dangers of drug abuse, the programs that help people get off drugs, and how to avoid drug use.

"Great for reports or reluctant readers." Booklist

Includes bibliographical references

Esherick, Joan

No more butts; kicking the tobacco habit. Mason Crest 2009 112p il (Tobacco: the deadly drug) lib bdg $26.95

Grades: 6 7 8 9 **616.86**

1. Smoking cessation programs

ISBN 978-1-4222-0236-4 lib bdg; 1-4222-0236-4 lib bdg

LC 2008-13215

Explains how difficult smoking cessation can be and offers tips on how to quit for good.

"The writing is professional but not at a level that causes readers to struggle. The information is made relevant to the everyday reader . . . [and] . . . it would be a strong addition to the nonfiction section of any library and is appropriate for a broad age level." Voice Youth Advocates

Includes glossary and bibliographical references

Hunter, David

Born to smoke; nicotine and genetics. Mason Crest 2009 112p il (Tobacco: the deadly drug) lib bdg $26.95

Grades: 6 7 8 9 **616.86**

1. Smoking 2. Tobacco habit 3. Behavior genetics

ISBN 978-1-4222-0243-2; 1-4222-0243-7

LC 2008-13218

Explains how genetics may affect an individual's susceptibility to nicotine addiction, and discusses the debate over genetic predisposition to nicotine addiction versus a person's upbringing.

"The writing is professional but not at a level that causes readers to struggle. The information is made relevant to the everyday reader . . . [and] . . . it would be a strong addition to the nonfiction section of any library and is appropriate for a broad age level." Voice Youth Advocates

Includes glossary and bibliographical references

Hyde, Margaret Oldroyd

★ **Smoking** 101; an overview for teens. [by] Margaret O. Hyde, John F. Setaro. Twenty-First Century Books 2006 128p il lib bdg $26.60

Grades: 8 9 10 11 12 **616.86**

1. Smoking 2. Tobacco

ISBN 0-7613-2835-1

LC 2004-22757

"The message is clear, the facts are well-presented, and the tone is insightful. These authors understand the teen audience and how to reach it." SLJ

Includes bibliographical references

Miller, Heather

Smoking. Cherry Lake Pub. 2009 32p il (Health at risk) lib bdg $27.07

Grades: 4 5 6 7 **616.86**

1. Smoking 2. Tobacco habit

ISBN 978-1-60279-286-9 lib bdg; 1-60279-286-0 lib bdg

LC 2008017501

This describes why smoking is dangerous, how difficult it is to stop once you start, and what efforts are underway to put the brakes on this habit.

"Great for reports or reluctant readers." Booklist

Includes bibliographical references

616.89 Mental disorders

★ **(Don't)** call me crazy; 33 voices start the conversation about mental health. edited by Kelly Jensen. Algonquin Young Readers 2018 240 p. (trade pbk. original : alk. paper) $16.95

Grades: 7 8 9 10 11 12 **616.89**

1. Mental health 2. Mental illness 3. Adolescent psychology 4. Mental health -- Case studies 5. Mental illness -- Case studies 6. Young adults -- Mental health -- Case studies

ISBN 9781616207816

LC 2018010861

Schneider Family Book Award Honor Book: Teens (2019)

In this book, edited by Kelly Jensen, "thirty-three actors, athletes, writers, and artists offer essays, lists, comics, and illustrations that explore a wide range of topics: their personal experiences with mental illness, how we do and don't talk about mental health,

help for better understanding how every person's brain is wired differently, and what, exactly, might make someone crazy." (Publisher's note)

Includes bibliographical references

Kent, Deborah

★ **Snake** pits, talking cures, & magic bullets; a history of mental illness. 21st Cent. Bks. (Brookfield) 2003 160p il lib bdg $26.90

Grades: 6 7 8 9 **616.89**

1. Mental illness

ISBN 0-7613-2704-5

LC 2002-11208

Looks at how the mentally ill have been treated throughout history, focusing on advances made in the 19th and 20th centuries regarding mental hospitals, medications, and social acceptance

"An excellent history peppered with fascinating accounts. . . . Black-and-white archival photographs and reproductions appear throughout. . . . This is a fine treatment of a topic not heavily covered for this audience." SLJ

Includes glossary and bibliographical references

Life inside my mind; 31 authors share their personal struggles. edited by Jessica Burkhart. Simon Pulse 2018 viii, 309 p.p (hardcover) $17.99

Grades: 8 9 10 11 12 **616.89**

1. Mental health 2. Depression (Psychology) 3. Mental illness

ISBN 9781481494663; 9781481494649; 1481494643

LC 2018930091

This book, edited by Jessica Burkhart, "is an anthology of true-life events from writers of this generation, for this generation. These essays tackle everything from neurodiversity to addiction to OCD to PTSD and much more. The goals of this book range from providing home to those who are feeling alone, awareness to those who are witnessing a friend or family member struggle, and to open the floodgates to conversation." (Publisher's note)

"These bold, brave essays will educate the uninformed and inspire hope in those who may feel alone in their suffering." Pub Wkly

Meisel, Abigail

Investigating depression and bipolar disorder; real facts for real lives. Enslow Publishers 2010 160p il (Investigating diseases) lib bdg $34.60

Grades: 6 7 8 9 10 **616.89**

1. Depression (Psychology) 2. Manic-depressive illness

ISBN 978-0-7660-3340-5; 0-7660-3340-6

LC 2008-50060

"Meisel discusses the history, science, diagnosis, and treatment of depression and bipolar disorder. In addition, she shows how these illnesses affect not just the patients, but their families, peers, and friends. She explains the science behind the two conditions, their possible causes, and the varying nature of the illnesses themselves. . . . This is an excellent book for persons from high school age to adults to read and become familiar with these important illnesses." Sci Books Films

Includes glossary and bibliographical references

★ **Mental** health information for teens; edited by Siva Ganesh Maharaja. 5th edition Omnigraphics 2017 448 p hardcover $69

Grades: 7 8 9 10 11 12 **616.89**

1. Mental health 2. Adolescent psychology 3. Teenagers -- Health and hygiene

ISBN 0780815734; 9780780815735

LC 2017028218

This book "presents facts about the causes, warning signs, and diagnosis of mental illnesses, and it explains how the adolescent brain differs from the adult brain. Some of the specific disorders described in detail include anxiety, depression, eating disorders, post-traumatic stress disorder, psychoses, schizophrenia, and impulse control disorders." (Publisher's note)

Parks, Peggy J., 1951-

Schizophrenia. ReferencePoint Press 2011 96p il (Compact research: diseases and disorders) $26.95

Grades: 7 8 9 10 11 12 **616.89**

1. Schizophrenia

ISBN 978-1-60152-140-8; 1-60152-140-5

LC 2010037253

"Fortified with contemporary individual case studies of both teens and adults [this] title . . . discusses variations of [schizophrenia], as well as the prevalence, symptoms, causes, effects, diagnoses, and treatment, drawing upon media interviews and commentary as well as clinical reports and research studies. . . . The clear design includes recent graphs and tables, color photos and diagrams, and lots of carefully documented primary-source quotes from patients, researchers, and scientists." Booklist

Includes bibliographical references

616.9 Other diseases

Allman, Toney

Infectious disease research; by Toney Allman. ReferencePoint Press 2012 96 p. (Inside science series) (hardback) $27.95

Grades: 6 7 8 9 10 11 12 **616.9**

1. Communicable diseases -- Encyclopedias 2. Communicable diseases

ISBN 1601521774; 9781601521774

LC 2011007745

This book, by Toney Allman, presents a research guide to infectious disease research. "Infectious diseases are responsible for untold global suffering and the loss of millions of human lives each year. This knowledge drives the research toward a fuller understanding of infectious microbial agents and the development of new treatment and prevention methods for infectious diseases." (Publisher's note)

Includes bibliographical references and index

Aronin, Miriam

Tuberculosis; the white plague! Bearport Pub. 2011 32p il map (Nightmare plagues) lib bdg $25.27

Grades: 4 5 6 7 **616.9**

1. Tuberculosis

ISBN 978-1-936088-06-5; 1-936088-06-1

LC 2010010679

Discover what causes tuberculosis and how it affects the body.

"The writing is accessible and interspersed with interesting photographs and fact boxes. . . . [The book relies] on an honest discussion of [tuberculosis and is an] . . . effective, easily navigated [introduction]." SLJ

Includes glossary and bibliographical references

Colligan, L. H.

★ **Tick** -borne illnesses. Marshall Cavendish Benchmark 2009 64p il (Health alert) $22.95

Grades: 4 5 6 7 **616.9**

1. Tick-borne diseases

ISBN 978-0-7614-2914-2; 0-7614-2914-X

LC 2007-38517

This "title features a handsome format, with well-chosen illustrations, a substantial amount of information, and some practical insights." Booklist

Includes glossary

Emmeluth, Donald

Botulism; consulting editor, Hilary Babcock; foreword by David L. Heymann. 2nd ed.; Chelsea House 2010 144p il map (Deadly diseases and epidemics) $34.95

Grades: 7 8 9 10 **616.9**

1. Botulism

ISBN 978-1-60413-235-9; 1-60413-235-3
LC 2010-8111

First published 2005

This book contains "information on this disease, exploring its history, causes, statistics, and . . . diagnostic and treatment breakthroughs. It also includes accounts of numerous recent outbreaks." Publisher's note

Includes glossary and bibliographical references

Green, Caroline

Drug resistance. New Forest Press 2010 64p il (Cutting-edge science) lib bdg $34.25

Grades: 7 8 9 10 **616.9**

1. Drug resistance

ISBN 978-1-84898-323-6; 1-84898-323-9

This addresses the topic of drug resistance, "touching on both scientific and societal issues . . . The underlying science is addressed, as well as the current state of scientific and ethical thinking. Stock color photographs and diagrams accompany the [text]. Sidebars provide biographical information on contemporary scientists as well as highlights of their research methods and studies." Horn Book Guide

Includes glossary and bibliographical references

Hoffmann, Gretchen

★ **Chicken** pox. Marshall Cavendish Benchmark 2009 62p il (Health alert) $22.95

Grades: 4 5 6 7 **616.9**

1. Chickenpox

ISBN 978-0-7614-2916-6; 0-7614-2916-6

This "title features a handsome format, with well-chosen illustrations, a substantial amount of information, and some practical insights." Booklist

Includes glossary

Kelly, Evelyn B.

Investigating tuberculosis and superbugs; real facts for real lives. [by] Evelyn B. Kelly, Ian Wilker, and Marylou Ambrose. Enslow Publishers 2010 160p il (Investigating diseases) lib bdg $34.60

Grades: 7 8 9 10 **616.9**

1. Tuberculosis 2. Drug resistance

ISBN 978-0-7660-3343-6; 0-7660-3343-0
LC 2009-37811

This "methodically presents medical and statistical information about major kinds of tuberculosis, malaria, AIDS/HIV, and other persistent bacterial, viral, and parasitic pandemics worldwide that are becoming ominously resistant to once-effective treatments. . . . [This is] massively documented with endnotes; supplemented by sidebar insertions, accounts of specific cases, and small color photos; and rounded off with digestible lists of relevant further sources." Booklist

Includes bibliographical references

Murphy, Jim

Invincible microbe; tuberculosis and the never-ending search for a cure. Jim Murphy, Alison Blank. Clarion Books 2012 149 p. (hardback) $18.99

Grades: 5 6 7 8 9 **616.9**

1. Tuberculosis 2. Lungs -- Diseases 3. Communicable diseases -- Treatment 4. Microorganisms

ISBN 0618535748; 9780618535743
LC 2011025951

This book looks at tuberculosis. It "starts with archeologists finding evidence of tuberculosis in a 500,000 year old skull and continues through to the present day. Various 'cures' such as the medieval 'king's touch' . . . , bloodletting of the 19th century, twentieth century sanatoriums and modern day drug cocktails are all discussed." Also "covered is the socioeconomic side of the disease, with a discussion of how treatment often varied depending on the race and economic status of the patient." (Children's Literature)

Includes bibliographical references

Newman, Patricia

Ebola; fears and facts. by Patricia Newman. Lerner Publishing Group, Inc. 2016 48 p. color illustrations, maps (lb : alk. paper) $31.99

Grades: 4 5 6 7 8 **616.9**

1. Ebola virus 2. Epidemics 3. Hemorrhagic diseases

ISBN 1467792403; 9781467792400
LC 2015001167

This juvenile reference book, by Patricia Newman, "takes you behind the sensational headlines to address questions and concerns about the [Ebola] virus. Learn about the history of the disease, its symptoms, and how it spreads. Find out how the 2014 epidemic compares to past Ebola outbreaks, as well as to outbreaks of other infectious diseases." (Publisher's note)

"Breaking new ground, Newman has written a truly excellent book for middle grade students that tackles the terrifying spector of Ebola. As the title suggests, readers will come away with more facts and less fears." SLJ

Parks, Peggy J., 1951-

HPV; Peggy J. Parks. 2nd edition Referencepoint Press Inc. 2015 96 p. col. ill., col. map $28.95

Grades: 7 8 9 10 11 12 **616.9**

1. Papillomaviruses

ISBN 1601526903; 9781601526908
LC 200844026

"A frank survey of medical statistics concerning HPV and the HPV vaccine, Parks's summation incorporates charts, photos, sidebars, research chronology, and primary sources to valorize the need for immunization. The fact-filled text covers the risks from cervical cancer as well as other types of sexually transmitted diseases, particularly the human immunodeficiency virus. Primary and secondary indexing leads the reader to specifics of population protection, including the Centers for Disease Control and Prevention and the National Cervical Cancer Coalition." (VOYA)

Includes bibliographical references and index

Sheen, Barbara

MRSA. Lucent Books 2010 104p il (Diseases and disorders series) $33.45

Grades: 7 8 9 10 **616.9**

1. Methicillin-Resistant Staphylococcus aureus

ISBN 978-1-4205-0144-5; 1-4205-0144-5
LC 2009-32644

This "offers a thorough explanation of [MRSA] giving a basic definition; a discussion of the causes, symptoms, and treatments; a description of living with the disease; and ideas of future treatment and diagnoses. Each volume lists source notes and organizations to contact. A glossary, index, and ideas for further reading are also included. The color photographs and sidebars help to make the information in the dense text more easily understood, and personal stories provide insight into how individuals deal with their disease." Voice Youth Advocates

Includes glossary and bibliographical references

Shmaefsky, Brian

Toxic shock syndrome; [by] Brian R. Shmaefsky; consulting editor, Hilary Babcock; foreword by David L. Heymann. 2nd ed.; Chelsea House 2010 127p il (Deadly diseases and epidemics) $34.95

Grades: 8 9 10 11 12 **616.9**

1. Toxic shock syndrome

ISBN 978-1-60413-243-4; 1-60413-243-4

LC 2010029222

First published 2003

This describes types of toxic shock syndrome, its causes, diagnosis and treatment.

Includes glossary and bibliographical references

★ **Stress** information for teens; edited by Siva Ganesh Maharaja. 3rd edition Omnigraphics 2017 400 p hardcover $69

Grades: 7 8 9 10 11 12 **616.9**

1. Stress management 2. Stress (Psychology) 3. Teenagers -- Health and hygiene

ISBN 9780780815896; 0780815890

LC 2017041421

This book "helps readers understand what stress is, recognize the different types of stressors, and realize how stress affects the adolescent mind, body, and behavior. Common causes of teen stress are discussed, and diseases and disorders having possible stress components (including asthma, back pain, chronic fatigue, peptic ulcers, eczema, hair loss, and eating disorders) are explained. Facts about successful practices, therapies, and techniques for handling anger, improving body image and self-esteem, and relieving stress . . . are also included." (Publisher's note)

616.95 Sexually transmitted diseases, zoonoses

Collins, Nicholas

Frequently asked questions about STDs; by Nicholas Collins and Samuel G. Woods. Rosen Pub. 2012 64 p. col. ill. (library) $31.95

Grades: 7 8 9 10 **616.95**

1. Teenagers -- Sexual behavior 2. Sexually transmitted diseases 3. Sexually transmitted diseases -- Miscellanea

ISBN 1448846307; 9781448846306

LC 2011000303

This book by Nicholas Collins looks at STDs. "Sexually transmitted diseases are clinically explained, including how they affect the body, how to recognize symptoms of infection, and how teens can protect themselves and their partner against, not only STDs, but HIV and AIDS as well." (Voice of Youth Advocates)

Includes bibliographical references (p. 83) and index.

Cozic, Charles P.

Herpes. ReferencePoint Press 2011 96p il (Compact research: diseases and disorders) $23.95

Grades: 7 8 9 10 11 12 **616.95**

1. Herpesvirus diseases

ISBN 978-1-60152-117-0; 1-60152-117-0

LC 2010030634

Introduces herpes and discusses the symptoms, possible health effects, and treatments for the virus.

Includes bibliographical references

Dougherty, Terri

Sexually transmitted diseases. Lucent Books 2010 96p il (Diseases and disorders series) $32.45

Grades: 7 8 9 10 **616.95**

1. Sexually transmitted diseases

ISBN 978-1-4205-0220-6

LC 2009-39583

"This book discusses the most common afflictions, diseases that are usually found in combinations, medical advances, and how the outlook for STDs is complicated by new trends such as drug-resistant strains. Information is also supplied about causes, prevention, diagnosis, and treatment. . . . A number of the photos show some of the horrific physical manifestations in individuals, including infants. . . . [This book] should be considered for first purchase." SLJ

Includes bibliographical references

Yancey, Diane

STDs. Twenty-First Century Books 2012 128p il (USA today health reports: diseases and disorders)

Grades: 7 8 9 10 11 12 **616.95**

1. Sexually transmitted diseases

ISBN 0-7613-5456-5; 978-0-7613-5456-7

LC 2010036514

"Yancey writes in a straightforward manner about sexually transmitted diseases, opening with the profiles of several teens coping with an STD. . . . The causes, symptoms, and treatments of the main STDs, . . . are thoroughly covered, from the emotional side effects of genital herpes to the dangers of ordering an HIV home sample collection kit online. . . . Students, teachers, and librarians looking to supplement health textbooks with current information will find this . . . valuable." Voice Youth Advocates

Includes bibliographical references

616.97 Diseases of immune system

Ballard, Carol

Explaining food allergies. Smart Apple Media 2010 45p il (Explaining) $23.95

Grades: 5 6 7 8 **616.97**

1. Food allergy

ISBN 978-1-59920-316-4; 1-59920-316-2

LC 2008049936

This "does an excellent job of discussing complex clinical science while showing what daily life is like for kids living with food allergies, from the signs and symptoms to the tests and treatments. . . . This blend of the technical and the personal will have wide appeal." Booklist

Ehrlich, Paul

Living with allergies; [by] Paul M. Ehrlich, with Elizabeth Shimer Bowers. Facts On File 2009 168p (Teen's guides) $34.95; pa $14.95

Grades: 7 8 9 10 11 12 **616.97**

1. Allergy

ISBN 9781438129976; 978-0-8160-7327-6; 0-8160-7327-9; 0-8160-7742-8 pa

LC 2008-34352

This "book addresses allergy triggers, preventing allergic reactions, what to expect from treatment, paying for care, and how to help yourself, friends, or family members who may have allergies." Publisher's note

Includes glossary and bibliographical references

Hillstrom, Kevin

Food allergies; by Kevin Hillstrom. Lucent Books 2012 96 p. col. ill. (Nutrition and health) (hardcover) $30.95

Grades: 7 8 9 10 11 12 **616.97**

1. Food allergy

ISBN 1420507206; 9781420507201

LC 2012002945

This book on food allergies by Kevin Hillstrom is part of the "Nutrition and Health" book series. It "discusses the rising numbers of allergic young people, the physiology of the symptoms (with a clear diagram of an anaphylactic reaction), the search for a cure, and the social stigma." (Booklist) "Doctors, researchers, and people living with food allergies are quoted throughout the text." (Publisher's note)

Includes bibliographical references (p. 81-84) and index.

James, Otto

AIDS. Smart Apple Media 2010 46p il (Voices) lib bdg $34.95

Grades: 7 8 9 10 11 12 **616.97**

1. AIDS (Disease)

ISBN 978-1-59920-282-2; 1-59920-282-4

LC 2009-5417

"AIDS looks at causes, prevention, treatment, and the chances of a cure and also discusses abstinence, safe sex, the cost of AIDS drugs, and much more. . . . [The] blend of current political debate with witnesses' close-up experiences told through photos, narratives, and quotes will draw browsers, and many will go on to find out more." Booklist

Includes glossary and bibliographical references

Marsico, Katie

HIV /AIDS. ABDO Pub. Co. 2010 112p il (Essential issues) lib bdg $22.95

Grades: 7 8 9 10 **616.97**

1. AIDS (Disease)

ISBN 978-1-60453-955-4; 1-60453-955-0

LC 2009-29954

This is "well-written, providing examples that put a human face to each problem. Quotes and facts are clearly attributed, and their sources are noted in the extensive back matter. . . . Sidebars provide further information, or, more compellingly, offer stories about those touched by the topic. . . . [This] will be of great assistance to students writing reports." SLJ

Includes glossary and bibliographical references

★ **Quicksand;** HIV/AIDS in our world. by Anonymous. Candlewick Press 2009 103p $15.99

Grades: 6 7 8 9 10 **616.97**

1. AIDS (Disease)

ISBN 978-0-7636-1589-5; 0-7636-1589-7

LC 2009-7761

"The anonymous author explains her motivation for writing this book by telling readers that ten years ago, when HIV/AIDS was still considered a taboo subject, her brother-in-law was diagnosed with the disease. She writes in a truthful, open manner, addressing common questions about HIV/AIDS and providing easy-to-understand and honest advice. . . . The author's personal insight is what makes this book an important addition. Topics address everything from the history of HIV/AIDS to how to protect oneself from the disease. She also provides suggestions on how to cope with hearing that a family or friend has HIV/AIDS. . . . The author's focus on how the disease affects all people, whether they have contracted HIV/AIDS or not, makes this book a must-have for all teen collections." Voice Youth Advocates

Includes glossary and bibliographical references

Sonenklar, Carol

AIDS. Twenty-First Century Books 2011 128p il (USA Today health reports: diseases and disorders) lib bdg $34.60

Grades: 8 9 10 11 12 **616.97**

1. AIDS (Disease)

ISBN 978-0-8225-8581-7 lib bdg; 0-8225-8581-2 lib bdg

LC 2010-37633

This book about AIDS will serve as "solid report fodder. . . . [The] volume has an introduction, a description of the condition, chapters on what it is like to live with it, and material on research and treatments. A healthy smattering of statistics and personal stories appear throughout." SLJ

Includes glossary and bibliographical references

Yount, Lisa

Luc Montagnier; identifying the AIDS virus. by Lisa Yount. Chelsea House 2011 xix, 123 p.p col.ill. (library) $35

Grades: 7 8 9 10 11 12 **616.97**

1. AIDS (Disease) 2. HIV (Viruses)

ISBN 1604136618; 9781604136616

LC 2010047006

This book by Lisa Yount is part of the Trailblazers in Science and Technology series and looks at Luc Montagnier. It "recounts the life and career of the Nobel Prize-winning French virologist whose contributions to the understanding of the nature of viruses led to a significant advance in cancer research and in discovering the HIV virus that causes AIDS." (Publisher's note)

Includes bibliographical references and index.

616.99 Tumors and miscellaneous communicable diseases

★ **Cancer** information for teens; edited by Greg Mullin. 4th edition Omnigraphics 2018 424 p hardcover $69

Grades: 7 8 9 10 11 12 **616.99**

1. Cancer

ISBN 9780780813199; 9780780816152 hardcover

LC 2017052247

This book "presents updated facts about cancer causes, prevention, diagnosis, and treatment. It explains how cancer occurs in the body and describes some warning signs; and provides information on coping with treatment side effects, changes in body image, and social and survivorship issues. Issues of concern to teens with friends or family members who have cancer are also addressed." (Publisher's note)

Goldsmith, Connie

Skin cancer. Twenty-First Century Books 2010 128p il (USA Today health reports: diseases and disorders) lib bdg $34.60

Grades: 7 8 9 10 11 12 **616.99**

1. Cancer 2. Skin -- Diseases

ISBN 978-0-7613-5469-7; 0-7613-5469-7

LC 2010-10003

This describes causes, prevention, and treatments of skin cancer.

This is "liberally sprinkled with relevant articles and 'snapshots' (graphs showing statistical breakdowns of the topic at hand) from the newspaper, providing a competent introduction to primary-source material." SLJ

Includes glossary and bibliographical references

Markle, Sandra

Leukemia; true survival stories. Lerner Publications 2010 48p il (Powerful medicine) lib bdg $27.93

Grades: 5 6 7 8 **616.99**

1. Leukemia

ISBN 978-0-8225-8700-2 lib bdg; 0-8225-8700-9 lib bdg

LC 2009-34441

This book about leukemia "will grab the attention of middle school readers. . . . The illustrations and photos are stunning with medically accurate captions. Real-life patients, whose photos are included in the text, are highlighted, with updates on their progress at the end of . . . [the] book. . . . This . . . fills the need for up-to-date books on medical topics using vocabulary that a young teenager can understand." Voice Youth Advocates

Includes glossary and bibliographical references

Parks, Peggy J., 1951-

Brain tumors. ReferencePoint Press 2011 96p il (Compact research: diseases and disorders) $26.95

Grades: 7 8 9 10 11 12 **616.99**

1. Brain -- Tumors

ISBN 978-1-60152-138-5; 1-60152-138-3

LC 2010040107

"Fortified with contemporary individual case studies of both teens and adults [this] title . . . discusses variations of [brain tumors], as well as the prevalence, symptoms, causes, effects, diagnoses, and treatment, drawing upon media interviews and commentary as well as clinical reports and research studies. . . . The clear design includes recent graphs and tables, color photos and diagrams, and lots of carefully documented primary-source quotes from patients, researchers, and scientists." Booklist

Includes bibliographical references

Sheen, Barbara

Prostate cancer; Barbara Sheen. Lucent Books 2008 104 p. col. ill. (hardcover) $34.95

Grades: 7 8 9 10 **616.99**

1. Prostate gland -- Cancer 2. Cancer 3. Prostate -- Cancer

ISBN 1590185935; 9781590185933

LC 2008003808

This book is part of the Diseases & Disorders series and looks at prostate cancer. The series "offers young readers and researchers a means of understanding ailments and their ramifications. Clear, careful explanations offer insight into what these conditions are, what causes them, how people live with them, and the latest information about treatment and prevention." (Publisher's note)

Includes bibliographical references (p. 85-90, 96-97) and index.

Silver, Marc

My parent has cancer and it really sucks; Marc Silver, Maya Silver. Sourcebooks Fire 2013 272 p. $14.99

Grades: 6 7 8 9 10 11 12 **616.99**

1. Cancer -- Psychological aspects 2. Children of cancer patients

ISBN 9781402273070; 140227307X

LC 2012039095

This handbook "aims to guide teens through the experience of having an ill parent. . . . Short chapters include 'Let's Talk: How to Keep Your Family Communication Lines Wide Open,' 'How Things Will Change During Cancer,' 'Dealing with Stress,' 'The Power (and the Limits) of Optimism and Faith,' 'Seeking Support,' 'Facing a Dire Prognosis,' and 'Losing a Parent to Cancer.'" (School Library Journal)

"Drawing on their experiences, the Silvers offer advice for finding solace in people who have been there and who have found ways to cope... It's admirable that the authors don't sugarcoat the realities of cancer and will speak with an honesty that teens will identify with and find comfort in." Booklist

617 Surgery, regional medicine, dentistry, ophthalmology, otology, audiology

Markle, Sandra

Wounded brains; true survival stories. Lerner Publications 2011 48p il (Powerful medicine) lib bdg $27.93

Grades: 5 6 7 8 **617**

1. Brain -- Wounds and injuries

ISBN 978-0-8225-8704-0 lib bdg; 0-8225-8704-1 lib bdg

LC 2009034440

Describes several true cases of traumatic brain injury and the medical treatment that followed.

This narrative reads "like information from the Discovery Health channel, for kids: part fascinating science, part human interest story, and part 'Eew, gross!'. . . Clear, straightforward prose is supplemented by definitions and explanations of medical techniques and jargon. The numerous color photos and medical images will satisfy readers' curiosity." SLJ

Includes glossary and bibliographical references

Murphy, Jim

★ **Breakthrough!** how three people saved "blue babies" and changed medicine forever. Jim Murphy. Clarion Books 2015 144 p. illustrations hardback $18.99; paperback $10.99

Grades: 4 5 6 7 8 **617**

1. Heart -- Surgery 2. Cardiovascular system -- Surgery 3. Surgeons -- Maryland -- Biography

ISBN 9780547821832; 9780358094258

LC 2015013601

In this book, author Jim Murphy details how "in 1944 a groundbreaking operation repaired the congenital heart defect known as blue baby syndrome. The operation's success brought the surgeon Alfred Blalock international fame and paved the way for open-heart surgery. But the technique had been painstakingly developed by Vivien Thomas, Blalock's African American lab assistant, who stood behind Blalock in the operating room to give him step-by-step instructions." (Publisher's note)

"Murphy's dramatic nonfiction narrative recounting of one of the first open heart surgeries ever performed is not to be missed—even reluctant readers will be hooked." SLJ

Townsend, John

★ **Scalpels,** stitches & scars; a history of surgery. Raintree 2005 56p il (Painful history of medicine) lib bdg $32.86; pa $9.90

Grades: 6 7 8 9 **617**

1. Surgery

ISBN 1-4109-1332-5 lib bdg; 1-4109-1337-6 pa

LC 2004-14248

A history of surgery from ancient times to the present

This is "packed with grisly facts and gory images. . . . But the science is accurate, and many readers will be intrigued by the medical drama. . . . The design, with lots of color pictures, captions, and boxes, will grab browsers, and the cover art is a thrilling story in itself." Booklist

Includes glossary and bibliographical references

Woog, Adam

The **bionic** hand. Norwood House Press 2009 48p il lib bdg $25.27

Grades: 3 4 5 6 **617**

1. Bionics 2. Artificial limbs

ISBN 978-1-59953-341-4 lib bdg; 1-59953-341-3 lib bdg

LC 2009-15640

"Explores the development and creation of the i-LIMB which is the first commercially available bionic hand." Publisher's note

617.1 Injuries and wounds

Lew, Kristi

Clot & scab; gross stuff about your scrapes, bumps, and bruises. illustrations by Michael Slack. Millbrook Press 2010 48p il (Gross body science) lib bdg $29.27

Grades: 4 5 6 **617.1**

1. Wounds and injuries

ISBN 978-0-8225-8965-5 lib bdg; 0-8225-8965-6 lib bdg

LC 2008-45626

"Solid information layered between sarcastic comments and kid-friendly terminology like fart, poop, barf, and puke will keep readers engaged. . . . Labeled, captioned (and graphic) photographs, cartoon-style illustrations, and micrographs add information." SLJ

Includes glossary and bibliographical references

Markle, Sandra

Bad burns; true survival stories. Lerner Publications 2010 48p il (Powerful medicine) lib bdg $27.93

Grades: 5 6 7 8 **617.1**

1. Burns and scalds

ISBN 978-0-8225-8702-6 lib bdg; 0-8225-8702-5 lib bdg

LC 2009034439

Explores how advancements in medicine and technology have helped victims of severe skin burns, and includes real-life stories of burn survivors and tips on burn prevention and treatment.

This narrative reads "like information from the Discovery Health channel, for kids: part fascinating science, part human interest story, and part 'Eew, gross!'. . . Clear, straightforward prose is supplemented by definitions and explanations of medical techniques and jargon. The numerous color photos and medical images will satisfy readers' curiosity." SLJ

Includes glossary and bibliographical references

Shattered bones; true survival stories. Lerner Publications 2010 48p il (Powerful medicine) lib bdg $27.93

Grades: 5 6 7 8 **617.1**

1. Bones 2. Fractures

ISBN 978-0-8225-8703-3 lib bdg; 0-8225-8703-3 lib bdg

LC 2009034442

Offers true stories of people who suffered broken bones, along with information on the skeleton, its structure and function, and the treatments doctors use for injuries.

This narrative reads "like information from the Discovery Health channel, for kids: part fascinating science, part human interest story, and part 'Eew, gross!'. . . Clear, straightforward prose is supplemented by definitions and explanations of medical techniques and jargon. The numerous color photos and medical images will satisfy readers' curiosity." SLJ

Includes glossary and bibliographical references

★ **Sports** injuries information for teens; edited by Siva Ganesh Maharaja. 4th edition Omnigraphics 2017 448 p. hardcover $69

Grades: 7 8 9 10 11 12 **617.1**

1. Wounds and injuries 2. Athletes -- Wounds and injuries 3. Teenagers -- Health and hygiene

ISBN 078081567X; 9780780815674

LC 2017029918

This book "offers teens a comprehensive, fact-based guide to being a healthy athlete. It includes guidelines for participating safely in sports and avoiding injury. It also discusses how to deal with injuries when they do occur. It explains diagnostic and treatment procedures and discusses issues related to rehabilitation, including suggestions for making decisions about returning to play." (Publisher's note)

617.4 Surgery by systems and regions

Goldsmith, Connie

Traumatic brain injury; from concussion to coma. Connie Goldsmith. Twenty-First Century Books 2014 88 p. illustrations (lib. bdg. : alk. paper) $34.60

Grades: 6 7 8 9 10 11 **617.4**

1. Nervous system 2. Brain -- Wounds and injuries

ISBN 1467713481; 9781467713481

LC 2013001346

This juvenile nonfiction book, by Connie Goldsmith, explores traumatic brain injury, including "the different types of TBIs, what causes them, and how they are diagnosed and treated. . . . [It also profiles] National Hockey League player Derek Boogaard and U.S. Representative Gabby Giffords, both of whom sustained TBIs, with dramatically different outcomes. . . . [Finally, it previews] medical technologies that help victims recover and promise hope for the future." (Publisher's note)

"Photographs, charts, and statistics are included, which expand the information. Appended are source notes, a glossary, a bibliography, and a list of websites and resources. The currency of this topic and its potential impact on teens make this a smart choice for school and public libraries." Booklist

Includes bibliographical references and index

McClafferty, Carla Killough

Fourth down and inches; concussions and football's make-or-break moment. by Carla Killough McClafferty. Carolrhoda Books 2013 96 p. (lib. bdg. : alk. paper) $20.95

Grades: 6 7 8 9 10 11 12 **617.4**

1. Brain -- Concussion 2. Football players -- Wounds and injuries 3. Football injuries 4. Head -- Wounds and injuries 5. Football players -- Health and hygiene

ISBN 1467710679; 9781467710671

LC 2013004192

This book by Carla Killough McClafferty presents a "warning about the dangers of playing football, especially at the youth level. . . . The author . . . presents story after poignant story of high school and professional players who suffered brain damage or worse. Among their profiles are details of research studies, photos of MRI images and damaged brain tissue, and explanations of chronic traumatic encephalopathy (CTE) and second-impact syndrome." (Publishers Weekly)

Includes bibliographical references and index

Yount, Lisa

Alfred Blalock, Helen Taussig, and Vivien Thomas; mending children's hearts. by Lisa Yount. Chelsea House 2012 xviii, 127 p.p col. ill. (Trailblazers in science and technology) (library) $35

Grades: 7 8 9 10 11 12 **617.4**

1. Heart -- Surgery 2. Surgeons 3. Pediatric cardiology -- History 4. Heart surgeons -- United States -- Biography

ISBN 1604136588; 9781604136586

LC 2010035656

This book, part of the Trailblazers in Science and Technology series, focuses on medical professionals Alfred Blalock, Helen Taussig, and Vivien Thomas. The book "recounts the lives and careers of three medical pioneers—a white male surgeon (Blalock), a white female cardiologist (Taussig), and an African-American male laboratory technician (Thomas)—who combined their skills in 1944 to create a groundbreaking operation" for pediatric cardiology. (Publisher's note)

"Sidebars and captioned color and archival photographs round out the dense, though clearly written, texts." SLJ

Includes bibliographical references and index.

617.5 Regional medicine

Ear, nose, and throat; edited by Kara Rogers. Britannica Educational Pub. in association with Rosen Educational Services 2012 xvii, 186 p.p col. ill.

Grades: 7 8 9 10 11 12 **617.5**

1. Ear 2. Nose 3. Throat 4. Otolaryngology -- Popular works

ISBN 1615306579; 9781615306572

LC 2011013432

Editor Kara Rogers presents a book on otolaryngology. "The interconnectedness of the ear, nose, and throat is evident when you consider how the smell . . . can affect your perception of their taste, or how a runny nose and scratchy throat can lead to an ear infection. In addition to enabling sensory perception, the ear, nose, and throat perform a number of vital functions in the human body. This incisive volume examines the structure of each in turn and in concert with the other, also exploring the diseases and disorders that sometimes afflict them." (Publisher's note)

Includes bibliographical references (p. 170-171) and index

617.7 Ophthalmology

Bender, Lionel

Explaining blindness. Smart Apple Media 2010 45p il (Explaining) lib bdg $34.25

Grades: 5 6 7 8 **617.7**

1. Blind

ISBN 978-1-59920-310-2 lib bdg; 1-59920-310-3 lib bdg

LC 2008-49286

Describes blindness, including its possible causes, the different types of visual impairment, current treatments and cures, and how blind and visually impaired people live everyday lives

"The incorporation of quotes and personal accounts in 'Case Notes' sidebars adds to the sensitive tone found throughout [the title]." SLJ

Includes glossary

Markle, Sandra

Lost sight; true survival stories. Lerner Publications 2010 48p il (Powerful medicine) lib bdg $27.93

Grades: 5 6 7 8 **617.7**

1. Eye 2. Blind 3. Vision

ISBN 978-0-8225-8701-9 lib bdg; 0-8225-8701-7 lib bdg

LC 2009-34443

This book about vision loss "will grab the attention of middle school readers. . . . The illustrations and photos are stunning with medically accurate captions. Real-life patients, whose photos are included in the text, are highlighted, with updates on their progress at the end of . . . [the] book." Voice Youth Advocates

Includes glossary and bibliographical references

Sheen, Barbara

Artificial eyes; by Barbara Sheen. Norwood House Press 2017 48 p. color illustrations (hardback : alk. paper) $26.60

Grades: 5 6 7 **617.7**

1. Eyes, Artificial 2. Medical technology 3. Medical innovations 4. Vision

ISBN 9781599537610

LC 2015027486

This book, in the Tech Bytes series by Barbara Sheen, describes the invention and development of artificial eyes. "Scientists have been perfecting artificial eyes for several centuries. From the most basic versions where artificial eyes were painted and worn over the eyelid, to today's versions that make it virtually impossible to tell a person has lost their eye. Correlates with STEM instruction. [The book] includes glossary, websites, and bibliography for further reading." (Publisher's note)

"The authors are more than just technology experts; they are also skilled writers for the youth market. What results is an easy-to-navigate series. Reluctant readers who like technology will love this series." VOYA

Includes bibliographical references (page 45) and index

617.8 Otology and audiology

Levete, Sarah

Explaining deafness. Smart Apple Media 2010 45p il (Explaining) lib bdg $34.25

Grades: 5 6 7 8 **617.8**

1. Deafness

ISBN 978-1-59920-313-3 lib bdg; 1-59920-313-8 lib bdg

LC 2008-49289

Discusses the history, diagnosis, and treatment of deafness, including ways to cope with living with the condition

"The incorporation of quotes and personal accounts in 'Case Notes' sidebars adds to the sensitive tone found throughout [the title]." SLJ

Includes glossary, bibliographical references and filmography

617.9 Operative surgery and special fields of surgery

Campbell, Andrew

Cosmetic surgery. Smart Apple Media 2010 44p il (Science in the news) lib bdg $34.25

Grades: 6 7 8 9 **617.9**

1. Plastic surgery

ISBN 978-1-59920-322-5 lib bdg; 1-59920-322-7 lib bdg

LC 2008-49274

This book about cosmetic surgery "move[s] smoothly, occasionally pausing for the definition of a term. [The title] boast[s] plenty of attractive photos, and a clean layout allows the information to be easily consumed. . . . Provides the information that younger teens need." SLJ

Includes glossary

Organ transplants. Smart Apple Media 2010 45p il (Science in the news) lib bdg $34.25

Grades: 6 7 8 9 **617.9**

1. Transplantation of organs, tissues, etc.

ISBN 978-1-59920-321-8 lib bdg; 1-59920-321-9 lib bdg

LC 2008-41436

"Discusses current practices of organ transplants, developments in science that make transplants possible, and the history of organ transplants as well as issues surrounding organ shortage and organ selling." Publisher's note

Includes glossary

Foran, Racquel

★ **Organ** transplants; Racquel Foran. Abdo Pub. Co. 2013 112 p. illustrations (chiefly color) $34.22

Grades: 6 7 8 9 10 **617.9**

1. Medical technology 2. Transplantation of organs, tissues, etc.

ISBN 1617839043; 9781617839047

LC 2013932976

Written by Racquel Foran and part of the Medical Marvels series, "This title follows the development of organ transplants, including early attempts at transplantation, groundbreaking discoveries and the doctors who made them, and where the science is heading in the future. . . . Sidebars, full-color photos, a glossary, and well-placed graphs, charts, and maps, enhance this . . . title." (Publisher's note)

"The book is handsomely designed, with interesting full-bleed photographs often facing a page of text. Sidebars, highlighted in yellow, pertain to the topic and never feel intrusive. Source notes and a bibliography . . . add to the title's usefulness for researchers." Booklist

Includes bibliographical references and index

Schwartz, Tina P.

Organ transplants; a survival guide for the entire family: the ultimate teen guide. Scarecrow Press 2005 243p il (It happened to me) $36.50

Grades: 7 8 9 10 **617.9**

1. Transplantation of organs, tissues, etc.

ISBN 0-8108-4924-0

LC 2004-21563

"The 13 chapters, written in a question-and-answer format, detail the steps involved from diagnosis and being placed on a waiting list to pre and post-surgery. . . .The well-written text is complemented by a comprehensive section of suggestions for additional information. . . . Texts with this breadth of coverage are rare." SLJ

Includes bibliographical references

618.2 Obstetrics

★ **Pregnancy** information for teens; edited by Keith Jones. 3rd edition Omnigraphics 2017 440 p hardcover $69

Grades: 7 8 9 10 11 12 **618.2**

1. Teenage parents 2. Teenage pregnancy 3. Teenagers -- Health and hygiene

ISBN 0780815572; 9780780815575

LC 2017007851

This book "provides information about prenatal care, nutrition, fetal development, and preparing for labor and delivery. It includes facts about abortion and adoption, as well as information for teens who choose to parent their infants, along with other helpful information." (Publisher's note)

618.92 Pediatrics

★ **Allergy** information for teens; health tips about allergic reactions to food, pollen, mold, and other substances, including facts about diagnosing, treating, and preventing allergic responses and complications. edited by Karen Bellenir. 2nd ed. Omnigraphics, Inc. 2013 xiii, 388 p.p ill. (hardcover) $69

Grades: 8 9 10 11 12 **618.92**

1. Allergy -- Encyclopedias 2. Teenagers -- Health and hygiene 3. Allergy 4. Food allergy 5. Insect allergy 6. Allergy in children

ISBN 0780812883; 9780780812888

LC 2012038514

This book is a "51-chapter resource for reliable information about the many kinds of allergic reactions, triggers, symptoms, tests, treatments, and management strategies. Each chapter presents topics in short sections, using a handy question-and-answer format interwoven with many diagrams and sidebars. The volume concludes with lists of 19 additional titles, 10 cookbooks, and 24 articles, many with 2005 publication dates." (School Library Journal)

Includes bibliographical references and index.

Chaloner, Kim

Diabetes and me; an essential guide for kids and parents. written by Kim Chaloner & illustrated by Nick Bertozzi. Hill and Wang, a division of Farrar, Straus, and Giroux 2013 176 p. illustrations (hardcover) $30

Grades: 4 5 6 7 8 9 10 11 12 Adult **618.92**

1. Diabetes 2. Diabetes in children

ISBN 0809028190; 9780809028191; 9780809038718; 9781466848481

LC 2012036543

In this book, author Kim Chaloner "gives kids the tools they need to take charge of their health and understand what it means to be diagnosed with diabetes. In this graphic guide, she walks four young people through the basics of diabetes, both Type 1 and Type 2. . . . Illustrated by the award-winning artist Nick Bertozzi." (Publisher's note)

"Bertozzi . . . ably depicts a diverse group of diabetics, detailed accounts of handling monitors during the course of the school day, and some apt metaphorical battles between sugars and insulin. This easy-to-read resource is a standout for its wealth of information and welcoming format." Booklist

Includes bibliographical references

Grossberg, Blythe

★ **Asperger's** rules! how to make sense of school and friends. by Blythe Grossberg. Magination Press 2012 127 p. col. ill. (paperback) $9.95; (hardcover) $14.95

Grades: 5 6 7 8 **618.92**

1. Life skills 2. Social skills 3. Asperger's syndrome 4. Autism in children 5. Autistic children -- Education 6. Asperger's syndrome -- Social aspects

ISBN 1433811286; 9781433811272; 9781433811289

LC 2011053483

This book by Blythe Grossberg presents a "guide for readers with Asperger's, covering feelings and emotions, teachers, asking for help, and dealing with bullies. Quizzes let readers reflect on their own approaches to situations like interacting with kids at school, and Grossberg also includes tips on how to interpret social situations. . . . Flowcharts illustrate how various conversations might progress, and other sections focus on dressing properly and eating healthful meals." (Publishers Weekly)

Kemper, Bitsy

Teens and phobias; by Bitsy Kemper. ReferencePoint Press, Inc. 2017 80 p. (Teen mental health) (hardback) $29.95
Grades: 8 9 10 11 **618.92**

1. Phobias 2. Adolescent psychology 3. Phobias in children
ISBN 9781682821299; 9781682821282

LC 2016035298

In this book in the Teen Mental Health series, by Bitsy Kemper, "phobias are a widespread group of anxiety disorders and a cause of much distress for teens. 'Teens and Phobias' examines the nature of these disorders, what causes them, what it is like to live with them, and how or whether they can be treated or cured." (Publisher's note)

"Extremely current in its coverage, this set not only recognizes the importance of such standard topics as eating disorders and suicide but also acknowledges less-covered disorders not often associated with adolescence . . . ." SLJ

Includes bibliographical references and index

Verdick, Elizabeth

The **survival** guide for kids with autism spectrum disorders (and their parents) by Elizabeth Verdick & Elizabeth Reeve ; illustrated by Nick Kobyluch. Free Spirit Pub. 2012 234 p. col. ill. (pbk.) $16.99
Grades: 5 6 7 8 Adult **618.92**

1. Autism 2. Autistic children 3. Parents of autistic children 4. Children with autism spectrum disorders 5. Autistic children -- Family relationships
ISBN 1575423855; 9781575423852; 9781575426747

LC 2011046520

This book "offers kids with autism spectrum disorders (ASDs) their own comprehensive resource for both understanding their condition and finding tools to cope with the challenges they face every day . . . with an emphasis on helping children gain new self-understanding and self-acceptance. Meant to be read with a parent, the book addresses questions . . . and provides strategies for communicating, making and keeping friends, and succeeding in school." (Publisher's note)

"This volume could become a treasured resource for families looking for help in successfully working through some of the problems faced by higher-functioning children with ASD." SLJ

620 Engineering and allied operations

Mercer, Bobby

Junk drawer engineering; 25 construction challenges that don't cost a thing. Bobby Mercer. Chicago Review Press Inc. 2017 224 p. (trade paper : alk. paper) $14.99
Grades: 4 5 6 7 8 **620**

1. Engineering 2. Science -- Experiments 3. Engineering -- Experiments
ISBN 9781613737163

LC 2016037089

In this activity book, in the Junk Drawer Science series, by Bobby Mercer, "there's no need for expensive, high-tech materials to test your engineering skills--you probably have all you need in your home junk drawer. . . . Each project has a suggested materials list, step-by-step instructions with illustrations for one possible solution, and suggestions on how to adapt each challenge for different ages and skill levels." (Publisher's note)

620.1 Engineering mechanics and materials

Hunt, Shannon

★ **Engineered!** engineering design at work. by Shannon Hunt, illustrated by James Gulliver Hancock. Kids Can Press 2017 48 p. color illustrations $17.99
Grades: 5 6 7 8 9 10 **620.1**

1. Engineering 2. Engineering -- Vocational guidance
ISBN 177138560X; 9781771385602

LC 2017035790

This book, by Shannon Hunt, illustrated by James Gulliver Hancock, presents nine real-life problems for which engineers designed inventive (and even crazy!) solutions. . . . A helpful seven-step flowchart of the engineering design process is also featured. . . . [and] these steps are highlighted in each chapter with helpful icons that refer back to the flowchart." (Publisher's note)

"Eye-opening, encouraging, and attractive—a winning trifecta" Kirkus.

Kassinger, Ruth

Glass; from Cinderella's slippers to fiber optics. [by] Ruth G. Kassinger. Twenty-First Century Bks. 2003 80p il lib bdg $25.90
Grades: 7 8 9 10 **620.1**

1. Glass
ISBN 0-7613-2109-8

LC 2002-5329

Describes the physical composition and characteristics of glass, and presents glassmaking techniques and the various uses made of glass throughout history

This "will catch the interest of a wide variety of readers. The color photographs are clear, interesting, and self-explanatory." Libr Media Connect

Includes bibliographical references

Morris, Neil

Glass. Amicus 2010 48p il (Materials that matter) lib bdg $28.50
Grades: 4 5 6 7 **620.1**

1. Glass
ISBN 978-1-60753-065-7 lib bdg; 1-60753-065-1 lib bdg

LC 2009029796

"The clean layout includes photographs and occasional charts, graphs, and technical illustrations against a range of pastel backgrounds. Inset boxes provide further detail, interesting extras, and recycling information. . . . [This book offers] easily accessible background information for report writers." SLJ

Includes glossary and bibliographical references

Other titles in this series are:

Metals
Paper
Plastics
Textiles
Wood

Metals. Amicus 2010 48p il (Materials that matter) lib bdg $28.50

Grades: 4 5 6 7 **620.1**

1. Metals

ISBN 978-1-60753-066-4 lib bdg; 1-60753-066-X lib bdg

LC 2009029797

"The clean layout includes photographs and occasional charts, graphs, and technical illustrations against a range of pastel backgrounds. Inset boxes provide further detail, interesting extras, and recycling information. . . . [This book offers] easily accessible background information for report writers." SLJ

Includes glossary and bibliographical references

Ward, David J.

Materials science; by D. J. Ward. Lerner Publications 2009 47p il (Cool science) lib bdg $26.60

Grades: 4 5 6 **620.1**

1. Materials

ISBN 978-0-8225-7588-7 lib bdg; 0-8225-7588-4 lib bdg

LC 2007042176

This describes how scientists study the microscopic parts of materials such as plastic, glass, or stainless steel, how they learn how each part makes something hard or soft, strong or weak, or good or bad at carrying heat, and how they use that knowledge to create supermaterials to help make better sports equipment, tinier computer chips, and more.

Includes glossary and bibliographical references

620.2 Sound and related vibrations

Claybourne, Anna

Ear -splitting sounds and other vile noises; by Anna Claybourne. Crabtree Pub Co 2013 32 p. (reinforced library binding : alk. paper) $27.60

Grades: 4 5 6 **620.2**

1. Noise 2. Sound 3. Science 4. Sounds

ISBN 0778709256; 9780778709251; 9780778709510

LC 2012043526

This book, by Anna Claybourne, part of the "disgusting and dreadful science" series, "features a look at the weird, revolting and shocking aspects of science for children at KS2." This volume focuses on sound and noise. "The books offer . . . fascinating facts, fun examples and true-life stories to provide ways in to understanding solid scientific principles." (Publisher's note)

"These brief and lively introductions provide a plethora of fun and gross facts. Sounds explains the science behind sound, how ears work, ultrasound, and more. It also includes a scientific explanation of how whoopee cushions work..." SLJ

Includes bibliographical references and index

Other titles in the series include:

Electric shocks and other energy evils (2013)

Glaring light and other eye-burning rays (2013)

Gut-wrenching gravity and other fatal forces (2013)

Rooney, Anne

Audio engineering and the science of soundwaves; Anne Rooney. Crabtree Publishing 2014 32 p. (Engineering in action) (reinforced library binding) $27.60

Grades: 5 6 7 8 **620.2**

1. Sound 2. Sound -- Recording and reproducing 3. Acoustical engineering 4. Sound -- Recording and reproducing

ISBN 077871196X; 9780778711964; 9780778712299

LC 2013035439

"From sound effects in video games and movies to surround-sound theatres, this fact-filled book [by Anne Rooney] explores the many ways audio engineers apply the science of sound. Readers will explore how sound travels and the characteristics of sound waves. Readers will also learn how to combine their understanding of sound science and the engineering design process to tackle a design challenge of their own." (Publisher's note)

"Books in the Engineering in Action series provide broad introductions to their respective fields in a colorfully illustrated, large-format package...Audio tackles the science of sound and hearing, the differences between analog and digital signals, and the varied work of audio engineers. Solid information for engineering-minded students." Booklist

Includes index

Other titles in the series include:

Aerospace engineering and the principles of flight (2013)

Chemical engineering and chain reactions (2014)

Civil engineering and the science of structures (2013)

Electrical engineering and the science of circuits (2013)

Environmental engineering and the science of sustainability (2014)

Mechanical engineering and simple machines (2013)

Optical engineering and the science of light (2014)

621 Applied physics

Sobey, Ed

Electric motor experiments. Enslow Publishers 2011 128p il (Cool science projects with technology) lib bdg $31.93

Grades: 6 7 8 9 **621**

1. Electric motors 2. Science -- Experiments

ISBN 978-0-7660-3306-1; 0-7660-3306-6

This explains how motors work and includes experiments in how to build and use a motor.

Includes glossary and bibliographical references

621.042 Energy engineering

Allen, John

Careers in environmental and energy technology; by John Allen. ReferencePoint Press, Inc. 2017 80 p. (High-tech careers) (hardback) $29.95

Grades: 7 8 9 10 **621.042**

1. Vocational guidance 2. Energy industries 3. Energy industries -- Vocational guidance 4. Environmental engineering -- Vocational guidance

ISBN 9781682821114; 9781682821107

LC 2016033948

In this book, by John Allen, "emphasis on environmental issues has made high-tech careers related to the environment and energy technology among the fastest growing occupations in the United States. Comments from people in the industry, current statistics and forecasts, and realistic descriptions provide a useful look at high-tech environmental and energy technology jobs ranging from fuel cell engineers to environmental analysts to renewable energy project developers." (Publisher's note)

"A few color photos, an interview with a renewable energy project developer, and a list of other jobs in the field round out this useful introduction for students with an interest in a career in the field." Booklist

Includes bibliographical references and index

Burgan, Michael

Energy; by Michael Burgan. Mason Crest 2017 64 p. color illustrations (hardback) $23.95

Grades: 6 7 8 9 10 **621.042**

1. STEM education 2. Energy development 3. Biomass energy 4. Energy industries 5. Renewable energy sources

ISBN 1422235890; 9781422235898

LC 2016004733

This juvenile book, by Michael Burgan, part of the "STEM in current events" series, explores developments in science, technology, engineering and mathematics within the energy sector. "'Text-Dependent Questions' and 'Research Project' sections help learners to re-engage with the text and topic—many even promote group work." (School Library Journal)

"A great fit for classroom or school libraries and a strong consideration for public libraries interested in the integration of STEM into everyday life." SLJ

Includes bibliographcial references (page 62) and index.

621.1 Fluid-power technologies

Collier, James Lincoln

The **steam** engine. Marshall Cavendish Benchmark 2006 112p il (Great inventions) lib bdg $37.07

Grades: 7 8 9 10 **621.1**

1. Steam engines

ISBN 0-7614-1880-6

This is a history of the steam engine and its influence on American history and culture.

This is presented "thoughfully yet conversationally. . . . [It] will reward steady reading." Horn Book Guide

Includes glossary and bibliographical references

O'Neal, Claire

How to use waste energy to heat and light your home. Mitchell Lane Publishers 2009 47p il (Tell your parents) lib bdg $21.50

Grades: 4 5 6 7 **621.1**

1. Recycling 2. Waste products as fuel

ISBN 978-1-58415-765-6 lib bdg; 1-58415-765-8 lib bdg

LC 2009-4483

Explores how to reduce the amount of trash produced and stored by reusing items and recycling materials, and describes how these efforts can help protect the environment

This title "offers numerous facts and statistics, all of which are cited. . . . Chapters cover present-day issues and . . . are interspersed with full-color photographs and short 'Did You Know' trivia boxes. . . . Back matter includes detailed resource lists and 'Try This!' experiments." SLJ

Includes glossary and bibliographical references

621.3 Electrical, magnetic, optical, communications, computer engineering; electronics, lighting

Swanson, Jennifer

Amazing feats of electrical engineering; Jennifer Swanson. Essential Library 2015 112 p. $35.64 **621.3**

1. Electrical engineering 2. Electricity

ISBN 1624034284; 9781624034282

LC 2014932576

This book by Jennifer Swanson "examines amazing feats of electrical engineering. Engaging text explores the global positioning system, solar power plants, and self-driving cars. It also examines the engineers who made these projects a reality and traces the history of the discipline. Relevant sidebars, stunning photos, and a glossary aid readers' understanding of the topic. A hands-on project and career-planning chart give readers a sense of what it takes to become an engineer." (Publisher's note)

Includes bibliographical references (pages 104-109) and index

Yount, Lisa

Nikola Tesla; harnessing electricity. by Lisa Yount. Chelsea House 2012 xviii, 128 p.p col. ill. (Trailblazers in science and technology) (library) $35

Grades: 7 8 9 10 11 12 **621.3**

1. Electricity 2. Tesla, Nikola, 1856-1943 3. Inventors -- United States -- Biography 4. Electrical engineers -- United States -- Biography

ISBN 1604136707; 9781604136708

LC 2010052627

This book by Lisa Yount is part of the Trailblazers in Science and Technology series and looks at Nikola Tesla. He "saw his fortunes reverse as many times." He "drew the attention of businessman George Westinghouse with his alternating current (AC), a method of delivering electricity more efficiently and over greater distances than Edison's direct current (DC). With Westinghouse's support, Tesla's method soon became dominant in the industry." (Publisher's note)

Includes bibliographical references and index.

621.31 Generation, modification, storage, transmission of electric power

Lew, Kristi

Goodbye, gasoline; the science of fuel cells. Compass Point Books 2009 48p il (Headline science) lib bdg $27.93

Grades: 5 6 7 8 **621.31**

1. Fuel cells

ISBN 978-0-7565-3521-6 lib bdg; 0-7565-3521-2 lib bdg

LC 2008011729

This "clearly examines the history and technology of hydrogen fuel cells, including the various types such as proton exchange membrane and alkaline cells. An excellent description of how the technology works gives readers an understanding of both the successes and problems relating to these promising energy sources. . . . The color illustrations and charts . . . are clear and helpful, and the text, although information rich, is not overly difficult." SLJ

O'Neal, Claire

How to use wind power to light and heat your home. Mitchell Lane Publishers 2009 47p il map (Tell your parents) lib bdg $21.50

Grades: 4 5 6 7 **621.31**

1. Wind power 2. Renewable energy resources

ISBN 978-1-58415-762-5 lib bdg; 1-58415-762-3 lib bdg

LC 2009-4530

Introduces wind power, including the history of harnessing the wind for work, how modern wind power generates electricity, and how to install a turbine to a home

This book "offers numerous facts and statistics, all of which are cited. . . . Chapters cover present-day issues and . . . are interspersed with full-color photographs and short 'Did You Know' trivia boxes. . . . Back matter includes detailed resource lists and 'Try This!' experiments." SLJ

Includes glossary and bibliographical references

Rusch, Elizabeth

★ The **next** wave; the quest to harness the power of the oceans. by Elizabeth Rusch. Houghton Mifflin Harcourt 2014 80 p. color illustrations (Scientists in the field) paperback $9.99; $18.99

Grades: 5 6 7 8 9 **621.31**

1. Ocean 2. Ocean energy resources 3. Renewable energy resources 4. Tidal power 5. Renewable energy sources

ISBN 9781328852328; 9780544099999

LC 2013050150

In this book, by Elizabeth Rusch, part of the Scientists in the Field series, readers "journey to the wave-battered coast of the Pacific Northwest to meet some of the engineers and scientists working to harness the punishing force of our oceans. . . . With an array of amazing devices that cling to the bottom of the sea floor and surf on the crests of waves, these explorers are using a combination of science, imagination, and innovation to try to capture wave energy." (Publisher's note)

"Rusch captures the determined, entrepreneurial spirit of the profiled engineers as well as the need for creative problem-solving and ingenuity. Photographs and illustrations feature prototypes in both small-scale laboratory and full-ocean tests." Horn Book

Includes bibliographical references and index

Spalding, Maddie

The **science** of wind energy; by Maddie Spalding. ReferencePoint Press, Inc. 2018 80 p. color illustrations (Science of renewable energy) (hardcover : alk. paper) $29.95

Grades: 7 8 9 10 11 12 **621.31**

1. Wind power 2. Renewable energy resources

ISBN 9781682823101; 9781682823095

LC 2017042008

In this book in the Science of Renewable Energy series, by Maddie Spalding, "every day, vast fields of wind turbines turn the energy of moving air into useful electricity. 'The Science of Wind Energy' examines the field of wind energy, including the underlying scientific concepts, its potential for replacing fossil fuels, examples of how it is used today, and prospective future developments." (Publisher's note)

Includes bibliographical references and index

621.32 Lighting

Collier, James Lincoln

Electricity and the light bulb; [by] James Lincoln Collier. Marshall Cavendish Benchmark 2006 112p il (Great inventions) lib bdg $37.07

Grades: 7 8 9 10 **621.32**

1. Electric power 2. Electric lighting

ISBN 0-7614-1878-4

LC 2004-21623

This is a history of electric power and the invention of the light bulb and their influence on American history and culture.

This is presented "thoughfully yet conversationally. . . . [It] will reward steady reading." Horn Book Guide

Includes glossary and bibliographical references

Sonneborn, Liz

The **electric** light; Thomas Edison's illuminating invention. Chelsea House 2007 120p il (Milestones in American history) lib bdg $35

Grades: 7 8 9 10 **621.32**

1. Inventors 2. Electric lighting

ISBN 978-0-7910-9350-4 lib bdg; 0-7910-9350-6 lib bdg

LC 2006-34432

This "accessible [volume captures] the hard work, perseverance, and natural talent of Edison. . . . The [text explores] the [man's life] along with providing information about the genesis and development of [electric light]. Many photographs, reproductions, and sidebars contribute to a clean design and help clarify topics." Horn Book Guide

Includes bibliographical references

621.36 Optical engineering

Bow, James

Lasers; James Bow. Gareth Stevens Publishing 2016 48 p. color illustrations (library binding) $31.95

Grades: 5 6 7 8 **621.36**

1. Lasers 2. Technology

ISBN 1482451581; 9781482451580; 9781482451641

This juvenile book, by James Bow, part of the "Cutting-Edge Technology" series, explores laser technology "from DVD players to laser pointers. . . . Even fiber optics communication and cutting devices use laser technology to produce great things. This book explores the possibilities of light, bringing amazing facts about lasers to the eyes of enthusiastic readers interested in this cutting-edge technology." (Publisher's note)

"Rock-solid choices that will update and deepen science and technology collections." SLJ

Includes bibliographical references (page 47) and index.

621.38 Electronics, communications engineering

Gregory, Josh

From butterfly wings to display technology; by Josh Gregory. Cherry Lake Publishing 2014 32 p. color illustrations (Innovations from Nature) (lib. bdg.) $28.50

Grades: 6 7 8 9 10 **621.38**

1. Biomimicry 2. Inventions 3. Butterflies 4. Inventions 5. Flat panel displays

ISBN 1624317545; 9781624317545; 9781624317606

LC 2013030377

This book, by Josh Gregory, part of the Innovations from Nature series, "explores how researchers take ideas from plants and animals and turn them into projects with practical applications. . . . [It] explains the concept of structural color, such as the iridescent colors formed by the ridged scales on a butterfly's wings. This concept has led to the development of IMOD display screens for electronic devices." (Booklist)

"These creative books use a pleasantly unusual angle to show how aspects of nature can inspire scientists and engineers. For instance, some scientists, inspired by the way a gecko's feet allow it to stick to surfaces, are attempting to create an adhesive tape using the structure of the lizard's foot. High-resolution photographs and a dark black and purple layout give the books a slick, stylish look, while the narrative is both fascinating and informative. Intriguing additions to science collections." SLJ

Includes bibliographical references and index

Other titles in the series include:
From African Plants to Vaccine Preservation (2014)
From Bats to Radar (2013)
From Birds to Aircraft (2013)
From Cats' Eyes to Reflectors (2013)
From Gecko Feet to Adhesive Tape (2014)
From Kingfishers to Bullet Trains (2013)
From Locusts to Automobile Anti-Collision Systems (2013)
From Sharks to Swimsuits (2013)
From Termite Den to Office Building (2014)
From Thistle Burrs to Velcro (2013)
From Woodpeckers to Helmets (2013)

621.381 Electronics

Electronics; edited by Sherman Hollar. Britannica Educational Pub. in association with Rosen Educational Services 2012 80 p. (Introduction to physics) (library binding) $31.70
Grades: 7 8 9 10 11 12 **621.381**
1. Electronics
ISBN 9781615306640; 1615306641
LC 2011017100

This book, edited by Sherman Hollar, is part of the Introduction to Physics series. It "examines various components, such as electron tubes and semiconductors, that have been essential to electronics over the years, as well as the history of the field in general and its applications in everyday life." (Publisher's note)

Includes bibliographical references and index

621.383 Specific communications systems

Coe, Lewis

The **telegraph**; a history of Morse's invention and its predecessors in the United States. McFarland & Co. 1993 184p il hardcover o.p. pa $29.95
Grades: 7 8 9 10 **621.383**
1. Artists 2. Painters 3. Inventors 4. Telegraph
ISBN 0-7864-1808-7 pa
LC 92-53597

This study of the development of the telegraph includes brief biographical sketches of Samuel Morse and other inventors

Includes bibliographical references

621.384 Radiotelephony

Kling, Andrew A.

Cell phones. Lucent Books 2010 112p il (Technology 360) $33.45
Grades: 8 9 10 11 12 **621.384**
1. Cellular telephones
ISBN 978-1-4205-0164-3; 1-4205-0164-X
LC 2009-6249

This book explores "the early development and advances of [cell phone] technology, its impact on society both positive and negative, and the importance it plays in our lives. . . . The history . . . progresses from the telegraph to the invention of the telephone, the merging of radio and telephone, and the implementation of computers to replace humans, eventually leading to wireless phones. Issues in regard to texting, the addition of cameras, video capabilities, disposal, safety, multimedia, and numerous other advances are addressed. . . . numerous color photos, diagrams, 'Bits & Bytes' boxes as well as many other additional text boxes create appeal and provide beneficial informative and complementary material to aid in understanding the technical details of the [text]." SLJ

Includes glossary and bibliographical references

Westphal, Michael

Cell phone science; what happens when you call and why. [by] Michele Sequeira, Michael Westphal. University of New Mexico Press 2010 174p il (Barbara Guth worlds of wonder science series for young readers) $24.95
Grades: 6 7 8 9 **621.384**
1. Cellular telephones 2. Wireless communication systems
ISBN 978-0-8263-4968-2; 0-8263-4968-4
LC 2010028600

"The book sets out to help readers understand the complex science behind . . . [cell phones]. . . . The book features clear explanations, easy-to-read text, and colorful photographs and illustrations on almost every page. Boxed areas and information in the margins supplement the text. Students interested in learning the story of the science behind their cell phone will be well rewarded with this title." SLJ

Includes glossary and bibliographical references

621.385 Telephony

Spilsbury, Richard

The **telephone**; [by] Richard and Louise Spilsbury. Heinemann Library 2011 32p il (Tales of invention) lib bdg $29; pa $7.99
Grades: 4 5 6 7 **621.385**
1. Telephone 2. Cellular telephones
ISBN 978-1-4329-3826-0 lib bdg; 1-4329-3826-6 lib bdg; 978-1-4329-3833-8 pa; 1-4329-3833-9 pa
LC 2009049027

"Beginning with the first telegraph, the book discusses how sound travels, how speech is transmitted by wire, and how Alexander Graham Bell's first telephones worked. Then the text quickly traces later technological developments, from transatlantic cables to early cell phones to the small, light, versatile models available today. . . . The many photographs and other illustrations include excellent labeled diagrams." Booklist

Includes bibliographical references

621.388 Television

Grabowski, John

Television. Lucent Books 2011 112p il (Technology 360) $33.45

Grades: 7 8 9 10 **621.388**

1. Television

ISBN 978-1-4205-0169-8; 1-4205-0169-0

LC 2010033525

This book offers "clean design with clear explanations of sometimes-complicated scientific subjects. . . . This brings the information [about television] up to date with flat screens and 3-D. . . . A strong [title] for report writers and students with a serious interest in technology and its inventions." Booklist

Includes bibliographical references

621.4 Prime movers and heat engineering

Woelfle, Gretchen

The **wind** at work; an activity guide to windmills. Gretchen Woelfle. 2nd ed. Chicago Review Press 2013 vii, 145 p.p ill. (paperback) $16.95

Grades: 4 5 6 **621.4**

1. Windmills 2. Science -- Experiments

ISBN 1613741006; 9781613741009

LC 2012046319

This introduction to windmills "discusses their history and function through modern times. . . . About one-third of the book is devoted to activities illustrating the properties of wind and the jobs performed by windmills. . . . The concluding chapters focus on windmills as a source of energy and suggest how to chart household energy use." (Booklist) Index. "Grades four to eight." (SLJ)

"The historical information is excellent, and includes Persian windmills of 1000 years ago, Dutch windmills of the 17th century, and modern wind turbines. Amusing anecdotes and intriguing facts are woven into the text, keeping it lively. . . . Black-and-white historical prints, photographs, and diagrams appear throughout." SLJ

Includes bibliographical references (pages 133-135) and index

621.43 Internal-combustion engines

Miller, Ron

Rockets. Lerner 2008 112p il (Space innovations) lib bdg $31.93

Grades: 7 8 9 10 **621.43**

1. Rocketry 2. Rockets (Aeronautics)

ISBN 978-0-8225-7153-7; 0-8225-7153-6

LC 2006-21220

The author "describes the history of rocket science, beginning in ancient China, where saltpeter, sulfur, and charcoal were first combined to create gunpowder. . . . The stories of the development of rockets through time are complemented by short biographies of important scientists such as Robert Goddard, stories of young model rocket makers, and sidebars explaining the science that makes rockets work. . . . It is a good choice for high school libraries, as well as for boys who are interested in science and nonfiction." Voice Youth Advocates

Includes bibliographical references

621.44 Geothermal engineering

Boyle, Jordan

Examining geothermal energy; Jordan Boyle. Clara House Books 2013 48 p. (Examining energy) (alk. paper) $24.95

Grades: 5 6 7 **621.44**

1. Geothermal resources 2. Geothermal engineering

ISBN 1934545414; 9781934545416

LC 2012035244

"This entry in the Examining Energy series presents . . . [an] overview of the advantages as well as past and present uses of geothermal energy. There are also glimpses of current research on future means of producing this energy in locales where no heat sources are conveniently near the earth's surface." It is "framed as a series of first-person conversations between a fictional student named Derek and likewise fictional scientists or tour guides at seven actual sites." (Booklist)

Includes bibliographical references and index

621.46 Electric and related motors

Gabrielson, Curt

Kinetic contraptions; build a hovercraft, airboat, and more with a hobby motor. Chicago Review Press 2010 176p il pa $16.95

Grades: 7 8 9 10 **621.46**

1. Airplanes -- Models 2. Motorboats -- Models 3. Automobiles -- Models

ISBN 978-1-55652-957-3; 1-55652-957-0

LC 2009-25695

The author "describes projects intended to foster in students a passion for electrical experimentation as they construct more than 20 motor-powered devices. With sections dedicated to creating machines that run on land, water, and air, as well as spinning machines (such as a snow globe) and bizarre machines (such as a bubble maker), the book has projects designed to appeal to everyone." Education Digest

621.47 Solar-energy engineering

Bearce, Stephanie

How to harness solar power for your home. Mitchell Lane Publishers 2009 47p il map (Tell your parents) lib bdg $21.50

Grades: 4 5 6 7 **621.47**

1. Solar energy

ISBN 978-1-58415-761-8 lib bdg; 1-58415-761-5 lib bdg

LC 2009-4529

This title about solar power "offers numerous facts and statistics, all of which are cited. . . . Chapters cover present-day issues and . . . are interspersed with full-color photographs and short 'Did You Know' trivia boxes. . . . Back matter includes detailed resource lists and 'Try This!' experiments." SLJ

Includes glossary and bibliographical references

Bright, Sandra

Examining solar energy; by Sandra Bright. Clara House Books 2013 48 p. (hardcover : alk. paper) $24.95

Grades: 5 6 7 8 **621.47**

1. Solar energy 2. Energy resources

ISBN 1934545457; 9781934545454

LC 2012035316

This book, by Sandra Bright, looks at solar energy through "fictitious research journals that examine the history, science, and future outlook of [energy resources]. Additional historical information, better scientific explanations, and extended future outlooks round-out the content." (Publisher's note)

Includes bibliographical references (pages 46-47) and index

Walker, Niki

Harnessing power from the sun; [by] Niki Walker. Crabtree Pub. Co. 2007 32p il map (Energy revolution) lib bdg $23.93; pa $8.95

Grades: 5 6 7 8 **621.47**

1. Solar energy

ISBN 978-0-7787-2912-9 lib bdg; 0-7787-2912-5 lib bdg; 978-0-7787-2926-6 pa; 0-7787-2926-5 pa

LC 2006014368

This describes various ways of gathering and distributing solar energy, and includes a brief history of solar power, and tips on energy conservation

"Vivid color photographs with informative captions extend the [text], showing diverse people and applications." SLJ

Includes glossary

621.48 Nuclear engineering

Kidd, J. S.

Nuclear power; the study of quarks and sparks. [by] J.S. Kidd and Renee A. Kidd. rev ed.; Chelsea House 2006 208p il (Science and society) $35

Grades: 7 8 9 10 **621.48**

1. Nuclear energy

ISBN 978-0-8160-5606-4; 0-8160-5606-4

LC 2005-52872

First published 1999 with title: Quarks and sparks: the story of nuclear power

Examines the people, events, and motivations leading up to modern-day discoveries and advances in nuclear physics

"Extensive scientific explanations are kept manageable, thanks to consistent references to their historical context; and descriptions of the nuclear race during the Second World War are especially riveting." Booklist [review of 1999 edition]

Includes bibliographical references

Mahaffey, James A.

Fusion; James A. Mahaffey. Facts on File 2012 x, 142 p.p (ebook) $45.00; (hardcover) $45.00

Grades: 7 8 9 10 11 12 **621.48**

1. Sun 2. Nuclear fusion 3. Big bang theory 4. Nuclear reactors 5. Fusion -- Popular works

ISBN 9781438138435; 0816076537; 9780816076536

LC 2011012505

This book, by author James A. Mahaffey, "deliver[s] complex information including background on the theories, applications, devices, and future of fusion. [Topics include] . . . hydrogen fusion in the Sun . . . the big bang nucleosynthesis . . . [and] the International Tokamak Experimental Reactor and the Demonstration Power Plant." (School Library Journal)

Includes bibliographical references and index.

Oxlade, Chris

Nuclear power. Smart Apple Media 2010 44p il map (Science in the news) lib bdg $34.25

Grades: 6 7 8 9 **621.48**

1. Nuclear energy 2. Nuclear engineering

ISBN 978-1-59920-320-1 lib bdg; 1-59920-320-0 lib bdg

LC 2008-49277

This book about nuclear power "move[s] smoothly, occasionally pausing for the definition of a term. [The title] boast[s] plenty of attractive photos, and a clean layout allows the information to be easily consumed. . . . Provides the information that younger teens need." SLJ

Includes glossary

621.5 Pneumatic, vacuum, low-temperature technologies

Pringle, Laurence, 1935-

Ice! the amazing history of the ice business. Laurence Pringle. Calkins Creek 2012 74 p. $17.95

Grades: 4 5 6 7 8 **621.5**

1. Ice 2. Refrigeration 3. Food -- Preservation

ISBN 159078801X; 9781590788011

LC 2012937320

This book looks at "iceboxes, icehouses, icemen, and . . . more about the history of the harvesting, storage, and delivery of ice." Author Laurence Pringle "briefly covers early food preservation . . . before delving into the rise of the ice industry in the early 1800s, and, in particular, the harvesting of the frozen stuff at pristine Rockland Lake in New York." (School Library Journal)

Includes bibliographical references and index.

621.9 Tools

Tomecek, Steve

Tools and machines; by Stephen M. Tomecek. Chelsea House Publishers 2010 182p il (Experimenting with everyday science) $35

Grades: 5 6 7 8 **621.9**

1. Tools 2. Machinery 3. Science -- Experiments

ISBN 978-1-60413-171-0; 1-60413-171-3

LC 2009-22332

This "offers 25 easy-to-perform activities that illuminate scientific principles. . . . [This] discusses levers, pulleys, and meters and explains how people use them in their daily lives. . . . Following each experiment are additional comments on the science behind the experiment and link to the one that follows. Photographs, simple diagrams and illustrations, and sample data tables appear throughout, and the [layout is] clear and colorful." SLJ

Includes bibliographical references

621.988 Additive manufacturing equipment

Bow, James

3 -D Printers; James Bow. Gareth Stevens Publishing 2016 48 p. color illustrations $31.95

Grades: 5 6 7 8 **621.988**

1. Three-dimensional printing

ISBN 1482451611; 9781482451610

This book in the Cutting-Edge Technology series, by James Bow, " explores the science behind . . . [3-D printers], including the history of 3-D printing and what scientists hope to achieve with these unique tools. Whether used for art, medicine, or just to make something cool at home, 3-D printing is poised to have a remarkable impact on our lives, and this book chronicles the technology's journey from concept to reality." (Publisher's note)

"Rock-solid choices that will update and deepen science and technology collections." SLJ

Includes bibliographical references (p. 47) and index.

Koch, Melissa

3D printing; the revolution in personalized manufacturing. by Melissa Koch. Twenty-First Century Books 2017 112 p. color illustrations (lb : alk. paper) $37.32

Grades: 7 8 9 10 11 12 **621.988**

1. Printing 2. Three-dimensional printing

ISBN 9781512467765; 9781512448603; 9781512415704

LC 2016033030

This book, Melissa Koch, focuses on 3D printing. "[T]here are many innovative uses for 3D printing. Yet 3D printing has drawbacks. Chemicals used in 3D printing can be toxic, and legal experts are not sure how to protect 3D printing inventions so that others do not steal ideas. Learn how 3D printing works and how we can keep up with the safety, health, and legal challenges that lie ahead." (Publisher's note)

"Student-report-friendly features and lots of color photos help to make this an attractive, timely, and popular addition to STEM collections." Booklist

Includes bibliographical references and index

622 Mining and related operations

Squire, Ann O.

Hydrofracking; the process that has changed America's energy needs. by Ann O. Squire. Children's Press, an imprint of Scholastic Inc. 2013 64 p. (Cornerstones of freedom) (library binding) $30

Grades: 4 5 6 **622**

1. Hydraulic fracturing 2. Shale gas 3. Gas well drilling

ISBN 0531236048; 9780531219621; 9780531236048

LC 2012034322

This book by Ann O. Squire is part of the "Cornerstones of Freedom" series, which provides "overviews of important national and global issues and their effects on current world development, especially in the United States." It "discusses the advantages and disadvantages of this method of extracting petroleum and natural gas, by pumping water and chemicals deep below the Earth's surface. Renewable energy sources are discussed as alternatives to this practice." (School Library Journal)

Includes bibliographical references (page 61) and index

622.342 Precious metals

McDonnell, Julia

How precious metals form; Julia McDonnell. Gareth Stevens Publishing 2017 32 p. illustrations (chiefly color) (library bound) $26.60; (ebook) $26.60

Grades: 5 6 7 **622.342**

1. Precious metals 2. Mines and mineral resources

ISBN 1482447304; 9781482447279; 9781482447293; 9781482447309; 9781482447323

LC 2016015519

This juvenile book, by Julia McDonnell, part of the "From the Earth: How Resources Are Made" series, "takes readers underground where they'll discover the processes and elements that shape precious metals. They'll learn about the features of metals that make them desirable, such as luster, ductility, and reactivity, and how certain metals are utilized." (Publisher's note)

"This series would be a great addition to school or public libraries, as it makes an often dull topic really shine." SLJ

Includes bibliographical references (page 31) and index.

623.4 Ordnance

Boos, Ben

Swords; an artist's devotion. written & illustrated by Ben Boos. Candlewick Press 2008 82p il $24.99; pa $12.99

Grades: 6 7 8 9 **623.4**

1. Swords

ISBN 978-0-7636-3148-2; 0-7636-3148-5; 978-0-7636-5098-8 pa

LC 2007-52333

"This absorbing, large-format collection of sketches, paintings, and historical notes on sword craft is not called an artist's devotion for nothing. Boos's treatment of his subject is reverential and his artwork is outstanding, combining meticulous attention to detail and a designer's sense for layout. The spare text provides just enough information but generally allows the illustrations to speak for themselves." SLJ

Includes bibliographical references

Collier, James Lincoln

Gunpowder and weaponry. Benchmark Bks. 2004 124p il (Great inventions) lib bdg $37.07

Grades: 6 7 8 9 **623.4**

1. Guns 2. Gunpowder 3. Military art and science 4. Firearms

ISBN 0-7614-1540-8

LC 2002-156289

This is a history of warfare and weaponry with emphasis on the significance of the invention of gunpowder

Includes bibliographical references

Diagram Group

The **new** weapons of the world encyclopedia; an international encyclopedia from 5000 B.C. to the 21st century. [by] the Diagram Group. rev ed.; St Martin's Press 2007 368p il pa $24.95

Grades: 8 9 10 11 12 Adult **623.4**

1. Reference books 2. Weapons -- History

ISBN 978-0-312-36832-6 pa; 0-312-36832-1 pa

First published 1980 with title: Weapons: an international encyclopedia from 5000 B.C. to 2000 A.D

This "guide covers the entire history of weapons, from the earliest, most primitive instruments up to remarkable advances in modern defense and warfare. . . . Includes weapons used in Kosovo, Afghanistan, Iraq and the Israel-Lebanon conflict. . . . [This book is] illustrated, with hundreds of color diagrams, charts [and] photographs." Publisher's note

Includes bibliographical references

Gurstelle, William

The **art** of the catapult; build Greek ballistae, Roman onagers, English trebuchets, and more ancient artillery. 2nd edition Chicago Review Press 2018 177 p il map paperback $16.99

Grades: 5 6 7 8 9 10 **623.4**

1. Catapult

ISBN 1-55652-526-5; 9780912777337 paperback

"This collection of 10 working catapult projects offers a fascinating look at world history, military strategy, and physics, related with an engaging yet lighthearted touch. . . . Instructions are clear, with full materials lists, helpful diagrams, and no skipped steps. . . . There's excellent booktalk potential here, and lively reading even for those who never get around to constructing a catapult." SLJ

Includes bibliographical references

Sheinkin, Steve

★ **Bomb**; the race to build and steal the world's most dangerous weapon. Steve Sheinkin. Roaring Brook Press 2012 266 p. ill. (hc) $19.99

Grades: 5 6 7 8 9 10 11 12 Adult **623.4**

1. Nuclear warfare 2. Nuclear weapons 3. World War, 1914-1918 -- Chemical warfare 4. Atomic bomb -- History 5. Operation Freshman, 1942 6. Atomic bomb -- Germany -- History 7. World War, 1939-1945 -- Secret service -- Soviet Union 8. World War, 1939-1945 -- Secret service -- Great Britain 9. World War, 1939-1945 -- Commando operations -- Norway -- Vemork

ISBN 1596434872; 9781596434875

LC 2011044096

YALSA Award for Excellence in Nonfiction for Young Adults (2013)

John Newbery Honor Book (2013); National Book Award Finalist: Young People's Literature (2012)

Robert F. Sibert Informational Book Medal (2013)

Author Steve Sheinkin's "story unfolds in three parts, covering American attempts to build the [atomic] bomb, how the Soviets tried to steal American designs and how the Americans tried to keep the Germans from building a bomb. It was the eve of World War II, and the fate of the world was at stake . . . all along the way spies in the United States were feeding sensitive information to the KGB." (Kirkus Reviews)

Includes bibliographical references (p. [243]-259) and index

623.7 Communications, vehicles, sanitation, related topics

101 great tanks; edited by Robert Jackson. Rosen Pub. 2010 112p il (The 101 greatest weapons of all times) lib bdg $31.95

Grades: 7 8 9 10 **623.7**

1. Military tanks

ISBN 978-1-4358-3595-5 lib bdg; 1-4358-3595-6 lib bdg

LC 2009-32880

Presents photographs and detailed information about 101 great tanks, from the very first British tank to ultramodern armored fighting vehicles.

Describes "why and when the type of vehicle was created, its advantages and disadvantages, when and where it served, countries that may have purchased or license-built it, and when it was removed from service. . . . Contains a detailed two-dimensional color drawing and black-and-white or color photo of the featured vehicle. . . . Back matter includes a listing of memorials and museums and an excellent further-reading list. A first purchase where the subject is popular." SLJ

Includes glossary

Mooney, Carla

Pilotless planes. Norwood House Press 2010 48p il (A great idea) lib bdg $25.27

Grades: 3 4 5 6 **623.7**

1. Drone aircraft 2. Military aeronautics

ISBN 978-1-59953-381-0 lib bdg; 1-59953-381-2 lib bdg

LC 2010008500

This "discusses the development and use of unmanned aerial vehicles, also called UAVs or drones, such as the Predator planes currently used by the U.S. Air Force. Looking beyond military uses, the last chapter also considers future public safety, environmental, and commercial applications. . . . Presenting specific, current information, [this book] will appeal to young people intrigued by inventions." Booklist

Includes glossary and bibliographical references

623.74 Vehicles

101 great bombers; Robert Jackson, editor. Rosen Pub. 2010 112p il (The 101 greatest weapons of all times) lib bdg $31.95

Grades: 7 8 9 10 **623.74**

1. Bombers

ISBN 978-1-4358-3594-8 lib bdg; 1-4358-3594-8 lib bdg

LC 2009-32090

Presents photographs and detailed information about 101 great bombers, from the early twentieth-century biplanes to ultramodern stealth bombers.

Describes "why and when the type of vehicle was created, its advantages and disadvantages, when and where it served, countries that may have purchased or license-built it, and when it was removed from service. . . . Contains a detailed two-dimensional color drawing and black-and-white or color photo of the featured vehicle. . . . Back matter includes a listing of memorials and museums and an excellent further-reading list. A first purchase where the subject is popular." SLJ

Includes glossary

101 great fighters; edited by Robert Jackson. Rosen Pub. 2010 112p il (The 101 greatest weapons of all times) lib bdg $31.95

Grades: 7 8 9 10 **623.74**

1. Fighter planes

ISBN 978-1-4358-3597-9 lib bdg; 1-4358-3597-2 lib bdg

LC 2009-32122

Presents photographs and detailed information about 101 great fighter planes, from the early twentieth-century biplanes to ultramodern jet fighters.

Describes "why and when the type of vehicle was created, its advantages and disadvantages, when and where it served, countries that may have purchased or license-built it, and when it was removed from service. . . . Contains a detailed two-dimensional color drawing and black-and-white or color photo of the featured vehicle. . . . Back matter includes a listing of memorials and museums and an excellent further-reading list. A first purchase where the subject is popular." SLJ

Includes glossary

Spilsbury, Richard

Drones; by Louise Spilsbury, Richard Spilsbury. Gareth Stevens Publishing 2016 48 p. color illustrations $31.95

Grades: 5 6 7 8 **623.74**

1. Drone aircraft 2. Technological innovations

ISBN 1482451565; 9781482451566; 9781482451627

LC 2016049387

This children's book, by Louise Spilsbury and Richard Spilsbury, part of the "Cutting-Edge Technology" series, "tackles the history of drone technology and where future development will take these exciting aircraft. . . . These pilotless flying machines are now used all over the world by ordinary people who love remote controlled vehicles. Today, drones of all shapes and sizes can achieve amazing things." (Publisher's note)

"Rock-solid choices that will update and deepen science and technology collections." SLJ

623.82 Nautical craft

101 great warships; Robert Jackson, editor. Rosen Pub. 2010 112p il (The 101 greatest weapons of all times) lib bdg $31.95

Grades: 7 8 9 10 **623.82**

1. Warships

ISBN 978-1-4358-3596-2 lib bdg; 1-4358-3596-4 lib bdg

LC 2009-32929

Presents photographs and detailed information about 101 great warship, from the early twentieth-century battleships to ultramodern aircraft carriers.

Describes "why and when the type of vehicle was created, its advantages and disadvantages, when and where it served, countries that may have purchased or license-built it, and when it was removed from service. . . . Contains a detailed two-dimensional color drawing and black-and-white or color photo of the featured vehicle. . . . Back matter includes a listing of memorials and museums and an excellent further-reading list. A first purchase where the subject is popular." SLJ

Includes glossary

Farndon, John

★ **Stickmen's** guide to watercraft; by John Farndon ; illustrated by John Paul de Quay. Lerner Pub Group 2016 32 p. illustrations (chiefly color) (ebook) $26.65; $7.99

Grades: 3 4 5 6 **623.82**

1. Ships 2. Aircraft carriers 3. Boats and boating

ISBN 9781467795944; 1467793620; 9781467793629; 9781467795937

LC 2015032760

This children's book in the Stickmen's Guides to How Everything Works, by John Farndon, illustrated by John Paul de Quay, answers questions such as "How does a giant cruise ship stay upright? Just how big is an aircraft carrier? How are submarines powered? Join the Stickmen for a close look at how watercrafts work, though be careful you may get into deep water!" (Publisher's note)

"Deeply informative and pleasantly approachable, this is sure to make a splash." Booklist

Macaulay, David

★ **Crossing** on time; steam engines, fast ships, and a journey to the New World. David Macaulay. Roaring Brook Press 2019 127 p. illustrations (hardcover) $24.99

Grades: 5 6 7 8 9 **623.82**

1. Steamboats 2. Ocean liners 3. Shipbuilding 4. Shipbuilding -- History 5. United States (Steamship) -- History 6. Ocean liners -- United States -- History

ISBN 9781596434776

LC 2018039860

In this book, author "David Macaulay . . . brings his signature curiosity and detailing to the story of the steamship. . . . Macaulay guides readers through the fascinating history that culminated in the building of the most advanced--and last--of these steamships: the SS United States. This book artfully explores the design and construction of the ship and the life of its designer and engineer, William Francis Gibbs." (Publisher's note)

Includes bibliographical references

Spilsbury, Richard

Robots underwater; Richard and Louise Spilsbury. Gareth Stevens Publishing 2016 48 p. color illustrations $31.95

Grades: 4 5 6 7 **623.82**

1. Robots 2. Underwater exploration

ISBN 1482430223; 9781482430226

LC 2014415766

In this book, by Richard and Louise Spilsbury, part of the Amazing Robots series, "without underwater robots, people never would have been able to explore the shipwreck of the Titanic as much as they have. From mapping the ocean floor to testing water quality, the jobs these robots can do are astounding. Through many examples and full-color photographs, readers dive deep with underwater robots, learning the technology behind these amazing machines and how they help people every day." (Publisher's note)

"The full-color photos of robots in action and the high-interest nature of robotics may catch the interest of science-minded kids." Booklist

623.89 Navigation

Williams, Linda D.

Navigational aids; [by] Linda Williams. Marshall Cavendish Benchmark 2007 128p il (Great inventions) lib bdg $27.95

Grades: 6 7 8 9 **623.89**

1. Navigation 2. Aids to navigation .

ISBN 978-0-7614-2599-1

LC 2006028959

"An examination of the origins, history, development, and impact of the various navigational aids humans have used through the centuries." Publisher's note

Includes glossary and bibliographical references

Young, Karen Romano

Across the wide ocean; the why, how, and where of navigation for humans and animals at sea. Greenwillow Books 2007 78p il $18.99; lib bdg $19.89

Grades: 4 5 6 7 **623.89**

1. Ocean 2. Navigation 3. Marine animals

ISBN 978-0-06-009086-9; 0-06-009086-3; 978-0-06-009087-6 lib bdg; 0-06-009087-1 lib bdg

LC 2005-46146

"Readers follow such disparate entities as a loggerhead sea turtle, a nuclear submarine, and a sailboat crew seeking scientific sightings of North Atlantic right whales as Young explores the concept of navigation. . . . Larded with photos, diagrams, and maps. . . . Deceptively simple in appearance, the informative text can push some intense mental activity." SLJ

624 Civil engineering

Aaseng, Nathan

Construction : building the impossible. Oliver Press (Minneapolis) 2000 144p il (Innovators) $21.95

Grades: 6 7 8 9 **624**

1. Generals 2. Pyramids 3. Inventors 4. Architects 5. Physicians 6. Panama Canal 7. Civil engineering 8. Hoover Dam (Ariz. and Nev.) 9. Civil engineers 10. Bridge engineers 11. Mechanical engineers 12. Structural engineers 13. Brooklyn Bridge (New York, N.Y.)

ISBN 1-88150-859-5

LC 98-51815

Profiles eight builders and their famous construction projects, including Imhotep and the Step Pyramid, Alexandre Eiffel and the Eiffel Tower, and William Lamb and the Empire State Building

"The prose is clear and engaging, with a layperson's approach to technical information. Sidebars feature related anecdotes, fun facts, and word definitions. Historical photos, drawings, and diagrams are fascinating and well chosen." Booklist

Includes glossary and bibliographical references

Caney, Steven

★ **Steven** Caney's ultimate building book. Running Press 2006 596p il $29.95

Grades: 4 5 6 7 8 **624**

1. Building 2. Civil engineering

ISBN 0-7624-0409-4

"Caney examines 'building' in its broadest sense, encompassing everything from skyscrapers and bridges to bird feeders and peanut-shell 'bricks.' Opening sections investigate the history and techniques of construction, with clearly written explanations supported by black-and-white photographs and diagrams. . . . The author reinforces important concepts of design in a way that is fascinating and effective." SLJ

Carmichael, L. E.

Amazing Feats of Civil Engineering; by L.E. Carmichael. Essential Library 2015 112 p. $35.64 **624**

1. Civil engineering 2. Structural engineering

ISBN 1624034276; 9781624034275

LC 2014932575

This book by L.E. Carmichael "examines amazing feats of civil engineering. Engaging text explores massive bridges, the world's tallest skyscraper, and the Panama Canal. It also examines the engineers who made these projects a reality and traces the history of the discipline. Relevant sidebars, stunning photos, and a glossary aid readers' understanding of the topic. A hands-on project and career-planning chart give readers a sense of what it takes to become an engineer." (Publisher's note)

Includes bibliographical references (pages 104-109) and index

Fantastic feats and failures; by the editors of YES magazine. Kids Can Press 2004 52p il hardcover o.p. pa $7.95

Grades: 4 5 6 7 **624**

1. Civil engineering

ISBN 1-55337-633-1; 1-55337-634-X pa

This "book spotlights 20 notable highs and lows in engineering. The 'feats' celebrated include the Sydney Opera House, the Brooklyn Bridge, and Canadarm (a huge, Canadian-built robotic arm used for repairs in space). Among the 'failures' are the space shuttle Challenger, the Tacoma Narrows Bridge, and the Chernobyl nuclear power plant. . . . Well organized and engagingly written. . . . Excellent photos . . . illustrate the places and events discussed, while colorful drawings visually represent concepts." Booklist

Levy, Matthys

Engineering the city; how infrastructure works: projects and principles for beginners. [by] Matthys Levy and Richard Panchyk. Chicago Review Press 2000 129p pa $14.95

Grades: 6 7 8 9 **624**

1. Civil engineering 2. Municipal engineering

ISBN 1-55652-419-6

LC 00-31774

"Combining a study of urban infrastructure with the history of human development, the authors examine the topics of water, transportation, waste and garbage disposal, and pollution. A wide variety of projects include scientific experiments and extension activities. . . . Containing scientific and historical information, this book will serve as a springboard for cross-curricular projects in history and science, with connections to math and language arts." Book Rep

Includes glossary and bibliographical references

Macaulay, David

★ **Underground**. Houghton Mifflin 1976 109p il hardcover o.p. pa $9.95

Grades: 5 6 7 8 9 **624**

1. Subways 2. Building 3. Sewerage 4. Electric lines 5. Public utilities 6. Civil engineering

ISBN 0-395-24739-X; 0-395-34065-9 pa

"Introduced by a visual index—a bird's eye view of a busy, hypothetical intersection with colored indicators marking the specific locations analyzed in subsequent pages—detailed illustrations are combined with a clear, precise narrative to make the subject comprehenssible and fascinating." Horn Book

Includes glossary

Roberts, Russell

The **Eiffel** Tower; by Russell Roberts. Purple Toad Pub Inc 2016 32 p. illustrations (some color) $26.50

Grades: 4 5 6 7 8 **624**

1. Eiffel Tower (Paris, France)

ISBN 1624692036; 9781624692031

LC 2016937176

This book, by Russell Roberts, presents "the story of how the Eiffel Tower was built, and the people who made it happen. Learn how they did it and see what materials they used in this real life building journey that kids who love to build in Lego and Minecraft will be thrilled to read." (Publisher's note)

"An enlightening look at this famous landmark." Booklist

Includes bibliographic references (page 29) and index.

Sullivan, George

★ **Built** to last; building America's amazing bridges, dams, tunnels, and skyscrapers. Scholastic Nonfiction 2005 128p il map $18.99

Grades: 5 6 7 8 **624**

1. Civil engineering

ISBN 0-439-51737-0

LC 2004-60996

This is a "survey of American building—from the Erie Canal to Boston's current 'Big Dig.' Chronological chapters describe the historical forces that helped drive each project as well as the specific technological feats linked to each pioneering structure. . . . The wide selection of captivating illustrations includes archival photos and engravings, architectural drawings, and color photos. . . . Sullivan's skillful integration of social and economic history distinguishes this clear, well-designed title." Booklist

624.1 Structural engineering and underground construction

Connolly, Sean

The **book** of massively epic engineering disasters; 33 thrilling experiments based on history's greatest blunders. Sean Connolly. Workman Pub Co 2017 241 p. illustrations (Irresponsible science) (hardcover) $14.95

Grades: 4 5 6 7 8 **624.1**

1. Disasters 2. Engineering -- Popular works 3. Engineering 4. Structural failures 5. Science -- Experiments 6. System failures (Engineering)

ISBN 9781523501953; 9780761183945; 0761183949

LC 2017037722

This book in the Irresponsibe Science series, by Sean Connolly, illustrates "the greatest engineering disasters in history. Each engineering disaster includes a simple . . .experiment . . . using everyday household items to explain the underlying science and put learning into action. . . . Stomp on a tube of toothpaste to demonstrate what happens to non-Newtonian fluids under pressure--and how a ruptured tank sent . . . molasses through the streets of Boston in 1919." (Publisher's note)

"A new collection from an old hand at designing intriguing STEM activities that will entertain as well as enlighten." Kirkus

Includes bibliographical references and index.

Graham, Ian

Tremendous tunnels. Amicus 2010 32p il (Superstructures) lib bdg $28.50

Grades: 5 6 7 8 **624.1**

1. Tunnels

ISBN 978-1-60753-134-0; 1-60753-134-8

LC 2009030865

"The vivid illustrations often help clarify points made in the text. . . . [This] colorful, informative [book offers] intriguing glimpses of notable engineering feats." Booklist

Includes glossary and bibliographical references

624.2 Bridges

Graham, Ian

Fabulous bridges. Amicus 2010 32p il (Superstructures) lib bdg $28.50

Grades: 5 6 7 8 **624.2**

1. Bridges

ISBN 978-1-60753-132-6; 1-60753-132-1

LC 2009030864

"The vivid illustrations often help clarify points made in the text. . . . [This] colorful, informative [book offers] intriguing glimpses of notable engineering feats." Booklist

Includes glossary and bibliographical references

Prentzas, G. S.

The **Brooklyn** Bridge. Chelsea House Publishers 2009 120p il (Building America: then and now) lib bdg $35

Grades: 6 7 8 9 **624.2**

1. Bridges 2. Brooklyn Bridge (New York, N.Y.)

ISBN 978-1-60413-073-7 lib bdg; 1-60413-073-3 lib bdg

LC 2008-25543

This describes the construction and impact of the Brooklyn Bridge

Includes glossary and bibliographical references

627 Hydraulic engineering

Aldridge, Rebecca

The **Hoover** Dam. Chelsea House 2009 119p il (Building America: then and now) lib bdg $35

Grades: 6 7 8 9 **627**

1. Dams 2. Hoover Dam (Ariz. and Nev.)

ISBN 978-1-60413-069-0 lib bdg; 1-60413-069-5 lib bdg

LC 2008-25545

This describes the history and impact of Hoover Dam

"Photos, maps, and informative sidebars supplement the densely detailed writing. American history buffs will find [this volume] useful for doing research." Horn Book Guide

Includes bibliographical references

Latham, Donna

Canals and dams; investigate feats of engineering. Nomad Press 2013 122 p. $21.95

Grades: 5 6 7 8 **627**

1. Dams 2. Canals

ISBN 1619301695; 9781619301696

This book "opens with an explanation of engineering, introduces the different types of engineers, and describes the problem-solving process they use. Canals and dams are given center stage as their structures and the scientific principles behind them are explained, history and examples are given, and disasters caused by or resulting from their construction or aging are shared." (School Library Journal)

Mann, Elizabeth

Hoover Dam; with illustrations by Alan Witschonke. Mikaya Press 2001 44p il (Wonders of the world) $19.95; pa $9.95

Grades: 4 5 6 7 **627**

1. Hoover Dam (Ariz. and Nev.)

ISBN 978-1-931414-02-9; 1-931414-02-5; 978-1-931414-13-5 pa; 1-931414-13-0 pa

LC 2001-34520

Describes the engineering, construction, and social and historical contexts of the Hoover Dam

"A wonderfully readable, well-organized book filled with fascinating detail." SLJ

627.8 Dams and reservoirs

Nagelhout, Ryan

How do dams work? Ryan Nagelhout. PowerKids Press 2016 32 p. (pbk.) $11.75

Grades: 4 5 6 **627.8**

1. Dams 2. Hydraulic engineering 3. Dams -- Environmental aspects 4. Dams -- Design and construction

ISBN 9781499419993; 9781499420005; 9781499420012

LC 2016013444

This children's book, in the STEM waterworks series, by Ryan Nagelhout, shows that "all dams rely on science to function properly. People first began damming rivers to stop flooding and provide water for irrigation. These early dams were made with simple techniques and technology. Today, dams are constructed to prevent flooding and to provide water for irrigation, hydroelectric power, and freshwater for large populations." (Publisher's note)

"The book ends with a hopeful outlook as scientists rethink ways to use dams to protect the environment. Colorful diagrams, panoramic views, and photos of dam construction not only relate the roles of these structures but show STEM in action." Booklist

628 Sanitary engineering

Hand, Carol

Amazing feats of environmental engineering; Carol Hand. Essential Library 2015 112 p. $35.64 **628**

1. Sanitary engineering 2. Environmental science 3. Environmental engineering

ISBN 1624034292; 9781624034299

LC 2014932584

This book by author Carol Hand "examines amazing feats of environmental engineering. Engaging text explores projects that supply water to impoverished areas, structures in the Netherlands that hold back the Atlantic Ocean, and the cleanup of contaminated areas. It also examines the engineers who made these projects a reality and traces the history of the discipline. Relevant sidebars, stunning photos, and a glossary aid readers' understanding of the topic." (Publisher's note)

Includes bibliographical references and index

Harmon, Dan

Jobs in environmental cleanup and emergency hazmat response; [by] Daniel E. Harmon. Rosen Pub. 2010 80p il (Green careers) lib bdg $30.60

Grades: 7 8 9 **628**

1. Hazardous wastes 2. Vocational guidance 3. Environmental sciences

ISBN 978-1-4358-3570-2; 1-4358-3570-0

LC 2009-14946

"Written in clear, concise language, . . . [this] features color pictures and boxes with supplementary information. Chapters and sections are broken into reasonable lengths suitable for reluctant readers, but interesting enough for advanced students." Libr Media Connect

Includes glossary and bibliographical references

Horn, Geoffrey

Environmental engineer; by Geoffrey M. Horn. Gareth Stevens Pub. 2010 32p il (Cool careers: cutting edge) lib bdg $26; pa $8.95

Grades: 4 5 6 **628**

1. Vocational guidance 2. Sanitary engineering 3. Environmental protection

ISBN 978-1-4339-1956-5 lib bdg; 1-4339-1956-7 lib bdg; 978-1-4339-2155-1 pa; 1-4339-2155-3 pa

LC 2009004746

This introduction to environmental engineering careers offers "clear, solid information in a large font. . . . [This] short [book is] packed with relevant, current material." SLJ

Includes glossary and bibliographical references

628.4 Waste technology, public toilets, street cleaning

Gardner, Robert

Recycle; green science projects for a sustainable planet. Enslow Publishers 2011 128p il (Team Green science projects) lib bdg $31.93

Grades: 6 7 8 9 10 **628.4**

1. Recycling 2. Science projects 3. Science -- Experiments

ISBN 978-0-7660-3648-2; 0-7660-3648-0

LC 2009-37903

This describes science projects about recycling, including experiments and information about plastics, solid waste and decomposition, composting, aluminum, and paper.

"Gardner provides plenty of information, well-designed experiments, and demonstrations, and then shares brief science-fair ideas. . . . Experiments and demonstrations are presented with clear step-by-step instructions and occasional illustrations and represent a wide range of complexity." SLJ

Includes glossary and bibliographical references

629 Other branches of engineering

Grove, Tim

Milestones of flight; From Hot-Air Balloons to SpaceShipOne. by Tim Grove. Abrams Books for Young Readers 2016 112 p. illustrations $21.95

Grades: 5 6 7 8 **629**

1. Aeronautics -- Flights 2. Aeronautics -- United States -- History 3. Aeronautics -- History -- Chronology

ISBN 9781419720031

LC 2015033040

This children's book by Tim Grove looks into America's contributions to aviation, "from the Wright brothers and their competitors to the military pilots who first circumnavigated the globe, from the initial space rocket to the moon walk, from the earliest man made satellite to today's spy drones. The book also describes what inventions—such as rocket propulsion, the wind tunnel, and the silicon chip—helped move flight upward and beyond." (Publisher's note)

"Period photographs, illustrations, and documents complement a crisply written and informative look at the past and present of flight, with glimpses of its future." Pub Wkly

Includes bibliographical references and index

629.1 Aerospace engineering

Hickam, Homer H.

★ **Rocket** boys; a memoir. [by] Homer H. Hickam, Jr. Delacorte Press 1998 368p $25.95; pa $14

Grades: 7 8 9 10 11 12 Adult **629.1**

1. Authors 2. Novelists 3. Aerospace engineers 4. Memoirists 5. West Virginia 6. Authors, American 7. Writers on science

ISBN 0-385-33320-X; 0-385-33321-8 pa

LC 98-19304

"Even if Hickam stretched the strict truth to metamorphose his memories into Stand By Me-like material for Hollywood . . . the embellishing only converts what is a good story into an absorbing, rapidly readable one that is unsentimental but artful about adolescence, high school, and family life." Booklist

Rooney, Anne

Aerospace engineering and the principles of flight; Anne Rooney. Crabtree Publishing Company 2013 32 p. (Engineering in action) (pbk. : alk. paper) $9.95

Grades: 5 6 7 8 **629.1**

1. Aeronautics 2. Aerospace engineering 3. Airplanes -- Design and construction 4. Flight

ISBN 0778775003; 9780778774952; 9780778775003

LC 2012040538

This book, "part of the Engineering in Action series, presents a "glimpse at the basics of flight and what aerospace engineers do. The initial sections are about the history of flight, including information about how engineers use flight dynamics for their designs. The following sections lead readers through the design process from brainstorming to the actual aircraft testing. Two simple activities are included." (Booklist)

Includes bibliographical references and index

Smibert, Angie

Amazing Feats of Aerospace Engineering; Angie Smibert. Essential Library 2015 112 p. illustrations (chiefly color) $35.64

Grades: 7 8 9 10 **629.1**

1. Aeronautics 2. Aerospace engineering

ISBN 162403425X; 9781624034251

LC 2014932565

This book by Angi Smibert "examines amazing feats of aerospace engineering. Engaging text explores the Saturn V moon rocket, the International Space Station, and the world's largest passenger jet. It also examines the engineers who made these projects a reality and traces the history of the discipline. Relevant sidebars, stunning photos, and a glossary aid readers' understanding of the topic. A hands-on project and career-planning chart give readers a sense of what it takes to become an engineer." (Publisher's note)

"These substantial books begin with a brief introduction and history, then validate the "Amazing Feats" label with remarkable projects including the International Space Station, a thought-controlled bionic leg, the Canadian Confederation Bridge, and the driverless car; challenges and problem-solving are emphasized. Illustrations include both color photos and diagrams. Career advice, facts, and a hands-on project are appended." Horn Book

Includes bibliographical references (pages 104-109) and index

Other titles in the series are:

Amazing Feats of Biological Engineering (2014)

Amazing Feats of Civil Engineering (2014)

Amazing Feats of Electrical Engineering (2014)

Amazing Feats of Environmental Engineering (2014)

Amazing Feats of Mechanical Engineering (2014)

629.13 Aeronautics

Finkelstein, Norman H.

Three across; the great transatlantic air race of 1927. [by] Norman H. Finkelstein. Calkins Creek 2008 134p il $17.95

Grades: 5 6 7 8 **629.13**

1. Admirals 2. Generals 3. Explorers 4. Air pilots 5. Memoirists 6. Travel writers 7. Air force officers 8. Aeronautics -- History 9. Metal industry executives 10. Aircraft industry executives

ISBN 978-1-59078-462-4; 1-59078-462-6

LC 2007-18345

"Framing the story in way that should enthrall any aviation fan, Finklestein traces the rise of aviation from Kitty Hawk to the 1927 Orteig Prize, a $25,000 award for the first person to fly nonstop across the Atlantic. This book focuses on the first three flights to pull it off: the Spirit of St. Louis, piloted by Charles Lindbergh; the Columbia, led by ambitious shyster Charles A. Levine; and the America, boasting Arctic explorer Richard E. Byrd at the controls." Booklist

Includes bibliographical references

Flight and motion; the history and science of flying. M.E. Sharpe 2008 5v il set $325

Grades: 6 7 8 9 10 **629.13**

1. Reference books 2. Flight -- Encyclopedias 3. Aeronautics -- Encyclopedias

ISBN 978-0-7656-8100-3 set; 0-7656-8100-5 set

LC 2007030815

"Report writers as well as those simply interested in browsing will find much to hold their interest in this set, which provides comprehensive coverage of the history of aviation, including spaceflight, as well as the science and technology on which it depends." Booklist

Includes bibliographical references

Hense, Mary

How fighter pilots use math; math curriculum consultant: Rhea A. Stewart. Chelsea Clubhouse 2010 32p il (Math in the real world) lib bdg $28

Grades: 4 5 6 **629.13**

1. Air pilots 2. Aeronautics 3. Mathematics 4. Vocational guidance

ISBN 978-1-60413-605-0 lib bdg; 1-60413-605-7 lib bdg

LC 2009-20242

This describes how fighter pilots use math to judge speed, attain altitude, and maintain safety, and includes relevant math problems and information about how to become a fighter pilot

Includes glossary and bibliographical references

Wilgus, Alison

Flying machines; how the Wright brothers soared. Alison Wilgus ; Molly Brooks. First Second 2017 113 p. chiefly ills. (some color) (Science comics) (hardcover) $19.99

Grades: 5 6 7 8 **629.13**

1. Aeronautics 2. Graphic novels 3. Airplanes -- United States -- History

ISBN 9781626721395; 9781626721401

LC 2016945553

In this book, by Alsion Wilgus, illustrated by Molly Brooks, "follow the famous aviators from their bicycle shop in Dayton, Ohio, to the fields of North Carolina where they were to make their famous flights. In an era of dirigibles and hot air balloons, the Wright Brothers were among the first innovators of heavier than air flight. But in the hotly competitive international race toward flight, Orville and Wilbur were up against a lot more than bad weather." (Publisher's note)

"An accessible and engaging introduction to the Wright brothers and how they ushered in the age of flight." Kirkus

Includes bibliographical references.

629.130 Biography of flight

Brown, Jeremy K.

Amelia Earhart; by Jeremy K. Brown. Chelsea House 2011 132p ill. (hardcover : acid-free paper) $35.00

Grades: 6 7 8 9 **629.130**

1. Biography 2. Women air pilots 3. Air pilots -- United States -- Biography 4. Women air pilots -- United States -- Biography 5. Cross-country flying -- History -- 20th century 6. Flights around the world -- History -- 20th century

ISBN 9781604139105

LC 2011000037

This book chronicles the life of female aviator Amelia Earhart. "From her . . . beginnings in a small Kansas town to her . . . solo flight across the Atlantic, Earhart defied expectations and rose to become the most famous female pilot of all time. Despite the restrictions placed on women of her era, she broke through barriers and refused to allow society to label her. As a result, she made history through her daring flights all over the world. In 1937, she disappeared without a trace while on a solo flight around the world." (Kids' Catalog Web)

Includes bibliographical references (p. 124-125) and index

629.133 Aircraft types

Greger, Margaret

Kites for everyone; how to make and fly them. diagrams by Del Greger. 3rd ed.; Dover Publications 2006 121p il pa $9.95

Grades: 7 8 9 10 11 12 Adult **629.133**

1. Kites

ISBN 978-0-4864-5295-1 pa; 0-4864-5295-6 pa

LC 2006048453

First published 1984 by Richland, WA

This is a "guide with . . . illustrated instructions for creating more than 50 . . . airborne objects—everything from simple bag kites to Vietnamese, Snake, Dutch, Dragon, Bullet, Delta, and Flowform flyers." Publisher's note

Includes bibliographical references

White, Rowland

Cleared for takeoff; The Ultimate Book of Flight. by Rowland White. Chronicle Books 2016 320 p. color ill., color maps (ebook) $22.09; (hardcover) $21.99

Grades: 4 5 6 7 8 **629.133**

1. Aeronautics -- History 2. Flying-machines -- History 3. Aeronautics -- History -- Pictorial works 4. Flying-machines -- History -- Pictorial works

ISBN 9781452143484; 9781452135502

LC 2014044858

This book on flight for young readers, by Rowland White, is "packed with stories of heroic and innovative pioneers, fascinating profiles of remarkable planes from Spitfires to space shuttles, and how-to instructions for making everything from origami helicopters to bottle rockets—all accompanied by sensational photographs, illustrations, and diagrams." (Publisher's note)

"For anybody with an interest in aviation, this will prove a fascinating resource for browsing. Wings up!" Kirkus

629.2 Motor land vehicles, cycles

Mara, Wil

From locusts to...automobile anti-collision systems; by Wil Mara. Cherry Lake Pub. 2012 32 p. col. ill. (Innovations from nature) (library) $28.50; (e-book) $28.50; (paperback) $14.21

Grades: 4 5 6 7 **629.2**

1. Biomimicry 2. Automobiles -- Collision avoidance systems 3. Locusts

ISBN 1610805011; 9781610805018; 9781610805889; 9781610806756

LC 2012011856

"This . . . entry in the '21st Century Skills Innovation Library: Innovations from Nature' series explores how automobile manufacturers and scientists are trying to develop . . . collision avoidance systems based on the instincts of the humble locust, which has the ability to avoid oncoming objects while in a swarm. . . . [Wil] Mara describes the science of biomimicry, or 'the practice of copying nature--plants and animals--to build or improve something.'" (Booklist)

Includes bibliographical references (p. 31) and index.

Smith, Miranda

Speed machines; and other record-breaking vehicles. Kingfisher 2009 63p il (Kingfisher knowledge) $12.95

Grades: 5 6 7 8 **629.2**

1. Speed 2. Vehicles

ISBN 978-0-7534-6287-4; 0-7534-6287-7

"This well-organized, full-color book is packed with facts, photos, and history. It covers all aspects in history dealing with humankind's quest for speed, including land, water and air. . . . There are short blocks of main text and sidebars or blurbs to add additional information. Besides the usual suspects in books that cover this topic—cars, motorcycles, and planes—this book includes boats, gliders, hot air balloons, trains, and windsurfing among other speed machines. . . . It is an essential purchase, especially where books about racing, cars, planes, trucks, motorcycles, etc. are popular." Voice Youth Advocates

Zettwoch, Dan

Cars; engines that move you. Dan Zettwoch. First Second 2019 128 p. color illustrations (Science comics) (hardcover) $19.99

Grades: 4 5 6 7 **629.2**

1. Automobiles

ISBN 9781626728219; 9781626728226

LC 2018944912

"In Dan Zettwoch's . . . [book], you'll learn where cars came from and how they work. When you pop the hood, what are you looking at? How does gasoline--or electric batteries, or even steam--make a car move? Rev up your motor and take look at the combustible history of the automobile and its explosive effects on our modern lives." (Publisher's note)

"The winding scenery that gives this journey warmth is historical anecdotes (the world's first getaway car?!?) and visual flourishes charting things like aesthetic transformations, land speed records, and weird cars. Illustrating all this data could make for unreadable clutter, but Zettwoch imbues his visually dense pages with personality and flow befitting his subject." Booklist

629.22 Types of vehicles

Balmer, Alden J.

Doc Fizzix mousetrap racers; the complete builder's manual. [by] Alden J. Balmer; [illustrations by Mike Harnisch] Fox Chapel 2008 142p il pa $14.95

Grades: 6 7 8 9 **629.22**

1. Physics 2. Automobiles -- Models

ISBN 978-1-56523-359-1; 1-56523-359-X

"Building a mousetrap-powered model racer is more complex than it first appears, and Balmer uses this project as a springboard for teaching principles of physics such as energy, forces, torque, friction, and traction. . . . The author's enthusiasm for the topic and for teaching are apparent throughout, and his focus on safety is consistent. The thorough instructions are complemented by clear, captioned, full-color photos and line drawings and diagrams that illustrate each step of the construction process." SLJ

629.222 Gasoline-powered, oil-powered, man-powered vehicles

Bearce, Stephanie

All about electric and hybrid cars; and who's driving them. Mitchell Lane Publishers 2009 47p il (Tell your parents) lib bdg $21.50

Grades: 4 5 6 7 **629.222**

1. Electric automobiles

ISBN 978-1-58415-763-2 lib bdg; 1-58415-763-1 lib bdg

LC 2009004528

This describes how hybrid and electric cars work and new inventions in the automotive industry, including vehicles powered by hydrogen and solar powered cars

Includes bibliographical references

Harmon, Dan

First car smarts; by Daniel E. Harmon. Rosen Pub. 2010 64p il (Get smart with your money) lib bdg $29.95; pa $12.95

Grades: 7 8 9 10 11 12 **629.222**

1. Automobiles

ISBN 978-1-4358-5269-3 lib bdg; 1-4358-5269-9 lib bdg; 978-1-4358-5544-1 pa; 1-4358-5544-2 pa

This is a guide to buying your first car and the costs of car ownership including maintanence and insurance.

This offers "practical information and advice. . . . The writing is accessible. . . . The [book is] heavily illustrated with large, clear, up-to-date photographs of teens." SLJ

Includes glossary and bibliographical references

Williams, Brian

Who invented the automobile? Arcturus Pub. 2010 46p il (Breakthroughs in science and technology) lib bdg $32.80

Grades: 5 6 7 8 **629.222**

1. Engines 2. Automobiles

ISBN 978-1-84837-681-6; 1-84837-681-2

LC 2010011019

Examines the history of the automobile.

This book is "divided into easy to read short chapters with large, colorful photographs and graphics on every page. . . . The added inserts provide additional information to engage readers and help them connect with the scientific details." Libr Media Connect

Woods, Bob

Hottest muscle cars; by Bob Woods. Enslow Publishers 2008 48p il (Wild wheels!) lib bdg $23.93; pa $7.95

Grades: 4 5 6 7 **629.222**

1. Automobiles

ISBN 978-0-7660-2872-2 lib bdg; 0-7660-2872-0 lib bdg; 978-0-7660-3611-6 pa; 0-7660-3611-1 pa

LC 2007007423

This focuses on "the beginning of America's love for muscle cars, and see why they are still loved today." Publisher's note

Includes glossary and bibliographical references

Hottest sports cars; by Bob Woods. Enslow Publishers 2008 48p il (Wild wheels!) lib bdg $23.93; pa $7.95

Grades: 4 5 6 7 **629.222**

1. Automobiles

ISBN 9780766028739 lib bdg; 9780766036093 pa

LC 2007007428

This focuses on "some of the world's most famous sports cars; how they began, and where they are going in the future." Publisher's note

Includes glossary and bibliographical references

629.227 Cycles

Farndon, John

Megafast motorcycles; by John Farndon ; illustrated by Mat Edwards and Jeremy Pyke. Hungry Tomato 2016 32 p. (pb : alk. paper) $7.99

Grades: 3 4 5 6 **629.227**

1. Motorcycles 2. Motorcycle racing 3. Superbikes 4. Motorcycles, Racing

ISBN 1467795836; 9781467793643; 9781467795838

LC 2015031655

This children's book, by John Farndon and illustrated by Mat Edwards and Jeremy Pyke, profiles high-performance racing motorcycles. "Motorcycles are made for speed but some get there louder and faster than others! . . . Hang on tight as detailed illustrations take you on the road, around the track, and across salt flats on these powerful bikes. Get the latest facts on how they reach those extreme speeds and stay on the road." (Publisher's note)

Lakin, Patricia

Bicycles; Patricia Lakin. Aladdin 2017 32 p. color illustrations (Made by hand) (hardback) $17.99

Grades: 3 4 5 6 7 **629.227**

1. Bicycles 2. Bicycles -- Design and construction

ISBN 9781481478960; 9781481478977

LC 2016034643

With this book, by Patricia Lakin, "go behind the scenes and learn how craftsman Aaron Dykstra makes one-of-a-kind bicycles by hand. . . . Aaron Dykstra of Six-Eleven Bicycles in Roanoke, Virginia, got his first job at a small local bike shop when he was fifteen and he spent the majority of his teen years riding and racing bikes. After a stint in the air force, Aaron realized his true passion was on land: making these beautiful machines." (Publisher's note)

"A must-have for school and public libraries in need of materials to support STEM curricula and maker spaces." School Library Journal.

Includes bibliographical references.

Smedman, Lisa

From boneshakers to choppers; the rip-roaring history of motorcycles. Annick Press 2007 120p il $24.95; pa $14.95

Grades: 5 6 7 8 **629.227**

1. Motorcycles

ISBN 978-1-55451-016-0; 1-55451-016-3; 978-1-55451-015-3 pa; 1-55451-015-5 pa

"Smedman defines 'motorcycles' broadly enough to include everything from Harleys to Vespas, and even bicycles, in this lively, wide-ranging history. . . . Illustrated with a generous array of action photos, historical shots, and period advertisements." Booklist

Includes bibliographical references

629.28 Tests, driving, maintenance, repair

Miller, Malinda

Modern mechanics; maintaining tomorrow's green vehicles. Mason Crest Publishers 2011 64p il (New careers for the 21st century: finding your role in the global renewal) lib bdg $22.95

Grades: 7 8 9 10 **629.28**

1. Machinery 2. Mechanics (Persons) 3. Vocational guidance
ISBN 978-1-4222-1818-1 lib bdg; 1-4222-1818-X lib bdg
LC 2010016870

"Chapters identify and emphasize specific careers-important strengths, necessary aptitudes and interests, education and training, projected earnings, closely related occupations, type of work environment, and predictions for the future of the field. . . . Color photos have a small role amid the many statistics, figures, graphs and charts that support and supplement the . . . [text]." SLJ

Includes bibliographical references

629.4 Astronautics

Benoit, Peter

The **space** race; by Peter Benoit. Children's Press 2012 64 p. ill. (some col.) (library) $30.00; (paperback) $8.95

Grades: 4 5 6 **629.4**

1. Astronautics -- United States 2. Space flight 3. Astronautics -- Soviet Union -- History 4. Astronautics -- United States -- History 5. Space race -- History 6. Space flight -- History
ISBN 0531281655; 9780531230657; 9780531281659
LC 2011031454

This book by Peter Benoit is part of the "Cornerstones of Freedom" series. It "attempts to provide an historical overview of the race between the United States and Soviet Union to explore space. . . . The book ends with a map . . . a . . . list of influential individuals, a timeline, and a glossary." (Children's Literature)

Includes bibliographical references (p. 60-61) and index.

Bortz, Alfred B.

Seven wonders of space technology; by Fred Bortz. Twenty-First Century Books 2011 80p il (Seven wonders) lib bdg $33.26; ebook $24.95

Grades: 5 6 7 8 **629.4**

1. Astronautics 2. Space vehicles 3. Outer space -- Exploration
ISBN 978-0-7613-5453-6 lib bdg; 0-7613-5453-0 lib bdg; 9780761372806
LC 2010-23996

This book examines the science involved in the Great Observatories, the International Space Station, New Horizons, Moon bases and lunar water, Mars rovers, rocketry, and weather satellites. Glossary. Index. "Grades seven to twelve." (Sci Books Films)

"Highlights some of astronomy's greatest technical advancements, from land observatories to spinning satellites to moon bases. . . . [This] volume makes basic concepts clear in lively, energetic language that, along with the mesmerizing color photos and artists' renderings of space, will easily captivate a young audience, while up-to-date examples, including discoveries made in the last five years, will only increase the sense of immediacy and excitement." Booklist

Includes glossary and bibliographical references

Carlisle, Rodney P.

Exploring space; rev ed.; Chelsea House 2010 120p il (Discovery and exploration) lib bdg $35

Grades: 7 8 9 10 **629.4**

1. Astronautics 2. Outer space -- Exploration
ISBN 978-1-60413-188-8; 1-60413-188-8
LC 2009-25585

First published 2005 by Facts on File

This describes the history of space exploration, from early astronomers to first steps into space by Germans, Soviets, and Americans, space flight to the Moon, space stations, space shuttles, unmanned space exploration, the Hubble space telescope, radio telescopes, and possible future explorations

Includes glossary and bibliographical references

Crompton, Samuel

Sputnik /Explorer 1; the race to conquer space. [by] Samuel Willard Crompton. Chelsea House 2007 106p il (Milestones in American history) lib bdg $35

Grades: 7 8 9 10 **629.4**

1. Astronautics 2. Space flight
ISBN 0-7910-9357-3 lib bdg; 978-0-7910-9357-3 lib bdg
LC 2006034127

"This book begins in 1957 with Russia's successful launch of the first artificial sattellite. With the Cold War as a backdrop, the text goes on to describe the space race between the United States and Russia. . . . Many photographs, quotations, and sidebars detail the roles played by key figures." Horn Book Guide

Includes bibliographical references

Harris, Joseph

Space exploration; impact of science and technology. Gareth Stevens Pub. 2010 64p il map (Pros and cons) lib bdg $35

Grades: 5 6 7 8 **629.4**

1. Astronautics 2. Outer space -- Exploration
ISBN 978-1-4339-1989-3 lib bdg; 1-4339-1989-3 lib bdg
LC 2009-12436

An "active layout that features color photographs, maps, graphs or charts on every spread, this . . . [book] has much to offer. . . . It conveniently outlines the range of views . . . helping students to learn how to view both sides of [the] issue[s]." SLJ

Includes glossary and bibliographical references

Jones, Tom

Ask the astronaut; a galaxy of astonishing answers to your questions on spaceflight. Tom Jones. Smithsonian Books 2016 224 p. illustrations $12.95

Grades: 5 6 7 8 **629.4**

1. Astronauts 2. Space flight 3. Children's questions and answers 4. Outer space -- Exploration 5. Space flight -- Physiological effect
ISBN 1588345378; 9781588345370
LC 2015037850

In this book author Tom Jones "answers every question you have ever had about space. His . . . blend of wit, personal experience, and technical expertise shines in each answer, and together all the answers illuminate the true space experience from start to finish. His engaging and informative responses remind readers of historic space achievements, acquaint them with exciting new ambitions, [and] make them feel like they have experienced space firsthand." (Publisher's note)

Includes bibliographical references

Mara, Wil

Space exploration; science, technology, and engineering. Wil Mara. Children's Press 2014 64 p. color illustrations (library binding) $30

Grades: 5 6 7 8 **629.4**

1. Space flight 2. Outer space -- Exploration 3. Astronautics 4.

Space flight -- History 5. Outer space -- Exploration -- History
ISBN 0531206157; 9780531206157; 9780531210741

LC 2014003569

In this children's book by Wil Mara "readers will learn about some of the greatest space missions in history and find out what today's top engineers and scientists are doing to advance space exploration to new heights. They will also find out what it takes to begin a career in space exploration and how different workers can fill a variety of roles in the quest to reach distant planets and stars." (Publisher's note)

"An appropriate series for middle schoolers searching for concrete career possibilities." SLJ

Includes bibliographical references (page 61) and index

McMahon, Peter

The **space** adventurer's guide; Your Passport to the Coolest Things to See and Do in the Universe. Peter McMahon ; illustrated by Josh Holinaty. Kids Can Press 2018 100 p. $17.99

Grades: 4 5 6 7 8 **629.4**

1. Astronautics 2. Space flight 3. Interplanetary voyages
ISBN 1771380322; 9781771380324

This book, by Peter McMahon, illustrated by Josh Holinaty, presents "a travel guide for kids to plan their own out-of-this-world journeys. Eight potential space vacations are described, one per chapter, complete with information about pre-trip preparations (like training to withstand extreme g-forces), accommodations and dining (hot dogs in zero gravity, anyone?), awesome activities (how about a real moon walk?) and so much more." (Publisher's note)

Royston, Angela

Space; Angela Royston. Smart Apple Media 2016 32 p. color illustrations $31.35

Grades: 4 5 6 7 **629.4**

1. Outer space
ISBN 1625881584; 9781625881588

LC 2015460990

This book on outer space, by Angela Royston, part of the Research on the Edge series, "is a gripping look the vital research scientists carry out in the final frontier, and the incredible technology that enables them to live and work in such a dangerous place. [It] also explains how this research can increase our understanding of other planets, expand our knowledge of the universe, and discover untapped resources." (Publisher's note)

"Readers who choose to explore these books... will be rewarded with rich portraits of innovative science in exciting locations." Booklist

Includes bibliographical references and index

Saari, Peggy

Space exploration, Primary sources; [by] Peggy Saari. U.X.L, Thomson Gale 2005 203p il (Space exploration reference library) $63

Grades: 7 8 9 10 **629.4**

1. Astronautics
ISBN 0-7876-9213-1

LC 2004-15879

This volume contains excerpts from 17 documents and speeches, beginning with a chapter from a Jules Verne book and ending with remarks made in early 2004 by George W. Bush on a new vision for space exploration. Each selection is introduced with material on the context, key points, and information on the author

Includes glossary and bibliographical references

Skurzynski, Gloria

★ **This** is rocket science; true stories of the risk-taking scientists who figure out ways to explore beyond Earth. National Geographic 2010 80p il $18.95; lib bdg $28.90

Grades: 5 6 7 8 **629.4**

1. Rocketry 2. Aeronautics 3. Aerospace engineers
ISBN 978-1-4263-0597-9; 1-4263-0597-4; 978-1-4263-0598-6 lib bdg; 1-4263-0598-2 lib bdg

LC 2009-20386

"This concise book provides a historical, as well as contemporary, introduction to the field of aeronautical engineering with a decidedly human interest perspective. . . . This text will be a great introduction to many of the significant contributors to the field of rocket science." Sci Books Films

Includes glossary and bibliographical references

Stott, Carole

Space exploration; written by Carole Stott; photographed by Steve Gorton. Dorling Kindersley 2009 71p il (DK eyewitness books) $16.99

Grades: 4 5 6 7 **629.4**

1. Astronautics 2. Outer space -- Exploration
ISBN 978-0-7566-5828-1; 0-7566-5828-4

First published 1997 by Knopf

Describes rockets, exploratory vehicles, and other technological aspects of space exploration, satellites, space stations, and the life and work of astronauts.

Young, Karen Romano

Space junk; the dangers of polluting earth's orbit. Karen Romano Young. Twenty-First Century Books 2016 64 p. color illustrations (lb : alk. paper) $33.32

Grades: 7 8 9 10 **629.4**

1. Space debris 2. Artificial satellites 3. Space pollution
ISBN 1467756008; 9781467756006

LC 2015013396

In this book, by Karen Romano Young, readers can " learn about the dangers of space junk collisions, how scientists track them, and how space agencies are working to develop new technologies to clean up the space junk. Along the way, [readers] hear from the scientists who are working to ensure that outer space remains a safe place to travel and explore." (Publisher's note)

"Clearly written and concise, the book lays out the problem without sensationalizing it, while including human-interest details, such as your odds of being stuck by falling space junk (at 'one in several trillion,' decidedly low). Small, well-captioned color photos, helpful diagrams, and interesting sidebars enhance the text. A natural for booktalking to STEM-minded kids, this slender volume belongs in many libraries." Booklist

Includes bibliographical references and index

Rhuday-Perkovich, Olugbemisola

Above and beyond; NASA's journey to tomorrow. Olugbemisola Rhuday-Perkovich. Feiwel & Friends 2018 160 p. (hardcover) $19.99

Grades: 5 6 7 8 **629.4**

1. Astronautics 2. United States. National Aeronautics and Space Administration
ISBN 9781250308467; 9781250308474

LC 2018936427

In this book, by Olugbemisola Rhuday-Perkovich, young readers "will learn how NASA started, how it faced challenges along the way, how much it has achieved, and how it will continue to move forward in the future. . . . 'Above and Beyond' aims to leave audiences hopeful and inspired about the future of our planet--and convinced that NASA is essential to our continued survival as we mark its important anniversaries and dream of new discoveries to come." (Publisher's note)

"Space nerds will be hooked; an extensive bibliography makes this a natural for report writers, and the format and generous artwork will attract browsers." (Booklist)

629.43 Unmanned space flight

Carson, Mary Kay

Mission to Pluto; The First Visit to an Ice Dwarf and the Kuiper Belt. Mary Kay Carson ; with photographs by Tom Uhlman. Houghton Mifflin Harcourt 2016 73 p. illustrations (chiefly color) $18.99; (ebook) $18.99

Grades: 5 6 7 8 **629.43**

1. Pluto (Dwarf planet) 2. Kuiper Belt 3. Space flight 4. Interplanetary voyages 5. New Horizons (Spacecraft) 6. Outer space -- Exploration

ISBN 9780544416710; 9780544868106

LC 2015037656

This book, by Mary Kay Carson, with photos by Tom Uhlman, "goes where no person or spacecraft has ever gone before. Follow along with the team of scientists as they build New Horizons, fly it across the solar system, and make new discoveries about a world three billion miles away." (Publisher's note)

"This enthusiastic, accessible look at both cutting-edge scientific discovery and the dynamic work behind the scenes will be an easy sell to space-mad kids and a valuable addition to any school library." Booklist

Includes bibliographical references (page 72) and index.

Siy, Alexandra

★ **Cars** on Mars; roving the red planet. Charlesbridge 2009 57p il $18.95

Grades: 5 6 7 8 **629.43**

1. Space vehicles 2. Mars (Planet) -- Exploration 3. Mars (Planet) 4. Roving vehicles (Astronautics)

ISBN 1-57091-462-1; 978-1-57091-462-1

LC 2008-40751

This is an introduction to the Mars Exploration Rovers, Spirit and Opportunity. Included are photographs of the Mars landscape taken over a five-year period as the rovers searched for water on the planet. Glossary. Bibliography. Index. "Grades three to eight." (Sci Books Films)

"This title will sweep readers up in an exploratory mission that has come closer than any other so far to finding sure signs of extraterrestrial life." SLJ

Includes glossary and bibliographical references

Spilsbury, Richard

Robots in space; Richard and Louise Spilsbury. Gareth Stevens Publishing 2016 48 p. color illustrations $31.95

Grades: 4 5 6 7 **629.43**

1. Robots 2. Outer space

ISBN 1482430142; 9781482430141

LC 2014415767

In this book, by Richard and Louise Spilsbury, part of the Amazing Robots series, "readers learn all about these incredible robots as well as other space technology including robotnauts, or robot astronauts! Examples of the robots used in space are shown in full-color photographs, complete with explanations of their abilities. The main content and sidebars delve into the technological and scientific side of creating robots and how important theyve become to space exploration." (Publisher's note)

"The full-color photos of robots in action and the high-interest nature of robotics may catch the interest of science-minded kids." Booklist

629.44 Auxiliary spacecraft

Cole, Michael D.

The **Columbia** space shuttle disaster; from first liftoff to tragic final flight. Enslow Pubs. 2003 48p il (Countdown to space) lib bdg $18.95

Grades: 4 5 6 **629.44**

1. Space vehicle accidents 2. Columbia (Space shuttle)

ISBN 0-7660-2295-1

LC 2003-4823

First published 1995 with title: Columbia

Details the first flight of the space shuttle Columbia, as well as its tragic final flight

"The account offers a lot of information, helping to make sense of a highly complicated subject. . . . The color and b&w photographs complement the story." Libr Media Connect

Includes glossary and bibliographical references

Holden, Henry M.

The **coolest** job in the universe; working aboard the International Space Station. Henry M. Holden. Enslow 2013 48 p. (American space missions, astronauts, exploration, and discovery) (hbk.) $23.93

Grades: 4 5 6 7 8 **629.44**

1. International Space Station 2. Space flight 3. Space sciences 4. Manned space flight 5. Space sciences -- Research

ISBN 0766040747; 9780766040748

LC 2012002222

This book, by Henry M. Holden, is part of the "American Space Missions: Astronauts, Exploration, and Discovery" series. In it the daily life of astronauts working on the International Space Station is explored. This book "focuses on the construction of the ISS, what life is like onboard, and the importance of the research projects conducted. . . . Throughout, the courage, dedication, and sacrifice of the astronauts are emphasized." (School Library Journal)

Includes bibliographical references (p. 43-45, 47) and index

Miller, Ron

Satellites; by Ron Miller. Twenty-First Century Books 2007 112p il (Space innovations) lib bdg $31.93

Grades: 7 8 9 10 **629.44**

1. Artificial satellites

ISBN 978-0-8225-7154-4

LC 2007001075

This "begins with the science of Newton, the history of rockets, and the vivid imaginations of nineteenth-century science-fiction writers. It traces the historical development of man-made satellites from Sputnik 1 to the Earth orbiters currently transmitting everything from Earth-based communications signals to images of the universe. . . . Illustrations include many small color photos and some paintings, diagrams, satellite images, and black-and-white photos. . . . Miller synthesizes his evident research into a well-organized discussion." Booklist

Includes bibliographical references

629.442 Space stations

Larson, Kirsten W.

International Space Station; Kirsten W. Larson. Rourke Pub Group 2017 48 p. $10.95

Grades: 4 5 6 7 **629.442**

1. International Space Station 2. Space stations 3. Artificial satellites

ISBN 168342459X; 9781683424598

This book in the Engineering Wonders series, by Kirsten W. Larson, "[offers] an in-depth overview of the engineering processes involved in constructing the international space station. Addresses the obstacles of construction, the impact on society, and the science of engineering such superstructures." (Publisher's note)

"Complete with glossaries, reading-comprehension questions, online resources, and—in Elevators and International Space Station—time lines, these comprehensive titles are a stellar resource for space-crazy or engineering-inclined middle-grade readers." Booklist

629.45 Manned space flight

Bodden, Valerie

Man walks on the Moon. Creative Education 2009 48p il map (Days of change) $32.80

Grades: 5 6 7 8 **629.45**

1. Space flight to the moon 2. Project Apollo

ISBN 9781608185283; 978-1-58341-735-5; 1-58341-735-4

LC 2008009166

"With elegant design and mature prose, the Days of Change series is an ideal starting point for all manner of school projects. . . . The very first page of Man Walks on the Moon questions whether or not the feat was worth the resources, before reveling in the tech-heavy details of spaceflight and offering up some telling photos." Booklist

Includes bibliographical references

To the moon; by Valerie Bodden. Creative Education 2011 48 p. col. ill. (Great expeditions) (paperback) $12.00; (hardcover) $34.25

Grades: 5 6 7 8 **629.45**

1. Apollo project 2. Space flight to the moon -- History 3. Project Apollo (U.S.) -- History

ISBN 1608180689; 9780898126662; 9781608180684

LC 2010033549

This book by Valerie Bodden on the 1969 moon landing is part of the "Great Expeditions" series. "This factual account is . . . accompanied with both black and white and color photographs. Profiles of four of the astronauts, reproductions of some of their significant journal entries, and inset boxes of supplemental information aid in understanding. Includes a table of contents, a timeline, end notes, a bibliography, and an index." (Children's Literature)

Includes bibliographical references (p. 46-47) and index.

Brown, Don, 1949-

Rocket to the moon! by Don Brown. Amulet Books 2019 136 p. illustrations (Big ideas that changed the world) (hardcover) $13.99

Grades: 3 4 5 6 7 **629.45**

1. Space flight to the moon 2. Apollo project 3. Project Apollo (U.S.)

ISBN 1419734040; 9781419734045

LC 2018022209

This book by Don Brown "explores the people and technology that made the moon landing possible. . . . [I]t focuses on the moon landing itself, showing the events leading up to it and how it changed the world. The book takes readers through the history of rocket building: from ancient Chinese rockets, to 'bombs bursting in air' during the War of 1812, to Russia's Sputnik program, to the moon landing." (Publisher's note)

Brown "uses restrained colors and loose, fluid modeling to give his mildly cartoonish depictions of figures and (then) cutting-edge technology an engagingly informal air. He doesn't gloss over Laika's sad fate or the ugly fact that Wernher von Braun built rockets for the Nazis with 'concentration-camp prisoners.' . . . A frank, often funny appreciation of our space program's high-water mark." Kirkus

Includes bibliographical references (pages 126-128) and index

Chaikin, Andrew

★ **Mission** control, this is Apollo; the story of the first voyages to the moon. [by] Andrew Chaikin, with Victoria Kohl; [with paintings by] Alan Bean. Penguin Group 2009 114p il $23.99

Grades: 5 6 7 8 9 **629.45**

1. Astronautics 2. Space flight to the moon 3. Project Apollo 4. Astronautics -- History

ISBN 0-670-01156-8; 978-0-670-01156-8

LC 2009000833

This is a "history of the piloted Apollo missions. . . . [Drawing on] interviews he conducted for his book for adults (A Man on the Moon), Chaikin covers each of the twelve missions in a separate chapter. [Index.] Intermediate." (Horn Book)

"Based on interviews with 28 astronauts, this history of the Apollo program masterfully describes the missions and personalizes them with astronauts' own words. Chaikin starts with a brief overview of its origins and of the Mercury and Gemini missions. He then highlights the significance of each manned Apollo mission in chronological chapters, with full-page sidebars on such topics as food, TV coverage, space sickness and going to the bathroom in space. The handsome design has many photographs, diagrams of the rockets and modules and more than 30 well-reproduced paintings by Apollo 12 astronaut Bean." Kirkus

Includes bibliographical references

Collins, Michael

Flying to the moon; an astronaut's story. Revised and updated edition Farrar, Straus & Giroux 2019 162p il hardcover $19.99

Grades: 5 6 7 8 **629.45**

1. Astronauts 2. Space flight to the moon

ISBN 0-374-42356-3; 9780374312022 hardcover

First published 1976 with title: Flying to the moon, and other strange places

The author recounts his early days as an Air Force test pilot, his NASA training and his experiences aboard Gemini 10 and the Apollo 11 mission to the moon. Collins also advocates continued exploration of the universe

"A well told tale, which includes a lot of easily explained science." BAYA Book Rev

Dell, Pamela

Man on the moon; how a photograph made anything seem possible. Compass Point Books 2011 64p il (Captured history) lib bdg $33.99

Grades: 6 7 8 9 **629.45**

1. Astronauts 2. Documentary photography 3. Space flight to the

moon 4. Project Apollo 5. Air force officers 6. Nonfiction writers
ISBN 978-0-7565-4396-9; 0-7565-4396-7

LC 2010038577

This book about the iconic photograph of Neil Armstrong walking on the moon, taken by fellow astronaut Buzz Aldrin, places the photo "in historical context, profiles the photographer, describes the conditions under which it was taken, and analyzes both its immediate and its continuing impact. The [text includes] ample background information and details and [is] enhanced by large photos and sidebars." SLJ

Includes glossary and bibliographical references

Dyson, Marianne J.

Home on the moon; living on a space frontier. National Geographic Soc. 2003 64p il $18.95

Grades: 4 5 6 7 **629.45**

1. Moon

ISBN 0-7922-7193-9

LC 2002-5280

Considers the moon as a frontier that has been only partially explored, looking at its history, geography, and weather, as well as what people would require to live and work there. Includes activities

"Clear writing, vivid images, interesting details, and quotes from astronauts and scientists make this a lively, fact-filled introduction." Booklist

Includes glossary and bibliographical references

Gibson, Karen Bush

Women in space; 23 stories of first flights, scientific missions, and gravity-breaking adventures. Karen Bush Gibson. Chicago Review Press 2014 240 p. (cloth) $19.95

Grades: 7 8 9 10 **629.45**

1. Women astronauts 2. Outer space -- Exploration 3. Women in astronautics 4. Women astronauts -- Biography

ISBN 9781613748442; 1613748442

LC 2013024950

This book, by Karen Bush Gibson, "profiles 23 pioneers, including Eileen Collins, the first woman to command the space shuttle; Peggy Whitson, who logged more than a year in orbit aboard the International Space Station; and Mae Jemison, the first African American woman in space; as well as astronauts from Japan, Canada, Italy, South Korea, France, and more." (Publisher's note)

Includes bibliographical references and index

Goodman, Susan E.

How do you burp in space? and other tips every space tourist needs to know. by Susan Goodman ; illustrated by Michael Slack. Bloomsbury Pub." 2013 80 p. (hardback) $16.99

Grades: 4 5 6 **629.45**

1. Space flight 2. Interplanetary voyages 3. Space tourism 4. Manned space flight

ISBN 1599900688; 9781599900681; 9781599909349

LC 2011035303

In this children's book, author Susan E. Goodman "gives readers who will be the first generation of true space tourists general advice about how to prepare for the trip, what to pack, what food and accommodations will be like, and recreational opportunities both in Earth's orbit and on the moon. She also highlights some hazards, such as drinking carbonated drinks: Burping in microgravity brings up more than just CO2." (Kirkus Reviews)

Ultimate field trip 5; blasting off to Space Academy. by Susan E. Goodman; photographs by Michael J. Doolittle. Atheneum Bks. for Young Readers 2001 41p il hardcover o.p. $17

Grades: 4 5 6 7 **629.45**

1. Astronauts 2. Space flight 3. U.S. Space Camp (Huntsville, Ala.)

ISBN 0-689-83044-0; 0-689-84863-3 pa

LC 00-38082

"This book follows student trainees through a weeklong session at the U.S. Space Academy in Huntsville, AL, as they are exposed to what it takes to become an astronaut and to the inner workings of the entire space program. . . . Varied-colored pages, replete with outstanding full-color, captioned photos, are artistically appealing as well as informative." SLJ

Includes glossary and bibliographical references

Green, Carl R.

Spacewalk; the astounding Gemini 4 mission. Carl R. Green. Enslow Publishers 2013 48 p. $23.93

Grades: 4 5 6 7 8 **629.45**

1. Gemini project 2. Outer space 3. Space flight 4. Project Gemini (U.S.) -- History

ISBN 0766040755; 9780766040755

LC 2011030869

This children's book, by Carl R. Green, "explores the astounding GEMINI 4 mission. . . . Pilot Ed White could see Hawaii, California, Texas, and Florida . . . while walking in space! . . . The first American spacewalk was a monumental achievement, and it helped push the space program toward its ultimate goal of landing men on the Moon." (Publisher's note)

Includes bibliographical references and index

Hartman, Eve

Mission to Mars; [by] Eve Hartman and Wendy Meshbesher. Raintree 2010 56p il (Science missions) lib bdg $33.50; pa $9.49

Grades: 5 6 7 8 **629.45**

1. Space flight to Mars 2. Mars (Planet)

ISBN 9781-4109-3821-3 lib bdg; 1-4109-3821-2 lib bdg; 978-1-4109-3996-8 pa; 1-4109-3996-0 pa

LC 2009-53209

""Will human beings ever explore Mars? Can it be colonized? Find out in this fascinating book on Martian exploration." (Publisher's note)

"Excellent black-and-white and color photos throughout are matched perfectly to the texts and well captioned. Good choices for reports and debates." SLJ

Includes glossary and bibliographical references

Hense, Mary

How astronauts use math; math curriculum consultant: Rhea A. Stewart. Chelsea Clubhouse 2010 32p il (Math in the real world) lib bdg $28

Grades: 4 5 6 **629.45**

1. Astronauts 2. Mathematics 3. Astronautics 4. Vocational guidance

ISBN 978-1-60413-610-4 lib bdg; 1-60413-610-3 lib bdg

LC 2009-23926

This describes how astronauts use math for such tasks as calculating distance, speed, and velocity, and includes relevant math problems and information about how to become an astronaut

Includes glossary and bibliographical references

Holden, Henry M.

Danger in space; surviving the Apollo 13 disaster. Henry M. Holden. Enslow Publishers 2013 48 p. $23.93

Grades: 4 5 6 7 8 **629.45**

1. Apollo project 2. Picture books for children 3. Apollo 13 (Spacecraft) 4. Project Apollo (U.S.) 5. Space vehicle accidents -- United States

ISBN 0766040720; 9780766040724

LC 2011037734

This children's picture book tells the story of the U.S. National Aerospace and Space Administration's Apollo 13 mission. "Soaring through space at twenty-five thousand miles per hour, Apollo 13 was on course for the Moon. Suddenly, the three astronauts aboard the spacecraft heard a loud bang. A strong vibration rumbled through the crew cabin. There had been an explosion in the oxygen tank! More than two hundred thousand miles from Earth, Apollo 13 was in grave danger." (Publisher's note)

Includes bibliographical references and index

Maurer, Richard

★ **Destination** moon; the remarkable and improbable voyage of Apollo 11. Richard Maurer. Roaring Brook Press 2019 400 p. (hardcover) $19.99

Grades: 6 7 8 9 10 11 **629.45**

ISBN 9781626727441; 9781626727458

LC 2018955851

This book, by Richard Maurer, presents "the history of NASA's Apollo program from Earth orbital missions to lunar landings in a propulsive nonfiction narrative. . . . Beginning with fighter pilots in World War II, Maurer traces the origins of the Apollo program to a few exceptional soldiers, a Nazi engineer, and a young eager man who would become president." (Publisher's note)

"Here's an absorbing, insightful, solidly informative resource for readers who want to understand the U.S. space program from the ground up." (Booklist)

Ross, Stewart

Moon : science, history, and mystery. Scholastic 2009 128p il lib bdg $18.99

Grades: 4 5 6 **629.45**

1. Astronautics 2. Space flight to the moon 3. Project Apollo 4. Moon -- Exploration

ISBN 978-0-545-12732-5 lib bdg; 0-545-12732-7 lib bdg

"Jam-packed with information, this colorful oversize volume chronicles the race to land a person on the Moon. Alternating chapters describe Moon mythologies and superstitions, the history of astronomical study, and the efforts involved in launching a lunar expedition. . . . The photographs pop with color and action. . . . The invaluable contribution of Muslim scientists is included. . . . [The book's] multicultural history will expand any collection." SLJ

Includes glossary

Sandler, Martin W.

Apollo 8; the mission that changed everything. Martin W. Sandler. Candlewick Press 2018 176 p. $24.99

Grades: 6 7 8 9 **629.45**

1. Astronautics 2. Apollo project 3. Space flight to the moon

ISBN 0763694894; 9780763694890

This book, by Martin W. Sandler, tells one of the historic chapters in the U.S. history, the success of Apollo 8, the second manned spaceflight mission in the United States Apollo space program. "In a volume full of astonishing full-color photographs, including the iconic Earthrise photo, . . . Sandler unfolds an incredible chapter in U.S. history: Apollo 8 wouldn't just orbit Earth, it would take American astronauts to see the dark side of the moon." (Publisher's note)

Stone, Tanya Lee

★ **Almost** astronauts; 13 women who dared to dream. Candlewick Press 2008 133p il $24.99; pa $17.99

Grades: 5 6 7 8 9 10 **629.45**

1. Women astronauts 2. Sex discrimination 3. Project Mercury -- History 4. Sex discrimination against women

ISBN 0-7636-3611-8; 0-7636-4502-8 pa; 978-0-7636-3611-1; 978-0-7636-4502-1 pa

LC 2008-17487

Boston Globe-Horn Book Award honor book: Nonfiction (2009)

This book "explores the little known experiences of 13 brave, inspiring women who dreamed of becoming astronauts in the very early days of NASA's training program and submitted themselves to many of the tests undertaken by their male counterparts, the Mercury 7." Tanya Lee Stone "brings together a variety of primary and secondary sources, including her interviews with some of the women involved, to provide a unique view of the challenges faced by the female pilots of the day." (School Library Journal)

"In 1960, thirteen American women passed the physical exams required to become astronauts as surely as any of the men already involved in NASA's early space flight endeavors, but they were disqualified solely because of their gender. This book is their story. . . . Any girl with an interest in space flight or the history of women's rights will enjoy this account and applaud these courageous pioneers." Voice Youth Advocates

Includes bibliographical references

Thimmesh, Catherine

★ **Team** moon; how 400,000 people landed Apollo 11 on the moon. Houghton Mifflin Company 2006 80p il $19.95

Grades: 5 6 7 8 **629.45**

1. Space flight to the moon 2. Apollo 11 (Spacecraft)

ISBN 0-618-50757-4

LC 2005-10755

"Thimmesh retraces the course of the space mission that landed an actual man, on the actual Moon. It's an oft-told tale, but the author tells it from the point of view not of astronauts or general observers, but of some of the 17,000 behind-the-scenes workers at Kennedy Space Center, the 7500 Grumman employees who built the lunar module, the 500 designers and seamstresses who actually constructed the space suits, and other low-profile contributors who made the historic flight possible. . . . This dramatic account will mesmerize even readers already familiar with the event. . . . This stirring, authoritative tribute to the collective effort . . . belongs in every collection." SLJ

Includes glossary and bibliographical references

629.8 Automatic control engineering

Chaffee, Joel

How to build a prize-winning robot. Rosen Central 2011 48p il (Robotics) lib bdg $26.50; pa $11.75

Grades: 5 6 7 8 **629.8**

1. Robots

ISBN 978-1-4488-1238-7 lib bdg; 1-4488-1238-0 lib bdg; 978-1-4488-2252-2 pa; 1-4488-2252-1 pa

LC 2010025748

"Kids who are fascinated with robots will want [this title] available." SLJ

Includes glossary and bibliographical references

Freedman, Jeri

Robots through history. Rosen Central 2011 48p il (Robotics) lib bdg $26.50; pa $11.75

Grades: 5 6 7 8 **629.8**

1. Robots

ISBN 978-1-4488-1236-3 lib bdg; 1-4488-1236-4 lib bdg; 978-1-4488-2250-8 pa; 1-4488-2250-5 pa

LC 2010024139

"Kids who are fascinated with robots will want [this title] available." SLJ

Includes glossary and bibliographical references

Graham, Ian

Robot technology. Smart Apple Media 2012 il (New technology)

Grades: 4 5 6 7 **629.8**

1. Robots

ISBN 1-599-20533-5; 978-1-599-20533-5

LC 2010044240

Describes current robotics technology, including the applications of robots in space, in the military, in industry, and around the house. Discusses the pros and cons of creating fully autonomous robots.

This "offers a fine overview for reports, and its attractive design may also entice middle-grade readers to learn more." Booklist

Koontz, Robin

Animal -inspired robots; Robin Koontz ; [edited by] Keli Sipperley. Rourke Educational Media 2018 48 p. $35.64

Grades: 4 5 6 7 8 **629.8**

1. Robots 2. Animal behavior

ISBN 9781641564571

LC 2018930485

In this book in the Nature-Inspired Innovations series, by Robin Koontz, edited by Keli Sipperley, "scientists and engineers study and learn from nature to help solve problems and improve the world. Learn how biomimics has contributed to robotics. This title supports NGSS for Engineering Design." (Publisher's note)

Mackay, Jenny

Robots. Lucent Books 2010 104p il (Technology 360) $32.45

Grades: 8 9 10 11 12 **629.8**

1. Robots

ISBN 978-1-4205-0168-1; 1-4205-0168-2

LC 2009045634

This book explores "the early development and advances of [robotics], its impact on society both positive and negative, and the importance it plays in our lives. . . . [It] describes the technical aspects of movement, artificial intelligence, and robots of the future. . . . Numerous color photos, diagrams, 'Bits & Bytes' boxes as well as many other additional text boxes create appeal and provide beneficial informative and complementary material to aid in understanding the technical details of the [text]." SLJ

Includes glossary and bibliographical references

Mercer, Bobby

The **Robot** book; build and control 20 electric gizmos, machines, and hacked toys. Bobby Mercer. Chicago Review Press Inc. 2014 208 p. illustrations (Science in motion) (trade paper) $14.95

Grades: 4 5 6 **629.8**

1. Machinery 2. Robots 3. Robotics 4. Personal robotics

ISBN 1556524072; 9781556524073

LC 2014015327

In this book author "Bobby Mercer will show you how to turn common household objects and repurposed materials into 20 easy-to-build robots for little or no cost. Every hands-on project contains a materials list and detailed step-by-step instructions with photos for easy assembly. Mercer also explains the science and technology behind each robot, including concepts such as friction, weight and mass, [and] center of gravity." (Publisher's note)

"A solid starting point for readers with an interest in circuitry or engineering—or who simply like to take things apart to see how they work." Publishers Weekly

Payment, Simone

Robotics careers; preparing for the future. Rosen Central 2011 48p il (Robotics) lib bdg $26.50; pa $11.75

Grades: 5 6 7 8 **629.8**

1. Robots 2. Vocational guidance

ISBN 978-1-4488-1239-4 lib bdg; 1-4488-1239-9 lib bdg; 978-1-4488-2253-9 pa; 1-4488-2253-X pa

LC 2010024134

"Kids who are fascinated with robots will want [this title] available." SLJ

Includes glossary and bibliographical references

Robot. DK Pub 2018 160 p. $19.99

Grades: 4 5 6 7 **629.8**

1. Robots

ISBN 1465475842; 9781465475848

This book, by DK Publishing, explores the latest technology in robotics. "In bold, clear graphics, readers are introduced to work robots like the 'six-legged scuttler,' robotic submersibles, space robots, and biomimetic robots such as a bionic kangaroo. Models show the interior circuitry of the robots, while readers can also see them in mid-motion as they perform their applications: a robot programmed to work on factory floors grasps an egg with its adjustable 'gripper.'" (Publisher's note)

Shea, Therese

The **robotics** club; teaming up to build robots. Rosen Central 2011 48p il (Robotics) lib bdg $26.50; pa $11.75

Grades: 5 6 7 8 **629.8**

1. Clubs 2. Robots

ISBN 978-1-4488-1237-0 lib bdg; 1-4488-1237-2 lib bdg; 978-1-4488-2251-5 pa; 1-4488-2251-3 pa

This title "will provide students with the information necessary to form a club and compete at making and using robots. Kids who are fascinated with robots will want [this title] available." SLJ

Smibert, Angie

Artificial intelligence; thinking machines and smart robots with science activities for kids. Angie Smibert ; illustrated by Alexis Cornell. Nomad Press 2018 122 p. $22.95

Grades: 5 6 7 8 **629.8**

1. Robotics 2. Inventions 3. Artificial intelligence

ISBN 1619306735; 9781619306738

In this book in the Build It Yourself series, by Angie Smibert, illustrated by Alexis Cornell readers ages 10 to 15 learn the early definitions of artificial intelligence or] AI and discover how these definitions, and the tests that are applied to determine whether a machine has AI or not, have changed as machines have grown increasingly competent in unexpected ways." (Publisher's note)

Sobey, Ed

Robot experiments. Enslow Publishers 2011 128p il (Cool science projects with technology) lib bdg $31.93

Grades: 6 7 8 9 **629.8**

1. Robots 2. Science projects 3. Science -- Experiments

ISBN 978-0-7660-3303-0; 0-7660-3303-1

LC 2009037897

While this book "includes some suggestions for science-fair projects and a few experiments throughout, it also provides a detailed description of each component and step-by-step instruction for building a robot. This highly complicated process is explained using understandable terms and in a well-organized manner and includes information as detailed as computer-programming codes." SLJ

Includes glossary and bibliographical references

Woog, Adam

SCRATCHbot. Norwood House Press 2010 48p il (A great idea) lib bdg $25.27

Grades: 3 4 5 6 **629.8**

1. Robots

ISBN 978-1-59953-380-3 lib bdg; 1-59953-380-4 lib bdg

LC 2010008502

"Woog introduces a small, rolling robot with prominent whiskers, used to mimic a rodent's ability to sense its surroundings through touch. Discussions include how inventors are inspired by nature and how this appealing robot might be useful. Presenting specific, current information, [this book] will appeal to young people intrigued by inventions." Booklist

Includes glossary and bibliographical references

629.892 Robots

Gilby, Nancy Benovich

FIRST robotics; by Nancy Benovich Gilby. Cherry Lake Publishing 2016 32 p. color illustrations (lib. bdg.) $29.93

Grades: 4 5 6 7 8 **629.892**

1. Robotics 2. Inventions

ISBN 9781633623781; 9781633624061

LC 2015013323

This juvenile book, by Nancy Benovich Gilby, focuses on robotics. In it "students learn more about this recent innovation through detailed explanations built to foster creativity and critical thinking. Fun, engaging text introduces readers to new ideas and builds on maker-related concepts they may already know." (Publisher's note)

"Though narrowly focused, each title presents enough basic concepts that students shouldn't have much trouble expanding beyond the fundamentals." Booklist

Includes bibliographical references and index

Sjonger, Rebecca

Robotics engineering and our automated world; Rebecca Sjonger. Crabtree Publishing Co. 2017 32 p. color illustrations (ebook) $41.40; (reinforced library binding : alk. paper) $27.60

Grades: 5 6 7 8 **629.892**

1. Robotics 2. Technological innovations

ISBN 9781427117861; 0778775372; 9780778775379; 9780778775416

LC 2016027282

In this book, by Rebecca Sjonger, "readers will learn how robotics engineers find new ways for robots to do work that would be dangerous, time-consuming, dull, or impossible for humans to perform. Real-life examples and a design challenge help students understand key concepts related to the engineering design process, and how robotics engineers play a vital role in expanding our knowledge of the universe." (Publisher's note)

"A fascinating and thoughtfully arranged presentation of modern engineering." Booklist

Includes bibliographical references (page 30) and index

Spilsbury, Louise

Robotics; by Louise Spilsbury, Richard Spilsbury. Gareth Stevens Publishing 2016 48 p. (library binding) $31.95; (ebook) $31.95

Grades: 5 6 7 8 **629.892**

1. Robots 2. Technological innovations

ISBN 1482451603; 9781482451665; 9781482451603; 9781482451542

LC 2016057303

This juvenile book, by Louise Spilsbury and Richard Spilsbury, part of the "Cutting-Edge Technology" series, "takes a look at the amazing developments in robotic technology, from the early days of robots to the varied landscape of robotics we see today. Readers will learn the differences between robots being developed to look just like humans and the complex thinking machines designed to play chess or build cars." (Publisher's note)

"Rock-solid choices that will update and deepen science and technology collections." SLJ

Spilsbury, Richard

Robots in industry; Richard and Louise Spilsbury. Gareth Stevens Publishing 2016 48 p. color illustrations $31.95

Grades: 4 5 6 7 **629.892**

1. Industrial robots

ISBN 9781482430028

LC 2014415754

In this book in the Amazing Robots series, by Richard and Louise Spilsbury, "readers learn how integral robots have become in many parts of industry, including in production, factories, and in situations dangerous for people. Full-color photographs provide readers with a unique look at a growing branch of science. The main content and sidebars highlight real-life examples of robots at work as well as understandable explanations of their technology." (Publisher's note)

"The full-color photos of robots in action and the high-interest nature of robotics may catch the interest of science-minded kids." Booklist

Robots in medicine; Richard and Louise Spilsbury. Gareth Stevens Publishing 2016 48 p. color illustrations $31.95

Grades: 4 5 6 7 **629.892**

1. Robots

ISBN 148243010X; 9781482430103

LC 2014415763

In this book, by Richard and Louise Spilsbury, part of the Amazing Robots series, "readers are introduced to cutting-edge medical technology with full-color photographs of robots actually used in hospitals and doctors offices today. The main content offers detailed, but understandable, information about the science of these incredible machines. Additionally, readers learn about the integration of these robots into many careers in medicine, technology, and science." (Publisher's note)

"The full-color photos of robots in action and the high-interest nature of robotics may catch the interest of science-minded kids." Booklist

Includes bibliographical references (page 47) and index.

630 Agriculture and related technologies

Mickelson, Trina

Free -range farming; by Trina Mickelson. Lerner Publications 2016 64 p. color illustrations (lb : alk. paper) $34.65; (ebook) $34.65

Grades: 5 6 7 8 **630**

1. Animal welfare 2. Organic farming 3. Sustainable agriculture 4. Livestock 5. Agricultural systems

ISBN 9781467793896; 9781467797108

LC 2015019694

This children's book, written by Trina Mickelson and part of the Growing Green series, "begins with a look at commercial farming, comparing the benefits of increased production and lower costs with negatives like pollution and animal cruelty. Then it goes on to explain the free-range movement." (Booklist)

"This series for upper-middle grades focusing on 'green' food and farming practices that have gained popularity covers what has sparked each movement, what its health and environmental benefits are, and what some of its challenges are." Horn Book

Includes bibliographical references and index

Perritano, John

Agriculture; by John Perritano. Mason Crest 2017 64 p. color illustrations (hardback) $23.95

Grades: 6 7 8 9 10 **630**

1. Agriculture 2. Agricultural innovations 3. Agricultural mathematics

ISBN 9781422235881; 9781422282892

LC 2016004741

In this book in the STEM in Current Events series, by John Perritano, "check out many stories from the world of Agriculture, including these breaking headlines: 'Science: Pond Scum Studies Aid Farmers Technology'; 'Texting to Track African Agriculture'; 'Engineering: Urban Rooftops Convert to Fertile Farms'; 'Math: Calculating Soil Erosion Saves Lives.' Find out how these stories and many more are making an impact on farmers, farming, and the food we eat." (Publisher's note)

"A great fit for classroom or school libraries and a strong consideration for public libraries interested in the integration of STEM into everyday life." SLJ

Richardson, Gillian

10 plants that shook the world; Gillian Richardson ; illustrated by Kim Rosen. Annick Press 2013 132 p. (hardcover) $24.95

Grades: 4 5 6 7 8 **630**

1. Plants 2. Agriculture -- History

ISBN 1554514452; 9781554514458

This book, by Gillian Richardson, illustrated by Kim Rosen, profiles ten plants with significant histories. It describes how "countries went to war to control trade centers for pepper . . . , a grass called papyrus became the first effective tool for sharing knowledge through writing . . . , Europeans in the 1600s cut down rainforests to grow sugar, contributing to soil erosion . . . [and] dependence on the potato caused one of the greatest tragedies in history." (Publisher's note)

"With bold, lively caricatures from Rosen throughout, it's an intriguing and well-designed study of the ways plants have helped start wars, cure diseases, and advance technology." Pub Wkly

Rosen, Michael J.

Our farm; four seasons with five kids on one family's farm. written and photographed by Michael J. Rosen. Darby Creek Pub. 2008 144p il $18.95

Grades: 4 5 6 7 8 **630**

1. Family life 2. Ohio 3. Farm life -- United States

ISBN 978-1-58196-067-9; 1-58196-067-0

A journal of one year on the Bennett farm in central Ohio. Shows how one family, with the help of relatives and friends, creates a life and livelihood on a 150-acre farm.

"This engaging book is an unsentimental, appreciative look into the world of one farm family." SLJ

Rothman, Julia

Farm anatomy; the curious parts & pieces of country life. Julia Rothman. Storey Pub. 2011 223 p. col. ill., col. maps

Grades: 7 8 9 10 11 12 **630**

1. Barns 2. Farms 3. Farm life 4. Farm produce 5. Domestic animals 6. Farm life -- Miscellanea 7. Farm life -- Pictorial works

ISBN 1603429816; 9781603429818

LC 2012360929

This book explains the "difference between a weanling and a yearling, or a farrow and a barrow . . . [in this] guide to the curious parts and pieces of rural living. Dissecting everything from tractors and pigs to fences, hay bales, crop rotation patterns, and farm tools, [Julia] Rothman gives a . . . tour of the quirky details of country life. From the shapes of squash varieties to the parts of a goat; from how a barn is constructed to what makes up a beehive, every corner of the barnyard is uncovered and celebrated." (Publisher's note)

Includes bibliographical references (p. 220-222).

631.4 Soil science

Graham, Ian

You wouldn't want to live without dirt; written by Ian Graham ; illustrated by Mark Bergin ; series created by David Salariya. Franklin Watts, an imprint of Scholastic Inc. 2016 32 p. color ill., color map (library binding) $29.00

Grades: 3 4 5 6 **631.4**

1. Soils

ISBN 9780531214886; 9780531224380

LC 2015030229

This book, by Ian Graham, illustrated by Mark Bergin, asks "what if we didn't have any dirt or soil? . . . The ground would look different and many of the plants, trees and animals we know today would disappear. Dirt, and or soil, supplies a surprising variety of raw materials for making things. Learn about the ways dirt and soil have been used by humans over the centuries, from cave paintings to crop farming, and the exciting prospects for dirt and soil we may see in the future." (Publisher's note)

"The books feature a time line and numerous ancillaries, but the myriad entertaining facts are the real hit. Who wouldn't want to read them?" Booklist

Hirsch, Rebecca E., 1969-

Soil; Rebecca E. Hirsch. Core Library 2015 48 p. color illustrations (hbk.) $32.79

Grades: 5 6 7 **631.4**

1. Soils 2. Soil ecology 3. Soil geomorphology

ISBN 1624033911; 9781624033919

LC 2014932352

This children's book by Rebecca E. Hirsch, part of the Rocks and Minerals book series, "presents information on the different types of soil, discussing why soil is important and the consequences of natural erosion." (Publisher's note)

"Aligned to Common Core and state standards, the series provides ample opportunity for additional research ('Stop and Think'), hands-on experimentation ('In the Field'), and critical thinking ('Changing Minds') that will have readers looking at the world around them with a better understanding of just what exactly they're seeing. Despite a few issues, these are solid choices." SLJ

Includes bibliographical references (page 47) and index

631.5 Cultivation and harvesting

Regis, Natalie

Genetically modified crops and food; edited by Natalie Regis. Britannica Educational Publishing in association with Rosen Educational Services 2016 xviii, 174 p.p illustrations (some color) (library bound) $39.75; (ebook) $29.95

Grades: 7 8 9 10 11 12 **631.5**

1. Transgenic plants 2. Food -- Biotechnology 3. Genetically modified foods 4. Crops -- Genetic engineering

ISBN 1622755782; 9781622755783; 9781622755790

LC 2014049175

This book in the Biotechnology Revolution series, edited by Natalie Regis, "explains the reactions of scientists, farmers, . . . and medical doctors to the scientific changes in agriculture, which have ranged from support to skepticism, and shows how different governments around the world view the inclusion of GMOs in food. The unbiased approach allows readers to decide for themselves whether GMOs are the answer to world hunger or could negatively impact . . . [world] health." (Publisher's note)

"The set up of the text is user-friendly with bold, colored fonts for the headings of each section lending to easy navigation of the text." VOYA

Includes bibliographical references (pages 157-167) and index

633.1 Cereals

Sobol, Richard

The **life** of rice; from seedling to supper. Candlewick Press 2010 36p il map (Traveling photographer) $17.99

Grades: 3 4 5 6 **633.1**

1. Rice 2. Thailand

ISBN 978-0-7636-3252-6; 0-7636-3252-X

LC 2009-15138

"Turning his lens to the rice fields of Thailand, Sobol begins this affectionate account with a description of the Royal Plowing Ceremony that kicks off the planting season and continues through cultivation and into the harvest. Brief explanations of the growing stages of rice are accompanied by beautiful color photographs of the fields in their various phases. . . . Sobol offers an interesting look at a country and its people, and their relationship to the land. The writing is accessible and lively, providing a unique, specific look at one of the world's most important staples." SLJ

633.5 Fiber crops

Meltzer, Milton

The **cotton** gin. Benchmark Bks. 2003 123p il (Great inventions) lib bdg $25.95

Grades: 6 7 8 9 **633.5**

1. Cotton

ISBN 0-7614-1537-8

LC 2002-15308

The author describes the invention of the cotton gin and its effects on history including "the influence of mechanized cotton processing on the growth of slavery in the United States and the increase in textile mills. . . . The author expertly describes a setting that is ripe for invention. Powerful photographs . . . historical artwork, and personal narratives make the times real and relevant to readers." SLJ

Includes bibliographical references

634.9 Forestry

Collard, Sneed B.

Fire birds; valuing natural wildfires and burned forests. Sneed B. Collard III. Bucking Horse Books 2015 48 p. color illustrations (alk. paper) $17

Grades: 4 5 6 7 8 **634.9**

1. Birds 2. Wildfires

ISBN 9780984446070

LC 2014945653

In this book, author Sneed B. Collard III "explores how a forest devastated by a fire slowly recuperates, focusing on the work of biologist Richard Hutto, who studies the birds that thrive in burned forests. . . . . Individual birds like the hairy woodpecker and mountain bluebird are profiled in sidebars, and a chart lists the birds that most frequently populate new burn areas." (Publishers Weekly)

"A book that will leave readers asking questions and challenging assumptions--and with a keener appreciation of our environment." SLJ

Includes bibliographical references and index.

Silverstein, Alvin

Wildfires; the science behind raging infernos. [by] Alvin and Virginia Silverstein and Laura Silverstein Nunn. Enslow Publishers 2010 48p il map (The science behind natural disasters) lib bdg $23.93

Grades: 4 5 6 **634.9**

1. Wildfires

ISBN 978-0-7660-2973-6 lib bdg; 0-7660-2973-5 lib bdg

LC 2008-48025

"Scientific explanations are accompanied by plentiful color diagrams that will help students to grasp causes and effects. . . . Photos . . . are effective, and are sometimes turned into helpful, lively diagrams by the addition of such features as wind-direction arrows." SLJ

Includes glossary and bibliographical references

635 Garden crops (Horticulture)

Cohen, Whitney

The **book** of gardening projects for kids; 101 ways to get kids outside, dirty, and having fun. Whitney Cohen and John Fisher. 1st ed. Timber Press 2012 264 p. col. ill. $29.95

Grades: Adult **635**

1. Gardening 2. Gardens -- Guidebooks 3. Gardens -- Activity projects 4. Gardening for children

ISBN 1604693738; 9781604692457

LC 2011036778

In this book, "Whitney Cohen and John Fisher draw on years of experience in the Life Lab Garden Classroom and gardening with their own children to teach parents how to integrate the garden into their family life, no matter its scope or scale. The book features . . . gardening advice, including how to design a play-friendly garden, ideas for fun-filled theme gardens, and how to cook and preserve the garden's bounty. 101 . . . garden activities are also featured." (Publisher's note)

Cornell, Kari

The **nitty** -gritty gardening book; fun projects for all seasons. Kari Cornell ; photography by Jennifer Larson. Millbrook Press 2015 48 p. color illustrations lib. bdg $26.65

Grades: 3 4 5 6 **635**

1. Gardening 2. Gardening for children

ISBN 9781467726474

LC 2014009384

This book, by Kari Cornell, focuses on gardening. "Become a gardener in any season with these fun and easy projects. You don't even need a garden space—many of these activities can be done by planting in containers to set on a porch or a patio or even in a window. Try your hand at growing potatoes and strawberries. Plant bright flowers that attract butterflies, birds, and bees. Learn how to get daffodils to bloom in the winter! You can even make your own compost." (Publisher's note)

"Pleasant photographs by Larson are supplemented with clear diagrams and stock photos." Kirkus

Includes bibliographical references and index.

Woolf, Alex

You wouldn't want to live without vegetables; written by Alex Woolf ; illustrated by David Antram ; series created by David Salariya. Franklin Watts, an imprint of Scholastic Inc. 2016 32 p. color illustrations (library binding) $29.00

Grades: 3 4 5 6 **635**

1. Vegetables

ISBN 9780531214909; 9780531224403

LC 2015035314

This book, by Alex Woolf, illustrated by David Antram, explains that "vegetables provide us with essential vitamins and minerals that make our bodies healthier and stop us from getting sick. They're also used to make things like dyes, lotions and adhesives. Learn how vegetables are grown and cultivated, and the often inspired innovations made with such humble foodstuffs as the potato and the carrot." (Publisher's note)

"The books feature a time line and numerous ancillaries, but the myriad entertaining facts are the real hit. Who wouldn't want to read them?" Booklist

636 Animal husbandry

Keenan, Sheila

Animals in the house; a history of pets and people. Scholastic Nonfiction 2007 112p il hardcover o.p.

Grades: 4 5 6 **636**

1. Pets

ISBN 978-0-439-69286-1; 9780670062720

"Keenan provides an overview of pets andtheir people. Beginning with statistics about pet ownership, the text goes on to describe how animals and humans came together . . . and discusses how this relationship has changed and deepened. . . . Eye-catchingly designed, the format uses Photoshop to best advantage, providing interesting graphics, popping borders, and plenty of pictures featuring adorable animals." Booklist

Includes bibliographical references

Matzke, Ann

★ **Hedgehog**; Ann Matzke ; [edited by] Keli Sipperley. Rourke Educational Media 2015 32 p. color illustrations (hardcover) $32.79

Grades: 3 4 5 6 **636**

1. Pets 2. Hedgehog

ISBN 9781634305334; 9781634304337

LC 2015931856

This children's book, Ann Matzke, edited by Keli Sipperley, part of the "You Have a Pet What!?" series, explores hedgehogs. "Hedgehogs are not your typical pet. These interesting and unusual nocturnal animals with bright eyes, sweet faces and prickly backs require special care and handling. . . . Learn . . . a lot more facts about these cute, quirky little pets and see if a hedgehog is the right pet for you." (Publisher's note)

"Well written, with a clean design, these titles will be useful for educators and popular with potential pet owners." SLJ

636.088 Animals for specific purposes

Halls, Kelly Milner

Saving the Baghdad Zoo; a true story of hope and heroes. by Kelly Milner Halls, with William Sumner. Greenwillow Books 2010 64p il map $17.99

Grades: 4 5 6 7 **636.088**

1. Zoos 2. Wildlife conservation 3. Baghdad (Iraq) 4. Baghdad Zoo (Iraq)

ISBN 978-0-06-177202-3; 0-06-177202-X

LC 2008-52820

"This eye-opening tale of compassion and cooperation chronicles the mission of an international team of military personnel, zoo staffers, veterinarians, and relief workers to rescue neglected animals in Baghdad. . . . Sobering and uplifting photographs—many taken by Sumner—underscore both the direness of the situation and the spirit of hope that drove the project." Publ Wkly

Includes bibliographical references

Laidlaw, Rob

Wild animals in captivity; [by] Rob Laidlaw. Fitzhenry & Whiteside 2008 48p il paperback $12.95

Grades: 4 5 6 7 8 **636.088**

1. Zoos 2. Animal welfare

ISBN 9781554553884 paperback; 978-1-55455-025-8

"A passionate, well-written, and well-researched argument against the practices of most zoos around the world. . . . Describes the damage done when animals are unnaturally confined and moved to inhospitable climates, and compares the wild and captive lives of polar bears, orcas, elephants, and great apes—the four species most harmed by captivity. . . . The issues raised in this important and powerful book will resonate with young and old." SLJ

Markle, Sandra

Animal heroes; true rescue stories. by Sandra Markle. Millbrook Press 2009 64p il lib bdg $29.27

Grades: 4 5 6 7 **636.088**

1. Pets 2. Animals 3. Rescue work

ISBN 978-0-8225-7884-0 lib bdg; 0-8225-7884-0 lib bdg

LC 2007-50435

"Nine stories, based on interviews with the grateful survivors, describe how brave animals rescued people in catastrophic circumstances. Each edgy retelling reveals details that only the participants could know, including sounds, smells, sights, and the knowledge that at any moment they could die, deepening the tension. Mixed in are Markle's broad and perfectly attuned insights about animal behavior." SLJ

Includes glossary and bibliographical references

O'Connell, Caitlin

Bridge to the wild; Behind the Scenes at the Zoo. written by Caitlin O'Connell ; with photographs by Caitlin O'Connell & Timothy Rodwell. Houghton Mifflin Harcourt 2016 208 p. color illustrations $18.99

Grades: 4 5 6 7 **636.088**

1. Zoos 2. Animal behavior 3. Human-animal relationships 4. Atlanta Zoo 5. Zoo animals 6. Zoo keepers

ISBN 9780544277397

LC 2015024535

"Over five days we meet a menagerie of magnificent animals—pandas, elephants, gorillas, meerkats, flamingos and more—alongside the longtime animal lover, scientist, and researcher Caitlin O'Connell. With inside access to the guidance and knowledge of their beloved zoo caretakers and with . . . photographs, we are able to see the day-to-day marvels—and sometimes misfortunes—behind the animals' enclosures that often go unseen by the everyday zoo visitor." (Publisher's note)

"Readers should find the book's facts and photos intriguing, and the collaborators' curiosity and passion inspiring." Pub Wkly

Includes bibliographical references and index.

636.089 Veterinary medicine

Jackson, Donna M.

★ **ER** vets; life in an animal emergency room. Houghton Mifflin 2005 88p il $17

Grades: 5 6 7 8 **636.089**

1. Veterinary medicine

ISBN 0-618-43663-4

"With plentiful, excellent-quality photographs, this highly visual book offers a behind-the-scenes look at an emergency animal hospital in Colorado. . . . A section on grief counseling for families with critically ill pets and a spread on how to put together a pet first-aid kit are included. Well-researched and well-written, ER Vets is an engaging book on a hot topic." SLJ

636.1 Horses

Clutton-Brock, Juliet

Horse; written by Juliet Clutton-Brock. DK Pub. 2008 72p il (DK eyewitness books) paperback $9.99; library $19.99

Grades: 4 5 6 7 **636.1**

1. Horses

ISBN 9781465451743 paperback; 9781465451750 library; 978-0-7566-3775-0

LC 2008276033

First published 2003 in the United Kingdom

Examines the anatomy, history, and breeds of horses, and discusses the different ways horses have been used throughout history

Crosby, Jeff

Harness horses, bucking broncos & pit ponies; a history of horse breeds. written and illustrated by Jeff Crosby and Shelley Ann Jackson. Tundra Books 2011 69p il map $21.99

Grades: 4 5 6 7 **636.1**

1. Horses

ISBN 978-0-88776-986-3; 0-88776-986-1

"After a brief introduction, the animals are grouped by the roles they have played in relation to people: 'Rapid Transit,' 'Military Advantage,' 'Horsepower,' 'Equine Entertainment,' and 'Feral Horses.' The concise and interesting information on each of the 43 breeds is accompanied by an illustration of the type as well as one of the horse in action and often includes a small map showing its origins. The excellent painterly pictures clearly capture the unique life of each horse." SLJ

Includes bibliographical references

Matzke, Ann H.

★ **Mini** horse; Ann Matzke ; [edited by] Keli Sipperley. Rourke Educational Media 2015 32 p. color illustrations (hardcover) $32.78

Grades: 3 4 5 6 **636.1**

1. Pets 2. Miniature horses

ISBN 9781634304344

LC 2015931857

This children's book, by Ann Matzke, edited by Keli Sipperley, part of the "You Have a Pet What?!" series, is an entry on miniature horses where the series focuses on "exotic pets . . . , covering history, natural habitat, care, and characteristics both positive and negative. . . . The animals' personalities are described, and information on bonding and communication is provided." (School Library Journal)

"Well written, with a clean design, these titles will be useful for educators and popular with potential pet owners." SLJ

Ransford, Sandy

The **Kingfisher** illustrated horse and pony encyclopedia; written by Sandy Ransford; photographed by Bob Langrish. Revised edition Kingfisher 2010 224p il hardcover $24.99

Grades: 4 5 6 7 **636.1**

1. Horses 2. Horsemanship

ISBN 9780753464854; 0753464853

"The first section focuses on the horse itself--breeds, life cycle, domestication, and anatomy. The next section covers many areas of horse management, including feeding, housing, grooming, health care and first aid, and equipment. The third section examines the various aspects of riding, both western and English, although the majority of the photos feature English saddlery." (SLJ)

636.2 Cattle and related animals

Freedman, Russell

In the days of the vaqueros; America's first true cowboys. Clarion Bks. 2001 70p il $18; pa $9.99

Grades: 4 5 6 7 **636.2**

1. Cowhands 2. Ranch life 3. Mexican Americans 4. Southwestern States

ISBN 0-395-96788-0; 978-0-395-96788-1; 978-0-547-13365-2 pa; 0-547-13365-0 pa

LC 2001-17357

The author "tells the story with depth, clarity, and a vigor that conveys the thrilling excitement of the work and the macho swagger of the culture. . . . The book's design is beautiful, with spacious type on thick paper, and the dazzling illustrations—prints, paintings, and photos on almost every page." Booklist

Includes glossary and bibliographical references

636.4 Swine

Reed, Cristie

★ **Mini** pig; Cristie Reed ; [edited by] Keli Sipperley. Rourke Educational Media 2015 32 p. color illustrations; color map (hardcover) $32.79

Grades: 3 4 5 6 **636.4**

1. Pets 2. Miniature pigs

ISBN 9781634304313

LC 2015931854

This children's book, by Cristie Reed, edited by Keli Sipperley, part of the 'You Have a Pet What?!' series, is an entry on miniature pigs where the series focuses on "exotic pets . . . , covering history, natural habitat, care, and characteristics both positive and negative. . . . The animals' personalities are described, and information on bonding and communication is provided." (School Library Journal)

"Well written, with a clean design, these titles will be useful for educators and popular with potential pet owners." SLJ

636.5 Chickens and other kinds of domestic birds

Caughey, Melissa

A **kid's** guide to keeping chickens; Best Breeds, Creating a Home, Care and Handling, Outdoor Fun, Crafts and Treats. Melissa Caughey. Storey Publishing 2015 137 p. color illustrations (hardcover with pull-out poster : alk. paper) $26.95

Grades: 4 5 6 7 8 **636.5**

1. Chickens 2. Eggs -- Production

ISBN 1612124186; 1612126480; 9781612124186; 9781612126487

LC 2014033788

This book, by Melissa Caughey, "provides all the information kids need to raise healthy chickens and have tons of fun doing it! Caughey shares her advice in an engaging way so that kids understand what it means to keep chickens and what kind of housing, food, equipment, and care the chickens will need to thrive. She also suggests lots of creative activities sure to spark enthusiasm and imagination." (Publisher's note)

"The book contains color photographs—including pictures of children working with chickens—and the text is broken into manageable chunks, with sidebar facts and testimonials. An index and other resources conclude. A good addition for public libraries." Booklist

636.7 Dogs

Castaldo, Nancy F.

Sniffer dogs; how dogs (and their noses) save the world. Nancy F. Castaldo. Houghton Mifflin Harcourt 2014 160 p. color illustrations $16.99

Grades: 4 5 6 7 8 **636.7**

1. Rescue dogs 2. Search dogs 3. Smell 4. Detector dogs 5. Dogs -- Sense organs

ISBN 054408893X; 9780544088931

LC 2013017612

This middle grade book by Nancy F. Castaldo describes how "some dogs work with police officers, soldiers and even scientists to put their 'sniffers' to work. Sniffer dogs make use of the amazing biology behind their noses to protect people from bombs, catch criminals smuggling drugs, or help researchers locate a hard to find snail in a forest." (Publisher's note)

"The attractive color photos that capture many of these canines in action and the accessible tone of the text make this an appealing read. A well-organized, thoughtfully written title that celebrates the achievements of these great dogs." SLJ

Includes bibliographical references and index

Frydenborg, Kay

★ A **dog** in the cave; the wolves who made us human. by Kay Frydenborg. Houghton Mifflin Harcourt 2017 ix, 246 p.p illustrations (chiefly color) (hardcover) $18.99

Grades: 7 8 9 10 **636.7**

1. Dogs 2. Human-animal relationships -- History 3. Coevolution 4. Dogs -- History 5. Dogs -- Evolution

ISBN 9781328694904; 9780544286566

LC 2016000217

In this book, author Kay Frydenborg discusses "growing evidence that we influenced dogs' evolution--and they, in turn, changed ours. . . . Combining history, paleontology, biology, and cutting-edge medical science, . . . Frydenborg paints a picture of how two different species became deeply entwined--and how we coevolved into the species we are today." (Publisher's note)

"The tone is inviting and accessible, the topic high interest, and the research impeccable. This narrative blend of history and science belongs on all shelves." Booklist

Includes bibliographical references (pages 239-240)and index.

Hirsch, Andy

Dogs; from predator to protector. Andy Hirsch. First Second 2017 128 p. chiefly color illustrations (Science comics) (hardcover) $19.99

Grades: 4 5 6 7 8 **636.7**

1. Comic books, strips, etc. 2. Dogs

ISBN 9781626727670; 9781626727687

LC 2016961597

"How well do you know our favorite furry companion? Did they really descend from wolves? What's the difference between a Chihuahua and a Saint Bernard? And just how smart are they? Join one friendly mutt on a journey to discover the secret origin of dogs, how genetics and evolution shape species, and where in the world his favorite ball bounced off to." (Publisher's note)

"Thorough, clearly presented scientific information is lightened by silly asides from dog-narrator Rudy to keep readers entertained and engaged as they learn a huge amount about the science of dogs." Kirkus

Includes bibliographical references

Houston, Dick

Bulu, African wonder dog. Random House 2010 323p il $15.99; lib bdg $18.99

Grades: 5 6 7 8 **636.7**

1. Dogs 2. Wildlife conservation 3. Zambia

ISBN 978-0-375-84723-3; 0-375-84723-5; 978-0-375-94720-9 lib bdg; 0-375-94720-5 lib bdg

LC 2009015804

"In the Nyanja language, bulu means 'wild dog,' and that's what Steve and Anna Tolan named the beloved little Jack Russell mix they adopted. Disregarding warnings about the dangers of raising a dog in the bush, the Tolans moved from England to rural Zambia to fulfill their lifelong dream of setting up an animal rescue and conservation center. . . . Bulu's energy, high spirits, and loyalty to his masters make the book read like a praise song to dogs. Houston's account is an animal-lover's delight, complete with the action-adventure of surviving the bush, fighting poachers, and spreading a message of conservation." Booklist

Laidlaw, Rob

No shelter here; Making the world a kinder place for dogs. Rob Laidlaw. Pajama Press 2012 63 p.

Grades: 3 4 5 6 7 8 **636.7**

1. Dogs 2. Animal rights 3. Animal welfare

ISBN 0986949558; 9780986949555

This book provides an "informative and visually varied introduction to problems affecting dogs worldwide. In a short, colorful volume with sidebars and photographs on nearly every page, professional dog advocate [Rob] Laidlaw . . . presents facts about how dogs live, provides an overview of the cruelty dogs face at the hands of humans and offers profiles of young activists who are working to better dogs' lives. . . . A list of animal welfare websites points interested readers toward further information." (Kirkus)

Includes bibliographical references and index.

MacLeod, Elizabeth

Top dogs; true stories of canines that made history. Elizabeth MacLeod. Annick Press 2017 102 p. illustrations (chiefly color) (paperback) $12.95

Grades: 5 6 7 **636.7**

1. Anecdotes 2. Working dogs 3. Dogs

ISBN 1554519063; 9781554519064

This book, by Elizabeth MacLeod, "tells the stories of 8 amazing canines through the ages whose actions influenced the course of history. . . . MacLeod's kid-friendly, narrative style captures the time and place when the events took place as well as the sense of adventure that colors every story. . . . Scattered throughout the book are side bars filled with information about the exploits of many other dogs as well as the history, habits, and characteristics of various breeds." (Publisher's note)

"The chapters are well organized and chock-full of photos and other design elements to keep readers' interest." SLJ

Sundance, Kyra

101 dog tricks, kids edition; fun and easy activities, games, and crafts. Kyra Sundance. Quarry Books 2014 191 p. color illustrations $19.99

Grades: 3 4 5 6 **636.7**

1. Dogs -- Training

ISBN 1592538932; 9781592538935

LC 2014014373

This book on dog tricks, by Kyra Sundance, "features full color step-by-step photos of every trick, making it easy to follow along. Real kids are featured in the photos, actually training dogs--you can do it too! Many tricks are simple enough that your dog can learn them in ten minutes." (Publisher's note)

"The tricks only require common household or easily accessible items, and they include helpful tips for preparation, troubleshooting, and what to expect. Many of the tips also differentiate for differently sized and more fearful or shy dogs." Booklist

Wadsworth, Ginger

Poop detectives; Working Dogs in the Field. by Ginger Wadsworth. Charlesbridge 2016 80 p. color illustrations (reinforced for library use) $17.95; (ebook) $9.99

Grades: 3 4 5 6 7 **636.7**

1. Working dogs -- Training 2. Detector dogs -- Training 3. Working Dogs for Conservation 4. Detector dogs

ISBN 9781580896504; 9781607346500

LC 2015026876

In this book, by Ginger Wadsworth, "scat-detection dogs like Wicket, Tucker, and Orbee are conservation heroes and pioneers in a cutting-edge field of science. Canine detectives use their super sense of smell to locate the scat of target animals. From loose bear dung to gooey whale poop, scat can tell scientists valuable information about an animal's sex, age, diet, and health--all without harming the animal or endangering the researcher." (Publisher's note)

"This book encourages readers to think about unconventional sources of information and the unusual methods of data collection necessary to scientific discovery." Booklist

Includes bibliographical references (pages 77-78) and index.

636.755 Terriers

Gagne, Tammy

West Highlands, Scotties, and other terriers; by Tammy Gagne. Capstone Press 2017 32 p. color illustrations (ebook) $27.99; (library binding) $27.99

Grades: 4 5 6 **636.755**

1. Dogs 2. Terriers 3. Dog breeds

ISBN 9781515703136; 9781515703044

LC 2015043106

In this book, by Tammy Gagne, "learn all about the characteristics of terrier dog breeds and much more! Packed with amazing photographs and fun facts, dog owners and fans will get an in-depth look at these intelligent canines." (Publisher's note)

"While Gagne points out positive qualities in each breed discussed, readers looking for a new pet will find the carefully phrased comments in the personality, training, and care paragraphs very useful in deciding whether to choose a terrier and, if so, which one. A solid choice for libraries." Booklist

Includes bibliographical references and index

636.8 Cats

Laidlaw, Rob

Cat champions; caring for our feline friends. By Rob Laidlaw. Orca Book Pub 2014 64 p. illustrations (chiefly color) $19.95

Grades: 4 5 6 7 8 **636.8**

1. Cats 2. Animal welfare 3. Voluntarism 4. Cats -- Health 5. Animal shelters

ISBN 1927485312; 9781927485316

In this book, readers "meet kids who are helping at shelters, fostering kittens, volunteering with sterilization programs and caring for abandoned cats. Animal advocate Rob Laidlaw brings readers a hopeful, inspiring look at the issues facing domesticated and feral cats, and the cat champions who are working to help them." (Publisher's note)

"The format is busy, but cat lovers probably won't mind so many photos, and the sidebars are all informative. The list of organizations where kids can learn about ways they can help is extensive and useful." Booklist

Myron, Vicki

Dewey the library cat; a true story. [by] Vicki Myron with Bret Witter. Little, Brown 2010 214p $16.99

Grades: 4 5 6 7 8 **636.8**

1. Cats 2. Libraries

ISBN 978-0-316-06871-0; 0-316-06871-3

Adapted from: Dewey: the small town library cat who touched the world, published 2008 by Grand Central Publisher for adults

"From the opening chapter, when librarian Vicki Myron finds a fragile, freezing kitten in the book return, children will be hooked on her heartwarming story about Dewey Readmore Books. . . . Anecdotes such as Dewey's fascination with rubber bands, his bizarre behavior during a bat invasion, and his finicky eating habits are ideal booktalk material. So are descriptions of Dewey's tender, intuitive interactions with people of all ages and backgrounds." Booklist

636.9 Other mammals

Kenney, Karen Latchana

★ **Sugar** glider; Karen Kenney; edited by Keli Sipperley. Rourke Educational Media 2015 32 p. color illustrations $32.79

Grades: 3 4 5 6 **636.9**

1. Marsupials 2. Sugar gliders as pets

ISBN 1634304365; 9781634304368

LC 2015931859

Author Karen Kenney presents this children's book on sugar gliders as pets "covering history, natural habitat, care, and characteristics both positive and negative. Restrictions on ownership and any special housing and health care requirements are carefully pointed out. The animals' personalities are described, and information on bonding and communication is provided. A short list of 'Things to Think About...' encapsulates all the issues." (School Library Journal)

"Though most kids will be (thankfully) dissuaded by the amount of specialized care these animals require, the beautifully reproduced photos of oddball pets are undeniably appealing, and there are enough fascinating and informative facts to keep readers enthralled. Highly recommended." Booklist

Reed, Cristie

Ferret; Cristie Reed. Rourke Educational Media 2015 32 p. color illustrations $32.79

Grades: 2 3 4 5 **636.9**

1. Ferrets 2. Pets

ISBN 1634304322; 9781634304320

LC 2015931855

This children's book by Cristie Reed on ferrets as pets "introduces these animals, covering history, natural habitat, care, and characteristics both positive and negative. Restrictions on ownership and any special housing and health care requirements are carefully pointed out. The animals' personalities are described, and information on bonding and communication is provided." (Publisher's note)

"Well written, with a clean design, these titles will be useful for educators and popular with potential pet owners." SLJ

636.92 Marsupials

Boruchowitz, David E.

Sugar gliders; David E. Boruchowitz ; [editor, Thomas Mazorlig] T.F.H. 2012 111 p. (Animal planet. Pet care library) (pbk. : alk. paper) $10.95

Grades: 4 5 6 7 **636.92**

1. Sugar glider 2. Sugar gliders as pets

ISBN 0793837111; 9780793837113

LC 2011049947

This book on sugar gliders by David E. Boruchowitz is part of the "Animal Planet Pet Care Library" series. "According to Boruchowitz, they make excellent house pets due to their affinity for cuddling in tiny places. . . . Every aspect of ownership is covered, from basic dietary requirements to grooming and socialization." (Booklist)

Includes bibliographical references and index

636.935 Rodents

Kenney, Karen Latchana

★ **Rat**; Karen Kenney; [edited by] Keli Sipperley. Rourke Educational Media 2015 32 p. color illustrations (hbk.) $32.79; (pbk.) $9.95

Grades: 3 4 5 6 **636.935**

1. Pets 2. Rats

ISBN 1634304357; 9781634304351; 9781634305358; 1634305353

LC 2015931858

Author Karen Kenney presents this children's book on rats as pets "covering history, natural habitat, care, and characteristics both positive and negative. Restrictions on ownership and any special housing and health care requirements are carefully pointed out. The animals' personalities are described, and information on bonding and communication is provided. A short list of 'Things to Think About...' encapsulates all the issues." (School Library Journal)

"Well written, with a clean design, these titles will be useful for educators and popular with potential pet owners." SLJ

Toor, Rachel

Misunderstood; why the humble rat may be your best pet ever. Rachel Toor ; [edited by] Wes Adams. Farrar, Straus & Giroux 2016 256 p. illustrations (hardcover) $17.99

Grades: 6 7 8 9 **636.935**

1. Rats 2. Rats as pets

ISBN 9780374303082; 9780374303099

LC 2016930725

This book about domesticated rats, by Rachel Toor, edited by Wes Adams, "blends history and science with profiles of interesting people and autobiographical anecdotes as it joyfully sets the record straight about why this reviled creature is actually a most amazing species. Readers will come away with a deeper understanding and appreciation of domestic rats--and may be convinced to adopt one themselves." (Publisher's note)

"A delightful addition to any library or classroom's creative nonfiction section." SLJ

Includes bibliographical references.

638 Insect culture

Buchmann, Stephen

Honey bees; letters from the hive. Delacorte Press 2010 212p il $16.99; paperback $8.99

Grades: 7 8 9 10 **638**

1. Bees 2. Honey

ISBN 978-0-385-73770-8; 9780385737715 paperback; 978-0-385-90683-8

LC 2010-6093

Based on the adult book, Letters from the hive: an intimate history of bees, honey, and humankind published by Delacorte Press in 2005

"This sweeping survey engagingly discusses bee biology and behavior and examines humanity's relationship with bees, from prehistoric times to the present, through their significant roles in art, religion, literature and medicine. Buchmann, a beekeeper and entomologist, also offers a great deal of information about honey. . . . The text is illustrated with black-and-white photographs and documented with source notes." Kirkus

Burns, Loree Griffin

The **hive** detectives; chronicle of a honey bee catastrophe. by Loree Griffin Burns with photographs by Ellen Harasimowicz. HMH Books for Young Readers 2010 80 p. il (Scientists in the field) $18.99

Grades: 5 6 7 8 9 10 **638**

1. Bees 2. Beekeeping 3. Insects -- Behavior 4. Honeybee 5. Bee culture

ISBN 0547152310; 9780547152318

LC 2009045249

In this book, author Loree Griffin Burns "profiles bee wranglers and bee scientists who have been working to understand colony collapse disorder, or CCD. In this dramatic and enlightening story, readers explore the lives of the fuzzy, buzzy insects and learn what might happen to us if they were gone." (Publisher's note)

"Not long after beekeepers encountered a devastating new problem in their hives in 2006, a team of bee scientists began working to discover the causes of colony collapse disorder (CCD), now attributed to a combination of factors possibly including pesticides, nutrition, mites and viruses. . . . Mock notebook pages break up the narrative with biographies of the individual scientists, information about who and what can be found inside the hive and the features of bee bodies. An appendix adds varied fascinating facts about bees—again using the format of an illustrated research journal. Harasimowicz's clear, beautifully reproduced photographs support and extend the text." Kirkus

Includes bibliographical references (p. 65) and index

Chadwick, Fergus

★ The **bee** book; Fergus Chadwick, Steve Alton, Emma Sarah Tennant, Bill Fitzmaurice, Judy Earl. DK Publishing 2016 221 p. illustrations (some color) $25

Grades: Adult **638**

1. Beekeeping 2. Bees 3. Honeybee 4. Bumblebees 5. Bee culture

ISBN 1465443835; 9781465443830

LC 2015458993

This book "shows you step-by-step how to create a bee-friendly garden, get started in beekeeping, and harness the power of honey for well-being. Fully illustrated with full-color photographs throughout, this . . . guide covers everything you need to know to start your own backyard hive, from setup to harvest. Practical beekeeping techniques are explained with clear step-by-step sequences, photos, and diagrams." (Publisher's note)

"This is a charming, information-rich book that should lead readers to appreciate bees and welcome them into their gardens and wild places and even encourage some to keep honeybees." Booklist

Harkins, Susan Sales

Design your own butterfly garden; by Susan Sales Harkins and William H. Harkins. Mitchell Lane Publishers 2008 48p il (Gardening for kids) lib bdg $29.95

Grades: 3 4 5 6 **638**

1. Butterfly gardens

ISBN 978-1-58415-638-3 lib bdg; 1-58415-638-4 lib bdg

LC 2008-2245

Introduces the principles of butterfly gardening, discussing how to plan the garden, what flowers to plant there, and how to maintain it in all seasons

"All the tasks delineated are well within the scope of children's abilities, and the items needed to complete them are not hard to find. . . . [The book has] excellent full-color photography and include[s] charts and diagrams to assist in the completion of the projects." SLJ

Includes bibliographical references

639.2 Commercial fishing, whaling, sealing

Foster, Mark

Whale port; a history of Tuckanucket. written by Mark Foster; illustrated by Gerald Foster. Houghton Mifflin Company 2007 64p il $18

Grades: 4 5 6 7 **639.2**

1. Whaling

ISBN 978-0-618-54722-7; 0-618-54722-3

LC 2006018772

This describes the history of whaling in New England through the fictional village of Tuckanucket and Zachariah Taber, his family and neighbors.

The village is "depicted in precisely detailed ink and crayon pictures. . . . The Fosters . . . have elegantly synthesized a tremendous amount of information into a beguiling format." Horn Book

Hand, Carol

Dead zones; why earth's waters are losing oxygen. by Carol Hand. Twenty-First Century Books 2016 80 p. color illustrations (lb : alk. paper) $35.99

Grades: 7 8 9 10 **639.2**

1. Anoxic zones 2. Marine pollution 3. Fish kills 4. Marine eutrophication 5. Nutrient pollution of water 6. Fishes -- Effect of water pollution on

ISBN 9781467775731

LC 2014041304

This juvenile book, by Carol Hand, explores how "currently the world has more than 400 identified dead zones. . . . The good news is that people can eliminate dead zones by changing agricultural practices and reducing pollution. Using real-world examples, this book looks at the impact of pollution on global water resources, and discusses the interconnectedness of ecosystems and organisms." (Publisher's note)

"A significant overview for serious eco-activists or any students interested in our planet's oceans and waterways." SLJ

McKissack, Pat, 1944-2017

Black hands, white sails; the story of African-American whalers. [by] Patricia C. McKissack & Fredrick L. McKissack. Scholastic Press 1999 xxiv, 152p il $17.95

Grades: 5 6 7 8 **639.2**

1. Whaling 2. Abolitionists 3. African Americans

ISBN 0-590-48313-7

LC 99-11439

A Coretta Scott King honor book for text, 2000

A history of African-American whalers between 1730 and 1880, describing their contributions to the whaling industry and their role in the abolitionist movement

"A well-researched and detailed book." SLJ

Includes bibliographical references

639.34 Fish culture in aquariums

Wood, Kathleen

The **101** best tropical fishes; how to choose & keep hardy, brilliant, fascinating species that will thrive in your home aquarium. by Kathleen Wood; with Mary E. Sweeney and Scott W. Michael. T.F.H. Publications 2007 192p il (Adventurous aquarist guide) $18.95

Grades: 6 7 8 9 **639.34**

1. Aquariums 2. Tropical fish

ISBN 978-1-8900-8793-7; 1-8900-8793-9

LC 2008-28294

"Presents 101 full-page species accounts of fishes that not only have high survival rates in captivity but also are appealing in appearance and behave well in community tanks. Also included are 33 species to avoid—fishes that most commonly wreak havoc in home aquariums because of their size or aggressiveness, or that tend to perish in the hands of inexperienced aquarists." Publisher's note

Includes bibliographical references

639.9 Conservation of biological resources

Coey, Julia

Animal Hospital; Rescuing Urban Wildlife. Julia Coey. Firefly Books Ltd 2015 64 p. color illustrations (hardcover) $19.95

Grades: 4 5 6 7 **639.9**

1. Wildlife rehabilitation 2. Animal rescue

ISBN 9781770855724; 1770855726

LC 2015458728

This juvenile book, by Julia Coey, "describes how injured and orphaned wild animals are rehabilitated and cared for after being rescued from perilous situations. It follows the activities of an urban animal rescue facility and the efforts of the trained professionals that rescue, treat, rehabilitate and release the animals." (Publisher's note)

"The author's suggestions for readers' involvement include reminders about appropriate trash disposal as well as names of organizations, and a concluding chapter describes three similar rehab centers around the world. A straightforward introduction to an appealing topic for upper-elementary and middle school readers." Kirkus

Includes bibliographical references and index.

Love, Ann

Rewilding; Giving Nature a Second Chance. by Jane Drake and Ann Love. Annick Press 2017 88 p. color illustrations (hardcover) $19.95

Grades: 5 6 7 8 **639.9**

1. Wildlife rehabilitation 2. Environmentalism 3. Wildlife reintroduction

ISBN 9781554519620; 9781554519644; 9781554519613; 1554519624

In this book, by Jane Drake and Ann Love, "rewilding is an important environmental movement to restore habitats to their natural state in order to support native species and make room for animals to move freely. In this comprehensive look at rewilding, the authors present examples from around the world where endangered animals have been rehabilitated and returned to their natural habitats." (Publisher's note)

"Clearly organized and accessibly written, this is a welcome overview." Kirkus

Includes bibliographical references and index.

Montgomery, Sy

★ **Kakapo** rescue; saving the world's strangest parrot. text by Sy Montgomery; photographs by Nic Bishop. Houghton Mifflin 2010 73p il map (Scientists in the field) $18

Grades: 4 5 6 7 **639.9**

1. Parrots 2. Endangered species 3. Wildlife conservation 4. New Zealand

ISBN 978-0-618-49417-0; 0-618-49417-0

LC 2009-45250

Awarded the Robert F. Sibert Medal, 2011

Montgomery and Bishop head "to a remote island off the southern tip of New Zealand, where they join a local government-sponsored research team that is working to save the Kakapo parrot from extinction. . . . Montgomery's delight in her subject is contagious, and throughout her enthusiastic text, she nimbly blends scientific and historical facts with immediate, sensory descriptions of fieldwork. Young readers will be fascinated. . . . Bishop's photos of the creatures and their habitat are stunning." Booklist

640 Home and family management

Walsh, Peter

It's all too much, so get it together; with illustrations by John Hendrix. Simon & Schuster BFYR 2009 278p il pa $12.99

Grades: 7 8 9 10 **640**

1. House cleaning 2. Conduct of life 3. Storage in the home

ISBN 978-1-4169-9549-4 pa; 1-4169-9549-8 pa

This book suggests ways for teens to get rid of clutter and lead more organized, less stressful lives.

This is "is fun and light in tone. . . . For teens who are as overwhelmed by their lives as they are by their stuff, the quizzes and fictional scenarios will be right on point and may help them approach what they own and why in a new way. In addition to the suggestions for managing clutter (physical and mental), Walsh also offers tips for clutter-free friendships, jobs, studying, and even family fights." Voice Youth Advocates

641.3 Food

Llewellyn, Claire

Cooking with fruits and vegetables; by Claire Llewellyn with recipes by Clare O'Shea. Rosen Central 2011 48p il (Cooking healthy) lib bdg $27.95

Grades: 5 6 7 8 **641.3**

1. Fruit 2. Cooking 3. Vegetables

ISBN 978-1-4488-4844-7; 1-4488-4844-X

LC 2010039333

This book pairs "facts about [fruits and vegetables], including where it is eaten, with eye-catching photos. . . . Each course (section) has an overview of the vegetable group . . . followed by recipes from all over the world. They vary in difficulty. . . . The cooking directions are clear and straightforward. . . . [The book is] profusely illustrated with full-color photos. Students who are learning to cook will appreciate [this] excellently organized [read]." SLJ

Includes bibliographical references

Menzel, Peter

What the world eats; photographed by Peter Menzel; written by Faith D'Aluisio. Tricycle Press 2008 160p il map $22.99

Grades: 4 5 6 7 8 **641.3**

1. Diet 2. Eating customs 3. Food -- Pictorial works

ISBN 978-1-58246-246-2; 1-58246-246-1

LC 2007-41439

An adaptation of Hungry Planet, published 2005 by Ten Speed Press for adults

"Stunning color photographs of mealtimes and daily activities illustrate the warm, informative, anecdotal narratives. . . . This is a fascinating, sobering, and instructive look at daily life around the world." Booklist

Includes bibliographical references

Reilly, Kathleen M.

Food; 25 amazing projects investigate the history and science of what we eat. illustrated by Farah Rizvi. Nomad Press 2010 124p il (Build it yourself) pa $15.95

Grades: 4 5 6 **641.3**

1. Food

ISBN 978-1-934670-59-0; 1-934670-59-6

"This broad overview of food touches on its history and future, production and packaging, social and cultural practices, and health and safety concerns. . . . The information presented and questions posed on food packaging, mega-farming, locally grown vs. commercially grown foods, free-range grazing, and healthy food choices make this a particularly up-to-date survey. . . . Every chapter concludes with two to three hands-on activities that range from cooking to science and art projects. . . . This soup-to-nuts look at the business and consumption of food will make a good addition to most collections." SLJ

Includes glossary and bibliographical references

Thornhill, Jan

Who wants pizza? the kids' guide to the history, science & culture of food. Maple Tree Press 2010 64p il $22.95; pa $10.95

Grades: 4 5 6 **641.3**

1. Food 2. Agriculture

ISBN 978-1-897349-96-0; 1-897349-96-3; 978-1-897349-97-7 pa; 1-897349-97-1 pa

This discusses "where food comes from and if there's enough to go around. Amid color photographs and sidebars, Thornhill writes concisely about hunter-gatherers, agriculture, processed foods, globalization, and poverty, among numerous other topics, providing a straightforward and balanced overview of the modern food industry, and the choices readers have when it comes to their own meals." Publ Wkly

641.5 Cooking

Arroyo, Sheri L.

How chefs use math; math curriculum consultant, Rhea A. Stewart. Chelsea Clubhouse 2010 32p il (Math in the real world) lib bdg $28

Grades: 4 5 6 **641.5**

1. Cooks 2. Cooking 3. Mathematics 4. Vocational guidance

ISBN 978-1-60413-608-1 lib bdg; 1-60413-608-1 lib bdg

LC 2009-14180

This describes how chefs use math for such tasks as measuring ingredients, watching temperatures, buying food, setting menu prices, and managing restaurant and catering businesses, and includes relevant math problems and information about how to become a chef

Includes glossary and bibliographical references

Batmanglij, Najmieh

Happy Nowruz; cooking with children to celebrate the Persian New Year. [by] Najmieh Batmanglij. Mage Publishers 2008 119p il $40

Grades: 4 5 6 7 8 **641.5**

1. New Year 2. Eating customs 3. Middle Eastern cooking 4. Iran -- Social life and customs

ISBN 1-933823-16-X; 978-1-933823-16-4

LC 2007-036047

"Combining a cookbook format with straightforward, informational text, this amply illustrated title offers a detailed introduction to the history and customs surrounding Nowruz, the Persian New Year. . . . The covered spiral binding allows pages to remain open while cooking, and the uncluttered, attractive format, featuring color photos of kids in the kitchen and whimsical illustrations, will attract interested browsers." Booklist

Carle, Megan

Teens cook; how to make what you want to eat. [by] Megan and Jill Carle with Judi Carle. Ten Speed Press 2004 146p il pa $19.95

Grades: 7 8 9 10 **641.5**

1. Cooking

ISBN 1-58008-584-9

This cookbook features "recipes for a variety of dishes including chocolate chip scones, potato skins, broccoli cheese soup, steak fajitas, baked macaroni and cheese, and toffee bars. Because Megan is a vegetarian, there are several vegetarian recipes or vegetarian substitutes. . . . Attractive, engaging, and told from a teen perspective, this cookbook will make an excellent addition to any nonfiction collection." Voice Youth Advocates

★ The **complete** cookbook for young chefs; America's Test Kitchen Kids. Sourcebooks Inc 2018 208 p. $19.99

Grades: 4 5 6 7 8 **641.5**

1. Cookbooks 2. Cooking

ISBN 1492670022; 9781492670025

IACP Award Winner: Children, Youth & Family (2019)

This cookbook, presents "recipes [that] were thoroughly tested by more than 750 kids to get them just right for cooks of all skill levels--including recipes for breakfast, snacks and beverages, dinners, desserts, and more. Step-by-step photos of tips and techniques will help young chefs feel like pros in their own kitchen." (Publisher's note)

"The inviting, encouraging tone, which never talks down to the audience; emphasis on introducing and reinforcing basic skills; and approachable, simplified recipes make this a notable standout among cookbooks for kids." Booklist

D'Amico, Joan

★ The **coming** to America cookbook; delicious recipes and fascinating stories from America's many cultures. [by] Joan D'Amico, Karen Eich Drummond. Wiley 2005 180p il pa $14.95

Grades: 5 6 7 8 **641.5**

1. Cooking 2. United States -- Immigration and emigration

ISBN 0-471-48335-4

LC 2004-14947

The authors "provide information about American immigrants from 18 nations as well as recipes representing each group. . . . Accompanied by line drawings of ethnic families choosing, preparing, and eating food, . . . chapters discuss each country's climate, history, major waves of emigration, and traditional foods. Typically, three recipes follow. . . . Teachers and students looking for recipes from American immigrant cultures will make good use of this handy resource." Booklist

Ejaz, Khadija

Recipe and craft guide to India. Mitchell Lane Publishers 2010 63p il map (World crafts and recipes) lib bdg $33.95

Grades: 4 5 6 7 8 **641.5**

1. Handicraft 2. Indic cooking

ISBN 978-1-58415-938-4 lib bdg; 1-58415-938-3 lib bdg

LC 2010008950

Provides recipes for several popular Indian dishes and includes instructions on creating colorful and traditional Indian crafts.

This provides "plenty of ideas for adding tasty treats and impressive visual aids to cultural reports or presentations." SLJ

Includes glossary and bibliographical references

Gold, Rozanne

★ **Eat** fresh food; awesome recipes for teen chefs. by Rozanne Gold and her all-star team; photographs by Phil Mansfield. Bloomsbury Children's Books 2009 160p il $21.99; pa $17.99

Grades: 6 7 8 9 10 **641.5**

1. Cooking

ISBN 1-59990-282-6; 1-59990-445-4 pa; 978-1-59990-282-1; 978-1-59990-445-0 pa

LC 2008-42443

"This joyful recipe book features fresh, healthful ingredients and encourages ambitious young chefs to collaborate on such mature dishes as Grape-and-Pignoli Breakfast Cake, Crunchy Wasabi-Lime Salmon with red cabbage and sugar snaps and orange-ginger sweet potato puree. . . . A prime pick for adventurous eaters and a potential catalyst for those in a junk food rut." Publ Wkly

How to cook; delicious dishes perfect for teen cooks. DK Pub. 2011 127p il $17.99

Grades: 7 8 9 10 **641.5**

1. Cooking

ISBN 978-0-7566-7214-0; 0-7566-7214-7

"This attractive book has dozens of recipes with an international flair. Some spreads feature a single dish, like lamb tagine, while others focus on several recipes using a single ingredient or technique. Experimentation is encouraged, and developing confidence is an unstated but obvious goal. This book is not for beginners, but teens with a bit of experience will enjoy trying the many tasty-sounding recipes for everything from jambalaya to macaroons. Vegetarian options are included throughout. Bright color photos show the finished dishes, and the pages are embellished with simple drawings showing processes and ingredients." SLJ

Includes glossary

Hughes, Meredith Sayles

Plants vs. meats; the health, history, and ethics of what we eat. Meredith Sayles Hughes. Twenty-First Century Books 2015 160 p. (ebook) $34.65; (lb : alk. paper) $34.65

Grades: 6 7 8 9 10 **641.5**

1. Diet 2. Vegetarianism 3. Food -- Social aspects 4. Vegetarian foods

ISBN 9781467795807; 9781467780117

LC 2015007494

This book, by Meredith Sayles Hughes, "is a timely, student-friendly primer on the historical, nutritional, and ethical impacts of what and how humans eat. Discussing popular diets, from paleo to locavore, as well as the history of the growth and consumption of food from prehistoric times to the present, this book presents facts from both sides of the vegetarian-omnivore debate, leaving readers to make their own food choices." (School Library Journal)

"This solid introduction to where food comes from and the consequences of its consumption and production is a worthy addition." SLJ

Includes bibliographical references (pages 90-93) and index.

LaRoche, Amelia

Recipe and craft guide to France. Mitchell Lane Publishers 2010 63p il map (World crafts and recipes) lib bdg $33.95

Grades: 4 5 6 7 8 **641.5**

1. Handicraft 2. French cooking

ISBN 978-1-58415-936-0 lib bdg; 1-58415-936-7 lib bdg

LC 2010008949

Provides recipes for several popular French dishes and includes instructions on creating crafts using household items.

This provides "plenty of ideas for adding tasty treats and impressive visual aids to cultural reports or presentations." SLJ

Includes glossary and bibliographical references

Lee, Frances

Fun with Chinese cooking. PowerKids Press 2009 32p il (Let's get cooking!) lib bdg $18.95; pa $11.75

Grades: 4 5 6 7 **641.5**

1. Chinese cooking

ISBN 978-1-4358-3453-8 lib bdg; 1-4358-3453-4 lib bdg; 978-1-4358-3475-0 pa; 1-4358-3475-5 pa

LC 2009010337

This includes recipes for such Chinese dishes as spring rolls and braised mushrooms, and highlights the history and dishes that surround the Chinese New Year.

"The photography is exceptional, with children engaged in the cooking process. . . . Children, and the adults who assist them, will spend hours together mastering the techniques." SLJ

Locricchio, Matthew

The **2nd** international cookbook for kids; photographs by Jack McConnell. Marshall Cavendish 2008 176p il $18.99

Grades: 5 6 7 8 **641.5**
1. Cooking
ISBN 978-0-7614-5513-4
LC 2008003178

The recipes are "presented in a challenging yet teen-friendly step-by-step sequence. The book is best for patient chefs with kitchen experience and adventurous appetites. Informative sidebars provide facts about the recipes and cultures." Horn Book Guide

The **international** cookbook for kids; by Matthew Locricchio; photographs by Jack McConnell. Reprint Marshall Cavendish 2012 175p il $12.99
Grades: 5 6 7 8 **641.5**
1. Cooking
ISBN 9780761463139
LC 2004-5894

This includes "60 classic recipes from Italy, France, China, and Mexico, . . . chef's tips discussing ingredients, nutrition, and technique, safety section discussing basic kitchen precautions, cooking terms and definitions." Publisher's note

★ **Teen** cuisine; new vegetarian. by Matthew Locricchio. Marshall Cavendish Children 2012 207 p. (hardcover) $24.95
Grades: 7 8 9 10 11 12 **641.5**
1. Vegetarian cooking 2. Teenagers -- Nutrition
ISBN 0761462589; 9780761462583; 9780761462590
LC 2011049502

This book, by Matthew Locricchio, is designed for teenagers and "speaks directly to today's most popular eating trends." The cookbook features "original step-by-step recipes for all times of day arranged into sections, [a] special sushi section, chef's tips, safety section, cooking terms, and ingredient definitions, [and] kitchen essentials and equipment." (Publisher's note)

"With this useful resource, delectable dishes made with fresh ingredients are within teens' reach. Everything from breakfasts to soups, salads, entrees, and desserts are featured. Few packaged or canned shortcuts are recommended, so these recipes may involve a little extra time and care; the rewards are evident, as shown in appetizing photographs." (Horn Book)

Mattern, Joanne

Recipe and craft guide to China. Mitchell Lane Publishers 2010 63p il map (World crafts and recipes) lib bdg $33.95
Grades: 4 5 6 7 8 **641.5**
1. Handicraft 2. Chinese cooking
ISBN 978-1-58415-937-7 lib bdg; 1-58415-937-5 lib bdg
LC 2010009242

Provides recipes for several popular Chinese dishes and includes instructions on creating crafts using household items.

This provides "plenty of ideas for adding tasty treats and impressive visual aids to cultural reports or presentations." SLJ

Includes glossary and bibliographical references

Mofford, Juliet Haines

Recipe and craft guide to Japan. Mitchell Lane Publishers 2010 63p il map (World crafts and recipes) lib bdg $33.95
Grades: 4 5 6 7 8 **641.5**
1. Handicraft 2. Japanese cooking
ISBN 978-1-58415-933-9 lib bdg; 1-58415-933-2 lib bdg
LC 2010008951

Provides recipes for several popular Japanese dishes and includes instructions on creating traditional Japanese crafts using household items.

This provides "plenty of ideas for adding tasty treats and impressive visual aids to cultural reports or presentations." SLJ

Includes glossary and bibliographical references

Recipe and craft guide to the Caribbean. Mitchell Lane Publishers 2010 64p il map (World crafts and recipes) lib bdg $33.95
Grades: 4 5 6 7 8 **641.5**
1. Handicraft 2. Caribbean cooking
ISBN 978-1-58415-935-3 lib bdg; 1-58415-935-9 lib bdg
LC 2010009240

Provides recipes for several popular Caribbean dishes and includes instructions on creating traditional Caribbean crafts using household items.

This provides "plenty of ideas for adding tasty treats and impressive visual aids to cultural reports or presentations." SLJ

Includes glossary and bibliographical references

Reusser, Kayleen

Recipe and craft guide to Indonesia. Mitchell Lane Publishers 2010 64p il map (World crafts and recipes) lib bdg $33.95
Grades: 4 5 6 7 8 **641.5**
1. Handicraft 2. Indonesian cooking
ISBN 978-1-58415-934-6 lib bdg; 1-58415-934-0 lib bdg
LC 2010009243

Provides recipes for several popular Indonesian dishes and includes instructions on creating crafts using household items.

This provides "plenty of ideas for adding tasty treats and impressive visual aids to cultural reports or presentations." SLJ

Includes glossary and bibliographical references

Sheen, Barbara

Foods of Chile. KidHaven Press 2011 64p il map (A taste of culture) $28.75
Grades: 4 5 6 **641.5**
1. Chilean cooking 2. Chile -- Social life and customs
ISBN 978-0-7377-5421-6; 0-7377-5421-4
LC 2010035995

"Demonstrating that a nation's cuisine springs from its geography, history, and traditions, [this volume explores Chile's background], the availability of fresh ingredients, and recipes that followed. . . . Culturally specific foods are described alongside some accompanying recipes and photos of people enjoying the dishes." Horn Book Guide

Includes glossary and bibliographical references

Foods of Cuba. KidHaven Press 2011 64p il map (A taste of culture) $28.75
Grades: 4 5 6 **641.5**
1. Cuban cooking 2. Cuba -- Social life and customs
ISBN 978-0-7377-5113-0; 0-7377-5113-4
LC 2010030795

"Demonstrating that a nation's cuisine springs from its geography, history, and traditions, [this volume explores Cuba's background], the availability of fresh ingredients, and recipes that followed. . . . Culturally specific foods are described alongside some accompanying recipes and photos of people enjoying the dishes." Horn Book Guide

Includes glossary and bibliographical references

Foods of Egypt. KidHaven Press 2010 64p il map (A taste of culture) $28.75

Grades: 4 5 6 **641.5**

1. Egyptian cooking 2. Egypt -- Social life and customs
ISBN 978-0-7377-4843-7; 0-7377-4843-5

LC 2009038461

"Sheen explores how different native dishes and types of local celebrations emerge from [Egypt's] culture and surroundings. [An] introductory [map] with a [key] to areas of food production illuminate the country's cuisine by identifying geographical landforms and climate. Traditions and tastes are described in accessible detail; key recipes are included and unfamiliar foods are pictured." Horn Book Guide

Includes glossary and bibliographical references

Foods of Ireland. KidHaven Press 2011 64p il map (A taste of culture) $28.75

Grades: 4 5 6 **641.5**

1. Irish cooking 2. Ireland -- Social life and customs
ISBN 978-0-7377-5114-7; 0-7377-5114-2

LC 2010018791

"Sheen explores how different native dishes and types of local celebrations emerge from [Ireland's] culture and surroundings. [An] introductory [map] with a [key] to areas of food production illuminate the country's cuisine by identifying geographical landforms and climate. Traditions and tastes are described in accessible detail; key recipes are included and unfamiliar foods are pictured." Horn Book Guide

Includes glossary and bibliographical references

Foods of Kenya. KidHaven Press 2010 64p il map (A taste of culture) $28.75

Grades: 4 5 6 **641.5**

1. African cooking 2. Kenyan cooking 3. Kenya -- Social life and customs
ISBN 978-0-7377-4813-0; 0-7377-4813-3

LC 2009048378

"Sheen explores how different native dishes and types of local celebrations emerge from [Kenya's] culture and surroundings. [An] introductory [map] with a [key] to areas of food production illuminate the country's cuisine by identifying geographical landforms and climate. Traditions and tastes are described in accessible detail; key recipes are included and unfamiliar foods are pictured." Horn Book Guide

Includes glossary and bibliographical references

Foods of Korea. KidHaven Press 2011 64p il map (A taste of culture) $26.75

Grades: 4 5 6 **641.5**

1. Korean cooking 2. Korea -- Social life and customs
ISBN 978-0-7377-5115-4; 0-7377-5115-0

LC 2010018789

"Demonstrating that a nation's cuisine springs from its geography, history, and traditions, [this volume explores Korea's background], the availability of fresh ingredients, and recipes that followed. . . . Culturally specific foods are described alongside some accompanying recipes and photos of people enjoying the dishes." Horn Book Guide

Includes glossary and bibliographical references

Foods of Peru. KidHaven Press 2011 64p il map (A taste of culture) $28.75

Grades: 4 5 6 **641.5**

1. Peruvian cooking 2. Peru -- Social life and customs
ISBN 978-0-7377-5346-2; 0-7377-5346-3

LC 2010032959

"Demonstrating that a nation's cuisine springs from its geography, history, and traditions, [this volume explores Peru's background], the availability of fresh ingredients, and recipes that followed. . . . Culturally specific foods are described alongside some accompanying recipes and photos of people enjoying the dishes." Horn Book Guide

Includes glossary and bibliographical references

Smart, Denise

The **cookbook** for girls; written by Denise Smart; photography by Howard Shooter. DK Pub. 2009 128p il $17.99

Grades: 4 5 6 **641.5**

1. Cooking
ISBN 978-0-7566-4500-7; 0-7566-4500-X

"The photos alone make this attractive cookbook worth the price of admission. . . . Most of these dishes will appeal to adventurous eaters and their foodie parents." SLJ

Stern, Sam

Sam Stern's get cooking. Candlewick Press 2009 144p $17.99

Grades: 6 7 8 9 **641.5**

1. Cooking
ISBN 978-0-7636-3926-6; 0-7636-3926-5

British teenage cook Sam Stern presents over 100 new recipes based on his own favorite ingredient, chocolate, and the favorite ingredients of seven of his friends.

"Stern does an excellent job of introducing teens to the kitchen. . . . Every page boasts bright colors and pictures with large print and a user-friendly ingredients list in sidebar format. The recipes run from very easy to a bit challenging, but the step-by-step directions will help even the most challenged cook find a way around the kitchen." Voice Youth Advocates

Tuminelly, Nancy

Cool meat-free recipes; delicious & fun foods without meat. Nancy Tuminelly. ABDO Pub. Co. 2013 32 p. (Checkerboard how-to library. Cool recipes for your health) $28.50

Grades: 3 4 5 6 7 8 **641.5**

1. Cooking 2. Vegetarian cooking
ISBN 161783582X; 9781617835827

LC 2012023989

Author Nancy Tuminelly's book "gives young readers the tools to make healthy, tasty--and safe--dishes for anybody, anytime. This book has kid-tested, easy meat-free recipes, perfect for those who follow a vegetarian or vegan diet. Basic baking techniques, tools, and ingredients are illustrated so kids can quickly prepare each recipe, such as Breakfast Bars and Sloppy Joes." (Publisher's note)

Includes bibliographical references and index

Warren, Rachel Meltzer

The **smart** girl's guide to going vegetarian; how to look great, feel fabulous, and be a better you. Rachel Meltzer Warren, MS, RDN. Sourcebooks Fire 2014 240 p. (alk. paper) $12.99

Grades: 7 8 9 10 11 12 **641.5**

1. Veganism 2. Eating habits 3. Vegetarianism 4. Vegetarian cooking 5. Teenagers -- Nutrition
ISBN 1402284918; 9781402284915

LC 2013023334

In this book, author Rachel Meltzer Warren "encourages readers who are considering changing their diet to begin by participating in Meatless Mondays. Chapters include information on nutrients that are crucial to a healthy diet and what foods they can be found in for all types of diets (vegan, lacto-ovo, pescetarian). The book also includes types of restaurants with vegetarian-friendly options and an explanation of how to use the choosemyplate.gov resource to practice planning a healthy meal." (Publisher's note)

"A vegetarian herself since age 12, Warren knows the questions that teen girls ask and the arguments their parents raise when kids want to experience vegetarianism or veganism. Here, she offers sound advice for girls who are considering being or have chosen to go vegetarian or vegan and for those who waver about where they stand on the topic... The catchy, accessible text is broken up by generous topic headings and questions. Overall, a sound guide for any teenager, really, and her or his parents." (Booklist)

Includes bibliographical references and index

A **teen's** guide to gut health; the low-FODMAP way to tame IBS, Crohn's, colitis, and other digestive disorders. Rachel Meltzer Warren, MS, RDN. The Experiment 2017 209 p. (pbk) $15.95

Grades: 7 8 9 10 **641.5**

1. Gastrointestinal system 2. Teenagers -- Health and hygiene 3. Teenagers -- Health and hygiene -- Popular works 4. Gastrointestinal system -- Diseases -- Diet therapy 5. Gastrointestinal system -- Diseases -- Popular works

ISBN 9781615193554; 9781615193547

LC 2016020920

"Fourteen percent of high school students have symptoms of IBS—such as pain, bloating, and frequent trips to the bathroom. Plus (as if that weren't bad enough!), poor gut health can mean missed school days and trips, awkward explanations, extra doctor's visits, and major cafeteria confusion. Here's the good news: In A Teen's Guide to Gut Health, registered dietitian Rachel Meltzer Warren explains how you can find relief—on a low-FODMAP diet." (Publisher's note)

"There is an abundance of scientific information (plentiful but not overwhelming) as well as sound steps for managing everyday situations." SLJ

Includes bibliographical references and index.

Webb, Lois Sinaiko

Holidays of the world cookbook for students; [by] Lois Sinaiko Webb and Lindsay Grace Roten. updated and rev.; Greenwood 2011 442p il map $95; pa $32.95

Grades: 5 6 7 8 9 10 **641.5**

1. Cooking 2. Holidays

ISBN 978-0-313-38393-9; 0-313-38393-6; 978-0-313-39790-5 pa; 0-313-39790-2 pa; 978-0-313-38394-6 ebook

LC 2011-8458

First published 1995 by Oryx Press

"The recipes appear with each country entry, and the countries are arranged in alphabetical order within each region: Africa, Asia and the South Pacific, the Caribbean, Europe, Latin America, the Middle East, and North America." Publisher's note

The **multicultural** cookbook for students; [by] Lois Sinaiko Webb and Lindsay Grace Roten. Updated & rev.; Greenwood Press 2009 354p map $85

Grades: 7 8 9 10 **641.5**

1. Cooking

ISBN 978-0-313-37558-3; 0-313-37558-5

LC 2009-26718

First published 1993 under the authorship of Carole Lisa Albyn

"This highly informative cookbook includes not only recipes, but also information on the country, its food staples, and ethnic and cultural divisions. Recipes are divided into seven sections according to geography: Africa, Asia and South Pacific, The Caribbean, Europe, Latin America, The Middle East, and North America. . . . Recipes are then divided by country with a description of the country concentrating on culinary information. A minimum of two recipes per country are also annotated with information about the ingredients or why the dish was important to the area. . . . This book is a great resource for cultural research even if the actual recipes will not be prepared. There is a comprehensive index by recipe name, country, and ingredients." Libr Media Connect

Includes glossary and bibliographical references

641.509 History, geographic treatment, biography

Abrams, Dennis

Julia Child, chef; by Dennis Abrams. Chelsea House 2011 134 p. ill. (some col.)

Grades: 6 7 8 9 **641.509**

1. Cooks -- United States -- Biography

ISBN 9781604139129

LC 2011000039

'This book offers a biography of chef "Julia Child . . . [who] started a cooking revolution when she burst onto television screens in the 1960s. Before long, Americans inspired by her example began cooking French food at home in droves and truly appreciating the pleasure that preparing good food can provide. Yet Child did not grow up knowing how to cook or even with an interest in fine cuisine. Her story is one of an American woman's quest to find herself, to find her passion, and then to find a way to share that passion with the world. It is the story of how Julia McWilliams of Pasadena, California, transformed herself into Julia Child, 'The French Chef.'" (Publisher's note)

Includes bibliographical references and index

641.59 Cooking characteristic of specific geographic environments, ethnic cooking

D'Amico, Joan

The **United** States cookbook; fabulous foods and fascinating facts from all 50 states. [by] Joan D'Amico and Karen Eich Drummond; illustrations by Jeff Cline and Tina Cash-Walsh. Wiley 2000 186p il pa $12.95

Grades: 5 6 7 8 **641.59**

1. Cooking

ISBN 0-471-35839-8

LC 99-39548

Provides information about the fifty states along with a recipe native to each of them, such as Boston baked beans from Massachusetts, crab cakes from Maryland, Key lime pie from Florida, corn dogs from Iowa, and taco soup from New Mexico

"There are helpful sections on the use of equipment; cooking skills, such as cutting, measuring, and mixing, and safety rules." SLJ

Locricchio, Matthew

The **cooking** of Brazil; Matthew Locricchio; with photos by Jack McConnell. 2nd ed. Marshall Cavendish Benchmark 2012 96 p. ill. (library) $35.64; (ebook) $35.64

Grades: 7 8 9 10 11 12 **641.59**

1. Cookbooks 2. Brazilian cooking 3. Cooking 4. Food -- Brazil 5. Cooking, Brazilian

ISBN 1608705498; 9781608705498; 9781608707379

LC 2011004948

This book, by Matthew Locricchio, "invites . . . readers to the kitchen to experience the satisfaction of preparing authentic [Brazilian] recipes." The book "opens with a . . . look at the . . . country and their culinary traditions and contributions to international cuisine. This cultural introduction is followed with an overview of kitchen safety, food handling, and common sense nutrition, then on to a wide variety of recipes that range from soups and salads to main entrees and desserts." (Publisher's note)

Includes bibliographical references and index.

The **cooking** of France; by Matthew Locricchio. Benchmark Books 2011 96 p. (Superchef) (print) $35.64

Grades: 4 5 6 7 8 **641.59**

1. Cookbooks 2. French cooking 3. Cooking, French 4. Food habits -- France

ISBN 160870551X; 9781608705511; 9781608707393

LC 2010052549

Author Matthew Locricchio presents a book on French cooking. "After a shared introduction about safety, [it] introduces . . . regional cuisines, mentioning festivals, traditions, and music to give readers a broader cultural view of [France]. Recipes, divided into categories such as soups and salads, main courses, and so on, make up the bulk of [the] book." (Booklist)

Includes bibliographical references and index

The **cooking** of Greece; Matthew Locricchio. Marshall Cavendish Benchmark 2011 96 p. (print) $35.64

Grades: 4 5 6 7 8 **641.59**

1. Cookbooks 2. Greek cooking 3. Cooking, Greek 4. Food habits -- Greece 5. Cooking, Mediterranean

ISBN 1608705528; 9781608705528; 9781608707409

LC 2010052548

In this book, author Matthew Locricchio "begins with a region-by-region overview of Greece, highlighting the natural produce of each area and the resulting cuisine, then groups his recipes by type–'Pies & Pitas,' 'Entrées,' etc. A section on kitchen safety . . . gives particulars on using knives. Fresh, healthful ingredients are emphasized, and suggestions are offered for adapting the recipes for vegetarians." (School Library Journal)

Includes bibliographical references and index

The **cooking** of Italy; by Matthew Locricchio. Marshall Cavendish Benchmark 2011 96 p. (print) $35.64

Grades: 4 5 6 7 8 **641.59**

1. Cookbooks 2. Italian cooking 3. Cooking, Italian 4. Food habits -- Italy

ISBN 1608705544; 9781608705542; 9781608707423

LC 2010051849

In this book, by Matthew Locricchio, Italian cooking recipes are presented. It also "discusses general safety rules in the kitchen as well as specific rules for using knives. Regions of Italy . . . are defined along with a description of how geography influences crops, celebrations, and traditions that flourish within each area. Cooking terms are [also] explained." (Publisher's note)

Includes bibliographical references and index

Mendez, Sean

One world kids cookbook; easy, healthy and affordable family meals. by Sean Mendez. Interlink 2011 96 p. $20

Grades: 5 6 7 8 **641.59**

1. Diet 2. Cookbooks 3. Eating habits

ISBN 1566568668; 9781566568661

Author Sean Mendez presents a cookbook "aimed at encouraging young people to think about what they eat through emphasizing the importance of a balanced diet. It contains kitchen tips and suggests vegetarian substitutes to the meat recipes. One World Kids Cookbook aims to instill a passion for good, wholesome, healthy food as well as a passion for life." (Publisher's note)

Sheen, Barbara

Foods of Australia; by Barbara Sheen. KidHaven Press 2010 64 p. (hardcover) $31.95

Grades: 4 5 6 **641.59**

1. Australian cooking 2. Australia -- Social life and customs 3. Cooking -- Australia 4. Cooking, Australian

ISBN 0737748125; 9780737748123

LC 2009032643

This book, by Barbara Sheen, "explores the foods, cooking traditions, customs, eating habits, and food sources of [Australia]. [It discusses] ingredients that form the staples of cooking . . ., the favorite dishes, the snacks and sweets, the traditional holiday meals, and the preparations and traditions associated with these foods." (Publisher's note)

Includes bibliographical references and index

Wagner, Lisa

Cool Mexican cooking; fun and tasty recipes for kids. by Lisa Wagner. Checkerboard Library 2011 32 p. (Cool world cooking) $28.50

Grades: 3 4 5 6 **641.59**

1. Mexican cooking 2. Cooking 3. Cooking, Mexican

ISBN 1617146625; 9781617146626

LC 2010022194

This book, by Lisa Wagner, "introduces readers to world geography and authentic, easy-to-make recipes [for Mexican cuisine]. Cooking teaches kids about food, math and measuring, and following directions. Each kid-tested recipe includes step-by-step instructions and how-to photos. Tools and ingredients lists are also provided, as well as pronunciation guides when needed." (Publisher's note)

641.594 European cooking

Wagner, Lisa

Cool French cooking; fun and tasty recipes for kids. by Lisa Wagner. Checkerboard Library 2011 32 p. $28.50

Grades: 3 4 5 6 **641.594**

1. French cooking 2. Cooking 3. Cooking, French

ISBN 1617146609; 9781617146602

LC 2010022192

This book, by Lisa Wagner, "introduces readers to world geography and authentic, easy-to-make recipes [for French cuisine]. Cooking teaches kids about food, math and measuring, and following directions. Each kid-tested recipe includes step-by-step instructions and how-to photos. Tools and ingredients lists are also provided, as well as pronunciation guides when needed." (Publisher's note)

Cool Italian cooking; fun and tasty recipes for kids. by Lisa Wagner. Checkerboard Library 2011 32 p. $28.50

Grades: 3 4 5 6 **641.594**

1. Italian cooking 2. Cooking 3. Cooking, Italian

ISBN 1617146617; 9781617146619

LC 2010022193

This book, by Lisa Wagner, "introduces readers to world geography and authentic, easy-to-make recipes [for Italian cuisine}. Cooking teaches kids about food, math and measuring, and following directions. Each kid-tested recipe includes step-by-step instructions and how-to photos. Tools and ingredients lists are also provided, as well as pronunciation guides when needed." (Publisher's note)

641.595 Asian cooking

Wagner, Lisa

Cool Chinese and Japanese cooking; fun and tasty recipes for kids. by Lisa Wagner. ABDO Pub. 2011 32 p. (Cool world cooking) $28.50

Grades: 3 4 5 6 **641.595**

1. Chinese cooking 2. Japanese cooking 3. Cooking 4. Cooking, Chinese 5. Cooking, Japanese

ISBN 1617146595; 9781617146596

LC 2010022191

This book, by Lisa Wagner, "introduces readers to world geography and authentic, easy-to-make recipes [for Chinese and Japanese cuisine]. Cooking teaches kids about food, math and measuring, and following directions. Each kid-tested recipe includes step-by-step instructions and how-to photos. Tools and ingredients lists are also provided, as well as pronunciation guides when needed." (Publisher's note)

641.6 Cooking specific materials

Llewellyn, Claire

Cooking with meat and fish; [by] Claire Llewellyn, Clare O'Shea. Rosen Central 2011 48p il map (Cooking healthy) lib bdg $27.95

Grades: 5 6 7 8 **641.6**

1. Meat 2. Cooking 3. Seafood

ISBN 978-1-4488-4845-4; 1-4488-4845-8

LC 2010039337

A description of each type of meat and fish, how to cook them in a healthy manner, and recipe examples of each.

This book pairs "facts about [meat and fish], including where it is eaten, with eye-catching photos. . . . Each course (section) has an overview of the . . . [meat] followed by recipes from all over the world. They vary in difficulty. . . . The cooking directions are clear and straightforward. . . . [The book is] profusely illustrated with full-color photos. Students who are learning to cook will appreciate [this] excellently organized [read]." SLJ

Includes glossary and bibliographical references

641.8 Cooking specific kinds of dishes and preparing beverages

Carle, Megan

Teens cook dessert; [by] Megan and Jill Carle, with Judi Carle. Ten Speed Press 2006 158p pa $19.95

Grades: 6 7 8 9 10 **641.8**

1. Cooking 2. Desserts

ISBN 978-1-58008-752-0; 1-58008-752-3

LC 2005-24343

The authors "start out with the all-around favorites, like classic chocolate chip cookies. There are holiday recipes for Halloween dirt pie, complete with cookie tombstones and gummy worms that seem to crawl out of the chocolate 'earth.' The final chapter has fancy foods like vanilla soufflt with chocolate sauce or fresh raspberry napoleons. . . . Not only do the recipes sound delicious, they look delicious in glossy color pictures. . . . The instructions are easy to understand." Voice Youth Advocates

Love, Ann

Sweet! the delicious story of candy. [by] Ann Love & Jane Drake; illustrated by Claudia Dávila. Tundra Books 2007 64p il map $19.95

Grades: 4 5 6 7 **641.8**

1. Candy

ISBN 978-0-88776-752-4

"This history of things sweet and sugary is a yummy feast. The prose is chatty and inviting. Color cartoon illustrations show multiethnic people in the process of making or enjoying everything from honey to ice cream to cotton candy (called candy floss here) to jelly beans and chocolate." SLJ

641.86 Desserts

Eboch, M. M.

Crave -worthy candy confections with a side of science; by M.M. Eboch. Capstone Press 2019 32 p. (hardcover) $31.32

Grades: 5 6 7 8 9 **641.86**

1. Candy 2. Desserts

ISBN 9781543510713

LC 2018011648

In this book in the Sweet Eats with a Side of Science 4D, by M.M. Eboch, "what makes some candy sticky? How does a spoonful of sugar turn into your favorite sweet? Budding chefs will discover the science behind making candy all while enjoying some sweet treats. Video tutorials and bonus materials offer an augmented reality experience through the free Capstone 4D app." (Publisher's note)

644.6 Plumbing

DiPiazza, Francesca Davis

Remaking the john; the invention and reinvention of the toilet. Francesca Davis DiPiazza. Twenty-First Century Books 2015 64 p. color illustrations (lib. bdg. : alk. paper) $34.60

Grades: 6 7 8 9 **644.6**

1. Toilets 2. Sewage disposal 3. Toilets -- History

ISBN 1467726451; 9781467726450

LC 2013040138

Readers of this book by Francesca Davis Dipiazza will "explore the many ways people across the globe and through the ages have invented--and reinvented--the toilet. You will learn about everything from ancient Roman sewers to the world's first flush toilets. You'll also find out about the twenty-first-century Reinvent the Toilet Challenge--an engineering contest designed to spur creation of an ecologically friendly, water-saving, inexpensive, and sanitary toilet." (Publisher's note)

"This honest, fact-filled little book should attract readers and researchers (who may even begin celebrating World Toilet Day every November 19)." SLJ

Includes bibliographical references (pages 58-59) and index

646.2 Sewing and related operations

Plumley, Amie Petronis

Sewing school; 21 sewing projects kids will love to make. [by] Amie Petronis Plumley & Andria Lisle; photography by Justin Fox Burks. Storey Pub. 2010 143p il $16.95

Grades: 3 4 5 6 **646.2**

1. Sewing

ISBN 978-1-60342-578-0; 1-60342-578-0

LC 2010022154

"This large-format book offers appealing projects illustrated with color photos of step-by-step directions as well as kids engaged in sewing and showing off work. The opening 12 lessons begin with topics such as threading a needle, knotting the thread, and making a basic running stitch. After covering basic knowledge and skills, the presentation moves on to instructions for fun easy projects." Booklist

646.7 Management of personal and family life

Buchholz, Rachel

How to survive anything; shark attack, quicksand, embarrassing parents, pop quizzes, and other perilous situations. illustrations by Chris Philpot. National Geographic 2011 176p il (National geographic kids) pa $12.95

Grades: 5 6 7 8 **646.7**

1. Life skills 2. Survival skills

ISBN 978-1-4263-0774-4; 1-4263-0774-8

LC 2010028045

"Buchholz doles out hilarious and handy advice for suffering though both natural and manmade catastrophes. Part survival guide and part self-help book, it provides honest, tongue-in-cheek answers to questions teens may be reluctant to ask out loud, in addition to imparting disaster preparedness strategies. It's a clever, winning combination. Superb full-color digital illustrations and photographs and a lively, conversational tone will catch and keep readers' attention, and the list-heavy layout is fun to read and easy to understand." SLJ

Clinton, Chelsea, 1980-

Start now! you can make a difference. Chelsea Clinton. Philomel Books 2018 144 p. (hardcover) $16.99

Grades: 4 5 6 7 8 **646.7**

1. Environmental protection 2. Children -- Conduct of life 3. Children -- Health and hygiene 4. Bullying

ISBN 9780525514367

LC 2018042716

In this book, author Chelsea Clinton "breaks down the concepts of health, hunger, climate change, endangered species and bullying, so that readers can understand the world around them, and how they can make a difference in their own lives . . . and the world at large. With . . . photographs of real live kids who are making a difference today, and lists of ways to get involved, this book is the perfect introduction to young activists who want to make the world a better place." (Publisher's note)

Ehrman, M. K.

★ **Taking** a stand; being a leader & helping others. ABDO Pub. Co. 2009 112p il (Essential health: strong beautiful girls) lib bdg $22.95

Grades: 6 7 8 9 **646.7**

1. Leadership 2. Life skills 3. Attitude (Psychology)

ISBN 978-1-60453-105-3 lib bdg; 1-60453-105-3 lib bdg

LC 2008-15211

This features fictional narratives paired with firsthand advice from a licensed psychologist to help preteen and teen girls evaluate success and build leadership skills. Topics include the challenges of competition, and taking on too much.

"The topics are well selected, the design is attractive, and the stories feature girls from a variety of cultures." Booklist

Includes glossary and bibliographical references

Fonseca, Christine

The **girl** guide; finding your place in a mixed-up world. by Christine Fonseca. Prufrock Press 2013 228 p. $14.95

Grades: 6 7 8 9 **646.7**

1. Girls 2. Teenagers

ISBN 1618210270; 9781618210272

This book, by Christine Fonseca, is designed "for girls in grades 6-8 as they enter the tumultuous world of adolescence. Worksheets and quizzes, as well as stories from older girls and women, [cover] everything a teenage girl needs to know on the journey toward her own identity. Proven strategies for dealing with stress management, confronting relational aggression, being safe online, navigating the changing mother-daughter relationship, and more make this [a] guide for any girl to get through the teen years." (Publisher's note)

"Sporting a sassy, appealing cover, The Girl Guide elbows its way into the already-crowded market of self-help and self-esteem-building books...There's a bit of genius at play here as the author gives the gift of time to her readers-time for reflection and for de-stressing through the act of creating. Teens should not rush through this book. No quick fixes are offered, just reasonable suggestions for maintaining true north through the turbulent teen years." (School Library Journal)

Fornay, Alfred

Born beautiful; the African American teenager's complete beauty guide. John Wiley & Sons 2002 166p il pa $14.95

Grades: 8 9 10 11 12 **646.7**

1. Personal grooming 2. Personal appearance 3. Teenagers -- Health and hygiene 4. African American women -- Health and hygiene

ISBN 0-471-40275-3

LC 2002-18131

This book on beauty and grooming for African American teenage girls includes information on makeup, hairstyles, nail and skin care, diet, and clothing.

Harris, Ashley Rae

★ **Is** this really my family? relating to your relatives. ABDO Pub. Co. 2009 112p il (Essential health: strong, beautiful girls) lib bdg $22.95

Grades: 6 7 8 9 **646.7**

1. Family 2. Parent-child relationship

ISBN 978-1-60453-101-5 lib bdg; 1-60453-101-0 lib bdg

LC 2008-12105

Presents character narratives and discussion questions to help teenage girls develop positive ways to build healthy relationships with members of their immediate family.

"The topics are well selected, the design is attractive, and the stories feature girls from a variety of cultures." Booklist

Includes glossary and bibliographical references

Heos, Bridget

A **career** as a hairstylist. Rosen 2010 80p il (Essential careers) lib bdg $30.60

Grades: 7 8 9 10 11 12 **646.7**

1. Hairstylists 2. Vocational guidance

ISBN 978-1-4358-9474-7 lib bdg; 1-4358-9474-X lib bdg

This title "is so informative it could be subtitled 'Everything You Want to Know about Becoming a Hair Stylist.'... After the basics, Heos discusses the nitty-gritty of finding a job, keeping it, and running one's own business. The history of hair-cutting careers follows, and there are even ethical discussions. . . . A must for career shelves." Booklist

Mayost, Eric

Amazing braids, buns, & twists; Eric Mayost ; photography by Roee Fainburg. Imagine! Publishing 2015 144 p. color illustrations (pbk.) $14.95

Grades: 8 9 10 11 12 **646.7**

1. Hair 2. Braids (Hairstyling) 3. Braids (Hairdressing)

ISBN 1623540666; 9781623540661

LC 2014033871

This hair-styling book, by Eric Mayost with photography by Roee Fainburg, presents "four classic and contemporary braids, buns, and twists styles with step-by-step tutorials for each one. Detailed photographs will take the guesswork out of styling, while glossy fashion photographs will demonstrate how to tailor and accessorize each hairdo." (Publisher's note)

"The 34 hairstyles contained in this guide will be the envy of many young women." Booklist

Morgenstern, Julie

Organizing from the inside out for teens; the foolproof system for organizing your room, your time, and your life. [by] Julie Morgenstern and Jessi Morgenstern-Colón; illustrations by Janet Pedersen. Holt & Co. 2002 238p il pa $15

Grades: 7 8 9 10 **646.7**

1. Life skills 2. Time management

ISBN 0-8050-6470-2

LC 2002-68552

The authors "offer practical advice to teenagers who want to get organized. After considering what might be holding them back and the three steps to success (analyze, strategize, attack), the discussion shifts to the two major areas of concern: managing space and managing time. . . . Useful advice in an accessible paperback format." Booklist

Peskowitz, Miriam

The **daring** book for girls; Andrea Buchanan, Miriam Peskowitz ; illustrated by Alexis Seabrook. 1st ed. Collins 2007 viii, 279 p.p ill. (some col.), col. map hardcover $16.99

Grades: 4 5 6 7 8 9 **646.7**

1. Girls 2. Amusements 3. Recreation 4. Curiosities and wonders 5. Girls in literature 6. Girls -- Conduct of life 7. Girls -- Life skills guides

ISBN 9780061472572; 9780062208965 hardcover

LC 2007031986

This book is "filled with interesting activities to try and important facts [girls] may not know, but are sure to keep them busy for hours. The authors cover everything from making a lemon-powered clock to the history of writing and cursive, from how to paddle a canoe to the Periodic Table of the Elements." (School Library Journal)

Includes bibliographical references (p. 274-276).

Rosenwald, Laurie

All the wrong people have self esteem; an inappropriate book for young ladies (or, frankly, anybody else) Bloomsbury Children's Books 2008 un il $16.99

Grades: 6 7 8 9 **646.7**

1. Life skills 2. Conduct of life

ISBN 978-1-59990-240-1; 1-59990-240-0

LC 2008-14386

Rosenwald "tackles political correctness, the follies of prevailing wisdom and her favorite peeves using all the tools in her arsenal: her spread-size collages feature fonts on sterioids, magazine cut-outs, photos and cartoons paired with witty diatribes confessions. . . . Funny, fresh and impossible not to read cover to cover." Publ Wkly

649 Child rearing; home care of people with disabilities and illnesses

Chasse, Jill D.

The **babysitter's** survival guide; fun games, cool crafts, and how to be the best babysitter in town. illustrated by Jessica Secheret. Sterling Pub. Co. 2010 107p il $12.95

Grades: 5 6 7 8 **649**

1. Babysitting

ISBN 978-1-4027-4654-3; 1-4027-4654-7

LC 2009-2538

"This useful, up-to-date handbook offers plenty of practical advice with a wise emphasis on safety, which makes it a good choice for new sitters as well as those with experience. Chassé starts with information on starting a business, including references, advertising, and interviewing. Child development is a main focus; suggested activities and tips on interaction with children at different developmental stages will be appreciated by sitters and parents alike. . . . Occasional two-color cartoons feature diverse children and sitters." SLJ

Includes bibliographical references

Crissey, Pat

Personal hygiene? What's that got to do with me? Jessica Kingsley 2005 94p il pa $19.95

Grades: 5 6 7 **649**

1. Autism 2. Hygiene 3. Asperger's syndrome

ISBN 978-1-8431-0796-5; 1-8431-0796-1

LC 2004-24966

Explains the importance of personal hygiene to children with autism and asperger's syndrome.

649.1 Child rearing

Bondy, Halley

Don't sit on the baby; the ultimate guide to sane, skilled, and safe babysitting. Halley Bondy. Zest Books 2012 127 p. (pbk.) $12.99

Grades: 7 8 9 10 11 12 **649.1**

1. Child care 2. Babysitting 3. Infants -- Care

ISBN 0982732236; 9780982732236

LC 2011942757

This book is a "how to guide [that] covers everything . . . that a teen might need to know to become a babysitter. The first section covers topics such as . . . what to expect from kids ages newborn to ten. Section two covers essential skills such as feeding, dressing, playing, bathing, bedtime, and keeping kids healthy. The final section includes tips on how to get a job, how to interview, how much to charge, and even how to quit a job." (Children's Literature)

Includes web resources and index.

650 Management and auxiliary services

Trueit, Trudi Strain

Animal trainer; Trudi Strain Trueit. Cavendish Square 2014 64 p. color illustrations $34.21

Grades: 6 7 8 9 10 **650**

1. Animal trainers 2. Vocational guidance 3. Animal trainers -- literature 4. Animal training -- Vocational guidance -- literature

ISBN 1627124616; 9780761480754; 9780761480822; 9781627124614

LC 2012027729

This book, by Trudi Strain Trueit, focuses on "professionals engaged in a wide range of careers with animals and . . . [describes] their daily work to bring to life numerous options for animal trainers and wildlife conservationists. After a general introduction to animal training, . . . [the author] includes focus chapters for those working with dogs, horses, and marine mammals." (School Library Journal)

"The books include color pictures and a section with more resources. There is enough information in each book to give students an idea of the working conditions and job requirements for each career." Lib Med Con

Includes bibliographical references and index

Wildlife Conservationist; Trudy Strain Trueit. Cavendish Square 2014 64 p. color illustrations (Careers with Animals) $34.21

Grades: 6 7 8 9 10 **650**

1. Vocational guidance 2. Wildlife conservation 3. Wildlife conservation -- Vocational guidance 4. Environmental protection -- Vocational guidance

ISBN 1627124675; 9781627124676

This children's book by Trudi Strain Trueit, part of the Careers with Animals series, discusses career options in the field of wildlife conservation. It aims to help readers to "Explore the job duties, career specialties, educational requirements, and job outlook in this growing field." (Publisher's note)

"While offering encouragement to animal lovers, Trueit does not minimize hard work and long hours involved, sometimes in adverse conditions. A list of relevant websites provides additional resources to expand the information supplied in these readable and realistic career overviews." SLJ

650.1 Personal success in business

Fischer, James

Earning money; jobs. Mason Crest Publishers 2011 64p il (Junior library of money) $22.95

Grades: 6 7 8 9 **650.1**

1. Work 2. Employment 3. Job hunting

ISBN 978-1-4222-1763-4; 1-4222-1763-9

LC 2010-28156

"Teens learn why working is important and how to find the right job, including what steps to take in preparation and what is expected of them once they have a job. . . . This . . . is stunning, with vivid color illustrations on every page. Each subtopic is covered in a two-page spread that features bold graphics and bright colors. This succinct and visually appealing coverage is sure to fit the attention span of students." Voice Youth Advocates

Includes glossary and bibliographical references

Harmon, Dan

First job smarts; by Daniel E. Harmon. Rosen Pub. 2010 64p il (Get smart with your money) lib bdg $29.95; pa $12.95

Grades: 7 8 9 10 11 12 **650.1**

1. Personal finance 2. Part-time employment 3. Teenagers -- Employment

ISBN 978-1-4358-5268-6 lib bdg; 1-4358-5268-0 lib bdg; 978-1-4358-5542-7 pa; 1-4358-5542-6 pa

LC 2008-42892

This offers information on topics such as income tax and saving and investing.

This offers "practical information and advice. The writing is accessible. . . . [The book is] heavily illustrated with large, clear, up-to-date photographs of teens." SLJ

Includes glossary and bibliographical references

652 Processes of written communication

Bell-Rehwoldt, Sheri

Speaking secret codes. Capstone Press 2010 32p il (Edge books: making and breaking codes) lib bdg $26.65

Grades: 4 5 6 7 **652**

1. Ciphers 2. Cryptography

ISBN 978-1-4296-4569-0 lib bdg; 1-4296-4569-5 lib bdg

LC 2010004163

"Spoken codes in history, including the Underground Railroad and POWs during the Vietnam War, are introduced by using various examples of word substitutions. Educators will appreciate the concise information provided by codes that have shaped world history. . . . Historical photographs, highlighted vocabulary words and definitions, and do-it-yourself suggestions will keep readers interested." SLJ

Includes glossary and bibliographical references

Gregory, Jillian

Breaking secret codes. Capstone Press 2010 32p il (Edge books: making and breaking codes) lib bdg $26.65

Grades: 4 5 6 7 **652**

1. Ciphers 2. Cryptography

ISBN 978-1-4296-4568-3 lib bdg; 1-4296-4568-7 lib bdg

LC 2010004162

"Educators will appreciate the concise information provided by codes that have shaped world history. Sample cryptographs are scattered throughout the pages, along with other noteworthy facts. Historical photographs, highlighted vocabulary words and definitions, and do-it-yourself suggestions will keep readers interested." SLJ

Includes glossary and bibliographical references

Making secret codes. Capstone Press 2010 32p il (Edge books: making and breaking codes) lib bdg $26.65

Grades: 4 5 6 7 **652**

1. Ciphers 2. Cryptography

ISBN 978-1-4296-4567-6 lib bdg; 1-4296-4567-9 lib bdg

LC 2010004161

"Educators will appreciate the concise information provided by codes that have shaped world history. Sample cryptographs are scattered throughout the pages, along with other noteworthy facts. Historical photographs, highlighted vocabulary words and definitions, and do-it-yourself suggestions will keep readers interested." SLJ

Includes glossary and bibliographical references

Mitchell, Susan K.

Spy codes and ciphers. Enslow Publishers 2011 48p il (The secret world of spies) lib bdg $23.93

Grades: 4 5 6 **652**

1. Spies 2. Ciphers 3. Espionage 4. Cryptography

ISBN 978-0-7660-3709-0

LC 2010006176

Discusses different methods of secret communications used by spies, such as Morse code, the Enigma machine, the Najavo language, and digital steganography, and includes career information.

Includes glossary and bibliographical references

Pincock, Stephen

Codebreaker; the history of codes and ciphers, from the ancient pharaohs to quantum cryptography. 1st U.S. ed; Walker 2006 176p il $19.95

Grades: 6 7 8 9 **652**

1. Ciphers 2. Cryptography

ISBN 978-0-8027-1547-0; 0-8027-1547-8

LC 2007310362

"Pincock's fascinating book reveals to the reader that codes and ciphers have been used by pharaohs, queens, generals, politicians, and lovers for at least 4,000 years. . . . Beautifully written, entertaining but never shallow, and replete with fascinating insights into the arcane world of cryptography, Codebreaker is that rare work—a nonfiction title that is as appealing as a fast-paced thriller. It should be an essential purchase for libraries serving young adults." Voice Youth Advocates

Includes bibliographical references

658 General management

Andrews, David

Business without borders; globalization. Heinemann Library 2010 56p il map (The global marketplace) lib bdg $33.50

Grades: 6 7 8 9 **658**

1. Globalization 2. International trade

ISBN 978-1-4329-3933-5 lib bdg; 1-4329-3933-5 lib bdg

LC 2010004097

This title covers "a wealth of material in concise paragraphs with pertinent subheadings. . . . [It has] clearly written, accessible content. It touches on currency, global trade, and purchasing power, and stresses that globalization is 'a process that is still going on today.'" SLJ

Includes glossary and bibliographical references

Bochner, Arthur Berg

The **new** totally awesome business book for kids (and their parents) with twenty super businesses you can start right now! [by] Arthur Bochner & Rose Bochner; foreword by Andriane G. Berg. rev and updated 3rd ed.; Newmarket Press 2007 188p il pa $9.95

Grades: 4 5 6 7 **658**

1. Small business 2. Money-making projects for children

ISBN 978-1-55704-757-1 pa; 1-55704-757-X pa

LC 2007002637

First published 1995 with title: The totally awesome business book for kids

A comprehensive look at the basic financial and management aspects of moneymaking businesses for children

"This book can certainly be thought provoking for young people with an entrepreneurial spirit. . . . The illustrations are lively and engaging, and the text non-threatening." Voice Youth Advocates

Includes bibliographical references

658.1 Organization and financial management

Cuban, Mark, 1958-

Kid start up; how you can be an entrepreneur. Mark Cuban, Shaan Patel, and Ian McCue. Diversion Books 2018 123 p. (hardback) $15

Grades: 4 5 6 7 8 **658.1**

1. Money-making projects for children 2. Entrepreneurship 3. New business enterprises

ISBN 9781635764727

LC 2018181784

In this book about entrepreneurship, by Mark Cuban, Shaan Patel and Ian McCue, "you don't have to be a grownup to launch your start-up. We'll show you how to discover a great business idea and get it off the ground. You can try one of our ten kid-friendly businesses, including timeless ventures like starting a lemonade stand to more modern-day endeavors like launching an Etsy art store, or create your own." (Publisher's note)

658.8 Management of marketing

Weinick, Suzanne

Increasing your tweets, likes, and ratings; marketing your digital business. Suzanne Weinick. 1st ed. Rosen Pub. 2013 64 p. col. ill. (Digital entrepreneurship in the age of apps, the web, and mobile devices) (library) $31.95; (paperback) $12.95

Grades: 8 9 10 11 12 **658.8**

1. Marketing 2. Social media 3. Internet marketing 4. Electronic commerce -- Marketing

ISBN 1448869285; 9781448869282; 9781448869763; 9781448869770

LC 2012006836

This "entry in the . . . Digital Entrepreneurship in the Age of Apps, the Web, and Mobile Devices series . . . focuses on marketing minutiae, including giving your app a savvy name, choosing a useful Twitter image, monitoring your Facebook page, vlogging, and knowing your SEO [search engine optimization] from your PPC [pay per click] and CPM [cost per impression]." (Booklist)

Includes bibliographical references (p. 57-62) and index.

659.1 Advertising

Beker, Jeanne

Strutting it! the grit behind the glamour. Tundra Books 2011 78p il pa $17.95

Grades: 6 7 8 9 **659.1**

1. Fashion models 2. Vocational guidance 3. Modeling

ISBN 978-1-77049-224-0 pa; 1-77049-224-0 pa

"Beker—for 25 years a host of Canada's Fashion Television—distills the essence of her many years of experience as a model-watcher into this slim but engaging combination of advice, history and truth-telling. Each chapter showcases a different aspect of a model's career development. . . . Blessedly responsible and sane, a worthy title for any career collection for teens and a must for aspiring models." Kirkus

659.19 Advertising specific kinds of organizations, products, services

Curtis, Andrea

Eat this! how fast food marketing gets you to buy junk (and how to fight back) Andrea Curtis ; illustrated by Peggy Collins. Firefly Books 2018 40 p. $16.95

Grades: 4 5 6 7 8 **659.19**

1. Junk food 2. Nutrition 3. Food industry

ISBN 9780889955325

This book by Andrea Curtis, illustrated by Peggy Collins "examines how fast food marketing gets you to buy junk and how you can fight back. It shows how marketers embed sales pitches in media to lure consumers to foods that can negatively impact the health of children. [It] explains what advertising is, discusses product placement and other tools used to sell products. Curtis provides careful insights into the fast food industry and ways in which young people can push back." (Publisher's note)

660.6 Biotechnology

Lachner, Elizabeth

Bioengineering; edited by Elizabeth Lachner. Britannica Educational Publishing in association with Rosen Educational Services 2016 xiv, 173 p.p color illustrations (ebook) $29.95; (library bound) $39.75

Grades: 7 8 9 10 11 12 **660.6**

1. Biotechnology 2. Bioengineering

ISBN 9781622755813; 9781622755806

LC 2014047675

In this book in the Biotechnology Revolution series, edited by Elizabeth Lachner, "recent advances in bioengineering have fundamentally changed both the world in which we live and the bodies within which we live. Among the topics covered in this invaluable compendium are homeostasis, biological and artificial control systems, diagnostic imaging, prostheses, biomaterials, environmental engineering, and various subfields of bioengineering." (Publisher's note)

"Each text has a table of contents, index, and full-color photographs and illustrations. The visual appeal of the books is high." VOYA

Includes bibliographical references (pages 168-170) and index

660.65 Genetic engineering

Colson, Mary

GMOs; Mary Colson. Gareth Stevens Publishing 2016 48 p. $31.95; (ebook) $31.95

Grades: 5 6 7 8 **660.65**

1. Food -- Biotechnology 2. Genetically modified foods

ISBN 1482451573; 9781482451573; 9781482451511

LC 2016040538

This book, in the Cutting-Edge Technology series by Mary Colson, "explores the pros and cons of these [laboratory] modified crops, such as corn, rice, and soybeans. While exploring what changes scientists make to these plants and how these changes impact their consumption, it also studies the potential risks of altering natural genetic material and how consuming GMOs impacts humans." (Publisher's note)

"Useful books for updating the engineering shelves." Booklist

664 Food technology

Aronson, Marc, 1950-

★ **Sugar** changed the world; a story of magic, spice, slavery, freedom, and science. by Marc Aronson and Marina Budhos. Clarion Books 2010 166p il map

Grades: 7 8 9 10 11 12 **664**

1. Slavery 2. World history 3. Sugar -- History 4. Sugar trade 5. Slavery -- History

ISBN 0618574921; 9780618574926

LC 2009033579

The book discusses the history of sweet substances. "Sugar was the substance that drove the bloody slave trade and caused the loss of countless lives but it also planted the seeds of revolution that led to freedom in the American colonies, Haiti, and France." (Publisher's note) Chronology. Bibliography. Index. "Grades seven to twelve." (Bull Cent Child Books)

"From 1600 to the 1800s, sugar drove the economies of Europe, the Americas, Asia and Africa and did more 'to reshape the world than any ruler, empire, or war had ever done.' Millions of people were taken from Africa and enslaved to work the sugar plantations throughout the Caribbean, worked to death to supply the demand for sugar in Europe. . . . Maps, photographs and archival illustrations, all with captions that are informative in their own right, richly complement the text, and superb documentation and an essay addressed to teachers round out the fascinating volume." Kirkus

Includes bibliographical references

Gardner, Robert

Ace your food science project; great science fair ideas. [by] Robert Gardner, Salvatore Tocci, and Thomas R. Rybolt. Enslow Publishers 2009 128p il (Ace your science project) lib bdg $31.93

Grades: 5 6 7 8 **664**

1. Food 2. Science projects 3. Science -- Experiments

ISBN 978-0-7660-3228-6 lib bdg; 0-7660-3228-0 lib bdg

LC 2008-49780

"Presents several science experiments and project ideas using food." Publisher's note

Includes bibliographical references

668.4 Plastics

Morris, Neil

Plastics. Amicus 2010 48p il (Materials that matter) lib bdg $28.50

Grades: 4 5 6 7 **668.4**

1. Plastics

ISBN 978-1-60753-068-8 lib bdg; 1-60753-068-6 lib bdg

LC 2009051435

"The clean layout includes photographs and occasional charts, graphs, and technical illustrations against a range of pastel backgrounds.

Inset boxes provide further detail, interesting extras, and recycling information. . . . [This book offers] easily accessible background information for report writers." SLJ

Includes glossary and bibliographical references

670 Manufacturing

Slavin, Bill

Transformed; how everyday things are made. written by Bill Slavin with Jim Slavin; illustrated by Bill Slavin. Kids Can Press 2005 160p il $24.95

Grades: 4 5 6 7 **670**

1. Manufactures

ISBN 1-55337-179-8

This describes the manufacture of such items "as baseballs, plastic dinosaurs, toothpaste, cereal, paper, and bricks. Each two-page spread covers the making of one of the 69 items in numbered paragraphs. The pictures are the best part—clear watercolor and ink images, made all the more engaging by folks in overalls directing the action." Booklist

Includes glossary and bibliographical references

671.5 Joining and cutting of metals

Nelson, David Erik

Soldering; by David Erik Nelson. Cherry Lake Publishing 2015 32 p. color illustrations (21st Century skills innovation library. Makers as innovators) (lib. bdg.) $28.50

Grades: 4 5 6 7 8 **671.5**

1. Soldering 2. Metal-work 3. Solder and soldering

ISBN 1631377744; 9781631377747; 9781631377945

LC 2014005538

This juvenile manual, by David Erik Nelson, part of the "21st Century Skills Innovation Library: Makers As Innovators" series, teaches "how to solder electronic components together and build your own devices. Readers will learn basic soldering skills, which will be useful in pursuing a variety of engineering projects." (Publisher's note)

"Though not the most obvious fit into the 21st Century Skills Innovation Library series, this introduction to soldering provides DIYers with basic guidelines to a skill still useful for a variety of projects, from jewelry making and plumbing to creating or repairing electronic circuits. ..Color photos depict gear, a soldered electronic board, and a young solderer at work. This quick but utilitarian guide closes with leads to several more detailed print and online resources." Booklist

Includes bibliographical references and index

Other titles in the series include:

3D Modeling (2015)
3D Printing (2014)
Arduino (2014)
Digital Badges (2013)
E-textiles (2013)
Game Design (2014)
Maker Faire (2014)
Makerspaces (2014)
Raspberry Pi (2014)
Squishy Circuits (2014)
Web Design with HTML5 (2015)

676 Pulp and paper technology

Morris, Neil

Paper. Amicus 2010 48p il (Materials that matter) lib bdg $28.50

Grades: 4 5 6 7 **676**

1. Paper

ISBN 978-1-60753-067-1 lib bdg; 1-60753-067-8 lib bdg

LC 2009051436

"The clean layout includes photographs and occasional charts, graphs, and technical illustrations against a range of pastel backgrounds. Inset boxes provide further detail, interesting extras, and recycling information. . . . [This book offers] easily accessible background information for report writers." SLJ

Includes glossary and bibliographical references

677 Textiles

Morris, Neil

Textiles. Amicus 2010 48p il (Materials that matter) lib bdg $28.50

Grades: 4 5 6 7 **677**

1. Fabrics

ISBN 978-1-60753-069-5 lib bdg; 1-60753-069-4 lib bdg

LC 2009051434

"The clean layout includes photographs and occasional charts, graphs, and technical illustrations against a range of pastel backgrounds. Inset boxes provide further detail, interesting extras, and recycling information. . . . [This book offers] easily accessible background information for report writers." SLJ

Includes glossary and bibliographical references

682 Small forge work (Blacksmithing)

Weitzman, David

★ **Skywalkers**; Mohawk ironworkers build the city. Roaring Brook Press/Flash Point 2010 124p il $19.99

Grades: 8 9 10 11 12 Adult **682**

1. Bridges 2. Building 3. Skyscrapers 4. Mohawk Indians 5. Steel construction 6. Construction workers 7. Skyscrapers -- History

ISBN 1-59643-162-8; 978-1-59643-162-1

Weitzman relates the history of Mohawks from Kahnawàke, Québec, known for their ability to navigate heights, who worked on the construction of bridges and tall buildings in Canada and New York City. "Intermediate, middle school." (Horn Book)

"Stunning photographs complement Weitzman's comprehensive research and clear text in this memorable tribute to Mohawk ironworkers. . . . Weitzman wisely intersperses passages of construction history and technical technique with numerous personal stories. . . . Plentiful black and white archival photographs . . . are chilling or breathtaking. Throughout, Weitzman's admiration and respect for the Mohawk people shine through." Voice Youth Advocates

Includes glossary and bibliographical references

683.4 Small firearms

Blumenthal, Karen

★ **Tommy**; the gun that changed America. by Karen Blumenthal. Roaring Brook Press 2015 240 p. (hardcover) $19.99

Grades: 7 8 9 10 **683.4**

1. Guns -- United States -- History 2. Thompson submachine gun -- History

ISBN 9781626720848

LC 2014040642

This book, by Karen Blumenthal, describes how "the Tommy gun became the weapon of choice for a generation of bootleggers and bank-robbing outlaws, and became a deadly American icon. Following a bloody decade--and eighty years before the mass shootings of our own time--Congress moved to take this weapon off the streets, igniting a national debate about gun control." (Publisher's note)

"This biography of a gun traces the Thompson submachine gun (a.k.a. the Tommy) from its 1918 invention--by former Army officer John Thompson as a potential military weapon--to its use by crooks and bootleggers terrorizing people throughout the next two decades. With thorough research and impeccable documentation, Blumenthal also examines the history of American gun laws, showing the complexity of gun culture. Bib., ind." Horn Book

Includes bibliographical references and index

688.7 Recreational equipment

Bedford, Allan

The **unofficial** LEGO builder's guide; by Allan Bedford. No Starch Press 2005 xviii, 319 p.p $24.95

Grades: 4 5 6 7 8 **688.7**

1. LEGO toys

ISBN 1593270542; 1593274416; 9781593274412

LC 2005013747

This is a handbook about building LEGO structures. "Starting with the basic structure, anatomy, and flexibility of the Lego system, readers are taught different building techniques to add stability and ideas to their creations. Much of the book is devoted to the kinds of scale used in the Lego world and provides mathematical explanations for one's work. Chapters on sculpting and mosaic-making are also" offered. (School Library Journal)

Oxlade, Chris

Gadgets and games; Chris Oxlade. Capstone Heinemann Library 2013 56 p. col. ill. (Design and engineering for STEM) (library) $33.50; (paperback) $9.49

Grades: 5 6 7 **688.7**

1. Electronics 2. Industrial design 3. Product life cycle 4. Toys -- Design and construction 5. Household appliances -- Design and construction 6. Electronic apparatus and appliances -- Design and construction

ISBN 1432970364; 9781432970314; 9781432970369

LC 2012013468

This book, part of the Design and Engineering for STEM series, looks at electronic devices and mobile games. It looks at the life cycle of these items, or "the stages from their design, manufacture, and sale to their use, maintenance, and disposal." Topics include "prototyping, the sourcing of components, the production process, the decisions made by designers and engineers, and recycling." (Publisher's note)

Includes bibliographical references (p. 54) and index.

Ross, Stewart

Sports technology. Smart Apple Media 2011 il (New technology)

Grades: 4 5 6 7 **688.7**

1. Sports

ISBN 1-599-20534-3; 978-1-599-20534-2

LC 2010044241

Describes the technological advances in the sports industry, including the technology used to create better equipment, sports wear, judging tools, and playing surfaces.

This "offers a fine overview for reports, and its attractive design may also entice middle-grade readers to learn more." Booklist

Rothrock, Megan

The **LEGO** adventure book; cars, castles, dinosaurs & more! Megan Rothrock. No Starch Press 2013 199 p. [Vol. 1] color illustrations $24.95

Grades: 4 5 6 7 8 9 **688.7**

1. LEGO toys 2. Models and modelmaking

ISBN 1593274424 (v. 1); 9781593274429 (v. 1)

LC 2012033902

This book on LEGO building, by Megan Rothrock, "is filled with bright visuals, step-by-step breakdowns of 25 models, and nearly 200 example models from the world's best builders. Learn to build robots, trains, medieval villages, spaceships, airplanes, and much more." (Publisher's note)

"—LEGO enthusiast Megs builds an Idea Lab for creating projects and, with its completion, travels by Transport-O-lux to see what others are inspired to make...This one certainly won't sit on shelves. A fun read for LEGO fans of all ages." SLJ

Stone, Tanya Lee

The **good,** the bad, and the Barbie; a doll's history and her impact on us. Viking 2010 130p il $19.99

Grades: 6 7 8 9 10 **688.7**

1. Barbie dolls 2. Mattel Inc. 3. Toy industry executives

ISBN 978-0-670-01187-2; 0-670-01187-8

LC 2010-7507

"Stone tantalizes with her brief and intriguing survey of Barbie. She begins with the history of Mattel, started by self-made businesswoman Ruth Handler in the 1940s, and moves onto materialism, body image, portrayals of ethnicity, nudity, taboo and art." Kirkus

Includes bibliographical references

Wulffson, Don L.

Toys! amazing stories behind some great inventions. [by] Don Wulffson; with illustrations by Laurie Keller. Revised and updated edition Holt & Co. 2014 137p il paperback $10.99

Grades: 4 5 6 7 **688.7**

1. Toys 2. Inventions

ISBN 0-8050-6196-7; 9781250034090 paperback

Originally published 2000

Describes the creation of a variety of toys and games, from seesaws to Silly Putty and toy soldiers to Trivial Pursuit

"Each of the 25 chapters is illustrated with small, humorous drawings and discusses a particular toy or game's origin and development. The book ends with a bibliography and a list of Web sites. Good, readable fare for browsing or light research." Booklist

Includes bibliographical references

688.72 Toys

Schwartz, Jordan

The **art** of LEGO design; creative ways to build amazing models. Jordan Schwartz. No Starch Press 2014 267 p. color illlustrations (pbk.) $24.95

Grades: 4 5 6 7 8 9 **688.72**

1. LEGO toys 2. LEGO toys -- Design and construction

ISBN 1593275536; 9781593275532

LC 2013048974

This book, by Jordan Schwartz, "explores LEGO as an artistic medium. This wide-ranging collection of creative techniques will help you craft your own amazing models as you learn to see the world through the eyes of some of the greatest LEGO builders. Each concept is presented with a collection of impressive models to spark your imagination, like fantastic dragons, futuristic spaceships, expressive characters, and elaborate dioramas." (Publisher's note)

"Part inspirational guide and part project design manual, the book encourages creativity and ingenuity while educating builders about the customs of the LEGO community (e.g., never paint LEGOs). There are helpful sections designed for novices that suggest how to organize workspace, find inspiration, select tools, and prepare for projects, while more advanced builders might embrace sections about developing personal style, sharing models publicly, and using feedback to enhance skills... The creative thinking process conveyed in the book is fascinating and could inspire non-LEGO builders (e.g., writers and painters) in their innovative efforts." VOYA

688.76 Equipment for outdoor sports and games

Swanson, Jennifer

Super gear; how the science of nanotechnology is changing sports. by Jennifer Swanson. Charlesbridge 2016 80 p. chiefly color illustrations (ebook) $52.99; (reinforced for library use) $17.95

Grades: 6 7 8 9 **688.76**

1. Sporting goods 2. Technological innovations 3. Sports sciences 4. Performance technology 5. Sports -- Technological innovations

ISBN 9781607348771; 9781580897204

LC 2015017347

This book, by Jennifer Swanson, presents "a close-up look at sports and nanotechnology, the cutting-edge science that manipulates objects at the atomic level. Nanotechnology is used to create high-tech swimsuits, tennis rackets, golf clubs, running shoes, and more. It is changing the face of sports as we know it." (Publisher's note)

"A highly engaging introduction to an exciting aspect of cutting-edge, real-world science for STEM collections." SLJ

Includes bibliographical references (pages 68-69) and index.

690 Construction of buildings

Byers, Ann

Jobs as green builders and planners. Rosen Pub. 2010 80p il (Green careers) lib bdg $30.60

Grades: 5 6 7 8 **690**

1. Building 2. Vocational guidance 3. Environmental science

ISBN 978-1-4358-3566-5 lib bdg; 1-4358-3566-2 lib bdg

LC 2009015517

This "well-conceived [introduction focuses] on various jobs in [building and construction planning], the education and experience required, and expected earnings. The [book is] well organized, making it easy to gain an overview of the major aspects of the work. . . . [This book] will make [a] good [addition] to career collections. Photographs from the field and website and contact information for professional organizations add value." SLJ

Includes glossary and bibliographical references

Dillon, Patrick

The **Story** of buildings; from the pyramids to the Sydney Opera House and beyond. Patrick Dillon, illustrated by Stephen Biesty. Candlewick Press 2014 96 p. $19.99

Grades: 5 6 7 8 **690**

1. Building 2. Buildings 3. Architecture 4. Architecture -- History

ISBN 0763669903; 9780763669904

LC 2013943096

This book, by Patrick Dillon and illustrated by Stephen Biesty, is a "narrative history of buildings. . . . Why and how did people start making buildings? How did they learn to make them stronger, bigger, and more comfortable? Why did they start to decorate them in different ways? . . . Dillon's stories of remarkable buildings—and the remarkable people who made them—celebrates the ingenuity of human creation." (Publisher's note)

"This large, handsome volume combines broad discussions of architectural history with exceptional drawings of significant buildings from ancient to modern times...Through his signature cross sections, details of interiors and construction can be seen as well. While the text, illustrations, and captions all provide information, it's the drawings of buildings that make this a valuable resource. " Booklist

Macaulay, David

★ **Unbuilding**. Houghton Mifflin 1980 78p il $18; pa $9.95

Grades: 4 5 6 7 8 9 **690**

1. Building 2. Skyscrapers 3. Empire State Building (New York, N.Y.)

ISBN 0-395-29457-6; 0-395-45425-5 pa

LC 80-15491

This fictional account of the dismantling and removal of the Empire State Building describes the structure of a skyscraper and explains how such an edifice would be demolished

"Save for the fact that one particularly stunning double-page spread is marred by tight binding, the book is a joy: accurate, informative, handsome, and eminently readable." Bull Cent Child Books

Miller, Malinda

Green construction; creating energy-efficient, low-impact buildings. Mason Crest Publishers 2010 64p il (New careers for the 21st century: finding your role in the global renewal) lib bdg $22.95

Grades: 7 8 9 10 **690**

1. Vocational guidance 2. Sustainable architecture

ISBN 978-1-4222-1815-0 lib bdg; 1-4222-1815-5 lib bdg

LC 2010010013

"Chapters identify and emphasize specific careers—important strengths, necessary aptitudes and interests, education and training, projected earnings, closely related occupations, type of work environment, and predictions for the future of the field. . . . Color photos have a small role amid the many statistics, figures, graphs and charts that support and supplement the . . . [text]." SLJ

Includes bibliographical references

Somervill, Barbara A.

Green general contractor. Cherry Lake Pub. 2011 32p il (Cool careers) lib bdg $27.07

Grades: 4 5 6 7 **690**

1. Building 2. Vocational guidance 3. Sustainable architecture
ISBN 978-1-60279-987-5; 1-60279-987-3

LC 2010029535

This book begins "with a personal story of a teen and then [segues] into the occupation [of general contractor]. . . . [It covers] the necessary training and skills for the job (and options for obtaining them), a typical day, salary expectations, and well-known professionals in the field. The [text is] accessible and clearly written. . . . The [volume has] a generous number of clear color photographs that depict people at work." SLJ

Includes glossary and bibliographical references

Woolf, Alex

Buildings; by Alex Woolf. Heinemann Library 2013 56 p. ill. (chiefly col.) (library) $33.50; (paperback) $9.49

Grades: 6 7 8 9 **690**

1. Building 2. Architecture
ISBN 1432970291; 9781432970291; 9781432970345

LC 2012013465

This book by Alex Woolf examines the life cycle of a building, covering "the stages from its design, construction, and opening to its use, maintenance, and demolition and disposal at the end of its useful life. This book explains what happens during these stages, such as planning, the sourcing of materials, the construction process, the decisions made by designers and engineers, and refurbishing and recycling." (Publisher's note)

"Books in the Design and Engineering for STEM series offer an up-to-date introduction to an industry in a time of change..Buildings emphasizes the impact of architecture, construction, and demolition on the environment and shows how that impact can be minimized at different stages. Appearing on nearly every page, illustrations include many color photos and the occasional graph, digital drawing, or map. This attractive, informative series tackles meaningful topics and doesn't talk down to readers." (Booklist)

Includes bibliographical references (page 55) and index.

696 Utilities

Gregory, Josh

Plumber. Cherry Lake Pub. 2011 32p il (Cool careers) lib bdg $27.07

Grades: 4 5 6 7 **696**

1. Plumbing 2. Vocational guidance
ISBN 978-1-60279-984-4; 1-60279-984-9

LC 2010029538

This book begins "with a personal story of a teen and then [segues] into the occupation [of plumber]. . . . [It covers] the necessary training and skills for the job (and options for obtaining them), a typical day, salary expectations, and wellknown professionals in the field. The [text is] accessible and clearly written. . . . The [volume has] a generous number of clear color photographs that depict people at work." SLJ

Includes glossary and bibliographical references

MacDonald, Fiona

You wouldn't want to live without toilets! Fiona Macdonald ; illustrated by David Antram. Franklin Watts, an imprint of Scholastic Inc. 2015 32 p. color illustrations library $29

Grades: 5 6 7 8 **696**

1. Toilets 2. Sewerage 3. Toilets -- History 4. Sewage disposal -- History
ISBN 0531212157; 9780531213063; 9780531212158

LC 2014039628

This children's book by Fiona MacDonald on toilets "takes us on a historical journey to see how people coped in the past, and how they developed ingenious ways to make life safer and more pleasant." (Publisher's note)

"Time lines chart the inventions' major developments and discoveries, providing a solid background for each subject, while brief yet interesting historical examples will appeal to even the most reluctant reader. " SLJ

Includes bibliographical references and index

700 THE ARTS

Makosz, Rory

Latino arts and their influence on the United States; songs, dreams, and dances. Mason Crest Publishers 2005 112p il (Hispanic heritage) $22.95

Grades: 7 8 9 10 **700**

1. Latin American art 2. Arts -- United States
ISBN 1-59084-938-8

LC 2004022968

This "book begins with a general discussion of the ways in which cultures express themselves through their arts. It goes on to discuss the arts of Latin American cultures and their growing prominence in the United States, with emphasis on dance and music. Writing, painting, theater arts, and holidays are also included. . . . [This is] an excellent resource both for students researching Latino arts for reports and for general readers." SLJ

Includes bibligraphical references

Robson, David

The **Black** arts movement. Lucent Books 2009 104p il (Lucent Library of Black History) $32.45

Grades: 7 8 9 10 **700**

1. African American arts 2. Arts -- United States
ISBN 978-1-4205-0053-0; 1-4205-0053-8

LC 2008016446

This focuses on African American literature, music, and art.

This is "highly accessible and [provides] cultural context to help readers understand [the] topic. . . . [The] book includes captioned color and black-and-white photographs and reproductions on every spread. Well-organized and clearly written." SLJ

Includes bibligraphical references

700.9 History, geographic treatment, biography of the arts

Flatt, Lizann

Arts and culture in the early Islamic world; Lizann Flatt. Crabtree Pub. Company 2012 48 p. col. ill., col. map (Life in the early Islamic world) (reinforced library binding : alk. paper) $30.60

Grades: 5 6 7 **700.9**

1. Islamic art 2. Islamic civilization

ISBN 0778721671; 9780778721673; 9780778721741; 9781427195609; 9781427198372

LC 2012000074

This book by Lizann Flatt is part of the "Life in the Early Islamic World" series. It "introduces the important roles that many of the arts, but especially calligraphy, architecture, and the decorative arts, have had in Islamic culture, in which art is meant to be 'useful as well as beautiful.'" (Booklist) "The main texts are supplemented with blue boxes of information, subsections, and many high-quality reproductions, maps, and paintings." (School Library Journal)

701 Philosophy and theory of fine and decorative arts

Dickins, Rosie

The **Usborne** art treasury; pictures, paintings, and projects. [by] Rosie Dickins; designed by Nicola Butler. Usborne 2007 94p il $19.99

Grades: 4 5 6 7 **701**

1. Painting 2. Art appreciation

ISBN 978-0-7945-1452-5

"Each project in this colorful, attractive compendium of art projects begins with a particular work of art. . . . Throughout the book, the excellent presentation of the projects makes them seem not only possible to complete but also worth doing. Illustrated step-by-step, the instructions are clearly written and practical." Booklist

Hensley, Laura

Art for all; what is public art? Raintree 2010 32p il (Culture in action) $29

Grades: 5 6 7 8 **701**

1. Art

ISBN 978-1-4109-3923-4; 1-4109-3923-5

LC 2009051126

This "briefly surveys public art, from murals and graffiti to obelisks and religious statues. . . . A world map shows the locations of 16 public artworks mentioned in the text. . . . The quality of the illustrations is fine. . . . Given the book's broad scope and few pages, it accomplishes a good deal. Three activities, a time line, a glossary, and a brief bibliography round out this attractive presentation." Booklist

Includes glossary and bibliographical references

Laidlaw, Jill

Fine art adventures; 36 creative, hands-on projects inspired by classic masterpieces. Maja Pitamic and Jill Laidlaw. Chicago Review Press 2017 144 p. $19.99

Grades: 5 6 7 8 **701**

1. Children's art 2. Art appreciation 3. Creative activities and seat work

ISBN 9780912777047

LC 2016054105

This book, by Maja Pitamic and Jill Laidlaw, "introduces young artists, ages 6 and up, to key masterpieces and interesting techniques, then lets them loose. Children will: create a Pointillist artwork with paints and a toothbrush, work with plaster to recreate a cave painting, use cardboard and coat hangers to design a mobile sculpture, build a dramatic jungle scene inside an old shoebox, and many more engaging, hands-on projects." (Publisher's note)

Tomecek, Steve

Art & architecture; by Stephen M. Tomecek. Chelsea House Publishers 2010 174p il (Experimenting with everyday science) $35

Grades: 4 5 6 7 **701**

1. Architecture 2. Art and science 3. Science -- Experiments 4. Art -- Study and teaching

ISBN 978-1-60413-168-0; 1-60413-168-3

LC 2009030195

"This fun and informative book features 25 simple experiments using common household items and foods such as blueberries, colored cellophane, food coloring, Magic Markers, miniature marshmallows, and wooden toothpicks to demonstrate principles and inspire creative thought about the intersection of science with the visual and mechanical arts. The six chapters include activities that illuminate certain scientific aspects of each respective subject. . . . Accessible for independent reading by children with a scientific bent or curiosity about how the world works, these experiments would also be useful for scout projects or science clubs." SLJ

Includes bibliographical references

702.8 Auxiliary techniques and procedures; apparatus, equipment, materials

Luxbacher, Irene

★ The **jumbo** book of art; written and illustrated by Irene Luxbacher. Kids Can Press 2003 208p il pa $14.95

Grades: 4 5 6 7 **702.8**

1. Color 2. Drawing 3. Painting 4. Sculpture 5. Art -- Study and teaching

ISBN 1-55074-762-2

"Each of the four chapters is devoted to instructing readers in the basics of one technique—drawing, creating with color, sculpture, and mixed-media projects, respectively—and then inspires those readers to let loose and have fun making something beautiful. . . . The book features clear layouts, well-written definitions of terms, full-color illustrations, and more than 90 projects. . . . This practical, lively, and smart package is a must-have for every art and elementary school classroom, and a welcome addition to most library collections." SLJ

Includes glossary

Meredith, Eleanor

Think and make like an artist; art activities for creative kids. Claudia Boldt and Eleanor Meredith. Thames & Hudson 2017 80 p. color illustrations (pbk.) $19.95

Grades: 3 4 5 6 7 8 **702.8**

1. Art -- Technique 2. Creative activities

ISBN 9780500650981

LC 2016955403

Written by Claudia Boldt and illustrated by Eleanor Meredith, this art activity book "encourages sophisticated thinking and gives budding artists a chance to develop their imaginations. . . . Children learn to experiment with different materials and ideas, make their own creative decisions, and produce their own unique artworks by way of engaging projects inspired by the work of eight contemporary artists working in media. . . ." (Publisher's note)

"This is an inspiring introduction to the concept of art as a vehicle to comment on or question the world." SLJ

Wenzel, Angela

13 art techniques children should know; Angela Wenzel ; translation by Cynthia Hall. Prestel Pub. Random House 2013 45 p. illustrations (some color) (13... children should know) $14.95

Grades: 4 5 6 **702.8**

1. Art -- Technique

ISBN 3791371363; 9783791371368

LC 2012953950

This book, by Angela Wenzel, "introduces young readers to a variety of important art techniques, explained through some of the world's most recognizable masterpieces. What's the difference between watercolor and gouache, or between a collage and an assemblage? How are frescoes and mosaics made? Why do prints look so different from each other? These questions and others are explored through major works of art in dazzling color reproductions." (Publisher's note)

704 Special topics in fine and decorative arts

Bolden, Tonya

Wake up our souls; a celebration of Black American artists. Published in association with Smithsonian American Art Museum. Harry N. Abrams 2004 128p il $24.95

Grades: 6 7 8 9 10 **704**

1. African American art

ISBN 0-8109-4527-4

Presents a history of African American visual arts and artists from the days of slavery to the present

"Bolden's writing is rich and lyrical. She smoothly incorporates the historical context, explaining pivotal events and relevant artistic movements clearly and succinctly." SLJ

Brooks, Susie

Get into Art! Enjoy Great Art--then Create Your Own! by Susie Brooks. Kingfisher 2013 31 p. col. ill. (hardcover) $14.99

Grades: 3 4 5 6 7 **704**

1. Art -- Guidebooks 2. Art 3. Picture books for children

ISBN 0753470586; 9780753470589

For this book, Susie Brooks' "goal is to convince her readers that art is not just something one observes, but rather something that one does. Using a topic beloved by many kids - animals - she presents 13 works by famous artists, each of which incorporates animals into its subject and theme. Each reproduced masterpiece occupies its own two-page spread, and Brooks explores one major art technique for each." (Booklist)

January, Brendan

★ **Native** American art & culture; [by] Brendan January. Raintree 2005 56p il map (World art & culture) lib bdg $23; pa $9.99

Grades: 5 6 7 8 **704**

1. Native Americans 2. Native American art

ISBN 978-1-4109-1108-7 lib bdg; 1-4109-1108-X lib bdg; 978-1-4109-2118-5 pa; 1-4109-2118-2 pa

LC 2004-8072

"January investigates the many art forms of the Native American tribes. . . . Chapters are dedicated to pottery, textiles, carving, and painting as well as body art, architecture, ceremonies, songs, and dances. . . . Numerous color photographs of both ancient and modern artwork are included on each spread, and they are exceptional. . . . This fresh look at Native American culture through its artwork will be a welcome alternative for reports and classroom discussion, and the popularity of the subject matter and appealing design will attract readers outside the classroom environment." SLJ

Includes bibliographical references

Raczka, Bob

Before they were famous; how seven artists got their start. Millbrook Press 2010 32p il (Art adventures) $25.26

Grades: 4 5 6 7 **704**

1. Artists 2. Creative ability

ISBN 978-0-7613-6077-3; 0-7613-6077-8

LC 2009049596

"Short biographies written in conversational, jargon-free text introduce seven great artists, as young beginners and then as creators of famous works. From Dürer and Michelangelo to Picasso and Dali, the featured artists are presented chronologically on uncluttered, open spreads that include beautiful full-page reproductions. . . . Great preparation for a gallery visit, this will appeal to older readers, too, for its exciting, never-condescending talk about the pictures and the artists who created them." Booklist

704.03 Ethnic and national groups

★ **Dreaming** in Indian; Contemporary Native American Voices. edited by Lisa Charleyboy and Mary Leatherdale. Annick Press 2014 128 p. color illustrations $19.95

Grades: PreK 7 8 9 10 11 12 **704.03**

1. Native Americans 2. Native American artists

ISBN 1554516870; 9781554516872

LC 2014045769

This book, edited by Lisa Charleyboy and Mary Leatherdale, is an "anthology from some of the most groundbreaking Native artists working in North America today. . . . Emerging and established Native artists, including acclaimed author Joseph Boyden, renowned visual artist Bunky Echo Hawk, and stand-up comedian Ryan McMahon, contribute thoughtful and heartfelt pieces on their experiences growing up Indigenous." (Publisher's note)

"Original and accessible, both an exuberant work of art and a uniquely valuable resource." Kirkus

Companion to Urban Tribes (2015)

704.9 Iconography

Stieff, Barbara

Earth, sea, sun, and sky; art in nature. translated from German by Cynthia Hall; illustrated by Michael Schmölzl. Prestel 2011 88p il lib bdg $14.95

Grades: 6 7 8 9 **704.9**

1. Art 2. Nature 3. Aesthetics

ISBN 978-3-7913-7048-4; 3-7913-7048-0

"A conversational writing style combines with many color photographs and drawings to convey information about art inspired by nature. In the beginning, Stieff describes the historical development of gardens and how they are an art form. She moves on to provide many examples of how art is found on land, in water, and in the air. The photographs, which range in size, further illuminate the text. Throughout the work, references are made to activities detailed in the final section. These projects, which include making daisy soup, learning some water games, forming seed balls, and creating pictures in water, encourage readers to look at or create art." SLJ

708 Galleries, museums, private collections of fine and decorative arts

An **eye** for art; focusing on great artists and their work. National Gallery of Art with Chicago Review Press, Incorporated 2013 180 p. (pbk.) $19.95

Grades: 4 5 6 7 8 9 10 11 12 **708**

1. Art 2. Art appreciation 3. National Gallery of Art (U.S.)

ISBN 1613748973; 9781613748978

LC 2013009403

This book is an "introduction to the works collected in the National Gallery of Art. More than 50 great artists are highlighted, from the 13th to the 21st centuries. The artists and their works and techniques are . . . arranged stylistically in categories that include 'Studying Nature,' 'Observing Everyday Life,' 'Exploring Places,' and 'Telling Stories.'" (School Library Journal)

709 History, geographic treatment, biography

Ayres, Charlie

Lives of the great artists. Thames & Hudson 2008 96p il $19.95

Grades: 5 6 7 8 **709**

1. Artists 2. Art -- History

ISBN 978-0-500-23853-0; 0-500-23853-7

LC 2008-91000

Presents illustrated and age-appropriate imaginary tours of the studios of famous artists from Leonardo da Vinci and Michelangelo to Monet and van Gogh, in an anecdotal reference that is complemented by reproductions of famous works and introductory portraits

This is "brightly written and augmented with activities, Web resources, and fun facts. . . . The works of art chosen to represent each artist are heavy on the drama and detail, resulting in high kid appeal and interesting captions. . . . The layout is clean and clear." SLJ

Children's book of art; an introduction to the world's most amazing paintings and sculptures. DK Pub. 2009 139p il $24.99

Grades: 4 5 6 7 **709**

1. Art appreciation 2. Art -- History

ISBN 978-0-7566-5511-2; 0-7566-5511-0

"From prehistoric to modern times, this expertly designed survey delivers a wealth of information. Much more than a mere time line, the focus shifts from artist to movement to medium with fluidity. Gallery pages examine how particular subjects are depicted in art from a variety of cultures and time periods. Hundreds of color reproductions are sure to hold readers' interest. . . . The vast amount of information presented is neither overwhelming nor superficial." SLJ

Finger, Brad

13 American artists children should know. Prestel 2010 46p il $14.95

Grades: 4 5 6 **709**

1. American art 2. Art appreciation 3. Artists -- United States

ISBN 978-3-7913-7036-1; 3-7913-7036-7

"Beginning with Winslow Homer and ending with Andy Warhol and Jasper Johns, this picture-book overview introduces 13 well-known American artists. On each double-page spread, short biographies combine with richly reproduced images of the artists' famous works. . . . Finger . . . writes with clarity and enthusiasm." Booklist

Includes glossary

Hockney, David, 1937-

A **history** of pictures for children; from cave paintings to computer drawings. by David Hockney and Martin Gayford ; illustrated by Rose Blake. Abrams Books for Young Readers 2018 128 p. (hc-pob with jacket) $24.99

Grades: 5 6 7 8 **709**

1. Historical literature 2. Art -- History

ISBN 9781419732119

LC 2017058996

This book, by David Hockney and Martin Gayford, illustrated by Rose Blake, "takes young readers on an adventure through art history. From cave paintings to video games, this book shows how and why pictures have been made, linking art to the human experience. Hockney and Gayford explain each piece of art in the book, helping young minds to grasp difficult concepts." (Publisher's note)

Includes bibliographical references and index

Raczka, Bob

★ **Name** that style; all about isms in art. by Bob Raczka. Millbrook Press 2008 32p il (Art adventures) lib bdg $25.26; pa $9.95

Grades: 5 6 7 8 **709**

1. Art -- History

ISBN 978-0-8225-7586-3 lib bdg; 0-8225-7586-8 lib bdg; 978-1-58013-824-6 pa; 1-58013-824-1 pa

LC 2008000312

"Beginning with naturalism and ending with photorealism, with many stops along the way, this compact overview documents the shifts, both in terms of technique as well as subject matter, that differentiate each style from its predecessors. Each 'ism' gets a two-page spread, with a beautifully reproduced example. . . . This is . . . indispensible for any middle-grade classrooms introducing art history." Booklist

Schumann, Bettina

13 women artists children should know; [by] Bettina Schumann; [translated from German by Jane Michael] Prestel 2009 46p il $14.95

Grades: 5 6 7 8 **709**

1. Women artists 2. Art appreciation

ISBN 978-3-7913-4333-4; 3-7913-4333-5

This is profiles women artists such as Sofonisba Anguissola, Maria Sybilla Merian, Mary Cassatt, Georgia O'Keeffe, Frida Kahlo, Louise Bourgeois, and Cindy Sherma

This "large-format, brightly colored [survey proves a] solid, even inspiring [introduction] to the art world. . . . Leading questions encourage budding artists to use the featured subjects and artworks as inspiration." Horn Book Guide

Includes glossary

Wenzel, Angela

13 artists children should know; [translation by Jane Michael] Prestel 2010 46p il $14.95

Grades: 4 5 6 **709**

1. Artists 2. Art appreciation 3. Art -- History

ISBN 978-3-7913-4173-6; 3-7913-4173-1

This profiles 13 artists such as Leondardo da Vinci, Vincent Van Gogh, Vermeer, and Henri Matisse

This "large-format, brightly colored [survey provides a] solid, even inspiring [introduction] to the art world. . . . Leading questions encourage budding artists to use the featured subjects and artworks as inspiration." Horn Book Guide

Includes glossary

Wood, Alix

Urban 'street' art; Alix Wood. Gareth Stevens Publishing 2015 32 p. illustrations (color) (But is it art?) (library binding) $26.60

Grades: 5 6 7 8 **709**

1. Graffiti 2. Street art 3. Outdoor art 4. Art and popular culture 5. Offenses against property

ISBN 9781482422948 ; 148242293X; 9781482422931; 9781482422955; 9781482422962

LC 2014033435

In this book, by Alix Wood, "not all art is displayed in a museum. For example, yarn bombing or guerilla knitting grew out of a movement in Texas to use up old yarn. Today, city dwellers might walk outside to find trees, bike racks, or even mail boxes covered by intricately knitted covers. The result is colorful, fun, and easily removed. However, other street art such as graffiti isn't seen as so harmless." (Publisher's note)

"Subjects include the thought-provoking, disturbing, whimsical, and unforgettable, from sidewalk 'gum art' to defaced stop signs to sunflowers planted in desolate urban areas to white 'ghost' bikes that honor fallen cyclists." SLJ

709.02 6th-15th centuries, 500-1499

Taylor, Diane C.

The **renaissance** artists; with history projects for kids. Diane C. Taylor. Nomad Press 2018 112 p. $22.95

Grades: 4 5 6 7 8 **709.02**

1. Renaissance 2. Italian artists

ISBN 1619306867; 9781619306868

This book in the Renaissance for Kids series, by Diane C. Taylor, "is a wonderfully enticing introduction to the Renaissance via the lives of five artists: Michelangelo, da Vinci, Titian, Botticelli, and Raphael. An accessible introduction offers a concise overview of just what exactly the Renaissance was, establishing social and historical context, and then five chapters explore the contributions and lasting impact of each painter." (Booklist)

709.03 Modern period, 1500-

Gunderson, Jessica

Impressionism; by Jessica Gunderson. Creative Education 2008 48p il (Movements in art) lib bdg $32.80

Grades: 6 7 8 9 **709.03**

1. Impressionism (Art)

ISBN 978-1-58341-611-2 lib bdg; 1-58341-611-0 lib bdg

LC 2007008493

This "discusses the leading Impressionist artists, their subjects, and their techniques. Quality reproductions of many paintings and occasional sepia photos of the painters and their settings illustrate the detailed, informative overview." Booklist

Includes glossary and bibliographical references

Realism; by Jessica Gunderson. 1st ed.; Creative Education 2009 48p il (Movements in art) lib bdg $32.80

Grades: 6 7 8 9 **709.03**

1. Realism in art

ISBN 978-1-58341-612-9 lib bdg; 1-58341-612-9 lib bdg

LC 2007008494

"Gunderson describes how art trends, politics, and inventions informed the work that was produced during [the Realism] movement. . . . [The] book provides an overview of the movement and its key players in continuous prose that is broken up by an occasional highlighted section of text. The color photographs, illustrations, and reproductions, many of them full page, are relevant and of high quality. . . . The [text delivers a] well-rounded [account] that students will find accessible." SLJ

Includes glossary and bibliographical references

Romanticism; [by] Jessica Gunderson. Creative Education 2009 48p il (Movements in art) lib bdg $32.80

Grades: 6 7 8 9 **709.03**

1. Romanticism in art

ISBN 978-1-58341-613-6; 1-58341-613-7

LC 2007008495

"Gunderson describes how art trends, politics, and inventions informed the work that was produced during [the Romantic] movement. . . . [The] book provides an overview of the movement and its key players in continuous prose that is broken up by an occasional highlighted section of text. The color photographs, illustrations, and reproductions, many of them full page, are relevant and of high quality. . . . The [text delivers a] well-rounded [account] that students will find accessible." SLJ

Includes glossary and bibliographical references

709.04 20th century, 1900-1999

Claybourne, Anna

Surrealism. Heinemann Library 2009 48p il (Art on the wall) lib bdg $32.86

Grades: 5 6 7 8 9 10 **709.04**

1. Surrealism 2. Modern art

ISBN 978-1-4329-1367-0; 1-4329-1367-0

LC 2008020316

This title succeeds "in presenting a bird's-eye view of [Surrealism] without oversimplification. Information on individual artists is included in the broader context of the movement. Visually exciting, with plenty of color, [the layout is] hip and should appeal to the target audience." SLJ

Includes glossary and bibliographical references

Laidlaw, Jill

★ **Modern** art adventures; 36 creative, hands-on projects inspired by artists from Monet to Banksy. Maja Pitamic and Jill Laidlaw. Chicago Review Press, Inc. 2015 144 p. illustrations (mostly color) (trade paper) $19.95

Grades: 5 6 7 8 9 **709.04**

1. Art 2. Art appreciation 3. Art, Modern -- 19th century 4. Art, Modern -- 20th century 5. Art, Modern -- 21st century

ISBN 1613731779; 9781613731772

LC 2014037521

This book, by Maja Pitamic and Jill Laidlaw, "introduces young artists to groundbreaking masterpieces and fresh techniques, then lets them loose to create their own works of art. . . . Children create two artworks based on the techniques and visual effects of the each featured piece of art and the projects cover a wide range of media, from tissue paper mosaics to stencils to comic cut-outs, with a variety of difficulty levels." (Publisher's note)

"This intriguing title introduces readers to modern art movements, from impressionism to contemporary street art, through child-friendly projects. Each movement includes examples of famous works of art, basic information (title, artist's name and nationality, and year painted) on the piece, and a brief discussion. . . . well-organized introduction to modern art concepts, perfect for classroom use." SLJ

Includes bibliographical references and index

Spilsbury, Richard

Pop art. Heinemann Library 2009 48p il (Art on the wall) lib bdg $23

Grades: 5 6 7 8 9 10 **709.04**

1. Pop art

ISBN 978-1-4329-1368-7 lib bdg; 1-4329-1368-9 lib bdg

LC 2008020358

This describes how Pop art began, some of the movement's artists, and the influence of Pop art

This title succeeds "in presenting a bird's-eye view of [Pop art] without oversimplification. Information on individual artists is included in the broader context of the movement. Visually exciting, with plenty of color, [the layout is] hip and should appeal to the target audience." SLJ

Includes glossary and bibliographical references

Yancey, Diane

Art deco. Lucent Books 2010 112p il (Eye on art) $33.45

Grades: 7 8 9 10 **709.04**

1. Art deco

ISBN 978-1-4205-0340-1; 1-4205-0340-5

LC 2010032961

"Presents an in-depth look at the art deco movement and its lasting legacy. . . . [It provides] a great deal of information, so middle school readers may not read them cover to cover; however, ample cover photos and quotes from artists will make this . . . appealing to students interested in art." Voice Youth Advocates

Includes glossary and bibliographical references

709.2 Biography

Herrera, Nicolas

High riders, saints and death cars; a life saved by art. Nicholas Herrera ; as told to Elisa Amado ; photos by John T. Denne. Groundwood Books/House of Anansi Press 2011 55p il

Grades: 9 10 11 12 **709.2**

1. Motorcycles 2. Art and religion 3. American folk art 4. Hispanic American artists -- Biography 5. Sculptors -- United States -- Biography 6. Artists 7. Sculptors 8. Artists -- United States 9. Hispanic Americans -- Biography

ISBN 0888998546; 9780888998545

"Nicholas Herrera did not plan to become an artist. He did poorly in school because he was not allowed to speak Spanish and was not recognized as being dyslexic. He became involved with drugs and alcohol, but after a life-threatening accident he turned to art. This book is his account of how he found a way to express himself and become productive. Herrera creates folk art, adding his own twist by incorporating fast cars, motorcycles, and other symbols from his life." (Library Media Connection)

"The subtitle of New Mexican folk artist Herrera's autobiography (told to and written by Amado) isn't hyperbole: even Herrera's mother wasn't sure he would survive his wild and self-destructive teenage years during the 1960s. . . . After emerging from a coma following an alcohol-related car accident, Herrera devotes his life to creating art. . . . Herrera's folk art sculptures . . . [blend] religious iconography with imagery from contemporary Hispanic and biker culture, as well as social and political commentary. . . . Never minimizing the gravity of Herrera's struggles, the book makes clear the concrete impact that art can have." Publ Wkly

Spence, David

Michelangelo; written by David Spence; editor, Guy Croton. North American ed. New Forest Press 2010 48 p. col. ill. (Great artists and their world) (library) $32.80

Grades: 6 7 8 9 **709.2**

1. Artists 2. Painters 3. Sculptors 4. Architects 5. Artists, Italian 6. Art, Renaissance -- Italy 7. Art -- 15th and 16th centuries

ISBN 1848983093; 9781848983090

"Offers biographical information [of Michelangelo Buonarroti] . . . interspersed with art history and criticism in an eye-catching format. . . . [Includes] a long introductory paragraph and four-to-six images with explanatory notes. . . . Spence . . . does a good job of explaining why art that might seem ordinary today was revolutionary at the time of its creation." SLJ

Includes bibliographical references and index.

709.3 Specific continents, countries, localities

Langley, Andrew

★ **Ancient** Greece. Raintree 2005 48p il (History in art) lib bdg $31.43; pa $8.99

Grades: 4 5 6 7 **709.3**

1. Greek art 2. Greece -- Civilization

ISBN 978-1-4109-0517-8 lib bdg; 1-4109-0517-9 lib bdg; 978-1-4109-2035-5 pa; 1-4109-2035-6 pa

LC 2004-7523

The author shows "how art provides primary-source information about everyday and family life, beliefs and religion, and philosophy and mythology in . . . ancient [Greece]. . . . The [book follows] a well-organized format that makes the history accessible for reports, but the [author takes the book] beyond a reports-only status. Captions for the two or three illustrations per spread are clear." SLJ

Includes glossary and bibliographical references

711 Area planning (Civic art)

Macaulay, David

★ **City** : a story of Roman planning and construction. Houghton Mifflin 1974 112p il $18; pa $10.99

Grades: 4 5 6 7 8 9 10 **711**

1. Civil engineering 2. Roman architecture 3. City planning -- Rome

ISBN 0-395-19492-X; 0-395-34922-2 pa

LC 74-4280

"By following the inception, construction, and development of an imaginary Roman city, the account traces the evolution of Verbonia from the selection of its site under religious auspices in 26 B.C. to its completion in 100 A.D." Horn Book

Includes glossary

720 Architecture

Barker, Geoff P.

Incredible skyscrapers. Amicus 2011 32p il (Superstructures) lib bdg $28.50

Grades: 5 6 7 8 **720**

1. Skyscrapers

ISBN 978-1-6075-3133-3; 1-6075-3133-X

LC 2009044044

"The vivid illustrations often help clarify points made in the text. . . . [This] colorful, informative [book offers] intriguing glimpses of notable engineering feats." Booklist

Includes bibliographical references

Finger, Brad

13 skyscrapers children should know; by Brad Finger. Prestel Pub 2016 45 p. illustrations (chiefly color) $14.95

Grades: 4 5 6 7 8 **720**

1. Skyscrapers

ISBN 3791372513; 9783791372518

This book, by Brad Finger, "takes young readers around the world to investigate how tall buildings are constructed. . . . There's something irresistible about a skyscraper. It can reshape an entire city skyline, and from the building's top floors, people can see the world from a different perspective. Travelling from New York City to Dubai, from London to Shanghai, and from Kuala Lumpur to Chicago, this colorful book features double-page spreads for each of the skyscrapers it profiles." (Publisher's note)

"Still, fascinating anecdotes about the state of the world during each building's inception make this an interesting read, and it provides plenty of valuable information, both at a glance and for more in-depth study." Booklist

Hosack, Karen

Buildings; [by] Karen Hosack. Raintree 2009 32p il map (What is art?) lib bdg $27.50

Grades: 5 6 7 8 **720**

1. Buildings 2. Architecture

ISBN 978-1-4109-3165-8 lib bdg; 1-4109-3165-X lib bdg

LC 2008-9700

This "features public spaces and private residences created from a variety of materials. Every page includes a paragraph about the structure with glossary terms in bold type. . . . [Title is] consistent in quality of design and content." SLJ

Includes glossary and bibliographical references

Macaulay, David

★ **Building** big. Houghton Mifflin 2000 192p il $30; pa $12.95

Grades: 5 6 7 8 9 10 **720**

1. Dams 2. Bridges 3. Tunnels 4. Engineering 5. Skyscrapers 6. Architecture

ISBN 0-395-96331-1; 0-618-46527-8 pa

LC 00-28116

"Macaulay combines his detailed yet vaguely whimsical illustrations with simple, straightforward prose that breaks down complex architectural and engineering accomplishments into easily digestible tidbits that don't insult the intelligence of the reader of any age." N Y Times Book Rev

Includes glossary

Paxmann, Christine

From mud huts to skyscrapers; architecture for children. by Christine Paxmann ; illustrated by Anne Ibelings. Prestel Pub. Random House 2012 64 p. ill. (hardcover) $19.95

Grades: 4 5 6 **720**

1. Architecture

ISBN 3791371134; 9783791371139

LC 2012939038

This book "takes readers on a journey through time, exploring well-known structures such as the pyramids, Hagia Sophia, Versailles, and the Guggenheim Museum. Each spread is dedicated to a single building; in addition to a detailed illustration of the structure, it also includes information about the architect, the architectural style, and/or definitions of particular details." (School Library Journal)

Roeder, Annette

13 buildings children should know; [translator, Jane Michael] Prestel 2009 46p il $14.95

Grades: 5 6 7 8 **720**

1. Architecture

ISBN 978-3-7913-4171-2; 3-7913-4171-5

"The famous buildings featured in this pictorial collection include Notre Dame cathedral in Paris, Neuschwanstein Castle in Germany, New York City's Guggenheim Museum and the Beijing National Stadium (built for the 2008 Olympics), each pictured in color photographs, cross-sections and/or ground plans, with time lines tracing the buildings' developments and changes over time. . . . A sound introduction to some impressive structures." Publ Wkly

Stern, Steven L.

Building greenscrapers; consultant, Frank Robbins. Bearport Pub. 2009 32p il (Going green) lib bdg $25.27

Grades: 4 5 6 7 **720**

1. Skyscrapers 2. Sustainable architecture

ISBN 978-1-59716-962-2 lib bdg; 1-59716-962-5 lib bdg

LC 2009-12494

"Color photographs (most full page) and a few diagrams accompany the informative text. . . . Overall, the [book] . . . is user-friendly and covers topics that are not easily found elsewhere." SLJ

Includes glossary and bibliographical references

724 Architecture from 1400

Alphin, Tom

The **LEGO** architect; by Tom Alphin. No Starch Press 2015 186 p. illustrations (hardcover) $24.95

Grades: 4 5 6 7 8 9 **724**

1. LEGO toys 2. Architecture -- History 3. Architectural models 4. Architecture, Modern -- Themes, motives

ISBN 9781593276133; 1593276133

LC 2015017603

This book, by Tom Alphin, "travel[s] through the history of architecture [reproduced with LEGO blocks.] . . . You'll learn about styles like Art Deco, Modernism, and High-Tech, and find inspiration in galleries of LEGO models. Then take your turn building 12 models in a variety of styles. Snap together some bricks and learn architecture the fun way!" (Publisher's note)

Includes bibliographical references

726 Buildings for religious and related purposes

Macaulay, David

★ **Mosque**. Houghton Mifflin 2003 96p il $18

Grades: 4 5 6 7 8 9 10 **726**

1. Mosques -- Design and construction

ISBN 0-618-24034-9

LC 2003-177

"Once again Macaulay uses clear words and exemplary drawings to explore a majestic structure's design and construction. . . . In his respectful, straightforward explanation of the mosque's design, Macaulay offers an unusual, inspiring perspective into Islamic society." Booklist

Includes glossary

★ **Pyramid**. Houghton Mifflin 1975 80p il $20; pa $9.95

Grades: 4 5 6 7 8 9 10 **726**

1. Pyramids 2. Egypt -- Civilization

ISBN 0-395-21407-6; 0-395-32121-2 pa

LC 75-9964

The construction of a pyramid in 25th century B.C. Egypt is described. "Information about selection of the site, drawing of the plans, calculating compass directions, clearing and leveling the ground, and quarrying and hauling the tremendous blocks of granite and limestone is conveyed as much by pictures as by text." Horn Book

Includes glossary

Mann, Elizabeth

The **Parthenon**; illustrations by Yuan Lee. Mikaya Press 2006 47p il (Wonders of the world) $22.95

Grades: 4 5 6 7 **726**

1. Athens (Greece) -- History 2. Greece -- Civilization 3. Parthenon (Athens, Greece)

ISBN 1-931414-15-7

This "volume introduces the history of ancient Athens culminating in the building of the Parthenon. . . . [The text is] well-researched and clearly written. . . . The color illustrations include an excellent map of Greece, photos of artifacts and sculptures, and many clearly deliniated, large-scale paintings." Booklist

726.6 Cathedrals

Macaulay, David

Building the book Cathedral. Houghton Mifflin 1999 112p il $29.95

Grades: 4 5 6 7 8 9 **726.6**

1. Cathedrals 2. Gothic architecture

ISBN 0-395-92147-3

LC 99-17975

"On its twenty-fifth anniversary, the author recounts the origins of his first book and suggests revisions he'd make in light of what he's learned. . . . Most of the original Cathedral: the story of it's construction is reproduced in this oversized celebratory volume, along with lots of preliminary sketches, new commentary, and revised, or newly deployed, art. . . . Touches of informal humor further enliven a book that's already mesmerizing for both its original content and its insights into this author-illustrator's incisive, ebulliently creative mind." Horn Book

728.8 Large and elaborate private dwellings

Humphrey, Paul

Building a castle; by Paul Humphrey. Arcturus Pub. 2012 32 p. col. ill. (library) $28.50

Grades: 4 5 6 **728.8**

1. Castles -- Design and construction 2. Castles -- Europe -- Design and construction

ISBN 1848585594; 9781848585591

LC 2011051450

This book by Paul Humphrey "takes readers on a journey from the very beginnings of castles as fortresses to the lavish tourist destinations of today." The text, along with "contextual photographs, staged reenactments, and detailed diagrams offers . . . [an] overview of how an architectural structure reveals the culture, class system, and daily life of the Middle Ages. Castles from the Czech Republic, Scotland, England, Turkey, and Holland are highlighted." (Children's Literature)

729 Design and decoration of structures and accessories

Macaulay, David

★ **Built** to last. Houghton Mifflin Harcourt 2010 272p il $24.99

Grades: 4 5 6 7 8 9 10 **729**

1. Castles 2. Cathedrals 3. Architecture 4. Mosques -- Design and construction

ISBN 978-0-547-34240-5; 0-547-34240-3

"Significantly updating the Caldecott Honor-winning Castle (1977) and Cathedral (1973) with new text and full-color illustrations, this hefty volume combines them with a very lightly revised Mosque (2003) for a three-in-one architectural spree. No mere colorization of the black-and-white originals of the first two books, . . . the all-new, often breathtaking images have been drawn by hand and then digitally colored to harmonize, beautifully with the look of Mosque. . . . Take a moment to mourn the originals, then celebrate this entirely worthy revision." Kirkus

730 Sculpture and related arts

Laidlaw, Jill

★ **Three** -dimensional art adventures; 36 Creative, Artist-Inspired Projects in Sculpture, Ceramics, Textiles, and More. Maja Pitamic and Jill Laidlaw. Chicago Review Press Inc. 2016 144 p. (trade paper) $19.99

Grades: 5 6 7 8 9 **730**

1. Sculpture 2. Sculpture -- Study and teaching (Elementary) -- Activity programs

ISBN 9781613736593

LC 2015048885

This book, by Maja Pitamic and Jill Laidlaw, "introduces young artists, ages 6 and up, to groundbreaking masterpieces and fresh techniques, then lets them loose. . . . [The authors] also explore the stories and meanings behind 18 well-known works of three-dimensional art as inspiration for these kid-tested, exciting, and creative projects. No prior knowledge of three-dimensional art is required—just enthusiasm for the subject and a willingness to discover." (Publisher's note)

"Like its predecessor, it's a book that succeeds for its ambition and breadth as it helps brings art out of the museum and makes it immediate and relevant in the lives of readers." Pub Wkly

731 Sculpture

Wenzel, Angela

13 sculptures children should know. Prestel 2010 il $14.95
Grades: 4 5 6 **731**

1. Sculpture 2. Art appreciation

ISBN 978-3-7913-7010-1; 3-7913-7010-3

This "large-format, brightly colored [survey provides a] well-oranized [introduction] to the . . . world [of sculpture]. [It] highlights a variety of works from antiquity to modern times. . . . Leading questions encourage budding artists to use the featured subjects and artworks as inspiration." Horn Book Guide

Includes glossary

736 Other plastic arts

Boursin, Didier

Easy origami. Firefly 2005 64p il $19.95; pa $9.95
Grades: 4 5 6 7 **736**

1. Origami

ISBN 1-55297-928-8; 1-55297-939-3 pa

This guide provides step-by-step instructions for 24 origami projects, ranked as very easy, easy, and detailed, and the book includes tips for best results

"Paper-folding novices in particular may be drawn to this collection by its unusually clean design and bright, inviting colors." SLJ

Nguyen, Duy

Zombigami; paper folding for the living dead. Sterling 2011 il pa $9.95
Grades: 5 6 7 8 **736**

1. Origami 2. Zombies

ISBN 978-1-4027-8646-4; 1-4027-8646-8

"Featuring both a detachable photo gallery of folded ghouls placed in atmospheric settings and a package of origami paper in suitably ominous colors and patterns, this collection of 13 undead figures may not survive intact for long but offers experienced paper folders hours of creepy fun. Nguyen opens with a tutorial of creases and folding symbology then . . . goes on to show how each figure is folded with plenty of carefully drawn and clearly labeled step diagrams. Nonetheless, most of these models are challenging projects." SLJ

Song, Sok

Origami accessories; A Foldable Fashion Guide. by Sok Song. Capstone Press 2016 47 p. color illustrations (Savvy. Fashion origami) (ebook) $31.99; (library binding) $31.99
Grades: 4 5 6 7 8 **736**

1. Origami 2. Fashion 3. Paper work 4. Dress accessories

ISBN 9781515716464; 1515716236; 9781515716235

LC 2016022940

With this book, by Sok Song, "transform a simple sheet of paper into a fashion-forward accent piece with easy-to-follow instructions and illustrated diagrams. Create accessories to amp up every outfit in your closet, including purses, shoes, and jewelry. With ten original, one-of-a-kind origami fashion accessories, even everyday outfits are sure to be runway-ready. All you have to do is fold it, shape it, and style it." (Publisher's note)

"Peppy printed papers and a mod-looking cover give this series lots of shelf appeal... Upgrade your origami section with these original models and excellent instructions." SLJ

Includes bibliographical references (page 48)

Stern, Joel

Jewish holiday origami; photographs by David Greenfield. Dover Publications 2006 64p il pa $5.95
Grades: 8 9 10 11 12 Adult **736**

1. Origami 2. Jewish holidays

ISBN 0-486-45076-7; 978-0-486-45076-6

LC 2005-56934

This book contains a "year's worth of holiday projects—from Chanukah dreidels and a menorah with candles, to Passover pyramids and an image of the Red Sea parting." Publisher's note

Temko, Florence

Origami holiday decorations for Christmas, Hanukkah, and Kwanzaa. Tuttle Pub. 2003 63p il pa $8.95
Grades: 5 6 7 8 **736**

1. Origami 2. Holiday decorations

ISBN 0-8048-3477-6 pa; 978-0-8048-3477-3 pa

LC 2002075060

"Among the 25 original projects are a Holiday Calendar, Jewish Star, Kwanzaa Bowl, and Santa Claus Table Decoration." Publisher's note

739.27 Jewelry

Macfarlane, Katherine

The **jeweler's** art; by Katherine Nell Macfarlane. Lucent Books 2007 112p il (Eye on art) lib bdg $32.45
Grades: 7 8 9 10 11 12 **739.27**

1. Jewelry

ISBN 978-1-59018-984-9

LC 2007-7804

A look at jewelry through the ages.

This "title is thoroughly researched and fully referenced, and contains quotations from artists and art historians. The writing is generally clear and fluid. . . . Many of the pages have good-quality photos of artwork and artists." SLJ

Includes bibliographical references

740 Graphic arts

Kidd, Chip

Go; a Kidd's guide to graphic design. Chip Kidd. Workman Publishing Company, Inc. 2013 160 p. (alk. paper) $17.95
Grades: 5 6 7 8 9 10 11 12 Adult **740**

1. Graphic design 2. Children and design 3. Graphic arts -- Technique

ISBN 076117219X; 9780761172192

LC 2013032394

YALSA Award for Excellence in Nonfiction for Young Adults: Finalist (2014)

This book is an introduction to graphic design. It introduces "the aspiring designer to the thought processes behind typography and visual organization. Among the topics are color, juxtaposition, typography, design history, and the use of design to convey concepts such as irony and metaphor." (Library Journal)

Includes bibliographical references and index

741.2 Techniques, procedures, apparatus, equipment, materials

Ames, Lee J.

Drawing with Lee Ames; from the bestselling, award-winning creator of the Draw 50 series, a proven step-by-step guide to the fundamentals of drawing for all ages. Doubleday 1990 262p il pa $21

Grades: 6 7 8 9 **741.2**

1. Drawing

ISBN 0-385-23701-4

LC 90-31436

The author "offers a compendium of samples for beginning artists. Ames explains his approach to beginning art instruction as a form of mimicry, where students copy samples in order to get a feel for the process of drawing. . . . This is definitely for the beginning student who possesses very little to no drawing experience. . . . Ames's approach offers a good base from which students can then move on to more in-depth instruction." Voice Youth Advocates

Includes bibliographical references

McMillan, Sue

How to improve at drawing. Crabtree Pub. Co. 2010 48p il (How to improve at) lib bdg $29.27; pa $9.95

Grades: 7 8 9 10 **741.2**

1. Drawing -- Technique

ISBN 978-0-7787-3576-2 lib bdg; 0-7787-3576-1 lib bdg; 978-0-7787-3598-4 pa; 0-7787-3598-2 pa

"McMillan begins [this] book with a spread each on the history of drawing, equipment, perspective, color and textures, and composition. . . . [The] book has step-by-step instructions for a variety of attractive projects. The . . . book has, for each project, a series of four to six preliminary sketches that show the progression from first line to complete outline, but it is left to the artist to add the final shading." SLJ

Includes glossary

Scott, Damion

★ **How** to draw hip-hop; [by] Damion Scott and Kris Ex. Watson-Guptill 2006 144p il pa $19.95

Grades: 7 8 9 10 **741.2**

1. Drawing 2. Hip-hop

ISBN 0-8230-1446-0

LC 2005-29156

"This book combines the bold and energetic lines of graffiti art with the bright colors of cel-shaded video games and an obvious Japanese manga influence. . . . [It discusses] genre-specific concepts like wild style lettering [and] hip-hop clothing. . . . There is no other book of this kind on the market, making it a necessary and relevant purchase." SLJ

Temple, Kathryn

★ **Drawing**; the only drawing book you'll ever need to be the artist you've always wanted to be. [by] Kathryn Temple. Lark Books 2005 112p il (Art for kids) $17.95

Grades: 5 6 7 8 **741.2**

1. Drawing

ISBN 1-57990-587-0

LC 2004-17909

This "introduction to essential drawing techniques builds from the starting points of lines and simple shapes. . . . Eight concise chapters explore seeing with artist's eyes, line drawing, light and shadow, proportion and scale, perspective, drawing faces, drawing bodies, and using imagination. The succinct text reads smoothly and is written in a clear, understandable style. Sample sketches and crisp, color photographs extend the text." SLJ

Drawing in color. Lark Books 2009 112p il (Art for kids) $17.95

Grades: 5 6 7 8 **741.2**

1. Color 2. Drawing

ISBN 978-1-57990-821-8; 1-57990-821-7

LC 2008050618

"This heavily illustrated guide encourages budding artists to learn some basic skills and decide what works for them. Before jumping into project ideas, Temple explains some drawing tools and the basics of color theory. She provides clear, step-by-step instructions while reminding children that there is no right or wrong way to draw. Then, in nine chapters that each cover a particular technique or type of subject. . . . Projects use a variety of mediums, including colored pencils, markers, and oil pastels. The balance of detailed text and color images is visually appealing. Children will enjoy honing their observation skills as they practice using color in new ways." SLJ

741.5 Cartoons, graphic novels, caricatures, comics

Abadzis, Nick

★ **Laika**. First Second Books 2007 205p il

Grades: 7 8 9 10 11 12 **741.5**

1. Graphic novels 2. Space flight -- Graphic novels 3. Soviet Union -- History -- 1953-1991 -- Graphic novels

ISBN 1-59643-101-6; 978-1-59643-101-0

LC 2006-51907

Laika was the abandoned puppy destined to become Earth's first space traveler. This is her journey. Along with Laika, there is Korolev, once a political prisoner and now a driven engineer at the top of the Soviet space program, and Yelena, the lab technician responsible for Laika's health and life. The book depicts the dedication and struggles of the scientists and technicians who worked in the Soviet space program, based on research Abadzis did before writing this book. The book includes a bibliography of books and websites.

"Abadzis's tear-inducing and solidly researched graphic novel treatment of Laika's surpassingly tragic story is a standout." Publ Wkly

Allison, John

Bad machinery; 1 the case of the team spirit. John Allison ; [edited by] James Lucas Jones. Oni Press 2013 112 p. chiefly color illustrations $19.99

Grades: 7 8 9 10 11 12 Adult **741.5**

1. Mystery graphic novels 2. School stories -- Graphic novels

ISBN 1620100843; 9781620100844

LC 2012953355

"Shauna. Charlotte. Mildred. Three schoolgirl sleuths. Jack. Linton. Sonny. Three schoolboy investigators. Tackleford. One mid-sized city with a history of countless mysteries. Is there enough room at Griswalds Grammar School for two groups of kid detectives? There better be, because once these kids have set their sights on solving a mystery there's nothing that can derail them. Nothing, except maybe gossip, classwork, new football player cards, torment from siblings, or any number of childhood distractions." (Publisher's note)

"Allison is a triple threat: he plots deftly, draws confidently, and writes dead-on adolescent dialogue. Set in a grammar school in a British working-class community, this first book in his Bad Machinery series--originally published as a webcomic--has three earnest boys vying against three sharp-tongued girls to solve mysteries." Pub Wkly

Other Bad Machinery volumes are:
The case of the good boy (2014)
The case of the simple soul (2014)
The case of the lonely one (2015)
The case of the fire inside (2016)
The case of the forked road (2017)

Anderson, Laurie Halse, 1961-

★ **Speak**; the graphic novel. Laurie Halse Anderson, illustrated by Emily Carrol. Farrar, Straus & Giroux 2018 384 p. illustrations (hardcover) $19.99

Grades: 7 8 9 10 11 12 **741.5**

1. Rape -- Fiction 2. High schools -- Fiction 3. Loneliness -- Comic books, strips, etc. 4. Teenage girls -- Comic books, strips, etc.

ISBN 9780374300289

LC 2017933387

Eisner Nominee: Best Adaptation from Another Medium (2019)

In this graphic novel, by Laurie Halse Anderson, illustrated by Emily Carrol, Melinda "is friendless--an outcast--because she busted an end-of-summer party by calling the cops, so now nobody will talk to her, let alone listen to her. . . . . Through her work on an art project, she is finally able to face what really happened that night: She was raped by an upperclassman, a guy who still attends Merryweather [High] and is still a threat to her." (Publisher's note)

"This potent retelling of the modern classic Speak blends words and images to create magic: a new representation of a teen whose voice is ripped from her, the battles she must wage to find it again, and the triumph of finally being able to speak out. Carroll's grayscale artwork perfectly depicts the starkness of Melinda's depression through strong ink lines and striking panels that rely on pencil and charcoal textural effects for the backgrounds." SLJ

Anderson, M. T., 1968-

Yvain; the Knight of the Lion. M.T. Anderson, illustrated by Andrea Offermann. Candlewick Press 2017 144 p. chiefly color illustrations $19.99

Grades: 7 8 9 10 **741.5**

1. Knights and knighthood -- Graphic novels

ISBN 0763659398; 9780763659394

In this graphic novel, by M.T. Anderson, illustrated by Andrea Offermann, "sir Yvain sets out from King Arthur's court and defeats a local lord in battle, unknowingly intertwining his future with the lives of two compelling women: Lady Laudine, the beautiful widow of the fallen lord, and her sly maid Lunette." (Publisher's note)

"This adaptation of Chrétien de Troyes' medieval poem beautifully ties together period art and imagery with stylish visual storytelling." Booklist

Appignanesi, Richard

A **midsummer** night's dream; illustrated by Kate Brown. Abrams 2008 207p (Manga Shakespeare) pa $9.95

Grades: 7 8 9 10 **741.5**

1. Poets 2. Authors 3. Dramatists 4. Graphic novels

ISBN 978-0-8109-9475-1; 0-8109-9475-5

Shakespeare's comedy of romance, Faerie, and shenanigans in the forest is adapted into a manga-style graphic novel. Hermia is in love with Lysander, while Demetrius is in love with Hermia, and Helen loves Demetrius. When mischievous fairy Puck decides to have some fun with the powerful love potion he has fetched for Fairy King Oberon, chaos reigns. While the human foursome needs to sort itself out, Oberon seeks revenge against his wife, Queen Titania, by having Puck use the love potion on her so she falls in love with the first creature she sees—who happens to be a yokel to whom Puck gave a donkey's head. The text takes dialog from the original play. The book includes a plot summary and a brief biography of Shakespeare.

Romeo and Juliet; by William Shakespeare; adapted by Richard Appignanesi; illustrated by Sonia Leong. Amulet Books 2007 195p (Manga Shakespeare) pa $9.95

Grades: 8 9 10 11 12 **741.5**

1. Poets 2. Authors 3. Dramatists 4. Graphic novels

ISBN 978-0-8109-9325-9; 0-8109-9325-2

LC 2006-100362

First published in the United Kingdom

Shakespeare's classic play of star-crossed young lovers gets the manga treatment. The book is set in modern Tokyo with rival yakuza gangs and uses somewhat abridged text from the play for the dialogue.

"Although the richness of the language may be lost, the script keeps the spirit of the story intact, hitting all the major speeches." Booklist

Arai, Kiyoko

Beauty Pop, Vol. 1; story and art by Kiyoko Arai. Viz Media/Shojo Beat 2006 194p il pa $8.99

Grades: 7 8 9 10 11 12 **741.5**

1. Manga 2. Shojo manga 3. Graphic novels 4. Hair -- Graphic novels

ISBN 978-1-4215-0575-6

At Kiri Koshiba's high school, three popular upper classmen do occasional "Scissors Projects," working makeovers on specially selected girls. Narumi Shogo, who cuts hair, wants to become the best beautician in Japan and has won every youth competition - except one, years ago, that a younger girl won. When girls who aren't already pretty ask Narumi for a makeover, he tells them they're too ugly. Kiri helps two of the girls, working a stylist's magic that makes the girls glow; she's not interested in competition, even though her family owns a salon. Narumi wants to know who dares to be the upstart and challenge him, and he sets up the school's cultural festival to be a haircutting duel. Will Kiri even bother to compete?

Volume 1 of 10

Arni, Samhita

Sita's Ramayana; Moyna Chitrakar, illustrator. Groundwood Books 2011 il $24.95

Grades: 5 6 7 8 **741.5**

1. Graphic novels 2. Ramayana 3. Hindu mythology -- Graphic novels

ISBN 978-1-55498-145-8; 1-55498-145-X

"The Ramayana is the story of the exiled prince Rama and his beautiful wife, Sita. When she is kidnapped by a love-struck demon king, her husband's efforts to rescue her result in a war that eventually involves not only demons and mortals, but also gods, monsters, and even animals. . . . Here, a Patua scroll painter has adapted it as a fast-paced, brilliantly bold graphic novel. All of the suspense, treachery, sorcery, and pathos of this epic is depicted in homemade natural dyes layered onto paper in energetic lines, rhythmic patterns, and fields of hot, bright colors. . . . This book would be a must-purchase based on the strength of its dramatic story and arresting art, enhanced by superior design and high-quality production. Brilliant and fresh." SLJ

Beagle, Peter S.

The **last** unicorn; original story by Peter S. Beagle; adaptation by Peter B. Gillis; art by Renae De Liz. IDW 2011 167p il rpt $16.00; $24.99

Grades: 6 7 8 9 10 **741.5**

1. Graphic novels 2. Unicorns -- Fiction

ISBN 9780451450524 rpt; 978-1-60010-851-8; 1-60010-851-2

Presents a graphic novel adaptation of the famous novel, in which a unicorn, alone in an enchanted wood, discovers she might be the last of her kind and sets out on a journey to find others like her.

"A beloved story is now a graphic novel in this excellent adaptation. . . . Much of the original novel's lyrical language has been included, and readers will be eager to find out if the unicorn will give up her quest for love, or if any of Schmendrick's spells will ever turn out right. . . . The illustrations are graceful and detailed, and inked in warm, glowing colors. This is a worthy successor to the classic novel and film." SLJ

Bell, Cece

★ **El** deafo; Cece Bell; color by David Lasky. Abrams Books 2014 233 p. color illustrations $21.95

Grades: 3 4 5 6 7 **741.5**

1. Deaf children 2. Autobiographical graphic novels 3. Schools 4. Friendship 5. Hearing aids for children

ISBN 1419710206; 9781419710209

LC 2013955590

Eisner Award: Best Publication for Kids (2015)

Newbery Honor Book (2015)

"In this . . . graphic novel memoir, author/illustrator Cece Bell chronicles her hearing loss at a young age and her subsequent experiences with the Phonic Ear, a very powerful--and very awkward--hearing aid. The Phonic Ear gives Cece the ability to hear--sometimes things she shouldn't--but also isolates her from her classmates." (Publisher's note)

"Bell's bold and blocky full-color cartoons perfectly complement her childhood stories--she often struggles to fit in and sometimes experiences bullying, but the cheerful illustrations promise a sunny future." Booklist

Black, Holly

The **Good** Neighbors; book one: Kin. Graphix 2008 117p (The Good Neighbors) $16.99

Grades: 7 8 9 10 11 12 **741.5**

1. Graphic novels 2. Fantasy graphic novels 3. Fairies -- Graphic novels

ISBN 978-0-439-85562-4; 0-439-85562-4

LC 2007-49008

Sixteen-year-old Rue has grown up in a world much like ours, except that the human world and the world of faerie have co-existed, as good neighbors, for a long time. When Rue's mother disappears and her professor father becomes the main suspect in the murder of a young woman, Rue's life turns strange. As she digs for information to figure out what is happening in her life, Rue discovers that her mother is a faerie and has returned to that realm because of a broken promise.

"This sophisticated tale is well served by Naifeh's stylish, angular illustrations." SLJ

Other titles in this series are:

Kith (2009)

Kind (2010)

Bowers, Rick

Superman vs. the Ku Klux Klan; the true story of how the iconic superhero battled the men of hate. by Rick Bowers. National Geographic 2012 160 p.

Grades: 7 8 9 10 11 12 **741.5**

1. Ku Klux Klan 2. Comic books, strips, etc. -- History and criticism 3. United States -- Social life and customs -- History 4. Superman (Comic strip) 5. Superman (Fictitious character) 6. Comic books, strips, etc. -- Social aspects

ISBN 1426309155; 1426309163; 9781426309151; 9781426309168

LC 2011024660

This book by Richard Bowers relates how "In 1946 . . . the powers behind the Superman franchise decided to use the superhero (in his radio incarnation) to take on a growing concern: the reemergence of the Ku Klux Klan . . . [Rick] Bowers begins with the story of Superman's creators, two Jewish kids who grew up in Cleveland. In alternating sections, he also follows the evolution of the Klan, from its beginnings after the Civil War to its renaissance . . . in the 1920s and beyond. A dual biography of both the hero and the hate group, this book also chronicles the early years of comics . . . and discusses how both Superman and the Klan came with values they wanted to impress upon young people." (Booklist)

Includes bibliographical references and index.

Brosgol, Vera

★ **Anya's** ghost. First Second 2011 221p il $19.99; pa $15.99

Grades: 6 7 8 9 10 **741.5**

1. Graphic novels 2. Ghosts -- Graphic novels 3. School stories -- Graphic novels

ISBN 978-1-59643-713-5; 1-59643-713-8; 978-1-59643-552-0 pa; 1-59643-552-6 pa

LC 2010036251

"A deliciously creepy page-turning gem from first-time writer and illustrator Brosgol. . . . A moodily atmospheric spectrum of grays washes over the clean, tidy panels, setting a distinct stage before the first words appear. . . . In addition to the supernatural elements, Brosgol interweaves some savvy insights about the illusion of perfection and outward appearance. . . . A book sure to haunt its reader long after the last page is turned—exquisitely eerie." Kirkus

★ **Be** prepared; Vera Brosgol ; color by Alec Longstreth. First Second 2018 256 p. chiefly color illustrations (hardcover) $22.99

Grades: 4 5 6 7 8 **741.5**

1. Camps -- Fiction 2. Friendship -- Fiction 3. Social acceptance -- Fiction

ISBN 9781626724440; 9781626724457

LC 2017946145

Eisner Nominee: Best Publication for Kids (2019)

In this book, by Vera Brosgol, "all Vera wants to do is fit in--but that's not easy for a Russian girl in the suburbs. Her friends live in fancy houses and their parents can afford to send them to the best summer camps. Vera's single mother can't afford that sort of luxury, but there's one summer camp in her price range--Russian summer camp. Vera is sure she's found the one place she can fit in, but camp is far from what she imagined." (Publisher's note)

"Brosgol's artwork has immense depth, from the facial expressions and gestures to the spot-on visual gags, and she strikes a perfect balance between heartfelt honesty and uproarious, self-deprecating humor." Booklist

Brown, Jeffrey

★ **Star** Wars; Jedi Academy. Jeffrey Brown ; [edited by] Rex Ogle. Scholastic, Inc 2013 160 p. illustrations (Star Wars: Jedi Academy) (paper over board) $12.99

Grades: 3 4 5 6 7 **741.5**

1. Outer space -- Fiction 2. Middle schools -- Fiction 3. Star Wars

-- Comic books, strips, etc.
ISBN 0545505178; 9780545505178; 9780545609999
LC 2013931939

In this book, by Jeffrey Brown, "Roan Novachez thought he was destined to attend Pilot Academy Middle School, just as his older brother and father did. His dreams are crushed when he is rejected by Pilot Academy and accepted into a sketchy new school called Coruscant Jedi Academy. . . . Confused and struggling to keep up, Roan tries to fly under the radar and passes the time drawing comics of his daily life at his strange boarding school." (Booklist)

"While it might be disappointing for those familiar with this world to see scant representation of beloved characters, it makes the book an easy starting point for new fans. There are plenty of references to other elements (the T-16 Skyhopper and Jedi training remotes, for example) for diehards to get excited about." SLJ

Other Jedi Academy titles by Brown are:
Return of the Padawan (2014)
The Phantom Bully (2015)

Cameron, Neill

Mega Robo Bros; by Neill Cameron ; additional coloring by Lisa Murphy. Scholastic Press 2018 96 p. chiefly color illustrations $8.99

Grades: 1 2 3 4 5 6 **741.5**

1. Science fiction 2. Robots -- Fiction 3. Brothers -- Fiction
ISBN 1338185950; 9781338185959

In this book in the Mega Robo Bros series, by Neill Cameron, "London! The future! Alex and Freddy are just like any other brothers. They squabble. They drive their parents crazy. There's only one difference... They're the most powerful robots on Earth! But Alex and Freddy will soon discover that they're not the only super-powered robots around. For an evil robotic mind is making sinister plans, and their lives won't stay peaceful for much longer." (Publisher' s note)

Camper, Cathy

Lowriders in space; book 1 by Cathy Camper ; illustrated by Raul Gonzalez III. Chronicle Books 2014 112 p. chiefly color illustrations (Lowriders) hc $22.99

Grades: 4 5 6 7 8 **741.5**

1. Space vehicles 2. Mechanics (Persons) 3. Automobiles -- Fiction 4. Graphic novels 5. Lowriders -- Fiction 6. Friendship -- Fiction 7. Mexican Americans -- Fiction 8. Competition (Psychology) -- Fiction 9. Lowriders -- Comic books, strips, etc
ISBN 9781452121550; 1452121559
LC 2013040709

Cathy Camper "introduces readers to Lupe Impala, Flapjack Octopus, and Elirio Malaria, three friends who love working with cars and dream of having their own garage shop. One day they see an opportunity to achieve their goal--a car competition. When they start working on a lowrider to prepare it for the competition, an out-of-this world journey begins." (School Library Journal)

"Raúl's snazzy panels--impressively drawn in only red, blue, and black ballpoint pen on tea-stained paper--resemble an amped-up Mighty Mouse cartoon rendered in anarchic yet skillful doodles. It's a joyfully explosive style, and it perfectly matches the Latino characters and barrio setting." Booklist

Other titles in this series are:
Lowriders to the center of the Earth (2016)
Lowriders blast from the past (2018)

Lowriders to the center of the Earth; by Cathy Camper ; illustrated by Raul the Third. Chronicle Books 2016 128 p. chiefly color illustrations hbk $22.99

Grades: 4 5 6 7 8 **741.5**

1. Cats -- Graphic novels 2. Automobiles -- Graphic novels 3. Mexican Americans -- Graphic novels 4. Gods and goddesses -- Graphic novels 5. Lowriders -- Fiction 6. Aztec gods -- Comic books, strips, etc
ISBN 1452138362; 9781452123431; 9781452138367; 1452123438
LC 2015021996

Pura Belpré Illustrator Award (2017)

"Lupe Impala, Elirio Malaria, and El Chavo Octopus are living their dream at last. They're the proud owners of their very own garage. But when their beloved cat Genie goes missing, they need to do everything they can to find him. Little do they know the trail will lead them to the realm of Mictlantecuhtli, the Aztec god of the Underworld, who is keeping Genie prisoner!" (Publisher's note)

"Raúl the Third's ultradetailed crosshatched artwork more than meets the demands of this cast-of-thousands comic opus." Kirkus

Carey, Mike

Re -Gifters; written by Mike Carey; art by Sonny Liew and Marc Hempel. DC Comics/Minx 2007 148p il pa $9.99

Grades: 7 8 9 10 11 12 **741.5**

1. Graphic novels 2. Romance graphic novels 3. Martial arts -- Graphic novels 4. School stories -- Graphic novels 5. High school students -- Graphic novels
ISBN 978-1-4012-0371-9 pa; 1-4109-0371-X pa

"Jen Dik Seong, or Dixie, is having trouble getting her ki focused. Normally an outstanding hapkido student, she finds that her crush on classmate Adam is affecting her ability to fight. This is not good, as the national competition is fast approaching, and her parents expect her to do well. . . . Dixie makes a series of poor choices. She decides to spend the entry fee . . . on an elaborate birthday present for Adam. . . . This is a terrific read that features complex characters dealing with internal and external conflicts that make them believable and endearing. Lively black-and-white illustrations bring action and emotion to the story." SLJ

Carroll, Emily

★ **Through** the woods; Emily Carroll. 1st ed Margaret K. McElderry Books 2014 208 p. chiefly color illustrations (trade paper) $14.99; (hardcover) $21.99

Grades: 8 9 10 11 12 Adult **741.5**

1. Horror fiction 2. Comic books, strips, etc. 3. Short stories 4. Graphic novels
ISBN 9781442465961; 9781442465954
LC 2013030969

Ignatz Award: Outstanding Artist (2015)

Eisner Award: Best Graphic Album--Reprint (2015)

In this book, Emily Carroll "crafts five unsettling tales in graphic-novel format inspired by common folkloric themes--from wolves in the woods to peculiar visitors to dark possessions. In 'Our Neighbor's House,' three sisters who find themselves alone in a cabin are taken, one by one, in the middle of the night by a smiling stranger. . . . 'The Nesting Place' focus on malevolent spirit possession." (Horn Book Magazine)

"All the tales in Carroll's debut graphic novel are fairly standard ghost stories, but it is her eerie illustrations--popping with bold color on black, glossy pages--that masterfully build terrifying tension and a keep-the-lights-on atmosphere." Booklist

Castellucci, Cecil

The **Plain** Janes; by Cecil Castellucci and Jim Rugg. DC Comics/Minx 2007 un il pa $9.99

Grades: 7 8 9 10 11 12 **741.5**

1. Graphic novels 2. Art -- Graphic novels 3. Friendship -- Graphic novels 4. School stories -- Graphic novels 5. High school students -- Graphic novels

ISBN 978-1-4012-1115-8

After a bomb attack in Metro City, Jane's parents move to suburban Kent Waters, where Jane feels lost. Then she meets three other Janes at the "reject" table in the high school lunch room, and she convinces them to help her form their own secret club: P.L.A.I.N.—People Loving Art in Neighborhoods. However, their "art attacks" cause the authorities to think that P.L.A.I.N. is a terrorist group.

"The art, inspired by Dan Clowes' work, is absolutely engaging. Packaged like manga this is a fresh, exciting use of the graphic-novel format." Booklist

Another title about the Janes is:

Janes in love (2008)

Chanani, Nidhi

Pashmina; Nidhi Chanani. First Second 2017 161 p. chiefly color illustrations (hardcover) $21.99

Grades: 4 5 6 7 8 **741.5**

1. India -- Fiction 2. Mother-daughter relationship -- Fiction

ISBN 1626720886; 9781626720879; 9781626720886

LC 2016961589

In this graphic novel, by Nidhi Chanani, "Priyanka Das has so many unanswered questions: Why did her mother abandon her home in India years ago? What was it like there? And most importantly, who is her father, and why did her mom leave him behind? But Pri's mom avoids these questions. . . . For Pri, her mother's homeland can only exist in her imagination. That is, until she finds a mysterious pashmina tucked away in a forgotten suitcase." (Publisher's note)

"Contemporary reality is shown in grayscale; the past in sepia hues; and Pri's imagined India in rich colors that radiate off the pages. Priyanka is a realistically complex, sometimes moody character, with depth shown through her varied interests and inquisitive musings." Horn Book

Chmakova, Svetlana

★ **Awkward**; by Svetlana Chmakova. Yen Press 2015 210 p. illustrations (chiefly color) $24

Grades: 5 6 7 8 **741.5**

1. Clubs -- Fiction 2. School stories -- Graphic novels 3. Middle schools -- Fiction 4. Graphic novels 5. Schools -- Fiction 6. Popularity -- Fiction

ISBN 0316381306; 0316381322; 9780316381307; 9780316381321

LC 2015945195

Eisner Nominee: Best Publication for Teens (2016)

In this middle grade book, by Svetlana Chmakova, "protagonist Peppi is fantastically imperfect. . . . She is the new girl at Berrybrook Middle School and is having a hard time fitting in because of her struggles with social anxiety. The work opens with the young teen pushing away the first person who tries to help her, Jaime, and it only gets more awkward from there." (School Library Journal)

★ **Brave**; Svetlana Chmakova. Yen Press 2017 238 p. chiefly color illustrations (hardcover) $24

Grades: 4 5 6 7 **741.5**

1. Popularity -- Fiction 2. Middle schools -- Fiction

ISBN 0316363170; 9780316363174; 9780316363181

LC 2017934376

In this book, by Svetlana Chmakova, "in his daydreams, Jensen is the biggest hero that ever was, saving the world and his friends on a daily basis. But his middle school reality is very different--math is hard, getting along with friends is hard. . . . And the pressure's on even more once the school newspaper's dynamic duo, Jenny and Akilah, draw Jensen into the whirlwind of school news, social-experiment projects, and behind-the-scenes club drama." (Publisher's note)

"This is a subtle, well-observed treatment of a kid who doesn't fit in. The various threads of friendship and belonging are woven masterfully and ring true, with a conclusion that brings everything together." SLJ

Crush; Svetlana Chmakova. Yen Press 2018 234 p. chiefly color illustrations (Berrybrook Middle School) (hardcover) $24

Grades: 5 6 7 8 **741.5**

1. Teenagers -- Fiction 2. Friendship -- Fiction 3. Interpersonal relations -- Fiction 4. Friendship -- Comic books, strips, etc. 5. Middle schools -- Comic books, strips, etc.

ISBN 0316363235; 9780316363235; 9780316363242

LC 2018948318

Eisner Nominee: Best Publication for Kids (2019)

"Jorge seems to have it all together. . . . The only time he ever really feels off his game is when he crosses paths with a certain girl... But when the group dynamic among the boys starts to shift, will Jorge be able to balance what his friends expect of him versus what he actually wants?" (Publisher's note)

"The character development is wonderful. With each page turn, everyone becomes more complex, and the situations they experience are timely and real. The artwork tends toward colorful pastels, and the backgrounds lighten and darken to reflect characters' emotions in a lovely, subtle way." SLJ

Cliff, Tony

Delilah Dirk and the Turkish Lieutenant; by Tony Cliff. First Second 2013 176 p. ill. (paperback) $15.99

Grades: 7 8 9 10 11 12 **741.5**

1. Adventure fiction 2. Historical fiction 3. Istanbul (Turkey) -- Fiction 4. Women adventurers -- Fiction

ISBN 1596438134; 9781596438132

LC 2013947230

In this book, "Delilah Dirk has abandoned conventional court life and become a globe-trotting soldier of fortune. She is captured and held prisoner in 1800s Constantinople. Eventually she escapes, taking along the astonished Turkish Lieutenant Erdemogul Selim, whose quiet life centers around a proper cup of tea. This unlikely pair embarks on a wild journey that includes flying a ship, outwitting the Evil Pirate Captain Zakul, and escaping burning buildings." (School Library Journal)

"Plenty of fight scenes will attract male readers, in addition to females looking for strong heroines. All in all, this is a carefree romp across the Ottoman Empire with an upbeat tone that is refreshing." Lib Med Con

Other titles in this series are:

Delilah Dirk and the King's Shilling (2016)

Delilah Dirk and the Pillars of Hercules (2018)

Colfer, Eoin

Artemis Fowl: the graphic novel; adapted by Eoin Colfer and Andrew Donkin; art by Giovanni Rigano; color by Paolo

Lammana. Hyperion Books for Children 2007 un il $18.99; pa $9.99

Grades: 4 5 6 7 8 9 **741.5**

1. Graphic novels 2. Fantasy graphic novels 3. Adventure graphic novels

ISBN 978-0-7868-4881-2; 0-7868-4881-2; 978-0-7868-4882-9 pa; 0-7868-4882-0 pa

Twelve-year-old genius and criminal mastermind Artemis Fowl runs his missing father's crime empire and gets his hands on a book that will give him access to the underground fairy world. This graphic novel adaptation gives the book a European look and color palette

"Excellent use of color and shading gives the panels a tremendous sense of light with enchanting effect. Characters are expressively brought to life with fun, exaggerated style." SLJ

Other Artemis Fowl graphic novels are:
Artemis Fowl: the Arctic incident (2009)
Artemis Fowl: the eternity code (2013)
Artemis Fowl: the opal deception (2014)

★ **Illegal**; Eoin Colfer, Andrew Donkin ; art by Giovanni Rigano ; lettering by Chris Dickey. Sourcebooks Inc 2018 144 p. chiefly illustrations $19.99

Grades: 5 6 7 8 9 **741.5**

1. Poor -- Fiction 2. Siblings -- Fiction 3. Undocumented immigrants -- Fiction

ISBN 1492662143; 9781492662143

In this book, by Eoin Colfer and Andrew Donkin, illustrated by Giovanni Rigano, "Ebo is alone. His brother, Kwame, has disappeared, and Ebo knows it can only be to attempt the hazardous journey to Europe, and a better life--the same journey their sister set out on months ago. . . . He sets out after Kwame and joins him on the quest to reach Europe. Ebo's epic journey takes him across the Sahara Desert to the dangerous streets of Tripoli, and finally out to the merciless sea." (Publisher's note)

"The format allows sensitive and difficult topics such as murder, death, and horrific, traumatizing conditions to unfold for children, Ebo's reactions speaking volumes and dramatic perspectives giving a sense of scope. A creators' note provides factual context, and an appendix offers an Eritrean refugee's minimemoir in graphic form." Kirkus

Collar, Orpheus

The **red** pyramid; the graphic novel. Rick Riordan ; adapted by Orpheus Collar ; lettered by Jared Fletcher. Disney/Hyperion Books 2012 un chiefly color illustrations (The Kane chronicles) pbk $12.99; hbk $21.99

Grades: 4 5 6 7 8 9 **741.5**

1. Magic -- Fiction 2. Egyptian mythology -- Fiction 3. Brothers and sisters -- Fiction

ISBN 1423150694 ; 1423150686 ; 9781423150695 ; 9781423150688

LC 2012007905

"Since their mother's death, Sadie and Carter have become near-strangers. While Sadie has lived with her grandparents in London, Carter has traveled the world with their father, the famed Egyptologist Dr. Julius Kane. One night, Dr. Kane brings the siblings to the British Museum, where he hopes to set things right for his family. Instead, he unleashes the Egyptian god Set, who banishes him to oblivion and forces the children to flee for their lives." (Publisher's note)

"Out of necessity, much of the dialogue is dedicated to explaining actions and events, but a constant stream of humor prevents the reader from getting bogged down by logistics. The colorful artwork has an almost painting-like quality, . . . and some clever visual jokes and thoughtful use of panels make good use of the format." VOYA

Corona, Jorge

Feathers; written & illustrated by Jorge Corona ; colors by Jen Hickman ; letters by Deron Bennett. Archaia 2015 160 p. chiefly illustrations (hardcover) $24.99

Grades: 5 6 7 8 **741.5**

1. Orphans -- Graphic novels 2. Monsters -- Graphic novels

ISBN 9781608867530; 1608867536

LC 2015055238

In this graphic novel, written & illustrated by Jorge Corona, "Poe has lived his entire eleven-year-old life hidden away under the protection of his adoptive father, Gabriel. He spends his days secretly helping . . . bands of orphans who roam the slums. . . . When Bianca, an overprotected girl from the wealthy City beyond the Wall, escapes into the Maze in search of adventure, their worlds collide." (Publisher's note)

"Poe is a true underdog hero, and Bianca's wish to be set free from her restricting life is something to which middle grades readers can relate. Stunning illustrations contrast the stark white orderly city with the dark and dangerous Maze." SLJ

Craft, Jerry

★ **New** kid; Jerry Craft ; with colors by Jim Callahan. HarperCollins 2019 256 p. chiefly color illustrations (hardback) $21.99

Grades: 4 5 6 7 **741.5**

1. Graphic novels 2. Racism -- Fiction 3. Private schools -- Fiction 4. Race -- Comic books, strips, etc. -- Fiction 5. Schools -- Comic books, strips, etc. -- Fiction 6. Private schools -- Comic books, strips, etc. -- Fiction 7. Parent and child -- Comic books, strips, etc. -- Fiction

ISBN 0062691201; 9780062691194; 9780062691200

LC 2018938256

In this graphic novel, by Jerry Craft, "seventh grader Jordan Banks . . . [was enrolled by] his parents . . . in a prestigious private school known for its academics, where Jordan is one of the few kids of color in his entire grade. As he makes the daily trip from his Washington Heights apartment to the upscale Riverdale Academy Day School, Jordan soon finds himself torn between two worlds--and not really fitting into either one." (Publisher's note)

"This school story stands out as a robust, contemporary depiction of a preteen navigating sometimes hostile spaces yet staying true to himself thanks to friends, family, and art." (Horn Book)

Ellis, Grace

★ **Lumberjanes**; Volume 1 Beware the kitten holy. written by Noelle Stevenson & Grace Ellis ; illustrated by Brooke Allen ; colors by Maarta Laiho ; letters by Aubrey Aiese ; created by Shannon Watters, Grace Ellis & Noelle Stevenson. Boom! Studios 2015 128 p. ill. (chiefly col.) (Lumberjanes) pbk $14.99

Grades: 6 7 8 9 10 11 12 Adult **741.5**

1. Camps -- Fiction 2. Adventure fiction 3. Summer -- Fiction 4. Monsters -- Fiction 5. Female friendship -- Graphic novels

ISBN 1608866874; 9781608866878

Eisner Award: Best New Series (2015)

Harvey Award: Best New Series (2015)

Eisner Award: Best Publication for Teens (2015)

Harvey Award: Best Original Graphic Publication For Young Readers (2015)

"[This] graphic novel begins mid-adventure as five campers are out after hours investigating a strange event that they all witnessed: a woman turning into a giant bear. This is just the first of many odd occurrences that Jo, April, Molly, Mal, and Ripley encounter at the summer camp for 'Hardcore Lady Types.' The Lumberjanes, as the scouts are called, band together to solve puzzles, defeat three-eyed creatures, and escape the ire of their watchful counselor Jen." (School Library Journal)

"Humorously riffing on everything from scout badges to the X-Men to feminist heroes . . ., it's a sharp, smart, and most of all fun celebration of sisterhood." Pub Wkly

Volume 1 of an ongoing series

Emerson, Sharon

Zebrafish; written by Sharon Emerson; drawn by Renee Kurilla. Atheneum Books for Young Readers 2010 119p il $16.99

Grades: 4 5 6 7 **741.5**

1. Graphic novels 2. Rock music -- Graphic novels

ISBN 978-1-4169-9525-8; 1-4169-9525-0

LC 2009-41683

When their rock band becomes popular, five middle schoolers use their new fame to generate awareness (and donations) for an important cause.

Explorer; the lost islands. edited by Kazu Kibuishi. Abrams Books 2013 128 p. (Explorer) (hardcover) $19.95; (pbk.) $10.95

Grades: 4 5 6 7 8 **741.5**

1. Islands 2. Graphic novels

ISBN 1419708813; 141970883X; 9781419708817; 9781419708831

LC 2013935794

In this follow-up to "Explorer: The Mystery Boxes," Kazu Kibuishi and a crew of cartoonists again take turns weaving seven tales based around a loose theme. This time the motif is islands, and the contributors are left to interpret it in illustrated shorts. Some, by using their strange and remote settings as microcosms, underscore the value of hard work . . . or finding one's niche . . . , while others examine more abstract concepts such as exploration and isolation." (Publishers Weekly)

Fairfield, Lesley

Tyranny. Tundra Books 2009 114p il pa $10.95

Grades: 8 9 10 11 12 **741.5**

1. Graphic novels 2. Eating disorders -- Graphic novels

ISBN 0-88776-903-9; 978-0-88776-903-0

This graphic novel portrays teenager Anna's struggle with anorexia, "personified as her tormentor, Tyranny." (Publisher's note) "Age eleven and up." (Quill Quire)

"This is one of the most moving and important graphic novels to come along in years. Many stories have been written about teens who try to change what they see in the mirror through anorexia and bulimia, but this one features a girl who is driven by her own personal demon. That demon is called Tyranny, and it is represented by an angry and chaotic swirl of lines that form the shape of a person. . . . Fairfield treats this important subject with intelligence and empathy. . . . The simple yet powerful black-and-white drawings do wonders in bringing the book's message to its readers." SLJ

Fajardo, Alexis E.

Kid Beowulf and the blood-bound oath. Bowler Hat 2008 il pa $14.95

Grades: 6 7 8 9 **741.5**

1. Graphic novels 2. Beowulf -- Graphic novels 3. Monsters -- Graphic novels

ISBN 978-0-9801419-1-7 pa; 0-9801419-1-5 pa

"In the standard Beowulf story, the character appears as a full-fledged hero, with little concept of how he actually became one. Fajardo tells the backstory, using a blend of humor and soap-opera plot twists. . . . The cartoon-style illustrations are lively and contain lots of visual humor." SLJ

Flight explorer; edited by Kazu Kibuiski. Villard 2008 112p il pa $10

Grades: 4 5 6 7 **741.5**

1. Graphic novels 2. Fantasy graphic novels 3. Humorous graphic novels 4. Adventure graphic novels 5. Science fiction graphic novels

ISBN 978-0-345-50313-8 pa; 0-345-50313-9 pa

This anthology includes stories that Kibuishi kept from Flight Volume 4 because they had all-ages appeal, as well as stories submitted especially for this volume. Kibuishi's own Copper and his talking dog cross a deep canyon by leaping onto mushrooms, only to discover the vegetation is intelligent. Kean Soo's Jellaby and his human friends frolic in the snow. Missile Mouse by Jake Parker defends a village on another planet, only to discover his coming was prophesied (this story includes two uses of the word "crap"). The other stories will appeal to younger readers, while some of the humor will also appeal to older readers. Other than the one bad word in "Missile Mouse" (noted above), there shouldn't be any other content that would keep this book out of most elementary and middle schools.

"Every story has a layout that promotes an acute sense of pacing and showcases the crisp, defined, full-color art." SLJ

Ford, Christopher

Stickman Odyssey; an epic doodle. Philomel Books 2011 200p il $12.99

Grades: 5 6 7 8 **741.5**

1. Graphic novels 2. Humorous graphic novels 3. Adventure graphic novels 4. Greek mythology -- Graphic novels

ISBN 978-0-399-25426-0; 0-399-25426-9

LC 2010-36900

In this humorous take on the Odyssey, Zozimos, banished from his country by his evil stepmother, has many adventures as he prepares to return home to reclaim the throne that is rightfully his.

"The black-and-white illustrations are occasionally simple to the point of hilarity. . . . There is subtlety and depth here, however, and the contrast between the intentionally plain characters and their seemingly larger-than-life (but ultimately universal) quests . . . makes the final product both the promised Greek epic tale and an examination of the ways in which modern humans are isolated and lost. . . . Ford balances allegory and madcap quest so perfectly that the book inspires reflection even while it is clearly a quick-reading, ridiculous, often gross adventure." Bull Cent Child Books

Furudate, Haruichi

Haikyu!! Volume 1 story and art by Haruichi Furudate ; translation, Adrienne Beck. Viz 2016 197 P. chiefly illustrations paperback $9.99

Grades: 7 8 9 10 11 12 **741.5**

1. Shonen manga 2. Volleyball -- Fiction 3. School stories -- Graphic novels

ISBN 9781421587660; 1421587661

"Ever since he saw the legendary player known as the 'Little Giant' compete at the national volleyball finals, Shoyo Hinata has been aiming to be the best volleyball player ever! After losing his first and last volleyball match against Tobio Kageyama, . . . Shoyo Hinata swears to become his rival after graduating middle school. But what happens when the guy he wants to defeat ends up being his teammate?!" (Publisher's note)

Volume 1 of an ongoing series

Gaiman, Neil, 1960-

★ The **graveyard** book graphic novel Volume 1; based on the novel by Neil Gaiman ; adapted by P. Craig Russell ; illustrated by Kevin Nowlan, P. Craig Russell, Tony Harris, Scott Hampton, Galen Showman, Jill Thompson, Stephen B. Scott ; colorist, Lovern Kindzierski ; letterer, Rick Parker. HarperCollins 2014 188 p. color illustrations $19.99

Grades: 5 6 7 8 9 10 **741.5**

1. Graphic novels 2. Orphans -- Fiction 3. Cemeteries -- Fiction

ISBN 9780062194817; 006219481X

LC 2013953799

This graphic novel is an adaptation of the "Newbery Medal-winning novel, [where] Bod is an unusual boy . . . , the only living resident of a graveyard. Raised from infancy by the ghosts, werewolves, and other cemetery denizens, Bod has learned the antiquated customs of his guardians' time as well as their ghostly teachings." (Publisher's note)

"Russell brings his decades of comics know-how to this lovely, lyrical adaptation of [Gaiman's] well-loved, Newbery Medal--winning book. Not content to rely exclusively on his own distinctive talents, Russell has enlisted some of the industry's greatest contemporary illustrators as contributors, who fill the panels with appropriately gothic tones. In order to give ample room to the novel's twists and turns, the adaptation has been divided into two parts." Booklist

★ The **graveyard** book graphic novel Volume 2; based on the novel by Neil Gaiman ; adapted by P. Craig Russell ; illustrated by David LaFuente, Scott Hampton, P. Craig Russell, Kevin Nowlan, Galen Showman ; colorist, Lovern Kindzierski ; letterer, Rick Parker. HarperCollins 2014 188 p. color illustrations (hardcover) $19.99

Grades: 5 6 7 8 9 10 **741.5**

1. Dead -- Fiction 2. Orphans -- Fiction 3. Cemeteries -- Fiction 4. Supernatural graphic novels 5. Graphic novels 6. Supernatural -- Fiction

ISBN 0062194836; 9780062194831

LC 2013497350

"Russell concludes the two-part adaptation of Gaiman's Newbery Medal winner, encompassing the final three chapters of the novel. Bod, raised by the ghostly denizens of a graveyard, is a young adult now, yearning for knowledge of the world of the living. After a showdown with a pair of school bullies . . . Bod finally confronts the ancient order who murdered his family and overcomes them with his supernatural know-how and his innate courage and cleverness." (Booklist)

"Russell and his team of illustrators continue to do this amazing story justice with images that lead readers down a path into Bod's dark and magical graveyard world. Gaiman has the ability to weave beauty and intrigue into a story that has a strong potential to frighten." VOYA

Hansel & Gretel; a Toon graphic. Neil Gaiman, Lorenzo Mattotti. Toon Books 2014 56 p. black and white illustrations hbk $16.95

Grades: 2 3 4 5 6 **741.5**

1. Folklore -- Germany 2. Fairy tales -- Graphic novels 3. Fairy tales 4. Graphic novels

ISBN 9781935179627; 1935179624

LC 2014000694

This graphic novel offers a retelling of the Germanic folk tale of Hansel and Gretel. "Hansel overhears his mother presenting her logical argument to abandon the children in the forest so that she and her husband might have some hope of surviving the famine caused by the war. He reluctantly agrees, but he is happy when the children outsmart the plan. However, as conditions worsen, their mother persuades their father to abandon them a second time." (Bulletin of the Center for Children's Books)

"Mattotti contributes elegant b&w ink spreads that alternate with spreads of text. His artistry flows from the movement of his brush and the play of light and shadow. . . . Gaiman makes the story's horrors feel very real and very human, and Mattotti's artwork is genuinely chilling." Pub Wkly

Includes bibliographical references

Garcia, Kami

Teen Titans; Raven. written by Kami Garcia ; illustrated by Gabriel Picolo ; with Jon Sommariva and Emma Kubert ; colorist, David Calderon ; letterer, Tom Napolitano ; Raven created by Marv Wolfman and George Pérez. DC Ink 2019 192 p. color illustrations $16.99

Grades: 7 8 9 10 11 12 **741.5**

1. Orphans -- Fiction 2. Psychic ability -- Fiction 3. Graphic novels

ISBN 1401286232; 9781401286231

LC 2018043961

"When a tragic accident takes the life of . . . Raven Roth's foster mom, . . . she moves to New Orleans to recover. . . . Starting over isn't easy. . . . But as she grows closer to her new friends, her foster sister, Max and Tommy Torres, a guy who accepts her for who she is now, Raven has to decide if she's ready to face what's buried in the past . . . and the darkness building inside her." (Publisher's note)

"Garcia makes great use of teenage emotion and drama in this origin story, and it's nicely carried out in Picolo's expressive artwork, largely in black, white, and gray. Calderon uses cool color washes, featuring lots of purple, for Raven, which emphasizes her powers and keeps the focus of the story on her." Booklist

Gillman, Melanie

★ **As** the crow flies; by Melanie Gillman. Iron Circus Comics 2017 272 p chiefly color illustrations paperback $30

Grades: 7 8 9 10 11 12 **741.5**

1. Gender identity -- Fiction 2. Teenagers -- Graphic novels 3. Religious camps -- Comic books, strips, etc.

ISBN 9781945820069; 1945820063

Stonewall Book Award Honor Book: Children's & Young Adult Literature (2018)

In this book, by Melanie Gillman, "Charlie Lamonte is thirteen years old, queer, black, and questioning what was once a firm belief in God. So naturally, she's spending a week of her summer vacation stuck at an all-white Christian youth backpacking camp. As the journey wears on and the rhetoric wears thin, she can't help but poke holes in the pious obliviousness of this storied sanctuary with little regard for people like herself . . . or her fellow camper, Sydney." (Publisher's note)

"This contemplative graphic novel, taken from Gillman's ongoing webcomic, perceptively explores race, gender, faith, and friendship. Elegantly composed, richly hued images vividly portray the lush forest setting and shy, thoughtful Charlie's inner turmoil as she yearns to voice her opinions." SLJ

Glass, Bryan J. L.

The **mice** templar, volume one: the prophecy; created by Bryan J.L. Glass & Michael Avon Oeming. Image Comics 2008 256p il $29.99

Grades: 6 7 8 9 10 11 12 Adult **741.5**

1. Graphic novels 2. Fantasy graphic novels 3. Adventure graphic novels 4. Mice -- Graphic novels

ISBN 978-1-58240-871-2; 1-58240-871-8

In a land populated by animals, the Mice Templar used to protect the people of the mouse kingdom, but a civil war destroyed them; the king now employs rat soldiers, and they prey upon the mouse villages. Young Karic still idolizes the Mice Templar, but everything he knows and believes is shattered when his village is raided by rats, burned, and his family captured as slaves. He survives, saved by a mysterious mouse named Pilot, who says he was once a Templar and offers to train Karic. The salmon in the river say that Karic is the one prophesied to restore the Templar, but can he truly be the one? The book includes considerable battle violence.

"Equal parts Norse myth, Arthurian legend, and Mrs. Frisby and the Rats of N.I.M.H., The Mice Templar series re-imagines the warrior animal tale with just enough of its own spin to make it well worth adding to the collection." Voice Youth Advocates

Other titles in this series are:
Destiny Part One (2010)
Destiny Part Two (2010)
Legend (2013)
A Midwinter Night's Dream (2012)

Gownley, Jimmy

Amelia rules!: the whole world's crazy! Renaissance Press 2003 176p $24.95; pa $14.95

Grades: 3 4 5 6 **741.5**

1. Graphic novels 2. Humorous graphic novels 3. Friendship -- Graphic novels 4. Family life -- Graphic novels

ISBN 0-9712169-3-2; 0-9712169-2-4 pa

"Amelia . . . is getting used to life with her newly divorced mom and her hip, young aunt Tanner; settling in at a strange new school; and finding a group of friends. Amelia is no sweet innocent, nor are her three G.A.S.P (Gathering of Awesome Superpals) buddies: Reggie, superhero in the making; Rhonda, Amelia's tough bete noire with a fourth-grade 'thing' for Reggie; and quiet, mysterious Pajamaman. Jealousy, meanness, sadness, and confusion, as well as surprising generosity, and love crisscross the pages in energetic, freewheeling, full-color cartoon art that unwraps a kid's-eye view of life honestly, poignantly, and with a hefty dollop of melodrama." Booklist

Other titles in this series are:
Amelia rules!: What makes you happy? (2004)
Amelia rules! Superheroes (2005)
Amelia rules! a very ninja Christmas (2009)
Amelia rules! When the past is a present (2010)
Amelia rules! The tweenage guide to not being unpopular (2010)
Amelia rules! True things (adults don't want kids to know (2010)
Amelia rules! The meaning of life. . . and other stuff (2011)
Amelia rules! Her permanent record (2012)

The **dumbest** idea ever! by Jimmy Gownley. Graphix / Scholastic 2014 240 p. color illustrations $24.99

Grades: 5 6 7 **741.5**

1. High school -- Graphic novels 2. Autobiographical graphic novels

ISBN 0545453461; 9780545453462; 9780545453479

LC 2013939128

In this graphic memoir by Jimmy Gownley, "at thirteen, Jimmy was popular, at the top of his class, and the leading scorer on his basketball team. But . . . when chicken pox forced him to miss the championship game . . . , he got pneumonia and missed . . . school. Before Jimmy knew it, his grades were sinking and nothing seemed to be going right. How would Jimmy turn things around, get back on top at school, and maybe even get a date with the cutest girl in school?" (Publisher's note)

"[Gownley] recounts his beginnings as a cartoonist. . . . Humble, endearing and utterly easy to relate to." Kirkus

Grayson, Devin

Uglies; Shay's story. created by Scott Westerfeld ; written by Scott Westerfeld and Devin Grayson ; illustrations by Steven Cummings. Del Rey 2012 160 p. chiefly ill. (prebind) $22.10; (paperback) $10.99

Grades: 7 8 9 10 **741.5**

1. Dystopian graphic novels 2. Conformity -- Graphic novels 3. Plastic surgery -- Graphic novels 4. Science fiction 5. Friendship -- Fiction 6. Beauty, Personal -- Fiction

ISBN 9780606264754; 0345527224; 9780345527226

LC 2012374898

This young adult graphic novel retells the story of author Scott Westerfeld's dystopia "Uglies" from "the point of view of recurring frenemy Shay." It is "set in a . . . future time when discord is suppressed through ruthlessly enforced conformity and obligatory plastic surgery at age 16. . . . Shay yearns for freedom. An encounter with the flawed and alluring David, a covert envoy from the Smoke, a secret community of nonconformists, may offer Shay the escape she craves." (Publishers Weekly)

Followed by:
Uglies: Cutters (2012)

Gulledge, Laura Lee

Will & whit; Laura Lee Gulledge. Abrams Book 2013 192 p. ill. (paperback) $12.95

Grades: 7 8 9 10 **741.5**

1. Grief -- Graphic novels 2. Fear of the dark -- Graphic novels

ISBN 1419705466; 9781419705465

LC 2012955192

In this graphic novel, by Laura Lee Gulledge, "Wilhelmina 'Will' Huxstep is a creative soul struggling to come to terms with a family tragedy. She crafts whimsical lamps, in part to deal with her fear of the dark. . . . She longs for unplugged adventures with her fellow creative friends, Autumn, Noel, and Reese. Little does she know that she will get her wish in the form of an arts carnival and a blackout . . . which forces Will to face her fear of darkness." (Publisher's note)

Hale, Nathan

Nathan Hale's hazardous tales; one dead spy. Nathan Hale. Amulet Books 2012 128 p. (hardcover) $12.95

Grades: 3 4 5 6 7 **741.5**

1. Storytelling -- Graphic novels 2. United States -- History -- Graphic novels

ISBN 141970396X; 9781419703966

LC 2012947189

In this graphic novel, historical figure "[Nathan] Hale, convicted of espionage, forestalls death by telling stories from American history. In this volume, he's helped by the hangman in telling the story of the early days of the revolution. He takes readers from his college days at Yale to the Boston Massacre, the Boston Tea Party, his joining the 7th Connecticut regiment, the Battle of Bunker Hill and other pivotal scenes in New England and New York City." (Kirkus)

Other titles in this series are:
Big bad ironclad! (2012)
Donner dinner party (2013)
Treaties, trenches, mud, and blood (2014)
The underground abductor (2015)
Alamo all-stars (2016)

Raid of no return (2017)
Lafayette! (2018)

★ The **underground** abductor; an abolitionist tale. Nathan Hale. Harry N Abrams Inc. 2015 125 p. illustrations (chiefly color) (Nathan Hale's Hazardous Tales) (hardcover) $12.95
Grades: 3 4 5 6 7 **741.5**
1. Biographical graphic novels 2. Underground Railroad -- Comic books, strips, etc. 3. Fugitive slaves -- United States -- Comic books, strips, etc.
ISBN 9781419715365; 1419715364
Eisner Nominee: Best Publication for Kids (2016)
In this graphic novel, "a fictionalized Nathan Hale (a patriot from the American Revolutionary War) tells stories about America's most extraordinary heroes and villains. In this installment, Hale tells his British captors about Harriet Tubman, the spy and nurse who helped hundreds of American slaves run away in the 1800s on the Underground Railroad." (School Library Journal)
Includes bibliographical references

Hale, Shannon
★ **Best** friends; Shannon Hale ; artwork by LeUyen Pham ; color by Hilary Sycamore. First Second 2019 239 p. chiefly color illustrations (hardcover) $21.99
Grades: 3 4 5 6 **741.5**
1. Peer pressure -- Fiction 2. Girls -- Fiction 3. Social acceptance -- Fiction 4. Peer pressure 5. Preteen girls 6. Social acceptance
ISBN 9781250317452; 9781250317469
LC 2018953553
"Sixth grade is supposed to be perfect. Shannon's got a sure spot in the in-crowd called The Group, and her best friend is their leader, Jen, the most popular girl in school. But the rules are always changing, and Shannon has to scramble to keep up. She never knows which TV shows are cool, what songs to listen to, and who she's allowed to talk to. Who makes these rules, anyway? And does Shannon have to follow them?" (Publisher's note)
"Pham's art is evocative in its simplicity; detailed facial expressions add emotional depth and accessibility for even the most reluctant readers. An author's note talks earnestly and age-appropriately about anxiety. Consider this a must-read for fans of Raina Telegmeier or Victoria Jamieson." Kirkus

★ **Rapunzel's** revenge; [by] Shannon and Dean Hale; illustrated by Nathan Hale. Bloomsbury 2008 144p il map $18.99; pa $14.99
Grades: 5 6 7 8 **741.5**
1. Graphic novels 2. Fantasy graphic novels 3. Humorous graphic novels 4. Fairy tales -- Graphic novels
ISBN 1-59990-070-X; 1-59990-288-5 pa; 978-1-59990-070-4; 978-1-59990-288-3 pa
LC 2007-37670
In this graphic novel, Rapunzel escapes "from the enchanted tree where Mother Gothel imprisoned her. Rapunzel sets off alone through the ghost towns and Badlands of Gothel's Reach. She is determined to find Gothel's Villa and teach Mother Gothel a long-overdue lesson for her years of treachery and lies, and help her real mother get out of the mine camps where Mother Gothel has kept her enslaved." (Publisher's note)
"The dialogue is witty, the story is an enticing departure from the original, and the illustrations are magically fun and expressive." SLJ
Another title about these characters is:
Calamity Jack (2009)

★ **Real** friends; Shannon Hale ; illustrated by LeUyen Pham. First Second 2017 224 p. color illustrations (hardcover) $21.99
Grades: 3 4 5 6 **741.5**
1. Bullies 2. Friendship
ISBN 9781626724167; 9781626727854
LC 2016945552
In this graphic memoir, by Shannon Hale, illustrated by LeUyen Pham, "Shannon and Adrienne have been best friends ever since they were little. But one day, Adrienne starts hanging out with Jen, the most popular girl in class and the leader of a circle of friends called The Group. Everyone in The Group wants to be Jen's #1, and some girls would do anything to stay on top . . . even if it means bullying others." (Publisher's note)
"The author reflects on her life from the vantage point of adulthood, displaying a mature awareness of her own flaws and an understanding of the behavior of unsympathetic kids such as Wendy and Jenny, and her accessible writing and hopeful tone will speak to readers. Pham's gentle cartoon images make effective use of perspective and composition to underscore Shannon's sense of alienation." SLJ

Harrell, Rob
Monster on the Hill; by Rob Harrell. Top Shelf Productions 2013 192 p. color illustrations pbk $19.95
Grades: 4 5 6 7 8 **741.5**
1. Monsters -- Graphic novels 2. Friendship -- Graphic novels
ISBN 1603090754; 9781603090759
This graphic novel by Rob Harrell is set in "1860s England [where] every . . . township is terrorized by a . . . monster - much to the townsfolk's delight! Each town's . . . monster is a source of local pride [and] tourism. Unfortunately, for . . . Stoker-on-Avon, their monster isn't quite as impressive. Can the morose Rayburn get a monstrous makeover and become a proper horror? It's up to the eccentric Dr. Charles Wilkie and plucky street urchin Timothy to get him up to snuff." (Publisher's note)

Hart, Christopher, 1957-
The **master** guide to drawing anime; how to draw original characters from simple templates. Christopher Hart. Sixth&Spring Books 2015 144 p. color illustrations pbk $19.95
Grades: 7 8 9 10 11 12 **741.5**
1. Manga -- Drawing 2. Cartooning -- Technique
ISBN 9781936096862; 1936096862
LC 2014030200
Nothing brings anime artists more satisfaction than creating original characters to use in a comic strip or graphic novel. . . . Christopher Hart helps them reach this goal by providing insight into the six most popular anime types: schoolgirls, schoolboys, preteens, vengeful bad guys, humorous personalities, and fantasy figures. He supplies templates for each; an extensive array of 'menus' of head and body types, outfits, and accessories; and detailed, accessible, step-by-step demonstrations and drawing exercises." (Publisher's note)

Hatke, Ben
Mighty Jack; Volume 1 Ben Hatke ; color by Alex Campbell and Hilary Sycamore. First Second 2016 203 p. chiefly color illustrations $14.99
Grades: 4 5 6 7 **741.5**
1. Fantasy fiction 2. Autistic children -- Fiction 3. Brothers and

sisters -- Fiction
ISBN 1626722641; 9781626722644

LC 2015951861

In this book, by Ben Hatke, "Jack might be the only kid in the world who's dreading summer. But he's got a good reason: summer is when his single mom takes a second job and leaves him at home to watch his autistic kid sister, Maddy. It's a lot of responsibility, and it's boring, too, because Maddy doesn't talk. Ever. But then, one day at the flea market, Maddy does talk—to tell Jack to trade their mom's car for a box of mysterious seeds. It's the best mistake Jack has ever made." (Publisher's note)

Another title in this series is:
Mighty Jack and the goblin king (2017)

Mighty Jack and the Goblin King; Ben Hatke. First Second 2017 208 p. chiefly color illustrations (pbk.) $14.99; (hardcover) $22.99

Grades: 4 5 6 7 **741.5**

1. Magic -- Fiction 2. Monsters -- Graphic novels 3. Siblings -- Graphic novels
ISBN 9781626722668; 9781626722675

LC 2016961549

"In this follow-up to Mighty Jack, the titular character and his friend Lilly travel through a portal in search of Jack's sister, Maddy, who has been kidnapped by an ogre. The duo are separated and must battle their own monsters, helped along the way by even more winsome and fantastical creatures than in the first volume." (School Library Journal)

Heuvel, Eric

A **family** secret; [English translation, Lorraine T. Miller] Farrar, Straus and Giroux 2009 62p il pa $9.99; $18.99

Grades: 7 8 9 10 11 12 **741.5**

1. Graphic novels 2. Jews -- Graphic novels 3. Grandmothers -- Graphic novels 4. Holocaust, 1933-1945 -- Graphic novels
ISBN 0-374-32271-6; 978-0-374-42265-3 pa; 0-374-42265-6 pa; 978-0-374-32271-7

LC 2009-13943

Original Dutch edition, 2003

While searching his Dutch grandmother's attic for yard sale items, Jeroen finds a scrapbook which leads Gran to tell of her experiences as a girl living in Amsterdam during the Holocaust, when her father was a Nazi sympathizer and Esther, her Jewish best friend, disappeared

This is a "moving graphic novel. . . . The art is in ink and watercolor, with very clear, highly detailed panels. . . . [A] gripping story." Booklist

Hicks, Faith Erin

The **divided** earth; Faith Erin Hicks ; color by Jordie Bellaire. First Second 2018 272 p. chiefly color illustrations (The nameless city) (hbk.) $21.99

Grades: 5 6 7 8 9 10 **741.5**

1. Fantasy fiction 2. Friendship -- Fiction 3. Cities and towns -- Fiction
ISBN 1626721610; 9781626721609; 9781626721616

LC 2017957143

Eisner Award: Best Publication for Kids (2019)

"The Nameless City--held by the rogue Dao prince Erzi--is under siege by a coalition of Dao and Yisun forces who are determined to end the war for the Nameless City once and for all. . . . Rat and Kai must infiltrate Erzi's palace and steal back the ancient and deadly formula for napatha, the ancient weapon of mass destruction Erzi has unearthed--before he can use it to destroy everything Rat and Kai hold dear!" (Publisher's note)

"Bold, dynamic drawings and rich, nuanced coloring heighten the drama; occasionally, the action breaks through the panel into the white space, as if the explosive force of Napatha and the energy and vitality of the heroic duo cannot be contained." VOYA

Friends with boys; Faith Erin Hicks. First Second 2012 un chiefly ill $16.99

Grades: 6 7 8 9 10 **741.5**

1. Ghost stories 2. Graphic novels 3. Teenagers -- Fiction
ISBN 9781596435568

LC 2011030470

In this graphic novel, "[the] youngest of four siblings and the only girl, Maggie is both excited and worried about starting high school after being home-schooled her whole life. . . . As Maggie makes friends with a perky indie girl named Lucy and her mysterious brother, Alistair, she broods over the loss of her mother, who recently left the family without much of an explanation, and tries to figure out what the ghost wants from her." (Bulletin of the Center for Children's Books)

★ The **Nameless** City; Faith Erin Hicks ; color by Jordie Bellaire. First Second 2016 240 p. chiefly color illustrations (trade pbk.) $14.99

Grades: 5 6 7 8 9 10 **741.5**

1. Friendship -- Fiction 2. Fantasy graphic novels 3. Survival skills -- Fiction 4. Cities and towns -- Fiction 5. Survival -- Fiction
ISBN 1626721564; 9781626721562; 9781626721579

LC 2015020651

"Every nation that invades the City gives it a new name. . . . The natives don't let themselves get caught up in the unending wars. To them, their home is the Nameless City. . . . Kaidu is . . . a Dao born and bred--a member of the latest occupying nation. Rat is a native of the Nameless City. At first, she hates Kai for everything he stands for, but his love of his new home may be the one thing that can bring these two unlikely friends together." (Publisher's note)

"With comprehensive world building, well-rounded characters, and entertaining action, this expertly executed story will find a home with a wide variety of readers, all of whom will be eagerly awaiting the next installment." Booklist

The **stone** heart; Faith Erin Hicks. First Second 2017 256 p. chiefly color illustrations (The nameless city) (hardcover) $21.99

Grades: 5 6 7 8 9 10 **741.5**

1. Magic -- Fiction 2. Adventure fiction 3. Fantasy fiction -- Graphic novels
ISBN 1626721599; 9781626721586; 9781626721593

LC 2016938731

In this book, by Faith Erin Hicks, "Kaidu and Rat have only just recovered from the assassination attempt on the General of All Blades when more chaos breaks loose in the Nameless City: deep conflicts within the Dao nation are making it impossible to find a political solution for the disputed territory of the City itself." (Publisher's note)

"Flourishing from the strong worldbuilding and characterization of the first installment, this middle volume . . . provides a vital and enthralling closer look at those readers have already met as well as unfurling more of the Chinese-inspired city's past, as colorist Bellaire brings all to stunning emotional life." Kirkus

The **war** at Ellsmere. Slave Labor Graphics 2008 156p il pa $12.95

Grades: 6 7 8 9 10 11 **741.5**

1. Graphic novels 2. Humorous graphic novels 3. Friendship --

Graphic novels 4. School stories -- Graphic novels
ISBN 1-59362-140-X; 978-1-59362-140-7

Juniper is the newest scholarship student at the prestigious Ellsmere Academy; she wanted to attend there in order to increase her chances of getting into a good medical school. She's on scholarship because her mom has had to raise her alone since her father died when she was young. Jun makes one friend at Ellsmere, Cassie, who calls herself the cliche of the poor little rich girl. Wealthy Emily calls Cassie "Orphan" because her parents ignore her, and chooses to call Jun "Project," as in Headmistress Ms. Bishop's latest project. Emily is also determined to get rid of Jun, especially when Jun encourages Cassie to work harder and even win the extra credit essay contest. Now it's war, or as Jun puts it, "It's like Upstairs Downstairs meets Lord of the Flies. In plaid skirts. And sweater vests." There's one incident when Jun punches Emily in the face.

"Hicks gives readers enough tension and quirky turns to satisfy and pleasantly surprise." Booklist

Hinds, Gareth, 1971-

Beowulf; adapted and illustrated by Gareth Hinds. Candlewick Press 2007 un il $21.99; pa $9.99

Grades: 8 9 10 11 12 Adult **741.5**

1. Graphic novels 2. Adventure graphic novels 3. Beowulf -- Graphic novels 4. Monsters -- Graphic novels
ISBN 978-0-7636-3022-5; 0-7636-3022-5; 978-0-7636-3023-2 pa; 0-7636-3023-3 pa

LC 2006-49023

Graphic novel adaptation of the Old English epic poem, Beowulf

"For fantasy fans both young and old, this makes an ideal introduction to a story without which the entire fantasy genre would look very different; many scenes may be too intense for very young readers." Publ Wkly

The **Iliad**; Gareth Hinds. Candlewick Press 2019 272 p. color illustrations $16.99

Grades: 7 8 9 10 11 12 **741.5**

1. Trojan War -- Graphic novels 2. Greek mythology -- Graphic novels
ISBN 0763696633; 9780763696634

LC 2018961357

"In this stunning graphic novel adaptation . . . , renowned illustrator Gareth Hinds captures all the grim glory of Homer's epic. Dynamic illustrations take readers directly to the plains of Troy, into the battle itself, and lay bare the complex emotions of the men, women, and gods whose struggles fueled the war and determined its outcome." (Publisher's note)

"The excellent visual guides, maps, and notes aid in this task and further contextualize the epic's time, place, and significance. The most striking scenes are the battles, presented in intimate detail and in awe-inspiring, sweeping overviews. Hinds's relatively plain language retains just enough meter to hint at the cadences of the work, and, together with the dynamic art, creates an accessible entrée to an enduring classic." Pub Wkly

Includes bibliographical references

★ **King** Lear; a play by William Shakespeare; adapted and illustrated by Gareth Hinds. Candlewick Press 2009 123p il $22.99; pa $11.99

Grades: 7 8 9 10 11 12 **741.5**

1. Poets 2. Authors 3. Dramatists 4. Graphic novels
ISBN 978-0-7636-4343-0; 0-7636-4343-2; 978-0-7636-4344-7 pa; 0-7636-4344-0 pa

A reissue of the title first published 2007 by Thecomic.com

"Employing a range of artistic styles that convey dramatic mood, the artist begins the play almost as a fairy tale, featuring bright, softly washed drawings. Once Cordelia is cast out and things sour, the images become darker and more compact. As the king descends into madness, the art becomes downright menacing, with Lear appearing as a jagged, ghostly figure drawn with white pencil on a dark background." (Kirkus)

The **merchant** of Venice; a play. by William Shakespeare; adapted and illustrated by Gareth Hinds. Candlewick Press 2008 68p il $21.99; pa $11.99

Grades: 8 9 10 11 12 Adult **741.5**

1. Poets 2. Authors 3. Dramatists 4. Graphic novels
ISBN 978-0-7636-3024-9; 978-0-7636-3025-6 pa

LC 2007-938349

Hinds uses a sketchy art style and blue and gray tones to illustrate his graphic adaptation of Shakespeare's controversial play. He sets the play in modern Venice and uses more modern language, including prose, at the beginning of the play and then gradually returns to Shakespeare's original language for the courtroom scenes. The play tells the story of a debt owed to a Jewish merchant of Venice, of a strong-willed young woman who is determined to choose her own husband, and of the quest to save a young man from the fate of having a pound of flesh cut from him.

"Fans of the play will find this an intriguing adaptation." Publ Wkly

The **most** excellent and lamentable tragedy of Romeo & Juliet; a play by William Shakespeare. by William Shakespeare, adapted and illustrated by Gareth Hinds. Candlewick Press 2013 128 p. (hardcover) $21.99; (pbk.) $12.99

Grades: 7 8 9 10 **741.5**

1. Graphic novels
ISBN 0763659487; 0763668079; 9780763659486; 9780763668075

LC 2012950561

This book by Gareth Hinds presents a graphic novel adaptation of William Shakespeare's play "Romeo and Juliet." "The most notable change between this story and Shakespeare's original is the creative license that Hinds takes with ethnicity--he makes the characters of African, Indian, and Caucasian descent in order to promote the universality of the story. The Shakespearean language is abridged but not adapted into contemporary English." (School Library Journal)

"Cleaving to Shakespeare's words and dramatic arc, Hinds (The Merchant of Venice) creates another splendid graphic novel, tracing each scene in taut, coherent dialogue. The characters, in period dress modified by a few more contemporary touches, are poignantly specific yet universal. Hinds delivers the play's essence and beauty, its glorious language, furious conflict, yearning love, and wrenching tragedy." (Horn Book)

★ The **Odyssey**; a graphic novel. by Gareth Hinds. Candlewick Press 2010 248 p. col. ill. $24.99

Grades: 7 8 9 10 11 12 Adult **741.5**

1. Poets 2. Authors 3. Graphic novels 4. Odyssey 5. Greek mythology -- Graphic novels 6. Mythology, Greek
ISBN 0763642665; 0763642681; 9780763642662; 9780763642686

LC 2010007512

"Retells, in graphic novel format, Homer's epic tale of Odysseus, the ancient Greek hero who encounters witches and other obstacles on his journey home after fighting in the Trojan War." (Publisher's note)

This is "the most lavish retelling of Homer yet. . . . Hinds lets the epic story take its time, with a slow build and pages that aren't afraid to alternate packed dialogue with titanic action. The sumptuous art, produced with grain, texture, and hue, evokes a time long past while detailing every line and drop of sweat on Odysseus' face and conveying the sheer grandeur of seeing a god rise out of the ocean." Booklist

Holm, Jennifer L.

★ **Sunny** side up; Jennifer L. Holm & Matthew Holm ; with color by Lark Pien. Graphix 2015 224 p. illustrations (jacketed hardcover) $23.99

Grades: 3 4 5 6 **741.5**

1. Adventure fiction 2. Summer -- Fiction 3. Florida -- Fiction 4. Friendship -- Fiction 5. Grandfathers -- Fiction

ISBN 0545741653 ; 9780545741651

LC 2014957906

Eisner Nominee: Best Publication for Kids (2016)

In this book, by Jennifer L. Holm, illustrated by Matthew Holm, "Sunny Lewin has been packed off to Florida to live with her grandfather for the summer. At first she thought Florida might be fun. . . . But the place where Gramps lives is no amusement park. It's full of . . . old people. Really old people. Luckily, Sunny isn't the only kid around. She meets Buzz, a boy who is completely obsessed with comic books, and soon they're having adventures of their own." (Publisher's note)

"Woven into the Florida frolic though, through dated flashback images, is the real reason for Sunny's last-minute visit: her older brother is struggling with addiction, and Sunny thinks she got him in trouble. Though Sunny will appeal to all kinds of readers, an authors' note shares the Holms' hope to let kids in similar situations know that it's OK to feel sad and to talk about it. Clear dialogue bubbles, plenty of wordless spreads, and Matthew's cartoons and beach-umbrella color palette keep Sunny's story an upbeat one that readers will easily stick with." Booklist

Other titles in this series are:

Swing it, Sunny (2017)

Sunny rolls the dice (2019)

Swing it, Sunny! Jennifer L. Holm & Matthew Holm ; with color by Lark Pien. Scholastic Press 2017 224 p. chiefly color illustrations (hardcover) $24.99; (pbk.) $12.99

Grades: 3 4 5 6 **741.5**

1. Middle schools -- Fiction 2. Family problems -- Fiction 3. Brothers and sisters -- Fiction 4. Graphic novels 5. Schools -- Fiction 6. Middle schools -- Fiction 7. Brothers and sisters -- Fiction 8. Dysfunctional families -- Fiction 9. Middle schools -- Comic books, strips, etc 10. Brothers and sisters -- Comic books, strips, etc 11. Dysfunctional families -- Comic books, strips, etc

ISBN 9780545741705; 9780545741729; 9780545741767

LC 2016054939

In this book, by Jennifer and Matthew Holm, "Summer's over and it's time for Sunny Lewin to enter the strange and unfriendly hallways of . . . middle school. When her Gramps calls her from Florida to ask how she's doing, she always tells him she's fine. But the truth? Sunny is NOT having the best time." (Publisher's note)

"Using a combination of short exchanges of dialogue and frequent wordless reaction shots, the Holms again leverage simply drawn scenes colored by Pien into a loosely autobiographical narrative that is poignant and hilarious in turn and emotionally rich throughout." Kirkus

Horikoshi, Kohei

★ **My** Hero Academia; Volume 1 story & art Kohei Horikoshi ; translation & English adaptation Caleb Cook. Viz 2015 187 p. chiefly illustrations $9.99

Grades: 7 8 9 10 11 12 **741.5**

1. Manga 2. Shonen manga 3. Superheroes -- Fiction 4. High schools -- Fiction 5. High school students -- Fiction

ISBN 1421582694; 9781421582696

"What would the world be like if 80 percent of the population manifested superpowers called 'Quirks' at age four? Heroes and villains would be battling it out everywhere! Being a hero would mean learning to use your power, but where would you go to study? The Hero Academy of course! But what would you do if you were one of the 20 percent who were born Quirkless? Middle school student Izuku Midoriya wants to be a hero more than anything, but he hasn't got an ounce of power in him. With no chance of ever getting into the prestigious U.A. High School for budding heroes, his life is looking more and more like a dead end. Then an encounter with All Might, the greatest hero of them all, gives him a chance to change his destiny." (Publisher's note)

Volume 1 of an ongoing series

Horowitz, Anthony

Stormbreaker : the graphic novel; [by] Anthony Horowitz; adapted Antony Johnston; illustrated by Kanako Damerum & Yusuru Takasaki. Philomel Books 2006 un il (Alex Rider) pa $14.99

Grades: 5 6 7 8 **741.5**

1. Graphic novels 2. Spies -- Graphic novels

ISBN 0-399-24633-9

In this graphic novel version on Horowitz's novel, fourteen-year-old Alex Rider is coerced into continuing his uncle's dangerous work for Britain's intelligence agency, MI6.

"If it's possible, this is even more rapidly paced than the novel. Alex remains an appealing hero here, and the idea of a heroic teen up against insidious adults continues to be an extremely powerful draw for readers." Booklist

Other graphic novel adaptations in this series are:

Point blank (2007)

Skeleton key (2009)

Eagle strike (2012)

Hosler, Jay

Clan Apis. Active Synapse 2000 158p il pa $15

Grades: 4 5 6 7 8 9 10 11 12 **741.5**

1. Graphic novels 2. Bees -- Graphic novels 3. Science -- Graphic novels

ISBN 0-9677255-0-X

"Opening with a creation myth . . . and working through the biological, sociological, and ecological changes affecting the life of Nyuki the bee, the text is a combination of authoritative science; appealing, detailed black-and-white drawings; and dialogue replete with humor, pubescent angst, political sloganeering, and more. Nyuki's colony undertakes migration to a new hive, is beset by a woodpecker, and hibernates through a winter that yields to a revitalizing spring." Booklist

Hotta, Yumi

Hikaru No Go, Volume 1; [by] Yumi Hotta and Takeshi Obata. Viz Media, LLC 2004 192p il pa $7.95

Grades: 5 6 7 8 9 10 11 12 **741.5**

1. Manga 2. Shonen manga 3. Graphic novels 4. Board games -- Graphic novels

ISBN 1-59116-222-X

Sixth-grade Hikaru Shindo's discovery of a bloodstained game board leads to an encounter with the ghost of Go master Fujiwara-no-Sai and the formation of an unbeatable Go team.

Volume 1 of 23

Humphries, Sam

Jonesy; Volume 1 by Sam Humphries & Caitlin Rose Boyle ; colors by Mickey Quinn ; letters by Corey Breen ; cover by Caitlin Rose Boyle. Boom! Studios 2016 112 p. chiefly color illustrations $9.99

Grades: 7 8 9 10 11 12 **741.5**

1. Fantasy fiction 2. Humorous fiction 3. Teenage girls -- Fiction
ISBN 1608868834; 9781608868834

"Jonesy is a self-described 'cool dork.' . . . But she has a secret nobody knows. She has the power to make people fall in love! . . . There's only one catch--it doesn't work on herself. She's gonna have to find love the old-fashioned way, and in the meantime, figure out how to distract herself from the real emotions she inevitably has to face when her powers go wrong." (Publisher's note)

Volume 1 of 3

Igarashi, Daisuke

Children of the sea, vol. 1. Viz Media/Viz Signature 2009 320p il pa $14.99

Grades: 7 8 9 10 11 12 **741.5**

1. Manga 2. Seinen manga 3. Graphic novels 4. Fantasy graphic novels 5. Mystery graphic novels 6. Adventure graphic novels 7. Ocean -- Graphic novels
ISBN 978-1-4215-2914-1; 1-4215-2914-9

"Igarashi's storytelling is quiet, thoughtful, and thought provoking, but it is his drawings that make this manga so amazing. Extremely detailed settings turn panels into mini-masterpieces." Booklist

Volume 1 of 5

Inzana, Ryan

Ichiro; written & illustrated by Ryan Inzana. Houghton Mifflin/Houghton Mifflin Harcourt 2012 288 p. ill. (chiefly col.)

Grades: 7 8 9 10 **741.5**

1. Fantasy graphic novels 2. Supernatural graphic novels 3. Japan -- History -- Graphic novels 4. Folklore -- Japan -- Graphic novels 5. Japanese Americans -- Graphic novels 6. Graphic novels 7. Japan -- Fiction 8. Monsters -- Fiction 9. Grandfathers -- Fiction 10. Supernatural -- Fiction 11. Gods and goddesses -- Fiction
ISBN 0547252692; 9780547252698

LC 2011277558

This graphic novel depicts the story of Ichiro, "a young American teen, son of a Japanese immigrant and an American soldier killed in combat, [who] goes to Japan with his mother for an extended visit and begins to grapple with sophisticated cultural complexities. . . . After his mother and Japanese grandfather tell him stories of Japanese history and folklore, Ichiro has a fantastical adventure involving the Japanese myth of the shape-shifting tanuki spirit." (Kirkus Reviews)

Jablonski, Carla

Resistance, book 1; art by Leland Purvis; color by Hilary Sycamore. First Second Books 2010 121p il (Resistance) pa $16.99

Grades: 6 7 8 9 10 11 12 **741.5**

1. Graphic novels 2. Adventure graphic novels 3. World War, 1939-1945 -- Jews -- Rescue -- Graphic novels 4. World War, 1939-1945 -- Underground movements -- Graphic novels 5. France -- History -- 1940-1945, German occupation -- Graphic novels
ISBN 978-1-59643-291-8; 1-59643-291-8

Paul and his younger sister Marie live in a small village in Vichy France during World War II. Thus far, the war hasn't really touched them, but now Nazi soldiers come, and Paul's friend, Henri, and his parents are Jews and therefore in danger. When Paul and Marie try to protect Henri, their secret leaks out to members of the Resistance. Although they are young, they soon become recruits in the Resistance. Paul's incessant sketching in his book turns out to be a valuable talent, but he and Marie, and then their older sister, Sylvie, don't quite realize just how dangerous things can get. The cover is very striking, with Paul aiming a slingshot at a Nazi soldier. The Author's Note at the end of the book talks about history, the Resistance, and why the events in France during World War II should not be depicted as black and white, heroic Resistance versus villainous Vichy.

Other titles in this series are:
Defiance (2011)
Victory (2012)

Jacques, Brian

Redwall : the graphic novel; by Brian Jacques; illustrated by Bret Blevins; adapted by Stuart Moore; lettering by Richard Starkings. Philomel Books 2007 143p il pa $12.99

Grades: 4 5 6 7 8 9 **741.5**

1. Graphic novels 2. Fantasy graphic novels 3. Adventure graphic novels 4. Mice -- Graphic novels
ISBN 978-0-399-24481-0; 0-399-24481-6

When Cluny the rat's army attacks Redwall Abbey, young Matthias the mouse follows in the footsteps of the long-ago hero Martin the Warrior to defend his home

"The story is a page-turner, and the detailed black-and-white drawings capture both the passion and the pathos." SLJ

Jamieson, Victoria

★ **All's** faire in middle school; Victoria Jamieson. Dial Books for Young Readers 2017 248 p. chiefly color illustrations (hardcover) $20.99; (pbk.) $12.99

Grades: 4 5 6 7 8 **741.5**

1. Friendship -- Fiction 2. Family life -- Fiction 3. Middle schools -- Fiction
ISBN 0525429999; 9780525429982; 9780525429999

LC 2016044190

In this book, by Victoria Jamieson, "eleven-year-old Imogene (Impy) has grown up with two parents working at the Renaissance Faire, and she's eager to begin her own training as a squire. First, though, she'll need to prove her bravery. Luckily Impy has just the quest in mind--she'll go to public school after a life of being homeschooled! But it's not easy to act like a noble knight-in-training in middle school. Impy falls in with a group of girls who seem really nice (until they don't)." (Publisher's note)

"Jamieson masterfully taps into the voice and concerns of middle-schoolers, and the offbeat setting of the Renaissance faire adds some lively texture." Booklist

★ **Roller** girl; by Victoria Jamieson. Dial Books 2015 240 p. chiefly color illustrations (paperback) $12.99

Grades: 4 5 6 7 8 **741.5**

1. Graphic novels 2. Friendship -- Fiction 3. Roller derby -- Fiction 4. Roller skating -- Fiction
ISBN 0803740166; 9780803740167

LC 2014011310

Newbery Honor Book (2016)
Eisner Nominee: Best Publication for Kids (2016)

This graphic novel, by Victoria Jamieson, is "about friendship and surviving junior high through the power of roller derby. For most of her twelve years, Astrid has done everything with her best friend Nicole. But after Astrid falls in love with roller derby and signs up for derby camp,

Nicole decides to go to dance camp instead. And so begins the most difficult summer of Astrid's life as she struggles to keep up with the older girls at camp." (Publisher's note)

"Jamieson captures this snapshot of preteen angst with a keenly decisive eye, brilliantly juxtaposing the nuances of roller derby with the twists and turns of adolescent girls' friendships." Kirkus

Johnson, Cathy G.

The **breakaways**; Cathy G. Johnson ; colors by Kevin Czap. First Second 2019 224 p. chiefly color illustrations (hardcover) $19.99

Grades: 4 5 6 7 8 **741.5**

1. Soccer -- Fiction 2. Schools -- Fiction 3. Middle schools -- Fiction

ISBN 9781250196941; 9781626723573

LC 2018938078

"Quiet, sensitive Faith starts middle school already worrying about how she will fit in. To her surprise, Amanda, a popular eighth grader, convinces her to join the school soccer team. . . . Having never played soccer in her life, Faith ends up on the C team. . . . Although they are awful at soccer, Faith and her teammates soon form a bond . . . that challenges their notions of loyalty, identity, friendship, and unity." (Publisher's note)

"Vignettes show the players' varied home lives, interests, and friendship dramas. Sketchy full-color artwork features characters with exaggerated expressions." SLJ

Keenan, Sheila

Dogs of war; by Sheila Keenan and illustrated by Nathan Fox. Graphix 2013 208 p. (hardcover) $22.99

Grades: 4 5 6 7 **741.5**

1. Dogs -- Fiction 2. War -- Graphic novels 3. Graphic novels 4. Dogs -- War use -- Fiction 5. World War, 1914-1918 -- Fiction 6. World War, 1939-1945 -- Fiction 7. Vietnam War, 1961-1975 -- Fiction

ISBN 0545128870; 9780545128872; 9780545128889

LC 2011006735

This graphic novel, by Sheila Keenan, "tells the stories of the canine military heroes of World War I, World War II, and the Vietnam War. This collection of three fictional stories was inspired by historic battles and real military practice. Each story tells the remarkable adventures of a soldier and his service dog . . . bringing to life the faithful dogs who braved bombs, barrages, and battles to save the lives of countless soldiers." (Publisher's note)

Includes bibliographical references

Kibuishi, Kazu

★ **Amulet,** book one: The Stonekeeper. Graphix 2008 185p $21.99; pa $9.99

Grades: 3 4 5 6 7 8 **741.5**

1. Graphic novels 2. Fantasy graphic novels 3. Mystery graphic novels 4. Adventure graphic novels

ISBN 0-439-84680-3; 0-439-84681-1 pa; 978-0-439-84680-6; 978-0-439-84681-3 pa

Emily and Narvin's mother is kidnapped and dragged into a strange world where, it seems, the children's great-grandfather had been before. It's up to the children to save their mother's life. "Grades three to five." (Bull Cent Child Books)

"Filled with excitement, monsters, robots, and mysteries, this fantasy adventure will appeal to many readers." SLJ

Other titles in this series are:

The Stonekeeper's curse (2009)
The Cloud Searchers (2010)
The Last Council (2011)
Prince of the elves (2012)
Escape from Lucien (2014)
Firelight (2016)
Supernova (2018)

Kim, Derek Kirk

Good as Lily; written by Derek Kirk Kim; illustrated by Jesse Hamm; lettering by Jared K. Fletcher. DC Comics/Minx 2007 un il pa $9.99

Grades: 7 8 9 10 11 12 **741.5**

1. Graphic novels 2. Fantasy graphic novels 3. Humorous graphic novels

ISBN 978-1-4012-1381-7

"On her eighteenth birthday, Korean American Grace suddenly finds herself surrounded by three very corporeal essences of herself: as a small child, as a 30-year-old woman, and as 'a cranky old fart.' Each of these incarnations is at an emotional precipice, which teenage Grace helps resolve, allowing the other self to quietly disappear. . . . Kim's pacing and plotting are excellent, and Hamm's black, white, and gray artwork is lively, witty, and full of appropriate comedy and melodrama." Booklist

Kitoh, Mohiro

Bokurano : Ours. Viz Media 2010 198p il pa $12.99

Grades: 6 7 8 9 **741.5**

1. Science fiction graphic novels 2. Robots -- Graphic novels

ISBN 978-1-4215-3361-2 pa; 1-4215-3361-8 pa

"After wandering into a cave by the sea, 15 kids meet Kokopelli, who invites them to play a video game that involves piloting a giant robot. They are asked to sign a contract, not knowing the deadly repercussions or that they will have to protect the planet. The cockpit consists of designated, floating chairs for each one while at the controls of the robot designed to defeat alien invaders. . . . Sound effects and large frames help create action and edginess on the pages. This story will intrigue readers." SLJ

Volume 1 of 11

Kovac, Tommy

Wonderland; written by Tommy Kovac; illustrated by Sonny Liew. Disney Press 2008 159p il $19.99

Grades: 4 5 6 7 8 **741.5**

1. Graphic novels 2. Fantasy graphic novels

ISBN 978-1-4231-0451-3; 1-4231-0451-X

First published as single-issue comics by SLG Publishing

"Ever wonder what happened in Wonderland after Alice left? Follow the quirky tale of Mary Ann, the meticulous and dutiful housekeeper for the White Rabbit, as she continues the tale. Her boss is now wanted for treason by the Queen of Hearts for allowing the Alice Monster to enter the kingdom–off with his head! On the run and fearing for their lives, Mary Ann and White Rabbit encounter the meddlesome Cheshire Cat, the ever-contentious troublemaker, sending the White Rabbit straight into the clutches of the queen and poor Mary Ann tumbling into the Treacle Well. . . . This is a terrific look at a great classic. The energetic, action-packed illustrations complement the story in Disney-cartoon style, making for a great read for all ages" SLJ

Krosoczka, Jarrett J., 1977-

★ **Hey,** kiddo; Jarrett J. Krosoczka. Graphix, an imprint of Scholastic 2018 320 p. chiefly color illustrations $24.99

Grades: 7 8 9 10 11 12 **741.5**

1. Absentee fathers 2. Dysfunctional families 3. Children of drug

addicts -- Biography
ISBN 0545902479; 9780545902472

YALSA Award for Excellence in Nonfiction for Young Adults: Finalist (2019)

National Book Award Finalist: Young People's Literature (2018)

This book is a memoir by Jarrett J. Krosoczka. "Jarrett's family is [a dysfunctional one]. His mom is an addict, in and out of rehab, and in and out of Jarrett's life. His father is a mystery -- Jarrett doesn't know where to find him, or even what his name is. Jarrett lives with his grandparents. . . . Only as a teenager can Jarrett begin to piece together the truth of his family, reckoning with his mother and tracking down his father." (Publisher's note)

"Krosoczka as an author generously and lovingly shows his flawed family members striving to do the best they can even as Krosoczka the character clearly aches for more. Honest, important, and timely." Kirkus

L'Engle, Madeleine, 1918-2007

A **wrinkle** in time; the graphic novel. Madeleine L'Engle ; adapted and illustrated by Hope Larson. Farrar Straus Giroux 2012 392 p. $19.99

Grades: 4 5 6 7 **741.5**

1. Time travel -- Fiction 2. Space and time -- Fiction 3. Graphic novels 4. Science fiction

ISBN 0374386153; 9780374386153

LC 2010044120

Hope Larson presents a graphic novel adaptation of Madeleine L'Engle's "allegorical fantasy in which a group of young people are guided through the universe by Mrs. Who, Mrs. Which and Mrs. What -- women who possess supernatural powers. They traverse fictitious regions, meet and face evil and demonstrate courage at the right moment. Religious allusions are secondary to the philosophical struggle designed to yield the meaning of life and one's place on earth." (Kirkus Reviews)

Langridge, Roger

Thor, the mighty avenger, v.1. writer, Roger Langridge; artist, Chris Samnee; colorist, Matthew Wilson. Marvel 2011 un il pa $14.99

Grades: 8 9 10 11 12 **741.5**

1. Graphic novels 2. Greek mythology -- Graphic novels

ISBN 978-0-7851-4121-1; 0-7851-4121-9

"Readers meet the mysterious blond-haired God of Thunder with no memory when historian Jane Foster watches him get tossed out of a Norse exhibition one day. After the gallant fellow helps her out and she takes him in, an utterly charming romance ensues. . . . Langridge deserves top marks for taking a character whose story possibilities might seem limited and imbuing him with a fresh and highly entertaining life. . . . Samnee's art grounds the vigorous superhero action with expressive faces, subtle lighting tones, and an individual style that makes the drama sing." Booklist

Volume 1 of 2

Larson, Hope

All summer long; by Hope Larson. Farrar, Straus & Giroux 2018 176 p. chiefly color illustrations (pbk.) $12.99

Grades: 5 6 7 8 **741.5**

1. Bildungsromans 2. Summer -- Fiction 3. Friendship -- Fiction

ISBN 0374310718; 9780374304850; 9780374310714

LC 2017956974

Eisner Nominee: Best Publication for Teens (2019)

In this book, by Hope Larson , "thirteen-year-old Bina has a long summer ahead of her. . . . [H]er best friend, Austin . . . [is] off to soccer camp for a month, and he's been acting kind of weird. . . . [When] Austin comes home from camp, . . . he's acting even weirder. . . . How Bina and Austin rise above their growing pains and reestablish their friendship and respect for their differences makes for a touching and funny coming-of-age story." (Publisher's note)

"Larson's panels are superb at revealing emotional conflict, subtext, and humor within the deceptively simple third-person limited plot, allowing characters to grow and develop emotionally over only a few spreads." Kirkus

Compass south; Hope Larson ; illustrated by Rebecca Mock. Margaret Ferguson Books/Farrar, Straus & Giroux 2016 224 p. chiefly color illustrations (hardcover) $17.99

Grades: 4 5 6 7 **741.5**

1. Siblings -- Fiction 2. Gangs -- Fiction 3. Juvenile delinquents -- Fiction 4. New Orleans (La.) -- Fiction 5. Graphic novels 6. Twins -- Fiction 7. Buried treasure -- Fiction 8. Voyages and travels -- Fiction 9. Brothers and sisters -- Fiction 10. Adventure and adventurers -- Fiction

ISBN 0374300437; 9780374300432

LC 2015039907

"When 12-year-old twins Alexander and Cleopatra's father disappears, they join the Black Hook Gang and are caught by the police pulling off a heist. They agree to reveal the identity of the gang in exchange for tickets to New Orleans. . . . Neither Alexander nor Cleo realizes the real danger they are in-they are being followed by pirates who think they hold the key to treasure." (Publisher's note)

"A variety of panel sizes keeps the pace brisk while allowing for the occasional pause to set the scene or linger in an emotional moment." Horn Book

Another title in this series is:
Knife's edge (2017)

★ **Mercury**. Atheneum Books for Young Readers 2010 234p il $19.99; pa $9.99

Grades: 8 9 10 11 12 **741.5**

1. Graphic novels 2. Supernatural graphic novels 3. Nova Scotia -- Graphic novels

ISBN 978-1-4169-3585-8; 1-4169-3585-1; 978-1-4169-3588-9 pa; 1-4169-3588-6 pa

LC 2009-903638

This book, "relates two coming-of-age stories in tandem, showing how the past interweaves with the present. In the present, Tara and her mother have lost their old farmhouse in a fire, and Tara's mother is struggling to support them from far away while Tara lives with relatives. . . . In 1859, Josey, Tara's ancestor, falls in love with a gold dowser who has convinced her father to open a mine. Her mother, who has supernatural sight, is sure that the dowser means no good." (School Library Journal)

"The storytelling, both in words and pictures, brilliantly offers details from Canadian history and modern life. The dialogue varies from funny to poignant. An excellent graphic novel." SLJ

Lat

★ **Kampung** boy. First Second 2006 141p il pa $16.95

Grades: 7 8 9 10 11 12 Adult **741.5**

1. Graphic novels 2. Muslims -- Graphic novels 3. Malaysia -- Graphic novels 4. Family life -- Graphic novels

ISBN 1-59643-121-0

LC 2005-34135

First published 1979 in Malaysia with title: Lat, the kampung boy

"Malaysian cartoonist Lat uses the graphic novel format to share the story of his childhood in a small village, or kampung. From his birth and adventures as a toddler to the enlargement of his world as he attends classes in the village, makes friends, and, finally, departs for a prestigious city boarding school, this autobiography is warm, authentic, and wholly engaging." Booklist

Another title about Lat is:
Town boy (2007)

Lee, Tony

Outlaw : the legend of Robin Hood; a graphic novel. written by Tony Lee; illustrated by Sam Hart; colored by Artur Fujita. Candlewick Press 2009 un il $21.99; pa $11.99

Grades: 7 8 9 10 11 12 **741.5**

1. Graphic novels 2. Adventure graphic novels 3. Robin Hood (Fictional character) 4. Great Britain -- History -- 1154-1399, Plantagenets -- Graphic novels

ISBN 978-0-7636-4399-7; 0-7636-4399-8; 978-0-7636-4400-0 pa; 0-7636-4400-5 pa

LC 2008-943331

In this retelling of the Robin Hood legend, it's the year 1192, and Robin of Loxley has returned home from the Crusades after receiving news of his father's death. The Sheriff of Nottingham and Sir Guy of Gisburn govern Nottingham at the pleasure of Prince John. When Gisburn treacherously stabs Robin in a murder attempt, Robin escapes to Sherwood Forest, where the outlaws befriend him. With the help of such men as Little John and Friar Tuck, he organizes the outlaws and they start hurting Prince John where it matters–in his moneybags.

"Lee's excellent rendition of the famed selfless hero goes hand-in-hand with Hart's expressive illustrations, featuring lots of closeups and dramatic lighting and a beautiful jewel-toned palette. Teens will get caught up in this exciting page-turner." SLJ

Libenson, Terri

Just Jaime; Terri Libenson. Balzer + Bray 2019 256 p. color illustrations (hardcover) $22.99

Grades: 3 4 5 6 **741.5**

1. Friendship -- Fiction 2. Best friends -- Fiction 3. Middle schools -- Fiction

ISBN 9780062851062; 9780062851079

LC 2018968544

In this book in the Emmie & Friends series, by Terri Libenson, "the last day of seventh grade has Jaime and Maya wondering who their real friends are. Jaime knows something is off with her friend group. They've started to exclude her and make fun of the way she dresses and the things she likes. At least she can count on her BFF, Maya, to have her back . . . right?" (Publisher's note)

"The emotional roller-coaster of navigating friendships as they change shape, particularly in middle school, is portrayed with admirable sincerity, gentle humor, heartbreaking pain, and of course plenty of texts and emojis." Booklist

Liu, Na

Little White Duck; a childhood in China. Na Liu and Andrés Vera Martínez. Graphic Universe 2012 96 p. col. ill. (lib. bdg. : alk. paper) $29.27; (pbk.) $9.95

Grades: 4 5 6 **741.5**

1. China -- History -- 1976- 2. Biographical graphic novels 3. Graphic novels

ISBN 0761365877; 9780761365877; 9780761381150; 0761381155

LC 2011005347

This graphic novel provides a "glimpse into Chinese girlhood during the 1970s and '80s." It begins with the 3-year-old narrator trying to understand the death of Chairman Mao. "From there, her life unfolds in short sketches. . . . She explains about the four pests that plague China . . . and her stomach-turning school assignment to catch rats and deliver the severed tails to her teacher . . . [as well as] the origins of Chinese New Year, her favorite holiday." (Kirkus Reviews)

"This picturesque treasure introduces Chinese culture through a personal perspective that is both delightful and thought-provoking." SLJ

Lowry, Lois, 1937-

The **giver**; by Lois Lowry ; adapted and illustrated by P. Craig Russell. Houghton Mifflin Harcourt 2019 192 p. chiefly illustrations $22.99

Grades: 6 7 8 9 **741.5**

1. Bildungsromans 2. Dystopian fiction 3. Memory -- Fiction 4. Dystopian comics 5. Comics adaptations 6. Ethics -- Comic books, strips, etc. 7. Memory -- Comic books, strips, etc.

ISBN 0544157885; 9780544157880

This graphic novel in the Giver Quartet series, by Lois Lowry, adapted and illustrated by P. Craig Russell, tells "the haunting story . . . [of] twelve-year-old Jonas, who lives in a seemingly ideal, if colorless, world of conformity and contentment. Not until he is given his life assignment as the Receiver of Memory does he begin to understand the dark, complex secrets behind his fragile community." (Publisher's note)

"This striking retelling of the modern classic blends words and images to create a brilliant new representation of Lowry's dystopian conflict between the ideals of free will and security. The artwork, rendered in blue pencil and grayscale, perfectly depicts Jonas's stark, dysfunctional society, and the measured introduction and brief glimpses of color keep readers hopeful for a brighter future." SLJ

Lutes, Jason

Houdini : the handcuff king. Hyperion Books for Children/ Jump at the Sun 2007 90p il (Center for Cartoon Studies presents) $16.99; pa $9.99

Grades: 4 5 6 7 8 9 10 **741.5**

1. Magicians 2. Graphic novels 3. Biographical graphic novels 4. Nonfiction writers 5. Magicians -- Graphic novels

ISBN 978-0-7868-3902-5; 978-0-7868-3903-2 pa

On May 1, 1908, magician Harry Houdini performed one of his famous handcuff escapes, this time in handcuffs and leg irons, while jumping off the Cambridge Bridge in Massachusetts into the frigid Boston River. This graphic novel takes the reader through Houdini's day, from 5:00 a.m. as he makes his preparations, makes a practice jump, coaches his wife Bess on how she's to help him, and then makes the jump.

This is a "fascinating graphic novel. . . . The format will instantly draw a lot of attention from readers and then hold on to it. Lutes and Bertozzi use grayscale comic panels to share their story about the life of Harry Houdini in a unique way. . . . The book resembles a hybrid between fiction and nonfiction, and the ingenious choice of format will appeal to a broad age range of readers." Voice Youth Advocates

Martin, Ann M.

★ The **Baby** -sitter's Club: Kristy's great idea; a graphic novel. story by Ann M. Martin ; adapted by Raina Telgemeier. Scholastic Graphix 2006 192p il paperback $10.99; $16.99; pa $8.99

Grades: 3 4 5 6 **741.5**

1. Graphic novels 2. Friendship -- Graphic novels 3. Babysitting -- Graphic novels

ISBN 9780545813877; 0-439-80241-5; 0-439-73933-0 pa

LC 2005-37749

Other Baby-sitters Club titles by Raina Telgemeier are:
The truth about Stacey (2006)
Mary Anne saves the day (2007)

Claudia and Mean Janine (2008)

McCann, Jim

Return of the Dapper Men; written by Jim McCann; art by Janet Lee; lettered by Dave Lanphear; edited by Stephen Christy. Archaia Comics 2010 un il $24.95

Grades: 4 5 6 7 8 **741.5**

1. Graphic novels 2. Science fiction graphic novels 3. Robots -- Graphic novels

ISBN 978-1-932386-90-5; 1-932386-90-4

"In the dreamy land of Anorev, children, all under age 11, live underground among intricate gear-work mechanisms, while elegant robots live in abandoned houses aboveground. . . . All are perpetually stuck in the same day, and time has, essentially, ceased to mean anything—until 314 Dapper Men rain from the sky and set in motion the impetus for change. . . . Where this book truly stands out is how well the story works in concert with Lee's stunning artwork, which employs an art nouveau sheen. . . . A true dazzler that speaks on multiple levels for both child and adult readers and one that gets richer with each read." Booklist

McCoola, Marika

Baba Yaga's assistant; Marika McCoola ; illustrated by Emily Carroll. Candlewick Press 2015 136 p. color illustrations $16.99

Grades: 4 5 6 7 **741.5**

1. Witches -- Graphic novels 2. Supernatural graphic novels 3. Fairy tales -- Graphic novels

ISBN 076366961X; 9780763669614

LC 2014951398

Eisner Nominee: Best Publication for Kids (2016)

In this graphic novel, by Marika McCoola and Emily Carroll, "Russian folklore icon Baba Yaga mentors a lonely teen. . . . Most children think twice before braving a haunted wood filled with terrifying beasties to match wits with a witch, but not Masha. Her beloved grandma taught her many things: that stories are useful, that magic is fickle, that nothing is too difficult or too dirty to clean. The fearsome witch of folklore needs an assistant, and Masha needs an adventure." (Publisher's note)

"McCoola's offering is a well-nuanced delight, satisfyingly blending fairy tale, legend, and thrills. As a perfect complement, Carroll's evocative art enthralls, capturing both the emotion and the magic of McCoola's yarn and breathing new life into an old folk tale." Kirkus

Meconis, Dylan

Queen of the sea; Dylan Meconis. Candlewick Press 2019 400 p. color illustrations $24.99

Grades: 5 6 7 8 **741.5**

1. Exiles -- Fiction 2. Queens -- Fiction 3. Orphans -- Fiction 4. Female friendship -- Fiction

ISBN 1536204986; 9781536204988

LC 2018962223

In this graphic novel, by Dylan Meconis, "when her sister seizes the throne, Queen Eleanor of Albion is banished to a tiny island off the coast of her kingdom, where the nuns of the convent spend their days peacefully praying, sewing, and gardening. But the island is also home to Margaret, a mysterious young orphan girl whose life is upturned when the cold, regal stranger arrives." (Publisher's note)

"It's a stunning visual package, and the slow-burning story of Margaret's gradually opening world is made all the more captivating by the well-researched historical setting, immersive world building, and engrossing characters." Booklist

Medley, Linda

Castle waiting; the definitive edition Fantagraphics 2006 456p il $29.95

Grades: 5 6 7 8 9 10 11 12 **741.5**

1. Graphic novels 2. Fantasy graphic novels 3. Fairy tales -- Graphic novels

ISBN 1-56097-747-7

All of Medley's previously self-published comics are collected here in one volume for the first time. The titular castle was the home of Sleeping Beauty, whose story is retold from the viewpoint of the flibbertigibbet ladies in waiting. After the flighty princess awakens with the kiss of a handsome but not too bright prince, the castle becomes a sanctuary for various misfits. Readers will find references to many fairy tales, folk tales, and nursery rhymes in Medley's book, and her clean, clear black-and-white art reflects the works of classic illustrators such as Arthur Rackham.

Mercado, Yehudi

Sci -fu; Book 1 Kick it off. Yehudi Mercado ; additional colors by David Wheeler ; edited by James Lucas Jones and Desiree Wilson ; designed by Kate Z. Stone. Oni Press 2018 144 p. chiefly color illustrations $12.99

Grades: 4 5 6 7 8 **741.5**

1. Robots -- Fiction 2. Disc jockeys -- Fiction 3. Teenage boys -- Fiction

ISBN 1620104725; 9781620104729

LC 2017948857

In this book, author Yehudi Mercado "sets his sights on 1980s Brooklyn and Wax, a young mix-master who scratches the perfect beat and accidentally summons a UFO that transports his family, best friend, and current crush to the robot-dominated planet of Discopia. Now Wax and his crew must master the intergalactic musical martial art of Sci-Fu to fight the power and save Earth. Word to your mother." (Publisher's note)

"Mercado uses onomatopoeia and visualized sound waves to emphasize that this is an aural adventure; color-coded speech balloons help readers keep track of who is spitting rhymes. His caricatured figures and dynamic layouts, coupled with a neon palette and graffiti flourishes, make for an entertaining story with a little something for everyone: hip-hop, tech-driven action, and romance." Pub Wkly

Meyer, Marissa, 1984-

Wires and nerve; Volume 1 Marissa Meyer ; art by Doug Holgate with Stephen Gilpin. Feiwel & Friends 2017 240 p. chiefly color illustrations (hardcover) $21.99

Grades: 7 8 9 10 11 12 **741.5**

1. Androids -- Fiction 2. Imaginary wars and battles-- Fiction 3. Cyborgs -- Comic books, strips, etc. 4. Imaginary wars and battles -- Comic books, strips, etc.

ISBN 9781250078261

LC 2016939440

"The 'Lunar Chronicles' continue in this entertaining graphic novel sequel to the existing volumes. This follow-up to the futuristic fairy-tale retellings centers on Iko, cyborg mechanic Cinder's best friend. Acclimating to her human body, the android is trying to help Queen Cinder of Luna ease tensions with Earth by hunting down rogue wolf-hybrid soldiers who were once enslaved by Cinder's evil stepmother and have now been banished to the green planet. Joined by other familiar characters (Cress, Winter, Thorne), loyal Iko defends the new queen against her enemies." (School Library Journal)

"Holgate's dynamic, stylized artwork handily balances the story's action and humor while bringing Meyer's world to vivid life." Pub Wkly

Followed by:

Wires and nerve Volume 2, Going rogue

MOONSHOT; The Indigenous Comics Collection. edited by Hope Nicholson. Alternate History Comics Inc 2015 176 p. chiefly illustrations $17.99

Grades: 6 7 8 9 10 11 12 Adult **741.5**

1. Graphic novels 2. American literature -- Native American authors

ISBN 0987715259; 9780987715258

This comic anthology, edited by Hope Nicholson, "from traditional stories to exciting new visions of the future, . . . presents some of the finest comic book and graphic novel work in North America. The traditional stories presented in the book are with the permission from the elders in their respective communities, making this a truly genuine, never-before-seen publication." (Publisher's note)

"This collection of folklore from a powerhouse team of Native authors, including Buffy Sainte-Marie and Richard Van Camp, will wow readers with traditional and futuristic tales based on tribal-specific cultural teachings. . . . The full-page illustrations in some selections and the bright colors in others add depth and understanding to the narratives. The artwork is as diverse as the stories collected." SLJ

Neri, Greg

★ **Yummy**; the last days of a Southside Shorty. by G. Neri; illustrated by Randy DuBurke. Lee & Low Books 2010 94p il pa $16.95

Grades: 8 9 10 11 12 **741.5**

1. Children 2. Graphic novels 3. Biographical graphic novels 4. Gang members 5. Murder victims 6. Gangs -- Graphic novels 7. Violence -- Graphic novels 8. Chicago (Ill.) -- Graphic novels 9. African Americans -- Graphic novels

ISBN 978-1-58430-267-4 pa; 1-58430-267-4 pa

LC 2006-17771

Coretta Scott King Author Award honor book, 2011

"In 1994, in the Roseland neighborhood of Chicago's South Side, a 14-year-old girl named Shavon Dean was killed by a stray bullet during a gang shooting. Her killer, Robert "Yummy" Sandifer, was 11 years old. Neri recounts Yummy's three days on the run from police (and, eventually, his own gang) through the eyes of Roger, a fictional classmate of Yummy's. Roger grapples with the unanswerable questions behind Yummy's situation, with the whys and hows of a failed system, a crime-riddled neighborhood, and a neglected community." (Publishers Weekly)

"Neri's straightforward, unadorned prose is the perfect complement to DuBurke's stark black-and-white inks; great slabs of shadow and masterfully rendered faces breathe real, tragic life into the players." Publ Wkly

Nguyen, Mai K.

Pilu of the woods; Mai K. Nguyen. Oni Press 2019 157 p. (hardback) $17.99

Grades: 4 5 6 7 **741.5**

1. Grief -- Fiction 2. Nature -- Fiction 3. Friendship -- Fiction 4. Mothers and daughters -- Fiction

ISBN 9781620105634; 9781620105511

LC 2018940556

"Willow loves the woods near her house. They're calm and quiet, so different from her own turbulent emotions. . . . When her emotions get the better of her one day, she decides to run away into the woods. There, she meets Pilu, a lost tree spirit who can't find her way back home. . . . Willow offers to help Pilu. . . . But the journey is long, and Pilu isn't sure she's ready to return home yet." (Publisher's note)

"The soft, muted colors are a perfect match to the sylvan atmosphere, and Nguyen's rounded, thick-lined cartoon artwork is cheerful enough to temper the message about grief and loss. The heavier aspects of Willow's experiences are very nicely handled, and though some kids might find the metaphor of the monsters a bit puzzling, the resolution should be crystal clear." Booklist

O'Connor, George

★ **Hermes**; tales of the trickster. George O'Connor. First Second 2018 76 p. chiefly color illustrations (Olympians) (pbk.) $10.99

Grades: 4 5 6 7 8 **741.5**

1. Greek mythology -- Fiction 2. Gods and goddesses -- Fiction

ISBN 9781626725249; 9781626725256; 9781626725263

LC 2017941162

In this book in the Olympians series, author "George O'Connor delves into the myth of Hermes, the trickster god. From his infancy, when he bewitches animals and bends them to his will (stealing a herd of Apollo's prize cattle in the bargain), to his adolescence and adulthood when he becomes father to the equally mischievous Pan, Hermes's story is wildly entertaining as he brings a little bit of chaos to everything he touches or creates." (Publisher's note)

"O'Connor illustrates the speedy god's mischievousness with cartoon slapstick flair, playing up his witty repartee and sly, impish appeal. O'Connor's artwork is as solid as ever, with muscle-bound deities and grotesque monsters aplenty." Booklist

Includes bibliographical references

★ **Zeus**; king of the gods. First Second 2010 76p il (Olympians) $16.99; pa $9.99

Grades: 5 6 7 8 **741.5**

1. Graphic novels 2. Classical mythology 3. Zeus (Greek deity)

ISBN 978-1-59643-431-8; 1-59643-625-5; 978-1-59643-432-5 pa; 1-59643-431-7 pa

"O'Connor unveils his new Olympians graphic-novel series with this story of the daddy of Greek gods. Most immediately striking about this, aside from the exciting artwork, is the care O'Connor takes to visualize the creation myth that begins with Gaea creating and taking as a husband the sky, Ouranos. Their children the Titans and other proto-Olympian entities are often neglected or at best murkily covered, but here they're vividly portrayed with all the magnificence of their beyond-good-and-evil power. After this breathtaking and lengthy sequence, Zeus enters the scene to grow from a feisty nymph-needling youth to a lightning bolt-wielding avenger." (Booklist)

"It's [the] balance between respect for myth and adherence to comic-book form that works so wonderfully well here." Bull Cent Child Books

Other titles in this series are:

Athena, grey-eyed goddess (2010)
Hera, the goddess and her glory (2011)
Hades, lord of the dead (2012)
Poseidon, earth shaker (2013)
Aphrodite, goddess of love (2013)
Ares, bringer of war (2015)
Apollo, the brilliant one (2016)
Artemis, wild goddess of the hunt (2017)
Hermes, tales of the trickster (2018)

O'Neill, Katie

Princess princess ever after; Katie O'Neill ; [edited by] Ari Yarwood. Oni Press 2016 56 p. chiefly color illustrations (hardcover) $12.99

Grades: 4 5 6 7 8 **741.5**

1. Magic -- Fiction 2. Fantasy graphic novels 3. LGBT people -- Fiction 4. Princesses -- Fiction

ISBN 1620103400; 9781620103401

LC 2016931407

In this book, by Katie O'Neill, "when the heroic princess Amira rescues the kind-hearted princess Sadie from her tower prison, neither expects to find a true friend in the bargain. Yet as they adventure across the kingdom, they discover that they bring out the very best in the other person. They'll need to join forces and use all the know-how, kindness, and bravery they have in order to defeat their greatest foe yet: a jealous sorceress." (Publisher's note)

"The princesses' affection for each other deepens with every challenge--and every round of snappy banter--and when wedding bells ring, they're for a couple who truly know and have freely chosen one another. O'Neill delivers an alternative fairy tale that challenges conventions with every twist of the plot but doesn't veer into heavy-handed preachiness that pulls readers out of the story." Kirkus

Oima, Yoshitoki

A **silent** voice; Volume 1 Yoshitoki Oima ; translation, lettering, Steven LeCroy. Kodansha 2015 186 p. chiefly illustrations (pbk.) $10.99

Grades: 7 8 9 10 **741.5**

1. Shonen manga 2. Bullies -- Graphic novels 3. Deaf children -- Graphic novels 4. School stories -- Graphic novels 5. Deaf children -- Comic books, strips, etc.

ISBN 163236056X; 9781632360564

Eisner Nominee: Best U.S. Edition of International Material--Asia (2016)

"Shoya is a bully. When Shoko, a girl who can't hear, enters his elementary school class, she becomes their favorite target. . . . But the children's cruelty goes too far. Shoko is forced to leave the school, and Shoya ends up shouldering all the blame. Six years later, the two meet again. Can Shoya make up for his past mistakes, or is it too late?" (Publisher's note)

Volume 1 of 7

Ottaviani, Jim

Primates; The Fearless Science of Jane Goodall, Dian Fossey, and Biruté Galdikas. Jim Ottaviani ; illustrated by Maris Wicks. First edition First Second 2013 133 p. chiefly color illustrations (hardcover) $19.99

Grades: 5 6 7 8 9 10 Adult **741.5**

1. Primates

ISBN 1596438657; 9781596438651

LC 2013427678

This book presents an "account of the three greatest primatologists of the last century: Jane Goodall, Dian Fossey, and Biruté Galdikas. These three ground-breaking researchers were all students of the great Louis Leakey, and each made profound contributions to primatology--and to our own understanding of ourselves." (Publisher's note)

"More story than study, the book provides an accessible introduction to Goodall's, Fossey's and Galdikas' lives and work." Kirkus

Includes bibliographical references, page 138

Paige, Danielle

Mera; tidebreaker. written by Danielle Paige ; illustrated by Stephen Byrne. DC Ink 2019 192 p. chiefly color illustrations (paperback) $16.99

Grades: 7 8 9 10 11 12 **741.5**

1. Arranged marriage -- Fiction 2. Princesses -- Graphic novels 3. Resistance to government -- Graphic novels 4. Graphic novels 5. Superheroes -- Comic books, strips, etc.

ISBN 9781401283391

LC 2018043960

In this book, by Danielle Paige, "Princess Mera is teenage royalty and heir to the throne of Xebel, a penal colony ruled by the other no-so-lost land under the sea, Atlantis. Her father, his court and the entire kingdom are expecting her to marry and introduce a new king. But Mera is destined to wear a different crown...." (Publisher's note)

"An exciting and romantic look at a lesser-known superhero, for DC comics followers and newcomers alike." (School Library Journal)

Pak, Greg

Mech Cadet Yu; Volume 1 written by Greg Pak ; illustrated by Takeshi Miyazawa ; colored by Triona Farrell. Simon & Schuster 2018 128 p. chiefly color illustrations $14.99

Grades: 4 5 6 7 8 **741.5**

1. Graphic novels 2. Robots -- Fiction 3. Extraterrestrial beings -- Fiction

ISBN 1684151953; 9781684151950

"Every year, giant sentient robots from outer space come to Earth and bond forever with a brand new crop of cadets at Sky Corps Academy to help keep the planet safe. But this year, instead of making a connection with a cadet, one of the mechs bonds with Stanford, a young kid working with his Mom as a janitor at Sky Corps. Stanford has the opportunity of a lifetime but he'll first have to earn the trust of his classmates if he's to defend the planet from the monstrous Sharg." (Publisher's note)

"Set in the near future in Arizona, the tale strikes the perfect balance between action and drama. The battle sequences are thrilling and the characterization, writing, and dialogue strong." SLJ

Volume 1 of 3

Peach-Pit (Group)

Shugo chara! Peach-Pit; translated by June Kato; adapted by David Walsh; lettered by North Market Street Graphics. Del Rey/Ballantine Books 2007 v1-v6 il v1 $10.95

Grades: 5 6 7 8 9 **741.5**

1. Graphic novels

ISBN 978-0-345-49745-1 v1

LC 2007296632

"Everybody at Seiyo Elementary thinks that stylish and super cool Amu has it all: But nobody knows the real Amu, a shy girl who wishes she had the courage to truly be herself. Changing Amu's life is going to take more than wishes and dreams--it's going to take a little magic! One morning, Amu finds a surprise in her bed: three strange little eggs. Each egg contains a Guardian Character, an angel-like being who can give her the power to be someone new." (Publisher's note)

"Readers should revel in the lightly romantic and comedic plot and delight in the adorably stylized characters, from brooding mysterious cat-eared boys to small, sweet doll-like girls. Fans of CLAMP's Cardcaptor Sakura (Tokyopop) will enjoy these adventures of another plucky fourth grader uncovering magical secrets and learning of her wondrous fantasy world. Sheer bubblegum fun." SLJ

Volume 1 of 12

Pearson, Luke

Hilda and the troll; Luke Pearson. Flying Eye Books 2013 40 p. chiefly color illustrations (Hildafolk) $18.95

Grades: 3 4 5 6 **741.5**

1. Adventure fiction 2. Trolls -- Fiction 3. Explorers -- Fiction

ISBN 1909263141; 9781909263147

Originally published 2010 as Hildafolk

This book, by Luke Pearson, is "about an adventurous little girl and her habit of befriending anything, no matter how curious it might seem. While on an expedition to illustrate the magical creatures of the mountains around her home, Hilda spots a mountain troll. As the blue-haired explorer sits and sketches, she slowly starts to nod off. By the time she wakes up, the troll has totally disappeared and, even worse, Hilda is lost in a snowstorm." (Publisher's note)

"The art is as whimsical as the protagonist, and the bright colors enhance this comic book's magical-realistic effect." Horn Book

Other titles about Hilda are:
Hilda and the Midnight Giant (2012)
Hilda and the Bird Parade (2013)
Hilda and the Black Hound (2014)
Hilda and the Stone Forest (2016)

Petersen, David E., 1977-

Mouse guard; volume 2 legends of the guard. Archaia Entertainment 2010 144 p. color illustrations (hbk.) $19.95
Grades: 5 6 7 8 **741.5**

1. Mice -- Fiction 2. Adventure fiction 3. Short stories -- Collections
ISBN 9781936393268 Vol. 2; 1936393263 Vol. 2
Harvey Nominee: Best Continuing or Limited Series (2014)
Eisner Nominee: Best Publication for Kids (2014)
Harvey Nominee: Best Anthology (2014)

"Inside the June Alley Inn, located in the western mouse city of Barkstone, mice gather to tell tales, each trying to outdo the other. A competition, of sorts, begins. The rules: Every story must contain one truth, one lie, and have never been told in that tavern before. With the winner getting his bar tab cleared, fantastic stories are spun throughout the evening!" (Publisher's note)

"The art styles of the ensuing stories are all over the map, from the elegant, tapestry-worthy The Battle of the Hawk's Mouse & the Fox's Mouse, by Jeremy Bastian, to the joltingly cartoony A Mouse Named Fox, from Katie Cook. In substance, the stories are equally varied, but all champion the heroism of the noble mouse warriors and even include a couple clever takes on classics." Booklist

★ **Mouse** Guard: Fall 1152. Archaia Studios Press 2007 un il $24.95
Grades: 5 6 7 8 **741.5**

1. Graphic novels 2. Fantasy graphic novels 3. Mice -- Graphic novels
ISBN 978-1-932386-57-8; 1-932386-57-2
Eisner Award: Best Publication for Kids (2008)

In a medieval world populated by animals, mice have their own civilization but live in constant peril from predators. They live in hidden towns protected by the Guard, who also escort travelers between towns. Three young members of the Guard, Lieam, Saxon, and Kenzie, go in search of a missing grain merchant. They find him dead in the belly of a snake who tried to eat them; but they also find evidence that the dead merchant is a traitor. Now they need to find out to whom he was betraying the Guard and why. While this story features animals and is suitable for most readers who can handle some fighting action, there's nothing cute or Disney-esque in the art. Characters die, this is a serious story, but readers who have read Bone or the Harry Potter series can handle the action in this book. This is the first in a series.

Followed by: Mouse Guard: Winter 1152 (2009)

Mouse Guard: Winter 1152; story & art by David Petersen. Archaia Studios Press 2009 un il $24.95
Grades: 5 6 7 8 **741.5**

1. Graphic novels 2. Fantasy graphic novels 3. Mice -- Graphic novels
ISBN 978-1-932386-74-5; 1-932386-74-2
Sequel to: Mouse Guard: Fall 1152 (2007)

"In the Winter of 1152, the Mouse Guard face a food and supply shortage threatening the lives of many mouse through a cold and icy season. Some of the Guard's finest--Saxon, Kenzie, Lieam, and Sadie, led by Celanawe, the legendary Black Axe--traverse the snow-blanketed territories acting as diplomats to improve relations between the mouse cities and the Guard, and find themselves on a race against time to deliver crucial medicines." (Publisher's note)

"Picking up where Fall 1152 . . . left off, Winter 1152 follows the darkening adventures of the brave troops of the Mouse Guard as they battle the elements, predators, and even other mice in order to secure their way of life. The high-quality artwork found in the first volume carries over into this one. The narrative . . . is fast paced and compelling. . . . Combining a tale of action, romance, comedy, and tragedy with the graphic-novel format results in a topnotch work with wide appeal." SLJ

Followed by: Mouse Guard: The black axe (2013)

Phelan, Matt

Around the world. Candlewick Press 2011 240p il $24.99
Grades: 4 5 6 7 **741.5**

1. Graphic novels 2. Voyages and travels
ISBN 978-0-7636-3619-7; 0-7636-3619-3
LC 2010043153

"Phelan presents three true stories of around-the-world adventures inspired by Jules Verne's Around the World in Eighty Days that, even though they were undertaken in the late 1800s, would be hardly less arduous today. Thomas Stevens, Joshua Slocum, and Nellie Bly saw the world from the seat of a bicycle, aboard a 36-foot sloop, and via trains and ships, respectively. The small, specific pleasures of Phelan's work . . . are showcased in panels laid out in horizontal bands, reinforcing the linear, ever-onward nature of each narrative. The use of limited color palettes enhances the artist's characteristic delicate, expressive pen-and-ink drawings without overpowering them, allowing each traveler's character to be the dominant story element. . . . Design elements such as borders and frames lend a jaunty festivity to a graphic novel that will appeal to aficionados of the form and any reader in search of engrossing true journeys." SLJ

Snow White; A Graphic Novel. by Matt Phelan. Candlewick Press 2016 216 p. chiefly ill. (some color) $19.99
Grades: 4 5 6 7 8 **741.5**

1. New York (N.Y.) -- Fiction 2. Depressions -- 1929 -- Fiction
ISBN 0763672335; 9780763672331

This graphic novel, by Matt Phelan, "delivers a darkly stylized noir Snow White set against the backdrop of Depression-era Manhattan. The scene: New York City. . . . Enter a cast of familiar characters: a young girl, Samantha White, returning after being sent away by her cruel stepmother, the Queen of the Follies, years earlier; her father, the King of Wall Street, who survives the stock market crash only to suffer a strange and sudden death; [and] seven street urchins." (Publisher's note)

"With a keen historical slant, a bit of action and intrigue, high visual interest, and the fairy-tale leaning, this will awe a wide readership. Brilliant." Kirkus

The **storm** in the barn. Candlewick Press 2009 201p il $24.99; pa $14.99
Grades: 4 5 6 7 8 9 **741.5**

1. Graphic novels 2. Adventure graphic novels 3. Kansas -- Graphic novels 4. Monsters -- Graphic novels 5. Dust storms -- Graphic novels 6. United States -- History -- 1933-1945 -- Graphic

novels
ISBN 978-0-7636-3618-0; 0-7636-3618-5; 978-0-7636-5290-6 pa; 0-7636-5290-3 pa

In Kansas of 1937, the land has been in the grip of the Dust Bowl for four years, and eleven-year-old Jack Carter has seen his family worn down by it. But the day Jack outruns a dust storm all the way home from town, he glimpses something odd in the abandoned Talbot barn, and he tries to find the courage to go into the barn and confront what is there.

"Children can read this as a work of historical fiction, a piece of folklore, a scary story, a graphic novel, or all four. Written with simple, direct language, it's an almost wordless book: the illustrations' shadowy grays and blurry lines eloquently depict the haze of the dust. A complex but accessible and fascinating book." SLJ

Pope, Paul

Battling Boy; Paul Pope ; colors by Hilary Sycamore. First Second 2013 208 p. chiefly ill. (paperback) $15.99; (hardcover) $24.99

Grades: 7 8 9 10 11 12 **741.5**

1. Fantasy graphic novels 2. Superhero graphic novels
ISBN 1596438053; 9781596431454; 9781596438057

LC 2013030815

Eisner Award: Best Publication for Teens (2014)

In this book, "the hero Haggard West helps battle the evil forces of Sadisto and his hooded ghouls. However, in a shocking turn of events, evil triumphs over good, and the metropolis is left without protection. In a world far, far away, a 13-year-old son of a god has been chosen to help Earth fight the onslaught of monsters as a rite of passage. Sent with only a few possessions, including an array of magical T-shirts, Battling Boy helps the city—but he finds he cannot do it alone." (Kirkus Reviews)

"This is a sophisticated tale for younger readers, but Pope manages to both grant full-scale wish fulfillment and acknowledge the limitations of young boys with equal aplomb. His art, meanwhile, looks like nothing else in comics, with ropy, sinewy figures, dynamic action, and gritty urban design all captured in panels that have the rough, subversive tone of classic punk album covers." Booklist

Pullman, Philip, 1946-

The **golden** compass; volume 1 the graphic novel. adapted by Stéphane Melchior, art by Clément Oubrerie ; coloring by Clément Oubrerie with Philippe Bruno ; translated by Annie Eaton. Alfred A. Knopf 2015 80 p. color illustrations (hardback) $18.99

Grades: 6 7 8 9 10 **741.5**

1. Fantasy graphic novels 2. Fantasy 3. Graphic novels
ISBN 9780553523867; 0553523724; 0553523864; 0553523716; 9780553523713; 9780553523720

LC 2015005828

In this graphic novel adaptation of the young adult fantasy by Philip Pullman, adapted and illustrated by Stéphane Melchior-Durand and Clément Oubrerie, "Lyra Belacqua is content to run wild among the scholars of Jordan College, with her daemon familiar always by her side. But the arrival of her fearsome uncle, Lord Asriel, draws her to the heart of a terrible struggle—a struggle born of Gobblers and stolen children, and a mysterious substance known as Dust." (Publisher's note)

Quintero, Isabel

Photographic; the life of Graciela Iturbide. Isabel Quintero + Zeke Pena. J. Paul Getty Museum 2018 95 p. illustrations (hardcover) $19.95

Grades: 7 8 9 10 11 12 **741.5**

1. Women photographers -- Biography 2. Artistic photography 3. Photography, Artistic 4. Photographers -- Mexico -- Biography
ISBN 9781947440005

LC 2017023891

Boston Globe–Horn Book Award: Nonfiction (2018)

This book, by by Isabel Quintero, illustrated by Zeke Peña, presents a biography of Mexican artistic photographer Graciela Iturbide. "Iturbide was born in Mexico City in 1942, the oldest of 13 children. When tragedy struck Iturbide as a young mother, she turned to photography for solace and understanding. From then on Iturbide embarked on a photographic journey that has taken her throughout her native Mexico . . . and beyond." (Publisher's note)

"Teens will come away with an evolved sense of how to look at a creator's life and work and how to think critically about art as a process." SLJ

Includes bibliographical references (page 91).

Reed, M. K.

Americus; written by MK Reed; art by Jonathan Hill. First Second 2011 215p il pa $14.99

Grades: 8 9 10 11 12 **741.5**

1. Graphic novels 2. Libraries -- Fiction 3. Censorship -- Fiction 4. Books and reading -- Fiction 5. Christian fundamentalism -- Fiction
ISBN 978-1-59643-601-5; 1-59643-601-8

LC 2010051586

"Neil Barton finds the transition from middle school to high school to be challenging. He finds solace reading and listening to music, and working at the library. A censorship challenge by a fundamentalist Christian group forces him to courageously stand up before the public library board." (Library Media Connection)

"The clever mix of fantasy and realistic fiction, thoughtful pacing, authentic dialogue, and expressive art perfectly captures the angst of a nerdy teen who is at first ostracized but then finds his niche as he finds his voice." Booklist

Renier, Aaron

The **unsinkable** Walker Bean; written and illustrated by Aaron Renier; colored by Alec Longstreth. First Second 2010 191p il pa $13.99

Grades: 5 6 7 8 **741.5**

1. Graphic novels 2. Adventure graphic novels
ISBN 978-1-59643-453-0 pa; 1-59643-453-8 pa

The story "centers around a cursed skull stolen from the lair of two deep-sea crustacean witches. Like all who look upon the skull, Walker's beloved grandpa falls deathly ill when he finds it, and the boy sets out to return the skull from whence it came. . . . The generous page size lets [the] reader dive into Renier's quavery and painstakingly detailed cartooning, and he really shows off his stuff with a bounty of full-splash dazzlers. . . . Exciting, deep, funny, and scary, with tremendous villains and valor galore." Booklist

Followed by:

The unsinkable Walker Bean and the knights of the waxing moon (2018)

Roman, Dave

Astronaut Academy: Zero gravity. First Second Books 2011 185p il pa $9.99; $16.99

Grades: 4 5 6 7 8 **741.5**

1. Graphic novels 2. Humorous graphic novels 3. Science fiction graphic novels 4. School life -- Graphic novels
ISBN 9781596436206; 9781596437562

LC 2010-941434

Hakata Soy has been the leader of a futuristic superhero team, but he has given that up and just wants to be a normal student at Astronaut Academy, a school on a space station, where students take such courses as anti-gravity gymnastics and fire-throwing. Other students include Doug Hiro, who always wears his space helmet, rich girl Maribelle Mellonbelly, Miyumi San (Maribelle's rival), and egotistical Billy Lee. Hakata Soy has some trouble adjusting to school life, and things get much worse when the villainous Gotcha Birds steal a robotic twin to Hakata Soy and reprogram it to kill him. The comics originally appeared as web comics, then as mini comics that Roman took to various comic cons; this is the first trade book collection of the stories. Middle grade students, boys and girls, will enjoy this book, which is full of humor and action with little actual violence.

"Students like the introspective Hakata Soy, the space-gymnastics-obsessed Doug Hiro, and the snooty rich girl Mirabelle Mellonbelly meet up at Astronaut Academy, a middle school where the zany mixes with the postmodern. . . . Silliness is high on the agenda, aided by minimal, cartoonish art that plays on manga tropes but also manages to build character into the simple lines of a face. . . . This is one for readers looking for more involved and complex comedy than a cursory glance at the images might lead one to expect." Booklist

Followed by: Astronaut academy: Re-entry (2013)

Russell, P. Craig

★ **Coraline**; based on the novel by Neil Gaiman; adapted and illustrated by P. Craig Russell; colorist, Lovern Kindzierski; letterer, Todd Klein. HarperCollins 2008 186p il $18.99; lib bdg $19.89

Grades: 4 5 6 7 **741.5**

1. Graphic novels 2. Horror graphic novels

ISBN 978-0-06-082543-0; 978-0-06-082544-7 lib bdg

LC 2007-930658

"An adaptation of Gaiman's 2002 novel Coraline, . . . a tale of childhood nightmares. As in the original story, Coraline wanders around her new house and discovers a door leading into a mirror place, where she finds her button-eyed 'other mother,' who is determined to secure Coraline's love one way or another. This version is a virtuoso adaptation. . . . A master of fantastical landscapes, Russell sharpens the realism of his imagery, perserving the humanity of the characters and heightening the horror." Booklist

Schrag, Ariel

Stuck in the middle; seventeen comics from an unpleasant age. edited by Ariel Schrag. Viking 2007 210p il hardcover o.p. pa O.P.

Grades: 7 8 9 10 11 12 **741.5**

1. Graphic novels 2. Teenagers -- Graphic novels 3. Middle schools -- Graphic novels

ISBN 978-0-670-06221-8

LC 2006-52581

Scott, Mairghread

The **city** on the other side; Mairghread Scott, illustrated by Robin Robinson. First Second 2018 224 p. chiefly color illustrations (hardcover) $23.99

Grades: 4 5 6 7 **741.5**

1. Magic -- Comic books, strips, etc. 2. Fairies -- Comic books, strips, etc. 3. Missing persons -- Comic books, strips, etc. 4. Imaginary wars and battles -- Comic books, strips, etc.

ISBN 9781250152558; 9781626724570

LC 2017941171

In this book, by Mairghread Scott, illustrated by Robin Robinson, "Isabel plays the part of a perfectly proper little girl. . . . She's . . . not the kind of girl who goes on adventures. But that all changes when Isabel breaches an invisible barrier and steps into another world. She discovers a city not unlike her own, but magical and dangerous. . . . Only Isabel, with the help of a magical necklace, . . . stands a chance of ending the war before it destroys the fairy world." (Publisher's note)

"Robinson's colorful, dynamic artwork crackles with spirited fun and portrays San Francisco and its fairy-realm equivalent in broad, evocative panels." Kirkus

Sell, Chad

★ The **cardboard** kingdom; by Chad Sell ; [with contributions by] Jay Fuller, David Demeo, Katie Schenkel, Manuel Betancourt, Molly Muldoon, Vid Alliger, Cloud Jacobs, Michael Cole, and Barbara Perez Marquez. Alfred A. Knopf 2018 288 p. chiefly color illustrations $20.99

Grades: 4 5 6 7 **741.5**

1. Costume -- Fiction 2. Friendship -- Fiction 3. Imagination -- Comic books, strips, etc.

ISBN 9781524719371

Eisner Nominee: Best Publication for Kids (2019)

"Welcome to a neighborhood of kids who transform ordinary boxes into colorful costumes, and their ordinary block into cardboard kingdom. This is the summer when sixteen kids encounter knights and rogues, robots and monsters--and their own inner demons--on one last quest before school starts again. In the Cardboard Kingdom, you can be anything you want to be--imagine that!" (Publisher's note)

"Sell's playful, expressive, and boldly colored artwork always keeps the mood fun, quickly shifting between the real world and the kids' imagined scenes in the Cardboard Kingdom. The blocky figures have a great cartoon quality, and, with a wide range of skin tones, genders, and family types, every kid reading will have someone to relate to." Booklist

Sfar, Joann

★ The **little** prince; adapted from the book by Antoine de Saint-Exupéry; translated by Sarah Ardizzone; colour by Brigitte Findakly. Houghton Mifflin Harcourt 2010 110p il $19.99

Grades: 5 6 7 8 9 **741.5**

1. Graphic novels 2. Fantasy graphic novels 3. Extraterrestrial beings -- Graphic novels

ISBN 978-0-547-33802-6; 0-547-33802-3

"On the surface, this is a straight graphic-novel retelling of the narrator pilot getting stranded in the desert, where he meets a curious little boy who claims to be from a wee planet very far away. . . . The ultimately tricky task is to honor the source but not sound like an adaptation (otherwise, why not just read the original?) and Sfar nails it on both counts. . . . Everything is handled with both reverence and ingenuity." Booklist

Shen, Prudence

Nothing Can Possibly Go Wrong; by Prudence Shen, illustrated by Faith Erin Hicks. First Second 2013 288 p. (paperback) $16.99

Grades: 7 8 9 10 **741.5**

1. Robots -- Fiction 2. Cheerleading -- Fiction 3. School stories -- Graphic novels

ISBN 159643659X; 9781596436596

"You wouldn't expect Nate and Charlie to be friends. Charlie's the laid-back captain of the basketball team, and Nate is the neurotic, scheming president of the robotics club. But they are friends, however unlikely--until Nate declares war on the cheerleaders. At stake is funding that will either cover a robotics competition or new cheerleading uniforms--but not both." (Publisher's note)

"Shen's plot ably balances drama, humor, angst, and robotic geekery, giving the book an immediate YA appeal, but one that's broad enough to be enjoyable to older readers, as well. Visually, Hicks's wide-eyed, inky b&w panels infuse the characters with real emotion and personality, capturing the book's heartfelt youthfulness." Pub Wkly

Shiga, Jason

Meanwhile. Abrams/Amulet 2010 un il $15.95

Grades: 4 5 6 7 8 9 **741.5**

1. Graphic novels 2. Science fiction graphic novels

ISBN 0-8109-8423-7; 978-0-8109-8423-3

LC 2009-39844

In this choose-your-own adventure graphic novel, a boy stumbles on the laboratory of a mad scientist who asks him to choose between testing a mind-reading device, a time machine, and a doomsday machine. (Bull Cent Child Books)

"In this graphic novel mind boggler . . . readers play the role of little Jimmy and on the first page make the seemingly innocuous decision of ordering a vanilla or chocolate ice-cream cone. Tubes connect panels in all directions and veer off into tabs to other pages, creating a head-spinningly tangled web of story. . . . The crux is that Jimmy stumbles into the lab of an affable mad scientist and is allowed to tinker with three inventions: a mind reader, a time machine, and the Killitron, which obliterates all life on earth aside from the user's. . . . It's maddening and challenging, all right, but that's precisely what makes it so crazy fun." Booklist

Shimura, Takako

Wandering son; Volume One Shimura Takako ; translated by Matt Thorn. Fantagraphics 2011 192 p. ill. (hardcover) $19.99

Grades: 7 8 9 10 11 12 Adult **741.5**

1. Manga 2. Seinen manga 3. Puberty -- Graphic novels 4. Bildungsromans -- Graphic novels 5. Transgender people -- Graphic novels

ISBN 1606994166; 9781606994160

This manga "tells the story of a friendship between Shuichi, a young boy who wishes he were a girl, and Yoshino, a young girl who wishes she were a boy. . . . Shuichi's impulses toward a female identity feel confusing and shameful to him, and it's the girls in his life—first Yoshino, and then Saori—who point out his difference and encourage it. . . . Both children are teased mercilessly by their classmates, whose sexual development, while perhaps more socially normative, is just as confusing to them." (Publishers Weekly)

"This literary manga is a lovely, sensitive portrayal of two tweens exploring their gender identity. The art has a spare, dreamy quality, while the plot focuses on the children's forthright curiosity rather than on angst." Booklist

Volume 1 of 15 (8 available in English)

Siddell, Thomas

★ **Gunnerkrigg** Court: orientation; [by] Tom Siddell. Archaia Studios Press 2009 296p il $26.95

Grades: 6 7 8 9 10 11 12 **741.5**

1. Graphic novels 2. Fantasy graphic novels

ISBN 978-1-932386-34-9; 1-932386-34-3

"Antimony Carver is a precocious and preternaturally self-possessed young girl starting her first year of school at gloomy Gunnerkrigg Court, a very British boarding school that has robots running around along side body-snatching demons, forest gods, and the odd mythical creature. The opening volume in the series follows Antimony through her orientation year: the people she meets, the strange things that happen, and the things she causes to happen as she and her new friend, Kat, unravel the mysteries of the Court and deal with the everyday adventures of growing up." (Publisher's note)

"The first 14 chapters of Siddell's popular webcomic are collected here in an alluring hardcover. The premise, best described as science-fantasy, involves a young girl named Antimony plopped into a strange boarding-school/industrial-complex which . . . she knows nothing about. Discrete chapters . . . all feature varying levels of jaw-dropping peculiarity, devilish bursts of humor, and sublime creativity that lurk at the ends of the school's corridors. The darkly hued artwork is deceptively simplistic and displays a flair for the crucial details of setting and atmosphere." Booklist

Other titles in this series are:

Vol. 2: Research (2009)

Vol. 3: Reason (2011)

Vol. 4: Materia (2013)

Vol. 5: Refine (2015)

Smith, Jeff

★ **Bone** : out from Boneville. Scholastic Graphix 2005 144p il paperback $12.99; hardcover $26.99

Grades: 4 5 6 7 8 9 10 11 12 **741.5**

1. Graphic novels 2. Fantasy graphic novels 3. Adventure graphic novels

ISBN 9780439706407; 0439706408; 0439706238; 9780439706230

"After being run out of Boneville, the three Bone cousins -- Fone Bone, Phoney Bone, and Smiley Bone -- are separated and lost in a vast, uncharted desert. One by one, they find their way into a deep, forested valley filled with wonderful and terrifying creatures. Eventually, the cousins are reunited at a farmstead run by tough Gran'ma Ben and her spirited granddaughter, Thorn. But little do the Bones know, there are dark forces conspiring against them and their adventures are only just beginning!" (Publisher's note)

"The nine-volume Bone graphic novel series was the toast of the comics world when it was published by Smith's own Cartoon Books beginning in the early 1990s; in this first volume of Scholastic's new edition, the original b&w art has been beautifully converted into color." Pub Wkly

Other titles in this series are:

Bone: the great cow race (vol. 2)

Bone: eyes of the storm (vol. 3)

Bone: the dragonslayer (vol. 4)

Bone: Rock Jaw: master of the Eastern border (vol. 5)

Bone: old man's cave (vol. 6)

Bone: ghost circles (vol. 7)

Bone: treasure hunters (vol. 8)

Bone: crown of horns (vol. 9)

Bone : Rose; by Jeff Smith ; with illustrations by Charles Vess. Scholastic Graphix 2009 138p il $21.99; pa $10.99

Grades: 4 5 6 7 8 **741.5**

1. Graphic novels 2. Fantasy graphic novels 3. Adventure graphic novels

ISBN 978-0-545-13542-9; 0-545-13542-7; 978-0-545-13543-6 pa; 0-545-13543-5 pa

"When a terrifying dragon attacks the small towns of the Northern Valley, a young Princess Rose (known later as Gran'ma Ben) must defeat it. The beast is actually the ancient evil, the Lord of the Locusts, and while Rose faces danger with honor, her elder sister, Princess Briar, follows a more sinister path." (Publisher's note)

"When a terrifying dragon attacks the small towns of the Northern Valley, a young Princess Rose (known later as Gran'ma Ben) must defeat it. The beast is actually the ancient evil, the Lord of the Locusts, and while Rose faces danger with honor, her elder sister, Princess Briar, follows a more sinister path." Publisher's note

Bone : tall tales; by Jeff Smith with Tom Sniegoski; color by Steve Hamaker. Graphix 2010 108p il $21.99; pa $10.99
Grades: 4 5 6 7 8 **741.5**

1. Graphic novels 2. Fantasy graphic novels 3. Adventure graphic novels

ISBN 978-0-545-14095-9; 0-545-14095-1; 978-0-545-14096-6 pa; 0-545-14096-X pa

"Long before the Bone cousins were ever lost in the uncharted desert on the outskirts of the Valley, Big Johnson Bone, the discoverer of the Rolling Bone River, founded Boneville. But little is known of the mighty explorer's adventures before he started his famous trading post. So when Smiley Bone sits down with a group of young campers to retell the legendary stories of Boneville's origin and its tough, no-nonsense founder, what they hear are tall tales in typical BONE fashion." (Publisher's note)

This "introduces Big Johnson Bone, the explorer who founded Boneville. A fearless Davey Crockett-like character, he defeats a cave bear when just a baby and grows up to best all manner of beasts, including a pack of ratlike creatures intent on taking over the forest. Big Johnson's recklessness in the face of danger results in much humor, as does the commentary of his terrified, sarcastic monkey companion. Smith's quick wit shines through in the exchanges between Johnson and his companions. The colorful art is jam-packed with action, and the characters are enhanced with exaggerated features and movements." SLJ

Soo, Kean

Jellaby; Volume 1 the lost monster. by Kean Soo. Stone Arch Books 2014 160 p. color illustrations (Jellaby) (pbk.) $12.95; (library binding) $19.99
Grades: 4 5 6 7 8 9 **741.5**

1. Monsters -- Fiction 2. Friendship -- Fiction 3. Extraterrestrial beings -- Fiction 4. Human-alien encounters -- Comic books, strips, etc

ISBN 1434291952; 9781434264206; 9781434291950

LC 2013037026

First published 2008

"Portia has just moved to a new neighborhood with her mom. Adjusting to life without a father is hard enough, but school is boring and her classmates are standoffish. . . . But things start to get better when Portia mounts a midnight excursion into the woods behind her house where she discovers a shy and sweet purple monster. Life with Jellaby is exciting, but Portia's purple friend has secrets of his own." (Publisher's note)

"Soo grounds the story in a fairly gritty contemporary reality, where kids deal with bullies and well-meaning adults try to help. Clear, clean lines and easy-to-follow panel layouts round out the package." Booklist

Jellaby : monster in the city. Hyperion Books 2009 172p il pa $9.99
Grades: 4 5 6 7 8 9 **741.5**

1. Graphic novels 2. Fantasy graphic novels 3. Monsters -- Graphic novels 4. Friendship -- Graphic novels

ISBN 1-4231-0565-6 pa; 978-1-4231-0565-7 pa

Beginning right where the first book ended, Portia, Jason, and Jellaby continue on their way to Toronto, walking after Portia panicked and they got off the train. They're searching for a way home for Jellaby, and they think a door somewhere in Exhibition Place, where the Canadian National Exhibition is taking place, holds a clue. Portia feels torn between wanting to help her friend yet not wanting to say goodbye forever, and her ambivalence causes a rift between her and Jason. When she doesn't want to trust a masked magician who seems to know too much about them and Jellaby, Portia leaves Jason. They all end up in the Automotive Building, where the masked man leads Jason and Jellaby down below the building, while Portia seems to find her long lost father. But is he really her father, and just what is waiting for Jason and Jellaby under the Automotive Building? Soo again uses a mostly purple color palette.

Steele, Hamish

★ **Deadendia**; the watcher's test. Hamish Steele. Nobrow Press 2018 240 p. chiefly color illustrations $14.95
Grades: 7 8 9 10 11 12 **741.5**

1. Horror fiction 2. LGBT people -- Fiction 3. Amusement parks -- Fiction 4. Transgender people -- Fiction

ISBN 1910620475; 9781910620472

"Barney and his best friend Norma are just trying to get by and keep their jobs, but working at the Dead End theme park also means battling demonic forces, time traveling wizards, and scariest of all--their love lives! Follow the lives of this diverse group of employees of a haunted house, which may or may not also serve as a portal to hell, in this hilarious and moving graphic novel, complete with talking pugs, vengeful ghosts and LBGTQIA love!" (Publisher's note)

"The art is imaginative and engaging, with rich, evocative color schemes. With time travel, demonic possession , monsters, magic spells, and fights between creatures of pure sadness and pure happiness, there is never a dull moment--but in the realm of human emotion, there are relatable ones." Kirkus

Stevenson, Noelle

★ **Nimona**; by Noelle Stevenson. HarperCollins Childrens Books 2015 272 p. $17.99
Grades: 7 8 9 10 11 12 **741.5**

1. Fantasy graphic novels 2. Magic -- Graphic novels 3. Good and evil -- Fiction 4. Heroes and heroines -- Graphic novels 5. Shapeshifting -- Comic books, strips, etc.

ISBN 0062278231; 9780062278234

National Book Award Finalist: Young People's Literature (2015)

Eisner Nominee: Best Digital/Web Comic (2015)

Eisner Award: Best Graphic Album--Reprint (2016)

In this graphic novel, by Noelle Stevenson, "Nimona is an impulsive young shapeshifter with a knack for villainy. Lord Ballister Blackheart is a villain with a vendetta. As sidekick and supervillain, Nimona and Lord Blackheart are about to wreak some serious havoc. Their mission: prove to the kingdom that Sir Ambrosius Goldenloin and his buddies at the Institution of Law Enforcement and Heroics aren't the heroes everyone thinks they are." (Publisher's note)

"This celebrated webcomic, a mash-up of medieval culture with modern science and technology, is now available in print. . . . Action scenes dominate as Nimona shifts with Hulk-like ferocity from frightful creatures such as a fire-breathing dragon to a docile cat or a timid child. Dialogue is fresh and witty with an abundance of clever lines." SLJ

Stroud, Jonathan

The **Amulet** of Samarkand; a Bartimaeus graphic novel. adapted by Jonathan Stroud and Andrew Donkin; art by Lee Sullivan; color by Nicolas Chapuis; lettering by Chris Dickey. Disney/Hyperion Books 2010 un il hardcover o.p. O.P.
Grades: 7 8 9 10 **741.5**

1. Graphic novels 2. Magic -- Graphic novels

ISBN 978-1-4231-1146-7; 1-4231-1146-X

LC 2010-35513

Boston Globe-Horn Book Award Honor: Fiction (2004)

Nathaniel, a magician's apprentice, summons up the djinni Bartimaeus and instructs him to steal the Amulet of Samarkand from the powerful magician Simon Lovelace.

"The artwork is lively, atmospheric, and exciting. . . .The depth of Stroud's alternate London, some complex political machinations, and the large cast of human and demon characters are all well realized here." Booklist

Sturm, James

★ **Satchel** Paige; striking out Jim Crow. by James Sturm & Rich Tommaso; with an introduction by Gerald Early. Jump at the Sun 2007 89p il $16.99; pa $9.99

Grades: 6 7 8 9 10 11 12 **741.5**

1. Graphic novels 2. Baseball players 3. Baseball -- Graphic novels

ISBN 0-7868-3900-7; 0-7868-3901-5 pa

LC 2007-61362

This graphic novel is "about fictional Emmet Wilson, a black farmer whose moment of glory as a player in the Negro Leagues came when he scored a run off the great pitcher, Satchel Paige. . . . This visually powerful, suspenseful, even profound story makes an excellent choice for readers interested in baseball or in the history of race relations." Booklist

Sutherland, Tui T.

Wings of fire : the graphic novel; Book 1 The dragonet prophecy. by Tui T. Sutherland ; adapted by Barry Deutsch ; art by Mike Holmes ; color by Maarta Laiho. Graphix 2018 224 p. color illustrations, map $24.99

Grades: 4 5 6 7 **741.5**

1. Dragons -- Fiction 2. Friendship -- Fiction 3. Imaginary wars and battles -- Fiction

ISBN 9780545942164

LC 2017955178

"Clay has grown up under the mountain, chosen along with four other dragonets to fulfill a . . . prophecy and end the war between the dragon tribes of Pyrrhia. . . . So when one of the dragonets is threatened, all five spring into action. Together, they will choose freedom over fate, leave the mountain, and fulfill their destiny -- on their own terms." (Publisher's note)

"Adapted from Sutherland's middle-grade series, the story is surprisingly riveting; the politics involved between the warring factions and dragon races makes for great world building, and the war-torn world, complete with gladiatorial-style fights and backstabbings, is an intriguing backdrop for the five dragons' development." Booklist

Other Wings of Fire graphic novels are:

The lost heir (2019)

The hidden kingdom (2019)

Takaya, Natsuki

Fruits Basket Collector's Edition; Volume 1. Natsuki Takaya ; translation, Sheldon Drzka ; lettering, Lys Blakeslee. Yen Press 2016 400 p. chiefly illustrations $20

Grades: 7 8 9 10 11 12 **741.5**

1. Shojo manga 2. Family -- Fiction 3. Secrets -- Fiction

ISBN 0316360163; 9780316360166

Originally published in the U.S. by Tokyopop in 23 volumes

"After a family tragedy turns her life upside down, plucky high schooler Tohru Honda takes matters into her own hands and moves out... into a tent! Unfortunately for her, she pitches her new home on private land belonging to the mysterious Sohma clan, and it isn't long before the owners discover her secret. But, as Tohru quickly finds out when the family offers to take her in, the Sohmas have a secret of their own--when touched by the opposite sex, they turn into the animals of the Chinese Zodiac!" (Publisher's note)

Volume 1 of 12

Tamaki, Mariko

★ **Emiko** superstar; written by Mariko Tamaki; illustrated by Steve Rolston. DC Comics/Minx 2008 149p il hardcover o.p. pa O.P.

Grades: 7 8 9 10 11 12 **741.5**

1. Graphic novels 2. Performance art -- Graphic novels 3. Racially mixed people -- Graphic novels

ISBN 978-1-4012-1536-1

"Emiko, a half-Japanese, half-Caucasian Canadian, is a self-described geek facing a summer of babysitting and isolation. Things change when she stumbles upon an underground performing art scene inspired by Andy Warhol's Factory. She eventually takes to the stage . . . and achieves minor celebrity. Soon, though, Emiko must face the troubling complexities in the lives of her new friends and the consequences of her own questionable actions. . . . Rolston's playful, vibrant b&w illustrations bring the characters to life." Publ Wkly

Skim; words by Mariko Tamaki; drawings by Jillian Tamaki. Groundwood Books 2008 144p il PB 12.95; HC $18.95

Grades: 7 8 9 10 11 12 **741.5**

1. Graphic novels 2. LGBT youth -- Fiction 3. Humorous graphic novels 4. Friendship -- Graphic novels 5. School stories -- Graphic novels

ISBN 088899964X; 0-88899-753-1; 9780888999641; 978-0-88899-753-1

Ignatz Award: Outstanding Graphic Novel (2008)

Skim is Kimberly Keiko Cameron, a not-slim half-Japanese would-be Wiccan goth who attends a private school. When classmate Katie Matthews' ex-boyfriend commits suicide, concerned guidance counselors descend upon the school because so many of the student body goes into mourning overdrive. The popular clique starts a new club, Girls Celebrate Life, and make Katie their project, especially after she falls off her roof and breaks both arms. Kim and her best friend Lisa observe all this, but counselors target Kim for her goth tendencies and are convinced she'll become suicidal any moment. All she is, is in love with her English teacher, Ms. Archer, who seems to reciprocate and then leaves the school. As Lisa starts to get sucked into the GLC, Kim and Katie tentatively begin a new friendship. There is only one rather chaste kiss between Kim and Ms. Archer. Artist Jillian Tamaki draws Kim to look like a classical Heian period Japanese woman.

★ **This** One Summer; Mariko Tamaki, [art by] Jillian Tamaki. First Second 2014 320 p. chiefly ill. pbk 17.99; hbk $21.99; pbk 17.99; hbk 21.99

Grades: 7 8 9 10 11 12 Adult **741.5**

1. Graphic novels 2. Vacations -- Fiction 3. Friendship -- Fiction

ISBN 159643774X; 9781626720947; 9781596437746; 1626720940

Ignatz Award: Outstanding Graphic Novel (2014)

Eisner Award: Best Graphic Album--New (2015)

Harvey Nominee: Best Artist (2015)

Harvey Nominee: Best Graphic Album of Original Work (2015)

Caldecott Honor Book (2015)

Harvey Nominee: Best Original Graphic Publication For Young Readers (2015)

Printz Honor Book (2015)

"Every summer, Rose goes with her mom and dad to a lake house in Awago Beach. . . . Rosie's friend Windy is always there, too, like the little sister she never had. But this summer is different. . . . It's a summer of secrets, and sorrow, and growing up, and it's a good thing Rose and Windy have each other." (Publisher's note)

"This captivating graphic novel presents a fully realized picture of a particular time in a young girl's life, an in-between summer filled with yearning and a sense of ephemerality." SLJ

Tan, Shaun

★ The **arrival**. Arthur A. Levine Books 2007 un il $19.99
Grades: 6 7 8 9 10 **741.5**

1. Graphic novels 2. Stories without words 3. Immigrants -- Graphic novels

ISBN 0-439-89529-4; 9780439895293

LC 2006-21706

Boston Globe-Horn Book Award special citation (2008)

In this wordless graphic novel, a man leaves his homeland and sets off for a new country, where he must build a new life for himself and his family.

"Young readers will be fascinated by the strange new world the artist creates. . . . They will linger over the details in the beautiful sepia pictures and will likely pick up the book to pore over it again and again." SLJ

Telgemeier, Raina

★ **Drama**; Raina Telgemeier ; with color by Gurihiru. 1st ed. Graphix 2012 233 p. chiefly ill. $23.99
Grades: 5 6 7 8 **741.5**

1. Graphic novels 2. School stories 3. LGBT youth -- Fiction 4. Middle schools -- Fiction 5. Children's plays -- Fiction 6. Schools -- Fiction 7. Theater -- Fiction 8. Interpersonal relations -- Fiction

ISBN 0545326982; 0545326990; 9780545326988; 9780545326995

LC 2011040748

Stonewall Honor Book (2013)

Author Raina Telgemeier's book focuses on a middle school drama production. "Callie loves theater . . . [S]he's the set designer for the stage crew, and this year she's determined to create a set worthy of Broadway on a middle-school budget. But how can she, when she doesn't know much about carpentry, ticket sales are down, and the crew members are having trouble working together?" (Publisher's note)

"In this realistic and sympathetic story, feelings and thoughts leap off the page, revealing Telgemeier's keen eye for young teen life." Booklist

Includes bibliographical references

★ **Ghosts**; Raina Telgemeier ; with color by Braden Lamb. Graphix, an imprint of Scholastic 2016 256 p. chiefly color illustrations pbk $10.99; hbk $24.99
Grades: 3 4 5 6 7 **741.5**

1. Ghost stories 2. Graphic novels 3. Ghosts -- Fiction 4. Sisters -- Fiction 5. Cystic fibrosis -- Fiction 6. Moving, Household -- Fiction 7. California, Northern -- Fiction 8. Ghosts -- Comic books, strips, etc 9. Sisters -- Comic books, strips, etc 10. Moving, Household -- Comic books, strips, etc 11. Family life -- California, Northern -- Fiction 12. California, Northern -- Comic books, strips, etc 13. Families -- California, Northern -- Comic books, strips, etc

ISBN 0545540623; 9780545540629; 9780545540612; 0545540615

LC 2016004672

Eisner Award: Best Publication for Kids (2017)

"Catrina and her family have just moved to Northern California. Bahía de la Luna is different from Cat's hometown--for one thing, everyone is obsessed with ghosts--but the sea air makes it easier for Cat's younger sister, Maya, who has cystic fibrosis (CF), to breathe. Carlos, a new friend and neighbor, introduces the girls to a different perspective on the spiritual world." (School Library Journal)

"In her treatment of illness and death, Telgemeier (Sisters) nudges readers toward the edge of their comfort zone, but she never leaves them alone there. The story is consistently engaging, the plot is tightly built, and--as always--Telgemeier excels at capturing facial expressions." Pub Wkly

★ **Guts**; Raina Telgemeier ; with color by Braden Lamb. Graphix, an imprint of Scholastic 2019 224 p. chiefly color illustrations paperback $12.99
Grades: 3 4 5 6 **741.5**

1. Fear in children 2. Stress (Physiology) 3. Emotions in children 4. Stress in children 5. Stomach -- Diseases 6. Children -- Physiology

ISBN 9780545852500; 9780545852517

LC 2018050676

"Raina wakes up one night with a terrible upset stomach. Her mom has one, too, so it's probably just a bug. Raina eventually returns to school, where she's dealing with the usual highs and lows: friends, not-friends, and classmates who think the school year is just one long gross-out session. It soon becomes clear that Raina's tummy trouble isn't going away... and it coincides with her worries about food, school, and changing friendships." (Publisher's note)

"After a particularly bad bout of the flu in fourth grade, Raina keeps having stomach aches and intense feelings about food and germs. The thought of being near a sick person sends her into a panic, and conflicts among her friends at school and embarrassment about bodily functions in general certainly don't help matters. In this third graphic memoir, Telgemeier describes her childhood anxiety in an approachable, nonjudgmental way and emphasizes how useful talk therapy can be." Booklist

★ **Sisters**; Raina Telgemeier; with color by Braden Lamb. First edition Graphix 2014 197 p. chiefly color illustrations hbk $24.99; pbk $10.99
Grades: 5 6 7 8 **741.5**

1. Siblings 2. Family life 3. Autobiographical graphic novels 4. Interpersonal relations

ISBN 9780545540599; 9780545540605

LC 2013008700

"Raina can't wait to be a big sister. But once Amara is born, things aren't quite how she expected them to be. . . . They are sisters, after all. Raina uses her signature humor . . . in both present-day narrative and perfectly placed flashbacks to tell the story of her relationship with her sister, which unfolds during the course of a road trip from their home in San Francisco to a family reunion in Colorado." (Publisher's note)

"The author's narrative style is fresh and sharp, and the combination of well-paced and well-placed flashbacks pull the plot together, moving the story forward and helping readers understand the characters' point of view. The volume captures preadolescence in an effortless and uncanny way and turns tough subjects, such as parental marriage problems, into experiences with which readers can identify." (School Library Journal)

★ **Smile**. Scholastic/Graphix 2010 213p il $21.99; pa $10.99
Grades: 5 6 7 8 **741.5**

1. Graphic novels 2. Autobiographical graphic novels 3. Dentistry -- Graphic novels 4. Friendship -- Graphic novels 5. Personal appearance -- Graphic novels

ISBN 978-0-545-13205-3; 0-545-13205-3; 978-0-545-13206-0 pa; 0-545-13206-1 pa

LC 2008-51782

Boston Globe-Horn Book Honor: Nonfiction (2010)

Eisner Award: Best Publication for Teens (2011)

"Raina just wants to be a normal sixth grader. But one night after Girl Scouts she trips and falls, severely injuring her two front teeth. What follows is a long and frustrating journey with on-again, off-again braces, surgery, embarrassing headgear, and even a retainer with fake teeth attached. And on top of all that, there's still more to deal with: a major earthquake, boy confusion, and friends who turn out to be not so friendly." (Publisher's note)

"Telgemeier has created an utterly charming graphic memoir of tooth trauma, first crushes and fickle friends, sweetly reminiscent of Judy Blume's work." Kirkus

TenNapel, Doug

Bad Island; created, written, and drawn by Doug TenNapel. Graphix 2011 218p il $24.99

Grades: 6 7 8 9 10 **741.5**

1. Adventure graphic novels 2. Family life -- Graphic novels 3. Extraterrestrial beings -- Graphic novels 4. Father-son relationship -- Graphic novels 5. Survival after airplane accidents, shipwrecks, etc. -- Graphic novels

ISBN 0545314798; 0545314801 pa; 9780545314794; 9780545314800 pa

LC 2011276008

"Dad has decided to take Reese, who is too cool for family outings, and his sister, Janine, on a fishing trip. The vacation takes an unexpected turn when their boat capsizes during a storm and they find themselves marooned on a strange island. To their horror, the family slowly realizes that the island is the submerged body of a giant creature, escaped from another world. The story alternates between the shipwreck survivors and the faraway world that created this "island." Both stories feature conflict between an adolescent son and his father. . . . Ultimately, both rebellious adolescents grow up and find their place as young men." (School Libr J)

"Though father, mother, teenage son, and tween daughter face the various dangers like a gang of Indiana Joneses, their family stresses are believable. . . . A clever, old-fashioned adventure with some modern twists and a lighthearted tone." Booklist

Cardboard; Doug TenNapel. Graphix / Scholastic 2012 288 p. $24.99

Grades: 5 6 7 8 **741.5**

1. Boxes -- Fiction 2. Gifts -- Graphic novels 3. Magic -- Graphic novels 4. Bullies -- Graphic novels 5. Father-son relationship -- Graphic novels

ISBN 0545418720; 9780545418720; 9780545418737

LC 2011934533

In this graphic novel, "Cam Howerton's out-of-work father is so broke, the best he can do for Cam's birthday is an empty cardboard box purchased from a toy seller with two mysterious rules: return every unused scrap of cardboard and don't ask for any more. . . . [T]he box becomes a project. What should father and son make out of the box? 'A boxer,' Cam suggests. . . . 'Boxer Bill,' created from inanimate material, comes alive. Unfortunately, Marcus, the neighborhood bully . . . steals the scrap materials, and begins turning out a whole evil empire of cardboard monsters. . . . [A]fter losing control of them he must unite with Cam and his father to defeat the massive cardboard army. . . . [Q] uestions are raised about what it means to be a man, what makes a good man, and what forms people's character." (Horn Book)

Ghostopolis; created, written, and drawn by Doug TenNapel. Graphix 2010 266 p. il pa $12.99; $24.99

Grades: 7 8 9 10 **741.5**

1. Graphic novels 2. Ghosts -- Graphic novels

ISBN 9780545210287; 9780545210270; 0545210275

LC 20090942984

This graphic novel tells the story of an "agent for the Supernatural Immigration Task Force, . . . Frank Gallows[, whose] . . . job [is] to catch ghosts on Earth and send them back to the afterlife. However, during one particularly tricky deportation, he accidentally zaps a young—living—boy. Garth Hale suddenly finds himself surrounded by mummies and goblins in a crumbling, ghastly city, with a skeleton horse and his long-departed grandfather as his only friends. Gallows comes crashing into the afterlife, as well, on a daring rescue mission. As this bumbling team tries to find a way home, they end up face to face with the evil ruler of Ghostopolis, who doesn't look too kindly upon mortals in his city." (Kirkus)

"When readers first meet Garth Hale, he is about to receive the fifth diagnosis that his disease is incurable. How fitting, then, that a boy who thinks about death more than other kids his age should be accidentally zapped into the afterlife. When washed-up ghost wrangler Frank Gallows realizes that he accidentally sent Garth through to the other side, he does everything in his power to rescue him. Meanwhile, Garth explores the spirit world. . . . TenNapel mixes emotional epiphanies with humor in a way that will appeal to a broad audience. Characters experience personal growth and learn lessons about themselves throughout the course of this book. . . . TenNapel's colorful illustrations are filled with energy and life, and they use shade and silhouettes to great advantage." SLJ

Thompson, Craig, 1975-

Space dumplins; Craig Thompson with color by Dave Stewart. Graphix / Scholastic 2015 320 p. color illustrations $24.99

Grades: 3 4 5 6 **741.5**

1. Missing persons -- Fiction 2. Interplanetary voyages -- Fiction 3. Father-daughter relationship -- Fiction

ISBN 0545565413; 9780545565417; 9780545565431

LC 2014956159

In this graphic novel by Craig Thompson, "for Violet Marlocke, family is the most important thing in the whole galaxy. So when her father goes missing while on a hazardous job, she can't just sit around and do nothing. To get him back, Violet throws caution to the stars and sets out with a group of misfit friends on a quest to find him. But space is vast and dangerous, and she soon discovers that her dad is in big, BIG trouble." (Publisher's note)

"Thompson's art is wild and busy, with overcrowded, unconventional panel structures. The worldbuilding is a strikingly imaginative pastiche that seamlessly blends biblical references, poop jokes, and social satire." Kirkus

Thrash, Maggie

Lost soul, be at peace; Maggie Thrash. Candlewick Press 2018 192 p. chiefly illustrations $18.99

Grades: 7 8 9 10 11 12 **741.5**

1. Bildungsromans 2. Lesbian teenagers -- Fiction 3. Depression (Psychology) -- Fiction

ISBN 0763694193; 9780763694197

"Picking up a year and a half after the events of her graphic memoir, Honor Girl, Thrash once again chronicles her adolescence, this time injecting her narrative with a dose of the supernatural. Growing up in Atlanta, 16-year-old Maggie feels invisible. She came out as a lesbian at the beginning of the school year, with barely any reaction from classmates, and though she is depressed, her stern father and her oblivious socialite mother are unaware of her anguish. Only her cat makes her smile, but her pet's disappearance sends her deeper into turmoil. Tommy, a ghost only she can see, enters the scene, and the two try to uncover his connection to Maggie and her family." (School Library Journal)

Tolstikova, Dasha

A **Year** Without Mom; by Dasha Tolstikova. Groundwood Books 2015 176 p. color illustrations $19.95
Grades: 5 6 7 8 **741.5**

1. Russia 2. Refugees 3. Mother-daughter relationship
ISBN 1554986923; 9781554986927

This book, by Dasha Tolstikova, "follows 12-year-old Dasha through a year full of turmoil after her mother leaves for America. It is the early 1990s in Moscow, and political change is in the air. But Dasha is more worried about her own challenges as she negotiates family, friendships and school without her mother. Just as she begins to find her own feet, she gets word that she is to join her mother in America — a place that seems impossibly far from everything and everyone she loves." (Publisher's note)

"Scribbly, childlike pencil drawings are filled in with gray wash and accentuated with red and the occasional pop of blue. They are deceptively simple, but with great narrative sophistication, they capture both the specificity of Dasha's experience and the universality of her emotions." Kirkus

The **TOON** treasury of classic children's comics; selected and edited by Art Spiegelman and Francoise Mouly; introduction by Jon Scieszka. Abrams ComicArts 2009 350p il $40
Grades: 3 4 5 6 **741.5**

1. Comic books, strips, etc.
ISBN 978-0-8109-5730-5; 0-8109-5730-2

LC 2009009830

"These stories are terrifically funny, joltingly exuberant, bafflingly bizarre, and best of all, compiled into one hearty, hefty, handsome volume." Booklist

Torres, J.

Lola : a ghost story; [by] J. Torres & [illustrated by] Elbert Or. Oni Press 2009 102p il $14.95
Grades: 4 5 6 7 8 **741.5**

1. Graphic novels 2. Ghosts -- Graphic novels 3. Family life -- Graphic novels 4. Philippines -- Graphic novels
ISBN 978-1-934964-33-0; 1-934964-33-6

"Lola ('grandmother' in Tagalog) has just died, and Jesse is reluctant to visit her home in the Philippines. He was afraid of her because she was rumored to have magical abilities, and because he thinks she tried to drown him when he was a baby. Jesse listens to family members tell stories about her as he tries to adjust to their strange mix of superstitions and religion. . . . Jesse is an unusually nuanced character. . . . When he sees something extraordinary, it's unclear if he is dreaming, hallucinating, or if he has inherited his grandmother's abilities. Torres's gradual revelation of details will keep readers hanging until they learn the truth. Or's artwork uses sepia tones and smooth lines, and features characters with cute button eyes. But the sweet images can quickly turn horrific when Jesse has his visions. " SLJ

Trondheim, Lewis

Tiny Tyrant; by Lewis Trondheim; translated from the French by Alexis Siegel; illustrated by Fabrice Parme. First Second Books 2007 124p il $12.95
Grades: 4 5 6 7 8 9 10 11 12 Adult **741.5**

1. Graphic novels 2. Humorous graphic novels
ISBN 978-1-59643-094-5

LC 2006021479

"Tiny child-king Ethelbert is spoiled and difficult, expecting to have his every whim fulfilled-or else. . . . In the end, though, he becomes a hero. The dynamic cartoons are filled with details and riddled with humor; most pages have between six and eight small pictures. . . . This title will have wide appeal. It's young and accessible enough for elementary-grade kids, but teens will also be charmed by the rascally king." SLJ

Varon, Sara

Bake sale. First Second 2011 157p il $19.99; pa $16.99
Grades: 3 4 5 6 7 8 **741.5**

1. Graphic novels 2. Cupcakes -- Graphic novels 3. Bakers and bakeries -- Graphic novels
ISBN 978-1-59643-740-1; 1-59643-740-5; 978-1-59643-419-6 pa; 1-59643-419-8 pa

LC 2010051587

"Cupcake's life is pretty good. He's got his bakery, and his band, and his best friend, Eggplant. His days are full of cooking, socializing, and playing music. But lately, Cupcake has been struggling in the kitchen. He's sure the solution to all his problems is out there somewhere. But maybe that solution is hiding closer to home." (Publisher's note)

Venditti, Robert

★ The **lightning** thief: the graphic novel; by Rick Riordan; adapted by Robert Venditti; art by Attila Futaki; color by Jose Villarrubia; layouts by Orpheus Collar; lettering by Chris Dickey. Disney/Hyperion Books 2010 un il (Percy Jackson and the Olympians) $19.99; pa $9.99
Grades: 5 6 7 8 **741.5**

1. Graphic novels 2. Greek mythology -- Graphic novels
ISBN 978-1-4231-1696-7; 1-4231-1696-8; 978-1-4231-1710-0 pa; 1-4231-1710-7 pa

LC 2010035512

After learning that he is the son of a mortal woman and Poseidon, god of the sea, twelve-year-old Percy is sent to a summer camp for demigods like himself, and joins his new friends on a quest to prevent a war between the gods.

This graphic novel adaptation of Rick Riordan's novel "succeeds in spectacular fashion. . . . The book retains the excellent pacing of the original and gives a face to Riordan's vision of the mythological made modern. Futaki's artwork is exemplary but what leaves such a lasting impression is Villarrubia's coloring, which reveals both subtlety and spectacle when needed." Publ Wkly

Other graphic adaptations in this series are:
The sea of monsters (2013)
The Titan's curse (2013)

Viney, Brigit

Frankenstein; [by] Mary Shelley; [adapted and illustrated by Brigit Viney] Lucent 2010 144p il (Classic comics) $32.45
Grades: 6 7 8 9 **741.5**

1. Graphic novels 2. Horror graphic novels
ISBN 978-1-4205-0374-6; 1-4205-0374-X

"Much of the power of Viney's adaptation of Mary Shelley's horror classic lies within the artwork. Action sequences jump off the page, while portraits of each character provide nuance and depth to the text. . . . This . . . wins points for a masterful rendition that adds much value to the original." Kirkus

Walden, Tillie

★ **Spinning**; Tillie Walden. First Second 2017 400 p. chiefly illustrations hardcover $22.99; paperback $17.99

Grades: 7 8 9 10 11 12 **741.5**

1. Graphic memoir 2. Lesbian teenagers 3. Figure skaters -- Biography

ISBN 9781626727724; 9781626729407

LC 2016961586

Eisner Award: Best Reality-Based Work (2018)

This graphic memoir, by Tillie Walden, "captures what it's like to come of age, come out, and come to terms with leaving behind everything you used to know. . . . For ten years, figure skating was . . . Walden's life. . . . But as she switched schools, got into art, and fell in love with her first girlfriend, she began to question how the close-minded world of figure skating fit in with the rest of her life, and whether all the work was worth it." (Publisher's note)

"Walden's cumulative growth and courage to speak up for what she actually wants are unmistakable and deeply satisfying. A stirring, gorgeously illustrated story of finding the strength to follow one's own path." Booklist

Wang, Jen, 1984-

★ The **prince** and the dressmaker; Jen Wang. First Second 2018 288 p. chiefly color illustrations (hardcover) $24.99

Grades: 7 8 9 10 11 12 **741.5**

1. Romance fiction 2. Fashion -- Fiction 3. Princes -- Fiction

ISBN 9781250159854; 9781626723634

LC 2017941173

Eisner Award: Best Publication for Teens (2019)

In this graphic novel, by Jen Wang, "Prince Sebastian is looking for a bride--or rather, his parents are looking for one for him. Sebastian is too busy hiding his secret life from everyone. At night he puts on daring dresses and takes Paris by storm as the fabulous Lady Crystallia--the hottest fashion icon in the world capital of fashion! Sebastian's secret weapon (and best friend) is the brilliant dressmaker Frances--one of only two people who know the truth: sometimes this boy wears dresses." (Publisher's note)

"Frances's daring designs shine in Wang's elegantly drafted and gorgeously colored illustrations, and the irreverently anachronistic approach to the setting provides a lovely and humorous counterbalance to the seriousness of the prince's situation." Pub Wkly

★ **Stargazing**; Jen Wang ; color by Lark Pien. First Second 2019 224 p. chiefly color illustrations (hardcover) $21.99

Grades: 3 4 5 6 **741.5**

1. Best friends -- Fiction 2. Individuality -- Fiction 3. Chinese Americans -- Fiction

ISBN 9781250183873; 9781250183880

LC 2018944915

In this graphic novel, by Jen Wang, "Moon is everything Christine isn't. She's confident, impulsive, artistic . . . and though they both grew up in the same Chinese-American suburb, Moon is somehow unlike anyone Christine has ever known. But after Moon moves in next door, these unlikely friends are soon best friends, sharing their favorite music videos and painting their toenails when Christine's strict parents aren't around." (Publisher's note)

"Wang tells a story that will ring true to just about any middle-schooler who's dealt with shifting friendships, but her additional insights into navigating differences within the Chinese American community will be a balm to readers in similar situations." Booklist

Weing, Drew

Set to sea. Fantagraphics 2010 un il hardcover o.p. O.P.

Grades: 8 9 10 11 12 **741.5**

1. Graphic novels 2. Poets -- Graphic novels 3. Sea stories -- Graphic novels 4. Seafaring life -- Graphic novels

ISBN 978-1-60699-368-2; 1-60699-368-2

The author "has produced a beautiful gem here, with minimal dialogue, one jolting battle scene, and each small page owned by a single panel filled with art whose figures have a comfortable roundness dredged up from the cartoon landscapes of our childhood unconscious, even as the intensely crosshatched shadings suggest the darkness that sometimes traces the edges of our lives. . . . [This book] is playful, atmospheric, dark, wistful, and wise." Booklist

Weinstein, Lauren

Girl stories; by Lauren R. Weinstein. Henry Holt 2006 237p il pa $16.95

Grades: 7 8 9 10 11 12 Adult **741.5**

1. Graphic novels 2. Humorous graphic novels 3. Girls -- Graphic novels 4. Friendship -- Graphic novels

ISBN 978-0-8050-7863-3; 0-8050-7863-0

LC 2005-46205

"Smart, creative Lauren sheds her geeky rep in high school in Weinstein's collection of comic strips, which have to intimacy of a teen's diary. The color-washed sketches have an edgy quality." Booklist

Wheeler, Andrew

Another castle; Grimoire. Andrew Wheeler, Paulina Ganucheau, edited by Ari Yarwood. Oni Press 2017 152 p. color illustrations $15.99

Grades: 7 8 9 10 11 12 Adult **741.5**

1. Friendship -- Fiction 2. Princesses -- Fiction 3. Good and evil -- Fiction 4. Heroes and heroines -- Fiction

ISBN 1620103117; 9781620103111

LC 2016950325

This book, by Andrew Wheeler and Paulina Ganucheau, edited by Ari Yarwood, "begins when Princess Misty of Beldora, . . . [was] captured by Lord Badlug, the ruler of the neighboring kingdom of Grimoire. He intends to marry her and conquer Beldora. . . . The people of Grimoire already suffer under his rule and desperately need a hero. . . . Together with the citizens of Grimoire, . . . Misty must fight to protect her kingdom and free both realms from Badlug's tyrannical rule." (Publisher's note)

"Ganucheau contributes some thrilling and bloody action sequences, and her candy-colored palette, suffused with bright pinks and purples, is an inspired touch, just one more way this story subverts expectations." Pub Wkly

Whitley, Jeremy

Princeless; Book One Save Yourself. Jeremy Whitley ; illustrated by M. Goodwin. Action Lab Entertainment 2012 116 p. ill. (paperback) $14.95

Grades: 4 5 6 7 8 **741.5**

1. Adventure graphic novels 2. Princesses -- Graphic novels

ISBN 1450798942; 9781450798945

This graphic novel collects "the first storyline of the multiple Eisner Award-nominated and multiple Glyph Award-winning series" from Jeremy Whitley. It follows "the adventures of Princess Adrienne, a princess who's tired of waiting to be rescued. Along with her guardian dragon, Sparky, they begin their own quest." (Publisher's note)

Other Princeless volumes are:

2, Get Over Yourself

3, The Pirate Princess

4, Be Yourself

5, Make Yourself 1

6, Make Yourself 2

7, Find Yourself
8, Princesses

Wood, Audrey

Into the volcano; a graphic novel. Blue Sky Press 2008 174p il map $18.99

Grades: 2 3 4 5 6 7 8 **741.5**

1. Graphic novels 2. Adventure graphic novels 3. Brothers -- Graphic novels

ISBN 978-0-439-72671-9; 0-439-72671-9

LC 2007-51084

While their parents are away doing research, brothers Duffy and Sumo Pugg go with their cousin, Mister Come-and-Go, to Kokalaha Island, where they meet Aunt Lulu and become trapped in an erupting volcano.

"The visual format combined with nonstop action will keep reluctant readers and adventure fans turning pages to the very end." Voice Youth Advocates

Yang, Gene Luen, 1973-

★ **American** born Chinese; by Gene Luen Yang ; color by Lark Pien. First Second 2006 233p il pa $16.95

Grades: 7 8 9 10 11 12 **741.5**

1. Graphic novels 2. Chinese Americans -- Graphic novels

ISBN 1-59643-152-0; 978-1-59643-152-2

LC 2005-58105

Eisner Award: Best Graphic Album--New (2007)
National Book Award Finalist: Young People's Literature (2006)
Printz Award (2007)

"Jin Wang is the only Asian American boy in his new school; Danny is a young man deeply embarrassed by his visiting Chinese cousin, portrayed deliberately by the author as an ethnic cliché; and the Monkey King, a figure from Chinese lore, is desperate to be treated like a god. This . . . story relates how three characters overcome hurdles to find satisfaction within themselves." (Library Journal)

"True to its origin as a Web comic, this story's clear, concise lines and expert coloring are deceptively simple yet expressive. Even when Yang slips in an occasional Chinese ideogram or myth, the sentiments he's depicting need no translation. Yang accomplishes the remarkable feat of practicing what he preaches with this book: accept who you are and you'll already have reached out to others." Publ Wkly

★ **Boxers**; Gene Luen Yang ; color by Lark Pien. First Second 2013 328 p. (pbk.) $18.99

Grades: 7 8 9 10 11 12 Adult **741.5**

1. Historical fiction 2. China -- History -- Boxer Rebellion, 1899-1901 -- Graphic novels

ISBN 1596433590; 9781596433595

LC 2013947229

National Book Award for Young People's Literature: Finalist (2013)
Boston Globe-Horn Book Honor: Fiction (2014)
Ignatz Nominee: Outstanding Graphic Novel (2014)

"Life in Little Bao's peaceful rural village is disrupted when . . . a priest and his phalanx of soldiers . . . arrive." They start "smashing the village god, appropriating property, and administering vicious beatings for no reason. Little Bao and his older brothers train in kung fu and swordplay." . . . Little Bao "becomes the leader of a peasant army, eventually marching to Beijing." (School Library Journal)

"China's Boxer Rebellion is the unlikely backdrop for this graphic treatment of young villagers on the opposite sides of history. Bao wants to drive out the white devils that poison his country with opium and Christianity. Four-Girl is an unwanted daughter who finds purpose in the missionary life. Their stories collide in a moment of grace that could only be penned by the Printz Award-winning author of 'American Born Chinese.'" LJ

★ **Saints**; by Gene Luen Yang ; color by Lark Pien. First Second 2013 170 p. (pbk.) $15.99

Grades: 7 8 9 10 11 12 Adult **741.5**

1. Historical fiction 2. China -- History -- Boxer Rebellion, 1899-1901 -- Graphic novels

ISBN 1596436891; 9781596436893

LC 2013947228

Ignatz Nominee: Outstanding Graphic Novel (2014)
Boston Globe-Horn Book Honor: Fiction (2014)
National Book Award for Young People's Literature: Finalist (2013)

This graphic novel, by Gene Luen Yang and Lark Pien, "follows a lonely girl . . . . Unwanted by her family, Four-Girl isn't even given a proper name until she converts to Catholicism and is baptized by the very same priest who bullies Little Bao's village. Four-Girl, now known as Vibiana, leaves home and finds fulfillment in service to the Church, while Little Bao roams the countryside committing acts of increasing violence as his army grows." (School Library Journal)

"Yang presents a 'diptych' of graphic novels set during China's Boxer Rebellion. Boxers follows Little Bao, who learns to harness the power of ancient gods to fight the spread of Christianity; Saints centers on Four-Girl, who sits squarely on the other side of the rebellion. Yang's characteristic infusions of magical realism, bursts of humor, and distinctively drawn characters make for a compelling read." (Horn Book)

Secret coders; Gene Luen Yang & Mike Holmes. First Second 2015 96 p. color illustrations (Secret coders) (hardcover) $17.99

Grades: 4 5 6 7 **741.5**

1. School stories -- Graphic novels 2. Computer programming -- Graphic novels

ISBN 9781626722767; 9781626720756; 1626722765

In this graphic novel, by Gene Yuen Lang and Mike Holmes, "Hopper, an enthusiastic 12-year-old girl . . . , has just started school at the creepy Stately Academy. After getting in a fight . . . with Eni . . . , Hopper and Eni become friends while unraveling the secrets of the school. Robotic birds, family troubles, and sinister, child-hating school administrators lead to a story both emotionally rich and rife with learning opportunities." (School Library Journal)

"Holmes' blocky cartoon illustrations, in black, white, and green, clearly depict basic programming concepts with tidy visual cues, such as grids of floor tiles. Yang and Holmes do such a great job explaining the concepts that even programming newbies will be likely to catch on." Booklist

Other titles in this series are:
Paths and portals (2016)
Secrets and sequences (2017)
Robots and repeats (2017)
Potions and parameters (2018)
Monsters and modules (2018)

The **Shadow** Hero; story by Gene Luen Yang ; art by Sonny Liew ; lettering by Janice Chiang. First Second 2014 176 p. chiefly color illustrations $17.99

Grades: 6 7 8 9 10 **741.5**

1. Superheroes -- Fiction 2. Comic books, strips, etc. 3. Chinese Americans -- Fiction

ISBN 1596436972; 9781596436978

This book, by Gene Luen Yang, is about "Green Turtle, a 1940s comic book hero. . . . The Green Turtle is cast as an unlikely 19-year-old young man, Hank, the son of Chinese immigrants who own a grocery store in 1940s America. When his mother is rescued by a superhero, the loving but overbearing woman decides that it's Hank's fate to become a hero himself, and she does everything in her power to push her son in that direction." (School Library Journal)

"Yang and Liew have crafted an origin story for the Green Turtle, a little-known . . . World War II-era comic superhero created by cartoonist Chu Hing in 1944. Much about the series remains a mystery, as Yang shares in an author's note, but according to rumors Hing wanted his star to be Chinese, and, not surprisingly for the era, his publishers balked at the idea. Now seventy years later, Yang and Liew vindicate the cartoonist by imagining the Green Turtle as 'perhaps . . . the first Asian American superhero.'" Horn Book

Yolen, Jane

Foiled; written by Jane Yolen; artwork by Mike Cavallaro. First Second 2010 160p il pa $15.99

Grades: 7 8 9 10 **741.5**

1. Graphic novels 2. Fantasy graphic novels 3. Fencing -- Graphic novels

ISBN 978-1-59643-279-6; 1-59643-279-9

"Besting competitors twice her age in tournaments, and keeping a strict routine of fencing practice, homework, and role-playing games, Aliera is a loner and likes it that way—until she becomes lab partners with the cutest boy in school. . . . Turns out her new ruby-handled foil is the key to his interest in her, and to the yet-unseen magical dimension she must keep in balance. . . . [Yolen] has created a strong, conflicted, and relatable girl hero. . . . Cavallaro's artwork suits Aliera's monochrome existence, but burst into life when she finally sees (in color!) the faerie beasties cheering her on." Booklist

741.6 Graphic design, illustration, commercial art

★ **Artist** to artist; 23 major illustrators talk to children about their art. Philomel Books 2007 105p il $30

Grades: 4 5 6 7 **741.6**

1. Illustrators 2. Illustration of books 3. Picture books for children

ISBN 978-0-399-24600-5

"This anthology celebrates and elucidates contemporary picture-book art. . . . Ashley Bryan, Quentin Blake, Leo Lionni, Alice Provensen, and Gennady Spirin are among the contributors, whose comments are formatted as signed letters illustrated with childhood photographs. . . . Each artist includes glorious self-portraits and a gatefold page that reveals a marvelous array of sketches, color mixes, and studio scenes. All readers will find something that piques curiosity or provides insight." Booklist

Ellabbad, Mohieddine

The **illustrator's** notebook; [translated from the Arabic by Sarah Quinn] Groundwood Books/House of Anansi Press 2006 30p il $16.95

Grades: 5 6 7 8 **741.6**

1. Illustrators 2. Illustration of books

ISBN 0-88899-700-0

"Part children's book, part autobiography, part design treatise, this hard-to-categorize Egyptian import is full of wonders from start to finish. Ellabbad uses excerpts from his notebooks to discuss ways of seeing art from an artist's perspective and as someone from an Arabic culture. Printed like the Egyptian edition—read right to left—the pages are magnificently and surprisingly illustrated, juxtaposing Arabic script (English translations appear in the margins), watercolor paintings, pasted-in photos and pictures from comic books, and all manner of characters from Eastern and Western cultures." SLJ

Flath, Camden

Media in the 21st century; artists, animators, and graphic designers. Mason Crest Publishers 2010 64p il (New careers for the 21st century: finding your role in the global renewal) lib bdg $22.95; pa $9.95

Grades: 7 8 9 10 **741.6**

1. Artists 2. Vocational guidance

ISBN 978-1-4222-1816-7 lib bdg; 1-4222-1816-3 lib bdg; 978-1-4222-2037-5 pa; 1-4222-2037-0 pa

LC 2010014935

"Chapters identify and emphasize specific careers—important strengths, necessary aptitudes and interests, education and training, projected earnings, closely related occupations, type of work environment, and predictions for the future of the field. . . . Color photos have a small role amid the many statistics, figures, graphs and charts that support and supplement the . . . [text]." SLJ

Includes bibliographical references

Marcus, Leonard S., 1950-

A **Caldecott** celebration; seven artists and their paths to the Caldecott medal. rev ed.; Walker & Co. 2008 55p il $19.95; lib bdg $20.85

Grades: Adult Professional **741.6**

1. Illustrators 2. Caldecott Medal 3. Illustration of books

ISBN 978-0-8027-9703-2; 0-8027-9703-2; 978-0-8027-9704-9 lib bdg; 0-8027-9704-0 lib bdg

LC 2007-23132

First published 1998

Profiles seven Caldecott award winning books and their authors, including Robert McCloskey's "Make Way for Ducklings," Marcia Brown's "Cinderella," Maurice Sendak's "Where the Wild Things Are," William Steig's "Sylvester and the Magic Pebble," Chris Van Allsburg's "Jumanji," David Wiesner's "Tuesday," and Mordicai Gerstein's "The Man Who Walked Between the Towers"

"The value of this volume is that Marcus makes these exceptional author/illustrators, and the processes by which they created their award-winning picture books, accessible to children and to adults who value children's literature." SLJ

Randolph Caldecott; the man who could not stop drawing. Leonard S. Marcus. Farrar, Straus & Giroux (BYR) 2013 64 p. (hardcover) $24.99

Grades: 5 6 7 8 **741.6**

1. Picture books for children 2. Illustrators -- England -- Biography

ISBN 0374310254; 9780374310257

LC 2012050406

This book is a biography of Randolph Caldecott, "the illustrator for whom the Caldecott Medal is named." Leonard S. Marcus begins by "describing the changes wrought in 19th-century Great Britain by the steam engine, which eased travel and greatly expanded distribution of media. He details Caldecott's early days clerking in a bank and his search for freelance illustration work, then describes how diligence and charm lead to his first book-illustrating assignment" and then to a career in illustration. (Publishers Weekly)

Tan, Shaun

The **bird** king; an artist's notebook. Shaun Tan. Arthur A. Levine Books 2013 128 p. (hardcover : alk. paper) $19.99

Grades: 3 4 5 6 7 741.6

1. Artists' notebooks

ISBN 0545465133; 9780545465137

LC 2012016625

This book by author and illustrator Shaun Tan "is a collection of sketches, random jottings, preliminary designs for book, film and theatre projects, sketchbook pages and drawings from life. Each of these represent some aspect of a working process, whereby stories generally evolve from visual research and free-wheeling doodles. They are also 'unfinished' pieces created in a single sitting, not originally intended for publication." (Publisher's note)

741.9 Collections of drawings

Volavkova, Hana

--I never saw another butterfly-- children's drawings and poems from Terezin concentration camp, 1942-1944. edited by Hana Volavková; foreword by Chaim Potok; afterword by Vaclav Havel. expanded 2nd ed; Schocken Bks. 1993 xxii, 106p il hardcover o.p. pa $17.50

Grades: 4 5 6 7 741.9

1. Child artists 2. Children's writings 3. Holocaust, 1933-1945 4. Terezin (Czechoslovakia: Concentration camp)

ISBN 0-8052-1015-6 pa

LC 92-50477

Original Czech edition, 1959; first American edition published 1964 by McGraw-Hill

"Of the 15,000 children who passed through Terezin before going to Auschwitz, only 100 lived. This book is a collection of poems and drawings by some of them. . . . This touching book adds another facet to library collections on the Holocaust." SLJ

742 Perspective in drawing

DuBosque, Doug

Draw 3-D; a step-by-step guide to perspective drawing. Peel Productions 1999 63p il pa $8.99

Grades: 6 7 8 9 10 742

1. Drawing 2. Perspective

ISBN 0-939217-14-7

LC 98-42174

"Using easy-to-follow, step-by-step sketches, DuBosque introduces readers to the techniques of three-dimensional drawing. Beginning with such elementary concepts as depth, he progresses logically through shading, reflections, and multiple vanishing points. The supportive tone encourages novices to keep trying and not become discouraged." SLJ

743 Drawing and drawings by subject

Ames, Lee J.

Draw 50 aliens, UFO's galaxy ghouls, milky way marauders, and other extra terrestrial creatures; [by] Lee J. Ames with Ric Estrada. Doubleday 1998 un il (Draw 50) hardcover o.p. pa $8.95

Grades: 4 5 6 7 743

1. Drawing

ISBN 978-0-385-49144-0; 0-385-49144-1; 978-0-385-49145-7 pa; 0-385-49145-X pa

LC 98-20077

A step-by-step guide to drawing outer space creatures

Draw 50 beasties and yugglies and turnover uglies and things that go bump in the night. Doubleday 1988 il (Draw 50) hardcover o.p. pa $8.95

Grades: 4 5 6 7 743

1. Drawing 2. Monsters in art

ISBN 978-0-385-24625-5; 0-385-24625-0; 978-0-385-26767-0 pa; 0-385-26767-3 pa

LC 88-16143

Provides step-by-step instructions for drawing monsters, goons, and gruesome beasts

Ames "encourages readers to take plenty of time and suggests very lightly sketching out the step-by-step drawings so that mistakes may be rectified. This one, with its popular subject of imaginative monsters and other nightmare inhabitants, will be a sure-fire circulator." SLJ

Other Draw 50 titles are:

Draw 50 animal 'toons

Draw 50 animals

Draw 50 athletes

Draw 50 buildings and other structures

Draw 50 boats, ships, trucks & trains

Draw 50 cats

Draw 50 dinosaurs and other prehistoric animals

Draw 50 dogs

Draw 50 horses

Draw 50 monsters, creeps, superheroes, demons, dragons, nerds, dirts, ghouls, giants, vampires, zombies, and other curiosa

Draw 50 baby animals

Draw 50 flowers, trees, and other plants

Draw 50 birds; [by] Lee J. Ames with Tony D'Adamo. Doubleday 1996 un il (Draw 50) hardcover o.p. pa $8.95

Grades: 4 5 6 7 743

1. Drawing 2. Birds in art

ISBN 978-0-385-47006-3; 0-385-47006-1; 978-0-385-47163-3 pa; 0-385-47163-7 pa

LC 96-27621

Draw 50 endangered animals; [by] Lee J. Ames with Warren Budd. Doubleday 1992 un il (Draw 50) hardcover o.p. pa $8.95

Grades: 4 5 6 7 743

1. Drawing 2. Animals in art 3. Animal painting and illustration

ISBN 978-0-385-41191-2; 0-385-41191-X; 978-0-385-46985-2 pa; 0-385-46985-3 pa

LC 92-23092

Step-by-step instructions on how to draw a variety of threatened species from all over the world

Draw 50 famous faces. Doubleday 1978 un il (Draw 50) hardcover o.p. pa $8.95

Grades: 4 5 6 7 743

1. Drawing 2. Portraits

ISBN 978-0-385-13217-6; 0-385-13217-4; 978-0-385-23432-0 pa; 0-385-23432-5 pa

LC 77-15878

Step-by-step instructions for drawing historical figures, statesmen, sports, stars, and entertainers

Draw 50 holiday decorations; [by] Lee J. Ames with Ray Burns. Doubleday 1987 un il (Draw 50) hardcover o.p. pa $8.95
Grades: 4 5 6 7 **743**

1. Drawing 2. Holiday decorations
ISBN 978-0-385-19057-2; 0-385-19057-3; 978-0-385-26770-0 pa; 0-385-26770-3 pa
LC 87-15581

Step-by-step instructions for drawing a variety of holiday subjects such as Baby New Year, Cupid and his arrow, July 4th rockets, turkey, pumpkin, Easter basket, Santa Claus, and a menorah

Draw 50 people; [by] Lee J. Ames with Creig Flessel. Doubleday 1993 un il (Draw 50) hardcover o.p. pa $8.95
Grades: 4 5 6 7 **743**

1. Portraits 2. Drawing -- Technique
ISBN 978-0-385-41193-6; 0-385-41193-6; 978-0-385-41194-3 pa; 0-385-41194-4 pa
LC 93-20631

Bergin, Mark

How to draw pets. PowerKids Press 2011 32p il (How to draw) lib bdg $25.25; pa $11.75
Grades: 4 5 6 7 **743**

1. Animals in art 2. Drawing -- Technique
ISBN 978-1-4488-4511-8 lib bdg; 978-1-4488-4517-0 pa
LC 2010049184

"The cover features sketches of a cat, dog, and rabbit, allowing children to see both structure as well as finished product. Inside, the book starts by showing pictures of animals drawn with different materials such as pencils, ink, charcoals, and pastels, and explains what each medium accomplishes. Next comes an introduction to perspective and looks at different parts of animals. The familiar circle method then gets kids drawing pets from head to tails. . . . The amount of information throughout is just right: thorough but not overwhelming." Booklist

Includes glossary

Butkus, Mike

How to draw zombies; discover the secrets to drawing, painting, and illustrating the undead. by Mike Butkus and Merrie Destefano. Walter Foster 2011 128p il map $48.95
Grades: 8 9 10 11 12 **743**

1. Zombies 2. Monsters in art 3. Drawing -- Technique
ISBN 978-1-936309-63-4; 1-936309-63-7
LC 2010052983

"For young artists fascinated by the living dead, this sophisticated drawing book gives step-by-step instructions for creating a variety of unexpected characters. . . . Most of the drawings are done in pencil, but acrylic paints are also occasionally featured. An added bonus is the instructions for giving a final digital touch to the drawings on the computer. . . . Extra bits of zombie lore are added. Fans of the truly terrifying will appreciate the fact that the featured pictures attain a high level of creepiness. . . . Those looking for a zombie drawing book with added bite will find hours of fun with this one." Booklist

Hodges, Jared

Draw furries; how to create anthropomorphic and fantasy animals. by Jared Hodges and Lindsay Cibos. IMPACT Books 2009 127p il pa $22.99
Grades: 7 8 9 10 **743**

1. Animals in art 2. Fantasy in art 3. Drawing -- Technique
ISBN 978-1-60061-417-0 pa; 1-60061-417-5 pa
LC 2009019609

"Hodges and Cibos have created a thorough guide. Describing creatures in terms of a sliding scale from human to animal, they begin with some tips on basic anatomy and style. . . . The instruction is grouped by the kind of animal portrayed. . . . Full-color spreads throughout show what can be achieved with practice, and the book concludes with chapters on color and perspective." SLJ

Masiello, Ralph

Ralph Masiello's ancient Egypt drawing book. Charlesbridge 2008 un $16.95; pa $7.95
Grades: 4 5 6 7 **743**

1. Drawing 2. Egypt -- Civilization
ISBN 978-1-57091-533-8; 978-1-57091-534-5 pa
LC 2007027023

"Masiello starts by showing readers how to draw the Great Pyramid of Khafre using simple shapes and lines. His easy-to-follow instructions gradually build in complexity, as he moves to ancient symbols, then Egyptian gods, Queen Nefertiti, and King Tutankhamen. The finished pictures are colored with mixed media. Concise paragraphs tell more about each subject, including historical context." Horn Book Guide

Includes bibliographical references

Miller, Steve

Dinosaurs : how to draw thunder lizards and other prehistoric beasts; [by] Steve Miller. Watson-Guptill Publications 2008 144p il pa $19.95
Grades: 8 9 10 11 12 Adult **743**

1. Drawing 2. Dinosaurs in art
ISBN 978-0-8230-9919-1 pa; 0-8230-9919-9 pa
LC 2008531195

First published 2005 with title: Thunder lizards; how to draw fantastic dinosaurs

This offers instruction in drawing dinosaurs based on scientific research and includes examples of the work of such artists as Arthur Adams, Bryan Baugh, Brett Booth, Scott Harman, Gregory S. Paul, and Bernie Wrightson

Includes bibliographical references

Peffer, Jessica

DragonArt; how to draw fantastic dragons and fantasy creatures. Impact Books 2005 127p il pa $19.99
Grades: 5 6 7 8 **743**

1. Dragons 2. Drawing 3. Mythical animals
ISBN 1-58180-657-4
LC 2005013013

This is a guide to drawing dragons and other mythical beasts such as griffins, guardian gargoyles, and deadly basilisks.

"This book has great writing and superb illustrations and manages to do everything right from the front cover to the index." SLJ

Stephens, Jay

Heroes! draw your own superheroes, gadget geeks & other do-gooders. [by] Jay Stephens. Lark Books 2007 64p il $12.95; pa $5.95

Grades: 4 5 6 7 **743**

1. Drawing 2. Superheroes 3. Cartoons and caricatures

ISBN 978-1-57990-934-5; 1-57990-934-5; 978-1-60059-179-2 pa; 1-60059-179-5 pa

LC 2006101661

"Stephens shows just how to draw [superheroes]. . . . Stephens does a good job organizing his material, beginning with a bit of history, then moving quickly to hero heads, . . . and on to masks, disguises, physical features, power effects, and action moves. The brightly colored illustrations offer plenty of how-to info and lots of great heroes, male and female, to use as models." Booklist

Other titles in this series are:

Monsters!

Robots!

745 Decorative arts

Major, John S.

★ **Caravan** to America; living arts of the Silk Road. [by] John S. Major and Betty J. Belanus. Cricket Bks. 2002 130p il map hardcover o.p. pa $15.95

Grades: 4 5 6 7 **745**

1. Arts 2. Cookbook writers 3. Cooking teachers

ISBN 0-8126-2666-4; 0-8126-2677-X pa

LC 2002-5477

Profiles eight artists and artisans now living in America who are originally from the "Silk Road," an ancient network of caravan trails through which trade goods, ideas, and arts pass between Asia and the Mediterranean

"Full of colorful and informative archival and contemporary photographs and drawings. . . . Each person's story is told in an interesting manner, and information about their specialty and its history is woven throughout the text. . . . Not only is the work informative, but it is handsome as well." SLJ

Includes glossary and bibliographical references

Tejubehan (Singer)

★ **Drawing** from the City; Teju Behan. Pgw 2012 28 p. $35.95

Grades: 3 4 5 6 7 8 **745**

1. India 2. Artists 3. Poverty

ISBN 9380340176; 9789380340173

This "autobiographical art book recounts self-taught artist Teju Behan's journey from an impoverished childhood in rural India, through her family's efforts to improve their lot in a tent city in Mumbai, and into her adulthood, when she lived as a singer and artist with her husband. . . . Hand-screen-printed illustrations comprised of intricate linework and patterns of dots underscore elements of the text." (Kirkus)

745.2 Industrial art and design

Arato, Rona

Design it! the ordinary things we use every day and the not-so-ordinary ways they came to be. illustrations by Claudia Newell. Tundra Books 2010 71p il pa $20.95

Grades: 4 5 6 7 **745.2**

1. Industrial design 2. Inventors 3. Inventions 4. Design, Industrial

ISBN 978-0-88776-846-0 pa; 0-88776-846-6 pa

"This book opens with an explanation of what industrial designers do and with whom they work to make better products. Brief chapters then cover such topics as home, communications, lighting, and toy design and include a good-design checklist that takes function, usability, ergonomics, aesthetics, and greenness into consideration. The language is chatty and inviting, and the pages are full of cartoon illustrations and text superimposed on colorful geometric backgrounds. Sidebars offer a wealth of further information." SLJ

Mooney, Carla

Industrial design; why smartphones aren't round and other mysteries with science activities for kids. by Carla Mooney ; illustrated by Tom Casteel. Nomad Press 2018 122 p. $22.95

Grades: 5 6 7 8 **745.2**

1. Engineering 2. Industrial design

ISBN 1619306700; 9781619306707

In this book in the Build It Yourself series, by Carla Mooney, illustrated by Tom Casteel, "readers ages 10-15 engage in and learn about the engineering design process from its earliest beginnings when individuals designed and crafted their own tools to today, when engineers work to find the best design for products that are then manufactured in bulk by automated machines." (Publisher's note)

"Industrial Design looks at the steps of the design process; how industrial design changed the world, as with sewer systems and electric lights; innovations in electronics and computer-aided design (e.g., 3-D printing); and considerations for the future, such as sustainable and user experience designs" (Booklist)

Welsbacher, Anne

Earth -friendly design; by Anne Welsbacher. Lerner Publications Company 2009 72p il (Saving our living Earth) lib bdg $30.60

Grades: 5 6 7 8 **745.2**

1. Industrial design 2. Environmental protection

ISBN 978-0-8225-7564-1 lib bdg; 0-8225-7564-7 lib bdg

LC 2007-35925

"Provides a thorough, interesting discussion of multiple aspects of [Earth-friendly design], including historical origins, the current situation, and potential solutions. . . . Photos from around the world accompany discussions. . . . [This is a] solid choice to replace outdated books." SLJ

Includes glossary and bibliographical references

745.5 Handicrafts

Blake, Susannah

Crafts for pampering yourself; Susannah Blake. Enslow Publishers, Inc. 2013 32 p. color illustrations (Eco chic) $22.60

Grades: 4 5 6 7 8 **745.5**

1. Cosmetics 2. Handicraft 3. Green products

ISBN 0766043142; 9780766043145

LC 2012045280

In this book, author Susannah Blake offers suggestions on how readers can "have an eco-friendly pampering party with these . . . craft ideas. From lip balm to bath infusion, this book offers easy step-by-step instructions to upcycle, customise and add sparkle to your bathroom routines." (Publisher's note)

"Numbered step-by-step illustrations; a fresh, tween-friendly design; explanations of basic craft skills; and instructions for throwing a 'pamper party' round out the beauty-meets-responsibility fun."

Carlson, Laurie

Knit, hook, and spin; a kid's activity guide to fiber arts and crafts. Laurie Carlson. Chicago Review Press Inc. 2016 144 p. illustrations (trade paper) $14.99

Grades: 4 5 6 7 **745.5**

1. Handicraft for children 2. Textile crafts

ISBN 9781613734001

LC 2015044783

This book, by Laurie Carlson, is an "activity book packed with over 70 projects across a variety of fiber arts including knitting, felting, knotting and braiding, spinning, weaving, crocheting, and dyeing. Clear instructions and illustrations guide you in creating these cute, useful crafts." (Publisher's note)

"From slippers to tote bags and from friendship bracelets to comfort dolls, there is something for almost anyone wanting to learn how to create from these very tactile sources." Kirkus

Dobson, Jolie

The **duct** tape book; 25 Projects to Make With Duct Tape. Firefly Books Ltd 2012 144 p. (paperback) $14.95

Grades: 7 8 9 10 11 12 **745.5**

1. Duct tape 2. Handicraft

ISBN 1770850988; 9781770850989

This book by Jolie Dobson on crafting with duct tape "contains 25 . . . projects" with "instructions and color photographs." The projects include a "bike pannier . . . vest . . . purse . . . piggy bank . . . wallet . . . bow ties . . . picture frames . . . knapsack . . . skirt and chaps . . . [and] tissue box." (Publisher's note)

Martin, Laura C.

Nature's art box; from t-shirts to twig baskets: 65 cool projects for crafty kids to make with natural materials you can find anywhere. written by Laura C. Martin; with drawings by David Cain. Storey Bks. 2003 215p il hardcover o.p. pa $16.95

Grades: 4 5 6 7 **745.5**

1. Nature craft

ISBN 1-58017-503-1; 1-58017-490-6 pa

LC 2002-154374

"Each chapter includes information about historical and ethnic uses for the natural substances. Activities are rated by level of difficulty; all have easy-to-follow instructions. Projects range from baskets, picture frames, wreaths, necklaces, and gift wrap to body paint, amulet bags, and painted stones. . . . The projects display a respect for nature and art, and a simple, subtle beauty." SLJ

Includes bibliographical references

Scheunemann, Pam

Trash to treasure; a kid's upcycling guide to crafts : fun, easy projects with paper, plastic, glass & ceramics, fabric, metal, and odds & ends. Pam Scheunemann. Scarletta Junior Readers 2013 144 p. color illustrations (pbk.) $15.95

Grades: 5 6 7 8 **745.5**

1. Handicraft 2. Recycling (Waste, etc.) 3. Salvage (Waste, etc.)

ISBN 9781938063183

LC 2013010144

This book, by Pam Scheunemann, "will help kids get creative and recycle and repurpose their trash into handmade treasures. All projects feature common everyday items to reuse in a fun new way. From bottle-top pop art to felted tin-can organizers, kids will love making useful crafts and helping the environment. Great tips and advice on reusing, garage sales, and spotting treasures are also provided." (Publisher's note)

Torres, Laura

Best friends forever! 199 crafts to make and share. Workman Pub. 2004 148p il pa $13.95

Grades: 5 6 7 8 **745.5**

1. Handicraft

ISBN 0-7611-3274-0

LC 2004-45635

"These projects are organized into seven categories: 'Photo Fun,' 'Cool Notes,' 'Gifts to Make Together,' 'Home and School,' 'Fashions,' 'Fun and Games,' and 'Jewelry.' . . . Using clear language, detailed directions, and bright color photos of the finished products, Torres has pulled together a wealth of craft ideas." SLJ

Warwick, Ellen

Everywear; written by Ellen Warwick; illustrated by Bernice Lum. Kids Can Press 2008 80p il (Planet girl) $14.95

Grades: 5 6 7 8 **745.5**

1. Handicraft 2. Fashion accessories 3. Dress accessories

ISBN 978-1-55337-799-3; 1-55337-799-0

"After several opening pages that introduce supplies, . . . very basic stitching skills, and terminology, girls turn to the . . . issue of hair: woven-ribbon bands, jazzed-up chopsticks; fabric-flower-bedecked combs; reversible ponytail wraps. Next come body adornments . . . followed by stuff to stow it in, of clutched, dangled, and toted varieties. Each project features a list of supplies, . . . clearly numbered steps with cartoon-styled illustrations . . . and full-color photograph of the finished item. . . . [This has] genuine sleepover appeal." Bull Cent Child Books

Wolf, Laurie Goldrich

Recyclo -gami; 40 crafts to make your friends green with envy! Running Press Teens 2010 112p il $14.95

Grades: 4 5 6 7 **745.5**

1. Recycling 2. Handicraft

ISBN 978-0-7624-4052-8; 0-7624-4052-X

"Wolf's fun, resourceful projects offer straightforward ways to reuse common materials to make accessories, jewelry, household decorations, games, and gifts. Leftover tissue or wrapping paper can be used to create decoupage plates; old crayons are melted and baked into molds to make multicolored crayons; and unused CDs and DVDs are transformed into funky, freeform bowls when melted in the oven. . . . The ease of most of the activities should inspire readers to see the recycling bin as a potential treasure trove." Publ Wkly

Wolfe, Brian

Extreme face painting; 50 friendly & fiendish demos. [by] Brian and Nick Wolfe. IMPACT Books 2010 127p il pa $24.99

Grades: 6 7 8 9 10 11 12 Adult **745.5**

1. Face painting

ISBN 978-1-4403-0270-1; 1-4403-0270-7

LC 2010-17861

"This is a guide for experienced artists ready to take their craft to the next level. . . . These instructions show how to use shading and highlights to shape a variety of frightening and whimsical forms. The authors open the book with basic information about materials, colors, and techniques. Then they demonstrate different projects. . . . Each entry has a full-page color photograph of the final product and smaller photos of each step in the painting process. Clearly written instructions appear below each photo. . . . Some of the fiendish visages are quite frightening. The book comes with an informative DVD where the authors demonstrate two of the face paintings from the book. . . . This is a great resource." SLJ

745.54 Papers

Diehn, Gwen

Making books that fly, fold, wrap, hide, pop up, twist, and turn; books for kids to make. Lark Bks. 1998 96p il hardcover o.p. pa $12.95

Grades: 4 5 6 7 **745.54**

1. Handicraft 2. Paper crafts

ISBN 1-57990-023-2; 978-1-57990-326-8 pa; 1-57990-326-6 pa

LC 97-41037

Presents instructions for making various kinds of books including those that carry messages across space and time as well as those that save words, ideas, and pictures

"Clear directions and diagrams and attractive full-color photographs of completed projects will make it easy for readers to duplicate 18 different folded, wrapped, and pop-up books." Booklist

Includes glossary

Latno, Mark

The **paper** boomerang book; build them, throw them, and get them to return every time. Chicago Review Press 2010 245p il pa $12.95

Grades: 5 6 7 8 **745.54**

1. Boomerangs 2. Paper crafts

ISBN 978-1-56976-282-0 pa; 1-56976-282-1 pa

LC 2010007251

"In a unique . . . guide Latno . . . [explains] how to make, fine-tune, and decorate a type of paper boomerang that can be constructed with commonly available materials and thrown with (relative) safety indoors. The instructions and simply drawn diagrams are embedded in a history of boomerangs and throwing sticks, a challenging technical discussion of the physics of boomerangs and gyroscopes, and very detailed descriptions of the characteristics of railroad board (Latno's preferred paper) and alternatives, plus art-and-craft materials that can be used to dress up finished models." SLJ

Includes glossary and bibliographical references

Phillips, Jennifer

Paper artist; creations kids can fold, tear, wear, or share. by Gail D. Green, Kara L. Laughlin, and Jennifer Phillips. Capstone 2013 112 p. col. ill. (pbk.) $12.95

Grades: 4 5 6 7 8 **745.54**

1. Paper crafts 2. Paper work

ISBN 1623700043; 9781623700041

LC 2012032454

"From the garland wind chimes on the front cover to the picture frame on the back cover, the book is filled with easy, creative paper projects set within a clear, mature, magazine design." (Booklist)

"The well-organized layout is stunning, with beautiful photographs and step-by-step instructions that are appealing and simple to follow. Useful extra tips are added if needed." SLJ

Turnbull, Stephanie

Cool stuff to make with paper; Stephanie Turnbull. Smart Apple Media 2015 32 p. color illustrations (Cool stuff) $31.35

Grades: 4 5 6 7 8 **745.54**

1. Paper crafts 2. Handicraft 3. Paper work 4. Party decorations

ISBN 1625881894; 9781625881892

LC 2013047372

This book, by Stephanie Turnbull, "offers kids the opportunity to master basic methods of papercraft while also allowing them to express their own creativity. Clear, approachable text and a colorful, magazine-style format make these titles inviting reads, while step-by-step instructions help ensure projects are easy to complete." (Publisher's note)

Includes bibliographical references (page 31) and index

745.592 Toys, models, miniatures, related objects

Aranzi Aronzo Inc.

Cute dolls; by Aranzi Aronzo! Vertical Inc. 2007 79p il (Let's make cute stuff) pa $14.95

Grades: 6 7 8 9 10 **745.592**

1. Dolls 2. Handicraft

ISBN 978-1-932234-78-7 pa; 1-932234-78-0 pa

Original Japanese edition 2002

"Familiarity with Japan's Aranzi Aronzo brand . . . won't be necessary to muster an audience for this doll-making book. The felt-trimmed, jersey-cloth, self-consciously cute 'mascots' will be an instant draw for manga-loving teens. . . . Those who attempt one of the 21 rag dolls, for which a sewing machine is recommended, will find the techniques well explained, as well as supported by and entertainingly extended by photographs and small cartoon representations of the doll characters." Booklist

Harbo, Christopher L.

Paper airplanes: Flight school, level 1. Capstone Press 2010 32p il (Edge books. Paper airplanes) lib bdg $26.65

Grades: 3 4 5 6 **745.592**

1. Paper crafts 2. Airplanes -- Models

ISBN 978-1-4296-4741-0 lib bdg; 1-4296-4741-8 lib bdg

LC 2010001005

This "includes a list of basic materials and an overview of folding instructions and techniques. . . . Along with hints on how to hold the plane for takeoff to maximize strengths are suggestions on conducting friendly competitions with the finished products. Sure to keep readers busy for hours." SLJ

Includes bibliographical references

Other titles in this series are:

Copilot, level 2

Pilot, level 3

Captain, level 4

Mercer, Bobby

The **flying** machine book; build and launch 35 rockets, gliders, helicopters, boomerangs, and more. Bobby Mercer. Chicago Review Press 2012 ix, 197 p.p ill. (pbk.) $14.95

Grades: 4 5 6 **745.592**

1. Flight 2. Aeronautics 3. Airplanes -- Models 4. Models and modelmaking 5. Paper airplanes 6. Flying-machines -- Models

ISBN 9781613740866

LC 2011041174

This book provides "step-by-step instructions for 35 aerodynamic projects . . . Physics teacher [Bobby] Mercer . . . here provides . . . directions for building a variety of flying machines including rockets, gliders, helicopters, boomerangs and assorted launchers. An opening chapter called 'Flight School' introduces the Bernoulli principle and four forces: lift, thrust, drag and weight. . . . Each subsequent chapter begins with more flight school, repeating the relevant principles and applying them to the different forms of flying machines described. Many of the constructions use similar techniques and most are not difficult. The models are made of common materials: card stock and old folders, drinking straws, rubber bands and duct tape." (Kirkus Reviews)

Rigsby, Mike

Amazing rubber band cars; easy-to-build wind-up racers, models, and toys. [by] Mike Rigsby. Chicago Review Press 2007 121p il lib bdg $12.95

Grades: 4 5 6 7 **745.592**

1. Toys 2. Handicraft 3. Automobiles -- Models

ISBN 978-1-55652-736-4 lib bdg; 1-55652-736-5 lib bdg

LC 2007013969

This offers instructions for making toy and model cars "using mostly cardboard, glue, pencils, rubber bands, and a few other easily obtainable materials. . . . Readers will learn about corrugated and flat cardboard, and how to use glue and work with templates. Excellent instructions are accompanied by black-and-white photos every step of the way. . . . These projects are fun to construct, and inquisitive minds will be fascinated by the moving cars." SLJ

745.593 Useful objects

Turnbull, Stephanie

Diaries and keepsakes; style secrets for girls. Stephanie Turnbull. Smart Apple Media 2014 32 p. color illustrations (Girl talk) (library binding) $31.35

Grades: 4 5 6 7 8 **745.593**

1. Diaries 2. Scrapbooking 3. Handicraft for children 4. Gift books 5. Book design

ISBN 1599209454; 9781599209456

LC 2012051570

This book, by Stephanie Turnbull, part of the "Girl Talk" series," is "for preteen and teen girls on crafty ways to make and keep memories of events. Includes information on decorating, writing in, and hiding a private diary. Also includes idea for using photos to create scrapbooks and other photo keepsakes, such as mugs." (Publisher's note)

Includes bibliographical references (page 31) and index

745.594 Decorative objects

Trusty, Brad

The **kids'** guide to balloon twisting; by Brad and Cindy Trusty. Capstone Press 2011 32p il (Kids' guides) lib bdg $26.65

Grades: 4 5 6 7 **745.594**

1. Balloons 2. Handicraft

ISBN 978-1-4296-5444-9; 1-4296-5444-9

LC 2010036470

Gives kids step-by-step instructions about how to twist balloon animals and other shapes.

"Rare is the kid not dazzled by the squeaking, twisting balloon maestros out there, and this brightly illustrated, step-by-step guide makes it easy—well, easy-ish." Booklist

Includes bibliographical references

Turnbull, Stephanie

Cards and gifts; style secrets for girls. by Stephanie Turnbull. Smart Apple Media 2014 32 p. color illustrations (Girl talk) (library binding) $31.35

Grades: 4 5 6 7 8 **745.594**

1. Greeting cards 2. Handicraft for children

ISBN 1599209446; 9781599209449; 9781625889959

LC 2012051546

This book, by Stephanie Turnbull, features "crafty ways to make and present gifts. Includes information on materials that work best and step-by-step instructions to create cards, envelopes, photo frames, cookies, and other treats for girls." (Publisher's note)

Includes bibliographical references (p. 31) and index

745.6 Calligraphy, heraldic design, illumination

Winters, Eleanor

Calligraphy for kids. Sterling Pub. Co. 2004 128p il $14.95

Grades: 6 7 8 9 **745.6**

1. Calligraphy

ISBN 1-4027-0664-2

LC 2003-23438

This "guide to calligraphy begins with a survey of materials, a glossary, and suggestions on posture and pen and paper positions. Succinct chapters showing how to create a variety of alphabets follow. Winters . . . folds fascinating history into her expert instructions. Her clean layouts showcase beautifully rendered examples and practical exercises." Booklist

746 Textile arts

Slee, Natasha

Planet fashion; 100 years of fashion history. Natasha Slee, illustrated by Cynthia Kittler. Motorbooks Intl 2019 64 p. $24.99

Grades: 4 5 6 7 8 **746**

1. Fashion -- History 2. Clothing and dress -- History

ISBN 1786031957; 9781786031952

In this book, by Natasha Slee, illustrated by Cynthia Kittler, "travel through 25 scenes in fashion history, circling the globe with your two young stylish travel companions--one boy and one girl, dressed the part in every picture. Each lavishly illustrated scene captures the mood and style of a unique time and place, accompanied by a trove of fashion history facts." (Publisher's note)

746.43 Knitting, crocheting, tatting

Bradberry, Sarah

★ **Kids** knit! simple steps to nifty projects. [by] Sarah Bradberry. Sterling Pub. Co. 2004 96p il hardcover o.p. pa $9.95

Grades: 5 6 7 8 **746.43**

1. Knitting

ISBN 0-8069-7733-7; 978-1-4027-4057-2 pa; 1-4027-4057-3 pa

LC 2004-19375

Presents basic knitting techniques and instructions for making a backpack, pillow, doll, and other simple projects

This "book works equally well for beginners and experienced knitters. . . . Besides the requisite information on knitting and purling, there are invaluable tips about finishing garments, fixing mistakes, and adding embellishments. The projects have been chosen with an eye toward simplicity, yet they have real appeal." Booklist

Rimoli, Ana Paula

Amigurumi world; seriously cute crochet. Martingale & Co. 2008 80p il $18.95

Grades: 7 8 9 10 11 12 Adult **746.43**

1. Toys 2. Crocheting

ISBN 978-1-5647-7847-5; 1-5647-7847-9

LC 2007041240

This offers instructions for crocheting toy animals such as baby monkeys, bears, owls, hedgehogs, and elephants.

Snow, Tamie

Tiny yarn animals; amigurumi friends to make and enjoy. Home 2008 61p il $12.95

Grades: 8 9 10 11 12 Adult **746.43**

1. Toys 2. Crocheting

ISBN 978-1-55788-530-2; 1-55788-530-3

LC 2008-013935

This is a "book of crocheted animal patterns. The 20 toys in the collection range from the expected (pig, lamb, and mouse) to the quirky (beaver, lemur, and hedgehog) and they are all cheery, colorful, and cute. A beginners' tutorial provides full-color photographic illustrations of basic crochet stitches, and the directions are clear enough for first-time crocheters to understand." Libr J

Turner, Sharon

Find your style and knit it too; by Sharon Turner. Wiley 2007 165p il pa $14.99

Grades: 6 7 8 9 **746.43**

1. Knitting

ISBN 978-0-470-13987-5 pa; 0-470-13987-0 pa

LC 2007028419

This is a "full-service knit book for teens and pre-teens. . . . The book works on every level. Beginning with knitting basics, Turner explains everything from choosing materials to fundamental how-tos . . . to fixing mistakes. . . . [This offers] easy-to-follow patterns, each illustrated by a crisp color photograph." Booklist

746.46 Patchwork and quilting

Rubin, Susan Goldman

The **quilts** of Gee's Bend; Susan Goldman Rubin. Abrams Books for Young Readers 2017 56 p. color illustrations, map (hardback) $21.95

Grades: 5 6 7 8 **746.46**

1. Quilts 2. African American art 3. African American women 4. Quilts -- Alabama -- Wilcox County -- History 5. African American women -- Alabama -- Wilcox County 6. African American quilts -- Alabama -- Wilcox County 7. African American quiltmakers -- Alabama -- Wilcox County

ISBN 9781419721311

LC 2016029253

This book, by Susan Goldman Rubin, explores the history and culture of the women of Gee's Bend in southern Alabama, as well as their quilting traditions. . . . "Rubin . . . look[s] at an important facet of African American art and culture. . . . [The book] shares specifics about this rare community and its rich traditions, allowing children to pause to consider history through the eyes of the people who lived it and through a legacy that is passed on to the next generation." (Publisher's note)

"Combining history, memoir, and quilting, this fascinating portrait of an indomitable community will appeal to readers, artists, and crafters of all ages." School Library Journal.

Includes bibliographical references and index

746.9 Other textile products

Bertoletti, John C.

How fashion designers use math; math curriculum consultant: Rhea A. Stewart. Chelsea Clubhouse 2010 32p il (Math in the real world) lib bdg $28

Grades: 4 5 6 **746.9**

1. Mathematics 2. Fashion design 3. Fashion -- Vocational guidance

ISBN 978-1-60413-606-7 lib bdg; 1-60413-606-5 lib bdg

LC 2009-22683

This describes how designers use math to measure, create, and produce their fashions, and includes problems to solve and information about how to become a fashion designer

"Color photos of designers in action combine with diagrams that further clarify the easily digestible text." Booklist

Includes glossary and bibliographical references

Black, Alexandra

The **fashion** book; author, Alexandra Black. DK Publishing 2014 160 p. ill. (chiefly col.)

Grades: 6 7 8 9 10 11 12 **746.9**

1. Fashion 2. Fashion -- History

ISBN 1465422846; 9781465422842

"From corsets and camis to tailoring and textiles, 'The Fashion Book' is a sassy style guide for teenage girls who want to discover the stories behind their favorite looks, find their own style, and learn what makes the fashion world tick. Packed with gorgeous images, this illustrated book for young adults takes a unique look at fashion. It reveals how modern-day looks, from catwalk to high-street fashions, draw on the styles of the past from the Middle Ages to the Renaissance and from the rebel attire of the 50s to the sport-inspired looks of the 80s." (Publisher's note)

Spilsbury, Richard

Hi -tech clothes; Richard Spilsbury. Capstone Heinemann Library 2013 56 p. (Design and engineering for STEM) (hb) $33.50

Grades: 5 6 7 **746.9**

1. Fashion 2. Clothing and dress 3. Fashion design 4. Product life cycle 5. Clothing factories -- Technological innovations

ISBN 1432970321; 9781432970321; 9781432970376

LC 2012013469

This book by Richard Spilsbury focuses on clothes, discussing "design, manufacture, and sale to their use, cleaning, and repair, and eventually their disposal. This book explains what happens during these stages, such as prototyping, the sourcing of materials and components, the manufacturing process, the decisions made by designers, and recycling." (Publisher's note)

Includes bibliographical references and index

★ The **teen** vogue handbook; an insider's guide to careers in fashion. Razorbill 2009 276p il pa $24.95
Grades: 7 8 9 10 11 12 **746.9**
1. Clothing industry 2. Fashion -- Vocational guidance
ISBN 978-1-59514-261-0; 1-59514-261-4
LC 2009-10626

"Any teen interested in a career in fashion should read this handbook. It is filled with advice from top designers, photographers, models, stylists, makeup artists, writers, and their interns and assistants. They share how they got started and give tips to those interested in a fashion career. This book looks and reads like a magazine on glossy pages filled with photographs and sidebars, but the interviews give pertinent information on every aspect of work in fashion." Voice Youth Advocates

Includes bibliographical references

Vendittelli, Marie

The **Fashion** Book; written by Marie Vendittelli ; illustrated by Sophie Griotto ; translated by Annie Barton ; edited by Jen Wainwright ; concept and design by Laëtitia Robaeys ; cover design by Barbara Ward. Trafalgar Square Books 2013 128 p. $15.99
Grades: 6 7 8 9 10 **746.9**
1. Fashion design 2. Fashion designers
ISBN 1780551134; 9781780551135

This book is a guide to becoming a confident fashion designer. Marie Vendittelli and Sophie Griotto offer "numerous ideas and tips for drawing, working with color and fabric, designing with the seasons in mind, and accessorizing. . . . There are brief profiles of famed designers, including Coco Chanel, Yves St. Laurent, and Alexander McQueen." (Publishers Weekly)

Wooster, Patricia

So, you want to work in fashion? how to break into the world of fashion and design. Patricia Wooster. Aladdin 2014 192 p. illustrations (Be what you want series) (hardcover) $19.99
Grades: 4 5 6 7 8 **746.9**
1. Clothing industry 2. Fashion -- Vocational guidance
ISBN 1582704538; 9781582704524; 9781582704531
LC 2014005268

"In addition to tips and interviews from a variety of fashion professionals, 'So, You Want to Work in Fashion?' includes inspiring stories from young people who are in the industry right now, as well as activities, a glossary, and resources to help you on your way to a successful career in fashion." (Publisher's note)

"A wonderfully comprehensive, accessible and realistic entree into the dynamic world of fashion." Kirkus

Includes bibliographical references

747 Interior decoration

Weaver, Janice

★ **It's** your room; a decorating guide for real kids. [by] Janice Weaver and Frieda Wishinsky; illustrated by Claudia Dávila. Tundra Books 2006 63p il pa $14.95
Grades: 5 6 7 8 **747**
1. Interior design
ISBN 0-88776-711-7

"Budding interior designers and readers who want to personalize their rooms will appreciate this title. It is filled with step-by-step guidelines for creating a budget, selecting paint colors and fabrics, organizing closets and desks, laying everything out, and adding finishing touches. The illustrations will be a hit with first-time decorators just starting to develop their own color sense." SLJ

750 Painting and paintings

Raczka, Bob

Unlikely pairs; fun with famous works of art. [by] Bob Raczka. Millbrook Press 2006 31p il lib bdg $23.93; pa $9.95
Grades: 4 5 6 7 **750**
1. Painting 2. Art appreciation
ISBN 0-7613-2936-6 lib bdg; 0-7613-2378-3 pa
LC 2003-14078

Invites the reader to discover fourteen funny stories produced by pairing twenty-eight paintings from different eras and styles

"Raczka deserves an A+ for cleverness. . . . Rodin's The Thinker is juxtaposed with Klee's modernistic painting of a chessboard so that the statue looks as if it is contemplating the next move. Siméon-Chardin's picture of a boy blowing soap bubbles seems to be creating Kandinsky's Several Circles. Each selection takes up a page and is reproduced in crisp color. . . . This book is an amusing way to introduce children to famous works of art." SLJ

751.4 Techniques and procedures

Peot, Margaret

★ **Inkblot**; drip, splat, and squish your way to creativity. Boyds Mills Press 2011 56p il $19.95
Grades: 4 5 6 7 **751.4**
1. Ink painting 2. Art -- Technique 3. Painting -- Technique
ISBN 1-59078-720-X; 978-1-59078-720-5
LC 22010-929541

This describes how to make inkblots and use them in art and as inspiration for writing and other forms of creativity.

"Peot's own entrancing inkblots . . . plus a few guest blots, illustrate every step, showing how the pure blot becomes a final artwork. . . . Readers get clear directions and lively encouragement." Kirkus

Includes bibliographical references

Self, Caroline

Chinese brush painting; [by] Caroline Self and Susan Self. 1st ed.; Tuttle 2007 64p il $16.95
Grades: 7 8 9 10 11 12 **751.4**
1. Calligraphy 2. Ink painting 3. Chinese painting
ISBN 978-0-8048-3877-1; 0-8048-3877-1
LC 2006037838

This "introduces readers to the art of Chinese calligraphy and brush painting. The text is fluid and graceful . . . and the authors wrap succinct accounts of Chinese history and lore around their clear, step-by-step, illustrated instructions." Booklist

Includes bibliographical references

751.7 Specific forms

Bingham, Jane

Graffiti. Raintree 2009 32p il (Culture in action) $28.21; pa $7.99

Grades: 5 6 7 8 **751.7**

1. Graffiti 2. Mural painting and decoration

ISBN 978-1-4109-3401-7; 1-4109-3401-2; 978-1-4109-3418-5 pa; 1-4109-3418-7 pa

LC 2008054323

"According to the time line in the . . . book, graffiti can be traced back to 60,000 BCE and paintings on cave walls. A note on the contents page states that it is illegal to draw on other people's property without permission. The different types of graffiti described are interesting, and some of the artwork is beautiful. A section on problems talks about ugly tags (short nicknames), the expense of cleanup, and how some cities have legal graffiti walls. . . . Well organized and with bright, colorful photography, [this] introductory [title gives] readers good basic knowledge." SLJ

Includes glossary and bibliographical references

Uschan, Michael V., 1948-

Graffiti. Lucent Books 2010 112p il (Eye on art) $33.45

Grades: 7 8 9 10 **751.7**

1. Graffiti

ISBN 978-1-4205-0324-1; 1-4205-0324-3

LC 2010028699

Looks at the history of painted graffiti and explores the work of early artists as well as current ones.

This provides "a great deal of information, so middle school readers may not read them cover to cover; however, ample color photos and quotes from artists will make this . . . appealing to students interested in art." Voice Youth Advocates

Includes glossary and bibliographical references

758 Nature, architectural subjects and cityscapes, other specific subjects

Lanza, Barbara

Enchanting elves; paint elven worlds and fantasy characters. IMPACT Books 2009 128p il pa $22.99

Grades: 7 8 9 10 **758**

1. Fantasy in art 2. Watercolor painting -- Technique

ISBN 978-1-60061-307-4; 1-60061-307-1

LC 2009014745

"Lanza includes watercolors of elves and similar creatures such as sprites, gnomes, and dwarves. Materials and basic skills are explained before moving on to chapters that explore faces, figures, and settings. This approach makes the projects accessible to artists who may not have worked with watercolor before. . . . Useful coloring instructions specify brush and color choices." SLJ

759 History, geographic treatment, biography

D'Harcourt, Claire

Masterpieces up close; Western Painting from the 14th to 20th Centuries. by Claire d'Harcourt. Chronicle Books Llc 2015 64 p. il $29.95

Grades: 4 5 6 7 8 **759**

1. Painting 2. Art appreciation 3. Painting -- Appreciation

ISBN 9781616894146 ; 1616894148

LC 200416341

This book, by Claire d'Harcourt, "will send readers on a journey through the world's most famous paintings from the Middle Ages to the twentieth century. They will see some familiar faces, like Leonardo's Mona Lisa and Warhol's Marilyn, and meet some that may be new to them, like the princess in Vel zquez's Las Meninas and the mysterious little girl in Rembrandt's Night Watch. Full-color reproductions of over 20 paintings provide the perfect hunting ground for over a hundred details." (Publisher's note)

"As in earlier entries in this series, readers are invited to find more than one hundred details in twenty-one well-known paintings, ranging from Giotto's frescoes to Warhol's Marilyns. The details are accompanied by statements of their artistic or symbolic significance, and each group of paintings (organized chronologically) is followed by a broader discussion of the works' context and importance." Horn Book

759.05 History 1800-1899

Sabbeth, Carol

★ **Monet** and the impressionists for kids; their lives and ideas, 21 activities. Chicago Review Press 2002 140p il pa $17.95

Grades: 5 6 7 8 **759.05**

1. Art appreciation 2. Impressionism (Art)

ISBN 1-55652-397-1

LC 2001-47191

Discusses the nineteenth-century French art movement known as Impressionism, focusing on the works of Monet, Renoir, Degas, Cassatt, Cezanne, Gauguin, and Seurat

"A beautifully designed introduction to Impressionism. . . . Sabbeth also includes 21 appealing extension activities such as recipes, crafts, games, and writing suggestions. Quality color reproductions on glossy pages, and varied, attractive layouts add to the book." SLJ

Includes glossary and bibliographical references

759.054 Impressionism

Heine, Florian

Impressionism; 13 artists children should know. by Florian Heine. Prestel Pub 2015 45 p. color illustrations (13... children should know) $14.95

Grades: 4 5 6 **759.054**

1. Artists 2. Impressionism (Art)

ISBN 3791372068; 9783791372068

This book, by Florian Heine, "shows young readers how painters from Claude Monet to John Singer Sargent introduced impressionist styles of painting and so changed the course of art. In this beautifully produced volume, young readers are given the opportunity to study masterpieces of Impressionist work in great detail." (Publisher's note)

759.06 1900-1999

Barsony, Piotr

The **stories** of the Mona Lisa; an imaginary museum tale about the history of modern art. Piotr Barsony ; translated from

the French by Joanna Oseman. Skyhorse Publishing 2012 55 p. (hardcover : alk. paper) $19.95
Grades: 5 6 7 8 **759.06**
1. Art -- History 2. Mona Lisa (Painting) 3. Art movements 4. Painting, Modern
ISBN 1620872285; 9781620872284
LC 2012015603
"As [this book by Pietr Barsony] begins, a little girl asks: 'Dad, will you tell me a story?' The story her painter father tells is a history of art with the Mona Lisa as its central character. . . . He takes daughter and readers both on a journey of discovery through an imaginary museum. . . . Each painting is of only the Mona Lisa. . . . They are his own responses to and interpretations of Leonardo's masterpiece as filtered through the vision of other artists and movements." (Kirkus Reviews)

759.13 United States

Lawrence, Jacob
The **great** migration; an American story. paintings by Jacob Lawrence; with a poem in appreciation by Walter Dean Myers. HarperCollins Pubs. 1993 un il hardcover o.p. pa $8.99
Grades: 4 5 6 7 **759.13**
1. African Americans in art
ISBN 0-06-023037-1; 0-06-443428-1 pa
LC 93-16788
"Lawrence is a storyteller with words as well as pictures: his captions and his own 1992 introduction to this book are the best commentary on his work." Booklist

759.9 Other geographic areas

Rubin, Susan Goldman
★ **Diego** Rivera; an artist for the people. by Susan Goldman Rubin. Abrams Books for Young Readers 2013 56 p. (reinforced) $21.95
Grades: 5 6 7 8 **759.9**
1. Mural painting and decoration 2. Painters -- Mexico -- Biography
ISBN 0810984113; 9780810984110
LC 2012010022
This book, by Susan Goldman Rubin, "offers young readers . . . insight into the life and artwork of the famous Mexican painter and muralist [Diego Rivera]. The book follows Rivera's career, looking at his influences and tracing the evolution of his style. His work often called attention to the culture and struggles of the Mexican working class. . . . The book contains a list of museums where you can see Rivera's art, a historical note, a glossary, and a bibliography." (Publisher's note)
Includes bibliographical references and index

Vry, Silke
Paul Klee for children; Silke Vry ; [translation, Jane Michael] Prestel 2011 95 p. $14.95
Grades: 4 5 6 **759.9**
1. Art -- Technique 2. Art appreciation
ISBN 3791370774; 9783791370774
LC 2011937220
This book, by SIlke Vry, is about the art work of Paul Klee. "Paul Klee's playful paintings are a natural introduction for children to the world of creativity and art. . . . The German artist was fascinated by children's drawings, and incorporated their energy and simplicity into his own work. This . . . introduction to Klee's paintings focuses on the artist's love of color and symbols, his lighthearted technique, and his belief that music and painting were inextricably linked." (Publisher's note)

769.56 Postage stamps and related devices

Postal Service guide to U.S. stamps. U.S. Postal Service il
Grades: 8 9 10 11 12 Adult **769.56**
1. Reference books 2. Postage stamps -- Catalogs
First published 1974 with title: United States stamps and stories. Revised annually
Contains reproductions and histories of U.S. postage stamps

770 Photography, computer art, cinematography, videography

Aronson, Marc, 1950-
Eyes of the world; Robert Capa, Gerda Taro, and the Invention of Modern Photojournalism. Marc Aronson and Marina Budhos. Hendry Holt & Co. 2017 304 p. illustrations (ebook) $60; (hardcover) $22.99
Grades: 7 8 9 10 **770**
1. Photojournalists -- Europe -- Biography 2. Photojournalism 3. War photographers -- Europe -- Biography 4. Spain -- History -- Civil War, 1936-1939 -- Biography 5. Spain -- History -- Civil War, 1936-1939 -- Photography
ISBN 9781250109675; 9780805098358
LC 2016020545
YALSA Honor Book for Excellence in Nonfiction for Young Adults (2018)
This book, by Marc Aronson and Marina Budhos, tells the inspiring story of "Robert Capa and Gerda Taro, . . . [two] young Jewish refugees, idealistic and in love. As photographers in the 1930s, they set off to capture their generation's most important struggle--the fight against fascism. Among the first to depict modern warfare, Capa, Taro, and their friend Chim took powerful photographs of the Spanish Civil War that went straight from the action to news magazines." (Publisher's note)
"Dense but never dull, this book exposes art and humanity in history." Booklist
Includes bibliographical references and index

Finger, Brad
13 photos children should know. Prestel 2011 45p il lib bdg $14.95
Grades: 4 5 6 **770**
1. Modern history 2. Documentary photography
ISBN 978-3-7913-7047-7; 3-7913-7047-2
Examines the history behind thirteen popular photographs, including the moon landing, the fall of the Berlin Wall, and the wedding of Prince Charles and Princess Diana.

Kallen, Stuart A.
Photography. Lucent Books 2007 112p il (Eye on art) $32.45
Grades: 7 8 9 10 11 12 **770**
1. Photography -- History
ISBN 978-1-59018-986-3
LC 2007015978

"This volume surveys the history of photography, from the ancient camera obscura to the digital camera. . . . This title offers a clear overview of an art form that many teens both practice and appreciate." Booklist

Includes bibliographical references

Meyerowitz, Joel

Seeing things; A Kid's Guide to Looking at Photographs. Joel Meyerowitz. Aperture Foundation 2016 80 p. illustrations (hardcover : alk. paper) $24.95

Grades: 6 7 8 9 10 11 12 **770**

1. Visual literacy 2. Photography 3. Artistic photography

ISBN 9781597113151

LC 2015953484

In this children's book, acclaimed photographer Joel Meyerowitz "takes readers on a journey through the power and magic of photography: its abilities to freeze time, tell a story, combine several layers into one frame and record life's fleeting and beautiful moments. The book features the work of masters such as William Eggleston, Mary Ellen Mark, Helen Levitt and Walker Evans, among many others." (Publisher's note)

"Meyerowitz's informative, enthusiastic tone will be perfectly engaging for teens interested in pursuing photography." Booklist

Proujansky, Alice

Go photo! An Activity Book for Kids. Alice Proujansky. Aperture 2016 108 p. color illustrations (hardcover : alk. paper) $19.95

Grades: 4 5 6 7 **770**

1. Creative activities 2. Photography

ISBN 9781597113557

LC 2015959630

This children's book by Alice Proujansky "features 25 hands-on and creative activities inspired by photography. Aimed at children between eight and twelve years old, this playful and fun collection of projects encourages young readers to experiment with their imaginations, get messy with materials and engage with the world in new and exciting ways. . . . Each project also features a series of pictures and handy tips to help guide the reader step-by-step." (Publisher's note)

"Proujansky touches on technical aspects of photography, such as composition and lighting... but her emphasis is generally on playful exploration, building readers' confidence behind the camera through an array of creative projects and ideas." Pub Wkly

Turnbull, Stephanie

Cool stuff to photograph; Stephanie Turnbull. Smart Apple Media 2015 32 p. color illustrations (Cool stuff) $31.35

Grades: 4 5 6 7 8 **770**

1. Digital cameras 2. Photography

ISBN 1625881908; 9781625881908

LC 2013047370

This book, by Stephanie Turnbull, "offers kids the opportunity to learn photography skills while also allowing them to express their own creativity. Clear, approachable text and a colorful, magazine-style format make these titles inviting reads, while step-by-step instructions help ensure projects are easy to complete." (Publisher's note)

Includes bibliographical references and index

770.9 History, geographical treatment, biography

Sandler, Martin W.

★ **America** through the lens; photographers who changed the nation. Henry Holt and Co. 2005 182p il $19.95

Grades: 6 7 8 9 **770.9**

1. Photography 2. Photographers

ISBN 0-8050-7367-1

"The photographs are stunning." SLJ

Includes bibliographical references

775 Digital photography

Johnson, Daniel

4 -H guide to digital photography. Voyageur Press 2009 176p $18.99

Grades: 5 6 7 8 **775**

1. Digital photography

ISBN 978-0-7603-3652-6; 0-7603-3652-0

LC 2009014679

This guide to digital photography offers "sound and comprehensive information. . . . [It] features numerous excellent photos that support the text. It explores types of digital cameras, how to take good photos, the complexities of lighting, managing images . . . and the importance of just enjoying this activity. Types of photography such as landscape and macro are explained. The author does an excellent job of discussing the importance of both technological details and artistic creativity." SLJ

Includes glossary

Rabbat, Suzy

Using digital images. Cherry Lake Pub. 2010 32p il (Super smart information strategies) lib bdg $27.07

Grades: 3 4 5 6 **775**

1. Digital photography

ISBN 978-1-60279-954-7 lib bdg; 1-60279-954-7 lib bdg

LC 2010018941

"The information on deciding between file formats and resolutions in Using Digital Images will be tremendously helpful, and some beginner techniques on taking and editing effective photos are a nice bonus." Booklist

Includes bibliographical references

778.5 Cinematography and videography

Green, Julie

Shooting video to make learning fun. Cherry Lake Pub. 2010 32p il (Super smart information strategies) lib bdg $27.07

Grades: 3 4 5 6 **778.5**

1. Digital video recording 2. Motion pictures -- Production and direction

ISBN 978-1-60279-955-4 lib bdg; 1-60279-955-5 lib bdg

LC 2010002022

"This books helps students learn how to harness the power of video to inform and entertain. Includes background information and practical hands on activities." Publisher's note

Includes bibliographical references

779 Photographic images

Delannoy, Isabelle

★ **Our** living Earth; a story of people, ecology, and preservation. by Isabelle Delannoy; photographs by Yann Arthus-Bertrand. Harry N. Abrams 2008 157p il $24.95

Grades: 5 6 7 8 **779**

1. Human geography 2. Aerial photography

ISBN 978-0-8109-7132-5; 0-8109-7132-1

LC 2008010324

"Wrapped around Arthus-Bertrand's magnificent aerial photographs from around the world, Delannoy's text is organized thematically, covering fresh water, biodiversity, oceans, land, cities, people, food, and climate. . . . Readers will find surprising information and images to ponder. Almost every page supports the overarching theme that social justice and environmental protection are inextricably related. . . . This volume raises awareness, and the striking images, astonishing statistics, and brief explanations will stimulate readers to investigate further and possibly to take action." SLJ

780 Music

Bourne, Joyce

The **concise** Oxford dictionary of music; [by] Michael Kennedy and Joyce Bourne Kennedy. 5th ed.; Oxford University Press 2007 839p il (Oxford paperback reference) pa $17.99

Grades: 8 9 10 11 12 Adult **780**

1. Reference books 2. Music -- Dictionaries 3. Musicians -- Dictionaries

ISBN 978-0-19-920383-3 pa; 0-19-920383-0 pa

LC 2007008461

First published 1952 as a condensation of the Oxford companion to music

This music "dictionary includes over 14,000 entries on terms from 'allegro' to 'zingaro,' and on works from 'Aida' to 'Tosca,' as well as instruments and their history, composers, librettists, musicians, singers, and orchestras. It also [includes] comprehensive works lists for major composers." Publisher's note

Hansen, Dee

The **music** and literacy connection; Dee Hansen, Elaine Bernstorf, and Gayle M. Stuber. Rowman & Littlefield 2014 314 p. illustrations, music (cloth : alk. paper) $80

Grades: Professional **780**

1. Reading 2. Music and literature 3. Reading (Primary) 4. School music -- Instruction and study 5. Interdisciplinary approach in education

ISBN 1475805985; 9781475805987; 9781475805994

LC 2014023926

This book, by Dee Hansen, , Elaine Bernstorf, and Gayle M. Stuber, looks at "the links between reading and music by examining those skills and learning processes that are directly parallel for music learning and language arts literacy in the pre-K, elementary, and secondary levels. This edition includes two new chapters: one dedicated to secondary music education and teacher evaluation, and another that offers a literature review of latest literacy research in education, neuroscience, and neuropsychology." (Publisher's note)

Includes bibliographical references and index

780.89 Ethnic and national groups

Tsoukanelis, Erika Alexia

The **Latin** music scene; the stars, the fans, the music. Enslow Publishers 2009 48p il (The music scene) lib bdg $23.93

Grades: 6 7 8 9 **780.89**

1. Music -- Latin America

ISBN 978-0-7660-3399-3 lib bdg; 0-7660-3399-6 lib bdg

LC 2008-48013

This describes the music, stars, clothes, contracts, and world of Latin music

Includes glossary and bibliographical references

780.92 Biography

Earls, Irene

Young musicians in world history. Greenwood Press 2002 139p il $44.95

Grades: 8 9 10 11 12 **780.92**

1. Musicians

ISBN 0-313-31442-X

LC 2001-40559

Profiles thirteen musicians who achieved high honors and fame before the age of twenty-five, representing many different time periods and musical styles

"A useful introduction to some of the musical giants of the last four centuries." SLJ

Includes glossary and bibliographical references

Roberts, Russell, 1953-

★ **Scott** Joplin; by Russell Roberts. Mitchell Lane Publishers 2012 47 p. ill. (chiefly col.) (library) $29.95

Grades: 6 7 8 9 **780.92**

1. Jazz music 2. Composers -- United States -- Biography

ISBN 1612282733; 9781612282732

LC 2012008633

This book by Russ Roberts is part of the American Jazz series and looks at musician Scott Joplin. Within each entry, "information about the subjects' childhoods and preparation for their musical careers is included, as are the positive and negative aspects of their adult lives. Their contributions to the world of jazz are . . . explored." (School Library Journal)

Includes bibliographical references (pages 44-45), chronology (pages 40-41) and index.

781.2 Elements of music

Tomecek, Steve

Music; [by] Stephen M. Tomecek. Chelsea House 2010 165p il (Experimenting with everyday science) $35

Grades: 5 6 7 8 **781.2**

1. Musical instruments 2. Science -- Experiments 3. Music -- Acoustics and physics

ISBN 978-1-60413-169-7; 1-60413-169-1

LC 2009-22333

This "offers 25 easy-to-perform activities that illuminate scientific principles. . . . Topics . . . include the history of music, various instruments, and how scientific principles explain the creation of sounds. . . . Following each experiment are additional comments on the science behind the experiment and link to the one that follows. Photographs, simple diagrams and illustrations, and sample data tables appear throughout, and the [layout is] clear and colorful." SLJ

Includes bibliographical references

781.6 Traditions of music

Kallen, Stuart A.

The **history** of classical music. Lucent Bks. 2002 112p il (Music library) $28.70

Grades: 6 7 8 9 **781.6**

1. Music -- History and criticism

ISBN 978-1-59018-123-2; 1-59018-123-9

LC 2002-3815

This follows classical music "from Medieval times into the present, closing with a description of avant-garde composer John Cage's 4′33″—4 minutes and 33 seconds of silence. . . . [The volume is] greatly enhanced by fascinating excerpts from primary material, including articles, letters, and diaries, often in the words of the composer or musician. . . . Students reading for reports or for personal interest will find much useful information." Booklist

Includes bibliographical references

781.642 Country music

Kallen, Stuart A.

The **history** of country music. Lucent Bks. 2002 112p il (Music library) $28.70

Grades: 6 7 8 9 **781.642**

1. Country music

ISBN 1-59018-124-7

LC 2002-664

A history of country music which discusses its roots, influences, and various types including bluegrass, honky tonk, cowboy music, western swing, and rockabilly

Includes bibliographical references

781.644 Soul

Mendelson, Aaron A.

★ **American** R & B; Gospel grooves, funky drummers, and soul power. Aaron Mendelson. Twenty-First Century Books 2013 64 p. (lib. bdg. : alk. paper) $30.60

Grades: 7 8 9 10 11 12 **781.644**

1. Blues music 2. American songs 3. African American music 4. Soul music -- History and criticism 5. Rhythm and blues music -- History and criticism

ISBN 0761345019; 9780761345015

LC 2011045636

Author Aaron Mendelson's book focuses on R&B music. "Rhythm and blues music evolved from all sorts of sounds: swinging jazz, gritty blues, and African American spiritual songs. The music's smooth mix of styles made it unique, and its passionate performers made it a sensation. Ever since Ray Charles hit the charts in the 1950s, R & B fans have held it down on dance floors. And R & B singers have belted out messages of love and calls for social change." (Publisher's note)

Includes bibliographical references and index.

Pinkney, Andrea Davis, 1963-

★ **Rhythm** ride; a road trip through the Motown sound. Andrea Davis Pinkney. Roaring Brook Press 2015 176 p. illustrations (hardback) $22.99

Grades: 5 6 7 8 9 **781.644**

1. Rhythm and blues music -- Sound recordings 2. Motown Record Corporation 3. Sound recording industry -- United States

ISBN 9781596439733; 1596439734

LC 2014045894

NAACP Image Award Nominee: Outstanding Literary Work- Youth/Teens (2016)

"Berry Gordy began Motown in 1959. . . . He converted the garage of a residential house into a studio and recruited teenagers . . . Smokey Robinson, Mary Wells, Marvin Gaye, Stevie Wonder, and Diana Ross to sing for his new label. Meanwhile, the country was on the brink of a cultural revolution, and one of the most powerful agents of change in the following decade would be this group of young black performers from urban Detroit." (Publisher's note)

"An ebullient, wonderfully told introduction to music that had an indelible influence on a generation and its times." Kirkus

781.646 Reggae

Neely, Daniel T.

The **reggae** scene; the stars, the fans, the music. [by] Peter Manuel and Daniel T. Neely. Enslow Publishers 2009 48p il (The music scene) lib bdg $23.93

Grades: 6 7 8 9 **781.646**

1. Reggae music

ISBN 978-0-7660-3400-6 lib bdg; 0-7660-3400-3 lib bdg

LC 2008-48014

This describes the music, stars, clothes, contracts, and world of reggae music

This "is clearly written, well organized, and copiously illustrated with full-color photographs of noted performers." SLJ

Includes glossary and bibliographical references

781.65 Jazz

Handyside, Chris

★ **Jazz**; [by] Christopher Handyside. Heinemann Library 2006 48p il (A history of American music) lib bdg $31.43

Grades: 5 6 7 8 **781.65**

1. Jazz music

ISBN 1-4034-8149-0

LC 2005019305

"This book charts the development of this uniquely American Music form from the 1600s through to the present. It also shows how social, economic, and regional factors have all helped to shape Jazz over time and, in turn, how this music has gone on to influence other genres." Publisher's note

Includes glossary and bibliographical references

Kallen, Stuart A.

The **history** of jazz. Lucent Bks. 2003 112p il (Music library) lib bdg $21.96

Grades: 6 7 8 9 **781.65**

1. Jazz music
ISBN 1-59018-125-5

LC 2002-2220

This follows jazz music's "evolution from its African roots through contemporary forms. [The volume is] greatly enhanced by fascinating excerpts from primary material, including articles, letters, and diaries, often in the words of the composer or musician. . . . Students reading for reports or for personal interest will find much useful information." Booklist

Includes bibliographical references

Marsalis, Wynton, 1961-

★ **Jazz** A-B-Z; [by] Wynton Marsalis and Paul Rogers; with biographical sketches by Phil Schaap. Candlewick Press 2005 un il $24.99

Grades: 5 6 7 8 9 10 **781.65**

1. Jazz music 2. Jazz musicians
ISBN 978-0-7636-3434-6

LC 2005-48448

This is an illustrated alphabetically arranged introduction to jazz musicians.

This is a "witty, stunningly designed alphabet catalog. . . . The biographical sketches and notes on poetic forms by Phil Schaap are concise and genuinely informative. . . . Rogers's pastiche full-page portraits, his use of expressive typography and the smaller vignettes he sprinkles throughout are bound to heighten any reader's appreciation of both the musicians and the music. . . . [Marsalis offers] clever . . . poems, wordplays, odes and limericks." N Y Times Book Rev

781.66 Rock (Rock 'n' roll)

Aberback, Brian

Black Sabbath; pioneers of heavy metal. Enslow Publishers 2010 112p il (Rebels of rock) lib bdg $31.93

Grades: 6 7 8 9 10 **781.66**

1. Rock musicians 2. Black Sabbath (Musical group)
ISBN 978-0-7660-3379-5 lib bdg; 0-7660-3379-1 lib bdg

LC 2009012295

"Refreshingly levelheaded and loaded with sourced quotes, [this is] that rare middle-grade biography . . . that is able to trace a band's history, revel in its rock awesomeness, and be blunt about such things as drug abuse, all the while keeping things at an age-appropriate keel. . . . Packed with pics, it's all here." Booklist

Includes bibliographical references

Bowe, Brian J.

The **Ramones**; American Punk Rock Band. Enslow Publishers 2010 128p il (Rebels of rock) lib bdg $31.93

Grades: 6 7 8 9 10 **781.66**

1. Rock musicians 2. Ramones (Musical group)
ISBN 978-0-7660-3233-0; 0-7660-3233-7

LC 2008040362

"Avid fans of rock music will find [this title] appealing, entertaining, and enlightening. [The] book begins with a brief introduction to the band through an account of a major musical event. Subsequent chapters include short biographies of the various band members. . . . Direct quotes add life to the well-written and lively [narrative]. . . . Descriptions and analyses of the music and albums offer insight into the impact [the] band had on today's rock music." SLJ

Includes bibliographical references

Burlingame, Jeff

Aerosmith; hard rock superstars. Enslow Publishers 2010 112p il (Rebels of rock) lib bdg $31.93

Grades: 6 7 8 9 10 **781.66**

1. Rock musicians 2. Aerosmith (Musical group)
ISBN 978-0-7660-3236-1; 0-7660-3236-1

LC 2009006469

"Avid fans of rock music will find [this title] appealing, entertaining, and enlightening. [The] book begins with a brief introduction to the band through an account of a major musical event. Subsequent chapters include short biographies of the various band members. . . . Direct quotes add life to the well-written and lively [narrative]. . . . Descriptions and analyses of the music and albums offer insight into the impact [the] band had on today's rock music." SLJ

Includes bibliographical references

George-Warren, Holly

Shake, rattle, & roll; the founders of rock & roll. words by Holly George-Warren; pictures by Laura Levine. Houghton Mifflin 2001 un il hardcover o.p. pa $5.95

Grades: 3 4 5 6 **781.66**

1. Musicians 2. Rock music
ISBN 0-618-05540-1; 0-618-43229-9 pa

LC 00-33480

"A wonderfully entertaining browsing book that will also fill a gap in most music collections." SLJ

Goodmark, Robyn

Girls rock; how to get your group together and make some noise. [by] Robyn Goodmark; illustrated by Adrienne Yan. Billboard Books 2008 178p il pa $13.95

Grades: 6 7 8 9 10 **781.66**

1. Rock music 2. Bands (Music) 3. Women musicians
ISBN 978-0-8230-9948-1; 0-8230-9948-2

LC 2008007386

This "shows the ins, outs, and good and bad things that come with starting a band and making it successful. . . . The conversational tone and quizzes throughout give the presentation the feel of a teen magazine. . . . Clever cartoon illustrations appear throughout. . . . Not only does this book provide the technical assistance newbie musicians might need, but it also provides advice on choosing a band name and more emotional topics like how to find creative inspiration. This is a wonderful guide for any girl who wants to start a band." SLJ

Guillain, Charlotte

Punk; music, fashion, attitude! Raintree 2011 32p il (Culture in action) lib bdg $29

Grades: 5 6 7 8 **781.66**

1. Punk rock music
ISBN 978-1-4109-3916-6; 1-4109-3916-2

LC 2009052585

"Guillain delves into the history of punk and follows its influence on modern art, fashion, and politics. . . . [This volume is] quick, interesting, up-to-date . . . with plenty of supportive, captioned, full-color photographs. [It] also [provides] related project suggestions." SLJ

Includes glossary and bibliographical references

Handyside, Chris

★ **Rock**. Heinemann Library 2006 48p il (A history of American music) lib bdg $31.43

Grades: 5 6 7 8 **781.66**

1. Rock music

ISBN 1-4034-8150-4

This history of rock music is an "excellent, clear [introduction]. . . . [It] opens with the mid-1950s advent of rock n roll and continues with surf music, girl groups, the British invasion, psychedelic rock, heavy metal, punk, and grunge. Featured musicians range from Elvis Presley to Kurt Cobain." SLJ

Includes bibliographical references

Mead, Wendy

The **alternative** rock scene; the stars, the fans, the music. [by] Wendy S. Mead. Enslow Publishers 2009 48p il (The music scene) lib bdg $23.93

Grades: 6 7 8 9 **781.66**

1. Rock music

ISBN 978-0-7660-3401-3 lib bdg; 0-7660-3401-1 lib bdg

LC 2008-48015

This describes the music, stars, clothes, contracts, and world of alternative rock music

This "is clearly written, well organized, and copiously illustrated with full-color photographs of noted performers." SLJ

Includes glossary and bibliographical references

Roberts, Jeremy

The **Beatles**; music revolutionaries. Twenty-First Century Books 2011 112p il (USA Today lifeline biographies) lib bdg $33.26

Grades: 6 7 8 9 10 **781.66**

1. Rock musicians 2. Beatles

ISBN 978-0-7613-6421-4; 0-7613-6421-8

LC 2010031041

This "takes readers on an accessible tour of the band's rollicking run from Liverpool's underground scene to its nearly decade-long perch atop the charts. Written in a straightforward, reportorial style, . . . the book offers a fine dissection of the Beatle phenomenon. . . . As easy on the eyes as it is fun to read." Booklist

Includes discography, filmography, and bibliographical references

Sanna, Ellyn

Hip -hop: a short history; [by] Rosa Waters. Mason Crest Publishers 2007 64p il (Hip-hop) lib bdg $22.95; pa $7.95

Grades: 4 5 6 7 **781.66**

1. Hip-hop 2. Rap music

ISBN 1-4222-0109-0 lib bdg; 978-1-4222-0109-1 lib bdg; 1-4222-0261-5 pa; 978-1-4222-0261-6 pa

LC 2006004320

"The book begins with a visually eye-popping time line, then moves quickly through the roots of hip-hop—through slavery, the civil rights movement, and the black church. Musical influences included gospel, blues, jazz, funk, and rock. . . . A wide-awake design, full-color photos, and a winning writing style put a positive spin on this musical phenomenon." Booklist

Includes glossary and bibliographical references

Witmer, Scott

Bookings & gigs. ABDO 2009 32p il (Rock band) lib bdg $27.07

Grades: 6 7 8 9 **781.66**

1. Rock music 2. Music industry -- Vocational guidance

ISBN 978-1-60453-689-8 lib bdg; 1-60453-689-6 lib bdg

LC 2009-6606

This offers advice to rock bands on how to find places to perform

"Copious examples and photos of bands drawn from a wide chronological and stylistic range ensure that every reader, from metalheads (Metallica) to Linkin Park fans will find something of interest here." SLJ

Includes glossary

History of rock bands. ABDO 2010 32p il (Rock band) lib bdg $27.07

Grades: 6 7 8 9 **781.66**

1. Rock music -- History and criticism

ISBN 978-1-60453-692-8 lib bdg; 1-60453-692-6 lib bdg

LC 2009-6609

This is a history of rock music

"Copious examples and photos of bands drawn from a wide chronological and stylistic range ensure that every reader, from metalheads (Metallica) to Linkin Park fans will find something of interest here." SLJ

Includes glossary

Managing your band. ABDO 2010 32p il (Rock band) lib bdg $27.07

Grades: 6 7 8 9 **781.66**

1. Rock music 2. Music industry -- Vocational guidance

ISBN 978-1-60453-693-5 lib bdg; 1-60453-693-4 lib bdg

LC 2009-6610

This offers information and advice about managing a rock music band

"Copious examples and photos of bands drawn from a wide chronological and stylistic range ensure that every reader, from metalheads (Metallica) to Linkin Park fans will find something of interest here." SLJ

Includes glossary

Recording. ABDO 2010 32p il (Rock band) lib bdg $27.07

Grades: 6 7 8 9 **781.66**

1. Rock music 2. Sound recordings 3. Music industry -- Vocational guidance

ISBN 978-1-60453-694-2 lib bdg; 1-60453-694-2 lib bdg

LC 2009-6611

This offers information and advice on recording for rock bands

"Copious examples and photos of bands drawn from a wide chronological and stylistic range ensure that every reader, from metalheads (Metallica) to Linkin Park fans will find something of interest here." SLJ

Includes glossary

The **show**. ABDO 2010 32p il (Rock band) lib bdg $27.07

Grades: 6 7 8 9 **781.66**

1. Rock music 2. Music industry -- Vocational guidance

ISBN 978-1-60453-695-9 lib bdg; 1-60453-695-0 lib bdg

LC 2009-6612

This offers information and advice about performing for rock bands

"Copious examples and photos of bands drawn from a wide chronological and stylistic range ensure that every reader, from metalheads (Metallica) to Linkin Park fans will find something of interest here." SLJ

Includes glossary

782.1 Vocal forms

Siberell, Anne

★ **Bravo!** brava! a night at the opera; behind the scenes with composers, cast, and crew. introduction by Frederica von Stade. Oxford Univ. Press 2001 64p il $19.95

Grades: 4 5 6 7 **782.1**

1. Opera

ISBN 0-19-513966-6

LC 2001-21206

"An excellent resource for reports, this unusual book has an exceptional range of topics for younger students and is an essential purchase for upper elementary and middle school music programs." SLJ

Includes glossary and bibliographical references

782.25 Small-scale vocal forms

Giovanni, Nikki

★ **On** my journey now; looking at African-American history through the spirituals. [by] Nikki Giovanni; foreword by Arthur C. Jones. 1st ed.; Candlewick Press 2007 116p $18.99; pa $8.99

Grades: 7 8 9 10 **782.25**

1. Spirituals (Songs) 2. African Americans -- History

ISBN 978-0-7636-2885-7; 0-7636-2885-9; 978-0-7636-4380-5 pa; 0-7636-4380-7 pa

LC 2006051695

"Personal and passionate, Giovanni's short narrative talks about the sacred songs first sung by slaves, tracing how the people in bondage created the great spirituals to tell their stories, and what the songs still mean to us today." Booklist

782.42 Songs

Crossingham, John

★ **Learn** to speak music; a guide to creating, performing, and promoting your songs. written by John Crossingham; illustrated by Jeff Kulak. OwlKids 2009 96p il $27.95; pa $17.95

Grades: 6 7 8 9 **782.42**

1. Songwriters and songwriting 2. Music industry -- Vocational guidance

ISBN 978-1-897349-64-9; 1-897349-64-5; 978-1-897349-65-6 pa; 1-897349-65-3 pa

This is an "incredibly readable book. Crossingham uses a comfortable, conversational tone with a sensibility that will appeal to teens and preteens alike. . . . The exceptional graphic design and illustrations . . . enhance and broaden the musical themes addressed with humor, wit, and style." SLJ

Guerinot, Jim

Legends, icons & rebels; music that changed the world. by Robbie Robertson, Jim Guerinot, Sebastian Robertson, and Jared Levine. Tundra Books 2013 128 p. (hardcover) $29

Grades: 6 7 8 9 10 11 12 **782.42**

1. Musicians 2. Music -- History and criticism

ISBN 1770495711; 9781770495715; 9781770495739

LC 2013931040

Authors Robbie Robertson, Jim Guerinot, Jared Levine, and Sebastian Robertson discuss "twenty-seven musical legends. Short profiles chronicle personal stories and achievements of extraordinarily talented artists whose innovations changed the landscape of music for generations to come. Carefully compiled like any great playlist, the line-up features . . . Ray Charles to Johnny Cash, Chuck Berry to Bob Dylan." (Publisher's note)

"In this oversize, weighty volume, music-industry-veteran authors offer collected anecdotal sketches, including personal memories, of twenty-seven music "risk-takers" such as Aretha Franklin, the Beatles, and Bob Dylan. Their meteoric careers, many touched by tragedy, are justly celebrated. A timeline of these artists' first recordings (1925-1968) ends the book; includes two CDs of sparkling audio quality with one iconic song by each." (Horn Book)

National anthems of the world; edited by Michael Jamieson Bristow. 11th ed.; Weidenfeld & Nicolson 2006 629p $90

Grades: 5 6 7 8 9 10 11 12 Adult **782.42**

1. National songs

ISBN 0-304-36826-1

First published 1943 in the United Kingdom with title: National anthems of the United Nations and France

This volume contains national anthems of about 198 nations, including melody and accompaniment. Words are presented in the native language with transliteration provided where necessary. English translations follow. Brief historical notes on the adoption of each anthem are included

"An essential reference resource for all libraries." Libr J

Quinn, Jason

The **Beatles**; Jason Quinn, illustrated by Lalit Kumar Sharma. Random House Inc. 2017 150 p. chiefly color illustrations $16.99

Grades: 7 8 9 10 **782.42**

1. Beatles 2. Rock music

ISBN 9381182221; 9789381182222

LC 2017004209

This book in the Campfire Graphic Novels series, by Jason Quinn, illustrated by Lalit Kumar Sharma, tells story of 'The Beatles' . . . the world's most enduring and biggest rock band ever! This is the story of their struggle for success. Taking us through the early days of rock 'n' roll, and their lives in Liverpool during the 1950s, we journey with them to Hamburg as they come of age and through grit, determination and masses of talent became the lads who made the sixties swing!" (Publisher's note)

"A lively and informal look at the young Beatles." Kirkus

Silverman, Jerry

Songs and stories of the Civil War. 21st Cent. Bks. (Brookfield) 2002 96p il lib bdg $30.60

Grades: 5 6 7 8 **782.42**

1. United States -- History -- 1861-1865, Civil War -- Songs

ISBN 0-7613-2305-8

LC 2001-35795

Provides a history of the music and lyrics of a dozen Civil War songs, describing the circumstances under which they were created and performed

"Black-and-white reproductions of period photos, engravings, paintings, and drawings illustrate the text. A good resource offering an interesting sidelight on the times." Booklist

Includes discography and bibliographical references

Stotts, Stuart

★ **We** shall overcome; a song that changed the world. by Stuart Stotts; foreword by Pete Seeger; with illustrations by Terrance Cummings. Clarion Books 2009 72p il $18

Grades: 5 6 7 8 **782.42**

1. African Americans -- Civil rights -- Songs

ISBN 978-0-547-18210-0; 0-547-18210-4

LC 2009022578

"This smart, effective telling has few missteps. From the informative black-and-white photographs to the solid back matter to the CD sung by Pete Seeger, it is a complete package." Booklist

Witmer, Scott

Songwriting. ABDO 2010 32p il (Rock band) lib bdg $27.07

Grades: 6 7 8 9 **782.42**

1. Rock music 2. Vocational guidance 3. Songwriters and songwriting

ISBN 978-1-60453-696-6 lib bdg; 1-60453-696-9 lib bdg

LC 2009-6613

This offers advice on songwriting for rock bands

"Copious examples and photos of bands drawn from a wide chronological and stylistic range ensure that every reader, from metalheads (Metallica) to Linkin Park fans will find something of interest here." SLJ

Includes glossary

Yolen, Jane

★ **Apple** for the teacher; thirty songs for singing while you work. collected and introduced by Jane Yolen; music arranged by Adam Stemple; art edited by Eileen Michaelis Smiles. Harry N. Abrams 2005 117p il $24.95

Grades: 4 5 6 7 **782.42**

1. Songs 2. Work -- Songs

ISBN 0-8109-4825-7

LC 2004-24404

"Yolen has brought together a collection of 30 work songs . . . which represent a wide variety of occupations. . . . She introduces each job, explaining unusual vocabulary and references in the songs. . . . The artwork . . . is elegant. Ranging from sculpture to paintings to needlework, each selection of Americana has been carefully matched to the occupation, beautifully reproduced on high-quality paper, and meticulously identified." Booklist

782.421 Folk songs

Cooper, Michael L.

★ **Slave** spirituals and the Jubilee Singers. Clarion Bks. 2001 86p il music $16

Grades: 7 8 9 10 **782.421**

1. Spirituals (Songs) 2. African American music 3. Jubilee Singers (Musical group)

ISBN 0-395-97829-7

LC 00-65854

"The first half of this book traces the development of spirituals from African musical traditions and discusses the place of religion in the lives of the slaves. The second half focuses on Fisk University's Jubilee Singers. . . . Illustrated with many archival prints and photographs, the book includes extensive annotated source notes and the words and music to seven of the spirituals popularized by the Jubilee Singers." SLJ

Includes bibliographical references

Schwartz, Heather E.

Taylor Swift; superstar singer and songwriter. Heather E. Schwartz. Lerner Publications 2019 48 p. (hardback) $31.99

Grades: 5 6 7 8 **782.421**

1. Country musicians 2. Singers -- United States 3. Singers -- United States -- Biography 4. Country musicians -- United States -- Biography

ISBN 9781541528857; 9781541528864

LC 2018003071

In this children's book in the Gateway Biographies series, by Heather E. Schwartz, "from her early career in country music to her chart-topping pop hits, learn more about singer-songwriter Taylor Swift, one of the best-selling musical artists of all time." (Publisher's note)

Includes bibliographical references and index

783 Music for single voices

Landau, Elaine

Is singing for you? Lerner Publications 2011 40p il (Ready to make music) lib bdg $27.93

Grades: 4 5 6 7 **783**

1. Singing

ISBN 978-0-7613-5427-7 lib bdg; 0-7613-5427-1 lib bdg

LC 2009052350

Helps readers explore the art of singing. This book covers the basics, including tips for getting started and info on vocal technique.

"Landau covers all the bases so that prospective musicians have the information they need. . . . Kids thinking about taking up an instrument will find . . . [this book] helpful in their decision-making process." SLJ

Includes glossary and bibliographical references

784.19 Instruments

Baines, Anthony

The **Oxford** companion to musical instruments; written and edited by Anthony Baines. Oxford University Press 1992 404p il $85

Grades: 8 9 10 11 12 Adult **784.19**

1. Reference books 2. Musical instruments -- Dictionaries

ISBN 0-19-311334-1

LC 92-8635

Based on The New Oxford companion to music (1983)

This volume presents alphabetically arranged entries for musical instruments. "The individual entries cover specific instruments and families thereof (e.g., Wind Instruments) as well as their representation in different countries (e.g., Africa) and time periods (e.g., Baroque). . . . Playing techniques, a brief history, and a list of the major repertory are [discussed]." Booklist

Helsby, Genevieve

★ **Those** amazing musical instruments; [by] Genevieve Helsby; with Marin Alsop as your guide. Sourcebooks Jabberwocky 2007 176p il $19.95

Grades: 4 5 6 7 8 9 **784.19**

1. Musical instruments

ISBN 978-1-4022-0825-6; 1-4022-0825-1

LC 2007013821

This is "a guide to instruments commonly found in an orchestra. . . . Utilizing large print; ample, colorful illustrations; and an open format, the book is logically organized into chapters about each of the musical instrument families, including keyboards, the voice, and modern electronic instruments. Throughout, readers are prompted to listen to the accompanying CD-ROM, which features more than 100 musical samples.

Information is clearly presented, and the author's enthusiasm for her subject is contagious." SLJ

Kallen, Stuart A.

The **instruments** of music. Lucent Bks. 2003 112p il (Music library) lib bdg $27.45

Grades: 6 7 8 9 **784.19**

1. Musical instruments

ISBN 1-59018-127-1

LC 2001-6609

This volume "includes history, cultural background, and the place of individual instruments in music from classical orchestra to rock and roll." Publisher's note

Includes bibliographical references

784.192 Techniques and procedures for instruments themselves

Pagliaro, Michael

The **musical** instrument desk reference; a guide to how band and orchestral instruments work. Michael J. Pagliaro. Scarecrow Press 2012 189 p. (cloth : alk. paper) $65

Grades: Adult Professional **784.192**

1. Musical instruments 2. Wind instruments -- Construction 3. Bowed stringed instruments -- Construction

ISBN 0810882701; 9780810882706; 9780810882713

LC 2012007244

This book "begins with an 'easy-reference quick start' section on woodwinds, followed by more in-depth chapters on the flute, clarinet, saxophone, oboe, and the bassoon. For the brass instruments, there are fingering charts, an expanded in-depth study chapter, and a chapter on functioning. Nonfretted string instruments . . . are also given a chapter on producing sound and an expanded in-depth study chapter. The final chapter consists of an overview of percussion instruments." (Booklist)

784.2 Full orchestra (Symphony orchestra)

Ganeri, Anita

★ The **young** person's guide to the orchestra; Benjamin Britten's composition on CD narrated by Ben Kingsley. book written by Anita Ganeri. Harcourt Brace & Co. 1996 56p il $25

Grades: 4 5 6 7 **784.2**

1. Orchestra 2. Music appreciation 3. Musical instruments

ISBN 0-15-201304-0

LC 95-41478

"Accompanying this book on orchestral music is a CD featuring Britten's A Young Person's Guide to the Orchestra . . . as well as Dukas' The Sorcerer's Apprentice. The book begins with an overview of the orchestra and then centers around groups of instruments, explaining a bit of their history and their sound's distinctive quality. . . . The book also introduces eight famous composers, world music, Benjamin Britten, and the background of The YoungPerson's Guide to the Orchestra. . . . Handsome and useful." Booklist

Includes glossary

784.4 Light orchestra

Bolden, Tonya

Take -off! American all-girl bands during WW II. Alfred A. Knopf 2007 76p il $18.99; lib bdg $21.99

Grades: 6 7 8 9 **784.4**

1. Jazz musicians 2. Women musicians

ISBN 978-0-375-82797-6; 0-375-82797-8; 978-0-375-92797-3 lib bdg; 0-375-92797-2 lib bdg

LC 2006-24523

"To appreciate this book, readers need at least a nodding acquaintance with swing music. The accompanying CD will help, and Bolden's introduction, which features opinions from Benny Goodman, Ella Fitzgerald, and others, gets things off to a good start. Then, using fascinating archival material . . . she goes on to discuss pioneering female jazz bands. . . . Bolden [uses] a fresh style of writing, as bouncy as the music." Booklist

Includes glossary and bibliographical references

785 Ensembles with only one instrument per part

Marx, Trish

Steel drumming at the Apollo; the road to Super Top Dog. by Trish Marx; photographs by Ellen B. Senisi. Lee & Low Books 2007 56p il $22

Grades: 4 5 6 7 **785**

1. Musicians 2. Bands (Music) 3. Steel drum (Musical instrument) 4. Apollo Theatre (New York, N.Y.)

ISBN 978-1-60060-124-8; 1-60060-124-3

LC 2007008947

"Marx traces the band's progress through the tiers of competition in clear evocative prose depicting the visceral experience of performing as well as the hard work of practice and composition. Senisi's color photographs enliven every page." SLJ

786 Specific instruments and their music

Witmer, Scott

Drums, keyboards, and other instruments. ABDO 2009 32p il (Rock band) lib bdg $27.07

Grades: 6 7 8 9 **786**

1. Drums 2. Rock music 3. Musical instruments 4. Keyboards (Electronics)

ISBN 978-1-60453-690-4 lib bdg; 1-60453-690-X lib bdg

LC 2009-6607

This offers information for rock bands about keyboards, drums, and other instruments

"Copious examples and photos of bands drawn from a wide chronological and stylistic range ensure that every reader, from metalheads (Metallica) to Linkin Park fans will find something of interest here." SLJ

Includes glossary

786.2 Keyboard instruments

Batten, Jack

Oscar Peterson; the man and his jazz. Jack Batten. Tundra Books of Northern New York 2012 165 p. (hardcover) $19.95

Grades: 6 7 8 **786.2**

1. Jazz music -- History and criticism

ISBN 1770492690; 9781770492691

LC 2011940582

This children's book, by Jack Batten, is a biography of the Jazz pianist Oscar Peterson. "Oscar Peterson released over 200 recordings, won seven Grammy Awards, received the Order of Canada and is considered to have been one of the greatest jazz pianists of all time. This new biography . . . is the story of a black kid from a Montreal ghetto who reached acclaim in the great music halls of the world." (Publisher's note)

786.9 Drums and devices used for percussive effects

Landau, Elaine

Are the drums for you? Lerner Publications 2011 40p il (Ready to make music) lib bdg $27.93

Grades: 4 5 6 7 **786.9**

1. Drums 2. Percussion instruments

ISBN 978-0-7613-5426-0 lib bdg; 0-7613-5426-3 lib bdg

LC 2009-48971

Hear what professional drummers like about their instrument, and learn what skills a good drummer needs.

"Landau covers all the bases so that prospective musicians have the information they need. . . . Kids thinking about taking up an instrument will find . . . [this book] helpful in their decision-making process." SLJ

Includes glossary and bibliographical references

787 Stringed instruments (Chordophones)

Ganeri, Anita

Stringed instruments. Smart Apple Media 2011 32p il (How the world makes music) lib bdg $28.50

Grades: 4 5 6 **787**

1. Stringed instruments

ISBN 978-1-599-20480-2

LC 2010042418

Describes various stringed instruments from around the world including familiar instruments such as the guitar and violin, along with other traditional instruments such as the Japanese Koto and Indian lutes.

787.2 Violins

Landau, Elaine

Is the violin for you? Lerner Publications 2011 40p il (Ready to make music) lib bdg $27.93

Grades: 4 5 6 7 **787.2**

1. Violins

ISBN 978-0-7613-5423-9 lib bdg; 0-7613-5423-9 lib bdg

LC 2009045609

Hear what professional violinists like about their instrument, and learn what skills a good violinist needs.

"Landau covers all the bases so that prospective musicians have the information they need. . . . Kids thinking about taking up an instrument will find . . . [this book] helpful in their decision-making process." SLJ

Includes glossary and bibliographical references

787.8 Plectral lute family

Ellis, Rex M.

With a banjo on my knee; a musical journey from slavery to freedom. Watts 2001 160p il lib bdg $28

Grades: 7 8 9 10 **787.8**

1. Banjos 2. African American music

ISBN 0-531-11747-2 lib bdg; 978-0-531-11747-7 lib bdg

LC 00-33035

This is a "well-written, attractive work, which unveils a segment of social history both powerful and far reaching." Booklist

Includes glossary, discography and bibliographical references

787.87 Guitars

Landau, Elaine

Is the guitar for you? Lerner Publications 2011 40p il (Ready to make music) lib bdg $27.93

Grades: 4 5 6 7 **787.87**

1. Guitars

ISBN 978-0-7613-5424-6 lib bdg; 0-7613-5424-7 lib bdg

LC 2009-48750

Hear what professional guitarists like about their instrument, and learn what skills a good guitarist needs.

"Landau covers all the bases so that prospective musicians have the information they need. . . . Kids thinking about taking up an instrument will find . . . [this book] helpful in their decision-making process." SLJ

Includes glossary and bibliographical references

Witmer, Scott

Guitars & bass. ABDO 2010 32p il (Rock band) lib bdg $27.07

Grades: 6 7 8 9 **787.87**

1. Guitars 2. Rock music

ISBN 978-1-60453-691-1 lib bdg; 1-60453-691-8 lib bdg

LC 2009-6608

This offers information about guitars and basses for rock bands

"Copious examples and photos of bands drawn from a wide chronological and stylistic range ensure that every reader, from metalheads (Metallica) to Linkin Park fans will find something of interest here." SLJ

Includes glossary

788 Wind instruments (Aerophones)

Landau, Elaine

Is the flute for you? Lerner Publications 2011 40p il (Ready to make music) lib bdg $27.93

Grades: 4 5 6 7 **788**

1. Flutes

ISBN 978-0-7613-5420-8 lib bdg; 0-7613-5420-4 lib bdg

LC 2009048970

Hear what professional flutists like about their instrument, and learn what skills a good flutist needs.

"Landau covers all the bases so that prospective musicians have the information they need. . . . Kids thinking about taking up an instrument will find . . . [this book] helpful in their decision-making process." SLJ

Includes glossary and bibliographical references

788.7 Saxophones

Golio, Gary

Spirit seeker; John Coltrane's musical journey. by Gary Golio ; paintings by Rudy Gutierrez. Clarion Books 2012 48 p. (hardcover) $17.99

Grades: 3 4 5 6 7 **788.7**

1. Music and religion 2. Creation (Literary, artistic, etc.) 3. Saxophonists -- United States -- Biography 4. Jazz musicians -- United States -- Biography

ISBN 0547239947; 9780547239941

LC 2011045948

Includes bibliographical references and discography.

This book, by Gary Golio, illustrated by Rudy Gutierrez, explores the musical career of Jazz saxophonist John Coltrane. "Growing up, John was a seeker. He wondered about spirit, and the meaning of life. And whether music could be a key to unlocking those mysteries. . . . This is the story of a shy, curious boy from a deeply religious family who grew up to find solace and inspiration in his own unique approach to both spirituality and music." (Publisher's note)

Rice, Earle

★ **Charlie** Parker; by Earle Rice Jr. Mitchell Lane Publishers 2012 47 p. ill. (library) $29.95

Grades: 6 7 8 9 **788.7**

1. Jazz musicians -- Biography 2. African American musicians -- Biography 3. Jazz musicians -- United States -- Biography

ISBN 1612282660; 9781612282664

LC 2012008628

This biography of musician Charlie Parker, part of the American Jazz series, presents an "account of Parker's drug-abuse-shortened life and stellar career--along with a . . . technical, specific analysis of his musical education and innovations." It includes "period photos of 'Bird' and his bandmates, plus a time line, a discography, and . . . sets of print and web resources for children and adults alike." (Booklist)

Includes discography (p. [41]), bibliographical references (p. 44), and index.

788.9 Brass instruments (Lip-reed instruments)

Landau, Elaine

Is the trumpet for you? Lerner Publications 2011 40p il (Ready to make music) lib bdg $27.93

Grades: 4 5 6 7 **788.9**

1. Trumpet

ISBN 978-0-7613-5422-2 lib bdg; 0-7613-5422-0 lib bdg

LC 2009048280

Hear what professional trumpeters like about their instrument, and learn what skills a good trumpeter needs.

"Landau covers all the bases so that prospective musicians have the information they need. . . . Kids thinking about taking up an instrument will find . . . [this book] helpful in their decision-making process." SLJ

Includes glossary and bibliographical references

790 Recreational and performing arts

Glenn, Joshua

Unbored; the essential field guide to serious fun. [compiled by] Joshua Glenn & Elizabeth Foy Larsen ; design by Tony Leone. Bloomsbury USA 2012 352 p. (hardback) $25

Grades: 5 6 7 **790**

1. Amusements 2. Games 3. Amusements 4. Handicraft 5. Recreation

ISBN 1608196410; 9781608196418

LC 2012012368

This activity book by Elizabeth Foy Larsen and Joshua Glen, illustrated by Heather Kasunick and Mister Reusch, "provides kids with information to round out their world view and inspire them to learn more. From how-tos on using the library or writing your representative to a graphic history of video games, the book isn't shy about teaching. Yet the bulk of the 350-page mega-resource presents hands-on activities." (Publisher's note)

790.1 General kinds of recreational activities

Ball, Jacqueline A.

Traveling green. Bearport Pub. 2009 32p il (Going green) lib bdg $25.27

Grades: 4 5 6 7 **790.1**

1. Travel -- Environmental aspects

ISBN 978-1-59716-964-6 lib bdg; 1-59716-964-1 lib bdg

LC 2009-19836

"Color photographs (most full page) and a few diagrams accompany the informative text[s]. . . . Overall, the [book] . . . is user-friendly and covers topics that are not easily found elsewhere." SLJ

Includes glossary and bibliographical references

Centore, Michael

Entertainment industry; by Michael Centore. Mason Crest 2017 64 p. color illustrations (hardback) $23.95

Grades: 6 7 8 9 10 **790.1**

1. STEM education 2. Cultural industries 3. Circus 4. Animal trainers 5. Computer graphics 6. Entertainment events 7. Television broadcasting -- Special effects

ISBN 1422235904; 9781422235904

LC 2016004738

This juvenile book, by Michael Centore, part of the "STEM in current events" series, explores developments in science, technology, engineering and mathematics within the entertainment industry. "'Text-Dependent Questions' and 'Research Project' sections help learners to re-engage with the text and topic—many even promote group work." (School Library Journal)

"A great fit for classroom or school libraries and a strong consideration for public libraries interested in the integration of STEM into everyday life." SLJ

Includes bibliographical references and index

Ferrer, J. J.

The **art** of stone skipping and other fun old-time games; stoopball, jacks, string games, coin flipping, line baseball, jump rope, and more. by J.J. Ferrer ; illustrated by Todd Dakins. Charlesbridge Pub., Inc. 2012 192 p. (paperback) $14.95

Grades: K 1 2 3 4 5 6 7 8 9 10 11 12 Adult **790.1**

1. Games

ISBN 1936140748; 9781936140749

LC 2012015052

This book, by J. J. Ferrer, offers a "collection of timeless games that guarantees kids a good time- by themselves, with a group of friends, or with family. Includes ball games . . . , card games . . . , sack races, and old favorites such as Duck, Duck, Goose and Red Rover. There is also a chapter for car games. Simple instructions explain the rules, how many people can play, the object of the game, and what you need." (Publisher's note)

Includes bibliographical references and index.

Hines-Stephens, Sarah

Show off; how to do absolutely everything one step at a time. [by] Sarah Hines Stephens and Bethany Mann. Candlewick Press 2009 224p il $18.99

Grades: 5 6 7 8 **790.1**

1. Amusements 2. Handicraft 3. Recreation

ISBN 978-0-7636-4599-1; 0-7636-4599-0

LC 2009015847

"This lively illustrated activity book delivers concise instructions for a variety of indoor and outdoor activities. Projects include crafts, pranks and magic tricks; ideas for nature exploration; and other purely entertaining feats. . . . The instructions are heavy on graphics and light on detail, making for an eye-catching but potentially frustrating experience. But readers should enjoy the irreverence and variety." Publ Wkly

Rowell, Victoria

Tag, toss & run; 40 classic lawn games. Paul Tukey & Victoria Rowell. Storey Pub. 2012 207 p. (pbk. : alk. paper) $14.95

Grades: Adult Professional **790.1**

1. Games 2. Outdoor recreation 3. Games 4. Outdoor games

ISBN 1603425608; 9781603425605

LC 2011049410

This book on "family lawn games" presents a "guide to 40 time-tested favorites -- from classics like capture the flag, croquet, badminton, and bocce to the lesser-known Cherokee marbles, cornhole, and Kubb. The authors offer a quick overview of the basic structure of each game, as well as strategies for playing and tips for creating fun variations." (Publisher's note)

Includes bibliographical references and index.

791 Public performances

Lusted, Marcia Amidon

Entertainment. ABDO Pub. Company 2011 112p il (Inside the industry) $23.95

Grades: 5 6 7 8 **791**

1. Performing arts -- Vocational guidance

ISBN 978-1-61714-799-9; 1-61714-799-0

LC 2010041255

This "well-designed [book describes] a variety of careers in [entertainment]. Because [it helps] readers assess if these positions are suitable for their personality types and backgrounds, the [title is a] good [choice] for career exploration and self-discovery. [It is] also useful for research and reports. . . . Sidebars and full-color photos appear throughout." SLJ

Includes bibliographical references

791.4 Motion pictures, radio, television

Gilbert, Sara D., 1943-

The **story** of Pixar; Sara Gilbert. Creative Education 2014 46 p. illustrations (chiefly color) (Built for success) (hardcover : alkaline paper) $37.10

Grades: 6 7 8 9 **791.4**

1. Animated films 2. Computer animation 3. Pixar (Firm) 4. Animated films -- United States 5. Computer animation -- United States

ISBN 1608183963; 9781608183968

LC 2013029615

This book, by Sara Gilbert, presents a "look at the origins, leaders, growth, and innovations of Pixar, the movie studio founded in 1986, which is one of the most successful producers of computer-animated films today." (Publisher's note)

"This series that profiles well-known businesses (previous books include The Story of Google, The Story of Microsoft, The Story of Amazon, and The Story of Nike, which SLJ called "interesting and well written") continues with some more winners. Though books on corporate America sound like a hard sell, the large, attractive photos and beautiful design will pull in readers, and these companies—focusing on music, movies, and social media—have a fairly high "cool" quotient. Well written and well organized, the text flows smoothly, providing comprehensive coverage." SLJ

Includes bibliographical references and index

Other titles in this series include:

The Story of Amazon.com (2013)
The Story of Apple (2012)
The Story of CNN (2013)
The Story of Coca-Cola (2009)
The Story of Disney (2009)
The Story of eBay (2012)
The Story of Facebook (2012)
The Story of Ford (2009)
The Story of Google (2009)
The Story of McDonald's (2009)
The Story of Microsoft (2009)
The Story of MTV (2015)
The Story of Nike (2009)
The Story of Starbucks (2008)
The Story of Target (2015)
The Story of the NFL (2012)
The Story of Twitter (2015)
The Story of Wal-Mart (2011)

791.43 Motion pictures

Bliss, John

Art that moves; animation around the world. Raintree 2011 32p il (Culture in action) lib bdg $29

Grades: 5 6 7 8 **791.43**

1. Animated films

ISBN 978-1-4109-3922-7; 1-4109-3922-7

LC 2009051125

This "is a good choice for children interested in animated movies. Bliss looks at techniques from the early beginnings to modern times and mentions recent film releases such as Cars (2006) and Where the Wild Things Are (2010). . . . [This volume is] quick, interesting, up-to-date . . . with plenty of supportive, captioned, full-color photographs. [It] also [provides] related project suggestions." SLJ

Includes bibliographical references

Cohn, Jessica

Animator. Gareth Stevens Pub. 2010 32p il (Cool careers: cutting edge) lib bdg $26; pa $8.95

Grades: 4 5 6 **791.43**

1. Vocational guidance 2. Animation (Cinematography)

ISBN 978-1-4339-1953-4 lib bdg; 1-4339-1953-2 lib bdg; 978-1-4339-2152-0 pa; 1-4339-2152-9 pa

LC 2009002006

Describes the work of an animator.

This title offers "clear, solid information in a large font. . . . [This] short [book is] packed with relevant, current material." SLJ

Includes glossary and bibliographical references

Finch, Christopher

The **art** of Walt Disney; Christopher Finch. New edition Harry N Abrams 2011 503 p illustrations hardcover $90

Grades: 7 8 9 10 11 12 Adult **791.43**

1. Walt Disney Company

ISBN 0810998149; 9780810998148

LC 2011007947

First published 1973

"This book was the first to reveal the wealth of concept art, animation drawings, and archival material created in the course of animating films. In this newly revised edition, author Christopher Finch has thoroughly reworked every chapter to incorporate the vast achievements of The Walt Disney Company in filmmaking, theater, and theme parks, from Walt's day to the present, including all-new exciting chapters on Pixar Animation Studio and Walt Disney Animation

Hill, Z. B.

Filmmaking & documentaries; Z.B. Hill. Mason Crest, an imprint of National Highlights 2014 64 p. (Art today!) (hardback) $23.95

Grades: 5 6 7 8 **791.43**

1. Vocational guidance 2. Motion pictures -- Production and direction 3. Documentary films -- Production and direction

ISBN 1422231712; 9781422231678; 9781422231715; 9781422287088

LC 2014011828

In this book, by Z. B. Hill, "[d]iscover the world of filmmaking, including the business behind both Hollywood hits and small films. Learn how you can get started on a career behind the camera!" (Publisher's note)

"This entry in the Art Today! series provides students interested in filmmaking with a solid introductory survey, including basic definitions of jobs and elements of the industry, a brief history of filmmaking and documentaries, the all-important business of profitability and funding, and realistic ways to get involved at a beginner's level...Though this offers more of a broad overview than detailed instruction, tweens who want to know where to start with filmmaking will find enough direction here. A "Find Out More" section, further reading, and a glossary append the text." Booklist

Filmmaking and documentaries

Indovino, Shaina Carmel

Dracula and beyond; famous vampires & werewolves in literature and film. Mason Crest Publishers 2011 63p il (The making of a monster: vampires & werewolves) lib bdg $22.95; pa $9.95

Grades: 7 8 9 10 **791.43**

1. Vampires 2. Werewolves 3. Vampires in literature 4. Horror fiction -- History and criticism

ISBN 978-1-4222-1803-7 lib bdg; 1-4222-1803-1 lib bdg; 978-1-4222-1956-0 pa; 1-4222-1956-9 pa

LC 2010020684

Explores portrayals of vampires and werewolves in literature and movies.

"The writing is engaging and accessible, and peppered easily with teen vernacular. . . . Large, clear photographs and period and contemporary drawings appear on every other page or so. . . . First-rate entertainment." SLJ

Includes glossary and bibliographical references

Reynolds, David West

Star Wars: the complete visual dictionary; written by David West Reynolds (episodes I, II and IV-VI) and James Luceno (episode III); updates and new material by Ryder Windham; special fabrications by Robert E. Barnes . . . [et. al.]; new photography by Alex Ivanov. 1st American ed.; DK Pub. 2006 270p il $40

Grades: 6 7 8 9 10 11 12 Adult **791.43**

1. Star Wars films

ISBN 0-7566-2238-7; 978-0-7566-2238-1

LC 2006298949

Material in this book was originally published in various DK Pub. publications, 1998-2005

"Star Wars Complete Visual Dictionary brings together all four . . . titles from The Visual Dictionary series (Episode I-III and the Trilogy) in one volume. . . . This book is [a] comprehensive visual guide to every character, weapon, starship, droid, creature and alien in the Star Wars universe." Publisher's note

Seba, Jaime

Gay characters in theatre, movies, and television: new roles, new attitudes; by Jaime A. Seba. Mason Crest Publishers 2011 64p il (Gallup's guide to modern gay, lesbian, and transgender lifestyle) lib bdg $22.95; pa $9.95

Grades: 8 9 10 11 12 **791.43**

1. Gay men 2. Lesbians 3. LGBT people 4. Homosexuality in literature 5. Homosexuality on television 6. Homosexuality in motion pictures

ISBN 978-1-4222-2012-2 lib bdg; 1-4222-2012-5 lib bdg; 978-1-4222-2013-9 pa; 1-4222-2013-3 pa

LC 2010017051

"This slender, accessible overview uses numerous examples, past and present, to show how the depiction of gay, lesbian, bisexual, and transgender (GLBT) characters in the entertainment industry affects popular culture and has helped push growing acceptance into the mainstream. . . . The book features an open, inviting format, and portraits, reproduced posters, and short profiles of GLTB stars . . . add to the title's browsability." Booklist

Includes bibliographical references

Woog, Adam

Vampires in the movies. ReferencePoint Press, Inc. 2010 80p il (The vampire library) $26.95

Grades: 7 8 9 10 **791.43**

1. Vampires 2. Motion pictures -- History and criticism

ISBN 978-1-60152-135-4; 1-60152-135-9

LC 2010017982

Examines different ways vampires have been presented throughout history in films, from the early-twentieth century for Lugosi films to the present-day mania for Twilight and other modern takes.

"Energetic and suprisingly educational, this lively [book] seizes upon a zietgeist topic and takes it as far as possible." Booklist

Includes bibliographical references

791.5 Puppetry and toy theaters

Kennedy, John E.

★ **Puppet** planet. North Light Books 2006 79p il $16.99

Grades: 4 5 6 7 **791.5**

1. Puppets and puppet plays

ISBN 978-1-58180-794-3; 1-58180-794-5

LC 2005033711

This book offers twelve "puppet projects, each using a variety of techniques, [and] features 'action panels' so readers can see how each puppet comes to life. [It also] Includes staging ideas to play up each project's uniqueness." Publisher's note

791.8 Animal performances

Collard III, Sneed B.

The **world** famous Miles City Bucking Horse Sale. Bucking Horse Books 2010 64p il $18

Grades: 5 6 7 8 **791.8**

1. Horses 2. Rodeos 3. Montana

ISBN 0984446001; 9780984446001; 978-0-9844460-0-1; 0-9844460-0-1

"Collard takes readers inside the Miles City [Montana] Bucking Horse Sale, a four-day event that draws visitors from across the country. Started in 1951 as a sale of wild horses, it's evolved into a jamboree of music, rodeo, food, contests, and a parade. . . . Plenty of action-filled color photographs break up the narrative. . . . Handsomely designed, . . . this is a fascinating look at a fresh topic." Booklist

Includes glossary

Grayson, Robert

Performers. Marshall Cavendish Benchmark 2010 64p il (Working animals) lib bdg $28.50

Grades: 4 5 6 7 **791.8**

1. Animals in entertainment

ISBN 978-1-60870-165-0 lib bdg; 1-60870-165-4 lib bdg

LC 2010006893

"Describes the role of animals in movies, sporting events, and various competitions." Publisher's note

Includes glossary and bibliographical references

Laidlaw, Rob

On parade; the hidden world of animals in entertainment. Fitzhenry & Whiteside 2010 55p il $19.95

Grades: 4 5 6 **791.8**

1. Zoos 2. Circus 3. Animal welfare 4. Animals in entertainment

ISBN 978-1-55455-143-9; 1-55455-143-9

This book examines animals at the zoo and circus, animals working in movies and television, violence in the world of performing animals and offers ways to improve conditions and prevent animal abuse.

The author's "clearly argued text; crisp, captioned color photos; and appended list of organizations make this an important source for animal advocates." Booklist

792 Stage presentations

Aliki

★ **William** Shakespeare & the Globe; written & illustrated by Aliki. HarperCollins Pubs. 1999 48p il hardcover o.p. pa $6.99

Grades: 4 5 6 7 8 9 **792**

1. Poets 2. Authors 3. Dramatists 4. Globe Theatre (London, England) 5. Shakespeare's Globe (London, England)

ISBN 0-06-027820-X; 0-06-443722-1 pa

LC 98-7903

"A logically organized and engaging text, plenty of detailed illustrations with informative captions, and a clean design provide a fine introduction to both bard and theater." Horn Book Guide

Becker, Helaine

Funny business; clowning around, practical jokes, cool comedy, cartooning, and more . . . illustrated by Claudia Dávila. Maple Tree 2005 160p il $21.95; pa $9.95

Grades: 5 6 7 8 **792**

1. Clowns 2. Cartooning 3. Wit and humor

ISBN 1-897066-40-6; 1-897066-41-4 pa

"Becker offers funny facts, an informative diagram showing what goes on in the body when you laugh, brief discussions of different types of humor (situation comedy, parody, farce, riddles, puns), a How Funny Are You? quiz, tips and timing for standup routines, body lingo, props, six improvisation games, clowning material, and more. For kids who want to learn how to juggle, tell jokes, or use sight-gag items, it's all here. Cartooning is explained as well." SLJ

Belli, Mary Lou

Acting for young actors; the ultimate teen guide. [by] Mary Lou Belli & Dinah Lenney. Back Stage Books 2006 205p il pa $16.96

Grades: 7 8 9 10 11 12 **792**

1. Acting

ISBN 978-0-8230-4947-9 pa; 0-8230-4947-7 pa

LC 2006007265

"Belli and Lenney, an Emmy-winning director of Girlfriends and a Yale-educated ER actress offer stagestruck teens trunks-full of sound advice packaged with a conversational tone and grounded experience. . . . The authors offer a series of questions for character analysis; suggested readings and viewings abound. . . . The handbook succeeds at communicating clearly without talking down to readers; engaging prose makes it an ideal text for classes and teens who want commonsense career prep and insight." Voice Youth Advocates

Includes bibliographical references

Kenney, Karen Latchana

Cool costumes; how to stage your very own show. ABDO Pub. Company 2010 32p il (Cool performances) lib bdg $17.95

Grades: 4 5 6 **792**

1. Costume 2. Theater

ISBN 978-1-60453-714-7 lib bdg; 1-60453-714-0 lib bdg

LC 2009-1751

Includes step-by-step instructions on how to create royalty robes, animal ears, baseball T-Shirts and more

"Simple language, colorful page design, and detailed step-by-step photos invite children to gather some easily available houselhold items, apply paint and some imagination, and put on a play—or just play." SLJ

Includes glossary and webliography

Other titles in this series are:
Cool makeup
Cool productions
Cool sets and props
Cool scripts and acting
Cool special effects

Lamedman, Debbie

The **ultimate** audition book for teens; 111 one-minute monologues. Smith & Kraus (Young actor series)
Grades: 7 8 9 10 11 12 **792**

1. Acting 2. Monologues

A series of collections of 111 original monologues, all about one minute long, to be used by male and female teenage actors in auditions.

"Some suggestive sexual situations described here will not be acceptable in some classrooms. Drama teachers may, however, welcome some of this material for beginning acting students." Book Rep [review of volume one]

Millennium monologs; 95 contemporary characterizations for young actors. edited by Gerald Lee Ratliff. Meriwether 2002 261p pa $15.95
Grades: 8 9 10 11 12 **792**

1. Acting 2. Monologues 3. American drama -- Collections
ISBN 1-56608-082-7

LC 2002-13009

An anthology of monologues by contemporary writers, divided into four categories: "Hope and Longing," "Spirit and Soul," "Fun and Fantasy," and "Doubt and Despair." Includes audition techniques

"This fine collection of American monologues is notable for its diversity as well as for the high quality of the material." Booklist

Rogers, Barb

Costumes, accessories, props, and stage illusions made easy. Meriwether Pub. 2005 205p il pa $19.95
Grades: 8 9 10 11 12 **792**

1. Costume 2. Theater -- Production and direction
ISBN 978-1-56608-103-0; 1-56608-103-3

LC 2005-4359

This book details ways to make theater "costumes with simple tools such as scissors, glue guns, and paint. In addition, there are chapters on how to make hats, gloves, armor, and animal heads, as well as other props and accessories from rummage-sale finds and a little imagination. . . . This is a useful volume for schools and community theaters with little or no budgets for costumes and props." SLJ

Includes bibliographical references

Schumacher, Thomas L.

How does the show go on? an introduction to the theater. by Thomas Schumacher with Jeff Kurtti. 2nd ed; Disney 2008 128p il $22.95
Grades: 4 5 6 7 **792**

1. Theater
ISBN 978-1-4231-2031-5; 1-4231-2031-0

"Filled with lavish color photos of Disney theater productions, this eye-catching volume has clever chapter titles, beginning with 'Overture,' which tells about 'styles of theaters' and 'kinds of shows.' In 'Act One' and 'Act Two,' aspects of the front and back of the house are discussed, including the marquee, the box office, props, special effects, and so on. Interspersed throughout the facts and photos are 'Stage Notes,' where bits of trivia are doled out." SLJ

Skog, Jason

Acting; a practical guide to pursuing the art. Compass Point Books 2010 48p il (Performing arts) lib bdg $28.65
Grades: 5 6 7 8 **792**

1. Acting 2. Vocational guidance
ISBN 978-0-7565-4364-8 lib bdg; 0-7565-4364-9 lib bdg

LC 2010012604

A guide for those interested in a career in acting, and includes tips on education, technique, and more.

"Meant for students contemplating a career in the field . . . [this book goes] beyond basic introductions and into more detail about what it takes to make it as a professional. . . . [The author maintains] . . . a frank, realistic tone, stressing the importance of hard work and dedication. Great [resource] . . . for those wanting to make their passions more than just a hobby." SLJ

Includes glossary and bibliographical references

Underwood, Deborah

Staging a play. Raintree 2009 32p il (Culture in action) $28.21; pa $7.99
Grades: 5 6 7 8 **792**

1. Theater -- Production and direction
ISBN 978-1-4109-3396-6; 1-4109-3396-2; 978-1-4109-3413-0 pa; 1-4109-3413-6 pa

LC 2009000417

This "discusses the various professionals involved in a production, such as actors, costume designers, prop masters, and stage handlers. Well organized and with bright, colorful photography, [this] introductory [title gives] readers good basic knowledge." SLJ

Includes glossary and bibliographical references

792.09 History, geographic treatment, biography

Currie, Stephen

An **actor** on the Elizabethan stage. Lucent Bks. 2003 96p il maps (Working life) $27.45
Grades: 6 7 8 9 **792.09**

1. Theater -- History 2. Great Britain -- History -- 1485-1603, Tudors
ISBN 1-59018-174-3

LC 2002-9460

Discusses various aspects of theatrical life, including staging and performance, financing, types of acting troupes, and social and economic influences

This is "well written and the [author draws on quotes] from many primary sources." Libr Media Connect

Includes bibliographical references

792.6 Musical plays

Amendola, Dana

★ A **day** at the New Amsterdam Theatre; photos by Gino Domenico; written by Dana Amendola. Disney Editions 2004 125p il $24.95
Grades: 4 5 6 7 **792.6**

1. Theater 2. New Amsterdam Theatre (New York, N.Y.)
ISBN 0-7868-5438-3

"This title covers a day in the life of Disney's The Lion King, the long-running Broadway musical. . . . A clock in a corner of each spread guides readers through the day as box-office personnel, makeup designers, dancers, actors, cleaning staff, and others do their jobs. Each spread includes several full-color photos that are often gritty, sometimes glamorous. . . . This unique volume provides an honest, realistic, eye-opening look at the behind-the-scenes work that goes into the running of a Broadway show." SLJ

Bezdecheck, Bethany

Directing. Rosen Pub. 2009 64p il (High school musicals) lib bdg $21.95

Grades: 7 8 9 10 **792.6**

1. Musicals -- Production and direction

ISBN 978-1-4358-5259-4 lib bdg; 1-4358-5259-1 lib bdg

LC 2008041598

"Bezdecheck lays out the process of directing a musical production, from play selection to auditions to dress rehearsals. . . . There's some good, practical advice here." Booklist

Includes bibliographical references

Michael, Ted

So you wanna be a superstar? the ultimate audition guide. by Ted Michael ; with contributions by Nic Cory & Mara Jill Herman ; introduction by Lea Salonga ; edited by Lisa Cheng. RP Kids 2012 151 p. (paperback: consumable) $10.95; (paperback) $10.95; (ebook) $10.95

Grades: 4 5 6 7 8 **792.6**

1. Auditions 2. Voice culture

ISBN 0762446102; 9780762446100; 9780762447015 pdf

LC 2012932845

This book by Ted Michael presents a guide for " hopeful musical theater, show choir, a cappella, and glee club singers" with advice designed to help readers "train [their] vocal cords, pick the right audition material, and become comfortable with the spotlight. Interactive quizzes . . . and words of advice from industry professionals" are also included. (Publisher's note)

792.8 Ballet and modern dance

Augustyn, Frank

★ **Footnotes**; dancing the world's best-loved ballets. [by] Frank Augustyn and Shelley Tanaka. Millbrook Press 2001 94p il $17.95

Grades: 5 6 7 8 **792.8**

1. Ballet

ISBN 0-7613-1646-9

LC 00-50075

"Fine photographs, most in color, add enormously to the book's appeal. A well-crafted, readable volume." Booklist

Balanchine, George, 1904-1983

101 stories of the great ballets; George Balanchine and Francis Mason. First edition Dolphin Books 1975 xiv, 541 p.p $18.95

Grades: 5 6 7 8 9 10 11 12 Adult **792.8**

1. Ballet -- Stories, plots, etc. 2. Ballets -- Stories, plots, etc

ISBN 0385033982; 9780385033985

LC 73009140

This book, by George Balanchine and Francis Mason, "includes scene-by-scene retellings of the most popular classic and contemporary ballets, as performed by the world's leading dance companies. Certain to delight long-time fans as well as those just discovering the beauty and drama of ballet." (Publisher's note)

"Accessible books on ballet are few and far between . . . [but] George Balanchine and Francis Mason's 101 Stories of the Great Ballets is considered the bible of ballet librettos." Christian Science Monitor

Froman, Kyle

In the wings; behind the scenes at the New York City Ballet. Kyle Froman. John Wiley & Sons 2007 ix, 118 p.p ill. (some col.) ;

Grades: 6 7 8 9 10 11 12 Adult **792.8**

1. Ballet 2. Anecdotes 3. New York City Ballet -- Anecdotes. 4. New York City Ballet -- Pictorial works.

ISBN 9780470173435 (cloth)

LC 2007024556

"Here is New York City Ballet as it really is- the good, the not so good, and the majestically beautiful. It's a true story, and it's told by someone who can honestly claim that he was there." (Publisher's Note)

"An 11-year veteran dancer for the New York City Ballet, Froman here documents life in the corps de ballet in a photo-album and diary-like format. Presenting a day in the life of the dancers, he takes readers through the stages of warming up, class, physical therapy, rehearsals, preparation, and, of course, the show. . . . An engaging point of view and an attractive layout make this an entertaining read. YAs may also find it a good introduction to the dance world as a possible career. Recommended for all libraries." LJ

Kupesic, Rajka

The **white** ballets. Tundra Books 2011 40p il $19.95

Grades: 4 5 6 7 **792.8**

1. Ballet -- Stories, plots, etc.

ISBN 978-0-88776-923-8; 0-88776-923-3

This retells the stories of Swan Lake, Giselle, and La Bayadère and includes information and comments on the three ballets.

"The tales are well told, and the author, a former ballerina, provides information on the history of the ballet. Each painting in gold leaf and oil represents a scene from one of the ballets. The richly colored illustrations are very stylized with graceful figures dressed in flowing, romantic costumes, and Kupesic elaborates on the details, symbols, and characters in her artwork. . . . For ballet enthusiasts this is a unique look at these classics." SLJ

Lee, Laura

A **child's** introduction to ballet; the stories, music and magic of classical dance. [by] Laura Lee; illustrated by Meredith Hamilton. Black Dog & Leventhal Publishers 2007 96p il $19.95

Grades: 4 5 6 7 8 **792.8**

1. Ballet

ISBN 978-1-57912-699-5; 1-57912-699-5

LC 2006048867

"This lively and attractive volume delves into the history of ballet from its beginnings in Italy through the 20th century. . . . Detailed and well-written descriptions of 25 of the most famous and influential ballets are provided along with colorful illustrations of scenes. A CD presents excerpts from them and the author poses some questions and gives some insights to think about as one listens to the music." SLJ

Marsico, Katie

Choreographer. Cherry Lake Pub. 2011 32p il (Cool arts careers) lib bdg $18.95

Grades: 4 5 6 7 **792.8**

1. Dance 2. Choreographers 3. Vocational guidance

ISBN 978-1-61080-136-2; 1-61080-136-9

LC 2011001170

"Illustrated with color photos of the famous, the young, and the fabulously festooned, this is a sturdy presentation of facts and case studies that will bring the process of professional choreography home to those students considering such a competitive and demanding career." Booklist

Includes bibliographical references

Miles, Lisa

Ballet spectacular; a young ballet lover's guide and an insight into a magical world. Lisa Miles. Barrons Educational Series, Inc. 2014 80 p. color illustrations $18.99

Grades: 4 5 6 7 8 **792.8**

1. Ballet 2. Ballet dancers 3. Royal Ballet

ISBN 0764167456; 9780764167454

LC 2014940905

Author Lisa Miles presents this "reference volume for children who love ballet. Featuring stunning full-color photos from The Royal Ballet's own collections and informative, fact-filled entries, it covers all things dance. Most intriguing to passionate young lovers of dance will be the exploration of a day in the life of a professional ballet dancer, images of beloved performers such as Margot Fonteyn, Darcey Bussell, and Carlos Acosta, detailed close-ups of costumes, and photos." (Publisher's note)

"Combining aspects of a coffee-table book and an introductory handbook, it provides a hodgepodge of basic information about ballet history, famous ballets, life in a major company, and the elements involved in a performance, such as choreography, music, sets, and costumes, while Britain's Royal Ballet Company and School are referenced throughout the book." Booklist

Minden, Eliza Gaynor

The **ballet** companion; a dancer's guide to the technique, traditions, and joys of ballet. Eliza Gaynor Minden. Touchstone Books 2005 xv, 331 p.p illustrations (some color) $29.95

Grades: 6 7 8 9 10 11 12 Adult **792.8**

1. Ballet 2. Ballet dancers 3. Ballet dancing -- Handbooks, manuals, etc

ISBN 9780743264075; 074326407X

LC 2005044102

This book, by Eliza Gaynor Minden "is a fresh, comprehensive, and thoroughly up-to-date reference book for the dancer. With 150 stunning photographs of ballet stars Maria Riccetto and Benjamin Millepied demonstrating perfect execution of positions and steps, this elegant volume brims with everything today's dance student needs" (Publisher's note)

"[The Author's] explanation of the differences between the six major ballet styles, along with the superb glossaries of terms and dance history timeline, make this book a valuable resource for dance studios and a great primer for dancers in the early stages of training." Publishers Weekly

Includes bibliographical references (p. [316]-317) and index

Schorer, Suki

Put your best foot forward; a young dancer's guide to life. by Suki Schorer and the School of American Ballet; illustrations by Donna Ingemanson. Workman Publishing 2005 96p il pa $9.95

Grades: 4 5 6 7 **792.8**

1. Ballet

ISBN 978-0-7611-3795-5 pa; 0-7611-3795-5 pa

LC 2005051428

"The words of counsel proffered by the author, who was a principal dancer for the New York City Ballet and is a teacher at the School of American Ballet, are engaging, imaginative, and right on target. . . . Practical tips such as essentials that need to be in your bag and behavioral advice such as being grateful for criticism are nicely woven into the book. The photographs, mainly of female dancers, are clear and colorful. These words of wisdom will keep dancers on their toes and stretching their minds and hearts." SLJ

792.9 Stage productions

Cox, Carole

Shakespeare kids; performing his plays, speaking his words. Libraries Unlimited 2010 xx, 126p il pa $30

Grades: Adult Professional **792.9**

1. Poets 2. Authors 3. Dramatists 4. Theater -- Production and direction

ISBN 978-1-59158-838-2 pa; 1-59158-838-3 pa

LC 2009041731

This is a "a practical guide for performing Shakespeare's plays, albeit in condensed form, without changing his poetic dialogue. . . . Cox gears her work to teachers of students in grades 3-8, librarians, or adults leading recreational programs, providing precise, detailed instructions on all facets of youth-oriented Shakespearean play production. . . . The text is clear and concise . . . Black-and-white photos capture specific moments that illustrate the performers' enthusiasm." SLJ

Includes bibliographical references

793.3 Social, folk, national dancing

Ancona, George

★ **Ole!** Flamenco. Lee & Low 2010 un il map $19.95

Grades: 5 6 7 8 **793.3**

1. Flamenco

ISBN 978-1-60060-361-7; 1-60060-361-0

LC 2010-22272

Ancona tells "the story of flamenco, an art form that's more than dancing and has been around for hundreds of years. He begins with a short introduction that chronicles his visit to Spain. . . . He then returns readers to Santa Fe, New Mexico, where a group of young people are learning flamenco. A helpful map traces the art form's roots, while the text explains both the history of the Gypsies and flamenco. Full-color photographs capture the excitement and dazzle. . . . All aspects of flamenco are explored, including movements, facial expressions, and sound effects." Booklist

Includes glossary and bibliographical references

Fishkin, Rebecca Love

Dance; a practical guide to pursuing the art. content adviser, Hannah Seidel and Chris Ferris and dancers; reading adviser, Alexa L. Sandmann. Compass Point Books 2011 48p il (Performing arts) lib bdg $28.65

Grades: 5 6 7 8 **793.3**

1. Dance 2. Vocational guidance

ISBN 978-0-7565-4363-1 lib bdg; 0-7565-4363-0 lib bdg

LC 2010012605

This guide about a career in dance includes tips on education, technique, and more.

"Meant for students contemplating a career in the field . . . [this book goes] beyond basic introductions and into more detail about what it takes to make it as a professional. . . . [The author maintains] . . . a frank, realistic tone, stressing the importance of hard work and dedication. Great [resource] . . . for those wanting to make their passions more than just a hobby." SLJ

Includes glossary and bibliographical references

Garofoli, Wendy

Hip -hop dancing. Capstone Press 2011 4v il lib bdg ea $30.65

Grades: 4 5 6 **793.3**

1. Dance 2. Hip-hop

ISBN 978-1-4296-5484-5 v1; 1-4296-5484-5 v1; 978-1-4296-5485-2 v2; 1-4296-5485-6 v2; 978-1-4296-5486-9 v3; 1-4296-5486-9 v3; 978-1-4296-5487-6 v4; 1-4296-5487-2 v4

LC 2010030394

Provides instructions for joining or starting a hip-hop dance crew, and includes information about real-life crews.

"These volumes cover the basic moves as well as more detailed movements often seen on television programs. . . . Everything about the set is jazzy and current. Sentences are short and direct, with a small-sized font detailing step-by-step instructions and fact boxes extending the information." Booklist

Includes bibliographical references

Haney, Johannah

Capoeira. Marshall Cavendish Benchmark 2011 47p il (Martial arts in action) $29.93

Grades: 4 5 6 7 **793.3**

1. Capoeira (Dance)

ISBN 978-0-7614-4932-4; 978-1-6087-0362-3 e-book

LC 2010013829

This describes the history, equipment, and technique of capoeira.

This treats "martial arts with the dignity that serious enthusiasts bring to the sport. . . . Illustrations include not only photos of modern gear and from films but also historical images." Booklist

Smith, Karen Lynn

Popular dance; from ballroom to hip-hop. consulting editor, Elizabeth A. Hanley; foreword by Jacques D'Amboisse. Chelsea House Publishers 2010 165p il (World of dance) lib bdg $35

Grades: 6 7 8 9 **793.3**

1. Dance

ISBN 978-1-60413-484-1; 1-60413-484-4

LC 2009053491

"Students who want a deeper and more comprehensive understanding of the origins and present status of various styles [of popular dance] will find this volume useful. It takes readers from the saltarello and galliard of the Renaissance to present-day hip-hop and zumba. . . . It has an encyclopedic approach as it identifies and defines the dances and touches on their cultural influences. . . . This volume would be a valuable resource for research and casual browsing." SLJ

Includes glossary and bibliographical references

793.38 Balls

Zimmerman Rutledge, Jill S.

Prom; the big night out. by Jill S. Zimmerman Rutledge, LCSW. Twenty-First Century Books 2017 80 p. color illustrations (lb : alk. paper) $35.99

Grades: 7 8 9 10 11 12 **793.38**

1. Proms 2. Dating (Social customs)

ISBN 9781512428506; 9781512439182; 9781512402674

LC 2016009114

This book, by Jill S. Zimmerman Rutledge, is "a brief but thorough overview of the history of the prom and how the event has evolved over the years. The book starts off with the first cotillions and debutante balls of the 20th century and progresses toward the more casual and diverse proms of the present day. The history-related text is alleviated by candid photos of teens, which keeps the tone conversational and amusing. . . . Prom-related tips and tricks are provided." (School Library Journal)

"The advice and history in this volume complement and enhance the prom magazines available each year." Kirkus

Includes bibliographical references and index.

793.73 Puzzles and puzzle games

Moscovich, Ivan

Big book of brain games; 1000 playthinks of art, mathematics & science. by Ivan Moscovich; foreword by Ian Stewart; illustrated by Tim Robinson. Workman Pub. 2006 420p il pa $22.95

Grades: 7 8 9 10 **793.73**

1. Scientific recreations

ISBN 0-7611-3466-2 pa; 978-0-7611-3466-4 pa

LC 2006299017

First published 2001 with title: 1000 playthinks: puzzles, paradoxes, illusions & games

This is a "collection of 1,000 challenges, puzzles, riddles, illusions. . . . Twelve basic categories include Geometry, Patterns, Numbers, Logic and Probability, and Perception. [A] key at the top of each game ranks its difficulty on a scale of 1 to 10, while indices in the back cross-reference the puzzles." Publisher's note

Includes bibliographical references

793.8 Magic and related activities

Banfield, Jake

★ **Magic** tricks with coins, cards, and everyday objects; Jake Banfield. QEB 2017 120 p. color illustrations $14.95

Grades: 4 5 6 7 8 **793.8**

1. Magicians 2. Magic tricks

ISBN 1682971511; 9781682971512

In this book, by Jake Banfield, "learn greatest magic tricks around and astound your friends and family, all without buying fancy props or equipment. From coins to muffins, you can make magic with anything you can get your hands on! With over 50 step-by-step magic tricks of varying levels of difficulty, this book is a great insight into the popular world of 'street magic'." (Publisher's note)

"Readers who are serious about learning magic will enjoy getting the inside scoop on its subtleties while gaining experience with the technical aspects of the craft." Pub Wkly

Jennings, Madeleine

Magic step-by-step; [by] Madeleine Jennings and Colin Francome. Rosen Central 2010 89p il (Skills in motion) lib bdg $31.95

Grades: 5 6 7 8 **793.8**

1. Magic tricks

ISBN 978-1-4358-3363-0; 1-4358-3363-5

LC 2009-13221

Presents step-by-step instructions on performing magic tricks, including card tricks, rope tricks, and sleight of hand.

"Colorful photographs show the entire movement of each skill presented, giving new meaning to the term 'step-by-step.' Progression borders at the bottom of the pages highlight the salient points to notice in performing each skill from beginning to end." SLJ

Includes bibliographical references

Noyes, Deborah

The **magician** and the spirits; Harry Houdini and the curious pastime of communicating with the dead. Deborah Noyes. Viking Books for Young Readers 2017 160 p. illustrations, portraits (hardback) $18.99

Grades: 6 7 8 **793.8**

1. Magicians 2. Spiritualism 3. Magicians -- United States -- Biography 4. Escape artists -- United States -- Biography

ISBN 9780803740181

LC 2016053762

In this book, by Deborah Noyes, "a century ago, the curious idea that spirits not only survive death but can be contacted on the 'other side' was widespread. Psychic mediums led countless séances, claiming to connect the grieving with their lost relations. . . . The craze caught Harry Houdini's attention. Well-known by then as most renowned magician and escape artist, he began to investigate these spiritual phenomena." (Publisher's note)

"Noyes' attention to Houdini's outsize personality—a key component of his campaign against spiritualists—adds compelling depth. A worthwhile addition to any nonfiction section, and ideal for kids intrigued by historical oddities." Booklist

793.93 Adventure games

Miller, John

★ **Unofficial** Minecraft Lab for Kids; Family-friendly projects for exploring and teaching math, science, history, and culture through creative building. John Miller and Chris Fornell Scott. Quarry 2017 144 p. color illustrations $22.99

Grades: 4 5 6 7 **793.93**

1. Handicraft 2. Video games 3. Computer games 4. Minecraft (game)

ISBN 9781631591174 ; 9781631591853

"Unofficial Minecraft Lab for Kids includes a variety of creative exercises that explore the game's aspects and uses them to teach fun, educational lessons." Publisher's note

"Family interaction is highly encouraged, although this could easily work as a library program or classroom lesson. Fans of the game will be pleased by the new skills acquired, while adults will appreciate the insight into kids' latest obsession." Booklist

Sciandra, Michael E.

The **modern** nerd's guide to LARPing; Mike Sciandra. Gareth Stevens Publishing 2018 32 p. (library bound) $26.6

Grades: 5 6 7 8 **793.93**

1. Role playing 2. Fantasy games 3. Acting games

ISBN 9781538212097; 9781538212103; 9781538212110

LC 2017033554

This book in the Geek Out! series, by Mike Sciandra, is about "LARPing, or live-action role playing, . . . one of the hottest hobbies today. Its devoted participants develop detailed characters, inventing names and personalities, as well as costumes and props. The improvisational nature and opportunity for creativity at LARP events makes for a new experience every time." (Publisher's note)

794.1 Chess

Basman, Michael

Chess for kids; written by Michael Basman. Dorling Kindersley 2001 45p il $12.99; pa $6.99

Grades: 4 5 6 7 **794.1**

1. Chess

ISBN 0-7894-6540-X; 0-7566-1807-X pa

LC 00-59018

This guide to chess explains the rudiments of the game, techniques and winning strategies

"A solid introduction for novices and good for skilled players wanting to develop their strategies and find out about chess clubs and tournaments." Booklist

King, Daniel

★ **Chess**; from first moves to checkmate. New ed.; Kingfisher 2010 64p il pa $8.99

Grades: 5 6 7 8 9 10 11 12 **794.1**

1. Chess

ISBN 978-0-7534-1930-4

First published 2000

Introduces the rules and strategies of chess, as well as its history and some of the great players and matches.

794.8 Electronic games

Adams, Suellen S.

Crash course in gaming; Suellen S. Adams. Libraries Unlimited, an imprint of ABC-CLIO, LLC 2014 xi, 125 p.p (Libraries unlimited crash course series) (pbk.) $45

Grades: Adult Professional **794.8**

1. Video games

ISBN 161069046X; 9781610690461

LC 2013031465

This book, by Suellen S. Adams, "discusses the pros and cons of gaming, the types of games and game systems, circulating collections, and game programs. It explains how a library's video game program can—and should—do much more than simply draw younger users to the library, providing examples of how everyone from parents to senior citizens can benefit from a patron-oriented computer gaming program." (Publisher's note)

"Librarians who are considering adding a circulating video-game collection will find guidance in this volume. It provides readers with information on evaluating video games, building a strong circulating collection, creating programming for all ages around that collection, and engaging children and teens with related literature...Libraries looking for guidance on building, maintaining, and growing a successful circulating collection for gamers will find this book invaluable, as will libraries with a need to overhaul their collections."

Includes bibliographical references (pages 121-122) and index

Egan, Jill

How video game designers use math; math curriculum consultant: Rhea A. Stewart. Chelsea Clubhouse 2010 32p il (Math in the real world) lib bdg $28

Grades: 4 5 6 **794.8**

1. Mathematics 2. Video games 3. Computer games 4. Computer animation 5. Vocational guidance

ISBN 978-1-60413-603-6 lib bdg; 1-60413-603-0 lib bdg

LC 2009-24173

This describes how video game designers use math to create and produce their games and includes relevant math problems and information about how to become a video game designer

Includes glossary and bibliographical references

Hansen, Dustin

Game on! Video Game History from Pong and Pac-Man to Mario, Minecraft, and More. Dustin Hansen. Feiwel & Friends 2016 368 p. illustrations (hardback) $19.99; (ebook) $60

Grades: 5 6 7 8 9 10 11 12 **794.8**

1. Video games -- History

ISBN 9781250080950; 9781250080967

LC 2016027564

In this book, by Dustin Hansen, "find out about the fast and furious growth and evolution of video games . . . by looking at some of the most popular, innovative, and influential games ever, from Pong, the very first arcade game ever, to modern hits like Uncharted. Learn about the creators and inspiration . . . , discover historical trivia and Easter eggs . . . , and explore the innovations that make each game special." (Publisher's note)

"This satisfyingly thorough and worthy addition to any collection is sure to please hard-core gamers and newbies alike." SLJ

Haugen, Hayley Mitchell, 1968-

Video games; by Hayley Mitchell Haugen. Norwood HousePress 2015 64 p. (Matters of Opinion) (library edition : alk. paper) $27.93

Grades: 5 6 7 8 9 **794.8**

1. Video games -- Social aspects

ISBN 1599536013; 9781599536019

LC 2014003798

This book, by Hayley Mitchell Haugen, "explores the pros and cons of several issues related to video games, including whether video games cause violence, discourage exercise, and proper regulation." (Publisher's note)

"Students will be interested in debating issues surrounding video games: whether the games lead to violence, health risks, and whether there should be regulation. In addition to pros and cons of each and a final writing assignment, three debate techniques--the author's credibility, deceptive arguments, and logical fallacies--are also analyzed. Sidebars and captioned photos support the choppy text. Reading list, timeline, websites. Glos., ind." Horn Book

Includes bibliographical references (page 60) and index

Jozefowicz, Chris

Video game developer. Gareth Stevens Pub. 2010 32p il (Cool careers: cutting edge) lib bdg $26; pa $8.95

Grades: 4 5 6 **794.8**

1. Video games 2. Computer games 3. Vocational guidance

ISBN 978-1-4339-1958-9 lib bdg; 1-4339-1958-3 lib bdg; 978-1-4339-2157-5 pa; 1-4339-2157-X pa

LC 2008053549

This introduction to video game developer careers offers "clear, solid information in a large font. . . . [This] short [book is] packed with relevant, current material." SLJ

Includes glossary and bibliographical references

Oxlade, Chris

Gaming technology. Smart Apple Media 2011 46p il (New technology) lib bdg $34.25

Grades: 4 5 6 7 **794.8**

1. Video games 2. Computer games

ISBN 9781599205311

LC 2010044239

Describes the technology used for creating and playing video games. Includes information on how different platforms work and the direction video game technology may be going.

This "offers a fine overview for reports, and its attractive design may also entice middle-grade readers to learn more." Booklist

Includes glossary and bibliographical references

Rauf, Don

Computer game designer; [by] Don Rauf and Monique Vescia. Ferguson 2007 un il (Virtual apprentice) lib bdg $29.95; pa $9.95

Grades: 6 7 8 9 **794.8**

1. Computer games 2. Vocational guidance

ISBN 978-0-8160-6754-1 lib bdg; 0-8160-6754-6 lib bdg; 0-8160-7550-6 pa; 978-0-8160-7550-8 pa

LC 2006036565

"This in-depth introduction to the field of computer-game design offers specific practical advice. . . . Following a basic history of computer games and information about game types and rating levels, chapters, which are illustrated with many color photos, profile contemporary professionals and delve into current trends and the day-to-day work of game creators." Booklist

796 Athletic and outdoor sports and games

Berman, Len

The **greatest** moments in sports; upsets and underdogs. Len Berman. Sourcebooks Jabberwocky 2012 iv, 124 p.p ill. (hardcover) $19.99

Grades: 5 6 7 8 **796**

1. Sports upsets -- History

ISBN 140227226X; 9781402272264

In this sports book, "[Len] Berman offers his take on 25 of the most unexpected victories. . . . Youngsters learn about Billy Mills's surprise win of Olympic Gold for the 10,000 meter run in 1964, and Mexico's Little League World Series win of 1957. Text boxes . . . [present] biographical information and quick glimpses into the records of the 'champions' versus the 'underdogs.' The accompanying CD offers additional insight from Berman on 10 of the upsets." (School Library Journal)

Blumenthal, Karen

★ **Let** me play; the story of Title IX, the law that changed the future of girls in America. Atheneum Books for Young Readers 2005 152p il $19.95

Grades: 6 7 8 9 10 **796**

1. Women athletes 2. Sex discrimination 3. Education Amendments

of 1972 -- Title IX
ISBN 0-689-85957-0

LC 2004-1450

Title IX legislation assured "that 'no one could be closed out of any educational program or activity receiving federal money simply because of sex.' After explaining the genesis of the legislation, . . . Blumenthal discusses how evolving guidelines and interpretations brought girls' school athletic programs into its purview. [Bibliography. Index.] Grades nine to twelve." (Bull Cent Child Books)

"The author looks at American women's evolving rights by focusing on the history and future of Title IX, which bans sex discrimination in U.S. education. . . . The images are . . . gripping, and relevant political cartoons and fact boxes add further interest. Few books cover the last few decades of American women's history with such clarity and detail." Booklist

Includes bibliographical references

Burgan, Michael

Olympic gold 1936; how the image of Jesse Owens crushed Hitler's evil myth. by Michael Burgan. Compass Point Books, a Capstone imprint 2017 64 p. illustrations (some color) (Captured history. Sports) (library binding) $34.65

Grades: 6 7 8 9 **796**

1. Olympic games 2. African American athletes 3. Documentary photography -- United States -- History 4. African American track and field athletes -- Biography -- Pictorial works 5. Track and field athletes -- United States -- Biography -- Pictorial works
ISBN 9780756555283; 9780756555320

LC 2016038562

This book, by Michael Burgan, describes how "Jesse Owens' gold-medal winning feats at the 1936 Olympics in Berlin struck a mighty propaganda blow against Adolf Hitler. The Nazi leader had planned to use the German games as a showcase of supposed Aryan superiority. Instead, there was American black athlete Owens on the podium being photographed by Hitler's personal photographer, Heinrich Hoffmann." (Publisher's note)

Includes bibliographical references and index

Connolly, Sean

The **Book** of Wildly Spectacular Sports Science; 54 All-Star Experiments. by Sean Connolly. Workman Pub Co 2016 256 p. color illustrations (ebook) $14.95; $14.95

Grades: 4 5 6 7 8 **796**

1. Sports 2. Science -- Experiments
ISBN 9780761189770; 0761189289; 9780761189282

This book, by Sean Connolly, presents "54 all-star experiments that demonstrate the scientific principles powering a wide variety of sports and activities. . . . Using common household objects, each project includes step-by-step instructions, tips, and a detailed explanation of how and why the experiment worked. It's a win-win." (Publisher's note)

"The chatty tone, clear scientific explanations, and broad range of athletics discussed mean there's something here for just about every kind of sports fan." Pub Wkly

Cronn-Mills, Kirstin

LGBTQ + athletes claim the field; Striving for Equality. Kirstin Cronn-Mills, with an introduction by Alex Jackson Nelson, MSW, LGSW. Twenty-First Century Books 2016 104 p. illustrations (some color) (lb : alk. paper) $34.65

Grades: 6 7 8 9 10 **796**

1. Gay athletes 2. Transgender athletes
ISBN 9781467780124

LC 2015036754

This book, by Kirstin Cronn-Mills, with introduction by Alex Jackson Nelson, "highlights the struggles of numerous LGBTQIA amateur and professional athletes across a wide variety of sports. . . . The section on transgender and intersex athletes is the most focused and includes high-profile Olympians like Caitlyn Jenner and Caster Semenya as well as lesser-known but similarly pioneering individuals in college athletics, Ironman competitions, tennis, and martial arts." (School Library Journal)

"Crisp color photographs, usually of athletes on or off the field, enhance the text throughout and visually reinforce the message that athletics are for everyone." SLJ

Includes bibliographical references and index

Doeden, Matt

The **Super** Bowl; chasing football immortality. Matt Doeden. Millbrook Press 2018 64 p. illustrations (chiefly color) (Spectacular sports) (lb : alk. paper) $33.32

Grades: 3 4 5 6 7 8 **796**

1. Super Bowl (Game) 2. Football -- United States -- History 3. Football -- History
ISBN 9781512427547

LC 2016042224

This book in the Spectacular Sports series, by Matt Doeden, "explores the history of the Super Bowl and covers the championship game's greatest moments, from Vince Lombardi leading the Green Bay Packers to victory in Super Bowl I to Tom Brady and the New England Patriots coming from 25 points behind to win Super Bowl LI. Don't miss the thrills and the fanfare of the biggest game of the year." (Publisher's note)

"From the beginning of the National Football League and the origins of the term Super Bowl to the transformation of the halftime show, this book provides a concise, informative history of the football's annual championship. Even better, though, are the lively descriptions of the noteworthy games and the most memorable moments in Super Bowl history, starting with the greatest upset (1969) and ending with the greatest comeback (2017)." Booklist

Includes bibliographical references and index

Fay, Gail

Sports; the ultimate teen guide. by Gail Fay. Scarecrow Press, Inc. 2012 338 p. (It happened to me) (cloth : alk. paper) $50

Grades: 7 8 9 10 11 12 **796**

1. Teenagers 2. School sports 3. Teenage athletes -- Training of 4. High school athletes -- Training of
ISBN 0810882175; 9780810882171; 9780810882188

LC 2012028320

This book, by Gail Fay, is "for high school athletes of all levels [and] provides up-to-date information on sports-related issues, practical tips, and valuable resources. Each chapter features quotes from current and former high school athletes who share their experiences related to the given topic. Issues discussed include choosing a sport to play, balancing all aspects of life as a student-athlete, [and] dealing with the pressures of competition." (Publisher's note)

Includes bibliographical references and index

Gifford, Clive

Sports. Amicus 2010 46p il (Healthy lifestyles) lib bdg $32.80

Grades: 7 8 9 10 **796**

1. Sports 2. Physical fitness
ISBN 978-1-60753-088-6; 1-60753-088-0

LC 2009-47567

This book is "well-written and satisfyingly informative. . . . [The] magazine-like format includes numerous sidebars, color photos, and charts." SLJ

Includes glossary and bibliographical references

Hile, Lori

Surviving extreme sports. Raintree 2011 56p il (Extreme survival) lib bdg $33.50

Grades: 4 5 6 7 **796**

1. Extreme sports 2. Wilderness survival
ISBN 978-1-4109-3968-5; 1-4109-3968-5

LC 2010028689

This book is "fun and informative. [This] well-organized title starts with an overview [of extreme sports], offers some specific examples, and includes additional facts or tips and resources. . . . [It features] dramatic archival and full-color photos on nearly every page. . . . [This is a book] that youngsters will enjoy and talk about." SLJ

Includes glossary and bibliographical references

Howell, Brian

Sports. ABDO Pub. Co. 2011 112p il (Inside the industry) lib bdg $23.95

Grades: 5 6 7 8 **796**

1. Sports -- Vocational guidance
ISBN 978-1-61714-804-0; 1-61714-804-0

LC 2010042558

This " well-designed [book describes] a variety of careers in [sports]. Because [it helps] readers assess if these positions are suitable for their personality types and backgrounds, the [title is a] good [choice] for career exploration and self-discovery. [It is] also useful for research and reports. . . . Sidebars and full-color photos appear throughout." SLJ

Includes bibliographical references

Mattern, Joanne

So, you want to work in sports? the ultimate guide to exploring the sports industry. Joanne Mattern. Aladdin/Beyond Words 2014 224 p. illustrations (Be what you want) (paperback) $9.99; (hardback) $18.99

Grades: 4 5 6 7 8 **796**

1. Sports 2. Vocational guidance
ISBN 1582704481; 158270449X; 9781582704487; 9781582704494

LC 2013025469

This book, by Joanne Mattern, is a "guide that can help you score a career in the sports industry. . . . From the popular careers of professional athlete, coach, sports broadcaster, and photographer, to the lesser-known professions of sports agent, statistician, sports therapist, and scout, [this book] delves into a wide variety of possible futures that are exciting and rewarding." (Publisher's note)

"Information is presented dynamically, with numerous sidebars ("Did you know "), graphs, lists, a career quiz, and hand-drawn illustrations. There are no photos. One of the book's strongest assets is its excellent resource section, including a six-page list of websites for professional organizations . . . and two pages of books and online documents." SLJ

Includes bibliographical references and index

Ralston, Birgitta

Snow play; how to make forts & slides & winter campfires plus the coolest Loch Ness monster and 23 other brrrilliant [i.e. brilliant] project in the snow. Artisan 2010 111p il $14.95

Grades: 4 5 6 7 8 9 10 11 12 Adult **796**

1. Snow 2. Outdoor recreation
ISBN 978-1-57965-405-4; 1-57965-405-3

"Opening with explanations of different types of snow and the various tools needed to work with it, this how-to book describes more than two dozen projects, most of which will require adult help and supervision. . . . Ratings of difficulty, the number of people and tools needed, the type of snow required, and the time frame are included with each project. Short snow-related facts appear throughout. . . . A brief listing of worldwide snow festivals, snow hotels and igloos, and an ice museum completes the package. While kids can certainly use this book to inspire ideas for winter fun, adults will find it equally useful, especially for generating ideas for family projects." SLJ

Rand, Casey

Graphing sports. Heinemann Library 2009 32p il (Real world data) $28.21; pa $7.99

Grades: 5 6 7 8 **796**

1. Graphic methods 2. Sports -- Statistics
ISBN 978-1-4329-2621-2; 1-4329-2621-7; 978-1-4329-2630-4 pa; 1-4329-2630-6 pa

LC 2009001189

This explains sports related concepts through charts and graphs.

"The writing is spot-on for the audience. Most importantly, the statistics used are well chosen and instantly understandable, and the text clearly explains how each type of graph can be used to best display different types of data." SLJ

Includes glossary and bibliographical references

Zuckerman, Gregory

Rising above; Gregory Zuckerman ; with Elijah and Gabriel Zuckerman. Philomel Books 2018 224 p. (hardback) $17.99

Grades: 6 7 8 **796**

1. African American women athletes -- Biography 2. Women athletes -- United States -- Biography 3. African American women athletes -- Biography
ISBN 9780399547478

LC 2017037902

This book, by Gregory Zuckerman, Elijah Zuckerman and Gabriel Zuckerman, presents "real-life stories of female superstar athletes Serena and Venus Williams, Simone Biles, Carli Lloyd, and more -- role models all. . . . The athletes featured in this book met earth-shaking challenges head on, and through hard work and perseverance, went on to conquer the sports world." (Publisher's note)

796.083 Young people – Outdoor recreation

Hewitt, Ben

The **young** adventurer's guide to (almost) everything; build a fort, camp like a champ, poop in the woods--45 action-packed outdoor activities. Ben and Penny Hewitt ; illustrations by Luke Boushee. Roost Books 2019 xx, 187 p.p (hardcover : alk. paper) $16.95

Grades: 7 8 9 10 11 12 **796.083**

1. Camping 2. Nature study 3. Outdoor recreation 4. Outdoor

recreation for children 5. Nature study -- Activity programs
ISBN 9781611805949

LC 2018013405

This book, by Ben and Penny Hewitt, illustrated by Luke Boushee, presents "45 step-by-step, illustrated activities that teach kids everything from how to see like an owl to build the world's coolest fort from sticks. . . . This survival guide is your ticket to getting down and dirty in nature and learning to make the coolest things with your own two hands." (Publisher's note)

"outdoor-adventure activities combine wisdom and fun in this practical guide to the wild A thoughtful introduction acknowledges the Native American origins of many of the skills introduced in the book." --Kirkus

796.097 Sports – North America

Doeden, Matt

Coming up clutch; the greatest upsets, comebacks, and finishes in sports history. Matt Doeden. Millbrook Press 2019 64 p. (lb : alk. paper) $34.65

Grades: 5 6 7 8 9 10 **796.097**

1. Sports -- History 2. Sports -- United States 3. Sports upsets -- History 4. Comebacks
ISBN 9781512427561

LC 2017047697

This book in the Spectacular Sports series, by Matt Doeden, presents the "most memorable buzzer-beating baskets, double-digit comebacks, and unexpected meltdowns [in the history of sports.] . . . From racing legend Man o' War's only career loss in 1919 to the 2017 Super Bowl's incredible finish, sports fans will have plenty to digest. Doeden also writes about the science behind clutch performances." (Publisher's note)

Includes bibliographical references and index

796.1 Miscellaneous games

Birmingham, Maria

Weird zone; sports. Maria Birmingham. Owlkids Books Inc. 2013 128 p. (Weird zone) $22.95

Grades: 4 5 6 7 **796.1**

1. Sports
ISBN 1926973607; 9781926973609

LC 2012948714

This book on unusual sports by Maria Birmingham is part of the "Weird Zone" book series. It includes such sports as "rolling down a hill in a plastic ball (aka 'zorbing') . . . professional-grade pillow fighting . . . lawn-mower racing . . . [and] extreme ironing. . . . Each sport gets a two-page spread." (Kirkus Reviews)

Sobey, Ed

Radio -controlled car experiments. Enslow Publishers 2011 128p il (Cool science projects with technology) lib bdg $31.93

Grades: 6 7 8 9 **796.1**

1. Science projects 2. Automobiles -- Models 3. Science -- Experiments
ISBN 978-0-7660-3304-7; 0-7660-3304-X

This explains how and why radio-controlled cars work, and offers experiments.

This book "is bursting with fast-paced experiments that have easy-to-follow instructions and are sure to interest young car enthusiasts." SLJ

Includes glossary and bibliographical references

796.2 Activities and games requiring equipment

Bell-Rehwoldt, Sheri

The **kids'** guide to jumping rope. Capstone Press 2011 32p il (Kids' guides) lib bdg $26.65

Grades: 4 5 6 7 **796.2**

1. Rope skipping
ISBN 978-1-4296-5443-2; 1-4296-5443-0

LC 2010035018

Describes the sport of jumping rope, including how-to information on jumps and tricks.

This includes "plentiful photos of giddy girls (and a few guys) madly skipping rope. . . . This makes jumping rope look like the best time in the world." Booklist

Includes bibliographical references

796.22 Skateboarding

Fitzpatrick, Jim

Skateboarding. Cherry Lake Pub. 2009 32p il (Innovation in sports) lib bdg $27.07

Grades: 4 5 6 7 **796.22**

1. Skateboarding
ISBN 978-1-60279-259-3 lib bdg; 1-60279-259-3 lib bdg

LC 2008007548

This describes skateboarding history, equipment, safety, and health benefits.

This "stands out by emphasizing monumental shifts and advances in the events themselves. . . . Concise and occasionally revelatory." Booklist

Includes glossary and bibliographical references

Lakin, Patricia

Skateboards; by Patricia Lakin. Aladdin 2017 32 p. color illustrations (Made by hand) (paper over board) $17.99

Grades: 3 4 5 6 7 **796.22**

1. Board books for children 2. Skateboarding -- History 3. Skateboards -- Design and construction 4. Board books
ISBN 9781481448338

LC 2016016442

This book in the Made by Hand series, by Patricia Lakin, follows Jake Eshelman's creative process, as he plans and constructs custom skateboards for his company. "Charts, infographics, and bold photographs make this a picture book for anyone who is curious about how a skateboard is made. This book also features a history of skateboarding, a timeline, and resources to inspire kids to make their own objects by hand." (Publisher's note)

Includes bibliographical references

Powell, Ben

Skateboarding skills; the rider's guide. Firefly Books 2008 128p il pa $16.95

Grades: 7 8 9 10 11 12 Adult **796.22**

1. Skateboarding

ISBN 978-1-55407-360-3; 1-55407-360-X

LC 2008-275044

The author "offers a colorful and useful manual for mastering numerous skateboard tricks. Intended for riders of all ages, the book presents step-by-step breakdowns of skills illustrated with photographs of children around age 12; each step of a trick features a picture and a written description." Libr J

796.3 Ball games

Chetwynd, Josh

The **secret** history of balls; Josh Chetwynd ; Illustrations by Emily Stackhouse. Perigee Trade 2011 xiv, 221p ill.

Grades: 7 8 9 10 11 12 Adult **796.3**

1. Ball games 2. Sporting goods 3. Sports -- History

ISBN 9780399536748

LC 2010054221

This book "mines the stories and lore of sports and recreation to offer insight into 60 balls - whether they're hollow, solid, full of air, or stuffed with twine or made of leather, metal, rubber, plastic, or polyurethane - that give us joy on playing fields and in every arena from backyards to stadiums around the globe." (Publishers' note)

796.323 Basketball

Bryant, Howard

Legends; the best players, games, and teams in basketball. Howard Bryant. Philomel Books 2016 368 p. (Legends)

Grades: 6 7 8 9 **796.323**

1. Basketball -- United States -- History 2. Basketball players -- United States -- Biography

ISBN 9780698175150; 9780399169052

LC 2016032754

In this book "featuring Top Ten Lists to chew on and debate, and a Top 40-style Timeline of Key Moments in Basektball History, this comprehensive collection includes the greatest dynasties, from the Bill Russell-era Celtics, to the Magic Jonson-led Lakers, to the Jordan-led Bulls, right up to the Tim Duncan-led Spurs. All the greats take flight toward the hoop in this perfect book for young fans who dream about stepping on an NBA court." Publisher's note

"Hoops fans will find a goldmine of information guaranteed to deepen their basketball knowledge and their understanding of the game." VOYA

Coy, John

Hoop genius; how a desperate teacher and a rowdy gym class invented basketball. by John Coy ; illustrated by Joe Morse. Carolrhoda Books 2013 32 p. (reinforced) $16.95

Grades: 2 3 4 5 6 **796.323**

1. Basketball 2. Picture books for children 3. Basketball -- United States -- History

ISBN 0761366172; 9780761366171

LC 2011021235

"In 1891, a teacher named James Naismith invented a game that was destined to become a national sensation. The boys' gym class at his school was particularly rowdy. He needed to find an indoor activity for the energetic lads that was fun, but not too rough. Inspired by a favorite childhood game, he stayed up late one night typing the rules of his new game." The class was captivated and the game's popularity spread. (School Library Journal)

Doeden, Matt

The **Final** Four; the pursuit of college basketball glory. Matt Doeden. Millbrook Press 2016 64 p. illustrations (lb : alk. paper) $33.32

Grades: 4 5 6 7 8 **796.323**

1. College basketball 2. Sports tournaments 3. NCAA Basketball Tournament -- History

ISBN 1467787809; 9781467787802

LC 2015025429

This book, by Matt Doeden, examines how "the NCAA men's basketball tournament is one of the most popular sports events in the United States. By the time the tournament of 68 teams has been whittled down to the Final Four, excitement reaches a fever pitch. From the first intercollegiate basketball game played in 1895 all the way to the thrills and drama of the most recent Final Four, read about the shocking moments and stunning upsets that give March Madness its name." (Publisher's note)

"Though the book's appeal will be limited to serious basketball fans, the historical perspective and engaging presentation make it a solid choice." SLJ

Includes bibliographical references and index

Gifford, Clive

Basketball; [by] Clive Gifford. PowerKids Press 2009 32p il (Personal best) lib bdg $25.25

Grades: 4 5 6 7 8 **796.323**

1. Basketball

ISBN 978-1-4042-4444-3 lib bdg; 1-4042-4444-1 lib bdg

LC 2007-42989

This guide to basketball "offers well-organized and easy-to-follow instructions, focusing on rules, clothing, specific skills, and competitions. . . . Informative, readable." SLJ

Includes bibliographical references

Labrecque, Ellen

Basketball; by Ellen Labrecque. Cherry Lake Pub. 2009 32p il (Innovation in sports) lib bdg $27.07

Grades: 4 5 6 7 **796.323**

1. Basketball

ISBN 978-1-60279-256-2 lib bdg; 1-60279-256-9 lib bdg

LC 2008002044

This describes basketball history, rules, equipment, training, and great players.

This "stands out by emphasizing monumental shifts and advances in the events themselves. . . . Concise and occasionally revelatory." Booklist

Includes glossary and bibliographical references

Robinson, Tom

Basketball. Norwood House Press 2010 64p il (Girls play to win) lib bdg $26.60

Grades: 4 5 6 7 **796.323**

1. Basketball

ISBN 978-1-59953-388-9; 1-59953-388-X

LC 2010009814

Covers the history, rules, fundamentals and significant personalities of the sport of women's basketball. Topics include: techniques, strategies, competitive events, and equipment.

"With an easy design and format, the [text is] highly accessible to even the most reluctant readers and [provides] great exposure and insight into the world of female professional sports." Horn Book Guide

Includes glossary and bibliographical references

Slade, Suzanne

Basketball; how it works. Capstone Press 2010 48p il (Science of sports) lib bdg $29.32; pa $7.95

Grades: 4 5 6 7 **796.323**

1. Basketball

ISBN 978-1-4296-4021-3 lib bdg; 1-4296-4021-9 lib bdg; 978-1-4296-4873-8 pa; 1-4296-4873-2 pa

The book's "photograph-heavy design works to engage its audience, while the easy-to-read [text explains] the science." Horn Book Guide

Includes glossary

Stewart, Mark

Swish; the quest for basketball's perfect shot. by Mark Stewart and Mike Kennedy. Millbrook Press 2009 64p il lib bdg $25.26

Grades: 5 6 7 8 **796.323**

1. Basketball

ISBN 978-0-8225-8752-1 lib bdg; 0-8225-8752-1 lib bdg

LC 2008-24958

"The wide pages offer plenty of room for well-spaced text, sidebars, and illustrations. Each page has at least one picture, with mostly color photos, and the many action shots make the book more exciting. With information on women's and men's basketball at both collegiate and professional levels, this is a nice addition to sports collections." Booklist

Includes bibliographical references

Thornley, Stew

Kevin Garnett; champion basketball star. by Stew Thornley. Enslow Publishers 2013 48 p. col. ill. (library) $23.93

Grades: 4 5 6 7 **796.323**

1. Picture books for children 2. Basketball players -- United States -- Biography

ISBN 0766040283; 9780766040281

LC 2011031517

This book by Stew Thornley is a children's picture book biography of professional basketball player Kevin Garnett. In his "career, Garnett has won MVP trophies and other individual awards, but his NBA championship ring is most important to him. The team has always come first for KG." (Publisher's note)

Includes bibliographical references (p. 47) and index.

Kobe Bryant; champion basketball star. by Stew Thornley. Enslow Publishers 2013 48 p. col. ill. (library) $23.93

Grades: 4 5 6 7 **796.323**

1. Picture books for children 2. Bryant, Kobe, 1978- 3. Basketball players -- United States -- Biography

ISBN 0766040291; 9780766040298

LC 2011038174

This picture book by Stew Thornley is a biography of professional basketball player Kobe Bryant. "He can swish shots from long range or drive to the basket for a vicious dunk. Bryant once scored 81 points in a single game! He can also dish it to his teammates and play lockdown defense. . . . The Los Angeles Lakers superstar has won five NBA titles since coming out of high school, and he has earned many individual awards." (Publisher's note)

Tim Duncan; champion basketball star. by Stew Thornley. Enslow Publishers 2013 48 p. col. ill. (Sports Star Champions) (library) $23.93

Grades: 4 5 6 7 **796.323**

1. Basketball players -- United States -- Biography

ISBN 0766040305; 9780766040304

LC 2011050440

This book by Stew Thornley is part of the Sports Star Champions series and looks at basketball player Tim Duncan. The texts "focus on the athletes' professional careers, with very little information about their personal lives. . . . Each book ends with career statistics, the player's address, and a brief list for further reading." (School Library Journal)

Includes bibliographical references (p. 47) and index.

Yancey, Diane

Basketball. Lucent Books 2011 112p il (Science behind sports) lib bdg $33.45

Grades: 5 6 7 8 **796.323**

1. Basketball

ISBN 978-1-4205-0293-0; 1-4205-0293-X

LC 2010035239

This "explores the scientific principles such as momentum, gravity, friction, and aerodynamics, plus many more, behind [basketball]. . . . [The author discusses the sport's] origins, history, and changes, . . . the biomechanics and physiology of playing, related health and medical concerns, and the causes and treatment of sports-related injuries. Additional information tells how exercise, diet and nutrition, warming up, and training relate to peak performance and enjoyment of the sport. . . . [The book] has features on possible side effects of anabolic steroid use; how MRIs work; and how various improvements to the courts, basketballs, shoes, and uniforms have affected the game. The action photography . . . is fantastic. . . . [A must-have] for sports fans, athletes, science students, and even anyone considering a career in sports-related medicine, coaching, or other connected fields." SLJ

Includes glossary and bibliographical references

796.325 Volleyball

Crisfield, Deborah

Winning volleyball for girls; [by] Deborah W. Crisfield, John Monteleone; foreword by Maria Nolan. 3rd ed.; Chelsea House 2009 189p il (Winning sports for girls) lib bdg $44.95; pa $11.96

Grades: 7 8 9 10 11 12 **796.325**

1. Volleyball

ISBN 978-0-8160-7720-5 lib bdg; 0-8160-7720-7 lib bdg; 978-0-8160-7721-2 pa; 0-8160-7721-5 pa

LC 2009-5733

First published 1995 by Facts on File

This includes a brief history of volleyball followed by descriptions of the rules, court and equipment, training, techniques such as the spike, the serve, the block, and the pass, offensive and defensive play, putting a team together, and game strategies.

Includes glossary and bibliographical references

McDougall, Chros

Volleyball. Norwood House Press 2010 64p il (Girls play to win) lib bdg $26.60

Grades: 4 5 6 7 **796.325**

1. Volleyball

ISBN 978-1-59953-392-6; 1-59953-392-8

LC 2010009810

Covers the history, rules, fundamentals and significant personalities of the sport of women's volleyball. Topics include: techniques, strategies, competitive events, and equipment.

"With an easy design and format, the [text is] highly accessible to even the most reluctant readers and [provides] great exposure and insight into the world of female professional sports." Horn Book Guide

Includes glossary and bibliographical references

796.332 American football

Bryant, Howard

Legends; the best players, games, and teams in football. Howard Bryant. Philomel Books 2015 xiv, 305 p.p $17.99

Grades: 6 7 8 9 **796.332**

1. Super Bowl (Game) 2. Football -- History 3. National Football League 4. National Football League -- History 5. Football -- United States -- History 6. Football teams -- United States -- Rating of 7. Football coaches -- United States -- Rating of 8. Football players -- United States -- Rating of

ISBN 9780399169045

LC 2015023192

This book, by Howard Bryant, "details twenty of the greatest Super Bowls in NFL history—and expands on their relevance within the larger scope of dynasties, giants of the coaching world, and marquee players making history. From the upsets to the blowouts to the nail-biting finishes, this is the perfect book for young fans eager to kick off their football schooling." (Publisher's note)

"The top moments, games, and players are designed to be discussed and debated as only true lovers of the game can, and a thorough index and photos contribute nicely." Booklist

Buckley, James

Ultimate guide to football; by James Buckley, Jr. Franklin Watts 2010 160p il $30; pa $7.99

Grades: 4 5 6 7 **796.332**

1. Football

ISBN 978-0-531-20752-9; 0-531-20752-8; 978-0-531-21023-9 pa; 0-531-21023-5 pa

LC 2009011003

This guide to football covers "historical highlights and delectable ephemera . . . with spreads covering each NFL team interspersed among chatty tales. . . . The highlighter-green color scheme matches the loud, vibrant layout and heightens the contrasting black-and-white player photos, while sporadic cartoons add some pep to the presentation." Booklist

Includes bibliographical references

Frederick, Shane

Football; the math of the game. Capstone Press 2011 il (Sports math) lib bdg $30.65; pa $7.95

Grades: 6 7 8 9 **796.332**

1. Football 2. Mathematics

ISBN 978-1-4296-6567-4 lib bdg; 1-4296-6567-X lib bdg; 978-1-4296-7319-8 pa; 1-4296-7319-2 pa

LC 2011007864

Presents the mathematical concepts involved with the sport of football.

This offers a "dazzling layout, which includes countless vivid photographs and overlays of facts and figures. . . . This takes its concept and runs all the way to the end zone with it—dense and heavy, but undoubtedly impressive." Booklist

Includes bibliographical references

Gigliotti, Jim

Football. Cherry Lake Pub. 2009 32p il (Innovation in sports) lib bdg $27.07

Grades: 4 5 6 7 **796.332**

1. Football

ISBN 978-1-60279-257-9 lib bdg; 1-60279-257-7 lib bdg

LC 2008002305

This describes football history, rules, equipment, training and strategy, and innovators

This "stands out by emphasizing monumental shifts and advances in the events themselves. . . . Concise and occasionally revelatory." Booklist

Includes glossary and bibliographical references

Gilbert, Sara

The **story** of the NFL. Creative Education 2011 un il (Built for success) $23.95

Grades: 6 7 8 9 **796.332**

1. Football 2. National Football League

ISBN 978-1-60818-063-9; 1-60818-063-8

LC 2010031224

A look at the origins, leaders, growth, and management of the NFL, the professional football league that was formed in 1920 and today governs 32 teams throughout the United States.

This book is "written in a lively style, yet with a minimum of fuss. . . . The slim, gleaming format, well-chosen photos, and the effort to explore what makes a company successful today [makes this title] unique." Booklist

Includes bibliographical references

Rappoport, Ken

Peyton Manning; champion football star. by Ken Rappoport. Enslow Publishers 2013 48 p. col. ill. (Sports Star Champions) (library) $23.93

Grades: 4 5 6 7 **796.332**

1. Quarterbacks (Football) 2. Football players -- United States -- Biography 3. Quarterbacks (Football) -- United States -- Biography

ISBN 0766040275; 9780766040274

LC 2011052759

This book is part of the Sports Star Champion series and looks at quarterback Peyton Manning. The "texts focus on the athletes' professional careers, with very little information about their personal lives. Occasional sidebars add additional interest, and each book ends with career statistics, the player's address, and a brief list for further reading." (School Library Journal)

Includes bibliographical references (p. 47) and index.

Sheinkin, Steve

★ **Undefeated**; Jim Thorpe and the Carlisle Indian School football team. Steve Sheinkin. Roaring Brook Press 2017 280 p. illustrations, portraits (hardback) $19.99

Grades: 6 7 8 9 10 11 12 **796.332**

1. Football -- History 2. Football -- United States -- History 3. United States Indian School (Carlisle, Pa.) -- Football 4. Indians,

Treatment of -- United States -- History -- 20th century
ISBN 9781596439559; 9781596439542

LC 2016009083

This book, by Steve Sheinkin, narrates how Jim Thorpe and Pop Warner "met in 1907 at the Carlisle Indian Industrial School in Pennsylvania, where they forged one of the winningest teams in American football history. . . . It's [also] an unflinching look at the U.S. government's violent persecution of Native Americans and the school that was designed to erase Indian cultures." (Publisher's note)

"Containing a generous collection of black-and-white period photographs, this is a model of research and documentation, as well as of stylish writing that tells an always absorbing story." Booklist

Includes bibliographical references and index.

Stewart, Mark

Touchdown; the power and precision of football's perfect play. by Mark Stewart and Mike Kennedy. Millbrook Press 2009 64p il lib bdg $27.93

Grades: 5 6 7 8 **796.332**

1. Football

ISBN 978-0-8225-8751-4 lib bdg; 0-8225-8751-3 lib bdg

LC 2008044295

"This attractive book opens with an intriguing history of American football. . . . Next, 10 double-page spreads feature 'Ten Unforgettable Touchdowns' in both professional and collegiate games from 1913 to 2006. After a chapter on 'touchdown makers,' spotlighting outstanding players . . . comes a short section on notable touchdown bloopers and another on trick plays and the element of surprise. . . . Photos, period prints, and reproductions of trading cards illustrate the text while adding color to the pages. . . . This nicely designed book provides plenty of on-the-field drama as well as pertinent information in a smoothly written overview of the touchdown." Booklist

796.334 Soccer (Association football)

Bazemore, Suzanne

Soccer : how it works. Capstone Press 2010 48p il (Science of sports) lib bdg $29.32; pa $7.95

Grades: 4 5 6 7 **796.334**

1. Soccer

ISBN 978-1-4296-4025-1 lib bdg; 1-4296-4025-1 lib bdg; 978-1-4296-4876-9 pa; 1-4296-4876-7 pa

The book's "photography-heavy design works to engage its audience, while the easy-to-read [text explains] the science." Horn Book Guide

Includes glossary

Berne, Emma Carlson

What a kick; How a Clutch World Cup Win Propelled Women's Soccer. by Emma Carlson Berne. Compass Point Books 2016 64 p. illustrations (some color) (library binding) $34.65; (ebook) $34.65

Grades: 6 7 8 9 **796.334**

1. Soccer players 2. Women athletes 3. World Cup (Soccer) 4. Soccer for women -- United States 5. Women soccer players -- United States

ISBN 9780756552930; 9780756552978; 9780756553012

LC 2015034468

This book, by Emma Carlson Berne, focuses on the "1999 womens World Cup soccer match. . . . Penalty kicks would decide the world champion. . . . Brandi Chastain was up. If she made her kick, the Americans would win the World Cup. Success! After her winning goal, Chastain dropped to the turf, whipped off her jersey, and screamed with joy." (Publisher's note)

"The many illustrations and large photos are a fascinating visual record of events before and after the captured moment." SLJ

Includes bibliographical references and index

Crisfield, Deborah

Winning soccer for girls; [by] Deborah W. Crisfield; foreword by Bill Hawkey and Patrick Murphy. 3rd ed.; Chelsea House 2010 164p il (Winning sports for girls) lib bdg $39.50; pa $14.95

Grades: 7 8 9 10 **796.334**

1. Soccer

ISBN 978-0-8160-7714-4 lib bdg; 0-8160-7714-2 lib bdg; 978-0-8160-7715-1 pa; 0-8160-7715-0 pa

LC 2008-50595

First published 1996 by Facts on File

This soccer guidebook contains "material on developing agility, power, and strength and improving ball control and handling. The history and rules of the game are also examined, and a glossary lists soccer terms." Publisher's note

Includes glossary and bibliographical references

Doeden, Matt

The **world** cup; soccer's global championship. By Matt Doeden. Millbrook Press 2018 64 p. (lb : alk. paper) $33.32

Grades: 5 6 7 8 9 10 **796.334**

1. Soccer 2. World Cup (Soccer)

ISBN 9781512427554

LC 2017009220

In this book in the Spectacular Sports series, "author Matt Doeden explores the history of international soccer and covers the World Cup's greatest moments, from the Save of the Century to Diego Maradona's Hand of God goal to the United States Women's National Team's dominance. The most shocking goals, the greatest upsets, and the fun and fanfare of soccer's biggest event are all here." (Publisher's note)

Includes bibliographical references and index

Gifford, Clive

The **Kingfisher** soccer encyclopedia. Kingfisher 2010 144p il $19.99

Grades: 5 6 7 8 **796.334**

1. Reference books 2. Soccer -- Encyclopedias

ISBN 978-0-7534-6397-0; 0-7534-6397-0

First published 2006

"Gifford does an excellent job of covering most aspects of the game from its history of a hundred-plus years to its current rules and tactics, teams, competitions, and famous players. Each section is clearly identified and provides additional information about the game. . . . Students involved in the sport or interested in specific teams or players will appreciate this book." Voice Youth Advocates

Includes glossary and bibliographical references

Hornby, Hugh

Soccer; written by Hugh Hornby; photographed by Andy Crawford. DK Pub. 2008 70p il (DK eyewitness books) $15.99

Grades: 4 5 6 7 **796.334**

1. Soccer

ISBN 978-0-7566-3779-8; 0-7566-3779-1

LC 2008276290

First published 2000

Examines all aspects of the game of soccer: its history, rules, techniques, tactics, equipment, playing fields, competitive play, and more.

Jennings, Madeleine

Soccer step-by-step; [by] Madeleine Jennings and Ian Howe. Rosen Central 2010 95p il (Skills in motion) lib bdg $31.95

Grades: 5 6 7 8 **796.334**

1. Soccer

ISBN 978-1-4358-3362-3; 1-4358-3362-7

LC 2009-12538

Presents instructions on the basic movements of soccer, including passing, shooting, and goalkeeping.

"Colorful photographs show the entire movement of each skill presented, giving new meaning to the term 'step-by-step.' Progression borders at the bottom of the pages highlight the salient points to notice in performing each skill from beginning to end." SLJ

Includes bibliographical references

Kassouf, Jeff

Soccer. Norwood House Press 2011 64p il (Girls play to win) lib bdg $26.60

Grades: 4 5 6 7 **796.334**

1. Soccer

ISBN 978-1-59953-464-0; 1-59953-464-9

LC 2011011037

Covers the history, rules, fundamentals, and significant personalities of the sport of women's soccer. Topics include: techniques, strategies, competitive events, and equipment.

Includes glossary and bibliographical references

Killion, Ann

Champions of women's soccer; Ann Killion. Philomel Books 2018 257 p. (hardback) $17.99

Grades: 4 5 6 7 8 **796.334**

1. Sports for women 2. Women soccer players -- United States -- Biography 3. Women soccer players -- Biography

ISBN 9780399549014

LC 2017037906

This book, by Ann Killion, is an "ultimate guide to Women's Soccer for young sports fans. . . . Featuring Top Ten Lists and stunning photos of history-making moments, this comprehensive collection catalogs the rise of women's soccer in America; the greatest American players such as Mia Hamm, Hope Solo, and Alex Morgan; the greatest international stars, including Marta and Homare Sawa; the future class of superstars; and the most thrilling World Cup and Olympic matches." (Publisher's note)

Luke, Andrew

History of the Cup; Andrew Luke. Mason Crest 2018 80 p. (Road to the world's most popular cup) (hardback) $24.95

Grades: 7 8 9 10 **796.334**

1. Soccer -- History 2. Sports -- History 3. World Cup (Soccer) -- History

ISBN 9781422278314; 9781422239490; 9781422239537

LC 2017046669

This book in the Road to the World's Most Popular Cup series, by Andrew Luke, "takes readers through the struggles of the early years and describes the players and the matches that brought the tournament, and the sport, to greatness. From the Maracanazo to the Game of the Century, all the best moments are here." (Publisher's note)

St. John, Warren

Outcasts united; the story of a refugee soccer team that changed a town. Warren St. John. Delacorte Press 2012 226 p. (trade hardcover) $16.99

Grades: 6 7 8 **796.334**

1. Refugees 2. Soccer teams 3. Soccer coaches 4. Refugees -- Africa 5. Refugee children -- Georgia -- Clarkston 6. Soccer coaches -- Georgia -- Clarkston -- Biography

ISBN 0385741944; 9780375988806; 9780375990335; 9780385741941

LC 2012001412

This book by Warren St. John "is the story of a refugee soccer team, a remarkable woman coach and a small southern town turned upside down by the process of refugee resettlement. It's a tale about resilience, the power of one person to make a difference and the daunting challenge of creating community in a place where people seem to have little in common." (Publisher's note)

Stewart, Mark

★ **Goal!** : the fire and fury of soccer's greatest moment; [by] Mark Stewart and Mike Kennedy. Millbrook Press 2010 64p il lib bdg $27.93

Grades: 5 6 7 8 **796.334**

1. Soccer

ISBN 978-0-8225-8754-5 lib bdg; 0-8225-8754-8 lib bdg

LC 2009014098

"This well-written book explores the nuances of scoring in the world's most popular sport. A quick history of the game lays the groundwork with details that may be new to even hard-core fans. The second chapter jumps right into the good stuff with descriptions of 10 of the most famous goals. . . . Also included is a rundown of the best male and female scorers from the early twentieth century to the present and weird anomalies and amusing anecdotes from soccer lore." Booklist

796.34 Racket games

Smolka, Bo

Lacrosse. Norwood House Press 2011 64p il (Girls play to win) lib bdg $26.60

Grades: 4 5 6 7 **796.34**

1. Lacrosse

ISBN 978-1-59953-463-3; 1-59953-463-0

LC 2011011050

Covers the history, rules, fundamentals, and significant personalities of the sport of women's lacrosse. Topics include: techniques, strategies, competitive events, and equipment.

Includes glossary and bibliographical references

Swissler, Becky

Winning lacrosse for girls; foreword by Katie Bergstrom. 2nd ed.; Chelsea House 2010 212p il (Winning sports for girls) lib bdg $44.95; pa $14.95

Grades: 7 8 9 10 **796.34**

1. Lacrosse

ISBN 978-0-8160-7712-0 lib bdg; 0-8160-7712-6 lib bdg; 978-0-8160-7713-7 pa; 0-8160-7713-4 pa

LC 2008-51346

First published 2004 by Facts on File

This lacrosse guidebook "teaches the game's basic skills, strategies, and drills and how to master them. Chapters cover the history of the game, the basics of stick handling, the rules of play, passing and receiving, offense and defense, key strategies, skills and tactics, conditioning, and . . . more." Publisher's note

Includes bibliographical references

796.342 Tennis (Lawn tennis)

Gifford, Clive

Tennis; [by] Clive Gifford. Sea-to-Sea Publications 2009 30p il (Know your sport) lib bdg $27.10

Grades: 5 6 7 8 **796.342**

1. Tennis

ISBN 978-1-59771-153-1 lib bdg; 1-59771-153-5 lib bdg

LC 2008-7322

"Describes the equipment, courts, training, moves, and competitions of tennis. Includes step-by-step descriptions of moves." Publisher's note

Includes glossary

796.352 Golf

Gifford, Clive

Golf : from tee to green; the essential guide for young golfers. Sea-to-Sea Publications 2010 64p il (Know your sport) $16.99

Grades: 5 6 7 8 **796.352**

1. Golf

ISBN 978-1-59771-217-0; 1-59771-217-5

LC 2008045861

Presents an instructional guide to the sport of golf, with information on different aspects of play and the equipment used.

"This book will be welcomed by young golf enthusiasts, whether they're beginners or experienced players. . . . A useful and attractive guide." Horn Book Guide

Includes bibliographical references

Kelley, K. C.

Golf. Cherry Lake Pub. 2009 32p il (Innovation in sports) lib bdg $27.07

Grades: 4 5 6 7 **796.352**

1. Golf

ISBN 978-1-60279-262-3 lib bdg; 1-60279-262-3 lib bdg

LC 2008002045

This describes golf history, rules, balls, and club technology, and innovators

This "stands out by emphasizing monumental shifts and advances in the events themselves. . . . Concise and occasionally revelatory." Booklist

Includes bibliographical references

796.357 Baseball

Adamson, Thomas K.

Baseball; the math of the game. Capstone Sports 2012 48p il (Sports math) lib bdg $30.65

Grades: 6 7 8 9 **796.357**

1. Baseball 2. Mathematics

ISBN 978-1-4296-6569-8

LC 2011004483

"Overall these books will appeal to serious sports fans who want to learn more about the numbers of the game." SLJ

Includes bibliographical references

Bryant, Howard

★ **Legends**; the best players, games, and teams in baseball. Howard Bryant. Philomel Books 2015 240 p. (Legends) $16.99

Grades: 6 7 8 9 **796.357**

1. Baseball 2. Baseball players 3. Baseball -- United States -- History 4. Baseball players -- United States -- Biography

ISBN 0399169032; 9780399169038

LC 2014031744

This book, by Howard Bryant, "is no traditional almanac of mundane statistics, but rather a storyteller's journey through baseball's storied game. . . . This collection covers some of the greatest players from Babe Ruth to Hank Aaron; the greatest teams to take the field and swing the bats; . . . the greatest playoff rivalries, including the 2004 showdown between the Red Sox and Yankees that turned into an instant classic; and . . . edge-of-your-seat World Series moments." (Publisher's note)

"Baseball fans are known for their mental repositories of statistics, facts, and figures, and this book will attract all manner of analysis and discussion among lovers of America's favorite pastime...Fans of other sports will cheer: this is only the first in a series devoted to sports legends, and a second volume, about football, will come out this fall."

Buckley, James

Ultimate guide to baseball. Shoreline Pub. 2010 160p il $30; pa $7.99

Grades: 4 5 6 7 **796.357**

1. Baseball

ISBN 978-0-531-20750-5; 0-531-20750-1; 978-0-531-21021-5 pa; 0-531-21021-9 pa

LC 2009043684

"This is a wide-ranging, brisk overview of the game. Sections briefly skim baseball history, hitting, pitching, defense and baserunning, and the World Series. Each major league team is introduced in a thumbnail sketch. . . . Other topics include baseball slang and nicknames, the 11 ways to get on base, and the author's choices for the best defensive players of all time. . . . Buckley writes with a lightly humorous touch that should appeal to fans and browsers." SLJ

Includes bibliographical references

Doeden, Matt

The **World** Series; baseball's biggest stage. by Matt Doeden. Millbrook Press, A division of Lerner Publishing Group, Inc. 2014 64 p. (lib. bdg. : alk. paper) $33.27

Grades: 4 5 6 7 **796.357**

1. Baseball 2. World Series (Baseball) 3. World Series (Baseball) -- History

ISBN 1467718963; 9781467718967

LC 2013018082

This book describes how "when the top teams face off in the World Series each season, team legacies and fans' hearts are on the line. Author Matt Doeden covers the century-long history of the World Series, from its humble beginnings to becoming a worldwide sensation. Discover the drama behind the statistics and record books that keeps the crowd enthralled!" (Publisher's note)

"This valentine to the Fall Classic opens with a quick history--though only through the 2012 series--then goes on in separate chapters to highlight renowned games, awesome individual performances, and memorable plays or incidents. . . . The color photos on every spread are almost all action shots and capture the excitement of each feat or moment." Booklist

Includes bibliographical references (p. 62) and index

Gitlin, Marty

Softball. Norwood House Press 2011 64p il (Girls play to win) lib bdg $26.60

Grades: 4 5 6 7 **796.357**

1. Softball

ISBN 978-1-59953-465-7; 1-59953-465-7

LC 2011011051

Covers the history, rules, fundamentals, and significant personalities of the sport of women's softball. Topics include: techniques, strategies, competitive events, and equipment.

Includes glossary and bibliographical references

Gola, Mark

Winning softball for girls; foreword by Gretchen Cammiso. 2nd ed.; Chelsea House 2009 220p il (Winning sports for girls) pa $14.95; lib bdg $44.95

Grades: 7 8 9 10 **796.357**

1. Softball

ISBN 0-8160-7716-9 lib bdg; 978-0-8160-7717-5 pa; 0-8160-7717-7 pa; 978-0-8160-7716-8 lib bdg

LC 2008-54453

First published 2002 by Facts on File

"Gola covers the history, rules of the game, and necessary equipment as well as tips for hitting, pitching, and base running. The fundamentals of defense and offense are covered, along with a number of drills in each area. In addition, the author details the various positions and gives advice on conditioning. . . . This title could prove useful in balancing baseball-laden collections." SLJ

Includes bibliographical references

Lipsyte, Robert

Heroes of baseball; the men who made it America's favorite game. [by] Robert Lipsyte. Atheneum Books for Young Readers 2006 92p il $19.95

Grades: 4 5 6 7 **796.357**

1. Baseball -- Biography

ISBN 0-689-86741-7; 978-0-689-86741-5

LC 2005010841

"Using as a focus some of baseball's greats—Big Al Spalding, Babe Ruth, Mickey Mantle, Jackie Robinson, Curt Flood . . . —Lipsyte offers a strong history of the game and its place in American culture. . . . Although much of this material, including the pictures, might be familiar to young readers already absorbed in the game, it is nicely laid out and colorfully formatted. Lipsyte has a clear, vivid style." Booklist

Includes glossary and bibliographical references

Thorn, John

First pitch; how baseball began. Beach Ball Books 2011 40p il pa $14.99

Grades: 4 5 6 7 **796.357**

1. Baseball -- History

ISBN 978-1-936310-04-3; 1-936310-04-X

"Packed with vintage images and photographs, this history of baseball takes readers from the origins of the sport to the present day. . . . Thorn . . . writes clearly and eloquently. . . . Fans who think they know baseball may discover they have much to learn." Publ Wkly

Wong, Stephen

Baseball treasures; by Stephen Wong; photographs by Susan Einstein. Collins 2007 58p il $16.99; lib bdg $17.89

Grades: 5 6 7 8 **796.357**

1. Baseball -- History 2. Baseball -- Collectibles

ISBN 978-0-06-114464-6; 0-06-114464-9; 978-0-06-114473-8 lib bdg; 0-06-114473-8 lib bdg

LC 2006036069

This describes collectibles connected with the history of baseball, including balls, gloves and bats, jerseys, baseball cards, World Series memorabilia, and trophies.

This is "a well-designed, well-illustrated book for kids. . . . The text manages to impart the essential information without becoming bogged down in too much detail." Booklist

796.4 Weight lifting, track and field, gymnastics

Bobrick, Benson

A **passion** for victory; the story of the Olympics in ancient and early modern times. Benson Bobrick. Alfred A. Knopf 2012 xvi, 143 p.p ill. (hardback) $19.99

Grades: 4 5 6 7 **796.4**

1. Olympic games 2. Sports tournaments 3. Olympics

ISBN 9780375868696; 9780375968693

LC 2011016036

The book offers an "account of the Olympic Games and their place in history. . . . [Athletes] Milo of Croton, Jim Thorpe, Johnny Weissmuller and Jesse Owens are given their due here. The photo-essay format conveys their stories . . . as well as the glory, shenanigans and pettiness of the Olympics throughout history. Almost every full-page spread includes at least one photograph, and the text . . . addresses the cultural context of the games." (Kirkus Reviews)

Includes bibliographical references.

796.42 Track and field

Gifford, Clive

Track and field; [by] Clive Gifford. PowerKids Press 2009 32p il (Personal best) lib bdg $25.25

Grades: 4 5 6 7 8 **796.42**

1. Track athletics

ISBN 978-1-4042-4442-9 lib bdg; 1-4042-4442-5 lib bdg

LC 2007-42984

This guide to track and field "offers well-organized and easy-to-follow instructions, focusing on rules, clothing, specific skills, and competitions. . . . Informative, readable." SLJ

Includes bibliographical references

Housewright, Ed

Winning track and field for girls; foreword by Jason-Lamont Jackson. 2nd ed.; Chelsea House 2009 194p il (Winning sports for girls) lib bdg $44.95; pa $11.96

Grades: 7 8 9 10 11 12 **796.42**

1. Track athletics

ISBN 978-0-8160-7718-2 lib bdg; 0-8160-7718-5 lib bdg; 978-0-8160-7719-9 pa; 0-8160-7719-3 pa

LC 2009-9019

First published 2004 by Facts on File

This includes a brief history of women's track, followed by topics including sprints, hurdles, middle and long distances, relays, jumping events, throwing events, the heptathlon, cross-country, and the triathlon, mental preparations and nutrition, stetches and weight lifting.

Includes bibliographical references

McDougall, Chros

Track & field. Norwood House Press 2011 64p il (Girls play to win) lib bdg $26.60

Grades: 4 5 6 7 **796.42**

1. Track athletics

ISBN 978-1-59953-467-1; 1-59953-467-3

LC 2011011053

Covers the history, rules, fundamentals, and significant personalities of the sport of women's track and field. Topics include: techniques, strategies, competitive events, and equipment.

Includes glossary and bibliographical references

796.44 Gymnastics

Raisman, Aly, 1994-

Fierce; how competing for myself changed everything. Aly Raisman, Blythe Lawrence. Little, Brown & Co. 2017 368 p. (hardcover) $18.99

Grades: 7 8 9 10 11 12 **796.44**

1. Women athletes -- Biography 2. Women Olympic athletes -- United States -- Biography

ISBN 9780316472678; 9780316472692; 9780316472708

LC 2017952905

In this memoir, gymnast and Olympian Aly Raisman "shows what it takes to be a champion on and off the floor, and takes readers on a behind-the-scenes journey before, during, and after her remarkable achievements in two Olympic Games--through her highest highs, lowest lows, and all the moments in between. . . . [E]nhanced with never-before-published photos, excerpts from [her] personal journals . . ., and hard-won advice for readers striving to rise above challenges." (Publisher's note)

Schwartz, Heather E.

Gymnastics. Lucent Books 2011 96p il (Science behind sports) lib bdg $33.45

Grades: 5 6 7 8 **796.44**

1. Gymnastics

ISBN 978-1-4205-0277-0; 1-4205-0277-8

LC 2010033544

This "explores the scientific principles such as momentum, gravity, friction, and aerodynamics, plus many more, behind [gymnastics]. . . . [The author discusses the sport's] origins, history, and changes, . . . the biomechanics and physiology of playing, related health and medical concerns, and the causes and treatment of sports-related injuries. Additional information tells how exercise, diet and nutrition, warming up, and training relate to peak performance and enjoyment of the sport. . . . One of the most interesting chapters . . . is 'The Psychology of Gymnastics,' which discusses fears, force of will, honing the competitive edge, and the pressure to succeed. . . . [This volume is] jam-packed full of information. [A must-have] for sports fans, athletes, science students, and even anyone considering a career in sports-related medicine, coaching, or other connected fields." SLJ

Includes glossary and bibliographical references

796.48 Olympic games

Butterfield, Moira

Events. Sea-to-Sea Publications 2011 32p il (The Olympics) lib bdg $19.95

Grades: 4 5 6 7 **796.48**

1. Olympic games

ISBN 978-1-5977-1321-4; 1-5977-1321-X

LC 2011006465

This describes events of the Olympics.

Includes glossary and bibliographical references

History. Sea-to-Sea Publications 2011 32p il (The Olympics) lib bdg $28.50

Grades: 4 5 6 7 **796.48**

1. Olympic games

ISBN 978-1-5977-1319-1; 1-5977-1319-8

LC 2011006470

This is a history of the Olympics.

Includes glossary and bibliographical references

Farrell, Courtney

Terror at the Munich Olympics. ABDO 2010 112p il map (Essential events) $22.95

Grades: 6 7 8 9 **796.48**

1. Terrorism 2. Olympic games, 1972 (Munich, Ger.)

ISBN 978-1-60453-945-5; 1-60453-945-3

LC 2009-30426

This offers "vivid detail as well as historical and political context. . . . Farrell starts with the Munich Olympics but quickly backtracks to offer an explanation of the conflicts in the Middle East surrounding the creation of the State of Israel, and the rise of terrorism in response to these conflicts. The kidnapping and murder of the Israeli athletes is then described, along with the apparent bungling of rescue efforts. The book concludes with chapters on the response to the killings by Israel, as well as attempts at brokering peace in the region among the various countries in conflict. . . . [This title has] pertinent sidebars with primary source material. Archival photos add to the dramatic [narrative]." SLJ

Includes bibliographical references

Hotchkiss, Ron

The **matchless** six; the story of Canada's first women's Olympic team. Tundra Books 2006 194p il pa $16.95

Grades: 7 8 9 10 **796.48**

1. Olympic games 2. Women athletes 3. Track athletics

ISBN 0-88776-738-9; 978-0-88776-738-8

"Hotchkiss provides detailed information on the six Canadian athletes who won the track-and-field event in 1928, the first Olympics that included women. The personalities and accomplishments of Jane Bell, Myrtle Cook, Bobbie Rosenfeld, Ethel Smith, Ethel Catherwood, and Jean Thompson are highlighted with biographical information. . . . Accuracy is supported by quotes from newspapers, sports writers, coaches, and managers. . . . Anyone interested in the history of the Olympics, the history of women in the Games, or of track and field will find the book worth reading." SLJ

Macy, Sue

★ **Swifter,** higher, stronger; a photographic history of the Summer Olympics. by Sue Macy; foreword by Bob Costas. updated for the 2008 Summer Olympics; National Geographic 2008 96p il $18.95; lib bdg $27.90

Grades: 4 5 6 7 **796.48**

1. Olympic games

ISBN 978-1-4263-0290-9; 1-4263-0290-8; 978-1-4263-0302-9 lib bdg; 1-4263-0302-5 lib bdg

First published 2004

A detailed look at the history of the Olympic Games, from their origins in Ancient Greece, through their rebirth in nineteenth century France, to the present, highlighting the contributions of individuals to the Games' success and popularity.

"While other books on the topic go into more depth on specific sports, athletes, or historical events, none are as enthusiastically broad or as enjoyable to read as this one. And, it's superbly illustrated with colorful, well-chosen, and enticing photographs." SLJ [review of 2004 ed.]

Includes bibliographical references

796.5 Outdoor life

George, Jean Craighead

★ **Pocket** guide to the outdoors; [by] Jean Craighead George; with Twig C. George . . . [et al.] Dutton Children's Books 2009 138p il pa $9.99

Grades: 5 6 7 8 **796.5**

1. Camping 2. Outdoor life 3. Wilderness survival

ISBN 978-0-525-42163-4 pa; 0-525-42163-7 pa

"This survival guide is the book to read before a wilderness adventure. In short, clearly written chapters, it provides practical tips about ways to enjoy nature and includes information about building shelters, starting fires, making a fishing line and cleaning a fish, outdoor cooking, identifying animal tracks and edible and poisonous plants, and the basics of orienteering. Safety is always considered. Drawings and clearly labeled sketches help with identification." SLJ

Includes bibliographical references

Paulsen, Gary

★ **Woodsong**. Bradbury Press 1990 132p map hardcover o.p. pa $6.99

Grades: 7 8 9 10 **796.5**

1. Outdoor life 2. Sled dog racing 3. Minnesota

ISBN 0-02-770221-9; 1-4169-3939-3 pa

LC 89-70835

ALA YALSA Margaret A. Edwards Award (1997)

For the author and his family, life in northern Minnesota is a wild experience involving wolves, deer, and the sled dogs that make their way of life possible. Includes an account of Paulsen's first Iditarod, a dogsled race across Alaska

"The book is packed with vignettes that range among various shades of terror and lyrical beauty." Voice Youth Advocates

Schofield, Jo

Make it wild; 101 things to make and do outdoors. [by] Jo Schofield and Fiona Danks. Frances Lincoln 2010 159p il pa $24.95

Grades: 4 5 6 7 8 **796.5**

1. Nature craft 2. Outdoor life

ISBN 978-0-7112-2885-6; 0-7112-2885-X

"Using the raw materials nature has to offer, the authors offer clear, concise instructions on how to create ephemeral art, outdoor toys, jewelry, sculptures, and dozens of other things using materials like clay, ice, leaves, sand, and wood. The instructions offer good guidance but also encourage children to use their own creativity and imagination to craft the final product. The projects range in level of difficulty and, depending on the age of the child, can be done individually or in collaboration with siblings, peers, or parents. The authors include safety instructions and recommendations for further resources on outdoor creative exercises. The activities will teach problem solving and commonsense, useful skills; instill a deeper appreciation of nature; and encourage creativity and ingenuity. An excellent choice for any library collection." Booklist

796.51 Walking

Hart, John, 1965-

Walking softly in the wilderness; the Sierra Club guide to backpacking. 4th ed, complete rev and updated; Sierra Club Books 2005 508p il map (Sierra Club outdoor adventure guide) pa $16.95

Grades: 8 9 10 11 12 Adult **796.51**

1. Backpacking 2. Wilderness areas

ISBN 1-57805-123-1

LC 2004-56554

First published 1977

This guide for both the novice and experienced hiker reflects the environmental concerns of the Sierra Club. Among topics covered are: clothing and equipment; making and breaking camp; problem animals and plants; hiking and camping with kids. Listings of conservation and wilderness travel organizations, map and equipment sources, land management agencies, and Internet contacts are appended.

Includes bibliographical references

796.52 Walking and exploring by kind of terrain

Aronson, Marc, 1950-

Rising water; the story of the Thai cave rescue. Marc Aronson. Atheneum Books For Young Readers, an imprint of Simon & Schuster Children's Publishing Division 2019 160 p. $17.99

Grades: 5 6 7 8 **796.52**

1. Rescue work 2. Natural disasters 3. Caving accidents -- Thailand -- Chiang Rai (Province) 4. Caving -- Search and rescue operations -- Thailand -- Chiang Rai (Province)

ISBN 9781534444133; 9781534444140

LC 2018047593

This book, by Marc Aronson, tells "the incredible true story of the twelve boys trapped with their coach in a flooded cave in Thailand and their inspiring rescue. . . . Aronson brings us the backstory behind how this astounding rescue took place. . . . [The book] highlights the creative thinking and technology that made a successful mission possible by examining the physical, environmental, and psychological factors surrounding the rescue." (Publisher's note)

"The story of the young Thai soccer players trapped in a cave for several days is one that gripped the world. Aronson makes the event feel new through his deeply detailed research and his ability to share pertinent information that news organizations may have ignored." (School Library Journal)

Bodden, Valerie

To the top of Mount Everest; by Valerie Bodden. 1st ed. Creative Education 2012 48 p. ill. (some col.) (Great Expeditions) (paperback) $12.00; (library) $34.25

Grades: 5 6 7 8 **796.52**

1. Exploration 2. Mount Everest (China and Nepal) 3. Mountaineering -- Everest, Mount (China and Nepal) -- History 4.

Mountaineers -- Everest, Mount (China and Nepal) -- Biography
ISBN 1608180700; 9780898126686; 9781608180707
LC 2010033553

This book by Valerie Bodden is part of the Great Expeditions series and looks at expeditions to the top of Mount Everest. "Bodden includes brief biographies of major people involved in each expedition, interspersed with the text. There are also numerous photographs or reproductions of paintings and woodcuts from the time of the expeditions." (Library Media Connection)

Includes bibliographical references and index.

Brennan, Kristine

Sir Edmund Hillary, modern day explorer. Chelsea House 2001 63p il (Explorers of new worlds) hardcover o.p. lib bdg $21.85

Grades: 4 5 6 7 **796.52**

1. Mountaineering 2. Mountaineers 3. Nonfiction writers 4. Mount Everest (China and Nepal)
ISBN 0-7910-5953-7 lib bdg; 0-7910-6163-9 pa
LC 00-43077

A biography of the New Zealander who, with his Sherpa climbing partner Tenzing Norgay, first reached the Summit of Mount Everest in 1953

"Accessible and well organized. . . . Fresh, appealing, and well written." SLJ

Includes glossary and bibliographical references

Cleare, John

Epic climbs. Kingfisher 2011 64p il (Epic adventure) $19.95

Grades: 5 6 7 8 **796.52**

1. Mountaineering
ISBN 978-0-7534-6573-8; 0-7534-6573-6

"Cleare gives the history of five of the most famous and dangerous mountains to climb: Eiger, K2, Everest, McKinley, and Matterhorn. Each section has a short, easy-to-read summary that gives the history of climbers who have conquered these peaks. Full-color photos include the view from the top and historical and contemporary climbing equipment." SLJ

Skreslet, Laurie

To the top of Everest; [by] Laurie Skreslet with Elizabeth MacLeod. Kids Can Press 2001 56p il hardcover o.p. pa $9.95

Grades: 4 5 6 7 **796.52**

1. Mountaineering 2. Mount Everest (China and Nepal)
ISBN 1-55074-721-5; 1-55074-814-9 pa

This is an account of Skreslet's "1982 trek up Everest when he became one of the first Canadians to make it to the top. Skreslet takes readers through every exciting, excruciating element of the climb. Beautiful color photographs abound." Booklist

Includes glossary

Wurdinger, Scott D.

Rock climbing; [by] Scott Wurdinger and Leslie Rapparlie. Creative Education 2007 48p il (Adventure sports) $31.35

Grades: 6 7 8 9 **796.52**

1. Mountaineering
ISBN 978-1-58341-394-4; 1-58341-394-4
LC 2005051785

This outlines "the history, gear, safety equipment, and competitions for [rock climbing]. . . . Large, full-color glossy photos . . . include action shots, closeup views of equipment and techniques, and pictures of exotic landscapes." SLJ

Includes bibliographical references

796.522 Mountains, hills, rocks

Athans, Sandra K.

Secrets of the sky caves; danger and discovery on Nepal's Mustang Cliffs. Sandra K. Athans. Millbrook Press 2014 64 p. color illustrations (lib. bdg. : alk. paper) $33.27

Grades: 4 5 6 7 **796.522**

1. Mountaineering 2. Nepal -- Description and travel 3. Caves -- Nepal -- Mustang (District) 4. Mustang (Nepal : District) -- Antiquities 5. Mountaineering -- Nepal -- Mustang (District) 6. Mustang (Nepal : District) -- Discovery and exploration
ISBN 1467700169; 9781467700160
LC 2013017736

"What's more dangerous than scaling Mount Everest? For mountaineer Pete Athans, the answer lies in the ancient kingdom of Mustang, a remote part of the Asian nation of Nepal. . . From 2007 to 2012, Pete explored Mustang's sky caves with a team that included scientists, mountain climbers, and even two children. They found mummies, murals, manuscripts, and other priceless artifacts." (Publisher's note)

"The author, sister of expedition leader Pete Athans, offers a wealth of information about this little-known archaeological wonder. Color photographs provide stunning visuals." Horn Book

Includes bibliographical references (pages 61-62) and index

Berne, Emma Carlson

Summiting Everest; how a photograph celebrates teamwork at the top of the world. by Emma Carlson Berne. Capstone Compass Point Books 2014 64 p. (Compass point books. Captured history.) (library binding) $33.99

Grades: 5 6 7 8 9 **796.522**

1. Mountaineering 2. Mount Everest (China and Nepal) 3. Portrait photography -- Everest, Mount (China and Nepal) 4. Mountaineering expeditions -- Everest, Mount (China and Nepal) -- Pictorial works
ISBN 0756547342; 9780756547349; 9780756547905
LC 2013027843

"Not far from the top, before their final hours of climbing, team photographer Alfred Gregory snapped a picture of [Edmund] Hillary and [Tenzing] Norgay, with the imposing Himalayas spread out behind them. It was the highest photograph anyone in human history had ever taken. With a click of his camera shutter in May 1953, Gregory opened up a hidden world for the rest of humanity to share." (Publisher's note)

Includes bibliographical references and index

796.525 Caves

Felix, Rebecca

Exploring caves; by Rebecca Felix. Essential Library 2014 144 p. color illustrations (Story of exploration) $35.64

Grades: 5 6 7 8 9 10 **796.525**

1. Caves 2. Exploration
ISBN 1624032494; 9781624032493
LC 2013946594

"This title offers a wonderful presentation about caves and exploration of them. The vivid photos provide a glimpse into various types of caves and aid in understanding the text, which offers plenty of information about the formation of caves, as well as the history of cave exploration. The author makes certain to impress upon the reader how far the study of these natural formations has come. The reader is also introduced to what caves can tell us about prehistoric civilizations." (VOYA)

Includes bibliographical references and index

796.54 Camping

Champion, Neil

Fire and cooking. Amicus 2010 32p il (Survive alive) lib bdg $19.95

Grades: 4 5 6 7 **796.54**

1. Fires 2. Camping 3. Wilderness survival

ISBN 978-1-60753-039-8 lib bdg; 1-60753-039-2 lib bdg

LC 2010001626

This offers survival tips for building a fire and cooking in the wild, including information on different kinds of fires. Also discusses how to know what to cook and utensils to use.

This "colorful [book contains] numerous photos and illustrations that effectively break the [text] into small, readable chucks. There's lots of practical, everyday information here. . . . Brief yet gripping real-life survival stories are interspersed throughout the [book]." SLJ

796.6 Cycling and related activities

Adamson, Thomas K.

BMX racing; Thomas K. Adamson. Bellwether Media, Inc. 2016 24 p. color illustrations (hardcover : alk. paper) $24.95

Grades: 3 4 5 6 7 **796.6**

1. Bicycle racing 2. Extreme sports 3. Bicycle motocross

ISBN 9781626172746; 1626172749

LC 2015007777

This children's book by Thomas K. Adamson is part of a series "on extreme sports, covering history, gear, events, and famous athletes. Each book begins with an account of a gold-winning performance. Graphics and color photos help convey each sport's difficulty and appeal. 'BMX Racing' notes that Olympic races usually finish in 40 seconds or less." (School Library Journal)

"The books' exciting tone and dynamic illustrations will draw kids into the world of extreme sports." Booklist

Includes bibliographical references (page 23) and index

Macy, Sue, 1954-

★ **Wheels** of change; how women rode the bicycle to freedom (with a few flat tires along the way) National Geographic 2011 96p il map $18.95; lib bdg $27.90

Grades: 4 5 6 7 8 **796.6**

1. Cycling 2. Bicycles 3. Gender role 4. Women athletes 5. Sex role 6. Feminism 7. Women -- United States -- History 8. Cycling for women

ISBN 978-1-4263-0761-4; 1-4263-0761-6; 978-1-4263-0762-1 lib bdg; 1-4263-0762-4 lib bdg

LC 2010-27141

This is an "engaging look at the emancipating impact that bikes had on late-nineteenth-century U.S. women. The eye-catching chapters, filled with archival images . . . zero in on the profound ways that bicycles subverted traditional notions of femininity. . . . Macy seamlessly weaves together research, direct quotes . . . and historical overviews that put the facts into context, while sidebars expand on related topics. . . . A strong, high-interest choice for both classroom and personal reading." Booklist

Includes bibliographical references

Robinson, Laura

★ **Cyclist** bikelist; a book for every rider. illustrated by Ramón K. Pérez. Tundra Books 2010 55p il pa $17.95

Grades: 4 5 6 7 **796.6**

1. Cycling 2. Bicycles

ISBN 978-0-88776-784-5; 0-88776-784-2

The author "covers a broad range of topics, from choosing and caring for a bike to differences in tires, how gear ratios work, and even proper dress and nutrition. She also provides a quick overview of the bicycle's history and inspiring sketches of several renowned racers. . . . Supplemented by photos of different types of bikes, Pérez's bright, cartoon-style pictures add both humor and . . . sharply drawn details. A first-rate guide." Booklist

796.72 Automobile racing

Blackwood, Gary L.

The **Great** Race; the amazing round-the-world auto race of 1908. [by] Gary Blackwood. Abrams Books for Young Readers 2008 141p il $19.95

Grades: 6 7 8 9 **796.72**

1. Automobile racing 2. Voyages around the world

ISBN 978-0-8109-9489-8; 0-8109-9489-5

LC 2007-22414

"In 1908, several car manufacturers sponsored a global race that was routed across America, then across Siberia and Europe, ending in Paris. . . . Blackwood presents an extremely well-researched and detailed account of this large-scale publicity stunt. . . . There's enough sheer adventure here, carried out by some eccentric characters, to attract almost every reader. Helping things along are the photographs from the event. . . . A fascinating account." Booklist

Kelley, K. C.

Hottest NASCAR machines; by K. C. Kelley. Enslow Publishers 2008 48p il (Wild wheels!) lib bdg $23.93

Grades: 4 5 6 7 **796.72**

1. Automobile racing 2. National Association for Stock Car Auto Racing

ISBN 978-0-7660-2869-2 lib bdg; 0-7660-2869-0 lib bdg

LC 2007007426

"Experience the thrill of a NASCAR race, and learn about the cars, personalities, and races associated with this sport." Publisher's note

Includes glossary and bibliographical references

Other titles in this series are:

Hottest muscle cars

Hottest sports cars

Morganelli, Adrianna

Formula One. Crabtree Pub. 2007 32p il (Automania!) lib bdg $25.20; pa $8.95

Grades: 4 5 6 **796.72**

1. Automobile racing

ISBN 978-0-7787-3009-5 lib bdg; 0-7787-3009-3 lib bdg; 978-0-7787-3031-6 pa; 0-7787-3031-X pa

LC 2006-14362

This book "traces the history of Grand Prix racing, the development of the cars and their equipment, qualifying and racing, the tracks, safety measures, racing teams, and dominant drivers, with a sidebar on women in F1 racing. . . . Morganelli's writing is . . . organized and . . . readable. . . . [This] book is an attractive introduction." SLJ

Includes glossary

Pimm, Nancy Roe

The **Daytona** 500; the thrill and thunder of the great American race. Milbrook Press 2011 64p il (Spectacular sports) lib bdg $29.27

Grades: 5 6 7 8 **796.72**

1. Automobile racing

ISBN 978-0-7613-6677-5; 0-7613-6677-6

LC 2010027263

"Pimm, who worked in the pit box during her husband Ed Pimm's NASCAR racing days, offers an informative introduction to the Daytona 500. Beginning in 1903 . . . this traces the event's history and discusses the cars, drivers, strategies, and memorable moments. Colorful photos illustrate the clear text, while the many sidebars spotlight related facts." Booklist

Includes bibliographical references

796.8 Combat sports

Bjorklund, Ruth

Aikido. Marshall Cavendish Benchmark 2011 47p il (Martial arts in action) $29.93

Grades: 4 5 6 7 **796.8**

1. Aikido

ISBN 978-0-7614-4931-7; 978-1-6087-0361-6 e-book

LC 2010013820

This describes the history, equipment, and technique of aikido.

This treats "martial arts with the dignity that serious enthusiasts bring to the sport. . . . Illustrations include not only photos of modern gear and from films but also historical images." Booklist

Ellis, Carol

Judo and jujitsu. Marshall Cavendish Benchmark 2011 47p il (Martial arts in action) $29.93

Grades: 4 5 6 7 **796.8**

1. Judo 2. Jiu-jitsu

ISBN 978-0-7614-4933-1; 978-1-6087-0363-0 e-book

LC 2010013821

This describes the history, equipment, and technique of judo and jujitsu.

This treats "martial arts with the dignity that serious enthusiasts bring to the sport. . . . Illustrations include not only photos of modern gear and from films but also historical images." Booklist

Kendo. Marshall Cavendish Benchmark 2010 47p il (Martial arts in action) $29.93

Grades: 4 5 6 7 **796.8**

1. Kendo

ISBN 978-0-7614-4935-5; 0-7614-4935-3

LC 2010013827

This book about kendo offers "an introduction, a brief history, and expectations for students who begin taking classes. . . . [This title is] outstanding, using an approachable voice without fictionalizing and presenting the history of [kendo] in a way that makes it feel relevant." SLJ

Includes glossary and bibliographical references

Wrestling. Marshall Cavendish Benchmark 2010 47p il (Martial arts in action) $29.93

Grades: 4 5 6 7 **796.8**

1. Wrestling

ISBN 978-0-7614-4941-6; 0-7614-4941-8

LC 2010013819

This book about wrestling offers "an introduction, a brief history, and expectations for students who begin taking classes. . . . [This title is] outstanding, using an approachable voice without fictionalizing and presenting the history of [wrestling] in a way that makes it feel relevant." SLJ

Includes glossary and bibliographical references

Haney-Withrow, Anna

Tae kwon do. Marshall Cavendish Benchmark 2011 47p il (Martial arts in action) $29.93

Grades: 4 5 6 7 **796.8**

1. Tae kwon do

ISBN 978-0-7614-4940-9; 978-1-6087-0368-5 e-book

LC 2010013828

This describes the history, equipment, and technique of tae kwon do.

This treats "martial arts with the dignity that serious enthusiasts bring to the sport. . . . Illustrations include not only photos of modern gear and from films but also historical images." Booklist

Inman, Roy

The **judo** handbook; [by] Roy Inman. North American ed.; Rosen Pub. 2008 256p il (Martial arts) lib bdg $39.95

Grades: 7 8 9 10 11 12 **796.8**

1. Judo

ISBN 978-1-4042-1393-7; 1-4042-1393-7

LC 2007-37742

This features "step-by-step descriptions of various moves, accompanied by detailed, full-color photographs. [This] volume offers a background on the history of the art and its use as a sport as well as a system for self-defense. [The] handbook features a concise description of the judo fundamentals, then begins describing the techniques: throwing techniques, combination and counter-techniques, ground techniques, and combination and counter-techniques against them. The book makes good use of the Japanese terms used in judo study, integrating their meanings seamlessly into the text." SLJ

Includes bibliographical references

Mack, Gail

Kickboxing. Marshall Cavendish Benchmark 2011 47p il lib bdg $29.93

Grades: 4 5 6 7 **796.8**

1. Kickboxing

ISBN 978-0-7614-4936-2; 978-1-6087-0366-1 e-book

LC 2010014798

This describes the history, equipment, and technique of kickboxing.

This treats "martial arts with the dignity that serious enthusiasts bring to the sport. . . . Illustrations include not only photos of modern gear and from films but also historical images." Booklist

Mason, Paul, 1967-

Boxing. Sea-to-Sea Publications 2011 32p il (Combat sports) lib bdg $28.50

Grades: 4 5 6 **796.8**

1. Boxing

ISBN 978-1-59771-273-6; 1-59771-273-6

"...[Provides] an inviting look for students who are learning about techniques and for examining records and statistics... Use to refresh an older collection." SLJ

Includes glossary and bibliographical references

Pawlett, Mark

The **tae** kwon do handbook; [by] Mark and Ray Pawlett. Rosen Pub. 2008 256p il (Martial arts) lib bdg $39.95

Grades: 7 8 9 10 11 12 **796.8**

1. Tae kwon do

ISBN 978-1-4042-1396-8; 1-4042-1396-1

LC 2007-31559

This features "step-by-step descriptions of various moves, accompanied by detailed, full-color photographs. [The] volume offers a background on the history of the art and its use as a sport as well as a system for self-defense. . . . [The book] spends about 150 pages on techniques, and also covers dietary recommendations, a history of Korea, a description of the I Ching, and other concepts. . . . It [includes] an excellent section on strength training . . . and the text devoted to basic fundamentals of the sport, such as stances and stepping, gives those building blocks appropriate importance." SLJ

Includes bibliographical references

Pawlett, Raymond

The **karate** handbook; [by] Ray Pawlett. Rosen Pub. Group 2008 256p il (Martial arts) $39.95

Grades: 7 8 9 10 11 12 **796.8**

1. Karate

ISBN 978-1-4042-1394-4; 1-4042-1394-5

LC 2007-32795

This "offers a thorough introduction to karate that covers both the underlying philosophy and the physical practice. A thoughtful, sophisticated history opens the book and discusses karate's roots in Zen Buddhism, the styles of karate, and dojo etiquette. Later spreads feature lucid, step-by-step instructions." Booklist

Includes bibliographical references

Ritschel, John

The **kickboxing** handbook; [by] John Ritschel. Rosen Pub. 2008 256p il (Martial arts) lib bdg $39.95

Grades: 7 8 9 10 11 12 **796.8**

1. Martial arts

ISBN 978-1-4042-1395-1; 1-4042-1395-3

LC 2007-37746

"This volume features step-by-step descriptions of various moves and strength-building exercises, accompanied by detailed, full-color photographs. . . . [This book] does emphasize safety, showing the correct way to punch in order to avoid injuring one's hand and displaying clear photographs on striking areas of the foot in order to perform kicks properly." SLJ

Whiting, Jim

Inside the cage; the greatest fights of mixed martial arts. Capstone Press 2010 48p il (Velocity. the world of mixed martial arts) lib bdg $27.99

Grades: 5 6 7 8 **796.8**

1. Martial arts

ISBN 978-1-4296-3426-7 lib bdg; 1-4296-3426-X lib bdg

LC 2009-7344

"Whiting provides information in fact boxes and in short bursts of text. Dramatic camera angles show sweating, bloody kickboxers, and cagefighters from just outside the ring. . . . The author also discusses how politics has entered into the viewing of competitions on network and pay-per-view television. Fans of the sport will be mesmerized." SLJ

Includes glossary and bibliographical references

796.815 Oriental martial arts forms

Mason, Paul, 1967-

Judo; [by] Paul Mason. Sea-to-Sea Publications 2009 30 p. col. ill. (Know your sport) (library) $27.10

Grades: 5 6 7 8 **796.815**

1. Judo

ISBN 978-1-59771-151-7; 1-59771-151-9

LC 2008007318

"Describes the equipment, training, moves, and competitions of judo. Includes step-by-step descriptions of moves." Publisher's note

Includes index.

796.91 Ice skating

McDougall, Chros

Figure skating. Norwood House Press 2010 64p il (Girls play to win) lib bdg $26.60

Grades: 4 5 6 7 **796.91**

1. Ice skating

ISBN 978-1-59953-389-6; 1-59953-389-8

LC 2010009809

"This begins with a look back at the origin of [figure skating] and the traces the young women who played a role in skating from the olden days to today. The first of six chapters describes skating basics . . . and then the progression of stars begins. . . . Color photos, sidebars, and boxed explanations break up the text. . . . A nicely compact history." Booklist

Includes glossary and bibliographical references

796.93 Skiing and snowboarding

Kenney, Karen Latchana

Skiing & snowboarding. Norwood House Press 2010 64p il (Girls play to win) lib bdg $26.60

Grades: 4 5 6 7 **796.93**

1. Skiing 2. Snowboarding

ISBN 978-1-59953-391-9; 1-59953-391-X

LC 2010009808

Covers the history, rules, fundamentals and significant personalities of the sports of women's skiing and snowboarding. Topics include: techniques, strategies, competitive events, and equipment.

"With an easy design and format, the [text is] highly accessible to even the most reluctant readers and [provides] great exposure and insight into the world of female professional sports." Horn Book Guide

Includes glossary and bibliographical references

Schwartz, Heather E.

Snowboarding. Lucent Books 2011 104p il (Science behind sports) $33.45

Grades: 5 6 7 8 **796.93**

1. Snowboarding

ISBN 978-1-4205-0322-7; 1-4205-0322-7

LC 2010033274

This "explores the scientific principles such as momentum, gravity, friction, and aerodynamics, plus many more, behind [snowbarding]. . . . [The author discusses the sport's] origins, history, and changes, . . . the biomechanics and physiology of playing, related health and medical concerns, and the causes and treatment of sports-related injuries. Additional information tells how exercise, diet and nutrition, warming up, and training relate to peak performance and enjoyment of the sport. . . . The action photography . . . is fantastic. . . . [This volume is] jam-packed full of information. [A must-have] for sports fans, athletes, science students, and even anyone considering a career in sports-related medicine, coaching, or other connected fields." SLJ

Includes glossary and bibliographical references

796.94 Snowmobiling

Woods, Bob

Snowmobile racers. Enslow Publishers 2010 48p il (Kid racers) lib bdg $23.93

Grades: 5 6 7 8 **796.94**

1. Snowmobiles

ISBN 978-0-7660-3487-7 lib bdg; 0-7660-3487-9 lib bdg

LC 2009020784

This describes snowmobiles and races for kids, discussing which snowmobiles qualify, how they are built and raced, who the best drivers are, what to look for in a snowmobile, safety, good sportsmanship, and how racing activities can be a good part of family life.

"The easily digestible text gets more visual weight on the page, but there are plenty of captioned color photos depicting different sorts of races as well as recreational snowmobiling." Booklist

Includes glossary and bibliographical references

796.962 Ice hockey

Adams, Carly

Queens of the ice; they were fast, they were fierce, they were teenage girls. Lorimer 2011 131p il (Record books) $16.95; pa $9.95

Grades: 5 6 7 8 **796.962**

1. Hockey 2. Women athletes

ISBN 978-1-55277-721-3; 1-55277-721-9; 978-1-55277-720-6 pa; 1-55277-720-0 pa

"Filled with exciting action, this . . . title . . . showcases the history of the Preston Rivulettes, a Canadian hockey team of teenage girls who played together for 10 seasons, from 1931 until 1940, without losing a game and at a time when many believed that girls could not play the sport and needed chaperones. . . . Adams deepens the story with the historical background of the Great Depression and the team's struggle to find money. Occasional achival photos and boxed inserts add to the clear, readable account." Booklist

Burgan, Michael

Miracle on ice; How a Stunning Upset United a Country. by Michael Burgan. An imprint of Capstone Press 2016 64 p. illustrations (some color) (Hardcover : alk. paper) $34.65

Grades: 6 7 8 9 **796.962**

1. Hockey -- History 2. Hockey -- Soviet Union -- History 3. Hockey -- United States -- History 4. Hockey teams -- Soviet Union -- History 5. Hockey teams -- United States -- History

ISBN 9780756552909; 9780756552947

LC 2015049427

In this book, by Michael Burgan, "the mighty Soviets were the favorites to win hockey gold at the 1980 Winter Olympics. But a team of U.S. college players had other ideas. The stunning upset of the Soviet hockey team by the young Americans has been called the greatest moment in international hockey. And to many people the victory was about much more than sports." (Publisher's note)

"The many illustrations and large photos are a fascinating visual record of events before and after the captured moment. This series is certain to entice sports fans to read about history." SLJ

Includes bibliographical references (page 63) and index.

Johnstone, Robb

Hockey; rev ed.; Weigl Publishers 2009 24p il (In the zone) $24.45; pa $8.95

Grades: 4 5 6 7 **796.962**

1. Hockey

ISBN 978-1-6059-6130-9; 1-6059-6130-2; 978-1-6059-6131-6 pa; 1-6059-6131-0 pa

LC 2009005607

First published 2001

"Colorful, informative. . . . For those just showing an interest in the bone-crushing sport, [this is] an excellent place to get their bearings. Using short, mostly two-page chapters, Johnstone explains the genesis of the sport, the gear needed, the rules, the positions, and the leagues, before concluding with biographies of eight legendary NHL players." Booklist

McKinley, Michael

Ice time; the story of hockey. Tundra Books 2006 80p il $18.95

Grades: 5 6 7 8 **796.962**

1. Hockey

ISBN 978-0-88776-762-3; 0-88776-762-1

"This straightforward history of hockey emphasizes the professional game and Canadian players. . . . Hockey enthusiasts will find this a welcome arrival." Booklist

McMahon, Dave

Hockey. Norwood House Press 2010 64p il (Girls play to win) lib bdg $26.60

Grades: 4 5 6 7 **796.962**

1. Hockey

ISBN 978-1-59953-390-2; 1-59953-390-1

LC 2010009811

Covers the history, rules, fundamentals and significant personalities of the sport of women's hockey. Topics include: techniques, strategies, competitive events, and equipment.

"With an easy design and format, the [text is] highly accessible to even the most reluctant readers and [provides] great exposure and insight into the world of female professional sports." Horn Book Guide

Includes glossary and bibliographical references

Sharp, Anne Wallace

Ice hockey. Lucent Books 2011 112p il map (Science behind sports) lib bdg $33.45

Grades: 5 6 7 8 **796.962**

1. Hockey

ISBN 978-1-4205-0281-7; 1-4205-0281-6

LC 2010025670

This book about ice hockey highlights "performance; chapter headings include topics such as 'Training and Nutrition,' 'High-Tech Equipment,' and 'Injuries and Treatments.' Physics, biology, and psychology concepts related to the [sport] are . . . wrapped into technical discussions of moves and techniques. Many photographs of pros and novices in action add interest." Horn Book Guide

Includes glossary and bibliographical references

Stewart, Mark

Score! the action and artistry of hockey's magnificent moment. Millbrook Press 2010 64p il $29.27

Grades: 5 6 7 8 **796.962**

1. Hockey

ISBN 978-0-8225-8753-8; 0-8225-8753-X

"Stewart and Kennedy take readers on a chatty, photo-studded tour of the art of scoring in the rink. This intermediate-level hockey book definitely isn't for beginners. . . . What savvy readers will get, however, is a bounty of information on the game's defining goals, goal scorers, and goal-scoring techniques. . . . This makes a worthy addition to any sports shelf." Booklist

797.1 Aquatic sports

Storey, Rita

Sailing. Sea-to-Sea Publications 2011 30p il (Know your sport) lib bdg $28.50

Grades: 4 5 6 **797.1**

1. Sailing

ISBN 978-1-59771-286-6

LC 2010003439

This "volume provides an introduction to the equipment, techniques, and safety measures for [sailing]. . . . Instructive photographs help illustrate such concepts as [tacking a sailboat], . . . while engaging stock images capture the excitement on the water. The [volume concludes] with racing information, profiling top racers, rules, and tactics." Horn Book Guide

Includes glossary

Thorpe, Yvonne

Canoeing and kayaking. Sea-to-Sea Publications 2011 30p il (Know your sport) $28.50

Grades: 4 5 6 **797.1**

1. Canoes and canoeing 2. Kayaks and kayaking

ISBN 9781597712859

LC 2010003438

This "volume provides an introduction to the equipment, techniques, and safety measures for [canoeing and kayaking]. . . . Instructive photographs help illustrate such concepts as . . . paddling a kayak, while engaging stock images capture the excitement on the water. The [volume concludes] with racing information, profiling top racers, rules, and tactics." Horn Book Guide

Includes glossary

Wurdinger, Scott D.

Kayaking; by Scott Wurdinger and Leslie Rapparlie. Creative Education 2006 48p il (Adventure sports) $21.95

Grades: 5 6 7 8 **797.1**

1. Kayaks and kayaking

ISBN 978-1-58341-397-5

LC 2005051057

"Strong, full-page color photographs illustrate this overview of kayaking. . . . Tracing the use of kayaks back thousands of years, the authors touch on the history of the boats before moving on to contemporary usage for sports and recreation. . . . The exciting views . . . will instantly draw browsers and serious readers alike." Booklist

Includes bibliographical references

797.12 Types of vessels

Brown, Daniel James

The **boys** in the boat; the true story of an American team's epic journey to win gold at the 1936 olympics. Daniel James Brown; adapted for young readers by Gregory Mone. Viking Childrens Books 2015 240 p. (hardcover) $17.99

Grades: 5 6 7 8 **797.12**

1. Olympic games, 1936 (Berlin, Ger.) 2. Rowing -- United States -- History 3. Rowers -- United States -- Biography 4. University of Washington -- Rowing -- History

ISBN 0451475925; 9780451475923

LC 2015006199

This juvenile book, by Daniel James Brown, tells "the astonishing tale of nine working-class boys from the American West who at the 1936 Olympics showed the world what true grit really meant. With rowers who were the sons of loggers, shipyard workers, and farmers, the University of Washington's eight-oar crew was never expected to defeat the elite East Coast teams, yet they did, going on to shock the world by challenging the German boat rowing for Adolf Hitler." (Publisher's note)

"Overcoming a difficult childhood, Joe Rantz made the freshman crew team at the University of Washington. There, he met equally determined boys and a coach driven to take the gold at the Olympics in Hitler's Germany. Each team member is profiled; the sport of rowing becomes comprehensible and compelling. This adaptation of the adult bestseller is liberally illustrated with black-and-white photographs." Horn Book

797.2 Swimming and diving

Gifford, Clive

Swimming; [by] Clive Gifford. PowerKids Press 2009 32p il (Personal best) lib bdg $25.25

Grades: 4 5 6 7 8 **797.2**

1. Swimming

ISBN 978-1-4042-4443-6 lib bdg; 1-4042-4443-3 lib bdg

LC 2007-43003

This guide to swimming "offers well-organized and easy-to-follow instructions, focusing on rules, clothing, specific skills, and competitions. . . . Informative, readable." SLJ

Hoblin, Paul

Swimming & diving. Norwood House Press 2011 64p il (Girls play to win) lib bdg $26.60

Grades: 4 5 6 7 **797.2**

1. Diving 2. Swimming

ISBN 978-1-59953-466-4; 1-59953-466-5

LC 2011011038

Covers the history, rules, fundamentals, and significant personalities of the sport of women's swimming and diving. Topics include: techniques, strategies, competitive events, and equipment.

Includes glossary and bibliographical references

797.5 Air sports

Blair, Margaret Whitman

The **roaring** 20; the first cross-country air race for women. National Geographic 2006 128p il map $21.95

Grades: 6 7 8 9 **797.5**

1. Airplane racing 2. Women air pilots

ISBN 0-7922-5389-2

LC 2005-05472

"This book offers a detailed look at the first 'Powder Puff Derby' run in the summer of 1929. . . . Starting in Santa Monica, California, and ending in Cleveland, Ohio, the women flew over deserts and mountains. . . . It was an all-star event with racers including Amelia Earhart, 'Pancho' Barnes, and Louise Thaden. . . . The photos of flyers, landscapes, and memorabilia bring the story to life. This book is a welcome addition." Voice Youth Advocates

Includes bibliographical references

798.4 Horse racing

Scanlan, Lawrence

The **big** red horse; the story of Secretariat and the loyal groom who loved him. with photos by Raymond Woolfe. Harper Trophy 2011 166p il pa $7.99

Grades: 4 5 6 7 **798.4**

1. Horse racing 2. Stablehands

ISBN 978-0-06-202669-9; 0-06-202669-0

"This biography of the legendary racehorse provides many intimate details about his daily life and incredible prowess. . . . His good looks and tremendous athletic ability enabled him to win the Triple Crown at a record-breaking pace and the hearts of the American people. Scanlan focuses on the special relationship between Secretariat and his groom, Eddie Sweat. . . . Black-and-white photos are scattered throughout. . . . This solid book will have special appeal for horse lovers." SLJ

Tate, Nikki

Behind the scenes: the racehorse. Fitzhenry & Whiteside 2008 72p il $22.95; pa $18.95

Grades: 5 6 7 8 **798.4**

1. Horse racing

ISBN 978-1-55455-018-0; 1-55455-018-1; 978-1-55455-032-6 pa; 1-55455-032-7 pa

"A short history of horse racing opens this attractive and informative book. Tate discusses the breeding, training, and care of the horses but devotes plenty of space to the people who are involved in the sport. . . . The many color photos . . . are quite clear and well matched to the text." Booklist

799.1 Fishing

Maas, Dave

★ **Kids'** guide to fishing; the young angler's guide to catching more and bigger fish. Dave Maas. Walter Foster Jr. 2017 96 p. illustrations (some color) (Ranger Rick kids' guides) (hardcover) $14.95

Grades: 4 5 6 7 8 **799.1**

1. Fishing 2. Outdoor recreation 3. Freshwater fishes 4. Fishes -- Identification 5. Fishing -- Equipment and supplies 6. Fishing -- Handbooks, manuals, etc.

ISBN 9781633223820; 9781942875741; 1633223825

This book in the Ranger Rick Kids' Guides series, by Dave Maas, presents "tips for catching all sorts of fish. This book is also filled with little-known fish facts, like: Did you know that some of the fish you catch are older than you? It' true! Just check out the fish age charts in this book! Also included is a real working compass to help you navigate through the wilderness." (Publisher's note)

"This informative title in the Ranger Rick Kids' Guides is made for young anglers, whether they are just beginning or looking to improve their technique." Booklist

799.2 Hunting

Peterson, Judy Monroe

Big game hunting. Rosen Central 2011 64p il map (Hunting: pursuing wild game!)) lib bdg $29.25; pa $12.95

Grades: 5 6 7 8 **799.2**

1. Hunting

ISBN 978-1-4488-1240-0 lib bdg; 1-4488-1240-2 lib bdg; 978-1-4488-2270-6 pa; 1-4488-2270-X pa

LC 2010006859

In this introduction to big game hunting "Peterson displays an impressive grasp of the pastime by throwing in almost everything: types of guns and bows, safety laws, licenses, land access, animal behavior, clothing, methods of hunting, and preparing harvested meat. . . . [The book] is jam-packed with info. . . . A green-heavy design, bright photos of hunters . . . and prey, and above average back matter close out this solid entry." Booklist

Includes bibliographical references

Wolny, Philip

Waterfowl. Rosen Central 2011 64p il (Hunting: pursuing wild game!) lib bdg $29.25; pa $12.95

Grades: 4 5 6 7 **799.2**

1. Hunting 2. Water birds

ISBN 978-1-4488-1243-1 lib bdg; 1-4488-1243-7 lib bdg; 978-1-4488-2273-7 pa; 1-4488-2273-4 pa

LC 2010017396

This guide to waterfowl hunting covers what to wear and pack, shooting strategies, the construction of duck blinds, gun safety, hunting permits and licenses, and other laws relating to hunting limits, seasons, and private and public property.

Includes bibliographical references

800 LITERATURE, RHETORIC & CRITICISM

803 Dictionaries, encyclopedias, concordances

Benet's reader's encyclopedia; edited by Bruce F. Murphy. 5th ed.; Collins 2008 1210p $60

Grades: 8 9 10 11 12 Adult **803**

1. Reference books 2. Literature -- Dictionaries

ISBN 978-0-06-089016-2

LC 2008-31430

First published 1948 under the editorship of William Rose Benet

This encyclopedia contains over 10,000 entries and covers world literature from early times to the present. Includes entries on authors, literary movements, principal characters, plot synopses, terms, awards, myths and legends, etc.

This is "an edifying staple for any literary library." Libr J

Brewer's dictionary of phrase & fable; edited by Susie Dent. 19th edition Brewer's 2013 1480 p $26.50

Grades: 6 7 8 9 10 11 12 Adult **803**

1. Reference books 2. Allusions 3. Mythology -- Dictionaries 4. Literature -- Dictionaries 5. English language -- Terms and phrases

ISBN 9780550107640

Provides definitions of typical phrases and words and explains their historical origins.

Lewis, Catherine

★ **Thrice** told tales; Catherine Lewis. Atheneum Books for Young Readers 2013 144 p. (hardcover) $16.99

Grades: 7 8 9 10 **803**

1. Literary style 2. Authorship -- Handbooks, manuals, etc. 3. Literature -- Terminology 4. Authorship

ISBN 1416957847; 9781416957843; 9781442460768

LC 2012010644

In this book, Catherine Lewis makes "use of the 'Three Blind Mice' nursery rhyme to illustrate nearly 100 elements of writing and literature—plot, dialogue, flashbacks, coincidence, and more. . . . Lewis expands on each term in brief 'Snip of the Tale' summaries and an extensive appendix." (Publishers Weekly)

"Three blind mice. See how they run—and how they take your writing to a new level. This clever review of literary terms will delight students and experts looking for a concise way to understand exposition and point-of-view or discern an epic from a bildungsroman." (Library Journal)

★ The **Oxford** dictionary of literary terms; [compiled by] Chris Baldick. 4th edition Oxford University Press 2015 392 p $18.95

Grades: 7 8 9 10 11 12 Adult **803**

1. Reference books 2. Literature -- Dictionaries 3. English language -- Terms and phrases

ISBN 9780198715443

First published 1990 with title: The concise Oxford dictionary of literary terms

"The bestselling Oxford Dictionary of Literary Terms provides clear and concise definitions of the most troublesome literary terms, from abjection to zeugma. It is an essential reference tool for students of literature in any language. Now expanded and in its fourth edition, it includes increased coverage of new terms from modern critical and theoretical movements, such as feminism, schools of American poetry, Spanish verse forms, life writing, and crime fiction." (Publisher's note)

808 Rhetoric and collections of literary texts from more than two literatures

Bauer, Marion Dane

A **writer's** story; from life to fiction. Clarion Bks. 1995 134p $14.95; pa $6.95

Grades: 7 8 9 10 **808**

1. Authors 2. Women authors 3. Authors, American 4. Children's authors

ISBN 0-395-72094-X; 0-395-75053-9 pa

LC 94-48800

"Drawing on her own experiences, the novelist examines the origins of inspiration and the subconscious drives that compel authors to write. She points out that many components of fiction—characters, settings, plot details—need not be autobiographical, yet the text does suggest that a story's meaning is directly linked to the unique experiences of its creator. . . . Bauer provides invaluable information for both writers and readers of fiction." Publ Wkly

Cornwall, Phyllis

Put it all together. Cherry Lake Pub. 2010 32p il (Super smart information strategies) lib bdg $27.97

Grades: 3 4 5 6 **808**

1. Report writing

ISBN 978-1-60279-643-0 lib bdg; 1-60279-643-2 lib bdg

LC 2009027806

"The appealing layout includes manageable paragraphs, a variety of engaging illustrations, and examples that clearly guide readers through each topic. In [this book], strategies include gathering resources, organizing information, and ways of presenting discoveries." SLJ

Includes glossary and bibliographical references

Flath, Camden

Freelance and technical writers; words for sale. Mason Crest Publishers 2010 64p il (New careers for the 21st century: finding your role in the global renewal) $22.95

Grades: 7 8 9 10 **808**

1. Authorship 2. Technical writing 3. Vocational guidance

ISBN 1-4222-1814-7; 978-1-4222-1814-3

LC 2010011419

"Each chapter divides information between general freelance writing and technical writing, with the latter painted as the way of the future. . . . Flath carefully details the highs and lows of self-employment, keeping readers abreast of freelancers' special concerns, including taxes, time management, networking, and health insurance. He also highlights which personality types might enjoy writing projects. . . . Overall, the information is helpful for anxious students concerned about job prospects." Booklist

Fletcher, Ralph

How to write your life story; [by] Ralph Fletcher. Collins 2007 102p $15.99; pa $5.99

Grades: 5 6 7 8 **808**

1. Authorship 2. Autobiography -- Authorship

ISBN 978-0-06-050770-1; 978-0-06-050769-5 pa

LC 2007010990

A guide to help write an autobiography

"Fletcher gives readers and educators many practical and supportive tips. . . . Interspersed within the text are interviews with Jack Gantos, Kathi Appelt, and Jerry Spinelli, along with passages from the author's own memoir." SLJ

How writers work; finding a process that works for you. HarperTrophy 2000 114p pa $4.99

Grades: 4 5 6 7 **808**

1. Authorship 2. Creative writing

ISBN 0-380-79702-X

LC 00-27573

Focuses on the skills and techniques necessary for good writing, with excerpts from established writers and samples of young people's work as examples

"The book makes youngsters feel good about their writing without making light of the work involved. . . . This is a useful resource." SLJ

Includes bibliographical references

Gaines, Ann

★ **Don't** steal copyrighted stuff! avoiding plagiarism and illegal internet downloading. [by] Ann Graham Gaines. Enslow Publishers 2008 192p il (Prime) $38.60

Grades: 7 8 9 10 **808**

1. Copyright 2. Plagiarism 3. Bibliographical citations

ISBN 978-0-7660-2861-6; 0-7660-2861-5

LC 2007-8370

"The first three chapters explain just what plagiarism is, the types of plagiarism, and what copyright and fair use are. Two chapters explain how to find sources, take notes properly, and construct a project or paper using proper citations in MLA format. . . . Every student should be required to read this. . . . Librarians and teachers who are looking for explanations of copyright and plagiarism and illustrative examples will find this book to be a good resource." Libr Media Connect

Includes bibliographical references

Gilbert, Sara D., 1943-

Write your own article; newspaper, magazine, online. by Sara Gilbert. Compass Point Books 2009 64p il (Write your own) lib bdg $33.26; pa $5.95

Grades: 6 7 8 9 **808**

1. Authorship 2. Journalism

ISBN 0-7565-3855-6 lib bdg; 0-7565-3945-5 pa; 978-0-7565-3855-2 lib bdg; 978-0-7565-3945-0 pa

LC 2008-13342

"There is much useful information provided. . . . [The book has] full-color photos, graphics, and tinted text boxes on nearly every page. [This is a solid selection] for aspiring writers." SLJ

Includes glossary and bibliographical references

Gutman, Dan

My weird writing tips; by Dan Gutman and illustrated by Jim Paillot. HarperCollins Publishers 2013 160 p. $5.99

Grades: 3 4 5 6 7 **808**

1. Language arts 2. English language -- Composition and exercises

ISBN 0062091069; 9780062091062; 9780062091079

LC 2012029985

This book by Dan Gutman "offers tricks for spelling hard words, understanding the difference between similar words like "its" and "it's," and conquering grammar stumbling blocks like commas and apostrophes. He also teaches readers how to write an engaging story, in line with the grades 2–5 Common Core goals for writing a narrative." (Publisher's note)

Harper, Elizabeth

Your name in print; a teen's guide to publishing for fun, profit, and academic success. [by] Elizabeth Harper and Timothy Harper. St. Martin's Griffin 2005 186p pa $13.95

Grades: 7 8 9 10 **808**

1. Authorship 2. Publishers and publishing

ISBN 0-312-33759-0

LC 2004-24675

The authors "offer chapters and features on a variety of subjects: writing outlets (such as local papers and blogs); article topics; workspaces; book publishing and agents; tips from pros; sample columns; [and] 'glances' at current teen writers. . . . This book will be a useful addition for most libraries." Voice Youth Advocates

Includes bibliographical references

Janeczko, Paul B.

★ **Writing** winning reports and essays. Scholastic Reference 2003 224p (Scholastic guides) lib bdg $16.95; pa $7.95

Grades: 5 6 7 8 **808**

1. Authorship 2. Report writing

ISBN 0-439-28717-0 lib bdg; 0-439-28718-9 pa

LC 2002-30543

Provides strategies for writing successful research reports and essays, including social studies reports, book reports, persuasive essays, personal essays, and descriptive essays

"A solid and useful resource." SLJ

Mack, James

Journals and blogging; [by] Jim Mack. Raintree 2009 32p il (Culture in action) $28.21; pa $7.99

Grades: 5 6 7 8 **808**

1. Blogs 2. Diaries 3. Weblogs

ISBN 978-1-4109-3406-2; 1-4109-3406-3; 978-1-4109-3423-9 pa; 1-4109-3423-3 pa

LC 2009000490

This "encourages readers to write as a way to express their feelings. It describes different types of journals and blogs. A page on Internet safety and the danger of downloading material encourages adult supervision. . . . Well organized and with bright, colorful photography, [this] introductory [title gives] readers good basic knowledge." SLJ

Includes glossary and bibliographical references

Miles, Liz

Writing a screenplay. Raintree 2009 32p il (Culture in action) $28.21; pa $7.99

Grades: 5 6 7 8 **808**

1. Drama -- Technique

ISBN 978-1-4109-3407-9; 1-4109-3407-1; 978-1-4109-3424-6 pa; 1-4109-3424-1 pa

This covers writing for "film and television. Plot, location, characters, dialogue, and mood are a few of the components discussed. . . . Well organized and with bright, colorful photography, [this] introductory [title gives] readers good basic knowledge." SLJ

Includes glossary and bibliographical references

Nobleman, Marc Tyler

★ **Extraordinary** e-mails, letters, and resumes; by Marc Tyler Nobleman. Watts 2005 128p il (F. W. Prep) $30.50

Grades: 7 8 9 10 **808**

1. E-mail 2. Letter writing 3. Résumés (Employment) 4. Electronic mail systems

ISBN 0-531-16759-3

This "builds a resume step-by-step, shows examples of different types of business letters, and addresses basic and not-so-basic netiquette. . . . [It is] laid out clearly and attractively, using bulleted lists, sample writings, and tables comparing examples of outstanding versus dull writing. The language is easy to follow, and the graphics and coloring enhances the books' readability." Voice Youth Advocates

Nuwer, Hank

To the young writer; nine writers talk about their craft. Watts 2002 111p il lib bdg $23 **808**

1. Authorship 2. Authors, American

ISBN 0-531-11591-7

LC 2001-24895

Nine writers, including a Hollywood screenwriter, a novelist, and a sportswriter, talk about their craft

"A concise, practical, and accessible guide. . . . A range of topics is discussed including the thrill of reporting, editing, storytelling, and writing for student publications, different audiences, and from personal experience. Also included are tips for aspiring writers. . . . This inspiring book offers a number of options for those considering the field." SLJ

Includes bibliographical references

Tadjo, Veronique

★ **Talking** drums; a selection of poems from Africa south of the Sahara. edited and illustrated by Véronique Tadjo. Bloomsbury Children's Books 2003 96p il map $15.95

Grades: 5 6 7 8 **808**

1. African poetry -- Collections

ISBN 1-58234-813-8

LC 2003-52173

A collection of traditional and twentieth-century poems from sub-Saharan Africa, written in or translated into English, that expresses the spirit and history of this region

"The contemporary and the traditional are both well represented in this lively anthology. . . . Illustrated with small, black-and-white folk-art drawings, the collection ranges widely, including poems of love, sorrow, and pride. . . . This [is a] fine resource for social studies and literature classes, which will also be great for reading aloud." Booklist

Includes glossary

Writing and publishing; the librarian's handbook. edited by Carol Smallwood. American Library Association 2010 189p (ALA guides for the busy librarian) pa $65

Grades: Adult Professional **808**

1. Authorship 2. Library science

ISBN 978-0-8389-0996-6; 0-8389-0996-5

LC 2009-25047

"This important writer's guide is readable from cover to cover or by bits and pieces and is a helpful and handy read for every librarian." Libr Media Connect

Includes bibliographical references

808.02 Authorship techniques, plagiarism, editorial techniques

Carter, Ally

★ **Dear** Ally, how do you write a book? Ally Carter. Scholastic 2019 336 p. $18.99

Grades: 7 8 9 10 11 12 **808.02**

1. Authorship 2. Creative writing

ISBN 1338212265; 9781338212266

LC 2019008162

"Whether you're writing for fun or to build a career, . . . [this book, by] Ally Carter is ready to help you make your work shine. With honesty, encouragement, and humor, Ally's ready here to answer the questions that writers struggle with the most. . . . It offers a behind-the-scenes look at how books get made, from idea to publication, and gives you insight into the writing processes of some of the biggest and most talented YA authors writing today." (Publisher's note)

"What Stephen King did for adult writers in On Writing (2000), popular YA novelist Carter does for aspiring teen authors in this guide to writing fiction. Chapters cover expected topics, such as getting started, world building, developing the plot, creating characters, and finding your process, while a Q&A format drives the content." Booklist

Gantos, Jack

★ **Writing** radar; using your journal to snoop out and craft great stories. Jack Gantos. Farrar, Straus & Giroux 2017 203 p. illustrations (hardcover) $17.99

Grades: 4 5 6 7 8 **808.02**

1. Advice literature 2. Creative writing 3. Diaries -- Authorship 4. Authorship -- Vocational guidance 5. Creative writing -- Vocational guidance

ISBN 9780374304560; 9780374304577

LC 2016057821

This book, by Jack Gantos, is a "funny and practical creative writing guide perfect for all kids who dream of seeing their name on the spine of a book. . . . [He] instructs young writers on using their 'writing radar' to unearth story ideas from their everyday lives. Incorporating his own misadventures as a developing writer, Gantos inspires readers to build confidence and establish good writing habits as they create, revise, and perfect their stories." (Publisher's note)

"A focused, fun, and uncommonly useful guide for young, aspiring writers." Booklist

Levine, Gail Carson, 1947-

Writer to writer; from think to ink. Gail Carson Levine. HarperCollins 2014 304 p. (hardback) $16.99

Grades: 5 6 7 8 **808.02**

1. Authorship 2. Creative writing

ISBN 0062275305; 9780062275301

LC 2014005858

In this book, author Gail Carson Levine "offers a behind-the-scenes take on writing and teaches you how to become a world-class author. Drawing from her popular blog, Gail answers readers' fiction- and poetry-writing questions and dives into how to make a story come alive. If you're interested in writing prose and poetry or just want to be a better and more rounded writer, this book will help you on your creative journey." (Publisher's note)

"Ella Enchanted author Levine offers writing advice and prompts, primarily for fiction writers. The chapters, mostly expanded from her blog, look in-depth at aspects of writing including large-scale character and plot concerns and more specific matters of style. A lengthy section focuses on poetry and its role in fiction. Levine's second book on writing (Writing Magic) takes budding authors' craft questions seriously." Horn Book

Myers, Walter Dean, 1937-2014

Just write; here's how. Walter Dean Myers. 1st ed. Collins 2012 161 p. (lib. bdg.) $17.99; (trade paperback) $7.99

Grades: 7 8 9 **808.02**

1. Authorship 2. Fiction -- Technique 3. Creative writing 4. Authorship -- Miscellanea

ISBN 0062203894; 9780062203892; 9780062203908

LC 2012931468

In this book, "[t]he third National Ambassador for Young People's Literature offers a how-to guide for young writing enthusiasts. . . . [Walter Dean] Myers tells about his own life and how he became a writer before moving on to the craft itself, offering advice on structuring fiction using a six-box outline and nonfiction with a four-box outline. Excerpts from his own notebooks and commentaries on his work with teen writer Ross Workman" are also presented. (Kirkus Reviews)

808.1 Rhetoric in specific literary forms

Fandel, Jennifer

Puns, allusions, and other word secrets; [by] Jennifer Fandel. Creative Education 2005 48p il (Understanding poetry) $21.95

Grades: 7 8 9 10 **808.1**

1. Poetics

ISBN 1-58341-341-3

LC 2004058229

This "deals with the importance of choosing the right word, the opportunity to create new words or strange combinations, point of view, and hidden meanings. An excellent choice of poems . . . enhances the discussion of these aspects of poetry. The text asks readers questions about their impressions and reactions to the various verses." SLJ

Includes bibliographical references

Rhyme, meter, and other word music; [by] Jennifer Fandel. Creative Education 2005 48p il (Understanding poetry) $21.95

Grades: 7 8 9 10 **808.1**

1. Poetics

ISBN 1-58341-342-1

LC 2004058230

This "title offers clear explanations and examples of perfect, slant, and internal rhymes. The various forms a poem can take, including haiku, limerick, and sonnet, are also described. . . . The selections will increase young peoples understanding and appreciation of this word music." SLJ

Includes bibliographical references

Fletcher, Ralph

Poetry matters; writing a poem from the inside out. HarperCollins Pubs. 2002 142p hardcover o.p. pa $4.99

Grades: 4 5 6 7 **808.1**

1. Poetics

ISBN 0-06-623599-5 lib bdg; 0-380-79703-8 pa

LC 2001-24640

"Chapters deal with images; creating 'music,' or sounds and rhythms; how to generate ideas for poems; the construction of the words on the page; and more. Tips on fine-tuning are also given. . . . Major poetic forms are defined, including haiku, ode, and free verse, and there is a section on ways to share your work. Interspersed are Fletcher's personal insights and interviews with three poets—Kristine O'Connell George, Janet S. Wong, and J. Patrick Lewis. . . . Since this thought-provoking book covers more of the internal, less-tangible aspects of poetry , it may be more suited for readers who have some experience with the genre." SLJ

Includes bibliographical references

The **Poetry** Friday Anthology for Middle School; Poems for the School Year with Connections to the Common Core State Standards (CCSS) for English Language Arts (ELA) Edited by Sylvia M. Vardell and Janet S. Wong. Pomelo Books 2013 284 p. $26.98

Grades: Professional **808.1**

1. Children's poetry 2. Common Core State Standards 3. Poetry -- study and teaching (elementary)

ISBN 193705778X; 9781937057787

Edited by Sylvia Vardell and Janet S. Wong, "The Poetry Friday Anthology is a series for K-5 and Middle School (6-8) designed to help teachers meet the Common Core State Standards (CCSS) in the English Language Arts (ELA). . . . Teaching tips for each poem provide step-by-step poetry lessons that address curriculum requirements. The poems . . . include examples of . . . metaphor and simile; personification; onomatopoeia; hyperbole; dramatic irony; and different forms." (Publisher's note)

Prelutsky, Jack

★ **Pizza,** pigs, and poetry; how to write a poem. Greenwillow Books 2008 191p il $16.99; pa $5.99

Grades: 4 5 6 **808.1**

1. Poetics

ISBN 978-0-06-143449-5; 0-06-143449-3; 978-0-06-143448-8 pa; 0-06-143448-5 pa

LC 2007-36738

"Along with easy-to-follow tips for creating verse, haiku, and concrete poetry, the reigning Children's Poet Laureate offers insights into his own thought processes, . . . glimpses of his childhood, and personal anecdotes. . . . Prelutsky tucks in more than a dozen examples of his own work, plus 10 two-and-part-of-a-third line 'poem starts.'" Booklist

Seeing the blue between; advice and inspiration for young poets. compiled by Paul B. Janeczko. Candlewick Press 2002 132p $18.99; pa $7.99

Grades: 7 8 9 10 **808.1**

1. Poetics 2. American poetry -- Collections

ISBN 0-7636-0881-5; 0-7636-2909-X pa

LC 2001-25882

"The letters are personal, friendly, and supportive. . . . A valuable addition to public and school libraries, with the potential for much classroom and personal use." SLJ

Wentworth, Marjory

★ **Out** of wonder; poems celebrating poets. Kwame Alexander with Chris Colderley and Marjory Wentworth ; illustrated by Ekua Holmes. Candlewick Press 2017 56 p. color illustrations $16.99

Grades: 3 4 5 6 7 8 **808.1**

1. Poetry -- Collections

ISBN 076368094X; 9780763680947

LC 2017931505

Coretta Scott King Illustrator Award (2018)

"Out of gratitude for the poet's art form, . . . author and poet Kwame Alexander, along with Chris Colderley and Marjory Wentworth, present original poems that pay homage to twenty famed poets who have made the authors' hearts sing and their minds wonder. . . . Mixed-media images by Ekua Holmes . . . complete the celebration and invite the reader to listen, wonder, and perhaps even pick up a pen." (Publisher's note)

"Each illustration captures not just the feeling of the poem but wakes readers up to life's excitements and small joys. Exemplary words and pictures make this a multicultural masterwork." Booklist

Wolf, Allan

Immersed in verse; an informative, slightly irreverent & totally tremendous guide to living the poet's life. [by] Allan Wolf; illustrated by Tuesday Mourning. Lark Books 2006 112p il $14.95

Grades: 5 6 7 8 **808.1**

1. Poetics

ISBN 1-57990-628-1

LC 2005024825

Contains advice, ideas, writing activities, and encouragement from a working poet for aspiring poets. Includes poems by a variety of poets from the unknown to the famous, including Langston Hughes, E.E. Cummings, Eve Merriam, and more

"This how-to guide—chock-full of examples—is sure to inspire and nurture young poets. The information is intensive without being overwhelming, wise without being didactic. Wolf's love of language is evident throughout." SLJ

Includes glossary and bibliographical references

808.2 Rhetoric of drama

Elish, Dan

Screenplays. Marshall Cavendish 2011 95p il (Craft of writing) $34.21

Grades: 7 8 9 10 **808.2**

1. Motion picture plays -- Technique

ISBN 1-6087-0501-3; 978-1-6087-0501-6

This "deftly explores the essentials of the form and function of storytelling for a visual medium. Beginning with an extensive history of filmmaking . . . young writers get a glimpse of the evolution of the writer's role. . . . Snippets of scripts and full-page film stills used to illustrate various stages of writing reinforce the thrilling idea that your work could come to life onscreen. . . . Writing exercises and a further-reading section are included." Booklist

Includes bibliographical references

Lawrence, Colton

Big fat paycheck; a young person's guide to writing for the movies. Bantam Bks. 2004 269p il hardcover o.p. $11.99

Grades: 7 8 9 10 **808.2**

1. Motion picture plays -- Technique

ISBN 0-553-13122-2; 0-553-13122-2 pa

"A lively, compelling, and concisely concrete guide for creative kids with big-screen dreams." SLJ

808.3 Rhetoric of fiction

Anderson, Jennifer Joline

Writing fantastic fiction; by Jennifer Joline Anderson. Lerner Publications 2015 56 p. illustrations (chiefly color) (lb : alk. paper) $33.32

Grades: 4 5 6 7 **808.3**

1. Creative writing 2. Authorship 3. Fiction -- Authorship

ISBN 9781467779081; 9781467782906

LC 2014044105

This book, by Jennifer Joline Anderson, "takes you through the steps of writing a story from beginning to end. Learn how to gather inspiration and develop a story's characters. Then visualize and organize your story's plot with a writing map. And after you've written a really rough draft, check out tips for revising your work. You'll also be inspired by unique writing exercises and storytelling insights from popular authors." (Publisher's note)

"Clearly presented and with a colorful design, this will work very well for middle-graders, but the advice is so good, older kids will find it extremely helpful as well. An especially inviting way to step into writing." Booklist

Includes bibliographical references and index

Bodden, Valerie

Creating the character; dialogue and characterization. [by] Valerie Bodden. Creative Education 2009 48p il (The art of creative prose) lib bdg $22.95

Grades: 6 7 8 9 **808.3**

1. Authorship 2. Creative writing 3. Characters and characteristics in literature 4. Fiction -- Technique

ISBN 978-1-58341-622-8 lib bdg; 1-58341-622-6 lib bdg

LC 2007-19611

"Young authors learn the importance of showing, rather than telling, when developing a character, as well as creating well-developed protagonists and antagonists, memorable minor characters, and natural-sounding dialogue. . . . Young writers who pick [this] up . . . will find valuable guidance." SLJ

Includes glossary and bibliographical references

Painting the picture; imagery and description. by Valerie Bodden. Creative Education 2009 48p il (The art of creative prose) lib bdg $22.95

Grades: 6 7 8 9 **808.3**

1. Authorship 2. Creative writing 3. Fiction -- Technique

ISBN 978-1-58341-623-5 lib bdg; 1-58341-623-4 lib bdg

LC 2007-18964

"Highlights the use of images that appeal to the senses, word choice, and figurative language. . . . Concludes with several suggested exercises. . . . Young writers who pick [this] up . . . will find valuable guidance." SLJ

Includes glossary and bibliographical references

Setting the style; wording and tone. [by] Valerie Bodden. Creative Education 2009 48p il (The art of creative prose) lib bdg $22.95

Grades: 6 7 8 9 **808.3**

1. Authorship 2. Creative writing 3. Fiction -- Technique

ISBN 978-1-58341-625-9 lib bdg; 1-58341-625-0 lib bdg

LC 2007-19609

"Encourages authors to find their own voice, explaining the difference between literary and direct styles and detailing the importance of rhythm, tone, and atmosphere in fiction writing. . . . Young writers who pick [this] up . . . will find valuable guidance." SLJ

Includes glossary and bibliographical references

Telling the tale; narration and point of view. [by] Valerie Bodden. Creative Education 2009 48p il (The art of creative prose) lib bdg $22.95

Grades: 6 7 8 9 **808.3**

1. Authorship 2. Creative writing 3. Fiction -- Technique

ISBN 978-1-58341-624-2 lib bdg; 1-58341-624-2 lib bdg

LC 2007-4198

"Covers the choice of a narrator and viewpoint, including multiple and unreliable narrators. . . . Young writers who pick [this] up . . . will find valuable guidance." SLJ

Includes glossary and bibliographical references

Brave the page; a young writer's guide to telling epic stories. by Rebecca Stern and Grant Faulkner ; introduction by Jason Reynolds. Viking 2019 288 p. $13.99

Grades: 5 6 7 8 9 **808.3**

1. Authorship 2. Creative writing

ISBN 0451480295; 9780451480293

"Partly a how-to guide on the nitty-gritty of writing, partly a collection of inspiration to set (and meet) ambitious goals, . . . [the book] is the go-to resource for middle-grade writers. Narrated in a fun, refreshingly kid-friendly voice, it champions . . . [National Novel Writing Month's] central mission that everyone's stories deserve to be told." (Publisher's note)

"Though specifically targeting young writers, this upbeat handbook is a wonderful instruction guide for writers of any age as well as a perfect text for any creative-writing classroom." --Kirkus

Farrell, Tish

Write your own fantasy story; by Tish Farrell. Compass Point Books 2006 64p il $31.93; pa $6.95

Grades: 4 5 6 7 **808.3**

1. Creative writing 2. Fantasy fiction -- Authorship

ISBN 0-7565-1639-0; 0-7565-1814-8 pa

LC 2005033654

"Full-color photographs, movie stills, and fun graphics enliven the [presentation]. . . . It's hard to think of a better way to hook emerging writers up with good advice about honing their skills." SLJ

Includes bibliographical references

Write your own mystery story; by Tish Farrell. Compass Point Books 2006 64p il $31.93; pa $6.95

Grades: 4 5 6 7 **808.3**

1. Creative writing 2. Mystery fiction -- Authorship

ISBN 0-7565-1641-2; 0-7565-1816-4 pa

LC 2005030730

"Full-color photographs, movie stills, and fun graphics enliven the [presentation]. . . . It's hard to think of a better way to hook emerging writers up with good advice about honing their skills." SLJ

Includes bibliographical references

Write your own science fiction story; by Tish Farrell. Compass Point Books 2006 64p il $31.93; pa $6.95

Grades: 4 5 6 7 **808.3**

1. Creative writing 2. Science fiction -- Authorship

ISBN 0-7565-1643-9; 0-7565-1818-0 pa

LC 2005030732

"Full-color photographs, movie stills, and fun graphics enliven the [presentation]. . . . It's hard to think of a better way to hook emerging writers up with good advice about honing their skills." SLJ

Includes bibliographical references

Giff, Patricia Reilly, 1935-

Writing with Rosie; you can write a story too. Patricia Reilly Giff. Holiday House 2016 73 p. (hardcover) $15.95; (ebook) $15.95

Grades: 3 4 5 6 7 8 **808.3**

1. Creative writing 2. Fiction -- Technique

ISBN 082343656X; 9780823436569; 9780823437504

LC 2015041844

In this book, author Patricia Reilly Giff "breaks down the process of writing fiction into steps, all while trying to cope with the constant distractions from her exuberant seventy-pound golden retriever puppy, Rosie. Citing examples from her award-winning novels she explains how to proceed with each step in chapter sections titled Can You See What I Did? Young writers can find the inspiration and tips they need to try their hand in sections called Your Turn." (Publisher's note)

"An excellent choice for writing classes or for individual inspiration." Booklist

Hanley, Victoria

★ **Seize** the story; a handbook for teens who like to write. [by] Victoria Hanley. Cottonwood Press 2008 213p il pa $15.95

Grades: 7 8 9 10 **808.3**

1. Authorship 2. Creative writing 3. Fiction -- Technique

ISBN 978-1-877673-81-8 pa; 1-877673-81-1 pa

A guide to fiction writing for teenagers with advice on approaching the young-adult market, and discusses dialogue, plot, and other related topics; and presents interviews with established authors such as T. A. Barron, Joan Bauer, and Chris Crutcher.

"Hanley uses examples from familiar novels and authors such as 'Harry Potter' and Stephenie Meyer's Twilight . . . to illustrate elements of writing. . . . This book is an excellent resource for creative writing classes as well as individuals." SLJ

Includes bibliographical references

Levine, Gail Carson

★ **Writing** magic; creating stories that fly. Collins 2006 167p $16.99; pa $5.99

Grades: 5 6 7 8 **808.3**

1. Authorship 2. Creative writing 3. Fiction -- Technique

ISBN 978-0-06-051961-2; 0-06-051969-4; 978-0-06-051960-5 pa; 0-06-051960-6 pa

LC 2006-00481

"Levine, best known for Ella Enchanted (1997), offers middle-graders ideas about making their own writing take flight. . . . Among the topics she covers are shaping character, beginnings and endings, revising, and finding ideas. . . . Each chapter concludes with writing exercises. . . . A terrific item to have on hand for writing groups or for individual young writers who want to improve." Booklist

Litwin, Laura Baskes

Write horror fiction in 5 simple steps; Laura Baskes Litwin. Enslow Publishers 2013 48 p. (Creative Writing in 5 Simple Steps) $23.93

Grades: 4 5 6 **808.3**

1. Horror fiction -- Authorship 2. Horror tales -- Technique 3. Horror tales -- Authorship

ISBN 076603836X; 9780766038363

LC 2010038776

This book by Laura Baskes Litwin, part of the Creative Writing in 5 Simple Steps series, "shows aspiring writers how to write a terrifying tale of horror. . . . A good horror story is like a good ride at an amusement park. Feeling scared without having to face real danger is exhilarating. The story builds with tantalizing ideas. The reader inches out on the coaster track, knowing the precarious drop is seconds away." (Publisher's note)

Includes bibliographical references, filmography and index

Mazer, Anne

★ **Spilling** ink; a young writer's handbook. by Anne Mazer and Ellen Potter; illustrated by Matt Phelan. Flash Point 2010 275p il $17.99; pa $9.99

Grades: 5 6 7 8 **808.3**

1. Authorship 2. Creative writing 3. Fiction -- Technique 4.

Authorship 5. Fiction -- Authorship
ISBN 978-1-59643-514-8; 1-59643-514-3; 978-1-59643-628-2 pa; 1-59643-628-X pa

"Two fine writers put their heads together and come up with an equally fine guide to their craft for beginners. . . . Mazer speaks to beginnings . . . while Potter tackles endings; and both have diverting things to say about everything that happens in between, whether it's the narrative voice or (eek) writer's block. [They are] always agreeable, practical, and commonsensical in their approach. . . . Their text is enlivened with sidebar features, personal anecdotes, and suggestions to readers for exercising their new skills. . . . Such devices, along with the authors' unfailing good humor, will go a long way to convincing their audience that writing can actually be fun! A notion that is nicely underscored by Phelan's engaging and always appealing illustrations." Booklist

Mlynowski, Sarah

See Jane write; a girl's guide to writing chick lit. by Sarah Mlynowski and Farrin Jacobs. Quirk Books 2006 191p il pa $14.95

Grades: 8 9 10 11 12 **808.3**

1. Authorship 2. Creative writing 3. Publishers and publishing 4. Fiction -- Technique
ISBN 1-59474-115-8

"Fun, inspiring, and organized in a clear and encouraging style, this book covers topics from what chick lit is to how to create believable characters, develop a plot, and set a tone. The authors discuss seeing a project through to the finish and getting it published. The writing style is quirky and the advice is sound." SLJ

Otfinoski, Steven

★ **Extraordinary** short story writing; by Steven Otfinoski. Franklin Watts 2005 128p il (F.W. prep) lib bdg $30.50; pa $9.95

Grades: 5 6 7 8 **808.3**

1. Authorship 2. Short story 3. Creative writing 4. Fiction -- Technique
ISBN 0-531-16760-7 lib bdg; 0-531-17578-2 pa

LC 2005006650

"In this excellent resource, specific ways to write different types of stories, project ideas, and resources are presented in such a way as to make short story assignments enjoyable. Readers are given many tips and practice activities in chapters that progress from gathering ideas to the final revision. Each section includes quotes from wellknown authors such as Edgar Allan Poe, Richard Peck, and Louis Sachar." SLJ

Includes bibliographical references

Rosinsky, Natalie M.

Write your own fairy tale; by Natalie M. Rosinsky. Compass Point Books 2008 64p il (Write your own) lib bdg $33.26; pa $6.95

Grades: 5 6 7 8 **808.3**

1. Creative writing 2. Fairy tales -- Authorship
ISBN 978-0-7565-3369-4 lib bdg; 0-7565-3369-4 lib bdg; 978-0-7565-3370-0 pa; 0-7565-3370-8 pa

LC 2007015720

This offers suggestions on how to write fairy tales, discussing settings, characters, viewpoint, plots, and style

Includes glossary and bibliographical references

Write your own myth; by Natalie M. Rosinsky. Compass Point Books 2008 64p il (Write your own) lib bdg $33.26; pa $6.95

Grades: 5 6 7 8 **808.3**

1. Creative writing 2. Authorship -- Myths
ISBN 978-0-7565-3372-4 lib bdg; 0-7565-3372-4 lib bdg; 978-0-7565-3373-1 pa; 0-7565-3373-2 pa

LC 2007011472

This offers suggestions for writing myths, discussing setting, characters, viewpoint, plots and style

Includes bibliographical references

Write your own tall tale; by Natalie M. Rosinsky. Compass Point Books 2008 64p il (Write your own) pa $6.95; lib bdg $33.26

Grades: 5 6 7 8 **808.3**

1. Creative writing 2. Tall tales -- Authorship
ISBN 978-0-7565-3376-2 pa; 0-7565-3376-7 pa; 978-0-7565-3375-5 lib bdg; 0-7565-3375-9 lib bdg

LC 2007012462

This offers suggestions for writing tall tales, discussing settings, characters, viewpoint, plots, and style

Includes glossary and bibliographical references

Stiefvater, Maggie

The **anatomy** of curiosity; by Tessa Gratton, Maggie Stiefvater, Brenna Yovanoff. Carolrhoda Lab 2015 296 p. (lb : alk. paper) $18.99

Grades: 8 9 10 11 **808.3**

1. Authorship 2. Creation (Literary, artistic, etc.) 3. Fiction -- Authorship 4. American fiction -- 21st century
ISBN 9781467723985

LC 2014046862

In this book, authors Tessa Gratton, Maggie Stiefvater, and Brenna Yovanoff "have assembled a new trio of vignettes. . . . Each short work sheds light on one aspect of writing: characterization, world-building, and the development of an idea." (School Library Journal)

"At its best, this is an accessible guidebook for creating fiction that illustrates the complexity of the process while offering practical tips for managing it." Kirkus

Includes bibliographical references and index

808.4 Rhetoric of essays

Orr, Tamra

★ **Extraordinary** essays. Franklin Watts 2005 128p il (F. W. Prep) $31; pa $9.95

Grades: 7 8 9 10 **808.4**

1. Essay 2. Authorship
ISBN 0-531-16761-5; 0-531-17576-6 pa

"This concise, appealingly designed writing guide offers practical advice to students on how to successfully complete essay assignments. Topics covered include choosing a topic, brainstorming, researching, crafting and defending a thesis statement, and revising." Booklist

Includes bibliographical references

808.5 Rhetoric of speech

Ryan, Margaret

★ **Extraordinary** oral presentations. Franklin Watts 2005 128p il (F. W. Prep) $31; pa $9.95

Grades: 7 8 9 10 **808.5**

1. Public speaking

ISBN 0-531-16758-5; 0-531-17577-4 pa

This offers advice on preparing oral presentations

This book provides "good, practical ideas for students." SLJ

Includes bibliographical references

808.8 Collections of literary texts from more than two literatures

Beware! R.L. Stine picks his favorite scary stories. HarperCollins Pubs. 2002 214p il $16.99; pa $5.99

Grades: 4 5 6 7 **808.8**

1. Horror fiction 2. Literature -- Collections

ISBN 0-06-623842-0; 0-06-055547-5 pa

LC 2002-18938

Stine "brings together 19 brief stories, folktales, poems, and cartoons from the likes of Ray Bradbury, William Sleator, Robert W. Service . . . Gahan Wilson, and Alvin Schwartz. . . . There's something in this diverse literary buffet for every taste—including enough genuine eeriness to make it a discomfiting choice for under-the-covers reading." Booklist

Classic horse stories; compiled by Christina Rossetti Darling and Blue Lantern Studio. Chronicle Books 2010 144p $19.99

Grades: 4 5 6 **808.8**

1. Horses 2. Literature -- Collections

ISBN 978-0-8118-6569-2; 0-8118-6569-X

LC 2010008550

"This compilation of stories, poems, and artwork celebrates the relationship between horses and their devotees. Darling pulls from a wide range of familiar, beloved material: excerpts from Steinbeck's The Red Pony, Farley's The Black Stallion, and Lewis's The Horse and His Boy join poetry from Shakespeare, Farjeon, and Stevenson. Varied paintings and illustrations from throughout the 20th century underscore the point that the book offers something for all tastes." Publ Wkly

Classic western stories; the most beloved stories. compiled by Cooper Edens. Chronicle Books 2009 140p il $19.99

Grades: 5 6 7 8 **808.8**

1. West (U.S.) 2. American literature -- Collections

ISBN 978-0-8118-6325-4

LC 2008009819

Stories, folktales, and poems with a western setting, including stories of Paul Bunyan, Pecos Bill, Indian legends, and tales of Lewis and Clark, among others.

"Colorful, often full-page, exquisitely produced illustrations by artists such as Frederic Remington, N. C. Wyeth, and Winslow Homer bring the words to life. Overall a visual delight, this stunning book is an excellent addition to art and literature collections." SLJ

The **Coyote** Road; trickster tales. edited by Ellen Datlow and Terri Windling; introduction by Terri Windling; decorations by Charles Vess. Viking Childrens Books 2007 523p il $19.99; pa $10.99

Grades: 7 8 9 10 11 12 **808.8**

1. Short stories 2. Literature -- Collections

ISBN 978-0-670-06194-5; 0-670-06194-8; 978-0-14-241300-5 pa; 0-14-241300-3 pa

LC 2007-12414

A collection of stories and poems about tricksters in all parts of the world by a variety of authors.

"This excellent collection is bound to find an audience among experienced readers of the genre but is attractive to less-able readers, as well, for the short, punchy stories and an always-engaging trickster character." SLJ

First kiss (then tell) [edited by] Cylin Busby. Bloomsbury Children's Books 2008 212p il $15.95; pa $8.95

Grades: 7 8 9 10 **808.8**

1. Kissing 2. Literature -- Collections

ISBN 978-1-59990-199-2; 978-1-59990-241-8 pa

LC 2007-42365

Twenty-five best-selling young adult authors share stories about their first kiss. Includes quotations, facts, advice, and illustrations.

This is an "entertaining collection. . . . These authors treat their own stories with the same freshness and respect with which they approach their YA novels. . . . Some stories are poems, one is a play, and a few are in comic form. . . . This is a good collection for browsing." Booklist

Flake, Sharon G.

You don't even know me; stories and poems about boys. Hyperion/Jump at the Sun 2010 195p $16.99

Grades: 7 8 9 10 **808.8**

1. Short stories 2. Boys -- Poetry 3. Boys -- Fiction 4. African Americans -- Poetry 5. African Americans -- Fiction

ISBN 978-1-4231-0014-0; 1-4231-0014-X

"This memorable collection of short stories and poems offers a glimpse into the urban lives of several African American boys. . . . Flake offers a vivid, unforgettable collection. . . . The voices ring true. . . . The stories and poetry are quite thought provoking." Voice Youth Advocates

Hip deep; opinions, essays, and vision from American teenagers. edited by Abe Louise Young. Next Generation Press 2006 164p pa $12.95 **808.8**

1. Teenagers' writings 2. American literature -- Collections

ISBN 0-9762706-2-5

"This collection of essays and poems by teens should inspire even the most reluctant writer to press on. By writing about their feelings on subjects ranging from frustration and anger to determination and renewal, these young people expose themselves from the inside out and launch themselves onto new paths." Voice Youth Advocates

I can't keep my own secrets; six-word memoirs by teens famous & obscure: from Smith magazine. edited by Rachel Fershleiser and Larry Smith. HarperTeen 2009 184p il pa $8.99

Grades: 7 8 9 10 **808.8**

1. Autobiographies 2. Teenagers' writings

ISBN 978-0-06-172684-2; 0-06-172684-2

LC 2009-14584

"The ruminations span from the haunting . . . to the funny . . . to the inspirational. . . . A razor focus is put on issues that hit youths the hardest. . . . It has just the right proportion of humor and heartbreak." Booklist

Jocelyn, Marthe

Scribbling women; true tales from astonishing lives. Tundra Books 2011 197p il $19.95

Grades: 6 7 8 9 10 **808.8**

1. Literature -- Biography 2. Literature -- Women authors 3.

Biography, Collective 5. Women authors -- Biography
ISBN 978-0-88776-952-8; 0-88776-952-7

Profiles women authors who have defied something that would have held others back, from societal convention to oppression, including Nellie Bly, Daisy Ashford, and Dang Thuy Tram.

"Liberally using each writer's own words, Jocelyn's lyrical prose takes us deep into their lives, but mostly into their spirits and courageous souls. Young readers can share the obstacles, joys, and/or sorrows each women faced," Kirkus

Includes bibliographical references

★ **Leaving** home: stories; selected by Hazel Rochman and Darlene Z. McCampbell. HarperCollins Pubs. 1997 231p hardcover o.p. pa $11.99

Grades: 6 7 8 9 10 **808.8**

1. Short stories 2. Youth -- Fiction
ISBN 0-06-440706-3

LC 96-28979

An international anthology that reflects the thoughts and feelings of young people as they make their way into the world. Authors represented include Amy Tan, Sandra Cisneros, Tim Wynne-Jones, and Toni Morrison

"The editors have varied the tones, the music, the voices, and the meanings of the pieces, which provide both humorous and heartbreaking stories of the meaning of adolescence." ALAN

Read all about it! great read-aloud stories, poems, and newspaper pieces for preteens and teens. edited by Jim Trelease. Penguin Bks. 1993 489p il pa $13.95

Grades: 8 9 10 11 12 **808.8**

1. Authors 2. Literature -- Collections
ISBN 0-14-014655-5

LC 93-21781

This is a collection of 52 selections of fiction, poetry, and nonfiction from newspapers, magazines, and books by such authors as Cynthia Rylant, Jerry Spinelli, Howard Pyle, Rudyard Kipling, Robert W. Service, Maya Angelou, Moss Hart, Pete Hamill, and Leon Garfield. Includes biographical information about the authors

Spinelli, Eileen

Today I will; a year of quotes, notes, and promises to myself. [by] Eileen & Jerry Spinelli; illustrated by Julia Rothman. Alfred A. Knopf 2009 un il $15.99; lib bdg $18.99

Grades: 5 6 7 8 **808.8**

1. Quotations 2. Conduct of life 3. American literature -- Collections
ISBN 978-0-375-84057-9; 0-375-84057-5; 978-0-375-96230-1 lib bdg; 0-375-96230-1 lib bdg

LC 2008047869

"The Spinellis turn their skills to inspiring readers with quotes and promises for every day of the year. There is a single-page entry for each day, and each one begins with a quote from children's literature. . . . Each quote is followed by an explanatory note. Each note is then summarized into a short promise on which readers can reflect. . . . The book covers a vast array of topics and themes, from serious to silly, and is inspiring and helpful." SLJ

808.81 Collections in specific forms

★ **Crush:** love poems. Word of Mouth Books/KA Productions 2007 72p pa $10

Grades: 8 9 10 11 12 **808.81**

1. Love poetry 2. Poetry -- Collections
ISBN 978-1-88801-840-0

"Alexander offers a cosmopolitan menu of tanka, haiku, long titles that lead into short first lines, verbal formulas that lead to sung discoveries, French phrases, prose poems, and poems written in Spanglish. The book is divided into three sections with various speakers, and a fourth section that includes poems by Sherman Alexie, Pablo Neruda, Nikki Giovanni, and the title poem, 'Crush' by Naomi Shihab Nye. . . . This well-crafted anthology will capture the interest of teens." SLJ

★ A **foot** in the mouth; poems to speak, sing, and shout. [edited by Paul B. Janeczko; illustrated by Chris Raschka] Candlewick Press 2009 64p il $17.99

Grades: 4 5 6 7 **808.81**

1. Poetry -- Collections
ISBN 978-0-7636-0663-3; 0-7636-0663-4

LC 2008-935581

"The poems in Janeczko and Raschka's collection . . . are not complacent, although plenty are funny and some are familiar. . . . Punchy collages flutter across airy white pages in loose visual arrangements; torn scraps of origami paper layer with fluid lines in tart color. Janeczko introduces the collection with the idea that 'Poetry is sound,' a pleasure to vocalize and memorize. . . . Readers will be emboldened to join in the 'song.'" Publ Wkly

Greenberg, Jan

★ **Side** by side; new poetry inspired by art from around our world. collected by Jan Greenberg. Abrams Books for Young Readers 2008 88p il $19.95

Grades: 8 9 10 11 12 **808.81**

1. Art -- Poetry 2. Poetry -- Collections
ISBN 978-0-8109-9471-3; 0-8109-9471-2

LC 2007-11973

This is an "anthology of accomplished poems inspired by artworks. . . . [Greenberg brings] together the work of poets and artists from around the globe. . . . The poems are grouped loosely into categories, defined in Greenberg's inspirational introduction. . . . Each spread features a poem in its original language, the English translation, and an artwork, usually from the same country or culture as the poem. With a few exceptions, the reproductions of the art, which ranges from ancient to contemporary work, are sharp and clear, and the moving, often startling poems invite readers to savor the words and then look closely at each image." Booklist

★ **I** feel a little jumpy around you; a book of her poems & his poems collected in pairs. [by] Naomi Shihab Nye and Paul B. Janeczko. Simon & Schuster Bks. for Young Readers 1996 256p hardcover o.p. pa $10

Grades: 7 8 9 10 **808.81**

1. Poetry -- Collections
ISBN 0-689-81341-4

LC 95-44904

A collection of poems, by male and female authors, presented in pairings that offer insight into how men and women look at the world, both separately and together.

"Though the gender counterpoint really plays little part in the juxtaposition, the pairings are piquant and provide a manageable way to start talking about a very large collection of poetry. An engaging marginal dialogue, taken from Nye's and Janeczko's collaborative fax correspondence, appears alongside the appendix and permits a revealing peek behind the scences. Highly readable notes from contributors are included, as is an index of poems and a gender-segregated index of poets." Bull Cent Child Books

★ **It's** a woman's world; a century of women's voices in poetry. edited by Neil Philip. Dutton Children's Bks. 2000 93p il $17.99
Grades: 7 8 9 10 **808.81**
1. Women poets 2. Poetry -- Collections
ISBN 0-525-46328-3
LC 99-88363

An anthology of poetry by twentieth-century women from around the world including, Sylvia Plath, Nigar Hanim, Sonia Sanchez, and Nellie Wong

"Beautifully reproduced black-and-white photos introduce each section. Overall, this book is dense, challenging, and provocative." SLJ

Janeczko, Paul B., 1945-

★ The **Death** of the Hat; A Brief History of Poetry in 50 Objects. selected by Paul B. Janeczko ; illustrated by Chris Raschka. Candlewick Press 2015 80 p. color illustrations $17.99
Grades: 3 4 5 6 7 **808.81**
1. Poetry -- Collections 2. Creation (Literary, artistic, etc.)
ISBN 0763669636; 9780763669638
LC 2013957308

This children's book, by Paul B. Janeczko, illustrated by Chris Raschka, focuses on "poems through history inspired by objects. . . . A book-eating moth in the early Middle Ages. A peach blossom during the Renaissance. A haunted palace in the Victorian era. A lament for the hat in contemporary times. Poetry has been a living form of artistic expression for thousands of years, and throughout that time poets have found inspiration in everything." (Publisher's note)

"Janeczko and Raschka's stellar fourth poetry collaboration, following A Poke in the I and other acclaimed titles, presents a chronological 'history' of the development of poetry, from the Middle Ages to the present. The highlighted poems are, ostensibly, about objects, but a cigar is rarely just a cigar. . . . Janeczko's substantial introduction gives an overview of poetry's evolution over the centuries, yet works like Lord Byron's 'A Riddle, on the Letter E' resonate powerfully on their own." Pub Wkly

Light-gathering poems; edited by Liz Rosenberg. Holt & Co. 2000 146p $15.95
Grades: 7 8 9 10 **808.81**
1. Poetry -- Collections
ISBN 0-8050-6223-8
LC 99-49231

Companion volume to Earth-shattering poems (1997)

"Poems were chosen for their ability to 'gather light,' some representing beauty, some joy, some fascinating imagery, and some the illusive light at the end of a dark tunnel. . . . Notable writers such as Robert Frost, Walt Whitman, Langston Hughes, Edna St. Vincent Millay, Emily Dickinson, and Allen Ginsberg share the spotlight with contemporaries such as Gary Soto, Kate Schmitt, Mary Oliver, Steven Dauer, and Henry M. Seiden." Voice Youth Advocates

Includes bibliographical references

The **new** Oxford book of war poetry; edited by Jon Stallworthy. Oxford University Press 2014 xl, 406 p.p
Grades: 8 9 10 11 12 Adult **808.81**
1. War poetry
ISBN 9780198704485; 9780198704478
LC 2013497520

"There can be no area of human experience that has generated a wider range of powerful feelings than war. Jon Stallworthy's classic and celebrated anthology spans centuries of human experience of war, from Homer's Iliad, through the First and Second World Wars, the Vietnam War, and the wars fought since. This new edition, published to mark the centenary of the outbreak of the First World War, includes a new introduction and additonal poems from David Harsent and Peter Wyton, among others. The new selection provides improved coverage of the two World Wars and the Vietnam War, and new coverage of the wars of the late twentieth and early twenty-first centuries." (Publisher's note)

Includes bibliographic references (pages 381-384) and index

Nye, Naomi Shihab

★ **What** have you lost? poems. selected by Naomi Shihab Nye; photographs by Michael Nye. Greenwillow Bks. 1999 206p hardcover o.p. pa $9.99
Grades: 7 8 9 10 **808.81**
1. Loss (Psychology) 2. Poetry -- Collections
ISBN 0-380-73307-2
LC 98-26674

The topic of loss is "explored by the one hundred and forty poets whose work is collected here in twenty-two unlabeled, thematically arranged sections. The poems focus on specific losses, including those we experience as we grow up, leave home or homeland, fall in love, grow old; what we suffer when someone dies suddenly—or slowly; what we're deprived of by acts of violence and anger; and losses accrued through travel and distance. The poets are all contemporary. {Index.} Young adult." (Horn Book)

In her "introduction, the anthologist-poet considers loss—its certainty, scope, and effect, and its ability to give rise to art. The topic is thoroughly explored by the one hundred and forty poets whose work is collected here in twenty-two unlabeled, thematically arranged sections. . . . The poets are all contemporary, with a dozen or so hailing from outside the United States." Horn Book

The **Oxford** book of story poems; [compiled by] Michael Harrison and Christopher Stuart-Clark. Oxford University Press 2006 175p il pa $18.95
Grades: 5 6 7 8 **808.81**
1. Poetry -- Collections
ISBN 978-0-19-276344-0 pa; 0-19-276344-X pa
LC 2007282711

First published 1990

This anthology contains "narrative verse by British and American poets, from traditional ballads such as 'Sir Patrick Spens' to contemporary poems such as Judith Nicholls' 'Storytime.' . . . The poets include Carroll, Keats, de la Mare, Kennedy, Lear, Lindsay, Longfellow, Noyes, Poe, Southey, and Tolkien. . . . A handy collection of story poems for reading aloud or alone." Booklist [review of 1990 edition]

★ **Poetry** speaks: who I am; poems of discovery, inspiration, independence, and everything else. Sourcebooks Jabberwocky 2010 136p $19.99
Grades: 5 6 7 8 9 10 **808.81**
1. Poetry -- Collections
ISBN 978-1-4022-1074-7; 1-4022-1074-4

This collection "aims at middle-grade readers with more than 100 strikingly diverse poems by writers including Poe, Frost, Nikki Giovanni, and Sandra Cisneros. The works are slotted together in mindful thematic order, beside occasional spot art. . . . Pairing a contemporary poem like Toi Derricotte's 'Fears of the Eighth Grade' alongside Keats's 'When I Have Fears That I May Cease to Be,' results in a refreshing lack of literary hierarchy that enables disparate works to build and reflect upon one another. An accompanying CD features recordings of 44 of the poems. . . . A sound and rewarding introduction to the joys of poetry." Publ Wkly

★ **River** of words; young poets and artists on the nature of things. edited by Pamela Michael; introduced by Robert Hass. Milkweed Editions 2008 298p il hardcover o.p. pa $18

Grades: 4 5 6 7 8 9 **808.81**

1. Nature poetry 2. Children's art 3. Children's writings 4. Teenagers' writings 5. Poetry -- Collections

ISBN 978-1-57131-685-1; 1-57131-685-X; 978-1-57131-680-6 pa; 1-57131-680-9 pa

"In 1995 Michael and Hass . . . cofounded the River of Words project, designed to connect students' art and poetry education to the natural world immediately around them. . . . The poems and pictures in this handsomely designed volume have been culled from yearly contests. . . . The works are startling, many of them dislocating and highly complex." Publ Wkly

Step lightly; poems for the journey. collected by Nancy Willard. Harcourt Brace & Co. 1998 99p hardcover o.p. pa $12

Grades: 7 8 9 10 **808.81**

1. Poetry -- Collections

ISBN 0-15-202052-7

LC 98-5228

A collection of poems celebrating the ordinary in an unordinary way, by such authors as Emily Dickinson, Theodore Roethke, and D. H. Lawrence

"Willard weaves an anthology in which readers can find happiness, insight, inspiration, and wisdom." SLJ

The **tree** that time built; a celebration of nature, science, and imagination. selected by Mary Ann Hoberman and Linda Winston; [illustrations by Barbara Fortin] Sourcebooks Jabberwocky 2009 209p il $19.99

Grades: 5 6 7 8 **808.81**

1. Nature poetry 2. Science -- Poetry 3. Poetry -- Collections

ISBN 978-1-4022-2517-8; 1-4022-2517-2

LC 2009032608

An anthology of more than 100 poems celebrating the wonders of the natural world and encouraging environmental awareness. Includes an audio CD that comprises readings of 44 of the poems, many performed by the poets themselves.

"Classic works by Walt Whitman, Emily Dickinson, Christina Rossetti, and the like, and selections from contemporary poets are included. . . . This handsome collection is especially appropriate for classroom use and instruction. . . . From the playful to the profound, the poems invite reflection and inspire further investigation." SLJ

Includes glossary and bibliographical references

★ **War** and the pity of war; edited by Neil Philip; illustrated by Michael McCurdy. Clarion Bks. 1998 96p il $20

Grades: 5 6 7 8 9 10 **808.81**

1. War poetry 2. Poetry -- Collections

ISBN 0-395-84982-9

LC 97-32897

"The selections, covering conflicts from ancient Persia to modern-day Bosnia, are by a wide variety of poets, from the well known (Tennyson, Whitman, Sandburg, Auden), to the obscure (Anakreon from ancient Greece and 11th-century Chinese poet Bunno). . . . The stark and simple scratchboard drawings are reminiscent of the Ernie Pyle illustrations from World War II and are as memorable as the best propaganda." SLJ

808.82 Collections of drama

Actor's choice; monologues for teens. edited by Erin Detrick. Playscripts 2008 131p pa $14.95

Grades: 6 7 8 9 10 **808.82**

1. Acting 2. Monologues 3. Drama -- Collections

ISBN 978-0-9709046-6-9; 0-9709046-6-5

LC 2007-50166

"This volume of highly entertaining monologues is gleaned from one-act and full-length plays published by Playscripts, Inc. . . . This is an excellent volume to help students prepare for competitions as well as to use in drama, speech, or English classes." SLJ

The **Book** of monologues for aspiring actors; [edited by] Marsh Cassady. NTC Pub. Group 1995 212p il pa $23.96

Grades: 7 8 9 10 **808.82**

1. Acting 2. Monologues 3. Drama -- Collections

ISBN 0-8442-5771-0

LC 94-66239

"The selections range from the classical Greeks to Sam Shepard and Oscar Wilde; they give YA's the opportunity to develop characters of like ages in many different settings. Several questions to probe the actors' imaginations appear at the end of each monologue." SLJ

Great monologues for young actors; Craig Slaight, Jack Sharrar, editors. Smith & Kraus 1992 3v v1 pa $11.95; v2-v3 pa ea $14.95

Grades: 8 9 10 11 12 **808.82**

1. Acting 2. Monologues 3. Drama -- Collections

ISBN 1-880399-03-2 v1; 0-57525-106-X v2; 1-57525-408-1 v3

These volumes provide an introduction and acting notes for monologues for men and women drawn from contemporary and classic works

★ **Great** scenes for young actors from the stage; Craig Slaight, Jack Sharrar, editors. Smith & Kraus 1991 256p 2v v1 pa $11.95; v2 pa $14.95

Grades: 7 8 9 10 **808.82**

1. Acting 2. Drama -- Collections

ISBN 0-9622722-6-4 v1; 1-57525-107-8 v2

Contains scenes from classic and contemporary plays. The selections, graded according to ability level, include a range of roles for men, women, and groups. Includes a brief synopsis of each play along with special notes

New audition scenes and monologs from contemporary playwrights; the best new cuttings from around the world. edited by Roger Ellis. Meriwether Pub. 2005 177p pa $15.95
Grades: 6 7 8 9 **808.82**

1. Acting 2. Monologues 3. Drama -- Collections
ISBN 1-56608-105-X

"This work presents a wide variety of scenes selected especially for performers aged 12 to 24. . . . Introductions to each scene are informative and were reviewed and approved with some reshaping by the authors. . . . A good choice for students who seek new ideas for drama, forensic, and writing classes." SLJ

Surface, Mary Hall

★ **More** short scenes and monologues for middle school students; inspired by literature, social studies, and real life. by Mary Hall Surface. 1st ed.; Smith and Kraus 2007 207p (Young actors series) pa $11.95
Grades: 6 7 8 9 **808.82**

1. Acting 2. Monologues 3. Drama -- Collections
ISBN 978-1-57525-560-6 pa; 1-57525-560-X pa
LC 2007281299

A collection of original scenes and monologues written especially for middle-school actors

"This volume stands out for its distinct voices, multicultural characters, and engaging scenes. The book is well organized. . . . This excellent book would be useful in a variety of classrooms including speech/communication, drama, English, and social studies." SLJ

Includes bibliographical references

★ **Short** scenes and monologues for middle school actors. Smith & Kraus 1999 183p (Young actors series) pa $11.95
Grades: 6 7 8 9 **808.82**

1. Acting 2. Monologues 3. Drama -- Collections
ISBN 1-57525-179-5
LC 99-52457

A collection of original scenes and monologues written especially for middle-school actors

"A welcome find for young actors in search of material for auditions." SLJ

Includes bibliographical references

808.83 Collections of fiction

Hague, Michael

The **Book** of dragons; selected and illustrated by Michael Hague. Morrow 1995 146p il hardcover o.p. pa $10.99
Grades: 5 6 7 8 **808.83**

1. Short stories 2. Fantasy fiction 3. Dragons -- Fiction
ISBN 0-688-10879-2; 0-06-075968-2 pa
LC 94-42958

This collection comprises an anonymous poem, "The Dragon of Wantley," and sixteen literary fairy tales and retellings of folktales and legends about dragons. The tales include "Kenneth Grahame's 'Reluctant Dragon,' Kan Pao's 'Li Chi Slays the Serpent,' J.R.R. Tolkien's 'Bilbo Baggins and Smaug,' the Grimms' 'Devil and His Grandmother,' and William H.H. Kingston's 'St. George and the Dragon.'" (Booklist) "Grades three to six." (SLJ)

"Excerpts from classic novels such as J. R. R. Tolkien's The Hobbit, C. S. Lewis's Voyage of the Dawn Treader, and short stories such as Kenneth Grahame's 'The Reluctant Dragon' are included. In addition, there are folktales from China, Italy, and Germany. Most of the heroes are men, but occasionally children are the only ones who can outsmart the dragon. . . . Hague's beautiful full-page watercolors reflect the different moods of the stories and the temperaments of the dragons depicted." SLJ

808.85 Collections of speeches

Lend me your ears; great speeches in history. selected and introduced by William Safire. Updated and expanded; W.W. Norton 2004 1157p $39.95
Grades: 8 9 10 11 12 Adult **808.85**

1. Speeches
ISBN 978-0-393-05931-1; 0-393-05931-6
LC 2004-13625

First published 1992

This "is a good addition for those . . . in need of modern speeches. With an excellent index." Libr J

808.88 Collections of miscellaneous writings

Alcorn, Stephen

A **gift** of days; the greatest words to live by. Atheneum Books for Young Readers 2009 115p il $21.99
Grades: 5 6 7 8 **808.88**

1. Quotations 2. Celebrities
ISBN 978-1-4169-6776-7; 1-4169-6776-1
LC 2007-48766

"Beautifully designed and imaginatively conceptualized, this volume presents 366 days and 366 quotations from famous people, tagged to the days they were born. Alcorn lays this out on each double-page spread with a stunning polychrome-relief block-print bordered with pattern on one leaf and, facing, a week of birthdays and quotes. These images are often brilliantly inventive. . . . Librarians, educators and historically minded kids will take much pleasure from looking up birthdays to see the associated wisdom from women and men across the ages." Kirkus

Bartlett, John

Bartlett's familiar quotations; a collection of passages, phrases, and proverbs traced to their sources in ancient and modern literature. by John Bartlett ; Geoffrey O'Brien, general editor. 18th ed. Little, Brown, and Co. 2012 lxi, 1438 p.p (hardcover) $50.00
Grades: 8 9 10 11 12 Adult **808.88**

1. Quotations 2. Quotations, English
ISBN 0316017590; 9780316017596
LC 2012019870

This book, in its 18th edition, presents a collection of quotations "from the times of ancient Egyptians to the present day." (Publisher's note) It "includes 2500 new quotes and more than 800 newcomers, from Julia Child to David Foster Wallace. Quotes have been culled to bring in more foreigners and women and more material from fiction and poetry." (Library Journal)

809 History, description, critical appraisal of more than two literatures

Bookmarked; teen essays on life and literature from Tolkien to Twilight. edited by Ann Camacho. Free Spirit Pub. 2012 215 p. $15.99

Grades: 6 7 8 **809**

1. Essays 2. Teenagers -- Conduct of life 3. Literature -- History and criticism 4. Life in literature 5. Literature and morals 6. Literature -- Appreciation 7. Teenagers -- Books and reading

ISBN 1575423960; 9781575423968

LC 2011043942

Edited by Ann Camacho, the book offers 50 essays in which "young people from a wide range of backgrounds reflect on how words from literature connect with and influence their lives, goals, and personal philosophies. Essays explore character building topics including suffering the death of a parent, facing a life-threatening illness, letting go of perfectionism, making friends, reaching goals, and grappling with questions of identity." (Publisher's note)

Campbell, Patricia J.

Campbell's scoop; reflections on young adult literature. [by] Patty Campbell. Scarecrow Press 2010 245p (Scarecrow studies in young adult literature) $40

Grades: Adult Professional **809**

1. Teenagers -- Books and reading 2. Young adult literature -- History and criticism

ISBN 978-0-8108-7293-6; 0-8108-7293-5

LC 2009-45563

"This resource represents the accumulated wisdom of a veteran librarian, author, speaker, critic, and pioneer of young adult services. Selected from several sources over many years, these essays and articles present a broad collection of critical writing. The articles are grouped into categories that include 'How We Got Here,' 'Trends and Tendencies,' 'Defining YA,' and 'Censorship Near and Far.' . . . Campbell's Scoop is a solidly useful professional title that weighs in on a diversity of topics. Unlike professional books that discuss and recommend specific YA titles, Campbell's Scoop is timeless. The information will not become dated and the breadth of the articles makes the collection relevant to a wide audience." Voice Youth Advocates

Includes bibliographical references

Hirschmann, Kris

Vampires in literature. ReferencePoint Press 2010 80p il (The vampire library) lib bdg $26.95

Grades: 7 8 9 10 **809**

1. Vampires in literature

ISBN 978-1-60152-134-7; 1-60152-134-0

LC 2010010104

Examines different ways vampires have been presented in literature from the first vampire novel in 1819 to the present-day.

"Energetic and surprisingly educational, this lively [book] seizes upon a zietgeist and takes it as far as possible." Booklist

Manglik, Gauri

Muslims in story; expanding multicultural understanding through children's and young adult literature. Gauri Manglik and Sadaf Siddique. ALA Editions 2018 xvi, 248 p.p illustrations $49.99

Grades: Adult Professional **809**

1. Children -- Books and reading 2. Children's literature -- Bibliography 3. Islam -- United States -- Bibliography 4. Muslims -- United States -- Bibliography

ISBN 9780838917411

LC 2018023567

This book, by Gauri Manglik and Sadaf Siddique, "is a timely and proactive approach to tackling . . . [Islamophobia], by engendering friendships and empathy through quality children's and young adult literature. Exposing children in their formative years to positive stories about Muslims can go a long way to creating a multicultural understanding by cementing ideas of tolerance, respect, and acceptance." (Publisher's note)

Includes bibliographical references

Sutton, Roger

A **family** of readers; the book lover's guide to children's and young adult literature. [by] Roger Sutton and Martha V. Parravano; foreword by Gregory Maguire. Candlewick Press 2010 350p il $22; pa $14.99

Grades: Adult Professional **809**

1. Children -- Books and reading 2. Teenagers -- Books and reading 3. Children's literature -- History and criticism

ISBN 978-0-7636-3280-9; 0-7636-3280-5; 978-0-7636-5755-0 pa; 0-7636-5755-7 pa

"This collection of essays from editors, reviewers, and authors emanates enthusiasm for books and reading. . . . Each section begins with an overview, followed by a selection of essays. The first chapter addresses the very smallest book lovers, and the last tackles the needs of young adults. Each chapter is followed by an annotated list of books. A complete bibliography and biographical sketches of the contributors are included in the end. . . . It should be required reading for every youth services librarian." Voice Youth Advocates

809.1 Literature in specific forms other than miscellaneous writings

Bodden, Valerie

Concrete poetry. Creative Education 2010 32p il (Poetry basics) $28.50

Grades: 5 6 7 8 **809.1**

1. Poetry -- History and criticism

ISBN 978-1-58341-775-1; 1-58341-775-3

LC 2008009156

This book describes concrete poetry's "history, characteristics, and variations. Many examples are provided as well as ideas for how children can write their own pieces. The information is accessible, and the writing is sufficiently lively to engage readers. The well-designed pages feature a variety of art reproductions from different literary eras and some photographs." Horn Book Guide

Includes glossary and bibliographical references

Haiku. Creative Education 2010 32p il (Poetry basics) $19.95

Grades: 5 6 7 8 **809.1**

1. Haiku

ISBN 978-1-58341-776-8; 1-58341-776-1

LC 2008-9158

Presents history and examples of the Japanese form of poetry called haiku.

"The information is accessible, and the writing is sufficiently lively to engage readers. The well-designed pages feature a variety of art reproductions from different literary eras and some photographs." Horn Book Guide

Includes glossary and bibliographical references

Limericks. Creative Education 2010 32p il (Poetry basics) $19.95

Grades: 5 6 7 8 **809.1**

1. Limericks

ISBN 978-1-58341-777-5; 1-58341-777-X

LC 2008-9159

This describes limericks' "history, characteristics, and variations. Many examples are provided as well as ideas for how children can write their own pieces. The information is accessible, and the writing is sufficiently lively to engage readers. The well-designed pages feature a variety of art reproductions from different literary eras and some photographs." Horn Book Guide

Includes glossary and bibliographical references

809.3 Fiction- criticism

★ **Brave** new words; the Oxford dictionary of science fiction. edited by Jeffrey Prucher; introduction by Gene Wolfe. Oxford University Press 2007 xxxi, 342p $29.95

Grades: 7 8 9 10 11 12 Adult **809.3**

1. Reference books 2. Science fiction -- Dictionaries

ISBN 978-0-19-530567-8; 0-19-530567-1

LC 2006-37280

This is a "dictionary of the language of science fiction based on historical principles. . . . Entries include part of speech, etymology, definition with cross references to related terms, usage status (e.g., historical, jocular, derogatory, obsolete), variant forms, and . . . dated citations and quotations illustrating the usage of the word over time." Libr J

Includes bibliographical references

810 Literatures of specific languages and language families

911: the book of help; edited by Michael Cart; with Marianne Carus and Marc Aronson. Cricket Bks. 2002 178p $17.95; pa $9.95

Grades: 8 9 10 11 12 **810**

1. Terrorism 2. September 11 terrorist attacks, 2001 3. American literature -- Collections

ISBN 0-8126-2659-1; 0-8126-2676-1 pa

LC 2002-4707

A collection of essays, poems, and short fiction, created in response to the terrorist attacks of September 11, 2001. Contributors include Katherine Paterson, Joan Bauer, Walter Dean Myers, Nikki Giovanni, Arnold Adoff, and Russell Freedman

This "stands out for its rich prose, its unusual reporting, its search for context, its reminder of wonders." NY Times Book Rev

Amend, Allison

Hispanic -American writers. Chelsea House 2010 128p il (Multicultural voices) $35

Grades: 7 8 9 10 11 12 **810**

1. Latino authors 2. Hispanic American authors 3. American literature -- Hispanic American authors -- History and criticism

ISBN 978-1-60413-312-7; 1-60413-312-0

LC 2009-46535

Profiles notable Hispanic Americans and their work in the field of literature, including Sandra Cisneros, Julia Alvarez, and Junot Diaz.

"This volume opens with a succinct yet thorough introduction to the historical and cultural context of eight authors. The overview explains the origins and uses of the terms Chicano, Hispanic, and Latino and sketches the histories of the nations where most Hispanic-Americans have their roots. Amend also identifies common themes in Hispanic-American literature such as language and family; however, she also notes each community's unique concerns. . . . Amend also suggests books by other Latino writers for further reading." SLJ

Includes bibliographical references

Aronson, Marc

Beyond the pale; new essays for a new era. Scarecrow Press 2003 145p (Scarecrow studies in young adult literature) $37.50

Grades: Adult Professional **810**

1. Books and reading 2. Young adult literature -- History and criticism

ISBN 0-8108-4638-1; 978-0-8108-4638-8

LC 2002-151299

"Teachers, librarians, and students of children's and young adult literature will appreciate the breadth and clarity of this book, as well as the impressive bibliographies of fantasy and of professional reading on it." SLJ

Includes bibliographical references

Crowe, Chris

More than a game; sports literature for young adults. [by] Chris Crowe. Scarecrow Press 2004 171p (Scarecrow studies in young adult literature) $45

Grades: Adult Professional **810**

1. Sports in literature 2. Young adult literature -- History and criticism

ISBN 0-8108-4900-3; 978-0-8108-4900-6

LC 2003-13561

"Readable and fascinating. . . . Categorizing and listing every sports-related book with teen appeal is an impossible feat, but the appendixes earn a medal for their impressive range. If only all professional reading could be so brainy and muscular." Voice Youth Advocates

Includes bibliographical references

Dude! stories and stuff for boys. edited by Sandy Asher and David Harrison. Dutton Childrens Books 2006 258p il $17.99

Grades: 4 5 6 7 **810**

1. Boys 2. American literature -- Collections

ISBN 0-525-47684-9

LC 2005025060

"These 18 original stories, plays, and poems by prizewinning writers range from entertaining to challenging and offer an array of characters and experiences. In Bill C. Davis' intimate, thought-provoking 'Family Meeting,' a boy whose stepbrother committed suicide discovers the value of life. Jamie Adoff's 'Twelve' is a rap poem about experiencing violence but still retaining hope. Jose Cruz Gonzalez's play Watermelon Kisses is an amusing, credible portrayal of brotherly love and squabbles. The selections, which include many well-written gems, will resonate with and also amuse middle-grade boys." Booklist

★ **Girls** got game; sports stories and poems. edited by Sue Macy. Holt & Co. 2001 152p $17.95
Grades: 6 7 8 9 **810**
1. Sports 2. Women athletes 3. American literature -- Collections
ISBN 0-8050-6568-7
LC 00-47297

A collection of short stories and poems written by and about young women in sports

"The lineup of authors includes heavy hitters such as Virginia Euwer Wolff and Jacqueline Woodson as well as some lesser-known talents. . . . This earnest and high-minded anthology can be dipped into or devoured in one sitting; however it is read, it should empower girls and guide them along their paths toward becoming strong, independent women." SLJ

★ **Growing** up Latino; memoirs and stories. edited with an introduction by Harold Augenbraum and Ilan Stavans; foreword by Ilan Stavans. Houghton Mifflin 1993 xxix, 344p hardcover o.p. pa $15
Grades: 6 7 8 9 10 **810**
1. American literature -- Hispanic American authors -- Collections
ISBN 0-395-66124-2
LC 92-32624

A collection of short stories and excerpts from novels and memoirs written by twenty-five Latino authors. Among the contributors are Julia Alvarez, Oscar Hijuelos, Denise Chávez, Rolando Hinojosa, and Sandra Cisneros.

Includes bibliographical references

★ **Guys** write for Guys Read; edited by Jon Scieszka. Viking 2005 272p il $16.99; pa $11.99
Grades: 6 7 8 9 10 **810**
1. American literature -- Collections
ISBN 0-670-06007-0; 0-670-01144-4 pa
LC 2004-28984

This is a collection of short stories, essays, columns, cartoons, anecdotes, and artwork by such writers and illustrators as Brian Jacques, Jerry Spinelli, Chris Crutcher, Mo Willems, Chris Van Allsburg, Matt Groening, and Neil Gaiman, selected by voters at the Guys Read web site.

This is "a diverse and fast-paced anthology . . . that deserves a permanent place in any collection . . . . There's something undeniably grand about this collective celebration of the intellectual life of the common boy." SLJ

Hill, Laban Carrick

★ **Harlem** stomp! a cultural history of the Harlem Renaissance. Little, Brown 2004 151p il hardcover o.p. pa $12.99
Grades: 7 8 9 10 **810**
1. Harlem Renaissance 2. African American arts 3. African Americans -- Intellectual life
ISBN 0-316-81411-3; 0-316-03424-X pa
LC 2002-73067

National Book Award Finalist: Young People's Literature (2004)

"The vibrancy, energy, and color of the Harlem Renaissance come to life in this gem of a book packed with poetry, prose, song lyrics, art, and photography created by some of the period's most influential figures. . . . Informative and highly entertaining, it deserves to be shelved in any library." Voice Youth Advocates

Includes bibliographical references

Hillstrom, Kevin

The **Harlem** Renaissance. Omnigraphics 2008 228p il map (Defining moments) $49
Grades: 7 8 9 10 **810**
1. Harlem Renaissance 2. African American arts
ISBN 978-0-7808-1027-3; 0-7808-1027-9
LC 2007-51132

"This an insightful, highly accessible subject primer for general collections." Libr J

Includes glossary and bibliographical references

Otfinoski, Steven

Native American writers. Chelsea House 2010 126p il (Multicultural voices) $35
Grades: 8 9 10 11 12 **810**
1. American literature -- Native American authors 2. Native American literature -- History and criticism
ISBN 978-1-60413-314-1; 1-60413-314-7
LC 2009-41334

"This title introduces 10 major Native American poets and writers, such as N. Scott Momaday, Louise Erdrich, James Welch, and Sherman Alexie. An overview preceding the author entries explains the impact of white settlers on the culture of Native Americans, as well as the utilization of Native American storytelling and traditions in their literature and development of their writings. . . . The easily accessible information and fascinating details of the lives and writings of these authors make this a useful resource for both informative reading and research." SLJ

Includes bibliographical references

Things I have to tell you; poems and writing by teenage girls. edited by Betsy Franco; photographs by Nina Nickles. Candlewick Press 2001 63p il hardcover o.p. pa $8.99
Grades: 7 8 9 10 **810**
1. Girls 2. Teenagers' writings 3. American literature -- Collections
ISBN 0-7636-0905-6; 0-7636-1035-6 pa
LC 99-46884

A collection of poems, stories, and essays written by girls twelve to eighteen years of age and revealing the secrets which enabled them to overcome the challenges they faced

Wachale! poetry and prose on growing up Latino in America; edited by Ilan Stavans. Cricket Publs. 2001 146p $16.95
Grades: 5 6 7 8 **810**
1. Latinos (U.S.) 2. Hispanic Americans 3. Bilingual books -- English-Spanish 4. American literature -- Hispanic American authors -- Collections
ISBN 0-8126-4750-5
LC 2001-47189

A bilingual collection of poems, stories, and other writings which celebrates diversity among Latinos.

"This collection would make a fine classroom text, great for reading aloud and for stimulating students from everywhere to write about their roots and celebrate their shifting places across borders." Booklist

Includes glossary and bibliographical references

Walking on earth and touching the sky; poetry and prose by Lakota youth at Red Cloud Indian School. edited by Timothy P. McLaughlin ; illustrations by S.D. Nelson ; with a foreword by Joseph M. Marshall III. Abrams Books for Young Readers 2012 80 p. $19.95
Grades: 6 7 8 **810**
1. Children's writings 2. Native American children 3. Poor children -- United States 4. Indian children's writings 5. American

literature -- Indian authors 6. Teton Indians -- Literary collections
ISBN 1419701797; 9781419701795

LC 2011036454

This book is an "anthology of work by children in grades five through eight." Poet "and teacher [Timothy P.] McLaughlin, after gradually connecting with his students at Red Cloud Indian School, provided them with creative-writing prompts that yielded sometimes-magical outcomes." The students, living in "the second-poorest county in the country," wrote on themes like the :Natural World" and "Family, Youth, and Dreams." (Kirkus)

Wilkin, Binnie Tate

African and African American images in Newbery Award winning titles; progress in portrayals. Scarecrow Press 2009 195p pa $40

Grades: Adult Professional **810**

1. Newbery Medal 2. African Americans in literature 3. Children's literature -- History and criticism
ISBN 978-0-8108-6959-2 pa; 0-8108-6959-4 pa

LC 2009017726

"The author has exhaustively examined all books that have won the Newbery Medal and been cited as honor books since the award's creation in 1922. Her purpose is to evaluate the representation of Africans and African Americans, and to describe how these groups are portrayed in each title's historical context.... Books with the most positive images are awarded three pluses, while books with marginal African-American characters are indicated with an 'M.'... An essential volume for scholars, teachers, and librarians." SLJ

Includes bibliographical references

WritersCorps

City of one; young writers speak to the world. from WritersCorps; foreword by Isabel Allende; edited by Collete DeDonato. Aunt Lute Books 2004 239p pa $10.95

Grades: 7 8 9 10 **810**

1. Teenagers' writings
ISBN 1-87996-069-9

LC 2004-45089

"This anthology celebrates the 10th anniversary of WritersCorps workshops, which bring creative-writing instruction to low-income kids from public schools, youth detention centers, halfway houses, and afterschool programs. More than 150 young people ranging in age from 9 to 23 write about their lives and the state of the world.... Poems about family, freedom, inner peace, self-identity, and the writing process round out this remarkable anthology." SLJ

810.8 American literature -- Collections

Rookie on love; Tavi Gevinson. Penguin Group USA 2018 288 p. $14.95

Grades: 7 8 9 10 11 12 **810.8**

1. Teenagers' writings 2. Interpersonal relations 3. Teenage girls -- Conduct of life
ISBN 0448493993; 9780448493992

This anthology, edited by Tavi Gevinson, is "about [love,] the heart's most powerful emotion.... Featuring exclusive, never-before-seen essays, poems, comics, and interviews from contributors like Jenny Zhang, Emma Straub, Hilton Als, Janet Mock, John Green, Rainbow Rowell, Gabourey Sidibe, Mitski, Alessia Cara, Etgar Keret, Margo Jefferson, Sarah Manguso, Durga Chew-Bose, and many more!" (Publisher's note)

811 American poetry

Adoff, Jaime

The **song** shoots out of my mouth; illustrated by Martin French. Dutton Children's Bks. 2002 48p il $17.99

Grades: 7 8 9 **811**

1. Music -- Poetry 2. Poetry -- By individual authors
ISBN 0-525-46949-4

LC 2002-284232

This is a "collection of 24 poems. Though free in form and diverse in mood and tone, all are about music, from Hip Hop to classical and from reggae to gospel. Another common element is the energy underscoring Adoff's language, which invites readers to move to the rhythm of the words.... All shine with the poet's obvious love of music and musicians." Booklist

Includes glossary and discography

African American Poetry; edited by Arnold Rampersad and Marcellus Blount ; illustrated by Karen Barbour. Sterling Pub Co Inc. 2013 48 p. ill. (hardcover) $14.95

Grades: 3 4 5 6 7 **811**

1. American poetry -- Asian American authors
ISBN 1402716893; 9781402716898

This book of poetry by African American authors"introduces 27 poets from the days of Phillis Wheatley to well-established poets writing in the 21st century. A four-page introduction outlines historical periods and influences. Presented chronologically, the entries begin with a paragraph describing the poet's life and work. Paul Laurence Dunbar, Countee Cullen, Langston Hughes, Lucille Clifton, Maya Angelou, and others are joined by George Moses Horton...and others." (School Library Journal)

Alexander, Elizabeth

Miss Crandall's School for Young Ladies and Little Misses of Color; poems. by Elizabeth Alexander and Marilyn Nelson; pictures by Floyd Cooper. Wordsong 2007 47p il $17.95

Grades: 7 8 9 10 **811**

1. Teachers 2. Abolitionists 3. Schools -- Poetry 4. African Americans -- Poetry 5. Poetry -- By individual authors
ISBN 978-1-59078-456-3; 1-59078-456-1

LC 2006-38985

"Twenty-four sonnets tell the story of Prudence Crandall and her efforts to educate young African-American women in Canterbury, CT, 1833-1834.... The sonnet format is challenging but compelling.... There are empty spaces in the pictures just as the language of the poetry leaves openness for readers' interpretation. A heartfelt, unusual presentation." SLJ

★ **America** at war; poems. selected by Lee Bennett Hopkins; illlustrated by Stephen Alcorn. Margaret K. McElderry Books 2008 84p il $21.99

Grades: 5 6 7 8 **811**

1. War poetry 2. American poetry -- Collections 3. United States -- History -- Poetry
ISBN 978-1-4169-1832-5; 1-4169-1832-9

LC 2006-08723

"This handsome anthology, expressing Americans' varied experience during wartime, is a fine selection of poems accessible to children. ... The poems will touch readers with their sharp poignancy and undeniable power. Throughout the well-designed book, the expressive watercolor artwork enhances the poetry." Booklist

Angelou, Maya

★ **Maya** Angelou; edited by Edwin Graves Wilson; illustrated by Jerome Lagarrigue. Sterling Pub. 2007 48 p. col. ill. (Poetry for young people) (hardcover) $14.95

Grades: 4 5 6 7 **811**

1. African American women 2. Poets, American 3. African Americans -- Poetry 4. Poetry -- By individual authors

ISBN 9781402720239; 1402720238

LC 2006013803

"Wilson's introduction . . . addresses how Angelou's life has informed her imagination. . . . Twenty-five poems show her concern with the African-American experience. . . . Dignity, pride, and resiliancy are at this collection's core. . . . Footnotes offer definitions of colloquialisms and difficult words. Lagarrigue's painterly artwork uses golds, greens, and violets to capture the luminescent quality of the poems. . . . This [is a] distinguished work." SLJ

Atkins, Jeannine

★ **Borrowed** names; poems about Laura Ingalls Wilder, Madam C. J. Walker, Marie Curie, and their daughters. Henry Holt & Co. 2010 209p il $16.99

Grades: 6 7 8 9 10 **811**

1. Authors 2. Chemists 3. Novelists 4. Physicists 5. Entrepreneurs 6. Philanthropists 7. Cosmeticians 8. Western writers 9. College teachers 10. Children's authors 11. Nonfiction writers 12. Patrons of the arts 13. Young adult authors 14. Nobel laureates for physics 15. Cosmetics industry executives 16. Nobel laureates for chemistry 17. Poetry -- By individual authors 18. Mother-daughter relationship -- Poetry

ISBN 978-0-8050-8934-9; 0-8050-8934-9

LC 2009-23446

"In 1867, three women who achieved great success were born: writer Laura Ingalls Wilder, entrepreneur Madam C. J. Walker, and scientist Marie Curie. All three had complicated relationships with their daughters, relationships that Atkins explores in this unusual volume of poetry. . . . In vivid scenes written with keen insight and subtle imagery, the poems offer a strong sense of each daughter's personality as well as the tensions and ties they shared with their notable mothers." Booklist

Bernier-Grand, Carmen T.

★ **Diego**; bigger than life. illustrated by David Diaz. Marshall Cavendish Children 2009 64p il $18.99

Grades: 8 9 10 11 12 **811**

1. Artists 2. Painters 3. Poetry -- By individual authors

ISBN 978-0-7614-5383-3; 0-7614-5383-0

LC 2007-13761

ALA ALSC Belpre Author Medal Honor Book (2010)

ALA ALSC Belpre Illustrator Medal Honor Book (2010)

This is a "well written and beautifully illustrated volume. . . . Almost all written in first-person from the artist's point of view, the poems convey information succinctly within a context of colorful narrative and clearly expressed emotion. . . . Apart from four reproductions of Rivera's paintings and one photo of the artist, the illustrations are mixed-media pictures by Diaz. Depicting Rivera and his world, these iconic images glow with warmth, light, and color." Booklist

Includes bibliographical references

★ **Frida**; viva la vida = long live life. by Carmen T. Bernier-Grand. Marshall Cavendish Children 2007 64 p. ill. $14.24

Grades: 8 9 10 11 12 **811**

1. Artists 2. Painters 3. Poetry -- By individual authors 4. Painters -- Mexico -- Biography

ISBN 9780761453369

LC 2006014479

In this book, "Frida Kahlo, a native of Mexico, is described . . . in biographical poems accompanied by her own artwork. Both text and images reveal the anguish and joy of her two marriages to muralist Diego Rivera, her life-long suffering from a crippling bus accident, and her thirst for life, even as she tasted death. . . . Back matter includes excerpts from Frida's diary and letters, a prose biography, a chronology of the artist's life, a glossary of Spanish words, sources, and notes." (Publisher's note)

"Bernier-Grand introduces a famous life with lyrical free-verse poems. Nearly every double-page spread pairs a well-reproduced painting by Frida Kahlo with an original poem that defines turning points in the artist's life. Bernier-Grand's words expertly extend the autobiographical imagery so evident in the art." Booklist

Includes bibliographical references (p. 61).

Borus, Audrey

A **student's** guide to Emily Dickinson. Enslow Publishers 2005 152p il (Understanding literature) $27.93

Grades: 7 8 9 10 **811**

1. Poets 2. Authors

ISBN 0-7660-2285-4

LC 2004-18098

"A short discussion of Dickinson's life and times is followed by a chapter on how to read and analyze her poems, which would be particularly useful for students reading her work for the first time. Subsequent chapters focus on particular themes in the poems such as death and eternity, truth, faith and reality, the natural world, and the influence of the Civil War." SLJ

Includes bibliographical references

Bryan, Ashley

Ashley Bryan's Puppets; Making Something from Everything. Ashley Bryan. Simon & Schuster 2014 80 p. $19.99

Grades: PreK K 1 2 3 4 5 6 **811**

1. Poetry 2. Waste products 3. Puppets and puppet plays 4. Children's poetry 5. Puppets -- Poetry 6. Found objects -- Poetry

ISBN 1442487283; 9781442487284

In this book, "storyteller and creator Ashley Bryan reveals the vibrant spirit of found objects in this . . . treasury of poetry and puppets. . . . For decades, Ashley has walked up and down the beach, stopping to pick up sea glass, weathered bones, a tangle of fishing net, an empty bottle, a doorknob. Treasure. And then, with glue and thread and paint and a sprinkling of African folklore, Ashley breathes new life into these materials." (Publisher's note)

"—Award-winning author and illustrator Bryan has combined his love of art and poetry in this captivating and beautifully designed book... Traditional African themes abound as the characters introduce themselves through their poems, and readers are invited into the world of puppets and poetry. Bryan has truly created a book for all to treasure.—" SLJ

Bulion, Leslie

At the sea floor cafe; odd ocean critter poems. written by Leslie Bulion; illustrated by Leslie Evans. Peachtree Publishers 2011 45p il $14.95

Grades: 5 6 7 8 **811**

1. Marine animals -- Poetry 2. Poetry -- By individual authors

ISBN 978-1-56145-565-2; 1-56145-565-2

LC 2010026691

"Using complex poetry forms and cleverly constructed lines, Bulion plays tribute to sea creatures. . . . Evans's spare, well-placed hand-colored linoleum block prints hold their own without overwhelming the text." Horn Book Guide

Burleigh, Robert

★ **Hoops**; illustrated by Stephen T. Johnson. Harcourt Brace & Co. 1997 un il hardcover o.p. pa $6

Grades: 6 7 8 9 **811**

1. Basketball -- Poetry 2. Poetry -- By individual authors

ISBN 0-15-201450-0; 0-15-216380-8 pa

LC 96-18440

Illustrations and poetic text describe the movement and feel of the game of basketball

"Burleigh's staccato text is well matched by Johnson's dynamic pastels. Muted colors and a strong sense of motion as bodies leap and lift, pounce and poke, aptly complement the words." SLJ

★ **Cool** salsa; bilingual poems on growing up Latino in the United States. edited by Lori M. Carlson; introduction by Oscar Hijuelos. Holt & Co. 1994 xx, 123p il hardcover o.p. pa $6.99

Grades: 5 6 7 8 9 10 **811**

1. Bilingual books -- English-Spanish 2. American poetry -- Hispanic American authors -- Collections

ISBN 0-8050-3135-9; 978-0-449-70436-3 pa; 0-449-70436-X pa

LC 93-45798

"This collection presents poems by 29 Mexican-American, Cuban-American, Puerto Rican, and other Central and South American poets, including Sandra Cisneros, Luis J. Rodriguez, Pat Mora, Gary Soto, Ana Castillo, Oscar Hijuelos, Ed J. Vega, Judith Ortiz-Cofer, and other Latino writers both contemporary and historical. Brief biographical notes on the authors are provided. All the poems deal with experiences of teenagers." Book Rep

Crisler, Curtis L.

★ **Tough** boy sonatas; illustrations by Floyd Cooper. Wordsong 2007 86p il $19.95

Grades: 8 9 10 11 12 **811**

1. Indiana -- Poetry 2. African Americans -- Poetry 3. City and town life -- Poetry 4. Poetry -- By individual authors

ISBN 978-1-932425-77-2; 1-932425-77-2

LC 2006-11836

"Crisler presents a collection of potent, hard-hitting poems about growing up in Gary, Indiana. Written mostly in voices of young African American males, the poems evoke the grit and ash of crumbling, burned-out streets as well as the realities of hardscrabble life. . . . Written with skillful manipulation of sound, rhythm, and form, the poems are filled with sophisticated imagery and graphic words . . . and Cooper's illustrations extend . . . the poems' impact. Created in sooty black and gray, the powerful drawings are mostly portraits of anguished young men." Booklist

Dickinson, Emily, 1830-1886

My letter to the world and other poems; with illustrations by Isabelle Arsenault. KCP Poetry 2008 un il (Visions in poetry) $17.95; pa $9.95

Grades: 7 8 9 10 11 12 **811**

1. Poets 2. Authors 3. Poetry -- By individual authors

ISBN 1-55453-103-9; 1-55453-339-2 pa; 978-1-55453-103-5; 978-1-55453-339-8 pa

This is an illustrated edition of seven Emily Dickinson poems. "Age ten and up." (N Y Times Book Rev)

"The long final biographical note about the introvert and recluse who gloried in being 'Nobody' will take readers back to the poetry, which speaks as a 'letter to the world,' as will the clear analysis of the mixed-media illustrations, in which Arsenault links the poet's repeated images of isolation with her intense connections to nature. . . . Dickinson's exploration of the difference between loneliness and rich solitude will resonate with teens." Booklist

Engle, Margarita

Soaring earth; a companion memoir to Enchanted air. Margarita Engle. Atheneum Books for Young Readers 2019 157 p. (hardback) $18.99

Grades: 8 9 10 11 12 **811**

1. Women authors 2. Narrative poetry 3. Cuban Americans -- Biography 4. Women authors, American -- 20th century -- Biography

ISBN 9781534429550; 9781534429536

LC 2018003603

In this book, author "Margarita Engle recounts her teenage years during the turbulent 1960s. . . . Engle's childhood straddled two worlds: the . . . island of Cuba and the . . . dream-soaked reality of Los Angeles. But the revolution has transformed Cuba into a mystery of impossibility, . . . then the shock waves of war reach America. . . . Amid the challenges of adolescence and a world steeped in conflict, Margarita finds hope . . . and love in the most unexpected of places." (Publisher's note)

"The author's evocative language, vivid imagery, and authentic portrayal will engage teens. Her bumpy and circuitous road filled with failures, homelessness, and eventual resolution and academic success will encourage young adults on their own paths." SLJ.

★ The **surrender** tree; poems of Cuba's struggle for freedom. Henry Holt and Co. 2008 169p $17.95

Grades: 7 8 9 10 11 12 **811**

1. Novels in verse 2. Cuba -- Fiction

ISBN 978-0-8050-8674-4; 0-8050-8674-9

LC 2007-27591

A Newbery Medal honor book, 2009

Pura Belpre Author Award, 2009

This "book is written in clear, short lines of stirring free verse. . . . [The author] draws on her own Cuban American roots . . . to describe those who fought in the nineteenth-century Cuban struggle for independence. At the center is Rosa, a traditional healer, who nurses runaway slaves and deserters in caves and other secret hideaways. . . . Many readers will be caught by the compelling narrative voices and want to pursue the historical accounts in Engle's bibliography." Booklist

Fields, Terri

After the death of Anna Gonzales. Holt & Co. 2002 100p $16.95

Grades: 7 8 9 10 **811**

1. Suicide -- Poetry 2. Poetry -- By individual authors

ISBN 0-8050-7127-X

LC 2002-24074

Poems written in the voices of forty-seven people, including students, teachers, and other school staff, record the aftermath of a high school student's suicide and the preoccupations of teen life

"A short book, easily read, which should generate serious thought and discussion." BAYA Book Rev

Fleischman, Paul

★ **Big** talk; poems for four voices. illustrated by Beppe Giacobbe. Candlewick Press 2000 44p il $17.99; pa $7.99

Grades: 4 5 6 7 **811**

1. Poetry -- By individual authors

ISBN 0-7636-0636-7; 0-7636-3805-6 pa

LC 99-46882

A collection of poems to be read aloud by four people, with color-coded text to indicate which lines are read by which readers

"Each poem is more demanding, and more rewarding, than the last. Giacobbe highlights the humor in strips of vignettes that run along the bottom of the page. This is 'toe-tapping, tongue-flapping fun.'" Horn Book Guide

★ **I** am phoenix: poems for two voices; illustrated by Ken Nutt. Harper & Row 1985 51p il hardcover o.p. pa $5.99

Grades: 4 5 6 7 **811**

1. Birds -- Poetry 2. Poetry -- By individual authors

ISBN 0-06-446092-4 pa

LC 85-42615

A collection of poems about birds to be read aloud by two voices

"Devotés of the almost lost art of choral reading should be among the first to appreciate this collection. . . . Printed in script form, the selections . . . have a cadenced pace and dignified flow; their combination of imaginative imagery and realistic detail is echoed by the combination of stylized fantasy and representational drawings in the black and white pictures, all soft line and strong nuance." Bull Cent Child Books

★ **Joyful** noise: poems for two voices; illustrated by Eric Beddows. Harper & Row 1988 44p il $15.99; lib bdg $16.89; pa $5.99

Grades: 4 5 6 7 **811**

1. Insects -- Poetry 2. Poetry -- By individual authors

ISBN 0-06-021852-5; 0-06-021853-3 lib bdg; 0-06-446093-2 pa

LC 87-45280

Awarded the Newbery Medal, 1989

"There are fourteen poems in the handsomely designed volume, with stylish endpapers and wonderfully interpretive black-and-white illustrations. Each selection is a gem, polished perfection." Horn Book

Forbes, Robert L.

Beast Friends Forever; by Robert L. Forbes ; illustrated by Ronald Searle. Penguin Group USA 2013 80 p. (hardcover) $19.95

Grades: 4 5 6 7 **811**

1. Animal courtship 2. Animals -- Poetry 3. Animals

ISBN 1590208080; 9781590208083

In this book of children's poetry by Robert Forbes, "animal courtship is infused with quirky human characteristics and some sneaky social commentary. Readers meet Lancelot the Ocelot, doing time for 'his romance turned to tragedy, ending in a crime.' And Babette the Skunk, having studied with 'Parisian perfumers,' has fashioned a new scent, 'packaged in black and called "In-d-scent,"/It's sure to enflame any white-striped gent.'" (School Library Journal)

Forler, Nan

Winterberries and apple blossoms; reflections and flavors of a Mennonite year. paintings by Peter Etril Snyder. Tundra Books 2011 39p il $22.95

Grades: 4 5 6 7 **811**

1. Cooking 2. Months -- Poetry 3. Mennonites -- Poetry 4. Poetry -- By individual authors

ISBN 978-1-77049-254-7; 1-77049-254-2

With a poem for every month of the year, young Naomi introduces us to her family and hosts a journey through the seasonal rhythms of her rural Mennonite community. Includes a recipe for each month of the year.

This includes "12 evocative poems. . . . Snyder . . . contributes smudgy, sunlit acrylic scenes that convey a close-knit family that works, plays, and prays together. Along with Forler's graceful verse, and recipes for every season, it all adds up to a warm portrait of a community seldom found in the spotlight." Publ Wkly

Frost, Robert

★ **Robert** Frost; edited by Gary D. Schmidt; illustrated by Henri Sorensen. Sterling 1994 48p il (Poetry for young people) $14.95; pa $6.95

Grades: 4 5 6 7 **811**

1. Poetry -- By individual authors

ISBN 0-8069-0633-2; 1-4027-5475-2 pa

LC 94-11161

This volume "contains a three-page overview of the poet's life, 29 poems selected and arranged around the seasons of the year, brief and apt commentaries on each, and a useful index of titles and subject matter. The realistic watercolor illustrations capture the delicate beauty of a New England spring and the glory of fall while still suggesting the around-the-corner chill of winter, a disquiet echoing throughout much of Frost's poetry." SLJ

George, Kristine O'Connell

★ **Swimming** upstream; middle school poems. illustrated by Debbie Tilley. Clarion Bks. 2002 79p il $14

Grades: 5 6 7 8 **811**

1. Schools -- Poetry 2. Poetry -- By individual authors

ISBN 0-618-15250-4

LC 2002-2746

A collection of poems capture the feelings and experiences of a girl in middle school

"Students will relate to this voice 'navigating upstream,' while they try to find their own place in the middle-school wilderness." SLJ

Giovanni, Nikki

Ego -tripping and other poems for young people; illustrations by George Ford; foreword by Virginia Hamilton. 2nd ed; Hill Bks. 1993 52p il hardcover o.p. pa $10.95

Grades: 5 6 7 8 **811**

1. African Americans -- Poetry 2. Poetry -- By individual authors

ISBN 1-55652-189-8; 1-55652-188-X pa

LC 93-29578

First published 1974

Giovanni has added 10 new poems to her earlier "collection of 23 poems for young people. Ford's illustrations in sepia shades are bold and full of character and dreaming. As Virginia Hamilton says in her foreword, Giovanni's voice is personal and warm, she 'celebrates ordinary folks' and writes of struggle and liberation. She's upbeat and celebratory without minimizing hard times." Booklist

Grandits, John

★ **Blue** lipstick; concrete poems. Clarion Books 2007 un il $15; pa $5.95

Grades: 5 6 7 8 9 10 **811**

1. Poetry -- By individual authors

ISBN 978-0-618-56860-4; 0-618-56860-3; 978-0-618-85132-4 pa; 0-618-85132-1 pa

LC 2006-23332

"This selection introduces readers to Jessie, who impulsively purchases blue lipstick, but later, regretfully decides to give it 'the kiss-off.' Jessie is big sister to Robert, who was featured in Grandits's Technically, It's Not My Fault (Clarion, 2004). As he did in that terrific collection, the author uses artful arrangements of text on the page, along with 54 different typefaces, to bring his images and ideas to life. . . . This irreverent, witty collection should resonate with a wide audience." SLJ

★ **Technically,** it's not my fault; concrete poems. by John Grandits. Clarion Books 2004 un il $15; pa $5.95

Grades: 5 6 7 8 **811**

1. Poetry -- By individual authors

ISBN 0-618-42833-X; 0-618-50361-7 pa

LC 2004-231

A collection of concrete poems on such topics as roller coasters, linguini, basketball, and sisters

"Grandits combines technical brilliance and goofy good humor to provide an accessible, fun-filled collection of poems, dramatically brought to life through a brilliant book design." SLJ

Grimes, Nikki

At Jerusalem's gate; poems of Easter. with woodcuts by David Frampton. Eerdmans Books for Young Readers 2005 un il $20

Grades: 5 6 7 8 **811**

1. American poetry 2. Easter -- Poetry 3. Easter -- Juvenile Poetry 4. Children's poetry, American 5. Poetry -- By individual authors

ISBN 0-8028-5183-5

LC 2003-1089

"Twenty-two poems trace the events celebrated by Christians as Easter Week, from Jesus' entry into Jerusalem through his appearance to disciples after the Resurrection. . . . Grades five to eight." (Bull Cent Child Books)

"Each poem is preceded by a brief synopsis of the event, often accompanied by the author's own musings and queries, which prompt readers to think and ask questions of their own. . . . Bold, handsome woodcuts reinforce the powerful drama depicted in poetry. An outstanding effort." SLJ

A **dime** a dozen; pictures by Angelo. Dial Bks. for Young Readers 1998 54p il $17.99

Grades: 5 6 7 8 **811**

1. African Americans -- Poetry 2. Poetry -- By individual authors

ISBN 0-8037-2227-3

LC 97-5798

A collection of poems about an African-American girl growing up in New York

"Free-flowing and very accessible, the poetry may inspire readers to distill their own life experiences into precise, imaginative words and phrases." Booklist

★ **One** last word; Wisdom from the Harlem Renaissance. Nikki Grimes ; Illustrated by Cozbi Cabrera [and 12 others] Bloomsbury USA Childrens 2017 128 p. color illustrations (hardback) $18.99; (ebook) $42

Grades: 5 6 7 8 **811**

1. American poetry -- African American authors -- Collections 2. African Americans -- Poetry

ISBN 9781619635548; 9781619635555

LC 2016016215

Boston Globe Horn Book Fiction & Poetry Honor (2017)

"In this collection of poetry, Nikki Grimes looks afresh at the poets of the Harlem Renaissance -- including voices like Langston Hughes, Georgia Douglas Johnson, and many more writers of importance and resonance from this era -- by combining their work with her own original poetry. Using 'The Golden Shovel' poetic method, Grimes has written a collection of poetry that is as gorgeous as it is thought-provoking." (Publisher's note)

"This anthology has plenty to offer, including effective introductions to Harlem Renaissance poets, well-expressed ideas and images, and, for young writers, a challenging way to turn admiration into inspiration." Booklist

Grover, Lorie Ann

Loose threads. Margaret K. McElderry Bks. 2002 296p $16.95 **811**

1. Breast cancer -- Poetry 2. Poetry -- By individual authors

ISBN 0-689-84419-0

LC 2001-44724

A series of poems describes how seventh-grader Kay Garber faces her grandmother's battle with breast cancer while living with her mother and great-grandmother and dealing with everyday junior high school concerns

"The poetic, spare language, written in Kay's self-possessed, first-person voice, is refreshingly frank about the disease. . . . Grover's book balances vivid emotional scenes with plenty of space between the words." Booklist

Includes bibliographical references

Harley, Avis

★ **African** acrostics; a word in edgeways. poems by Avis Harley; photographs by Deborah Noyes. Candlewick Press 2009 un il $17.99; pa $6.99

Grades: 4 5 6 7 **811**

1. Acrostics 2. Children's poetry 3. Animals -- Africa 4. Animals -- Poetry 5. Animals 6. Poetry -- By individual authors

ISBN 978-0-7636-3621-0; 0-7636-3621-5; 978-0-7636-5818-2 pa

LC 2008017916

This volume depicts "such wild animals as giraffes, zebras, and lions, in poems written to contain acrostics, in which beginning or ending letters from the poetry lines can be used to spell other words." (Publisher's note) "Grades four to six." (Bull Cent Child Books)

"Harley has written 18 poems, each one featuring a different animal. All are written as acrostics, with most of them based on the first letter of each line, but several with more unusual patterns. . . . Much of Harley's poetry consists of carefully crafted descriptive word imagery that is right on target. . . . Most of the full-page, full-color photos of the animals are perfect companions to the facing selections." SLJ

Haskins-Bookser, Laura

The **softer** side of hip-hop; poetic reflections on love, family, and relationships. by Laura Haskins-Bookser; illustrated by Jami Moffett. Morning Glory Press 2008 il pa $9.95

Grades: 8 9 10 11 12 **811**

1. Teenage mothers -- Poetry 2. Poetry -- By individual authors

ISBN 978-1-932538-83-0 pa; 1-932538-83-6 pa

"Haskins-Bookser brings her hip-hop sensibility to a genre—poetry—that is really at the heart and soul of both hip-hop and rap. She voices the hopes, fears, and joys of a single teen mother. . . . Her poems are at once cautionary, but are tales of hope and transcendence as well. Each poem is heartfelt and well crafted. This is a lovely treasure, enhanced by Moffett's beautifully executed drawings and quotes from teen mothers." SLJ

★ **Heart** to heart; new poems inspired by twentieth-century American art. edited by Jan Greenberg. Abrams 2001 80p il map $19.95

Grades: 5 6 7 8 9 10 **811**

1. American art 2. Art -- 20th century 3. American poetry -- Collections

ISBN 0-8109-4386-7

LC 99-462335

Michael L. Printz Award honor book, 2002

A compilation of poems by Americans writing about American art in the twentieth century, including such writers as Nancy Willard, Jane Yolen, and X. J. Kennedy.

"From a tight diamante and pantoum to lyrical free verse, the range of poetic styles will speak to a wide age group. . . . Concluding with biographical notes on each poet and artist, this rich resource is an obvious choice for teachers, and the exciting interplay between art and the written word will encourage many readers to return again and again to the book." Booklist

Hemphill, Stephanie

Your own, Sylvia; a verse portrait of Sylvia Plath. Alfred A. Knopf 2007 261p $15.99; lib bdg $18.99

Grades: 8 9 10 11 12 **811**

1. Poets 2. Authors 3. Novelists 4. Children's poetry 5. Poetry -- By individual authors

ISBN 978-0-375-83799-9; 978-0-375-93799-6 lib bdg

LC 2006-07253

Michael L. Printz Award honor book, 2008

These poems are "written from the viewpoint of the people in Sylvia's life or in a third-person imagining of Plath's own experience. . . . Grade nine and up." (Bull Cent Child Books)

"Hemphill's verse, like Plath's, is completely compelling: every word, every line, worth reading." Horn Book

Includes bibliographical references

Herrera, Juan Felipe

★ **Laughing** out loud, I fly; poems in English and Spanish. drawings by Karen Barbour. HarperCollins Pubs. 1998 un il $15.99

Grades: 6 7 8 9 **811**

1. Mexican Americans -- Poetry 2. Poetry -- By individual authors 3. Bilingual books -- English-Spanish

ISBN 0-06-027604-5

LC 96-45476

A collection of poems in Spanish and English about childhood, place, and identity

"Barbour's black-and-white drawings accompany each poem, delicately underlining its images but allowing the strong sensuality of the words to seep into readers' minds." SLJ

Holbrook, Sara

More than friends; poems from him and her. [by] Sara Holbrook and Allan Wolf. Wordsong 2008 64p il $16.95

Grades: 6 7 8 9 10 **811**

1. Love poetry 2. Poetry -- By individual authors

ISBN 978-1-59078-587-4; 1-59078-587-8

LC 2007-50282

"In these parallel poems, a boy and a girl describe their progression from friendship to romance. . . . The simple language expresses strong feelings in a variety of poetic forms. . . . Small black-and-white photos never get in the way of the words, which tell the edgy truth of romance in all its joy and confusion." Booklist

Hopkins, Lee Bennett

Been to yesterdays: poems of a life; illustrations by Charlene Rendeiro. Wordsong 1995 64p il $15.95; pa $9.95

Grades: 4 5 6 7 **811**

1. Poetry -- By individual authors

ISBN 1-56397-467-3; 1-56397-808-3 pa

LC 94-73320

"Hopkins distills the experience of his middle-grade years into 28 poems of poignant clarity. . . . Good reading and an excellent, unconventional choice for teachers doing units on poetry and autobiography." Booklist

Hovey, Kate

★ **Ancient** voices; written by Kate Hovey; with illustrations by Murray Kimber. Margaret McElderry Books 2004 un il $18.95

Grades: 6 7 8 9 **811**

1. Classical mythology -- Poetry 2. Poetry -- By individual authors

ISBN 0-689-83342-3

LC 00-28359

Twenty-three poems give voice to a variety of goddesses, gods, and mortals from Greek and Roman mythology

"These lyrical poems and dramatic picture-book-size illustrations humanize the Greek myths with flashes of contemporary realism. . . . The poetry here is both intense and accessible, with unobtrusive rhyme that adds to the music of the lines." Booklist

Hughes, Langston

★ The **dream** keeper and other poems; including seven additional poems. [by] Langston Hughes; illustrated by Brian Pinkney. 75th anniversary ed.; Alfred A. Knopf 2007 83p il $16.99

Grades: 4 5 6 7 **811**

1. African Americans -- Poetry 2. Poetry -- By individual authors

ISBN 978-0-679-84421-1

First published 1932; this is a reissue of the 1994 edition

A collection of sixty-six poems, selected by the author for young readers, including lyrical poems, songs, and blues, many exploring the black experience

"Black-and-white scratchboard illustrations in Pinkney's signature style express the emotion and beat of the poetry. . . . The poems are . . . colloquial and direct yet mysterious and complex." Booklist

★ **Langston** Hughes; edited by Arnold Rampersad & David Roessel; illustrations by Benny Andrews. Sterling Pub. 2006 48p il (Poetry for young people) $14.95

Grades: 5 6 7 8 **811**

1. African Americans -- Poetry 2. Poetry -- By individual authors

ISBN 1-4027-1845-4; 978-1-4027-1845-8

LC 2005025369

A brief profile of African American poet Langston Hughes accompanies some of his better known poems for children.

"This charming collection of 26 poems is vibrantly illustrated with depictions of African Americans in varied settings. . . . This will be a welcome introduction to Hughes's poetry for elementary students, and it includes sufficient detail to make it useful and enjoyable for older students." SLJ

★ **I** am the darker brother; an anthology of modern poems by African Americans. edited and with an afterword by Arnold Adoff; drawings by Benny Andrews; introduction by Rudine Sims Bishop; foreword by Nikki Giovanni. rev ed; Simon & Schuster Bks. for Young Readers 1997 208p il hard-cover o.p. pa $5.99
Grades: 6 7 8 9 10 **811**
1. American poetry -- African American authors -- Collections
ISBN 0-689-81241-8; 0-689-80869-0 pa
LC 97-144181
First published 1968
This anthology presents "the African-American experience through poetry that speaks for itself. . . . Because of the historical context of many of the poems, the book will be much in demand during Black History Month, but it should be used and treasured as part of the larger canon of literature to be enjoyed by all Americans at all times of the year. An indispensable addition to library collections." SLJ

★ **I**, too, sing America; three centuries of African American poetry. [selected and annotated by] Catherine Clinton; illustrated by Stephen Alcorn. Houghton Mifflin 1998 128p il $21
Grades: 6 7 8 9 **811**
1. African Americans -- Poetry 2. American poetry -- African American authors -- Collections
ISBN 0-395-89599-5
LC 97-46137
"For each poet, Clinton provides a biography and a brief, insightful commentary on the poem(s) she has chosen, including a discussion of political as well as literary connections. Alcorn's dramatic, full-page, full-color illustrations opposite each poem evoke the quiltlike patterns and rhythmic figures of folk art." Booklist

Indivisible; poems for social justice. edited by Gail Bush & Randy Meyer ; foreword by Common. Norwood House Press 2013 94 p. (pbk. : alk. paper) $14.60
Grades: 7 8 9 10 11 12 **811**
1. Poetry 2. Social justice 3. Social problems 4. Social justice -- Poetry 5. Social problems -- Poetry
ISBN 9781603574174
LC 2012021600
In this book of poetry, editors Gail Bush and Randy Meyer "have selected 54 previously published works by twentieth-century poets. The work represents a broad variety of races, cultures, and ethnicities and deals with such issues as bigotry and injustice, as well as with freedom, equality, and comity. Divided into five sections, the poems essentially chart a course from outside our culture to an inside where we can celebrate common dreams." (Booklist)
"From Langston Hughes and Amiri Baraka to Joy Harjo and Toi Derricotte, the poets discuss perspective, misguided pity, stereotyping, patriarchy, and thousands of other sticky issues. This carefully selected collection is not only poetically breathtaking, but will undoubtedly prove useful time and again as we seek to provide resources for educating empathetic global citizens.—" (School Library Journal)
Includes bibliographical references and index.

The **Invisible** ladder; an anthology of contemporary American poems for young readers with the poets' own photos and commentary. edited by Liz Rosenberg. Holt & Co. 1996 210p il $21.95
Grades: 7 8 9 10 **811**
1. Poets, American 2. American poetry -- Collections
ISBN 0-8050-3836-1
LC 96-12361
Features such poets as Robert Bly, Allen Ginsberg, Nikki Giovanni, and Galway Kinnell by including photos, selections of their work, and comments on their poetry
Rosenberg "introduces many exciting new adult voices to young people. Some of the poets' commentaries are sophisticated, some are pretentious; but most are immediate and extraordinarily moving, nearly as powerful as the poetry they lead into." Booklist

Johnston, Tony

Voice from afar; poems of peace. by Tony Johnston; paintings by Susan Guevara. Holiday House 2008 32p il $16.95
Grades: 5 6 7 8 **811**
1. War poetry 2. Poetry -- By individual authors
ISBN 978-0-8234-2012-4; 0-8234-2012-4
LC 2007031434
"Johnston offers thoughtful responses to war's senseless violence. Her free-verse word pictures call to mind scenes of terrible devastation. . . .Yet Johnston finds cause for hope amid the grimness. . . . Johnston adds her own voice, the sympathetic observer from afar, sending prayers for peace. Guevara's paintings, crafted with acrylic and oil paint with collage on textured canvas, feature subdued, neutral colors and haunting images." SLJ

Katz, Bobbi

Trailblazers; poems of exploration. by Bobbi Katz; illustrations by Carin Berger. Greenwillow Books 2007 208p il $18.99; lib bdg $19.89
Grades: 5 6 7 8 **811**
1. Explorers -- Poetry 2. Poetry -- By individual authors
ISBN 978-0-688-16533-8; 0-688-16533-8; 978-0-688-16534-5 lib bdg; 0-688-16534-6 lib bdg
LC 2006016696
This is a collection of poems about "the lives of more than 120 explorers, from ancient times to the present. . . . Katz challenges readers to consider not only the courage of these individuals, but also to broaden their horizons in terms of the definition of exploration and the motivations behind it. . . . All the selections encourage reading aloud, especially the poems for two voices. The few black-and-white illustrations scattered throughout are small and iconic." SLJ
Includes bibliographical references

★ A **kick** in the head; selected by Paul B. Janeczko; illustrated by Chris Raschka. Candlewick Press 2005 61p il $17.99; pa $9.99
Grades: 4 5 6 7 **811**
1. American poetry -- Collections
ISBN 978-0-7636-0662-6; 0-7636-0662-6; 978-0-7636-4132-0 pa; 0-7636-4132-4 pa
LC 2004-48508
"Raschka's high-spirited, spare torn-paper-and-paint collages ingeniously broaden the poems' wide-ranging emotional tones. . . . Clear, very brief explanations of poetic forms . . . accompany each entry; a fine introduction and appended notes offer further information. . . . This is the introduction that will ignite enthusiasm." Booklist

Kirk, Connie Ann

A **student's** guide to Robert Frost. Enslow Pubs. 2006 160p il (Understanding literature) $27.93

Grades: 7 8 9 10 **811**

1. Poets 2. Authors

ISBN 0-7660-2434-2

LC 2005-13392

In this book, "the career of this literary giant is examined. . . . Poems are put into historical and biographical context, with special emphasis placed on curriculum-related works, including 'Stopping by Woods on a Snowy Evening,' 'The Road Not Taken,' 'The Gift Outright,' and 'Fire and Ice.'" Publisher's note

Lawson, JonArno

Black stars in a white night sky; [by] JonArno Lawson; illustrated by Sherwin Tjia. Wordsong 2008 118p il $16.95

Grades: 4 5 6 7 **811**

1. Humorous poetry 2. Poetry -- By individual authors

ISBN 978-1-59078-521-8

LC 2007018927

First published 2006 in Canada

"This uproarious collection blends slapstick, puns, parodies, and sheer absurdity with lots of wry ideas. . . . Tjia's surreal art, in black-and-white silhouettes, is as rhythmic and absurd as the verse, which is perfect for reading aloud." Booklist

Think again; written by JonArno Lawson; illustrated by Julie Morstad. Kids Can Press 2010 62p il $16.95

Grades: 6 7 8 9 **811**

1. Children's poetry 2. Poetry -- By individual authors 3. Interpersonal relations -- Poetry

ISBN 978-1-55453-423-4; 1-55453-423-2

"More than 40 introspective poems and accompanying illustrations explore the complexity of close relationships. . . . Ever playful, the poet's pithy quatrains distill relational truths to their essence. . . . The illustrator's spare grayscale drawings . . . effectively amplify the tension they masterfully depict. An entirely rewarding combination." Kirkus

Levy, Debbie

★ The **year** of goodbyes; a true story of friendship, family and farewells. Disney-Hyperion Books 2010 136p il $16.99

Grades: 5 6 7 8 **811**

1. Jews -- Poetry 2. Holocaust, 1933-1945 -- Poetry 3. Poetry -- By individual authors

ISBN 1-4231-2901-6; 978-1-4231-2901-1

LC 2009-18671

"In 1930s Germany, it was common for young girls to keep poesiealbums, or autograph books, in which friends could write poems, draw pictures, or offer wishes to the owner. Levy has based this novel in verse on the actual poesiealbum kept by her mother, Jutta Salzberg, when she was twelve years old. . . . Grades four to seven." (Bull Cent Child Books)

"Artfully weaving together her mother's poesiealbum (autograph/poetry album), diary, and her own verse, Levy crafts a poignant portrait of her Jewish mother's life in 1938 Nazi Germany that crackles with adolescent vitality." Publ Wkly

Lewis, J. Patrick

★ **Black** cat bone; [by] J. Patrick Lewis; illustrations by Gary Kelley. Creative Editions 2006 48p il $19.95

Grades: 6 7 8 9 10 **811**

1. Singers 2. Guitarists 3. Blues musicians 4. Songwriters 5. Blues music -- Poetry 6. Mississippi -- Poetry 7. Poetry -- By individual authors 8. African American musicians -- Poetry

ISBN 978-1-56846-194-6

LC 2005-52298

"Robert Johnson, the celebrated blues musician, is said to have sold his soul to the devil for his skills on the guitar. . . . Lewis's verse echoes Johnson's music. . . . A single line of text parades ghostlike across the bottom of each page, explaining the aspect of the man's life that the poem sings of, and becoming a cumulative mini-bio in itself. A couple of Johnson's own lyrics appear with the sequence of Lewis's poems where they add to the narrative tension. Kelley's mixed-media illustrations in blues and browns add to the mood and enliven the layout." SLJ

★ The **brothers'** war; Civil War voices in verse. including photographs by Civil War photographers. National Geographic 2007 31p il $17.95; lib bdg $20.90

Grades: 5 6 7 8 9 10 **811**

1. Poetry -- By individual authors 2. United States -- History -- 1861-1865, Civil War -- Poetry

ISBN 978-1-4263-0036-3; 978-1-4263-0037-0 lib bdg

LC 2006-103275

"This heartrending collection of original poems paired with photographs by Civil War photographers makes real what statistics about war cannot—that the casualties of any war have human faces. Lewis . . . writes poignantly and lyrically. . . . An elegant design of gold, silver and black handsomely frames the text and photographs." Publ Wkly

Countdown to summer; a poems for every day of the school year. illustrations by Ethan Long. Little, Brown and Co. 2009 un il $15.99

Grades: 4 5 6 **811**

1. Schools -- Poetry 2. Poetry -- By individual authors

ISBN 978-0-316-02089-3; 0-316-02089-3

LC 2008016772

"180 poems are here gathered to be enjoyed on a vitamin-like one-a-day basis. . . . Some verses are long, some short, some thought-provoking, some laugh-provoking. Long's penciled spot art provides an agreeable visual accompaniment." Kirkus

The **house**; illustrated by Roberto Innocenti. Creative Editions 2009 un il $19.95

Grades: 4 5 6 7 **811**

1. Houses -- Poetry 2. Poetry -- By individual authors

ISBN 978-1-56846-201-1; 1-56846-201-8

"The walls in a stone farmhouse literally talk in this first-person narrative that deals with the ravages of time and their effects on the structure and its inhabitants. After a brief history, the house (constructed in 1656, 'a plague year') fast forwards to the dawn of the 20th century, when children discover its ruins. The quatrains, one to a spread, alternate between an AABB and ABBA rhyme scheme, thus avoiding singsong predictability. . . . Children will pore over Innocenti's marvelously detailed spreads, composed in an oversize, vertical format and set in an Italian hill town. . . . In the subset of books dealing intelligently with the effects of time on a single location, this is a provocative choice." SLJ

★ **Monumental** verses. National Geographic 2005 31p il $16.95; lib bdg $25.90

Grades: 5 6 7 8 **811**

1. Monuments -- Poetry 2. Poetry -- By individual authors

ISBN 0-7922-7135-1; 0-7922-7139-4 lib bdg

"Lewis offers 14 poems celebrating monumental structures. From the remnants of civilizations at Stonehenge, Easter Island, and Machu Picchu to the more modern achievements of the Taj Mahal, the Eiffel

Tower, and the Statue of Liberty, the subjects are varied and the accompanying photos are striking." Booklist

★ **Self** -portrait with seven fingers; the life of Marc Chagall in verse. [by] J. Patrick Lewis &Jane Yolen. Creative Editions 2011 38p il $18.99
Grades: 5 6 7 8 **811**
1. Artists 2. Painters 3. Jews -- Poetry 4. Artists -- Poetry 5. Jews -- Biography
ISBN 978-1-56846-211-0; 1-56846-211-5
LC 2009034767

"Lewis and Yolen pair 14 poems about Marc Chagall (1887–1985) with reproductions of more than a dozen of his paintings (as well as vintage photographs) in this moving account of the artist's Jewish upbringing in what is now Belarus, . . . his ascent in the art world, and his loves and losses, including arrest by the Nazis while living in Paris. . . . The duo's emphatic and empathetic verse is put into context by informative biographical sidebars that appear beneath each poem. A study in resilience, dedication, and wide-ranging talent." Publ Wkly

Includes bibliographical references

★ **Lives:** poems about famous Americans; selected by Lee Bennett Hopkins; illustrated by Leslie Staub. HarperCollins Pubs. 1999 31p il $15.99
Grades: 4 5 6 7 **811**
1. American poetry -- Collections 2. United States -- Biography -- Poetry
ISBN 0-06-027767-X; 0-06-027768-8 lib bdg
LC 98-29851

A collection of poetic portraits of sixteen famous Americans from Paul Revere to Neil Armstrong, by such authors as Jane Yolen, Nikki Grimes, and X. J. Kennedy

"Hopkins's eloquent introduction praises the power of poetry. Concluding 'Notes on the Lives' give readers useful biographical information. Full-page portraits feature Staub's distinctive, flat, primitive style, and their backgrounds have details particular to the subject. . . . A winning combination of poems and illustrations." SLJ

Longfellow, Henry Wadsworth

★ **Henry** Wadsworth Longfellow; edited by Frances Schoonmaker; illustrated by Chad Wallace. Sterling 1998 48p il (Poetry for young people) $14.95
Grades: 4 5 6 7 **811**
1. Children's poetry, American 2. Poetry -- By individual authors
ISBN 0-8069-9417-7
LC 98-14833

A collection of 27 poems, "among them, 'The Village Blacksmith,' 'The Wreck of the Hesperus.' 'The Children's Hour,' 'Paul Revere's Ride,' and 'Hiawatha's Childhood' from 'The Song of Hiawatha.' A several-page introduction to Longfellow's life also includes some of the stories behind the poems." Booklist

Hiawatha and Megissogwon; illustrated by Jeffrey Thompson; afterword by Joseph Bruchac. National Geographic Soc. 2001 un il $16.95
Grades: 5 6 7 8 **811**
1. Native Americans -- Poetry 2. Poetry -- By individual authors
ISBN 0-7922-6676-5
LC 00-12719

"Readers who persevere through the no-longer-familiar poem will be rewarded for their efforts by Hiawatha's exciting adventures, ferocious battles, and victorious homecoming. The text has been capably illustrated in a complex process utilizing original drawings, black-and-white scratchboard, and a computer program for color." SLJ

Maddox, Marjorie

Rules of the game; baseball poems. illustrated by John Sandford. Wordsong 2009 32p il $16.95
Grades: 5 6 7 8 **811**
1. Baseball -- Poetry 2. Poetry -- By individual authors
ISBN 978-1-59078-603-1; 1-59078-603-3
LC 2008-19018

"Sports fans will find themselves nodding in recognition of Maddox's sophisticated grasp of the game's intricacies, while language mavens will appreciate her joyous wordplay and dead-on command of poetic devices. . . . Sandford's charcoal pencil drawings, backed by sepia-toned pages . . . impart a classy timelessness to the book that's a nice match to its subject." Booklist

Meltzer, Milton

★ **Walt** Whitman; a biography. 21st Cent. Bks. (Brookfield) 2002 160p il lib bdg $31.90
Grades: 7 8 9 10 **811**
1. Poets 2. Authors 3. Essayists 4. Poets, American
ISBN 0-7613-2272-8
LC 2001-27798

"The book honestly explores Whitman's character and actions, including his racial prejudice and his tendency to write anonymous (and effective) praises of his own writing. Ultimately, this has a definite edge and relevance that gives it more resonance than blander overviews of the poet. . . . Photographs of Whitman and his family, images of his work, and reproductions of period illustrations . . . liven up the formatting." Bull Cent Child Books

Includes bibliographical references

Mora, Pat

Dizzy in your eyes; poems about love. Alfred A. Knopf 2010 165p il $15.99; lib bdg $18.99
Grades: 7 8 9 10 **811**
1. Love poetry 2. Poetry -- By individual authors
ISBN 978-0-375-84375-4; 0-375-84375-2; 978-0-375-94565-6 lib bdg; 0-375-94565-2 lib bdg
LC 2009-04300

"From family and school to dating and being dumped, the subjects in these 50 poems cover teens' experiences of love in many voices and situations. . . . Mora writes in free verse, as well as a variety of classic poetic forms—including haiku, clerihew, sonnet, cinquain, and blank verse—and for each form, there is an unobtrusive explanatory note on the facing page. The tight structures intensify the strong feelings in the poems, which teens will enjoy reading on their own or hearing aloud in the classroom." Booklist

★ **My** America; a poetry atlas of the United States. selected by Lee Bennett Hopkins; illustrated by Stephen Alcorn. Simon & Schuster Bks. for Young Readers 2000 83p il $21.95
Grades: 4 5 6 7 **811**
1. United States -- Poetry 2. American poetry -- Collections
ISBN 0-689-81247-7
LC 98-47402

A collection of poems evocative of seven geographical regions of the United States, including the Northeast, Southeast, Great Lakes, Plains, Mountain, Southwest, and Pacific Coast States.

"Some poems are purposive, but the best . . . capture places and people in all their diversity. Stephen Alcorn's handsome, multi-textured pictures . . . avoid literal interpretation and capture the sweep of the land and the rhythm of the words." Booklist

My black me; a beginning book of black poetry. edited by Arnold Adoff. [rev ed.]; Dutton Children's Bks. 1994 83p hardcover o.p. pa $6.99

Grades: 5 6 7 8 **811**

1. African Americans -- Poetry 2. American poetry -- African American authors -- Collections

ISBN 0-525-45216-8; 0-14-037443-4 pa

First published 1974

A compilation of poems reflecting thoughts on being black by such authors as Langston Hughes, Lucille Clifton, Nikki Giovanni, and Imamu Amiri Baraka

Myers, Walter Dean, 1937-2014

★ **Harlem**; a poem. pictures by Christopher Myers. Scholastic 1997 un il $16.95

Grades: 5 6 7 8 9 10 **811**

1. African Americans -- Poetry 2. Poetry -- By individual authors 3. Harlem (New York, N.Y.) -- Poetry

ISBN 0-590-54340-7

LC 96-8108

A Caldecott Medal honor book, 1998

A poem celebrating the people, sights, and sounds of Harlem

"Myers's paean to Harlem sings, dances, and swaggers across the pages, conveying the myriad sounds on the streets. . . . Christopher Myers's collages add an edge to his father's words, vividly bringing to life the sights and scenes of Lenox Avenue." Horn Book Guide

Here in Harlem; poems in many voices. written by Walter Dean Myers. Holiday House 2004 88p il $16.95

Grades: 7 8 9 10 **811**

1. African Americans -- Poetry 2. Poetry -- By individual authors 3. Harlem (New York, N.Y.) -- Poetry

ISBN 0-8234-1853-7

LC 2003-67605

"In each poem here, a resident of Harlem speaks in a distinctive voice, offering a story, a thought, a reflection, or a memory. The poetic forms are varied and well chosen. . . . Expressive period photos from Myers' collection accompany the text of this handsome book." Booklist

National Council of Teachers of English

A **Jar** of tiny stars: poems by NCTE award-winning poets; Bernice E. Cullinan, editor; illustrations by Andi MacLeod; portraits by Marc Nadel. Wordsong 1996 94p il $17.95

Grades: 4 5 6 7 **811**

1. American poetry -- Collections

ISBN 1-56397-087-2

LC 93-60466

"Each poet who has won the NCTE Poetry Award—David McCord, Aileen Fisher, Karla Kuskin, Myra Cohn Livingston, Eve Merriam, John Ciardi, Lilian Moore, Arnold Adoff, Valerie Worth, and Barbara Esbensen—is pictured at the beginning of a section that includes several representative poems and a significant quote. The portraits are watercolor renditions from photographs, with cheerful pen-and-ink sketches accompanying the verse; all are in black and white." Bull Cent Child Books

Nelson, Marilyn

Carver, a life in poems. Front St. 2001 103p il $16.95

Grades: 7 8 9 10 **811**

1. Botanists 2. Poetry -- By individual authors

ISBN 1-88691-053-7

LC 00-63624

Boston Globe-Horn Book Award: Fiction and Poetry (2001)

National Book Award Finalist: Young People's Literature (2001)

"A series of fifty-nine poems portrays George Washington Carver as a private, scholarly man of great personal faith and social purpose. Nelson fills in the trajectory of Carver's life with details of the cultural and political contexts that shaped him even as he shaped history. As individual works, each poem stands as a finely wrought whole of . . . high caliber." Horn Book Guide

★ **Fortune's** bones; the manumission requiem. Front Street 2004 32p il $16.95

Grades: 7 8 9 10 **811**

1. Slavery -- Poetry 2. African Americans -- Poetry 3. Poetry -- By individual authors

ISBN 1-932425-12-8

LC 2004-46917

"This requiem honors a slave who died in Connecticut in 1798. His owner, a doctor, dissected his body, boiling down his bones to preserve them for anatomy studies. The skeleton . . . hung in a local museum until 1970. . . . The museum . . . uncovered the skeleton's provenance, created a new exhibit, and led to the commissioning of these six poems. The selections . . . arc from grief to triumph. . . . The facts inform the verse and open up a full appreciation of its rich imagery and rhythmic, lyrical language." SLJ

Includes bibliographical references

★ The **freedom** business; including a narrative of the life & adventures of Venture, a native of Africa. Wordsong 2008 72p il $18.95

Grades: 8 9 10 11 12 **811**

1. Slavery -- Poetry 2. Connecticut -- Poetry 3. African Americans -- Poetry

ISBN 978-1-932425-57-4; 1-932425-57-8

LC 2008-04437

"Venture Smith, born Broteer Furro in Guinea, was captured and enslaved at the age of six and brought to America in 1738. . . . His narrative, published in 1798, appears continuously on the left-hand page of each spread; Nelson's luminous poems appear on the right. Both are thrown into relief by Dancy's mixed-media artwork, which includes images of birds, ropes, chains and blood to heighten the visceral emotions of both texts. . . . Tragic, important, breathtaking." Kirkus

★ **How** I discovered poetry; by Marilyn Nelson and illustrated by Hadley Hooper. Dial Books 2014 112 p. (hardcover : alk. paper) $17.99

Grades: 7 8 9 10 11 12 **811**

1. American poets 2. Civil rights -- United States -- History 3. Authorship -- Poetry 4. Poetry -- Authorship

ISBN 0803733046; 9780803733046

LC 2013005289

Coretta Scott King Author Award Honor Book (2015)

In this memoir, author Marilyn Nelson "tells the story of her development as an artist and young woman through fifty eye-opening poems. Readers are given an intimate portrait of her growing self-awareness and artistic inspiration along with a larger view of the world around her: racial tensions, the Cold War era, and the first stirrings of the feminist movement." (Publisher's note)

"In this fictionalized memoir in verse, renowned poet Nelson lyrically recounts her passage from ages 4 to 14, from numerous military base homes; through friends, schools, and dogs; and from developmental stages of initiative through industry to identity..Hooper's line-and-shade illustrations, along with Nelson's family photos, set a quiet and respectful tone and offer readers the feeling of taking an unsolicited peek behind a heavy curtain. For fans of Nelson's impressive body of children's and adult poetry, including the brilliant A Wreath for Emmett Till (2005), this insight into her modulated memories gratifies that heartfelt belief that here writes a woman of great substance." (Booklist)

★ **My** Seneca Village; by Marilyn Nelson. Namelos 2015 98 p. $21.95

Grades: 6 7 8 9 10 **811**

1. Central Park (New York, N.Y.) 2. American poetry -- African American authors

ISBN 1608981967; 9781608981960

LC 2016007993

Los Angeles Times Book Prize: Young Adult Literature (2015)

In this poetry collection, author Marilyn Nelson "recreates the long lost community of Seneca Village. A multi-racial, multi-ethnic neighborhood in the center of Manhattan, it thrived in the middle years of the 19th century. . . . Then work crews arrived to build Central Park, and Seneca Village disappeared. Illustrated in the poet's own words -- with brief prose descriptions of what she sees inside her poems -- this collection takes readers back in time." (Publisher's note)

"Nelson chooses prose narrative to connect these 40-some lyric fictional portraits that include schoolchildren, a mariner, a bootblack, a hairdresser, a musician, bar owners, lovers, and a fortuneteller, among others, along with poignant snapshots of famous historical figures Frederick Douglass and Maria Stewart, the first African-American woman to lecture on politics and religion." Kirkus

★ **Sweethearts** of rhythm; the story of the greatest all-girl swing band in the world. written by Marilyn Nelson; illustrated by Jerry Pinkney. Dial Books 2009 un il $21.99

Grades: 4 5 6 7 **811**

1. Women musicians 2. Jazz music -- Poetry 3. Jazz 4. Poetry -- By individual authors 5. International Sweethearts of Rhythm

ISBN 0-8037-3187-6; 978-0-8037-3187-5

LC 2008-46255

This is a study of the racially mixed group the International Sweethearts of Rhythm. Bibliography. "Grades six to nine." (Bull Cent Child Books)

"On all fronts, a resonant performance." Publ Wkly

★ A **wreath** for Emmett Till; illustrated by Philippe Lardy. Houghton Mifflin 2005 un il $17

Grades: 8 9 10 11 12 **811**

1. Children 2. Murder victims 3. Lynching -- Poetry 4. Mississippi -- Poetry 5. African Americans -- Poetry 6. Poetry -- By individual authors

ISBN 0-618-39752-3

LC 2004-9205

Michael L. Printz Award honor book, 2006

Boston Globe-Horn Book Honor: Fiction (2005)

This is a "poetry collection about Till's brutal, racially motivated murder. The poems form a heroic crown of sonnets—a sequence in which the last line of one poem becomes the first line of the next. . . . The rigid form distills the words' overwhelming emotion into potent, heart-stopping lines that speak from changing perspectives. . . . When matched with Lardy's gripping, spare, symbolic paintings of tree trunks, blood-red roots, and wreaths of thorns, these poems are a powerful achievement that teens and adults will want to discuss together." Booklist

Nye, Naomi Shihab

★ **19** varieties of gazelle; poems of the Middle East. Greenwillow Bks. 2002 142p $16.95; pa $6.99

Grades: 7 8 9 10 **811**

1. Middle East -- Poetry 2. Poetry -- By individual authors

ISBN 0-06-009765-5; 0-06-050404-8 pa

LC 2002-771

National Book Award Finalist: Young People's Literature (2002)

In this "volume, Nye collects her poems about growing up as an Arab American (her ancestry is Palestinian), including previously published poems and newly written pieces. This rich and varied volume offers insights into the experience of childhood in two very different worlds. . . . This volume will fill a need for classroom use, for young people seeking a more personal understanding of the Middle East, and for readers seeking a connection with their own Middle Eastern background." Bull Cent Child Books

★ **Honeybee**; poems & short prose. Greenwillow Books 2008 164p $16.99; lib bdg $17.89

Grades: 8 9 10 11 12 **811**

1. Poetry -- By individual authors

ISBN 978-0-06-085390-7; 0-06-085390-5; 978-0-06-085391-4 lib bdg; 0-06-085391-3 lib bdg

LC 2007-36742

This poetry "anthology is a rallying cry, a call for us to rediscover such beelike traits as interconnectedness, strong community, and honest communication. . . . Teens at the very start of their questioning years will recognize their own angst in Nye's sense of irony, their idealistic optimism in her simple wonder." SLJ

A **maze** me; poems for girls. pictures by Terre Maher. 1st ed; Greenwillow Books 2005 118p il $16.99; lib bdg $17.89

Grades: 7 8 9 10 **811**

1. Girls -- Poetry 2. Poetry -- By individual authors

ISBN 0-06-058189-1; 0-06-058190-5 lib bdg

LC 2004-3283

These "poems draw from Nye's observations about nature, home, school, and neighborhood to make connections to a girl's inner world. . . . Most poems . . . speak with a powerful immediacy. . . . A wide age range will respond to these deeply felt poems about everyday experiences." Booklist

Salting the ocean; 100 poems by young poets. selected by Naomi Shihab Nye; pictures by Ashley Bryan. Greenwillow Bks. 2000 111p il $16.99

Grades: 4 5 6 7 **811**

1. Children's writings 2. American poetry -- Collections

ISBN 0-688-16193-6

LC 99-30590

"While working within various school systems during the 1970s, Nye collected and saved these poems written by students in grades 1-12. . . . The collection is divided into four sections, each of which has approximately 25 poems. . . . In 'The Self and the Inner World,' the young poets express their thoughts about growing up, how they feel about their bodies . . . and make observations about people and events that surround them. 'Where We Live' looks at the trees, birds, sounds, and other aspects of the community in which the children live. 'Anybody's Family' includes poems about ethnicity, members of the students' households, and their feelings toward family members. In 'The Wide Imagination,' the poets . . . write about such topics as mirrors, history, time, words, and love." (SLJ) Index. "Grades four to twelve." (Booklist)

"These poems are divided into four topics: The Self and the Inner World, Where We Live, Anybody's Family, and the Wide Imagination." Horn Book Guide

Includes bibliographical references

Voices in the air; poems for listeners. Naomi Shihab Nye ; illustrated by Dawn Henning. Greenwillow Books 2018 208 p. (hardcover) $17.99

Grades: 8 9 10 11 **811**

1. Hope 2. Poetry -- Collections 3. Hope -- Juvenile poetry 4. Inspiration -- Juvenile poetry

ISBN 9780062691842

LC 2017046142

This book "is a collection of almost one hundred original poems written by the award-winning poet Naomi Shihab Nye in honor of the artists, writers, poets, historical figures, ordinary people, and diverse luminaries from past and present who have inspired her. Full of words of encouragement, solace, and hope, this collection offers a message of peace and empathy." (Publisher's note)

Includes bibliographical references and indexes

Orgill, Roxane

★ **Jazz** Day; The Making of a Famous Photograph. Roxane Orgill ; illustrated by Francis Vallejo. Candlewick Press 2016 66 p. color illustrations $18.99

Grades: 4 5 6 7 8 **811**

1. Jazz musicians 2. Poetry -- Collections 3. Harlem (New York, N.Y.) 4. Jazz music

ISBN 0763669547; 9780763669546

LC 2015933243

Boston Globe-Horn Book Award: Picture Book (2016)

"When Esquire magazine planned an issue to salute the American jazz scene in 1958, graphic designer Art Kane pitched a crazy idea: how about gathering a group of beloved jazz musicians and photographing them? He didn't own a good camera, didn't know if any musicians would show up, and insisted on setting up the shoot in front of a Harlem brownstone. Could he pull it off?" (Publisher's note)

"In 21 poems, Orgill introduces Art Kane's iconic 1958 Harlem photograph to young readers, spotlighting many of the 57 jazz musicians pictured. . . . Vallejo's acrylic-and-pastel paintings vividly capture the shoot's vignettes and the skittish excitement of neighborhood kids." Kirkus

Includes bibliographical references (pages 54-55)

The **Oxford** book of American poetry; chosen and edited by David Lehman; associate editor, John Brehm. Oxford University Press 2006 lvii, 1132p $35

Grades: 8 9 10 11 12 Adult **811**

1. American poetry -- Collections

ISBN 0-19-516251-X; 978-0-19-516251-6

LC 2005-36590

First published 1950 with title: The Oxford book of American verse

"The book is not only a sound historical survey, but also gives the reader a powerful taste of poetry's impact upon the wider world." Economist

Includes bibliographical references

The **Oxford** book of children's verse in America; edited by Donald Hall. Oxford University Press 1985 xxxviii, 319p $39.95; pa $19.95

Grades: 5 6 7 8 9 10 11 12 Adult **811**

1. American poetry -- Collections

ISBN 0-19-503539-9; 0-19-506761-4 pa

LC 84-20755

"A fine and carefully winnowed collection of American poetry is gathered in a book that will interest students of children's literature and young people who simply enjoy browsing." Horn Book

Pinkney, Andrea Davis, 1963-

Martin rising; requiem for a King. by Andrea Davis Pinkney ; paintings by Brian Pinkney. Scholastic Press 2018 127 p. illustrations (chiefly color) (hardcover : acid-free paper) $19.99

Grades: 4 5 6 7 8 **811**

1. Civil rights workers -- United States -- Biography -- Juvenile poetry

ISBN 9780545702546; 9780545702539

LC 2016031408

This book, by Andrea Davis Pinkney, with paintings by Brian Pinkney, "brings a fresh perspective to Martin Luther King, the Gandhi-like, peace-loving activist whose dream of equality--and whose courage to make it happen--changed the course of American history. And even in his death, he continues to transform and inspire all of us who share his dream." (Publisher's note)

"Written with an eye toward choral reading, this is a unique and remarkable resource." Pub Wkly

Includes bibliographical references (pages 126-127).

★ The **Place** my words are looking for; what poets say about and through their work. selected by Paul B. Janeczko. Bradbury Press 1990 150p il $17.95

Grades: 4 5 6 7 **811**

1. Poetics 2. American poetry -- Collections

ISBN 0-02-747671-5

LC 89-39331

"More than forty contemporary poets are included: Eve Merriam, X. J. Kennedy, Felice Holman, Gary Soto, Mark Vinz, Karla Kuskin, and John Updike, among others. Their contributions vary widely in theme and mood and style, though the preponderance of the pieces are written in modern idiom and unrhymed meter. The accompanying comments frequently are as insightful and eloquent as the poems themselves." Horn Book

Poe, Edgar Allan

The **raven**; with illustrations by Ryan Price. KCP Poetry 2006 un il (Visions in poetry) $17.95

Grades: 7 8 9 10 **811**

1. Poetry -- By individual authors

ISBN 978-1-55337-473-2; 1-55337-473-8

This poem originally published by Poe in 1845 is presented with illustrations by Price that "suggest a background story shaped by the narrator's guilt, embodied in the terrifying figure of the raven. . . . Ages ten and up." (Publisher's note)

"Originally published in 1845, the poem is narrated by a melancholy scholar brooding over Lenore, a woman he loved who is now lost to him. One bleak December at midnight, a raven with fiery eyes visits the scholar and perches above his chamber door. Struggling to understand the meaning of the word his winged visitant repeats 'Nevermore!' the narrator descends by stages into madness." Publisher's note

★ A **Poem** of her own; voices of American women yesterday and today. edited by Catherine Clinton; illustrated by Stephen Alcorn. Abrams 2003 79p il $17.95

Grades: 6 7 8 9 **811**

1. American poetry -- Women authors -- Collections

ISBN 0-8109-4240-2

LC 2002-12851

Presents a collection of more than twenty poems by American women published between 1678 and 2001. Includes poems by Phillis Wheatley, Gertrude Stein, Lucille Clifton, Sandra Cisneros, and Naomi Shihab Nye

"The intelligent selection is matched by the fresh, open design, highlighted by Alcorn's exciting paintings, executed in light-fast casein paint." Booklist

Poetry for kids; Robert Frost. edited by Jay Parini ; illustrated by Michael Paraskevas. MoonDance Press 2017 48 p. (hardback) $14.95

Grades: 5 6 7 8 **811**

1. Poetry -- Collections 2. American poetry -- Collections

ISBN 1633222209; 9781633222205

LC 2017010647

This book in the Poetry for Kids series, edited by Jay Parini, illustrated by Michael Paraskevas is "a collection [of poems by Robert Frost] specially curated for young readers which won't just be read, but consumed, experienced, and treasured for a lifetime... This stunning celebration of... [Frost's] best-loved work includes 35 poems specially chosen for children ages 8 to 14 by... Parini." (Publisher's note)

Poetry from the masters: the pioneers; edited by Wade Hudson; illustrated by Stephan J. Hudson. Just Us Books 2003 88p il pa $9.95

Grades: 7 8 9 10 **811**

1. African American authors 2. American poetry -- African American authors -- Collections

ISBN 0-940975-96-3

This book "focuses on a particular group of black poets, 'trailblazers' who forged a path by overcoming 'almost impossible obstacles.' Hudson puts these writers in perspective and provides a social and literary context. Eleven poets are profiled, starting with Phillis Wheatley and ending with Gwendolyn Brooks. . . . Each writer is introduced with a brief biographical sketch that highlights his or her literary significance and contributions, followed by the full text of two or more poems. . . . This is an excellent resource for students seeking research materials or just looking for wonderful examples of poetry to read." SLJ

Includes bibliographical references

★ A **Poke** in the I; [selected by] Paul Janeczko; illustrated by Chris Raschka. Candlewick Press 2001 35p il hardcover o.p. pa $7.99

Grades: 4 5 6 7 8 9 10 **811**

1. American poetry -- Collections

ISBN 0-7636-0661-8; 0-7636-2376-8 pa

LC 00-33675

"Thirty concrete poems of all shapes and sizes are carefully laid on large white spreads, extended by Raschka's quirky watercolor and paper-collage illustrations. . . . Beautiful and playful, this title should find use in storytimes, in the classroom, and just for pleasure anywhere." SLJ

★ The **Random** House book of poetry for children; selected and introduced by Jack Prelutsky; illustrated by Arnold Lobel. Random House 1983 248p il $19.95; lib bdg $21.99

Grades: 3 4 5 6 **811**

1. English poetry -- Collections 2. American poetry -- Collections

ISBN 0-394-85010-6; 0-394-95010-0 lib bdg

LC 83-2990

In this anthology emphasis "is placed on humor and light verse; but serious and thoughtful poems are also included. . . . Approximately two thirds of the selections were written within the past forty years—the splendid contributions of such writers as John Ciardi, Aileen Fisher, Dennis Lee, Myra Cohn Livingston, David McCord, Eve Merriam, and Lilian Moore. [There are] . . . samplings of earlier poets from Shakespeare and Blake to Emily Dickinson and Walter de la Mare." Horn Book

★ **Reflections** on a gift of watermelon pickle--and other modern verse; [compiled by] Stephen Dunning, Edward Lueders, Hugh Smith. Lothrop, Lee & Shepard Bks. 1967 139p il $19.99

Grades: 6 7 8 9 10 **811**

1. American poetry -- Collections

ISBN 0-688-41231-9

First published 1966 by Scott, Foresman in a text edition

"Although some of the [114] selections are by recognized modern writers, many are by minor or unknown poets, and few will be familiar to the reader. Nearly all are fresh in approach and contemporary in expression. . . . Striking photographs complementing or illuminating many of the poems enhance the attractiveness of the volume." Booklist

Rosen, Michael J.

The **horse's** haiku; Michael J. Rosen ; Stan Fellows. Candlewick Press 2018 48 p. $17.99

Grades: 3 4 5 6 7 **811**

1. Haiku 2. Animals -- Poetry 3. Children's poetry

ISBN 0763689165; 9780763689162

In this book of poetry, "from field to stable, from rest to riding, poet Michael J. Rosen captures the nature of horses with spare and graceful haiku. Filled with Stan Fellows's evocative artwork, this collection celebrates the beauty of horses while peacefully grazing or in all their powerful and dynamic action." (Publisher's note)

Rylant, Cynthia

Something permanent; photographs by Walker Evans; poetry by Cynthia Rylant. Harcourt Brace & Co. 1994 61p il $18

Grades: 7 8 9 10 **811**

1. Poetry -- By individual authors

ISBN 0-15-277090-9

LC 93-3861

"For students in junior high and high school, the juxtaposition of Evans' photos and Rylant's poems will demonstrate how emotions can be rooted in objects and how, to dig them out, you need to use strong, sturdy words." Booklist

Sendak, Maurice, 1928-2012

★ **My** brother's book; Maurice Sendak ; [edited by] Michael di Capua. HarperCollins 2013 32 p. (hardcover bdg.) $18.95

Grades: 4 5 6 7 8 **811**

1. Poetry 2. Poetry -- Collections

ISBN 0062234897; 9780062234896

LC 2012942549

In this book, "with influences from Shakespeare and William Blake, [Maurice] Sendak pays homage to his late brother, Jack, whom he credited for his passion for writing and drawing. Pairing Sendak's . . . poetry with his . . . artwork, . . . Sendak's tribute to his brother is an expression of both grief and love. . . . Pulitzer Prize--winning literary critic and Shakespearean scholar Stephen Greenblatt contributes a[n] . . . introduction." (Publisher's note)

Service, Robert W.

★ The **cremation** of Sam McGee; by Robert W. Service; paintings by Ted Harrison; introduction by Pierre Berton. 20th anniversary ed.; Kids Can Press 2006 un il $17.95

Grades: 4 5 6 7 **811**

1. Yukon Territory -- Poetry 2. Poetry -- By individual authors

ISBN 978-1-55453-092-2; 1-55453-092-X

Text first published 1907. This is a reissue of the edition first published 1986 in Canada and 1987 in the United States by Greenwillow Bks.

This poem "has gripped readers and listeners for decades. . . . [The illustrator] obviously appreciates the humor inherent in the text. . . . As Pierre Berton observes in his introduction, [Harrison's] 'style is unique: part Oriental, part native American, part Ted Harrison.'" Horn Book

Shange, Ntozake

★ **Freedom's** a-callin' me; poems by Ntozake Shange; paintings by Rod Brown. Amisatd/Collins 2012 il $16.99

Grades: 4 5 6 7 **811**

1. Slavery -- Poetry 2. African Americans -- Poetry 3. Underground railroad -- Poetry

ISBN 978-0-06-133741-3; 0-06-133741-2

LC 2010050515

The author and illustrator present "a series of poems and paintings that express the hope and frustration of enslaved people trying to navigate the Underground Railroad. Using dialect to convey a Southern cadence, Shange's poems communicate powerful emotions. . . . These poems are a cry from the heart. . . . The expressive, impressionistic paintings capture attention with their bold strokes and vivid coloring." SLJ

★ **We** troubled the waters; poems by Ntozake Shange; paintings by Rod Brown. Amistad/Collins 2009 un il $16.99; lib bdg $17.89

Grades: 4 5 6 7 8 9 10 **811**

1. Poetry -- By individual authors 2. African Americans -- Civil rights -- Poetry

ISBN 978-0-06-133735-2; 0-06-133735-8; 978-0-06-133737-6 lib bdg; 0-06-133737-4 lib bdg

LC 2008025360

"Each spread pairs a poem with blurred, expressive acrylic paintings, and the pages feature both well-known civil rights leaders and ordinary people who endured oppression. . . . The messages are haunting. . . . The colloquial lines, indelible images, and comparisons between then and now will keep readers talking." Booklist

Shields, Carol Diggory

English, fresh squeezed! 40 thirst-for-knowledge-quenching poems. by Carol Diggory Shields; illustrations by Tony Ross. Handprint Books 2004 80p il $14.95

Grades: 4 5 6 7 **811**

1. English language -- Poetry 2. Poetry -- By individual authors

ISBN 1-59354-053-1

LC 2004-53905

"Shields presents humorous poems both celebrating and bemoaning parts of speech, grammatical rules, and other annoyances of English class. Her rhyming verse is generally snappy and pointed. . . . Ross's spot illustrations in black and white with a blue tone add visual amusement without overwhelming." SLJ

★ **Shimmy** shimmy shimmy like my sister Kate; looking at the Harlem Renaissance through poems. [edited by] Nikki Giovanni. Holt & Co. 1995 186p $17.95

Grades: 8 9 10 11 12 **811**

1. Harlem Renaissance 2. American poetry -- African American authors -- Collections

ISBN 0-8050-3494-3

LC 95-38617

This anthology includes poems by such authors as Paul Laurence Dunbar, Langston Hughes, Countee Cullen, Gwendolyn Brooks, and Amiri Baraka. Commentary and a discussion of the development of African American arts known as the Harlem Renaissance is provided by editor Giovanni

Includes bibliographical references

Sidman, Joyce

★ **What** the Heart Knows; chants, charms, and blessings. written by Joyce Sidman and illustrated by Pamela Zagarenski. Houghton Mifflin Harcourt 2013 80 p. $16.99

Grades: 6 7 8 9 10 11 12 **811**

1. Children's poetry 2. Blessing and cursing 3. Children's poetry, American

ISBN 0544106164; 9780544106161

LC 2012047836

This book, by Joyce Sidman and illustrated by Pamela Zagarenski, "is a collection of poems to provide comfort, courage, and humor at difficult or daunting moments in life. It conjures forth laments, spells, invocations, chants, blessings, promises, songs, and charms. Here are pleas on how to repair a friendship, wishes to transform one's life or to slow down time, charms to face the shame of a disapproving crowd, invocations to ask for forgiveness, [and] to understand the mysteries of happiness." (Publisher's note)

"Sidman and Zagarenski present "Chants & Charms," "Spells & Invocations," "Laments & Remembrances," and "Praise Songs & Blessings" in a variety of poetic forms. Each poem speaks directly from Sidman's heart to the reader's, addressing subjects of deep importance: forgiveness, friendship, bravery, death, illness, moving. Zagarenski's illustrations beautifully extend the poems with her dreamy style and deft use of white space, symbolism, and images." (Horn Book)

Silverstein, Shel

★ **Every** thing on it; poems and drawings by Shel Silverstein. Harper 2011 194p il $19.99; lib bdg $20.89

Grades: 3 4 5 6 **811**

1. Humorous poetry 2. Nonsense verses 3. Poetry -- By individual authors

ISBN 978-0-06-199816-4; 0-06-199816-8; 978-0-06-199817-1 lib bdg; 0-06-199817-6 lib bdg

The second original book to be published since Silverstein's passing in 1999, this poetry collection includes more than one hundred and thirty never-before-seen poems and drawings completed by the cherished American artist and selected by his family from his archives.

"Silverstein's inspired word play and impish sense of humor are in abundant evidence. His signature line drawings accompany many of the poems and complete the jokes of some. . . . Adults who grew up with Uncle Shelby will find themselves wiping their eyes by the time they get to the end of this collection; children new to the master will find themselves hooked." Kirkus

Falling up; poems and drawings by Shel Silverstein. HarperCollins Pubs. 1996 171p il $17.99; lib bdg $18.89

Grades: 3 4 5 6 **811**

1. Humorous poetry 2. Nonsense verses 3. Poetry -- By individual authors

ISBN 0-06-024802-5; 0-06-024803-3 lib bdg

LC 96-75736

This "collection includes more than 150 poems. . . . As always, Silverstein has a direct line to what kids like, and he gives them poems celebrating the gross, the scary, the absurd, and the comical. The drawings are much more than decoration. They often extend a poem's meaning and, in many cases, add some great comedy." Booklist

★ A **light** in the attic; Special edition; Harper 2009 185p il $18.99

Grades: 3 4 5 6 **811**

1. Humorous poetry 2. Nonsense verses 3. Poetry -- By individual authors

ISBN 978-0-06-190585-8; 0-06-190585-2

First published 1981

This collection of more than one hundred poems "will delight lovers of Silverstein's raucous, rollicking verse and his often tender, whimsical, philosophical advice. . . . The poems are tuned in to kids' most hidden feelings, dark wishes and enjoyment of the silly. . . . The witty line drawings are a full half of the treat of this wholly satisfying anthology by the modern successor to Edward Lear and Hilaire Belloc." SLJ [review of 1981 edition]

★ **Where** the sidewalk ends; the poems & drawings of Shel Silverstein. 30th anniversary special ed; HarperCollins 2004 183p il $17.99; lib bdg $18.89

Grades: 3 4 5 6 7 8 9 10 **811**

1. Humorous poetry 2. Nonsense verses 3. Poetry -- By individual authors

ISBN 0-06-057234-5; 0-06-058653-2 lib bdg

LC 2004-269335

First published 1974

"There are skillful, sometimes grotesque line drawings with each of the 127 poems, which run in length from a few lines to a couple of pages. The poems are tender, funny, sentimental, philosophical, and ridiculous in turn, and they're for all ages." Sat Rev

Singer, Marilyn

★ **Central** heating; poems about fire and warmth. illustrated by Meilo So. Alfred A. Knopf 2005 41p il $15.95; lib bdg $17.99

Grades: 4 5 6 7 **811**

1. Fire -- Poetry 2. Heat -- Poetry 3. Poetry -- By individual authors

ISBN 0-375-82912-1; 0-375-92912-6 lib bdg

LC 2004-4274

"The complicated nature of fire is explored in Singer's energetic short poems and So's deceptively simple single-color illustrations. . . . This title . . . belongs on library shelves everywhere." SLJ

Smith, Charles R., Jr., 1969-

★ **Hoop** queens; poems. Candlewick Press 2003 35p il hardcover o.p. pa $5.99

Grades: 4 5 6 7 **811**

1. Basketball -- Poetry 2. Women athletes -- Poetry 3. Poetry -- By individual authors

ISBN 0-7636-1422-X; 0-7636-3561-8 pa

LC 2002-41111

A collection of twelve poems that celebrate contemporary women basketball stars, including Yolanda Griffith, Chamique Holdsclaw, and Natalie Williams

"Action photos of the athletes are pasted large on colorful, dynamic backgrounds that barely hold the motion-filled poems to the page. Notes about each player and poem communicate the joy Smith finds both in watching the game and writing poetry. Pure pleasure for basketball fans and inspiration for kids who doubted poetry was alive." SLJ

Smith, Hope Anita

★ **Mother** poems; words and pictures by Hope Anita Smith. Henry Holt and Co. 2009 72p il $16.95

Grades: 4 5 6 7 **811**

1. Death -- Poetry 2. Mothers -- Poetry 3. Bereavement -- Poetry 4. African Americans -- Poetry 5. Poetry -- By individual authors

ISBN 978-0-8050-8231-9; 0-8050-8231-X

LC 2008-18342

"Smith writes about an African American child's grief at the sudden death of her mother. . . . Like the poetry, Smith's simple, torn-paper collages in a folk-art style show the close embraces and vignettes without overwhelming the words." Booklist

Soto, Gary

Canto familiar; [illustrated by Annika Nelson] Harcourt Brace & Co. 1995 79p il $18; pa $5.95

Grades: 4 5 6 **811**

1. Mexican Americans -- Poetry 2. Poetry -- By individual authors

ISBN 978-0-15-200067-7; 0-15-200067-4; 978-0-15-205885-2 pa; 0-15-205885-0 pa

LC 94-24218

"This collection of simple free verse captures common childhood moments at home, at school, and in the street. Many of the experiences are Mexican American . . . and occasional Spanish words are part of the easy, colloquial, short lines. . . . The occasional full-page, richly colored woodcuts by Annika Nelson capture the child's imaginative take on ordinary things." Booklist

★ A **fire** in my hands; poems by Gary Soto. rev and expanded ed.; Harcourt 2006 74p $16

Grades: 6 7 8 9 **811**

1. Mexican Americans -- Poetry 2. Poetry -- By individual authors

ISBN 0-15-205564-9

LC 2005024610

First published 1991 by Scholastic

"Half the poems are new to this expanded edition of a collection first published 15 years ago, including some great ones from Soto's adult books that speak about feeling stuck at home and growing up poor, Catholic, and Mexican American. Soto's chatty introduction about writing poetry that celebrates small, common things will appeal to both readers and writers, as will the informal questions and answers at the back of the book and the brief autobiographical notes Soto includes with each poem." Booklist

A **natural** man. Chronicle Bks. 2000 71p pa $13.95

Grades: 7 8 9 10 **811**

1. Mexican Americans -- Poetry 2. Poetry -- By individual authors
ISBN 0-8118-2518-3

LC 99-18353

"This poetry anthology offers a photographic glimpse into the lives of California's Chicanos. But although the titles and use of Spanish words create a very particular setting, the characters, stories, and truths of these selections have a universal resonance." SLJ

★ **Neighborhood** odes; illustrated by David Diaz. Harcourt Brace Jovanovich 1992 68p il hardcover o.p. pa $5.95
Grades: 4 5 6 **811**

1. Hispanic Americans -- Poetry 2. Poetry -- By individual authors
ISBN 0-15-256879-4; 0-15-205364-6 pa

LC 91-20710

"Twenty-one poems, all odes, celebrate life in a Hispanic neighborhood. Other than the small details of daily life—peoples' names or the foods they eat—these poems could be about any neighborhood. With humor, sensitivity, and insight, Soto explores the lives of children. . . . David Diaz's contemporary black-and-white illustrations, which often resemble cut paper, effortlessly capture the varied moods—happiness, fear, longing, shame, and greed—of this remarkable collection. With a glossary of thirty Spanish words and phrases." Horn Book

Partly cloudy; poems of love and longing. Harcourt 2009 100p $16
Grades: 7 8 9 10 **811**

1. Love poetry 2. Poetry -- By individual authors
ISBN 978-0-15-206301-6; 0-15-206301-3

LC 2008-22267

Poet Gary Soto captures the voices of young people as they venture toward their first kiss, brood over bruised hearts, and feel the thrill of first love.

"Soto's new book of verse about adolescent love is remarkable. . . . The language of the poems is spare but evocative, with not one word wasted. . . . Teens will find these poems very engaging and will relate to how the emotion of love is expressed in everyday moments." Voice Youth Advocates

★ **Soul** looks back in wonder; [illustrated by] Tom Feelings. Dial Bks. 1993 un il hardcover o.p. pa $7.99
Grades: 4 5 6 7 **811**

1. African Americans -- Poetry 2. American poetry -- African American authors -- Collections
ISBN 0-8037-1001-1; 0-14-056501-9 pa

LC 93-824

Coretta Scott King Award for illustration

Artwork and poems by such writers as Maya Angelou, Langston Hughes, and Askia Toure portray the creativity, strength, and beauty of their African American heritage

"This thoughtful collection of poetry is unique. . . . Feelings selected sketches done while he was in West Africa, South America, and at home in America. The original drawings were enhanced with colored pencils, colored papers, stencil cut-outs, and other techniques to give a collage effect. Marbled textures bring vibrancy to the work." Horn Book

Spires, Elizabeth

★ **I** heard God talking to me; William Edmondson and his stone carvings. Farrar, Straus and Giroux 2009 56p il $17.95
Grades: 8 9 10 11 12 Adult **811**

1. Artists 2. Sculptors 3. Religious poetry 4. Artists -- Poetry 5. Sculpture -- Poetry 6. African Americans -- Poetry 7. Poetry -- By individual authors
ISBN 978-0-374-33528-1; 0-374-33528-1

LC 2008-02343

"Moved by a religious vision at age 57, Nashville janitor William Edmondson began carving tombstones and whimsical figures out of stone in 1931 and went on to attract the attention of international collectors, eventually becoming the first African American artist to have a solo show at the Museum of Modern Art in New York. This handsome picture-book-sized poetry collection pairs full-page, black-and-white photos of Edmondson and his works with poems inspired by the images. . . . Supported by an appended prose biography, these playful, thought-provoking poems introduce a fascinating artist." Booklist

Tell the world; teen poems from WritersCorps. HarperTeen 2008 116p $16.99; pa $8.99
Grades: 7 8 9 10 11 12 **811**

1. Teenagers' writings 2. American poetry -- Collections
ISBN 978-0-06-134505-0; 0-06-134505-9; 978-0-06-134504-3 pa; 0-06-134504-0 pa

LC 2007-49577

"This worthy collection of brief poems offers an array of teen voices. . . . An essay by WritersCorps teacher Michelle Matz adds a vivid picture of her students and their lives. This fine collection should inspire creativity and resonate with teens who find their own hopes, fears, and dreams eloquently voiced in the works of these young poets." SLJ

Testa, Maria

Something about America. Candlewick Press 2005 84p $14.99
Grades: 6 7 8 9 **811**

1. Immigrants -- Poetry 2. Burns and scalds -- Poetry 3. Serbian Americans -- Poetry 4. Poetry -- By individual authors
ISBN 0-7636-2528-0

LC 2005-47064

"Testa's distilled poetry never seems forced, and her stirring words enhance a sense of the characters' experiences and emotions. . . . Based on an actual incident, this is an excellent choice for readers' theater and classroom discussion." Booklist

Thayer, Ernest Lawrence

Casey at the bat; written by Ernest L. Thayer; with illustrations by Joe Morse. Kids Can Press 2006 un il (Visions in poetry) $16.95
Grades: 5 6 7 8 **811**

1. Baseball -- Poetry 2. Poetry -- By individual authors
ISBN 1-55337-827-X; 978-1-55337-827-3

"Morse updates Thayer's baseball classic to a modern, urban setting with a multiracial cast filling the familiar roles. As tall buildings loom above them, metallic fences confine the players who seem pensive and watchful. The figures are strikingly rendered in oils and acrylics, their features sharply limned in thick black lines and smudges of neutral color." SLJ

★ **Time** you let me in; 25 poets under 25. selected by Naomi Shihab Nye. Greenwillow Books 2010 236p $16.99; lib bdg $17.89
Grades: 8 9 10 11 12 **811**

1. American poetry -- Collections
ISBN 978-0-06-189637-8; 0-06-189637-3; 978-0-06-189638-5 lib bdg; 0-06-189638-1 lib bdg

LC 2009-19387

"This lively collection by young contemporary writers is rooted in the strong, emotional particulars of family, friendship, childhood memories, school, dislocation, war, and more. . . . Teens will connect with the passionate, unmoderated feelings that are given clarity and shape in each poem." Booklist

Includes bibliographical references

Weatherford, Carole Boston, 1956-

Remember the bridge; poems of a people. designed by Semador Megged. Philomel Bks. 2002 53p il $17.99

Grades: 5 6 7 8 **811**

1. African Americans -- Poetry 2. Poetry -- By individual authors

ISBN 0-399-23726-7

LC 2001-36161

"The author evokes imagined and actual individual experiences of the people . . . in the historical black-and-white photos, drawings, and etchings. . . . This celebratory, visually striking book will be appreciated in most collections." SLJ

You can fly; the Tuskegee Airmen. Carole Boston Weatherford ; art by Jeffery Boston Weatherford. Atheneum Books for Young Readers 2015 96 p. illustrations (hardcover : alk. paper) $16.99

Grades: 4 5 6 7 8 **811**

1. African American soldiers 2. World War, 1939-1945 -- Aerial operations 3. Tuskegee Army Air Field (Ala.) -- Juvenile poetry 4. African American air pilots -- History -- Juvenile poetry 5. World War, 1939-1945 -- Campaigns -- Western Front -- Juvenile poetry 6. World War, 1939-1945 -- Aerial operations, American -- Juvenile poetry 7. World War, 1939-1945 -- Participation, African American -- Juvenile poetry 8. United States. Army Air Forces. Fighter Squadron, 99th -- History -- Juvenile poetry

ISBN 9781481449380; 9781481449397

LC 2015012393

This book, by Carole Boston Weatherford and Jeffery Boston Weatherford, "celebrates the story of the Tuskegee Airmen. . . . From training days in Alabama to combat on the front lines in Europe, this is the story of the Tuskegee Airmen, the groundbreaking African-American pilots of World War II." (Publisher's note)

" This excellent treatment is enhanced with useful backmatter: author's note, timeline, and list of additional resources. Jeffery Boston Weatherford's scratchboard illustrations complement the text. A masterful, inspiring evocation of an era." Kirkus

Includes bibliographical references

Whipple, Laura

If the shoe fits; voices from Cinderella. illustrations by Laura Beingessner. Margaret K. McElderry Bks. 2002 67p il $17.95

Grades: 5 6 7 8 **811**

1. Cinderella -- Poetry 2. Fairy tales -- Poetry 3. Poetry -- By individual authors

ISBN 0-689-84070-5

LC 2001-30778

In this version of the fairy tale "the characters tell the story in blank verses. . . . The story unfolds just as it always does, but the multiple points of view—from Cinderella's to the prince's to the rat's to the queen's—enlarge and enrich the familiar tale to win a more sophisticated audience. . . . Paintings by Beingessner achieve just the right mixture of sorrow, beauty, and humor." Booklist

Whisper and shout; poems to memorize. edited by Patrice Vecchione. Cricket Bks. 2002 120p $16.95

Grades: 4 5 6 7 **811**

1. American poetry -- Collections

ISBN 0-8126-2656-7

LC 2002-591

A collection of poems on different subjects and in different styles, that lend themselves to memorization. Among the poets represented are Jack Prelutsky, Edward Lear, Ogden Nash, T. S. Eliot, Edna St. Vincent Millay, Christina Rossetti, and Lewis Carroll

"With a lengthy, enthusiastic introduction and a generous final section of resources and biographies, this anthology will get as much use in the classroom as with individual readers." Booklist

Includes bibliographical references

Whitman, Walt

★ **Walt** Whitman; edited by Jonathan Levin; illustrated by Jim Burke. Sterling 1997 48p il (Poetry for young people) $14.95; pa $6.95

Grades: 5 6 7 8 9 **811**

1. Children's poetry, American 2. Poetry -- By individual authors

ISBN 0-8069-9530-0; 1-4027-5477-9 pa

LC 97-433

An illustrated collection of twenty-six poems and excerpts from longer poems by the renowned nineteenth-century poet

"An outstanding introduction to Whitman's life and work. . . . This superb volume can be used to teach literature or to show a variety of poetic devices and style." SLJ

Wicked poems; edited by Roger McGough; illustrated by Neal Layton. Bloomsbury Children's Books 2004 208p il $15

Grades: 4 5 6 7 **811**

1. Good and evil -- Poetry 2. American poetry -- Collections

ISBN 1-58234-854-5

LC 2002-38551

"The 134 poems in this . . . collection focus on people exhibiting various degrees of wickedness. The book includes works from well-known poets . . . and children's authors such as Shel Silverstein, Eve Merriam, Myra Cohn Livingston, and Jack Prelutsky. . . . Childlike, black-and-white cartoons are laugh-out-loud funny. . . . A perfect choice for reading aloud as well as independent browsing." SLJ

Williams, William Carlos

William Carlos Williams; edited by Christopher MacGowan; illustrated by Robert Crockett. Sterling Pub. Co. 2004 48p il (Poetry for young people) $14.95

Grades: 7 8 9 10 **811**

1. Poetry -- By individual authors

ISBN 1-4027-0006-7

LC 2003-6885

A collection of thirty poems with illustrations and brief introductory remarks

"The introduction and commentary that MacGowan . . . provides not only fills in biographical details but expertly illuminates the craft and sensibility behind these 31 deceptively simple imagist poems . . . Despite its simple language and clear imagery, Williams' poetry is not widely available to young readers. This gathering should help to remedy that." Booklist

Words with wings; a treasury of African-American poetry and art. selected by Belinda Rochelle. HarperCollins Pubs. 2001 un il lib bdg $18.99
Grades: 4 5 6 7 **811**
1. African Americans in art 2. African Americans -- Poetry 3. American poetry -- African American authors -- Collections
ISBN 0-688-16415-3
LC 00-26864

Pairs twenty works of art by African-American artists such as Horace Pippin and Jacob Lawrence with twenty poems by African-American poets such as Langston Hughes, Countee Cullen, and Lucille Clifton

"Most of the combinations are stunning. . . . Short biographical paragraphs on each poet and artist round out this moving presentation." SLJ

Worth, Valerie

Pug and other animal poems; Valerie Worth ; pictures by Steve Jenkins. Margaret Ferguson Books, Farrar Straus Giroux 2012 40 p. $16.99
Grades: 2 3 4 5 **811**
1. Animals -- Poetry 2. Children's poetry 3. Animals -- Juvenile poetry 4. Children's poetry, American
ISBN 0374350248; 9780374350246
LC 2010034300

This juvenile poetry collection, by Valerie Worth, illustrated by Steve Jenkins, "examines a wide range of animal behavior, from the fleetingness of a fly sipping spilled milk to the constant steely presence of a powerful bull; the greedy meal of a street rat to a cat's quiet gift of a dead mouse on the doorstep." (Publisher's note)

WritersCorps

Paint me like I am; teen poems from WritersCorps. HarperTempest 2003 128p hardcover o.p. pa $6.99
Grades: 7 8 9 10 **811**
1. Teenagers' writings 2. American poetry -- Collections
ISBN 0-06-029288-1; 0-06-447264-7 pa
LC 2002-5942

"The teen voices in these poems, collected from the WritersCorps youth program, are LOUD—raging, defiant, giddy, lusty, and hopeful. Grouped into arbitrary categories, the poems explore identity, creative expressions, family, neighborhood, drugs, and relationships. . . . A foreword from Nikki Giovanni rounds out this moving collection, which also includes a few thoughtful writing exercises." Booklist

Yolen, Jane

The **Emily** sonnets; the life of Emily Dickinson. by Jane Yolen ; illustrations by Gary Kelley. 1st ed. Creative Editions 2012 40 p. col. ill. (reinforced) $19.99
Grades: 5 6 7 **811**
1. Dickinson, Emily, 1830-1886 -- Poetry
ISBN 1568462158; 9781568462158
LC 2011040841

This book by Jane Yolen presents 15 sonnets about poet Emily Dickinson. "The selections are constructed in various voices. . . . In the first five pieces, Emily speaks of the family's brick house, her close relationship with her sister Vinnie, her schooling, her variance with her family's religious beliefs, and the companionship of her dog. . . . The other speakers . . . tell of her always dressing in white, her life as a recluse, and her work." (School Library Journal)

★ **Sacred** places; illustrated by David Shannon. Harcourt Brace & Co. 1996 38p il $16
Grades: 4 5 6 7 **811**
1. Religious poetry 2. Poetry -- By individual authors
ISBN 0-15-269953-8
LC 92-30323

"The hazy moodiness of Shannon's paintings capture the mystery Yolen explores in her text, while his dense figures and literal interpretations of a passage from each poem draw Yolen's mystical flights back down to solid ground. Appended notes offer historical information on each sacred place." Bull Cent Child Books

Young, Ed

Beyond the great mountains; a visual poem about China. Chronicle Books 2005 32p il $17.95
Grades: 4 5 6 7 **811**
1. China -- Poetry 2. Poetry -- By individual authors
ISBN 0-8118-4343-2

"The book is comprised of 14 lines, each of which is accompanied by its own double-page illustration, done in cut and torn-paper collage. Young also provides the ancient characters for the images he presents. . . . Designed to be read vertically, each page is flipped up to reveal the accompanying illustration. In this way, the entire book becomes a piece of art, a visual treat of sublime colors and textures that joins with text and characters to describe the vastness and beauty of China." SLJ

812 American drama in English

Acting out; six one-act plays!: six Newbery stars! edited by Justin Chanda; featuring the playwrights, Avi . . . [et. al.] Atheneum Books for Young Readers 2008 175p il $16.99
Grades: 5 6 7 8 9 **812**
1. One act plays 2. American drama -- Collections
ISBN 978-1-4169-3848-4; 1-4169-3848-6

Contains six original one-act plays by Newbery Award-winning children's authors, including Sharon Creech, Susan Cooper, Avi, Patricia Maclachlan, Katherine Paterson, and Richard Peck

"Each play was inspired by a theater-improv game in which the authors started with the selection of a single word. The pieces all include the following words: 'dollop,' 'hoodwink,' 'Justin,' 'knuckleball,' 'panhandle,' and 'raven.'. . . An engaging choice for literature and acting classes as well as general reading." SLJ

Includes bibliographical references

Black, Ann N.

Readers theatre for middle school boys; investigating the strange and mysterious. illustrated by Cody Rust. Teachers Idea Press 2008 190p il (Readers theatre) pa $30
Grades: Adult Professional **812**
1. Readers' theater 2. Drama -- Collections
ISBN 978-1-59158-535-0 pa; 1-59158-535-X pa
LC 2007034923

"This book provides solid offerings of Readers Theater scripts for educators working with middle school boys. Selections include adaptations of such creepy classics as 'The Legend of Sleepy Hollow,' 'The Masque of the Red Death,' . . . and 'The Monkey's Paw.' The scripts have a new, fresh feel, and contain plenty of elements to capture and maintain adolescent males' attention." Libr Media Connect

Includes bibliographical references

Children's Theatre Company (Minneapolis, Minn.)

Fierce & true; plays for teen audiences. Peter & Elissa Adams, editors; The Children's Theatre Company. University of Minnesota Press 2010 219p il pa $17.95

Grades: 7 8 9 10 11 12 **812**

1. Drama -- Collections

ISBN 978-0-8166-7311-7; 0-8166-7311-X

The Children's Theatre Company "located in Minneapolis, wanted to broaden its audience, so it commissioned four playwrights to create works with young people (ages 12-18) specifically in mind. The results are the full-length plays in this anthology. . . . 'Anon(ymous)' is a contemporary retelling of Homer's Odyssey, set in a dirty North American city, and 'Five Fingers of Funk' is a mature musical celebrating the roots of hip-hop while dealing with issues of poverty and drugs. In 'The Lost Boys of Sudan,' three Dinka refugees flee the horrors of war and begin a harrowing yet humorous journey that takes them to Fargo, ND. And 'Prom' is played out as a frenetic battle between students and chaperones. Each of these selections has a distinctive voice, honoring adolescents as both actor and audience capable of understanding and engaging in today's complex issues." SLJ

Dunkleberger, Amy

A **student's** guide to Arthur Miller. Enslow Publs. 2005 160p il (Understanding literature) lib bdg $27.93

Grades: 7 8 9 10 **812**

1. Authors 2. Dramatists 3. Screenwriters

ISBN 0-7660-2432-6

This discusses the life of Arthur Miller and his works All My Sons, Death of a Salesman, The Crucible, A View From the Bridge, After the Fall, Incident at Vichy, and The Price

"Engaging and informative. . . . The very accessible format and the solid information make [this book] useful to students, and the engaging style should interest casual readers." SLJ

Includes glossary and bibliographical references

Hermann, Spring

A **student's** guide to Eugene O'Neill. Enslow Publishers 2009 176p il (Understanding literature) lib bdg $27.93

Grades: 7 8 9 10 **812**

1. Authors 2. Dramatists 3. Nobel laureates for literature

ISBN 978-0-7660-2886-9; 0-7660-2886-0

LC 2008-14599

"An introduction to the work of Eugene O'Neill for . . . students, which includes relevant biographical background on the author, explanations of various literary devices and techniques, and literary criticism for the novice reader." Publisher's note

Includes glossary and bibliographical references

Levine, Karen

★ **Hana's** suitcase on stage; original story by Karen Levine; play by Emil Sher. Second Story 2007 171p il (Holocaust remembrance book for young readers) pa $18.95

Grades: 5 6 7 8 **812**

1. Holocaust victims 2. Holocaust, 1933-1945 -- Drama

ISBN 978-1-89718-705-0 pa; 1-89718-705-X pa

"Set in the Tokyo Holocaust Center, the two-act play opens with the woman and two of her student helpers questioning and searching for answers to the suitcase's history. . . . Act II blends characters of Ishioka and her students with Hana and her family, each group individually recounting their stories in alternating voices. As with the original book, this title succeeds in recreating a striking representation of one child's tragic and beautiful life in a terrifying world of hate and prejudice. This volume will serve as one of the most effective teaching models for Holocaust curriculums available. Photographs and facsimiles of Nazi documents are included." SLJ

Loos, Pamela

A **reader's** guide to Lorraine Hansberry's A raisin in the sun. Enslow Publishers 2008 128p il (Multicultural literature) lib bdg $31.93

Grades: 7 8 9 10 **812**

1. Authors 2. Dramatists 3. African Americans in literature 4. Essayists 5. Newspaper editors 6. Nonfiction writers 7. American drama -- History and criticism

ISBN 978-0-7660-2830-2; 0-7660-2830-5

LC 2006-17900

"A Raisin in the Sun has become part of the literary canon and is required reading for many students. This guide is intended to help them better appreciate the social milieu out of which this play emerged . . . making this volume a fine resource." SLJ

Includes bibliographical references

Soto, Gary

★ **Novio** boy; a play. Harcourt 2006 78p pa $5.95

Grades: 7 8 9 10 **812**

1. Mexican Americans -- Drama 2. Dating (Social customs) -- Drama

ISBN 978-0-15-205863-0; 0-15-205863-X

LC 2007-271308

First published 1997

Rudy anxiously prepares for and then goes out on a first date with an attractive girl who is older than he is.

Stuyvesant High School (New York, N.Y.)

With their eyes; September 11th: the view from a high school at ground zero. edited by Annie Thoms; created by Taresh Batra [et. al.]; photos by Ethan Moses. HarperTempest 2002 228p il hardcover o.p. pa $6.99

Grades: 7 8 9 10 **812**

1. Teenagers' writings 2. American drama -- Collections 3. Stuyvesant High School (New York, N.Y.) 4. September 11 terrorist attacks, 2001 -- Drama

ISBN 0-06-051806-5; 0-06-051718-2 pa

LC 2002-4552

"The speakers reveal their emotions with painful honesty. . . . The book is an obvious choice for reader's theater and for use across the curriculum; its deeply affecting contents will also make compelling personal-interest reading." Booklist

Theatre for young audiences; 20 great plays for children. edited by Coleman A. Jennings; foreword by Maurice Sendak. St. Martin's Press 1998 604p il $35; pa $19.95 **812**

1. Drama -- Collections

ISBN 0-312-18194-9; 0-312-33714-0 pa

LC 97-36542

A collection of plays, many of which are based on favorite children's tales, including such titles as: "Charlotte's Web," "Really Rosie," "Wiley and the Hairy Man," "Wise Men of Chelm," and "The Crane Wife"

"Highly recommended for school and public libraries and anyone interested in a substantial collection of plays for children." Booklist

813 American fiction in English

Blasingame, James B.

Gary Paulsen. Greenwood Press 2007 164p (Teen reads: student companions to young adult literature) $45

Grades: 7 8 9 10 11 12 **813**

1. Authors 2. Sled dog racers 3. Children's authors 4. Short story writers 5. Young adult authors

ISBN 978-0-313-33532-7; 0-313-33532-X

LC 2007-21446

"This volume examines a sample of . . . books by Paulsen. A biographical chapter demonstrates how Paulsen's life experiences, notably the Iditarod, have influenced his writing. Each book is analyzed for plot, characterization, setting, and themes." Publisher's note

Includes bibliographical references

Bodart, Joni Richards

They suck, they bite, they eat, they kill; the psychological meaning of supernatural monsters in young adult fiction. Joni Richards Bodart. Scarecrow Press 2012 xxxi, 268 p.p (Scarecrow studies in young adult literature) $45

Grades: Adult Professional **813**

1. Folklore in literature 2. Monsters in literature 3. Supernatural in literature 4. Literature -- Psychological aspects

ISBN 9780810882270

LC 2011029544

This book examines the "rise of paranormal young adult fiction" and "focuses on popular contemporary titles lightly contextualized in a historical frame. . . . The book is divided into four sections: 'Vampires: The Aristocratic Monster'; 'Shapeshifters: The Transforming Monster'; 'Zombies: The Reanimated, Resurrected Monster'; and 'Angels, Unicorns, Demons: The Unexpectedly Deadly Monsters.' Each section opens with an overview of the literary and, when applicable, folkloric history of each supernatural being." (School Libr J) "Chapters focusing on individual authors follow . . . . [T]he chapters serve both as a tour through each invented universe and as a study of the author's relationship to the books, drawn mostly through existing interviews." (Booklist)

Includes bibliographical references

Cammarano, Rita

Betsy Byars. Chelsea House 2002 106p il (Who wrote that?) lib bdg $30

Grades: 4 5 6 7 **813**

1. Authors 2. Women authors 3. Authors, American 4. Children's authors

ISBN 0-7910-6720-3

LC 2001-8337

Describes the personal life and successful writing career of the Newbery Award-winning author, whose memorable characters include Bingo Brown, Herculeah Jones, and the Golly sisters

"An excellent resource for author studies and creative writing classes." Book Rep

Includes bibliographical references

Carroll, Pamela S.

Sharon Creech; [by] Pamela Sissi Carroll. Greenwood Press 2007 195p (Teen reads: student companions to young adult literature) lib bdg $45

Grades: 7 8 9 10 11 12 **813**

1. Authors 2. Novelists 3. Authors, American 4. Children's authors 5. Young adult authors 6. Young adult literature -- History and criticism

ISBN 978-0-313-33598-3 lib bdg; 0-313-33598-2 lib bdg

LC 2007-21470

This focuses on Sharon Creech's "work as a teacher and shows how she uses the practice of journal-keeping to create an emotional experience for both character and reader. Of special interest are the chapters on Creech's life and those that discuss Absolutely Normal Chaos, Bloomability, and The Wanderer." Voice Youth Advocates

Includes bibliographical references

Cart, Michael

The **heart** has its reasons; young adult literature with gay/lesbian/queer content, 1969-2004. [by] Michael Cart [and] Christine A. Jenkins. Scarecrow Press 2006 207p (Scarecrow studies in young adult literature) $42

Grades: Adult Professional **813**

1. LGBT literature 2. Homosexuality in literature 3. Teenagers -- Books and reading 4. Young adult literature -- History and criticism

ISBN 0-8108-5071-0

LC 2005-31320

"Both a comprehensive overview and a lively, detailed discussion of individual landmark books, this highly readable title . . . discusses 35 years of YA books with gay, lesbian, bisexual, transgender, and queer/questioning (GLBTQ) content. . . . With fully annotated bibliographies, including a chronological list, this is a valuable YA and adult resource, sure to be in great demand for personal reference and group discussion." Booklist

Includes bibliographical references

Cook, Judy

Natural writer: a story about Marjorie Kinnan Rawlings; by Judy Cook and Laura Lee Smith; illustrated by Laurie Harden. Carolrhoda Bks. 2001 64p il (Creative minds biography) lib bdg $21.27

Grades: 4 5 6 **813**

1. Authors 2. Novelists 3. Women authors 4. Frontier and pioneer life 5. Authors, American 6. Children's authors 7. Short story writers

ISBN 1-57505-468-X

LC 00-9657

"This biography begins with Rawling's childhood in the early 1900s and shows her development as a writer through her death. . . . This easy-to-read biography has an attractive cover and a full-page charcoal illustration in each chapter." SLJ

Includes bibliographical references

Crayton, Lisa A.

A **student's** guide to Toni Morrison. Enslow Publs. 2006 160p il (Understanding literature) lib bdg $27.93

Grades: 7 8 9 10 **813**

1. Authors 2. Novelists 3. Dramatists 4. Essayists 5. College teachers 6. Literary critics 7. Nobel laureates for literature

ISBN 0-7660-2436-9

LC 2005-19069

"Each work is placed in historical and biographical context, with special emphasis placed on curriculum-related material, including The Bluest Eye, Song of Solomon, and Beloved, along with several other noteworthy works." Publisher's note

Includes glossary and bibliographical references

Crew, Hilary S.

Experiencing America's story through fiction; historical novels for grades 7-12. Hilary Crew. ALA Editions, An imprint of the American Library Association 2014 xii, 193 p.p (paper) $57

Grades: Professional **813**

1. Library science 2. American fiction -- Bibliography 3. Historical fiction -- Bibliography 4. Historical fiction, American 5. Historical fiction, American -- Bibliography 6. Young adult fiction, American -- Bibliography 7. United States -- In literature -- Bibliography 8. Teenagers -- Books and reading -- United States 9. United States -- History -- Fiction -- Bibliography

ISBN 0838912257; 9780838912256

LC 2014008471

This annotated bibliography by Hillary Susan Crew "highlights more than 150 titles of historical fiction published since 2000 appropriate for seventh to twelfth graders." (Publisher's note)

"Historical fiction is a popular and effective way to connect literature to curriculum. Although the new Common Core Curriculum emphasizes informational texts, fiction can introduce different viewpoints and provide unique opportunities for evaluation and critical thinking. This book seeks to help history teachers and school and public librarians discover new historical fiction (most of the titles included were published between 2000 and 2013) and find ways to effectively use these titles to support their curriculum...The selection of books embodies a multitude of perspectives and truly represents the diversity of the United States. This outstanding bibliography is perfect for teachers, librarians, or history fans searching for just the right book." Horn Book

Includes bibliographical references (pages 183-185) and index

Dean, Tanya

Theodor Geisel. Chelsea House 2002 112p il (Who wrote that?) $22.95

Grades: 4 5 6 7 **813**

1. Artists 2. Authors 3. Humorists 4. Illustrators 5. Authors, American 6. Children's authors

ISBN 0-7910-6724-6

LC 2002-166

Describes the life and career of the author and illustrator known as Dr. Seuss who created such popular children's picture books as The cat in the hat, How the Grinch stole Christmas, and Horton hears a Who

"Well organized and clearly written." Booklist

Includes bibliographical references

Diorio, Mary Ann L.

A **student's** guide to Herman Melville. Enslow Publs. 2006 160p il (Understanding literature) lib bdg $27.93

Grades: 7 8 9 10 **813**

1. Authors 2. Novelists

ISBN 0-7660-2435-0

LC 2005-10159

"Each work is placed in historical and biographical context, with special emphasis placed on curriculum-related works, including his masterpiece, Moby Dick, along with Billy Budd, several of his short stories, including 'Bartleby the Scrivener,' and several of his poetic works." Publisher's note

Includes glossary and bibliographical references

A **student's** guide to Mark Twain; [by] Mary Ann L. Diorio. Enslow Publishers 2007 160p il (Understanding literature) $27.93

Grades: 7 8 9 10 **813**

1. Authors 2. Humorists 3. Novelists 4. Essayists 5. Satirists 6. Memoirists 7. Travel writers 8. Short story writers

ISBN 978-0-7660-2438-0; 0-7660-2438-5

LC 2006005888

"After a brief account of the writer's life, Diorio discusses 11 of his major works in chronological order, starting with 'The Jumping Frog' and ending with The Tragedy of Pudd'nhead Wilson. For each highlighted selection, she gives a bare-bones plot summary and a brief discussion of major themes, characters, and literary devices. . . . The book is nicely formatted, with readable font on uncluttered pages. There are a few black-and-white photographs of Twain and some relevant reproductions." SLJ

Includes bibliographical references

Don, Katherine

Real courage; the story of Harper Lee. by Katherine Don. Morgan Reynolds Pub. 2013 128 p. ill. (some col.) $28.95

Grades: 7 8 9 10 **813**

1. Women -- Biography 2. American authors -- Biography 3. Authors, American -- 20th century -- Biography

ISBN 9781599353487; 9781599353494

LC 2012016871

This book examines author Nelle Harper Lee and "the publication and film adaptation of her novel 'To Kill a Mockingbird.'" The book looks at "the turbulent 1960's civil rights movement and how Lee's book, which spoke of racial injustice, struck a nerve with the public. Lee grew up in a small Mississippi town that experienced segregation, which she later used as the fictional setting for 'Mockingbird.' The biography describes Lee's rise to fame and the legacy she left." (Voice of Youth Advocates)

"Students and teachers looking for a solid, accessible biography will find this to be a fine choice as the writing is straightforward and engaging." SLJ

Includes bibliographical references and index

Gallo, Donald R.

Richard Peck; the past is paramount. [by] Donald R. Gallo, Wendy J. Glenn. Scarecrow Press 2009 208p (Scarecrow studies in young adult literature) $35

Grades: 7 8 9 10 Adult Professional **813**

1. Authors 2. Novelists 3. Children's authors 4. Young adult authors

ISBN 978-0-8108-5848-0; 0-8108-5848-7

LC 2008036524

"Gallo and Wendy J. Glenn recount the highlights of Peck's life, focusing on his world travels, his accomplishments as a teacher and his renowned writing career. Gallo and Glenn examine Peck's 30 novels, as well as his short stories and children's books, poems, essays and other nonfiction." Publisher's note

Includes bibliographical references

Gantos, Jack

★ **Hole** in my life. Farrar, Straus & Giroux 2002 199p il $16; pa $8

Grades: 7 8 9 10 **813**

1. Authors 2. College teachers 3. Authors, American 4. Children's authors

ISBN 0-374-39988-3; 0-374-43089-6 pa

LC 2001-40957

Michael L. Printz Award honor book, 2003

The author relates how, as a young adult, he became a drug user and smuggler, was arrested, did time in prison, and eventually got out and went to college, all the while hoping to become a writer

"Gantos' spare narrative style and straightforward revelation of the truth have, together, a cumulative power that will capture not only a reader's attention but also empathy and imagination." Booklist

The girl who was on fire; your favorite authors on Suzanne Collins' Hunger games trilogy. edited by Leah Wilson. BenBella Books 2011 211p pa $12.95

Grades: Adult Professional **813**

1. Authors 2. Novelists 3. Fantasy writers 4. Young adult authors

ISBN 978-1-935618-04-1; 1-935618-04-0

LC 2011007180

"Fans of the trilogy will undoubtedly enjoy exploring elements of the series through the eyes of the author's contemporaries, each with a different expertise. The selections address the deeper social and political issues as well as the development of multilayered characters through witty and sometimes raw essays that ask readers to look deeper. . . . Essays explore . . . subjects from within Katniss's world of Panem with humor, irreverence, and social understanding. This thought-provoking text will be especially useful for educators or librarians utilizing the multidiscplinary themes in this trilogy with their students." SLJ

Includes bibliographical references

Glenn, Wendy J.

Sarah Dessen; from burritos to box office. [by] Wendy J. Glenn. Scarecrow Press 2005 147p (Scarecrow studies in young adult literature) $45

Grades: 7 8 9 10 Adult Professional **813**

1. Authors 2. Novelists 3. Young adult authors

ISBN 0-8108-5325-6; 978-0-8108-5325-6

LC 2004016058

This offers literary criticism of the works of Sarah Dessen, author of such young adult novels as The Truth About Forever, and Lock and Key

"Glenn's book is an excellent example of the kind of meaning-making exploration that students can examine in a work of literature written for adolescents. . . . Informative and lively." Voice Youth Advocates

Includes bibliographical references

Hamilton, Virginia

★ **Virginia** Hamilton: speeches, essays, and conversations; edited by Arnold Adoff & Kacy Cook. Blue Sky Press 2010 368p $29.99

Grades: 8 9 10 11 12 Adult Professional **813**

1. Authorship 2. Children's literature -- History and criticism

ISBN 978-0-439-27193-6; 0-439-27193-2

LC 2009031676

"A groundbreaking writer of children's fiction, folktales, biography, and picture books, Hamilton won every major award, and much of this book is made up of her acceptance speeches, including those for the Newbery, Hans Christian Andersen, and Coretta Scott King awards, as well as her Arbuthnot and Zena Sutherland lectures. Aimed at a general audience, the book employs a tone both scholarly and informal, as Hamilton talks about her career as a woman and a black writer in America and about the form and content of her work in general and with particular titles. . . . Many speeches include introductions by children's literature scholars and editors, who add perspective on Hamilton's lasting influence, while family members fill in biographical details. A must for YAs who love her books, this will also appeal to librarians, teachers, and children's literature students." Booklist

Includes bibliographical references

Hickam, Homer H.

The **Coalwood** way; by Homer H. Hickam, Jr. Delacorte Press 2000 318p hardcover o.p. pa $6.99

Grades: 7 8 9 10 11 12 Adult **813**

1. Authors 2. Novelists 3. Aerospace engineers 4. Memoirists 5. West Virginia 6. Authors, American 7. Writers on science

ISBN 0-440-23716-5

LC 00-35884

This sequel to Rocket boys "continues the author's life story with his senior year in high school, 1959, in the declining West Virginia mining town of Coalwood. The rocket club, featured in the last book, is pushed to the periphery, and the focus shifts to Hickam's teenage problems, which include his parents, girls, and a sadness whose cause he cannot divine." Booklist

Hinds, Maurene J.

A **reader's** guide to Richard Wright's Black boy. Enslow Publishers 2010 128p il (Multicultural literature) lib bdg $31.93

Grades: 6 7 8 9 **813**

1. Authors 2. Novelists 3. Dramatists 4. Essayists 5. Nonfiction writers 6. Short story writers 7. American literature -- African American authors

ISBN 978-0-7660-3165-4 lib bdg; 0-7660-3165-9 lib bdg

LC 2008-36473

"An introduction to Richard Wright's novel Black Boy . . . which includes relevant biographical background on the author, explanations of various literary devices and techniques, and literary criticism for the novice reader." Publisher's note

Includes glossary and bibliographical references

Hinton, KaaVonia

Angela Johnson; poetic prose. [by] KaaVonia Hinton. Scarecrow Press 2006 107p (Scarecrow studies in young adult literature) $35

Grades: 7 8 9 10 Adult Professional **813**

1. Poets 2. Authors 3. Novelists 4. Children's authors 5. Short story writers 6. Young adult authors

ISBN 978-0-8108-5092-7; 0-8108-5092-3

LC 2006001893

The examines the life and works of Angela Johnson, author of such novels as Toning the Sweep and A Cool Moonlight

"This book is a well-researched biography suitable for reports or even thoughtful fans. Certainly teachers seeking to use Johnson's books in their classes should find the literary criticism very useful." Voice Youth Advocates

Includes bibliographical references

Sharon M. Draper; embracing literacy. [by] KaaVonia Hinton. Scarecrow Press 2009 131p (Scarecrow studies in young adult literature) $35

Grades: 7 8 9 10 Adult Professional **813**

1. Authors 2. Teachers 3. Novelists 4. Children's authors 5. Young adult authors

ISBN 978-0-8108-5985-2; 0-8108-5985-8

LC 2008036695

"Author KaaVonia Hinton reveals how Draper became an exceptional teacher and writer, and how she uses her writing to urge young people to embrace literacy. Hinton also explores how Draper has made a lasting contribution to the field of young adult literature. This book-length study examines both her life and work." Publisher's note

Includes bibliographical references

Hirschmann, Kris

Frankenstein. ReferencePoint Press 2011 80p il (Monsters and mythical creatures) $27.95

Grades: 6 7 8 9 **813**

1. Authors 2. Novelists 3. Monsters in literature

ISBN 978-1-60152-180-4; 1-60152-180-4

LC 2011002145

This is "an ideal starting point for young researchers interested in the weird, mysterious, and paranormal. Using fleet, descriptive prose to communicate the impressively researched (and sourced) information, [this] medium-length [work manages] to rope in just about everything, from folklore to history to pop culture. The bulk of Frankenstein focuses upon Mary Shelley's masterpiece, not just the infamous contest for which it was written but also the reception and critical analysis, both then and now. . . . The illustrations are fine and varied, the sidebars always illuminating, and the back matter robust." Booklist

Includes bibliographical references

Hogan, Walter

★ **Humor** in young adult literature; a time to laugh. Scarecrow Press 2005 223p (Scarecrow studies in young adult literature) $40

Grades: Adult Professional **813**

1. Teenagers -- Books and reading 2. Wit and humor -- History and criticism

ISBN 0-8108-5072-9

LC 2004-18903

"As a reader's advisory tool, this book is invaluable, paving the way for many laughter-filled hours to come." Voice Youth Advocates

Includes bibliographical references

Jocelyn, Marthe

A **Big** Dose of Lucky; Marthe Jocelyn. Orca Book Publishers 2015 264 p. $14.95

Grades: 7 8 9 10 11 12 **813**

1. Orphans -- Fiction 2. Teenage girls -- Fiction 3. Racially mixed people -- Fiction

ISBN 1459806689; 9781459806689

LC 2015935534

In this novel, by Marthe Jocelyn, "Malou has just turned sixteen . . . and all she knows for sure is that she's of mixed race and that she was left at an orphanage as a newborn. When the orphanage burns to the ground, she finds out that she may have been born in a small town in Ontario. Parry Sound turns out to have quite a few young brown faces, but Malou can't believe they might be related to her. After she finds work . . . an Aboriginal boy . . . helps her find answers to her questions." (Publisher's note)

"Sharp writing keeps this dramatic coming-of-age story from taking a turn toward the saccharine or melodramatic, despite the casual and not-so-casual racism Malou endures outside the sheltered confines of the orphanage. Lovely and easily digestible historical fiction." Booklist

Other titles in this series are:

Innocent (2015)

Shattered Glass (2015)

My Life Before Me (2015)

Stones on a Grave (2015)

Small Bones (2015)

Jones, Jen

A **reader's** guide to Gary Soto's Taking sides. Enslow Publishers 2010 127p il (Multicultural literature) lib bdg $31.93

Grades: 8 9 10 11 12 **813**

1. Poets 2. Authors 3. Novelists 4. Hispanic Americans in literature 5. Essayists 6. College teachers 7. Children's authors 8. Young adult authors

ISBN 978-0-7660-3168-5 lib bdg; 0-7660-3168-3 lib bdg

LC 2008-38587

An introduction to Gary Soto's novel Taking sides for high school students, which includes biographical background on the author, explanations of various literary devices and techniques, and literary criticism for the novice reader.

Includes glossary and bibliographical references

Juster, Norton

The **annotated** Phantom tollbooth; by Norton Juster; illustrations by Jules Feiffer; introduction and notes by Leonard Marcus. Alfred A. Knopf 2011 284p il $29.99; lib bdg $32.22

Grades: Adult Professional **813**

1. Authors 2. Architects 3. Children's authors

ISBN 978-0-375-85715-7; 0-375-85715-X; 978-0-375-95715-4 lib bdg; 0-375-95715-4 lib bdg

LC 2011013174

"Still ferrying dazzled readers to Dictionopolis and beyond 50 years after his first appearance, young Milo is accompanied this time through by encyclopedic commentary from our generation's leading (and most readable) expert on the history of children's literature and publishing. . . . Leonard opens with typically lucid and well-organized pictures of both Juster's and Feiffer's formative years and later careers, interwoven with accounts of the book's conception, publication and critical response. In notes running alongside the ensuing facsimile, he puts on an intellectual show. . . . he delivers notes on topics as diverse as the etymological origins of "BALDERDASH!" and mimetic architecture to textual parallels with the Wizard of Oz and echoes of Winsor McKay and George Grosz in the art. Family photos, scrawled notes and images of handwritten and typescript manuscript pages further gloss a work that never ages nor fails to astonish." Kirkus

Kramer, Barbara

Toni Morrison; a biography of a nobel prize-winning writer. by Barbara Kramer. Enslow Publishers 2012 104 p. (library) $26.60

Grades: 7 8 9 10 **813**

1. Morrison, Toni 2. African American novelists -- Biography 3. Novelists, American -- 20th century -- Biography

ISBN 0766039897; 9780766039896

LC 2011024344

In this biography of African American author Toni Morrison, "Barbara Kramer explores the life and career of this talented writer. From her childhood in Loraine, Ohio, to her creative expressions of African-American culture, Morrison has always remembered her past. She has taught at several universities, as well as being the author of novels, short stories essays, and a play." (Publisher's note)

Includes bibliographical references (p. 88-99) and index.

Lazo, Caroline Evensen

F. Scott Fitzgerald; voice of the Jazz Age. {by} Caroline Lazo. Lerner Publs. 2003 128p il (Lerner long biographies) lib bdg $25.26 **813**

1. Authors 2. Novelists 3. Screenwriters 4. Authors, American 5. Short story writers

ISBN 0-8225-0074-4

LC 2001-7210

"This well-documented book offers a fascinating glimpse into the acclaimed author's early years, unremarkable academic record, extravagant lifestyle, and work." SLJ

Includes bibliographical references (p. 118-119) and index

Litwin, Laura Baskes

A **reader's** guide to Zora Neale Hurston's Their eyes were watching god. Enslow Publishers 2010 128p il (Multicultural literature) lib bdg $31.93

Grades: 8 9 10 11 12 **813**

1. Authors 2. Novelists 3. Dramatists 4. African Americans in literature 5. Memoirists 6. Folklorists 7. Short story writers

ISBN 978-0-7660-3164-7; 0-7660-3164-0

LC 2008-38524

An introduction to Zora Neale Hurston's novel Their eyes were watching God for high school students, which includes biographical background on the author, explanations of various literary devices and techniques, and literary criticism for the novice reader.

Includes glossary and bibliographical references

Loos, Pamela

A **reader's** guide to Amy Tan's The joy luck club. Enslow Publishers 2008 112p il (Multicultural literature) $31.93

Grades: 6 7 8 9 **813**

1. Authors 2. Novelists 3. Mother-daughter relationships in literature 4. Essayists 5. Children's authors 6. Short story writers 7. Literature -- Women authors 8. American literature -- Asian American authors

ISBN 978-0-7660-2832-6; 0-7660-2832-1

LC 2006102440

The book is "an excellent resource for the student wanting to do more in depth research. . . . [The] photos . . . chosen are of good quality. . . . The [volume is] well organized, clearly written, and simple to understand." Voice Youth Advocates

Includes bibliographical references

Lukes, Bonnie L.

Soldier's courage: the story of Stephen Crane. Morgan Reynolds 2002 144p il lib bdg $21.95

Grades: 7 8 9 10 **813**

1. Authors 2. Novelists 3. Authors, American

ISBN 1-88384-694-3

LC 2002-5095

"Lukes's gift for storytelling and her stirring prose result in a thoroughly readable and informative volume." SLJ

Includes bibliographical references

Marler, Myrna Dee

Walter Dean Myers. Greenwood Press 2008 198p (Teen reads: student companions to young adult literature) $45

Grades: 8 9 10 11 12 Adult Professional **813**

1. Poets 2. Authors 3. Novelists 4. Editors 5. Children's authors 6. Young adult authors

ISBN 978-0-313-33628-7; 0-313-33628-8

LC 2008010070

"Marler analyzes the life and works of the accomplished author. The first two chapters are devoted to a brief biography and the historical and cultural influences on Myers's writing. The remainder of the volume looks at his books, including comparisons of plots and characters as well as thematic development within each novel." SLJ

Includes bibliographical references

McArthur, Debra

A **student's** guide to Edgar Allan Poe. Enslow Publishers 2006 160p il por (Understanding literature) lib bdg $27.93

Grades: 7 8 9 10 **813**

1. Poets 2. Authors 3. Essayists 4. Short story writers

ISBN 0-7660-2437-7

LC 2005024273

This examines the life and career of Edgar Allan Poe, discussing such works as The Raven, The Fall of the House of Usher, and The Tell-TaleHeart.

Includes glossary and bibliographical references

A **student's** guide to William Faulkner; [by] Debra A. McArthur. Enslow Publishers 2009 160p il (Understanding literature) lib bdg $27.93

Grades: 7 8 9 10 **813**

1. Authors 2. Novelists 3. Screenwriters 4. Short story writers 5. Nobel laureates for literature

ISBN 978-0-7660-2885-2; 0-7660-2885-2

LC 2008-3010

"An introduction to the work of William Faulkner for . . . students, which includes relevant biographical background on the author, explanations of various literary devices and techniques, and literary criticism for the novice reader." Publisher's note

Includes glossary and bibliographical references

McClellan, Marilyn

Madeleine L'Engle; banned, challenged, and censored. Enslow Publishers 2008 160p il (Authors of banned books) $25.95

Grades: 8 9 10 11 12 **813**

1. Authors 2. Novelists 3. Essayists 4. Memoirists 5. Mystery writers 6. Children's authors 7. Books -- Censorship 8. Short story writers 9. Writers on religion 10. Young adult authors 11. Science fiction writers

ISBN 978-0-7660-2708-4; 0-7660-2708-2

LC 2007015134

This "uses the attacks on one classic yet frequently challenged book, L'Engle's 1963 Newbery Medal winner, A Wrinkle in Time, to draw teens into a dynamic discussion of general censorship history and issues. McClellan describes the objections, frequently Christian fundamentalists citing the book's 'satanic content,' and counters them with comments from the other side. . . . Readers will also find a succinct biography of L'Engle. . . . occasional photos, a chapter of literary analysis, and summaries of both Wrinkle and L'Engle's Many Waters (1986)." Booklist

Includes bibliographical references

Myers, Walter Dean, 1937-2014

★ **Bad** boy; a memoir. HarperCollins Pubs. 2001 214p $15.95; pa $6.99

Grades: 7 8 9 10 **813**

1. Poets 2. Authors 3. Novelists 4. African American authors 5. Editors 6. Authors, American 7. Children's authors 8. Young adult authors

ISBN 0-06-029523-6; 0-06-447288-4 pa

LC 00-52978

This "is a story full of funny anecdotes, lofty ideals, and tender moments." SLJ

Napoli, Donna Jo

Zel. Dutton Children's Bks. 1996 227p hardcover o.p. pa $5.99

Grades: 7 8 9 10 **813**

1. Fairy tales 2. Mother-daughter relationship -- Fiction
ISBN 0-525-45612-0; 0-14-130116-3 pa

LC 96-15135

Based on the fairy tale Rapunzel, the story is told in alternating chapters from the point of view of Zel, her mother, and the prince, and delves into the psychological motivations of the characters

"This version, with its Faustian overtones, will challenge readers to think about this old story on a deeper level. It begs for discussion in literature classes." SLJ

Paulsen, Gary

★ **Guts**; the true stories behind Hatchet and the Brian books. Delacorte Press 2001 148p hardcover o.p. pa $5.50

Grades: 6 7 8 9 **813**

1. Authors 2. Hunting 3. Wilderness survival 4. Sled dog racers 5. Authors, American 6. Children's authors 7. Short story writers 8. Young adult authors 9. Children's stories -- Authorship 10. Authors, American -- 20th century -- Biography
ISBN 0385326505; 0440407125

LC 00-34061

The author relates incidents in his life and how they inspired parts of his books about the character, Brian Robeson

"Readers squeamish about hunting or the death of animals will find many of the stories disturbing . . . but those who embrace the sport or have enjoyed the novels will see in Paulsen a responsible role model—a man who respects life and death as equal partners." Booklist

★ **How** Angel Peterson got his name; and other outrageous tales about extreme sports. Wendy Lamb Bks. 2003 111p hardcover o.p. pa $5.99

Grades: 5 6 7 8 **813**

1. Authors 2. Sled dog racers 3. Authors, American 4. Children's authors 5. Short story writers 6. Young adult authors
ISBN 0-385-72949-9; 0-385-90090-2 lib bdg; 978-0-440-22935-3 pa; 0-440-22935-9 pa

LC 2002-7668

Author Gary Paulsen relates tales from his youth in a small town in northwestern Minnesota in the late 1940s and early 1950s, such as skiing behind a souped-up car and imitating daredevil Evel Knievel

"Writing with humor and sensitivity, Paulsen shows boys moving into adolescence believing they can do anything. . . . None of them dies (amazingly), and even if Paulsen exaggerates the teensiest bit, his tales are side-splittingly funny and more than a little frightening." Booklist

★ **My** life in dog years; with drawings by Ruth Wright Paulsen. Delacorte Press 1998 137p il $15.95; pa $6.50

Grades: 4 5 6 7 **813**

1. Dogs 2. Authors 3. Sled dog racers 4. Authors, American 5. Children's authors 6. Short story writers 7. Young adult authors
ISBN 0-385-32570-3; 0-440-41471-7 pa

LC 97-40254

The author describes some of the dogs that have had special places in his life, including his first dog, Snowball, in the Philippines; Dirk, who protected him from bullies; and Cookie, who saved his life

"Paulsen differentiates his canine friends beautifully, as only a keen observer and lover of dogs can. At the same time, he presents an intimate glimpse of himself, a lonely child of alcoholic parents, who drew strength and solace from his four-legged companions and a love of the great outdoors. Poignant but never saccharine, honest, and open." Booklist

Pingelton, Timothy J.

A **student's** guide to Ernest Hemingway. Enslow Publishers 2005 160p il map (Understanding literature) lib bdg $27.93

Grades: 7 8 9 10 **813**

1. Poets 2. Authors 3. Novelists 4. Short story writers 5. Nobel laureates for literature
ISBN 0-7660-2431-8

This discusses Hemingway's life and his novels In Our Time, The Sun Also Rises, A Farewell to Arms, and The Old Man and the Sea

"Engaging and informative. . . . The very accessible format and the solid information make [this book] useful to students, and the engaging style should interest casual readers." SLJ

Includes glossary and bibliographical references

Reef, Catherine

★ **John** Steinbeck. Clarion Bks. 1996 163p il $17.95; pa $8.95

Grades: 7 8 9 10 **813**

1. Authors 2. Novelists 3. Screenwriters 4. Authors, American 5. Nobel laureates for literature
ISBN 0-395-71278-5; 0-618-43244-2 pa

LC 95-11500

"The book traces Steinbeck's life from his childhood in California, to his burgeoning writing career and his passion for social justice, to his worldwide recognition. Reef does an excellent job of synthesizing Steinbeck's work, his private life, and his politics and philosophy." Bull Cent Child Books

Includes bibliographical references

Reid, Suzanne Elizabeth

Virginia Euwer Wolff; capturing the music of young voices. [by] Suzanne Elizabeth Reid. Scarecrow Press 2003 137p il (Scarecrow studies in young adult literature) $49

Grades: 8 9 10 11 12 Adult Professional **813**

1. Authors 2. Children's authors 3. Young adult authors
ISBN 978-0-8108-4858-0; 0-8108-4858-9

LC 2003-10897

"In five short chapters, Reid provides an intriguing exploration of this popular author's personal life along with an in-depth summary and analysis of five of her young adult novels." Voice Youth Advocates

Includes bibliographical references

Ross-Stroud, Catherine

Janet McDonald; the original project girl. [by] Catherine Ross-Stroud. Scarecrow Press 2009 137p il (Scarecrow studies in young adult literature) $35

Grades: 7 8 9 10 Adult Professional **813**

1. Authors 2. Lawyers 3. Novelists 4. Young adult authors
ISBN 978-0-8108-5802-2; 0-8108-5802-9

LC 2008030712

This "is a bio-critical study of McDonald and her work as it relates to the contributions she has made to the genre of teen fiction." Publisher's note

Includes bibliographical references

Schroeder, Heather Lee

A **reader's** guide to Marjane Satrapi's Persepolis. Enslow Publishers 2010 152p il map (Multicultural literature) lib bdg $34.60

Grades: 8 9 10 11 12 **813**

1. Artists 2. Authors 3. Novelists 4. Cartoonists 5. Memoirists
ISBN 978-0-7660-3166-1; 0-7660-3166-7

LC 2008-51820

An introduction to Marjane Satrapi's graphic novel Persepolis for high school students, which includes biographical background on the author, explanations of various literary devices and techniques, and literary criticism for the novice reader.

Includes glossary and bibliographical references

Stefoff, Rebecca

Jack London; an American original. Oxford Univ. Press 2002 127p il maps (Oxford portraits) lib bdg $28

Grades: 7 8 9 10 **813**

1. Authors 2. Novelists 3. Authors, American 4. Short story writers
ISBN 0-19-512223-2

LC 2001-53087

"This volume does an excellent job of illuminating London's extraordinary life and career. The narrative is exciting and accessible. . . . The text is supplemented by interesting and informative illustrations, and includes excerpts from primary-source material." SLJ

Includes bibliographical references

Stover, Lois T.

Jacqueline Woodson; the real thing. [by] Lois Thomas Stover. Scarecrow Press 2003 189p (Scarecrow studies in young adult literature) $49

Grades: 8 9 10 11 12 Adult Professional **813**

1. Authors 2. Novelists 3. College teachers 4. Children's authors 5. Young adult authors
ISBN 978-0-8108-4857-3; 0-8108-4857-0

LC 2003-9881

"Students who are interested in learning more about this particular author will find plenty of information that will illuminate second and deeper readings of her works. Teachers searching for ways to help make connections among the books will find Stover's work of great value." Voice Youth Advocates

Includes bibliographical references

Tighe, Mary Ann

Sharon Creech; the words we choose to say. Scarecrow Press 2006 123p (Scarecrow studies in young adult literature) $35

Grades: 7 8 9 10 **813**

1. Authors 2. Novelists 3. Children's authors 4. Young adult authors
ISBN 978-0-8108-5086-6; 0-8108-5086-9

LC 2005037615

"Tighe bills her resource as a 'biocritical volume' on Sharon Creech, beginning with a chronology of her life before continuing with a more complete look, as well as the influence of her life experiences on her writing. . . . Tighe does an admirable and complete job of examining Creech's body of work." Voice Youth Advocates

Includes bibliographical references

Tyson, Edith S.

Orson Scott Card; writer of the terrible choice. Scarecrow Press 2003 xxv, 187p (Scarecrow studies in young adult literature) $40

Grades: 8 9 10 11 12 Adult Professional **813**

1. Authors 2. Novelists 3. Editors 4. Fantasy writers 5. Short story writers 6. Science fiction writers
ISBN 0-8108-4790-6

LC 2003-5730

"Tyson begins her book with a . . . preface gleaned from Card's own explanation of the purpose of his writing, followed by a light biographical skimming of his life and development as a writer. The best features of the book are Tyson's excellent analyses of Card's books. Each book is summarized . . . and then enriched with different perspectives on the meaning, or some relevant background information, or something that Card himself wrote about that particular book. The sequence and interrelatedness of his books are also well documented. This book is a must-have for both professional and circulating collections." Voice Youth Advocates

Includes bibliographical references

★ The **wand** in the word; conversations with writers of fantasy. compiled and edited by Leonard S. Marcus. Candlewick Press 2006 202p il $19.99

Grades: 6 7 8 9 **813**

1. Authors, English 2. Authors, American 3. Fantasy fiction -- History and criticism
ISBN 0-7636-2625-2

LC 2005-46913

"Marcus presents interviews with 13 fantasy luminaries, including Lloyd Alexander, Susan Cooper, Nancy Farmer, Brian Jacques, Garth Nix, Tamora Pierce, and Philip Pullman. The writers' distinct personalities and career paths emerge, as do intriguing similarities. . . . Each profile includes a black-and-white author's photo, a reading list, and a bit of ephemera, often a handwritten manuscript page. . . . [This is] a rich resource that will be consulted as frequently by children's literature professionals as by genre fans themselves." Booklist

Winchell, Mike

Been There, Done That; Writing Stories from Life. edited by Mike Winchell. Penguin Group USA 2015 304 p. illustrations $17.99

Grades: 4 5 6 7 Professional **813**

1. Authorship 2. Creative writing 3. Creation (Literary, artistic, etc.)
ISBN 0448486725; 9780448486727

LC 2015026311

This anthology, edited by Mike Winchell, " looks at the process of taking real-life experiences and turning them into works of engaging fiction. The collection features award-winning and bestselling middle-grade authors who provide both original fictional short stories as well as the nonfiction accounts that inspired them. The contributing authors include Julia Alvarez, Karen Cushman, [and] Margarita Engle." (Publisher's note)

"Each story is prefaced with the author's account of what really happened, proving that the old adage 'Write what you know' can take a story in so many rich directions. This collection offers a little something for everyone and plenty of opportunities for classroom writing exercises." Booklist

814 American essays in English

Kirk, Andrew

Understanding Thoreau's Civil disobedience. Rosen Pub. 2010 128p il (Words that changed the world) lib bdg $31.95

Grades: 7 8 9 10 **814**

1. Authors 2. Naturalists 3. Resistance to government 4. Essayists 5. Pacifists 6. Writers on nature 7. Nonfiction writers

ISBN 978-1-4488-1671-2; 1-4488-1671-8

LC 2010-10221

First published 2004 by Barrons with title: Civil disobedience

This considers Thoreau's Civil Disobedience, including its "'Context and Creator,' 'Immediate Impact,' 'Legacy,' and 'Aftermath.' . . . [Exploring] the historical context of transcendentalism and resistance to big government. . . . [The] author provides a balance of deep context, expressive writing, and pertinent information." SLJ

Includes glossary and bibliographical references

Red; the next generation of American writers--teenage girls--on what fires up their lives today. edited by Amy Goldwasser. Hudson Street Press 2007 267p $21.95

Grades: 8 9 10 11 12 Adult **814**

1. Girls 2. Essays 3. Teenagers' writings

ISBN 978-1-59463-040-8; 1-59463-040-2

LC 2007027247

"The authors are complicated and real, with interests and concerns of immense scope. . . . It will be a surefire hit for girls." Voice Youth Advocates

814.6 American essays – 2000-

Chack, Erin

This is really happening; true stories. by Erin Chack. Razorbill 2017 234 p. (hardcover) $17.99

Grades: 7 8 9 10 11 12 **814.6**

1. Cancer 2. Women -- Biography 3. Women authors -- Biography 4. Generation Y

ISBN 9780448493589; 9780448493596; 9780448493602; 0448493586

LC 2017288655

"[Erin] Chack, a senior writer at BuzzFeed, pens a smart, fast-paced exploration of her later teen years in this collection of short personal stories. From first periods and loves to college and a cancer diagnosis at age 19, Chack chronicles her experiences with wit and honesty, presenting an unromanticized look at her illness and her own mortality." (School Library Journal)

"With a knack for infusing the most dire or painfully awkward circumstances with a heaping dose of humor and infectious enthusiasm, Chack and her candidly conversational, meandering approach will quickly convert readers into chuckling confidants. A heartfelt celebration of goofiness in all its glory." Booklist

815 American speeches in English

★ **American** Heritage book of great American speeches for young people; edited by Suzanne McIntire. Wiley 2001 292p il pa $14.95

Grades: 7 8 9 10 **815**

1. American speeches

ISBN 0-471-38942-0

LC 00-43749

This is a "compendium of more than 100 speeches that span nearly 400 years of American history, from Powhatan (1609) to Senator Charles Robb (2000). Prominent orators include Patrick Henry, Thomas Jefferson, John Kennedy, Richard Nixon, Martin Luther King, Jr., and Malcolm X. . . . The speeches inform readers and provide examples of how the spoken word has affected Americans throughout our past." SLJ

★ **U-X-L** Asian American voices; edited by Deborah Gillan Straub. 2nd ed; U.X.L 2004 xxv, 315p il $58

Grades: 7 8 9 10 11 12 **815**

1. Asian Americans 2. American speeches

ISBN 0-7876-7600-4

LC 2003-110048

First published 1997 with title: Asian American voices

This "reference presents full or excerpted speeches, sermons, orations, poems, testimony and other notable spoken words of Asian Americans. Each entry is accompanied by an introduction and boxes explaining terms and events to which the speech refers. The volume is illustrated with photographs and drawings." Publisher's note

817 American humor and satire in English

Cleary, Brian P.

The **laugh** stand; adventures in humor. by Brian P. Cleary; illustrated by J.P. Sandy. Millbrook Press 2008 48p il lib bdg $16.95

Grades: 4 5 6 **817**

1. Word games 2. Wit and humor

ISBN 978-0-8225-7849-9

LC 2007021889

Cleary "promotes fun with words in 13 small sections that toy with puns, anagrams, daffynitions, Tom Swifties, and more. . . . Sandy's ideally matched cartoons are a google-eyed cast that includes humans, animals, food items with faces, and societal icons. This team marries humor with sublime learning." SLJ

Includes bibliographical references

818 American miscellaneous writings in English

★ **Guys** read; true stories. edited and with an introduction by Jon Scieszka ; stories by Candace Fleming, Douglas Florian, Nathan Hale, Thanhha Lai, Sy Montgomery, Jim Murphy, T. Edward Nickens, Elizabeth Partridge, Steve Sheinkin, and James Sturm ; with illustrations by Brian Floca. Walden Pond Press 2014 272 p. (Guys read) (hardback) $16.99

Grades: 4 5 6 7 8 **818**

1. Essays 2. Short stories 3. American prose literature 4. American prose literature -- 21st century

ISBN 0061963828; 9780061963810; 9780061963827

LC 2014010024

Part of the Guys Read series, edited by Jon Scieszka, this book "features ten stories that are 100% amazing, 100% adventurous, 100% unbelievable--and 100% true. A star-studded group of award-winning nonfiction authors and journalists provides something for every reader, all aligned with the Common Core State Standards." (Publisher's note)

"Ten terrifically told true stories demonstrate the wide range of subjects and formats available for young readers of nonfiction. This fifth anthology in the Guys Read series stars some of the best-known names in informational writing today. . . . Selected, edited, and neatly introduced by Scieszka, National Ambassador for Young People's Literature emeritus, these appetite-whetting accounts are accompanied by occasional illustrations by Floca (not seen). You certainly don't have to be a guy to appreciate these morsels of fact-based storytelling and then beg for more." Booklist

Hargrave, John

Sir John Hargrave's mischief maker's manual; by Sir John Hargrave. Grosset & Dunlap 2009 270p il $15.99

Grades: 7 8 9 10 **818**

1. Practical jokes

ISBN 978-0-448-44982-1; 0-448-44982-X

LC 2008-34518

Presents a definitive guide to pulling off such perfect pranks as making crank calls and freezing worms inside ice cubes, divided into five specific sections.

"Pranks include making a 'Screaming Cabinet' (using the device from musical greeting cards), creating the 'World's Largest Butt Photo' and faking an alien landing. What's most appealing, however, is the emphasis on being clever, creative and funny while making mischief." Publ Wkly

Mark Twain; Todd Howard, book editor. Greenhaven Press 2002 190p il (People who made history) lib bdg $34.95; pa $23.70 **818**

1. Authors 2. Humorists 3. Novelists 4. Essayists 5. Satirists 6. Memoirists 7. Travel writers 8. Authors, American 9. Short story writers

ISBN 0-7377-0897-2 lib bdg; 0-7377-0896-4 pa

LC 2001-28923

A collection of essays about the American author and humorist with primary source documents

Includes bibliographical references

McCurdy, Michael

Walden then & now; an alphabetical tour of Henry Thoreau's pond. Charlesbridge 2010 un il lib bdg $16.95

Grades: 4 5 6 7 **818**

1. Authors 2. Alphabet 3. Naturalists 4. Essayists 5. Pacifists 6. Writers on nature 7. Nonfiction writers 8. Natural history -- Massachusetts

ISBN 978-1-58089-253-7 lib bdg; 1-58089-253-1 lib bdg

LC 2009-26645

"Elegiac woodcarvings evoke the setting of Henry Thoreau's Walden Pond as the text weaves past and present in this lengthy alphabet poem. On each spread, consecutive letters face one another, making a couplet of the lines. A dark, but not somber, woodcarving illustrates each letter, and an explanatory paragraph expands upon the information in the verse. . . . The book ends with entries from Thoreau's diary and McCurdy's inspiration and starting point for this book. Purchase as an introduction to Thoreau and for poetry shelves." SLJ

Paulsen, Gary

★ **Caught** by the sea; my life on boats. Delacorte Press 2001 103p maps $15.95; pa $5.50

Grades: 5 6 7 8 **818**

1. Authors 2. Ocean travel 3. Boats and boating 4. Sled dog racers 5. Authors, American 6. Children's authors 7. Short story writers 8. Young adult authors

ISBN 0-385-32645-9; 0-440-40716-8 pa

LC 2001-17336

"Paulsen traces his life at sea, from buying his first sailboat to getting lost in the Pacific to encountering sharks. . . . His sometimes comic, sometimes near-fatal sea-going errors make for absorbing, captivating reading." Booklist

821 English poetry

Blake, William

William Blake; edited by John Maynard; illustrated by Alessandra Cimatoribus. Sterling Pub. 2006 48p il (Poetry for young people) $14.95

Grades: 5 6 7 8 **821**

1. Children's poetry, English. 2. Poetry -- By individual authors

ISBN 978-0-8069-3647-5; 0-8069-3647-9

LC 2006013858

"The book begins with a heroic attempt to explain some of [Blake's] themes and philosophy in a four-page introduction. Maynard speaks of the poet with insight, eloquence, and obvious admiration. . . . He prefaces each poem with explanatory comments that are also thought-provoking and illuminating. . . . The artwork is well matched to the tone of the poems. Cimatoribus's illustrations are at the same time childlike and surreal." SLJ

Carroll, Lewis, 1832-1898

★ **Jabberwocky**; the classic poem from Lewis Carroll's Through the looking glass, and what Alice found there. reimagined and illustrated by Chistopher Myers. 1st ed. Jump at the Sun/Hyperion Books for Children 2007 1 v. (unpaged) col. ill. $15.99

Grades: 4 5 6 7 **821**

1. Nonsense verses 2. Poetry -- By individual authors

ISBN 978-1-4231-0372-1; 1-4231-0372-6

LC 2007018337

This reinterpretation of Lewis Carroll's poem about the Jabberwock uses a basketball court as setting. "Ages five to nine." (N Y Times Book Rev)

"Myers cleverly translates Carroll's nonsense poem into a contemporary tale through sports imagery. . . . The spectacular paintings have silhouetted figures on vibrant backgrounds. . . . The jaunty text is in capital letters in an extra-large black font, with some words highlighted in color." SLJ

Classic poetry; an illustrated collection. selected by Michael Rosen; pictures by Paul Howard. Candlewick Press 1998 160p il $21.99; pa $12.99

Grades: 7 8 9 10 **821**

1. Poetry -- Collections

ISBN 978-1-56402-890-7; 1-56402-890-9; 978-0-7636-4210-5 pa; 0-7636-4210-X pa

LC 98-18282

A collection of favorite poems by such writers as William Shakespeare, Emily Dickinson, Edward Lear, Walt Whitman, and Langston Hughes, with portraits of the poets, brief biographical background, and illustrations

"This handsome edition introduces major poets through works accessible to young people. Each section begins with a portrait of the author and a short summary of his or her life, followed by one or two poems or parts of poems. Each spread includes at least one illustration evocative of the tone of the poetry as well as the times of the poet. . . . Illustrator Paul Howard's gifts are not diminished by the smaller size of some pictures, for some of his best work here is in miniature. . . . Few anthologies for this age group include such a fine selection of works from beyond the childhood classics, introduce the poets so vividly, or provide such a rich collection of haunting illustrations." Booklist

Cohen, Barbara

★ **Canterbury** tales; [by] Geoffrey Chaucer; selected, translated, and adapted by Barbara Cohen; illustrated by Trina Schart Hyman. Lothrop, Lee & Shepard Bks. 1988 87p il $24.99

Grades: 4 5 6 7 **821**

1. Poets 2. Authors 3. Middle Ages 4. Poetry -- By individual authors

ISBN 0-688-06201-6

LC 86-21045

"Cohen's evident love and respect for Chaucer's writing keep her close to the text. Her writing retains the flavor of the times and the spirit of Chaucer's words while her prose retelling, enriched by Hyman's lively full-color paintings, enhances the book's appeal to young people. . . . An excellent introduction to The Canterbury Tales for young readers." Booklist

Coleridge, Samuel Taylor

Samuel Taylor Coleridge; edited by James Engell; illustrated by Harvey Chan. Sterling 2003 48p il (Poetry for young people) $14.95

Grades: 7 8 9 10 **821**

1. Poetry -- By individual authors

ISBN 0-8069-6951-2

LC 2003-6549

Introduces the life of author Samuel Taylor Coleridge and presents a sample of his poetry, including complete works and excerpts, with a brief, explanatory introduction to each

"Chan's enchanting paintings embellish the text and do a nice job of capturing the mood of the poetry without dominating it. . . . A useful purchase for any collection." SLJ

The **Kingfisher** book of funny poems; selected by Roger McGough; illustrated by Caroline Holden. Kingfisher (NY) 2002 256p il $18.95

Grades: 4 5 6 7 **821**

1. Humorous poetry 2. English poetry -- Collections 3. American poetry -- Collections

ISBN 0-7534-5480-7

LC 2001-38942

A collection of over 200 poems, limericks, and verses from such authors as Emily Dickinson, Lewis Carroll, and Shel Silverstein

"This collection is chock-full of wacky, witty, and whimsical poems that will hook readers from the first stanza to the last. . . . What really brings out the humor are the equally zany black-and-white drawings that appear on almost every page." SLJ

Kipling, Rudyard, 1865-1936

If; a father's advice to his son. [by] Rudyard Kipling; photographs by Charles R. Smith. Atheneum Books for Young Readers 2007 un il $14.99

Grades: 4 5 6 **821**

1. Poetry -- By individual authors

ISBN 978-0-689-87799-5; 0-689-87799-4

LC 2006005312

"Kipling's powerful poem comes to life for a contemporary audience in atmospheric photographs that use the metaphor of sports. A lovely shot of a boy heading a soccer ball accompanies the opening couplet: 'If you can keep your head/when all about you/are losing theirs/and blaming it on you.' The mood and actions in most of the illustrations clearly invoke the verse." SLJ

Lear, Edward

The **owl** and the pussycat; illustrations by Stephane Jorisch. KCP Poetry 2007 un il (Visions in poetry) $16.95; pa $9.95

Grades: 5 6 7 8 **821**

1. Nonsense verses 2. Cats -- Poetry 3. Owls -- Poetry 4. Poetry -- By individual authors

ISBN 978-1-55337-828-0; 1-55337-828-8; 978-1-55453-232-2 pa; 1-55453-232-9 pa

"This striking entry in an aptly named series envisions a darker subtext to Lear's well-known poem. Jorisch consulted Lear's own drawings when preparing his winsome watercolor and ink illustrations, noting the melancholy quality of the title characters. The light verse is transformed by the artist's vision into a mismatched couple seeking a place of acceptance. . . . For older readers, this book shows true artistic vision and a great example of the power of personal interpretation and inspiration." SLJ

Love and longing; a collection of classic poetry and prose. introduced by Jacqueline Wilson; edited by Kate Agnew. Totem 2011 128p pa $9.95

Grades: 8 9 10 11 12 **821**

1. Love poetry 2. English poetry -- Collections

ISBN 978-1-840-46523-5; 1-840-46523-9

First published 2004 in the United Kingdom

This collection "features love poems and prose excerpts by writers including Sappho, Shakespeare, Milton, the Brontës, and Wordsworth. Works are loosely arranged according to chapter headings drawn from particular poems. . . . creating an engaging interchange of images and ideas. . . . This is a resonant sampling of both standards and lesser-known gems." Publ Wkly

Noyes, Alfred

The **highwayman**; [by] Alfred Noyes; with illustrations by Murray Kimber. Kids Can Press 2005 un il (Visions in poetry) $17.95

Grades: 7 8 9 10 **821**

1. Thieves -- Poetry 2. Poetry -- By individual authors

ISBN 978-1-55337-425-1; 1-55337-425-8

"Painting in an art deco style and film noir palette, Kimber casts a motorcycle-riding rebel as the highwayman; a curvaceous glamour girl as Bess; and tommy-gun toting cops as the soldiers who intrude upon the lovers' tryst. . . . The dramatic artwork plays up the elements teens will find most rewarding—particularly the protagonists' defiance of authority and the unblushingly melodramatic conclusion." Booklist

Poems to learn by heart; [selected by] Caroline Kennedy ; paintings by Jon J Muth. Disney-Hyperion 2012 192 p. (hardcover) $19.99

Grades: 2 3 4 5 6 7 8 **821**

1. Poetry -- Collections 2. English poetry 3. American poetry

ISBN 1423108051; 9781423108054

LC 2011022651

This anthology, by Caroline Kennedy, illustrated by John J. Muth, offers "more than a hundred poems that speak to all of us: the young and young at heart, readers new to poetry and devoted fans. These poems explore deep emotions, as well as ordinary experiences. They cover the range of human experience and imagination. Divided into sections about nature, sports, monsters and fairies, friendship and family." (Publisher's note)

Tennyson, Alfred Tennyson

The **Lady** of Shalott; illustrated by Geneviève Côtè. Kids Can Press 2005 un il (Visions in poetry) $16.95

Grades: 7 8 9 10 **821**

1. Arthurian romances 2. Poetry -- By individual authors

ISBN 978-1-55337-874-7; 1-55337-874-1

"The pictures in this small book bring an early-twentieth-century urban setting to Tennyson's classic Arthurian poem, written in 1842, about a young woman imprisoned in a tower, endlessly weaving what she sees in the mirror, until she dares to break free and look outside. . . . Cote's quiet line-and-watercolor and pastel artwork opens up the story, preserving the romance and mystery without filling in too much." Booklist

Williams, Marcia

★ **Chaucer's** Canterbury Tales; retold and illustrated by Marcia Williams. Candlewick Press 2007 45p il $16.99

Grades: 4 5 6 7 **821**

1. Poets 2. Authors 3. Middle Ages 4. Poetry -- By individual authors

ISBN 978-0-7636-3197-0; 0-7636-3197-3

A retelling in comic strip form of Geoffrey Chaucer's famous work in which a group of pilgrims in fourteenth-century England tell each other stories as they travel on a pilgrimage to the cathedral at Canterbury

"Chaucer's pilgrims come to life in the energetic retelling of nine tales. . . . The watercolor-and-ink cartoon-art displayed in a comic-book format is a perfect match for the raucous and sometimes-raw humor." SLJ

Wordsworth, William

William Wordsworth; edited by Alan Liu; illustrated by James Muir. Sterling 2003 48p il (Poetry for young people) $14.95

Grades: 7 8 9 10 **821**

1. Poetry -- By individual authors

ISBN 0-8069-8277-2

LC 2003-6163

An illustrated collection of nineteen popular poems by William Wordsworth, who was the poet laureate of England in the mid-nineteenth century. Includes an introduction to the poet's life and work

The editor has "chosen well, bringing together about 20 of [the] great poet's most accessible, compelling poems. . . . The full color paintings on each page are beautiful." Booklist

822.3 Drama of Elizabethan period, 1558-1625

Coville, Bruce

William Shakespeare's A midsummer night's dream. Dial Bks. 1996 un $17.95; pa $7.99

Grades: 5 6 7 8 9 **822.3**

1. Poets 2. Authors 3. Audiobooks 4. Dramatists

ISBN 0-8037-1784-9; 0-14-250168-9 pa

LC 94-12600

A simplified prose retelling of Shakespeare's play about the strange events that take place in a forest inhabited by fairies who magically transform the romantic fate of two young couples.

"Coville introduces the story and also conveys something of the poetry and drama. Nolan's framed graphite and watercolor paintings express the dreaminess and absurdity of the play, and the pictures have a theatrical flair." Booklist

William Shakespeare's Romeo and Juliet; retold by Bruce Coville; pictures by Dennis Nolan. Dial Bks. 1999 un il $16.99

Grades: 5 6 7 8 9 **822.3**

1. Poets 2. Authors 3. Dramatists

ISBN 0-8037-2462-4

LC 98-36178

A simplified prose retelling of Shakespeare's play about two young people who defy their warring families' prejudices and dare to fall in love

"Coville's treatment is generally faithful to the original and is nicely enhanced by Dennis Nolan's lushly romantic illustrations. . . . This is an accessible and enticing introduction to one of Shakespeare's most popular works." Booklist

Krueger, Susan Heidi

The **tempest**; [by] Susan H. Krueger; introduction by Joseph Sobran. Marshall Cavendish Benchmark 2009 127p il (Shakespeare explained) lib bdg $29.93

Grades: 7 8 9 10 11 12 **822.3**

1. Poets 2. Authors 3. Dramatists

ISBN 978-0-7614-3423-8; 0-7614-3423-2

LC 2009-2587

This book offers an "engaging [introduction] to the Bard's work. . . . Krueger's lively, opinionated, and knowledgeable analysis of the complex play . . . will easily draw students into further discussion." Booklist

Includes glossary and bibliographical references

McDermott, Kristen

William Shakespeare; his life and times. [by] Kristen McDermott, and Ari Berk; including extracts from the works of William Shakespeare. Candlewick Press 2010 un il $19.99

Grades: 6 7 8 9 **822.3**

1. Poets 2. Authors 3. Dramatists

ISBN 978-0-7636-4794-0; 0-7636-4794-2

"This fictionalized amalgamation of original and secondary source materials is presented with panache. . . . The authors succintly sum up Shakespeare's life and works with the help of snippets from his plays. Contemporaneous images and literary excerpts, in addition to pop-ups, foldouts, and removable letters, help set the scene for readers." Horn Book Guide

McKeown, Adam

Julius Caesar; a retelling by Adam McKeown; illustrated by Janet Hamlin. Sterling Pub. Co. 2008 80p il (Young reader's Shakespeare) $14.95

Grades: 6 7 8 9 **822.3**

1. Poets 2. Authors 3. Statesmen 4. Dramatists 5. Historians 6. Rome -- History -- Fiction

ISBN 978-1-4027-3579-0; 1-4027-3579-0

LC 2007030733

"This handsomely illustrated retelling . . . stays true both to the rousing action of [Shakespeare's] play and to the characters' inner conflicts. McKeown's clear, stimulating introduction raises the complex moral issues. . . . Hamlin's dramatic, full-color art . . . ably captures the personal torment as well as the dynamics of the battlefield." Booklist

Mussari, Mark

Othello; [by] Mark Mussari; introduction by Joseph Sobran. Marshall Cavendish Benchmark 2009 111p il (Shakespeare explained) lib bdg $29.95

Grades: 7 8 9 10 11 12 **822.3**

1. Poets 2. Authors 3. Dramatists

ISBN 978-0-7614-3422-1; 0-7614-3422-4

LC 2008-37506

"A literary analysis of the play Othello. Includes information on the history and culture of Elizabethan England." Publisher's note

Includes glossary and bibliographical references

Nettleton, Pamela Hill

William Shakespeare; playwright and poet. by Pamela Hill Nettleton. Compass Point Books 2005 112p il map (Signature lives) lib bdg $30.60

Grades: 5 6 7 8 **822.3**

1. Poets 2. Authors 3. Dramatists

ISBN 0-7565-0816-9

LC 2004-23081

Profiles the life and work of William Shakespeare

"This biography is one of the best available for younger students. Nettleton supplements what little is actually known about the bard's life with detailed and accurate information about everyday life in England during the period, the theater, and publishing practices of the time. The text is enhanced by full-color illustrations and black-and-white reproductions." SLJ

Includes bibliographical references

Packer, Tina

★ **Tales** from Shakespeare; retold by Tina Packer; illustrated by Gail de Marcken . . . [et al.] Scholastic Press 2004 192p il $24.95

Grades: 5 6 7 8 **822.3**

1. Poets 2. Authors 3. Dramatists

ISBN 0-439-32107-7

LC 2003-42710

Tina Packer retells ten of Shakespeare's plays. The stories are illustrated by various artists: Macbeth by Barry Moser, The Tempest by Mark Teague, Othello by Kadir Nelson, Twelfth Night by Chesley McLaren, Romeo and Juliet by David Shannon, Much Ado About Nothing by Mary GrandPre, King Lear by Leo and Diane Dillon, As You Like It by Barbara McClintock, A Midsummer Night's Dream by Gail De Marcken, and Hamlet by P.J. Lynch

This is "a treasure trove of well-told tales. In these adaptations, Packer captures the essence of the playwright's words and ideas, placing them in concise and clearly told stories. . . . Each illustrator sets the appropriate tone for and conveys the mood of the tale, and the breadth of artistic interpretations gives the book appeal to a wide audience." SLJ

Raum, Elizabeth

Twenty -first-century Shakespeare. Raintree 2011 32p il (Culture in action) lib bdg $29

Grades: 5 6 7 8 **822.3**

1. Poets 2. Authors 3. Dramatists 4. Dramatists, English 5. Authors, English

ISBN 978-1-4109-3920-3; 1-4109-3920-0

LC 2009050693

This "discusses modern adaptations of the Bard's classic works; teachers may find this a useful resource to help students see how Shakespeare remains a part of today's culture. [This volume is] quick, interesting, up-to-date . . . with plenty of supportive, captioned, full-color photographs. [It] also [provides] related project suggestions." SLJ

Includes glossary and bibliographical references

Shakespeare, William, 1564-1616

One hundred and eleven Shakespeare monologues; the ultimate audition book for teens. edited by Lisa Bansavage and L. E. McCullough; introduction by Jill K. Swanson. Smith & Kraus 2003 176p (Young actors series) pa $11.95

Grades: 7 8 9 10 11 12 **822.3**

1. Acting 2. Monologues

ISBN 1-57525-356-9

"These monologues are divided into three sections: those for female actors, male actors, or either. They are further subdivided into comedies, histories, and tragedies. . . . The genius of this book is in the introduction, which offers a wealth of information for teens who have never encountered Shakespeare." SLJ

Sobran, Joseph

A **midsummer** night's dream; Joseph Sobran. Marshall Cavendish Benchmark 2008 111p. ill. (some col.) lib bdg $29.95

Grades: 7 8 9 10 11 12 **822.3**

1. Poets 2. Authors 3. Dramatists

ISBN 978-0-7614-3030-8; 0-7614-3030-X

LC 2008007079

"A literary analysis of the play A Midsummer Night's Dream. Includes information on the history and culture of Elizabethan England." Publisher's note

"[This book] provides practical information, skillfully presented, making the complexities of Shakespearean theater accessible to present-day students. [The] author's contagious enthusiasm and attractive presentation make [it] imminently useful for high school and public libraries.—" VOYA

Includes glossary and bibliographical references

Stanley, Diane

★ **Bard** of Avon: the story of William Shakespeare; by Diane Stanley and Peter Vennema; illustrated by Diane Stanley. Morrow Junior Bks. 1992 un il hardcover o.p. pa $6.99

Grades: 4 5 6 7 **822.3**

1. Poets 2. Authors 3. Dramatists

ISBN 0-688-09108-3; 0-688-09109-1 lib bdg; 0-688-16294-0 pa

LC 90-46564

A brief biography of the world's most famous playwright, using only historically correct information

"A remarkably rounded picture of Shakespeare's life and the period in which he lived is presented . . . together with a thoughtful attempt to relate circumstances in his personal life to the content of his plays. . . . The text is splendidly supported by the illustrations, which are stylized, yet recognizable, and present a clear view of life in the late sixteenth century. A discerning, knowledgeable biography, rising far above the ordinary." Horn Book

Includes bibliographical references

823 English fiction

Bruton, Catherine

We can be heroes; by Catherine Bruton. Egmont Books 2011 496 p. illustrations (pbk.) $10.99

Grades: 5 6 7 8 9 **823**

1. September 11 terrorist attacks, 2001 -- Fiction

ISBN 1405256524; 9781405256520

This book, by Catherine Bruton, is "about the summer my mom went away. The summer that me and Jed and Priti tried to catch a suicide bomber and prevent an honor killing. There's stuff about how we built a tree house and joined the bomb squad. . . . So it's not really about 9/11 but, then again, none of those things would have happened if it hadn't been for that day. So I guess it's all back to front, sort of." (Publisher's note)

Colbert, David

The **magical** worlds of Harry Potter; David Colbert. Updated and complete ed. Berkley Books 2008 xi, 209 p.p ill. (paperback) $14.00

Grades: 5 6 7 8 **823**

1. Authors 2. Novelists 3. Fantasy writers 4. Children's authors 5. Young adult authors 6. Fantasy fiction -- History and criticism

ISBN 0425223183; 9780425223185

LC 2008274096

First published 2001 in the United Kingdom; first United States edition 2002

Explores the sources and meanings of aspects of the literary world of Harry Potter within myths, legends, and history.

"Long after the enthusiasm for Harry and friends has abated, this small volume will serve as a resource to answer questions that may result from reading other stories in the genre." SLJ [review of 2002 edition]

Includes bibliographical references (p. 317-318) and index.

Cooling, Wendy

D is for Dahl; a gloriumptious A-Z guide to the world of Roald Dahl. illustrations by Quentin Blake; compiled by Wendy Cooling. Viking 2005 149p il hardcover o.p. pa $5.99

Grades: 4 5 6 7 **823**

1. Authors 2. Children's authors 3. Short story writers

ISBN 0-670-06023-2; 0-14-240934-0 pa

This is an alphabetically arranged collection of facts about the life and work of the popular author of children's books

"This dictionary-of-sorts is entertaining, insightful, and of particular interest to Dahl's fans. . . . The writing is clear, wicked, and fun. An occasional black-and-white photograph complements Blake's illustrations." SLJ

Gribbin, Mary

The **science** of Philip Pullman's His Dark Materials; [by] Mary and John Gribbon; with an introduction by Philip Pullman. Knopf 2005 203p il $15.95; lib bdg $17.99; pa $5.99

Grades: 6 7 8 9 **823**

1. Authors 2. Science 3. Novelists 4. Fantasy writers 5. Young adult authors

ISBN 0-375-83144-4; 0-375-93144-9 lib bdg; 0-375-83146-0 pa

LC 2004-57731

"The Gribbins show how concepts are the real magic of Pullman's trilogy. Each chapter begins with a quote drawn from the books, which leads to an elegantly written explanation of the science. . . . The authors do an amazing job teasing an introduction to string theory from Will's 'subtle knife.' . . . Naturally, fans of the series will be the best audience, but the book offers much to readers simply interested in the advanced sciences, who then may be led back to His Dark Materials." Booklist

Jones, Diana Wynne, 1934-2011

Reflections; on the magic of writing. by Diana Wynne Jones. Greenwillow Books 2012 368 p. (hardback) $24.99

Grades: 7 8 9 10 11 12 **823**

1. Fantasy fiction -- Authorship 2. Children's stories -- Authorship

ISBN 0062219898; 9780062219893

LC 2012018080

This book, by Diana Wynne Jones, was arranged "after being informed that she had terminal cancer in 2010." It "pull[s] together" a "group of essays, lectures, and articles . . . about writing fantasy for children. . . . The selected pieces are thematically arranged, beginning with . . . a contemplative piece about watching children at play that sets the stage for her subsequent arguments regarding the importance of imagination and creativity." (Bulletin of the Center for Children's Books)

Includes bibliographical references and index

Latham, Don

David Almond; memory and magic. Scarecrow Press 2006 151p (Scarecrow studies in young adult literature) $40

Grades: 7 8 9 10 11 12 Adult Professional **823**

1. Authors 2. Novelists 3. Short story writers 4. Young adult authors

ISBN 978-0-8108-5500-7; 0-8108-5500-3

LC 2006002300

This "explores the writings of the critically acclaimed YA author best known for Skellig . . . and Kit's Wilderness. . . . After a brief biography and thematic overview, Latham addresses Almond's published works one by one. . . . Weaving his explorations almost as seamlessly as Almond wove the original stories, Latham clearly illustrates the novels' inherent depth and teachability." Voice Youth Advocates

Includes bibliographical references

Nardo, Don

Understanding Frankenstein. Lucent Bks. 2003 128p il (Understanding great literature) lib bdg $27.45

Grades: 7 8 9 10 **823**

1. Authors 2. Novelists

ISBN 1-59018-147-6

LC 2002-12560

Discusses Mary Shelley's sources of ideas for the compelling plot, well-developed characters, and universal themes of "Frankenstein" which have led to its enduring popularity.

"The text is easy to understand. A solid introduction for middle school students." SLJ

Includes bibliographical references

Pascal, Janet B.

Arthur Conan Doyle; beyond Baker Street. Oxford Univ. Press 1999 158p il (Oxford portraits) $28

Grades: 7 8 9 10 **823**

1. Authors 2. Novelists 3. Authors, Scottish 4. Mystery writers

ISBN 0-19-512262-3

LC 99-36643

"Pascal does a fine job of conveying the era in which her object lived." SLJ

Includes bibliographical references (p. 151-154) and index

Shea, George

A **reader's** guide to Chinua Achebe's Things fall apart; [by] George Shea. Enslow Publishers 2008 128p il (Multicultural literature) lib bdg $31.93

Grades: 7 8 9 10 **823**

1. Poets 2. Authors 3. Novelists 4. Essayists 5. Short story writers

ISBN 978-0-7660-2831-9 lib bdg; 0-7660-2831-3 lib bdg

LC 2006038486

"Shea explores why many consider the book to be the greatest African novel ever written. . . . Extensive back matter includes a chronology, glossary, chapter notes, and a bibliography of books and Web sites." Booklist

Includes glossary and bibliographical references

Wells-Cole, Catherine

Charles Dickens; England's most captivating storyteller. written by Catherine Wells-Cole ; including extracts from the works of Charles Dickens. 1st U.S. ed. Candlewick/Templar Books 2011 28 p. ill., maps (some col.) (Historical notebook) (hardcover) $19.99

Grades: 7 8 9 10 11 12 **823**

1. Authors 2. Novelists 3. Authors, English 4. London (England) -- Social life and customs -- 19th century

ISBN 0763655678; 9780763655679

LC 2011013677

This book by Catherine Wells-Cole "provides a . . . glimpse into the life" of author Charles Dickens. "Like a scrapbook, the book includes excerpts from Dickens' personal letters, illustrations from his original books, family photos, and other images from the Victorian age. . . . Double-page spreads focus on Dickens' childhood, family life, and fame. Other spreads focus on topics that influenced his writing, including schools, prisons, and workhouses." (Library Media Connection)

"In this scrapbook homage to Dickens, each page teems with images and reproductions, from letters to book excerpts to maps, all pertaining to a different area of Dickens's life and work. The topics range widely, skimming the surface of both the esteemed author's life and the subjects that interested him most. . . . The gorgeous, high-quality reproductions make a strong visual impact, and while the flaps, folds, and envelopes make readers work to uncover information, most will be quickly drawn into the hunt for more treasured tidbits about Dickens and his time." SLJ

828 English miscellaneous writings

Jones, Diana Wynne

★ The **tough** guide to Fantasyland; rev and updated ed.; Firebird 2006 234p pa $9.99

Grades: 8 9 10 11 12 **828**

1. Fantasy fiction

ISBN 0-14-240722-4

LC 2006041153

First published 1996

This "book contains alphabetic entries for people, places, and events in a fantasy world and information on how travelers can best find their way to the epic final battle. Icons conveniently identify lodging, food, and other necessary elements that travelers will need in their journey. . . . This brilliantly written satire perfectly celebrates and skewers the clichés of the fantasy genre." Voice Youth Advocates

Means, A. L.

A **student's** guide to George Orwell. Enslow Pubs. 2005 176p il (Understanding literature) lib bdg $27.93

Grades: 7 8 9 10 **828**

1. Authors 2. Novelists 3. Essayists

ISBN 0-7660-2433-4

An introduction to the life and work of the author of 1984, Animal Farm and other works

Includes glossary and bibliographical references

Neimark, Anne E.

Myth maker: J.R.R. Tolkien; illustrated by Brad Weinman. Harcourt Brace & Co. 1996 118p il rpt $12.99 **828**

1. Authors 2. Novelists 3. Linguists 4. Philologists 5. Fantasy writers 6. Authors, English 7. Children's authors

ISBN 0-15-298847-5; 9780547997346 rpt

LC 96-4196

Follows the life and work of the renowned fantasy writer, creator of hobbits and Middle Earth and "The Lord of the Rings."

843 French fiction

Schoell, William

Remarkable journeys: the story of Jules Verne. Morgan Reynolds 2002 112p il (World writers) lib bdg $21.95 **843**

1. Authors 2. Novelists 3. Authors, French 4. Children's authors 5. Science fiction writers

ISBN 1-88384-692-7

LC 2002-2016

A biography of the nineteenth-century Frenchman whose childhood love of literature, science, and adventure, along with his vivid imagination, led him to become a highly successful science fiction author

"Thanks to Schoell's smooth, crisp writing, this fascinating, approachable biography, which lends insight into Verne's eccentric characters and relatives, proves nearly as exciting as the writer's best stories." Booklist

Includes bibliographical references

860 Literatures of Spanish, Portuguese, Galician languages

Cofer, Judith Ortiz

Riding low on the streets of gold; Latino literature for young adults. edited, with an introduction, by Judith Ortiz Cofer. Arte Publico Press 2003 p. cm

Grades: 7 8 9 10 11 12 **860**

ISBN 1-558-85380-4 (alk. paper)

LC 2003-61231

"These 11 poems and 12 stories explore growing up, recognizing one's place in the world, and living the bilingual immigrant experience. The collection blends works of familiar authors, including José Martí, Tomás Rivera, Victor Villaseñor, and Pat Mora, with the writings of newcomers. Mike Padilla's 'Carrying Sergei' relates the story of a

Mexican girl who befriends a Russian immigrant boy after pushing him down a flight of stairs and breaking his leg. Through visits to his home, she discovers much about him and even more about herself. Friendship is also the theme of Daniel Chacón's 'Too White,' in which the protagonist faces the decision of admitting his friendship with a white boy or choosing to be part of the local Mexican gang. In Jesús Salvador Treviño's 'The Fabulous Sinkhole,' the personalities of an entire neighborhood are revealed as various individuals react to the emergence of a giant hole in Mrs. Romero's front yard. The poems are well chosen and blend well with the prose. The stories could be a starting point for interesting discussion topics, but the gritty language in a few of them may keep the book from being an assigned text. A photograph and brief biography of the author precede each work. Several poems in Spanish are accompanied by the English translation. Unfortunately, there are a handful of Spanish terms that are not defined within the text and there is no glossary. However, this is a minor detraction from this solid introduction to Latino literature." SLJ

"In this vibrant collection, Cofer collects memoir, poetry, and fiction by Latino writers who muse on las luchas, or struggles, of young people's daily lives: the universal coming-of-age experiences and the specific issues of Latino youth. Set in diverse locations . . . Teens of all cultural backgrounds will find much to connect with and contemplate in these rich offerings." Booklist

The **literature** of Spain and Latin America; edited by J.E. Luebering. Britannica Educational Publishing, in association with Rosen Educational Services 2010 317 p. (The Britannica Guide to World Literature) (lib. bdg.) $46

Grades: 8 9 10 11 12 **860**

1. Spanish literature -- History and criticism 2. Latin American literature -- History and criticism 3. Spanish American literature -- History and criticism

ISBN 1615301054; 9781615301058

LC 2009045098

This book, edited by J.E. Luebering, "examines the vibrant prose and dynamic range of both Spanish and Latin American authors, whose narratives are informed as much by their imaginations as the turbulent histories of these native lands. Influenced by a plethora of diverse cultures, these tales truly tell a global story." (Publisher's note)

Includes bibliographical references and index

★ The **Tree** is older than you are; a bilingual gathering of poems & stories from Mexico with paintings by Mexican artists. selected by Naomi Shihab Nye. Simon & Schuster Bks. for Young Readers 1995 111p il hardcover o.p. pa $13.95

Grades: 7 8 9 10 **860**

1. Mexican literature -- Collections 2. Bilingual books -- English-Spanish

ISBN 0-689-82097-8; 0-689-82087-9 pa

LC 95-1565

"This bilingual anthology of poems, stories, and paintings by Mexican writers and artists brims over with a sense of wonder and playful exuberance, its themes as varied and inventive as a child's imagination." Voice Youth Advocates

861 Spanish poetry

Argueta, Jorge

Somos Como Las Nubes / We Are Like the Clouds; by Jorge Argueta, illustrated by Alfonso Ruano. Groundwood Books 2016 36 p. color illustrations $18.95

Grades: 4 5 6 7 8 **861**

1. Refugees 2. Central America

ISBN 1554988497; 9781554988495

This book, by Jorge Argueta, illustrated by Alfonso Ruano, asks "why are young people leaving their country to walk to the United States to seek a new, safe home? Over 100,000 such children have left Central America. . . . A refugee from El Salvador's war in the eighties, Argueta was born to explain the tragic choice confronting young Central Americans today who are saying goodbye to everything they know because they fear for their lives. This book brings home their situation." (Publisher's note)

"The scarcity of Latino children's and young-adult books that center on Central American experiences makes this poignant poetry collection extremely vital." Booklist

880 Classical Greek literature and literatures of related Hellenic languages

Classical authors; 500 BCE to 1100 CE. edited by Kathleen Kuiper. Britannica Educational Publishing, in association with Rosen Educational Services 2014 xvii, 310 p.p color illustrations (The Britannica guide to authors) $54

Grades: 8 9 10 11 12 **880**

1. Authors -- Biography 2. Classical literature 3. Authors, Classical -- Biography 4. Authorship -- History -- To 1500 5. Literature, Ancient -- History and criticism 6. Classical literature -- History and criticism

ISBN 1615309977; 9781615309979

LC 2012043651

In this book, edited by Kathleen Kuiper, "since ancient times, storytelling has been a valued art form that enables traditions, beliefs, and lessons to be transmitted from one generation to the next. . . . The individuals and works profiled in this absorbing volume have withstood the test of time, remaining culturally significant and influencing authors and readers alike for centuries." (Publisher's note)

Includes bibliographical references (pages 302-305), glossary, and index

883 Classical Greek epic poetry and fiction

Cross, Gillian, 1945-

The **Iliad**; Gillian Cross. Candlewick Press 2015 151 p. color ill., color maps

Grades: 6 7 8 9 **883**

1. Greek mythology 2. Trojan War -- Fiction

ISBN 9780763678326

LC 2014952487

This book, by Gillian Cross and illustrated by Neil Packer, presents a newly illustrated retelling of Homer's the Iliad. "After nine years of war between the Greeks and Trojans, . . . two proud and powerful Greeks, King Agamemnon and legendary warrior Achilles, quarrel over a beautiful maiden, causing Achilles and his myrmidons to drop out of the fight. Meanwhile, fueled by rage and pride, honor and greed, soldiers on both sides . . . perform heroic deeds, attempting to end the war." (Publisher's note)

"The striking mixed-media artwork varies from large, richly colored scenes to others using a minimum of color very effectively. Packer uses forms, particularly human forms, in expressive, inventive ways. An eye-catching introduction to the classic story." Booklist

Homer

The **Iliad**; translated by Robert Fagles; introduction and notes by Bernard Knox. Viking 1990 683p $40; pa $15.95

Grades: 8 9 10 11 12 Adult **883**

1. Poetry -- By individual authors

ISBN 978-0-670-83510-2; 978-0-14-027536-0 pa

LC 89-70695

Homer's epic of the Trojan War.

"Fagles gives us a stark and terrible poem, an Iliad about, as its first word announces, rage. He conveys, far better than either Lattimore or Fitzgerald, the psychological experience of combat and war." Classical World

The **Odyssey**; translated by Robert Fagles; introduction and notes by Bernard Knox. Viking 1996 541p $35; pa $16

Grades: 8 9 10 11 12 Adult **883**

1. Poetry -- By individual authors

ISBN 978-0-670-82162-4; 978-0-14-026886-7 pa

LC 96-17280

This is a verse translation of Homer's epic poem

"Fagles' Odyssey is the one to put into the hands of younger, first-time readers, not least because of its paucity of notes, which, though sometimes frustrating, is a sign that translation has been used to do the work of explanation. Altogether, an outstanding piece of work." Booklist

Includes bibliographical references

Landmann, Bimba

★ The **fate** of Achilles. Getty 2011 36p il $19.95

Grades: 4 5 6 7 **883**

1. Poets 2. Authors

ISBN 978-1-60606-085-8; 1-60606-085-6

"Landmann (The Incredible Voyage of Ulysses) continues her retelling of Homer's epics with this haunting version of the Iliad. Ghostly, Giacometti-style figures accompany the story of Achilles's life, from his baptism in the river Styx . . . to his departure for Troy, . . . the death of his dearest friend, . . . and his reconciliation with the father of the enemy he has slain. . . . Readers with the patience to sit through saga-length narratives will be fascinated by her prose, which moves easily through the sprawling epic without feeling ponderous or hurried. These kinds of retellings are few and far between, and hers are magic." Publ Wkly

The **incredible** voyage of Ulysses; text and illustrations by Bimba Landmann. Getty Publications 2010 un il $19.95

Grades: 4 5 6 7 **883**

1. Poets 2. Authors

ISBN 978-1-60606-012-4; 1-60606-012-0

"With narrative restraint and illustrative power, Landmann's . . . retelling of Homer's Odyssey follows Ulysses as he battles frightening creatures and endures the treachery of the gods while sailing home to Ithaca. . . . The paintings, worked with swift, bold strokes, combine the solemn stiffness of Greek statuary with the prophetic sweep of William Blake's imaginings." Publ Wkly

Lister, Robin

The **odyssey**; retold by Robin Lister; illustrated by Alan Baker. reformatted ed.; Kingfisher 2004 175p il (Kingfisher epics) pa $7.95

Grades: 5 6 7 8 **883**

1. Poets 2. Authors 3. Odysseus (Greek mythology)

ISBN 0-7534-5723-7

First published 1988

A retelling of Homer's epic poem that describes the wanderings of Odysseus after the fall of Troy.

Osborne, Mary Pope

The **gray** -eyed goddess; with artwork by Troy Howell. Hyperion Bks. for Children 2003 120p il (Mary Pope Osborne's Tales from the Odyssey) hardcover o.p. pa $4.99

Grades: 4 5 6 7 **883**

1. Poets 2. Authors 3. Odysseus (Greek mythology)

ISBN 0-7868-0773-3; 0-7868-0931-0 pa

Retells a part of the Odyssey in which Odysseus' wife, Penelope, and their son, Telemachus, are desperately warding off the men who want to marry her. Then a visit from a mysterious stranger gives Telemachus the courage to confront the suitors, and to search for his long-lost father

The **land** of the dead; illustrated by Troy Howell. Hyperion Bks. for Children 2002 105p il (Mary Pope Osborne's Tales from the Odyssey) $9.99; pa $4.99

Grades: 4 5 6 7 **883**

1. Poets 2. Authors 3. Odysseus (Greek mythology)

ISBN 0-7868-0771-7; 0-7868-0929-9 pa

LC 2002-69078

A retelling of part of the Odyssey in which Odysseus and his fleet continue their journey and encounter giant cannibals, a beautiful witch, and the Land of the Dead

"Osborne's simple, engaging narrative will surely capture interest as it presents a great hero in bold, yet human, dimensions." Booklist

The **one** -eyed giant; with artwork by Troy Howell. Hyperion Bks. for Children 2002 105p il (Mary Pope Osborne's Tales from the Odyssey) hardcover o.p. pa $4.99

Grades: 4 5 6 7 **883**

1. Poets 2. Authors 3. Odysseus (Greek mythology)

ISBN 0-7868-0770-9; 0-7868-0928-0 pa

LC 2002-68539

Retells a part of the Odyssey in which King Odysseus fights the cyclops

"In brief chapters and concise sentences, Osborne pares down . . . [this adventure] into easily absorbed, swiftly paced episodes." Publ Wkly

Return to Ithaca; with artwork by Troy Howell. Hyperion Books for Children 2004 105p (Mary Pope Osborne's Tales from the Odyssey) $9.99

Grades: 4 5 6 7 **883**

1. Poets 2. Authors 3. Odysseus (Greek mythology)

ISBN 0-7868-0774-1

LC 2003-60355

Retells part of Homer's Odyssey in which Odysseus, with the help of the goddess Athena, plans to get revenge on those who have plagued his wife and son during his absence

895.1 Chinese literature

Liu Siyu

★ A **thousand** peaks; poems from China. [by] Siyu Liu and Orel Protopopescu; illustrated by Siyu Liu. Pacific View Press 2002 52p il $19.95

Grades: 5 6 7 8 9 10 **895.1**

1. Chinese poetry 2. Bilingual books -- English-Chinese

ISBN 1-88189-624-2

LC 2001-34008

A collection of thirty-five poems spanning nineteen centuries, representing both famous and lesser-known poets, including both the Chinese text and a literal translation.

This "is an anthology of considerable fascination and broad utility. . . . The layout is neat, tidily fitting each poem's material on a single page and adding a line drawing featuring a relevant Chinese character. The wealth of material here provides a more stimulating entree to Chinese history than any dry textbook." Bull Cent Child Books

Includes bibliographical references

897 Literatures of North American native languages

★ **Dancing** teepees: poems of American Indian youth; selected by Virginia Driving Hawk Sneve, with art by Stephen Gammell. Holiday House 1989 32p il $17.95; pa $8.95

Grades: 4 5 6 **897**

1. Native Americans -- Poetry

ISBN 0-8234-0724-1; 0-8234-0879-5 pa

LC 88-11075

An illustrated collection of poems from the oral tradition of Native Americans

This is an "eclectic collection, drawn from a variety of tribal traditions. Printed on heavy paper, the book is illustrated with a catalogue of marvelously rendered designs and motifs, ranging from those of the Northwest Coast to the intricate beadwork patterns of the Great Lakes and the zigzag geometric borders of Southwestern pottery." N Y Times Book Rev

900 HISTORY

901 Philosophy and theory of history

Beller, Susan Provost

★ The **history** puzzle; how we know what we know about the past. [by] Susan Provost Beller. Twenty-First Century Books 2006 128p il lib bdg $26.60

Grades: 7 8 9 10 **901**

1. History -- Philosophy

ISBN 978-0-7613-2877-3; 0-7613-2877-7

LC 2005017745

"Beller looks at more than 20 historical sites or archaeological excavations . . . in order to present the varying interpretations of history and how they have been colored by tradition, socioeconomic factors, and religious beliefs. . . . Frequent, well-placed sepia-toned photographs and period reproductions serve to enhance the text, and the source notes, further reading, and list of Web sites give students an ample list of resources for further study." SLJ

Includes bibliographical references

902 Miscellany of history

Hughes, Susan

Case closed? nine mysteries unlocked by modern science. written by Susan Hughes; illustrated by Michael Wandelmaier. Kids Can Press 2010 88p il map $17.95

Grades: 6 7 8 9 **902**

1. Archeology 2. Technological innovations 3. History -- Miscellanea

ISBN 978-1-55453-362-6; 1-55453-362-7

Examines how developments in modern science, such as DNA analysis and spectroscopy, have helped to re-open archaeological mysteries about ancient cities, Egypt's first female pharaoh, a missing expedition to find the Northwest Passage, and more.

"The writing is clear and engaging. The full-color illustrations are a mix of photographs, maps, and flat, animation-style art." SLJ

Includes glossary

904 Collected accounts of events

Beyer, Rick

The **greatest** stories never told; 100 tales from history to astonish, bewilder, & stupefy. HarperResource 2003 214p il $17.95

Grades: 7 8 9 10 **904**

1. History -- Miscellanea

ISBN 0-06-001401-6

LC 2004-296419

"Beginning with the year 46 B.C. and ending in 1990, Beyer presents a chronological account of one hundred unknown, partially known, and familar tales about an array of people and events that have shaped the world. . . . They range from the mundane to the fantastic. . . . Extensive research went into the production of this charming work. Primary documents in the form of letters, laws, illustrations, and photographs bring to life these unique and incredible anecdotes." Voice Youth Advocates

Includes bibliographical references

Guiberson, Brenda Z.

★ **Disasters**; natural and man-made catastrophes through the centuries. Henry Holt and Company 2010 228p il $18.99

Grades: 5 6 7 8 9 **904**

1. Disasters 2. Natural disasters

ISBN 978-0-8050-8170-1; 0-8050-8170-4

LC 2009018908

"The subtitle provides an accurate outline of the contents of this lively treatment of disasters from smallpox to Hurricane Katrina. In each chapter, Guiberson outlines the sources of the disaster, the results, and means of obviating the problems that caused these tragedies. For example, the chapter on the Great Chicago Fire begins with the construction of the city over unstable marshland. . . . This kind of exhaustive background serves to create an understanding of the contributory issues and demonstrates possible preventive steps. Guiberson's compellingly written exegesis is equally good in the other nine chapters. Well-placed, black-and-white reproductions and photos extend the text. A perfect example of solid historical research coupled with engaging writing." SLJ

Includes bibliographical references

Meissner, David

Call of the Klondike; a true gold rush adventure. by David Meissner and Kim Richardson. Calkins Creek 2013 168 p. (reinforced) $16.95

Grades: 6 7 8 **904**

1. Alaska -- Gold discoveries 2. Klondike River valley (Yukon) -- Gold discoveries

ISBN 1590788230; 9781590788233

LC 2013931060

Here, the authors share the experience of two 20-something Yale graduates from 1897, Stanley Pearce and Marshall Bond, who participated in the Klondike gold rush. Their letters are offered along with "diary entries, telegrams and Pearce's articles for the Denver Republican." The book also incorporates "pull-out quotes, maps, posters, documents and many . . . captioned photographs, including one of Jack London, who camped near Pearce and Bond's cabin." (Kirkus Reviews)

909 World history

Adams, Simon

★ The **Kingfisher** atlas of world history; a pictorial guide to the world's people and events, 10,000 BCE-present. Kingfisher 2010 181p il map $24.99

Grades: 4 5 6 7 **909**

1. World history 2. Historical geography

ISBN 978-0-7534-6388-8; 0-7534-6388-1

"This colorful and fact-packed book is not only informative but well organized. Sections cover 'The Ancient World,' 'The Medieval World,' 'Exploration and Empire,' and 'The Modern World,' and each section contains 15 or 16 thematic maps presented in chronological order. . . . It is very useful and entertaining as well as data-filled." Booklist

Badcott, Nicholas

Pocket timeline of Islamic civilizations. Interlink 2009 32p il $13.95

Grades: 7 8 9 10 **909**

1. Reference books 2. Islamic civilization -- Chronology

ISBN 978-1-56656-758-9; 1-56656-758-0

"Badcott takes readers on a colorful and captivating tour of Islamic civilizations from the 7th to the 20th century. He discusses the rise and fall of dynasties, along with their achievements and contributions in art, medicine, architecture, commerce, and science. . . . The writing style is easy to read. . . . Attractive color photographs of buildings, pottery, jewelry, art, and inventions help maintain readers' interest throughout." SLJ

Includes bibliographical references

Eamer, Claire

Traitors' Gate and other doorways to the past. Annick Press 2008 154p il $24.95; pa $12.95

Grades: 6 7 8 9 **909**

1. Doorways 2. World history

ISBN 978-1-55451-145-7; 1-55451-145-3; 978-1-55451-144-0 pa; 1-55451-144-5 pa

"Eamer uses the concrete image of doorways to introduce famous (and not-so-famous) structures. She begins with perhaps the most amazing one, located in Petra, Jordan. Al-Khazner is hidden in a sandstone cliff. . . . Among the other structures discussed are Cape Coast Castle in Ghana, through whose doorway Africans were led to slave ships; the six doors of the Kremlin's Holy Antechamber; . . . and Spruce Tree House, an ancient cliff house in Colorado. . . . The many photographs are nicely reproduced, and Eamer's text is always solid and sometimes soars." Booklist

Includes bibliographical references

Hinds, Kathryn, 1962-

★ The **city**; by Kathryn Hinds. Marshall Cavendish Benchmark 2008 96 p. col. ill., maps (library) $8.66

Grades: 6 7 8 9 10 **909**

1. Middle Ages 2. City and town life 3. Medieval civilization 4. Islamic countries

ISBN 076143089X; 9780761430896

LC 2008019432

"A social history of the Islamic world from the eighth through the mid-thirteenth century, with a focus on life in the cities" Publisher's note

Includes bibliographical references and index.

★ The **countryside**; by Kathryn Hinds. Marshall Cavendish Benchmark 2008 95 p. col. ill. (library) $8.66

Grades: 6 7 8 9 10 **909**

1. Deserts 2. Middle Ages 3. Country life 4. Medieval civilization 5. Islamic countries

ISBN 0761430911; 9780761430919

LC 2008019266

"Presents a social history of the Islamic world from the eighth through the mid-thirteenth century, with a focus on life in the desert and countryside." Publisher's note

Includes bibliographical references and index.

Hussain, Saima S.

The **Arab** world thought of it; inventions, innovations, and amazing facts. Saima S. Hussain. Annick Press 2013 48 p. $21.95

Grades: 6 7 8 **909**

1. Arab civilization 2. Arab countries -- History

ISBN 1554514770; 9781554514779

This book is an "introduction to the Arab world through the arts and sciences developed in the many countries of the Middle East and North Africa and other regions where Arab culture flourished." Topics include "education, astronomy, weaponry, architecture, food, medical discoveries, arts and crafts, religion, and everyday inventions such as mattresses and hard soap." (Kirkus Reviews)

Kennedy, Susan

History year by year; written by Peter Chrisp, Joe Fullman, and Susan Kennedy ; consultant, Philip Parker. DK Publishing 2013 320 p. col. ill., col. maps $24.99

Grades: 4 5 6 7 8 9 **909**

1. Anthropology 2. World history 3. Chronology, Historical

ISBN 1465414185; 9781465414182

LC 2012286068

This book "presents the world through a detailed timeline, letting children follow the influences, patterns, and connections between historical events.Beginning with prehistory and running up to the Arab Spring, budding historians will learn about the history of humans across the world. Spreads highlight major historical eras . . . while quotations from primary and secondary sources alongside insight from experts give proper historical context." (Publisher's note)

"Every few pages, a particular subtopic gets extra attention. . . . Features such as these make this an excellent browsing book, but students can still pull information from the text. A brief history of both the United States and Canada is appended. A good addition to most collections, both for the information it offers and for its appealing format." SLJ

Moore, Christopher, 1957-

From then to now; a short history of the world. illustrated by Andrej Krystoforski. Tundra Books 2011 188p il map $25.95

Grades: 7 8 9 10 **909**

1. World history 2. Civilization -- History

ISBN 978-0-88776-540-7; 0-88776-540-8

"Capably told and uniquely illustrated, From Then to Now explains how imaginative human cultures have produced an intellectually and socially dynamic world. The work follows the course of human history from hunter-gatherer beginnings, through expansion and contact, to a modern, tightly interconnected global world. Along the way, Moore tackles how humanity, through agricultural and industrial innovations, has shaped and been shaped by environmental obstacles. Full-color spot art appears occasionally, and color sidebars provide information on a number of subjects. . . . This exceptional history of humanity is a breath of fresh air." SLJ

National Geographic concise history of the world; an illustrated timeline. edited by Neil Kagan. Revised edition National Geographic Society 2013 416 p. ill. (some col.), maps $40

Grades: 6 7 8 9 10 11 12 Adult **909**

1. World history 2. Historical chronology

ISBN 1426211783; 9781426211782

LC 2015430064

"For readers of all ages, world history is easily accessible, depicted as never before—so that events occurring simultaneously around the world can be viewed at-a-glance together. . . . The book's innovative time line truly sets it apart, allowing readers to scan across a spread and explore a single area or compare contemporary societies across the globe." (Publisher's note)

Includes bibliographical references (pages 405-406) and index

Smith, Tom

Discovery of the Americas, 1492-1800; rev ed.; Chelsea House 2010 134p il map (Discovery and exploration) lib bdg $35

Grades: 7 8 9 10 11 **909**

1. Explorers 2. America -- Exploration

ISBN 978-1-60413-195-6; 1-60413-195-0

LC 2009-22330

First published 2005

"The chapters are well-illustrated with color and black and white historic photos, illustrations and maps. Chapter layout is clearly organized with helpful subtitles; sidebars develop related themes in eye-catching colors." Libr Media Connect

Includes glossary and bibliographical references

909.07 General historical periods

Currie, Stephen

The **Medieval** crusades; by Stephen Currie. Lucent Books 2009 96 p. ill. (chiefly col.), col. map (library) $34.95

Grades: 6 7 8 9 **909.07**

1. Middle Ages 2. Crusades 3. Civilization, Medieval

ISBN 1420500627; 9781420500622

LC 2008046532

This book by Stephen Currie is part of the World History series and looks at the medieval crusades. It "begins with an explanation of early Christendom and Islam and the schisms that existed within each religion. . . . The focus of the book falls on the long-term effects of the Crusades, creating European awareness of other countries and cultures that led to increased commerce and trade, which in turn led to the Age of Exploration and the Renaissance." (Voice of Youth Advocates)

Includes bibliographical references and index.

Hinds, Kathryn, 1962-

★ The **palace**; [by] Kathryn Hinds. Marshall Cavendish Benchmark 2008 96p il map (Life in the Medieval Muslim world) lib bdg $23.95

Grades: 6 7 8 9 10 **909.07**

1. Middle Ages 2. Medieval civilization 3. Elite (Social sciences) 4. Islamic countries

ISBN 978-0-7614-3088-9 lib bdg; 0-7614-3088-1 lib bdg

LC 2008010734

"Richly illustrated with art reproductions, maps, photos, and ornate Islamic border designs, [this] . . . will entice visual learners." Libr Media Connect

Includes glossary and bibliographical references

Knight, Judson

Middle ages: almanac; edited by Judy Galens. U.X.L 2001 lxv, 226p il map (Middle Ages reference library) $60

Grades: 8 9 10 11 12 **909.07**

1. Middle Ages 2. World history 3. Reference books 4. Medieval civilization

ISBN 0-7876-4856-6

LC 00-59442

This reference's 19 chapters review world history from the fall of the Roman Empire in 500 A.D. to the beginning of the Renaissance in 1500 A.D.

"The volume's strength is its broad coverage; it includes material on India, Southeast Asia, China, Japan, the Americas, and Africa as well as Europe and the Middle East, making it unique among other books for this age group." SLJ

Includes bibliographical references

Middle ages: primary sources; [compiled by] Judson Knight; Judy Galens, editor. U.X.L 2000 xxxiv, 161p il (Middle Ages reference library) $60

Grades: 8 9 10 11 12 **909.07**

1. Middle Ages

ISBN 0-7876-4860-4

LC 00-59441

This volume contains "19 full or excerpted documents written during this period, including the work of celebrated writers such as St. Augustine, Marco Polo, and Dante as well as less familiar individuals such as Anna Comnena and Lo Kuan-chung. Each selection is placed in its historical context and followed by a section entitled 'What happened next'. . . . Unfamiliar words or terms are defined in sidebars. Each entry has a box profiling the author of the documents and at least two illustrations." Booklist

Includes bibliographical references

909.08 Modern history, 1450/1500-

Huff, Toby E.

★ An **age** of science and revolutions, 1600-1800; [by] Toby Huff. Oxford University Press 2005 173p il map (Medieval & early modern world) lib bdg $32.95

Grades: 7 8 9 10 **909.08**

1. Europe -- Civilization 2. World history -- 17th century 3. World

history -- 18th century
ISBN 0-19-517724-X
LC 2004-21612

This volume "looks at 200 years of world history. . . . [It includes] overview chapters on China, India, and the Middle East . . . [and] discusses the Enlightenment in Europe in some depth. . . . [This is a] useful book, which may spark discussion about current controversies about connections between science and religion." Booklist

Includes bibliographical references

Wiesner, Merry E.

★ An **age** of voyages, 1350-1600; [by] Merry E. Wiesner-Hanks. Oxford University Press 2005 189p il map (Medieval & early modern world) $32.95

Grades: 7 8 9 10 **909.08**

1. Middle Ages 2. World history -- 16th century
ISBN 0-19-517672-3; 978-0-19-517672-8
LC 2004021178

"In accessible language supported by prolific illustrations and primary sources, [this volume describes an era] that transformed the world." SLJ

Includes bibliographical references

909.8 World history--1800-

Winkler, Allan M.

The **Cold** War; a history in documents. by Allan M. Winkler. 2nd ed. Oxford University Press 2011 ix, 160 p.p ill., maps (Pages from History) (paperback) $34.95; (hardcover) $42.95

Grades: 8 9 10 11 12 **909.8**

1. Cold War 2. United States -- Foreign relations -- Soviet Union 3. Cold War -- Sources 4. World politics -- 1945-1989 -- Sources 5. Russia -- Foreign relations -- United States -- Sources 6. United States -- Foreign relations -- Russia -- Sources
ISBN 0199765995; 9780199765980; 9780199765997
LC 2010049111

This book by Allan M. Winkler is part of the Pages from History series and "traces the evolution of the Cold War . . . . By addressing the key issues of the Cold War via documents, the author provides a . . . look into a time that set the table for the modern era. Topics such as nuclear proliferation, McCarthyism, censorship, the Vietnam War and the Civil Rights Movement are all" addressed. (Children's Literature)

Includes bibliographical references and index.

909.82 World history--20th century, 1900-1999

Grant, R. G.

The **Cold** War. Arcturus Pub. 2011 46p il (Secret history) lib bdg $32.80 **909.82**

1. Cold war
ISBN 978-1-84837-696-0; 1-84837-696-0
LC 2010011765

This book explores the secrets of the Cold War. The superpowers never fought openly on a battlefield. Instead, they attacked one another by underhand means-spying, propaganda, secret operations, and guerrilla wars.

"The title of the Secret History series will grab readers, even reluctant ones, and they won't be disappointed by the intriguing info regarding codes and code breakers, spies, terrorists, and double agents, with profiles of heroes and traitors on all sides. . . . The readable design, with clear type on thick, high-quality paper, includes lots of sidebars, photos, screens, and quotes." Booklist

Includes bibliographical references

Harrison, Paul

Why did the Cold War happen? Gareth Stevens Pub. 2011 48p il map (Moments in history) lib bdg $31.95; pa $14.05

Grades: 6 7 8 9 **909.82**

1. Cold war 2. World politics -- 1945-1991
ISBN 978-1-4339-4166-5 lib bdg; 1-4339-4166-X lib bdg; 978-1-4339-4167-2 pa; 1-4339-4167-8 pa
LC 2010012456

"Examines the events that served as . . . [precursors to the Cold War]. . . . Brightly colored pullout boxes highlight important turning points, the perspective of the everyday man, and further information on why specific events occurred. Numerous photographs help readers visualize concepts more fully. . . . Students should be able to easily use this resource." Libr Media Connect

Includes glossary and bibliographical references

Kaufman, Michael T.

★ **1968**. Roaring Brook Press 2009 148p il $22.95

Grades: 7 8 9 10 11 12 **909.82**

1. World history -- 20th century
ISBN 978-1-59643-428-8; 1-59643-428-7
LC 2008-15471

Kaufman "expertly draws young readers into the worldwide events of a single, watershed year: 1968. . . . Each chapter focuses on a different hot spot around the globe, beginning with the Tet Offensive and the Vietnam War and moving through uprisings in New York, Paris, Prague, Chicago, and Mexico City, as well as the assassinations of Martin Luther King Jr. and Robert F. Kennedy. . . . The images, drawn from the [New York] Times archives, are riveting and will easily draw young people into the fascinating, often horrifying events." Booklist

909.83 World history--21st century, 2000-2099

Lace, William W.

The **Indian** Ocean tsunami of 2004. Chelsea House 2008 127p il map (Great historic disasters) $35

Grades: 7 8 9 10 **909.83**

1. Indian Ocean earthquake and tsunami, 2004
ISBN 978-0-7910-9642-0; 0-7910-9642-4
LC 2007-36950

"The author explains in detail the seismic activities that caused the 2004 Indian Ocean tsunami, as well as the lack of systems in place to quickly notify those in danger. Also included are many well-captioned photos . . . and short but interesting personal stories of both survivors and victims." Horn Book Guide

Includes glossary and bibliographical references

Torres, John Albert

Disaster in the Indian Ocean, Tsunami 2004; [by] John A. Torres. Mitchell Lane 2005 48p il map (Monumental milestones) lib bdg $19.95

Grades: 5 6 7 8 **909.83**

1. Indian Ocean earthquake and tsunami, 2004
ISBN 1-58415-344-X

This "emerges from the author's personal trip to Indonesia after the December 26, 2004, catastrophe. . . . Primary-source accounts, many taken from Torres' own interviews, chillingly recreate the tsunami's initial strike, its chaotic aftermath, and the challenges of recovery." Booklist

Includes bibliographical references

910 Geography and travel

Belmont, Helen

★ **Looking** at aerial photographs; [by] Helen Belmont. Smart Apple Media 2008 46p il map (Geography skills) $22.95

Grades: 6 7 8 9 **910**

1. Geography 2. Aerial photography

ISBN 978-1-59920-048-4; 1-59920-048-1

LC 2006036139

"The text is easy to follow. . . . The examples given in the text that involve places are almost always accompanied by excellent photographs. . . . Maps, block diagrams, tables, and graphs are clearly presented and easy to interpret." Sci Books Films

Includes glossary and bibliographical references

Dumont-Le Cornec, Elisabeth

Wonders of the world; natural and man-made majesties. by Elisabeth Dumont-Le Cornec; illustrated by Laureen Topalian and Kristel Riethmuller. Abrams Books for Young Readers 2007 151p il $24.95

Grades: 6 7 8 9 **910**

1. Antiquities 2. Civilization 3. Historic sites 4. Natural monuments 5. Curiosities and wonders

ISBN 978-0-8109-9417-1; 0-8109-9417-8

LC 2007016198

This "volume features 71 natural and man-made wonders selected from sites on the UNESCO World Heritage list. . . . This visually stunning book presents each selected site on a double-page spread. Most of the spread is devoted to an excellent color photo reproduced on heavy, glossy paper and accompanied by several paragraphs of explanatory text, good captions, and a small washed drawing. . . . A rich visual experience." Booklist

Elliott, Lynne

Exploration in the Renaissance; [by] Lynne Elliott. Crabtree 2009 32p il pa $8.95; lib bdg $26.60

Grades: 6 7 8 9 **910**

1. Renaissance 2. America -- Exploration 3. Discoveries in geography -- European

ISBN 978-0-7787-4613-3 pa; 978-0-7787-4593-8 lib bdg

LC 2008-52601

"Ideal introductions to concepts, people, and events of the Renaissance... succinct and thorough." SLJ

Goodman, Joan E.

A **long** and uncertain journey: the 27,000 mile voyage of Vasco da Gama; by Joan Elizabeth Goodman; illustrated by Tom McNeely. Mikaya Press 2001 47p il map (Great explorers book) $22.95

Grades: 4 5 6 7 **910**

1. Explorers

ISBN 0-9650493-7-X

LC 00-63795

"McNeely's full-page illustrations, which vibrate with life and action, lighten the format, and quotations from the diary of an anonymous sailor on the voyage add fascinating detail and vivid description. . . . A good resource for reports, but the book is also intelligently written and exciting." Booklist

Jennings, Ken

Maps and geography; by Ken Jennings ; illustrated by Mike Lowery. Little Simon, an imprint of Simon & Schuster Children's Pub. Division 2014 160 p. (The junior genius guides) $18.99

Grades: 3 4 5 6 **910**

1. Maps 2. Geography

ISBN 144249848X; 9781442473287; 9781442498488

LC 2012050862

This book, by Ken Jennings and illustrated by Mike Lowery, is part of the "Junior Genius Guides" series. "With this . . . guide to maps and geography, you'll become an expert and wow your friends and teachers with clever facts. . . . With great illustrations, cool trivia, and fun quizzes to test your knowledge, this guide will have you on your way to whiz-kid status in no time!" (Publisher's note)

"The new line of Junior Genius Guide books kicks off with a stellar collection of facts about climate, national flags, maps, and more, all in an engaging, arch tone. Jeopardy! champ and author Jennings, making his first foray into books for children, arranges the trivia in chapters that lightly satirize a school-day schedule, including a lunch period offering an ingenious and easy recipe for an edible map, a craft project in art class, and an official certification exam before the dismissal bell... Lowery's black-and-white spot illustrations help explain concepts, such as cartographic projections, and add the overall levity, making this a successful nonfiction package as well as pure reading fun. Published simultaneously with the second in the series, Greek Mythology." Booklist

Includes bibliographical references and index

Kerley, Barbara

★ The **world** is waiting for you; by Barbara Kerley. National Geographic 2013 48 p. (hardcover : alk. paper) $17.95

Grades: 1 2 3 4 5 6 **910**

1. Vocational guidance 2. Discoveries in geography

ISBN 1426311141; 9781426311147; 9781426311154

LC 2012026526

This book, by Barbara Kerley, "shows kids a pathway from their current interests and talents to a future career or interest. And in so doing, it also encourages adventure, exploration, and discovery, three core principles of National Geographic's mission. Selected photos make the connections compelling and the future real for kids, then rich back matter brings the message home with inspirational quotes from the real-life adventurers pictured in the images." (Publisher's note)

Richards, Jon

Planet Earth; by Jon Richards and illustrated by Ed Simkins. Owl Kids 2013 32 p. $15.95

Grades: 3 4 5 6 **910**

1. Graphic design 2. Signs and symbols

ISBN 1926973755; 9781926973753

In this book by Jon Richards "explores planet Earth using a wide variety of icons, graphics, and pictograms." Readers can "compare the tallest mountains from each continent, see the entire volume of water on the Earth poured into one glass, stack up Eiffel Towers and compare the height of the world's tallest waterfall." (Publisher's note)

Wojtanik, Andrew, 1989-

The **National** Geographic Bee ultimate fact book; countries A to Z. Andrew Wojtanik. National Geographic 2012 384 p. maps (pbk.) $21.90; (reinforced library binding) $21.90

Grades: 5 6 7 8 9 10 **910**

1. Atlases 2. Nations 3. Geography 4. Geography -- Encyclopedias

ISBN 1426309473; 1426309635; 9781426309472; 9781426309632

LC 2011282873

This book "provides statistical information for the world's 195 countries at a glance. The book starts off with a world map and full-page continental maps. Individual entries for countries are listed alphabetically. . . . A glossary explains terms that may be unfamiliar to students . . . . Each country entry includes a map with longitude and latitude and basic facts: continent, size, population, and capital." (Voice of Youth Advocates)

Includes bibliographical references (p. 382)

910.3 Geography--Dictionaries, encyclopedias, concordances, gazetteers

Gifford, Clive

The **Kingfisher** geography encyclopedia; 2nd ed., rev. and updated ed.; Kingfisher 2011 487p il map $34.99

Grades: 4 5 6 7 **910.3**

1. Reference books 2. Geography -- Encyclopedias

ISBN 978-0-7534-6575-2; 0-7534-6575-2

Statistics, text, and color maps reveal the physical geography, peoples, politics, governments, languages, religions, and currencies of each nation of the world.

"The geographical descriptions are well written and include striking photos. The text is large and easy to read. . . . It is a great book to keep around the library for students to browse and dream about their next journey." Voice Youth Advocates

910.4 Accounts of travel and facilities for travelers

Adams, Simon

Titanic; by Simon Adams. Updated edition DK 2014 72 p. color illustrations (DK Eyewitness) hbk $19.99; pbk $9.99

Grades: 4 5 6 7 **910.4**

1. Shipwrecks 2. Titanic (Steamship)

ISBN 1465420576; 1465420991; 9781465420992; 9781465420572

LC 2015302651

First published 1999

In this book about the Titanic, readers "discover the triumphs and tragedies of this 'unsinkable' luxury liner. Detailed images and text highlight all aspects of this fateful journey including how the ship was built and equipped, what kind of passengers and crew she carried, what facilities she offered onboard, how she struck an iceberg, why she sank so quickly, how many people were saved, and how many lives were lost." (Publisher's note)

Anderson, Harry S.

Exploring the polar regions; rev ed.; Chelsea House 2010 116p il map (Discovery and exploration) lib bdg $35

Grades: 7 8 9 10 **910.4**

1. Polar regions -- Exploration

ISBN 978-1-60413-190-1; 1-60413-190-X

LC 2009-22863

First published 2004 by Facts on File

Covers exploration and discovery of the Arctic and Antarctic regions.

"The chapters are well-illustrated with color and black and white historic photos, illustrations and maps. Chapter layout is clearly organized with helpful subtitles; sidebars develop related themes in eye-catching colors. . . . [This book] attractively and effectively surveys an important . . . area in world studies." Libr Media Connect

Includes glossary and bibliographical references

Aronson, Marc

★ The **world** made new; why the Age of Exploration happened & how it changed the world. [by] Marc Aronson & John W. Glenn. National Geographic 2007 64p il map $17.95; lib bdg $27.90

Grades: 4 5 6 7 **910.4**

1. Explorers 2. Exploration

ISBN 978-0-7922-6454-5; 978-0-7922-6978-6 lib bdg

LC 2006022091

"This highly pictorial, readable overview provides significant depth of coverage. . . . The illustrations, most in full color, make ample and appropriate use of period prints as well as contemporary illustrations and photographs. The result is a visual feast that fleshes out the . . . remarkably evenhanded narrative." SLJ

Includes glossary and bibliographical references

Bergreen, Laurence

Magellan; over the edge of the world. Laurence Bergreen. Roaring Brook Press 2017 xii, 211 p.p illustrations, maps (hardback) $19.99

Grades: 7 8 9 **910.4**

1. Explorers -- Portugal -- History 2. Voyages around the world 3. Explorers -- Portugal -- Biography 4. Voyages around the world -- History -- 16th century

ISBN 9781626721210; 9781626721203

LC 2015035814

This book is "a middle-grade adaptation of Laurence Bergreen's adult bestseller, about Magellan's historic voyage around the globe. On September 6, 1522, a horribly battered ship manned by eighteen malnourished, scurvy-ridden sailors appeared on the horizon near a Spanish port. . . . How did Ferdinand Magellan's voyage to circle the world—one of the largest and best-equipped expeditions ever mounted--turn into this ghost ship?" (Publisher's note)

"Bergreen ably adapts his book for adults Over the Edge of the World: Magellan's Terrifying Circumnavigation of the Globe (2003) into a gripping and harrowing true adventure story for young readers." Kirkus

Includes bibliographical references (pages 189-199) and index.

Bristow, David

★ **Sky** sailors; true stories of the balloon era. [by] David L. Bristow. Farrar Straus Giroux 2010 134p il $18.99

Grades: 4 5 6 7 **910.4**

1. Balloons

ISBN 978-0-374-37014-5; 0-374-37014-1

LC 2009037285

"This lively look at escapades of daring men—and a surprising number of women—who risked their lives flying in balloons will appeal to adventure, history and science buffs—and perhaps steampunk fans as well. Each of the nine chapters, which are chronologically arranged, focuses on an exciting story, starting with the first confirmed human balloon flight in 1783 . . . and ending with Dolly Shepherd, a young British woman in the early 1900s who parachuted out of balloons, hanging onto a trapeze. . . . Useful captions accompany many full-color illustrations of artwork and photographs." Kirkus

Includes bibliographical references

Burlingame, Jeff

The **Titanic** tragedy. Marshall Cavendish Benchmark 2011 111p il (Perspectives on) lib bdg $33.93

Grades: 8 9 10 11 12 **910.4**

1. Shipwrecks 2. Titanic (Steamship)

ISBN 978-1-60870-450-7 lib bdg; 1-60870-450-5 lib bdg; 978-1-60870-722-5 ebook

LC 2010041560

This tltle offers "excellent, thorough, and accurate information for reports or for general reading. [It] examines safety issues in the shipping industry in relation to the importance of profit, the historical background of the Gilded Age, the effects of privilege on the survivors of the disaster, the economic impact on those less well off, and the way the disaster affected future regulation of the shipping industry." SLJ

Includes bibliographical references

Cerullo, Mary M.

Shipwrecks; exploring sunken cities beneath the sea. [by] Mary M. Cerullo. Dutton Children's Books 2009 64p il $18.99

Grades: 5 6 7 8 **910.4**

1. Shipwrecks 2. Portland (Steamer) 3. Henrietta Marie (Ship)

ISBN 978-0-525-47968-0; 0-525-47968-6

LC 2008-48967

This focuses "on two wrecks: the Henrietta Marie, sunk in 1700 near the Florida Keys, and the Portland, sunk in 1898 off the coast of Massachusetts. The book makes the convincing case that these wrecks are important not only for historical reasons but also for the underwater ecosystems their structures now host. . . . This delivers both education and shivers." Booklist

Clifford, Barry

Real pirates; the untold story of the Whydah from slave ship to pirate ship. by Barry Clifford and Kenneth J. Kinkor with Sharon Simpson; photography by Kenneth Garrett. National Geographic 2008 175p il map $16.95

Grades: 4 5 6 7 **910.4**

1. Pirates 2. Archeology 3. Shipwrecks 4. Slave trade 5. Whidah (Ship) 6. Cape Cod (Mass.)

ISBN 978-1-4263-0279-4; 1-4263-0279-7

LC 2008299778

"Clifford, an underwater archaeological explorer, used research and the artifacts recovered from the Whydah to tell the story of its life as a slave galley and pirate ship. In the process, he dispels many myths about buccaneers. . . . Photographs of artifacts . . . and the recovery crew at work combine with large visually appealing paintings of dramatic battle, storm, and courtroom scenes. . . . The book is a fascinating blend of history, ocean-diving recovery, and archaeology, and demonstrates archaeology in action and the role artifacts play in informing us about the past." SLJ

Includes bibliographical references

Denenberg, Barry

★ **Titanic** sinks! Viking 2011 72p il $19.99

Grades: 5 6 7 8 **910.4**

1. Shipwrecks 2. Titanic (Steamship)

ISBN 0670012432; 9780670012435

LC 2011012040

This is a "gripping recounting of the Titanic's doomed maiden voyage, chronicled in the tabloid-style pages of a fictional magazine. . . . Melding fact and fiction, the book compiles dramatic headlines, articles that range from news bulletins about the building of the ship to a chatty tour of its lavish interior, and an array of stunning period photographs." Publ Wkly

Gilkerson, William

A **thousand** years of pirates. Tundra Books 2009 96p il map $32.95

Grades: 6 7 8 9 10 **910.4**

1. Pirates

ISBN 978-0-88776-924-5; 0-88776-924-1

"Pirates are given scholarly scrutiny in this handsome and invigorating overview. Short but dense chapters introduce the major factions, characters, and incidents that connect the scattered history of seagoing bandits. . . . Gilkerson's grasp of the politics surrounding each nation's pirates . . . is most impressive." Booklist

Includes bibliographical references

Grove, Tim

First flight around the world; the adventures of the American fliers who won the race. by Tim Grove. Abrams Books for Young Readers, in assoc. w/Smithsonian Ntl. Air & Space Museum 2015 96 p. col. ill.; maps (hardcover) $21.95

Grades: 5 6 7 8 **910.4**

1. Aeronautics -- Flights 2. Voyages around the world 3. World records 4. Flights around the world 5. United States. Army. Air Corps

ISBN 1419714821; 9781419714825

LC 2014024665

YALSA Award for Excellence in Nonfiction for Young Adults: Shortlist (2016)

This children's book, by Tim Grove, "documents the exciting journey of four American planes--the Chicago, Boston, New Orleans, and Seattle--and their crews on a race around the world. The trip held many challenges: extreme weather, tricky navigation, unfamiliar cultures, fragile planes, and few airfields. The world fliers risked their lives for the sake of national pride." (Publisher's note)

"This gripping, well-designed title details the United States' 1924 successful attempt to become the first nation to circumnavigate the globe by flight. . . . Offering a look at a lesser-known historical event, this beautiful, well-written book is an essential addition for all collections." SLJ

Includes bibliographical references

Hagglund, Betty

Epic treks. Kingfisher 2011 64p il (Epic adventure) $19.99

Grades: 5 6 7 8 **910.4**

1. Explorers 2. Voyages and travels

ISBN 978-0-7534-6668-1; 0-7534-6668-6

LC 2011041638

"The graphics will grab readers in [this] exciting, extra-large-size [title] . . . packed with high-quality color photos on every double-page spread. Just as gripping are the narratives, captions, and technical details of exploration, adventure, and survival. . . . Epic Treks covers Lewis and Clark, Livingston and Stanley, Burk and Wells, and Amundsen and

Scott, each journey an exciting adventure filled with details about what they endured and what they found, as well as their failures and shortcomings." Booklist

Includes glossary

Hanel, Rachael

Pirates; [by] Rachael Hanel. Creative Education 2008 48p il map (Fearsome fighters) $31.35

Grades: 4 5 6 **910.4**

1. Pirates

ISBN 978-1-58341-537-5; 1-58341-537-8

LC 2006021844

"This book explores 'the golden age of piracy' from the sixteenth through the nineteenth centuries. Hanel discusses battles, types of ships and weapons, and attire and behavior. Vignettes of well-known male and female pirates are included. Archival reproductions and sidebars provide additional information." Horn Book Guide

Includes glossary and bibliographical references

Hopkinson, Deborah, 1942-

★ **Titanic**; voices from the disaster. by Deborah Hopkinson. Scholastic Press 2012 289 p. (hardcover) $17.99

Grades: 5 6 7 8 **910.4**

1. Titanic (Steamship) 2. Shipwrecks

ISBN 0545116740; 9780545116749

LC 2011006695

Robert F. Sibert Honor Book (2013)

YALSA Award for Excellence in Nonfiction for Young Adults Finalist (2013)

In this book about the sinking of the Titanic, author Deborah "Hopkinson begins with a description of the ship . . . and introduces some of the passengers who embarked on its maiden voyage. The narrative shifts . . . to the disaster itself with a litany of things gone wrong. . . . [M] emoirs . . . are interlaced throughout the text, as survivors testified . . . on the relative chaos or calm, heroism or cowardice, of passengers and crew." (Bulletin of the Center for Children's Books)

Includes bibliographical references

Hunter, Nick

Pirate treasure; by Nick Hunter. Raintree 2013 48 p. (hb) $29.33

Grades: 5 6 7 8 **910.4**

1. Pirates 2. Buried treasure 3. Treasure troves

ISBN 1410949532; 9781410949530; 9781410949608

LC 2012012890

This book, by Nick Hunter, "examines the hunt for treasures lost or hidden by pirates, and examines whether any of the legends of buried treasure could really be true. Part of the Treasure Hunters series, 'Pirate Treasure' offers a crosscurricular mix of science & technology and history & civilizations. Pirate treasures covered in the book include those of the famous Blackbeard and Captain Kidd, the pirate shipwreck the Whydah, and the mysterious Oak Island Money Pit." (Publisher's note)

Includes bibliographical references and index

Lavery, Brian

The **conquest** of the ocean; the illustrated history of seafaring. Brian Lavery. Dk Pub 2013 400 p. $30

Grades: 8 9 10 11 12 **910.4**

1. Seafaring life 2. Maritime history

ISBN 146540841X; 9781465408419

This book offers a "survey of humanity's history on the seas." It "begins about 30,000 years ago with Polynesian seafarers' colonization of Pacific islands and continues through to address harrowing accounts of modern-day piracy. Ports of call between these distant coasts include the treasure voyages of Ming official Zheng He, the discovery of the New World, the invention of the Fresnel lens, the Battle of Midway, and many others." (Publishers Weekly)

Lawlor, Laurie

Magnificent voyage; an American adventurer on Captain James Cook's final expedition. Holiday House 2002 236p il maps $22.95

Grades: 7 8 9 10 **910.4**

1. Explorers 2. Oceania 3. Naval officers 4. Travel writers 5. Resolution (Ship)

ISBN 0-8234-1575-9

LC 2002-17148

Based on the writings of John Ledyard, an American cook on the ship Resolution, tells of explorer James Cook's final voyage in search of the Northwest Passage, discovery of the Hawaiian Islands, and murder

"The author's detailed picture of the voyage, and of Ledyard's relatively brief career, makes engrossing, if gloomy, reading." Booklist

Includes bibliographical references (p. 226-229) and index

Marschall, Ken

Inside the Titanic; illustrated by Ken Marschall; text by Hugh Brewster. Little, Brown 1997 32p il $19.95

Grades: 4 5 6 7 **910.4**

1. Shipwrecks 2. Titanic (Steamship)

ISBN 0-316-55716-1

LC 97-382

"Color cutaway paintings of the Titanic in this oversize book allow readers to view every deck as they follow two 12-year-old boys exploring the vessel, and to see how the liner struck the iceberg and sank." Booklist

Includes glossary and bibliographical references

McPherson, Stephanie Sammartino

★ **Iceberg** right ahead! the tragedy of the Titanic. Twenty-First Century Books 2011 112p il lib bdg $33.26

Grades: 4 5 6 7 8 **910.4**

1. Shipwrecks 2. Titanic (Steamship)

ISBN 9780761367567

LC 2011002352

"With innumerable books, movies, documentaries, novels, and biographies all telling versions of the Titanic story, it would seem that there is little more to learn, yet by providing more details and some of the most up-to-date research, McPherson's compelling, thoughtful narrative proves otherwise. . . . The layout includes plenty of period photographs, diagrams, artwork, and sidebars with interesting tangential tidbits, making for a thorough resource. . . . A comprehensive, well-written, thoroughly researched title." SLJ

Includes bibliographical references

Morris, Neil

Voyages of discovery. Zak Books 2009 48p il map (History of the world) lib bdg $34.25

Grades: 7 8 9 10 **910.4**

1. Explorers 2. Exploration

ISBN 978-88-6098-154-7 lib bdg; 88-6098-154-9 lib bdg

LC 2008-8409

The "effectiveness lies in the combination of lush illustrations, well-chosen, captioned photographs of contemporary artifacts, and . . . [a] reasoned, concise [narrative]. Succinct time lines border most pages, and . . . the proper amount of white space, and clear dark print maintain organization and clarity. A superior choice." SLJ

Includes glossary

Mosco, Rosemary

The **Atlas** Obscura explorer's guide for the world's most adventurous kid; Dylan Thuras and Rosemary Mosco, illustrated by Joy Ang. Workman Pub Co 2018 112 p. $19.95

Grades: 4 5 6 7 8 **910.4**

1. Curiosities and wonders 2. Voyages and travels 3. Voyages around the world

ISBN 1523503548; 9781523503544

This book, in the Atlas Obscura's series, by Dylan Thuras and Rosemary Mosco, illustrated by Joy Ang, "is a thrilling expedition to 100 of the most surprising, mysterious, and weird-but-true places on earth. . . . As you climb mountains, zip-line over forests, and dive into oceans, this book is your passport to a world of hidden wonders, illuminated by gorgeous art." (Publisher's note)

Mundy, Robyn

Epic voyages. Kingfisher 2011 64p il (Epic adventure) $19.99

Grades: 5 6 7 8 **910.4**

1. Explorers

ISBN 978-0-7534-6574-5; 0-7534-6574-4

"The graphics will grab readers in [this] exciting, extra-large-size [title] . . . packed with high-quality color photos on every double-page spread. Just as gripping are the narratives, captions, and technical details of exploration, adventure, and survival. . . . [This] book covers Magellan, Cook, Shackleton, Heyedahl and also Chichester, who, in 1966, sailed alone around the world." Booklist

Nardo, Don

Polar explorations; by Don Nardo. Lucent Books 2011 104 p. ill., col. maps, photographs (library) $34.95

Grades: 6 7 8 9 **910.4**

1. Polar regions -- Exploration 2. Exploration 3. Explorers -- Polar regions -- Biography 4. Polar regions -- Discovery and exploration

ISBN 142050360X; 9781420503609

LC 2010039667

This book by Don Nardo is part of the World History series and looks at polar explorations. The series "examines the eras, events, civilizations, and movements that have shaped human history, providing readers with insight into the past and its many legacies. Vivid writing, full-color photographs and extensive use of fully cited primary and secondary source quotations provide a sense of immediacy." (Publisher's note)

Includes bibliographical references and (p. 95-97) index.

Philbrick, Nathaniel

★ **Revenge** of the whale; the true story of the whaleship Essex. Putnam 2002 164p il maps $16.99; pa $7.99

Grades: 7 8 9 10 **910.4**

1. Whaling 2. Shipwrecks 3. Essex (Whaleship)

ISBN 0-399-23795-X; 0-14-240068-8 pa

LC 2002-667

Boston Globe-Horn Book Award Honor: Nonfiction (2003)

Recounts the 1820 sinking of the whaleship "Essex" by an enraged sperm whale and how the crew of young men survived against impossible odds. Based on the author's adult book "In the heart of the sea"

"The story of the Essex crew is a compelling saga of desperation and survival that will appeal to young people. The grisly details of cannibalism necessary to the telling of the story may provoke shivers but should not give anyone nightmares." SLJ

Includes bibliographical references

Rose, Jamaica

The **book** of pirates; a guide to plundering, pillaging, and other pursuits. [by] Jamaica Rose & Michael MacLeod. Gibbs Smith 2010 224p il map $12.99

Grades: 6 7 8 9 10 **910.4**

1. Pirates

ISBN 978-1-4236-0670-3; 1-4236-0670-1

LC 2010009086

"This delightful book, written partly in pirate dialect, is full of creative activities, interspersed with plenty of fascinating historical facts. . . . The introduction defines piracy. The opening chapter is a true-or-false account of some of the many well-known myths about pirates. . . . The authors discuss the origins and history of these rogues, the lives of famous pirates (including females), rules and codes and behavior, and present-day piracy. Those planning to attend an event as a pirate can follow the instructions for proper attire, along with diagrams and directions for makeup and the construction of a foam cutlass. . . . Jokes, games, songs, and a recipe for making cannonballs (from peanut butter) add to the fun." SLJ

Includes glossary

Ross, Stewart

★ **Into** the unknown; how great explorers found their way by land, sea, and air. illustrated by Stephen Biesty. Candlewick Press 2011 un il map $19.99

Grades: 4 5 6 7 **910.4**

1. Explorers 2. Discoveries in geography

ISBN 978-0-7636-4948-7; 0-7636-4948-1

LC 2010038720

Boston Globe-Horn Book Honor: Nonfiction (2011)

"Biesty's trademark amusing, informatively detailed illustrations are a highlight of this entertaining examination of several voyages of exploration. . . . Chapters cover an impressive range of exploration. In addition to the usual suspects, they include a 340 B.C.E. Greek voyage to the Arctic Circle; Chinese Admiral Zheng He to India; [and] David Livingston and Mary Kingsley into the African interior. . . . Each chapter includes a fold-out section of illustrations with a map of the journey and a cross-section of the method of transportation. . . . An altogether agreeable package for armchair explorers." Kirkus

Sandler, Martin W.

The **Whydah**; a pirate ship feared, wrecked, and found. Martin W. Sandler. Candlewick Press 2017 170 p. illustrations, maps (hardcover) $19.99

Grades: 6 7 8 9 **910.4**

1. Pirates 2. Shipwrecks 3. Slave trade -- History 4. Whidah (Ship)

ISBN 9780763680336; 9780763693732

LC 2017931938

YALSA Honor Book for Excellence in Nonfiction for Young Adults (2018)

This book, by Martin W. Sandler, presents the "story of the captaincy, wreck, and discovery of the Whydah--the only pirate ship ever found--and the incredible mysteries it revealed. . . . The Whydah was . . . built to ply the Triangular Trade route, which it did until one of the greediest pirates of all, Black Sam Bellamy, commandeered it. Filling the ship to capacity with treasure, Bellamy hoped to retire with his bounty--but in 1717 the ship sank in a storm off Cape Cod." (Publisher's note)

"The author weaves a fascinating story about piracy and the legendary 18th-century pirate ship Whydah, which sunk off the coast of Cape Cod on April 24, 1717, during a perfect storm." SLJ

Includes bibliographical references (pages 165-166) and index.

Sherman, Casey

The **finest** hours; the true story of a heroic sea rescue. Michael J. Tougias and Casey Sherman. Christy Ottaviano Books 2014 176 p. illustrations (hardback) $17.99

Grades: 4 5 6 7 8 **910.4**

1. Shipwrecks 2. Survival after airplane accidents, shipwrecks, etc. 3. CG36500 (Lifeboat) 4. Pendleton (Tanker) 5. Shipwrecks -- Massachusetts 6. Shipwreck survival -- History

ISBN 0805097643; 9780805097641; 9781250044235

LC 2013030661

This book by Michael J. Tougias and Casey Sherman "tells the story of a harrowing Coast Guard rescue when four men in a tiny lifeboat overcame insurmountable odds and saved more than 30 stranded sailors." In this book, the events of the February 18, 1952 wreck of two oil tankers near Cape Cod are adapted for middle-grade readers. (Publisher's note)

"The accounts of each rescue's logistics—-for example, sailors trying to time their leaps from their destroyed tanker to the rescue boat amid rocking waves—-are nail-biting, and they are relayed by the authors with an effectively sober, just-the-facts terseness." Booklist

Includes bibliographical references

Vail, Martha

Exploring the Pacific; [by] Martha Vail; John S. Bowman and Maurice Isserman, general editors. rev ed.; Chelsea House 2010 120p il map (Discovery and exploration) $35

Grades: 7 8 9 10 **910.4**

1. Explorers 2. Pacific Ocean

ISBN 978-1-60413-197-0; 1-60413-197-7

LC 2009-22106

First published 2005 by Facts on File

"The chapters are well-illustrated with color and black and white historic photos, illustrations, and maps. Chapter layout is clearly organized with helpful subtitles; sidebars develop related themes in catching colors." Libr Media Connect

Includes glossary and bibliographical references

Wallace, Rich

Bound by ice; a true North Pole survival story. Sandra Neil Wallace and Rich Wallace. Calkins Creek 2017 191 p. illustrations, maps (hardcover) $17.95

Grades: 6 7 8 9 10 **910.4**

1. North Pole -- Exploration 2. Polar regions -- Exploration 3. Jeannette (Ship) 4. Discoveries in geography 5. North Pole -- Discovery and exploration -- American 6. Arctic regions -- Discovery and exploration -- American

ISBN 9781629799155; 9781629794280

LC 2017937776

This book, by Sandra Neil Wallace and Rich Wallace, "follows the journey of George Washington De Long and the crew of the USS Jeannette, who departed San Francisco in the summer of 1879 hoping to find a route to the North Pole. . . [I]n mid-September the ship became locked in ice north of Siberia and drifted for nearly two years before it was crushed by ice and sank. De Long and his men escaped the ship and began a . . . journey in extreme polar conditions." (Publisher's note)

"Abundant archival illustrations, bibliography, and source notes bolster this gripping, accessible account." Pub Wkly

Includes bibliographical references and index.

Weatherly, Myra

Women of the sea; ten pirate stories. Morgan Reynolds 2006 160p il map lib bdg $26.95

Grades: 7 8 9 10 **910.4**

1. Women pirates

ISBN 1-931798-80-X

A revised edition of Women pirates: eight stories of adventure (1998)

This is a collective biography of such women pirates as Lady Killigrew, Lai Choi San, and Maria Cobham

Includes glossary and bibliographical references

White, Pamela

Exploration in the world of the Middle Ages, 500-1500; Pamela White, John S. Bowman, and Maurice Isserman, general editors. Rev. ed.; Chelsea House 2010 132p il map (Discovery and exploration) $35

Grades: 7 8 9 10 **910.4**

1. Explorers 2. Exploration 3. Middle Ages

ISBN 978-1-60413-193-2; 1-60413-193-4

LC 2009-30202

First published 2005 by Facts On File

This describes world exploration in the Middle Ages by pilgrims and missionaries, the Vikings, Muslim travelers, Europeans seeking Asia, Marco Polo, and Portuguese sailors, and describes Medieval legends of mythical monsters and lands

Includes glossary and bibliographical references

910.92 Geographers, travelers, explorers regardless of country of origin

Fritz, Jean

Around the world in a hundred years; from Henry the Navigator to Magellan. illustrated by Anthony Bacon Venti. Putnam 1994 128p il map hardcover o.p. pa $8.99

Grades: 4 5 6 7 **910.92**

1. Princes 2. Explorers 3. Colonial administrators

ISBN 0-399-22527-7; 0-698-11638-0 pa

LC 92-27042

"Fritz examines the voyages of ten explorers, acknowledging that their contributions, though deserving of recognition, were dearly bought. Opening and closing chapters summarize the fourteenth-century world view and indicate later expansion of geographic understanding. As always, Fritz tempers scholarship with humor in this brief volume—illustrated with drawings in pencil—which reads like an adventure story." Horn Book Guide

Includes bibliographical references

911 Historical geography

Leacock, Elspeth

Places in time; a new atlas of American history. [by] Elspeth Leacock and Susan Buckley; illustrations by Randy Jones. Houghton Mifflin 2001 48p il $15; pa $6.95

Grades: 4 5 6 7 **911**

1. Reference books 2. United States -- Historical geography

ISBN 0-395-97958-7; 0-618-3113-0 pa

LC 00-59741

This book presents "20 sites in American history at the moment of their historical significance, beginning in 1200 (Cahokia) and ending in 1953. Places and times include New Plymouth—1627, Charlestown—1739, Saratoga—1777, Philadelphia—1787, Abilene—1871, and Chicago—1893. The detailed cutaway views of homes, forts, and mills are impressive enough to keep readers looking again and again. These fascinating slices of life stir the imagination and lead to questions and further research." SLJ

Includes bibliographical references

Todras, Ellen H.

Explorers, trappers, and pioneers; by Ellen H. Todras. Kingfisher 2012 32 p. ill. (All About America) (paperback) $9.99

Grades: 4 5 6 **911**

1. America -- Exploration 2. Frontier and pioneer life -- United States

ISBN 0753465159; 9780753465158

This book by Ellen H. Todras is part of the "All About America" series. It "begins with the Vikings landing in Newfoundland 1,000 years ago and concludes with the Oklahoma Land Rush in 1889." It "offers 13 highly illustrated double-page spreads that present topics using a few paragraphs of information, related text boxes, and several color illustrations and five or more captioned illustrations." (Booklist)

912 Graphic representations of surface of earth and of extraterrestrial worlds

Hollingum, Ben

Maps and mapping the world; [Ben Hollingum, editor] Gareth Stevens Pub. 2010 48p il map (Understanding maps of our world) lib bdg $31; pa $14.95

Grades: 6 7 8 9 **912**

1. Maps

ISBN 978-1-4339-3498-8 lib bdg; 1-4339-3498-1 lib bdg; 978-1-4339-3501-5 pa; 1-4339-3501-5 pa

LC 2009-37275

"These fascinating books open with an identical whirlwind time line of cartographic history, beginning with a map of the world as 15th-century Europeans knew it and ending with the first photos of Earth taken from space...Related events and topics also spring up... The books' further-reading lists, which include print and Web materials, are particularly extensive. Wonderful resources." SLJ

Includes glossary and bibliographical references

Travel maps; [Ben Hollingum, editor] Gareth Stevens Pub. 2010 48p il map (Understanding maps of our world) lib bdg $31; pa $14.95

Grades: 6 7 8 9 **912**

1. Maps

ISBN 978-1-4339-3506-0 lib bdg; 1-4339-3506-6 lib bdg; 978-1-4339-3507-7 pa; 1-4339-3507-4 pa

LC 2009-37277

"These fascinating books open with an identical whirlwind time line of cartographic history...descriptions of cartographic challenges, old and new, result in a lot of valuable extras–. Wonderful resources." SLJ

Includes glossary and bibliographical references

★ **National** Geographic atlas of the world; 11th edition National Geographic Society 2019 153 p color maps $215

Grades: 4 5 6 7 8 9 10 11 12 Adult **912**

1. Atlases

ISBN 9781426213540; 9781426220586

"National Geographic's flagship Atlas of the World, now in its 11th edition, provides authoritative maps of every country, ocean, and region of the world, as well as thematic maps and accompanying graphics showing important population, environmental, and economic patterns. Organized by continent and reflecting today's political boundaries and identities, this authoritative atlas is an indispensable reference for schools and libraries, as well as the latest resource for home browsing and study." (Publisher's note)

National Geographic Kids student world atlas; your fact-filled reference for school and home. 5th edition National Geographic Society Children's Books 2019 143 p. color illustrations hardcover $19.99

Grades: 5 6 7 8 9 10 **912**

1. Atlases

ISBN 9781426334801 hardcover; 9781426317750; 9781426317774 ; 9781426317767

Previously titled Student Atlas of the World

"From the cartographic experts at National Geographic comes the latest edition of its award-winning student atlas, with everything kids want and need to know about our changing world. Dynamic, user-friendly content includes photos, facts, charts, graphics, and full-color political, physical, and thematic maps on important topics. Completely updated maps and statistics ensure that kids have all the latest information as they learn more about current events and become global citizens." (Publisher's note)

★ **National** Geographic United States atlas for young explorers; 3rd ed.; National Geographic 2008 175p il map $24.95

Grades: 4 5 6 7 **912**

1. Atlases 2. Reference books 3. United States -- Maps

ISBN 978-1-4263-0255-8; 1-4263-0255-X

First published 1999

This atlas offers maps of each of the states in the United States, divided into five geographical regions, plus U.S. territories. Each state map indicates physical features such as mountains and rivers, national forests, cities, major interstate roads, and industries, and is accompanied by color photos and facts about the state. An introductory section describes how to use the companion web site for more information, maps of the United States biomes, climates, natural hazards, political states, population, ethnic diversity, and energy use.

★ **Oxford** Atlas of the world. Oxford University Press 448 p. il map

Grades: 7 8 9 10 11 12 Adult **912**

1. Atlases 2. Earth -- Maps 3. Physical geography 4. Reference books

First published 1992. Updated annually. Variant title: Atlas of the world

"The only world atlas updated annually, guaranteeing that users will find the most current geographic information, Oxford's Atlas of the World is the most authoritative atlas on the market. Full of crisp, clear cartography of urban areas and virtually uninhabited landscapes around the globe, the Atlas is filled with maps of cities and regions at carefully selected scales that give a striking view of the Earth's surface." (Publisher's note)

Panchyk, Richard

Charting the world; geography and maps from cave paintings to GPS with 21 activities. by Richard Panchyk. Chicago Review Press 2011 xi, 132 p.p ill., maps (some col.) (paperback) $18.95

Grades: 7 8 9 10 **912**

1. Maps 2. Cartography -- Maps 3. Cartography 4. Map reading 5. Maps -- History

ISBN 1569763445; 9781569763445

LC 2011019317

Author "[Richard] Panchyk's book helps explain why maps are exciting, how they expand our world, and have done so for generations. . . . Maps document the lay of the land, the placement of cities, and the height of mountains, among many other things. Panchyk walks us through these mapmaking skills, offering activities along the way. . . .Panchyk also provides sidebars about such notable explorers as Amerigo Vespucci, for whom America was named." (Children's Literature)

Includes bibliographical references (p. 126-127) and index.

Rand McNally Goode's World Atlas; edited by Howard Veregin. 23rd ed. Rand McNally 2009 400 p. paperback $56.80

Grades: 7 8 9 10 11 12 Adult **912**

1. Maps 2. Atlases

ISBN 9780528877544; 9780133864649 paperback

"Goode's World Atlas by Rand McNally helps students navigate through global and regional landscapes with ease. With color-coded headings and charts, brief introductions to each section, and more than 60 new reference and thematic maps, the 23rd edition gives you a comprehensive view of the world and its changing population and physical characteristics." (Publisher's note)

Ross, Val

The **road** to there; mapmakers and their stories. Tundra Books 2003 146p il map $22.95; pa $15.95

Grades: 6 7 8 9 **912**

1. Maps

ISBN 0-88776-621-8; 0-88776-933-0 pa

"Ross presents an intriguing look at several mapmakers and the way that their work reflected not only physical boundaries, but also important aspects of their lives and the times in which they lived. . . . The tone of the text is chatty, sometimes humorous, and never dry. . . . Filled with details and insights and written with a storyteller's touch, this book will simultaneously inform and fascinate readers." SLJ

Student atlas; Dorling Kindersley, Inc. 8th edition DK Pub. 2015 176 p. ill. hardcover $14.99

Grades: 5 6 7 8 **912**

1. Atlases 2. Geography

ISBN 9781465438768 hardcover

This book from DK Publishing is part of the Student Atlas series. It is a "single-volume guide to the nations of the world. [It's] fully revised and updated, and packed with clear, detailed maps highlighting landscape, industry, land use, population, climate and environmental issues." (Publisher's note)

Taylor, Barbara

Looking at maps; [by] Barbara Taylor. Smart Apple Media 2008 46p il map (Geography skills) $22.95

Grades: 6 7 8 9 **912**

1. Maps

ISBN 1-59920-050-3; 978-1-59920-050-7

LC 2006100224

"The text is easy to follow. . . . The examples given in the text that involve places are almost always accompanied by excellent photographs. . . . Maps, block diagrams, tables, and graphs are clearly presented and easy to interpret." Sci Books Films

Includes glossary and bibliographical references

916 Geography of and travel in Africa

Bodden, Valerie

To the heart of Africa; by Valerie Bodden. Creative Education 2011 48 p. col. ill. (Great Expeditions) (library) $34.25

Grades: 5 6 7 8 **916**

1. Exploration 2. Africa -- Exploration 3. Explorers -- Scotland -- Biography 4. Explorers -- Africa, Southern -- Biography 5. Africa, Sub-Saharan -- Discovery and exploration 6. Missionaries, Medical -- Africa, Southern -- Biography

ISBN 1608180662; 9781608180660

LC 2010033414

This book by Valerie Bodden is part of the Great Expeditions series and looks at expeditions into Africa. "Bodden includes brief biographies of major people involved in each expedition, interspersed with the text. There are also numerous photographs or reproductions of paintings and woodcuts from the time of the expeditions." (Library Media Connection)

Includes bibliographical references (p. 46-47) and index.

917 Geography of and travel in North America

Butts, Edward

Shipwrecks, monsters, and mysteries of the Great Lakes; [by] Ed Butts. Tundra Books 2010 80p il pa $14.95

Grades: 4 5 6 7 **917**

1. Shipwrecks 2. Great Lakes

ISBN 978-1-77049-206-6 pa; 1-77049-206-2 pa

"In 1679, a French ship called the Griffon left Green Bay on Lake Michigan, bound for Niagara with a cargo of furs. Neither the Griffon nor the five-man crew was ever seen again. . . . Its disappearance was probably the result of the first shipwreck on a Great Lake. Since then, more than six thousand vessels, large and small, have met tragic ends. . . . Shoals and reefs, uncharted rocks, and sandbars could snare a ship or rip open a hull. Unpredictable winds could capsize a vessel at any moment. . . . The wreckage of ships and the bones of the people who sail them litter the bottoms of the five lakes: Ontario, Erie, Huron, Michigan, and Superior. Ed Butts has gathered stories and lake lore in this [volume]." (Publisher's note) "Ages nine to twelve." (Quill Quire)

Includes bibliographical references

Clark, William

Off the map; the journals of Lewis and Clark. edited by Peter and Connie Roop; illustrations by Tim Tanner. Walker & Co. 1993 40p il hardcover o.p. pa $8.95

Grades: 5 6 7 8 **917**

1. Lewis and Clark Expedition (1804-1806) 2. West (U.S.) -- Exploration

ISBN 0-8027-7546-2

LC 92-18340

A compilation of entries and excerpts from the journals of William Clark and Meriwether Lewis, describing their historic expedition

"The full-color illustrations, mainly in warm earth tones, give the pages an attractive look, but the most vivid pictures come from the journals themselves. . . . This vivid source material would be a welcome part of any classroom study of the subject." Booklist

Stille, Darlene R., 1942-

The **journals** of Lewis and Clark; by Darlene R. Stille. Heinemann Library 2012 48 p. ill. (some col.), col. map (Documenting U.S. History) (library) $32; (paperback) $8.99

Grades: 4 5 6 **917**

1. United States -- History -- Sources 2. Lewis and Clark Expedition (1804-1806) 3. Explorers -- West (U.S.) -- Diaries 4. West (U.S.) -- Description and travel 5. Journals of the Lewis and Clark Expedition

ISBN 1432967541; 9781432967543; 9781432967635

LC 2011037783

This book on the journals of Meriwether Lewis and William Clark by Darlene R. Stille is part of the "Documenting U.S. History" series. It answers such questions as "What writing materials did Lewis and Clark take on their expedition? What types of plants and animals did Lewis and Clark describe in their journals? [and] where can the journals be seen and read today?" (Publisher's note)

Includes bibliographical references and index

Sutton, Patricia

Capsized! the forgotten story of the SS Eastland disaster. Patricia Sutton. Chicago Review Press 2018 xx, 155 p.p (hardback) $17.99

Grades: 5 6 7 8 **917**

1. Shipwrecks 2. Marine accidents -- History 3. Eastland (Ship) 4. Shipwrecks -- Illinois -- Chicago River

ISBN 9781613739433

LC 2017051163

This book, by Patricia Sutton, "details the events leading up to the . . . [capsizing of SS Eastland on July 24, 1915] and provides a nail-biting, minute-by-minute account of the ship's capsizing. From the courage of the survivors to the despair of families who lost loved ones, . . . Sutton brings to light the stories of ordinary working people enduring the unthinkable." (Publisher's note)

"In a tautly written, vividly detailed, suspenseful narrative, Sutton chronicles the event that stands today as the greatest loss of life on the Great Lakes...Her fast-paced account makes ample use of primary sources, plaiting them into her narrative naturally as dialogue. A true disaster story rivetingly told" --Kirkus Reviews 2018 May #2

Includes bibliographical references and index

917.804 West (U.S.) – Travel

Bertozzi, Nick

★ **Lewis** & Clark. First Second 2011 144 p. ill., map (pbk.) $16.99

Grades: 5 6 7 8 **917.804**

1. Explorers 2. Graphic novels 3. Lewis and Clark Expedition (1804-1806) 4. Explorers -- Fiction 5. Territorial governors 6. United States -- History -- 1783-1865 -- Graphic novels

ISBN 1596434503; 9781596434509

LC 2010036255

This book presents, in graphic novel format, the adventures of explorers Lewis and Clark during their journey from St. Louis to the Pacific Ocean. Bibliography. "Grades six to ten." (Bull Cent Child Books)

Bertozzi "brings new life to the epic westward journey of explorers Lewis and Clark in this graphic novel perfect for history buffs. . . . Lewis's . . . deteriorating mental state throughout the expedition and particularly on the return trip is eloquently drawn, with Bertozzi managing to combine both history lesson and character study in strong, gripping drawings." SLJ

919 Geography of and travel in Australasia, Pacific Ocean islands, Atlantic Ocean islands, Arctic islands, Antarctica and on extraterrestrial worlds

Armstrong, Jennifer

★ **Shipwreck** at the bottom of the world; the extraordinary true story of Shackleton and the Endurance. Crown 1998 134p il maps pbk $12.95

Grades: 7 8 9 10 11 12 **919**

1. Explorers 2. Endurance (Ship) 3. Imperial Trans-Antarctic Expedition (1914-1917) 1914-1917:

ISBN 0-517-80014-4; 9780375810497

LC 97-52063

This book describes the events of the 1914 Shackleton Antarctic expedition when, after being trapped in a frozen sea for nine months, their ship, Endurance, was finally crushed, forcing Shackleton and his men to make a very long and perilous journey across ice and stormy seas to reach inhabited land. (Booklist)

A book that will capture the attention and imagination of any reader." SLJ

Includes bibliographical references and index

919.89 Antarctica – geography

Bertozzi, Nick

Shackleton; Antarctic odyssey. Nick Bertozzi. First edition First Second 2014 128 p. illustrations, maps $16.99

Grades: 5 6 7 8 9 10 **919.89**

1. Antarctica -- Exploration 2. Graphic novels 3. Explorers -- Great Britain -- Biography 4. Antarctica -- Discovery and exploration -- British

ISBN 1596434511; 9781596434516

This book by Nick Bertozzi describes how "Ernest Shackleton was one of the last great Antarctic explorers, and he led one of the most ambitious Antarctic expeditions ever undertaken. This is his story, and the story of the dozens of men who threw in their lot with him--many of whom nearly died in the unimaginably harsh conditions of the journey." (Publisher's note)

"Bertozzi eschews all narrative explanation, relying solely on dialogue among the crew and the detailed black-and-white panels to tell the story. The snow- and ice-bound journey is the perfect match for Bertozzi's minimal style--vast stretches of white become gasp-worthy, desolate vistas." Booklist

Bodden, Valerie

To the South Pole; by Valerie Bodden. Creative Education 2011 48 p. col. ill. (Great Expeditions) (library) $34.25

Grades: 5 6 7 8 **919.89**

1. South Pole -- Exploration 2. Amundsen, Roald, 1872-1928 3. Explorers -- Norway -- Biography 4. South Pole -- Discovery and

exploration
ISBN 1608180697; 9781608180691

LC 2010033552

This book by Valerie Bodden, part of the "Great Expeditions" series, presents "a history of Roald Amundsen's . . . 1911 trip to the South Pole, detailing the challenges encountered, the individuals involved, the discoveries made, and how the expedition left its mark upon the world." (Publisher's note) . Major historical milestones and details about the search for the southernmost tip of the world are related in" addition to "profiles of four of the major explorers". (Children's Literature)

Includes bibliographical references (p. 46-47) and index.

92 Biography

Abbott, Berenice, 1898-1991

★ Sullivan, George. **Berenice** Abbott, photographer; an independent vision. Clarion Books 2006 170p il $20

Grades: 7 8 9 10 **92**

1. Photographers 2. Women photographers
ISBN 978-0-618-44026-9; 0-618-44026-7

LC 2005-30736

A biography of Berenice Abbott, who was a pioneer in the field of professional photography and is particularly acclaimed for her photographs of the streets and buildings of New York City before they were replaced by skyscrapers during a building boom in the 1920s and early 1930s.

"Sullivan brings together an enormous amount of information about Abbott and presents it in a clear, thoughtful manner. . . . Large, clear reproductions of Abbott's photos appear throughout the book." Booklist

Includes bibliographical references

Abdul-Jabbar, Kareem, 1947-

★ Obstfeld, Raymond. **Becoming** Kareem; growing up on and off the court. Kareem Abdul-Jabbar and Raymond Obstfeld. Little, Brown & Co. 2017 xii, 289 p.p illustrations (hardback) $17.99

Grades: 7 8 9 10 11 12 **92**

1. Basketball players -- United States -- Biography 2. African Americans -- Biography 3. Social reformers -- United States
ISBN 9780316478137; 9780316555333; 9780316555388

LC 2017036942

In this memoir, by Kareem Abdul-Jabbar and Raymond Obstfeld, "at one time, Lew Alcindor was just another kid from New York City with all the usual problems: He struggled with fitting in, with pleasing a strict father, and with overcoming shyness that made him feel socially awkward. But with a talent for basketball, and an unmatched team of supporters, Lew Alcindor was able to transform and to become Kareem Abdul-Jabbar." (Publisher's note)

"One of the greatest basketball players of all time reminisces on the lessons that pushed him into a life of personal reinvention." Kirkus

Abu al-Qasim Khalaf ibn Abbas al-Zahrawi, d. 1013?

Ramen, Fred. **Albucasis** (Abu al-Qasim al-Zahrawi) renowned Muslim surgeon of the Tenth Century. [by] Fred Ramen. Rosen Pub. Group 2006 112p il map (Great Muslim philosophers and scientists of the Middle Ages) lib bdg $33.25

Grades: 5 6 7 8 **92**

1. Arabs 2. Surgeons 3. Physicians 4. Medieval civilization 5. Spain -- History 6. Writers on medicine
ISBN 1-4042-0510-1

LC 2005015786

"Acknowledging the skimpy historical record on his subject, Ramen fleshes out this profile of an influential Spanish physician with sweeping histories of ancient Mediterranean civilizations, early medicine, the rise of Islam, and the rise and fall of Muslim culture in Spain. Readers will come away impressed by the surgeon's contributions to medicine, which ranged from an encyclopedic surgical text to the invention of the forceps to the pioneering use of sutures. The information is buttressed by color photos of architectural remains and manuscript pages." Booklist

Includes glossary and bibliographical references

Acevedo, Sylvia

Acevedo, Sylvia. **Path** to the stars; my journey from Girl Scout to rocket scientist. Sylvia Acevedo. Clarion Books, Houghton Mifflin Harcourt 2018 320 p. (hardcover) $17.99

Grades: 4 5 6 7 8 **92**

1. Engineers -- United States 2. Girl Scouts of the United States of America 3. Hispanic American women -- Biography 4. Engineers -- United States -- Biography 5. Hispanic American scientists -- Biography 6. Women engineers -- United States -- Biography 7. Girl Scouts of the United States of America -- Officials and employees
ISBN 9781328809568

LC 2018005790

This book, by Sylvia Acevedo, is an "inspiring memoir for young readers about a Latina rocket scientist whose early life was transformed by joining the Girl Scouts and who currently serves as CEO of the Girl Scouts of the USA. . . . Young Sylvia's life transformed when she joined the Brownies. The Girl Scouts taught her how to take control of her world and nourished her love of numbers and science." (Publisher's note)

Adams, Ansel, 1902-1984

West, Krista. **Ansel** Adams. Chelsea House 2011 124p il map (Conservation heroes) lib bdg $35

Grades: 6 7 8 9 **92**

1. Photographers
ISBN 978-1-60413-946-4; 1-60413-946-3

LC 2010030591

This is a biography of the American photographer and environmentalist, best known for his black-and-white photographs of the American West,

"Captivating, richly informative. . . . The scope of [this book] is comprehensive. . . . [The book is] engaging as [it is] educational and will be ideal for research and reports." SLJ

Includes glossary and bibliographical references

Addams, Jane, 1860-1935

Caravantes, Peggy. **Waging** peace; the story of Jane Addams. [by] Peggy Caravantes. rev ed; Morgan Reynolds Publishing 2004 144p il lib bdg $23.95

Grades: 5 6 7 8 **92**

1. Authors 2. Philanthropists 3. Essayists 4. Pacifists 5. Social welfare leaders 6. Nobel laureates for peace
ISBN 1-93179-840-0

LC 2004-8357

This is a "biography of the social reformer, humanitarian, and winner of the 1931 Nobel Peace Prize. . . . Archival black-and-white photos . . . grace the book. This is a solid addition to women's history collections." SLJ

Includes bibliographical references

Fradin, Judith Bloom. **Jane** Addams; champion of democracy. by Judith Bloom Fradin and Dennis Brindell Fradin. Clarion Books 2006 216p il $21
Grades: 7 8 9 10 **92**

1. Authors 2. Philanthropists 3. Hull House (Chicago, Ill.) 4. Essayists 5. Pacifists 6. Social welfare leaders 7. Nobel laureates for peace 8. Chicago (Ill.) -- Social conditions
ISBN 0-618-50436-1

A biography of the social activist, pacifist, author, founder of Hull House in Chicago, and winner of the Nobel Peace Prize.

"A fascinating and rich life is related in strong, unfussy prose." Booklist

Includes bibliographical references

Aguirre, Hank, 1932-1994

Copley, Bob. The **tall** Mexican: the life of Hank Aguirre, all-star pitcher, businessman, humanitarian; with a foreword by Jose F. Niño. Piñata Bks. 1998 159p il hardcover o.p. pa $9.95
Grades: 7 8 9 10 **92**

1. Businesspeople 2. Baseball players 3. Automobile executives 4. Baseball -- Biography
ISBN 1-55885-294-8

LC 98-3185

A biography of the All-Star major-league pitcher whose commitment to his Hispanic heritage led him to found Mexican Industries to help provide economic opportunities to the inner-city Detroit community

"Myriad reminiscences from friends, family, employees, colleagues, and fellow athletes provide readers with the sense of true admiration felt for the subject." SLJ

Alcott, Louisa May, 1832-1888

Meigs, Cornelia Lynde. **Invincible** Louisa; the story of the author of Little Women. with a new introduction by the author. Little, Brown 1995 195p il hardcover o.p. pa $6.95; $9 **92**

1. Authors 2. Novelists 3. Women authors 4. Authors, American 5. Young adult authors
ISBN 0-316-56594-6 pa; 9780316565943
First published 1933
Awarded the Newbery Medal, 1934

This biography "is to be praised still for its straightforward account of a life of struggle and success. . . . If you want to know about Louisa's external life, and trace there the events which gave rise to the internal urges and passions that produced 'Little Women,' this book will serve well." N Y Times Book Rev

Silverthorne, Elizabeth. **Louisa** May Alcott; foreword by Kyle Zimmer. 2nd ed; Chelsea House 2011 117p il (Who wrote that?) lib bdg $35
Grades: 6 7 8 9 **92**

1. Authors 2. Novelists 3. Women authors 4. Authors, American 5. Young adult authors
ISBN 978-1-60413-760-6; 1-60413-760-6
First published 2002

"Silverthorne covers Alcott's life from her birth in 1832 to her death in 1888, with information about her writing life and major titles. The author creates a clear picture of the period and of a determined, diligent, and loyal woman who was shocked at the popularity of her most famous work." SLJ [review of 2002 edition]

Includes bibliographical references

Alexander, the Great, 356-323 B.C.

★ Adams, Simon. **Alexander**; the boy soldier who conquered the world. National Geographic 2005 64p il map (World history biographies) $17.95; lib bdg $27.90
Grades: 4 5 6 7 **92**

1. Ancient civilization 2. Kings
ISBN 0-7922-3660-2; 0-7922-3661-0 lib bdg

This describes the life and times of Alexander the Great.

This is a "handsomely designed [book]. . . . illustrated with maps and many color photographs of art and sculpture that give substance to [the era]. . . . Adams does not downplay Alexander's brutality or all-consuming ambition and includes examples of both." SLJ

Includes bibliographical references

Alhazen, 965-1039

Steffens, Bradley. **Ibn** al-Haytham; first scientist. Morgan Reynolds Pub. 2007 128p il (Profiles in science) lib bdg $27.95
Grades: 7 8 9 10 **92**

1. Physicists 2. Scientists 3. Mathematicians
ISBN 978-1-59935-024-0; 1-59935-024-6

LC 2006-23970

The author "has organized what is known of his subject's life and work into a coherent narrative. . . . Like the history of mathematics, the history of science is incomplete without an acknowledgment of early scholars in the Middle East. This clearly written introduction to al-Haytham, his society, and his contributions does that." Booklist

Includes bibliographical references

Ali, Muhammad, 1942-2016

Burgan, Michael. **Ali's** knockout punch; how a photograph stunned the boxing world. by Michael Burgan. Capstone Point Books, A Capstone imprint 2017 64 p. illustrations (some color) (Captured history. Sports) (library binding) $34.65
Grades: 6 7 8 9 **92**

1. Documentary photography 2. Documentary photography -- United States -- History
ISBN 9780756555276; 9780756555313

LC 2016038560

This book, by Michael Burgan, focuses on "one of the most famous sports images of all time. Former heavyweight boxing champion Sonny Liston is sprawled on his back in the boxing rim. Muhammad Ali stands over Liston, holding his right hand as if ready to throw another punch. The reigning world champion had just thrown a short, right-handed punch to the side of Liston's head." (Publisher's note)

Includes bibliographical references and index

Micklos, John. **Muhammad** Ali; I am the greatest. [by] John Micklos, Jr. Enslow Publishers 2010 160p il (American rebels) lib bdg $34.60
Grades: 6 7 8 9 10 **92**

1. African American athletes 2. Boxers (Persons) 3. Boxing -- Biography
ISBN 978-0-7660-3381-8; 0-7660-3381-3

LC 2009-17593

"This biography of the three-time heavyweight world champion, Vietnam War protester, and Nobel Peace Prize nominee includes useful context-setting background; Micklos's play-by-play descriptions of Ali's bouts provide just enough detail for boxing fans." Horn Book Guide

Includes bibliographical references

Myers, Walter Dean, 1937-2014. The **greatest** : Muhammad Ali. Scholastic 2001 172p il hardcover o.p. pa $4.99
Grades: 7 8 9 10 **92**

1. African American athletes 2. Boxers (Persons) 3. Boxing -- Biography

ISBN 0-590-54342-3; 0-590-54343-1 pa

This is a biography of the boxer. Bibliography. Index. "Middle school." (Horn Book)

In this biography Myers combines "reportage of Ali's major fights (especially against Sonny Liston, Joe Frazier, and George Foreman) with his own reflections about the sport's destructiveness and about Ali's unpopular views." Horn Book

★ Smith, Charles R., Jr., 1969- **Twelve** rounds to glory: the story of Muhammad Ali; illustrated by Bryan Collier. Candlewick Press 2007 80p il $19.99
Grades: 5 6 7 8 **92**

1. African American athletes 2. Boxers (Persons) 3. Boxing -- Biography

ISBN 978-0-7636-1692-2; 0-7636-1692-3

LC 2007-25998

"Rap-style cadences perfectly capture the drama that has always surrounded the boxer's life. . . . Collier's compelling watercolor collages with their brown overtones beautifully portray Ali's determination and strength." SLJ

Ali, Rubina

Ali, Rubina. **Slumgirl** dreaming; Rubina's journey to the stars. [by] Rubina Ali in collaboration with Anne Berthod and Divya Dugar. Delacorte Press 2009 187p il pa $9.99
Grades: 5 6 7 8 **92**

1. Actors 2. Children 3. India 4. Slumdog millionaire (Motion picture)

ISBN 978-0-385-73908-5 pa; 0-385-73908-7 pa

LC 2009029305

The young actress describes her life growing up in the slums of Mumbai, her experiences on the set of the film "Slumdog Millionaire," and how her life has changed as a result of her role in the film

"The writing here has a journalistic feel. It is not poetic or especially nuanced. But in a sea of cookie-cutter biography series, this book stands out. It has heart, and is aimed at an age group that will identify with Ali in essential ways." SLJ

Allende, Isabel

Axelrod-Contrada, Joan. **Isabel** Allende. Marshall Cavendish Benchmark 2010 159p il (Today's writers and their works) $42.79
Grades: 8 9 10 11 12 **92**

1. Authors 2. Novelists 3. Dramatists 4. Journalists 5. Women authors 6. Authors, Chilean 7. Children's authors

ISBN 978-0-7614-4116-8; 0-7614-4116-6

This biography of Isabel Allende places the author in the context of her times and discusses her work.

This book provides "excellent information for reports. . . . [The text is] organized well, lending [itself] to be read in [its] entirety or used as needed for research, and [includes] full-color photos and illustrations." SLJ

Includes bibliographical references

Alonso, Alicia

★ Bernier-Grand, Carmen T. **Alicia** Alonso; prima ballerina. illustrated by Raúl Colón. Marshall Cavendish Children's 2011 64p il $19.99
Grades: 4 5 6 7 **92**

1. Cubans 2. Ballet dancers 3. Choreographers 4. Dance directors

ISBN 978-0-7614-5562-2; 0-7614-5562-0

LC 2010018269

"An informative, beautifully illustrated introduction to the world-renowned dancer. Alonso's focused life and illustrious career are made even more remarkable by the fact that she lost her peripheral vision at age 19 and had to learn to visualize both the stage set and the dance itself in order to execute spins and lifts, and to choreograph ballets. Each one is presented as a titled one-page piece in abbreviated poetic prose; many face full-page textured paintings rendered in Colón's distinctive mix of watercolor, colored, and lithograph pencils." SLJ

Includes bibliographical references

Alvarez, Julia, 1950-

Aykroyd, Clarissa. **Julia** Alvarez; novelist and poet. by Clarissa Aykroyd. Lucent Books 2008 104p il (The twentieth century's most influential Hispanics) $32.45
Grades: 7 8 9 10 **92**

1. Poets 2. Authors 3. Novelists 4. Women authors 5. Hispanic American women 6. Essayists 7. Poets, American 8. College teachers 9. Children's authors

ISBN 978-1-4205-0022-6; 1-4205-0022-8

LC 2007025974

"This introduction to author Alvarez gives a comprehensive look at the Dominican American writer's life and literary career. The lively writing . . . is supported by numerous quotes from Alvarez and details . . . that will pique kids' interest." Booklist

Includes bibliographical references

Andersen, Hans Christian, 1805-1875

Varmer, Hjordis. **Hans** Christian Andersen; his fairy tale life. illustrated by Lilian Brogger; translated by Tiina Nunnally. Groundwood Books 2005 111p il $19.95
Grades: 5 6 7 8 **92**

1. Authors 2. Novelists 3. Dramatists 4. Authors, Danish 5. Children's authors 6. Short story writers

ISBN 0-88899-690-X

"Most of this book describes Andersen's childhood and belated schooling, showing his poverty and the grief he experienced over the death of his beloved father, as well as several horrifying events such as being forced by a teacher to witness the beheading of three young people. . . . The biography is divided into 11 chapters, set up as if they were stories. . . . The writing flows smoothly, with many details provided to help students picture the places and events. Brøgger's haunting, mixed-media illustrations add to the somber and at times surreal feeling of the text." SLJ

Anderson, Laurie Halse

★ Anderson, Laurie Halse, 1961- **Shout**; Laurie Halse Anderson. Penguin Group USA 2019 304 p. $17.99
Grades: 7 8 9 10 11 12 **92**

1. Rape 2. Free verse 3. Sexual harassment 4. Poetry -- Collections

ISBN 0670012106; 9780670012107

LC 2019002852

Author Laurie Halse Anderson "has written a poetry memoir that is as vulnerable as it is rallying, as timely as it is timeless. In free verse, Anderson shares reflections, rants, and calls to action woven between deeply personal stories from her life. . . . This important memoir is a denouncement of our society's failures and a love letter to all the people with the courage to say #MeToo and #TimesUp, whether aloud, online, or only in their own hearts." (Publisher's note)

"But more than that, it is a captivating, powerful read about clawing your way out of trauma, reclaiming your body, and undoing lifetimes of lessons in order to use your voice as the weapon it is. Fervent and deafening." Booklist

Glenn, Wendy J. **Laurie** Halse Anderson; speaking in tongues. Scarecrow Press 2010 169p (Scarecrow studies in young adult literature) $40

Grades: 8 9 10 11 12 **92**

1. Authors 2. Novelists 3. Women authors 4. Authors, American 5. Young adult authors

ISBN 978-0-8108-7281-3

LC 2009-30545

"This book is a comprehensive look at the life, work, and thoughts of Laurie Halse Anderson. . . . Any teen with a research paper on Laurie Halse Anderson who is lucky enough to have access to this title will walk away with a high mark." Voice Youth Advocates

Includes bibliographical references

Anderson, Marian, 1897-1993

★ Freedman, Russell. The **voice** that challenged a nation; Marian Anderson and the struggle for equal rights. Clarion Books 2004 114p il $18

Grades: 5 6 7 8 **92**

1. African American singers 2. Opera singers 3. African Americans -- Civil rights 4. African American women -- Biography

ISBN 0-618-15976-2

LC 2003-19558

A Newbery Medal honor book, 2005

In the mid-1930s, Marian Anderson was a famed vocalist who had been applauded by European royalty and welcomed at the White House. But, because of her race, she was denied the right to sing at Constitution Hall in Washington, D.C. This is the story of her resulting involvement in the civil rights movement of the time.

"In his signature prose, plain yet eloquent, Freedman tells Anderson's triumphant story, with numerous black-and-white photos and prints that convey her personal struggle, professional artistry, and landmark civil rights role." Booklist

Includes bibliographical references

Andrews, Roy Chapman, 1884-1960

★ Bausum, Ann. **Dragon** bones and dinosaur eggs: a photobiography of Roy Chapman Andrews. National Geographic Soc. 2000 64p il map $17.95

Grades: 5 6 7 8 **92**

1. Fossils 2. Dinosaurs 3. Explorers 4. Zoologists 5. Naturalists 6. Travel writers 7. Writers on nature 8. Writers on science 9. Museum administrators

ISBN 0-7922-7123-8

LC 99-38363

A biography of the great explorer-adventurer, who discovered huge finds of dinosaur bones in Mongolia, pioneered modern paleontology field research, and became the director of the American Museum of Natural History

"Bausum's account reads smoothly, and a layout dense with captioned sepia photographs and quotes from Andrews provides plenty of oases for readers as they follow him through the desert." Bull Cent Child Books

Includes bibliographical references

Anthony, Susan B. (Susan Brownell), 1820-1906

Colman, Penny. **Elizabeth** Cady Stanton and Susan B. Anthony; a friendship that changed the world. Henry Holt and Company 2011 256p il $18.99

Grades: 7 8 9 10 **92**

1. Feminism 2. Suffragists 3. Women -- Suffrage 4. Biography, Individual

ISBN 978-0-8050-8293-7; 0-8050-8293-X

LC 2010-39762

"Elizabeth Cady Stanton, a married mother of four boys at the time they met, and Susan B. Anthony, an unmarried schoolteacher, formed a friendship that lasted until Elizabeth's death more than 50 years later. Their tireless work, including advocacy, speeches, organizing and writing, placed them at the center of tumultuous events in the middle of the 19th century. . . . This [is a] lively, very readable narrative. . . . This thoughtful portrayal to two complex women is . . . enhanced by comprehensive backmatter, making this an invaluable addition to the literature of suffrage." Kirkus

Includes bibliographical references

Kanefield, Teri, 1960- **Susan** B. Anthony; Teri Kanefield. Abrams Books for Young Readers 2019 240 p. (hardcover with jacket) $16.99

Grades: 6 7 8 9 **92**

1. Feminists 2. Women's rights -- United States 3. Suffragists -- United States -- Biography 4. Feminists -- United States -- Biography

ISBN 9781419734014

LC 2018034261

"In the fourth installment in the Making of America series, Susan B. Anthony, Teri Kanefield examines the life of America's famous suffragette. . . . As Anthony saw the situation, 'Women's subsistence is in the hands of men, and most arbitrarily and unjustly does he exercise his consequent power.' She began her public career as a radical abolitionist, and after the Civil War, she became an international figurehead of the women's suffrage movement." (Publisher's note)

"Susan B. Anthony was among the earliest proponents of women's rights and devoted most of her life to the cause. In an in-depth biography of this important historical figure, Kanefield relies heavily on primary-source materials, especially Anthony's own revealing words." (Kirkus Reviews)

Includes bibliographical references and index

Appleseed, Johnny, 1774-1845

Worth, Richard. **Johnny** Appleseed; select good seeds and plant them in good ground. Enslow Publishers 2010 128p il map (Americans: the spirit of a nation) $23.95

Grades: 4 5 6 7 **92**

1. Apples 2. Frontier and pioneer life 3. Pioneers 4. Fruit growers

ISBN 978-0-7660-3352-8; 0-7660-3352-X

LC 2008048701

"This nicely illustrated and sourced [biography] . . . includes full-page sidebars." Booklist

Includes glossary and bibliographical references

Archimedes, ca. 287-212 B.C.

Hightower, Paul. The **greatest** mathematician; Archimedes and his eureka! moment. Enslow Publishers 2010 128p il (Great minds of ancient science and math) lib bdg $31.93

Grades: 5 6 7 8 **92**

1. Mathematicians 2. Greece -- History 3. Writers on science
ISBN 978-0-7660-3408-2 lib bdg; 0-7660-3408-9 lib bdg
LC 2008051818

This biography is a "solid [choice], as . . . [it provides] a good overview of the cultural and political landscape of the times, as well as pictures." SLJ

Includes glossary and bibliographical references

Aristotle, 384-322 B.C.

Gow, Mary. The **great** thinker: Aristotle and the foundations of science. Enslow Publishers 2010 128p il (Great minds of ancient science and math) lib bdg $31.93

Grades: 6 7 8 9 **92**

1. Philosophy 2. Scientists 3. Philosophers 4. Writers on science
ISBN 978-0-7660-3121-0; 0-7660-3121-7
LC 2009023813

"Presents a biography of the fourth-century B.C.E. Greek philosopher and scientist Aristotle, whose writings on logic, metaphysics, ethics, politics, and literary criticism influenced Western thought for hundreds of years. . . . [This] colorful, attractive book includes simple, straightforward text with nice illustrations and appendixes of suggested activities, a supplemental chronology, chapter notes, and glossary." Voice Youth Advocates

Includes glossary and bibliographical references

Katz Cooper, Sharon. **Aristotle**; philosopher, teacher, and scientist. Compass Point Books 2006 112p il (Signature lives) $31.93

Grades: 6 7 8 9 **92**

1. Philosophers 2. Writers on science
ISBN 978-0-7565-1873-8; 0-7565-1873-3
LC 2006005403

Includes glossary and bibliographical references

Armstrong, Louis, 1901-1971

★ Orr, Tamra. **Louis** Armstrong; by Tamra Orr. Mitchell Lane Publishers 2012 47 p. ill. (chiefly col.) (library) $29.95

Grades: 6 7 8 9 **92**

1. Jazz musicians -- United States -- Biography
ISBN 1612282644; 9781612282640
LC 2012008631

This book by Tamra Orr is part of the American Jazz series and looks at musician Louis Armstrong. Within each entry, "information about the subjects' childhoods and preparation for their musical careers is included, as are the positive and negative aspects of their adult lives. Their contributions to the world of jazz are . . . explored." (School Library Journal)

Includes bibliographical references (pages 44-45) and index.

Partridge, Kenneth. **Louis** Armstrong; musician. Chelsea House 2011 110p il (Black Americans of achievement) lib bdg $35

Grades: 6 7 8 9 **92**

1. Singers 2. Jazz musicians 3. African American musicians 4. Band leaders 5. Trumpet players
ISBN 978-1-60413-833-7; 1-60413-833-5

This "is a sweet, touching biography that looks at the extraordinary life of a musical genius. The writing is clear and engaging, with a light, humorous touch. . . . Readers are treated to an overview of a unique personality." SLJ

Includes bibliographical references

Arnold, Benedict, 1741-1801

Fritz, Jean. **Traitor** : the case of Benedict Arnold. Putnam 1981 191p il hardcover o.p. pa $5.99

Grades: 5 6 7 8 **92**

1. Spies 2. Generals 3. Army officers 4. United States -- History -- 1775-1783, Revolution
ISBN 0-399-20834-8; 0-698-11553-8 pa
LC 81-10584

"The writing is smooth, the material carefully organized and used in the best of biographical style—that is, Arnold is presented accurately and the reader is left to judge the strength and weaknesses of his character rather than being told by the author." Bull Cent Child Books

Includes bibliographical references

★ Murphy, Jim. The **real** Benedict Arnold. Clarion Books 2007 264p il map $20

Grades: 7 8 9 10 **92**

1. Spies 2. Generals 3. Army officers 4. United States -- History -- 1775-1783, Revolution
ISBN 978-0-395-77609-4; 0-395-77609-0
LC 2007-5700

"Using Arnold's surviving military journals and political documents, Murphy carefully contrasts popular myth with historical fact. . . . As far as possible, he meticulously traces Arnold's life, revealing a complex man who was actually as much admired as he was loathed." Booklist

Includes bibliographical references

★ Sheinkin, Steve. The **notorious** Benedict Arnold; a true story of adventure, heroism, & treachery. Steve Sheinkin. Roaring Brook Press 2010 337p. ill. $19.99

Grades: 7 8 9 10 **92**

1. Spies 2. Generals 3. American Loyalists 4. Army officers 5. United States -- Continental Army 6. Biography, Individual 7. United States -- History -- 1775-1783, Revolution
ISBN 1-59643-486-4; 978-1-59643-486-8
LC 201034797

Boston Globe-Horn Book Awards: Nonfiction (2012)
YALSA Award for Excellence in Nonfiction for Young Adults (2012)

This is a biography of the Continental Army officer who won battles for the Americans during the Revolutionary War but felt ill-used and unappreciated by the Continental Congress. He obtained command of the fort at West Point, New York, and plotted to surrender it to the British. After the plot was exposed in September 1780, he was commissioned into the British Army. Bibliography. Index. "Middle school, high school." (Horn Book)

"Sheinkin sees Arnold as America's 'original action hero' and succeeds in writing a brilliant, fast-paced biography that reads like an adventure novel. . . . The author's obvious mastery of his material, lively prose and abundant use of eyewitness accounts make this one of the most exciting biographies young readers will find." Kirkus

Includes bibliographical references

Asimov, Isaac, 1920-1992

Hoppa, Jocelyn. **Isaac** Asimov; science fiction trailblazer. [by] Jocelyn Hoppa. Enslow Publishers 2009 104p il (Authors teens love) lib bdg $31.93

Grades: 6 7 8 9 **92**

1. Authors 2. Novelists 3. Biochemists 4. Authors, American 5. Children's authors 6. Writers on science 7. Short story writers 8. Young adult authors 9. Science fiction writers

ISBN 978-0-7660-2961-3; 0-7660-2961-1

LC 2008-12299

"A biography of Russian-American science-fiction author Isaac Asimov." Publisher's note

Includes bibliographical references

Attila, King of the Huns, d. 453

★ Price, Sean Stewart. **Attila** the Hun; leader of the barbarian hordes. [by] Sean Stewart Price. Revised edition Franklin Watts 2015 128p il (A wicked history) paperback $9.95

Grades: 6 7 8 9 **92**

1. Huns 2. Kings and rulers 3. Tribal leaders

ISBN 978-0-531-20737-6; 9780531223291 paperback; 978-0-531-21801-3

LC 2015019345

First published 2009

"In fascinating detail, the book not only introduces Attila, but gives the backstory on what made the rise of the Huns possible. The exciting yet concise writing brings readers close to the battlefield, but the fighting and intrigue are neatly set against the sweep of history." Booklist

Includes bibliographical references

Audubon, John James, 1785-1851

Plain, Nancy. **This** strange wilderness; the life and art of John James Audubon. Nancy Plain. University of Nebraska Press 2015 136 p. illustrations (chiefly color) (pbk. : alk. paper) $19.95

Grades: 5 6 7 8 9 10 **92**

1. Bird watching 2. Naturalists -- Biography 3. Naturalists -- United States -- Biography 4. Ornithologists -- United States -- Biography

ISBN 0803248849; 9780803248847; 9780803284012; 9780803284029; 9780803284036

LC 2014020552

YALSA Award for Excellence in Nonfiction for Young Adults: Shortlist (2016)

This book, by Nancy Plain, focuses on the founder of modern ornithology John James Audubon. "His masterpiece, 'The Birds of America' depicts almost five hundred North American bird species, each image - lifelike and life size - rendered in vibrant color. . . . Plain brings together the amazing story of this American icon's career and the beautiful images that are his legacy." (Publisher's note)

"This narrative of the life of a dedicated and hard-working figure is the story of an amazing individual and a glimpse into the natural history of the early United States." SLJ

Includes bibliographical references and index

Sherman, Pat. **John** James Audubon. Chelsea House 2010 152p il map (Conservation heroes) lib bdg $35

Grades: 6 7 8 9 10 **92**

1. Artists 2. Painters 3. Naturalists 4. Ornithologists 5. Writers on science 6. Birds -- United States 7. Artists -- United States

ISBN 978-1-60413-953-2; 1-60413-953-6

LC 2010026480

A biography of the French American ornithologist and artist famous for his paintings and study of American birds.

"Captivating, richly informative. . . . The scope of [this book] is comprehensive. . . . [The book is] engaging as [it is] educational and will be ideal for research and reports." SLJ

Includes glossary and bibliographical references

Aung San Suu Kyi

O'Keefe, Sherry. **Champion** of freedom; Aung San Suu Kyi. Sherry O'Keefe. Morgan Reynolds Pub. 2011 160 p. ill. (some col.), col. maps $28.95

Grades: 7 8 9 10 11 12 **92**

1. Myanmar 2. Political activists 3. Democracy -- Burma 4. Burma -- Politics and government -- 1988- 5. Women Nobel Prize winners -- Burma -- Biography 6. Women political activists -- Burma -- Biography 7. Women political prisoners -- Burma -- Biography

ISBN 1599351684; 9781599351681; 9781599353142

LC 2011035740

Author Sherry O'Keefe tells the story of politician Aung San Suu Kyi. "Knowing that the military regime will not allow her to return if she leaves, the Nobel Peace Prize laureate has remained in Burma, enduring extreme isolation, the threat of death, and personal pain and sacrifice, including the chance to see her dying husband one last time. . . . [Suu Kyi] remains as determined as ever to see Burma emerge from its isolation and join the family of democratic nations in the world." (Publisher's note)

Includes bibliographical references and index.

Rose, Simon. **Aung** San Suu Kyi. 2011 24p il por (Remarkable people) $27.13; pa $12.95

Grades: 4 5 6 7 **92**

1. Political prisoners 2. Women political activists 3. Dissenters 4. Political leaders 5. Nonfiction writers 6. Human rights activists 7. Nobel laureates for peace 8. Myanmar -- Politics and government

ISBN 978-1-61690-833-1; 1-61690-833-5; 978-1-61690-834-8 pa; 1-61690-834-3 pa

LC 2011011584

This looks at Aung San Suu Kyi's "life, accomplishments, and challenges while including a page of quotes, an annotated list of contemporaries and influences, starter suggestions for writing a paper, and a time line and glossary. [The book] looks into the Nobel Peace Prize– winning Myanmar activist, whose struggle for democracy has landed her under house arrest multiple times." Booklist

Austen, Jane, 1775-1817

★ Reef, Catherine. **Jane** Austen; a life revealed. Clarion Books 2011 192p il $18.99

Grades: 6 7 8 9 10 **92**

1. Authors 2. Novelists 3. Women authors 4. Novelists, English 5. Biography, Individual

ISBN 0-547-37021-0; 978-0-547-37021-7

LC 2011008146

In this biography of the English novelist, Reef "combines firsthand accounts of Austen written by relatives and friends, historical information about Britain in the late 1700s, the basic facts of Austen's life, . . . and Austen's own novels and surviving letters. . . . A family tree, notes, a selected bibliography, a list of Austen's work, and an index are appended. . . . Middle school, high school." (Horn Book)

Reef "combines firsthand accounts of Austen written by relatives and friends, historical information about Britain in the late 1700s, the basic facts of Austen's life that are readily known, and Austen's own novels and surviving letters, presented in a chronological format. . . . Reef's account also focuses on Austen's large family and many friends, highlighting the connections between Austen's novels and her life. . . .

For devout Janeites it's fascinating to see all this information combined, and for others it's a worthwhile introduction to a masterful writer's life." Horn Book

Includes bibliographical references

Baker, Ella, 1903-1986

Bohannon, Lisa Frederiksen. **Freedom** cannot rest; Ella Baker and the civil rights movement. [by] Lisa Frederiksen Bohannon. 1st ed; Morgan Reynolds Pub. 2005 176p il map (Portraits of Black Americans) lib bdg $26.95

Grades: 7 8 9 10 **92**

1. Essayists 2. Political leaders 3. Civil rights activists 4. African Americans -- Civil rights

ISBN 978-1-931798-71-6; 1-931798-71-0

LC 2005007156

"Baker was a major player in the Civil Rights movement of the 1960s. She was the principal organizer of SNCC, the Student Nonviolent Coordinating Committee.... Bohannon ... makes good use of vintage photographs, artwork, and text boxes that further explain historical events. . . . Her biography might be a good place to start to get a good overview of Baker's life and the times in which she lived." SLJ

Includes bibliographical references

Barakat, Ibtisam

★ Barakat, Ibtisam. **Tasting** the sky; a Palestinian childhood. Farrar, Straus & Giroux 2007 176p $16

Grades: 6 7 8 9 10 **92**

1. Poets 2. Authors 3. Palestinian Arabs 4. Israel-Arab conflicts 5. Memoirists 6. College teachers 7. Young adult authors

ISBN 0-374-35733-1; 978-0-374-35733-7

LC 2006-41265

"In 1981 the author, then in high school, boarded a bus bound for Ramallah. The bus was detained by Israeli soldiers at a checkpoint on the West Bank, and she was taken to a detention center before being released. The episode triggers sometimes heart-wrenching memories of herself as a young child, at the start of the 1967 Six Days' War, as Israeli soldiers conducted raids, their planes bombed her home, and she fled with her family across the border to Jordan. . . . What makes the memoir so compelling is the immediacy of the child's viewpoint, which depicts both conflict and daily life without exploitation or sentimentality." Booklist

Barnum, P. T. (Phineas Taylor), 1810-1891

★ Fleming, Candace. The **great** and only Barnum; the tremendous, stupendous life of showman P.T. Barnum. illustrated by Ray Fenwick. Schwartz & Wade Books 2009 151p il $18.99; lib bdg $21.99

Grades: 5 6 7 8 **92**

1. Circus 2. Circus executives

ISBN 978-0-375-84197-2; 0-375-84197-0; 978-0-375-94597-7 lib bdg; 0-375-94597-0 lib bdg

LC 2008-45847

"In this sweeping yet cohesive biography, Fleming so finely tunes Barnum's legendary ballyhoo that you can practically hear the hucksterism and smell the sawdust.... The material is inherently juicy, but credit Fleming's vivacious prose, bountiful period illustrations, and copious source notes for fashioning a full picture on one of the forebearers of modern celebrity." Booklist

Includes bibliographical references

Barton, Clara, 1821-1912

Hamen, Susan E. **Clara** Barton; Civil War hero & American Red Cross founder. ABDO Pub. 2010 112p il map (Military heroes) lib bdg $22.95

Grades: 7 8 9 **92**

1. Nurses 2. American Red Cross 3. Red Cross officials 4. Social welfare leaders

ISBN 978-1-60453-960-8; 1-60453-960-7

LC 2009-32363

"The rush of literary adrenalin will hook readers immediately and keep them enthralled until the end.... Given the dynamic topic [and] .. . appealing layout . . . [this is] likely to attract reluctant readers. In addition, sources are plentiful and well documented." SLJ

Includes glossary and bibliographical references

Krensky, Stephen. **Clara** Barton. DK Pub. 2011 128p il (DK biography) $14.99; pa $5.99

Grades: 5 6 7 8 **92**

1. Nurses 2. American Red Cross 3. Red Cross officials 4. Social welfare leaders

ISBN 978-0-7566-7279-9; 0-7566-7279-1; 978-0-7566-7278-2 pa; 0-7566-7278-3 pa

Describes the life and accomplishments of Clara Barton, a teacher who organized efforts to bring nursing care to wounded soldiers during the Civil War and who went on to become the founder of the American Red Cross.

"Barton is placed in historical context, and key concepts, such as the causes of the Civil War, the struggle for women's suffrage, and the importance of the Geneva Convention, are explained. Compact in form, the text is complemented by full-color and archival photographs and reproductions on every spread.... An excellent resource for reports that will also appeal to fans of biography." SLJ

Includes bibliographical references

Beals, Melba

Beals, Melba Pattillo, 1941- **March** forward, girl; from young warrior to Little Rock Nine. by Melba Pattillo Beals ; illustrated by Frank Morrison. Houghton Mifflin Harcourt 2018 224 p. $16.99

Grades: 6 7 8 9 10 **92**

1. School integration 2. Southern States -- Race relations 3. African American civil rights workers -- Biography

ISBN 1328882128; 9781328882127

In this memoir, Melba Pattillo Beals, with Frank Morrison recounts her "growing up [years] while facing adversity in the Jim Crow South. . . . [It] paints a vivid picture of Beals' powerful early journey on the road to becoming a champion for equal rights, an acclaimed journalist, a best-selling author, and the recipient of this country's highest recognition, the Congressional Gold Medal." (Publisher's note)

Beecher family

★ Fritz, Jean. **Harriet** Beecher Stowe and the Beecher preachers. Putnam 1994 144p il $15.99; pa $5.99

Grades: 5 6 7 8 **92**

1. Authors 2. Novelists 3. Abolitionists 4. Women authors 5. Authors, American 6. Children's authors 7. Nonfiction writers 8. Short story writers

ISBN 0-399-22666-4; 0-698-11660-7 pa

LC 93-6408

This is a biography of the abolitionist author of "Uncle Tom's Cabin" with an emphasis on the influence of her preacher father and her family on her life and work.

"Written with vivacity and insight, this readable and engrossing biography is an important contribution to women's history as well as to the history of American letters." Horn Book

Includes bibliographical references

Beethoven, Ludwig van, 1770-1827

Bauer, Helen. **Beethoven** for kids; his life and music with 21 activities. Chicago Review Press 2011 129p il pa $16.95

Grades: 4 5 6 7 **92**

1. Composers 2. Composers, Austrian

ISBN 1-56976-711-4; 978-1-56976-711-5

LC 2011018131

"This introduction to the towering classical composer sets the story of his life and work in the context of the revolutionary events of early-19th-century Europe. . . . The author's own extensive musical experience contributes to the breadth of this title. Sidebars and historical prints add further information about musical forms and instruments, historical events and people mentioned. . . . This will be particularly useful for parents and classroom teachers hoping to make the study of great music more interesting." Kirkus

Includes bibliographical references

Martin, Russell. The **mysteries** of Beethoven's hair; [by Russell Martin and Lydia Nibley] Charlesbridge 2009 120p il lib bdg $15.95

Grades: 5 6 7 8 **92**

1. Composers

ISBN 978-1-57091-714-1 lib bdg; 1-57091-714-0 lib bdg

LC 2008-07257

"Based on Martin's adult book Beethoven's Hair: An Extraordinary Historical Odyssey and Scientific Mystery Solved (Broadway, 2000), this reworking for a young audience presents an intriguing interdisciplinary story. Martin and Nibley trace the labyrinthine journey of a lock of Beethoven's hair encased in a glass and wooden locket from the 18th century to the present. . . . This is a most unusual, thoroughly researched detective story written in a clearly accessible and lively tone. Black-and-white photos and reproductions appear throughout. . . . It is . . . an incredibly readable and absorbing selection that demonstrates the multidimensional nature of true scholarship." SLJ

Bell, Alexander Graham, 1847-1922

Carson, Mary Kay. **Alexander** Graham Bell; giving voice to the world. [by] Mary Kay Carson. Sterling 2007 124p il (Sterling biographies) lib bdg $12.95; pa $5.95

Grades: 6 7 8 9 **92**

1. Inventors 2. Teachers of the deaf 3. Telecommunications executives

ISBN 978-1-4027-4951-3 lib bdg; 1-4027-4951-1 lib bdg; 1-4027-3230-9 pa; 978-1-4027-3230-0 pa

LC 2007003502

"Carson introduces Bell's life, giving readers an excellent picture of why this man became so famous. . . . [The book provides] clear, concise information in an easy-to-follow format with captioned photographs and illustrations on most pages." SLJ

Includes glossary and bibliographical references

Carson, Mary Kay. **Alexander** Graham Bell for kids; his life and inventions, with 21 activities. Mary Kay Carson. Chicago Review Press 2018 144 p. illustrations $16.99

Grades: 4 5 6 7 8 **92**

1. Telephone -- History 2. Inventors -- United States -- Biography 3. Deaf -- Means of communication 4. Telephone -- United States -- History

ISBN 9780912777139

LC 2017027641

This book in the For Kids series, by Mary Kay Carson presents a biography of telephone inventor Alexander Graham Bell. "Bell invented not only the telephone, but also early versions of the phonograph, the metal detector, airplanes, and hydrofoil boats. This Scottish immigrant was also a pioneering speech teacher and a champion of educating those with hearing impairments, work he felt was his most important contribution to society." (Publisher's note)

"The inventor of the telephone gets extensive treatment in this book, which combines biography, history, and activities for children. . . . Many of the activities featured throughout the chapters, such as making an ear trumpet and feeling sound vibrations, use materials readers likely have at home, fairly easily giving them a taste of the devices used during Bell's time and illustrating properties of sound." Kirkus

Includes bibliographical references and index

Bell, Cool Papa, 1903-1991

McCormack, Shaun. **Cool** Papa Bell. Rosen Pub. Group 2002 112p il (Baseball Hall of Famers of the Negro leagues) lib bdg $29.25

Grades: 5 6 7 8 **92**

1. Baseball players 2. African American athletes 3. Baseball -- Biography

ISBN 0-8239-3474-8

LC 2001-3121

This is a biography of the African American who played in the Negro Leagues and was elected to the Baseball Hall of Fame in 1974

This "title presents an unvarnished picture of the racism in this country and how it impacted amateur and professional baseball from 1868 onward. . . . The layout . . . is attractive, the style . . . is engaging, and the b&w photographs enhance the narrative." Book Rep

Includes glossary and bibliographical references

Bernstein, Leonard, 1918-1990

★ Rubin, Susan Goldman. **Music** was IT: young Leonard Bernstein. Charlesbridge 2011 178p il lib bdg $19.95

Grades: 5 6 7 8 **92**

1. Composers 2. Conductors (Music) 3. Jews -- Biography 4. Biography, Individual

ISBN 1-58089-344-9 lib bdg; 978-1-58089-344-2 lib bdg; 978-1-60734-276-2 e-book

LC 2010-07584

This is a biography of composer and conductor Leonard Bernstein. Bibliography. Index. "Grades five to nine." (Bull Cent Child Books)

"An impeccably researched and told biography of Leonard Bernstein's musical apprenticeship, from toddlerhood to his conducting debut with the New York Philharmonic at age 25. . . . Drawn from interviews, family memoirs and other print resources, quotations are well-integrated and assiduously attributed. Photos, concert programs, early doodles and letters, excerpts from musical scores and other primary documentation enhance the text. Excellent bookmaking—from type to trim size—complements a remarkable celebration of a uniquely American musical genius." Kirkus

Bezos, Jeffrey, 1964-

Robinson, Tom. **Jeff** Bezos; Amazon.com architect. ABDO Pub. Co. 2010 112p il (Publishing pioneers) $22.95

Grades: 5 6 7 8 **92**

1. Businessmen 2. Internet marketing 3. Booksellers and bookselling 4. Amazon.com Inc. 5. Retail executives 6. Internet

executives
ISBN 978-1-60453-759-8; 1-60453-759-0
LC 2009015989

In this biography of Amazon.com executive Jeff Bezos "the research is solid and there are extensive source notes. . . . With marbled borders and an array of photographs, maps, diagrams, and document reproductions, [this book has] an engaging and pleasing design. " SLJ

Includes glossary and bibliographical references

Scally, Robert. **Jeff** Bezos; founder of Amazon and the Kindle. by Robert D. Scally. Morgan Reynolds Pub. 2011 112p il (Business leaders) $28.95
Grades: 7 8 9 10 11 12 **92**

1. Businessmen 2. Amazon.com Inc. 3. Retail executives 4. Internet executives
ISBN 978-1-59935-178-0; 1-59935-178-1; 978-1-59935-214-5 e-book
LC 2011015611

This biography of Jeff Bezos, founder of Amazon and Kindle, "will grab YAs. . . . The design is browsable, with clear type and lots of color screens and informal photos of young people at work." Booklist

Includes bibliographical references

Bhutto, Benazir

Naden, Corinne J. **Benazir** Bhutto. Marshall Cavendish Benchmark 2010 96p il (Leading women) $39.93
Grades: 5 6 7 8 **92**

1. Prime ministers 2. Women politicians 3. Political leaders 4. Pakistan -- Politics and government
ISBN 978-0-7614-4952-2; 0-7614-4952-3

In this biography "readers learn about Bhutto's student years at Radcliffe College and her rise to prime minister of Pakistan, the first woman to lead a Muslim state. . . . The [woman's life is] revealed within the political and historical context of [her] times and [includes] quotes from autobiographical material. . . . Color and black-and-white photos are included. . . . The compact size, chronological organization, and accessible writing [style makes this biography a] good [resource] for reports." SLJ

Includes bibliographical references

★ Price, Sean. **Benazir** Bhutto. Heinemann Library 2009 112p il map (Front-page lives) $38.93
Grades: 6 7 8 9 10 **92**

1. Prime ministers 2. Political leaders 3. Women -- Pakistan 4. Prime ministers -- Pakistan 5. Pakistan -- Politics and government
ISBN 978-1-43293-222-0; 1-43293-222-5
LC 2009018315

"This volume, on the assassinated leader of Pakistan, is particularly well done, thanks to Price's clear and compelling text. . . . The many color photographs are particularly crisp and colorful, and the sidebars briefly but effectively deal with important topics." Booklist

Includes bibliographical references

Bieber, Justin, 1994-

Bieber, Justin. **Justin** Bieber: first step 2 forever; my story. HarperCollins Children's Books 2010 236p il $21.99
Grades: 4 5 6 7 **92**

1. Singers 2. Pop musicians
ISBN 978-0-06-203974-3; 0-06-203974-1

"Bieber, the platinum-selling singer/songwriter . . . debuts with an account of his 16-year-old life that's cheeky yet entirely in line with his safe and wholesome image. . . . The book covers his upbringing in Ontario, his early introduction to music, YouTube stardom, his love of pranks, and the stratospheric success he now enjoys—all interspersed with lyrics, tweets, and numerous full-bleed photographs of Bieber." Publ Wkly

Binstock, Melissa

Binstock, Melissa. **Nourishment**; feeding my starving soul when my mind and body betrayed me. Health Communications 2011 276p pa $14.95
Grades: 7 8 9 10 **92**

1. Students 2. Mentally ill 3. Tourette syndrome 4. Learning disabilities 5. Attention deficit disorder 6. Obsessive-compulsive disorder 7. Memoirists 8. Anorexia nervosa -- Personal narratives
ISBN 978-0-7573-1542-8 pa; 0-7573-1542-9 pa; 978-0-7573-9193-4 ebook; 0-7573-9193-1 ebook
LC 2010039690

"This unforgettable memoir chronicles the torment and challenges that plague the author. She is diagnosed with various psychological and neurological disorders by the young age of eleven years. . . . Melissa becomes acquainted with a new-type of therapy through her equestrian accomplishments. Soon however, . . . Melissa's fragile system, sends Melissa into a serious bout of mental illness and anorexia nervosa. . . . Once inside this facility, Melissa generously allows readers to eavesdrop into the day-to-day world of those who suffer from this plight. . . . This is a great read for teenagers who suffer from mental illness, peer acceptance issues, and eating disorders." Voice Youth Advocates

Black Elk, 1863-1950

★ Nelson, S. D. **Black** Elk's vision; a Lakota story. Abrams Books for Young Readers 2010 47p il $19.95
Grades: 5 6 7 8 **92**

1. Shamans 2. Oglala Indians 3. Indian leaders 4. Native Americans -- Biography
ISBN 978-0-8109-8399-1; 0-8109-8399-0
LC 2009-9392

"This handsomely designed, large-format book tells the story of Black Elk (1863-1950), a Lakota man who saw many changes come to his people. . . . Often quoting from Black Elk Speaks (1932), Nelson makes vivid the painful ways life changed for the Lakotain in the 1800s. . . . Colorful, imaginative artwork, created using pencils and acrylic paints, is interspersed with nineteenth-century photos, underscoring that this dramatic account reflects the experiences of a man who witnessed history." Booklist

Blake, William, 1757-1827

Bedard, Michael. **William** Blake; the gates of paradise. Tundra Books 2006 192p il $28.99
Grades: 8 9 10 11 12 **92**

1. Poets 2. Artists 3. Authors 4. Engravers 5. Illustrators 6. Poets, English
ISBN 978-0-88776-763-0; 0-88776-763-X

"Bedard provides a satisfying biography of English artist, poet, and visionary William Blake. . . . Illustrated with drawings, paintings, engravings, and photos of sites and artifacts, the book is handsomely produced. . . . Bedard writes with precision, simplicity, and grace." Booklist

Includes bibliographical references

Bly, Nellie, 1864-1922

Bankston, John. **Nellie** Bly; journalist. John Bankston. Chelsea House 2011 155 p. ill. (hc) $35.00
Grades: 7 8 9 10 **92**

1. Women journalists 2. Journalists -- United States -- Biography

3. Women journalists -- United States -- Biography
ISBN 1604139080; 9781604139082

LC 2011000040

This book offers a biography journalist Elizabeth Cochrane, better known as Nellie Bly. An angry letter she wrote in response to a newspaper article about the role of women "earned her a job and a new name: Nellie Bly. As her alter ego, she gave a voice to women who worked in factories and were being treated in asylums. And she would travel around the world faster than anyone ever had. By the time she was 25, Nellie Bly was the most famous reporter in the world." (Google Books)

Includes bibliographical references (p. 144-147) and index

★ Macy, Sue. **Bylines** : a photobiography of Nellie Bly; foreword by Linda Ellerbee. National Geographic 2009 64p il map $19.95; lib bdg $28.90

Grades: 5 6 7 8 **92**

1. Authors 2. Journalists 3. Women journalists 4. Nonfiction writers
ISBN 978-1-4263-0513-9; 1-4263-0513-3; 978-1-4263-0514-6 lib bdg; 1-4263-0514-1 lib bdg

LC 2008-52329

This is a biography of the American reporter. Index. "Grades five to nine." (Bull Cent Child Books)

"This detailed biography of the trailblazing 19th-century journalist incorporates photographs of Bly and her subjects. The extensive text explores the details of a life spent seeking justice. . . . A thorough introduction to the life of a fascinating figure." Publ Wkly

Bohr, Niels

Spangenburg, Ray. **Niels** Bohr; atomic theorist. [by] Ray Spangenburg and Diane Kit Moser. Rev ed; Chelsea House 2008 141p bibl il (Makers of modern science) $35

Grades: 7 8 9 10 11 12 **92**

1. Scientists
ISBN 978-0-8160-6178-5; 0-8160-6178-5

LC 2008-1196

"Spangenburg and Moser delve into Bohr's background and present him as a loving, talkative, and inquisitive person who liked soccer. He was also concerned about the consequences of his work with nuclear weapons and was involved in many humanitarian efforts... New content includes informational sidebars and a discussion of string theory." SLJ

Includes bibliographical references

Bolt, Usain, 1986-

Cantor, George. **Usain** Bolt; by George Cantor. Lucent Books 2011 96 p. col. ill. (People in the News) (hardcover) $33.95

Grades: 6 7 8 9 **92**

1. Sprinters 2. Olympic athletes 3. Track and field athletes -- Jamaica -- Biography
ISBN 1420503413; 9781420503418

LC 2011006980

This book offers a biography of Olympic sprinter Usain Bolt, a Jamaican athlete who set several world records, by author George Cantor. It is part of the "People in the News" series, which "profiles the lives and careers of some of today's most prominent newsmakers. Whether covering contributions and achievements or notorious deeds, books in this series examine why these well-known individuals garnered public attention." (Publisher's note)

Includes bibliographical references and index

Bolívar, Simón, 1783-1830

Reis, Ronald A. **Simon** Bolivar. Chelsea House 2010 120p il (The great Hispanic heritage) $30

Grades: 6 7 8 9 **92**

1. Generals 2. Statesmen 3. Revolutionaries 4. South America -- History
ISBN 978-1-60413-731-6; 1-60413-731-2

LC 2010-9485

This "offers a balanced view of El Liberator, who shed his privileged youth in a wealthy Creole Venezuelan family and became a military strategist determined to create independent Latin American states. . . . A selection of well-chosen images, a chronology, chapter notes, and [a] suggested reading [list] round out [this] engaging [title] in a sure-to-be popular [book] for reports and personal interest." Booklist

Includes bibliographical references

Bonhoeffer, Dietrich, 1906-1945

★ Hendrix, John. The **faithful** spy; Dietrich Bonhoeffer and the plot to kill Hitler. John Hendrix. Amulet Books 2018 176 p. (hardback) $24.99

Grades: 6 7 8 9 10 11 12 **92**

1. World War, 1939-1945 -- Underground movements 2. Hitler, Adolf, 1889-1945 -- Assassination attempts 3. Theologians -- Germany -- Biography 4. Anti-Nazi movement -- Germany -- Biography 5. Church and state -- Germany -- History -- 20th century 6. Government, Resistance to -- Germany -- History -- 20th century
ISBN 9781419728389

LC 2017032171

YALSA Award for Excellence in Nonfiction for Young Adults: Finalist (2019

This book, by John Hendrix, tells the story of Dietrich Bonhoeffer, a pastor who free the German people from oppression during World War II. "Adolf Hitler's Nazi party is gaining strength and becoming more menacing every day. . . . Bonhoeffer . . . forms a breakaway church to speak out against the established political and religious authorities. . . . Bonhoeffer decides that Hitler must be stopped by any means possible!" (Publisher's note)

"Biographies of key figures from WWII are plentiful in kids books, but Hendrix's captivating account of the life of Dietrich Bonhoeffer is a standout." (Booklist)

Martin, Michael J. **Champion** of freedom; Dietrich Bonhoeffer. by Michael Martin. Morgan Reynolds Pub. 2012 144 p. ill. (some col.) (hbk.) $28.95

Grades: 7 8 9 10 11 12 **92**

1. Clergy 2. Theologians
ISBN 1599351692; 9781599351698

LC 2010049095

This book looks at "Dietrich Bonhoeffer [who in 1943] was arrested and imprisoned by the Gestapo for crimes [against] the government. . . . [This] German Lutheran Pastor was integrally involved in the plot to assassinate Adolf Hitler. During his two years of imprisonment, Bonhoeffer manages extreme circumstances, including interrogation and isolation, but is able to protect both himself and his co-conspirators through careful rhetorical practices. How does a pastor and a loyal German justify his involvement in the plot? . . . How could a pastor who penned a book titled Ethics, ethically justify his actions? This book considers some of those questions and is for theologians, ethicists, and rhetoricians as it examines the intersection of faith, politics, and classic rhetorical theory. (Amazon.com)

Includes bibliographical references (p. 140) and index.

McCormick, Patricia, 1956- The **plot** to kill Hitler; Dietrich Bonhoeffer: Pastor, Spy, Unlikely Hero. Patricia McCormick ; [edited by] Alessandra Balzer. Balzer + Bray 2016 192 p. illustrations (hardback) $18.99

Grades: 6 7 8 9 **92**

1. World War, 1939-1945 -- Underground movements

ISBN 9780062411082

LC 2016936295

This book, by Patricia McCormick, is a "narrative about Dietrich Bonhoeffer, a pastor and pacifist who became an unlikely hero during World War II and took part in a plot to kill Hitler. . . . It takes readers from his privileged early childhood to the studies and travel that would introduce him to peace activists around the world--eventually putting this gentle, scholarly pacifist on a deadly course to assassinate one of the most ruthless dictators in history." (Publisher's note)

Includes bibliographical references (pages 165-166) and index.

Boone, Daniel, 1734-1820

Sanford, William R. **Daniel** Boone; courageous frontiersman. by William R. Sanford and Carl R. Green. Enslow Publishers 2013 48 p. col. ill., map (library) $21.26; (paperback) $7.95

Grades: 5 6 7 8 **92**

1. Frontier and pioneer life -- United States 2. Kentucky -- Biography 3. Pioneers -- Kentucky -- Biography 4. Frontier and pioneer life -- Kentucky

ISBN 076604002X; 9780766040021; 9781464400858; 9781464509926; 9781464609923

LC 2011037736

This book by William Sanford is part of the Courageous Heroes of the American West series and focuses on Daniel Boone. "Through the untamed wilderness, Daniel Boone marched forward. He was leading a group of workers to carve out the Wilderness Road. Over hills, through dense forests, along stony paths, and fending off American Indian attacks, Boone never quit. He opened the way for thousands of settlers to move west, establishing the settlement of Boonesborough in 1775." (Publisher's note)

Includes bibliographical references (p. 47) and index.

Borges, Jorge Luis, 1899-1986

McNeese, Tim. **Jorge** Luis Borges; [by] Tim McNeese. Chelsea House 2008 119p il (The great Hispanic heritage) $30

Grades: 6 7 8 9 **92**

1. Poets 2. Authors 3. Novelists 4. Authors, Argentine 5. Essayists 6. Translators 7. Literary critics 8. Short story writers

ISBN 978-0-7910-9665-9; 0-7910-9665-3

LC 2007032008

This biography provides a "substantive [portrait], including background information and historical context, of . . . beloved writer Borges. . . . The well-documented [text] effectively [combines] anecdotes, quotations, and historical details. Many photographs and sidebars are also included." Horn Book Guide

Includes bibliographical references

Bornstein, Michael, 1940-

Bornstein, Michael. **Survivors** club; the true story of a very young prisoner of Auschwitz. Michael Bornstein, Debbie Bornstein Holinstat. Farrar, Straus Giroux Books for Young Readers 2017 352 p. (hardback) $16.99

Grades: 5 6 7 8 **92**

1. Jewish children in the Holocaust 2. Auschwitz (Poland: Concentration camp) 3. Holocaust, 1939-1945 -- Personal narratives 4. Auschwitz (Concentration camp) 5. Żarki (Poland) -- Biography 6. Jews -- Poland -- Żarki -- Biography 7. Jewish children in the Holocaust -- Poland -- Żarki -- Biography 8. Holocaust, Jewish (1939-1945) -- Poland -- Żarki -- Personal narratives

ISBN 9780374305710; 9781250118752

LC 2016028010

This book, by Michael Bornstein and Debbie Bornstein Holinstat, "tells the unforgettable story of how a father's courageous wit, a mother's fierce love, and one perfectly timed illness saved his life, and how others in his family from Zarki, Poland, dodged death at the hands of the Nazis time and again with incredible deftness. Working from his own recollections, . . . Michael relates his inspirational Holocaust survival story with the help of his daughter, Debbie." (Publisher's note)

Bourgeois, Louise, 1911-2010

★ Greenberg, Jan. **Runaway** girl: the artist Louise Bourgeois; [by] Jan Greenberg and Sandra Jordan. Abrams 2003 80p il $19.95

Grades: 7 8 9 10 **92**

1. Artists 2. Sculptors 3. Women artists 4. Artists -- United States

ISBN 0-8109-4237-2

LC 2002-11922

Introduces the life of renowned modern artist Louise Bourgeois, who is known primarily for her sculptures

"In clear, elegant prose, bolstered with numerous quotes from the artist, the authors seamlessly juxtapose stories of Bourgeois' life with relevant artworks. . . . Beautifully reproduced photographs, printed on well-designed pages, offer an excellent mix of the artist's personal life and her art." Booklist

Includes bibliographical references

Bradbury, Ray, 1920-

Bankston, John. **Ray** Bradbury; foreword by Kyle Zimmer. Chelsea House 2011 140p il (Who wrote that?) lib bdg $35.00

Grades: 6 7 8 9 10 **92**

1. Authors 2. Novelists 3. Screenwriters 4. Authors, American 5. Children's authors 6. Short story writers 7. Science fiction writers

ISBN 1-60413-778-9; 978-1-60413-778-1

This discusses the life and work of author Ray Bradbury.

Includes bibliographical references

Braille, Louis, 1809-1852

★ Freedman, Russell. **Out** of darkness: the story of Louis Braille; illustrated by Kate Kiesler. Clarion Bks. 1997 81p il $16.95; pa $7.95

Grades: 4 5 6 7 **92**

1. Blind 2. Inventors 3. Teachers of the blind 4. Blind -- Books and reading

ISBN 0-395-77516-7; 0-395-96888-7 pa

LC 95-52353

"Without melodrama, Freedman tells the momentous story in quiet chapters in his best plain style, making the facts immediate and personal. . . . A diagram explains how the Braille alphabet works, and Kate Kessler's full-page shaded pencil illustrations are part of the understated poignant drama." Booklist

Brave Bird, Mary

Brave Bird, Mary. **Lakota** woman; by Mary Crow Dog and Richard Erdoes. 1st HarperPerennial ed; HarperPerennial 1991 263p il rpt $14.95

Grades: 8 9 10 11 12 Adult **92**

1. Dakota Indians 2. Political activists 3. Memoirists 4. Indian leaders 5. American Indian Movement 6. Native Americans -- Biography

ISBN 0-06-097389-7; 9780802145420 rpt

LC 90-55980

First published 1990 by Grove Weidenfeld

"Born in 1955 and raised in poverty on the Rosebud Reservation, Mary Crow Dog escaped an oppressive Catholic boarding school but fell into a marginal life of urban shoplifting and barhopping. A 1971 encounter with AIM (the American Indian Movement), participation in the 1972 Trail of Broken Treaties march on Washington, and giving birth to her first child while under fire at the 1973 siege of Wounded Knee radicalized her." Libr J

Breckinridge, Mary, 1881-1965

★ Wells, Rosemary. **Mary** on horseback; three mountain stories. pictures by Peter McCarty. Dial Bks. for Young Readers 1998 53p il $16.99; pa $4.99

Grades: 4 5 6 7 **92**

1. Nurses 2. Midwives

ISBN 0-670-88923-7; 0-14-130815-X pa

LC 97-43409

Tells the stories of three families who were helped by the work of Mary Breckinridge, the first nurse to go into the Appalachian Mountains and give medical care to the isolated inhabitants. Includes an afterword with facts about Breckinridge and the Frontier Nursing Service she founded

"These beautifully written stories will remain with the reader long after the book is closed." Booklist

Bridgman, Laura Dewey, 1829-1889

Alexander, Sally Hobart. **She** touched the world: Laura Bridgman, deaf-blind pioneer; by Sally Hobart Alexander and Robert Alexander. Clarion Books 2008 100p il $18

Grades: 5 6 7 8 **92**

1. Deaf 2. Blind 3. Students 4. Physicians 5. Philanthropists 6. Humanitarians 7. Teachers of the blind

ISBN 978-0-618-85299-4; 0-618-85299-9

"At the age of three, in 1832, Laura Bridgman contracted scarlet fever and lost her sight, her hearing, her sense of smell, and much of her sense of taste. Her family sent her to Dr. Samuel [Gridley] Howe at the New England Institute for the Education of the Blind, and by the age of 10, Laura was world-famous for her accomplishments. . . . Alexander . . . presents a well-written and thoroughly researched biography of this remarkable woman, with numerous black-and-white photos." Booklist

Includes bibliographical references

Brin, Sergey

Sapet, Kerrily. **Google** founders: Larry Page and Sergey Brin. Morgan Reynolds Pub. 2011 112p il (Business leaders) $28.95

Grades: 7 8 9 10 11 12 **92**

1. Businesspeople 2. Web search engines 3. Computer scientists 4. Google, Inc. 5. Internet executives 6. Information technology executives

ISBN 978-1-59935-177-3; 1-59935-177-3; 978-1-59935-213-8 e-book

LC 2011014665

This biography of Google founders Larry Page and Sergey Bring "will grab YAs. . . . The design is browsable, with clear type and lots of color screens and informal photos of young people at work." Booklist

Includes bibliographical references

Brown, John, 1800-1859

★ Hendrix, John. **John** Brown; his fight for freedom. written and illustrated by John Hendrix. Abrams Books for Young Readers 2009 39p il $18.95

Grades: 4 5 6 7 **92**

1. Abolitionists 2. Slavery -- United States

ISBN 978-0-8109-3798-7; 0-8109-3798-0

LC 2008-45969

The author "traces how John Brown went from conducting slaves along the Underground Railroad to espousing violent insurrection as a means to end slavery. . . . Reinforcing Brown as a larger-than-life folk hero, the pictures are exhilarating. . . . By embracing Brown's complexity, especially in the well-argued afterword, Hendrix sows acres of fertile ground for discussion." Booklist

Marrin, Albert, 1936- A **volcano** beneath the snow; John Brown's war against slavery. Albert Marrin. Alfred A. Knopf 2014 256 p. illustrations, maps (trade) $19.99

Grades: 8 9 10 11 12 **92**

1. United States -- Biography 2. Abolitionists -- United States 3. Harpers Ferry (W. Va.) -- History -- John Brown's Raid, 1859 4. Abolitionists -- United States -- Biography

ISBN 0307981525; 9780307981523; 9780307981530

LC 2012043231

This book, by Albert Marrin, focuses on John Brown. "Deeply religious, Brown believed that God had chosen him to right the wrong of slavery. He was willing to kill and die for something modern Americans unanimously agree was a just cause. And yet he was a religious fanatic and a staunch believer in 'righteous violence,' an unapologetic committer of domestic terrorism." (Publisher's note)

"Chapters present the history of the 'peculiar institution' (slavery) both here and abroad, details of Brown's life and family, his relationship with the abolitionists, his radicalization leading to the killings at Pottawatomie, Kansas, and, eventually, the uprising at Harper's Ferry and his trial and hanging. . . . black-and-white illustrations include period photos, portraits, artwork, maps, fliers, and posters. Extensive notes and further-reading suggestions are included." SLJ

Includes bibliographical references

Bruchac, Joseph, 1942-

★ Bruchac, Joseph. **Bowman's** store; a journey to myself. 1st Lee & Low ed; Lee & Low Books 2001 315p il pa $9.95

Grades: 7 8 9 10 **92**

1. Poets 2. Authors 3. Abnaki Indians 4. Storytellers 5. College teachers 6. Magazine editors 7. Authors, American 8. Children's authors 9. Nonfiction writers 10. Native Americans -- Biography

ISBN 1-58430-027-2; 978-1-58430-027-4

LC 2001-16435

A reissue of the title first published 1997 by Dial Books

"Each episode is constructed with a true storyteller's attention to language and plot development. Students of modern Native American cultures will find plenty of food for thought." Booklist

Buchanan, James, 1791-1868

Burgan, Michael. **James** Buchanan. Marshall Cavendish Benchmark 2011 112p il (Presidents and their times) lib bdg $23.95

Grades: 5 6 7 8 **92**

1. Presidents 2. Senators 3. Members of Congress 4. Secretaries of state 5. Presidents -- United States

ISBN 978-0-7614-4810-5; 0-7614-4810-1

LC 2009025933

This offers information on President James Buchanan and places him within his historical and cultural context. Also explored are the formative events of his times and how he responded.

"The abundant sidebars provide a good deal of background information that will be helpful to students. . . . Attractive . . . as well as useful." Booklist

Includes glossary and bibliographical references

Buffalo Bill, 1846-1917

Fleming, Candace, 1962- **Presenting** Buffalo Bill; The Man Who Invented the Wild West. Candace Fleming. Roaring Brook Press 2016 288 p. illustrations (hardcover) $19.99; (ebook) $60

Grades: 6 7 8 9 10 **92**

1. Buffalo Bill's Wild West Show 2. Pioneers -- West (U.S.) -- Biography 3. West (U.S.) -- Biography 4. Buffalo Bill's Wild West Show -- History 5. Entertainers -- United States -- Biography

ISBN 9781596437630; 9781626727472

LC 2015035540

In this book, by Candace Fleming, "everyone knows the name Buffalo Bill, but few these days know what he did or, in some cases, didn't do. . . . This [is] the first significant biography of Buffalo Bill Cody for younger readers in many years. . . . With copious archival illustrations and a handsome design, [it] makes the great showman come alive for new generations. Extensive back matter, bibliography, and source notes complete the package." (Publisher's note)

"Illustrated with archival material and supplemented with extensive backmatter, this is a thoroughly engaging portrait of a fascinating, larger-than-life figure." Kirkus

Includes bibliographical references

Sanford, William R. **Buffalo** Bill Cody; courageous wild west showman. by William R. Sanford and Carl R. Green. Enslow Publishers 2013 48 p. ill., map (library) $21.26; (paperback) $7.95

Grades: 5 6 7 8 **92**

1. Buffalo Bill's Wild West Show 2. Frontier and pioneer life -- West (U.S.) 3. West (U.S.) -- Biography 4. Pioneers -- West (U.S.) -- Biography 5. Buffalo Bill's Wild West Show -- History 6. Entertainers -- United States -- Biography

ISBN 0766040070; 9780766040076; 9781464400902

LC 2011031052

This book by William Sanford and Carl R. Green is part of the "Courageious Heroes of the American West" series. It presents a biography of Buffalo Bill Cody, who "had many jobs--Pony Express rider, scout, soldier, buffalo hunter. But he was most famous for entertaining audiences with his Wild West show. Many Americans and others around the world could not travel to see the real Wild West, so Buffalo Bill Brought it to them." (Publisher's note)

Includes bibliographical references (p. 47) and index.

Bullard, Eugene Jacques, 1894-1961

Greenly, Larry. **Eugene** Bullard; world's first Black fighter pilot. Larry W. Greenly. Junebug Books 2012 160 p. illustrations $19.95

Grades: 8 9 10 11 12 **92**

1. Fighter pilots -- France -- Biography 2. African American fighter pilots -- Biography 3. World War, 1914-1918 -- Aerial operations, French 4. World War, 1939-1945 -- Aerial operations, French 5. African American fighter pilots -- France -- Biography 6. Race discrimination -- United States -- History -- 20th century

ISBN 158838280X; 9781588382801

LC 2012036425

This book, by Larry Greenly, "tells the story of pioneering black aviator Eugene Bullard from his birth in 1895 to his combat experiences in both World War I and II and, finally, his return to America. . . . He ran away from home at twelve and eventually made his way to France, where he joined the French Foreign Legion and later the Lafayette Flying Corps, to become the world's first black fighter pilot." (Publisher's note)

"The incredible story of Eugene Bullard—an African American honored by the French, yet shunned by the Americans—is one too long neglected. . . . Though his heroic deeds brought recognition from the French, a white American doctor in Paris became a constant stumbling block for further progress in Eugene's life and career. . . . Using Bullard's memoirs and other sparse information about him, Greenly crafts a moving, novelistic biography that portrays Bullard's courage throughout his life. Meanwhile, the black-and-white photos, of everything from a teenage Bullard boxing to wartime aircrafts, add plenty of historical flavor." Booklist

Includes bibliographical references

Burns, Anthony, 1834-1862

★ Hamilton, Virginia. **Anthony** Burns: the defeat and triumph of a fugitive slave. Knopf 1988 193p hardcover o.p. pa $5.50

Grades: 5 6 7 8 **92**

1. Slaves 2. Slavery -- United States 3. African Americans -- Biography

ISBN 0-679-83997-6 pa

LC 87-38063

A biography of the slave who escaped to Boston in 1854, was arrested at the instigation of his owner, and whose trial caused a furor between abolitionists and those determined to enforce the Fugitive Slave Act

"This book does exactly what good biography for children ought to do: takes readers directly into the life of the subject and makes them feel what it was like to be that person in those times." Horn Book

Includes bibliographical references

Burr, Aaron, 1756-1836

★ St. George, Judith. The **duel** : the parallel lives of Alexander Hamilton and Aaron Burr. Viking 2009 97p il $16.99

Grades: 6 7 8 9 10 **92**

1. Statesmen 2. Vice-presidents 3. Secretaries of the treasury 4. Politicians -- United States

ISBN 978-0-670-01124-7; 0-670-01124-X

LC 2009-5660

"After a prologue following the steps of Alexander Hamilton and Aaron Burr on the morning of their famous duel, St. George backtracks to trace the 'parallel lives' mentioned in the subtitle. . . . Well researched and organized, the book offers insights into the personalities, lives, and times of Burr and Hamilton." Booklist

Busby, Cylin, 1970-

★ Busby, Cylin. The **year** we disappeared; a father-daughter memoir. [by] Cylin Busby & John Busby. Bloomsbury 2008 329p $16.99

Grades: 8 9 10 11 12 **92**

1. Police 2. Authors 3. Violence 4. Father-daughter relationship 5. Magazine editors 6. Children's authors

ISBN 978-1-59990-141-1; 1-59990-141-2

LC 2008017215

"No one with even a marginal interest in true crime writing should miss this page-turner, by turns shocking and almost unbearably sad. In 1979, in an underworld-style hit, a gunman shot John Busby, a policeman in Cape Cod; a fluke saved John's life, but he was permanently disfigured and disabled, and the family placed under 24-hour protection. Eventually the family went into hiding in Tennessee, but arguably their 'disappearance' takes place long before they move—as John and his daughter, Cylin, alternately narrate, readers can see how the shooting erased the family's sense of themselves. . . . Where John's chapters provide the grim facts, it is Cylin's authentically childlike perspective that, in revealing the cost to her innocence, renders the tragic experience most searingly." Publ Wkly

Includes bibliographical references

Busby, John, 1942-

★ Busby, Cylin. The **year** we disappeared; a father-daughter memoir. [by] Cylin Busby & John Busby. Bloomsbury 2008 329p $16.99

Grades: 8 9 10 11 12 **92**

1. Police 2. Authors 3. Violence 4. Father-daughter relationship 5. Magazine editors 6. Children's authors

ISBN 978-1-59990-141-1; 1-59990-141-2

LC 2008017215

"No one with even a marginal interest in true crime writing should miss this page-turner, by turns shocking and almost unbearably sad. In 1979, in an underworld-style hit, a gunman shot John Busby, a policeman in Cape Cod; a fluke saved John's life, but he was permanently disfigured and disabled, and the family placed under 24-hour protection. Eventually the family went into hiding in Tennessee, but arguably their 'disappearance' takes place long before they move—as John and his daughter, Cylin, alternately narrate, readers can see how the shooting erased the family's sense of themselves. . . . Where John's chapters provide the grim facts, it is Cylin's authentically childlike perspective that, in revealing the cost to her innocence, renders the tragic experience most searingly." Publ Wkly

Includes bibliographical references

Caesar, Julius, 100-44 B.C.

Galford, Ellen. **Julius** Caesar; the boy who conquered an empire. [by] Ellen Galford. National Geographic 2007 64p il map (World history biographies) $17.95; lib bdg $27.90

Grades: 5 6 7 8 **92**

1. Statesmen 2. Historians 3. Rome -- History 4. Emperors -- Rome

ISBN 978-1-4263-0064-6; 978-1-4263-0065-3 lib bdg

LC 2006020777

A biography of the Roman emperor

This "visually appealing [title is] packed with excellent photographs and reproductions, interesting sidebars, and [has] a time line running along the bottom of every page. . . . [This book is] useful, well-written." SLJ

Includes glossary and bibliographical references

Calamity Jane, 1852-1903

Sanford, William R. **Calamity** Jane; courageous wild west woman. by William R. Sanford and Carl R. Green. Enslow Publishers 2013 48 p. ill., map (library) $21.26; (paperback) $7.95

Grades: 5 6 7 8 **92**

1. Cowgirls 2. West (U.S.) -- Biography 3. Pioneers -- West (U.S.) -- Biography 4. Women pioneers -- West (U.S.) -- Biography

ISBN 0766040100; 9780766040106; 9781464400933

LC 2011033840

This book by William Sanford is part of the Courageous Heroes of the American West series and focuses on Calamity Jane. "The truth and myth are difficult to separate in the wild life of Calamity Jane. An independent spirit, she never stayed in one place for long. She worked as a gold prospector, bullwhacker, nurse, and had many other jobs, Calamity Jane refused to conform to the typical roles of a nineteenth-century woman." (Publisher's note)

Includes bibliographical references (p. 47) and index.

Calcines, Eduardo F., 1955-

★ Calcines, Eduardo F. **Leaving** Glorytown; one boy's struggle under Castro. Farrar, Straus & Giroux 2009 221p il $17.95

Grades: 7 8 9 10 **92**

1. Businesspeople 2. Cuban refugees 3. Memoirists 4. Cuba -- History -- 1959- 5. Biography, Individual

ISBN 0-374-34394-2; 978-0-374-34394-1

LC 2008-7506

Eduardo F. Calcines was "three years old when Castro came to power in January 1959. After that, everything changed for his family and his country. When he was ten, his family applied for an exit visa to emigrate to America. . . . His father was sent to an agricultural cultural reform camp to do hard labor as punishment for daring to want to leave Cuba. During the years to come, as he grew up in Glorytown, a neighborhood in the city of Cienfuegos, Eduardo hoped . . . that their exit visa would be granted before he turned fifteen, the age at which he would be drafted into the army. In [this memoir, Calcines] . . . recounts his boyhood and chronicles the conditions that led him to wish above all else to leave behind his beloved extended family and his home." (Publisher's note) "Grades seven to ten." (Bull Cent Child Books)

"Calcines's spirited memoir captures the political tension, economic hardship, family stress, and personal anxiety of growing up during the early years of the Castro regime in Cuba. . . . The author shares startling, clear memories about his life in the Glorytown barrio of Cienfuegos. . . . Calcines writes about Cuba with immediacy, nostalgia, and passion. This personal account will acquaint readers with the oppressive and ironic effects of communism." SLJ

Canaletto, 1697-1768

Rice, Earle. **Canaletto**; by Earle Rice Jr. Mitchell Lane Publishers 2007 48p il (Art profiles for kids) lib bdg $29.95

Grades: 7 8 9 10 **92**

1. Artists 2. Painters 3. Artists, Italian

ISBN 978-1-58415-561-4 lib bdg; 1-58415-561-2 lib bdg

LC 2007023412

This offers "well-documented information for teens doing reports. [The] volume covers the painter's childhood, training, travels, influences, and historical context. The chronological chapters build a survey of the [artist's] oeuvres, including the style and subject matter of [his] works and past and present critical reaction." SLJ

Includes glossary and bibliographical references

Carr, Emily, 1871-1945

★ Debon, Nicolas. **Four** pictures by Emily Carr. Douglas & McIntyre 2003 un il $15.95

Grades: 4 5 6 7 **92**

1. Artists 2. Painters 3. Women artists 4. Artists, Canadian 5. Diarists 6. Memoirists

ISBN 0-88899-532-6

"Debon has distilled four periods in the Canadian artist's life (1871-1945) into enticing vignettes that illuminate her passions, determination, health problems, relationships with fellow Group of Seven artists, and, most of all, her dramatic progression as a painter. . . . Engaging artwork and brisk storytelling make this a consideration for most libraries." SLJ

Carroll, Lewis, 1832-1898

Rubin, C. M. The **real** Alice in Wonderland; a role model for the ages. [by] C.M. Rubin with Gabriella Rose Rubin. AuthorHouse 2010 134p il $29.95

Grades: 7 8 9 10 **92**

1. Authors 2. Children 3. Novelists 4. Mathematicians 5. Characters and characteristics in literature 6. Children's authors 7. Writers on science

ISBN 978-1-4490-8131-7; 1-4490-8131-2

LC 2010-901865

"Readers will follow this title down the rabbit hole to discover the world of the real Alice who inspired Lewis Carroll's Alice in Wonderland. The book moves seamlessly through the life of Alice Pleasance Liddell. . . . This offering paints a full picture of Alice, not only as a child who has captivated literature but also as a woman who was truly ahead of her time. This is a purchase that will do well with a range of people and should be offered as a standard accompaniment to Alice in Wonderland. The illustrations and pictures will make it quite popular in a public library." Voice Youth Advocates

Includes bibliographical references

Carson, Rachel, 1907-1964

Scherer, Glenn. **Who** on earth is Rachel Carson? mother of the environmental movement. [by] Glenn Scherer and Marty Fletcher. Enslow Publishers 2009 112p il (Scientists saving the earth) lib bdg $31.93

Grades: 5 6 7 8 **92**

1. Authors 2. Biologists 3. Conservationists 4. Women scientists 5. Environmentalists 6. College teachers 7. Marine biologists 8. Writers on nature 9. Writers on science

ISBN 978-1-59845-116-0 lib bdg; 1-59845-116-2 lib bdg

LC 2008028498

"The writing is clear and informative. . . . Color photographs are relevant and of good quality." SLJ

Includes bibliographical references

Carver, George Washington, 1864?-1943

Harness, Cheryl. The **groundbreaking,** chance-taking life of George Washington Carver and science & invention in America; by Cheryl Harness. National Geographic 2008 143p il map (Cherly Harness histories) $16.95; lib bdg $25.90

Grades: 4 5 6 7 **92**

1. Botanists 2. Scientists 3. African Americans -- Biography

ISBN 978-1-4263-0196-4; 1-4263-0196-0; 978-1-4263-0197-1 lib bdg; 1-4263-0197-9 lib bdg

LC 2007029316

"Harness presents Carver as a man who, regardless of constant hardship and racial prejudice, persevered to become a beloved teacher and devoted scientist. . . . The author raises challenging questions throughout. . . . The lively prose style conveys his sense of passion and adventure about the man and his intellectual pursuits, and the simple black-and-white drawings add a further sense of drama." SLJ

Includes bibliographical references

Thomas, Peggy. **George** Washington Carver for kids; his life and discoveries with 21 activities. Peggy Thomas. Chicago Review Press Incorporated 2019 144 p. (trade paper) $16.99

Grades: 4 5 6 7 8 **92**

1. African American agriculturists -- Biography 2. Scientists -- Biography 3. Tuskegee Institute -- History 4. African American scientists -- Biography 5. Agriculturists -- United States -- Biography

ISBN 9780915864003

LC 2018035154

This book in the For Kids series, by Peggy Thomas, presents a biography of George Washington Carver. "Carver was a scientist, . . . and humanitarian. Born into slavery during the Civil War, he later pursued an education and would become the first black graduate from Iowa Agricultural College. Carver then took a teaching position at the Tuskegee Institute. . . . There, Carver taught poor Southern farmers how to nourish the soil, conserve resources, and feed their families." (Publisher's note)

"Carver's life and work are explored in meticulous detail in this activity-filled biography" (Kirkus Reviews).

Includes bibliographical references and index

Cash, Johnny

Willett, Edward. **Johnny** Cash; the man in black. Enslow Publishers 2010 160p il (American rebels) lib bdg $34.60

Grades: 6 7 8 9 **92**

1. Singers 2. Country music 3. Country musicians 4. Songwriters

ISBN 978-0-7660-3386-3 lib bdg; 0-7660-3386-4 lib bdg

LC 2009017346

This "fascinating, well-organized [portrait of the country music singer] . . . opens with the infamous 1968 live-album recording at California's Folsom State Prison. . . . Skillfully chosen photos, chapter notes, and [a] suggested-reading [list completes this] well-researched, wholly engaging [introduction]." Booklist

Includes bibliographical references

Castle, James, 1900-1977

★ Say, Allen. **Silent** days, silent dreams; Allen Say. Arthur A. Levine Books 2017 64 p. color illustrations (hardback) $21.99

Grades: 3 4 5 6 7 8 **92**

1. Deaf -- Fiction 2. Artists -- Fiction 3. People with disabilities -- Fiction

ISBN 9780545927611; 9781338214420

LC 2017017323

Schneider Family Book Award for Young Children, 2018.

ALA Notable Children's Book, 2018.

In this book, author Allen Say "takes readers through an imagined look at [deaf-mute artist James] Castle's childhood, allows them to experience his emergence as an artist despite the overwhelming difficulties he faced, and ultimately reveals the triumphs that he would go on to achieve." (Publisher's note)

"With sensitive text and powerful illustrations, Say brings this remarkable, inspiring life to poignant reality." Kirkus

Includes bibliographical references

Castro, Fidel, 1926-2016

Wheeler, Jill C., 1964- **Fidel** Castro; Cuban revolutionary leader. Jill C. Wheeler. Abdo Pub. 2018 48 p.
Grades: 4 5 6 7 **92**

1. Heads of state -- Cuba -- Biography 2. Revolutionaries -- Cuba -- Biography
ISBN 9781532111808

LC 2017930439

This book in the Newsmakers series, by Jill C. Wheeler, features Fidel Castro, who "took control of the Cuban government [in 1959] and became its new leader. [It] explores the early life of Castro and his rise to power. Easy-to-read text, vivid images, and helpful back matter give readers a clear look at this subject." (Publisher's note)

Catherine II, the Great, Empress of Russia, 1729-1796

★ Vincent, Zu. **Catherine** the Great; Empress of Russia. Franklin Watts 2009 128p il map (A wicked history) $30; pa $5.95
Grades: 6 7 8 9 **92**

1. Empresses 2. Russia -- History 3. Russia -- Kings and rulers
ISBN 978-0-531-21802-0 lib bdg; 0-531-21802-3 lib bdg; 978-0-531-20738-3 pa; 0-531-20738-2 pa

LC 2008041543

"Catherine the Great might be . . . known as a cruel dictator with lots of lovers, but author Vincent shows how the Empress of Russia actually took on her position (well, after she had her husband murdered) with some good intentions. . . . Young readers will find the manipulation of Catherine's early days particularly interesting." Booklist

Includes bibliographical references

Catherine, Duchess of Cambridge, 1982-

Doeden, Matt. **Prince** William & Kate; a royal romance. Lerner Publications 2011 48p il lib bdg $26.60
Grades: 5 6 7 8 **92**

1. Princes 2. Princesses
ISBN 978-0-7613-8029-0; 0-7613-8029-9

LC 2011003413

"This short and sweet volume accents what down-to-earth and normal newlyweds Prince William and Kate Middleton are really like. After a brief recap of the couple's engagement interview, the book goes on to profile the pair individually and then as a duo. . . . This is an upbeat, readable narrative about a handsome, appealing couple. The color photographs are well chosen." Booklist

Includes glossary and bibliographical references

Catlin, George, 1796-1872

★ Reich, Susanna. **Painting** the wild frontier: the art and adventures of George Catlin. Clarion Books 2008 160p il map $21
Grades: 7 8 9 10 11 12 **92**

1. Artists 2. Painters 3. West (U.S.) in art 4. Native Americans in art 5. Artists -- United States
ISBN 978-0-618-71470-4; 0-618-71470-7

LC 2007-38847

This is a "biography of nineteenth-century painter George Catlin, famous for his portraits of Native American life. . . . A great introduction to Catlin's work as well as an excellent title to use in social studies, history, and art classes." Booklist

Includes bibliographical references

Cezanne, Paul, 1839-1906

Burleigh, Robert. **Paul** Cezanne; a painter's journey. H.N. Abrams 2006 31p il $17.95
Grades: 4 5 6 7 **92**

1. Artists 2. Painters 3. Artists, French
ISBN 0-8109-5784-1

LC 2005011779

"Burleigh offers brief insights into Cézanne's personal life, such as his relationship with his father, who did not support his sons interest in art. However, the emphasis is on interpreting some individual paintings and understanding the artist's various styles, including the impact of the Impressionists and his evolution to a freer and simpler manner of expression in his later years. . . . The high-quality reproductions demonstrate Burleigh's points. . . . A solid, lively introduction." SLJ

Spence, David. **Cezanne**. New Forest Press 2010 48p il (Great artists and their world) lib bdg $32.80
Grades: 6 7 8 9 **92**

1. Artists 2. Painters 3. Artists, French
ISBN 978-1-84898-315-1; 1-84898-315-8

"Offers biographical information [of Paul Cezanne] . . . interspersed with art history and criticism in an eye-catching format. . . . [Includes] a long introductory paragraph and four-to-six images with explanatory notes. . . . Spence . . . does a good job of explaining why art that might seem ordinary today was revolutionary at the time of its creation." SLJ

Includes glossary

Chaplin, Charlie, 1889-1977

★ Fleischman, Sid. **Sir** Charlie; Chaplin, the funniest man in the world. Greenwillow Books 2010 268p il $19.99; lib bdg $20.89
Grades: 5 6 7 8 9 **92**

1. Actors 2. Comedians 3. Motion pictures 4. Motion picture directors 5. Motion picture producers 6. Biography, Individual
ISBN 0-06-189640-3; 0-06-189641-1 lib bdg; 978-0-06-189640-8; 978-0-06-189641-5 lib bdg

LC 2009019689

This is a biography of the actor and director who starred in such films as City Lights (1931), Modern Times (1940), The Great Dictator (1947) and Limelight (1952). Chronology. Bibliography. Index. "Grades six to ten." (Bull Cent Child Books)

"This lively and engaging account of a poor Cockney boy who became the world's greatest silent-movie comedian is a must for biography collections. . . . Brief, easily digestible chapters, an extensive time line, and plenty of photos make the book's well-researched content accessible and appealing." SLJ

Charles, Ray

★ Woog, Adam. **Ray** Charles and the birth of soul; [by] Adam Woog. Lucent Books 2006 112p il (Lucent library of Black history) lib bdg $28.70
Grades: 7 8 9 10 **92**

1. Blind 2. Singers 3. Pianists 4. Soul music 5. Blues musicians 6. African American singers
ISBN 1-59018-844-6

LC 2005022586

"Woog does an excellent job of describing Charles's rare talent and the trajectory of his long and legendary career. . . . The text is clearly written and well organized. Black-and-white photographs illustrate and inform." SLJ

Includes bibliographical references

Chavez, Cesar, 1927-1993

Stavans, Ilan, 1961- **Cesar** Chavez; a photographic essay. Cinco Puntos Press 2010 91p il pa $13.95

Grades: 7 8 9 10 **92**

1. Agricultural laborers 2. Migrant agricultural laborers 3. Labor leaders 4. Mexican Americans -- Biography

ISBN 1-933693-22-3; 978-1-933693-22-4

LC 2009044179

"Chavez secured better working conditions for thousands with his 1970 victory for the United Farm Workers Union by bargaining with the table-grape growers. This photo-biography covers the high points of his career, including ample and pointed quotes by him and touching on his global recognition and interactions with activist Fred Ross Jr., Dolores Huerta, Pope Paul VI, and Senator Robert F. Kennedy. The full-page black-and-white photos give a sense of the man at various ages, of the migrant workers' lives, and of being on the road demonstrating and striking. The book also includes a comprehensive time line. It is an excellent introduction to social activism from the 1950s through the 1980s." SLJ

Child, Julia

Abrams, Dennis. **Julia** Child, Chef; by Dennis Abrams. Chelsea House 2011 134 p. ill. (some col.) (Women of achievement) lib bdg $35

Grades: 6 7 8 9 **92**

1. Cooks 2. Television personalities 3. Cookbook writers 4. Cooks -- United States -- Biography

ISBN 1604139129; 9781604139129

LC 2011000039

'This book offers a biography of chef "Julia Child . . . [who] started a cooking revolution when she burst onto television screens in the 1960s. Before long, Americans inspired by her example began cooking French food at home in droves and truly appreciating the pleasure that preparing good food can provide. Yet Child did not grow up knowing how to cook or even with an interest in fine cuisine. Her story is one of an American woman's quest to find herself, to find her passion, and then to find a way to share that passion with the world. It is the story of how Julia McWilliams of Pasadena, California, transformed herself into Julia Child, 'The French Chef.'" (Publisher's note)

This "provides an engaging introduction to the chef as a privileged but the individualistic woman who took some time to find her way in life but eventually shared her passion for French cooking with the world. . . . Solid fare for the biography collection." Booklist

Includes bibliographical references and index

Chisholm, Shirley, 1924-2005

Raatma, Lucia. **Shirley** Chisholm. Marshall Cavendish Benchmark 2010 96p il (Leading women) $39.93

Grades: 4 5 6 7 **92**

1. Women politicians 2. Members of Congress 3. Presidential candidates 4. African American women -- Biography

ISBN 978-0-7614-4953-9; 0-7614-4953-1

"The arresting portrait on the cover will guide readers right into this well-written [biography of] . . . the first African American woman to enter Congress. . . . Raatma vividly explains what was happening in the country at the time and uses those events effectively as a backdrop. The many photos, both black and white and color, are good choices for the well-designed book." Booklist

Includes bibliographical references

Cho, Margaret, 1968-

Tiger, Caroline. **Margaret** Cho. Chelsea House 2007 111p bibl il por (Asian Americans of achievement) lib bdg $30

Grades: 7 8 9 10 **92**

1. Comedians 2. Korean Americans -- Biography

ISBN 0-7910-9275-5; 978-0-7910-9275-0

LC 2006028385

This is "a lively introduction to the comedian, from her rebellious childhood and teen years to her current successes. . . . The frequent quotes from Cho's funny insightful material will guide readers to seek out her performances." Booklist

Includes glossary and bibliographical references

Choo, Jimmy, 1961-

Sapet, Kerrily. **Jimmy** Choo. Morgan Reynolds Pub. 2010 112p il (Profiles in fashion) $28.95

Grades: 7 8 9 10 **92**

1. Shoemakers 2. Fashion designers 3. Shoe designers

ISBN 978-1-59935-151-3; 1-59935-151-X

LC 2010018813

"Malaysian-born Choo has shod some of the most famous feet in the world. . . . Sapet provides insider details about Choo's remarkable career. . . . Explanations of shoe-biz terms, as well as Asian concepts such as feng shui, enliven the text, and the eye-catching design includes many color photos of both the shoes and their celebrity fans. . . . This [is an] engrossing introduction to both an exemplary designer and to the fashion business." Booklist

Includes bibliographical references

Christo, 1935-

★ Greenberg, Jan. **Christo** & Jeanne-Claude; through the Gates and beyond. [by] Jan Greenberg and Sandra Jordan. Roaring Brook Press 2008 50p il $19.95

Grades: 6 7 8 9 **92**

1. Artists 2. Artists -- Biography 3. Gates: Project for Central Park, New York

ISBN 978-1-59643-071-6; 1-59643-071-0

LC 2007-19951

"In 2005, the dull gray of a New York City winter was interrupted when two indominable artists, Christo and his partner, Jeanne-Claude, brought Central Park brilliantly to life with their outdoor work The Gates. . . . This book, chronicling both The Gates as well as the artists' other projects, is as thoughtful, eye-opening, and meticulous as the work it celebrates." Booklist

Includes bibliographical references

Christo, Jeanne-Claude, 1935-2009

★ Greenberg, Jan. **Christo** & Jeanne-Claude; through the Gates and beyond. [by] Jan Greenberg and Sandra Jordan. Roaring Brook Press 2008 50p il $19.95

Grades: 6 7 8 9 **92**

1. Artists 2. Artists -- Biography 3. Gates: Project for Central Park, New York

ISBN 978-1-59643-071-6; 1-59643-071-0

LC 2007-19951

"In 2005, the dull gray of a New York City winter was interrupted when two indominable artists, Christo and his partner, Jeanne-Claude, brought Central Park brilliantly to life with their outdoor work The Gates. . . . This book, chronicling both The Gates as well as the artists' other projects, is as thoughtful, eye-opening, and meticulous as the work it celebrates." Booklist

Includes bibliographical references

Churchill, Winston Sir, 1874-1965

★ Severance, John B. **Winston** Churchill; soldier, statesman, artist. Clarion Bks. 1996 144p il map $17.95

Grades: 5 6 7 8 **92**

1. Statesmen 2. Historians 3. Prime ministers 4. Memoirists 5. Cabinet members 6. Members of Parliament 7. Nobel laureates for literature 8. Prime ministers -- Great Britain 9. Great Britain -- Politics and government -- 20th century

ISBN 0-395-69853-7

LC 94-25129

This is a biography of the British "Prime Minister. Although Severance focuses on Churchill's contributions during World War II, he also describes the statesman's boyhood, Boer War adventures, and political ascendancy." (SLJ) Bibliography. Index. "Grades five to eight." (Booklist)

This "biography presents an affectionate portrait of Britain's renowned Prime Minister. Although Severance focuses on Churchill's contributions during World War II, he also describes the statesman's boyhood, Boer War adventures, and political ascendancy." SLJ

Includes bibliographical references

Cisneros, Sandra

Warrick, Karen Clemens. **Sandra** Cisneros; inspiring Latina author. Enslow Publishers 2009 128p il (Latino biography library) $31.93

Grades: 6 7 8 9 **92**

1. Poets 2. Authors 3. Novelists 4. Women authors 5. Mexican American authors 6. Essayists 7. Authors, American 8. Short story writers

ISBN 978-0-7660-3162-3; 0-7660-3162-4

LC 2008041798

Discusses the life of Latina author Sandra Cisneros, including her childhood in Chicago, her path to becoming an accomplished author, and her work in the Latino community.

"Warrick brings originality to Cisnero's story by explaining how the facts of the novelist's life provide a foundation for her advocacy on behalf of others. . . . The text is well documented. . . . This straightforward, thorough biography is a solid addition to most collections." SLJ

Includes bibliographical references

Clark, William, 1770-1838

Crompton, Samuel. **Lewis** and Clark; [by] Samuel Willard Crompton. Chelsea House 2009 116p il map (Great explorers) lib bdg $30

Grades: 6 7 8 9 **92**

1. Explorers 2. Lewis and Clark Expedition (1804-1806) 3. West (U.S.) 4. Territorial governors

ISBN 978-1-60413-418-6 lib bdg; 1-60413-418-6 lib bdg

LC 2009-8687

Biography of the explorers Lewis and Clark

"The information . . . is presented in such a way as to attract and maintain readers' interest. . . . With a full complement of maps, photographs (where available), illustrations, time lines, and document reproductions, a full story is told. Well-written and throughly researched, this . . . will make a solid addition." SLJ

Includes glossary and bibliographical references

Cleary, Beverly

Cleary, Beverly. A **girl** from Yamhill: a memoir. Morrow 1988 279p il hardcover o.p. pa $12.99

Grades: 6 7 8 9 **92**

1. Authors 2. Women authors 3. Authors, American 4. Children's authors

ISBN 0-688-07800-1; 0-380-72740-4 pa

LC 87-31554

Follows the popular children's author from her childhood years in Oregon through high school and into young adulthood, highlighting her family life and her growing interest in writing

"The author sees her child self with the same clarity and objectivity as she has seen her fictional characters, and her reminiscences have a resultant integrity and candor." Bull Cent Child Books

Clemente, Roberto, 1934-1972

Freedman, Lew. **Roberto** Clemente; baseball star & humanitarian. ABDO Pub. Co. 2011 112p il (Legendary athletes) lib bdg $34.22

Grades: 6 7 8 9 **92**

1. Baseball players 2. Baseball -- Biography 3. Puerto Ricans -- Biography

ISBN 978-1-61714-754-8; 1-61714-754-0

LC 2010041161

This biography of baseball star Roberto Clemente "goes beyond merely discussing [his] accomplishments. . . . [It] also [explores] the social and political [influence he] had on society as a whole. In addition, [it introduces] historical events in the context of [his life]. . . . This . . . is teeming with information and is a must-purchase for sports fans and readers interested in social activism." SLJ

Includes glossary and bibliographical references

Cleopatra, Queen of Egypt, d. 30 B.C.

Blackaby, Susan. **Cleopatra**; Egypt's last and greatest queen. Sterling Pub. 2009 124p il (Sterling biographies) $12.95; pa $5.95

Grades: 5 6 7 8 **92**

1. Queens 2. Egypt -- History

ISBN 978-1-4027-6540-7; 1-4027-6540-1; 978-1-4027-5710-5 pa; 1-4027-5710-7 pa

LC 2008030146

"Villainess or goddess, a great queen or a selfish and overly ambitious woman—readers get to decide. They will be drawn into this biography by a description of a legendary magnificent banquet given by Mark Antony for Cleopatra. The lively narrative maintains interest from her birth in 69 BCE to her death in 31 BCE. . . . Sidebars, color photographs, and reproductions appear throughout. . . . This book leaves readers fascinated and eager to learn more about her time in history." SLJ

Includes glossary and bibliographical references

Shecter, Vicky Alvear. **Cleopatra** rules! the amazing life of the original teen queen. Boyds Mills Press 2010 128p il map $17.95

Grades: 5 6 7 8 **92**

1. Queens 2. Egypt -- History 3. Biography, Individual

ISBN 1590787188; 9781590787182

LC 2009-26737

This is a biography of "Cleopatra VII, the last pharaoh of Egypt." (Publisher's note) Bibliography. Index. "Grades six to ten." (Bull Cent Child Books)

"This attractive book presents Cleopatra's story through an unusual text, informative sidebars, and excellent color illustrations. . . . Calling attention to the writing as much as its story, the text includes puns, informal language, and contemporary metaphors. . . . Shecter's solid research is evident." Booklist

Includes glossary and bibliographical references

Clinton, Hillary Rodham, 1947-

Blashfield, Jean F. **Hillary** Clinton. Marshall Cavendish Benchmark 2010 112p il (Leading women) $39.93

Grades: 4 5 6 7 **92**

1. Lawyers 2. Women politicians 3. Senators 4. Secretaries of state 5. Spouses of presidents 6. Presidential candidates 7. Presidents' spouses -- United States

ISBN 978-0-7614-4954-6; 0-7614-4954-X

A biography of the Secretary of State and former Senator, presidential candidate, and First Lady.

Includes bibliographical references

Blumenthal, Karen. **Hillary** Rodham Clinton; a woman living history. Karen Blumenthal. Feiwel & Friends 2016 448 p. illustrations (hardcover) $18.99

Grades: 7 8 9 10 11 12 **92**

1. Women politicians 2. Legislators -- United States -- Biography 3. United States. Congress. Senate -- Biography 4. Cabinet officers -- United States -- Biography 5. United States. Department of State -- Biography 6. Women legislators -- United States -- Biography 7. Presidents' spouses -- United States -- Biography 8. Women cabinet officers -- United States -- Biography 9. Presidential candidates -- United States -- Biography 10. Women presidential candidates -- United States -- Biography

ISBN 1250060141; 9781250060143

LC 2015026916

YALSA Award for Excellence in Nonfiction for Young Adults: Finalist (2017)

In this biography "author Karen Blumenthal gives . . . an intimate and unflinching look at the public and personal life of Hillary Rodham Clinton. Illustrated throughout with black-and-white photographs and political cartoons, this is a . . . biography about a woman who has fascinated--and divided--the public, who continues to push boundaries, and who isn't afraid to reach for one more goal." (Publisher's note)

"As astounding as Clinton's many accomplishments are, readers receive a balanced, wholly human portrait with all the flaws it entails. A richly detailed study that is as perceptive as it is engaging." Kirkus

Levinson, Cynthia. **Hillary** Rodham Clinton; Do All the Good You Can. Cynthia Levinson. Balzer + Bray 2016 352 p. 8 leaves of plates; ill. $16.99

Grades: 5 6 7 8 **92**

1. Women politicians

ISBN 0062387308; 9780062387301

LC 2015940617

Author Cynthia Levinson presents this "meticulously researched middle grade biography of Hillary Rodham Clinton--First Lady, senator, secretary of state, and Democratic candidate for president in 2016. Levinson creates a compelling and personal portrait of Hillary's historic journey from her childhood to her service as secretary of state and beyond. Includes a timeline of Hillary Rodham Clinton's life and an eight-page photo insert." (Publisher's note)

"A respectful, insightful, and inspiring portrait of a fiercely ambitious, remarkably successful woman who has changed the face of American politics." Kirkus

Includes bibliographical references (pages 293-322) and index.

Tracy, Kathleen. The **Clinton** view; the historic fight for the 2008 Democratic presidential nomination. Mitchell Lane Publishers 2009 48p il (Monumental milestones) lib bdg $29.95

Grades: 6 7 8 9 **92**

1. Lawyers 2. Women politicians 3. Senators 4. Secretaries of state 5. Spouses of presidents 6. Presidential candidates 7. Presidents' spouses -- United States 8. Presidents -- United States -- Election -- 2008

ISBN 978-1-58415-731-1; 1-58415-731-3

LC 2008053545

This looks at the 2008 presidential campaign from the point of view of candidate Hillary Clinton

This "begins with the Iowa caucus, the effect the loss had on front-runner Clinton, and how her win in New Hampshire made her the second Clinton 'comeback kid.' Then, the book goes back to Clinton's early years, her academic successes, and her tenures as First Lady and senator. Tracy captures some of the excitement of the campaign. . . . The design is lively and colorful, and the photos will draw readers." Booklist

Includes bibliographical references

Collard, Sneed B

Collard, Sneed B. **Snakes,** Alligators, and Broken Hearts; journeys of a biologist's son. Sneed B. Collard III. Mountain Press 2015 176 p. illustrations $17

Grades: 5 6 7 8 **92**

1. American authors -- Biography

ISBN 0984446060; 9780984446063

This book, by Sneed B. Collard III, "recounts the author's adventures and experiences growing up as the son of a biologist during the 1960s and 70s. With humor and compassion, the author describes the innocence of his early childhood, the heartbreak of his parents' divorce, and his rocky journey through adolescence all against the backdrop of animals, travel, and his poignant relationship with his father." (Publisher's note)

"Collard proceeds to lay the groundwork for his future as a writer and observer of the natural world, describing similarly vivid animal encounters alongside otherwise fairly typical accounts of schooling, Scouting, brushes with girls, and growing up in the increasingly troubled 1960s." Booklist

Collins, Michael, 1930-

Schyffert, Bea Uusma. The **man** who went to the far side of the moon: the story of Apollo 11 astronaut Michael Collins. Chronicle 2003 77p il $14.95

Grades: 5 6 7 8 **92**

1. Astronauts 2. Space flight 3. Aerospace consultants 4. Museum administrators

ISBN 0-8118-4007-7

Boston Globe-Horn Book Award Honor: Nonfiction (2004)

A biography of the astronaut, Michael Collins, who circled the moon in the Apollo 12 space capsule while his colleagues Neil Armstrong and Buzz Aldrin landed the lunar module and walked on the moon.

"This excellent book—illustrated scrapbook-style with a cleverly presented mix of photographs, illustrations, and charts—communicates the excitement of space travel." Booklist

Colvin, Claudette

★ Hoose, Phillip. **Claudette** Colvin; twice toward justice. by Phillip Hoose. Melanie Kroupa Books 2009 133p il $19.95

Grades: 6 7 8 9 10 **92**

1. Civil rights activists 2. African Americans -- Civil rights 3. African American women -- Biography 4. Biography, Individual 5. Civil rights movements 5. African Americans -- Civil rights

-- History
ISBN 978-0-374-31322-7; 0-374-31322-9

LC 2008-05435

National Book Award: Young People's Literature (2009)
ALA ALSC Newbery Medal Honor Book (2010)

"Teenager Claudette Colvin's significant contribution to the struggle for equal accommodation is presented in this biography that smoothly weaves excerpts from Hoose's extensive interviews with Colvin and his own supplementary commentary. . . . [Readers learn] why her arrest for refusing to give up her bus seat to a white passenger never became the crucial incident to spark the Montgomery Bus Boycott. . . . Plenty of black-and-white photographs and well-deployed sidebars enhance the text." Bull Cent Child Books

Includes bibliographical references

Cone, Claribel, 1864-1929

★ Fillion, Susan. **Miss** Etta and Dr. Claribel; Bringing Matisse to America. David R. Godine 2011 83p il $18.95

Grades: 4 5 6 7 **92**

1. Artists 2. Painters 3. Physicians 4. Art collectors 5. Art -- Collectors and collecting
ISBN 978-1-56792-434-3; 1-56792-434-4

LC 2010048937

"An affectionate, lively examination of the reciprocal relationship between a great artist and two great art lovers. Etta and Claribel Cone, unmarried sisters from a wealthy Baltimore family . . . [were] discerning collectors of modern art, particularly that of Henri Matisse. . . . Their account is lavishly illustrated in full color by reproductions from the Cone Collection at the Baltimore Museum of Art and Matisse-inflected paintings by the author, who drew extensively on the Cone archive that is also housed at the museum. . . . This appealing work stands as both a portrait of two unconventional women and a celebration of the possibilties of arts patronage." Kirkus

Cone, Etta, 1870-1949

★ Fillion, Susan. **Miss** Etta and Dr. Claribel; Bringing Matisse to America. David R. Godine 2011 83p il $18.95

Grades: 4 5 6 7 **92**

1. Artists 2. Painters 3. Physicians 4. Art collectors 5. Art -- Collectors and collecting
ISBN 978-1-56792-434-3; 1-56792-434-4

LC 2010048937

"An affectionate, lively examination of the reciprocal relationship between a great artist and two great art lovers. Etta and Claribel Cone, unmarried sisters from a wealthy Baltimore family . . . [were] discerning collectors of modern art, particularly that of Henri Matisse. . . . Their account is lavishly illustrated in full color by reproductions from the Cone Collection at the Baltimore Museum of Art and Matisse-inflected paintings by the author, who drew extensively on the Cone archive that is also housed at the museum. . . . This appealing work stands as both a portrait of two unconventional women and a celebration of the possibilties of arts patronage." Kirkus

Cook, James, 1728-1779

Feinstein, Stephen. **Captain** Cook; great explorer of the Pacific. Enslow 2010 112p il (Great explorers of the world) lib bdg $31.93

Grades: 6 7 8 9 **92**

1. Explorers 2. Voyages around the world 3. Naval officers 4. Travel writers 5. Oceania -- Exploration
ISBN 978-1-59845-102-3; 1-59845-102-2

LC 2009006503

Examines the life of Captain James Cook, a British explorer and scientist, including his early life, his many Pacific voyages, and his death and legacy

This "provides a harrowing and enlightening account of Cook's discoveries. . . . Cook is portrayed as an intelligent and thoughtful man who regretted some of these negative impacts. Each volume is well organized, with text that is easy to read. . . . This . . . would serve as a useful resource for middle and elementary school students and may inspire them to read further." Voice Youth Advocates

Includes glossary and bibliographical references

Copeland, Misty

Copeland, Misty, 1982- **Life** in motion; an unlikely ballerina. Misty Copeland with Brandy Colbert. Young Readers edition Aladdin 2016 186 p. illustrations (hardcover : alk. paper) $17.99; (pbk : alk. paper) $7.99

Grades: 5 6 7 8 9 **92**

1. Ballet dancers 2. African American dancers -- Biography 3. Ballerinas -- United States -- Biography
ISBN 9781481479790; 9781481479806; 1481479806; 1481479792

LC 2016036841

"As the first African-American principal dancer at the American Ballet Theatre, Misty Copeland has been breaking down all kinds of barriers in the world of dance. But when she first started dancing--at the late age of thirteen--no one would have guessed the shy, underprivileged girl would one day make history in her field." (Publisher's note)

"In this young readers' edition of her 2014 memoir of the same name and with Colbert's assistance, Copeland writes in a conversational tone. She devotes much space to her innate abilities, her ABT career, and her overwhelming desire to succeed and be an inspiration." Kirkus

Includes bibliographical references and index

Copernicus, Nicolaus, 1473-1543

Andronik, Catherine M. **Copernicus**; founder of modern astronomy. rev ed; Enslow Publishers 2009 128p bibl il (Great minds of science) lib bdg $31.93

Grades: 5 6 7 8 **92**

1. Astronomers
ISBN 978-0-7660-3013-8 lib bdg; 0-7660-3013-X lib bdg

LC 2008-23940

First published 2002

"A highly readable book that presents a good balance between the biographical information needed to understand Copernicus as a man and the scientific explanations necessary to understand his work. . . . Good-quality, black-and-white reproductions, illustrations, and photographs add interest to the clearly written text." SLJ [review of 2002 edition]

Includes glossary and bibliographical references

Cormier, Robert

Beckman, Wendy Hart. **Robert** Cormier; banned, challenged, and censored. Enslow Publishers 2008 160p bibl il por (Authors of banned books) lib bdg $34.60

Grades: 6 7 8 9 10 **92**

1. Authors 2. Novelists 3. Censorship 4. Authors, American 5. Young adult authors
ISBN 978-0-7660-2691-9; 0-7660-2691-4

LC 2007-28003

"Cormier is generally cited as one of the finest and most challenged writers for teens. This combination of biography and literary criticism explains his appeal to readers as well as the most common objections to his works from parents and school districts. A history of other censorship, including several recent court cases involving the First Amendment, and a biographical sketch of Cormier precede the discussion of The Chocolate War (1974), I Am the Cheese (1977), and After the First Death (1979, all Knopf). . . . A helpful overview of the works of a major YA author." SLJ

Includes glossary and bibliographical references

Corwin, Jeff

Corwin, Jeff. **Jeff** Corwin: a wild life; the authorized biography. Penguin Group 2009 100p il pa $6.99

Grades: 4 5 6 7 **92**

1. Biologists 2. Naturalists 3. Conservationists 4. Television personalities

ISBN 978-0-14-241403-3 pa; 0-14-241403-4 pa

LC 2009008092

"The host of Animal Planet . . . and other popular TV programs blends his exciting adventure in the wild with his passionate call for conservation. . . . An insert of beautifully reproduced color photos from his global travels show him with a giraffe in Kenya, a moose in Alaska, and more. . . . The adventures are thrilling, and the messages are urgent." Booklist

Cosgrove, Miranda, 1993-

Yasuda, Anita. **Miranda** Cosgrove. Weigl 2011 24p il (Remarkable people) $27.13; pa $12.95

Grades: 4 5 6 7 **92**

1. Actors 2. Singers

ISBN 978-1-6169-0668-9; 1-6169-0668-5; 978-1-6169-0673-3 pa; 1-6169-0673-1 pa

LC 2010051144

A biography of actress and singer Miranda Cosgrove

Cousteau, Jacques Yves, 1910-1997

Knowles, Jo. **Jacques** Cousteau. Chelsea House 2011 117p il (Conservation heroes) lib bdg $35

Grades: 6 7 8 9 10 **92**

1. Ocean 2. Authors 3. Scientists 4. Skin diving 5. Divers 6. Naval officers 7. Oceanographers 8. Nonfiction writers

ISBN 978-1-60413-947-1; 1-60413-947-1

LC 2010030584

A biography of the French undersea explorer and conservationist.

"Captivating, richly informative. . . . The scope of [this book] is comprehensive. . . . [The book is] engaging as [it is] educational and will be ideal for research and reports." SLJ

Includes glossary and bibliographical references

Coville, Bruce

Marcovitz, Hal. **Bruce** Coville. Chelsea House 2006 124p bibl il por (Who wrote that?) $30

Grades: 6 7 8 9 **92**

1. Authors 2. Authors, American 3. Children's authors

ISBN 0-7910-8656-9

LC 2005008182

A biography of the popular author of children's and young adult fantasy and science fiction books.

Includes bibliographical references

Crandall, Prudence, 1803-1890

★ Jurmain, Suzanne. The **forbidden** schoolhouse; the true and dramatic story of Prudence Crandall and her students. Houghton Mifflin 2005 150p il $18

Grades: 5 6 7 8 **92**

1. Teachers 2. Educators 3. Abolitionists 4. African Americans -- Education

ISBN 0-618-47302-5

This is the story of Prudence Crandall, who, in 1831, opened a school for African American girls in Canterbury, Connecticut.

"A compelling, highly readable book. . . . Writing with a sense of drama that propels readers forward . . . Jurmain makes painfully clear what Crandall and her students faced. . . . Including a number of sepia-toned and color photographs as well as historical engravings, the book's look will draw in readers." Booklist

Includes bibliographical references

Crazy Horse, Sioux Chief, ca. 1842-1877

★ Freedman, Russell. The **life** and death of Crazy Horse; drawings by Amos Bad Heart Bull. Holiday House 1996 166p il maps $22.95

Grades: 5 6 7 8 9 10 **92**

1. Oglala Indians 2. Indian chiefs 3. Native Americans -- Biography

ISBN 0-8234-1219-9

LC 95-33303

A biography of the Oglala Indian leader who relentlessly resisted the white man's attempt to take over Indian lands.

This is "a compelling biography that is based on primary source documents and illustrated with pictographs by a Sioux band historian." Voice Youth Advocates

Includes bibliographical references

Creech, Sharon

Baptiste, Tracey. **Sharon** Creech; foreword by Kyle Zimmer. Chelsea House 2011 118p il (Who wrote that?) lib bdg $35

Grades: 6 7 8 9 **92**

1. Authors 2. Novelists 3. Women authors 4. Authors, American 5. Children's authors 6. Young adult authors

ISBN 978-1-60413-774-3; 1-60413-774-6

LC 2010030595

A biography of the author of Walk Two Moons and Absolutely Normal Chaos.

Includes bibliographical references

Cromwell, Oliver, 1599-1658

Aronson, Marc. **John** Winthrop, Oliver Cromwell, and the Land of Promise. Clarion Books 2004 205p il map $20

Grades: 7 8 9 10 **92**

1. Clergy 2. Puritans 3. Heads of state 4. Revolutionaries 5. Government officials 6. Colonial administrators 7. Great Britain -- History -- 1603-1714, Stuarts 8. Massachusetts -- History -- 1600-1775, Colonial period

ISBN 0-618-18177-6

LC 2003-16418

"The accessible text is accompanied by excerpts from primary source documents and vivid illustrations. The author's passion for the period comes across in his writing. Aronson provides an excellent source for historical and biographical data." Voice Youth Advocates

Includes bibliographical references

Crutcher, Chris, 1946-

★ Crutcher, Chris. **King** of the mild frontier: an ill-advised autobiography. Greenwillow Bks. 2003 260p il $16.99; pa $6.99

Grades: 8 9 10 11 12 **92**

1. Authors 2. Novelists 3. Authors, American 4. Young adult authors

ISBN 0-06-050249-5; 0-06-050251-7 pa

LC 2002-11224

Chris Crutcher, author of young adult novels such as "Ironman" and "Whale Talk," as well as short stories, tells of growing up in Cascade, Idaho, and becoming a writer

"Like his novels, Crutcher's autobiography is full of heartbreak, poignancy, and hilarity. . . . This honest, insightful, revealing autobiography is a joy to read." Booklist

Cruz, Celia, 1929-2003

Cartlidge, Cherese. **Celia** Cruz. Chelsea House Publishers 2010 112p il (The great Hispanic heritage) lib bdg $30

Grades: 6 7 8 9 **92**

1. Singers 2. Salsa musicians

ISBN 978-1-60413-771-2; 1-60413-771-1

LC 2010007809

This "delves frankly into the Cuban-born singer-songwriter's life, including her blatant rejection of Fidel Castro and her subsequent immigration to the U.S., where President Clinton eventually honored her with a Presidential Medal. . . . A selection of well-chosen images, a chronology, chapter notes, and [a] suggested reading [list] round out [this] engaging and sure-to-be-popular [book] for reports and personal interest." Booklist

Cummings, E. E. (Edward Estlin), 1894-1962

Reef, Catherine. **E.** E. Cummings. Clarion Books 2006 149p il $21

Grades: 7 8 9 10 11 12 **92**

1. Poets 2. Authors 3. Poets, American

ISBN 978-0-618-56849-9; 0-618-56849-2

LC 2006-10453

"Reef explores the interaction of events and poetry to portray a man whose story would not be complete without an understanding of both. She makes clear that the king of experimental poetry was deeply grounded in the very structure he subverted. Black-and-white photographs vivify the facts, while the spacious format gives Cummings's words room to spread out. List of major works, source notes. Bib., glos., ind." (Horn Book)

Includes bibliographical references

Curie, Marie, 1867-1934

Borzendowski, Janice. **Marie** Curie; mother of modern physics. Sterling Pub 2009 124p il map (Sterling biographies) $12.95; pa $5.95

Grades: 7 8 9 10 **92**

1. Chemists 2. Physicists 3. Women scientists 4. Nobel laureates for physics

ISBN 978-1-4027-6543-8; 1-4027-6543-6; 978-1-4027-5318-3 pa; 1-4027-5318-7 pa

LC 2008-30701

"This interesting, informative biography of the scientist and Nobel Prize winner explores both Curie's personal and professional life. It includes numerous archival and modern photos and reproductions. . . . The book is far more thorough and satisfying than most biographies of Curie for teens." SLJ

Includes bibliographical references

★ Krull, Kathleen. **Marie** Curie; [illustrations by] Boris Kulikov. Viking 2007 128p il (Giants of science) $15.99

Grades: 5 6 7 8 **92**

1. Chemists 2. Physicists 3. Women scientists 4. Nobel laureates for physics

ISBN 978-0-670-05894-5; 0-670-05894-7

LC 2007-24251

"The compelling and conversational narrative (ably assisted by Kulikov's black-and-white drawings) portrays a brilliant . . . woman with plenty of idiosyncrasies, and the story of her discovery of radium . . . is as engaging as any of her personal dramas and challenges." Horn Book

MacLeod, Elizabeth. **Marie** Curie; a brilliant life. written by Elizabeth MacLeod. Kids Can Press 2004 32p il $14.95; pa $6.95

Grades: 5 6 7 8 **92**

1. Chemists 2. Physicists 3. Women scientists 4. Nobel laureates for physics

ISBN 1-55337-570-X; 1-55337-571-8 pa

"The drive and self-sacrifice that enabled Marie Curie to win two Nobel Prizes and become the most acclaimed female scientist to date are explored in this accessible biography, which covers Curie's personal and professional lives. Illustrated with well-chosen archival photos." Horn Book Guide

Dahl, Roald

★ Dahl, Roald. **Boy** : tales of childhood. Farrar, Straus & Giroux 1984 160p il hardcover o.p. rpt $6.99

Grades: 4 5 6 7 8 9 **92**

1. Authors 2. Authors, English 3. Children's authors 4. Short story writers

ISBN 0-14-130305-0; 9780142413814 rpt

LC 84-48462

"In these memoirs, Dahl reminisces about growing up in a large Norwegian family living in Wales during the 1920s and 1930s. The text is illustrated with sketches, old photographs and excerpts of letters he wrote as a boy." SLJ

Dahl, Roald. **More** about Boy; Roald Dahl's tales from childhood. Farrar, Straus, and Giroux 2009 229p il $16.99

Grades: 5 6 7 8 **92**

1. Authors 2. Authors, English 3. Children's authors 4. Short story writers

ISBN 978-0-374-35055-0; 0-374-35055-8

LC 2009016118

First published 2008 in the United Kingdom

"Containing the entire text and artwork from Dahl's 1984 autobiography Boy, this reworked and expanded version also incorporates previously unpublished materials from the Roald Dahl Museum and Story Centre in England, as well as excerpts that have appeared in earlier books. . . . Dahl's revealing writing, open and full of wicked humor, is certain to endear the beloved writer . . . to a new generation." Publ Wkly

Dalai Lama XIV, 1935-

Kimmel, Elizabeth Cody. **Boy** on the lion throne; the childhood of the 14th Dalai Lama. with a foreword by His Holiness the Dalai Lama. Roaring Brook Press 2009 146p il map $18.95

Grades: 4 5 6 7 **92**

1. Buddhism 2. Tibet (China) 3. Buddhist leaders 4. Political leaders 5. Nobel laureates for peace

ISBN 978-1-59643-394-6; 1-59643-394-9

Follows the childhood of Lhamo Thondup, who was identified at the age of two as the fourteenth reincarnation of the Dalai Lama, describing the humble life he was born into and how his life changed after he was recognized

"Kimmel is reverent without being adulatory, and her explanation of the Dalai Lama's relationship with Maoist China is presented in simple, clear language. This is a strange and fascinating story told in an engaging style, and young readers will find lots to keep them turning the pages." Bull Cent Child Books

Includes bibliographical references

Dalí, Salvador, 1904-1989

McNeese, Tim. **Salvador** Dali; [by] Tim McNeese. Chelsea House Publishers 2006 122p il (Great Hispanic heritage) lib bdg $30

Grades: 7 8 9 10 **92**

1. Artists 2. Painters 3. Artists, Spanish

ISBN 0-7910-8837-5

LC 2005025998

A biography of the 20th century surrealist painter.

"McNeese does a wonderful job of describing [this man's life] and, more importantly, the times in which [he] lived. . . . [The book is] expertly researched." SLJ

Includes bibliographical references

Dandridge, Dorothy

Herringshaw, DeAnn. **Dorothy** Dandridge; singer & actress. ABDO Pub. Co. 2011 112p il (Essential lives) $23.95

Grades: 6 7 8 9 10 **92**

1. Actors 2. Singers 3. African American actors

ISBN 978-1-61714-779-1; 1-61714-779-6

LC 2010042150

"This volume profiles the life of . . . actress Dorothy Dandridge . . . Dandridge's life reads much like a screenplay. . . . Students will be captivated by Dandridge's guts and by the naked hypocrisy of the racisim that she faced even as a movie star." Booklist

Includes bibliographical references

Darwin, Charles, 1809-1882

★ Eldredge, Niles. **Charles** Darwin and the mystery of mysteries; by Niles Eldredge and Susan Pearson. Rb Flash Point 2010 135p il map lib bdg $19.99

Grades: 7 8 9 10 **92**

1. Naturalists 2. Travel writers 3. Writers on science 4. Beagle Expedition (1831-1836)

ISBN 978-1-59643-374-8; 1-59643-374-4

Follows Charles Darwin on his journey aboard the HMS Beagle and presents the thinking that led him to the theory of evolution and the writing of The origin of the species. Includes historical photographs and passages from Darwin's personal diary.

"Numerous quotations from Darwin's works and correspondence bring his voice to readers. . . . Eldredge and Pearson have done a fine job of summarizing both Darwin's life and work." SLJ

★ Heiligman, Deborah. **Charles** and Emma; the Darwins' leap of faith. Henry Holt and Company 2009 268p il $18.95

Grades: 7 8 9 10 11 12 **92**

1. Naturalists 2. Travel writers 3. Writers on science 4. Spouses of prominent persons

ISBN 978-0-8050-8721-5; 0-8050-8721-4

LC 2008-26091

National Book Award Finalist: Young People's Literature (2009)

"This rewarding biography of Charles Darwin investigates his marriage to his cousin Emma Wedgwood. . . . Embracing the paradoxes in her subjects' personalities, the author unfolds a sympathetic and illuminating account, bolstered by quotations from their personal writings as well as significant research into the historical context." Publ Wkly

Includes bibliographical references

★ Krull, Kathleen. **Charles** Darwin; illustrated by Boris Kulikov. Viking 2010 144p il (Giants of science) $15.99

Grades: 5 6 7 8 **92**

1. Evolution 2. Naturalists 3. Travel writers 4. Writers on science

ISBN 978-0-670-06335-2; 0-670-06335-5

LC 2010-07315

"Krull once again offers an illuminating, humanizing portrait of a famous scientist. . . . Krull . . . writes in easily paced, lively, conversational prose, knitting together interesting facts, anecdotes, and historical overviews into a fascinating whole. She offers clear definitions of not only Darwin's theories but also how his discoveries built on previous scientists' work. . . . Kulikov's whimsical ink drawings and well-culled list of resources round out this strong entry in the series." Booklist

Schanzer, Rosalyn. **What** Darwin saw; the journey that changed the world. National Geographic 2009 47p il map $17.95; lib bdg $26.90

Grades: 3 4 5 6 **92**

1. Evolution 2. Naturalists 3. Travel writers 4. Writers on science 5. Beagle Expedition (1831-1836)

ISBN 978-1-4263-0396-8; 1-4263-0396-3; 978-1-4263-0397-5 lib bdg; 1-4263-0397-1 lib bdg

LC 2008-39809

"Schanzer uses Darwin's own words, taken from his journals, books, and letters, in the speech balloons of her graphic depiction of the voyage of the Beagle. This is not a full biography, but begins with Darwin's acceptance of the offer to sail on the expedition and ends with the presentation of his theory of evolution in 1860. Bright, watercolor cartoons accurately portray landscapes and specimens while also creating a vivid sense of adventure." SLJ

Includes bibligraphical references

Darwin, Emma Wedgwood, 1808-1896

★ Heiligman, Deborah. **Charles** and Emma; the Darwins' leap of faith. Henry Holt and Company 2009 268p il $18.95

Grades: 7 8 9 10 11 12 **92**

1. Naturalists 2. Travel writers 3. Writers on science 4. Spouses of prominent persons

ISBN 978-0-8050-8721-5; 0-8050-8721-4

LC 2008-26091

National Book Award Finalist: Young People's Literature (2009)

"This rewarding biography of Charles Darwin investigates his marriage to his cousin Emma Wedgwood. . . . Embracing the paradoxes in her subjects' personalities, the author unfolds a sympathetic and illuminating account, bolstered by quotations from their personal writings as well as significant research into the historical context." Publ Wkly

Includes bibliographical references

Dave, fl. 1834-1864

Cheng, Andrea. **Etched** in clay; the life of Dave, enslaved potter and poet. Andrea Cheng ; with woodcuts by the author. Lee & Low Books 2012 144 p. (hardcover : alk. paper) $17.95

Grades: 4 5 6 **92**

1. Slaves 2. Potters 3. African American poets 4. African American potters 5. Slaves -- South Carolina

ISBN 160060451X; 9781600604515; 9781600608933

LC 2012027280

In this children's biography in verse, Caldecott Honor-winner Andrea Cheng looks at the "life of the enslaved potter Dave," who wrote poetry. "Records indicate Dave, who was born in the United States in 1801, was most likely purchased at a slave auction at age 17 by Harvey Drake, who, with his uncles, held the Pottersville Stoneware Manufactory in South Carolina. Dave took to the wheel within weeks and went on to become one of the most accomplished potters in the region." (Kirkus Reviews)

Davis, Benjamin O., Jr.

★ Earl, Sari. **Benjamin** O. Davis, Jr. Air Force general & Tuskegee Airmen leader. ABDO Pub. Co. 2010 111p il map (Military heroes) lib bdg $22.95

Grades: 7 8 9 **92**

1. Generals 2. Air force officers 3. United States -- Air Force

ISBN 978-1-60453-961-5; 1-60453-961-5

LC 2009-32339

Biography of Benjamin O. Davis Jr.

"The rush of literary adrenalin will hook readers immediately and keep them enthralled until the end. . . . Given the dynamic topic [and] . . . appealing layout . . . [this is] likely to attract reluctant readers. In addition, sources are plentiful and well documented." SLJ

Includes glossary and bibliographical references

Davis, Miles

★ Orr, Tamra. **Miles** Davis; by Tamra Orr. Mitchell Lane Publishers 2012 47 p. ill. (library) $29.95

Grades: 6 7 8 9 **92**

1. Jazz musicians -- United States

ISBN 1612282652; 9781612282657

LC 2012008632

This book by Tamra Orr is part of the American Jazz series and looks at Miles Davis. "Known to jazz lovers around the world as the Prince of Darkness, Miles Davis lived a roller-coaster life of highs and lows. . . . You can follow his lows of grappling with the power of drug and alcohol addiction and racial prejudice to his highs of achieving world fame and appreciation, plus becoming a husband, father, and grandfather." (Publisher's note)

Includes discography (pages 41-42), bibliographical references (pages 44-45), and index.

De la Renta, Oscar

Darraj, Susan Muaddi. **Oscar** de la Renta. Chelsea House 2010 116p il (The great Hispanic heritage) lib bdg $30

Grades: 6 7 8 9 **92**

1. Fashion designers

ISBN 978-1-60413-733-0; 1-60413-733-9

LC 2010009488

This "presents a warm, almost fawning account of the wildly successful fashion designer, who maintains a home in and close ties to his native Dominican Republic. . . . A selection of well-chosen images, a chronology, chapter notes, and [a] suggested reading [list] round out [this] engaging [title] in a sure-to-be-popular [book] for reports and personal interest." Booklist

Includes bibliographical references

Délano, Poli, 1936-

Délano, Poli. **When** I was a boy Neruda called me Policarpo; illustrated by Manuel Monroy. Groundwood Books/House of Anansi Press 2006 84p il $15.95

Grades: 5 6 7 8 **92**

1. Poets 2. Authors 3. Diplomats 4. Novelists 5. Poets, Chilean 6. Mexico 7. Memoirists 8. Short story writers 9. Nobel laureates for peace 10. Nobel laureates for literature 11. Biography, Individual

ISBN 0-88899-726-4

In this book, the author ¿offers seven vignettes, interspersed with six of Neruda's . . . poems and biographical information, to give middle-grade readers a sense of what it was like to grow up in the constant presence of a kindly, though spoiled and eccentric, celebrity. . . . Grades four to six.¿ (MultiCult Rev)

"Based on the author's childhood remembrances of when he and his diplomat parents lived with Tío Pablo [Neruda] in Mexico, these seven chapters reveal both the genius and the eccentricities of the Nobel Prize-winning Chilean poet. . . . The chapters are short, well written, and filled with interesting details that will open up a new and exotic world. . . . Monroy's pen-and-sepia-toned drawings are . . . at times humorous, at times dramatic, but always enticing." SLJ

Degas, Edgar, 1834-1917

Spence, David. **Degas**. New Forest Press 2010 48p il (Great artists and their world) lib bdg $32.80

Grades: 6 7 8 9 **92**

1. Artists 2. Painters 3. Artists, French

ISBN 978-1-84898-318-2; 1-84898-318-2

"Offers biographical information [of Edgar Degas] . . . interspersed with art history and criticism in an eye-catching format. . . . [Includes] a long introductory paragraph and four-to-six images with explanatory notes. . . . Spence . . . does a good job of explaining why art that might seem ordinary today was revolutionary at the time of its creation." SLJ

Includes glossary

Democritus

Macfarlane, Katherine. The **father** of the atom; Democritus and the nature of matter. Enslow Publishers 2010 112p il map (Great minds of ancient science and math) lib bdg $31.93

Grades: 5 6 7 8 **92**

1. Atoms 2. Matter 3. Mathematics 4. Philosophers 5. Writers on science

ISBN 978-0-7660-3410-5 lib bdg; 0-7660-3410-0 lib bdg

LC 2008-46265

This biography is a "solid [choice], as . . . [it provides] a good overview of the cultural and political landscape of the times, as well as pictures." SLJ

Includes glossary and bibliographical references

Diakité, Baba Wagué

A **gift** from childhood; memories of an African boyhood. Groundwood Books 2010 134p il $18.95

Grades: 5 6 7 8 **92**

1. Artists 2. Authors 3. Illustrators 4. Mali 5. Children's authors 6. Africa

ISBN 0-88899-931-3; 978-0-88899-931-3

This is a memoir about growing up in a small village in Mali. "Age ten and up." (N Y Times Book Rev)

"Diakite's . . . illustrated memoir focuses on his childhood in a small Malian village. . . . Interspersed with Diakite's recounting of his youth . . . are stories about his grandfather's brokering peaceful relations with the French, a blacksmith who stymies Death, and others. . . . Diakite's precise language and vibrant illustrations, created on earthenware tiles, form an engrossing story of community life. Studded with Malian proverbs, metaphors, and morals . . . it's a memoir alive with far more voices than just that of the author." Publ Wkly

Dickens, Charles, 1812-1870

★ Rosen, Michael, 1946- **Dickens**; his work and his world. illustrated by Robert Ingpen. Candlewick Press 2005 95p il $19.99

Grades: 5 6 7 8 **92**

1. Authors 2. Novelists 3. Authors, English 4. Biography, Individual

ISBN 0-7636-2752-6

LC 2004-61847

"The art adds to the richness of a volume designed and written with care." Booklist

★ Warren, Andrea. **Charles** Dickens and the street children of London. Houghton Mifflin Books for Children/Houghton Mifflin Harcourt 2011 144p il $18.99

Grades: 6 7 8 9 10 **92**

1. Authors 2. Novelists 3. Children in literature 4. Authors, English 5. London (England) 6. Poor -- Great Britain 7. Great Britain -- History -- 19th century

ISBN 978-0-547-39574-6; 0-547-39574-4

LC 2011003450

"This absorbing book introduces Dickens within the context of his times. . . . Chapters about his life and his novels alternate with related chapters describing the plight of the poor (especially children) in Victorian England (especially London). . . . Glimpses of his world are offered in reproductions of illustrations from Dickens' novels as well as period portraits and photos of people and places that appear throughout the book. . . . Warren writes in a clear, direct, vivid manner that brings it all to life." Booklist

Dickinson, Emily, 1830-1886

Goddu, Krystyna Poray. **Becoming** Emily; the life of Emily Dickinson. Krystyna Poray Goddu. Chicago Review Press 2019 192 p. illustrations $17.99

Grades: 5 6 7 8 **92**

1. Women poets -- Biography 2. American women poets -- Biography 3. Women poets, American -- 19th century -- Biography

ISBN 9780897330039

LC 2018024637

In this book, by Krystyna Poray Goddu, "young readers will learn how . . . [author Emily] Dickinson was a lively social being with a warm family life. Highly educated for a girl of her era, she actively engaged in both the academic and social aspects of the schools she attended until she was nearly eighteen. Her family and friends were important to her, and she was a prolific, thoughtful, and witty correspondent who shared many poems with her closest friends and relatives." (Publisher's note)

"Archival photographs enhance the telling. With select poems, revealing passages from letters, and a richly detailed narrative, this thorough study is sure to entice middle-grade readers to explore one of the 19th century's greatest poets." Kirkus

Includes bibliographical references and index

Dorsey, Jack

Smith, Chris. **Twitter**; Jack Dorsey, Biz Stone and Evan Williams. [by] Chris Smith and Marci McGrath. Morgan Reynolds Pub. 2011 112p il (Business leaders) $28.95

Grades: 7 8 9 10 11 12 **92**

1. Online social networks 2. Twitter, Inc. 3. Internet executives 4. Computer programmers 5. Computer software executives

ISBN 978-1-59935-179-7; 1-59935-179-X; 978-1-59935-216-9 e-book

LC 2011024699

This biography of the founders of Twitter "will grab YAs. . . . The design is browsable, with clear type and lots of color screens and informal photos of young people at work." Booklist

Includes bibliographical references

Douglass, Frederick, 1818-1895

★ Adler, David A. **Frederick** Douglass; a noble life. Holiday House 2010 138p il $18.95

Grades: 7 8 9 10 **92**

1. Slaves 2. Authors 3. Abolitionists 4. Memoirists 5. African Americans -- Biography

ISBN 978-0-8234-2056-8; 0-8234-2056-6

LC 2009-29970

A biography of Frederick Douglass, who was born into slavery in 1818 and raised on a Maryland plantation under brutal conditions and who grew up to become a famous orator, journalist, author, and adviser to U.S. presidents.

This is "a thoroughly researched, lucidly written biography. . . . Adler does an excellent job of exploring the atrocities and dehumanizing indignities . . . visited on those who lived in slavery." Booklist

Includes bibliographical references

★ Bolden, Tonya. **Facing** Frederick; the life of Frederick Douglass, a monumental American man. Tonya Bolden. Abrams Books for Young Readers 2017 vii, 200 p.p illustrations (some color) (hardcover with jacket : alk. paper) $19.99

Grades: 6 7 8 9 10 **92**

1. African American abolitionists -- Biography 2. Antislavery movements -- United States -- History -- 19th century 3. Antislavery movements -- United States 4. Abolitionists -- United States -- Biography

ISBN 9781683351177; 9781419725463

LC 2017009962

This biography, by Tonya Bolden, tells the life of "Frederick Douglass . . . [who] is best known for the telling of his own emancipation. . . . [It] captures the whole complicated, and at times perplexing, person that he was. Statesman, suffragist, writer, and newspaperman, this book focuses on Douglass the man rather than the historical icon." (Publisher's note)

"A spirited biography that fully honors its redoubtable subject." Kirkus

Includes bibliographical references and index

Cline-Ransome, Lesa. **Words** set me free; the story of young Frederick Douglass. Lesa Cline-Ransome ; illustrated by James E. Ransome. Simon & Schuster Books for Young Readers 2012 32 p. (hardback) $17.99

Grades: 6 7 8 **92**

1. Abolitionists 2. Slaves -- Emancipation 3. African Americans -- Biography 4. Slaves -- United States -- Biography 5. Abolitionists -- United States -- Biography 6. African American abolitionists -- Biography 7. Antislavery movements -- United States -- History -- 19th century

ISBN 9781416959038

LC 2011013323

Frederick Douglass "relates his early years, from first vague memories of his mother . . . through his childhood, with his service leased to the Auld family of Baltimore; to his first attempt to make an escape from Talbot County, Maryland. The narration is . . . focused on the way learning to read both inspired and enabled young Frederick to plan for a life of freedom in the North . . . This chapter in Douglass' story concludes with his forgery of a pass, written 'in a firm and steady hand,' which

would allow him to 'walk right out of Talbot County and into freedom up north.'" (Bulletin of the Center for Children's Books)
Includes bibliographical references and index

Esty, Amos. **Unbound** and unbroken: the story of Frederick Douglass. Morgan Reynolds Pub. 2010 143p il map (Civil rights leaders) lib bdg $28.95
Grades: 7 8 9 10 **92**
1. Slaves 2. Authors 3. Abolitionists 4. Memoirists 5. African Americans -- Biography
ISBN 978-1-59935-136-0; 1-59935-136-6
LC 2009-54287
Traces the life and historical impact of the noted abolitionist, detailing his birth into slavery and harsh upbringing, his subsequent escape, and his emergence as a leader.
"Multiple biographies have been written about Douglass; however, few capture the depth of his intellect as an orator and writer. Through interwoven quotes from his autobiography, speeches, and pictures, this story also serves as prime research material. Douglass's ingenious case for the Constitution and fifth of July speech make the biography accessible from cover to cover." Voice Youth Advocates
Includes bibliographical references

Du Bois, W. E. B. (William Edward Burghardt), 1868-1963
Bolden, Tonya. **W.E.B.** Du Bois; a twentieth-century life. Viking Children's Books 2008 224p il (Up close) $16.99
Grades: 7 8 9 10 **92**
1. Authors 2. Novelists 3. Historians 4. Editors 5. Essayists 6. Sociologists 7. Nonfiction writers 8. Civil rights activists 9. African Americans -- Biography 10. African Americans -- Civil rights
ISBN 978-0-670-06302-4; 0-670-06302-9
LC 2007-52380
"The author covers her subject's life, which spanned 95 years, from Reconstruction to the modern Civil Rights Movement. . . . This balanced, lively account records his many contributions as a teacher, speaker, Civil Rights activist, sociologist, writer, and cofounder of several organizations, including the NAACP, as well as his failings." SLJ
Includes bibliographical references

Whiting, Jim. **W.E.B.** Du Bois; civil rights activist, author, historian. Mason Crest Publishers 2010 64p il (Transcending race in America: biographies of biracial achievers) $22.95; pa $9.95
Grades: 5 6 7 8 **92**
1. Authors 2. Novelists 3. Historians 4. Editors 5. Essayists 6. Sociologists 7. Nonfiction writers 8. Civil rights activists 9. African Americans -- Biography 10. African Americans -- Civil rights
ISBN 978-1-4222-1618-7; 1-4222-1618-7; 978-1-4222-1632-3 pa; 1-4222-1632-2 pa
LC 2009022049
"The author openly discusses Du Bois' political and ideological struggles, which concluded with his move to Ghana and admittance into the Communist Party. . . . The book . . . provides solid information about Du Bois." Booklist
Includes glossary and bibliographical references

Dvorak, Antonín, 1841-1904
Horowitz, Joseph. **Dvorak** in America; in search of the New World. Cricket Bks. 2003 158p il $17.95
Grades: 7 8 9 10 **92**
1. Composers
ISBN 0-8126-2681-8
LC 2002-151456
An account of Antonin Dvorak's 1890s stay in America, where he took the essences of Indian drums, slave spirituals, and other musical forms and created from them a distinctly new music
"A welcome addition to music and biography collections." SLJ
Includes bibliographical references

Earhart, Amelia, 1898-1937
Brown, Jeremy K. **Amelia** Earhart. Chelsea House 2011 132p il lib bdg $35
Grades: 6 7 8 **92**
1. Air pilots 2. Missing persons 3. Women air pilots 4. Memoirists
ISBN 978-1-60413-910-5; 1-60413-910-2
This "supplies an evenhanded account of Earhart's personal life, her challenges as a woman in aviation, and her many achievements in flight. . . . Solid fare for the biography collection." Booklist

★ Fleming, Candace, 1962- **Amelia** lost: the life and disappearance of Amelia Earhart. Schwartz & Wade Books 2011 118p il map
Grades: 4 5 6 7 **92**
1. Air pilots 2. Missing persons 3. Women air pilots 4. Memoirists 5. Biography, Individual
ISBN 0-375-84198-9; 0-375-94598-9 lib bdg; 978-0-375-84198-9; 978-0-375-94598-4 lib bdg
LC 2010-05279
Fleming "offers a fresh look at this famous aviatrix. Employing dual narratives—straightforward biographical chapters alternating with a chilling recounting of Earhart's final flight and the search that followed—Fleming seeks to uncover the 'history of the hype,' pointing out numerous examples in which Earhart took an active role in mythologizing her own life. . . . Frequent sidebars, well-chosen maps, archival documents, and photos further clarify textual references without disturbing the overall narrative flow." Booklist

Tanaka, Shelley. **Amelia** Earhart; the legend of the lost aviator. by Shelley Tanaka; illustrated by David Craig. Abrams Books for Young Readers 2008 48p il map $18.95
Grades: 3 4 5 6 **92**
1. Air pilots 2. Missing persons 3. Women air pilots 4. Memoirists
ISBN 978-0-8109-7095-3; 0-8109-7095-3
LC 2007-39749
NCTE Orbis Pictus Award (2009)
This is an account of the life of aviator Amelia Earhart from her childhood up to the time she disappeared on a flight in 1937.
"This title is notable . . . for its smooth, powerful storytelling, ample gallery of well-chosen photographs, and nicely placed sidebar information on such topics as flight delays, navigation, and around-the-world flight records." Bull Cent Child Books
Includes bibliographical references

Earle, Sylvia A., 1935-
Reichard, Susan E. **Who** on earth is Sylvia Earle? undersea explorer of the ocean. Enslow Publishers 2009 112p il (Scientists saving the earth) lib bdg $31.93
Grades: 5 6 7 8 **92**
1. Botanists 2. Marine biology 3. Women scientists 4. Underwater

exploration 5. Divers 6. Marine biologists
ISBN 978-1-59845-118-4 lib bdg; 1-59845-118-9 lib bdg
LC 2008032014

"The writing is clear and informative. . . . Color photographs are relevant and of good quality." SLJ

Includes glossary and bibliographical references

Edison, Thomas A. (Thomas Alva), 1847-1931

Hardyman, Robyn. **Nikola** Tesla and Thomas Edison; Robyn Hardyman. Gareth Stevens Publishing 2014 48 p. illustrations (some color) $31.95

Grades: 4 5 6 **92**

1. Tesla, Nikola, 1856-1943
ISBN 1482414732; 9781482414738

This children's book by Robyn Hardyman on scientists Nikola Tesla and Thomas Edison is part of a series known for its "graphics and ability to make complex concepts accessible. The authors have . . . select[ed] key quotes from the scientists' writings that young readers can understand (provided in sidebars titled 'In Their Own Words')." (School Library Journal)

"The dual biography is a particularly ingenious feature. Readers learn that Alfred Russel Wallace and Darwin, rivals as well as supporters, shared much of the same information, making similar discoveries. Reading their parallel stories will let children see how different people solve the same problems. Original takes on science biographies." SLJ

Krieg, Katherine. **Thomas** Edison; world-changing inventor. by Katherine Krieg. Core Library, an imprint of Abdo Publishing 2015 48 p. illustrations (some color) (hbk) $32.79

Grades: 4 5 6 **92**

1. Inventors 2. Inventors -- United States -- Biography 3. Businessmen -- United States -- Biography 4. Electrical engineers -- United States -- Biography
ISBN 1624033784; 9781624033780
LC 2014932578

This children's book by Katherine Krieg on Thomas Edison "chronicles the life and career of the genius inventor, from his time inventing for Western Union to his creation of the lightbulb and phonograph." (Publisher's note)

"Students will learn about the different accomplishments of each scientist while joining them on the often tumultuous journey to success. A staple for libraries." SLJ

Includes bibliographical references (page 47) and index

Woodside, Martin. **Thomas** A. Edison; the man who lit up the world. [by] Martin Woodside. Sterling 2007 124p (Sterling biographies) lib bdg $12.95; pa $5.95

Grades: 5 6 7 8 **92**

1. Inventors
ISBN 978-1-4027-4955-1 lib bdg; 1-4027-4955-4 lib bdg; 978-1-4027-3229-4 pa; 1-4027-3229-5 pa
LC 2007003509

"Woodside presents the life, struggles, failures, and successes of a man whose motto was 'the most important way to succeed is always to try one more time.' [The book provides] clear, concise information in an easy-to-read format with captioned photographs and illustrations on most pages." SLJ

Includes glossary and bibliographical references

Einstein, Albert, 1879-1955

Anderson, Jennifer Joline. **Albert** Einstein; Revolutionary Physicist. Jennifer Joline Anderson. Core Library 2014 48 pp. illustrations (Great Minds of Science) $32.79

Grades: 4 5 6 **92**

1. Physics
ISBN 1629684791; 9781629684796; 9781624033797; 1624033792

This children's book by Jennifer Joline Anderson, part of the Great Minds of Science series, chronicles the life and career of the genius physicist [Albert Einstein], from his youth in Germany to his groundbreaking work on relativity, gravity, space, and time." (Publisher's note)

★ Delano, Marfe Ferguson. **Genius**; a photobiography of Albert Einstein. National Geographic 2005 64p il $17.95; lib bdg $27.90; pa $7.95

Grades: 5 6 7 8 **92**

1. Physicists 2. Nobel laureates for physics
ISBN 0-7922-9544-7; 0-7922-9545-5 lib bdg; 1-4263-0294-0 pa
LC 2004-15001

A biography of the German American physicist.

This "combines a solid text with a particularly attractive format. . . . Delano offers just enough information about Einstein's theories to give a sense of his work. . . . Oversize and filled with well-selected photographs, the book is very handsome." Booklist

★ Krull, Kathleen. **Albert** Einstein; illustrated by Boris Kulikov. Viking 2009 141p il (Giants of science) $15.99

Grades: 5 6 7 8 **92**

1. Physicists 2. Nobel laureates for physics
ISBN 978-0-670-06332-1; 0-670-06332-0
LC 2009-16037

"Krull delivers a splendidly humane biography of that gold standard of brilliance, Albert Einstein. . . . Drawing extensively on Einstein's writings, she presents a fully rounded portrait of a man whose genius combined with a bad temper and arrogance, to the detriment of his own professional advancement, not to mention his relationships with women and his children. Using concrete examples, the author brings such mind-bending notions as his General Theory of Relativity within the grasp of child readers." Kirkus

Eisenhower, Dwight D. (Dwight David), 1890-1969

Mara, Wil. **Dwight** Eisenhower. Marshall Cavendish Benchmark 2011 112p il (Presidents and their times) lib bdg $34.21

Grades: 5 6 7 8 **92**

1. Generals 2. Presidents 3. College presidents 4. Presidents -- United States
ISBN 978-0-7614-4812-9; 0-7614-4812-8
LC 2009033042

"The size makes it ideal for that one-hundred page biography assignment; the readability makes the titles accessible to reluctant readers in high school; the succinct, well-presented information makes the volumes fitting for initial research at both the middle and high school level." Voice Youth Advocates

Includes glossary and bibliographical references

Eisner, Will, 1917-2005

Johns, Geoff, 1973- **Will** Eisner; [by] Robert Greenberger. Rosen Pub. Group 2005 112p il (Library of graphic novelists) lib bdg $31.95

Grades: 6 7 8 9 **92**

1. Authors 2. Cartoonists 3. Cartoons and caricatures 4. Comic book writers 5. Publishing executives

ISBN 1-4042-0286-2

LC 2004-16656

This "book focuses on the artist's work rather than on his life. It sketches in major events, . . . but dwells heavily on the characters he created and his influence on the graphic-novel format. This is a well-organized and easy-to-read volume." SLJ

Includes bibliographical references

Eleanor, of Aquitaine, Queen, consort of Henry II, King of England, 1122?-1204

★ Kramer, Ann. **Eleanor** of Aquitaine; the queen who rode off to battle. National Geographic 2006 64p il map (World history biographies) $17.95; lib bdg $27.90

Grades: 5 6 7 8 **92**

1. Queens 2. France -- History -- 0-1328 3. Great Britain -- History -- 1154-1399, Plantagenets

ISBN 0-7922-5895-9; 0-7922-5896-7 lib bdg

An illustrated biography of the medieval queen who traveled to the Crusades with her first husband King Louis VII of France and later married King Henry II of England.

Includes glossary and bibliographical references

Elizabeth I, Queen of England, 1533-1603

★ Adams, Simon. **Elizabeth** I; the outcast who became England's queen. [by] Simon Adams. National Geographic 2005 64p il map (World history biographies) $17.95; lib bdg $27.90

Grades: 4 5 6 7 **92**

1. Queens 2. Great Britain -- Kings and rulers 3. Great Britain -- History -- 1485-1603, Tudors

ISBN 0-7922-3649-1; 0-7922-3654-8 lib bdg

LC 2005001359

An illustrated introduction to the life and times of the 16th century queen of England

"Accomplishments and hardships are clearly explained with supporting quotes and facts. . . . Beautifully illustrated and visually appealing." SLJ

Includes glossary and bibliographical references

Ellington, Duke, 1899-1974

Stein, Stephanie. **Duke** Ellington; his life in jazz with 21 activities. [by] Stephanie Stein Crease. Chicago Review Press 2009 148p il (For kids) pa $16.95

Grades: 5 6 7 8 **92**

1. Composers 2. Jazz musicians 3. Band leaders

ISBN 978-1-55652-724-1; 1-55652-724-1

LC 2008-23742

"This large-format book combines an illustrated biography of Duke Ellington with activities designed to offer insights into Ellington s era and his music. An informative account in an attractive...format." Booklist

Includes bibliographical references, discography, and filmography

Emerson, Ralph Waldo, 1803-1882

Caravantes, Peggy. **Self** -reliance: the story of Ralph Waldo Emerson. Morgan Reynolds Pub. 2010 143p il map (World writers) lib bdg $28.95

Grades: 7 8 9 10 **92**

1. Poets 2. Authors 3. Philosophers 4. Essayists 5. Authors, American

ISBN 978-1-59935-124-7; 1-59935-124-2

LC 2010-8143

Presents the life and career of the eighteenth century New England essayist, poet, and lecturer who advocated a philosophy of self-reliance and individualism and was an important figure in the American Transcendental Movement.

This volume treats "young adult readers with respect and . . . [works] to ease them into scholarly research and writing in an engaging manner." Voice Youth Advocates

Includes bibliographical references

Engle, Margarita

★ Engle, Margarita, 1951. **Enchanted** air; a Cold War memoir. Margarita Engle. Atheneum Books for Young Readers 2015 208 p. illustrations (hardcover) $17.99

Grades: 6 7 8 9 10 **92**

1. Cuban Americans 2. Cuban Americans -- Biography 3. Women authors, American -- 20th century -- Biography

ISBN 9781481435222; 9781481435239

LC 2014017408

YALSA Award for Excellence in Nonfiction for Young Adults: Shortlist (2016)

Pura Belpre Author Award (2016)

This book is a memoir in poetry by Margarita Engle. "She narrates growing up in Los Angeles in the 1950s and early '60s torn by her love of two countries: the United States, where she was born and raised, and Cuba, where her mother was from and where she spent vacations visiting family. Woven into the fabric of her childhood is the anxiety of deteriorating relations between the two countries as the Cuban revolution takes place, affecting both her family and the two countries at large." (Kirkus Reviews)

"A deeply personal memoir-in-verse filled with Engle's trademark intricately woven lyricism. . . . Engle captures the heart of a quiet, young girl torn between two cultures." SLJ

Followed by Soaring earth (2019)

Eratosthenes, 3rd cent. B.C.

Gow, Mary. **Measuring** the Earth; Eratosthenes and his celestial geometry. Enslow 2010 128p il (Great minds of ancient science and math) lib bdg $31.93

Grades: 5 6 7 8 **92**

1. Astronomers 2. Mathematicians 3. Geographers 4. Writers on science

ISBN 978-0-7660-3120-3 lib bdg; 0-7660-3120-9 lib bdg

LC 2008-38523

This biography is a "solid [choice], as . . . [it provides] a good overview of the cultural and political landscape of the times, as well as pictures." SLJ

Includes glossary and bibliographical references

Ericsson, Aprille, 1963-

Waxman, Laura Hamilton. **Aerospace** engineer Aprille Ericsson; by Laura Hamilton Waxman. Lerner Publications 2015 32 p. color illustrations (STEM trailblazer bios) (lib. bdg. : alk. paper) $26.60

Grades: 4 5 6 7 **92**

1. Women engineers 2. Aerospace engineers -- United States -- Biography 3. African American women aerospace engineers --

United States -- Biography
ISBN 1467757934; 9781467757935; 9781467761185
LC 2014013767

In this biography by Laura Hamilton Waxman, readers learn how "Aprille Ericsson's passion for science has helped her pave the way for future engineers. Ericsson was one of the few girls in her middle school who loved math and science. Years later, she became the first woman to receive a PhD in mechanical engineering from Howard University. At NASA, she's helped build spacecraft that can map the moon, monitor climate change, or even bring soil and rocks back from Mars." (Publisher's note)

"Highly recommended, especially where current biographies, particularly of those involved in STEM careers, are needed and requested; strong supplemental reading for science classes, too." SLJ

Includes bibliographical references and index

Euclid

Hightower, Paul. The **father** of geometry: Euclid and his 3D world. Enslow Publishers 2010 112p il (Great minds of ancient science and math) lib bdg $31.93

Grades: 6 7 8 9 **92**

1. Geometry 2. Mathematicians 3. Writers on science
ISBN 978-0-7660-3409-9 lib bdg; 0-7660-3409-7 lib bdg
LC 2009-23814

"Describes the life of another fourth-century B.C.E. man who would ultimately become known as the 'father of geometry.' He was not famous like the philosophers of his time, but his book The Elements totally revised what was known of mathematics at the time. . . . Includes simple, straightforward text with nice illustrations and appendixes of suggested activities, a supplemental chronology, chapter notes, and glossary." Voice Youth Advocates

Includes glossary and bibliographical references

Farmer, Paul, 1959-

★ Kidder, Tracy. **Mountains** beyond mountains; the quest of Dr. Paul Farmer, a man who would cure the world. by Tracy Kidder ; adapted for young people by Michael French. Delacorte Press 2013 288 p. hardcover o.p. (hardcover trade) $16.99

Grades: 7 8 9 10 11 12 Adult **92**

1. Physicians 2. Access to health care 3. Human rights 4. Right to health 5. Poor -- Medical care 6. Physicians -- Biography 7. Missionaries, Medical -- Biography
ISBN 0385743181; 9780307980885; 9780375990991; 9780385743181
LC 2012024905

This book is a study of Paul Farmer, an American doctor who opened a healthcare center for the poor in Haiti. "By Farmer's decree, no patient can be turned away. But medical aid alone is not enough. He also emphasizes the need to eliminate problems that contribute to illness: dirty water, inadequate nutrition, poor sanitation, illiteracy. . . . Encouraged by the success of his clinic, Farmer wants to replicate it as 'a laboratory for the world.'" (Christian Science Monitor)

This is a "portrait of Paul Farmer (MacArthur 'genius' grant, 1993), a driven, dedicated, rigidly idealistic doctor who commutes between Harvard and Haiti, where he works . . . to relieve the suffering of some of the poorest people on earth." N Y Times Book Rev

Includes bibliographical references

Ferrera, America, 1984-

Abrams, Dennis. **America** Ferrera. Chelsea House Publishers 2010 107p il (The great Hispanic heritage) lib bdg $30

Grades: 6 7 8 9 **92**

1. Actors
ISBN 978-1-60413-967-9; 1-60413-967-6
LC 2010009481

A biography of the actress best known for her roles in television's Ugly Betty and in films such as Real Women Have Curves and The Sisterhood of the Traveling Pants.

Fey, Tina, 1970-

Friedman, Lauri S. **Tina** Fey. Lucent Books 2010 96p il (People in the news) $33.45

Grades: 7 8 9 10 **92**

1. Actors 2. Comedians 3. Screenwriters 4. Television scriptwriters
ISBN 978-1-4205-0238-1; 1-4205-0238-7
LC 2009039362

A biography of writer, producer and Saturday Night Live funnygirl Tina Fey.

"With color photos of the actress at work throughout, this . . . does an excellent job of contexualizing Fey's comedy in the stream of current events. . . . This offers plenty of insight and inspiration for budding comedians, actors, and writers as well as researchers." Booklist

Includes bibliographical references

Feynman, Richard Phillips, 1918-1988

★ Henderson, Harry. **Richard** Feynman; quarks, bombs, and bongos. Chelsea House 2010 138p il (Makers of modern science) $35

Grades: 7 8 9 10 **92**

1. Authors 2. Physicists 3. Writers on science 4. Nobel laureates for physics
ISBN 978-0-8160-6176-1; 0-8160-6176-9

A biography of physicist Richard Feyman.

"The mark of a good biography is when it makes people you may never have heard of, in fields you might not be interested in, fascinating. [This book] does this with [a] well-chosen [subject], engaging writing, plenty of sidebars that take the text in new directions, and perhaps most importantly, the determination to present a fully-rounded person, not just a scientist." Booklist

Filipovic, Zlata

Filipovic, Zlata. **Zlata's** diary; a child's life in Sarajevo. with an introduction by Janine Di Giovanni; translated with notes by Christina Pribichevich-Zoric. Penguin Books 2006 195p il pa $13

Grades: 6 7 8 9 **92**

1. Children 2. Diarists 3. Sarajevo (Bosnia and Hercegovina)
ISBN 0-14-303687-4

A reissue with a new preface of the title first published 1994 by Viking

"Filipovic's diary personalizes the tragedy in war-torn Sarajevo." Booklist

Fitzgerald, Ella

★ Stone, Tanya Lee. **Ella** Fitzgerald. Viking 2008 203p il (Up close) $16.99

Grades: 7 8 9 10 **92**

1. Singers 2. African American singers 3. Pop musicians 4. African American women -- Biography
ISBN 978-0-670-06149-5; 0-670-06149-2
LC 2007-23117

This is a "strong biography [of the African American singer]. . . . Stone's smooth, straightforward narrative draws from authoritative sources. . . . The abundant quotes from Fitzgerald and her musician peers greatly develop the narrative." Booklist

Includes bibliographical references

Fleischman, Sid, 1920-2010

★ Fleischman, Sid. The **abracadabra** kid; a writer's life. Greenwillow Bks. 1996 198p il hardcover o.p. $16.99

Grades: 5 6 7 8 **92**

1. Authors 2. Magicians 3. Magazine editors 4. Authors, American 5. Children's authors 6. Young adult authors

ISBN 0-688-14859-X; 0-688-15855-2 pa

LC 95-47382

This autobiography, "turns real life into a story complete with cliff-hangers. And it's a classic boy's story, from card tricks and traveling magic shows to World War II naval experiences and screen-writing gigs for John Wayne movies. En route, we learn how Fleischman learned the craft of writing." Bull Cent Child Books

Includes bibliographical references

Freedman, Jeri. **Sid** Fleischman; [by] Jeri Freedman. Rosen Pub. Group 2004 112p (Library of author biographies) lib bdg $31.95

Grades: 5 6 7 8 **92**

1. Authors 2. Magicians 3. Authorship 4. Magazine editors 5. Authors, American 6. Children's authors 7. Young adult authors

ISBN 0-8239-4019-5

LC 2003-5203

Discusses the life and work of this popular author, including his writing process and methods, inspirations, a critical discussion of his books, biographical timeline, and awards

"Libraries looking to expand their biography section will be well served by [this] informative [title]." SLJ

Includes bibliographical references

Ford, Henry, 1863-1947

Mitchell, Don. **Driven**; a photobiography of Henry Ford. foreword by Lee Iacocca. National Geographic 2010 64p il map $18.95; lib bdg $27.90

Grades: 5 6 7 8 **92**

1. Businessmen 2. Philanthropists 3. Automobile industry 4. Automobile executives

ISBN 978-1-4263-0155-1; 1-4263-0155-3; 978-1-4263-0156-8 lib bdg; 1-4263-0156-1 lib bdg

LC 2009-07136

"Mitchell introduces readers to the founder of the auto company. . . . Thoughts, feelings, and quotes abound, and they are well sourced. . . . The writing is clear, and the organization is chronological. . . . Driven combines fine photography and an inviting text to depict Ford's life and his impact on the world." SLJ

Includes bibliographical references

Fossey, Dian

Doak, Robin S. **Dian** Fossey; friend to Africa's gorillas. Robin S. Doak. Heinemann Library 2015 48 p. illustrations; color maps (hardcover) $32.65

Grades: 5 6 7 8 **92**

1. Gorillas 2. Conservationists 3. Gorilla -- Rwanda 4. Primatologists -- United States -- Biography 5. Women primatologists -- United States -- Biography

ISBN 1484604687; 1484604733; 9781484604687; 9781484604731

LC 2013040521

This book "takes an engaging look at the work of ground-breaking conservationist Dian Fossey and her work with mountain gorillas. It covers Fossey's inspiration, her methods, findings, and the impact of her work in Africa." (Publisher's note)

"Students will appreciate her dedication—2000 hours of observing gorillas. The graphics present a time line of primate development and maps that are as excellent and informative as the rest of this must-have series." SLJ

Includes bibliographical references (pages 46-47) and index

Kushner, Jill Menkes. **Who** on earth is Dian Fossey? defender of the mountain gorillas. Enslow Publishers 2009 112p il (Scientists saving the earth) lib bdg $31.93

Grades: 5 6 7 8 **92**

1. Authors 2. Gorillas 3. Women scientists 4. Murder victims 5. Primatologists 6. Writers on science

ISBN 1-59845-117-0 lib bdg; 978-1-59845-117-7 lib bdg

LC 2008029376

"The book is filled with factual information, yet is written in a manner that makes both Fossey and her gorillas come to life for the reader." Sci Books Films

Includes glossary and bibliographical references

France, Diane L.

★ Hopping, Lorraine Jean. **Bone** detective; the story of forensic anthropologist Diane France. Franklin Watts 2005 118p il (Women's adventures in science) lib bdg $31.50

Grades: 7 8 9 10 **92**

1. Anthropologists 2. Women scientists 3. Forensic anthropology 4. Forensic scientists 5. Forensic sciences 6. Biography, Individual

ISBN 0-531-16776-3

LC 2005-0784

This book by Lorraine Jean Hopping is part of the Women's Adventures in Science series. It presents a biography of forensic anthropologist Diane France. "The book describes her marriages and divorce, a battle with cancer, experiences with sexism on the job, working at the World Trade Center site, and how one must learn to put personal feelings 'in a box' when working on forensic cases." (SB&F: Your Guide to Science Resources for All Ages)

This "introduces the life and work of a contemporary forensic anthropologist, from her rural childhood to her work identifying the victims of the 9/11 tragedies. . . . The extensive detail gives readers a vivid sense of the daily work of a 'bone detective,' and clear explanations of the science will intrigue and inspire readers." Booklist

Includes glossary and bibliographical references

Frank, Anne, 1929-1945

★ Frank, Anne. The **diary** of a young girl: the definitive edition; edited by Otto H. Frank and Mirjam Pressler; translated by Susan Massotty. Bantam 1997 340p $29.95; pa $7.99

Grades: 5 6 7 8 9 10 11 12 Adult **92**

1. Children 2. Diarists 3. Holocaust victims 4. Jews -- Netherlands 5. Holocaust, 1933-1945 6. World War, 1939-1945 -- Jews 7. Netherlands -- History -- 1940-1945, German occupation

ISBN 0-385-47378-8; 9780553577129

LC 94-41379

"This new translation of Frank's famous diary includes material about her emerging sexuality and her relationship with her mother that was originally excised by Frank's father, the only family member to survive the Holocaust." Libr J

★ Metselaar, Menno. **Anne** Frank: her life in words and pictures; from the archives of The Anne Frank House. [by] Menno Metselaar and Ruud van der Rol; translated by Arnold J. Pomerans. Roaring Brook Press 2009 215p il map pa $12.99
Grades: 5 6 7 8 **92**

1. Children 2. Diarists 3. Holocaust victims 4. Jews -- Netherlands 5. Holocaust, 1933-1945 6. World War, 1939-1945 -- Jews 7. Netherlands -- History -- 1940-1945, German occupation
ISBN 978-1-59643-546-9; 1-59643-546-1; 978-1-59643-547-6 pa; 1-59643-547-X pa

First published 2004 in the Netherlands with title: The story of Anne Frank

Boston Globe-Horn Book Award honor book: Nonfiction (2010)

"Beginning with a single photograph of the cover of Anne Frank's diary and the quote, 'One of my nicest presents,' this small, beautifully formatted book is accessible, compelling, and richly pictorial. . . . The book immediately immerses readers in the girl's life via a series of family photographs, many previously unpublished. Divided chronologically, the accompanying text is enhanced by diary entries, resulting in a historically succinct yet descriptive presentation. . . . Even for those collections where Anne Frank is well represented, this is a moving and valuable book." SLJ

Müller, Melissa, 1967- **Anne** Frank; the biography. by Melissa Muller ; translated by Rita and Robert Kimber. 2nd U.S. ed. Metropolitan Books/Henry Holt and Company 2013 480 p. hardcover o.p. (hardcover) $35
Grades: 7 8 9 10 11 12 Adult **92**

1. Children 2. Amsterdam (Netherlands) -- Biography 3. Jewish children in the Holocaust -- Biography 4. Jews -- Netherlands -- Amsterdam -- Biography 5. Holocaust, Jewish (1939-1945) -- Netherlands -- Amsterdam -- Biography
ISBN 0805087311; 9780805087314

LC 2013000297

This biography of Anne Frank "was originally published in 1998, but this expanded edition takes into account diary entries that had previously been redacted by Anne's father [Otto], as well as recently discovered letters from Otto to relatives in the United States and unpublished documents provided to [Melissa] Müller during interviews with those who knew Anne and her family." (Publishers Weekly)

"Müller includes a family tree; a family history; and considerable insight into the character, personality, and quality of life of Anne's parents, relatives, and friends. Interviews with many of these surviving people give a clearer idea of the situation and Anne's reactions to it." SLJ

Franklin, Benjamin, 1706-1790

★ Adler, David A. **B.** Franklin, printer. Holiday House 2001 126p il lib bdg $19.95
Grades: 4 5 6 7 **92**

1. Authors 2. Diplomats 3. Inventors 4. Statesmen 5. Scientists 6. Writers on science 7. Members of Congress 8. Statesmen -- United States
ISBN 0-8234-1675-5

LC 2001-24535

This "surveys Benjamin Franklin's life as a printer, a scientist, an inventor, a writer, and a statesman. . . . Throughout the book, details, anecdotes, and quotations bring the man's portrait into clearer focus, while period illustrations . . . help readers envision the background of his times." Booklist

Includes bibliographical references

★ Dash, Joan. A **dangerous** engine; Benjamin Franklin, from scientist to diplomat. pictures by Dusan Petricic. Frances Foster Books 2006 246p il $17
Grades: 7 8 9 10 **92**

1. Authors 2. Diplomats 3. Inventors 4. Statesmen 5. Scientists 6. Writers on science 7. Members of Congress 8. Statesmen -- United States
ISBN 0-374-30669-9

LC 2004-63204

"Franklin's long, productive, and interesting life is vividly recounted in a lively manner. Familiar aspects are covered, from his days as a printer in Philadelphia to his diplomatic service and his role in the development of the fledgling United States democracy. What may be new to some readers is Franklin's dedication to, and life-long love of, science and invention. . . . Witty pen-and-ink illustrations appear throughout." SLJ

★ Fleming, Candace. **Ben** Franklin's almanac; being a true account of the good gentleman's life. Atheneum Bks. for Young Readers 2003 120p il $19.95
Grades: 5 6 7 8 **92**

1. Authors 2. Diplomats 3. Inventors 4. Statesmen 5. Scientists 6. Writers on science 7. Members of Congress 8. Statesmen -- United States
ISBN 0-689-83549-3

LC 2002-6136

Brings together eighteenth century etchings, artifacts, and quotations to create the effect of a scrapbook of the life of Benjamin Franklin

"An authoritative work of depth, humor, and interest, presenting Franklin in all his complexity, ranging from the heroic to the vulgar, the saintly to the callous." SLJ

★ Freedman, Russell, 1929-2018. **Becoming** Ben Franklin; how a candle-maker's son helped light the flame of liberty. Russell Freedman. 1st ed. Holiday House 2013 86 p. col. ill. (hardcover) $24.95
Grades: 5 6 7 8 **92**

1. Franklin, Benjamin, 1706-1790 2. Founding Fathers of the United States 3. Printers -- United States -- Biography 4. Inventors -- United States -- Biography 5. Statesmen -- United States -- Biography 6. Scientists -- United States -- Biography
ISBN 0823423743; 9780823423743

LC 2012002971

This book is a biography of Ben Franklin. Russell Freedman "chose episodes that reflect how the young man, disgruntled with being his brother's apprentice, made a life for himself . . . . By describing the obstacles Franklin overcame in establishing his print shop in Philadelphia, Freedman delineates a . . . path between his subject's early ambition and his ease with people to his success in business and then to his later roles as a diplomat, revolutionary, and public servant." (School Library Journal)

Includes bibliographical references (p. 78-82) and index.

Krull, Kathleen. **Benjamin** Franklin; by Kathleen Krull ; illustrated by Boris Kulikov. Viking 2013 121 p. (Giants of science) (hardcover) $15.99
Grades: 5 6 7 8 **92**

1. Inventors 2. Scientists 3. Franklin, Benjamin, 1706-1790 4. Inventors -- United States -- Biography 5. Scientists -- United States -- Biography
ISBN 0670012874; 9780670012879

LC 2013018404

This book, by Kathleen Krull, part of the Giants of Science series, "explains the many ways that Franklin was the American manifestation of the European Enlightenment, putting his discoveries in clear historical context. Known as 'natural philosophers' in the eighteenth century, scientists like Franklin specialized in the kind of theoretical thinking that could result in inventions to make life better, from lightning rods to efficient heating stoves." (Booklist)

"The majority of this helpful book deals with Franklin's innovative scientific processes and his reasoning behind such inventions as the Franklin stove and the lightning rod; he coined words (still in use today) with definitions specific to the field, such as positive, negative, and charge. Kulikov's occasional black-and-white illustrations add sly humor to the account." (Horn Book)

Includes bibliographical references and index

Miller, Brandon Marie. **Benjamin** Franklin, American genius; his life and ideas, with 21 activities. Chicago Review Press 2009 125p il pa $16.95

Grades: 4 5 6 7 **92**

1. Authors 2. Diplomats 3. Inventors 4. Statesmen 5. Scientists 6. Writers on science 7. Members of Congress

ISBN 978-1-55652-757-9 pa; 1-55652-757-8 pa

LC 2009012456

"Miller does an excellent job of presenting a synopsis of Franklin's life in a highly readable manner. . . . Imbedded in each chapter are asides that further elaborate on Franklin's life and times and activities that coordinate with the text or the historical facts presented. The directions are easy to follow and enhance the overall presentation, especially in terms of classroom connections. Illustrations accompany each project and reproductions of primary documents, renderings, and paintings provide added value." SLJ

Includes glossary and bibliographical references

Franklin, Rosalind, 1920-1958

Polcovar, Jane. **Rosalind** Franklin and the structure of life. Morgan Reynolds 2006 144p il lib bdg $26.95

Grades: 7 8 9 10 **92**

1. DNA 2. Chemists 3. Biologists 4. Women scientists 5. Geochemists

ISBN 978-1-59935-022-6; 1-59935-022-X

LC 2006-16864

A biography of the scientist whose unpublished research led to the discovery of the structure of DNA

"Polcovar writes a rattling good story on two fronts: a woman becoming a scientist in an age when that was still unusual and the complex dynamics of personalities in a field sometimes thought of as impersonal." Booklist

Includes bibliographical references

Friedman, Cory

Patterson, James. **Med** head; my knock-down, drag-out, drugged-up battle with my brain. as told by James Patterson & Hal Friedman. Little Brown & Co. 2010 302p il pa $8.99

Grades: 6 7 8 9 10 **92**

1. Mentally ill 2. Tourette syndrome 3. Obsessive-compulsive disorder

ISBN 978-0-316-076173 pa; 0-316-07617-1 pa

The story of Cory Friedman and his family's decades-long struggle to determine the cause of Cory's neurological disease.

"Based on detailed notes on medications, physician appointments, and school visits, this is a page-turning examination of what could have been a wasted, despairing life. . . . While nonfiction resources can provide the facts on mental disorders, this excellent biography puts them into a context that promotes compassion. " Voice Youth Advocates

Friedman, Milton, 1912-2006

Crain, Cynthia D. **Milton** Friedman; by Cynthia D. Crain and Dwight R. Lee. Morgan Reynolds Pub. 2009 144p il (Profiles in economics) lib bdg $28.95

Grades: 8 9 10 11 12 **92**

1. Economists 2. College teachers 3. Nobel laureates for economic sciences

ISBN 978-1-59935-108-7 lib bdg; 1-59935-108-0 lib bdg

LC 2009-169

Biography of the economist Milton Friedman

"Relationships, education, early influences, and family life are all described . . . [and] economic theory is closely tied to cultural and political events. . . . The writing is straightforward, the . . . [author] assume[s] a certain level of knowledge about world events." SLJ

Includes bibliographical references

Fritz, Jean

★ Fritz, Jean. **Homesick** : my own story; illustrated with drawings by Margot Tomes and photographs. Putnam 1982 163p il $16.99; pa $5.99

Grades: 5 6 7 8 **92**

1. Authors 2. Women authors 3. China 4. Children's authors

ISBN 0-399-20933-6; 0-698-11782-4 pa

LC 82-7646

Companion volume to China homecoming

A Newbery Medal honor book, 1983

"The descriptions of places and the times are vivid in a book that brings to the reader, with sharp clarity and candor, the yearnings and fears and ambivalent loyalties of a young girl." Bull Cent Child Books

Frost, Robert, 1874-1963

★ Caravantes, Peggy. **Deep** woods; the story of Robert Frost. Morgan Reynolds 2006 176p il (World writers) lib bdg $27.95

Grades: 7 8 9 10 **92**

1. Poets 2. Authors 3. Poets, American

ISBN 978-1-931798-92-1; 1-931798-92-3

LC 2005037514

This "introduces poet Robert Frost. . . . Though focused on the man, Caravantes' presentation includes a few short selections from Frost's verse and, in sidebars, a bit of information about poetic forms. . . . Well organized and clearly written, the book offers a very readable account of Frost's often troubled life as an individual, a family man, a poet, and a public figure." Booklist

Includes bibliographical references

Wooten, Sara McIntosh. **Robert** Frost; the life of America's poet. Enslow Publishers 2006 128p (People to know today) lib bdg $31.93

Grades: 6 7 8 9 **92**

1. Poets 2. Authors 3. Poets, American

ISBN 0-7660-2627-2 lib bdg; 978-0-7660-2627-8 lib bdg

LC 2005034882

"In this insightful biography, Wooten recounts Frost's difficult life from his childhood with an abusive, alcoholic father, through his many financial challenges as he tried to establish a career, to his constant struggle with shyness and depression. . . . Her book is thoroughly researched." SLJ

Includes bibliographical references

Fry, Varian, 1907-1967

★ McClafferty, Carla Killough. **In** defiance of Hitler; the secret mission of Varian Fry. Farrar, Straus & Giroux 2008 196p il $19.95

Grades: 7 8 9 10 11 12 **92**

1. Journalists 2. Editors 3. Classicists 4. Humanitarians 5. Holocaust, 1933-1945 6. World War, 1939-1945 -- France 7. World War, 1939-1945 -- Jews -- Rescue

ISBN 978-0-374-38204-9; 0-374-38204-2

LC 2007-33271

"This stirring account of a young New York City journalist who secretly helped more than 2,000 refugees escape Nazi-occupied France blends exciting adventure with the grim history. . . . The author begins with a brief overview of Hitler's rise and the threat to the Jews, and then draws heavily on Fry's autobiography and his letters home." Booklist

Gaines, Ernest J., 1933-

Abrams, Dennis. **Ernest** J. Gaines. Chelsea House 2010 120p il (Who wrote that?) lib bdg $30

Grades: 6 7 8 9 **92**

1. Authors 2. Novelists 3. African American authors 4. Authors, American 5. Children's authors 6. Short story writers

ISBN 978-1-60413-683-8; 1-60413-683-9

LC 2009022340

This discusses the life and work of author Ernest J. Gaines.

Includes bibliographical references

Galen, ca. 129-ca. 200

Yount, Lisa. The **father** of anatomy; Galen and his dissections. Enslow Publishers 2010 128p il (Great minds of ancient science and math) lib bdg $31.93

Grades: 6 7 8 9 **92**

1. Physicians 2. Human anatomy 3. Writers on medicine

ISBN 978-0-7660-3380-1; 0-7660-3380-5

LC 2008-29633

"A biography of ancient Greek physician Galen, whose dissections of animals led to discoveries about human anatomy. He was the authority on medical knowledge in the Western world for more than fifteen hundred years." Publisher's note

Includes glossary and bibliographical references

Galilei, Galileo, 1564-1642

★ Panchyk, Richard. **Galileo** for kids; his life and ideas: 25 activities. foreword by Buzz Aldrin. Chicago Review Press 2005 166p il map pa $16.95

Grades: 5 6 7 8 **92**

1. Astronomers 2. Writers on science

ISBN 1-55652-566-4

LC 2004-22936

A biography of the Renaissance scientist and his times with related activities

"Clear . . . writing places Galileo squarely within the historical context of the turbulent Italian Renaissance. . . . Panchyk's title is a good choice for those interested in integrating history and science curriculums." SLJ

Includes bibliographical references

★ Steele, Philip. **Galileo**; the genius who faced the Inquisition. National Geographic 2005 64p il (World history biographies) $17.95; lib bdg $27.90

Grades: 4 5 6 7 **92**

1. Astronomers 2. Writers on science

ISBN 0-7922-3656-4; 0-7922-3657-2 lib bdg

LC 2005-01357

An illustrated introduction to the 16th century astronomer and his times

"Accomplishments and hardships are clearly explained with supporting quotes and facts. . . . Beautifully illustrated and visually appealing." SLJ

Gama, Vasco da, 1469-1524

★ Calvert, Patricia. **Vasco** da Gama; so strong a spirit. [by] Patricia Calvert. Benchmark Books 2005 96p il map (Great explorations) lib bdg $29.93

Grades: 5 6 7 8 **92**

1. Explorers

ISBN 0-7614-1611-0

LC 2003-22946

Recounts the voyages undertaken by fifteenth-century Portuguese explorer Vasco da Gama to strengthen his nation's power by establishing a sea trade route to India.

Includes bibliographical references

Gandhi, Indira, 1917-1984

Schupack, Sara. **Indira** Gandhi; by Sara Schupack. Marshall Cavendish Benchmark 2012 96 p. (print) $39.93

Grades: 6 7 8 9 **92**

1. Prime ministers -- India 2. Prime ministers -- India -- Biography 3. Women prime ministers -- India -- Biography 4. India -- Politics and government -- 20th century

ISBN 0761449558; 9780761449553; 9781608707126

LC 2011009224

Author Sara Schupack presents a biography of former Indian Prime Minister Indira Ghandi. Part of the "Leading Women series [which] focus on the background and political achievements of twentieth-century women, . . . [it] also include[s] helpful sidebars that provide context on related people, organizations, and events mentioned in the text." (Booklist)

Includes bibliographical references and index

Gandhi, Mahatma, 1869-1948

De Lambilly, Elisabeth. **Gandhi**; his life, his struggles, his words. written by Elisabeth de Lambilly; illustrated by Severine Cordier; [translated by Robert Brent] Enchanted Lion Books 2010 67p il (Great spiritual leaders of modern times)

Grades: 6 7 8 9 **92**

1. Authors 2. Pacifism 3. Journalists 4. Nonviolence 5. Resistance to government 6. Essayists 7. Pacifists 8. Memoirists 9. Political leaders 10. Statesmen -- India 11. Writers on politics 12. India -- Politics and government

ISBN 1-59270-094-2; 978-1-59270-094-3

LC 2010025235

Original French edition, 2007

"The historical facts are as compelling as the biographical story, and the message of nonviolence will spark intense debate about political action, then and now." Booklist

Includes bibliographical references

Ebine, Kazuki. **Gandhi** : a manga biography. Penguin 2011 192p il pa $15

Grades: 7 8 9 10 **92**

1. Manga 2. Authors 3. Journalists 4. Graphic novels 5. Essayists

6. Pacifists 7. Memoirists 8. Political leaders 9. Statesmen -- India 10. Writers on politics 11. India -- Politics and government
ISBN 978-0-14-312024-7; 0-14-312024-7

"Ebine's nicely drawn manga biography is a clear and concise introduction to Gandhi's life. The biography not only touches upon Gandhi's major accomplishements . . . but also humanizes Gandhi by showing his struggles with insecurity as a young man. . . . This title is a great addition to social studies curricula, and it will have special appeal to budding young activists and idealists." Booklist

Sawyer, Kem Knapp. **Mohandas** Gandhi. Morgan Reynolds Pub. 2011 144p il (Champion of freedom) lib bdg $28.95
Grades: 6 7 8 9 10 **92**

1. Authors 2. Journalists 3. Essayists 4. Pacifists 5. Memoirists 6. Political leaders 7. Statesmen -- India 8. Writers on politics 9. India -- Politics and government
ISBN 978-1-59935-166-7; 1-59935-166-8

LC 2010047904

This title "starts with an overview of the British Raj at the time of Mohandas Gandhi's birth and what life was like for those living under it. The thorough biography then goes on to trace the key events, philosophical influences, and personal relationships that shaped the life of a man who spread the doctrine of nonviolence. Interesting anecdotes, explanations of Indian culture, and an engaging, well-organized narrative make this a solid resource." Booklist

Includes bibliographical references

★ Wilkinson, Philip. **Gandhi**; the young protester who founded a nation. National Geographic 2005 64p il (World history biographies) $17.95; lib bdg $27.90
Grades: 4 5 6 7 **92**

1. Authors 2. Journalists 3. Passive resistance 4. Essayists 5. Pacifists 6. Memoirists 7. Political leaders 8. Writers on politics 9. India -- Politics and government
ISBN 0-7922-3647-5; 0-7922-3648-3 lib bdg

"Double-page spreads describe phases in Gandhi's life, from childhood to his tragic death, detailed in Wilkinson's straightforward, succinct language and in anecdotes, which will capture young people's attention and also humanize the great leader." Booklist

Includes glossary and bibliographical references

García Márquez, Gabriel, 1928-

Darraj, Susan Muaddi. **Gabriel** Garcia Marquez. Chelsea House 2006 112p bibl il por (Great Hispanic heritage) lib bdg $30
Grades: 6 7 8 9 **92**

1. Authors 2. Novelists 3. Journalists 4. Authors, Colombian 5. Short story writers 6. Nobel laureates for literature
ISBN 0-7910-8839-1

LC 2006010615

A biography of the Colombian novelist who won the Nobel Prize for Literature in 1982

"A great deal of biographical information and some historical context is imparted in [this volume]. . . . Scattered throughout are many photographs and helpful boxed historical asides." Horn Book Guide

Includes bibliographical references

Garrison, William Lloyd, 1805-1879

Esty, Amos. The **liberator** : the story of William Lloyd Garrison. Morgan Reynolds Pub. 2010 144p il (Civil rights leaders) lib bdg $28.95
Grades: 7 8 9 10 **92**

1. Abolitionists 2. Newspaper editors 3. Slavery -- United States
ISBN 978-1-59935-137-7; 1-59935-137-4

LC 2009-54290

This biography of abolitionist William Lloyd Garrison "will hook readers with discussions of the larger political issues as well as [Garrison's] personal struggles. . . . The design . . . is readable, with spacious type and many kinds of illustrations, including color and sepia photos, paintings, and reproductions of famous documents." Booklist

Includes bibliographical references

Garvey, Marcus, 1887-1940

Kallen, Stuart A. **Marcus** Garvey and the Back to Africa Movement. Lucent Books 2006 112p il map (Lucent library of Black history) $32.45
Grades: 7 8 9 10 **92**

1. Writers on politics 2. Civil rights activists 3. African Americans -- Civil rights
ISBN 1-59018-838-1

LC 2005027286

"Kallen seeks . . . to discuss and expand on [Garvey's] contributions to Black Nationalism, and to place his particular movement within the context of his times. Here, Garvey emerges as a man who anticipated those later movements that centered on black pride and black power. In an exceptionally evenhanded manner, the author also shows Garvey to have been naive, unrealistic, and lacking in management skills. A superb speechmaker, a charismatic leader, and an excellent propagandist, he seemed ill prepared to deal with the powerful enemies he made. . . . Kallen describes this all in clear, well-written prose. Archival photographs are placed throughout to good advantage." SLJ

Includes bibliographical references

Gates, Bill, 1955-

Aronson, Marc. **Bill** Gates; a twentieth-century life. Penguin Group 2008 192p il (Up close) $16.99
Grades: 7 8 9 10 **92**

1. Businesspeople 2. Computer software industry 3. Microsoft Corporation 4. Computer software executives
ISBN 978-0-670-06348-2; 0-670-06348-7

LC 2008-15552

This is a biography of the businessman who co-founded Microsoft.

"Well researched, thought-provoking, and up-to-date, this biography . . . offers insights into Gates' character as well as an engaging account of his life." Booklist

Isaacs, Sally Senzell. **Bill** and Melinda Gates; [by] Sally Isaacs. Heinemann Library 2010 112p il (Front-page lives) $38.93
Grades: 6 7 8 9 10 **92**

1. Businesspeople 2. Philanthropists 3. Computer industry 4. Foundation officials 5. Computer software executives 6. Spouses of prominent persons 7. Microsoft Corporation -- History 8. Bill and Melinda Gates Foundation
ISBN 978-1-4329-3220-6; 1-4329-3220-9

LC 2009-18180

A biography of Microsoft founder and billionaire Bill Gates and his wife, Melinda who, through the Bill and Melinda Gates Foundation, have helped people around the world by donating billions of dollars to solve global health problems and other issues.

"The subjects' lives are presented with depth and breadth and in such a way as to make clear how their actions impacted the world and why they are or were so important. . . . The writing is accessible and engaging, with color and black-and-white photographs." SLJ

Includes glossary and bibliographical references

Lesinski, Jeanne M. **Bill** Gates; entrepreneur and philanthropist. rev ed; Twenty-First Century Books 2009 112p il (Lifeline biographies) lib bdg $33.26

Grades: 6 7 8 9 **92**

1. Businesspeople 2. Computer software industry 3. Microsoft Corporation 4. Computer software executives

ISBN 978-1-58013-570-2; 1-58013-570-6

LC 2008008565

A revised edition of the title first published 2000

This biography "boasts lively, credible writing and a compelling layout. Particularly interesting are the reprints of USA Today articles found throughout, which flesh out the [narrative] in a unique and appealing manner. . . . Full-color and black-and-white photos appear on almost every spread." SLJ

Includes bibliographical references

Gates, Melinda French

Isaacs, Sally Senzell. **Bill** and Melinda Gates; [by] Sally Isaacs. Heinemann Library 2010 112p il (Front-page lives) $38.93

Grades: 6 7 8 9 10 **92**

1. Businesspeople 2. Philanthropists 3. Computer industry 4. Foundation officials 5. Computer software executives 6. Spouses of prominent persons 7. Microsoft Corporation -- History 8. Bill and Melinda Gates Foundation

ISBN 978-1-4329-3220-6; 1-4329-3220-9

LC 2009-18180

A biography of Microsoft founder and billionaire Bill Gates and his wife, Melinda who, through the Bill and Melinda Gates Foundation, have helped people around the world by donating billions of dollars to solve global health problems and other issues.

"The subjects' lives are presented with depth and breadth and in such a way as to make clear how their actions impacted the world and why they are or were so important. . . . The writing is accessible and engaging, with color and black-and-white photographs." SLJ

Includes glossary and bibliographical references

Gauguin, Paul, 1848-1903

Spence, David. **Gauguin**. New Forest Press 2010 48p il map (Great artists and their world) lib bdg $32.80

Grades: 6 7 8 9 **92**

1. Artists 2. Painters 3. Artists, French

ISBN 978-1-84898-316-8; 1-84898-316-6

"Offers biographical information [of Paul Gauguin] . . . interspersed with art history and criticism in an eye-catching format. . . . [Includes] a long introductory paragraph and four-to-six images with explanatory notes. . . . Spence . . . does a good job of explaining why art that might seem ordinary today was revolutionary at the time of its creation." SLJ

Includes glossary

Gehrig, Lou, 1903-1941

Buckley, James. **Lou** Gehrig; Iron Horse of baseball. Sterling 2010 124p il (Sterling biographies) pa $5.95

Grades: 6 7 8 9 **92**

1. Baseball players 2. Baseball -- Biography

ISBN 978-1-4027-7151-4 pa; 1-4027-7151-7 pa

This biography of Lou Gehrig is "studded with quotes and illustrated with photos. . . . Lou Gehrig is today inextricably linked with ALS, the progressive nerve disease that ended his baseball career and ultimately his life, but he is also remembered as the Iron Horse of baseball, the legendary slugger who played a phenomenal 2,130 consecutive games for the Yankees. Written in a straightforward, journalistic style, [this biography presents a] very readable [account] of the [life] of [an athlete] who made [his mark] on American culture." Booklist

Includes glossary and bibliographical references

Gehry, Frank

Bodden, Valerie. **Frank** Gehry. Creative Education 2009 48p il (Xtraordinary artists) lib bdg $32.80

Grades: 4 5 6 7 **92**

1. Architects

ISBN 978-1-58341-662-4 lib bdg; 1-58341-662-5 lib bdg

LC 2007004201

This is a biography of architect Frank Gehry

This offers an "interesting [layout]; big, high-quality reproductions and photographs on heavy paper; insightful quotes from diverse sources; and . . . an excerpt from an essay about [Gehry] at the end of the book. Readers get a strong sense of [the] artist's personality along with an excellent survey of his work." SLJ

Includes bibliographical references

Geronimo, Apache Chief, 1829-1909

Sullivan, George. **Geronimo**; Apache renegade. Sterling 2010 124p il map (Sterling biographies) lib bdg $12.95; pa $5.95

Grades: 7 8 9 10 **92**

1. Apache Indians 2. Indian chiefs 3. Native Americans -- Biography

ISBN 978-1-4027-6843-9 lib bdg; 1-4027-6843-5 lib bdg; 978-1-4027-6279-6 pa; 1-4027-6279-8 pa

LC 2009-24135

"Geronmino describes how the Apache leader was feared and hated as he led violent clashes with whites, pursuing bloody vengeance for the massacre of his family and all that his people had lost, an identity far from the romanticized image that glorified him. . . . [The] spacious design is highly scannable, with color background screens, photos, maps, and historic prints throughout." Booklist

Includes glossary and bibliographical references

Gibson, Josh, 1911-1947

Twemlow, Nick. **Josh** Gibson. Rosen Pub. Group 2002 112p il (Baseball Hall of Famers of the Negro leagues) lib bdg $29.25

Grades: 5 6 7 8 **92**

1. Baseball players 2. African American athletes 3. Baseball -- Biography

ISBN 0-8239-3475-6

LC 2001-4143

Presents a biography of the powerful home run hitter and chronicles the history of African American participation in organized baseball, the formation of the Negro leagues, and racial politics in America

Includes glossary and bibliographical references

Giff, Patricia Reilly

Giff, Patricia Reilly. **Don't** tell the girls; a family memoir. by Patricia Reilly Giff. Holiday House 2005 131p il $16.95

Grades: 4 5 6 7 **92**

1. Authors 2. Teachers 3. Women authors 4. Authors, American

5. Children's authors
ISBN 0-8234-1813-8

LC 2004-47452

"Giff reflects on her childhood and her family, going back through several generations. Spotlighting her two grandmothers, she lovingly relates remembered conversations and incidents involving the one she knew well before turning to the other grandmother, whom she never met. . . . This little book has much to offer thoughtful children. . . . With . . . sharply reproduced family photos and documents, this handsome book's small format reflects its intimate, conversational style." Booklist

Gillespie, Dizzy, 1917-1993

★ Boone, Mary. **Dizzy** Gillespie; by Mary Boone. Mitchell Lane Publishers 2013 47 p. ill. (some col.) (library) $29.95
Grades: 6 7 8 9 **92**

1. Jazz musicians -- Biography 2. Gillespie, Dizzy, 1917-1993 3. Bop (Music) -- History and criticism 4. Jazz musicians -- United States -- Biography
ISBN 9781612282725

LC 2012008630

This book by Mary Boone, part of the "American Jazz" series, presents a "biography of Jazz great Dizzy Gillespie written for intermediate through middle school age readers. . . . Gillespie owed much of his success to an elementary school teacher who worked to harness his energy and anger by recruiting him for the school band. . . . In the 1940s, the trumpet virtuoso and respected improviser teamed up with musician Charlie Parker to lay the foundations for bebop." (Publisher's note)

Includes discography (p. 42), bibliographical references (p. 44-45), and index.

Ginsberg, Blaze

Ginsberg, Blaze. **Episodes**; my life as I see it. Roaring Brook Press 2009 274p $16.99
Grades: 6 7 8 9 10 **92**

1. Autism 2. Teenagers' writings 3. Memoirists
ISBN 978-1-59643-461-5; 1-59643-461-9

"The high-functioning spectrum-disorder child portrayed in his mother Debra's Raising Blaze (2002) steps up to offer his own views of high school and after. He structures his memoir . . . as thumbnail summaries of concurrent or successive TV series. . . . He writes in a distant but often humorous voice about feelings, fixations, and the seemingly aimless way people move in and out of his life. . . . This book provides memorable insight into the author's distinctive mind and spirit." Booklist

Ginsburg, Ruth Bader

★ Ortiz, Victoria. **Dissenter** on the bench; Ruth Bader Ginsburg's life and work. Victoria Ortiz. Clarion Books 2019 208 p. (hardback) $18.99
Grades: 6 7 8 9 10 11 12 **92**

1. Dissenting opinions -- United States 2. Judges -- United States -- Biography 3. Women lawyers -- United States -- Biography 4. United States. Supreme Court -- Officials and employees
ISBN 9780544973640

LC 2018035167

This book, by Victoria Ortiz, discusses the "life and career of the fiercely principled Supreme Court Justice. . . . Dramatically narrated case histories from Justice Ginsburg's stellar career are interwoven with an account of RBG's life--childhood, family, beliefs, education, marriage, legal and judicial career, children, and achievements--and her many-faceted personality is captured." (Publisher's note)

"Ortiz offers detailed accounts of cases Ginsburg either heard as a Supreme Court justice or argued as a lawyer defending individuals' rights under the Constitution. The descriptions of noteworthy legal cases and significant court decisions are particularly well done." (Booklist)

Gogh, Vincent van, 1853-1890

Bodden, Valerie. **Vincent** van Gogh. Creative Education 2009 48p il (Xtraordinary artists) lib bdg $32.80
Grades: 4 5 6 7 **92**

1. Artists 2. Painters 3. Artists, Dutch
ISBN 978-1-58341-663-1 lib bdg; 1-58341-663-3 lib bdg

LC 2007002118

This biography of the artist offers an "interesting [layout]; big, high-quality reproductions and photographs on heavy paper; insightful quotes from diverse sources; and meaty selections of the artist's own writing . . . at the end of the book. Readers get a strong sense of [the] artist's personality along with an excellent survey of his work." SLJ

Includes bibliographical references

Crispino, Enrica. **Van** Gogh; illustrated by Simone Boni . . . [et. al.]; [English translation, Susan Ashley] Oliver Press 2008 64p il (Art masters) $27.95
Grades: 6 7 8 9 10 **92**

1. Artists 2. Painters 3. Artists, Dutch
ISBN 978-1-934545-05-8; 1-934545-05-8

"Using generous, colorful, and cleanly designed two-page spreads, Crispino situates Van Gogh among other artists within certain time periods and locations, portraying his work and life as a counterpoint to various traditions and trends. Most topics are centered by an original drawing that is surrounded by photographs, paintings, artifacts, and descriptions. . . . Consider this volume the equivalent of an unusually insightful museum tour guide." Booklist

Whiting, Jim. **Vincent** Van Gogh; by Jim Whiting. Mitchell Lane 2007 48p il (Art profiles for kids) lib bdg $29.95
Grades: 7 8 9 10 **92**

1. Artists 2. Painters 3. Artists, Dutch
ISBN 978-1-58415-564-5 lib bdg; 1-58415-564-7 lib bdg

LC 2007000662

This offers "well-documented information for teens doing reports. [The] volume covers the painter's childhood, training, travels, influences, and historical context. The chronological chapters build a survey of the [artist's] oeuvres, including the style and subject matter of [his] works and past and present critical reaction." SLJ

Includes glossary and bibliographical references

Goh, Chan Hon, 1969-

Goh, Chan Hon. **Beyond** the dance; a ballerina's life. [by] Chan Hon Goh with Cary Fagan. Tundra Bks. 2002 151p lib bdg $15.95
Grades: 6 7 8 9 **92**

1. Ballet 2. Authors 3. Ballet dancers 4. Children's authors
ISBN 0-88776-596-3

LC 2002-101724

This "autobiography introduces a prima ballerina with the National Ballet of Canada. Goh was born in Beijing but raised in Vancouver by her dancer parents. She discusses the events in her homeland that led her family to emigrate, their adjustment to life in Vancouver, and her parents' struggles to build the Goh Ballet Company. . . . The book is lavishly illustrated with black-and-white photographs, and balletomanes will enjoy poring over every detail." SLJ

Goodall, Jane, 1934-

Silvey, Anita. **Untamed**; the wild life of Jane Goodall. Anita Silvey ; foreword by Jane Goodall. National Geographic Books 2015 96 p. col. illustrations, col. maps (library binding : alk. paper) $28.90

Grades: 4 5 6 7 8 **92**

1. Primates -- Behavior 2. Primatology 3. Chimpanzees -- Behavior 4. Primatologists -- England -- Biography 5. Women primatologists -- England -- Biography

ISBN 1426315198; 9781426315183; 9781426315190

LC 2014017715

This children's book by Anita Silvey profiles "Jane Goodall, one of the most recognized scientists in the Western world, [who] became internationally famous because of her ability to observe and connect with another species. She began tirelessly fighting to protect the environment so that chimpanzees and other animals will continue have a place and a future on our planet." (Publisher's note)

"Silvey (The Plant Hunters) adeptly chronicles the life of Goodall from her childhood fascination with animal behavior to her groundbreaking field research of chimpanzees in Africa and her work to preserve endangered animals' habitats." Publishers Weekly

Welty, Tara. **Jane** Goodall. Chelsea House 2011 124p il (Conservation heroes) lib bdg $35

Grades: 6 7 8 9 **92**

1. Chimpanzees 2. Women scientists 3. Primatologists 4. Writers on nature 5. Nonfiction writers

ISBN 978-1-60413-952-5; 1-60413-952-8

LC 2010030583

This is a biography of primatologist and conservationist Jane Goodall, who studied the chimpanzees of Tanzania.

"Captivating, richly informative. . . . The scope of [this book] is comprehensive. . . . [The book is] engaging as [it is] educational and will be ideal for research and reports." SLJ

Includes glossary and bibliographical references

Goodman, Benny, 1909-1986

★ Mattern, Joanne. **Benny** Goodman; by Joanne Mattern. Mitchell Lane Publishers 2013 47 p. ill. (some col.) (library) $29.95

Grades: 6 7 8 9 **92**

1. Jazz musicians 2. Clarinetists -- United States -- Biography 3. Jazz musicians -- United States -- Biography

ISBN 1612282695; 9781612282695

LC 2012008483

This book by Joanne Mattern is part of the American Jazz series and looks at musician Benny Goodman. Within each entry, "information about the subjects' childhoods and preparation for their musical careers is included, as are the positive and negative aspects of their adult lives. Their contributions to the world of jazz are . . . explored." (School Library Journal)

Includes bibliographical references (p. 44-45) and index.

Gore, Al, 1948-

Baptiste, Tracey. **Al** Gore. Chelsea House 2011 119p il (Conservation heroes) lib bdg $35

Grades: 6 7 8 9 **92**

1. Vice-presidents 2. Conservationists 3. Environmentalists 4. Senators 5. Members of Congress 6. Presidential candidates 7. Nobel laureates for peace 8. Vice-presidents -- United States

ISBN 978-1-60413-949-5; 1-60413-949-8

LC 2010030592

A biography of the environmentalist and former vice-president.

"Captivating, richly informative. . . . The scope of [this book] is comprehensive. . . . [The book is] engaging as [it is] educational and will be ideal for research and reports." SLJ

Includes glossary and bibliographical references

Graham, Martha

★ Freedman, Russell. **Martha** Graham, a dancer's life. Clarion Bks. 1998 175p il $18

Grades: 7 8 9 10 **92**

1. Dancers 2. Modern dance 3. Choreographers 4. Dance teachers

ISBN 0-395-74655-8

LC 97-15832

A photo-biography of the American dancer, teacher, and choreographer who was born in Pittsburgh in 1895 and who became a leading figure in the world of modern dance

"A showstopping biography that captures its dynamic subject's personality, vision, and artistry." SLJ

Includes bibliographical references

Grandin, Temple

Montgomery, Sy. **Temple** Grandin; how the girl who loved cows embraced autism and changed the world. by Sy Montgomery. Houghton Mifflin Harcourt 2012 147 p. col. ill. $17.99

Grades: 4 5 6 7 8 **92**

1. Autism 2. Cattle 3. Biography 4. Women scientists -- Biography 5. Animal welfare -- United States 6. Livestock -- Housing -- United States 7. Livestock -- Handling -- United States 8. Autistic people -- United States -- Biography 9. Animal scientists -- United States -- Biography 10. Animal specialists -- United States -- Biography 11. Women animal specialists -- United States -- Biography

ISBN 0547443153; 9780547443157

LC 2011039911

AAAS/Subaru SB&F Prize for Excellence in Science Books: Middle Grade Science Book (2013)

This book by Sy Montgomery presents a biography of autistic animal scientist Temple Grandin. Sy Montgomery argues that "though one never outgrows autism, it doesn't condemn those who have it to unproductive lives, and an appendix, 'Temple's Advice for Kids on the Spectrum,' provides first-hand wisdom. Photos and diagrams depict Grandin's work as well as documenting her early life and career." (Kirkus Reviews)

Includes bibliographical references and index.

Sepahban, Lois. **Temple** Grandin; inspiring animal-behavior scientist. Lois Sepahban. Core Library 2015 48 p. colour illustrations $32.79

Grades: 4 5 6 **92**

1. Animal behavior 2. Animal welfare -- United States 3. Autistic people -- United States -- Biography 4. Animal scientists -- United States -- Biography

ISBN 1624033806; 9781624033803

LC 2014932491

This children's book by Lois Sepahban, part of the Great Minds of Science series, "chronicles the life and career of the animal scientist, from her work to help others with autism to her lobbying for animal welfare." (Publisher's note)

"Students will learn about the different accomplishments of each scientist while joining them on the often tumultuous journey to success. A staple for libraries." SLJ

Includes bibliographical references (page 47) and index

Greenberg, Hank, 1911-1986

Sommer, Shelley. **Hammerin'** Hank Greenberg; baseball pioneer. Calkins Creek 2011 135p il $17.95

Grades: 5 6 7 8 **92**

1. Baseball players 2. Jews -- Biography 3. Baseball -- Biography
ISBN 1-59078-452-9; 978-1-59078-452-5

"Greenberg grew up in an Orthodox Jewish family in New York and went on to be a Hall-of-Fame first baseman and left fielder, playing most of his career with the Detroit Tigers in the 1930s and 1940s. . . . Sommer presents a fast-moving, straightforward biography. . . . Numerous black-and-white photos enhance the text. . . . An excellent choice for kids who enjoy delving into baseball history." Booklist

Grimberg, Tina

Grimberg, Tina. **Out** of line; growing up Soviet. Tundra Books 2007 117p il $22.95

Grades: 7 8 9 10 **92**

1. Rabbis 2. Memoirists 3. Soviet Union 4. Jews -- Russia 5. Jews -- Biography 6. Children's authors
ISBN 978-0-88776-803-3; 0-88776-803-2

"In this warm memoir, Grimberg recalls her childhood in Kiev during the '60s and '70s. She shares the difficulties of Soviet life and explains how members of her family coped with challenges such as shortages. . . . Interwoven with her own experience of growing up in a Jewish family are the stories of her maternal and paternal grandparents. . . . The book is an exemplar of clear, graceful writing and fine storytelling skills." SLJ

Groening, Matt

Kallen, Stuart A. **Matt** Groening; the Simpsons. by Stuart A. Kallen. ReferencePoint Press, Inc. 2015 80 p. (hardback) $28.95

Grades: 6 7 8 9 **92**

1. Cartoonists -- Biography 2. Cartoonists -- United States -- Biography
ISBN 1601527845; 9781601527844

LC 2014035198

This book, by Stuart A. Kallen, part of the "Contemporary cartoon creators series," profiles the maker of the popular television show "The Simpsons." "Cartoonist Matt Groening . . . has a talent for mocking, criticizing, and exposing the foolishness of modern culture. This talent has resulted in financial success, critical acclaim, and the longest-running show in television history." (Publisher's note)

"Complemented by color photos of the cartoonists and their groundbreaking characters, the books draw attention to the social commentary often seen in these shows and how their creators have responded to criticism and controversy. They're scholarly enough for serious biography studies yet plenty of fun for leisurely readers." Booklist

Includes bibliographical references and index

Gross, Elly Berkovits, 1929-

Gross, Elly Berkovits. **Elly**; my true story of the Holocaust. [by] Elly Berkovits Gross. Scholastic Press 2009 125p il $14.99

Grades: 4 5 6 7 **92**

1. Poets 2. Authors 3. Holocaust survivors 4. Memoirists 5. Jews -- Romania 6. Holocaust, 1933-1945 -- Personal narratives
ISBN 978-0-545-07494-0; 0-545-07494-0

Relates how the author was torn from her happy home and sent to Birkenau by the Nazis, describing how she worked long hours and fought for survival before being set free at the end of the war and beginning a new life in America.

"As a powerful reminder of man's capacity for inhumanity, this memoir is essential reading." Booklist

Guevara, Ernesto, 1928-1967

Abrams, Dennis. **Ernesto** Che Guevara. Chelsea House Publishers 2010 128p il (The great Hispanic heritage) lib bdg $30

Grades: 6 7 8 9 **92**

1. Guerrillas 2. Physicians 3. Revolutionaries 4. Cuba -- History -- 1959-
ISBN 978-1-60413-732-3; 1-60413-732-0

This "begins with Guevara's childhood as the son of Argentinean aristocrats and gives a balanced portrait of the controversial figure, from his famous worldwide revolutionary efforts to his assassination at the age of 39. . . . A selection of well-chosen images, a chronology, chapter notes, and [a] suggested reading [list] round out [this] engaging [title] in a sure-to-be popular [book] for reports and personal interest." Booklist

Includes bibliographical references

★ Miller, Calvin Craig. **Che** Guevara; in search of revolution. Morgan Reynolds Pub. 2006 192p il map (World leaders) lib bdg $27.95

Grades: 7 8 9 10 **92**

1. Guerrillas 2. Physicians 3. Revolutionaries 4. Cuba -- History -- 1959-
ISBN 978-1-931798-93-8; 1-931798-93-1

LC 2006-5975

This biography of the guerilla leader is "woven into . . . [an] account of the global politics of his day, including his role in the Cuban revolution and the showdown with the U.S. The design is appealing, with clear type, occasional photos, and maps, and teens will be drawn to the account of the young leader who made a difference in spite of an inglorious defeat." Booklist

Includes bibliographical references

Kallen, Stuart A. **Che** Guevara; by Stuart A. Kallen. Twenty-First Century Books 2013 88 p. (lib. bdg. : alk. paper) $33.27

Grades: 8 9 10 11 12 **92**

1. Cuba -- History -- 1958-1959, Revolution 2. Cuba -- History -- 1959-1990 3. Revolutionaries -- Cuba -- Biography 4. Latin America -- History -- 1948-1980 5. Guerrillas -- Latin America -- Biography
ISBN 0822590352; 9780822590354

LC 2011045480

In author Stuart A. Kallen's book on Che Guevara, "the charismatic Argentinian revolutionary had been leading guerilla fighters in the jungles of Bolivia and was captured by the Bolivian army. Mario Terán, a sergeant in the Bolivian army, volunteered to execute the prisoner. He carried out the bloody assignment with nine point-blank shots to Guevara's body . . . In this chronicle of an assassination, find out what inspired the myth of Che Guevara and what brought him to this bloody crossroads of history." (Publisher's note)

Includes bibliographical references and index.

Gunther, John, 1929-1947

Gunther, John. **Death** be not proud; a memoir. Harper & Row 1949 261p il hardcover o.p. pa $13.95

Grades: 7 8 9 10 **92**

1. Sick 2. Cancer 3. Brain -- Tumors
ISBN 0-06-123097-9

A memoir of John Gunther's seventeen-year-old son, who died after a series of operations for a brain tumor. Not only a tribute to a remarkable boy but an account of a brave fight against disease

Guthrie, Woody, 1912-1967

★ Partridge, Elizabeth. **This** land was made for you and me; the life and songs of Woody Guthrie. Viking 2002 217p il $21.99

Grades: 7 8 9 10 **92**

1. Singers 2. Folk musicians 3. Memoirists 4. Songwriters

ISBN 0-670-03535-1

LC 2001-46770

National Book Award Finalist: Young People's Literature (2002)

Boston Globe-Horn Book Award: Nonfiction (2002)

A biography of Woody Guthrie, a singer who wrote over 3,000 folk songs and ballads as he traveled around the United States, including "This Land is Your Land" and "So Long It's Been Good to Know Yuh"

This "presents an unflinchingly accurate portrait of a rambling and unpredictable man. . . . In addition to a panoply of archival photographs, which add realism to this engrossing story of a life, the book includes carefully selected quotes from songs, acquaintances, and documents to punctuate the story with authenticating detail without detracting from the momentum of the narrative." Bull Cent Child Books

Includes bibliographical references

Halvorsen, Gail

★ Tunnell, Michael. **Candy** bomber; the story of the Berlin airlift's chocolate pilot. Charlesbridge 2010 110p il $18.95; pa $9.95

Grades: 4 5 6 7 **92**

1. Air pilots 2. Air force officers 3. Biography, Individual 4. Berlin (Germany) -- History -- Blockade, 1948-1949

ISBN 1-58089-336-8; 1-58089-337-6 pa; 978-1-58089-336-7; 978-1-58089-337-4 pa

This book takes place "[i]n 1948, after World War II, [in] Berlin, . . . [where Michael] Tunnell tells us that pilot Gail Halvorsen spent a night in the city, noticing kids behind a fence watching the planes land. He offered sticks of Doublemint gum to two of the kids, who passed them around so their pals could get a whiff. . . . Soon people all over began sending candy-and-handkerchief parachutes to Halvorsen and other pilots to drop over Berlin." (School Library Journal)

"Curious about the city into which he ferried goods during the Berlin Airlift in 1948, pilot Gail Halvorsen stayed over to visit, met some children, and offered to drop candy and gum when he next flew over. This simple idea grew into a massive project with reverberations today. Tunnell tell this appealing story . . . clearly and chronologically, weaving just enough background for twenty-first century readers and illustrating almost every page with black-and-white photographs, many from Halvorsen's own collection." Booklist

Includes bibliographical references

Hamilton, Alexander, 1757-1804

★ Fritz, Jean, 1915-2017. **Alexander** Hamilton; the outsider. illustrations by Ian Schoenherr. G.P. Putnam's Sons 2011 144p il $16.99

Grades: 5 6 7 8 **92**

1. Statesmen 2. Statesmen -- United States 3. Secretaries of the treasury 4. United States -- History -- 1775-1783, Revolution 5. United States -- Politics and government -- 1783-1809

ISBN 039925546X; 9780399255465

LC 2010006008

Fritz "provides a brisk, well-written account introducing Founding Father Alexander Hamilton as an outsider to America. . . . Fast moving and engaging, this straightforward biography acknowledges Hamilton's flaws while portraying him as an intelligent, energetic man who rose to the challenge of his times. . . . In addition to the black-and-white reproductions of period paintings and prints that illustrate the text, Schoenherr's striking, engraving-like images of Hamilton as scholar, soldier, aide-decamp, statesman, and duelist introduce each section." Booklist

Includes bibliographical references

Kanefield, Teri, 1960- **Alexander** Hamilton; the making of America. by Teri Kanefield. Abrams Books for Young Readers 2017 208 p. illustrations (hardback) $16.95

Grades: 5 6 7 8 **92**

1. Statesmen -- United States 2. Statesmen -- United States -- Biography 3. United States -- Politics and government -- 1783-1809

ISBN 9781419725784

LC 2016046103

This book on Alexander Hamilton, by Teri Kanefield, "is the story that epitomizes the American dream—a poor immigrant who made good in America. In the end, Hamilton rose from poverty through his intelligence and ability, and did more to shape our country than any of his contemporaries." (Publisher's note)

"A great addition to upper elementary and middle school libraries." Kirkus.

Includes bibliographical references and index.

★ St. George, Judith. The **duel** : the parallel lives of Alexander Hamilton and Aaron Burr. Viking 2009 97p il $16.99

Grades: 6 7 8 9 10 **92**

1. Statesmen 2. Vice-presidents 3. Secretaries of the treasury 4. Politicians -- United States

ISBN 978-0-670-01124-7; 0-670-01124-X

LC 2009-5660

"After a prologue following the steps of Alexander Hamilton and Aaron Burr on the morning of their famous duel, St. George backtracks to trace the 'parallel lives' mentioned in the subtitle. . . . Well researched and organized, the book offers insights into the personalities, lives, and times of Burr and Hamilton." Booklist

Hammel, Heidi B.

★ Bortz, Fred. **Beyond** Jupiter; the story of planetary astronomer Heidi Hammel. [by] Fred Bortz. Franklin Watts 2005 110p il (Women's adventures in science) lib bdg $31.50

Grades: 7 8 9 10 **92**

1. Astronomers 2. Women astronomers 3. College teachers 4. Biography, Individual

ISBN 0-531-16775-5

LC 2005-0778

This book by Fred Bortz is part of the Women's Adventures in Science series. It profiles "Heidi Hammel . . . a planetary astronomer, a scientist who uses the world's most powerful telescopes to learn about planets. By making remarkable discoveries in the farthest reaches of our solar system, Heidi also helps us better understand the planet we call home. The giant planets Neptune and Uranus are Heidi's specialties." (Publisher's note)

The author "has captured some of the engaging qualities of Heidi Hammel's personality through extensive work with her and with the cooperation of her friends and family." Sci Books Films

Includes glossary and bibliographical references

Handel, George Frideric, 1685-1759

Lee, Lavina. **Handel's** world; [by] Lavina Lee. Rosen Pub. Group 2008 64p il (Music throughout history) lib bdg $29.25

Grades: 5 6 7 8 **92**

1. Composers

ISBN 978-1-4042-0726-4 lib bdg; 1-4042-0726-0 lib bdg

LC 2005030127

This "book begins with an introduction briefly addressing social issues of the day, historical background, or other significant information. . . . Successive chapters discuss the [man's] early [life], family background, social status, personality characteristics, musical training and education, obstacles or challenges, and influences. A chapter . . . focuses on the musician's well-known compositions, describing through lively and colorful language some of the musical elements employed." SLJ

Includes glossary and bibliographical references

Hannibal, 247-183 B.C.

Mills, Cliff. **Hannibal**; [by] Cliff Mills. Chelsea House 2008 120p bibl il map (Ancient world leaders) lib bdg $30

Grades: 6 7 8 9 **92**

1. Generals 2. Rome -- History

ISBN 978-0-7910-9580-5 lib bdg; 0-7910-9580-0 lib bdg

LC 2007-50493

"Mills's informative biography starts with Hannibal preparing to attack the Romans and then goes back in time to explain the founding of Carthage and the history of its conflict with Rome, mainly focusing on the Second Punic War and the subject's journey and battles during that time. . . . Frequent inserts add extra information . . . without distracting readers from the narrative. Colorful reproductions are also interspersed throughout. . . . [This offers] clear, descriptive writing." SLJ

Includes bibliographical references

Hargreaves, Alice Pleasance Liddell, 1852-1934

Rubin, C. M. The **real** Alice in Wonderland; a role model for the ages. [by] C.M. Rubin with Gabriella Rose Rubin. AuthorHouse 2010 134p il $29.95

Grades: 7 8 9 10 **92**

1. Authors 2. Children 3. Novelists 4. Mathematicians 5. Characters and characteristics in literature 6. Children's authors 7. Writers on science

ISBN 978-1-4490-8131-7; 1-4490-8131-2

LC 2010-901865

"Readers will follow this title down the rabbit hole to discover the world of the real Alice who inspired Lewis Carroll's Alice in Wonderland. The book moves seamlessly through the life of Alice Pleasance Liddell. . . . This offering paints a full picture of Alice, not only as a child who has captivated literature but also as a woman who was truly ahead of her time. This is a purchase that will do well with a range of people and should be offered as a standard accompaniment to Alice in Wonderland. The illustrations and pictures will make it quite popular in a public library." Voice Youth Advocates

Includes bibliographical references

Hatshepsut, Queen of Egypt

★ Galford, Ellen. **Hatshepsut**; the princess who became king. National Geographic 2005 64p il map (World history biographies) $17.95; lib bdg $27.90

Grades: 4 5 6 7 **92**

1. Queens 2. Kings and rulers 3. Egypt -- History 4. Egypt -- Civilization

ISBN 0-7922-3645-9; 0-7922-3646-7 lib bdg

This "presents the life of Queen Hatshepsut, who ruled Egypt as pharaoh during the New Kingdom, around 3500 years ago. Illustrated with clear, color photos of artifacts and sites as well as colorful maps, the text discusses aspects of Egyptian life such as education and religion in Hatshepsut's life. . . . With a clearly written text and many handsome photos, this provides an accessible introduction to Hatshepsut and her times." Booklist

Hawking, Stephen W., 1942-2018

★ Bankston, John. **Stephen** Hawking; breaking the boundaries of time and space. [by] John Bankston. Enslow Publishers 2005 128p il (Great minds of science) $26.60

Grades: 5 6 7 8 **92**

1. Physicists 2. People with disabilities 3. People with physical disabilities 4. College teachers 5. Writers on science

ISBN 0-7660-2281-1

LC 2004-9193

This biography of the English physicist, who suffers from amyotrophic lateral sclerosis, includes explanations of his theories and experiments

"This excellent book features large font size and double spacing that makes it easy for any one to read. . . . The activities part of the book is outstanding." Sci Books Films

Includes glossary and bibliographical references

Hawthorne, Nathaniel, 1804-1864

Meltzer, Milton. **Nathaniel** Hawthorne; a biography. Twenty-First Century Books 2007 160p il (American literary greats) lib bdg $31.93

Grades: 7 8 9 10 **92**

1. Authors 2. Novelists 3. Authors, American 4. Short story writers

ISBN 978-0-7613-3459-0 lib bdg; 0-7613-3459-9 lib bdg

LC 2005000018

"The legendary novelist's life is portrayed as being as dramatic as the plotlines of his novels, and readers will be captivated by the detailed accounts of the family tragedies that made up his childhood and the financial and literary vicissitudes of his adult life. Meltzer provides sufficient background about New England at the time as well as accounts of the historical events that were shaping the country." SLJ

Includes bibliographical references

Hemingway, Ernest, 1899-1961

★ Reef, Catherine. **Ernest** Hemingway; a writer's life. Clarion Books 2009 183p il $20

Grades: 8 9 10 11 12 **92**

1. Poets 2. Authors 3. Novelists 4. Authors, American 5. Short story writers 6. Nobel laureates for literature

ISBN 978-0-618-98705-4; 0-618-98705-3

LC 2008-32885

"Reef creates a memorable portrait of the writer and his times, and even readers too young for most of Hemingway's oeuvre will enjoy armchair traveling to the bullfights in Spain, fishing expeditions to the Dry Tortugas and the Marquesas Keys, big-game hunting on the Serengeti and covering the Spanish Civil War. Along the way, they will gain a sense of the writer and his times and will even pick up some writing tips." Kirkus

Includes bibliographical references

Hendrix, Jimi

Willett, Edward. **Jimi** Hendrix; kiss the sky. Enslow Publishers 2006 160p bibl por (American rebels) lib bdg $27.93

Grades: 7 8 9 10 **92**

1. Singers 2. Guitarists 3. Rock musicians 4. African American musicians

ISBN 0-7660-2449-0

LC 2005033751

"This biography introduces electric-guitar virtuouso Jimi Hendrix. . . . [This is a] good, basic introduction to Hendrix's life and the reasons for his enduring fame." Booklist

Includes bibliographical references

Henry, John William, 1847?-ca. 1875

★ Nelson, Scott Reynolds. **Ain't** nothing but a man; my quest to find the real John Henry. [by] Scott Reynolds Nelson with Marc Aronson. National Geographic 2008 64p il $18.95; lib bdg $27.90

Grades: 4 5 6 7 8 **92**

1. Railroad workers 2. Railroads -- History 3. African Americans -- Biography 4. John Henry (Legendary character)

ISBN 978-1-4263-0000-4; 1-4263-0000-X; 978-1-4263-0001-1 lib bdg; 1-4263-0001-8 lib bdg

LC 2007-12446

This describes the author's research to find the real man who inspired the songs and legends about the African American steel-driving hero.

"The layout is attractive, with a sepia and beige background for the text and sepia-toned photographs. . . . This is an excellent example of how much detective work is needed for original research." SLJ

Includes bibliographical references

Henson, Matthew Alexander, 1866-1955

★ Johnson, Dolores. **Onward**; a photobiography of African-American polar explorer Matthew Henson. National Geographic 2006 64p il $17.95

Grades: 5 6 7 8 **92**

1. Explorers 2. North Pole 3. African Americans -- Biography

ISBN 0-7922-7914-X

LC 2005-05837

"The quest to be the first to reach the North Pole is an exciting adventure story, and Henson got there first, as part of the ninth expedition led by Robert Peary in 1909. But Henson was African American, labeled as Peary's 'Negro manservant,' and he did not get full recognition until 2001. This . . . focuses on the physical details of the dangerous Arctic journeys . . . the repeated failures and the teamwork, as well as Henson's skills, stamina, and essential role in forging relationships with the Inuit. . . . The book design is beautiful: thick paper, spacious type, and stirring photos that capture the icy storms as well as the people involved in the history." Booklist

Hillary, Edmund Sir

Crompton, Samuel. **Sir** Edmund Hillary; [by] Samuel Willard Crompton. Chelsea House 2009 112p il map (Great explorers) lib bdg $30

Grades: 6 7 8 9 10 11 12 **92**

1. Mountaineering 2. Mountaineers 3. Nonfiction writers 4. Mount Everest (China and Nepal)

ISBN 978-1-60413-420-9 lib bdg; 1-60413-420-8 lib bdg

LC 2009-8688

Biography of the explorer Sir Edmund Hillary

"The information . . . is presented in such a way as to attract and maintain readers' interest. . . . With a full complement of maps, photographs (where available), illustrations, time lines, and document reproductions, a full story is told. Well-written and throughly researched, this . . . will make a solid addition." SLJ

Includes glossary and bibliographical references

★ Elish, Dan. **Edmund** Hillary; first to the top. [by] Dan Elish. Marshall Cavendish Benchmark 2007 80p il map (Great explorations) lib bdg $32.79

Grades: 5 6 7 8 **92**

1. Mountaineering 2. Mountaineers 3. Nonfiction writers 4. Mount Everest (China and Nepal)

ISBN 978-0-7614-2224-2 lib bdg; 0-7614-2224-2 lib bdg

LC 2005027929

This "appealing [title features] readable [text], solid research, and variety of color illustrations." SLJ

Includes bibliographical references

Hinton, S. E.

★ Kjelle, Marylou Morano. **S.E.** Hinton; author of The outsiders. Enslow Publishers 2007 112p bibl il por (Authors teens love) lib bdg $31.93

Grades: 6 7 8 9 **92**

1. Authors 2. Novelists 3. Women authors 4. Authors, American 5. Children's authors 6. Young adult authors

ISBN 978-0-7660-2720-6 lib bdg; 0-7660-2720-1 lib bdg

LC 2006036820

"This well-written and informative biography weaves facts about Hinton's life with analyses of and reflections on her novels." SLJ

Includes glossary and bibliographical references

Hippocrates

Gow, Mary. The **greatest** doctor of ancient times: Hippocrates and his oath. Enslow Publishers 2009 128p il map (Great minds of ancient science and math) lib bdg $31.93

Grades: 5 6 7 8 **92**

1. Physicians 2. Medicine -- History 3. Writers on medicine 4. Greece -- Civilization

ISBN 978-0-7660-3118-0 lib bdg; 0-7660-3118-7 lib bdg

LC 2008029630

"This interesting take on medicine concludes with several activities. . . . Photographs on sepia-colored pages are a good match for the subject." Booklist

Includes glossary and bibliographical references

Hitler, Adolf, 1889-1945

★ Giblin, James Cross, 1933-2016. The **life** and death of Adolf Hitler; by James Cross Giblin. Clarion Bks. 2002 246p il maps $20

Grades: 7 8 9 10 **92**

1. Dictators 2. Heads of state 3. National socialism 4. Nazi leaders 5. Germany -- History -- 1918-1933 6. Germany -- History -- 1933-1945

ISBN 0-395-90371-8

LC 2001-47091

"In a time when people, young and old, are unaware or have forgotten that people like Hitler, his nation of followers, and his high command existed, Giblin's carefully researched account is more important than ever. It is so readable that it should hold younger readers and educate older ones who may need their brains refilled with the facts of history. An essential purchase." Kirkus

Includes glossary and bibliographical references

Hodgman, Ann

Hodgman, Ann. **How** to die of embarrassment every day. Henry Holt and Co. 2011 208p il $16.99

Grades: 5 6 7 8 **92**

1. Authors 2. Women authors 3. Cookbook writers 4. Authors, American 5. Children's authors

ISBN 978-0-8050-8705-5; 0-8050-8705-2

LC 2010-49004

Hodgman offers a "chatty personal narrative . . . focusing on her childhood years and her tendency to land herself into humiliating situations. . . . The generous supply of spot art and relevant images from Hodgman's childhood adds to the browsibility. . . . There's . . . plenty of humor . . . but more importantly there's a tacit message about the survivability of embarrassment and the fact that we all, even seemingly perfect and polished adults, spend our lives goofing up." Bull Cent Child Books

Hopper, Edward, 1882-1967

★ Rubin, Susan Goldman. **Edward** Hopper; painter of light and shadow. Abrams Books for Young Readers 2007 47p il $18.95

Grades: 5 6 7 8 **92**

1. Artists 2. Painters 3. Artists -- United States

ISBN 978-0-8109-9347-1; 0-8109-9347-3

LC 2006-31978

"On every page of this beautifully designed biography, readers will find a reproduction of Hopper's work, matched to clear, eloquent commentary. . . . Readers . . . will come back to read about the man and look at his art again and again." Booklist

Includes bibliographical references

Houdini, Harry, 1874-1926

Biskup, Agnieszka. **Houdini**; the life of the great escape artist. illustrated by Pat Kinsella. Capstone Press 2011 32p il (Graphic library: American graphic) lib bdg $29.32; pa $7.95

Grades: 4 5 6 7 **92**

1. Magicians 2. Biographical graphic novels 3. Nonfiction writers

ISBN 978-1-4296-5474-6 lib bdg; 1-4296-5474-0 lib bdg; 978-1-4296-6268-0 pa; 1-4296-6268-9 pa

LC 2010024848

In graphic novel format, explores the life of Harry Houdini and describes some of his most daring escapes.

"The illustrations are eye-catching and the narration is presented simply, yet compellingly. . . . Fact-filled, entertaining, and accessible." SLJ

Includes bibliographical references

Carlson, Laurie M. **Harry** Houdini for kids; his life and adventures with 21 magic tricks and illusions. Chicago Review Press 2009 136p il pa $16.95

Grades: 4 5 6 7 **92**

1. Magicians 2. Magic tricks 3. Nonfiction writers

ISBN 978-1-55652-782-1 pa; 1-55652-782-9 pa

LC 2008021404

"Reluctant readers (as well as budding troublemakers) will flock to this biography/handbook hybrid about one of the most famous magicians who ever lived. Even for those familiar with Houdini's fascinating story, Carlson's snappy writing gives it new life. . . . Nearly every page is enlivened with period photographs, boxed sections containing biographies and definitions, and, most important, 21 magic tricks that will have readers breaking out their deck of cards and practicing their sleight of hand." Booklist

★ Fleischman, Sid. **Escape!** the story of the great Houdini. Greenwillow Books 2006 210p il $18.99; lib bdg $19.89

Grades: 5 6 7 8 **92**

1. Magicians 2. Nonfiction writers

ISBN 978-0-06-085094-4; 0-06-085094-9; 978-0-06-085095-1 lib bdg; 0-06-0850957-1 lib bdg

LC 2005052631

"Fleischman looks at Houdini's life through his own eyes, as a fellow magician. . . . Fleischman's tone is lively and he develops a relationship with readers by revealing just enough truth behind Houdini's razzle-dazzle to keep the legend alive. . . . Engaging and fascinating." SLJ

Includes bibliographical references

Houston, Samuel, 1793-1863

Bodden, Valerie. **Samuel** Houston; Army leader & historic politician. ABDO Pub. Co. 2010 112p il map (Military heroes) lib bdg $22.95

Grades: 7 8 9 **92**

1. Governors 2. Statesmen 3. Senators 4. Army officers 5. Texas -- History 6. Politicians -- United States

ISBN 978-1-60453-962-2; 1-60453-962-3

LC 2009-32373

Biography of Samuel Houston.

"The rush of literary adrenalin will hook readers immediately and keep them enthralled until the end. . . . Given the dynamic topic [and] . . . appealing layout . . . [this is] likely to attract reluctant readers. In addition, sources are plentiful and well documented." SLJ

Includes glossary and bibliographical references

Howe, Samuel Gridley, 1801-1876

Alexander, Sally Hobart. **She** touched the world: Laura Bridgman, deaf-blind pioneer; by Sally Hobart Alexander and Robert Alexander. Clarion Books 2008 100p il $18

Grades: 5 6 7 8 **92**

1. Deaf 2. Blind 3. Students 4. Physicians 5. Philanthropists 6. Humanitarians 7. Teachers of the blind

ISBN 978-0-618-85299-4; 0-618-85299-9

"At the age of three, in 1832, Laura Bridgman contracted scarlet fever and lost her sight, her hearing, her sense of smell, and much of her sense of taste. Her family sent her to Dr. Samuel [Gridley] Howe at the New England Institute for the Education of the Blind, and by the age of 10, Laura was world-famous for her accomplishments. . . . Alexander . . . presents a well-written and thoroughly researched biography of this remarkable woman, with numerous black-and-white photos." Booklist

Includes bibliographical references

Hubble, Edwin Powell, 1889-1953

Datnow, Claire L. **Edwin** Hubble; discoverer of galaxies. rev ed; Enslow Publishers 2007 128p il (Great minds of science) lib bdg $31.93

Grades: 5 6 7 8 **92**

1. Astronomers

ISBN 978-0-7660-2791-6 lib bdg; 0-7660-2791-0 lib bdg

LC 2006-20111

First published 1997

Traces the life and work of the man whose study of galaxies led to a new understanding of the universe

Includes glossary and bibliographical references

Hudson, Henry, d. 1611

★ Otfinoski, Steven. **Henry** Hudson; in search of the Northwest Passage. [by] Steven Otfinoski. Marshall Cavendish Benchmark 2006 80p il map (Great explorations) lib bdg $32.79

Grades: 5 6 7 8 **92**

1. Explorers 2. America -- Exploration

ISBN 978-0-7614-2225-9 lib bdg; 0-7614-2225-0 lib bdg

"An examination of the life and accomplishments of the famed explorer who lent his name to several geographic locations in North America" Publisher's note

Includes bibliographical references

★ Weaver, Janice. **Hudson**; written by Janice Weaver; illustrated by David Craig. Tundra Books 2010 47p il map $22.95

Grades: 3 4 5 6 **92**

1. Explorers 2. Biography, Individual 3. America -- Exploration 4. Canada -- Discovery and exploration -- British 5. America -- Discovery and exploration

ISBN 978-0-88776-814-9; 0-88776-814-8

This is a biography of the explorer. "The grandson of a trader, Hudson sailed under both British and Dutch flags, looking for a northern route to China. Although none of his voyages led to the discovery of a northwest passage, he did explore what is now Hudson's Bay and what is now New York City." (Publisher's note) Index. "Ages eight to twelve." (Quill Quire)

"This dramatic picture-book biography about Henry Hudson, who discovered neither the new land nor the passage to Asia he sought, makes the explorer's lack of success a gripping read. . . . Weaver is clear about what is fact and what is supposition, and the tumultuous early-seventeenth-century history is meticulously documented. . . . Craig's glowing period portraits, landscapes, and watercolors of the ship in dangerous seas intensify the drama, and archival prints and maps add interest." Booklist

Includes bibliographical references

Huerta, Dolores, 1930-

Brill, Marlene Targ **Dolores** Huerta stands strong; the woman who demanded justice. Marlene Targ Brill. Ohio University Press 2018 104 p. (pb : alk. paper) $14.95

Grades: 5 6 7 8 **92**

1. Migrant agricultural laborers 2. Women labor leaders -- United States -- Biography 3. Mexican American women labor union members -- Biography 4. Migrant agricultural laborers -- Labor unions -- United States -- History 5. Mexican American migrant agricultural laborers -- Labor unions -- Organizing -- History

ISBN 9780821423295; 9780821423301

LC 2018019627

This book in the Biographies for Young Readers series, by Marlene Targ Brill, follows the life of Dolores Huerta, cofounder of the National Farmworkers Association, "from the mining communities of the Southwest where her father toiled, to the vineyards and fields of California, and across the country to the present day. As she worked for fair treatment for others, Dolores earned the nation's highest honors. More important, she found her voice." (Publisher's note)

Includes bibliographical references

Hunter, Clementine, 1886?-1988

Whitehead, Kathy. **Art** from her heart: folk artist Clementine Hunter; [illustrated by] Shane Evans. G.P. Putnam's Sons 2008 un il $16.99

Grades: 4 5 6 7 **92**

1. Artists 2. Folk art 3. Painters 4. Women artists 5. African American artists 6. Centenarians 7. Biography, Individual

ISBN 0-399-24219-8; 978-0-399-24219-9

LC 2006-34458

This is a biography of Louisiana artist Clementine Hunter, who depicted life on a plantation. Bibliography. "Ages five to eight." (Bull Cent Child Books) "In the 1950s, segregation laws denied artist Clementine Hunter admission to the gallery that exhibited her work. . . . Hunter was not stopped by self-pity, and she did not wait for 'the perfect time to paint.' She had no canvas, so she made art with whatever she could find--window shades, glass bottles, old boards." (Booklist)

"Whitehead's lyrical text speaks of Hunter's perseverance and talent as well as of the simplicity, love of nature, and caring of friends and family that informed her work. Evans bolsters Whitehead's words with bold mixed-media illustrations that portray Hunter in hard times and in good." SLJ

Hunter-Gault, Charlayne

Hunter-Gault, Charlayne, 1942- **To** the mountaintop! Charlayne Hunter-Gault. Roaring Brook Press 2012 v, 198 p.p ill

Grades: 6 7 8 9 10 11 12 **92**

1. Colleges and universities 2. Women political activists 3. African Americans -- Civil rights 4. Southern States -- Race relations 5. African American journalists -- Biography 6. Journalists -- United States -- Biography 7. Civil rights movements -- Southern States -- History -- 20th century 8. African Americans -- Civil rights -- Southern States -- History -- 20th century

ISBN 9781596436053

LC 2011020894

This book is written by Charlayne "Hunter-Gault . . . [who along with her] classmate Hamilton Holmes . . . [was one of] the first African Americans to be admitted to the University of Georgia, Athens. . . . [It] recalls the turbulent years from 1959, when she was first approached to challenge the system by seeking admission, through two years of legal battles for her admission to be finalized, through the campus protests and challenges unleashed by her actual enrollment, to graduation and her full-time position in 1965 at the 'New Yorker.' Organized by year, Hunter-Gault's personal experiences are set within the context of the larger civil rights movement." (Bulletin of the Center for Children's Books)

Includes bibliographical references and index

Hurston, Zora Neale, 1891-1960

★ Fradin, Dennis Brindell. **Zora!** the life of Zora Neal Hurston. Judith Bloom Fradin and Dennis Brindell Fradin. Clarion Books 2012 xi, 180 p.p ill. $17.99

Grades: 5 6 7 8 **92**

1. African American authors -- Biography 2. African American women -- Biography 3. Folklorists -- United States – Biography 4. Authors, American -- 20th century -- Biography

ISBN 0547006950; 9780547006956

LC 2011025949

This book by Dennis Brindell Fradin and Judith Bloom Fradin presents a "biography of . . . African-American author . . . [Zora Neale] Hurston. . . . Beginning with a . . . scene of the 59-year-old Hurston, already a well-known author, working as a white family's domestic helper because she needed a paycheck, the Fradins . . . establish the complexities of Zora's inner and external worlds, before offering highlights of her life in chronological order." (Publishers Weekly)

Includes bibliographical references and index.

★ Litwin, Laura Baskes. **Zora** Neale Hurston; I have been in sorrow's kitchen. Enslow Publishers 2007 128p bibl il por (African-American biography library) lib bdg $23.95

Grades: 7 8 9 10 **92**

1. Authors 2. Novelists 3. Dramatists 4. Women authors 5. African American authors 6. Memoirists 7. Folklorists 8. Short story writers

ISBN 978-0-7660-2536-5 lib bdg; 0-7660-2536-5 lib bdg

LC 2005034881

Litwin "offers an engaging portrait of legendary author and folklorist Zora Neale Hurston. . . . Well-paced . . . chapters follow Hurston through her remarkable career. . . . Generously sprinkled with excerpts from Hurston's own works and illustrated with numerous black-and-white portraits of Hurston and her prominent friends and collaborators." Booklist

Includes bibliographical references

★ Lyons, Mary E. **Sorrow's** kitchen; the life and folklore of Zora Neale Hurston. 1st Collier Books ed; Collier Books 1993 144p il (Great achievers) pa $7.99

Grades: 7 8 9 10 **92**

1. Authors 2. Novelists 3. Dramatists 4. Women authors 5. African American authors 6. Memoirists 7. Folklorists 8. Short story writers

ISBN 0-02-044445-1

LC 92-30600

First published 1990 by Scribner

This biography details "Hurston's migration from Florida to Baltimore, Washington, D.C., and finally Harlem as well as her travels through the West Indies to collect folklore. The text contains eleven excerpts from Hurston's books. . . . Lyons has created a prime example of biography—fascinating, enlightening, stimulating, and satisfying." Horn Book

Includes bibliographical references

Inouye, Daniel K.

Slavicek, Louise Chipley. **Daniel** Inouye. Chelsea House 2007 128p bibl il por (Asian Americans of achievement) lib bdg $30

Grades: 6 7 8 9 **92**

1. Lawyers 2. Senators 3. State legislators 4. District attorneys 5. Members of Congress 6. Statesmen -- United States 7. Asian Americans -- Biography

ISBN 978-0-7910-9271-2 lib bdg; 0-7910-9271-2 lib bdg

LC 2006026062

A biography of the Senator from Hawaii

This is "well-researched . . . attractive . . . solid." SLJ

Includes glossary and bibliographical references

IraqiGirl

IraqiGirl. **IraqiGirl**; diary of a teenage girl in Iraq. Haymarket 2009 205p pa $13

Grades: 6 7 8 9 10 **92**

1. Blogs 2. Iraq War, 2003-2011 3. Weblogs 4. Bloggers 5. Iraq War, 2003-2011 -- Personal narratives

ISBN 978-1-931859-73-8; 1-931859-73-6

"In 2004 in Mosul (the third largest city in Iraq), a 15-year-old girl started a blog detailing her life in the midst of the Iraq War. Her journal encompasses the day-to-day trauma the American invasion has caused her city, her family and friends. . . . [The author's] authentically teenage voice, emotional struggles and concerns make her story all the more resonant." Publ Wkly

Irwin, Bindi, 1998-

Breguet, Amy. **Steve** and Bindi Irwin. Chelsea House 2011 140p il map (Conservation heroes) lib bdg $35

Grades: 6 7 8 9 **92**

1. Conservationists 2. Wildlife conservation 3. Television personalities 4. Zoo directors 5. Herpetologists 6. Children of prominent persons

ISBN 978-1-60413-957-0; 1-60413-957-9

A biography of Steve Irwin, Australian star of The Crocodile Hunter, who died in 2006, and his daughter, Bindi.

"Captivating, richly informative. . . . The scope of [this book] is comprehensive. . . . [The book is] engaging as [it is] educational and will be ideal for research and reports." SLJ

Irwin, Steve, 1962-2006

Breguet, Amy. **Steve** and Bindi Irwin. Chelsea House 2011 140p il map (Conservation heroes) lib bdg $35

Grades: 6 7 8 9 **92**

1. Conservationists 2. Wildlife conservation 3. Television personalities 4. Zoo directors 5. Herpetologists 6. Children of prominent persons

ISBN 978-1-60413-957-0; 1-60413-957-9

A biography of Steve Irwin, Australian star of The Crocodile Hunter, who died in 2006, and his daughter, Bindi.

"Captivating, richly informative. . . . The scope of [this book] is comprehensive. . . . [The book is] engaging as [it is] educational and will be ideal for research and reports." SLJ

Jackson, Robert Houghwout, 1892-1954

Jarrow, Gail. **Robert** H. Jackson; New Deal lawyer, Supreme Court Justice, Nuremberg prosecutor. Calkins Creek 2008 128p il $18.95

Grades: 7 8 9 10 **92**

1. Judges 2. Lawyers 3. Nuremberg Trial of Major German War Criminals, 1945-1946 4. Attorneys general 5. Government officials 6. Supreme Court justices

ISBN 978-1-59078-511-9

LC 2007-18858

"Framed by Jackson's famous speech as chief American prosecutor at the 1945 international Nuremberg trial of Nazi war criminals, this detailed biography sets his law career within the history and politics of his time and raises essential issues of human rights." Booklist

Includes bibliographical references

Jacobs, Jane, 1916-2006

Lang, Glenna. **Genius** of common sense; Jane Jacobs and the story of The death and life of great American cities. [by] Glenna Lang & Marjory Wunsch. David R. Godine 2009 127p il map $17.95

Grades: 7 8 9 10 11 12 **92**

1. Authors 2. City planning 3. Urban sociology 4. Urban planners 5. Nonfiction writers 6. New York (State) -- History

ISBN 978-1-56792-384-1; 1-56792-384-4

LC 2009-08304

"This is the story of a remarkable woman, brought up during the Depression and with no college education, who single-handedly changed the way America viewed its cities. . . . At 18, she moved to New York to pursue her career as a writer and fell in love with the city. It was there that she had her infamous battles with Robert Moses over urban renewal and did the research for her most famous book, The Death and Life of Great American Cities. Black-and-white photographs, maps, and political cartoons and other reproductions appear on most pages. . . . Lang and Wunsch are to be commended for introducing a fascinating female role model." SLJ

Includes bibliographical references

Jacobs, Marc, 1963-

Branscomb, Leslie Wolf. **Marc** Jacobs. Morgan Reynolds Pub. 2011 112p il (Profiles in fashion) $28.95

Grades: 7 8 9 10 **92**

1. Fashion designers

ISBN 978-1-59935-153-7; 1-59935-153-6

LC 2010022226

This biography of Marc Jacobs describes "the personal [life] and economic details of the multimillion-dollar business of [this] high-profile [designer]. [It discusses] the designer's cultural background, childhood, family, work history and education. The . . . [author describes] the early influences that inspired the [designer] to pursue this career and [provides] details of the philosophy [the] designer uses to make [his] clothing unique. . . . The writing is clear and well organized. Color photos are included and give readers a feel for the time period and the types of clothing and accessories the [designer] created." Voice Youth Advocates

Includes bibliographical references

Jalāl ad-Dīn Rūmī Maulana, 1207-1273

★ Demi. **Rumi**; whirling dervish. written and illustrated by Demi. Marshall Cavendish Children 2009 31p il $19.99

Grades: 4 5 6 7 **92**

1. Poets 2. Persian poetry

ISBN 978-0-7614-5527-1; 0-7614-5527-2

LC 2008012920

"Demi presents this picture-book introduction to the thirteenth-century mystical poet. . . . Demi condenses her famous subject's life into a brief but substantive text. . . . She adds frequent excerpts from Rumi's poems and writings. . . . In an introductory note, Demi cites Turkish miniatures as her inspiration for the small-scale, elaborately patterned pictures, rendered in Turkish and Chinese inks with gold overlay. . . . The gilded, celebratory pictures create shimmering beauty from the smallest details." Booklist

James, LeBron

Yasuda, Anita. **Lebron** James. 2011 24p il (Remarkable people) $27.13; pa $12.95

Grades: 4 5 6 7 **92**

1. Basketball players 2. Basketball -- Biography

ISBN 978-1-6169-0669-6; 1-6169-0669-3; 978-1-6169-0674-0 pa; 1-6169-0674-X pa

LC 2010051003

This looks at Lebron James' "life, accomplishments, and challenges while including a page of quotes, an annotated list of contemporaries and influences, starter suggestions for writing a paper, and a time line and glossary. . . . [This book] follows basketball's 'King James' from his early life with a single teen mother to his splashy entry into the NBA at age 19." Booklist

Jay-Z, 1969-

Spilsbury, Richard. **Jay** -Z; Richard Spilsbury. Heinemann Library 2013 48 p. (Titans of business) (pbk.) $8.99

Grades: 4 5 6 7 **92**

1. Businessmen 2. Rap musicians 3. Success in business 4. Rap musicians -- United States -- Biography

ISBN 1432964305; 1432964372; 9781432964306; 9781432964375

LC 2011050758

This book, part of the Titans of Business series, looks at rapper and entrepreneur Jay-Z. "Starting with Jay-Z's early life as Shawn Corey Carter in a poor Brooklyn neighborhood, the biography recounts how he overcame his difficult adolescence as a drug dealer with his desire to be a musician." (Booklist)

Includes bibliographical references and index

Jefferson, Thomas, 1743-1826

Miller, Brandon Marie. **Thomas** Jefferson for kids; his life and times, with 21 activities. Chicago Review Press 2011 ix, 132p il $16.95

Grades: 4 5 6 7 **92**

1. Architects 2. Presidents 3. Vice-presidents 4. Essayists 5. Presidents -- United States

ISBN 978-1-56976-348-3; 1-56976-348-8

LC 2011019318

"Miller offers a thorough and methodical overview of Jefferson's life and political career. . . . The presentation is expecially forthright about Jefferson's ownership of slaves and his fathering of children with Sally Hemmings. . . . The volume offers the chance to delve into Jefferson's life and be inspired by the range of his interests." Kirkus

Includes bibliographical references

Jemison, Mae C.

Jemison, Mae C. **Find** where the wind goes; moments from my life. [by] Mae Jemison. Scholastic Press 2001 196p il hardcover o.p. $16.95

Grades: 5 6 7 8 **92**

1. Astronauts 2. Physicians 3. African American women -- Biography

ISBN 0-439-13195-2; 0-439-13196-0 pa

LC 00-41008

"Mae Jemsion, doctor, scientist, astronaut, and professor, here tells of the formative incidents of her life. . . . The author discusses her youth—her days in the South, her family's move to Chicago's South Side, school experiences, and growing up—as well as her later life and her place in the space program. . . . Grades five to eight." (Bull Cent Child Books)

"Dr. Jemison, the first woman of color to travel in space, shares her life story in this autobiographical selection." Book Rep

Jobs, Steve, 1955-2011

Blumenthal, Karen. **Steve** Jobs; the man who thought different : a biography. by Karen Blumenthal. Feiwel and Friends 2012 310 p. ill., ports.

Grades: 7 8 9 10 **92**

1. Apple Inc. 2. Inventors -- United States -- Biography 3. Businesspeople -- United States -- Biography 4. Computer industry -- United States -- History 5. Apple Computer, Inc. -- History 6. Inventors -- United States -- Biography 7. Businesspeople -- United States -- Biography

ISBN 125001445X; 125001557X; 9781250014450; 9781250015570

LC 2012376637

YALSA Award for Excellence in Nonfiction for Young Adults Finalist (2013)

This book is a biography of technology executive Steve Jobs. "[Karen] Blumenthal weaves her portrait on the thematic frame used by Jobs himself in his autobiographical 2005 Stanford commencement address." She chronicles "his adoption as an infant through his 'phone phreaking' days to a spectacular rise and just as meteoric fall from corporate grace in the 1980s. Following a decade of diminished fortunes and largely self-inflicted complications in personal relationships, he returned to Apple." (Kirkus)

Includes bibliographical references (p. [278]-283) and index

Goldsworthy, Steve. **Steve** Jobs. Weigl 2011 24p il (Remarkable people) $27.13; pa $12.95 **92**

1. Entrepreneurs 2. Businesspeople 3. Computer industry 4. Computer scientists 5. Apple Computer Inc. 6. Computer industry executives 7. Electronics industry executives

ISBN 978-1-6169-0670-2; 1-6169-0670-7; 978-1-6169-0675-7 pa; 1-6169-0675-8 pa

LC 2010050999

This looks at Steve Jobs' "life, accomplishments, and challenges while including a page of quotes, an annotated list of contemporaries and influences, starter suggestions for writing a paper, and a time line and glossary. . . . [This book] kicks off as current as possible with a picture of the bearded Apple CEO displaying an iPad, before getting into the ups (he became a multimillionaire in just two years) and downs (his struggle with cancer)." Booklist

Quinn, Jason. **Steve** Jobs; genius by design. by Jason Quinn ; illustrated by Amit Tayal. Random House Inc 2012 104 p. ill. (chiefly col.) $12.99

Grades: 7 8 9 10 11 12 Adult **92**

1. Computer industry 2. Biographical graphic novels

ISBN 9380028768; 9789380028767

This graphic novel, by Jason Quinn, illustrated by Amit Tayal, presents a biography of the 20th-century technology entrepreneur and Apple Inc. founder Steve Jobs. "Steve Jobs and his inventions changed the world we live in." The book ranges "from his birth and his adoption, through the advent of the computer age and on into the digital age. Forced out of the company he created, his indomitable vision allowed him to change the world of computers, movies, music and telecommunications." (Publisher's note)

"This cleverly designed volume provides a concise but well-balanced view of Steve Jobs the wunderkind, including his difficult personality and complex genius." Booklist

Johnson, Earvin, 1959-

Roselius, J Chris. **Magic** Johnson; basketball star and entrepreneur. ABDO Pub. Co. 2011 112p il (Legendary athletes) lib bdg $34.22

Grades: 6 7 8 9 **92**

1. African American athletes 2. Basketball coaches 3. Basketball players 4. Real estate developers 5. Basketball -- Biography

ISBN 978-1-61714-756-2; 1-61714-756-7

LC 2010046696

This biography of basketball star Magic Johnson "goes beyond merely discussing [his] accomplishments. . . . [It] also [explores] the social and political [influence he] had on society as a whole. In addition, [it introduces] historical events in the context of [his life]. . . . This . . . is teeming with information and is a must-purchase for sports fans and readers interested in social activism." SLJ

Includes glossary and bibliographical references

Johnson, Mamie, 1935-

★ Green, Michelle Y. A **strong** right arm: the story of Mamie Peanut Johnson; introduction by Mamie Johnson. Dial Bks. for Young Readers 2002 111p il $15.99; pa $5.99

Grades: 4 5 6 7 **92**

1. Women athletes 2. Baseball players 3. African American athletes 4. Collectibles dealers 5. Baseball -- Biography

ISBN 0-8037-2661-9; 0-14-240072-6 pa

LC 2001-28616

"Johnson was a pitcher with the Negro Leagues' Indianapolis Clowns from 1953 to 1955. In the introduction, Johnson speaks directly and movingly to the reader about her meeting with author Green, who then lets the famous ballplayer tell her own story in a lively first-person narrative. Johnson's ebullient personality and determination fairly leap off the page." Booklist

Includes bibliographical references

Jolie, Angelina

Abrams, Dennis. **Angelina** Jolie; actress and activist. Chelsea House 2011 146p il (Women of achievement) $35

Grades: 6 7 8 9 **92**

1. Actors

ISBN 978-1-60413-909-9; 1-60413-909-9

This "focuses on the superstar's troubled youth, her award-winning performances as an actress, and her work on behalf of refugees around the world. Abrams is frank in discussing Jolie's fascination, in her younger years, with knives, cutting, and blood. . . . Solid fare for the biography collection." Booklist

Jones, John Paul, 1747-1792

Cooper, Michael L. **Hero** of the high seas; John Paul Jones and the American Revolution. National Geographic 2006 128p il map $21.95; lib bdg $32.90

Grades: 5 6 7 8 **92**

1. Admirals 2. Naval officers 3. United States -- History -- 1775-1783, Revolution

ISBN 0-7922-5547-X; 0-7922-5548-8 lib bdg

LC 2005-36256

"Cooper charts his subject's life from a scandal-ridden Scottish captain on a trading ship to a man of self-invention who came to the American colonies to start a new life and became a naval hero. Jones is presented as a loyal captain, an arrogant leader, a determined sailor, and a flagrant social climber. The narrative style will appeal to reluctant readers, for it reads like a chronicle of thrilling naval adventures. . . . The text is clear and understandable." SLJ

Includes bibliographical references

Jordan, Barbara, 1936-1996

Raatma, Lucia. **Barbara** Jordan; Lucia Raatma. Marshall Cavendish 2012 96 p. (Leading women) (print) $39.93

Grades: 7 8 9 **92**

1. Women political activists 2. Civil rights -- United States 3. Legislators -- United States -- Biography 4. Texas -- Politics and government -- 1951- 5. United States. Congress. House -- Biography 6. African American women legislators -- Texas -- Biography 7. African American women legislators -- United States -- Biography

ISBN 0761449566; 9780761449560; 9781608707133

LC 2011003470

This biography of Barbara Jordan by Lucia Raatma is part of the Leading Women series. The books "focus on the background and political achievements of twentieth-century women, including those well known in America and those lesser known, too. Each woman's story is told in a narrative, chronological style, illustrated by photographs. . . . Barbara Jordan's connection to the civil rights movement" is noted. (Booklist)

Includes bibliographical references and index

Joseph, Nez Percé Chief, 1840-1904

Biskup, Agnieszka. **Thunder** rolling down the mountain; the story of Chief Joseph and the Nez Perce. illustrated by Rusty Zimmerman. Capstone Press 2011 32p il (Graphic library: American graphic) lib bdg $29.32; pa $7.95

Grades: 4 5 6 7 **92**

1. Biographical graphic novels 2. Indian chiefs 3. Nez Percé Indians

ISBN 978-1-4296-5472-2 lib bdg; 1-4296-5472-4 lib bdg; 978-1-4296-6270-3 pa; 1-4296-6270-0 pa

LC 2010027914

In graphic novel format, explores the battles and hardships faced by Chief Joseph and the Nez Perce when they were forced to leave their homelands.

"The illustrations are eye-catching and the narration is presented simply, yet compellingly. . . . Fact-filled, entertaining, and accessible." SLJ

Includes bibliographical references

Hopping, Lorraine Jean. **Chief** Joseph; the voice for peace. Sterling 2010 124p il map (Sterling biographies) lib bdg $12.95

Grades: 7 8 9 10 **92**

1. Indian chiefs 2. Nez Percé Indians 3. Native Americans -- Biography

ISBN 978-1-4027-6842-2; 1-4027-6842-7

LC 2009-24132

This biography is "packed with fast action and detailed analysis. . . . Hopping tells of Joseph's painful decision to leave his land to save Nez Percé lives, choosing peace because he knew they could not win against the U.S. . . . [The] spacious design is highly scannable, with color background screens, photos, maps, and historic prints throughout." Booklist

Includes glossary and bibliographical references

Judge, Oney

★ Dunbar, Erica Armstrong. **Never** caught, the story of Ona Judge; George and Martha Washington's courageous slave who dared to run away. by Erica Armstrong Dunbar and Kathleen Van Cleve. Young readers edition Aladdin 2019 272 p. illustrations $18.99

Grades: 4 5 6 7 8 **92**

1. Fugitive slaves 2. Slavery -- History 3. African American women -- Biography 4. Slaves -- United States -- Biography 5. Fugitive slaves -- United States -- Biography 6. Slavery -- Pennsylvania -- Philadelphia -- History -- 18th century

ISBN 9781534416178

LC 2018043941

"Erica Armstrong Dunbar reveals a fascinating and heartbreaking behind-the-scenes look at the Washingtons when they were the First Family--and an in-depth look at their slave, Ona Judge, who dared to escape from one of the nation's Founding Fathers. . . . When she was told that she was going to be given as a wedding gift to Martha Washington's granddaughter, Ona made the bold and brave decision to flee to the north." (Publisher's note)

"The accessible narrative, clear context, and intricately recorded details of the lives of the enslaved provide much-needed understanding of the complexities and contradictions of the country's founding." Kirkus

Includes bibliographical references and index

Julian, Percy L., 1899-1975

Stille, Darlene R. **Percy** Lavon Julian; pioneering chemist. Compass Point Books 2009 112p il map (Signature lives) lib bdg $34.65

Grades: 6 7 8 9 10 **92**

1. Chemists 2. Pharmaceutical executives

ISBN 978-0-7565-4089-0; 0-7565-4089-5

LC 2008-38462

Details the life of chemist Percy Lavon Julian and his accomplishments

The "inviting page design features photos and boxed screens on each spread, and . . . includes a detailed bibliography, source notes, time line and glossary." Booklist

Includes glossary and bibliographical references

Juárez, Benito, 1806-1872

Stein, R. Conrad. **Benito** Juarez and the French intervention; [by] R. Conrad Stein. Morgan Reynolds Pub. 2008 160p il map (The story of Mexico) lib bdg $27.95

Grades: 6 7 8 9 **92**

1. Presidents 2. Mexico -- History

ISBN 978-1-59935-052-3 lib bdg; 1-59935-052-1 lib bdg

LC 2007016005

The book provides "detailed information in a readable format, and [a] lively writing style. . . . Colorful reproductions and photographs help to maintain interest. [This] title tells the story of Juárez, a Zapotec Indian, and his rise to political leadership. Born into poverty in 1806, he became Mexico's first Indian president, presiding over a country in turmoil." SLJ

Includes glossary and bibliographical references

Kahlo, Frida, 1907-1954

Hillstrom, Laurie. **Frida** Kahlo; painter. by Laurie Collier Hillstrom. Lucent Books 2008 104p il (The twentieth century's most influential Hispanics) lib bdg $32.45

Grades: 6 7 8 9 10 **92**

1. Artists 2. Painters 3. Women artists 4. Artists, Mexican

ISBN 978-1-4205-0019-6 lib bdg; 1-4205-0019-8 lib bdg

LC 2007-32106

"Kahlo's life . . . is chronicled as are the influences of her marriage to Rivera and her physical pain on on her art. . . . The layout draws the eye with colorful chapter headings and highlighted quotes." Lib Media Connect

Includes bibliographical references

Kamkwamba, William, 1987-

Mealer, Bryan. The **boy** who harnessed the wind; William Kamkwamba and Bryan Mealer ; illustrated by Anna Hymas. Young Readers' Edition Dial Books for Young Readers 2015 293 p. col. ill., col. map $8.99; $16.99

Grades: 4 5 6 7 **92**

1. Windmills 2. Irrigation 3. Inventors

ISBN 9780147510426 ; 0803740808; 0147510422 ; 9780803740808

"When a terrible drought struck William Kamkwamba's tiny village in Malawi, his family lost all of the season's crops, leaving them with nothing to eat and nothing to sell. William began to explore science books in his village library, looking for a solution. There, he came up with the idea that would change his family's life forever: he could build a windmill. Made out of scrap metal and old bicycle parts, William's windmill brought electricity to his home and helped his family pump the water they needed to farm the land." (Publisher's note)

"This youth edition of the original adult book of the same title has been skillfully adapted for middle grade readers." SLJ

Kazerooni, Abbas

Kazerooni, Abbas. **On** two feet and wings; one boy's amazing story of survival. Abbas Kazerooni. Skyscape 2014 199 p. (trade pbk : alk. paper) $16.99

Grades: 5 6 7 8 **92**

1. Refugees 2. Children and war 3. Iran-Iraq War, 1980-1988
ISBN 1477847839; 9781477847831

LC 2014933778

Abbas Kazerooni's memoir is set when "the Iran-Iraq war is at its bloodiest, and the Ayatollahs who rule Iran have reduced the recruitment age for the army. If Abbas doesn't escape, it's almost certain that he will be drafted and die fighting for a regime that has stripped his family of all they have. On his own in the strange, often frightening city of Istanbul, Abbas grows up fast." (Publisher's note)

"Young readers will understand [Kazerooni's] overwhelming loneliness and fear as well as his satisfaction at managing on his own. With child immigrants so much in the news, Kazerooni's unusual, compelling story is especially timely." Booklist

Keat, Nawuth, 1964-

Keat, Nawuth. **Alive** in the killing fields; surviving the Khmer Rouge genocide. by Nawuth Keat with Martha E. Kendall. National Geographic 2009 127p il map $15.95; lib bdg $23.90

Grades: 7 8 9 10 11 **92**

1. Authors 2. Cambodian refugees 3. Political refugees 4. Young adult authors
ISBN 978-1-4263-0515-3; 1-4263-0515-X; 978-1-4263-0516-0 lib bdg; 1-4263-0516-8 lib bdg

LC 2008-39805

"Told with stark simplicity, Nawuth's narrative is memorable yet accessible to young readers." Voice Youth Advocates

Includes bibliographical references

Keckley, Elizabeth, ca. 1818-1907

Jones, Lynda. **Mrs.** Lincoln's dressmaker: the unlikely friendship of Elizabeth Keckley and Mary Todd Lincoln; by Lynda D. Jones. National Geographic 2009 80p il $18.95; lib bdg $27.90

Grades: 5 6 7 8 **92**

1. Memoirists 2. Dressmakers 3. Spouses of presidents 4. Slavery -- United States 5. United States -- Race relations 6. African American women -- Biography 7. Presidents' spouses -- United States 8. Washington (D.C.) -- Social life and customs
ISBN 978-1-4263-0377-7; 1-4263-0377-7; 978-1-4263-0378-4 lib bdg; 1-4263-0378-5 lib bdg

LC 2008-29314

"Readers may be familiar with the ups and downs of Lincoln's life, but details of Keckley's story . . . will give them new insights into the life of a slave, in this case, one who was educated and had a profession." Booklist

Includes bibliographical references

Kellar, Harry, 1849-1922

★ Jarrow, Gail. The **amazing** Harry Kellar; great American magician. Gail G. Jarrow. Calkins Creek 2012 96 p. col. ill. $17.95

Grades: 3 4 5 6 7 8 **92**

1. Magicians 2. Optical illusions
ISBN 1590788656; 9781590788653

LC 2011940465

This book is a biography of Harry Keller (later Kellar), "the first dean of the Society of American Magicians, a man [magician Harry] Houdini regarded as a mentor. . . . Few secrets of the illusions are revealed here, but [Gail] Jarrow makes it clear that it was Kellar's art that made them seem like real magic." The book also includes "[d]ozens of . . . Kellar posters" and a "timeline, bibliography, [and] annotated sources." (Kirkus)

Keller, Helen, 1880-1968

Delano, Marfe Ferguson. **Helen's** eyes; a photobiography of Annie Sullivan, Helen Keller's teacher. [foreword by Keller Johnson Thompson] National Geographic 2008 63p il map $17.95; lib bdg $27.90

Grades: 4 5 6 7 **92**

1. Deaf 2. Blind 3. Authors 4. Teachers 5. Memoirists 6. Humanitarians 7. Teachers of the deaf 8. Inspirational writers 9. Teachers of the blind 10. Social welfare leaders
ISBN 978-1-4263-02-9-1; 1-4263-0209-6; 978-1-4263-0210-7 lib bdg; 1-4263-0210-X lib bdg

"There are many biographies of Helen Keller and Annie Sullivan, but this one is very nicely done. . . . The book is honest in its portrayals, especially of Sullivan. . . . What makes this oversize book so appealing is the clean design, with large typeface. The many fascinating photographs are sometimes placed over historical documents." Booklist

Includes bibliographical references

★ Keller, Helen. The **story** of my life; edited and with a preface by James Berger. The restored ed.; Modern Library 2003 xlvi, 343p il hardcover o.p. pa $9.95

Grades: 8 9 10 11 12 Adult **92**

1. Deaf 2. Blind 3. Authors 4. Memoirists 5. Humanitarians 6. Inspirational writers 7. Social welfare leaders
ISBN 0-679-64287-0; 0-8129-6886-7 pa

LC 2002-40971

First published 1903

This biography of the inspirational Keller contains accounts of her home life and her relationship with her devoted teacher Anne Sullivan.

Includes bibliographical references

Lawlor, Laurie. **Helen** Keller: rebellious spirit. Holiday House 2001 168p il $22.95

Grades: 5 6 7 8 **92**

1. Deaf 2. Blind 3. Authors 4. Memoirists 5. Humanitarians 6. Inspirational writers 7. Social welfare leaders
ISBN 0-8234-1588-0

LC 00-36950

A "biography of the most famous deaf and blind person in history. Drawing on social and scientific studies of deafness and blindness as well as on American history texts, Lawlor puts Keller's experiences in context. . . . At the same time, readers get a strong feel for Keller's personality and for the personalities of Annie Sullivan, Alexander Graham Bell, and other major figures in her life. Aided by numerous well-chosen photographs and excerpts from Keller's writings." Horn Book

Includes bibliographical references

Sullivan, George. **Helen** Keller; her life in pictures. foreword by Keller Johnson Thompson. Scholastic Nonfiction 2007 80p il $17.99

Grades: 4 5 6 7 **92**

1. Deaf 2. Blind 3. Authors 4. Memoirists 5. Humanitarians 6. Inspirational writers 7. Social welfare leaders

ISBN 0-439-91815-4; 978-0-439-91815-2

LC 2006-51401

"Accompanied by brief, simply phrased commentary from Sullivan, this suite of photos portrays Keller from early childhood into her 80s. . . . This profile will serve equally well as an introduction, or as supplementary reading for confirmed admirers." Booklist

Includes bibliographical references

Kennedy, John F. (John Fitzgerald), 1917-1963

★ Cooper, Ilene. **Jack**; the early years of John F. Kennedy. by Ilene Cooper. 1st ed. Penguin Group USA 2013 168 p. ill. (paperback) $12.99

Grades: 5 6 7 8 9 10 11 12 **92**

1. Catholics 2. Presidents 3. Presidents -- United States

ISBN 0147510317; 9780147510310

LC 2002075912

This book by Ilene Cooper offers a "portrait of [John F.] Kennedy's "youth and the forces that shaped it. . . . Readers discover what it was like for Jack to grow up under the paradoxical influences of privilege and prejudice. His father's wealth . . . couldn't remove the perceived taint of the family's Irish Catholic heritage . . . . To compensate, Joseph and Rose Kennedy pushed their children to excel at everything they did," leading to rivalry between Jack and his brother Joe. (Horn Book Magazine)

"Intelligent design and numerous fabulous, well-placed, and well-captioned black-and-white photographs enrich Cooper's clear prose. . . . This sensitive, well-researched biography will enhance any collection." Voice Youth Advocates

Includes bibliographical references and index.

★ Heiligman, Deborah. **High** hopes; a photobiography of John F. Kennedy. National Geographic 2003 63p il map $17.95

Grades: 4 5 6 7 **92**

1. Presidents 2. Senators 3. Members of Congress 4. Presidents -- United States

ISBN 0-7922-6141-0

LC 2003-7819

Photographs and text trace the life of President John F. Kennedy.

The text "successfully captures the spirit that makes Kennedy an enduring figure in our history. . . . This well-designed book features large, well-chosen, black-and-white photographs." SLJ

Includes bibliographical references

Sandler, Martin W. **Kennedy** through the lens; how photography and television revealed and shaped an extraordinary leader. Walker & Co. 2011 96p il

Grades: 6 7 8 9 10 **92**

1. Presidents 2. Senators 3. Members of Congress 4. Presidents -- United States 5. United States -- History -- 1961-1974 -- Pictorial works

ISBN 0802721605; 0802721613; 9780802721600; 9780802721617

LC 2010-11103

This book describes how John F. Kennedy used the medium of television and advances in photography to mold his image and further his political agenda. Index. "Grades five to nine." (Bull Cent Child Books)

"Sandler offers a fascinating photo-essay examining how images shaped public perceptions of John F. Kennedy. . . . The book begins with an overview of Kennedy's life and the role photography and television played in his career. Subsequent spreads are chronological, covering Kennedy's life from childhood through assassination. . . . Kennedy's life and administration were documented with a groundbreaking intimacy the public had never known before, making this an accessible, insightful perspective on one of America's most famous presidents." Kirkus

Kennedy, Robert F., 1925-1968

Aronson, Marc. **Robert** F. Kennedy; a twentieth-century life. Viking 2007 204p il (Up close) $15.99

Grades: 8 9 10 11 12 **92**

1. Senators 2. Attorneys general 3. Siblings of presidents 4. Presidential candidates 5. Politicians -- United States

ISBN 978-0-670-06066-5; 0-670-06066-6

LC 2006-102150

Explores Robert F. Kennedy's life from his childhood to his adult years as Attorney General, New York state senator, and candidate for the presidency of the United States.

"Aronson draws on a wide variety of sources and is very honest in examining his subject as a complete human being, warts and all. . . . This text stands as an unbiased and illuminating resource." SLJ

Includes bibliographical references

Keynes, John Maynard, 1883-1946

Crain, Cynthia D. **John** Maynard Keynes; by Cynthia D. Crain and Dwight R. Lee. Morgan Reynolds Pub. 2009 144p il (Profiles in economics) lib bdg $28.95

Grades: 8 9 10 11 12 **92**

1. Economists 2. Nonfiction writers 3. Patrons of the arts

ISBN 978-1-59935-109-4 lib bdg; 1-59935-109-9 lib bdg

LC 2009-168

Biography of the economist John Maynard Keynes

"Relationships, education, early influences, and family life are all described . . . [and] economic theory is closely tied to cultural and political events. . . . The writing is straightforward, the . . . [author] assume[s] a certain level of knowledge about world events." SLJ

Includes bibliographical references

Kim, Jong Il, 1942-2011

Wyborny, Sheila. **Kim** Jong Il; by Sheila Wyborny. Lucent Books 2009 104 p. ill. (some col.), map (People in the News) (library) $35.95

Grades: 6 7 8 9 **92**

ISBN 9781420500912; 1420500910

LC 2008049567

This book by Sheila Wyborny is part of the People in the News series and focuses on late North Korean leader Kim Jong Il. The series "profiles the lives and careers of some of today's most prominent newsmakers. Whether covering contributions and achievements or notorious deeds, books in this series examine why these well-known people garner public attention." (Publisher's note)

Includes bibliographical references (p. 90-91) and index.

King, Billie Jean

Gitlin, Marty. **Billie** Jean King; tennis star and social activist. ABDO Pub. Co. 2011 112p il (Legendary athletes) lib bdg $34.22

Grades: 6 7 8 9 **92**

1. Women athletes 2. Sportscasters 3. Tennis players 4. Tennis -- Biography

ISBN 978-1-61714-757-9; 1-61714-757-5

LC 2010046584

This biography of tennis champion Billie Jean King "goes beyond merely discussing [her] accomplishments. . . . [It] also [explores] the social and political [influence she] had on society as a whole. In addition, [it introduces] historical events in the context of [her life]. . . . This . . . is teeming with information and is a must-purchase for sports fans and readers interested in social activism." SLJ

Includes glossary and bibliographical references

King, Coretta Scott, 1927-2006

Gelfand, Dale Evva. **Coretta** Scott King; civil rights activist. Legacy ed; Chelsea House 2006 137p bibl il por (Black Americans of achievement) lib bdg $30

Grades: 7 8 9 10 **92**

1. African Americans -- Civil rights

ISBN 0-7910-9522-3

LC 2006022651

First published 1997 under the authorship of Lisa Renee Rhodes

A biography of the civil rights activist and widow of Martin Luther King

Includes bibliographical references

King, Martin Luther, Jr., 1929-1968

★ Aretha, David. **Martin** Luther King Jr. and the 1963 March on Washington; by David Aretha. Morgan Reynolds Pub. 2014 112 p. illustrations (some color) $28.95

Grades: 7 8 9 10 11 12 **92**

1. African Americans -- Civil rights 2. March on Washington for Jobs and Freedom (1963 : Washington, D.C.) 3. Civil rights demonstrations -- Washington (D.C.) -- History -- 20th century

ISBN 1599353725; 9781599353722

LC 2012035355

In this book, author David "Aretha begins his look at the historic 1963 March on Washington with a review of Jim Crow in the American South and the early days of the modern Civil Rights Movement. . . . Aretha offers considerable detail about the march, including the peaceful, racially integrated crowd and the rousing speeches, which culminated with Dr. King's 'Dream' speech." (Publisher's note)

"Black-and-white archival photographs, boxed quotes, and excerpts from notable speeches enhance this series documenting pivotal laws and incidents of the civil rights movement. Each title builds up to the featured event, though Brown more successfully sets the stage with historical context and what follows. Both are well researched additions to library collections. Timeline, websites. Bib., ind." (Horn Book)

Includes bibliographical references

★ Bolden, Tonya. **M.L.K.** journey of a King. photography editor, Bob Adelman. Abrams Books for Young Readers 2006 128p il $19.95

Grades: 7 8 9 10 **92**

1. Clergy 2. Nonfiction writers 3. Civil rights activists 4. Nobel laureates for peace 5. African Americans -- Biography 6. African Americans -- Civil rights

ISBN 978-0-8109-5476-2; 0-8109-5476-1

LC 2006-13332

"Do libraries need another biography of King? Yes, if it's as good as this one, which will reach a wide audience. . . . Stirring, beautifully reproduced, well-captioned photos . . . accompany the text." Booklist

King, Stephen, 1947-

Stefoff, Rebecca, 1951- **Stephen** King. Marshall Cavendish Benchmark 2010 175p il (Today's writers and their works) lib bdg $42.79

Grades: 8 9 10 11 12 **92**

1. Authors 2. Novelists 3. Authors, American 4. Short story writers 5. Science fiction writers

ISBN 0-7614-4122-0; 978-0-7614-4122-9

This biography of Stephen King places the author in the context of his times and discusses his work.

This book provides "excellent information for reports." SLJ

Includes bibliographical references

Koehl, Mimi, 1948-

Parks, Deborah. **Nature's** machines; the story of biomechanist Mimi Koehl. by Deborah Amel Parks. Joseph Henry Press 2005 118p il (Women's adventures in science) lib bdg $31; pa $9.95

Grades: 7 8 9 10 **92**

1. Biologists 2. Ergonomics 3. Women scientists 4. Bioengineers 5. College teachers 6. Human engineering

ISBN 0-531-16780-1 lib bdg; 0-309-09559-X pa

LC 2005-10201

Mimi Koehl "wanted to know more about sea anemones, particularly how they survive the turbulent surf on rocky beaches. Her inquiries and experiments led to discoveries in a new field, biomechanics, in which scientists examine how form determines movement and function in the animal kingdom. . . . This [book] should spark the curiosity of any reader." Voice Youth Advocates

Includes bibliographical references

Korematsu, Fred, 1919-2005

Yogi, Stan. **Fred** Korematsu speaks up; by Laura Atkins and Stan Yogi ; illustrations by Yutaka Houlette. Heyday 2016 112 p. illustrations (hardcover) $18

Grades: 4 5 6 7 8 **92**

1. Japanese Americans 2. Japanese Americans -- Evacuation and relocation, 1942-1945 3. Japanese Americans -- Civil rights -- History -- 20th century

ISBN 9781597143684

LC 2016008098

"When Fred Korematsu, a young Japanese-American man, defied U.S. governmental orders by refusing to report to prison camps during World War II, he and his allies set in motion a landmark civil liberties case." (Kirkus)

Includes bibliographical references and index

L'Engle, Madeleine

Voiklis, Charlotte Jones. **Becoming** Madeleine L'Engle; a biography by her granddaughters. Charlotte Jones Voiklis and Léna Roy. Farrar, Straus & Giroux Books for Young Readers 2018 162 p. (hardcover) $19.99

Grades: 4 5 6 7 8 **92**

1. Biography 2. American authors -- 20th century -- Biography

ISBN 9780374307646

LC 2017014004

"This elegant and insightful biography of Madeleine L'Engle . . . was written by her granddaughters, Charlotte Jones Voiklis and Léna Roy. . . . [H]er granddaughters weave together an in-depth and unique view of the famous writer. It is a story of overcoming obstacles--a lonely childhood, financial insecurity, and countless rejections of her writing--and eventual triumph." (Publisher's note)

La Salle, Robert Cavelier, sieur de, 1643-1687

Crompton, Samuel. **Robert** de La Salle; [by] Samuel Willard Crompton. Chelsea House 2009 110p il map (Great explorers) lib bdg $30

Grades: 6 7 8 9 **92**

1. Explorers

ISBN 978-1-60413-419-3 lib bdg; 1-60413-419-4 lib bdg

LC 2009014166

Bipgraphy of the explorer Robert de La Salle

"The information . . . is presented in such a way as to attract and maintain readers' interest. . . . With a full complement of maps, photographs (where available), illustrations, time lines, and document reproductions, a full story is told. Well-written and throughly researched, this . . . will make a solid addition." SLJ

Includes glossary and bibliographical references

Lafayette, Marie Joseph Paul Yves Roch Gilbert du Motier, marquis de, 1757-1834

★ Freedman, Russell. **Lafayette** and the American Revolution. Holiday House 2010 88p il $24.95

Grades: 6 7 8 9 **92**

1. Generals 2. Statesmen 3. United States -- History -- 1775-1783, Revolution

ISBN 978-0-8234-2182-4; 0-8234-2182-1

LC 2009052342

A Robert F. Sibert Medal honor book, 2011

A biography of the French general who fought Cornwallis' troops at Yorktown in the American Revolution.

"In this solidly researched and smoothly written biography, Freeman creates a vivid portrait of Lafayette. . . . Handsomely designed with a spacious format and good use of color, the book includes many clearly reproduced paintings and prints." Booklist

Includes bibliographical references

Lang, Lang, 1982-

★ Lang, Lang. **Lang** Lang; playing with flying keys. by Lang Lang with Michael French; introduction by Daniel Barenboim. Delacorte Press 2008 215p il $16.99; lib bdg $19.99

Grades: 7 8 9 10 **92**

1. Pianists 2. China 3. Classical musicians

ISBN 978-0-385-73578-0; 0-385-73578-2; 978-0-385-90564-0 lib bdg; 0-385-90564-5 lib bdg

LC 2007-51597

"Although he is only 26, Chinese-born Lang is recognized as one of the world's most accomplished classical pianists. This smoothly paced, often rivetingly candid autobiography . . . follows the musician through his first encounters with the keyboard and grueling training to his triumphant debut concerts with the Chicago Symphony." Booklist

Lauren, Ralph

Mattern, Joanne. **Ralph** Lauren. Chelsea House 2011 101p il (Famous fashion designers) lib bdg $35

Grades: 6 7 8 9 10 **92**

1. Fashion designers

ISBN 978-1-60413-978-5; 1-60413-978-1

LC 2010036192

This is a biography of fashion designer Ralph Lauren.

Includes glossary and bibliographical references

Lavoisier, Antoine Laurent, 1743-1794

Van Gorp, Lynn. **Antoine** Lavoisier; and his impact on modern chemistry. Compass Point Books 2009 40p il (Mission: Science) lib bdg $26.60

Grades: 4 5 6 7 **92**

1. Chemists 2. Scientists

ISBN 978-0-7565-3959-7 lib bdg; 0-7565-3959-5 lib bdg

LC 2008007283

Profiles the life and career of the Frenchman who is considered the founder of chemistry

"Color photographs, reproductions, diagrams, and maps are liberally sprinkled throughout [this] attractive [book]. Numerous sidebars offer tangential information." SLJ

Lawrence, Jacob, 1917-2000

★ Duggleby, John. **Story** painter: the life of Jacob Lawrence. Chronicle Bks. 1998 55p il $16.95

Grades: 4 5 6 7 **92**

1. Artists 2. Painters 3. Illustrators 4. African American artists 5. African American painters -- Biography 6. African Americans in art

ISBN 0-8118-2082-3

LC 98-4513

This is a biography of the twentieth-century African American painter. Bibliography. "Grades four to eight." (SLJ)

"Lawrence's expressionistic, stark paintings, in excellent full-page color reproduction . . . nicely complement Duggleby's measured account of a materially poor but culturally rich childhood and Lawrence's subsequent struggles and successes." Publ Wkly

Includes bibliographical references

Layson, Annelex Hofstra

Layson, Annelex Hofstra. **Lost** childhood; my life in a Japanese prison camp during World War II. [by] Annelex Hofstra Layson; with Herman Viola. National Geographic 2008 111p il $15.95; lib bdg $23.90

Grades: 5 6 7 8 9 **92**

1. Prisoners of war 2. Memoirists 3. World War, 1939-1945 -- Personal narratives 4. World War, 1939-1945 -- Prisoners and prisons

ISBN 978-1-4263-0321-0; 1-4263-0321-1; 978-1-4263-0322-7 lib bdg; 1-4263-0322-X lib bdg

LC 2008-11671

In a shockingly honest narrative, a former prisoner-of-war tells how her family, along with ten thousand other Dutch residents living in the Dutch East Indies were shipped off to interment camps where food rationing, terrible sanitary conditions, and an uncertain future were the norms for more than three years

The author's narrative is warm and enthralling. . . . Layson's voice captivates and engages. Libr Media Connect

Includes bibliographical references

Le Guin, Ursula K., 1929-

Brown, Jeremy K. **Ursula** K. Le Guin; foreword by Kyle Zimmer. Chelsea House Publishers 2010 128p il (Who wrote that?) lib bdg $35

Grades: 6 7 8 9 10 **92**

1. Authors 2. Novelists 3. Women authors 4. Fantasy writers 5. College teachers 6. Authors, American 7. Children's authors 8. Short story writers 9. Science fiction writers

ISBN 978-1-60413-724-8; 1-60413-724-X

LC 2010006600

"Le Guin's work raises questions about identity and morality, and Brown explores her treatment of these themes in a way that readers, whether they're reading for pleasure or for reports, will appreciate. . . . This title does a fine job of conveying both the story of an author's long career and the vision that fuels it." SLJ

Includes bibliographical references

Lee, Harper, 1926-2016

★ Madden, Kerry. **Harper** Lee; a twentieth-century life. Viking Children's Books 2009 223p il map (Up close) $16.99

Grades: 7 8 9 10 **92**

1. Authors 2. Novelists 3. Women authors 4. Essayists 5. Authors, American 6. Short story writers

ISBN 978-0-670-01095-0; 0-670-01095-2

LC 2008-53911

"A narrative both well paced and richly detailed . . . this biography will appeal to fans of the novel and to newcomers. . . . Extensive source notes and an excellent bibliography round out this superb biography." Kirkus

Includes bibliographical references

Shields, Charles J., 1951- **I** am Scout: the biography of Harper Lee. Henry Holt & Co. 2008 245p il $18.95

Grades: 7 8 9 10 **92**

1. Authors 2. Novelists 3. Women authors 4. Essayists 5. Authors, American 6. Short story writers 7. Biography, Individual

ISBN 0-8050-8334-0; 978-0-8050-8334-7

LC 2007-27572

This is a biography of the author of To Kill a Mockingbird (1960). It is an abridged version of Shields's adult biography Mockingbird (2006). Bibliography. Index. "Grades seven to ten." (Bull Cent Child Books)

Shields "offers a fascinating look at the unconventional Lee, which captures his elusive subject and her lifelong friend, Truman Capote. . . . Shields' formidable research . . . will impress any student who has ever written a term paper." Booklist

Includes bibliographical references

Lee, Robert E. (Robert Edward), 1807-1870

Robertson, James I. **Robert** E. Lee; Virginian soldier, American citizen. [by] James I. Robertson, Jr. Atheneum Books for Young Readers 2005 159p il maps $21.95

Grades: 7 8 9 10 **92**

1. Generals 2. College presidents 3. United States -- History -- 1861-1865, Civil War

ISBN 0-689-85731-4

LC 2003-22108

This portrait of the Confederate general "puts particular emphasis on his life during the Civil War years but provides plenty of information on his youth, his early military career, and his postwar years. . . . Useful for reports and interesting in its own right, this well-researched biography will be a solid addition to library collections." Booklist

Includes bibliographical references

Leif Eriksson, fl. 1000

DeFries, Cheryl L. **Leif** Eriksson; Viking explorer of the New World. Enslow Publishers 2010 112p il map (Great explorers of the world) lib bdg $31.93

Grades: 6 7 8 9 **92**

1. Vikings 2. Explorers 3. America -- Exploration

ISBN 978-1-59845-126-9; 1-59845-126-X

This "provides some interesting stories from the Vikings' family history. Readers will be intrigued by the folklore and legends. The mystery behind [Ericksson's] discovery of America is explored briefly, as well as his impact on navigation, law, and culture. Photographs of Viking artifacts bring provide an interesting glimpse into the past. . . . This . . . would serve as a useful resource for middle and elementary school students and may inspire them to read further." Voice Youth Advocates

Includes glossary and bibliographical references

Lennon, John, 1940-1980

Behnke, Alison Marie. **Death** of a dreamer; the assassination of John Lennon. Alison Marie Behnke. Twenty-First Century Books 2012 96 p.

Grades: 5 6 7 8 **92**

1. Assassination 2. Rock musicians -- Political activity 3. Rock musicians -- England -- Biography 4. Rock musicians 5. Murder -- New York (State) -- New York 6. Murderers -- New York (State) -- Biography

ISBN 0822590360; 9780822590361

LC 2010005550

"Twin narratives converge in New York City on December 8, 1980, when John Lennon was murdered by Mark David Chapman. [Alison Marie] Behnke calls the murder an assassination, and by the general definition of the word--'to murder (a usually prominent person) by sudden or secret attack, often for political reasons'--the murder of John Lennon might qualify. Lennon was political by the end of his life, writing 'Give Peace a Chance,' which became the anthem of the peace movement, but he was hardly a revolutionary, as Behnke terms him. Chapman was not especially political, and he didn't really seem to know why he attacked Lennon; it was certainly not from any well-thought-out political motives, as the author herself describes." (Kirkus)

Includes bibliographical references (p. 92), discography (p. 93), filmography (p. 93), and index

Burlingame, Jeff. **John** Lennon; Imagine. Enslow Publishers 2010 160p il (American rebels) lib bdg $34.60

Grades: 6 7 8 9 **92**

1. Singers 2. Rock musicians 3. Beatles 4. Songwriters

ISBN 978-0-7660-3675-8 lib bdg; 0-7660-3675-8 lib bdg

LC 2009040045

A biography of the rock musician and peace-activist John Lennon.

"This attractive biography includes sidebars, wide margins, large type, and many photographs throughout. Burlingame maintains readers' interest." SLJ

Includes bibliographical references

★ Partridge, Elizabeth. **John** Lennon; all I want is the truth. a photographic biography by Elizabeth Partridge. Viking 2005 232p il $24.99

Grades: 8 9 10 11 12 **92**

1. Singers 2. Rock musicians 3. Beatles 4. Songwriters

ISBN 0-670-05954-4

LC 2005-11850

Michael L. Printz Award honor book, 2006

"This handsome book will be eagerly received by both Beatles fans, who are legion, and their elders, who will enjoy reliving the glory days of the Fab Four and exploring the inner workings of a creative talent." SLJ

Includes bibliographical references

★ Rappaport, Doreen. **John's** secret dreams; the life of John Lennon. written by Doreen Rappaport; illustrated by Bryan Collier. Hyperion Books for Children 2004 un il $16.99

Grades: 4 5 6 7 **92**

1. Singers 2. Rock musicians 3. Beatles 4. Songwriters
ISBN 0-7868-0817-9

LC 2003-57116

"Using a combination of simple prose, song lyrics, and illustration, this heartfelt picture-book biography traces Lennon's life from his childhood to his death. Striking in both its simplicity and complexity, it captures this enigmatic singer, artist, songwriter, and folk hero in a way that will move and fascinate those too young to remember the man but are surrounded by his music and myth." SLJ

Leonard, Buck, 1907-1997

Payment, Simone. **Buck** Leonard. Rosen Pub. Group 2002 112p il (Baseball Hall of Famers of the Negro leagues) lib bdg $29.25

Grades: 5 6 7 8 **92**

1. Baseball players 2. African American athletes 3. Baseball -- Biography
ISBN 0-8239-3473-X

LC 2001-3151

A biography of first-baseman who played in the Negro Leagues and was inducted into the Baseball Hall of Fame in 1972

This "title presents an unvarnished picture of the racism in this country and how it impacted amateur and professional baseball from 1868 onward. . . . The layout . . . is attractive, the style . . . is engaging." Book Rep

Includes glossary and bibliographical references

Leonardo, da Vinci, 1452-1519

Anderson, Maxine. **Amazing** Leonardo da Vinci inventions you can build yourself. Nomad Press 2006 122p il map (Learn some hands-on history) pa $14.95

Grades: 5 6 7 8 **92**

1. Artists 2. Painters 3. Handicraft 4. Inventions 5. Scientists 6. Renaissance 7. Artists, Italian 8. Writers on science
ISBN 0-9749344-2-9

"Anderson has combined biography with doable activities that mirror ideas found in Leonardo's notebooks. Using common household objects (duct tape, foil, cereal boxes, paper-towel tubes, etc.), readers can make a parachute, hydrometer, invisible ink, walk-on-water shoes, etc. Anderson introduces each project with an explanation of why Leonardo came up with the idea and whether he created just the sketch or the sketch and the object. Detailed steps and illustrations provide clarity." SLJ

★ Krull, Kathleen. **Leonardo** da Vinci; illustrated by Boris Kulikov. Viking 2005 128p il (Giants of science) $15.99

Grades: 5 6 7 8 **92**

1. Artists 2. Painters 3. Scientists 4. Renaissance 5. Artists, Italian 6. Writers on science
ISBN 0-670-05920-X

This is a "biography of Leonardo da Vinci that highlights his scientific approach to understanding the physical world. The first half of the book describes Leonardo's apprenticeship and his work as an artist in Milan. The second half relates events in his later life, emphasizing his observation and investigation of the human body and nature. . . . Six excellent ink drawings illustrate this attractive volume. A very readable, vivid portrait set against the backdrop of remarkable times." Booklist

Includes bibliographical references

Phillips, John. **Leonardo** da Vinci; the genius who defined the Renaissance. National Geographic 2006 64p bibl il (World history biographies) $17.95; lib bdg $27.90; pa $6.95

Grades: 5 6 7 8 **92**

1. Artists 2. Painters 3. Scientists 4. Renaissance 5. Artists, Italian 6. Writers on science
ISBN 978-0-7922-5385-3; 0-7922-5385-X; 978-0-7922-5386-0 lib bdg; 0-7922-5386-8 lib bdg; 978-1-4263-0248-0 pa; 1-4263-0249-7 pa

Examines the life of Renaissance genius Leonardo da Vinci, discussing his inquiries and accomplishments in art and various fields of science

Includes bibliographical references

Levine, Gail Carson, 1947-

Abrams, Dennis. **Gail** Carson Levine; [by] Dennis Abrams; foreword by Kyle Zimmer. Chelsea House 2007 120p bibl il por (Who wrote that?) $30

Grades: 6 7 8 9 **92**

1. Authors 2. Women authors 3. Authors, American 4. Children's authors
ISBN 978-0-7910-8970-5; 0-7910-8970-3

LC 2007019449

This biography examines the "writer's life, including the inspiration behind some of [her] works. [The] volume includes photographs and quotations from interviews, as well as descriptions of main characters and annotated lists of books and awards. Useful for aspiring authors as well as book report writers." Horn Book Guide

Includes bibliographical references

Lewis, C. S. (Clive Staples), 1898-1963

Hamilton, Janet. **C.** S. Lewis; twentieth century pilgrim. Morgan Reynolds Pub. 2010 128p il (World writers) lib bdg $28.95

Grades: 7 8 9 10 **92**

1. Authors 2. Novelists 3. Theologians 4. Essayists 5. Satirists 6. Authors, English 7. Literary critics 8. Children's authors
ISBN 978-1-59935-112-4; 1-59935-112-9

LC 2009-7134

In this biography of the British author, "Lewis' childhood is well-documented, as is his love of literature as an escape from the real world. Hamilton clearly shows the importance religion played in Lewis's life. The impact that war, and the resulting loss of the imaginative worlds he could find in literature, and his struggle with religious belief are tied directly to his writing." Voice Youth Advocates

Includes bibliographical references

Lewis, John, 1940

★ Lewis, John R., 1940- **March**; Book One. John Lewis ; [co-written by] Andrew Aydin ; [art by] Nate Powell. Top Shelf Productions 2013 121 p. chiefly ill. (acid-free paper) $14.95

Grades: 8 9 10 11 12 Adult **92**

1. African Americans -- Civil rights -- Graphic novels 2. Civil rights movements -- United States -- Comic books, strips, etc
ISBN 9781603093002

LC 2013218903

Coretta Scott King (Author) Honor Book (2014)

This graphic novel, by U.S. congressman John Lewis, "in collaboration with co-writer Andrew Aydin and New York Times best-selling artist Nate Powell . . . spans John Lewis' youth in rural Alabama, his life-changing meeting with Martin Luther King, Jr., the birth of the Nashville Student Movement, and their battle to tear down segregation through nonviolent lunch counter sit-ins, building to a . . . climax on the steps of City Hall." (Publisher's note)

"This is superb visual storytelling that establishes a convincing, definitive record of a key eyewitness to significant social change." SLJ

★ Lewis, John. **March**; Book Two. by John Lewis and Andrew Aydin ; illustrated by Nate Powell. Top Shelf Productions 2015 192 p. chiefly ill. (pbk) $19.95

Grades: 8 9 10 11 12 Adult **92**

1. African Americans -- Civil rights -- Graphic novels 2. Civil rights movements 3. African American legislators 4. Legislators -- United States 5. African Americans -- Civil rights 6. African American civil rights workers 7. Civil rights workers -- United States 8. Autobiographical comic books, strips, etc.

ISBN 9781603094009; 1603094008

LC 2015004150

Eisner Nominee: Best Publication for Teens (2016)

Eisner Award: Best Reality-Based Work (2016)

Ignatz Nominee: Outstanding Series (2015)

This graphic novel, by John Lewis and Andrew Aydin, illustrated by Nate Powell, "takes us behind the scenes of some of the most pivotal moments of the Civil Rights Movement. . . . After the success of the Nashville sit-in campaign, John Lewis is more committed than ever to changing the world through nonviolence -- but as he and his fellow Freedom Riders board a bus into the vicious heart of the deep south, they will be tested like never before." (Publisher's note)

"Heroism and steadiness of purpose continue to light up Lewis' frank, harrowing account of the civil rights movement's climactic days. . . . The contrast between the dignified marchers and the vicious, hate-filled actions and expressions of their tormentors will leave a deep impression on readers." Kirkus

★ Lewis, John R., 1940- **March**; Book Three. by John Lewis and Andrew Aydin ; illustrated by Nate Powell. Top Shelf Productions 2016 256 p. chiefly illustrations pbk $19.99

Grades: 8 9 10 11 12 Adult **92**

1. Civil rights -- United States

ISBN 9781603094023; 1603094024

National Book Award: Young People's Literature (2016)

Eisner Award: Best Reality-Based Work (2017)

YALSA Award for Excellence in Nonfiction for Young Adults (2017)

Printz Award (2017)

Sibert Informational Book Award (2017)

Coretta Scott King (Author) Book Award (2017)

This book is the "conclusion of the award-winning and best-selling March trilogy. Congressman John Lewis, an American icon and one of the key figures of the civil rights movement, joins co-writer Andrew Aydin and artist Nate Powell to bring the lessons of history to vivid life for a new generation, urgently relevant for today's world." (Publisher's note)

"Though Lewis and Aydin throw a lot at readers in this volume, their message, helped along seamlessly and splendidly by Powell's fantastic, cinematic artwork, is abundantly clear: the victories of the civil rights movement, symbolized in particular by Barack Obama's inauguration, are hard-won and only succeeded through the dogged dedication of a wide variety of people." Booklist

Sapet, Kerrily. **John** Lewis. Morgan Reynolds Pub. 2009 128p il (Political profiles) lib bdg $28.95

Grades: 6 7 8 9 **92**

1. Members of Congress 2. Civil rights activists 3. African Americans -- Civil rights 4. Southern States -- Race relations

ISBN 978-1-59935-130-8 lib bdg; 1-59935-130-7 lib bdg

LC 2009027748

A biography of African American civil rights activist John Lewis

This is "solid, evenhanded, and wonderfully helpful. . . . Particularly interesting is the section of the book that describes Lewis' congressional race against fellow civil rights activist Julian Bond. . . . Unusually well-chosen photos, fine notes, and [a list] of further sources add to the usefulness and appeal of this [book]." Booklist

Includes bibliographical references

Lewis, Meriwether, 1774-1809

Crompton, Samuel. **Lewis** and Clark; [by] Samuel Willard Crompton. Chelsea House 2009 116p il map (Great explorers) lib bdg $30

Grades: 6 7 8 9 **92**

1. Explorers 2. Lewis and Clark Expedition (1804-1806) 3. West (U.S.) 4. Territorial governors

ISBN 978-1-60413-418-6 lib bdg; 1-60413-418-6 lib bdg

LC 2009-8687

Biography of the explorers Lewis and Clark

"The information . . . is presented in such a way as to attract and maintain readers' interest. . . . With a full complement of maps, photographs (where available), illustrations, time lines, and document reproductions, a full story is told. Well-written and throughly researched, this . . . will make a solid addition." SLJ

Includes glossary and bibliographical references

Leyson, Leon, 1929-2013

★ Leyson, Leon, 1929-2013. The **boy** on the wooden box; Leon Leyson ; with Marilyn J Harran and Elisabeth B Leyson. Atheneum Books for Young Readers 2013 240 p. (hardcover) $16.99

Grades: 6 7 8 9 **92**

1. Holocaust survivors 2. World War, 1939-1945 -- Jews -- Rescue 3. Narewka (Poland) -- Biography 4. Jews -- Poland -- Narewka -- Biography 5. Płaszów (Concentration camp) 6. Concentration camp inmates -- Poland -- Płaszów -- Biography 7. Jewish children in the Holocaust -- Poland -- Kraków -- Biography 8. Holocaust, Jewish (1939-1945) -- Poland -- Kraków -- Personal narratives

ISBN 1442497815; 9781442497818; 9781442497832

LC 2013017987

In this book, "Leon Leyson (born Leib Lezjon) was only ten years old when the Nazis invaded Poland and his family was forced to relocate to the Krakow ghetto. With incredible luck, perseverance, and grit, Leyson was able to survive the sadism of the Nazis, including that of the demonic Amon Goeth, commandant of Plaszow, the concentration camp outside Krakow. Ultimately, it was the generosity and cunning of one man, a man named Oskar Schindler, who saved Leon Leyson's life, and the lives of his mother, his father, and two of his four siblings, by adding their names to his list of workers in his factory—a list that became world renowned: Schindler's List." (Publisher's Note)

"This powerful memoir of one of the youngest boys on Schindler's list deserves to be shared...This memoir is a natural curriculum addition to WWII units for upper-elementary- and middle-school readers. Be sure to have additional materials on hand about Oskar Schindler, as readers will want to do more research into Leyson's story." (Booklist)

Li Cunxin

Li Cunxin. **Mao's** last dancer; [by] Li Cunxin. Young readers' ed.; Walker & Co. 2008 290p il map $16.99

Grades: 6 7 8 9 **92**

1. Defectors 2. Ballet dancers 3. Securities brokers 4. China -- History -- 1949-1976

ISBN 978-0-8027-9779-7; 0-8027-9779-2

LC 2008-6104

An adaptation of the title published 2003 by Putnam for adults

Chosen from millions of children to serve in Mao's cultural revolution by studying at the Beijing Dance Academy, Li knew ballet would be his family's best opportunity to escape the bitter poverty in his rural China home. From one hardship to another, Li persevered, never forgetting the family he left behind.

"Cunxin's tale is a wonderfully crafted coming-of-age story. . . . He paints a clear picture of harsh realities of life in communist China but does so without being overly negative. . . . Photographs provide readers with a glimpse of varying aspects of Cunxin's life, a short note on the history of China, and a time line of China in the twentieth century." Voice Youth Advocates

Li, Moying, 1954-

★ Moying Li. **Snow** falling in spring; coming of age in China during the cultural revolution. Farrar, Straus and Giroux 2008 176p $16

Grades: 7 8 9 10 11 12 **92**

1. Memoirists 2. Financial consultants 3. Biography, Individual 4. China -- History -- 1949-1976 -- Personal narratives

ISBN 978-0-374-39922-1; 0-374-39922-0

LC 2006-38356

"This memoir . . . offers a highly personal look at China's Cultural Revolution. The author is four years old when Mao initiates the Great Leap Forward in 1958. . . . Li effectively builds the climate of fear that accompanies the rise of the Red Guard, while accounts of her headmaster's suicide and the pulping of her father's book collection give a harrowing, closeup view of the persecution. Sketches about her grandparents root the narrative within a broader context of Chinese traditions as well as her own family's values." Publ Wkly

Li, Zhongmei

Bernstein, Richard. A **girl** named Faithful Plum; Richard Bernstein. Alfred A. Knopf Books for Young Readers 2011 270p. ill. $15.99; lib bdg $18.99

Grades: 7 8 9 10 11 12 **92**

1. Dancers 2. Arts -- China 3. Dance directors 4. China -- Biography

ISBN 978-0-375-86960-0; 0-375-86960-3; 978-0-375-96960-7 lib bdg; 0-375-96960-8 lib bdg

LC 2010048722

"In 1978, an 11-year-old girl fights poverty and prejudice with gutsy perseverance and talent to fulfill her dream of studying at the Beijing Dance Academy. . . . Faithful Plum, or Zhongmei, lives in a remote area of China near Siberia. . . . She loves to dance, though, and upon hearing that the Academy is holding national auditions she sets her mind on going. . . . After a horrific three-day journey by trains and buses, Zhongmei comes through the difficult audition only to face an extreme daily regimen of exercise and instruction, an appallingly rigid dormitory supervisor and a ballet teacher scarred by the Cultural Revolution. . . . The conversations ring true, albeit 'imagined,' and events have been compressed to keep the pace flowing. A fascinating and memorable account of a life and times difficult to imagine today." Kirkus

Lichtenstein, Roy, 1923-1997

★ Rubin, Susan Goldman. **Whaam!** : the art & life of Roy Lichtenstein. Abrams 2008 47p il $18.95

Grades: 4 5 6 7 **92**

1. Artists 2. Pop art 3. Painters 4. Sculptors 5. Printmakers 6. Artists -- United States

ISBN 978-0-8109-9492-8; 0-8109-9492-5

LC 2007-42048

"Rubin presents an overview of a modern master with clear writing and an abundance of his eye-popping works, all framed on pages that mirror the artist's signature use of primary colors and Benday dots." Booklist

Lin, Maya Ying

Rubin, Susan Goldman. **Maya** Lin; thinking with her hands. by Susan Goldman Rubin. Chronicle Books 2017 99 p. illustrations (some color) (hardback) $17.99

Grades: 5 6 7 8 **92**

1. Chinese Americans 2. Women architects -- Biography 3. Artists -- United States -- Biography 4. Architects -- United States -- Biography 5. Women architects -- United States -- Biography 6. Chinese American artists -- United States -- Biography 7. Chinese American architects -- United States -- Biography

ISBN 9781452140896; 9781452108377

LC 2016058584

In this book, by Susan Goldman Rubin, "the Vietnam Veterans Memorial in Washington, D.C., is one of the most famous pieces of civic architecture in the world. But most people are not as familiar with the reserved college student who entered and won the design competition to build it. This accessible biography tells the story of Maya Lin, from her struggle to stick with her vision of the memorial to the wide variety of works she has created since then." (Publisher's note)

"A finely designed, endlessly compelling examination of the life and work of one of America's most notable architects." Booklist

Includes bibliographical references and index.

Lincoln family

★ Holzer, Harold. **Father** Abraham; Lincoln and his sons. Calkins Creek 2011 231p il $17.95

Grades: 6 7 8 9 **92**

1. Lawyers 2. Presidents 3. Pioneers 4. State legislators 5. Members of Congress 6. Presidents -- United States 7. Biography, Individual

ISBN 1590783034; 9781590783030

This biography "looks at the lives of Abraham Lincoln and his family, including the relationship between the president and his sons." (Publisher's note) Bibliography. Index. "Middle school, high school." (Horn Book)

"This profile of 'the clan that might have become America's royal family but instead became America's cursed family' offers both a wagonload of fascinating period photos and a case study in domestic tragedy and dysfunction. . . . If the author sometimes hobbles his narrative with fussy details, he also tucks in such intimate touches as samples of homely verse from both parents and children and finishes off with quick looks at all of the direct descendants." Kirkus

Lincoln, Abraham, 1809-1865

Aronson, Billy. **Abraham** Lincoln. Marshall Cavendish Benchmark 2009 112p il (Presidents and their times) lib bdg $23.95

Grades: 5 6 7 8 **92**

1. Lawyers 2. Presidents 3. State legislators 4. Members of Congress 5. Presidents -- United States 6. United States -- History

-- 1861-1865, Civil War
ISBN 978-0-7614-2839-8 lib bdg; 0-7614-2839-9 lib bdg
LC 2007019190

This provides "information on President Abraham Lincoln and places him within his historical and cultural context. Also explored are the formative events of his times and how he responded." Publisher's note

Includes glossary and bibliographical references

★ Denenberg, Barry. **Lincoln** shot! a president's life remembered. chief writer, Barry Denenberg; artist, Christopher Bing. Feiwel and Friends 2008 40p il $24.95

Grades: 5 6 7 8 **92**

1. Lawyers 2. Presidents 3. State legislators 4. Members of Congress 5. Presidents -- United States 6. United States -- History -- 1861-1865, Civil War
ISBN 978-0-312-37013-8; 0-312-37013-X
LC 2007-48851

"The concept is that this is a commemorative edition of 'The National News' published one year after Lincoln's death . . . Also included is an engaging, readable yet detailed account of Lincoln's life. . . . [This book] is an example of how high-quality bookmaking can turn a history lesson into an authentic experience." Booklist

★ Fleming, Candace. The **Lincolns**; a scrapbook look at Abraham and Mary. Schwartz & Wade Books 2008 177p il map $24.99; lib bdg $28.99

Grades: 7 8 9 10 11 12 **92**

1. Lawyers 2. Presidents 3. State legislators 4. Members of Congress 5. Spouses of presidents 6. Presidents -- United States 7. Presidents' spouses -- United States 8. United States -- History -- 1861-1865, Civil War
ISBN 978-0-375-83618-3; 0-375-83618-7; 978-0-375-93618-0 lib bdg; 0-375-93618-1 lib bdg
LC 2007-44113

Boston Globe-Horn Book Award: Nonfiction (2009)

Fleming twines "accounts of two lives—Abraham and Mary Todd Lincoln—into one fascinating whole. On spreads that combine well-chosen visuals with blocks of headlined text, Fleming gives a full, birth-to-death view of the 'inextricably bound' Lincolns." Booklist

★ Freedman, Russell Bruce, 1929-2018. **Abraham** Lincoln and Frederick Douglass; the story behind an American friendship. by Russell Freedman. Houghton Mifflin Harcourt 2012 119 p. $18.99

Grades: 4 5 6 7 8 **92**

1. Friendship 2. Abolitionists -- United States 3. United States -- History -- 1861-1865, Civil War -- Biography 4. Friendship -- United States 5. Presidents -- United States -- Biography 6. African American abolitionists -- Biography
ISBN 9780547385624
LC 2011025953

This book tells the story of Abraham Lincoln, "the 16th president, . . . [along] with his friend and ally, abolitionist Frederick Douglass. The story opens with Douglass anxiously waiting to meet Lincoln for the first time to air grievances about the treatment of African-American soldiers during the Civil War. . . . Subsequent chapters detail the leaders' often parallel biographies. Both were self-made and shared a passion for reading, rising from poverty to prominence." (Publishers Weekly)

Includes bibliographical references (p. [108]-109) and index

★ Freedman, Russell. **Lincoln** : a photobiography. Clarion Bks. 1987 149p il $18; pa $7.95

Grades: 5 6 7 8 9 10 **92**

1. Lawyers 2. Presidents 3. State legislators 4. Members of Congress 5. Presidents -- United States 6. United States -- History -- 1861-1865, Civil War
ISBN 0-89919-380-3; 0-395-51848-2 pa
LC 86-33379

Awarded the Newbery Medal, 1988

This is "a balanced work, elegantly designed and enhanced by dozens of period photographs and drawings, some familiar, some refreshingly unfamiliar." Publ Wkly

Includes bibliographical references

Giblin, James. **Good** brother, bad brother; the story of Edwin Booth and John Wilkes Booth. Clarion Books 2005 244p il $22

Grades: 5 6 7 8 **92**

1. United States -- History -- 1861-1865, Civil War
ISBN 0-618-09642-6
LC 2004-21260

Boston Globe-Horn Book Honor: Nonfiction (2005)

This is a dual biography of John Wilkes Booth, who assassinated Abraham Lincoln, and his brother, Edwin, an actor. (Horn Book)

Giblin "frames the intertwined tale of two brothers with accounts of their families, friends, the Civil War, and nineteenth-century theater. . . . Alcoholism and depression afflicted the family, but Giblin is brilliant at showing that darkness was only one part of a life. . . . Giblin's book will engross readers until the very last footnote." Booklist

Includes bibliographical references

★ Holzer, Harold. **Father** Abraham; Lincoln and his sons. Calkins Creek 2011 231p il $17.95

Grades: 6 7 8 9 **92**

1. Lawyers 2. Presidents 3. Pioneers 4. State legislators 5. Members of Congress 6. Presidents -- United States 7. Biography, Individual
ISBN 1590783034; 9781590783030

This biography "looks at the lives of Abraham Lincoln and his family, including the relationship between the president and his sons." (Publisher's note) Bibliography. Index. "Middle school, high school." (Horn Book)

"This profile of 'the clan that might have become America's royal family but instead became America's cursed family' offers both a wagonload of fascinating period photos and a case study in domestic tragedy and dysfunction. . . . If the author sometimes hobbles his narrative with fussy details, he also tucks in such intimate touches as samples of homely verse from both parents and children and finishes off with quick looks at all of the direct descendants." Kirkus

Lincoln, Abraham. **Abraham** Lincoln the writer; a treasury of his greatest speeches and letters. compiled and edited by Harold Holzer. Boyds Mills Press 2000 106p il lib bdg $15.95

Grades: 7 8 9 10 **92**

1. Lawyers 2. Presidents 3. State legislators 4. Members of Congress 5. Presidents -- United States 6. United States -- History -- 1861-1865, Civil War
ISBN 1-56397-772-9
LC 99-66551

"Lincoln's writings include personal letters, notes on the law, excerpts from speeches, debates, and inaugural addresses, letters to parents of fallen soldiers, and telegrams to his family. Reproductions of period photos, portraits, and documents illustrate the text effectively. . .

. Highly interesting and a fine resource for students seeking quotations or for those wanting to meet Lincoln through his own words." Booklist

★ Sandler, Martin W. **Lincoln** through the lens; how photography revealed and shaped an extraordinary life. Walker Pub. Co. 2008 97p il $19.99; lib bdg $20.89

Grades: 6 7 8 9 10 **92**

1. Lawyers 2. Presidents 3. State legislators 4. Members of Congress 5. Photography -- History 6. Presidents -- United States 7. United States -- History -- 1861-1865, Civil War -- Pictorial works

ISBN 978-0-8027-9666-0; 0-8027-9666-4; 978-0-8027-9667-7 lib bdg; 0-8027-9667-2 lib bdg

LC 2008-0219

"When Lincoln became president, photography was new and he joined the 'very first generation of human beings ever to be photographed.' . . . This extraordinary book is a tribute to the way contemporary and future generations came to view Lincoln. . . . Part biography, part history of of the Civil War, the book touches on many interesting topics. . . . Every step of the way there are fascinating photographs. . . . Although it's the pictures that provide the 'wow factor,' Sandler's perceptive words have their own elegance." Booklist

★ Zeller, Bob. **Lincoln** in 3-D; by Bob Zeller and John Richter. Chronicle Books 2010 223p il $35

Grades: 6 7 8 9 **92**

1. Lawyers 2. Presidents 3. Three-dimensional photography 4. State legislators 5. Members of Congress 6. Three dimensional photography 7. United States -- History -- 1861-1865, Civil War -- Pictorial works

ISBN 978-0-8118-7231-7; 0-8118-7231-9

LC 2010013792

"This visually striking volume is built around 185 stereoscopic photographs from the Civil War era. Glasses included in the back give the full three-dimensional effect. . . . The introduction offers fascinating background on stereoscopic pictures, followed by a narrative text tracing Lincoln's life and the stages of the war. All of the photos include informative captions that give context even for images not mentioned in the text. . . . The striking images make this a powerful visual depiction of Lincoln and his times." SLJ

Includes bibliographical references

Lincoln, Mary Todd, 1818-1882

Jones, Lynda. **Mrs.** Lincoln's dressmaker: the unlikely friendship of Elizabeth Keckley and Mary Todd Lincoln; by Lynda D. Jones. National Geographic 2009 80p il $18.95; lib bdg $27.90

Grades: 5 6 7 8 **92**

1. Memoirists 2. Dressmakers 3. Spouses of presidents 4. Slavery -- United States 5. United States -- Race relations 6. African American women -- Biography 7. Presidents' spouses -- United States 8. Washington (D.C.) -- Social life and customs

ISBN 978-1-4263-0377-7; 1-4263-0377-7; 978-1-4263-0378-4 lib bdg; 1-4263-0378-5 lib bdg

LC 2008-29314

"Readers may be familiar with the ups and downs of Lincoln's life, but details of Keckley's story . . . will give them new insights into the life of a slave, in this case, one who was educated and had a profession." Booklist

Includes bibliographical references

Lindbergh, Anne Morrow, 1906-2001

Gherman, Beverly. **Anne** Morrow Lindbergh; between the sea and the stars. [by] Beverly Gherman. Twenty-first Century Books 2008 160p (Lerner biography) lib bdg $27.93

Grades: 6 7 8 9 **92**

1. Poets 2. Authors 3. Generals 4. Novelists 5. Air pilots 6. Women air pilots 7. Diarists 8. Essayists 9. Memoirists 10. Air force officers 11. Spouses of prominent persons

ISBN 978-0-8225-5970-2 lib bdg; 0-8225-5970-6 lib bdg

LC 2005022498

Explores the life and career of Anne Morrow Lindbergh, including her marriage to Charles Lindbergh, flying experiences, and success as an author.

"Clearly written and illustrated with frequent, clear black-and-white photos, the book is strongest in demonstrating Gherman's thorough understanding of Anne's emotional core. . . . A solid resource for reports as well as a fascinating portrait for biography fans." Booklist

Includes bibliographical references

Lindbergh, Charles, 1902-1974

Gherman, Beverly. **Anne** Morrow Lindbergh; between the sea and the stars. [by] Beverly Gherman. Twenty-first Century Books 2008 160p (Lerner biography) lib bdg $27.93

Grades: 6 7 8 9 **92**

1. Poets 2. Authors 3. Generals 4. Novelists 5. Air pilots 6. Women air pilots 7. Diarists 8. Essayists 9. Memoirists 10. Air force officers 11. Spouses of prominent persons

ISBN 978-0-8225-5970-2 lib bdg; 0-8225-5970-6 lib bdg

LC 2005022498

Explores the life and career of Anne Morrow Lindbergh, including her marriage to Charles Lindbergh, flying experiences, and success as an author.

"Clearly written and illustrated with frequent, clear black-and-white photos, the book is strongest in demonstrating Gherman's thorough understanding of Anne's emotional core. . . . A solid resource for reports as well as a fascinating portrait for biography fans." Booklist

Includes bibliographical references

Giblin, James. **Charles** A. Lindbergh; a human hero. [by] James Cross Giblin. Clarion Bks. 1997 212p il $22

Grades: 6 7 8 9 **92**

1. Generals 2. Air pilots 3. Memoirists 4. Air force officers

ISBN 0-395-63389-3

LC 96-9501

A biography of the pilot whose life was full of controversy and tragedy, but also fulfilling achievements

"This sympathetic and informed account (beautifully illustrated with contemporary photographs) is an excellent introduction to Lindbergh and also to the early years of the celebrity society in which we live now." N Y Times Book Rev

Includes bibliographical references

Lockwood, Belva Ann, 1830-1917

Norgren, Jill. **Belva** Lockwood; equal rights pioneer. by Jill Norgren. Twenty-First Century Books 2009 112p il (Trailblazer biography) lib bdg $31.93

Grades: 6 7 8 9 **92**

1. Lawyers 2. Suffragists 3. Women lawyers 4. Women's rights 5. Lecturers 6. Presidential candidates

ISBN 978-0-8225-9068-2 lib bdg; 0-8225-9068-9 lib bdg

LC 2007-50265

First published 2007 by New York University Press with title: Belva Lockwood: the woman who would be president

"Through a clear and engaging text, this biography shows how Lockwood, a relatively unknown historical figure, was an inspiring pioneer of the equal-rights movement." SLJ

Includes bibliographical references

Long, Jessica Tatiana

Long, Jessica. **Unsinkable**; from Russian orphan to paralympic swimming world champion. by Jessica Long, with Hannah Long. Houghton Mifflin Harcourt 2018 104 p. (alk. paper) $16.99

Grades: 5 6 7 8 **92**

1. Biography 2. Athletes with disabilities -- Biography 3. Women swimmers -- United States -- Biography 4. Swimmers -- United States -- Biography 5. Athletes with disabilities -- United States -- Biography

ISBN 9781328707253

LC 2017041724

In this book, Paralympic swimmer "Jessica Long delivers an inspirational photographic memoir. Born in Siberia with fibular hemimelia, Jessica Long was adopted from a Russian orphanage at thirteen months old and has since become the second most decorated U.S. Paralympic athlete of all time. Now, Jessica shares all the moments in her life . . . that led to her domination in the Paralympic swimming world." (Publisher's note)

"Jessica Long tells her story through short chapters devoted to self-defined life-changing moments, with an engaging narrative helped along by plenty of family and professional photos...Unique in its coverage of Paralympians, and inspirational on so many levels, this is a great addition for middle-school collections." Booklist

Includes bibliographical references and index

Louis, Joe, 1914-1981

Sullivan, George. **Knockout!** : a photobiography of boxer Joe Louis. National Geographic 2008 64p il $17.95; lib bdg $27.90

Grades: 6 7 8 9 **92**

1. Soldiers 2. African American athletes 3. Boxers (Persons) 4. Boxing -- Biography

ISBN 978-1-4263-0328-9; 1-4263-0328-9; 978-1-4263-0329-6 lib bdg; 1-4263-0329-7 lib bdg

LC 2008-25036

"This oversize biography of Joe Louis is just the thing for getting the blood of reluctant readers and sports fans pumping. Using copious period photographs . . . and full-color reproductions of fight posters and memoriblia, Sullivan relays in straightforward language the rags-to-riches saga of the 'Brown Bomber,' and sets the story against the rampant racism of 1920s America. . . . Sullivan's fight recaps are clear and vivid." Booklist

Includes bibliographical references

Love, Nat, 1854-1921

Bloom, Barbara Lee. **Nat** Love. Chelsea House 2010 102p il (Legends of the Wild West) lib bdg $35

Grades: 6 7 8 9 **92**

1. Cowhands 2. Cowboys 3. Porters 4. West (U.S.) -- History 5. African Americans -- Biography

ISBN 978-1-60413-599-2; 1-60413-599-9

A biography of Nat Love, who was born in a log cabin in Tennessee in 1854 as the slave of Robert Love and who, in 1869, four years after the slaves had been freed, moved out West to find work as a cowhand.

Bloom "does a fine job chronicling [Love's] exploits as a black cowboy and beyond. . . . Weaving historical context throughout in related sidebars and lengthy captions, the book features black-and-white and color photos, paintings, and other illustrations." Booklist

Includes glossary and bibliographical references

★ McKissack, Fredrick, 1939-2013. **Best** shot in the West; the adventures of Nat Love. by Patricia C. McKissack and Fredrick L. McKissack, Jr. ; illustrated by Randy DuBurke. Chronicle Books 2012 129 p. chiefly col. ill., col. map $19.99

Grades: 7 8 9 10 11 12 **92**

1. Cowhands -- Graphic novels 2. Railroads -- United States 3. West (U.S.) -- History -- Graphic novels 4. African Americans -- Biography -- Graphic novels 5. Cartoons and comics 6. West (U.S.) -- Cartoons and comics 7. Cowboys -- West (U.S.) -- Cartoons and comics 8. African American cowboys -- West (U.S.) -- Cartoons and comics 9. African Americans -- West (U.S.) -- Biography -- Cartoons and comics 10. West (U.S.) -- Biography -- Comic books, strips, etc. 11. Cowboys -- West (U.S.) -- Biography -- Comic books, strips, etc. 12. African American cowboys -- West (U.S.) -- Biography -- Comic books, strips, etc.

ISBN 0811857492; 9780811857499

LC 2007021419

In this graphic novel, "Nat Love's cattle-driving days are long over and America is a much tamer place when the black cowboy, now a Pullman porter, runs into Bugler, a man he knew back in the day. Bugler's son is a publisher . . . of . . . stories from the Wild West, and Love is persuaded to contribute his memoirs. From this . . . story, . . . [Patricia C. and Frederick L.] McKissack . . . segue into Love's adventures, based on his autobiography." (Bulletin of the Center for Children's Books)

Low, Juliette Gordon, 1860-1927

★ Wadsworth, Ginger. **First** Girl Scout; Ginger Wadsworth. Clarion Books 2012 xiii, 210p ill. $17.99

Grades: 7 8 9 10 11 12 **92**

1. Biography 2. Girl Scouts 3. Philanthropists 4. Scout leaders 5. Girl Scouts of the United States of America

ISBN 978-0-547-24394-8; 0-547-24394-4

LC 2011009642

This book offers a biography of the founder of the Girl Scouts organization. "Juliette (Daisy) Gordon Low [who] was a . . . woman with ideas that were ahead of her time. She witnessed important eras in U.S. history, from the Civil War and Reconstruction to westward expansion to post–World War I. And she made history by founding the first national organization to bring girls from all backgrounds into the out-of-doors. Daisy created controversy by encouraging them to prepare not only for traditional homemaking but also for roles as professional women—in the arts, sciences, and business—and for active citizenship outside the home. Her group also welcomed girls with disabilities at a time when they were usually excluded." (Publisher's note)

"Low's personality really comes to life through the details in the narrative. Wadsworth shows readers that this remarkable woman was a skilled leader and hostess in spite of having suffered severe hearing loss that made conversation difficult. . . . The attractive book design features chapter headings that look like Girl Scout badges, and most spreads include period photos or reproductions of primary-source documents." SLJ

Includes bibliographical references (p. 201-204) and index.

Lowry, Lois

Bankston, John. **Lois** Lowry; [by] John Bankston. Chelsea House 2009 127p bibl il (Who wrote that?) lib bdg $30

Grades: 6 7 8 9 **92**

1. Authors 2. Novelists 3. Women authors 4. Authors, American 5. Young adult authors

ISBN 978-1-6041-3335-6 lib bdg; 1-6041-3335-X lib bdg

LC 2008035039

This examines the life and work of the popular author for children and young adults

"Lowry's road to publication was a winding one, with her first novel, A Summer to Die (1977), published at age 40. She went on to become the two-time Newbery Medal winner—Number the Stars (1989) and The Giver (1993)—that most kids remember from classroom encounters. This generous entry into the Who Wrote That? series answers not only the series title but also how Lowry wrote and why it matters. . . . Among the highlights is the focus on Lowry's willingness to broach controversial topics, which make her a perennial on ALA's challenged-books list. This is a welcome addition to a rather small pool of biographies on this prolific author." Booklist

Includes bibliographical references

★ Lowry, Lois, 1937- **Looking** back; a book of memories. Lois Lowry. 2nd edition Houghton Mifflin Harcourt 2016 259 p illustrations hbk $18.99

Grades: 4 5 6 7 8 **92**

1. Women authors -- 20th century -- Biography

ISBN 0544807960; 9780544807969

Originally published 1998

"In an updated edition of her photographic memoir originally published in 1998, Lowry offers reflections on life, work, and literature." (Kirkus)

Lugovskaia, Nina, 1918-1993

Lugovskaia, Nina. **I** want to live; the diary of a young girl in Stalin's Russia. translated by Andrew Bromfield. Houghton Mifflin 2006 280p il $17.99

Grades: 7 8 9 10 11 12 **92**

1. Artists 2. Painters 3. Persecution 4. Diarists 5. Soviet Union -- Politics and government

ISBN 978-0-618-60575-0; 0-618-60575-4

Original Russian edition, 2003

Reveals the life of a teenage girl in Stalin's Russia, where fear of arrest was a fact of daily life.

"Lugovskaya's diary, which was found in the NKVD archives, stands as a compelling historical artifact and Nina's story gives a moving—if relentlessly melancholy—personal account of life in Communist Russia." Publ Wkly

Includes bibliographical references

Lyons, Maritcha Rémond, 1848-1929

★ Bolden, Tonya. **Maritcha**; a nineteenth-century American girl. Abrams 2005 47p il $17.95

Grades: 4 5 6 7 8 9 10 **92**

1. Teachers 2. Civic leaders 3. New York (N.Y.) -- Race relations 4. African American women -- Biography 5. African Americans -- New York (N.Y.)

ISBN 0-8109-5045-6

LC 2004-05849

"The high quality of writing and the excellent documentation make this a first choice for all collections." SLJ

Ma, Yo-Yo, 1955-

Worth, Richard. **Yo** -Yo Ma. Chelsea House 2006 119p bibl il por (Asian Americans of achievement) lib bdg $30

Grades: 7 8 9 10 **92**

1. Chinese Americans 2. Cellists 3. Violoncellists 4. Classical musicians

ISBN 978-0-7910-9270-5 lib bdg; 0-7910-9270-4 lib bdg

LC 2006026335

"World-famous cellist Ma was born in Paris to a family originally from China. He was taught the cello at the age of four by his father, and early on it became obvious that he was a musical genius. The book has information about Ma's teachers, influences, and favorite composers." (School Library Journal)

This is "well-researched . . . attractive . . . solid." SLJ

Includes glossary and bibliographical references

MacMillan, Donald, 1874-1970

Cowan, Mary Morton. **Captain** Mac: the life of Donald Baxter MacMillan, Arctic explorer. Calkins Creek 2010 208p il $17.95

Grades: 6 7 8 9 **92**

1. Explorers 2. Arctic regions 3. Biography, Individual

ISBN 1-59078-709-9; 978-1-59078-709-0

LC 2009-36113

"From 1908 until 1954, Donald Baxter MacMillan spent nearly 50 years exploring the Arctic. . . . Cowan focuses on the . . . role MacMillan played in Robert Peary's 1908-09 North Pole Expedition, as well as his relationships with explorers Peary, Matthew Henson, and Richard Byrd. [Index.] Age ten and up." (Publisher's note)

"This biography, written with obvious respect and admiration, covers the life and achievements of the Arctic explorer. . . . The author skillfully weaves primary-source quotes with short, action-oriented sentences. . . . This engaging biography is also a solid overview of an era of exploration that still captivates adventurous youths." SLJ

Includes bibliographical references

Magellan, Ferdinand, 1480?-1521

Aretha, David. **Magellan**; first to circle the globe. Enslow Publishers 2009 112p il map (Great explorers of the world) lib bdg $31.93

Grades: 6 7 8 9 **92**

1. Explorers

ISBN 978-1-59845-097-2 lib bdg; 1-59845-097-2 lib bdg

LC 2008-13550

This "biography of Magellan reads like an adventure, detailing his life, while intriguing the reader with the danger and adversity surrounding his career. . . . Antique and current maps punctuate the text together with modern photographs and historic illustrations. The monumental implications of Magellan's life and voyage make this true adventure a winner." Libr Media Connect

Includes glosaary and bibliographical references

Malcolm X, 1925-1965

Burlingame, Jeff. **Malcolm** X. Enslow Publishers 2010 160p il lib bdg $34.60

Grades: 6 7 8 9 **92**

1. Black Muslims 2. Black Muslim leaders 3. Civil rights activists 4. African Americans -- Biography 5. African Americans -- Civil rights

ISBN 978-0-7660-3384-9; 0-7660-3384-8

LC 2009017597

In this biography the life of Malcolm X is "effectively explored to provide an understanding of [the] man's ideals, values, and perspectives on society as well as his reactions to pivotal events. . . . [The book] highlights the development of the human-rights activist's philosophy by exploring the impact of several childhood tragedies, causing him to question authority and to encourage others to do so as well. . . . [This title is] clear and concise and [includes] many images and descriptions of important events and people that [Malcolm X] interacted with and [was] impacted by." SLJ

Gunderson, Jessica. **X** : the biography of Malcolm X; illustrated by Seitu Hayden. Graphic Library 2011 32p il (Graphic library: American graphic) lib bdg $29.32; pa $7.95
Grades: 4 5 6 7 **92**

1. Black Muslims 2. Biographical graphic novels 3. Black Muslim leaders 4. Civil rights activists 5. African Americans -- Biography
ISBN 978-1-4296-5471-5 lib bdg; 1-4296-5471-6 lib bdg; 978-1-4296-6267-3 pa; 1-4296-6267-0 pa
LC 2010037029

In graphic novel format, explores the life and death of Malcolm X.

"The illustrations are eye-catching and the narration is presented simply, yet compellingly. . . . Fact-filled, entertaining, and accessible." SLJ

Includes glossary and bibliographical references

★ Sharp, Anne Wallace. **Malcolm** X and Black pride. Lucent Books 2010 104p il (Lucent library of black history) $32.45
Grades: 6 7 8 9 **92**

1. Black Muslims 2. Black Muslim leaders 3. Civil rights activists 4. African Americans -- Biography 5. African Americans -- Civil rights
ISBN 978-1-4205-0123-0; 1-4205-0123-2
LC 2009038463

This book takes "a frank, balanced, and compelling look at the man who was born Malcolm Little and whose furious insistence on equality for African Americans continues to both inspire and provoke controversy. . . . Supported by well-selected photos, extensive chapter notes, and further-reading suggestions, this is a strong choice for student research." Booklist

Includes bibliographical references

Mandela, Nelson, 1918-2013

Catel, Patrick. **Nelson** Mandela. Heinemann Library 2010 112p il map (Front-page lives) $38.93
Grades: 6 7 8 9 10 **92**

1. Presidents 2. Political prisoners 3. Political leaders 4. Human rights activists 5. Nobel laureates for peace 6. South Africa -- Politics and government
ISBN 978-1-4329-3219-0; 1-4329-3219-5
LC 2009-18178

The life of South African President Nelson Mandela is "presented with depth and breadth. . . . The writing is accessible and engaging, with color and black-and-white photographs and . . . color maps complementing the text." SLJ

Includes glossary and bibliographical references

Gormley, Beatrice. **Nelson** Mandela; South African revolutionary. by Beatrice Gormley. Aladdin 2014 256 p. illustrations (Real-life story) (hardback) $17.99
Grades: 5 6 7 8 **92**

1. Presidents -- South Africa -- Biography
ISBN 1481420593; 9781481420594; 9781481420600
LC 2014019020

This book, by Beatrice Gormley, is a "comprehensive biography that tells the complete life story of internationally renowned peacemaker Nelson Mandela. . . . Born in 1918 in South Africa, he grew up in a culture of government-enforced racism and became involved in the anti-apartheid movement at a young age. Deeply committed to nonviolent activism, Mandela directed a peaceful campaign against the racist policies of his South African government, and spent 27 years in prison as a result." (Publisher's note)

"More than a year after his death, the influence of Nelson Mandela is still felt keenly by people around the world. This timely biography provides a complete picture of a complex man...This book is an understandable and multifaceted tribute to an icon of defiance and optimism in the face of tribulation." Booklist

Includes bibliographical references and index

Keller, Bill. **Tree** shaker; the story of Nelson Mandela. Kingfisher 2008 128p il $17.95
Grades: 8 9 10 11 12 **92**

1. Presidents 2. Political prisoners 3. Political leaders 4. Human rights activists 5. Nobel laureates for peace 6. South Africa -- Race relations 7. South Africa -- Politics and government
ISBN 978-0-7534-5992-8; 0-7534-5992-2
LC 2007-03559

The author "offers a balanced, thoughtful account of Mandela's political activism and accomplishments and his pivotal role in South Africa's modern history. . . . [The book is] packed with dramatic photos, swathes of paint, handprints and images of the African continent." Publ Wkly

Includes bibliographical references

Manet, Édouard, 1832-1883

Spence, David. **Manet**. New Forest Press 2010 48p il (Great artists and their world) lib bdg $32.80
Grades: 6 7 8 9 **92**

1. Artists 2. Painters 3. Artists, French
ISBN 978-1-84898-313-7; 1-84898-313-1

"Offers biographical information [of Edouard Manet] . . . interspersed with art history and criticism in an eye-catching format. . . . [Includes] a long introductory paragraph and four-to-six images with explanatory notes. . . . Spence . . . does a good job of explaining why art that might seem ordinary today was revolutionary at the time of its creation." SLJ

Includes glossary

Mankiller, Wilma

Sonneborn, Liz. **Wilma** Mankiller. Marshall Cavendish Benchmark 2010 112p il (Leading women) $39.93
Grades: 5 6 7 8 **92**

1. Cherokee Indians 2. Indian chiefs
ISBN 978-0-7614-4959-1; 0-7614-4959-0
LC 2009029399

"The story of Mankiller's lifelong work for the Cherokee Nation and her role as its first female principal chief will absorb readers. The [woman's life is] revealed within the political and historical context of [her] times and [includes] quotes from autobiographical material. . . . Color and black-and-white photos are included. . . . The compact size, chronological organization, and accessible writing [style makes this biography a] good [resource] for reports." SLJ

Manzano, Juan Francisco, 1797-1854

Engle, Margarita, 1951. The **poet** slave of Cuba: a biography of Juan Francisco Manzano; art by Sean Qualls. Henry Holt 2006 183p il $16.95

Grades: 7 8 9 10 **92**

1. Poets 2. Slaves 3. Authors 4. Slavery -- Cuba 5. Biography, Individual

ISBN 0-8050-7706-5; 978-0-8050-7706-3

LC 2005-46200

Awarded the Pura Belpré Author Award, 2008

This is a "biography of a Cuban slave who escaped to become a celebrated poet." (Publisher's note) "Grades seven to twelve." (Bull Cent Child Books)

"This is a book that should be read by young and old, black and white, Anglo and Latino." SLJ

Manzano, Sonia

★ Manzano, Sonia. **Becoming** Maria; love and chaos in the South Bronx. Sonia Manzano. Scholastic Press 2015 272 p. illustrations (black & white) (hardback) $17.99

Grades: 9 10 11 12 **92**

1. Hispanic American women 2. Hispanic American women -- Biography 3. Coming of age -- Bronx (New York, N.Y.) 4. Television writers -- United States -- Biography. 5. Television actors and actresses -- United States -- Biography

ISBN 9780545621847; 9780545621854; 9780545621861

LC 2015007490

In this memoir, "actress Manzano, best known as Maria from Sesame Street, provides a[n] . . . account of her tough Nuyorican upbringing in the South Bronx. Split into three parts, this touching memoir is a chronological series of vignettes in the author's life, starting with her earliest memories as a diaper-clad toddler witnessing her father's drunken outbursts and meeting a mysterious 'dark little girl,' who turns out to be her older half sister." (Kirkus Reviews)

"This beautifully rendered coming-of-age story calls to mind Betty Smith's classic A Tree Grows in Brooklyn. Though it's a bit slow moving at times and would have benefited from a time line to help ground readers, this is nevertheless an inspiring portrait of resiliency and a time capsule for a New York that now feels like a distant memory." Booklist

Mao Zedong, 1893-1976

Heuston, Kimberley Burton. **Mao** Zedong; [by] Kimberley Heuston. Franklin Watts 2010 128p il map (Wicked history) lib bdg $30

Grades: 5 6 7 8 **92**

1. Heads of state 2. Communist leaders 3. Political leaders 4. China -- History -- 1949-1976

ISBN 978-0-531-20756-7; 0-531-20756-0

LC 2009034157

"...short enough not to intimidate yet long enough to impart the enormity of the tyrant's atrocities. Opening with a description of Zedong's ruthlessness as an early revolutionary, Heuston follows him through the 82 years of his life, describing his devastating impact on China. Black-and-white photos, maps of Uganda and of China, time lines of the men's lives, and labeled webs showing their allies and enemies... make the books accessible." SLJ

Includes glossary and bibliographical references

Naden, Corinne J. **Mao** Zedong and the Chinese Revolution. Morgan Reynolds Pub. 2009 144p il map (World leaders) lib bdg $28.95

Grades: 7 8 9 10 11 12 **92**

1. Heads of state 2. Communist leaders 3. Political leaders 4. China -- History -- 1949-1976

ISBN 978-1-59935-100-1; 1-59935-100-5

LC 2008-27829

This "discusses Chariman Mao Zedong's rise to power and his crucial role in national and international history. . . . Naden's analysis of the significant role of young people will draw YA readers for reports and for personal interest. The readable design, with clear type and lots of historic color photos as well as screens and detailed maps, includes spacious back matter." Booklist

Includes bibliographical references

Slavicek, Louise Chipley. **Mao** Zedong. Chelsea House 2004 116p il (Great military leaders of the 20th century) lib bdg $23.95

Grades: 6 7 8 9 **92**

1. Heads of state 2. Communist leaders 3. Political leaders 4. China -- History -- 1949-1976

ISBN 0-7910-7407-2

LC 2003-6929

A biography of Chinese leader Mao Zedong, discussing the battles that helped shape him and reasons behind his popularity among his countrymen

"Slavicek blends personal, philosophical, and historical information to trace Mao's journey to power. Clear accounts of the communist movement, the Long March, and the eventual battle with the Nationalists and Japanese are included." SLJ

Includes bibliographical references

Marley, Bob

★ Medina, Tony. **I** and I; Bob Marley. illustrated by Jesse Joshua Watson. Lee & Low Books 2009 un il $19.95

Grades: 4 5 6 **92**

1. Singers 2. Jamaica 3. Reggae musicians

ISBN 978-1-60060-257-3; 1-60060-257-6

LC 2008-33485

"In the words and rhythms of Jamaican patois, Medina's lyrical, direct lines make the most sense when read in tandem with the extensive appended notes. . . . Like the words, Watson's beautifully expressive acrylic paintings evoke a strong sense of Marley's remarkable life and his Caribbean homeland." Booklist

Includes bibliographical references

Paprocki, Sherry Beck. **Bob** Marley; musician. [by] Sherry Beck Paprocki. legacy ed.; Chelsea House 2006 111p bibl il por (Black Americans of achievement) lib bdg $30

Grades: 6 7 8 9 **92**

1. Singers 2. Musicians 3. Reggae music 4. Reggae musicians

ISBN 0-7910-9213-5

LC 2006004578

A biography of the Jamaican reggae musician.

The book goes "beyond the typical personal information to provide some social history revelant to the subject's time. Captioned photographs and boxed inserts enhance the conversational [text]." Horn Book Guide

Includes bibliographical references

Marshall, Thurgood, 1908-1993

Crowe, Chris. **Thurgood** Marshall; a twentieth-century life. Viking 2008 248p il (Up close) $16.99

Grades: 6 7 8 9 10 **92**

1. Judges 2. Lawyers 3. Solicitors general 4. Civil rights activists 5. Supreme Court justices 6. African Americans -- Biography 7. United States -- Supreme Court

ISBN 978-0-670-06228-7; 0-670-06228-6

LC 2007-042794

"This is a captivating portrait of a heroic champion of justice that also offers great insight into the most pivotal moments of the Civil Rights Movement." Kirkus

Marx, Karl, 1818-1883

Rossig, Wolfgang. **Karl** Marx. Morgan Reynolds 2009 112p il (Profiles in economics) lib bdg $28.95

Grades: 8 9 10 **92**

1. Philosophers 2. Writers on politics 3. Political and social philosophers

ISBN 978-1-59935-132-2; 1-59935-132-3

LC 2009-29563

"This book presents the life of Karl Marx and places his social and economic theories within the useful context of his youth in a prosperous German family. . . . [The author] provides a well-researched account of Marx's life and his work." Booklist

Includes bibliographical references

Mason, Biddy, 1818-1891

White, Arisa. **Biddy** Mason speaks up; by Arisa White and Laura Atkins ; illustrations by Laura Freeman. Heyday 2019 112 p. (hardcover : alk. paper) $18

Grades: 5 6 7 8 9 **92**

1. African American women -- Biography 2. Slaves -- United States -- Biography 3. Overland journeys to the Pacific 4. Freedmen -- California -- Biography 5. Frontier and pioneer life -- California 6. Women slaves -- United States -- Biography 7. African American women -- California -- Biography 8. African American midwives -- California -- Biography

ISBN 9781597144032

LC 2018010807

This book in the Fighting for Justice series, by Arisa White and Laura Atkins, illustrated by Laura Freeman, "introduces young readers to another real-life champion for civil rights: Bridget 'Biddy' Mason, an African American philanthropist, healer, and midwife who was born into slavery. . . . [The book also examines] slavery, racism, and community healing in the United States." (Publisher's note)

Includes bibliographical references and index

Matisse, Henri

★ Fillion, Susan. **Miss** Etta and Dr. Claribel; Bringing Matisse to America. David R. Godine 2011 83p il $18.95

Grades: 4 5 6 7 **92**

1. Artists 2. Painters 3. Physicians 4. Art collectors 5. Art -- Collectors and collecting

ISBN 978-1-56792-434-3; 1-56792-434-4

LC 2010048937

"An affectionate, lively examination of the reciprocal relationship between a great artist and two great art lovers. Etta and Claribel Cone, unmarried sisters from a wealthy Baltimore family . . . [were] discerning collectors of modern art, particularly that of Henri Matisse. . . . Their account is lavishly illustrated in full color by reproductions from the Cone Collection at the Baltimore Museum of Art and Matisse-inflected paintings by the author, who drew extensively on the Cone archive that is also housed at the museum. . . . This appealing work stands as both a portrait of two unconventional women and a celebration of the possibilties of arts patronage." Kirkus

Mawson, Douglas Sir, 1882-1958

Bredeson, Carmen. **After** the last dog died; the true-life, hair-raising adventure of Douglas Mawson and his 1912 Antarctic Expedition. National Geographic 2003 63p il map $18.95

Grades: 5 6 7 8 **92**

1. Explorers 2. Geologists 3. Mountaineers 4. Antarctica -- Exploration

ISBN 0-7922-6140-2

LC 2003-0756

Describes the life and career of the Australian explorer, Sir Douglas Mawson, focusing on his 1912 scientific expedition to Antarctica

"Bredson's compelling story of courage and survival draws heavily on quotes from Mawson and other primary source documents; there are also charts, maps, and many photographs." Booklist

McCain, John S., 1936-2018

Robinson, Tom. **John** McCain; POW & statesman. ABDO Pub. 2010 112p il map (Military heroes) lib bdg $22.95

Grades: 7 8 9 **92**

1. Prisoners of war 2. Senators 3. Members of Congress 4. Presidential candidates 5. Politicians -- United States 6. United States -- Congress -- Senate

ISBN 978-1-60453-963-9; 1-60453-963-1

LC 2009-32369

"The rush of literary adrenalin will hook readers immediately and keep them enthralled until the end. . . . Given the dynamic topic [and] . . . appealing layout . . . [this is] likely to attract reluctant readers. In addition, sources are plentiful and well documented." SLJ

Includes glossary and bibliographical references

McCarthy, Joseph, 1908-1957

★ Giblin, James Cross, 1933-2016. The **rise** and fall of Senator Joe McCarthy; [by] James Cross Giblin. Clarion Books 2009 294p il $22.00

Grades: 8 9 10 11 12 **92**

1. Anticommunist movements 2. Senators 3. United States -- History -- 1953-1961 4. Biography, Individual

ISBN 0-618-61058-8; 978-0-618-61058-7

LC 2009015005

Giblin examines the life of Joseph Mccarthy, the junior senator from Wisconsin. The book "discusses the Cold War tensions that shaped his beliefs and the unconstitutional methods he used to further his ends." (Publisher's note) Bibliography. Index. "Grades eight to twelve." (Bull Cent Child Books)

"YAs will see the contemporary parallels in this biography of the anti-Communist crusader who rose to power over 50 years ago. . . . Giblin's title, formatted with an open, photo-filled design and written in easy, direct style, makes no superficial connections, and the afterword, 'Another McCarthy?' will prompt discussion about the accusations of terrorism in the aftermath of 9/11. Just as memorable is the scathing commentary from famous journalist Edward Murrow about the differences between dissent and disloyalty." Booklist

Includes bibliographical references

McCartney, Stella

Aldridge, Rebecca. **Stella** McCartney. Chelsea House 2011 112p il (Famous fashion designers) lib bdg $35

Grades: 6 7 8 9 10 **92**

1. Fashion designers

ISBN 978-1-60413-982-2; 1-60413-982-X

LC 2010033972

A biography of fashion designer Stella McCartney.

"Biography collections in need of a bit of sprucing up should find [this title] helpful." SLJ

Includes glossary and bibliographical references

McClintock, Barbara

Spangenburg, Ray. **Barbara** McClintock; pioneering geneticist. by Ray Spangenburg and Diane Kit Moser. Chelsea House 2008 xxi, 136p il (Makers of modern science) $29.95
Grades: 8 9 10 11 12 **92**

1. Genetics 2. Women scientists 3. Geneticists 4. Nobel laureates for physiology or medicine
ISBN 978-0-8160-6172-3; 0-8160-6172-6
LC 2006032356

A biography of the Nobel Prize winning geneticist.
Includes glossary and bibliographical references

McMullan, James, 1934-

McMullan, James. **Leaving** China; an artist paints his World War II childhood. James McMullan. Algonquin Young Readers 2014 128 p. color illustrations (alk. paper) $19.95
Grades: 7 8 9 10 11 12 **92**

1. Artists 2. World War, 1939-1945 -- Art and the war 3. China -- History -- 1937-1945 -- Anecdotes 4. Illustrators -- United States -- Biography 5. Children of missionaries -- China -- Biography 6. World War, 1939-1945 -- Personal narratives, American
ISBN 1616202556; 9781616202552
LC 2013035241

"A memoir of celebrated artist McMullan's early years, from age 2 to 11. His was a hopscotch childhood, thanks to WWII. Born in 1934 in Tsingtao, China, he subsequently lived in Shanghai, Canada, India, then China and Canada again and, finally, in the U.S. . . . The book consists of 54 chronologically arranged full-page illustrations, each accompanied by a facing page of text. The exquisite full-color pictures are filled with air and space, reminiscent of the Chinese scrolls that fascinated McMullan as a child. These pictures and the evocative text are a happy exercise in harmony." Booklist

Includes bibliographical references and index

Mead, Margaret, 1901-1978

Mark, Joan T. **Margaret** Mead; coming of age in America. [by] Joan Mark. Oxford Univ. Press 1998 110p il (Oxford portraits in science) $28
Grades: 7 8 9 10 **92**

1. Anthropologists 2. Curators 3. Writers on science
ISBN 0-19-511679-8
LC 98-18604

This is a biography of the American anthropologist who wrote Coming of Age in Samoa. Bibliography. Index. "Grades six to ten." (Libr J)

An "account of the life and works of the influential, pioneering anthropologist. . . . Mark does a fine job of abstracting Mead's research and published works and showing why they were both critically acclaimed and criticized. The reader-friendly prose is peppered with fascinating anecdotes and photos. Mead herself is presented as a complex, intriguing figure, with fascinating, often contradictory, public and private lives." Booklist

Includes bibliographical references

Meir, Golda, 1898-1978

Blashfield, Jean F. **Golda** Meir. Marshall Cavendish Benchmark 2010 112p il (Leading women) $39.93
Grades: 5 6 7 8 **92**

1. Diplomats 2. Prime ministers 3. Women politicians 4. Cabinet members 5. Israel -- History 6. Jews -- Biography
ISBN 978-0-7614-4960-7; 0-7614-4960-4

"Meir survived pogroms in Russia as a child and became prime minister of Israel. . . . The [woman's life is] revealed within the political and historical context of [her] times and [includes] quotes from autobiographical material. . . . Color and black-and-white photos are included. . . . The compact size, chronological organization, and accessible writing [style makes this biography a] good [resource] for reports." SLJ

Includes bibliographical references

Meltzer, Milton, 1915-2009

★ Meltzer, Milton. **Milton** Meltzer; writing matters. Franklin Watts 2004 160p il lib bdg $29
Grades: 7 8 9 10 **92**

1. Authors 2. Historians 3. Biographers 4. Authors, American 5. Children's authors 6. Nonfiction writers
ISBN 0-531-12257-3
LC 2004-2947

"The author includes clear, interesting explanations about the American historical and economic events that influenced his life. While this book is a pleasure to read for general interest, it would also supplement units on American history." SLJ

Includes bibliographical references

Menchú, Rigoberta

Kallen, Stuart A. **Rigoberta** Menchu, Indian rights activist; by Stuart A. Kallen. Lucent Books 2007 104p il (The 20th century's most influential Hispanics) $31.20
Grades: 6 7 8 9 **92**

1. Mayas 2. Guatemala 3. Memoirists 4. Indian leaders 5. Human rights activists 6. Nobel laureates for peace 7. Native Americans -- Civil rights
ISBN 1-59018-975-2
LC 2006025690

Presents the life and accomplishments of the human rights activist who won the Noble Peace Prize in 1992 for her work to stop the oppression of her people, the Mayas of Guatemala.

This is a "stirring biography. . . . The selection of photos and captions enhance the text." SLJ

Includes bibliographical references

Mendes, Chico

Murphy, Alexa Gordon. **Chico** Mendes. Chelsea House 2011 126p il (Conservation heroes) lib bdg $35
Grades: 6 7 8 9 **92**

1. Rubber 2. Rain forests 3. Conservationists 4. Social activists 5. Amazon River valley
ISBN 978-1-60413-951-8; 1-60413-951-X
LC 2010030590

A biography of the Brazilian rubber tapper, trade union leader and environmentalist who fought to preserve the Amazon rainforest

"Captivating, richly informative. . . . The scope of [this book] is comprehensive. . . . [The book is] engaging as [it is] educational and will be ideal for research and reports." SLJ

Includes glossary and bibliographical references

Mercator, Gerardus, 1512-1594

Heinrichs, Ann. **Gerardus** Mercator; father of modern mapmaking. by Ann Heinrichs. Compass Point Books 2008 112p il map (Signature lives) lib bdg $31.93
Grades: 6 7 8 9 **92**

1. Maps 2. Cartographers
ISBN 978-0-7565-3312-0 lib bdg; 0-7565-3312-0 lib bdg
LC 2007004902

A biography of the sixteenth-century geographer who created a world map in 1569 which introduced a new way of showing the spherical earth on a flat sheet of paper.

"Clear explanations of scientific thought and fact are presented in conversational tones and illuminated by easily grasped examples. . . . [The book includes] sidebars, maps, and well-captioned illustrations." SLJ

Includes glossary and bibliographical references

Merian, Maria Sibylla, 1647-1717

★ Sidman, Joyce. The **girl** who drew butterflies; how Maria Merian's art changed science. Joyce Sidman. Houghton Mifflin Harcourt 2018 120 p. illustrations (chiefly color) (hardcover) $17.99

Grades: 4 5 6 7 **92**

1. Insects -- Metamorphosis 2. Naturalists -- Biography 3. Women scientists 4. Scientists -- Germany -- Biography 5. Scientific illustrators -- Biography 6. Entomologists -- Germany -- Biography 7. Women naturalists -- Germany -- Biography 8. Entomology -- Germany -- History -- 17th century 9. Scientific illustration -- Germany -- History -- 17th century

ISBN 9781328830289; 9780544717138

LC 2016057731

Robert F. Sibert Informational Book Award (2019)

In this book, by Joyce Sidman, "one of the first naturalists to observe live insects directly, Maria Sibylla Merian was also one of the first to document the metamorphosis of the butterfly. In this visual nonfiction biography, richly illustrated throughout with full-color original paintings by Merian herself, . . . Sidman paints her own picture of one of the first female entomologists and a woman who flouted convention in the pursuit of knowledge and her passion for insects." (Publisher's note)

"An exceptionally crafted visual biography of a pioneering entomologist and naturalist who lived a life devoted to discovery." Kirkus

Includes bibliographical references and index.

Mexia, Ynes, 1870-1938

Anema, Durlynn. **Ynes** Mexia, botanist and adventurer; [by] Durlynn Anema. 1st ed; Morgan Reynolds Pub. 2005 144p il (Women adventurers) lib bdg $26.95

Grades: 6 7 8 9 **92**

1. Botanists 2. Explorers 3. Women scientists 4. Mexican Americans -- Biography

ISBN 1-931798-67-2; 978-1-931798-67-9

LC 2005010694

A biography of the botanist who traveled on expeditions throughout South America and Mexico during the 1920s and collected over 500 new plant species.

"An interesting and colorful look at a Mexican-American scientist. The easy-to-read narrative draws on the woman's correspondences." SLJ

Includes bibliographical references

Michelangelo Buonarroti, 1475-1564

Spence, David. **Michelangelo**; [written by David Spence]; editor Guy Croton. North American ed.; New Forest Press 2010 48p il map (Great artists & their world) lib bdg $32.80

Grades: 6 7 8 9 **92**

1. Artists 2. Painters 3. Sculptors 4. Architects 5. Artists, Italian 6. Art -- 15th and 16th centuries

ISBN 978-1-84898-309-0; 1-84898-309-3

LC 2010925210

Explores the world, art, and life of the great Italian artist.

Includes glossary and bibliographical references

Milk, Harvey

Aretha, David. **No** compromise: the story of Harvey Milk. Morgan Reynolds 2010 128p il (Civil rights leaders) lib bdg $28.95

Grades: 7 8 9 10 11 12 **92**

1. Gay rights activists 2. Gay men -- Civil rights 3. Local government officials

ISBN 1-59935-129-3; 978-1-59935-129-2

LC 2009-25708

This is a biography of the gay-rights activist and San Francisco politician who was killed in 1973.

This is written "with simple and engaging prose. . . . Full-color and black-and-white photos are interspersed thoughout, giving a sense of the time period." SLJ

Minamoto, Yoshitsune, 1159-1189

★ Turner, Pamela S. **Samurai** rising; the epic life of Minamoto Yoshitsune. Pamela S. Turner ; with illustrations by Gareth Hinds. Charlesbridge 2015 256 p. illustrations, maps (reinforced for library use) $16.95

Grades: 7 8 9 10 **92**

1. Samurai 2. Japan -- History 3. Samurai -- Japan -- Biography 4. Generals -- Japan -- Biography 5. Japan -- History -- Heian period, 794-1185

ISBN 1580895840; 9781580895842

LC 2014049179

YALSA Award for Excellence in Nonfiction for Young Adults: Finalist (2017)

This book, by Pamela S. Turner, illustrated by Gareth Hinds, is an "epic tale of warriors and bravery, rebellion and revenge. . . . When Yoshitsune was just a baby, his father went to war with a rival samurai family—and lost. His father was killed, his mother captured, and his brothers sent away. Yoshitsune was raised in his enemy's household. . . . But . . . when the time came for the Minamoto to rise up against their enemy once again, Yoshitsune was there." (Publisher's note)

"The back cover warns: 'Very few people in this story die of natural causes.' Turner delivers on the promise of that hook, and it will leave lovers of military history clamoring for more of this type." Horn Book

Mitchell, Maria, 1818-1889

Gormley, Beatrice. **Maria** Mitchell; the soul of an astronomer. [by] Beatrice Gormley. Eerdmans Books for Young Readers 2004 137p il pa $12

Grades: 7 8 9 10 **92**

1. Astronomers 2. Women astronomers 3. College teachers

ISBN 978-0-8028-5264-9 pa; 0-8028-5264-5 pa

First published 1995

A biography of the first female science professor at Vassar College and the first American woman astronomer

"With a smoothly flowing and lively style, this biography introduces readers to the 19th-century astronomer. Well-chosen, primary-source quotations and quality black-and-white photos add authenticity to the text, and contribute greatly to the author's objective and comprehensive description of Mitchell's accomplishments." SLJ [review of 1995 edition]

Includes bibliographical references

Mizrahi, Isaac

Petrillo, Lisa. **Isaac** Mizrahi. Morgan Reynolds Pub. 2011 111p il $28.95

Grades: 7 8 9 10 **92**

1. Fashion designers 2. Television personalities 3. Talk show hosts
ISBN 978-1-59935-152-0; 1-59935-152-8

LC 2010018312

This biography of Isaac Mizrahi discusses "the designer's cultural background, childhood, family, work history and education. The [author describes] the early influences that inspired the [designer] to pursue this career and [provides] details of the philosophy [the] designer uses to make [his] clothing unique. . . . The writing is clear and well organized. Color photos are included and give readers a feel for the time period and the types of clothing and accessories the [designer] created." Voice Youth Advocates

Includes bibliographical references

Mohapatra, Jyotirmayee, 1978-

Woog, Adam. **Jyotirmayee** Mohapatra; by Adam Woog. KidHaven Press 2006 48p il $24.95

Grades: 4 5 6 7 **92**

1. Social action 2. Feminists 3. Women -- India 4. Children's rights advocates
ISBN 0-7377-3611-9

LC 2006009121

"Mohapatra grew up in a rural village in India and became a leader in the fight for the rights of girls and women. . . . The power of one individual to inspire others to action is clearly expressed in this well-written profile. Full-color photos and a map enhance the presentation." SLJ

Includes bibliographical references

Molnar, Haya Leah

Molnar, Haya Leah. **Under** a red sky; memoir of a childhood in Communist Romania. Farrar Straus Giroux 2010 302p il $17.99

Grades: 6 7 8 9 10 **92**

1. Copywriters 2. Jews -- Romania 3. Advertising executives
ISBN 978-0-374-31840-6; 0-374-31840-9

LC 2008055562

"Molnar began life as Eva Zimmerman . . . in Bucharest, Romania. . . . It came as a huge shock to Molnar when she learned in 1958 that her entire family had applied to emigrate to Israel and that she was Jewish. . . . As Eva pieces together her family's history, a vivid story emerges, ranging from funny, tender moments of family life to the horrific revelations of the Romanian holocaust. . . . Black-and-white family photos illustrate this poignant, memorable offering." Booklist

Monaque, Mathilde

Monaque, Mathilde. **Trouble** in my head; a young girl's fight with depression. translated by Lorenza Garcia. Trafalgar Square 2009 167p pa $15.95

Grades: 7 8 9 10 **92**

1. Depression (Psychology)
ISBN 978-0-09-191723-4 pa; 0-09-191723-9 pa

"Monaque tells her own story of depression, which began at age 14. Recounting her experience from memory, the teen attempts to discern what caused the illness as well as to explain the process she went through to overcome it. . . . She is bright and articulate and paints a vivid picture of what depression feels like from the inside." SLJ

Monet, Claude, 1840-1926

Spence, David. **Monet**. New Forest Press 2010 48p il (Great artists and their world) lib bdg $32.80

Grades: 6 7 8 9 **92**

1. Artists 2. Painters 3. Artists, French
ISBN 978-1-848983-12-0; 1-848983-12-3

"This slender title offers a thorough introduction to Oscar Claude Monet, who, before helping to found the French Impressionist movement, was known for his sharp-eyed, witty caricature drawings. . . . The spreads cover a wide range of topics, all presented in short paragraphs and long captions that accompany the multiple, mostly well-reproduced artwork and archival photos on every page." Booklist

Monroe, James, 1758-1831

Naden, Corinne J. **James** Monroe; [by] Corinne J. Naden and Rose Blue. Marshall Cavendish Benchmark 2009 96p il map (Presidents and their times) lib bdg $34.21

Grades: 5 6 7 8 **92**

1. Presidents 2. Secretaries of state 3. Presidents -- United States
ISBN 978-0-7614-2838-1 lib bdg; 0-7614-2838-0 lib bdg

LC 2007-29480

"Provides comprehensive information on President James Monroe and places him within his historical and cultural context. Also explored are the formative events of his times and how he responded." Publisher's note

Includes glossary and bibliographical references

Montgomery, L. M. (Lucy Maud), 1874-1942

Rosenberg, Liz. **House** of dreams; the life of L. M. Montgomery. Liz Rosenberg, Julie Morstad [illustrator] Candlewick Press 2018 352 p. $17.99

Grades: 6 7 8 9 10 **92**

1. Women novelists -- Biography 2. Canadian novelists -- Biography
ISBN 0763660574; 9780763660574

"An affecting biography of [L. M. Montgomery], the author of 'Anne of Green Gables,' [by Liz Rosenberg, illustrated by Julie Morstad] is the first for young readers to include revelations about her last days and to encompass the complexity of a brilliant and sometimes troubled life. . . . Through this revealing and deeply moving biography, kindred spirits of all ages . . . will be captivated anew by the words of this remarkable woman." (Publisher's note)

Mora, Pat

Marcovitz, Hal. **Pat** Mora; [by] Hal Marcovitz; forward by Kyle Zimmer. Chelsea House 2008 134p il (Who wrote that?) $30

Grades: 6 7 8 9 **92**

1. Poets 2. Authors 3. Women authors 4. Mexican American authors 5. Essayists 6. Poets, American 7. College teachers 8. Children's authors 9. Young adult authors 10. Museum administrators 11. College administrators 12. Mexican Americans -- Biography
ISBN 978-0-7910-9528-7; 0-7910-9528-2

LC 2007019452

This biography examines the "writer's life, including the inspiration behind some of [her] works. [The] volume includes photographs and quotations from interviews, as well as descriptions of main characters and annotated lists of books and awards. Useful for aspiring authors as well as book report writers." Horn Book Guide

Includes bibliographical references

Mozart, Wolfgang Amadeus, 1756-1791

Riggs, Kate. **Wolfgang** Amadeus Mozart. Creative Education 2009 48p il (Xtraordinary artists) lib bdg $32.80

Grades: 4 5 6 7 **92**

1. Composers

ISBN 978-1-58341-664-8 lib bdg; 1-58341-664-1 lib bdg

LC 2007008963

This biography of the composer offers an "interesting [layout]; big, high-quality reproductions and photographs on heavy paper; insightful quotes from diverse sources; and meaty selections of the artist's own writing . . . at the end of the book. Readers get a strong sense of [Mozart's] personality along with an excellent survey of his work." SLJ

Includes bibliographical references

Weeks, Marcus. **Mozart**; the boy who changed the world with his music. [by] Marcus Weeks. National Geographic 2007 64p il map (World history biographies) $17.95; lib bdg $27.90

Grades: 5 6 7 8 **92**

1. Composers

ISBN 978-1-4263-0002-8; 1-4263-0002-6; 978-1-4263-0003-5 lib bdg; 1-4263-0003-4 lib bdg

LC 2006020783

An introduction to the life and music of the composer and musician Mozart.

This "visually appealing [title is] packed with excellent photographs and reproductions, interesting sidebars, and have a time line running along the bottom of every page. . . . [The book is] useful, well-written." SLJ

Includes bibliographical references

Muhammad, Ibtihaj, 1985-

★ Muhammad, Ibtihaj, 1985- **Proud**; living my American dream. Ibtihaj Muhammad. Little, Brown & Co. 2018 304 p. (hardcover) $17.99

Grades: 6 7 8 9 10 11 12 **92**

1. Olympic athletes 2. Hijab (Islamic clothing) 3. Muslims -- United States -- Biography 4. Fencers -- United States -- Biography 5. Women fencers -- United States -- Biography 6. Women Olympic athletes -- United States -- Biography

ISBN 9780316477000

LC 2018013877

This book, by Ibtihaj Muhammad, tells "the inspiring all-American story of . . . Olympic fencer, activist, and Time '100 Most Influential People' honoree Ibtihaj Muhammad. At the 2016 Rio Olympics, Ibtihaj Muhammad . . . [was] the first American to compete wearing hijab, and made history as the first Muslim-American woman to medal. . . . [Her] journey from a young outsider to an Olympic hero is . . . uniquely American tale of hard work, determination, and self-reliance." (Publisher's note)

"Muhammad describes her struggles with classmates, teammates, referees, and even the public at large, who only saw her as an outsider. She also relates how finding a community of fencers of color, supportive family and trainers, perseverance, and, above all, her faith helped her overcome adversity." (Booklist)

Muir, John, 1838-1914

Goldstein, Natalie. **John** Muir. Chelsea House 2011 139p il (Conservation heroes) lib bdg $35

Grades: 6 7 8 9 **92**

1. Authors 2. Naturalists 3. Conservationists 4. Nature conservation 5. Writers on nature

ISBN 978-1-60413-945-7; 1-60413-945-5

LC 2010030582

This is a biography of naturalist John Muir, who founded the Sierra Club and helped save forest areas in the American West.

"Captivating, richly informative. . . . The scope of [this book] is comprehensive. . . . [The book is] engaging as [it is] educational and will be ideal for research and reports." SLJ

Includes glossary and bibliographical references

Munch, Edvard, 1863-1944

Whiting, Jim. **Edvard** Munch; by Jim Whiting. Mitchell Lane 2009 48p il (Art profiles for kids) lib bdg $20.95

Grades: 7 8 9 10 **92**

1. Artists 2. Painters 3. Artists, Norwegian

ISBN 978-1-58415-712-0; 1-58415-712-7

LC 2008-2250

"The profile of Munch explains how the artist attempted to convey his deep feelings of anxiety in his paintings. . . . [Goes] beyond basic facts, providing historical context and significance of the art and the artist. . . . Provide[s] plenty of information for reports in a reader-friendly format." SLJ

Includes glossary and bibliographical references

Murakami, Haruki, 1949-

Mussari, Mark. **Haruki** Murakami. Marshall Cavendish Benchmark 2010 127p il (Today's writers and their works) lib bdg $42.79

Grades: 8 9 10 11 12 **92**

1. Authors 2. Novelists 3. Authors, Japanese 4. Nonfiction writers 5. Short story writers

ISBN 978-0-7614-4124-3; 0-7614-4124-7

This biography of Haruki Murakami places the author in the context of his times and discusses his work.

Includes bibliographical references

Myers, Walter Dean, 1937-

Sickels, Amy. **Walter** Dean Myers; [by] Amy Sickels. Chelsea House 2008 128p il (Who wrote that?) $30

Grades: 6 7 8 9 **92**

1. Poets 2. Authors 3. Novelists 4. African American authors 5. Editors 6. Authors, American 7. Children's authors 8. Young adult authors

ISBN 978-0-7910-9524-9; 0-7910-9524-X

LC 2007045507

This biography examines the "writer's life, including the inspiration behind some if [his] works. [The] volume includes photographs and quotations from interviews, as well as descriptions of main characters and annotated lists of books and awards. Useful for aspiring authors as well as book report writers." Horn Book Guide

Includes bibliographical references

Nakahama, Manjirō, 1827-1898

★ Blumberg, Rhoda. **Shipwrecked!** : the true adventures of a Japanese boy. HarperCollins Pubs. 2000 80p il map hardcover o.p. pa $7.99

Grades: 5 6 7 8 **92**

1. Survival after airplane accidents, shipwrecks, etc. 2. Interpreters 3. Japan -- History 4. Japan -- Foreign relations -- United States 5. United States -- Foreign relations -- Japan

ISBN 0-688-17484-1; 0-688-17485-X pa

LC 99-86664

In 1841, rescued by an American whaler after a terrible shipwreck leaves him and his four companions castaways on a remote island, fourteen-year-old Manjiro learns new laws and customs as he becomes the first Japanese person to set foot in the United States

"Exemplary in both her research and writing, Blumberg hooks readers with anecdotes that astonish without sensationalizing, and she uses language that's elegant and challenging, yet always clear. Particularly notable is the well-chosen reproductions of original artwork." Booklist

Includes bibliographical references

Napoleon I, Emperor of the French, 1769-1821

Burleigh, Robert. **Napoleon**; the story of the little corporal. Abrams Books for Young Readers 2007 43p il map $18.95

Grades: 4 5 6 7 **92**

1. Emperors 2. France -- Kings and rulers 3. France -- History -- 1799-1815

ISBN 978-0-8109-1378-3; 0-8109-1378-X

LC 2006-23610

"Burleigh's straightforward style and clear focus make accessible this account of the rapid rise and fall of the skilled military leader and emperor of France. The period artwork, accompanied by helpful captions, enhances the cleanly designed presentation." Horn Book Guide

Nefertiti, Queen, consort of Akhenaton, King of Egypt, 14th cent. B.C.

Lange, Brenda. **Nefertiti.** Chelsea House Publishers 2009 108p bibl il (Ancient world leaders) lib bdg $30

Grades: 6 7 8 9 **92**

1. Queens 2. Egypt -- History

ISBN 978-0-7910-9581-2 lib bdg; 0-7910-9581-9 lib bdg

LC 2008004869

This biography of Nefertiti "deals less with the specifics of the [ancient Egyptian queen] and more with [her world] and times, including religious and political issues. The [author uses] speculation, derived from both tradition and scholarship, as to who [this] ancient [leader] may have been and how [she] might have governed." SLJ

Includes bibliographical references

Neruda, Pablo, 1904-1973

Délano, Poli. **When** I was a boy Neruda called me Policarpo; illustrated by Manuel Monroy. Groundwood Books/House of Anansi Press 2006 84p il $15.95

Grades: 5 6 7 8 **92**

1. Poets 2. Authors 3. Diplomats 4. Novelists 5. Poets, Chilean 6. Mexico 7. Memoirists 8. Short story writers 9. Nobel laureates for peace 10. Nobel laureates for literature 11. Biography, Individual

ISBN 0-88899-726-4

In this book, the author offers seven vignettes, interspersed with six of Neruda's . . . poems and biographical information, to give middle-grade readers a sense of what it was like to grow up in the constant presence of a kindly, though spoiled and eccentric, celebrity. . . . Grades four to six. (MultiCult Rev)

"Based on the author's childhood remembrances of when he and his diplomat parents lived with Tío Pablo [Neruda] in Mexico, these seven chapters reveal both the genius and the eccentricities of the Nobel Prize-winning Chilean poet. . . . The chapters are short, well written, and filled with interesting details that will open up a new and exotic world. . . . Monroy's pen-and-sepia-toned drawings are . . . at times humorous, at times dramatic, but always enticing." SLJ

Shull, Jodie A. **Pablo** Neruda; passion, poetry, politics. [by] Jodie A. Shull. Enslow Publishers 2009 128p bibl il por (Latino biography library) lib bdg $31.93

Grades: 6 7 8 9 **92**

1. Poets 2. Authors 3. Diplomats 4. Novelists 5. Poets, Chilean 6. Nobel laureates for peace 7. Nobel laureates for literature

ISBN 978-0-7660-2966-8; 0-7660-2966-2

LC 2008008698

This book contains information about Pablo Neruda: "After openly denouncing the president of Chile in 1948, Pablo Neruda was declared an enemy of his own country. Despite being forced into exile for three years, Neruda maintained his political views. Nothing could deter Neruda from these beliefs or his most celebrated passion-poetry. Author Jodie A. Shull explores the life of this talented writer from his childhood in the Chilean rainforests to winning the Nobel Prize for Literature." (Publisher's note)

Includes bibliographical references

Newton, Isaac Sir, 1642-1727

Hollihan, Kerrie Logan. **Isaac** Newton and physics for kids; his life and ideas with 21 activities. Chicago Review Press 2009 131p il map pa $16.95

Grades: 4 5 6 7 **92**

1. Physicists 2. Scientists 3. Mathematicians 4. Writers on science

ISBN 978-1-55652-778-4 pa; 1-55652-778-0 pa

LC 2008048635

"Hollihan introduces readers to the scientific brilliance, as well as the social isolation, of this giant figure, blending a readable narrative with an attractive format that incorporates maps, diagrams, historical photographs, and physics activities." Booklist

Includes bibliographical references

★ Krull, Kathleen. **Isaac** Newton; illustrated by Boris Kulikov. Viking 2006 126p il (Giants of science) $15.99

Grades: 5 6 7 8 **92**

1. Physicists 2. Scientists 3. Mathematicians 4. Writers on science

ISBN 0-670-05921-8

LC 2005017741

This "profiles Sir Isaac Newton, the secretive, obsessive, and brilliant English scientist who invented calculus, built the first reflecting telescope, developed the modern scientific method, and discerned many of our laws of physics and optics. . . . The lively, conversational style will appeal to readers. . . . Kulikov's humorous pen-and-ink drawings complement the lighthearted text of this fascinating introduction." Booklist

Losure, Mary. **Isaac** the Alchemist; Secrets of Isaac Newton, Reveal'd. by Mary Losure. Candlewick Press 2017 176 p. illustrations (ebook) $19.99; $19.99

Grades: 5 6 7 8 9 **92**

1. Alchemy

ISBN 9780763680473; 0763670634; 9780763670634

LC 2015934464

In this book, by Mary Losure, a "surprising true story of Isaac Newton's boyhood suggests an intellectual development owing as much to magic as science. Before Isaac Newton became the father of physics, an accomplished mathematician, or a leader of the scientific revolution, he was a boy living in an apothecary's house, observing and experimenting, recording his observations of the world in a tiny notebook." (Publisher's note)

"Narrative nonfiction at its best and most convincing." Kirkus
Includes bibliographical references and index.

Steele, Philip. **Isaac** Newton; the scientist who changed everything. [by] Philip Steele. National Geographic Society 2007 64p il map (World history biographies) $17.95; lib bdg $27.90
Grades: 4 5 6 7 **92**
1. Physicists 2. Scientists 3. Mathematicians 4. Writers on science
ISBN 978-1-4263-0114-8; 978-1-4263-0115-5 lib bdg
LC 2006020772
"The cradle-to-grave text includes vivid descriptions of Newton's youth. . . . The dynamic format is a draw; numerous mostly archival images . . . and a time-line border add interest and cultural context on each spacious page." Booklist
Includes bibliographical references

Nezahualcóyotl, King of Texcoco, 1402-1472

★ Serrano, Francisco. The **poet** king of Tezcoco; a great leader of Ancient Mexico. illustrated by Pablo Serrano; biography translated and adapted by Trudy Balch; poetry translated by Jo Anne Engelbert. Groundwood Books/House of Anansi Press 2007 35p il $18.95
Grades: 4 5 6 7 **92**
1. Aztecs 2. Kings 3. Mexico -- History
ISBN 978-0-88899-787-6; 0-88899-787-6
"In the fifteenth century, the land where Mexico City now sprawls was a vast, green kingdom called Tezcoco. This . . . introduces one of Tezcoco's greatest rulers, a Toltec royal named Nezahualcoyotl. . . . The folk-art inspired illustrations echo the area's artistic traditions with beautiful patterning and symbolic imagery and flat , simplified characters reminiscent of hieroglyphics. Groundbreaking in its coverage of exciting history, this book offers details that are rarely presented to young people." Booklist

Nightingale, Florence, 1820-1910

★ Reef, Catherine. **Florence** Nightingale; The Courageous Life of the Legendary Nurse. Catherine Reef. Clarion Books 2017 192 p. illustrations (some color) (ebook) $18.99; (hardcover) $18.99
Grades: 7 8 9 10 11 12 **92**
1. Nurses -- England -- Biography 2. Nightingale, Florence, 1820-1910
ISBN 9780544535824; 9780544535800
LC 2015045606
This book by Catherine Reef "explores the exceptional life of a woman who defied the stifling conventions of Victorian society to pursue what was considered an undesirable vocation. She is best known for her work during the Crimean War, when she vastly improved gruesome and deadly conditions and made nightly rounds to visit patients, becoming known around the world as the Lady with the Lamp. . . . Her modern methods in nursing became the defining standards still used today." (Publisher's note)
"A captivating and inspiring study of one woman's perseverance and the good that came from it." Booklist
Includes bibliographical references and index

Nixon, Richard M. (Richard Milhous), 1913-1994

★ Aronson, Billy. **Richard** M. Nixon; [by] Billy Aronson. Marshall Cavendish Benchmark 2007 96p il (Presidents and their times) lib bdg $22.95
Grades: 5 6 7 8 **92**
1. Presidents 2. Vice-presidents 3. Senators 4. Nonfiction writers 5. Members of Congress 6. Presidents -- United States
ISBN 978-0-7614-2428-4
LC 2006013839
Aronson "is able to paint a picture so full that readers will come away feeling that they know the man and understand at least some of the forces that shaped him. . . . The narrative moves chronologically, marching through the war years, Nixon's tenure in Congress and as vice-president, his presidential loss to JFK, his successful efforts to remake himself as a politician, and his years as president. . . . The typeface is clear, the photographs are well chosen." Booklist
Includes glossary and bibliographical references

Noguchi, Isamu, 1904-1988

Tiger, Caroline. **Isamu** Noguchi. Chelsea House 2007 112p bibl il por (Asian Americans of achievement) lib bdg $30
Grades: 6 7 8 9 **92**
1. Artists 2. Sculptors 3. Industrial designers 4. Japanese Americans -- Biography
ISBN 0-7910-9276-3 lib bdg; 978-0-7910-9276-7 lib bdg
LC 2006026230
A biography of the artist, born in 1904 to an American mother and a Japanese poet father, who created sculpture, furniture, stage sets, and public gardens.
"This engaging account of the prolific and diverse artist will add depth to any biography collection." SLJ
Includes bibliographical references

Northup, Solomon, b. 1808

Fradin, Dennis. **Stolen** into slavery; the true story of Solomon Northup. by Judy and Dennis Fradin. National Geographic Society 2012 120 p.
Grades: 6 7 8 **92**
1. Plantation life 2. Louisiana -- History 3. African Americans -- Biography 4. Slavery -- United States -- History 5. Louisiana -- History -- 19th century 6. Slaves -- United States -- Biography 7. Slavery -- Louisiana -- History -- 19th century 8. Plantation life -- Louisiana -- History -- 19th century
ISBN 9781426309373; 9781426309380
LC 2011024664
"Drawn away from his upstate New York home and family in 1841 by a fake offer of well-paid temporary work, Solomon Northup awoke in a foul Washington D.C. cell, unable to prove that he was a freeman. His abductors sold him into slavery, and after managing to get a message off to his wife explaining what had happened, he was sold in New Orleans to owners who changed his name and controlled his fate for the next twelve years." (Bulletin of the Center for Children's Books)
Includes bibliographical references and index

Nuñez Cabeza de Vaca, Alvar, 16th cent.

Lourie, Peter. **On** the Texas trail of Cabeza de Vaca; 1st ed.; Boyds Mills Press 2008 48p il map $17.95
Grades: 4 5 6 7 **92**
1. Explorers 2. Historians 3. Travel writers 4. Texas -- History 5. Mexico -- History 6. Government officials 7. America -- Exploration 8. Colonial administrators
ISBN 978-1-59078-492-1; 1-59078-492-8
LC 2007049180
"In 1527, Governor Pánfilo de Narváez sailed westward from Spain to explore the land that stretched between present-day Florida and Mexico, colonizing and conquering. With him, as his treasurer and sheriff,

was Cabeza de Vaca. . . . He [returned] with a wealth of information, codified in La Relación , his account of his experience. Then, 475 years later, Lourie set out to follow Cabeza de Vaca's trail through Texas. . . . This well-researched, beautifully composed book is the result. Using primary sources and period reproductions as well as the author's experiences and contemporary pictures, it highlights historical information within the context of current circumstances. Beautifully placed photos, reproductions, maps, and sidebars enhance the fluid text." SLJ

Includes bibliographical references

Nye, Naomi Shihab, 1952-

Nye, Naomi Shihab. **I'll** ask you three times, are you ok? tales of driving and being driven. Greenwillow Books 2007 242p $15.99; lib bdg $16.89

Grades: 7 8 9 10 11 12 **92**

1. Poets 2. Authors 3. Voyages and travels 4. Editors 5. Essayists 6. Children's authors

ISBN 978-0-06-085392-1; 978-0-06-085393-8 lib bdg

LC 2006-36548

The author "writes about sudden intimate connections with strangers, especially taxi drivers, who often yield glimpses of family and exile that can sometimes change us. . . . The prose is chatty, fast, and unpretentious, and teens will enjoy the driving stuff and the idea of her kissing in the backseat, and they'll feel her sense of control when she is behind the wheel herself." Booklist

O'Connor, Sandra Day

Abrams, Dennis. **Sandra** Day O'Connor; U.S. Supreme Court Justice. Chelsea House 2009 136p il (Women of achievement) $30

Grades: 6 7 8 9 **92**

1. Judges 2. Supreme Court justices

ISBN 978-1-60413-337-0; 1-60413-337-6

LC 2008055367

A biography of the first woman U. S. Supreme Court Justice.

Includes bibliographical references

O'Dell, Scott, 1898-1989

Marcovitz, Hal. **Scott** O'Dell; [by] Hal Marcovitz; foreword by Kyle Zimmer. Chelsea House 2008 128p il (Who wrote that?) lib bdg $30

Grades: 6 7 8 9 **92**

1. Authors 2. Novelists 3. Authors, American 4. Children's authors 5. Nonfiction writers 6. Short story writers 7. Young adult authors

ISBN 978-0-7910-9526-3 lib bdg; 0-7910-9526-6 lib bdg

LC 2007019577

This biography examines the "writer's life, including the inspiration behind some of [his] works. [The] volume includes photographs and quotations from interviews, as well as descriptions of main characters and annotated lists of books and awards. Useful for aspiring authors as well as book report writers." Horn Book Guide

Includes bibliographical references

O'Keeffe, Georgia, 1887-1986

Rubin, Susan Goldman. **Wideness** and wonder: the life and art of Georgia O'Keeffe. Chronicle Books 2011 117p il $16.99

Grades: 6 7 8 9 **92**

1. Artists 2. Painters 3. Women artists 4. Artists -- United States 5. Biography, Individual

ISBN 0-8118-6983-0; 978-0-8118-6983-6

LC 2010008256

This is a biography of the American artist and a study of her work. Index. "Intermediate, middle school." (Horn Book)

Rubin "here looks at the life and work of Georgia O'Keeffe. Nicely illustrated with family photos, portrait photos by Stieglitz, and many reproductions of the artist's drawings and paintings, the book builds a convincing portrayal of O'Keeffe from her student days to her ultimate recognition as an important American artist. The book's design is striking." Booklist

Includes bibliographical references

Oakley, Annie, 1860-1926

Koestler-Grack, Rachel A. **Annie** Oakley. Chelsea House 2010 102p bibl il por (Legends of the wild west) lib bdg $30

Grades: 6 7 8 9 **92**

1. Entertainers 2. Marksmen 3. West (U.S.) -- History

ISBN 978-1-60413-594-7; 1-60413-594-8

LC 2009041338

Includes glossary and bibliographical references

Wills, Charles A. **Annie** Oakley: a photographic story of a life; [by] Chuck Wills. DK Pub. 2007 128p il (DK biography) $14.99

Grades: 4 5 6 7 **92**

1. Entertainers 2. Marksmen

ISBN 978-0-7566-2986-1

A biography of the sharp-shooter in Buffalo Bill's Wild West Show, from her humble Quaker heritage, her childhood filled with poverty and abuse, to her rise to international fame.

"This highly readable book has a rich layout of photographs and illustrations on every spread." SLJ

Obama, Barack, 1961-

Abramson, Jill. **Obama**; the historic journey. Young reader's ed.; Callaway 2009 94p il map $24.95

Grades: 5 6 7 8 **92**

1. Lawyers 2. Presidents 3. Racially mixed people 4. Senators 5. State legislators 6. Nobel laureates for peace 7. Presidents -- United States 8. African Americans -- Biography

ISBN 978-0-670-01208-4; 0-670-01208-4

LC 2009-5051

"This scaled down, teen-friendly version of The New York Times's adult biography is geared for middle school students. Containing many of the same photos, it provides a brief overview of the President's life, information that has been revealed over the election year and during his administration. . . . Its allure is in the many photographs with captions, sidebars, speech quotes, and charts. The book is nicely organized. The writing is direct and simple, explaining things such as convention delegates. . . . The book should entice young readers to explore his life further." Voice Youth Advocates

Burgan, Michael. **Barack** Obama. Heinemann Library 2010 112p il (Front-page lives) $38.93

Grades: 6 7 8 9 10 **92**

1. Lawyers 2. Presidents 3. Racially mixed people 4. Senators 5. State legislators 6. Nobel laureates for peace 7. Presidents -- United States 8. African Americans -- Biography

ISBN 978-1-4329-3218-3; 1-4329-3218-7

LC 2009-18176

President Obama's life is "presented with depth and breadth. . . . The writing is accessible and engaging, with color and black-and-white photographs." SLJ

Includes glossary and bibliographical references

Gibson, Karen Bush. The **Obama** view; the historic fight for the 2008 Democratic presidential nomination. Mitchell Lane Publishers 2009 il (Monumental milestones) lib bdg $20.95

Grades: 6 7 8 9 **92**

1. Lawyers 2. Presidents 3. Racially mixed people 4. Senators 5. State legislators 6. Nobel laureates for peace 7. African Americans -- Biography 8. Presidents -- United States -- Election -- 2008

ISBN 978-1-5841-5732-8; 1-5841-5732-1

LC 2008053464

This book is "clearly and crisply written. Starting with Obama's career in Illinois politics, the book then details his unlikely journey to the presidency, starting with his childhood in Hawaii and Indonesia. The final chapter deals with the presidential election and doesn't shy away from such issues as the way race was an election subtext. . . . The design is lively and colorful, and the photos will draw readers." Booklist

Includes bibliographical references

Krensky, Stephen. **Barack** Obama. DK Pub. 2010 128p il map (DK biography) $14.99; pa $5.99

Grades: 6 7 8 9 **92**

1. Lawyers 2. Presidents 3. Racially mixed people 4. Senators 5. State legislators 6. Nobel laureates for peace 7. Presidents -- United States 8. African Americans -- Biography

ISBN 978-0-7566-5804-5; 0-7566-5804-7; 978-0-7566-5805-2 pa; 0-7566-5805-5 pa

LC 2010277785

Presents the life of Barack Obama, including his childhood in the United States and abroad, careers as a community organizer and lawyer, and his election as the forty-four president.

"Krensky excels at providing context not only for Obama's election, but also for his unlikely rise to prominence. . . . DK's powerful photographic format and the usual blurbs and sidebars work well at keeping this age group's interest." SLJ

Includes bibliographical references

Obama, Barack. **Dreams** from my father; a story of race and inheritance. Crown Publishers 2007 442p $25.95

Grades: 7 8 9 10 11 12 Adult **92**

1. Lawyers 2. Presidents 3. Racially mixed people 4. Senators 5. State legislators 6. Nobel laureates for peace 7. Presidents -- United States 8. African Americans -- Biography

ISBN 978-0-307-38341-9

LC 2007-271892

First published 1995 by Times Books

This is the autobiography of the Illinois senator who would later become the 44th president of the United States.

The author "offers an account of his life's journey that reflects brilliantly on the power of race consciousness in America. . . . Obama writes well; his account is sensitive, probing, and compelling." Choice [review of 1995 edition]

Thomas, Garen Eileen. **Yes** we can: a biography of Barack Obama. Feiwel and Friends 2009 236p il map pa $6.99

Grades: 6 7 8 9 **92**

1. Lawyers 2. Presidents 3. Racially mixed people 4. Senators 5. State legislators 6. Nobel laureates for peace 7. Presidents -- United States 8. African Americans -- Biography

ISBN 978-0-312-58639-3 pa; 0-312-58639-6 pa

"The updated edition of this bestselling biography of Barack Obama covers his life from birth through the 2008 Presidential election. . . . [This] is a nice, fast introduction to the nation's current president for those who want more than an encyclopedia article and less then the autobiographical volumes and speeches." Voice Youth Advocates

Includes bibliographical references

Zeiger, Jennifer. **Barack** Obama; by Jennifer Zeiger. Children's Press 2012 64 p. ill. (chiefly col.), col. map (library binding) $30.00; (paperback) $8.95

Grades: 4 5 6 **92**

1. Presidents -- United States -- Biography 2. Racially mixed people -- United States -- Biography

ISBN 0531230503; 0531281507; 9780531230503; 9780531281505

LC 2011031124

This book presents a "nonfiction account of President [Barack] Obama's life for middle school students. . . . The book includes many color photographs of the President as a young boy and young adult. It gives the details of his life in Indonesia and Hawaii and traces his career up to the 2012 re-election campaign. His education is a focus of the biography and there is ample discussion of his educational career and how it has helped to shape him into the man he is today." (Children's Literature)

Includes bibliographical references (p. 61) and index.

Obama, Michelle

Brophy, David. **Michelle** Obama; meet the First Lady. by David Bergen Brophy. HarperCollins 2009 114p il $16.99; pa $6.99

Grades: 5 6 7 8 **92**

1. Lawyers 2. Spouses of presidents 3. Hospital administrators 4. African American women -- Biography 5. Presidents' spouses -- United States

ISBN 978-0-06-177991-6; 0-06-177991-1; 978-0-06-177990-9 pa; 0-06-177990-3 pa

A brief biography of Michelle Obama, wife of President Barack Obama

"The author . . . mixes personal data with information about the political process that brought the Obamas to the White House. . . . This biography is a must-have for all school libraries." Voice Youth Advocates

Includes glossary

Colbert, David. **Michelle** Obama; an American story. Houghton Mifflin Harcourt 2009 151p il $16

Grades: 5 6 7 8 **92**

1. Lawyers 2. Spouses of presidents 3. Hospital administrators 4. African American women -- Biography 5. Presidents' spouses -- United States

ISBN 978-0-547-24941-4; 0-547-24941-1

This biography delves into "the subject of The First Lady's family roots. . . . It offers a strong sense of who Obama was as a child, her solid upbringing, and her adult choices, all bolstered with numerous quotes from Obama and those who know her best. . . . Two sections of color photos and appended source notes for direct quotes complete this timely, highly readable biography." Booklist

Uschan, Michael V., 1948- **Michelle** Obama. Lucent Books 2010 112p il (People in the news) $32.45

Grades: 8 9 10 11 12 **92**

1. Lawyers 2. Spouses of presidents 3. Hospital administrators 4. African American women -- Biography 5. Presidents' spouses -- United States

ISBN 978-1-4205-0209-1; 1-4205-0209-3

LC 2009036557

"This biography is enjoyable reading for those writing reports and for those who simply want to learn more about the First Lady. As well as covering her life with Barack Obama and in the White House, Uschan discusses her family life, education, and early career and includes sidebars on such topics as her experience as a black student at mostly white Ivy League schools. Quotes from interviews with Obama reveal her intelligence, humor, and down-to-earth sensibility." SLJ

Includes bibliographical references

Ocampo, Adriana C., 1955-

Hopping, Lorraine Jean. **Space** rocks; the story of planetary geologist Adriana Ocampo. Franklin Watts 2005 118p il (Women's adventures in science) $9.95

Grades: 7 8 9 10 **92**

1. Geologists 2. Women scientists

ISBN 0-531-16783-6

LC 2005006644

"Adriana Ocampo grew up in Argentina. . . . When her father moved the family to the United States. . . . her enthusiasm for satellite design and interest in geology eventually led to a job [with NASA]. First helping to design a Mars rover, she then got involved in the search for a crater created by a massive asteroid collision that evidently caused mass extinctions in the age of dinosaurs. She now examines photos of distant planets taken by 'flyby' space probes and [plans] new geological expeditions." Voice Youth Advocates

Includes bibliographical references

Ochoa, Ellen, 1958-

Schraff, Anne E. **Ellen** Ochoa; astronaut and inventor. [by] Anne Schraff. Enslow Publishers 2010 128p il (Latino biography library) lib bdg $31.93

Grades: 6 7 8 9 **92**

1. Inventors 2. Astronauts 3. Women inventors 4. Women astronauts 5. NASA officials 6. Hispanic Americans -- Biography

ISBN 978-0-7660-3163-0; 0-7660-3163-2

LC 2008-40349

"Explores the life of Ellen Ochoa, including her childhood in California, her rise through the ranks in NASA, several space shuttle missions, and becoming the first Latino woman in space." Publisher's note

Includes bibliographical references

Ohr, George E., 1857-1918

Greenberg, Jan. The **mad** potter; George E. Ohr, eccentric genius. Jan Greenberg and Sandra Jordan. Roaring Brook Press 2013 56 p. (hardcover : alk. paper) $17.99

Grades: 4 5 6 7 8 **92**

1. American pottery 2. Potters -- United States -- Biography 3. Art pottery, American -- Mississippi -- Biloxi

ISBN 159643810X; 9781596438101

LC 2012047601

Robert F. Sibert Honor Book (2014)

This children's book is a biography of American potter George E. Ohr. "Ohr's eccentricities and his penchant for self-promotion are clearly presented. . . . What makes a George E. Ohr vase sell at auction nowadays for $84,000, and is he really America's greatest art potter? Certainly his work is whimsical . . . vases tilting like leaning towers, a teapot with a spout like an open-mouthed serpent, and all manner of wrinkled, twisted and squashed vessels." (Kirkus Reviews)

Includes bibliographical references and index

Osceola, Seminole chief, 1804-1838

Sanford, William R. **Seminole** chief Osceola; by William R. Sanford. Enslow Publishers 2013 48 p. (library) $21.26

Grades: 6 7 8 9 **92**

1. Native Americans -- United States 2. Seminole Indians -- Kings and rulers -- Biography

ISBN 0766041174; 9780766041172

LC 2011050996

This book is part of the Native American Chiefs and Warriors series and looks at Seminole Chief Osceola. "Osceola led his people, the Seminoles, in one of the longest struggles of the Indian Wars. In a game of hide and seek in the Florida wetlands, the Seminoles struck deadly blows to the U.S. Army. Osceoloa was never defeated, but was finally double-crossed and captured." (Publisher's note)

Includes bibliographical references and index.

Owens, Jesse, 1913-1980

Burlingame, Jeff. **Jesse** Owens; I always loved running. Enslow Publishers 2011 128p il (African-American biography library) lib bdg $31.93

Grades: 6 7 8 9 **92**

1. Track athletics 2. African American athletes 3. Olympic athletes 4. Runners (Athletes)

ISBN 978-0-7660-3497-6; 0-7660-3497-6

LC 2010015697

"This book opens with Jesse Owens' celebrated victory in the 1936 Olympics in Berlin, when he triumphed in the 100-meter dash and Hitler refused to congratulate him. In a more nuanced historical account than many books offer, Burlingame looks at different interpretations of the day's events and comments on how Owens' own account changed over time. . . . After the dramatic opening chapter, the book offers a chronological account of Owens' life. . . . On every page, color brightens the headings, backgrounds, bordered photos, sidebars, and boxed quotes." Booklist

Includes bibliographical references

Gigliotti, Jim. **Jesse** Owens; gold medal hero. Sterling 2010 124p il $12.95; pa $5.95

Grades: 6 7 8 9 **92**

1. Track athletics 2. African American athletes 3. Olympic athletes 4. Runners (Athletes)

ISBN 978-1-4027-7149-1; 1-4027-7149-5; 978-1-4027-6361-8 pa; 1-4027-6361-1 pa

LC 2009024221

A biography of African-American runner Jesse Owens, whose success in the 1936 Berlin Olympic games was a victory for equality and an affront to Nazi leader Adolf Hitler's view of Aryan supremacy.

"Opinionated yet informative, . . . [this blends] anecdotes, quotations, and facts to create [an] engaging [portrait]. . . . Photographs and sidebars are incorporated into [a] reader-friendly [design]." Horn Book Guide

Includes glossary and bibliographical references

McDougall, Chros. **Jesse** Owens; trailblazing sprinter. ABDO Pub. Co. 2011 112p il (Legendary athletes) lib bdg $34.22

Grades: 6 7 8 9 **92**

1. Track athletics 2. African American athletes 3. Olympic athletes

4. Runners (Athletes)
ISBN 978-1-61714-758-6; 1-61714-758-3
LC 2010046697

This biography of track star Jesse Owens "goes beyond merely discussing [his] accomplishments. . . . [It] also [explores] the social and political [influence he] had on society as a whole. In addition, [it introduces] historical events in the context of [his life]. . . . This . . . is teeming with information and is a must-purchase for sports fans and readers interested in social activism." SLJ

Includes glossary and bibliographical references

Page, Larry

Sapet, Kerrily. **Google** founders: Larry Page and Sergey Brin. Morgan Reynolds Pub. 2011 112p il (Business leaders) $28.95

Grades: 7 8 9 10 11 12 **92**

1. Businesspeople 2. Web search engines 3. Computer scientists 4. Google, Inc. 5. Internet executives 6. Information technology executives
ISBN 978-1-59935-177-3; 1-59935-177-3; 978-1-59935-213-8 e-book
LC 2011014665

This biography of Google founders Larry Page and Sergey Bring "will grab YAs. . . . The design is browsable, with clear type and lots of color screens and informal photos of young people at work." Booklist

Includes bibliographical references

Paolini, Christopher

Bankston, John. **Christopher** Paolini; foreword by Kyle Zimmer. Chelsea House Publishers 2010 132p il (Who wrote that?) lib bdg $35

Grades: 6 7 8 9 10 **92**

1. Authors 2. Novelists 3. Fantasy writers 4. Authors, American 5. Young adult authors
ISBN 978-1-60413-727-9; 1-60413-727-4
LC 2010001366

This discusses the life and work of author Christopher Paolini.

Includes bibliographical references

Parks, Rosa, 1913-2005

★ Parks, Rosa. **Rosa** Parks: my story; by Rosa Parks with Jim Haskins. Dial Bks. 1992 192p il $17.99; pa $6.99

Grades: 5 6 7 8 **92**

1. Civil rights activists 2. African Americans -- Civil rights 3. African American women -- Biography 4. Montgomery (Ala.) -- Race relations
ISBN 0-8037-0673-1; 0-14-130120-1 pa
LC 89-1124

Rosa Parks describes her early life and experiences with race discrimination, and her participation in the Montgomery bus boycott and the civil rights movement

"A remarkable story, a record of quiet bravery and modesty, a document of social significance, a taut drama told with candor." Bull Cent Child Books

Tracy, Kathleen. The **life** and times of Rosa Parks. Mitchell Lane Publishers 2009 48p il (Profiles in American history) lib bdg $29.95

Grades: 6 7 8 9 **92**

1. Civil rights activists 2. African Americans -- Civil rights 3. African American women -- Biography 4. Montgomery (Ala.) -- Race relations
ISBN 978-1-58415-666-6 lib bdg; 1-58415-666-X lib bdg
LC 2008020927

This a biography of the American American seamstress who refused to give up her seat on a Montgomery, Albama, city bus to a white passenger, which led to challenging the constitutionality of Montgomery's bus segregation laws

This offers "a wealth of concise and well-organized information. . . . [The] book is fair and balanced and includes viewpoints from those who opposed or disagreed with [Parks'] accomplishments. The design is crisp and colorful without overwhelming the words on the page." SLJ

Includes glossary and bibliographical references

Paterson, Katherine

Bankston, John. **Katherine** Paterson. Chelsea House 2010 128p il (Who wrote that?) lib bdg $30

Grades: 6 7 8 9 **92**

1. Authors 2. Novelists 3. Women authors 4. Authors, American 5. Young adult authors
ISBN 978-1-60413-499-5; 1-60413-499-2
LC 2009022345

This discusses the life and work of author Katherine Paterson.

Includes bibliographical references

Patrick, Danica, 1982-

★ Sirvaitis, Karen. **Danica** Patrick; racing's trailblazer. Twenty-First Century Books 2010 112p il (USA Today: lifeline biographies) lib bdg $33.26

Grades: 7 8 9 10 11 12 **92**

1. Women athletes 2. Automobile racing 3. Automobile racing drivers
ISBN 978-0-7613-5222-8; 0-7613-5222-8
LC 2009-45846

This biography is "both informative and eye-catching. . . . Even young readers with little interest in car racing will be caught up in the story behind Danica Patrick. . . . This involving story does more than recount the high times. Teammates are killed, loyalties switch, and personal criticism is a fact of life in the limelight." Booklist

Patton, George S. (George Smith), 1885-1945

Gitlin, Marty. **George** S. Patton; World War II general & military innovator. ABDO Pub. Co. 2010 112p il (Military heroes) lib bdg $22.95

Grades: 7 8 9 10 **92**

1. Generals 2. Army officers 3. World War, 1939-1945 -- Campaigns
ISBN 978-1-60453-964-6; 1-60453-964-X
LC 2009032371

This volume "offers a solid introduction to the controversial World War II commander, chronicling Patton's life from his childhood through his untimely death from injuries suffered in an automobile accident. . . . Quoting primary sources, Gitlin effectively portrays Patton as an aggressive, ambitious, courageous, often reckless, and occasionally visionary military commander. The volume is illustrated throughout with black-and-white photographs." Booklist

Includes bibliographical references

Paul, Alice, 1885-1977

Kops, Deborah. **Alice** Paul and the fight for women's rights; from the vote to the equal rights amendment. Deborah Kops. Calkins Creek 2017 216 p. illustrations $17.95; (ebook) $9.99

Grades: 7 8 9 10 11 12 **92**

1. United States -- History 2. Women political activists 3. Women -- Suffrage -- United States
ISBN 9781629793238; 9781629797953

LC 2016951184

This book, by Deborah Kops, tells the "story of extraordinary leader Alice Paul, from the woman suffrage movement--the long struggle for votes for women--to the 'second wave,' when women demanded full equality with men. . . . She reignited the sleepy suffrage moment with dramatic demonstrations and provocative banners. After women won the vote in 1920, Paul wrote the Equal Rights Amendment (ERA), which would make all the laws that discriminated against women unconstitutional." (Publisher's note)

"A rich, fascinating, and inspiring account of a tireless champion for women's rights." Kirkus

Includes bibliographical references and index.

Paulsen, Gary

Paulsen, Gary, 1939- **This** side of wild; mutts, mares, and laughing dinosaurs. Gary Paulsen. Simon & Schuster Books for Young Readers 2015 120 p. illustrations (hardcover) $16.99

Grades: 4 5 6 7 8 **92**

1. Human-animal relationships -- History 2. Human-animal relationships 3. Authors, American -- 20th century -- Biography
ISBN 1481451502; 9781481451505; 9781481451512

LC 2015004132

In this children's book, author Gary Paulsen shares "true stories about his relationship with animals, highlighting their compassion, intellect, intuition, and sense of adventure." (Publisher's note)

"For anyone who loves the natural world and excellent writing, this is a must-read." Booklist

Pavlov, Ivan Petrovich, 1849-1936

Saunders, Barbara R. **Ivan** Pavlov; exploring the mysteries of behavior. Enslow Publishers 2006 112p il por (Great minds of science) lib bdg $31.93

Grades: 5 6 7 8 **92**

1. Scientists 2. Behaviorism 3. Physiologists 4. Writers on medicine 5. Nobel laureates for physiology or medicine
ISBN 0-7660-2506-3

LC 2005031648

This is a biography of Russian scientist Ivan Pavlov, best known for his experiments with dogs, which were key to the development of behaviorism, and who won the 1904 Nobel Prize for his research on digestion

"The accessible [text has] an inviting, open format and [offers] many anecdotes. . . . Good-quality photos and illustrations complement the [narrative]." SLJ

Includes glossary and bibliographical references

Peary, Marie Ahnighito, 1893-1978

Kirkpatrick, Katherine. **Snow** baby; the Arctic childhood of Admiral Robert E. Peary's daring daughter. [by] Katherine Kirkpatrick. Holiday House 2007 50p il map $16.95

Grades: 5 6 7 8 **92**

1. Admirals 2. Explorers 3. Arctic regions 4. Children of prominent persons 5. Biography, Individual
ISBN 0-8234-1973-8; 978-0-8234-1973-9

LC 2006-02016

This is a biography of Marie Peary, the daughter of the discoverer of the North Pole. Chronology. Bibliography. Index. "Grades four to seven." (Bull Cent Child Books)

"Born north of the Arctic Circle in 1893, Marie Ahnighito Peary published her own version of her youth in 1934 (The Snowbaby's Own Story), on which this book is based. Kirkpatrick's engaging text captures the girl's adventurous spirit and the opportunities that her father's life as an explorer presented, as well as her love of the North and her Inuit friends." SLJ

Peary, Robert Edwin, 1856-1920

Kirkpatrick, Katherine. **Snow** baby; the Arctic childhood of Admiral Robert E. Peary's daring daughter. [by] Katherine Kirkpatrick. Holiday House 2007 50p il map $16.95

Grades: 5 6 7 8 **92**

1. Admirals 2. Explorers 3. Arctic regions 4. Children of prominent persons 5. Biography, Individual
ISBN 0-8234-1973-8; 978-0-8234-1973-9

LC 2006-02016

This is a biography of Marie Peary, the daughter of the discoverer of the North Pole. Chronology. Bibliography. Index. "Grades four to seven." (Bull Cent Child Books)

"Born north of the Arctic Circle in 1893, Marie Ahnighito Peary published her own version of her youth in 1934 (The Snowbaby's Own Story), on which this book is based. Kirkpatrick's engaging text captures the girl's adventurous spirit and the opportunities that her father's life as an explorer presented, as well as her love of the North and her Inuit friends." SLJ

Peck, Richard, 1934-

Campbell, Kimberly. **Richard** Peck; a spellbinding storyteller. Enslow Publishers 2008 112p bibl por (Authors teens love) lib bdg $31.93

Grades: 6 7 8 9 **92**

1. Authors 2. Novelists 3. Authors, American 4. Children's authors 5. Young adult authors
ISBN 978-0-7660-2723-7 lib bdg; 0-7660-2723-6 lib bdg

LC 2006034069

A biography of the 2001 Newbery-winning book, A Year Down Yonder

Includes bibliographical references

Peet, Bill

★ Peet, Bill. **Bill** Peet: an autobiography. Houghton Mifflin 1989 190p il hardcover o.p. pa $15

Grades: 4 5 6 7 **92**

1. Artists 2. Authors 3. Illustrators 4. Authors, American 5. Children's authors 6. Walt Disney Productions
ISBN 0-395-50932-7; 0-395-68982-1 pa

LC 88-37067

A Caldecott Medal honor book, 1990

"Every page of this oversized book is illustrated with Peet's unmistakable black-and-white drawings of himself and the people, places, and events described in the text. Familiar characters from his books and movies appear often." SLJ

Pei, I. M., 1917-2019

★ Rubalcaba, Jill. **I.M.** Pei; architect of time, place, and purpose. Marshall Cavendish 2011 92p il map $23.99; ebook $23.99

Grades: 6 7 8 9 10 11 12 **92**

1. Architects 2. Chinese Americans
ISBN 978-0-7614-5973-6; 0-7614-5973-1; 978-0-7614-6081-7 ebook; 0-7614-6081-0 ebook

LC 2011001910

"An exquisite package, much like one of Pei's buildings." Kirkus
Includes bibliographical references

Slavicek, Louise Chipley. **I.M.** Pei. Chelsea House 2009 120p bibl il por (Asian Americans of achievement) lib bdg $30
Grades: 6 7 8 9 **92**
1. Architects 2. Chinese Americans
ISBN 978-1-60413-567-1; 1-60413-567-0
LC 2009014609

"A fascinating look at the world-renowned architect. . . . Slavecek deftly covers Pei's life, including his childhood and political events that were going on in China at the time. . . . The narrative is easy to read, the sidebars are informative, and the chronology and glossary are very helpful. A solid choice for most libraries." SLJ

Includes glossary and bibliographical references

Pelosi, Nancy, 1940-

Marcovitz, Hal. **Nancy** Pelosi; politician. Chelsea House Publishers 2009 144p il (Women of achievement) lib bdg $30
Grades: 7 8 9 10 **92**
1. Women politicians 2. Members of Congress 3. Speakers of the House
ISBN 978-1-60413-075-1 lib bdg; 1-60413-075-X lib bdg
LC 2008-34674

This is a biography of the first woman to serve as speaker of the U.S. House of Representatives

Includes bibliographical references

Pelé, 1940-

Buckley, James. **Pele**. DK Pub. 2007 128p il (DK biography) $14.99; pa $4.99
Grades: 6 7 8 9 **92**
1. Soccer players 2. Soccer -- Biography
ISBN 978-0-7566-2996-0; 978-0-7566-2987-8 pa

This "introduces Edson Arantes do Nascimento, know to the world as soccer legend Pelé. The chapters stretch from Pelé's Brazilian youth . . . through is astonishing career and his current retirement. . . . Buckley grounds his enthusiasm with well-integrated facts and quotes. . . . Crisply reproduced photographs appear on every page." Booklist

Includes bibliographical references

Simon, Eddy. **Pele**; the king of soccer. written by Eddy Simon ; illustrated by Vincent Brascaglia ; English translation by Joe Johnson. First Second 2017 144 p. chiefly color illustrations (pbk.) $15.99
Grades: 4 5 6 7 8 9 **92**
1. Soccer players -- Biography
ISBN 9781626727557; 9781626729797
LC 2016961595

"Edson Arantes do Nascimento, known to his schoolmates as Pelé, grew up in poverty in the Sao Paulo region of Brazil. He was too poor to afford a real soccer ball, so he played with a ball of newspaper. . . . He dominated the youth leagues and signed his first professional soccer contract at the age of fifteen. Within two years he was celebrated internationally, when he led Brazil to victory at the world cup." (Publisher's note)

"This particularly smart delineation of Pelé has it all: his career, his blunders, decency, and goodness. And his gift." Kirkus

Perkins, Frances, 1882-1965

Keller, Emily. **Frances** Perkins; first woman cabinet member. Morgan Reynolds Pub. 2006 160p il lib bdg $27.95
Grades: 8 9 10 11 12 **92**
1. Cabinet officers 2. Women politicians 3. College teachers 4. Secretaries of labor 5. State government officials
ISBN 978-1-931798-91-4 lib bdg; 1-931798-91-5 lib bdg
LC 2006023971

"This clearly written title highlights the groundbreaking accomplishments of the woman who served under Franklin D. Roosevelt as the U.S. Secretary of Labor. . . . The narrative is well researched and includes numerous quotes that are cited in a source notes section. Good-quality photographs depict many of the individuals mentioned in the text and illustrate the historical period." SLJ

Includes bibliographical references

Perón, Eva, 1919-1952

Favor, Lesli J. **Eva** Peron. Marshall Cavendish Benchmark 2010 112p il (Leading women) $39.93
Grades: 5 6 7 8 **92**
1. Women politicians 2. Argentina -- History 3. Spouses of presidents
ISBN 978-0-7614-4962-1; 0-7614-4962-0

A biography of the influential and admired First Lady of Argentina.

Includes bibliographical references

Picasso, Pablo, 1881-1973

Bernier-Grand, Carmen T. **Pablo** Picasso; I the king, yo el rey. by Carmen T. Bernier-Grand ; illustrated by David Diaz. 1st ed. Marshall Cavendish 2012 64 p. ill. (hardcover) $19.99
Grades: 7 8 9 10 **92**
1. Art -- History
ISBN 0761461779; 9780761461777
LC 2011032177

This biography of painter Pablo Picasso is written "in free-verse style. . . . The artist's strong will and drive are demonstrated in his decision to wander Madrid with sketchbook in lieu of attending art school; by his insistent attempts to develop his own style (e.g., his Blue Period; his fascination with masklike faces; his creation of Cubism); by his move to Paris; and his insatiable desire for women." (School Library Journal)

Spence, David. **Picasso**. New Forest Press 2010 48p il (Great artists and their world) lib bdg $32.80
Grades: 6 7 8 9 **92**
1. Cubism 2. Artists 3. Painters 4. Artists, French
ISBN 978-1-848983-14-4; 1-848983-14-X

"Offers biographical information [of Pablo Picasso] . . . interspersed with art history and criticism in an eye-catching format. . . . [Includes] a long introductory paragraph and four-to-six images with explanatory notes. . . . Spence . . . does a good job of explaining why art that might seem ordinary today was revolutionary at the time of its creation." SLJ

Includes glossary

Pierce, Tamora, 1954-

Dailey, Donna. **Tamora** Pierce; foreword by Kyle Zimmer. Chelsea House Publishers 2006 146p bibl il por (Who wrote that?) lib bdg $30
Grades: 6 7 8 9 **92**
1. Authors 2. Novelists 3. Women authors 4. Fantasy writers 5. College teachers 6. Authors, American 7. Children's authors
ISBN 978-0-7910-8795-4 lib bdg; 0-7910-8795-6 lib bdg
LC 2005025041

This biography, which examines the "writer's personal life and writing career, [is] ideal for fans. . . . The synopses of most popular books, and lists of works, well-known characters, and major awards may help report writers." Horn Book Guide

Includes bibliographical references

Pike, Zebulon Montgomery, 1779-1813

Sanford, William R. **Zebulon** Pike; courageous Rocky Mountain explorer. by William R. Sanford and Carl R. Green. Enslow Publishers 2013 48 p. ill. (library) $21.26; (paperback) $7.95

Grades: 5 6 7 8 **92**

1. Exploration 2. West (U.S.) -- Biography 3. West (U.S.) -- History -- To 1848 4. Explorers -- West (U.S.) -- Biography 5. West (U.S.) -- Discovery and exploration

ISBN 1464400954; 9780766040120; 9781464400957

LC 2011051629

This book by William R. Sanford is part of the Courageous Heroes of the American West series and looks at Zebulon Pike. "After the United States purchased the Louisiana Territory in 1803, the young nation needed brave pioneers to explore this vast uncharted land. Zebulon Pike . . . led an expedition across rolling prairies before arriving at the towering mountains" and being the first to explore the southern Rocky Mountains. (Publisher's note)

Includes bibliographical references (p. 47) and index.

Pocahontas, d. 1617

Jones, Victoria Garrett. **Pocahontas**; a life in two worlds. Sterling 2010 124p il map (Sterling biographies) lib bdg $12.95; pa $9.95

Grades: 7 8 9 10 **92**

1. Princesses 2. Powhatan Indians 3. Jamestown (Va.) -- History 4. Native Americans -- Biography

ISBN 978-1-4027-6844-6 lib bdg; 1-4027-6844-3 lib bdg; 978-1-4027-5158-5 pa; 1-4027-5158-3 pa

LC 2009-24136

A biography of the daughter of Chief Powhatan and her friendship with the colonists of the Jamestown settlement.

Includes glossary and bibliographical references

Poe, Edgar Allan, 1809-1849

Lange, Karen E. **Nevermore**; a photobiography of Edgar Allan Poe. National Geographic 2009 64p il $19.95; lib bdg $28.90

Grades: 6 7 8 9 **92**

1. Poets 2. Authors 3. Essayists 4. Authors, American 5. Short story writers 6. Biography, Individual

ISBN 978-1-4263-0398-2; 1-4263-0398-X; 978-1-4263-0399-9 lib bdg; 1-4263-0399-8 lib bdg

LC 2008-39833

In text and photographs, this volume depicts the life of the poet and short story writer. Chronology. Index. "Grades five to nine." (Bull Cent Child Books)

"The drama of Poe's tortured life unfolds in accessible prose. Textual information is interspersed with photos, artistic interpretations, and revealing quotations presented in script. . . . This volume offers a fairly complete and thoroughly readable description of Poe's life and his importance to literature." SLJ

Includes bibliographical references

Polo, Marco, 1254-1323?

Demi. **Marco** Polo; written and illustrated by Demi. Marshall Cavendish 2008 un il map $19.99

Grades: 4 5 6 7 **92**

1. Explorers 2. Travelers 3. Voyages and travels 4. Travel writers

ISBN 978-0-7614-5433-5; 0-7614-5433-0

"This elegant, scholarly picture-book biography brings the explorer's fantastic journey to life. . . . Demi weaves her subject's own accounts into a seamless tale of wonder. . . . The delicately rendered illustrations, painted with Chinese inks and gold overlays . . . capture the exotic beauty of 13th-century China." SLJ

Feinstein, Stephen. **Marco** Polo; amazing adventures in China. Enslow Publishers 2009 112p il (Great explorers of the world) lib bdg $31.93

Grades: 6 7 8 9 **92**

1. Explorers 2. Travelers 3. Voyages and travels 4. Travel writers

ISBN 978-1-59845-103-0 lib bdg; 1-59845-103-0 lib bdg

LC 2008-40344

"Examines the life of Italian explorer Marco Polo, including a childhood in Venice, his travels in China and the Mongol empire, his service to Kublai Khan, and his imprisonment in Genoa." Publisher's note

Includes glossary and bibliographical references

Twist, Clint. **Marco** Polo; history's great adventurer. Candlewick Press 2011 un il (Historical notebooks) $19.99

Grades: 5 6 7 8 **92**

1. Explorers 2. Travelers 3. Voyages and travels 4. Travel writers

ISBN 978-0-7636-5286-9; 0-7636-5286-5

LC 2010040131

First published 2010 in the United Kingdom with title: Marco Polo; geographer of distant lands

"In this sumptuous scrapbook, excerpts from Marco Polo's own account of his travels are paired with beautiful maps, drawings, and illustrations. . . . This volume is well suited to browsing, and many readers will want to spend time poring over the many details." SLJ

Powell, Barbara Johns, 1935-1991

Kanefield, Teri, 1960- The **girl** from the tar paper school; Barbara Rose Johns and the advent of the civil rights movement. by Teri Kanefield. Abrams Books for Young Readers 2013 56 p. (alk. paper) $19.95

Grades: 5 6 7 8 **92**

1. Segregation in education 2. African Americans -- Civil rights 3. Civil rights -- United States -- History 4. Civil rights workers -- United States -- Biography 5. Virginia -- Race relations -- History -- 20th century 6. Women civil rights workers -- United States -- Biography 7. Segregation in education -- Virginia -- History -- 20th century 8. Civil rights movements -- United States -- History -- 20th century

ISBN 1419707965; 9781419707964

LC 2012040990

This book, by Teri Kanefield, focuses on "Barbara Rose Johns. . . . In 1951, witnessing the unfair conditions in her racially segregated high school, Barbara Johns led a walkout . . . jumpstarting the American civil rights movement. Ridiculed by the white superintendent and school board . . . Barbara and her classmates held firm and did not give up. Her school's case went all the way to the Supreme Court and helped end segregation as part of Brown v. Board of Education." (Publisher's note)

"A heartfelt tribute to Barbara Rose Johns, a lesser-known heroine of the early civil rights movement. In 1951 Virginia, black Robert R. Moton High School and white Farmville High were separate but definitely not equal, and quiet Barbara and her classmates decided to strike.

Profuse details, some extraneous, threaten to overtake the inspiring story of bravery." (Horn Book)

Includes bibliographical references and index

Powell, Colin L., 1937-

Vander Hook, Sue. **Colin** Powell; general & statesman. ABDO Pub. Co. 2010 112p il (Military heroes) lib bdg $22.95

Grades: 7 8 9 10 **92**

1. Generals 2. Statesmen 3. Secretaries of state 4. African Americans -- Biography

ISBN 978-1-60453-965-3; 1-60453-965-8

LC 2009032364

This biography of Colin Powell covers Powell's service in the Vietnam War, his role as a White House fellow, a four-star general, and commander-in-chief of Forces Command and Powell's service to the U.S. presidents as the chairman of the Joint Chiefs of Staff and the secretary of state.

"The rush of literary adrenalin will hook readers immediately and keep them enthralled until the end. . . . Given the dynamic topic . . . [and] appealing layout [this book is] likely to appeal to reluctant readers. In addition, sources are plentiful and well-documented, making the [title] suitable for research projects." SLJ

Includes bibliographical references

Presley, Elvis, 1935-1977

Collins, Terry. **Elvis**; a graphic novel. illustrated by Michele Melcher. Capstone Press 2011 32p il (Graphic library: American graphic) lib bdg $29.32; pa $7.95

Grades: 4 5 6 7 **92**

1. Actors 2. Singers 3. Rock musicians 4. Biographical graphic novels

ISBN 978-1-4296-5476-0 lib bdg; 1-4296-5476-7 lib bdg; 978-1-4296-6266-6 pa; 1-4296-6266-2 pa

LC 2010024847

In graphic novel format, explores the life of Elvis Presley and describes his return to stardom through his '68 Comeback Special.

"The illustrations are eye-catching and the narration is presented simply, yet compellingly. . . . Fact-filled, entertaining, and accessible." SLJ

Includes glossary and bibliographical references

Micklos, John. **Elvis** Presley; I want to entertain people. [by] John Micklos, Jr. Enslow Publishers 2010 160p il (American rebels) lib bdg $34.60

Grades: 6 7 8 9 **92**

1. Actors 2. Singers 3. Rock musicians

ISBN 978-0-7660-3382-5 lib bdg; 0-7660-3382-1 lib bdg

LC 2009017595

The first chapter of this "fascinating, well-organized [portrait of the the rock musician] . . . describes the King's 1956 Ed Sullivan Show appearance, which was watched by a screaming audience of 60 million home viewers. . . . Skillfully chosen photos, chapter notes, and [a] suggested-reading [list completes this] well-researched, wholly engaging [introduction]." Booklist

Includes bibliographical references

Puente, Tito, 1923-2000

McNeese, Tim. **Tito** Puente; [by] Tim McNeese. Chelsea House 2008 118p il (The great Hispanic heritage) lib bdg $30

Grades: 6 7 8 9 **92**

1. Composers 2. Musicians 3. Band leaders 4. Percussionists 5. Music arrangers 6. Puerto Ricans -- Biography

ISBN 978-0-7910-9666-6 lib bdg; 0-7910-9666-1 lib bdg

LC 2007031984

This biography provides a "substantive [portrait], including background information and historical context of . . . charismatic band leader Puente. . . . The well-documented [text] effectively [combines] anecdotes, quotations, and historical details. Many photographs and sidebars are also included." Horn Book Guide

Includes bibliographical references

Pujols, Albert, 1980-

Needham, Tom. **Albert** Pujols; MVP on and off the field. Enslow Publishers 2007 128p bibl por (Sports stars with heart) lib bdg $23.95

Grades: 4 5 6 7 **92**

1. Baseball players 2. Baseball -- Biography

ISBN 978-0-7660-2866-1 lib bdg; 0-7660-2866-6 lib bdg

LC 2006031843

"Baseball fans know Pujols from his outstanding record: Rookie of the Year, a National League MVP, a team leader helping the St. Louis Cardinals win the World Series in 2006. However, with its combination of sharp writing, eye-catching design, and well-chosen photos, this . . . is so pleasing that even those who don't follow baseball will enjoy learning about Pujols." Booklist

Includes bibliographical references

Pullman, Philip, 1946-

Speaker-Yuan, Margaret. **Philip** Pullman. Chelsea House 2006 118p il (Who wrote that?) lib bdg $30

Grades: 6 7 8 9 **92**

1. Authors 2. Novelists 3. Fantasy writers 4. Authors, English 5. Young adult authors

ISBN 0-7910-8658-5

LC 2005-8184

This "draws upon an impressive array of sources—particularly Pullman's own writings—to present the groundbreaking author's life and work. . . . What may thrill readers most . . . are the insights into the writing process." Booklist

Includes bibliographical references

Raisman, Aly, 1994-

Leigh, Anna. **Aly** Raisman; athlete and activist. Anna Leigh. Lerner Publications 2019 48 p. (lb : alk. paper) $31.99

Grades: 5 6 7 8 **92**

1. Women Olympic athletes -- United States -- Biography 2. Women political activists -- United States -- Biography 3. Women gymnasts -- United States -- Biography 4. Sexual abuse victims -- United States -- Biography

ISBN 9781541542617; 9781541546370

LC 2018027289

This children's book in the Gateway Biographies series, by Anna Leigh, features US Olympian Aly Raisman. Gymnast "Raisman is a leader on and off the mat. She is an outspoken voice against sexual assault. Learn about the most fascinating details of her life as a gold-winning gymnast." (Publisher's note)

"Sharp photographs and a judicious use of sidebars make for an attractive format that adds to the books' appeal." Booklist

Includes bibliographical references and index

Ramirez, Manny, 1972-

Friedman, Ian C. **Manny** Ramirez. Chelsea House Publishers 2010 111p il (The great Hispanic heritage) lib bdg $30

Grades: 6 7 8 9 **92**

1. Baseball players 2. Baseball -- Biography

ISBN 978-1-60413-730-9; 1-60413-730-4

LC 2010007813

A biography of the baseball player.

Includes bibliographical references

Ramses II, King of Egypt

Fitzgerald, Stephanie J. **Ramses** II; Egyptian pharaoh, warrior, and builder. Compass Point Books 2009 112p il map (Signature lives) lib bdg $34.60

Grades: 6 7 8 9 **92**

1. Kings and rulers 2. Kings 3. Egypt -- History 4. Egypt -- Civilization

ISBN 978-0-7565-3836-1 lib bdg; 0-7565-3836-X lib bdg

LC 2008005726

This biography of the pharaoh Ramses II offers "details about the history and daily life of Egypt's New Kingdom era. . . . [The texts is] accompanied by high-quality photographs of artifacts, maps, and floor plans. [The] book's detailed time line, comparing events in Egypt to those throughout the world, is helpful for placing the lives of the pharaohs in context." SLJ

Includes glossary and bibliographical references

Randolph, Asa Philip, 1889-1979

Miller, Calvin Craig. **A.** Philip Randolph and the African American labor movement. Morgan Reynolds 2005 160p il (Portraits of Black Americans) $24.95

Grades: 8 9 10 11 12 **92**

1. Labor unions 2. Labor leaders 3. Civil rights activists 4. African Americans -- Biography 5. African Americans -- Civil rights

ISBN 1-931798-50-8

LC 2004-23706

A biography of the African American leader

"Miller lucidly traces Randolph's spectacular career while presenting a case study in the effective use of hard-nosed rhetoric and nonviolent tactics to achieve breakthroughs in the fight against segregation. Profusely illustrated with photographs, sometimes in color, and capped by resource lists." Booklist

Includes bibliographical references

Rankin, Jeannette, 1880-1973

Naden, Corinne J. **Jeanette** Rankin; Corinne J. Naden. Marshall Cavendish Benchmark 2012 96 p. (print) $39.93

Grades: 2 **92**

1. Legislators 2. Suffragists -- Montana -- Biography 3. Women pacifists -- United States -- Biography 4. Women legislators -- United States -- Biography

ISBN 0761449639; 9780761449638; 9781608707171

LC 2010047559

This biography of Jeannette Rankin by Corinne J. Naden is part of the Leading Women series. The books' "focus on the background and political achievements of twentieth-century women, including those well known in America and those lesser known, too. Each woman's story is told in a narrative, chronological style, illustrated by photographs." (Booklist)

Includes bibliographical references and index

Rasputin, Grigori Efimovich, 1871-1916

Goldberg, Enid A. **Grigory** Rasputin; holy man or mad monk? [by] Enid A. Goldberg & Norman Itzkowitz. Scholastic 2008 128p il map (Wicked history) lib bdg $30

Grades: 6 7 8 9 **92**

1. Monks 2. Courtiers 3. Russia -- History

ISBN 978-0-531-12594-6 lib bdg; 0-531-12594-7 lib bdg

LC 2007001692

"This engaging, thought-provoking book provides a chronological account of Rasputin's life as well as the historical background necessary to understand it in context. Was Rasputin a holy man, or was he simply a philandering charlatan who rose to power because of his unique relationship with Tsar Nicholas and Tsarina Alexandra? . . . Captioned, black-and-white period photographs enhance the text. Recommended for both curricular pursuits and pleasure reading." SLJ

Includes glossary and bibliographical references

Ray, Rachael

★ Abrams, Dennis. **Rachael** Ray; food entrepreneur. Chelsea House Publishers 2009 128p bibl il por (Women of achievement) lib bdg $30

Grades: 6 7 8 9 **92**

1. Cooks 2. Television personalities 3. Talk show hosts 4. Cookbook writers

ISBN 978-1-60413-078-2 lib bdg; 1-60413-078-4 lib bdg

LC 2008034642

"Rachael Ray will be familiar to kids for her talk show and other television appearances, and that will draw them in. But once there, they'll respond to the story of Ray. . . . As a cook who never went to culinary school, Ray knows that her career is an unlikely one. Abrams does a particularly good job of capturing that unpredictability as well as Ray's uniquely exuberant personality. . . . Enjoyable and useful." Booklist

Includes bibliographical references

Reagan, Ronald, 1911-2004

Burgan, Michael. **Ronald** Reagan; a photographic story of a life. DK Pub. 2011 128p il (DK biography) $14.99; pa $5.99

Grades: 5 6 7 8 **92**

1. Actors 2. Governors 3. Presidents 4. Presidents -- United States

ISBN 978-0-7566-7075-7; 0-7566-7075-6; 978-0-7566-7074-0 pa; 0-7566-7074-8 pa

"Burgan's survey covers the basic facts in a positive but not propagandistic introduction. . . . Featuring small but clear photos or boxed commentary on every page and capped with a substantial . . . multimedia resource list, this compact volume . . . gives readers a broad picture of his achievements and a sense of his compelling personal style." Booklist

Includes bibliographical references

Marsico, Katie. **Ronald** Reagan. Marshall Cavendish Benchmark 2011 112p il (Presidents and their times) lib bdg $23.95

Grades: 5 6 7 8 **92**

1. Actors 2. Governors 3. Presidents 4. Presidents -- United States

ISBN 978-0-7614-4814-3; 0-7614-4814-4

LC 2009044590

This offers information on President Ronald Reagan and places him within his historical and cultural context. Also explored are the formative events of his times and how he responded.

"The abundant sidebars provide a good deal of background information that will be helpful to students. . . . Attractive . . . as well as useful." Booklist

Includes glossary and bibliographical references

Rector, Sarah, 1902-1967

Bolden, Tonya. **Searching** for Sarah Rector; the richest black girl in America. Tonya Bolden. Abrams Books for Young Readers 2014 80 p. $21.95

Grades: 4 5 6 7 8 **92**

1. Rich 2. African American women 3. Creek County (Okla.) -- Biography 4. Creek Indians -- Oklahoma -- Creek County -- Biography 5. Women millionaires -- Oklahoma -- Creek County -- Biography 6. Petroleum industry and trade -- Oklahoma -- History -- 20th century 7. African American women -- Oklahoma -- Creek County -- Biography

ISBN 1419708465; 9781419708466

LC 2012039254

Author Tonya Bolden presents a biography of Sarah Rector, who "turned 18 in 1920, [and] the young black woman had amassed a fortune estimated at $1 million. In telling her story, Bolden makes a largely unknown portion of American history accessible to young readers. Rector and her family were 'Creek freedmen,' black citizens of the Creek Indian nation." (School Library Journal)

Includes bibliographical references and index

Red Cloud, 1822-1909

★ Nelson, S. D. **Red** Cloud; a Lakota story of war and surrender. by S.D. Nelson. Abrams Books for Young Readers 2017 56 p. color ills., maps, portraits (hardcover) $19.95

Grades: 4 5 6 7 **92**

1. Lakota Indians -- History 2. Red Cloud's War, 1866-1867 3. Oglala Indians -- Kings and rulers -- Biography

ISBN 9781683350545; 9781419723131

LC 2016048744

This children's book, by S. D. Nelson, tells the story of "Chief Red Cloud [who] deeply opposed white expansion into Native American territory. . . . Red Cloud recognized that continued conflict would only bring destruction to his people. He made the controversial decision to make an agreement with the U.S. government, and moved his people to a reservation. The effects of his decision . . . shaped much of the history of Native American relations with the U.S. in years to come." (Publisher's note)

"An impressive amount of information movingly and handsomely conveyed." Kirkus

Includes bibliographical references (pages 54-55) and index.

Reiss, Johanna

Reiss, Johanna. The **journey** back. Crowell 1976 212p hardcover o.p. pa $17.95

Grades: 5 6 7 8 9 10 **92**

1. Authors 2. Holocaust survivors 3. Children's authors 4. Jews -- Netherlands

ISBN 978-0-690-01252-1; 978-0-59543-050-5 pa

Sequel to The upstairs room

"The journey is the return home in the spring of 1945 for thirteen-year-old Annie and her older sister Sini. . . . The background of the early years is recapitulated. . . . The book offers an intensely provocative story, recalling many personal crises and tests of human nature cruelly beset by the dangers and deprivations of war." Horn Book

★ Reiss, Johanna. The **upstairs** room. Crowell 1972 273p hardcover o.p. pa $5.99

Grades: 3 4 5 6 7 8 **92**

1. Authors 2. Holocaust survivors 3. Children's authors 4. Jews -- Netherlands 5. World War, 1939-1945 -- Jews 6. Holocaust, 1933-1945 -- Personal narratives 7. Netherlands -- History -- 1940-1945, German occupation

ISBN 0-690-85127-8; 0-06-440370-X pa

A Newbery Medal honor book, 1973

"In a vital, moving account the author recalls her experiences as a Jewish child hiding from the Germans occupying her native Holland during World War II. . . . Ten-year-old Annie and her twenty-year-old sister Sini, . . . are taken in by a Dutch farmer, his wife, and mother who hide the girls in an upstairs room of the farm house. Written from the perspective of a child the story affords a child's-eye-view of the war." Booklist

Followed by The journey back

Rembrandt Harmenszoon van Rijn, 1606-1669

Roberts, Russell. **Rembrandt**; [by] Russell Roberts. Mitchell Lane 2009 48p il (Art profiles for kids) lib bdg $20.95

Grades: 7 8 9 10 **92**

1. Artists 2. Etchers 3. Painters 4. Artists, Dutch 5. Drafters

ISBN 978-1-58415-710-6 lib bdg; 1-58415-710-0 lib bdg

LC 2008-2241

"Tracks the artist's rise to fame and the bitter years and bankruptcy that followed. . . . [Goes] beyond basic facts, providing historical context and significance of the art and the artist. . . . Provide[s] plenty of information for reports in a reader-friendly format." SLJ

Includes glossary and bibliographical references

Renoir, Auguste, 1841-1919

Spence, David. **Renoir**. New Forest Press 2010 48p il (Great artists and their world) lib bdg $32.80

Grades: 6 7 8 9 **92**

1. Artists 2. Painters 3. Artists, French 4. Impressionism (Art)

ISBN 978-1-848983-15-5; 1-848983-17-4

"Offers biographical information [of Auguste Renoir] . . . interspersed with art history and criticism in an eye-catching format. . . . [Includes] a long introductory paragraph and four-to-six images with explanatory notes. . . . Spence . . . does a good job of explaining why art that might seem ordinary today was revolutionary at the time of its creation." SLJ

Includes glossary

Revere, Paul, 1735-1818

★ Giblin, James. The **many** rides of Paul Revere; by James Cross Giblin. Scholastic Press 2007 85p il map $17.99

Grades: 4 5 6 7 **92**

1. Artisans 2. Metalworkers 3. Revolutionaries 4. United States -- History -- 1775-1783, Revolution

ISBN 978-0-439-57290-3; 0-439-57290-8

LC 2006-38369

"This well-organized biography presents a lucid account of Revere's childhood, his limited education, his training in his father's workshop, his brief military career, and his adult life as a silversmith, family man, and Revolutionary War leader. . . . Giblin presents salient facts and intriguing details to create a well-rounded and credible image of the man. Among the many illustrations are period portraits, narrative paintings, engravings, drawings, and maps as well as photos of significant sites and artifacts." Booklist

Includes bibliographical references

Rhodes-Courter, Ashley Marie

Rhodes-Courter, Ashley Marie. **Three** little words; a memoir. Atheneum Books for Young Readers 2008 304p il $17.99; pa $9.99

Grades: 8 9 10 11 12 Adult **92**

1. Foster children 2. Adopted children 3. Foster home care 4. Memoirists 5. Child benefactors

ISBN 978-1-4169-4806-3; 1-4169-4806-6; 978-1-4169-4807-0 pa; 1-4169-4807-4 pa

LC 2007-21629

"This memoir lends a powerful voice to thousands of 'boomerang kids' who repeatedly wind up back in foster care." SLJ

Rice, Condoleezza, 1954-

Hubbard-Brown, Janet. **Condoleezza** Rice; stateswoman. Chelsea House Publishers 2008 113p il (Black Americans of achievement) lib bdg $30

Grades: 6 7 8 9 **92**

1. Women politicians 2. College teachers 3. Government officials 4. Political scientists 5. Secretaries of state 6. Presidential advisers 7. College administrators 8. African American women -- Biography

ISBN 978-0-7910-9715-1; 0-7910-9715-3

LC 2007035678

This biography details the African American stateswoman's "rise from adversity to . . . recognition. The [book goes] beyond the typical personal information to provide some social history relevant to the subject's time. Captioned photographs and boxed inserts enhance the conversational [text]." Horn Book Guide

Includes bibliographical references

Ride, Sally

Macy, Sue, 1954- **Sally** Ride; life on a mission. by Sue Macy. Aladdin 2014 160 p. illustrations (Real-life story) (hardback) $17.99

Grades: 4 5 6 7 8 **92**

1. Astronauts 2. Women astronauts 3. Physicists

ISBN 1442488549; 9781442488540; 9781442488557

LC 2014016685

"Sally Ride was more than the first woman in space--she was a real-life explorer and adventurer whose life story is a true inspiration for all those who dream big. . . . She was also a nationally ranked tennis player, a physicist who enjoyed reading Shakespeare, a university professor, the founder of a company that helped inspire girls . . . , and a recipient of the Presidential Medal of Freedom." (Publisher's note)

"The extensive backmatter provides scholarly data, while the writing imparts the drive and character of this famous woman. Macy's slim, empathetic account makes readers see the woman behind the achievement." Kirkus

Includes bibliographical references and index

O'Shaughnessy, Tam. **Sally** Ride; a photo biography of America's pioneering woman in space. Tam O'Shaughnessy. Roaring Brook Press 2015 153 p. illustrations (some color) (hardcover) $19.99

Grades: 4 5 6 7 8 **92**

1. Women astronauts 2. Astronauts -- United States -- Biography 3. Astronauts -- United States -- Pictorial works 4. Women astronauts -- United States -- Biography 5. Women astronauts -- United States -- Pictorial works

ISBN 9781596439948; 1596439947

LC 2015004913

This biography of Sally Ride, by Tam O'Shaughnessey, "is an intimate journey from her formative years to her final moments. Before she earned a Ph.D. in physics, she was called an underachiever by her high school classmates. After her first historic space flight-she took a second in 1984-Sally continued to break ground as an inspirational advocate for space exploration, public policy, and science education." (Publisher's note)

"Ride was notoriously private, and this glimpse into her life and background will be both eye-opening and inspiring for many young readers. The irresistible photos and appealing page layouts make it an especially good pick for reluctant readers." Booklist

Riis, Jacob A. (Jacob August), 1849-1914

Burgan, Michael. **Exposing** hidden worlds; how Jacob Riis' photos became tools for social reform. by Michael Burgan. Compass Point Books, a Capstone imprint 2018 64 p. illustrations (Captured history) (library binding) $34.65

Grades: 5 6 7 8 **92**

1. Journalists -- Biography 2. Photographers -- United States -- Biography 3. Journalists -- New York (State) -- New York -- Biography 4. Photographers -- New York (State) -- New York -- Biography

ISBN 9780756556181; 9780756556204

LC 2017010277

This book in the Captured History series, by Michael Burgan, features social reformer Jacob Riis and his photographs that became tools for social reforms in the U.S. "The book focused on the difficult time immigrants faced as thousands of newcomers flooded into the United States each year. Riis called for reform and hoped to prod government officials to help the poor people who were forced to live under horrible conditions." (Publisher's note)

"Burgan writes persuasively about Riis . . . whose work has lasting power as well as historical significance. Burgan's informative text, detailed captions, and illustrated sidebars give readers the background knowledge needed to understand the historical context and appreciate Riis' work." Booklist

Includes bibliographical references (page 63) and index

Rivera, Diego, 1886-1957

Hillstrom, Kevin. **Diego** Rivera; muralist. by Kevin Hillstrom. Lucent Books 2008 104p il (The twentieth century's most influential Hispanics) lib bdg $32.45

Grades: 6 7 8 9 10 **92**

1. Artists 2. Painters 3. Artists, Mexican

ISBN 978-1-4205-0018-9 lib bdg; 1-4205-0018-X lib bdg

LC 2007-32104

"Rivera's life, beginnning with his childhood, is placed in the context of the artistic, political, and economic influences on family and his career. . . . The layout draws the eye with colorful headings and highlighted quotes." Libr Media Connect

Includes bibliographical references

Rizal, José, 1861-1896

Arruda, Suzanne Middendorf. **Freedom's** martyr; the story of Jose Rizal, national hero of the Phillipines. [by] Suzanne Middendorf Arruda. Avisson Press 2003 106p il (Avisson young adult series) pa $19.95

Grades: 7 8 9 10 **92**

1. Authors 2. Novelists 3. Physicians 4. Philippines 5. Revolutionaries 6. Political leaders

ISBN 1-88810-555-0

LC 2003-45320

"Born in the Philippines on June 19, 1861, Rizal was executed by the Spanish for treason on December 30, 1896. . . . Rizal wanted representation for native peoples in the Spanish government and wrote three novels and several poems detailing their plight. . . . This well-written, readable biography will prove useful for reports and background information on the history of the Philippines." SLJ

Includes bibliographical references

Robeson, Paul, 1898-1976

Slavicek, Louise Chipley. **Paul** Robeson; entertainer and activist. Chelsea House 2011 112p il (Black Americans of achievement) lib bdg $35

Grades: 6 7 8 9 10 **92**

1. Actors 2. Singers 3. Football players 4. African American actors 5. African American singers 6. Civil rights activists 7. African Americans -- Biography

ISBN 978-1-60413-843-6; 1-60413-843-2

This biography of the African American singer, actor, and activist "chronicles Robeson's struggles to overcome racial prejudice, leading to his staunch support of communism—a stand that caused him to lose favor in Hollywood and contributed to his eventual reclusion. Slavicek delves deeply into Robeson's story, giving readers a strong sense of the challenges Robeson faced, as well as the complex, courageous individual behind the legend. Archival black-and-white photos further lend a sense of intimacy, while 'did you know' sidebars expand on related topics." Booklist

Includes bibliographical references

Robinson, Jackie, 1919-1972

★ Robinson, Sharon. **Promises** to keep: how Jackie Robinson changed America. Scholastic 2004 64p il $16.95

Grades: 4 5 6 7 **92**

1. Baseball players 2. African American athletes 3. Army officers 4. Baseball -- Biography

ISBN 0-439-42592-1

LC 2003-42709

"Robinson's daughter, Sharon, describes her father's youth, his rise to become major-league baseball's first African American player, and his involvement in the civil rights movement. . . . Her private view of her father's accomplishments, placed within the context of American sports and social history, makes for absorbing reading. An excellent selection of family and team photographs and other materials . . . illustrate this fine tribute." Booklist

Wukovits, John F. **Jackie** Robinson and the integration of baseball; [by] John F. Wukovits. Lucent Books 2007 104p il (Lucent library of Black history) $28.70

Grades: 7 8 9 10 **92**

1. Baseball players 2. African American athletes 3. Army officers 4. Baseball -- Biography

ISBN 1-59018-913-2; 978-1-59018-913-9

LC 2006010831

"Wukovits does a credible job of adding historical perspective to a straightforward account of Robinson's life and accomplishments. He sets the stage by focusing on baseball's history of racial exclusion, and on the discrimination faced by the athlete and his family. He covers Robinson's military career and his brief stint in the Negro Leagues before he signed with the Brooklyn Dodgers. Robinson's triumphant career in the major leagues and his later life are detailed as well. This is a well-researched and concise account." SLJ

Includes bibliographical references

Roosevelt, Eleanor, 1884-1962

Cooper, Ilene. **Eleanor** Roosevelt; her impact on the civil rights movement, the White House, and the world. by Ilene Cooper. Abrams Books for Young Readers 2018 192 p. (hardcover with jacket) $17.99

Grades: 5 6 7 8 9 **92**

1. Civil rights workers -- Biography 2. Presidents' spouses -- United States -- Biography 3. Civil rights workers -- United States -- Biography 4. Women civil rights workers -- United States -- Biography 5. Civil rights movements -- United States -- History -- 20th century

ISBN 9781419722950

LC 2017058795

This biography of Eleanor Roosevelt, by Ilene Cooper, "shows . . . how the former First Lady evolved from a poor little rich girl to a protector and advocate for those without a voice. . . . [Eleanor] was a woman deeply insecure about her looks and her role in the world. But by recognizing her fears and constantly striving to overcome her prejudices, she used her proximity to presidents and her own power to aid in the fight for Civil Rights and other important causes." (Publisher's note)

Includes bibliographical references and index

★ Fleming, Candace. **Our** Eleanor; a scrapbook look at Eleanor Roosevelt's remarkable life. Atheneum Books for Young Readers 2005 176p il $19.95

Grades: 5 6 7 8 **92**

1. Diplomats 2. Columnists 3. Humanitarians 4. Social activists 5. Spouses of presidents 6. United Nations officials 7. Presidents' spouses -- United States

ISBN 0-689-86544-9

LC 2004-22825

Told in scrapbook style, this biography looks behind the politics to present First Lady Eleanor Roosevelt in her many roles: wife and mother, United Nations delegate, popular columnist, civil rights crusader, and champion of the underprivileged.

"Each of the seven chapters leads readers through the subject's busy life with short sections of text filled with well-documented first-person accounts and direct quotes. . . . Not a spread goes by without incredible archival photographs or reproductions, newspaper and magazine clippings, handwritten letters, and diary entries. . . . They all provide relevant and fascinating insight." SLJ

Roosevelt, Franklin D. (Franklin Delano), 1882-1945

Panchyk, Richard. **Franklin** Delano Roosevelt for kids; his life and times with 21 activities. [by] Richard Panchyk. Chicago Review Press 2007 147p il pa $14.95

Grades: 4 5 6 7 **92**

1. Governors 2. Presidents 3. People with disabilities 4. Philatelists 5. Presidents -- United States 6. United States -- Politics and government -- 1933-1945

ISBN 978-1-55652-657-2 pa; 1-55652-657-1 pa

LC 2007003484

"There are many interesting photos . . . and they are all sufficiently captioned. . . . Information about the Roosevelts [is] presented in a lively, engaging manner." SLJ

Includes bibliographical references

Roosevelt, Theodore, 1858-1919

Adler, David A., 1947- **Colonel** Theodore Roosevelt; David A. Adler. Holiday House 2014 138 p. (hardcover) $18.95

Grades: 4 5 6 92

1. Presidents -- United States -- Biography

ISBN 9780823429509

LC 2013018852

In this biography, author David A. Adler has created a meticulously researched portrayal of the 26th president of the United States. . . . Some called him the cowboy president because of his experiences as a Dakota Territory rancher, adventurer, and head of Rough Rider Regiment in the Spanish-American War. Yet as president, he was anything but a hayseed. He increased the country's stature in the international sphere, built the Panama canal, and won the Nobel Peace Prize." (Publisher's note)

★ Cooper, Michael L. **Theodore** Roosevelt; a twentieth-century life. Viking 2009 208p il (Up close) $16.99

Grades: 7 8 9 10 92

1. Governors 2. Presidents 3. Vice-presidents 4. Nobel laureates for peace 5. Presidents -- United States

ISBN 978-0-670-01134-6; 0-670-01134-7

LC 2010-279534

"This biography presents an evenhanded account of the life and presidency of Theodore Roosevelt. . . . This clearly written biography includes many anecdotes and well-chosen quotes that help bring Roosevelt to life. . . . Cooper offers a solid portrayal of this noteworthy American president." Booklist

Includes biblographical references

Fitzpatrick, Brad. **Theodore** Roosevelt. Chelsea House 2011 142p il (Conservation heroes) lib bdg $35

Grades: 6 7 8 9 10 92

1. Governors 2. Presidents 3. Vice-presidents 4. Nobel laureates for peace 5. Presidents -- United States

ISBN 978-1-60413-948-8; 1-60413-948-X

LC 2010026475

A biography of President Theodore Roosevelt which concentrates on his contributions to environmental conservation.

"Captivating, richly informative. . . . The scope of [this book] is comprehensive. . . . [The book is] engaging as [it is] educational and will be ideal for research and reports." SLJ

Includes glossary and bibliographical references

★ Fritz, Jean. **Bully** for you, Teddy Roosevelt! illustrations by Mike Wimmer. Putnam 1991 127p il hardcover o.p. pa $5.99

Grades: 5 6 7 8 92

1. Governors 2. Presidents 3. Vice-presidents 4. Nobel laureates for peace 5. Presidents -- United States

ISBN 0-399-21769-X; 0-698-11609-7 pa

LC 90-8142

Follows the life of the twenty-sixth president, discussing his conservation work, hunting expeditions, family life, and political career

"Jean Fritz gives a rounded picture of her subject and deftly blends the story of a person and a picture of an era." Bull Cent Child Books

Includes bibliographical references

Hollihan, Kerrie Logan. **Theodore** Roosevelt for kids; his life and times + 21 activities. Chicago Review Press 2010 133p il pa $16.95

Grades: 5 6 7 8 92

1. Governors 2. Handicraft 3. Presidents 4. Vice-presidents 5. Nobel laureates for peace 6. Presidents -- United States 7. United States -- Politics and government -- 1898-1919

ISBN 978-1-55652-955-9 pa; 1-55652-955-4 pa

"What stands out in this volume is the writing, which presents history as an engaging and informative story. . . . The projects are interesting and accessible. . . . Both useful and entertaining, this is a worthy addition to most collections." SLJ

Rappaport, Doreen, 1939- **To** dare mighty things; the life of Theodore Roosevelt. written by Doreen Rappaport ; illustrated by C. F. Payne. Disney-Hyperion 2013 48 p. (hardback) $17.99

Grades: 2 3 4 5 6 92

1. Presidents -- United States 2. Presidents -- United States -- Biography

ISBN 142312488X; 9781423124887

LC 2013010691

This picture book, by Doreen Rappaport and illustrated by C. F. Payne, is a biography of American president Theodore Roosevelt. "As an American president, he left [a] . . . mark upon his country. He promised a 'square deal' to all citizens, he tamed big businesses, and protected the nation's wildlife and natural beauty. His . . . leadership assured that he would always be remembered." (Publisher's note).

Rowling, J. K.

Peterson-Hilleque, Victoria. **J.K.** Rowling, extraordinary author. ABDO Pub. Company 2010 112p il (Essential lives) $32.79

Grades: 5 6 7 8 92

1. Authors 2. Novelists 3. Women authors 4. Fantasy writers 5. Authors, English 6. Children's authors 7. Young adult authors

ISBN 978-1-61613-517-1; 1-61613-517-4

LC 2010000503

This biography of author J. K. Rowling "toggles between the subject's personal and professional life. . . . [The book] offers sidebar . . . definitions of particular characters or events in the 'Harry Potter' series. The writing is accessible, the format is open, and full-color photos appear throughout." SLJ

Includes glossary and bibliographical references

Rudolph, Wilma, 1940-1994

Anderson, Jennifer Joline. **Wilma** Rudolph; track and field inspiration. ABDO Pub. Co. 2011 112p il (Legendary athletes) lib bdg $34.22

Grades: 6 7 8 9 92

1. Women athletes 2. Track athletics 3. Olympic athletes 4. Runners (Athletes)

ISBN 978-1-61714-759-3; 1-61714-759-1

LC 2010046698

This biography of track star Wilma Rudolph "goes beyond merely discussing [her] accomplishments. . . . [It] also [explores] the social and political [influence she] had on society as a whole. In addition, [it introduces] historical events in the context of [her life]. . . . This . . . is teeming with information and is a must-purchase for sports fans and readers interested in social activism." SLJ

Includes glossary and bibliographical references

Runyon, Brent

Runyon, Brent. The **burn** journals. Alfred A. Knopf 2004 373p hardcover o.p. pa $13.95

Grades: 7 8 9 10 92

1. Authors 2. Suicide 3. Burns and scalds 4. Essayists 5. Memoirists

ISBN 0-375-82621-1; 1-4000-9642-1 pa

LC 2004-5643

"One February day in 1991, Runyon came home from eighth grade . . . and set himself on fire. . . . The dialogue between Runyon and his nurses, parents, and especially his hapless psychotherapists is natural and believable, and his inner dialogue is flip, often funny, and sometimes raw. . . . The authentically adolescent voice of the journals will engage even those reluctant to read such a dark story." SLJ

Rustin, Bayard, 1910-1987

★ Brimner, Larry Dane. **We** are one: the story of Bayard Rustin. Calkins Creek 2007 48p il $17.95

Grades: 5 6 7 8 **92**

1. Civil rights activists 2. African Americans -- Biography 3. African Americans -- Civil rights

ISBN 1-59078-498-7

"Brimner sets Rustin's personal story against the history of segregation in his time and focuses on his leadership role . . . in the struggle for civil rights. On each page, the clearly written, informal text is accompanied by eloquently captioned archival photos." Booklist

Includes bibliographical references

★ Miller, Calvin Craig. **No** easy answers; Bayard Rustin and the civil rights movement. Morgan Reynolds Pub. 2005 160p il lib bdg $24.95

Grades: 7 8 9 10 **92**

1. Civil rights activists 2. African Americans -- Biography 3. African Americans -- Civil rights

ISBN 1-931798-43-5

LC 2004-18518

"Miller combines the life story of a great social activist with the history of the struggle for civil rights in the U.S. The politics are exciting, with details of the radical campaigns in the 1940s and 1950s, Rustin's impassioned call for nonviolent protest, and his role in organizing both the Montgomery Bus Boycott and the 1963 March on Washington." Booklist

Includes bibliographical references

Ruth, Babe, 1895-1948

Yomtov, Nelson. The **Bambino** : the story of Babe Ruth's legendary 1927 season; illustrated by Tim Foley. Capstone Press 2011 32p il (Graphic library: American graphic) lib bdg $29.32; pa $7.95

Grades: 4 5 6 7 **92**

1. Baseball players 2. Biographical graphic novels 3. Baseball -- Biography

ISBN 978-1-4296-5473-9 lib bdg; 1-4296-5473-2 lib bdg; 978-1-4296-6265-9 pa; 1-4296-6265-4 pa

LC 2010024764

In graphic novel format, follows Babe Ruth through the 1927 season and describes his attempt to break his own home run record.

"The illustrations are eye-catching and the narration is presented simply, yet compellingly. . . . Fact-filled, entertaining, and accessible." SLJ

Includes glossary and bibliographical references

Sacagawea, ca. 1788-ca. 1812

Berne, Emma Carlson. **Sacagawea**; crossing the continent with Lewis & Clark. Sterling 2010 124p il map (Sterling biographies) lib bdg $12.95; pa $5.95

Grades: 7 8 9 10 **92**

1. Shoshoni Indians 2. Lewis and Clark Expedition (1804-1806) 3. Interpreters 4. Guides (Persons) 5. Shoshone Indians 6. West (U.S.) -- Exploration 7. Native Americans -- Biography

ISBN 978-1-4027-6845-3 lib bdg; 1-4027-6845-1 lib bdg; 978-1-4027-5738-9 pa; 1-4027-5738-7 pa

LC 2009-24139

"Contrary to myth, Sacagawea explains that the Shoshone teen was not a princess, her relationship with Clark was platonic, and she was a peace symbol rather than a guide until they finally reached the Shoshone tribe. . . . [The] spacious design is highly scannable, with color background screens, photos, maps, and historic prints throughout." Booklist

Includes glossary and bibliographical references

Sanford, William R. **Sacagawea**; courageous American Indian guide. by William R. Sanford and Carl R. Green. Enslow Publishers 2013 48 p. ill., map (library) $21.26

Grades: 5 6 7 8 **92**

1. Native Americans -- United States 2. Shoshoni women -- Biography 3. Shoshoni Indians -- Biography

ISBN 0766040062; 9780766040069

LC 2011048291

This book, part of the Courageous Heroes of the American West series, looks at Sacagawea. "Throughout Lewis and Clark's journey in the uncharted American West, this young America Indian woman proved to be an invaluable member of the expedition. Sacagawea served as translator and guide, all while caring for her infant son." (Publisher's note)

Includes bibliographical references (p. 47) and index.

Saint-Georges, Joseph Boulogne, chevalier de, 1745-1799

Brewster, Hugh. The **other** Mozart; the life of the famous Chevalier de Saint George. [by] Hugh Brewster; illustrated by Eric Velasquez. Abrams Books for Young Readers 2007 48p il $18.95

Grades: 4 5 6 7 **92**

1. Nobility 2. Composers 3. Violinists 4. Racially mixed people

ISBN 978-0-8109-5720-6; 0-8109-5720-5

LC 2006-07488

"Born to a white plantation owner and a black slave in eighteenth-century Guadeloupe, Joseph Bologne grew up to become the Chevalier de Saint-George, one of France's most accomplished composers. In this picture-book biography for middle-graders, Brewster introduces his subject's fascinating life. . . . Archival images and Velasquez's arresting full-page portraits will captivate many young readers." Booklist

Salisbury, Graham, 1944-

★ Gill, David Macinnis. **Graham** Salisbury; island boy. David Macinnis Gill. Scarecrow Press 2005 109p (Scarecrow studies in young adult literature) $35

Grades: 7 8 9 10 **92**

1. Authors 2. Novelists 3. Authors, American 4. Children's authors 5. Short story writers

ISBN 0-8108-5338-8

LC 2004031042

"Part literary analysis and part biography, this is a well-balanced look at an unusual talent, a writer who has an eye for the frailties of life and the rites of adolescence. Gill discusses how growing up in Hawaii in the '50s influenced Salisbury's writing and does a fine job of showing the complexity of his work." SLJ

Includes bibliographical references

Salk, Jonas, 1914-1995

Sherrow, Victoria. **Jonas** Salk; beyond the microscope. 2nd rev ed; Chelsea House 2008 146p il (Makers of modern science) $35

Grades: 7 8 9 10 **92**

1. Physicians 2. Scientists 3. Poliomyelitis vaccine 4. Microbiologists 5. Writers on medicine

ISBN 978-0-8160-6180-8; 0-8160-6180-7

LC 2006-33429

First published 1993 by Facts on File

This biography of Jonas Salk "describes this respected immunologist's medical research and his lifelong efforts to promote scientific and human progress on a global scale." Publisher's note

Includes glossary and bibliographical references

Samanci, Özge, 1975-

Samanci, Özge. **Dare** to disappoint; growing up in Turkey. Özge Samancı. Farrar, Straus & Giroux 2015 190 p. illustrations (paperback) $16.99

Grades: 6 7 8 9 10 **92**

1. Turkey 2. Artists 3. Family life 4. Turkey -- History -- 1960- 5. Artists -- Turkey -- Biography 6. Turkey -- History -- 1960- -- Comic books, strips, etc 7. Artists -- Turkey -- Biography -- Comic books, strips, etc

ISBN 0374316988; 9780374316983

LC 2015000704

In this graphic memoir, author Ozge Samanci "recounts her story using inventive collages, weaving together images of the sea, politics, science, and friendship.Growing up on the Aegean Coast, Ozge loved the sea and imagined a life of adventure while her parents and society demanded predictability. Her dad expected Ozge, like her sister, to become an engineer. She tried to hear her own voice over his and the religious and militaristic tensions of Turkey and the conflicts between secularism and fundamentalism." (Publisher's Note)

"In the growing body of graphic novel memoirs, this one is a standout." SLJ

Santa Anna, Antonio López de, 1794-1876

Lange, Brenda. **Antonio** Lopez de Santa Anna. Chelsea House Publishers 2010 102p il map (The great Hispanic heritage) lib bdg $30

Grades: 6 7 8 9 **92**

1. Generals 2. Presidents 3. Texas -- History 4. Mexico -- History

ISBN 978-1-60413-734-7; 1-60413-734-7

LC 2010007515

A biography the Mexican general and president who is well-known for his part in the Battle of the Alamo during the U.S. Mexican War.

Includes bibliographical references

Santana, Carlos, 1947-

Slavicek, Louise Chipley. **Carlos** Santana. Chelsea House Publishers 2006 120p il (Great Hispanic heritage) lib bdg $30

Grades: 6 7 8 9 **92**

1. Guitarists 2. Rock musicians 3. Band leaders 4. Mexican Americans -- Biography

ISBN 978-0-7910-8844-9 lib bdg; 0-7910-8844-8 lib bdg

LC 2005026000

This biography of rock musician Santana is filled "with excellent details—music and familial [history sheds] light on the man's roots and focus strongly on his humanitarian efforts. . . . Color photos and sidebars add interest, and quotes from magazines, newspapers, and interviews are meticulously cited in the endnotes." SLJ

Includes bibliographical references

Say, Allen

Say, Allen. The **Inker's** Shadow; by Allen Say. Scholastic Press 2015 80 p. illustrations (some color) $19.99

Grades: 5 6 7 8 **92**

1. Schools 2. Japanese 3. Bildungsromans 4. Father-son relationship

ISBN 0545437768; 9780545437769

In this book, by Allen Say, "life as teen in Southern California was a cold existence. His father, one of the leading hamburger salesmen in Japan, ran a booming burger business, much like McDonald's, and sent Allen to an American military academy, so that his son could learn English and 'become a success in life.' As the school's first and only Japanese student, he experienced immediate racism among his fellow cadets and his teachers." (Publisher's note)

"A deceptively simple story, given depth by technically excellent illustrations that require a sophisticated level of visual and cultural literacy to successfully interpret." SLJ

Schaller, George B.

★ Turner, Pamela S. A **life** in the wild; George Schaller's struggle to save the last great beasts. Farrar, Straus and Giroux 2008 103p il map $21.95

Grades: 5 6 7 8 **92**

1. Zoologists 2. Wildlife conservation 3. Nonfiction writers

ISBN 978-0-374-34578-5; 0-374-34578-3

LC 2007-42844

"The author interviewed Schaller and had access to his photos, which allowed her to capture beautifully the spirit of Schaller's work. The book is organized chronologically, and each chapter covers a geographic area and the principal animals that Schaller studied there. . . . Animal lovers and conservation-minded students will enjoy this excellent introduction to Schaller and his ideals." Voice Youth Advocates

Includes bibliographical references

Schiaparelli, Elsa, 1890-1973

Rubin, Susan Goldman. **Hot** pink; the life and fashions of Elsa Schiaparelli. Susan Goldman Rubin. Abrams Books For Young Readers 2015 56 p. illustrations (chiefly color) (hardcover) $21.95

Grades: 5 6 7 8 9 **92**

1. Fashion design 2. Fashion -- France -- History -- 20th century 3. Fashion design -- France -- History -- 20th century

ISBN 9781419716423

LC 2014032527

This book, by Susan Goldman Rubin, explores how "shocking pink—hot pink, as it is called today—was the signature color of Elsa Schiaparelli (1890–1973) and perhaps her greatest contribution to the fashion world. Schiaparelli was one of the most innovative designers in the early 20th century. Many design elements that are taken for granted today she created and brought to the forefront of fashion." (Publisher's note)

"With accessible text, an inviting format, and a comprehensive list of multimedia resources in the back matter, this concise biography is well suited to classroom use, particularly for students who prefer to approach history through art." Booklist

Schindler, Oskar, 1908-1974

★ Leyson, Leon, 1929-2013. The **boy** on the wooden box; Leon Leyson ; with Marilyn J Harran and Elisabeth B Leyson. Atheneum Books for Young Readers 2013 240 p. (hardcover) $16.99

Grades: 6 7 8 9 **92**

1. Holocaust survivors 2. World War, 1939-1945 -- Jews -- Rescue 3. Narewka (Poland) -- Biography 4. Jews -- Poland -- Narewka -- Biography 5. Płaszów (Concentration camp) 6. Concentration camp inmates -- Poland -- Płaszów -- Biography 7. Jewish children in the Holocaust -- Poland -- Kraków -- Biography 8. Holocaust, Jewish (1939-1945) -- Poland -- Kraków -- Personal narratives

ISBN 1442497815; 9781442497818; 9781442497832

LC 2013017987

In this book, "Leon Leyson (born Leib Lezjon) was only ten years old when the Nazis invaded Poland and his family was forced to relocate to the Krakow ghetto. With incredible luck, perseverance, and grit, Leyson was able to survive the sadism of the Nazis, including that of the demonic Amon Goeth, commandant of Plaszow, the concentration camp outside Krakow. Ultimately, it was the generosity and cunning of one man, a man named Oskar Schindler, who saved Leon Leyson's life, and the lives of his mother, his father, and two of his four siblings, by adding their names to his list of workers in his factory—a list that became world renowned: Schindler's List." (Publisher's Note)

"This powerful memoir of one of the youngest boys on Schindler's list deserves to be shared...This memoir is a natural curriculum addition to WWII units for upper-elementary- and middle-school readers. Be sure to have additional materials on hand about Oskar Schindler, as readers will want to do more research into Leyson's story." (Booklist)

Schliemann, Heinrich, 1822-1890

★ Schlitz, Laura Amy. The **hero** Schliemann; the dreamer who dug for Troy. illustrated by Robert Byrd. Candlewick Press 2006 72p il $12.23

Grades: 4 5 6 **92**

1. Archeologists 2. Excavations (Archeology) 3. Archaeologists 4. Troy (Extinct city)

ISBN 0-7636-2283-4

LC 2005046916

This is a biography of the archaeologist who rediscovered ancient Troy. "Intermediate." (Horn Book)

"In this slim biography, Schlitz introduces Heinrich Schliemann, a nineteenth-century 'storyteller, archaeologist, and crook,' who led a search for the lost cities of Homer's epic poems." Booklist

Schulz, Charles M.

★ Gherman, Beverly. **Sparky** : the life and art of Charles Schulz. Chronicle Books 2010 125p il $16.99

Grades: 5 6 7 8 **92**

1. Cartoonists

ISBN 978-0-8118-6790-0; 0-8118-6790-0

A look at the life and influences of Charles Schulz, creator of the beloved comic strip Peanuts.

"Gherman's clear and direct prose is just right for portraying the life of the famous cartoonist for young readers. The splashy, bright design, with multicolored pages and several of Schulz's cartoons included, makes this a cheery read that may well introduce the Peanuts comic strip to a new generation, who likely know Charlie Brown mostly through the holiday TV specials. An informative yet lighthearted look at the life of an American icon." Kirkus

Schumann, Clara, 1819-1896

★ Reich, Susanna. **Clara** Schumann; piano virtuoso. Clarion Bks. 1999 118p il $18; pa $9.95

Grades: 5 6 7 8 **92**

1. Pianists 2. Women composers

ISBN 0-395-89119-1; 0-618-55160-3 pa

LC 98-24510

Describes the life of the German pianist and composer who made her professional debut at age nine and who devoted her life to music and to her family

"This thoroughly researched book draws on primary sources, both Clara's own diaries and her voluminous correspondence with her husband. . . . Reich's lucid, quietly passionate biography is liberally illustrated with photographs and reproductions." Horn Book Guide

Shichtman, Sandra H. The **joy** of creation; the story of Clara Schumann. by Sandra Shichtman and Dorothy Indenbaum. Morgan Reynolds 2011 159p il (Classical composers) lib bdg $28.95

Grades: 6 7 8 9 10 **92**

1. Pianists 2. Composers

ISBN 978-1-59935-123-0; 1-59935-123-4

LC 2009054289

This title "provides a detailed account of the acclaimed nineteenth-century German pianist and composer Clara Schumann. . . . Adundant quotes, many from Schumann's diary, add intimacy to the straightforward, sometimes dense narrative, which also provides historical context and background to her notable life and legacy. The attractively designed volume intersperses color and black-and-white illustrations." Booklist

Includes bibliographical references

Schutz, Samantha, 1978-

Schutz, Samantha. **I** don't want to be crazy; a memoir of anxiety disorder. PUSH Books 2006 280p $16.99

Grades: 8 9 10 11 12 **92**

1. Anxiety 2. Panic disorders 3. Editors 4. Memoirists

ISBN 0-439-80518-X

LC 2005028964

"In this moving memoir, Schutz details her struggle with anxiety disorder. . . . Written in verse, this memoir successfully conveys what it is like to suffer from panic attacks." Voice Youth Advocates

Scieszka, Jon, 1954-

Scieszka, Jon. **Knucklehead**; tall tales and mostly true stories of growing up Scieszka. Viking 2008 106p il $16.99; pa $12.99

Grades: 4 5 6 7 **92**

1. Authors 2. Authors, American 3. Children's authors

ISBN 978-0-670-01106-3; 0-670-01106-1; 978-0-670-01138-4 pa; 0-670-01138-X pa

LC 2008-16870

"Scieszka . . . has written an autobiography about boys, for boys and anyone else interested in baseball, fire and peeing on stuff. . . . The text is divided into two- to three- page nonsequential chapters and peppered with scrapbook snapshots and comic-book-ad reproductions. . . . By themselves, the chapters entertain with abrupt, vulgar fun. Taken together, they offer a look at the makings of one very funny author." Booklist

Seeger, Pete, 1919-2014

Silvey, Anita. **Let** your voice be heard; The Life and Times of Pete Seeger. Anita Silvey. Clarion Books 2016 112 p. illustrations (hardcover) $17.99

Grades: 5 6 7 8 **92**

1. Folk musicians 2. Folk singers -- United States -- Biography
ISBN 9780547330129

LC 2015034787

In this book by Anita Silvey, "Pete Seeger, the iconic folk musician and multiple Grammy winner, discovered early in life that what he wanted to do was make music. His amazing career as singer, songwriter, and banjo player spanned seven decades. . . . An activist and protester, Seeger crusaded for the rights of labor, the rights of people of color, and the First Amendment right to let his voice be heard, and launched the successful campaign to clean up the Hudson River." (Publisher's note)

"A lively, unique contribution to the biography shelves." Booklist

Includes bibliographical references and index

Seguin, Juan Nepomuceno, 1806-1890

Chemerka, William R. **Juan** Seguin; Tejano leader. William R. Chemerka ; illustrations by Don Collins. Bright Sky Press 2012 64 p. ill. $16.95

Grades: 3 4 5 6 **92**

1. Texas -- History 2. Political activists 3. Soldiers -- Texas -- Biography 4. Politicians -- Texas -- Biography 5. Texas -- History -- Republic, 1836-1846 6. Alamo (San Antonio, Tex.) -- Siege, 1836 7. Texas -- History -- Revolution, 1835-1836 -- Biography
ISBN 1933979798; 9781933979793

LC 2011052720

This book is a biography of Texan Juan Seguin by William R. Chemerka. Despite "having been forced to flee to Mexico and die in obscurity, Tejano Juan Seguin is recognised as a Texas hero. From his family's early support of settlers such as Stephen F. Austin to his years in the Texas Senate and as mayor of Bexar, this biography celebrates the life of Juan Seguin and his . . . efforts in securing Texas' independence." (WorldCat)

Selkirk, Alexander, 1676-1721

Kraske, Robert. **Marooned**; the strange but true adventures of Alexander Selkirk, the real Robinson Crusoe. illustrated by Robert Andrew Parker. Clarion Books 2005 120p il map $15

Grades: 5 6 7 8 **92**

1. Sailors 2. Survival after airplane accidents, shipwrecks, etc.
ISBN 0-618-56843-3

LC 2004-28769

"In 1704, English sailing master Alexander Selkirk was marooned on Juan Fernandez, an isolated Pacific island. . . . In 1709, two English ships rescued him, hired him as a second mate, and later captured a Spanish treasure ship. . . . Kraske offers a well-focused look at life in several quite different settings during the early eighteenth century as well as an absorbing telling of Selkirk's story." Booklist

Includes glossary and bibliographical references

Sellins, Fannie, 1872-1919

Farrell, Mary Cronk. **Fannie** never flinched; One Woman's Courage in the Struggle for American Labor Union Rights. Mary Cronk Farrell. Abrams Books for Young Readers 2016 56 p. illustrations (ebook) $15.54; (hardcover) $19.95

Grades: 4 5 6 7 8 **92**

1. Labor -- United States -- History 2. Women labor leaders -- United States -- Biography 3. Labor unions -- United States -- History 4. Labor unions -- Organizing -- United States -- History
ISBN 9781613129722; 9781419718847

LC 2015040020

This book by Mary Cronk Farrell is about "Fannie Sellins (1872–1919), [who] lived during the Gilded Age of American Industrialization, when the Carnegies and Morgans wore jewels while their laborers wore rags. Fannie dreamed that America could achieve its ideals of equality and justice for all, and she sacrificed her life to help that dream come true. Fannie became a union activist, helping to create St. Louis, Missouri, Local 67 of the United Garment Workers of America. (Publisher's note)

"A cogent, well-documented, handsomely designed treatment of a heretofore forgotten hero of labor." Kirkus

Includes bibliographical references and index

Sendlerowa, Irena, 1910-2008

Mazzeo, Tilar J. **Irena's** children; Young Readers Edition; A True Story of Courage. adapted by Mary Cronk Farrell. Margaret K. McElderry Books 2016 272 p. illustrations (hardcover : alk. paper) $17.99

Grades: 7 8 9 10 11 12 **92**

1. Jews -- Poland 2. World War, 1939-1945 -- Poland 3. Jewish children in the Holocaust 4. World War, 1939-1945 -- Jews -- Rescue 5. Holocaust, 1939-1945 6. World War, 1939-1945 7. Warsaw (Poland) -- Biography 8. Holocaust, Jewish (1939-1945) -- Poland 9. World War, 1939-1945 -- Poland -- Warsaw 10. World War, 1939-1945 -- Jews -- Rescue -- Poland 11. Jews -- Poland -- Warsaw -- History -- 20th century 12. Jewish children in the Holocaust -- Poland -- Warsaw 13. Righteous Gentiles in the Holocaust -- Poland -- Biography
ISBN 1481449915; 9781481449915; 9781481449922; 9781481449939

LC 2016004169

This book, adapted by Mary Cronk Farrell, presents "the extraordinary and long forgotten story of Irena Sendler—the 'female Oskar Schindler'—who took staggering risks to save 2,500 children from death and deportation in Nazi-occupied Poland during World War II." (Publisher's note)

"She was short in stature but had immense courage and didn't consider herself a hero: 'What I did was not an extraordinary thing.' The children Sendler saved and the readers of this moving biography would undoubtedly disagree." Booklist

Includes bibliographical references and index

Seuss, Dr.

Anderson, Tanya. **Dr.** Seuss (Theodor Geisel) foreword by Kyle Zimmer. 2nd ed; Chelsea House 2011 128p il (Who wrote that?) lib bdg $35

Grades: 6 7 8 9 **92**

1. Artists 2. Authors 3. Humorists 4. Illustrators 5. Authors, American 6. Children's authors
ISBN 978-1-60413-750-7; 1-60413-750-9

LC 2010030589

This discusses the life and work of author Theodor Geisel, known as Dr. Seuss.

Includes bibliographical references

Shackleton, Ernest Henry Sir, 1874-1922

Koestler-Grack, Rachel A. **Sir** Ernest Shackleton; [by] Linda Davis. Chelsea House 2009 143p il (Great explorers) lib bdg $30

Grades: 6 7 8 9 **92**

1. Explorers 2. Antarctica -- Exploration
ISBN 978-1-60413-421-6 lib bdg; 1-60413-421-6 lib bdg

LC 2009-14164

Biography of Sir Ernest Shackleton

"The information . . . is presented in such a way as to attract and maintain readers' interest. . . . With a full complement of maps, photographs (where available), illustrations, time lines, and document reproductions, a full story is told. Well-written and throughly researched, this . . . will make a solid addition." SLJ

Includes glossary and bibliographical references

Shakur, Tupac

★ Golus, Carrie. **Tupac** Shakur; hip-hop idol. Twenty-First Century Books 2010 112p il (USA Today: lifeline biographies) lib bdg $33.26

Grades: 7 8 9 10 11 12 **92**

1. Poets 2. Actors 3. Rap music 4. African American musicians 5. Rap musicians

ISBN 978-0-7613-5473-4; 0-7613-5473-5

LC 2009-38127

"The story told in Tupac Shakur will be inspirational for some and a cautionary tale for others. Born into poverty, Shakur became one of hip-hop's biggest stars. But even as he climbed up the ladder of success, drugs and violence were always there to pull him back down." Booklist

Includes bibliographical references

Harris, Ashley Rae. **Tupac** Shakur; multi-platinum rapper. ABDO Pub. Co. 2010 112p il (Lives cut short) lib bdg $32.79

Grades: 5 6 7 8 **92**

1. Poets 2. Actors 3. Hip-hop 4. Rap music 5. African American musicians 6. Rap musicians

ISBN 978-1-60453-791-8; 1-60453-791-4

This discusses Tupac Shakur's early life, "providing details that give insight into later success and troubles and maintaining a laudatory tone that focuses on the individual's artistic achievements and hard work to achieve fame. Details [such as] explaining . . . that Tupac Shakur was a standout student in high school are bound to resonate with readers. Numerous photos and sidebars appear throughout. [A] worthwhile [resource] for reports as well as popular reading." SLJ

Sheba, Queen of

Lucks, Naomi. **Queen** of Sheba. Chelsea House Publishers 2009 112p il (Ancient world leaders) lib bdg $30

Grades: 6 7 8 9 **92**

1. Queens 2. Biblical characters

ISBN 978-0-7910-9579-9 lib bdg; 0-7910-9579-9 lib bdg

LC 2008004872

This biography of the Queen of Sheba "references various oral traditions from Europe, the Middle East, and Ethiopia to reveal aspects of the woman's personality. Classical paintings and full-color photographs of sculptures, landscapes, and archaeological finds complement the text. . . . The [text is] easily digestible and appropriate for the intended age group." SLJ

Includes glossary and bibliographical references

Shelley, Mary Wollstonecraft, 1797-1851

Wells, Catherine. **Strange** creatures: the story of Mary Shelley. Morgan Reynolds 2009 160p il (World writers) $28.95

Grades: 7 8 9 10 **92**

1. Authors 2. Novelists 3. Women authors 4. Authors, English

ISBN 978-1-59935-092-9; 1-59935-092-0

LC 2008039042

"This engaging biography limns [Mary Shelley's] unconventional life, focusing on her love affair (and later marriage) with poet Percy Bysshe Shelley, the writing of Frankenstein when she was still a teenager, and the novel's infamy and lasting influence. Period illustrations and photographs appear throughout." Horn Book Guide

Includes bibliographical references

Sheppard, Ella, 1851-1914

Lowinger, Kathy. **Give** Me Wings; How a Choir of Former Slaves Took on the World. Kathy Lowinger. Firefly Books Ltd 2015 144 p. illustrations, portraits (hardcover) $21.95

Grades: 6 7 8 9 **92**

1. Freedmen 2. Choirs (Music)

ISBN 1554517478; 9781554517473

This book, by Kathy Lowinger, tells the story of Ella Sheppard, a former slave who "became a founding member of a traveling choir, the Jubilee Singers, to help raise funds for the Fisk Free Colored School, later known as Fisk University. The Jubilee Singers traveled from Cincinnati to New York, following the path of the Underground Railroad. With every performance they endangered their lives . . . , but they also broke down barriers between blacks and whites." (Publisher's note)

"Lowinger does not shy away from the more unpleasant aspects of that history and grounds it in the very human and relatively little-known story of Sheppard and the Jubilee Singers, which makes the struggle all the more touching and real." SLJ

Includes bibliographical references and index.

Sherman, Cindy

★ Greenberg, Jan. **Meet** Cindy Sherman; artist, photographer, chameleon. by Jan Greenberg and Sandra Jordan. Roaring Brook Press 2017 64 p. illustrations (some color) (hardcover) $19.99

Grades: 5 6 7 8 **92**

1. Photographers -- Biography 2. Photography, Artistic 3. Women photographers -- United States -- Biography

ISBN 9781250199065; 9781626725201

LC 2016058238

This book, by Sandra Jordan and Jan Greenberg, is "an unconventional biography, that much like Cindy Sherman's famous photographs, has something a little more meaningful under the surface. Infusing the narrative with Sherman's photographs, as well as children's first impressions of the photographs, this is a biography that goes beyond birth, middle age, and later life. It's a look at how we look at art." (Publisher's note)

"This masterfully executed biography of a fascinating working artist, written in a tone ideal for its target audience, will be invaluable for libraries hoping to enliven their arts collections." Booklist

Includes bibliographical references

Shiner, Michael, 1805-1880

Bolden, Tonya. **Capital** days; Michael Shiner's journal and the growth of our nation's capital. by Tonya Bolden. Abrams Books for Young Readers 2015 90 p. (hardback) $21.95

Grades: 4 5 6 **92**

1. Washington (D.C.) -- History 2. African Americans -- Biography 3. Washington (D.C.) -- Biography 4. Slaves -- Maryland -- Biography 5. Freedmen -- Washington (D.C.) -- Biography 6. Washington (D.C.) -- History -- 19th century 7. African Americans -- Washington (D.C.) -- Biography 8. Washington (D.C.) -- Race relations -- History -- 19th century

ISBN 1419707337; 9781419707339

LC 2014024668

This book, by Tonya Bolden, "introduces young readers to Washington, D.C., during the early to mid-19th century. Spanning more than 60 years, the story of Michael Shiner (c. 1804–1880) highlights a period of immense change in our country and its capital." Topics include the burning of the city during the War of 1812, the rebuilding of the Capitol and White House, the raising of the Washington Monument . . . the Civil War, [and] the end of slavery." (Publisher's note)

Includes bibliographical references and index

Shivack, Nadia

Shivack, Nadia. **Inside** out; portrait of an eating disorder. written and illustrated by Nadia Shivack. Atheneum Books for Young Readers 2007 un il $17.99

Grades: 7 8 9 10 11 12 **92**

1. Graphic novels 2. Memoirists 3. Bulimia -- Graphic novels 4. Bulimia -- Patients -- United States -- Biography -- Comic books, strips, etc.

ISBN 0-689-85216-9; 978-0-689-85216-9

LC 2004016096

In this book the author gives readers a harrowing look inside her battle with anorexia and bulimia through pictures and captions.

"In this heartfelt, honest memoir, the author uses a graphic novel format to reveal her anguished, ongoing struggle with bulimia. . . . Though intensely personal and—perhaps of necessity—repetitious, this harrowing chronicle may well provide support and solace to teens facing a similar crisis." Publ Wkly

Siegal, Aranka

Siegal, Aranka. **Memories** of Babi; stories. Farrar, Straus & Giroux 2008 116p $16

Grades: 4 5 6 7 **92**

1. Authors 2. Farm life 3. Grandmothers 4. Holocaust survivors 5. Ukraine 6. Jews -- Biography 7. Children's authors

ISBN 978-0-374-39978-8; 0-374-39978-6

LC 2007007002

Siegal's "Upon the Head of the Goat (1981) is about her childhood in Hungary as Hitler comes to power. In this follow-up, written in nine wry sketches, she remembers the years before that—especially her close relationship with her Jewish grandmother, who lived on a small farm just across the Hungarian border in Ukraine." Booklist

★ Siegal, Aranka. **Upon** the head of the goat: a childhood in Hungary, 1939-1944. Farrar, Straus & Giroux 1981 213p hardcover o.p. pa $5.95

Grades: 6 7 8 9 **92**

1. Authors 2. Holocaust survivors 3. Jews -- Hungary 4. Children's authors 5. World War, 1939-1945 -- Jews 6. Holocaust, 1933-1945 -- Personal narratives

ISBN 0-374-38059-7; 0-374-48079-6 pa

LC 81-12642

A Newbery Medal honor book, 1982

"The story is familiar . . . but a few pages into Aranka Siegal's fine memoir . . . you feel the power and interest of her particular experience and remember that this story cannot be told too often." Newsweek

Silverstein, Shel

Baughan, Michael Gray. **Shel** Silverstein; [by] Michael Gray Baughan. Chelsea House 2008 120p il (Who wrote that?) lib bdg $30

Grades: 6 7 8 9 **92**

1. Poets 2. Authors 3. Singers 4. Cartoonists 5. Songwriters 6. Authors, American 7. Children's authors

ISBN 978-0-7910-9676-5 lib bdg; 0-7910-9676-9 lib bdg

LC 2007045336

This biography of the popular author of Where the Sidewalk Ends examines the writer's "life, including the inspiration behind some of [his] works. [The] volume includes photographs and quotations from interviews, as well as descriptions of main characters and annotations lists of books and awards. Useful for aspiring authors as well as book report writers." Horn Book Guide

Includes bibliographical references

Simmons, Russell, 1957-

Lommel, Cookie. **Russell** Simmons. Chelsea House 2007 104p bibl il por (Hip-hop stars) lib bdg $30

Grades: 7 8 9 10 **92**

1. Record producers 2. Broadcasting executives 3. Motion picture executives 4. Recording industry executives

ISBN 978-0-7910-9467-9 lib bdg; 0-7910-9467-7 lib bdg

LC 2007001463

This "weaves a concise history of hip-hop music and culture into a solid biography of one of its originators, Def Jam Records founder Russell Simmons. . . . [This is an] inspiring title that's sure to find wide circulation among hip-hop fans." Booklist

Includes glossary and bibliographical references

Sís, Peter, 1949-

★ Sis, Peter, 1949- The **wall**; growing up behind the Iron Curtain. Farrar, Straus and Giroux 2007 un il $18

Grades: 4 5 6 7 8 9 10 **92**

1. Artists 2. Authors 3. Cold war 4. Animators 5. Illustrators 6. Set designers 7. Children's authors 8. Prague (Czech Republic) 9. Biography, Individual

ISBN 978-0-374-34701-7; 0-374-34701-8

LC 2006-49149

Boston Globe-Horn Book Award: Nonfiction (2008)

"The author pairs his remarkable artistry with journal entries, historical context and period photography to create a powerful account of his childhood in Cold War-era Prague." Publ Wkly

Sitting Bull, Dakota Chief, 1831-1890

★ Nelson, S. D. **Sitting** Bull; Lakota warrior and defender of his people. by S. D. Nelson. Abrams Books for Young Readers 2015 55 p. illustrations (chiefly color) (hardcover) $19.95

Grades: 4 5 6 **92**

1. Dakota Indians 2. Hunkpapa Indians -- History 3. Hunkpapa Indians -- Kings and rulers -- Biography

ISBN 9781419707315

LC 2014045761

In this children's book, S. D. Nelson, "an enrolled member of the Standing Rock Sioux Tribe in the Dakotas, presents Sitting Bull's life as an entry point into that period of history. . . . The book is . . . told in the first person, with Sitting Bull describing his childhood training to be a warrior and a hunter." (School Library Journal)

"A tragic true story told in powerfully subdued tones." Booklist

Stanley, George Edward. **Sitting** Bull; great Sioux hero. Sterling 2010 124p il map (Sterling biographies) lib bdg $12.95

Grades: 7 8 9 10 **92**

1. Dakota Indians 2. Indian chiefs 3. Native Americans -- Biography

ISBN 978-1-4027-6846-0 lib bdg; 1-4027-6846-X lib bdg

LC 2009-24141

This is a biography of the Sioux Indian chief.

Includes glossary and bibliographical references

Smith, Adam, 1723-1790

Crain, Cynthia D. **Adam** Smith; by Cynthia D. Crain and Dwight R. Lee. Morgan Reynolds Pub. 2009 160p il map (Profiles in economics) lib bdg $28.95

Grades: 8 9 10 11 12 **92**

1. Economists 2. Nonfiction writers

ISBN 978-1-59935-107-0 lib bdg; 1-59935-107-2 lib bdg

LC 2009-138

Biography of the economist Adam Smith

"Relationships, education, early influences, and family life are all described . . . [and] economic theory is closely tied to cultural and political events. . . . The writing is straightforward, the . . . [author] assume[s] a certain level of knowledge about world events." SLJ

Includes bibliographical references

Snicket, Lemony, 1970-

Abrams, Dennis. **Lemony** Snicket (Daniel Handler) foreword by Kyle Zimmer. Chelsea House Publishers 2010 117p il (Who wrote that?) lib bdg $35

Grades: 6 7 8 9 10 **92**

1. Authors 2. Novelists 3. Authors, American 4. Children's authors

ISBN 978-1-60413-726-2; 1-60413-726-6

LC 2010006599

A biography of the author of the A Series of Unfortunate Events series.

"Abrams delivers a witty account of his subject. . . . He presents a substantive look at Snicket/Handler, including synopses of and reactions to his adult books, his major influences, and musical interests. Abundant secondary-source quotes, full-color photos and film stills, and a chapter devoted to the series that made him famous will appeal to many readers. This lively biography will not disappoint." SLJ

Includes bibliographical references

Snyder, Grace, 1882-1982

Warren, Andrea. **Pioneer** girl; a true story of growing up on the prairie. with a new afterword by the author. University of Nebraska Press 2009 104p il map pa $14.95

Grades: 5 6 7 8 **92**

1. Frontier and pioneer life 2. Quiltmakers 3. Centenarians

ISBN 978-0-8032-2526-8 pa; 0-8032-2526-1 pa

LC 2009-20883

First published 1998 by Morrow Junior Books

Biography of Nebraska homesteader, Grace McCance Snyder

"This new edition offers an afterword that includes information about black homesteaders, Native Americans, and the specific tasks of women, especially quilting. . . . Although it is written for younger readers than a teen audience, readability and intense subject matter should make the book popular with those readers." Voice Youth Advocates

Includes bibliographical references

Son, Thi Anh Tuyet

Skrypuch, Marsha Forchuk, 1954- **One** Step at a Time; A Vietnamese Child Finds Her Way. by Marsha Forchuk Skrypuch. Pajama Press 2013 vii, 93 p.p (hardcover) $17.95

Grades: 6 7 8 **92**

1. Orphans 2. Poliomyelitis

ISBN 1927485010; 9781927485019

In this true story, Marsha Forchuk Skrypuch "continues the story of Tuyet, an eight-year-old Vietnamese refugee and polio survivor with a damaged leg, whose rescue she narrated in 'Last Airlift: A Vietnamese Orphan's Rescue from War.' Adopted by an unconditionally loving and supportive Canadian family, unable to understand or express much in English, Tuyet begins a difficult journey through surgeries and arduous physical therapy to repair her leg." (Publishers Weekly)

Soto, Gary

Abrams, Dennis. **Gary** Soto; foreword by Kyle Zimmer. Chelsea House Pubs. 2008 120p bibl il por (Who wrote that?) $30

Grades: 5 6 7 8 **92**

1. Poets 2. Authors 3. Novelists 4. Mexican American authors 5. Essayists 6. College teachers 7. Authors, American 8. Children's authors 9. Young adult authors 10. Mexican Americans -- Biography

ISBN 978-0-7910-9529-4; 0-7910-9529-0

LC 2007045509

A biography of the popular Mexican American author for children and young adults.

Includes bibliographical references

Soto, Hernando de, ca. 1500-1542

Young, Jeff C. **Hernando** de Soto; Spanish conquistador in the Americas. Enslow Publishers 2009 112p il (Great explorers of the world) lib bdg $31.93

Grades: 6 7 8 9 **92**

1. Explorers 2. America -- Exploration 3. Colonial administrators 4. Mississippi River valley

ISBN 978-1-59845-104-7 lib bdg; 1-59845-104-9 lib bdg

LC 2008-30753

"Discusses the life of Spanish explorer Hernando de Soto, including his travels in the Americas, the claim of Florida for Spain, and his eventual discovery of the Mississippi River." Publisher's note

Includes glossary and bibliographical references

Sotomayor, Sonia, 1954-

Gitlin, Marty. **Sonia** Sotomayor; Supreme Court justice. by Martin Gitlin. ABDO Pub. Co. 2011 112p il (Essential lives) $32.79

Grades: 5 6 7 8 **92**

1. Judges 2. Women judges 3. District attorneys 4. Supreme Court justices 5. Hispanic Americans -- Biography

ISBN 978-1-61613-518-8; 1-61613-518-2

LC 2010000499

This biography of Supreme Court Justice Sonia Sotomayor "toggles between the subject's personal and professional life; [it] offers sidebar explanations of legal issues. . . . The writing is accessible, the format is open, and full-color photos appear throughout." SLJ

Includes glossary and bibliographical references

McElroy, Lisa Tucker. **Sonia** Sotomayor; first Hispanic U.S. Supreme Court justice. Lerner Publications 2010 48p il lib bdg $26.60

Grades: 5 6 7 8 **92**

1. Judges 2. Women judges 3. District attorneys 4. Supreme Court justices 5. Hispanic Americans -- Biography

ISBN 978-0-7613-5861-9 lib bdg; 0-7613-5861-7 lib bdg

LC 2009037703

"Well organized and straightforward, this biography is appealing with its bright photographs and bold, easy-to-read font. Starting with Sotomayor's childhood in the Bronx, the author covers the justice's life and career up to her nomination to the Supreme Court. . . . An informative, interesting, and, most of all, inspiring read." SLJ

Includes bibliographical references

Sotomayor, Sonia, 1954- The **beloved** world of Sonia Sotomayor; Sonia Sotomayor. Delacorte Books for Young Readers 2018 352 p. (hardback) $17.99

Grades: 6 7 8 9 **92**

1. Hispanic American women 2. Women judges -- United States -- Biography 3. Hispanic American women -- Biography 4. Judges -- United States -- Biography 5. Hispanic American judges -- Biography 6. United States. Supreme Court -- Officials and employees -- Biography

ISBN 9781524771140; 9781524771157

LC 2018014386

YALSA Award for Excellence in Nonfiction for Young Adults: Finalist (2019

In this memoir of U.S. Justice Sonia Sotomayor, readers will "discover the inspiring life of... Sotomayor, the first Latina and third woman appointed to the United States Supreme Court. . . . Sonia did not let the hardships of her background--which included growing up in the rough housing projects of New York City's South Bronx, dealing with juvenile diabetes, coping with parents who argued and fought personal demons, and worrying about money--stand in her way." (Publisher's note)

Spade, Kate

Freistadt, Margo. **Kate** Spade. Morgan Reynolds Pub. 2011 112p il (Profiles in fashion) $28.95

Grades: 7 8 9 10 **92**

1. Fashion designers

ISBN 978-1-59935-154-4; 1-59935-154-4

LC 2010022227

A biography of Kate Spade, designer of handbags, luggage, stationery, shoes, eyeglasses, homewares and other products.

Includes bibliographical references

Spinelli, Jerry

★ Spinelli, Jerry, 1941- **Knots** in my yo-yo string; the autobiography of a kid. Knopf 1998 148p il hardcover o.p. pa $10.95

Grades: 4 5 6 7 **92**

1. Authors 2. Magazine editors 3. Authors, American 4. Children's authors 5. Biography, Individual

ISBN 0-679-88791-1 pa; 0-679-98791-6

LC 97-30827

This Italian-American Newbery Medalist presents a humorous account of his childhood and youth in Norristown, Pennsylvania

"There is an 'everyboy' universality to Spinelli's experiences, but his keen powers of observation and recall turn the story into a richly rewarding personal history." Horn Book Guide

Standish, Myles, 1584-1656

Harness, Cheryl. The **adventurous** life of Myles Standish; and the amazing-but-true survival story of Plymouth Colony. painstakingly written and illustrated by Cheryl Harness. National Geographic 2006 144p il map (Cheryl Harness history) $16.95; lib bdg $25.90

Grades: 4 5 6 7 **92**

1. Pilgrims (New England colonists) 2. Colonists 3. Pilgrim fathers 4. Colonial leaders 5. Massachusetts -- History -- 1600-1775, Colonial period

ISBN 978-0-7922-5918-3; 0-7922-5918-1; 978-0-7922-5919-0 lib bdg; 0-7922-5919-X lib bdg

"Harness chronicles the history of the Plymouth Pilgrims from their troubles in England to their first years in North America, with the focus on Standish. Separating documented history from speculation, the narrative explains religious movements, introduces key figures, and gives a balanced account of Pilgrim-Indian relationships. . . . The tone is casual. . . . A reader-friendly approach to history." Booklist

Includes bibliographical references

Stanton, Elizabeth Cady, 1815-1902

Colman, Penny. **Elizabeth** Cady Stanton and Susan B. Anthony; a friendship that changed the world. Henry Holt and Company 2011 256p il $18.99

Grades: 7 8 9 10 **92**

1. Feminism 2. Suffragists 3. Women -- Suffrage 4. Biography, Individual

ISBN 978-0-8050-8293-7; 0-8050-8293-X

LC 2010-39762

"Elizabeth Cady Stanton, a married mother of four boys at the time they met, and Susan B. Anthony, an unmarried schoolteacher, formed a friendship that lasted until Elizabeth's death more than 50 years later. Their tireless work, including advocacy, speeches, organizing and writing, placed them at the center of tumultuous events in the middle of the 19th century. . . . This [is a] lively, very readable narrative. . . . This thoughtful portrayal to two complex women is . . . enhanced by comprehensive backmatter, making this an invaluable addition to the literature of suffrage." Kirkus

Includes bibliographical references

Steiner, Matt

Warren, Andrea. **Escape** from Saigon; how a Vietnam War orphan became an American boy. Farrar, Straus and Giroux 2004 110p il map hardcover o.p. pa $9.95

Grades: 6 7 8 9 10 **92**

1. Refugees 2. Physicians 3. Interracial adoption 4. Vietnamese Americans 5. Racially mixed people 6. Vietnam War, 1961-1975

ISBN 978-0-374-32224-3; 0-374-32224-4; 978-0-374-40023-1 pa; 0-374-40023-7 pa

LC 2003-60672

Chronicles the experiences of Matt Steiner, an orphaned Amerasian boy, from his birth and early childhood in Saigon through his departure from Vietnam in the 1975 Operation Babylift and his subsequent life as the adopted son of an American family in Ohio.

"The child-at-war story and the facts about the Operation Babylift rescue are tense and exciting. Just as gripping is the boy's personal conflict." Booklist

Steller, Georg Wilhelm, 1700-1746

Arnold, Ann. **Sea** cows, shamans, and scurvy: Alaska's first naturalist: Georg Wilhelm Steller. Farrar, Straus & Giroux 2008 227p il map $21

Grades: 6 7 8 9 **92**

1. Explorers 2. Naturalists 3. Alaska

ISBN 978-0-374-39947-4; 0-374-39947-6

LC 2006037400

"This is a detailed and lavishly illustrated biography of Georg Wilhelm Steller (1707-1746), Alaska's first naturalist. . . . He is the only scientist ever to describe, dissect, and eat the flightless spectacled cormorant. Species bear his name, including Steller's albatross, eider, jay, sculpin, sea cow, sea eagle, and sea lion. Arnold's exciting, harrowing account is personalized by excerpts from Steller's journal." KLIATT

Includes bibliographical references

Stine, R. L., 1943-

Marcovitz, Hal. **R.L.** Stine; foreword by Kyle Zimmer. Chelsea House Publishers 2006 134p bibl il por (Who wrote that?) lib bdg $30

Grades: 6 7 8 9 **92**

1. Authors 2. Magazine editors 3. Authors, American 4. Children's authors

ISBN 0-7910-8659-3

LC 2005008186

A biography of the popular author of Goosebumps and other children's horror stories.

Includes bibliographical references

Stone, Biz

Smith, Chris. **Twitter**; Jack Dorsey, Biz Stone and Evan Williams. [by] Chris Smith and Marci McGrath. Morgan Reynolds Pub. 2011 112p il (Business leaders) $28.95

Grades: 7 8 9 10 11 12 **92**

1. Online social networks 2. Twitter, Inc. 3. Internet executives 4. Computer programmers 5. Computer software executives

ISBN 978-1-59935-179-7; 1-59935-179-X; 978-1-59935-216-9 e-book

LC 2011024699

This biography of the founders of Twitter "will grab YAs. . . . The design is browsable, with clear type and lots of color screens and informal photos of young people at work." Booklist

Includes bibliographical references

Stowe, Harriet Beecher, 1811-1896

★ Fritz, Jean. **Harriet** Beecher Stowe and the Beecher preachers. Putnam 1994 144p il $15.99; pa $5.99

Grades: 5 6 7 8 **92**

1. Authors 2. Novelists 3. Abolitionists 4. Women authors 5. Authors, American 6. Children's authors 7. Nonfiction writers 8. Short story writers

ISBN 0-399-22666-4; 0-698-11660-7 pa

LC 93-6408

This is a biography of the abolitionist author of "Uncle Tom's Cabin" with an emphasis on the influence of her preacher father and her family on her life and work.

"Written with vivacity and insight, this readable and engrossing biography is an important contribution to women's history as well as to the history of American letters." Horn Book

Includes bibliographical references

Stringfield, Bessie, 1911-1993

Gill, Joel Christian. **Bessie** Stringfield; tales of the talented tenth. words and pictures by Joel Christian Gill. Fulcrum Publishing 2016 122 p. color illustrations, color map (Tales of the talented tenth) (paperback) $23.95

Grades: 5 6 7 8 9 10 **92**

1. Women motorcyclists -- United States -- Biography -- Comic books, strips, etc 2. Graphic novels 3. African Americans -- Biography -- Comic books, strips, etc 4. African American women -- Biography -- Comic books, strips, etc 5. United States -- Description and travel -- Comic books, strips, etc 6. Messengers -- United States -- Biography -- Comic books, strips, etc 7. Motorcyclists -- United States -- Biography -- Comic books, strips, etc 8. United States. Army -- Civilian employees -- Biography -- Comic books, strips, etc

ISBN 9781938486944

LC 2016030231

This biography, by Joel Christian Gill, tells the 'true story of Bessie Stringfield, the woman known today as The Motorcycle Queen of Miami and the first black woman to be inducted into the American Motorcyclist Association Hall of Fame and the Harley Davidson Hall of Fame. Stringfield was a pioneer in motorcycling during her lifetime; she rode as a civilian courier for the US military and founded the Iron Horse Motorcycle Club in Miami." (Publisher's note)

"An incredible true story that has as much power as Bessie and the motorcycles she rode." Kirkus

Includes bibliographical references (pages 120-121).

Su, Shih, 1036, 7-1101

Demi. **Su** Dongpo; Chinese genius. Lee & Low Books 2006 un il map $24

Grades: 4 5 6 7 **92**

1. Poets 2. Authors 3. Authors, Chinese 4. Calligraphers

ISBN 978-1-58430-256-8; 1-58430-256-9

LC 2005030437

"In reverent tribute to a 'statesman, philosopher, poet, painter, engineer, architect, and humanitarian' born nearly ten centuries ago, Demi offers a text in which quoted passages of poetry and references to 'mystical painting skills' mingle with biographical detail. She pairs this with her trademark scenes of dignified, finely detailed figures floating through luminescent clouds in traditional dress. Though she sounds a false note near the end with a dismissive description of Hainan Island as 'a place inhabited only by natives,' this portrait of a 'knight-errant,' who shone brightly in both the literary and political arenas while surviving several severe reversals of fortune, presents an exemplary role model. In the author's view, he still stands at the 'heart and soul of Chinese culture.'" Kirkus

Sullivan, Anne, 1866-1936

Delano, Marfe Ferguson. **Helen's** eyes; a photobiography of Annie Sullivan, Helen Keller's teacher. [foreword by Keller Johnson Thompson] National Geographic 2008 63p il map $17.95; lib bdg $27.90

Grades: 4 5 6 7 **92**

1. Deaf 2. Blind 3. Authors 4. Teachers 5. Memoirists 6. Humanitarians 7. Teachers of the deaf 8. Inspirational writers 9. Teachers of the blind 10. Social welfare leaders

ISBN 978-1-4263-02-9-1; 1-4263-0209-6; 978-1-4263-0210-7 lib bdg; 1-4263-0210-X lib bdg

"There are many biographies of Helen Keller and Annie Sullivan, but this one is very nicely done. . . . The book is honest in its portrayals, especially of Sullivan. . . . What makes this oversize book so appealing is the clean design, with large typeface. The many fascinating photographs are sometimes placed over historical documents." Booklist

Includes bibliographical references

Tan, Amy

Mussari, Mark. **Amy** Tan. Marshall Cavendish Benchmark 2010 125p il (Today's writers and their works) lib bdg $42.79

Grades: 8 9 10 11 12 **92**

1. Authors 2. Novelists 3. Women authors 4. Essayists 5. Authors, American 6. Children's authors 7. Short story writers 8. Chinese Americans -- Biography

ISBN 978-0-7614-4127-4; 0-7614-4127-1

This biography of Amy Tan places the author in the context of her times and discusses her work.

Includes bibliographical references

O'Keefe, Sherry. **From** China to America; the story of Amy Tan. Morgan Reynolds Pub. 2011 112p il lib bdg $28.95

Grades: 7 8 9 10 **92**

1. Authors 2. Novelists 3. Women authors 4. Essayists 5. Authors, American 6. Children's authors 7. Short story writers 8. Chinese Americans -- Biography

ISBN 978-1-59935-138-4; 1-59935-138-2

LC 2010-7594

"Born in California, the daughter of Chinese immigrants, Tan grew up as an American on the outside and Chinese on the inside. . . . Growing up, Tan faced the loss of her brother and father and the morbid outlook of her mother. Their tumultuous relationship led her to write stories about mother-and-daughter conflict, which later became the basis for The Joy Luck Club. This book gives readers a brief overview of the novelist's life and a greater understanding of the inspiration behind her novels." SLJ

Includes bibliographical references

Tarbell, Ida M. (Ida Minerva), 1857-1944

McCully, Emily Arnold, 1939- **Ida** M. Tarbell; the woman who challenged big business--and won! by Emily Arnold McCully. Clarion Books/Houghton Mifflin Harcourt 2014 288 p. illustrations (hardcover) $18.99

Grades: 7 8 9 10 **92**

1. Women journalists 2. Journalists -- Biography 3. Journalists 4. Women -- Biography 5. Journalists -- United States -- Biography

ISBN 0547290926; 9780547290928

LC 2012039650

YALSA Award for Excellence in Nonfiction for Young Adults: Finalist (2015)

"Born in 1857 and raised in oil country, Ida M. Tarbell was one of the first investigative journalists and probably the most influential in her time. Her series of articles on the Standard Oil Trust, a complicated business empire run by John D. Rockefeller, revealed to readers the underhanded, even illegal practices that had led to Rockefeller's success." (Publisher's note)

"McCully expertly brings to life the story of a unique and determined woman in this well-written and thoroughly researched biography, filled with numerous and pertinent photographs." SLJ

Includes bibliographical references and index

Taylor, Major, 1878-1932

Brill, Marlene Targ. **Marshall** Major Taylor; world champion bicyclist, 1899-1901. by Marlene Targ Brill. Twenty-First Century Books 2008 112p il (Trailblazer biography) lib bdg $31.93

Grades: 5 6 7 8 **92**

1. Bicycle racing 2. African American athletes 3. Cyclists

ISBN 978-0-8225-6610-6 lib bdg; 0-8225-6610-9 lib bdg

LC 2006003883

"Marshall Taylor, an African American bicyclist who, despite facing prejudice in racing and in life, achieved world renown at the turn of the last century. . . . Brill's accessible, personable prose vividly relates Taylor's experiences." Booklist

Includes bibliographical references

Tecumseh, Shawnee Chief, 1768-1813

Zimmerman, Dwight Jon. **Tecumseh**; shooting star of the Shawnee. Sterling 2010 124p il map (Sterling biographies) lib bdg $12.95

Grades: 7 8 9 10 **92**

1. Shawnee Indians 2. Indian chiefs 3. Native Americans -- Biography

ISBN 978-1-4027-6847-7; 1-4027-6847-8

LC 2009-24142

"Lots of detailed physical battles dominate Tecumseh, with a strong focus on the Shawnee's brutal displacement by white settlers and the Indians caught up in the tensions between the U.S. and Great Britain. . . . [The] spacious design is highly scannable, with color background screens, photos, maps, and historic prints throughout." Booklist

Includes glossary and bibliographical references

Teresa, Mother, 1910-1997

Slavicek, Louise Chipley. **Mother** Teresa; caring for the world's poor. Chelsea House 2007 113p bibl il por (Modern peacemakers) lib bdg $30

Grades: 7 8 9 10 **92**

1. Nuns 2. Missionaries 3. Nobel laureates for peace

ISBN 0-7910-9433-2 lib bdg; 978-0-7910-9433-4 lib bdg

LC 2006028383

A biography of the nun who won the Nobel Peace Prize for her work with the poor of India

This "book is well organized and well written, and reads like a story. It is balanced in that it points out the critics of Mother Teresa's selection for the Nobel Peace Prize . . . as well as her admirers." SLJ

Includes bibliographical references

Tesla, Nikola, 1856-1943

Hardyman, Robyn. **Nikola** Tesla and Thomas Edison; Robyn Hardyman. Gareth Stevens Publishing 2014 48 p. illustrations (some color) $31.95

Grades: 4 5 6 **92**

1. Tesla, Nikola, 1856-1943

ISBN 1482414732; 9781482414738

This children's book by Robyn Hardyman on scientists Nikola Tesla and Thomas Edison is part of a series known for its "graphics and ability to make complex concepts accessible. The authors have . . . select[ed] key quotes from the scientists' writings that young readers can understand (provided in sidebars titled 'In Their Own Words')." (School Library Journal)

"The dual biography is a particularly ingenious feature. Readers learn that Alfred Russel Wallace and Darwin, rivals as well as supporters, shared much of the same information, making similar discoveries. Reading their parallel stories will let children see how different people solve the same problems. Original takes on science biographies." SLJ

Thoreau, Henry David, 1817-1862

★ Meltzer, Milton. **Henry** David Thoreau; a biography. Twenty-First Century Books 2007 160p il lib bdg $31.93

Grades: 7 8 9 10 11 12 **92**

1. Authors 2. Naturalists 3. Essayists 4. Pacifists 5. Authors, American 6. Writers on nature 7. Nonfiction writers

ISBN 978-0-8225-5893-4 lib bdg; 0-8225-5893-9 lib bdg

LC 2006013747

In this biography "readers see Thoreau through a variety of lenses—brother, friend, pencil maker, abolitionist, naturalist, and transcendentalist—to name only a few. Meltzer's clear and succinct writing style is punctuated with well-chosen and good-quality photographs and reproductions. . . . A first-rate choice for any student seeking a well-organized introduction to the life of the author and philosopher." SLJ

Includes bibliographical references

Thorpe, Jim, 1888-1953

Labrecque, Ellen. **Jim** Thorpe; an athlete for the ages. Sterling 2010 124p il (Sterling biographies) $12.95

Grades: 7 8 9 10 **92**

1. Athletes 2. Decathletes 3. Pentathletes 4. Olympic athletes 5. Native Americans -- Biography

ISBN 978-1-4027-7150-7; 1-4027-7150-9

This biography of Native American athlete Jim Thorpe is "studded with quotes and illustrated with photos. . . . [It] details his taking of Olympic gold in the 1912 decathlon and pentathlon events, though he was forced to return the medals the following year amid charges of professionalism, a matter resolved in his favor 70 years later. Written in a straightforward, journalistic style, [this biography presents a] very readable [account] of the [life] of [an athlete] who made [his mark] on American culture." Booklist

Tillage, Leon, 1936-2011

★ Tillage, Leon. **Leon's** story; [by] Leon Walter Tillage; collage art by Susan L. Roth. Farrar, Straus & Giroux 1997 107p il hardcover o.p. pa $6.95

Grades: 4 5 6 7 8 9 10 **92**

1. African Americans -- Biography 2. North Carolina -- Race relations

ISBN 0-374-34379-9; 0-374-44330-0 pa

LC 96-43544

The son of a North Carolina sharecropper recalls the hard times faced by his family and other African Americans in the first half of the twentieth century and the changes that the civil rights movement helped bring about

The author's "voice is direct, the words are simple. There is no rhetoric, no commentary, no bitterness. . . . This quiet drama will move readers of all ages . . . and may encourage them to record their own family stories." Booklist

Tolkien, J. R. R. (John Ronald Reuel), 1892-1973

Willett, Edward. **J.R.R.** Tolkien; master of imaginary worlds. Enslow Publishers 2004 128p il (Authors teens love) lib bdg $26.60

Grades: 6 7 8 9 **92**

1. Authors 2. Novelists 3. Linguists 4. Philologists 5. Fantasy writers 6. Authors, English 7. Children's authors

ISBN 0-7660-2246-3

LC 2003-15657

Examines the personal life and literary career of the author of the Lord of the Rings trilogy

This "clearly goes a step beyond the typical series book, offering a more perceptive and more detailed, satisfying portrayal of its subject. . . . [The] volume includes a great deal of back matter: a time line, a list of selected works, a glossary, detailed chapter notes, and lists of recommended books and Internet sites." Booklist

Includes bibliographical references

Tom Thumb, 1838-1883

★ Sullivan, George. **Tom** Thumb; the remarkable true story of a man in miniature. Clarion Books 2010 200p il $20

Grades: 6 7 8 9 **92**

1. Circus 2. Dwarfs 3. Little people 4. Circus performers 5. Biography, Individual

ISBN 0-547-18203-1; 978-0-547-18203-2

LC 2009-52910

This is a biography of the circus performer who was part of the P.T. Barnum troupe. Index. "Grades five to eight." (Bull Cent Child Books)

"Insets on dwarfism appear early in the text, elucidating Tom Thumb's condition for readers without seriously interrupting to genial flow of the narration. Generous leading and a large stock of photographs and period reproductions will entice readers who shy away from longer works of nonfiction." Bull Cent Child Books

Toussaint Louverture, 1743?-1803

★ Rockwell, Anne F., 1934- **Open** the door to liberty!: a biography of Toussaint L'Ouverture; illustrated by R. Gregory Christie. Houghton Mifflin Books for Children 2009 64p il $18

Grades: 5 6 7 8 **92**

1. Generals 2. Revolutionaries 3. Haiti -- History 4. Blacks -- Biography 5. Slavery -- West Indies

ISBN 978-0-618-60570-5; 0-618-60570-3

LC 2007-25746

"In this eye-opening biography, Rockwell makes a strong case that Toussaint L'Ouverture is one of the most overlooked heroes of the eighteenth century. A freed slave of the French colony of St. Domingue (what we now know as Haiti), L'Ouverture was 48 when he was so inspired by his people's uprising against the French that he joined them and, through his oratory and strategical skills, became their leader. In 1793, he led history's first triumphant slave rebellion, but the resulting freedom would not last long. . . . Evocative paintings in primary colors help tell the story." Booklist

Includes bibliographical references

Truth, Sojourner, 1797-1883

Horn, Geoffrey M. **Sojourner** Truth; speaking up for freedom. by Geoffrey Michael Horn. Crabtree Pub. Co. 2010 64 p. ill. (some col.) (pbk. : alk. paper) $10.95

Grades: 4 5 6 7 8 **92**

1. Abolitionists -- United States -- Biography 2. African American women -- Biography 3. African American abolitionists -- Biography 4. Social reformers -- United States -- Biography

ISBN 0778748405; 9780778748243; 9780778748403

LC 2009022428

This children's picture book by Geoffrey M. Horn in the Voices for Freedom: Abolitionist Views series looks at abolitionist Sojourner Truth. It "relates and details Truth's life and times, from her often-brutal treatment as a slave, named Isabella at birth, to her freedom, religious influences, and self-determination . . . and path to outspoken, sometimes provocative, and influential traveling speaker on a mission to raise awareness of and support for abolitionism." (Booklist)

"Combining accessible, lively prose and abundant visuals, this title . . . offers an engaging, informative introduction to the early advocate for the rights of African Americans and women." Booklist

Tubman, Harriet, 1820?-1913

★ Allen, Thomas B. **Harriet** Tubman, secret agent; how daring slaves and free Blacks spied for the Union during the Civil War. featuring illustrations by Carla Bauer. National Geographic Society 2006 191p il map $16.95; lib bdg $25.90

Grades: 6 7 8 9 **92**

1. Abolitionists 2. Underground railroad 3. Slavery -- United States 4. African American women -- Biography

ISBN 0-7922-7889-5; 0-7922-7890-9 lib bdg

LC 2005030927

"Allen brings readers much more than the usual biography of the brave rescuer on the Underground Railroad. This small, packed volume tells of Harriet Tubman's astonishing roles as spy, secret agent, and military leader, and it combines her personal story with a history of the abolitionist movement and the Civil War, focusing on how ex-slaves and free blacks served the Union cause. . . . The dense history is illustrated with numerous archival images, maps, and woodcuts, and the documentation is meticulous." Booklist

Includes bibliographical references

Petry, Ann, 1908-1997. **Harriet** Tubman; conductor on the Underground Railroad. Ann Lane Petry. Harpercollins Childrens Books 2018 257 p. illustrations $16.99

Grades: 4 5 6 **92**

1. Abolitionists -- Biography

ISBN 0062691309; 9780062691309

Originally published 1955

This book, by Ann Lane Petry, tells the story of Harriet Tubman, the heroic woman who guided more than 300 slaves to freedom. "Harriet was born a slave and dreamed of being free. She was willing to risk everything--including her own life--to see that dream come true. After her daring escape, Harriet became a conductor on the secret Underground Railroad, helping others make the dangerous journey to freedom." (Publisher's note)

Sawyer, Kem Knapp. **Harriet** Tubman. DK Publishing 2010 128p il (DK biography) pa $5.99

Grades: 6 7 8 9 **92**

1. Abolitionists 2. Underground railroad 3. Slavery -- United States 4. African American women -- Biography

ISBN 978-0-7566-5806-9; 0-7566-5806-3

An illustrated exploration of the life of Harriet Tubman that covers her childhood, experiences as a slave, escape to freedom, work on the Underground Railroad, antislavery activism, and other topics.

"Meticulous about what is known and what is 'not confirmed,' the simple prose is eloquent in describing how Tubman started as a passenger on the Underground Railroad and went on to become one of its most famous conductors. . . . Highly readable, the series design, with highly legible type on thick paper, includes color photographs and prints on every spread." Booklist

Includes bibliographical references

Turing, Alan Mathison, 1912-1954

Corrigan, Jim. **Alan** Turing. Morgan Reynolds Pub. 2008 112p il (Profiles in mathematics) lib bdg $27.95

Grades: 7 8 9 10 **92**

1. Mathematicians

ISBN 978-1-59935-064-6; 1-59935-064-5

LC 2007-11704

"Corrigan's descriptions of English mathematician Turing as sporting 'ragged, wrinkled clothes' and few social graces will fit many readers' mental image of a numbers genius. But other aspects of this portrait push against stereotypes. . . . Throughout, candid mentions of Turing's homosexuality help readers contextualize the scandal he endured after running afoul of the era's discriminatory legislation. Equal sensitivity distinguishes Corringan's handling of Turing's death, officially (but not decisively) a suicide." Booklist

Includes bibliographical references

★ Henderson, Harry. **Alan** Turing; computing genius and wartime code breaker. Chelsea House 2011 133p il (Makers of modern science) $35

Grades: 7 8 9 10 **92**

1. Mathematicians

ISBN 978-0-8160-6175-4; 0-8160-6175-0

LC 2010-15798

A biography of code breaker and computer pioneer Alan Turing.

"The mark of a good biography is when it makes people you may never have heard of, in fields you might not be interested in, fascinating. [This book] does this with [a] well-chosen [subject], engaging writing, plenty of sidebars that take the text in new directions, and perhaps most importantly, the determination to present a fully-rounded person, not just a scientist." Booklist

Includes bibliographical references

Tutankhamen, King of Egypt

★ Demi. **Tutankhamun**; written and illustrated by Demi. Marshall Cavendish Children 2009 un il map $19.99

Grades: 4 5 6 7 **92**

1. Kings and rulers 2. Kings 3. Egypt -- History

ISBN 978-0-7614-5558-5; 0-7614-5558-2

LC 2008029313

"The unmistakable designs and opulent glitter of ancient Egyptian art gleam on every page of Demi's picture-book introduction to Tutankhamun. Beginning with King Tut's great-grandfather, Demi presents the broad historical context surrounding the young monarch's reign. . . . Demi's language, organized into brief but pithy paragraphs, is clear. . . . It's the beautiful illustrations that will attract and hold a young audience most, and as usual, Demi incorporates artistic motifs and materials appropriate to her subject." Booklist

Twain, Mark, 1835-1910

Caravantes, Peggy. A **great** and sublime fool; the story of Mark Twain. Morgan Reynolds Pub. 2009 176p il map (World writers) lib bdg $28.95

Grades: 7 8 9 10 **92**

1. Authors 2. Humorists 3. Novelists 4. Essayists 5. Satirists 6. Memoirists 7. Travel writers 8. Authors, American 9. Short story writers

ISBN 978-1-599-35088-2; 1-599-35088-2

LC 2008-34139

This "offers a workmanlike but readable account of one of America's first great writers. . . . A nice selection of photographs and artwork complement the narrative. . . . Detailed source notes and an in-depth time line round out this even and reliable . . . biography." Booklist

Includes bibliographical references

★ Fleischman, Sid. The **trouble** begins at 8; a life of Mark Twain in the wild, wild West. Greenwillow Books 2008 224p il $18.99; lib bdg $19.89

Grades: 5 6 7 8 **92**

1. Authors 2. Humorists 3. Novelists 4. Essayists 5. Satirists 6. Memoirists 7. Travel writers 8. Authors, American 9. Short story writers 10. Biography, Individual

ISBN 0-06-134431-1; 0-06-134432-X lib bdg; 978-0-06-134431-2; 978-0-06-134432-9 lib bdg

LC 2007-37891

This biography of Mark Twain focuses on his travels. Chronology. Index. "Grades five to nine." (Bull Cent Child Books)

"Fleischman writes a charming biography of Samuel Clemens before he became Mark Twain, the great American novelist. . . . Written with a sense of humor and wit that honors Twain, this book is sprinkled with famous Twain quotes, excerpts of his writing, and pictures of Twain and other primary documents from the era Clemens spent both on the Mississippi River and in the West." Voice Youth Advocates

Includes bibliographical references

Sonneborn, Liz. **Mark** Twain; foreword by Kyle Zimmer. Chelsea House Publishers 2010 125p il (Who wrote that?) lib bdg $35

Grades: 6 7 8 9 10 **92**

1. Authors 2. Humorists 3. Novelists 4. Essayists 5. Satirists 6. Memoirists 7. Travel writers 8. Authors, American 9. Short story writers

ISBN 978-1-60413-728-6; 1-60413-728-2

LC 2010006601

This biography of Mark Twain "begins with the writer's memorable visit to his Missouri hometown in 1902, then tracks back to his early days and his well-known transformation from Sam Clemens to Mark Twain. Sonneborn deals with her material well, hitting all the highlights and keeping the narrative moving along. Good use of details adds interest. . . . A solid purchase." SLJ

Includes bibliographical references

Typhoid Mary, 1869-1938

Bartoletti, Susan Campbell. **Terrible** typhoid Mary; the most harmless and yet most dangerous woman in America : a true story of the deadliest cook in America. by Susan Campbell Bartoletti. Houghton Mifflin Harcourt 2015 240 p. illustrations $17.99

Grades: 6 7 8 9 10 **92**

1. Typhoid fever 2. Communicable diseases 3. Cooks -- New York (State) -- New York -- Biography 4. Quarantine -- New York (State) -- New York -- History 5. Typhoid fever -- New York (State) -- New York -- History

ISBN 0544313674; 9780544313675

LC 2014023057

This biography of Mary Mallon, by Susan Campbell Bartoletti, "looks beyond the tabloid scandal of Mary's controversial life. How she was treated by medical and legal officials reveals a lesser-known story of human and constitutional rights, entangled with the science of pathology and enduring questions about who Mary Mallon really was. How did her name become synonymous with deadly disease? And who is really responsible for the lasting legacy of Typhoid Mary?" (Publisher's note)

"This well-researched biography of Mary Mallon, also known as Typhoid Mary, begins in 1906, when Mallon was hired as a cook for a wealthy family vacationing in Oyster Bay, Long Island. The outbreak of typhoid that swept through the household a few weeks later turned out to be a pivotal event that forever changed her life. . . . Middle grade biography lovers will gravitate toward this compelling title." SLJ

Includes bibliographical references

Uwiringiyimana, Sandra

Pesta, Abigail. **How** dare the sun rise; memoirs of a war child. Sandra Uwiringiyimana ; with Abigail Pesta. Katherine Tegen Books 2017 288 p. color illustrations (hardcover) $19.99

Grades: 7 8 9 10 11 12 **92**

1. Massacres 2. Refugees -- Biography 3. Refugees 4. Rochester (N.Y.) -- Biography 5. Refugees -- United States -- Biography 6. Massacres -- Burundi -- Bujumbura Region 7. Refugees -- Congo (Democratic Republic) -- Biography

ISBN 9780062470157; 9780062470164; 9780062470140

LC 2016957991

"This profoundly moving memoir is the remarkable and inspiring true story of Sandra Uwiringiyimana, a girl from the Democratic Republic of the Congo who tells the tale of how she survived a massacre, immigrated to America, and overcame her trauma through art and activism. Sandra was just ten years old when she found herself with a gun pointed at her head. She had watched as rebels gunned down her mother and six-year-old sister in a refugee camp." (Publisher's note)

"The title is a critical piece of literature, contributing to the larger refugee narrative in a way that is complex and nuanced but still accessible for a YA audience." SLJ

Valentino

Reis, Ronald A. **Valentino**. Chelsea House 2011 119p il (Famous fashion designers) lib bdg $35

Grades: 6 7 8 9 10 **92**

1. Fashion designers

ISBN 978-1-60413-983-9; 1-60413-983-8

LC 2010034101

This is a biography of fashion designer Valentino.

Includes glossary and bibliographical references

Vedder, Amy

Ebersole, Rene. **Gorilla** mountain; the story of wildlife biologist, Amy Vedder. [by] Rene Ebersole. F. Watts 2005 118p il (Women's adventures in science) lib bdg $31

Grades: 7 8 9 10 **92**

1. Gorillas 2. Conservationists 3. Women scientists 4. Biography, Individual

ISBN 0-531-16779-8

LC 2005-00823

This is a biography of wildlife conservationist Amy Vedder. Glossary. Index. "Grades seven to twelve." (Sci Books Fiilms)

This is "interesting, substantive, and eminently readable." SLJ

Includes bibliographical references

Versace, Gianni, 1946-1997

Davis, Daniel K. **Versace**. Chelsea House 2011 116p il (Famous fashion designers) lib bdg $35

Grades: 6 7 8 9 10 **92**

1. Fashion designers

ISBN 978-1-60413-980-8; 1-60413-980-3

LC 2010034103

This is a biography of fashion designer Gianni Versace.

"Biography collections in need of a bit of sprucing up should find [this title] helpful." SLJ

Includes glossary and bibliographical references

Victoria, Queen of Great Britain, 1819-1901

Reef, Catherine. **Victoria**; portrait of a queen. Catherine Reef. Clarion Books 2017 256 p. $18.99

Grades: 7 8 9 **92**

1. Queens -- Great Britain 2. Great Britain -- Kings and rulers

ISBN 9780544716148

LC 2016050621

This book, by Catherine Reef, presents an "illustrated account of a confident, strong-minded, and influential woman. Victoria woke one morning at the age of eighteen to discover that her uncle had died and she was now queen. She went on to rule for sixty-three years, with an influence so far-reaching that the decades of her reign now bear her name--the Victorian period." (Publisher's note)

"Victoria's personality comes through in the lively narrative, though Reef never shies from the public and personal controversies that Victoria brought on herself. All the necessary context for understanding her life and times is woven through without ever getting in the way." Kirkus

Vincent, Erin

Vincent, Erin. **Grief** girl; my true story. Delacorte Press 2007 306p $15.99; lib bdg $18.99

Grades: 8 9 10 11 12 **92**

1. Authors 2. Bereavement 3. Memoirists

ISBN 978-0-385-73353-3; 0-385-73353-4; 978-0-385-90368-4 lib bdg; 0-385-90368-5 lib bdg

LC 2006-11650

"In 1983, Vincent, then 14, lost both her parents in a road accident. In this poignant memoir, she chronicles her rocky journey through adolescence as she, her 17-year-old sister, Tracy, and their brother, Trent, learn to cope on their own." Booklist

Wald, Lillian D., 1867-1940

Kaplan, Paul M. **Lillian** Wald; America's great social and healthcare reformer. Paul M. Kaplan. Pelican Publishing Company 2018 112 p. (hardcover : alk. paper) $14.95

Grades: 7 8 9 10 11 12 **92**

1. Social reformers -- United States -- Biography 2. Henry Street Settlement (New York, N.Y.) 3. Social reformers -- New York (State) -- New York 4. Public health nurses -- New York (State) -- New York

ISBN 9781455623495

LC 2017033545

In this biography book for children, author "Paul Kaplan follows powerful activist Lillian Wald, a social and education reformer dedicated to helping less fortunate citizens in New York. While living there, Wald began campaigning for healthcare, which lead her to inserting herself into the social climate of her patients. . . . Lillian Wald was not only a revolutionary reformer but also an advocate for women's suffrage, racial integration, and worker's rights." (Publisher's note)

Includes bibliographical references and index

Waldman, Neil, 1947-

★ Waldman, Neil. **Out** of the shadows; an artist's journey. Boyds Mills Press 2006 144p il $21.95

Grades: 5 6 7 8 **92**

1. Artists 2. Authors 3. Illustrators 4. Jews -- Biography 5. Children's authors 6. Artists -- United States

ISBN 1-59078-411-1

Neil Waldman reveals how his passion for art emerged in the kitchen of his family's apartment, where he discovered the work of Vincent Van Gogh and the ability to use illustration as a means to escape the sadness that plagued his home.

"Young artists, as well as readers who wonder about the person behind the pictures they have seen, will appreciate every element of this book: well-constructed story, visual richness, and uncompromising honesty." Booklist

Walker, C. J., Madame, 1867-1919

Bundles, A'Lelia P. **Madam** C.J. Walker; entrepreneur. [by] A'Lelia Bundles. Legacy ed; Chelsea House Publishers 2008 103p (Black Americans of achievement) lib bdg $30

Grades: 6 7 8 9 **92**

1. Philanthropists 2. African American businesspeople 3. Cosmeticians 4. Cosmetics industry executives 5. African American women -- Biography

ISBN 978-1-60413-072-0 lib bdg; 1-60413-072-5 lib bdg

LC 2008008429

First published 1991

A biography of the African American businesswoman whose invention of facial creams and other cosmetics led to great financial success

The book goes "beyond the typical personal information to provide some social history relevant to the subject's time. Captioned photographs and boxed inserts enhance the conversational [text]." Horn Book Guide

Includes bibliographical references

Walker, Maggie Lena, 1867-1934

Ransom, Candice F. **Maggie** L. Walker; pioneering banker and community leader. Twenty-First Century Books 2009 112p il (Trailblazer biographies) lib bdg $31.93

Grades: 6 7 8 9 **92**

1. African American businesspeople 2. Bankers 3. African American women -- Biography

ISBN 978-0-8225-6611-3 lib bdg; 0-8225-6611-7 lib bdg

LC 2007-42906

Retells the life and career of Maggie L. Walker, who founded the St. Luke Penny Savings Bank, the first bank established specifically for African Americans.

"The text is thoroughly researched and well organized. . . . Good-quality archival photographs add interest and clarity. A solid selection for report writers." SLJ

Includes bibliographical references

Walker, Mary Edwards, 1832-1919

Goldsmith, Bonnie Zucker. **Dr.** Mary Edwards Walker; Civil War surgeon & medal of honor recipient. [by] Bonnie Z. Goldsmith. ABDO Pub. 2010 112p il (Military heroes) lib bdg $22.65

Grades: 7 8 9 **92**

1. Physicians 2. Suffragists 3. Women physicians 4. Feminists 5. United States -- History -- 1861-1865, Civil War -- Women 6. United States -- History -- 1861-1865, Civil War -- Medical care

ISBN 978-1-60453-966-0; 1-60453-966-6

LC 2009-32367

Biography of suffragist and physician, Dr. Mary Edwards Walker.

"The rush of literary adrenalin will hook readers immediately and keep them enthralled until the end. . . . Given the dynamic topic [and] . . . appealing layout . . . [this is] likely to attract reluctant readers. In addition, sources are plentiful and well documented." SLJ

Includes glossary and bibliographical references

Wallace, Perry

Maraniss, Andrew. **Strong** inside; the true story of how Perry Wallace broke college basketball's color line. Andrew Maraniss. Philomel Books 2016 262 p. illustrations $17.99

Grades: 7 8 9 10 **92**

1. Basketball 2. Civil rights

ISBN 0399548343; 9780399548345

LC 2017288156

This book, by Andrew Maraniss, tells the story of an athlete Perry Wallace. "Wallace was born at an historic crossroads in U.S. history. He entered kindergarten the year that the Brown v. Board of Education decision led to integrated schools, allowing blacks and whites to learn side by side. . . . When Vanderbilt University recruited Wallace to play basketball, he courageously accepted the assignment to desegregate the Southeastern Conference." (Publisher's note)

"This moving biography is thought-provoking, riveting and heart-wrenching, though it remains hopeful as it takes readers into the midst of the basketball and civil rights action." Booklist.

Includes bibliographical references and index.

Wallenberg, Raoul

★ Borden, Louise, 1949- **His** name was Raoul Wallenberg. Houghton Mifflin 2012 135p il $18.99

Grades: 7 8 9 10 11 12 **92**

1. Diplomats 2. Missing persons 3. Political prisoners 4. Humanitarians 5. Holocaust, 1933-1945 6. World War, 1939-1945 -- Jews -- Rescue

ISBN 0-618-50755-8; 978-0-618-50755-9

This book offers a "biography . . . of Raoul Wallenberg, a Swedish businessman who dedicated the latter part of his life to helping Hungarian Jews escape from Budapest at the end of the Second World War. . . . Wallenberg's business dealings in Hungary made him an ideal candidate when the American-based War Refugee Board came to Sweden seeking someone for a mission to Hungary, to provide assistance to Jews who were being deported to Auschwitz by the trainload. Upon arrival in Budapest, Wallenberg invented the 'schutzpasse' system, wherein falsified documents connected Hungarian Jews to neutral Sweden and subsequently saved the lives of thousands." (Bulletin of the Center for Children's Books)

"Based on Borden's years of intensive personal research, including interviews and archival sources, this account written in rapid-reading free verse . . . is presented in a spacious, accessible format that includes lots of historic and personal photos, documents, and profiles of victims and heroes. Borden skillfully places the biographical story in historical context. . . . This is an important addition to the Holocaust curriculum." Booklist

Walton, Sam

Blumenthal, Karen. **Mr.** Sam; how Sam Walton built Wal-Mart and became America's richest man. Penguin Group 2011 183p il $17.99

Grades: 5 6 7 8 **92**

1. Businessmen 2. Discount stores 3. Retail executives 4. Wal-Mart Stores, Inc. 5. Biography, Individual

ISBN 978-0-670-01177-3; 0-670-01177-0

LC 2010049520

"This spectacular success story tracks Walton's rise from lower-middle-class origins to, by the mid-1980s, the top of the 'America's Richest' list. . . . Written in a fluid, journalistic style and enhanced by photos, boxed-out 'Sam stories,' charts tracking changes in Americans' spending habits, and a lavish source list, this account of the man who created what is today the world's largest company makes compelling reading." Booklist

Wang, Vera

Petrillo, Lisa. **Vera** Wang. Morgan Reynolds 2010 112p il (Profiles in fashion) $28.95

Grades: 7 8 9 10 **92**

1. Fashion designers 2. Magazine editors

ISBN 978-159935-150-6; 1-59935-150-1

This discusses the fashion "designer's cultural background, childhood, family, work history and education. . . . The writing is clear and well organized. Color photos are included and give readers a feel for the time period and the types of clothing and accessories the [designer] created." Voice Youth Advocates

Todd, Anne M. **Vera** Wang; [by] Anne M. Todd. Chelsea House 2007 120p bibl il por (Asian Americans of achievement) lib bdg $30

Grades: 7 8 9 10 **92**

1. Fashion designers 2. Magazine editors

ISBN 978-0-7910-9272-9 lib bdg; 0-7910-9272-0 lib bdg

LC 2006028386

A biography of the fashion designer

This is "well-researched . . . attractive . . . solid." SLJ

Warhol, Andy, 1928-1987

★ Rubin, Susan Goldman. **Andy** Warhol; pop art painter. H.N. Abrams 2006 48p il $18.95

Grades: 4 5 6 7 **92**

1. Artists 2. Pop art 3. Artists -- United States 4. Motion picture directors

ISBN 0-8109-5477-X

LC 2005-13238

"Andy Warhol was a colorful figure who revolutionized how the world looks at art. Rubin's coherent and interesting narrative is filled with quotes by the artist and people who knew him. . . . Excellent-quality black-and-white and full-color photographs of Warhol and his family and reproductions of his paintings and those of others who influenced him appear throughout." SLJ

Willett, Edward. **Andy** Warhol; everyone will be famous for 15 minutes. Enslow Publishers 2010 160p il (American rebels) lib bdg $34.60

Grades: 6 7 8 9 **92**

1. Artists 2. Pop art 3. Artists -- United States 4. Motion picture directors

ISBN 978-0-7660-3385-6 lib bdg; 0-7660-3385-6 lib bdg

LC 2009017596

This "fascinating, well organized [portrait] . . . starts with the 1962 L.A. art exhibition at which the artist first presented his iconic paintings of Campbell Soup cans that kicked off the pop-art movement into high gear. . . . Skillfully chosen photos, chapter notes, and [a] suggested-reading [list completes this] well-researched, wholly engaging [introduction]." Booklist

Includes bibliographical references

Warren, Earl, 1891-1974

Branscomb, Leslie Wolf. **Earl** Warren. Morgan Reynolds Pub. 2011 112p il (Supreme Court justices) lib bdg $28.95

Grades: 7 8 9 10 **92**

1. Judges 2. Governors 3. Supreme Court justices

ISBN 978-1-59935158-2; 1-59935158-7

LC 2010020403

This "offers a balanced look at the life and career of Earl Warren. . . . He was appointed chief justice of the U.S. Supreme Court in 1953. Branscomb includes Warren's mistakes but portrays him as a fair-minded man who led the court ably through a series of controversial and significant decisions. . . . Well-chosen boxed quotes and period photos appear throughout the book, with color used sparingly but effectively. This well-researched and clearly written volume offers a good introduction to Warren." Booklist

Includes bibliographical references

Wasdin, Howard E.

★ Wasdin, Howard E. **I** am a SEAL Team Six warrior; memoirs of an American soldier. Howard E. Wasdin and Stephen Templin. 1st ed. St. Martin's Griffin 2012 vi, 182 p.p ill. (paperback) $7.99

Grades: 8 9 10 11 12 **92**

1. Snipers -- United States -- Biography 2. United States. Navy.

SEALs -- Biography 3. United States. Navy -- Commando troops -- Biography
ISBN 1250016436; 9781250016430

LC 2012376658

This book offers an "[a]bridged, . . . young-readers version of an ex-SEAL sniper's account ('SEAL Team Six,' 2011) of his training and combat experiences in Operation Desert Storm and the first Battle of Mogadishu. . . . In later chapters he retraces his long, difficult physical and emotional recovery from serious wounds received during the 'Black Hawk Down' operation, his increasing focus on faith and family after divorce and remarriage and his second career as a chiropractor." (Kirkus Reviews)

Includes bibliographical references (p. [181]-182).

Washington, Booker T., 1856-1915

★ Washington, Booker T. **Up** from slavery; edited with an introduction and notes by William L. Andrews. Oxford University Press 2008 xxvii, 196p (Oxford world's classics) pa $9.95
Grades: 7 8 9 10 11 12 Adult **92**

1. Slaves 2. Authors 3. Educators 4. African American educators 5. Memoirists 6. Nonfiction writers 7. Tuskegee Institute 8. Civil rights activists 9. African Americans -- Biography
ISBN 978-0-19-955239-9

LC 2008-279129

First published 1901

"The classic autobiography of the man who, though born in slavery, educated himself and went on to found Tuskegee Institute." N Y Public Libr

Includes bibliographical references

Washington, George, 1732-1799

Earl, Sari. **George** Washington; revolutionary leader & founding father. by Sari K. Earl. ABDO Pub. 2010 112p il map (Military heroes) lib bdg $22.95
Grades: 7 8 9 **92**

1. Generals 2. Presidents 3. Presidents -- United States 4. United States -- Continental Army
ISBN 978-1-60453-967-7; 1-60453-967-4

LC 2009-32372

"The rush of literary adrenalin will hook readers immediately and keep them enthralled until the end. . . . Given the dynamic topic [and] . . . appealing layout . . . [this is] likely to attract reluctant readers. In addition, sources are plentiful and well documented." SLJ

Includes glossary and bibliographical references

★ McClafferty, Carla Killough. The **many** faces of George Washington; remaking a presidential icon. Carolrhoda Books 2011 120p il lib bdg $20.95
Grades: 6 7 8 9 **92**

1. Generals 2. Presidents 3. Presidents -- United States 4. Biography, Individual
ISBN 978-0-7613-5608-0; 0-7613-5608-8

LC 2010-28178

"With the goal of boosting interest in George Washington, in 2005 Mount Vernon commissioned three life-size reproductions of him at ages 19, 45 and 57. Enthusiastic prose and informative photographs convey in considerable detail the work on this project by a variety of experts, including sculptors, archaeologists, historians, dentists, painters, taxidermists and more. . . . Quotations from Washington and his contemporaries add a personal note, while reproductions of portraits, statues and artifacts supply visual interest. Color photographs show some of the steps in the reconstruction." Kirkus

Includes bibliographical references

Mooney, Carla. **George** Washington; 25 great projects you can build yourself. illustrated by Samuel Carbaugh. Nomad 2011 121p il (Build it yourself) $21.95; pa $15.95
Grades: 4 5 6 7 **92**

1. Generals 2. Handicraft 3. Presidents 4. Presidents -- United States
ISBN 978-1-934670-64-4; 1-934670-64-2; 978-1-934670-63-7 pa pa; 1-934670-63-4 pa

"The life of George Washington lends itself remarkably well to a variety of kid-friendly crafts that don't require old-fashioned materials or 18th-century skills. . . . The projects separate biographical chapters that are thorough and clear. . . . Sidebars with vocabulary words, quotes, interesting facts about the man and his time, and 'What if?' questions regarding pivotal moments in Washington's life add to the text. These sidebars, as well as amusing cartoon illustrations, make the subject light and approachable." SLJ

Includes glossary and bibliographical references

Van Lente, Fred. **George** Washington; Fred Van Lente, illustrated by Ryan Dunlavey. HarperCollins 2018 128 p. chiefly color illustrations (Action presidents) (hardcover) $9.99
Grades: 4 5 6 7 8 **92**

1. Biography 2. Presidents -- United States
ISBN 9780062394057

LC 2017950229

Includes bibliographical references

In this book in the Action Presidents series, by Fred Van Lente, illustrated by Ryan Dunlavey, "we all know that George Washington was our first president and a hero of the American Revolution, but did you also know that he didn't want to be president and had teeth so bad that he hated to smile? . . . U.S. history comes to life like never before! Historically accurate and highly entertaining . . . [w]ith timelines, maps, charts, and more." (Publisher's note)

"Van Lente aims to contextualize historical figures who are often blindly lionized . . ., a goal that comes through clearly amid a flurry of gags and jokes." Pub Wkly

Weber, EdNah New Rider

Weber, EdNah New Rider. **Rattlesnake** Mesa; stories from a native American childhood. by EdNah New Rider Weber; photographs by Richela Renkun. Lee & Low Books 2004 132p il $18.95
Grades: 4 5 6 7 **92**

1. Artisans 2. Memoirists 3. Storytellers 4. Native Americans -- Biography
ISBN 1-58430-231-3

LC 2004-2385

"Weber describes her experiences with warmth and affection in this unusually compelling memoir. Striking black-and-white photos . . . add to the book's appeal." Horn Book Guide

Webster, Noah, 1758-1843

Reef, Catherine. **Noah** Webster; man of many words. Catherine Reef. Clarion Books, an imprint of Houghton Mifflin Harcourt 2015 224 p. illustrations, map (hardback) $18.99
Grades: 7 8 9 **92**

1. English language -- Lexicography -- United States 2. Founding Fathers of the United States 3. Educators -- United States --

Biography 4. Lexicographers -- United States -- Biography
ISBN 0544129830; 9780544129832

LC 2014027803

In this biography for children, author Catherine Reef "guides [readers] through [Noah] Webster's remarkable life, from boyhood on a Connecticut farm through the fight for American independence to his days as a writer and political activist who greatly influenced our Founding Fathers and the direction of the young United States." (Publisher's note)

"Though the narrative is occasionally dry, the abundance of information and accessible writing are undeniable, and with a helpful time line, photos and reproductions of primary documents, and a list of additional resources, this volume will be very useful for students working on American history reports." Booklist

Includes bibliographical references (pages 189-195) and index.

Wells, H. G. (Herbert George), 1866-1946

Abrams, Dennis. **H.G.** Wells; foreword by Kyle Zimmer. Chelsea House 2011 128p il (Who wrote that?) lib bdg $35
Grades: 6 7 8 9 10 **92**

1. Authors 2. Novelists 3. Historians 4. Authors, English 5. Writers on science 6. Writers on politics 7. Science fiction writers
ISBN 978-1-60413-770-5; 1-60413-770-3

LC 2010030588

This discusses the life and work of author H. G. Wells.

Includes bibliographical references

Wells-Barnett, Ida B., 1862-1931

Hinman, Bonnie. **Eternal** vigilance: the story of Ida B. Wells-Barnett. Morgan Reynolds Pub. 2010 128p il (Civil rights leaders) $28.95
Grades: 7 8 9 10 **92**

1. Authors 2. Lynching 3. Journalists 4. Women journalists 5. African American educators 6. Essayists 7. Nonfiction writers 8. Newspaper executives 9. Civil rights activists 10. United States -- Race relations 11. African Americans -- Civil rights 12. African American women -- Biography 13. African Americans -- Social conditions
ISBN 978-1-59935-111-7; 1-59935-111-0

LC 2010-8144

"Hinman tells of Wells-Barnett's tireless efforts as an antilynching crusader and civil rights advocate. . . . Hinman paints an engaging portrait of the activist who was instrumental in the formation of the NAACP. Each stage of Wells-Barnett's life is placed in historical context, providing students with a better understanding of the world in which she lived. Well-chosen black-and-white photographs and other period materials are included throughout the text." SLJ

Includes bibliographical references

Wharton, Edith, 1862-1937

★ Wooldridge, Connie Nordhielm. The **brave** escape of Edith Wharton; a biography. Clarion Books 2010 184p il $20
Grades: 7 8 9 10 **92**

1. Authors 2. Novelists 3. Women authors 4. Authors, American 5. Nonfiction writers 6. Short story writers
ISBN 978-0-547-23630-8; 0-547-23630-1

LC 2009-33574

"In this thoroughly researched, humanizing biography, Wooldridge writes with lively specifics about both the author and her time. . . . Frequent, well-woven quotes from Wharton's family and friends contribute to a strong sense of an energetic, groundbreaking, and ferociously intelligent writer, but it's the many quotes in Wharton's own voice that leave the most indelible impact." Booklist

Whitfield, Simon, 1975-

Whitfield, Simon. **Simon** says gold: Simon Whitfield's pursuit of athletic excellence; by Simon Whitfield with Cleve Dheensaw. Orca Publishers 2009 118p il pa $14
Grades: 5 6 7 8 **92**

1. Athletes 2. Track athletics 3. Triathletes
ISBN 978-1-55469-141-8 pa; 1-55469-141-9 pa

"In 2000, Whitfield won a gold medal in the inaugural triathlon race held in the Sydney Summer Olympics. . . . He tells his story with candor, and he sheds light on the dark side of early success and the pressures athletes face. Sidebars offer more information on the sport of triathlon, and scrapbook-style color photographs enliven the tale." SLJ

Whitman, Narcissa Prentiss, 1808-1847

Harness, Cheryl. The **tragic** tale of Narcissa Whitman and a faithful history of the Oregon Trail; written and illustrated by Cheryl Harness. National Geographic Society 2006 144p il map (Cheryl Harness history) $16.95; lib bdg $25.90
Grades: 4 5 6 7 **92**

1. Frontier and pioneer life 2. Overland journeys to the Pacific 3. Pioneers 4. Missionaries
ISBN 0-7922-5920-3; 0-7922-7890-9 lib bdg

LC 2005-30930

This "introduces a nineteenth-century pioneer and missionary. . . . [She and her husband Marcus Whitman] journeyed along the Oregon Trail to the Waiilatpu Mission, where they ministered to the Cayuse. . . . Harness' chatty, conversational style makes the pair accessible to modern readers, and frequent quotes from Narcissa's diaries and letters and a time line help to frame the story in light of world and national events. Harness' black-line illustrations . . . help to break up the text for younger readers." Booklist

Includes bibliographical references

Whitman, Walt, 1819-1892

Kerley, Barbara. **Walt** Whitman; words for America. illustrated by Brian Selznick. Scholastic Press 2004 un il $16.95
Grades: 4 5 6 7 **92**

1. Poets 2. Authors 3. Essayists 4. Poets, American
ISBN 0-439-35791-8

LC 2003-20085

A biography of the American poet whose compassion led him to nurse soldiers during the Civil War, to give voice to the nation's grief at Lincoln's assassination, and to capture the true American spirit in verse

"Delightfully old-fashioned in design, [the book's] oversized pages are replete with graceful illustrations and snippets of poetry. The brilliantly inventive paintings add vibrant testimonial to the nuanced text." SLJ

Wiesel, Elie, 1928-2016

Koestler-Grack, Rachel A. **Elie** Wiesel; witness for humanity. by Rachel Koestler-Grack. Gareth Stevens Pub. 2009 112p il map (Life portraits) lib bdg $34
Grades: 7 8 9 10 **92**

1. Authors 2. Novelists 3. Journalists 4. Holocaust survivors 5. Jews -- Romania 6. Holocaust, 1933-1945 7. Human rights activists 8. Nobel laureates for peace
ISBN 978-1-4339-0054-9 lib bdg; 1-4339-0054-8 lib bdg

LC 2008-31630

"Recounts the struggles . . . [Wiesel] experienced as a Holocaust survivor and as someone who still works to end all violence against humanity. . . . Many photos, images, and sidebars, as well as the expected back matter contribute . . . without being didactic and educate without preaching." Voice Youth Advocates

Includes glossary and bibliographical references

Wiesenthal, Simon

★ Rubin, Susan Goldman. The **Anne** Frank Case: Simon Wiesenthal's search for the truth; illustrated by Bill Farnsworth. Holiday House 2009 40p il $18.95

Grades: 4 5 6 7 **92**

1. Authors 2. Architects 3. Holocaust survivors 4. Essayists 5. Memoirists 6. Nazi hunters 7. Jewish leaders 8. Jews -- Biography 9. Holocaust, 1933-1945

ISBN 978-0-8234-2109-1; 0-8234-2109-0

LC 2007-28396

"Even those who have heard of Wiesenthal will be thrilled by this account. . . . Farnsworth's stirring full-page oil paintings are filled with emotion." Booklist

Includes glossary and bibliographical references

Wilder, Laura Ingalls, 1867-1957

Berne, Emma Carlson. **Laura** Ingalls Wilder; by Emma Carlson Berne. ABDO Pub. 2008 112p il map $22.95

Grades: 4 5 6 7 **92**

1. Authors 2. Novelists 3. Women authors 4. Frontier and pioneer life 5. Western writers 6. Authors, American 7. Children's authors 8. Young adult authors

ISBN 978-1-59928-843-7; 1-59928-843-5

LC 2007012513

"Beginning in 1929 with the events that led up to the publication of Little House in the Big Woods , this readable biography further amplifies Wilder's life and correlates it with her books. . . . This volume is packed with relevant material, a time line, archival photographs, quotes from primary sources, and an official Web site." SLJ

Includes glossary and bibliographical references

Wilder, Laura Ingalls. A **Little** House traveler; writings from Laura Ingalls Wilder's journeys across America. by Laura Ingalls Wilder. HarperCollins 2006 344p il $16.99; pa $7.99

Grades: 5 6 7 8 **92**

1. Authors 2. Novelists 3. Women authors 4. Western writers 5. Authors, American 6. Children's authors 7. Young adult authors 8. United States -- Description and travel

ISBN 978-0-06-072491-7; 0-06-072491-9; 978-0-06-072492-4 pa; 0-06-072492-7 pa

LC 2005014975

"This volume combines three Wilder travel diaries: On the Way Home, recounting the 1894 trip from South Dakota to Missouri, with husband Almanzo and daughter Rose; West from Home, featuring letters written by Laura to Almanzo during her 1915 solo visit to Rose in San Francisco; and The Road Back, highlighting Laura's previously unpublished record of a 1931 trip with Almanzo to De Smet, South Dakota, and the Black Hills. . . . This offers an amazing look at a beloved author, as well as a fascinating account of travel before interstate highways and air-conditioning." Booklist

William, Prince, Duke of Cambridge, 1982-

Doeden, Matt. **Prince** William & Kate; a royal romance. Lerner Publications 2011 48p il lib bdg $26.60

Grades: 5 6 7 8 **92**

1. Princes 2. Princesses

ISBN 978-0-7613-8029-0; 0-7613-8029-9

LC 2011003413

"This short and sweet volume accents what down-to-earth and normal newlyweds Prince William and Kate Middleton are really like. After a brief recap of the couple's engagement interview, the book goes on to profile the pair individually and then as a duo. . . . This is an upbeat, readable narrative about a handsome, appealing couple. The color photographs are well chosen." Booklist

Includes glossary and bibliographical references

Williams, Evan

Smith, Chris. **Twitter**; Jack Dorsey, Biz Stone and Evan Williams. [by] Chris Smith and Marci McGrath. Morgan Reynolds Pub. 2011 112p il (Business leaders) $28.95

Grades: 7 8 9 10 11 12 **92**

1. Online social networks 2. Twitter, Inc. 3. Internet executives 4. Computer programmers 5. Computer software executives

ISBN 978-1-59935-179-7; 1-59935-179-X; 978-1-59935-216-9 e-book

LC 2011024699

This biography of the founders of Twitter "will grab YAs. . . . The design is browsable, with clear type and lots of color screens and informal photos of young people at work." Booklist

Includes bibliographical references

Williams, Serena, 1981-

Williams, Venus. **Venus** & Serena; serving from the hip, ten rules for living, loving, and winning. [by] Venus and Serena Williams with Hilary Beard. Houghton Mifflin 2005 133p il pa $14

Grades: 7 8 9 10 **92**

1. Women athletes 2. African American athletes 3. Tennis players 4. Tennis -- Biography

ISBN 0-618-57653-3

LC 2004-13204

"The sisters and tennis players . . . give teens advice on everyday living, showing them how to aim high and reach their goals. The 10 rules for success include building a 'dream team' (people who support your goals), doing well in school, learning self-respect, valuing friendships, taking care of yourself emotionally and physically, obtaining financial security, and overcoming setbacks. The final chapter discusses the virtues of volunteerism and charity. . . . Never preachy and always practical, this is a welcome addition to most collections." SLJ

Williams, Venus, 1980-

Williams, Venus. **Venus** & Serena; serving from the hip, ten rules for living, loving, and winning. [by] Venus and Serena Williams with Hilary Beard. Houghton Mifflin 2005 133p il pa $14

Grades: 7 8 9 10 **92**

1. Women athletes 2. African American athletes 3. Tennis players 4. Tennis -- Biography

ISBN 0-618-57653-3

LC 2004-13204

"The sisters and tennis players . . . give teens advice on everyday living, showing them how to aim high and reach their goals. The 10 rules for success include building a 'dream team' (people who support your goals), doing well in school, learning self-respect, valuing friendships, taking care of yourself emotionally and physically, obtaining financial security, and overcoming setbacks. The final chapter discusses the virtues of volunteerism and charity. . . . Never preachy and always practical, this is a welcome addition to most collections." SLJ

Wilson, Jacqueline

Bankston, John. **Jacqueline** Wilson. Chelsea House 2011 128p il (Who wrote that?) lib bdg $35

Grades: 6 7 8 9 10 **92**

1. Authors 2. Novelists 3. Women authors 4. Authors, American
ISBN 978-1-60413-773-6; 1-60413-773-8

LC 2010047679

"Wilson knew from an early age that writing was her calling. Growing up in a turbulent home and dropping out of school at 16 pushed her to start writing for Jackie, a magazine for teenage girls. This well-written biography includes a quick-paced, fact-filled synopsis of her life." SLJ

Includes bibliographical references

Wilson, Woodrow, 1856-1924

Marsico, Katie. **Woodrow** Wilson. Marshall Cavendish Benchmark 2011 112p il (Presidents and their times) $23.95

Grades: 5 6 7 8 **92**

1. Governors 2. Presidents 3. College presidents 4. Nobel laureates for peace 5. Presidents -- United States
ISBN 978-0-7614-4815-0; 0-7614-4815-2

LC 2009041116

This offers information on President Woodrow Wilson and places him within his historical and cultural context. Also explored are the formative events of his times and how he responded.

"The abundant sidebars provide a good deal of background information that will be helpful to students. . . . Attractive . . . as well as useful." Booklist

Includes glossary and bibliographical references

Winthrop, John, 1588-1649

Aronson, Marc. **John** Winthrop, Oliver Cromwell, and the Land of Promise. Clarion Books 2004 205p il map $20

Grades: 7 8 9 10 **92**

1. Clergy 2. Puritans 3. Heads of state 4. Revolutionaries 5. Government officials 6. Colonial administrators 7. Great Britain -- History -- 1603-1714, Stuarts 8. Massachusetts -- History -- 1600-1775, Colonial period
ISBN 0-618-18177-6

LC 2003-16418

"The accessible text is accompanied by excerpts from primary source documents and vivid illustrations. The author's passion for the period comes across in his writing. Aronson provides an excellent source for historical and biographical data." Voice Youth Advocates

Includes bibliographical references

Woodhull, Victoria C., 1838-1927

Havelin, Kate. **Victoria** Woodhull. Twenty-First Century Books 2007 112p (Trailblazer biography) lib bdg $30.60

Grades: 7 8 9 10 **92**

1. Feminism 2. Suffragists 3. Feminists 4. Presidential candidates
ISBN 978-0-8225-5986-3 lib bdg; 0-8225-5986-2 lib bdg

LC 2005022824

A biography of the nineteenth century feminist who became the first woman to run for president of the U.S.

"A well-researched, well-organized biography. . . . [Woodhull's] fascinating and full life is expertly detailed in this narrative." SLJ

Includes bibliographical references

Woods, Tiger, 1975-

Roberts, Jeremy. **Tiger** Woods; golf's master. by Jeremy Roberts. Twenty-First Century Books 2009 112p il (Lifeline biographies) lib bdg $33.26

Grades: 6 7 8 9 **92**

1. Golf 2. Golfers
ISBN 978-1-58013-569-6 lib bdg; 1-58013-569-2 lib bdg

LC 2008-3098

"There are a number of biographies about the world's best golfer, but this one is particularly good. Not only does it chronicle the life of Woods but it offers a solid look at family influences, various tournaments, and personal relationships. . . . Color photographs are well chosen." Booklist

Includes bibliographical references

Woodson, Jacqueline

Hinton, KaaVonia. **Jacqueline** Woodson; by KaaVonia Hinton. Mitchell Lane Publishers 2008 48p il (Classic storytellers) lib bdg $29.95

Grades: 5 6 7 8 **92**

1. Authors 2. Novelists 3. Women authors 4. African American authors 5. College teachers
ISBN 978-1-58415-533-1 lib bdg; 1-58415-533-7 lib bdg

LC 2007-669

"This biography details the life of a popular African-American author. It covers her childhood, the challenges she faced growing up during the height of the Civil Rights Movement, what inspired her to begin to write, and her many literary successes. The book is filled with photos of the writer at various stages of her life and the covers of some of her books. Young people should find inspiration in Woodson's story." SLJ

Includes glossary and bibliographical references

★ Woodson, Jacqueline, 1963- **Brown** girl dreaming; Jacqueline Woodson. Nancy Paulsen Books 2014 336 p. illustrations, photographs (hardback) $16.99

Grades: 4 5 6 7 8 **92**

1. African American women -- Biography 2. American poetry -- African American authors 3. African American women authors -- Biography -- Poetry 4. Authors, American -- 20th century -- Biography -- Poetry
ISBN 0399252517; 9780399252518

LC 2014021346

Newbery Honor Book (2015)
Boston Globe-Horn Book Honor: Nonfiction (2015)
Coretta Scott King Author Award (2015)
National Book Award: Young People's Literature (2014)
Robert F. Sibert Honor Book (2015)

"Raised in South Carolina and New York, [author Jacqueline] Woodson always felt halfway home in each place. In vivid poems, she shares what it was like to grow up as an African American in the 1960s and 1970s, living with the remnants of Jim Crow and her growing awareness of the Civil Rights movement." (Publisher's note)

"Here is a memoir-in-verse so immediate that readers will feel they are experiencing the author's childhood right along with her." Horn Book

Wright, Orville, 1871-1948

★ Collins, Mary. **Airborne** : a photobiography of Wilbur and Orville Wright. National Geographic Soc. 2003 63p il maps $18.95

Grades: 4 5 6 7 **92**

1. Inventors 2. Aeronautics -- History 3. Aircraft industry executives
ISBN 0-7922-6957-8

LC 2002-5279

Examines the lives of the Wright brothers and discusses their experiments and triumphs in the field of flight

"The well-chosen photos give readers a feel for Kitty Hawk—windy, sandy, solitary. This is an exceptionally well-informed picture of the Wright brothers and what their 100-year-old achievement really meant." SLJ

★ Freedman, Russell. The **Wright** brothers: how they invented the airplane; with original photographs by Wilbur and Orville Wright. Holiday House 1991 129p il hardcover o.p. pa $14.95

Grades: 5 6 7 8 9 10 **92**

1. Inventors 2. Aeronautics -- History 3. Aircraft industry executives

ISBN 0-8234-0875-2; 0-8234-1082-X pa

LC 90-48440

A Newbery Medal honor book, 1992

In this "combination of photography and text, Freedman reveals the frustrating, exciting, and ultimately successful journey of these two brothers from their bicycle shop in Dayton, Ohio, to their Kitty Hawk flights and beyond. . . . An essential purchase for younger YAs." Voice Youth Advocates

Includes bibliographical references

Wright, Richard, 1908-1960

Hart, Joyce. **Native** son: the story of Richard Wright. Morgan Reynolds 2002 128p il (World writers) lib bdg $21.95

Grades: 7 8 9 10 **92**

1. Authors 2. Novelists 3. Dramatists 4. African American authors 5. Essayists 6. Authors, American 7. Nonfiction writers 8. Short story writers

ISBN 1-931798-06-0

LC 2002-13686

"The writing is accessible and flows smoothly." SLJ

Includes bibliographical references

Levy, Debbie. **Richard** Wright. Twenty-First Century Books 2008 160p (Literary greats) $33.26

Grades: 7 8 9 10 11 12 **92**

1. Authors 2. Novelists 3. Dramatists 4. African American authors 5. Essayists 6. Nonfiction writers 7. Short story writers

ISBN 978-0-8225-6793-6

LC 2006-101189

A biography of the African American author of Native Son and Black Boy

This "absorbing biography . . . does a fine job of placing Wright's personal life in the context of black history. . . . Cleanly designed and featuring a small photo on every double-page spread." Booklist

Includes bibliographical references

Wright, Susanna, 1697-1784

Kanefield, Teri, 1960- The **extraordinary** Suzy Wright; a colonial woman on the frontier. by Teri Kanefield. Abrams Books for Young Readers 2015 64 p. illustrations, maps (hardcover) $19.95

Grades: 5 6 7 8 9 10 **92**

1. Society of Friends 2. Pennsylvania -- History 3. Frontier and pioneer life -- United States 4. Columbia (Pa.) -- Biography 5. Clerks of court -- Pennsylvania -- Biography 6. Poets -- Pennsylvania -- Columbia -- Biography 7. Women -- Pennsylvania -- Columbia -- Biography 8. Quakers -- Pennsylvania -- Columbia -- Biography 9. Frontier and pioneer life -- Pennsylvania -- Columbia 10. Pennsylvania -- History -- Colonial period, ca. 1600-1775

ISBN 9781419718663

LC 2015019813

This book, by Teri Kanefield, tells "the little-known story of Quaker Susanna (Suzy) Wright (1697–1784), a renowned poet and political activist. Suzy helped settle the Pennsylvania frontier, where she acted as legal counselor to her less literate neighbors. . . . Surviving documents and correspondence between Suzy and a host of her contemporaries . . . reveal that Suzy, from her home on the frontier, exerted considerable influence in the highest circles of Pennsylvania government." (Publisher's note)

"These primary materials, including Suzy's poems and letters, give her a voice that time had threatened to still. Fine source notes and references, along with an afterword that helps explain how Suzy and the Quaker movement influenced American history into the 20th century, add valuable context. An excellent resource that shines a spotlight on a previously little-known but highly meritorious woman." Kirkus

Includes bibliographical references and index

Wright, Wilbur, 1867-1912

★ Collins, Mary. **Airborne** : a photobiography of Wilbur and Orville Wright. National Geographic Soc. 2003 63p il maps $18.95

Grades: 4 5 6 7 **92**

1. Inventors 2. Aeronautics -- History 3. Aircraft industry executives

ISBN 0-7922-6957-8

LC 2002-5279

Examines the lives of the Wright brothers and discusses their experiments and triumphs in the field of flight

"The well-chosen photos give readers a feel for Kitty Hawk—windy, sandy, solitary. This is an exceptionally well-informed picture of the Wright brothers and what their 100-year-old achievement really meant." SLJ

★ Freedman, Russell. The **Wright** brothers: how they invented the airplane; with original photographs by Wilbur and Orville Wright. Holiday House 1991 129p il hardcover o.p. pa $14.95

Grades: 5 6 7 8 9 10 **92**

1. Inventors 2. Aeronautics -- History 3. Aircraft industry executives

ISBN 0-8234-0875-2; 0-8234-1082-X pa

LC 90-48440

A Newbery Medal honor book, 1992

In this "combination of photography and text, Freedman reveals the frustrating, exciting, and ultimately successful journey of these two brothers from their bicycle shop in Dayton, Ohio, to their Kitty Hawk flights and beyond. . . . An essential purchase for younger YAs." Voice Youth Advocates

Includes bibliographical references

Yasui, Sachiko

★ Stelson, Caren. **Sachiko**; A Nagasaki Bomb Survivor's Story. by Caren B. Stelson. Carolrhoda Books 2016 144 p. illustrations (some color) (lb : alk. paper) $19.99; (ebook) $19.99

Grades: 5 6 7 8 **92**

1. Atomic bomb victims 2. World War, 1939-1945 -- Japan 3. Nagasaki (Japan) -- Bombardment, 1945 4. Nagasaki-shi (Japan) -- History -- Bombardment, 1945 5. World War, 1939-1945 -- Japan -- Nagasaki-shi (Japan) 6. Atomic bomb victims -- Japan -- Nagasaki-

shi -- Biography
ISBN 9781467789035; 9781512408935
LC 2015043908

Sibert Honor Book (2017)

This book, by Caren B. Stelson, "tells the true story of six-year-old Sachiko Yasui's survival of the Nagasaki atomic bomb on August 9, 1945, and the heartbreaking and lifelong aftermath. Having conducted extensive interviews with Sachiko Yasui,... Stelson chronicles Sachiko s trauma and loss as well as her long journey to find peace." (Publisher's note)

"This powerful narrative account of one person finding her voice after insufferable trauma encapsulates a grim era in global history." Pub Wkly

Includes bibliographical references and index

Yep, Laurence

Marcovitz, Hal. **Laurence** Yep; [by] Hal Marcovitz. Chelsea House 2008 136p il (Who wrote that?) $30

Grades: 6 7 8 9 **92**

1. Authors 2. Novelists 3. College teachers 4. Authors, American 5. Children's authors 6. Young adult authors 7. Chinese Americans -- Biography

ISBN 978-0-7910-9527-0; 0-7910-9527-4
LC 2007045508

This biography of the Chinese American author examines the "writer's life, including the inspiration behind some of [his] works. [The] volume includes photographs and quotations from interviews, as well as descriptions of main characters and annotated lists of books and awards. Useful for aspiring authors as well as book report writers." Horn Book Guide

Includes bibliographical references

Yolen, Jane

Carpan, Carolyn. **Jane** Yolen; [by] Carolyn Carpan. Chelsea House 2006 128p bibl il (Who wrote that?) lib bdg $30

Grades: 6 7 8 9 **92**

1. Authors 2. Novelists 3. Women authors 4. Editors 5. Fantasy writers 6. Authors, American 7. Children's authors 8. Science fiction writers

ISBN 978-0-7910-8660-5 lib bdg; 0-7910-8660-7 lib bdg
LC 2005007828

This describes the life and work of author Jane Yolen

"The photographs that illustrate the text show places from the author's life or period photos. . . . The extensive quotes from Yolen share her feelings as she wrote full time and published more than 250 books while raising a family. . . . [The book includes] extensive notes, a chronology, works by the author listed by publication date, major awards, and most wellknown characters." Voice Youth Advocates

Includes bibliographical references

Yousafzai, Malala, 1997-

Aretha, David. **Malala** Yousafzai and the girls of Pakistan; by David Aretha. Morgan Reynolds Publishing 2014 64 p. color illustrations (Out in front) $27.45

Grades: 5 6 7 8 **92**

1. Women political activists 2. Taliban 3. Girls -- Education -- Pakistan 4. Political activists -- Pakistan 5. Women social reformers -- Pakistan 6. Girls -- Violence against -- Pakistan 7. Sex discrimination in education -- Pakistan

ISBN 1599354543; 9781599354545
LC 2013044510

This book, by David Aretha, offers "the story of Malala Yousafzai's life. . . . By the time she was 11, she wrote candidly about the Taliban and their efforts to block girls' access to schools. Two years later, she was nominated for the International Children's Peace Prize but less than a year after that she was shot in the face by a Taliban assassin. . . . Yousafzai's eventual recovery and continued activism is a demonstration of bravery and conviction." (School Library Journal)

"This biography of the Pakistani girl who survived an assassination attempt by the Taliban provides geographical, historical, and sociopolitical context for Yousafzai's dedication to education activism. Captioned color photographs pair well with the concise and factual text. Important quotes are printed in red, which is difficult to read on some backgrounds. Significant terms are defined in the text. Websites. Bib., ind." Horn Book

Includes bibliographical references and index

McCormick, Patricia, 1956- **I** am Malala; how one girl stood up for education and changed the world. Malala Yousafzai with Patricia McCormick. Young readers edition Little Brown & Co 2014 230 p. illustrations, map (hardback) $17

Grades: 5 6 7 8 **92**

1. Women -- Education 2. Children's rights -- Pakistan 3. Young women -- Education -- Pakistan -- Biography

ISBN 031632793X; 9780316327930
LC 2014015881

"Malala Yousafzai was only ten years old when the Taliban took control of her region. . . . They said girls couldn't go to school. Raised in a once-peaceful area of Pakistan transformed by terrorism, Malala was taught to stand up for what she believes. So she fought for her right to be educated." (Publisher's note)

"Young education activist and Taliban victim Malala Yousafzai recounts her Pakistani childhood in this deftly adapted memoir. Domestic and academic tales illustrate her unusual maturity and resilience in the face of increasing Taliban threats. Yousafzai's moving narrative and engaging, sincere voice may provide an entryway to international awareness for middle-grade readers; a map and a thorough timeline provide additional political context." Horn Book

Zaharias, Babe Didrikson, 1911-1956

Freedman, Russell. **Babe** Didrikson Zaharias; the making of a champion. Clarion Bks. 1999 192p il hardcover o.p.; pbk $10.99

Grades: 5 6 7 8 9 10 **92**

1. Women athletes 2. Golfers 3. Hurdlers 4. High jumpers 5. Javelin throwers 6. Olympic athletes

ISBN 0-395-63367-2; 9780544104914 ; 0544104919
LC 98-50208

A biography of Babe Didrikson, who broke records in golf, track and field, and other sports, at a time when there were few opportunities for female athletes

"Freedman's measured yet lively style captures the spirit of the great athlete. . . . Plenty of black-and-white photos capture Babe's spirit and dashing good looks; the documentation . . . is impeccable." Horn Book

Includes bibliographical references

Lobby, Mackenzie. **Babe** Didrikson Zaharias; groundbreaking all-around athlete. ABDO Pub. Co. 2011 112p il (Legendary athletes) lib bdg $34.22

Grades: 6 7 8 9 **92**

1. Women athletes 2. Golfers 3. Hurdlers 4. High jumpers 5. Javelin throwers 6. Olympic athletes

ISBN 978-1-61714-755-5; 1-61714-755-9
LC 2010041158

This biography of athlete Babe Didrikson Zaharias "goes beyond merely discussing [her] accomplishments. . . . [It] also [explores] the social and political [influence she] had on society as a whole. In addition, [it introduces] historical events in the context of [her life]. . . . This . . . is teeming with information and is a must-purchase for sports fans and readers interested in social activism." SLJ

Includes glossary and bibliographical references

Van Natta, Don, 1964- **Wonder** girl; the magnificent sporting life of Babe Didrikson Zaharias. Little, Brown and Co. 2011 403p il $27.99

Grades: 5 6 7 8 **92**

1. Women athletes 2. Golfers 3. Hurdlers 4. High jumpers 5. Javelin throwers 6. Olympic athletes

ISBN 978-0-316-05699-1; 0-316-05699-5

LC 2010041794

Describes the life and times of LPGA founder Babe Didrikson, the Texas woman who achieved All-American status in basketball, won gold medals in track and field in the 1932 Olympics, and became the first woman to play against men in a PGA tournament.

This is an "engaging biography. . . . Van Natta marvelously narrates the forgotten life of the 'greatest all-around athlete of all time,' a story that every American sport fan should relish." Publ Wkly

Includes bibliographical references

Wallace, Rich. **Babe** conquers the world; the legendary life of Babe Didrikson Zaharias. Rich Wallace, Sandra Neil Wallace. Calkins Creek 2014 272 p. (Includes bibliographical references (page 266-268) and index.) $16.95

Grades: 4 5 6 7 8 **92**

1. Women athletes -- Biography

ISBN 1590789814; 9781590789810

LC 2013953471

This book, by Rich Wallace and Sandra Neil Wallace, is a biography of Babe Didrikson Zaharias. "A champion basketball player, an Olympic track-and-field star, and career golfer, Babe didn't let obstacles stand in the way of her success. The authors detail her trajectory from the daughter of a Norwegian immigrant born in a working-class Texas neighborhood to record wins at the 1932 Olympics (still not broken to this day) to her last days as she fought cancer." (School Library Journal)

"Babe Didrikson Zaharias is perhaps the most accomplished athlete that young people have never heard of. She was an Olympic track star in the 1932 games, a noted professional basketball player, and a formative member of the LPGA...This is part sports journalism, part narrative nonfiction, and part proof that professional athletes can be exemplary role models for young people." Booklist

Zapata, Emiliano, 1879-1919

Stein, R. Conrad. **Emiliano** Zapata and the Mexican Revolution. Morgan Reynolds Pub. 2011 144p il map (The story of Mexico) $28.95

Grades: 6 7 8 9 **92**

1. Generals 2. Revolutionaries 3. Mexico -- History -- Revolution, 1910-1920

ISBN 978-1-5993-5163-6; 1-5993-5163-3

LC 2010041616

This traces the life and impact of Zapata and his revolutionary movement on the history of Mexico.

"Stein organizes and clearly presents a great deal of information. . . . The . . . format features a chronological text supplemented with useful sidebars and brightened with color illustrations, including many photos, artifacts, and period artworks." Booklist

Includes bibliographical references

Zenatti, Valérie, 1970-

Zenatti, Valerie. **When** I was a soldier; a memoir. translated by Adriana Hunter. Bloomsbury Children's Books 2005 235p $16.95

Grades: 7 8 9 10 **92**

1. Authors 2. Soldiers 3. Novelists 4. Women soldiers 5. Israel 6. Memoirists 7. Translators 8. Children's authors

ISBN 1-58234-978-9

A "fast, wry, present-tense memoir. . . . Readers on all sides of the war-peace continuum, here and there, will find much to talk about." Booklist

Zuckerberg, Mark

Hasday, Judy L. **Facebook** and Mark Zuckerberg. Morgan Reynolds Pub. 2011 112p il (Business leaders) $28.95

Grades: 7 8 9 10 11 12 **92**

1. Businessmen 2. Online social networks 3. Facebook Inc. 4. Internet executives

ISBN 978-1-59935-176-6; 1-59935-176-5; 978-1-59935-215-2 e-book

LC 2011023210

This biography of Mark Zuckerberg and how he started Facebook "will grab YAs. . . . The design is browsable, with clear type and lots of color screens and informal photos of young people at work." Booklist

Includes bibliographical references

Woog, Adam. **Mark** Zuckerberg, Facebook creator. KidHaven Press 2009 48p il map (Innovators) $28.25

Grades: 4 5 6 7 **92**

1. Businesspeople 2. Facebook Inc. 3. Internet executives

ISBN 978-0-7377-4566-5; 0-7377-4566-5

LC 2009013458

"This brisk, readable [biography the creator of Facebook] . . . presents an appealing picture of the shy, lonely future billionaire . . . This is fascinating and relevant stuff." Booklist

Includes bibliographical references

920 Biography, genealogy, insignia

Aaseng, Nathan

Business builders in sweets and treats; [by] Nathan Aaseng. Oliver Press 2005 160p il (Business builders) $24.95

Grades: 5 6 7 8 **920**

1. Food industry 2. Businesspeople

ISBN 1-881508-84-6

LC 2003-64984

This is a "study of Hershey and chocolate, Wrigley and chewing gum, Ben and Jerry and ice cream, and others who make things we love to eat. . . . A few well-chosen sidebars document sweets that don't get a whole chapter. Excellent sources and citations, boxed facts, a lively style, and sometimes mouthwatering pictures finish the package." Booklist

Includes bibliographical references

Bagieu, Pénélope

★ **Brazen**; rebel ladies who rocked the world. Pénélope Bagieu. First Second 2018 304 p. chiefly color illustrations (pbk.) $17.99

Grades: 8 9 10 11 12 Adult **920**

1. Biography 2. Women -- Biography
ISBN 9781626728684; 9781626728691

LC 2017941160

Eisner Award: Best U.S. Edition of International Material (2019)

"With her characteristic wit and dazzling drawings, celebrated graphic novelist Pénélope Bagieu profiles the lives of . . . feisty female role models, some world famous, some little known. From Nellie Bly to Mae Jemison or Josephine Baker to Naziq al-Abid, the stories in this comic biography are sure to inspire the next generation of rebel ladies." (Publisher's note)

"Both art and text are clever, smart, and distilled for maximum impact. The women are not idealized, nor are their flaws ignored. Instead, they are treated with wit and empathy. . . . A fresh and joyous look at women's history that is sure to delight even the most jaded readers." LJ

Baker, Rosalie F.

Ancient Egyptians; people of the pyramids. [by] Rosalie F. and Charles F. Baker. Oxford Univ. Press 2001 189p il maps (Oxford profiles) $50

Grades: 7 8 9 10 **920**

1. Egypt -- Biography 2. Egypt -- Civilization
ISBN 0-19-512221-6

LC 2001-21209

"Divided into five periods from the Old Kingdom, about 2686 B.C., to the declining New Kingdom, about 245 B.C., this book profiles some 30 Egyptian leaders, devoting a three- to seven-page chapter to each one. . . . The entries are well written and researched. . . . A useful addition for report writers and subject enthusiasts." SLJ

Includes glossary and bibliographical references

Bausum, Ann

Our country's first ladies; [by] Ann Bausum; with a foreword by First Lady Laura Bush. National Geographic 2007 127p il $19.95; lib bdg $28.90

Grades: 5 6 7 8 **920**

1. Presidents' spouses -- United States
ISBN 978-1-4263-0006-6; 978-1-4263-0007-3 lib bdg

LC 2006021284

"A well-researched, thoughtfully written, attractive account. Fact boxes provide basic information such as birth and death dates, marriage dates, and children's names; a 'Did You Know' section shares interesting personal tidbits. Periodic time lines help to place the women's lives within the broader events of history. There is enough information here for simple reports. Interesting facts and anecdotes will hold readers' attention. . . . An excellent layout and clear, colorful photographs and reproductions will further entice readers." SLJ

Includes bibliographical references

Beccia, Carlyn

They lost their heads! what happened to Washington's teeth, Einstein's brain, and other famous body parts. by Carlyn Beccia. Bloomsbury 2018 192 p. (hardcover) $18.99

Grades: 5 6 7 8 **920**

1. Human body 2. Celebrities -- Anecdotes 3. Human body -- Anecdotes
ISBN 0802737455; 9780802737458

LC 2017024255

In this book, author Carlyn Beccia "explores the misadventures of noteworthy body parts through history and springboards to exploring STEM topics such as forensics, DNA testing, brain science, organ donation, and cloning. The engaging tone, wonderfully creepy subject matter, and delightfully detailed art are sure to capture even the most reluctant readers." (Publisher's note)

Benjamin, Michelle

Nobel's women of peace; by Michelle Benjamin and Maggie Mooney. Second Story Press 2008 146p il (Women's Hall of fame) pa $10.95

Grades: 6 7 8 9 **920**

1. Nobel Prizes 2. Women -- Biography
ISBN 978-1-897187-38-8; 1-897187-38-6 pa

Profiles the twelve female recipients of the Nobel Peace Prize since its creation, including how they became activists for peace and their accomplishments before and after winning the prestigious award.

"Substantive enough to support basic reports, the profiles include many women who are rarely featured in books for youth. . . . The international stories of individuals dedicating their lives to humanitarian efforts will inspire young activists, who will want to move on to the extensive list of appended resources." Booklist

Includes bibliographical references

Benson, Sonia

Korean War: biographies; [by] Sonia G. Benson; Gerda-Ann Raffaelle, editor. U.X.L 2002 xxx, 268p il pa $60

Grades: 7 8 9 10 **920**

1. Korean War, 1950-1953 -- Biography
ISBN 0-7876-5692-5

LC 2001-44241

Presents biographies of twenty-six men and women who participated in or were affected by the Korean War, including politicians, military leaders, journalists, and nurses

"An excellent starting point for researching the . . . people of the Korean War." Booklist

Includes bibliographical references

Bolden, Tonya

★ **Pathfinders**; The Journeys of 16 Extraordinary Black Souls. Tonya Bolden. Abrams Books for Young Readers 2017 124 p. $24.95; (ebook) $18.65

Grades: 5 6 7 8 **920**

1. African Americans -- Biography 2. Successful people -- United States -- Biography
ISBN 9781419714559; 9781613129739

LC 2015043356

This book, by Tonya Bolden, "is a collective biography of sixteen diverse American men and women of African descent who made their mark on American history in the 18th to 20th centuries. . . . Bolden offers an insightful look at these figures, from Venture Smith, who bought his freedom; to Sadie Alexander, who contributed to the Civil Rights movement in the United States; to Katherine Johnson, who helped the United States land on the moon." (Publisher's note)

"A well-researched book introducing a varied group of African Americans who excelled in their own, individual ways." Booklist

Includes bibliographical references and index

Portraits of African-American heroes; paintings by Ansel Pitcairn. Dutton Children's Books 2003 88p il $18.99; pa $11.99

Grades: 4 5 6 7 **920**

1. African Americans -- Biography

ISBN 0-525-47043-3; 0-14-240473-X pa

LC 2002-75911

"Each profile lists expected biographical information, but offers even more by way of keen insights into a subject's personality based on interviews and information drawn from personal memoirs. . . . Pitcairn's beautifully rendered sepia-toned portraits make each subject jump from the page, beckoning children to come ever closer and learn." Booklist

Bragg, Georgia

How they choked; failures, flops, and flaws of the awfully famous. by Georgia Bragg ; illustrated by Kevin O'Malley. Bloomsbury/Walker 2014 208 p. (pbk.) $18.89

Grades: 5 6 7 8 **920**

1. Inventions 2. Celebrities 3. Decision making 4. Celebrities -- Conduct of life 5. History -- Errors, inventions, etc.

ISBN 0802734898; 9780802734884; 9780802734891

LC 2013039127

This book, by Georgia Bragg, "knocks fourteen famous achievers off their pedestals to reveal the human side of history. Successful 'failures' include: Marco Polo, Queen Isabella of Spain, Montezuma II, Ferdinand Magellan, Anne Boleyn, Isaac Newton, Benedict Arnold, Susan B. Anthony, George Armstrong Custer, Thomas Alva Edison, Vincent Van Gogh, J. Bruce Ismay, 'Shoeless Joe' Jackson, [and] Amelia M. Earhart." (Publisher's note)

"On the heels of How They Croaked: The Awful Ends of the Awfully Famous (2011), Bragg seeks to reconcile what she sees as a major flaw of the biography genre—that authors ignore the human potential for error. Her compendium is unapologetically full of bad news, criticism, and belly flops...The snarkily entertaining narratives are illustrated with caricatures of each subject. For better or worse, subjects are rarely as one-dimensional as most biographies paint them, and this book proves that nobody is perfect." Booklist

★ **How** they croaked; the awful ends of the awfully famous. Walker & Co. 2011 178p il $17.99; lib bdg $18.89

Grades: 5 6 7 8 **920**

1. Death 2. Biography 3. Celebrities -- Death 4. Biography, Collective

ISBN 978-0-8027-9817-6; 0-8027-9817-9; 978-0-8027-9818-3 lib bdg; 0-8027-9818-7 lib bdg

LC 2010-08659

"Bragg chronicles with ghoulish glee the chronic or fatal maladies that afflicted 19 historical figures. Nonsqueamish readers will by entranced by her riveting descriptions. . . . The author tucks quick notes on at least marginally relevant topics, such as leeching, scurvy, presidential assassins, and mummy eyes . . . between the chapters. . . . O'Malley's cartoon portraits and spot art add just the right notes of humor to keep the contents from becoming too gross." Booklist

Butts, Edward

She dared; true stories of heroines, scoundrels, and renegades. [by] Ed Butts; illustrated by Heather Collins. Tundra Bks. 2005 121p il pa $8.95

Grades: 6 7 8 9 10 **920**

1. Women -- Biography 2. Canada -- Biography

ISBN 0-88776-718-4

This "details the lives of some of Canada's most famous and infamous women. The stories showcase explorers, spies, criminals, and pioneers in a variety of career fields. Organized chronologically from the 16th to the mid-20th century, this 12-chapter offering is historically sound and well researched." SLJ

Castro, Ivan A.

★ **100** hispanics you should know. Libraries Unlimited 2007 303p bibl il $55

Grades: 6 7 8 9 **920**

1. Hispanic Americans -- Biography

ISBN 1-59158-327-6

"This eye-opening and valuable reference is one of the few biographical compilations for young people that address the achievements of Spanish-speaking individuals across the world and throughout history, especially in the sciences, arts, politics, and military. The alphabetically arranged entries begin with key information about the individuals, such as birthplaces, birth and death dates, career highlights, and b&w portraits; then continue with important contributions; and end with bibliographies." Libr Media Connect

Chemistry, Earth, and space sciences; edited by Derek Hall. Brown Bear Books 2010 64p il (Facts at your fingertips) lib bdg $35.65

Grades: 8 9 10 11 **920**

1. Chemists 2. Scientists 3. Astronomers 4. Space sciences 5. Science -- History 6. Chemistry -- History

ISBN 978-1-933834-47-4 lib bdg; 1-933834-47-1 lib bdg

LC 2009-13342

Profiles the lives and work of nine scientists and chemists who have made significant contributions to modern science, including Nicolaus Copernicus, Antoine Lavoisier, Dmitri Mendeleev, and Stephen Hawking

This provides "explanations about important discoveries, related work, and social and political influences that impacted the subjects' work. . . . The approximately six-to-eight page entries include important dates, photographs, diagrams, and sidebars on relevant scientists. The writing is often highly technical and some knowledge of the basics is assumed." SLJ

Includes glossary and bibliographical references

Chin-Lee, Cynthia

★ **Amelia** to Zora; twenty-six women who changed the world. illustrated by Megan Halsey and Sean Addy. Charlesbridge 2005 32p il $15.95

Grades: 4 5 6 7 **920**

1. Women -- Biography

ISBN 1-57091-522-9

"The illustrations are done in a remarkable mix of media. . . . The text portions are short . . . but they are enticing. By choosing her subjects from every culture, the author introduces children to the scope of the struggles and achievements of women from many times and many places." Booklist

Colson, Mary

Albert Einstein and Sir Arthur Eddington; Mary Colson. Gareth Stevens Publishing 2014 48 p. illustrations (some color) (Dynamic Duos of Science) $31.95

Grades: 4 5 6 **920**

1. Scientists 2. Physicists

ISBN 1482414708; 9781482414707

This book by Mary Colson focuses on scientists Albert Einstein and Arthur Eddington and is part of a series known for "graphics and [the] ability to make complex concepts accessible. The authors have [selected] key quotes from the scientists' writings that young readers can understand (provided in sidebars titled 'In Their Own Words')." (School Library Journal)

D'Agnese, Joseph

Signing their rights away; the fame and misfortune of the men who signed the United States Constitution. by Denise Kiernan & Joseph D'Agnese. Quirk Books 2011 254p il $19.95
Grades: 8 9 10 11 12 Adult **920**

1. Statesmen -- United States 2. Presidents -- United States 3. United States -- Constitution 4. United States -- History -- 1775-1783, Revolution -- Biography 5. United States -- Politics and government -- 1775-1783, Revolution

ISBN 978-1-59474-520-1

Presents the lives, deaths, and scandals involving the thirty-nine signers of the United States Constitution, including Benjamin Franklin, Alexander Hamilton, and James McHenry.

"For readers of American history, this is both educational and entertaining." Booklist

Includes bibliographical references

Davis, Kenneth C.

In the Shadow of Liberty; the hidden history of slavery, four presidents, and five black lives. Kenneth C. Davis. Henry Holt & Co. 2016 304 p. $17.99
Grades: 6 7 8 9 10 **920**

1. Slavery -- United States 2. Presidents -- United States 3. United States -- Race relations -- History 4. African Americans -- Biography 5. Slaves -- United States -- Biography 6. Presidents -- Relations with African Americans -- History

ISBN 1627793119; 9781627793117

LC 2015035204

YALSA Award for Excellence in Nonfiction for Young Adults: Finalist (2017)

This book, by Kenneth C. Davis, shares "the stories of five enslaved people who witnessed the birth of America: Billy Lee, valet to George Washington; Ona Judge, who escaped from Martha Washington; Isaac Granger, servant of Thomas Jefferson; Paul Jennings, who witnessed the War of 1812 in James Madison's White House; and Alfred Jackson, 'owned' by Andrew Jackson." (Publisher's note)

"This well-researched book offers a chronological history of slavery in America and features five enslaved people and the four U.S. presidents who owned them. . . . Always referring to enslaved people rather than slaves, Davis organizes a great deal of factual material, personal accounts, and quotes into a very readable history book." Booklist

Includes bibliographical references and index

Drucker, Malka

Portraits of Jewish American heroes; by Malka Drucker; illustrated by Elizabeth Rosen. Dutton Children's Books 2008 96p il $22.99
Grades: 4 5 6 **920**

1. Jews -- United States -- Biography

ISBN 978-0-525-47771-6; 0-525-47771-3

LC 2007-028481

"From Albert Einstein and Bella Abzug to Ruth Bader Ginsburg, Hank Greenberg, and Steven Spielberg, this invitingly illustrated collective biography celebrates 20 Jewish American heroes in all their diversity. . . . The nicely designed volume includes full-page portraits of the subjects in various media. . . . Drucker's eloquent, chatty style opens up big issues about Judaism as a source of idealism and for a just, compassionate society." Booklist

Includes bibliographical references

Dublin, Anne

Dynamic women dancers. Second Story Press 2009 128p il (The women's hall of fame) pa $10.95
Grades: 6 7 8 9 **920**

1. Dancers

ISBN 978-1-897187-56-2 pa; 1-897187-56-4 pa

"Profiles ten dancers, each from different countries and backgrounds. Most of the dancers performed ballet or modern dance, but a flamenco dancer and a South Indian classical dancer are also included. Entries are brief, detailing their backgrounds, studies, and the challenges each woman faced. . . . Black-and-white pictures help break up the text, and a few inset boxes offer supplemental quotes or information. . . . Present[s] information well, and the lives profiled are both interesting and inspirational." Voice Youth Advocates

Includes glossary and bibliographical references

Edwards, Sue Bradford

Hidden human computers; the black women of NASA. by Sue Bradford Edwards and Duchess Harris and Duchess Harris, JDm PHD. Essential Library 2016 112 p. illustrations, portraits (Hidden heroes) (library binding) $35.64
Grades: 7 8 9 10 11 12 **920**

1. African American women 2. United States. National Aeronautics and Space Administration 3. African American mathematicians -- Biography 4. Women mathematicians -- United States -- Biography

ISBN 1680783874; 9781680783872

LC 2016910293

This book, by Sue Bradford Edwards, "discusses how in the 1950s, black women made critical contributions to NASA by performing calculations that made it possible for the nation's astronauts to fly into space and return safely to Earth. Aligned to Common Core Standards and correlated to state standards." (Publisher's note)

"An essential purchase for STEM collections." Booklist

Includes bibliographical references (pages 106-109) and index.

Fradin, Dennis B.

The **founders**; the 39 stories behind the U.S. Constitution. [by] Dennis Brindell Fradin; illustrated by Michael McCurdy. Walker & Co. 2005 162p il map $22.95; lib bdg $23.95
Grades: 4 5 6 7 **920**

1. Statesmen -- United States 2. United States -- Constitution 3. United States -- Politics and government -- 1783-1809

ISBN 0-8027-8972-2; 0-8027-8973-0 lib bdg

"The makers of the U.S. Constitution are profiled in two or three pages each, in sections introduced by a brief note about their home states. McCurdy's black-and-white scratchboard illustrations are properly stately and engaging. Readers will find great nuggets of fact." Booklist

Includes bibliographical references

★ **Funny** business; conversations with writers of comedy. compiled and edited by Leonard S. Marcus. Candlewick Press 2009 214p il $21.99
Grades: 5 6 7 8 9 10 **920**

1. Authors 2. Authorship 3. Wit and humor

ISBN 978-0-7636-3254-0; 0-7636-3254-6

This book comprises interviews with writers of humorous books for young people: Judy Blume, Beverly Cleary, Sharon Creech, Christopher Paul Curtis, Anne Fine, Daniel Handler, Carl Hiaasen, Norton Juster, Dick King-Smith, Hilary McKay, Daniel Pinkwater, Louis Sachar, and Jon Scieszka. Index. "Intermediate, middle school." (Horn Book)

"In 12 entertaining interviews . . . Marcus's compilation explores the childhoods, writing processes and senses of humor of well-known writers for children, including Judy Blume, Beverly Cleary, Daniel Handler, Norton Juster and Jon Scieszka. Marcus's evident knowledge of his subjects' writing makes for some intriguing questions and answers. . . . Photographs, manuscript pages and even e-mail chains between the writers and their editors add fascinating tidbits." Publ Wkly

Goldstone, Lawrence

Higher, steeper, faster; The daredevils who conquered the skies. Lawrence Goldstone. Little, Brown & Co. 2017 243 p. (hardcover) $18.99

Grades: 4 5 6 7 **920**

1. Aeronautics -- History 2. Air pilots -- Biography 3. Flight -- History 4. Air pilots -- History 5. Daredevils -- History 6. Air pilots -- Biography

ISBN 9780316350235

LC 2016016576

This book, by Lawrence Goldstone, "takes readers inside the world of the brave men and women who popularized flying through their deadly stunts and paved the way for modern aviation. With heart-stopping accounts of the action-packed race to conquer the skies, plus photographs and fascinating archival documents, this book will exhilarate readers as they fly through the pages." (Publisher's note)

Includes bibliographical references (pages 231-234) and index

Gourse, Leslie

Sophisticated ladies; the great women of jazz. illustrated by Martin French. Dutton Children's Books/Penguin Young Readers Group 2007 64p il $19.99

Grades: 7 8 9 10 11 12 **920**

1. Singers 2. Jazz music 3. Women -- Biography

ISBN 978-0-525-47198-1; 0-525-47198-7

LC 2006-14852

"This lively collective biography of 14 singers begins in the 1920s with Bessie Smith and Ethel Waters and moves on through current performers Cassandra Wilson and Diana Krall. A vibrant, full-page portrait opens each chapter, depicting the performer with bold vitality, in a style suggestive of a theater poster." SLJ

Includes discography and bibliographical references

Haskins, James

African American religious leaders; [by] Jim Haskins and Kathleen Benson. Wiley 2008 162p il (Black stars) lib bdg $24.95

Grades: 6 7 8 9 10 11 12 Adult **920**

1. African Americans -- Religion 2. African Americans -- Biography

ISBN 978-0-471-73632-5; 0-471-73632-5

LC 2007-27347

"It's great to have all these figures between two covers, and even a sampling of the entries captures the importance of religion, and its leaders, in African American life." Booklist

Includes bibliographical references

Heiligman, Deborah

★ **Vincent** and Theo; the Van Gogh brothers. Deborah Heiligman. Henry Holt 2017 454 p. illustrations (some color) $19.99

Grades: 7 8 9 **920**

1. Brothers 2. Painters -- Biography

ISBN 9780805093391

LC 2016009017

YALSA Award for Excellence in Nonfiction for Young Adults (2018)

Printz Honor Book (2018)

"A meticulously researched account of the relationship between brothers Theo and Vincent van Gogh draws on hundreds of letters written by the master artist that illuminate how Theo supported Vincent throughout the latter's creative and interpersonal struggles." (Publisher's note)

"In fittingly painterly language, Heiligman offers vivid descriptions of Vincent's artwork and life, which grow more detailed and colorful as Vincent's own artistic style becomes richer and more refined, particularly during the intense, almost manic flurry of work he produced in his last few years. This illuminating glimpse into the Van Goghs' turbulent lives and historical period will add compelling depth to readers' understanding of the iconic painter." Booklist

Heine, Florian

13 architects children should know; by Florian Heine ; translation by Paul Kelly. Prestel 2014 45 p. chiefly color illustrations (13... children should know) $14.95

Grades: 4 5 6 **920**

1. Architects 2. Architecture

ISBN 3791371843; 9783791371849

This book, by Florian Heine, "opens a door into the fascinating world of architecture. Buildings of every shape and size, and from all corners of the world, populate this colorful and beautifully produced book that introduces children to history's most iconic architectural feats and the people behind them." (Publisher's note)

Henderson, Harry

Larry Page and Sergey Brin; information at your fingertips. author, Harry Henderson. Chelsea House 2012 134 p. (Trailblazers in science and technology) (library) $35

Grades: 7 8 9 10 11 12 **920**

1. Google 2. Google (Firm) 3. Web search engines 4. Webmasters -- United States -- Biography 5. Businesspeople -- United States -- Biography 6. Computer programmers -- United States -- Biography 7. Internet programming -- United States -- Biography 8. Telecommunications engineers -- United States -- Biography

ISBN 1604136766; 9781604136760

LC 2011032584

This book, by Harry Henderson, is a biography of the founders of the Internet company Google Inc. as part of the "Trailblazers in Science and Technology" series. "When . . . Larry Page and Sergey Brin collaborated on the search engine Google, they didn't realize that their invention would soon become so ingrained in Web culture that its name would be used as a verb." (Publisher's note)

Includes bibliographical references and index

Herrera, Juan Felipe, 1948-

★ **Portraits** of Hispanic American heroes; by Juan Felipe Herrera ; pictures by Raul Colon. Dial Books for Young Readers 2014 96 p. color illustrations (hardback) $19.99

Grades: 4 5 6 7 8 **920**

1. Biography 2. Latinos (U.S.)

ISBN 0803738099; 9780803738096

LC 2013044661

Pura Belpré (Author) Honor Book (2015)

This book by Juan Felipe Herrera "showcases twenty Hispanic and Latino American men and women who have made outstanding contributions to the arts, politics, science, humanitarianism, and athletics.

Biographies of Cesar Chavez, Sonia Sotomayor, Ellen Ochoa, Roberto Clemente, and many more [are included]." (Publisher's note)

"Herrera packs relevant info and kid-appropriate details . . . without overwhelming the work, infusing the narratives with engaging text. Colon's portraits are luminous." SLJ

Includes bibliographical references

Hodgkins, Fran

Champions of the ocean; illustrations by Cris Arbo. Dawn Publications 2009 144p il (Earth heroes) pa $11.95

Grades: 5 6 7 8 **920**

1. Scientists 2. Oceanography 3. Environmentalists

ISBN 978-1-58469-119-8 pa; 1-58469-119-0 pa

LC 2009-17926

This is a collective biography of oceanographers William Beebe, Archie Carr, Jacques-Yves Cousteau, Margaret Wentworth Owings, Eugenie Clark, Roger Payne, Sylvia Earle, and Tierney Thys.

This is illustrated with "black-and-white photographs and illustrations. [The book] provides young readers with fascinating facts and insights. . . . This volume is an excellent introduction to the biography genre, as well as a terrific research book." Sci Books Films

Includes bibliographical references

Hoose, Phillip M., 1947-

★ **Attucks!** Oscar Robertson and the basketball team that awakened a city. Phillip Hoose. Farrar, Straus & Giroux Books for Young Readers 2018 224 p. (hardcover) $19.99

Grades: 7 8 9 10 11 12 **920**

1. Biography 2. Basketball players -- United States -- Biography 3. Crispus Attucks Tigers (Basketball team) -- History

ISBN 9780374306120

LC 2018002809

This book, by Phillip Hoose, presents "the true story of the all-black high school basketball team that broke the color barrier in segregated 1950s Indiana. . . . Anchored by . . . Oscar Robertson, a future college and NBA star, the Crispus Attucks Tigers went down in history as the first state champions from Indianapolis and the first all-black team in U.S. history to win a racially open championship tournament--an integration they had forced with their on-court prowess." (Publisher's note)

"Acclaimed author Hoose (The Boys Who Challenged Hitler, 2015, etc.) returns to his home state with the true story of the all-black high school basketball team that broke the color barrier in segregated 1950s Indianapolis, anchored by one of the greatest players of all time." (Kirkus Reviews)

Includes bibliographical references and index

Ignotofsky, Rachel

Women in sports; 50 fearless athletes who played to win. Rachel Ignotofsky. Ten Speed Press 2017 128 p. color illustrations (hardback) $16.99

Grades: 4 5 6 7 8 **920**

1. Biography 2. Sports for women 3. Women athletes -- Biography 4. Women athletes -- History 5. Women Olympic athletes -- History 6. Women Olympic athletes -- Biography

ISBN 9781607749783

LC 2016055531

Amelia Bloomer Lists: Middle Graders Nonfiction (2018)

This book, by Rachel Ignotofsky, "highlights the achievements and stories of fifty notable women athletes from the 1800s to today. . . . [They] include well-known figures like tennis player Billie Jean King and gymnast Simone Biles. . . . The book also contains infographics on topics that sporty women want to know about such as muscle anatomy, a timeline of women's participation in sports, pay and media statistics for female athletes, and influential women's teams." (Publisher's note)

"The writing is accessible to a wide range of readers, and the material is concise and orderly, often leaving readers wanting more. Fortunately, a thorough bibliography is appended, making it easy to dive deeper into the lives of some of these fascinating trailblazers." SLJ

Includes bibliographical references and index

Jokulsson, Illugi

Stars of all time; Illugi Jökulsson. Abbeville Press Publishers 2017 64 p. (hardcover) $13.95

Grades: 5 6 7 8 **920**

1. Soccer 2. Soccer players 3. Soccer -- History 4. Soccer players -- Biography

ISBN 9780789212955

LC 2017020776

This book in the World Soccer Legends series, by Illugi Jökulsson, "highlights both iconic pioneers of world soccer, including Pelé, Johan Cruyff, and Maradona, and more recent all-star players, such as Messi and Ronaldo. Young readers will learn about where each player grew up, how he made it to the top, and what makes his playing style unique." (Publisher's note)

"The worldwide scope of the players represented is impressive, and it also gives a sense of world history, as in the entry on Mozambique's Eusébio, who played for then-imperial overlord Portugal. Joyful, enthusiastic, well-versed, and uplifting." (Kirkus)

Kane, Joseph Nathan

★ **Facts** about the presidents; a compilation of biographical and historical information. Joseph Nathan Kane, Janet Podell [editors] 8th ed; Wilson, H.W. 2009 720p $150

Grades: 8 9 10 11 12 Adult **920**

1. Reference books 2. Presidents -- United States

ISBN 9780824210878

LC 2008056016

First published 1959

The main part of this work provides an individual chapter on each President, from Washington through Barack Obama, presenting such information as family, education, election, Vice President, main events and accomplishments of his administration, and First Lady. Part two contains tables and lists presenting comparative data on all the Presidents

Kennedy, John F.

Profiles in courage. HarperCollins Pubs. 2003 xxii, 245p $19.95; pa $13.95

Grades: 7 8 9 10 11 12 Adult **920**

1. Judges 2. Courage 3. Lawyers 4. Governors 5. Statesmen 6. Presidents 7. Senators 8. Army officers 9. Political leaders 10. State legislators 11. Members of Congress 12. Newspaper executives 13. Secretaries of state 14. Territorial governors 15. Supreme Court justices 16. Presidential candidates 17. Secretaries of the interior 18. Politicians -- United States

ISBN 0-06-053062-6; 0-06-085493-6 pa

LC 2003-40676

A reissue of the title first published 1956

This series of profiles of Americans who took courageous stands at crucial moments in public life includes John Quincy Adams, Daniel Webster, Thomas Hart Benton, Sam Houston, Edmund G. Ross, Lucius Q. C. Lamar, George Norris, Robert A. Taft and others.

Includes bibliographical references

Kiernan, Denise

★ **Signing** our lives away; the fame and misfortune of the men who signed the Declaration of Independence. by Denise Kiernan & Joseph D'Agnese. Quirk 2009 255p $19.95

Grades: 5 6 7 8 **920**

1. Statesmen -- United States 2. United States -- Declaration of Independence 3. United States -- Politics and government -- 1775-1783, Revolution

ISBN 978-1-59474-330-6; 1-59474-330-4

"Kiernan and D'Agnese present readers with astonishing individual portraits of all the signers [of the Declaration of Independence] in an attempt both to dispel some of the mythology surrounding the document as well as to establish a place in the historical discourse for those men not named Jefferson, Hancock, Franklin, or Adams. The marvelously arranged work lends itself to either straightforward reading or skipping around. . . . An entertaining and effective narrative of about three to five pages per individual is presented." SLJ

Includes bibliographical references

Killam, G. D.

Student encyclopedia of African literature; [by] Douglas Killam and Alicia L. Kerfoot. Greenwood Press 2008 xxiii, 339p $85

Grades: 8 9 10 11 12 **920**

1. Reference books 2. African literature -- Encyclopedias

ISBN 978-0-313-33580-8; 0-313-33580-X

LC 2007-35356

"This alphabetically arranged volume provides brief information about authors, individual works, and issues related to the literature of the African continent, and a few themed articles that cover the literature of its diaspora. The articles are concise, if academic, and the coverage reasonably comprehensive." SLJ

Kimmel, Elizabeth Cody

Ladies first; 40 daring American women who were second to none. [by] Elizabeth Cody Kimmel; foreword by Stacy Allison. National Geographic 2006 192p il $18.95

Grades: 5 6 7 8 **920**

1. Women -- Biography 2. United States -- Biography

ISBN 0-7922-5393-0

LC 2005005113

This offers "introductions to forty of America's most brilliant and courageous women. Each essay is three pages in length and includes a fourth full-page portrait of the woman being introduced. . . . The women chosen achieved greatness in a wide range of endeavors, from athletics to the arts to politics. . . . Students will find these excellent essays useful as an introduction to the women portrayed and as a good jumping off point for further research." Voice Youth Advocates

Includes bibliographical references

Krull, Kathleen

Lives of the explorers; discoveries, disasters (and what the neighbors thought) Kathleen Krull ; illustrated by Kathryn Hewitt. HMH Books for Young Readers 2014 96 p. col. ill., col. maps (hardback) $20.99

Grades: 4 5 6 7 **920**

1. Explorers 2. Exploration 3. United States -- Exploration 4. Discoveries in geography 5. Adventure and adventurers

ISBN 0152059105; 9780152059101

LC 2013037697

"Krull introduces middle-grade readers to a diverse cast of 17 explorers in this latest offering from her series. A short, two-to five page chapter is devoted to each explorer, incorporating a biographical sketch and a short discussion of the explorer's contributions. The subjects are presented chronologically, beginning in the medieval period with the Norseman Leif Ericson and finishing with the astronaut Sally Ride." (School Library Journal)

"The straightforward, accessible prose makes for fast reading, and Krull doesn't shy away from some deplorable, stomach-turning facts, which kids will devour and use to spice up staid homework assignments." Kirkus

Includes bibliographical references

Lives of the presidents; fame, shame (and what the neighbors thought) written by Kathleen Krull; illustrated by Kathryn Hewitt. updated ed.; Harcourt Children's Books 2011 104p il $21

Grades: 4 5 6 7 **920**

1. Presidents -- United States

ISBN 978-0-547-49809-6; 0-547-49809-8

First published 1998

"This new edition is sure to be even more popular than the original title (Harcourt, 1998) as it includes Presidents George W. Bush and Barack Obama, who are given the same cheeky-but-respectful treatment as their predecessors. . . . [Krull] provides further information on ex-Presidential activity since 1998, such as Jimmy Carter's Nobel Prize, Ronald Reagan's passing, and the Clintons' post-White House work. All other entries and art are virtually unaltered. Guaranteed to inject some levity into the ubiquitous presidential biography assignment, the 2011 Lives of the Presidents is a must-have for elementary schools and public libraries." SLJ

Includes bibliographical references

Langley, Wanda

Women of the wind; early women aviators. [by] Wanda Langley. Morgan Reynolds Pub. 2006 160p il map lib bdg $26.95

Grades: 6 7 8 9 **920**

1. Women air pilots

ISBN 978-1-931798-81-5; 1-931798-81-8

LC 2005022951

"This collective biography celebrates the accomplishments of nine American women who pioneered in the field of aviation: Harriet Quimby, Katherine Stinson, Ruth Law, Bessie Coleman, Amelia Earhart, Ruth Nichols, Louise Thaden, Anne Morrow Lindbergh, and Jacqueline Cochran. . . . Well reproduced and often in color, the illustrations include a great many photos, as well as maps and period advertisements. . . . Langley . . . offers information, anecdotes, and inspiring stories." Booklist

Includes bibliographical references

Lawlor, Laurie

★ **Super** women; six scientists who changed the world. by Laurie Lawlor. Holiday House 2017 48 p. illustrations, portraits (hardcover) $17.95

Grades: 7 8 9 10 **920**

1. Women scientists -- Biography 2. Scientists -- Biography

ISBN 9780823436750

LC 2016027036

This book, by Laurie Lawlor, "celebrates the scientific as well as the social significance of six incredible women who broke new ground with their research, busted through glass ceilings with their careers, and advanced humanity's understanding of our world in the process. These amazing women defied prejudice to succeed in the sciences using genius, ambition, and perseverance." (Publisher's note)

"This compilation of short biographies of six pioneering women scientists is a welcome and fascinating addition to STEM resources." SLJ

Lawrence, Sandra

Anthology of amazing women; trailblazers who dared to be different. written by Sandra Lawrence ; illustrated by Nathan Collins. Little Bee Books 2018 128 p. color illustrations $17.99

Grades: 4 5 6 7 **920**

1. Biography 2. Women -- History 3. Women -- Biography

ISBN 1499806906; 9781499806908

This book, by Sandra Lawrence, illustrated by Nathan Collins, "tells the awe-inspiring stories of 50 women who have pushed the boundaries of human excellence and endeavor. Featuring familiar icons like Elizabeth I and Malala Yousafzai, and introducing hidden figures like Chien-Shiung Wu and Aud the Deep-Minded, kids will be fascinated reading about these women's achievements in science, sports, the arts, politics, and history." (Publisher's note)

"Lawrence has selected individuals who have left indelible marks upon history. Featured trailblazers include Beyoncé, Georgia O'Keeffe, and Mary Jackson. Lawrence also highlights many other women who aren't typically covered in history texts for this audience." SLJ

Life sciences; edited by Derek Hall. Brown Bear Books 2010 64p il (Facts at your fingertips) lib bdg $35.65

Grades: 8 9 10 11 **920**

1. Scientists 2. Life sciences

ISBN 978-1-933834-45-0 lib bdg; 1-933834-45-5 lib bdg

LC 2009-13343

Profiles the lives and work of famous life scientists, including Charles Darwin, Louis Pasteur, and Alexander Fleming

This provides "explanations about important discoveries, related work, and social and political influences that impacted the subjects' work. . . . The approximately six-to-eight page entries include important dates, photographs, diagrams, and sidebars on relevant scientists. The writing is often highly technical and some knowledge of the basics is assumed." SLJ

Includes glossary and bibliographical references

Malnor, Bruce

Champions of the wilderness; by Bruce and Carol L. Malnor; illustrated by Anisa Claire Hovemann. Dawn Publications 2009 143p il (Earth heroes) pa $11.95

Grades: 5 6 7 8 **920**

1. Environmentalists

ISBN 978-1-58469-116-7 pa; 1-58469-116-6 pa

LC 2008-53670

"This is a short gem of a book that includes short biographies of eight 'heroes' who have championed the preservation and/or conservation of wilderness areas around the world over the past two centuries. Henry David Thoreau, John Muir, Teddy Roosevelt, Aldo Leopold, Richard St. Barbe Baker, Mardy Murie, David Suzuki, and Wangari Maathai are the heroes in question. The storytelling is fluent and engaging." Sci Books Films

Includes bibliographical references

Malnor, Carol

Champions of wild animals; by Carol L. and Bruce Malnor; illustrations by Anisa Claire Hovemann. Dawn Publications 2010 144p il (Earth heroes) pa $11.95

Grades: 5 6 7 8 **920**

1. Naturalists 2. Endangered species 3. Wildlife conservation

ISBN 978-1-58469-123-5 pa; 1-58469-123-9 pa

LC 2010-16030

This describes "the youth and careers of eight of the world's greatest environmentalists who championed the protection of wildlife, including William Hornaday (saved the bison from extinction), Ding Darling (A Duck's Best Friend), Rachel Carson (author of Silent Spring), Roger Tory Peterson (Inventor of the Modern Field Guide), R.D. Lawrence (Storyteller for Wolves), E.O. Wilson (Lord of the Ants), Jane Goodall (Champion for Chimps), and Ian and Saba Douglas-Hamilton (Saving the Elephants)." Publisher's note

Includes bibliographical references

Mattern, Joanne

Mystics and psychics. Morgan Reynolds Pub. 2011 128p il (World religions and beliefs) $28.95

Grades: 6 7 8 9 **920**

1. Mysticism 2. Extrasensory perception

ISBN 978-1-59935-148-3; 1-59935-148-X

LC 2010008690

"Mattern offers an evenhanded look at some of the most famous (and controversial) of those with otherworldly powers. The mystics are Hildegard of Bingen, a twelfth-century German anchoress, and Padre Pio, and Italian monk who died in 1968. . . . Others profiled include Nostradamus; Edgar Cayce . . . ; Jeanne Dixon . . . ; and Peter Hurkos. . . . The profiles are interspersed with comments from skeptics and other reasons for visions. . . . Good illustrations and excellent back matter extend the well-written text." Booklist

Includes bibliographical references

Maydell, Natalie

★ **Extraordinary** women from the Muslim world. Global Content Publishing 2008 117p il map $16.95

Grades: 5 6 7 8 **920**

1. Muslim women 2. Women -- Biography

ISBN 978-0-97999-010-6; 0-97999-010-6

This "is an illustrative introduction to 13 Muslim women in history who have lived extraordinary lives and influenced their communities in a positive way, often overcoming extreme hardship and inaccurate stereotypes that have been placed on the role of women in Islam." Publisher's note

McCann, Michelle Roehm

Girls who rocked the world; heroines from Sacagawea to Natalie Portman. Michelle Roehm McCann and Amelie Welden. Simon & Schuster 2012 p. cm. (hardcover : alk. paper) $18.99

Grades: 5 6 7 8 **920**

1. Feminism 2. Women -- History 3. Women -- Biography 4. Girls -- Biography 5. Heros -- Biography 6. Women heros -- Biography

ISBN 9781582703022; 9781582703619

LC 2011050502

Author Michelle Roehm McCann presents "examples of strong, independent female role models, all of whom first impacted the world as teenagers or younger." The book "spans a variety of achievements, interests, and backgrounds, from Harriet Tubman and Coco Chanel to

S.E. Hinton and Maya Lin--each with her own incredible story of how she created life-changing opportunities for herself and the world." (Publisher's note)

Includes bibliographical references and index.

More girls who rocked the world; heroines from Ada Lovelace to Misty Copeland. Michelle Roehm McCann ; illustrated by David Hahn. Aladdin/Beyond Words 2017 ix, 309 p.p illustrations (hardback) $21.99

Grades: 5 6 7 8 **920**

1. Women -- Biography 2. Heroes and heroines 3. Girls -- Biography 4. Heroes -- Biography 5. Women heroes -- Biography

ISBN 9781481496889; 9781582706405; 9781582706412

LC 2017006516

Sequel to: Girls Who Rocked the World (2012)

This book, by Michelle Roehm McCann, illustrated by David Hahn, "offers a fun and uplifting collection of influential stories with forty-five more movers and shakers who made a difference before turning twenty. From Annie Oakley and Queen Victoria to Malala Yousafzai and Adele--each with her own incredible story of how she created life-changing opportunities for herself and the world--you'll get to know these capable queens of empires and courageous icons of entertainment." (Publisher's note)

"A diverse compendium that will entertain, inform, and inspire." Kirkus

Includes bibliographical references (pages 271-309).

Nathan, Amy

Meet the dancers; from ballet, broadway, and beyond. Henry Holt 2008 231p il $18.95

Grades: 5 6 7 8 **920**

1. Dance 2. Dancers

ISBN 978-0-8050-8071-1; 0-8050-8071-6

LC 2007-27589

"This collective biography reveals the paths that 16 diverse dancers followed to become professionals and to join prestigious companies. . . . The tone of the text is conversational. . . . The pictures dramatically capture how talented these performers are. Anyone, whether considering a career in dance or not, will be inspired and educated by these up-close-and-personal accounts." SLJ

Noyce, Pendred E.

Remarkable Minds; Seventeen More Pioneering Women in Science and Medicine. Penny Noyce. Tumblehome Learning, Inc 2015 192 p. illustrations $18.95

Grades: 6 7 8 9 10 **920**

1. Women scientists 2. Women in medicine

ISBN 0990782905; 9780990782902

LC 2015907841

This book, by Penny Noyce, "introduces the lives, sayings, and dreams of 16 women over four centuries and chronicles their contributions to mathematics, physics, chemistry, astronomy, and medicine. Some of the notable women portrayed in the book include French mathematician Marie-Sophie Germain . . . Scottish chemist Elizabeth Fulhame, . . . and Rita Levi-Montalcini, who . . . received the 1986 Nobel Prize in Physiology or Medicine for [the] discovery of nerve growth factor." (Publisher's note)

"This scholarly look at 17 remarkable, intelligent women devoted to research in science and medicine will round out science or biography collections." SLJ

Open the unusual door; true life stories of challenge, adventure, and success by black Americans. edited and with an introduction by Barbara Summers. Graphia 2005 206p pa $7.99

Grades: 7 8 9 10 **920**

1. African Americans -- Biography

ISBN 0-618-58531-1

"A wonderful cross section of excerpts from published autobiographies. The 16 stories tell of challenges met and opportunities recognized and realized. Colin Powell's recollection of his introduction to the military life at City College in New York City stands alongside Russell Simmons's retelling of the turning point in his life when, at 16 years of age, he shot at and missed a fellow drug dealer. . . . This little gem of a book should be a first purchase for public and school libraries." SLJ

Orgill, Roxane

Shout, sister, shout! the girl singers who shaped a century. Margaret K. McElderry Bks. 2001 148p il hardcover o.p. pa $12.95

Grades: 6 7 8 9 **920**

1. Actors 2. Singers 3. Popular music 4. Folk musicians 5. Jazz musicians 6. Blues musicians 7. Songwriters 8. Pop musicians 9. Children's authors 10. Women -- Biography

ISBN 0-689-81991-9; 978-1-4169-6391-2 pa; 1-4169-6391-X pa

LC 99-54374

"The lives of ten 'girl singers,' representing different genres of popular music, from vaudeville to blues to jazz to country, are arranged by decade. Profiles of Sophie Tucker, Ma Rainey, Bessie Smith, Ethel Merman, Judy Garland, Anita O'Day, Joan Baez, Bette Midler, Madonna, and Lucinda Williams are included." Voice Youth Advocates

Includes discography and bibliographical references

Ottaviani, Jim

Dignifying science; stories about women scientists. written by Jim Ottaviani and illustrated by Donna Barr . . . [et al.] 3rd ed; G.T. Labs 2009 142p il pa $16.95

Grades: 6 7 8 9 10 11 12 **920**

1. Graphic novels 2. Biographical graphic novels 3. Women scientists -- Graphic novels

ISBN 978-0-9788037-3-5; 0-9788037-3-5

First published 1999

Ottaviani provides biographical sketches of women scientists such as Lise Meitner, Rosalind Franklin, Barbara McClintock, and Hedy Lamarr (yes, the actress was also an inventor); all the stories are illustrated by women comics artists, including Lea Hernandez, Linda Medley, Anne Timmons, and others.

★ **Philosophy,** invention, and engineering; edited by Derek Hall. Brown Bear Books 2009 64p il (Facts at your fingertips) lib bdg $35.65

Grades: 8 9 10 11 12 **920**

1. Inventors 2. Inventions 3. Scientists 4. Philosophers

ISBN 978-1-93383-448-1 lib bdg; 1-93383-448-X lib bdg

LC 2009013344

"The book provides a multitude of facts—and fairly deep content—about Artistotle, James Watt, Charles Babbage and Ada Lovelace, Turing, and Jonas Salk. . . . Rich in synthesized information, this book encompasses a wealth of knowledge and gives a clear overall picture of the world at the time of each scientist's life." Booklist

Physical sciences; edited by Derek Hall. Brown Bear Books 2010 64p il (Facts at your fingertips) lib bdg $35.65
Grades: 8 9 10 11 **920**

1. Chemists 2. Physicists 3. Scientists
ISBN 978-1-933834-46-7; 1-933834-46-3

LC 2009-13345

Profiles the lives and work of people who have made significant contributions in physical sciences, including Isaac Newton, Marie and Pierre Curie, Albert Einstein and Richard Feynman.

This provides "explanations about important discoveries, related work, and social and political influences that impacted the subjects' work. . . . The approximately six-to-eight page entries include important dates, photographs, diagrams, and sidebars on relevant scientists. The writing is often highly technical and some knowledge of the basics is assumed." SLJ

Includes glossary and bibliographical references

Pinkney, Andrea Davis, 1963-

★ **Let** it shine; stories of Black women freedom fighters. illustrated by Stephen Alcorn. Harcourt 2000 107p il $20
Grades: 4 5 6 7 **920**

1. Slaves 2. Authors 3. Midwives 4. Educators 5. Journalists 6. Abolitionists 7. Philanthropists 8. Essayists 9. Memoirists 10. Political leaders 11. Nonfiction writers 12. Members of Congress 13. Newspaper executives 14. Presidential advisers 15. African American women 16. Civil rights activists 17. Organization officials 18. Political party leaders 19. Presidential candidates 20. United States -- Race relations 21. African Americans -- Civil rights 22. African American women -- Biography 23. African Americans -- Civil rights -- History 24. African American women civil rights workers -- Biography
ISBN 0-15-201005-X

LC 99-42806

This is a collection of "sketches celebrating the contributions of 10 women who moved forward the cause of civil rights in America. . . . They include Harriet Tubman, Mary McLeod Bethune and Rosa Parks, as well as Biddy Mason, Ida B. Wells-Barnett, Ella Josephine Baker, Dorothy Irene Height and Fannie Lou Hamer." (SLJ) Bibliography. "Grades three to six." (Bull Cent Child Books)

This "collective biography tells of 10 extraordinary black women. From Sojourner Truth to Shirley Chisholm, this is also a view of African American history through individual lives. . . . Stephen Alcorn's allegorical oil portraits are dramatic and beautiful. . . . The immediacy of the text and the spacious design of the large volume make this a natural for reading aloud." Booklist

Includes bibliographical references

Reef, Catherine

★ The **Bronte** sisters; the brief lives of Charlotte, Emily and Anne. by Catherine Reef. Clarion Books 2012 240 p. ill. (hardcover) $18.99
Grades: 7 8 9 10 **920**

1. Bronte family 2. Women authors -- Biography 3. Women authors, English -- Biography 4. Sisters -- England -- Yorkshire -- Biography 5. Authors, English -- 19th century -- Biography
ISBN 0547579667; 9780547579665

LC 2011043559

"This collective biography of the Brontë family fills in . . . detail of their personal and public lives: what they wrote, their family stories as a minister's unmarried daughters, how they published under men's names, and how their groundbreaking novels were received at a time when women were expected to 'stay home and be quiet.'" (Booklist)

"A solid and captivating look at these remarkable pioneers of modern fiction." Kirkus

Includes bibliographical references (p. 212-217) and index.

Frida & Diego; art, love, life. Catherine Reef. Houghton Mifflin Harcourt 2014 176 p. illustrations (some color) (hardcover) $18.99
Grades: 7 8 9 10 **920**

1. Artists -- Biography 2. Painters -- Mexico -- Biography 3. Artist couples -- Mexico -- Biography
ISBN 0547821840; 9780547821849

LC 2013021340

"Nontraditional, controversial, rebellious, and politically volatile, the Mexican artists Frida Kahlo and Diego Rivera are remembered for their provocative paintings as well as for their deep love for each other. Their marriage was one of the most tumultuous and infamous in history--filled with passion, pain, betrayal, revolution, and, above all, art that helped define the twentieth century." (Publisher's note)

"Reef points out each individual's artistic development and unique qualities as a painter. Archival photos and color reproductions of artworks further enhance the narrative. Writing a dual biography is challenging, but in this case, the portrayal of each person would seem incomplete without an understanding of the other." Booklist

Includes bibliographical references and index

Roberts, Cokie, 1943-2019

★ **Founding** mothers; remembering the ladies. by Cokie Roberts and illustrated by Diane Goode and edited by Alyson Day. HarperCollins 2014 40 p. (hardcover bdg.) $17.99
Grades: 3 4 5 6 7 **920**

1. Women -- United States -- History 2. United States -- History -- 1775-1783, Revolution
ISBN 0060780029; 9780060780029; 9780060780036

LC 2013936887

This book, by Cokie Roberts and illustrated by Diane Goode, "reveals the incredible accomplishments of the women who orchestrated the American Revolution behind the scenes. Roberts traces the stories of heroic, patriotic women such as Abigail Adams, Martha Washington, Phillis Wheatley, Mercy Otis Warren, Sarah Livingston Jay, and others. Details are gleaned from their letters, private journals, lists, and ledgers." (Publisher's note)

"Most children know that the "Founding Fathers" are the men who helped the 13 colonies develop into the United States. What about the women of the time period?...Grammarians may not appreciate the author's colloquial style, but the conversational tone is appealing. Beautifully intricate illustrations, rendered with antique pens, sepia ink, and watercolors, suit the text well. Thoughtful design, well-chosen facts, and an approachable format combine to make a book readers will enjoy and appreciate.—" (SLJ)

Rubin, Susan Goldman

Everybody paints! the lives and art of the Wyeth family. by Susan Goldman Rubin. Chronicle Books 2013 105 p. illustrations (chiefly color) (alk. paper) $16.99
Grades: 6 7 8 9 10 **920**

1. American painting 2. Artists -- United States -- Biography 3. Wyeth family
ISBN 0811869849; 9780811869843

LC 2013006595

Author Susan Goldman Rubin "shares the . . . story of the Wyeths--N.C., Andrew, and Jamie--three generations of painters and arguably the First Family of American Art. The . . . text traces the events that shaped their art and the ways their art influenced them in return, while the . . . design showcases . . . reproductions of the works that have made the Wyeth family legendary." (Publisher's note)

"This small-trim book celebrates the artistic Wyeth family, mostly the work of revered illustrator N. C. Wyeth; his son Andrew, popular modern realist best-known for Christina's World; and grandson Jamie, an acclaimed painter working today. Rubin's prose is fluid, and seamlessly worked-in quotes from her subjects add to the narrative's personal feel. The handsome, clean design showcases the excellent reproductions." Horn Book

Schatz, Kate

Rad American women A-Z; written by Kate Schatz ; illustrated by Miriam Klein Stahl. City Lights Books 2015 64 p. color illustrations, portraits $14.95

Grades: 6 7 8 9 **920**

1. Women -- United States -- Biography 2. Women -- United States -- Biography

ISBN 0872866831; 9780872866836

LC 2014037930

This book on American women, written by Kate Schatz and illustrated by Miriam Klein Stahl, features "26 diverse individuals. There are artists and abolitionists, scientists and suffragettes, rock stars and rabble-rousers, and agents of change of all kinds. The book includes an introduction that discusses what it means to be 'rad' and 'radical,' an afterword with 26 suggestions for how you can be 'rad,' and a Resource Guide with ideas for further learning and reading." (Publisher's note)

"Colorful and hip potraitures create a visual sensation that immediately draws in readers. Profiled are 26 American women from the 18th through 21st centuries, who have made—or are still making—history as artists, writers, teachers, lawyers, or athletes...Classes across the curriculum can utilize this informative book." SLJ

Simoni, Suzanne

Fantastic women filmmakers. Second Story Press 2008 122p il (Women's hall of fame) pa $10.95

Grades: 7 8 9 10 **920**

1. Women in the motion picture industry 2. Motion picture producers and directors -- Biography

ISBN 978-1-897187-36-4 pa; 1-897187-36-X pa

"Includes profiles of earlier filmmakers such as Nell Shipman and Ida Lupiano as well as contemporary directors like Deepa Mehta, Patricia Rozema, and Mira Nair. The author includes filmmakers who found varied and unique ways to navigate the industry. . . . The profiles . . . are revealing, inspiring, and insightful." Voice Youth Advocates

Includes glossary and bibliographical references

Sullivan, Otha Richard

African American millionaires. John Wiley & Sons 2004 158p il (Black stars) $24.95

Grades: 6 7 8 9 **920**

1. African Americans -- Biography

ISBN 0-471-46928-9

LC 2004-14694

This profiles 25 African American millionaires

"Sullivan offers an exemplary compilation of a relatively unexplored subject area. . . . The book is well organized, highly readable, and inspiring." SLJ

Includes bibliographical references

Tate, Eleanora E.

African American musicians; Jim Haskins, general editor. Wiley 2000 70p il (Black stars) $24.95

Grades: 6 7 8 9 **920**

1. African American musicians

ISBN 0-471-25356-1

LC 99-51360

"Many genres and skills are represented from spirituals, gospel, ragtime, blues, jazz, and soul. Scott Joplin, Marian Anderson, Duke Ellington, and Aretha Franklin are here as well as Michael Jackson and a few lesser-known individuals. Each entry includes a black-and-white photo or reproduction and sidebars on pertinent topics." SLJ

Includes bibliographical references

Thimmesh, Catherine

Girls think of everything; stories of ingenious inventions by women. by Catherine Thimmesh ; illustrated by Melissa Sweet. Updated edition Houghton Mifflin 2018 106 p color illustrations $17.99

Grades: 5 6 7 8 **920**

1. Women -- Biography 2. Inventions -- United States -- History 3. Inventors -- United States -- Biography 4. Women inventors -- United States -- Biography

ISBN 9781328772534

"This updated edition of the bestselling 'Girls Think of Everything,' by Sibert-winner Catherine Thimmesh and Caldecott Honor winner Melissa Sweet, retains all the integrity of the original but includes expanded coverage of inventions (and inventors) to better reflect our diverse and technological world. . . . [It offers] readers stories about inventions that are full of hope and vitality--empowering them to think big, especially in the face of adversity." (Publisher's note)

Includes bibliographical references (pages 96-99) and index

Waldherr, Kris

Bad princess; true tales from behind the tiara. Kris Waldherr. Scholastic Inc. 2018 128 p. illustrations (some color) (hardcover) $12.99

Grades: 4 5 6 7 8 **920**

1. Biography 2. Princesses 3. Princesses -- Biography 4. Princesses -- Social life and customs

ISBN 9781338047998; 9781338047981

LC 2017032549

This book, by Kris Waldherr, "explores more than 30 true princess stories, going beyond the glitz and glamour to find out what life was really like for young royals throughout history. A mix of royal biography, pop culture, art, style, and pure fun, 'Bad Princess' is a whip-smart, tongue-in-cheek spin on the traditional princess narrative, proving that it takes more than a pretty crown to be a great leader." (Publisher's note)

"This absorbing, thought-provoking, and intriguing exploration of a perennially popular topic will both entertain and inform." Booklist

Wilson, Jamia

★ **Young,** gifted and black; meet 52 black heroes from past and present. Jamia Wilson, illustrated by Andrea Pippins. Motorbooks Intl 2018 64 p. $22.99

Grades: 3 4 5 6 7 **920**

1. Blacks -- Biography 2. African Americans -- Biography

ISBN 1786031582; 9781786031587

"Meet 52 icons of color from the past and present in this celebration of inspirational achievement--a collection of stories about changemakers to encourage, inspire and empower the next generation of changemakers. Jamia Wilson has carefully curated this range of black icons and the book is stylishly brought together by Andrea Pippins' colorful and celebratory illustrations." (Publisher's note)

Winter, Jonah

Peaceful heroes; illustrated by Sean Addy. Arthur A. Levine Books 2009 56p il $17.99
Grades: 4 5 6 7 **920**

1. Peace 2. Heroes and heroines
ISBN 978-0-439-62307-0; 0-439-62307-3
LC 2008-48311

"Starting off with Jesus, Gandhi, King, and Sojourner Truth, this collective biography goes on to profile many less well-known peace activists across the world. . . . The detailed portraits never deny the horrifying realities that the peace-seeking leaders are fighting against. With the chatty interactive text, there are handsome full-page pictures of each activist, rendered in oil, acrylic, and collage in shades of red and brown." Booklist

Yolen, Jane

Sea queens; women pirates around the world. illustrated by Christine Joy Pratt. Charlesbridge 2008 103p il $18.95
Grades: 4 5 6 7 **920**

1. Women pirates 2. Women -- Biography
ISBN 978-1-58089-131-8; 1-58089-131-4
LC 2007026983

This offers "12 portraits of sword-swinging, seafaring women throughout history, from Artemisia, in 500 B.C.E. Persia, to Madame Ching, an early nineteenth-century Chinese woman and named here as 'the most successful pirate in the world.' . . . The scratchboard illustrations work well as portraits. . . . The book is filled with fascinating, dramatically told stories and sidebars." Booklist

Includes bibliographical references

Young, Jeff C.

Brilliant African-American scientists; 9 exceptional lives. MyReportLinks.com Books 2009 128p il (Great scientists and famous inventors) lib bdg $33.27
Grades: 5 6 7 8 **920**

1. Scientists 2. African Americans -- Biography
ISBN 978-1-59845-083-5 lib bdg; 1-59845-083-2 lib bdg
LC 2008053924

"Each chapter provides a graphic time line of the milestones in each of the scientists' lives and relates details on their early life, education, research and accomplishments. Several disciplines and science-related careers are highlighted. . . . Each of the chapters contains an inset that provides a link to a website for information on the scientist. A listing of Internet sites and brief descriptions of them are included, as are a glossary, chapter notes, and suggestions for further reading." Sci Books Films

Includes glossary and bibliographical references

Inspiring African-American inventors; 9 extraordinary lives. Enslow Publishers 2009 128p il (Great scientists and famous inventors) lib bdg $33.27
Grades: 5 6 7 **920**

1. African American inventors
ISBN 978-1-59845-080-4 lib bdg; 1-59845-080-8 lib bdg
LC 2007-22937

"This collective biography . . . profiles nine African American inventors: Lewis Howard Latimer, Jan E. Matziliger, Granville T. Woods, George Washington Carver, Madam C. J. Walker, Garrett A. Morgan, Percy Lavon Julian, Patricia Era Bath, and Lonnie G. Johnson. . . . Clearly written and logically organized, this volume provides a useful guide to the subject." Booklist

Includes glossary and bibliographical references

920.003 Dictionaries, encyclopedias, concordances of biography as a discipline

American Indian biographies; edited by Carole Barrett, Harvey Markowitz, project editor, R. Kent Rasmussen. rev ed.; Salem Press 2005 623p il map (Magill's choice) $62
Grades: 8 9 10 11 12 Adult **920.003**

1. Reference books 2. Native Americans -- Biography
ISBN 1-58765-233-1; 978-1-58765-233-2
LC 2004-28872

First published 1999; some essays originally appeared in Dictionary of world biography, Great lives from history: the Renaissance & early modern era, 1454-1600 (2005), and American ethnic writers (2000)

"The book contains essays on religious, social, and political leaders; warriors; and reformers from the past as well as modern activists, writers, artists, entertainers, scientists, and athletes. . . . A great bargain and an asset in any library that supports an American history curriculum." Booklist

Includes bibliographical references

Great athletes; edited by The Editors of Salem Press; special consultant Rafer Johnson. Salem Press 2010 13v il set $1,020
Grades: 7 8 9 10 11 12 **920.003**

1. Reference books 2. Athletes -- Dictionaries
ISBN 978-1-58765-473-2; 1-58765-473-3
LC 2009-21905

"This massive undertaking totals 1,470 entries covering athletes in baseball, basketball, boxing, football, golf, auto racing, soccer, tennis, and Olympic sports. Additionally, well-known athletes in other, less recognized sports—such as cycling, skateboarding, stunt riding, martial-arts and chess—are included. . . . Overall, this is a well-put-together and wide-ranging set." Booklist

Includes bibliographical references

Lifelines in world history; general editor, Mounir A. Farah. Sharpe Reference 2009 4v il map set $299
Grades: 6 7 8 9 10 11 12 **920.003**

1. World history 2. Reference books 3. Civilization -- History 4. Biography -- Dictionaries
ISBN 978-0-7656-8125-6; 0-7656-8125-0
LC 2008-16288

"This set provides profiles of influential world leaders. Each volume contains 15 to 20 sketches that include basic biographical information, an overview of the subject's achievements, and analysis of the 'interplay' between the person and the 'political, economic, and social circumstances' in which he or she lived. . . . Entries range in length from five to eight pages and offer well-captioned color reproductions, photos, and maps. . . . This attractive set provides well-illustrated, objective information in a global context." SLJ

Includes bibliographical references

The **Lincoln** Library of Sports Champions; 9th edition Lincoln Library 2013 14 v. illustrations $523
Grades: 7 8 9 10 11 12 **920.003**

1. Sports 2. Athletes
ISBN 0912168005; 9780912168005

First published 1975

Presents brief, alphabetically arranged biographies of nearly 300 great sports personalities, past and present, from around the world. Features a table of contents arranged by sport and a supplementary reading list.

Riley, Sam G.

African Americans in the media today; an encyclopedia. [by] Sam G. Riley. Greenwood Press 2007 581p 2v set$175

Grades: 7 8 9 10 11 12 **920.003**

1. Mass media 2. Reference books 3. African Americans in television broadcasting 4. African Americans -- Biography -- Dictionaries

ISBN 978-0-313-33679-9; 0-313-33679-2 set; 978-0-313-33680-5 v1; 0-313-33680-6 v1; 978-0-313-33681-2 v2; 0-313-33681-4 v2

LC 2007008192

"This concise, alphabetically arranged work describes hundreds of people . . . in various fields of communications. It includes, for example, reporters, anchormen and women, talk-show hosts, and television producers. . . . Each of the mostly one to two-page entries includes biographical information, . . . work experience, awards, and, in some cases, includes anecdotes or articles by or about the individual. . . . A worthwhile resource for biography or communications projects." SLJ

Includes bibliographical references

Rockman, Connie C.

Tenth book of junior authors and illustrators; edited by Connie C. Rockman. Wilson, H.W. 2008 803p autog il por (Junior authors & illustrators series) hardcover o.p. $120

Grades: Adult Professional **920.003**

1. Reference books 2. Authors -- Dictionaries 3. Illustrators -- Dictionaries 4. Children's literature -- Bio-bibliography

ISBN 978-0-8242-1066-3; 0-8242-1066-2

LC 2008043312

This volume covers some 200 authors and illustrators of books for children and young adults including David Almond, Blue Balliett, Terry Pratchett, and Laura Vaccaro Seeger. For 17 authors and artists whose careers include significant new works and honors since their profile in earlier editions of the series, newly written entries are featured

"Standard resource for libraries serving young readers and students studying children's and young adult literature." Booklist

Includes bibliographical references

Something about the author; facts and pictures about authors and illustrators of books for young people. Gale Res. il

Grades: Adult Professional **920.003**

1. Reference books 2. Authors -- Dictionaries 3. Illustrators -- Dictionaries 4. Children's literature -- Bio-bibliography

First published 1971. Frequency varies

"This important series gives comprehensive coverage of the individuals who write and illustrate books for children. Each new volume adds about 100 profiles. Entries include career and personal data, a bibliography of the author's works, information on works in progress and references to further information." Safford. Guide to Ref Materials for Sch Libr Media Cent. 5th edition

Something about the author: autobiography series. Gale Res. il

Grades: Adult Professional **920.003**

1. Reference books 2. Authors -- Dictionaries 3. Illustrators -- Dictionaries 4. Children's literature -- Bio-bibliography

First published 1986

An "ongoing series in which juvenile authors discuss their lives, careers, and published works. Each volume contains essays by 20 established writers or illustrators (e.g., Evaline Ness, Nonny Hogrogian, Betsy Byars, Jean Fritz) who represent all types of literature, preschool to young adult. . . . Some articles focus on biographical information, while others emphasize the writing career. Most, however, address young readers and provide family background, discuss the writing experience, and cite some factors that influenced it. Illustrations include portraits of the authors as children and more recent action pictures and portraits. There are cumulative indexes by authors, important published works, and geographical locations mentioned in the essays." Safford. Guide to Ref Books for Sch Libr Media Cent. 5th edition

Sonneborn, Liz

★ **A to Z of American Indian women**; rev ed; Facts on File 2007 320p il map (Facts on File library of American history) $60

Grades: 8 9 10 11 12 **920.003**

1. Reference books 2. Native American women -- Dictionaries

ISBN 978-0-8160-6694-0

LC 2007-8162

First published 1998 with title: A to Z of Native American women

"This resource is of exceptionally high quality." SLJ

Includes bibliographical references

Yount, Lisa

A to Z of women in science and math; rev ed; Facts on File 2007 368p il (Facts on File library of world history) $60

Grades: 8 9 10 11 12 **920.003**

1. Reference books 2. Women scientists -- Dictionaries 3. Women mathematicians -- Dictionaries

ISBN 978-0-8160-6695-7; 0-8160-6695-7

LC 2007-23966

First published 1999

"More than 195 alphabetically arranged articles detail the lives of women from antiquity through modern day, including well-known scientists and mathematicians and less well-documented individuals. . . . The usefulness of this resource lies not only in the balanced group of profiles that have been assembled, providing a valuable tool for teachers and curriculum developers, but also in the readable and engaging entries themselves." Booklist

Includes bibliographical references

920.02 General collections of biography

Swartz, Clay

Who wins? 100 Historical Figures Go Head-to-Head and You Decide the Winner! created by Clay Swartz ; illustrated by Tom Booth. Workman Publishing Co., Inc. 2016 52 p. color illustrations (alk. paper) $14.95

Grades: 5 6 7 8 **920.02**

1. Educational games 2. Celebrities -- Biography 3. Biography -- Study and teaching

ISBN 9780761185444

LC 2015040316

This book, by Clay Swartz, illustrated by Tom Booth, "turns history into a compelling game, which means kids learn while having fun in the process. Each of the famous people is given a short bio and ranked in six categories—bravery, leadership, artistry, wealth, wisdom, and fitness." (Publisher's note)

"History with a hilarious spin and a cinch to provoke vigorous debates aplenty." Kirkus

Includes bibliographical references and index

920.72 Women

León, Vicki

Outrageous women of the Middle Ages; by Vicki Leon. Wiley 1998 ix, 118 p.p ill., maps hardcover o.p. (paperback) $14.95; (prebind) $23.95

Grades: 4 5 6 7 8 **920.72**

1. Middle Ages 2. Women -- History 3. Women -- Biography 4. Women -- History -- Middle Ages, 500-1500 5. Civilization, Medieval -- 6. Biography -- Middle Ages, 500-1500

ISBN 9780471170044; 9781435280090

LC 97030307

In this book, Vicki Leon looks at women of the Middle Ages. She "tells of a Viking killed by a severed head, a queen who knew the meaning of congregating frogs, and much more. The stories and sidebars provide a detailed picture of the times. . . . The women profiled lived in the 6th through 14th centuries in Europe, Asia, and Africa. Their spheres included everything from astronomy to warfare. They were nomads and empresses." (School Library Journal)

Includes bibliographical references (p. 115-117).

Schatz, Kate

Rad girls can; stories of bold, brave, and brilliant young women. Kate Schatz ; illustrated by Miriam Klein Stahl. Ten Speed Press 2018 112 p. (hardback) $16.99

Grades: 9 10 11 12 **920.72**

1. Women -- History 2. Women -- Biography 3. Girls -- Biography

ISBN 9780399581106

LC 2017049166

In this book, by Kate Schatz, illustrated by Miriam Klein Stahl, "you'll learn about a diverse group of young women who are living rad lives, whether excelling in male-dominated sports like boxing, rock climbing, or skateboarding; speaking out against injustice and discrimination; expressing themselves through dance, writing, and music; or advocating for girls around the world. Each profile is paired with the dynamic paper-cut art." (Publisher's note)

Includes bibliographical references and index

Rad women worldwide; Artists and Athletes, Pirates and Punks, and Other Revolutionaries Who Shaped History. by Kate Schatz ; illustrated by Miriam Klein Stahl. Ten Speed Press 2016 112 p. illustrations (ebook) $47.97; (hardback) $15.99

Grades: 6 7 8 9 Adult **920.72**

1. Women -- History 2. Women -- Biography

ISBN 9780399578878; 9780399578861

LC 2016012179

This book by Kate Schatz, illustrated by Miriam Klein Stahl, offers "tales of perseverance and radical success by pairing well researched . . . biographies with . . . cut-paper portraits. From 430 BCE to 2016, . . . the book features an array of diverse figures, including Hatshepsut (. . . who ruled Egypt peacefully for two decades) and Malala Yousafzi (the youngest person to win the Nobel Peace Prize) to Poly Styrene (legendary teenage punk and lead singer of X-Ray Spex)." (Publisher's note)

"Readers of either gender could well find a role model in the India-born U.S. astronaut Kalpana Chawla, or in Wangari Maathai, whose Green Belt Movement in Africa resulted in the planting of more than 30 million environment-reviving trees." Booklist

Includes bibliographical references and index

929 Genealogy, names, insignia

Ollhoff, Jim

Beginning genealogy; expert tips to help you trace your own ancestors. ABDO Pub. Co. 2011 32p il (Your family tree) $18.95

Grades: 4 5 6 7 **929**

1. Research 2. Genealogy

ISBN 978-1-61613-460-0; 1-61613-460-7

LC 2009050812

This is "great . . . for kids interested in genealogy. . . . [It does] a wonderful job of presenting the fundamentals of genealogical research in a clear and exciting manner. . . . Understanding and properly using primary documents is stressed throughout. . . . [An] attractive, spacious [layout]; full-color, sharp images; clearly labeled diagrams; and scattered maps add information and appeal." SLJ

Includes glossary

Collecting primary records. ABDO Pub. Co. 2011 32p il (Your family tree) $18.95

Grades: 4 5 6 7 **929**

1. Research 2. Genealogy

ISBN 978-1-61613-461-7; 1-61613-461-5

LC 2009050811

This describes how to collect primary records for geneological research.

This is "great . . . for kids interested in genealogy. . . . [It does] a wonderful job of presenting the fundamentals of genealogical research in a clear and exciting manner. . . . Understanding and properly using primary documents is stressed throughout. . . . [An] attractive, spacious [layout]; full-color, sharp images; clearly labeled diagrams; and scattered maps add information and appeal." SLJ

Includes glossary

DNA; window to the past: how science can help untangle your family roots. ABDO Pub. Co. 2011 32p il map (Your family tree) $18.95

Grades: 4 5 6 7 **929**

1. Genetics 2. Genealogy

ISBN 978-1-61613-462-4; 1-61613-462-3

LC 2009050808

This explains how DNA is used in geneology.

This is "great . . . for kids interested in genealogy. . . . [It does] a wonderful job of presenting the fundamentals of genealogical research in a clear and exciting manner. . . . Understanding and properly using primary documents is stressed throughout. . . . [An] attractive, spacious [layout]; full-color, sharp images; clearly labeled diagrams; and scattered maps add information and appeal." SLJ

Includes glossary

Filling the family tree. ABDO Pub. Co. 2011 32p il (Your family tree) lib bdg $18.95

Grades: 4 5 6 7 **929**

1. Research 2. Genealogy

ISBN 978-1-61613-464-8; 1-61613-464-X

LC 2009050806

This is "great . . . for kids interested in genealogy. . . . [It does] a wonderful job of presenting the fundamentals of genealogical research in a clear and exciting manner. . . . Understanding and properly using primary documents is stressed throughout. . . . [An] attractive, spacious [layout]; full-color, sharp images; clearly labeled diagrams; and scattered maps add information and appeal." SLJ

Using your research; how to check your facts and use your information. ABDO Pub. Co. 2011 32p il (Your family tree) lib bdg $18.95

Grades: 4 5 6 7 **929**

1. Research 2. Genealogy

ISBN 978-1-61613-465-5; 1-61613-465-8

LC 2009050805

Presents a brief guide on how to check facts and use other information in genealogical research.

This is "great . . . for kids interested in genealogy. . . . [It does] a wonderful job of presenting the fundamentals of genealogical research in a clear and exciting manner. . . . Understanding and properly using primary documents is stressed throughout. . . . [An] attractive, spacious [layout]; full-color, sharp images; clearly labeled diagrams; and scattered maps add information and appeal." SLJ

Includes glossary

Resler, T. J.

National Geographic Kids guide to genealogy; tips & tricks on how to uncover your roots and build your family tree! by T.J. Resler. Natl Geographic Soc Childrens books 2018 160 p. (pbk.) $14.99

Grades: 5 6 7 8 **929**

1. DNA 2. Genealogy

ISBN 1426329830; 9781426329845; 9781426329838

LC 2017050028

This children's book, by T. J. Resler, "helps readers dig into the past and learn more about their own family history. . . . This lively guide will get you started on researching your family's past and let you in on the newest and most up-to-date technology for genealogy research. Get tips on how to interview family members, create a family tree, and much more." (Publisher's note)

929.9 Forms of insignia and identification

Bateman, Teresa

Red, white, blue, and Uncle who? the stories behind some of America's patriotic symbols. illustrated by John O'Brien. Holiday House 2001 64p il $16.95; pa $6.95

Grades: 4 5 6 7 **929.9**

1. National emblems 2. National monuments

ISBN 0-8234-1285-7; 0-8234-1784-0 pa

LC 00-57258

This "volume presents 17 'patriotic symbols,' an umbrella term that encompasses everything from the flag to Uncle Sam, from Mount Rushmore to the Korean War Memorial. Bateman finds plenty of interesting information to share about each symbol or site, and browsers will be entertained by the many stories of origination, construction, and history." Booklist

Includes bibliographical references

Shearer, Benjamin F.

State names, seals, flags, and symbols; a historical guide. [by] Benjamin F. Shearer and Barbara S. Shearer. 3rd ed, rev and expanded; Greenwood Press 2001 495p il $73.95

Grades: 8 9 10 11 12 Adult **929.9**

1. Reference books 2. Seals (Numismatics) 3. Flags -- United States 4. Geographic names -- United States

ISBN 0-313-31534-5

LC 2001-23525

First published 1987

"Chapters on mottoes, flowers, trees, birds, songs, holidays, and license plates are just a sampling of what is covered, and the format is such that the concisely written material can be found as expeditiously as possible. Even though the book is touted predominantly as a reference tool, the information provided makes fascinating and enlightening reading." Libr J [review of 1994 edition]

Includes bibliographical references

Znamierowski, Alfred, 1940-

The **World** Encyclopedia of Flags; The definitive guide to international, flags, banners, standards and ensigns, with over 1400 illustration. by Alfred Znamierowski. Lorenz Books 2019 256 p. hardcover $25

Grades: 5 6 7 8 9 10 11 12 Adult **929.9**

1. Flags

ISBN 9780754834809 hardcover; 9780754826293

This book, by Alred Znamierowski, presents "a directory of flags and a fascinating history of their development and usage, featuring over 600 flags including military signs, royal standards, civic flags, ensigns and national flags, expertly illustrated throughout." (Publisher's note)

930 History of ancient world (to ca. 499)

Adams, Simon

The **Kingfisher** atlas of the ancient world; illustrated by Katherine Baxter. Kingfisher 2006 44p il $15.95

Grades: 4 5 6 7 **930**

1. Reference books 2. Ancient civilization 3. Historical geography

ISBN 978-0-7534-5914-0; 0-7534-5914-0

"Featuring seventeen . . . hand-illustrated maps and . . . with . . . information about ancient civilizations and peoples, this is [a] . . . pictorial guide to what the world was like between 10,000 B.C. and A.D. 1000. Each . . . map shows the major sites from a particular civilization or group of civilizations. . . . Feature spreads use photographs of cultural and architectural artifacts, as well as additional information, to focus in greater depth on the key cultures of Egypt, Greece, and Rome." Publisher's note

Morris, Neil

Prehistory. Zak Books 2009 48p il map (History of the world) lib bdg $34.25

Grades: 7 8 9 10 **930**

1. History 2. Prehistoric peoples

ISBN 978-88-6098-156-1 lib bdg; 88-6098-156-5 lib bdg

LC 2008-8399

The "effectiveness lies in the combination of lush illustrations, well-chosen, captioned photographs of contemporary artifacts, and . . . [a] reasoned, concise [narrative]. Succinct time lines border most pages, . . .

the proper amount of white space, and clear dark print maintain organization and clarity. A superior choice." SLJ

Includes glossary

Shuter, Jane

Ancient China; Jane Shuter. Revised edition Capstone 2016 48 p color illustrations, color map (Excavating the past) paperback $8.99

Grades: 4 5 6 7 **930**

1. China 2. China -- Antiquities 3. China -- Civilization

ISBN 9781484636459; 9781484636770

"Through archeological excavations and artifacts, readers get the real story of life in ancient civilizations including common experiences for children and adults, as well as comparisons between the lives of different societal classes. Each book explores the idiosyncrasies of daily life in an ancient civilization from religion, to government, to warfare." (Publisher's note)

The **world** in ancient times; primary sources and reference volume. Ronald Mellor & Amanda Podany, general editors. Oxford University Press 2005 188p il map (World in ancient times) $32.95

Grades: 7 8 9 10 **930**

1. Ancient history 2. Reference books 3. Ancient civilization

ISBN 978-0-19-522220-3; 0-19-522220-2

LC 2004026578

"An excellent introduction to the use of primary resources in historical research. The 76 selections include poems, letters, inscriptions, and other contemporary accounts from antiquity as well as more modern descriptions and excerpts. Materials from Asia, Europe, and the Americas are highlighted." SLJ

Includes bibliograghical references

930.1 Archaeology

Barber, Nicola

Lost cities; by Nicola Barber. Capstone Raintree 2013 48 p. col. ill. (Treasure hunters) (hardcover) $29.33; (paperback) $8.99

Grades: 5 6 7 8 **930.1**

1. Picture books for children 2. Extinct cities 3. Legends 4. Civilization, Ancient 5. Archaeology -- History

ISBN 1410949524; 1410949591; 9781410949523; 9781410949592

LC 2012012891

This book by Nicola Barber is part of the Treasure Hunters series and looks at lost cities. This entry "examines the search for lost cities and the important artefacts within them that can offer us an extraordinary window on to the past. . . . Cities covered in the book include Pompeii, Troy, the desert city of Ubar, and the Inca city of Machu Picchu." (Publisher's note)

Includes bibliographical references (p. 46-47) and index.

Tomb explorers; by Nicola Barber. Capstone Raintree 2013 48 p. ill. (mostly col.) (Treasure hunters) (library) $29.33; (paperback) $8.99

Grades: 5 6 7 8 **930.1**

1. Tombs 2. Archeology 3. Antiquities 4. Treasure troves 5. Civilization, Ancient 6. Archaeology -- History

ISBN 1410949559; 9781410949554; 9781410949622

LC 2012012894

This book by Nicola Barber "examines the hunt for and discovery of ancient tombs, and the valuable treasures they hold. . . . Part of the Treasure Hunters series, 'Tomb Explorers' offers a crosscurricular mix of science & technology and history & civilizations. . . .Tombs covered in the book include that of Tutankhamun, the Sumerian royal tombs of Ur, the Terracotta Army of ancient China, and the Mayan tombs of Palanque in the Mexican Rainforest, and the Oseberg ship burial." (Publisher's note)

Includes bibliographical references and index.

Croy, Anita

Exploring the past. Marshall Cavendish Benchmark 2010 48p il (Invisible worlds) $28.50

Grades: 4 5 6 7 **930.1**

1. Fossils 2. Archeology 3. Human origins 4. Prehistoric peoples 5. Ancient civilization

ISBN 978-0-7614-4194-6; 0-7614-4194-8

The narrative is "clear, well written, broken down into manageable pieces, and peppered with eye-opening facts. The numerous photographs are so phenomenal that they will inspire kids to read the text . . . so that they can wrap their minds around what they see." SLJ

Includes glossary and bibliographical references

Hunter, Nick

Ancient treasures; by Nick Hunter ; edited by Laura Knowles ... [et al.] ; illustrated by Martin Bustamante. Raintree 2013 48 p. col. ill., col. maps (Treasure hunters) (hardcover) $29.33; (paperback) $8.99

Grades: 5 6 7 8 **930.1**

1. Archeology 2. Buried treasure 3. Ancient civilization 4. Treasure troves 5. Civilization, Ancient 6. Archaeology -- History

ISBN 1410949508; 9781410949509; 9781410949578

LC 2012012757

"Part of the Treasure Hunters series, 'Ancient Treasures' offers a crosscurricular mix of science & technology and history. . . .Treasures covered in the book include the Roman Hoxne Hoard, the Anglo-Saxon Staffordshire Hoard, the extraordinary discoveries of the Rosetta Stone and Dead Sea Scrolls, and the South American treasures of Lake Guatavita. The book also looks at the motives for these searches, and the importance of responsible archaeology." (Publisher's note)

Includes bibliographical references (p. 46-47) and index.

Rubalcaba, Jill

Every bone tells a story; hominid discoveries, deductions, and debates. [by] Jill Rubalcaba and Peter Robertshaw. Charlesbridge 2010 185p il map lib bdg $18.95

Grades: 8 9 10 11 12 **930.1**

1. Archeology 2. Fossil hominids 3. Prehistoric peoples 4. Excavations (Archeology)

ISBN 978-1-58089-164-6; 1-58089-164-0

LC 2008-26961

"Archaeology and paleontology are the exciting focus in this accessible account of four hominins who lived long before recorded history. . . . The informal style never oversimplifies the engaging science and technology, and the authors raise as many questions as they answer in the detailed chapters." Booklist

931 China to 420

Ball, Jacqueline A.

★ **Ancient** China; archaeology unlocks the secrets of China's past. by Jacqueline Ball and Richard Levey, Robert Murowchick, consultant. National Geographic 2006 64p il (National Geographic investigates) hardcover o.p. lib bdg $27.90; $17.95

Grades: 5 6 7 8 **931**

1. China -- Antiquities 2. China -- Civilization

ISBN 9780792278566 lib bdg; 9780792277835

"This volume spotlights archaeological finds from Ancient China. . . . While the discussions of archaeology will hold readers' interest, the accompanying illustrations steal the show." Booklist

Kleeman, Terry F.

The **ancient** Chinese world; [by] Terry Kleeman & Tracy Barrett. Oxford University Press 2005 174p il map (World in ancient times) $32.95

Grades: 7 8 9 10 **931**

1. China -- History

ISBN 0-19-517102-0

LC 2004-14408

"Readers seriously interested in history, in archaeology—or in China—will be well served by this engrossing book." SLJ

Includes bibliographical references

Liu-Perkins, Christine

At home in her tomb; Lady Dai and the ancient Chinese treasures of Mawangdui. Christine Liu-Perkins ; illustrated by Sarah Brannen. Charlesbridge 2013 80 p. (reinforced for library use) $19.95

Grades: 5 6 7 8 **931**

1. Tombs 2. Excavations (Archeology) -- China 3. China -- History -- Han dynasty, 202 B.C.-220 A.D. 4. Treasure troves -- China -- Changsha (Hunan Sheng) 5. Material culture -- China -- Changsha (Hunan Sheng) 6. Excavations (Archaeology) -- China -- Changsha (Hunan Sheng) 7. Human remains (Archaeology) -- China -- Changsha (Hunan Sheng)

ISBN 1580893708; 9781580893701; 9781607346159

LC 2012024630

This book, by Christine Liu-Perkins, "unearths the mysteries of the Mawangdui tombs, one of China's top archaeological finds of the last century. Miniature servants, mysterious silk paintings, scrolls of long-lost secrets, and the best preserved mummy in the world (the body of Lady Dai) are just some of the artifacts that shed light upon life in China during the Han dynasty." (Publisher's note)

"In 1971, the tomb of "Lady Dai" was discovered, virtually intact and of enormous archaeological significance. Here, buried in 158 BCE, was her still-soft body and more than a thousand artifacts. Liu-Perkins describes the discovery in fascinating detail; brief imagined scenes supplement the evidence. Illustrative materials include maps and well-captioned photos as well as Brannen's watercolors of the fictionalized scenes. Timeline. Bib., glos., ind." Horn Book

Includes bibliographical references and index

O'Connor, Jane

★ The **emperor's** silent army; terracotta warriors of Ancient China. Viking 2002 48p il $17.99

Grades: 4 5 6 7 **931**

1. Emperors 2. China -- Antiquities

ISBN 0-670-03512-2

LC 2001-46900

Describes the archaeological discovery of thousands of life-sized terracotta warrior statues in northern China in 1974, and discusses the emperor who had them created and placed near his tomb

"This intriguing book is enhanced by beautiful illustrations—pictures of stone engravings, colorful paintings, drawings, and maps—while numerous photographs show the clay soldiers from different perspectives. . . . The author's writing style is entertaining, yet informative." Book Rep

Includes bibliographical references

932 Egypt to 640

Ancient Egypt; edited by Sherman Hollar. Britannica Educational Pub. in association with Rosen Educational Services 2011 87p il map (Ancient civilizations) lib bdg $31.70

Grades: 5 6 7 8 **932**

1. Egypt -- History 2. Egypt -- Civilization

ISBN 978-1-61530-523-0; 1-61530-523-8

LC 2011004714

This book provides "enough information about the development, way of life, accomplishments, and decline of [Ancient Egypt] without overwhelming readers. Maps; full-color illustrations and photographs, many full page; and sidebars provide additional focus. . . . The use of the Nile and its influence on the development of this civilization is emphasized. . . . The building of the great pyramids and the art of mummification are also mentioned. A detailed discussion of the everyday lives of the rich and the poor provide valuable insight." SLJ

Includes glossary and bibliographical references

Berger, Melvin

★ **Mummies** of the pharaohs; exploring the Valley of the Kings. [by] Melvin Berger & Gilda Berger. National Geographic Soc. 2001 64p il $17.95

Grades: 4 5 6 7 **932**

1. Mummies 2. Egypt -- Antiquities

ISBN 0-7922-7223-4

LC 00-55411

This offers "stunning photographs and clear, compelling text. . . . A fascinating historical resource that kids will read straight through for pleasure and also find useful for report writing." Booklist

George, Charles, 1949-

The **pyramids** of Giza; by Charles and Linda George. ReferencePoint Press 2012 80 p. (Ancient Egyptian wonders) (hardcover) $28.95

Grades: 8 9 10 11 12 **932**

1. Pyramids 2. Egypt -- Antiquities 3. Pyramids of Giza (Egypt) 4. Jīzah (Egypt) -- Antiquities

ISBN 1601522584; 9781601522580

LC 2012000282

This book by Charles George is part of the Ancient Egyptian Wonders series and looks at the pyramids of Giza. "Three of the grandest of all the pyramids built by the pharaohs of Egypt still stand on the Giza Plateau. These monuments serve as reminders of their builders but also of the glory and grandeur that was ancient Egypt." (Publisher's note)

Includes bibliographical references and index.

Kerrigan, Michael

Egyptians. Marshall Cavendish Benchmark 2010 64p il (Ancients in their own words) $32.79

Grades: 5 6 7 8 **932**

1. Egypt -- Civilization

ISBN 978-1-60870-064-6; 1-60870-064-X

Features "Numerous photographs provide visual interest, with text describing the images to give details and background. Translations of the writings offer primary sources to accompany the secondary material presented. . . . The text is interesting enough to read cover to cover while the table of contents' descriptive chapter titles and the comprehensive index enable the . . . [book] to be used for specific research." Libr Media Connect

Includes bibliographical references

Lace, William

King Tut's curse; by William W. Lace. ReferencePoint Press 2012 80 p. ill. (Ancient Egyptian wonders series.) (hardcover) $27.95

Grades: 8 9 10 11 12 **932**

1. Egypt -- Antiquities 2. Tutankhamen, King of Egypt -- Tombs 3. Valley of the Kings (Egypt) -- Antiquities 4. Excavations (Archaeology) -- Egypt -- Valley of the Kings

ISBN 1601522509; 9781601522504

LC 2011048987

This book by William W. Lace is part of the Ancient Egyptian Wonders series and looks at King Tut's curse. Topics include "its origin, how it spread, and the remaining mysteries and search for answers. The title opens with Lord Carnarvon's 1923 death . . . and continues on to discuss Tutankhamen's life, rule, and death (including recent DNA testing, which indicates he had malaria) as well as the endeavors of those involved in the tomb's discovery." (Booklist)

This "explores Egyptian history, mummy making, the discovery and opening of the tomb of Tutankhamen in 1922, and the events that happened after that. Much of the book is based on archaeologist Howard Carter's diaries and letters, and on period newspaper articles. The color photographs in [this attractive [book] are excellent, and the readable [text is] interesting." SLJ

Mummification and death rituals of ancient Egypt; by William W. Lace. ReferencePoint Press, Inc. 2013 80 p. (Ancient Egyptian wonders) (hardcover) $27.95

Grades: 8 9 10 11 12 **932**

1. Egypt -- Antiquities 2. Ancient civilization 3. Mummies -- Egypt 4. Egypt -- Civilization -- 332-30 B.C. 5. Funeral rites and ceremonies -- Egypt -- History

ISBN 1601522541; 9781601522542

LC 2012011481

This book is part of the Ancient Egyptian Wonders series and focuses on mummification and death rituals of ancient Egypt. "Each book contains a timeline, important facts highlighted in sidebars, and websites." Each book "includes quotes from experts and ancient texts." (Library Media Connection)

Includes bibliographical references and index.

The **new** cultural atlas of Egypt; edited by Leon Gray. Marshall Cavendish References 2010 192p il map lib bdg $99.93

Grades: 7 8 9 10 **932**

1. Atlases 2. Egypt -- History 3. Egypt -- Antiquities 4. Egypt -- Civilization

ISBN 978-0-7614-7877-5; 0-7614-7877-9

This title offers "students a wealth of information on all aspects of [Ancient Egyptian civilization]. . . . Packed with well-chosen, pertinent photos and artwork that add stunning detail to the study of [this culture] . . . [this book stands] out with excellent maps inserted within lucid, relevant text." SLJ

Includes glossary and bibliographical references

Rubalcaba, Jill

★ **Ancient** Egypt; archaeology unlocks the secrets of Egypt's past. by Jill Rubalcaba. National Geographic 2007 64p il map (National Geographic investigates) $17.95; lib bdg $27.90

Grades: 5 6 7 8 **932**

1. Egypt -- Antiquities 2. Egypt -- Civilization 3. Excavations (Archeology) -- Egypt

ISBN 0-7922-7784-8; 978-0-7922-7784-2; 0-7922-7857-7 lib bdg; 978-0-7922-7857-3 lib bdg

LC 2006032111

This describes how archeologists have learned about Ancient Egypt.

This offers "the beautiful photography and illustrations characteristic of the National Geographic Society, [a] well-written [text] and sidebars, and information on recent archaeological finds." SLJ

Includes bibliographical references

Weitzman, David L.

Pharaoh's boat; written and illustrated by David Weitzman. Houghton Mifflin Harcourt 2009 un il map $17

Grades: 4 5 6 7 **932**

1. Ships 2. Kings 3. Egypt -- Civilization

ISBN 978-0-547-05341-7; 0-547-05341-X

LC 2008036081

"Weitzman recounts the construction of a boat made for the Pharaoh Cheops and discusses its rediscovery and restoration in the 20th century. He weaves the history, texts, mythology, and customs of ancient Egypt into an effective narrative. . . . The volume's stylized illustrations are inspired by the two-dimensional depictions from ancient Egyptian art. The paintings' earth tones, accentuated by bright greens and blues, are both appropriate for the subject matter and pleasing to the eye." SLJ

932.01 Egypt--Early history to 332 B.C.

Kallen, Stuart A.

★ **Pharaohs** of Egypt; by Stuart A Kallen. ReferencePoint Press, Inc. 2013 80 p. (Ancient Egyptian wonders series) (hardcover) $27.95

Grades: 8 9 10 11 12 **932.01**

1. Pharaohs -- Egypt 2. Egypt -- Civilization 3. Pharaohs -- History 4. Egypt -- Antiquities 5. Egypt -- Civilization -- To 332 B.C 6. Egypt -- Politics and government -- To 332 B.C

ISBN 1601522568; 9781601522566

LC 2012000360

This book is part of the Ancient Egyptian Wonders series and looks at the pharaohs of Egypt. The series provides an "overview of ancient Egyptian civilization. . . . Each book contains a timeline, important facts highlighted in sidebars, and websites." Photographs and artwork are included. (Library Media Connection)

Includes bibliographical references and index

Nardo, Don

Ancient Egypt; by Don Nardo. ReferencePoint Press, Inc. 2018 80 p. (Cause & effect: ancient civilizations) (hardback) $29.95

Grades: 7 8 9 10 11 12 **932.01**

1. Ancient history 2. Egypt -- History 3. Egypt -- Civilization 4. Egypt -- History -- 332-30 B.C. 5. Egypt -- History -- To 332 B.C.

ISBN 1682821501; 9781682821503

LC 2016045977

This book in the Cause & Effect: Ancient Civilizations series, by Don Nardo, "offers a brief history of ancient Egypt and discusses the earliest civilization that developed across the Nile River Valley, the building of the pyramids, religious beliefs, and Cleopatra's role in Egypt's fall to the Romans." (Publisher's note)

"Well-written examinations of the factors that created, sustained, and eventually destroyed ancient civilizations distinguish this set." SLJ

Includes bibliographical references

Whiting, Jim

Life along the ancient Nile; by Jim Whiting. ReferencePoint Press, Inc. 2013 80 p. (Ancient Egyptian wonders series.) (hardcover) $27.95

Grades: 8 9 10 11 12 **932.01**

1. Egypt -- History 2. Ancient civilization 3. Nile River Valley -- Civilization 4. Egypt -- Civilization -- To 332 B.C

ISBN 1601522525; 9781601522528

LC 2012000358

This book is part of the Ancient Egyptian Wonders series and focuses on life along the ancient Nile. It offers "coverage of marriage, fashion, medicine, and social classes" as well as dental procedures and wild parties. "Each book contains a timeline, important facts highlighted in sidebars, and websites." (Library Media Connection)

Includes bibliographical references and index.

935 Mesopotamia to 637 and Iranian Plateau to 637

Gruber, Beth

★ **Ancient** Iraq; archaeology unlocks the secrets of Iraq's past. by Beth Gruber; Tony Wilkinson, consultant. National Geographic 2007 64p il map (National Geographic investigates) $17.95; lib bdg $27.90

Grades: 5 6 7 8 **935**

1. Iraq -- Antiquities 2. Iraq -- Civilization 3. Excavations (Archeology) -- Iraq

ISBN 978-0-7922-5382-2; 978-0-7922-5383-9 lib bdg

LC 2006032109

This explores the "world of ancient Iraq, in the region once known as Mesopotamia, the cradle of civilization. Join scientists as they study the Citadel in northern Iraq; explore the ancient city of Nineveh; and see how ancient treasures help scientists reassemble the mosaic-like puzzle of Iraq's past." Publisher's note

Includes bibliographical references

Kerrigan, Michael

Mesopotamians. Marshall Cavendish Benchmark 2010 64p il (Ancients in their own words) lib bdg $32.79

Grades: 5 6 7 8 **935**

1. Iraq -- Civilization

ISBN 978-1-60870-066-0; 1-60870-066-6

"Numerous photographs provide visual interest, with text describing the images to give details and background. Translations of the writings offer primary sources to accompany the secondary material presented. . . . The text is interesting enough to read cover to cover while the table of contents' descriptive chapter titles and the comprehensive index enable the . . . [book] to be used for specific research." Libr Media Connect

Includes bibliographical references

Nardo, Don

Ancient Mesopotamia; by Don Nardo. ReferencePoint Press, Inc. 2018 80 p. (Cause & effect: ancient civilizations) (hardback) $29.95

Grades: 7 8 9 10 11 12 **935**

1. Ancient history 2. Ancient civilization 3. Iraq -- Civilization 4. Iraq -- Civilization -- To 634

ISBN 1682821587; 9781682821589

LC 2016045952

This book in the Cause & Effect: Ancient Civilizations series, by Don Nardo, "introduces ancient Mesopotamian civilization, describing the introduction of agriculture, the rise of urban culture, the development of writing, and a brief history of the successive kingdoms that occupied the region." (Publisher's note)

"Well-written examinations of the factors that created, sustained, and eventually destroyed ancient civilizations distinguish this set." SLJ

Includes bibliographical references and index

936 Europe north and west of Italian Peninsula to ca. 499

Aronson, Marc

★ **If** stones could speak; unlocking the secrets of Stonehenge. by Marc Aronson; with Mike Parker Pearson and the Riverside Project. National Geographic 2010 64p il map $17.95; lib bdg $26.90

Grades: 4 5 6 7 **936**

1. Archeology 2. Archaeologists 3. College teachers 4. Stonehenge (England) 5. Excavations (Archeology) -- England

ISBN 978-1-4263-0599-3; 1-4263-0599-0; 978-1-4263-0600-6 lib bdg; 1-4263-0600-8 lib bdg

"Aronson investigates the work of archaeologist Mike Parker Pearson and his controversial theory that Stonehenge is but one end of a memorial ritual pathway that would have had an equivalent wood structure at the other end. . . . Time lines, resource lists, and photos of researchers at work add even more value to this informative, thought-provoking study. A uniquely perceptive look at how real science works." Booklist

Includes bibliographical references

Green, Jen

★ **Ancient** Celts; archaeology unlocks the secrets of the Celts' past. by Jen Green; Bettina Arnold, consultant. National Geographic 2008 64p il map (National Geographic investigates) $17.95; lib bdg $27.90

Grades: 4 5 6 7 **936**

1. Celts 2. Celtic civilization 3. Ireland -- Antiquities 4. Great Britain -- Antiquities 5. Excavations (Archeology) -- Europe

ISBN 978-1-4263-0225-1; 1-4263-0225-8; 978-1-4263-0226-8 lib bdg; 1-4263-0226-6 lib bdg

LC 2007047836

This describes ancient Celtic civilization and how archeologists have found out about it.

"With excellent-quality photographs and a well-written text, this is a thorough presentation of the most up-to-date knowledge about this ancient European culture." SLJ

Includes glossary and bibliographical references

Hinds, Kathryn, 1962-

Ancient Celts. Marshall Cavendish Benchmark 2009 79p il map (Barbarians!) lib bdg $35.64

Grades: 6 7 8 9 **936**

1. Celts

ISBN 978-0-7614-4062-8 lib bdg; 0-7614-4062-3 lib bdg

LC 2008-35976

This book has "wonderful photographs of contemporaneous and more recent artwork and sculpture, which bring the . . . [Ancient Celts] to life for the modern reader." Voice Youth Advocates

Includes glossary and bibliographical references

Early Germans. Marshall Cavendish Benchmark 2009 80p il (Barbarians!) lib bdg $35.64

Grades: 6 7 8 9 **936**

1. Germanic peoples 2. Rome -- History 3. Germany -- History

ISBN 978-0-7614-4064-2 lib bdg; 0-7614-4064-X lib bdg

LC 2008055789

"This . . . devotes excellent coverage and exposure to the emergence, development, and legacy of [the early Germans]." Libr Media Connect

Includes glossary and bibliographical references

Goths. Marshall Cavendish Benchmark 2009 80p il (Barbarians!) lib bdg $35.64

Grades: 6 7 8 9 **936**

1. Goths 2. Rome -- History

ISBN 978-07614-4065-9 lib bdg; 0-7614-4065-8 lib bdg

LC 2009014114

This has "wonderful photographs of contemporaneous and more recent artwork and sculpture, which bring the . . . [Goths] to life for the modern reader." Voice Youth Advocates

Includes glossary and bibliographical references

Huns. Marshall Cavendish Benchmark 2009 80p il (Barbarians!) lib bdg $35.64

Grades: 6 7 8 9 **936**

1. Huns 2. Nomads 3. Tribal leaders 4. Asia -- History 5. Europe -- History

ISBN 978-0-7614-4066-6 lib bdg; 0-7614-4066-6 lib bdg

LC 2008054828

"This . . . devotes excellent coverage and exposure to the emergence, development, and legacy of [the Huns]." Libr Media Connect

Includes glossary and bibliographical references

Millard, Anne

A **street** through time; written by Anne Millard; illustrated by Steve Noon. Revised ed. DK Pub. 2012 32p col il $17.99

Grades: 4 5 6 7 **936**

1. Cities and towns

ISBN 0-7894-3426-1

LC 98-3226

Traces the development of one street from the Stone Age to the present day, from dirt track to the rebuilding of inns as wine bars, showing how people lived and what they did all day

"The time-line construct is a useful demonstration for children, and the busy vistas would make a fine spring-board for encouraging students to create scenes of local history." Horn Book Guide

Includes glossary

937 Italian Peninsula to 476 and adjacent territories to 476

Ancient Rome; edited by Anita Croy. Brown Bear Books 2010 64p il map (Facts at your fingertips) lib bdg $35.65

Grades: 6 7 8 9 **937**

1. Rome -- Civilization

ISBN 978-1-933834-56-6 lib bdg; 1-933834-56-0 lib bdg

LC 2009-16805

Presents an introduction to ancient Rome, discussing its history, wars, system of government, provinces, and final decline

This begins "with an introduction accompanied by a striking full-page photo, followed by a two-page time line, and a two-paged spread for each topic. This format makes information easily accessible. Beautiful color photos of ancient ruins, drawings, maps, diagrams, and re-creations create appeal and enhance the information. . . . Whether for recreational browsing or serious research, this . . . will certainly prove useful for students." Libr Media Connect

Includes glossary and bibliographical references

Deckker, Zilah

★ **Ancient** Rome; archaeology unlocks the secrets of Rome's past. by Zilah Deckker; Robert Lindley Vann, Consultant. National Geographic 2007 64p il map (National Geographic investigates) $17.95; lib bdg $27.90

Grades: 4 5 6 7 **937**

1. Archeology 2. Rome -- Antiquities 3. Rome -- Civilization

ISBN 978-1-4263-0128-5; 978-1-4263-0129-2 lib bdg

LC 2007024795

This describes what archeologists have learned about Ancient Rome

Includes glossary and bibliographical references

Deem, James M.

★ **Bodies** from the ash. Houghton Mifflin 2005 50p il $16

Grades: 4 5 6 7 **937**

1. Pompeii (Extinct city)

ISBN 0-618-47308-4

LC 2004-26553

"On August 24, 79 C.E., the long-silent Mt. Vesuvius erupted, and volcanic ash rained down on the 20,000 residents of Pompeii. This photo-essay explains what happened when the volcano exploded—and how the results of this disaster were discovered hundreds of years later. . . . [This offers an] enormous amount of information. . . . But the jewels here are the numerous . . . photographs, especially those featuring the plaster casts and skeletons of people in their death throes. . . . Excellent for browsers as well as researchers." Booklist

Hanel, Rachael

Gladiators. Creative Education 2008 48p il (Fearsome fighters) lib bdg $31.35

Grades: 4 5 6 **937**

1. Gladiators 2. Rome -- Civilization

ISBN 978-1-58341-535-1 lib bdg; 1-58341-535-1 lib bdg

LC 2006021842

This "recounts the brutality and cruelty of fighting for sport celebrated during Roman times. . . . [The book does] an adequate job of covering fighting techniques, weapons, and history. Photographs and archival reproductions enhance the [presentation]; sidebars provide additional information." Horn Book Guide

Includes glossary and bibliographical references

Hinds, Kathryn, 1962-

Everyday life in the Roman Empire. Marshall Cavendish Benchmark 2010 320p il lib bdg $42.79

Grades: 7 8 9 10 **937**

1. Holy Roman Empire 2. Rome -- History

ISBN 978-0-7614-4484-8; 0-7614-4484-X

LC 2009-5913

A compilation of four titles in the Everyday Life in the Roman Empire series, published 2004: The city; The countryside; The Patricians; Religion

This book combines "clear, bold text with vivid reproductions of period paintings, frescoes, and sculptures, making for [a] stunning [presentation]." SLJ

Includes glossary and bibliographical references

Kerrigan, Michael

Romans. Marshall Cavendish Benchmark 2010 64p il (Ancients in their own words) lib bdg $32.79

Grades: 5 6 7 8 **937**

1. Rome -- Civilization

ISBN 978-1-60870-067-7; 1-60870-067-4

"Numerous photographs provide visual interest, with text describing the images to give details and background. Translations of the writings offer primary sources to accompany the secondary material presented. . . . The text is interesting enough to read cover to cover while the table of contents' descriptive chapter titles and the comprehensive index enable the . . . [book] to be used for specific research." Libr Media Connect

Includes bibliographical references

Lassieur, Allison

★ The **ancient** Romans; written by Allison Lassieur. Franklin Watts 2004 112p il map (People of the ancient world) lib bdg $30.50; pa $9.95

Grades: 5 6 7 8 **937**

1. Rome -- Civilization

ISBN 0-531-12338-3 lib bdg; 0-531-16742-9 pa

LC 2004-1955

"This attractive, thorough, and comprehensible book . . . offers a stellar introduction to life in ancient Rome." Booklist

Includes bibliographical references

Mann, Elizabeth

The **Roman** Colosseum; with illustrations by Michael Racz. Mikaya Press 1998 45p il (Wonders of the world) $19.95

Grades: 4 5 6 **937**

1. Rome -- Antiquities 2. Colosseum (Rome, Italy)

ISBN 0-9650493-3-7

LC 98-20060

Describes the building of the Colosseum in ancient Rome, and tells how it was used

This offers "a clear, well-written text and full-color drawings and paintings." SLJ

Includes glossary

Moser, Barry

Ashen sky; the letters of Pliny the Younger on the eruption of Vesuvius. illustrated by Barry Moser; written and translated by Benedicte Gilman. The J. Paul Getty Museum 2007 39p il map $19.95

Grades: 7 8 9 10 11 12 Adult **937**

1. Pompeii (Extinct city)

ISBN 978-0-89236-900-3; 0-89236-900-0

LC 2007-2781

This is a "handsome volume. Using an advanced vocabulary and sophisticated sentence structure, the text sets the event in historical context and gives brief biographical information about the elder and younger Pliny and Tacitus. . . . Moser's engravings reflect the darkness described in the text as day was turned to night by clouds of ash." SLJ

Includes bibliographical references

Nardo, Don

Classical civilization; by Don Nardo. Morgan Reynolds Pub. 2011 128 p. col. ill., maps (World history) (library) $28.95

Grades: 6 7 8 9 **937**

1. Rome -- History 2. Rome -- Civilization

ISBN 1599351749; 9781599351742

LC 2011005672

This book by Don Nardo on ancient Rome is part of the World History series. "Nardo provides a framework of history, then discusses aspects of the culture with far-reaching effects, such as its government, laws, architecture, roads, and language. The section called 'The First Urban Civilization' reveals surprising similarities between ancient Roman cities and their modern counterparts." (Booklist)

Includes bibliographical references (p. 120-121) and index.

Words of the ancient Romans; primary sources. Don Nardo, editor. Lucent Books 2003 128p il (The Lucent library of historical eras, Ancient Rome) $27.45

Grades: 6 7 8 9 **937**

1. Rome -- History 2. Rome -- History -- Sources

ISBN 1-59018-318-5

LC 2003-1645

"Excerpts from historians such as Plutarch, Livy, and Suetonius, as well as the satires of Juvenal and poetry of Ovid, are included in this history of ancient Rome as told through the words of those who lived at the time. Various chapters cover the founding of the city, Julius Caesar's life, the reign of Augustus, home and family life, entertainment, leisure, and religion. . . . Each chapter . . . [begins] with an introduction that helps to put the subject in perspective for modern readers." SLJ

Park, Louise

The **Roman** gladiators; by Louise Park and Timothy Love. Marshall Cavendish Benchmark 2009 32p il (Ancient and medieval people) $19.95

Grades: 4 5 6 **937**

1. Gladiators 2. Rome -- History 3. Rome -- Social life and customs

ISBN 978-0-7614-4443-5; 0-7614-4443-2

This title has "a simple and elegant design with the proper balance of quality writing and quantity of information. . . . Handy time lines, well-chosen photos of ruins and artifacts, quality illustrations, inset 'Quick Facts,' and 'What You Should Know About' features will grab reluctant readers and captivate even those with short attention spans." SLJ

Includes glossary

938 Greece to 323

Ancient Greece; edited by Michael Anderson. Britannica Educational Pub. in association with Rosen Educational Services 2012 88p il (Ancient civilizations) lib bdg $31.70
Grades: 5 6 7 8 **938**
1. Greece -- Civilization
ISBN 978-1-61530-513-1; 1-61530-513-0
LC 2011000086
This book provides "enough information about the development, way of life, accomplishments, and decline of [Ancient Greece] without overwhelming readers. Maps; full-color illustrations and photographs, many full page; and sidebars provide additional focus. . . . The system of city-states is explained. Literature, art, and architecture and their lasting influence are described in detail." SLJ
Includes glossary and bibliographical references

Kerrigan, Michael
Greeks. Marshall Cavendish Benchmark 2010 64p il (Ancients in their own words) lib bdg $32.79
Grades: 5 6 7 8 **938**
1. Greece -- Civilization
ISBN 978-1-60870-065-3; 1-60870-065-8
"Numerous photographs provide visual interest, with text describing the images to give details and background. Translations of the writings offer primary sources to accompany the secondary material presented. . . . The text is interesting enough to read cover to cover while the table of contents' descriptive chapter titles and the comprehensive index enable the . . . [book] to be used for specific research." Libr Media Connect
Includes bibliographical references

Marcovitz, Hal
★ **Ancient** Greece; by Hal Marcovitz. ReferencePoint Press 2012 96 p. (Understanding world history) (hardcover) $27.95
Grades: 7 8 9 10 **938**
1. Greece -- History 2. Greece -- Civilization 3. Greece -- Civilization -- To 146 B.C.
ISBN 9781601522849; 1601522843
LC 2011048991
This book on ancient Greece by Hal Marcovitz is part of "Understanding World History, a series that surveys the political, social, and cultural trends of major periods and events in world history."(Publisher's note) It "combines mythology, history, and politics and provides an enlightening perspective on the treatment of women in the cultures of Athens and Sparta." (Booklist)
Includes bibliographical references and index.

McGee, Marni
★ **Ancient** Greece; archaeology unlocks the secrets of Greece's past. by Marni McGee; Michael Shanks, consultant. National Geographic 2007 64p il map (National Geographic investigates) $17.95; lib bdg $27.90
Grades: 5 6 7 8 **938**
1. Greece -- Antiquities 2. Greece -- Civilization 3. Excavations (Archeology) -- Greece
ISBN 978-0-7922-7826-9; 0-7922-7826-7; 978-0-7922-7872-6 lib bdg; 0-7922-7872-0 lib bdg
LC 2006032108
This describes how archeologists have found out about Ancient Greek civilization
This offers "the beautiful photography and illustrations characteristic of the National Geographic Society, [a] well-written [text] and sidebars, and information on recent archaeological finds." SLJ
Includes bibliographical references

Nardo, Don
Classical civilization; by Don Nardo. Morgan Reynolds Pub. 2011 112 p. ill. (some col.), col. map (World history) (library) $28.95
Grades: 6 7 8 9 **938**
1. Greece -- History 2. Greece -- Civilization 3. Greece -- History -- To 146 B.C. 4. Greece -- Civilization -- To 146 B.C.
ISBN 1599351730; 9781599351735
LC 2011000235
This book by Don Nardo on ancient Greece is part of the World History series. It "encompasses not only political history but also influential developments in political thinking, philosophy, science, literature, architecture, sports, and the military. The section on the Olympics debunks the notion that early Olympic athletes were amateurs without financial backing." (Booklist)
Includes bibliographical references and index.

The **new** cultural atlas of the Greek world; edited by Tim Cooke. Marshall Cavendish Reference 2010 192p il map lib bdg $99.93
Grades: 7 8 9 10 **938**
1. Atlases 2. Greece -- History 3. Greece -- Antiquities 4. Greece -- Civilization
ISBN 978-0-7614-7878-2; 0-7614-7878-7
This offers "students a wealth of information on all aspects of . . . ancient [Greek civilization]. . . . Packed with well-chosen, pertinent photos and artwork that add stunning detail to the study of [this culture] . . . [this book stands] out with excellent maps inserted within lucid, relevant text." SLJ
Includes glossary and bibliographical references

Park, Louise
The **Spartan** hoplites; by Louise Park and Timothy Love. Marshall Cavendish Benchmark 2009 32p il map (Ancient and medieval people) $19.95
Grades: 4 5 6 **938**
1. Soldiers 2. Sparta (Extinct city) 3. Athens (Greece) -- History
ISBN 978-0-7614-4449-7; 0-7614-4449-1
LC 2008-55779
This title has "a simple and elegant design with the proper balance of quality writing and quantity of information. . . . Handy time lines, well-chosen photos of ruins and artifacts, quality illustrations, inset 'Quick Facts', and 'What You Should Know About' features will grab reluctant readers and captivate even those with short attention spans." SLJ
Includes glossary

Powell, Anton
Ancient Greece; 3rd ed.; Chelsea House 2007 96p il map (Cultural atlas for young people) $35
Grades: 5 6 7 8 **938**
1. Greece -- Civilization 2. Greece -- History -- 0-323
ISBN 978-0-8160-6821-0; 0-8160-6821-6
First published 1989
Maps, charts, illustrations, and text trace the history and culture of ancient Greece.
"Filled with excellent captioned, color maps, photographs, and illustrations of primary source materials. There are sidebars, gazetteers,

and timelines of events in politics, war, art, technology, etc." Libr Media Connect

Includes glossary and bibliographical references

Roberts, Jennifer Tolbert

The **ancient** Greek world. Oxford University Press 2004 190p il map $32.95

Grades: 7 8 9 10 **938**

1. Greece -- Civilization 2. Greece -- History -- 0-323

ISBN 0-19-515696-X

Introduces the history, culture, and people of ancient Greece and examines its many contributions to the development of Western society

"A thoroughly researched political and cultural history. . . . Extensive quotes from primary sources, attractive page layouts, numerous good-quality color photographs of ruins and artifacts, plus the infusion of humor make for a palatable, solid resource for any collection. " SLJ

Villing, Alexandra

The **ancient** Greeks; their lives and their world. J. Paul Getty Museum 2010 80p il $17.95

Grades: 7 8 9 10 **938**

1. Greece -- Civilization

ISBN 978-0-89236-985-0; 0-89236-985-X

"This volume provides a colorful overview of life in ancient Greece. Each chapter covers a different topic and, though short, contains lots of information. Numerous photographs of art and artifacts, along with accompanying captions, illustrate the bygone culture." Horn Book Guide

939 Other parts of ancient world

Cline, Eric H., 1960-

★ **Digging** for Troy; from Homer to Hisarlik. [by] Jill Rubalcaba and Eric H. Cline; with illustrations by Sarah S. Brannen. Charlesbridge 2011 74p il map $17.95; pa $9.95

Grades: 5 6 7 8 **939**

1. Trojan War 2. Troy (Extinct city) 3. Greece -- Civilization 4. Excavations (Archaeology) -- Turkey 5. Archaeologists 6. Civilization, Mycenaean 6. Excavations (Archaeology) -- Turkey -- Troy (Extinct city)

ISBN 978-1-58089-326-8; 1-58089-326-0; 978-1-58089-327-5 pa; 1-58089-327-9 pa

LC 2010-07586

"Rubalcaba teams up with a noted archaeologist to make sense of the complicated, controversial, contradictory history and remains of the Turkish site called Hisarlik, better known as Troy. . . . The book begins with a brief but exciting retelling of the Trojan War . . . and goes on to profile Heinrich Schliemann. . . . After Schliemann, generations of archaeologists have excavated Hisarlik: along with the history of the excavations, readers are given an overview of technological developments in the field. . . . Source notes and an impressive bibliography attest to meticulous research and guide readers to journal articles, books, and online museum exhibits. Elegant illustrations mimicking Greek red-figure pottery are lovely and appropriate. Extraordinarily readable, gracefully laid out, and speckled with lines from The Iliad, this book will inspire young people interested in solving the mysteries of the past." SLJ

Includes bibliographical references

Hinds, Kathryn, 1962-

Scythians and Sarmatians. Marshall Cavendish Benchmark 2009 80p il map (Barbarians!) lib bdg $35.64

Grades: 6 7 8 9 **939**

1. Horses 2. Nomads 3. Scythians 4. Sarmatians

ISBN 978-0-7614-4072-7 lib bdg; 0-7614-4072-0 lib bdg

LC 2009016496

"This . . . devotes excellent coverage and exposure to the emergence, development, and legacy of [the Scythians and Sarmatians]." Libr Media Connect

Includes glossary and bibliographical references

Podany, Amanda H.

The **ancient** Near Eastern world; [by] Amanda H. Podany & Marni McGee. Oxford University Press 2005 174p il map (World in ancient times) $32.95

Grades: 7 8 9 10 **939**

1. Middle East -- Antiquities 2. Middle East -- Civilization

ISBN 0-19-516159-9

LC 2004-13622

This "traces the history of the Fertile Crescent until Alexander the Great's conquest in 330 B.C.E. . . . The text is matched with a great deal of supporting matter including time lines, maps, dramatis personae, high-quality photos, and artists' renderings. [This] fine [volume is a] worthy [addition] to most libraries." SLJ

Includes bibliographical references

Sherrow, Victoria

Ancient Africa; archaeology unlocks the secrets of Africa's past. by Victoria Sherrow; James Denbow, consultant. National Geographic Society 2007 64p il map (National Geographic investigates) $17.95

Grades: 4 5 6 7 **939**

1. Africa -- Antiquities 2. Africa -- Civilization

ISBN 978-0-7922-5384-6; 0-7922-5384-1

LC 2007277594

This describes archeological discoveries about ancient peoples of Africa including the Dogon people of Mali, the ancient city of Jenne-jeno, and the Kushite temples at Jebel Barkal.

Includes bibliographical references

940.1 Europe--Early history to 1453

Corbishley, Mike

The **Middle** Ages; 3rd ed.; Chelsea House 2007 96p il map (Cultural atlas for young people) $35

Grades: 5 6 7 8 **940.1**

1. Middle Ages 2. Medieval civilization

ISBN 978-0-8160-6825-8; 0-8160-6825-9

First published 1989

Maps, charts, illustrations, and text explore the history and culture of the Middle Ages.

"The maps are excellent, precise, clear, and easy to read and understand, and the illustrations, particularly those of works of art, are wonderful. . . . This attractive volume provides an intriguing cross-cultural look at the medieval world. An excellent addition." SLJ

Includes glossary and bibliographical references

Durman, Laura

Castle life; by Laura Durman. Arcturus Pub. 2013 32 p. col. ill. (library) $28.50

Grades: 4 5 6 **940.1**

1. Castles 2. Medieval civilization 3. Civilization, Medieval
ISBN 1848585608; 9781848585607

LC 2011051440

In this book, author "[Laura] Durman presents young readers with a . . . view of what life was really like for everyday people in the Middle Ages. Bound by the strict societal system known as feudalism, peasants, knights, and nobles shared space . . . in castles. Readers take a room by room tour, learning how castles functioned both day-to-day, when under siege, and at times of feasting and banqueting." (Children's Literature)

Knights; by Laura Durman. Arcturus Pub. 2012 32 p. col. ill. (Knights and castles) (library) $28.50

Grades: 4 5 6 **940.1**

1. Picture books for children 2. Knights and knighthood 3. Civilization, Medieval
ISBN 1848585616; 9781848585614

LC 2011051452

This book by Laura Durman is part of the Knights and Castles series and looks at knights. The "books cover a wide range of topics such as weapons, castle construction, food, religion, and the structure and hierarchy of society." Full-color photographs and illustrations are included. (School Library Journal)

Includes bibliographical references (p. 31) and index.

Helget, Nicole

Barbarians; Nicole Helget. Creative Education 2012 48 p. (alk. paper) $35.65

Grades: 5 6 7 8 **940.1**

1. Huns 2. Nomads 3. Vikings 4. Teutonic peoples 5. Classical civilization 6. Middle Ages 7. Migrations of nations 8. Europe -- History -- 392-814
ISBN 1608181820; 9781608181827

LC 2011035798

This book by Nicole Lea Helget "focuses on the transient, adaptable Gelts, Franks, Goths, Huns, and Vikings, collectively known as 'barbarians,' and their differing warring skills against the Greek and Roman Empires." (Booklist) "Viewed as threats by the Romans in particular, the barbarian people were often co-opted or conquered and then integrated into the Empire. Eventually, as the Roman Empire waned, the pressure of nomadic barbarians proved too much to withstand and Rome fell." (Children's Literature)

Includes bibliographical references and index

Hinds, Kathryn, 1962-

★ **Everyday** life in medieval Europe. Marshall Cavendish Benchmark 2009 285p il lib bdg $42.79

Grades: 6 7 8 9 **940.1**

1. Middle Ages 2. Medieval civilization 3. Europe -- Social conditions 4. Europe -- Economic conditions 5. Europe -- History -- 476-1492 6. Europe -- Social life and customs
ISBN 978-0-7614-3927-1; 0-7614-3927-7

LC 2008012748

"Fluid, approachable, beautifully illustrated, and fascinatingly detailed." Booklist

Includes glossary and bibliographical references

Langley, Andrew

Medieval life; written by Andrew Langley; photographed by Geoff Brightling. rev ed; DK Pub. 2011 72p il (DK eyewitness books) lib bdg $19.99

Grades: 4 5 6 7 **940.1**

1. Medieval civilization
ISBN 9780756682828 lib bdg
First published 1996 by Knopf

An illustrated look at various aspects of life in medieval Europe, covering everyday life, religion, royalty, and more.

Malam, John

Early medieval times. Zak Books 2009 48p il map (History of the world) lib bdg $34.25

Grades: 7 8 9 10 **940.1**

1. Middle Ages 2. Medieval civilization 3. Europe -- History -- 476-1492
ISBN 978-88-6098-150-9 lib bdg; 88-6098-150-6 lib bdg

LC 2008-8405

The "effectiveness lies in the combination of lush illustrations, well-chosen, captioned photographs of contemporary artifacts, and . . . [a] reasoned, concise [narrative]. Succinct time lines border most pages, and . . . the proper amount of white space, and clear dark print maintain organization and clarity. A superior choice." SLJ

Includes glossary

Morris, Neil

Late medieval Europe. Zak Books 2009 48p il map (History of the world) lib bdg $34.25

Grades: 7 8 9 10 **940.1**

1. Middle Ages 2. Medieval civilization 3. Europe -- History -- 476-1492
ISBN 978-88-6098-152-3 lib bdg; 88-6098-152-2 lib bdg

LC 2008-8407

The "effectiveness lies in the combination of lush illustrations, well-chosen, captioned photographs of contemporary artifacts, and . . . [a] reasoned, concise [narrative]. Succinct time lines border most pages, and . . . the proper amount of white space, and clear dark print maintain organization and clarity. A superior choice." SLJ

Includes glossary

Nardo, Don

Medieval Europe; by Don Nardo. 1st ed. Morgan Reynolds Pub. 2011 128 p. col. ill., maps (World history) (library) $28.95

Grades: 6 7 8 9 **940.1**

1. Middle Ages 2. Great Britain -- History -- 1066-1485, Medieval period 3. Civilization, Medieval 4. Europe -- History -- 476-1492 5. Europe -- Social life and customs
ISBN 1599351722; 9781599351728

LC 2010054477

This book by Don Nardo, part of the World History series, focuses on Medieval Europe. Medieval Europe "was the bridge that led from the ancient world to the modern one." Topics include the Roman Catholic Church, the stone castles built by kings and nobles, the Crusades, and the Renaissance. (Publisher's note)

Includes bibliographical references (p. 120-121) and index.

Park, Louise

The **medieval** knights; by Louise Park and Timothy Love. Marshall Cavendish Benchmark 2009 32p il map (Ancient and medieval people) $19.95

Grades: 4 5 6 **940.1**

1. Medieval civilization 2. Knights and knighthood
ISBN 978-0-7614-4444-2; 0-7614-4444-0

LC 2008-55777

This title has "a simple and elegant design with the proper balance of quality writing and quantity of information. . . . Handy time lines, well-chosen photos of ruins and artifacts, quality illustrations, inset 'Quick Facts', and 'What You Should Know About' features will grab reluctant readers and captivate even those with short attention spans." SLJ

Includes glossary

Schlitz, Laura Amy

★ **Good** masters! Sweet ladies! voices from a medieval village. [by] Laura Amy Schlitz; illustrated by Robert Byrd. Candlewick Press 2007 85p il $19.99; pa $9.99

Grades: 5 6 7 8 **940.1**

1. Monologues 2. Middle Ages -- Drama

ISBN 978-0-7636-1578-9; 0-7636-1578-1; 978-0-7636-4332-4 pa; 0-7636-4332-7 pa

Awarded the Newbery Medal, 2008

A collection of short one-person plays featuring characters, between ten and fifteen years old, who live in or near a thirteenth-century English manor

"Designed for performance and excellent for use in interdisciplinary history classrooms, the book offers students an incredibly approachable format for learning about the Middle Ages that makes the period both realistic and relevant. . . . Byrd's illustrations evoke the era and give dramatists ideas for appropriate costuming and props." SLJ

940.2 Europe--1453-

Claybourne, Anna

The **Renaissance**; [by] Anna Claybourne. Raintree 2008 64p il map (Time travel guide) lib bdg $34.29; pa $9.99

Grades: 6 7 8 9 **940.2**

1. Renaissance

ISBN 978-1-4109-2910-5 lib bdg; 978-1-4109-2916-7 pa

LC 2007006027

This describes life in 15th and 16th century Europe in the form of travel guide.

The book "is chock-full of color photographs and reproductions, maps, sidebars, and age-appropriate humor. . . . The [author has] done a commendable job of writing [text] that [measures] up to the rich visual layout." SLJ

Includes bibliographical references

Currie, Stephen

★ The **Renaissance**; by Stephen Currie. ReferencePoint Press, Inc. 2012 96 p. (hardcover) $27.95

Grades: 7 8 9 10 **940.2**

1. Renaissance

ISBN 1601521898; 9781601521897

LC 2011048993

This book by Stephen Currie is part of the "Understanding World History" series. It "opens with an . . . overview of the circumstances that came together to inspire a Renaissance." (School Library Journal) It profiles "artists and philosophers . . . along with scientists like [Isaac] Newton. Also discussed is the tension between religion and humanism." (Booklist)

Includes bibliographical references and index.

Elliott, Lynne

The **Renaissance** in Europe; [by] Lynne Elliott. Crabtree Pub. Co. 2009 32p il lib bdg $26.60; pa $8.95

Grades: 6 7 8 9 **940.2**

1. Renaissance 2. Europe -- Civilization

ISBN 978-0-7787-4591-4 lib bdg; 0-7787-4591-0 lib bdg; 978-0-7787-4611-9 pa; 0-7787-4611-9 pa

LC 2008-52410

"Ideal introductions to concepts, people, and events of the Renaissance... succinct and thorough. "SLJ

Encyclopedia of women in the Renaissance; Italy, France, and England. Diana Robin, Anne R. Larsen, Carole Levin, editors. ABC-CLIO 2007 xx, 459p il $95

Grades: 7 8 9 10 11 12 **940.2**

1. Renaissance 2. Women -- Europe 3. Women -- History

ISBN 1-85109-772-4; 978-1-85109-772-2

LC 2006038854

"This work covers how women of the [Renaissance] lived; how they were treated and viewed; and literary, artistic musical, social, political, scientific, and religious contributions they made. Most of the roughly 150 entries are biographies. . . . Each of the alphabetically arranged essays is about one-half to two pages long, and is signed, concise, and well written. . . . An excellent addition." SLJ

Includes bibliographical references

Grant, Neil

Renaissance Europe. Zak Books 2009 48p il map (History of the world) lib bdg $34.25

Grades: 7 8 9 10 **940.2**

1. Renaissance 2. Medieval civilization 3. Europe -- History -- 476-1492 4. Europe -- History -- 1492-1789

ISBN 978-88-6098-153-0 lib bdg; 88-6098-153-0 lib bdg

LC 2008-8408

The "effectiveness lies in the combination of lush illustrations, well-chosen, captioned photographs of contemporary artifacts, and . . . [a] reasoned, concise [narrative]. Succinct time lines border most pages, and . . . clear dark print maintain organization and clarity. A superior choice." SLJ

Includes glossary

Hinds, Kathryn, 1962-

★ **Everyday** life in the Renaissance. Marshall Cavendish Benchmark 2010 327p il lib bdg $42.79

Grades: 7 8 9 10 **940.2**

1. Renaissance 2. Europe -- Civilization

ISBN 978-0-7614-4483-1; 0-7614-4483-1

LC 2008-54829

A compilation of four titles in the Everyday Life in the Renaissance series, published 2004: The church; The city; The countryside; The court

This book combines "clear, bold text with vivid reproductions of period paintings, frescoes, and sculptures, making for [a] stunning [presentation]." SLJ

Includes glossary and bibliographical references

Malam, John

The **birth** of modern nations. Zak Books 2009 48p il map (History of the world) lib bdg $34.25

Grades: 7 8 9 10 **940.2**

1. Europe -- History -- 17th century

ISBN 978-88-6098-155-4 lib bdg; 88-6098-155-7 lib bdg

LC 2008-8570

The "effectiveness lies in the combination of lush illustrations, well-chosen, captioned photographs of contemporary artifacts, and . . . [a] reasoned, concise [narrative]. Succinct time lines border most pages, and . . . the proper amount of white space, and clear dark print maintain organization and clarity. A superior choice." SLJ

Includes glossary

940.3 World War I, 1914-1918

Adams, Simon

World War I; written by Simon Adams; photographed by Andy Crawford. rev ed.; DK Pub. 2007 72p il (DK eyewitness books) $15.99

Grades: 4 5 6 7 **940.3**

1. World War, 1914-1918

ISBN 978-0-7566-3007-2; 0-7566-3007-X

LC 2007279476

First published 2001

This look at World War I examines life in the trenches and the devastation of Europe by the Great War

Barber, Nicola

World War I; by Nicola Barber. Heinemann Library 2012 80 p. ill. (some col.), col. maps (Living through) (library) $36.50; (paperback) $10.99

Grades: 6 7 8 9 **940.3**

1. World War, 1914-1918

ISBN 1432960105; 9781432960018; 9781432960100

LC 2011015931

In this book on World War I, part of the "Living Through" series, "[Nicola] Barber explains the European political powder keg of the late 1800s and the turn of the last century before telling of the assassination of Archduke Franz Ferdinand." (VOYA) Other topics include " the role of women in the war, propaganda, and the misalignment of the Peace Treaty of Versailles." (Children's Literature)

Includes bibliographical references (p. 76-78) and index.

Batten, Jack

The **war** to end all wars; the story of World War I. Tundra Books 2009 154p il $22.95

Grades: 7 8 9 10 11 12 **940.3**

1. World War, 1914-1918

ISBN 978-0-88776-879-8; 0-88776-879-2

"More than six million soldiers perished in World War I . . . and this beautifully designed, highly readable photo-essay combines a few of their personal stories with the larger picture of politics and military strategies on all sides. . . . Young people with a particular interest in the war will be enthralled." Booklist

Bausum, Ann

★ **Unraveling** freedom; the battle for democracy on the home front during World War I. National Geographic 2010 88p il $19.95; lib bdg $28.90

Grades: 7 8 9 10 **940.3**

1. Civil rights 2. German Americans 3. World War, 1914-1918 -- United States 4. United States -- Politics and government -- 1898-1919

ISBN 978-1-4263-0702-7; 1-4263-0702-0; 978-1-4263-0703-4 lib bdg; 1-4263-0703-9 lib bdg

LC 2010-10631

"Bausum describes the events that would eventually lead the U.S. into the European conflict that ultimately led to World War I. She then turns her attention to describing the destruction of civil liberties by President Wilson, Congress, and those in control of political power during the country's campaign to 'make the world safe for democracy.' . . . Black-and-white archival photos and political cartoons are arranged in an artistic manner with informative captions. Appropriate quotations by various people of the time are displayed in elegant fonts. Make this unique and timely offering a definite first purchase." SLJ

Includes bibliographical references

Carlisle, Rodney P.

World War I. Facts on File 2006 454p il map (Eyewitness history) $75

Grades: 8 9 10 11 12 **940.3**

1. World War, 1914-1918 -- Personal narratives

ISBN 0-8160-6061-4; 978-0-8160-6061-0

LC 2005-27236

First published 1992 under the authorship of Joe H. Kirchberger with title: The First World War

This book "provides hundreds of firsthand accounts—from diary entries, letters, speeches, and newspaper accounts—that focus on different warfare issues and on the social and cultural impacts of the war on Europe and the United States. . . . This volume also includes critical documents related to this topic, as well as capsule biographies of key figures, narrative sections, eyewitness testimonies, 102 black-and-white photographs, maps and graphs, a bibliography, notes, a glossary, chronologies, appendixes, and an index." Publisher's note

Includes bibliographical references

Coetzee, Marilyn Shevin

World War I; a history in documents. [by] Marilyn Shevin-Coetzee and Frans Coetzee. 2nd ed; Oxford University Press 2011 182p il (Pages from history) $39.95; pa $24.95

Grades: 7 8 9 10 **940.3**

1. World War, 1914-1918 -- Sources

ISBN 978-0-19-973151-0; 978-0-19-973152-7 pa

LC 2009049519

First published 2002 with authors' names in reverse order

Offering an "account of the war as more than a purely military phenomenon, . . . [this book] also addresses its profound social, cultural, and economic implications. Authors Marilyn Shevin-Coetzee and Frans Coetzee use editorials, memoirs, newspaper articles, poems, and letters to recreate the many facets of the war." Publisher's note

Includes bibliographical references

Freedman, Russell

★ The **war** to end all wars; World War I. Clarion Books 2010 176p il map $22

Grades: 6 7 8 9 10 **940.3**

1. World War, 1914-1918

ISBN 978-0-547-02686-2; 0-547-02686-2

LC 2009-28971

"In his signature lucid style, Freedman offers a photo-essay that examines World War I, the first global war in which modern weapons inflicted mass slaughter and an estimated 20 million people were killed. Interwoven into the big picture of the war's causes and consequences are unforgettable vignettes of German and Allied soldiers, drawn from reports, letters, and diaries, and the personal details are heartbreaking." Booklist

Grant, R. G.

Why did World War I happen? Gareth Stevens Pub. 2011 48p il map (Moments in history) lib bdg $31.95; pa $14.05

Grades: 6 7 8 9 **940.3**

1. World War, 1914-1918

ISBN 978-1-4339-4181-8 lib bdg; 1-4339-4181-3 lib bdg; 978-1-4339-4182-5 pa; 1-4339-4182-1 pa

LC 2010012459

"Examines the events that served as . . . [precursors to World War I]. . . . Brightly colored pull-out boxes highlight important turning points, the perspective of the everyday man, and further information on why specific events occurred. Numerous photographs help readers visualize concepts more fully. . . . Students should be able to easily use this resource." Libr Media Connect

Includes glossary and bibliographical references

Osborne, Linda Barrett

★ **Come** on in, America; the United States in World War I. Linda Barrett Osborne. Abrams Books for Young Readers 2017 176 p. b&w illustrations, map $17.95

Grades: 5 6 7 8 9 **940.3**

1. World War, 1914-1918 -- United States 2. World War, 1914-1918

ISBN 9781419723780

LC 2016036830

In this book, by Linda Barrett Osborne, examines the decision of the U.S. to be involved in the First World War. "On April 6, 1917, the United States declared war on Germany. . . . German submarine attacks on American ships in March 1917 were the overt motive for declaring war, but the underlying reasons were far more complex. [Osborne] explores not only how and why the United States joined World War I, but also the events . . . that changed the course of American history." (Publisher's note)

Includes bibliographical references and index

Swain, Gwenyth

World War I; an interactive history adventure. by Gwenyth Swain ; consultant: Timothy Solie. Capstone Press 2012 112 p. ill. (some col.) (library) $31.32; (paperback) $6.95

Grades: 3 4 5 6 **940.3**

1. World War, 1914-1918

ISBN 1429679972; 9781429660204; 9781429679978

LC 2011033624

This book by Gwenyth Swain is part of the You Choose series. "At the bottom of many pages, you are asked to make a decision about what to do or where to go. Subsequent decisions take you to the adventure's end, at which point readers may choose to go back and begin again and find out where an alternate path might have led. . . . [In] Belgium . . . student nurses must decide whether to stay at their hospital or flee. Later, a British teen has to choose whether to enlist or wait." (Booklist)

Includes bibliographical references (p. 111) and index.

940.4 Military history of World War I

Bascomb, Neal

The **grand** escape; the greatest prison breakout of the 20th century. Neal Bascomb. Arthur A. Levine Books 2018 275 p. (hardback) $18.99

Grades: 7 8 9 10 **940.4**

1. Escapes 2. Prisoners of war 3. World War, 1914-1918 4. Prisoners of war -- Great Britain -- Biography 5. Prisoner-of-war escapes -- Germany -- Holzminden 6. World War, 1914-1918 -- Prisoners and prisons, German 7. Prisoners of war -- Germany -- Holzminden -- Biography

ISBN 9781338140354; 9781338140347

LC 2018016857

In this book, by Neal Bascomb, "at the height of World War I, as battles raged in the trenches and in the air, another struggle for survival was being waged in the most notorious POW camp in all of Germany: Holzminden. . . . It was home to the most troublesome Allied prisoners--and the most talented at escape. 'The Grand Escape' tells the remarkable tale of a band of pilots who pulled off an ingenious plan and made it out of enemy territory in the biggest breakout of WWI." (Publisher's note)

Includes bibliographical references and index

Greatest breakout of the 20th century

Bausum, Ann

Stubby the War Dog; The True Story of World War I's Bravest Dog. by Ann Bausum. Natl Geographic Soc Childrens books 2014 80 p. $26.90

Grades: 4 5 6 7 **940.4**

1. Dogs -- War use 2. World War, 1914-1918 -- United States 3. Stubby (Dog) 4. Dogs -- War use -- United States 5. United States. Army. Infantry Regiment, 102nd -- Mascots

ISBN 1426314868; 1426314876; 9781426314865; 9781426314872

This book, by Ann Bausum, is the story of "Stubby, a terrier of unknown origin, [who] found his way to the training grounds in New Haven, CT, as recruits were preparing to ship off to . . . World War I. . . . He attached himself to J. Robert Conroy, one of the recruits, and they became an inseparable team for the rest of Stubby's life. . . . [T] he dog lived the life of any soldier: sleeping in trenches, dodging bullets in the heat of battle, and ferreting out enemy combatants." (School Library Journal)

"The popularity of tales about dogs in war stems from the inherent poignancy—sweet, loyal, sad-eyed canines entered into the mad chaos of man-made destruction. But enter they occasionally do, and none more famously than Stubby... The speedy story is surrounded by evocative period photos, including plenty of the goofy-faced Stubby, and leads up to his later careers as a vaudeville star and a football mascot, and his eventual taxidermied inclusion in the Smithsonian. A triumph on three fronts: educational, emotional, and inspirational. For older teens, suggest Bausman's adult title, Sergeant Stubby." Booklist

Murphy, Jim

★ **Truce**; the day the soldiers stopped fighting. Scholastic Press 2009 116p il map $19.99

Grades: 5 6 7 8 **940.4**

1. World War, 1914-1918

ISBN 978-0-545-13049-3; 0-545-13049-2

LC 2008-40500

"By December 1918, the western front of World War I featured two parallel trenches stretching from the North Sea to the Alps. . . . On Christmas Day, an informal peace broke out in many locations along the front. . . . Murphy's excellent telling of this unusual war story begins with an account of the events that led to WWI and follows the shift in the soldiers' mind-sets. . . . Printed in tones of sepia, the illustrations in this handsome volume include many period photos as well as paintings and maps. . . . Well organized and clearly written, this presentation vividly portrays the context and events of the Christmas Truce." Booklist

Includes bibliographical references

940.53 World War II, 1939-1945

Adams, Simon

World War II; written by Simon Adams; photographed by Andy Crawford. rev ed.; DK Pub. 2007 72p il (DK eyewitness books) $16.99

Grades: 4 5 6 7 **940.53**

1. World War, 1939-1945

ISBN 978-0-7566-3008-9; 0-7566-3008-8

LC 2008273315

First published 2000

Provides a concise history of World War II including information about the Holocaust, the code-breaking Enigma, and the deadly V2 rocket

Altman, Linda Jacobs

Escape --teens on the run; primary sources from the Holocaust. Holocaust research by Margaret Shannon. Enslow Publishers 2010 128p il map (True stories of teens in the Holocaust) lib bdg $31.93

Grades: 7 8 9 10 11 12 **940.53**

1. Holocaust, 1933-1945 2. World War, 1939-1945 -- Children 3. World War, 1939-1945 -- Refugees

ISBN 978-0-7660-3270-5 lib bdg; 0-7660-3270-1 lib bdg

LC 2009021378

Discusses children and teens on the run during the Holocaust in Europe, including the different ways young people escaped the Nazis, places of refuge in Europe, and hiding and resistance.

The "book provides historical background, but the narratives rest upon the recollections, making the material immediate and horrifyingly real." SLJ

Includes glossary and bibliographical references

Hidden teens, hidden lives; primary sources from the Holocaust. Enslow Publishers 2010 128p il (True stories of teens in the Holocaust) lib bdg $31.93

Grades: 8 9 10 11 12 **940.53**

1. Holocaust survivors 2. Holocaust, 1933-1945 3. World War, 1939-1945 -- Children 4. World War, 1939-1945 -- Personal narratives

ISBN 978-0-7660-3271-2; 0-7660-3271-X

LC 2009-6504

"Explores the lives of children and teens who went into hiding during the Holocaust; looks at various places used as hiding spots, such as barns and attics, and different ways to hide, like assuming false identities, and how these were used as a tool to survive." Publisher's note

Includes bibliographical references

Shattered youth in Nazi Germany; primary sources from the Holocaust. Holocaust research by Margaret Shannon. Enslow Publishers 2010 128p il map (True stories of teens in the Holocaust) lib bdg $31.93

Grades: 8 9 10 11 12 **940.53**

1. National socialism 2. Hitler-Jugend 3. Holocaust, 1933-1945 4. Germany -- Politics and government -- 1933-1945

ISBN 978-0-7660-3268-2 lib bdg; 0-7660-3268-X lib bdg

LC 2008048002

Examines the lives of children and teens living in Germany before and during the Holocaust, including the rise of Nazism, growing persecution of Jews, and the Hitler Youth

The "book provides historical background, but the narratives rest upon the recollections, making the material immediate and horrifyingly real." SLJ

Includes glossary and bibliographical references

The **Warsaw** Ghetto Uprising; striking a blow against the Nazis. Enslow 2011 128p il map (The Holocaust through primary sources) lib bdg $31.93

Grades: 7 8 9 10 11 12 **940.53**

1. Jews -- Poland 2. Holocaust, 1933-1945 3. Warsaw (Poland) -- History -- Uprising of 1943

ISBN 978-0-7660-3320-7; 0-7660-3320-1

LC 2010021596

Examines the Warsaw ghetto uprising, including the roots of the resistance in the Warsaw ghetto, stories from the participants in the uprising, how the battle ended, and how the small group of fighters became heroes during the Holocaust

Includes glossary and bibliographical references

Ambrose, Stephen E.

★ The **good** fight; how World War II was won. Atheneum Bks. for Young Readers 2001 96p il maps $19.95

Grades: 5 6 7 8 **940.53**

1. World War, 1939-1945

ISBN 0-689-84361-5

LC 00-49600

"An excellent balance between the big picture and the humanizing details, well supported by fact boxes, tinted photographs, and battlefield maps that are both simple and clear. . . . Ambrose's style is authoritative and warm." Booklist

Includes glossary and bibliographical references

Bitton-Jackson, Livia

★ **I** have lived a thousand years; growing up in the Holocaust. by Livia E. Bitton-Jackson. Simon & Schuster Bks. for Young Readers 1997 224p hardcover o.p. pa $5.99

Grades: 7 8 9 10 **940.53**

1. Jews -- Hungary 2. Holocaust, 1933-1945 -- Personal narratives

ISBN 0-689-81022-9; 0-689-82395-9 pa

LC 96-19971

Based on the author's book for adults, Elli: coming of age in the Holocaust (1980)

"This is a memorable addition to the searing accounts of Holocaust survivors." Horn Book

Includes glossary

My bridges of hope; searching for life and love after Auschwitz. Simon & Schuster Bks. for Young Readers 1999 258p hardcover o.p. pa $4.99

Grades: 7 8 9 10 **940.53**

1. Holocaust survivors 2. Hebraists 3. Memoirists 4. College teachers

ISBN 0-689-84898-6 pa

LC 98-8046

In 1945, after surviving a harrowing year in Auschwitz, fourteen-year-old Elli returns, along with her mother and brother, to the family home, now part of Slovakia, where they try to find a way to rebuild their shattered lives

The author's "story is utterly involving, and adds an important chapter to the ongoing attempt to understand the Holocaust and its consequences." Publ Wkly

Includes glossary

Byers, Ann

Saving children from the Holocaust; the Kindertransport. Enslow Publishers 2011 128p il (The Holocaust through primary sources) lib bdg $31.93

Grades: 7 8 9 10 11 12 **940.53**

1. Holocaust, 1933-1945 2. World War, 1939-1945 -- Jews -- Rescue

ISBN 978-0-7660-3323-8; 0-7660-3323-6

LC 2010014215

Discusses the Kindertransport, including the people who organized the operation, how the transports worked, the children's lives who escaped on a transport, and how ten thousand children were saved from the Holocaust.

Includes glossary and bibliographical references

Trapped --youth in the Nazi ghettos; primary sources from the Holocaust. Holocaust research by Margaret Shannon. Enslow Publishers 2010 128p il (True stories of teens in the Holocaust) lib bdg $31.95

Grades: 8 9 10 11 12 **940.53**

1. Holocaust, 1933-1945 2. World War, 1939-1945 -- Children 3. World War, 1939-1945 -- Personal narratives

ISBN 978-0-7660-3272-9; 0-7660-3272-8

LC 2009013475

Examines the lives of Jewish children and teens in the ghettos during the Holocaust, including the formation of the ghettos, the miserable conditions, hard labor, and the deportations to camps.

The "book provides historical background, but the narratives rest upon the recollections, making the material immediate and horrifyingly real." SLJ

Includes glossary and bibliographical references

Callery, Sean

World War II; Visual history of the world's darkest days. by Sean Callery. 1st ed. Scholastic 2013 105 p. ill. (some col.), col. maps (paperback) $15.99

Grades: 5 6 7 8 **940.53**

1. Military history 2. World War, 1939-1945

ISBN 0545479754; 9780545479752

LC 2012285678

This book presents "World War II in a nutshell. The text is divided into five chapters: 'The Path to War,' 'Europe & the Atlantic War,' the Pacific theater, Africa & the Middle East, and the end of the war. Each section is divided into several two-page topics. The title page of each chapter asks three questions that are answered in the text. It is followed by a two-page time line with boxed information and vintage photos." (School Library Journal)

Deem, James M.

Auschwitz; voices from the death camp. Enslow Publishers 2011 128p il map (The Holocaust through primary sources) lib bdg $31.93

Grades: 7 8 9 10 11 12 **940.53**

1. Holocaust, 1933-1945 2. Jews -- Persecutions 3. Auschwitz (Poland: Concentration camp)

ISBN 978-0-7660-3322-1; 0-7660-3322-8

LC 2010003064

Examines Auschwitz, a death camp during the Holocaust, including its construction and daily workings, true accounts from prisoners of the camp and Nazi perpetrators, and how more than 1 million people were murdered there.

Includes glossary and bibliographical references

Kristallnacht; the Nazi terror that began the Holocaust. Enslow Publishers 2011 128p il (The Holocaust through primary sources) lib bdg $31.93

Grades: 7 8 9 10 11 12 **940.53**

1. Kristallnacht, 1938 2. Jews -- Germany 3. Holocaust, 1933-1945 4. Jews -- Persecutions

ISBN 978-0-7660-3324-5; 0-7660-3324-4

LC 2010015696

Discusses Kristallnacht, a four-day pogrom instigated by the Nazis against Germany's Jews, including stories from the victims, witnesses and perpetrators of the attack, and how it marked the beginning of the Holocaust.

"Personal testimony is a powerful way to tell history. . . . These accounts . . . are tightly edited, drawing on the memories of victims, perpetrators, and witnesses. . . . Each chapter blends an individual's testimony with historical background and commentary as well as photos of the witness and of the brutal events." Booklist

Includes glossary and bibliographical references

The **prisoners** of Breendonk; personal histories from a World War II concentration camp. written by James M. Deem. Houghton Mifflin Harcourt 2015 352 p. illustrations, maps $18.99

Grades: 8 9 10 11 12 **940.53**

1. Concentration camps 2. World War, 1939-1945 -- Prisoners and prisons, German 3. Breendonk (Concentration camp) 4. Concentration camps -- Belgium -- Willebroek 5. Concentration camp inmates -- Belgium -- Biography 6. World War, 1939-1945 -- Prisoners and prisons, German -- Biography 7. World War, 1939-1945 -- Concentration camps -- Belgium -- Willebroek

ISBN 9780544096646

LC 2015010722

This book, by James M. Deem, looks at Breendonk, a Nazi concentration camp which "held about 3,600 prisoners between 1940 and 1945. Jews, communists, common criminals, and freedom fighters all found themselves subject to incarceration. Life in Breendonk was no different than that in any of the better-known camps. . . . This narrative is told through the lives of various prisoners who lived (and died) there." (School Library Journal)

"The overall quality of this volume makes this title about a little-known camp a strong choice." SLJ

Downing, David

★ The **origins** of the Holocaust; [by] David Downing. World Almanac Library 2006 48p il map (World Almanac Library of the Holocaust) lib bdg $30

Grades: 7 8 9 10 **940.53**

1. Antisemitism 2. Holocaust, 1933-1945

ISBN 0-8368-5943-X

LC 2005042114

This "adds essential background history to the many accounts of the Nazi genocide. Downing goes back nearly 2,000 years to show the roots of antiSemitism and the long persecution of the Jews. . . . The clear overview connects that history with the rise of the Nazi Party and Hitler's vision of the Aryan master race. . . . The book design is spacious, with many photos, clear maps, and boxed insets." Booklist

Includes glossary and bibliographical references

Edsel, Robert M.

The **greatest** treasure hunt in history; the story of the Monuments Men. by Robert M. Edsel. Scholastic Focus, an imprint of Scholastic Inc. 2019 368 p. $18.99

Grades: 7 8 9 10 **940.53**

1. Art thefts 2. Cultural property -- Protection 3. World War, 1939-1945 -- Art and the war 4. Art thefts -- Germany -- History -- 20th century 5. Art treasures in war -- Europe -- History -- 20th century 6. World War, 1939-1945 -- Destruction and pillage -- Europe 7. Allied Forces. Supreme Headquarters. Monuments, Fine Arts and Archives Section -- History 8. World War, 1939-1945 -- Confiscations and contributions -- Germany 9. Cultural property -- Protection -- Europe -- History -- 20th century

ISBN 9781338251197

LC 2018016710

This book, by Robert M. Edsel, "recounts the astonishing true story of 11 men and one woman who risked their lives amidst the bloodshed of World War II to preserve churches, libraries, monuments, and works of art that for centuries defined the heritage of Western civilization. As the war raged, these American and British volunteers . . . found themselves in a desperate race against time to . . . save the many priceless treasures . . . stolen by Adolf Hitler and the Nazis." (Publisher's note)

Includes bibliographical references and index

Fishkin, Rebecca Love

Heroes of the Holocaust. Compass Point Books 2011 64p il (The holocaust) lib bdg $33.32; pa $8.95

Grades: 6 7 8 9 **940.53**

1. Holocaust, 1933-1945 2. World War, 1939-1945 -- Jews -- Rescue 3. World War, 1939-1945 -- Underground movements

ISBN 978-0-7565-4391-4 lib bdg; 0-7565-4391-6 lib bdg; 978-0-7565-4443-0 pa; 0-7565-4443-2 pa

LC 2010026492

This book tells the stories of those who defied and resisted the Nazis. Some helped one person or family, some saved dozens, and others organized efforts that helped thousands.

This volume "succeeds in outlining a horrific chapter in history without oversimplifying. . . . [This] book features multiple quotes from survivors about their wartime experiences, providing voices with which young people can identify." SLJ

Includes glossary and bibliographical references

Fox, Anne L.

Ten thousand children; true stories told by children who escaped the Holocaust on the Kindertransport. by Anne L. Fox and Eva Abraham-Podietz. Behrman House 1998 128p il pa $11.75

Grades: 5 6 7 8 **940.53**

1. Jewish refugees 2. Holocaust, 1933-1945 -- Personal narratives

ISBN 0-87441-648-5

LC 98-33600

Tells the true stories of children who escaped Nazi Germany on the Kindertransport, a rescue mission led by concerned British to save Jewish children from the Holocaust

"The design is like an open scrapbook, with different size typefaces, snapshots, news photos, and marginal notes; and the combination of the general overview with personal memories will bring readers, from middle grades through adult, close to the experience." Booklist

Frank, Anne, 1929-1945

★ **Anne** Frank's diary; the graphic adaptation. Anne Frank ; adapted by Ari Folman ; illustrations by David Polonsky. Pantheon Books 2018 160 p. chiefly illustrations hardcover $24.95

Grades: 8 9 10 11 12 **940.53**

1. Holocaust, 1939-1945 2. Jews -- Persecutions 3. Jewish children in the Holocaust -- Biography 4. Amsterdam (Netherlands) -- Biography -- Biography -- Comic books, strips, etc 5. Jews -- Persecutions -- Netherlands -- Amsterdam -- Biography -- Comic books, strips, etc 6. Jewish children in the Holocaust -- Netherlands -- Amsterdam -- Biography -- Comic books, strips, etc

ISBN 9781101871805; 9781101871799

LC 2017034415

Eisner Nominee: Best Adaptation from Another Medium (2019)

This book "is the first graphic edition of 'The Diary [of a Young Girl]' and includes extensive quotation directly from the definitive edition. It remains faithful to the original, while the stunning illustrations interpret and add layers of visual meaning . . . to this classic work of Holocaust literature." (Publisher's note)

"The classic, original text of Frank's diary is, as Folman writes in his adapter's note, impossible to improve upon; instead, he and Polonsky (cocreators of the film Waltz with Bashir) focus on illuminating its humor, insight, and supporting cast in this spirited graphic adaptation, authorized by the Anne Frank Foundation." Pub Wkly

Friedman, Ina R.

★ The **other** victims; first-person stories of non-Jews persecuted by the Nazis. Houghton Mifflin 1990 214p hardcover o.p. pa $6.95

Grades: 6 7 8 9 **940.53**

1. Holocaust survivors 2. Holocaust, 1933-1945 -- Personal narratives

ISBN 0-395-74515-2 pa

LC 89-27036

Personal narratives of Christians, Gypsies, deaf people, homosexuals, and blacks who suffered at the hands of the Nazis before and during World War II.

"Well organized and edited, the tales are harrowing, though they all end happily, often with escape or immigration to America and highly successful careers. Friedman points out that these were the lucky ones, and her book serves as a much-needed reminder that the Nazi nightmare extended far beyond Europe's Jewish population." Bull Cent Child Books

Includes bibliographical references

Hillman, Laura

I will plant you a lilac tree; a memoir of a Schindler's list survivor. Atheneum Books for Young Readers 2005 243p il map $16.95

Grades: 7 8 9 10 **940.53**

1. Jews -- Germany 2. Holocaust, 1933-1945 -- Personal narratives

ISBN 0-689-86980-0

LC 2004-10534

"In 1942 Berlin, Hannelore, 16, bravely volunteers to be deported with her mother and two younger brothers to Poland. . . . They are soon separated, and during the next three years Hannelore is moved through eight concentration camps. In clipped, first-person narrative, she remembers the worst. . . . She tells it as she endured it, quietly relaying the facts without sensationalism or sentimentality." Booklist

Hodge, Deborah

Rescuing the children; the story of the kindertransport. Deborah Hodge. Tundra Books of Northern New York 2012 60 p. (hardcover) $17.95

Grades: 4 5 6 **940.53**

1. Holocaust, 1939-1945 2. Jewish children in the Holocaust 3. World War, 1939-1945 -- Children 4. World War, 1939-1945 -- Refugees 5. Child refugees -- Great Britain -- History

ISBN 1770492569; 9781770492561

LC 2011938776

This children's book, by Deborah Hodge, "tells the story of how ten thousand Jewish children were rescued out of Nazi Europe just before the outbreak of World War 2. They were saved by the Kindertransport--a rescue mission that transported the children (or Kinder) from Nazi-ruled countries to safety in Britain. The book includes real-life accounts of the children and is illustrated with archival photographs . . . and original art by the Kinder commemorating their rescue." (Publisher's note)

Hoffman, Betty N.

Liberation; stories of survival from the Holocaust. Enslow Publishers 2011 128p il map (The Holocaust through primary sources) lib bdg $31.93

Grades: 7 8 9 10 11 12 **940.53**

1. Immigrants 2. Jewish refugees 3. Holocaust survivors 4. Jews -- Europe 5. Holocaust, 1933-1945 6. World War, 1939-1945 -- Europe 7. World War, 1939-1945 -- Refugees

ISBN 978-0-7660-3319-1; 0-7660-3319-8

LC 2010007234

Discusses the liberation of Europe and the aftermath of the Holocaust, including the displaced persons camps, primary source accounts from Holocaust survivors, and how those survivors started new lives in new countries

Includes glossary and bibliographical references

Hoose, Phillip M., 1947-

★ The **boys** who challenged Hitler; Knud Pedersen and the Churchill Club. Phillip Hoose. First edition Farrar, Straus, Giroux 2015 208 p. illustrations (hardback) $19.99

Grades: 7 8 9 10 11 12 **940.53**

1. Resistance to government 2. World War, 1939-1945 -- Underground movements 3. Heroes -- Denmark -- Biography 4. Sabotage -- Denmark -- History -- 20th century 5. Boys -- Political activity -- Denmark -- Biography 6. Denmark -- History -- German occupation, 1940-1945 7. Churchill-klubben (Ålborg, Denmark) -- History 8. World War, 1939-1945 -- Underground movements -- Denmark 9. Government, Resistance to -- Denmark -- History -- 20th century 10. Middle school students -- Political activity -- Denmark -- Biography

ISBN 0374300224; 9780374300227

LC 2014026101

Robert F. Sibert Honor Book (2016)

This book, by Phillip Hoose, describes how "at the outset of World War II, Denmark did not resist German occupation. Deeply ashamed of his nation's leaders, fifteen-year-old Knud Pedersen resolved with his brother and a handful of schoolmates to take action against the Nazis if the adults would not. . . . The boys' exploits and eventual imprisonment helped spark a full-blown Danish resistance." (Publisher's note)

"Hoose brilliantly weaves Pedersen's own words into the larger narrative of Denmark's stormy social and political wartime climate, showing how the astonishing bravery of otherwise ordinary Danish teens started something extraordinary." Horn Book

Includes bibliographical references and index

Hopkinson, Deborah, 1942-

Courage & defiance: stories of spies, saboteurs, and survivors in World War II Denmark; stories of spies, saboteurs, and survivors in World War II Denmark. Deborah Hopkinson. Scholastic Press 2015 352 p. illustrations (hardback) $17.99

Grades: 5 6 7 8 **940.53**

1. Jews -- Denmark 2. Denmark -- History 3. World War, 1939-1945 -- Underground movements 4. Denmark -- History -- German occupation, 1940-1945 5. World War, 1939-1945 -- Underground movements -- Denmark

ISBN 0545592208; 9780545592208

LC 2014046786

This book, by Deborah Hopkinson, "brings to bold life the remarkable story of the Danish resistance and rescue of over 7,000 Jews during WWII. When the Nazis invaded Denmark on Tuesday, April 9, 1940, the people of this tiny country to the north of Germany awoke to a devastating surprise. The government of Denmark surrendered quietly, and the Danes were ordered to go about their daily lives as if nothing had changed. But everything had changed." (Publisher's note)

Includes bibliographical references (pages 303-309) and index.

Houston, Jeanne Wakatsuki

★ **Farewell** to Manzanar; a true story of Japanese American experience during and after the World War II internment. [by] Jeanne Wakatsuki Houston and James D. Houston. Houghton Mifflin 2002 188p $15

Grades: 7 8 9 10 **940.53**

1. Manzanar War Relocation Center 2. World War, 1939-1945 -- United States 3. Japanese Americans -- Evacuation and relocation, 1942-1945

ISBN 0-618-21620-0

LC 2002-727748

A reissue with a new afterword of the title first published 1973

"A spare, powerful memoir." Rochman. Against borders

Isserman, Maurice

★ **World** War II; John S. Bowman, general editor. rev ed; Chelsea House 2010 256p il map (America at war) lib bdg $45

Grades: 8 9 10 11 12 **940.53**

1. United States -- History -- 1933-1945 2. World War, 1939-1945 -- United States

ISBN 978-0-8160-8185-1; 0-8160-8185-9

LC 2009-52541

First published 1991

This book describes and interprets the role of the United States in World War II.

Includes glossary and bibliographical references

Kacer, Kathy

Hiding Edith; a true story. Second Story 2006 120p (Holocaust remembrance book for young readers) pa $10.95

Grades: 4 5 6 7 **940.53**

1. Holocaust survivors 2. Jews -- France 3. Holocaust, 1933-1945

ISBN 1-897187-06-8

"Kacer recounts some extraordinary history: in Moissac, France, under Nazi occupation, a French Jewish couple hid 100 Jewish refugee children—with the support of the townspeople. Kacer, who based her account on interviews, tells the story of one child, Edith Schwalb. Captioned black-and-white photos on almost every page show Edith at home in Vienna before the war, then in Belgium, and then, separated from her parents, living with the rescuers." Booklist

Kent, Deborah

The **tragic** history of the Japanese-American internment camps; [by] Deborah Kent. Enslow Pub. 2007 128p il (From many cultures, one history) lib bdg $31.93

Grades: 6 7 8 9 **940.53**

1. World War, 1939-1945 -- United States 2. Japanese Americans -- Evacuation and relocation, 1942-1945

ISBN 978-0-7660-2797-8 lib bdg; 0-7660-2797-X lib bdg

LC 2007015125

This "will provide clear, easy-to-understand facts with critical analysis and will be useful for reports." Libr Media Connect

Includes glossary and bibliographical references

Kris, 1972-

A **bag** of marbles; based on the memoir by Joseph Joffo ; adapted by Kris ; illustrated by Vincent Bailly ; translated by Edward Gauvin. Graphic Universe 2013 126 p. color illustrations (pbk) $9.95

Grades: 6 7 8 9 10 **940.53**

1. Holocaust, 1939-1945 2. Children and war -- Fiction 3. World War, 1939-1945 -- France 4. Graphic novels 5. Jews -- France -- Fiction 6. World War, 1939-1945 -- France -- Fiction 7. Holocaust, Jewish (1939-1945) -- France -- Fiction 8. France -- History -- German occupation, 1940-1945 -- Fiction

ISBN 1467715166; 9781467707008; 9781467715164; 9781467716512

LC 2013002284

"Ten years old at the start of the story, Joffo recalls his Jewish family planning their escape from Occupied France during World War II. Tension runs through the story as he and his brother set off on the long journey to the Free Zone, where they plan to meet up with their older brothers. Along the way the boys must hide their Jewish identity, evade train security, and find a passeur, or guide, to take them past guard posts and fences to safe territory." (School Library Journal)

"This graphic-novel adaptation of Joffo's 1973 memoir of the same name succeeds in melding sensitive and accurate imagery with the original narrative flow of a young secular Jewish boy's experiences in occupied France." Booklist

Langley, Andrew

World War II; by Andrew Langley. Heinemann Library 2012 80 p. ill. (some col.), col. maps (Living through) (library) $36.50; (paperback) $10.99

Grades: 6 7 8 9 **940.53**

1. World War, 1939-1945

ISBN 1432960024; 9781432960025; 9781432960117

LC 2011016056

This book by Andrew Langley is part of the Living Through series and looks at World War II. It answers questions including "why was World War II so devastating, and how had the world become so divided into armed camps? How did the war affect people on both sides of the conflict, and why are its consequences still felt today?" (Publisher's note)

Includes bibliographical references (p. 76-78) and index.

Lee, Carol Ann

Anne Frank and the children of the Holocaust. Viking 2006 242p il map $16.99

Grades: 6 7 8 9 10 **940.53**

1. Children 2. Diarists 3. Holocaust victims 4. Holocaust, 1933-1945

ISBN 0-670-06107-7

"This book will still serve as an excellent overview in the classroom and for personal reading." Booklist

Includes bibliographical references

Levine, Karen

★ **Hana's** suitcase; a true story. Whitman, A. 2003 111p il lib bdg $15.95

Grades: 4 5 6 7 **940.53**

1. Holocaust victims 2. Holocaust, 1933-1945

ISBN 0-8075-3148-0

LC 2002-27439

First published 2002 in Canada

A biography of a Czech girl who died in the Holocaust, told in alternating chapters with an account of how the curator of a Japanese Holocaust center learned about her life after Hana's suitcase was sent to her

"The account, based on a radio documentary Levine did in Canada . . . is part history, part suspenseful mystery, and always anguished family drama, with an incredible climactic revelation." Booklist

Marrin, Albert, 1936-

★ **Uprooted**; The Japanese American Experience During World War II. Albert Marrin. Alfred A. Knopf 2016 256 p. illustrations, maps hbk $17.99; (lib. bdg.) $20.99

Grades: 7 8 9 10 11 12 **940.53**

1. Japanese Americans -- Evacuation and relocation, 1942-1945 2. World War, 1939-1945 -- Japanese Americans

ISBN 9780553509366; 9780553509373

LC 2015025406

Sibert Honor Book (2017)

This book, by Albert Marrin, presents a "look at the internment of Japanese Americans during World War II. . . . [It] takes a close look at the history of racism in America and carefully follows the treacherous path that led one of our nation's most beloved presidents to make this decision. Meanwhile, it also illuminates the history of Japan and its own struggles with racism and xenophobia, which led to the bombing of Pearl Harbor, ultimately tying the two countries together." (Publisher's note)

"A final chapter draws a connection to the treatment of Muslim Americans in the aftermath of twenty-first-century terrorist attacks and discusses the uneasy tension between liberty and security during wartime. Generous quotations and photographs are integrated throughout the text, providing the immediacy that comes with primary sources." Horn Book

Meltzer, Milton

★ **Rescue** : the story of how Gentiles saved Jews in the Holocaust. Harper & Row 1988 168p maps hardcover o.p. pa $9.99

Grades: 6 7 8 9 **940.53**

1. Holocaust, 1933-1945 2. World War, 1939-1945 -- Jews -- Rescue

ISBN 0-06-024210-8; 0-06-446117-3 pa

LC 87-47816

A recounting drawn from historic source material of the many individual acts of heroism performed by righteous gentiles who sought to thwart the extermination of the Jews during the Holocaust

"This is an excellent portrayal of a difficult topic. Meltzer manages to both explain without accusing, and to laud without glorifying. . . . The discussion of the complicated relations between countries are clear, but not simplistic. An impressive aspect of this book is its lack of didacticism." Voice Youth Advocates

Includes bibliographical references

Mullenbach, Cheryl

★ **Double** victory; how African American women broke race and gender barriers to help win World War II. Cheryl Mullenbach. Chicago Review Press 2012 272 p. (Women of action) (hardcover) $19.95

Grades: 7 8 9 10 11 12 **940.53**

1. World War, 1939-1945 -- Women 2. African American women -- Biography 3. United States -- Race relations -- History 4. African Americans -- Employment 5. African Americans -- Civil rights 6. World War, 1939-1945 -- African Americans 7. World War, 1939-1945 -- Women -- United States 8. African American women -- History -- 20th century 9. United States -- Race relations -- History -- 20th century 10. African American women -- Employment -- History -- 20th century 11. African American women -- Civil rights -- History -- 20th century

ISBN 1569768080; 9781569768082

LC 2012021343

Amelia Bloomer Project (2014)

This book, by Cheryl Mullenbach, is part of the "Women of Action" series. "African American women . . . did extraordinary things to help their country during World War II. In these pages young readers meet a range of remarkable women: war workers, political activists, military women, volunteers, and entertainers. . . . But many others fought discrimination at home and abroad in order to contribute to the war effort." (Publisher's note)

Includes bibliographical references and index

Opdyke, Irene Gut

★ **In** my hands; memories of a Holocaust rescuer. [by] Irene Gut Opdyke with Jennifer Armstrong. Knopf 1999 276p il hardcover o.p. pa $12

Grades: 7 8 9 10 **940.53**

1. World War, 1939-1945 -- Poland 2. World War, 1939-1945 -- Jews -- Rescue 3. Holocaust, 1933-1945 -- Personal narratives 4. World War, 1939-1945 -- Personal narratives

ISBN 0-679-89181-1; 0-385-72032-7 pa

LC 98-54095

Recounts the experiences of the author who, as a young Polish girl, hid and saved Jews during the Holocaust

"No matter how many Holocaust stories one has read, this one is a must, for its impact is so powerful. . . . Opdyke's remarkable story is simply told, with clarity and feeling." SLJ

Oppenheim, Joanne

★ **Dear** Miss Breed; true stories of the Japanese American incarceration during World War II and a librarian who made a difference. foreword by Elizabeth Kikuchi Yamada; afterword by Snowden Becker. Scholastic 2006 287p il $22.99

Grades: 7 8 9 10 **940.53**

1. Librarians 2. World War, 1939-1945 -- United States 3. Japanese Americans -- Evacuation and relocation, 1942-1945

ISBN 0-439-56992-3; 978-0-439-56992-7

LC 2004-59009

This "account focuses on Clara Breed, a children's librarian at the San Diego Public Library, and the Japanese-American children she served prior to World War II and whom she continued to serve after their families were sent to an Arizona internment camp. . . . Illustrated with numerous photographs . . . and incorporating copious letters and documents, the book is . . . compelling." Horn Book

Includes bibliographical references

Perl, Lila

Four perfect pebbles; a Holocaust story. by Lila Perl and Marion Blumenthal Lazan. Greenwillow Bks. 1996 130p il $16.99; pa $5.99

Grades: 6 7 8 9 **940.53**

1. Jews -- Germany 2. Holocaust, 1933-1945 -- Personal narratives

ISBN 0-688-14294-X; 0-380-73188-6 pa

LC 95-9752

"This book warrants attention both for the uncommon experiences it records and for the fullness of that record. . . . Quotes from Lazan's 87-year-old mother are invaluable—her memories of the family's experiences afford Marion's story a precision and wholeness rarely available to child survivors." Publ Wkly

Includes bibliographical references

Prins, Marcel

Hidden like Anne Frank; fourteen true stories of survival. Marcel Prins and Peter Henk Steenhuis ; translated by Laura Watkinson. Arthur A. Levine Books, An Imprint of Scholastic Inc. 2014 256 p. illustrations, maps (hardback) $16.99

Grades: 7 8 9 10 11 12 **940.53**

1. Holocaust, 1939-1945 2. Hidden children (Holocaust) 3. Jewish children in the Holocaust 4. World War, 1939-1945 -- Children 5. Netherlands -- Biography 6. Hidden children (Holocaust) -- Netherlands -- Biography 7. World War, 1939-1945 -- Netherlands -- Personal narratives 8. Jewish children in the Holocaust -- Netherlands -- Biography 9. Holocaust, Jewish (1939-1945) -- Netherlands -- Personal narratives

ISBN 0545543622; 9780545543620; 9780545543637; 9780545543644

LC 2013040908

This book, by Marcel Prins and Peter Henk Steenhuis, presents "fourteen . . . true stories of children hidden away during World War II. . . . Some children were only three or four years old when they were hidden; some were teenagers. Some hid with neighbors or family, while many were with complete strangers. But all know the pain of losing their homes, their families, even their own names. They describe the secret network of brave people who kept them safe." (Publisher's note)

"This volume includes compelling first-person accounts of survival during the Holocaust and WWII in Holland, including coauthor Prins's mother's experience. Readers will encounter incredible acts of courage, both from the subjects themselves and the Resistance fighters and ordinary people willing to risk their lives. Family photos and archival images appear throughout; a glossary and pictures of the survivors today are appended." Horn Book

Rappaport, Doreen, 1939-

★ **Beyond** courage; the untold story of Jewish resistance during the Holocaust. by Doreen Rappaport. 1st ed. Candlewick Press 2012 228 p. ill., maps (hardcover) $22.99

Grades: 6 7 8 9 10 11 12 **940.53**

1. Biography 2. Jews -- History 3. Resistance to government 4. Holocaust, Jewish (1939-1945) 5. Righteous Gentiles in the Holocaust 6. World War, 1939-1945 -- Jews -- Rescue 7. World War, 1939-1945 -- Jewish resistance

ISBN 0763629766; 9780763629762

LC 2011048116

In this book, Doreen Rappaport offers "more than 20 stories of Jewish resistance to the Holocaust, some never before told. From all corners of Nazi-occupied Europe, these harrowing accounts . . . pay tribute to the brave thousands who defied their oppressors in ways large and small. In one, 12-year-old Mordechai Shlayan . . . blows up a hotel where German officers are dining. In another, 22-year-old Marianne Cohn is caught smuggling children into Switzerland." (Publishers Weekly)

Includes bibliographical references (p. 209-221) and index.

Rogasky, Barbara

Smoke and ashes; the story of the Holocaust. rev and expanded ed; Holiday House 2002 256p il maps hardcover o.p. O.P.; pa O.P.

Grades: 6 7 8 9 **940.53**

1. Holocaust, 1933-1945

ISBN 0-8234-1612-7; 0-8234-1677-1 pa

LC 2001-16797

First published 1988

The author "details the dark horror of Nazism—from the beginning pogroms the Nazis organized against German Jews to the setting up of concentration camps and death factories. . . . In clear and simple prose, she relates how the Jews lived and died in the camps . . . and how a small number of non-Jews helped them in their struggle. She concludes with an account of the Nuremburg Trials and the many instances of contemporary anti-Semitism that have outlived Hitler." SLJ [review of 1988 edition]

Includes bibliographical references

Rol, Ruud van der

★ **Anne** Frank, beyond the diary; a photographic remembrance. by Ruud van der Rol and Rian Verhoeven; in association with the Anne Frank House; translated by Tony Langham and Plym Peters; with an introduction by Anna Quindlen. Viking 1993 113p il map hardcover o.p. pa $10.99

Grades: 5 6 7 8 **940.53**

1. Children 2. Diarists 3. Holocaust victims 4. Jews -- Netherlands 5. Holocaust, 1933-1945 6. World War, 1939-1945 -- Jews 7. Netherlands -- History -- 1940-1945, German occupation

ISBN 0-670-84932-4; 0-14-036926-0 pa

LC 92-41528

Original Dutch edition, 1992

Photographs, illustrations, and maps accompany historical essays, diary excerpts, and interviews, providing an insight to Anne Frank and the massive upheaval which tore apart her world

"Readers will become absorbed in the richness of the detail and careful explanation which revisit and expand the familiar, well-loved story." Horn Book

Rubin, Susan Goldman

The **cat** with the yellow star; coming of age in Terezin. [by] Susan Goldman Rubin, with Ela Weissberger. Holiday House 2006 40p il hardcover o.p. $16.95; $17.99

Grades: 3 4 5 6 7 **940.53**

1. Holocaust, 1933-1945 2. Jews -- Czechoslovakia 3. Terezin (Czechoslovakia: Concentration camp)

ISBN 0-8234-1831-6; 9781518228032

LC 2004-57582

This is a memoir of Ela Stein's experiences as a child. "Stein was eleven years old in February of 1942 when she was sent to the Terezin concentration camp. While there, a children's opera called Brundibar was performed, and Ela was chosen to play the pivotal role of the cat. [Index.] Grades three to six." (Bull Cent Child Books)

"In 1942, at age 11, Ela Weissberger was transported with her Czech family to the Nazi concentration camp Terezin. She survived, and now, based on extensive personal interviews, Rubin tells Weissberger's story of being a Jewish child in that camp, including how the young prisoners rehearsed and performed the opera Brundibar." Booklist

Samuels, Charlie

Home front; by Charlie Samuels. Brown Bear Books 2012 48 p. ill. (some col.) (World War II sourcebook) (library) $35.65

Grades: 5 6 7 8 **940.53**

1. Military history 2. World War, 1939-1945 3. World War, 1939-1945 -- Social aspects 4. World War, 1939-1945 -- Economic aspects

ISBN 1936333228; 9781936333226

LC 2011007054

This book by Charlie Samuels is part of the World War II Sourcebook series and focuses on the home front. "Each page is illustrated. Little-known facts and, sometimes, direct narratives are presented with the information given to the reader. . . . Each book has the same timeline of World War II, maps of both the European and Pacific theaters, interesting biographical snapshots of people involved, and a list of websites that students may use to further explore World War II." (Library Media Connection)

Life under occupation; by Charlie Samuels. Brown Bear Books 2011 48 p. ill. (chiefly col.), col. maps (World War II sourcebook) (library) $35.65

Grades: 5 6 7 8 **940.53**

1. World War, 1939-1945 2. World War, 1939-1945 -- Occupied territories 3. World War, 1939-1945 -- Europe 4. World War, 1939-1945 -- Atrocities 5. World War, 1939-1945 -- Pacific Area 6. World War, 1939-1945 -- Occupied territories

ISBN 1936333260; 9781936333264

LC 2011007055

This book by Charlie Samuels, part of the World War II Sourcebook series, and focuses on life under occupation. "Each page is illustrated. Little-known facts and, sometimes, direct narratives are presented with the information given to the reader. . . . Each book has the same timeline of World War II, maps of both the European and Pacific theaters, . . . biographical snapshots of people involved, and a list of websites." (Library Media Connection)

Includes bibliographical references and index.

Sandler, Martin W.

Imprisoned; the betrayal of Japanese Americans during World War II. by Martin W. Sandler. Walker Books For Young Readers 2013 176 p. (hardcover) $22.99; (library) $23.89

Grades: 7 8 9 10 **940.53**

1. World War, 1939-1945 2. Japanese Americans -- Evacuation and relocation, 1942-1945 3. World War, 1939-1945 -- Japanese Americans 4. Japanese Americans -- History -- 20th century

ISBN 0802722776; 0802722784; 9780802722775; 9780802722782

LC 2012032295

YALSA Award for Excellence in Nonfiction for Young Adults: Finalist (2014)

This book offers a "survey of Executive Order 9066 and its aftermath. The order authorized the U.S. military to relocate over 100,000 Japanese-Americans--many were U.S. citizens--from their homes in Washington, Oregon and California to detention camps. . . . A few government officials did object to the order, questioning its constitutionality." (Kirkus Reviews)

"Sandler's earnest telling is complemented by well-chosen primary sources, not just the words . . . but also the black-and-white photographs that present striking images." Horn Book

Sender, Ruth Minsky

The **cage**. Macmillan 1986 245p hardcover o.p. pa $5.99
Grades: 7 8 9 10 **940.53**

1. Jews -- Poland 2. Holocaust, 1933-1945 -- Personal narratives
ISBN 0-02-781830-6; 0-689-81321-X pa

LC 86-8562

This "Holocaust memoir presents a series of brief scenes from 1939, when the author was 12 and Hitler invaded Poland, through the Russian liberation of the Mitelsteine labor camp in 1945. . . . Older students with previous knowledge of the subject will find Sender's narrative moving and thought provoking." SLJ

Senker, Cath

Why did World War II happen? Gareth Stevens Pub. 2011 48p il map (Moments in history) lib bdg $31.95; pa $14.05
Grades: 6 7 8 9 **940.53**

1. World War, 1939-1945
ISBN 978-1-4339-4184-9 lib bdg; 1-4339-4184-8 lib bdg; 978-1-4339-4185-6 pa; 1-4339-4185-6 pa

LC 2010015834

"Examines the events that served as . . . [precursors to World War II]. . . . Brightly colored pull-out boxes highlight important turning points, the perspective of the everyday man, and further information on why specific events occurred. Numerous photographs help readers visualize concepts more fully. . . . Students should be able to easily use this resource." Libr Media Connect

Includes glossary and bibliographical references

Spiegelman, Art

★ **Maus**; a survivor's tale. Art Spiegelman. 25th anniversary ed. Pantheon Bks. 1996 295 p. 2v in 1 ill., maps (some col.) $35
Grades: 7 8 9 10 11 12 Adult **940.53**

1. Graphic novels 2. Biographical graphic novels 3. Holocaust, 1933-1945 -- Graphic novels
ISBN 0-679-40641-7

LC 96-32796

A combined edition of Maus I : My father bleeds history (1986) and Maus II : And here my troubles began (1991)

Los Angeles Times Book Prize: Fiction (1992) for Maus II

Pulitzer Prize Special Award (1992)

Eisner Award: Best Graphic Album--Reprint for Maus II

Harvey Award: Best Graphic Album of Previously Published Material (1992) for Maus II

"An undisputed classic and award-winning title (including a Pulitzer Prize in 1992) in which renowned cartoonist Spiegelman depicts his father's experiences as a World War II Nazi concentration camp survivor. The memoir is also a chronicle of Spiegelman's relationship with his father as we witness their visits and disagreements. The black-and-white drawings are straightforward, but with an interesting twist: all of the Jews are depicted as mice and the Nazis as cats." LJ

In this work "Spiegelman takes the comic book to a new level of seriousness, portraying Jews as mice and Nazis as cats. Depicting himself being told about the Holocaust by his Polish survivor father, Spiegelman not only explores the concentration-camp experience, but also the guilt, love, and anger between father and son." Rochman. Against borders

Taylor, Peter Lane

The **secret** of Priest's Grotto; a Holocaust survival story. [by] Peter Lane Taylor with Christos Nicola. Kar-Ben Pub. 2007 64p il map lib bdg $10.95; pa $8.95
Grades: 5 6 7 8 9 10 11 12 **940.53**

1. Caves 2. Jews -- Ukraine 3. Holocaust, 1933-1945
ISBN 978-1-58013-260-2 lib bdg; 1-58013-260-X lib bdg; 978-1-58013-261-9 pa; 1-58013-261-8 pa

LC 2006-21709

"This volume relays the tale of 38 Ukrainian Jews who sought refuge in a local cave to escape the invading Nazis in fall of 1942 and remained there for 344 days. . . . At once sobering and uplifting, this is an astounding story of survival, powerfully told." Publ Wkly

Thomson, Ruth

★ **Terezin**; voices from the Holocaust. Candlewick Press 2011 64p il $18.99
Grades: 5 6 7 8 **940.53**

1. Jews -- Czechoslovakia 2. Holocaust, 1933-1945 -- Personal narratives 3. Holocaust, Jewish (1939-1945) 4. Terezín (Czech Republic: Concentration camp)
ISBN 0-7636-4963-5; 978-0-7636-4963-0

LC 2010-39164

"Between 1941 and 1945, Nazi Germany turned the small town of Terezín, Czechoslovakia, into a ghetto, and then into a transit camp for thousands of Jewish people. It was a 'show' camp, where inmates were forced to use their artistic talents to fool the world about the truth of gas chambers and horrific living conditions for imprisoned Jews. Here is their story, told through the firsthand accounts of those who were there." (Publisher's note) Index. "Grades five to eight." (Bull Cent Child Books)

"Two years after the Nazi invasion of Czechoslovakia, the small fortress village of Terezin was converted into a Jewish ghetto, and over the next four years, ten of thousands of Jews were transported there while in transit to death camps in the east. The history of Terezin is fascinating: the camp housed many noted artists. . . . Much of the art created at Terezin survived the Holocaust, and a generous sampling is included in this volume. Thomson opts to tell the story of Terezin almost entirely in the voices of those who lived there. . . . This is an accessible, carefully researched work that effectively uses primary-source material to make the experience of the Jews of Terezin come alive for today's students." Bull Cent Child Books

Includes glossary and bibliographical references

Voices from the Second World War; stories of war as told to children of today. Candlewick Press 2018 320 p. $24.99
Grades: 4 5 6 7 8 **940.53**

1. Historical literature 2. Military history 3. World War, 1939-1945
ISBN 0763694924; 9780763694920

"In . . . [this] intergenerational keepsake volume, [from Candlewick Press,] witnesses to World War II share their memories with young interviewers so that their experiences will never be forgotten. . . . In a unique collection, RAF pilots, evacuees, resistance fighters, Land Girls, U.S. Navy sailors, and survivors of the Holocaust and the Hiroshima bombing all tell their stories, passing on the lessons learned to a new generation." (Publisher's note)

"This title will help readers understand that war affects real-life people, including children. A solid choice for collections that serve middle school students." SLJ

Warren, Andrea

Enemy child; the story of Norman Mineta, a boy imprisoned in a Japanese American internment camp during World War II. Andrea Warren. Holiday House 2019 244 p. (hardback) $22.99

Grades: 5 6 7 8 9 **940.53**

1. Historical fiction 2. World War, 1939-1945 -- Evacuation of civilians -- Fiction 3. Japanese Americans -- Evacuation and relocation, 1942-1945 -- Fiction 4. Legislators -- United States -- Biography 5. World War, 1939-1945 -- Children -- United States -- Biography 6. Heart Mountain Relocation Center (Wyo.) -- Children -- Biography 7. World War, 1939-1945 -- Japanese Americans -- Children -- Biography 8. Japanese Americans -- Evacuation and relocation, 1942-1945 -- Children -- Biography

ISBN 9780823441976; 9780823441518

LC 2018009814

In this book, by Andrea Warren, "it's 1941 and ten-year-old Norman Mineta is a carefree fourth grader in San Jose, California. . . . But when Japanese forces attack Pearl Harbor, Norm's world is turned upside down. . . . He and his Japanese American family . . . , along with everyone else of Japanese ancestry living on the West Coast, are forced by the government to move to internment camps, leaving everything they have known behind." (Publisher's note)

Includes bibliographical references and index

Surviving Hitler; a boy in the Nazi death camps. HarperCollins Pubs. 2001 146p il hardcover o.p. pa $6.99

Grades: 5 6 7 8 **940.53**

1. Holocaust, 1933-1945

ISBN 0-688-17497-3; 0-06-029218-0 lib bdg; 0-06-000767-2 pa

LC 00-38899

"Simply told, Warren's powerful story blends the personal testimony of Holocaust survivor Jack Mandelbaum with the history of his time, documented by stirring photos from the archives of the U.S. Holocaust Memorial Museum. . . . An excellent introduction for readers who don't know much about the history." Booklist

Includes bibliographical references

940.54 Military history of World War II

Allen, Thomas B.

★ **Remember** Pearl Harbor; American and Japanese survivors tell their stories. foreword by Robert D. Ballard. National Geographic Soc. 2001 57p il maps $17.95

Grades: 5 6 7 8 **940.54**

1. Pearl Harbor (Oahu, Hawaii), Attack on, 1941 2. World War, 1939-1945 -- Personal narratives

ISBN 0-7922-6690-0

LC 2001-796

Personal accounts of the Japanese attack on Pearl Harbor, with background information.

"Eyewitness testimony of Japanese and American men and women from various backgrounds enriches this balanced treatment of World War II. . . . The first-person voices along with dozens of black-and-white photos and several full-color maps make this a draw for both browsers and World War II buffs." Booklist

Includes bibliographical references

Allport, Alan

The **Battle** of Britain; by Alan Allport. Chelsea House 2012 128 p. (Milestones in modern world history) (hardcover) $35

Grades: 7 8 9 10 11 12 **940.54**

1. Britain, Battle of, 1940 2. World War, 1939-1945 -- Aerial operations 3. World War, 1939-1945 -- Great Britain 4. Britain, Battle of, Great Britain, 1940

ISBN 160413920X; 9781604139204

LC 2011023053

This book, part of the Milestones in Modern World History series, "describes the air campaign waged by the Luftwaffe (German air force) against England's Royal Air Force during WWII. It starts with a look at [Adolph] Hitler's rise to power and continues with such pivotal conflicts as the Blitz. The author also notes how important the burgeoning radar technology of the time aided England's defense." (Booklist)

Includes bibliographical references and index

Atkinson, Rick, 1952-

D -Day; the invasion of Normandy, 1944. Rick Atkinson with Kate Waters. Henry Holt & Co. 2014 224 p. (hardcover) $18.99

Grades: 6 7 8 9 10 11 12 **940.54**

1. World War, 1939-1945 2. Normandy (France), Attack on, 1944 3. World War, 1939-1945 -- Campaigns -- France -- Normandy

ISBN 1627791116; 9781627791113; 9781627791120

LC 2014005162

Written by Rick Atkinson, "Adapted for young readers from . . . 'The Guns at Last Light,' 'D-Day' captures the events and the spirit of that day--June 6, 1944--the day that led to the liberation of western Europe from Nazi Germany's control. They came by sea and by sky to reclaim freedom from the occupying Germans, turning the tide of World War II." (Publisher's note)

"With Kate Waters. Adapted from Atkinson's adult book The Guns at Last Light, this young readers' edition focuses, effectively and excitingly, on the invasion of Normandy but provides enough context for WWII both before and after June 6, 1944. Copious photographs and a vibrant design will invite war buffs in; appended lists of interesting facts add appeal. Reading list, timeline, websites. Bib., glos., ind." Horn Book

Includes bibliographical references and index

The **attack** on Pearl Harbor; David Haugen and Susan Musser, book editors. Greenhaven Press 2011 204p il map (Perspectives on modern world history) lib bdg $39.70

Grades: 8 9 10 11 12 **940.54**

1. Pearl Harbor (Oahu, Hawaii), Attack on, 1941

ISBN 978-0-7377-5004-1; 0-7377-5004-9

LC 2010033590

In "discussing the events of December 7, 1941. . . [this] well-organized [volume presents] a wealth of clearly written analyses from a rich variety of viewpoints. With the inclusion of historical background, firsthand experiences, and discussions of particular points of controversy, [it helps] to familiarize readers with the [attack on Pearl Harbor] and [serves] as [an exercise] in the development of analytical thinking skills." SLJ

Includes bibliographical references

Atwood, Kathryn

Women heroes of World War II; 26 stories of espionage, sabotage, resistance, and rescue. Chicago Review Press 2011 266p il map $19.95

Grades: 7 8 9 10 **940.54**

1. World War, 1939-1945 -- Women 2. World War, 1939-1945 -- Underground movements

ISBN 978-1-55652-961-0; 1-55652-961-9

LC 2010-41830

"The 26 women profiled in this collective biography served on the front lines and behind enemy lines in Europe as correspondents, couriers, propagandists, Resistance fighters, saboteurs and spies. . . . Atwood's admiration and enthusiasm for her subjects is apparent in these engaging profiles, and readers will likely be inspired to investigate these fascinating women further." Kirkus

Includes glossary and bibliographical references

Bascomb, Neal

Sabotage; the mission to destroy Hitler's atomic bomb. Neal Bascomb. Arthur A. Levine Books, an imprint of Scholastic Inc. 2016 307 p. illustrations, maps (hardcover : alk. paper) $17.99

Grades: 8 9 10 11 12 **940.54**

1. Sabotage 2. World War, 1939-1945 3. Atomic bomb -- History 4. Atomic bomb -- Germany -- History 5. Sabotage -- Norway -- History -- 20th century 6. World War, 1939-1945 -- Germany -- Technology 7. World War, 1939-1945 -- Commando operations -- Norway 8. World War, 1939-1945 -- Underground movements -- Norway

ISBN 9780545735339; 9780545732437

LC 2015043455

This book, by Neal Bascomb, is the "true story of spies and survival. The invasion begins at night, with German cruisers slipping into harbor, and soon the Nazis occupy all of Norway. They station soldiers throughout the country. They institute martial rule. And at Vemork, an industrial fortress high above a dizzying gorge, they gain access to an essential ingredient for the weapon that could end World War II: Hitler's very own nuclear bomb." (Publisher's note)

"Bascomb's clear-eyed account of the thrilling mission and its many challenges, cast against the backdrop of WWII—and helped along by photos, maps, and diagrams—will handily engage teens." Booklist

Includes bibliographical references and index

Bradley, James

Flags of our fathers; heroes of Iwo Jima. [by] James Bradley with Ron Powers; adapted for young people by Michael French. Delacorte Press 2001 211p il $15.95; pa $8.95

Grades: 7 8 9 10 **940.54**

1. Iwo Jima, Battle of, 1945 2. Photojournalists 3. United States -- Marine Corps

ISBN 0-385-72932-4; 0-385-73064-0 pa

LC 00-50914

"A journalistic, accessible adaptation of the earlier book for adult readers, this account by a survivor's son centers on [Rosenthal's] famous photo of six Marines raising a U.S. flag on Iwo Jima. The accurate, engaging text provides the men's pre-war backgrounds, their war service to that time, what they actually did on the island and afterward, and the consequences of the famous photo." Horn Book Guide

Includes bibliographical references

Burgan, Michael

Hiroshima; birth of the nuclear age. Marshall Cavendish Benchmark 2009 128p il (Perspectives on) lib bdg $27.95

Grades: 8 9 10 11 12 **940.54**

1. Atomic bomb 2. Hiroshima (Japan) -- Bombardment, 1945

ISBN 978-0-7614-4023-9; 0-7614-4023-2

LC 2008-29249

This provides information on the Manhattan Project, the bombing of Hiroshima, and its legacy.

"Utilizing an unbiased and chronological narrative, [the author delves] deeply into the [topic], providing an overall representation as well as a substantial degree of insight. . . . The potency of [this title] lies in the excellent arrangement of numerous well-chosen sidebars and photos, and fluent, concise prose." SLJ

Includes bibliographical references

Raising the flag; how a photograph gave a nation hope in wartime. Compass Point Books 2011 64p il (Captured history) lib bdg $33.99; pa $8.95

Grades: 6 7 8 9 **940.54**

1. World War, 1939-1945 2. Documentary photography 3. Iwo Jima, Battle of, 1945 4. Photojournalists

ISBN 978-0-7565-4395-2; 0-7565-4395-9; 978-0-7565-4449-2 pa; 0-7565-4449-1 pa

LC 2010038572

This book about the iconic Joe Rosenthal photograph of American soldiers raising the flag at Iwo Jima places the photo "in historical context, profiles the photographer, describes the conditions under which it was taken, and analyzes both its immediate and its continuing impact. The [text includes] ample background information and details and [is] enhanced by large photos and sidebars." SLJ

Includes glossary and bibliographical references

Chrisp, Peter

World War II: fighting for freedom; the story of the conflict that changed the world 1939-1945. Scholastic 2010 63p il map $12.99

Grades: 4 5 6 7 **940.54**

1. World War, 1939-1945

ISBN 978-0-545-24984-3; 0-545-24984-8

Provides information and facts on events leading up to the war, important battles and campaigns, political and military leaders, and life on the home fronts.

"Fascinating photographs dominate each spread, but there are also maps, quotations, diagrams, and interesting text box features. . . . This book provides a solid overview of World War II, but it is the visual aspect that makes it stand out." Libr Media Connect

Includes glossary

Cornioley, Pearl Witherington

Code name Pauline; memoirs of a World War II special agent. Pearl Witherington Cornioley with Hervé Larroque ; edited by Kathryn J. Atwood. Chicago Review Press 2013 208 p. (Women of action) (hardback) $19.95

Grades: 8 9 10 11 12 **940.54**

1. World War, 1939-1945 -- Secret service 2. World War, 1939-1945 -- Underground movements -- France 3. World War, 1939-1945 -- Secret service -- Great Britain 4. World War, 1939-1945 -- Underground movements -- France

ISBN 1613744870; 9781613744871

LC 2013008734

In this memoir, "one of the most celebrated female World War II resistance fighters shares . . . her experiences as a special agent for the British Special Operations Executive. French-born British citizen [Pearl Witherington] Cornioley tells her story through a series of reminiscences, including . . . her recruitment and training as a special agent, and parachuting into a remote, rural area of occupied France." (Kirkus Reviews)

"Cornioley's detailed account of her time as a British special agent in Nazi-occupied France is suited for readers already familiar with the basic events of World War II. She narrates with short sentences and a matter-of-fact tone that keeps readers at a distance from her story, but the material is well documented and thorough. Appropriate for students needing primary source material. " (Horn Book)

Includes bibliographical references and index

Drez, Ronald J.

★ **Remember** D-day; the plan, the invasion, survivor stories. National Geographic Books 2004 61p il map $17.95; lib bdg $27.90

Grades: 5 6 7 8 **940.54**

1. World War, 1939-1945 -- Campaigns -- France

ISBN 0-7922-6666-8; 0-7922-6965-9 lib bdg

LC 2003-17733

Discusses the events and personalities involved in the momentous Allied invasion of France on June 6, 1944

"This well-organized, clearly written account provides a solid overview for readers unfamiliar with the subject. A first-rate purchase." SLJ

Includes bibliographical references

Farrell, Mary Cronk

Pure grit; how American World War II nurses survived battle and prison camp in the Pacific. by Mary Cronk Farrell. Abrams Books for Young Readers 2014 160 p. illustrations, color maps (hardcover : alk. paper) $24.95

Grades: 7 8 9 10 11 12 **940.54**

1. Nurses 2. Military medicine 3. World War, 1939-1945 -- Medical care 4. World War, 1939-1945 -- Prisoners and prisons 5. Prisoners of war -- Philippines 6. Prisoners of war -- United States 7. Military nursing -- United States -- History 8. World War, 1939-1945 -- Campaigns -- Philippines 9. Nurses -- United States -- History -- 20th century 10. World War, 1939-1945 -- Medical care -- United States 11. World War, 1939-1945 -- Prisoners and prisons, Japanese

ISBN 1419710281; 9781419710285

LC 2013017134

This book, by Mary Cronk Farrell, focuses on American World War II Navy and Army nurses who were stationed in the Pacific. "Nurses, deeply engaged in caring for desperately wounded soldiers, were sent to Bataan. After living on near-starvation rations, the nurses on Bataan were evacuated to Corregidor. . . . A few were rescued from Corregidor before it too fell to enemy forces. . . . The remaining nurses were then imprisoned . . . and not released until late winter of 1945." (Kirkus Reviews)

"Using historical interviews and modern correspondence with the subjects' relatives, Farrell presents a fascinating account of the more than one hundred army and navy nurses who served in the South Pacific in WWII. Through every battle and retreat, and even in POW camps, these nurses cared for the injured under the most primitive of conditions. The book's utilitarian design features archival photographs." Horn Book

Includes bibliographical references and index

Standing up against hate; how black women in the Army helped change the course of WWII. Mary Cronk Farrell. Abrams Books for Young Readers 2018 208 p. (hardcover with jacket) $17.99

Grades: 5 6 7 8 **940.54**

1. World War, 1939-1945 2. African American women 3. African American women -- Biography 4. Women soldiers -- United States -- Biography 5. World War, 1939-1945 -- Participation, Female 6. World War, 1939-1945 -- Participation, African American 7. United States. Army. Women's Army Corps -- African American officers -- Biography 8. United States. Army. Women's Army Auxiliary Corps -- African American officers -- Biography

ISBN 9781419731600

LC 2018009606

This book, by Mary Cronk Farrell, "tells the stories of the African American women who enlisted in the newly formed Women's Army Auxiliary Corps (WAAC) in World War II. . . . The book centers around Charity Adams, who commanded the only black WAAC battalion sent overseas and became the highest ranking African American woman in the military by the end of the war. Along with Adams's story are those of other black women who played a crucial role in integrating the armed forces." (Publisher's note)

Includes bibliographical references

Grant, R. G.

Why did Hiroshima happen? Gareth Stevens Pub. 2010 48p il map (Moments in history) lib bdg $31.95; pa $14.05

Grades: 6 7 8 9 **940.54**

1. Atomic bomb 2. World War, 1939-1945 -- Japan 3. World War, 1939-1945 -- United States 4. Hiroshima (Japan) -- Bombardment, 1945

ISBN 978-1-4339-4163-4 lib bdg; 1-4339-4163-5 lib bdg; 978-1-4339-4164-1 pa; 1-4339-4164-3 pa

LC 2010012464

This "explains the before, during, and after of [the bombing of Hiroshima]. . . . Sidebars include meticulously cited eyewitness quotes or extra insight on particularly important events. Even more information is contained in the maps, period photographs, and well-placed captions that grace every page." SLJ

Includes glossary and bibliographical references

Hama, Larry

The **battle** of Iwo Jima; guerilla warfare in the Pacific. by Larry Hama; illustrated by Anthony Williams. Rosen Pub. 2007 48p il map (Graphic battles of World War II) lib bdg $29.25

Grades: 5 6 7 8 9 **940.54**

1. Graphic novels 2. World War, 1939-1945 -- Graphic novels 3. Iwo Jima, Battle of, 1945 -- Graphic novels

ISBN 978-1-4042-0781-3 lib bdg; 1-4042-0781-3 lib bdg

LC 2006007645

"Using a graphic novel to introduce the battle for Iwo Jima makes it very accessible. Before the graphic-novel section of the book begins, Hama provides a short, informative background piece describing the run-up to World War II, the significance of the Japanese war machine, and the importance of the tiny island of Iwo Jima. Then the graphic novel, illustrated by Williams in camouflage colors, does a terrific job of examining the ups and downs of the battle as well as the horror of so many losses—on both sides." Booklist

Includes bibliographical references

Hillstrom, Laurie

The **attack** on Pearl Harbor; [by] Laurie Collier Hillstrom. Omnigraphics 2009 237p il (Defining moments) $49

Grades: 7 8 9 10 11 12 **940.54**

1. Reference books 2. Pearl Harbor (Oahu, Hawaii), Attack on, 1941

ISBN 978-0-7808-1069-3; 0-7808-1069-4

LC 2009-4236

"This book is divided into three well-organized sections. Part one provides a narrative overview detailing the events leading up to the attack, the attack itself, and the aftermath, including the U.S. victory in the Pacific as well as the occupation and reconstruction of Japan after World War II. Part two is composed of eight two to three-page biographies of the important figures such as Yamamoto, Roosevelt, and Doris Miller, the first African-American to receive the Navy Cross. A final section of primary documents from the Japanese attack plan to Truman's announcement of the end of the war provides insight into the war in the Pacific. . . . This work is a must-have for reports and assignments." SLJ

Includes glossary and bibliographical references

Holm, Tom

Code talkers and warriors; Native Americans and World War II. Chelsea House 2007 168p il map (Landmark events in Native American history) $35

Grades: 7 8 9 10 **940.54**

1. World War, 1939-1945 -- Native Americans
ISBN 978-0-7910-9340-5; 0-7910-9340-9

LC 2006102263

"In this title about Native Americans in World War II, Holm . . . expands considerably on his specific topic to highlight significant miliary roles played by Native Americans in conflicts dating back to the sixteenth century. . . . [This is] outstanding. . . . [A] valuable resource." Booklist

Includes bibliographical references

Hopkinson, Deborah, 1942-

D -Day; the WWII invasion that changed history. by Deborah Hopkinson. Scholastic Focus 2018 400 p. $16.99

Grades: 5 6 7 8 9 10 **940.54**

1. Military history 2. Operation Overlord 3. World War, 1939-1945 -- Campaigns -- France 4. Normandy (France) -- History, Military 5. World War, 1939-1945 -- Campaigns -- France -- Normandy
ISBN 9780545682480

LC 2017057211

This book, by Deborah Hopkinson, offers information on "the WWII invasion known as D-Day, [which] was [considered] the largest military endeavor in history. . . . The goal of D-Day was the total defeat of Hitler's regime, and the defense of free democracies everywhere. . . . Hopkinson weaves together the contributions of not only D-Day's famous players, but African Americans, women, journalists, and service members." (Publisher's note)

Includes bibliographical references and index

Dive! World War II Stories of Sailors & Submarines in the Pacific: The Incredible Story of U.S. Submarines in WWII. by Deborah Hopkinson. Scholastic Press 2016 384 p. illustrations, map $17.99

Grades: 4 5 6 7 8 **940.54**

1. World War, 1939-1945 2. World War, 1939-1945 -- Campaigns -- Pacific Ocean 3. World War, 1939-1945 -- Naval operations -- Submarine 4. World War, 1939-1945 -- Naval operations, American
ISBN 9780545425582

LC 2015040229

This book by Deborah Hopkinson "tells the incredible story of America's little known 'war within a war' -- US submarine warfare during World War II. Following the attack on Pearl Harbor, the US entered World War II in December 1941 with only 44 Naval submarines -- many of them dating from the 1920s. With the Pacific battleship fleet decimated after Pearl Harbor, it was up to the feisty and heroic sailors aboard the US submarines to stop the Japanese invasion across the Pacific." (Publisher's note)

"With a fascinating blend of submarine mechanics and tales of courage, readers will dive in deep." Booklist

Includes bibliographical references and index

Kuhn, Betsy

Angels of mercy; the Army nurses of World War II. Atheneum Bks. for Young Readers 1999 114p il map $18

Grades: 5 6 7 8 **940.54**

1. Women in the armed forces 2. World War, 1939-1945 -- Women 3. United States -- Army Nurse Corps
ISBN 0-689-82044-5

LC 98-36610

Relates the experiences of World War II Army nurses, who brought medical skills, courage, and cheer to hospitals throughout Europe, North Africa, and the Pacific

"Excellent reproductions, maps and a time line accompany the clear, well-written text." SLJ

Includes bibliographical references

Moore, Kate

The **Battle** of Britain. Osprey 2010 200p il map $29.95

Grades: 7 8 9 10 **940.54**

1. Britain, Battle of, 1940 2. World War, 1939-1945 -- Great Britain
ISBN 978-1-84603-474-9; 1-84603-474-4

"In the summer and autumn of 1940, Britain faced an unparalleled challenge. Forced to beat a quick retreat from Dunkirk with the German Luftwaffe in hot pursuit, the British dug in for what was to be one of the most remarkable feats in the history of human endurance. In this spectacular oversize volume, Moore recounts with notable lucidity and depth the events and characters from both the British and German home fronts during this critical moment in world history and offers an excellent analysis of prewar preparations by both sides. The most outstanding feature of the work is without a doubt the stunning visuals. The book is packed with a fantastic range of archival photos, maps, and war posters." SLJ

Mullenbach, Cheryl

Torpedoed! a World War II story of a sinking passenger ship and two children's survival at sea. Cheryl Mullenbach. Chicago Review Press 2017 xiii, 158 p.p illustrations (hardcover) $17.99

Grades: 4 5 6 7 8 **940.54**

1. Athenia (Steamship) 2. Shipwreck survival 3. Children and war -- United States 4. Shipwrecks -- North Atlantic Ocean 5. World War, 1939-1945 -- Naval operations, German 6. World War, 1939-1945 -- Children -- United States 7. World War, 1939-1945 -- Naval operations -- Submarine 8. Passenger ships -- Great Britain -- History -- 20th century
ISBN 9781613738245; 9781613738276

LC 2017000468

This book, by Cheryl Mullenbach, "vividly re-creates the events surrounding the attack on the Athenia, the first ship lost in the battle of the Atlantic. . . . [She] brings to life the prewar environment in America and Europe, the anxious days leading up to the surprise attack, the frantic rush to escape the sinking ship, and the long, terrifying night that Russell, Florence, and others spent in churning lifeboats battling the elements and imagining the worst." (Publisher's note)

"An engaging, sometimes-harrowing account of the first casualty in what became known as the Battle of the Atlantic." Kirkus

Includes bibliographical references and index

Nathan, Amy

Yankee doodle gals; women pilots of World War II. foreword by Eileen Collins. National Geographic Soc. 2001 86p il maps $21

Grades: 6 7 8 9 **940.54**

1. Women air pilots 2. World War, 1939-1945 -- Aerial operations
ISBN 0-7922-8216-7

LC 2001-560

This describes the Women's Air Force Service Pilots of World War II

"There's plenty of action to involve readers, and the women's perseverance in the face of obstacles is inspiring. Wonderful black-and-white photos extend the text." Booklist

Includes bibliographical references

Nelson, Pete

Left for dead; a young man's search for justice for the USS Indianapolis. [by] Peter Nelson; with a preface by Hunter Scott. Delacorte Press 2002 xx, 201p il hardcover o.p. pa $8.95

Grades: 7 8 9 10 **940.54**

1. Children 2. Students 3. Naval officers 4. Indianapolis (Cruiser) 5. World War, 1939-1945 -- Naval operations
ISBN 0-385-72959-6; 0-385-73091-8 pa

LC 2001-53774

Recalls the sinking of the U.S.S. Indianapolis at the end of World War II, the navy cover-up and unfair court martial of the ship's captain, and how a young boy helped the survivors set the record straight fifty-five years later.

"Written in simple chronological order, it tells a powerful story." Book Rep

Includes bibliographical references

Olson, Tod

Lost in the Pacific, 1942; not a drop to drink. Tod Olson. Scholastic Inc. 2016 vii, 168 p.p illustrations $12.99

Grades: 6 7 8 9 **940.54**

1. World War, 1939-1945 2. Survival at sea -- Pacific Ocean 3. Survival after airplane accidents, shipwrecks, etc. 4. Aircraft accidents -- Pacific Ocean 5. Airplane crash survival -- Pacific Ocean 6. World War, 1939-1945 -- Aerial operations, American
ISBN 0545928117; 9780545928083; 9780545928113

LC 2016006972

This juvenile book, by Tod Olson, begins on "October 21, 1942, and somewhere over the Pacific Ocean a lone B-17 runs low on fuel. In order to avert a crash, the pilot and copilot choose to attempt to land the plane on the surface of the ocean . . . and thus begins the survival struggle of eight men in three tiny life rafts." (School Library Journal)

"A riveting, completely engrossing true survival story." Kirkus

Includes bibliographical references

Pearson, P. O'Connell

Fly girls; the daring American women pilots who helped win WWII. P. O'Connell Pearson. Simon & Schuster Books for Young Readers 2018 208 p. (hardcover) $16.99

Grades: 5 6 7 8 9 **940.54**

1. World War, 1939-1945 -- Women 2. Women air pilots 3. World War, 1939-1945 4. Women air pilots -- United States 5. Women Airforce Service Pilots (U.S.) 6. Air pilots, Military -- United States 7. World War, 1939-1945 -- Participation, Female 8. World War, 1939-1945 -- Aerial operations, American
ISBN 9781534404106; 9781534404113

LC 2017011062

In this book, "author Patricia Pearson offers a beautifully written account of the remarkable but often forgotten group of female fighter pilots who answered their country's call in its time of need during World War II. . . . Through grit and pure determination, 1,100 of these female pilots . . . were finally allowed to ferry planes from factories to bases, to tow targets for live ammunition artillery training, to test repaired planes and new equipment, and more." (Publisher's note)

Samuels, Charlie

Propaganda; by Charlie Samuels. Brown Bear Books 2011 48 p. ill. (chiefly col.), col. maps (World War II sourcebook) (library) $35.65

Grades: 5 6 7 8 **940.54**

1. World War, 1939-1945 -- Propaganda 2. World War, 1939-1945
ISBN 1936333236; 9781936333233

LC 2011010241

This book by Charlie Samuels on propaganda is part of the World War II Sourcebook series. "Each page is illustrated. Little-known facts and, sometimes, direct narratives are presented with the information given to the reader. . . . Each book has the same timeline of World War II, maps of both the European and Pacific theaters, interesting biographical snapshots of people involved, and a list of websites that students may use to further explore World War II." (Library Media Connection)

Includes bibliographical references and index.

Soldiers; [Charlie Samuels] Brown Bear Books 2011 48 p. ill. (some col.), maps (col.) (World War II sourcebook) (library binding) $35.65

Grades: 5 6 7 8 **940.54**

1. Soldiers 2. World War, 1939-1945 3. Soldiers -- History -- 20th century
ISBN 1936333244; 9781936333240

LC 2011007057

This book by Charlie Samuels, part of the World War II Sourcebook series, "Describes the life of a soldier in World War II, from recruitment efforts around the world, to the daily life during the fighting." (Publisher's note)

Includes bibliographical references (p. 47) and index

Sheinkin, Steve

★ The **Port** Chicago 50; disaster, mutiny, and the fight for civil rights. Steve Sheinkin. Roaring Brook Press 2014 208 p. illustrations (hardcover : alk. paper) $19.99

Grades: 5 6 7 8 9 **940.54**

1. United States. Navy 2. African American sailors 3. African Americans -- Civil rights 4. World War, 1939-1945 5. Port Chicago Mutiny, Port Chicago, Calif., 1944
ISBN 1596437960; 9781596437968

LC 2013013452

National Book Award Shortlist: Young People's Literature (2014)

YALSA Award for Excellence in Nonfiction for Young Adults: Finalist (2015)

Boston Globe-Horn Book Award: Nonfiction (2014)

Author Steve Sheinkin tells how "on July 17, 1944, a massive explosion rocked the segregated Navy base at Port Chicago, California. On August 9th, 244 men refused to go back to work until unsafe and unfair conditions at the docks were addressed. Fifty were charged with mutiny." (Publisher's note)

"An unusual entry point for the study of WWII and the nascent civil rights movement. Photographs are helpful, and documentation is thorough." (Horn Book)

Includes bibliographical references and index

Stone, Tanya Lee

★ **Courage** has no color, the true story of the Triple Nickles; America's first black paratroopers. Tanya Lee Stone. Candlewick Press 2013 160 p. $24.99

Grades: 5 6 7 8 **940.54**

1. Parachute troops 2. United States. Army 3. World War, 1939-1945 4. African American soldiers

ISBN 0763651176; 9780763651176

LC 2012942315

Orbis Pictus Awards Honor Book (2014)

YALSA Award for Excellence in Nonfiction for Young Adults: Finalist (2014)

This book tells the "untold story of the 555th Parachute Infantry Battalion, America's first black paratroopers." Enlisted black men "faced the tyranny of racial discrimination on the homefront. . . . When 1st Sgt. Walter Morris, whose men served as guards at The Parachute School at Fort Benning, saw white soldiers training to be paratroopers, he knew his men would have to train and act like them to be treated like soldiers." (Kirkus Reviews)

Torres, John Albert

The **Battle** of Midway; by John A. Torres. Mitchell Lane Publishers 2011 48p il map (Technologies and strategies in battle) lib bdg $29.95

Grades: 6 7 8 9 **940.54**

1. Midway, Battle of, 1942 2. World War, 1939-1945 -- Campaigns

ISBN 978-1-61228-078-3; 1-61228-078-1

LC 2011002746

This "is an in-depth account of the 1942 Battle of Midway, detailing how it was fought by sea and air by the U.S. and Japan. . . . This useful research source packs a wealth of information into its straightforward narrative. This colorful layout intersperses abundant visuals, including maps and archival photos as well as sidebars." Booklist

Includes glossary and bibliographical references

Wukovits, John F., 1944-

The **bombing** of Pearl Harbor; by John F. Wukovits. Lucent Books 2011 112 p. ill. (some col.), photographs (World history) (library) $34.95

Grades: 6 7 8 9 **940.54**

1. World War, 1939-1945 -- Causes 2. Pearl Harbor (Oahu, Hawaii), Attack on, 1941

ISBN 1420503308; 9781420503302

LC 2010035993

This book by John Wukovits is part of the World History series and looks at the bombing of Pearl Harbor. Each book in the series offers an "overview of an important historical event or period. The series is designed both to acquaint readers with the basics of history and to make them aware that their lives and their own historical era are an intimate part of the ongoing human saga." (Publisher's note)

Includes bibliographical references (p. 97-100) and index.

941 British Isles

Dillon, Patrick

The **story** of Britain from the Norman Conquest to the European Union; illustrated by P.J. Lynch. Candlewick Press 2011 341p il map $21.99

Grades: 5 6 7 8 **941**

1. Great Britain -- History

ISBN 978-0-7636-5122-0; 0-7636-5122-2

LC 2010038883

"This well-written, thoughtfully illustrated volume [is] an indispensible tool for European history buffs." Horn Book Guide

Indovino, Shaina C.

United Kingdom; by Rae Simons and Shaina C. Indovino. Mason Crest Publishers 2012 64 p. col. ill., col. maps (library) $22.95

Grades: 5 6 7 8 **941**

1. Great Britain 2. Northern Ireland 3. European Union -- Great Britain 4. European Union -- Northern Ireland

ISBN 1422222616; 9781422222614; 9781422222928

LC 2010051852

This book on the United Kingdom by Rae Simons and Shaina Carmel Indovino "covers Modern Issues, History and Government, The Economy, People and Culture, and Looking to the Future. . . Identical information on "The Formation of the European Union" appears in every book" in the series. (Library Media Connection) Also covered are "issues like immigration and the global financial crisis". (Publisher's note)

Includes bibliographical references (p. 60) and index.

941.081 British Isles--Reign of Victoria, 1837-1901

Schomp, Virginia

Victoria and her court. Marshall Cavendish Benchmark 2010 80p il (Life in Victorian England) lib bdg $34.21

Grades: 6 7 8 9 **941.081**

1. Queens 2. Courts and courtiers 3. Great Britain -- History -- 19th century

ISBN 978-1-60870-028-8 lib bdg; 1-60870-028-3 lib bdg

A social history of Victorian England, focusing on the upper echelons of society during the reign of Queen Victoria (1837-1901)

This "is clearly written, thorough, and informative. The visually rich layout includes photographs and paintings from the time period, full-page illustrations, and attention-grabbing sidebars. Most appealing are the primary source quotations, which are plentiful and relevant.." Libr Media Connect

Includes glossary and bibliographical references

941.1 Scotland

Waldron, Melanie

Scotland; by Melanie Waldron. Heinemann Library 2012 48 p. col. ill., col. maps (Countries around the world) (library) $32.65; (paperback) $8.99

Grades: 6 7 8 9 **941.1**

1. Culture 2. Scotland

ISBN 1432952161; 9781432952167; 9781432952419

LC 2010044776

This book by Melanie Waldron is part of the Countries Around the World series and looks at Scotland. This entry "offers complete coverage of this . . . country, including sections on history, geography, wildlife, infrastructure and government, and culture. It also includes a detailed fact file, maps and charts, and a traceable flag." (Publisher's note)

Includes bibliographical references (p. 44) and index.

941.5 Ireland

Feed the children first; Irish memories of the Great Hunger. edited by Mary E. Lyons. Atheneum Bks. for Young Readers 2002 43p il pbk. $22.99

Grades: 5 6 7 8 **941.5**

1. Famines 2. Ireland -- History

ISBN 9781442482920

LC 00-49606

The editor presents extracts from memoirs of the Irish famine period. Bibliography. "Intermediate, middle school." (Horn Book)

Lyons "compiles quotations from Irish citizens on the devastating effects of the potato famine that ravaged Ireland between 1845 and 1852." Publ Wkly

Includes bibliographical references

Fradin, Dennis Brindell

The **Irish** potato famine; by Dennis Fradin. Marshall Cavendish Benchmark 2012 32 p. (Great escapes) (library) $34.21

Grades: 5 6 7 8 **941.5**

1. Famines 2. Ireland -- History -- Famine, 1845-1852 3. Escapes -- Ireland -- History -- 19th century 4. Irish -- Migrations -- History -- 19th century 5. Disaster victims -- Ireland -- History -- 19th century 6. Ireland -- Emigration and immigration -- History -- 19th century

ISBN 1608704734; 9781608704736

LC 2010018788

This book, part of the Great Escapes series, focuses on the Irish Potato Famine. "Each book begins with an introduction to an individual who escaped, followed by the history of the precipitating events, the escape itself, and a follow-up on what happened after the escape. Each title includes a timeline, notes, and additional information on the topic." (Library Media Connection)

Includes bibliographical references and index.

941.7 Republic of Ireland

Blashfield, Jean F.

Ireland; Enchantment of the World. by Jean F. Blashfield. Children's Press ; an imprint of Scholastic Inc. 2014 144 p. (Enchantment of the world--second series) (library binding) $40

Grades: 5 6 7 8 **941.7**

1. Ireland

ISBN 0531236765; 9780531236765

LC 2013002015

This book, by Jean F. Blashfield, focuses on Ireland. The book focuses on "country's culture, history, and geography are explored in detail. . . . Sidebars highlight especially interesting people, places, and events. . . . Recipes give readers the opportunity to experience foreign cuisine." (Publisher's note)

"Many students turn to the Internet for writing reports, but for reliably accurate, attractively presented and well-calibrated information, the long-standing Enchantment of the World series remains a superior choice. Each volume has been completely rewritten from a previous edition —in many cases to startling effect given recent political events. Although the basic structure holds true to past versions, the updated photographs are truly eye-popping and take care to portray the countries as modern often opting for showing, say, a surgeon at work rather than a rural farmer. It might not be necessary for libraries to replace Ireland, since it hasn't changed radically, but this is a solid offering with updated statistics. Each volume in this reliable series includes extensive back matter with a detailed index." Booklist.

Includes bibliographical references and index

942 England and Wales

Banting, Erinn

England; by Erinn Banting ; edited by Sarah Cairns ; illustrated by Jeff Crosby, Dianne Eastman, and David Wysotski. Revised ed. Crabtree Pub. Co. 2012 32 p. ill. (some col.) (Lands, peoples, and cultures) (library) $26.60; (paperback) $8.95; (ebook) $26.60

Grades: 4 5 6 **942**

1. Culture 2. England 3. England -- Civilization 4. England -- Social life and customs

ISBN 0778798283; 9780778798286; 9780778798316; 9781427180056 pdf

LC 2012013776

This book by Erinn Banting is part of the Lands, Peoples and Cultural Series and looks at the culture of England. The books offer information about "folktales, sports, and history." Also included are "a table of contents, short glossary (words highlighted in test) and index." (Catholic Library World)

Includes index

942.02 England--Norman period, 1066-1154

Hamilton, Janice

The **Norman** conquest of England; by Janice Hamilton. Twenty-First Century Books 2008 un il map (Pivotal moments in history) lib bdg $38.60

Grades: 7 8 9 10 **942.02**

1. Normans 2. Kings 3. Great Britain -- History -- 1066-1154, Norman period

ISBN 978-0-8225-5902-3

LC 2006102629

This is an account of the invasion and conquest of England by the Normans in 1066 and its consequences.

This is "clearly written and interesting enough for browsers as well as report writers. Maps, full-color and black-and-white photos, and reproductions of manuscripts contribute to the attractive format and make the subject matter come alive." SLJ

Includes glossary and bibliographical references

942.03 England--Period of House of Plantagenet, 1154-1399

Levy, Debbie

The **signing** of the Magna Carta. Twenty-First Century Books 2008 160p il map (Pivotal moments in history) lib bdg $38.60

Grades: 7 8 9 10 11 12 **942.03**

1. Magna Carta 2. Great Britain -- History -- 1154-1399, Plantagenets

ISBN 978-0-8225-5917-7 lib bdg; 0-8225-5917-X lib bdg

LC 2005-20971

This "research source explains the intent of the treaty of 1215 that became the Magna Carta, the factors that produced it, as well as its evolution, historical significance, and relevance today. . . . The clear explanation of the 'Great Charter's' historical context accompanied by informative inserts and beautiful, relevant illustrations make this a book to dip into as well as to read through." Voice Youth Advocates

Includes glossary and bibliographical references

942.05 England--Period of House of Tudor, 1485-1603

Hollihan, Kerrie Logan

Elizabeth I--the people's queen; her life and times: 21 activities. Chicago Review Press 2011 129p il (For kids) pa $16.95

Grades: 4 5 6 7 8 **942.05**

1. Queens 2. Great Britain -- History -- 1485-1603, Tudors

ISBN 978-1-56976-349-0; 1-56976-349-6

LC 2010047647

This is an interactive biography of Queen Elizabeth I.

"The writing is clear and suited to readers with no previous knowledge of the topic. The activities vary in difficulty, from reading The Faerie Queen, to creating a family coat of arms, to growing a knot garden. The book is well illustrated with black-and-white reproductions of portraits, engravings, and paintings depicting major events in the Tudors' lives. . . . This well-organized book succeeds at being interesting and scholarly at the same time." SLJ

Includes bibliographical references

Kallen, Stuart A.

★ **Elizabethan** England; by Stuart A. Kallen. ReferencePoint Press 2013 96 p. (Understanding world history series) (hardcover) $27.95

Grades: 7 8 9 10 **942.05**

1. Great Britain -- History -- 1558-1603, Elizabeth 2. England -- Civilization -- 16th century 3. England -- Social conditions -- 16th century 4. Great Britain -- History -- Elizabeth, 1558-1603

ISBN 1601524846; 9781601524843

LC 2012026174

This book, part of the Understanding World History series, looks at Elizabethan England. It "relates Queen Elizabeth I's advance to power and considers the hardships of life in London, the rise of the arts during the Renaissance, and Elizabeth's role as 'pirate queen,' endorsing privateering, slave trading, and the defeat of the Spanish Armanda." (Booklist)

Includes bibliographical references and index

943 Germany and neighboring central European countries

Burgan, Michael

The **Berlin** airlift; by Michael Burgan. Compass Point Books 2007 48 p. ill. (some col.) (We the people) (paperback) $7.95; (library) $27.99

Grades: 4 5 6 7 **943**

1. Berlin (Germany) -- History -- Blockade, 1948-1949

ISBN 9780756520366; 0756520363; 075652024X; 9780756520243

LC 2006006766

Examines the joint effort of the United States and Great Britain who flew in around the clock to deliver supplies to Berlin during the Soviet blockade of 1948-49.

"The writing is clear and concise and the vocabulary is age-appropriate. [This] title contains excellent contemporary photographs." SLJ

Includes bibliographical references (p. 46-47) and index.

Freedman, Russell, 1929-2018

We will not be silent; the White Rose student resistance movement that defied Adolf Hitler. Russell Freedman. Clarion Books 2016 112 p. illustrations (hardback) $17.99

Grades: 5 6 7 8 **943**

1. Students -- Political activity 2. Germany -- History -- 1933-1945 3. World War, 1939-1945 -- Underground movements 4. Weisse Rose (Resistance group) 5. Anti-Nazi movement -- Germany -- Munich 6. Munich (Germany) -- History -- 20th century 7. Universität München -- Riot, 1943 8. College students -- Political activity -- Germany -- Munich -- History -- 20th century

ISBN 0544223799; 9780544223790

LC 2015020439

Sibert Honor Book (2017)

This book, authored by Russell Freedman, "tells the story of Austrian-born Hans Scholl and his sister Sophie. They belonged to Hitler Youth as young children, but began to doubt the Nazi regime. As older students, the Scholls and a few friends formed the White Rose, a campaign of active resistance to Hitler and the Nazis. Risking imprisonment or even execution, the White Rose members distributed leaflets urging Germans to defy the Nazi government." (Publisher's note)

"A thorough and accessible introduction to the Holocaust and the students who dared to take a stand against evil." Kirkus

Includes bibliographical references (pages 93-95) and index.

Indovino, Shaina C.

Germany; by Ida Walker and Shaina C. Indovino. Mason Crest Publishers 2013 64 p. ill. (some col.), col. maps (Major European nations) (library) $22.95

Grades: 5 6 7 8 **943**

1. Germany 2. Germany -- Politics and government 3. Germany -- History 4. European Union -- Germany 5. German -- Description and travel 6. Germany -- Social life and customs

ISBN 1422222438; 9781422222430

LC 2010051291

This book on Germany by Ida Walker and Shaina Carmel Indovino is part of the "Major European Nations" series, which "stresses the modern relationships, goals, and problems of the European Union. . . . Chapters begin with 'Modern Issues' and a brief summary of the country's history and government, followed by chapters on economy, people and culture, and 'Looking to the Future.' In addition, there is a time line and a few suggestions for finding out more." (School Library Journal)

Nardo, Don

Hitler in Paris; how a photograph shocked a world at war. by Don Nardo. Compass Point Books 2014 64 p. (library binding) $33.99

Grades: 6 7 8 9 **943**

1. World War, 1939-1945 -- France -- Paris 2. France -- History -- 1940-1945, German occupation 3. Photographs -- Political aspects

ISBN 0756547334; 9780756547332; 9780756547899

LC 2013030415

This book, by Don Nardo, focuses on a photograph of dictator Adolf Hitler in Paris, France during World War II. "Only days before, on June 14, 1940, German soldiers had overrun the city, shocking the world. . . . He posed for a photo in front of the Eiffel Tower, the beloved symbol of France and the country's free, democratic people. The photo, taken by his personal photographer, Heinrich Hoffmann, would show the world that Nazi Germany had triumphed over its bitter enemy." (Publisher's note)

"Analyzing visual images and setting them in a larger historical and cultural context is an important skill. This volume uses Heinrich Hoffmann's 1940 photograph of Hitler in front of the Eiffel Tower to discuss the dictator's rise to power and Hoffmann's image-crafting of his subject. A spacious page design, which includes plenty of photos, enhances the presentation. Reading list, timeline. Bib., glos., ind." Horn Book

Includes bibliographical references (page 63) and index

Other titles in the series include:
Assassination and its Aftermath (2014)
The Blue Marble (2014)
Breaker Boys (2012)
Civil War Witness (2014)
Little Rock Girl 1957 (2012)
Man on the Moon (2011)
Migrant Mother (2011)
Raising the Flag (2011)
Summiting Everest (2014)
Tank Man (2014)

943.085 Period of Weimar Republic, 1918-1933

Freeman, Charles

Why did the rise of the Nazis happen? Gareth Stevens Pub. 2011 48p il map (Moments in history) lib bdg $31.75; pa $14.05

Grades: 6 7 8 9 **943.085**

1. Heads of state 2. National socialism 3. Nazi leaders 4. Germany -- Politics and government -- 1918-1933

ISBN 978-1-4339-4175-7 lib bdg; 1-4339-4175-9 lib bdg; 978-1-4339-4176-4 pa; 1-4339-4176-7 pa

LC 2010017229

"Examines the events that served as . . . [precursors to the rise of the Nazis]. . . . Brightly colored pullout boxes highlight important turning points, the perspective of the everyday man, and further information on why specific events occurred. Numerous photographs help readers visualize concepts more fully. . . . Students should be able to easily use this resource." Libr Media Connect

Includes glossary and bibliographical references

943.086 Germany--Period of Third Reich, 1933-1945

Bartoletti, Susan Campbell

★ **Hitler** Youth; growing up in Hitler's shadow. Scholastic Nonfiction 2005 176p il map $19.95

Grades: 7 8 9 10 **943.086**

1. National socialism 2. Holocaust, 1933-1945 3. Germany -- History -- 1933-1945

ISBN 0-439-35379-3

LC 2004-51040

A Newbery Medal honor book, 2006

"Bartoletti draws on oral histories, diaries, letters, and her own extensive interviews with Holocaust survivors, Hitler Youth, resisters, and bystanders to tell the history from the viewpoints of people who were there. . . . The stirring photos tell more of the story. . . . The extensive back matter is a part of the gripping narrative." Booklist

Includes bibliographical references

Living in Nazi Germany; Elaine Halleck, book editor. Greenhaven Press 2004 158p il map (Exploring cultural history) $29.95; pa $21.20

Grades: 7 8 9 10 **943.086**

1. National socialism 2. Germany -- Politics and government -- 1933-1945

ISBN 0-7377-1731-9; 0-7377-1732-7 pa

LC 2003-57961

This includes "eyewitness accounts from victims of Hitler's brutality as well as from those who found places in the Nazi machine. . . . Most of the accounts are from less well known sources, and many are compelling. Excerpts from a few familiar volumes, such as Albert Speer's memoirs and the wartime diaries of Joseph Goebbels, also appear. . . . An effective, insightful look at aspects of the Nazi system." Booklist

Includes bibliographical references

943.8 Poland

Docalavich, Heather

Poland; by Healther Docalavich and Shaina C. Indovino. Mason Crest Publishers 2013 64 p. col. ill., col. maps (library) $22.95

Grades: 5 6 7 8 **943.8**

1. Poland 2. European Union -- Poland

ISBN 1422222543; 9781422222546

LC 2010051465

This book by Heather Docalavich and Shaina C. Indovino is part of the Major European Union Nations series and looks at Poland. "It joined the EU in 2004 . . . . For long time, Poland has been home to scientific thinkers, artists, and musicians. Today, it is one of the countries that have weathered the global recession the best, proving this nation's strength." (Publisher's note)

Includes bibliographical references and index

Kadziolka, Jan

Poland; [by] Jan Kadziolka, Tadeusz Wojciechowski. Oliver Press 2011 48p il map (Looking at Europe) lib bdg $24.95

Grades: 7 8 9 10 **943.8**

1. Poland

ISBN 978-1-881508-89-2; 1-881508-89-7

LC 2009035350

This describes Poland today, its history, cities, transportation, culture, education, economy, cuisine, tourism, and natural environment.

This will "best suit students with good vocabularies and some knowledge of European history. . . . [It is] clearly written and well organized. . . . [It includes] many clear photos as well as colorful sidebars. . . . Attractive, informative." Booklist

Includes glossary and bibliographical references

Mara, Wil

Poland; by Wil Mara. Children's Press, an imprint of Scholastic Inc. 2014 144 p. illustrations and maps (library binding) $40

Grades: 5 6 7 8 **943.8**

1. Poland

ISBN 0531220168; 9780531220160

LC 2013026061

This book, by Wil Mara, focuses on Poland. The book discusses the "country's culture, history, and geography are explored in detail, allowing readers a chance to see how people live. . . . Sidebars highlight especially interesting people, places, and events . . . [and] easy recipes give readers the opportunity to experience foreign cuisine first-hand." (Publisher's note)

Includes bibliographical references and index

944 France and Monaco

Elliott, David

Voices; the final hours of Joan of Arc. by David Elliott. Houghton Mifflin Harcourt 2019 208 p. (hardcover) $17.99

Grades: 7 8 9 10 **944**

1. Christian saints -- Biography 2. Soldiers -- France -- Biography 3. Women soldiers -- France -- Biography 4. Christian saints -- France -- Biography 5. Christian women saints -- France -- Biography

ISBN 9781328987594

LC 2018025855

In this book, author David Elliott "explores how Joan of Arc changed the course of history and remains a figure of fascination centuries after her extraordinary life and death. Told through medieval poetic forms and in the voices of the people and objects in Joan of Arc's life, (including her family and even the trees, clothes, cows, and candles of her childhood), 'Voices' offers an unforgettable perspective on an extraordinary young woman." (Publisher's note)

"An elegant, spirited introduction to classical poetry and to a woman fighting not just for a cause but for a place in a world that undervalued her voice." (Booklist)

Indovino, Shaina C.

France; by Jeanine Sanna and Shaina C. Indovino. Mason Crest Publishers 2013 64 p. col. ill., col. maps (hardcover) $22.95

Grades: 5 6 7 8 **944**

1. France

ISBN 142222242X; 9781422222423

LC 2010051290

Presents an introduction to France, discussing its history, system of government, economy, education, culture, and prospects for the future.

Includes bibliographical references (p. 59) and index.

Sonneborn, Liz

France; by Liz Sonneborn. Children's Press 2013 144 p. ill., maps (library) $40

Grades: 5 6 7 8 **944**

1. France

ISBN 0531256006; 9780531256008

LC 2012047113

This book by Liz Sonneborn is part of the Enchantment of the World series and looks at France. It covers "history, government, geography, natural resources, economics, the arts, and culture. . . . Maps, charts, sidebars highlighting items of interest, a time line, and a 'Fast Facts' section add to the presentation." (School Library Journal)

Includes bibliographical references (page 134) and index

944.04 France since 1789

Riggs, Kate

The **French** Revolution. Creative Education 2009 48p il map (Days of change) lib bdg $32.80

Grades: 5 6 7 8 **944.04**

1. France -- History -- 1789-1799, Revolution

ISBN 978-1-58341-734-8 lib bdg; 1-58341-734-6 lib bdg

LC 2008009728

"With elegant design and mature prose, the Days of Change series is an ideal starting point for all manner of school projects. . . . The political pressures at the center of The French Revolution are difficult to dramatize, but Riggs carefully lays out the factions and civil disobedience that led to the Declaration of the Rights of Man and of The Citizen—and then the emperor's reign that overthrew everything." Booklist

Includes bibliographical references

945 Italy, San Marino, Vatican City, Malta

Blashfield, Jean F.

Italy; by Jean F. Blashfield. Children's Press, an imprint of Scholastic Inc. 2014 144 p. (library binding) $40

Grades: 5 6 7 8 **945**

1. Italy 2. Italy -- History 3. Italy -- Civilization 4. Italy -- Economic conditions 5. Italy -- Politics and government 6. Italy -- Social life and customs

ISBN 0531236773; 9780531236772

LC 2013000087

This book, by Jean F. Blashfield, focuses on Italy. The book discusses the "country's culture, history, and geography are explored in detail, allowing readers a chance to see how people live. . . . Sidebars highlight especially interesting people, places, and events . . . [and] recipes give readers the opportunity to experience foreign cuisine firsthand." (Publisher's note)

"Many students turn to the Internet for writing reports, but for reliably accurate, attractively presented and well-calibrated information, the long-standing Enchantment of the World series remains a superior choice. Each volume has been completely rewritten from a previous edition —in many cases to startling effect given recent political events. Although the basic structure holds true to past versions, the updated photographs are truly eye-popping and take care to portray the countries as modern often opting for showing, say, a surgeon at work rather than a rural farmer. It might not be necessary for libraries to replace [this title], since it hasn't changed radically, but this is a solid offering with updated statistics. Each volume in this reliable series includes extensive back matter with a detailed index." Booklist

Includes bibliographical references and index

946 Spain, Andorra, Gibraltar, Portugal

Augustin, Byron

Andorra; by Byron D. Augustin. Marshall Cavendish Benchmark 2009 144p il map (Cultures of the world) lib bdg $42.79

Grades: 5 6 7 8 **946**

1. Andorra

ISBN 978-0-7614-3122-0 lib bdg; 0-7614-3122-5 lib bdg

LC 2007040356

"Provides comprehensive information on the geography, history, governmental structure, economy, cultural diversity, peoples, religion, and culture of Andorra." Publisher's note

Includes glossary and bibliographical references

947 Russia and neighboring east European countries

Gottfried, Ted

The **road** to Communism; illustrated by Melanie Reim. 21st Cent. Bks. (Brookfield) 2002 144p il lib bdg $28.90

Grades: 8 9 10 11 12 **947**

1. Soviet Union -- History -- 1917-1921, Revolution

ISBN 0-7613-2557-3

LC 2001-52252

Chronicles the Czarist Russian Empire in the 1800s, the birth of Bolshevism, events leading to the Russian Revolution of 1917, and the development of new political structures in its aftermath

"Gottfried writes with clarity and distance even as he narrates the dramatic details of the political conflict and the emotion of the 'dream that failed.'" Booklist

Includes glossary and bibliographical references

947.08 Russia since 1855

Fleming, Candace, 1962-

★ The **family** Romanov; murder, rebellion, and the fall of imperial Russia. Candace Fleming. Schwartz & Wade Books 2014 304 p. il, maps, genealogical table $18.99

Grades: 7 8 9 10 11 12 **947.08**

1. Russia -- History -- 1917-1921, Revolution 2. Russia -- History -- Nicholas II, 1894-1917 3. Soviet Union -- History -- Revolution, 1917-1921

ISBN 0375867821; 9780375867828; 9780375967825

LC 2013037904

Robert F. Sibert Honor Book (2015)

Boston Globe-Horn Book Award: Nonfiction (2015)

YALSA Award for Excellence in Nonfiction for Young Adults: Finalist (2015)

This book, by Candace Fleming, describes how "when Russia's last tsar, Nicholas II, inherited the throne in 1894, he was unprepared to do so. With their four daughters (including Anastasia) and only son, a hemophiliac, Nicholas and his reclusive wife, Alexandra, buried their heads in the sand, living a life of opulence as World War I raged outside their door and political unrest grew into the Russian Revolution." (Publisher's note)

"Fleming crafts an exciting narrative from this complicated history and its intriguing personalities. It is full of rich details about the Romanovs, insights into figures such as Vladimir Lenin and firsthand accounts from ordinary Russians affected by the tumultuous events. A variety of photographs adds a solid visual dimension." Kirkus

Includes bibliographical references and index

947.084 Russia (Soviet Union)--1917-1991

The **Rise** of the Soviet Union; Tom Streissguth, book editor. Greenhaven Press 2002 256p (Turning points in world history) hardcover o.p. pa $23.70

Grades: 7 8 9 10 **947.084**

1. Soviet Union -- History

ISBN 0-7377-0929-4; 0-7377-0928-6 pa

LC 2001-40866

A collection of essays concerning the social, economic and political issues in the history of the Soviet Union

Includes bibliographical references

947.085 Russia (Soviet Union)--1953-1991

Langley, Andrew

The **collapse** of the Soviet Union; the end of an empire. Compass Point Books 2006 96p il map (Snapshots in history) lib bdg $31.93

Grades: 7 8 9 10 **947.085**

1. Soviet Union -- History

ISBN 978-0-7565-2009-0; 0-7565-2009-6

LC 2006003003

This "describes leaders, their plans, and their ultimate downfalls, from the removal of Tsar Nicholas II to the problems of present-day Russia. [This book is] great for research . . . brief but comprehensive." SLJ

Includes glossary and bibliographical references

947.5 Caucasus

Dhilawala, Sakina

★ **Armenia**; Sakina Dhilawala, Debbie Nevins. 3rd edition Marshall Cavendish Benchmark 2017 144p il map (Cultures of the world) library $47.07

Grades: 5 6 7 8 **947.5**

1. Armenia

ISBN 9781502627407 library

First published 1997

"Provides comprehensive information on the geography, history, wildlife, governmental structure, economy, cultural diversity, peoples, religion, and culture of Armenia." Publisher's note

Includes glossary and bibliographical references

948 Scandinavia

Allan, Tony

Exploring the life, myth, and art of the Vikings; Tony Allan. Rosen Pub. 2012 144 p. (Civilizations of the world)

Grades: 7 8 9 10 11 **948**

1. Vikings 2. Viking art 3. Norse mythology 4. Viking civilization 5. Art, Viking 6. Mythology, Norse 7. Civilization, Viking

ISBN 9781448848331

LC 2011008856

This book on the Vikings "offers an informative overview of . . . political and social history as well as its art, architecture, and mythology, all bolstered with plenty of . . . details and narratives. . . . [T]he illustrations include artworks, documents, and handsome maps as well as photos of significant sites and artifacts. . . . "Vikings" explores heritage that the Norse people shared and their history as traders, raiders, and settlers in other lands." (Booklist) The book "put[s] the art . . . in context, explaining how a society's religious beliefs, legends, and cultural traditions manifest themselves through images and iconography. The . . . layout features full-color photographs of architecture, sculpture, and painting on every page, accompanied by informative captions." (School Libr J)

Includes bibliographical references (p. 136-137) and index

Hinds, Kathryn, 1962-

Vikings; masters of the sea. Marshall Cavendish Benchmark 2009 79p il (Barbarians!) lib bdg $24.95

Grades: 6 7 8 9 **948**

1. Vikings

ISBN 978-0-7614-4074-1 lib bdg; 0-7614-4074-7 lib bdg

LC 2008039052

"This . . . devotes excellent coverage and exposure to the emergence, development, and legacy of [the Vikings]." Libr Media Connect

Includes glossary and bibliographical references

Nardo, Don

The **Vikings**. Lucent Books 2010 112p il (World history) lib bdg $33.45

Grades: 6 7 8 9 **948**

1. Vikings

ISBN 978-1-4205-0316-6; 1-4205-0316-2

LC 2010010500

This is an introduction to Viking civilization.

This "shines as it provides a contemporaneous writing as well as work by scholars that offer plenty of drama—and lots of facts too. . . . [It also] provides a solid time line, plenty of photographs, sourced quotes, and a list of books and websites for further investigation. Excellent for reports and research." Booklist

Includes bibliographical references

948.5 Sweden

Heinrichs, Ann

Sweden; by Ann Heinrichs. Children's Press, an Imprint of Scholastic Inc. 2014 144 p. color illustrations (library binding) $40

Grades: 5 6 7 8 **948.5**

1. Sweden

ISBN 0531220176; 9780531220177

LC 2013022562

This book, by Ann Heinrichs, focuses on Sweden. The "country's culture, history, and geography are explored in detail, allowing readers a chance to see how people live. . . . Sidebars highlight especially interesting people, places, and events [and] recipes give readers the opportunity to experience foreign cuisine first-hand." (Publisher's note)

"Introduces Sweden, describing its geography, history, animals, government, economy, food, religion, cities, culture, and family life." Baker & Taylor

Includes bibliographical references and index

Phillips, Charles

★ **Sweden**; [by] Charles Phillips; Susan C. Brantly and Eric Clark consultants. National Geographic 2009 64p il map (Countries of the world) lib bdg $27.90

Grades: 4 5 6 7 **948.5**

1. Sweden

ISBN 978-1-4263-0389-0 lib bdg; 1-4263-0389-0 lib bdg

LC 2009275585

This describes the geography, nature, history, people & culture, and government & economy of Sweden

Includes glossary and bibliographical references

948.97 Finland

Tan, Chung Lee

Finland; writers, Chung Lee Tan, Elizabeth Schmermund. 3rd edition Cavendish Square 2017 144p il map (Cultures of the world) library $47.07

Grades: 5 6 7 8 **948.97**

1. Finland

ISBN 9781502622273 library

LC 2016041208

First published 1996

This provides "information on the geography, history, governmental structure, economy, cultural diversity, peoples, religion, and culture of Finland." Publisher's note

Includes glossary and bibliographical references

949.35 Luxembourg

Sheehan, Patricia

Luxembourg; by Patricia Sheehan & Sakina Dhilawala. 3rd edition Cavendish Square 2017 144p il map (Cultures of the world) library $47.07

Grades: 5 6 7 8 **949.35**

1. Luxembourg

ISBN 9781502627438 library

First published 1997

Discusses the geography, history, government, economy, and customs of the smallest of the Benelux countries

Includes glossary and bibliographical references

949.4 Switzerland

Rogers Seavey, Lura

Switzerland; by Lura Rogers Seavey. Children's Press, an imprint of Scholastic Inc. 2017 144 p. color ill., color maps (library binding) $40

Grades: 5 6 7 8 **949.4**

1. Switzerland

ISBN 0531218872; 9780531218877

LC 2016000985

In this book, by Lura Rogers Seavey, "Switzerland has become known as a place of peace and prosperity. Readers will explore this European nation's fascinating history and find out how it came to occupy such a unique position in the world. They will learn how the country is governed and what makes its economy so strong. They will also explore its beautiful cities and mountainous landscapes and sample its rich culture." (Publisher's note)

"With stunning, high-quality photos that reflect the richness of cultures around the globe, the Enchantment of the World series earns its name." Booklist

Includes bibliographical references and index

949.5 Greece

Feldman, Ruth Tenzer

The **fall** of Constantinople. Twenty-First Century Books 2008 160p il map (Pivotal moments in history) lib bdg $38.60

Grades: 7 8 9 10 **949.5**

1. Byzantine Empire 2. Istanbul (Turkey) -- History -- Siege, 1453

ISBN 978-0-8225-5918-4 lib bdg; 0-8225-5918-8 lib bdg

LC 2006037501

"This volume examines the fall of Constantinople, marking the end of the Middle Ages. Sure to satisfy history buffs, the book not only relates military facts but also delves into the events leading up to Constantinople's defeat as well as exploring its effects throughout history. Numerous sidebars, illustrations, maps, and art reproductions provide additional information." Horn Book Guide

Includes glossary and bibliographical references

Green, Jen

★ **Greece**; [by] Greg Anderson and Kostas Vlassopoulos, consultants. National Geographic 2009 64p il map (Countries of the world) lib bdg $27.90

Grades: 4 5 6 7 **949.5**

1. Greece

ISBN 978-1-4263-0470-5 lib bdg; 1-4263-0470-6 lib bdg

This describes the geography, nature, history, people and culture, government and economy of Greece

Includes glossary and bibliographical references

Vanvoorst, Jennifer Fretland

The **Byzantine** Empire; by Jenny Fretland VanVoorst. Compass Point Books 2013 48 p. ill. (chiefly col.), col. map (library) $28.65; (paperback) $8.95

Grades: 6 7 8 **949.5**

1. Byzantine Empire -- Civilization

ISBN 075654565X; 0756545862; 9780756545659; 9780756545864

LC 2012001994

This children's nonfiction book, by Jennifer Fretland VanVoorst, profiles the Byzantine Empire as part of the "Exploring the Ancient World" series. "The Byzantine Empire, which thrived from 395 to 1453, was a fascinating place. Its people thought of themselves as Romans, spoke Greek, and hailed from all across Europe and Asia. . . . It was a Christian empire that preserved and developed Europe's intellectual heritage at a time when western Europe was in decline." (Publisher's note)

Includes bibliographical references (p. 46-47) and index.

949.7 Serbia, Croatia, Slovenia, Bosnia and Hercegovina, Montenegro, Macedonia

Halilbegovich, Nadja

My childhood under fire; a Sarajevo diary. Kids Can Press 2006 120p il $14.95

Grades: 5 6 7 8 **949.7**

1. Yugoslav War, 1991-1995 2. Sarajevo (Bosnia and Hercegovina)

ISBN 1-55337-797-4

"In 1992, when the bombing started in Sarajevo, Halilbegovich, 12, kept a diary of her terrifying daily life under siege. Her terse vignettes replay the horror of her comfortable home torn apart." Booklist

949.9 Bulgaria

Prazdny, Bronja

Bulgaria. Oliver Press 2011 48p il map (Looking at Europe) lib bdg $24.95

Grades: 7 8 9 10 **949.9**

1. Bulgaria

ISBN 978-1-881508-85-4; 1-881508-85-4

LC 2009032670

This describes Bulgaria today, its history, cities, transportation, culture, education, economy, cuisine, tourism, and natural environment.

This will "best suit students with good vocabularies and some knowledge of European history. . . . [It is] clearly written and well organized. . . . [It includes] many clear photos as well as colorful sidebars. . . . Attractive, informative." Booklist

Includes glossary and bibliographical references

950 History of Asia

Campbell, Rusty

Atlas of Asia; [by] Rusty Campbell, Malcolm Porter, and Keith Lye. Rosen Central 2010 il map lib bdg $26.50; pa $11.75

Grades: 4 5 6 7 **950**

1. Asia

ISBN 978-1-4358-8455-7 lib bdg; 1-4358-8455-8 lib bdg; 978-1-4358-9112-8 pa; 1-4358-9112-0 pa

"Most of the spreads cover a region or one of the continent's bigger countries and provide large, clear maps and columns of almanac data surrounded by short chapters on famous people, animals, industries, cities, sports, and more, all accompanied by color illustrations or photographs and informative sidebars... with guidance [children] will encounter some absorbing and informative material." SLJ

Galloway, Priscilla

★ **Adventures** on the ancient Silk Road; [by] Priscilla Galloway with Dawn Hunter. Annick Press 2009 164p il pa $14.95; $24.95

Grades: 6 7 8 9 **950**

1. Explorers 2. Travelers 3. Voyages and travels 4. Kings 5. Buddhist monks 6. Travel writers 7. Asia -- Description and travel

ISBN 1-55451-197-6 pa; 1-55451-198-4; 978-1-55451-197-6 pa; 978-1-55451-198-3

"The monk Xuanzang, the conqueror Genghis Khan, and the merchant Marco Polo each traveled the Silk Road, years apart. Their journeys, by different routes and for different motives, are gripping historical narratives, sensitively and excitingly fictionalized here, in language that is lively and descriptive, clear but not oversimplified. Vibrant reproductions of art and photos of artifacts leap off every colorful page." SLJ

Helget, Nicole

Mongols; Nicole Helget. Creative Education 2013 48 p. (Fearsome fighters) (alk. paper) $35.65

Grades: 5 6 7 8 **950**

1. Mongols 2. Asia -- History 3. Military art and science -- History 4. Mongols -- History 5. Mongols -- Warfare 6. Military art and science -- Mongolia -- History -- To 1500

ISBN 1608181847; 9781608181841

LC 2011035800

Author Nicole Helget presents a book on the history of the people of Mongolia, their influence on world culture, and their impact on society. The book presents a "look at the Mongols, including how they built the most widespread empire in history, their lifestyle, their weapons, and how they remain a part of today's culture through books and film." (Publisher's note)

Includes bibliographical references (p. 48) and index

Morris, Neil

Asian civilizations. Zak Books 2009 48p il map (History of the world) lib bdg $34.25

Grades: 7 8 9 10 **950**

1. Ancient civilization 2. Asia -- History 3. Asia -- Civilization
ISBN 978-88-6098-160-8 lib bdg; 88-6098-160-3 lib bdg

LC 2008-8403

The "effectiveness lies in the combination of lush illustrations, well-chosen, captioned photographs of contemporary artifacts, and . . . [a] reasoned, concise [narrative]. Succinct time lines border most pages, and . . . the proper amount of white space, and clear dark print maintain organization and clarity. A superior choice." SLJ

Includes glossary

Nardo, Don

Genghis Khan and the Mongol Empire. Lucent Books 2011 96p il map (World history) $33.45

Grades: 5 6 7 8 9 **950**

1. Mongols
ISBN 978-1-4205-0326-5; 1-4205-0326-X

LC 2010032960

"Using new scholarship, Nardo paints a more nuanced and sophisticated picture of a man who united several nomadic clans and then went on to found history's largest empire. Starting with his early childhood and ending with the death of his grandson, Kublai Khan, the book focuses on Genghis Khan's empire building and leadership, including his code of laws and justice. The book features several color photographs of present-day Mongolia period reenactments, as well as artistic representations from the era. . . . Nardo includes quotations from several scholars while still keeping the book engaging and accessible for a wide variety of readers." SLJ

Includes glossary and bibliographical references

951 China and adjacent areas

Bardoe, Cheryl

China; a history. by Cheryl Bardoe. Abrams Books for Young Readers 2018 176 p. (hardcover, jacketed, picture) $22.99

Grades: 5 6 7 8 **951**

1. China -- History 2. China -- Civilization 3. Historical literature 4. China -- History -- Exhibitions 5. China -- Civilization -- Exhibitions 6. Cyrus Tang Hall of China -- Exhibitions
ISBN 9781419721212

LC 2017046786

This book, by Cheryl Bardoe, "traces the 7,000-year story of . . . [China]. Full-color maps, photos, and illustrations of the people, landscape, artifacts, and rare objects bring the history of this nation to life! Young readers learn about prehistoric China, follow the reign of emperors and dynasties, and come to understand how China became the world power that it is today." (Publisher's note)

"A bit dry for casual readers but nonetheless an excellent resource and a beautifully presented, nuanced introduction to pre-20th-century Chinese history." (Kirkus Reviews)

Includes bibliographical references and index

Marx, Trish

Elephants and golden thrones; inside China's Forbidden City. written by Trish Marx; photographs and photograph selection by Ellen B. Senisi; foreword by Li Ji. Abrams Books for Young Readers 2008 48p il $18.95

Grades: 4 5 6 7 **951**

1. China 2. Forbidden City (Beijing, China)
ISBN 978-0-8109-9485-0; 0-8109-9485-2

LC 2007-022413

Introduces Beijing's Forbidden City, recounting some of the most famous incidents from its past, and describing its rooms, their function, and some of the daily rituals of palace life.

The author "brings the Forbidden City to life by telling stories about six different royal inhabitants from Zhengde, 'one of the worst emperors in Chinese history,' to Puyi, who became a pawn of the invading Japanese. . . . Beautiful drawings and photographs, some provided by the Palace Museum and some taken for this book, lend color and provide additional information. Of particular note are the photos of the interiors of buildings, a number of which are not regularly open to the public." Booklist

Includes bibliographical references

Pelleschi, Andrea

China. ABDO 2012 144p. il (Countries of the world) lib bdg $35.64

Grades: 6 7 8 9 **951**

1. China
ISBN 978-1-61783-107-2

LC 2011019959

" Chapters then cover all the expected details for report-writers... Vivid photographs and useful maps in an eye-pleasing design enliven the presentation." Horn Book

Includes glossary and bibliographical references

Sis, Peter

★ **Tibet**; through the red box. Farrar, Straus & Giroux 1998 un il maps $25

Grades: 4 5 6 7 **951**

1. Tibet (China)
ISBN 0-374-37552-6

LC 97-50175

A Caldecott Medal honor book, 1999

"When Sis opens the red lacquered box that has sat on his father's table for decades, he finds the diary his father kept when he was lost in Tibet in the mid-1950s. The text replicates the diary's spidery handwriting, while the illustrations depict elaborate mazes and mandalas, along with dreamlike spreads that are filled with fragmented details of the father's and son's lives. . . . Impeccably designed and beautifully made, the book has a dreamlike quality that will keep readers of many ages coming back to find more in its pages." Booklist

Ting, Renee

Chinese history stories; edited by Renee Ting; translated from Chinese by Qian Jifang. Shens Books 2009 2v il ea $19.95

Grades: 6 7 8 9 **951**

1. China -- History
ISBN 978-1-885008-37-4 v1; 1-885008-37-6 v1; 978-1885008-38-1 v2; 1-885008-38-4 v2

LC 2009027288

"These first two entries in a planned series of 12 volumes offer gripping introductions to China's cultural narratives. From the initial two-page condensation of 3000 years of history to the suggestions to 'Learn More' after (often more useful to read before), the well-told stories and the attractively varied illustrations are riveting. . . . Multiple illustrators provide changing art styles and historical allusions, but all are detailed, lively, and colorful." SLJ

Yomtov, Nelson

China; by Nel Yomtov. Children's Press, an imprint of Scholastic Inc. 2018 144 p. (library binding : alk. paper) $40

Grades: 5 6 7 8 **951**

1. China -- History 2. China -- Description and travel 3. China -- Social life and customs 4. China

ISBN 0531235718; 9780531235713

LC 2016056323

In this book in the Enchantment of the World series, by Nel Yomtov, "with a history dating back thousands of years, . . . [China is] one of the world's oldest civilizations. Readers will tour this geographically diverse nation from its most remote natural landscapes to its most populated cities. Along the way, they will learn about China's history and traditions, get a taste of the local culture, take a close look at the many plants and animals found there, and much more." (Publisher's note)

Includes bibliographical references (page 134) and index

951.05 China--Period of People's Republic, 1949-

Burgan, Michael

Tank man; how a photograph defined China's protest movement. by Michael Burgan. Compass Point Books 2014 64 p. (Captured history) (library binding) $33.99

Grades: 6 7 8 9 **951.05**

1. Demonstrations 2. Tiananmen Square Incident, Beijing (China), 1989 3. Photojournalism -- China 4. China -- History -- Tiananmen Square Incident, 1989 -- Pictorial works

ISBN 0756547318; 9780756547318; 9780756547875

LC 2013031196

"This middle grades book by Michael Burgan describes how "For almost two months in spring 1989, Beijing's Tiananmen Square had been the site of growing protests against China's hardline communist government. In early June, China's leaders had had enough. In a matter of days soldiers cleared the square. . . . As tanks rumbled through the streets near Tiananmen Square, a man in a white shirt came suddenly into view. He held up his right hand." (Publisher's note)

"Analyzing visual images and setting them in a larger historical and cultural context is an important skill. In this volume Burgan uses the iconic photograph of a Tiananmen Square protester facing down a tank to discuss the 1989 student protest in China and the Communist government's violent retaliation. A spacious page design, which includes plenty of photos, enhances the presentation. Reading list, timeline. Bib., glos., ind." Horn Book

Includes bibliographical references (page 63) and index

Other titles in the series include:

Assassination and its Aftermath (2014)
The Blue Marble (2014)
Breaker Boys (2012)
Civil War Witness (2014)
Hitler in Paris (2014)
Little Rock Girl 1957 (2012)
Man on the Moon (2012)
Migrant Mother (2011)
Raising the Flag (2011)
Summiting Everest (2014)

The **diary** of Ma Yan; the struggles and hopes of a Chinese schoolgirl. edited and introduced by Pierre Haski; translated from the French by Lisa Appignanesi. HarperCollins 2005 166p $15.99; lib bdg $16.89

Grades: 5 6 7 8 **951.05**

1. China 2. Diarists 3. Students

ISBN 0-06-076496-1; 0-06-076497-X lib bdg

LC 2004-16136

Original French edition, 2002

This book, edited by Pierre Haski offers "Ma Yan's . . . diary chronicles her struggle to escape hardship and bring prosperity to her family through her persistent, sometimes desperate, attempts to continue her schooling." The book discusses her efforts to continue schooling despite the hunger and poverty she endures in rural China. (Publisher's note)

"In 2001, while a French journalist was visiting remote Ningxia province in northwest China, a Muslim woman wearing the white headscarf of the Hui people thrust the diaries of her daughter into his hands. The three small notebooks described the girl's struggle to get an education despite extreme poverty. . . . The girl's feelings for her mother were powerful and complex, and she alternated between overwhelming love and rage at the injustices she suffered." SLJ

Jiang, Ji-li

★ **Red** scarf girl; a memoir of the Cultural Revolution. foreword by David Henry Hwang. HarperCollins Pubs. 1997 285p $16.99; pa $6.99

Grades: 6 7 8 9 10 **951.05**

1. Communism -- China 2. China -- History -- 1949-1976 -- Personal narratives

ISBN 0-06-027585-5; 0-06-446208-0 pa

LC 97-5089

"This is an autobiographical account of growing up during Mao's Cultural Revolution in China in 1966. . . . Jiang describes in terrifying detail the ordeals of her family and those like them, including unauthorized search and seizure, persecution, arrest and torture, hunger, and public humiliation. . . . Her voice is that of an intelligent, confused adolescent, and her focus on the effects of the revolution on herself, her family, and her friends provides an emotional focal point for the book, and will allow even those with limited knowledge of Chinese history to access the text." Bull Cent Child Books

Slavicek, Louise Chipley

The **Chinese** Cultural Revolution. Chelsea House Publishers 2010 128p il (Milestones in modern world history) lib bdg $35

Grades: 8 9 10 11 12 **951.05**

1. China -- History -- 1949-1976

ISBN 978-1-60413-278-6; 1-60413-278-7

LC 2008-54885

"From the cover photo onward, young people are front and center in [this book,] . . . which focuses on the Red Guards who heard the anti-establishment call of their leader, Mao Zedong, in 1966. This political upheaval led to the deaths of up to four million Chinese over 10 years." Booklist

Includes bibliographical references

The **Tiananmen** Square protests of 1989; Jeff Hay, editor. Greenhaven Press 2010 177p il map (Perspectives on modern world history) lib bdg $39.70

Grades: 7 8 9 10 **951.05**

1. Tiananmen Square Incident, Beijing (China), 1989

ISBN 978-0-7377-4796-6; 0-7377-4796-X

LC 2009041850

Offers basic historical information about the Tiananmen Square protests of 1989 , examining the controversies surrounding this event and providing first-person narratives from people who lived through or were impacted by it.

"The book has numerous full-color photographs, sidebars to enhance the text, and illustrations. This is a highly readable book and would be a good addition to the library's world history collection." Libr Media Connect

Includes glossary and bibliographical references

Yu Chun

Little Green; growing up during the Chinese Cultural Revolution. [by] Chun Yu. Simon & Schuster Books for Young Readers 2005 112p il $15.95

Grades: 6 7 8 9 **951.05**

1. China -- History -- 1949-1976

ISBN 0-689-86943-6

LC 2003-27433

"Chun Yu was born in China in 1966, the year the Great Cultural Revolution began, and in spare poetry she remembers the first 10 years of her life. True to a child's bewildered viewpoint and augmented by occasional, small black-and-white family photos, Yu gets across the grief at home and the school indoctrination." Booklist

951.25 Hong Kong

Kagda, Falaq

Hong Kong; Falaq Kagda, Magdalene Koh, Debbie Nevins. 3rd edition Cavendish Square 2018 144p il map (Cultures of the world) library $47.07

Grades: 5 6 7 8 **951.25**

1. Hong Kong (China)

ISBN 9781502632395 library

LC 2017040196

First published 1998

Surveys the geography, history, government, economy, and culture of Hong Kong

Includes glossary and bibliographical references

951.5 Tibet Autonomous Region (China)

Sonneborn, Liz

Tibet; by Liz Sonneborn. Children's Press, an imprint of Scholastic Inc. 2017 144 p. color ill., color maps (library binding) $40

Grades: 5 6 7 8 **951.5**

1. Tibet (China) 2. Tibet Autonomous Region (China)

ISBN 9780531218884

LC 2015048619

In this children's book in the Enchantment of the World series, by Liz Sonneborn, "despite Tibet's official status as a part of China, the country's people widely consider it to be an independent nation. Readers will trace Tibet's long history to discover how this conflict came to be. Along the way, they will find out how Tibet's people live, how the region is governed, and much more. They will also get a close-up look at its beautiful landscapes and diverse wildlife." (Publisher's note)

"With stunning, high-quality photos that reflect the richness of cultures around the globe, the Enchantment of the World series earns its name." Booklist

Includes bibliographical references and index

951.7 Mongolia

Pang, Guek-Cheng, 1950-

Mongolia; Henrietta Toth and Pang Guek Cheng. 3rd edition Cavendish Square 2019 144 p. col. ill., col. maps (Cultures of the world) library $47.07

Grades: 5 6 7 8 **951.7**

1. Mongolia

ISBN 9781502641298 library

This describes the geography, history, wildlife, governmental structure, economy, cultural diversity, peoples, religion, and culture of Mongolia

Includes bibliographical references and index.

951.73 Outer Mongolia (Mongolian People's Republic)

Bjorklund, Ruth

Mongolia; by Ruth Bjorklund. Children's Press, an Imprint of Scholastic Inc. 2017 144 p. color ill., color maps (library binding : alk. paper) $40

Grades: 5 6 7 8 **951.73**

1. Mongolia

ISBN 0531218848; 9780531218846

LC 2015043526

This book, by Ruth Bjorklund, focuses on Mongolia. "Situated directly between China and Russia, the country of Mongolia long had close ties to its larger neighbors. However, since the early 1990s it has become increasingly independent, and many Mongolians have worked to rediscover a national culture that existed long before Chinese or Russian rule. Readers will explore this Mongolia's amazing history and find out what makes its culture so unique." (Publisher's note)

"With stunning, high-quality photos that reflect the richness of cultures around the globe, the Enchantment of the World series earns its name." Booklist

Includes bibliographical references and index

951.9 Korea

Bowler, Ann Martin

All about Korea; stories, songs, crafts, and more. illustrated by Soosoonam Barg. Periplus Editions 2011 64p il $16.95

Grades: 3 4 5 6 **951.9**

1. Korea

ISBN 978-0-8048-4012-5; 0-8048-4012-1 (hardcover)

LC 2010040845

Reece, Richard

The **Korean** War. ABDO Pub. 2011 112p il map (Essential events) lib bdg $23.95

Grades: 7 8 9 10 11 12 **951.9**

1. Korean War, 1950-1953

ISBN 978-1-61714-766-1; 1-61714-766-4

LC 2010044661

This describes the Korean War and discusses the political and social issues pertaining to it.

Includes glossary and bibliographical references

Senker, Cath

★ **North** Korea and South Korea; by Cath Senker. 1st ed. Rosen Pub. 2013 48 p. col. ill. (library) $29.25

Grades: 6 7 8 **951.9**

1. Korea (North) 2. Korea (South) 3. Korea (North) -- History 4. Korea (South) -- History 5. Korea (North) -- Social conditions 6. Korea (South) -- Social conditions

ISBN 1448860296; 9781448860296

LC 2012010617

This book by Cath Senker is part of the Our World Divided series and looks at North Korea and South Korea. "Each of these volumes begins with a recent news event pertaining to the featured conflict and then looks back at the origin and milestones of the discord. . . . 'Viewpoints' sidebars are . . . supplementary features. They showcase quotations about a specific matter from individuals on opposing sides." (School Library Journal)

Includes bibliographical references (p. 46) and index.

951.93 North Korea (People's Democratic Republic of Korea)

Sonneborn, Liz

North Korea; by Liz Sonneborn. Children's Press ; an imprint of Scholastic Inc. 2014 144 p. illustrations. maps (Enchantment of the world. Second series) (library binding) $40

Grades: 5 6 7 8 **951.93**

1. Korea (North)

ISBN 0531236781; 9780531236789

LC 2013003650

This book, by Liz Sonneborn, is part of the Enchantment of the World Series. "Each volume has been completely rewritten from a previous edition. . . . 'North Korea' has a new author and a strong political focus, discussing life under the new leader, Kim Jong-un. . . . Each volume in this . . . series includes extensive back matter with a detailed index." (Booklist)

Includes bibliographical references and index

952 Japan

Bjorklund, Ruth

Japan; by Ruth Bjorklund. Children's Press, an imprint of Scholastic Inc. 2018 144 p. (library binding : alkaline paper) $40

Grades: 5 6 7 8 **952**

1. Japan -- History 2. Japan -- Description and travel 3. Japan -- Social life and customs 4. Japan

ISBN 0531235696; 9780531235690

LC 2016052309

In this book in the Enchantment of the World series, by Ruth Bjorklund, "Japan is a country of towering mountains, beautiful farmland, and huge cities. Despite its relatively small size, it is home to one of the world's most powerful economies and plays a major role in global politics. Readers will learn all about Japan's rich history, culture, and traditions. They will also find out how the country is governed, . . . what it is like to live there today, and much more." (Publisher's note)

Includes bibliographical references (pages 134) and index

Blumberg, Rhoda

★ **Commodore** Perry in the land of the Shogun. Lothrop, Lee & Shepard Bks. 1985 144p il map $21.99; pa $8.99

Grades: 5 6 7 8 **952**

1. Naval officers 2. Japan -- History 3. Japan -- Foreign relations -- United States 4. United States -- Foreign relations -- Japan 5. United States Naval Expedition to Japan (1852-1854)

ISBN 0-688-03723-2; 0-06-008625-4 pa

LC 84-21800

A Newbery Medal honor book, 1986

This "is a well-written story of Matthew Perry's expedition to open Japan to American trade and whaling ports. The account is sensitive to the extreme cultural differences that both the Japanese and Americans had to overcome. Especially good are the chapters and paragraphs explaining Japanese feudal society and culture. The text is marvelously complemented by the illustrations, almost all reproductions of contemporary Japanese art." SLJ

Includes bibliographical references

Moore, Willamarie

All about Japan; stories, songs, crafts, and more. illustrated by Kazumi Wilds. Tuttle Pub. 2011 63p il $16.95

Grades: 3 4 5 6 **952**

1. Japan

ISBN 978-4-8053-1077-9; 4-8053-1077-4

LC 2010040843

"In this treasure-trove of information, two children, one a Tokyo urbanite and the other from a rural village, introduce readers to their country and its culture, including geography, language, traditional arts, costume, etiquette, sports, and festivals. The dual narrators' conversational descriptions of their homes and daily routines will engage young readers while highlighting the differences between the Westernized big-city existence and the traditional way of life in Japan's countryside, deftly demonstrating the rich variety of lifestyles within this island nation. The scope of this book is remarkably comprehensive, covering almost anything a child would want to know." SLJ

Niz, Xavier

Samurai; a guide to the feudal knights. by Xavier W. Niz. Capstone Press 2012 48p il map (History's greatest warriors) lib bdg $30.65

Grades: 6 7 8 **952**

1. Samurai

ISBN 978-1-4296-6601-5 lib bdg; 1-4296-6601-3 lib bdg

LC 2011004956

"...Focuses [more] on relaying facts about the four groups of exceptional fighters than on a narrative... [and has] extensive modern cultural references to which students will relate." SLJ

Includes bibliographical references

Somervill, Barbara A.

Japan; by Barbara A. Somervill. Children's Press 2012 144 p. ill., maps (library) $40

Grades: 5 6 7 8 **952**

1. Japan 2. Japan -- Social life and customs

ISBN 0531253546; 9780531253540

LC 2011009503

This book is part of the Enchantment of the World series and focuses on Japan. "Topics such as climate, wildlife, history, government, pop culture, and the arts are all addressed, providing a . . . look at Japan's past and present. With content revised considerably from previous editions, this book goes beyond facts and statistics to give readers an intimate glimpse at typical Japanese youth through fictionalized anecdotes detailing moments in their daily lives." (School Library Journal)

Includes bibliographical references and index.

Turnbull, Stephen R.

The **most** daring raid of the samurai. Rosen Pub. 2011 64p il map (The most daring raids in history) lib bdg $29.25

Grades: 7 8 9 10 **952**

1. Samurai 2. Japan -- History

ISBN 978-1-4488-1872-3; 1-4488-1872-9

LC 2010030843

First published 2009 in the United Kingdom with title: The samurai capture a king

In 1609, the Samurai from the Shimazu clan of Satsuma took control of the independent kingdom of Ryukyu. This audacious military campaign brought an end to centuries of warfare between the Shimazu clan and the king of Ryukyu.

This book is "packed with facts, covering the details of the action, the people involved, and the tools used, in engaging prose. The authors cite their sources thoroughly. . . . Diagrams, . . . and maps make the action easy to follow and provide visual context for the raids. . . . This . . . is sure to find a large readership." SLJ

Includes glossary and bibliographical references

953 Arabian Peninsula and adjacent areas

King, David C.

★ The **United** Arab Emirates; [by] David C. King. 2nd ed; Marshall Cavendish Benchmark 2008 144p il map (Cultures of the world) lib bdg $42.79

Grades: 5 6 7 8 **953**

1. United Arab Emirates

ISBN 978-0-7614-2565-6

LC 2006030237

This describes the geography, history, government, economy, environment, people, and culture of the United Arab Emirates.

Includes glossary and bibliographical references

953.3 Yemen

Hestler, Anna

Yemen; by Anna Hestler and Jo-Ann Spilling. 2nd ed.; Marshall Cavendish Benchmark 2010 144p il map (Cultures of the world) lib bdg $42.79

Grades: 5 6 7 8 **953.3**

1. Yemen

ISBN 978-0-7614-4850-1 lib bdg; 0-7614-4850-0 lib bdg

LC 2009021200

First published 1999

This describes the geography, history, wildlife, governmental structure, economy, cultural diversity, peoples, religion, and culture of Yemen

Includes glossary and bibliographical references

O'Neal, Claire

We visit Yemen; by Claire O'Neal. Mitchell Lane Publishers 2012 63 p. ill. (chiefly col.), col. maps (library) $33.95; (ebook) $33.95

Grades: 4 5 6 7 8 **953.3**

1. Yemen -- Description and travel 2. Yemen (Republic)

ISBN 1584159618; 1612281060; 9781584159612; 9781612281063

LC 2011016773

This book on Yemen by Claire O'Neal is part of the "Your Land and My Land: The Middle East" series, which "provides an . . . introduction to the history and geography of several Middle Eastern and Southeast Asian countries from a tourist's perspective." Also included are a "recipe and a . . . craft project representing the country." (Booklist)

Includes bibliographical references and index.

953.53 Oman

Ejaz, Khadija

We visit Oman; by Khadija Ejaz. Mitchell Lane Publishers 2012 63 p. col. ill., col. maps (library) $33.95; (ebook) $33.95

Grades: 4 5 6 7 8 **953.53**

1. Oman -- Description and travel 2. Oman

ISBN 1584159626; 1612281044; 9781584159629; 9781612281049

LC 2011000724

This book on Oman by Khadija Ejaz is part of the "Your Land and My Land: The Middle East" series, which "provides an . . . introduction to the history and geography of several Middle Eastern and Southeast Asian countries from a tourist's perspective." Also included are a "recipe and a . . . craft project representing the country." (Booklist)

Includes bibliographical references (p. 59-61) and index.

953.57 United Arab Emirates

Somervill, Barbara A.

★ **United** Arab Emirates; by Barbara A. Somervill. Children's Press 2016 144 p. color illustrations (Enchantment of the world) library $40

Grades: 5 6 7 8 **953.57**

1. United Arab Emirates

ISBN 9780531232989 library

LC 2015020051

"A desert land located along the east coast of the Arabian Peninsula, the area now known as the United Arab Emirates was once occupied mainly by groups of roaming nomads. Today, it is home to sprawling modern cityscapes, with luxurious accommodations that draw tourists and businesspeople from all around the world. Readers will find out how the United Arab Emirates has grown and changed over time. They will learn what life is like for the country's people, how its government is run, what the natural landscape is like, and much more." (Publisher's note)

Includes bibliographical references (page 134) and index

953.6 Persian Gulf States

Cooper, Robert

Bahrain; [by] Robert Cooper and Jo-Ann Spilling. 2nd ed.; Marshall Cavendish Benchmark 2011 144p il map (Cultures of the world) lib bdg $42.79

Grades: 5 6 7 8 **953.6**

1. Bahrain

ISBN 978-1-6087-0213-8; 1-6087-0213-8

LC 2010019621

First published 2000

Provides information on the geography, history, wildlife, governmental structure, economy, cultural diversity, peoples, religion, and culture of Bahrain.

Includes glossary and bibliographical references

953.67 Kuwait

O'Shea, Maria

Kuwait; by Maria O'Shea and Michael Spilling. 2nd ed.; Marshall Cavendish Benchmark 2010 144p il map (Cultures of the world) lib bdg $42.79

Grades: 5 6 7 8 **953.67**

1. Kuwait

ISBN 978-0-7614-4479-4 lib bdg; 0-7614-4479-3 lib bdg

LC 2009007069

First published 1999

Provides information on the geography, history, wildlife, governmental structure, economy, cultural diversity, peoples, religion, and culture of Kuwait

Includes glossary and bibliographical references

Sonneborn, Liz

Kuwait; Enchantment of the World. by Liz Sonneborn. Children's Press, an imprint of Scholastic Inc. 2014 144 p. ill., maps. (library binding) $40

Grades: 5 6 7 8 **953.67**

1. Kuwait 2. Kuwait -- Fiction

ISBN 053122015X; 9780531220153

LC 2013026062

This book, by Liz Sonneborn, focuses on Kuwait. The book discusses the "country's culture, history, and geography are explored in detail, allowing readers a chance to see how people live. . . . Sidebars highlight especially interesting people, places, and events . . . [and] easy recipes give readers the opportunity to experience foreign cuisine firsthand." (Publisher's note)

"Many students turn to the Internet for writing reports, but for reliably accurate, attractively presented and well-calibrated information, the long-standing Enchantment of the World series remains a superior choice. Each volume has been completely rewritten from a previous edition—in many cases to startling effect given recent political events. Although the basic structure holds true to past versions, the updated photographs are truly eye-popping and take care to portray the countries as modern often opting for showing, say, a surgeon at work rather than a rural farmer. It might not be necessary for libraries to replace [this title], since it hasn't changed radically, but this is a solid offering with updated statistics. Each volume in this reliable series includes extensive back matter with a detailed index." Booklist.

Includes bibliographical references and index

Tracy, Kathleen

We visit Kuwait; by Kathleen Tracy. Mitchell Lane Publishers 2012 63 p. ill. (chiefly col.), col. maps (Your land and my land. The Middle East) (library bound) $33.95; (ebook) $33.95

Grades: 4 5 6 7 8 **953.67**

1. Kuwait -- Description and travel 2. Kuwait

ISBN 1584159588; 1612281001; 9781584159582; 9781612281001

LC 2011002756

This book on Kuwait by Kathleen Tracy is part of the "Your Land and My Land: The Middle East" series, which "provides an . . . introduction to the history and geography of several Middle Eastern and Southeast Asian countries from a tourist's perspective." Also included are a "recipe and a . . . craft project representing the country." (Booklist)

Includes bibliographical references (p. 58-61) and index.

953.8 Saudi Arabia

Tracy, Kathleen

We visit Saudi Arabia; by Kathleen Tracy. Mitchell Lane Publishers 2011 63 p. col. ill., map (library) $33.95

Grades: 4 5 6 7 8 **953.8**

1. Persian Gulf region 2. Saudi Arabia

ISBN 1584159634; 9781584159636

LC 2011000728

This book by Kathleen Tracy is part of the Social Studies series and looks at Saudi Arabia. "One of the most socially conservative countries on earth, Saudi Arabia is defined by Islam and ancient traditions. At the same time, its vast oil fields have helped build glistening, modern cities filled with world-class restaurants and designer shops." (Publisher's note)

Includes bibliographical references and index.

954 India and neighboring south Asian countries

Gibson, Karen Bush

The **Taj** Mahal; Karen Gibson. Purple Toad Pub Inc 2016 32 p. color ill., color maps $26.50

Grades: 4 5 6 7 8 **954**

1. Taj Mahal (Agra, India)

ISBN 1624692117; 9781624692116

LC 2016046156

This book, by Karen Gibson, presents "story of how the Taj Mahal was built, and the people who made it happen. Learn how they did it and see what materials they used in this real life building journey that kids who love to build in Lego and Minecraft will be thrilled to read." (Publisher's note)

"Clearly written narratives and informative graphics tell the stories of the conception, construction, and symbolic importance of some of the world's most magnificent structures." SLJ

Includes bibliographical references (page 29) and index.

Mann, Elizabeth

★ **Taj** Mahal; a story of love and empire. by Elizabeth Mann; with illustrations by Alan Witschonke. Mikaya 2008 47p il (Wonders of the world) $22.95

Grades: 4 5 6 7 **954**

1. Mogul Empire 2. Taj Mahal (Agra, India)

ISBN 1-931414-20-3; 978-1-931414-20-3

LC 2008060054

This is a "dramatic retelling of the construction of the Taj Mahal. Mann begins with two pages of prose that relay the commonly told legend, but then proceeds to explode that legend with descriptive writing, colorful illustrations, ancient paintings, maps, and photographs." Booklist

Includes bibliographical references

954.9 Other jurisdictions

NgCheong-Lum, Roseline, 1962-

Maldives; 2nd ed.; Marshall Cavendish Benchmark 2011 144p il map (Cultures of the world) lib bdg $42.79

Grades: 5 6 7 8 **954.9**

1. Maldives

ISBN 978-1-6087-0217-6; 1-6087-0217-0

LC 2010019746

First published 2001

Provides information on the geography, history, wildlife, governmental structure, economy, cultural diversity, peoples, religion, and culture of Maldives.

Includes glossary and bibliographical references

Taylor-Butler, Christine

Sacred mountain; Everest. Lee & Low Books 2009 48p il $19.95

Grades: 5 6 7 8 **954.9**

1. Mount Everest (China and Nepal)

ISBN 978-1-60060-255-9; 1-60060-255-X

LC 2008-30423

"The informative text is amply illustrated with well-chosen black-and-white and color photographs." SLJ

Includes glossary

954.91 Pakistan

Hinman, Bonnie

We visit Pakistan; by Bonnie Hinman. Mitchell Lane Publishers 2012 63 p. ill. (chiefly col.), col. maps (Your land and my land. The Middle East) (library) $33.95

Grades: 4 5 6 7 8 **954.91**

1. Pakistan

ISBN 158415960X; 9781584159605

LC 2011030763

This book on Pakistan by Bonnie Hinman is part of the "Your Land and My Land: The Middle East" series, which "provides an . . . introduction to the history and geography of several Middle Eastern and Southeast Asian countries from a tourist's perspective." Topics such as "terrorism and al-Qaeda" are covered along with "descriptions of the country's history and attractions." Also included are a "recipe and a . . . craft project representing the country." (Booklist)

Includes bibliographical references (p. 59-61) and index.

Sonneborn, Liz

Pakistan; by Liz Sonneborn. Children's Press 2013 144 p. ill. (mostly col.), col. maps. (Enchantment of the world, second series) (library) $40

Grades: 5 6 7 8 **954.91**

1. Pakistan 2. Pakistan -- Description and travel

ISBN 0531275442; 9780531275443

LC 2012000505

This book, by Liz Sonneborn, is part of the "Enchantment of the World" series. In it the author provides information and photographs showcasing the people, places and events surrounding the South Asian country of Pakistan. Contents include photographs of Pakistani cities and landscapes, statistics describing the nation's features, and traditional Pakistani recipes.

Includes bibliographical references and index

954.92 Bangladesh

Orr, Tamra

Bangladesh; by Tamra B. Orr. 2nd edition Children's Press 2018 144p il map (Enchantment of the world, second series) library $40

Grades: 5 6 7 8 **954.92**

1. Bangladesh

ISBN 9780531130506 library

LC 2017057578

Describes the geography, people, government, culture, history, religion, economy, and wildlife of Bagladesh

"The strong design features highly readable type and beautiful, color photos on almost every page. . . . Includes clear maps and useful end matter." Booklist

Includes bibliographical references

954.96 Nepal

Sangma, Angela

Everest; Sangma Francis, illustrated by Lisk Feng. Flying Eye Books 2018 80 p. $24

Grades: 4 5 6 7 8 **954.96**

1. Himalaya Mountains 2. Mount Everest (China and Nepal)

ISBN 1911171992; 9781911171997

This picture book, by Sangma Francis, illustrated by Lisk Feng, presents facts about Mount Everest, the world's highest mountain. "Hundreds of people dare to climb Mount Everest every year . . . hoping to experience Earth's highest peak. But there is so much more to this mountain. . . . Travel back to its ancient origins, learn about the flowers and plants that grow upon this great peak, and discover the rich history of religions, myths, and legends that surround . . . [it]." (Publisher's note)

955 Iran

DiPrimio, Pete

We visit Iran; by Pete DiPrimio. Mitchell Lane Publishers 2012 63 p. col. ill., maps (library) $33.95

Grades: 4 5 6 7 8 **955**

1. Iran -- History 2. Iran

ISBN 1584159545; 9781584159544

LC 2011016765

This book by Pete DiPrimio looks at Iran. "It is a Middle Eastern country with European (not Arabian) founders. It was the home of one of the ancient world's greatest empires, the Persian Empire. Its many ancient ruins include the palace complex of Persepolis, which was so big it took 150 years to finish. While the nation develops nuclear technology, its government—called an Islamic Republic—dictates people's lives, from the clothing they wear to the news they hear." (Publisher's note)

Includes bibliographical references and index.

Steele, Philip

★ **Iran** and the West; by Philip Steele. 1st ed. Rosen Pub. 2013 48 p. col. ill. (library) $29.25

Grades: 6 7 8 **955**

1. Iran -- Foreign relations 2. Iran 3. Iran -- History
ISBN 1448860318; 9781448860319

LC 2012010613

In this book, readers "explore the long history and culture of Iran—the rise of the Ayatollah, the election of current president Mahmoud Ahmadinejad, diplomatic relations with countries in Europe and the United States, and the importance of Iran in the global economy." Photographs, illustrations, maps, and further reading are included. (Publisher's note)

Includes bibliographical references (p. 46) and index.

Wagner, Heather Lehr

The **Iranian** Revolution. Chelsea House 2010 111p il (Milestones in modern world history) lib bdg $35

Grades: 7 8 9 10 11 12 **955**

1. Iran -- History -- 1941-1979
ISBN 978-1-60413-490-2; 1-60413-490-9

LC 2009-22336

"Chapters cover the origin of the Pahlavi dynasty, [Ayatollah] Khomeini's early life and how he came to symbolize opposition to the shah's regime, and the shah's aggressive campaigns of reform and Westernization. . . . A solid addition to the series." SLJ

Includes bibliographical references

956 Middle East (Near East)

Abbott, David

Conflict in the Middle East. Arcturus Pub. 2011 46p il (Secret history) lib bdg $32.80

Grades: 7 8 9 10 **956**

1. Spies 2. Espionage 3. Israel-Arab conflicts 4. Middle East -- Politics and government
ISBN 978-1-8483-7697-7; 1-8483-7697-9

LC 2010011001

This book explores the secrets of the Arab-Israeli conflict. Both sides in this war have made use of spies, surveillance, special operations, and secret weapons. Even the peace talks have their own secret history.

"The title of the Secret History series will grab readers, even reluctant ones, and they won't be disappointed by the intriguing info regarding codes and code breakers, spies, terrorists, and double agents, with profiles of heroes and traitors on all sides. . . . The readable design, with clear type on thick, high-quality paper, includes lots of sidebars, photos, screens, and quotes." Booklist

Includes bibliographical references

The **Middle** East: opposing viewpoints; David M. Haugen, Susan Musser and Kacy Lovelace, book editors. Greenhaven Press 2009 261p il map (Opposing viewpoints series) lib bdg $38.50; pa $26.75

Grades: 8 9 10 11 12 **956**

1. Middle East -- Politics and government 2. Middle East -- Foreign relations -- United States 3. United States -- Foreign relations -- Middle East
ISBN 978-0-7377-4532-0 lib bdg; 0-7377-4532-0 lib bdg; 978-0-7377-4533-7 pa; 0-7377-4533-9 pa

LC 2008-55848

The articles in this anthology cover such topics as U.S. relations with Middle Eastern nations, the Israeli/Palestinian conflict, whether Iran is a threat to the United States, and counterterrorism efforts in Middle Eastern nations.

Includes bibliographical references

956.04 Middle East--1945-1980

Woolf, Alex

The **Arab** -Israeli War since 1948; by Alex Woolf. 1st ed. Heinemann Library 2011 80 p. ill. (some col.), col. maps (library) $36.50; (paperback) $10.99

Grades: 6 7 8 9 **956.04**

1. Israel-Arab conflicts 2. Arab-Israeli conflict
ISBN 1432959956; 9781432959951; 9781432960049

LC 2011015920

"In this volume of the illustrated 'Living Through' series, readers are given a . . . summary of the critical events that shaped what we now think of as the Arab-Israeli Wars. . . . Readers will encounter some of the individuals, causes, and ongoing contradictions that make this international issue so seemingly unsolvable." (Children's Literature)

Includes bibliographical references (p. 76-78) and index.

956.1 Turkey

Lace, William W.

★ The **unholy** crusade; the ransacking of medieval Constantinople. [by] William W. Lace. Lucent Books 2007 104p il map (Lucent library of historical eras, Middle Ages) lib bdg $32.45

Grades: 6 7 8 9 **956.1**

1. Crusades 2. Middle Ages 3. Istanbul (Turkey)
ISBN 978-1-59018-846-0 lib bdg; 1-59018-846-2 lib bdg

LC 2006002572

"Lace gives equal attention to the events leading up to the destruction of Constantinople and traces the planning and plotting of the Crusades. . . . [The book has] numerous color reproductions. Clear, concise writing makes [it] highly readable, while the scholarship makes [it a] valuable [resource]." SLJ

Includes bibliographical references

LaRoche, Amelia

We visit Turkey; by Amelia LaRoche. Mitchell Lane Publishers 2012 63 p. ill. (chiefly col.), col. maps (library) $33.95

Grades: 4 5 6 7 8 **956.1**

1. Turkey -- Description and travel 2. Turkey
ISBN 1584159561; 9781584159568

LC 2011030765

This book on Turkey by Amelia Laroche is part of the "Your Land and My Land: The Middle East" series, which "provides an . . . introduction to the history and geography of several Middle Eastern and Southeast Asian countries from a tourist's perspective." It "similarly mentions but does not dwell upon the rise of Islam and the hijab controversy." Also included are a "recipe and a . . . craft project representing the country." (Booklist)

Includes bibliographical references (p, 59-61) and index.

Shields, Sarah D.

★ **Turkey**; [by] Sarah Shields. National Geographic 2009 64p il map (Countries of the world) lib bdg $27.90

Grades: 4 5 6 7 **956.1**

1. Turkey

ISBN 978-1-4263-0387-6 lib bdg; 1-4263-0387-4 lib bdg

LC 2009275583

This describes the geography, nature, history, people and culture, government and economy of Turkey

Includes glossary and bibliographical references

956.7 Iraq

Adams, Simon

The **Iraq** War. Arcturus Pub. 2011 46p il map (Secret history) lib bdg $32.80

Grades: 7 8 9 10 **956.7**

1. Iraq War, 2003-2011

ISBN 978-1-84837-698-4; 1-84837-698-7

LC 2010011764

This examines the Iraq War, including "from propaganda and intelligence to technology and sacrifice. . . . Archival photographs combine with a busy but well-organized design to present an engaging perspective. . . . Both reluctant readers and history buffs in need of a fresh approach to events will appreciate this [book]." Horn Book Guide

Includes bibliographical references

Bingham, Jane

The **Gulf** wars with Iraq; by Jane Bingham. Heinemann Library 2012 80 p. ill., maps (library) $36.50; (paperback) $10.99

Grades: 6 7 8 9 **956.7**

1. Iraq War, 2003-2011 2. Persian Gulf War, 1991

ISBN 1432959972; 9781432959975; 9781432960063

LC 2011015922

This book by Jane Bingham is part of the Living Through series and looks at the U.S. Gulf Wars with Iraq. Here, "Bingham takes her readers back through the twists and turns of fact and fiction that are part and parcel of these connected conflicts." Topics include "the falsification of intelligence linked to Saddam Hussein's weapons program, the ruthless nature of the Iraqi dictator and his family, and the human cost of these two wars." (Children's Literature)

Includes bibliographical references (p. 77-78) and index.

Ellis, Deborah

★ **Children** of war; voices of Iraqi refugees. Groundwood Books 2009 128p il $15.95; pa $9.95

Grades: 7 8 9 10 11 12 **956.7**

1. Refugees 2. Children and war 3. Iraq War, 2003-2011

ISBN 978-0-88899-907-8; 0-88899-907-0; 978-0-88899-908-5 pa; 0-88899-908-9 pa

Ellis "interviews child refugees from Iraq, now living in Jordan, and a few who have made it to Canada. . . . Accompanying each of the . . . interviews with young people is a brief introduction and a photo. . . . What is haunting are their graphic recent memories of what they witnessed. . . . An important, current title that will have lasting significance." Booklist

Includes glossary

Mason, Paul, 1967-

The **Iraq** War. Arcturus Pub. 2011 48p il map (Secret history) lib bdg $32.80

Grades: 7 8 9 10 **956.7**

1. Iraq War, 2003-2011 2. Iraq -- Politics and government

ISBN 978-1-84837-639-7; 1-84837-639-1

LC 2009051266

"The title of the Secret History series will grab readers, even reluctant ones, and they won't be disappointed by the intriguing info regarding codes and code breakers, spies, terrorists, and double agents, with profiles of heroes and traitors on all sides. . . . The readable design, with clear type on thick, high-quality paper, includes lots of sidebars, photos, screens, and quotes." Booklist

Includes bibliographical references

O'Neal, Claire

We visit Iraq; by Claire O'Neal. Mitchell Lane Publishers 2012 63 p. ill. (chiefly col.), col. maps (library bound) $33.95

Grades: 4 5 6 7 8 **956.7**

1. Persian Gulf region 2. Iraq

ISBN 1584159553; 9781584159551

LC 2011016771

This book by Claire O'Neal is part of the Social Studies series and looks at Iraq. "Iraq's Tigris and Euphrates rivers turned this Middle Eastern desert into the world's first farmland. Over six millenia, Iraq's civilizations have laid foundations for the rest of the world. They built great stone ziggurats and soaring mosques. They invented the wheel, the calendar, and the written word. With their riches, they also attracted war." (Publisher's note)

Includes bibliographical references (p. 59-61) and index.

Samuel, Charlie

★ **Iraq**; [by] Charlie Samuels; Sarah Shields and Shakir Mustafa, consultants. National Geographic 2007 64p il map (Countries of the world) lib bdg $27.90

Grades: 4 5 6 7 **956.7**

1. Iraq

ISBN 978-1-4263-0061-5

LC 2007024675

This describes the geography, nature, history, people and culture, government and economy of Iraq.

Includes glossary and bibliographical references

Smithson, Ryan

Ghosts of war; my tour of duty. HarperTeen 2009 321p il $16.99; lib bdg $17.89

Grades: 8 9 10 11 12 **956.7**

1. Soldiers -- United States 2. Iraq War, 2003-2011 -- Personal narratives

ISBN 978-0-06-166468-7; 0-06-166468-5; 978-0-06-166470-0 lib bdg; 0-06-166470-7 lib bdg

LC 2008-35420

"Ryan Smithson was a typical 16-year-old high-school student until 9/11. . . . Smithson enlisted in the Army Reserve the following year and, a year into the Iraq war, was deployed to an Army engineer unit as a heavy-equipment operator. His poignant, often harrowing account, especially vivid in sensory details, chronicles his experiences in basic training and in Iraq. . . . This memoir is a remarkable, deeply penetrating read that will compel teens to reflect on their own thoughts about duty, patriotism and sacrifice." Kirkus

Includes glossary and bibliographical references

Yomtov, Nelson

Iraq; by Nel Yomtov. Children's Press, an imprint of Scholastic Inc. 2018 144 p. (library binding) $40

Grades: 5 6 7 8 **956.7**

1. Iraq -- History 2. Iraq -- Civilization 3. Iraq

ISBN 0531235904; 9780531235904

LC 2017025777

In this book in the Enchantment of the World series, by Nel Yomtov, "home to some of humankind's first great civilizations and the birthplace of many of our most important intellectual achievements, the land that is now Iraq has a long and remarkable history. Readers will discover . . . what life is like for the average Iraqi citizen, from what people eat to where they work and what they do for fun, and learn about the country's government, economy, and more." (Publisher's note)

Includes bibliographical references and index

956.91 Syria

Gelfand, Dale Evva

Syria; by Dale Evva Gelfand. ABDO Pub. Co. 2013 144 p. (library) $35.64

Grades: 8 9 10 11 12 **956.91**

1. Syria

ISBN 1617836397; 9781617836398

LC 2012946084

This book by Dale Ewa Gelfant is part of the Countries of the World series and looks at Syria. It "introduces Syria's history, geography, culture, climate, government, economy, and other significant features. Sidebars, maps, fact pages, a glossary, a timeline, historic images and full-color photos" are included. (Publisher's note)

Yomtov, Nel

Syria; Nel Yomtov. Children's Press, an imprint of Scholastic Inc. 2013 144 p. color illustrations (library binding) $40

Grades: 5 6 7 8 **956.91**

1. Syria

ISBN 053123679X; 9780531236796

LC 2013000088

This book, by Nel Yomtov, focuses on Syria. The "country's culture, history, and geography are explored in detail, allowing readers a chance to see how people live. . . . Sidebars highlight especially interesting people, places, and events [and] recipes give readers the opportunity to experience foreign cuisine first-hand." (Publisher's note)

"Many students turn to the Internet for writing reports, but for reliably accurate, attractively presented and well-calibrated information, the long-standing Enchantment of the World series remains a superior choice. Each volume has been completely rewritten from a previous edition—in many cases to startling effect given recent political events. Although the basic structure holds true to past versions, the updated photographs are truly eye-popping and take care to portray the countries as modern—often opting for showing, say, a surgeon at work rather than a rural farmer. Syria obviously can't be completely up-to-date because of the ongoing rebellion, but it does a good job of explaining the roots of the unrest, along with the usual topics of food, religion, and customs. Each volume in this reliable series includes extensive back matter with a detailed index." Booklist

Includes bibliographical references and index

956.92 Lebanon

Sheehan, Sean

Lebanon; Sean Sheehan, Zawiah Abdul Latif, and Elizabeth Schmermund. 3rd edition Cavendish Square 2017 144p il map (Cultures of the world) library $47.07

Grades: 5 6 7 8 **956.92**

1. Lebanon

ISBN 9781502626127 library

LC 2016049579

First published 1997

"Provides comprehensive information on the geography, history, wildlife, governmental structure, economy, cultural diversity, peoples, religion, and culture of Lebanon." Publisher's note

Includes bibliographical references

956.93 Cyprus

Spilling, Michael

Cyprus; Michael and Jo-Ann Spilling, and Fiona Young-Brown. 3rd edition Cavendish Square 2019 144p il map (Cultures of the world) library $47.07

Grades: 5 6 7 8 **956.93**

1. Cyprus

ISBN 9781502647320 library

First published 2000

This offers information on the geography, history, wildlife, governmental structure, economy, cultural diversity, peoples, religion, and culture of Cyprus

Includes glossary and bibliographical references

956.94 Palestine; Israel

Ellis, Deborah

★ **Three** wishes; Palestinian and Israeli children speak. Groundwood Bks. 2004 110p il map hardcover o.p. pa $9.99

Grades: 5 6 7 8 **956.94**

1. Palestinian Arabs 2. Israel-Arab conflicts

ISBN 0-88899-608-X; 0-88899-645-4 pa

"An excellent presentation of a confusing historic struggle, told within a palpable, perceptive and empathetic format." SLJ

Includes bibliographical references

Frank, Mitch

Understanding the Holy Land; answering questions about the Israeli-Palestinian Conflict. Viking 2005 152p il map (paperback) $8.99

Grades: 6 7 8 9 10 **956.94**

1. Israel-Arab conflicts

ISBN 0670060437; 9780670060436

LC 2004014973

The author "tackles the complex subject of the Israeli-Palestinian conflict, making it comprehensible, if not any less horrific. . . . He uses a simple yet wonderfully effective technique to present the information: questions and answers. . . . Evenhanded and honest." Booklist

Includes bibliographical references

Immell, Myra

Israel : opposing viewpoints; Myra Immell, book editor. Greenhaven Press 2011 193p map (Opposing viewpoints series) $41.70; pa $28.90

Grades: 8 9 10 11 12 **956.94**

1. Israel-Arab conflicts

ISBN 978-0-7377-4974-8; 0-7377-4974-1; 978-0-7377-4975-5 pa; 0-7377-4975-X pa

LC 2010022999

Articles in this anthology discuss Israel's right to exist, key issues in the conflict between Israel and Palestine, and what U.S. policy should be regarding Israel.

Includes bibliographical references

Owings, Lisa

Israel; by Lisa Owings. ABDO Pub. Co. 2013 144 p. (library) $35.64

Grades: 8 9 10 11 12 **956.94**

1. Israel

ISBN 1617836303; 9781617836305

LC 2012946075

This book by Lisa Owings is part of the Countries of the World series and looks at Israel. It "introduces Israel's history, geography, culture, climate, government, economy, and other significant features. Sidebars, maps, fact pages, a glossary, a timeline, historic images and full-color photos, and well-placed graphs and charts" are included. (Publisher's note)

Robinson, Anthony

Young Palestinians speak; living under occupation. Anthony Robinson & Annemarie Young ; with photography by Anthony Robinson. Interlink Books, an imprint of Interlink Publishing Group, Inc. 2017 118 p. color ills., color maps (hardcover) $19.99

Grades: 6 7 8 9 10 11 12 **956.94**

1. Intifada, 2000- 2. Palestinian Arabs 3. West Bank -- History 4. Arab-Israeli conflict 5. Gaza Strip -- History 6. Children, Palestinian Arab -- Interviews

ISBN 9781566560153

LC 2016042874

This book, by Anthony Robinson and Annemarie Young, focuses on "Palestine today, [where] a second generation of children and young people is growing up experiencing life under occupation. These are children who know only fear when they see an Israeli soldier or come across a roadblock. This book provides a platform for young people, from all over this occupied land, to speak in their own voices about the day-to-day experience of living under occupation." (Publisher's note)

"A poignant, powerful, and insightful collection of voices seldom heard." Kirkus

Includes bibliographical references.

Saul, Laya

We visit Israel; by Laya Saul. Mitchell Lane Publishers 2012 63 p. ill., maps (library) $33.95

Grades: 4 5 6 7 8 **956.94**

1. Israel -- Description and travel 2. Israel

ISBN 158415957X; 9781584159575

LC 2011024706

This book on Israel by Laya Saul is part of the "Your Land and My Land: The Middle East" series, which "provides an . . . introduction to the history and geography of several Middle Eastern and Southeast Asian countries from a tourist's perspective. . . . 'We Visit Israel' is clearly written from a Jewish Israeli perspective, but Saul makes sure to mention areas of conflict and controversy." Also included are a "recipe and a . . . craft project representing the country." (Booklist)

Includes bibliographical references (p. 60-61) and index.

956.95 Jordan and West Bank

Perdew, Laura

Understanding Jordan today; by Laura Perdew. Mitchell Lane Publishers 2014 63 p. (A kid's guide to the Middle East) $33.95

Grades: 4 5 6 7 **956.95**

1. Jordan

ISBN 1612286542; 9781612286549

LC 2014020462

This children's book, by Laura Perdew, part of the "Kid's Guide to the Middle East" series, "is an accurate and contemporary presentation that explores the Middle Eastern nation of Jordan with a focus on the country as it is today: current issues, culture, and lifestyle. The book is written in an easy-to-read enjoyable narrative form for elementary readers grades 3-6." (Publisher's note)

"Trying to sort through the Middle East can be difficult for even the most educated adults, but the titles in A Kid's Guide to the Middle East series breaks down the culture and ongoing conflict into manageable portions...Extensive back matter includes a recipe, craft, time line, glossary, and area facts. An essential series to help children appreciate and understand the rich diversity of this region." Booklist

Includes bibliographical references and index

Other recommended titles in the series are:

Understanding Afghanistan Today (2014)
Understanding Iran Today (2014)
Understanding Iraq Today (2014)
Understanding Israel Today (2014)
Understanding Lebanon Today (2015)
Understanding Palestine Today (2015)
Understanding Saudi Arabia Today (2014)
Understanding Syria Today (2014)
Understanding Turkey Today (2015)

958.1 Afghanistan

Bjorklund, Ruth

Afghanistan; by Ruth Bjorklund. Children's Press, an imprint of Scholastic Inc. 2018 144 p. illustrations, maps (Enchantment of the world) (library binding) $40

Grades: 5 6 7 8 **958.1**

1. Islamic countries 2. Afghanistan -- History 3. Afghanistan -- Description and travel 4. Afghanistan

ISBN 0531235874; 9780531235874

LC 2017025769

This book provides information on "Afghanistan, . . . a land of great turmoil. It has seen conflicts between internal factions and wars involving foreign nations. . . . Readers will get an up-close look at life in Afghanistan, from what people eat and do for fun to where they live and what kinds of jobs they do. They will also learn about Afghanistan's history, government, economy, traditions, and more." (Publisher's note)

Includes bibliographical references (page 134) and index

Hunter, Dawn

Beyond bullets; a photo journal of Afghanistan. by Rafal Gerszak, with Dawn Hunter; photographs by Rafal Gerszak. Annick Press 2011 127p il $19.95

Grades: 7 8 9 10 11 12 **958.1**

1. Photographers 2. Photojournalism 3. Afghan War, 2001- 4. Afghanistan

ISBN 978-1-55451-293-5; 1-55451-293-X

"Photographer Rafal Gerszak spent a year embedded with the American military in Afghanistan, where he used his camera to document everyday life in the wartorn country. While there, he developed a deep affection for the land and its people, and he later returned on his own. Framed by journal entries that relate his experiences on two levels—as a foreigner looking for a deeper connection to a country that has stirred him and as a journalist looking for another side to the story—Beyond Bullets addresses the volatile situation in Afghanistan." (Publisher's note) "Age twelve and up." (Quill Quire)

"Author/photographer Gerszak first went to Afghanistan to spend a year embedded with an American military unit documenting house searches, disputes with village elders and the aftermath of battles. He returned as an unaffiliated photographer without a military escort, determined to document civilian life. This 'photo journal' features images from both trips to Afghanistan, accompanied by diarylike accounts of his travels. Gerszak's frank and descriptive observations effectively convey the ugliness, monotony and tragedy of war." Kirkus

Lunis, Natalie

The **takedown** of Osama bin Laden; by Natalie Lunis. Bearport Publishing 2012 32 p. (Special ops) (lib. bdg.) $25.27

Grades: 4 5 6 7 **958.1**

1. United States. Navy 2. Terrorism 3. Terrorists -- Biography 4. United States. Navy. SEALs

ISBN 1617724599; 9781617724596

LC 2011040472

In this book by Natalie Lunis on U.S. Navy SEALs "young readers will follow this elite group of soldiers on their raid and explore the context for their mission, from the 9/11 attacks by Al Qaeda to the war against terrorists in Afghanistan. Large, full-color photos, grade-appropriate text, and a narrative format [are designed to] keep kids turning the pages as they learn about [the U.S.] military." (Publisher's note)

Includes bibliographical references (p. 31) and index

Lusted, Marcia Amidon

The **capture** and killing of Osama bin Laden. ABDO Pub. Co. 2012 112p il (Essential events) lib bdg $23.95

Grades: 6 7 8 **958.1**

1. Terrorism 2. Terrorists 3. Al Qaeda (Organization)

ISBN 978-1-61783-180-5; 1-61783-180-8

LC 2011025479

"Lusted explores Osama bin Laden's early life and the influences leading to his radicalization...The hunt for and eventual killing of bin Laden are not sensationalized." Horn Book

Includes glossary and bibliographical references

Steele, Philip

★ **Afghanistan**; from war to peace? by Philip Steele. 1st ed. Rosen Central 2012 48 p. col. ill., col. maps (library) $29.25

Grades: 6 7 8 **958.1**

1. Afghanistan -- History 2. Afghanistan -- Foreign relations 3. Afghanistan -- Politics and government 4. Afghanistan 5. Afghanistan -- History, Military

ISBN 9781448860302

LC 2012010616

This book by Philip Steele " examine[s] the history of Afghanistan, including its wars with the British Empire through its present-day occupation by American and NATO forces. Issues explored include the rise of the Taliban, the 9/11 attacks and the subsequent U.S. military ouster of the Taliban, the war of insurgency, and the plan for military withdrawal." (Publisher's note)

Includes bibliographical references and index.

Whitfield, Susan

★ **Afghanistan**; [by] Susan Whitfield; Thomas Barfield and Maliha Zulfacar, consultants. National Geographic 2008 64p il map (Countries of the world) lib bdg $27.90

Grades: 4 5 6 7 **958.1**

1. Afghanistan

ISBN 978-1-4263-0256-5 lib bdg; 1-4263-0256-8 lib bdg

This describes the geography, nature, history, people and culture, government, and economy of Aghanistan.

Includes glossary and bibliographical references

958.104 Afghanistan--1919-

Elish, Dan

Inside the situation room; how a photograph showed America defeating Osama bin Laden. by Dan Elish. Compass Point Books 2019 64 p. $8.95

Grades: 5 6 7 8 **958.104**

1. Terrorism -- Prevention -- United States 2. Bin Laden, Osama, 1957-2011 -- Assassination 3. United States. -- Navy. -- SEALs -- History -- 21st century 4. War on Terrorism, 2001-2009 5. Terrorism -- United States -- Prevention 6. Special operations (Military science) -- Pakistan 7. United States. Navy. SEALs -- History -- 21st century 8. Middle East -- Politics and government -- 21st century 9. Special operations (Military science) -- United States

ISBN 9780756558796; 9780756558819

LC 2018018480

This book in the Captured History series, by Dan Elish, presents "on-point historical photographs combined with strong narration [to] bring the story of the raid that captured [Osama] bin Laden to life. Kids will feel as though they are in the room with President Barack Obama, Secretary of State Hillary Clinton, and the others in the cabinet who called for and monitored the raid." (Publisher's note)

958.4 Turkestan

Pang, Guek-Cheng, 1950-

Kazakhstan; 2nd ed.; Marshall Cavendish Benchmark 2011 144p il map (Cultures of the world) lib bdg $42.79

Grades: 5 6 7 8 **958.4**

1. Kazakhstan

ISBN 978-1-6087-0455-2; 1-6087-0455-6

First published 2001

This offers information on the geography, history, wildlife, governmental structure, economy, cultural diversity, peoples, religion, and culture of Kazakhstan.

959.4 Laos

Dalal, A. Kamala

★ **Laos**; [by] A. Kamala Dalal. National Geographic 2009 64p il (Countries of the world) lib bdg $27.90

Grades: 4 5 6 7 **959.4**

1. Laos

ISBN 978-1-4263-0388-3 lib bdg; 1-4263-0388-2 lib bdg

This describes the geography, nature, history, people and culture, and govenment and economy of Laos

Includes glossary and bibliographical references

959.6 Cambodia

Sonneborn, Liz

The **Khmer** Rouge; by Liz Sonneborn. Marshall Cavendish Benchmark 2012 80 p. ill. (some col.), col. map (library) $34.21; (ebook) $34.21

Grades: 5 6 7 8 **959.6**

1. Dith Pran, 1942-2008 2. Genocide -- Cambodia 3. Cambodia -- History -- 1975- 4. Parti communiste du Kampuchea 5. Cambodia -- History -- 1975-1979 6. Political atrocities -- Cambodia 7. Journalists -- Cambodia -- Biography 8. Political refugees -- Cambodia -- Biography

ISBN 1608704742; 9781608704743; 9781608706952 pdf

LC 2011005595

This book "tells the story of Dith Pran, a Cambodian journalist and translator who provided support to Sydney Schanberg, a New York Times correspondent. . . . Sadly, when Schanberg evacuated, Pran was forced to remain behind where he fell into captivity. Over a three year time period Dith Pran survived horrendous conditions but ultimately escaped and fled to Thailand. There, in a refugee camp, Pran was rescued by Schanberg and relocated to the United States." (Children's Literature)

Includes bibliographical references and index.

959.7 Vietnam

Green, Jen

★ **Vietnam**; [by] Jen Green. National Geographic 2008 64p il map (Countries of the world) lib bdg $27.90

Grades: 4 5 6 7 **959.7**

1. Vietnam

ISBN 978-1-4263-0202-2

LC 2007047832

This describes the geography, nature, history, people and culture, government, and economy of Vietnam.

Includes glossary and bibliographical references

959.704 Vietnam--1945-

Caputo, Philip

★ **10,000** days of thunder; a history of the Vietnam War. [by] Philip Caputo. 1st ed; Atheneum Books for Young Readers 2005 128p il $22.95

Grades: 6 7 8 9 **959.704**

1. Vietnam War, 1961-1975

ISBN 0-689-86231-8

LC 2004-15468

In this history of the Vietnam War "Caputo has produced what is at once an overview and a sensitive, resonant picture of the war as seen and experienced by American soldiers, the Viet Cong, North Vietnamese guerrillas, and the citizens of both South Vietnam and the United States. . . . Caputo's prose is clear and direct, and the award-winning photos . . . add an immediacy that sets this title apart from more conventional treatments." SLJ

Includes glossary and bibliographical references

DiConsiglio, John

Vietnam; the bloodbath at Hamburger Hill. Franklin Watts 2010 64p il map (24/7: goes to war) lib bdg $27; pa $7.95

Grades: 6 7 8 9 **959.704**

1. Hamburger Hill, Battle of, Vietnam, 1969

ISBN 978-0-531-25526-1 lib bdg; 0-531-25526-3 lib bdg; 978-0-531-25451-6 pa; 0-531-25451-8 pa

LC 2009-14912

Describes the eight-day battle in May 1969 where American forces struggled to capture a tiny piece of the Vietnam countryside, considered a watershed turning point in the Vietnam War

This "will appeal to these readers, because . . . [it tells] a story while presenting the facts. . . . The first chapter gives the historic details concerning the war up to the particular battle, with the story of the battle told from a first-person perspective. A mixture of news photos and photos taken by the men involved appear throughout the book." Libr Media Connect

Includes glossary and bibliographical references

Freedman, Russell, 1929-2018

★ **Vietnam**; A History of the War. Russell Freedman. Holiday House 2016 160 p. illustrations, map (ebook) $20; (hardcover) $20.00

Grades: 6 7 8 9 **959.704**

1. Vietnam War, 1961-1975

ISBN 9780823437481; 9780823436583

LC 2016001051

This book, by Russell Freedman, focuses on the Vietnam War. "In words and photographs he chronicles the unfolding events in Vietnam and at home as increasing numbers of young men were sent into the jungles to fight. After assessing the catastrophic damage, Freedman concludes the book with a hopeful epilogue on Vietnam today. A glossary, source notes, bibliography and index are included." (Publisher's note)

"Solid history that doesn't shy away from difficult truths and important moral and political lessons." Kirkus

Includes bibliographical references

Gifford, Clive

Why did the Vietnam War happen? Gareth Stevens 2011 48p il map (Moments in history) lib bdg $31.95; pa $14.05

Grades: 6 7 8 9 **959.704**

1. Vietnam War, 1961-1975

ISBN 978-1-4339-4178-8 lib bdg; 1-4339-4178-3 lib bdg; 978-1-4339-4179-5 pa; 1-4339-4179-1 pa

LC 2010015835

This book looks at the causes of the Vietnam War and surrounding controversies.

"Brightly colored pull-out boxes highlight important turning points, the perspective of the everyday man, and further information on why specific events occurred. Numerous photographs help readers visualize concepts more fully. . . . Students should be able to easily use this resource." Libr Media Connect

Includes glossary and bibliographical references

Gitlin, Marty

U.S. involvement in Vietnam; by Martin Gitlin; content consultant Clarence R. Wyatt. ABDO Pub. Co. 2010 112p il map (Essential events) lib bdg $32.79

Grades: 6 7 8 9 **959.704**

1. Vietnam War, 1961-1975 2. United States -- History -- 1961-1974

ISBN 978-1-60453-949-3; 1-60453-949-6

LC 2009-31071

This title examines an important historic event, the U.S. involvement in Vietnam. Readers will learn about the events leading up to this, including Communist North Vietnam taking military action over South Vietnam, the United States sending aid to South Vietnam.

"The writing is accessible and is richer than a lot of history writing, allowing the reader to become engaged in the text as a story, and the layout provides enought white space to allow lower level readers to feel confident." Libr Media Connect

Includes glossary and bibliographical references

McNab, Chris

50 things you should know about the Vietnam War; Chris McNab. Motorbooks Intl 2016 80 p. color ill., color maps $15.95

Grades: 4 5 6 7 8 **959.704**

1. Military history 2. Vietnam War, 1961-1975

ISBN 1609929616; 9781609929619

This children's book by Chris McNab from the "50 Things You Should Know About" series "is packed full of infographics, illustrations, maps, and color photographs from the period. Not only identifying major political and military figures from both sides of the conflict with the 'Who's Who' pages, this title also documents the significance of medical workers, protesters, and civilians caught in the crossfire." (Publisher's note)

"An excellent starting point for understanding the Vietnam War, presented as a conflict that commenced with French colonial occupation and continues even today." Kirkus

Partridge, Elizabeth

★ **Boots** on the ground; America's war in Vietnam. Elizabeth Partridge. Viking 2018 213 p. illustrations, maps (hardcover) $22.99

Grades: 7 8 9 10 11 12 **959.704**

1. Vietnam War, 1961-1975 -- Biography 2. Vietnam War, 1961-1975 -- United States

ISBN 9780425291788; 9780142423752; 9780670785063

LC 2017013227

YALSA Award for Excellence in Nonfiction for Young Adults: Finalist (2019

This book, by Elizabeth Partridge, tells the experiences of six American soldiers, one American military nurse, and one Vietnamese refugee during the Vietnam War. "From dense jungles and terrifying firefights to chaotic helicopter rescues and harrowing escapes, each individual experience reveals a different facet of the war and moves us forward in time. Alternating with these chapters are profiles of key American leaders and events." (Publisher's note)

"With an impressive amount of well-chosen photographs, this is a necessary, conscientious look at a factious time in American and world history." Booklist

Includes bibliographical references and index.

Senker, Cath

The **Vietnam** War; by Cath Senker. Heinemann Library 2012 80 p. ill. (some col.), col. maps (Living through) (library) $36.50; (paperback) $10.99

Grades: 6 7 8 9 **959.704**

1. Vietnam War, 1961-1975

ISBN 1432960008; 9781432960001; 9781432960094

LC 2011015928

In this book on the Vietnam War, part of the "Living Through" series, author "[Cath] Senker begins her story with the French colonization of Southeast Asia and ends it with an analysis of why the war ended the way it did. In between, Senker takes her readers back to a time in American history when policies went awry and the nation imposed terrible destruction on foreign lands and its own people." (Children's Literature)

Includes bibliographical references (p. 76-77) and index

Sheinkin, Steve

★ **Most** dangerous; Steve Sheinkin. Roaring Brook Press 2015 384 p. illustrations, map (hardback) $19.99

Grades: 7 8 9 10 11 12 **959.704**

1. Vietnam War, 1961-1975 2. Pentagon Papers 3. Vietnam War, 1961-1975 -- United States 4. Rand Corporation -- Employees -- Biography 5. United States -- Politics and government -- 1969-1974

ISBN 1596439521; 9781596439528

LC 2014040761

National Book Award Finalist: Young People's Literature (2015)

Boston Globe-Horn Book Nonfiction Award (2016)

YALSA Award for Excellence in Nonfiction for Young Adults (2016)

Author Steve Sheinkin presents this "exploration of . . . how Daniel Ellsberg transformed from obscure government analyst into 'the most dangerous man in America,' and risked everything to expose the government's deceit. [The] book . . . interrogates the meanings of patriotism, freedom, and integrity." (Publisher's note)

"In this thoroughly researched, thoughtfully produced, and beautifully written book, Sheinkin delves into the life of Daniel Ellsberg, former Pentagon consultant and a self-described 'cold warrior,' who gradually made an about-face with regard to America's presence in Vietnam. . . . A timely and extraordinary addition to every library." SLJ

Includes bibliographical references and index

Skrypuch, Marsha Forchuk, 1954-

Last airlift; a Vietnamese orphan's rescue from war. Marsha Forchuk Skrypuch. Pajama Press 2012 120 p. $17.95

Grades: 3 4 5 6 **959.704**

1. Orphans 2. Aeronautics -- Flights 3. International adoption 4. Evacuation of civilians -- Vietnam 5. Vietnam War, 1961-1975 -- Children

ISBN 098694954X; 9780986949548

This book "tells the story of the last Canadian airlift [from Vietnam] through the memories of one child, Son Thi Anh Tuyet. Nearly 8 years old, the sad-eyed girl . . . had lived nearly all her life in a Catholic orphanage." When "she and a number of the institution babies were taken away, placed on an airplane and flown to a new world. . . . she assumed that John and Dorothy Morris had chosen her to help with their three children; instead, she had acquired a family." (Kirkus Reviews)

Young, Marilyn Blatt

The **Vietnam** War: a history in documents; [by] Marilyn B. Young, John J. Fitzgerald, A. Tom Grunfeld. Oxford Univ. Press 2002 175p il maps (Pages from history) lib bdg $32.95; pa $19.95

Grades: 7 8 9 10 **959.704**

1. Vietnam War, 1961-1975

ISBN 0-19-512278-X lib bdg; 0-19-516635-3 pa

LC 2001-52338

"The documents are skillfully tied together by brief text that gives good background information. . . . The book is well balanced in showing both sides. . . . Good-quality, black-and-white photos and illustrations are plentiful and informative." SLJ

Includes glossary and bibliographical references

960 History of Africa

Bowden, Rob, 1973-

★ **African** culture; [by] Rob Bowden and Rosie Wilson. Heinemann Library 2009 48p il map (Africa focus) $30; pa $8.99

Grades: 4 5 6 **960**

1. Africa -- Civilization 2. Africa -- Social life and customs

ISBN 978-1-4329-2440-9; 1-4329-2440-0; 978-1-4329-2445-4 pa; 1-4329-2445-1 pa

LC 2008-48310

This book "presents a clear and timely overview of the diverse and complex continent. The full-color photographs are of exceptional quality. [The] book also includes interesting fact boxes, sidebars, maps, and a time line. [It] focuses on traditions and how they are relevant for today. Highlights include family and daily life; religion, beliefs, and customs; and the performing and visual arts." SLJ

Includes bibliographical references

Habeeb, William Mark

Africa; Facts and Figures. by William Mark Habeeb. Mason Crest Publishers 2012 87 p. ill. (chiefly col.), col. map (The Evolution of Africa's Major Nations) (library) $22.95

Grades: 7 8 9 10 **960**

1. Africa -- History 2. Africa -- Social conditions 3. Africa -- Politics and government 4. Africa

ISBN 1422221768; 9781422221761

LC 2010048000

This book is "[t]he first of a new series, 'Continent in the Balance: Africa,' . . . introduces the continent in all its geographical and cultural diversity. . . . [H]istorian [William Mark] Habeeb discusses the huge contemporary problems in many countries, including poverty and AIDS, and examines how colonialism carved up the continent with arbitrary borders that have resulted in devastating ethnic and religious conflicts that exist even today." (Booklist)

This is an "excellent, detailed overview. . . . The attractive, open design, with clear type, beautiful photos, maps, and lots of extras in lists and insets, manages to pack in an extraordinary amount of information." Booklist

Includes bibliographical references (p. 82-83) and index.

Mooney, Carla

Amazing Africa; projects you can build yourself. illustrated by Megan Stearns. Nomad Press 2010 122p il (Build it yourself) pa $15.95

Grades: 4 5 6 7 **960**

1. Handicraft 2. Africa

ISBN 978-1-934670-41-5; 1-934670-41-3

"Casual and informative, this large, attractive, browsable paperback . . . offers a view of contemporary African life that reaches far beyond the usual scenery-and-wildlife tourists' perspective. Blending history, culture, and tradition with politics and life in both cities and rural areas, the chapters begin with a look at natural wonders and dangerous wildlife that will grab readers, then move on to historical discussions of humankind's birthplace and early civilizations. . . . The open design includes sketches on every page. . . . The craft projects [include making] your own Maasai beaded necklace, kente cloth, woven basket, galimoto doll, and . . . more." Booklist

Murray, Jocelyn

Africa; updated by Brian A. Stewart. 3rd ed.; Chelsea House 2007 96p il map (Cultural atlas for young people) $35

Grades: 5 6 7 8 **960**

1. Africa -- History 2. Africa -- Civilization

ISBN 978-0-8160-6826-5; 0-8160-6826-7

First published 1990

Presents information on the history and various regions and cultures of Africa.

Includes glossary and bibliographical references

Peoples and cultures of Africa; edited by Peter Mitchell. Chelsea House 2006 6v il map set $234

Grades: 5 6 7 8 **960**

1. Reference books 2. Ethnology -- Africa 3. Africa -- Civilization

ISBN 0-8160-6260-9 set; 978-0-8160-6261-4 v1; 978-0-8160-6262-1 v2; 978-0-8160-6263-8 v3; 978-0-8160-6264-5 v4; 978-0-8160-6265-2 v5; 978-0-8160-6266-9 v6

LC 2006040011

"This attractive and informative set provides well-written, well-researched introductory information about African geography and culture. Each of the first five volumes covers a region within the continent . . . and opens with introductory information on that area's physical features, biomes, religions, languages, and cultures, and includes an extensive time line. It is followed by color-coded, alphabetically arranged entries examining the region's tribal and ethnic groups; art, sculpture, and textiles; performing arts and literature; and religion and individual cultures in further detail. . . . The final volume is devoted to single-page geographic and economic profiles of Africa's nations. . . . This quality set will give report writers a solid introduction to the diversity of Africa." SLJ

Includes bibliographical references

961.1 Tunisia

Brown, Roslind Varghese

Tunisia; Rosalind Varghese Brown, Michael Spilling, Debbie Nevins. 3rd edition Cavendish Square 2018 144p il map (Cultures of the world) library $47.07

Grades: 5 6 7 8 **961.1**

1. Tunisia

ISBN 9781502632357 library

LC 2017034825

First published 1998

"Provides comprehensive information on the geography, history, wildlife, governmental structure, economy, cultural diversity, peoples, religion, and culture of Tunisia." Publisher note

Includes glossary and bibliographical references

962 Egypt, Sudan, South Sudan

Heinrichs, Ann

The **Nile**. Marshall Cavendish Benchmark 2008 96p il map (Nature's wonders) lib bdg $24.95

Grades: 5 6 7 8 **962**

1. Nile River 2. Nile River valley

ISBN 978-0-7614-2854-1

LC 2007019187

"It's tough to make a river interesting, but this . . . does an admirable job of it. . . . Crisp, full-color photos and original artwork decorate nearly every page. . . . [This is a] well-thought-out natural history." Booklist

Includes glossary and bibliographical references

962.4 Sudan and South Sudan

Brownlie, Ali

Sudan in our world; by Ali Brownlie Bojang. Smart Apple Media 2010 32p il (Countries in our world) lib bdg $28.50

Grades: 5 6 7 8 **962.4**

1. Sudan

ISBN 978-1-59920-434-5 lib bdg; 1-59920-434-7 lib bdg

LC 2009052421

"Issues such as Civil War, fighting in Darfur, the government, and millions of displaced refugees continue to cripple the country and impede its advancement. While Sudan is rich in resources, its future remains uncertain. [This title] will appeal to children interested in learning more about Africa and those needing factual information for reports." SLJ

Includes glossary and bibliographical references

The **crisis** in Darfur; Jeff Hay, book editor. Greenhaven Press 2011 165p il map (Perspectives on modern world history) $39.70

Grades: 8 9 10 11 12 **962.4**

1. Sudan -- History -- Darfur conflict, 2003-

ISBN 978-0-7377-5257-1; 0-7377-5257-2

LC 2010033168

In discussing "the continuing human tragedy in Darfur, [this] well-organized [volume presents] a wealth of clearly written analyses from a rich variety of viewpoints. With the inclusion of historical background, firsthand experiences, and discussions of particular points of controversy, [it helps] to familiarize readers with the [topic] . . . and [serves] as [an exercise] in the development of analytical thinking skills." SLJ

Includes bibliographical references

Dau, John Bul

Lost boy, lost girl; escaping civil war in Sudan. by John Bul Dau and Martha Arual Akech; with Michael Sweeney and K. M. Kostyal. National Geographic 2010 159p il map $15.95; lib bdg $23.90

Grades: 7 8 9 10 **962.4**

1. Refugees 2. Sudan -- History -- Civil War, 1983-2005

ISBN 978-1-4263-0708-9; 1-4263-0708-X; 978-1-4263-0709-6 lib bdg; 1-4263-0709-8 lib bdg

LC 2010-17960

"The tragic story of Sudan's Lost Boys and Lost [Girls] is told in simple language by two survivors. . . . In 1987, when Dau was 13 and Akech was 6, war came to their village. Both traveled hundreds of miles to a UN refugee camp in Ethiopia. After a few years of safety, the refugees were forced to move again. . . . Teens who know little about Sudan and its problems will be drawn into this moving, inspiration story." SLJ

Steele, Philip

★ **Sudan,** Darfur and the nomadic conflicts; by Philip Steele. 1st ed. Rosen Pub. 2013 48 p. col. ill. (library) $29.25

Grades: 6 7 8 **962.4**

1. Current events 2. Sudan -- History -- Darfur conflict, 2003- 3. Sudan -- History 4. Sudan -- Ethnic relations

ISBN 1448860288; 9781448860289

LC 2012010639

This book by Philip Steele is part of the Our World Divided series and looks at Sudan, Darfur, and the nomadic conflicts. "Each of these volumes begins with a recent news event pertaining to the featured conflict and then looks back at the origin and milestones of the discord. . . . 'Viewpoints' sidebars . . . showcase quotations about a specific matter from individuals on opposing sides." (School Library Journal)

Includes bibliographical references (p. 46) and index.

Xavier, John

★ **Darfur**; African genocide. [by] John Xavier. 1st ed.; Rosen Pub. Group 2008 64p il map (In the news) $29.95

Grades: 6 7 8 9 **962.4**

1. Genocide 2. Sudan -- History -- Darfur conflict, 2003-

ISBN 978-1-4042-1912-0; 1-4042-1912-9

LC 2007002909

An overview of the crisis in Darfur, its history and why it matters.

"Informative reflection of today's headlines. . . . In-depth exploration of the crisis in Darfur, the history of the conflict, and why it matters to the rest of the world. . . . The glossaries and Web sites at the end of each are most helpful." Voice Youth Advocates

Includes glossary and bibliographical references

963 Ethiopia and Eritrea

Gish, Steven

Ethiopia; writers: Steven Gish, Winnie Thay, Zawiah Abdul Latif ; Debbie Nevins. 3rd edition Cavendish Square 2017 144p il map (Cultures of the world) library $47.07

Grades: 5 6 7 8 **963**

1. Ethiopia

ISBN 9781502622099 library

LC 2016030325

First published 1996

This provides "information on the geography, history, governmental structure, economy, cultural diversity, peoples, religion, and culture of Ethiopia." Publisher's note

Includes glossary and bibliographical references

963.5 Eritrea

NgCheong-Lum, Roseline, 1962-

Eritrea; 2nd ed.; Marshall Cavendish Benchmark 2011 144p il map (Cultures of the world) lib bdg $42.79

Grades: 5 6 7 8 **963.5**

1. Eritrea

ISBN 978-1-6087-0454-5; 1-6087-0454-8

LC 2010035973

First published 2001

Provides information on the geography, history, wildlife, governmental structure, economy, cultural diversity, peoples, religion, and culture of Eritea.

"Plentiful color photographs accompany substantial amounts of information." SLJ

Includes glossary and bibliographical references

964 Morocco, Ceuta, Melilla, Western Sahara, Canary Islands

Seward, Pat

Morocco; Pat Seward, Orin Hargraves, and Ruth Bjorklund. 3rd edition Cavendish Square 2016 144p il map (Cultures of the world) library $47.07

Grades: 5 6 7 8 **964**

1. Morocco

ISBN 9781502616999 library

LC 2015681104

First published 1995

Describes the geography, history, government, economy, people, and culture of Morocco

Includes glossary and bibliographical references

965 Algeria

Kagda, Falaq

Algeria; Falaq Kagda, Zawiah Abdul Latif, Debbie Nevins. 3rd edition Cavendish Square 2018 144p il map (Cultures of the world) library $47.07

Grades: 5 6 7 8 **965**

1. Algeria

ISBN 9781502627421 library

LC 2016054483

First published 1997

"Provides comprehensive information on the geography, history, wildlife, governmental structure, economy, cultural diversity, peoples, religion, and culture of Algeria." Publisher's note

Includes glossary and bibliographical references

Wagner, Heather Lehr

The **Algerian** war; by Heather Lehr Wagner. Chelsea House 2012 120 p. (Milestones in modern world history) (hardcover) $35

Grades: 7 8 9 10 11 12 **965**

1. France -- Foreign relations -- Algeria 2. Algeria -- History -- 1954-1962, Revolution 3. France -- Colonies -- Africa -- History 4. National liberation movements -- Algeria

ISBN 1604139234; 9781604139235

LC 2011023060

This book, part of the Milestones in Modern World History series, "opens with a triumphant France celebrating its freedom at the end of WWII while citizens of its colony, Algeria, were denied their own equality and freedom. Following an overview of Algerian possession, the text outlines French injustices toward Algeria, most notably discrimination of its Muslim population and the rise of revolution." (Booklist)

Includes bibliographical references and index

966 West Africa and offshore islands

Haywood, John

West African kingdoms; [by] John Haywood. Raintree 2008 64p il map (Time travel guide) lib bdg $34.29; pa $9.99

Grades: 6 7 8 9 **966**

1. West Africa 2. Ghana Empire 3. Songhai Empire 4. Mali -- History

ISBN 978-1-4109-2912-9 lib bdg; 978-1-4109-2918-1 pa

LC 2007006053

This describes life in West Africa between 1200 and 1600 AD, including the kingdoms of Mali, Songhai, and Benin, in the form of a travel guide.

Includes glossary and bibliographical references

966.1 Mauritania

Blauer, Ettagale

Mauritania; [by] Ettagale Blauer & Jason Lauré. Marshall Cavendish Benchmark 2009 144p il map (Cultures of the world) lib bdg $42.79

Grades: 5 6 7 8 **966.1**

1. Mauritania

ISBN 978-0-7614-3116-9

This describes the geography, history, government, economy, environment, people, and culture of Mauritania

966.2 Mali, Burkina Faso, Niger

Blauer, Ettagale

Mali; [by] Ettagale Blauer & Jason Lauré. 2nd ed.; Marshall Cavendish Benchmark 2008 144p il map (Cultures of the world) lib bdg $42.79

Grades: 5 6 7 8 **966.2**

1. Mali

ISBN 978-0-7614-2568-7

First published 1997

This describes the geography, history, government, economy, environment, people, and culture of Mali

Includes glossary and bibliographical references

McKissack, Pat, 1944-2017

The **royal** kingdoms of Ghana, Mali, and Songhay; life in medieval Africa. [by] Patricia and Fredrick McKissack. Holt & Co. 1993 142p il maps hardcover o.p. pa $12.99

Grades: 5 6 7 8 **966.2**

1. Ghana Empire 2. Songhai Empire 3. Mali -- History

ISBN 0-8050-4259-8 pa

LC 93-4838

Examines the civilizations of the Western Sudan which flourished from 700 to 1700 A.D., acquiring such vast wealth that they became centers of trade and culture for a continent

"The McKissacks are careful to distinguish what is known from what is surmised; they draw on the oral tradition, eyewitness accounts, and contemporary scholarship; and chapter source notes discuss various conflicting views of events." Booklist

Includes bibliographical references

966.3 Senegal

Berg, Elizabeth

Senegal; Elizabeth L. Berg, Ruth Lau, Debbie Nevins. 3rd edition Cavendish Square 2019 144p il map (Cultures of the world) library $47.07

Grades: 5 6 7 8 **966.3**

1. Senegal

ISBN 9781502636423 library

LC 2018016358

First published 1999

Describes the geography, history, wildlife, governmental structure, economy, cultural diversity, peoples, religion, and culture of Senegal

Includes glossary and bibliographical references

Mulroy, Tanya

Senegal; [by] Tanya Mulroy. Mason Crest Publishers 2008 79p il map (Africa: continent in the balance) lib bdg $21.95

Grades: 5 6 7 8 **966.3**

1. Senegal

ISBN 978-1-4222-0091-9 lib bdg; 1-4222-0091-4 lib bdg

LC 2006-17341

This book is "clear and concise, and the authors' easy-to-read texts impart a good deal of up-to-date information. . . . Chapters . . . cover the . . . country's history; politics and government; economy; and people, including discussions of family life, education, ethnic groups, health care, sports, and the arts, with the focus being on the largest cities." SLJ

Includes glossary and bibliographical references

966.4 Sierra Leone

Fowler, Will

Counterterrorism in West Africa; the most dangerous SAS assault. Rosen Pub. 2011 64p il map (The most daring raids in history) lib bdg $29.25

Grades: 7 8 9 10 **966.4**

1. Rescue work 2. Sierra Leone -- History -- Civil War, 1991- 3. Great Britain -- Army -- Special Air Service Regiment

ISBN 978-1-4488-1871-6; 1-4488-1871-0

LC 2010029621

This book offers a scene-by-scene account of the SAS (Special Air Service) and Operation Barras in Sierra Leone in 2000.

This book is "packed with facts, covering the details of the action, the people involved, and the tools used, in engaging prose. The authors cite their sources thoroughly. . . . Diagrams, photos, . . . and maps make the action easy to follow and provide visual context for the raids. . . . This . . . is sure to find a large readership." SLJ

Includes glossary and bibliographical references

Hasday, Judy L.

Sierra Leone; [by] Judy Hasday. Mason Crest Publishers 2008 79p il map (Africa: continent in the balance) lib bdg $21.95

Grades: 5 6 7 8 **966.4**

1. Sierra Leone

ISBN 978-1-4222-0092-6; 1-4222-0092-2

LC 2006-17342

This book features the country's "history; politics and government; economy; and people, including discussions of family life, education, ethnic groups, health care, sports, and the arts, with the focus being on the largest cities. . . . Interspersed throughout are numerous color and some black-and-white photographs, with descriptive captions, as well as 'Quick Facts' regarding geography, the economy, and the people. . . . The information is presented in an engaging manner." SLJ

Includes glossary and bibliographical references

LeVert, Suzanne

Sierra Leone; [by] Suzanne LeVert. Marshall Cavendish Benchmark 2007 144p il map (Cultures of the world) lib bdg $42.79

Grades: 5 6 7 8 **966.4**

1. Sierra Leone

ISBN 978-0-7614-2334-8 lib bdg; 0-7614-2334-6 lib bdg

LC 2005035964

This provides "information on the geography, history, governmental structure, economy, cultural diversity, peoples, religion, and culture of Sierra Leone." Publisher's note

Includes glossary and bibliographical references

966.68 Côte d'Ivoire (Ivory Coast)

Sheehan, Patricia

Cote d'Ivoire; [by] Patricia Sheehan and Jacqueline Ong. 2nd ed.; Marshall Cavendish Benchmark 2010 144p il map (Cultures of the world) lib bdg $42.79

Grades: 5 6 7 8 **966.68**

1. Ivory Coast

ISBN 978-0-7614-4854-9 lib bdg; 0-7614-4854-3 lib bdg

LC 2009045688

First published 2000

This offers information on the geography, history, wildlife, governmental structure, economy, cultural diversity, peoples, religion, and culture of Cote d'Ivoire

Includes glossary and bibliographical references

966.7 Ghana

Levy, Patricia

Ghana; Peg Robinson, Patricia Levy, and Winnie Wong. 3rd edition Cavendish Square 2019 144p il map (Cultures of the world) library $47.07

Grades: 5 6 7 8 **966.7**

1. Ghana

ISBN 9781502640727 library

First published 1999

Introduces the geography, history, government, economy, culture, and people of Ghana

Includes glossary and bibliographical references

966.9 Nigeria

Giles, Bridget

Nigeria; [by] Bridget Giles. National Geographic 2007 64p il map (Countries of the world) lib bdg $27.90

Grades: 4 5 6 7 **966.9**

1. Nigeria

ISBN 978-1-4263-0124-7

LC 2007024729

This describes the geography, nature, history, people and culture, government, and economy of Nigeria

"What helps [this book] stand out from the pack is [its] high-quality, rich photography. . . . The photos provide as much information as the [text]. . . . The writing is straightforward and solid." SLJ

Includes glossary and bibliographical references

Walker, Ida

★ **Nigeria**; Ida Walker. Mason Crest Publishers 2013 79 p. (hardcover : alk. paper) $22.95

Grades: 5 6 7 8 9 10 11 **966.9**

1. Nigeria

ISBN 1422222004; 9781422222003; 9781422222287; 9781422294406

LC 2010047767

This book, by Ida Walker, focuses on the country of Nigeria. "With a population of more than 133 million people, Nigeria is Africa's most populous country. Military leaders have ruled Nigeria for much of its history as an independent country, and it was not until 1999 that a civilian government was restored. However, this has not ensured peace. . . . Although Nigeria controls great reserves of oil, and is one of the largest exporters of oil to the United States, most Nigerians are very poor." (Publisher's note)

"This series is a needed collection for high school media centers. It fills a void by supplying up-to-date books on African countries that incorporates both an historical and modern perspective. Each book covers the land, government, economy, culture, people, religion, holidays, and festivals...These books will be useful for researchers and browsers alike." (Library Media Connection)

Includes bibliographical references and index

967.11 Cameroon

Sheehan, Sean

Cameroon; [by] Sean Sheehan and Josie Elias. 2nd ed.; Marshall Cavendish Benchmark 2011 144p il map (Cultures of the world) lib bdg $42.79

Grades: 5 6 7 8 **967.11**

1. Cameroon

ISBN 978-1-6087-0214-5; 1-6087-0214-6

LC 2010019623

First published 2001

Provides information on the geography, history, wildlife, governmental structure, economy, cultural diversity, peoples, religion, and culture of Cameroon.

Includes glossary and bibliographical references

967.51 Democratic Republic of the Congo

Heale, Jay

Democratic Republic of the Congo; Jay Heale, Yong Jui Lin, Debbie Nevins. 3rd edition Cavendish Square 2018 144p il map (Cultures of the world) library $47.07

Grades: 5 6 7 8 **967.51**

1. Congo (Republic)

ISBN 9781502636386 library

LC 2018004543

First published 1999

Describes the geography, history, government, economy, people, lifestyle, religion, languages, arts, leisure, festivals, and food of The Democratic Republic of the Congo

Includes glossary and bibliographical references

967.57 Rwanda and Burundi

Koopmans, Andy

Rwanda; Andy Koopmans. Mason Crest Publishers, Inc. 2013 87 p. color illustrations (hardcover) $22.95

Grades: 5 6 7 8 **967.57**

1. Rwanda 2. Africa -- Social life and customs

ISBN 1422221830; 9781422221839; 9781422222119; 9781422294246

LC 2010048004

Presents facts about Rwanda, including geography, history, politics, and economy.

Includes bibliographical references and index

967.571 Rwanda

Bankston, John

We visit Rwanda; by John Bankston. Mitchell Lane Publishers 2013 63 p. color illustrations (library bound) $33.95

Grades: 4 5 6 7 **967.571**

1. Rwanda

ISBN 9781612283074

LC 2012009881

Describes the history, natural features, geography, government, people, and culture of Rwanda, including different animals native to the country and the increased role of women in government.

Includes bibliographical references (p. 61) and index

Nardo, Don

The **Rwandan** genocide; by Don Nardo. Lucent Books 2011 104 p. ill. (hardcover) $34.95

Grades: 6 7 8 9 **967.571**

1. Genocide 2. Ethnic relations 3. Rwanda -- History 4. Rwanda -- History -- Civil War, 1994 5. Genocide -- Rwanda -- History -- 20th century 6. Ethnic conflict -- Rwanda -- History -- 20th century 7. Rwanda -- Ethnic relations -- History -- 20th century

ISBN 142050567X; 9781420505672

LC 2010039533

This book by Don Nardo is part of the World History series and looks at the Rwandan Genocide. The series "examines the eras, events, civilizations, and movements that have shaped human history, providing readers with insight into the past and its many legacies." Photographs, timelines, sidebars, and annotated bibliographies are included. (Publisher's note)

Includes bibliographical references and index.

967.61 Uganda

Barlas, Robert

Uganda; Robert Barlas, Yong Jui Lin, and Brett Griffin. 3rd edition Cavendish Square 2019 144p il map (Cultures of the world) library binding $47.07

Grades: 5 6 7 8 **967.61**
1. Uganda
ISBN 9781502647405
First published 2000
This offers information on the geography, history, wildlife, governmental structure, economy, cultural diversity, peoples, religion, and culture of Uganda
Includes glossary and bibliographical references

Dunstan, Simon
Entebbe; the most daring raid of Israel's special forces. Rosen Pub. 2011 64p il map (The most daring raids in history) lib bdg $29.25
Grades: 7 8 9 10 **967.61**
1. Israel -- History
ISBN 978-1-4488-1868-6; 1-4488-1868-0
LC 2010029622
The Israeli Forces operation at Entebbe was one of the most daring counter-terrorist assaults of all time. This book explores this important piece of history with narration and illustrations and diagrams.

This book is "packed with facts, covering the details of the action, the people involved, and the tools used, in engaging prose. The authors cite their sources thoroughly. . . . Diagrams, photos (where available), and maps make the action easy to follow and provide visual context for the raids. . . . This . . . is sure to find a large readership." SLJ
Includes glossary and bibliographical references

967.62 Kenya

Broberg, Catherine
Kenya in pictures; rev and expanded; Lerner Publs. 2003 80p il map (Visual geography series) lib bdg $31.93
Grades: 5 6 7 8 **967.62**
1. Kenya
ISBN 0-8225-1957-7
LC 2001-3829
First published 1988 under the authorship of Joel Reuben
A brief overview of Kenya's land, history, government, people, and culture
The book is "visually appealing with photos and sidebars that complement the text." Libr Media Connect
Includes bibliographical references

967.73 Somalia

Hassig, Susan M.
Somalia; Susan M. Hassig, Zawiah Abdul Latif, and Ruth Bjorklund. 3rd edition Cavendish Square 2017 144p il map (Cultures of the world) library $47.07
Grades: 5 6 7 8 **967.73**
1. Somalia
ISBN 9781502626073 library
LC 2016057403
First published 1997
"Provides comprehensive information on the geography, history, wildlife, governmental structure, economy, cultural diversity, peoples, religion, and culture of Somalia." Publisher's note
Includes glossary and bibliographical references

967.8 Tanzania

Heale, Jay
Tanzania; by Jay Heale, Winnie Wong, and Kelly Spence. 3rd edition Cavendish Square 2018 144p il map (Cultures of the world) library $47.07
Grades: 5 6 7 8 **967.8**
1. Tanzania
ISBN 9781502636324 library
LC 2017059789
First published 1998
"Provides comprehensive information on the geography, history, wildlife, governmental structure, economy, cultural diversity, peoples, religion, and culture of Tanzania." Publisher's note
Includes glossary and bibliographical references

MacDonald, Joan Vos
Tanzania; Joan Vos MacDonald. Mason Crest Publishers, Inc. 2013 87 p. illustrations, map (The evolution of Africa's major nations. East) (hardcover) $22.95
Grades: 5 6 7 8 **967.8**
1. Tanzania 2. Africa -- Social life and customs
ISBN 1422221865; 9781422221860; 9781422222140; 9781422294277
LC 2010048002
Author Joan Vos MacDonald describes how "the United Republic of Tanzania was created in the 1960s by the merger of two independent countries: Tanganyika, a territory on mainland East Africa, and the Zanzibar islands in the Indian Ocean. " (Publisher's note)
Includes bibliographical references (p. 84) and index

967.9 Mozambique

Mulroy, Tanya
Mozambique; Tanya Mulroy. Mason Crest Publishers, Inc. 2013 87 p. color illustrations (hardcover) $22.95
Grades: 5 6 7 8 **967.9**
1. Mozambique 2. Geography
ISBN 1422221822; 9781422221822; 9781422222102; 9781422294239
LC 2011018504
Presents facts about Mozambique, including its geography, history, politics, and economy.
Includes bibliographical references and index

968 Republic of South Africa and neighboring southern African countries

Coster, Patience
The **struggle** against apartheid. Arcturus Pub. 2010 48p il (Timelines) lib bdg $34.25
Grades: 7 8 9 10 **968**
1. Apartheid 2. South Africa -- History 3. South Africa -- Race relations
ISBN 978-1-84837-640-3; 1-84837-640-5
LC 2009051269
Discusses events in South Africa that lead up to and followed the end of apartheid, beginning with the peace treaty of Vereeniging and continuing through the election of Jacob Zuma.

"Background information about major figures is appended. The many images are relevant and well-placed." Horn Book Guide

Includes glossary and bibliographical references

Downing, David

★ **Apartheid** in South Africa; [by] David Downing. Heinemann Library 2004 56p il (Witness to history) $31.36

Grades: 7 8 9 10 **968**

1. Apartheid 2. South Africa -- Race relations

ISBN 1-4034-4870-1; 9780431170619

LC 2003-18235

Examines the historical forces that led to the development of the system of apartheid, what life was like under the system for both blacks and whites, and the efforts that caused the end of this system

"This dense volume is an excellent narrative overview of the apartheid struggle, drawing extensively on primary sources that provide depth, detail, drama, and authenticity." Booklist

Weltig, Matthew Scott

The **aftermath** of the Anglo-Zulu war; by Matthew S. Weltig. Twenty-First Century Books 2008 160p il (Aftermath of history) lib bdg $38.60

Grades: 6 7 8 9 10 **968**

1. Zulu War, 1879 2. Zulu (African people) 3. South Africa -- History

ISBN 978-0-8225-7599-3; 0-8225-7599-X

LC 2007-50826

"The well–written text provides a detailed account of the devastation and ruin brought to Zululand by the British government and by Boer settlers, replete with text boxes that provide clarification and further explanation of what are often complex and confusing issues and events. Illustrations consist of both period photographs and paintings of the fierce fighting. Reckless bravery, treachery, cruelty, betrayal, and greed are all here, resulting in an absorbing, but tragic story." SLJ

Includes glossary and bibliographical references

968.06 South Africa--Period as Republic, 1961-

Brownlie, Ali

South Africa in our world; [by] Ali Brownlie Bojang. Smart Apple Media 2010 32p il (Countries in our world) lib bdg $28.50

Grades: 5 6 7 8 **968.06**

1. South Africa

ISBN 978-1-59920-444-4 lib bdg; 1-59920-444-4 lib bdg

LC 2009043163

This "contains relevant information presented in a visually appealing layout. Large colorful photographs inform readers about the past, present, and future of the country. . . . The book gives an honest view of apartheid, poverty, and government conflicts. At the same time, it is hopeful about recent changes, such as the hosting of the World Cup and the growing economy." SLJ

Includes glossary and bibliographical references

Sonneborn, Liz

★ The **end** of apartheid in South Africa. Chelsea House Publishers 2010 120p il (Milestones in modern world history) lib bdg $35

Grades: 8 9 10 11 12 **968.06**

1. Apartheid 2. Anti-apartheid movement 3. South Africa -- Race relations

ISBN 978-1-60413-409-4; 1-60413-409-7

LC 2008-54805

This is "an excellent in-depth overview, one of the best on the subject, with chapters on the early history before the establishment of the apartheid regime and with profiles of many important leaders (not just Nelson Mandela), as well as clear discussion of present-day politics, the role of the Truth and Reconciliation Commission, and the ongoing inequality. Never simplistic, it is an outstanding overview for teens new to the subject; for those who know something of the history, it fills in the big picture with depth and detail about both leaders and ordinary people, what has changed, and how much still needs to be done." Booklist

Includes bibliographical references

Wright, Adrienne

Hector; a boy, a protest, and the photograph that changed apartheid. Adrienne Wright. Page Street Publishing 2019 48 p. chiefly color illustrations (hardcover) $18.99

Grades: 4 5 6 7 **968.06**

1. Apartheid -- South Africa 2. Children -- South Africa -- Biography 3. Journalism, Pictorial -- South Africa 4. South Africa -- History -- Soweto Uprising, 1976

ISBN 1624146910; 9781624146916

LC 2018061595

In this book, author Adrienne Wright describes how, "on June 16, 1976, Hector Pieterson, an ordinary boy, lost his life after getting caught up in what was supposed to be a peaceful protest. Black South African students were marching against a new law requiring that they be taught half of their subjects in Afrikaans, the language of the White government. The story's events unfold from the perspectives of Hector, his sister, and the photographer who captured their photo." (Publisher's note)

"A gentle palette of tawny sepia and cobalt chalk pastel lends a softness that complements Hector's sweet disposition and contrasts with the bloody events of the day. Nzima's powerful photograph—the one that caught the world's attention—is distinct yet seamlessly integrated in this unique account." Booklist

Includes bibliographical references

968.83 Botswana

Wittmann, Kelly

Botswana; Kelly Wittmann. Mason Crest Publishers, Inc. 2013 79 p. ill. (some col.), col. map (hardcover) $22.95

Grades: 5 6 7 8 **968.83**

1. Botswana 2. Geography

ISBN 1422221938; 9781422221938; 9781422222218; 9781422294338

LC 2011018530

This book "covers the land, government, economy, culture, people, religion, holidays, and festivals" of Botswana. (Library Media Connection)

968.91 Zimbabwe

Arnold, James R.

Robert Mugabe's Zimbabwe; by James R. Arnold and Roberta Wiener. Twenty-First Century Books 2008 160p (Dictatorships) lib bdg $38.60

Grades: 7 8 9 10 **968.91**

1. Presidents 2. Prime ministers 3. Zimbabwe
ISBN 978-0-8225-7283-1

LC 2006-100765

This history of Zimbabwe under the dictatorship of Robert Mugabe gives "students a glimpse into the repression and daily struggle for survival under [this] brutal [government]." SLJ

Includes glossary and bibliographical references

Hall, Martin

Great Zimbabwe; [by] Martin Hall and Rebecca Stefoff. 1st ed.; Oxford University Press 2006 47p il map (Digging for the past) $23

Grades: 7 8 9 10 **968.91**

1. Archeology 2. Shona (African people) 3. Zimbabwe
ISBN 978-0-19-515773-4; 0-19-515773-7

LC 2005014607

This "explores a ruined fourteenth-century stone city in Zimbabwe and covers controversies over its origin, its artifacts, and theories about its former inhabitants. The well-written text will spur readers' curiosity, while archival and modern photos, ancient maps, and European explorers' notes add a fascinating variety to the book's visual presentation." Horn Book Guide

Includes glossary and bibliographical references

968.94 Zambia

Holmes, Timothy

Zambia; Timothy Holmes, Winnie Wong, Debbie Nevins. 3rd edition Cavendish Square 2018 144p il map (Cultures of the world) library $47.07

Grades: 5 6 7 8 **968.94**

1. Zambia
ISBN 9781502632432 library

LC 2017044406

First published 1998

Describes the geography, history, government, economy, people, lifestyle, religion, language, arts, leisure, festivals, and food of Zambia

Includes glossary and bibliographical references

969.1 Madagascar

Heale, Jay

Madagascar; Jay Heale, Zawiah Abdul Latif, Debbie Nevins. 3rd edition Cavendish Square 2018 144p il map (Cultures of the world) library $47.07

Grades: 5 6 7 8 **969.1**

1. Madagascar
ISBN 9781502632425 library

LC 2017041694

First published 1998

"Provides comprehensive information on the geography, history, wildlife, governmental structure, economy, cultural diversity, peoples, religion, and culture of Madagascar." Publisher's note

Includes glossary and bibliographical references

970 History of North America

Desaulniers, Kristi L.

Northern America; [by] Kristi L. Desaulniers and Charles F. Gritzner. Chelsea House 2006 128p il map (Modern world cultures) lib bdg $30

Grades: 7 8 9 10 **970**

1. North America
ISBN 0-7910-8141-9

LC 2005031766

This describes the geography, history, culture, population, politics, economy, regions, and possible future of The United States and Canada.

Includes bibliographical references

970.004 North American native peoples

Bial, Raymond

The **Crow**. Marshall Cavendish Benchmark 2006 124p il map (Lifeways) lib bdg $38.50

Grades: 5 6 7 8 **970.004**

1. Crow Indians 2. Native Americans
ISBN 978-0-7614-1901-3; 0-7614-1901-2

LC 2004-22235

Discusses the history, culture, beliefs, changing ways, and notable people of the Crow.

Includes glossary and bibliographical references

The **Shoshone**. Benchmark Bks. 2001 128p il (Lifeways) lib bdg $38.50

Grades: 5 6 7 8 **970.004**

1. Shoshoni Indians
ISBN 978-0-7614-1211-3; 0-7614-1211-5

LC 2001-18496

This examines the origins, villages and camps, lifeways, beliefs, history, language, and social conditions of The Shoshone Indians

Includes glossary and bibliographical references

Bjornlund, Lydia D.

The **Trail** of Tears; the relocation of the Cherokee Nation. Lucent Books 2010 104p il map (American history) lib bdg $33.45

Grades: 5 6 7 8 **970.004**

1. Cherokee Indians 2. Native Americans -- Relocation
ISBN 978-1-4205-0211-4; 1-4205-0211-5

LC 2010001549

Describes the Federal government's seizure of Cherokee lands in Georgia and the forced migration of the Cherokee Nation to Oklahoma along the route that came to be known as the Trail of Tears.

This is "well written and [includes] primary sources, photographs, reproductions, and maps." SLJ

Includes bibliographical references

Brown, Dee Alexander

★ **Bury** my heart at Wounded Knee; an Indian history of the American West. [by] Dee Brown. Thirtieth anniversary ed; Holt & Co. 2001 487p il hardcover o.p. pa $16

Grades: 8 9 10 11 12 Adult **970.004**

1. Generals 2. Civil engineers 3. Government officials 4. West (U.S.) -- History 5. Native Americans -- Wars 6. Native Americans

-- West (U.S.)
ISBN 0-8050-6634-9; 0-8050-6669-1 pa
LC 00-40958

First published 1970

This is an account of the experience of the American Indian during the white man's expansion westward.

Includes bibliographical references

Connolly, Sean

The **Americas** and the Pacific. Zak Books 2009 48p il map (History of the world) lib bdg $34.25

Grades: 4 5 6 7 8 **970.004**

1. Maoris 2. Aboriginal Australians 3. Native Americans -- History
ISBN 978-88-60981-61-5 lib bdg; 88-60981-61-1 lib bdg
LC 2008008404

"Artists' renderings show groups of people engaged in representative activities, but it's the reproductions of artifacts . . . that will pull readers and browsers most. . . . [This is an] engaging overview." Booklist

Includes bibliographical references

Denetdale, Jennifer

★ The **Long** Walk; the forced Navajo exile. [by] Jennifer Denetdale. Chelsea House 2007 143p il map (Landmark events in Native American history) lib bdg $30

Grades: 7 8 9 10 **970.004**

1. Navajo Indians
ISBN 978-0-7910-9344-3 lib bdg; 0-7910-9344-1 lib bdg
LC 2007021723

"In 1863, the Diné (Navajo) faced transformations to their way of life with the Americans' determination to first subjugate and then remove them to a reservation. . . . This book exposes the series of events that facilitated the Navajo's removal from their homeland, their experiences during the Long Walk, their time at the Bosque Redondo reservation, their return home, and the ways in which they remember the Long Walk and the Bosque Redondo." Publisher's note

Includes bibliographical references

Dolan, Edward F.

The **American** Indian wars; [by] Edward F. Dolan. Millbrook Press 2003 112p il map lib bdg $29.90

Grades: 5 6 7 8 **970.004**

1. Native Americans -- Wars
ISBN 0-7613-1968-9
LC 2002-153012

Examines the battles and treaties between native peoples and early European settlers of what was to become the United States, as conflicts arose primarily over land, but also over food and other issues

"Period drawings, paintings, and photographs effectively illustrate a text packed with history." Booklist

Includes bibliographical references

Dunbar-Ortiz, Roxanne

An **indigenous** peoples' history of the United States for young people; Roxanne Dunbar-Ortiz ; adapted by Jean Mendoza and Debbie Reese. Beacon Press 2019 ix, 270 p.p (pbk. : alk. paper) $18.95

Grades: 8 9 10 11 12 **970.004**

1. Native Americans -- North America 2. United States -- Politics and government 3. United States -- Race relations -- History 4. United States -- Colonization 5. United States -- Race relations 6. Indians of North America -- Colonization 7. United States -- Politics and government 8. Indians of North America -- Historiography 9. Indians, Treatment of -- United States -- History
ISBN 9780807049396
LC 2019004266

This book in the ReVisioning American History for Young People series, by Roxanne Dunbar-Ortiz, adapted by Debbie Reese and Jean Mendoza, "examines the legacy of Indigenous peoples' resistance, resilience, and steadfast fight against imperialism. . . . Dunbar-Ortiz reveals the roles that settler colonialism and policies of American Indian genocide played in forming our national identity." (Publisher's note)

"Maps, photographs, informative sidebars, points for discussion, and a recommended book list round out this accessible, engaging, and necessary addition to school libraries and classrooms. An excellent read, dismantling American mythologies and fostering critical reasoning about history and current events." --Kirkus 05/2019

Includes bibliographical references and index

Edwards, Judith

The **history** of the American Indians and the reservation; [by] Judith Edwards. Enslow Publishers 2008 128p il map (From many cultures, one history) lib bdg $31.93

Grades: 6 7 8 9 **970.004**

1. Native Americans -- History
ISBN 978-0-7660-2798-5 lib bdg; 0-7660-2798-8 lib bdg
LC 2007028275

"Explores the difficult changes American Indians were forced to make, including moving off their land, adapting to like on reservations, and how those reservations have changed since their creation." Publisher's note

Includes glossary and bibliographical references

Ehrlich, Amy

★ **Wounded** Knee: an Indian history of the American West; adapted for young readers by Amy Ehrlich from Dee Brown's Bury my heart at Wounded Knee. Holt & Co. 1974 202p il maps hardcover o.p. pa $13.95

Grades: 6 7 8 9 **970.004**

1. Generals 2. Ghost dance 3. Apache Indians 4. Dakota Indians 5. Navajo Indians 6. Arapaho Indians 7. Cheyenne Indians 8. Sand Creek, Battle of, 1864 9. Indian chiefs 10. Civil engineers 11. Government officials 12. West (U.S.) -- History 13. Native Americans -- Wars 14. Native Americans -- West (U.S.)
ISBN 0-8050-2700-9 pa

This book traces the plight of the Navaho, Apache, Cheyenne and Sioux Indians in their struggles against the white man in the West between 1860 and 1890. It recounts battles and their causes, participants, and consequences during this era

"Some chapters [of the original] have been deleted, others condensed, and in some instances sentence structure and language have been simplified. The editing is good, and this version is interesting, readable, and smooth." SLJ

Includes bibliographical references

Elish, Dan

★ The **Trail** of Tears; the story of the Cherokee removal. Benchmark Books 2002 96p il map (Great journeys) lib bdg $32.79

Grades: 5 6 7 8 **970.004**

1. Cherokee Indians 2. Native Americans -- Relocation
ISBN 0-7614-1228-X
LC 00-52902

This "is particularly moving. Elish does a fine job introducing the Cherokee nation. . . . Filled with crisp, well-selected photographs and historical illustrations." Booklist

Includes bibliographical references

Encyclopedia of Native American wars and warfare; general editors, William B. Kessel, Robert Wooster. Facts on File 2005 398p il map $75; pa $21.95

Grades: 7 8 9 10 **970.004**

1. Reference books 2. Native Americans -- Wars -- Encyclopedias

ISBN 0-8160-3337-4; 0-8160-6430-X pa

LC 00-56200

"This encyclopedia offers readers a wide range of information about Native American history in North America after 1492." Choice

Includes bibliographical references

★ **Encyclopedia** of the American Indian; Stories, Timelines, Maps, and More. National Geographic Kids 2019 304 p. (hardcover) $24.99

Grades: 5 6 7 8 **970.004**

1. Native Americans

ISBN 9781426334535; 9781426334542

LC 2018031435

"More than 160 tribes are featured in this outstanding new encyclopedia, which presents a comprehensive overview of the history of North America's Native peoples. From the Apache to the Zuni, readers will learn about each tribe's history, traditions, and culture, including the impact of European expansion across the land and how tribes live today. Features include maps of ancestral lands; timelines of important dates and events; fact boxes for each tribe; bios of influential American Indians such as Sitting Bull; sidebars on daily life, homes, food, clothing, jewelry, and games; Did You Know facts with photographs; and traditional Native stories. The design is compelling and colorful, packed with full-color photographs." (Publisher's note)

Gibson, Karen Bush

Native American history for kids; with 21 activities. Chicago Review Press 2010 127p il pa $16.95

Grades: 6 7 8 9 10 **970.004**

1. Native Americans

ISBN 978-1-56976-280-6 pa; 1-56976-280-5 pa

LC 2010005695

"This gripping, highly readable overview will draw teens and even some adults into the history of Native Americans, from early times and the arrival of European settlers up to the present. The examples of racism are horrifying. . . . Also horrifying are the accounts of forced assimilation." Booklist

Includes glossary and bibliographical references

Gitlin, Marty

Wounded Knee Massacre. Greenwood 2011 xxiii, 185p il (Landmarks of the American mosaic) $35; e-book $35

Grades: 7 8 9 10 **970.004**

1. Wounded Knee Creek, Battle of, 1890 2. Native Americans -- West (U.S.)

ISBN 978-1-59884-409-2; 1-59884-409-1; 978-1-59884-410-8 e-book; 1-59884-410-5 e-book

LC 2010035200

"This concise, chronologically arranged text places the massacre in context by concisely examining the 'seeds of conflict' into the late 1860s; the fallout from Little Big Horn; the reemergence of the Ghost Dance; and, ultimately, the worst slaughter of Native men, women, and children in American history. . . . Substantial back matter includes lucid biographies of key figures and 13 primary documents." SLJ

Includes glossary and bibliographical references

Jastrzembski, Joseph C.

The **Apache** wars; the final resistance. Chelsea House Publishers 2007 133p il map (Landmark events in Native American history) lib bdg $35

Grades: 7 8 9 10 **970.004**

1. Apache Indians

ISBN 978-0-7910-9343-6; 0-7910-9343-3

LC 2007-990

This account features "lively writing and direct quotes, and [is] enhanced by many color and black-and-white photos, drawings, and illustrations." SLJ

Includes bibliographical references

Keoke, Emory Dean

★ **American** Indian contributions to the world; [by] Emory Dean Keoke and Kay Marie Porterfield. Facts on File 2005 5v il map set$175

Grades: 7 8 9 10 **970.004**

1. Native Americans

ISBN 0-8160-5392-8

This set "focuses on the many significant contributions that members of North, Central, and South American tribes have made to both United States and world culture. . . . The appendixes are well organized. . . . This set would be an excellent addition to any school media center's collection." Voice Youth Advocates

Includes glossary and bibliographical references

King, David C.

First people; an illustrated history of American Indians. DK Pub. 2008 192p il map $19.99

Grades: 5 6 7 8 **970.004**

1. Native Americans

ISBN 978-0-7566-4092-7; 0-7566-4092-X

"This rich pictorial work serves as an entertaining, informative, and visually appealing introduction to American Indian culture and history. Each of the seven chapters covers a different time period in chronological order. . . . The glossy photographs, colorful drawings, and easily accessible paragraphs . . . make for an easy-to-use overall package." SLJ

National Museum of the American Indian (U.S.)

Do all Indians live in tipis? questions and answers. from the National Museum of the American Indian; foreword by Rick West; introduction by Wilma Mankiller. Collins, in association with the National Museum of the American Indian, Smithsonian Institution 2007 239p il pa $14.95

Grades: 8 9 10 11 12 **970.004**

1. Native Americans

ISBN 978-0-06-115301-3; 0-06-115301-X

LC 2007-60874

"This highly accessible and informative book aims to dispel some of the major myths and stereotypes still surrounding Native people in the United States and Canada. . . . The straightforward questions were compiled from actual phone calls, emails, letters, and in-person visits to the George Gustav Heye Center in New York, a major branch of the National Museum of the American Indian. The Native American writers who answered them did so concisely with hints of humor and an abundance of research and experience. . . . This is a topnotch resource for both people just learning about Native American cultures and those who think they know the facts." SLJ

Schomp, Virginia

The **Native** Americans; [by] Virginia Schomp. Marshall Cavendish Benchmark 2007 96p il map (Myths of the world) lib bdg $34.21

Grades: 6 7 8 9 **970.004**

1. Native Americans

ISBN 978-0-7614-2550-2 lib bdg; 0-7614-2550-0 lib bdg

LC 2007013511

"With [its] beautiful illustrations, high-quality production, and focus on source material, the [book] should whet the interest of readers." SLJ

Includes glossary and bibliographical references

Vander Hook, Sue

Trail of Tears. ABDO Pub. 2010 112p il map (Essential events) lib bdg $32.79

Grades: 6 7 8 9 **970.004**

1. Cherokee Indians 2. Native Americans -- Relocation

ISBN 978-1-60453-946-2; 1-60453-946-1

LC 2009-31066

This title examines an important historic event, the Trail of Tears. Readers will learn the background of European settlement in Native American lands, relations between the groups, and how this led to the Trail of Tears.

"The writing is accessible and is richer than a lot of history writing, allowing the reader to become engaged in the text as a story, and the layout provides enough white space to allow lower level readers to feel confident." Libr Media Connect

Includes glossary and bibliographical references

Yue, Charlotte

★ The **wigwam** and the longhouse; [by] Charlotte and David Yue. Houghton Mifflin 2000 118p il $15

Grades: 4 5 6 7 **970.004**

1. Woodland Indians

ISBN 0-395-84169-0

LC 98-28971

Describes the history, customs, religion, government, homes, and present-day status of the various native peoples that inhabited the eastern woodlands since before the coming of the Europeans

Includes bibliographical references

Zimmerman, Dwight Jon

Saga of the Sioux; an adaptation of Dee Brown's Bury My Heart at Wounded Knee. [adapted] by Dwight Jon Zimmerman. Henry Holt and Company 2011 208p il map $18.99

Grades: 5 6 7 8 **970.004**

1. Dakota Indians 2. West (U.S.) -- History 3. Native Americans -- Wars

ISBN 978-0-8050-9364-3; 0-8050-9364-8

LC 2011004792

"Dwight Jon Zimmerman has created a masterful adaptation of Dee Brown's Bury My Heart at Wounded Knee, presenting late nineteenth century history from a Native American viewpoint. While Brown's book traces the fates of several Native American tribes in the western United States, Zimmerman's adaptation focuses solely on the Sioux. . . . Historical figures central to the narrative, both Native American and white, are portrayed as real people, rather than caricatures. Rather than simply describing what happened, the book looks at why it happened. Individuals' motivations, strengths, and flaws are all explored in relation to how historical events unfolded. The book includes numerous photographs, illustrations, and maps that aid understanding and create visual appeal. . . . This is a must-have addition to any United States history collection serving teens." Voice Youth Advocates

Includes glossary and bibliographical references

Zimmerman, Larry J.

Exploring the life, myth, and art of Native Americans. Rosen Pub. 2009 144p il map (Civilizations of the world) lib bdg $29.95

Grades: 7 8 9 10 11 12 **970.004**

1. Native Americans -- Art 2. Native Americans -- Religion

ISBN 978-1-4358-5614-1; 1-4358-5614-7

LC 2009-9268

This book describes the cultures, myths, and art of Native Americans.

"This beautifully illustrated and well-written [title] . . . is perfect for those assignments where students must look at the culture of a civilization. Artwork and pictures blend seamlessly with the information and the reader is taken on a journey of discovery. Myths are used as the story of how the people view themselves, blended with the discussion of the reality of life. Everyday life is tied to the belief systems and is explained in light of those beliefs. The pictures are beautifully done and there is almost as much information in the captions as there is in the text." Libr Media Connect

Includes glossary and bibliographical references

970.01 North America--Early history to 1599

Freedman, Russell

★ **Who** was first? discovering the Americas. Clarion Books 2007 88p il map $19

Grades: 6 7 8 9 **970.01**

1. Explorers 2. America -- Exploration

ISBN 978-0-618-66391-0

LC 2006-102485

This "looks at various ideas about the discovery of the Americas. . . . Beyond the very readable presentation of facts and theories, the book's main accomplishment is in showing that history is . . . an evolving process of logically interpreted evidence continually questioned, disputed, and revised. . . . The illustrations, many in color, include many excellent maps as well as reproductions of period drawings, paintings, engravings, and photos. . . . A well-researched, intelligent account." Booklist

Includes bibliographical references

Gunderson, Jessica

Conquistadors; by Jessica Gunderson. Creative Education 2011 48 p. (alk. paper) $35.65

Grades: 5 6 7 8 **970.01**

1. United States -- History 2. Soldiers 3. Military art and science -- History 4. Soldiers -- Spain -- History 5. America -- Discovery and exploration -- Spanish

ISBN 1608181839; 9781608181834

LC 2011035799

Author Jessica Gunderson's book "covers the beginnings of the people, weaponry, war tactics, and famous leaders, and examines the current perception of the group in popular culture in an appealing, detailed, and evenhanded manner. Historical reproductions, primary documents, photographs, maps, and film stills appear throughout" the "explorations of history." (Publisher's note)

Includes bibliographical references and index

Harrison, David L.

Mammoth bones and broken stones; the mystery of North America's first people. with illustrations by Richard Hilliard and archaeological photographs. Boyds Mills Press 2010 48p il map $18.95

Grades: 4 5 6 7 **970.01**

1. Prehistoric peoples 2. North America -- Antiquities
ISBN 978-1-59078-561-4; 1-59078-561-4

LC 2009020247

"How and when the Western Hemisphere . . . came to be populated continues to be both mysterious and controversial for scientists. . . . Harrison does a good job setting the issue in context. He describes the earliest efforts to identify the original inhabitants of the continents, exploring the Clovis culture. . . . After clearly explaining how scholars decided that they were the first, he then lists the arguments against this hypothesis. . . . The narrative is aided by both photographs and original illustrations that imagine scenes from both the distant past and the field experiences." Kirkus

Includes glossary and bibliographical references

Huey, Lois Miner

American archaeology uncovers the Vikings. Marshall Cavendish Benchmark 2009 64p il map (American archaeology) lib bdg $21.95

Grades: 4 5 6 7 **970.01**

1. America -- Antiquities 2. America -- Exploration 3. Vikings -- North America 4. Excavations (Archeology) -- Canada 5. Excavations (Archeology) -- United States
ISBN 978-0-7614-4270-7 lib bdg; 0-7614-4270-7 lib bdg

LC 2008050266

This describes how archeologists have learned about the Vikings in America.

This is "both intriguing and engaging for young readers. . . . A welcomed addition to classroom and school libraries." Libr Media Connect

Includes glossary and bibliographical references

Mann, Charles C.

★ **Before** Columbus; the Americas of 1491. Atheneum Books for Young Readers 2009 117p il map $24.99

Grades: 5 6 7 8 9 10 **970.01**

1. America -- Antiquities 2. Native Americans -- Origin 3. Native Americans -- History
ISBN 978-1-4169-4900-8; 1-4169-4900-3

LC 2009007691

Adapted from 1491, published 2006 by Knopf for adults

"Mann paints a superb picture of pre-Columbian America. In the process, he overturns the misconceived image of Natives as simple, widely scattered savages with minimal impact on their surroundings. Well-chosen, vividly colored graphics and photographs of mummies, pyramids, artifacts, and landscapes as well as the author's skillful storytelling will command the attention of even the most reluctant readers." SLJ

Includes glossary and bibliographical references

Mooney, Carla

Explorers of the New World; discover the golden age of exploration; with 22 projects. illustrated by Tom Casteel. Nomad 2011 120p il map (Build it yourself) pa $15.95 **970.01**

1. Explorers 2. America -- Exploration
ISBN 978-1-936313-44-0; 1-936313-44-8

Provides twenty-two step-by-step projects to help readers learn about the explorers that discovered America and their voyages.

"This informative, entertaining activity book takes readers on a fascinating voyage of their own. . . . Each chapter concludes with 'Make Your Own' activities that bring life to the history with instructions for the construction of a logbook, clay activities, recipes, games, etc. Some may require the assistance of an adult but are not complicated or time consuming." SLJ

Includes glossary and bibliographical references

Peterson, Cris

Birchbark brigade; a fur trade history. Calkins Creek 2009 135p il $18.95

Grades: 7 8 9 10 **970.01**

1. Fur trade 2. Frontier and pioneer life 3. America -- Exploration 4. Native Americans -- History
ISBN 978-1-59078-426-6; 1-59078-426-X

LC 2008055109

"Peterson first provides a history of the military, political and economic development of the [fur] trade and then gives readers a snapshot of the lives of the Indians and voyageurs who did the actual work. She relies on a wealth of primary-source material, from archival illustrations to quotes from players both large and small. . . . The author's enthusiasm for her subject will communicate itself to readers, even those who never dreamed they'd be interested, making this the best kind of discovery." Kirkus

Includes bibliographical references

Walker, Sally M.

★ **Their** skeletons speak; Kennewick man and the Paleoamerican world. by Sally M. Walker and Douglas W. Owsley. Carolrhoda Books 2012 136 p. (lib. bdg. : alk. paper) $22.95

Grades: 8 9 10 11 12 **970.01**

1. Kennewick Man 2. Paleo-Indians 3. Human remains (Archeology) 4. Washington (State) -- Antiquities 5. Paleo-Indians -- Washington (State) -- Origin 6. Human remains (Archaeology) -- Washington (State) 7. Paleo-Indians -- Anthropometry -- Washington (State)
ISBN 0761374574; 9780761374572

LC 2011051329

This book by Sally M. Walker and Douglas W. Owsley presents a "detailed study of the discovery and forensic evaluation of the skeleton dubbed 'Kennewick Man.' . . . From his accidental discovery in 1996 through multiple examinations by scientists with ever-improving forensic tools . . . an actual human being emerges from a time long gone, speaking to us through his bones. . . . A final facial reconstruction leaves readers face-to-face with a real person." (School Library Journal)

Includes bibliographical references and index.

Wulffson, Don L.

Before Columbus; early voyages to the Americas. by Don Wulffson. Twenty-First Century Books 2008 128p il map lib bdg $30.60

Grades: 6 7 8 9 **970.01**

1. Explorers 2. America -- Antiquities 3. America -- Exploration
ISBN 978-0-8225-5978-8 lib bdg; 0-8225-5978-1 lib bdg

LC 2005-24487

"This engaging presentation of early exploration of the Americas offers both fact and speculation on who, when, and why voyagers came; how they traveled; and what evidence they left behind. . . . Citing legends and sagas, oral and written histories, and archaeological discoveries, Wulffson presents an intriguing array of possibilities. . . . The stories and unanswered questions about pre-Columbian voyagers will capture the imaginations of many readers, offer fascinating glimpses of different cultural groups, [and] stimulate further research." SLJ

Includes bibliographical references

970.1 North American native peoples

Ellis, Deborah

Looks Like Daylight; Voices of Indigenous Kids. by Deborah Ellis, with a foreword by Loriene Roy. Pgw 2013 256 p. $15.95

Grades: 6 7 8 9 10 11 12 **970.1**

1. Interviews 2. Native American children

ISBN 1554981204; 9781554981205

This book, by Deborah Ellis, "is a . . . collection of interviews with [native] children aged nine to eighteen. They come from all over the continent, from Iqaluit to Texas, Haida Gwaai to North Carolina. . . . Many of these children are living with the legacy of the residential schools; many have lived through the cycle of foster care. Many others have found something in their roots that sustains them, have found their place in the arts, the sciences, athletics." (Publisher's note)

"In this cultural undertaking, Ellis interviews Native American and aboriginal children and teens, ages nine to eighteen. Whether heart-wrenching or uplifting, each first-person narrative is compelling, insightful, and incredibly moving. Introductory matter sheds painful light on the historically horrific treatment of North America's indigenous peoples, as well as the challenges they face still. An extensive list of charitable and informational organizations is appended." (Horn Book)

Yellowhorn, Eldon

Turtle Island; the story of North America's first people. Eldon Yellowhorn and Kathy Lowinger. Annick Press 2017 116 p. illustrations (chiefly color) (hardcover) $24.95

Grades: 4 5 6 7 **970.1**

1. Historical literature 2. Indigenous peoples 3. Native Americans -- History 4. Indians of North America -- History

ISBN 9781554519460; 9781554519446; 9781554519439; 1554519446

This book, by Eldon Yellowhorn and Kathy Lowinger, "goes back to the Ice Age to give young readers a glimpse of what life was like pre-contact. . . . The authors take the reader back as far as 14,000 years ago to imagine moments in time. A wide variety of topics are featured, from the animals that came and disappeared over time, to what people ate, how they expressed themselves through art, and how they adapted to their surroundings." (Publisher's note)

"The multifaceted history of the Indigenous peoples of North American before and after European contact is made accessible in a well-written, fluid narrative complemented by appealing graphics." SLJ

Includes bibliographical references and index.

971 Canada

Baker, Stuart

In the Arctic. Marshall Cavendish Benchmark 2010 32p il map (Climate change) lib bdg $19.95

Grades: 5 6 7 8 **971**

1. Arctic regions 2. Greenhouse effect

ISBN 978-0-7614-4437-4 lib bdg; 0-7614-4437-8 lib bdg

LC 2009-5767

The book about climate change in the Arctic "is perfectly organized for students. . . . Unique layout features serve as signposts and will help focus readers' attention. . . . [The book] features an outstanding chart of possible effects of global warming on the area in question, listing 'Possible Event,' 'Predicted Result,' and 'Impact' in short, bulleted statements." SLJ

Includes glossary

Ferry, Steven

Ontario. Lucent Books 2003 112p il map (Exploring Canada) $29.95

Grades: 6 7 8 9 **971**

1. Canada 2. Ontario

ISBN 978-1-59018-050-1; 1-59018-050-X

LC 2002-14351

Examines the history, geography, climate, industries, people, and culture of what is by far the most populous of Canada's provinces

Includes bibliographical references

Quebec. Lucent Books 2003 112p il map (Exploring Canada) $29.95

Grades: 6 7 8 9 **971**

1. Canada 2. Québec (Province)

ISBN 978-1-59018-051-8; 1-59018-051-8

LC 2002-4111

Examines the history, geography, climate, industries, people, culture, and ongoing separatist struggle of Canada's largest province

Includes bibliographical references

Yukon Territory; by Steven Ferry, Blake Harris, and Liz Szynkowski. Lucent Books 2003 112p il map (Exploring Canada) $29.95

Grades: 6 7 8 9 **971**

1. Canada 2. Yukon Territory

ISBN 978-1-59018-053-2; 1-59018-053-4

LC 2002-4110

Examines the history, geography, climate, industries, people, and culture of Canada's most remote and untamed region.

Includes bibliographical references

Junior Worldmark encyclopedia of the Canadian provinces; [Timothy L. Gall and Susan Bevan Gall, editors] 5th ed.; U.X.L 2007 294p il map $70

Grades: 5 6 7 8 9 10 **971**

1. Reference books 2. Canada

ISBN 978-1-4144-1060-9; 1-4144-1060-3

LC 2007003908

First published 1997

"Arranged by 40 . . . subheadings . . . this . . . resource provides . . . information on all of Canada's provinces and territories. [It includes] details on Canada's arts, climate, government, health, languages, notable persons, ethnic groups and . . . more." Publisher's note

Includes bibliographical references

Laws, Gordon D.

Alberta; by Gordon D. Laws and Lauren M. Laws. Lucent Books 2003 112p il map (Exploring Canada) $29.95

Grades: 6 7 8 9 **971**

1. Canada 2. Alberta

ISBN 978-1-59018-045-7; 1-59018-045-3

LC 2002-9880

Explains the history, geography, climate, industry, people, and culture of Canada's princess province, having been named after the daughter of Queen Victoria.

Includes bibliographical references

Manitoba; by Gordon D. Laws and Lauren M. Laws. Lucent Books 2003 112p il map (Exploring Canada) $29.95

Grades: 6 7 8 9 **971**

1. Canada 2. Manitoba

ISBN 978-1-59018-047-1; 1-59018-047-X

LC 2002-14364

Examines the history, geography, climate, industries, people, and culture of one of the most diverse of Canada's provinces

Includes bibliographical references

The **Northwest** Territories; by Gordon Laws and Lauren M. Laws. Lucent Books 2004 112p il map (Exploring Canada) $29.95

Grades: 6 7 8 9 **971**

1. Canada 2. Northwest Territories

ISBN 978-1-59018-049-5; 1-59018-049-6

LC 2002-156055

Examines the history, geography, climate, industries, people, and culture of Canada's Northwest Territories

Includes bibliographical references

Mara, Wil

Canada; by Wil Mara. Children's Press, an imprint of Scholastic Inc. 2018 144 p. illustrations, maps (Enchantment of the world) (library binding) $40

Grades: 5 6 7 8 **971**

1. Canada -- History 2. Canada -- Description and travel 3. Canada -- Social life and customs 4. Canada

ISBN 0531235726; 9780531235720

LC 2016050354

"Located directly north of the United States, Canada is one of the world's largest countries. . . . Readers will experience all sides of this North American nation as they explore its history and learn more about its people. They will find themselves immersed in Canadian culture as they learn about the country's government, economy, traditions, and much more." (Publisher's note)

Includes bibliographical references (page 134) and index

Mayell, Mark

Newfoundland. Lucent Books 2003 112p il map (Exploring Canada) $29.95

Grades: 6 7 8 9 **971**

1. Canada 2. Newfoundland

ISBN 978-1-59018-048-8; 1-59018-048-8

LC 2003-2060

Examines the history, geography, climate, industries, people, and culture of Canada's Newfoundland

Includes bibliographical references

Saskatchewan. Lucent Books 2003 128p il map (Exploring Canada) $29.95

Grades: 6 7 8 9 **971**

1. Canada 2. Saskatchewan

ISBN 978-1-59018-052-5; 1-59018-052-6

LC 2003-43346

Examines the history, geography, climate, industries, people, and culture of the central province known as Canada's breadbasket

Includes bibliographical references

Palana, Brett J.

British Columbia. Lucent Books 2003 112p il map (Exploring Canada) $29.95

Grades: 6 7 8 9 **971**

1. Canada 2. British Columbia

ISBN 978-1-59018-046-4; 1-59018-046-1

LC 2002-4112

Examines the history, geography, climate, industries, people, and culture of Canada's westernmost province

Includes bibliographical references

Walker, Sally M.

★ **Blizzard** of glass; the Halifax explosion of 1917. Henry Holt 2011 xii, 145p il $18.99

Grades: 5 6 7 8 **971**

1. World War, 1914-1918 -- Naval operations 2. Halifax (N.S.) -- History -- Explosion, 1917

ISBN 978-0-8050-8945-5; 0-8050-8945-4

LC 2011005914

"The text reads smoothly with unfamiliar words defined in the text. Illustrations consist of two full-page maps and numerous black-and-white photos. The final chapter revisits the featured families and their descendants, thus tying up the loose ends. . . . This tragic, but well-told story belongs in most collections." SLJ

Includes bibliographical references

Wallace, Mary

Inuksuk journey; an artist at the top of the world. Maple Tree Press 2008 64p il $24.95

Grades: 5 6 7 8 **971**

1. Inuit 2. Canada 3. Arctic regions

ISBN 978-1-897349-26-7; 1-897349-26-2

"Nunavut, an Arctic territory in northern Canada, is a cold, open space where inuksuk, piles of stone in the shape of a person used to 'mark a family home, welcome guests, guide travelers, and ensure safe passage,' are commonly found. Wallace has developed a passion for these ancient messengers, and here she presents a journal of her week-long trek to Inuksugassait, a place where countless numbers of the stone markers stand. . . . Wallace includes personal photos, sketches, and comments that give readers an intimate portrait of life in this place. Over a dozen vibrant oil paintings depicting scenes from her journey are scattered throughout. . . . Readers will be fascinated by this firsthand account of true adventure." SLJ

Weaver, Janice

Mirror with a memory; a nation's story in photographs. Tundra Books 2007 159p il $29.95

Grades: 6 7 8 9 **971**

1. Canada -- History

ISBN 0-88776-747-8; 978-0-88776-747-0

"Defining moments in Canadian history are thematically presented in this photography collection. . . . In the conversational commentary that accompanies each image, Weaver provides historical context. Thought-provoking media literacy issues are also raised. . . . A great visual retrospective of a nation's people, places, and events." SLJ

Williams, Brian

★ **Canada**; [by] Brian Williams; Tom Carter and Ben Cecil, consultants. National Geographic 2007 64p il map (Countries of the world) lib bdg $27.90; pa $12.95

Grades: 4 5 6 7 **971**

1. Canada

ISBN 978-1-4263-0025-7 lib bdg; 978-1-4263-0573-3 pa

LC 2007296572

A basic overview of the history, geography, climate and culture of Canada

This "clear, succinct [overview] will support assignments without overwhelming casual readers. . . . A good selection of recent, high-quality color photographs gives the [book] visual appeal." SLJ

Includes glossary and bibliographical references

971.004 Canada – First Nations

Gray Smith, Monique

★ **Speaking** our truth; a journey of reconciliation. Monique Gray Smith. Orca Book Publishers 2017 159 p. illustrations, color map (hardcover) $29.95

Grades: 6 7 8 9 10 **971.004**

1. First Nations 2. Reconciliation 3. Canada -- Race relations

ISBN 9781459815841; 9781459815858; 9781459815834

LC 2017933028

This book, by Monique Gray Smith, looks at how "Canada's relationship with its Indigenous people has suffered as a result of both the residential school system and the lack of understanding of the historical and current impact of those schools. Healing and repairing that relationship requires education, awareness and increased understanding of the legacy and the impacts still being felt by Survivors and their families." (Publisher's note)

"A sensitive and extensive insight into the experiences of Indigenous people in Canada. Smith traces the historical events, movements, and laws affecting people of the First Nations and connects this history to the impact still resonating generations later." SLJ

Includes bibliographical references and index.

971.01 Early history to 1763

Worth, Richard

New France, 1534-1763; featuring the region that now includes all or parts of Michigan, Minnesota, Wisconsin, Illinois, Indiana, Ohio, Pennsylvania, Vermont, Maine, and Canada from Manitoba to Newfoundland. by Richard Worth. National Geographic Society 2007 109p il map (Voices from colonial America) $21.95; lib bdg $32.90

Grades: 5 6 7 8 **971.01**

1. Mississippi River valley -- History 2. Canada -- History -- 0-1763 (New France)

ISBN 978-1-4263-0147-6; 1-4263-0147-2; 978-1-4263-0148-3 lib bdg; 1-4263-0148-0 lib bdg

LC 2007-29544

"Worth presents the history of the vast French colony known as New France. Clearly written, the book is studded with quotes from people living in the colony and illustrated with colorful paintings, prints, and maps from a variety of periods. . . . This nicely designed introduction to a historically significant area fills a gap in many colonial history series and library collections." Booklist

Includes bibliographical references

971.5 Atlantic Provinces

Laws, Gordon D.

The **Maritime** Provinces; by Gordon D. Laws and Lauren M. Laws. Lucent Books 2004 112p il map (Exploring Canada) $29.95

Grades: 6 7 8 9 **971.5**

1. Canada 2. Maritime Provinces

ISBN 978-1-59018-335-9; 1-59018-335-5

LC 2003-5440

Examines the history, geography, climate, industries, people, and culture of Canada's Maritime Provinces

Includes bibliographical references

972 Mexico, Central America, West Indies, Bermuda

Ancient Aztec and Maya; edited by Anita Croy. Brown Bear Books 2010 64p il map (Facts at your fingertips) lib bdg $35.65

Grades: 6 7 8 9 **972**

1. Mayas 2. Aztecs

ISBN 978-1-933834-58-0 lib bdg; 1-933834-58-7 lib bdg

LC 2009-17295

Examines the leading Indian civilizations of Latin America and native North Americans, discussing their history, culture, food and shelter, government and trade, and geographical information

This begins "with an introduction accompanied by a striking full-page photo, followed by a two-page time line, and a two-paged spread for each topic. This format makes information easily accessible. Beautiful color photos of ancient ruins, drawings, maps, diagrams, and recreations create appeal and enhance the information. . . . Whether for recreational browsing or serious research, this . . . will certainly prove useful for students." Libr Media Connect

Includes glossary and bibliographical references

Bingham, Jane

The **Aztec** empire; [by] Jane Bingham. Raintree 2007 64p il map (Time travel guide) lib bdg $34.29; pa $9.99

Grades: 6 7 8 9 **972**

1. Aztecs 2. Mexico -- Civilization

ISBN 978-1-4109-2730-9 lib bdg; 1-4109-2730-X lib bdg; 978-1-4109-2737-8 pa; 1-4109-2737-7 pa

LC 2006033875

A description of life in the Aztec empire written in the form of a travel guide.

Includes glossary and bibliographical references

Cooke, Tim

★ **Ancient** Aztec; archaeology unlocks the secrets of Mexico's past. National Geographic 2007 64p il map (National Geographic investigates) $17.95; lib bdg $27.90

Grades: 4 5 6 7 **972**

1. Aztecs 2. Mexico -- Antiquities 3. Excavations (Archeology)

-- Mexico
ISBN 978-1-4263-0072-1; 1-4263-0072-7; 978-1-4263-0073-8 lib bdg; 1-4263-0073-5 lib bdg

LC 2007024813

This describes ancient Aztec origins, technology, major archeological sites, civilization, and connections to the present

"Pithy and appealing. . . . Aerial photos, time [line], informative sidebars, an interview with an archaeologist, and excellent maps augment rigorously supported [text] that [asks] and [answers] interesting questions." SLJ

George, Charles

Maya civilization; [by] Charles and Linda George. Lucent Books 2010 96p il (World history) lib bdg $33.45

Grades: 6 7 8 9 **972**

1. Mayas 2. Mexico -- Civilization 3. Central America -- Civilization
ISBN 978-1-4205-0240-4; 1-4205-0240-9

LC 2009053266

This is an introduction to Mayan civilization, including research which explains some of its mysteries.

This "shines as it provides a contemporaneous writing as well as work by scholars that offer plenty of drama—and lots of facts too. . . . [It also] provides a solid time line, plenty of photographs, sourced quotes, and a list of books and websites for further investigation. Excellent for reports and research." Booklist

Includes bibliographical references

Gruber, Beth

★ **Mexico**; [by] Beth Gruber; Gary S. Elbow and Jorge Zamora, consultants. National Geographic 2007 64p il map (Countries of the world) lib bdg $27.90; pa $12.95

Grades: 4 5 6 7 **972**

1. Mexico
ISBN 0-7922-7669-8 lib bdg; 1-4263-0566-4 pa

LC 2004026452

"This volume introduces Mexico's geography, history, wildlife, culture, and government. The many excellent color photos and maps are a striking feature of the series. . . . This will be a useful addition to many libraries." Booklist

Includes glossary and bibliographical references

Harris, Nathaniel

★ **Ancient** Maya; archaeology unlocks the secrets to the Maya's past. by Nathaniel Harris; Elizabeth Graham, consultant. National Geographic 2008 64p il map (National Geographic investigates) $17.95; lib bdg $27.90

Grades: 4 5 6 7 **972**

1. Mayas 2. Mexico -- Antiquities 3. Excavations (Archeology) -- Mexico
ISBN 978-1-4263-0227-5; 1-4263-0227-4; 978-1-4263-0228-2 lib bdg; 1-4263-0228-2 lib bdg

LC 2007047837

This describes ancient Mayan civilization and how archeologists found out about it.

Includes glossary and bibliographical references

Heinrichs, Ann

The **Aztecs**; by Ann Heinrichs. Benchmark Books 2011 64 p. (Technology of the ancients) (print) $32.79

Grades: 4 5 6 7 **972**

1. Aztecs 2. Technological innovations -- History
ISBN 1608707652; 9781608707539; 9781608707652

LC 2011018348

This book, by Ann Heinrichs, includes "presentations of [the Aztec's] ancient cultures, emphasiz[ing] governance and material culture (clothing, crafts, architecture). The book [does] not cover the origins of the empires or try to explain how they became so powerful." (School Library Journal)

Junior Worldmark encyclopedia of the Mexican states; [Timothy L. Gall and Susan Bevan Gall, editors] 2nd ed.; U.X.L,Thomson/Gale 2007 423p il map $70

Grades: 5 6 7 8 9 10 **972**

1. Reference books 2. Mexico
ISBN 978-1-4144-1112-5

LC 2007003906

First published 2004

"Arranged by 28 . . . subheadings . . . Junior Worldmark Encyclopedia of the Mexican States provides . . . information on each of Mexico's 31 states. Topics covered include climate, plants and animals, population and ethnic groups, religions, transportation, history, state and local governments, political parties, judicial system, economy, education, arts, media, tourism, sports, famous people and . . . more." Publisher's note

Includes bibliographical references

Kops, Deborah

Palenque; by Deborah Kops. Twenty-First Century Books 2008 80p il (Unearthing ancient worlds) lib bdg $30.60

Grades: 5 6 7 8 **972**

1. Mayas 2. Mexico -- Antiquities 3. Palenque site (Mexico) 4. Excavations (Archeology) -- Mexico
ISBN 978-0-8225-7504-7 lib bdg; 0-8225-7504-3 lib bdg

LC 2007021323

This describes the discovery of the ancient Mayan site of Palenque in 1840 by John Stephens and Frederick Catherwood, and the mid-20th century excavations of the site by Alberto Ruz Lhuillier, who discovered the tomb of the Mayan king Pakal, who died in 683 A.D., inside a pyramid

This "clearly written [title is] illustrated with large photographs and period artwork, and the pages are broken up with text boxes featuring quotes and interesting anecdotes." SLJ

Includes glossary and bibliographical references

Lourie, Peter

★ **Hidden** world of the Aztec. Boyds Mills Press 2006 48p il map $17.95

Grades: 4 5 6 7 **972**

1. Aztecs 2. Excavations (Archeology) -- Mexico
ISBN 978-1-59078-069-5; 1-59078-069-8

The author takes a "look at the Aztecs from the perspective of archaeological digs at the Great Temple in modern-day Mexico City and at the Pyramid of the Moon in Teotihuacan. . . . The writing style is clear, informative, and interesting." SLJ

Includes glossary and bibliographical references

Nardo, Don

Aztec civilization. Lucent Books 2010 104p il map (World history) lib bdg $33.45

Grades: 6 7 8 9 **972**

1. Aztecs

ISBN 978-1-4205-0242-8; 1-4205-0242-5

LC 2009040802

This is an introduction to Aztec civilization, including its rise and fall and the role of women.

This "shines as it provides a contemporaneous writing as well as work by scholars that offer plenty of drama—and lots of facts too. . . . [It also] provides a solid time line, plenty of photographs, sourced quotes, and a list of books and websites for further investigation. Excellent for reports and research." Booklist

Includes bibliographical references

Schomp, Virginia

The **Aztecs**; [by] Virginia Schomp. Marshall Cavendish Benchmark 2009 96p il map (Myths of the world) lib bdg $23.95

Grades: 6 7 8 9 **972**

1. Aztecs

ISBN 978-0-7614-3096-4 lib bdg; 0-7614-3096-2 lib bdg

LC 2008007082

"A retelling of several key Aztec myths, with background information describing the history, geography, belief systems, and customs of the Aztecs." Publisher's note

Includes glossary and bibliographical references

Sonneborn, Liz

Mexico; by Liz Sonneborn. Children's Press, an imprint of Scholastic Inc. 2018 144 p. (library binding) $40

Grades: 5 6 7 8 **972**

1. Mexico -- History 2. Mexico -- Description and travel 3. Mexico -- Social life and customs 4. Mexico

ISBN 053123570X; 9780531235706

LC 2016054005

In this book in the Enchantment of the World series," by Liz Sonneborn, "among the largest and most populous of the Latin American nations, Mexico is a land of great contrasts. . . . Readers will explore the many sides of Mexico as they venture into the heart of this amazing country. They will learn about its long history and unique culture, find out what life is like for its people, examine some of its most incredible wildlife, and much more." (Publisher's note)

Includes bibliographical references (pages 134-135) and index

Stein, R. Conrad, 1937-

Ancient Mexico. Morgan Reynolds Pub. 2011 144p il map (The story of Mexico) $28.95

Grades: 6 7 8 9 **972**

1. Mexico -- History 2. Native Americans -- Mexico

ISBN 1-59935-161-7; 978-1-59935-161-2

LC 2010041379

"Stein organizes and clearly presents a great deal of information. . . . The . . . format features a chonological text supplemented with useful sidebars and brightened with color illustrations, including many photos, artifacts, and period artworks. . . . [The book] provides a historical survey of Mexico's early inhabitants, from the arrival of Paleo-Indians through civilizations such as the Olmecs, the Maya, and Toltecs, and the Aztecs." Booklist

Includes bibliographical references

Cortes and the Spanish Conquest; [by] R. Conrad Stein. 1st ed.; Morgan Reynolds Pub. 2008 160p il map (The story of Mexico) lib bdg $27.95

Grades: 6 7 8 9 10 **972**

1. Aztecs 2. Explorers 3. Mexico -- History 4. Colonial administrators

ISBN 978-1-59935-053-0 lib bdg; 1-59935-053-X lib bdg

LC 2007016004

This "identifies the 'encounter' between the Spanish and Aztecs as one that 'would put the human character itself on trial.' The author provides a look at both societies, tracing the Aztecs' rise to power and the Spaniards' interest in exploration. The Spanish conquest of the Aztecs, led by Hernando Cortés, is related in great depth, and the book ends with a discussion of its legacy. [An] excellent [introduction] to Mexican history." SLJ

Includes bibliographical references

The **Mexican** Revolution. Morgan Reynolds Pub. 2008 160p il map (The story of Mexico) lib bdg $27.95

Grades: 6 7 8 9 10 **972**

1. Mexico -- History

ISBN 978-1-59935-051-6; 1-59935-051-3

LC 2007-22136

"Opening with Porfirio Díaz's presidency (beginning in 1876), [this book] explains how Indian land was expropriated and allotted to rich hacienda owners, describes resistance movements led by Emiliano Zapata and Pancho Villa, and details 10 years of political upheaval and violent uprisings (1910-1920), ending with Alvaro Obregó's election as president of Mexico. . . . [The book has] a lively narrative style. . . . Pertinent illustrations, including photographs, historical paintings, and maps are sprinkled throughout. . . . Well-written and well-researched." SLJ

Includes bibliographical references

The **Mexican** War of Independence; [by] R. Conrad Stein. Morgan Reynolds Pub. 2008 144p il map (The story of Mexico) lib bdg $27.95

Grades: 6 7 8 9 10 **972**

1. Mexico -- History

ISBN 978-1-59935-054-7 lib bdg; 1-59935-054-8 lib bdg

LC 2007022137

This "covers the years between 1521, when Hernando Cortés completed his conquest of the Aztec empire, and 1855, when Antonio Lopez Santa Anna was overthrown. The book provides excellent background information about three centuries of Spain's rule over Mexico. . . . [The book has] a lively narrative style. . . . Pertinent illustrations, including photographs, historical paintings, and maps are sprinkled throughout. . . . Well-written and well-researched." SLJ

Includes bibliographical references

972.08 Mexico since 1867

Stein, R. Conrad

Modern Mexico. Morgan Reynolds Pub. 2011 144p il map (The story of Mexico) $28.95

Grades: 6 7 8 9 **972.08**

1. Mexico -- History 2. Mexico -- Politics and government

ISBN 978-1-5993-5162-9; 1-5993-5162-5

LC 2010053630

"Stein organizes and clearly presents a great deal of information. . . . The . . . format features a chronological text supplemented with useful sidebars and brightened with color illustrations, including many photos, artifacts, and period artworks. . . . [The book] looks at events in

Mexico since 1920, focusing primarily on presidential administrations, economic problems, political unrest, and emigration." Booklist

Includes bibliographical references

972.81 Guatemala

Croy, Anita

★ **Guatemala**. National Geographic 2009 64p il map (Countries of the world) lib bdg $27.90

Grades: 4 5 6 7 **972.81**

1. Guatemala

ISBN 978-1-4263-0471-2 lib bdg; 1-4263-0471-4 lib bdg

This describes the geography, nature, history, people and culture, government and economy of Guatemala

Includes glossary and bibliographical references

Laughton, Timothy

Exploring the life, myth, and art of the Maya; Timothy Laughton. Rosen Pub. 2012 144 p. (Civilizations of the world)

Grades: 7 8 9 10 11 **972.81**

1. Mayan art 2. Mayas -- History 3. Mayas -- Folklore 4. Mayas -- Social life and customs 5. Maya art

ISBN 9781448848324

LC 2011009790

This book on the Maya "offers an informative overview of . . . political and social history as well as its art, architecture, and mythology, all bolstered with plenty of . . . details and narratives. . . . [T]he illustrations include artworks, documents, and handsome maps as well as photos of significant sites and artifacts. . . . In "Maya," [Timothy] Laughton shows how archaeology and scholarship have shifted accepted views on this culture over the last century." (Booklist) The book "put[s] the art . . . in context, explaining how a society's religious beliefs, legends, and cultural traditions manifest themselves through images and iconography. The . . . layout features full-color photographs of architecture, sculpture, and painting on every page, accompanied by informative captions." (School Libr J)

Includes bibliographical references (p. 138) and index

Sheehan, Sean

Guatemala; Sean Sheehan, Magdalene Koh, and Alex Tessman. 3rd edition Cavendish Square 2018 128p il maps (Cultures of the world) library $47.07

Grades: 5 6 7 8 **972.81**

1. Guatemala

ISBN 9781502636249 library

LC 2017048025

Introduces the geography, history, religion, government, economy, and culture of Guatemala

"A good-quality full-color photograph, reproduction, or map appears on most pages. This [is a] solid volume." SLJ

Includes glossary and bibliographical references

Vanvoorst, Jennifer Fretland

The **ancient** Maya; by Jenny Fretland VanVoorst. Compass Point Books 2013 48 p. col. ill. (library) $28.65; (paperback) $8.95

Grades: 4 5 6 7 8 **972.81**

1. Mayas 2. Civilization, Ancient 3. Mexico -- Civilization 4. Central America -- Civilization 5. Mayas -- Social life and customs

ISBN 0756545641; 0756545846; 9780756545642; 9780756545840

LC 2012001966

This children's nonfiction book, by Jennifer Fretland VanVoorst, profiles the Mayan civilization as part of the "Exploring the Ancient World" series. "The civilization of the . . . Maya reached its peak about 2,000 years ago. The Maya held a complex religious view of the world. In an effort to maintain order by pleasing their many gods, they built imposing stone temples, developed a written language, and played a ball game with life-or-death consequences." (Publisher's note)

Includes bibliographical references (p. 46) and index.

972.82 Belize

Jermyn, Leslie

Belize; [by] Leslie Jermyn and Yong Jui Lin. 2nd ed.; Marshall Cavendish Benchmark 2012 144p il map (Cultures of the world) lib bdg $42.79

Grades: 5 6 7 8 **972.82**

1. Belize

ISBN 978-1-60870-452-1; 1-60870-452-1

LC 2010035966

Provides information on the geography, history, wildlife, governmental structure, economy, cultural diversity, peoples, religion, and culture of Belize.

"The concise writing offers enough material for report writers without overwhelming them. Numerous full-color and black-and-white photos of interest, a clean layout, and use of pastels to highlight headings and sidebars contribute to the attractiveness of . . . [this presentation]." SLJ

Includes glossary and bibliographical references

972.83 Honduras

McGaffey, Leta

Honduras; Lauren Wehner, Leta McGaffey and Michael Spilling. 3rd edition Cavendish Square 2019 144p il map (Cultures of the world) library $47.07

Grades: 5 6 7 8 **972.83**

1. Honduras

ISBN 9781502641021 library

First published 1999

"Provides comprehensive information on the geography, history, wildlife, governmental structure, economy, cultural diversity, peoples, religion, and culture of Honduras." Publisher's note

Includes glossary and bibliographical references

Shields, Charles J., 1951-

Honduras; Charles J. Shields. Mason Crest Publishers 2016 64 p. illustrations, map (library binding) $22.95

Grades: 5 6 7 8 **972.83**

1. Honduras 2. Geography

ISBN 9781422232903

"Once a center for the Mayan civilization, Honduras was colonized by Spain during the 16th century. Three centuries of colonial rule produced a civilization that blended Spanish and native customs and culture. Since gaining independence from Spain in 1821, Honduras has experienced a great deal of political instability." (Publisher's note)

972.84 El Salvador

Foley, Erin

El Salvador; Erin Foley, Rafiz Hapipi and Debbie Nevins. 3rd edition Cavendish Square 2016 144p il map (Cultures of the world) library $47.07

Grades: 5 6 7 8 **972.84**

1. El Salvador

ISBN 9781502608086 library

LC 2015034167

First published 1994

This describes the geography, history, government, economy, environment, people, lifestyle, religion, language, arts, leisure, festivals, and food of El Salvador

Includes glossary and bibliographical references

972.85 Nicaragua

Kallen, Stuart A.

The **aftermath** of the Sandinista Revolution. Twenty-First Century Books 2009 160p il (Aftermath of history) lib bdg $38.60

Grades: 8 9 10 11 12 **972.85**

1. Nicaragua -- Politics and government

ISBN 978-0-8225-9091-0; 0-8225-9091-3

LC 2008-25356

"The 1979 overthrow of the corrupt Nicaraguan government by the Marxist Sandinistas brought change to one of the poorest countries in the Americas and instilled in the U.S. new fears about the spread of Communism. . . . Kallen offers a good overview of one of the Latin American theaters of the Cold War." SLJ

Includes glossary and bibliographical references

Kott, Jennifer

Nicaragua; Jennifer Kott, Kristi Streiffert, Debbie Nevins. 3rd edition Cavendish Square 2016 144p il map (Cultures of the world) library $47.07

Grades: 5 6 7 8 **972.85**

1. Nicaragua

ISBN 9781502608062 library

LC 2015031033

First published 1994

An illustrated overview of the geography, economy, history, government, politics, and culture of Nicaragua

Includes glossary and bibliographical references

972.86 Costa Rica

Foley, Erin

Costa Rica; Erin Foley, Barbara Cooke, and Tatiana Ryckman. 3rd edition Cavendish Square 2018 144p il map (Cultures of the world) library 47.07

Grades: 5 6 7 8 **972.86**

1. Costa Rica

ISBN 9781502626103 library

LC 2016057411

First published 1997

This offers "information on the geography, history, wildlife, governmental structure, economy, cultural diversity, peoples, religion, and culture of Costa Rica." Publisher's note

Includes glossary and bibliographical references

Yomtov, Nel

★ **Costa** Rica; by Nel Yomtov. Scholastic Library Pub 2014 144 p. illustrations, color maps (library binding) $40

Grades: 5 6 7 8 **972.86**

1. Costa Rica 2. Costa Rica

ISBN 0531220141; 9780531220146

LC 2013022563

This book, by Nel Yomtov, focuses on Costa Rica. The "country's culture, history, and geography are explored in detail, allowing readers a chance to see how people live in faraway nations. . . . Sidebars highlight especially interesting people, places, and events . . . [and] easy recipes give readers the opportunity to experience foreign cuisine first-hand." (Publisher's note)

Includes bibliographical references and index

972.87 Panama

Hassig, Susan M.

★ **Panama**; writers, Susan Hassig, Lynette Quek, Debbie Nevins. 3rd edition Cavendish Square 2017 144p il map (Cultures of the world) $42.79; library $47.07

Grades: 5 6 7 8 **972.87**

1. Panama

ISBN ; 9781502622150 library

LC 2016036878

First published 1996

This provides "information on the geography, history, wildlife, governmental structure, economy, cultural diversity, peoples, religion, and culture of Panama." Publisher's note

Includes glossary and bibliographical references

Vander Hook, Sue

Building the Panama Canal. ABDO Pub. Co. 2010 112p il map (Essential events) lib bdg $32.79

Grades: 6 7 8 9 **972.87**

1. Panama Canal

ISBN 978-1-60453-942-4; 1-60453-942-9

LC 2009-30373

Readers will learn about the historic quests to find a pathway between the Atlantic and Pacific oceans, France's pursuit in building a canal, and the United States' first trials in building the Panama Canal.

"The writing is accessible and is richer than a lot of history writing, allowing the reader to become engaged in the text as a story, and the layout provides enough white space to allow lower level readers to feel confident." Libr Media Connect

Includes glossary and bibliographical references

972.9 West Indies (Antilles) and Bermuda

Kras, Sara Louise

Antigua and Barbuda; [by] Sara Louise Kras. Marshall Cavendish Benchmark 2008 144p il map (Cultures of the world) lib bdg $42.79

Grades: 5 6 7 8 **972.9**

1. Antigua and Barbuda

ISBN 978-0-7614-2570-0

LC 2006031537

This describes the geography, history, government, economy, environment, people, and culture of Antigua and Barbuda

Includes glossary and bibliographical references

972.91 Cuba

Sheehan, Sean

Cuba; Sean Sheehan. 3rd edition Cavendish Square 2016 144p il map (Cultures of the world) library $47.07

Grades: 5 6 7 8 **972.91**

1. Cuba

ISBN 9781502608000 library

LC 2015031032

First published 1994

This describes the geography, history, government, economy, population, lifestyle, religion, language, arts, leisure, festivals, and food of Cuba

Includes glossary and bibliographical references

Smith-Llera, Danielle

Che Guevara's face; How a Cuban Photographer's Image Became a Cultural Icon. by Danielle Smith-Llera. Compass Point Books, a capstone imprint 2017 64 p. illustrations (library binding) $34.65; (ebook) $34.65

Grades: 6 7 8 9 **972.91**

1. Guerrillas -- Latin America -- Biography 2. Cuba -- History -- 1959-1990

ISBN 9780756554408; 9780756554422; 9780756554446

LC 2016008219

This book, by Danielle Smith-Llera, describes how "Alberto Korda transformed a simple photo into a world famous portrait of a larger than life revolutionary. Korda's 1960 photo of Che Guevara's defiant face has traveled the world in many forms. It shows up wherever people struggle for freedom and human rights. And in the 21st century, the controversial photo continues to inspire, entertain, and even infuriate." (Publisher's note)

"The books in the series are handsomely designed and visually do their subjects justice. The fact-filled texts are inviting but never talk down to the audience. Mark this series as a great way to discuss history, photography, and the way both shape public perception." Booklist

Includes bibliographical references and index

Stein, R. Conrad

Cuban Missile Crisis; in the shadow of nuclear war. Enslow Publishers 2009 128p il map (America's living history) lib bdg $31.93

Grades: 5 6 7 8 **972.91**

1. Cuban Missile Crisis, 1962 2. Soviet Union -- Foreign relations -- United States 3. United States -- Foreign relations -- Soviet Union

ISBN 978-0-7660-2905-7 lib bdg; 0-7660-2905-0 lib bdg

LC 2008-4703

"This engaging account provides a thorough discussion of events. . . . Archival photographs, maps, sidebars, and many primary sources effectively depict key figures, political posturing, and the nation's anxiety." Horn Book Guide

Includes glossary and bibliographical references

Tracy, Kathleen

We visit Cuba. Mitchell Lane Publishers 2010 63p il (Your land and my land) lib bdg $33.95

Grades: 4 5 6 7 **972.91**

1. Cuba

ISBN 978-1-58415-890-5 lib bdg; 1-58415-890-5 lib bdg

LC 2010006558

"With an inviting format that includes bright color photos on every spread, this title . . . offers an appealing overview of Cuba's history, geography, culture and lifestyle, politics, economics, and more. . . . A good starting point for research as well as for personal interest." Booklist

Includes glossary and bibliographical references

Wright, David K.

Cuba; by David K. Wright. Children's Press 2009 144p il map (Enchantment of the world, second series) lib bdg $38

Grades: 5 6 7 8 **972.91**

1. Cuba

ISBN 978-0-531-12096-5 lib bdg; 0-531-12096-1 lib bdg

LC 2008008423

This describes the geography, history, culture, people, and government of Cuba

Includes bibliographical references

972.92 Jamaica and Cayman Islands

Green, Jen

★ **Jamaica**; [by] Jen Green; David J. Howard and Joel Frater, consultants. National Geographic 2008 64p il map (Countries of the world) lib bdg $27.90

Grades: 4 5 6 7 **972.92**

1. Jamaica

ISBN 978-1-4263-0300-5 lib bdg; 1-4263-0300-9 lib bdg

This describes the geography, nature, history, people and culture, government, and economy of Jamaica.

Includes glossary and bibligraphical references

Sheehan, Sean

Jamaica; Sean Sheehan, Debbie Nevins, Angela Black. Cavendish Square Publishing 2015 144 p. (library binding) $47.07

Grades: 5 6 7 8 **972.92**

1. Jamaica 2. Geography

ISBN 1502600773; 9781502600776

LC 2014037926

Introduces the geography, history, religion, government, economy, and culture of Jamaica

Includes bibliographical references and index

972.93 Dominican Republic

Foley, Erin

Dominican Republic; Erin Foley, Leslie Jermyn, and Debbie Nevins. 3rd edition Cavendish Square 2016 144p color illustrations (Cultures of the world) library $47.07

Grades: 5 6 7 8 **972.93**

1. Dominican Republic

ISBN 9781502608048 library

LC 2015032397

First published 1995

"The material is well organized in easily readable sections, accurately illustrated with well-placed, full-color photographs on every page." SLJ

Rogers Seavey, Lura

Dominican Republic; by Lura Rogers and Barbara Radcliffe Rogers. Children's Press 2009 144p il map (Enchantment of the world, second series) lib bdg $37

Grades: 5 6 7 8 **972.93**

1. Dominican Republic

ISBN 978-0-531-12097-2 lib bdg; 0-531-12097-X lib bdg

LC 2008000087

Describes the geography, history, culture, religion, and people of the Caribbean island nation of the Dominican Republic

Includes bibliographical references

972.94 Haiti

Aronin, Miriam

Earthquake in Haiti. Bearport Pub. 2011 32p il map (Code red) lib bdg $25.27

Grades: 4 5 6 7 **972.94**

1. Earthquakes 2. Haiti

ISBN 978-1-936088-66-9; 1-936088-66-5

LC 2010011126

Describes the devastating earthquake that occurred in Haiti on January 12, 2010.

"The text is written from the points of view of some of the people involved, including primary source direct quotes. Some of the pictures are necessarily graphic, which adds to the authenticity. . . . This title will be used for browsing as well as for reports." Libr Media Connect

Includes glossary and bibliographical references

NgCheong-Lum, Roseline, 1962-

Haiti; Roseline NgCheong-Lum, Leslie Jermyn and Debbie Nevins. 3rd edition Cavendish Square 2016 144p il map (Cultures of the world) library $47.07

Grades: 5 6 7 8 **972.94**

1. Haiti

ISBN 9781502608024 library

LC 2015035323

First published 1995

Describes the geography, history, government, economy, culture, peoples, and religion of Haiti

Includes glossary and bibliographical references

Sonneborn, Liz

Haiti; by Liz Sonneborn. Children's Press, an imprint of Scholastic Inc. 2019 144 p. (library binding : alk. paper) $40

Grades: 5 6 7 8 **972.94**

1. Haiti -- History 2. Haiti Earthquake, Haiti, 2010 3. Haiti -- Description and travel 4. Haiti

ISBN 0531130487; 9780531130483

LC 2018016142

In this book in the Enchantment of the World series, by Liz Sonneborn, "the tiny Caribbean nation of Haiti was devastated by a massive earthquake. Since then, it has struggled to make a complete recovery, suffering setbacks such as a 2016 hurricane that left thousands dead. . . . Readers will learn all about Haitian history and culture. They will also find out how the country is governed, what drives its economy, and more." (Publisher's note)

Includes bibliographical references and index

972.95 Puerto Rico

Schwabacher, Martin

Puerto Rico; by Martin Schwabacher and Steve Otfinoski. 2nd ed.; Marshall Cavendish Benchmark 2010 144p il map (Celebrate the states) $42.79

Grades: 5 6 7 8 **972.95**

1. Puerto Rico

ISBN 978-0-7614-4734-4; 0-7614-4734-2

LC 2009007066

First published 2001

This offers information on the geography, history, wildlife, governmental structure, economy, cultural diversity, peoples, religion, and landmarks of Puerto Rico.

Includes bibliographical references

Stille, Darlene R., 1942-

Puerto Rico; by Darlene R. Stille. Revised edition Children's Press, an Imprint of Scholastic Inc. 2014 144 p. illustrations, maps (library binding : alk. paper) $40

Grades: 4 5 6 7 **972.95**

1. Puerto Rico 2. United States -- History

ISBN 0531282902; 9780531282908

LC 2013044805

"Not quite an independent nation, yet not quite a state, either, Puerto Rico enjoys a unique relationship with the United States. Readers will learn how Puerto Rico was first settled and how it came to be a part of the United States. They will also learn about its rich cultural heritage and how its people live today. In addition, detailed descriptions of the island's topography and wildlife give readers an up-close tour of Puerto Rico's wilderness." (Publisher's note)

Includes bibliographical references(pages 133-137)and index

Worth, Richard

Puerto Rico in American history. Enslow Publishers 2008 128p il map (From many cultures, one history) lib bdg $23.95

Grades: 6 7 8 9 10 **972.95**

1. Puerto Rico

ISBN 978-0-7660-2836-4; 0-7660-2836-4

LC 2006-37087

This is a "book about the ties between Puerto Rico and the U.S. . . . Worth's overview will help to acclimate readers new to the island's history. . . . Writing in short, plain sentences, the author touches upon the commonwealth's ongoing struggle with poverty, migration, and language and the current conflicts about statehood and independence. The book's clean design is inviting, with lots of color-screened boxes, full-color photos, archival artwork, and maps." Booklist

Includes glossary and bibliographical references

972.96 Bahama Islands

Hintz, Martin

The **Bahamas**; by Martin Hintz. Children's Press 2013 144 p. col. ill., col. maps (Enchantment of the world. Second series) (library) $40

Grades: 5 6 7 8 **972.96**

1. Bahamas 2. Bahamas -- Description and travel
ISBN 0531275418; 9780531275412
LC 2012000513

This book, by Martin Hintz, is part of the "Enchantment of the World" series. In it the author provides information and photographs showcasing the people, places and events surrounding the Caribbean island chain of the Bahamas. Contents include photographs of Bahaman cities and landscapes, statistics describing the islands' features, and traditional Bahaman recipes.

Includes bibliographical references and index

972.98 Windward and other southern islands

Orr, Tamra

Saint Lucia; [by] Tamra Orr. 2nd ed.; Marshall Cavendish Benchmark 2008 144p il map (Cultures of the world) lib bdg $42.79

Grades: 5 6 7 8 **972.98**

1. Saint Lucia
ISBN 978-0-7614-2569-4
First published 1997

This describes the geography, history, government, economy, environment, people, and culture of Saint Lucia

Includes glossary and bibliographical references

Pang, Guek-Cheng, 1950-

Grenada; 2nd ed.; Marshall Cavendish Benchmark 2011 144p il map (Cultures of the world) lib bdg $42.79

Grades: 5 6 7 8 **972.98**

1. Grenada
ISBN 978-1-6087-0216-9; 1-6087-0216-2
LC 2010019807

First published 2001

Provides information on the geography, history, wildlife, governmental structure, economy, cultural diversity, peoples, religion, and culture of Grenada.

Includes glossary and bibliographical references

973 United States

Addasi, Maha

A **kid's** guide to Arab American history; more than 50 activities. by Yvonne Wakim Dennis and Maha Addasi. 1st ed. Chicago Review Press 2013 xx, 204 p.p ill. (paperback) $16.95

Grades: 4 5 6 7 **973**

1. Arab Americans -- History 2. Arab Americans -- Social life and customs 3. Arab Americans -- History -- Study and teaching -- Activity programs
ISBN 1613740174; 9781613740170
LC 2012035758

This book by Yvonne Wakim Dennis and Maha Addasi "provides a contemporary as well as historical look at the people and experiences that have shaped Arab American culture. Each chapter focuses on a different group of Arab Americans including those of Lebanese, Syrian, Palestinian, Jordanian, Egyptian, Iraqi, and Yemeni descent and features more than 50 fun activities that highlight their distinct arts, games, clothing, and food." (Publisher's note)

Africa to America; from the Middle Passage through the 1930s. edited by Jeff Wallenfeldt, Manager, Geography and History. Britannica Educational Pub. 2010 268 p. (library binding) $45.00

Grades: 6 7 8 **973**

1. Slavery 2. Human rights 3. Harlem Renaissance 4. African Americans -- History 5. African Americans -- Biography 6. African Americans -- Intellectual life
ISBN 1615301267; 9781615301263
LC 2009054299

Editor Jeff Wallenfeldt offers a history of African Americans. "At the expense of basic human rights, dignity, and decency, Africans were torn from their native countries and first brought to the United State as slaves. Yet even in the face of injustice and hardship they have endured since then, African Americans have been bolstered by the sacrifices, leadership, and determination of courageous individuals . . . [Wallenfeldt captures] the history of African Americans . . . from origins on the African continent to the end of the Harlem Renaissance." (Barnes & Noble)

Includes bibliographical references and index

Armstrong, Jennifer

★ The **American** story; 100 true tales from American history. illustrated by Roger Roth. Alfred A. Knopf 2006 358p il map $34.95; lib bdg $39.99

Grades: 4 5 6 7 **973**

1. United States -- History
ISBN 0-375-81256-3; 0-375-91256-8 lib bdg
LC 2005-34822

"This large, fully illustrated compendium features 100 stories, familiar and lesser known, drawn from America's past and arranged in chronological order. . . . Thanks to writing that is consistently good and sometimes excellent, the tales will certainly hold readers' attention, and brightening nearly every page are lively drawings enhanced by watercolor washes." Booklist

Includes bibliographical references

Bausum, Ann

★ **Our** country's presidents; a complete encyclopedia of the U.S. presidency. written by Ann Bausum. National Geographic Partners 2017 224 p. illustrations (some color) (hardcover) $24.95; (reinforced library edition) $28.90; (hardcover) $24.95; (reinforced library edition) $28.90

Grades: 4 5 6 7 **973**

1. Presidents -- United States -- Biography 2. United States -- Politics and government -- History 3. United States -- History 4. Presidents -- Biography -- Encyclopedias 5. Presidents -- United States -- History
ISBN 142632944X; 9781426326851; 9781426326868; 9781426329449; 1426326858; 1426326866
LC 2017286164

This encyclopedia, by Ann Bausum, "presents the 43 individuals who have led the U.S., plus America's newest commander-in-chief, in this up-to-date, authoritative, and lavishly illustrated family, school, and library reference. It features comprehensive profiles of the 43 former presidents along with timelines and descriptions of crucial events during their terms. Information about the 2016 president-elect is also included." (Publisher's note)

"A clear, colorful design; a variety of sidebars; and rich historical material make this a solid, go-to resource for information on the presidents."--School Library Journal

Includes bibliographical references and index

Benson, Sonia

★ **UXL** encyclopedia of U.S. history; [by] Sonia Benson, Daniel E. Brannen Jr., and Rebecca Valentine; Lawrence W. Baker and Sarah Hermsen, project editors. U.X.L 2008 8v il map set$485

Grades: 6 7 8 9 10 11 12 **973**

1. Reference books 2. United States -- History -- Encyclopedias

ISBN 978-1-4144-3043-0

LC 2008022347

"This set offers more than 700 entries addressing various cultural, political, economic, and social events, trends, movements, and developments that shaped American history. . . . Black-and-white illustrations, reproductions, archival photographs, maps, sidebars, and inserts accompany the text. . . . Most school and public library collections that serve students in grades 6 through 12 will want to have this recommended resource." Booklist

Includes bibliographical references

Bockenhauer, Mark H.

Our fifty states; by Mark H. Bockenhauer and Stephen F. Cunha; foreword by former president Jimmy Carter. National Geographic Society 2004 239p il map $25.95; lib bdg $45.90

Grades: 4 5 6 7 **973**

1. Reference books 2. United States

ISBN 0-7922-6402-9; 0-7922-6992-6 lib bdg

LC 2004-1190

This "book is organized by regions: the Northeast, Southeast, Midwest, Southwest, and West, with a map of each region and a short history. Four pages are devoted to each state and include basic facts and a map. The full-color photographs are outstanding. Reproductions of archival illustrations depict four important events from each state's history. The final sections offer a paragraph about each of the territories and a page of facts and figures about the United States." SLJ

Includes bibliographical references

Bolden, Tonya

How to build a museum; Tonya Bolden. Viking Childrens Books 2016 64 p. color illustrations (hardcover) $17.99; (ebook) $53.97

Grades: 5 6 7 8 **973**

1. Historical museums -- Washington (D.C.) 2. African Americans -- Museums -- Washington (D.C.) 3. National Museum of African American History and Culture (U.S.) 4. Historical museums -- Washington (D.C.) -- Design and construction

ISBN 9780451476371; 9780698403826

LC 2016011612

In this book, author Tonya Bolden explains that "the campaign to set up a museum honoring black citizens is nearly 100 years old. . . . Assembling its incredibly far-reaching collections is a modern story that involves all kinds of people, from educators and activists, to politicians, architects, curators, construction workers, and ordinary Americans who donated cherished belongings to be included in NMAAHC's thematically-organized exhibits." (Publisher's note)

"A well-organized and informative book introducing this significant new historical center." Booklist

Buckley, Susan

★ **Journeys** for freedom; a new look at America's story. [by] Susan Buckley and Elspeth Leacock; illustrations by Rodica Prato. Houghton Mifflin Co. 2006 48p il map $17

Grades: 4 5 6 7 **973**

1. United States -- History

ISBN 978-0-618-22323-7; 0-618-22323-1

LC 2004000974

This "history focuses on 20 individuals' quest for freedom across U.S. history. Some . . . will be familiar, but most will not. The stories, both varied and fascinating, often go beyond the personal. . . . Running along the bottom of each double-page spread is a pictorial map keyed to the text. . . . The authors make excellent use of primary sources. . . . As powerful as it is useful." Booklist

Kids make history; a new look at America's story. [by] Susan Buckley and Elspeth Leacock; Illustrations by Randy Jones. Houghton Mifflin 2006 48p il $17

Grades: 4 5 6 7 **973**

1. United States -- History

ISBN 978-0-618-22329-9; 0-618-22329-0

LC 2005036309

"This book introduces 20 children in extraordinary times, starting in 1607 with Pocahontas and ending in 2001 with 9/11 as experienced by high school senior Jukay Hsu. Laura Ingalls Wilder; John Rankin, Jr.; and Susie Baker, a young slave celebrating her independence in 1863, are among those included. The text and the highly detailed watercolor illustrations are married with numbers in small red boxes keyed to both elements for clarification. . . . A good browsing choice for children interested in American history." SLJ

Croy, Elden

United States. National Geographic 2010 64p il map (Countries of the world) lib bdg $27.90

Grades: 4 5 6 7 **973**

1. United States

ISBN 978-1-4263-0632-7 lib bdg; 1-4263-0632-6 lib bdg

This describes the geography, nature, history, people and culture, government and economy of the United States.

"The information is substantial but not overwhelming. The [text is] clear, and the discussion points are well chosen. . . . [The text is] complemented with stunning photographs." SLJ

David Rubel

★ **Scholastic** encyclopedia of the presidents and their times; David Rubel ; with a foreword by James M. McPherson. Updated edition Scholastic 2013 248 p. illustrations, maps $24.99

Grades: 5 6 7 8 **973**

1. United States -- History 2. Presidents -- United States

ISBN 9780545499859

This encyclopedia "documents the tenure of each of the American presidents. It also includes information about the headlines, people, and fads that defined America during each presidency." (Publisher's note)

Eggers, Dave, 1970-

★ **Her** right foot; written by Dave Eggers ; art by Shawn Harris. Chronicle Books 2017 104 p. color illustrations (hardcover) $19.99

Grades: 3 4 5 6 7 8 **973**

1. Statue of Liberty (New York, N.Y.) 2. Art criticism 3. Monuments -- United States 4. Historic sites -- United States 5. Emigration and immigration in art 6. Statue of Liberty National Monument (N.Y. and N.J.) -- Appreciation

ISBN 9781452162812; 9781452162935

LC 2016057953

NCTE Orbis Pictus Honor Book, 2018

ALA Notable Children's Book, 2018.

In this book, "Dave Eggers and Shawn Harris investigate a seemingly small trait of America's most emblematic statue. What they find is about more than history, more than art. What they find in the Statue of Liberty's right foot is the powerful message of acceptance that is essential of an entire country's creation." (Publisher's note)

"This beautifully designed and conversational yet sophisticated book about the history of the iconic statue is also filled with humor and interesting trivia." SLJ

Includes bibliographical references.

Exploring American history: from colonial times to 1877; editors, Tom Lansford, Thomas E. Woods, Jr. Marshall Cavendish Reference 2008 11v il map set$359.95

Grades: 6 7 8 9 **973**

1. Reference books 2. United States -- History -- 1775-1783, Revolution -- Encyclopedias 3. United States -- History -- 1600-1775, Colonial period -- Encyclopedias

ISBN 978-0-7614-7746-4; 0-7614-7746-2

LC 2007060896

"This set contains 219 signed articles on the nearly 250 years of American life. . . . The articles have a uniform format and are color coded to indicate broad subject areas—culture, government, laws, people, or places. . . . The articles present a solid overview of current research as well as a rich array of information. . . . The set is thoughtfully arranged, easy to use, and accessible for a wide range of students." Booklist

Includes bibliographical references

Hoose, Phillip M.

★ **We** were there, too! young people in U.S. history. [by] Phillip Hoose. Farrar, Straus & Giroux 2001 264p il $28

Grades: 5 6 7 8 **973**

1. Youth 2. Children 3. United States -- History

ISBN 0-374-38252-2

LC 99-89052

National Book Award Finalist: Young People's Literature (2001)

Biographies of dozens of young people who made a mark in American history, including explorers, planters, spies, cowpunchers, sweatshop workers, and civil rights workers

"A treasure chest of history come to life, this is an inspired collection. . . . Because the book is packed with historical documents, evocatively illustrated . . . and full of eyewitness quotations, it should prove valuable to young historians and researchers." SLJ

Includes bibliographical references

Johnston, Robert D.

★ The **making** of America; the history of the United States from 1492 to the present. Robert D. Johnston ; with a foreword by Douglas Brinkley. Revised ed. National Geographic 2010 240 p. ill. (chiefly col.), col. maps (hardcover) $29.95; (library) $38.90

Grades: 5 6 7 8 **973**

1. United States -- History

ISBN 9781426306631; 1426306636; 9781426306655; 1426306652

LC 2011401219

First published 2002

Includes bibliographical references (p. 226-234) and index.

"This energetically written and profusely illustrated history remains one of the top-drawer single-volume accounts of the founding and growth of the U.S. for middle grade students. The previous edition ended with 9/11; here, into the same page count, Johnston fits Hurricane Katrina, the wars in Iraq and Afghanistan, Barack Obama's election, and other major events." Booklist

Krasner, Barbara

Jewish immigrants; in their shoes. Barbara Krasner. Childs World 2019 32 p. (library reinforced : alk. paper) $28.50

Grades: 4 5 6 7 **973**

1. Jews -- United States 2. Jews -- Social conditions 3. United States -- Immigration and emigration

ISBN 9781503827998

LC 2018944221

This book in the Immigrant Experiences series, by Barbara Krasner, "offers readers a compelling look into the lives, challenges, and successes of Jewish immigrants. Additional features include a Fast Facts page, a timeline, informative photo captions, critical-thinking questions, primary source quotes and accompanying source notes, a phonetic glossary, additional resources for further study, and an index." (Publisher's note)

"Jewish Immigrants gives three historical views of Jews fleeing Brazil in 1654, Bavaria in 1842, and Russia in 1891 because of religious intolerance." (Kirkus)

Lake, Matthew

Weird U.S. a freaky field trip through the 50 states. [by] Matt Lake and Randy Fairbanks. Sterling Pub. 2011 128p il $14.95

Grades: 6 7 8 9 **973**

1. Curiosities and wonders 2. United States -- History 3. Folklore -- United States 4. United States -- Guidebooks

ISBN 978-1-4027-5462-3; 1-4027-5462-0

LC 2010027019

"Imagine the kitsch of a field trip to the world's largest ball of twine and multiple it by about a thousand and you'll begin to appreciate the imaginative and colorful romp through the United States' weirdest roadside attractions. Each site . . . is described in detail with full-color photographs. . . . Sure to be a hit with students that pore over the Guiness Book of World Records and Ripley's Believe It or Not!." Booklist

Miller, Marilyn

Words that built a nation; voices of democracy that have shaped America's history. Marilyn Miller and Ellen Scordato. St. Martin's Press 2018 208 p. $18.99

Grades: 5 6 7 8 **973**

1. United States -- History 2. United States -- Politics and government -- History

ISBN 1635651883; 9781635651881

This book, by Marilyn Miller and Ellen Scordato, presents "United States' most important historical essays, speeches, and documents into one accessible collection for kids. . . . From the Constitution and the Gettysburg Address to the 2015 Supreme Court ruling on same-sex marriage, the updated collection preserves the documents of the first edition and introduces the landmark statements that are impacting our nation today." (Publisher's note)

Panchyk, Richard

★ The **keys** to American history; understanding our most important historic documents. Chicago Review Press 2009 241p il map $24.95; pa $19.95

Grades: 7 8 9 10 11 12 **973**

1. United States -- History -- Sources

ISBN 978-1-55652-716-6; 1-55652-716-0; 978-1-55652-804-0 pa; 1-55652-804-3 pa

"This impressive collection is a valuable resource for gaining a greater appreciation for and understanding of our nation's dynamic history." SLJ

Includes bibliographical references

Pinkney, Andrea Davis, 1963-

Hand in hand; ten Black men who changed America. by Andrea Davis Pinkney ; paintings by Brian Pinkney. Disney/Jump at the Sun 2012 243 p. $19.99

Grades: 4 5 6 7 **973**

1. Biography 2. United States -- History 3. African Americans -- Biography 4. African American men -- Biography 5. Social change -- United States -- History

ISBN 1423142578; 9781423142577

LC 2011051348

Coretta Scott King Author Book Award (2013)

Boston Globe-Horn Book Honor: Nonfiction (2013).

In this book, Andrea Davis Pinkney profiles "ten influential black men--including Frederick Douglass, W.E.B. Du Bois, Thurgood Marshall, Jackie Robinson, and Martin Luther King Jr." She presents "descriptions of each man's influence on civil rights, culture, art, or politics. . . . An examination of Barack Obama's life and presidential election carries readers into the present day, placing the achievements of those who came before him into perspective." (Publishers Weekly)

Includes bibliographical references and index.

Tarrant-Reid, Linda

Discovering Black America; from the age of exploration to the twenty-first century. Linda Tarrant-Reid. Abrams Books for Young Readers 2012 xi, 244 p.p ill. (some col.), col. maps (hardcover) $29.95

Grades: 5 6 7 8 9 10 **973**

1. Blacks -- History 2. United States -- History -- 1775-1783, Revolution 3. United States -- History -- 1861-1865, Civil War 4. African Americans -- History 5. African Americans -- Biography

ISBN 0810970988; 9780810970984

LC 2011052201

Author Linda Tarrant-Reid presents a book on "African-American history, beginning with accounts of black explorers before the settlement of North America . . . [The book] includes major historical events . . . [such as] the American Revolution . . . [and] the period following the Civil War and Reconstruction . . . The societal changes brought on by World War II and the civil rights movement [are presented] . . . [E]xchanges between Malcolm X and Martin Luther King . . . [and] the election of President Barack Obama and the challenges facing the first black president" are also described. (Kirkus)

Includes bibliographical references and index.

973.03 United States – Encyclopedias

★ **Junior** worldmark encyclopedia of the states; Drew Johnson and Cynthia Johnson, editors ; Kathleen J. Edgar, project editor. 6th edition UXL 2013 4v illustrations (set : alk. paper) $354

Grades: 5 6 7 8 9 10 **973.03**

1. Reference books 2. United States -- Encyclopedias

ISBN 9781414498645; 9781414498591

LC 2012050641

First published 1996

This encyclopedia, edited by Drew Johnson, Cynthia Johnson, and Kathleen J. Edgar, explores the states of the United States as well as its dependencies and broader territories. "Entries cover the geography, history, politics, economy and other facts about each state or area profiled. Alphabetically arranged entries feature consistent subheadings for each state so students can quickly find comparative information." (Publisher's note)

King, David C.

★ **Children's** encyclopedia of American history; by David C. King. Revised and updated DK Publishing, in association with the Smithsonian Institution 2014 320 p. illustrations (some color) (hardcover) $29.99

Grades: 4 5 6 **973.03**

1. United States -- History 2. United States -- History -- Encyclopedias, Juvenile

ISBN 1465428437; 9781465428431

LC 2015302320

"This revised edition takes a look at U.S. history, from the exploration of the New World in the 1400s to the present day. . . . New content includes the Boston bombing of 2013, the War on Terror, the death of Osama Bin Laden, and a focus on globalization and sports. Natural disasters, such as Hurricane Katrina, and additional environmental concerns are detailed. Presidential coverage is expanded to incorporate the election of Barack Obama, while other new topics include the growth of the Tea Party Movement and controversy regarding guns." SLJ

American history

973.09 Presidents--United States

Bausum, Ann

★ **Our** Country's Presidents; All You Need to Know About the Presidents, From George Washington to Barack Obama. by Ann Bausum; foreword by President Barack Obama. 4th ed. National Geographic 2013 223 p. ill., maps (hardcover) $24.95

Grades: 5 6 7 8 **973.09**

1. Presidents -- United States -- Encyclopedias 2. Presidents -- United States

ISBN 1426310897; 9781426310898

LC 2009290293

First published 2001

This book by Ann Bausum looks at U.S. presidents. The text shares "facts about the men's personal lives, humorous incidents, political backgrounds, records, struggles, battles, successes, what they are most famous for, events that occurred during their administrations, and memorable quotes." (School Library Journal)

"This exceedingly attractive offering is . . . chock-full of information, presented . . . in such an inviting manner that children will enjoy paging through, even if there's no school report looming. . . . Full of interesting tidbits as well as solid information." Booklist

Includes bibliographical references

Krull, Kathleen

A **kid's** guide to America's first ladies; Kathleen Krull ; illustrated by Anna Divito. HarperCollins 2017 256 p. illustrations (hardcover) $16.99; (ebook) $6.99

Grades: 4 5 6 7 8 **973.09**

1. Women -- United States -- Biography 2. Presidents' spouses -- United States -- Biography

ISBN 9780062381064; 9780062381071; 9780062381088

LC 2016940933

This book in the Kids' Guide to American History series, by Kathleen Krull, illustrated by Anna Divito, "introduces readers to the women of the White House. . . . Find out what our country's First Ladies thought, did, and advocated for as they moved into the White House. Why did the Patriots love Martha Washington? What causes did Eleanor Roosevelt support and lead? What did Jacqueline Kennedy do to establish her legacy long after she left the White House?" (Publisher's note)

"Gathering momentum as it rolls along chronologically through American history, this lively book profiles the women who have enjoyed, to varying degrees, the unique privileges and challenges of being first lady." Booklist

Includes bibliographical references (pages 239-240) and index.

★ The **presidency** A to Z; Gerhard Peters, editor ; John T. Woolley, editor. 5th ed. CQ Press 2012 xix, 715 p.p ill. (hardcover) $125

Grades: 8 9 10 11 12 Adult **973.09**

1. Presidents -- United States -- Biography 2. Presidents -- United States -- Encyclopedias

ISBN 1608719081; 9781608719082

LC 2012023290

This book, by Gerhard Peters, presents a dictionary of the U.S. presidency. The book is a "tool for understanding the presidency, both historically and today and for appraising how it and the executive branch have responded to the challenges facing the nation. It provides readers with quick information and in-depth background on the presidency through a comprehensive encyclopedia of over 300 easy-to-read entries." (Publisher's note)

"At over 700 pages and also available online, this core title. . . provid[es] a comprehensive encyclopedic treatment of the U.S. presidency. . . . A recommended purchase for all libraries and a required one for those with earlier editions, which it supplants." LJ

Includes bibliographical references (p. 684-690) and index.

Rhatigan, Joe

White House kids; the perks, pleasures, problems, and pratfalls of the Presidents' children. Joe Rhatigan ; with illustrations by Jay Shin. Charlesbridge Pub. 2012 96 p. ill. (chiefly col.) $14.95

Grades: 5 6 7 8 **973.09**

1. United States. White House Office 2. Presidents -- United States -- Family 3. Presidents -- United States -- Children 4. Children of presidents -- United States 5. Children of presidents -- United States -- Biography

ISBN 1936140802; 9781936140800

LC 2011045090

This book presents "an overview of the young occupants of the White House . . . [and] details the perks and downfalls of being a president's child. Information on pets, favorite games and activities . . . and education of presidential offspring is . . . presented. [Joe] Rhatigan explores the press's and the public's fascination with the children . . . as well as the scrutiny and negative press endured by Amy Carter and Chelsea Clinton." (School Library Journal)

"An inviting collection of insightful, interesting and often wacky and weird facts and stories about U.S. presidents and their families." Kirkus

Includes bibliographical references and index

973.2 United States--Colonial period, 1607-1775

Cappacio, George

The **Countryside** in colonial America; George Capaccio. Cavendish Square Publishing 2014 80 p. (library binding) $35.64

Grades: 6 7 8 **973.2**

1. United States -- History -- 1600-1775, Colonial period 2. United States -- History -- Colonial period, ca. 1600-1775 3. Indians of North America -- History -- Colonial period, ca. 1600-1775

ISBN 1627128859; 9781627128858

LC 2014006063

This book, by George Cappacio, part of the Life in colonial America series, "describes in rich detail the lives of Native Americans, African Americans, and white settlers, including children, women, and criminals. The introductory material that prefaces each title is of particular value, as it demonstrates that the colonists were part of a larger world picture." (Publisher's note)

"Thoroughly researched and expertly executed, this series describes in rich detail the lives of Native Americans, African Americans, and white settlers, including children, women, and criminals. The introductory material that prefaces each title is of particular value, as it demonstrates that the colonists were part of a larger world picture...Content in each title incorporates quotes from period letters and journals as well as a plethora of well-chosen, colorful illustrations. Strong, attractive titles for those looking for more coverage of Colonial America." SLJ

Gray, Edward G.

Colonial America; a history in documents. 2nd ed.; Oxford University Press 2011 211p il map (Pages from history) $39.95; pa $24.95

Grades: 7 8 9 10 **973.2**

1. United States -- History -- 1600-1775, Colonial period -- Sources

ISBN 978-0-19-976594-2; 978-0-19-976595-9 pa

LC 2010038458

First published 2003

This collection of primary sources examines "the lives of the colonists through their own words—in diaries, letters, sermons, newspaper columns, and poems." Publisher's note

Includes bibliographical references

Huey, Lois Miner

American archaeology uncovers the earliest English colonies. Marshall Cavendish Benchmark 2009 64p il map (American archaeology) lib bdg $31.36

Grades: 4 5 6 7 **973.2**

1. America -- Antiquities 2. America -- Exploration 3. Jamestown (Va.) -- History 4. Roanoke Island (N.C.) -- History 5. Great Britain -- Colonies -- America 6. Excavations (Archeology) -- United States

ISBN 978-0-7614-4264-6 lib bdg; 0-7614-4264-2 lib bdg

LC 2008050259

This describes how archeologists have learned about the history of early English colonists in America at Jamestown, Popham Colony, and Roanoke

"Huey enthusiastically brings . . . [this era] to life through artifacts and field research. . . . [The volume begins with an] introduction that defines 'historical archaeology' and explains its value in terms simple enough for lower-elementary readers to comprehend, yet detailed enough for older children to enjoy, an approach followed in the remaining chapters. . . . Huey's focus on American history, which is broken down into small, manageable chunks, is sure to entice budding historians." SLJ

Includes glossary and bibliographical references

Mandell, Daniel R.

King Philip's war; the conflict over New England. Chelsea House 2007 144p il map (Landmark events in Native American history) lib bdg $35

Grades: 7 8 9 10 **973.2**

1. Wampanoag Indians 2. King Philip's War, 1675-1676 3. New England -- History -- 1600-1775, Colonial period

ISBN 978-0-7910-9346-7; 0-7910-9346-8

LC 2006-102258

This account features "lively writing and direct quotes, and [is] enhanced by many color and black-and-white photos, drawings, and illustrations." SLJ

Includes bibliographical references

McNeese, Tim

Colonial America, 1543-1763. Chelsea House 2010 136p il map (Discovering U.S. history) $35

Grades: 5 6 7 8 **973.2**

1. United States -- History -- 1600-1775, Colonial period

ISBN 978-1-60413-349-3; 1-60413-349-X

LC 2008055170

This history of Colonial America "begins with a chapter on 'Rivals for North America' and ends with 'The Fight for the Ohio Country.' . . . [The] book has an excellent chronology; rich sidebars; and numerous well-captioned illustrations, maps, and photos that enhance the texts. [This book provides a] satisfying [introduction] to American history for students." SLJ

Includes glossary and bibliographical references

Nardo, Don

Daily life in colonial America. Lucent Books 2010 96p il (Lucent library of historical eras) $32.45

Grades: 6 7 8 9 **973.2**

1. United States -- History -- 1600-1775, Colonial period 2. United States -- Social life and customs -- 1600-1775, Colonial period

ISBN 978-1-4205-0264-0; 1-4205-0264-6

LC 2009045636

Presents an introduction to life in colonial America, discussing family and home life, occupations, education, recreation, medicine, and laws.

Includes bibliographical references

The **establishment** of the thirteen colonies. Lucent Books 2010 96p il (Lucent library of historical eras) lib bdg $32.45

Grades: 6 7 8 9 **973.2**

1. United States -- History -- 1600-1775, Colonial period

ISBN 978-1-4205-0267-1 lib bdg; 1-4205-0267-0 lib bdg

In this history of the establishment of the thirteen colonies in North America, "the detailed text is interspersed with sidebars of primary and secondary quotations and historical color illustrations that add both substance and visual interest. With its long paragraphs and dutiful citations, this is a fairy advanced take on the topic." Booklist

Includes bibliographical references

Government and social class in colonial America. Lucent Books 2010 96p il map (Lucent library of historical eras) lib bdg $32.45

Grades: 6 7 8 9 **973.2**

1. Social classes 2. United States -- History -- 1600-1775, Colonial period

ISBN 978-1-4205-0265-7; 1-4205-0265-4

LC 2009043640

"The detailed text is interspersed with sidebars of primary and secondary quotations and historical color illustrations that add both substance and visual interest. With its long paragraphs and dutiful citations, this is a fairly advanced take on the topic." Booklist

Includes bibliographical references

Pederson, Charles E.

The **French** & Indian War. ABDO Pub. Co. 2010 112p il map (Essential events) lib bdg $32.79

Grades: 6 7 8 9 **973.2**

1. United States -- History -- 1755-1763, French and Indian War

ISBN 978-1-60453-943-1; 1-60453-943-7

LC 2009-30425

This title examines an important historic event, the French & Indian War. Readers will learn the background of French and British settlement on Native American land and how conflict developed as a result.

"The writing is accessible and is richer than a lot of history writing, allowing the reader to become engaged in the text as a story, and the layout provides enough white space to allow lower level readers to feel confident." Libr Media Connect

Includes glossary and bibliographical references

Philbrick, Nathaniel

The **Mayflower** and the Pilgrims' New World. G.P. Putnam's Sons 2008 338p il map $19.99

Grades: 7 8 9 10 11 12 **973.2**

1. Farmers 2. Historians 3. Native Americans 4. Pilgrims (New England colonists) 5. Colonists 6. Carpenters 7. Army officers 8. Pilgrim fathers 9. Massachusetts -- History -- 1600-1775, Colonial period

ISBN 978-0-399-24795-8; 0-399-24795-5

LC 2007-30669

An adaptation of Mayflower: a story of community, courage, and war, published 2006 by Viking for adults

"This volume highlights both the Pilgrims' determination to find and settle a home where they could worship freely and the perilous journey that it took to make that happen. In accessible prose, the author shatters the American myth of the landing at Plymouth Rock and the first Thanksgiving. . . . The various maps, reproductions of historical documents, photographs of significant locations, and illustrations all come together with the text to help separate fact from legend and create a realistic, readable portrayal of the Pilgrims and their first 50 years in America." SLJ

Includes bibliographical references

Saari, Peggy

Colonial America: primary sources; Julie Carnagie, editor. U.X.L 1999 297p il (Colonial America reference library) $67

Grades: 8 9 10 11 12 **973.2**

1. United States -- History -- 1600-1775, Colonial period

ISBN 0-7876-3766-1

LC 99-34460

Presents the historical events and social issues of colonial America through twenty-four primary documents, including diary entries, poems, and personal narratives

"Each chapter adds helpful material before and after the excerpt to explain its importance. Illustrations and sidebars are used in this volume also, and difficult words are defined." Booklist

Stefoff, Rebecca

★ **American** voices from Colonial life. Benchmark Bks. 2003 119p (American voices from--) lib bdg $32.79

Grades: 6 7 8 9 **973.2**

1. United States -- History -- 1600-1775, Colonial period
ISBN 0-7614-1205-0

LC 2002-3223

Presents the history of the British colonies in North America, beginning with the Jamestown settlement, through excerpts from letters, pamphlets, journal entries, and other documents of the time

Includes glossary and bibliographical references

973.3 United States--Periods of Revolution and Confederation, 1775-1789

Allen, Thomas B.

Remember Valley Forge; patriots, Tories, and Redcoats tell their stories. [by] Thomas B. Allen. National Geographic 2007 61p il map $17.95; lib bdg $27.90

Grades: 5 6 7 8 **973.3**

1. Generals 2. Presidents 3. Valley Forge (Pa.) -- History 4. United States -- History -- 1775-1783, Revolution
ISBN 978-1-4263-0149-0; 978-1-4263-0150-6 lib bdg

LC 2007024821

The author "recounts here the activities of Washington and his soldiers during the winter of 1777-8, spent regrouping at Valley Forge, Pennsylvania. . . . Allen's strength is his attention to military details and strategies, but his account is clearly presented and succinctly written as well. . . . Illustrated with reproductions of period artwork, drawings, maps, and a few contemporary photographs." Booklist

American Revolution: primary sources; [compiled by] Linda Schmittroth; Lawrence W. Baker and Stacy A. McConnell, editors. U.X.L 2000 xxxiii, 264p il lib bdg $60

Grades: 8 9 10 11 12 **973.3**

1. United States -- History -- 1775-1783, Revolution
ISBN 0-7876-3790-4

LC 99-46940

This volume "presents 32 excerpted documents, beginning with the 1765 Stamp Act and ending with Washington's farewell address to the Continental Army in 1783. Each entry has helpful material to give the context for the document. The adjoining margins contain definitions of terms that may be unfamiliar. . . . [This volume] is attractive and easy to use." Booklist

Includes bibliographical references

The **American** revolutionaries: a history in their own words, 1750-1800; edited by Milton Meltzer. Crowell 1987 210p il hardcover o.p. pa $8.99

Grades: 6 7 8 9 **973.3**

1. United States -- History -- 1775-1783, Revolution 2. United States -- History -- 1755-1763, French and Indian War
ISBN 0-06-446145-9 pa

LC 86-47846

"Meltzer has assembled a collage of eyewitness accounts, speech and diary excerpts, letters, and other documents for a chronological account of the half century that included the American Revolution. . . . The voices of women who accompanied the troops and of blacks who fought with the army are both represented." Bull Cent Child Books

Aronson, Marc

★ The **real** revolution; the global story of American independence. Clarion Books 2005 238p il map lib bdg $21

Grades: 7 8 9 10 **973.3**

1. United States -- History -- 1775-1783, Revolution
ISBN 0-618-18179-2

LC 2005-1088

In this "volume, Aronson investigates the origins of the American Revolution and discovers some startling global connections. The colonies' quest for independence is tied to such seemingly unrelated incidents as Robert Clive's triumph over the French in India in 1750 and John Wilkes's accusations against the king in his newspaper, The North Briton, in the 1760s. . . . This outstanding work is highly compelling reading and belongs in every library." SLJ

Includes bibliographical references

Blair, Margaret Whitman

Liberty or death; the surprising story of runaway slaves who sided with the British during the American Revolution. National Geographic 2010 64p il map lib bdg $27.90

Grades: 5 6 7 8 **973.3**

1. African American soldiers 2. Slavery -- United States 3. United States -- History -- 1775-1783, Revolution
ISBN 978-1-4263-0590-0 lib bdg; 1-4263-0590-7 lib bdg

LC 2009-26853

"Blair provides a well-researched account of slaves in Virginia who, beginning in 1775, fled to the British. . . . Though told in a matter-of-fact tone, the story is often heart-wrenching. . . . Colorful reproductions of period paintings, prints, and documents illustrate the clearly written text. . . . A fine and singular addition to American history collections." Booklist

Includes bibliographical references

Casey, Susan

Women heroes of the American Revolution; 20 stories of espionage, sabotage, defiance, and rescue. Susan Casey. Chicago Review Press 2015 240 p. illustrations (Women of action) (hardback) $19.95

Grades: 7 8 9 10 **973.3**

1. Women -- United States -- History 2. United States -- History -- 1775-1783, Revolution 3. Women -- United States -- History -- 18th century 4. United States -- History -- Revolution, 1775-1783 -- Women 5. United States -- History -- Revolution, 1775-1783 -- Participation, Female
ISBN 1613745834; 9781613745830

LC 2014032760

Author Susan Casey's book on the American Revolution looks at how "women took action in many ways: as spies, soldiers, nurses, water carriers, fundraisers, writers, couriers, and more. Women Heroes of the American Revolution brings a fresh new perspective to their stories resulting from interviews with historians and with descendants of participants of the Revolution and features ample excerpts from primary source documents. Also included are contextualizing sidebars, images, source notes, and a bibliography." (Publisher's note)

"Extensive source notes are appended. The many black-and-white illustrations include reproductions of archival portraits, prints and drawings, letters, and newspaper advertisements. A fine, useful resource for students of American history." Booklist

Includes bibliographical references and index

Driver, Stephanie Schwartz

Understanding the Declaration of Independence. Rosen Pub. 2010 128p il (Words that changed the world) lib bdg $31.95

Grades: 7 8 9 10 **973.3**

1. Architects 2. Presidents 3. Vice-presidents 4. Essayists 5. United States -- Declaration of Independence 6. United States -- Politics and government -- 1775-1783, Revolution

ISBN 978-1-4488-1669-9; 1-4488-1669-6

LC 2010-10371

This surveys The Declaration of Independence, considering the "document's 'Context and Creator,' 'Immediate Impact,' 'Legacy,' and 'Aftermath.' . . . Exploring the colonial crisis leading to America's formal separation from the British Empire, . . . [the] author provides a balance of deep context, expressive writing, and pertinent information. Scattered throughout the [text] are a good number of well-captioned, color illustrations and photos. [This book is a] valuable [resource] for teachers and students doing research projects across the curriculum." SLJ

Includes glossary and bibliographical references

Fleming, Thomas J.

★ **Everybody's** revolution; a new look at the people who won America's freedom. [by] Thomas Fleming. Scholastic Nonfiction 2006 96p il $19.99

Grades: 4 5 6 7 **973.3**

1. United States -- History -- 1775-1783, Revolution

ISBN 0-439-63404-0

LC 2005051814

A history of the American Revolution, focusing on the roles played by women, young people, and various ethnic groups.

"With an open layout and clean typeface, this clearly written title is attractive and inviting. . . . Fleming's sound offering is an excellent starting point for discussions of the implications of the Revolutionary War in terms of freedom for all people." SLJ

Includes glossary and bibliographical references

Freedman, Russell

★ **Washington** at Valley Forge. Holiday House 2008 100p il map $24.95

Grades: 5 6 7 8 9 **973.3**

1. Generals 2. Presidents 3. Pennsylvania -- History 4. Valley Forge (Pa.) -- History 5. United States -- History -- 1775-1783, Revolution

ISBN 978-0-8234-2069-8; 0-8234-2069-8

LC 2007-52467

NCTE Orbis Pictus Award honor book (2009)

"With his usual clarity of focus and keen eye for telling quotations, Freedman documents how Washington struggled to maintain morale despite hunger, near-nakedness, and freezing conditions. . . . Throughout, high-quality reproductions depict Washington among the men, and with the numerous other influential people who played crucial roles." Booklist

Kostyal, K. M.

1776; a new look at revolutionary Williamsburg. by K.M. Kostyal with the Colonial Williamsburg Foundation; photographs by Lori Epstein. National Geographic 2009 48p il $17.95; lib bdg $27.90

Grades: 4 5 6 **973.3**

1. United States -- History -- 1775-1783, Revolution

ISBN 978-1-4263-0517-7; 1-4263-0517-6; 978-1-4263-0518-4 lib bdg; 1-4263-0518-4 lib bdg

LC 2009-18002

"Clear, distinctive photos add visual appeal to this short history of the American Revolution, written from the point of view of those living in Williamsburg, Virginia's capital in 1776. Kostyal blends political and social history into a readable account of the period, bolstered by informative sidebars, a chronology, and a closing note about the restoration of colonial Williamsburg. . . . The increasing inclusion of nonwhite colonists in the illustrations as well as the text is a welcome trend." Booklist

Includes bibliographical references

Murphy, Jim

★ The **crossing**; how George Washington saved the American Revolution. Scholastic Press 2010 96p il map $21.99

Grades: 5 6 7 8 **973.3**

1. Generals 2. Presidents 3. Trenton (N.J.), Battle of, 1776 4. United States -- History -- 1775-1783, Revolution

ISBN 978-0-439-69186-4; 0-439-69186-9

LC 2009-11561

Murphy "again digs into the well of history, this time emerging with a well-researched, absorbing account of the early battles of the Revolutionary War with General George Washington at their center. Enhanced by numerous sepia maps of troop movements, prints, paintings, and portraits of prominent figures, the blow-by-blow narrative begins with the shots fired at Lexington and Concord in 1775 and continues until the tide-turning battles at Trenton and Princeton in early 1777." Publ Wkly

Includes bibliographical references

A **young** patriot; the American Revolution as experienced by one boy. Clarion Bks. 1996 101p il maps $16; pa $7.95

Grades: 5 6 7 8 **973.3**

1. Soldiers 2. United States -- History -- 1775-1783, Revolution

ISBN 0-395-60523-7; 0-395-90019-0 pa

LC 93-38789

"Using Joseph Plumb Martin's first person account of his participation in the Revolutionary War as primary source material, Murphy intertwines this story of one teenager's life as a soldier with broader information about the Revolution, to put Martin's story in context. The handsome, informative, and fascinating look at American history is illustrated with many period reproductions." Horn Book Guide

Includes bibliographical references

Nash, Gary B.

Landmarks of the American Revolution. Oxford University Press 2003 158p il map (American landmarks) lib bdg $30

Grades: 6 7 8 9 **973.3**

1. Historic sites 2. United States -- History -- 1775-1783, Revolution

ISBN 0-19-512849-4

LC 2002-14152

"Written with the idea that historic sites can be considered primary sources, this book skillfully demonstrates the 'power of places.' Traditional documents, such as excerpts from letters, broadsides, and maps, as well as well-placed quotes, are incorporated into the text. The places include churches, halls, homes, and battlefields, covering the many facets of the Revolution: political, religious, and actual battles. . . . This well-organized book includes clear, full-color photographs or reproductions and a small inset map for each site." SLJ

Includes bibliographical references

Otfinoski, Steven

The **new** republic: 1760-1840s. Marshall Cavendish Benchmark 2009 79p il map (Hispanic America) lib bdg $23.95

Grades: 4 5 6 7 **973.3**

1. Latinos (U.S.) 2. Mexico -- History 3. Florida -- History 4. Hispanic Americans 5. Spaniards -- United States 6. United States -- History -- 1775-1783, Revolution

ISBN 978-0-7614-2938-8 lib bdg; 0-7614-2938-7 lib bdg

LC 2007-45958

"Provides comprehensive information on the history of the Spanish exploring the United States." Publisher's note

Includes glossary and bibliographical references

Sanders, Nancy I.

America's black founders; revolutionary heroes & early leaders with 21 activities. Chicago Review Press 2010 150p il $16.95

Grades: 4 5 6 7 **973.3**

1. African Americans -- History 2. United States -- History -- 1775-1783, Revolution

ISBN 978-1-55652-811-8; 1-55652-811-6

"This activity-based guide reveals how African Americans played crucial roles in helping the United States gain its independence. Sanders includes well-known figures such as Phillis Wheatley, Crispus Attucks, and James Forten in her narrative, but also enriches traditional accounts of the period by explaining the contributions of lesser-known patriots. . . . Most of the activities help make this period real to young people. . . . Sanders makes excellent use of primary sources." SLJ

973.4 United States--Constitutional period, 1789-1809

Lanier, Shannon

Jefferson's children; the story of one American family. by Shannon Lanier and Jane Feldman; with photographs by Jane Feldman; and an introduction by Lucian K. Truscott IV. Random House 2000 144p il hardcover o.p. pa $16.95

Grades: 7 8 9 10 **973.4**

1. Slaves 2. Architects 3. Presidents 4. Vice-presidents 5. Racially mixed people 6. Essayists 7. Mistresses 8. African Americans -- Biography 9. United States -- Race relations

ISBN 0-375-80597-4; 0-375-82168-6 pa

LC 00-44551

This is an "anthology of personal meditations by a variety of Jefferson's living descendants. Edited by Shannon Lanier, a descendant through Sally's son Madison Hemings's line, the portraits that emerge are as generous and jumbled as America itself. The statements range from hostile to conciliatory to indifferent to eloquent." NY Times Book Rev

Includes bibliographical references

McNeese, Tim

Early national America, 1790-1850. Chelsea House 2010 136p il map (Discovering U.S. history) $35

Grades: 5 6 7 8 **973.4**

1. United States -- History -- 1783-1865

ISBN 978-1-60413-351-6; 1-60413-351-1

LC 2009003679

McNeese "discusses the people, politics, economic conditions, and foreign affairs of [the U.S. from 1790 to 1850], objectively explaining how the attitudes, perceptions, and expectations of the American people and their leaders shaped the development of the country. . . . Color period art and photos, maps, and cutaway drawings supplement the [text]." SLJ

Includes glossary and bibliographical references

Stefoff, Rebecca

★ **American** voices from the new republic, 1783-1830. Benchmark Books 2004 xxiii, 116p (American voices from--) lib bdg $34.21

Grades: 6 7 8 9 10 **973.4**

1. United States -- History -- 1783-1865

ISBN 0-7614-1695-1

LC 2004-11391

Describes, through excerpts from diaries, speeches, newspaper articles, and other documents of the time, United States history from 1783 to 1830. Includes review questions.

973.5 United States--1809-1845

Bowes, John P.

Black Hawk and the War of 1832; removal in the north. [by] John P. Bowes. Chelsea House 2007 131p bibl il map (Landmark events in Native American history) lib bdg $35

Grades: 6 7 8 9 **973.5**

1. Sauk Indians 2. Black Hawk War, 1832 3. Indian chiefs 4. Native Americans -- Biography

ISBN 978-0-7910-9342-9 lib bdg; 0-7910-9342-5 lib bdg

LC 2007004927

This "provides a clear overview of early American expansion in the Northwest Territory, from the 1780s through the 1930s, detailing government actions and policies of Indian Removal and how they specifically affected the Sauks and Mesquakies, now known as the Sac and Fox tribes. . . . The battles that ensued (both intertribal and against the U.S. forces) are described, as are the policies created during this period. . . . Attractive color paintings, maps, and photographs appear throughout." SLJ

Includes bibliographical references

Macleod, D. Peter

Four Wars of 1812; One War, Four Perspectives. by D. Peter MacLeod. Pgw 2012 95 p. ill. (paperback) $19.95

Grades: 6 7 8 **973.5**

1. War of 1812

ISBN 1771000503; 9781771000505

This book on the war of 1812 "examine[s] the viewpoints, goals, and outcomes for its four major participants: Britain, Canada, the United States, and Native American nations. . . , Its four chapters, each focused on one combatant, are made up of spreads that feature either a color photo of period artifacts and weapons or reproductions of artwork . . . on one side and a[n] . . . essay that describes how it illustrates a . . . perspective about the war on the other." (School Library Journal)

Stewart, Mark

The **Indian** Removal Act; forced relocation. Compass Point Books 2007 96p il map (Snapshots in history) $23.95

Grades: 6 7 8 9 **973.5**

1. Cherokee Indians 2. Native Americans -- Relocation

ISBN 978-0-7565-2452-4; 0-7565-2452-0

LC 2006027084

Profiles the "Trail of Tears," the forced removal of five Southeastern Native American tribes to land west of the Mississippi River during the winter of 1838 and 1839.

"The book organizes a good deal of historical information into a cogent presentation. . . . Illustrations, many in color, include photos and maps as well as period engravings, portraits, and documents." Booklist

Includes glossary and bibliographical references

973.6 United States--1845-1861

Carey, Charles W.

The **Mexican** War; Mr. Polk's war. [by] Charles W. Carey, Jr. Enslow Pubs. 2002 128p il (American war series) lib bdg $26.60

Grades: 6 7 8 9 **973.6**

1. Mexican War, 1846-1848

ISBN 0-7660-1853-9

LC 2001-817

This "account of the 1846-1848 war addresses the origins, strategies, battles, and people involved in the conflict. The ramifications of the war for each country are discussed in separate chapters. . . . [This volume has] numerous black-and-white illustrations, a time line, solid footnotes, and chapters that begin with relevant quotes." SLJ

Includes bibliographical references

DiConsiglio, John

The **Mexican** -American War; by John DiConsiglio. Heinemann Library 2012 80 p. ill. (some col.), col. maps (library) $36.50; (paperback) $10.99

Grades: 6 7 8 9 **973.6**

1. Mexican War, 1846-1848

ISBN 1432959980; 9781432959982; 9781432960070

LC 2011016817

This book on the Mexican-American War by John DiConsiglio is part of the "Living Through" series. It "provid[e]s . . . an overview of the causes, events, and leading personalities that shaped this 19th century conflict" as well as "snapshots of the daily life of soldiers and civilians. . . . Issues linked to the legitimacy of the American invasion of Mexico, the dictatorial leadership of Mexican commanders, and the shifting course of military fortunes all are presented." (Children's Literature)

Includes bibliographical references (p. 76-77) and index.

Stein, R. Conrad

The **Mexican** -American War. Morgan Reynolds Pub. 2011 144p il map (The story of Mexico) $28.95

Grades: 6 7 8 9 **973.6**

1. Mexican War, 1846-1848

ISBN 978-1-5993-5160-5; 1-5993-5160-9

LC 2010041378

"Stein organizes and clearly presents a great deal of information. . . . The . . . format features a chronological text supplemented with useful sidebars and brightened with color illustrations, including many photos, artifacts, and period artworks. . . . [The book] explains the war's causes, its progress, and it aftermath in both countries." Booklist

Includes bibliographical references

973.7 Administration of Abraham Lincoln, 1861-1865

Adler, David A., 1947-

Harriet Tubman and the Underground Railroad; by David A. Adler. Holiday House 2013 140 p. ill. (hardcover) $18.95

Grades: 5 6 7 8 **973.7**

1. Underground Railroad 2. African American women -- Biography 3. Slaves -- United States -- Biography

ISBN 0823423654; 9780823423651

LC 2012006582

This book, by David A. Adler, gives a biography of the ex-slave Harriet Tubman. "She escaped from her owners in Maryland on the Underground Railroad in 1849 and then fearlessly returned . . . to help guide . . . others to freedom as the most famous conductor of the Underground Railroad. . . . During and after the war, she helped hundreds of freed slaves begin new lives, and she later founded a home for elderly former slaves and became active in the women's suffrage movement." (Publisher's note)

Includes bibliographical references

Allen, Roger MacBride

★ **Mr.** Lincoln's High-Tech War; how the North used the telegraph, railroads, surveillance balloons, ironclads, high-powered weapons, and more to win the Civil War. [by] Thomas B. Allen & Roger MacBride Allen. National Geographic Society 2009 144p il $18.95; lib bdg $25.90

Grades: 5 6 7 8 9 10 **973.7**

1. Lawyers 2. Presidents 3. State legislators 4. Members of Congress 5. Technology -- History 6. United States -- Army 7. United States -- History -- 1861-1865, Civil War 8. Technology -- United States -- History

ISBN 1-4263-0379-3; 1-4263-0380-7 lib bdg; 978-1-4263-0379-1; 978-1-4263-0380-7 lib bdg

LC 2008-24546

This book contends that "President Lincoln's appreciation for the power of technology played a critical role in the North's Civil War victory over the less developed South, and discusses the specific technologies used by the North in the war." (Publisher's note) Bibliography. Index. "Grades nine to twelve." (Publisher's note)

"Well researched and clearly written, the book discusses the course of the Civil War in terms of new technology, from the ironclad and the submarine to the rapid-fire, repeating rifle and the use of railroads to carry troops and supplies. . . . The many illustrations include captioned black-and-white reproductions of period prints, paintings, and photos as well as clearly labeled drawings. . . . [Readers] will gain a fascinating perspective on why the war progressed as it did and how it was ultimately won." Booklist

Includes bibliographical references

Anderson, Maxine

Great Civil War Projects; You Can Build Yourself. by Maxine Anderson. Sesquicentennial Edition Nomad Press 2012 120 p. illustrations, map $21.95

Grades: 7 8 9 10 **973.7**

1. Handicraft for children 2. United States -- History -- 1861-1865, Civil War 3. Handicraft 4. Inventions

ISBN 9781936749461 ; 1936749467

This book, by Maxine Anderson, "explores the Civil War era through hands-on building projects and activities using common household and craft store items. Detailed step-by-step instructions, diagrams, and templates for creating 25 Civil War projects, combined with historical background, facts and anecdotes, and biographies and trivia, give kids a hands-on way to experience the fascinating history of one of the most important eras in American history." (Publisher's note)

Includes bibliographical references and index

Armstrong, Jennifer

Photo by Brady; a picture of the Civil War. Atheneum Books For Young Readers 2005 160p il $18.95

Grades: 6 7 8 9 10 **973.7**

1. Photographers 2. Photography -- History 3. United States -- History -- 1861-1865, Civil War

ISBN 0-689-85785-3

LC 2004-8967

"Armstrong chronicles the Civil War from Lincoln's election to his death with both a storylike narrative of events and a photo-essay. . . . This book is also a look at early photographic techniques and offers a description of [Mathew] Brady's rare collection. . . . When readers remember that the pictures are more than 100 years old, they should recognize their exquisiteness, grandeur, and genius." SLJ

Includes bibliographical references

Beller, Susan Provost

Billy Yank and Johnny Reb; soldiering in the Civil War. Twenty-First Century Books 2008 112p il map (Soldiers on the battlefront) lib bdg $33.26

Grades: 5 6 7 8 **973.7**

1. Soldiers -- United States 2. United States -- History -- 1861-1865, Civil War

ISBN 978-0-8225-6803-2 lib bdg; 0-8225-6803-9 lib bdg

LC 2006010240

First published 2000

Describes military life for the average soldier in the Civil War, including camp life, diseases, and conditions for the wounded and prisoners of war. Includes excerpts from first-person accounts, letters, and diaries

The author "presents a good deal of solid information in an interesting manner. . . . Good black-and-white reproductions, mainly of photographs from the 1860s, appear throughout the book." Booklist [review of 2000 ed]

Includes bibliographical references

Benoit, Peter

The **surrender** at Appomattox; by Peter Benoit. Children's Press 2012 64 p. chiefly col. ill., col. map (library) $30.00; (paperback) $8.95

Grades: 4 5 6 **973.7**

1. Appomattox Campaign, 1865 2. United States -- History -- 1861-1865, Civil War -- Peace

ISBN 0531250415; 9780531250419; 9780531265666

LC 2011011967

This book by Peter Benoit, part of the "Cornerstones of Freedom" series, describes the events leading up to the end of the U.S. Civil War. It "sketches the events of the Battle of the Wilderness and the capture of Richmond as well as the meeting between [Ulysses S.] Grant and [Robert E.] Lee on April 9, 1865." (School Library Journal)

Includes bibliographical references (p. 61) and index.

Bobrick, Benson

The **Battle** of Nashville; General George H. Thomas & the most decisive battle of the Civil War. Alfred A. Knopf 2010 132p il map $19.99; lib bdg $22.99

Grades: 7 8 9 10 **973.7**

1. Nashville (Tenn.), Battle of, 1864 2. United States -- History -- 1861-1865, Civil War

ISBN 978-0-375-84887-2; 0-375-84887-8; 978-0-375-94887-9 lib bdg; 0-375-94887-2 lib bdg

"Background, strategies, and key individuals involved in the 1864 battle of Nashville come to life in this engaging piece of history. Starting on the eve of the fighting, the narrative then shifts back to examine the complex series of events leading to that moment, outlining the causes of the Civil War, key developments, and major figures. . . . Battle scenes are vivid, capturing the chaos and emotion involved, and military strategies, such as the innovative use of cavalry, are explained clearly. Plentiful illustrations from the period, including many portraits and several dramatic two-page paintings, help bring the period to life." SLJ

Includes bibliographical references

Bolden, Tonya

★ **Emancipation** Proclamation; Lincoln and the dawn of liberty. Tonya Bolden. Abrams Books for Young Readers 2012 128 p. (alk. paper) $24.95

Grades: 6 7 8 9 **973.7**

1. Slaves -- Emancipation 2. Emancipation Proclamation 3. United States -- History -- 1861-1865, Civil War 4. Slaves -- Emancipation -- United States 5. United States -- Politics and government -- 1861-1865 6. United States. President (1861-1865 : Lincoln). Emancipation Proclamation

ISBN 1419703900; 9781419703904

LC 2012000845

This book offers a "depiction of the issues and tensions surrounding abolition and the development of [Abraham] Lincoln's responses to them as the United States plunged into the Civil War. . . . The author tracks rising tides of both rhetoric and violence, as well as the evolution of President Abraham Lincoln's determined efforts to forge a policy that would serve military, political and moral necessities alike." (Kirkus Reviews)

Includes bibliographical references and index

Burgan, Michael

North over South; final victory in the Civil War. Compass Point Books 2011 64p il map (The Civil War) lib bdg $33.32; pa $6.95

Grades: 5 6 7 8 **973.7**

1. United States -- History -- 1861-1865, Civil War

ISBN 978-0-7565-4369-3 lib bdg; 0-7565-4369-X lib bdg; 978-0-7565-4413-3 pa; 0-7565-4413-0 pa

LC 2010001018

Recounts the end of the Civil War with insight into the key victories at Gettysburg and Vicksburg.

The layout is "clean and attractive, with a large font and reproductions of period illustrations and photos. . . . This . . . will help students understand the era's most important issues and events. A quality choice for reports." SLJ

Includes glossary and bibliographical references

Carlisle, Rodney P.

Civil War and Reconstruction. Facts on File 2008 452p il map (Eyewitness history) $75

Grades: 7 8 9 10 **973.7**

1. Reconstruction (1865-1876) 2. United States -- History -- 1861-1865, Civil War -- Sources

ISBN 978-0-8160-6347-5

LC 2006-35425

First published 1991 under the authorship of Joe H. Kirchberger

"This illustrated chronology of the Civil War contains over 100 black-and-white photographs (mostly from the Library of Congress Prints and Photographs Division), 16 maps, and biographies of 50 key figures in the era. Each period-based chapter offers a narrative that delves into deeper issues of the causation of war; a chronicle of events, detailed to the week; and eyewitness testimony, including diaries, journals, correspondence, editorials, and news accounts." Choice

Includes bibliographical references

A **Civil** War scrapbook; I was there too! History Colorado. Fulcrum Pub. 2012 64 p. ill. (some col.), maps (paperback) $14.95

Grades: 4 5 6 7 8 **973.7**

1. United States -- History -- 1861-1865, Civil War

ISBN 1555916686; 9781555916688

LC 2011042043

This book is "a multicultural Civil War history for children. The book . . . feature[es] chronological information" and "focus[es] on the different types of people and their place in the war. This . . . book emphasizes the roles of the children, women, minorities, and even pets that became mascots in the war." Also included are "historical photographs, drawings, maps, games, and primary quotes from children." (Publisher's Note)

Includes bibliographical references (p. 62-63) and index.

★ The **Civil** War: a visual history. DK Pub. 2011 360p il map $40

Grades: 5 6 7 8 **973.7**

1. United States -- History -- 1815-1861 2. United States -- History -- 1865-1898 3. United States -- History -- 1861-1865, Civil War -- Pictorial works

ISBN 978-0-7566-7185-3; 0-7566-7185-X

"A stunning, large-format pictorial history. The seven chapters are arranged chronologically, beginning with an overview of slavery in the United States, 1815 to 1860, and ending with a survey of the legacies of the conflict during the period 1865 to 1877. . . . Chapter introductions are followed by illustrated time lines and by short topical divisions that include biographies, maps, original documents or eyewitness accounts, illustrations, historical photographs, artifacts, and reproductions of paintings. Page layouts and the use of color are superb, and sidebars abound, adding to this extraordinary book." SLJ

DeFord, Deborah H.

African Americans during the Civil War; [by] Deborah H. DeFord. Chelsea House 2006 112p il map (Slavery in the Americas) $35

Grades: 6 7 8 9 **973.7**

1. African American soldiers 2. African Americans -- History 3. United States -- History -- 1861-1865, Civil War

ISBN 0-8160-6138-6

LC 2005021497

This "covers not only African Americans but also the forces that created the 'U.S. Colored Troops' and the spread of rights during and after the war. . . . Clearly written, accessible, and well organized, [this] volume is illustrated with black-and-white drawings, period photographs, and explanatory text boxes." SLJ

Includes bibliographical references

Gourley, Catherine

The **horrors** of Andersonville; life and death inside a Civil War prison. Twenty-First Century Books 2010 193p il lib bdg $38.60

Grades: 8 9 10 11 12 **973.7**

1. War criminals 2. Prisoners of war 3. Army officers 4. Andersonville Prison 5. United States -- History -- 1861-1865, Civil War -- Prisoners and prisons

ISBN 978-0-7613-4212-0; 0-7613-4212-5

LC 2008-46595

"This well-researched book describes the notorious Confederate prison camp known as Andersonville, where more than 45,000 Union soldiers lived in deplorable conditions and some 13,000 died, beginning in 1864. . . . Illustrated with many captioned photos and prints and enlivened with quotes from firsthand accounts, this book provides a balanced, informative introduction to Andersonville." Booklist

Includes bibliographical references

Gregory, Josh

Gettysburg; by Josh Gregory. Children's Press 2012 64 p. chiefly col. ill. (library) $30.00; (paperback) $8.95

Grades: 4 5 6 **973.7**

1. Gettysburg (Pa.), Battle of, 1863

ISBN 0531250342; 9780531250341; 9780531265598

LC 2011010751

In this book on the 1863 Battle of Gettysburg, "[Josh] Gregory takes his readers back to the precursor events that set the stage for this meeting engagement pitting General [Robert E.] Lee's Army of Northern Virginia against General [George] Meade's oft times defeated Union Army of the Potomac. In the end the efforts of Lee's seemingly indomitable veterans were not enough to overcome the forces of fate and tactics." (Children's Literature)

Includes bibliographical references (p. 61) and index.

Hernandez, Roger E.

The **Civil** War, 1840s-1890s. Marshall Cavendish Benchmark 2008 80p il map (Hispanic America) lib bdg $34.21

Grades: 4 5 6 7 **973.7**

1. Latinos (U.S.) 2. Hispanic Americans 3. United States -- Ethnic relations 4. United States -- History -- 1861-1865, Civil War

ISBN 978-0-7614-2939-5 lib bdg; 0-7614-2939-5 lib bdg

LC 2007049525

Discusses Hispanic participation during the Civil War

Includes glossary and bibliographical references

Hillstrom, Kevin

American Civil War: primary sources; [by] Kevin Hillstrom and Laurie Collier Hillstrom; Lawrence W. Baker, editor. U.X.L 2000 xxxi, 176, xxxiii-xliiip il $60

Grades: 8 9 10 11 12 **973.7**

1. United States -- History -- 1861-1865, Civil War -- Sources

ISBN 0-7876-3824-2

LC 99-46919

This volume "offers 14 full or excerpted speeches and written works. Each entry provides context, telling students what to keep in mind while reading the sources, as well as 'what happened next.' The speeches and writings come from Frederick Douglass, Abraham Lincoln, William Tecumseh Sherman, and Harriet Beecher Stowe, among others." Booklist

Howse, Jennifer

The **Civil** War. Weigl Publishers 2009 48p il map (African American history) lib bdg $29.05; pa $10.95

Grades: 6 7 8 9 **973.7**

1. African American soldiers 2. African Americans -- History 3. United States -- History -- 1861-1865, Civil War 4. United States

-- Army -- African American troops -- History
ISBN 978-1-59036-876-3 lib bdg; 1-59036-876-2 lib bdg; 978-1-59036-877-0 pa; 1-59036-877-0 pa
LC 2008-42478

"Howse creates a broad picture of the foundations leading to war, Afican Americans' role during the war, and finally the aftermath of the war, touching upon the civil rights movement. . . . This . . . is fabulous for students interested in or researching history. Glossy pictures, quick facts, technology links, and sidebars of information interrupt the text, giving readers interesting and important information without overwhelming them." Voice Youth Advocates

Includes glossary and bibliographical references

Huey, Lois Miner

American archaeology uncovers the Underground Railroad. Marshall Cavendish Benchmark 2009 64p il map (American archaeology) lib bdg $21.95
Grades: 4 5 6 7 **973.7**

1. Abolitionists 2. Underground railroad 3. Slavery -- United States 4. Excavations (Archeology) -- United States
ISBN 978-0-7614-4267-7 lib bdg; 0-7614-4267-7 lib bdg
LC 2009003168

This describes how archeologists have learned about the history of the Underground Railroad.

This is "both intriguing and engaging for young readers. . . . A welcomed addition to classroom and school libraries." Libr Media Connect

Includes glossary and bibliographical references

Jarrow, Gail

Lincoln's flying spies; Thaddeus Lowe and the Civil War Balloon Corp. Calkins Creek 2010 109p il $18.95
Grades: 7 8 9 10 **973.7**

1. Spies 2. Balloons 3. Inventors 4. United States -- History -- 1861-1865, Civil War
ISBN 978-1-59078-719-9; 1-59078-719-6

"This well-researched volume introduces American aeronaut and showman Thaddeus Lowe, who convinced President Lincoln that hydrogen-filled balloons, rising high above the countryside, could provide Union generals with useful information about the position, strength, and movements of Confederate troops and artillery. . . . The text offers a detailed account of [Lowe's] contribution to the Union war effort. Many period photos, prints, and drawings illustrate the book in black and white. . . . Jarrow provides a solid introduction to an intriguing aspect of Civil War history." Booklist

Includes bibliographical references

Johnson, Jennifer

Gettysburg; the bloodiest battle of the Civil War. Franklin Watts 2009 64p il map (24/7 goes to war) lib bdg $27; pa $7.95
Grades: 4 5 6 **973.7**

1. Gettysburg (Pa.), Battle of, 1863
ISBN 978-0-531-25528-5 lib bdg; 0-531-25528-X lib bdg; 978-0-531-25453-0 pa; 0-531-25453-4 pa
LC 2009016545

The author has done "a remarkable job of discussing and describing [the Civil War Battle of Gettysburg] in a limited number of pages. . . . The [book provides a] solid [introduction], followed by three chapters, one of which is based on the personal experiences of a named soldier, and the other two covering broader historical details and strategies of the battle. . . . Excellent maps and plenty of paintings and vintage photos enhance the [text]." SLJ

Includes bibliographical references

McNeese, Tim

Civil War battles. Chelsea House Publishers 2009 140p il (Civil War: a nation divided) lib bdg $35
Grades: 6 7 8 9 **973.7**

1. United States -- History -- 1861-1865, Civil War -- Campaigns
ISBN 978-1-60413-034-8 lib bdg; 1-60413-034-2 lib bdg
LC 2008-26561

This describes battles of the Civil War

Includes glossary and bibliographical references

The **Civil** War era, 1851-1865; consulting editor, Richard Jensen. Chelsea House 2010 144p il map (Discovering U.S. history) $35
Grades: 5 6 7 8 **973.7**

1. United States -- History -- 1861-1865, Civil War
ISBN 978-1-60413-352-3; 1-60413-352-X
LC 2009-3660

"The information is accurate and easy to understand. Pictures are well placed, and primary sources are included. . . . The maps are well done and there are sidebars with additional information. . . . [This would be good] to have on hand for reports as it is well laid out and easy to use." Libr Media Connect

Includes glossary and bibliographical references

Civil War leaders. Chelsea House Publishers 2009 144p il (Civil War: a nation divided) lib bdg $35
Grades: 6 7 8 9 **973.7**

1. United States -- History -- 1861-1865, Civil War -- Biography
ISBN 978-1-60413-033-1 lib bdg; 1-60413-033-4 lib bdg
LC 2009-655

This "features Abraham Lincoln, Jefferson Davis, Robert E. Lee, Ulysses S. Grant, Thomas 'Stonewall' Jackson, and Frederick Douglass. A short biography is followed by a brief description of the individual's part in the Civil War. . . . [The book includes] many black-and-white and color photographs and reproductions. . . . [This] well-organized [volume is a] first-rate [introduction] for students beginning their study of the era, or for those who want a basic review." SLJ

Includes glossary and bibliographical references

Mountjoy, Shane

Causes of the Civil War; the differences between the North and South. Chelsea House Publishers 2009 136p il (Civil War: a nation divided) lib bdg $35
Grades: 6 7 8 9 **973.7**

1. United States -- History -- 1861-1865, Civil War -- Causes
ISBN 978-1-60413-036-2 lib bdg; 1-60413-036-9 lib bdg
LC 2008-30242

Examines the sectional rivalries that surfaced in the early 19th century and intensified in the decades leading up to the war

This "is especially well written. Its eight chapters outline the economic, social, and political causes of the war. There are careful explanations of the importance of slavery to southern states, nullification and states' rights, the controversy of slavery expanding to western territories, and the impact of Lincoln's election to the presidency in 1860. [The book includes] many black-and-white and color photographs and reproductions." SLJ

Includes glossary and bibliographical references

Technology and the Civil War. Chelsea House Publishers 2009 136p il (Civil War: a nation divided) lib bdg $35

Grades: 6 7 8 9 **973.7**

1. Technology -- History 2. United States -- History -- 1861-1865, Civil War

ISBN 978-1-60413-037-9 lib bdg; 1-60413-037-7 lib bdg

LC 2008-26563

This "describes advancements sparked by the Civil War: the creation of new ships and weaponry, the use of the railroad to move troops and supplies, and of the telegraph to speed dispersal of information, and improvements in medicine and photography. The book also outlines how many of the inventions and innovations of the period laid the foundation for America's economic growth in the following decades. . . . Sidebars, quotes from primary sources, color and black-and-white illustrations, and historical photographs are scattered throughout [this] clearly written, well-organized [text]." SLJ

Includes glossary and bibliographical references

Murphy, Jim

The **boys'** war; Confederate and Union soldiers talk about the Civil War. Clarion Bks. 1990 110p il hardcover o.p. pa $8.95

Grades: 5 6 7 8 9 10 **973.7**

1. United States -- History -- 1861-1865, Civil War

ISBN 0-89919-893-7; 0-395-66412-8 pa

LC 89-23959

This book includes diary entries, personal letters, and archival photographs to describe the experiences of boys, sixteen years old or younger, who fought in the Civil War.

"An excellent selection of more than 45 sepia-toned contemporary photographs augment the text of this informative, moving work." SLJ

Includes bibliographical references

★ A **savage** thunder; Antietam and the bloody road to freedom. Margaret K. McElderry Books 2009 103p il map $17.99

Grades: 5 6 7 8 9 **973.7**

1. Generals 2. Governors 3. Antietam (Md.), Battle of, 1862 4. College presidents 5. Presidential candidates 6. United States -- History -- 1861-1865, Civil War

ISBN 978-0-689-87633-2; 0-689-87633-5

LC 2008-32738

"Murphy provides readers with a lucid and compelling narrative, drawn mainly from firsthand accounts. . . . Replete with excellent-quality archival photos, reproductions, and maps, this is an outstanding account of a battle." SLJ

Includes bibliographical references

Nardo, Don

Bull Run to Gettysburg; early battles of the Civil War. Compass Point Books 2011 64p il map (The Civil War) lib bdg $33.32; pa $6.95

Grades: 5 6 7 8 **973.7**

1. United States -- History -- 1861-1865, Civil War -- Campaigns

ISBN 978-0-7565-4368-6 lib bdg; 0-7565-4368-1 lib bdg; 978-0-7565-4411-9 pa; 0-7565-4411-4 pa

LC 2010001017

Reviews the early battles of the Civil War from the attack on Fort Sumter and the battle of the ironclads to Bull Run and Gettysburg.

The layout is "clean and attractive, with a large font and reproductions of period illustrations and photos. . . . This . . . will help students understand the era's most important issues and events. A quality choice for reports." SLJ

Includes glossary and bibliographical references

A **nation** divided; the long road to the Civil War. Compass Point Books 2010 64p il map (The Civil War) lib bdg $33.32

Grades: 5 6 7 8 **973.7**

1. Southern States -- History 2. United States -- History -- 1861-1865, Civil War -- Causes

ISBN 978-0-7565-4367-9 lib bdg; 0-7565-4367-3 lib bdg

LC 2010001016

Recounts events leading up to the Civil War and provides insight into the economic, cultural, and educational differences of the Northerners and Southerners.

The layout is "clean and attractive, with a large font and reproductions of period illustrations and photos. . . . This . . . will help students understand the era's most important issues and events. A quality choice for reports." SLJ

Includes glossary and bibliographical references

O'Connor, Jim

What was the Battle of Gettysburg? by Jim O'Connor ; illustrated by John Mantha. Grosset & Dunlap 2013 106 p. (hc) $15.99

Grades: 3 4 5 6 **973.7**

1. Gettysburg (Pa.), Battle of, 1863 2. United States -- History -- 1861-1865, Civil War

ISBN 0448465752; 9780448462868; 9780448465753

LC 2012027557

This book, by Jim O'Connor, John Mantha, and James Bennett, "offers a strongly contextualized account of the bloodiest engagement of the Civil War and a mostly chronological discussion of the battle. Chapters, each beginning with a historical date, tell the story in a narrative format, but the story is effectively broken up with boxed biographies of such figures as Mathew Brady, Jeb Stuart, and Abraham Lincoln." (Booklist)

Includes bibliographical references (p. 106)

Osborne, Linda Barrett

★ **Traveling** the freedom road; from slavery and the Civil War through Reconstruction. Abrams Books for Young Readers 2009 128p il map $24.95

Grades: 6 7 8 9 10 **973.7**

1. Reconstruction (1865-1876) 2. Slavery -- United States 3. African Americans -- History 4. United States -- History -- 1861-1865, Civil War 5. United States -- Politics and government -- 1783-1865 6. United States -- Politics and government -- 1865-1898

ISBN 0-8109-8338-9; 978-0-8109-8338-0

LC 2008-22298

"This fascinating, well-designed volume offers an essential introduction to the experiences of African Americans between 1800 and 1877. . . . Osborne moves from . . . personal stories to broader historical milestones, and in highly accessible language, she provides basic background even as she challenges readers with philosophical questions. . . . This fluid exchange between political events and intimate, human stories creates a highly absorbing whole." Booklist

Otfinoski, Steven, 1949-

The **Civil** War; by Steven Otfinoski. Children's Press, an imprint of Scholastic Inc. 2017 144 p. illustrations, maps (Step into history) (library binding) $36

Grades: 6 7 8 9 **973.7**

1. United States -- History -- 1861-1865, Civil War 2. United States -- History -- Civil War, 1861-1865 -- Influence 3. United States -- History -- Civil War, 1861-1865 -- Social aspects

ISBN 9780531225691; 9780531243633

LC 2016031160

In this book, by Steven Otfinoski, part of the Step Into History series, "in 1860, the United States was split in two. . . . As President Abraham Lincoln attempted to hold the country together, war broke out between the Union and the Confederates. Readers will discover why the southern states seceded, how the war affected the people of the United States, and what lasting effect the conflict had." (Publisher's note)

"Maps, a list of the Union and Confederate states, and useful back matter make this well-designed and thorough historical account one that kids will actually enjoy reading." Booklist

Includes bibliographical references (page 142) and index.

Porterfield, Jason

The **Lincoln** -Douglas senatorial debates of 1858; a primary source investigation. [by] Jason Porterfield. 1st ed; Rosen Central Primary Sources 2005 64p il map (Great historic debates and speeches) lib bdg $29.25

Grades: 5 6 7 8 **973.7**

1. Lawyers 2. Presidents 3. Senators 4. Political leaders 5. State legislators 6. Members of Congress 7. Presidential candidates

ISBN 1-4042-0153-X

LC 2003-25408

Discusses the debates between Lincoln and Douglas and how they influenced political campaigns throughout history.

This "readable [text provides a] balanced [overview]. Primary-source materials include archival maps, photos, reproductions, letters, and speeches that are examined in context." SLJ

Includes bibliographical references

Raatma, Lucia

The **Underground** Railroad; by Lucia Raatma. Children's Press 2011 64 p. col. ill. (library) $30.00; (paperback) $8.95

Grades: 4 5 6 **973.7**

1. Fugitive slaves 2. Underground Railroad 3. Fugitive slaves -- United States -- History -- 19th century 4. Antislavery movements -- United States -- History -- 19th century

ISBN 0531250431; 9780531250433; 9780531265680

LC 2011009493

This book by Lucia Raatma is part of the Cornerstones of Freedom series and looks at the Underground Railroad. The entry "explains how the system worked, the journey, and important people who guided slaves such as Harriet Tubman and Levi and Catherine White Coffin of Indiana, who helped about 2,000 slaves reach freedom." (School Library Journal)

Includes bibliographical references (p. 61) and index.

Rees, Bob

The **Civil** War; by Bob Rees. Heinemann Library 2012 80 p. ill. (some col.), col. maps (library) $36.50; (paperback) $10.99

Grades: 6 7 8 9 **973.7**

1. United States -- History -- 1861-1865, Civil War 2. United States -- History -- Civil War, 1861-1865

ISBN 1432959964; 9781432959968; 9781432960056

LC 2011018258

This book by Bob Rees is part of the Living Through . . . series and looks at the U.S. Civil War. The "set summarizes events in major conflicts using brief first-person accounts, sidebars, short biographies, color and archival photos, maps, and other graphics." The authors include "views from multiple perspectives." (School Library Journal)

Includes bibliographical references (p. 76) and index.

Reis, Ronald A.

African Americans and the Civil War. Chelsea House Publishers 2009 134p il (The Civil War: a nation divided) lib bdg $35

Grades: 6 7 8 9 **973.7**

1. African American soldiers 2. Slavery -- United States 3. United States -- History -- 1861-1865, Civil War

ISBN 978-1-60413-038-6 lib bdg; 1-60413-038-5 lib bdg

LC 2008-25665

This describes the roles African Americans played in the Civil War

Includes glossary and bibliographical references

Rottman, Gordon L.

The **most** daring raid of the Civil War; the great locomotive chase. Rosen Pub. 2011 64p il map (The most daring raids in history) lib bdg $29.25

Grades: 7 8 9 10 **973.7**

1. Chattanooga, Battle of, 1863 2. United States -- History -- 1861-1865, Civil War

ISBN 978-1-4488-1870-9; 1-4488-1870-2

LC 2010030195

In a daring attempt to cut off the supply lines of Confederate forces, Union soldiers planned to steal a train and disable the line as they traveled to Chattanooga, TN. One man's daring pursuit led to their ultimate failure. This book tells the story of how the raid was planned, and how it ultimately fell apart.

This book is "packed with facts, covering the details of the action, the people involved, and the tools used, in engaging prose. The authors cite their sources thoroughly. . . . Diagrams, . . . and maps make the action easy to follow and provide visual context for the raids. . . . This . . . is sure to find a large readership." SLJ

Includes glossary and bibliographical references

Sheinkin, Steve

Lincoln's Grave Robbers. Scholastic 2013 224 p. $16.99

Grades: 5 6 7 8 **973.7**

1. Grave robbing 2. Counterfeits and counterfeiting

ISBN 0545405726; 9780545405720

This book is an "account of the attempted heist of Abraham Lincoln's body in 1876." Steve Sheinkin first "delv[es] into the history of counterfeiting. . . . James Kennally, leader of one of the largest counterfeiting rings in the Midwest, masterminded the plot to steal the late president's body from the Lincoln Monument," intending "to ransom the purloined corpse" and extort "the government for a tidy sum of money and the freedom of his jailed, top-notch engraver." (Publishers Weekly)

Shepard, Ray Anthony

Now or never! 54th Massachusetts Infantry's war to end slavery. Ray Anthony Shepard. Calkins Creek 2017 144 p. illustrations, map (hardcover) $17.95

Grades: 6 7 8 9 10 11 12 **973.7**

1. Massachusetts -- History 2. Slavery -- United States -- History 3. United States -- History -- 1861-1865, Civil War 4. Soldiers -- Massachusetts -- Biography 5. African Americans -- History -- 1863-1877 6. Massachusetts -- History -- Civil War, 1861-1865 7. United States -- History -- Civil War, 1861-1865 8. United States.

Army. Massachusetts Infantry Regiment, 54th (1863-1865)
ISBN 9781629799162; 9781629793405

LC 2017937779

This book, by Ray Anthony Shepard, is the "riveting dual biography of two little-known but extraordinary men in Civil War history—George E. Stephens and James Henry Gooding. These Union soldiers not only served in the Massachusetts 54th Infantry, the well-known black regiment, but were also war correspondents who published eyewitness reports of the battlefields." (Publisher's note)

"This is a powerful use of primary resources, one that illuminates the lives of its subjects but never gets in the way of their remarkable stories." Kirkus

Includes bibliographical references (pages 136-139) and index.

Silvey, Anita

★ **I'll** pass for your comrade; women soldiers in the Civil War. Clarion Books 2008 115p il map $17

Grades: 6 7 8 9 **973.7**

1. Women soldiers 2. United States -- History -- 1861-1865, Civil War

ISBN 978-0-618-57491-9; 0-618-57491-3

LC 2008018053

This "spotlights Union and Confederate women who fought on the battlefields. . . . Period photos, prints, drawings, and documents are among the many illustrations. . . . Well researched and clearly written, this attractive book illuminates an aspect of the Civil War that is often overlooked." Booklist

Includes bibliographical references

Slavicek, Louise Chipley

Women and the Civil War. Chelsea House Publishers 2009 128p il (The Civil War: a nation divided) lib bdg $35

Grades: 6 7 8 9 **973.7**

1. Women -- United States -- History 2. United States -- History -- 1861-1865, Civil War -- Women

ISBN 978-1-60413-040-9 lib bdg; 1-60413-040-7 lib bdg

LC 2008-26562

"After a historical overview, six chapters . . . present information on female roles during the [Civil] war. . . . Women worked as nurses and caregivers and organized aid and relief societies. . . . Hundreds disguised themselves as men to fight and others worked as spies and saboteurs. They were forced to oversee and run family farms and plantations or to find employment in factories or government offices. A chapter on African-American women reviews how the war impacted their lives and mentions significant figures such as Harriet Tubman. Sidebars, quotes from primary sources, color and black-and-white illustrations, and historical photographs are scattered throughout [this] clearly written, well-organized [text]." SLJ

Includes glossary and bibliographical references

Stein, R. Conrad

Escaping slavery on the Underground Railroad; [by] R. Conrad Stein. Enslow Publishers 2008 128p il (From many cultures, one history) lib bdg $31.93

Grades: 6 7 8 9 **973.7**

1. Abolitionists 2. Underground railroad 3. Slavery -- United States

ISBN 978-0-7660-2799-2 lib bdg; 0-7660-2799-6 lib bdg

LC 2007015124

This is an account of American slavery, the Abolitionist movement, and escapes from slavery on the The Underground Railroad.

This "will provide clear, easy-to-understand facts with critical analysis and will be useful for reports." Libr Media Connect

Includes glossary and bibliographical references

Swanson, James L.

★ **Bloody** times; the funeral of Abraham Lincoln and the manhunt for Jefferson Davis. Collins 2011 196p il $16.99

Grades: 6 7 8 9 **973.7**

1. Lawyers 2. Statesmen 3. Presidents 4. Senators 5. Political leaders 6. State legislators 7. Secretaries of war 8. Members of Congress 9. United States -- History -- 1861-1865, Civil War

ISBN 978-0-06-156089-7; 0-06-156089-8

LC 2010045611

An adaptation for young people of Bloody Crimes, published 2010 by William Morrow for adults

This tells "the story of Lincoln's assassination, detailing the funeral and the return of the body for burial in Springfield, IL. Juxtaposed with this compelling drama is that of Jefferson Davis, president of the Confederate States of America, as he learned of Lee's surrender and traveled across the South trying to keep the Confederacy alive while being pursued by Federal forces bent on his arrest. . . . Lincoln's body was placed aboard a train that retraced the route taken by Lincoln as he traveled to the capital as president-elect. Readers will be fascinated by the details needed to plan this trip and the people involved. . . . Just as riveting is Davis's fruitless effort to avoid arrest. . . . A brilliant book that is sure to be hit with history aficionados." SLJ

Includes glossary and bibliographical references

★ **Chasing** Lincoln's killer; the search for John Wilkes Booth. Scholastic Press 2009 194p il map $16.99

Grades: 7 8 9 10 **973.7**

1. Actors 2. Lawyers 3. Presidents 4. Murderers 5. State legislators 6. Members of Congress 7. United States -- History -- 1861-1865, Civil War

ISBN 978-0-439-90354-7; 0-439-90354-8

LC 2008-17994

"This volume is an adaptation of Swanson's Manhunt: The 12-Day Chase for Lincoln's Killer (HarperCollins, 2006). Divided into 14 chapters and an epilogue, the sentences are shorter and chapters are condensed from the original but the rich details and suspense are ever present. . . . Excellent black-and-white illustrations complement the text. . . . Readers will be engrossed by the almost hour-by-hour search and by the many people who encountered the killer as he tried to escape. It is a tale of intrigue and an engrossing mystery." SLJ

Wagner, Heather Lehr

Spies in the Civil War. Chelsea House Publishers 2009 112p il (The Civil War: a nation divided) lib bdg $35

Grades: 6 7 8 9 **973.7**

1. Spies 2. United States -- History -- 1861-1865, Civil War

ISBN 978-1-60413-039-3 lib bdg; 1-60413-039-3 lib bdg

LC 2008-26568

This describes the work of Civil War spies Allan Pinkerton, Elizabeth Van Lew, Belle Boyd, and Rose O'Neal Greenhow and others

Includes glossary and bibliographical references

Walker, Sally M.

Secrets of a Civil War submarine; solving the mysteries of the H.L. Hunley. Carolrhoda Books 2005 112p il lib bdg $17.95

Grades: 7 8 9 10 **973.7**

1. Shipwrecks 2. Submarines 3. Underwater exploration 4.

Hunley (Submarine) 5. United States -- History -- 1861-1865, Civil War -- Naval operations
ISBN 1-57505-830-8

LC 2004-19646

This discusses "the Confederate submarine H. L. Hunley. . . . Walker begins with the history of the Hunley's design and construction as well as its place in Civil War and naval history. She really hits her stride, though, in explaining the complex techniques and loving care used in raising the craft, recovering its contents, and even reconstructing models of the crewmembers' bodies. . . . Thoroughly researched, nicely designed, and well illustrated with clear, color photos." Booklist

Includes glossary and bibliographical references

Warren, Andrea

★ **Under** siege! three children at the Civil War battle for Vicksburg. Melanie Kroupa Books 2009 166p il map $21.95

Grades: 7 8 9 10 **973.7**

1. Vicksburg (Miss.) -- Siege, 1863 2. United States -- History -- 1861-1865, Civil War
ISBN 978-0-374-31255-8; 0-374-31255-9

LC 2008-1136

"Warren creates a compelling account of the 1863 siege at Vicksburg that follows three young people from December 1862 through the aftermath of the surrender on July 4, 1863. . . . The author uses primary sources throughout, including scores of quotes, many attributed to the children themselves, period photographs, maps, and paintings. . . . The back matter is extensive, including an annotated list of recommended Civil War books, a longer bibliography of sources, and extensive endnotes and illustration credits." Voice Youth Advocates

Includes bibliographical references and index

Watkins, Samuel R.

The **diary** of Sam Watkins, a confederate soldier; edited by Ruth Ashby; illustrations by Laszlo Kubinyi. Benchmark Bks. 2004 95p il (In my own words) lib bdg $18.95

Grades: 5 6 7 8 **973.7**

1. Soldiers 2. United States -- History -- 1861-1865, Civil War
ISBN 0-7614-1646-3

LC 2003-1478

Excerpts from the diary of a Confederate soldier from Tennessee, describing the battles he fought in during the Civil War

This offers "an engaging history lesson." Horn Book Guide

Includes bibliographical references

Weber, Jennifer L.

Summer's bloodiest days; the Battle of Gettysburg as told from all sides. foreword by James M. McPherson. National Geographic 2010 61p il map $17.95; lib bdg $27.90

Grades: 5 6 7 8 **973.7**

1. Gettysburg (Pa.), Battle of, 1863 2. United States -- History -- 1861-1865, Civil War
ISBN 978-1-4263-0706-5; 1-4263-0706-3; 978-1-4263-0707-2 lib bdg; 1-4263-0707-1 lib bdg

"This colorful book tells of the Battle of Gettysburg, a dramatic event that becomes even more compelling because the text is laced with pertinent quotes from those who were there. Weber's vivid, pithy writing packs a great deal of information and many anecdotes into a relatively short account. . . . Many battle maps, short, informative sidebars, and the use of modern realistic paintings and photos of artifacts as well as period photographs . . . illustrate the book." Booklist

Includes bibliographical references

Williams, Carla

The **Underground** Railroad. Child's World 2009 32p il (Journey to freedom) lib bdg $28.50

Grades: 4 5 6 **973.7**

1. Underground railroad 2. Slavery -- United States
ISBN 978-1-60253-139-0 lib bdg; 1-60253-139-0 lib bdg

LC 2008031946

"Underground Railroad describes how this secret system worked and introduces key figures. Williams discusses relevant laws and amendments as well as the advent and conclusion of the Civil War. The facts, presented through stories, historical news accounts, and biographical sketches of Harriet Tubman and Levi Weeks, capture the desperation of the enslaved as well as the abolitionists' commitment to them. The [book is] concise and direct, yet the writing remains sophisticated. Vibrant personal stories accompanied by striking photographs of historical figures and artifacts provide a sense of the subjects' hopes and dreams." SLJ

Includes glossary and bibliographical references

Woog, Adam

The **Emancipation** Proclamation; ending slavery in America. Chelsea House Publishers 2009 117p il (Milestones in American history) lib bdg $35

Grades: 6 7 8 9 **973.7**

1. Slavery -- United States 2. Emancipation Proclamation (1863) 3. United States -- History -- 1861-1865, Civil War
ISBN 978-1-60413-307-3 lib bdg; 1-60413-307-4 lib bdg

LC 2008030742

This explores Lincoln's proclamation which ended slavery during the Civil War

This offers "short, clearly written chapters. . . . [It is] amply illustrated with black-and-white and color photographs and reproductions and supported with biographical sketches and excerpts from primary documents." Horn Book Guide

Includes bibliographical references

973.8 United States--Reconstruction period, 1865-1901

Custer's last stand; Thomas Streissguth, book editor. Greenhaven Press 2003 142p il maps (At issue in history) lib bdg $21.96; pa $14.96

Grades: 7 8 9 10 **973.8**

1. Generals 2. Little Bighorn, Battle of the, 1876 3. Army officers
ISBN 0-7377-1358-5 lib bdg; 0-7377-1359-3 pa

LC 2002-27875

"Using primary and secondary sources, this volume examines the controversial history of the Battle at the Little Bighorn in June, 1876. . . . Each of the 11 entries is preceded by a summary of the author's main points and conclusions. This excellent volume helps students understand the 'what' and 'why' of history." SLJ

Includes bibliographical references

Fitzgerald, Stephanie

Reconstruction; rebuilding America after the Civil War. Compass Point Books 2011 64p il map (The Civil War) lib bdg $33.32; pa $6.95

Grades: 5 6 7 8 **973.8**

1. Reconstruction (1865-1876) 2. United States -- History -- 1865-

1898
ISBN 978-0-7565-4370-9 lib bdg; 0-7565-4370-3 lib bdg; 978-0-7565-4414-0 pa; 0-7565-4414-9 pa
LC 2010001019

Recounts the history of the Reconstruction, as the United States government and people worked to recover from the effects of the Civil War.

The layout is "clean and attractive, with a large font and reproductions of period illustrations and photos. . . . This . . . will help students understand the era's most important issues and events. A quality choice for reports." SLJ

Includes glossary and bibliographical references

The **Gilded** Age: a history in documents; [compiled by] Janette Thomas Greenwood. Oxford Univ. Press 2000 191p il map (Pages from history) $39.95; pa $24.95
Grades: 7 8 9 10 **973.8**
1. United States -- History -- 1865-1898
ISBN 978-0-19-510523-0; 0-19-510523-0; 978-0-19-516638-5 pa; 0-19-516638-8 pa
LC 99-98194

Uses a wide variety of documents to show how Americans dealt with an age of extremes from 1887 to 1900, including rapid industrialization, unemployment, unprecedented wealth, and immigration

"There's plenty to absorb and much to capture the imagination. . . . Greenwood presents the history as a seamless tapestry sewn by the people who lived it." Booklist

Includes bibliographical references

Hillstrom, Kevin
American Indian removal and the trail to Wounded Knee; [by] Kevin Hillstrom and Laurie Collier Hillstrom. Omnigraphics 2010 250p il (Defining moments) lib bdg $55
Grades: 8 9 10 11 12 **973.8**
1. Wounded Knee Creek, Battle of, 1890 2. Native Americans -- Relocation 3. Native Americans -- Great Plains
ISBN 978-0-7808-1129-4; 0-7808-1129-1
LC 2010-4676

"This well-written volume effectively explores a topic of intense historical debate. Fascinating sidebars add significantly to the text." SLJ

Includes glossary and bibliographical references

McNeese, Tim
The **Gilded** Age and Progressivism, 1891-1913; Tim McNeese ; consulting editor, Richard Jensen. Chelsea House 2010 136 p. ill. (some col.) (Discovering U.S. history) (library) $35.00
Grades: 5 6 7 8 **973.8**
1. Progressivism (United States politics) 2. United States -- History -- 1865-1921 3. United States -- Social conditions -- 1865-1918 4. United States -- Politics and government -- 1901-1953 5. Progressivism (United States politics) -- History -- 19th century 6. Progressivism (United States politics) -- History -- 20th century
ISBN 1604133554; 9781604133554
LC 2009015012

McNeese "discusses the people, politics, economic conditions, and foreign affairs of [the U.S. from 1891 to 1913], objectively explaining how the attitudes, perceptions, and expectations of the American people and their leaders shaped the development of the country. . . . Color period art and photos, maps, and cutaway drawings supplement the [text]." SLJ

Includes bibliographical references and index.

Ruggiero, Adriane
American voices from Reconstruction. Marshall Cavendish Benchmark 2006 103p il (American voices from--) lib bdg $37.07
Grades: 6 7 8 9 10 11 12 **973.8**
1. Reconstruction (1865-1876)
ISBN 978-0-7614-2168-9 lib bdg; 0-7614-2168-8 lib bdg
LC 2005-24949

This "does an excellent job of bringing history close. . . . The spacious design . . . is very approachable, and the combination of voices and commentary will readers think critically." Booklist

Includes glossary and bibliographical references

Sanders, Nancy I.
Frederick Douglass for kids; his life and times with 21 activities. Nancy I. Sanders. Chicago Review Press 2012 ix, 145 p.p ill. (paperback) $16.95; (ebook) $11.99; (prebind) $25.95
Grades: 5 6 7 **973.8**
1. Biography 2. Slavery -- History 3. African Americans -- Biography 4. Abolitionists -- United States -- Biography 5. African American abolitionists -- Biography 6. Antislavery movements -- United States -- Study and teaching -- Activity programs 7. Antislavery movements -- United States -- History -- 19th century
ISBN 1569767173; 9781569767177; 9781613743560; 9781451774788
LC 2011050092

Author Nancy I. Sanders presents information on Frederick Douglass. "Born on a plantation, he later escaped slavery and helped others to freedom via the Underground Railroad. In time he became a bestselling author, an outspoken newspaper editor, a brilliant orator, a tireless abolitionist, and a brave civil rights leader. He was famous on both sides of the Atlantic in the years leading up to the Civil War, and when war broke out, Abraham Lincoln invited him to the White House for counsel and advice." (Publisher's note)

Includes bibliographical references (p. 136-137) and index.

Telgen, Diane
The **Gilded** Age; Diane Telgen. Omnigraphics 2012 xvi, 252 p.p ill. (hardcover : alk. paper) $16.99
Grades: 7 8 9 10 11 12 **973.8**
1. United States -- History -- 1865-1898 2. United States -- History -- 1865-1921 -- Sources 3. United States -- History -- 1865-1921 4. United States -- Politics and government -- 1865-1933 -- Sources 5. United States -- History -- 1865-1921 -- Biography 6. United States -- Politics and government -- 1865-1933
ISBN 0780812387; 9780780812383
LC 2011048642

This book by Diane Telgen "surveys America's rapid economic, social, demographic, and political changes from the end of the Civil War to the dawn of the twentieth century. . . . The volume also explains how various hallmarks of this era -- including rapid industrialization and urbanization, the economic divide between rich and poor, political corruption and reform, and social and religious activism -- laid the groundwork for the United States we live in today." (Publisher's note)

Includes bibliographical references (p. 237-242) and index

Walker, Paul Robert
★ **Remember** Little Bighorn; Indians, soldiers, and scouts tell their stories. [by] Paul Robert Walker; [foreword by John A. Doerner] National Geographic Society 2006 61p il map $17.95; lib bdg $27.90

Grades: 5 6 7 8 **973.8**

1. Little Bighorn, Battle of the, 1876
ISBN 0-7922-5521-6; 0-7922-5522-4 lib bdg
LC 2005030929

This "volume gives an almost blow-by-blow account of the famous battle that came to be known as Custer's Last Stand. Walker concentrates on the battle itself, fought on the Great Plains in 1876, and the book includes diagrams of each side's tactics. . . . Walker's exhaustive research . . . [brings] together the conflicting viewpoints of the whites and the Lakota Sioux, Cheyenne, and Arapaho fighters, documenting everything in source notes. The handsome book design, with thick paper, clear type, maps, stirring photos, and archival images, will attract readers to the battle story and then start them thinking about lasting historical issues." Booklist

Includes bibliographical references

Worth, Richard

African Americans during Reconstruction; [by] Richard Worth. Chelsea House 2006 112p il map (Slavery in the Americas) $35

Grades: 6 7 8 9 **973.8**

1. Reconstruction (1865-1876) 2. African Americans -- Civil rights
ISBN 0-81606-139-4
LC 2005015720

Tells the history of African Americans from the end of the Civil War through the nation's reconstruction.

Includes bibliographical references

973.9 United States--1901-

Brill, Marlene Targ

America in the 1900s. Twenty-First Century Books 2010 144p il (The decades of twentieth-century America) lib bdg $38.60

Grades: 7 8 9 10 **973.9**

1. United States -- History -- 1898-1919
ISBN 978-0-8225-3436-5 lib bdg; 0-8225-3436-3 lib bdg
LC 2007-40983

This is an overview of the 1900's

"The text is clear but not condescending, with unfamiliar terms defined in parentheses. Frequent, mostly black-and-white photographs punctuate pages with clear print and lots of white space. Time lines recap major events, while 'To Learn More' suggests not only books but also Web sites and films. . . . A worthwhile addition." Voice Youth Advocates

Includes bibliographical references

Sandler, Martin W.

★ The **Dust** Bowl through the lens; how photography revealed and helped remedy a national disaster. Walker & Co. 2008 96p il map $15.99; lib bdg $20.89

Grades: 5 6 7 8 **973.9**

1. Dust storms 2. Documentary photography 3. Great Plains -- History
ISBN 978-0-8027-9547-2; 0-8027-9547-1; 978-0-8027-9548-9 lib bdg; 0-8027-9548-X lib bdg
LC 2008-55979

"This excellent photo-essay traces the history of the Dust Bowl from its causes to its resolution. In tandem, Sandler treats the role of the budding field of photojournalism. Forty-four spreads feature a page of clear, direct text with a large, well-reproduced image, many of which are set on color pages. . . . Seldom has the connection between the arts and the general quality of life been made so clear. The text deals equally with those who fled the decimated Bread Basket for California and those who waited out the devastation and dust. Throughout, the use of primary sources is superb, with quotations from affected citizens, the photojournalists themselves, political and entertainment figures, and writers, giving a multifaceted picture of a seminal time in United States history." SLJ

973.91 United States--1901-1953

Bingham, Jane

The **Great** Depression; the Jazz Age, Prohibition, and the Great Depression, 1921-1937. Chelsea House 2011 64p il (A cultural history of women in America) $35

Grades: 5 6 7 8 **973.91**

1. Great Depression, 1929-1939 2. Women -- United States 3. Women -- United States -- History
ISBN 978-1-60413-933-4; 1-60413-933-1
LC 2010044889

An "eye-catching [layout] with good use of color, photographs, and informative sidebars, many of which use primary-source quotations, are the highlights of [this] appealing [volume]. . . . After a succinct overview of contemporary events, the chapters describe women's lives at home, at work, in education, in politics, in the arts, and their role in the general culture. . . . [This book] surveys an era after women won the right to vote and when the nation's economic crash placed new hardships on families." SLJ

Includes glossary and bibliographical references

Brill, Marlene Targ

America in the 1910s; by Marlee Richards. Twenty-First Century Books 2010 144p il (The decades of twentieth-century America) lib bdg $38.60

Grades: 7 8 9 10 **973.91**

1. United States -- History -- 1898-1919
ISBN 978-0-8225-3437-2 lib bdg; 0-8225-3437-1 lib bdg
LC 2007-42905

Presents the social, political, economical, and technological changes in the United States during the nineteen tens, including World War I, the Prohibition era, and the birth of the skyscraper.

The text is "enlivened with quotes and excerpts from primary sources, period photos, and two sets of sidebars. 'Profiles' provides biographical sketches of important people and 'Turning Points' explains the significance of important events. . . . A solid choice for readers and researchers." SLJ

Includes bibliographical references and filmography

Corrigan, Jim

The **1900s** decade in photos; a decade of discovery. Enslow Publishers 2010 64p il (Amazing decades in photos) lib bdg $27.93

Grades: 4 5 6 7 **973.91**

1. United States -- History -- 20th century
ISBN 978-0-7660-3129-6 lib bdg; 0-7660-3129-2 lib bdg
LC 2008042900

This highlights the important world, national, and cultural developments of the 1900s.

This is illustrated with "large, well-chosen black-and-white and color photos. . . . Captions provide specific information about the photos and supplement, rather than repeat, information in the [narrative]. Attractive and readable, this . . . will be popular with browsers and beginning researchers." SLJ

Includes glossary and bibliographical references

The **1910s** decade in photos; a decade that shook the world. Enslow Publishers 2010 64p il (Amazing decades in photos) lib bdg $27.93

Grades: 4 5 6 7 **973.91**

1. United States -- History -- 20th century

ISBN 978-0-7660-3130-2 lib bdg; 0-7660-3130-6 lib bdg

LC 2008042902

This highlights the important world, national, and cultural developments of the decade 1910-1919, including the sinking of the Titanic, the establishment of the Boy Scouts and Girl Scouts, immigration, income tax, Hollywood feature films, World War I, the Lusitania sinking, and more.

Includes glossary and bibliographical references

The **1920s** decade in photos; the Roaring Twenties. Enslow Publishers 2010 64p il (Amazing decades in photos) lib bdg $27.93

Grades: 4 5 6 7 **973.91**

1. United States -- History -- 1919-1933

ISBN 978-0-7660-3131-9 lib bdg; 0-7660-3131-4 lib bdg

LC 2008042903

This highlights the important world, national, and cultural developments of the decade 1920-1929, including Prohibition, jazz music, women's suffrage, the rise of Mussolini, flappers fashions, the KKK, U.S. Presidents Harding and Coolidge, the Teapot Dome Scandal, the rise of the Nazi Party, and more.

Includes glossary and bibliographical references

Davis, Barbara J.

The **Teapot** Dome Scandal; corruption rocks 1920s America. by Barbara J. Davis. Compass Point Books 2008 96p il map (Snapshots in history) lib bdg $31.93

Grades: 6 7 8 9 **973.91**

1. Teapot Dome Scandal, 1921-1924

ISBN 978-0-7565-3336-6 lib bdg; 0-7565-3336-8 lib bdg

LC 2007004920

"Describes the signature scandal of the 1920s, through which political appointees and personal friends of President Warren G. Harding used their positions to solicit bribes from powerful oil companies in return for rich Western oil leases. . . . [This] volume includes a minimal glossary, a helpful time line, and suggestions for further reading." Voice Youth Advocates

Includes glossary

Favreau, Marc

Crash; the Great Depression and the fall and rise of America. Marc Favreau. Little, Brown Books for Young Readers 2018 240 p. (hardback) $18.99

Grades: 5 6 7 8 **973.91**

1. New Deal, 1933-1939 2. United States -- History 3. Great Depression, 1929-1939 4. New Deal, 1933-1939 -- Sources 5. Depressions, 1929 -- United States 6. United States -- History -- 1919-1933 7. United States -- History -- 1933-1945 8. Depressions, 1929 -- United States -- Sources 9. United States -- History -- 1919-1933 -- Sources 10. United States -- History -- 1933-1945 -- Sources 11. United States -- Economic conditions -- 1918-1945 12. United States -- Economic conditions -- 1918-1945 -- Sources

ISBN 9780316464895; 9780316545860

LC 2016056930

This book, by Marc Favreau, "tells the story of the Great Depression, from the sweeping fallout of the market collapse to the more personal stories of those caught up in the aftermath. Packed with photographs, primary documents, and firsthand accounts, 'Crash' shines a spotlight on pivotal moments and figures across ethnic, gender, racial, social, and geographic divides, reflecting many different experiences of one of the most turbulent decades in American history." (Publisher's note)

Lindop, Edmund

America in the 1920s; by Edmund Lindop and Margaret J. Goldstein. Twenty-First Century Books 2010 144p il (The decades of twentieth-century America) lib bdg $38.60

Grades: 7 8 9 10 **973.91**

1. United States -- History -- 1919-1933

ISBN 978-0-7613-2831-5 lib bdg; 0-7613-2831-9 lib bdg

LC 2009-703

Outlines life in the United States in the 1920s, including Prohibition, the stock market crash, and advances in technology and entertainment such as the first radios and first talking movies

The text is "enlivened with quotes and excerpts from primary sources, period photos, and two sets of sidebars. 'Profiles' provides biographical sketches of important people and 'Turning Points' explains the significance of important events. . . . A solid choice for readers and researchers." SLJ

Includes bibliographical references

McElvaine, Robert S., 1947-

★ The **Depression** and New Deal; a history in documents. Oxford Univ. Press 2000 192p il (Pages from history) hardcover o.p. pa $19.95

Grades: 7 8 9 10 **973.91**

1. Great Depression, 1929-1939 2. United States -- Economic conditions -- 1933-1945

ISBN 0-19-510493-5; 0-19-516636-1 pa

LC 99-36644

"A vast assortment of diary entries, newspaper articles, campaign memos and speeches, political cartoons, songs, poetry, art, advertisements, photographs, and personal letters provide students with a political, economic, and social picture of this nation during the Depression. . . . [This] provides a balanced, inclusive picture of the period through the senses of the people who lived it." SLJ

Includes bibliographical references

973.917 Administration of Franklin Delano Roosevelt, 1933-1945

Bolden, Tonya

★ **FDR's** alphabet soup; New Deal America, 1932-1939. Alfred A. Knopf 2010 136p il $19.99; lib bdg $22.99

Grades: 5 6 7 8 **973.917**

1. Governors 2. Presidents 3. New Deal, 1933-1939 4. People with disabilities 5. Philatelists 6. People with Disabilities 7. United States -- History -- 1933-1945

ISBN 978-0-375-85214-5; 0-375-85214-X; 978-0-375-95214-2 lib bdg; 0-375-95214-4 lib bdg

LC 2009-10362

"Retracing the course of New Deal intiatives from the newly elected Roosevelt's 'famous First Hundred Days of action! action! action!' to his creation of the powerful Executive Office of the President in 1939, [Bolden] presents a coherent account of how FDR and his adminstration successfully (mostly) battled political, ideological, and legal challenges to create a sweeping recovery agenda. . . . Generally illustrated with period photos . . . this lively look back both invites and equips readers to ponder the pros and cons of 'gumptious government' in any era." Booklist

Includes glossary and bibliographical references

Corrigan, Jim

The **1930s** decade in photos; Depression and hope. Enslow Publishers 2010 64p il (Amazing decades in photos) lib bdg $27.93

Grades: 4 5 6 7 **973.917**

1. Great Depression, 1929-1939 2. United States -- History -- 1919-1933 3. United States -- History -- 1933-1945

ISBN 978-0-7660-3132-6 lib bdg; 0-7660-3132-2 lib bdg

LC 2008042904

This highlights the important world, national, and cultural developments of the decade 1930-1939, including the Great Depression, the Lindbergh kidnapping, the administration of FDR, the New Deal, jazz and swing music, the rise of Nazism, the repeal of Prohibition and more.

Includes glossary and bibliographical references

The **1940s** decade in photos; a world at war. Enslow Publishers 2010 64p il (Amazing decades in photos) lib bdg $27.93

Grades: 4 5 6 7 **973.917**

1. World War, 1939-1945 2. United States -- History -- 1933-1945 3. United States -- History -- 1945-1953

ISBN 978-0-7660-3133-3 lib bdg; 0-7660-3133-0 lib bdg

LC 2008042910

This covers the important world, national, and cultural developments of the decade 1940-1949, focusing on World War II.

This is illustrated with "large, well-chosen black-and-white and color photos. . . . Captions provide specific information about the photos and supplement, rather than repeat, information in the [narrative]. Attractive and readable, this . . . will be popular with browsers and beginning researchers." SLJ

Includes glossary and bibliographical references

Lindop, Edmund

America in the 1930s; [by] Edmund Lindop and Margaret J. Goldstein. Twenty-First Century Books 2010 144p il (The decades of twentieth-century America) lib bdg $38.60

Grades: 7 8 9 10 **973.917**

1. New Deal, 1933-1939 2. United States -- History -- 1933-1945

ISBN 978-0-7613-2832-2 lib bdg; 0-7613-2832-7 lib bdg

LC 2007-42902

The text is "enlivened with quotes and excerpts from primary sources, period photos, and two sets of sidebars. 'Profiles' provides biographical sketches of important people and 'Turning Points' explains the significance of important events. . . . A solid choice for readers and researchers." SLJ

Includes bibliographical references and filmography

America in the 1940s; by Edmund Lindop and Margaret J. Goldstein. Twenty-First Century Books 2010 144p il (The decades of twentieth-century America) lib bdg $38.60

Grades: 7 8 9 10 **973.917**

1. United States -- History -- 1933-1945 2. United States -- History -- 1945-1953

ISBN 978-0-7613-2945-9 lib bdg; 0-7613-2945-5 lib bdg

LC 2007-42904

Discusses the political, economic, social, cultural, and technology landscape of the United States in the fifth decade of the 20th century

The text is "enlivened with quotes and excerpts from primary sources, period photos, and two sets of sidebars. 'Profiles' provides biographical sketches of important people and 'Turning Points' explains the significance of important events. . . . A solid choice for readers and researchers." SLJ

Includes bibliographical references

McNeese, Tim

The **Great** Depression, 1929-1940; consulting editor Richard Jensen. Chelsea House 2010 136p il map (Discovering U.S. history) $35

Grades: 5 6 7 8 **973.917**

1. Economic conditions 2. Great Depression, 1929-1939 3. United States -- History -- 1933-1945

ISBN 978-1-60413-357-8; 1-60413-357-0

LC 2009-22090

"The information is accurate and easy to understand. Pictures are well placed, and primary sources are included. . . . The maps are well done and there are sidebars with additional information. . . . [This would be good] to have on hand for reports as it is well laid out and easy to use." Libr Media Connect

Includes glossary and bibliographical references

Nardo, Don

★ **Migrant** mother; how a photograph defined the Great Depression. Compass Point Books 2011 64p il (Captured history) lib bdg $33.99

Grades: 6 7 8 9 **973.917**

1. Photographers 2. Documentary photography 3. Great Depression, 1929-1939

ISBN 978-0-7565-4397-6; 0-7565-4397-5

LC 2010038578

This describes the significance of the iconic Dorothea Lange photograph of a migrant mother during the Great Depression and places it "in historical context, profiles the photographer, describes the conditions under which it was taken, and analyzes both its immediate and continuing impact. The [text includes] ample background information and details and [is] enhanced by large photos and sidebars." SLJ

Includes glossary and bibliographical references

Ruggiero, Adriane

★ **American** voices from The Great Depression. Benchmark Books 2004 xxi, 116p il (American voices from--) lib bdg $32.21

Grades: 6 7 8 9 **973.917**

1. Great Depression, 1929-1939 2. United States -- Economic conditions -- 1919-1933 3. United States -- Economic conditions -- 1933-1945

ISBN 0-7614-1696-X

LC 2004-865

Presents the history of the Great Depression through excerpts from letters, newspaper articles, speeches, and songs dating from the period. Includes review questions.

This "excellent [resource stands] out . . . because [it deals] strictly with primary sources, [contains] topnotch illustrations, and [enables] students to grasp the concepts without being overwhelmed." SLJ

Includes glossary and bibliographical references

973.92 United States--1953-2001

Brill, Marlene Targ

America in the 1970s. Lerner 2009 144p il (The decades of twentieth-century America) lib bdg $38.60

Grades: 7 8 9 10 **973.92**

1. United States -- Social conditions 2. United States -- History -- 1961-1974 3. United States -- History -- 1974-1989

ISBN 978-0-8225-3438-9; 0-8225-3438-X

LC 2007-38570

This is "a tightly constructed, smoothly phrased overview of the tumultuous 1970s. . . . The serviceable text is bolstered by skillful connections between events and movements, well-chosen representative quotes . . . and occasional snappy headlines . . . while sidebars profiling individuals and historical turning points . . . and a well-edited selection of photos add more interest." Booklist

America in the 1990s. Twenty-First Century Books 2010 144p il (The decades of twentieth-century America) lib bdg $38.60

Grades: 7 8 9 10 **973.92**

1. United States -- History -- 1989-

ISBN 978-0-8225-7603-7 lib bdg; 0-8225-7603-1 lib bdg

LC 2009-11628

Presents the social, political, economical, and technological changes in the United States during the 1990's

The text is "enlivened with quotes and excerpts from primary sources, period photos, and two sets of sidebars. 'Profiles' provides biographical sketches of important people and 'Turning Points' explains the significance of important events. . . . A solid choice for readers and researchers." SLJ

Includes bibliographical references and filmography

Corrigan, Jim

The **1990s** decade in photos; the rise of technology. Enslow Publishers 2010 64p il (Amazing decades in photos) lib bdg $27.93

Grades: 4 5 6 7 **973.92**

1. World history -- 20th century 2. United States -- History -- 1989-

ISBN 978-0-7660-3138-8 lib bdg; 0-7660-3138-1 lib bdg

LC 2008054648

This highlights the important world, national, and cultural developments of the decade 1990-1999, including Operation Desert Storm in 1991, race riots in Los Angeles, the election of President Clinton, the 1993 bombing of the World Trade Center, the Human Genome Project, the end of Apartheid, massacres in Bosnia and Rwanda, the Oklahoma City bombing, the O.J. Simpson murder trial, the Columbine High School shootings, and more

Includes glossary and bibliographical references

Lindop, Edmund

America in the 1950s; by Edmund Lindop; with Sarah Decapua. Twenty-First Century Books 2010 144p il (The decades of twentieth-century America) lib bdg $38.60

Grades: 7 8 9 10 **973.92**

1. United States -- History -- 1945-1953 2. United States -- History -- 1953-1961

ISBN 978-0-8225-7642-6 lib bdg; 0-8225-7642-2 lib bdg

LC 2008-40127

Presents the social, political, economical, and technological changes in the United States during the 1950s, including school integration, the Cold War, and the popularization of rock and roll

The text is "enlivened with quotes and excerpts from primary sources, period photos, and two sets of sidebars. 'Profiles' provides biographical sketches of important people and 'Turning Points' explains the significance of important events. . . . A solid choice for readers and researchers." SLJ

Includes bibliographical references and filmography

McNeese, Tim

Modern America, 1964-present; consulting editor, Richard Jensen. Chelsea House 2010 144p il map (Discovering U.S. history) $35

Grades: 5 6 7 8 **973.92**

1. United States -- History -- 1989- 2. United States -- History -- 1961-1974 3. United States -- History -- 1974-1989

ISBN 978-1-60413-361-5; 1-60413-361-9

"Through a good balance of social and political topics, McNeese capably covers a diverse range of subjects in [this] volume. . . . Modern America discusses civil rights, terrorism, and Barack Obama's first year as president. [The] book has an excellent chronology; rich sidebars; and numerous well-captioned illustrations, maps, and photos that enhance the [text]. [This book provides a] satisfying [introduction] to American history for students." SLJ

Includes glossary and bibliographical references

Wallace, Rich

Blood brother; Jonathan Daniels and His Sacrifice for Civil Rights. Rich Wallace, Sandra Neil Wallace. Calkins Creek 2016 352 p. illustrations $18.95

Grades: 6 7 8 9 10 **973.92**

1. Civil rights demonstrations -- Alabama 2. Civil rights -- United States -- History

ISBN 162979094X; 9781629790947

LC 2016932211

In this book, by Rich Wallace and Sandra Neil Wallace, "Jonathan Daniels, a white seminary student from New Hampshire, traveled to Selma, Alabama, in 1965 to help with voter registration of black residents. After the voting rights marches, he remained in Alabama, in the area known as 'Bloody Lowndes,' an extremely dangerous area, . . . to assist civil rights workers. Five months later, Jonathan Daniels was shot and killed while saving the life of Ruby Sales, a black teenager." (Publisher's note)

"An unusually inspiring story skillfully told." Kirkus

Includes bibliographical references (pages 329-337) and index.

973.921 Administration of Dwight David Eisenhower, 1953-1961

Corrigan, Jim

The **1950s** decade in photos; the American decade. Enslow Publishers 2010 64p il (Amazing decades in photos) lib bdg $27.93

Grades: 4 5 6 7 **973.921**

1. United States -- History -- 1945-1953 2. United States -- History -- 1953-1961

ISBN 978-0-7660-3134-0 lib bdg; 0-7660-3134-9 lib bdg

LC 2008042994

This highlights the important world, national, and cultural developments of the decade 1950-1959, including the Korean War, McCarthyism, the Baby Boom generation, the execution of the Rosenbergs, the Beat Generation, the polio epidemic and vaccine, the Montgomery Bus

Boycott, the Suez Crisis, the beginning of rock music, the launching of Sputnik, and the Cuban Revolution

Includes glossary and bibliographical references

Fitzgerald, Brian

McCarthyism; the red scare. Compass Point Books 2007 96p il map (Snapshots in history) lib bdg $31.93

Grades: 7 8 9 10 **973.921**

1. Cold war 2. Senators 3. Communism -- United States 4. United States -- History -- 1945-1953

ISBN 978-0-7565-2007-6 lib bdg; 0-7565-2007-X lib bdg

LC 2006003005

This "vividly portrays the fear of Communism in the U.S., beginning after the Russian Revolution. This book shows, in clear language, how McCarthy spread paranoia throughout the country and ruined many lives and careers." SLJ

Includes glossary and bibliographical references

973.922 Administration of John Fitzgerald Kennedy, 1961-1963

Nardo, Don

Assassination and its aftermath; how a photograph reassured a shocked nation. by Don Nardo. Compass Point Books, a Capstone imprint 2013 64 p. (Captured history) (library binding) $33.99

Grades: 6 7 8 9 **973.922**

1. Presidents -- United States -- Pictorial works 2. Kennedy, John F. (John Fitzgerald), 1917-1963 -- Assassination 3. Photojournalists -- United States -- History -- 20th century 4. Presidents -- Succession -- United States -- History -- 20th century

ISBN 0756546923; 9780756546922; 9780756546984

LC 2012051716

In this book, by Don Nardo, "vice president, Lyndon Baines Johnson, took the presidential oath of office on Air Force One just hours after the assassination [of U.S. President John F. Kennedy] . . . Cecil Stoughton's iconic photo [of this moment] showed the world that the smooth and orderly transfer of power called for in the U.S. Constitution had occurred." According to the book, "his photo helped ease the shock, tension, and fear in an anxious country." (Publisher's note)

Includes bibliographical references and index

O'Reilly, Bill, 1949-

Kennedy's last days; the assassination that defined a generation. by Bill O'Reilly. 1st ed. Henry Holt and Co. 2013 336 p. (hardcover) $19.99

Grades: 6 7 8 9 **973.922**

1. Assassination

ISBN 080509802X; 9780805098020

LC 2013009026

This book by Bill O'Reilly "chronicles John F. Kennedy's course from PT-109 through a challenging presidency and positively harps on Lee Harvey Oswald's determined but doomed quest to become a 'great man.' . . . News photos or snapshots on nearly every page provide views of the Kennedy and Oswald families over time, as well as important figures, places and major world events." (Kirkus Reviews)

Includes bibliographical references and index.

Stockland, Patricia M.

The **assassination** of John F. Kennedy; by Patricia M. Stockland. ABDO Pub. Co. 2008 112 p. ill. (some col.), map (library) $34.22

Grades: 7 8 9 10 **973.922**

1. Kennedy, John F. (John Fitzgerald), 1917-1963 -- Assassination

ISBN 1599288486; 9781599288482

LC 2007011999

This book by Patricia Stockland is part of the Essential Events series and looks at the assassination of former U.S. President John F. (Fitzgerald) Kennedy. The series "explores historic happenings around the globe and how those events have sculpted societies, the sciences, and politics." (Publisher's note)

Includes bibliographical references (p. 102) and index.

Swanson, James L.

★ The **President** Has Been Shot! The Assassination of John F. Kennedy. James L. Swanson. Scholastic Press 2013 336 p. (hbk.) $18.99

Grades: 6 7 8 9 10 11 12 **973.922**

1. Kennedy, John F. (John Fitzgerald), 1917-1963 -- Assassination

ISBN 0545490073; 9780545490078; 9780545496544

LC 2012041167

YALSA Award for Excellence in Nonfiction for Young Adults: Finalist (2014)

This book by James L. Swanson is a "young-adult book on the Kennedy assassination" in which the author "transport[s] readers back to one of the most shocking, sad, and terrifying events in American history. . . . The book [is] illustrated with archival photos, . . . diagrams, source notes, bibliography, places to visit, and index." (Publisher's note)

"Swanson's clear, concisely written, and riveting narrative highlights the key events of the Kennedy administration before focusing on the moment-by-moment details of JFK's assassination. Also included are an exploration of Lee Harvey Oswald's background, an aerial-view photograph of Dealey Plaza in Dallas, a detailed map of the motorcade route, and images of the Texas School Book Depository, where Oswald perched, rifle in hand." (Horn Book)

973.923 Administration of Lyndon Baines Johnson, 1963-1969

Corrigan, Jim

The **1960s** decade in photos; love, freedom, and flower power. Enslow Publishers 2010 64p il (Amazing decades in photos) lib bdg $27.93

Grades: 4 5 6 7 **973.923**

1. United States -- History -- 1961-1974

ISBN 978-0-7660-3135-7 lib bdg; 0-7660-3135-7 lib bdg

LC 2008042996

This highlights the important world, national, and cultural developments of the decade 1960-1969, including the U-2 spy plane, the election and assassination of JFK, the beginnings of manned space exploration, the Bay of Pigs invasion, the Vietnam War, the Cuban Missile Crisis, the British invasion in rock music, the Civil Rights movement, the Six-Day War in the Middle East, the assassinations of RFK and Martin Luther King, and Hippie culture

Includes glossary and bibliographical references

Lindop, Edmund

America in the 1960s; [by] Edmund Lindop; with Margaret J. Goldstein. Twenty-First Century Books 2009 144p il (Decades of twentieth century America) lib bdg $38.60

Grades: 7 8 9 10 **973.923**

1. United States -- History -- 1961-1974

ISBN 978-0-7613-3453-8 lib bdg; 0-7613-3453-X lib bdg

LC 2007-38028

Presents the social, political, economic, and technological changes in the United States during the nineteen sixties, including the civil rights movement, the popularization of rock music, and the expedition to the Moon

The text is "enlivened with quotes and excerpts from primary sources, period photos, and two sets of sidebars. 'Profiles' provides biographical sketches of important people and 'Turning Points' explains the significance of important events. . . . A solid choice for readers and researchers." SLJ

Includes bibliographical references and filmography

973.924 Administration of Richard Milhous Nixon, 1969-1974

Burgan, Michael

Death at Kent State; How a Photograph Brought the Vietnam War Home to America. by Michael Burgan, Content Adviser: Alan Canfora, Director, Kent May 4 Center. Compass Point Books, Capstone Press 2017 64 p. illustrations (ebook) $34.65; (library binding) $34.65

Grades: 6 7 8 9 **973.924**

1. Students -- Political activity 2. Kent State Shootings, Kent, Ohio, 1970 3. Vietnam War, 1961-1975 -- Protest movements -- United States 4. Kent State University -- Students -- Political activity -- History -- 20th century

ISBN 9780756554286; 9780756554248; 9780756554262

LC 2016008213

In this book in the Captured History series, by Michael Burgan, recalls how in 1970, "the shootings at Kent State University would shock the nation and spark a mass student strike across the country, the only one in U.S. history. A photojournalism student's photograph of a teen girl crying in anguish over a victim's dead body would win the Pulitzer Prize and become a symbol of the antiwar movement." (Publisher's note)

"The approachable text, appealing layout, and fascinating lens through which to explore history are all bolstered by extensive source notes and additional resources." Booklist

Includes bibliographical references and index

Corrigan, Jim

The **1970s** decade in photos; protest and change. Enslow Publishers 2010 64p il (Amazing decades in photos) lib bdg $27.93

Grades: 4 5 6 7 **973.924**

1. United States -- History -- 1961-1974 2. United States -- History -- 1974-1989

ISBN 978-0-7660-3136-4 lib bdg; 0-7660-3136-5 lib bdg

LC 2008042998

This highlights the important world, national, and cultural developments of the decade 1970-1979, including protests against the Vietnam War, terrorist airplane hijackings, the thawing of the Cold War, the deaths of rock musicians Jimi Hendrix, Janice Joplin, and Jim Morrison, the attack at the Munich Olympics, Watergate and the resignation of President Nixon, Three Mile Island, and more.

Includes glossary and bibliographical references

973.927 Administration of Ronald Reagan, 1981-1989

Brill, Marlene Targ

America in the 1980s. Twenty-First Century Books 2009 144p il (The decades of twentieth-century America) lib bdg $38.60

Grades: 7 8 9 10 **973.927**

1. Actors 2. Governors 3. Presidents 4. United States -- History -- 1974-1989

ISBN 978-0-8225-7602-0 lib bdg; 0-8225-7602-3 lib bdg

LC 2008-50116

Presents the social, political, economical, and technological changes in the United States during the 1980's

The text is "enlivened with quotes and excerpts from primary sources, period photos, and two sets of sidebars. 'Profiles' provides biographical sketches of important people and 'Turning Points' explains the significance of important events. . . . A solid choice for readers and researchers." SLJ

Includes bibliographical references

Corrigan, Jim

The **1980s** decade in photos; the triumph of democracy. Enslow Publishers 2010 64p il (Amazing decades in photos) lib bdg $27.93

Grades: 4 5 6 7 **973.927**

1. World history -- 20th century 2. United States -- History -- 1974-1989

ISBN 978-0-7660-3137-1 lib bdg; 0-7660-3137-3 lib bdg

LC 2008052627

This highlights the important world, national, and cultural developments of the decade 1980-1989, including the 1980 Winter Olympics, the presidency of Ronald Reagan, the Iran hostage crisis, the Space Shuttle, MTV, the War on Drugs, AIDS, the rise of the computer, fashion, the Chernobyl nuclear disaster, the Iran-Contra Affair, the massacre in Tiananmen Square, the fall of the Berlin Wall, and the U.S. invasion of Panama

Includes glossary and bibliographical references

973.93 United States--2001-

Corrigan, Jim

The **2000s** decade in photos; a new millennium. Enslow Publishers 2010 64p il (Amazing decades in photos) lib bdg $27.93

Grades: 4 5 6 7 **973.93**

1. World history -- 21st century 2. United States -- History -- 21st century

ISBN 978-0-7660-3139-5 lib bdg; 0-7660-3139-X lib bdg

LC 2008054644

This highlights the important world, national, and cultural developments of the first decade of the 21st century, including the disputed presidential election of 2000, the attacks of September 11, 2001, the Iraq War, digital technology and gadgets, the drop in stock market prices of internet companies, steroid use in sports, the Space Shuttle disaster of

2003, the tsumani of 2004, Hurricane Katrina, the massacre at Virginia Tech, the energy crisis, and the 2008 presidential election

Includes glossary and bibliographical references

Sutherland, James

The **ten** -year century; explaining the first decade of the new millennium. Viking 2010 152p il $18.99

Grades: 7 8 9 10 **973.93**

1. Modern history 2. United States -- History -- 21st century 3. United States -- Politics and government -- 2001-

ISBN 978-0-670-01223-7; 0-670-01223-8

LC 2010007314

"This overview of the first 10 years of the new millennium focuses on significant developments that have shaped life in the United States today. . . . The lucid, balanced narration results in a nuanced representation of a rapidly changing era." Publ Wkly

Includes bibliographical references

973.931 Administration of George W. Bush, 2001-2009

Abbott, David

The **Twin** Towers. Arcturus Pub. 2011 46p il (A place in history) lib bdg $34.25

Grades: 7 8 9 10 **973.931**

1. Terrorism 2. September 11 terrorist attacks, 2001 3. World Trade Center terrorist attack, 2001

ISBN 978-1-84837-677-9; 1-84837-677-4

LC 2010014195

"A recap of American Airlines Flight 11 just before it struck the north tower of the World Trade Center opens this thorough coverage of the events leading up to the attack and its affect on the nation. Following a look at the Twin Towers, this . . . title focuses on the motivation behind the terrorist attacks by addressing the rise of Islam, anti-Americanism, and al-Qaeda. . . . Additional quotes from Osama bin Laden and individuals affected by the attacks; related facts . . .; and attention-getting photos . . . make this a solid choice for U.S. studies." Booklist

Includes bibliographical references

Benoit, Peter

September 11 we will never forget; by Peter Benoit. Children's Press 2012 64 p. col. ill., col. map (ornerstones of freedom) (library) $30.00; (paperback) $8.95

Grades: 4 5 6 7 **973.931**

1. September 11 terrorist attacks, 2001 2. Terrorism -- United States

ISBN 0531250407; 9780531250402; 9780531265659

LC 2011009586

This book presents an "overview of the events of September 11, 2001 and the impact the day continues to have on present day life. . . . Boxed text adds information about international reaction, and the life of Osama Bin Laden, and other topics throughout the book. . . . .The immediate emergency responses at each site are described as well as government actions such as immediate grounding of planes . . . and military initiatives in the Middle East." (Children's Literature)

Includes bibliographical references (p. 61) and index.

Burgan, Michael

George W. Bush; Michael Burgan. Marshall Cavendish Benchmark 2012 112 p. $34.21

Grades: 5 6 7 8 **973.931**

1. Terrorism 2. Presidents -- United States 3. Presidents -- United States -- Biography

ISBN 1608701840; 9781608701841

LC 2010014801

This book "in the 'Presidents and Their Times' series provides . . . information about George W. Bush and how he handled critical situations (e.g., domestic spying vis-a-vis telephone records to highlight the difficulty battling terrorism and the effect of Bush's response to Hurricane Katrina). . . . Personal information is also provided about his early years, including his marriage to Laura, entry into politics, relationships with other family members, a decision to stop drinking, and his choice to become a Christian fundamentalist." Also included are "color and older black and white photos" and back matter such as "a timeline, chapter notes with complete citations, a glossary, books and websites for additional information, bibliography (books, articles, media), and index." (Children's Literature)

Includes bibliographical references and index

Hillstrom, Kevin

The **September** 11 terrorist attacks; by Kevin Hillstrom. Omnigraphics 2012 xv, 268 p.p (Defining moments) (hardcover : alk. paper) $55

Grades: 8 9 10 11 12 **973.931**

1. Qaida (Organization) 2. September 11 terrorist attacks, 2001 3. Terrorism -- United States

ISBN 0780812409; 9780780812406

LC 2011050673

This teen nonfiction reference book, by Kevin Hillstrom, is part of the "Defining Moments" series. It "opens with a lengthy overview that traces the origins and evolution of radical Islam, the birth and growth of Al Qaeda and its early attacks on the West, the events of September 11th, and the lasting . . . effects of the attack. The next section provides brief biographical sketches of eight terrorists and American . . . officials." (School Library Journal)

Includes bibliographical references and index

Wachtel, Alan

★ **September** 11; a primary source history. Gareth Stevens Pub. 2009 48p il (In their own words) lib bdg $27

Grades: 5 6 7 8 **973.931**

1. Terrorism 2. September 11 terrorist attacks, 2001

ISBN 978-1-4339-0048-8; 1-4339-0048-3

LC 2008045132

"The horror of September 11 feels very immediate, and uses both quotes from those who lived through it and stills from the attacks. The book does a fine job of chronicling the events, up to and including the controversies surrounding the New York memorial. The use of transcripts of phone conversations that took place aboard the doomed planes gives the book's beginning an almost 'you are there' effect. Later chapters feature such diverse sources as text from the Patriot Act and lyrics from Neil Young's song 'Let's Roll' to amplify the mood of the country." Booklist

Includes bibliographical references

Williams, Brian

The **war** on terror. Arcturus Pub. 2011 46p il (Secret history) lib bdg $32.80

Grades: 7 8 9 10 **973.931**

1. Terrorism 2. September 11 terrorist attacks, 2001 3. War on terrorism

ISBN 978-1-84837-699-1; 1-84837-699-5

LC 2010011013

This book explores the secrets of the War on Terror. It began with the terrorist attacks of 9/11, but the War on Terror is mostly fought in secret. Its fighters are spies, analysts, moles, and informers. Its weapons are phone taps, satellites, and killer drones.

"The title of the Secret History series will grab readers, even reluctant ones, and they won't be disappointed by the intriguing info regarding codes and code breakers, spies, terrorists, and double agents, with profiles of heroes and traitors on all sides. . . . The readable design, with clear type on thick, high-quality paper, includes lots of sidebars, photos, screens, and quotes." Booklist

Includes bibliographical references

974 Specific states of United States

Bial, Raymond

The **Delaware**. Marshall Cavendish Benchmark 2005 127p il map (Lifeways) lib bdg $38.50

Grades: 5 6 7 8 **974**

1. Delaware Indians 2. Native Americans

ISBN 978-0-7614-1904-4; 0-7614-1904-7

LC 2004-3088

Discusses the history, culture, beliefs, changing ways, and notable people of the Delaware.

Includes glossary and bibliographical references

Johnson, Claudia Durst

Daily life in colonial New England; [by] Claudia Durst Johnson. Greenwood Press 2002 xxvii, 215p (Daily life through history) $49.95

Grades: 7 8 9 10 **974**

1. New England -- History 2. New England -- Social life and customs -- To 1775 3. United States -- Social life and customs -- 1600-1775, Colonial period

ISBN 0-313-31458-6

LC 00-61721

This description of colonial life in New England covers such topics as the clergy and the church, crime and punishment, government and law, labor, shelter and attire, food and health, marriage and sex, arts and amusements, and Native Americans and Africans in New England

"In this excellent volume, Johnson draws a remarkably clear and complete picture of the day-to-day existence of the first European settlers in New England." Voice Youth Advocates

Includes bibliographical references

Rylant, Cynthia

★ **Appalachia**; the voices of sleeping birds. illustrated by Barry Moser. Harcourt Brace Jovanovich 1991 21p il $17; pa $6

Grades: 4 5 6 7 **974**

1. Appalachian region

ISBN 0-15-201605-8; 0-15-201893-X pa

LC 90-36798

"Taking her subtitle from a passage by James Agee, the author conveys with a marvelous economy of words the essence of the very special part of America where she was raised. A poetic text projects emotion as well as information. . . . Moser's watercolors capture the scene perfectly. . . . The book is a treasure—simply a beautiful combination of text and art." Horn Book

974.1 Maine

Dornfeld, Margaret

Maine; by Margaret Dornfeld and Joyce Hart. 2nd ed.; Marshall Cavendish Benchmark 2010 144p il map (Celebrate the states) lib bdg $42.79

Grades: 5 6 7 8 **974.1**

1. Maine

ISBN 978-0-7614-4726-9; 0-7614-4726-1

LC 2009002583

This offers information on the geography, history, wildlife, governmental structure, economy, cultural diversity, peoples, religion, and landmarks of Maine.

Includes bibliographical references

Heinrichs, Ann

Maine; By Ann Heinrichs. Revised edition Children's Press, A Division of Scholastic Inc. 2014 144 p. (library binding) $40

Grades: 4 5 6 7 **974.1**

1. Maine 2. Geography

ISBN 0531248879; 9780531248874

LC 2013032187

"Located in the far northeast corner of the country, Maine is known for its breathtaking natural beauty. Readers will trace the history of this remarkable state from its earliest settlement to its latest developments. They will also dive into the local culture, see the state's many fascinating sights, and learn about its economy." (Publisher's note)

Includes bibliographical references and index

974.2 New Hampshire

Auden, Scott

New Hampshire, 1603-1776; [by] Scott Auden ; with Alan Taylor, consultant. National Geographic Society 2007 109p il map (Voices from colonial America) $21.95; lib bdg $32.90

Grades: 5 6 7 8 **974.2**

1. New Hampshire -- History

ISBN 978-1-4263-0034-9; 1-4263-0034-4; 978-1-4263-0035-6 lib bdg; 1-4263-0035-2 lib bdg

LC 2006-36055

Provides a look at the long and changing colonial history of the state of New Hampshire through a review of its borders, founding fathers, motto, and more, complete with archival images, period maps, and various first-person accounts.

Offers " thorough, well-documented information about the struggles and successes of early non-native settlers [in New Hampshire]. . . . Many reproductions of period illustrations (both color and sepia) and some photos of archival documents and maps enhance the text." Horn Book Guide

Includes bibliographical references

Kent, Deborah, 1948-

New Hampshire; Deborah Kent. Revised edition Children's Press, an imprint of Scholastic Inc. 2015 144 p. illustrations, maps (library binding : alk. paper) $40

Grades: 4 5 6 7 **974.2**

1. New Hampshire 2. United States -- History

ISBN 0531282848; 9780531282847

LC 2013044358

"As one of the earliest English colonies in North America, New Hampshire played a major role in the formation of the United States. Readers will learn how this small New England state impacted the nation's development and why it remains a vital part of the country today. They will also tour New Hampshire's beautiful towns and wilderness areas, discover the local wildlife, and sample the state's rich traditions." (Publisher's note)

Includes bibliographical references(pages 133-137)and index

Otfinoski, Steven

New Hampshire; [by] Steve Otfinoski. 2nd ed.; Marshall Cavendish Benchmark 2008 144p il map (Celebrate the states) lib bdg $39.93

Grades: 4 5 6 7 **974.2**

1. New Hampshire

ISBN 978-0-7614-2718-6; 0-7614-2718-X

LC 2007-9944

First published 1999

"Provides comprehensive information on the geography, history, wildlife, governmental structure, economy, cultural diversity, peoples, religion, and landmarks of New Hampshire." Publisher's note

Includes bibliographical references

974.3 Vermont

Heinrichs, Ann

Vermont; by Ann Heinrichs. Revised edition Children's Press 2015 144 p. illustrations, maps (library binding : alk. paper) $40

Grades: 4 5 6 7 **974.3**

1. Vermont 2. Geography

ISBN 9780531282960 ; 0531282961

LC 2013046228

"A small state of small towns, Vermont preserves a New England heritage that reaches back many generations. Readers will find out what it is like to make homemade maple syrup and attend county fairs as they explore Vermont's history and culture. They will also learn about the state's government, wildlife, and economy." (Publisher's note)

Includes bibliographical references and index

974.4 Massachusetts

Doherty, Kieran

William Bradford; rock of Plymouth. 21st Cent. Bks. (Brookfield) 1999 192p il lib bdg $24.90

Grades: 6 7 8 9 **974.4**

1. Historians 2. Pilgrims (New England colonists) 3. Colonists 4. Pilgrim fathers 5. Massachusetts -- History -- 1600-1775, Colonial period

ISBN 0-7613-1304-4

LC 99-10631

A biography of one of the founders of the Plymouth Colony in Massachusetts and a history of the Pilgrims' difficult times during their early years in the New World

Includes bibliographical references

Edwards, Judith

The **Plymouth** Colony and the Pilgrim adventure in American history. Enslow Pubs. 2003 128p il map (In American history) lib bdg $26.60

Grades: 7 8 9 10 **974.4**

1. Pilgrims (New England colonists) 2. Massachusetts -- History -- 1600-1775, Colonial period

ISBN 0-7660-1989-6

LC 2002-12809

Traces the dangers and adventures surrounding the history of the Pilgrim settlement at Plymouth, Massachusetts, highlighting the roles played by William Brewster, Miles Standish, and other individuals

Includes bibliographical references

Trueit, Trudi Strain

Massachusetts; by Trudi Strain Trueit. Revised edition Children's Press, a Division of Scholastic Inc. 2014 144 p. (library binding) $40

Grades: 4 5 6 7 **974.4**

1. Massachusetts 2. Geography

ISBN 0531248895; 9780531248898

LC 2013032353

"As the origin point of the American Revolution, Massachusetts is home to some of the nation's oldest and most treasured historical sites. Readers will trace the history of this remarkable state from its earliest settlement to its latest developments. They will also dive into the local culture, see the state's many fascinating sights, and learn about its economy." (Publisher's note)

Includes bibliographical references and index

974.5 Rhode Island

Burgan, Michael

Rhode Island; by Michael Burgan. Revised edition Children's Press, a Division of Scholastic Inc. 2014 144 p. illustrations, maps (library binding : alk. paper) $40

Grades: 4 5 6 7 **974.5**

1. Rhode Island 2. United States -- History

ISBN 0531282910; 9780531282915

LC 2013044802

"Nestled between Connecticut and Massachusetts along the Atlantic Coast, Rhode Island is the smallest state in the nation. Readers will visit the state's lush forests, rocky coastline, and charming towns. They will find out how the state was settled and how it is governed today. They will also get a taste of Rhode Island's cuisine and culture as they learn about some of the state's local heroes." (Publisher's note)

Includes bibliographical references and index

Klein, Ted

Rhode Island; by Ted Klein. 2nd ed.; Marshall Cavendish Benchmark 2008 144p il map (Celebrate the states) lib bdg $39.93

Grades: 4 5 6 7 **974.5**

1. Rhode Island

ISBN 978-0-7614-2560-1; 0-7614-2560-8

LC 2006-36490

First published 1999

"Provides comprehensive information on the geography, history, wildlife, governmental structure, economy, cultural diversity, peoples, religion, and landmarks of Rhode Island." Publisher's note

Includes bibliographical references

974.6 Connecticut

Burgan, Michael

Connecticut, 1614-1776. National Geographic Society 2007 109p il map (Voices from colonial America) $21.95; lib bdg $32.90

Grades: 5 6 7 8 **974.6**

1. Connecticut -- History -- 1600-1775, Colonial period

ISBN 978-1-4263-0068-4; 1-4263-0068-9; 978-1-4263-0069-1 lib bdg; 1-4263-0069-7 lib bdg

LC 2007-3123

A history of Connecticut from its beginning as an English colony to 1788 when it became the fifth state.

Offers " thorough, well-documented information about the struggles and successes of early colonial settlers and settlements. . . . Many reproductions of period illustrations and some photographs of period documents and maps with relevant captions are included." Horn Book Guide

Includes bibliographical references

Kent, Zachary

Connecticut; by Zachary Kent. Revised edition Children's Press, an Imprint of Scholastic Inc. 2014 144 p. color illustrations, maps (library binding) $40

Grades: 4 5 6 7 **974.6**

1. Connecticut

ISBN 0531248798; 9780531248799

LC 2013031193

"Connecticut takes its name from a Native American word meaning 'land on the long tidal river.' Readers will trace the history of this remarkable state from its earliest settlement to its latest developments. They will also dive into the local culture, see the state's many fascinating sights, and learn about its economy." (Publisher's note)

Includes bibliographical references (page 138) and index

974.7 New York

Bial, Raymond

★ **Tenement**; immigrant life on the Lower East Side. Houghton Mifflin 2002 48p il $16

Grades: 4 5 6 7 **974.7**

1. Poor 2. Immigrants -- United States 3. Lower East Side (New York, N.Y.)

ISBN 0-618-13849-8

LC 2002-00407

Presents a view of New York City's tenements during the peak years of foreign immigration, discussing living conditions, laws pertaining to tenements, and the occupations of their residents

"The writing is particularly clear and sharp. Calling upon and quoting the writing of reformer Jacob Riis (and featuring his compelling photographs), Bial explains simply, yet engagingly, what tenement life was like. . . . Along with Riis' photographs, Bial provides some of his own, taken at the Lower East Side Tenement Museum in New York City." Booklist

Includes bibliographical references

Burgan, Michael

New York, 1609-1776; [by] Michael Burgan ; with Timothy J. Shannon, consultant. National Geographic Society 2006 109p il map (Voices from colonial America) $21.95; lib bdg $32.90

Grades: 5 6 7 8 **974.7**

1. New York (State) -- History

ISBN 978-0-7922-6390-6; 0-7922-6390-1; 978-0-7922-6860-4 lib bdg; 0-7922-6860-1 lib bdg

LC 2005-22033

Presents a brief history of colonial New York, from 1609 to 1776, and contains illustrations, historical maps, and first-person accounts from explorers, Native Americans, and colonists on early settlements.

Includes bibliographical references

Getzinger, Donna

★ The **Triangle** Shirtwaist Factory fire. Morgan Reynolds Pub. 2008 128p il map (American workers) $27.95

Grades: 7 8 9 10 **974.7**

1. New York (N.Y.) -- History 2. Labor -- Law and legislation 3. Triangle Shirtwaist Company, Inc.

ISBN 978-1-59935-099-8; 1-59935-099-8

LC 2008-4077

"Beginning with a brief account of the disaster, a description of the popular shirtwaist and the fabric used to make the blouse, the women who lost their lives, and the impact of the lack of communication among the workers, the first chapter is sure to hook readers. Successive chapters look more closely at New York City's growth, the varied immigrant population at that time, overcrowded factory conditions, the failure to enforce building regulations, and the many sweatshops developed from the desire of contractors to make money. . . . Archival photos and diagrams with captions add to the meaning of this devastating and important event in the history of labor." SLJ

Includes bibliographical references

Hansen, Joyce

★ **Breaking** ground, breaking silence; the story of New York's African burial ground. by Joyce Hansen and Gary McGowan. Holt & Co. 1998 130p il maps $19.95

Grades: 8 9 10 11 12 Adult **974.7**

1. Cemeteries 2. Excavations (Archeology) 3. African Americans -- History 4. New York (N.Y.) -- Antiquities

ISBN 0-8050-5012-4

LC 97-19105

Describes the discovery and study of the African burial site found in Manhattan in 1991, while excavating for a new building, and what it reveals about the lives of black people in Colonial times

"This book is well written and attractively designed, and readers should have access to it in social studies classrooms as well as in libraries. It will generate lots of class discussion and writing projects." Voice Youth Advocates

Huey, Lois Miner

American archaeology uncovers the Dutch colonies. Marshall Cavendish Benchmark 2009 64p il map (American archaeology) lib bdg $21.95

Grades: 4 5 6 7 **974.7**

1. Dutch Americans 2. America -- Antiquities 3. Netherlands -- Colonies -- America 4. Excavations (Archeology) -- United States

ISBN 978-0-7614-4263-9 lib bdg; 0-7614-4263-4 lib bdg

LC 2008050187

This describes how archeologists have learned about the history of Dutch settlers in America

"The text is quite chatty in this attractive title. . . . An inviting design with clear type includes several paintings of the period by a modern artist as well as maps and photos of excavation sites." Booklist

Includes glossary and bibliographical references

Mann, Elizabeth

Statue of Liberty; a tale of two countries. with illustrations by Alan Witschonke. Mikaya Press 2011 47p il map (Wonders of the world) $22.95

Grades: 4 5 6 7 **974.7**

1. Artists 2. Authors 3. Lawyers 4. Sculptors 5. National monuments 6. Children's authors 7. Fairy tale writers 8. Members of Parliament 9. Statue of Liberty (New York, N.Y.)

ISBN 978-1-931414-43-2; 1-931414-43-2

"The story of how Lady Liberty was conceived, constructed and bestowed makes a compelling tale. Pointing to the disparate long-term outcomes of the American and French revolutions to explain why the U.S. system of government became so admired in France, Mann takes the statue from Edouard Laboulaye's pie-in-the-sky proposal at a dinner party in 1865 to the massive opening ceremonies in 1886. . . . Witschonke supplements an array of period photos and prints with full-page or larger painted reconstructions of Bartholdi's studio and workshop, of the statue's piecemeal creation and finally of the Lady herself, properly copper colored as she initially was, presiding of New York's crowded harbor. As she still does." Kirkus

Includes bibliographical references

Marrin, Albert, 1936-

★ **Flesh** & blood so cheap; the Triangle fire and its legacy. Alfred A. Knopf 2011 182p il map $19.99; lib bdg $22.99

Grades: 5 6 7 8 **974.7**

1. Fires 2. Italian Americans 3. Jews -- United States 4. Labor -- United States 5. New York (N.Y.) -- History 6. Triangle Shirtwaist Company, Inc. 7. Industrial safety 8. United States -- Immigration and emigration

ISBN 978-0-375-86889-4; 0-375-86889-5; 978-0-375-96889-1 lib bdg; 0-375-96889-X lib bdg

LC 2010-21533

National Book Award Finalist: Young People's Literature (2011)

"Published to coincide with the centennial anniversary of the 1911 fire that erupted in the Triangle Shirtwaist Factory, this powerful chronicle examines the circumstances surrounding the disaster, which resulted in the deaths of 146 workers, mostly young Italian and Jewish women. . . . B&W photographs and illustrations reveal immigrant families' impoverished living environments, while testimonials describe the 'humiliating' work rules and unsafe conditions of factories like Triangle. . . . A concluding description of a Bangladeshi garment factory fire in 2010 offers contemporary parallels. Marrin's message that protecting human dignity is our shared responsibility is vitally resonant." Publ Wkly

Includes bibliographical references

Marsico, Katie

The **Triangle** Shirtwaist Factory fire; its legacy of labor rights. Marshall Cavendish Benchmark 2010 112p il (Perspectives on) lib bdg $27.95

Grades: 7 8 9 10 **974.7**

1. Fires 2. New York (N.Y.) -- History 3. Triangle Shirtwaist Company, Inc.

ISBN 978-0-7614-4027-7; 0-7614-4027-5

LC 2008-23267

"This well-written title examines many of the details preceding the 1911 disaster, the conditions that caused it, and the impact the incident continues to have on labor and businesses today. Historical accounts of the event, told through numerous direct quotes and shown in black-and-white photos of sweatshops and descriptions of tenement living conditions, reveal that poor labor laws and factory regulations were to blame. . . . Color photos and full-page sidebars provide additional information." SLJ

Includes bibliographical references

Murphy, Jim

★ The **giant** and how he humbugged America; by Jim Murphy. Scholastic Press 2012 112 p. (hardcover : alk. paper) $19.99

Grades: 5 6 7 8 **974.7**

1. Relics 2. Sculpture 3. Impostors and imposture 4. Cardiff giant 5. Cardiff (N.Y.) -- Antiquities 6. New York (State) -- Antiquities 7. Forgery of antiquities -- New York (State) -- Cardiff

ISBN 0439691842; 9780439691840

LC 2011036798

In this book, "[Jim] Murphy traces the checkered career of the 'Cardiff Giant,' a 10-foot-long stone figure unearthed in 1869 in an upstate New York farmyard. The giant was a national sensation until its unmasking as a hoax a few months later. Almost from the outset, both educated and popular opinion was divided over whether the figure was a fossilized human or a carving, an ancient relic or a modern 'humbug.' Murphy shows how the controversy itself fueled the giant's notoriety." (Booklist)

Includes bibliographical references and index

Platt, Richard

New York City; an illustrated history of the Big Apple. illustrated by Manuela Cappon. Kingfisher 2010 45p il map (Through time) $16.99

Grades: 4 5 6 7 **974.7**

1. New York (N.Y.) -- History

ISBN 978-0-7534-6416-8; 0-7534-6416-0

This is a history of New York City from its Native American origins to the present.

"In this magnificently illustrated work, historical happenings and intriguing offshoots are showcased like stars on Broadway. . . . A wealth of information in an engaging format." Booklist

Schomp, Virginia

New York; [by] Virginia Schomp. 2nd ed.; Benchmark Books 2006 144p il map (Celebrate the states) lib bdg $39.93

Grades: 4 5 6 7 **974.7**

1. New York (State)

ISBN 978-0-7614-1738-5; 0-7614-1738-9

LC 2004-853

First published 1997

This book about New York covers "standard facts: geography, history, government, economy, landmarks, and regions. . . . [It is] attractively illustrated with clear maps, charts, and pie graphs. Photos and reproductions of original documents add to overall effectiveness. . . . . Excellent additions for reports or general interest." SLJ

Includes bibliographical references

Slavicek, Louise Chipley

New York City's Central Park. Chelsea House Publishers 2009 120p il (Building America, then and now) lib bdg $35

Grades: 6 7 8 9 **974.7**

1. Central Park (New York, N.Y.)

ISBN 978-1-60413-044-7 lib bdg; 1-60413-044-X lib bdg

LC 2008-25548

This describes the history and impact of New York City's Central Park

"Photos, maps, and informative sidebars supplement the densely detailed writing. American history buffs will find [this volume] useful for doing research." Horn Book Guide

Includes glossary and bibliographical references

Somervill, Barbara A.

New York; by Barbara A. Somervill. Revised edition Children's Press 2014 144 p. illustrations, maps (library binding) $40

Grades: 4 5 6 7 **974.7**

1. New York (State) 2. United States -- History

ISBN 053124895X; 9780531248959

LC 2013032830

"Located in the northeastern United States, along the border with Canada, New York is home to the country's largest city. Readers will trace the history of this remarkable state from its earliest settlement to its latest developments. They will also dive into the local culture, see the state's many fascinating sights, and learn about its economy." (Publisher's note)

Includes bibliographical references and index

Talbott, Hudson

★ **River** of dreams; the story of the Hudson River. G. P. Putnam's Sons 2009 un il map $17.99

Grades: 4 5 6 7 **974.7**

1. Hudson River (N.Y. and N.J.)

ISBN 978-0-399-24521-3; 0-399-24521-9

Talbott offers a "compelling blend of political and natural history in this beautifully illustrated celebration of the Hudson River. Combining delicate watercolor-and-pencil illustrations with accessible text, the spreads move briskly through the Hudson's River's history." Booklist

974.8 Pennsylvania

Koestler-Grack, Rachel A.

The **Johnstown** flood of 1889. Chelsea House 2008 101p il (Great historic disasters) lib bdg $35

Grades: 6 7 8 9 **974.8**

1. Floods 2. Pennsylvania -- History

ISBN 978-0-7910-9763-2 lib bdg; 0-7910-9763-3 lib bdg

LC 2008-4894

This is a history of the flood of May 31, 1889 in Johnstown Pennsylvania

"Combining first-hand accounts, photographs, and other primary sources with a detailed and lively text, [this] fact-packed [resource offers] much to both report writers and history buffs." Horn Book Guide

Includes glossary and bibliographical references

Peters, Stephen

Pennsylvania; by Stephen Peters and Joyce Hart. 2nd ed.; Marshall Cavendish Benchmark 2009 144p il map (Celebrate the states) lib bdg $42.79

Grades: 4 5 6 7 **974.8**

1. Pennsylvania

ISBN 978-0-7614-3403-0; 0-7614-3403-8

LC 2008-8032

First published 2000

"Provides comprehensive information on the geography, history, wildlife, governmental structure, economy, cultural diversity, peoples, religion, and landmarks of Pennsylvania." Publisher's note

Includes bibliographical references

Somervill, Barbara A.

Pennsylvania; by Barbara A. Somervill. Revised edition Children's Press, A Division of Scholastic Inc. 2015 144 p. illustrations, maps (library binding : alk. paper) $40

Grades: 4 5 6 7 **974.8**

1. Pennsylvania 2. United States -- History

ISBN 0531282899; 9780531282892

LC 2013044801

"On July 4, 1776, members of the Continental Congress signed the Declaration of Independence in Philadelphia, making Pennsylvania the birthplace of the United States. Since then, Pennsylvania has continued to play an integral role in the nation's history. Readers will learn how the state has changed over time, how it is governed, and what it is like to live there today. They will also explore its breathtaking outdoor areas and vibrant cities." (Publisher's note)

Includes bibliographical references (page 138) and index

Walker, Sally M.

★ **Boundaries**; how the Mason-Dixon line settled a family feud and divided a nation. Sally M Walker. Candlewick Press 2014 208 p. ill., maps. $24.99

Grades: 7 8 9 10 11 12 **974.8**

1. Mason-Dixon Line 2. Surveying -- United States -- History -- 18th century

ISBN 0763656127; 9780763656126

LC 2013946612

This book, by Sally M. Walker, details the "Mason-Dixon Line's history, replete with property disputes, persecution, and ideological conflicts. . . . Walker traces the tale of the Mason-Dixon Line through family feuds, brave exploration, scientific excellence, and the struggle to define a cohesive country. But above all, this [is a] . . . story of surveying, marking, and respecting lines of demarcation." (Publisher's note)

"This thoroughly researched account of the Mason—Dixon Line encompasses a broad span of time and place, from sixteenth-century England to twentieth-century America... Walker's latest book offers a good deal of pertinent information on the subject at hand, as well as some interesting sidelights on American history." (Booklist)

974.9 New Jersey

Doak, Robin S.

New Jersey 1609-1776; y. [by] Robin Doak with Brendan McConville. National Geographic 2005 109p il map (Voices from colonial America) $21.95; lib bdg $32.90

Grades: 5 6 7 8 **974.9**

1. New Jersey -- History

ISBN 978-0-7922-6385-2; 0-7922-6385-5; 978-0-7922-6680-8 lib bdg; 0-7922-6680-3 lib bdg

LC 2004-26242

"This book gives detailed descriptions of family life and working in a Colonial village and the fight for independence. It also includes information about the Native people, early settlers, and first developments. . . . Paintings, maps, woodcuts, portraits, and reproductions accompany the well-written text. . . . An excellent resource." SLJ

Includes bibliographical references

Kent, Deborah, 1948-

New Jersey; by Deborah Kent. Revised edition Children's Press 2014 144 p. illustrations, maps (library binding) $40

Grades: 4 5 6 7 **974.9**

1. New Jersey 2. United States -- History

ISBN 0531248941; 9780531248942

LC 2013032829

"Though New Jersey is nicknamed the Garden State, it is actually one of the most urban and densely populated states in the country. Readers will trace the history of this remarkable state from its earliest settlement to its latest developments. They will also dive into the local culture, see the state's many fascinating sights, and learn about its economy." (Publisher's note)

Includes bibliographical references and index

Moragne, Wendy

New Jersey; by Wendy Moragne and Tamra B. Orr. 2nd ed.; Marshall Cavendish Benchmark 2009 144p il map (Celebrate the states) lib bdg $39.93

Grades: 4 5 6 7 **974.9**

1. New Jersey

ISBN 978-0-7614-3006-3; 0-7614-3006-7

LC 2007-38642

First published 2000

"Provides comprehensive information on the geography, history, wildlife, governmental structure, economy, cultural diversity, peoples, religion, and landmarks of New Jersey." Publisher's note

Includes bibliographical references

975.1 Delaware

Price, Karen

Delaware, 1638-1776; [by] Karen Hossell, with Karin Wulf, consultant. National Geographic Society 2006 109p il map (Voices from colonial America) $21.95; lib bdg $32.90

Grades: 5 6 7 8 **975.1**

1. Delaware -- History

ISBN 978-0-7922-6408-8; 0-7922-6408-8; 978-0-7922-6864-2 lib bdg; 0-7922-6864-4 lib bdg

LC 2006-13444

"Discusses the Native American massacre of the first European settlers in the Delaware region, and follows the events that helped the area develop into a thriving colony as it changed from Swedish to Dutch to British control." Publisher's note

Includes bibliographical references

Schuman, Michael

Delaware; by Michael Schuman and Marlee Richards. 2nd ed.; Marshall Cavendish Benchmark 2009 144p il map (Celebrate the states) lib bdg $42.79

Grades: 4 5 6 7 **975.1**

1. Delaware

ISBN 978-0-7614-3399-6; 0-7614-3399-6

LC 2008-5369

First published 2000

"Provides comprehensive information on the geography, history, wildlife, governmental structure, economy, cultural diversity, peoples, religion, and landmarks of Delaware." Publisher's note

Includes bibliographical references

975.2 Maryland

Blashfield, Jean F.

Maryland; By Jean F. Blashfield. Revised edition Children's Press, A Division of Scholastic Inc. 2014 144 p. color illustrations (library binding) $40

Grades: 4 5 6 7 **975.2**

1. Maryland 2. Geography

ISBN 0531248887; 9780531248881

LC 2013032188

"From the dense population of Baltimore to the untouched forests of the Appalachian region, Maryland is a land of incredible diversity. Readers will trace the history of this remarkable state from its earliest settlement to its latest developments. They will also dive into the local culture, see the state's many fascinating sights, and learn about its economy." (Publisher's note)

Includes bibliographical references and index

Doak, Robin S.

Maryland, 1634-1776. National Geographic 2007 105p il map (Voices from colonial America) $21.95; lib bdg $32.90

Grades: 5 6 7 8 **975.2**

1. Maryland -- History

ISBN 978-1-4263-0143-8; 1-4263-0143-x; 978-1-4263-0144-5 lib bdg; 1-4263-0144-8 lib bdg

LC 2007-27886

Offers "thorough, well-documented information about the struggles and successes of early colonial settlers and settlements. . . . Many reproductions of period illustrations and some photographs of period documents and maps with relevant captions are included." Horn Book Guide

Includes bibliographical references

Moore, Wes, 1978-

Discovering Wes Moore; Wes Moore. Delacorte Press 2012 160 p. (hardcover) $15.99

Grades: 7 8 9 10 11 12 **975.2**

1. Family life 2. Conduct of life 3. Blacks -- Biography 4. Youth -- Conduct of life 5. African American men -- Biography 6. Baltimore (Maryland) -- Biography 7. Bronx (New York, N.Y.) -- Biography 8. Soldiers -- United States -- Biography 9. Criminals -- Maryland -- Baltimore -- Biography 10. African Americans -- Maryland -- Baltimore -- Social conditions -- 20th century 11. African Americans -- Bronx (New York, N.Y.) -- Social conditions -- 20th century

ISBN 0385741677; 9780375986703; 9780375990182; 9780385741675

LC 2011049135

Author Wes Moore describes his experiences growing up. "After receiving poor grades and falling in with a bad crowd, his family pooled their limited finances to send him to Valley Forge Military Academy, where he found positive role models and became a Corps commander and star athlete. After earning an undergraduate degree, Wes attended Oxford as a Rhodes Scholar. When the author read about the conviction of another Wes Moore for armed robbery and killing a police officer, he wanted to find out how two youths . . . could take such divergent paths." (Kirkus)

Pietrzyk, Leslie

Maryland; by Leslie Rauth and Martha Kneib. 2nd ed.; Marshall Cavendish Benchmark 2008 144p il map (Celebrate the states) lib bdg $39.93

Grades: 4 5 6 7 **975.2**

1. Maryland

ISBN 978-0-7614-3004-9; 0-7614-3004-0

LC 2007-29497

First published 2000

"Provides comprehensive information on the geography, history, wildlife, governmental structure, economy, cultural diversity, peoples, religion, and landmarks of Maryland." Publisher's note

Includes bibliographical references

975.3 District of Columbia (Washington)

Aretha, David

The **story** of the civil rights march on Washington for jobs and freedom in photographs; David Aretha. Enslow Publishers, Inc. 2014 48 p. illustrations (some color) (The story of the civil rights movement in photographs) library $25.27

Grades: 5 6 7 8 **975.3**

1. March on Washington for Jobs and Freedom (1963 : Washington, D.C.) 2. African Americans -- Civil rights 3. Civil rights demonstrations -- Washington (D.C.) 4. March on Washington for Jobs and Freedom (1963 : Washington, D.C.) -- Pictorial works

ISBN 0766042383; 9780766042384

LC 2013004860

Author "David Aretha explores the 'greatest demonstration for freedom' in American history. On August 28, 1963, more than 250,000 people descended on Washington, D.C. They came by bus, car, and bicycle. Some even walked hundreds of miles to be there. On that day, the massive crowd gathered to march, protest, sing, and support the Civil Rights Movement and to demonstrate that the time had come to end segregation in the South." (Publisher's note)

"This series explores key events of the Civil Rights Movement through historical primary source pictures and documents. The books dramatically carry the reader from early 1963 Birmingham to sit-ins, marches, and protests. Through dramatic photographs along with descriptive captions, the reader feels the raw emotions of the times." Lib Med Con

House, Katherine L.

The **White** House for kids; a history of a home, office, and national symbol : with 21 activities. Katherine L. House. Chicago Review Press 2014 144 p. illustrations, plans (For kids series) (pbk.) $16.95

Grades: 4 5 6 7 **975.3**

1. Presidents -- United States 2. White House (Washington, D.C.) 3. Washington (D.C.) -- Buildings, structures, etc.

ISBN 1613744617; 9781613744611

LC 2013038108

This children's book, by Katherine L. House, offers an "educates young readers on the White House. Blending facts from numerous primary sources with engaging anecdotes . . . , this book provides the complete story of the presidents' home. Details on the many changes, updates, renovations, and redecorations that have occurred over the years are featured as well as a look at the daily lives of the White House's inhabitants." (Publisher's note)

"Chapter organization enhances interest by covering seven subjects and including examples from multiple historical periods. From the purposes and architecture of the building to the nature of multiple jobs performed, this book shows the varied functions of the White House." VOYA

Includes bibliographical references and index

Kent, Deborah, 1948-

Washington, D.C. by Deborah Kent. Revised edition Children's Press 2015 144 p. illustrations, maps (library binding) $40

Grades: 4 5 6 7 **975.3**

1. Washington (D.C.) 2. Geography

ISBN 9780531282984 ; 0531282988

LC 2013044317

"The nation's capital city is located in a small space between Virginia and Maryland, but it is not a part of either state. Readers will discover why the District of Columbia was chosen to be the center of the U.S. government and how the city was planned and constructed. They will also learn about the vibrant local culture and traditions as they find out what it is like to live in D.C. today." (Publisher's note)

Includes bibliographical references and index

★ **Our** White House; looking in, looking out. created by The National Children's Book and Literacy Alliance; introduction by David McCullough. Candlewick Press 2008 241p il $29.99

Grades: 5 6 7 8 **975.3**

1. White House (Washington, D.C.) 2. Washington (D.C.) 3. Short stories -- Collections 4. Presidents -- United States -- Family 5. United States -- Politics and government

ISBN 0-7636-2067-X; 978-0-7636-2067-7

This is a collection of essays, personal accounts, historical fiction, and poetry devoted to the history of the White House. Index. "Age ten and up." (N Y Times Book Rev)

"The White House is the focus of this handsome, large-format compendium of writings, both factual and fictional, and illustrations. . . . Poems and essays, stories and memoirs—all combine to create a mosaic of impressions of the house's residents and visitors and of the important events that occurred there. . . . The often-spectacular, beautifully reproduced on glossy paper, is particularly striking." Booklist

975.4 West Virginia

Hoffman, Nancy

West Virginia; [by] Nancy Hoffman and Joyce Hart. 2nd ed.; Marshall Cavendish Benchmark 2007 144p il map (Celebrate the states) lib bdg $39.93

Grades: 4 5 6 7 **975.4**

1. West Virginia

ISBN 978-0-7614-2562-5; 0-7614-2562-4

LC 2006-29393

First published 1999

Relates the history and describes the geographic features, places of interest, government, industry, environmental concerns, and life of the people of West Virginia.

Includes bibliographical references

975.5 Virginia

Kent, Deborah, 1948-

Virginia; by Deborah Kent. Revised edition Children's Press 2014 144 p. illustrations, maps (library binding) $40

Grades: 4 5 6 7 **975.5**

1. Virginia 2. Geography

ISBN 9780531248997 ; 0531248992

LC 2013033044

"First colonized by Europeans with the founding of Jamestown in 1607, Virginia is home to some of the oldest continuous settlements in the country. Readers will trace the history of this remarkable state from its earliest settlement to its latest developments. They will also dive into the local culture, see the state's many fascinating sights, and learn about its economy." (Publisher's note)

Includes bibliographical references and index

Pobst, Sandy

Virginia, 1607-1776; [by] Sandy Pobst with Kevin D. Roberts, consultant. National Geographic Society 2005 109p il map (Voices from colonial America) $21.95; lib bdg $32.90

Grades: 5 6 7 8 **975.5**

1. Virginia -- History

ISBN 978-0-7922-6388-3; 0-7922-6388-X; 978-0-7922-6771-3 lib bdg; 0-7922-6771-0 lib bdg

LC 2005-8885

"This title discusses the colony's founding, life on the Tidewater plantations, the struggles to survive, and the desire for independence. Full of period maps; portraits; photographs; and first-person accounts from masters and slaves, explorers, Native Americans, servants, and other residents, this is narrative nonfiction at its best. . . . An excellent resource." SLJ

Includes bibliographical references

975.6 North Carolina

Cannavale, Matthew C.

North Carolina, 1524-1776; by Matthew C. Cannavale; with Patrick Griffith, consultant. National Geographic Society 2007 109p il map (Voices from colonial America) $21.95; lib bdg $32.90

Grades: 5 6 7 8 **975.6**

1. North Carolina -- History

ISBN 978-1-4263-0032-5; 1-4263-0032-8; 978-1-4263-0033-2 lib bdg; 1-4263-0033-6 lib bdg

LC 2006-36004

A history of colonial North Carolina.

Includes bibliographical references

Heinrichs, Ann

North Carolina; by Ann Heinrichs. Revised edition Children's Press 2014 144 p. illustrations, maps (library binding) $40

Grades: 4 5 6 7 **975.6**

1. North Carolina 2. United States -- History

ISBN 0531248968; 9780531248966

LC 2013032831

"From its wet marshlands and the towering Appalachian Mountains to cities such as Raleigh and Charlotte, North Carolina is home to a diverse range of environments. Readers will trace the history of this remarkable state from its earliest settlement to its latest developments. They will also dive into the local culture, see the state's many fascinating sights, and learn about its economy." (Publisher's note)

Includes bibliographical references (p. 138) and index

Miller, Lee

Roanoke; the mystery of the Lost Colony. Scholastic Nonfiction 2007 112p il map $18.99

Grades: 4 5 6 7 **975.6**

1. Roanoke Island (N.C.) -- History 2. United States -- History -- 1600-1775, Colonial period

ISBN 0-439-71266-1; 978-0-439-71266-8

LC 2005-51820

"Miller, author of Roanoke: solving the mystery of the Lost Colony (2001), here reprises for a young audience her historical theory that a certain man sabotaged the expedition eventually known as the Lost Colony. . . . Miller does an exceptional job of preseneting the Native American culture and viewpoint. . . . This handsomely designed book features one or two illustrations on each spread, many in color, including reproductions or period drawings, paintings, and maps, as well as modern photos of sites and wildlife." Booklist

Includes bibliographical references

Shirley, David

North Carolina; by David Shirley and Joyce Hart. 2nd ed.; Marshall Cavendish Benchmark 2010 144p il map (Celebrate the states) lib bdg $43.79

Grades: 5 6 7 8 **975.6**

1. North Carolina

ISBN 978-0-7614-4729-0; 0-7614-4729-6

LC 2009007139

First published 2001

This offers information on the geography, history, wildlife, governmental structure, economy, cultural diversity, peoples, religion, and landmarks of North Carolina.

Includes bibliographical references

975.7 South Carolina

Doak, Robin S.

South Carolina, 1540-1776; by Robin Doak with Robert Olwell. National Geographic Society 2007 109p il map (Voices from colonial America) $21.95; lib bdg $32.90

Grades: 5 6 7 8 **975.7**

1. South Carolina -- History

ISBN 978-1-4263-0066-0; 1-4263-0066-2; 978-1-4263-0067-7 lib bdg; 1-4263-0067-0 lib bdg

LC 2007-3120

A history of South Carolina from its beginning as an English colony to 1788 when it became the eighth state.

Offers "thorough, well-documented information about the struggles and successes of early colonial settlers and settlements. . . . Many reproductions of period illustrations and some photographs of period documents and maps with relevant captions are included" Horn Book Guide

Includes bibliographical references

Hoffman, Nancy

South Carolina; by Nancy Hoffman and Joyce Hart. 2nd ed.; Marshall Cavendish Benchmark 2010 144p il map (Celebrate the states) lib bdg $42.79

Grades: 5 6 7 8 **975.7**

1. South Carolina

ISBN 978-0-7614-4034-5; 0-7614-4034-8

LC 2008038266

First published 2001

This offers information on the geography, history, wildlife, governmental structure, economy, cultural diversity, peoples, religion, and landmarks of South Carolina.

Includes bibliographical references

975.8 Georgia

Doak, Robin S.

Georgia, 1521-1776. National Geographic Society 2006 109p il map (Voices from colonial America) $21.95; lib bdg $32.90

Grades: 5 6 7 8 **975.8**

1. Georgia -- History

ISBN 978-0-7922-6389-0; 0-7922-6389-8; 978-0-7922-6858-1 lib bdg; 0-7922-6858-X lib bdg

LC 2005-22141

Provides a history of Georgia from the arrival of European explorers in the sixteenth century to its becoming a state in 1788.

Includes bibliographical references

Otfinoski, Steven

Georgia; 2nd ed.; Marshall Cavendish Benchmark 2010 144p il map (Celebrate the states) lib bdg $42.79

Grades: 5 6 7 8 **975.8**

1. Georgia

ISBN 978-0-7614-4031-4; 0-7614-4031-3

LC 2008041711

First published 2001

This offers information on the geography, history, wildlife, governmental structure, economy, cultural diversity, peoples, religion, and landmarks of Georgia.

Includes bibliographical references

Prentzas, G. S.

Georgia; by G.S. Prentzas. Revised ed. Children's Press 2014 144 p. ill. (chiefly col.), col. maps $40

Grades: 4 5 6 7 **975.8**

1. Georgia 2. United States -- History

ISBN 053124881X; 9780531248812

"The last of the 13 original colonies to be established, Georgia is the largest state east of the Mississippi River. Readers will trace the history of this remarkable state from its earliest settlement to its latest developments. They will also dive into the local culture, see the state's many fascinating sights, and learn about its economy." (Publisher's note)

Includes bibliographical references and index

975.9 Florida

Cannavale, Matthew C.

Florida, 1513-1821; [by] Matthew C. Cannavale with Robert Olwell, consultant. National Geographic 2006 109p il map (Voices from colonial America) $21.95; lib bdg $32.90

Grades: 5 6 7 8 **975.9**

1. Florida -- History

ISBN 978-0-7922-6409-5; 0-7922-6409-6; 978-0-7922-6866-6 lib bdg; 0-7922-6866-0 lib bdg

LC 2006-20505

Offers "thorough, well-documented information about the struggles and successes of early nonnative settlers [in Florida]. . . . Many reproductions of period illustrations (both color and sepia) and some photos of archival documents and maps enhance the text." Horn Book Guide

Includes bibliographical references

Hart, Joyce

Florida; [by] Perry Chang and Joyce Hart. 2nd ed.; Marshall Cavendish Benchmark 2007 144p il map (Celebrate the states) lib bdg $39.93

Grades: 4 5 6 7 **975.9**

1. Florida

ISBN 978-0-7614-2348-5; 0-7614-2348-6

LC 2006-8174

First published 1998

"Provides comprehensive information on the geography, history, wildlife, governmental structure, economy, cultural diversity, peoples, religion, and landmarks of Florida." Publisher's note

Includes bibliographical references

Orr, Tamra B.

Florida; by Tamra B. Orr. Revised edition Children's Press 2014 144 p. ill. (chiefly col.), col. maps (America the beautiful, third series) $40

Grades: 4 5 6 7 **975.9**

1. Florida

ISBN 0531248801; 9780531248805

"Thanks to its warm weather and plentiful beaches, Florida is often called the Sunshine State. Readers will trace the history of this remarkable state from its earliest settlement to its latest developments. They will also dive into the local culture, see the state's many fascinating sights, and learn about its economy." (Publisher's note)

Includes bibliographical references (p. 137-138) and index

Turner, Glennette Tilley

★ **Fort** Mose; and the story of the man who built the first free black settlement in Colonial America. Abrams Books for Young Readers 2010 42p il map $18.95

Grades: 5 6 7 8 **975.9**

1. Army officers 2. Florida -- History 3. Fort Mose site (Fla.) 4. Slavery -- United States 5. African Americans -- History 6. United States -- History -- 1600-1775, Colonial period

ISBN 978-0-8109-4056-7; 0-8109-4056-6

LC 2009-52205

"In the 18th century, some Africans escaped slavery in England's southern colonies to find freedom in the Spanish colony of Florida. As a leader of St. Augustine's community, African-born Francisco Menendez helped establish Fort Mose, the first free black community on North American soil. Turner does an excellent job of explaining how the residents of Fort Mose probably blended African, English, and Spanish traditions to create a unique—and uniquely American—culture." SLJ

Includes glossary and bibliographical references

976 South central United States

Gillette, Robert H.

Escape to Virginia; From Nazi Germany to Thalhimer's Farm. Robert H. Gillette. Arcadia Publishing 2016 256 p. illustrations $19.99

Grades: 7 8 9 10 **976**

1. Persecution 2. Germans -- United States 3. World War, 1939-

1945 -- Jews
ISBN 1626199124; 9781626199125
LC 2015947683

This book, by Robert H. Gillette, tells how "Jewish teenagers Eva and Töpper desperately searched for an escape from the stranglehold of 1930s Nazi Germany. Richmond department store owner William B. Thalhimer created a safe haven on a rural Virginia farm where Eva and Töpper would find refuge. Discover the remarkable true story of two young German Jews who endured the emotional torture of their adolescence, journeyed to freedom and ultimately confronted the evil that could not destroy their spirit." (Publisher's note)

"Gillette calls his narrative 'creative history'—though his account is not fictionalized, he nonetheless strives to make it read like a novel. Mostly, he succeeds: Gillette is an excellent storyteller, and the details he uses so illustratively are from primary sources, such as letters, diaries, photos, and other personal narratives. Although Eva sometimes seems too good to be true, overall, this is an engrossing and informative study of a less familiar corner of a much-covered period. Ample source notes make this a solid choice for student research." Booklist

976.1 Alabama

Somervill, Barbara A.

Alabama; by Barbara A. Somervill. Revised edition Children's Press, an imprint of Scholastic, Inc. 2014 144 p. color illustrations, maps (library binding) $40

Grades: 4 5 6 7 **976.1**

1. Alabama
ISBN 0531248755; 9780531248751
LC 2013030720

"Nicknamed the "Heart of Dixie,' Alabama is one of the first states that comes to mind when most people think about the southern United States. Readers will trace the history of this remarkable state from its earliest settlement to its latest developments. They will also dive into the local culture, see the state's many fascinating sights, and learn about its economy." (Publisher's note)

Includes bibliographical references (page 138) and index

976.2 Mississippi

Dell, Pamela

Mississippi; by Pamela Dell. Revised edition Children's Press, A Division of Scholastic Inc. 2014 144 p. (library binding) $40

Grades: 4 5 6 7 **976.2**

1. Mississippi 2. Geography
ISBN 0531248917; 9780531248911
LC 2013032478

"Bordered by the incredible river than shares its name, Mississippi a land of small towns and sprawling farmland. Readers will trace the history of this remarkable state from its earliest settlement to its latest developments. They will also dive into the local culture, see the state's many fascinating sights, and learn about its economy." (Publisher's note)

Includes bibliographical references and index

Ribeiro, Myra

The **assassination** of Medgar Evers. Rosen Pub. Group 2002 64p il (Library of political assassinations) $26.50

Grades: 5 6 7 8 **976.2**

1. Civil rights activists 2. African Americans -- Civil rights
ISBN 0-8239-3544-2
LC 2001-2389

The author "does a good job of introducing the inspiring leader and the cause he fought for." Booklist

Includes glossary and bibliographical references

Shirley, David

Mississippi; [by] David Shirley and Patricia K. Kummer. Marshall Cavendish Benchmark 2008 144p il map (Celebrate the states) lib bdg $39.93

Grades: 4 5 6 7 **976.2**

1. Mississippi
ISBN 978-0-7614-2717-9; 0-7614-2717-1
LC 2007-7868

First published 1999

"Provides comprehensive information on the geography, history, wildlife, governmental structure, economy, cultural diversity, peoples, religion, and landmarks of Mississippi." Publisher's note

Includes bibliographical references

976.3 Louisiana

Goldstone, Lawrence

Unpunished murder; massacre at Colfax and the quest for justice. by Lawrence Goldstone. Scholastic Focus 2018 288 p. $17.99

Grades: 7 8 9 10 11 12 **976.3**

1. Massacres -- Louisiana -- Colfax 2. African Americans -- Crimes against 3. Constitutional law -- United States 4. Reconstruction (U.S. history, 1865-1877) -- Louisiana 5. United States. Supreme Court -- History -- 19th century 6. African Americans -- Crimes against -- Louisiana -- Colfax -- History -- 19th century
ISBN 9781338239454
LC 2017055119

This book, by Lawrence Goldstone, narrates how, "on Easter Sunday of 1873, just eight years after the Civil War ended, a band of white supremacists marched into Grant Parish, Louisiana, and massacred over one hundred unarmed African Americans. The court case that followed reached the highest court in the land. Yet, following one of the most ghastly incidents of mass murder in American history, not one person was convicted." (Publisher's note)

Includes bibliographical references and index

Lassieur, Allison

Louisiana; by Allison Lassieur. Revised edition Children's Press, A Division of Scholastic Inc. 2014 144 p. (library binding) $40

Grades: 4 5 6 7 **976.3**

1. Louisiana 2. Geography
ISBN 0531248860; 9780531248867
LC 2013032186

"In 2005, Louisiana met with disaster when Hurricane Katrina struck the Gulf Coast. Since then, the state has been working to rebuild and recover. Readers will trace the history of this remarkable state from its earliest settlement to its latest developments. They will also dive into the local culture, see the state's many fascinating sights, and learn about its economy." (Publisher's note)

Includes bibliographical references and index

Worth, Richard

Louisiana, 1682-1803. National Geographic Society 2005 109p il map (Voices from colonial America) $21.95; lib bdg $32.90

Grades: 5 6 7 8 **976.3**

1. Louisiana -- History

ISBN 978-0-7922-6544-3; 0-7922-6544-0; 978-0-7922-6850-5 lib bdg; 0-7922-6850-4 lib bdg

LC 2005-16225

This "history of Louisiana begins in 1682 when Sieur de La Salle claimed the region for France. After that time, the region was governed under several different flags, including France, Spain, and Great Britain. . . . Thomas Jefferson purchased the land for the United States in 1803." Publisher's note

Includes bibliographical references

976.4 Texas

Green, Carl R.

Sam Houston; courageous Texas hero. by William R. Sanford and Carl R. Green. Enslow Publishers 2013 48 p. ill., map (library) $21.26; (paperback) $7.95

Grades: 5 6 7 8 **976.4**

1. Picture books for children 2. Governors -- Texas -- Biography 3. Legislators -- United States -- Biography 4. United States. Congress. Senate -- Biography

ISBN 0766040097; 9780766040090; 9781464400926

LC 2011051265

This book, part of the Courageous Heroes of the American West series, looks at Sam Houston. "One of the founders of Texas, Sam Houston served the state as governor and senator—but he is most remembered as an American hero" for defeating the Mexican army. "Surprising the Mexican troops with their bold attack, . . . the fiery Texans rallied to an overwhelming victory, claiming their independence." (Publisher's note)

Includes bibliographical references (p. 47) and index.

Haley, James L.

Stephen F. Austin and the founding of Texas. PowerPlus Bks. 2003 112p il map (Library of American lives and times) lib bdg $31.95 **976.4**

1. Pioneers 2. Frontier and pioneer life -- Texas

ISBN 0-8239-5738-1

LC 2001-4955

Surveys the life of Stephen Austin, an American pioneer, who later became one of the founders of Texas

"Clear and engaging.... The good-quality illustrations are almost all reproductions of period paintings, maps, and documents." SLJ

Includes glossary and bibliographical references

Levy, Janey

The **Alamo**; a primary source history of the legendary Texas mission. Rosen Central Primary Source 2003 64p il maps (Primary sources in American history) lib bdg $29.25

Grades: 7 8 9 10 **976.4**

1. Texas -- History 2. Alamo (San Antonio, Tex.)

ISBN 0-8239-3681-3

LC 2002-2368

A collection of primary source materials highlights the story behind the Alamo and its place in the history of San Antonio, Texas

This "will be extremely effective when introducing students to primary source material." Libr Media Connect

Includes bibliographical references

Newton, Michael

★ The **Texas** Rangers. Chelsea House Publishers 2011 128p il (Law enforcement agencies) lib bdg $35

Grades: 6 7 8 9 **976.4**

1. Law enforcement 2. Texas Rangers 3. Texas -- History

ISBN 978-1-60413-626-5; 1-60413-626-X

"Solidly and comprehensively researched. . . . In The Texas Rangers, a group that has long excited the country's imagination gets a full treatment, including its appearances on screen. An attractive design, plenty of photos, and solid back matter complete [the] package. Extremely useful for students and appealing for browsers." Booklist

Includes bibliographical references

Sanford, William R.

Davy Crockett; courageous hero of the Alamo. by William R. Sanford and Carl R. Green. Rev. ed. Enslow Publishers 2013 48 p. col. ill., map (library) $21.26; (paperback) $7.95

Grades: 5 6 7 8 **976.4**

1. Alamo (San Antonio, Tex.) -- History -- Siege, 1836 2. Alamo (San Antonio, Tex.) -- Siege, 1836 3. Pioneers -- Tennessee -- Biography 4. Legislators -- United States -- Biography 5. United States. Congress. House -- Biography

ISBN 0766040054; 9780766040052; 9781464400865

LC 2011037749

This book by William Sanford is part of the Courageous Heroes of the American West series and focuses on Davy Crockett. "The courageous Texans chose to defend the fort in San Antonio against more than two thousands Mexican soldiers. . . . Although his brave deeds at the Alamo made him legendary, Crockett had already gained fame as a hunter, soldier, and U.S. Congressman." (Publisher's note)

Includes bibliographical references (p. 47) and index.

Somervill, Barbara A.

Texas; by Barbara A. Somervill. Revised edition Children's Press 2014 144 p. illustrations, maps (library binding) $40

Grades: 4 5 6 7 **976.4**

1. Texas 2. United States -- History

ISBN 0531248984; 9780531248980

LC 2013033041

"Second in size only to Alaska, Texas is famed for its huge cattle ranches, oil fields, and several major cities. Readers will trace the history of this remarkable state from its earliest settlement to its latest developments. They will also dive into the local culture, see the state's many fascinating sights, and learn about its economy." (Publisher's note)

Includes bibliographical references and index

Teitelbaum, Michael

Texas, 1527-1836. National Geographic Society 2005 109p il map (Voices from colonial America) $21.95; lib bdg $32.90

Grades: 5 6 7 8 **976.4**

1. Texas -- History

ISBN 978-0-7922-6387-6; 0-7922-6387-1; 978-0-7922-6682-2 lib bdg; 0-7922-6682-X lib bdg

LC 2005-11450

"Presents the history of Texas, including life in Spanish Texas, the arrival of American settlers, and The Texas Republic and statehood." Publisher's note

Includes bibliographical references

Wade, Mary Dodson

Henrietta King, la patrona; by Mary Dodson Wade ; illustrated by Bill Farnsworth. Bright Sky Press 2012 23 p. $16.95

Grades: 4 5 6 7 **976.4**

1. Women ranchers -- Biography 2. Women philanthropists -- Biography 3. King Ranch (Tex.) 4. Texas -- Biography 5. Ranchers -- Texas -- Biography 6. Women ranchers -- Texas -- Biography 7. Philanthropists -- Texas -- Biography 8. Women philanthropists -- Texas -- Biography

ISBN 1933979631; 9781933979632

LC 2011052721

This book by Mary Dodson Wade "examines the . . . life of one of Texas's foremost frontier women and philanthropists, Henrietta Maria Morse Chamberlain King. . . . Henrietta accompanied her missionary father on his travels and later settled with her husband Richard King in the untamed frontiers of the south Texas gulf coast. . . . Under her stewardship, the family ranch went from . . . $500,000 in debt at her husband's death to a debt-free enterprise of more than one million acres." (Publisher's note)

Walker, Paul Robert

Remember the Alamo; Texians, Tejanos, and Mexicans tell their stories. by Paul Robert Walker. National Geographic 2007 61p il map $17.95; lib bdg $27.90

Grades: 5 6 7 8 **976.4**

1. Texas -- History 2. Alamo (San Antonio, Tex.)

ISBN 978-1-4263-0010-3; 978-1-4263-0011-0 lib bdg

LC 2006034497

"Opening with clear context about why tensions between Texas residents and the Mexican government were brought to a head, the book then chronicles events directly leading to the siege of the Alamo and its immediate aftermath, following up with an epilogue on the decisive battle of San Jacinto 10 months later. Bringing the history to life is a healthy selection of dramatic, modern paintings along with plenty of archival drawings, maps, and old photos." Booklist

Includes bibliographical references

Warrick, Karen Clemens

Alamo; victory or death on the Texas frontier. Enslow Publishers 2008 128p il map (America's living history) lib bdg $31.93

Grades: 5 6 7 8 **976.4**

1. Texas -- History 2. Alamo (San Antonio, Tex.)

ISBN 978-0-7660-2937-8; 0-7660-2937-9

LC 2007038458

"Archival photographs, reproductions, maps, and sidebars combine with vivid [text] to provide [a] comprehensive [introduction] to [the siege and battle of the Alamo]. . . . [This] engaging [volume] vividly [brings its] time [period] to life." Horn Book Guide

Includes glossary and bibliographical references

Worth, Richard

The **Texas** war of independence: the 1800s; by Richard Worth. Marshall Cavendish Benchmark 2009 79p il map (Hispanic America) lib bdg $23.95

Grades: 6 7 8 9 **976.4**

1. Mexican Americans 2. Mexican War, 1846-1848 3. Texas -- History

ISBN 978-0-7614-2934-0

LC 2007029478

This "provides a solid overview of these pivotal events in Hispanic American history. Illustrated throughout with maps and archival images." Booklist

Includes glossary and bibliographical references

976.6 Oklahoma

Baldwin, Guy

Oklahoma; by Guy Baldwin and Joyce Hart. 2nd ed.; Marshall Cavendish Benchmark 2009 144p il map (Celebrate the states) lib bdg $42.79

Grades: 5 6 7 8 **976.6**

1. Oklahoma

ISBN 978-0-7614-4032-1; 0-7614-4032-1

LC 2008044261

First published 2001

This offers information on the geography, history, wildlife, governmental structure, economy, cultural diversity, peoples, religion, and landmarks of Oklahoma.

Includes bibliographical references

Orr, Tamra B.

Oklahoma; by Tamra B. Orr. Revised edition Children's Press, an imprint of Scholastic Inc. 2014 144 p. illustrations, maps (lib. bdg.) $40

Grades: 4 5 6 7 **976.6**

1. Oklahoma 2. United States -- History

ISBN 0531248976; 9780531248973

LC 2013033040

"Admitted in 1907 as the 46th state in the union, Oklahoma is home to one of the country''s largest Native American populations. Readers will trace the history of this remarkable state from its earliest settlement to its latest developments. They will also dive into the local culture, see the state's many fascinating sights, and learn about its economy." (Publisher's note)

Includes bibliographical references (page 138) and index

976.8 Tennessee

Barrett, Tracy

Tennessee; by Tracy Barrett. 2nd ed.; Marshall Cavendish Benchmark 2006 144p il map (Celebrate the states) lib bdg $39.93

Grades: 4 5 6 7 **976.8**

1. Tennessee

ISBN 978-0-7614-2151-1; 0-7614-2151-3

LC 2005-24055

First published 1998

"Provides comprehensive information on the geography, history, wildlife, governmental structure, economy, cultural diversity, peoples, religion, and landmarks of Tennessee." Publisher's note

Includes bibliographical references

Somervill, Barbara A.

Tennessee; by Barbara A. Somervill. Revised edition Children's Press, an Imprint of Scholastic Inc. 2014 144 p. illustrations, maps (library binding : alk. paper) $40

Grades: 4 5 6 7 **976.8**

1. Tennessee 2. United States -- History

ISBN 0531282945; 9780531282946

LC 2013046226

"Known for its diverse and robust music scene, down-home cooking, and breathtaking vistas, Tennessee has developed a rich and unique culture throughout its history. Readers will journey through the state's most exciting locations as they learn about its history, geography, and government. They will also read about the state's most famous residents and local tradition." (Publisher's note)

Includes bibliographical references and index

976.9 Kentucky

Barrett, Tracy

Kentucky; [by] Tracy Barrett. 2nd ed.; Marshall Cavendish Benchmark 2008 144p il map (Celebrate the states) lib bdg $39.93

Grades: 4 5 6 7 **976.9**

1. Kentucky

ISBN 978-0-7614-2715-5; 0-7614-2715-5

LC 2007-6388

First published 1999

"Provides comprehensive information on the geography, history, wildlife, governmental structure, economy, cultural diversity, peoples, religion, and landmarks of Kentucky." Publisher's note

Includes bibliographical references

Santella, Andrew

Kentucky; by Andrew Santella. Revised edition Children's Press 2014 144 p. col. ill., col. maps (library binding) $40

Grades: 4 5 6 7 **976.9**

1. Kentucky 2. Geography

ISBN 0531248852; 9780531248850

LC 2013031928

"Kentucky is famed for its horse races and rolling expanses of farmland. Readers will trace the history of this remarkable state from its earliest settlement to its latest developments. They will also dive into the local culture, see the state's many fascinating sights, and learn about its economy." (Publisher's note)

Includes bibliographical references and index

977 North central United States

Kummer, Patricia K.

The **Great** Lakes; [by] Patricia K. Kummer. Marshall Cavendish Benchmark 2008 96p il map (Nature's wonders) lib bdg $35.64

Grades: 5 6 7 8 **977**

1. Great Lakes

ISBN 978-0-7614-2853-4 lib bdg; 0-7614-2853-4 lib bdg

LC 2007019728

"Provides comprehensive information on the geography, history, wildlife, peoples, and environmental issues of the Great Lakes." Publisher's note

Includes glossary and bibliographical references

977.1 Ohio

Sherrow, Victoria

Ohio; [by] Victoria Sherrow. 2nd. ed.; Marshall Cavendish Benchmark 2008 144p il map (Celebrate the states) lib bdg $39.93

Grades: 4 5 6 7 **977.1**

1. Ohio

ISBN 978-0-7614-2558-8; 0-7614-2558-6

LC 2006-34103

First published 1999

"Provides comprehensive information on the geography, history, wildlife, governmental structure, economy, cultural diversity, peoples, religion, and landmarks of Ohio." Publisher's note

Includes bibliographical references

977.2 Indiana

Stille, Darlene R., 1942-

Indiana; by Darlene R. Stille. Revised edition Children's Press 2014 144 p. col. ill., col. maps (library binding) $40

Grades: 4 5 6 7 **977.2**

1. Indiana 2. Geography

ISBN 0531248844; 9780531248843

LC 2013031926

"Located in the heart of the Midwest, Indiana is often described as the Crossroads of America. Readers will trace the history of this remarkable state from its earliest settlement to its latest developments. They will also dive into the local culture, see the state's many fascinating sights, and learn about its economy." (Publisher's note)

Includes bibliographical references and index

977.3 Illinois

Burgan, Michael

Illinois; by Michael Burgan. Revised edition Children's Press, a division of Scholastic Inc. 2014 144 p. ill. (chiefly color), col. map (lib. bdg.) $40

Grades: 4 5 6 7 **977.3**

1. Illinois 2. Geography

ISBN 0531248836; 9780531248836

LC 2013031925

"As the home state of one of the nation's most beloved presidents, Illinois is nicknamed the Land of Lincoln. Readers will trace the history of this remarkable state from its earliest settlement to its latest developments. They will also dive into the local culture, see the state's many fascinating sights, and learn about its economy." (Publisher's note)

Includes bibliographical references (page 138) and index

Hurd, Owen

Chicago history for kids; triumphs and tragedies of the Windy city, includes 21 activities. [by] Owen Hurd. Chicago Review Press 2007 182p il map $14.95

Grades: 5 6 7 8 977.3
1. Chicago (Ill.) -- History
ISBN 978-1-55652-654-1; 1-55652-654-7
LC 2006031807

"This attractive overview begins with geography and moves to the colorful stories that characterize the city. Hurd tapped local experts and collections, using primary and secondary sources and the responses of young readers to craft this engaging resource. . . . Excellent-quality photos, maps, illustrations, or boxed facts appear on every page." SLJ

Includes bibliographical references

Murphy, Jim

★ The **great** fire. Scholastic 1995 144p il maps $16.95; pa $12.99

Grades: 5 6 7 8 9 10 977.3
1. Fires -- Chicago (Ill.)
ISBN 0-590-47267-4; 0-439-20307-4 pa
LC 94-9963

Newbery honor book, 1996

"Firsthand descriptions by persons who lived through the 1871 Chicago fire are woven into a gripping account of this famous disaster. Murphy also examines the origins of the fire, the errors of judgment that delayed the effective response, the organizational problems of the city's firefighters, and the postfire efforts to rebuild the city. Newspaper lithographs and a few historical photographs convey the magnitude of human suffering and confusion." Horn Book Guide

Includes bibliographical references

977.4 Michigan

Bial, Raymond

The **Menominee**. Marshall Cavendish Benchmark 2006 127p il map (Lifeways) lib bdg $38.50

Grades: 5 6 7 8 977.4
1. Native Americans 2. Menominee Indians
ISBN 978-0-7614-1903-7; 0-7614-1903-9
LC 2004-22392

Discusses the history, culture, beliefs, changing ways, and notable people of the Menominee.

Includes glossary and bibliographical references

Brill, Marlene Targ

Michigan; by Marlene Targ Brill. 2d ed.; Marshall Cavendish Benchmark 2007 144p il map (Celebrate the states) lib bdg $39.93

Grades: 4 5 6 7 977.4
1. Michigan
ISBN 978-0-7614-2351-5; 0-7614-2351-6
LC 2006-8181

First published 1998

"Provides comprehensive information on the geography, history, wildlife, governmental structure, economy, cultural diversity, peoples, religion, and landmarks of Michigan." Publisher's note

Includes bibliographical references

Raatma, Lucia

Michigan; by Lucia Raatma. Revised edition Children's Press 2014 144 p. ill. (chiefly col.), col maps (library binding) $40

Grades: 4 5 6 7 977.4
1. Michigan 2. Geography
ISBN 0531248909; 9780531248904
LC 2013032355

"Located amid the waters of the Great Lakes, Michigan takes its name from a Native American word meaning "large lake." Readers will trace the history of this remarkable state from its earliest settlement to its latest developments. They will also dive into the local culture, see the state's many fascinating sights, and learn about its economy." (Publisher's note)

Includes bibliographical references and index

977.5 Wisconsin

Blashfield, Jean F.

Wisconsin; by Jean F. Blashfield. Revised edition Children's Press 2014 144 p. illustrations, maps (library binding) $40

Grades: 4 5 6 7 977.5
1. Wisconsin 2. Geography
ISBN 9780531248744 ; 0531248747
LC 2013033045

"Thanks to its large number of dairy farms, Wisconsin is the nation's top cheese producer. Readers will trace the history of this remarkable state from its earliest settlement to its latest developments. They will also dive into the local culture, see the state's many fascinating sights, and learn about its economy." (Publisher's note)

Includes bibliographical references and index

977.6 Minnesota

Schwabacher, Martin

Minnesota; [by] Martin Schwabacher and Patricia K. Kummer. 2nd ed.; Marshall Cavendish Benchmark 2008 144p il map (Celebrate the states) lib bdg $39.93

Grades: 4 5 6 7 977.6
1. Minnesota
ISBN 978-0-7614-2716-2; 0-7614-2716-3
LC 2007-2895

First published 1999

"Provides comprehensive information on the geography, history, wildlife, governmental structure, economy, cultural diversity, peoples, religion, and landmarks of Minnesota." Publisher's note

Includes bibliographical references

977.7 Iowa

Blashfield, Jean F.

Iowa; by Jean F. Blashfield. Revised edition Children's Press, an Imprint of Scholastic Inc. 2015 144 p. illustrations, maps (library binding) $40

Grades: 4 5 6 7 977.7
1. Iowa 2. Geography
ISBN 0531282791; 9780531282793
LC 2013044318

"Flanked on either side by two of the nation's mightiest rivers, Iowa's fertile rolling hills have made it one of the country's leading sources of agriculture. Readers will discover what grows in Iowa's vast, sprawling fields. They will also learn how the state was founded, what role it has played in U.S. history, and what life is like today in the Hawkeye State." (Publisher's note)

Includes bibliographical references (page 138) and index

Morrice, Polly Alison

Iowa; by Polly Morrice and Joyce Hart. 2nd ed.; Marshall Cavendish Benchmark 2007 144p il map (Celebrate the states) lib bdg $39.93

Grades: 4 5 6 7 **977.7**

1. Iowa

ISBN 978-0-7614-2350-8; 0-7614-2350-8

LC 2006-13620

First published 1998

"Provides comprehensive information on the geography, history, wildlife, governmental structure, economy, cultural diversity, peoples, religion, and landmarks of Iowa." Publisher's note

Includes bibliographical references

977.8 Missouri

Blashfield, Jean F.

Missouri; by Jean F. Blashfield. Revised edition Children's Press, A Division of Scholastic Inc. 2015 144 p. (library binding : alk. paper) $40

Grades: 4 5 6 7 **977.8**

1. Missouri 2. Geography

ISBN 0531282821; 9780531282823

LC 2013044325

"From the skyscrapers of St. Louis and Kansas City to the sprawling natural landscapes of the Ozarks and the Osage Prairie, Missouri is home to a breathtaking range of environments. Readers will learn how the area was first settled thousands of years ago by Native Americans and how it came to be part of the United States. They will also learn what it is like to live there today." (Publisher's note)

Includes bibliographical references(pages 138) and index

978 Western United States

Bodden, Valerie

Through the American West; by Valerie Bodden. Creative Education 2011 48 p. col. ill. (Great Expeditions) (library) $34.25

Grades: 5 6 7 8 **978**

1. Lewis and Clark Expedition (1804-1806) 2. West (U.S.) -- Discovery and exploration

ISBN 1608180654; 9781608180653

LC 2010033413

This book by Valerie Bodden is part of the "Great Expeditions" series. It describes an expedition "led by William Clark and Meriwether Lewis to explore the wilderness to the west and look for an all water route to the Pacific Ocean. They were aided by Sacagawea, a Shoshone Indian. The adventures and hardships of the arduous three-year journey include both the achievements and the disappointments encountered along the way". (Children's Literature)

Includes bibliographical references (p. 46-47) and index.

Brown, Don, 1949-

★ The **great** American dust bowl; by Don Brown. Houghton Mifflin Harcourt 2013 80 p. $18.99

Grades: 5 6 7 8 9 **978**

1. Dust storms -- Graphic novels 2. Dust Bowl Era, 1931-1939

ISBN 0547815506; 9780547815503

Author Don Brown presents a "graphic novel of one of America's most catastrophic natural events: the Dust Bowl. On a clear, warm Sunday, April 14, 1935, a wild wind whipped up millions upon millions of these specks of dust to form a duster, a savage storm on America's high southern plains." (Publisher's note)

"In this bleak yet compelling graphic-novel-style glimpse at the Dirty Thirties, Brown crisply paces the narrative with fascinating glimpses of the sociological and geological causes of the Dust Bowl. The color brown is a recurring theme here, as Brown relies, aptly, almost entirely on shades of brown throughout. Primary source material is used liberally, as characters speak directly to the reader, documentary-style." (Horn Book)

Croy, Anita

★ **Ancient** Pueblo; archaeology unlocks the secrets of America's past. by Anita Croy; J. Jefferson Reid, consultant. National Geographic 2007 64p il map (National Geographic investigates) $17.95; lib bdg $27.90

Grades: 4 5 6 7 **978**

1. Archeology 2. Pueblo Indians 3. Southwestern States -- Antiquities

ISBN 978-1-4263-0130-8; 978-1-4263-0131-5 lib bdg

LC 2007024800

This describes the prehistoric sites of the American Southwest, and what archeologists have learned from them about the lives of ancient Pueblo peoples.

Includes glossary and bibliographical references

George-Warren, Holly

The **cowgirl** way; hats off to America's women of the West. Houghton Mifflin Books for Children 2010 112p il $18

Grades: 4 5 6 7 **978**

1. Cowhands 2. Women -- West (U.S.)

ISBN 978-0-618-73738-3; 0-618-73738-3

"With ample dynamic photos and lively quotes throughout, George-Warren presents a thoroughly absorbing overview of the history of cowgirls up to the present. . . . Famous figures such as Belle Starr, Calamity Jane, and Annie Oakley are discussed in brief, but the real delights here are the anecdotes on lesser-known figures such as Lucille Mulhall, the first woman to be dubbed a cowgirl in print. . . . The introduction of women as rodeo and trick riders and their contributions to the sports in the 1920s and '30s are covered in fascinating detail, as are the film and singing sensations of the 1940s and '50s." SLJ

Huey, Lois Miner

American archaeology uncovers the westward movement. Marshall Cavendish Benchmark 2009 64p il map (American archaeology) lib bdg $21.95

Grades: 4 5 6 7 **978**

1. Historical geography 2. West (U.S.) -- History 3. United States -- Territorial expansion 4. Frontier and pioneer life -- West (U.S.) 5. Excavations (Archeology) -- United States

ISBN 978-0-7614-4265-3 lib bdg; 0-7614-4265-0 lib bdg

LC 2009003167

This describes how archeologists have learned about the history of the American West.

"The visually pleasing . . . [book is] replete with maps, paintings, and photographs, all appropriately placed and thoughtfully captioned. . . . Huey's focus on American history, which is broken down into small, manageable chunks, is sure to entice budding historians." SLJ

Includes glossary and bibliographical references

Marrin, Albert

★ **Years** of dust; the story of the Dust Bowl. Dutton Children's Books 2009 128p il map $22.99

Grades: 6 7 8 9 10 **978**

1. Droughts 2. Dust storms 3. Great Depression, 1929-1939 4. Great Plains -- History

ISBN 978-0-525-42077-4; 0-525-42077-0

LC 2008-13898

"The engaging narrative includes quotes from a variety of primary sources, and it is abundantly illustrated throughout with photographs and other archival material, making this a reader-friendly, insightful work of history." Kirkus

Includes glossary and bibliographical references

Miller, Brandon Marie

Women of the frontier; 16 tales of trailblazing homesteaders, entrepreneurs, and rabble-rousers. Brandon Marie Miller. Chicago Review Press 2013 256 p. (hardcover) $19.95

Grades: 7 8 9 10 11 12 **978**

1. Women -- United States 2. Frontier and pioneer life -- United States 3. West (U.S.) -- History -- Biography 4. Women pioneers -- West (U.S.) -- History -- Biography

ISBN 1883052971; 9781883052973

LC 2012035756

This book, part of the Women of Action series, is a collection of "tales of women's trials and triumphs during the years of settlement in the [U.S.] West. . . . [The section] 'Many a Weary Mile' describes the trip west by wagon; 'Oh Give Me a Home' explores early pioneering experiences. 'A Woman Can Work,' 'And Now the Fun Begins' and 'Great Expectations for the Future' all examine the careers of women who stepped out of typical female roles of the era." (Kirkus)

Includes bibliographical references and index

★ The **Old** West: history and heritage. Marshall Cavendish Reference 2009 11v il map set$359.95

Grades: 6 7 8 9 **978**

1. Reference books 2. West (U.S.) -- History -- Encyclopedias

ISBN 978-0-7614-7829-4; 0-7614-7829-9

LC 2008062302

In this set "each volume contains about 100 pages with 18 to 21 signed articles that vary in length from 3 to 10 pages and are arranged in an easy-to-use alphabetical sequence. The overall style is lively and enticing. The scope of the 193 articles includes the Canadian West and the Mexican territory and deals with the time period from 1787 to 1912. . . . The set is thoughtfully arranged and can be used by a wide range of students. The articles are interesting and enlightening." Booklist

Includes glossary and bibliographical references

Olson, Tod

How to get rich on a Texas cattle drive; afterword by Marc Aronson; illustrations by Scott Allred & Gregory Proch. National Geographic 2010 47p il map $18.95

Grades: 4 5 6 7 **978**

1. Cowhands 2. West (U.S.) -- History 3. Frontier and pioneer life -- West (U.S.)

ISBN 978-1-4263-0524-5; 1-4263-0524-9

"This book provides one of the better true-to-life insider accounts of what happens on a cattle drive: why the cattle are being driven, where they're being driven to and from, and the multitude of daily chores and unforeseen obstacles along the way. Period photos and artwork, as well as original drawings, make for a lively design, and an ongoing ledger keeps track of the main character's mostly modest finances." Booklist

★ **How** to get rich on the Oregon Trail; my adventures among cows, crooks & heroes on the road to fame and fortune. [illustrations by Scott Allred & Gregory Proch; afterword by Marc Anonson] National Geographic 2009 47p il (How to get rich) $18.95; lib bdg $27.90

Grades: 4 5 6 7 **978**

1. Oregon Trail 2. Frontier and pioneer life 3. Overland journeys to the Pacific 4. West (U.S.) -- History 5. Oregon Trail -- History 6. Western States -- Discovery and exploration

ISBN 1-4263-0412-9; 1-4263-0413-7 lib bdg; 978-1-4263-0412-5; 978-1-4263-0413-2 lib bdg

This is a follow-up to How to Get Rich in the California Gold Rush (2008). "The fictional William Reed gives readers a historical portrait of the hardships of life on the journey west, as well as the ingenuity, skill, and trickery used to overcome such challenges." (Publisher's note) "Grades four to seven." (Bull Cent Child Books)

"The action follows young Will Reed and his family as they set off from Illinois to find their fortune along the 2,000-mile Oregon Trail. . . . Informing Will's impish sketches and wry journal entries is a wealth of information about life along the trail. . . . An ongoing ledger calculates the family's balance as it fluctuates from $10.70 to $3,021.70, but it's clear that this journey is more about survival than riches. The illustrations, historical anecdotes, and run-ins with everyone from the Mormons to escaped slaves to Abraham Lincoln form a perfect blend of history and humbuggery." Booklist

Patent, Dorothy Hinshaw

The **horse** and the Plains Indians; a powerful partnership. Dorothy Hinshaw Patent ; photographs by William Munoz. Clarion Books 2012 xiii, 98 p.p ill. (chiefly col.) $17.99

Grades: 4 5 6 7 8 **978**

1. Horses 2. Domestic animals 3. Native Americans -- Great Plains 4. Horses -- Great Plains -- History 5. Human-animal relationships -- Great Plains -- History 6. Indians of North America -- Domestic animals -- Great Plains

ISBN 9780547125510

LC 2011025954

This book explores the relationship between Plains Indians and horses. The "Plains Indians and the horse were not always inseparable. Once, Native Americans used dogs to help carry their goods, and even after the Spaniards introduced the horse to the Americas," the Spanish hoarded the valuable animals. But "soon horses escaped from Spanish settlements, and Native Americans quickly learned how valuable the horse could be as a hunting mount, beast of burden, and military steed." (Publisher's note)

Includes bibliographical references and index

Pendergast, Tom

Westward expansion: primary sources; [by] Tom Pendergast and Sara Pendergast; Christine Slovey, editor. U.X.L 2001 xxix, 260p (Westward expansion reference library) $60

Grades: 7 8 9 10 **978**

1. West (U.S.) -- History 2. United States -- Territorial expansion

ISBN 0-7876-4864-7

LC 00-107861

This volume provides "full text or excerpts from diaries, books, letters and many other documents." Publisher's note

Includes bibliographical references

Schlissel, Lillian

Black frontiers; a history of African American heroes in the Old West. Simon & Schuster Bks. for Young Readers 1995 80p il hardcover o.p. pa $7.99

Grades: 5 6 7 8 **978**

1. West (U.S.) -- History 2. African Americans -- History 3. Frontier and pioneer life -- West (U.S.)

ISBN 0-689-80285-4; 0-689-83315-6 pa

LC 92-120

Focuses on the experiences of blacks as mountain men, soldiers, homesteaders, and scouts on the frontiers of the American West

"Good-quality period photos and black-and-white reproductions appear on nearly every page, adding human interest and realism to the text. An excellent addition to black history or westward movement units." Booklist

Includes bibliographical references

Sheinkin, Steve

Which way to the wild West? everything your schoolbooks didn't tell you about America's westward expansion. illustrated by Tim Robinson. Roaring Brook Press 2009 260p il map $19.95

Grades: 5 6 7 8 **978**

1. West (U.S.) -- History 2. United States -- Territorial expansion 3. Frontier and pioneer life -- West (U.S.)

ISBN 978-1-59643-321-2; 1-59643-321-3

Presents the greatest adventures of America's Westward expansion, from the Louisiana Purchase and the gold rush to the Indian wars and life of the cowboy, as well as the everyday happenings that defined living on the frontier

"An engaging storyteller, the author uses humor and little-known anecdotes to make such subjects as Manifest Destiny, the Mexican-American War, the Gold Rush and Custer's Last Stand entertaining for readers. His chatty, informal style . . . will appeal to young readers turned off to history by stale textbooks. Robinson's cartoons complement the text. . . . An accessible and engaging historical overview." Kirkus

Includes bibliographical references

Stefoff, Rebecca

★ **American** voices from the opening of the West. Benchmark Bks. 2002 105p (American voices from--) lib bdg $32.79

Grades: 6 7 8 9 **978**

1. West (U.S.) -- History 2. Frontier and pioneer life -- West (U.S.)

ISBN 0-7614-1201-8

LC 2001-8681

Presents the history of the westward expansion of the United States in the eighteenth and nineteenth centuries through excerpts from letters, newspaper articles, journal entries, and laws of the time

Includes glossary and bibliographical references

★ **American** voices from the Wild West. Marshall Cavendish Benchmark 2007 111p (American voices from--) lib bdg $37.07

Grades: 6 7 8 9 **978**

1. West (U.S.) -- History

ISBN 978-0-7614-2170-2 lib bdg; 0-7614-2170-X lib bdg

LC 2005028192

"Presents the history of the Wild West through a variety of primary source images and documents, such as diary entries, newspaper accounts, public speeches, popular literature, and personal letters." Publisher's note

Includes glossary and bibliographical references

Tunis, Edwin

★ **Frontier** living; written and illustrated by Edwin Tunis. Lyons Press 2000 165p il map pa $18.95

Grades: 5 6 7 8 9 10 **978**

1. West (U.S.) -- History 2. Frontier and pioneer life -- West (U.S.)

ISBN 1-58574-137-X

LC 00-710694

First published 1961 by World Publishing Company

This volume "portrays the manners and customs of the frontiersman and his family from the beginning of the westward movement through the 19th century in . . . text and more than 200 drawings." Wis Libr Bull

Vivian, R. Gwinn

Chaco Canyon; [by] R. Gwinn Vivian and Margaret Anderson. Oxford University Press 2002 47p il maps (Digging for the past) $19.95

Grades: 5 6 7 8 **978**

1. Archeology 2. Pueblo Indians 3. Cliff dwellers and cliff dwellings 4. Chaco Culture National Historical Park (N.M.)

ISBN 0-19-514280-2

LC 2001-54855

Relates the nineteenth-century discovery of cliff dwellings in the Chaco Canyon of northwest New Mexico, the excavations of the ancient ruins, and what the artifacts reveal about the civilization of the ancient Pueblo Indians

This "brings young readers up close to the field of archaeology. . . . Sharp color photos show the sites, artifacts, and the scientists at work." Booklist

Includes glossary and bibliographical references

978.004 Western United States--American native peoples

Langley, Andrew

The **Plains** Indian wars 1864-1890; by Andrew Langley. Heinemann Library 2012 80 p. ill. (some col.), col. maps (hardcover) $36.50; (paperback) $10.99

Grades: 6 7 8 9 **978.004**

1. United States -- Military history 2. Native Americans -- Wars

ISBN 1432959999; 9781432959999; 9781432960087

LC 2011015925

This book by Andrew Langley is part of the Living Through series and focuses on the Plains Indian Wars. "The Plains Indian Wars were not like most other wars. There were few large battles, and they took place across a huge but sparsely populated region over several decades. . . . The Living Through series relates the overall chronology of major wars and shows their impact on everyday lives." (Publisher's note)

Includes bibliographical references (p. 76-78) and index.

Sanford, William R.

Comanche Chief Quanah Parker; by William R. Sanford. Enslow Publishers 2013 48 p. ill., map (library) $21.26

Grades: 6 7 8 9 **978.004**

1. Parker, Quanah, 1845?-1911 2. Comanche Indians -- History 3. Comanche Indians -- Wars 4. Comanche Indians -- Kings and

rulers -- Biography
ISBN 076604095X; 9780766040953

LC 2011048762

This book by William R. Sanford is part of the Native American Chiefs and Warriors series. It "tells how Quanah, the last Comanche chief, at first drew controversy for surrendering to the U.S. government and agreeing to live on a reservation. He later earned praise for effectively bridging both cultures." (Booklist)

Includes bibliographical references and index.

Oglala Lakota Chief Red Cloud; by William R. Sanford. Enslow Publishers 2013 48 p. (library) $21.26

Grades: 6 7 8 9 **978.004**

1. Oglala Indians -- Wars 2. Oglala Indians -- Kings and rulers -- Biography
ISBN 0766040968; 9780766040960

LC 2011048760

This book is part of the Native American Chiefs and Warriors series and looks at Oglala Lakota Chief Red Cloud. Each title "focuses on the U.S. government's infringement upon Native American land and how these leaders responded." This entry "recounts Red Cloud's fight to prevent whites from traveling along the Bozeman and Oregon Trails, his meeting with President Ulysses Grant, and his band's forced move to a reservation." (Booklist)

Includes bibliographical references and index.

Oglala Sioux Chief Crazy Horse; by William R. Sanford. Enslow Publishers 2013 48 p. (library) $21.26

Grades: 6 7 8 9 **978.004**

1. Little Bighorn, Battle of the, Mont., 1876 2. Oglala Indians -- Kings and rulers -- Biography
ISBN 0766040941; 9780766040946

LC 2011048758

This book is part of the Native American Chiefs and Warriors series and looks at Oglala Sioux Chief Crazy Horse. Each title "focuses on the U.S. government's infringement upon Native American land and how these leaders responded." This entry "describes Crazy Horse's success as a chief and warrior, particularly during the Battle of the Little Bighorn, and the resulting jealousy among other Sioux leaders that led to his contentious death." (Booklist)

Includes bibliographical references (p. 46) and index.

978.1 Kansas

Bjorklund, Ruth

Kansas; by Ruth Bjorklund and Trudi Strain Trueit. 2nd ed.; Marshall Cavendish Benchmark 2009 144p il map (Celebrate the states) lib bdg $42.79

Grades: 4 5 6 7 **978.1**

1. Kansas
ISBN 978-0-7614-3400-9; 0-7614-3400-3

LC 2008-5537

"Provides comprehensive information on the geography, history, wildlife, governmental structure, economy, cultural diversity, peoples, religion, and landmarks of Kansas." Publisher's note

Includes bibliographical references

Cannarella, Deborah

Kansas; by Deborah Cannarella. Revised edition Children's Press, a Division of Scholastic Inc. 2014 144 p. ill. (chiefly col.), col. map (library binding) $40

Grades: 4 5 6 7 **978.1**

1. Kansas 2. Geography
ISBN 0531282805; 9780531282809

LC 2013044321

"Lying in the heart of the United States, Kansas is a sprawling landscape of rolling prairies and rugged hills. Readers will learn how the state was first settled thousands of years ago by ancient Paleo-Indians and find out how it came to be part of the United States. They will also explore the rich and varied culture of modern Kansas, from the crowded streets of Kansas City to the rural farms of the Great Plains." (Publisher's note)

Includes bibliographical references (pages 133-137)and index

McArthur, Debra

The **Kansas** -Nebraska Act and Bleeding Kansas in American history. Enslow Pubs. 2003 128p il map (In American history) lib bdg $26.60

Grades: 6 7 8 9 **978.1**

1. Abolitionists 2. Kansas -- History 3. Slavery -- United States
ISBN 0-7660-1988-8

LC 2002-152064

Describes the violent period of Kansas Territory history, prior to statehood and the Civil War, when abolitionists and pro-slavery factions openly murdered in defense of their cause

Includes bibliographical references

978.2 Nebraska

Bjorklund, Ruth

Nebraska; [by] Ruth Bjorklund and Marlee Richards. 2nd ed.; Marshall Cavendish Benchmark 2010 144p il map (Celebrate the states) $42.79

Grades: 5 6 7 8 **978.2**

1. Nebraska
ISBN 978-0-7614-4732-0; 0-7614-4732-6

"Every school library should purchase this." Voice Youth Advocates

Heinrichs, Ann

Nebraska; by Ann Heinrichs. Revised edition Children's Press 2014 144 p. (library binding) $40

Grades: 4 5 6 7 **978.2**

1. Nebraska 2. Geography
ISBN 0531248925; 9780531248928

LC 2013032479

"Known for its wide expanses of flat farmlands, Nebraska is one of the most sparsely populated states in the country. Readers will trace the history of this remarkable state from its earliest settlement to its latest developments. They will also dive into the local culture, see the state's many fascinating sights, and learn about its economy." (Publisher's note)

Includes bibliographical references (p. 138) and index

978.4 North Dakota

McDaniel, Melissa

North Dakota; by Melissa McDaniel and Sara Louise Kras. 2nd ed.; Marshall Cavendish Benchmark 2010 144p il map (Celebrate the states) lib bdg $42.79

Grades: 5 6 7 8 **978.4**

1. North Dakota

ISBN 978-0-7614-4733-7; 0-7614-4733-4

LC 2009002584

First published 2001

This offers information on the geography, history, wildlife, governmental structure, economy, cultural diversity, peoples, religion, and landmarks of North Dakota.

Includes bibliographical references

978.6 Montana

Bennett, Clayton

Montana; by Clayton Bennett and Wendy Mead. 2nd ed.; Marshall Cavendish Benchmark 2010 144p il map (Celebrate the states) $42.79

Grades: 5 6 7 8 **978.6**

1. Montana

ISBN 978-0-7614-4731-3; 0-7614-4731-8

LC 2009007939

First published 2001

This offers information on the geography, history, wildlife, governmental structure, economy, cultural diversity, peoples, religion, and landmarks of Montana.

Includes bibliographical references

Stein, R. Conrad

Montana; by R. Conrad Stein. Revised edition Children's Press, an Imprint of Scholastic Inc. 2014 144 p. (library binding : alk. paper) $40

Grades: 4 5 6 7 **978.6**

1. Montana 2. Geography

ISBN 053128283X; 9780531282830

LC 2013044324

"Montana is one of the nation's largest states, but it is home to very few large towns or cities. Rather, it is defined by its vast wilderness areas, which range from the high peaks of the Rocky Mountains to the rolling hills and flatlands of the Great Plains. Readers will find out how Montana was settled and what role it has played in U.S. history. They will also explore the state's rich culture and traditions." (Publisher's note)

Includes bibliographical references and index

978.7 Wyoming

Baldwin, Guy

Wyoming; [by] Guy Baldwin and Joyce Hart. 2nd ed.; Marshall Cavendish Benchmark 2008 144p il map (Celebrate the states) lib bdg $39.93

Grades: 4 5 6 7 **978.7**

1. Wyoming

ISBN 978-0-7614-2563-2; 0-7614-2563-2

LC 2007-19560

First publsihed 1999

"Provides comprehensive information on the geography, history, wildlife, governmental structure, economy, cultural diversity, peoples, religion, and landmarks of Wyoming." Publisher's note

Includes bibliographical references

Peabody, Erin

A **weird** and wild beauty; the story of Yellowstone, the world's first national park. Erin Peabody. Skyhorse Publishing, Inc. 2016 192 p. color illustrations (print) $14.99

Grades: 6 7 8 9 10 **978.7**

1. Yellowstone National Park -- History 2. National parks and reserves -- United States 3. Landscape protection -- United States -- History 4. Yellowstone National Park -- Environmental conditions 5. Yellowstone National Park -- Discovery and exploration 6. National parks and reserves -- United States -- History

ISBN 1634502043; 9781634502047

LC 2015035831

This book, by Erin Peabody, "tells the story of one of the first scientific expeditions into the vast Western wilderness surrounding the Yellowstone River. In 1871, Ferdinand Hayden led an expedition of geologists, naturalists, artists, photographers, soldiers, and adventurers into a remote corner of what was then the Montana Territory. The expedition's documentation . . . ultimately culminated in the passage of the Yellowstone Park Bill." (School Library Journal)

"By emphasizing the uniqueness of Yellowstone through the eyes of men like Hayden, who experienced it in its rawest form, this is a call for conservation neatly packaged as a high-interest historical narrative." Booklist

Includes bibliographical references and index

Prentzas, G. S.

Wyoming; by G.S. Prentzas. Revised edition Children's Press 2015 144 p. illustrations, maps (library binding : alk. paper) $40

Grades: 4 5 6 7 **978.7**

1. Wyoming 2. Geography

ISBN 9780531283004 ; 0531283003

LC 2013046232

"From the amazing geysers of Yellowstone National Park and the heights of the Rocky Mountains to the sprawling grasslands of the Great Plains, Wyoming offers some of the most incredible sights the United States has to offer. Readers will learn about the state's history, government, and economy as they tour its towns, cities, and wilderness. They will also explore the state's culture and cuisine as they see what it is like to live in Wyoming today." (Publisher's note)

Includes bibliographical references and index

978.8 Colorado

Somervill, Barbara A.

Colorado; by Barbara A. Somervill. Revised edition Children's Press 2014 144 p. (library binding) $40

Grades: 4 5 6 7 **978.8**

1. Colorado

ISBN 053124878X; 9780531248782

LC 2013031192

"With half of its territory lying within the Rocky Mountains, Colorado is known for its breathtaking natural features. Readers will trace the history of this remarkable state from its earliest settlement to its latest developments. They will also dive into the local culture, see the state's many fascinating sights, and learn about its economy." (Publisher's note)

Includes bibliographical references and index

978.9 New Mexico

Burgan, Michael

New Mexico; by Michael Burgan. Revised edition Children's Press, a division of Scholastic Inc. 2014 144 p. illustrations, maps (library binding : alk. paper) $40

Grades: 4 5 6 7 **978.9**

1. New Mexico 2. United States -- History

ISBN 0531282856; 9780531282854

LC 2013044359

"Located along the Mexican border in the southwestern United States, New Mexico is home to some of the country's largest Hispanic and Native American populations. Readers will explore the history and culture of this diverse state, from its settlement by Native Americans thousands of years ago to its important position within the United States today." (Publisher's note)

Includes bibliographical references (page 138) and index

979.1 Arizona

Hernandez, Daniel

They call me a hero; a memoir of my youth. Daniel Hernandez and Susan Goldman Rubin. Simon & Schuster Books for Young Readers 2013 240 p. (hardcover) $17.99

Grades: 7 8 9 10 11 12 **979.1**

1. Courage 2. Interns -- United States -- Biography 3. Heroes -- Arizona -- Tucson -- Biography 4. Tucson (Ariz.) -- History -- 21st century 5. Sexual minorities -- Civil rights -- Arizona -- Tucson 6. Tucson (Ariz.) -- Officials and employees -- Biography 7. Courage -- Arizona -- Tucson -- History -- 21st century

ISBN 1442462280; 9781442462281; 9781442462380

LC 2012019829

This book, by Daniel Hernandez, with Susan Gldman Rubin, is a memoir about heroism. "Daniel Hernandez was . . . working as an intern for U.S. Representative Gabrielle Giffords. On January 8, 2011, . . . Giffords was shot. Daniel Hernandez's quick thinking saved Giffords's life. . . . But while that may have been his most well-known moment in the spotlight, Daniel Hernandez, Jr. . . . [had] already accomplished much in his young life, and is working to achieve much more." (Publisher's note)

McDaniel, Melissa

Arizona; by Melissa McDaniel and Wendy Mead. 2nd ed.; Marshall Cavendish Benchmark 2009 144p il map (Celebrate the states) lib bdg $39.93

Grades: 4 5 6 7 **979.1**

1. Arizona

ISBN 978-0-7614-3398-9; 0-7614-3398-8

LC 2008-6212

First published 2000

"Provides comprehensive information on the geography, history, wildlife, governmental structure, economy, cultural diversity, peoples, religion, and landmarks of Arizona." Publisher's note

Includes bibliographical references

979.2 Utah

Kent, Deborah, 1948-

Utah; by Deborah Kent. Revised edition Children's Press 2015 144 p. illustrations, maps (library binding : alk. paper) $40

Grades: 4 5 6 7 **979.2**

1. Utah 2. Geography

ISBN 9780531282953 ; 0531282953

LC 2013046227

"Utah's dazzling rock formations and stunning canyons make it one of the highlights of the Southwestern United States. Readers will find out how the state was settled, first by ancient Paleo-Indians and later by Spanish Missionaries and Mormon travelers. They will tour some of the state's most interesting locations, meet its most influential residents, and learn how it is governed. They will also get a close look at the state's wildlife and a taste of its local culture." (Publisher's note)

Includes bibliographical references and index

Stefoff, Rebecca

Utah; by Rebecca Stefoff and Wendy Mead. 2nd ed.; Marshall Cavendish Benchmark 2010 144p il map (Celebrate the states) lib bdg $42.79

Grades: 5 6 7 8 **979.2**

1. Utah

ISBN 978-0-7614-4035-2; 0-7614-4035-6

LC 2008040026

This offers information on the geography, history, wildlife, governmental structure, economy, cultural diversity, peoples, religion, and landmarks of Utah.

Includes bibliographical references

979.3 Nevada

Heinrichs, Ann

Nevada; Ann Heinrichs. Revised edition Children's Press 2014 144 p. (library binding) $40

Grades: 4 5 6 7 **979.3**

1. Nevada 2. United States -- History

ISBN 0531248933; 9780531248935

LC 2013032828

"As one of the driest states in the country, Nevada has few residents outside of cities such as Las Vegas and Reno. Readers will trace the history of this remarkable state from its earliest settlement to its latest developments. They will also dive into the local culture, see the state's many fascinating sights, and learn about its economy." (Publisher's note)

Includes bibliographical references and index

979.4 California

Brimner, Larry Dane, 1949-

The **Rain** Wizard; The Amazing, Mysterious, True Life of Charles Mallory Hatfield. Larry Dane Brimner. Calkins Creek 2015 80 p. illustrations (some color) $16.95

Grades: 5 6 7 8 9 **979.4**

1. Rain 2. San Diego (Calif.) -- Fiction

ISBN 1590789903; 9781590789902

LC 2015931581

This book by Larry Dane Brimner describes how "In December 1915, San Diego's leaders claimed the town's reservoirs were nearly dry. Knowing the city would not survive and grow unless it had water, they hired Charles Mallory Hatfield, whose skills at making rain were legendary. But when torrents and torrents of rain came, disaster struck. Roads were closed, people drowned, and dams burst. The town elders blamed Hatfield and refused to pay him." (Publisher's note)

"The generously leaded text is set within wide margins and accompanied by copious archival illustrations; both decisions keep the relatively complex text accessible. An engaging, intriguing story of a fascinating man." Kirkus

Includes bibliographical references (pages 106-114) and index.

Calabro, Marian

★ The **perilous** journey of the Donner Party. Clarion Bks. 1999 192p il maps $20

Grades: 5 6 7 8 **979.4**

1. Donner party 2. Overland journeys to the Pacific 3. Frontier and pioneer life -- West (U.S.)

ISBN 0-395-86610-3

LC 98-29610

Uses materials from letters and diaries written by survivors of the Donner Party to relate the experiences of that ill-fated group as they endured horrific circumstances on their way to California in 1846-47

"Calabro's offering is a fine addition to the Donner Party canon and particularly well suited to its young audience, for whom the story of hardship and survival will be nothing short of riveting. . . . From the haunting cover with its lonely campfire to the recounting of a survivors' reunion, this is a page-turner." Booklist

Includes bibliographical references

Doak, Robin S.

California, 1542-1850; by Robin Doak; Andres Resendez, consultant. National Geographic Society 2006 109p map il (Voices from colonial America) $21.95; lib bdg $32.90

Grades: 5 6 7 8 **979.4**

1. California -- History

ISBN 978-0-7922-6391-3; 0-7922-6391-X; 978-0-7922-6861-1 lib bdg; 0-7922-6861-X lib bdg

LC 2005-30920

"Traces California's history from its origins as a sparsely populated outpost of the Spanish empire in the sixteenth century to the frenzied westward migration of the 1850s." Publisher's note

Includes bibliograhical references

Freedman, Russell, 1929-2018

★ **Angel** Island; gateway to Gold Mountain. Russell Freedman ; Chinese poems translated by Evans Chan. Clarion Books 2013 96 p. (hardcover) $17.99

Grades: 4 5 6 7 8 **979.4**

1. Immigrants -- United States 2. Angel Island Immigration Station (San Francisco, Calif.) 3. Angel Island (Calif.) -- History 4. Asia -- Emigration and immigration -- History 5. Angel Island Immigration Station (Calif.) -- History 6. United States -- Emigration and immigration -- History 7. San Francisco Bay Area (Calif.) -- Emigration and immigration -- History

ISBN 0547903782; 9780547903781

LC 2012036532

This book is a "history of Angel Island and its legacy in the American immigration narrative. Detailed descriptions of the island, the actual building, the events that took place there, and the people who passed through its doors are sprinkled with the emotional poems, quotes, and other writings that were discovered covering the walls of the areas where the detainees were housed." (School Library Journal)

Includes bibliographical references

Hale, Nathan

Donner dinner party; by Nathan Hale. Harry N Abrams Inc 2013 123 p. (Nathan Hale's Hazardous Tales) $12.95

Grades: 5 6 7 8 **979.4**

1. Donner party 2. Sierra Nevada Mountains

ISBN 1419708562; 9781419708565

In this graphic novel, author Nathan Hale "tells the harrowing story of the ill-fated Donner party. Beginning with their departure from Springfield, Illinois, in 1846, Hale depicts the party's progress . . . and includes lots of factual details, such as a roster of everyone in the party, how they died, and a helpful map showing just how . . . close they came to California before meeting their grisly end." (Booklist)

"This informative graphic novel capitalizes on enticingly gross history to great effect, balancing raw facts with strong storytelling." Booklist

McNeese, Tim

The **Donner** Party; a doomed journey. [by] Tim McNeese. Chelsea House 2009 146p il (Milestones in American history) lib bdg $35

Grades: 6 7 8 9 10 **979.4**

1. Donner party 2. Overland journeys to the Pacific 3. Frontier and pioneer life -- California 4. Frontier and pioneer life -- West (U.S.)

ISBN 978-1-60413-025-6 lib bdg; 1-60413-025-3 lib bdg

LC 2008-29652

"McNeese presents a thoroughly researched, clearly written account of the ill-fated Donner Party and the events and decisions that conspired against this early wagon train headed from Springfield, IL, to California. . . . Photos, reproductions, drawings, and primary-source documents as well as a detailed chronology make this an excellent resource." SLJ

Includes bibliographical references

Olson, Tod

★ **How** to get rich in the California Gold Rush; an adventurer's guide to the fabulous riches discovered in 1848 . . . illustrations by Scott Allred; afterword by Marc Aronson. National Geographic 2008 47p il map (How to get rich) $16.95; lib bdg $25.90

Grades: 4 5 6 7 **979.4**

1. Gold mines and mining 2. California -- Gold discoveries 3. Prospecting 4. Frontier and pioneer life -- California 5. California -- History

ISBN 1-4263-0315-7; 1-4263-0316-5 lib bdg; 978-1-4263-0315-9; 978-1-4263-0316-6 lib bdg

LC 2008-19601

This is a personal account of the California Gold Rush from the point-of-view of the fictitious character Thomas Hartley. "Grades four to seven." (Bull Cent Child Books)

This "deftly blends story with history to not only give readers an understanding of a gold rush but also to provide a lighthearted and engaging entry point into frontier life. . . . Period lithographs are reproduced alongside original illustrations. . . . A ledger on each page tracks the young men's finances in a genuinely exciting way, adding a sly element of math to this well-conceived and compulsively appealing book." Booklist

Includes bibliographical references

Orr, Tamra B.

California; by Tamra B. Orr. Revised edition Children's Press 2014 144 p. ill. (chiefly col.), col. maps $40

Grades: 4 5 6 7 **979.4**

1. California

ISBN 9780531248775 ; 0531248771

"Located along the coast of the Pacific Ocean, California is famed for its sunny weather, beaches, and incredible cities. Readers will trace the history of this remarkable state from its earliest settlement to its latest developments. They will also dive into the local culture, see the state's many fascinating sights, and learn about its economy." (Publisher's note)

Includes bibliographical references (page 138) and index

Slavicek, Louise Chipley

The **San** Francisco earthquake and fire of 1906; [by] Louise Chipley Slavicek. Chelsea House 2008 128p il (Great historic disasters) lib bdg $35

Grades: 5 6 7 8 **979.4**

1. Fires 2. Earthquakes -- California 3. San Francisco (Calif.) -- History

ISBN 978-0-7910-9650-5; 0-7910-9650-5

LC 2008-4896

This is a history of the 1906 earthquake and fire in San Francisco.

"Combining first-hand accounts, photographs, and other primary sources with a detailed and lively text, [this] fact-packed [resource offers] much to both report writers and history buffs." Horn Book Guide

Includes glossary and bibliographical references

Yep, Laurence, 1948-

★ The **lost** garden; by Laurence Yep. Messner 1991 xi, 117 p.p ill. (In my own words) (library) $14.98; (hardcover) $12.95

Grades: 6 7 8 9 10 11 12 **979.4**

1. Authors 2. Novelists 3. College teachers 4. Authors, American 5. Children's authors 6. Young adult authors 7. Chinese Americans -- Biography

ISBN 9780671741594; 9780671741600

LC 90040647

This is a volume in the In My Own Words series. The author of Dragonwings (BRD 1976), Child of The Owl (BRD 1977), The Rainbow People (BRD 1989), and The Star Fisher (BRD 1991) discusses his life and his writing. "Grades six to twelve." (SLJ)

"The writing is warm, wry, and humorous. . . . The Lost Garden will be welcomed as a literary autobiography for children and, more, a thoughtful probing into what it means to be an American." SLJ

979.5 Oregon

Kent, Deborah, 1948-

Oregon; by Deborah Kent. Revised edition Children's Press, an imprint of Scholastic Inc. 2014 144 p. illustrations, maps (library binding : alk. paper) $40

Grades: 4 5 6 7 **979.5**

1. Oregon 2. United States -- History

ISBN 0531282880; 9780531282885

LC 2013044361

"From the peak of Mount Hood to the depths of Crater Lake, Oregon is home to some of the United States' most beautiful outdoor areas. Readers will take a tour of the state as they learn about its history, geography, and wildlife. They will also learn what life is like for the people of Oregon, whether they live in a big city such as Portland or a rural farm east of the Cascade Range." (Publisher's note)

Includes bibliographical references (pages 133-137) and index

979.6 Idaho

Kent, Deborah, 1948-

Idaho; by Deborah Kent. Revised edition Children's Press, an Imprint of Scholastic Inc. 2015 144 p. col. ill., col. maps $40

Grades: 4 5 6 7 **979.6**

1. Idaho 2. Geography

ISBN 9780531282786; 0531282783

LC 2013044327

"As the country's leading potato provider, Idaho produces around 12 billion pounds of spuds every year. Readers will travel through Idaho's remarkable farms, as well as its cities, forests, and mountains, as they explore the state's rich history. They will also get a taste of modern Idaho culture as they learn about the state's traditions, cuisine, and local heroes." (Publisher's note

Includes bibliographical references (page 138) and index

Stefoff, Rebecca

Idaho; by Rebecca Stefoff. 2nd ed.; Marshall Cavendish Benchmark 2008 144p il map (Celebrate the states) lib bdg $39.93

Grades: 4 5 6 7 **979.6**

1. Idaho

ISBN 978-0-7614-3003-2; 0-7614-3003-2

LC 2007-29496

First published 2000

"Provides comprehensive information on the geography, history, wildlife, governmental structure, economy, cultural diversity, peoples, religion, and landmarks of Idaho." Publisher's note

Includes bibliographical references

979.7 Washington

Kirkpatrick, Katherine

★ **Mysterious** bones; the story of Kennewick Man. by Katherine Kirkpatrick; illustrated by Emma Stevenson. Holiday House 2011 60p il map $17.95

Grades: 6 7 8 9 **979.7**

1. Skeleton 2. Kennewick Man 3. Native Americans 4. Washington (State) 5. North America -- Antiquities

ISBN 978-0-8234-2187-9; 0-8234-2187-2

LC 2009025575

Kennewick Man "was found in remarkable condition near the Columbia River in Washington . . . in 1996—one of the oldest and most complete skeletons found in America. Kirkpatrick addresses the controversy surrounding the treatment of his remains. . . . Excellent illustrations accompany the story, with crisp line-drawings of tools, skeletons, maps and possible facial reconstructions." Kirkus

Includes glossary and bibliographical references

Stefoff, Rebecca

Washington; [by] Rebecca Stefoff. 2nd ed.; Marshall Cavendish Benchmark 2008 144p il map (Celebrate the states) lib bdg $39.93

Grades: 4 5 6 7 **979.7**

1. Washington (State)

ISBN 978-0-7614-2561-8; 0-7614-2561-6

LC 2006-32436

First published 1999

"Provides comprehensive information on the geography, history, wildlife, governmental structure, economy, cultural diversity, peoples, religion, and landmarks of Washington." Publisher's note

Includes bibliographical references

979.8 Alaska

Orr, Tamra B.

Alaska; Tamra B. Orr. Revised edition Children's Press 2014 144 p. color illustrations (library binding) $40

Grades: 4 5 6 7 **979.8**

1. Alaska

ISBN 0531248763; 9780531248768

LC 2013030722

"Far to the north of the rest of the country, Alaska became the union's 49th state in 1959. Readers will trace the history of this remarkable state from its earliest settlement to its latest developments. They will also dive into the local culture, see the state's many fascinating sights, and learn about its economy." (Publisher's note)

Includes bibliographical references and index

980 History of South America

Gorrell, Gena K.

★ **In** the land of the jaguar; South America and its people. illustrated by Andrej Krystoforski. Tundra Books 2007 149p il $22.95

Grades: 5 6 7 8 9 **980**

1. South America

ISBN 978-0-88776-756-2

"This beautifully designed volume, with an engaging narrative, combines a highly informative overview of the continent with country-by-country detail. . . . The spacious design includes big maps, clear type on thick paper, and small, beautiful, fully captioned illustrations." Booklist

981 Brazil

Berkenkamp, Lauri

Discover the Amazon; the world's largest rainforest. illustrated by Blair Shedd. Nomad Press 2008 90p il map pa $16.95

Grades: 4 5 6 7 **981**

1. Amazon River valley

ISBN 978-1-9346702-7-9 pa; 1-9346702-7-8 pa

"Berkenkamp's introduction to the [Amazon] river basin incorporates maps, drawings, and photos in various shades of green and brown on recycled paper. . . . The conversational style provides a 'you are there' feeling, conveying information and anecdotes while stressing outdoor survival skills. . . . Even readers who never travel to Amazonia will appreciate the region's complexity and significance after perusing this book." SLJ

Deckker, Zilah

Brazil; [by] Zilah Deckker; David Robinson and Joao Cezar de Castro Rocha, consultants. National Geographic 2008 64p il (Countries of the world) lib bdg $27.90

Grades: 4 5 6 7 **981**

1. Brazil

ISBN 978-1-4263-0298-5 lib bdg; 1-4263-0298-3 lib bdg

This describes the geography, nature, history, people and culture, government, and economy of Brazil.

Includes glossary and bibliographical references

Heinrichs, Ann

The **Amazon** rain forest. Marshall Cavendish Benchmark 2009 96p il (Nature's wonders) lib bdg $35.64

Grades: 6 7 8 9 **981**

1. Rain forests 2. Amazon River valley

ISBN 978-0-7614-3932-5; 0-7614-3932-3

LC 2008017562

Provides information on the geography, history, wildlife, peoples, and environmental issues of the Amazon Rain Forest.

Includes glossary and bibliographical references

★ **Brazil**; by Ann Heinrichs. Children's Press, an imprint of Scholastic Inc. 2013 144 p. illustrations, color maps (library binding) $40

Grades: 5 6 7 8 **981**

1. Brazil

ISBN 0531236757; 9780531236758

LC 2013000089

This book, by Ann Heinrichs, focuses on Brazil. The "country's culture, history, and geography are explored in detail, allowing readers a chance to see how people live. . . . Sidebars highlight especially interesting people, places, and events . . . [and] recipes give readers the opportunity to experience foreign cuisine first-hand." (Publisher's note)

"Many students turn to the Internet for writing reports, but for reliably accurate, attractively presented and well-calibrated information, the long-standing Enchantment of the World series remains a superior choice...Each volume in this reliable series includes extensive back matter with a detailed index." Booklist

Includes bibliographical references (page 134), filmography (page 134), and index.

982 Argentina

Blashfield, Jean F.

Argentina; Jean F. Blashfield. 2nd edition Children's Press/Scholastic 2015 144 p ill. (chiefly col.), maps (Enchantment of the World) library $40

Grades: 4 5 6 7 **982**

1. Argentina

ISBN 0531212505; 9780531212509

LC 2014031836

Introduces Argentina, describing the country's food, people, culture, and geography.

Includes bibliographical references (page 134) and index

Fearns, Les

Argentina; [by] Les and Daisy Fearns. Facts on File 2005 61p il map (Countries of the world) $30

Grades: 7 8 9 10 **982**

1. Argentina

ISBN 0-8160-6008-8

LC 2005040675

This is an introduction to Argentina's "culture, history, geography, government, and economy. [It is] competently written and [contains] current information. [The text is] clear but the level of vocabulary is quite high, which might prove challenging for less competent readers. Visually, the [book is] quite impressive, with full-color photographs, maps, tables, and graphs distributed throughout." SLJ

Includes bibliographical references

983 Chile

Burgan, Michael

Chile; by Michael Burgan. Children's Press, an imprint of Scholastic Inc. 2017 144 p. color ill., color maps (library binding) $40

Grades: 5 6 7 8 **983**

1. Chile

ISBN 0531218856; 9780531218853

LC 2015048543

This book on Chile, by Michael Burgan, part of the Enchantment of the World series, "includes maps, timelines, fast facts, charts, vivid four-color photographs, and a to find out more section. . . . Straightforward, unbiased, and probing prose will provoke readers to think like historians; engaging text will take readers on a virtual tour of the country." (Publisher's note)

"With stunning, high-quality photos that reflect the richness of cultures around the globe, the Enchantment of the World series earns its name." Booklist

Includes bibliographical references and index

985 Peru

Bingham, Jane

The **Inca** empire; [by] Jane Bingham. Raintree 2007 64p il map (Time travel guide) lib bdg $34.29; pa $9.99

Grades: 6 7 8 9 **985**

1. Incas 2. Peru

ISBN 978-1-4109-2731-6 lib bdg; 1-4109-2731-8 lib bdg; 978-1-4109-2738-5 pa; 1-4109-2738-5 pa

LC 2006033877

This describes life in the ancient Inca empire in the form of a travel guide.

Includes glossary and bibliographical references

Calvert, Patricia

★ The **ancient** Inca; written by Patricia Calvert. Franklin Watts 2004 128p il (People of the ancient world) lib bdg $30.50; pa $9.95

Grades: 5 6 7 8 **985**

1. Incas

ISBN 0-531-12358-8 lib bdg; 0-531-16740-2 pa

LC 2004-1956

This "well-written, attractive [title has] extensive collections of quality color photographs of ruins and artifacts." SLJ

Includes bibliographical references

Falconer, Kieran

★ **Peru**; [by] Kieran Falconer & Lynette Quek. 2nd ed.; Marshall Cavendish Benchmark 2006 144p il map (Cultures of the world) lib bdg $42.79

Grades: 5 6 7 8 **985**

1. Peru

ISBN 978-0-7614-2068-2 lib bdg; 0-7614-2068-1 lib bdg

First published 1995

This provides "information on the geography, history, governmental structure, economy, cultural diversity, peoples, religion, and culture of Peru." Publisher's note

Includes glossary and bibliographical references

Gruber, Beth

★ **Ancient** Inca; archaeology unlocks the secrets of the Inca's past. by Beth Gruber; Johan Reinhard, consultant. National Geographic 2007 64p il map (National Geographic investigates) $17.95; lib bdg $27.90

Grades: 5 6 7 8 **985**

1. Incas 2. Peru -- Antiquities 3. Excavations (Archeology) -- Peru

ISBN 978-0-7922-7827-6; 978-0-7922-7873-3 lib bdg

LC 2006032104

This describes how archeologists have found out about ancient Incan civilization.

This offers "the beautiful photography and illustrations characteristic of the National Geographic Society, [a] well-written [text] and sidebars, and information on recent archaeological finds." SLJ

Includes bibliographical references

986.1 Colombia

Croy, Anita

Colombia; [by] Anita Croy; Ulrich Oslender and Mauricio Pardo, consultants. National Geographic 2008 64p il map (Countries of the world) lib bdg $27.90

Grades: 4 5 6 7 **986.1**

1. Colombia

ISBN 978-1-4263-0257-2 lib bdg; 1-4263-0257-6 lib bdg

This describes the geography, nature, history, people and culture, government, and economy of Colombia

Includes glossary and bibliographical references

Yomtov, Nel

★ **Colombia**; by Nel Yomtov. Children's Press, an imprint of Scholastic Inc. 2014 144 p. illustrations, color maps (library binding) $40

Grades: 5 6 7 8 **986.1**

1. Colombia 2. Colombia

ISBN 0531220133; 9780531220139

LC 2013026060

This book, by Nel Yomtov, focuses on Colombia. The "country's culture, history, and geography are explored in detail, allowing readers a chance to see how people live in faraway nations. . . . Sidebars highlight especially interesting people, places, and events . . . [and] easy recipes give readers the opportunity to experience foreign cuisine first-hand." (Publisher's note)

Includes bibliographical references and index

986.6 Ecuador

Foley, Erin

★ **Ecuador**; Third Edition Marshall Cavendish Benchmark 2016 144p chiefly color illustrations lib bdg $47.07; (ebook) $47.07

Grades: 5 6 7 8 **986.6**

1. Ecuador

ISBN 9781502617019; 9781502617026

LC 2005022671

"Situated in South America very close to the Equator, Ecuador is a country known for its vibrant culture and ecotourism. This book discusses the history of Ecuador, what its people and cities are like, and examines how it became the country it is today" (Publisher's Note)

Includes bibliographical references (pages 141-142) and index.

Kras, Sara Louise

The **Galapagos** Islands; [by] Sara Louise Kras. Marshall Cavendish Benchmark 2008 96p il map (Nature's wonders) lib bdg $35.64

Grades: 5 6 7 8 **986.6**

1. Galapagos Islands

ISBN 978-0-7614-2856-5 lib bdg; 0-7614-2856-9 lib bdg

LC 2007020416

"Provides comprehensive information on the geography, history, wildlife, peoples, and environmental issues of the Galapagos Islands." Publisher's note

Includes glossary and bibliographical references

Lourie, Peter

★ **Lost** treasure of the Inca. Boyds Mills Press 1999 48p il map $18.95

Grades: 4 5 6 7 **986.6**

1. Incas 2. Buried treasure 3. Ecuador

ISBN 1-56397-743-5

The author describes his search in the mountains of Ecuador for gold hidden by the Incas

Lourie "succumbed to altitude sickness and had to descend without discovering a glimmer of the gold. But he did return with a ripping good yarn to tell . . . and some breathtaking photographs of the mist-shrouded volcanic peaks. This should be a hot pick for armchair travelers." Bull Cent Child Books

Includes glossary

988.1 Guyana

Jermyn, Leslie

Guyana; by Leslie Jermyn and Winnie Wong. Marshall Cavendish Benchmark 2010 144 p. col. ill., col. maps (library) $47.07

Grades: 5 6 7 8 **988.1**

1. Guyana

ISBN 1608700232; 9781608700233

LC 2010000724

This book by Leslie Jermyn is part of the Cultures of the World series and looks at the South American nation of Guyana. "Touching upon everything from its history to religion to architecture, this book . . . highlights the country's rich diversity and unique qualities. With a population that includes many different ethnic groups, the author . . . examines the contributions of each to Guyana's development and to its present culture." (Children's Literature)

Includes bibliographical references (p.142) and index.

Morrison, Marion

Guyana. Children's Press 2003 144p il map (Enchantment of the world, Second series) lib bdg $38

Grades: 5 6 7 8 **988.1**

1. Guyana

ISBN 978-0-516-22377-3 lib bdg; 0-516-22377-1 lib bdg

LC 2001-6915

Describes the geography, history, culture, religion, and people of Guyana

Includes bibliographical references

989.2 Paraguay

Jermyn, Leslie

Paraguay; [by] Leslie Jermyn and Yong Jui Lin. 2nd ed.; Marshall Cavendish Benchmark 2010 144p il map (Cultures of the world) lib bdg $42.79

Grades: 5 6 7 8 **989.2**

1. Paraguay

ISBN 978-0-7614-4858-7 lib bdg; 0-7614-4858-6 lib bdg

LC 2009046495

First published 2000

This offers information on the geography, history, wildlife, governmental structure, economy, cultural diversity, peoples, religion, and culture of Paraguay

Includes glossary and bibliographical references

989.5 Uruguay

Jermyn, Leslie

Uruguay; Leslie Jermyn, Winnie Wong, Debbie Nevins. 3rd edition Cavendish Square 2019 144p il map (Cultures of the world) library $47.07

Grades: 5 6 7 8 **989.5**

1. Uruguay

ISBN 9781502636447 library

LC 2018018147

First published 1999

Provides information on the geography, history, wildlife, governmental structure, economy, cultural diversity, peoples, religion, and culture of Uruguay

Includes glossary and bibliographical references

993 New Zealand

Gillespie, Carol Ann

New Zealand; [by] Carol Ann Gillespie. updated ed.; Chelsea House Publishers 2005 100p il map (Modern world nations) lib bdg $30

Grades: 7 8 9 10 **993**

1. New Zealand

ISBN 0-7910-8708-5

LC 2005045445

First published 1992

This describes the natural landscapes, unique plant and animal life, history, culture, people, government and politics, and future outlook of New Zealand

Includes bibliographical references

Jackson, Barbara

★ **New** Zealand; [by] Barbara Jackson; Vaughan Wood and Simon Milne, consultants. National Geographic 2008 64p il map (Countries of the world) lib bdg $27.90

Grades: 4 5 6 7 **993**

1. New Zealand

ISBN 978-1-4263-0301-2 lib bdg; 1-4263-0301-7 lib bdg

This describes the geography, nature, history, people and culture, government, and economy of New Zealand.

Smelt, Roselynn

New Zealand; Roselynn Smelt, Yong Jui Lin, and Joel Newsome. 3rd edition Cavendish Square 2019 128p il map (Cultures of the world) library $47.07

Grades: 5 6 7 8 **993**

1. New Zealand

ISBN 9781502636287

LC 2017059330

First published 1998

"Provides comprehensive information on the geography, history, wildlife, governmental structure, economy, cultural diversity, peoples, religion, and culture of New Zealand." Publisher's note

Includes glossary and bibliographical references

994 Australia

Arnold, Caroline

★ **Uluru,** Australia's Aboriginal heart; photographs by Arthur Arnold. Clarion Books 2003 64p il $16

Grades: 5 6 7 8 **994**

1. Aboriginal Australians 2. Australia 3. Uluru-Kata Tjuta National Park (Australia)

ISBN 0-618-18181-4

LC 2002-15542

Describes Uluru, formerly known as Ayers Rock, in Australia's Uluru-Kata Tjuta National Park, its plant and animal life, and the country's Aboriginal people for whom the site is sacred

"The book's greatest accomplishment . . . is to give readers a sense of the ongoing spiritual importance of Uluru to the Anangu, who have lived around it for 10,000 years. Clear, colorful photos of Uluru and its surroundings appear on nearly every page, illustrating the text with beauty and finesse." Booklist

Einfeld, Jann

Life in the Australian Outback. Lucent Bks. 2003 112p il map (Way people live) lib bdg $21.96

Grades: 6 7 8 9 **994**

1. Australia 2. Australian aborigines

ISBN 1-59018-014-3

LC 2001-7504

"An in-depth look at a unique culture that exists in Australia's remote interior. Well detailed and meticulously documented, this book does an excellent job of illustrating the diversity of the outback population as well as the challenges faced by its inhabitants." SLJ

Includes glossary and bibliographical references

Leppman, Elizabeth J.

Australia and the Pacific; series consulting editor Charles F. Gritzner. Chelsea House Pubs. 2006 118p il map (Modern world cultures) lib bdg $30

Grades: 7 8 9 10 **994**

1. Oceania 2. Australia

ISBN 0-7910-8150-8

This describes the natural landscapes, history, people, culture, geopolitics, economy, regional contrasts, and future outlook of Australia and the Pacific.

Includes bibliographical references

Turner, Kate

★ **Australia**; [by] Kate Turner; Elaine Stratford and Joseph Powell, consultants. National Geographic 2007 64p il map (Countries of the world) lib bdg $27.90

Grades: 4 5 6 7 **994**

1. Australia

ISBN 978-1-4263-0055-4

Describes the geography, nature, history, people and culture, government and economy of Australia

This "appealing [title has] wonderful photographs and maps. . . . [This book is a] reliable [source] for country research, and the interesting current material hold browsing potential as well." SLJ

Includes glossary and bibliographical references

995.3 Papua New Guinea

Gascoigne, Ingrid

Papua New Guinea; Ingrid Gascoigne and Cassandra Schumacher. 3rd edition Cavendish Square 2018 144p il map (Cultures of the world) library $47.07

Grades: 5 6 7 8 **995.3**

1. Papua New Guinea

ISBN 9781502636300

LC 2017046637

First published 1998

"Provides comprehensive information on the geography, history, wildlife, governmental structure, economy, cultural diversity, peoples, religion, and culture of Papua New Guinea." Publisher's note

Includes glossary and bibliographical references

996 Polynesia and other Pacific Ocean islands

NgCheong-Lum, Roseline, 1962-

Tahiti; writers, Roseline NgCheong-Lum, Debbie Nevins. 3rd edition Cavendish Square 2017 144p il map (Cultures of the world) library $47.07

Grades: 5 6 7 8 **996**

1. Tahiti (French Polynesia)

ISBN 9781502627414

"Provides comprehensive information on the geography, history, wildlife, governmental structure, economy, cultural diversity, peoples, religion, and culture of Tahiti." Publisher's note

Includes glossary and bibliographical references

Pelta, Kathy

Rediscovering Easter Island. Lerner Publs. 2000 112p il maps (How history is invented) lib bdg $23.93

Grades: 5 6 7 8 **996**

1. Easter Island

ISBN 0-8225-4890-9

LC 00-9163

Discusses the many visits made by explorers, missionaries, businessmen, scientists, and others to Easter Island since the late 1600s and what they revealed about life on this remote Pacific island

"Coverage is serious, generally evenhanded, and smoothly presented, making this a fine foundation for readers who enjoy digging up the past." Bull Cent Child Books

Includes bibliographical references

996.9 Hawaii and neighboring north central Pacific Ocean islands

Kent, Deborah

Hawai'i; by Deborah Kent. Revised edition Children's Press 2014 144 p. col ill, col maps $40

Grades: 4 5 6 7 **996.9**

1. Hawaii 2. United States -- Geography

ISBN 0531248828; 9780531248829

Includes bibliographical references (page 138) and index

"Added to the union in August 1959, Hawaii is the youngest member of the United States. Readers will trace the history of this remarkable state from its earliest settlement to its latest developments. They will also dive into the local culture, see the state's many fascinating sights, and learn about its economy." (Publisher's note)

998 Arctic islands and Antarctica

Bledsoe, Lucy Jane

★ **How** to survive in Antarctica; written and photographed by Lucy Jane Bledsoe. Holiday House 2006 101p il map $16.95

Grades: 5 6 7 8 **998**

1. Antarctica

ISBN 0-8234-1890-1

LC 2004-60639

"Bledsoe, who made three trips to study Antarctica, bases her informal, chatty narrative on her thrilling adventure, bringing close the amazing science and geography as well as the gritty facts of human survival in the frigid environment. . . . Bledsoe's own black-and-white photos . . . will grab students across the curriculum." Booklist

Includes glossary

Latta, Sara L.

Ice scientist; careers in the frozen Antarctic. Enslow Publishers 2009 128p il (Wild science careers) lib bdg $31.93

Grades: 5 6 7 8 **998**

1. Scientists 2. Vocational guidance 3. Antarctica -- Exploration

ISBN 978-0-7660-3048-0 lib bdg; 0-7660-3048-2 lib bdg

LC 2008-4652

The book's "greatest strength is in the variety of firsthand accounts and the scientists' breadth of experience. [The book has] appealing color photographs and an attractive design." SLJ

Includes glossary and bibliographical references

Lourie, Peter

Arctic thaw; the people of the whale in a changing climate. Boyds Mills Press 2007 47p il map $17.95

Grades: 5 6 7 8 **998**

1. Inupiat 2. Whaling 3. Human ecology 4. Alaska 5. Greenhouse effect

ISBN 978-1-59078-436-5; 1-59078-436-7

LC 2006-20045

"A somewhat sobering, yet upbeat examination of the probable effects of global warming on the culture of the Iñupiaq whale hunters of Alaska's North Slope. . . . [Lourie's] lively, straightforward text describes the mixture of traditional and modern ways of the present-day Iñupiaq, as well as the work of [Paul] Shepson and his team to record weather and climate changes and to predict what effect they will have locally and globally." SLJ

Includes bibliographical references

Lynch, Wayne

Arctic; text and photographs by Wayne Lynch; assisted by Aubrey Lang. NorthWord Books for Young Readers 2007 64p il map (Our wild world: ecosystems) hardcover o.p. pa $8.95

Grades: 4 5 6 7 **998**

1. Arctic regions 2. Animals -- Arctic regions

ISBN 978-1-55971-960-5; 978-1-55971-961-2 pa

LC 2006021920

"With accessible first-person writing, Lynch describes the Arctic ecosystem, discussing both the high and low Arctic. . . . Stunning photographs include close-ups and more expansive views." Horn Book Guide

Includes bibliographical references

Myers, Walter Dean, 1937-2014

★ **Antarctica**; journeys to the South Pole. Scholastic Press 2004 134p il maps $18.95

Grades: 6 7 8 9 **998**

1. Antarctica

ISBN 0-439-22001-7

LC 2004-2501

This book tracks "the explorers of the South Pole—including James Cook, Ernest Shackleton, and Richard Evelyn Byrd—and the dangers they encountered there, as well as their contributions to science." (Publisher's note) Index. "Grades five to nine." (Bull Cent Child Books)

This is "a lucid, well-written text." SLJ

Includes bibliographical references

Revkin, Andrew

★ The **North** Pole was here; puzzles and perils at the top of the world. [by] Andrew C. Revkin. 1st ed.; Kingfisher 2006 128p il map $15.95

Grades: 7 8 9 10 **998**

1. North Pole 2. Arctic regions 3. Greenhouse effect

ISBN 0-7534-5993-0; 978-0-7534-5993-5

LC 2005-24307

The author "relates his journey to the top of the world in the company of scientists studying climate changes. The informative chapters weave together accounts of his experiences and observations with details about the environment, its exploration, and scientific concepts. . . . The illustrations include full-color photographs of the author's trek, archival reproductions and photos of previous excursions, original diagrams that clarify concepts, and maps. . . . The wonderfully written narrative will pull youngsters into the book and hold them there willingly until the last page." SLJ

Includes bibliographical references

Tulloch, Coral

Antarctica; the heart of the world. 1st American ed.; Enchanted Lion Books 2006 48p il map $17.95

Grades: 6 7 8 9 **998**

1. Antarctica

ISBN 1-59270-054-3

LC 2005-40162

"Tulloch writes out of her experiences as a voyager on an Antarctic resupply ship to illuminate the continent's geologic history, its flora and fauna, and its importance to the global ecosystem. She also addresses the early and continuing human explorations and their impact on the region as well as the area's rich potential and possible future problems. The writing is clear, and the science is comprehensible without the slightest sense of talking down to youthful readers." Voice Youth Advocates

Includes bibliographical references

Wade, Rosalyn

Polar worlds. Simon & Schuster Books for Young Readers 2011 64p il (Insiders) $16.99

Grades: 4 5 6 7 **998**

1. Antarctica 2. Arctic regions

ISBN 978-1-4424-3275-8; 1-4424-3275-6

This "takes a look at the nether regions of the globe in this browser-friendly resource. . . . 'Introducing' opens with a geographic look at the Arctic and Antarctic regions, then moves on to the related topics of icebergs, plant and animal life, exploration, survival measures, and environmental threats. The 'In Focus' section zeroes in on 12 specific animals found in polar regions. . . . Each spread is dominated by a sharply rendered, often dramatic digital illustration. . . . A fine introduction to the world's deep freezers." Booklist

Walker, Sally M.

★ **Frozen** secrets; Antarctica revealed. Carolrhoda Books 2010 104p il map $20.95

Grades: 7 8 9 10 **998**

1. Antarctica

ISBN 978-1-58013-607-5; 1-58013-607-9

LC 2009-34282

This is an "account of the rich scientific findings coming out of the planet's southernmost continent. . . . It's an excellent overview that manages to pack a lot of technical and scientific information into a small space, but it's sufficiently well structured conceptually and well laid out visually . . . that it all goes down pretty easily. The photographic images reveal the stunning beauty of the continent in shot after shot, but there are also illuminating views of the scientists at work, and diagrams and maps round out the view." Bull Cent Child Books

Fic FICTION

50 Cent, 1975-

Playground; with Aura Moser. Razorbill 2011 314p $17.99

Grades: 7 8 9 10 **Fic**

1. Bullies -- Fiction

ISBN 978-1-59514-434-8; 1-59514-434-X

Thirteen-year-old Butterball doesn't have much going for him. He's teased about his weight. He hates the Long Island suburb his mom moved them to so she could go to nursing school and start her life over. He wishes he still lived with his dad in New York City where there's always something happening, even if his dad doesn't have much time for him. Still, that's not why he beat up Maurice on the playground.

"Readers who were ever confused about having a gay parent, or being overweight, or going through a parental breakup, or just wanting to fit in and be accepted by their peers, will relate to Butterball. 50 Cent's debut young adult novel is a quick read that will be great for discussions on a variety of important and timely topics." VOYA

Abawi, Atia

★ A **land** of permanent goodbyes; Atia Abawi. Philomel Books 2018 279 p. (hardback) $17.99

Grades: 7 8 9 10 11 12 **Fic**

1. Muslims -- Fiction 2. Bombings -- Fiction 3. Refugees -- Fiction 4. Syria -- Fiction 5. IS (Organization) -- Fiction 6. Family life -- Syria -- Fiction

ISBN 9780399546839; 9780399546846

LC 2017021847

In this novel, by Atia Abawi, "in a country ripped apart by war, Tareq lives with his . . . family . . . until the bombs strike. His city is in ruins. His life is destroyed. . . . In the wake of destruction, he's threatened by Daesh fighters and witnesses a public beheading. . . . As they travel as refugees from Syria to Turkey to Greece, facing danger at every turn, Tareq must find the resilience and courage to complete his harrowing journey." (Publisher's note)

"A heartbreaking, haunting, and necessary story that offers hope while laying bare the bleakness of the world Tareq leaves and the new one he seeks to join." Kirkus

Abbott, Tony, 1952-

Denis ever after; Tony Abbott. Katherine Tegen Books 2018 320 p. (hardcover) $16.99

Grades: 5 6 7 8 **Fic**

1. Horror fiction 2. Death -- Fiction 3. Siblings -- Fiction

ISBN 9780062491220

LC 2017951444

Edgar Finalist (2019)

"Denis Egan is dead. He's okay with that. . . . [T]he place where souls go is actually pretty nice. . . . [But h]is twin brother Matt can't let go of him, and as long as the living are holding on to his memory, Denis can't rest in peace. To uncover the truth about what happened that day five years before, Denis returns to his hometown and teams up with Matt. But visiting for too long has painful consequences for Denis." (Publisher's note)

The **forbidden** stone; by Tony Abbott. Katherine Tegen Books, an imprint of HarperCollinsPublishers 2014 432 p. (The Copernicus legacy) (hardback) $16.99

Grades: 4 5 6 7 **Fic**

1. Antiquities -- Fiction 2. Secret societies -- Fiction 3. Voyages

and travels -- Fiction 4. Adventure and adventurers -- Fiction
ISBN 006219447X; 9780062194473

LC 2013038560

"Four precocious preteens and a distracted astrophysicist travel to Europe to unravel a mystery that has already claimed several lives. . . . Filled with riddles and ciphers, this first of 12 installments will keep readers intellectually stimulated as well as entertained. The stepbrothers' bond, a budding crush and a mystery that plays off of real historical figures and facts make this more than a pedestrian whodunit. With engaging characters, a globe-trotting plot and dangerous villains, it is hard to find something not to like. Equal parts edge-of-your-seat suspense and heartfelt coming-of-age." (Kirkus)

Other titles in this series are:
The serpent's curse (2014)
The golden vendetta (2015)
The crown of fire (2016)

The **great** Jeff; by Tony Abbott. Little, Brown & Co. 2019 288 p. (hardcover) $16.99

Grades: 5 6 7 8 **Fic**

1. Poverty -- Fiction 2. Schools -- Fiction 3. Middle schools -- Fiction 4. Homeless persons -- Fiction 5. Single-parent families -- Fiction
ISBN 9780316479691

LC 2018020156

In this children's novel, by Tony Abbott, "life hasn't been great for Jeff Hicks. After years at his beloved St. Catherine's, he's forced to spend eighth grade in the public middle school, which he hates. He's no longer speaking to his former best friend, Tom Bender, because of 'that burned girl' Jessica Feeney. But worst of all, his family is changing, and it's not for the better." (Publisher's note)

Lunch -box dream. Farrar Straus Giroux 2011 178p $16.99

Grades: 6 7 8 9 **Fic**

1. Family life -- Fiction 2. Segregation -- Fiction 3. Race relations -- Fiction 4. Southern States -- Fiction 5. Missing children -- Fiction 6. African Americans -- Fiction 7. Voyages and travels -- Fiction
ISBN 978-0-374-34673-7; 0-374-34673-9

LC 2010-33105

Told from multiple points of view, a white family on a 1959 road trip between Ohio and Florida, visiting Civil War battlefields along the way, crosses paths with a black family near Atlanta, where one of their children has gone missing.

"Throughout, Abbott . . . builds an increasingly disturbing undercurrent of racial conflict, sibling distrust, and marital discord. Although beautifully crafted and written, the book's emotional complexity and unsettling tone will likely prove challenging." Publ Wkly

The **summer** of Owen Todd; Tony Abbott. Farrar, Straus & Giroux 2017 217 p. (hardcover) $17.99

Grades: 5 6 7 8 **Fic**

1. Friendship -- Fiction 2. Cape Cod (Mass.) -- Fiction 3. Child sexual abuse -- Fiction 4. Best friends -- Fiction 5. Sexual abuse -- Fiction
ISBN 9780374305529; 9780374305505

LC 2016058780

In this book, by Tony Abbott, "Owen and his best friend, Sean, are both eleven years old. They've lived on Cape Cod all their lives, and now that they're a little older, they'll finally be free to spend some time on their own. But Sean's mother has a different idea—she hires a babysitter to look after Sean. Paul is in his twenties, and a well-liked guy from church." (Publisher's note)

"Abbott has done a fine job of dramatizing the book's central problem. Books about abuse, especially of boys, are rare for this age group, so happily, this is a good example, and one hopes that it will spark much-needed discussion." Booklist

Wade and the scorpion's claw; by Tony Abbott. Katherine Tegen Books/HarperCollins 2014 224 p. illustrations (The Copernicus archives) (paperback) $3.99

Grades: 4 5 6 7 **Fic**

1. Adventure fiction 2. Relics -- Fiction 3. Antiquities -- Fiction 4. Secret societies -- Fiction 5. Voyages and travels -- Fiction 6. Adventure and adventurers -- Fiction
ISBN 0062314726; 9780062314727

LC 2014010026

"'Wade and the Scorpion's Claw' picks up right where 'The Copernicus Legacy: The Forbidden Stone' left off, with the Kaplan family seeking the next Copernicus relic. Now Wade, the curious, analytical, yet starry-eyed member of the group, leads the chase for another relic through the busy streets of San Francisco while on the run from one of Galina Krause's most treacherous henchmen." (Publisher's note)

"This first in a string of novellas is intended to link each of the six full-length novels in the Copernicus Legacy series. . . . This fast-paced adventure features vivid settings, difficult brainteasers and likable characters." Kirkus

Another title in this series is:
Becca and the prisoner's cross (2015)

Abdel-Fattah, Randa

★ **Does** my head look big in this? Orchard Books 2007 360p $16.99

Grades: 7 8 9 10 11 12 **Fic**

1. School stories 2. Muslims -- Fiction 3. Australia -- Fiction 4. Clothing and dress -- Fiction
ISBN 0-439-91947-9; 978-0-439-91947-0

LC 2006-29117

Year Eleven at an exclusive prep school in the suburbs of Melbourne, Australia, would be tough enough, but it is further complicated for Amal when she decides to wear the hijab, the Muslim head scarf, full-time as a badge of her faith—without losing her identity or sense of style. "Grades seven to ten." (Bull Cent Child Books)

"While the novel deals with a number of serious issues, it is extremely funny and entertaining." SLJ

★ **Where** the streets had a name; Randa Abdel-Fattah. Scholastic Press 2010 313p (reinforced binding) $17.99

Grades: 5 6 7 8 **Fic**

1. Jerusalem -- Fiction 2. Voyages and travels -- Fiction 3. Jewish-Arab relations -- Fiction 4. Israel -- Fiction 5. Muslims -- Fiction 6. West Bank -- Fiction 7. Family life -- Fiction 8. Palestinian Arabs -- Fiction 9. Israel-Arab conflicts -- Fiction
ISBN 0545172926; 9780545172929; 978-0-545-17292-9; 0-545-17292-6

LC 2009043122

This book tells the story of 13-year-old Hayaat, who "lives behind the Israeli-built Separation Wall in the West Bank City of Bethlehem. When her beloved grandmother falls ill . . . [she] decides to make her way to Jerusalem to fill an empty hummus jar with soil from the land of her grandmother's ancestral home. She is certain that this will mend her heart. Unfortunately, although Jerusalem is merely minutes away, curfews, checkpoints, and an identity card that doesn't allow her to cross the border mean that Hayaat and her soccer-loving, troublemaker friend

Samy face a perilous journey." (School Lib J) "At the many checkpoints, the friends encounter soldiers, both brutal and kind, and also an Israeli peacenik couple who helps the kids get past the towering barriers." (Booklist)

"Hayaat chronicles this life-altering journey in the first-person, present tense, giving readers an intimate glimpse into the life of her warm, eccentric Muslim family, who survive despite the volatile political environment. A refreshing and hopeful teen perspective on the Israeli-Palestinian dilemma." Kirkus

Abrahams, Peter, 1947-

Down the rabbit hole; an Echo Falls mystery. Laura Geringer Books 2005 375p $15.99; lib bdg $16.89; pa $6.99

Grades: 6 7 8 **Fic**

1. Mystery fiction

ISBN 0-06-073701-8; 0-06-073702-6 lib bdg; 0-06-073703-4 pa

LC 2004-14778

"Ingrid Levin-Hill . . . has just been cast as the lead in Alice in Wonderland when she finds herself in a different role—murder detective. The corpse is that of 'Cracked-Up Katie,' whom Ingrid encountered when she attempted to get from her orthodontist to soccer practice." Publ Wkly

Other Echo Falls mysteries are:
Behind the curtain (2006)
Into the dark (2008)

Reality check. HarperTeen 2009 330p $16.99; lib bdg $17.89; pa $8.99

Grades: 7 8 9 10 **Fic**

1. School stories 2. Gambling -- Fiction 3. Social classes -- Fiction 4. Missing persons -- Fiction

ISBN 978-0-06-122766-0; 0-06-122766-8; 978-0-06-122767-7 lib bdg; 0-06-122767-6 lib bdg; 978-0-06-122768-4 pa; 0-06-122768-4 pa

LC 2008-22593

After a knee injury destroys sixteen-year-old Cody's college hopes, he drops out of high school and gets a job in his small Montana town, but when his ex-girlfriend disappears from her Vermont boarding school, Cody travels cross-country to join the search.

"Abrahams writes a fine thriller that is pitched to attract everyone from reluctant readers to sports fans to romantic idealists." Voice Youth Advocates

Robbie Forester and the outlaws of Sherwood street; magic strikes. Peter Abrahams. Philomel Books 2011 320 p. $16.99

Grades: 5 6 7 8 **Fic**

1. Occult fiction -- Fiction 2. Fantasy fiction 3. Magic -- Fiction 4. Justice -- Fiction 5. Schools -- Fiction 6. Neighborhoods -- Fiction 7. Conduct of life -- Fiction 8. Brooklyn (New York, N.Y.) -- Fiction 9. Family life -- New York (State) -- New York -- Fiction

ISBN 0399255028; 9780399255021

LC 2010042330

In this book, when seventh-grader Robbie "accidentally acquires a homeless woman's charm bracelet, she discovers it's a catalyst for magical powers that engage only when justice is being denied. She and three friends . . . use their unique capabilities to uncover and thwart an evil real estate developer pushing small businesses and social services out of the borough." (School Library Journal)

Another title in the series is:
Giving to the poor (2013)

Acampora, Paul

Confusion is nothing new; Paul Acampora. Scholastic Press 2018 192 p. (hardcover) $16.99

Grades: 5 6 7 8 **Fic**

1. Single-parent families -- Fiction 2. Father-daughter relationship -- Fiction 3. Mother-daughter relationship -- Fiction 4. Bildungsromans 5. Schools -- Fiction 6. Friendship -- Fiction 7. Bands (Music) -- Fiction 8. Marching bands -- Fiction 9. Catholic schools -- Fiction

ISBN 9781338209990

LC 2017055121

In this book, by Paul Acampora, "Ellie Magari just learned that her mother is dead. Perhaps that would be sad if Ellie had ever met the woman. Exactly who was Ellie's mom? Does it even matter that she's gone? Perhaps a dead mom can still help Ellie figure out what it means to be a girl in the world today. Either way, Ellie wouldn't mind a role model beyond her master chef Dad." (Publisher's note)

Rachel Spinelli punched me in the face. Roaring Brook Press 2011 168p $15.99

Grades: 5 6 7 8 **Fic**

1. Moving -- Fiction 2. Trumpet -- Fiction 3. Musicians -- Fiction 4. Friendship -- Fiction 5. Connecticut -- Fiction 6. Family life -- Fiction 7. Single parent family -- Fiction

ISBN 978-1-59643-548-3; 1-59643-548-8

LC 2010027436

When fourteen-year-old Zachary and his father move to Falls, Connecticut, he spends a summer falling in love, coming to terms with his mother's absence, and forming eclectic friendships.

"Realistic dialogue and poignantly amusing situations . . . all come together to gently flesh out a few months in the lives of people readers will savor getting to know. . . . An outstanding, humane coming-of-age tale of loss, yearning and forgiveness." Kirkus

Adams, Douglas

★ The **hitchhiker's** guide to the galaxy; 25th anniversary illustrated collector's ed.; Harmony Books 2004 271p il $35

Grades: 7 8 9 10 11 12 Adult **Fic**

1. Science fiction

ISBN 1-4000-5293-9

LC 2004-558987

First published 1980

"Based on a BBC radio series, . . . this is the episodic story of Arthur Dent, a contemporary Englishman who discovers first that his unpretentious house is about to be demolished to make way for a bypass, and second that a good friend is actually an alien galactic hitchhiker who announces that Earth itself will soon be demolished to make way for an intergalactic speedway. A suitably bewildered Dent soon finds himself hitching . . . rides throughout space, aided by a . . . reference book, The Hitchhiker's Guide to the Galaxy, a compendium of 'facts,' philosophies, and wild advice." Libr J

Other titles in this series are:
Life, the universe, and everything
The restaurant at the end of the universe
So long, and thanks for all the fish
Mostly harmless

Life, the universe, and everything. Harmony Bks. 1982 227p hardcover o.p. pa $12.95

Grades: 11 12 Adult **Fic**

1. Science fiction

ISBN 0-517-54874-7; 0-345-41890-6 pa

LC 82-15470

Third volume in The hitchhiker's series

"Arthur Dent and his motley crew do tie up most of the loose ends and manage to prevent the destruction of the universe, but the first two novels . . . 'must' be read to understand the situation, and even then it's confusing." Libr J

Followed by So long, and thanks for all the fish

Mostly harmless. Harmony Bks. 1992 277p hardcover o.p. pa $12.95

Grades: 11 12 Adult **Fic**

1. Science fiction

ISBN 0-517-57740-2; 0-345-37933-0 pa

LC 92-25457

"A Grebulon reconnaissance ship with faulty programming, a news reporter suffering from a bad case of missed opportunities, a fugitive from the new 'improved' offices of the Hitchhiker's Guide to the Galaxy, and a hitchhiker lost in a parallel universe come together in grand style in the fifth installment of Adams's best-selling 'trilogy.'" Libr J

The **restaurant** at the end of the universe. Harmony Bks. 1981 250p hardcover o.p. pa $12.95

Grades: 11 12 Adult **Fic**

1. Satire 2. Wit and humor 3. Science fiction 4. Interplanetary voyages

ISBN 0-517-54535-7; 0-345-41892-1 pa

LC 81-6563

Second volume in The hitchhiker's series

First published 1980 in the United Kingdom

"Poor uprooted Arthur Dent finds himself swept along in the wake of Zaphod Beeblebrox, former President of the Galaxy, as Zaphod searches for the man who rules the Universe. They and their companions tumble from one scrape into another, with the erratic aid of Zaphod's dead great-grandfather and Marvin, their perpetually depressed robot. Adams's lively sense of the ridiculous has concocted many hilarious episodes, though the inspired lunacy of the first book has become rather uneven here. Still, this is one of the best pieces of sf humor available." Libr J

Followed by Life, the universe, and everything

So long, and thanks for all the fish. Harmony Bks. 1985 204p hardcover o.p. pa $7.99

Grades: 11 12 Adult **Fic**

1. Satire 2. Wit and humor 3. Science fiction 4. Interplanetary voyages

ISBN 0-517-55439-9; 0-345-39183-4 pa

LC 84-19350

Fourth volume in The hitchhiker's series

Arthur Dent "returns to a supposedly destroyed Earth to build a hyperspace bypass. The night of his return, Arthur falls in love with a sedated girl (her brother says she's 'barking mad'), only to lose her, then accidentally find her twice more. She is Fenchurch, the girl who in . . . 'Guide' . . . discovered the secret of Earth's potential happiness moments before it was demolished. Her 'madness' stems from the time when Earth should have been destroyed, and wasn't, but when all the dolphins disappeared. . . . The humor is still off-the-wall, but less forced and more gentle than the other books. . . . The series seems to be winding down, but it is still an addictive commodity to its fans." SLJ

Followed by Mostly harmless

Adams, Richard

Watership Down; Scribner classics ed.; Scribner 1996 429p $30; pa $15

Grades: 6 7 8 9 10 **Fic**

1. Allegories 2. Rabbits -- Fiction

ISBN 0-684-83605-X; 0-7432-7770-8 pa

First published 1972 in the United Kingdom; first United States edition 1974 by Macmillan

"Faced with the annihilation of its warren, a small group of male rabbits sets out across the English downs in search of a new home. Internal struggles for power surface in this intricately woven, realistically told adult adventure when the protagonists must coordinate tactics in order to defeat an enemy rabbit fortress. It is clear that the author has done research on rabbit behavior, for this tale is truly authentic." Shapiro Fic for Youth. 3d edition

Adams, S. J.

Sparks; the epic, completely true blue, (almost) holy quest of Debbie. 1; Flux 2011 256p pa $9.95

Grades: 8 9 10 11 12 **Fic**

1. Iowa -- Fiction 2. Lesbians -- Fiction 3. Religion -- Fiction

ISBN 978-0-7387-2676-2; 0-7387-2676-1

LC 2011022913

Stonewall Honor Book (2013)

A sixteen-year-old lesbian tries to get over a crush on her religious best friend by embarking on a 'holy quest' with a couple of misfits who have invented a wacky, made-up faith called the Church of Blue.

"Adams has an easy sense of humor . . . and Debbie and her offbeat cohorts are nuanced and authentic as they follow a circuitous path to greater self-awareness and self-reliance." Publ Wkly

Adlington, L. J.

★ The **diary** of Pelly D. Greenwillow Books 2005 282p hardcover o.p. pa $8.99

Grades: 7 8 9 10 **Fic**

1. Science fiction

ISBN 0-06-076615-8; 0-06-076617-4 pa

LC 2004-52258

"On the planet Home From Home, Toni V is a brute laborer, a barely educated member of the Demolition Crew that is busy pulverizing the bombed-out remains of City Five's central plaza. Pelly D is a hip member of the swank elite who used to live in an exclusive apartment fronting the plaza. Their stories come together when Toni V uncovers Pelly D's diary in the debris. . . . Middle school, high school." (Horn Book)

"Adlington has crafted an original and disturbing dystopian fantasy told in a smart and sympathetic teen voice." Booklist

Agard, John

★ The **young** inferno; written by John Agard; illustrated by Satoshi Kitamura. Frances Lincoln Children's 2009 un il $19.95

Grades: 8 9 10 11 12 **Fic**

1. Novels in verse 2. Hell -- Fiction

ISBN 978-1-84507-769-3; 1-84507-769-5

"The narrative poems in this short book are accessible and have important things to say about the state of the human race. . . . The hoodie-wearing protagonist . . . awakens in a strange and frightening forest. A dark man appears and introduces himself as the tale-teller Aesop: he is to be the teen's escort through Hell. . . . As the pair travels through the Circles of Hell, they see the sins of mankind. . . . The scribbled, heavy-lined black ink and watercolor illustrations convey exactly the right mood for a book about a modern-day expedition into Hell. This will be a great book to pair with a discussion about Dante's Inferno and/or poetic structure." SLJ

Agosín, Marjorie, 1955-

★ **I** lived on Butterfly Hill; Marjorie Agosín ; translated by E.M. O'Connor ; illustrated by Lee White. Atheneum Books for Young Readers 2014 464 p. illustrations $16.99

Grades: 5 6 7 8 **Fic**

1. Chile -- Fiction 2. Political refugees -- Fiction 3. Refugees -- Fiction 4. Separation (Psychology) -- Fiction 5. Valparaíso (Chile) -- Fiction

ISBN 1416953442; 9781416953449; 9781442494763

LC 2013018099

Pura Belpré (Author) Award (2015)

National Jewish Book Award Finalist: Children's and Young Adult (2014)

In this novel, by Marjorie Agosin, illustrated by Lee White, "Celeste Marconi . . . lives peacefully among friends and neighbors and family in the idyllic town of Valparaiso, Chile. . . . Celeste's parents--her educated, generous, kind parents--must go into hiding. . . . To protect their daughter, they send her to America. As Celeste adapts to her new life in Maine, she never stops dreaming of Chile. But even after democracy is restored to her home country, questions remain." (Publisher's note)

"The language is poetic and full of imagery and, while the book is long, it moves at a smooth pace. Occasional illustrations reflect the mood of each phase of the story." SLJ

Aguiar, Nadia

The **lost** island of Tamarind; [by] Nadia Aguiar. Feiwel and Friends 2008 437p il map (The Book of Tamarind) $17.95

Grades: 5 6 7 8 **Fic**

1. War stories 2. Adventure fiction 3. Magic -- Fiction 4. Giants -- Fiction 5. Islands -- Fiction 6. Pirates -- Fiction 7. Siblings -- Fiction

ISBN 978-0-312-38029-8; 0-312-38029-1

LC 2008-5623

Thirteen-year-old Maya, who has spent her life at sea with her marine biologist parents, yearns for a normal life, but when a storm washes her parents overboard, life becomes anything but normal for Maya, her younger brother and baby sister, as they land at a mysterious, uncharted island filled with danger.

"Each detail of this fantasy is crafted with care; readers will be drawn into this dangerous, magical world where anything is possible and nothing can be fully explained." SLJ

Other titles in this series are:

Secrets of Tamarind (2010)

The great wave of Tamarind (2016)

Ahdieh, Renée

Flame in the mist; Renee Ahdieh. G.P. Putnam's Sons 2017 392 p. (Flame in the Mist) (Hardcover) $17.99

Grades: 7 8 9 10 11 12 **Fic**

1. Adventure fiction 2. Alchemy -- Fiction 3. Samurai -- Fiction 4. Arranged marriage -- Fiction

ISBN 9780399171635

LC 2016057273

In this book, by Renee Ahdieh, "the daughter of a prominent samurai, Mariko has long known her place—she may be an accomplished alchemist, . . .but because she is not a boy, her future has always been out of her hands. At just seventeen years old, Mariko is promised to Minamoto Raiden, the son of the emperor's favorite consort—a political marriage that will elevate her family's standing. But en route to the imperial city of Inako, Mariko narrowly escapes a bloody ambush." (Publisher's note)

"Ahdieh delivers an elaborate fantasy set in feudal Japan, where a resilient young woman defies class conventions and gender roles in a quest for vengeance and autonomy." Pub Wkly

Another title in this series is:

Smoke in the sun (2018)

Smoke in the sun; Ahdieh, Renée. G.P. Putnam's Sons 2018 432 p. (hardback) $18.99

Grades: 7 8 9 10 11 12 **Fic**

1. Samurai -- Fiction 2. Siblings -- Fiction 3. Courts and courtiers -- Fiction 4. Sex role -- Fiction 5. Weddings -- Fiction 6. Conduct of life -- Fiction 7. Brothers and sisters -- Fiction 8. Japan -- History -- Tokugawa period, 1600-1868 -- Fiction

ISBN 9781524738143

LC 2018007928

Sequel to: Flame in the mist

In this novel in the Flame in the Mist series, by Renée Ahdieh, "after Okami is captured in the Jukai forest, Mariko has no choice--to rescue him, she must return to Inako and face the dangers that have been waiting for her in the Heian Castle. She tricks her brother, Kenshin, and betrothed, Raiden, into thinking she was being held by the Black Clan against her will, playing the part of the dutiful bride-to-be to infiltrate the emperor's ranks." (Publisher's note)

Ahmed, Samira

★ **Internment**; Samira Ahmed. Little, Brown & Co. 2019 400 p. (hardcover) $17.99

Grades: 7 8 9 10 11 **Fic**

1. Muslims -- Fiction 2. Prejudices -- Fiction 3. Concentration camps -- Fiction 4. Science fiction 5. Revolutionaries -- Fiction 6. Muslims -- United States -- Fiction

ISBN 9780316522694

LC 2018017615

In this book, by Samira Ahmed, "set in a horrifying near-future United States, seventeen-year-old Layla Amin and her parents are forced into an internment camp for Muslim American citizens. With the help of newly made friends also trapped within the internment camp, her boyfriend on the outside, and an unexpected alliance, Layla begins a journey to fight for freedom, leading a revolution against the internment camp's Director and his guards." (Publisher's note)

"Set shortly after the 2016 presidential election, Ahmed's novel presents a chilling depiction of America, in which U.S. citizens allow themselves to be controlled by prejudice and fear and succumb to the hateful rhetoric of a populist leader." (Booklist)

Love, hate & other filters; Samira Ahmed. Soho Teen 2018 281 p. illustrations (hardback) $18.99

Grades: 8 9 10 11 **Fic**

1. Muslims -- Fiction 2. Terrorism -- Fiction 3. High schools -- Fiction 4. East Indian Americans -- Fiction 5. Dating (Social customs) -- Fiction 6. Schools -- Fiction 7. Chicago (Ill.) -- Fiction 8. Family life -- Illinois -- Chicago -- Fiction

ISBN 9781616958473; 9781616958480

LC 2017021616

In this book, by Samira Ahmed, "American-born seventeen-year-old Maya Aziz is torn between worlds. There's the proper one her parents expect for their good Indian daughter: attending a college close to their suburban Chicago home, and being paired off with an older Muslim boy her mom deems 'suitable.' And then there is the world of her dreams: going to film school and living in New York City—and maybe (just maybe) pursuing a boy she's known from afar since grade." (Publisher's note)

"A well-crafted plot with interesting revelations about living as a secular Muslim teen in today's climate." Kirkus

Aiken, Joan

Black hearts in Battersea. Houghton Mifflin Co 1999 234p pa $7.99

Grades: 5 6 7 8 **Fic**

1. Orphans -- Fiction 2. London (England) -- Fiction

ISBN 978-0-395-97128-4; 0-395-97128-4

A reissue of the title first published 1964 by Doubleday

Simon arrives in London to meet an old friend and pursue the study of painting, but he finds himself in the middle of a wicked crew's plan to overthrow good King James and the Duke and Duchess of Battersea.

The **Witch** of Clatteringshaws. Delacorte Press 2005 131p pa $8.25

Grades: 5 6 7 8 **Fic**

1. Adventure fiction 2. Witches -- Fiction 3. Great Britain -- Fiction

ISBN 0-385-73226-0; 0-385-90252-2 lib bdg; 978-0-099-46406-8 pa

LC 2003027091

Dido travels to Scotland and, aided by Woodlouse and by Father Sam's cousin Malise, the Witch of Clatteringshaws, seeks another heir to the throne who can relieve her friend Simon of the burden of being king of England.

"Aiken somehow brings this story off with panache. Readers soon realize that her characters are just as amused by events as they are, swinging the story away from the ludicrous into a jolly romp of a fantasy." SLJ

★ The **wolves** of Willoughby Chase; illustrated by Pat Marriott. Delacorte Press 2000 181p il hardcover o.p. pa $6.99

Grades: 5 6 7 8 **Fic**

1. Great Britain -- Fiction

ISBN 0-385-32790-0; 0-440-49603-9 pa

First published 1962 in the United Kingdom; first United States edition 1963 by Doubleday

"Wicked wolves and a grim governess threaten Bonnie and her cousin Sylvia when Bonnie's parents leave Willoughby Chase for a sea voyage. Left in the care of the cruel Miss Slighcarp, the girls can hardly believe what is happening to their once happy home. The servants are dismissed, the furniture is sold, and Bonnie and Sylvia are sent to a prison-like orphan school. It seems as if the endless hours of drudgery will never cease. With the help of Simon the gooseboy and his flock, they escape. But how will they ever get Willoughby Chase free from the clutches of the evil Miss Slighcarp?" (Publisher's note)

"Plot, characterization, and background blend perfectly into an amazing whole. . . . Highly recommended." SLJ

Other titles in this series are:

Black hearts in Battersea (1964)
Cold Shoulder Road (1996)
The cuckoo tree (1971)
Dangerous games (1999)
Is underground (1993)
Midwinter nightingale (2003)
Nightbirds on Nantucket (1966)
The stolen lake (1981)
The witch of Clatteringshaws (2005)

Al-Mansour, Haifaa, 1974-

The **green** bicycle; Haifaa Al Mansour. Chronicle Books LLC 2015 352 p. (hardback) $16.99

Grades: 5 6 7 8 **Fic**

1. Girls -- Fiction 2. Bicycles -- Fiction 3. Sex role -- Fiction 4. Saudi Arabia -- Fiction 5. Coming of age -- Fiction 6. Bicycles and bicycling -- Fiction

ISBN 0525428062; 9780525428060

LC 2015014551

This children's story, by Haifaa Al Mansour, is a "Middle Eastern coming-of-age story is told with warmth, spirit, and a mischievous sense of humor. Spunky eleven-year-old Wadjda lives in Riyadh, Saudi Arabia with her parents. She desperately wants a bicycle so that she can race her friend Abdullah, even though it is considered improper for girls to ride bikes. . . . With the bicycle so closely in her sights, she will stop at nothing to get what she wants." (Publisher's note)

"Young readers will easily sympathize with Wadjda's wish for a bike, and they will come away with a deeper understanding of a faraway culture." Booklist

Alban, Andrea

Anya's war. Feiwel and Friends 2011 188p $16.99

Grades: 7 8 9 10 **Fic**

1. China -- Fiction 2. Jews -- China -- Fiction 3. Jewish refugees -- Fiction 4. Shanghai (China) -- Fiction 5. Abandoned children -- Fiction 6. Sino-Japanese Conflict, 1937-1945 -- Fiction

ISBN 978-0-312-37093-0; 0-312-37093-8

LC 2010-37089

In 1937, the privileged and relatively carefee life of a fourteen-year-old Jewish girl, whose family emigrated from Odessa, Ukraine, to Shanghai, China, comes to an end when she finds an abandoned baby, her hero, Amelia Earhart, goes missing, and war breaks out with Japan. Based on the author's family history.

"Most moving are the scenes with the full cast of family characters, who are irritating, irritable, funny, surprising, mean, and prejudiced. Alban also explores the complexities of Anya's Jewish community. . . . An important addition to literature about WWII refugees." Booklist

Alcott, Louisa May

Little women; illustrated by Scott McKowen. Sterling Pub. 2004 525p il $9.95

Grades: 5 6 7 8 **Fic**

1. Sisters -- Fiction 2. Family life -- Fiction 3. New England -- Fiction

ISBN 978-1-4027-1458-0; 1-4027-1458-0

LC 2004-15669

First published 1868

Chronicles the joys and sorrows of the four March sisters as they grow into young women in mid-nineteenth-century New England.

Other titles about members of the March family are:

Eight cousins (1875)
Jo's boys (1886)
Little men (1871)
Rose in bloom (1876)

Aldredge, Betsy

Sasquatch, love, and other imaginary things; Betsy Aldredge and Carrie DuBois-Shaw. Simon Pulse 2017 272 p. (hardcover) $19.99

Grades: 7 8 9 10 **Fic**

1. Yeti -- Fiction 2. Family life -- Fiction 3. Jews -- United States -- Fiction 4. Competition (Psychology) -- Fiction 5. Reality

television programs -- Fiction 6. Social classes -- Fiction 7. Television -- Production and direction -- Fiction
ISBN 9781507202814; 1507202806; 9781507202807
LC 2017009581

This book, by Betsy Aldredge and Carrie DuBois-Shaw, is "about a loving, quirky family on the hunt for the mythical Sasquatch. . . . It's bad enough that Samantha's parents . . . have dragged their daughter . . . hunting for yetis. But now they're doing it on national TV, and worse, in front of an aristocratic prep-school crew including a boy who disdains Samantha's family. But when he scorns her humble Ohio roots, she becomes determined to take him down." (Publisher's note)

"Samantha's first-person narration is marked by her sarcastic, wry, and delightfully snarky humor. 'Squatching' doesn't get any funnier than this." Kirkus

Alegria, Malin

Estrella's quinceanera. Simon & Schuster Books for Young Readers 2006 272p $14.95

Grades: 7 8 9 10 **Fic**

1. Mexican Americans -- Fiction 2. Quinceañera (Social custom) -- Fiction
ISBN 0-689-87809-5

Estrella's mother and aunt are planning a gaudy, traditional quinceañera for her, even though it is the last thing she wants.

"Alegria writes about Mexican American culture, first love, family, and of moving between worlds with poignant, sharp-sighted humor and authentic dialogue." Booklist

Alender, Katie

The **dead** girls of Hysteria Hall; Katie Alender. Point, an imprint of Scholastic Inc. 2015 336 p. (jacketed hardcover) $18.99

Grades: 7 8 9 10 11 12 **Fic**

1. Ghost stories 2. Horror fiction 3. Secrets -- Fiction 4. Family life -- Fiction 5. Pennsylvania -- Fiction 6. Haunted houses -- Fiction 7. Psychiatric hospitals -- Fiction 8. Horror tales 9. Horror stories 10. Ghosts -- Fiction 11. Sisters -- Fiction 12. Asylums -- Fiction 13. Secrecy -- Fiction
ISBN 9780545639996
LC 2014046681

In this book, by Katie Alender, "Delia's new house isn't just a house. Long ago, it was the Piven Institute for the Care and Correction of Troubled Females -- an insane asylum. . . . However, many of the inmates were not insane, just defiant and strong willed. Kind of like Delia herself. But the house still wants to keep "troubled" girls locked away. So, in the most horrifying way, Delia becomes trapped. And that's when she learns that the house is also haunted." (Publisher's note)

"Alender creates a fascinating, eerie world that turns on a nicely original use of time and features constantly interesting characters." Kirkus

Alexander, Kwame, 1968-

★ **Booked**; Kwame Alexander. Houghton Mifflin Harcourt 2016 320 p. (hardback) $16.99

Grades: 5 6 7 8 9 **Fic**

1. Soccer -- Fiction 2. Friendship -- Fiction 3. Books and reading -- Fiction
ISBN 9780544570986; 0544570987
LC 2015033312

In this novel by Kwame Alexander "soccer, family, love, and friendship, take center stage as twelve-year-old Nick learns the power of words as he wrestles with problems at home, stands up to a bully, and tries to impress the girl of his dreams. Helping him along are his best friend and sometimes teammate Coby, and The Mac, a rapping librarian who gives Nick inspiring books to read." (Publisher's note)

"Alexander scores again with this sports-themed verse novel, a companion to his Newbery Medal-winning The Crossover. . . . Emotionally resonant and with a pace like a player on a breakaway." Pub Wkly

★ The **crossover**; a basketball novel. by Kwame Alexander ; illustrated by Dawud Anyabwile. Houghton Mifflin Harcourt 2014 224 p. hardcover $16.99

Grades: 6 7 8 9 10 **Fic**

1. Novels in verse 2. Brothers -- Fiction 3. Basketball -- Fiction 4. Twins -- Fiction 5. Fathers and sons -- Fiction 6. African Americans -- Fiction
ISBN 9780544107717; 9780358064725
LC 2013013810

Coretta Scott King Honor Book (2015)
Newbery Medal (2015)

"The Bell twins are stars on the basketball court and comrades in life. While there are some differences—Josh shaves his head and Jordan loves his locks—both twins adhere to the Bell basketball rules: In this game of life, your family is the court, and the ball is your heart. With a former professional basketball player dad and an assistant principal mom, there is an intensely strong home front supporting sports and education in equal measures. When life intervenes in the form of a hot new girl, the balance shifts and growing apart proves painful." (Booklist)

"Despite his immaturity, Josh is a likable, funny, and authentic character. Underscoring the sports and the fraternal tension is a portrait of a family that truly loves and supports one another. Alexander has crafted a story that vibrates with energy and heart and begs to be read aloud." SLJ

★ **Rebound**; Kwame Alexander, illustrations by Dawud Anyabwile. Houghton Mifflin Harcourt 2018 416 p. illustrations (Crossover) (hardback) $16.99

Grades: 6 7 8 9 10 **Fic**

1. Family life 2. Basketball -- Fiction 3. African Americans -- Fiction 4. Novels in verse 5. Families -- Fiction 6. Washington (D.C.) -- History -- 20th century -- Fiction
ISBN 0544868137; 9780544868137
LC 2017061480

"In this 1988-set prequel to The Crossover, twelve-year-old Charlie Bell is spending the summer with his grandparents following the sudden death of his father. He finds solace on the basketball court. This story of realistic family dynamics, a search for confidence, and first romance is propelled by energetic, staccato poetry and elevated by a visceral exploration of grief." (Horn Book)

"The novel in verse is enhanced by Anyabwile's art, which reinforces Charlie's love for comics. An eminently satisfying story of family, recovery, and growing into manhood." Kirkus

Alexander, Lloyd, 1924-2007

The **Black** Cauldron; [by] Lloyd Alexander. rev. ed.; H. Holt 1999 182p (Chronicles of Prydain) $19.95

Grades: 5 6 7 8 **Fic**

1. Fantasy fiction
ISBN 0-8050-6131-2; 978-08050-6131-4
LC 98040896

First published 1965

Taran, Assistant Pig-Keeper of Prydain, faces even more dangers as he seeks the magical black cauldron, the chief implement of the evil powers of Arawn, lord of the Land of Death.

★ The **book** of three; rev ed.; Holt & Co. 1999 190p (Chronicles of Prydain) $19.95; pa $6.99
Grades: 5 6 7 8 **Fic**

1. Fantasy fiction 2. Fantasy
ISBN 0-8050-6132-0; 0-8050-8048-1 pa; 978-0-8050-6132-1; 978-0-8050-8048-3 pa

LC 98-40901

First published 1964

"Related in a simple, direct style, this fast-paced tale of high adventure has a well-balanced blend of fantasy, realism, and humor." SLJ

Other titles about the mythical land of Prydain are:
The black cauldron (1965)
The castle of Llyr (1966)
The foundling and other tales of Prydain (1999)
The high king (1968)
Taran Wanderer (1967)

The **castle** of Llyr; [by] Lloyd Alexander. rev.ed.; H. Holt 1999 172p (Chronicles of Prydain) $19.95
Grades: 5 6 7 8 **Fic**

1. Fantasy fiction
ISBN 0-8050-6133-9

LC 98040897

First published 1966

When Princess Eilonwy is sent to the Isle of Mona for training, she is bewitched by the evil enchantress Achren, so Taran and other friends must try to rescue her.

★ The **golden** dream of Carlo Chuchio. Henry Holt & Co. 2007 306p il $16.95
Grades: 5 6 7 8 9 **Fic**

1. Fantasy fiction 2. Middle East -- Fiction 3. Buried treasure -- Fiction 4. Voyages and travels -- Fiction
ISBN 978-0-8050-8333-0; 0-8050-8333-2

LC 2006-49710

Naive and bumbling Carlo, his shady camel-puller Baksheesh, and Shira, a girl determined to return home, follow a treasure map through the deserts and cities of the infamous Golden Road, as mysterious strangers try in vain to point them toward real treasures

This "is an exuberant and compassionate tale of adventure." Publ Wkly

The **high** king; rev ed; Holt & Co. 1999 253p (Chronicles of Prydain) $19.95
Grades: 5 6 7 8 **Fic**

1. Fantasy fiction
ISBN 0-8050-6135-5

LC 98-40900

Concluding title in the chronicles of Prydain which include: The book of three, The black cauldron, The castle of Llyr, and Taran Wanderer

First published 1968

Awarded The Newbery Medal, 1969

"The fantasy has the depth and richness of a medieval tapestry, infinitely detailed and imaginative." Saturday Rev

★ The **iron** ring. Dutton Children's Bks. 1997 283p hardcover o.p. pa $5.99
Grades: 5 6 7 8 **Fic**

1. Adventure fiction 2. India -- Fiction
ISBN 0-14-130348-4 pa

LC 96-29730

"Young Tamar, ruler of a small Indian kingdom, wagers with a visiting king and loses his kingdom and his freedom. Traveling to the king's land to make good on his debt, he collects quite an entourage and eventually overcomes his enemies with his friends' help. This tale offers delightful characters, a philosophical interest in the meaning of life, a thoughtful look at the caste system, and a clever use of Indian animal folktales." Horn Book Guide

★ The **remarkable** journey of Prince Jen. Dutton Children's Bks. 1991 273p hardcover o.p. pa $6.99
Grades: 5 6 7 8 **Fic**

1. Adventure fiction 2. China -- Fiction
ISBN 0-14-240225-7 pa

LC 91-13720

Bearing six unusual gifts, young Prince Jen in Tang Dynasty China embarks on a perilous quest and emerges triumphantly into manhood

"Alexander satisfies the taste for excitement, but his vivid characters and the food for thought he offers will nourish long after the last page is turned." SLJ

Taran Wanderer; [by] Lloyd Alexander. rev ed.; H. Holt 1999 222p (Chronicles of Prydain) $19.95
Grades: 5 6 7 8 **Fic**

1. Fantasy fiction
ISBN 0-8050-6134-7

LC 98040904

The fourth book of the Prydain cycle tells of the adventures that befell Taran when he went in search of his birthright and the truth about himself.

★ **Westmark**. Dutton 1981 184p hardcover o.p. pa $5.99
Grades: 5 6 7 8 **Fic**

1. Adventure fiction
ISBN 0-14-131068-5

A boy fleeing from criminal charges falls in with a charlatan, his dwarf attendant, and an urchin girl, travels with them about the kingdom of Westmark, and ultimately arrives at the palace where the king is grieving over the loss of his daughter

The author "peoples his tale with a marvelous cast of individuals, and weaves an intricate story of high adventure that climaxes in a superbly conceived conclusion, which, though predictable, is reached through carefully built tension and subtly added comic relief." Booklist

Other titles in this series are:
The Beggar Queen (1984)
The Kestrel (1982)

Alexander, William

Ambassador; William Alexander. Margaret K. McElderry Books 2014 240 p. (hardcover) $16.99
Grades: 5 6 7 8 **Fic**

1. Science fiction 2. Human-alien encounters -- Fiction 3. Ambassadors -- Fiction 4. Illegal aliens -- Fiction 5. Mexican Americans -- Fiction
ISBN 1442497645; 9781442497641; 9781442497658

LC 2013037333

In this middle grade book by William Alexander, "Gabe Fuentes is reading under the covers one summer night when he is interrupted by a creature who looks like a purple sock puppet. The sock puppet introduces himself as the Envoy and asks if Gabe wants to be Earth's ambassador to the galaxy. What sane eleven-year-old could refuse?" (Publisher's note)

"A shape-shifting creature called 'the Envoy' informs eleven-year-old Gabe that it has appointed him Earth's ambassador to 'everyone else.' Gabe travels across space (while he's asleep) to the Embassy. When he wakes up back home, he discovers his father is to be deported to Mexico the next day--and one of the other ambassadors is trying to kill Gabe. A meaty and entertaining novel." Horn Book

Another title in this series is:
Nomad (2015)

Goblin secrets; William Alexander. Margaret K. McElderry Books 2012 223 p.
Grades: 5 6 7 8 **Fic**

1. Fantasy fiction 2. Goblins -- Fiction 3. Witches -- Fiction 4. Brothers -- Fiction 5. Missing persons -- Fiction 6. Fantasy 7. Magic -- Fiction 8. Masks -- Fiction 9. Entertainers -- Fiction
ISBN 9781442427266; 9781442427280

LC 2011015491

National Book Award: Young People's Literature (2012)

In this book, a "tempestuous river divides the city of Zombay into two parts: the wealthy, aristocratic Northside, run by the Mayor and his gearworked Guard, and the Southside, whose impoverished residents are under the control of Graba, a powerful, cruel witch who takes in orphans to be her servants. . . . Rownie . . . learns that [his brother] Rowan was to play an essential part in a ritual meant to save the town from an impending flood." (Bulletin of the Center for Children's Books)

Nomad. Simon & Schuster 2015 272 p. $16.99
Grades: 5 6 7 8 **Fic**

1. Space warfare -- Fiction 2. Human-alien encounters -- Fiction
ISBN 144249767X; 9781442497672

"When we last left Earth's Ambassador, Gabe Fuentes, he was stranded on the moon. And when he's rescued by Kaen, another Ambassador, things don't get better: It turns out that the Outlasta race of aliens that has been systematically wiping out all other creatures--are coming. And they've set their sights on Earth. Enter Nadia. She was Earth's Ambassador before Gabe, but left her post in order to stop the Outlast. Nadia has discovered that the Outlast can conquer worlds by travelling fast through lanes created by the mysterious Machinae." (Publisher's note)

"'Alexander is clearly passionate about science, space exploration, and social justice, but he never allows that passion to shortchange the crackerjack adventure." Kirkus

Alexie, Sherman, 1966-

★ The **absolutely** true diary of a part-time Indian; art by Ellen Forney. Little, Brown 2007 229p il $18.99
Grades: 8 9 10 **Fic**

1. School stories 2. Friendship -- Fiction 3. Family life -- Fiction 4. Native Americans -- Fiction
ISBN 0316013684; 9780316013680

LC 2007-22799

Boston Globe-Horn Book Award: Fiction and Poetry (2008)
National Book Award: Young People's Literature (2007)

Budding cartoonist Junior leaves his troubled school on the Spokane Indian Reservation to attend an all-white farm town school where the only other Indian is the school mascot. "Grades seven to ten." (Bull Cent Child Books)

"The many characters, on and off the rez, with whom he has dealings are portrayed with compassion and verve. . . . Forney's simple pencil cartoons fit perfectly within the story and reflect the burgeoning artist within Junior." Booklist

Ali, S. K.

Love from A to Z; S.K. Ali. Salaam Reads 2019 384 p. (hardback) $18.99
Grades: 8 9 10 11 12 **Fic**

1. Arabs -- Fiction 2. Qatar -- Fiction 3. Muslims -- Fiction 4. Schools -- Fiction 5. Prejudices -- Fiction 6. High schools -- Fiction 7. Multiple sclerosis -- Fiction 8. Dawḥah (Qatar) -- Fiction
ISBN 9781534442726

LC 2018056836

"Heartfelt, honest, and featuring characters readers will fall in love with, this is sure to become a beloved book for many." (School Library Journal)

Allen, Kate

★ The **line** tender; by Kate Allen. Dutton Books for Young Readers 2019 384 p. illustrations (hardcover) $17.99
Grades: 6 7 8 9 **Fic**

1. Grief -- Fiction 2. Friendship -- Fiction 3. Sharks -- Fiction 4. Rockport (Mass.) -- Fiction 5. Loss (Psychology) -- Fiction 6. Single-parent families -- Fiction 7. Family life -- Massachusetts -- Rockport -- Fiction
ISBN 0735231605; 9780735231603

LC 2018017872

This book, by Kate Allen, tells "the story of Lucy, the daughter of a marine biologist and a rescue diver, and the summer that changes her life. If she ever wants to lift the cloud of grief over her family and community, she must complete the research her late mother began. She must follow the sharks." (Publisher's note)

"Allen offers, through Lucy's voice, a look at the intersection of art, science, friendship, and love in a way that is impressively nuanced and realistic while offering the reassurance of connection." Kirkus

Allison, Jennifer

★ **Gilda** Joyce, psychic investigator. Sleuth/Dutton 2005 321p pa $6.99; $13.99
Grades: 5 6 7 8 **Fic**

1. Mystery fiction 2. Cousins -- Fiction
ISBN 0-14-240698-8 pa; 0-525-47375-0; 978-0-14-240698-4 pa; 978-0-525-47375-6

LC 2004-10834

During the summer before ninth grade, intrepid Gilda Joyce invites herself to the San Francisco mansion of distant cousin Lester Splinter and his thirteen-year-old daughter, where she uses her purported psychic abilities and detective skills to solve the mystery of the mansion's boarded-up tower.

"Allison pulls off something special here. She not only offers a credible mystery . . . but also . . . provides particularly strong characterizations." Booklist

Other titles about Gilda Joyce are:
Gilda Joyce: the Ladies of the Lake (2006)
Gilda Joyce: the ghost sonata (2007)
Gilda Joyce: the dead drop (2009)
Gilda Joyce: the bones of the holy (2011)

Almond, David, 1951-

The **Boy** who swam with piranhas; David Almond, illustrated by Oliver Jeffers. Candlewick Press 2013 256 p. $15.99
Grades: 4 5 6 7 **Fic**

1. Orphans -- Fiction 2. Carnivals -- Fiction 3. Runaway children -- Fiction
ISBN 0763661694; 9780763661694

LC 2012947721

"Stanley Potts's uncle Ernie has developed an over-the-top fascination with canning fish in the house, and life at 69 Fish Quay Lane has turned barmy. But there's darkness in the madness, and when Uncle Ernie's obsession takes an unexpectedly cruel turn, Stan has no choice but to leave. As he journeys away from the life he's always known, he mingles with a carnival full of eccentric characters and meets the legendary Pancho Pirelli, the man who swims in a tank full of perilous piranhas." (Publisher's note)

"After his parents' deaths, Stanley Potts runs away with a carnival. He meets Pancho Pirelli, who performs the death-defying act of swimming with piranhas. Pirelli takes Stan under his wing, grooming him to become his sidekick and successor. Almond offers up some lighthearted fare, complete with old-fashioned intrusive narrator and numerous spot illustrations. The silliness is tempered by unsentimental, clear-eyed wisdom." Horn Book

Clay. Delacorte Press 2006 247p hardcover o.p. pa $8.99
Grades: 7 8 9 10 **Fic**

1. Horror fiction 2. Supernatural -- Fiction
ISBN 0-385-73171-X; 0-440-42013-X pa
LC 2005-22681

The developing relationship between teenager Davie and a mysterious new boy in town morphs into something darker and more sinister when Davie learns firsthand of the boy's supernatural powers.

"Rooted in the ordinariness of a community and in one boy's chance to play God, this story will grab readers with its gripping action and its important ideas." Booklist

★ **Kit's** wilderness; 10th-anniversary edition; Delacorte Press 2009 229p $16.99
Grades: 6 7 8 9 10 **Fic**

1. Ghost stories 2. Great Britain -- Fiction 3. Coal mines and mining -- Fiction
ISBN 978-0-385-32665-0; 0-385-32665-3
First published 1999
Michael L. Printz Award, 2001

Thirteen-year-old Kit goes to live with his grandfather in the decaying coal mining town of Stoneygate, England, and finds both the old man and the town haunted by ghosts of the past

The author "explores the power of friendship and family, the importance of memory, and the role of magic in our lives. This is a highly satisfying literary experience." SLJ

Mouse bird snake wolf; David Almond, illustrated by David McKean. Candlewick Press 2013 80 p. (reinforced) $17.99
Grades: 4 5 6 7 **Fic**

1. Animals -- Fiction 2. Fantasy fiction
ISBN 0763659126; 9780763659127
LC 2012950556

In this book, "Harry, Sue, and Little Ben live in a world whose lazy gods have made creatures like whales and camels but have given up their work, leaving blank spaces .... The children discover that they can create animals themselves, using sticks, leaves, and clay; Little Ben makes a mouse; Sue, a bird; and Harry, a snake. But Harry and Sue aren't satisfied. They create a terrifying wolf that turns on them and eats them, and Little Ben must summon the courage to save them." (Publishers Weekly)

★ **My** name is Mina. Delacorte Press 2011 300p $15.99; lib bdg $18.99
Grades: 5 6 7 8 **Fic**

1. Authorship -- Fiction
ISBN 978-0-385-74073-9; 0-385-74073-5; 978-0-375-98964-3 lib bdg; 0-375-98964-1 lib bdg; 978-0-375-98965-0 e-book
LC 2010040143

Prequel to: Skellig

"This intimate prequel to Skellig is built around Mina McKee, the curious and brilliant home-schooled child who eventually befriends that book's protagonist, Michael. Mina, a budding writer, reveals her love of words in her journal; most of the book unfolds in a handwritten-looking font, with Mina's more emphatic entries exploding onto the pages in massive display type. Her lyrical, nonlinear prose records her reflections on her past, existential musings . . . and self-directed writing exercises. . . . Almond gives readers a vivid picture of the joyfully freeform workings of Mina's mind and her mixed emotions about being an isolated child. Her gradual emergence from the protective shell of home is beautifully portrayed. . . . This novel will inspire children to let their imaginations soar." Publ Wkly

★ The **savage**; illustrated by Dave McKean. Candlewick Press 2008 79p il $17.99
Grades: 5 6 7 8 **Fic**

1. Death -- Fiction 2. Fathers -- Fiction
ISBN 978-0-7636-3932-7; 0-7636-3932-X
LC 2008-928388

A boy tells about a story he wrote when dealing with his father's death about a savage kid living in a ruined chapel in the woods-and the tale about the savage kid coming to life in the real world.

"This illustrated novella, a graphic novel within a novel, will satisfy Almond's fans and newcomers alike. McKean's illustrations-ink and watercolor in black, blues, and greens-add an appropriately eerie touch." Horn Book Guide

★ **Skellig**; 10th anniversary ed.; Delacorte Press 2009 182p $16.99; pa $6.99
Grades: 5 6 7 8 9 10 **Fic**

1. Fantasy fiction
ISBN 978-0-385-32653-7; 0-385-32653-X; 978-0-440-41602-9 pa; 0-440-41602-7 pa

First published 1998 in the United Kingdom; first United States edition 1999

Michael L. Printz Award honor book

Unhappy about his baby sister's illness and the chaos of moving into a dilapidated old house, Michael retreats to the garage and finds a mysterious stranger who is something like a bird and something like an angel.

"The plot is beautifully paced and the characters are drawn with a graceful, careful hand. . . . A lovingly done, thought-provoking novel." SLJ

Slog's dad; illustrated by Dave McKean. Candlewick Press 2011 52p il $15.99
Grades: 5 6 7 8 **Fic**

1. Death -- Fiction 2. Future life -- Fiction 3. Great Britain -- Fiction 4. Father-son relationship -- Fiction
ISBN 978-0-7636-4940-1; 0-7636-4940-6
LC 2010-38700

When Slog's father died he promised to return for one last visit in the spring, but when Slog spots a scruffy man on a bench outside the butcher shop and identifies him as his father, his best friend Davie is skeptical.

"This grief-strafed wonder tale is brilliantly matched by some of McKean's most moving artwork yet. Text pages, featuring a voice steeped on Northern English flavor, are counterpoised against wordless illustration sequences that move readers from heaven to earth and back again, beginning with a celestial descent from the sky to a park bench by a man trailing clouds of watercolor glory." Bull Cent Child Books

Alvarez, Jennifer Lynn

Starfire; by Jennifer Lynn Alvarez. HarperCollins 2014 245 p. (Guardian Herd) (hardback) $16.99

Grades: 5 6 7 **Fic**

1. Fantasy fiction 2. Adventure fiction 3. Horses -- Fiction 4. Mythical animals -- Fiction 5. Fantasy 6. Animals, Mythical -- Fiction 7. Animals -- Abnormalities -- Fiction 8. Adventure and adventurers -- Fiction

ISBN 0062286064; 9780062286062

LC 2014001890

This book, by Jennifer Lynn Alvarez, is the "first book in a . . . fantasy series about winged horses. . . . Once every hundred years, a black foal is born, prophesied to either unite or destroy the five herds of flying horses that live in Anok - fated to become the most powerful pegasus in all of the land. Star is this black foal. Even though Star has malformed wings that make him unable to fly, the leaders of each herd will take no risks and want to execute Star before his first birthday." (Publisher's note)

"Born the dark foal of Anok, Star is different from other pegasi--he can't fly, and on his first birthday the light of the Hundred Year Star will empower him to heal or destroy. Thunderwing, the herd's over-stallion, has vowed to kill him first. Scenes of adolescent pegasus bullying are overwrought, but the magical frame makes strong scaffolding for the well-executed plot." Horn Book

Alvarez, Julia, 1950-

★ **Before** we were free. Knopf 2002 167p $15.95; lib bdg $17.99; pa $5.99

Grades: 7 8 9 10 **Fic**

1. Generals 2. Presidents 3. Family life -- Fiction 4. Dominican Republic -- Fiction 5. Dominican Republic -- History -- 1930-1961 -- Fiction

ISBN 0-375-81544-9; 0-375-91544-3 lib bdg; 0-440-23784-X pa

LC 2001-50520

In the early 1960s in the Dominican Republic, twelve-year-old Anita learns that her family is involved in the underground movement to end the bloody rule of the dictator, General Trujillo

This "is a realistic and compelling account of a girl growing up too quickly while coming to terms with the cost of freedom." Horn Book

★ **How** Tia Lola came to visit/stay. Knopf 2001 147p $15.95; pa $5.50

Grades: 4 5 6 7 **Fic**

1. Aunts -- Fiction 2. Divorce -- Fiction 3. Vermont -- Fiction 4. Dominican Americans -- Fiction

ISBN 0-375-80215-0; 0-440-41870-4 pa

LC 00-62932

Although ten-year-old Miguel is at first embarrassed by his colorful aunt, Tia Lola, when she comes to Vermont from the Dominican Republic to stay with his mother, his sister, and him after his parents' divorce, he learns to love her.

"Readers will enjoy the funny situations, identify with the developing relationships and conflicting feelings of the characters, and will get a spicy taste of Caribbean culture in the bargain." SLJ

Other titles about Tia Lola are:

How Tia Lola learned to teach (2010)

How Tia Lola saved the summer (2011)

How Tia Lola ended up starting over (2011)

★ **Return** to sender. Alfred A. Knopf 2009 325p $16.99; lib bdg $19.99

Grades: 4 5 6 7 **Fic**

1. Vermont -- Fiction 2. Farm life -- Fiction 3. Friendship -- Fiction 4. Migrant labor -- Fiction 5. Illegal aliens -- Fiction

ISBN 978-0-375-85838-3; 0-375-85838-5; 978-0-375-95838-0 lib bdg; 0-375-95838-X lib bdg

LC 2008-23520

Awarded the Belpre Author Medal (2010)

After his family hires migrant Mexican workers to help save their Vermont farm from foreclosure, eleven-year-old Tyler befriends the oldest daughter, but when he discovers they may not be in the country legally, he realizes that real friendship knows no borders.

"Readers will be moved by small moments. . . . A tender, well-constructed book." Publ Wkly

Amateau, Gigi

A **certain** strain of peculiar. Candlewick Press 2009 261p $16.99

Grades: 6 7 8 9 **Fic**

1. Ranch life -- Fiction 2. Grandmothers -- Fiction

ISBN 978-0-7636-3009-6; 0-7636-3009-8

Tired of the miserable life she lives, Mary Harold leaves her mother behind and moves back to Alabama and her grandmother, where she receives support and love and starts to gain confidence in herself and her abilities.

"Mary Harold is a wonderfully complex and honest character. . . . [Her] narrative is heartfelt and poignant, and the message that being 'different' is nothing to be ashamed of will resonate with readers." Voice Youth Advocates

An Na

★ A **step** from heaven. Front St. 2000 156p $15.95

Grades: 7 8 9 10 **Fic**

1. Family life 2. Korean Americans 3. Emigration and immigration

ISBN 1-88691-058-8

LC 00-41083

National Book Award Finalist: Young People's Literature (2001)

Michael L. Printz Award, 2002

A young Korean girl and her family find it difficult to learn English and adjust to life in America. "Age ten and up." (N Y Times Book Rev)

"This isn't a quick read, especially at the beginning when the child is trying to decipher American words and customs, but the coming-of-age drama will grab teens and make them think of their own conflicts between home and outside. As in the best writing, the particulars make the story universal." Booklist

Anderson, Jodi Lynn

May Bird among the stars; book two. [by] Jodi Lynn Anderson. 1st ed.; Atheneum Books for Young Readers 2006 260p $16.95

Grades: 5 6 7 8 **Fic**

1. Fantasy fiction

ISBN 978-0-689-86924-2; 0-689-86924-X

LC 2005028832

Sequel to May Bird and The Ever After (2005)

Still trapped in The Ever After, ten-year-old May Bird struggles to decide whether to save the world of her ghostly friends from the evil Bo Cleevil or to return to her West Virginia home.

"Anderson has clearly had a great deal of fun creating a world not so different from our own where spirits go after death, and readers will love her humorous jabs at popular culture." SLJ

Followed by May Bird, warrior princess (2007)

My diary from the edge of the world; by Jodi Lynn Anderson. Aladdin 2015 432 p. $16.99

Grades: 4 5 6 7 **Fic**

1. Magic -- Fiction 2. Adventure fiction 3. Death -- Fiction 4. Diaries -- Fiction 5. Family life -- Fiction 6. Supernatural -- Fiction 7. Automobile travel -- Fiction

ISBN 1442483873; 9781442483873; 9781442483880

LC 2014039910

In this novel by Jodi Lynn Anderson "Gracie Lockwood has lived in Cliffden, Maine, her whole life. She's a typical girl in an atypical world: one where sasquatches helped to win the Civil War, where dragons glide over Route 1 on their way south for the winter . . . and where Dark Clouds come for people when they die. A Cloud comes looking for her little brother Sam. Her parents pack the family into a used Winnebago and set out on an epic search for a safe place that most people say doesn't exist: The Extraordinary World." (Publishers' note)

"An endearing narrator, a beguiling world that accommodates both mermaids and Pixy Stix, and a genuinely moving family story propel this adventure." Kirkus

★ **Tiger** Lily; Jodi Lynn Anderson. HarperTeen 2012 304 p. (trade bdg.) $17.99

Grades: 8 9 10 11 **Fic**

1. Romance fiction 2. Jealousy -- Fiction 3. Fairy tales -- Fiction 4. Love -- Fiction 5. Magic -- Fiction 6. Fairies -- Fiction

ISBN 0062003259; 9780062003256

LC 2011032659

This is the story of Tiger Lily, the girl Peter Pan spurned for Wendy. "Told from the perspective of Tinker Bell, the novel explores how Tiger Lily meets and falls in love with Peter, despite being betrothed to another villager, a man Tiger Lily despises. Tiger Lily and Peter's complicated inner conflicts emerge as they sort out their feelings about freedom, power, loyalty, and responsibility. When a girl from England arrives, Tiger Lily" feels jealous for the first time. (Publishers Weekly)

Anderson, John David

Minion; John David Anderson. Walden Pond Press, an imprint of HarperCollins 2014 288 p. (hardback) $16.99

Grades: 4 5 6 7 **Fic**

1. Adoption -- Fiction 2. Criminals -- Fiction 3. Superheroes -- Fiction 4. Good and evil -- Fiction 5. Supervillains -- Fiction

ISBN 006213311X; 9780062133113

LC 2013043188

In this book, by John David Anderson, "Michael Morn might be a villain, but he's really not a bad guy. When you live in New Liberty, known across the country as the City without a Super, there are only two kinds of people, after all: those who turn to crime and those who suffer. Michael and his adoptive father spend their days building boxes -special devices with mysterious abilities. . . . But then a Super comes to town, and Michael's world is thrown into disarray." (Publisher's note)

"Michael is as complex as the best Marvel and DC characters, and his dialogue is just as funny. The author trusts his readers enough to keep the characters ambiguous and to leave some mysteries unexplained at the end of the book." Kirkus

Ms. Bixby's Last Day; by John David Anderson. Harpercollins Childrens Books 2016 320 p. $16.99

Grades: 4 5 6 7 **Fic**

1. Teachers -- Fiction

ISBN 006233817X; 9780062338174

LC 2015947628

In this book, by John David Anderson, "Ms. Bixby is . . . the sort of teacher who makes you feel like school is somehow worthwhile. Who recognizes something in you that sometimes you don't even see in yourself. . . . Topher, Brand, and Steve know this better than anyone. And so when Ms. Bixby unexpectedly announces that she won't be able to finish the school year, they come up with a risky plan—more of a quest, really—to give Ms. Bixby the last day she deserves." (Publisher's note)

"Through their individual, interwoven narratives, these well-developed characters become the most intriguing elements of the story. A smart, funny, ultimately moving novel." Booklist

★ **Posted**; by John David Anderson. Harpercollins Childrens Books 2017 384 p. $16.99

Grades: 5 6 7 8 **Fic**

1. Bullies -- Fiction 2. Middle schools -- Fiction 3. Written communication -- Fiction

ISBN 006233820X; 9780062338204

This book, by John David Anderson, is "story about bullying, broken friendships, and the failures of communication between kids. . . . When cell phones are banned at Branton Middle School, Frost and his friends Deedee, Wolf, and Bench come up with a new way to communicate: leaving sticky notes for each other all around the school. It catches on, and soon all the kids in school are leaving notes—though for every kind and friendly one, there is a cutting and cruel one as well." (Publisher's note)

★ **Sidekicked**; John David Anderson. Walden Pond Press, an imprint of HarperCollinsPublishers 2013 384 p. (hardback) $16.99

Grades: 4 5 6 7 **Fic**

1. Adolescence -- Fiction 2. Superheroes -- Fiction 3. Humorous stories 4. Ability -- Fiction 5. Schools -- Fiction 6. Identity -- Fiction 7. Middle schools -- Fiction 8. Self-confidence -- Fiction 9. Adventure and adventurers -- Fiction

ISBN 0062133144; 9780062133144

LC 2012025495

In this book, "the main character is a sidekick named Andrew Bean. Like the best superheroes, he's down on his luck, always forgetting his utility belt when he needs it. Andrew is part of a school environmental club, H.E.R.O., that . . . doubles as a training program for sidekicks (motto: 'WE KEEP THE TRASH OFF THE STREETS'). Andrew's mentor is the Titan, an aging hero who'd rather go out drinking than fight crime." (Kirkus Reviews)

★ **Standard** hero behavior; [by] John David Anderson. Clarion Books 2007 273p $16

Grades: 6 7 8 **Fic**

1. Fantasy fiction 2. Adventure fiction 3. Heroes and heroines -- Fiction

ISBN 0-618-75920-4; 978-0-618-75920-0

LC 2007013059

When fifteen-year-old Mason Quayle finds out that their town of Darlington is about to be attacked by orcs, goblins, ogres, and trolls, he goes in search of some heroes to save the day.

"Mason is thoroughly believable. . . . Using imaginative details, witty language with a scattering of modern idiom, and lots of allusions, Anderson manages the difficult task of constructing a satisfying story while poking large fun at all genre traditions. Fantasy fans are ensured a good laugh." Booklist

Anderson, Katie D.

Kiss & Make Up. Amazon Childrens Pub 2012 307 p. (hardcover) $16.99

Grades: 7 8 9 10 **Fic**

1. School stories 2. Paranormal fiction

ISBN 076146316X; 9780761463160

This book focuses on Emerson Taylor, who "has a gift—or a curse. She can read a person's mind with the lightest of kisses. When her financially strapped aunt announces that Emerson will not be attending private school the following year if her grades don't improve, Emerson initializes Operation Liplock. She will begin study sessions with the geeky Ivys—those destined to attend Ivy League colleges—where she will kiss them, allowing their knowledge to transfer to her mind." (School Library Journal)

Anderson, Laurie Halse, 1961-

★ **Ashes**; Laurie Halse Anderson. Atheneum Books for Young Readers 2016 304 p. map (The seeds of America trilogy) (hardback) $16.99; (ebook) $15.99

Grades: 6 7 8 9 10 **Fic**

1. Slavery -- Fiction 2. African Americans -- Fiction 3. United States -- History -- 1775-1783, Revolution -- Fiction

ISBN 9781416961468; 9781416961475; 9781442445086

LC 2016002474

Sequel to: Forge

In this book, in the The Seeds of America Trilogy series by Laurie Halse Anderson, "as the Revolutionary War rages on, Isabel and Curzon have narrowly escaped Valley Forge--but their relief is short-lived. Before long they are reported as runaways. . . . With purpose and faith, Isabel and Curzon march on, . . . determined to find Isabel's little sister Ruth. . . . Heroism and heartbreak pave their path, but Isabel and Curzon won't stop until they reach Ruth, and then freedom." (Publisher's note)

"It's a gripping finish to an epic journey that speaks resoundingly to the human capacity to persevere." Pub Wkly

★ **Chains**; seeds of America. Simon & Schuster Books for Young Readers 2008 316p $17.99

Grades: 6 7 8 9 10 **Fic**

1. Spies -- Fiction 2. Slavery -- Fiction 3. New York (N.Y.) -- Fiction 4. African Americans -- Fiction 5. United States -- History -- 1775-1783, Revolution -- Fiction

ISBN 1-4169-0585-5; 1-4169-0586-3 pa; 978-1-4169-0585-1; 978-1-4169-0586-8 pa

LC 2007-52139

National Book Award Finalist: Young People's Literature (2008)

After being sold to a cruel couple in New York City, a slave named Isabel spies for the rebels during the Revolutionary War. "Grades seven to ten." (Bull Cent Child Books)

"This gripping novel offers readers a startlingly provocative view of the Revolutionary War. . . . [Anderson's] solidly researched exploration of British and Patriot treatment of slaves during a war for freedom is nuanced and evenhanded, presented in service of a fast-moving, emotionally involving plot." Publ Wkly

Followed by: Forge (2010)

★ **Fever,** 1793. Simon & Schuster Bks. for Young Readers 2000 251p $17.99; pa $6.99

Grades: 5 6 7 8 9 **Fic**

1. Epidemics -- Fiction 2. Yellow fever -- Fiction 3. Philadelphia (Pa.) -- Fiction 4. Pennsylvania -- History -- 1775-1865 5. Yellow fever -- Pennsylvania -- Philadelphia

ISBN 0689838581; 0689848919 pa; 9780689838583; 9780689848919 pa

LC 00-32238

ALA YALSA Margaret A. Edwards Award (2009)

In 1793 Philadelphia, sixteen-year-old Matilda Cook, separated from her sick mother, learns about perseverance and self-reliance when she is forced to cope with the horrors of a yellow fever epidemic. ¿Age ten and up.¿ (N Y Times Book Rev)

"A vivid work, rich with well-drawn and believable characters. Unexpected events pepper the top-flight novel that combines accurate historical detail with a spellbinding story line." Voice Youth Advocates

★ **Forge**. Atheneum Books for Young Readers 2010 297p (Seeds of America) $16.99

Grades: 6 7 8 9 10 **Fic**

1. Slavery -- Fiction 2. Soldiers -- Fiction 3. Pennsylvania -- Fiction 4. African Americans -- Fiction 5. United States -- History -- 1775-1783, Revolution -- Fiction

ISBN 978-1-4169-6144-4; 1-4169-6144-5

LC 2010-15971

Sequel to: Chains (2008)

Separated from his friend Isabel after their daring escape from slavery, fifteen-year-old Curzon serves as a free man in the Continental Army at Valley Forge until he and Isabel are thrown together again, as slaves once more.

"Weaving a huge amount of historical detail seamlessly into the story, Anderson creates a vivid setting, believable characters both good and despicable and a clear portrayal of the moral ambiguity of the Revolutionary age. Not only can this sequel stand alone, for many readers it will be one of the best novels they have ever read." Kirkus

Speak; 10th anniversary ed.; Speak 2009 197p pa $11.99

Grades: 7 8 9 10 **Fic**

1. School stories 2. Rape -- Fiction

ISBN 978-0-14-241473-6

LC 2009-502164

First published 1999

A traumatic event near the end of the summer has a devastating effect on Melinda's freshman year in high school.

The novel is "keenly aware of the corrosive details of outsiderhood and the gap between home and daily life at high school; kids whose exclusion may have less concrete cause than Melinda's will nonetheless find the picture recognizable. This is a gripping account of personal wounding and recovery." Bull Cent Child Books

★ **Wintergirls**. Viking 2009 288p $17.99

Grades: 8 9 10 11 12 **Fic**

1. Death -- Fiction 2. Friendship -- Fiction 3. Self-mutilation -- Fiction 4. Anorexia nervosa -- Fiction

ISBN 0-670-01110-X; 978-0-670-01110-0

LC 2008-37452

Eighteen-year-old Lia comes to terms with her best friend's death from anorexia as she struggles with the same disorder.

"As events play out, Lia's guilt, her need to be thin, and her fight for acceptance unravel in an almost poetic stream of consciousness in this startlingly crisp and pitch-perfect first-person narrative." SLJ

Anderson, M. T., 1968-

The **chamber** in the sky. Scholastic Press 2012 282 p. (hardcover) $17.99

Grades: 5 6 7 8 **Fic**

1. American satire 2. Fantasy fiction 3. Human-alien encounters

-- Fiction

ISBN 0545334934; 9780545334938

This novel, by National Book Award and Printz Honor winner M. T. Anderson, is book four of "The Norumbegan Quartet" series. "Brian and Gregory have . . . . gone to investigate intergalactic suburban sprawl that was infringing on the Vermont forests, and landed in the empire of New Norumbega inside the huge body of an alien. They've escaped certain death . . . and wreaked small amounts of havoc of their own. And finally, they're going to make sense of all their travels and adventures." (Publisher's note)

The **empire** of gut and bone. Scholastic 2011 324p (The Norumbegan quartet) $17.99

Grades: 5 6 7 8 **Fic**

1. Games -- Fiction 2. Supernatural -- Fiction

ISBN 978-0-545-13884-0; 0-545-13884-1

Sequel to: Suburb beyond the stars (2010)

"Bent on tracking down the elven Norumbegans in order to save Vermont from an invasion of dream-sucking Thusser, Brian, Gregory and the mechanical troll Kalgrash pass through an interdimensional curtain—to find themselves inside an organic alien body. . . . Returning fans will find the unapologetically intellectual looniness uncannily, happily familiar." Kirkus

Feed. Candlewick Press 2002 237p hardcover o.p. pa $7.99

Grades: 8 9 10 11 12 **Fic**

1. Satire 2. Science fiction

ISBN 0-7636-1726-1; 0-7636-2259-1 pa

LC 2002-23738

National Book Award Finalist: Young People's Literature (2002)

Boston Globe-Horn Book Award Honor: Fiction (2003)

Margaret A. Edwards Award (2019)

In a future where most people have computer implants in their heads to control their environment, a boy meets an unusual girl who is in serious trouble

"An ingenious satire of corporate America and our present-day value system." Horn Book Guide

The **Game** of Sunken Places; [by] M. T. Anderson. Scholastic Press 2004 260p (The Norumbegan quartet) $16.95; pa $5.99

Grades: 5 6 7 8 **Fic**

1. Games -- Fiction 2. Vermont -- Fiction

ISBN 0-439-41660-4; 0-439-41661-2 pa

LC 2003-20055

When two boys stay with an eccentric relative at his mansion in rural Vermont, they discover an old-fashioned board game that draws them into a mysterious adventure.

"Deliciously scary, often funny, and crowned by a pair of deeply satisfying surprises, this tour de force leaves one marveling at Anderson's ability to slip between genres as fluidly as his middle-grade heroes straddle worlds." Booklist

Other titles in this series are:

The suburb beyond the stars (2010)

The empire of gut and bone (2011)

The chamber in the sky (2012)

He laughed with his other mouths; M.T. Anderson ; illustrations by Kurt Cyrus. First edition Beach Lane Books 2014 304 p. illustrations (Pals in peril) (hardcover) $17.99

Grades: 4 5 6 7 **Fic**

1. Adventure fiction 2. Outer space -- Fiction 3. Humorous stories 4. Extraterrestrial beings -- Fiction 5. Adventure and adventurers -- Fiction

ISBN 1442451106; 9781442451100; 9781442451117

LC 2013034710

"In this action-packed conclusion to the celebrated Pals in Peril series, Jasper Dash soars to unprecedented heights--as in, intergalactic, out-of-this-world dimensions--in order to locate the father he's never known." (Publisher's note)

"The novel doesn't transcend the wacky sci-fi of old that inspired it but rather embraces it and dissects it, celebrating it and exploring why so many people fell in love with these silly worlds and gee-whiz heroes in the first place." Kirkus

The **suburb** beyond the stars. Scholastic Press 2010 223p (The Norumbegan quartet) $17.99

Grades: 5 6 7 8 **Fic**

1. Games -- Fiction 2. Vermont -- Fiction 3. Supernatural -- Fiction

ISBN 978-0-545-13882-6; 0-545-13882-5

LC 2009051836

Sequel to: The Game of Sunken Places (2004)

Friends Brian and Gregory have survived the Game of Sunken Places, but are once again drawn back to cousin Prudence's house in Vermont, where they discover that something has gone very wrong with time, people have disappeared, and danger is lurking everywhere.

"This is a fun and gripping read, with action, suspense, and creepy monsters." SLJ

Followed by: The empire of gut and bone (2011)

★ **Whales** on stilts; illustrations by Kurt Cyrus. Harcourt 2005 188p il (Pals in peril) $15; pa $5.95

Grades: 4 5 6 7 **Fic**

1. Science fiction

ISBN 0-15-205340-9; 0-15-205394-8 pa

LC 2004-17754

Racing against the clock, shy middle-school student Lily and her best friends, Katie and Jasper, must foil the plot of her father's conniving boss to conquer the world using an army of whales.

"A story written with the author's tongue shoved firmly into his cheek. . . . It's full of witty pokes at other series novels and Jasper's nutty inventions." SLJ

Other titles in this series are:

The clue of the linoleum lederhosen (2006)

Jasper Dash and the Flame-pits of Delaware (2009)

Agent Q., or the smell of danger! (2010)

Zombie mommy (2011)

He laughed with his other mouths (2012)

Anderson, Natalie C.

★ **City** of saints & thieves; Natalie C. Anderson. Penguin Group USA 2017 432 p. $18.99

Grades: 7 8 9 10 **Fic**

1. Gangs -- Fiction 2. Murder -- Fiction 3. Orphans -- Fiction 4. Sisters -- Fiction 5. Refugees -- Fiction

ISBN 0399547584; 9780399547584

LC 2016027799

In this novel, by Natalie C. Anderson, "after fleeing the Congo as refugees, Tina and her mother arrived in Kenya . . . to build a new life and home. Her mother quickly found work as a maid for a prominent family, headed by Roland Greyhill, . . . [whose] fortune was made from a life of corruption and crime. So when her mother is found shot to death in Mr. Greyhill's personal study, she knows exactly who's behind it." (Publisher's note)

"The novel is peppered with Swahili words and phrases, and Anderson makes an effort to paint a picture of the country. A story full of twists and turns, proving nothing is ever as black and white as it may seem." Kirkus

Anderson, Sophie

The **house** with chicken legs; Sophie Anderson. Scholastic 2018 272 p. $16.99

Grades: 4 5 6 7 **Fic**

1. Friendship -- Fiction 2. Grandmothers -- Fiction

ISBN 1338209965; 9781338209969

In this book, by Sophie Anderson, "all 12-year-old Marinka wants is a friend. A real friend. Not like her house with chicken legs. Sure, the house can play games like tag and hide-and-seek, but Marinka longs for a human companion. . . . But that's tough when your grandmother is a Yaga, a guardian who guides the dead into the afterlife. It's even harder when you live in a house that wanders all over the world . . . carrying you with it." (Publisher's note)

Andrews, Jesse

Me & Earl & the dying girl; by Jesse Andrews. Amulet Books 2012 295 p. $16.95

Grades: 8 9 10 **Fic**

1. Leukemia -- Fiction 2. Friendship -- Fiction 3. Family life -- Fiction 4. Pittsburgh (Pa.) -- Fiction 5. High school students -- Fiction 6. Humorous stories 7. Schools -- Fiction 8. High schools -- Fiction 9. Jews -- United States -- Fiction 10. Family life -- Pennsylvania -- Fiction

ISBN 9781419701764

LC 2011031796

This book is a "confessional from a teen narrator who won't be able to convince readers he's as unlikable as he wants them to believe." It covers "[h]is filmmaking ambitions . . . his unlikely friendship with the . . . Earl of the title. And his unlikelier friendship with Rachel, the titular 'dying girl'. . . . He chronicles his senior year, in which his mother guilt-trips him into hanging out with Rachel, who has acute myelogenous leukemia." (Kirkus Reviews)

Munmun; Jesse Andrews. Amulet Books 2018 404 p. illustrations (hardcover with jacket) $18.99

Grades: 7 8 9 10 11 12 **Fic**

1. Size -- Fiction 2. Siblings -- Fiction 3. Social classes -- Fiction 4. Brothers and sisters -- Fiction

ISBN 9781683352617; 9781419728716

LC 2017043773

In this book, by Jesse Andrews, "Warner and his sister Prayer are destitute--and tiny. Their size is not just demeaning, but dangerous: day and night they face mortal dangers that bigger richer people don't ever have to think about, from being mauled by cats to their house getting stepped on. There are no cars or phones built small enough for them, or schools or hospitals, for that matter. . . . [H]ow can two littlepoors survive in a world built against them?" (Publisher's note)

"Brilliant, savage, hilarious, a riveting journey through a harsh world that mirrors our own." Kirkus

Angleberger, Tom

Darth Paper strikes back; an Origami Yoda book. Tom Angleberger. Amulet Books 2011 159p il $12.95

Grades: 4 5 6 7 **Fic**

1. School stories 2. Origami -- Fiction 3. Puppets and puppet plays -- Fiction 4. Eccentrics and eccentricities -- Fiction

ISBN 978-1-4197-0027-9; 1-4197-0027-8

LC 2011010388

Harvey, upset when his Darth Paper finger puppet brings humiliation, gets Dwight suspended, but Origami Yoda asks Tommy and Kellan, now in seventh grade, to make a new casefile to persuade the School Board to reinstate Dwight.

This is "a satisfying tale of friendship and just resistance to authority. Pitch-perfect middle-school milieu and enough Star Wars references (and laughs) to satisfy fans and win new ones." Kirkus

Emperor Pickletine rides the bus; Tom Angleberger. Amulet Books 2014 205 p. illustrations (hardback) $13.95

Grades: 4 5 6 7 **Fic**

1. School stories 2. Origami -- Fiction 3. Humorous stories 4. Bus travel -- Fiction 5. Finger puppets -- Fiction 6. Washington (D.C.) -- Fiction 7. School field trips -- Fiction 8. Interpersonal relations -- Fiction 9. Eccentrics and eccentricities -- Fiction

ISBN 141970933X; 9781419709333

LC 2014012574

Origami Yoda

This middle grade novel by Tom Angleberger is "the final Origami Yoda case file from the kids at McQuarrie Middle School! After successfully fighting to save their field trip in 'Princess Labelmaker to the Rescue!,' Tommy and the gang prepare for a well-earned day of fun and adventure in Washington, DC . . . but of course it won't be that easy! This trip to the nation's capital will be full of shifting alliances and betrayals, carsickness and sugar rushes." (Publisher's note)

"The seventh grade of McQuarrie Middle School hits Washington, D.C., in this final installment of the popular Origami Yoda series. Exciting as a field trip is, the Rebel Alliance is reeling because Principal Rabbski has banned origami for the entire trip! . . . Origami Yoda has an earth-shattering revelation or two to impart before the book's end, making for a fitting series conclusion." Booklist

Horton Halfpott; or, The fiendish mystery of Smugwick Manor, or, The loosening of M'Lady Luggertuck's corset. Tom Angleberger with illustrations by the author. Amulet Books 2011 206p il $14.95

Grades: 4 5 6 7 **Fic**

1. Mystery fiction 2. Social classes -- Fiction 3. Household employees -- Fiction 4. Eccentrics and eccentricities -- Fiction 5. Great Britain -- History -- 19th century -- Fiction

ISBN 978-0-8109-9715-8; 0-8109-9715-0

LC 2010-38096

Horton, an upstanding kitchen boy in a castle in nineteenth-century England, becomes embroiled in a mystery surrounding a series of thefts. "Grades four to six." (Bull Cent Child Books)

"Readers will enjoy Angleberger's . . . penchant for the absurd as well as his many droll asides. . . . The ending satisfies, and with Angleberger's many eclectic characters, his wild-and-witty storytelling, and a lighthearted but perplexing mystery . . . readers are in for a treat." Publ Wkly

Princess Labelmaker to the rescue! an Origami Yoda book. by Tom Angleberger. Harry N. Abrams Inc. 2014 208 p. $13.95

Grades: 4 5 6 7 **Fic**

1. School stories 2. Star Wars films 3. Origami -- Fiction 4. Schools -- Fiction 5. Finger puppets -- Fiction 6. Interpersonal relations -- Fiction 7. Eccentrics and eccentricities -- Fiction

ISBN 1419710524; 9781419710520

LC 2013047291

In this book, part of the Origami Yoda series, by Tom Angleberger, "At McQuarrie Middle School, the war against the FunTime Menace--aka test prep--wages on. . . . To defeat the Dark Standardized Testing Forces they're going to need an even bigger, even more surprising ally: Principal Rabbski. But with great forces--aka the school board--pushing her from above, will the gang's former enemy don a finger puppet and join the Rebellion--or will her transformation to Empress Rabbski, Dark Lord of the Sith, be complete?" (Publisher's note)

"Angleberger continues to develop authentic and engaging voices in these 'case files.'" Horn Book

The **strange** case of Origami Yoda; Tom Angleberger. Amulet Books 2010 141p il $12.95

Grades: 4 5 6 7 **Fic**

1. School stories 2. Origami -- Fiction 3. Puppets and puppet plays -- Fiction 4. Eccentrics and eccentricities -- Fiction

ISBN 978-0-8109-8425-7; 0-8109-8425-3

LC 2009-39748

Tommy and his friends describe their experiences with a paper puppet of Yoda, made by their sixth-grade classmate Dwight, as they try to decide whether or not the puppet can really predict the future.

"The situations that Yoda has a hand in are pretty authentic, and the setting is broad enough to be any school. The plot is age-old but with the twist of being presented on crumpled pages with cartoon sketches, supposed hand printing, and varying typefaces. Kids should love it." SLJ

Other Origami Yoda books are:

Darth Paper strikes back (2011)

The secret of the fortune Wookiee (2012)

The surprise attack of Jabba the Puppett (2013)

Princess Labelmaker to the rescue! (2014)

Emperor Pickletine rides the bus (2014)

Angus, Jennifer

In search of Goliathus hercules; by Jennifer Angus. Albert Whitman 2012 350 p. (hardcover) $17.99

Grades: 3 4 5 6 7 **Fic**

1. Fantasy fiction 2. Insects -- Fiction 3. Human-animal communication -- Fiction 4. Metamorphosis -- Fiction

ISBN 0807529907; 9780807529904

LC 2011037135

In this novel, by Jennifer Angus, "Henri Bell, . . . in 1890 . . . strikes up a conversation with a friendly fly on the windowsill and discovers he possesses the astounding ability to speak with insects. Thus commences an epic journey for Henri as he manages a flea circus, commands an army of beetles, and ultimately sets out to British Malaya to find the mythical giant insect known as Goliathus Hercules." (Publisher's note)

Angus, Sam

A **Horse** Called Hero; by Sam Angus. Feiwel & Friends 2014 304 p. $16.99

Grades: 5 6 7 8 **Fic**

1. Horses -- Fiction 2. Brothers and sisters -- Fiction 3. World War, 1939-1945 -- Children

ISBN 1250045088; 9781250045089

In this book, by Sam Angus, "on the brink of World War II, a family forced out of their London home flees to the country. Wolfie and his older sister Dodo are devastated to leave behind everything they've ever known. . . . One day, they come across an orphaned fowl, which they raise as Hero, a strong and beautiful horse who lives up to his name when he saves the children from a fire. . . . One night, Hero is stolen, and the children are shattered." (Publisher's note)

"With London steeled for World War II, eight-year-old Wolfie and his older sister Dodo are sent to the countryside. It's difficult being city kids among strangers, but an orphaned foal named Hero helps the children adjust. In a parallel story line, the children's father has been accused of desertion. Angus's story is a big, satisfying tale of friendship, family, and war." Horn Book

Ansari, Rebecca K. S.

★ The **missing** piece of Charlie O'Reilly; Rebecca K. S. Ansari. Harpercollins Childrens Books 2019 400 p. $16.99

Grades: 4 5 6 7 8 **Fic**

1. Brothers -- Fiction 2. Friendship -- Fiction 3. Missing children -- Fiction

ISBN 006267966X; 9780062679666

In this novel, by Rebecca K. S. Ansari, "Charlie O'Reilly has lost his little brother. He wished him away the night before his birthday, and now he is missing. The worst part is that no one, including his parents, believes Liam ever existed. . . . His only solace is his friend Ana, who vows to help him find Liam, even though she can't remember him either." (School Library Journal)

"Ansari trusts her audience with a complex narrative that traverses the breadth of time and the depths of self. The weave of guilt, family struggle, and forgiveness both complicates and complements questions of love and self-acceptance." Kirkus

Anstey, Cindy

Carols and chaos; by Cindy Anstey. Swoon Reads 2018 336 p. (pbk.) $10.99

Grades: 7 8 9 10 **Fic**

1. Romance fiction 2. Christmas -- Fiction 3. Counterfeits and counterfeiting -- Fiction 4. Love -- Fiction 5. Household employees -- Fiction 6. Great Britain -- History -- George III, 1760-1820 -- Fiction

ISBN 9781250174871

LC 2018003012

Sequel to: Suitors and sabotage

In this book, by Cindy Anstey, "1817. The happy chaos of the Yuletide season has descended upon the country estate of Shackleford Park in full force, but lady's maid Kate Darby barely has the time to notice. . . . Matt Harlow is also rather busy. . . . Falling in love would be a disaster for either of them. But . . . when a devious counterfeiting scheme reaches the gates of Shackleford Park, . . . Kate and Matt are unwittingly swept up in the intrigue." (Publisher's note)

Love, lies and spies; Cindy Anstey. Swoon Reads 2016 368 p. (paperback) $10.99

Grades: 8 9 10 11 **Fic**

1. Romance fiction 2. Spies -- Fiction 3. Great Britain -- History -- 1789-1820 -- Fiction 4. London (England) -- History -- 19th century -- Fiction 5. Love -- Fiction

ISBN 9781250084033; 9781250084064

LC 2015026917

In this novel, by Cindy Anstey, "in spite of the trappings of her time, Juliana is a lady of education and scientific interests thanks to her father. In London for her first season, she meets a young man who at first thinks she may be mixed up in some shady dealings that he's in town to investigate." (School Library Journal)

"A cute premise and cover make this a solid purchase for budding historical romance readers." SLJ

Appelbaum, Susannah

The **Hollow** Bettle; illustrated by Jennifer Taylor. Alfred A. Knopf 2009 399p il (The Poisons of Caux) $16.99; lib bdg $19.99

Grades: 4 5 6 7 **Fic**

1. Fantasy fiction 2. Uncles -- Fiction 3. Poisons and poisoning -- Fiction

ISBN 978-0-375-85173-5; 0-375-85173-9; 978-0-375-95173-2 lib bdg; 0-375-95173-3 lib bdg

LC 2008-22626

Eleven-year-old Ivy Manx sets out with her new friend, a young "taster," to find her missing uncle, an outlawed healer, in the dangerous kingdom of Caux where magic, herbs, and poisons rule.

This "is a deeply satisfying, humor-laced quest with elements of wizardry and herbology, deeds of a dastardly nature, and, ultimately, redemption." Booklist

Other titles in this series are:

The Taster's Guild (2010)

The Shepherd of Weeds (2011)

Appelfeld, Aharon, 1932-2018

★ **Adam** and Thomas; by Aharon Appelfeld ; translated from Hebrew by Jeffrey Green ; illustrated by Philippe Dumas. Seven Stories Press 2015 160 p. color illustrations (hardback) $18.95

Grades: 4 5 6 7 8 **Fic**

1. Jews -- Fiction 2. Survival skills -- Fiction 3. Holocaust, 1939-1945 -- Fiction 4. World War, 1939-1945 -- Fiction 5. Refugees -- Fiction 6. Survival -- Fiction 7. Holocaust, Jewish (1939-1945) -- Fiction

ISBN 1609806344; 9781609806347

LC 2015010371

Mildred L. Batchelder Honor Book (2016)

This book, by Aharon Appelfeld, "is the story of two nine-year-old Jewish boys who survive World War II by banding together in the forest. They are alone, visited only furtively, every few days by Mina, a mercurial girl who herself has found refuge from the war by living with a peasant family. She makes secret journeys and brings the boys parcels of food at her own risk." (Publisher's note)

"Translated from the original Hebrew text and accompanied by Dumas' moving illustrations, the story is one of quiet perseverance and growing friendship between two very different boys experiencing the world together in a horrific time and place." Booklist

Appelt, Kathi, 1954-

★ **Keeper**; illustrations by August Hall. Atheneum Books for Young Readers 2010 399p il $16.99

Grades: 5 6 7 8 **Fic**

1. Ocean -- Fiction 2. Sailing -- Fiction 3. Mermaids and mermen -- Fiction 4. Mother-daughter relationship -- Fiction

ISBN 978-1-4169-5060-8; 1-4169-5060-5

LC 2010000795

On the night of the blue moon when mermaids are said to gather on a sandbar in the Gulf of Mexico, ten-year-old Keeper sets out in a small boat, with her dog BD and a seagull named Captain, determined to find her mother, a mermaid, as Keeper has always believed, who left long ago to return to the sea.

"Deftly spinning together mermaid lore, local legend and natural history, this stunning tale proves 'every landscape has its magical beings,' and the most unlikely ones can form a perfect family. Hall's black-and-white illustrations lend perspective and immediacy. Beautiful and evocative—an absolute 'keeper.' " Kirkus

Maybe a Fox; Kathi Appelt and Alison McGhee. Simon & Schuster 2016 272 p. (hardback) $16.99

Grades: 4 5 6 7 8 **Fic**

1. Foxes -- Fiction 2. Grief -- Fiction

ISBN 9781442482432; 9781442482425; 1442482427

LC 2015033463

In this juvenile novel, by Kathi Appelt and Alison McGhee, "a fox kit born with a deep spiritual connection to a rural Vermont legend has a special bond with 11-year-old Jules. . . . In the opening chapters, impulsive Sylvie makes a dash to throw a wishing rock into the Slip, . . . it is Jules who discovers that Sylvie tripped on a tree root, sliding in March snow to her death. Meanwhile, Jules' kind friend Sam . . . and aches for his war-veteran brother, who mourns Zeke, who didn't return from Afghanistan." (Kirkus Reviews)

"A good cry can be cathartic, and this book about nourishing one's soul during times of great sadness does the trick." Horn Book

★ The **true** blue scouts of Sugarman Swamp; by Kathi Appelt. 1st ed. Atheneum Books for Young Readers 2013 336 p. (hardcover) $16.99

Grades: 5 6 7 8 **Fic**

1. Swamps -- Fiction 2. Raccoons -- Fiction 3. Humorous stories 4. Swamp animals -- Fiction 5. Land developers -- Fiction 6. Scouting (Youth activity) -- Fiction

ISBN 1442421053; 9781442421059; 9781442481213

LC 2012023723

National Book Award Finalist: Young People's Literature (2013)

This book is "told from the perspectives of animals and humans. . . .The main concern of Bingo and Jeremiah, two raccoon Swamp Scouts, is the approaching brood of feral hogs, which could destroy the precious canebrake sugar used to make fried pies at the local Paradise Pies cafe. Meanwhile, 12-year-old Chap Brayburn, the cafe proprietor's son, is worried about rich, horrible Sonny Boy Beaucoup, who wants to turn the swamp into the 'Gator World Wrestling Arena and Theme Park.'" (Publishers Weekly)

★ The **underneath**; illustrated by David Small. Atheneum Books for Young Readers 2008 313p il $16.99; pa $7.99

Grades: 3 4 5 6 **Fic**

1. Cats -- Fiction 2. Dogs -- Fiction

ISBN 978-1-4169-5058-5; 1-4169-5058-3; 978-1-4169-5059-2 pa; 1-4169-5059-1 pa

LC 2007031969

A Newbery Medal honor book, 2009

National Book Award Finalist: Young People's Literature (2008)

An abandoned "calico cat, about to have kittens, hears the lonely howl of [Ranger], a chained-up hound deep in the backwaters of the bayou. . . . Ranger urges the cat to hide underneath the porch, to raise her kittens there because Gar-Face, the man living inside the house, will surely use them as alligator bait should he find them." (Publisher's note) "Intemediate." (Horn Book)

"Well realized in Small's excellent full-page drawings, this fine book is most of all distinguished by the originality of the story and the fresh beauty of its author's voice." Horn Book

Applegate, Katherine, 1956-

★ **Home** of the brave. Feiwel & Friends 2007 249p $16.95

Grades: 5 6 7 8 **Fic**

1. Novels in verse 2. Cattle -- Fiction 3. Africans -- Fiction 4. Refugees -- Fiction 5. Minnesota -- Fiction 6. Immigrants -- Fiction

ISBN 0-312-36765-1; 978-0-312-36765-7

LC 2006-32053

Kek, an African refugee, is confronted by many strange things at the Minneapolis home of his aunt and cousin, as well as in his fifth grade classroom, and longs for his missing mother, but finds comfort in the company of a cow and her owner.

"This beautiful story of hope and resilience is written in free verse." Voice Youth Advocates

★ The **one** and only Ivan; illustrated by Patricia Castelao. Harper 2012 il $16.99

Grades: 3 4 5 6 **Fic**

1. Gorillas -- Fiction 2. Elephants -- Fiction 3. Animal welfare -- Fiction

ISBN 978-0-06-199225-4; 0-06-199225-9

LC 2011010034

John Newbery Medal (2013)

"Ivan narrates his tale in short, image-rich sentences and acute, sometimes humorous, observations that are all the more heartbreaking for their simple delivery. . . . Spot art captures poignant moments throughout. Utterly believable, this bittersweet story, complete with an author's note identifying the real Ivan, will inspire a new generation of advocates." Kirkus

★ **Wishtree**; Katherine Applegate. Feiwel & Friends 2017 224 p. ebook $60.00; (hardcover) $16.99

Grades: 4 5 6 7 8 **Fic**

1. Wishes -- Fiction 2. Friendship -- Fiction 3. Immigrants -- Fiction

ISBN 9781250143037; 9781250043221

LC 2016058768

In this book, by Katherine Applegate, "Red is an oak tree who is many rings old. Red is the neighborhood 'wishtree'--people write their wishes on pieces of cloth and tie them to Red's branches. Along with her crow friend Bongo and other animals who seek refuge in Red's hollows, this 'wishtree' watches over the neighborhood." (Publisher's note)

"Even those who shy away from books with talking animals will find this believable fantasy elegant and poignant. Widening the appeal is a sparse word count, making this a great choice for a family or classroom read-aloud and an inviting option for reluctant readers." (SLJ)

Arbuthnott, Gill

The **Keepers'** tattoo. Chicken House 2010 425p $17.99

Grades: 6 7 8 9 **Fic**

1. Fantasy fiction 2. Dreams -- Fiction 3. Uncles -- Fiction 4. Tattooing -- Fiction 5. Identity (Psychology) -- Fiction

ISBN 978-0-545-17166-3; 0-545-17166-0

LC 2009-26327

Months before her fifteenth birthday, Nyssa learns that she is a special member of a legendary clan, the Keepers of Knowledge, as she and her uncle try to escape from Alaric, the White Wolf, who wants to use lines tattooed on her to destroy the rest of her people.

Arbuthnott "writes with restraint and thoughtfulness, never condescending to her readers. Nyssa is a convincing mixture of ignorance, courage, and resourcefulness." Publ Wkly

Arden, Katherine

Small spaces; Katherine Arden. G.P. Putnam's Sons Books for Young Readers 2018 224 p. (hardback) $16.99

Grades: 4 5 6 7 8 **Fic**

1. Horror fiction 2. Paranormal fiction 3. Friendship -- Fiction 4. Survival -- Fiction 5. Supernatural -- Fiction 6. Books and reading -- Fiction 7. Forests and forestry -- Fiction

ISBN 9780525515029

LC 2018010780

In this novel, author Katherine Arden "shrouds her Halloween-time story in autumnal mists, introducing a...cast of ominous figures, from ghosts to shapeshifters and scarecrow minions. Ollie is a relatable heroine who finds strength through trusting in friendship, while her ghostly adventures lead her to learn an important truth: sometimes, the best way to honor the memory of a loved one is by moving forward, bravely, and with love." (Publishers Weekly)

Armistead, Cal

Being Henry David; by Cal Armistead. Albert Whitman 2013 312 p. (hardcover) $16.99

Grades: 8 9 10 11 12 **Fic**

1. Mystery fiction 2. Amnesia -- Fiction 3. Guilt -- Fiction 4. Runaways -- Fiction 5. Concord (Mass.) -- Fiction 6. Family problems -- Fiction 7. New York (N.Y.) -- Fiction 8. Street children -- Fiction

ISBN 080750615X; 9780807506158

LC 2012017377

In this book, a "boy wakes up in Penn Station, remembering nothing. He guesses that he's about 17, he has a head injury, and he is carrying only 10 dollars. Near at hand is a copy of Walden, so for want of anything better he calls himself Henry David (Hank). He heads to Concord, Massachusetts, to find, he hopes, some clues at Walden Pond. As his memories slowly return, he remembers who he was; as he copes with the memories, he discovers who he is and can be." (School Library Journal)

Armstrong, Alan

Looking for Marco Polo; illustrated by Tim Jessell. Random House 2009 286p $16.99

Grades: 4 5 6 7 **Fic**

1. Travelers 2. Travel writers 3. Venice (Italy) -- Fiction 4. Missing persons -- Fiction

ISBN 978-0-375-83321-2; 0-375-83321-8

When they lose touch with his father's Gobi Desert expedition, eleven-year-old Mark accompanies his mother to Venice, Italy, and there, while waiting for news of his father, learns about the legendary Marco Polo and his adventures in the Far East.

"Armstrong ably conjures up the atmosphere of damp, foggy Venice in late December while blowing some dust off of the accounts of Marco Polo's travels with his lively storytelling. . . . Whether or not readers know the specifics of Marco Polo's voyages, they will enjoy this entertaining blend of contemporary and historical adventure." Booklist

Whittington; illustrated by S. D. Schindler. Random House 2005 191p il $14.95; lib bdg $16.99; pa $6.50

Grades: 4 5 6 **Fic**

1. Cats -- Fiction 2. Domestic animals -- Fiction

ISBN 0-375-82864-8; 0-375-92864-2 lib bdg; 0-375-82865-6 pa

LC 2004-05789

A Newbery Medal honor book, 2006

"A battered cat who calls himself Whittington takes up residence in a shabby barn already inhabited by a variety of scruffy livestock, owned by Bernie. . . . Bernie offers refuge not only to his animals but also to his parentless grandchildren, Abby and Ben, who carry burdens of their own. The children [can] communicate . . . with the animals, so Abby and Ben join the audience when Whittington the cat retells the story of Dick Whittington and his cat." (Bull Cent Child Books) "Intermediate, middle school." (Horn Book)

"The story works beautifully, both as historical fiction about medieval street life and commerce and as a witty, engaging tale of barnyard camaraderie and survival." Booklist

Armstrong, Kelley, 1968-

Aftermath; Kelley Armstrong. Crown 2018 371 p. (hardcover) $17.99

Grades: 7 8 9 10 **Fic**

1. Brothers -- Fiction 2. Teenagers -- Fiction 3. School shootings -- Fiction 4. Best friends -- Fiction 5. Brothers -- Death -- Fiction 6. High school students -- Fiction 7. Mass murder investigation -- Fiction

ISBN 0399550364; 9780399550362; 9780399550386

In this book, by Kelley Armstrong, "three years after losing her brother Luka in a school shooting, Skye Gilchrist is moving home. But there's no sympathy for Skye and her family because Luka wasn't a victim; he was a shooter. Jesse Mandal knows all too well that the scars of the past don't heal easily. The shooting cost Jesse his brother and his best friend--Skye. Ripped apart by tragedy, Jesse and Skye can't resist reopening the mysteries of their past." (Publisher's note)

The **gathering**. Harper 2011 359p (Darkness rising) $17.99

Grades: 7 8 9 10 **Fic**

1. School stories 2. Canada -- Fiction 3. Witchcraft -- Fiction 4. Family life -- Fiction 5. Supernatural -- Fiction 6. Vancouver Island (B.C.) -- Fiction

ISBN 978-0-06-179702-6 Harper; 0-06-179702-2 Harper; 978-0-385-66851-4 Doubleday Canada

LC 2010-32229

Sixteen-year-old Maya suspects there may be a relationship between her paw-print birthmark, her connection with wild animals, and strange events occurring in her tiny Vancouver Island community, where a medical research facility harbors big secrets.

"Comfortably mixing science, myth, and mystery, Armstrong creates a vivid world highlighted by appealing characters." Publ Wkly

Other titles in this series are:

The calling (2012)

The rising (2013)

The **summoning**. HarperCollinsPublishers 2008 390p (Darkest powers) $17.99; lib bdg $18.89

Grades: 7 8 9 10 **Fic**

1. Ghost stories 2. Supernatural -- Fiction

ISBN 978-0-06-166269-0; 0-06-166269-0; 978-0-06-166272-0 lib bdg; 0-06-166272-0 lib bdg

LC 2008-14221

After fifteen-year-old Chloe starts seeing ghosts and is sent to Lyle House, a mysterious group home for mentally disturbed teenagers, she soon discovers that neither Lyle House nor its inhabitants are exactly what they seem, and that she and her new friends are in danger.

"Suspenseful, well-written, and engaging, this page-turning . . . [novel] will be a hit." Voice Youth Advocates

Other titles in this series are:

The awakening (2009)

The reckoning (2010)

Armstrong, William Howard

★ **Sounder**; [by] William H. Armstrong; illustrations by James Barkley. Harper & Row 1969 116p il $15.99; pa $5.99

Grades: 5 6 7 8 **Fic**

1. Dogs -- Fiction 2. Family life -- Fiction 3. African Americans -- Fiction

ISBN 0-06-020143-6; 0-06-440020-4 pa

Awarded the Newbery Medal, 1970

"Set in the South in the era of sharecropping and segregation, this succinctly told tale poignantly describes the courage of a father who steals a ham in order to feed his undernourished family; the determination of the eldest son, who searches for his father despite the apathy of prison authorities; and the devotion of a coon dog named Sounder." Shapiro. Fic for Youth. 3d edition

Arnold, Elana K.

Far from fair; Elana K. Arnold. Houghton Mifflin Harcourt 2016 240 p. (hardcover) $16.99

Grades: 5 6 7 **Fic**

1. Dogs -- Fiction 2. Anger -- Fiction 3. Family life -- Fiction 4. Family problems -- Fiction 5. Recreational vehicles -- Fiction

ISBN 9780544602274

LC 2015013893

In this children's novel, by Elana K. Arnold, "Odette Zyskoski's life is being ruined by her parents' decision to sell their house and head north in an RV they've dubbed the Coach. . . . By using a third-person narration that keeps Odette at a slight remove from her family, Arnold captures the loneliness of a young teenager's inability to express the emotions that accompany life's upheavals." (Kirkus Reviews)

Arnold "deals with the many bumps in the road honestly, yet maintains an onward-and-upward outlook on life." Booklist

The **question** of miracles; by Elana K. Arnold. Houghton Mifflin Harcourt 2015 240 p. (hardback) $16.99

Grades: 4 5 6 7 **Fic**

1. Miracles -- Fiction 2. Friendship -- Fiction 3. Grief -- Fiction 4. Corvallis (Or.) -- Fiction 5. Moving, Household -- Fiction

ISBN 0544334647; 9780544334649

LC 2014000738

In this novel by Elana K. Arnold, "Iris is starting sixth grade in a new school in Oregon-new house, new people, new life. Her parents want to distract her from the recent death of her best friend in California. . . . She turns away from potential friends, seeking instead someone she can barely tolerate--so that she must only endure minimal interaction. His name is Boris, and while he is obviously an outcast, Iris prefers to be on the outskirts." (School Library Journal)

"This is a realistic view of grief, with particular emphasis on the agonizing longing to know if a lost loved one is truly out there somewhere." SLJ

Arnston, Steven

★ The **Wikkeling**; illustrated by Daniela Jaglenka Terrazzini. Running Press Kids 2011 256p il $18

Grades: 4 5 6 **Fic**

1. Science fiction

ISBN 978-0-7624-3903-4; 0-7624-3903-3

"In Henrietta's world, every part of life is monitored and regulated by computers. House cats are considered wild and dangerous animals. Old houses and old books can make children sick. The girl's orderly and safe life is disrupted the day she discovers a secret attic above her bedroom. . . . Soon after this discovery, she starts seeing the Wikkeling, a menacing yellow creature that gives children headaches with the touch of a finger. . . . Arntson has created a detailed and fascinating dystopian world that seems eerily similar to our own, and Terrazzini's illustrations strike just the right note." SLJ

Aronson, Sarah

Beyond lucky. Dial Books for Young Readers 2011 250p $16.99

Grades: 4 5 6 7 **Fic**

1. Mystery fiction 2. Chance -- Fiction 3. Soccer -- Fiction 4. Brothers -- Fiction 5. Jews -- United States -- Fiction

ISBN 978-0-8037-3520-0; 0-8037-3520-0

LC 2010-28800

Twelve-year-old Ari Fish is sure that the rare trading card he found has changed his luck and that of his soccer team, but after the card is stolen he comes to know that we make our own luck, and that heroes can be fallible.

"Aronson skillfully dodges the predictability of sports-themed books by creating multilayered characters and an intriguing whodunit. . . . Aronson . . . includes a lot of fun on-field action, but the off-field story is just as interesting. . . . Aronson's graceful storytelling will keep even nonsoccer buffs turning pages." Publ Wkly

Asher, Jay

Thirteen reasons why; a novel. Razorbill 2007 288p $16.99

Grades: 8 9 10 11 12 **Fic**

1. School stories 2. Suicide -- Fiction

ISBN 9781595141712

LC 2007-03097

When high school student Clay Jenkins receives a box in the mail containing thirteen cassette tapes recorded by his classmate Hannah, who committed suicide, he spends a bewildering and heartbreaking night crisscrossing their town, listening to Hannah's voice recounting the events leading up to her death.

"Clay's pain is palpable and exquisitely drawn in gripping casually poetic prose. The complex and soulful characters expose astoundingly rich and singularly teenage inner lives." SLJ

What light; Jay Asher. Penguin Group USA 2016 272 p. $18.99; (ebook) $56.97

Grades: 7 8 9 10 **Fic**

1. Christmas -- Fiction 2. Teenagers -- Fiction 3. Love -- Fiction

ISBN 1595145516; 9781595145512; 9780448493657

LC 2016038795

In this book, by Jay Asher, "Sierra's family runs a Christmas tree farm in Oregon—it's a bucolic setting for a girl to grow up in, except that every year, they pack up and move to California to set up their Christmas tree lot for the season. So Sierra lives two lives: her life in Oregon and her life at Christmas. And leaving one always means missing the other. Until this particular Christmas, when Sierra meets Caleb, and one life eclipses the other." (Publisher's note)

"Sierra's story provides an interesting window into alternative schooling and living arrangements facing some teens whose families work in agriculture. Certain to please readers seeking an escapist, feel-good holiday read." Booklist

Atkins, Jeannine

Finding wonders; Three Girls Who Changed Science. Jeannine Atkins. Atheneum Books for Young Readers 2016 208 p. illustrations (hardcover : alk. paper) $16.99

Grades: 5 6 7 8 **Fic**

1. Women scientists -- Fiction 2. Sex role -- Fiction 3. Scientists -- Fiction 4. Astronomers -- Fiction 5. Naturalists -- Fiction 6. Paleontologists -- Fiction

ISBN 9781481465656; 9781481465663

LC 2015036450

This book by Jeannine Atkins is a "novel in verse about three girls . . . who grew up to become groundbreaking scientists. Maria Merian . . . discovered the truth about metamorphosis and documented her findings in gorgeous paintings of the life cycles of insects. . . . Mary Anning . . . discovered fossils that would change people's vision of the past. . . . Maria Mitchell . . . longed to discover a new comet—and after years of studying the night sky, she finally did." (Publisher's note)

"Science is woven through the narratives, but within the fabric of the characters' daily lives and family struggles. While the Mary Anning narrative is the most haunting, each of these three perceptive portrayals is original and memorable." Booklist

Includes bibliographical references

Atkinson, Elizabeth

From Alice to Zen and everyone in between; a novel. Carolrhoda Books 2008 247p $16.95

Grades: 5 6 7 **Fic**

1. School stories 2. Moving -- Fiction 3. Popularity -- Fiction 4. Family life -- Fiction 5. Massachusetts -- Fiction 6. Eccentrics and eccentricities -- Fiction

ISBN 978-0-8225-7271-8; 0-8225-7271-0

LC 2007-9659

Upon moving from Boston to the suburbs, eleven-year-old tomboy Alice meets Zen, a very strange neighbor who is determined to help her become popular when they both begin middle school, although he himself is a loner.

"Atkinson describes Alice's ethical development credibly and engagingly." Booklist

★ **I,** Emma Freke; [by] Elizabeth Atkinson. Carolrhoda Books 2010 234p $16.95

Grades: 4 5 6 7 **Fic**

1. Wisconsin -- Fiction 2. Family life -- Fiction 3. Massachusetts -- Fiction 4. Family reunions -- Fiction 5. Single parent family -- Fiction 6. Eccentrics and eccentricities -- Fiction

ISBN 978-0-7613-5604-2; 0-7613-5604-5

LC 2009-38923

Growing up near Boston with her free-spirited mother and old-world grandfather, twelve-year-old Emma has always felt out of place but when she attends the family reunion her father's family holds annually in Wisconsin, she is in for some surprises.

"This rich story of self-acceptance offers readers much to think about. . . . The first-person narrative moves along briskly, with believable dialogue and plenty of humor." Booklist

Atwater-Rhodes, Amelia

Persistence of memory. Delacorte Press 2008 212p $15.99; lib bdg $18.99; pa $8.99

Grades: 8 9 10 11 12 **Fic**

1. Witches -- Fiction 2. Vampires -- Fiction 3. Supernatural -- Fiction 4. Schizophrenia -- Fiction

ISBN 978-0-385-73437-0; 0-385-73437-9; 978-0-385-90443-8 lib bdg; 0-385-90443-6 lib bdg; 978-0-440-24004-4 pa; 0-440-24004-2 pa

LC 2008-16062

Diagnosed with schizophrenia as a child, sixteen-year-old Erin has spent half of her life in therapy and on drugs, but now must face the possibility of weird things in the real world, including shapeshifting friends and her "alter," a centuries-old vampire.

"What sets this novel apart . . . are the two narrators—Erin, grown used to, and even comfortable with, the idea that she is mentally ill; and Shevaun, willing to do anything to protect the family she's cobbled together. Secondary characters are equally compelling, and the world that Atwater-Rhodes has created is believable and intriguing." SLJ

Auch, Mary Jane

Guitar boy. Henry Holt 2010 260p $16.99

Grades: 6 7 8 9 **Fic**

1. Guitars -- Fiction 2. Musicians -- Fiction 3. Family life -- Fiction 4. Adirondack Mountains (N.Y.) -- Fiction

ISBN 978-0-8050-9112-0; 0-8050-9112-2

LC 2009-50782

After his mother is severely injured in an accident and his father kicks him out of the house, thirteen-year-old Travis attempts to survive on his own until he meets a guitar maker and some musicians who take him in and help him regain his confidence so that he can try to patch his family back together.

"Budding musicians will be fascinated by the details, but all readers will find their heartstrings plucked by this story." Booklist

Wing nut; [by] MJ Auch. Henry Holt & Co. 2005 231p $16.95

Grades: 4 5 6 **Fic**

1. Birds -- Fiction 2. Moving -- Fiction 3. Old age -- Fiction

ISBN 0-8050-7531-3

LC 2004-54046

When twelve-year-old Grady and his mother relocate yet again, they find work taking care of an elderly man, who teaches Grady about cars, birds, and what it means to have a home

"Auch's story . . . is engaging. . . . What will attract readers . . . is the author's careful integration of bird lore and the unusual challenges of creating and maintaining a purple martin colony." Booklist

Austen, Catherine

All good children. Orca Book Publishers 2011 300p $19.95

Grades: 7 8 9 10 11 12 **Fic**

1. Siblings -- Fiction 2. Individualism -- Fiction 3. Totalitarianism -- Fiction

ISBN 978-1-55469-824-0; 1-55469-824-3

In the not-too-distant future, Max tries to maintain his identity in a world where the only way to survive is to conform and obey.

"Action packed, terrifying, and believable, this entertaining novel will provoke important discussions about subservience, resistance, and individual freedom." Booklist

Walking backward. Orca 2009 167p pa $9.95

Grades: 6 7 8 9 **Fic**

1. Bereavement -- Fiction

ISBN 978-1-55469-147-0 pa; 1-55469-147-8 pa

After his mother dies in a phobia-related car crash, twelve-year-old Josh tries to make sense of this grief while he looks after his little brother and watches his father retreat into a fantasy world

"In this impressive debut novel, Josh keeps a journal to chart his feelings and thoughts, allowing readers to follow his journey from sadness to acceptance and the eventual return of cohesion in his family. Given the subject matter, the story is never maudlin, and Josh's voice rings natural and true. An elegantly crafted volume of lasting power." Kirkus

Auxier, Jonathan

The **Night** Gardener; by Jonathan Auxier. Amulet Books 2014 368 p. (hardback) $16.95

Grades: 4 5 6 7 **Fic**

1. Ghost stories 2. Horror stories 3. Ghosts -- Fiction 4. Orphans -- Fiction 5. Dwellings -- Fiction 6. Storytelling -- Fiction 7. Household employees -- Fiction 8. Blessing and cursing -- Fiction 9. Brothers and sisters -- Fiction

ISBN 141971144X; 9781419711442

LC 2013047655

"'The Night Gardener' follows two abandoned Irish siblings who travel to work as servants at a creepy, crumbling English manor house. But the house and its family are not quite what they seem. Soon the children are confronted by a mysterious spectre and an ancient curse that threatens their very lives." (Publisher's note)

"Molly's whimsical tales illustrate life's essential lessons even as they entertain. As the characters face the unhealthy pull of the tree's allurements, they grow and change, revealing unexpected personality traits. Storytelling as a force to cope with life's challenges is subtly expressed and adds complexity to the fast-paced plot." SLJ

Peter Nimble and his fantastic eyes; a story. Amulet Books 2011 381p il $16.95

Grades: 4 5 6 7 **Fic**

1. Eye -- Fiction 2. Blind -- Fiction 3. Magic -- Fiction 4. Orphans -- Fiction 5. Thieves -- Fiction

ISBN 978-1-4197-0025-5; 1-4197-0025-1

LC 2010048692

Raised to be a thief, blind orphan Peter Nimble, age ten, steals from a mysterious stranger three pairs of magical eyes, that lead him to a hidden island where he must decide to become a hero or resume his life of crime.

"The fast-paced, episodic story, accompanied by Auxier's occasional pen-and-ink drawings, is inventive, unpredictable, and—like its hero—nimble." Publ Wkly

★ **Sophie** Quire and the last Storyguard; by Jonathan Auxier. Amulet Books 2016 464 p. illustrations (hardback) $18.95

Grades: 4 5 6 7 **Fic**

1. Fantasy fiction 2. Books and reading -- Fiction 3. Magic -- Fiction 4. Adventure and adventurers -- Fiction

ISBN 9781419717475

LC 2015039272

Sequel to: Peter Nimble and His Fantastic Eyes (2011)

"Sophie knows little beyond the four walls of her father's bookshop, where she repairs old books and dreams of escaping the confines of her dull life. But when a strange boy and his talking cat/horse companion show up with a rare and mysterious book, she finds herself pulled into an adventure beyond anything she has ever read." (Publisher's note)

"Ultimately, this affecting, compelling story stands on its own, embodying and highlighting the power and impact of tales well told--and why they endure." Booklist

★ **Sweep**; the story of a girl and her monster. by Jonathan Auxier. Amulet Books 2018 368 p. (hardback) $18.99

Grades: 4 5 6 7 8 **Fic**

1. Golem -- Fiction 2. Orphans -- Fiction 3. Homeless persons -- Fiction 4. Great Britain -- History -- 19th century -- Fiction

ISBN 9781419731402

LC 2018014305

Sydney Taylor Book Award: Older Readers (2019)

In this novel, by Jonathan Auxier, "it's been five years since the Sweep disappeared. Orphaned and alone, Nan Sparrow had no other choice but to work for a ruthless chimney sweep named Wilkie Crudd. . . . When Nan gets stuck in a chimney fire, she fears the end has come. Instead, she wakes to find herself unharmed in an abandoned attic. And she is not alone. Huddled in the corner is a mysterious creature--a golem--made from soot and ash." (Publisher's note)

"Auxier wipes away the grime from a bleak chapter in history where children were forced to work dangerous jobs that claimed many lives.

He questions what makes one a monster and applauds helping others, activism, education, earthly marvels, and the possibility of magic. Nan's fiery personality will attract readers like moths, and Auxier's unusual blend of mythology and history will keep them transfixed." Booklist

Avery, Tom

Not as we know it; Tom Avery. Schwartz & Wade Books 2016 176 p. (hbk.) $16.99

Grades: 5 6 7 8 9 **Fic**

1. Cystic fibrosis -- Fiction 2. Mythical animals -- Fiction 3. Twins -- Fiction 4. Beaches -- Fiction 5. Brothers -- Fiction 6. Imaginary creatures -- Fiction

ISBN 9780553535099; 0553535099; 9780553535105

LC 2015010810

In this middle-grade novel by Tom Avery, "twins Jamie and Ned do everything together, from watching their favorite show, Star Trek, to riding their bikes, to beachcombing after a storm. But Ned is sick with cystic fibrosis, and he may someday leave Jamie behind. One day the boys find a strange animal on the beach: smooth flesh on one end, scales at the other, and short arms and legs with long webbed fingers and toes. Could it be a merman, like in the old stories?" (Publisher's note)

"Through Jamie's thoughtful narration, readers are treated to a hauntingly beautiful story about brotherly bonds, wrenching grief, and the untethered hope that everything will somehow work out." Pub Wkly

Aveyard, Victoria

King's cage; Victoria Aveyard. HarperTeen, an imprint of HarperCollins Publishers 2017 512 p. (Red queen) (hardcover) $19.99

Grades: 7 8 9 10 **Fic**

1. Blood -- Fiction 2. Princesses -- Fiction 3. Resistance to government -- Fiction 4. Ability -- Fiction 5. Social classes -- Fiction 6. Courts and courtiers -- Fiction

ISBN 9780062310712; 9780062310699

LC 2016478470

"In this breathless third installment to Victoria Aveyard's . . . Red Queen series, rebellion is rising and allegiances will be tested on every side. Mare Barrow is a prisoner. . . . She lives at the mercy of a boy she once loved. . . . Now a king, Maven Calore . . . attempt[s] to maintain control over his country--and his prisoner. As Mare bears the weight of Silent Stone in the palace, her . . . band of newbloods and Reds continue organizing, training, and expanding." (Publisher's note)

Red queen; Victoria Aveyard. First edition HarperTeen, an imprint of HarperCollins Publishers 2015 388 p. $17.99

Grades: 8 9 10 11 **Fic**

1. Ability -- Fiction 2. Princesses -- Fiction 3. Teenage girls -- Fiction 4. Kings and rulers -- Fiction 5. Resistance to government -- Fiction 6. Blood -- Fiction

ISBN 0062310631; 9780062310637

LC 2014952542

This book, by Victoria Aveyard, is the "sweeping tale of seventeen-year-old Mare, a common girl whose once-latent magical power draws her into the dangerous intrigue of the king's palace. Mare Barrow's world is divided by blood--those with common, Red blood serve the Silver- blooded elite, who are gifted with superhuman abilities. Mare is a Red, scraping by as a thief in a poor, rural village, until a twist of fate throws her in front of the Silver court." (Publisher's note)

"First-time author Aveyard has created a volatile world with a dynamic heroine, and while there are moments of romance, they refreshingly take a backseat to the action. Anticipation is already high for this debut, and with the movie rights already acquired and two sequels to come, it will likely only grow." Booklist

Other titles in this series are:
Glass sword (2016)
King's cage (2017)
War storm (2018)

Avi, 1937-

The **Book** Without Words; a fable of medieval magic. Hyperion Books for Children 2005 203p hardcover o.p. pa $5.99

Grades: 5 6 7 8 **Fic**

1. Magic -- Fiction 2. Middle Ages -- Fiction 3. Supernatural -- Fiction 4. Great Britain -- History -- 0-1066 -- Fiction

ISBN 0-7868-0829-2; 0-7868-1659-7 pa

"At the dawning of the Middle Ages, Thorston, an old alchemist, works feverishly to create gold and to dose himself with a concoction that will enable him to live forever. The key to his success lies in a mysterious book with blank pages that can only be read by desperate, green-eyed people. . . . Avi's compelling language creates a dreary foreboding. . . . Clearly this is a story with a message, a true fable. Thoughtful readers will devour its absorbing plot and humorous elements, and learn a 'useful truth' along the way." SLJ

Catch you later, traitor; a novel. by Avi. Algonquin Young Readers 2015 304 p. hbk $16.95

Grades: 4 5 6 7 **Fic**

1. Mystery fiction 2. Communism -- Fiction 3. Families -- Fiction 4. Brooklyn (New York, N.Y.) -- History -- 20th century -- Fiction

ISBN 1616203595; 9781616203597

LC 2014031983

This novel by Avi is set in 1951 Brooklyn, New York. "Pete Collison is a regular kid who loves Sam Spade detective books and radio crime dramas, but when an FBI agent shows up at Pete's doorstep accusing his father of being a Communist, Pete finds himself caught in a real-life mystery. Could there really be Commies in Pete's family? As Pete follows the quickly accumulating clues, he begins to wonder if the truth could put his family's livelihood--and even their freedom--at risk." (Publisher's note)

"Avi's tale of one Brooklyn family living in a time of intolerance effectively explores the natures of suspicion, loyalty, and freedom, following a young protagonist who comes to learn the importance of freedom of speech and 'staying true to your own thoughts.'" Horn Book

Includes bibliographical references

★ **City** of orphans; with illustrations by Greg Ruth. Atheneum Books for Young Readers 2011 350p il $16.99

Grades: 5 6 7 8 **Fic**

1. Mystery fiction 2. Gangs -- Fiction 3. Immigrants -- Fiction 4. Family life -- Fiction 5. New York (N.Y.) -- Fiction 6. Homeless persons -- Fiction 7. Waldorf-Astoria Hotel (New York, N.Y.) -- Fiction.

ISBN 978-1-4169-7102-3; 1-4169-7102-5

LC 2010049229

In 1893 New York, thirteen-year-old Maks, a newsboy, teams up with Willa, a homeless girl, to clear his older sister, Emma, from charges that she stole from the brand new Waldorf Hotel, where she works. Includes historical notes.

"Avi's vivid recreation of the sights and sounds of that time and place is spot on, masterfully weaving accurate historical details with Maks' experiences." Kirkus

Includes bibliographical references

Crispin at the edge of the world. Hyperion Books for Children 2006 234p $16.99

Grades: 5 6 7 8 Fic

1. Orphans -- Fiction 2. Middle Ages -- Fiction 3. Great Britain -- History -- 1154-1399, Plantagenets -- Fiction

ISBN 0-7868-5152-X

LC 2006-41111

Sequel to Crispin: the cross of lead (2002)

Branded as traitors by the king's authorities, Crispin and his guardian, Bear, flee to coastal towns in fourteenth-century England, where they perform a musical juggling act and bond as a family after befriending a disfigured girl.

"Along with plenty of action and adventure, this displays a solid emotional base." Booklist

Followed by Crispin: the end of time (2010)

★ **Crispin** : the cross of lead. Hyperion Bks. for Children 2002 $15.99; pa $6.99

Grades: 5 6 7 8 Fic

1. Orphans -- Fiction 2. Middle Ages -- Fiction 3. Great Britain -- History -- 1154-1399, Plantagenets -- Fiction

ISBN 0-7868-0828-4; 0-7868-1658-9 pa

LC 2001-51829

Awarded the Newbery Medal, 2001

Falsely accused of theft and murder, an orphaned peasant boy in fourteenth-century England flees his village and meets a larger-than-life juggler who holds a dangerous secret

This "book is a page-turner from beginning to end. . . . A meticulously crafted story, full of adventure, mystery, and action." SLJ

Other titles in this series are:

Crispin at the edge of the world (2006)

Crispin: the end of time (2010)

Crispin : the end of time. Balzer + Bray 2010 223p $16.99; lib bdg $17.89

Grades: 5 6 7 8 Fic

1. Orphans -- Fiction 2. Middle Ages -- Fiction

ISBN 978-0-06-174080-0; 0-06-174080-2; 978-0-06-174082-4 lib bdg; 0-06-174082-9 lib bdg

Sequel to: Crispin at the edge of the world (2006)

"Still grieving for the fatherly protector they called Bear, Crispin and his friend Troth wander northward through the fourteenth-century French countryside . . . hoping to journey to Iceland. They arrive at a convent where the nuns value Troth's skill with healing herbs, and she decides to stay. Alone and near starvation, Crispin joins a troupe of traveling musicians who prove to be a band of murderous thieves. . . . Even readers new to the series will find this a compelling, first-person narrative." Booklist

★ **Don't** you know there's a war on? HarperCollins Pubs. 2001 200p hardcover o.p. pa $5.99

Grades: 4 5 6 7 Fic

1. Teachers -- Fiction 2. World War, 1939-1945 -- Fiction 3. Brooklyn (New York, N.Y.) -- Fiction

ISBN 0-380-97863-6; 0-380-81544-3 pa

LC 00-46102

In wartime Brooklyn in 1943, eleven-year-old Howie Crispers mounts a campaign to save his favorite teacher from being fired

"The 1943 Brooklyn setting is well evoked in Howie's lively, slang-spangled narration. The novel's uncomplicated, compact structure invites reading aloud." Horn Book Guide

The **fighting** ground. Lippincott 1984 157p hardcover o.p. lib bdg $16.89; pa $5.99; rpt $5.99

Grades: 5 6 7 8 Fic

1. United States -- History -- 1775-1783, Revolution -- Fiction

ISBN 0-397-32073-6; 0-397-32074-4 lib bdg; 0-06-440185-5 pa; 9780064401852 rpt

LC 82-47719

"It's April 1776, and the fighting ground is both the farm country of Pennsylvania and the heart of a boy which is 'wonderful ripe for war.' Twenty-four hours transform Jonathan from a cocky 13-year-old, eager to take on the British, into a young man who now knows the horror, the pathos, the ambiguities of war." Voice Youth Advocates

★ **Iron** thunder; the battle between the Monitor and the Merrimac, a civil war novel. Hyperion 2007 205p il $15.99; pa $5.99

Grades: 4 5 6 Fic

1. Ships -- Fiction 2. Brooklyn (New York, N.Y.) -- Fiction 3. United States -- History -- 1861-1865, Civil War -- Fiction

ISBN 978-1-4231-0446-9; 1-4231-0446-3; 978-1-4231-0518-3 pa; 1-4231-0518-4 pa

"This fascinating adventure taken from U.S. history begins in Brooklyn in 1862, when Tom Carroll, 13, is hired at the Iron Works in Greenpoint for a secret project, derisively known around the borough as Ericsson's Folly. John Ericsson, a Swedish inventor, is trying to build an ironclad ship that can battle the Merrimac, a Confederate ship being outfitted with metal plates in Virginia. . . . Illustrated with period engravings, this is gripping historical fiction from a keenly imagined perspective." Publ Wkly

The **man** who was Poe; a novel. Orchard Bks. 1989 208p hardcover o.p. pa $5.99

Grades: 4 5 6 7 Fic

1. Poets 2. Authors 3. Mystery fiction 4. Essayists 5. Short story writers

ISBN 0-531-08433-7; 0-380-73022-7 pa

LC 89-42537

Edmund "finds himself alone in 1848 Providence. Both his aunt and his sister have vanished under mysterious circumstances. Through a chance encounter, Edmund enlists the help of a man he comes to know as Auguste Dupin. . . . Dupin is in fact Poe." (SLJ) "Grades six to nine." (Bull Cent Child Books)

Avi blends "drama, history, and mystery without a hint of pastiche or calculation. And, as in the best mystery stories, readers will be left in the end with both the comfort of puzzles solved and the unease of mysteries remaining." Bull Cent Child Books

Midnight magic. Scholastic Press 1999 249p hardcover o.p. pa $5.99

Grades: 5 6 7 8 Fic

1. Italy -- Fiction 2. Magicians -- Fiction 3. Renaissance -- Fiction

ISBN 0-590-36035-3; 0-439-24219-3 pa

LC 98-50192

In Italy in 1491, Mangus the magician and his apprentice are summoned to the castle of Duke Claudio to determine if his daughter is indeed being haunted by a ghost.

An "entertaining tale of mystery and intrigue." SLJ

Another title about Mangus and Fabrizio is:

Murder at midnight (2009)

★ **Nothing** but the truth; a documentary novel. Scholastic Inc. 2010 177p pa $6.99

Grades: 6 7 8 9 **Fic**

1. School stories

ISBN 978-0-545-17415-2

First published 1991 by Orchard Bks.

A Newbery Medal honor book, 1992

A ninth-grader's suspension for singing "The Star-Spangled Banner" during homeroom becomes a national news story.

"The book is effectively set entirely in monologue or dialogue; conversations, memos, letters, diary entries, talk-radio transcripts, and newspaper articles are all interwoven to present an uninterrupted plot. The construction is nearly flawless; the characters seem painfully human and typically ordinary. . . . A powerful, explosive novel that involves the reader from start to finish." Horn Book

★ The **seer** of shadows. HarperCollinsPublishers 2008 202p $16.99; lib bdg $17.89; pa $6.99

Grades: 4 5 6 7 **Fic**

1. Ghost stories 2. Photography -- Fiction 3. New York (N.Y.) -- Fiction 4. Swindlers and swindling -- Fiction

ISBN 978-0-06-000015-8; 0-06-000015-5; 978-0-06-000016-5 lib bdg; 0-06-000016-3 lib bdg; 978-0-06-000017-2 pa; 0-06-000017-1 pa

LC 2007-10891

In New York City in 1872, fourteen-year-old Horace, a photographer's apprentice, becomes entangled in a plot to create fraudulent spirit photographs, but when Horace accidentally frees the real ghost of a dead girl bent on revenge, his life takes a frightening turn.

"Fast-paced yet haunting. . . . This engaging novel has great immediacy and strong narrative drive." Booklist

★ **Sophia's** war; a tale of the Revolution. Avi. Beach Lane Books 2012 302 p. (hardcover) $16.99

Grades: 5 6 7 8 **Fic**

1. Traitors -- Fiction 2. Women spies -- Fiction 3. United States -- History -- 1775-1783, Revolution -- Fiction 4. Spies -- Fiction 5. United States -- History -- Revolution, 1775-1783 -- Fiction 6. New York (N.Y.) -- History -- Revolution, 1775-1783 -- Fiction

ISBN 1442414413; 9781442414419; 9781442414426; 9781442414433

LC 2012007962

In this novel by Avi "Sophia Calderwood witnesses the execution of Nathan Hale in New York City, which is newly occupied by the British army . . . in 1776. . . . Recruited as a spy, . . . she becomes aware that someone in the American army might be switching sides, and she uncovers a plot that will grievously damage the Americans if it succeeds. But the identity of the would-be traitor is so shocking that no one believes her, and so Sophia decides to stop the treacherous plot herself." (Publisher's note)

Includes bibliographical references

★ The **true** confessions of Charlotte Doyle; decorations by Ruth E. Murray. Orchard Bks. 1990 215p $16.95; pa $5.99; rpt $16.99

Grades: 5 6 7 **Fic**

1. Sea stories

ISBN 0-531-05893-X; 0-380-72885-0 pa; 9780545477116 rpt

LC 90-30624

A Newbery Medal honor book, 1991

"Charlotte Doyle, thirteen, returning from school in England to join her family in Rhode Island, is deposited on a seedy ship with a ruthless, mad captain and a mutinous crew. Refusing to heed warnings about Captain Jaggery's brutality, Charlotte seeks his guidance and approval only to become his victim." (SLJ)

The author has "fashioned an intriguing, suspenseful, carefully crafted tale, with nonstop action on the high seas." Booklist

The **unexpected** life of Oliver Cromwell Pitts; being an absolutely accurate autobiographical account of my follies, fortune & fate. Avi. Algonquin Young Readers 2017 314 p. $16.95

Grades: 4 5 6 7 **Fic**

1. Runaways -- Fiction 2. Criminals -- Fiction 3. Voyages and travels -- Fiction 4. Great Britain -- History -- George I, 1714-1727 -- Fiction

ISBN 9781616205645

LC 2016042923

In this novel, by Avi, "in the seaside town of Melcombe Regis, England, 1724, Oliver Cromwell Pitts wakes to find his father missing and his house flooded by a recent storm. . . . Oliver's father has left, . . . he's gone to London, where Oliver's sister, Charity, is in trouble. . . . Oliver flees, following the trail of his father and sister. The journey is full of thieves, adventurers, and treachery--and London might be the most dangerous place of all." (Publisher's note)

"An ingeniously plotted Dickensian story filled with suspense, surprises, and ultimately satisfaction." Booklist.

Followed by:

The end of the world and beyond (2019)

Axelrod, Amy

Your friend in fashion, Abby Shapiro. Holiday House 2011 261p il $17.95

Grades: 4 5 6 **Fic**

1. Editors 2. Socialites 3. Letters -- Fiction 4. Spouses of presidents 5. Family life -- Fiction 6. Massachusetts -- Fiction 7. Fashion designers -- Fiction 8. Jews -- United States -- Fiction

ISBN 978-0-8234-2340-8; 0-8234-2340-9

LC 2010-24185

Beginning in 1959, Abby, nearly eleven, writes a series of letters to Jackie Kennedy, each with sketches of outfits she has designed, as she faces family problems, concerns about neighbors, and her own desperate desire for both her first bra and a Barbie doll.

"Abby is an especially memorable protagonist, but all [Axelrod's] characters vibrate with life. . . . Funny, lively, sensitive—a real winner." Kirkus

Ayres, Katherine

Macaroni boy. Delacorte Press 2003 182p hardcover o.p. pa $5.99

Grades: 5 6 7 8 **Fic**

1. School stories 2. Great Depression, 1929-1939 -- Fiction

ISBN 0-385-73016-0; 0-440-41884-4 pa

LC 2002-6768

In Pittsburgh in 1933, sixth-grader Mike Costa notices a connection between several strange occurrences, but the only way he can find out the truth about what's happening is to be nice to the class bully. Includes historical facts

"Actual places and events are interwoven with a heartwarming story of a close-knit family facing difficult times." Voice Youth Advocates

North by night; a story of the Underground Railroad. Delacorte Press 1998 176p hardcover o.p. pa $4.99

Grades: 6 7 8 9 **Fic**

1. Slavery -- Fiction 2. Underground railroad -- Fiction

ISBN 0-385-32564-9; 0-440-22747-x pa

LC 98-10039

Presents the journal of Lucinda, a sixteen-year-old girl whose family operates a stop on the Underground Railroad

This "is an absorbing tale. Ayres slips in a lot of evocative detail about the hard work of running a farm and a household before the Civil War, as well as some rather charming musing about kissing and its myriad effects on the psyche." Booklist

Azad, Nafiza

The **candle** and the flame; Nafiza Azad. Scholastic Press 2019 391 p. (hardback) $18.99

Grades: 8 9 10 11 **Fic**

1. Good and evil 2. Magic -- Fiction 3. Spirits -- Fiction 4. Identity (Psychology) -- Fiction 5. Genies -- Fiction 6. Identity -- Fiction 7. Silk Road -- Fiction 8. Good and evil -- Fiction 9. Jinn -- Fiction

ISBN 9781338306057; 9781338306040

LC 2018041274

In this novel, by Nafiza Azad, "Fatima lives in the city of Noor, a thriving stop along the Silk Road. There the music of myriad languages fills the air, and people of all faiths weave their lives together. . . . But when one of the most potent of the Ifrit dies, Fatima is changed in ways she cannot fathom. . . . Oud in hand, Fatima is drawn into the intrigues of the maharajah and his sister, the affairs of Zulfikar and the djinn, and the dangers of a magical battlefield." (Publisher's note)

"Azad combines Islamic concepts and Middle Eastern mythology with a variety of other traditions to create a magical treatise on identity, community, friendship, and love. Readers will identify with female characters who struggle against limiting societal expectations. The themes of trauma and grief are treated with care. Azad's vivid depiction of the details of Noor's sights and sounds make the city come alive." SLJ.

Babbitt, Natalie, 1932-2016

The **moon** over High Street; Natalie Babbitt. Scholastic 2012 148 p. (alk. paper) $15.95

Grades: 3 4 5 6 7 **Fic**

1. Family -- Fiction 2. Friendship -- Fiction 3. Decision making -- Fiction 4. Adopted children -- Fiction

ISBN 054537636X; 9780545376365

LC 2011926886

This children's novel by Natalie Babbitt "presents 12-year-old Joe. . . . Orphaned shortly after his birth, Joe, who loves the moon, has been raised by his Gran, but after she breaks a hip, he's sent to spend some of the summer with his father's cousin. . . . In nearly idyllic Midville, . . . he inadvertently comes to the attention of the very wealthy factory owner Mr. Boulderwall . . . who decides that he will adopt Joe and raise him to take over his company." (Kirkus)

★ **Tuck** everlasting. Farrar, Straus & Giroux 1975 139p $16; pa $6.99

Grades: 5 6 7 8 **Fic**

1. Fantasy fiction

ISBN 0-374-37848-7; 0-312-36981-6 pa

"Doomed to - or blessed with - eternal life after drinking from a magic spring, the Tuck family wanders about trying to live as inconspicuously and comfortably as they can. When ten-year-old Winnie Foster stumbles on their secret, the Tucks take her home and explain why living forever at one age is less a blessing that it might seem. Complications arise when Winnie is followed by a stranger who wants to market the spring water for a fortune." (Publisher's note)

Baccalario, Pierdomenico

Ring of fire; translated by Leah D. Janeczko; illustrations by Iacopo Bruno. Random House 2009 293p il (Century quartet) $16.99; lib bdg $19.99

Grades: 5 6 7 8 **Fic**

1. Italy -- Fiction 2. Rome (Italy) -- Fiction 3. Good and evil -- Fiction

ISBN 978-0-375-85895-6; 0-375-85895-4; 978-0-375-95895-3 lib bdg; 0-375-95895-9 lib bdg

LC 2009-08204

Original Italian edition, 2006

Four seemingly unrelated children are brought together in a Rome hotel where they discover that they are destined to become involved in a deep and ancient mystery involving a briefcase full of artifacts that expose them to great danger

"There are some genuinely exciting moments and the premise is intriguing." Publ Wkly

Other titles in this series are:

Star of Stone (2010)

City of Wind (2011)

Dragon of Seas (2012)

Bacigalupi, Paolo

★ The **drowned** cities; by Paolo Bacigalupi. Little, Brown and Company 2012 448p. paperback $11.00

Grades: 9 10 11 12 **Fic**

1. Science fiction 2. Apocalyptic fiction 3. Refugees -- Fiction 4. War -- Fiction 5. Orphans -- Fiction 6. Soldiers -- Fiction 7. Survival -- Fiction 8. Conduct of life -- Fiction 9. Genetic engineering -- Fiction

ISBN 9780316056243; 9780316056229 paperback

LC 2011031762

This book takes place "[i]n a dark future America where violence, terror, and grief touch everyone, young refugees Mahlia and Mouse have managed to leave behind the war-torn lands of the Drowned Cities by escaping into the jungle outskirts. But when they discover a wounded half-man--a bioengineered war beast named Tool--who is being hunted by a vengeful band of soldiers, their fragile existence quickly collapses." (Publisher's note)

★ **Ship** Breaker; Bacigalupi, Paolo. Little, Brown and Co. 2010 326p $17.99

Grades: 8 9 10 11 12 **Fic**

1. Science fiction 2. Recycling -- Fiction

ISBN 0316056219; 9780316056212

LC 2009-34424

National Book Award Finalist: Young People's Literature (2010)

Printz Award (2011)

In a futuristic world, teenaged Nailer scavenges copper wiring from grounded oil tankers for a living, but when he finds a beached clipper ship with a girl in the wreckage, he has to decide if he should strip the ship for its wealth or rescue the girl.

"Bacigalupi's cast is ethnically and morally diverse, and the book's message never overshadows the storytelling, action-packed pacing, or intricate world-building. At its core, the novel is an exploration of Nailer's discovery of the nature of the world around him and his ability to transcend that world's expectations." Publ Wkly

Other titles in this series are:

The Drowned Cities (2012)

Tool of War (2017)

Tool of war; Paolo Bacigalupi. Little, Brown & Co. 2017 377 p. (Ship breaker) (hardcover) $17.99

Grades: 8 9 10 11 12 **Fic**

1. Soldiers -- Fiction 2. Obedience -- Fiction 3. Genetic engineering -- Fiction 4. Science fiction 5. Survival -- Fiction

ISBN 9780316220835; 9780316364775

LC 2016051846

In this book in the Ship Breaker series, by Paolo Bacigalupi, "Tool, a half-man/half-beast designed for combat, is capable of so much more than his creators had ever dreamed. . . . But he is hunted relentlessly by someone determined to destroy him, who knows an alarming secret: Tool has found the way to resist his genetically ingrained impulses of submission and loyalty toward his masters..." (Publisher's note)

"Tool is at center stage at last as readers move through Bacigalupi's exploration of the intricate relationships connecting hunter and prey, master and enslaved, human and monster. Masterful." Kirkus

Zombie baseball beatdown; by Paolo Bacigalupi. Little, Brown and Co. 2013 304 p. $17

Grades: 5 6 7 8 **Fic**

1. Zombies -- Fiction 2. Packing-houses -- Fiction 3. Hispanic Americans -- Fiction 4. East Indian Americans -- Fiction 5. Racially mixed people -- Fiction

ISBN 0316220787; 9780316220781

LC 2012041463

In this book, middle school friends "Rabi, Miguel, and Joe literally smell trouble wafting from their small town's meatpacking plant, where they find cows living in filthy conditions and behaving oddly. Then the boys' baseball coach turns up moaning 'Brainsssss!' and tries to bite Rabi. When the children discover that meat from the sick cows is being packaged and sent to local supermarkets, they are on their own to prevent a zombie cow apocalypse because no one believes their story." (School Library Journal)

Baggott, Julianna

The **Prince** of Fenway Park. HarperCollinsPublishers 2009 322p $16.99; lib bdg $17.89

Grades: 4 5 6 7 **Fic**

1. Orphans -- Fiction 2. Baseball -- Fiction 3. Supernatural -- Fiction 4. Father-son relationship -- Fiction 5. Fenway Park (Boston, Mass.) -- Fiction 6. Boston Red Sox (Baseball team) -- Fiction

ISBN 978-0-06-087242-7; 0-06-087242-X; 978-0-06-087243-4 lib bdg; 0-06-087243-8 lib bdg

LC 2008-19666

In the fall of 2004, twelve-year-old Oscar Egg is sent to live with his father in a strange netherworld under Boston's Fenway Park, where he joins the fairies, pooka, banshee, and other beings that are trapped there, waiting for someone to break the eighty-six-year-old curse that has prevented the Boston Red Sox from winning a World Series

"Both whimsical and provocative (the 'N' word crops up in some historical references), this story will engage readers who like clever tales, and also those who enjoy chewing over controversial themes." SLJ

Bailey, Kristin

Legacy of the clockwork key; by Kristin Bailey. Simon Pulse 2013 416 p. (alk. paper) $17.99

Grades: 7 8 9 10 **Fic**

1. Inventions 2. Love -- Fiction 3. Science fiction 4. Orphans -- Fiction 5. Secret societies -- Fiction 6. London (England) -- History -- 19th century -- Fiction 7. Great Britain -- History -- Victoria, 1837-1901 -- Fiction

ISBN 1442440260; 9781442440265

LC 2011049871

In this book, "a teen girl unravels the mysteries of a secret society and their most dangerous invention. . . . When a fire consumes Meg's home, killing her parents . . . all she has left is the tarnished pocket watch she rescued from the ashes. But this is no ordinary timepiece. The clock turns out to be a mechanical key--a key that only Meg can use--which unlocks a series of deadly secrets and intricate clues that Meg has no choice but to follow." (Publisher's note)

Other titles in the series include:

Rise of the Arcane Fire (2014)

Shadow of the War Machine (2015)

Baker, Matthew

If you find this; by Matthew Baker. Little, Brown & Co. 2015 368 p. illustrations (hardcover) $17

Grades: 4 5 6 7 **Fic**

1. Old age -- Fiction 2. Heirlooms -- Fiction 3. Friendship -- Fiction 4. Grandfathers -- Fiction 5. Lost and found possessions -- Fiction

ISBN 0316240087; 9780316240086

LC 2013044749

In this book, by Matthew Baker, "Nicholas is a math and music genius with no friends and a huge problem: His father has lost his job, and they'll have to sell their house, which holds the only memory Nicholas has of his younger brother. Just in time, Nicholas's senile grandfather arrives, filled with tales of priceless treasure he has hidden somewhere in town--but where?" (Publisher's note)

"The vivid setting, complex characters, and original writing style result in a story with lasting impact. Reminiscent of Louis Sachar's Holes (1998), this is a rich, captivating tale about family and redemption that redefines the meaning of treasure." Booklist

Baldwin, James

Go tell it on the mountain. Knopf 1953 303p $15.95; pa $6.99

Grades: 8 9 10 11 12 Adult **Fic**

1. Family life -- Fiction 2. African Americans -- Fiction 3. Harlem (New York, N.Y.) -- Fiction

ISBN 0-679-60154-6; 0-440-33007-6 pa

This novel is an "autobiographical story of a Harlem child's relationship with his father against the background of his being saved in the pentecostal church." Benet's Reader's Ency of Am Lit

Balliett, Blue

★ **Chasing** Vermeer; illustrated by Brett Helquist. Scholastic Press 2004 254p il $16.95

Grades: 5 6 7 8 **Fic**

1. Artists 2. Painters 3. Mystery fiction 4. Art -- Fiction

ISBN 0-439-37294-1

LC 2002-152106

When seemingly unrelated and strange events start to happen and a precious Vermeer painting disappears, eleven-year-olds Petra and Calder combine their talents to solve an international art scandal.

Balliett's purpose "seems to be to get children to think—about relationships, connections, coincidences, and the subtle language of artwork. . . . [This is] a book that offers children something new upon each reading. . . . Helquist . . . outdoes himself here, providing an interactive mystery in his pictures." Booklist

Other titles about Petra and Calder are:

The Wright 3 (2006)

The Calder game (2008)

★ The **Danger** Box. Scholastic Press 2010 306p $16.99
Grades: 5 6 7 8 **Fic**

1. Naturalists 2. Travel writers 3. Diaries -- Fiction 4. Writers on science 5. Antiques -- Fiction 6. Michigan -- Fiction 7. Family life -- Fiction 8. Grandparents -- Fiction

ISBN 978-0-439-85209-8; 0-439-85209-9

LC 2010-16622

In small-town Michigan, twelve-year-old Zoomy and his new friend Lorrol investigate the journal found inside a mysterious box and find family secrets and a more valuable treasure, while a dangerous stranger watches and waits.

"This highly satisfying story will enlighten readers even as it inspires them to think about their own danger boxes." SLJ

★ **Hold** fast; by Blue Balliett. Scholastic Press 2013 288 p. (jacketed hardcover) $17.99
Grades: 3 4 5 6 **Fic**

1. Theft -- Fiction 2. Mystery fiction 3. Smuggling -- Fiction 4. Kidnapping -- Fiction 5. Chicago (Ill.) -- Fiction 6. Missing persons -- Fiction 7. Homeless persons -- Fiction 8. Mystery and detective stories

ISBN 0545299888; 9780545299886

LC 2012041035

This book focuses on "the Pearl family: Dash, Summer, 11-year-old Early, and the little Jubie. Do they have a lot? Well, yes, they have Dash's love of words, their devotion to each other, and their dream: to have a home. Trying to help that dream along, Dash, a page at the Chicago Public Library, makes extra money inventorying a private collection of old books. One . . . day, Dash disappears, and the family must move to a shelter after an odd robbery sees their . . . apartment destroyed." (Booklist)

Pieces and players; Blue Balliett ; [edited by] David Levithan. Scholastic Press 2015 320 p. illustrations $17.99
Grades: 5 6 7 8 **Fic**

1. Mystery fiction 2. Art thefts -- Fiction 3. Art museums -- Fiction

ISBN 054529990X; 9780545299909

LC 2014947736

In this children's book, by Blue Balliett, "thirteen extremely valuable pieces of art have been stolen from one of the most secretive museums in the world. A Vermeer has vanished. A Manet is missing. And nobody has any idea where they and the other eleven artworks might be . . . or who might have stolen them. . . . Calder, Petra, and Tommy are no strangers to heists and puzzles. Now they've been matched with two new sleuths -- Zoomy . . . and Early." (Publisher's note)

"This time it's a small family museum and 13 missing pieces of art providing the mystery that brings back characters met in previous titles. Tommy, Petra, and Calder are joined by Early Pearl and Zoomy Chamberlain. With all five kids led by their teacher Mrs. Hussey, each of the detective's special skills add to their understanding and help them arrive at the solution. Fans of the previous books will be delighted as these characters continue with their familiar predilections such as Calder's pentominoes clacking in his pockets. . . . Fun and engaging; a fitting addition for readers addicted to these art mysteries." SLJ

Baltazar, Armand

Diego and the Rangers of the Vastlantic; Armand Baltazar. Katherine Tegen Books, an imprint of HarperCollinsPublishers 2016 624 p. (hardback) $19.99
Grades: 5 6 7 8 **Fic**

1. Father-son relationship -- Fiction 2. Science fiction 3. Rescues -- Fiction 4. Friendship -- Fiction 5. Fathers and sons -- Fiction

ISBN 9780062402363

LC 2016013199

This book in the Timeless series, by Armand Baltazar, "explores a world painted new by the Time Collision. . . . This is the world Diego Ribera was born into. The past, present, and future coexisting together. . . . On his thirteenth birthday, Diego learns of a special gift he has within. . . . When his father, New Chicago's top engineer, is taken by the Aeternum, Diego must rescue him and prevent this evil group from disrupting the fragile peace humanity has forged." (Publisher's note)

Bancks, Tristan

Mac Slater hunts the cool. Simon & Schuster Books for Young Readers 2010 203p $15.99
Grades: 6 7 8 9 **Fic**

1. School stories 2. Beaches -- Fiction 3. Weblogs -- Fiction 4. Australia -- Fiction 5. Video recording -- Fiction

ISBN 978-1-4169-8574-7; 1-4169-8574-3

LC 2009-00152

Mac, an Australian youth, has one week to prove that he can be a "coolhunter," identifying emerging trends and posting images on a website, but he is competing against a classmate on whom he has a crush and dealing with resistance from his best friend and his own confusion over what "cool" means.

"Mac is a likable character who will appeal to a wide range of readers." Booklist

Followed by: Mac Slater vs. the city (2011)

Bannen, Megan

The **bird** and the blade; Megan Bannen. Harpercollins Childrens Books 2018 432 p. $17.99
Grades: 7 8 9 10 11 12 **Fic**

1. Riddles -- Fiction 2. Secrecy -- Fiction 3. Slavery -- Fiction 4. Kings and rulers -- Fiction

ISBN 0062674153; 9780062674159

In this novel, by Megan Bannen, "enslaved in Kipchak Khanate, Jinghua has lost everything: her home, her family, her freedom . . . until the kingdom is conquered by enemy forces and she finds herself an unlikely conspirator in the escape of Prince Khalaf and his . . . father across the vast Mongol Empire. . . . Jinghua hatches a scheme to use the Kipchaks' exile to return home, a plan that becomes increasingly fraught as her feelings for Khalaf evolve into an impossible love." (Publisher's note)

Bao, Karen

Dove arising; Karen Bao. Viking Books for Young Readers 2015 324 p. (Dove Chronicles) hardcover $17.99
Grades: 7 8 9 10 **Fic**

1. Space colonies 2. Militia movements -- Fiction 3. Children of prisoners -- Fiction 4. Moon -- Fiction 5. Science fiction 6. Youths' writings 7. Space colonies -- Fiction 8. Government, Resistance to -- Fiction

ISBN 0451469011; 9780451469014; 9780451476289

LC 2013041198

"Phaet Theta has lived her whole life in a colony on the Moon. She's barely spoken since her father died in an accident nine years ago. She cultivates the plants in Greenhouse 22, lets her best friend talk for her, and stays off the government's radar. Then her mother is arrested. The only way to save her younger siblings from the degrading Shelter is by enlisting in the Militia, the faceless army that polices the Lunar bases and protects them from attacks by desperate Earth dwellers. Training is brutal, but it's where Phaet forms an uneasy but meaningful alliance with the preternaturally accomplished Wes, a fellow outsider. Rank high, save her siblings, free her mom: that's the plan. Until Phaet's logically ordered world begins to crumble." (Publisher's note)

Other titles in this series are:
Dove exiled (2016)
Dove alight (2017)

Baptiste, Tracey

The **jumbies**; Tracey Baptiste. Algonquin Young Readers 2015 240 p. $15.95

Grades: 4 5 6 7 **Fic**

1. Supernatural -- Fiction 2. Imaginary creatures -- Fiction 3. Horror stories 4. Magic -- Fiction 5. Spirits -- Fiction 6. Caribbean Area -- Fiction 7. Blacks -- Caribbean Area -- Fiction

ISBN 1616204141; 9781616204143

LC 2014038605

In this children's novel by Tracey Baptiste "Corinne La Me . . . knows that jumbies aren't real; they're just creatures parents make up to frighten their children. Corinne begins to notice odd occurrences. She spots a beautiful stranger speaking to the town witch. Then this same beauty, called Severine, turns up at Corinne's house. Bewitching Corinne's father is the first step in Severine's plan to claim the entire island for the jumbies. Corinne must call on . . . ancient magic to stop Severine." (Publisher's note)

Another title in this series is:
Rise of the jumbies (2017)

Rise of the jumbies; Tracey Baptiste. Algonquin Young Readers 2017 266 p. (hardcover) $16.95

Grades: 4 5 6 7 **Fic**

1. Friendship -- Fiction 2. Caribbean region -- Fiction 3. Missing children -- Fiction 4. Horror stories 5. Spirits -- Fiction 6. Caribbean Area -- Fiction 7. Blacks -- Caribbean Area -- Fiction

ISBN 9781616207649; 9781616206659

LC 2017020557

Sequel to: The Jumbies (2015)

In this book, by Tracey Baptiste, "Corinne LaMer defeated the wicked jumbie Severine months ago, but things haven't exactly gone back to normal in her Caribbean island home. Everyone knows Corinne is half-jumbie, and many of her neighbors treat her with mistrust. When local children begin to go missing, snatched from the beach and vanishing into wells, suspicious eyes turn to Corinne." (Publisher's note)

"Baptiste allows her characters to find and create ways to grapple with uncomfortable truths. A stirring and mystical tale sure to keep readers thinking past the final page." Kirkus

Bardugo, Leigh

★ **King** of scars; Leigh Bardugo. Imprint 2019 528 p. (hardcover) $19.99

Grades: 8 9 10 11 12 **Fic**

1. Magic -- Fiction 2. Demonology -- Fiction 3. Kings and rulers -- Fiction

ISBN 9781250142276; 9781250142283

LC 2018944972

In this book in the King of Scars Duology series, by Leigh Bardugo, "the dashing young king, Nikolai Lantsov, has always had a gift for the impossible. No one knows what he endured in his country's bloody civil war--and he intends to keep it that way. Now, as enemies gather at his weakened borders, Nikolai must find a way to refill Ravka's coffers, forge new alliances, and stop a rising threat to the once-great Grisha Army." (Publisher's note)

Ruin and rising; Leigh Bardugo. Henry Holt and Co. 2014 432 p. (Grisha trilogy) (hardback) $18.99

Grades: 8 9 10 11 12 **Fic**

1. Fantasy fiction 2. Princes -- Fiction 3. Love stories

ISBN 080509461X; 9780805094619

LC 2013049306

In this young adult fantasy novel by Leigh Bardugo, part of the Grisha Trilogy, "Deep in an ancient network of tunnels and caverns, a weakened Alina must submit to the dubious protection of the Apparat and the zealots who worship her as a Saint. Yet her plans lie elsewhere, with the hunt for the elusive firebird and the hope that an outlaw prince still survives." (Publisher's note)

"Alina and company have only one hope: if they can kill the Firebird, its magical bones can be used to break the Darkling's chokehold on Ravka. In this concluding volume, Alina must rely on her childhood friend Mal's preternatural tracking ability. Bardugo's longstanding theme of "power corrupts" is developed organically; the magic she invents will surprise and delight readers." Horn Book

Shadow and bone; Leigh Bardugo. Henry Holt 2012 358 p. (Grisha trilogy) (hc) $17.99

Grades: 8 9 10 11 **Fic**

1. Fantasy fiction 2. Magic -- Fiction 3. Folklore -- Russia 4. Monsters -- Fiction 5. Slavic mythology -- Fiction 6. Ability -- Fiction 7. Orphans -- Fiction

ISBN 0805094598; 9780805094596

LC 2011034012

In this young adult novel, "[Leigh] Bardugo draws inspiration from Russian and Slavic myth and culture to kick off her 'Grisha' trilogy. In the nation of Ravka, Alina Starkov is a junior cartographer's assistant in the army, while her best friend Mai is an expert tracker. When a perilous mission into the magically created Shadow Fold goes wrong, Mai is gravely wounded and Alina manifests the rare ability to summon light. Immediately recruited into the order of the magic-using Grisha, Alina is taken under the wing of its intimidating and powerful leader, the Darkling, and heralded as the potential destroyer of the Shadow Fold. As she navigates Grisha politics and uncovers well-hidden secrets, she realizes that the fate of the nation rests on her shoulders and she may be in grave danger." (Publishers Weekly)

Other titles in this series are:
Siege and storm (2013)
Ruin and rising (2014)

Siege and storm; Leigh Bardugo. 1st ed. Henry Holt and Co. 2013 448 p. (Grisha trilogy) (hardcover) $17.99

Grades: 8 9 10 11 12 **Fic**

1. Fantasy fiction 2. Russia -- Fiction 3. Monsters -- Fiction 4. Fantasy 5. Magic -- Fiction 6. Orphans -- Fiction

ISBN 0805094601; 9780805094602

LC 2012046361

This fantasy novel, by Leigh Bardugo, is book 2 of the "Grisha Trilogy." "Alina must try to make a life with Mal in an unfamiliar land, all while keeping her identity as the Sun Summoner a secret. But she can't outrun her past or her destiny for long. The Darkling has emerged from the Shadow Fold with a terrifying new power and a dangerous plan that will test the very boundaries of the natural world." (Publisher's note)

Wonder Woman; Warbringer. Leigh Bardugo. Random House 2017 369 p. (DC icons) (hardback) $18.99

Grades: 6 7 8 9 10 **Fic**

1. Bildungsromans 2. Brothers and sisters -- Fiction 3. Female

friendship -- Fiction
ISBN 9780399549731; 9780399549748; 9780399549755
LC 2016044698

In this first book in the DC Icons series, by Leigh Bardugo, "Diana longs to prove herself to her legendary warrior sisters. But when the opportunity finally comes, she throws away her chance at glory and breaks Amazon law--risking exile--to save a mere mortal. Even worse, Alia Keralis is no ordinary girl and with this single brave act, Diana may have doomed the world." (Publisher's note)

"Bardugo breathes zippy new life into the story with a twisty plot, whip-smart characters, and her trademark masterful writing." Booklist

Barker, M. P.

Mending horses; by M.P. Barker. Holiday House 2014 309 p. (hardcover) $17.95
Grades: 5 6 7 8 **Fic**
1. Orphans -- Fiction 2. Prejudices -- Fiction 3. Child abuse -- Fiction 4. Irish Americans -- Fiction 5. Peddlars -- Fiction 6. Sex role -- Fiction 7. New England -- History -- 1775-1865 -- Fiction
ISBN 0823429482; 9780823429486
LC 2013019208

In this book, by M.P. Barker, "Daniel Linnehan is an indentured servant no more. He has his papers, his beloved horse, Ivy, and a new direction in life. But an Irish teenager, wearing fine clothes and riding an even finer horse, is asking for trouble. After a terrible misunderstanding leaves Daniel beaten, the peddler Jonathan Stocking takes Daniel under his wing. But Billy, another Irish youngster traveling with Mr. Stocking, is not thrilled that the two must work together." (Publisher's note)

Barnaby, Hannah

Wonder show; by Hannah Barnaby. Houghton Mifflin Books for Children 2012 viii, 274 p.p $16.99
Grades: 7 8 9 10 11 12 **Fic**
1. Carnivals -- Fiction 3. Orphanages -- Fiction 4. Runaway children -- Fiction 5. Fathers -- Fiction 5. Depressions -- 1929 -- United States -- Fiction
ISBN 0547599803; 9780547599809
LC 2011052426

William C. Morris Award Finalist (2013)

In this book by Hannah Barnaby, "Portia Remini, 13 . . . escapes . . . from the McGreavey Home for Wayward Girls to search for her father. . . . She joins a carnival. . . . On the lam from sinister 'Mister,' who runs McGreavey's, Portia learns the stories of some of the carnival's strange troupe. . . . But . . . when Mister's dragnet closes in, Portia decides that to find the answers she seeks she must return to the horror of The Home." (School Library Journal)

Barnes, Jennifer

The **Squad** : killer spirit; [by] Jennifer Lynn Barnes. 1st Laurel-Leaf ed.; Laurel Leaf Books 2008 324p pa $6.99
Grades: 7 8 9 10 **Fic**
1. School stories 2. Spies -- Fiction 3. Computers -- Fiction 4. Cheerleading -- Fiction
ISBN 978-0-385-73455-4
LC 2007017733

Sequel to: The Squad: perfect cover (2008)

As if it were not bad enough that sophomore computer hacker Toby Klein has to be a cheerleader to be part of the elite group of government operatives called the Squad, now she is part of the Homecoming court and has agreed to attend the dance with the most popular boy in school.

The **Squad** : perfect cover. Delacorte Press 2008 275p pa $6.99
Grades: 7 8 9 10 **Fic**
1. School stories 2. Spies -- Fiction 3. Computers -- Fiction 4. Cheerleading -- Fiction
ISBN 978-0-385-73454-7 pa; 0-385-73454-9 pa
LC 2007-09352

High school sophomore Toby Klein enjoys computer hacking and wearing combat boots, so she thinks it is a joke when she is invited to join the cheerleading squad but soon learns cheering is just a cover for an elite group of government operatives known as the Squad.

"In addition to offering crafty plotting and time-honored, typical teen conflicts and rivalries, Barnes maintains a sharp sense of humor in this action-adventure series." Bull Cent Child Books

Another title in this series is:
The Squad: killer spirit (2008)

Barnhill, Kelly Regan

★ The **girl** who drank the moon; Kelly Barnhill. Algonquin Young Readers 2016 400 p. $16.95
Grades: 5 6 7 8 **Fic**
1. Magic -- Fiction 2. Witches -- Fiction 3. Friendship -- Fiction 4. Friendship in children -- Fiction
ISBN 9781616205676; 1616205679
LC 2016006542

Newbery Medal (2017)

In this book, by Kelly Barnhill, "every year, the people of the Protectorate leave a baby as an offering to the witch who lives in the forest. They hope this sacrifice will keep her from terrorizing their town. But the witch in the Forest, Xan, is kind. She shares her home with a wise Swamp Monster and a Perfectly Tiny Dragon. Xan rescues the children and delivers them to welcoming families on the other side of the forest, nourishing the babies with starlight on the journey." (Publisher's note)

"The swiftly paced, highly imaginative plot draws a myriad of threads together to form a web of characters, magic, and integrated lives. Spiritual overtones encompass much of the storytelling with love as the glue that holds it all together." SLJ

★ The **mostly** true story of Jack; by Kelly Barnhill. Little, Brown 2011 323p il $16.99
Grades: 5 6 7 8 **Fic**
1. Iowa -- Fiction 2. Magic -- Fiction 3. Friendship -- Fiction 4. Family life -- Fiction
ISBN 978-0-316-05670-0; 0-316-05670-7
LC 2010044934

Jack is practically invisible at home, but when his parents send him to Hazelwood, Iowa, to spend a summer with his odd aunt and uncle, he suddenly makes friends, is beaten up by the town bully, and is plotted against by the richest man in town.

"A truly splendid amalgamation of mystery, magic and creeping horror will spellbind the middle-grade set. . . . The mystery deepens with each chapter, revealing exactly the right amount with each step. Answers are doled out so meticulously that readers will be continually intrigued rather than frustrated. The result is the ultime page-turner." Kirkus

★ The **witch's** boy; Kelly Barnhill. Algonquin Young Readers 2014 384 p. $16.95
Grades: 5 6 7 8 **Fic**
1. Fantasy 2. Magic -- Fiction 3. Twins -- Fiction 4. Witches -- Fiction 5. Brothers -- Fiction 6. Friendship -- Fiction 7. Robbers

and outlaws -- Fiction
ISBN 9781616203511

LC 2014014704

In this juvenile fantasy novel, by Kelly Regan Barnhill, "when Ned and his identical twin brother tumble from their raft into a raging river, only Ned survives. Villagers are convinced the wrong boy lived. But when a Bandit King comes to steal the magic Ned's mother, a witch, is meant to protect, it's Ned who safeguards the magic and summons the strength to protect his family and community." (Publisher's note)

"The writing is beautiful and lyrical, but keeps pace with an action-packed story. Powerful themes of grief, redemption, forgiveness, sacrifice, and generosity are all present." VOYA

Barnholdt, Lauren

Girl meets ghost; by Lauren Barnholdt. Aladdin 2013 224 p. (alk. paper) $15.99

Grades: 4 5 6 7 **Fic**

1. Dead -- Fiction 2. Ghosts -- Fiction 3. Schools -- Fiction 4. Middle schools -- Fiction 5. Psychic ability -- Fiction 6. Mystery and detective stories

ISBN 1442442468; 9781442442467

LC 2012032234

In this children's story, by Lauren Barnholt, "a tween girl becomes a reluctant medium. . . . There's an old saying that 'dead men tell no tales'--but that saying is definitely not true. Just ask twelve-year-old Kendall Williams, who can't get dead people to stop talking to her. . . . It's pretty frustrating being able to hear and see people that no one else can. . . . But Kendall is going to have to learn how to deal, because the only way to quiet the dead is to help them." (Publisher's note)

Sometimes it happens. Simon Pulse 2011 312p $16.99

Grades: 7 8 9 10 **Fic**

1. School stories 2. Dating (Social customs) -- Fiction

ISBN 978-1-4424-1314-6; 1-4424-1314-X

With help from her best friend Ava and Ava's boyfriend Noah, Hannah is recovering from being dumped by her boyfriend Sebastian, but on the first day of their senior year in high school, Ava learns that Hannah and Noah betrayed her while she was away.

"The writing style is smooth, featuring believable dialogue and first-person narration from Hannah's perspective. Hannah is a sympathetic character struggling with a relatable dilemma of liking your friend's significant other, yet wanting to be a faithful friend. The underlying message is captured by the title, Sometimes It Happens, as Hannah grows to understand that part of being human is hurting people without meaning to and then needing to ask for forgiveness." Voice Youth Advocates

Barratt, Mark

Joe Rat. Eerdmans Books for Young Readers 2009 307p pa $9

Grades: 7 8 9 10 **Fic**

1. Crime -- Fiction 2. Orphans -- Fiction 3. Mental illness -- Fiction 4. London (England) -- Fiction 5. Great Britain -- History -- 19th century -- Fiction

ISBN 978-0-8028-5356-1; 0-8028-5356-0

LC 2008055972

First published 2008 in the United Kingdom

In the dark, dank sewers of Victorian London, a boy known as Joe Rat scrounges for valuables which he gives to "Mother," a criminal mastermind who considers him a favorite, but a chance meeting with a runaway girl and "the Madman" transforms all their lives.

"The unraveling of the Madman's identity is but one of the pleasures of Barratt's leisurely and convincing historical fiction." Booklist

Followed by: The wild man (2010)

The **wild** man. Eerdmans Books for Young Readers 2010 341p pa $9

Grades: 7 8 9 10 **Fic**

1. Crime -- Fiction 2. Fathers -- Fiction 3. Orphans -- Fiction 4. Social classes -- Fiction 5. London (England) -- Fiction 6. Impostors and imposture -- Fiction 7. Great Britain -- History -- 19th century -- Fiction

ISBN 978-0-8028-5377-6 pa; 0-8028-5377-3 pa

LC 2010010937

Sequel to: Joe Rat (2009)

In Victorian England, Joe Rat has escaped the clutches of the criminal mastermind, Mother, and is trying to make an honest living in a better part of London, but when a rich philanthropist tracks down a man claiming to be Joe's missing father—a British army deserter—he must determine where his loyalties lie.

"Barratt writes as if he is keeping an adjacent berth to Dickens; here's hoping scrappy Joe has a few more tricks up his ratty sleeves." Booklist

Barrett, Tracy

The **100** -year-old secret. Henry Holt and Co. 2008 157p (The Sherlock files) $15.95

Grades: 4 5 6 7 **Fic**

1. Mystery fiction 2. Siblings -- Fiction 3. Great Britain -- Fiction

ISBN 978-0-8050-8340-8; 0-8050-8340-5

LC 2007034004

Xena and Xander Holmes, an American brother and sister living in London for a year, discover that Sherlock Holmes was their great-great-great grandfather when they are inducted into the Society for the Preservation of Famous Detectives and given his unsolved casebook, from which they attempt to solve the case of a famous missing painting

"The main characters are observant, bright, and gifted with powers of deduction." SLJ

Other titles in this series are:

The beast of Blackslope (2009)

The case that time forgot (2010)

The missing heir (2011)

The **Beast** of Blackslope. Henry Holt 2009 174p $15.99

Grades: 4 5 6 7 **Fic**

1. Mystery fiction 2. Siblings -- Fiction 3. Great Britain -- Fiction

ISBN 978-0-8050-8341-5; 0-8050-8341-3

LC 2008036941

Xena and Xander Holmes, an American brother and sister spending a year in England, use clues in their ancestor Sherlock Holmes' casebook as they try to solve the mystery of a monster threatening a peaceful country village where a documentary film is being made.

"Xena's methodical and calm rationality balances with Xander's intuitive imaginativeness so that they complement one another." SLJ

The **case** that time forgot. Henry Holt and Company 2010 158p (The Sherlock files) $15.99

Grades: 4 5 6 7 **Fic**

1. Mystery fiction 2. Siblings -- Fiction 3. Great Britain -- Fiction

ISBN 978-0-8050-8046-9; 0-8050-8046-5

"American kids living in London with their parents, Xena and Xander are not just the descendants of Sherlock Holmes. They have his notebook of unsolved cases, and they're not afraid to use it. . . . After a classmate of Egyptian descent asks for help finding an ancient amulet, the young sleuths spring into action. . . . The third mystery in the Sherlock

Files series will please fans intrigued by ancient Egypt, codes, danger, and the tantalizing possibility of magic." Booklist

King of Ithaka. Henry Holt and Company 2010 261p map $16.99
Grades: 7 8 9 10 **Fic**

1. Classical mythology -- Fiction 2. Odysseus (Greek mythology) -- Fiction
ISBN 978-0-8050-8969-1; 0-8050-8969-1

LC 2009-50770

Sixteen-year-old Telemachos and his two best friends leave their life of privilege to undertake a quest to find Telemachos's father Odysseus. "Grades six to ten." (Bull Cent Child Books)

"The exotic climes and vivid descriptions . . . give the story a sense of immediacy and color." Booklist

The **Stepsister's** Tale; by Tracy Barrett. Harlequin Books 2014 272 p. $16.99
Grades: 7 8 9 10 **Fic**

1. Romance fiction 2. Stepsisters -- Fiction 3. Poor 4. Fantasy 5. Stepfamilies 6. Fantasy fiction
ISBN 037321121X; 9780373211210

In this novel, by Tracy Barrett, "Jane Montjoy is tired of . . . pretending to live up to the standards of her mother's noble family--especially now that the family's wealth is gone. . . . When her stepfather suddenly dies, leaving nothing but debts and a bereaved daughter behind, it seems to Jane that her family is destined for eternal unhappiness. But a mysterious boy from the woods and an invitation to a royal ball are certain to change her fate." (Publisher's note)

"Sometimes it feels like fairy-tale retellings are a dime a dozen, and this is certainly not the first or the last account of a misunderstood antagonist. But, Barrett's comparably quiet account of a household of women working to survive together as a family, sometimes in spite of one another, shines with soft, bucolic realism...Overall, this is an enjoyable read. The inclusion of discussion questions in the back makes it a solid choice for book clubs." VOYA

Barron, T. A.

The **book** of magic; illustrated by August Hall. Philomel Books 2011 il (Merlin) $17.99 **Fic**

1. Fantasy fiction 2. Magic -- Fiction 3. Merlin (Legendary character) -- Fiction
ISBN 978-0-399-24741-5; 0-399-24741-6

LC 2011013552

A compendium of maps, character descriptions, magical terms, timelines, and other tidbits from the author's Merlin saga.

"Guides to long-running series have two important jobs. They should remind fans of all the things they particularly love about the books, and they should whet the appetites of newcomers, thus creating more fans. Barron's guide to his 12-book saga about Merlin succeeds in both objectives." SLJ

Doomraga's revenge. Philomel Books 2009 238p map (Merlin's dragon) $19.99
Grades: 6 7 8 9 **Fic**

1. Fantasy fiction 2. Magic -- Fiction 3. Dragons -- Fiction
ISBN 978-0-399-25212-9; 0-399-25212-6

LC 2008055872

Sequel to: Merlin's dragon (2008)

The dragon Basil, now grown mighty in strength, size, and courage, addresses and seeks the cause of a new series of crises that threaten the stability of Avalon, while his friend Merlin is distracted by problems with his son, Krystallus.

"No one can compare to Barron when writing about Merlin or Avalon. Once again, he brings texture, color, and love to the seven realms. His many fans will gobble up this . . . offering." SLJ

Followed by: Ultimate magic (2010)

The **fires** of Merlin. Philomel Bks. 1998 261p $20.99; pa $5.99
Grades: 5 6 7 8 **Fic**

1. Fantasy fiction 2. Merlin (Legendary character) -- Fiction
ISBN 0-399-23020-3; 0-441-00957-3 pa

LC 97-49561

Sequel to: The seven songs of Merlin (1997)

This is the third volume in the trilogy about Merlin's youth. Having voyaged to the Otherworld in his quest to find himself, the young wizard Merlin must face fire in many different forms and deal with the possibility of losing his own magical power

This "saga just keeps getting richer in characterization, ambience, and Celtic lore." Booklist

Followed by: the mirror of Merlin (1999)

★ The **lost** years of Merlin. Philomel Bks. 1996 326p pa $7.99; $19.99
Grades: 5 6 7 8 **Fic**

1. Fantasy fiction 2. Merlin (Legendary character) -- Fiction
ISBN 9780441006687 pa; 9780399230189

LC 96-33920

"A boy, hurled on the rocks by the sea, regains consciousness unable to remember anything—not his parents, not his own name. He is sure that the secretive Branwen is not his mother, despite her claims, and that Emrys is not his real name. The two soon find themselves feared because of Branwen's healing abilities and Emrys' growing powers. . . . Barron has created not only a magical land populated by remarkable beings but also a completely magical tale, filled with ancient Celtic and Druidic lore, that will enchant readers." Booklist

Other titles in this series are:
The seven songs of Merlin (1997)
The fires of Merlin (1998)
The mirror of Merlin (1999)
The wings of Merlin (2000)

Merlin's dragon. Philomel Books 2008 305p (Merlin's dragon) $19.99
Grades: 6 7 8 9 **Fic**

1. Fantasy fiction 2. Magic -- Fiction 3. Dragons -- Fiction
ISBN 978-0-399-24750-7; 0-399-24750-5

LC 2008-2469

Basil, a small, flying lizard who is searching for others like himself, discovers that there is more to him than he knows, as he becomes engaged in Avalon's great war between the evil Rhita Gawr and the forces of good.

"Basil is an appealing, complex character. . . . This first book in a new series will captivate readers already familiar with the fantasist's Merlin chronicles." Booklist

Other titles in this series are:
Doomraga's revenge (2009)
Utlimate magic (2010)

The **mirror** of Merlin. Philomel Bks. 1999 245p il $20.99; pa $7.99

Grades: 5 6 7 8 **Fic**

1. Fantasy fiction 2. Merlin (Legendary character)
ISBN 0-399-23455-1; 0-441-00846-1 pa

LC 99-13043

Sequel to: The fires of Merlin (1998)

This is the fourth volume in the author's series about Merlin's youth. Through adventures involving a haunted marsh, talking trees, and the creature called the ballymag, the young wizard Merlin continues to experience both his growing powers and his essential humanity

"With lots of surprises and some laugh-out-loud humor to leaven the palpable feeling of doom, this should be eagerly devoured by the saga's fans." Booklist

Followed by: The wings of Merlin (2000)

The **seven** songs of Merlin. Philomel Bks. 1997 306p $19.99; pa $7.99

Grades: 5 6 7 8 **Fic**

1. Fantasy fiction 2. Merlin (Legendary character) -- Fiction
ISBN 0-399-23019-X; 0-441-00701-5 pa

LC 97-9619

Sequel to: The lost years of Merlin (1996)

This is the second volume in the author's series about Merlin's youth. Having stumbled upon his hidden powers, the young wizard Merlin voyages to the Otherworld in his quest to find himself and the way to the realm of the spirit

"The tale is spellbinding (pun intended), and readers will relish not only the action and the well-crafted setting but also Merlin's growth from a callow youth to a wiser, more caring wizard-in-training." Booklist

Followed by: The fires of Merlin (1998)

Ultimate magic. Philomel Books 2010 223p (Merlin's dragon) $19.99

Grades: 6 7 8 9 **Fic**

1. Fantasy fiction 2. Magic -- Fiction 3. Dragons -- Fiction
ISBN 978-0-399-25217-4; 0-399-25217-7

LC 2009041645

Sequel to: Doomraga's revenge (2008)

The dragon Basilgarrad leads the ultimate battle to save the land of Avalon, and finally must decide whether to obey his dear friend Merlin's request, even though it means giving up his powers as a warrior.

"The many fans of Barron's various Merlin sagas will not be disappointed." Booklist

The **wings** of Merlin. Philomel Books 2000 352p $21.99; pa $7.99

Grades: 5 6 7 8 **Fic**

1. Fantasy fiction 2. Merlin (Legendary character) -- Fiction
ISBN 0-399-23456-X; 0-441-00988-3 pa

LC 00-27553

Sequel to: The mirror of Merlin (1999)

Merlin's fragile home on the isle of Fincayra is threatened by the attack of a mysterious warrior with swords for arms and by the escape of Stangmar from his imprisonment, as Merlin continues to move toward his ultimate destiny.

"Barron brings his Lost Years of Merlin saga to a resounding, satisfying close with this fifth volume." Booklist

Barrow, Randi G.

Saving Zasha; by Randi Barrow. Scholastic Press 2011 229p $16.99

Grades: 4 5 6 7 **Fic**

1. Dogs -- Fiction 2. Russia -- Fiction 3. Journalists -- Fiction 4. Single parent family -- Fiction 5. World War, 1939-1945 -- Fiction
ISBN 978-0-545-20632-7; 0-545-20632-4

LC 2010-16899

In 1945 Russia, those who own German shepherds are considered traitors, but thirteen-year-old Mikhail and his family are determined to keep the dog a dying man brought them, while his classmate Katia strives to learn his secret.

"Mikhail's sense of humor, concern for his family, and love of Zasha are all readily apparent in his narration, which smoothly incorporates background information for readers unfamiliar with 20th-century Russian life and history. . . . Barrow's novel is quick reading yet weighty, and captures the prejudices and aftereffects of war." Publ Wkly

Barry, Dave, 1947-

The **bridge** to Never Land; [by] Dave Barry and Ridley Pearson. Disney/Hyperion 2011 438p $18.99

Grades: 5 6 7 **Fic**

1. Fairy tales 2. Adventure fiction
ISBN 978-1-4231-3865-5; 1-4231-3865-1

Sequel to: Peter and the Sword of Mercy

"Bringing the Starcatchers series into the twenty-first century, this novel features Sarah and her brother, Aidan, who find a cryptic note in an antique desk and follow the clues to London, Princeton, and Orlando. Along the way, they clash with evil Lord Ombra, find an ally in Molly Darling's great-great-great nephew, and discover Einstein's part in the plan. The plot is a thrill ride of action and adventure, with plenty of chase scenes and (no surprise here) a trip to Never Land." Booklist

Peter & the shadow thieves; by Dave Barry and Ridley Pearson; illustrations by Greg Call. Disney Editions/Hyperion Books for Children 2006 556p il $18.99

Grades: 5 6 7 **Fic**

1. Fairy tales 2. Adventure fiction
ISBN 0-7868-3787-X

LC 2005-56033

Sequel to Peter and the starcatchers (2004)

Realizing that Molly and the other Starcatchers are in danger when the sinister being Lord Ombra visits the island and seems to control people through their shadows, Peter and Tinker Bell travel to England to help save the stardust. "Age ten and up." (N Y Times Book Rev)

This "is filled with enough rollicking, death-defying adventure to satisfy anyone." SLJ

Followed by Peter and the secret of Rundoon (2007)

Peter and the secret of Rundoon; by Dave Barry and Ridley Pearson; illustrations by Greg Call. Disney Editions/Hyperion Books for Children 2007 482p il $18.99

Grades: 5 6 7 **Fic**

1. Fairy tales 2. Adventure fiction
ISBN 0-7868-3788-8; 978-0-7868-3788-5

LC 2007006306

Sequel to Peter and the shadow thieves (2006)

Fearing that the sinister Lord Ombra was not destroyed, Peter and Molly travel to the land of Rundoon, which is ruled by the evil King Zarboff.

"This is a fun, intense, and totally worthwhile adventure." SLJ

Followed by Peter and the Sword of Mercy (2009)

Peter and the starcatchers; by Dave Barry and Ridley Pearson; illustrations by Greg Call. Hyperion 2004 451p il $17.99; pa $7.99
Grades: 5 6 7 **Fic**

1. Fairy tales 2. Adventure fiction 3. Pirates -- Fiction
ISBN 0-7868-5445-6; 0-7868-4907-X pa

LC 2004-55275

Soon after Peter, an orphan, sets sail from England on the ship Never Land, he befriends Molly, a young Starcatcher, whose mission is to guard a trunk of magical stardust from a greedy pirate and the native inhabitants of a remote island. "Age ten and up." (N Y Times Book Rev)

"The authors plait multiple story lines together in short, fast-moving chapters. . . . Capitalizing on familiar material, this adventure is carefully crafted to set the stage for Peter's later exploits. This smoothly written page-turner just might send readers back to the original." SLJ

Other titles in this series are:
Peter and the shadow thieves (2006)
Peter and the secret of Rundoon (2007)
Peter and the sword of mercy (2009)
The bridge to Never Land (2011)

Peter and the Sword of Mercy; by Dave Barry and Ridley Pearson; illustrations by Greg Call. Disney/Hyperion Books 2009 515p il $18.99
Grades: 5 6 7 **Fic**

1. Fairy tales 2. Adventure fiction
ISBN 978-1-4231-2134-3; 1-4231-2134-1

Sequel to: Peter and the secret of Rundoon (2007)

James, one of Peter's original Lost Boys, is now working for Scotland Yard and suspects that the heir to England's throne, Prince Albert Edward, is under the influence of shadow creatures who are after starstuff hidden in an underground vault which has only one key: the Sword of Mercy.

"This adventure is fast and intense, and readers will feel compelled to find out what happens next." VOYA

Followed by: The bridge to Never Land (2011)

The **worst** class trip ever; Dave Barry. First edition Disney-Hyperion Books 2015 214 p. illustrations, map $13.99
Grades: 5 6 7 **Fic**

1. Field trips -- Fiction 2. Terrorism -- Prevention -- Fiction 3. Washington (D.C.) -- Description and travel 4. Humorous stories 5. Terrorism -- Fiction 6. Conduct of life -- Fiction 7. Washington (D.C.) -- Fiction 8. School field trips -- Fiction
ISBN 1484708490; 9781484708491

LC 2014013171

"On a class trip to Washington, DC, eighth grader Wyatt Palmer and his best friend Matt believe that they have uncovered a terrorist plot. During a scuffle with these passengers, Matt removes an odd device from one man's backpack. This event gets Matt and Wyatt into trouble with their teacher. For the rest of their trip, Wyatt, Matt, and a few more of their classmates . . . avoid bad guys, sneak away from the rest of their class, and conceal the whole situation from their chaperones." (Publisher's note)

"With its wacky humor and mildly suspenseful scenarios, this appealing book will be a good fit for most libraries." SLJ

Another title in this series is:
The worst night ever (2016)

Bartlett, Claire Eliza

★ **We** rule the night; Claire Eliza Bartlett. Little, Brown and Co. 2019 400 p. (hardcover) $17.99
Grades: 8 9 10 11 12 **Fic**

1. War stories 2. Magic -- Fiction 3. Air pilots -- Fiction 4. Fantasy 5. War -- Fiction 6. Women air pilots -- Fiction
ISBN 0316417270; 9780316417273

LC 2018022805

In this book, by Claire Eliza Bartlett, "the richly textured world, painted in snow and fire, filled with disparate, diverse people who all want to win the war, is background to a powerful, slow burning story that develops Linné and Revna's reluctant friendship, their growing understanding of the world, and their emerging identities as soldiers who may not entirely trust the country they are willing to die for." (Kirkus Reviews)

"Rich characterizations and an enemy that, while it looms in the background, never feels quite as threatening as the country the girls are fighting for complete a story set against the bright, brutal backdrop of war. A breathless series starter from a new voice to watch." Booklist

Bartoletti, Susan Campbell

★ The **boy** who dared. Scholastic Press 2008 202p $16.99
Grades: 5 6 7 8 **Fic**

1. Courage -- Fiction 2. Underground leaders 3. National socialism -- Fiction 4. Germany -- History -- 1933-1945 -- Fiction
ISBN 0-439-68013-1; 978-0-439-68013-4

LC 2007014166

In October, 1942, seventeen-year-old Helmuth Hübener, imprisoned for distributing anti-Nazi leaflets, recalls his past life and how he came to dedicate himself to bringing the truth about Hitler and the war to the German people.

Bartoletti "does and excellent job of conveying the political climate surrounding Hitler's ascent to power, seamlessly integrating a complex range of socioeconomic conditions into her absorbing drama." Publ Wkly

Barwin, Steven

Hardball; Steven Barwin. Orca Book Publishers 2014 192 p. (Orca sports) (pbk.) $9.95
Grades: 7 8 9 10 **Fic**

1. Cousins -- Fiction 2. Baseball -- Fiction 3. School sports -- Fiction 4. Hazing 5. Cousins 6. Baseball players
ISBN 1459804414; 9781459804418; 9781459804425; 9781459804432

LC 2014935389

"Griffin has college in his sights and plans to land himself a baseball scholarship. His determination causes him to turn a blind eye to the hazing of new players by the team captain, Wade. But when Griffin senses that his cousin Carson is getting the brunt of Wade's aggression, Griffin finally stands up to him." (Publisher's note)

"Short, fast-paced chapters keep the narrative moving with a mix of baseball play-by-plays and sleuthing. A drug-dealing subplot adds a layer of suspense and raises the stakes well beyond troubles on the ball field. Ideal for reluctant readers, this book's gritty undertones will appeal to the intended high/low audience of sports fans." Booklist

Barzak, Christopher

The **gone** away place; Christopher Barzak. Alfred A. Knopf 2018 295 p. (hardcover) $17.99
Grades: 7 8 9 10 **Fic**

1. Ghost stories 2. Dead -- Fiction 3. Tornadoes -- Fiction 4. Family life -- Fiction 5. Ohio -- Fiction 6. Memory -- Fiction 7. Friendship -- Fiction 8. Family life -- Ohio -- Fiction 9. Dating (Social customs) -- Fiction
ISBN 9780399556098; 9780399556104

LC 2017044047

In this book, by Christopher Barzak, "since the day when a rash of powerful tornadoes touched down in Newfoundland, Ohio--killing more than half of the students in . . . [Ellie's] school, . . . she's been haunted: by the ghosts of her best friends. . . . [Then] a chance encounter with one ghost leads Ellie to discover a way to free the spirits that have been lingering since the storm, and she learns that she's not the only one seeing the ghosts--it's a town-wide epidemic." (Publisher's note)

Bashardoust, Melissa

Girls made of snow and glass; Melissa Bashardoust. Flatiron Books 2017 375 p. (hardback) $18.99

Grades: 7 8 9 10 **Fic**

1. Fantasy fiction 2. Magic -- Fiction 3. Stepmothers -- Fiction 4. Queens -- Fiction 5. Mothers and daughters -- Fiction

ISBN 9781250077745; 9781250077738

LC 2017022388

In this book, by Melissa Bashardoust, "at sixteen, Mina's mother is dead, her magician father is vicious, and her silent heart has never beat with love for anyone. . . . Fifteen-year-old Lynet looks just like her late mother, and one day she discovers why. . . . [The book] traces the relationship of two young women doomed to be rivals from the start. Only one can win all, while the other must lose everything--unless both can find a way to reshape themselves and their story." (Publisher's note)

"Compellingly flawed characters, vivid world building, and pitch-perfect pacing make this utterly superb." Booklist

Baskin, Nora Raleigh, 1961-

All we know of love. Candlewick Press 2008 201p $16.99

Grades: 6 7 8 9 10 **Fic**

1. Mothers -- Fiction 2. Loss (Psychology) -- Fiction 3. Voyages and travels -- Fiction

ISBN 978-0-7636-3623-4; 0-7636-3623-1

LC 2007-22396

Natalie, almost sixteen, sneaks away from her Connecticut home and takes the bus to Florida, looking for the mother who abandoned her father and her when she was ten years old.

"Baskin takes a familiar story line and examines it in a new and interesting way that will engage readers." Voice Youth Advocates

★ **Anything** but typical. Simon & Schuster Books for Young Readers 2009 195p il $15.99

Grades: 4 5 6 7 **Fic**

1. School stories 2. Autism -- Fiction 3. Authorship -- Fiction 4. Family life -- Fiction

ISBN 1416963782; 9781416963783

LC 2008-20994

ALA Schneider Family Book Award Honor Book (2010)

Jason, a twelve-year-old who wants to become a writer, relates what life is like as he tries to make sense of his world. "Grades six to nine." (Bull Cent Child Books)

"This is an enormously difficult subject, but Baskin, without dramatics or sentimentality, makes it universal." Booklist

Nine, ten; a September 11 story. Nora Raleigh Baskin. Atheneum Books for Young Readers 2016 208 p. (hardcover) $16.99

Grades: 4 5 6 7 8 **Fic**

1. Middle schools -- Fiction 2. September 11 terrorist attacks, 2001 -- Fiction

ISBN 9781442485068; 9781442485075

LC 2015011934

This book, by Nora Raleigh Baskin, presents a "look at the days leading up to the tragic events of September 11, 2001, and how that day impacted the lives of four middle schoolers. . . . Sergio . . . is struggling to come to terms with the absentee father he hates. . . . Will's father is gone, too, killed in a car accident. . . . Naheed has never before felt uncomfortable about being Muslim. . . . Aimee is starting a new school in a new city and missing her mom." (Publisher's note)

"Adults may be chilled by key names and places and what they portend, but children may gain a small sense of the magnitude of the changes that day wrought on our world. Tense, disturbing, and thought-provoking." Kirkus

Ruby on the outside; Nora Raleigh Baskin. First edition Simon & Schuster Books for Young Readers 2015 176 p. (hardcover) $16.99

Grades: 4 5 6 7 8 **Fic**

1. Aunts -- Fiction 2. Friendship -- Fiction 3. Best friends -- Fiction 4. Prisoners' families -- Fiction 5. Mothers and daughters -- Fiction

ISBN 1442485035; 9781442485037; 9781442485044

LC 2014018268

In this novel, by Nora Raleigh Baskin, "Ruby's mom is in prison, and to tell anyone the truth is to risk true friendship. . . . Eleven-year-old Ruby Danes is about to start middle school, and only her aunt knows her deepest, darkest, most secret secret: her mother is in prison. Then Margalit Tipps moves into Ruby's condo complex, and the two immediately hit it off. Ruby thinks she's found her first true-blue friend--but can she tell Margalit the truth about her mom?" (Publisher's note)

"This lyrical novel explores multiple aspects of the effects of incarceration on family—guilt, fear, anger, loneliness, and heavy responsibility. Baskin's plot structure, which flows from the present to periodic flashbacks, keeps the story from being unbearably dark. Margalit may be too good to be true, but she is just what the doctor ordered for Ruby's healing." Booklist

Runt; Nora Raleigh Baskin. Simon & Schuster Books for Young Readers 2013 208 p. (hardback) $15.99

Grades: 5 6 7 8 **Fic**

1. School stories -- Fiction 2. Female friendship -- Fiction 3. Dogs -- Fiction 4. Schools -- Fiction 5. Bullying -- Fiction 6. Popularity -- Fiction 7. Middle schools -- Fiction 8. Online social networks -- Fiction

ISBN 1442458070; 9781442458079; 9781442458086

LC 2012049461

This book shows "the day-to-day torments of students in a sixth-grade class. In a series of brief vignettes, [Nora Raleigh Baskin] moves between classmates including 'Smelly-Girl' Elizabeth, who can't shake the lingering scent (or shed hair) of her mother's dog-sitting business; Elizabeth's nemesis, Maggie, who . . . hasn't been able to repair her fallout with her artistically talented former best friend Freida; and Stewart and Matthew, two athletes whose rivalry leads to a fight." (Publishers Weekly)

★ The **summer** before boys. Simon & Schuster Books for Young Readers 2011 196p $15.99

Grades: 6 7 8 **Fic**

1. Girls -- Fiction 2. Friendship -- Fiction 3. Dating (Social customs) -- Fiction

ISBN 978-1-4169-8673-7; 1-4169-8673-1

LC 2010045688

Twelve-year-old best friends and relatives, Julia and Eliza are happy to spend the summer together while Julia's mother is serving in the National Guard in Iraq but when they meet a neighborhood boy, their close relationship begins to change.

"A poignant story of children on the homefront and the ways that a first love can break up longtime friendships and change things forever." Booklist

The **truth** about my Bat Mitzvah. Simon & Schuster Books for Young Readers 2008 138p $15.99; pa $5.99
Grades: 5 6 7 8 **Fic**

1. Jews -- Fiction 2. Bat mitzvah -- Fiction 3. Grandmothers -- Fiction
ISBN 978-1-4169-3558-2; 1-4169-3558-4; 978-1-4169-7469-7 pa; 1-4169-7469-5 pa

LC 2007-01248

After her beloved grandmother, Nana, dies, non-religious twelve-year-old Caroline becomes curious about her mother's Jewish ancestry.

"Readers will identify with Caroline and her preoccupations. . . . This quick read will be a hit with preteens contemplating their own identities." Booklist

Bass, Karen, 1962-

Graffiti knight. Orca Book Publishers 2014 272 p. $14.95
Grades: 7 8 9 10 **Fic**

1. Graffiti -- Fiction 2. Family life -- Fiction 3. Communist countries -- Fiction 4. Resistance to government -- Fiction
ISBN 1927485533; 9781927485538

In this book, "after a childhood cut short by war and the harsh strictures of Nazi Germany, sixteen-year-old Wilm is finally tasting freedom. . . . It's dangerous, of course, to be sneaking out at night to leave messages on police buildings. But it's exciting, too, and Wilm feels justified, considering his family's suffering. Until one mission goes too far, and Wilm finds he's endangered the very people he most wants to protect." (Publisher's note)

"Just as Ruta Sepetys revealed a different perspective of the Holocaust in Between Shades of Gray (2011), Bass introduces another view of history unknown to many American readers...This eye-opening story shows that war's end is never tidy." (Booklist)

Bassoff, Leah

★ **Lost** Girl Found; by Leah Bassoff and Laura DeLuca. Pgw 2014 192 p. maps $16.95
Grades: 6 7 8 9 10 **Fic**

1. Refugees -- Fiction 2. Mother-daughter relationship -- Fiction 3. Sudan -- History -- Civil War, 1983-2005 -- Fiction
ISBN 1554984165; 9781554984169

LC bl2014008921

In this book, by Leah Bassoff and Laura DeLuca, "Poni . . . [lives in a] small village in southern Sudan. . . . Then the war comes and there is only one thing for Poni to do. Run. . . . [She is] driven by the sheer will to survive and the hope that she can . . . make it to the Kakuma refugee camp in Kenya. . . . In Kakuma she is almost overwhelmed by the misery that surrounds her. Poni realizes that she must leave the camp at any cost. Her destination is a compound in Nairobi." (Publisher's note)

"After her southern Sudan village is bombed, Poni arrives at a Kenyan refugee camp, where conditions are brutal. Poni wants to finish her education, and she has a chance to do so when she escapes the refugee camp. Poni is a fully realized and sympathetic character. This fast-paced novel covers a lot of ground and incorporates a good deal of historical background." Horn Book

Bastedo, Jamie

On thin ice. Red Deer Press 2006 348p pa $10.95
Grades: 8 9 10 11 12 **Fic**

1. Inuit -- Fiction 2. Polar bear -- Fiction 3. Arctic regions -- Fiction 4. Greenhouse effect -- Fiction
ISBN 978-0-88995-337-6; 0-88995-337-6

"Set in the remote Arctic village of Nanurtalik, this novel follows Ashley as she journeys on the shaman path chosen for her through the Inuit line of her father. Disturbed by haunting—sometimes frightening—dreams of a gigantic polar bear that seems bent on destroying her, Ashley furiously draws her dreams onto paper, capturing the very essence of the bear within. . . . This novel is told with richness of language, culture, and emotion, but its sense of place sparkles brightest." Voice Youth Advocates

Followed by: Sila's revenge (2010)

Basye, Dale E.

Heck; where the bad kids go. by Dale E. Basye; illustrated by Bob Dob. Random House 2008 304p il $16.99; lib bdg $19.99
Grades: 5 6 7 8 **Fic**

1. School stories 2. Siblings -- Fiction 3. Future life -- Fiction
ISBN 978-0-375-84075-3; 0-375-84075-3; 978-0-375-94075-0 lib bdg; 0-375-94075-8 lib bdg

LC 2007-8379

When timid Milton and his older, scofflaw sister Marlo die in a marshmallow bear explosion at Grizzly Mall, they are sent to Heck, an otherworldly reform school from which they are determined to escape.

"The author's umpteen clever allusions—characters' eternal fates are decided by standardized 'Soul Aptitude Tests'; Mr. R. Nixon teaches ethics to evildoers in room 1972—make this book truly sparkle." Publ Wkly

Other titles in this series are:
Rapacia: the second circle of Heck (2009)
Blimpo: the third circle of Heck (2010)
Fibble: the fourth circle of Heck (2011)

Bateson, Catherine

★ **Being** Bee. Holiday House 2007 126p il $16.95; pa $7.95
Grades: 4 5 6 **Fic**

1. Australia -- Fiction 2. Family life -- Fiction 3. Guinea pigs -- Fiction 4. Father-daughter relationship -- Fiction
ISBN 978-0-8234-2104-6; 0-8234-2104-X; 978-0-8234-2208-1 pa; 0-8234-2208-9 pa

LC 2006-101561

Bee faces friction at home and at school when her widowed father begins seriously dating Jazzi, who seems to take over the house and their lives, but as shared secrets and common interests finally begin to draw them together, Jazzi accidentally makes a terrible mistake.

"Bee's emotions are perspectives are honest and clearly presented. . . . She is a likable, believable character." SLJ

Magenta McPhee. Holiday House 2010 170p $16.95
Grades: 4 5 6 7 **Fic**

1. Australia -- Fiction 2. Authorship -- Fiction 3. Single parent family -- Fiction 4. Dating (Social customs) -- Fiction 5. Father-daughter relationship -- Fiction
ISBN 978-0-8234-2253-1; 0-8234-2253-4

LC 2009-10854

First published 2009 in Australia

Thinking her father needs a new interest in his life after he is laid-off of work, teenaged Magenta, who envisions herself as a future fantasy author, decides to dabble in matchmaking which brings unexpected results.

"With a personality as colorful as her name, Bateson's . . . eponymous heroine has a narrative voice that is smart, wry, and down-to-earth. . . . This [is a] real and ultimately reassuring story." Publ Wkly

Battle, Craig

Camp average; Craig Battle. Owlkids Books 2019 240 p. (Camp average) (hardcover) $16.95

Grades: 4 5 6 7 8 **Fic**

1. Sports -- Fiction 2. Camps -- Fiction 3. Friendship -- Fiction

ISBN 9781771473057

LC 2018946402

In this book in the Camp Average series, by Craig Battle, "a group of 11-year-olds arrives to spend six weeks playing sports at Camp Avalon--which they affectionately call Camp Average, because they never win at any sport. And that's the way they like it. But this summer, new camp director Winston--who hates losing--has some hyper-competitive ideas about how to improve their performance, whether they want to or not!" (Publisher's note)

"Hilarious, irreverent, and timely, highly recommended for sports fans, summer-camp alums, and preteen-years survivors." Kirkus

Baucom, Ian

Through the skylight; a Venice tale. Ian Baucom. 1st ed. Atheneum Books for Young Readers 2013 400 p. ill. (hardcover) $17.99

Grades: 5 6 7 8 **Fic**

1. Fantasy fiction 2. Time travel -- Fiction 3. Venice (Italy) -- Fiction 4. Italy -- Fiction 5. Magic -- Fiction 6. Americans -- Italy -- Fiction 7. Mystery and detective stories 8. Brothers and sisters -- Fiction

ISBN 1416917772; 9781416917779

LC 2012010642

In this juvenile novel, by Ian Baucom, illustrated by Justin Gerard, "when Jared, Shireen, and Miranda are each given one glittering gift from an old Venetian shopkeeper, they never fathom the powers they are now able to unleash. . . . For in another time, centuries earlier, another trio . . . have been kidnapped and, along with hundreds of other children, will be sold into child slavery. Unless, that is, they can find some way to save them all." (Publisher's note)

"Frequent black-and-white illustrations support the narrative. Baucom's familiarity with the setting and use of Italian words heighten the atmosphere. . . . The mix of protagonists' genders, historical details, and interesting magic creates a story with broad appeal and a message about the power of words. . ." SLJ

Bauer, A. C. E.

★ **Come** Fall. Random House 2010 231p $15.99; lib bdg $18.99

Grades: 4 5 6 7 **Fic**

1. School stories 2. Crows -- Fiction 3. Fairies -- Fiction 4. Friendship -- Fiction 5. Foster home care -- Fiction

ISBN 978-0-375-85825-3; 0-375-85825-3; 978-0-375-95855-7 lib bdg; 0-375-95855-X lib bdg

LC 2009-32419

Drawn together by a mentoring program and an unusual crow, middle school misfits Salman, Lu, and Blos form a strong friendship despite teasing by fellow students and the maneuverings of fairies Oberon, Titania, and Puck.

"Weaving in magic, dreams, doubles, contrasts, and other elements from the original play, Bauer spins an enticing variant." Booklist

No castles here. Random House 2007 270p $15.99; lib bdg $18.99

Grades: 4 5 6 7 **Fic**

1. Magic -- Fiction 2. New Jersey -- Fiction 3. Choirs (Music) -- Fiction 4. Books and reading -- Fiction 5. City and town life -- Fiction

ISBN 978-0-375-83921-4; 978-0-375-93921-1 lib bdg

LC 2006023601

Eleven-year-old Augie Boretski dreams of escaping his rundown Camden, New Jersey, neighborhood, but things start to turn around with help from a Big Brother, a music teacher, and a mysterious bookstore owner, so when his school is in trouble, he pulls the community together to save it

This is a "heartwarming novel." Booklist

Bauer, Joan

Almost home; by Joan Bauer. Viking 2012 264 p. (hardcover) $16.99

Grades: 5 6 7 8 **Fic**

1. Pets -- Fiction 2. Homeless persons -- Fiction 3. Mother-daughter relationship -- Fiction 4. Mothers and daughters -- Fiction

ISBN 0670012890; 9780670012893

LC 2011050483

In this book by Joan Bauer, "when twelve-year-old Sugar's grandfather dies and her gambling father takes off yet again, Sugar and her mother . . . head to Chicago for a fresh start, only to discover that fresh starts aren't so easy to come by for the homeless. . . .With the help of a rescue dog . . . a foster family . . . and her own grace and good humor, Sugar comes to understand that while she can't control the hand life deals her, she can control how she responds." (Publisher's note)

Close to famous. Viking 2011 250p $16.99

Grades: 5 6 7 8 **Fic**

1. Baking -- Fiction 2. Literacy -- Fiction 3. Country life -- Fiction 4. West Virginia -- Fiction 5. Single parent family -- Fiction

ISBN 0-670-01282-3; 978-0-670-01282-4

LC 2010030022

Twelve-year-old Foster McFee and her mother escape from her mother's abusive boyfriend and end up in the small town of Culpepper, West Virginia, where they use their strengths and challenge themselves to build a new life, with the help of the friends they make there.

"Bauer skillfully brings readers to the heart of Culpepper with rich depictions of contemporary small town and its residents and rhythms." Publ Wkly

★ **Peeled**. G.P. Putnam's Sons 2008 256p $16.99

Grades: 6 7 8 9 10 **Fic**

1. Ghost stories 2. School stories 3. Farm life -- Fiction 4. Journalism -- Fiction 5. New York (State) -- Fiction

ISBN 978-0-399-23475-0; 0-399-23475-6

LC 2007-42835

In an upstate New York farming community, high school reporter Hildy Biddle investigates a series of strange occurrences at a house rumored to be haunted.

This is "a warm and funny story full of likable, offbeat characters led by a strongly voiced, independently minded female protagonist on her way to genuine, well-earned maturity." SLJ

Soar; Joan Bauer. Viking 2016 304 p. (hardcover) $16.99

Grades: 5 6 7 8 **Fic**

1. Baseball -- Coaching 2. Moving, Household -- Fiction 3. Adoption -- Fiction 4. Baseball -- Fiction 5. Teamwork (Sports)

-- Fiction 6. Heart -- Transplantation -- Fiction
ISBN 9780451470348; 0451470346

LC 2015013293

In this novel, by Joan Bauer, when Jeremiah is "told he can't play baseball following an operation on his heart, Jeremiah decides he'll do the next best thing and become a coach. Hillcrest, where Jeremiah and his father Walt have just moved, is a town known for its championship baseball team. But Jeremiah finds the town caught up in a scandal and about ready to give up on baseball. It's up to Jeremiah and his can-do spirit to get the town – and the team – back in the game." (Publisher's note)

"An outstanding, tender exploration of courage and the true nature of heroism and, for good measure, a fine homage to America's game, as well." Kirkus

Stand tall. Putnam 2002 182p $16.99; pa $6.99
Grades: 5 6 7 8 **Fic**

1. Divorce -- Fiction 2. Grandfathers -- Fiction
ISBN 0-399-23473-X; 0-14-240148-X pa

LC 2002-23876

Tree, a six-foot-three-inch twelve-year-old, copes with his parents' recent divorce and his failure as an athlete by helping his grandfather, a Vietnam vet and recent amputee, and Sophie, a new girl at school

The "swiftly paced story artfully blends poignant and outright funny moments, resulting in a triumphant tale that will resonate with many young readers." Publ Wkly

Bauer, Marion Dane

Little dog, lost; Marion Dane Bauer ; with illustrations by Jennifer Bell. Atheneum Books for Young Readers 2012 197 p. ill. (hardcover) $14.99
Grades: 4 5 6 7 **Fic**

1. Dogs -- Fiction 2. Picture books for children 3. Interpersonal relations -- Fiction 4. Novels in verse 5. Parks -- Fiction 6. Loneliness -- Fiction 7. City and town life -- Fiction
ISBN 1442434236; 9781442434233; 9781442434257

LC 2011034024

This book tells the tale of "three needy creatures." Buddy the dog is "re-homed with a clueless though kind woman" after her family moves; Mark "feels his life is empty without the dog he desperately needs but his mother won't permit"; and "Charles Larue, the aging caretaker of a nearby mansion . . . spends his lonely days waiting for something—anything—to bring meaning to his life." The story is written in "[l]ong, thin lines of free-verse text." Additionally, "black-and-white illustrations" are included. (Kirkus)

★ **On** my honor. Clarion Bks. 1986 90p $15
Grades: 4 5 6 7 **Fic**

1. Accidents -- Fiction
ISBN 0-89919-439-7

LC 86-2679

A Newbery Medal honor book, 1987

When his best friend drowns while they are both swimming in a treacherous river that they had promised never to go near, Joel is devastated and terrified at having to tell both sets of parents the terrible consequences of their disobedience

"Bauer's association of Joel's guilt with the smell of the polluted river on his skin is particularly noteworthy. Its miasma almost rises off the pages. Descriptions are vivid, characterization and dialogue natural, and the style taut but unforced. A powerful, moving book." SLJ

Bayard, Louis

★ **Lucky** strikes; Louis Bayard. Henry Holt & Co. 2016 320 p. (hardback) $16.99
Grades: 6 7 8 9 **Fic**

1. Orphans -- Fiction 2. Poverty -- Fiction 3. Siblings -- Fiction 4. Depressions -- 1929 -- Fiction 5. Virginia -- History -- 20th century -- Fiction 6. Brothers and sisters -- Fiction
ISBN 9781627793902

LC 2015023829

In this novel, by Louis Bayard, "with her mama recently dead and her pa sight unseen since birth, Amelia is suddenly in charge of her younger brother and sister--and of the family gas station. Harley Blevins . . . is in hot pursuit to clinch his fuel monopoly. To keep him at bay and keep her family out of foster care, Melia must come up with a father--and fast. And so when a hobo rolls out of a passing truck, Melia grabs opportunity by its beard." (Publisher's note)

"Her foible-ridden supporting cast features more adults than kids, and in an interesting twist, they give young readers insight into grown-up issues that transcend those usually found in youth books. Most of all, though, this is a darn good yarn with plenty of room for rooting and more than a few laughs." Booklist

Beasley, Cassie

Circus Mirandus; by Cassie Beasley. Dial Books for Young Readers, an imprint of Penguin Group (USA) Inc. 2015 304 p. (hardcover) $17.99
Grades: 4 5 6 **Fic**

1. Magic -- Fiction 2. Circus -- Fiction 3. Grandfathers -- Fiction 4. Sick -- Fiction 5. Orphans -- Fiction 6. Friendship -- Fiction 7. Great aunts -- Fiction
ISBN 0525428437; 9780525428435

LC 2014031463

In this novel by Cassie Beasley "even though his awful Great-Aunt Gertrudis doesn't approve, Micah believes in the stories his dying Grandpa Ephraim tells him of the magical Circus Mirandus: the invisible tiger guarding the gates . . . and the magician . . . the Man Who Bends Light. Finally, Grandpa Ephraim offers proof. The Circus is real. And the Lightbender owes Ephraim a miracle. Micah sets out to find the Circus and the man he believes will save his grandfather." (Publisher's note)

Beatty, Robert

Serafina and the Twisted Staff; Robert Beatty. Disney-Hyperion 2016 384 p. (hardback) $16.99
Grades: 5 6 7 **Fic**

1. Good and evil -- Fiction 2. Mystery fiction 3. Paranormal fiction 4. Horror stories 5. Identity -- Fiction 6. Supernatural -- Fiction 7. Shapeshifting -- Fiction 8. Biltmore Estate (Asheville, N.C.) -- Fiction
ISBN 9781484775035

LC 2016006654

Sequel to: Serafina and the black cloak

In this novel in the Serafina series by Robert Beatty, "Serafina finds herself caught between two worlds: she's too wild for Biltmore Estate's beautifully dressed ladies and formal customs, and too human to fully join her forest kin. Late one night, she encounters a strange and terrifying figure, and then she's attacked by the vicious wolfhounds under his control. . . . She's convinced that the stranger is not alone, that he has sent his accomplice into Biltmore in disguise." (Publisher's note)

"Even better than its predecessor, a sequel that delivers nonstop thrills from beginning to end." Kirkus

Beaty, Andrea

Dorko the magnificent; by Andrea Beaty. Amulet Books 2013 213 p. (hardcover) $16.95

Grades: 3 4 5 6 **Fic**

1. Magicians -- Fiction 2. Grandmothers -- Fiction 3. Humorous stories 4. Family life -- Fiction 5. Magic tricks -- Fiction
ISBN 1419706381; 9781419706387

LC 2012045674

In this book by Andrea Beaty "Robbie loves magic and he's good at it—sort of. When Grandma Melvyn moves in and takes over his room, Robbie discovers that she was once an internationally renowned magician and learns about the heartache that turned her into a bitter woman. Against all odds, Robbie and Grandma Melvyn form an uneasy alliance to show the world—or at least the kids of Hobson Elementary School—that he is a true magician." (Publisher's note)

Beaufrand, M. J.

★ **Useless** Bay; M. J. Beaufrand. Amulet Books 2016 240 p. (hardback) $17.95

Grades: 8 9 10 11 **Fic**

1. Mystery fiction 2. Islands -- Fiction 3. Family secrets -- Fiction 4. Brothers and sisters -- Fiction 5. Quintuplets -- Fiction 6. Missing children -- Fiction 7. Mystery and detective stories
ISBN 9781419721380

LC 2016007659

In this novel, by M.J. Beaufrand, "on Whidbey Island, the Gray quintuplets are the stuff of legend. . . . Together, they serve as an unofficial search-and-rescue team for the island, saving tourists and locals alike from the forces of wind and sea. But, when a young boy goes missing, the mysteries start to pile up. While searching for him, they find his mother's dead body instead—and realize that something sinister is in their midst." (Publisher's note)

"Short in length but long on atmosphere, it's a gripping mystery with a supernatural overlay that makes its setting all the more haunting. But it's the irresistible Gray quints, subject to their own rumors and local mythos, who steal the show. " Pub Wkly

Beck, Ian

The **secret** history of Tom Trueheart. Greenwillow Books 2007 341p il hardcover o.p. lib bdg $17.89; pa $6.99

Grades: 4 5 6 7 **Fic**

1. Fairy tales 2. Brothers -- Fiction 3. Storytelling -- Fiction
ISBN 978-0-06-115210-8; 0-06-115210-2; 978-0-06-115211-5 lib bdg; 0-06-115211-0 lib bdg; 978-0-06-115212-2 pa; 0-06-115212-9 pa

LC 2006043362

When young Tom Trueheart's seven older brothers all go missing during their adventures in the Land of Stories, he embarks on a perilous mission to save them and to capture the rogue story-writer who wants to do away with the heroes.

This "is a charming twist on fairy tales. . . . Silhouette drawings interspersed throughout add a wonderfully nostalgic touch." SLJ

Another title about Tom Trueheart is:
Tom Trueheart and the Land of Dark Stories (2008)

Tom Trueheart and the Land of Dark Stories. Greenwillow Books 2008 369p il $16.99; lib bdg $17.89

Grades: 4 5 6 7 **Fic**

1. Fairy tales 2. Brothers -- Fiction 3. Storytelling -- Fiction
ISBN 978-0-06-115213-9; 0-06-115213-7; 978-0-06-115214-6 lib bdg; 0-06-115214-5 lib bdg

"The Land of Dark Stories is guarded by the lighthouse of doom. Wolves and goblins patrol every forest and road. Here, the most frightening tales unfold. . . . When the villain Ormestone kidnaps Tom's six older brothers and their princess brides, Tom knows he must make the journey to the dark land." Publisher's note

Beckhorn, Susan Williams

The **wolf's** boy; by Susan Williams Beckhorn. Disney-Hyperion 2016 240 p. $16.99

Grades: 4 5 6 7 **Fic**

1. Wolves -- Fiction 2. Prehistoric peoples -- Fiction 3. Wilderness survival -- Fiction 4. Survival -- Fiction
ISBN 9781484725535

LC 2015016834

In this book, by Susan Williams Beckhorn, "Kai burns to become a hunter and to earn a rightful place among his people. But that can never be. He was born with a clubfoot. It is forbidden for him to use or even touch a hunter's sacred weapons. Shunned by the other boys, Kai turns to his true friends, the yellow wolves, for companionship. They have not forgotten the young human they nurtured as an abandoned infant." (Publisher's note)

"The bond between boy and canine—even one that's just learning to be a dog—is timeless, and animal-lovers in particular will be touched by this telling." Booklist

Bedford, Martyn

★ **Flip**. Wendy Lamb Books 2011 261p $16.99; lib bdg $19.99; ebook $10.99

Grades: 8 9 10 11 12 **Fic**

1. Supernatural -- Fiction 2. Great Britain -- Fiction
ISBN 978-0-385-73990-0; 0-385-73990-7; 978-0-385-90808-5 lib bdg; 0-385-90808-3 lib bdg; 978-0-375-89855-6 ebook; 0-375-89855-7 ebook

LC 2010-13158

A teenager wakes up inside another boy's body and faces a life-or-death quest to return to his true self or be trapped forever in the wrong existence.

"Bedford packs so much exhilarating action and cleanly cut characterizations into his teen debut that readers will be catapulted head-first into Alex's strange new world." Kirkus

Behar, Ruth

Lucky broken girl; Ruth Behar. Nancy Paulsen Books 2017 256 p. illustrations (hardback) $16.99

Grades: 5 6 7 8 **Fic**

1. Neighbors -- Fiction 2. Immigrants -- Fiction 3. Cuban Americans -- Fiction 4. Fractures -- Fiction 5. Family life -- New York (State) -- New York -- Fiction 6. Queens (New York, N.Y.) -- History -- 20th century -- Fiction
ISBN 9780399546440

LC 2016022378

Pura Belpré Award: Author (2018)

This novel, by Ruth Behar, is an "unforgettable multicultural coming-of-age narrative--based on the author's childhood in the 1960s--a young Cuban-Jewish immigrant girl is adjusting to her new life in New York City when her American dream is suddenly derailed. Ruthie's plight will intrigue readers, and her powerful story of strength and resilience, full of color, light, and poignancy, will stay with them for a long time." (Publisher's note)

Beil, Michael D.

The **Red** Blazer Girls: the mistaken masterpiece. Alfred A. Knopf 2011 309p $16.99; lib bdg $19.99

Grades: 5 6 7 8 **Fic**

1. School stories 2. Mystery fiction 3. Puzzles -- Fiction 4. Art thefts -- Fiction

ISBN 978-0-375-86740-8; 0-375-86740-6; 978-0-375-96740-5 lib bdg; 0-375-96740-0 lib bdg

LC 2010030006

Sophie and her friends, who call themselves The Red Blazer Girls, embark on solving a case involving mistaken identities, switched paintings, and some priceless family heirlooms.

"Sophie narrates with humor and self-effacing aplomb. Visual evidence inserted in the text invites reader participation." Kirkus

★ The **Red** Blazer Girls: the ring of Rocamadour. Alfred A. Knopf 2009 299p $15.99; lib bdg $18.99

Grades: 5 6 7 8 **Fic**

1. School stories 2. Mystery fiction 3. Puzzles -- Fiction 4. Friendship -- Fiction

ISBN 978-0-375-84814-8; 0-375-84814-2; 978-0-375-94814-5 lib bdg; 0-375-94814-7 lib bdg

LC 2008-25254

Catholic-schooled seventh-graders Sophie, Margaret, Rebecca, and Leigh Ann help an elderly neighbor solve a puzzle her father left for her estranged daughter twenty years ago.

"The dialogue is fast and funny, the clues are often solvable." Booklist

Other titles about the Red Blazer Girls are:

The Red Blazer Girls: the vanishing violin (2010)

The Red Blazer Girls: the mistaken masterpiece (2011)

The **Red** Blazer Girls: The vanishing violin. Alfred A. Knopf 2010 329p $16.99; lib bdg $19.99

Grades: 5 6 7 8 **Fic**

1. Mystery fiction 2. Violins -- Fiction

ISBN 978-0-375-86103-1; 0-375-86103-3; 978-0-375-96103-8 lib bdg; 0-375-96103-8 lib bdg

"Sophie, Margaret, Rebecca, and Leigh Ann . . . find themselves in the midst of several interlocking mysteries, mostly involving violins. . . . Beil has lost none of his edge when it comes to setting up sleuthing scenarios and offering kids codes and clues that will intrigue (or drive them crazy). Smartly plotted, smartly played." Booklist

Bell, Braden

The **kindling**; Braden Bell. Sweetwater Books 2012 291 p. (alk. paper) $14.99

Grades: 5 6 7 8 9 **Fic**

1. Paranormal fiction 2. Puberty -- Fiction 3. Magic -- Fiction 4. Kidnapping -- Fiction 5. Middle schools -- Fiction

ISBN 1462110274; 9781462110278

LC 2012011285

In this book, the three pubescent main characters discover they have magic powers. "This trio, under the watchful eyes of their teachers, is 'kindling,' meaning special powers they did not know they had are igniting. They are slated to join their teachers as Magi, Warriors of the Light, and will need to learn the tricks of the trade from them to fight off the darkhands from the Otherwhere, who have been kidnapping random children." (Voice of Youth Advocates)

Bell, Cathleen Davitt

Little blog on the prairie. Bloomsbury 2010 276p $16.99

Grades: 6 7 8 **Fic**

1. Camps -- Fiction 2. Weblogs -- Fiction 3. Wyoming -- Fiction 4. Frontier and pioneer life -- Fiction

ISBN 978-1-59990-286-9; 1-59990-286-9

LC 2009-46897

Thirteen-year-old Genevieve's summer at a frontier family history camp in Laramie, Wyoming, with her parents and brother is filled with surprises, which she reports to friends back home on the cell phone she sneaked in, and which they turn into a blog.

This is a "a lively journey with empathetic characters." Publ Wkly

Bell, Hilari

Crown of earth. Aladdin 2009 160p (The shield, sword and crown) $16.99

Grades: 6 7 8 9 **Fic**

1. Fantasy fiction 2. Adventure fiction 3. Pirates -- Fiction

ISBN 978-1-4169-0598-1; 1-4169-0598-7

LC 2009000912

Sequel to: Sword of waters (2008)

Fifteen-year-old Prince Ederan and fourteen-year-olds Arisa and Weasel finally realize the true meaning and value of the symbols of power in Deorthas when the Falcon demands the sword and shield in exchange for Weasel's life.

The "adventures (rescues, living undercover with fishermen, sailing) provide plenty of interest, but the real depth arrives during Bell's swift and surprising climax." Kirkus

Fall of a kingdom; by Hilari Bell. Simon Pulse 2005 422 p. map (Simon Pulse teen fantasy) (paperback) $6.99

Grades: 7 8 9 10 **Fic**

1. Fantasy fiction 2. Persian mythology -- Fiction

ISBN 0689854145; 9780689854149

LC 2005588003

This is the first book in Hilari Bell's Farsala trilogy. "Stories are told of a hero who will come to Farsala's aid when the need is greatest. But for thousands of years the prosperous land of Farsala has felt no such need. . . . Three young people are less sure of Farsala's invincibility. Jiaan, Soraya, and Kavi see Time's Wheel turning, with Farsala headed toward the Flames of Destruction. What they cannot see is how inextricably their lives are linked to Farsala's fate." (Publisher's note)

Forging the sword. Simon & Schuster Books for Young Readers 2006 494p (Farsala trilogy) $17.99

Grades: 7 8 9 10 **Fic**

1. Fantasy fiction

ISBN 978-0-689-85416-3; 0-689-85416-1

LC 2005017730

Farsalans, including Lady Soraya and her half-brother, Jiaan, Kavi, and others, work relentlessly and often secretly in their shared strategies regarding the ultimate defeat of the Hrum.

"Bell brings the Farsala Trilogy to a rousing conclusion. . . . The author maintains the complexity of her main characters and the intensity of the story line." Booklist

The **Goblin** Gate. HarperTeen 2010 377p map $16.99

Grades: 5 6 7 8 **Fic**

1. Fantasy fiction 2. Magic -- Fiction 3. Witches -- Fiction 4. Knights and knighthood -- Fiction

ISBN 978-0-06-165102-1; 0-06-165102-8

Sequel to: The Goblin Wood (2003)

Jeriah uncovers a web of political intrigue while trying to obtain a spell from Master Lazure that might allow him to rescue his brother

Tobin from the Otherworld, where he was taken by the beguiling hedge-witch Makenna and her legion of goblins.

"Author Bell has long shown herself adept in portraying social systems and political intrigues; here that talent is married to sympathetic characters struggling through challenges both external and internal." Horn Book

Followed by: The Goblin war (2011)

The **Goblin** War. HarperTeen 2011 314p $17.99
Grades: 5 6 7 8 **Fic**

1. War stories 2. Fantasy fiction 3. Magic -- Fiction 4. Goblins -- Fiction

ISBN 978-0-06-165105-2; 0-06-165105-2; 978-0-06-165106-9 lib bdg; 0-06-165106-0 lib bdg

LC 2010040322

Sequel to: The Goblin Gate (2010)

After crossing over from the Otherworld where they have been trapped in mortal danger, Tobin and Makenna must figure out how to stop an army of barbarians from taking over their Realm.

"Picking up at the immediate end of the previous novel, Bell ratchets up the suspense immediately and makes this finale a true page turner. . . . This rewarding resolution caps off a fascinating, engaging trilogy that holds appeal for a diverse fantasy audience." Kirkus

The **Goblin** Wood. Eos/HarperCollins Pubs. 2003 294p hardcover o.p. pa $7.99
Grades: 5 6 7 8 **Fic**

1. Fantasy fiction

ISBN 0-06-051371-3; 0-06-51373-3 pa

LC 2002-15281

A young Hedgewitch, an idealistic knight, and an army of clever goblins fight against the ruling hierarchy that is trying to rid the land of all magical creatures.

"Leavened by humor and a dollop of romance, this well-crafted fantasy adventure demonstrates Bell's talent for creating enduring characters and worlds." Booklist

Other titles in this trilogy are:

The Goblin Gate (2010)

The Goblin War (2011)

★ The **last** knight. Eos 2007 357p (Knight and rogue) $16.99; lib bdg $17.89
Grades: 7 8 9 10 **Fic**

1. Fantasy fiction 2. Knights and knighthood -- Fiction

ISBN 978-0-06-082503-4; 0-06-082503-0; 978-0-06-082504-1 lib bdg; 0-06-082504-9 lib bdg

LC 2006-36427

In alternate chapters, eighteen-year-old Sir Michael Sevenson, an anachronistic knight errant, and seventeen-year-old Fisk, his streetwise squire, tell of their noble quest to bring Lady Ceciel to justice while trying to solve her husband's murder.

"The novel is brimming with saved-by-a-hair escapades and fast-paced realistic action. . . . This well-created fantasy is a great read with worthwhile moral issues pertinent to its intended audience." SLJ

Other titles in this series are:

Rogue's home (2008)

Player's ruse (2010)

Player's ruse. Eos 2010 377p (Knight and rogue) $17.99; $18.89
Grades: 7 8 9 10 **Fic**

1. Fantasy fiction 2. Knights and knighthood -- Fiction

ISBN 978-0-06-082509-6; 0-06-082509-X; 978-0-06-082510-2 lib bdg; 0-06-082510-3 lib bdg

LC 2008046905

In alternate chapters, eighteen-year-old Sir Michael Sevenson, an anachronistic knight errant, and seventeen-year-old Fisk, his street-wise squire, relate their journey to Huckerston, a port town where dangerous bandits are raiding merchant ships.

"A blend of fantasy, adventure, and mystery, with a large cast of characters and a fast-paced plot, this installment will appeal most to fans of the previous titles." SLJ

Rogue's home. Eos 2008 422p (Knight and rogue) $17.99; lib bdg $18.89
Grades: 7 8 9 10 **Fic**

1. Fantasy fiction 2. Knights and knighthood -- Fiction

ISBN 978-0-06-082506-5; 0-06-082506-5; 978-0-06-082507-2 lib bdg; 0-06-082507-3 lib bdg

LC 2007-41728

Sequel to: The last knight (2007)

In alternate chapters, eighteen-year-old Sir Michael Sevenson, an anachronistic knight errant, and seventeen-year-old Fisk, his street-wise squire, tell of their journey to Ruesport, Fisk's home town, to investigate blackmail and a series of suspicious fires.

"In a story that's part buddy comedy, part Don Quixote, and part mystery novel, Bell outdoes herself with this intrepid pair. . . . Count on this book's humor, suspense, and plot twists to keep readers coming back for future installments." SLJ

Followed by: Player's ruse (2010)

Sword of waters. Simon & Schuster Books for Young Readers 2008 363p (The shield, sword and crown) $16.99; pa $6.99
Grades: 6 7 8 9 **Fic**

1. Fantasy fiction

ISBN 978-1-4169-0596-7; 1-4169-0596-0; 978-1-4169-0597-4 pa; 1-4169-0597-9 pa

LC 2007052081

Sequel to: Shield of stars (2007)

When fourteen-year-old Arisa, aided by Prince Edoran and Weasel, tries to find the long-lost sword, she faces betrayal of the worst kind.

"Fans of the first book will be captivated as the layers begin to unfurl and plots and deceptions are exposed that could not have been predicted." SLJ

Followed by: Crown of earth (2009)

Bell, Joanne

Juggling fire. Orca Book Publishers 2009 171p pa $12.95
Grades: 7 8 9 10 **Fic**

1. Missing persons -- Fiction 2. Wilderness survival -- Fiction 3. Father-daughter relationship -- Fiction 4. Yukon River valley (Yukon and Alaska) -- Fiction

ISBN 978-1-55469-094-7; 1-55469-094-3

"Sixteen-year-old Rachel's father disappeared years earlier from her family's home in the Yukon wilderness. . . . The teen sets off on a trek through the tundra and forest with only her dog as a companion, hoping to find clues about her father's disappearance. . . . Bell beautifully captures the natural world through descriptions of the mountainous terrain as well as nail-biting encounters with bears and wolves. Rachel is a smart, resourceful narrator." SLJ

Bell, Juliet

Kepler's dream; Juliet Bell. G. P. Putnam's Sons 2012 242 p. (hardcover) $16.99

Grades: 5 6 7 8 **Fic**

1. Mystery fiction 2. Leukemia -- Fiction 3. Dysfunctional families -- Fiction 4. Cancer -- Fiction 5. Grandmothers -- Fiction 6. Books and reading -- Fiction 7. Albuquerque (N.M.) -- Fiction 8. Mystery and detective stories 9. Swindlers and swindling -- Fiction 10. Family life -- New Mexico -- Fiction

ISBN 0399256458; 9780399256455

LC 2011024136

This book tells the story of "Ella Mackenzie, a . . . fifth-going-on-sixth grader, [who] is sent to what she calls Broken Family Camp. Ella's family is broken . . . . Her mother has leukemia . . . and is about to have a stem cell transplant. Her father, who works as a guide at an outdoor travel adventure company, has literally gone fishing, as he has for most of Ella's childhood. . . . Ella is forced to spend the summer with the paternal grandmother she has never met." (New York Times)

Bell, Ted

★ **Nick** of time. St. Martin's Griffin 2008 434p il (Nick McIver time adventure) $17.95; pa $7.99

Grades: 6 7 8 **Fic**

1. Admirals 2. Statesmen 3. Historians 4. Fantasy fiction 5. Prime ministers 6. Adventure fiction 7. Memoirists 8. Cabinet members 9. Pirates -- Fiction 10. Members of Parliament 11. Nobel laureates for literature 12. World War, 1939-1945 -- Fiction 13. France -- History -- 1799-1815 -- Fiction

ISBN 978-0-312-38068-7; 0-312-38068-2; 978-0-312-58143-5 pa; 0-312-58143-2 pa

LC 2008-13634

First published 2000 by Xlibris

This novel is set in "England, 1939, on the eve of war. [12-year-old] Nick and his younger sister, Kate, live in a lighthouse on the smallest of the Channel Islands. Nick and Kate come to the aid of their father who is engaged in a . . . war of espionage with German U-boat wolf packs." (Publisher's note) "Grades five to eight." (Bull Cent Child Books)

"This is an immensely appealing book. . . . [The book is filled] with great battle scenes; lots of nautical jargon; and themes of courage, integrity, and honor." SLJ

Bellairs, John

★ The **curse** of the blue figurine. Dial Bks. for Young Readers 1983 200p hardcover o.p. pa $5.99

Grades: 5 6 7 8 **Fic**

1. Mystery fiction

ISBN 0-8446-7138-4; 0-14-240258-3 pa

LC 82-73217

The author "intertwines real concerns with sorcery in a seamless fashion, bringing dimension to his characters and events with expert timing and sharply honed atmosphere." Booklist

Other titles about Johnny Dixon and Professor Childermass are:
The chessmen of doom (1989)
The eyes of the killer robot (1986)
The mummy, the will and the crypt (1983)
The revenge of the wizard's ghost (1985)
The secret of the underground room (1990)
The spell of the sorcerer's skull (1984)
The trolley to yesterday (1989)

Belleza, Rhoda

Empress of a thousand skies; Rhoda Belleza. Razorbill, an imprint of Penguin Random House 2017 313 p. (Empress of a Thousand Skies) (hardcover) $17.99

Grades: 7 8 9 10 11 12 **Fic**

1. Science fiction 2. Princesses -- Fiction 3. Fugitives from justice -- Fiction

ISBN 1101999101; 9781101999103; 9781101999127

LC 2016053016

In this novel, by Rhoda Belleza, "Rhee, also known as Crown Princess Rhiannon Ta'an, is the sole surviving heir to a powerful dynasty. She'll stop at nothing to avenge her family and claim her throne. . . . [When] Aly[,] . . . [the] star of a DroneVision show[,]. . . . [was] falsely accused of killing Rhee, he's forced to prove his innocence to save his reputation--and his life." (Publisher's note)

"This is a multiplanet, multiculture, multitech world and a timely tale. An exceptionally satisfying series opener." Kirkus

Followed by:
Blood of a thousand stars (2018)

Bemis, John Claude

The **nine** pound hammer. Random House 2009 357p (The clockwork dark) $16.99; lib bdg $19.99

Grades: 6 7 8 9 **Fic**

1. Fantasy fiction 2. Orphans -- Fiction 3. Siblings -- Fiction 4. John Henry (Legendary character)

ISBN 978-0-375-85564-1; 0-375-85564-5; 978-0-375-95564-8 lib bdg; 0-375-95564-X lib bdg; 978-0-375-85565-8 pa; 0-375-85565-3 pa

LC 2008-22503

Drawn by the lodestone his father gave him years before, twelve-year-old orphan Ray travels south, meeting along the way various characters from folklore who are battling against an evil industry baron known as the Gog.

"If readers still possess a twinkle of wonder for the step-right-up days of side-show hucksterism, Bemis' debut will shock and amaze them." Booklist

Other books in this series are:
The Wolf Tree (2010)
The White City (2011)

The **White** City. Random House 2011 386p (The clockwork dark) $17.99; lib bdg $20.99

Grades: 6 7 8 **Fic**

1. Fantasy fiction 2. Adventure fiction 3. World's Columbian Exposition (1893: Chicago, Ill.) -- Fiction

ISBN 978-0-375-85568-9; 0-375-85568-8; 978-0-375-95568-6 lib bdg; 0-375-95568-2 lib bdg

LC 2010014252

Sequel to: The Wolf Tree (2010)

Ray, Conker, and their Rambler friends face the Gog and his Machine in a final struggle at the 1893 Chicago Exposition.

"This third book focuses the complicated plots of the trilogy into a consistent conclusion that forces the reader to consider nature's strengths and technology's dangers. . . . [Fans] will find more than enough action and thought for their . . . tastes." Voice Youth Advocates

The **Wolf** Tree. Random House 2010 385p (The clockwork dark) $16.99

Grades: 6 7 8 **Fic**

1. Fantasy fiction 2. Orphans -- Fiction

ISBN 978-0-375-85566-5; 0-375-85566-1

Sequel to: The nine pound hammer (2009)

Ray Cobb and the rest of the Ramblers must cross into the Gloaming and destroy the Gog's machine, which has started to spread a darkness over the land.

Benjamin, Ali

★ The **next** great Paulie Fink; Ali Benjamin. Little, Brown & Co. 2019 368 p. (hardcover) $16.99

Grades: 4 5 6 7 8 **Fic**

1. School stories 2. Bullies -- Fiction 3. Contests -- Fiction 4. Friendship -- Fiction 5. Luck -- Fiction 6. Schools -- Fiction 7. Behavior -- Fiction

ISBN 9780316380881

LC 2018032813

In this book, by Ali Benjamin, "when Caitlyn Breen begins her disorienting new life at the rural Mitchell School-- . . . where there are only ten other students in the entire seventh grade--it seems like nobody can stop talking about some kid named Paulie Fink. . . . The kid was totally legendary. Now he's disappeared, and Caitlyn finds herself leading a reality-show-style competition to find the school's next great Paulie Fink." (Publisher's note)

"Frequently laugh-out-loud funny, the novel captures the quirks and traditions of a small community, and what it's like to enter such a community after its social dynamics are established." Horn Book

★ The **thing** about jellyfish; by Ali Benjamin. Little, Brown & Co. 2015 352 p. (hardcover) $17

Grades: 4 5 6 7 8 9 **Fic**

1. Grief -- Fiction 2. Jellyfishes -- Fiction 3. Friendship -- Fiction 4. Best friends -- Fiction

ISBN 0316380865; 9780316380867

LC 2014044025

National Book Award Finalist: Young People's Literature (2015)

In this novel by Ali Benjamin "after her best friend dies in a drowning accident, Suzy is convinced that the true cause of the tragedy was a rare jellyfish sting. Retreating into a silent world of imagination, she crafts a plan to prove her theory--even if it means traveling the globe, alone. Suzy's achingly heartfelt journey explores life, death, the astonishing wonder of the universe...and the potential for love and hope right next door." (Publisher's note)

"Benjamin's inverse approach to tragedy, placing the death at the beginning of the novel and storytelling through the grieving process, transcends the trope, as the story triumphs in the affecting realities of emotional response and resilience." SLJ

Benko, Kamilla

Secret in the stone; Kamilla Benko. Bloomsbury 2019 336 p. (Unicorn Quest) (hardcover) $16.99

Grades: 4 5 6 7 **Fic**

1. Magic -- Fiction 2. Sisters -- Fiction 3. Unicorns -- Fiction 4. Fantasy 5. Adventure and adventurers -- Fiction

ISBN 9781681192475

LC 2018026348

The second book in the Unicorn Quest fantasy series, by Kamilla Benko, is "about a real-world girl and her sister in a land full of magic and strange creatures. Claire Martinson and her sister Sophie have decided to stay in Arden--the magical land they discovered by climbing up a chimney in their great-aunt's manor. If what they've learned is true, the sisters are the last descendants of the royal family, and only a true heir of Arden [who] . . . can awaken the unicorns." (Publisher's note)

"Claire and Sophie's traverse across the magical world of Arden continues in this exciting continuation of The Unicorn Quest series." Booklist

Bennett, Holly

Shapeshifter. Orca Book Publishers 2010 244p il pa $9.95

Grades: 7 8 9 10 **Fic**

1. Fantasy fiction

ISBN 978-1-55469-158-6; 1-55469-158-3

In order to escape the sorceror who wants to control her gift of song, Sive must transform herself into a deer, leave the Otherworld and find refuge in Eire, the land of mortals.

This is a "rich, slightly revisionist retelling of an ancient Irish legend. Basic human emotions—fear, love, greed—move the tale along, and short first-person narratives that personalize the action are interspersed throughout." Booklist

Bennett, Olivia

The **Allegra** Biscotti collection. Sourcebooks 2010 246p pa $8.99

Grades: 5 6 7 8 **Fic**

1. School stories 2. Fashion -- Fiction

ISBN 978-1-4022-4391-2; 1-4022-4391-X

By day, Emma Rose is a quiet, under-the-radar student who doesn't mix with the popular set. But when school's out, she becomes Queen of the Runway—whipping up cutting-edge designs.

"Credible characterizations and dialogue keep the novel real. . . . Bennett slips in detailed descriptions of the teens' outfits and Emma's designs, which appear in spot art." Publ Wkly

Followed by: Who what wear (2011)

Who what wear; illustrated by Georgia Rucker. Sourcebooks Jabberwocky 2011 231p il (The Allegra Biscotti collection) pa $8.99

Grades: 5 6 7 8 **Fic**

1. Fashion designers -- Fiction

ISBN 978-1-4022-4392-9; 1-4022-4392-8

"Emma Rose, 14, is still trying to hide her identity as New York City's up-and-coming fashion designer, Allegra Biscotti, while juggling the pitfalls of friendship and middle school. . . . The novel . . . comes to a satisfying, if predictable, conclusion. Interspersed throughout are illustrations of Allegra's designs. . . . Who What Wear is a great recommendation for kids who dream of a career in fashion." SLJ

Benway, Robin, 1978-

★ **Far** from the tree; Robin Benway. HarperTeen 2017 384 p. hardcover $17.99

Grades: 7 8 9 10 11 12 **Fic**

1. Family secrets -- Fiction 2. Adopted children -- Fiction

ISBN 0062330624; 9780062330628; 9780062330642

National Book Award: Young People's Literature (2017)

In this book, by Robin Benway, "being the middle child has its ups and downs. But for Grace, an only child who was adopted at birth, discovering that she is a middle child is a different ride altogether. After putting her own baby up for adoption, she goes looking for her biological family. . . . And when her adopted family's long-buried problems begin to explode to the surface, Maya can't help but wonder where exactly it is that she belongs." (Publisher's note)

Benway "delves into the souls of these characters as they wrestle to overcome feelings of inadequacy, abandonment, and betrayal, gradually coming to understand themselves and each other." Pub Wkly

Benwell, Sarah

★ The **last** leaves falling; by Sarah Benwell. Simon & Schuster 2015 368 p. (hardcover) $17.99

Grades: 7 8 9 10 11 12 **Fic**

1. Friendship -- Fiction 2. Terminally ill -- Fiction 3. Amyotrophic lateral sclerosis 4. Single-parent families -- Fiction 5. Mother-son relationship -- Fiction 6. Japan -- Fiction 7. Assisted suicide -- Fiction 8. Mothers and sons -- Fiction 9. Online chat groups -- Fiction 10. Amyotrophic lateral sclerosis -- Fiction

ISBN 9781481430654; 9781481430661

LC 2014022950

This novel, by Sarah Benwell, is "infused with the haunting grace of samurai death poetry and the noble importance of friendship. Abe Sora is going to die, and he's only seventeen years old. Diagnosed with ALS (Lou Gehrig's disease), he's already lost the use of his legs, which means he can no longer attend school." (Publisher's note)

"References to samurai culture and snippets of poetry will leave readers at peace with the drifting ending. Benwell's gentle treatment of friendship and death with dignity will touch fans of John Green's The Fault in Our Stars (2012)." Kirkus

Berk, Ari

Death watch. Simon & Schuster Books for Young Readers 2011 527p (The Undertaken trilogy) $17.99

Grades: 7 8 9 10 **Fic**

1. Fantasy fiction 2. Father-son relationship -- Fiction

ISBN 978-1-4169-9115-1; 1-4169-9115-8

LC 2011006332

When seventeen-year-old Silas Umber's father disappears, Silas is sure it is connected to the powerful artifact he discovers, combined with his father's hidden hometown history, which compels Silas to pursue the path leading to his destiny and ultimately, to the discovery of his father, dead or alive.

"Berk's setting is atmospheric and creepy, fleshed out with a wealth of funereal traditions and folklore." Publ Wkly

Other titles in this series are:

Mistle child (2013)

Lych way (2014)

Berk, Josh

Strike three, you're dead; Josh Berk. Knopf Books for Young Readers 2013 256 p. (hardback) $16.99

Grades: 3 4 5 6 7 **Fic**

1. Mystery fiction 2. Baseball -- Fiction 3. Friendship -- Fiction 4. Murder -- Fiction 5. Best friends -- Fiction 6. Philadelphia Phillies (Baseball team) -- Fiction

ISBN 0375870083; 9780375870088; 9780375970085; 9780375987366

LC 2012023892

Edgar Award Finalist: Best Juvenile (2014)

In this mystery, by Josh Berk, twelve-year-old "Lenny, with the help of his buddies Mike and Other Mike, enters and wins a contest to guest-announce a Philadelphia Phillies game. When the hot rookie pitcher drops dead, the kids suspect that it's more than a previously undetected heart condition. They join another local sports fan and begin investigating the crime . . . while meeting their hero, flashy catcher Ramon Famosa, and other players in the process." (Publishers Weekly)

"Baseball aficionados will appreciate all the trivia Berk works into the story, with references to famous players and Phillies history scattered throughout. The wisecracking interplay between the boys is a strong point, though the solution to the mystery is really never in doubt." Pub Wkly

Berkeley, Jon

The **lightning** key. HarperCollins Pub. 2009 399p (The Wednesday tales) $16.99

Grades: 4 5 6 7 **Fic**

1. Adventure fiction 2. Angels -- Fiction 3. Orphans -- Fiction

ISBN 978-0-06-075513-3; 0-06-075513-X

Sequel to: The tiger's egg (2007)

Now that Miles Wednesday has discovered his link to a magical Tiger's Egg, he's suddenly at the wheel of a great voyage. Determined to recover the stolen stone and free the trapped soul within, Miles sets off with Little, a Song Angel, and the wisecracking blind explorer Baltinglass of Araby.

"Middle and junior high students will delight in this story, the most lyrical and sharply written of the series." Voice Youth Advocates

The **tiger's** egg; [by] Jon Berkeley; illustrated by Brandon Dorman. HarperCollinsPublishers 2007 400p il (The Wednesday tales) $16.99; lib bdg $17.89

Grades: 4 5 6 7 **Fic**

1. Adventure fiction 2. Angels -- Fiction 3. Circus -- Fiction 4. Tigers -- Fiction 5. Orphans -- Fiction

ISBN 978-0-06-075510-2; 0-06-075510-5; 978-0-06-075511-9 lib bdg; 0-06-075511-3 lib bdg

LC 2006039842

Sequel to: The Palace of Laughter (2006)

While working for the newly revamped circus, orphaned eleven-year-old Miles gains information about his past and sets off with his angel companion, Little, on a quest to find a mystical tiger's egg before it falls into the hands of their nemesis, Cortado.

"This novel is engaging from beginning to end. Fantasy lovers will enjoy a variety of plot twists that will surprise even the most perceptive reader." Voice Youth Advocates

Followed by: The lightning key (2009)

Berlin, Eric

The **potato** chip puzzles; Eric Berlin; [drawings by Katrina Damkoehler] G.P. Putnam's Sons 2009 244p il $16.99; pa $7.99

Grades: 4 5 6 7 **Fic**

1. Mystery fiction 2. Puzzles -- Fiction 3. Contests -- Fiction

ISBN 978-0-399-25198-6; 0-399-25198-7; 978-0-14-241637-2 pa; 0-14-241637-1 pa

LC 2008-33698

Sequel to: The puzzling world of Winston Breen (2007)

Winston and his friends enter an all-day puzzle contest to win fifty-thousand dollars for their school, but they must also figure out who is trying to keep them from winning. Puzzles for the reader to solve are included throughout the text.

"The pace is suspenseful but allows for pauses for problem-solving. The joy for both contestants and readers of this brain-teasing mystery will be in the process." Kirkus

★ The **puzzling** world of Winston Breen; the secret in the box. Putnam 2007 215p il $16.99; pa $7.99

Grades: 4 5 6 7 **Fic**

1. Mystery fiction 2. Puzzles -- Fiction 3. Siblings -- Fiction

ISBN 978-0-399-24693-7; 0-399-24693-2; 978-0-14-241388-3 pa; 0-14-241388-7 pa

LC 2006-20531

Puzzle-crazy, twelve-year-old Winston and his ten-year-old sister Katie find themselves involved in a dangerous mystery involving a hidden ring. Puzzles for the reader to solve are included throughout the text

"A delightfully clever mystery. . . . There is plenty of suspense to engage readers." SLJ

Followed by: The potato chip puzzles (2009)

Bernard, Romily

Find me; Romily Bernard. HarperTeen, an imprint of HarperCollinsPublishers 2013 320 p. (hardback) $17.99

Grades: 7 8 9 10 11 12 **Fic**

1. Foster children -- Fiction 2. Teenagers -- Suicide -- Fiction 3. Computer hackers -- Fiction 4. Foster home care -- Fiction 5. Mystery and detective stories

ISBN 0062229036; 9780062229038

LC 2013021519

In this book, "Tessa Waye was Wicket Tate's best friend until five years ago when Wick's drug-dealing father drove them apart. When Tessa commits suicide and her diary is left on the teen's front steps, Wick suspects there might be a dark reason she jumped to her death. Wick and her sister, Lily, are now free of their criminal father, living a shiny new life on the ritzy side of town with their foster parents. But Wick . . . fears her father will come back for them." (School Library Journal)

Other titles in this series are:

Remember me (2014)

Trust me (2016)

Berry, Julie

All the truth that's in me; by Julie Berry. Viking 2013 288 p. (hardcover : alk. paper) $17.99

Grades: 7 8 9 10 11 12 **Fic**

1. Truth -- Fiction 2. Kidnapping -- Fiction 3. Community life -- Fiction 4. War -- Fiction 5. Selective mutism -- Fiction

ISBN 0670786152; 9780670786152

LC 2012043218

In this book by Julie Berry, "sixteen-year-old Judith is still in love with Lucas, even after his father held her prisoner for two years and violently silenced her by cutting out part of her tongue. Another girl went missing at the same time and her body was found washed down a stream. Only Judith knows the truth of what happened to Lottie, but her muteness leaves her an outcast in the village, even from her own mother, and the truth stays bottled up inside her." (School Library Journal)

"Berry's novel is set in a claustrophobic village that seems to resemble an early American colonial settlement. Readers gradually learn "all the truth" from eighteen-year-old narrator Judith, who speaks directly (though only in her head) to her love, Lucas. Berry keeps readers on edge, tantalizing us with pieces of the puzzle right up until the gripping conclusion." (Horn Book)

★ The **passion** of Dolssa; by Julie Berry. Penguin Group 2016 496 p. (hardcover) $18.99

Grades: 7 8 9 10 **Fic**

1. Faith -- Fiction 2. France -- Fiction 3. Christian heresies 4. Friendship -- Fiction 5. Inquisition -- Fiction 6. Albigenses -- Fiction 7. Christian heresies -- Fiction 8. France -- History -- Louis IX, 1226-1270 -- Fiction 9. Provence (France) -- History -- 13th century -- Fiction

ISBN 0451469925; 9780451469922

LC 2015020814

Printz Honor Book (2017)

"Dolssa is an upper-crust city girl with a secret lover and an uncanny gift. Branded a heretic, she's on the run from the friar who condemned her mother to death by fire. . . . Botille is a matchmaker and a tavern-keeper, struggling to keep herself and her sisters on the right side of the law in their seaside town of Bajas. When their lives collide . . . Botille rescues a dying Dolssa and conceals her in the tavern." (Publisher's note)

"A (fictional) Catholic mystic, Dolssa de Stigata, escapes being burned as a heretic in 1241 France; mostly, this is the story of Botille, an enterprising young matchmaker from a tiny fishing village who rescues Dolssa. Botille's spirited character, the heart-rending suspense of events, and the terrifying context of the Inquisition in medieval Europe all render the novel irresistibly compelling." Horn Book

Includes bibliographical references

The **scandalous** sisterhood of Prickwillow Place; Julie Berry. Roaring Brook Press 2014 368 p. illustrations (hardback) $15.99

Grades: 6 7 8 **Fic**

1. School stories 2. Humorous fiction 3. Murder -- Fiction 4. Humorous stories 5. Schools -- Fiction 6. Boarding schools -- Fiction 7. Mystery and detective stories 8. Ely (England) -- History -- 19th century -- Fiction 9. Great Britain -- History -- Victoria, 1837-1901 -- Fiction

ISBN 1596439564; 9781596439566

LC 2014003249

In this middle grades book by Julie Berry, "the students of St. Etheldreda's School for Girls face a bothersome dilemma. Their irascible headmistress, Mrs. Plackett, and her surly brother, Mr. Godding, have been most inconveniently poisoned at Sunday dinner. Now the school will almost certainly be closed and the girls sent home--unless these seven very proper young ladies can hide the murders and convince their neighbors that nothing is wrong." (Publisher's note)

"Overall, this is a well-researched, clever, and deliciously dark comedy with an emphasis on female empowerment." SLJ

Includes bibliographical references

Bickle, Laura

The **hallowed** ones; Laura Bickle. Graphia 2012 311 p. (paperback) $8.99

Grades: 7 8 9 10 11 12 **Fic**

1. Horror stories 2. Amish -- Fiction 3. Terrorism -- Fiction 4. Family life -- Fiction 5. Bioterrorism -- Fiction 6. Coming of age -- Fiction 7. Christian life -- Fiction 8. Communicable diseases -- Fiction

ISBN 0547859260; 9780547859262

LC 2012014800

This book follows "Katie [who] is [about] to taste the freedom of rumspringa, [when] the elders close the gates of her small Amish community. . . . Katie daringly ventures Outside to find true horror: vampires have decimated a small nearby town and apparently much of the world's population. . . . Her situation is further complicated when she rescues Alex, a handsome Outsider who may or may not be a carrier of the contagion that seemingly caused the vampirism epidemic." (Bulletin of the Center for Children's Books)

The **outside**; Laura Bickle. Houghton Mifflin Harcourt 2013 320 p. (hardcover) $16.99

Grades: 7 8 9 10 11 12 **Fic**

1. Horror fiction 2. Paranormal fiction 3. Vampires -- Fiction 4. Horror stories 5. Amish -- Fiction 6. Coming of age -- Fiction 7. Christian life -- Fiction

ISBN 0544000137; 9780544000131

LC 2012040065

Sequel to: The hallowed ones

This book is a sequel to Laura Bickle's "The Hallowed Ones." Katie, an exile from an Amish community, travels with "Alex and Ginger, the two outsiders she's befriended, seeking other survivors of the vampire plague that's unmade their world. . . . Discovering a group that's genetically engineered with immunity to vampires raises tension between them, pitting science against religion: Are these vampires aliens or mutants spawned in labs, rather than manifestations of demonic evil?" (Kirkus Reviews)

Bigelow, Lisa Jenn

Drum roll, please; Lisa Jenn Bigelow. HarperCollins 2018 320 p. (hardcover) $16.99

Grades: 4 5 6 7 8 **Fic**

1. Camps -- Fiction 2. Drums -- Fiction 3. Friendship -- Fiction
ISBN 9780062791146

LC 2018933338

In this book, by Lisa Jenn Bigelow, "Melly only joined the school band because her best friend, Olivia, begged her to. But to her surprise, quiet Melly loves playing the drums. . . . Now she and Olivia are about to spend the next two weeks at Camp Rockaway . . . in the Michigan woods. But this summer brings a lot of big changes for Melly: her parents split up, her best friend ditches her, and Melly finds herself unexpectedly falling for another girl at camp." (Publisher's note)

Starting from here; by Lisa Jenn Bigelow. Marshall Cavendish Children 2012 282 p. (hardcover) $16.99

Grades: 8 9 10 11 12 **Fic**

1. School stories 2. Lesbians -- Fiction 3. Self-realization -- Fiction 4. Dogs -- Fiction 5. Schools -- Fiction 6. High schools -- Fiction 7. Fathers and daughters -- Fiction 8. Dating (Social customs) -- Fiction
ISBN 0761462333; 9780761462330; 9780761462347

LC 2011040129

In this book by Lisa Jenn Bigelow, "Colby is about ready to give up on people: her girlfriend Rachel dumps her and immediately moves onto Colby's opposite (a nice Jewish guy who does well in school), her mom is dead, and her dad is a frequently absent truck driver to whom she still hasn't come out. Only her best friend, Van, can bring her out of her shell. Then she adopts Mo, a friendly but wary stray dog, and life starts to move again." (Bulletin of the Center for Children's Books)

Billingsley, Franny

★ **Chime**. Dial Books for Young Readers 2011 361p $17.99

Grades: 7 8 9 10 11 12 **Fic**

1. Guilt -- Fiction 2. Twins -- Fiction 3. Sisters -- Fiction 4. Stepmothers -- Fiction 5. Supernatural -- Fiction
ISBN 0-8037-3552-9; 978-0-8037-3552-1

LC 2010-12140

National Book Award Finalist: Young People's Literature (2011); Boston Globe-Horn Book Award Honor: Fiction (2011)

"Since her stepmother's recent death, 17-year-old Briony Larkin knows that if she can keep two secrets--that she is a witch and that she is responsible for the accident that left Rose, her identical twin, mentally compromised--and remember to hate herself always, no other harm will befall her family in their Swampsea parsonage at the beginning of the twentieth century. The arrival of Mr. Clayborne, a city engineer, and his university-dropout son, Eldric, makes Briony's task difficult." (Booklist)

"Filled with eccentric characters—self-hating Briony foremost—and oddly beautiful language, this is a darkly beguiling fantasy." Publ Wkly

The **Folk** Keeper. Atheneum Bks. for Young Readers 1999 162p hardcover o.p. pa $4.99; pa $5.99

Grades: 5 6 7 8 **Fic**

1. Fantasy fiction
ISBN 0-689-82876-4; 0-689-84461-1 pa; 9780689844614 pa

LC 98-48778

Boston Globe Horn Book Winner (2000)

Orphaned Corinna disguises herself as a boy to pose as a Folk Keeper, one who keeps the supernatural Folk underground at bay. She discovers her heritage as a seal maiden when she is summoned to become the Folk Keeper for a wealthy family in their manor by the sea. "Ages ten to fourteen." (N Y Times Book Rev)

"The intricate plot, vibrant characters, dangerous intrigue, and fantastical elements combine into a truly remarkable novel steeped in atmosphere." Horn Book

Binding, Tim

★ **Sylvie** and the songman; with illustrations by Angela Barrett. Random House 2009 339p il $15.99; lib bdg $18.99

Grades: 5 6 7 8 **Fic**

1. Fantasy fiction
ISBN 978-0-385-75157-5; 0-385-75159-1; 978-0-385-75159-9 lib bdg; 0-385-75159-1 lib bdg

"Sylvie's composer father . . . goes missing and that's the first odd thing that interrupts her happy routine. Next, the animals seem to have lost their voices. The third is the arrival of the eerie, malevolent Woodpecker Man. . . . The dense narrative is packed with surreal imagery. . . . It's a testament to Binding's assured writing that the abstractions become visceral thrills, like a dream you just can't shake. . . . An unforgettable tale." Booklist

Bingham, Kelly

★ **Shark** girl. Candlewick Press 2007 276p $16.99; pa $8.99

Grades: 7 8 9 10 **Fic**

1. Novels in verse 2. Artists -- Fiction 3. Amputees -- Fiction
ISBN 978-0-7636-3207-6; 0-7636-3207-4; 978-0-7636-4627-1 pa; 0-7636-4627-X pa

LC 2006049120

After a shark attack causes the amputation of her right arm, fifteen-year-old Jane, an aspiring artist, struggles to come to terms with her loss and the changes it imposes on her day-to-day life and her plans for the future.

"In carefully constructed, sparsely crafted free verse, Bingham's debut novel offers a strong view of a teenager struggling to survive and learn to live again." Booklist

Binns, Barbara

Courage; Barbara Binns. HarperCollins 2018 368 p. (hardcover) $16.99

Grades: 4 5 6 7 **Fic**

1. Diving -- Fiction 2. Racism -- Fiction 3. Brothers -- Fiction
ISBN 9780062561657

LC 2018933336

In this book, by Barbara Binns, "ever since T'Shawn's dad died, his mother has been struggling to keep the family afloat. So when he's offered a spot on a prestigious diving team at the local private swim club, he knows that joining would only add another bill to the pile. But T studies hard and never gets into trouble, so he thinks his mom might be willing to bear the cost . . . until he finds out that his older brother, Lamont, is getting released early from prison." (Publisher's note)

Birdsall, Jeanne

★ The **Penderwicks**; a summer tale of four sisters, two rabbits, and a very interesting boy. Knopf 2005 262p (The Penderwicks) $15.95; lib bdg $17.77; pa $6.99

Grades: 3 4 5 6 **Fic**

1. Sisters -- Fiction 2. Single parent family -- Fiction
ISBN 0-375-83143-6; 0-375-93143-0 lib bdg; 0-440-42047-4 pa

LC 2004-20364

National Book Award: Young People's Literature (2005)

"Four sisters—Rosalind, Skye, Jane, and Batty—spend a few weeks with their father and dog at a cottage on the grounds of a stately home in the Berkshires, where they complicate the lives of a handsome gardener, a lonely boy, and the boy's officious mother. . . . Grades four to seven." (Bull Cent Child Books)

"This comforting family story . . . [offers] . . . four marvelously appealing sisters, true childhood behavior . . . , and a writing style that will draw readers close." Booklist

Other titles in this series are:
The Penderwicks on Gardam Street (2008)
The Penderwicks at Point Mouette (2011)
The Penderwicks in spring (2015)
The Penderwicks at last (2018)

The **Penderwicks** at Last; Jeanne Birdsall. Random House Childrens Books 2018 304 p. $16.99

Grades: 4 5 6 7 **Fic**

1. Siblings -- Fiction 2. Weddings -- Fiction 3. Family life -- Fiction

ISBN 038575566X; 9780385755665

In this book in The Penderwicks series, by Jeanne Birdsall, "it's summertime, and eleven-year-old Lydia is dancing at the bus stop, waiting for big sister Batty to get home from college. This is a very important dance and a very important wait because the two youngest sisters are about to arrive home to find out that the Penderwicks will all be returning to Arundel this summer. . . . And better still is the occasion: a good old-fashioned, homemade-by-Penderwicks wedding." (Publisher's note)

The **Penderwicks** at Point Mouette. Alfred A. Knopf 2011 295p (The Penderwicks) $16.99

Grades: 4 5 6 7 **Fic**

1. Maine -- Fiction 2. Summer -- Fiction 3. Vacations -- Fiction 4. Family life -- Fiction

ISBN 978-0-375-85851-2; 0-375-85851-2

This is the third book about the Penderwick family, who appeared previously in The Penderwicks (2005) and The Penderwicks on Gardam Street (2008). "When summer comes around, it's off to the beach for Rosalind . . . and off to Maine with Aunt Claire for the rest of the Penderwick girls, as well as their old friend, Jeffrey. That leaves Skye as OAP (oldest available Penderwick). . . . Things look good as they settle into their cozy cottage. . . . But can Skye hold it together long enough to figure out Rosalind's directions about not letting Batty explode? Will Jane's Love Survey come to a tragic conclusion after she meets the alluring Dominic? . . . And will Jeffrey be able to keep peace between the girls?" (Publisher's note) "Intermediate." (Horn Book)

"Balancing the novel's comedy is an affecting, neatly crafted subplot that builds up to the emotionally charged revelation involving Jeffrey. From start to finish, this is a summer holiday to savor." Publ Wkly

The **Penderwicks** in spring; Jeanne Birdsall. Knopf Books for Young Readers 2015 352 p. (The Penderwicks) (hardback) $16.99; (lib. bdg.) $19.99

Grades: 4 5 6 7 **Fic**

1. Birthdays -- Fiction 2. Family life -- Fiction 3. Massachusetts -- Fiction 4. Money-making projects for children -- Fiction 5. Singing -- Fiction 6. Surprise -- Fiction 7. Moneymaking projects -- Fiction 8. Single-parent families -- Fiction 9. Family life -- Massachusetts -- Fiction

ISBN 0375870776; 9780375870774; 9780375970771
LC 2014023537

Sequel to: The Penderwicks at Point Mouette (2011)

In this book, by Jeanne Birdsall, "springtime is finally arriving on Gardam Street, and there are surprises in store for each member of the family. Some surprises are just wonderful, like neighbor Nick Geiger coming home from war. And some are ridiculous, like Batty's new dog-walking business. Batty is saving up her dog-walking money for an extra-special surprise for her family, which she plans to present on her upcoming birthday." (Publisher's note)

"[T]he compelling story line examines the guilt that Batty feels over both the death of her mother and her inability to keep the family dog, Hound, alive--and it does so in touching ways. Batty is the narrator most of the time, but younger Ben takes over on occasion, and 2-year-old Lydia is an eccentric presence." Booklist

The **Penderwicks** on Gardam Street; [illustrations by David Frankland] Alfred A. Knopf 2008 307p il $15.99; lib bdg $18.99

Grades: 3 4 5 6 7 **Fic**

1. Sisters -- Fiction 2. Family life -- Fiction 3. Massachusetts -- Fiction 4. Dating (Social customs) -- Fiction

ISBN 978-0-3758-4090-6; 978-0-375-94090-3 lib bdg
LC 2007-49232

Sequel to: The Penderwicks (2005)

The four Penderwick sisters are faced with the unimaginable prospect of their widowed father dating, and they hatch a plot to stop him.

"Laugh-out-loud moments abound and the humor comes naturally from the characters and situations. . . . This is a book to cherish." SLJ

Birdseye, Tom

Storm Mountain. Holiday House 2010 135p $16.95

Grades: 4 5 6 7 **Fic**

1. Adventure fiction 2. Cousins -- Fiction 3. Blizzards -- Fiction 4. Mountaineering -- Fiction 5. Washington (State) -- Fiction 6. Wilderness survival -- Fiction

ISBN 978-0-8234-2130-5; 0-8234-2130-9
LC 2010005768

Two thirteen-year-old cousins Cat and Ty are trapped in a blizzard on the same treacherous mountain in the Cascades that claimed the lives of their world-famous, mountain-climber, twin fathers exactly two years earlier.

"Birdseye's prose, full of careening action, melodrama and overwrought similes, reflects Ty's bulldozing personality. Add believable characters, the author's mountain-climbing expertise and a tear-jerking conclusion, and there's plenty here for young adventure enthusiasts." Kirkus

Black, Holly, 1971-

Black heart; Holly Black. Margaret K. McElderry Books 2012 296 p. (The curse workers) (hardcover) $17.99

Grades: 7 8 9 10 **Fic**

1. Romance fiction 2. Science fiction 3. Brothers -- Fiction 4. Organized crime -- Fiction 5. Love -- Fiction 6. Criminals -- Fiction

ISBN 9781442403468; 9781442403482
LC 2011028143

This book, the final volume of the Curse Workers trilogy, continues to follow "Cassel . . . [who has] figured out the truth about himself and signed on as a Fed-in-training, as has his charming and utterly unreliable older brother. But of course things don't go as planned; there are a lot of long cons Cassel has set in play or disrupted whose ripples are still being felt. And there's Lila, Cassel's best friend and the love of his life, who is also the rising head of a crime family" and who hates Cassel's guts." (Kirkus)

The **copper** gauntlet; Holly Black and Cassandra Clare ; with illustrations by Scott Fischer. Scholastic Press 2015 272 p. illustrations (Magisterium) (jacketed hardcover) $17.99
Grades: 5 6 7 8 **Fic**

1. Adventure fiction 2. Magic -- Fiction 3. Wolves -- Fiction 4. Secrets -- Fiction
ISBN 0545522285; 9780545522281
LC 2015015713

In this book, Holly Black and Cassandra Clare, "Callum Hunt's summer break isn't like other kids'. His closest companion is a Chaos-ridden wolf, Havoc. His father suspects him of being secretly evil. And, of course, most kids aren't heading back to the magical world of the Magisterium in the fall. It's not easy for Call . . . and it gets even harder after he checks out his basement and discovers that his dad might be trying to destroy both him and Havoc." (publisher's note)

"The third-person narration, filtered through Callum's delightfully insecure-and-overcompensating-with-snarky-bravado perspective, carries a tone that will likely have readers chortling in recognition. A promising beginning to a complex exploration of good and evil, as well as friendship's loyalty." Kirkus

Sequel to "The Iron Trial"

★ **Doll** bones; Holly Black. 1st ed. Margaret K. McElderry Books 2013 256 p. (hardcover) $16.99
Grades: 5 6 7 8 **Fic**

1. Ghost stories 2. Dolls -- Fiction 3. Adventure fiction 4. Ghosts -- Fiction 5. Friendship -- Fiction 6. Family problems -- Fiction 7. Adventure and adventurers -- Fiction
ISBN 1416963987; 9781416963981; 9781442474871
LC 2012018299

Newberry Honor Book (2104)

In this book, by Holly Black, illustrated by Eliza Wheeler, "a doll that may be haunted leads three friends on a thrilling adventure. . . . Zach, Poppy, and Alice have been . . . playing one continuous, ever-changing game. . . . Ruling over all is the Great Queen, . . . cursing those who displease her. . . . Zach and Alice and Poppy set off on one last adventure to lay the Queen's ghost to rest. But nothing goes according to plan, and . . . creepy things begin to happen." (Publisher's note)

"Veteran Black packs both heft and depth into a deceptively simple (and convincingly uncanny) narrative. . . . A few rich metaphors . . . are woven throughout the story, as every encounter redraws the blurry lines between childishness and maturity, truth and lies, secrecy and honesty, magic and madness. Spooky, melancholy, elegiac and ultimately hopeful; a small gem." Kirkus

The **iron** trial; Holly Black, Cassandra Clare. First edition Scholastic Press 2014 304 p. illustrations (Magisterium) (hardcover) $17.99
Grades: 4 5 6 7 8 **Fic**

1. Fantasy fiction 2. Magic -- Fiction
ISBN 0545522250; 9780545522250
LC 2014937300

In this fantasy novel by Holly Black and Cassandra Clare, part of the Magisterium series, "most kids would do anything to pass the Iron Trial. Not Callum Hunt. He wants to fail. All his life, Call has been warned by his father to stay away from magic. If he succeeds at the Iron Trial and is admitted into the Magisterium, he is sure it can only mean bad things for him." (Publisher's note)

"The third-person narration, filtered through Callum's delightfully insecure-and-overcompensating-with-snarky-bravado perspective, carries a tone that will likely have readers chortling in recognition. A promising beginning to a complex exploration of good and evil, as well as friendship's loyalty." Kirkus

Other titles in this series are:
The copper gauntlet (2015)
The bronze key (2016)
The silver mask (2017)

Red glove. Margaret K. McElderry Books 2011 325p (The curse workers) $17.99
Grades: 7 8 9 10 **Fic**

1. Science fiction 2. Magic -- Fiction 3. Brothers -- Fiction 4. Criminals -- Fiction 5. Swindlers and swindling -- Fiction
ISBN 1-4424-0339-X; 978-1-4424-0339-0
LC 2010-31884

Sequel to: White cat (2010)

When federal agents learn that seventeen-year-old Cassel Sharpe, a powerful transformation worker, may be of use to them, they offer him a deal to join them rather than the mobsters for whom his brothers work.

This offers "a sleek a stylish blend of urban fantasy and crime noir." Booklist

★ The **white** cat. Margaret K. McElderry Books 2010 310p (The curse workers) $17.99
Grades: 7 8 9 10 **Fic**

1. Science fiction 2. Memory -- Fiction 3. Brothers -- Fiction 4. Criminals -- Fiction 5. Swindlers and swindling -- Fiction
ISBN 978-1-416-96396-7; 1-416-96396-0
LC 2009-33979

When Cassel Sharpe discovers that his older brothers have used him to carry out their criminal schemes and then stolen his memories, he figures out a way to turn their evil machinations against them.

This "starts out with spine-tingling terror, and information is initially dispensed so sparingly, readers will be hooked." Booklist

Other titles in this series are:
Red glove (2011)
Black heart (2012)

Black, Peter Jay

Urban outlaws; Peter Jay Black. Bloomsbury USA Childrens 2014 288 p. illustration (hardback) $16.99
Grades: 5 6 7 8 **Fic**

1. Science fiction 2. Ability -- Fiction 3. Orphans -- Fiction 4. Criminals -- Fiction 5. Adventure and adventurers 6. Computers -- Fiction 7. Adventure and adventurers -- Fiction
ISBN 1619634007; 9781619634008
LC 2014005604

In this middle-grades book, by Peter Jay Black, "deep beneath the city live five extraordinary kids: world-famous hacker Jack, gadget geek Charlie, free runner Slink, communications chief Obi, and decoy expert Wren. Orphans bonded over their shared sense of justice, the kids have formed the Urban Outlaws, a group dedicated to outsmarting criminals and handing out their stolen money through Random Acts of Kindness (R.A.K.s)." (Publisher's note)

"Five orphans—Jack, Charlie, Wren, Obi, and Slink—have made a home for themselves in a WWII bunker under the London subway. They are skilled in various ways—technological savvy, surveillance, and physical prowess in particular—and work together as the Urban Outlaws, using their knowledge to play Robin Hood against local criminals and sharing the benefits of their activities with those less fortunate than themselves...The characters are warm and well developed and will appeal to reluctant readers across middle school. This new series will be an excellent choice for younger fans of Alex Rider." Booklist

Other titles in the series are:
Blackout (2015)

Blackstone, Matt

Sorry you're lost; Matt Blackstone. Farrar Straus & Giroux 2014 312 p. (hardback) $15.99

Grades: 6 7 8 9 **Fic**

1. Grief -- Fiction 2. Middle schools -- Fiction 3. Dating (Social customs) -- Fiction 4. Children -- Conduct of life -- Fiction 5. Schools -- Fiction 6. Popularity -- Fiction 7. Conduct of life -- Fiction 8. Fathers and sons -- Fiction

ISBN 0374380651; 9780374380656

LC 2013021215

In this book, by Matt Blackstone, "Denny "Donuts" Murphy's mother dies [and] he becomes the world's biggest class clown. But deep down, Donuts just wants a normal life. . . . And so Donuts tries to get back into the groove by helping his best friend with their plan to get dates for the end-of-the-year school dance. When their scheme backfires, he learns that laughter is not the best medicine for all of his problems. Sometimes it's just as important to be true to yourself." (Publisher's note)

"Ever since his mother died, seventh grader Denny 'Donuts' Murphy has felt alone and small. So he intentionally develops a big persona, making everything into a joke. With the help of friends and a budding romance, Donuts sheds his manic showman exterior. The first-person narrative is a perfect vehicle to reveal Donuts's inner self in this story of substance and hope." Horn Book

Blackwood, Gary

Around the world in 100 days; [by] Gary Blackwood. Dutton Children's Books 2010 358p

Grades: 6 7 8 9 **Fic**

1. Adventure fiction 2. Automobiles -- Fiction 3. Journalists -- Fiction 4. Automobile travel -- Fiction 5. Voyages around the world -- Fiction 7. Great Britain -- History -- 19th century -- Fiction

ISBN 0-525-42295-1; 978-0-525-42295-2

LC 2009-53236

When seventeen-year-old Harry Fogg undertakes a race against time to win a wager with a member of his famous father's club, he puts to good use the recklessness and fascination with all things mechanical that have caused him trouble in Victorian England.

"The journey is fun and suspenseful." Booklist

Curiosity; by Gary Blackwood. Dial Books for Young Readers, an imprint of Penguin Group (USA) Inc. 2014 320 p. (hardcover) $16.99

Grades: 5 6 7 8 **Fic**

1. Chess -- Fiction 2. Robots -- Fiction 3. Historical fiction 4. Poverty -- Fiction 5. Apprentices -- Fiction 6. Philadelphia (Pa.) -- History -- 19th century -- Fiction

ISBN 0803739249; 9780803739246

LC 2013013438

This novel, by Gary Blackwood, begins in "Philadelphia, PA, 1835. Rufus, a twelve-year-old chess prodigy, is recruited by a shady showman named Maelzel to secretly operate a mechanical chess player called the Turk. . . . But Rufus's job working the automaton must be kept secret, and he fears he may never be able to escape his unscrupulous master. And what has happened to the previous operators of the Turk, who seem to disappear as soon as Maelzel no longer needs them?" (Publisher's note)

"Blackwood excels in writing historical fiction that is as informative as it is entertaining." Horn Book

★ The **Shakespeare** stealer; [by] Gary Blackwood. Dutton Children's Bks. 1998 216p $15.99; pa $5.99

Grades: 5 6 7 8 **Fic**

1. Poets 2. Authors 3. Dramatists 4. Orphans -- Fiction 5. Theater -- Fiction 6. Great Britain -- History -- 1485-1603, Tudors -- Fiction

ISBN 0-525-45863-8; 0-14-130595-9 pa

LC 97-42987

A young orphan boy is ordered by his master to infiltrate Shakespeare's acting troupe in order to steal the script of "Hamlet," but he discovers instead the meaning of friendship and loyalty

"Wry humor, cliffhanger chapter endings, and a plucky protagonist make this a fitting introduction to Shakespeare's world." Horn Book

Other titles in this series are:
Shakespeare's scribe (2000)
Shakespeare's spy (2003)

Shakespeare's scribe; [by] Gary Blackwood. Dutton Children's Bks. 2000 265p hardcover o.p. pa $6.99

Grades: 5 6 7 8 **Fic**

1. Poets 2. Authors 3. Dramatists 4. Orphans -- Fiction 5. Theater -- Fiction 6. Great Britain -- History -- 1485-1603, Tudors -- Fiction

ISBN 0-525-46444-1; 978-0-14-230066-4 pa; 0-14-230066-7 pa

LC 00-34603

In plague-ridden 1602 England, Widge, a fifteen-year-old orphan boy, who has become an apprentice actor, goes on the road with Shakespeare's troupe, and finds out more about his parents along the way

"The story is extremely well structured, with several interesting subplots. . . . The characters are well developed, with Widge being particularly memorable. The dialogue is realistic, and the humorous plays on words add another level of interest." SLJ

Followed by: Shakespeare's spy (2003)

Shakespeare's spy; [by] Gary Blackwood. Dutton Children's Bks. 2003 281p $16.99; pa $6.99

Grades: 5 6 7 8 **Fic**

1. Orphans -- Fiction 2. Theater -- Fiction 3. Great Britain -- History -- 1485-1603, Tudors -- Fiction

ISBN 0-525-47145-6; 0-14-240311-3 pa

LC 2003-61659

The winter of 1602 brings many changes for Widge, a young apprentice at London's Globe Theatre, as he becomes infatuated with Shakespeare's daughter Judith, attempts to write a play, learns more about his past, endangers himself to help a friend, acquires a new identity, and finds a new purpose in life

"Blackwood's well-integrated plot and intriguing subplots ensure a fast-paced tale of Elizabethan England that fans of the earlier novels will love." SLJ

The **year** of the hangman; [by] Gary Blackwood. Dutton Children's Bks. 2002 261p $16.99; pa $5.99

Grades: 8 9 10 11 12 **Fic**

1. United States -- History -- 1775-1783, Revolution -- Fiction

ISBN 0-525-46921-4; 0-14-240078-5 pa

LC 2002-67498

In 1777, having been kidnapped and taken forcibly from England to the American colonies, fifteen-year-old Creighton becomes part of developments in the political unrest there that may spell defeat for the patriots and change the course of history

"Packed with action, convincing historical speculation, and compelling portrayals of real-life and fictional characters, this page-turner will appeal to fans of both history and fantasy." SLJ

Blackwood, Sage

★ **Jinx**; Sage Blackwood. Harper 2013 368 p. (Jinx) (trade bdg.) $16.99
Grades: 4 5 6 7 **Fic**

1. Fantasy fiction 2. Magic -- Fiction 3. Voyages and travels -- Fiction 4. Fantasy
ISBN 0062129902; 9780062129901
LC 2012005249

This fantasy book is set "in the Urwald, an enormous, sentient forest where humans exist on sufferance . . . . After Jinx's brutal stepfather decides to abandon him in the forest, the boy is saved by a crusty, morally ambiguous wizard named Simon, who takes him in as a servant, eventually teaching him some magic. Years later, a 12-year-old Jinx and two new friends set off to find another wizard, the monstrous Bonemaster, in hopes he can help them overcome their respective magical troubles." (Publishers Weekly)

Followed by Jinx's magic (2014) and Jinx's fire (2015)

Jinx's fire; Sage Blackwood. Katherine Tegen Books, an imprint of HarperCollinsPublishers 2015 400 p. map (hardback) $16.99
Grades: 4 5 6 7 **Fic**

1. Fantasy fiction 2. Wizards -- Fiction 3. Forests and forestry -- Fiction 4. Fantasy 5. Magic -- Fiction 6. Orphans -- Fiction
ISBN 0062129961; 9780062129963
LC 2014022688

Sequel to: Jinx's magic

In this novel by Sage Blackwood, "the young wizard Jinx concludes his suspenseful and dryly humorous adventures in the magical forest of the Urwald with this third installment in the series. . . . The forest is under attack and its magic is fading. Can Jinx summon enough of his magic . . . to rescue Simon, defeat the Bonemaster, unite the Urwald, and fight off the invaders?" (Publisher's note)

"In this concluding volume of Blackwood's critically acclaimed series, Jinx is nearly 15, and he finally rescues his mentor, Simon, from the fate the evil Bonemaster wrought in Jinx's Magic (2014). . . . Series fans will be elated to have another outing with the sweetly sardonic hero, whose conscience is almost as troublesome as his grasp of spells. Fans of Cornelia Funke should add this to their stacks." Booklist

Jinx's magic; Sage Blackwood. Katherine Tegen Books 2014 400 p. (hardcover) $16.99
Grades: 4 5 6 7 **Fic**

1. Fantasy 2. Magic -- Fiction 3. Wizards -- Fiction 4. Orphans -- Fiction 5. Forests and forestry -- Fiction
ISBN 9780062129932; 0062129937
LC 2013010171

Sequel to: Jinx

"Jinx knows he can do magic. But he doesn't know why he's being stalked by a werewolf with a notebook, why the trees are starting to take back the only safe paths through the Urwald, or why the elves think Jinx and the evil Bonemaster are somehow connected." (Publisher's note)

"The plot is a little convoluted, wrapping up loose ends from the first volume and setting up elements for the next before finally establishing its own internal tension, but the unique setting, smart pace, likable characters, and sprightly voice hold the narrative together." Horn Book

Miss Ellicott's school for the magically minded; Sage Blackwood, edited by Melissa Miller. Katherine Tegen Books 2017 368 p. illustrations (ebook) $15.99; (hardcover) $16.99
Grades: 4 5 6 7 8 **Fic**

1. Magic -- Fiction 2. Missing persons -- Fiction 3. Private schools -- Fiction
ISBN 9780062402653; 9780062402639
LC 2016935939

In this book, by Sage Blackwood, edited by Melissa Miller, "Chantel would much rather focus on her magic than on curtsying, which is why she often finds herself in trouble at Miss Ellicott's School for Magical Maidens. But when Miss Ellicott mysteriously disappears along with all the other sorceresses in the city, Chantel's behavior becomes the least of her problems. Without any magic protecting the city, it is up to Chantel and her friends to save the Kingdom." (Publisher's note)

"This clever fantasy is a strong purchase for most middle grade collections." SLJ

Blair, Kate

Tangled planet; Kate Blair. Dancing Cat Books, an imprint of Cormorant Books Inc. 2018 259 p. (pbk. : alk. paper) $14.95
Grades: 8 9 10 11 12 **Fic**

1. Life on other planets -- Fiction 2. Interplanetary voyages -- Fiction 3. Murder -- Investigation -- Fiction 4. Colonization -- Fiction 5. Space travelers -- Fiction
ISBN 9781770865051; 1770865047; 9781770865044
LC 2017945945

In this book, by Kate Blair, "starship Venture has finally arrived at . . . Beta Earth, an uninhabited . . . planet. The first night seventeen-year-old engineer Ursa is on Beta Earth, she encounters a dead body. She's positive she saw a large creature with sharp teeth. . . . As injuries and bodies start piling up, Ursa must figure out who to trust when her fellow crewmates start taking sides between maintaining Venture's safety and the hope of creating a home on Beta Earth." (Publisher's note)

"A robust cast of secondary characters, each layered with their own motivations, histories, and perspectives, round out the novel and propel its fierce pace." SLJ

Blake, Ashley Herring

★ **Ivy** Aberdeen's letter to the world; Ashley Herring Blake. Little, Brown & Co. 2018 310 p. (hardcover) $16.99
Grades: 4 5 6 7 8 **Fic**

1. Lesbians -- Fiction 2. Tornadoes -- Fiction 3. Coming out (Sexual orientation) -- Fiction 4. Artists -- Fiction 5. Friendship -- Fiction 6. Family life -- Fiction
ISBN 9780316515481; 9780316515467
LC 2017019242

Stonewall Honor Book (2019)

In this novel, by Ashley Herring Blake, "when a tornado rips through town, twelve-year-old Ivy Aberdeen's house is destroyed and her family of five is displaced. Ivy feels invisible and ignored in the aftermath of the storm--and what's worse, her notebook filled with secret drawings of girls holding hands has gone missing. Mysteriously, Ivy's drawings begin to reappear in her locker with notes from someone telling her to open up about her identity." (Publisher's note)

"This necessary and emotionally complex addition to the body of middle-grade literature offers readers a positive, complex, and courageous portrayal of burgeoning sexuality and relationships within the world of junior high." Booklist

★ The **mighty** heart of Sunny St. James; Ashley Herring Blake. Little, Brown & Co. 2019 384 p. (hardcover) $16.99
Grades: 4 5 6 7 8 **Fic**

1. Friendship -- Fiction 2. Heart -- Transplantation -- Fiction 3. Mother-daughter relationship -- Fiction 4. Sexual orientation --

Fiction 5. Mothers and daughters -- Fiction
ISBN 9780316515535

LC 2018017613

In this book, by Ashley Herring Blake, "Sunny St. James receives a new heart, [and] decides to set off on a 'New Life Plan': 1) do awesome amazing things she could never do before; 2) find a new best friend; and 3) kiss a boy for the first time. . . . But when she meets her new best friend Quinn, Sunny questions whether she really wants to kiss a boy at all. With the reemergence of her mother, Sunny begins a journey to becoming the new Sunny St. James." (Publisher's note)

"A sweet and gentle story of self-discovery and a beautiful addition to the growing genre of middle-grade realism featuring girls who like girls." Kirkus

Blake, Kendare

★ **Anna** Dressed in Blood. Tor 2011 320p $17.99
Grades: 8 9 10 11 12 **Fic**

1. Ghost stories 2. Horror fiction 3. Cats -- Fiction 4. Witches -- Fiction
ISBN 978-0-7653-2865-6; 0-7653-2865-8

LC 2011018985

"Blake populates the story with a nice mixture of personalities, including Anna, and spices it with plenty of gallows humor, all the while keeping the suspense pounding. . . . Abundantly original, marvelously inventive and enormous fun, this can stand alongside the best horror fiction out there. We demand sequels." Kirkus

Blakemore, Megan Frazer

The **spy** catchers of Maple Hill; by Megan Frazer Blakemore. Bloomsbury 2014 320 p. (hardback) $16.99
Grades: 4 5 6 7 **Fic**

1. Mystery fiction 2. Vermont -- Fiction 3. Country life -- Fiction 4. Spies -- Fiction 5. Cold War -- Fiction 6. Friendship -- Fiction 7. City and town life -- Vermont -- Fiction 8. Vermont -- History -- 20th century -- Fiction
ISBN 1619633485; 9781619633483

LC 2013039857

In this children's novel by Megan Frazer Blakemore, "Hazel Kaplansky is a firm believer in the pursuit of knowledge and truth--and she also happens to love a good mystery. When suspicions swirl that a Russian spy has infiltrated her small town of Maple Hill, Vermont, amidst the fervor of Cold War era McCarthyism, Hazel knows it's up to her to find a suspect starting with Mr. Jones, the quietly suspicious grave digger." (Publisher's note)

"The book does a wonderful job of displaying the way in which the fear inherent in the McCarthy era turned neighbor against neighbor. While the heart of the story lies within the issues of trust and truth, the writing is never preachy, using Hazel's innate humor to deflect moments that veer close to saccarine or preachy. A strong work of historical fiction for mystery fans." SLJ Reviews

The **Water** Castle; by Megan Frazer Blakemore. Walker 2013 352 p. (hardback) $16.99
Grades: 3 4 5 6 7 **Fic**

1. Magic -- Fiction 2. Castles -- Fiction 3. Family secrets -- Fiction 4. Maine -- Fiction 5. Families -- Fiction 6. Dwellings -- Fiction 7. Moving, Household -- Fiction 8. Discoveries in science -- Fiction
ISBN 0802728391; 9780802728395

LC 2012016442

In this novel by Megan Frazer Blakemore "Ephraim Appledore-Smith is an ordinary boy, and up until his father's stroke he lived an ordinary life. But all that changes when his family moves to the Water Castle. . . . Mallory Green's family has always been the caretakers of the Water Castle. . . . She has been raised to protect the legendary Fountain of Youth, hidden on the estate grounds. When Ephraim learns of the Fountain, he's sure finding it can cure his dad." (Publisher's note)

Blazanin, Jan

A & L do summer. Egmont USA 2011 273p pa $8.99
Grades: 7 8 9 10 **Fic**

1. Iowa -- Fiction 2. Summer -- Fiction 3. Bullies -- Fiction 4. Friendship -- Fiction 5. Family life -- Fiction 6. Domestic animals -- Fiction
ISBN 978-1-60684-191-4 pa; 1-60684-191-2 pa; 978-1-60684-243-0 ebook

LC 2010-43616

In Iowa farm country, sixteen-year-old Aspen and her friend Laurel plan to get noticed the summer before their senior year and are unwittingly aided by pig triplets, a skunk, a chicken, bullies, a rookie policeman, and potential boyfriends.

"A series of mishaps add hilarity to the story. . . . All's well that ends well in this read perfectly suited for light refreshment on a hot summer day." Booklist

Block, Francesca Lia

The **island** of excess love; Francesca Lia Block. Henry Holt Books for Young Readers 2014 240 p. (hardback) $16.99
Grades: 8 9 10 11 12 **Fic**

1. Roman mythology 2. Adventure fiction 3. Love -- Fiction 4. Science fiction 5. Visions -- Fiction 6. Survival -- Fiction 7. Friendship -- Fiction 8. Los Angeles (Calif.) -- Fiction
ISBN 0805096310; 9780805096316

LC 2014005284

Companion to: Love in the Time of Global Warming

"Pen has lost her parents. She's lost her eye. But she has fought Kronen; she has won back her fragile friends and her beloved brother. Now Pen, Hex, Ash, Ez, and Venice are living in the pink house by the sea, getting by on hard work, companionship, and dreams. Until the day a foreboding ship appears in the harbor across from their home." (Publisher's note) The book is a companion to "Love in the Time of Global Warming."

"Just as Block's earlier novel was loosely based on The Odyssey, this is even more loosely based on The Aeneid. The result is a mesmerizing, magical, and mysterious tale of love and loss, stories and visions, and betrayal and redemption, all told in the author's signature lyrical voice." Booklist

★ **Love** in the time of global warming; Francesca Lia Block. Henry Holt and Co. 2013 240 p. (hardcover) $16.99
Grades: 8 9 10 11 12 **Fic**

1. Apocalyptic fiction 2. Voyages and travels -- Fiction 3. Love -- Fiction 4. Science fiction 5. Families -- Fiction 6. Survival -- Fiction 7. Earthquakes -- Fiction 8. Los Angeles (Calif.) -- Fiction
ISBN 0805096272; 9780805096279

LC 2012047808

Rainbow List (2014)

In this book, after "an earthquake and tidal wave destroy much of Los Angeles, Penelope—now going by Pen—sets out to find her family. In the course of a journey that explicitly parallels the one described in Homer's Odyssey, Pen navigates the blighted landscape with a crew of three other searchers. . . . Eventually they arrive in Las Vegas (the contemporary stand-in for the land of the dead) where Pen confronts the evil genius behind her world's destruction." (Publishers Weekly)

"In this Odyssey-inspired story, after the devastating Earth Shaker, Penelope sets out into the brutal Los Angeles landscape in search of her family. She meets an intriguing boy named Hex who joins her on her journey. Block's imagery is remarkable in this sophisticated melding of post-apocalyptic setting, re-imagined classic, and her signature magical realism." (Horn Book)

The **waters** & the wild. HarperTeen 2009 113p $16.99; lib bdg $17.89
Grades: 7 8 9 10 **Fic**

1. School stories 2. Fairies -- Fiction 3. Los Angeles (Calif.) -- Fiction
ISBN 978-0-06-145244-4; 0-06-145244-0; 978-0-06-145245-1 lib bdg; 0-06-145245-9 lib bdg

LC 2008031452

Thirteen-year-old Bee realizes that she is a fairy who has been switched at birth with another girl who now wants her life back.

"Fragments of poems by Yeats and Shelley are eerily apropos (and may provide an irresistible invitation for further reading). Haunting and thought provoking." Publ Wkly

Bloor, Edward

★ **Taken**. Alfred A. Knopf 2007 247p $17; pa $8.99
Grades: 6 7 8 9 10 **Fic**

1. Science fiction 2. Kidnapping -- Fiction 3. Social classes -- Fiction
ISBN 978-0-375-83636-7; 0-375-83636-5; 978-0-440-42128-3 pa; 0-440-42128-4 pa

LC 2006-35561

In 2036 kidnapping rich children has become an industry, but when thirteen-year-old Charity Meyers is taken and held for ransom, she soon discovers that this particular kidnapping is not what it seems.

"Deftly constructed, this is as riveting as it is thought-provoking." Publ Wkly

★ **Tangerine**. Harcourt Brace & Co. 1997 294p $17
Grades: 7 8 9 10 **Fic**

1. Soccer -- Fiction 2. Florida -- Fiction 3. Brothers -- Fiction
ISBN 0-15-201246-X

LC 96-34182

Twelve-year-old Paul, who lives in the shadow of his football hero brother Erik, fights for the right to play soccer despite his near blindness and slowly begins to remember the incident that damaged his eyesight

"Readers will cheer for this bright, funny, decent kid." Horn Book Guide

Blos, Joan W.

★ **Letters** from the corrugated castle; a novel of gold rush California, 1850-1852. Atheneum Books for Young Readers 2007 310p $17.99; pa $5.99
Grades: 5 6 7 8 **Fic**

1. California -- Fiction 2. Mexican Americans -- Fiction 3. Gold mines and mining -- Fiction 4. Frontier and pioneer life -- Fiction 5. Mother-daughter relationship -- Fiction
ISBN 978-0-689-87077-4; 0-689-87077-9; 978-0-689-87078-1 pa; 0-689-87078-7 pa

LC 2007-02673

A series of letters and newspaper articles reveals life in California in the 1850s, especially for thirteen-year-old Eldora, who was raised in Massachusetts as an orphan only to meet her influential mother in San Francisco, and Luke, who hopes to find a fortune in gold.

"It is Blos' sturdy characters, whose experiences reveal the complexity of human relationships and wisdom about 'the salt and the sweet of life,' who will make this last." Booklist

Blume, Judy, 1938-

★ **Are** you there God?, it's me, Margaret; rev format ed.; Atheneum 2001 149p hc $17.99
Grades: 4 5 6 7 **Fic**

1. Bildungsromans 2. Puberty -- Fiction 3. Religion -- Fiction
ISBN 0-689-84158-2; 9781481413978

A reissue of the title first published 1970 by Bradbury Press

A "story about the emotional, physical, and spiritual ups and downs experienced by 12-year-old Margaret, child of a Jewish-Protestant union." Natl Counc of Teach of Engl. Adventuring with Books. 2d edition

BFF* * best friends forever; two novels. Delacorte Press 496p $18.99 **Fic**

1. Friendship -- Fiction. 2. Family problems -- Fiction. 3. Gifted children -- Fiction. 4. Brothers and sisters -- Fiction. 5. Interpersonal relations -- Fiction.
ISBN 978-0-385-73407-3

A compilation of two previously published novels: Just as long and we're together (1987) and Here's to you Rachel Robinson (1993)

Here's to you, Rachel Robinson. Orchard Bks. 1993 196p hardcover o.p. pa $5.99
Grades: 5 6 7 8 **Fic**

1. Siblings -- Fiction 2. Friendship -- Fiction 3. Gifted children -- Fiction
ISBN 0-531-06801-3; 0-440-21974-4 pa

LC 93-9631

Expelled from boarding school, Charles' presence at home proves disruptive, especially for sister Rachel, a gifted seventh grader juggling friendships and school activities

"Blume once again demonstrates her ability to shape multidimensional characters and to explore—often through very convincing dialogue—the tangled interactions of believable, complex people." Publ Wkly

Tiger eyes; a novel. Bradbury Press 1981 206p $16.95; pa $6.99
Grades: 7 8 9 10 **Fic**

1. Death -- Fiction
ISBN 9781481413879; 9781481414395; 0-689-85872-8; 0-440-98469-6 pa

LC 81-6152

Resettled in the "Bomb City" with her mother and brother, Davey Wexler recovers from the shock of her father's death during a holdup of his 7-Eleven store in Atlantic City

"The plot is strong, interesting and believable. . . . The story though intense and complicated flows smoothly and easily." Voice Youth Advocates

Blume, Lesley M. M.

Julia and the art of practical travel; Lesley M.M. Blume. First edition Alfred A. Knopf 2015 192 p. illustrations $16.99
Grades: 4 5 6 **Fic**

1. Aunts -- Fiction 2. Automobile travel 3. Mother-daughter relationship -- Fiction 4. Missing persons -- Fiction 5. Automobile travel -- Fiction 6. United States -- History -- 1961-1969 -- Fiction
ISBN 0385752822; 9780385752824; 9780385752831

LC 2013044490

In this book by Lesley M. M. Blume, "after Julia's wealthy grandmother dies, and the family estate in the Hudson Valley is sold, Julia and her Aunt Constance hit the road, determined to track down Julia's mother, who disappeared three years before. In an old station wagon full of family heirlooms like a silver tea set and oriental carpets--'practical travel things,' according to Aunt Constance--they travel from New York to California." (Publishers Weekly)

"Each character is delightful and quirky, and readers will enjoy all of them. The story comes to a somewhat predictable conclusion, but it hardly matters. This book is filled with familial love and the joy of traveling, and readers will appreciate Julia's journey." SLJ

★ The **rising** star of Rusty Nail; [by] Lesley M.M. Blume. Alfred A. Knopf 2007 270p $15.99; lib bdg $18.99; pa $6.50

Grades: 4 5 6 **Fic**

1. Pianists -- Fiction 2. Minnesota -- Fiction 3. Musicians -- Fiction 4. Russian Americans -- Fiction

ISBN 978-0-375-83524-7; 978-0-375-93524-4 lib bdg; 978-0-440-42111-5 pa

LC 2006024252

In the small town of Rusty Nail, Minnesota, in the early 1950s, musically talented ten-year-old Franny wants to take advanced piano lessons from newcomer Olga Malenkov, a famous Russian musician suspected of being a communist spy by gossipy members of the community

"Blume has skillfully combined humor, history, and music to create an enjoyable novel that builds to a surprising crescendo." SLJ

Blumenthal, Deborah

Mafia girl; Deborah Blumenthal. Albert Whitman & Company 2014 256 p. (hardcover) $16.99

Grades: 8 9 10 11 **Fic**

1. Mafia -- Fiction 2. Family -- Fiction 3. Identity -- Fiction 4. Father-daughter relationship -- Fiction 5. Families -- Fiction

ISBN 0807549118; 9780807549117

LC 2013028440

In this book, by Deborah Blumenthal, "seventeen-year-old Gia is the most hated/loved girl in school. Why? Her father doesn't have a boss. He is the boss - the capo di tutti cappi, boss of all bosses. Not that Gia cares. But life gets complicated when she meets a cop she calls 'Officer Hottie' and feels a suprising chemistry. Then Vogue magazine wants to feature Gia in a fashion spread about real-life bad girls. On top of this, she's running for class president." (Publisher's note)

"Gia, the prized daughter of a New York Mafia boss, enjoys the carefree lifestyle her father's money and connections afford her. When the feds begin to close in on the family business, Gia must find an identity outside of Don's Daughter. Gia's voice is an entertaining, effervescent stream-of-consciousness, but the book's frantic pace muddles too many competing plot lines." Horn Book

Blundell, Judy

A **city** tossed and broken; the diary of Minnie Bonner. Judy Blundell. Scholastic Inc. 2013 224 p. (paper over board) $12.99

Grades: 4 5 6 7 **Fic**

1. Historical fiction 2. Household employees -- Fiction 3. San Francisco (Calif.) -- History -- Fiction 4. Diaries -- Fiction 5. Earthquakes -- Fiction 6. Family life -- California -- Fiction 7. San Francisco Earthquake and Fire, Calif., 1906 -- Fiction

ISBN 0545310229; 9780545310222

LC 2012014742

This novel, by Judy Blundell, presents the diary of the girl Minnie Bonner during the San Francisco, California earthquake of 1906 as part of the "Dear America" series. A "wealthy gentleman . . . offers Minnie a chance to work as a lady's maid. . . . But when a powerful earthquake strikes, Minnie finds herself the sole survivor among them. . . . Minnie has turned into an heiress overnight . . . and she is soon wrapped up in a deception that leads her down a dangerous path." (Publisher's note)

"The author deftly incorporates true events, circumstances and key historical figures into the rapidly unfolding fictional plot... Exciting, suspenseful, absorbing and informative." Kirkus

Strings attached. Scholastic Press 2011 310p $17.99

Grades: 7 8 9 10 **Fic**

1. Dance -- Fiction 2. Mafia -- Fiction 3. Homicide -- Fiction 4. New York (N.Y.) -- Fiction 5. Italian Americans -- Fiction

ISBN 978-0-545-22126-9; 0-545-22126-9

LC 2010-41078

Blundell "successfully constructs a complex web of intrigue that connects characters in unexpected ways. History and theater buffs will especially appreciate her attention to detail—Blundell again demonstrates she can turn out first-rate historical fiction." Publ Wkly

★ **What** I saw and how I lied. Scholastic Press 2008 284p $16.99

Grades: 8 9 10 11 12 **Fic**

1. Mystery fiction 2. Florida -- Fiction

ISBN 978-0-439-90346-2; 0-439-90346-7

LC 2008-08503

National Book Award: Young People's Literature (2008)

In 1947, with her jovial stepfather Joe back from the war and family life returning to normal, teenage Evie, smitten by the handsome young ex-GI who seems to have a secret hold on Joe, finds herself caught in a complicated web of lies whose devastating outcome change her life and that of her family forever.

"Using pitch-perfect dialogue and short sentences filled with meaning, Blundell has crafted a suspenseful, historical mystery." Booklist

Bobet, Leah

An **inheritance** of ashes; by Leah Bobet. Clarion Books 2015 400 p. map (hardback) $17.99

Grades: 7 8 9 10 11 12 **Fic**

1. War stories 2. Fantasy fiction 3. Secrets -- Fiction 4. Sisters -- Fiction 5. Monsters -- Fiction 6. Farm life -- Fiction 7. Fantasy 8. War -- Fiction

ISBN 9780544281110

LC 2015006823

In this book, by Leah Bobet, the "strange war down south—with its rumors of gods and monsters—is over. And while sixteen-year-old Hallie and her sister wait to see who will return from the distant battlefield, they struggle to maintain their family farm. When Hallie hires a veteran to help them, the war comes home in ways no one could have imagined, and soon Hallie is taking dangerous risks—and keeping desperate secrets." (Publisher's note)

"Bobet repeatedly emphasizes the importance family—of blood or of choice—plays in surviving calamity. The satisfying yet realistic ending will leave readers hoping for more." Booklist

Bock, Caroline

★ **LIE**. St. Martin's Griffin 2011 211p pa $9.99

Grades: 8 9 10 11 12 **Fic**

1. Homicide -- Fiction 2. Violence -- Fiction 3. Immigrants -- Fiction 4. Prejudices -- Fiction

ISBN 978-0-312-66832-7; 0-312-66832-5

LC 2011019824

Seventeen-year-old Skylar Thompson is being questioned by the police. Her boyfriend, Jimmy, stands accused of brutally assaulting two young El Salvadoran immigrants from a neighboring town, and she's the prime witness.

"This effective, character-driven, episodic story examines the consequences of a hate crime on the teens involved in it. . . . Realistic and devastatingly insightful, this novel can serve as a springboard to classroom and family discussions. Unusual and important." Kirkus

Bodeen, S. A.

The **Compound**. Feiwel and Friends 2008 248p $16.95; pa $8.99

Grades: 7 8 9 10 **Fic**

1. Twins -- Fiction 2. Fathers -- Fiction 3. Survival after airplane accidents, shipwrecks, etc. -- Fiction

ISBN 0-312-37015-6; 0-312-57860-1 pa; 978-0-312-37015-2; 978-0-312-57860-2 pa

LC 2007-36148

After his parents, two sisters, and he have spent six years in a vast underground compound built by his wealthy father to protect them from a nuclear holocaust, fifteen-year-old Eli, whose twin brother and grandmother were left behind, discovers that his father has perpetrated a monstrous hoax on them all.

"The audience will feel the pressure closing in on them as they, like the characters, race through hairpin turns in the plot toward a breathless climax." Publ Wkly

The **raft**; S.A. Bodeen. Feiwel and Friends 2012 231 p. $16.99

Grades: 7 8 9 10 **Fic**

1. Survival skills -- Fiction 2. Wilderness survival -- Fiction 3. Survival after airplane accidents, shipwrecks, etc. -- Fiction

ISBN 0312650108; 9780312650100

This novel, by S. A. Bodeen, is a plane crash survival story. "All systems are go until a storm hits during the flight. The only passenger, Robie doesn't panic until the engine suddenly cuts out and Max shouts at her to put on a life jacket. . . . And then . . . she's in the water. Fighting for her life. Max pulls her onto the raft. . . . They have no water. Their only food is a bag of Skittles. There are sharks. There is an island. But there's no sign of help on the way." (Publisher's note)

Shipwreck Island; by S. A. Bodeen. Feiwel & Friends 2014 192 p. hc $16.99

Grades: 5 6 7 8 **Fic**

1. Islands -- Fiction 2. Shipwrecks -- Fiction 3. Family life -- Fiction 4. Stepmothers -- Fiction

ISBN 9781250027771; 1250027772

In this book, by S. A. Bodeen, "Sarah is not happy that her dad has married again, forcing her to deal with a new stepmom and two new brothers. To help them bond, Sarah's dad and stepmom decide to take everyone on a vacation to Tahiti, rent a yacht, and cruise to their own private island. They sail right into a terrible storm, the captain is swept overboard, and the yacht runs aground on a deserted island.." (Library Media Connection)

"These very human protagonists respond in believable ways to their new family situation while encountering freakish animals, bizarrely dangerous weather, and a creepy, empty house." SLJ

Boie, Kirsten

The **princess** plot; translated by David Henry Wilson. Scholastic 2009 378p $17.99

Grades: 5 6 7 8 **Fic**

1. Princesses -- Fiction 2. Conspiracies -- Fiction

ISBN 978-0-545-03220-9; 0-545-03220-2

LC 2008-24403

Original German edition, 2005

Believing that she is on a film set after auditioning and winning the role of a princess, fourteen-year-old Jenna becomes the unsuspecting pawn in a royal conspiracy

"This novel takes simple, straightforward writing and layers it with kidnappings, political intrigue, and an abundance of secret plots. Readers will enjoy leisurely uncovering the mystery of Jenna's heritage, right along with Jenna herself." Booklist

Another title about Jenna is:

The princess trap (2010)

The **princess** trap; translated by David Henry Wilson. Chicken House/Scholastic 2010 405p $17.99

Grades: 5 6 7 8 **Fic**

1. School stories 2. Princesses -- Fiction

ISBN 978-0-545-22261-7; 0-545-22261-3

LC 2010010072

Sequel to: The princess plot (2009)

Original German edition, 2007

Palace rules, boarding school, and paparazzi have Jenna, princess of the newly unified kingdom of Scandia, longing for her former anonymity, but when she runs away she finds herself in grave danger—and in a position to prevent the outbreak of civil war.

Bolden, Tonya

★ **Crossing** Ebenezer Creek; by Tonya Bolden. Bloomsbury 2017 230 p. (hardback) $17.99

Grades: 7 8 9 10 11 12 **Fic**

1. Slavery -- Fiction 2. Siblings -- Fiction 3. Love -- Fiction 4. Freedmen -- Fiction 5. African Americans -- Fiction 6. Brothers and sisters -- Fiction 6. Sherman's March to the Sea -- Fiction 7. United States -- History -- Civil War, 1861-1865 -- Fiction

ISBN 9781619630550; 9781599903194

LC 2016037742

In this book, by Tonya Bolden, "when Mariah and her young brother Zeke are suddenly freed from slavery, they join Sherman's march through Georgia. . . . [Then] she meets a free black named Caleb, [and] Mariah dreams in a way she never dared . . . of a future worth living and the possibility of true love. But even hope comes at a cost, and as the difficult march continues toward the churning waters of Ebenezer Creek, Mariah's dreams are as vulnerable as ever." (Publisher's note)

"A poetic, raw, and extraordinary imagining of a little-known, shameful chapter in American history." Kirkus

Includes bibliographical references, pages [225]-227.

★ **Finding** family. Bloomsbury 2010 181p il $15.99

Grades: 4 5 6 7 **Fic**

1. Aunts -- Fiction 2. Family life -- Fiction 3. Grandfathers -- Fiction 4. West Virginia -- Fiction 5. African Americans -- Fiction

ISBN 978-1-59990-318-7; 1-59990-318-0

LC 2010-00535

Raised in Charleston, West Virginia, at the turn of the twentieth century by her grandfather and aunt on off-putting tales of family members she has never met, twelve-year-old Delana is shocked when, after Aunt Tilley dies, she learns the truth about her parents and some of her other relatives.

"This richly lyrical and historically persuasive coming-of-age story explores the ties that bind, break and renew an affuent African-American family. . . . Period photographic portraits from Bolden's personal collection illustrate the book. Each carefully posed subject is a fascinating enigma." Kirkus

Inventing Victoria; by Tonya Bolden. Bloomsbury 2019 272 p. (hardcover) $17.99

Grades: 8 9 10 11 12 **Fic**

1. Identity -- Fiction 2. African Americans -- Fiction 3. Reconstruction (1865-1876) -- Fiction 4. Reconstruction (U.S. history, 1865-1877) -- Fiction 5. Savannah (Ga.) -- History -- 19th century -- Fiction 6. Washington (D.C.) -- History -- 19th century -- Fiction

ISBN 9781681198071

LC 2018024642

In this novel, by Tonya Bolden, "as a young black woman in 1880s Savannah, Essie's dreams are very much at odds with her reality. Ashamed of her beginnings, but unwilling to accept the path currently available to her, Essie is trapped between the life she has and the life she wants. Until she meets a lady named Dorcas Vashon, the richest and most cultured black woman she's ever encountered." (Publisher's note)

Boles, Philana Marie

Little divas. Amistad 2006 164p $15.99; lib bdg $16.89; pa $5.99

Grades: 5 6 7 8 **Fic**

1. Cousins -- Fiction 2. Divorce -- Fiction 3. African Americans -- Fiction 4. Father-daughter relationship -- Fiction

ISBN 0-06-073299-7; 0-06-073300-4 lib bdg; 0-06-073301-2 pa

The summer before seventh grade, Cassidy Carter must come to terms with living with her father, practically a stranger, as well as her relationships with her cousins, all amidst the overall confusion of adolescence.

"Boles portrays this variable age well, and readers will feel for Cassidy's trials." SLJ

Bond, Victoria

Zora and me; the song of Ivory. [by] Victoria Bond and T. R. Simon. Candlewick Press 2010 170p $16.99; pa $6.99

Grades: 4 5 6 7 **Fic**

1. Authors 2. Novelists 3. Dramatists 4. Memoirists 5. Folklorists 6. Short story writers 7. Race relations -- Fiction 8. African Americans -- Fiction

ISBN 978-0-7636-4300-3; 0-7636-4300-9; 978-0-7636-5814-4 pa; 0-7636-5814-6 pa

LC 2009-47410

Coretta Scott King/John Steptoe New Talent Award (Author), 2011

This is a fictionalized account of Zora Neale Hurston's childhood with her best friend Carrie, in Eatonville, Florida. Annotated bibliography. "Grades four to seven." (Bull Cent Child Books)

"The brilliance of this novel is its rendering of African-American child life during the Jim Crow era as a time of wonder and imagination, while also attending to its harsh realities. Absolutely outstanding." Kirkus

Followed by:

The cursed ground (2018)

Bondoux, Anne-Laure

★ A **time** of miracles; translated from the French by Y. Maudet. Delacorte Press 2010 180p map $17.99; lib bdg $20.99

Grades: 6 7 8 9 **Fic**

1. War stories 2. Europe -- Fiction 3. Refugees -- Fiction

ISBN 978-0-385-73922-1; 0-385-73922-2; 978-0-385-90777-4 lib bdg; 0-385-90777-X lib bdg

LC 2010008539

"Readers will find themselves mesmerized not only by the eloquent language but by a plot every bit as harrowing and surprising as Koumail's cherished bedtime story." Horn Book

Boniface, William

The **great** powers outage; [by] William Boniface; illustrations by Stephen Gilpin. 1st ed.; HarperCollins 2008 342p il (The extraordinary adventures of Ordinary Boy) $16.99; lib bdg $17.89

Grades: 4 5 6 7 **Fic**

1. Superheroes -- Fiction

ISBN 978-0-06-077470-7; 0-06-077470-3; 978-0-06-077471-4 lib bdg; 0-06-077471-1 lib bdg

LC 2007049579

When the citizens of Superopolis begin to mysteriously lose their superpowers, Ordinary Boy and his friends investigate the world of master villains.

"Boniface has cleverly interlaced bits and pieces of story lines from past novels with this one to expand his wacky world with enough history and political overtones to appeal to those readers savvy enough to understand the satire behind the silliness. Reluctant readers can enjoy the comic graphic-novel essence of the text as well as Gilpin's humorous sketches." SLJ

The **hero** revealed; [by] William Boniface; illustrations by Stephen Gilpin. HarperCollins Pub. 2006 294p il (The extraordinary adventures of Ordinary Boy) $15.99; lib bdg $16.89; pa $6.99

Grades: 4 5 6 7 **Fic**

1. Superheroes -- Fiction

ISBN 978-0-06-077464-6; 0-06-077464-9; 978-0-06-077465-3 lib bdg; 0-06-077465-7 lib bdg; 978-0-06-077466-0 pa; 0-06-077466-5 pa

LC 2005018676

Ordinary Boy, the only resident of Superopolis without a superpower, uncovers and foils a sinister plot to destroy the town

"This first book in a new series is great fun. . . . Boniface wields a cynical, but definitely kid-friendly, sense of humor, and Gilpin's illustrations are sharp and witty." SLJ

Other titles in this series are:

The return of Meteor Boy? (2007)

The great powers outage (2008)

The **return** of Meteor Boy? [by] William Boniface; illustrations by Stephen Gilpin. 1st ed.; HarperCollinsPublishers 2007 344p (The extraordinary adventures of Ordinary Boy) $16.99; lib bdg $17.89

Grades: 4 5 6 7 **Fic**

1. Superheroes -- Fiction

ISBN 978-0-06-077467-7; 0-06-077467-3; 978-0-06-077468-4 lib bdg; 0-06-077468-1 lib bdg

LC 2006029877

Sequel to: The hero revealed (2006)

While working on a time machine for the Spring Science Fair, Ordinary Boy discovers the true identity of long-lost Superopolis hero Meteor Boy.

"This second book in the series will appeal to superhero and comic-book readers. . . . The conversational style and full black-and-white cartoon illustrations . . . add to the silly mood." Booklist

Followed by: The great powers outage (2008)

Booraem, Ellen

★ **Small** persons with wings. Dial Books for Young Readers 2011 302p $16.99

Grades: 4 5 6 7 **Fic**

1. Fantasy fiction 2. Magic -- Fiction 3. Fairies -- Fiction 4. Grandfathers -- Fiction 5. Lost and found possessions -- Fiction
ISBN 978-0-8037-3471-5; 0-8037-3471-9

LC 2010008400

When Mellie Turpin's grandfather dies and leaves her family his run-down inn and bar, she learns that for generations her family members have been fairy guardians. "Grades five to eight." (Bull Cent Child Books)

"In a fairy story that's wistful, humorous, and clever, Booraem . . . suggests that the real world—with its disappointments and failings—is still better than living with illusions. . . . The theme of making progress, rather than ignoring problems, is a strong one, gently presented." Publ Wkly

Texting the underworld; by Ellen Booraem. Dial Books for Young Readers 2013 319 p. (hardcover) $16.99

Grades: 5 6 7 8 **Fic**

1. Banshees -- Fiction 2. School stories -- Fiction 3. Fantasy fiction 4. Death -- Fiction 5. Humorous stories 6. Schools -- Fiction 7. Supernatural -- Fiction
ISBN 0803737041; 9780803737044

LC 2012032488

In this book by Ellen Booraem, "Conor O'Neill is a smart but timid seventh-grader. . . . When a banshee straight out of his Irish-born grandfather's stories appears in Conor's room, he's terrified that someone he loves is going to die soon. The banshee, Ashling, is new at her job, and . . . she's curious about the present day, [so] she masquerades as a new student at Conor's school." (Publishers Weekly)

Boos, Ben

Fantasy : an artist's realm. Candlewick Press 2010 83p il $19.99

Grades: 6 7 8 9 **Fic**

1. Fantasy fiction
ISBN 978-0-7636-4056-9; 0-7636-4056-5

LC 2010007511

"This tour of New Perigord begins by presenting the fictional realm's geography, warriors, enemies, common weapons, and mages, including full details of their abilities and spells. . . . [Boos] reveals 'commonly encountered spirits,' such as elves, undines, and banshees. . . . The large spreads are filled with authentically ancient-looking, digitally produced pictures of the many imagined inhabitants and elements, all described in densely packed, short blocks of text. . . . This offers plenty of entertainment for even those with a more casual interest in the fantasy genre." Booklist

Booth, Coe

Kinda like brothers; Coe Booth. Scholastic Press 2014 256 p. (hardcover) $17.99

Grades: 4 5 6 7 8 **Fic**

1. Brothers -- Fiction 2. Foster home care -- Fiction 3. Foster home care 4. African Americans 5. Interpersonal relations
ISBN 0545224969; 9780545224963

LC 2014937301

This book by Coe Booth "introduces an African-American family in Newark who open their home to foster children. By the time Kevon, 12, and his two-year-old sister, Treasure, arrive in the middle of the night, 11-year-old Jarrett has had enough of his mother's charity. Jarrett is forced to share a room with Kevon, who acts distant and ungrateful, and he's also annoyed to be attending summer school, with the threat of having to repeat the sixth grade." (Publishers Weekly)

Booth, Molly

Saving Hamlet; Molly Booth. Disner-Hyperion 2016 352 p. (hardcover) $17.99

Grades: 7 8 9 10 **Fic**

1. Theater -- Fiction 2. Time travel -- Fiction 3. Shakespeare, William, 1564-1616 -- Fiction
ISBN 1484752740; 9781484752746

LC 2015045426

In this book, by Molly Booth, "Emma Allen couldn't be more excited to start her sophomore year. Not only is she the assistant stage manager for the drama club's production of Hamlet, but her crush Brandon is directing. . . . But soon after school starts, everything goes haywire. Emma's promoted to stage manager with zero experience, her best friend Lulu stops talking to her, and Josh--the adorable soccer boy who's cast as the lead--turns out to be a disaster. It's up to Emma to fix it all." (Publisher's note)

"Emma is an easy-to-root-for heroine whose struggles will resonate with teens, drama geeks or otherwise, and her forays into Shakespeare's London add insight into gender identity in the theater. A fun, imaginative debut." Booklist

Bouwman, H. M.

A **crack** in the sea; H.M. Bouwman. G.P. Putnam's Sons 2017 357 p. (hardback) $16.99

Grades: 5 6 7 8 **Fic**

1. Fantasy fiction 2. Sea monsters -- Fiction 3. Fantasy 4. Kraken -- Fiction 5. Slavery -- Fiction 6. Refugees -- Fiction 7. Adventure and adventurers -- Fiction
ISBN 9780399545191; 9780399545207

LC 2016008734

In this children's historical fantasy story, by H. M. Bauwman and illustrated by Yuko Shimizu, "the doorway between worlds opens only when least expected. The Raft King is desperate to change that by finding the doorway that will finally take him and the people of Raftworld back home. To do it, he needs Pip, a young boy with an incredible gift. . . . Pip's sister Kinchen, though, is determined to rescue her brother and foil the Raft King's plans." (Publisher's note)

"This novel touches on sensitive and tragic moments in history and gives them fantastical remediation for a provocative, immersive read." Kirkus

Includes bibliographical references

A **tear** in the ocean; H.M. Bouwman ; illustrations, Yuko Shimizu. G.P. Putnam's Sons 2019 304 p. illustrations (hardback) $16.99

Grades: 5 6 7 8 **Fic**

1. Fantasy fiction 2. Adventure fiction 3. Friendship -- Fiction 4. Fantasy
ISBN 9780399545221

LC 2018025578

"Putnam, the future king of Raftworld, wants . . . to prove himself. When the water in the Second World starts to become salty . . . , Putnam sees his chance. He steals a boat and sneaks off toward the source of the salty water. He doesn't know he has a stowaway onboard, an island girl named Artie. . . . [A]s the two face uncertainty and danger in their shared adventure, an extraordinary friendship forms." (Publisher's note)

"An intentional folkloric sensibility is palpable throughout as they encounter fantastical beings and places along their journeys, shown in Shimizu's occasional, dramatic black-and-white illustrations. This is an engaging and original coming-of-age story with an unpredictable and adventurous plot, sure to captivate middle-grade and middle-school fantasy buffs." Horn Book

Bow, Erin

★ **Plain** Kate. Arthur A. Levine Books 2010 314p $17.99
Grades: 7 8 9 10 **Fic**

1. Fantasy fiction 2. Cats -- Fiction 3. Magic -- Fiction 4. Orphans -- Fiction 5. Witchcraft -- Fiction 6. Wood carving -- Fiction
ISBN 978-0-545-16664-5; 0-545-16664-0

LC 2009-32652

Plain Kate's odd appearance and expertise as a woodcarver cause some to think her a witch, but friendship with a talking cat and, later, with humans help her to survive and even thrive in a world of magic, charms, and fear.

"Despite the talking animal . . . and graceful writing . . . this is a dark and complex tale, full of violence—knives cut a lot more than wood. . . . Kate is undeniably a sympathetic character deserving of happiness." Publ Wkly

★ **Sorrow's** knot; Erin Bow. Arthur A. Levine Books 2013 368 p. (hardcover : alk. paper) $17.99
Grades: 8 9 10 11 12 **Fic**

1. Dead -- Fiction 2. Magic -- Fiction 3. Knots and splices -- Fiction 4. Identity -- Fiction 5. Fate and fatalism -- Fiction
ISBN 0545166667; 9780545166669; 9780545166676; 9780545578004

LC 2013007855

In this book, by Erin Bow, "the dead do not rest easy. Every patch of shadow might be home to something hungry, something deadly. Most of the people of this world live on the sunlit, treeless prairies. But a few carve out an uneasy living in the forest towns, keeping the dead at bay with wards made from magically knotted cords. The women who tie these knots are called binders. And Otter's mother, Willow, is one of the greatest binders her people have ever known." (Publisher's note)

"Sorrow's Knot is a dystopian novel that does not deal with the destruction of the broader world. Rather, it delves into the mythology of a group of people and how their prejudices and resistance to change came to be. Readers of suspense will love the dark tension of the story line, an ebb and flow that carries through to the very end." SLJ

Bowen, Fred

Quarterback season; written by Fred Bowen. Peachtree 2011 132p pa $5.95
Grades: 4 5 6 7 **Fic**

1. Diaries -- Fiction 2. Football -- Fiction
ISBN 978-1-56145-594-2; 1-56145-594-6

LC 2011002673

As a school assignment, eighth-grader Matt Monroe keeps a journal about his team's football season.

This is "another absorbing sports tale from the prolific and dependable Bowen. . . . The author expertly balances the subplots and football action." Booklist

Bowler, Tim

Fighting back. Philomel Books 2011 $16.99
Grades: 7 8 9 10 **Fic**

1. Gangs -- Fiction 2. Homicide -- Fiction 3. Violence -- Fiction 4. Homeless persons -- Fiction
ISBN 978-0-399-25431-4; 0-399-25431-5

LC 2010005392

First published in the United Kingdom

When streetwise fourteen-year-old Blade returns to "the Beast," the city he left years before, to find young Jaz and bring her to safety, he is forced to confront his own demons.

Bowles, David

They call me Guero; a border kid's poems. David Bowles. Cinco Puntos Press 2018 160 p. (cloth) $16.95
Grades: 5 6 7 8 **Fic**

1. Novels in verse 2. Boys -- Fiction 3. Mexican Americans -- Fiction
ISBN 9781947627062; 9781947627079

LC 2018027137

Pura Belpré Author Honor Book (2019)

In this book, by David Bowles, "Ğero is a Mexican American border kid with nerdy tastes, pale skin, and red hair. Wishing he had been born with a darker complexion so no one would question his Mexican American heritage, Ğero 's family tells him to be grateful for the advantages his lighter hair and skin. . . . Ğero 's voice carries this novel through a playful array of poetic forms, from sonnets to raps, free verse to haiku." (School Library Journal)

Bowling, Dusti

Insignificant events in the life of a cactus; by Dusti Bowling. Sterling Children's Books 2017 262 p. (hardcover) $14.95
Grades: 5 6 7 8 **Fic**

1. Friendship -- Fiction 2. Children with disabilities -- Fiction 3. Adoption -- Fiction 4. Amusement parks -- Fiction 5. Moving, Household -- Fiction 6. Tourette syndrome -- Fiction 7. Overweight persons -- Fiction 8. People with disabilities -- Fiction.
ISBN 9781454923459; 1454923458

LC 2017021165

In this novel, by Dusti Bowling, "Aven Green loves to tell people that she lost her arms in an alligator wrestling match, . . . but the truth is she was born without them. And when her parents take a job running Stagecoach Pass, a rundown western theme park in Arizona, . . . her new life takes an unexpected turn when she bonds with Connor, a classmate who also feels isolated because of his own disability." (Publisher's note)

"The tale of Stagecoach Pass is just as compelling as the story of Aven, and the setting, like the many colorful characters who people this novel, is so vivid and quirky that it's practically cinematic." SLJ

Bowman, Akemi Dawn

Starfish; Akemi Dawn Bowman. Simon Pulse 2017 352 p. (hardback) $17.99
Grades: 7 8 9 10 **Fic**

1. Family problems -- Fiction 2. Racially mixed people -- Fiction 3. Mother-daughter relationship -- Fiction 4. Artists -- Fiction 5. Identity -- Fiction 6. Sexual abuse -- Fiction 7. Self-perception -- Fiction 8. Mothers and daughters -- Fiction
ISBN 9781481487726

LC 2016045829

William C. Morris Honor Book (2018)

In this novel, by Akemi Dawn Bowman, Kiko Himura's mother "makes her feel unremarkable and . . . [with] a half-Japanese heritage she doesn't quite understand, Kiko prefers to keep her head down. . . . When she receives an invitation from her childhood friend to leave her small town and tour art schools on the west coast, Kiko jumps at the opportunity in spite of the anxieties and fears that attempt to hold her back." (Publisher's note)

"The story will resonate deeply with readers who have experienced abuse of any kind, or who have been held back by social anxiety. This is a stunningly beautiful, highly nuanced debut." (Booklist)

Summer bird blue; Akemi Dawn Bowman. Simon Pulse 2018 384 p. (jacketed hardcover) $18.99

Grades: 7 8 9 10 11 12 **Fic**

1. Death -- Fiction 2. Grief -- Fiction 3. Hawaii -- Fiction 4. Sisters -- Fiction 5. Composers -- Fiction 6. Mothers and daughters -- Fiction

ISBN 9781481487757

LC 2017048136

In this novel, by Akemi Dawn Bowman, "[Rumi Seto] wants to spend the rest of her life writing music with her younger sister, Lea. Then Lea dies in a car accident, and her mother sends her away to live with her aunt in Hawaii while she deals with her own grief. . . . With the help of . . . a teenage surfer named Kai . . . and an eighty-year-old named George Watanabe, . . . Rumi attempts to find her way back to her music." (Publisher's note)

Bradbury, Jennifer

★ **Shift**. Atheneum Books for Young Readers 2008 245p $16.99

Grades: 7 8 9 10 11 12 **Fic**

1. Travel -- Fiction 2. Cycling -- Fiction 3. Friendship -- Fiction 4. Missing persons -- Fiction

ISBN 978-1-4169-4732-5; 1-4169-4732-9

LC 2007-23558

When best friends Chris and Win go on a cross country bicycle trek the summer after graduating and only one returns, the FBI wants to know what happened.

"Bradbury's keen details . . . add wonderful texture to this exciting [novel.] . . . Best of all is the friendship story." Booklist

Wrapped. Atheneum Books for Young Readers 2011 309p $16.99

Grades: 7 8 9 10 **Fic**

1. Mystery fiction 2. Spies -- Fiction 3. Supernatural -- Fiction 4. Great Britain -- History -- 19th century -- Fiction

ISBN 978-1-4169-9007-9; 1-4169-9007-0

"An 1815 parlor diversion leads to a fizzy, frothy caper. Agnes is a Regency debutante. . . . When she pockets the trinket she finds among the linens at her neighbor's mummy-wrapping party, she unwittingly sets off a series of catastrophes . . . that include burglaries, violent attacks and murder. . . . Bradbury weaves Egyptology, Napoleanic conquest and a flirtation with the supernatural into a spy thriller." Kirkus

Bradbury, Ray, 1920-2013

The **Halloween** tree; [by] Ray Bradbury; illustrated by Joseph Mugnaini. Alfred A. Knopf 2007 145p il $15.99

Grades: 6 7 8 9 **Fic**

1. Fantasy fiction 2. Halloween -- Fiction

ISBN 0-394-82409-1; 978-0-394-82409-3

A reissue of the title first published 1972

A group of boys meet a spirit-being and are carried back in time to the origins of Halloween celebrations.

This is "fast-moving, genuinely eerie." Booklist

Something wicked this way comes. Avon Bks. 1999 293p $15.95; pa $7.99

Grades: 7 8 9 10 **Fic**

1. Horror fiction 2. Fantasy fiction

ISBN 0-380-97727-3; 0-380-72940-7 pa

A reissue of the title first published 1962 by Simon and Schuster

"We read here of the loss of innocence, the recognition of evil, the bond between generations, and the purely fantastic. These forces enter Green Town, Illinois, on the wheels of Cooger and Dark's Pandemonium Shadow Show. Will Halloway and Jim Nightshade, two 13-year-olds, explore the sinister carnival for excitement, which becomes desperation as the forces of the dark threaten to engulf-them. Bradbury's gentle humanism and lyric style serve this fantasy well." Shapiro. Fic for Youth. 3d edition

Braden, Ann

The **benefits** of being an octopus; Ann Braden. Sky Pony Press 2018 254 p. (hardback) $16.99

Grades: 4 5 6 7 8 **Fic**

1. Poverty -- Fiction 2. Friendship -- Fiction 3. Self-esteem -- Fiction 4. Schools -- Fiction 5. Middle schools -- Fiction 6. Social classes -- Fiction 7. Family problems -- Fiction 8. Brothers and sisters -- Fiction 9. Debates and debating -- Fiction

ISBN 9781510737525; 9781510737488

LC 2018016762

In this novel, by Ann Braden, "seventh-grader Zoey has her hands full as she takes care of her much younger siblings after school every day while her mom works her shift at the pizza parlor. . . . Zoey thinks how much easier everything would be if she were an octopus: eight arms to do eight things at once. . . . [This] explores the cultural divides around class and the gun debate through the eyes of one girl, living on the edges of society, trying to find her way forward." (Publisher's note)

Bradford, Chris

Young samurai: the way of the sword. Disney-Hyperion Books 2010 422p $16.99

Grades: 4 5 6 7 **Fic**

1. Adventure fiction 2. Japan -- Fiction 3. Ninja -- Fiction 4. Orphans -- Fiction 5. Samurai -- Fiction 6. Martial arts -- Fiction

ISBN 978-1-4231-2025-4; 1-4231-2025-6

LC 2009008309

Sequel to: Young samurai: the way of the warrior (2009)

In 1611 Japan, English orphan Jack Fletcher continues his difficult training at Niten Ichi Ryu Samurai School, while also trying to get back the rutter, his father's navigational logbook, that an evil ninja wants to possess.

"With straightforward prose, [Bradford] has managed to pen lively and exciting fight sequences and is slowly beginning to develop a keen edge to his cast of characters, laying significant groundwork for future installments." Booklist

★ **Young** samurai: the way of the warrior. Hyperion Books for Children 2009 359p $16.99

Grades: 4 5 6 7 **Fic**

1. Adventure fiction 2. Japan -- Fiction 3. Samurai -- Fiction 4. Martial arts -- Fiction

ISBN 978-1-4231-1871-8; 1-4231-1871-5

LC 2008-46180

First published 2008 in the United Kingdom

Orphaned by a ninja pirate attack off the coast of Japan in 1611, twelve-year-old English lad Jack Fletcher is determined to prove himself, despite the bullying of fellow students, when the legendary sword master who rescued him begins training him as a samurai warrior.

"Jack's story alone makes for a page-turner, but coupling it with intriguing bits of Japanese history and culture, Bradford produces an adventure novel to rank among the genre's best." Publ Wkly

Includes bibliographical references

Followed by: Young samurai: the way of the sword (2010)

Bradford, Michael

Button Hill; Michael Bradford. Orca Book Publishers 2015 264 p. (pbk.) $9.95

Grades: 6 7 8 **Fic**

1. Parapsychology -- Fiction 2. Missing children -- Fiction 3. Brothers and sisters -- Fiction

ISBN 1459807553; 9781459807556; 9781459807563; 9781459807570

LC 2014952055

In Michael Bradford's novel "Dekker isn't happy that he and his little sister, Riley, are stuck in Button Hill with their weird old great-aunt Primrose. When he discovers an old clock in the cellar, made entirely of bones and with a skull for a face, he doesn't think much about it. But when Riley goes missing, a strange boy named Cobb appears in Button Hill. He tells Dekker that Button Hill sits on the border between Nightside and Dayside--and that Riley is in Nightside." (Publisher's note)

"Dekker discovers a mysterious clock in the cellar beneath the basement of his great aunt Primrose's old house. After twisting the skull that decorates the Nightclock and unknowingly opening the border between the living world (Dayside) and that of the dead (Nightside), mischievous Dekker inadvertently allows a sinister, pointy-toothed boy named Cobb to kidnap his sister and hide her in Nightside...An additional purchase for those who like their fantasy with plenty of skeletons (and a soft-hearted zombie)."

Bradley, Kimberly Brubaker

★ **Jefferson's** sons; a founding father's secret children. Dial Books for Young Readers 2011 368p $17.99

Grades: 5 6 7 8 **Fic**

1. Slaves 2. Architects 3. Presidents 4. Vice-presidents 5. Essayists 6. Mistresses 7. Slavery -- Fiction 8. Virginia -- Fiction 9. African Americans -- Fiction

ISBN 978-0-8037-3499-9; 0-8037-3499-9

LC 2010049650

"The characters spring to life. . . . [This is a] fascinating story of an American family that represents so many of the contradictions of our history. The afterword is as fascinating as the novel." Kirkus

The **lacemaker** and the princess. Margaret K. McElderry Books 2007 199p $16.99; pa $6.99

Grades: 4 5 6 7 8 **Fic**

1. Queens 2. Friendship -- Fiction 3. Lace and lace making -- Fiction 4. France -- History -- 1789-1799, Revolution -- Fiction

ISBN 978-1-4169-1920-9; 1-4169-1920-1; 978-1-4169-8583-9 pa; 1-4169-8583-2 pa

In 1788, eleven-year-old Isabelle, living with her lacemaker grandmother and mother near the palace of Versailles, becomes close friends with Marie Antoinette's daughter, Princess Therese, and finds their relationship complicated not only by their different social class but by the growing political unrest and resentment of the French people.

"Skillfully integrated historical facts frame this engrossing, believable story." Booklist

★ The **war** that saved my life; by Kimberly Brubaker Bradley. Dial Books for Young Readers 2015 320 p. (hardcover) $16.99

Grades: 4 5 6 7 **Fic**

1. Brothers and sisters -- Fiction 2. People with disabilities -- Fiction 3. Great Britain -- History -- 20th century -- Fiction 4. World War, 1939-1945 -- Evacuation of civilians -- Fiction 5. Great Britain -- History -- George VI, 1936-1952 -- Fiction

ISBN 0803740816; 9780803740815

LC 2014002168

ALA Notable Children's Book, 2016
ALSC Notable Children's Recording, 2016.
Newbery Honor Book, 2016.
Odyssey Award for Excellence in Audiobook Production, 2016.
Schneider Family Book Award for Middle School, 2016.
Josette Frank Award, 2016.

In this book, by Kimberly Brubaker Bradley, "[n]ine-year-old Ada has never left her one-room apartment. Her mother is too humiliated by Ada's twisted foot to let her outside. So when her little brother Jamie is shipped out of London to escape the war, Ada doesn't waste a minute - she sneaks out to join him. So begins a new adventure of Ada, and for Susan Smith, the woman who is forced to take the two kids in." (Publisher's note)

"When word starts to spread about Germans bombing London, Ada's mother decides to send her little brother, Jamie, to the country. Not 11-year-old Ada, though—she was born with a crippling clubfoot, and her cruel mother treats her like a slave...The home-front realities of WWII, as well as Ada's realistic anger and fear, come to life in Bradley's affecting and austerely told story, and readers will cheer for steadfast Ada as she triumphs over despair." Booklist

Followed by The war I finally won (2017)

Brahmachari, Sita

Jasmine Skies; by Sita Brahmachari. Albert Whitman & Company 2012 336 p. $16.99

Grades: 6 7 8 9 **Fic**

1. India -- Fiction 2. Family secrets -- Fiction 3. Interpersonal relations -- Fiction 4. Secrecy 5. Families -- India 6. Voyages and travels 7. Dysfunctional families 8. Dating (social customs)

ISBN 0807537829; 1447205189; 9780807537824; 9781447205180

LC 2014013302

"Mira Levenson is excited to visit India for the first time. But upon arriving she is hurled into new sights, sounds, sweltering heat and deeply buried family secrets. From the moment Mira meets Janu she feels an instant connection to him. Nothing is as she imagined it--and suddenly home feels a long way away. But Mira is determined to uncover the truth about her family, and she must also make a decision that will break someone's heart." (Publisher's note)

"Vivid descriptions of the exotic setting, an emotionally honest (if naive and stubborn) narrator, and a sweet romance should captivate readers." Booklist

Mira in the present tense; Sita Brahmachari. Albert Whitman & Co 2013 284 p. $16.99

Grades: 5 6 7 8 **Fic**

1. Grief -- Fiction 2. Teenage girls -- Fiction 3. Diaries -- Fiction 4. Secrecy -- Fiction 5. Families -- Fiction

ISBN 080755149X; 9780807551493

In this middle grades book by Sita Brahmachari, "Twelve-year-old Mira comes from a chaotic, artistic, and outspoken family in which it's not always easy to be heard. As her beloved Nana Josie's health declines, Mira begins to discover the secrets of those around her and also starts to keep some of her own. She is drawn to mysterious Jide, a boy who is clearly hiding a troubled past." (Publisher's note)

"Mira narrates her story through a diary she receives for her twelfth birthday. She lives in London, is half Jewish and one-quarter Indian, and has joined a writing club at school. A few too many events and characters crowd the otherwise engaging story, which focuses on Mira's loving relationship with her Nana Josie, who is dying from cancer. " Horn Book

Brande, Robin

Evolution, me, & other freaks of nature. Alfred A. Knopf 2007 268p hardcover o.p. pa $7.99

Grades: 7 8 9 10 **Fic**

1. School stories 2. Evolution -- Fiction 3. Christian life -- Fiction
ISBN 978-0-375-84349-5; 0-375-84349-3; 978-0-375-94349-2 lib bdg; 0-375-94349-8 lib bdg; 978-0-440-24030-3 pa; 0-440-24030-1 pa

LC 2006-34158

Following her conscience leads high school freshman Mena to clash with her parents and former friends from their conservative Christian church, but might result in better things when she stands up for a teacher who refuses to include "Intelligent Design" in lessons on evolution.

"Readers will appreciate this vulnerable but ultimately resilient protagonist who sees no conflict between science and her own deeply rooted faith." Booklist

Brandeis, Gayle

My life with the Lincolns. Holt & Co. 2010 248p $16.99
Grades: 4 5 6 7 **Fic**

1. Family life -- Fiction 2. Race relations -- Fiction 3. African Americans -- Fiction
ISBN 978-0-8050-9013-0; 0-8050-9013-4

LC 2009-24151

"Twelve-year-old Mina Edelman is convinced that her family members are the Lincolns reincarnate, and she has many coincidences to back her up. . . . The strong theme of social justice creates a unifying thread in this informative, clear, personal, and passionate novel." Booklist

Brant, Wendy

★ **Zenn** diagram; Wendy Brant. Kids Can Press 2017 315 p. (hardcover) $17.95
Grades: 8 9 10 11 12 **Fic**

1. Psychic ability -- Fiction 2. Tutors and tutoring -- Fiction 3. Extrasensory perception -- Fiction
ISBN 9781771388566; 9781771387927; 1771387920

In this novel, by Wendy Brant, "Eva Walker is a seventeen-year-old math genius. And if that doesn't do wonders for her popularity, there's another thing that makes it even worse: when she touches another person or anything that belongs to them from clothes to textbooks to cell phones she sees a vision of their emotions. She can read a person's fears and anxieties. . . . Then one day a new student walks into Eva's life." (Publisher's note)

"Though the plot coincidences stretch belief at times, they are forgiven in light of the strengths of the story, which include a unique premise, natural dialogue, and complex characters." Booklist

Brashares, Ann

The **sisterhood** of the traveling pants. Delacorte Press 2001 294p $14.95; pa $8.95; pa $9.99
Grades: 8 9 10 **Fic**

1. Friendship -- Fiction
ISBN 0-385-72933-2; 0-385-73058-6 pa; 9780385730587 pa

LC 2002-282046

"Four teenagers—best friends since babyhood—have different destinations for the summer and are distressed about disbanding. When they find a pair of 'magic pants'—secondhand jeans that fit each girl perfectly, despite their different body types—they take a solemn vow that the Pants 'will travel to all the places we're going, and they will keep us together when we are apart.' . . . Middle school, high school." (Horn Book)

"Four lifelong high-school friends and a magical pair of jeans take summer journeys to discover love, disappointment, and self-realization." Booklist

Brashear, Amy

The **incredible** true story of the making of the Eve of destruction; Amy Brashear. Soho Teen 2018 312 p. (hardback) $18.99
Grades: 8 9 10 11 12 **Fic**

1. Family life 2. Nuclear reactor accidents -- Fiction 3. Motion pictures -- Production and direction -- Fiction 4. Nuclear accidents -- Fiction
ISBN 9781616959036

LC 2018027722

In this book, by Amy Brashear, "when sixteen-year-old Laura Ratliff wins a walk-on role . . . thanks to a radio call-in contest, she is more relieved than excited. Mingling with Hollywood stars on the set of a phony nuclear war is a perfect distraction from being the only child in her real nuclear family. . . . Her father, an officer in the Strategic Air Command, is absent . . . except when he phones at odd hours to hint at an impending catastrophe. But isn't that his job?" (Publisher's note)

Bray, Libba

★ **Beauty** queens. Scholastic Press 2011 396p $18.99
Grades: 8 9 10 11 12 **Fic**

1. Beauty contests -- Fiction 2. Survival after airplane accidents, shipwrecks, etc. -- Fiction
ISBN 978-0-439-89597-2; 0-439-89597-9

LC 2011-02321

In this book by Libba Bray, "on their way to the Miss Teen Dream competition, a planeload of beauty pageant contestants crashes on what appears to be a deserted island. While the surviving Teen Dreamers valiantly cope with the basics (finding food, water, and shelter; practicing their pageant skills), they become pawns in a massive global conspiracy involving a rogue former Miss Teen Dream winner; a megalomaniacal dictator; and a Big Brother-ish pageant sponsor, The Corporation." (Horn Book Magazine)

"A full-scale send-up of consumer culture, beauty pageants, and reality television: . . . it makes readers really examine their own values while they are laughing, and shaking their heads at the hyperbolic absurdity of those values gone seriously awry." Bull Cent Child Books

Breen, M. E.

★ **Darkwood**. Bloomsbury 2009 273p il $16.99
Grades: 5 6 7 8 **Fic**

1. Fantasy fiction 2. Adventure fiction 3. Wolves -- Fiction 4. Orphans -- Fiction 5. Sisters -- Fiction
ISBN 978-1-59990-259-3; 1-59990-259-1

LC 2008-44413

A clever and fearless orphan endures increasing danger while trying to escape from greedy, lawless men and elude the terrifying "kinderstalks"—animals who steal children—before discovering her true destiny.

"Breen's finely tuned storytelling—pithy description, quick and keen emotion, broad trust of readers' intelligence—offers equal gratification whether readers spot clues and connections early or late. Both grounded and wondrous." Kirkus

Brenna, Beverly

Waiting for no one. Red Deer 2011 187p pa $12.95
Grades: 7 8 9 10 **Fic**

1. Asperger's syndrome -- Fiction
ISBN 978-0-88995-437-3; 0-88995-437-2
Sequel to Wild orchid (2006)

Taylor Jane Smith is "taking a biology class at college and applying for a job at a local bookstore. Her Asperger's syndrome gives her an advantage in the class, but it's making the job-application process torture. . . . Taylor, with her flinty, exasperated approach to the world, remains a fascinating character and narrator." Bull Cent Child Books

Brennan, Caitlin

House of the star. Tor 2010 282p $17.99

Grades: 7 8 9 10 **Fic**

1. Fantasy fiction 2. Magic -- Fiction 3. Horses -- Fiction 4. Arizona -- Fiction 5. Princesses -- Fiction 6. Ranch life -- Fiction

ISBN 978-0-7653-2037-7; 0-7653-2037-1

LC 2010-36678

"Princess Elen of Ymbria has always wanted to be a rider of a worldrunner—a magical horse that can travel safely on faerie roads between worlds. She is invited to Earth to stay at the House of Star, an Arizona ranch where these animals are bred. The only catch is that someone from the royal family of Caledon has been invited as well. . . . Brennan creates a magical world based around a realistic ranch setting. The two main characters are complex and avoid the common clichés about princesses. Fans of fantasy and horses will find an intriguing premise and a galloping plot." SLJ

Brennan, Herbie

The **Doomsday** Box; a Shadow Project adventure. Balzer & Bray 2011 328p $16.99

Grades: 6 7 8 9 **Fic**

1. Spies -- Fiction 2. Plague -- Fiction 3. Cold war -- Fiction 4. Time travel -- Fiction 5. Extrasensory perception -- Fiction

ISBN 978-0-06-175647-4; 0-06-175647-4

LC 2010-15947

Sequel to: The Shadow Project (2010)

Working on a highly-classified espionage project, four English teenagers go back in time to the Cold War in 1962 to prevent a global outbreak of the bubonic plague in the twenty-first century.

"Readers who enjoy their action/adventure laced with weird science and real politics will enjoy this fast-paced, exciting second in the series." Bull Cent Child Books

The **secret** prophecy; Herbie Brennan. Balzer + Bray 2012 322 p. (hardback) $27.95

Grades: 5 6 7 8 **Fic**

1. Murder -- Fiction 2. England -- Fiction 3. Conspiracies -- Fiction 4. Secret societies -- Fiction 5. Mystery and detective stories

ISBN 0691155895; 9780062071804

LC 2012024991

In this book, "teenager Em Goverton gets two major shocks in quick succession: the sudden death of his father and the overheard suggestion that it might have been murder. After a short vacation in France with a childhood friend and her family leads to additional suspicious events, Em returns home to find his mother institutionalized and their house ransacked. Em's attempt to evade corrupt social services workers takes him to a homeless shelter and a helpful man named Victor." (Publishers Weekly)

The **Shadow** Project. Balzer & Bray 2010 355p $16.99

Grades: 6 7 8 9 **Fic**

1. Spies -- Fiction 2. Supernatural -- Fiction 3. Great Britain -- Fiction

ISBN 978-0-06-175642-9; 0-06-175642-3

LC 2009-14276

A young English thief stumbles on, and subsequently is recruited for, a super-secret operation that trains teenagers in remote viewing and astral projection techniques in order to engage in spying.

"The action has a ready-for-its-close-up cinematic quality, and there's a manageable blend of stock and original, fully fleshed characters to guarantee investment and relatability. This is the kind of mind candy that action/adventure junkies will gobble right up." Bull Cent Child Books

Followed by: The Doomsday Box (2011)

Brennan, Sarah Rees

Unspoken; by Sarah Rees Brennan. Random House Books for Young Readers 2012 373 p. (The Lynburn legacy) (hardcover) $18.99

Grades: 7 8 9 10 **Fic**

1. Gothic novels -- Fiction 3. Fantasy fiction -- Fiction 4. Mystery fiction -- Fiction 5. Horror stories 6. Magic -- Fiction 7. England -- Fiction 8. Magicians -- Fiction

ISBN 9780375870415; 9780375970412

LC 2012001954

"Kami Glass knows that she could be a great reporter. . . . The aristocratic, secretive Lynburns are coming home, . . . and Kami is determined . . . [to] get the scoop. Soon, two gorgeous, near-identical Lynburn cousins . . . join her journalistic team--not to mention Kami's imaginary best friend, . . . who turns out to be not quite so imaginary after all. And that's when the grisly murders start." (Kirkus Reviews)

Other titles in this series are:
Untold (2013)
Unmade (2014)

Brewer, Zac

The **chronicles** of Vladimir Tod: eighth grade bites. Dutton Children's Books 2007 182p (The chronicles of Vladimir Tod) $16.99

Grades: 6 7 8 9 **Fic**

1. School stories 2. Orphans -- Fiction 3. Vampires -- Fiction

ISBN 978-0-525-47811-9; 0-525-47811-6

LC 2006030455

For thirteen years, Vlad, aided by his aunt and best friend, has kept secret that he is half-vampire, but when his missing teacher is replaced by a sinister substitute, he learns that there is more to being a vampire, and to his parents' deaths, than he could have guessed.

This "is an exceptional current-day vampire story. The mix of typical teen angst and dealing with growing vampiric urges make for a fast-moving, engaging story." Voice Youth Advocates

Other in this series are:
Ninth grade slays (2008)
Tenth grade bleeds (2009)
Eleventh grade burns (2010)
Twelfth grade kills (2010)

First kill. Dial Books for Young Readers 2011 309p il (The Slayer chronicles) $17.99

Grades: 6 7 8 9 **Fic**

1. Horror fiction 2. Vampires -- Fiction

ISBN 0-8037-3741-6; 978-0-8037-3741-9

LC 2011006061

The summer before ninth grade, when Joss sets off to meet his uncle and hunt down the beast that murdered his younger sister three years earlier, he learns he is destined to join the Slayer Society.

"This companion volume to Brewer's Vlad Tod series (Twelfth Grade Kills, 2010, etc.) provides a simple entry point into the opposite side of the vampire world--those tasked with killing the undead. . . . Action flows seamlessly into drama, and a betrayal comes after a series of clever misdirections." Kirkus

Other titles in this series are:
Second chance (2012)
Third strike (2014)

Brewster, Alicia Wright

Echo; Alicia Wright Brewster. Dragonfairy Press 2013 291 p. (paperback) $14.95
Grades: 7 8 9 10 11 12 **Fic**

1. Magic -- Fiction 2. End of the world -- Fiction
ISBN 0985023023; 9780985023027
LC 2012951596

In this book by Alicia Wright Brewster, "Earth-Two . . . will end in 10 days. Calling up all elemental practitioners to help, the Council elders have averted catastrophe only by repeatedly rewinding time back 10 days before the end. With each rewind, they become weakened echoes of their original selves. . . . Their efforts focus on eliminating the Mages--formerly human 'ether manipulators' whose elemental energies have consumed their humanity--causing the crisis." (Kirkus Reviews)

"Fully realized characters from Asha to the walk-ons lend their intense authenticity to the plot, which straddles the line between fantasy and science fiction, and deflect attention from the rubber science. This world has depth, mirroring the memorable characters who populate it." Kirkus

Brezenoff, Steve

Brooklyn, burning. Carolrhoda Lab 2011 202p $17.95
Grades: 8 9 10 11 **Fic**

1. Musicians -- Fiction 2. Runaway teenagers -- Fiction 3. Brooklyn (New York, N.Y.) -- Fiction
ISBN 978-0-7613-7526-5
LC 2010051447

"Homelessness, queerness and the rougher sides of living on the street are handled without a whiff of sensationalism, and the moments between Kid, the first-person narrator, and Scout, addressed as 'you,' are described in language so natural and vibrant that readers may not even notice that neither character's gender is ever specified. . . . Overall, the tone is as raw, down-to-earth and transcendent as the music Scout and Kid ultimately make together." Kirkus

Briant, Ed

Choppy socky blues. Flux 2010 259p pa $9.95
Grades: 7 8 9 10 **Fic**

1. Karate -- Fiction 2. Great Britain -- Fiction 3. Dating (Social customs) -- Fiction 4. Father-son relationship -- Fiction
ISBN 978-0-7387-1897-2; 0-7387-1897-1
LC 2009-30491

In the South of England, fourteen-year-old Jay resumes contact with his father, a movie stuntman and karate instructor, after two years of estrangement to impress a girl who turns out to be the girlfriend of Jay's former best friend.

"Jason's insecurities, resentment toward (and gradual peacemaking with) his father, and obsession with girls are believably rendered—he's the kind of awkward hero readers will be glad to see come into his own." Publ Wkly

I am (not) the walrus; Ed Briant. 1st ed. Flux 2012 280 p. (pbk.) $9.95
Grades: 8 9 10 11 **Fic**

1. Romance fiction 2. Rock music -- Fiction 3. Bands (Music) -- Fiction
ISBN 073873246X; 9780738732466
LC 2012004314

This novel, by Ed Briant, describes how "Toby and Zack's first gig could make or break their Beatles cover band, the Nowhere Men. But ever since getting dumped by his girlfriend, lead singer Toby can't quite pull off the Beatles' feel-good vibe. When Toby finds a note hidden inside his brother's bass claiming the instrument was stolen, he embarks on a quest to find the true owner--and hopes a girl named Michelle will help him recover his lost mojo along the way." (Publisher's note)

Bridges, Robin

The **gathering** storm. Delacorte Press 2012 (The Katerina trilogy) $17.99; lib bdg $20.99; ebook $10.99
Grades: 7 8 9 10 **Fic**

1. Russia -- Fiction 2. Vampires -- Fiction 3. Supernatural -- Fiction 4. Good and evil -- Fiction 5. Courts and courtiers -- Fiction
ISBN 978-0-385-74022-7; 0-385-74022-0; 978-0-385-90829-0 lib bdg; 0-385-90829-6 lib bdg; 978-0-375-89901-0 ebook
LC 2011026175

In St. Petersburg, Russia, in 1888, royal debutante Katerina Alexandrovna, Duchess of Oldenburg, tries to hide a dark secret—that she has the ability to raise the dead—but when she uses her special skill to protect a member of the Imperial Family, she finds herself caught in a web of intrigue.

"The fully realized setting, a fantastical version of pre-revolutionary Russia, adds a level of believability to this [book]. . . . An atmospheric and complicated vampire tale." Kirkus

Brignull, Irena

★ The **Hawkweed** Prophecy; Irena Brignull. Weinstein Books 2016 368 p. (ebook) $11.99; $18.00
Grades: 7 8 9 10 **Fic**

1. Magic -- Fiction 2. Witches -- Fiction 3. Individuality -- Fiction 4. Female friendship -- Fiction
ISBN 9781602863019; 1602863008; 9781602863002
LC 2016037295

In this novel, by Irena Brignull, "Poppy Hooper and Ember Hawkweed couldn't lead more different lives. Poppy is a troubled teen, . . . causing chaos wherever she goes. . . . Ember is a young witch, struggling to find a place within her coven and prove her worth. Both are outsiders: feeling like they don't belong and seeking escape. Poppy and Ember soon become friends, and secretly share knowledge of their two worlds. Little do they know that destiny has brought them together." (Publisher's note)

"The third-person narration switches focus from character to character as they make frustrating, heart-rending, totally believable choices. Fantasy and nonfantasy readers alike will appreciate this gritty and intriguing coming-of-age story." Kirkus

Britt, Fanny

Jane, the fox & me; [written by] Fanny Britt ; [illustrated by] Isabelle Arsenault ; translated by Christine Morelli and Susan Ouriou. Pgw 2013 101 p. $19.95
Grades: 5 6 7 8 9 **Fic**

1. Teenage girls -- Fiction 2. Alienation (Social psychology) -- Fiction
ISBN 1554983606; 9781554983605
Eisner Nominee: Best Publication for Children (2014)
Governor General's Award: Children's Illustration (2013)

Written by Fanny Britt, illustrated by Isabelle Arsentault, and translated by Christine Morelli and Susan Ouriou, this "graphic novel reveals the casual brutality of which children are capable, but also assures readers that redemption can be found through connecting with another, whether the other is a friend, a fictional character or even, amazingly, a fox." (Publisher's note) It "centers on Hélène, ostracized by her former friends and now a loner at school." (Horn Book Magazine)

"Britt's well-constructed narrative is achieved sensitively through Arsenault's impressionistic artwork. . . . An elegant and accessible approach to an important topic." Booklist

Brittain, Bill

The **wish** giver; three tales of Coven Tree. drawings by Andrew Glass. Harper & Row 1983 181p il $16.89; pa $5.99

Grades: 5 6 7 8 **Fic**

1. Magic -- Fiction 2. Wishes -- Fiction

ISBN 0-06-020687-X; 0-06-440168-5 pa

LC 82-48264

A Newbery Medal honor book, 1984

"Captivating, fresh, and infused with homespun humor." Horn Book

Other titles about Coven Tree are:

Dr. Dredd's wagon of wonders (1987)

Professor Popkin's prodigious polish (1990)

Broach, Elise

★ **Masterpiece**; illustrated by Kelly Murphy. Henry Holt & Co. 2008 292p il $16.95

Grades: 4 5 6 7 **Fic**

1. Mystery fiction 2. Artists -- Fiction 3. Beetles -- Fiction 4. New York (N.Y.) -- Fiction

ISBN 978-0-8050-8270-8; 0-8050-8270-0

After Marvin, a beetle, makes a miniature drawing as an eleventh birthday gift for James, a human with whom he shares a house, the two new friends work together to help recover a Durer drawing stolen from the Metropolitan Museum of Art.

Broach "packs this fast-moving story with perennially seductive themes: hidden lives and secret friendships, miniature worlds lost to disbelievers. . . . Loosely implying rather than imitating the Old Masters they reference, the finely hatched drawings depict the settings realistically and the characters, especially the beetles, with joyful comic license." Publ Wkly

★ **Shakespeare's** secret; [by] Elise Broach. Henry Holt 2005 250p il $16.95; pa $5.99

Grades: 5 6 7 8 **Fic**

1. Mystery fiction

ISBN 0-8050-7387-6; 0-312-37132-2 pa

LC 2004-54020

Named after a character in a Shakespeare play, misfit sixth-grader Hero becomes interested in exploring this unusual connection because of a valuable diamond supposedly hidden in her new house, an intriguing neighbor, and the unexpected attention of the most popular boy in school.

"The mystery alone will engage readers. . . . The main characters are all well developed, and the dialogue is both realistic and well planned." SLJ

The **wolf** keepers; Elise Broach ; with illustrations by Alice Ratterree. Henry Holt & Co. 2016 352 p. illustrations, maps (ebook) $60; (hardback) $16.99

Grades: 4 5 6 7 8 **Fic**

1. Zoos -- Fiction 2. Wolves -- Fiction 3. Friendship -- Fiction 4. Mystery fiction -- Fiction 5. Runaways -- Fiction 6. Friendship -- Fiction 7. Mystery and detective stories

ISBN 9781250113047; 0805098992; 9780805098990

LC 2015049899

In this children's novel by Elise Broach, illustrated by Alice Ratterree, "Lizzie Durango and her dad have always had a zoo to call their home. . . . One afternoon . . . she finds Tyler Briggs, a runaway who has secretly made the zoo his makeshift home. The two become friends and . . . stumble into a covert investigation involving the zoo wolves who are suddenly dying. . . . This mystery will draw them into a high-stakes historical adventure involving the legend of John Muir." (Publisher's note)

"Tyler's wry comments about his race add further dimensions to a thoughtful, well-told tale, as do the pencil drawings. John Muir's spirit hums along under a well-developed plot with likable characters." Kirkus

Broaddus, Maurice

The **usual** suspects; Maurice Broaddus. Katherine Tegen Books 2019 288 p. (hardcover) $16.99

Grades: 5 6 7 8 **Fic**

1. Guns -- Fiction 2. Mystery fiction 3. Special education -- Fiction

ISBN 9780062796318

LC 2018962176

In this middle-grade novel, by Maurice Broaddus, "Thelonius Mitchell is tired of being labeled. He's in special ed, separated from the 'normal' kids at school who don't have any issues.' That's enough to make all the teachers and students look at him and his friends with a constant side-eye. (Although his disruptive antics and pranks have given him a rep too.) When a gun is found at a neighborhood hangout, Thelonius and his pals become instant suspects." (Publisher's note)

"Broaddus spins a hilarious, honest tale that sees Thelonius wrestle with circumstances beyond his control and grow into a leader while doing so. His cleareyed narration describes an unjust system too many kids know intimately." Kirkus

Brodien-Jones, Christine

The **glass** puzzle; Christine Brodien-Jones. Delacorte Press 2013 336 p. (hc) $16.99

Grades: 4 5 6 7 **Fic**

1. Horror fiction -- Fiction 2. Fantasy fiction -- Fiction 3. Wales -- Fiction 4. Cousins -- Fiction 5. Time travel -- Fiction 6. Supernatural -- Fiction 7. Tenby (Wales) -- Fiction 8. Adventure and adventurers -- Fiction 9. Wales -- History -- 1063-1284 -- Fiction

ISBN 0385742975; 9780307979933; 9780375990878; 9780385742979; 9780385742986

LC 2012015999

In this book, Zoé Badger and her cousin find an antique glass puzzle and unwittingly release Scravens—evil creatures with a craterous third eye and massive wings—into Tenby. The cousins, in turn, are magically transported to Wythernsea, an island long submerged underwater, whence the Scravens come. There they learn that Scravens are taking over the bodies of Tenby inhabitants—as well as terrorizing Wythernsea—and that they must save both towns from the creatures." (Kirkus Reviews)

Brody, Jessica

Unremembered; Jessica Brody. Farrar Straus & Giroux 2013 320 p. (hardcover) $17.99

Grades: 7 8 9 10 **Fic**

1. Amnesia -- Fiction 2. Survival after airplane accidents, shipwrecks, etc. -- Fiction 3. Science fiction 4. Space and time -- Fiction 5. Foster home care -- Fiction 6. Aircraft accidents -- Fiction 7. Genetic engineering -- Fiction

ISBN 0374379912; 9780374379919

LC 2012004545

In this young adult science fiction novel, by Jessica Brody, "when Freedom Airlines flight 121 went down . . . , the sixteen-year-old girl discovered floating among the wreckage . . . is making headlines across the globe. . . . Her body is miraculously unharmed and she has no memories. . . . No one knows how she survived. No one knows why she wasn't on the passenger manifest. And no one can explain why her DNA and fingerprints can't be found in a single database in the world." (Publisher's note)

"The amnesiac sole survivor of a plane crash, Sera learns that she's a human experiment with sinister forces tracking her down; Zen, who tells her that he's her pre-memory-wipe soul mate, tries to keep her safe. Sera is too much of a blank slate to make a compelling focal point, but the fated romance and intriguing time-travel elements will attract readers." Horn Book

Brooks, Bruce

The **moves** make the man; a novel. HarperCollins Pubs. 1984 280p hardcover o.p. pa $6.99

Grades: 7 8 9 10 11 12 **Fic**

1. Friendship -- Fiction 2. African Americans -- Fiction

ISBN 0-06-020679-9; 0-06-440564-8 pa

A Newbery Medal honor book, 1985

This is an "excellent novel about values and the way people relate to one another." N Y Times Book Rev

What hearts. HarperCollins Pubs. 1992 194p $14/ Can$18.75; lib bdg $13.89; rpt $6.99

Grades: 5 6 7 8 **Fic**

1. Remarriage -- Fiction

ISBN 0-06-021131-8; 0-06-021132-6 lib bdg; 9780064471275 rpt

LC 92-5305

Newbery Honor Book (1993)

"This novel is composed of four short stories that begin when the main character, Asa, is just graduating from the first grade and ends when Asa is an adolescent. The stories are about love—within a family, among friends, between boy and girl, husband and wife. . . . Age twelve and up." (Horn Book)

"This present-day saga traces the formative years of Asa, who has spent most of his life moving from one town to another with his emotionally fragile mother and bullying stepfather. . . . Asa takes on the role of protector as he chooses to make sacrifices in order to save his mother's marriage or prevent her from falling into a depressive state." Publ Wkly

Brooks, Laurie

Selkie girl; a novel. Alfred A. Knopf 2008 262p $15.99; lib bdg $18.99

Grades: 7 8 9 10 **Fic**

1. Fantasy fiction 2. Scotland -- Fiction 3. Seals (Animals) -- Fiction

ISBN 978-0-375-85170-4; 0-375-85170-4; 978-0-375-95170-1 lib bdg; 0-375-95170-9 lib bdg

LC 2008-03547

When sixteen-year-old Elin Jean finds a seal pelt hidden at home and realizes that her mother is actually a selkie, she returns the pelt to her mother, only to find her life taking many unexpected turns.

"An extraordinary, beautifully written tale about belonging, love, and the laws of nature. . . . Brooks's rich prose reverberates with vivid, cinematic images." SLJ

Brooks, Martha

★ **Mistik** Lake. Farrar, Straus and Giroux 2007 207p $16

Grades: 8 9 10 **Fic**

1. Mothers -- Fiction 2. Manitoba -- Fiction 3. Family life -- Fiction

ISBN 978-0-374-34985-1; 0-374-34985-1

LC 2006-37391

After Odella's mother leaves her, her sisters, and their father in Manitoba and moves to Iceland with another man, she then dies there, and the family finally learns some of the secrets that have haunted them for two generations. "Grades seven to ten." (Bull Cent Child Books)

"All of the characters seem distinct and real, thanks to the author's exceptional skill with details." Publ Wkly

★ **Queen** of hearts. Farrar Straus Giroux 2011 224p $16.99

Grades: 7 8 9 10 **Fic**

1. Sick -- Fiction 2. Manitoba -- Fiction 3. Hospitals -- Fiction 4. Family life -- Fiction 5. Tuberculosis -- Fiction

ISBN 978-0-374-34229-6; 0-374-34229-6

LC 2010-52661

Shortly after her first kiss but before her sixteenth birthday in December, 1941, Marie Claire and her younger brother and sister are sent to a tuberculosis sanatorium near their Manitoba farm.

"Readers will be held by the story's heartbreaking truths, right to the end." Booklist

Brothers, Meagan

★ **Debbie** Harry sings in French. Henry Holt 2008 232p $16.95

Grades: 8 9 10 11 12 **Fic**

1. Cross-dressers -- Fiction 2. Rock music -- Fiction

ISBN 978-0-8050-8080-3; 0-8050-8080-5

LC 2007-27322

When Johnny completes an alcohol rehabilitation program and his mother sends him to live with his uncle in North Carolina, he meets Maria, who seems to understand his fascination with the new wave band Blondie, and he learns about his deceased father's youthful forays into "glam rock," which gives him perspective on himself, his past, and his current life.

"The brisk pace and the strong-willed, empathetic narrator will keep readers fully engaged." Publ Wkly

Brouwer, Sigmund

Devil's pass; Sigmund Brouwer. Orca Book Publishers 2012 237 p. ill., map (pbk) $9.95

Grades: 6 7 8 9 10 **Fic**

1. Grandfathers -- Fiction 2. Voyages and travels -- Fiction 3. Grandparent-grandchild relationship -- Fiction 4. Canada -- Fiction 5. Street musicians -- Fiction 6. Canol Heritage Trail (N.W.T.) -- Fiction

ISBN 155469938X; 9781554699384

LC 2012938220

In author Sigmund Brouwer's book, "seventeen-year-old Webb's abusive stepfather has made it impossible for him to live at home, so Webb survives on the streets of Toronto. . . . When Webb's grandfather dies, his will stipulates that his grandsons fulfill specific requests. Webb's task takes him to the Canol Trail in Canada's Far North. . . . With a Native guide, two German tourists and his guitar for company, Webb is forced to confront terrible events in his grandfather's past and somehow deal with the pain and confusion of his own life." (Publisher's note)

Another title in this series is:

Barracuda (2016)

Brown, Gavin

Josh Baxter levels up; by Gavin Brown. Scholastic Press 2016 192 p. illustrations $12.99

Grades: 4 5 6 7 8 **Fic**

1. Moving -- Fiction 2. Families -- Fiction 3. Video games -- Fiction 4. Middle schools -- Fiction 5. Schools -- Fiction 6. Bullying -- Fiction 7. Family life -- Fiction
ISBN 9780545772945

LC 2015016236

In this book, by author Gavin Brown, "Josh Baxter is sick and tired of hitting the reset button. It's not easy being the new kid for the third time in two years. . . . Josh knows that his best bet is to keep his head down and stay under the radar. . . . But when Josh's mom sees his terrible grades and takes away his video games, it's clear his strategy has failed. Josh needs a new plan, or he'll never make it to the next level, let alone the next grade." (Publisher's note)

"Smartly paced and emotionally engaging, a book even those who have never held a controller will enjoy." Kirkus

Brown, Skila

★ **Caminar**; Skila Brown. Candlewick Press 2014 208 p. $15.99

Grades: 6 7 8 9 **Fic**

1. War stories 2. Guatemala -- Fiction 3. Novels in verse 4. Guatemala -- History -- Civil War, 1960-1996 -- fiction
ISBN 0763665169; 9780763665166

LC 2013946611

This book, by Skila Brown, is "set in 1981 Guatemala. . . . Carlos knows that when the soldiers arrive with warnings about the Communist rebels, it is time to be a man and defend the village, keep everyone safe. But Mama tells him not yet. . . . Numb and alone, he must join a band of guerillas as they trek to the top of the mountain where Carlos's abuela lives. Will he be in time, and brave enough, to warn them about the soldiers? What will he do then?" (Publisher's note)

"—Unlike many novels in verse, which can read like conventional narratives with line breaks, Caminar contributes poetry that elevates the genre. In this story of a decimated Guatemalan village in 1981, readers will encounter a range of imagery, repetition, rhythms, and visual effects that bring to life the psychological experience of Carlos, a young boy caught in the violent clash between the government's army and the people's rebels...This is a much-needed addition to Latin American-themed middle grade fiction." SLJ

To stay alive; Skila Brown. Candlewick Press 2016 304 p. $17.99

Grades: 6 7 8 9 10 **Fic**

1. Weather -- Fiction 2. Donner party -- Fiction 3. Wilderness survival -- Fiction 4. Novels in verse
ISBN 9780763678111

LC 2016946911

"The journey west by wagon train promises to be long and arduous for nineteen-year-old Mary Ann Graves and her parents and eight siblings. Yet she is hopeful about their new life in California: freedom from the demands of family, maybe some romance, better opportunities for all. But when winter comes early to the Sierra Nevada and their group gets a late start, the Graves family, traveling alongside the Donner and Reed parties, must endure one of the most harrowing and storied journeys in American history. Amid the pain of loss and the constant threat of death from starvation or cold, Mary Ann's is a narrative, told beautifully in verse, of a girl learning what it means to be part of a family, to make sacrifices for those we love, and above all to persevere." (Publisher's note)

"The strong novel in verse uses beautiful, descriptive words to depict the vastness of the landscape and the emotional and mental toll of perpetual suffering. This is a well-crafted narrative in which readers get to know and empathize with Mary Ann as her adventure shifts to survival. However, it might be difficult to stomach the travelers' desperate choices: the book does not shy away from the Donner Party's well-known resort to cannibalism." SLJ

Bruchac, Joseph, 1942-

Bearwalker; [by] Joseph Bruchac; illustrations by Sally Wern Comport. HarperCollinsPublishers 2007 208p il $15.99; lib bdg $16.89; pa $5.99

Grades: 5 6 7 8 **Fic**

1. Bears -- Fiction 2. Camping -- Fiction 3. Mohawk Indians -- Fiction 4. Adirondack Mountains (N.Y.) -- Fiction
ISBN 978-0-06-112309-2; 0-06-112309-9; 978-0-06-112311-5 lib bdg; 0-06-112311-0 lib bdg; 978-0-06-112315-3 pa; 0-06-112315-3 pa

LC 2006-30420

Although the littlest student in his class, thirteen-year-old Baron Braun calls upon the strength and wisdom of his Mohawk ancestors to face both man and beast when he tries to get help for his classmates, who are being terrorized during a school field trip in the Adirondacks.

"This exciting horror story, illustrated with b/w drawings, is based on Native American folklore." Kliatt

★ **Code** talker; a novel about the Navajo Marines of World War Two. Dial 2005 240p $16.99

Grades: 6 7 8 9 10 **Fic**

1. Navajo Indians -- Fiction 2. World War, 1939-1945 -- Fiction
ISBN 0-8037-2921-9

After being taught in a boarding school run by whites that Navajo is a useless language, Ned Begay and other Navajo men are recruited by the Marines to become Code Talkers, sending messages during World War II in their native tongue.

"Bruchac's gentle prose presents a clear historical picture of young men in wartime. . . . Nonsensational and accurate, Bruchac's tale is quietly inspiring." SLJ

Includes bibliographical references

Dragon castle. Dial Books for Young Readers 2011 346p $16.99

Grades: 4 5 6 7 **Fic**

1. Fairy tales 2. Dragons -- Fiction 3. Princes -- Fiction 4. Kings and rulers -- Fiction
ISBN 978-0-8037-3376-3; 0-8037-3376-3

LC 2010028798

Young prince Rashko, aided by wise old Georgi, must channel the power of his ancestor, Pavol the great, and harness a magical dragon to face the evil Baron Temny after the foolish King and Queen go missing.

Bruchac "spins a good-natured and humorous fairy tale. . . . With its subtle focus on peaceful resistance and use of classic folk-tale elements, this story exudes a gentle sense of fun." Publ Wkly

Killer of enemies; Joseph Bruchac. Tu Books, an imprint of Lee & Low Books, Inc. 2013 400 p. (hardcover : alk. paper) $19.95

Grades: 7 8 9 10 11 12 **Fic**

1. Dystopian fiction 2. Native Americans -- Fiction 3. Heroes and heroines -- Fiction 4. Science fiction 5. Hunting -- Fiction 6.

Hostages -- Fiction 7. Survival -- Fiction 8. Chiricahua Indians -- Fiction 9. Genetic engineering -- Fiction 10. Extrasensory perception -- Fiction

ISBN 1620141434; 9781620141434; 9781620141441

LC 2013023567

American Indian Youth Literature Award Winner (2014)

In this dystopian young adult novel by Joseph Bruchac, "seventeen year old Apache hunter Lozen and her family lives in a world of haves and have-nots. There were the Ones (people so augmented with technology and genetic enhancements that they were barely human) and there was everyone else who served the Ones. . . . She hunts monsters for the Ones who survived the apocalyptic events of the Cloud, which ensures the safety of her kidnapped family." (Publisher's note)

"A deadly assassin with extrasensory powers, Lozen (named for an Apache-Chiricahua warrior-woman forebear) takes out genetically modified superbeasts; her family is being held hostage to ensure her continued service. Bruchac devises ever-more-dangerous battles for his protagonist in the increasingly suspenseful story. What really makes the narrative vibrate is Lozen's sardonic voice, capturing both gallows humor and a very human vulnerability." (Horn Book)

Trail of the Dead (2015)

Arrow of Lightning (2017)

Talking leaves; by Joseph Bruchac. Dial Books for Young Readers 2016 256 p. illustrations (hardback) $16.99

Grades: 4 5 6 7 8 **Fic**

1. Cherokee Indians -- Fiction 2. Native Americans -- Fiction 3. Language and languages -- Fiction 4. Indians of North America -- Fiction

ISBN 9780803735088

LC 2015035887

In this book, by Joseph Bruchac, "thirteen-year-old Uwohali has not seen his father, Sequoyah, for many years. So when Sequoyah returns to the village, Uwohali is eager to reconnect. But Sequoyah's new obsession with making strange markings causes friends and neighbors in their tribe to wonder whether he is crazy, or worse—practicing witchcraft. What they don't know, and what Uwohali discovers, is that Sequoyah is a genius and his strange markings are actually an alphabet." (Publisher's note)

"An illuminating read for middle graders; purchase anywhere historical fiction is in demand." SLJ

Walking two worlds; Joseph Bruchac ; illustrated by David Fadden. 7th Generation 2015 120 p. (pbk.) $9.95

Grades: 5 6 7 8 9 **Fic**

1. Racism -- Fiction 2. Education -- Fiction 3. Seneca Indians -- Fiction 4. Native Americans -- Fiction

ISBN 9781939053107; 9781939053138

LC 2014046212

This book, by Joseph Bruchac, illustrated by David Fadden, and part of the Pathfinders series, is the "story of the early education of a famous Native American who gained greatness in the white man's world while staying true to his Seneca people. Hasanoanda was his Indian name. But in mission school he became Ely. He encountered racism and deceit but, against all odds, did not give up on his quest to walk between two worlds." (Publisher's note)

"Though the book lacks formal resources and references, and the time frame of events, including Ely's birth date, is occasionally unclear, Ely's challenges and successes are supportively portrayed, and may inspire readers to learn more about his life and times. An afterword provides some information on his later years." Booklist

★ The **winter** people. Dial Bks. 2002 168p $16.99; pa $5.99

Grades: 5 6 7 8 **Fic**

1. Abnaki Indians -- Fiction 2. United States -- History -- 1755-1763, French and Indian War -- Fiction

ISBN 0-8037-2694-5; 0-14-240229-X pa

LC 2002-338

As the French and Indian War rages in October of 1759, Saxso, a fourteen-year-old Abenaki boy, pursues the English rangers who have attacked his village and taken his mother and sisters hostage

"The narrative itself is thrilling, its spiritual aspects enlightening." Booklist

Wolf mark. Lee & Low/Tu Books 2011 377p $17.95

Grades: 6 7 8 9 **Fic**

1. Spies -- Fiction 2. Supernatural -- Fiction 3. Native Americans -- Fiction 4. Father-son relationship -- Fiction

ISBN 1-60060-661-X; 978-1-60060-661-8; 978-1-60060-878-0 e-book

LC 2011014252

When Lucas King's covert-ops father is kidnapped and his best friend Meena is put in danger, Luke's only chance to save them—a skin that will let him walk as a wolf—is hidden away in an abandoned mansion guarded by monsters.

"Bruchac has created a tense, readable novel. He combines Native American lore, supernatural elements, genetic engineering, romance, geopolitics, and adventure in one story. . . . The mystery and edge-of-your-seat action are enough to keep readers hooked." SLJ

Bruton, Catherine

I Predict a Riot; Catherine Bruton. Trafalgar Square Books 2014 304 p. $12.99

Grades: 7 8 9 10 **Fic**

1. Gangs -- Fiction 2. Motion picture producers and directors -- Fiction

ISBN 1405267194; 9781405267199

This novel by Catherine Bruton is set on "Coronation Road--a kaleidoscope of clashing cultures and parallel lives. Amateur film-maker Maggie prefers to watch life through the lens of her camera. In Tokes, she finds a great subject for her new film. And when violence erupts, led by the Starfish gang, Maggie has the perfect backdrop. But as the world explodes around her, Maggie can't hide behind the lens anymore." (Publisher's note)

Maggie's video camera seems to represent all the stories that aren't told in the media, making this searing tale one that will get readers talking." Booklist

Pop! Catherine Bruton. Egmont Books 2012 496 p. (pbk.) $10.99

Grades: 4 5 6 7 **Fic**

1. Fame -- Fiction 2. Reality television programs -- Fiction

ISBN 1405261331; 9781405261333

This novel, by Catherine Bruton, "mixes social issues with the absurdity of reality TV. The first round of auditions was a bit crazy. All these wannabe popstars sitting around trying to look wacky/soulful/tragic (delete as appropriate) to catch the attention of the TV cameras. The story of [the narrator], Agnes, Jimmy, and baby Alfie too; the tears, the tragedy, the broken homes and feuding families, the star-crossed lovers. And only some of it was made up." (Publisher's note)

Bryant, Jen

Kaleidoscope eyes; [by] Jen Bryant. Alfred A. Knopf 2009 264p $15.99; lib bdg $18.99

Grades: 5 6 7 8 **Fic**

1. Mystery fiction 2. Novels in verse 3. New Jersey -- Fiction 4. Buried treasure -- Fiction 5. Vietnam War, 1961-1975 -- Fiction

ISBN 0-375-84048-6; 0-375-94048-0 lib bdg; 978-0-375-84048-7; 978-0-375-94048-4 lib bdg

LC 2008027345

In 1968, with the Vietnam War raging, thirteen-year-old Lyza inherits a project from her deceased grandfather, who had been using his knowledge of maps and the geography of Lyza's New Jersey hometown to locate the lost treasure of Captain Kidd.

"Bryant weaves an emotional novel in poems based on a true story of buried treasure. Tensions among families are drawn with heart-wrenching prose, and her depiction of segregation is flawless. . . . The characters are witty and well developed." Voice Youth Advocates

★ **Ringside,** 1925; views from the Scopes trial, a novel. [by] Jen Bryant. Alfred A. Knopf 2008 228p $15.99; lib bdg $18.99

Grades: 8 9 10 11 12 **Fic**

1. Geologists 2. Novels in verse 3. Science teachers 4. Tennessee -- Fiction 5. Evolution -- Study and teaching -- Fiction

ISBN 978-0-375-84047-0; 0-375-84047-8; 978-0-375-94047-7 lib bdg; 0-375-94047-2 lib bdg

LC 2007-7177

Visitors, spectators, and residents of Dayton, Tennessee, in 1925 describe, in a series of free-verse poems, the Scopes 'monkey trial' and its effects on that small town and its citizens.

"Bryant offers readers a ringside seat in this compelling and well-researched novel. It is fast-paced, interesting, and relevant to many current first-amendment challenges." SLJ

Bryce, Celia

Anthem for Jackson Dawes; by Celia Bryce. Bloomsbury USA Childrens 2013 240 p. (hardback) $16.99

Grades: 7 8 9 10 **Fic**

1. Hospitals -- Fiction 2. Cancer patients -- Fiction 3. Cancer -- Fiction 4. Friendship -- Fiction 5. Family life -- Fiction 6. Medical care -- Fiction

ISBN 1599909758; 9781599909752

LC 2012024989

In this book, "after 13-year-old Megan Bright is diagnosed with a cancerous brain tumor, she's . . . determined to have everything remain as normal as possible during her time in the hospital. . . . Megan gets closer to the only other teenager there . . . and begins to acknowledge the emotions she's been keeping buried. Initially, Jackson rubs her the wrong way, but his positivity and determined interest in Megan teach her about optimism and taking control of what she can." (Publishers Weekly)

"Sensitive and honest, this novel addresses meaningful questions concerning mortality and soul searching, and its content is appropriate for younger teens." SLJ

Buckingham, Royce Scott

The **terminals**; Royce Scott Buckingham. First edition Thomas Dunne Books, St. Martin's Griffin 2014 288 p. (hardback) $18.99

Grades: 7 8 9 10 **Fic**

1. Spy stories 2. Adventure fiction 3. Terminally ill -- Fiction 4. Spies -- Fiction 5. Ability -- Fiction 6. Adventure and adventurers -- Fiction

ISBN 1250011558; 9781250011558

LC 2014031142

This young adult adventure novel, by Royce Scott Buckingham, "tells the . . . story of a covert team of young, terminally ill teens who spend their last year alive running dangerous missions as super-spies. . . . Cam joins this extreme spy team, and . . . as his teammates fall around him, he starts to receive cryptic messages from a haggard survivor of last year's class hiding in the forest. She reveals that the program isn't what it claims to be." (Publisher's note)

"Buckingham's above-average writing and exotic settings are plenty appealing. Fans of Robert Muchamore's Cherub series will eat up this sf-tinged espionage thriller." Booklist

Buckley-Archer, Linda

The **many** lives of John Stone; Linda Buckley-Archer. SSBFYR 2015 544 p. illustrations (hardcover) $17.99

Grades: 8 9 10 11 **Fic**

1. England -- Fiction 2. Identity -- Fiction 3. Supernatural -- Fiction 4. Summer employment -- Fiction 5. Longevity -- Fiction

ISBN 9781481426374; 9781481426381

LC 2014035641

In this book, by Linda Buckley-Archer, "Stella Park (Spark for short) has found summer work cataloging historical archives in John Stone's remote and beautiful house in Suffolk, England. . . . [W]hat kind of people live in the twenty-first century without using electricity, telephones, or even a washing machine? Additionally, the notebooks she's organizing span centuries—they begin in the court of Louis XIV in Versailles—but are written in the same hand." (Publisher's note)

"Spark's contemporary coming-of-age story is brilliantly heightened by the reader's understanding of her secret connection to John Stone. Exceptionally well orchestrated and a simply magnificent story." Booklist

Budhos, Marina

Ask me no questions; [by] Marina Budhos. Atheneum Books for Young Readers 2006 162p $16.95; pa $8.99

Grades: 7 8 9 10 **Fic**

1. School stories 2. Family life -- Fiction 3. Asian Americans -- Fiction 4. New York (N.Y.) -- Fiction

ISBN 1-4169-0351-8; 1-4169-4920-8 pa

LC 2005-1831

Fourteen-year-old Nadira, her sister, and their parents leave Bangladesh for New York City, but the expiration of their visas and the events of September 11, 2001, bring frustration, sorrow, and terror for the whole family.

"Nadira and Aisha's strategies for surviving and succeeding in high school offer sharp insight into the narrow margins between belonging and not belonging." Horn Book Guide

Tell us we're home; [by] Marina Budhos. Atheneum 2010 297p $16.95

Grades: 6 7 8 9 10 **Fic**

1. Immigrants -- Fiction 2. New Jersey -- Fiction 3. Social classes -- Fiction 4. Household employees -- Fiction 5. Mother-daughter relationship -- Fiction

ISBN 978-1-4169-0352-9; 1-4169-0352-6

LC 2009-27386

Three immigrant girls from different parts of the world meet and become close friends in a small New Jersey town where their mothers have found domestic work, but their relationships are tested when one girl's mother is accused of stealing a precious heirloom.

"These fully realized heroines are full of heart, and their passionate struggles against systemic injustice only make them more inspiring. Keenly necessary." Kirkus

Watched; Marina Budhos. Wendy Lamb Books 2016 272 p. (hbk.) $17.99
Grades: 9 10 11 12 **Fic**
1. Muslims -- Fiction 2. New York (N.Y.) -- Fiction 3. Undercover operations -- Fiction 4. Bangladeshi Americans -- Fiction
ISBN 9780553534184; 9780553534214; 9780553534191
LC 2015046828
"Naeem is far from the 'model teen.' Moving fast in his immigrant neighborhood in Queens is the only way he can outrun the eyes of his hardworking Bangladeshi parents and their gossipy neighbors. Even worse, they're not the only ones watching. Cameras on poles. Mosques infiltrated. Everyone knows: Be careful what you say and who you say it to. Anyone might be a watcher. Naeem thinks he can charm his way through anything, until his mistakes catch up with him and the cops offer a dark deal." (Publisher's note)
"Action takes second place to a deeper message, and room is left for readers to speculate on the fates of certain characters. While the absence of certainty may frustrate some readers, it also speaks to the underlying takeaway: you can never be sure what others' intentions are, even if you have made it your job to study them." Kirkus

Bukiet, Melvin Jules
Undertown; Melvin Jules Bukiet. Amulet Books 2013 304 p. (hardcover) $16.95
Grades: 6 7 8 **Fic**
1. Sewerage -- Fiction 2. Adventure fiction 3. Sailing -- Fiction 4. New York (N.Y.) -- Fiction 5. Homeless persons -- Fiction 6. Adventure and adventurers -- Fiction
ISBN 141970589X; 9781419705892
LC 2012039246
In this adventure novel, by Melvin Jules Bukiet, "Timothy and Jessamyn are towed through the streets of Manhattan riding in Timothy's family's sailboat, . . . The teens . . . then fall down a huge construction site hole and into the vast sewer system below. . . . The kids navigate waterfalls and rapids as they travel through the rain sewers. They meet a graffiti artist their own age, a homeless person named You, and rats the size of large dogs." (Publisher's note)
"Bukiet's first children's outing veers between language carefully designed to appeal to its intended audience and occasionally sophisticated sentence structure and subjects that should instead engage far older readers. Dramatic and imaginative, this will probably most appeal to readers with a taste for the esoteric." BookList

Bullen, Alexandra
Wish; a novel. Point 2010 323p $17.99
Grades: 8 9 10 11 12 **Fic**
1. Fantasy fiction 2. Magic -- Fiction 3. Twins -- Fiction 4. Wishes -- Fiction 5. Sisters -- Fiction 6. Bereavement -- Fiction 7. San Francisco (Calif.) -- Fiction
ISBN 978-0-545-13905-2; 0-545-13905-8
LC 2009-22730
After her vivacious twin sister dies, a shy teenaged girl moves with her parents to San Francisco, where she meets a magical seamstress who grants her one wish.
"The detailed descriptions of San Francisco and above all the sisters' relationship provide solid grounding for a touching, enjoyable read." Kirkus
Followed by: Wishful thinking (2011)

Bunce, Elizabeth C.
★ A **curse** dark as gold; [by] Elizabeth C. Bunce. Arthur A. Levine Books 2008 395p $17.99
Grades: 7 8 9 10 **Fic**
1. Magic -- Fiction 2. Uncles -- Fiction 3. Orphans -- Fiction 4. Sisters -- Fiction 5. Factories -- Fiction
ISBN 978-0-439-89576-7; 0-439-89576-6
LC 2007019759
ALA YALSA Morris Award, 2009
Upon the death of her father, seventeen-year-old Charlotte struggles to keep the family's woolen mill running in the face of an overwhelming mortgage and what the local villagers believe is a curse, but when a man capable of spinning straw into gold appears on the scene she must decide if his help is worth the price.
"This is a rich, compelling story that fleshes out the fairy tale, setting it in the nonspecific past of the Industrial Revolution. Readers unfamiliar with 'Rumplestilskin' will not be at a disadvantage here." KLIATT

Liar's moon. Arthur A. Levine Books 2011 356p $17.99
Grades: 8 9 10 11 12 **Fic**
1. Fantasy fiction 2. Mystery fiction 3. Magic -- Fiction 4. Thieves -- Fiction 5. Homicide -- Fiction 6. Social classes -- Fiction
ISBN 978-0-545-13608-2; 0-545-13608-3
LC 2011005071
"A solid fantasy sequel embroils its irresistible heroine in mystery, intrigue and romance. . . . A darn good read." Kirkus

★ **Star** crossed. Arthur A. Levine Books 2010 359p $17.99
Grades: 8 9 10 11 12 **Fic**
1. Fantasy fiction 2. Magic -- Fiction 3. Thieves -- Fiction 4. Religion -- Fiction 5. Social classes -- Fiction 6. Kings and rulers -- Fiction
ISBN 978-0-545-13605-1; 0-545-13605-9
LC 2010-730
In a kingdom dominated by religious intolerance, sixteen-year-old Digger, a street thief, has always avoided attention, but when she learns that her friends are plotting against the throne she must decide whether to join them or turn them in.
"Couching her characters and setting in top-notch writing, Bunce . . . hooks readers into an intelligent page-turner with strong themes of growth, determination, and friendship." Publ Wkly
Followed by: Liar's moon (2011)

Bunker, Lisa
Felix Yz; Lisa Bunker. Viking 2017 288 p. (hardback) $16.99
Grades: 5 6 7 8 9 **Fic**
1. Science fiction 2. Family life -- Fiction 3. Extraterrestrial beings -- Fiction 4. People with disabilities -- Fiction 5. Blogs -- Fiction 6. Schools -- Fiction
ISBN 9780425288504
LC 2016029068
In this book, by Lisa Bunker, "when Felix Yz was three years old, a hyperintelligent fourth-dimensional being became fused inside him after one of his father's science experiments went terribly wrong. The creature is friendly, but Felix—now thirteen—won't be able to grow to adulthood while they're still melded together. So a risky Procedure is planned to separate them . . . but it may end up killing them both instead." (Publisher's note)
"Joyful, heartbreaking, completely bonkers, and exuberantly alive." Kirkus.

Bunting, Eve

Blackwater. HarperCollins Pubs. 1999 146p hardcover o.p. pa $5.99

Grades: 5 6 7 8 **Fic**

1. Death -- Fiction 2. Guilt -- Fiction

ISBN 0-06-027843-9 lib bdg; 0-06-440890-6 pa

LC 99-24895

When a boy and girl are drowned in the Blackwater River, thirteen-year-old Brodie must decide whether to confess that he may have caused the accident

"Bunting's thought-provoking theme, solid characterization and skillful juggling of suspense and pathos make this a top-notch choice." Publ Wkly

The **pirate** captain's daughter; written by Eve Bunting. Sleeping Bear Press 2011 208p $15.95; pa $8.95

Grades: 7 8 9 10 **Fic**

1. Pirates -- Fiction 2. Sex role -- Fiction 3. Seafaring life -- Fiction 4. Father-daughter relationship -- Fiction

ISBN 978-1-58536-526-5; 1-58536-526-2; 978-1-58536-525-8 pa; 1-58536-525-4 pa

LC 2010032409

Upon her mother's death, fifteen-year-old Catherine puts her courage and strength to the test by disguising herself as a boy to join her father, a pirate captain, on a ship whose crew includes men who are trying to steal a treasure from him.

"This is a gripping and entertaining novel that will have readers sucked in until the last page. Even teens who are not fond of historical fiction will enjoy." Voice Youth Advocates

Burg, Ann

★ **All** the broken pieces; a novel in verse. Scholastic Press 2009 218p $16.99

Grades: 7 8 9 10 **Fic**

1. Novels in verse 2. Adoption -- Fiction 3. Vietnamese Americans -- Fiction 4. Vietnam War, 1961-1975 -- Fiction

ISBN 978-0-545-08092-7; 0-545-08092-4

LC 2008-12381

In this novel, by Ann Burg, "Matt Pin would like to forget: war torn Vietnam, bombs that fell like dead crows, and the terrible secret he left behind. But now that he is living with a caring adoptive family in the United States, he finds himself forced to confront his past. And that means choosing between silence and candor, blame and forgiveness, fear and freedom." (Publisher's note)

This is written "in rapid, simple free verse. . . . The intensity of the simple words . . . will make readers want to rush to the end and then return to the beginning again to make connections between past and present, friends and enemies." Booklist

Serafina's promise; by Ann E. Burg. Scholastic Press 2013 304 p. (alk. paper) $16.99

Grades: 5 6 7 8 **Fic**

1. Girls -- Fiction 2. Floods -- Fiction 3. Haiti -- Social conditions 4. Novels in verse 5. Haiti -- Fiction 6. Earthquakes -- Fiction 7. Brothers and sisters -- Fiction 8. Family life -- Haiti -- Fiction 9. Port-au-Prince (Haiti) -- Fiction

ISBN 0545535646; 9780545535649

LC 2012045609

Parents' Choice: Gold Medal Fiction (2013)

In this book, by Ann E. Burg, "Serafina is an 11-year-old Haitian struggling to keep her dream of becoming a doctor alive. Living in a desolate mountain village, Serafina toils at her daily chores while planning to attend school . Serafina has a warm family . . . who all come to support her vision. Then a flood washes away the family home, and the roaring stampede of an earthquake devastates the city of Port-au-Prince, where Serafina's father works." (Publisher's note)

Unbound; a novel in verse. Ann E. Burg. Scholastic Press 2016 352 p. (hardcover : alk. paper) $16.99; (ebook) $16.99

Grades: 4 5 6 7 **Fic**

1. Fugitive slaves -- Fiction 2. Slaves -- United States -- Fiction 3. African American families -- Fiction 4. Dismal Swamp (N.C. and Va.) -- Fiction 5. Novels in verse 6. Slavery -- Fiction 7. Family life -- Fiction 8. Southern States -- History -- 1775-1865 -- Fiction

ISBN 0545934273; 9780545934275; 9780545937870

LC 2016022923

In this middle grade novel by Ann E Burg, "the day Grace is called from the slave cabins to work in the Big House, Mama makes her promise to keep her eyes down. . . . But the more Grace sees of the heartless Master and hateful Missus, the more a rightiness voice clamors in her head-asking how come white folks can own other people, sell them on the auction block, and separate families forever. When that voice escapes without warning, it sets off a terrible chain of events." (Publisher's note)

"Grace's story of familial love, community, and hope is a moving, sensitive read." Pub Wkly

Burg, Shana

A **thousand** never evers. Delacorte Press 2008 301p $15.99; lib bdg $18.99

Grades: 6 7 8 9 **Fic**

1. Race relations -- Fiction 2. African Americans -- Fiction

ISBN 978-0-385-73470-7; 978-0-385-90468-1 lib bdg

As the civil rights movement in the South gains momentum in 1963—and violence against African Americans intensifies—the black residents, including seventh-grader Addie Ann Pickett, in the small town of Kuckachoo, Mississippi, begin their own courageous struggle for racial justice.

This is "gripping. . . . References to significant historical events . . . add authenticity and depth, while Addie's frank, expertly modulated voice delivers an emotional wallop." Publ Wkly

Burgis, Stephanie

The **girl** with the dragon heart; Stephanie Burgis. Bloomsbury 2018 288 p. (hardcover) $16.99

Grades: 4 5 6 7 **Fic**

1. Fantasy 2. Magic -- Fiction 3. Spies -- Fiction 4. Dragons -- Fiction 5. Fairies -- Fiction 6. Chocolate -- Fiction 7. Kings, queens, rulers, etc. -- Fiction

ISBN 9781681196978

LC 2018005069

In this book, by Stephanie Burgis, "Silke gets the opportunity she's been waiting for: the Crown Princess personally asks her to spy on the Elfenwald royal family during their first visit to the kingdom. In return, Silke will have the home she's always wanted in the secure palace. But Silke has her own dark, secret reasons for not trusting fairies . . . and her mission isn't as simple as she hoped. Soon, she discovers that her city is in danger." (Publisher's note)

Kat, incorrigible. Atheneum Books for Young Readers 2011 298p (The unladylike adventures of Kat Stephenson) $16.99

Grades: 6 7 8 9 10 **Fic**

1. Magic -- Fiction 2. Sisters -- Fiction 3. Great Britain -- History

-- 19th century -- Fiction
ISBN 1416994475; 9781416994473
LC 2009032543

In Regency England, when twelve-year-old Kat discovers she has magical powers, she tries to use them to rescue her sister from marrying a man she does not love.

"Regency romance and fantasy adventure all in one, this is a satisfying read and a promising beginning to a trilogy that is sure to be popular with middle school girls." SLJ

Other titles in this series are:
Renegade magic (2011)
Stolen magic (2012)

Burkinshaw, Kathleen

The **Last** Cherry Blossom; by Kathleen Burkinshaw. Sky Pony Press 2016 240 p. illustrations $16.99
Grades: 6 7 8 **Fic**

1. Japan -- Fiction 2. Historical fiction 3. World War, 1939-1945 -- Fiction 4. Hiroshima (Japan) -- Bombardment, 1945 -- Fiction
ISBN 1634506936; 9781634506939

In this book, by Kathleen Burkinshaw, "Yuriko is happy growing up in Hiroshima when it's just her and Papa. But her aunt Kimiko and her cousin Genji are living with them now, and the family is only getting bigger with talk of a double marriage! And while things are changing at home, the world beyond their doors is even more unpredictable. World War II is coming to an end, and Japan's fate is not entirely clear, with any battle losses being hidden from its people." (Publisher's note)

"Hiroshima proves nightmarishly horrifying, and readers will readily empathize with Yuriko's losses and will to survive." Pub Wkly

Includes bibliographical references (page 220).

Burnett, Frances Hodgson

The **secret** garden; illustrated by Inga Moore. Candlewick Press 2008 278p il $21.99
Grades: 3 4 5 6 **Fic**

1. Gardens -- Fiction 2. Orphans -- Fiction 3. Great Britain -- Fiction
ISBN 0-7636-3161-2; 978-0-7636-3161-1
LC 2006051838

First published 1911

A ten-year-old orphan comes to live in a lonely house on the Yorkshire moors where she discovers an invalid cousin and the mysteries of a locked garden.

"Burnett's tale . . . is presented in an elegant, oversize volume and handsomely illustrated with Moore's detailed ink and watercolor paintings. Cleanly laid-out text pages are balanced by artwork ranging from delicate spot images to full-page renderings." SLJ

Burtenshaw, Jenna

Shadowcry. Greenwillow Books 2010 311p (The secrets of Wintercraft) $16.99
Grades: 8 9 10 11 12 **Fic**

1. Fantasy fiction 2. Dead -- Fiction
ISBN 978-0-06-202642-2; 0-06-202642-9
LC 2010025823

Pursued by two ruthless men of the High Council of Albiom, fifteen-year-old Kate Winters discovers that she is one of the Skilled, a rare person who can see through the veil between the living and the dead.

"Elegant, complex prose sweeps readers along." Horn Book

Other titles in this series are:
Blackwatch (2012)
Winterveil (2013)

Burton, Rebecca

Leaving Jetty Road; [by] Rebecca Burton. 1st ed.; Knopf 2006 248p $15.95; lib bdg $17.99
Grades: 8 9 10 11 12 **Fic**

1. School stories 2. Australia -- Fiction 3. Friendship -- Fiction 4. Anorexia nervosa -- Fiction
ISBN 0-375-83488-5; 0-375-93488-X lib bdg
LC 2005018140

"In their final year of high school, best friends Lise, Nat, and Sofia make a New Year's resolution to become vegetarians. . . . As they prepare for the next steps in their lives, the girls become so wrapped up in themselves that they fail to see how their friends are growing, changing, and . . . hurting. Burton does an effective job of weaving the symptoms and personality characteristics of anorexia into an absorbing story about the tug and pull of old friendships as a teen's world expands." Booklist

Butcher, Kristin

Cheat; written by Kristin Butcher. Orca Book Publishers 2010 107p (Orca currents) pa $9.95
Grades: 7 8 9 10 **Fic**

1. School stories 2. Cheating (Education) -- Fiction
ISBN 978-1-55469-274-3; 1-55469-274-1

Laurel investigates a cheating scam at her high school.

"This novel is a realistic portrayal of high school students' attitudes towards cheating. . . . This is a well-written narrative that will challenge readers to make a decision about what's right and what's wrong." Libr Media Connect

Butler, Dori Hillestad

The **truth** about Truman School; by Dori Hillestad Butler. Albert Whitman 2008 170p $15.95; pa $7.99
Grades: 5 6 7 8 **Fic**

1. School stories 2. Bullies -- Fiction 3. Journalism -- Fiction 4. Newspapers -- Fiction
ISBN 978-0-8075-8095-0; 0-8075-8095-3; 978-0-8075-8096-7 pa; 0-8075-8096-1 pa
LC 2007-29977

Tired of being told what to write by the school newspaper's advisor, Zibby and her friend Amr start an underground newspaper online where everyone is free to post anything, but things spiral out of control when a cyberbully starts using the site to harrass one popular girl.

"The story moves at a good pace and the timely subject of cyberbullying will be relevant to readers. The language is accessible and the students' voices ring true." SLJ

Buyea, Rob

★ **Because** of Mr. Terupt. Delacorte Press 2010 269p $16.99; lib bdg $19.99
Grades: 4 5 6 **Fic**

1. School stories 2. Teachers -- Fiction 3. Connecticut -- Fiction 4. Family life -- Fiction
ISBN 0-385-73882-X; 0-385-90749-4 lib bdg; 978-0-385-73882-8; 978-0-385-90749-1 lib bdg
LC 2010-03414

Seven fifth-graders at Snow Hill School in Connecticut relate how their lives are changed for the better by "rookie teacher" Mr. Terupt. "Grades four to six." (Bull Cent Child Books)

"Introducing characters and conflicts that will be familiar to any middle-school student, this powerful and emotional story is likely to spur discussion." Publ Wkly

Other titles in this series are:
Mr. Terupt falls again (2012)

Saving Mr. Terupt (2015)

Mr. Terupt falls again; Rob Buyea. Delacorte Press 2012 356 p. (hc) $16.99

Grades: 4 5 6 **Fic**

1. School stories 2. Romance fiction 3. Teacher-student relationship -- Fiction 4. Summer -- Fiction 5. Classrooms -- Fiction 6. Moving, Household -- Fiction

ISBN 0385742053; 9780375989100; 9780375990380; 9780385742054

LC 2012010897

This book is a follow-up to Rob Buyea's "Because of Mr. Terupt." Here, "looping with his students into sixth grade, Mr. Terupt continues to surprise them with challenging projects and perfect reading suggestions." For the seven students who narrate the story, "family worries go along with lingering questions about the health of their teacher. Sixth-grade relationships and a grown-up romance" are also explored. (Kirkus)

The **perfect** score; Rob Buyea. Delacorte Press 2017 368 p. (trade hardcover) $16.99

Grades: 5 6 7 8 **Fic**

1. Examinations -- Fiction 2. Middle schools -- Fiction 3. Cheating (Education) -- Fiction 4. Schools -- Fiction 5. Cheating -- Fiction 6. Interpersonal relations -- Fiction

ISBN 9781101938256; 9781101938270

LC 2017017571

In this novel, by Rob Buyea, "no one likes or wants to take the statewide assessment tests. Not the students in Mrs. Woods's sixth-grade class. Not even Mrs. Woods. It's not as if the kids don't already have things to worry about. . . . Under pressure to be the top gymnast her mother expects her to be, RANDI starts to wonder what her destiny truly holds. Football-crazy GAVIN has always struggled with reading and feels as dumb as his high school-dropout father." (Publisher's note)

"Told through five students' perspectives, this novel is a heartfelt look at social interactions in middle school, a pointed commentary on standardized testing, and an entertaining read." (Booklist)

The perfect secret (2018)

Saving Mr. Terupt; Rob Buyea. Delacorte Press 2015 384 p. (hc) $16.99

Grades: 4 5 6 7 **Fic**

1. School stories 2. Teacher-student relationship -- Fiction 3. Schools -- Fiction 4. Teachers -- Fiction 5. Interpersonal relations -- Fiction 6. Teacher-student relationships -- Fiction

ISBN 9780375991202; 9780385743556

LC 2014031776

In this young adult novel, by Rob Buyea, "the kids from Mr. Terupt's fifth- and sixth-grade classes are entering their first year of junior high school. . . . Everyone is missing Mr. Terupt. When a fight threatens to break up the group forever, they think their favorite teacher is the only one who can help them. But the kids soon find out that it's Mr. Terupt who needs saving." (Publisher's note)

"Necessary background is deftly woven in, making this third in the series as easy for new readers to pick up as it is for returning fans. A warmly gracious invitation to a convincing middle school world." Kirkus

Saving Mister Terupt

Buzbee, Lewis

The **haunting** of Charles Dickens; [illustrated by] Greg Ruth. Feiwel and Friends 2009 357p il $17.99

Grades: 5 6 7 8 **Fic**

1. Authors 2. Novelists 3. Mystery fiction 4. Authors -- Fiction 5. Kidnapping -- Fiction 6. Family life -- Fiction 7. Missing persons -- Fiction 8. London (England) -- Fiction 9. Great Britain -- History -- 19th century -- Fiction

ISBN 978-0-312-38256-8; 0-312-38256-1

LC 2008028553

Twelve-year-old Meg travels the rooftops and streets of 1862 London, England, in search of her missing brother, Orion, accompanied by a family friend, the famed author Charles Dickens, whose quest is to find his next novel.

"Buzbee creates solid characters . . . and an authentic flavor of Dickensian London, enhanced by Ruth's striking and evocative b&w drawings . . . , while addressing issues of feminism, the search for identity, and child abuse." Publ Wkly

Byars, Betsy Cromer

Cracker Jackson; [by] Betsy Byars. Viking Kestrel 1985 147p hardcover o.p. pa $5.99

Grades: 5 6 7 8 **Fic**

1. Wife abuse -- Fiction 2. Child abuse -- Fiction

ISBN 0-670-80546-7; 0-14-031881-X pa

LC 84-24684

"Suspense, danger, near-tragedy, heartbreak and tension-relieving, unwittingly comic efforts at seriously heroic action mark this as the best of middle-grade fiction to highlight the problems of wife-battering and child abuse." SLJ

★ The **dark** stairs; a Herculeah Jones mystery. by Betsy Byars. Viking 1994 130p hardcover o.p. pa $5.99

Grades: 4 5 6 **Fic**

1. Mystery fiction

ISBN 0-670-85487-5; 0-14-240592-2 pa

LC 94-14012

The intrepid Herculeah Jones helps her mother, a private investigator, solve a puzzling and frightening case

"There is plenty to laugh at in this book, including classic chapter headings guaranteed to cause shivers for the uninitiated; practiced mystery readers may feel that they are in on a bit of a joke and appreciate the hint of parody. This is a page-turner that is sure to entice the most reluctant readers." SLJ

Other titles about Herculeah Jones are:

Tarot says beware (1995)
Dead letter (1996)
Death's door (1997)
Disappearing acts (1998)
The black tower (2006)
King of murder (2006)

The **keeper** of the doves; by Betsy Byars. Viking 2002 121p $14.99; pa $5.99

Grades: 4 5 6 7 **Fic**

1. Sisters -- Fiction 2. Kentucky -- Fiction 3. Family life -- Fiction

ISBN 0-670-03576-9; 0-14-240063-7 pa

LC 2002-9283

In the late 1800s in Kentucky, Amie McBee and her four sisters both fear and torment the reclusive and seemingly sinister Mr. Tominski, but their father continues to provide for his needs

"This is Byars at her best—witty, appealing, thought-provoking." Horn Book

Cabot, Meg

Airhead. Scholastic/Point 2008 340p $16.99
Grades: 7 8 9 10 **Fic**
1. Fashion models -- Fiction 2. New York (N.Y.) -- Fiction 3. Transplantation of organs, tissues, etc. -- Fiction
ISBN 978-0-545-04052-5; 0-545-04052-3
LC 2007-38269

Sixteen-year-old Emerson Watts, an advanced placement student with a disdain for fashion, is the recipient of a "whole body transplant"; and finds herself transformed into one of the world's most famous teen supermodels.

"Cabot's portrayal of Emerson is brilliant. . . . Pure fun, this first series installment will leave readers clamoring for the next." Publ Wkly

Other titles in this series are:
Being Nikki (2009)
Runaway (2010)

All -American girl. HarperCollins Pubs. 2002 247p hardcover o.p. pa $7.99
Grades: 7 8 9 10 **Fic**
1. Presidents -- Fiction
ISBN 0-06-029469-8; 0-06-029470-1 lib bdg; 0-06-147989-6 pa
LC 2002-19049

A sophomore girl stops a presidential assassination attempt, is appointed Teen Ambassador to the United Nations, and catches the eye of the very cute First Son. "Grades six to ten." (Bull Cent Child Books)

There's "surprising depth in the characters and plenty of authenticity in the cultural details and the teenage voices—particularly in Sam's poignant, laugh-out-loud narration." Booklist

Another title in this series is:
Ready or not (2005)

From the notebooks of a middle school princess; written & illustrated by Meg Cabot. First edition Feiwel & Friends 2015 192 p. illustrations (hardback) $16.99
Grades: 4 5 6 7 **Fic**
1. Orphans -- Fiction 2. Princesses -- Fiction 3. School stories 4. Diaries -- Fiction 5. Schools -- Fiction 6. Families -- Fiction 7. Middle schools -- Fiction
ISBN 1250066026; 9781250066022
LC 2014043845

"Olivia Grace Clarisse Mignonette Harrison is a completely average twelve-year-old. The only things about her that aren't average are her name . . . and the fact that she is a half-orphan who has never met her father. Then one completely average day . . . a limo containing Princess Mia Thermopolis of Genovia pulls up to invite her to New York to finally meet her father, who promptly invites her to come live with him." (Publisher's note)

"Cabot manages to combine wit and lavish details to po sitive effect, as evidenced by a royal grandmother who manages to be both familiar and surprising. While readers who already know the Princess Diaries might find this fairy tale a bit too retold, young newcomers to the Cabot magic will be charmed. A sweet fantasy, both funny and highly satisfying." Kirkus

Other titles in this series are:
Royal wedding disaster (2016)
Royal crush (2017)
Royal crown (2018)

★ The **princess** diaries. Avon Bks. 2000 238p lib bdg $15.89; pa $6.99; $15.95
Grades: 7 8 9 10 **Fic**
1. Diaries 2. Identity 3. Princesses 4. New York (N.Y.) 5. Fathers and daughters
ISBN 0-06-029210-5 lib bdg; 0-380-81402-1 pa; 0-380-97848-2
LC 99-46479

Fourteen-year-old Mia, who is trying to lead a normal life as a teenage girl in New York City, is shocked to learn that her father is the Prince of Genovia, a small European principality, and that she is a princess and the heir to the throne. "Grades five to nine." (Bull Cent Child Books)

"Readers will relate to Mia's bubbly, chatty voice and enjoy the humor of this unlikely fairy tale." SLJ

Other titles about Mia are:
Princess in the spotlight (2001)
Princess in love (2002)
Princess in waiting (2003)
Project princess (2003)
Princess in pink (2004)
The princess present (2004)
Princess in training (2005)
Party princess (2006)
Sweet sixteen princess (2006)
Valentine princess (2006)
Princess on the brink (2007)
Princess Mia (2008)
Forever princess (2009)
Royal wedding (2015)

Caine, Rachel

Ink and bone; the Great Library. Rachel Caine. New American Library 2015 355 p. (The Great Library) (hardcover) $17.99
Grades: 8 9 10 11 12 **Fic**
1. Dystopian fiction 2. Libraries -- Fiction 3. Alternative histories 4. Alexandrian Library -- Fiction
ISBN 9780451472397; 045147239X
LC 2015001509

In this young adult alternative history novel, by Rachel Caine, "the Great Library [of Alexandria] is now a presence in every major city, governing the flow of knowledge to the masses. . . . When he inadvertently commits heresy by creating a device that could change the world, Jess discovers that those who control the Great Library believe that knowledge is more valuable than any human life--and soon both heretics and books will burn." (Publisher's note)

"Caine has created a Dickensian future with an odd mix of technologies and elements of sorcery. A strong cast of characters and nail-biting intensity make for a promising start to this new series." SLJ

Otherr titles in this series are:
Paper and fire (2016)
Ash and quill (2017)
Smoke and iron (2018)

Cala, Caroline

Best babysitters ever; Caroline Cala. Houghton Mifflin Harcourt 2019 272 p. (hardback) $13.99
Grades: 4 5 6 7 8 **Fic**
1. Humorous fiction 2. Friendship -- Fiction 3. Babysitters -- Fiction 4. Clubs -- Fiction 5. Humorous stories 6. Best friends -- Fiction 7. Moneymaking projects -- Fiction
ISBN 9781328850898
LC 2018021264

"A girl named Kristy Thomas had a great idea: to form The Baby-Sitters Club with her best friends. And now twelve-year-old Malia Twiggs has had a great idea too. Technically, she had Kristy's idea. .

. . After a little convincing, Malia and her friends Dot and Bree start a babysitting club to earn funds for an epic birthday bash. But babysitting definitely isn't what they thought it would be." (Publisher's note)

Other titles in this series are:

The good, the bad, and the bossy (2019)

Calejo, Ryan

Charlie Hernández and the league of shadows; by Ryan Calejo. Aladdin 2018 336 p. (hardback) $17.99

Grades: 5 6 7 8 **Fic**

1. Shapeshifting -- Fiction 2. Secret societies -- Fiction 3. Hispanic Americans -- Fiction 4. Good and evil -- Fiction 5. Missing persons -- Fiction 6. Folklore -- Latin America -- Fiction

ISBN 9781534426580

LC 2018014304

In this book, by Ryan Calejo, "Charlie Hernández . . . possesses an almost encyclopedic knowledge of the monsters and ghouls . . . haunting the imaginations of children all across the Iberian Peninsula, . . . Central and South America. . . . But when Charlie begins to experience freaky bodily manifestations . . . he is suddenly swept up in a world where . . . mythical beings . . . seem to be walking straight out of the pages of Hispanic folklore and into his life." (Publisher's note)

Other titles in this series are:

Charlie Hernandez & the castle of bones (2019)

Caletti, Deb

★ The **last** forever; Deb Caletti. Simon Pulse 2014 336 p. (hardback) $17.99

Grades: 8 9 10 11 12 **Fic**

1. Love -- Fiction 2. Death -- Fiction 3. Grief -- Fiction 4. Father-daughter relationship -- Fiction 5. Friendship -- Fiction

ISBN 1442450002; 9781442450004

LC 2013031010

This book, by Deb Caletti, is a "novel of love and loss. . . . Nothing lasts forever, and no one gets that more than Tessa. After her mother died, it's all she can do to keep her friends, her boyfriend, her happiness from slipping away. And then there's her dad. He's stuck in his own daze, and it's hard to feel like a family when their house no longer seems like a home. Her father's solution? An impromptu road trip that lands them in a small coastal town." (Publisher's note)

"After a trying bout with cancer, Tess's mother has died, but she's left behind a one-of-a-kind pixiebell plant. "My mother vowed that the last pixiebell would never die on her watch, and now that I have it, it isn't going to die on mine, either," Tess vows... Featuring sharp-witted first-person narration, some fascinating facts about plants and seeds, relatable characters, and evocative settings, Caletti's (The Story of Us) inspiring novel eloquently depicts the nature of mutability. As with her previous books, this love story reverberates with honesty and emotion." (Publishers Weekly)

Callender, Kheryn

★ **Hurricane** child; by Kheryn Callender. Scholastic Press 2018 224 p. (jacketed hardcover : alk. paper) $17.99

Grades: 4 5 6 7 **Fic**

1. Friendship -- Fiction 2. Hurricanes -- Fiction 3. African American girls -- Fiction 4. Lesbians -- Fiction 5. Missing persons -- Fiction 6. Mothers and daughters -- Fiction 7. United States Virgin Islands -- Fiction

ISBN 9781338129304

LC 2017032545

Stonewall Book Award: Young Adult (2019)

In this book, by Kheryn Callender, "being born during a hurricane is unlucky, and twelve-year-old Caroline has had her share of bad luck lately. She's hated and bullied by everyone in her small school. . . . But when a new student named Kalinda arrives, Caroline's luck begins to turn around. . . . Now, Caroline must find the strength to confront her feelings for Kalinda, brave the spirit stalking her through the islands, and face the reason her mother abandoned her." (Publisher's note)

"An excellent and nuanced coming-of-age tale with a dash of magical realism for readers who enjoy character-driven novels, especially those with middle grade LGBTQ+ characterizations." SLJ

Cameron, Sharon

The **Forgetting**; by Sharon Cameron. Scholastic 2016 416 p. hardcover $18.99

Grades: 8 9 10 11 12 **Fic**

1. Science fiction 2. Memory -- Fiction 3. Amnesia -- Fiction 4. Friendship -- Fiction

ISBN 0545945216; 9780545945219

LC 2016007978

In this book, by Sharon Cameron, "what isn't written, isn't remembered. Even your crimes. Nadia lives in the city of Canaan, where life is safe and structured, hemmed in by white stone walls and no memory of what came before. But every twelve years the city descends into the bloody chaos of the Forgetting, a day of no remorse, when each person's memories -- of parents, children, love, life, and self -- are lost. Unless they have been written." (Publisher's note)

"Effective worldbuilding and strong characterization (even minor players have emotional depth) add substance to the fast-paced plot. A cosmetic resemblance to blockbuster teen dystopias allows Cameron to toy slyly with readers' expectations, but this is no retread." Kirkus

Another title in this series is:

The Knowing (2017)

Rook; Sharon Cameron. Scholastic Press 2015 456 p. (jacketed hardcover) $17.99

Grades: 7 8 9 10 11 12 **Fic**

1. Romance fiction 2. Suspense fiction 3. Revolutions -- Fiction 4. Adventure stories 5. France -- Fiction 6. Rescues -- Fiction 7. Secrets -- Fiction 8. Paris (France) -- Fiction

ISBN 0545675995; 9780545675994

LC 2014038853

In this novel, by Sharon Cameron, "centuries after a shifting of the Earth's poles, the Sunken City that was once Paris is in the grips of a revolution. All who oppose the new regime are put to the blade, except for those who disappear from their prison cells, a red-tipped rook feather left in their place. Is the mysterious Red Rook a savior of the innocent or a criminal? When the search for the Red Rook comes straight to her doorstep, Sophia discovers that her fiancé is not all he seems. Which is only fair, because neither is she." (Publisher's note)

"Still, the novel's 456 pages mostly fly by thanks to the nonstop intrigue and the occasional swoon-worthy kiss. Full of derring-do and double crosses, this romantic adventure is thoroughly engrossing." Kirkus

Cameron, Sophie

Last bus to Everland; Sophie Cameron. Roaring Brook Press 2019 336 p. (hardcover) $17.99

Grades: 7 8 9 10 11 12 **Fic**

ISBN 9781250149923; 9781250149930

LC 2018955879

In this book, by Sophie Cameron, "Brody Fair feels like nobody gets him: not his overworked parents, not his genius older brother, and definitely not the girls in the projects set on making his life miserable. Then he meets Nico, an art student who takes Brody to Everland . . . that opens at 11:21pm each Thursday for Nico and his band of present-day misfits and miscreants. Here Brody finds his tribe and a weekly respite from a world where he feels out of place." (Publisher's note)

"Everland is a lovely conceit amid beautifully realized worlds and wonderfully individual, empathetic characters." (Booklist)

Out of the blue; Sophie Cameron. Roaring Brook Press 2018 280 p. (hardcover) $17.99

Grades: 7 8 9 10 11 12 **Fic**

1. Grief -- Fiction 2. Angels -- Fiction 3. Mothers -- Fiction 4. Paranormal fiction

ISBN 1250149916; 9781250149909; 9781250149916

LC 2017957297

In this novel, by Sophie Cameron, "Jaya's life has completely fallen apart. Her mother is dead, her dad is on an obsessive wild goose chase, and mysterious winged beings are falling from the sky. For the past nine months, none of the them have survived the plummet to Earth, but when a female being lands near Jaya--and is still alive--she doesn't call the authorities. She hides the being and tries to nurse her back to health." (Publisher's note)

"A strong infusion of magic and wonder distinguish this debut novel." Kirkus

Camlot, Heather

Clutch; by Heather Camlot. Red Deer Press 2017 240 p. (paperback) $12.95

Grades: 4 5 6 7 8 **Fic**

1. Bildungsromans 2. Baseball -- Fiction 3. Jewish children -- Fiction 4. Montréal (Québec) 5. Jewish children -- Québec (Province) -- Montréal -- Fiction

ISBN 9780889955486; 0889955484

In this book, by Heather Camlot, "it is 1946 in a poor Jewish neighborhood in Montreal where a few dollars equals a fortune, and no matter where you go you will find the best home cooking anywhere on Earth. It is also a million miles away from the posh mansions on the other side of town. But a 12-year-old boy can still hope. On the other side of town something incredible is happening. Jackie Robinson is playing for the Montreal Royals. And he's going to change the world." (Publisher's note)

"Readers will be completely enthralled with Joey's world and root for him all the way. Powerful, moving, and wonderful." Kirkus

Includes bibliographical references (page 232).

Canales, Viola

★ The **tequila** worm. Wendy Lamb Books 2005 199p hardcover o.p. pa $7.99

Grades: 6 7 8 9 10 **Fic**

1. Texas -- Fiction 2. Mexican Americans -- Fiction

ISBN 0-375-84089-3 pa; 0-385-74674-1

LC 2004-24533

Sofia grows up in the close-knit community of the barrio in McAllen, Texas, then finds that her experiences as a scholarship student at an Episcopal boarding school in Austin only strengthen her ties to family and her "comadres."

"The explanations of cultural traditions . . . are always rooted in immediate, authentic family emotions, and in Canales' exuberant storytelling, which . . . finds both humor and absurdity in sharply observed, painful situations." Booklist

Cao, Wenxuan, 1954-

Bronze and sunflower; by Cao Wenxuan, illustrated by Meilo So, translated byHelen Wang. Candlewick Press 2017 400 p. illustrations (ebook) $16.99; $16.99

Grades: 4 5 6 7 8 **Fic**

1. Domestic fiction 2. Adoption -- Fiction 3. Friendship -- Fiction

ISBN 9780763693688; 0763688169; 9780763688165

LC 2017005320

Kirkus Prize Finalist: Young Readers' Literature (2017)

In this book, by Cao Wenxuan, illustrated by Meilo So, and translated by Helen Wang, "Sunflower is an only child, and when . . . her father tragically drowns, Sunflower is taken in by the poorest family in . . . [a rural] village, a family with a son named Bronze. . . . [Bronze] hasn't spoken a word since he was traumatized by a terrible fire. Bronze and Sunflower become inseparable, understanding each other as only the closest friends can." (Publisher's note)

Carbone, Elisa

Stealing freedom; [by] Elisa Carbone. Knopf 1998 258p hardcover o.p.

Grades: 6 7 8 9 **Fic**

1. Slavery -- Fiction 2. African Americans -- Fiction 3. Underground railroad -- Fiction

ISBN 0440417074; 0679893075

LC 98-36929

This historical novel is "based on the life of Ann Maria Weems, who was born into slavery in Maryland in the 1840s. . . . Her master's debts are many and so her beloved brothers are sold without warning. Abolitionists are able to buy the freedom of the rest of her family, but the master refuses to part with Ann Maria. . . . She surreptitiously teaches herself to read and falls in love with a neighbor's slave, Alfred. She promises never to leave without him, but there is nothing she can do when she is 'kidnapped' by abolitionists and has no way to contact him." (SLJ) "Grades seven to ten." (Booklist)

"This is a fine piece of historical fiction with a strong, appealing heroine." SLJ

Carbone, Elisa Lynn

Blood on the river; James Town 1607. [by] Elisa Carbone. Viking 2006 237p $16.99; pa $6.99

Grades: 5 6 7 8 **Fic**

1. Powhatan Indians -- Fiction 2. Jamestown (Va.) -- History -- Fiction 3. United States -- History -- 1600-1775, Colonial period -- Fiction

ISBN 0-670-06060-7; 0-14-240932-4 pa

LC 2005023646

Traveling to the New World in 1606 as the page to Captain John Smith, twelve-year-old orphan Samuel Collier settles in the new colony of James Town, where he must quickly learn to distinguish between friend and foe.

"A strong, visceral story of the hardship and peril settlers faced, as well as the brutal realities of colonial conquest." Booklist

Card, Orson Scott

★ **Ender's** game. TOR Bks. 1991 xxi, 226p $24.95; pa $6.99

Grades: 7 8 9 10 11 12 Adult **Fic**

1. Science fiction 2. Interplanetary voyages -- Fiction

ISBN 0-312-93208-1; 0-8125-5070-6 pa

A reissue of the title first published 1985

ALA YALSA Margaret A. Edwards Award (2008)

"The key, of course, is Ender Wiggin himself. Mr. Card never makes the mistake of patronizing or sentimentalizing his hero. Alternately likable and insufferable, he is a convincing little Napoleon in short pants." N Y Times Book Rev

Other titles in the author's distant future series about Ender Wiggin include:

Children of the mind (1996)
Ender in exile (2008)
Ender's shadow (1999)
Shadow of the giant (2005)
Shadow of the Hegemon (2001)
Shadow of the giant (2005)
Shadow puppets (2002)
Speaker for the dead (1986)
A war of gifts (2007)
Xenocide (1991)

Carey, Benedict

Poison most vial; a mystery. by Benedict Carey. Amulet Books 2012 215 p. (hardcover) $16.95
Grades: 5 6 7 8 **Fic**

1. Mystery fiction 2. Forensic sciences -- Fiction 3. Murder -- Fiction 4. Neighbors -- Fiction 5. Mystery and detective stories 6. Fathers and daughters -- Fiction
ISBN 1419700316; 9781419700316
LC 2011038222

In this novel by Benedict Carey "Ruby's janitor father becomes the prime suspect in a murder . . . [of] [f]orensics expert Dr. Ramachandran . . . [and] the eighth grader decides it's up to her to clear his name. . . . [She] enlists the aid of her large, Jamaican buddy, Rex, and reclusive, retired toxicologist Clara Whitmore, who lives in Ruby's building. What with hacking into computers, evading gangs and like spy-jinx, the mystery demands a lot of brain work." (Kirkus)

The **unknowns**. Amulet Books 2009 259p il map $16.95
Grades: 6 7 8 9 **Fic**

1. Mystery fiction 2. Mathematics -- Fiction 3. Conspiracies -- Fiction 4. Missing persons -- Fiction
ISBN 978-0-8109-7991-8; 0-8109-7991-8
LC 2008-33914

When people start vanishing from a godforsaken trailer park next to the Folsom Energy Plant, two eleven-year-olds investigate using mathematical clues that were hastily planted by their friend Mrs. Clarke before she disappeared.

"Successfully working in the concepts of pi and the Pythagorean theorem into an adventure story is no easy task, but . . . Carey succeeds because of his lively and unique writing." Voice Youth Advocates

Carey, Edward

Heap House; The Iremonger Trilogy. by Edward Carey. Overlook Press 2014 416 p. illustrations $16.99
Grades: 5 6 7 8 9 10 **Fic**

1. Boys -- Fiction 2. Houses -- Fiction 3. London (England) -- Fiction 4. Great Britain -- History -- Victoria, 1837-1901 -- Fiction 5. Dwellings 6. London (England) 7. Orphans -- Fiction 8. Family secrets -- Fiction
ISBN 1468309536; 9781468309539

In this book, by Edward Carey, "Clod is an Iremonger. He lives in the Heaps, a vast sea of lost and discarded items collected from all over London. At the centre is Heap House, a puzzle of houses, castles, homes and mysteries reclaimed from the city and built into a living maze of staircases and scurrying rats. The Iremongers are a mean and cruel family, robust and hardworking, but Clod has an illness. He can hear the objects whispering." (Publisher's note)

"Living among sentient trash heaps, Clod Iremonger has always been able to hear the voices of the objects that his family members carry, but the arrival of serving girl Lucy imbues the objects with a new and dangerous energy. Descriptive prose and black-and-white portraits create a unique cast of characters in a bleak, dilapidated home. Fans of Joan Aiken will flock to this dark mystery." Horn Book

Other titles in this series are:
Foulsham (2015)
Lungdon (2015)

Carey, Janet Lee

The **beast** of Noor. Atheneum Books for Young Readers 2006 497p $16.95
Grades: 6 7 8 9 **Fic**

1. Fantasy fiction
ISBN 978-0-689-87644-8; 0-689-87644-0
LC 2005-17731

Fifteen-year-old Miles Ferrell uses the rare and special gift he is given to break the curse of the Shriker, a murderous creature reportedly brought to Shalem Wood by his family's clan centuries

"Carey delivers an eerie, atmospheric tale, full of terror and courage, set in a convincingly realized magical realm." Booklist

Followed by: The dragons of Noor (2010)

Dragon's Keep. Harcourt 2007 302p $17
Grades: 7 8 9 10 **Fic**

1. Fantasy fiction 2. Dragons -- Fiction 3. Princesses -- Fiction 4. Mother-daughter relationship -- Fiction 5. Great Britain -- History -- 1066-1154, Norman period -- Fiction
ISBN 978-0-15-205926-2; 0-15-205926-1
LC 2006-24669

In 1145 A.D., as foretold by Merlin, fourteen-year-old Rosalind, who will be the twenty-first Pendragon Queen of Wilde Island, has much to accomplish to fulfill her destiny, while hiding from her people the dragon's claw she was born with that reflects only one of her mother's dark secrets.

This is told "in stunning, lyrical prose. . . . Carey smoothly blends many traditional fantasy tropes here, but her telling is fresh as well as thoroughly compelling." Booklist

Dragonswood; by Janet Lee Carey. Dial Books 2012 403p.
Grades: 7 8 9 **Fic**

1. Fantasy fiction 2. Romance fiction 3. Paranormal fiction 4. Fantasy 5. Dragons -- Fiction 6. Fairies -- Fiction 7. British Isles -- History -- 12th century -- Fiction
ISBN 9780803735040
LC 2011021638

"Wilde Island is not at peace. The kingdom mourns the dead Pendragon king and awaits the return of his heir; the uneasy pact between dragons, fairies, and humans is strained; and the regent is funding a bloodthirsty witch hunt, hoping to rid the island of half-fey maidens. Tess, daughter of a blacksmith, has visions of the future, but she still doesn't expect to be accused of witchcraft, forced to flee with her two best friends, or offered shelter by the handsome and enigmatic Garth Huntsman, a warden for Dragonswood. But Garth is the younger prince in disguise and Tess soon learns that her true father was fey." (Publisher's note)

Carlson, Caroline

The **world's** greatest detective; Caroline Carlson. HarperCollins 2017 351 p. (hardcover) $16.99
Grades: 4 5 6 7 **Fic**

1. Mystery fiction 2. Murder -- Fiction 3. Detectives -- Fiction 4. Detective and mystery stories
ISBN 9780062368294; 9780062368270
LC 2016957943

This book, by Caroline Carlson, is "a story of crime, tricks, and hilarity. . . . Detectives' Row is full of talented investigators, but Toby Montrose isn't one of them. He's only an assistant at his uncle's detective agency. . . . Toby's friend Ivy is the best sleuth around--or at least she thinks so. They both see their chance to prove themselves when the famed Hugh Abernathy announces a contest to choose the World's Greatest Detective." (Publisher's note)

"The witty dialogue, clever characters, and twists and turns are sure to keep young sleuths riveted." Booklist

Carman, Patrick

The **Dark** Hills divide; [by] Patrick Carman. Orchard Books 2005 253p (The land of Elyon) $11.95

Grades: 4 5 6 7 **Fic**

1. Fantasy fiction
ISBN 0-439-70093-0

LC 2004-16312

When she finds the key to a secret passageway leading out of the walled city of Bridewell, twelve-year-old Alexa realizes her lifelong wish to explore the mysterious forests and mountains that lie beyond the wall

"Narrator Aasne Vigesaa clearly portrays Alexa's thoughtful, inquisitive nature and unsettled feelings. . . . Vigesaa's excellent use of pace, pitch, and tone help differentiate each character." SLJ

Other titles in this series are:
Beyond the Valley of Thorns (2005)
The tenth city (2006)
Into the mist (2007)
Stargazer (2008)

The **house** of power. Little, Brown & Co. 2007 330p il (Atherton) $16.99; $16.99; pa $5.99

Grades: 5 6 7 8 **Fic**

1. Science fiction 2. Orphans -- Fiction 3. Friendship -- Fiction 4. Earthquakes -- Fiction 5. Social classes -- Fiction
ISBN 978-0-316-16670-6; 0-316-16670-7; 978-0-316-16671-3 pa; 0-316-16671-5 pa

LC 2006025976

Edgar, an eleven-year-old orphan, finds a book that reveals significant secrets about Atherton, the strictly divided world on which he lives, even as geological changes threaten to shift the power structure that allows a select few to live off the labor of others.

This "is a fast-paced novel with a unique setting, fascinating plot, and cliffhanger ending. It shines because of the author's imagination and skill." SLJ

Other titles in this series are:
Rivers of fire (2008)
The dark planet (2009)

Carmichael, Clay

★ **Wild** things; [written and illustrated by Clay Carmichael] Front Street 2009 248p il $18.95

Grades: 5 6 7 8 **Fic**

1. Cats -- Fiction 2. Uncles -- Fiction 3. Artists -- Fiction 4. Orphans -- Fiction 5. Family life -- Fiction
ISBN 978-1-59078-627-7; 1-59078-627-0

LC 2007-49911

Stubborn, self-reliant, eleven-year-old Zoe, recently orphaned, moves to the country to live with her prickly half-uncle, a famous doctor and sculptor, and together they learn about trust and the strength of family

"Carmichael gives a familiar plot a fresh new life in this touching story with a finely crafted sense of place." Booklist

Carriger, Gail

★ **Curtsies** & conspiracies; Gail Carriger. Little, Brown and Co. 2013 320 p. (Finishing school) $18

Grades: 7 8 9 10 11 12 **Fic**

1. Steampunk fiction 2. Espionage -- Fiction 3. Conspiracies -- Fiction 4. Science fiction 5. Robots -- Fiction 6. Schools -- Fiction 7. Etiquette -- Fiction 8. Boarding schools -- Fiction 9. Great Britain -- History -- George VI, 1936-1952 -- Fiction
ISBN 031619011X; 9780316190114

LC 2012048520

In this book, by Gail Carriger, "Sophronia's first year at Mademoiselle Geraldine's Finishing Academy for Young Ladies of Quality . . . is training her to be a spy. A conspiracy is afoot--one with dire implications for both supernaturals and humans. Sophronia must rely on her training to discover who is behind the dangerous plot-and survive the London Season with a full dance card." (Publisher's note)

"With the school's dirigible heading toward London for a liaison with an inventor studying aetherospheric travel, Sophronia (Etiquette & Espionage) is convinced that her professors are Up To Something. Is the academy affiliated with vampire hives, werewolf packs, the anti-supernatural Picklemen, or the Crown--all of whom would benefit from controlling aether technology? A witty and suspenseful steampunk romp." (Horn Book)

★ **Etiquette** & espionage; by Gail Carriger. Little, Brown 2013 320 p. (Finishing school) (alk. paper) $17.99

Grades: 7 8 9 10 11 12 **Fic**

1. Spy stories 2. School stories 3. Assassins -- Fiction 4. Science fiction 5. Robots -- Fiction 6. Schools -- Fiction 7. Espionage -- Fiction 7. Etiquette -- Fiction 9. Boarding schools -- Fiction 10. Great Britain -- History -- George VI, 1936-1952 -- Fiction
ISBN 031619008X; 9780316190084

LC 2012005498

In this book, Sophronia's mother is "desperate for her daughter to become a proper lady. So she enrolls Sophronia in Mademoiselle Geraldine's Finishing Academy for Young Ladies of Quality. But Sophronia soon realizes the school is not quite what her mother might have hoped. At Mademoiselle Geraldine's, young ladies learn to finish . . . everything. Certainly, they learn the fine arts of dance, dress, and etiquette, but they also learn to deal out death, diversion, and espionage." (Publisher's note)

Other titles in this series are:
Curtsies & conspiracies (2013)
Waistcoats & weaponry (2014)
Manners & mutiny (2015)

Carroll, Emma

In Darkling Wood; Emma Carroll. Delacorte Press 2017 231 p. $16.99

Grades: 5 6 7 8 9 **Fic**

1. Fantasy fiction 2. Magic -- Fiction 3. Fairies -- Fiction 4. Friendship -- Fiction 5. Brothers and sisters -- Fiction
ISBN 039955601X; 9780399556012

LC 2015049623

In this book, by Emma Carroll, "when Alice is suddenly bundled off to her estranged grandmother's Nell's house, there's nothing good about it, except the beautiful Darkling Wood, . . . but Nell wants to have it cut down. Alice feels at home there. She even finds a friend, a girl named Flo. But Flo doesn't go to the local school, and no one in town has heard of her. When Flo shows Alice the surprising secrets of Darkling Wood, Alice starts to wonder: What is real? And can she find out in time to save the wood from destruction?" (Publisher's note)

"A haunting and poignant exploration of family, loss, and redemption." Booklist.

Strange star; Emma Carroll. Delacorte Press 2018 240 p. (hc) $16.99
Grades: 4 5 6 7 8 **Fic**

1. Fairy tales 2. Ghost stories 3. Science fiction 4. Friendship -- Fiction 5. Horror stories 6. Adoption -- Fiction 7. Storytelling -- Fiction 8. Supernatural -- Fiction 9. Household employees -- Fiction 10. Switzerland -- History -- 19th century -- Fiction
ISBN 9780399556050; 9780399556067

LC 2017038517

In this novel, by Emma Carroll, "five friends meet at . . . the summer home of Lord Byron. After dinner is served, they challenge each other to tell ghost stories that will freeze the blood. But one of the guests--Mary Shelley--is stuck for a story to share. Then there's an unexpected knock at the front door. Collapsed on the doorstep is a girl with strange scars on her face. She has traveled a long way with her own tale to tell, and now they all must listen." (Publisher's note)

Carson, Rae

★ The **bitter** kingdom; by Rae Carson. Greenwillow Books 2013 448 p. (hardcover) $17.99
Grades: 8 9 10 11 12 **Fic**

1. Fantasy fiction 2. Magic -- Fiction 3. Queens -- Fiction 4. Love -- Fiction 5. Prophecies -- Fiction 6. Kings, queens, rulers, etc. -- Fiction
ISBN 0062026542; 9780062026545

LC 2013011912

Sequel to: The crown of embers

This is the final book in Rae Carson's Girl of Fire and Thorns trilogy. Here, "young Queen Elisa and her companions trek into enemy territory to rescue the man she loves, while a traitor back home attempts to overthrow her. Elisa's journeys take her to . . . Invierne, where she hopes to destroy the source of the Invierno' magic and bargain for peace; to the Basajuan desert, where only her most audacious plans have any chance to stop the war; and home to try to regain her throne." (Publishers Weekly)

★ The **crown** of embers; by Rae Carson. Greenwillow Books 2012 410 p. (hardcover) $17.99
Grades: 8 9 10 11 12 **Fic**

1. Adventure fiction 2. Love -- Fiction 3. Magic -- Fiction 4. Prophecies -- Fiction 5. Kings, queens, rulers, etc. -- Fiction
ISBN 0062026518; 9780062026514

LC 2012014125

This young adult fantasy novel, by Rae Carson, is the sequel to the Morris, Cybils, and Andre Norton Award finalist book "The Girl of Fire and Thorns." "Elisa is a hero. . . . [But] to conquer the power she bears once and for all, Elisa must follow the trail of long-forgotten--and forbidden--clues from the deep, undiscovered catacombs of her own city to the treacherous seas. With her goes a one-eyed spy, a traitor, and the man who--despite everything--she is falling in love with." (Publisher's note)

★ The **girl** of fire and thorns. Greenwillow Books 2011 423p $17.99
Grades: 8 9 10 11 12 **Fic**

1. Fantasy fiction 2. Magic -- Fiction 3. Prophecies -- Fiction 4. Kings and rulers -- Fiction
ISBN 978-0-06-202648-4; 0-06-202648-8

LC 2010042021

Morris Award Finalist (2012)

"The first book in the acclaimed and award winning New York Times bestselling trilogy. The Girl of Fire and Thorns is a remarkable novel full of adventure, sorcery, heartbreak, and power...Once a century, one person is chosen for greatness. Elisa is the chosen one. But she is also the younger of two princesses. The one who has never done anything remarkable, and can't see how she ever will. Now, on her sixteenth birthday, she has become the secret wife of a handsome and worldly king...And he's not the only one who seeks her. Savage enemies, seething with dark magic, are hunting her. A daring, determined revolutionary thinks she could be his people's savior. Soon it is not just her life, but her very heart that is at stake." (Publisher's Note)

"This fast-moving and exciting novel is rife with political conspiracies and machinations." SLJ

Walk on Earth a Stranger; Rae Carson. Greenwillow books 2015 448 p. map $17.99
Grades: 7 8 9 10 **Fic**

1. Magic -- Fiction 2. California -- Gold discoveries
ISBN 0062242911; 9780062242914

LC 2015015751

In Rae Carson's novel "Lee Westfall has a secret. She can sense the presence of gold in the world around her. Veins deep beneath the earth, pebbles in the river, nuggets dug up from the forest floor. The buzz of gold means warmth and life and home--until everything is ripped away by a man who wants to control her. Lee disguises herself as a boy and takes to the trail across the country. Gold was discovered in California, and where else could such a magical girl find herself, find safety?" (Publisher's note)

"Carson's story is simply terrific--tense and exciting, while gently and honestly addressing the brutal hardships of the westward migration. Even minor characters are fully three-dimensional, but it's Leah who rightfully takes center stage as a smart, resourceful, determined, and realistic heroine who embodies the age-old philosophy that it isn't what happens to you, but how you react to it that matters." Pub Wkly

Other titles in this series are:
Like a River Glorious (2016)
Into the Bright Unknown (2017)

Cartaya, Pablo

Each tiny spark; by Pablo Cartaya. Kokila 2019 315 p. (hardback) $16.99
Grades: 4 5 6 7 **Fic**

1. Hispanic Americans -- Fiction 2. Attention deficit disorder -- Fiction 3. Father-daughter relationship -- Fiction 4. Georgia -- Fiction 5. Schools -- Fiction 6. Middle schools -- Fiction 7. Fathers and daughters -- Fiction 8. Family life -- Georgia -- Fiction 9. Attention-deficit hyperactivity disorder -- Fiction
ISBN 9780451479723

LC 2019013145

This "deeply moving middle grade novel[, by Pablo Cartaya, is] about a daughter and father finding their way back to each other in the face of their changing family and community. . . [It] is a tender story about asking big questions and being brave enough to reckon with the answers." (Publisher's note)

"A pitch-perfect middle-grade novel that insightfully explores timely topics with authenticity and warmth." --Kirkus

The **epic** fail of Arturo Zamora; Pablo Cartaya. Viking 2017 236 p. (hardcover) $16.99
Grades: 5 6 7 **Fic**

1. Community life -- Fiction 2. Latinos (U.S.) -- Fiction 3. Cities

and towns -- Fiction
ISBN 1101997230; 9781101997239; 9781101997246
LC 2016052204

Pura Belpré Honor Book: Author (2018)

In this book, by Pablo Cartaya, "for Arturo, summertime in Miami means playing basketball until dark, sipping mango smoothies, and keeping cool under banyan trees. And maybe a few shifts as junior lunchtime dishwasher at Abuela's restaurant. Maybe. But this summer also includes Carmen, a cute poetry enthusiast who moves into Arturo's apartment complex and turns his stomach into a deep fryer." (Publisher's note)

"At turns funny, beautiful, and heartbreaking, this engrossing story will get kids cheering for triumphant, relatable Arturo and his powerful connections to family, tradition, and community." Booklist

Marcus Vega doesn't speak Spanish; Pablo Cartaya. Viking 2018 272 p. (hardcover) $16.99
Grades: 4 5 6 7 8 **Fic**

1. Family life -- Fiction 2. Down syndrome -- Fiction 3. Middle schools -- Fiction 4. Schools -- Fiction 5. Families -- Fiction 6. Puerto Rico -- Fiction 7. Puerto Ricans -- United States -- Fiction 8. People with mental disabilities -- Fiction
ISBN 9781101997260
LC 2017052895

In this book, by Pablo Cartaya, "after a fight at school leaves Marcus facing suspension, Marcus's mom decides it's time for a change of environment. She takes Marcus and his younger brother to Puerto Rico. . . . But Marcus can't focus knowing that his father--who walked out of their lives ten years ago--is somewhere on the island. . . . Marcus doesn't know if he'll ever find his father, but what he ultimately discovers changes his life." (Publisher's note)

Carter, Ally

All fall down; Ally Carter ; [edited by] David Levithan. Scholastic Press 2015 320 p. (Embassy row) $17.99
Grades: 7 8 9 10 **Fic**

1. Murder -- Fiction 2. Revenge -- Fiction 3. Ambassadors -- Fiction 4. Mother-daughter relationship -- Fiction
ISBN 0545654742; 9780545654746
LC 2014947739

In this book, by Ally Carter, "Grace Blakely is absolutely certain of three things: 1. She is not crazy. 2. Her mother was murdered. 3. Someday she is going to find the killer and make him pay. As certain as Grace is about these facts, nobody else believes her -- so there's no one she can completely trust. Not her grandfather, a powerful ambassador. Not her new friends, who all live on Embassy Row. . . . But they can't control Grace." (Publisher's note)

"This exciting first book in the Embassy Row series features sixteen-year-old Grace, who has moved into the United States Embassy on the coast of Adria with her ambassador grandfather. It is the first time in three years that she has been back to Adria, since her mother's tragic death in a fire... Her quest to find the truth is one that readers will love to follow, through the twists and turns of Embassy Row and with a diverse array of characters. Some help her, and some stand in her way . . . but Grace is a fighter, and she will stop at nothing to find out what happened to her mother. Readers will love this first book in what promises to be an exciting, thrilling mystery series from best-selling author Carter." VOYA

Other titles in this series are:
See how they run (2015)
Take the key and lock her up (2016)

Heist Society. Hyperion 2010 287p il map
Grades: 7 8 9 10 **Fic**

1. Thieves -- Fiction
ISBN 1-4231-1639-9; 978-1-4231-1639-4
LC 2009-40377

A group of teenagers conspire to re-steal several priceless paintings and save Kat Bishop's father from a vengeful collector who is accusing him of art theft. "Grades six to ten." (Bull Cent Child Books)

Carter "skillfully maintains suspense. . . . This is a thoroughly enjoyable, cinema-ready adventure." Booklist

Other titles about Kat are:
Uncommon criminals (2011)
Perfect scoundrels (2013)

Not if I save you first; Ally Carter. Scholastic Press 2018 293 p. (hardcover) $18.99
Grades: 8 9 10 11 **Fic**

1. Kidnapping -- Fiction 2. Best friends -- Fiction 3. Father-daughter relationship -- Fiction 4. Alaska -- Fiction 5. Rescues -- Fiction 6. Survival -- Fiction 7. Friendship -- Fiction 8. Forgiveness -- Fiction 9. Fathers and daughters -- Fiction 10. Wilderness survival -- Fiction
ISBN 9781338134148; 9781338134162
LC 2017049072

In this book, by Ally Carter, "Maddie thought she and Logan would be friends forever. But when your dad is a Secret Service agent and your best friend is the president's son, sometimes life has other plans. Before she knows it, Maddie's dad is dragging her to a cabin in the middle of the Alaskan wilderness." (Publisher's note)

"A tightly plotted thriller helmed by a firecracker that never loses her spark." Kirkus

Carter, Caela

Forever, or a long, long time; Caela Carter ; [edited by] Karen Chalpin. HarperCollins 2017 320 p. (ebook) $15.99; (hardcover) $16.99
Grades: 5 6 7 **Fic**

1. Adoption -- Fiction 2. Foster children -- Fiction 3. Brothers and sisters -- Fiction
ISBN 9780062385703; 9780062385680
LC 2016949993

This book, by Caela Carter, is a "story about two foster children who want desperately to believe that they've found their forever home. . . . Flora and her brother, Julian, . . . can't remember where they came from. And even now that they've been adopted, Flora still struggles to believe in forever. So along with their new mother, Flora and Julian begin a journey to go back and discover their past—for only then can they really begin to build their future." (Publisher's note)

"Poetic and meditative, this emotionally enthralling novel undresses assumptions with purpose and hope." Kirkus

Carvell, Marlene

Sweetgrass basket. Dutton Childrens Books 2005 243p $16.99
Grades: 7 8 9 10 **Fic**

1. School stories 2. Sisters -- Fiction 3. Mohawk Indians -- Fiction
ISBN 0-525-47547-8
LC 2004-24374

In alternating passages, two Mohawk sisters describe their lives at the Carlisle Indian Industrial School, established in 1879 to educate Native Americans, as they try to assimilate into white culture and one of them is falsely accused of stealing.

"Carvell has put together a compelling, authentic, and sensitive portrayal of a part of our history that is still not made accurately available to young readers." SLJ

Cashore, Kristin

★ **Fire**; a novel. Kristin Cashore. Dial Books 2009 461p map $17.99

Grades: 9 10 11 12 **Fic**

1. Fantasy fiction

ISBN 978-0-8037-3461-6; 0-8037-3461-1

LC 2009-5187

In a kingdom called the Dells, Fire is the last human-shaped monster, with unimaginable beauty and the ability to control the minds of those around her, but even with these gifts she cannot escape the strife that overcomes her world.

"Many twists propel the action . . . [and] Cashore's conclusion satisfies, but readers will clamor for a sequel to the prequel—a book bridging the gap between this one and Graceling." Publ Wkly

★ **Graceling**. Harcourt 2008 471p map $17; pa $9.99

Grades: 8 9 10 11 12 **Fic**

1. Fantasy fiction

ISBN 978-0-15-206396-2; 0-15-206396-X; 978-0-547-25830-0 pa; 0-547-25830-5 pa

LC 2007045436

ALA YALSA Morris Award Finalist, 2009

In a world where some people are born with extreme skills called Graces, Katsa struggles for redemption from her own horrifying Grace, the Grace of killing. She teams up with another young fighter to save their land from a corrupt king. "Age fourteen and up." (N Y Times Book Rev)

"This is gorgeous storytelling: exciting, stirring, and accessible. Fantasy and romance readers will be thrilled." SLJ

Other titles in this series are:

Fire (2009)

Bitterblue (2012)

Jane, unlimited; Kristin Cashore. Kathy Dawson Books 2017 453 p. illustrations, maps (hardcover) $18.99

Grades: 8 9 10 11 12 **Fic**

1. Grief -- Fiction 2. Orphans -- Fiction 3. Decision making -- Fiction 4. Islands -- Fiction

ISBN 0803741499; 9780698158894; 9780803741492

LC 2017030463

In this novel, by Kristin Cashore, "Jane has lived an ordinary life, raised by her aunt Magnolia--an adjunct professor and deep sea photographer. . . . But Aunt Magnolia was lost a few months ago in Antarctica on one of her expeditions. Now, with no direction, a year out of high school, and obsessed with making umbrellas that look like her own dreams (but mostly just mourning her aunt), she is easily swept away by Kiran Thrash--a glamorous, capricious acquaintance." (Publisher's note)

"Creation, compassion, and choice repeatedly emerge as themes in this ambitious, mind-expanding novel." Booklist

Castellucci, Cecil

Boy proof. Candlewick Press 2005 203p $15.99

Grades: 7 8 9 10 **Fic**

1. Motion pictures -- Fiction 2. Los Angeles (Calif.) -- Fiction

ISBN 978-0763627966

LC 2004-50256

Feeling alienated from everyone around her, Los Angeles high school senior and cinephile Victoria Denton hides behind the identity of a favorite movie character until an interesting new boy arrives at school and helps her realize that there is more to life than just the movies.

This "novel's clipped, funny, first-person, present-tense narrative will grab teens . . . with its romance and the screwball special effects, and with the story of an outsider's struggle both to belong and to be true to herself." Booklist

Catanese, P. W.

Dragon games. Aladdin 2010 373p il (The books of Umber) $16.99

Grades: 5 6 7 8 **Fic**

1. Fantasy fiction 2. Adventure fiction

ISBN 1-4169-7521-7; 978-1-4169-7521-2

LC 2009018743

Sequel to: Happenstance found (2009)

This is a sequel to Happenstance Found (2009). Having learned more about his mysterious past, Happenstance accompanies Lord Umber on a journey that could affect the future of Kuraharen. "Grades seven to ten." (Bull Cent Child Books)

"The fast-paced and high-energy action of this video-game-like quest will please fantasy adventure fans." Kirkus

The **End** of Time; The Books of Umber, Book 3. Aladdin 2011 (The Books of Umber) $16.99

Grades: 5 6 7 8 **Fic**

ISBN 9781416975205; 1416975209

1. Fantasy fiction 2. Adventure fiction 3. Magic -- Fiction

"As Happenstance struggles to master his unusual abilities, he realizes that time is running out--because Umber's rivals threaten to undo all the good he has achieved, while an unexpected new enemy with terrible destructive power approaches the kingdom." (Publisher's note)

Happenstance found. Aladdin 2009 342p il (The books of Umber) $16.99

Grades: 5 6 7 8 **Fic**

1. Fantasy fiction 2. Adventure fiction 3. Magic -- Fiction

ISBN 978-1-4169-7519-9; 1-4169-7519-5

LC 2008-45966

A boy awakens, blindfolded, with no memory of even his name, but soon meets Lord Umber, an adventurer and inventor, who calls him Happenstance and tells him that he has a very important destiny—and a powerful enemy.

"Catanese packs a lot into the book: rich characterizations, . . . well-choreographed action sequences and genuinely surprising twists at the end." Publ Wkly

Other titles in this series are:

Dragon games (2010)

The end of time (2011)

Catmull, Katherine

The **radiant** road; a novel. by Katherine Catmull. Dutton Books, an imprint of Penguin Random House LLC 2016 368 p. (hardcover) $17.99

Grades: 7 8 9 10 **Fic**

1. Magic -- Fiction 2. Fairies -- Fiction 3. Identity -- Fiction 4. Good and evil -- Fiction

ISBN 9780525953470

LC 2015020678

In this book, by Katherine Catmull, "Clare Macleod and her father are returning to Ireland, where they'll inhabit the house Clare was born in—a house built into a green hillside with a tree for a wall. For Clare, the house is not only full of memories of her mother, but also of a mysterious boy with raven-dark hair and dreamlike nights filled with stars and magic. Clare soon discovers that the boy is as real as the fairy-making magic." (Publisher's note)

"Catmull has created an eerily lovely story, writing with an old-fashioned style that at times sings like a lullaby. An excellent addition to either teen or juvenile collections of all sizes." Booklist

Cavanaugh, Nancy J.

This journal belongs to Ratchet; by Nancy J. Cavanaugh. Sourcebooks Jabberwocky 2013 320 p. (hardcover) $12.99

Grades: 4 5 6 7 **Fic**

1. Diaries -- Fiction 2. Home schooling -- Fiction 3. Father-daughter relationship -- Fiction 4. Self-acceptance -- Fiction 5. Fathers and daughters -- Fiction 6. Environmental protection -- Fiction

ISBN 1402281064; 9781402281068

LC 2012041339

This juvenile novel, by Nancy Cavanaugh, begins on "the first day of school for all the kids in the neighborhood. But not for me. I'm home-schooled. . . . The best I've got is this notebook. I'm supposed to use it for my writing assignments, but my dad never checks. Here's what I'm really going to use it for: Ratchet's Top Secret Plan . . . : turn my old, recycled, freakish, friendless, motherless life into something shiny and new." (Publisher's note)

"At first it seems artificial, with observations that are too on-the-nose. But as the novel's unexpectedly multifaceted plot comes together, it becomes increasingly compelling, suspenseful and moving. Triumphant enough to make readers cheer; touching enough to make them cry." Kirkus

Cerra, Kerry O'Malley

Just a drop of water; Kerry O'Malley Cerra. Skyhorse Publishing, Inc. 2014 320 p. (hardback) $14.95

Grades: 5 6 7 8 9 **Fic**

1. School stories 2. Friendship -- Fiction 3. September 11 terrorist attacks, 2001 -- Fiction 4. Muslims -- Fiction 5. Best friends -- Fiction 6. Arab Americans -- Fiction 7. Family life -- Florida -- Fiction 8. September 11 Terrorist Attacks, 2001 -- Fiction

ISBN 1629146137; 9781629146133

LC 2014015987

Kerry O'Malley Cerra's "historical novel takes place in . . . the days leading up to and after September 11, 2001. Jake Green struggles with the knowledge that one of the hijackers was living in his town prior to the attacks. His best friend and neighbor, Sam Medina, an Arab Muslim, is targeted by boys in their class. [When] Sam's father is taken into FBI custody after the discovery that he serviced the hijacker at the bank he worked . . . Jake soon finds himself at odds with his immediate family." (School Library Journal)

"The tragedy of 9/11 forces a 13-year-old Florida boy who has always lived with a comfortable, straightforward code of conduct to explore the issues of loyalty, patriotism and fair play... Cerra does a good job of re-creating the combination of fear, confusion, patriotism, prejudice and community spirit the attack engendered, and readers should identify with Jake's plight. A perceptive exploration of an event its audience already sees as history." Kirkus

Cervantes, Angela

Gaby, Lost and Found. Scholastic Inc. 2013 224 p. $16.99

Grades: 5 6 7 **Fic**

1. Bullies -- Fiction 2. Immigrants -- Fiction

ISBN 0545489458; 9780545489454

In this book, Gaby's mother is deported to Honduras, "Though she lives with her dad, Gaby basically parents herself with the help of her friend Alma's family. Her physical and emotional needs are barely met at home. Gaby's world brightens when her class begins a long-term volunteer project at the Furry Friends animal shelter. Like her mom, Gaby is an animal lover, and she develops her writing talent by crafting adoption profiles for the cats and dogs." (Kirkus Reviews)

Cervantes, Jennifer

The **storm** runner; J.C. Cervantes. Disney-Hyperion 2018 431 p. (hardback) $16.99

Grades: 5 6 7 8 **Fic**

1. Maya mythology -- Fiction 2. Father-son relationship -- Fiction 3. People with disabilities -- Fiction 4. Maya gods -- Fiction

ISBN 9781368016346; 9781368026840; 9781368023603

LC 2017048842

In this novel, by J. C. Cervantes, "Zane is an instantly relatable character: he's frustrated by his circumstances and wants to do the right thing, though he often gets into trouble for fighting bullies or wandering off alone. Cervantes wastes no time getting right into the action, and her conversational tone and suspenseful pacing will keep the pages turning. . . . Plentiful references to Mayan mythology and culture are bound to send readers searching for more background info." (Booklist)

Other titles in this series are:

The fire keeper (2019)

Tortilla sun. Chronicle Books 2010 224p $16.99

Grades: 5 6 7 8 **Fic**

1. New Mexico -- Fiction 2. Grandmothers -- Fiction 3. Father-daughter relationship -- Fiction

ISBN 0-8118-7015-4; 978-0-8118-7015-3

While spending a summer in New Mexico with her grandmother, twelve-year-old Izzy makes new friends, learns to cook, and for the first time hears stories about her father, who died before she was born.

"Cervantes evokes the beauty of the setting and develops a memorable cast of characters, brought to life through Izzy's heartfelt narration. A beautiful and engaging debut novel." Kirkus

Chabon, Michael

Summerland. Hyperion Bks. for Children 2002 500p hardcover o.p. pa $8.95

Grades: 5 6 7 8 **Fic**

1. Fantasy fiction 2. Magic -- Fiction 3. Baseball -- Fiction

ISBN 0-7868-0877-2; 0-7868-1615-5 pa

LC 2002-27497

Ethan Feld, the worst baseball player in the history of the game, finds himself recruited by a 100-year-old scout to help a band of fairies triumph over an ancient enemy

"Much of the prose is beautifully descriptive as Chabon navigates vividly imagined other worlds and offers up some timeless themes." Horn Book

Chaltas, Thalia

Because I am furniture. Viking Children's Books 2009 352p $16.99

Grades: 8 9 10 11 **Fic**

1. School stories 2. Novels in verse 3. Guilt -- Fiction 4. Child abuse -- Fiction 5. Child sexual abuse -- Fiction

ISBN 978-0-670-06298-0; 0-670-06298-7

LC 2008-23235

The youngest of three siblings, fourteen-year-old Anke feels both relieved and neglected that her father abuses her brother and sister but ignores her, but when she catches him with one of her friends, she finally becomes angry enough to take action.

"Incendiary, devastating, yet—in total—offering empowerment and hope, Chaltas's poems leave an indelible mark." Publ Wkly

Chan, Crystal

All that I can fix; by Crystal Chan. Simon Pulse 2018 314 p. (jacketed hardcover) $18.99

Grades: 7 8 9 10 11 **Fic**

1. Family life -- Fiction 2. Family problems -- Fiction 3. Racially mixed people -- Fiction
ISBN 9781534408906; 9781534408883

LC 2017039196

In this novel, by Crystal Chan, "in Makersville, Indiana, people know all about Ronney--he's from that mixed-race family with the dad who tried to kill himself, the pill-popping mom, and the genius kid sister. . . . [Then t]he local eccentric at the edge of town decided one night to open up all the cages of his exotic zoo . . . and then shoot himself dead. . . . Can Ronney figure out a way to hold it together as all his worlds fall apart?" (Publisher's note)

"A superbly entertaining read that weaves issues of mental health and gun control with adolescent angst." Kirkus

Chan, Gillian

The **disappearance**; Gillian Chan. Annick Press 2017 ix, 197 p.p (hardcover) $15.99

Grades: 8 9 10 11 12 **Fic**

1. Friendship -- Fiction 2. Group homes -- Fiction 3. Selective mutism -- Fiction 4. Scars -- Fiction 5. Mutism -- Fiction 6. Brothers -- Death -- Fiction
ISBN 9781554519835; 9781554519859; 9781554519842; 9781554519828; 1554519837

This novel, by Gillian Chan, "centers on the unlikely friendship between two boys, Jacob Mueller and Mike McCallum. . . . After mystifying experts and doctors, who finally decide that he is an elective mute, Jacob ends up in a juvenile group home, isolated and withdrawn. . . . Mike exists in his own private hell. Scarred physically and emotionally after the murder of his younger brother, his one aim is to survive the system until he is legally old enough to get out." (Publisher's note)

"Reluctant highly capable readers will be enticed, as will fans of R. L. Stine, Ripley's Believe It or Not, and ghost stories." VOYA

Chandler, Kristen

Wolves, boys, & other things that might kill me. Viking 2010 371p $17.99; pa $8.99

Grades: 7 8 9 10 11 12 **Fic**

1. Wolves -- Fiction 2. Yellowstone National Park -- Fiction
ISBN 978-0-670-01142-1; 0-670-01142-8; 978-0-14-241883-3 pa; 0-14-241883-8 pa

LC 2009-30179

Two teenagers become close as the citizens of their town fight over the packs of wolves that have been reintroduced into the nearby Yellowstone National Park.

This "is a lively drama, saturated with multifaceted characters and an environmental undercurrent. She writes persuasively about the great outdoors, smalltown dynamics and politics, and young love." Publ Wkly

Chapman, Fern Schumer

★ **Is** it night or day? Farrar, Straus, Giroux 2010 205p $17.99

Grades: 6 7 8 9 10 **Fic**

1. Chicago (Ill.) -- Fiction 2. Jewish refugees -- Fiction 3. Jews -- Germany -- Fiction 4. Holocaust, 1933-1945 -- Fiction 5. World War, 1939-1945 -- Fiction 6. Jews -- United States -- Fiction
ISBN 0-374-17744-9; 978-0-374-17744-7

LC 2008055602

In 1938, Edith Westerfeld, a young German Jew, is sent by her parents to Chicago, Illinois, where she lives with an aunt and uncle and tries to assimilate into American culture, while worrying about her parents and mourning the loss of everything she has ever known. Based on the author's mother's experience, includes an afterword about a little-known program that brought twelve hundred Jewish children to safety during World War II.

"In Edith's bewildered, sad, angry voice, the words are eloquent and powerful." Booklist

Charbonneau, Joelle

Graduation day; Joelle Charbonneau. Houghton Mifflin Harcourt 2014 304 p. (hardback) $17.99

Grades: 7 8 9 10 11 12 **Fic**

1. Dystopian fiction 2. Love -- Fiction 3. Loyalty -- Fiction 4. Survival -- Fiction 5. Adventure and adventurers -- Fiction 6. Government, Resistance to -- Fiction
ISBN 0547959214; 9780547959214

LC 2013034743

In this book, by Joelle Charbonneau, "The United Commonwealth teeters on the brink of all-out civil war. The rebel resistance plots against a government that rules with cruelty and cunning. Gifted student and Testing survivor, Cia Vale, vows to fight. . . . This is the chance to lead that Cia has trained for -- but who will follow? Plunging through layers of danger and deception, Cia must risk the lives of those she loves--and gamble on the loyalty of her lethal classmates." (Publisher's note)

"Charbonneau concludes her dystopian Testing trilogy with this action-packed finale, which sees Cia Vale secretly tasked by the President of the United Commonwealth to remove the officials behind the lethal Testing process that has claimed so many young lives...As in the previous books, Charbonneau remains focused on philosophical worries and moral tests over spectacle and bloodshed, with multiple layers and twists to keep readers forever guessing. Enough potential threads are left dangling to leave room for future stories." (Publishers Weekly)

Independent study; by Joelle Charbonneau. Houghton Mifflin, Houghton Mifflin Harcourt 2014 320 p. (The testing) (hardback) $17.99

Grades: 7 8 9 10 11 12 **Fic**

1. Love -- Fiction 2. Survival -- Fiction 3. Examinations -- Fiction 4. Government, Resistance to -- Fiction 5. Universities and colleges -- Fiction
ISBN 0547959206; 9780547959207

LC 2013004815

In this book, by Joelle Charbonneau, "sixteen-year-old Cia Vale was chosen by the United Commonwealth government as one of the best and brightest graduates of all the colonies. . . . [Now], Cia is a freshman at the University in Tosu City with her hometown sweetheart, Tomas—and though the government has tried to erase her memory of the brutal horrors of The Testing, Cia remembers. Her attempts to expose the ugly truth behind the government's murderous programs put her . . . in a world of danger." (Publisher's note)

"—In this sequel to The Testing (Houghton Harcourt, 2013), Cia is drawn deeper into the political machinations of Tosu City as she enters the University...Fans of The Testing will be thrilled with this new installment and will be anxiously waiting for the story's conclusion." (School Library Journal)

★ The **Testing**; by Joelle Charbonneau. Houghton Mifflin Harcourt 2013 344 p. (hardcover) $17.99

Grades: 7 8 9 10 11 12 **Fic**

1. Examinations -- Fiction 2. Survival skills -- Fiction 3. Schools -- Fiction 4. Missing persons -- Fiction 5. Graduation (School) -- Fiction 6. Universities and colleges -- Fiction

ISBN 0547959109; 9780547959108

LC 2012018090

In this book by Joelle Charbonneau, "Cia Vale is one of four teens chosen to represent her small colony at the annual Testing, an intensive mental and physical examination aimed at identifying the best and brightest, who will go on to the University and help rebuild their shattered world. Forewarned not to trust anyone, Cia nonetheless forms a tentative partnership with resourceful Tomas, with whom she shares an unexpected emotional connection." (Publishers Weekly)

Other titles in this series are:
Independent Study (2014)
Graduation Day (2014)

Chari, Sheela

Finding Mighty; Sheela Chari. Amulet Books 2017 320 p. (hardback) $16.95

Grades: 4 5 6 7 **Fic**

1. Graffiti -- Fiction 2. Family life -- Fiction 3. Racially mixed people -- Fiction 4. Parkour -- Fiction 5. Dobbs Ferry (N.Y.) -- Fiction 6. Mystery and detective stories 7. East Indian Americans -- Fiction 8. Family life -- New York (State) -- Fiction

ISBN 9781419722967

LC 2016042022

In this book, by Sheela Chari, "along the train lines north of New York City, twelve-year-old neighbors Myla and Peter search for the link between Myla's necklace and the disappearance of Peter's brother, Randall. Thrown into a world of parkour, graffiti, and diamond-smuggling, Myla and Peter encounter a band of thugs who are after the same thing as Randall. Can Myla and Peter find Randall before it's too late, and their shared family secrets threaten to destroy them all?" (Publisher's note)

Charles, Tami

Like Vanessa; Tami Charles, illustrated by Vanessa Brantley-Newton. Charlesbridge 2018 288 p. (reinforced for library use) $16.99

Grades: 5 6 7 8 **Fic**

1. Beauty contests -- Fiction 2. African American girls -- Fiction 3. Schools -- Fiction 4. Beauty contests -- Fiction 5. Family problems -- Fiction 6. Self-confidence -- Fiction 7. African Americans -- Fiction 8. Self-confidence -- Fiction 9. Nineteen eighties -- Fiction 10. Family life -- New Jersey -- Newark -- Fiction 11. Newark (N.J.) -- History -- 20th century -- Fiction 12. Urban schools -- New Jersey -- Newark -- Fiction 13. African American girls -- New Jersey -- Newark -- Fiction 14. Dysfunctional families -- New Jersey -- Newark -- Fiction

ISBN 9781580897778

LC 2016053961

In this novel, by Tami Charles, illustrated by Vanessa Brantley-Newton, "Vanessa Martin's real-life reality of living with family in public housing in Newark, New Jersey is a far cry from the glamorous Miss America stage. . . . But when a new teacher at school coordinates a beauty pageant and convinces Vanessa to enter, Vanessa's view of her own world begins to change." (Publisher's note)

Chase, Paula

Dough boys; Paula Chase. Greenwillow Books, an imprint of HarperCollins Publishers 2019 327 p. (hardback) $16.99

Grades: 5 6 7 8 **Fic**

1. Gangs -- Fiction 2. Friendship -- Fiction 3. African Americans -- Fiction 4. Brothers -- Fiction 5. Basketball -- Fiction 6. Best friends -- Fiction

ISBN 9780062691811

LC 2018052590

This book, by Paula Chase, presents "a memorably vivid story about the complex friendship between two African American boys whose lives are heading down very different paths. . . . Chase explores universal themes of friendship and budding romance, while also exploring complex issues that affect many young teens." (Publisher's note)

"Chase displays her signature flair for conveying black youths' language of intimacy even as she refuses the inaccurate yet popular theory that complex ethical entanglements cannot be engaged in middle-grade fiction. A thoughtful exploration of the soul-fulfilling heaviness of life in black urban communities." --Kirkus

So done; Paula Chase. Greenwillow Books, an imprint of HarperCollinsPublishers 2018 304 p. (hardback) $16.99

Grades: 5 6 7 8 **Fic**

1. Schools -- Fiction 2. Auditions -- Fiction 3. Friendship -- Fiction 4. Best friends -- Fiction 5. Middle schools -- Fiction 6. Family problems -- Fiction 7. African Americans -- Fiction 8. Racially-mixed people -- Fiction

ISBN 9780062691781

LC 2018022297

In this novel, by Paula Chase, "Jamila Phillips and Tai Johnson have been inseparable since they were toddlers, having grown up across the street from each other in Pirates Cove, a low-income housing project. As summer comes to an end, Tai can't wait for Mila to return from spending a month with her aunt in the suburbs. But both girls are grappling with secrets, and when Mila returns she's more focused on her upcoming dance auditions than hanging out with Tai." (Publisher's note)

Chee, Traci

★ The **Reader**; by Traci Chee. Penguin 2016 464 p. (Sea of ink and gold) hardcover $19.99

Grades: 8 9 10 11 12 **Fic**

1. Fantasy fiction 2. Adventure fiction 3. Murder -- Fiction 4. Kidnapping -- Fiction

ISBN 0399176772; 9780399176777

LC 2015039924

Kirkus Prize Finalist: Young Readers' Literature (2016)

"Fleeing into the wilderness after her father's brutal murder, Sefia learns how to hunt, track and steal in order to survive before embarking on a quest to rescue the beloved aunt who is her mentor, an effort that is shaped by a magnificent book that is unheard of in her otherwise illiterate society." (Publisher's note)

"This cleverly layered fantasy leaves more questions than it answers, but fortunately, it's only the first of what promises to be an enchanting series." Kirkus

Other titles in this series are:
The Speaker (2017)
The Storyteller (2018)

The **speaker**; Traci Chee. G.P. Putnam's Sons 2017 487 p. map (Sea of ink and gold) (hardback) $19.99

Grades: 8 9 10 11 12 **Fic**

1. Fantasy fiction 2. Orphans -- Fiction 3. Kidnapping -- Fiction 4. Nightmares -- Fiction 5. Books and reading -- Fiction

ISBN 9780698410633; 0399176780; 9780399176784

LC 2017016556

In this book, by Traci Chee, "having barely escaped the clutches of the Guard, Sefia and Archer are back on the run, slipping into the safety of the forest to tend to their wounds and plan their next move. Haunted by painful memories, Archer struggles to overcome the trauma of his past with the impressors, whose cruelty plagues him whenever he closes his eyes. But when Sefia and Archer happen upon a crew of impressors in the wilderness, Archer finally finds a way to combat his nightmares." (Publisher's note)

"Filled with even more magic and intrigue than its predecessor, this is a gripping follow-up that will leave readers speculating and wanting more." Kirkus

The **storyteller**; Traci Chee. G.P. Putnam's Sons 2018 544 p. (hardback) $19.99

Grades: 8 9 10 11 12 **Fic**

1. Fantasy fiction 2. Romance fiction 3. Orphans -- Fiction 4. Fantasy 5. War -- Fiction 6. Love -- Fiction 7. Books and reading -- Fiction 8. Adventure and adventurers -- Fiction

ISBN 9780399176791

LC 2018028167

In this book in the Reader series, by Traci Chee, "Sefia is determined to keep Archer out of the Guard's clutches and their plans for war between the Five Kingdoms. The Book, the ancient, infinite codex of the past, present and future, tells of a prophecy that will plunge Kelanna in that bloody war, but it requires a boy--Archer--and Sefia will stop at nothing to ensure his safety." (Publisher's note)

Chen, Justina

Return to me; by Justina Chen. Little, Brown and Co. 2013 352 p. (hardcover) $17.99

Grades: 7 8 9 10 **Fic**

1. Moving -- Fiction 2. Family life -- Fiction 3. Clairvoyance -- Fiction 4. Love -- Fiction 5. Architecture -- Fiction 6. Family problems -- Fiction 7. Moving, Household -- Fiction 8. Self-actualization (Psychology) -- Fiction

ISBN 0316102555; 9780316102551

LC 2012001549

In this book, "moving away from her Washington home seems to be a logical part of Reb's life plan; after the summer, she'll start at Columbia University, studying to be a corporate architect in the family firm, while her family moves to New Jersey for her father's new job. All that unravels upon their arrival on the East Coast, when her father announces that he's leaving the family to be with another woman, forcing Reb to question everything." (Bulletin of the Center for Children's Books)

Cheng, Jack

See you in the Cosmos; by Jack Cheng. Dial Books 2017 320 p. (ebook) $50.97; (hardback) $16.99

Grades: 5 6 7 8 **Fic**

1. Friendship -- Fiction 2. Family life -- Fiction 3. Rockets (Aeronautics) -- Fiction 4. Resilience (Personality trait) -- Fiction

ISBN 9780399186394; 9780399186370

LC 2016032255

In this novel, by Jack Cheng, "Alex Petroski loves space and rockets. . . . All he wants is to launch his golden iPod into space the way [astronomer] Carl Sagan . . . launched his Golden Record on the Voyager spacecraft in 1977. From Colorado to New Mexico, Las Vegas to L.A., Alex records a journey on his iPod. . . . But his destination keeps changing. And the . . . remarkable people he meets along the way can only partially prepare him for the secrets he'll uncover." (Publisher's note)

"Riveting, inspiring, and sometimes hilarious." Kirkus

Chibbaro, Julie

Deadly; illustrations by Jean-Marc Superville Sovak. Atheneum Books for Young Readers 2011 293 p. $16.99

Grades: 6 7 8 9 10 **Fic**

1. Sick 2. Domestics 3. Diaries -- Fiction 4. Sex role -- Fiction 5. Epidemiology -- Fiction 6. Typhoid fever -- Fiction 7. New York (N.Y.) -- Fiction 8. Interpersonal relations -- Fiction 9. New York (N.Y.) -- History -- 1898-1951 -- Fiction

ISBN 0689857381; 9780689857386; 978-0-689-85738-6; 0-689-85738-1

LC 2010002291

"Sixteen-year-old Prudence lives in a New York City tenement with her mother and attends a school where she feels like a misfit. Haunted by memories of her brother's painful dying and by unanswered questions about her father, who never returned from the Spanish-American War, she longs to fight death itself. Prudence takes a job with the health department, where she helps track down the source of a typhoid outbreak, a healthy carrier now remembered as Typhoid Mary." (Booklist)

"A deeply personal coming-of-age story set in an era of tumultuous social change, this is topnotch historical fiction that highlights the struggle between rational science and popular opinion as shaped by a sensational, reactionary press." SLJ

Childs, Tera Lynn

Sweet venom. Katherine Tegen Books 2011 345p (Medusa girls) $17.99

Grades: 7 8 9 10 **Fic**

1. Sisters -- Fiction 2. Monsters -- Fiction 3. Fate and fatalism -- Fiction 4. Classical mythology -- Fiction 5. San Francisco (Calif.) -- Fiction 6. Medusa (Greek mythology) -- Fiction

ISBN 978-0-06-200181-8; 0-06-200181-7

LC 2010050525

As monsters walk the streets of San Francisco, unseen by humans, three teenaged descendants of Medusa, the once-beautiful gorgon maligned in Greek mythology, must reunite and embrace their fates.

"Childs clearly has a sequel (or more) in mind and uses this book to ably set up an appealing conflict, introduce quite likable characters, and get readers ready for intrigue in the romance and fate-of-the-world departments." Booklist

Other titles in this series are:
Sweet shadows (2012)
Sweet legacy (2013)

Chilton, Andrew S.

The **goblin's** puzzle; the adventures of a boy with no name and two girls called Alice. by Andrew S. Chilton ; illustrations by Jensine Eckwall. Alfred A. Knopf 2016 288 p. illustrations (hardback) $16.99

Grades: 4 5 6 7 8 **Fic**

1. Humorous fiction 2. Fantasy

ISBN 9780553520705; 9780553520712

LC 2015013261

In this juvenile fantasy novel, by Andrew S. Chilton, with illustrations by Jensine Eckwall, "a nameless slave on a mission to uncover his true destiny . . . , [a] goblin . . . too tricky to be trusted . . . , a bookish peasant girl . . . and Princess Alice . . . are tangled up in a sinister plot to take over the kingdom, and together they must face kind monsters, a cruel magician, and dozens of deathly boring palace bureaucrats." (Publisher's note)

"An emphasis on questioning fate, societal rules, and traditions as well as the importance of wit and logic rather than brawn renders this lighthearted adventure fresh." Kirkus

Chima, Cinda Williams

★ The **Demon** King; a Seven Realms novel. Disney Hyperion 2009 506p map (Seven Realms) $17.99
Grades: 7 8 9 10 11 12 **Fic**

1. Fantasy fiction 2. Princesses -- Fiction 3. Witchcraft -- Fiction
ISBN 978-1-4231-1823-7; 1-4231-1823-5

LC 2008-46178

Relates the intertwining fates of former street gang leader Han Alister and headstrong Princess Raisa, as Han takes possession of an amulet that once belonged to an evil wizard and Raisa uncovers a conspiracy in the Grey Wolf Court.

"With full-blooded, endearing heroes, a well-developed supporting cast and a detail-rich setting, Chima explores the lives of two young adults, one at the top of the world and the other at the bottom, struggling to find their place and protect those they love." Publ Wkly

Other titles in this series are:
The Exiled Queen (2010)
The Gray Wolf Throne (2011)
The Crimson Crown (2012)

★ The **warrior** heir. Hyperion Books for Children 2006 426p hardcover o.p.
Grades: 7 8 9 10 11 12 **Fic**

1. Fantasy fiction 2. Magic -- Fiction
ISBN 0-7868-3916-3; 0-7868-3917-1 pa; 978-0-7868-3916-2; 978-0-7868-3917-9 pa

LC 2005-52720

After learning about his magical ancestry and his own warrior powers, sixteen-year-old Jack embarks on a training program to fight enemy wizards. "Grades seven to ten." (Bull Cent Child Books)

"Twists and turns abound in this remarkable, nearly flawless debut novel that mixes a young man's coming-of-age with fantasy and adventure. Fast paced and brilliantly plotted." Voice Youth Advocates

Other titles in this series are:
The dragon heir (2008)
The wizard heir (2007)

Choi, Sook Nyul

★ **Year** of impossible goodbyes. Houghton Mifflin 1991 171p hardcover o.p. pa $5.99
Grades: 5 6 7 8 **Fic**

1. Korea -- Fiction
ISBN 0-395-57419-6; 978-0-440-40759-1 pa

LC 91-10502

This is the story "of Sookan, a young girl living in northern Korea during the turbulent period of the Second World War. As the war rages, ten-year-old Sookan, her mother, and her younger brother courageously endure the cruelties of the Japanese military occupying Korea. Forced to work for the war effort, Sookan dreams of a time of peace and liberty for herself and her family. . . . With the end of the war in 1945, Sookan's hopes for freedom are dashed as she watches the superpowers divide her country and the Communist Russian troops take control of North Korea, coercing its citizens to adopt the Communist lifestyle. . . . Dangerous as it is, Sookan's family comes to believe that escape is their only chance for a happy future." (Publisher's note) "Grades five to nine." (Bull Cent Child Books)

"Tragedies are not masked here, but neither are they overdramatized. . . . The observations are honest, the details authentic, the characterizations vividly developed." Bull Cent Child Books

Chokshi, Roshani

★ **Aru** Shah and the end of time; Roshani Chokshi. Disney-Hyperion 2018 368 p. (hardcover) $16.99
Grades: 3 4 5 6 7 **Fic**

1. Honesty -- Fiction 2. Museums -- Fiction 3. Demonology -- Fiction 4. Antiquities -- Fiction 5. Supernatural -- Fiction 6. Mythology, Indic -- Fiction 7. Blessing and cursing -- Fiction
ISBN 9781368012355

LC 2017025506

This boo is "about twelve-year-old Aru Shah, who has a tendency to stretch the truth in order to fit in at school. While her classmates are jetting off to family vacations in exotic locales, she'll be spending her autumn break at home, in the Museum of Ancient Indian Art and Culture, waiting for her mom to return from her latest archaeological trip." (Publisher's note)

Chokshi "spins a fantastical narrative that seamlessly intertwines Hindu cosmology and folklore, feminism, and witty dialogue for an uproarious novel for young readers." Kirkus

Other titles in this series are:
Aru Shah and the song of death (2019)

Aru Shah and the song of death; by Roshani Chokshi. Disney-Hyperion 2019 400 p. (Pandava) $16.99
Grades: 3 4 5 6 7 **Fic**

1. Adventure fiction 2. Supernatural -- Fiction 3. Hindu mythology -- Fiction 4. Adventure and adventurers -- Fiction
ISBN 9781368013840

LC 2018045095

In this book in the Pandava Series, by Roshani Chokshi, "Aru is only just getting the hang of this whole Pandava thing when the Otherworld goes into full panic mode. The god of love's bow and arrow have gone missing, and the thief isn't playing Cupid. Instead, they're turning people into heartless fighting-machine zombies. . . . [S]omehow Aru gets framed as the thief. If she doesn't find the arrow by the next full moon, she'll be kicked out of the Otherworld. For good." (Publisher's note)

"The most compelling feature of the novel, however, is the complexity of its characters, who, despite their divinity or semidivinity, are at their core very human." Kirkus

Choldenko, Gennifer

★ **Al** Capone does my shirts. G.P. Putnam's Sons 2004 225p il $15.99; pa $6.99
Grades: 5 6 7 8 **Fic**

1. Autism -- Fiction 2. Siblings -- Fiction 3. Alcatraz Island (Calif.) -- Fiction
ISBN 0-399-23861-1; 0-14-240370-9 pa

LC 2002-31766

A Newbery Medal honor book, 2005

A twelve-year-old boy named Moose moves to Alcatraz Island in 1935 when guards' families were housed there, and has to contend with his extraordinary new environment in addition to life with his autistic sister.

"With its unique setting and well-developed characters, this warm, engaging coming-of-age story has plenty of appeal, and Choldenko offers some fascinating historical background on Alcatraz Island in an afterword." Booklist

Other titles in this series are:
Al Capone shines my shoes (2009)
Al Capone does my homework (2013)
Al Capone throws me a curve (2018)

Al Capone throws me a curve; Gennifer Choldenko. Wendy Lamb Books 2018 240 p. (trade) $17.99

Grades: 5 6 7 8 **Fic**

1. Autism -- Fiction 2. Prisons -- Fiction 3. Siblings -- Fiction 4. Brothers and sisters -- Fiction 5. Alcatraz Island (Calif.) -- History -- 20th century -- Fiction 6. United States Penitentiary, Alcatraz Island, California -- Fiction

ISBN 9781101938133; 9781101938140; 9781101938164

LC 2017026933

Sequel to: Al Capone does my homework

In this book in the Tales from Alcatraz series, by Gennifer Choldenko, "Moose Flanagan lives on a famous island in California: Alcatraz, home to some of the most dangerous prisoners in the United States in the 1930s. It's the summer before he starts high school, and Moose is going to play a lot of baseball and win a spot on the high school team. But he still needs to watch his . . . sister, Natalie--and then the warden asks Moose to look after his . . . daughter, Piper." (Publisher's note)

Chasing secrets; Gennifer Choldenko. Wendy Lamb Books, an imprint of Random House Children's Books 2015 288 p. (trade) $16.99

Grades: 5 6 7 8 **Fic**

1. San Francisco (Calif.) -- Fiction 2. Historical fiction 3. Father-daughter relationship -- Fiction 4. Plague -- Fiction 5. Friendship -- Fiction 6. Quarantine -- Fiction 7. Chinese Americans -- Fiction 8. Fathers and daughters -- Fiction 9. San Francisco (Calif.) -- History -- 20th century -- Fiction

ISBN 0385742533; 9780375990632; 9780385742535; 9780385742542

LC 2014040329

This novel, by Gennifer Choldenko, is set in "San Francisco, 1900. . . . A fantastic time to be alive for lots of people . . . but not thirteen-year-old Lizzie Kennedy. . . . Lizzie's secret passion is science, an unsuitable subject for finishing-school girls. Lizzie lives to go on house calls with her physician father. On those visits to his patients, she discovers a hidden dark side of the city--a side that¿s full of secrets, rats, and rumors of the plague." (Publisher's note)

"Thirteen-year-old Lizzie is a smart, scientifically-minded girl, out of place in a San Francisco finishing school in 1900. Applying the scientific method to rumors of the bubonic plague in Chinatown, Lizzie faces the power of the media and racist political schemes as she attempts to rescue her Chinese housekeeper from quarantine. Appealing, convincing characters and a detail-rich setting keep the light mystery afloat." Horn Book

Notes from a liar and her dog. Putnam 2001 216p hardcover o.p. pa $5.99

Grades: 5 6 7 8 **Fic**

1. Family life -- Fiction 2. Truthfulness and falsehood -- Fiction

ISBN 0-399-23591-4; 0-14-250068-2 pa

LC 00-55354

Eleven-year-old Ant, stuck in a family that she does not like, copes by pretending that her "real" parents are coming to rescue her, by loving her dog Pistachio, by volunteering at the zoo, and by bending the truth and telling lies

"Choldenko's writing is snappy and tender, depicting both Ant's bravado and her isolation with sympathy." Bull Cent Child Books

Chotjewitz, David

Daniel half human; and the good Nazi. translated by Doris Orgel. Atheneum Books for Young Readers 2004 298p hardcover o.p. pa $6.99

Grades: 7 8 9 10 **Fic**

1. Jews -- Fiction 2. Germany -- Fiction 3. National socialism -- Fiction

ISBN 0-689-85747-0; 0-689-85748-9 pa

LC 2003-25554

In 1933, best friends Daniel and Armin admire Hitler, but as anti-Semitism buoys Hitler to power, Daniel learns he is half Jewish, threatening the friendship even as life in their beloved Hamburg, Germany, is becoming nightmarish. Also details Daniel and Armin's reunion in 1945 in interspersed chapters.

"Orgel's translation reads smoothly and movingly. An outstanding addition to the large body of World War II/Holocaust fiction." SLJ

Christopher, John

When the Tripods came. Dutton 1988 151p hardcover o.p. pa $5.99

Grades: 5 6 7 8 **Fic**

1. Science fiction

ISBN 0-525-44397-5; 978-0-689-85762-1 pa; 0-689-85762-4 pa

LC 88-478

"A prequel to the author's well-known White Mountains trilogy . . . this relates how the Tripods came to Earth and imposed a new subservient order on its population. The protagonist is Laurie Corday, who, with his friend Andy, witnesses the first arrival of these towering metallic creatures. . . . The story's scenario exudes a chill; Laurie lives in the present, not some futuristic world, and the Tripods' insidious rise to power seems quite reasonable in the context of the story." Booklist

★ The **White** Mountains; 35th anniversary ed; Simon & Schuster Bks. for Young Readers 2003 164p hardcover o.p. pa $5.99

Grades: 5 6 7 8 **Fic**

1. Science fiction

ISBN 0-689-85504-4; 0-689-85672-5 pa

LC 2002-70808

A reissue of the title first published 1967 by Macmillan

Young Will Parker and his companions make a perilous journey toward an outpost of freedom where they hope to escape from the ruling Tripods, who capture mature human beings and make them docile, obedient servants

This "remarkable story . . . belongs to the school of science-fiction which puts philosophy before technology and is not afraid of telling an exciting story." Times Lit Suppl

Other titles about the Tripods are:

The city of gold and lead (2003 c1967)

The pool of fire (2003 c1968)

When the Tripods came (2003 c1988)

Christopher, Lucy

Flyaway; Lucy Christopher. Chicken House 2011 314p $16.99

Grades: 5 6 7 8 **Fic**

1. Sick -- Fiction 2. Swans -- Fiction 3. Hospitals -- Fiction 4. Wildlife conservation -- Fiction 5. Father-daughter relationship -- Fiction

ISBN 0545317711; 9780545317719

LC 2010051425

In this young adult novel, "when newly constructed power lines ruin the annual return of the whooping swans Isla and her father rise early to witness, the death of several of the wild creatures and her father's sudden and severe illness both confound Isla and emphasize her loneliness. At the hospital where her father awaits a heart operation, Harry, waiting there for a bone-marrow transplant, befriends Isla and points out the young swan he can see from his bed. . . . News broadcasts . . . about deadly outbreaks of bird flu contrast with the small unfolding of Isla's widowed grandfather's stiff grief as he helps her construct an art project--a harness and wings from an ancient stuffed swan--and innocent romance flutters between Isla and Harry even as the young swan regains flight and her father begins to recover." (Kirkus)

Christopher offers "readers a quiet but compelling story with several well-realized, idiosyncratic characters. She skillfully develops the novel's varied elements and weaves them into a unified narrative. . . . This sensitive novel will resonate with many readers." Booklist

Cisneros, Sandra, 1954-

★ The **house** on Mango Street. Knopf 1994 134p $24

Grades: 7 8 9 10 **Fic**

1. Chicago (Ill.) -- Fiction 2. Mexican Americans -- Fiction

ISBN 0-679-43335-X

LC 93-43564

Originally published by Arte Público Press in 1984

In this book by Sandra Cisneros, "Esperanza Cordero, a girl coming of age in the Hispanic quarter of Chicago, uses poems and stories to express thoughts and emotions about her . . . environment." (Publishers Weekly) It is "told in a series of vignettes--sometimes heartbreaking, sometimes deeply joyous". (Publisher's note)

This is "a composite of evocative snapshots that manages to passionately recreate the milieu of the poor quarters of Chicago." Commonweal

Clare, Cassandra, 1973-

City of bones. Margaret K. McElderry Books 2007 485p (The mortal instruments) $17.99; pa $9.99

Grades: 8 9 10 11 12 **Fic**

1. Horror fiction 2. Devil -- Fiction 3. Supernatural -- Fiction 4. New York (N.Y.) -- Fiction

ISBN 1-4169-1428-5; 1-4169-5507-0 pa; 978-1-4169-1428-0; 978-1-4169-5507-8 pa

LC 2006-08108

Suddenly able to see demons and the Darkhunters who are dedicated to returning them to their own dimension, fifteen-year-old Clary Fray is drawn into this bizzare world when her mother disappears and Clary herself is almost killed by a monster.

"This version of New York, full of Buffyesque teens who are trying to save the world, is entertaining and will have fantasy readers anxiously awaiting the next book in the series." SLJ

Other titles in the series include:

City of Ashes (2008)

City of Glass (2009)

City of Fallen Angels (2011)

City of Lost Souls (2012)

City of Heavenly Fire (2014)

Clockwork angel; by Cassandra Clare. Margaret K. McElderry Books 2010 479 p. (The infernal devices) hbk $24.99

Grades: 9 10 11 12 **Fic**

1. Fantasy fiction 2. Steampunk fiction 3. Fantasy graphic novels 4. Orphans -- Fiction 5. Demonology -- Fiction 6. Supernatural -- Fiction 7. London (England) -- Fiction 8. Secret societies -- Fiction

ISBN 1416975861 ; 9781416975861

LC 2012359456

"When sixteen-year-old Tessa Gray crosses the ocean to find her brother, her destination is England, the time is the reign of Queen Victoria, and something terrifying is waiting for her in London's Downworld, where vampires, warlocks and other supernatural folk stalk the gaslit streets. Only the Shadowhunters, warriors dedicated to ridding the world of demons, keep order amidst the chaos. . . . Tessa soon learns that she herself is a Downworlder with a rare ability: the power to transform, at will, into another person." (Publisher's note)

"Mysteries, misdirection, and riddles abound, and while there are some gruesome moments, they never feel gratuitous. Fans of the Mortal Instruments series and newcomers alike won't be disappointed." Publ Wkly

Other titles in this series are:

Clockwork prince (2011)

Clockwork princess (2013)

Clark, Henry

What we found in the sofa (and how it saved the world) by Henry Clark ; illustrated by Jeremy Holmes. Little, Brown and Co. 2013 368 p. $17

Grades: 3 4 5 6 7 **Fic**

1. Fantasy fiction 2. Science fiction 3. Humorous stories 4. Adventure and adventurers -- Fiction 5. Eccentrics and eccentricities -- Fiction

ISBN 0316206660; 9780316206662

LC 2012032467

"When River, Freak, and Fiona discover a mysterious sofa sitting at their bus stop, their search for loose change produces a rare zucchini-colored crayon. Little do they know this peculiar treasure is about to launch them into the middle of a plot to conquer the world!" (Publisher's note)

Cleary, Beverly

Dear Mr. Henshaw; illustrated by Paul O. Zelinsky. Morrow 1983 133p il $15.99; lib bdg $16.89; pa $5.99

Grades: 4 5 6 7 **Fic**

1. School stories 2. Divorce -- Fiction 3. Parent-child relationship -- Fiction

ISBN 0-688-02405-X; 0-688-02406-8 lib bdg; 0-380-70958-9 pa

LC 83-5372

Awarded the Newbery Medal, 1984

"Leigh Botts lives with his recently divorced mother and writes to his favorite author, Boyd Henshaw. When Henshaw answers his letters and encourages him to keep a journal, he does so, and in the process solves the mystery of who is stealing food from his lunchbox, tries to write a novel, and in the end, writes a prize-winning short story about an experience with his father. . . . Grades four to seven." (SLJ)

"Leigh Botts started writing letters to his favorite author, Boyd Henshaw, in the second grade. Now, Leigh is in the sixth grade, in a new school, and his parents are recently divorced. This year he writes many letters to Mr. Henshaw, and also keeps a journal. Through these the reader learns how Leigh adjusts to new situations, and of his triumphs." Child Book Rev Serv

Followed by: Strider (1991)

Strider; illustrated by Paul O. Zelinsky. Morrow Junior Bks. 1991 179p il hardcover o.p. lib bdg $16.89; pa $5.99

Grades: 4 5 6 7 **Fic**

1. Dogs -- Fiction 2. Divorce -- Fiction

ISBN 0-688-09900-9; 0-688-09901-7 lib bdg; 0-380-71236-9 pa

LC 90-6608

Sequel to Dear Mr. Henshaw

In a series of diary entries, Leigh tells how he comes to terms with his parents' divorce, acquires joint custody of an abandoned dog, and joins the track team at school

"The development of the narrative is vintage Beverly Cleary, an inimitable blend of comic and poignant moments." Horn Book

Cleaver, Vera

Where the lillies bloom; [by] Vera & Bill Cleaver; illustrated by Jim Spanfeller. Lippincott 1969 174p il hardcover o.p. pa $5.99

Grades: 5 6 7 8 **Fic**

1. Orphans -- Fiction 2. Siblings -- Fiction 3. Appalachian region -- Fiction

ISBN 0-397-31111-7; 0-06-447005-9 pa

"The setting is fascinating, the characterization good, and the style of the first-person story distinctive." Bull Cent Child Books

Followed by Trial Valley (1977)

Clement-Moore, Rosemary

Texas gothic. Delacorte Press 2011 406p $17.99; lib bdg $20.99

Grades: 6 7 8 9 10 **Fic**

1. Ghost stories 2. Texas -- Fiction 3. Sisters -- Fiction 4. Farm life -- Fiction 5. Witchcraft -- Fiction

ISBN 978-0-385-73693-0; 0-385-73693-2; 978-0-385-90636-4 lib bdg; 0-385-90636-6 lib bdg

LC 2010-47923

"The one person in the magic-practicing Goodnight family who strives for normality, Amy (short for Amaryllis) is happy for a summer of plain old hard work running Aunt Hyacinth's Texas ranch, leaving her sister Phin to her supernatural science experiments. She should have known better. Ghosts are nothing new for the Goodnight girls -- Hyacinth's late husband Burt has been a friendly presence for years -- but the deathly cold apparition in Amy's bedroom pulls them into a dangerous mystery." (Horn Book)

"This engaging mystery has plenty of both paranormal and romance, spiced with loving families and satisfyingly packed with self-sufficient, competent girls." Kirkus

Clements, Andrew

Extra credit; illustrations by Mark Elliott. Atheneum Books for Young Readers 2009 183p il $16.99

Grades: 4 5 6 **Fic**

1. Letters -- Fiction 2. Illinois -- Fiction 3. Afghanistan -- Fiction 4. Family life -- Fiction

ISBN 978-1-4169-4929-9; 1-4169-4929-1

LC 2008-42877

"Unless [Abby] wants to repeat the sixth grade, she'll have to meet some specific conditions, including taking on an extra-credit project: find a pen pal in a foreign country. Simple enough (even for a girl who hates homework). Abby's first letter arrives at a small school in Afghanistan, and Sadeed Bayat is chosen to be her pen pal.... Well, kind of. He is the best writer, but he is also a boy, and in his village it is not appropriate for a boy to correspond with a girl. So his younger sister dictates and signs the letter. Until Sadeed decides what his sister is telling Abby isn't what he'd like Abby to know." (Publisher's note) "Grades four to seven." (Bull Cent Child Books)

Clements "successfully bridges two cultures in this timely and insightful dual-perspective story." Publ Wkly

Things not seen. Philomel Bks. 2002 251p $15.99; pa $5.99

Grades: 7 8 9 10 **Fic**

1. Science fiction 2. Blind -- Fiction

ISBN 0-399-23626-0; 0-14-240076-9 pa

LC 00-69900

When fifteen-year-old Bobby wakes up and finds himself invisible, he and his parents and his new blind friend Alicia try to find out what caused his condition and how to reverse it.

"The author spins a convincing and affecting story." Publ Wkly

Other titles in this series are:

Things hoped for (2006)

Things that are (2008)

Troublemaker; Andrew Clements ; illustrated by Mark Elliott. Atheneum Books for Young Readers 2011 p. cm. $16.99

Grades: 4 5 6 7 **Fic**

1. Schools -- Fiction 2. Behavior -- Fiction 3. Brothers -- Fiction

ISBN 978-1-4169-4930-5; 1-4169-4930-5; 1416949305; 9781416949305

LC 2010045018

When his older brother gets in serious trouble, sixth-grader Clay decides to change his own mischief-making ways, but he cannot seem to shake his reputation as a troublemaker.

"Clements here enters into provocative territory and pulls it off like the pro he is. Kids will easily relate to Clay, and the secondary characters come alive as well." Kirkus

Cline-Ransome, Lesa

★ **Finding** Langston; by Lesa Cline-Ransome. Holiday House 2018 112 p. (hardcover) $16.99

Grades: 4 5 6 7 **Fic**

1. Poetry -- Fiction 2. Bullying -- Fiction 3. African Americans -- Fiction 4. Books and reading -- Fiction 5. Moving, Household -- Fiction 6. Single-parent families -- Fiction 7. Chicago (Ill.) -- History -- 20th century -- Fiction

ISBN 9780823439607

LC 2017030385

Coretta Scott King (Author) Honor Book (2019)

In this book, by Lesa Cline-Ransome, "when . . . Langston's mother dies in 1946, he and his father leave rural Alabama for Chicago's brown belt as a part of what came to be known as the Great Migration. It's lonely in the small apartment . . . and at school Langston is bullied. But his new . . . [home's] local public library welcomes everyone. There, . . . Langston discovers another Langston, a poet whom he learns inspired his mother enough to name her only son after him." (Publisher's note)

"Cline-Ransome, lauded for her picture books, including Booklist's 2017 Top of the List title Before She Was Harriet, proves herself an adept novelist, one with keen insight into the human condition. Every character, child and adult, is layered, a feat made more remarkable by the fact that the writing is spare." (Booklist)

Clinton, Cathryn

A **stone** in my hand. Candlewick Press 2002 191p hardcover o.p. pa $6.99

Grades: 8 9 10 11 **Fic**

1. Family life -- Fiction 2. Palestinian Arabs -- Fiction

ISBN 0-7636-1388-6; 0-7636-4772-1 pa

LC 2001-58423

Eleven-year-old Malaak and her family are touched by the violence in Gaza between Jews and Palestinians when first her father disappears and then her older brother is drawn to the Islamic Jihad

"With a sharp eye for nuances of culture and the political situation in the Middle East, Clinton has created a rich, colorful cast of characters and created an emotionally charged novel." SLJ

Cluess, Jessica

A **poison** dark and drowning; Jessica Cluess. Random House 2017 417 p. (Kingdom on fire) (hardcover) $17.99
Grades: 7 8 9 10 **Fic**

1. Magic -- Fiction 2. Demonology -- Fiction 3. Great Britain -- History -- Victoria, 1837-1901 -- Fiction
ISBN 9780553535945; 9780553535952; 9780553535969
LC 2016043364

Sequel to: A Shadow Bright and Burning (2016)

In this book in the Kingdom on Fire series, author "Jessica Cluess delivers her signature mix of magic, passion, and teen warriors fighting for survival. Henrietta doesn't need a prophecy to know that she's in danger. She came to London to be named the . . . first female sorcerer in centuries, . . . who would defeat the Ancients. Instead, she discovered . . . [that she] is not the chosen one. Still, she must play the role in order to keep herself and Rook . . . safe." (Publisher's note)

"As in the previous volume, Cluess keeps the action moving in the right direction. Fans will anxiously wait for the conclusion to this romantic and magical fantasy series." SLJ

★ A **shadow** bright and burning; Jessica Cluess. Random House 2016 416 p. (Kingdom on fire) (hardcover) $17.99; (ebook) $53.97
Grades: 7 8 9 10 **Fic**

1. Fantasy fiction 2. Magic -- Fiction 3. Fantasy
ISBN 9780553535907; 9780553535914; 9780553535921
LC 2015014593

In this novel, by Jessica Cluess, "Henrietta Howel can burst into flames. Forced to reveal her power to save a friend, she's shocked when instead of being executed, she's invited to train as one of Her Majesty's royal sorcerers. Thrust into the glamour of Victorian London, Henrietta is declared the chosen one, the girl who will defeat the Ancients, bloodthirsty demons terrorizing humanity. " (Publisher's note)

"Cluess' clever prose employs Dickensian names and rolls along at a speedy and compelling clip." Booklist

Other titles in this series are:
A poison dark and drowning (2017)
A sorrow fierce and falling (2018)

Coakley, Lena

Witchlanders. Atheneum Books for Young Readers 2011 400p $16.99
Grades: 7 8 9 10 11 12 **Fic**

1. War stories 2. Fantasy fiction 3. Witches -- Fiction
ISBN 978-1-4424-2004-5; 1-4424-2004-9
LC 2010051922

After the prediction of Ryder's mother, once a great prophet and powerful witch, comes true and their village is destroyed by a deadly assassin, Ryder embarks on a quest that takes him into the mountains in search of the destroyer.

"Plot twists unfold at a riveting pace, the boys' characters are compellingly sketched, and Coakley explores her subject matter masterfully without falling prey to safe plot choices." Publ Wkly

Coats, J. Anderson

The **wicked** and the just; by Jillian Anderson Coats. Harcourt 2012 344 p. $16.99
Grades: 7 8 9 10 11 12 **Fic**

1. Daughters -- Fiction 2. Prejudices -- Fiction 3. Middle Ages -- Fiction 4. Wales -- History -- Fiction 5. Household employees -- Fiction 6. Wales -- History -- 1284-1536 -- Fiction
ISBN 0547688377; 9780547688374
LC 2011027315

In this young adult historical novel, "two girls of very different degree are brought together unwillingly by the English conquest of Wales. Cecily is in a pet at having to leave the home of her youth . . . and relocate to the Welsh frontier. . . . Cecily hates Caernarvon. She hates its weather, its primitive appointments and its natives, especially Gwinny, the servant girl who doesn't obey, and the young man who stares at her." (Kirkus Review)

Cody, Matthew

Powerless; Matthew Cody. Alfred A. Knopf 2009 279p (Supers of Noble's Green) $15.99; lib bdg $18.99
Grades: 5 6 7 8 **Fic**

1. School stories 2. Moving -- Fiction 3. Bullies -- Fiction 4. Family life -- Fiction 5. Superheroes -- Fiction 6. Pennsylvania -- Fiction 7. Supernatural -- Fiction
ISBN 978-0-375-85595-5; 0-375-85595-5; 978-0-375-95595-2 lib bdg; 0-375-95595-X lib bdg
LC 2008-40885

Soon after moving to Noble's Green, Pennsylvania, twelve-year-old Daniel learns that his new friends have super powers that they will lose when they turn thirteen, unless he can use his brain power to protect them.

"This first novel has an intriguing premise, appealing characters, and a straightforward narrative arc with plenty of action as well as some serious moments." Booklist

Other titles in this series are:
Super (2012)
Villainous (2014)

Coggin, Linda

The **dog,** Ray; Linda Coggin. Candlewick Press 2016 208 p. $15.99
Grades: 4 5 6 7 **Fic**

1. Dogs -- Fiction 2. Death -- Fiction 3. Reincarnation -- Fiction
ISBN 9780763679385
LC 2016947247

In this book, by Linda Coggin, "Daisy, age twelve, has died in a car accident. She finds herself in the afterworld, which resembles nothing more than a job center. Her soul is being returned to Earth, but not as a human being—she's returning as a dog. A dog who retains Daisy's thoughts and pluck and is determined to get back to her parents and to get back home." (Publisher's note)

"A tender and heartfelt tale that is sure to delight dog-loving readers or anyone who likes their happy endings to be hard-earned." SLJ

Cohen, Marina

The **Inn** Between; by Marina Cohen ; illustrations by Sarah Watts. Roaring Brook Press 2016 208 p. (hardcover) $16.99
Grades: 5 6 7 8 **Fic**

1. Ghost stories 2. Horror fiction 3. Friendship -- Fiction 4. Hotels and motels -- Fiction 5. Horror tales 6. Horror stories 7. Ghosts -- Fiction 8. Best friends -- Fiction 9. Haunted places -- Fiction
ISBN 9781626722026
LC 2015004042

In this book, by Marina Cohen, "Quinn's best friend Kara has to move away [and] she goes on one last trip with Kara and her family. They stop over at the first hotel they see, a Victorian inn that instantly gives Quinn the creeps, and she begins to notice strange things happening around them. When Kara's parents and then brother disappear without a trace, the girls are stranded." (Publisher's note)

"Readers looking for a mystery with heart, humor, and hairy moments will be captivated" Kirkus

Colfer, Eoin

★ **Airman**; [by] Eoin Colfer. Hyperion Books for Children 2008 412p $17.99; pa $7.99

Grades: 5 6 7 8 9 **Fic**

1. Adventure fiction 2. Ireland -- Fiction 3. Airplanes -- Fiction 4. Inventors -- Fiction 5. Prisoners -- Fiction

ISBN 978-1-4231-0750-7; 1-4231-0750-0; 978-1-4231-0751-4 pa; 1-4231-0751-9 pa

LC 2007-38415

In the late nineteenth century, when Conor Broekhart discovers a conspiracy to overthrow the king, he is branded a traitor, imprisoned, and forced to mine for diamonds under brutal conditions while he plans a daring escape from Little Saltee prison by way of a flying machine that he must design, build, and, hardest of all, trust to carry him to safety.

This is "polished, sophisticated storytelling. . . . A tour de force." Publ Wkly

★ **Artemis** Fowl. Hyperion Bks. for Children 2001 277p $16.95; pa $7.99

Grades: 5 6 7 8 **Fic**

1. Fantasy fiction 2. Fairies -- Fiction

ISBN 0-7868-0801-2; 1-4231-2452-9 pa

LC 2001-16632

When a twelve-year-old evil genius tries to restore his family fortune by capturing a fairy and demanding a ransom in gold, the fairies fight back with magic, technology, and a particularly nasty troll

"Colfer's antihero, techno fantasy is cleverly written and filled to the brim with action, suspense, and humor." SLJ

Other Artemis Fowl books are:
The Arctic incident (2002)
The eternity code (2003)
The Opal deception (2005)
The lost colony (2006)
The time paradox (2008)
The Atlantis complex (2010)
The last guardian (2012)

Iron man; the gauntlet. Eoin Colfer. Marvel Press 2016 288 p. (hardcover) $16.99; (ebook) $16.99

Grades: 4 5 6 7 **Fic**

1. Superheroes -- Fiction

ISBN 9781484741603; 9781484744321

LC 2016943368

In this book, by Eoin Colfer, illustrated by Owen Richardson, "Tony Stark is known throughout the world as many things: billionaire, inventor, Avenger. But mainly for being the Invincible Iron Man. Just when Tony is about to add his pizzazz to an international eco-summit in Ireland, someone close to him forces him to question his role in making the world a more dangerous place with his high-tech weaponry. But Stark doesn't have much time to reflect before an old enemy presents him with an even greater challenge." (Publisher's note)

"Best of all, the author successfully captures the vulnerability and infuriatingly seductive arrogance of Stark, who polices the world to atone for his father's sins. Ideal for readers who are breathlessly awaiting the next film in the Marvel superhero franchise." Kirkus

The **reluctant** assassin; Eoin Colfer. Hyperion Book CH 2013 352 p. (W.A.R.P.) (hardcover) $17.99

Grades: 5 6 7 8 **Fic**

1. Time travel -- Fiction 2. Science fiction 3. Assassins -- Fiction 4. London (England) -- History -- 19th century -- Fiction 5. Great Britain -- History -- Victoria, 1837-1901 -- Fiction

ISBN 1423161629; 9781423161622

LC 2012048160

This is the first book in the time-travel W.A.R.P. series from Eoin Colfer. "After a bungled mission, [FBI agent] Chevie has been sent to London where she is 'babysitting a metal capsule,' which she learns is one end of a wormhole to the year 1898, when [young assassin] Riley (and a corpse) materialize, direct from the Victorian era." (Publishers Weekly)

Other titles in this series are:
The hangman's revolution (2014)
The forever man (2015)

Collier, James Lincoln

★ **My** brother Sam is dead; by James Lincoln Collier and Christopher Collier. Four Winds Press 1985 216p $17.95

Grades: 6 7 8 9 **Fic**

1. United States -- History -- 1775-1783, Revolution -- Fiction

ISBN 0-02-722980-7

LC 84-28787

A reissue of the title first published 1974

A Newbery Medal honor book, 1975

"In 1775 the Meeker family lived in Redding, Connecticut, a Tory community. Sam, the eldest son, allied himself with the Patriots. The youngest son, Tim, watched a rift in the family grow because of his brother's decision. Before the war was over the Meeker family had suffered at the hands of both the British and the Patriots." Shapiro. Fic for Youth. 3d edition

Collins, Suzanne, 1962-

★ **Catching** fire. Scholastic Press 2009 391p $17.99

Grades: 7 8 9 10 **Fic**

1. Science fiction

ISBN 978-0-439-02349-8; 0-439-02349-1

LC 2008-50493

Sequel to: Hunger Games (2008)

This dystopian young adult novel, volume 2 of the Hunger Games trilogy, takes place after a televised, state-sponsored duel known as the Hunger Games. "Katniss Everdeen has won . . . with fellow district tribute Peeta Mellark. But it was a victory won by defiance of the Capitol and their harsh rules. Katniss and Peeta should be happy. After all, they have just won for themselves and their families a life of safety and plenty. But there are rumors of rebellion among the subjects, and Katniss and Peeta, to their horror, are the faces of that rebellion." (Publisher's note)

"Beyond the expert world building, the acute social commentary and the large cast of fully realized characters, there's action, intrigue, romance and some amount of hope in a story readers will find completely engrossing." Kirkus

Followed by: Mockingjay (2010)

Gregor the Overlander. Scholastic Press 2003 311p (Underland chronicles) $16.95; pa $5.99

Grades: 4 5 6 7 **Fic**

1. Fantasy fiction

ISBN 0-439-43536-6; 0-439-67813-7 pa

LC 2002-155865

When eleven-year-old Gregor and his two-year-old sister are pulled into a strange underground world, they trigger an epic battle involving men, rats, cockroaches, and spiders while on a quest foretold by ancient prophecy. "Grades four to six." (Bull Cent Child Books)

"Collins creates a fascinating, vivid, highly original world and a superb story to go along with it." Booklist

Other titles in this series are:
Gregor and the prophecy of Bane (2004)
Gregor and the curse of the warmbloods (2005)
Gregor and the marks of secret (2006)
Gregor and the code of claw (2007)

★ The **Hunger** Games. Scholastic Press 2008 374p $17.99; pa $8.99
Grades: 7 8 9 10 **Fic**

1. Science fiction

ISBN 978-0-439-02348-1; 0-439-02348-3; 978-0-439-02352-8 pa; 0-439-02352-1 pa

LC 2007-39987

In this dystopian young adult novel, "in the ruins of a place once known as North America lies the nation of Panem, a shining Capitol surrounded by twelve outlaying districts. The Capitol . . . keeps the districts in line by forcing them all to send one girl and one boy between the ages of twelve and eighteen to participate in the annual Hunger Games, a fight to the death on live TV. Sixteen-year-old Katniss Everdeen . . . regards it as a death sentence when she is forced to represent her district in the Games." (Publisher's note)

"Collins's characters are completely realistic and sympathetic. . . . The plot is tense, dramatic, and engrossing." SLJ

Mockingjay. Scholastic Press 2010 390p (Hunger Games) $17.99
Grades: 7 8 9 10 **Fic**

1. Science fiction

ISBN 978-0-439-02351-1; 0-439-02351-3

LC 2008-50493

Sequel to: Catching fire (2009)

This dystopian novel, volume 3 of the Hunger Games trilogy, takes place after heroine Katniss Everdeen has "survived the Hunger Games twice. But now that she's made it out of the bloody arena alive, she's still not safe. . . . The Capitol wants revenge. Who do they think should pay for the unrest? Katniss. And what's worse, President Snow has made it clear that no one else is safe either. Not Katniss's family, not her friends, not the people of District 12." (Publisher's note)

"This concluding volume in Collins's Hunger Games trilogy accomplishes a rare feat, the last installment being the best yet, a beautifully orchestrated and intelligent novel that succeeds on every level." Publ Wkly

Collins, Tim

Notes from a totally lame vampire; because the undead have feelings too. written by Tim Collins; illustrated by Andrew Pinder. Aladdin 2010 328p il $12.99
Grades: 6 7 8 9 **Fic**

1. School stories 2. Love -- Fiction 3. Diaries -- Fiction 4. Vampires -- Fiction 5. Great Britain -- Fiction

ISBN 978-1-4424-1183-8; 1-4424-1183-X

LC 2010-10634

Published in the United Kingdom with title: Diary of a wimpy vampire

Nigel Mullet, a 100-year-old vampire doomed to spend eternity in the body of a socially awkward fifteen-year-old boy, records his attempts to impress the love of his life, Chloe, while battling an embarrassingly overwhelming desire to sink his fangs into her.

"This book has a witty, laugh-out-loud story line and cartoon illustrations that are liberally sprinkled throughout. Readers will sympathize with Nigel and his teen angst, and the great ending makes this a satisfying and entertaining read." SLJ

Other titles in this series are:
Prince of dorkness (2011)
Notes from a hairy-not-scary werewolf (2013)
Fangs a lot (2014)

Columbus, Chris, 1958-

House of secrets; Chris Columbus ; Ned Vizzini. 1st ed. Balzer + Bray 2013 496 p. (hardcover) $17.99
Grades: 5 6 7 8 **Fic**

1. Haunted houses -- Fiction 2. Adventure fiction 3. Fantasy 4. Dwellings -- Fiction 5. Supernatural -- Fiction 6. Books and reading -- Fiction 7. Brothers and sisters -- Fiction 8. Adventure and adventurers -- Fiction

ISBN 0062192469; 9780062192462

LC 2012051815

In this juvenile fantasy story, by Chris Columbus and Ned Vizzini, three siblings "relocate to an old Victorian house that used to be the home of occult novelist Denver Kristoff. . . . By the time the Walkers realize that one of their neighbors has sinister plans for them, they're banished to a primeval forest way off the grid. . . . Bloodthirsty medieval warriors patrol the woods around them, supernatural pirates roam the neighboring seas, and a power-hungry queen rules the land." (Publisher's note)

Other titles in this series are:
Battle of the beasts (2014)
Clash of the worlds (2016)

Combres, Elisabeth

Broken memory; a novel of Rwanda. translated by Shelley Tanaka. Groundwood Books/House of Anansi Press 2009 139p $17.95
Grades: 6 7 8 9 10 **Fic**

1. Rwanda -- Fiction 2. Orphans -- Fiction 3. Genocide -- Fiction 4. Hutu (African people) -- Fiction 5. Tutsi (African people) -- Fiction

ISBN 978-0-88899-892-7; 0-88899-892-9

Original French edition, 2007

"This is a quiet, reflective story; neither laden with detail nor full of historical descriptions, it is simply one girl's horrific tale of personal tragedy. . . . Combres' story offers readers intimate access to this chapter of history as well as considerable potential for discussion." Bull Cent Child Books

Compestine, Ying Chang

Revolution is not a dinner party; a novel. Henry Holt and Company 2007 256p map $16.95; pa $7.99
Grades: 5 6 7 8 **Fic**

1. Communism -- Fiction 2. Persecution -- Fiction 3. China -- History -- 1949-1976 -- Fiction

ISBN 978-0-8050-8207-4; 0-8050-8207-7; 978-0-312-58149-7 pa; 0-312-58149-1 pa

LC 2006035465

Starting in 1972 when she is nine years old, Ling, the daughter of two doctors, struggles to make sense of the communists' Cultural Revolution, which empties stores of food, homes of appliances deemed "bourgeois," and people of laughter.

"Readers should remain rapt by Compestine's storytelling throughout this gripping account of life during China's Cultural Revolution." Publ Wkly

Condie, Ally

The **last** voyage of Poe Blythe; Ally Condie. Dutton Books for Young Readers 2019 336 p. (hardback) $18.99

Grades: 7 8 9 10 11 12 **Fic**

1. Revenge -- Fiction 2. Boats and boating -- Fiction 3. Gold mines and mining -- Fiction 4. Self-confidence -- Fiction

ISBN 9780525426455

LC 2018042052

In this novel, by Ally Condie, "Poe has vowed to annihilate the river raiders who robbed her of everything two years ago. But as she navigates the treacherous waters of the Serpentine and realizes there might be a traitor among her crew, she must also reckon with who she has become, who she wants to be, and the ways love can change and shape you. Even--and especially--when you think all is lost." (Publisher's note)

"The plot moves across a well-thought-out dystopian backdrop, offering enough surprises to both intrigue and excite. Fans of Condie's Matched should find this a welcome and satisfying return to the author's YA roots." (Publishers Weekly)

★ **Matched**; Ally Condie. Dutton Books 2010 369p $17.99

Grades: 7 8 9 10 **Fic**

1. Fantasy fiction

ISBN 978-0-525-42364-5; 0-525-42364-8

All her life, Cassia has never had a choice. The Society dictates everything: when and how to play, where to work, where to live, what to eat and wear, when to die, and most importantly to Cassia as she turns 17, who to marry. When she is Matched with her best friend Xander, things couldn't be more perfect. But why did her neighbor Ky's face show up on her match disk as well?

"Condie's enthralling and twisty dystopian plot is well served by her intriguing characters and fine writing. While the ending is unresolved . . . , Cassia's metamorphosis is gripping and satisfying." Publ Wkly

Other titles in this series are:

Crossed (2011)

Reached (2012)

Connelly, Neil

Into the hurricane; Neil Connelly. Arthur A. Levine Books, an imprint of Scholastic inc. 2017 228 p. (hardcover : alk. paper) $17.99

Grades: 7 8 9 10 **Fic**

1. Suicide -- Fiction 2. Hurricanes -- Fiction 3. Interpersonal relations -- Fiction 4. Survival -- Fiction 5. Friendship -- Fiction 6. Louisiana -- Fiction

ISBN 9780545853873; 9780545853811

LC 2017009604

In this book, by Neil Connelly, "Eli and Max both have good reasons to go to the lighthouse on Shackles Island. For Max, it's . . . the right place to scatter her dad's ashes. For Eli, it . . . [has] the clearest view of the rocks where his sister died--so it's the right place to end his own life as well. But neither of them expected the other, nor the storm." (Publisher's note)

Connor, Leslie

All Rise for the Honorable Perry T. Cook; Leslie Connor. Harpercollins Childrens Books 2016 400 p. (hardcover) $16.99

Grades: 4 5 6 7 8 **Fic**

1. Children of prisoners -- Fiction 2. Mother-son relationship -- Fiction

ISBN 0062333461; 9780062333469

LC 2015940765

In this middle-grade novel, by Leslie Connor, "Eleven-year-old Perry was born and raised by his mom at the Blue River Co-ed Correctional Facility in tiny Surprise, Nebraska. His mom is a resident on Cell Block C. . . . That is, until a new district attorney discovers the truth—and Perry is removed from the facility and forced into a foster home. . . . Desperate to be reunited with his mom, Perry goes on a quest for answers about her past crime." (Publisher's note)

"With complex, memorable characters, a situation that demands sympathy, and a story that's shown, not just told, this is fresh and affecting. Well-crafted, warm, and wonderful." Kirkus

★ **Crunch**. Katherine Tegen Books 2010 330p $16.99; lib bdg $17.89

Grades: 5 6 7 8 **Fic**

1. Bicycles -- Fiction 2. Siblings -- Fiction 3. Family life -- Fiction 4. New England -- Fiction 5. Energy conservation -- Fiction 6. Business enterprises -- Fiction

ISBN 0-06-169229-8; 0-06-169233-6 lib bdg; 978-0-06-169229-1; 978-0-06-169233-8 lib bdg

LC 2009-24339

Dewey Marriss "never guessed that the gas pumps would run dry the same week he promised to manage the family's bicycle-repair business. Suddenly everyone needs a bike. And nobody wants to wait. Meanwhile, the crunch has stranded Dewey's parents far up north with an empty fuel tank and no way home. It's up to Dewey and his sister, Lil, to look after their younger siblings and run the bike shop on their own. . . . Age ten and up." (Publisher's note)

This novel concerns "the trials and tribulations of 14-year-old Dewey Mariss and his family. His parents are away from home, unable to return because of a gasoline shortage. Running their small family business, the Bike Barn, with his younger brother and helping older sister Lil look after the five-year-old twins keeps Dewey plenty busy. . . . Characters are colorful but believable, dialogue crisp and amusing. The New England setting is attractively realized, and the underlying energy crisis treated seriously but not sensationally." Kirkus

★ The **truth** as told by Mason Buttle; Leslie Connor ; [edited by] Katherine Tegen. Katherine Tegen Books 2018 336 p. (hardcover) $16.99

Grades: 4 5 6 7 8 **Fic**

1. Grief -- Fiction 2. Bullies -- Fiction 3. Friendship -- Fiction

ISBN 9780062491435

LC 2017934896

Schneider Family Book Award: Middle Grades (2019)

National Book Award Finalist: Young People's Literature (2018)

"Mason's learning disabilities are compounded by grief. Fifteen months ago, Mason's best friend, Benny Kilmartin, turned up dead in the Buttle family's orchard. . . . [Now], Mason and his new friend, tiny Calvin Chumsky, are . . . [bullied] in their neighborhood, so they create an underground club space for themselves. When Calvin goes missing, Mason finds himself in trouble again." (Publisher's note)

"Throughout this realistic problem novel, Connor's portrayal of Mason is spot-on, and the seventh-grader's honesty shines through as his greatest attribute. Laced throughout the story, and evident at the end, is hope for a brighter future, both for the entire family and the community." Booklist

★ **Waiting** for normal. Katherine Tegen Books 2008 290p $16.99; lib bdg $17.89

Grades: 5 6 7 8 **Fic**

1. Mothers -- Fiction 2. Family life -- Fiction 3. New York (State) -- Fiction

ISBN 978-0-06-089088-9; 0-06-089088-6; 978-0-06-089089-6 lib bdg; 0-06-089089-4 lib bdg

LC 2007-06881

Twelve-year-old Addie tries to cope with her mother's erratic behavior and being separated from her beloved stepfather and half-sisters when she and her mother go to live in a small trailer by the railroad tracks on the outskirts of Schenectady, New York.

"Connor . . . treats the subject of child neglect with honesty and grace in this poignant story. . . . Characters as persuasively optimistic as Addie are rare, and readers will gravitate to her." Publ Wkly

Constable, Kate

The **singer** of all songs. Arthur A. Levine Books 2004 297p hardcover o.p. pa $6.99

Grades: 7 8 9 10 **Fic**

1. Fantasy fiction 2. Magic -- Fiction

ISBN 0-439-55478-0; 0-439-55479-9 pa

LC 2003-9034

First published 2002 in Australia

Calwyn, a young priestess of ice magic, or chantment, joins with other chanters who have different magical skills to fight a sorcerer who wants to claim all powers for his own

"An impressive debut by an author who clearly has much to contribute to the fantasy genre." Booklist

Other available titles in this series are:

The waterless sea (2005)

The tenth power (2006)

Coombs, Kate

The **runaway** princess. Farrar, Straus and Giroux 2006 279p $17

Grades: 5 6 7 8 **Fic**

1. Fairy tales 2. Dragons -- Fiction 3. Princesses -- Fiction

ISBN 0-374-35546-0

LC 2005-51225

Fifteen-year-old Princess Meg uses magic and her wits to rescue a baby dragon and escape the unwanted attentions of princes hoping to gain her hand in marriage through a contest arranged by her father, the king.

"This witty, humorous tale will be popular with fantasy buffs who enjoy takeoffs on fairy tales." Booklist

Another title about Princess Meg is:

The runaway dragon (2009)

Cooney, Caroline B., 1947-

The **face** on the milk carton. Delacorte Press 2006 184p $15.95; pa $6.99

Grades: 7 8 9 10 **Fic**

1. Kidnapping -- Fiction

ISBN 978-0-385-32328-4; 0-385-32328-X; 978-0-440-22065-7 pa; 0-440-22065-3 pa

A reissue of the title first published 1990 by Bantam Books

A photograph of a missing girl on a milk carton leads Janie on a search for her real identity.

Cooney "demonstrates an excellent ear for dialogue and a gift for portraying responsible middle-class teenagers trying to come to terms with very real concerns." SLJ

Other titles in this series are:

Whatever happened to Janie (1993)

The voice on the radio (1996)

What Janie found (2000)

Janie face to face (2013)

Janie face to face; Caroline B. Cooney. Delacorte Press 2013 352 p. (Janie Johnson) (ebk) $20.99; (trade hardcover) $17.99

Grades: 7 8 9 10 **Fic**

1. Romance fiction 2. Kidnapping -- Fiction 3. Family life -- Fiction 4. Love -- Fiction 5. Identity -- Fiction 6. Authorship -- Fiction 7. New York (N.Y.) -- Fiction 8. Universities and colleges -- Fiction

ISBN 0385742061; 9780375979972; 9780375990397; 9780385742061

LC 2012006145

This book, by Caroline B. Cooney, is the conclusion to the "Janie Johnson" series which begun in 1990. "All will be revealed as readers find out if Janie and Reeve's love has endured, and whether or not the person who brought Janie and her family so much emotional pain and suffering is brought to justice." (Publisher's note)

Cooper, Abby

Sticks & stones; Abby Cooper. Farrar, Straus & Giroux 2016 288 p. (hardback) $16.99

Grades: 4 5 6 7 8 **Fic**

1. School stories 2. Self-acceptance -- Fiction 3. Schools -- Fiction 4. Diseases -- Fiction 5. Friendship -- Fiction 6. Middle schools -- Fiction

ISBN 0374302871; 9780374302870

LC 2015039454

In this juvenile novel, by Abby Cooper, "Elyse . . . has to deal with cognadjivisibilitis, or CAV: a disease that causes words to appear all over her body whenever they're spoken aloud. . . . As if that's not embarrassing enough, Elyse has just discovered that anything she thinks about herself (positive or negative) shows up, too. Now somebody at her school is sending her secret notes, claiming to want to help her with her predicament." (School Library Journal)

"Without being heavy-handed or sad, the book encourages resilience and addresses the pervasive self-esteem issues that plague so many young people today." Booklist

Cooper, Michelle

★ A **brief** history of Montmaray. Alfred A. Knopf 2009 296p $16.99; lib bdg $19.99

Grades: 7 8 9 10 **Fic**

1. Europe -- Fiction 2. Diaries -- Fiction 3. Islands -- Fiction 4. Princesses -- Fiction 5. Family life -- Fiction

ISBN 0-375-85864-4; 0-375-95864-9 lib bdg; 978-0-375-85864-2; 978-0-375-95864-9 lib bdg

LC 2008-49800

This book features "Sophie FitzOsborne [who] lives in a crumbling castle in the tiny island kingdom of Montmaray, along with her tomboy younger sister Henry, her beautiful, intellectual cousin Veronica, and Veronica's father, the completely mad King John. When Sophie receives a leather journal for her sixteenth birthday, she decides to write about her life on the island. But it is 1936 and bigger events are on the horizon." (Publisher's note)

"Cooper has crafted a sort of updated Gothic romance where sweeping adventure play equal with fluttering hearts." Booklist

Other titles in this series are:

The FitzOsbornes in exile (2011)
The FitzOsbornes at war (2012)

Cooper, Susan, 1935-

The **Boggart**. Margaret K. McElderry Bks. 1993 196p hardcover o.p. pa $5.99

Grades: 4 5 6 7 **Fic**

1. Canada -- Fiction 2. Scotland -- Fiction 3. Supernatural -- Fiction

ISBN 0-689-50576-0; 0-689-86930-4 pa

LC 92-15527

After visiting the castle in Scotland which her family has inherited and returning home to Canada, twelve-year-old Emily finds that she has accidentally brought back with her a boggart, an invisible and mischievous spirit with a fondness for practical jokes

"Using both electronics and theater as metaphors for magic, Cooper has extended the world of high fantasy into contemporary children's lives through scenes superimposing the ordinary and the extraordinary." Bull Cent Child Books

Other titles in this series are:
The Boggart and the monster (1997)
The Boggart fights back (2018)

★ The **dark** is rising. Simon Pulse 2007 244p il pa $8.99

Grades: 4 5 6 7 **Fic**

1. Fantasy fiction 2. Good and evil -- Fiction 3. Great Britain -- Fiction

ISBN 978-1-416-94965-7; 1-416-94965-8

Sequel to: Over sea, under stone

A reissue of the title first published 1973

On his eleventh birthday, Will Stanton discovers that he is the last of the Old Ones, destined to seek the six magical Signs that will enable the Old Ones to triumph over the evil forces of the Dark.

Ghost Hawk; by Susan Cooper. 1st ed. Margaret K. McElderry Books 2013 328 p. map (hardcover) $16.99

Grades: 5 6 7 8 **Fic**

1. Friendship -- Fiction 2. Native Americans -- North America 3. Native Americans -- Relations with early settlers 4. Ghosts -- Fiction 5. Survival -- Fiction 6. Coming of age -- Fiction 7. Wampanoag Indians -- Fiction 8. Massachusetts -- History -- New Plymouth, 1620-1691 -- Fiction

ISBN 1442481412; 9781442481411; 9781442481435

LC 2012039892

This novel is "a story of adventure and friendship between a young Native American and a colonial New England settler. Little Hawk is sent into the woods alone [and] if [he] survives three moons by himself, he will be a man. John Wakely is only ten when his father dies. . . . John sees how quickly the relationships between settlers and natives are deteriorating. His friendship with Little Hawk will put both boys in grave danger." (Publisher's note)

Greenwitch. Simon Pulse 2007 147p pa $8.99

Grades: 4 5 6 7 **Fic**

1. Fantasy fiction 2. Good and evil -- Fiction 3. Great Britain -- Fiction

ISBN 978-1-416-94966-4; 1-416-94966-6

Sequel to: The dark is rising

A reissue of the title first published 1974

Jane's invitation to witness the making of the Greenwitch begins a series of sinister events in which she and her two brothers help the Old Ones recover the grail stolen by the Dark.

The **grey** king; illustrated by Michael Heslop. Atheneum Pubs. 1975 208p il $19.99; pa $8.99

Grades: 5 6 7 8 **Fic**

1. Fantasy fiction 2. Wales -- Fiction 3. Good and evil -- Fiction

ISBN 0-689-50029-7; 1-4169-4967-4 pa

Awarded the Newbery Medal, 1976

"So well-crafted that it stands as an entity in itself, the novel . . . is nevertheless strengthened by its relationship to the preceding volumes—as the individual legends within the Arthurian cycles take on deeper significance in the context of the whole. A spellbinding tour de force." Horn Book

King of shadows. Margaret K. McElderry Bks. 1999 186p $16; pa $4.99; pa $6.99

Grades: 5 6 7 8 **Fic**

1. Poets 2. Authors 3. Dramatists 4. Actors -- Fiction 5. Globe Theatre (London, England) -- Fiction

ISBN 0-689-82817-9; 0-689-84445-X pa; 9780689844454 pa

LC 98-51127

Boston Globe Horn Book Honor Book (2000)

"Nat Field is thrilled when theater director Richard Babbage chooses him to become a player in the Company of Boys, an American summer drama troupe that will appear in Shakespeare's A Midsummer Night's Dream at the new replica of the Globe Theater in London. Shortly after his arrival in England, though, Nat feels ill and falls into a troubled sleep. To the doctor's astonishment, he seems to be suffering from the effects of the bubonic plague. He awakens in 1599 as another Nat Field, a child actor from St. Paul's School who is about to go to the Globe to rehearse A Midsummer Night's Dream in the role of Puck." (Booklist) "Grades six to nine." (Bull Cent Child Books)

"Cleverly explicating old and new acting and performance techniques, Susan Cooper entertains her contemporary readers while giving them a first-rate theatrical education." N Y Times Book Rev

★ **Over** sea, under stone; illustrated by Margery Gill. Harcourt Brace Jovanovich 1966 252p il $19; pa $5.99

Grades: 5 6 7 8 **Fic**

1. Fantasy fiction 2. Good and evil -- Fiction 3. Great Britain -- Fiction

ISBN 0-15-259034-X; 0-689-84035-7 pa

First published 1965 in the United Kingdom

Three children on a holiday in Cornwall find an ancient manuscript which sends them on a dangerous quest for a grail that would reveal the true story of King Arthur and that entraps them in the eternal battle between the forces of the Light and the forces of the Dark.

"The air of mysticism and the allegorical quality of the continual contest between good and evil add much value to a fine plot, setting, and characterization." Horn Book

Other titles in this series are:
The dark is rising (1973)
Greenwitch (1974)
The grey king (1975)
Silver on the tree (1977)

Silver on the tree. Atheneum Pubs. 1977 ix, 269p $19.99; pa $8.99

Grades: 5 6 7 8 **Fic**

1. Fantasy fiction 2. Wales -- Fiction
ISBN 0-689-50088-2; 978-1-416-94968-8 pa
LC 77-5361

In this conclusion of the tale begun in "Over Sea, Under Stone," Will Stanton, the Welsh boy Bran, and the Drew children try to locate the crystal sword that alone can vanquish the strong forces of Dark

Cormier, Robert

★ **After** the first death. Dell Publishing 1991 233p pa $6.50

Grades: 7 8 9 10 **Fic**

1. Terrorism -- Fiction
ISBN 0-440-20835-1
First published 1979 by Pantheon Bks.
ALA YALSA Margaret A. Edwards Award (1991)

"A busload of children is hijacked by a band of terrorists whose demands include the exposure of a military brainwashing project. The narrative line moves from the teenage terrorist Milo to Kate the bus driver and the involvement of Ben, whose father is the head of the military operation, in this confrontation. The conclusion has a shocking twist." Shapiro. Fic for Youth. 2d edition

Beyond the chocolate war; a novel. Dell 1986 278p pa $6.99

Grades: 9 10 11 12 **Fic**

1. School stories
ISBN 0-440-90580-X
First published 1985

Dark deeds continue at Trinity High School, climaxing in a public demonstration of one student's homemade guillotine. Sequel to "The Chocolate War."

★ The **chocolate** war; a novel. Pantheon Bks. 1974 253p rpt $8.99; $19.95

Grades: 7 8 9 10 **Fic**

1. School stories
ISBN 9780375829871 rpt; 0-394-82805-4
ALA YALSA Margaret A. Edwards Award (1991)

"In the Trinity School for Boys the environment is completely dominated by an underground gang, the Vigils. During a chocolate candy sale Brother Leon, the acting headmaster of the school, defers to the Vigils, who reign with terror in the school. Jerry Renault is first a pawn for the Vigils' evil deeds and finally their victim." Shapiro. Fic for Youth. 3d edition

Followed by Beyond the chocolate war (1985)

★ **I** am the cheese; a novel. Pantheon Bks. 1977 233p hardcover o.p. pa $6.50

Grades: 7 8 9 10 11 12 Adult **Fic**

1. Intelligence service -- Fiction
ISBN 0-394-83462-3; 0-440-94060-5 pa
LC 76-55948
ALA YALSA Margaret A. Edwards Award (1991)

"The suspense builds relentlessly to an ending that, although shocking, is entirely plausible." Booklist

Cornwell, Betsy

Mechanica; Betsy Cornwell. Houghton Mifflin Harcourt 2015 320 p. paperback $8.99; hardcover $17.99

Grades: 5 6 7 8 9 10 **Fic**

1. Inventors -- Fiction 2. Fractured fairy tales 3. Fairy tales 4. Magic -- Fiction 5. Inventions -- Fiction
ISBN 9780544668683; 9780547927718
LC 2015001336

This young adult novel, by Betsy Cornwell, is a retelling of the story of Cinderella. "Nicolette's awful stepsisters call her 'Mechanica.' . . . When she discovers a secret workshop in the cellar on her sixteenth birthday--and befriends Jules, a tiny magical metal horse--Nicolette starts to imagine a new life for herself. . . . Determined to invent her own happily-ever-after, Mechanica seeks to wow the prince and eager entrepreneurs alike." (Publisher's note)

Another title in this series is:
Venturess (2017)

Venturess; Betsy Cornwell. Clarion Books/Houghton Mifflin Harcourt 2017 311 p. (hardcover) $17.99

Grades: 5 6 7 8 9 10 **Fic**

1. Fairy tales 2. Magic -- Fiction 3. Inventors -- Fiction
ISBN 9780544319271; 9780544319295
LC 2016032623

Sequel to: Mechanica (2015)

In this book, by Betsy Cornwell, "inventor Nicolette Lampton is living her own fairy-tale happy ending. She's free of her horrible stepfamily, running a successful business, and is uninterested in marrying the handsome prince, Fin. Instead, she, Fin, and their friend Caro venture to the lush land of Faerie, where they seek to put an end to the bloody war their kingdom is waging." (Publisher's note)

"This unexpected sequel hits a sweet spot for fairy tale and steampunk lovers alike." Booklist

Corrigan, Eireann

Accomplice. Scholastic Press 2010 296p $17.99

Grades: 7 8 9 10 **Fic**

1. School stories 2. Fraud -- Fiction 3. Friendship -- Fiction 4. New Jersey -- Fiction
ISBN 978-0-545-05236-8; 0-545-05236-X
LC 2009-53869

High school juniors and best friends Finn and Chloe hatch a daring plot to fake Chloe's disappearance from their rural New Jersey town in order to have something compelling to put on their college applications, but unforeseen events complicate matters.

"Corrigan has crafted a complex, heart-wrenchingly plausible YA thriller. . . . A fascinating character study of individuals and an entire town, this tension-filled story will entice readers with a single booktalk." Booklist

Cotler, Steve

Cheesie Mack is not a genius or anything; illustrated by Adam McCauley. Random House 2011 229p il $15.99; lib bdg $18.99

Grades: 4 5 6 **Fic**

1. Mystery fiction 2. Summer -- Fiction 3. Friendship -- Fiction
ISBN 978-0-375-86437-7; 0-375-86437-7; 978-0-375-96437-4 lib bdg; 0-375-96437-1 lib bdg; 978-0-375-89570-8 e-book
LC 2009-33329

Ronald, aka Cheesie, Mack and his best friend Georgie find opportunies for summertime mischief "when Georgie finds a nearly century-old letter containing a worn penny and a locket, a mystery that eventually leads the pals to the Haunted Toad, a local rundown mansion. . . . Cheesie's . . . easygoing, accessible voice will certainly appeal to middle-grade readers. . . . The action . . . is all fun and games. . . . A light-hearted and fast-moving read for kids looking for middle-school shenanigans." Bull Cent Child Books

Other titles in this series are:

Cheesie Mack is cool in a duel (2012)
Cheesie Mack is running like crazy! (2013)
Cheesie Mack is not exactly famous (2014)
Cheesie Mack is sort of freaked out (2014)

Cottrell Boyce, Frank, 1959-

Cosmic. Walden Pond Press 2010 311p $16.99; lib bdg $17.89

Grades: 4 5 6 7 **Fic**

1. Size -- Fiction 2. Outer space -- Exploration -- Fiction

ISBN 978-0-06-183683-1; 0-06-183683-4; 978-0-06-183686-2 lib bdg; 0-06-183686-9 lib bdg

LC 2008277816

Boyce "knows how to tell a compellingly good story. But in his latest extravagantly imaginative and marvelously good-natured novel he has also written one that is bound to win readers' hearts." Booklist

Sputnik's guide to life on Earth; by Frank Cottrell Boyce. Walden Pond Press 2017 321 p. illustrations (hardcover) $16.99

Grades: 4 5 6 7 **Fic**

1. Boys -- Fiction 2. Human-alien encounters -- Fiction 3. Science fiction

ISBN 0062643622; 9780062643629; 9780062643643

In this book, by Frank Cottrell Boyce, "Prez knows that the best way to keep track of things is to make a list. . . . Prez is still learning to fit in at his new home when he . . . [met] Sputnik--a kid who is more than a little strange. First, he can hear what Prez is thinking. Second, he looks like a dog to everyone except Prez. Third, he can manipulate the laws of space and time. Sputnik, it turns out is an alien, and he's got a mission that requires Prez's help." (Publisher's note)

"A stellar exploration of the meaning of home and the earthly wonders all around us." Booklist

The **unforgotten** coat; Frank Cottrell Boyce ; photographs by Carl Hunter and Clare Heney. Candlewick Press 2011 112p il $15.99

Grades: 3 4 5 6 **Fic**

1. Mongols -- Fiction 2. Brothers -- Fiction 3. Refugees -- Fiction 4. Friendship -- Fiction 5. Immigrants -- Fiction 6. Great Britain -- Fiction

ISBN 978-0-7636-5729-1; 0-7636-5729-8

LC 2010048224

"When two Mongolian brothers inexplicably appear one morning in Julie's sixth grade class, no one, least of all Julie, knows what to do with them. But when Chingis, the older of the two brothers, proclaims Julie as their 'Good Guide'--a nomadic tradition of welcoming strangers to a new land--Julie must somehow navigate them through soccer, school uniforms, and British slang, all while trying to win Shocky's attention and perhaps also an invitation to her friend Mimi's house." (Publisher's note)

This is "a tight, powerful story--brimming with humor, mystery, and pathos--about illegal immigration and the price it exacts on children." Publ Wkly

Coulthurst, Audrey

★ **Of** Fire and Stars; by Audrey Coulthurst, illustrated by Jordan Saia. Harpercollins Childrens Books 2016 400 p. illustrations, map $17.99; (ebook) $16.99

Grades: 8 9 10 11 **Fic**

1. Fire -- Fiction 2. Magic -- Fiction 3. Princesses -- Fiction 4. Man-woman relationships -- Fiction

ISBN 0062433253; 9780062433251; 9780062433275

In this book, by Audrey Coulthurst, illustrated by Jordan Saia, Princess Dennaleia, "betrothed since childhood to the prince of Mynaria, . . . has always known what her future holds. Her marriage will seal the alliance between Mynaria and her homeland, protecting her people from other hostile kingdoms. But Denna has a secret. She possesses an Affinity for fire--a dangerous gift for the future queen of a land where magic is forbidden." (Publisher's note)

"A worthy debut that succeeds as both an adventure and a romance." Booklist

Other titles in this series are:
Of ice and shadows (2019)

Cousins, Dave

Waiting for Gonzo; Dave Cousins. First U.S. edition Flux 2015 288 p. $9.99

Grades: 7 8 9 10 **Fic**

1. Moving -- Fiction 2. Family life -- Fiction 3. High schools -- Fiction 4. Practical jokes -- Fiction 5. Brothers and sisters -- Fiction 6. England -- Fiction 7. Schools -- Fiction 8. Pregnancy -- Fiction 9. Moving, Household -- Fiction 10. Family life -- England -- Fiction

ISBN 073874199X; 9780738741994

LC 2014031277

In this book, by Dave Cousins, "[t]hings could be going better for Oz. He's just moved miles from all his friends. A prank at his new school puts him in the crosshairs of 'Psycho' Isobel Skinner, a bully who also happens to be his mum's new best friend. And he's driven off the only other kid who will have anything to do with him: a Tolkien-obsessed boy in desperate need of a decent playlist." (Publisher's note)

"In a darkly comic story written as Marcus's monologue to his unborn nephew (whom he nicknames Gonzo), Cousins (15 Days Without a Head) offers a vibrant, highly visual account of teen angst and backfiring schemes. Marcus makes more than a few mistakes at school and at home, but readers will never doubt that his heart is in the right place." Publishers Weekly

Coville, Bruce

★ **Aliens** ate my homework; illustrated by Katherine Coville. Pocket Bks. 1993 179p il hardcover o.p. pa $5.99

Grades: 4 5 6 **Fic**

1. Science fiction 2. Extraterrestrial beings -- Fiction

ISBN 1-4169-3883-4 pa

LC 93-3945

Rod is surprised when a miniature spaceship lands in his school science project and reveals five tiny aliens, who ask his help in apprehending an interstellar criminal

"A funny and suspenseful romp, with appealing illustrations throughout." Horn Book Guide

Other titles in this series are:
Aliens stole my body (1998)
I left my sneakers in dimension X (1994)
The search for Snout (1995)

★ **Juliet** Dove, Queen of Love; a magic shop book. Harcourt 2003 190p $17; pa $5.95

Grades: 4 5 6 **Fic**

1. Magic -- Fiction 2. Classical mythology -- Fiction

ISBN 0-15-204561-9; 0-15-205217-8 pa

LC 2003-11846

A shy twelve-year-old girl must solve a puzzle involving characters from Greek mythology to free herself from a spell which makes her irresistible to boys

"Although humorous, the story has surprising depth. . . . Coville capably interweaves mythological characters with realistic modern ones, keeping readers truly absorbed." SLJ

★ The **skull** of truth; a magic shop book. illustrated by Gary A. Lippincott. Harcourt Brace & Co. 1997 195p il $17
Grades: 4 5 6 7 **Fic**

1. Fantasy fiction 2. Truthfulness and falsehood -- Fiction
ISBN 0-15-275457-1

LC 97-9264

Charlie, a sixth-grader with a compulsion to tell lies, acquires a mysterious skull that forces its owner to tell only the truth, causing some awkward moments before he understands its power

"Coville has structured the story very carefully, with a great deal of sensitivity to children's thought processes and emotions. The mood shifts from scary to funny to serious are fused with understandable language and sentence structures." SLJ

Cox, Suzy

The **Dead** Girls Detective Agency; Suzy Cox. Harper 2012 355 p. (trade bdg.) $9.99
Grades: 7 8 9 10 **Fic**

1. Future life -- Fiction 3. Ghost stories -- Fiction 4. Mystery fiction -- Fiction 5. Dead -- Fiction 6. Murder -- Fiction 7. New York (N.Y.) -- Fiction 8. Mystery and detective stories
ISBN 0-06-202064-1; 9780062020642

LC 2012006567

This novel, by Suzy Cox, follows the ghost of a teenager seeking to solve her own murder. "Meet the Dead Girls Detective Agency: Nancy, Lorna, and Tess--not to mention Edison, the really cute if slightly hostile dead boy. Apparently, the only way out of this limbo is to figure out who killed me, or I'll have to spend eternity playing Nancy Drew. Considering I was fairly invisible in life, who could hate me enough to want me dead? And what if my murderer is someone I never would have suspected?" (Publisher's note)

Creech, Sharon

Absolutely normal chaos. HarperCollins Pubs. 1995 230p $16.99; pa $5.99
Grades: 5 6 7 8 **Fic**

1. Family life -- Fiction
ISBN 0-06-026989-8; 0-06-440632-6 pa

LC 95-22448

First published 1990 in the United Kingdom

"Those in search of a light, humorous read will find it; those in search of something a little deeper will also be rewarded." SLJ

Hate that cat. Joanna Cotler Books 2008 153p $15.99; lib bdg $16.89
Grades: 4 5 6 7 **Fic**

1. School stories 2. Novels in verse 3. Poetry -- Fiction
ISBN 978-0-06-143092-3; 978-0-06-143093-0 lib bdg

LC 2007044182

Jack is studying poetry again in school, and he continues to write poems reflecting his understanding of famous poems and how they relate to his life.

"Creech employs sensitivity and spare verse to carve an indelible portrait of a boy who discovers the power of self-expression." Booklist

Love that dog. HarperCollins Pubs. 2001 86p $15.99; lib bdg $14.89; pa $5.99
Grades: 4 5 6 7 **Fic**

1. School stories 2. Poetry 3. Poetry -- Fiction
ISBN 0-06-029287-3; 0-06-029289-X lib bdg; 0-06-440959-7 pa

LC 00-54233

"Jack thinks that boys don't write poetry. . . . The trouble is that his teacher, Ms. Stretchberry, keeps insisting that he read more and more poetry. Worse, she keeps insisting that he write poems, as well! . . . This book comes to us in the form of journal entries in Jack's own freeverse." (Christ Sci Monit) "Ages eight to twelve." (N Y Times Book Rev)

"Creech has created a poignant, funny picture of a child's encounter with the power of poetry. . . . This book is a tiny treasure." SLJ

Another title about Jack is:
Hate that cat (2008)

★ **Moo**; A Novel. Sharon Creech. Harpercollins Childrens Books 2016 288 p. (hardcover) $16.99
Grades: 4 5 6 7 **Fic**

1. Country life -- Fiction 2. Domestic animals -- Fiction
ISBN 9780062415240; 0062415247

This novel by Sharon Creech follows "one family's . . . move from the city to rural [country]. . . . When Reena, her little brother, Luke, and their parents first move to Maine, Reena doesn't know what to expect. She's ready for beaches, blueberries, and all the lobster she can eat. Instead, her parents 'volunteer' Reena and Luke to work for an eccentric neighbor named Mrs. Falala, who has a pig named Paulie, a cat named China, a snake named Edna—and that stubborn cow, Zora." (Publisher's note)

"A heartfelt tale that will be embraced by Creech's fans, work well as a classroom read-aloud, and find a spot in book groups." SLJ

The **unfinished** angel. Joanna Cotler Books 2009 164p
Grades: 4 5 6 **Fic**

1. Angels -- Fiction 2. Orphans -- Fiction 3. Villages -- Fiction 4. Switzerland -- Fiction
ISBN 0-06-143095-1; 0-06-143096-X lib bdg; 0-06-143097-8 pa; 978-0-06-143095-4; 978-0-06-143096-1 lib bdg; 978-0-06-143097-8 pa

LC 2009-02796

In a tiny village in the Swiss Alps, an angel meets an American girl named Zola who has come with her father to open a school, and together Zola and the angel rescue a group of homeless orphans. "Ages eight to twelve." (Publisher's note)

"Some books are absolute magic, and this is one of them. . . . Creech's protagonist is hugely likable. . . . Creech's offering deserves to be read out loud and more than once to truly enjoy the angel's hilarious malapropisms and outright invented words, and to appreciate the book's tender, comical celebration of the human spirit." SLJ

★ **Walk** two moons. HarperCollins Pubs. 1994 280p $16.99; lib bdg $17.89; pa $6.99
Grades: 6 7 8 9 **Fic**

1. Death -- Fiction 2. Friendship -- Fiction 3. Family life -- Fiction 4. Grandparents -- Fiction
ISBN 0-06-023334-6; 0-06-023337-0 lib bdg; 0-06-440517-6 pa

LC 93-31277

Awarded the Newbery Medal, 1995

After her mother leaves home suddenly, thirteen-year-old Sal and her grandparents take a car trip retracing her mother's route. Along the way, Sal recounts the story of her friend Phoebe, whose mother also left

"An engaging story of love and loss, told with humor and suspense. . . . A richly layered novel about real and metaphorical journeys." SLJ

Crockett, S. D.

After the snow; S. D. Crockett. Feiwel & Friends 2012 304 p. (hardback) $22.55

Grades: 6 7 8 9 10 11 12 **Fic**

1. Science fiction 2. Adventure fiction 3. Winter -- Fiction 4. Missing persons -- Fiction 5. Children and war -- Fiction 6. Survival -- Fiction 7. Voyages and travels -- Fiction 8. Adventure and adventurers -- Fiction

ISBN 9780312641696

LC 2011036122

William C. Morris Award Finalist (2013)

In this book, "Willo's father can still remember what life was like in Great Britain before the country entered a new ice age. . . . When his father and the rest of his family mysteriously disappear, Willo leaves the scant safety of home to search for them. . . . [He] saves a . . . girl he encounters along the way, and together they find their way into the city, in which a long-dormant resistance movement is preparing for a final desperate exodus." (Bulletin of the Center for Children's Books)

Cross, Gillian, 1945-

Where I belong. Holiday House 2011 245p $17.95

Grades: 7 8 9 10 **Fic**

1. Somalia -- Fiction 2. Refugees -- Fiction 3. Kidnapping -- Fiction 4. London (England) -- Fiction 5. Fashion designers -- Fiction

ISBN 978-0-8234-2332-3; 0-8234-2332-8

LC 2010-23671

This is a "fast-paced adventure. . . . The fashion element will engage readers who would otherwise not read this genre. . . . This broadly appealing title has an engaging cover and is a worthy addition to any collection." SLJ

Crossan, Sarah

One; by Sarah Crossan. Greenwillow Books, an imprint of HarperCollinsPublishers 2015 400 p. (trade ed.) $17.99

Grades: 8 9 10 11 12 **Fic**

1. Novels in verse 2. Conjoined twins -- Fiction 3. Twins -- Fiction 4. Schools -- Fiction 5. Sisters -- Fiction 6. High schools -- Fiction 7. Family problems -- Fiction

ISBN 9780062118752; 0062118757

LC 2015004714

"Life for 16-year-old Grace and her sister Tippi hasn't been easy: they're conjoined twins--literally joined at the hip. They've spent their lives dealing with staring strangers and invasive questions, but the girls are happy together and wouldn't have it any other way. Grace and Tippi have been home-schooled until now, but when the state decides to pay for the girls to attend a private high school instead, they begin their junior year among peers. . . . When Grace is diagnosed with a bad heart, the twins have a difficult decision to make: risk the dangerous separation surgery so Grace can qualify for a transplant, or stay together and get sicker until they both die." (Kirkus)

"Crossan trusts her characters and her readers to find their better selves through her gently paced story." Booklist

★ The **Weight** of Water; by Sarah Crossan. Bloomsbury USA 2013 224 p. $16.99

Grades: 5 6 7 8 **Fic**

1. Immigrants -- Fiction 2. School stories -- Fiction 3. Novels in verse 4. England -- Fiction 6. Swimming -- Fiction 5. Race relations -- Fiction 6. Swimming -- Fiction 7. Coventry (England) -- Fiction 8. Immigrants -- England -- Fiction 9. Mothers and daughters -- Fiction

ISBN 1599909677; 9781599909677

LC 2012038645

In this book, "12-year-old Kasienka moves with Mama from Gdansk, Poland, to Coventry, England, to find Tata, her father. The adjustment is difficult. At school, Kasienka is ostracized. At home, she questions why they are searching for a man who ran from them. When Kasienka complains, Mama questions her love. Kasienka feels powerful only when she swims at the pool—something Tata taught her to do. That is also where William, a schoolmate, first notices her." (Kirkus Reviews)

Crowder, Melanie

★ A **nearer** moon; Melanie Crowder. Atheneum Books for Young Readers 2015 160 p. (hardcover) $16.99

Grades: 4 5 6 7 8 **Fic**

1. Magic -- Fiction 2. Rivers -- Fiction 3. Sisters -- Fiction 4. Family life -- Fiction 5. Water spirits -- Fiction

ISBN 1481441485; 9781481441483

LC 2014043590

In this book, by Melanie Crowder, "[a]long a lively river, in a village raised on stilts, lives a girl named Luna. All her life she has heard tales of the time before the dam appeared, when sprites danced in the currents and no one got the mysterious wasting illness from a mouthful of river water. . . . [W]hen Luna's little sister falls ill with the river sickness, . . . Luna is determined to find a cure for her beloved sister, no matter what it takes.." (Publisher's note)

"Luna's brave journey to save her sister takes her to places her mother told her never to go and to the very heart of the dark magic. Told in alternating chapters of the past fairy time and Luna's present, this lyrical tale highlights the power of sisterly love in a truly enchanting way." SLJ

Crowe, Chris

Mississippi trial, 1955. Penguin Putnam 2002 231p pa $5.99; $17.99

Grades: 7 8 9 10 **Fic**

1. Children 2. Racism 3. Grandfathers 4. Murder victims 5. Fathers and sons 6. Mississippi -- Race relations

ISBN 0-14-250192-1 pa; 0-8037-2745-3

LC 2001-40221

In Mississippi in 1955, a sixteen-year-old finds himself at odds with his grandfather over issues surrounding the kidnapping and murder of a fourteen-year-old African American from Chicago. "Grades seven to ten." (Bull Cent Child Books)

"By combining real events with their impact upon a single fictional character, Crowe makes the issues in this novel hard-hitting and personal. The characters are complex." Voice Youth Advocates

Crowley, Cath

Words in deep blue; Cath Crowley. First American edition Alfred A. Knopf 2017 269 p. (hardcover) $17.99

Grades: 8 9 10 11 **Fic**

1. Romance fiction 2. Australia -- Fiction 3. Bookstores -- Fiction 4. Love -- Fiction

ISBN 9781101937662; 9781101937648; 9781101937655

LC 2016001071

In this book, by Cath Crowley, "years ago, Rachel had a crush on Henry Jones. The day before she moved away, she tucked a love letter into his favorite book in his family's bookshop. She waited. But Henry never came. Now Rachel has returned to the city--and to the bookshop--to work alongside the boy she'd rather not see, if at all possible, for the rest of her life. But Rachel needs the distraction. Her brother drowned months ago, and she can't feel anything anymore." (Publisher's note)

"This journey is original, wise, and essential . . . This love story is an ode to words and life." Kirkus

Crowley, Kieran Mark

The **misfits** club; Kieran Crowley. Feiwel and Friends 2018 320 p. (hardcover) $16.99

Grades: 4 5 6 7 Fic

1. Suspense fiction 2. Friendship -- Fiction 3. Girls' clubs -- Fiction

ISBN 9781250079268; 9781250079275

LC 2017944815

In this book, by Kieran Crowley, "nothing exciting ever happens in the small town of Newpark where Brian, Hannah, and twins Chris and Sam live. . . . The Misfits Club, a club they started when they were 8 years old, is disbanding and they still haven't managed to solve any real mysteries. But when they persuade new club member Amelia to go and investigate a spooky old house, they unexpectedly discover some stolen goods. Could this be their chance for one last adventure?" (Publisher's note)

"Filled with adventure until the very last page, and with incredible humor that will have readers laughing out loud, this action-packed, entertaining read is perfect for mystery fans." Booklist

Crutcher, Chris

★ **Deadline**. Greenwillow Books 2007 316p $16.99; lib bdg $17.89; pa $8.99

Grades: 8 9 10 11 12 Fic

1. School stories 2. Death -- Fiction 3. Terminally ill -- Fiction

ISBN 978-0-06-085089-0; 0-06-085089-2; 978-0-06-085090-6 lib bdg; 0-06-085090-6 lib bdg; 978-0-06-085091-3 pa; 0-06-085091-4 pa

LC 2006-31526

Given the medical diagnosis of one year to live, high school senior Ben Wolf decides to fulfill his greatest fantasies, ponders his life's purpose and legacy, and converses through dreams with a spiritual guide known as "Hey-Soos."

"Ben's sensitive voice uses self-deprecating humor, philosophical pondering, and effective dramatic irony." Voice Youth Advocates

Running loose. Greenwillow Bks. 1983 190p hardcover o.p. pa $8.99; pa $6.99

Grades: 7 8 9 10 Fic

1. School stories

ISBN 9780060094911 pa; 0-688-02002-X; 0-06-009491-5 pa

LC 82-20935

ALA YALSA Margaret A. Edwards Award (2000)

"Louie Banks tells what happened to him in his senior year in a small town Idaho high school. Besides falling in love with Becky and losing her in a senseless accident, Louie takes a stand against the coach when he sets the team up to injure a black player on an opposing team, and learns that you can't be honorable with dishonorable men. . . . Grade seven and up." (Voice Youth Advocates)

"Louie Banks tells what happened to him in his senior year in a small town Idaho high school. Besides falling in love with Becky and losing her in a senseless accident, Louie takes a stand against the coach when he sets the team up to injure a black player on an opposing team, and learns that you can't be honorable with dishonorable men." Voice Youth Advocates

Staying fat for Sarah Byrnes. Greenwillow Bks. 1993 216p hardcover o.p. pa $6.99

Grades: 7 8 9 10 Fic

1. Obesity -- Fiction 2. Swimming -- Fiction 3. Friendship -- Fiction 4. Child abuse -- Fiction

ISBN 0-688-11552-7; 0-06-009489-3 pa

LC 91-40097

ALA YALSA Margaret A. Edwards Award (2000)

"An obese boy and a disfigured girl suffer the emotional scars of years of mockery at the hands of their peers. They share a hard-boiled view of the world until events in their senior year hurl them in very different directions. A story about a friendship with staying power, written with pathos and pointed humor." SLJ

Whale talk. Greenwillow Bks. 2001 220p $15.99; pa $8.99

Grades: 7 8 9 10 Fic

1. School stories 2. Swimming -- Fiction 3. Racially mixed people -- Fiction

ISBN 0-688-18019-1; 0-06-177131-7 pa

LC 00-59292

Intellectually and athletically gifted, TJ, a multiracial, adopted teenager, shuns organized sports and the gung-ho athletes at his high school until he agrees to form a swimming team and recruits some of the school's less popular students

"This remarkable novel is vintage Crutcher: heart-pounding athletic competitions, raw emotion, an insufferable high school atmosphere that allows bullying and reveres athletes, and a larger-than-life teen hero who champions the underdog while skewering both racists and abusers with his rapier-sharp wit." Book Rep

Cummings, Priscilla

Blindsided. Dutton Children's Books 2010 226p $16.99

Grades: 7 8 9 10 Fic

1. School stories 2. Blind -- Fiction 3. Maryland -- Fiction

ISBN 978-0-525-42161-0; 0-525-42161-0

LC 2009-25092

"Natalie, 14, knows that her future is becoming dimmer as the loss of her eyesight is a nightmare she can't avoid. . . . Part of going from denial to acceptance is attending a boarding school for the blind. . . . Natalie is a credible character and her fear is palpable and painful. . . . Readers will enjoy the high drama and heroics." SLJ

Currier, Katrina Saltonstall

Kai's journey to Gold Mountain; an Angel Island story. illustrated by Gabhor Utomo. Angel Island Association 2005 39p il $16.95

Grades: 4 5 6 7 Fic

1. Immigrants -- Fiction 2. Chinese Americans -- Fiction 3. Los Angeles (Calif.) -- Fiction

ISBN 0-9667352-4-2

LC 2004-14821

In 1934, twelve-year-old Kai leaves China to join his father in America, but first he must take a long sea voyage, then endure weeks of crowded conditions and harsh examinations on Angel Island, fearing that he or his new friend will be sent home.

"The character Kai is based on a real person, whose photos, then and now, are part of the historical notes at the back of the book. Opposite each page of the intensely moving, detailed text are beautiful full-page watercolor-and-pencil illustrations that capture the crowded holding place, and, in unforgettable closeups, the characters' heartbreak and strength." Booklist

Curry, Jane Louise

The **Black** Canary. Margaret K. McElderry Books 2005 279p $16.95

Grades: 5 6 7 8 **Fic**

1. Generals 2. Courtiers 3. Conspirators 4. Royal favorites 5. Singers -- Fiction 6. London (England) -- Fiction 7. Racially mixed people -- Fiction 8. Great Britain -- History -- 1485-1603, Tudors -- Fiction

ISBN 0-689-86478-7

LC 2003-26150

As the child of two musicians, twelve-year-old James has no interest in music until he discovers a portal to seventeenth-century London in his uncle's basement, and finds himself in a situation where his beautiful voice and the fact that he is biracial might serve him well.

"A genuinely good story that conveys a sense of darkness and mystery in the textured backdrop of a storied time and place." Booklist

Curtis, Christopher Paul, 1953-

★ **Bud,** not Buddy. Delacorte Press 1999 245p $16.95; pa $6.50

Grades: 4 5 6 7 **Fic**

1. Orphans -- Fiction 2. African Americans -- Fiction 3. Great Depression, 1929-1939 -- Fiction

ISBN 0-385-32306-9; 0-440-41328-1 pa

LC 99-10614

Coretta Scott King Award for text

Awarded the Newbery Medal, 2000

Ten-year-old Bud, a motherless boy living in Flint, Michigan, during the Great Depression, escapes a bad foster home and sets out in search of the man he believes to be his father—the renowned bandleader, H. E. Calloway of Grand Rapids

"Curtis says in a afterword that some of the characters are based on real people, including his own grandfathers, so it's not surprising that the rich blend of tall tale, slapstick, sorrow, and sweetness has the wry, teasing warmth of family folklore." Booklist

★ **Elijah** of Buxton. Scholastic 2007 341p $16.99; pa $7.99

Grades: 5 6 7 8 **Fic**

1. Canada -- Fiction 2. Slavery -- Fiction

ISBN 0-439-02344-0; 978-0-439-02344-3; 0-439-02345-9 pa; 978-0-439-02345-0 pa

LC 2007-05181

A Newbery Medal honor book, 2008

In 1859, eleven-year-old Elijah Freeman, the first freeborn child in Buxton, Canada, which is a haven for slaves fleeing the American south, uses his wits and skills to try to bring to justice the lying preacher who has stolen money that was to be used to buy a family's freedom.

"Many readers drawn to the book by humor will find themselves at times on the edges of their seats in suspense and, at other moments, moved to tears." Booklist

★ The **journey** of little Charlie; Christopher Paul Curtis. Scholastic Press 2018 234 p. (hardcover) $16.99

Grades: 4 5 6 7 8 **Fic**

1. Slavery -- Fiction 2. Sharecroppers -- Fiction 3. Race relations -- Fiction 4. Fugitive slaves -- Fiction 5. African Americans -- Fiction 6. Fugitive slaves -- South Carolina -- Fiction

ISBN 9781338164008; 9780545156677; 9780545156660

LC 2017020256

National Book Award Finalist: Young People's Literature (2018)

In this children's book, by Christopher Paul Curtis, "twelve-year-old Charlie is down on his luck: His sharecropper father just died and Cap'n Buck. . . has come to collect a debt. Fearing for his life, Charlie strikes a deal with Cap'n Buck and agrees to track down some folks accused of stealing from the cap'n and his boss. It's not too bad of a bargain for Charlie... until he comes face-to-face with the fugitives and discovers their true identities." (Publisher's note)

"A characteristically lively and complex addition to the historical fiction of the era from Curtis." Kirkus

Includes bibliographical references.

★ The **madman** of Piney Woods; Christopher Paul Curtis. Scholastic Press 2014 384 p. $16.99

Grades: 4 5 6 7 **Fic**

1. Adventure fiction 2. Freedmen -- Fiction 3. Veterans -- Fiction 4. Immigrants -- Fiction 5. Irish -- Canada -- Fiction 6. Blacks -- Canada -- Fiction 7. Canada -- History -- 1867-1914 -- Fiction 8. Post-traumatic stress disorder -- Fiction 9. Chatham (Ont.) -- History -- 20th century -- Fiction 10. North Buxton (Ont.) -- History -- 20th century -- Fiction

ISBN 0545156645; 9780545156646; 9780545156653; 9780545633765

LC 2014003493

"Benji and Red couldn't be more different. They aren't friends. They don't even live in the same town. But their fates are entwined. A chance meeting leads the boys to discover that they have more in common than meets the eye. Both of them have encountered a strange presence in the forest, watching them, tracking them. Could the Madman of Piney Woods be real?" (Publisher's note)

★ The **Watsons** go to Birmingham--1963; a novel. Delacorte Press 1995 210p $16.95; pa $6.50

Grades: 4 5 6 7 **Fic**

1. Prejudices -- Fiction 2. Family life -- Fiction 3. African Americans -- Fiction

ISBN 0-385-32175-9; 0-440-41412-1 pa

LC 95-7091

A Newbery Medal honor book, 1996

The ordinary interactions and everyday routines of the Watsons, an African American family living in Flint, Michigan, are drastically changed after they go to visit Grandma in Alabama in the summer of 1963

"Curtis's ability to switch from fun and funky to pinpoint-accurate psychological imagery works unusually well. . . . Ribald humor, sly sibling digs, and a totally believable child's view of the world will make this book an instant hit." SLJ

Cushman, Karen

★ **Alchemy** and Meggy Swann. Clarion Books 2010 167p $16

Grades: 5 6 7 8 **Fic**

1. Alchemy -- Fiction 2. Poverty -- Fiction 3. London (England) -- Fiction 4. People with Disabilities -- Fiction 5. Father-daughter relationship -- Fiction 6. Great Britain -- History -- 1485-1603, Tudors -- Fiction

ISBN 978-0-547-23184-6; 0-547-23184-9

LC 2009-16387

In 1573, the crippled, scorned, and destitute Meggy Swann goes to London, where she meets her father, an impoverished alchemist, and eventually discovers that although her legs are bent and weak, she has many other strengths.

"Writing with admirable economy and a lively ability to recreate the past believably, Cushman creates a memorable portrayal of a troubled, rather mulish girl who begins to use her strong will in positive ways." Booklist

The **ballad** of Lucy Whipple. Clarion Bks. 1996 195p $15; $16.00
Grades: 5 6 7 8 **Fic**
1. Family life -- Fiction 2. Frontier and pioneer life -- Fiction 3. California -- Gold discoveries -- Fiction
ISBN 0-395-72806-1; 9780395728062
LC 95-45257

"Twelve-year-old Lucy is taken by her mother from their comfortable 19th-century home in Massachusetts to the rough-and-tumble California goldfields. Lucy's younger siblings don't object to this new life, but Lucy dislikes the dirt, hard work, and lack of civilization—especially reading material. When not helping Mama run Mr. Scatter's boarding house for miners, Lucy spends her time complaining or scheming a return to her beloved Massachusetts. Despite the losses she suffers in the makeshift town of Lucky Diggins, Lucy makes some surprising discoveries about herself and what she's gained in the West." (Christ Sci Monit) "Grades five to eight." (Booklist)

"Cushman's heroine is a delightful character, and the historical setting is authentically portrayed." SLJ

★ **Catherine,** called Birdy. Clarion Bks. 1994 169p $16
Grades: 6 7 8 9 **Fic**
1. Middle Ages -- Fiction 2. Great Britain -- Fiction
ISBN 0-395-68186-3
LC 93-23333

A Newbery Medal honor book, 1995

The year is 1290 and the thirteen-year-old daughter of an English county knight keeps a journal in which she records the events of her life, particularly her longing for adventures beyond the usual role of women and her efforts to avoid being married off. "Grades six to nine." (Booklist)

"In the process of telling the routines of her young life, Birdy lays before readers a feast of details about medieval England. . . . Superb historical fiction." SLJ

The **loud** silence of Francine Green. Clarion Books 2006 225p $16
Grades: 6 7 8 9 **Fic**
1. School stories 2. Family life -- Fiction 3. Los Angeles (Calif.) -- Fiction 4. United States -- Politics and government -- 1945-1953 -- Fiction
ISBN 978-0-618-50455-8; 0-618-50455-9
LC 2005-29774

In 1949, thirteen-year-old Francine goes to Catholic school in Los Angeles where she becomes best friends with a girl who questions authority and is frequently punished by the nuns, causing Francine to question her own values.

Readers will "savor the story of friends and family tensions, the sly humor, and the questions about patriotism, activism, and freedom." Booklist

★ The **midwife's** apprentice. Clarion Bks. 1995 122p $12; pa $5.99
Grades: 6 7 8 9 **Fic**
1. Midwives -- Fiction 2. Middle Ages -- Fiction 3. Great Britain -- Fiction
ISBN 0-395-69229-6; 0-06-440630-X pa
LC 94-13792

Awarded the Newbery Medal, 1996

In medieval England, a nameless, homeless girl is taken in by a sharp-tempered midwife, and in spite of obstacles and hardship, eventually gains the three things she most wants: a full belly, a contented heart, and a place in this world

"Earthy humor, the foibles of humans both high and low, and a fascinating mix of superstition and genuinely helpful herbal remedies attached to childbirth make this a truly delightful introduction to a world seldom seen in children's literature." SLJ

★ **Rodzina**. Clarion Bks. 2003 215p $16; pa $6.50
Grades: 5 6 7 8 **Fic**
1. Orphans -- Fiction 2. Polish Americans -- Fiction
ISBN 0-618-13351-8; 0-440-41993-X pa
LC 2002-15976

A twelve-year-old Polish American girl is boarded onto an orphan train in Chicago with fears about traveling to the West and a life of unpaid slavery

"The story features engaging characters, a vivid setting, and a prickly but endearing heroine. . . . Rodzina's musings and observations provide poignancy, humor, and a keen sense of the human and topographical landscape." SLJ

Includes bibliographical references

Will Sparrow's road; Karen Cushman. Clarion Books 2012 216 p. (hardback) $16.99
Grades: 5 6 7 8 **Fic**
1. Historical fiction 2. Runaway children -- Fiction 3. Swindlers and swindling -- Fiction 4. Runaways -- Fiction 5. Freak shows -- Fiction 6. Conduct of life -- Fiction 7. Great Britain -- History -- Elizabeth, 1558-1603 -- Fiction
ISBN 0547739621; 9780547739625
LC 2011045898

In this book by Karen Cushman, set in Elizabethan England, "Will Sparrow, liar and thief, becomes a runaway. On the road, he encounters a series of con artists . . . and learns that others are more adept than he at lying and thieving. Then he reluctantly joins a traveling troupe of 'oddities,' including a dwarf and a cat-faced girl. . . . At last Will is forced to understand that appearances are misleading and that he has been his own worst deceiver." (Publisher's note)

Includes bibliographical references.

Cypess, Leah

Death sworn; by Leah Cypess. Greenwillow Books, an imprint of HarperCollinsPublishers 2014 352 p. (hardback) $17.99
Grades: 7 8 9 10 11 12 **Fic**
1. Fantasy fiction 2. Romance fiction 3. Magic -- Fiction 4. Assassins -- Fiction 5. Love -- Fiction 6. Secrets -- Fiction
ISBN 0062221213; 9780062221216
LC 2013037379

Sequel: Death Marked (2015)

In this book, by Leah Cypress, "when a young sorceress is exiled to teach magic to a clan of assassins, she will find that secrets can be even deadlier than swords. . . . Ileni is losing her magic. And that means she's losing everything: her position as the rising star of her people, her purpose in life, and even the young man she loves. . . . Sent to the assassins' cave, . . . she'll find an ally in Sorin, the deadly young man who could be the assassins' next leader. . . . Sparks--magical and romantic--will fly." (Publisher's note)

"As seventeen-year-old Ileni's magic begins to fade, she's sent to the Black Mountain to tutor assassins in sorcery. With the help of Sorin, her student and assigned protector, she must discover who killed her predecessors before someone kills her. Ileni proves a compelling protagonist, and the blend of romance, assassins, magic, and murder-mystery consistently raises the stakes." Horn Book

Mistwood. Greenwillow Books 2010 304p $16.99
Grades: 7 8 9 10 **Fic**

1. Fantasy fiction 2. Magic -- Fiction 3. Kings and rulers -- Fiction
ISBN 978-0-06-195699-7; 0-06-195699-6
LC 2009-23051

Brought back from the Mistwood to protect the royal family, a girl who has no memory of being a shape-shifter encounters political and magical intrigue as she struggles with her growing feelings for the prince.

"A traditional premise is transformed into a graceful meditation on the ramifications of loyalty, duty and purpose. . . . Astonishing and inspiring." Kirkus

Nightspell. Greenwillow Books 2011 326p $16.99
Grades: 7 8 9 10 **Fic**

1. Ghost stories 2. Dead -- Fiction 3. Sisters -- Fiction 4. Kings and rulers -- Fiction
ISBN 978-0-06-195702-4; 0-06-195702-X
LC 2010012637

Sent by her father, the king of Raellia, who is trying to forge an empire out of warring tribes, Darri arrives in Ghostland and discovers that her sister, whom she planned to rescue, may not want to leave this land where the dead mingle freely with the living.

"Swordfights, blood, and double-dealing pack the pages as this action-filled story races to a surprising conclusion." Booklist

Cyprus, Naomi

Sisters of Glass; by Naomi Cyprus. Harpercollins Childrens Books 2017 377 p. (hardcover) $16.99
Grades: 4 5 6 7 **Fic**

1. Fantasy fiction 2. Magic -- Fiction 3. Sisters -- Fiction 4. Princesses -- Fiction
ISBN 9780062458483; 9780062458476; 0062458477

In this book, by Naomi Cyprus, "Halan is a powerless princess. She is heir to the Magi Kingdom, a blazing desert land ruled by ancient magic. But unlike every royal before her, Halan has no magical powers of her own. Nalah is a powerful pauper. The glassblower's daughter, she lives in the land of New Hadar, where magic is strictly outlawed. But Nalah has a powerful force growing within her—one she can't always control." (Publisher's note)

"First in the Shard series, this romp will hook readers with its appealing tween characters, exotic settings that blend old and modern, and empowering fight between right and wrong." Booklist

Another title in this series is:
Daughters of steel (2018)

D'Adamo, Francesco

Iqbal; a novel. written by Francesco D'Adamo; translated by Ann Leonori. Atheneum Bks. for Young Readers 2003 120p $15.95; pa $4.99
Grades: 5 6 7 8 **Fic**

1. Murder victims 2. Factory workers 3. Pakistan -- Fiction 4. Child labor -- Fiction 5. Children's rights advocates
ISBN 0-689-85445-5; 1-4169-0329-1 pa
LC 2002-153498

Original Italian edition, 2001

A fictionalized account of the Pakistani child who escaped from bondage in a carpet factory and went on to help liberate other children like him before being gunned down at the age of thirteen

"The situation and setting are made clear in this novel. Readers cannot help but be moved by the plight of these youngsters. . . . This readable book will certainly add breadth to most collections." SLJ

D'Lacey, Chris

Dark fire. Orchard Books 2010 567p (The last dragon chronicles) $17.99
Grades: 6 7 8 9 **Fic**

1. Fantasy fiction 2. Dragons -- Fiction
ISBN 978-0-545-10272-8; 0-545-10272-3
Sequel to: The fire eternal
First published 2009 in the United Kingdom

Lucy and the Pennykettle dragons try to find and destroy a drop of dark fire before it is discovered and used to birth a darkling, while in the Arctic, enshrouded in mist, hide dragons that have at last returned to Earth.

Followed by: Fire world

The **fire** ascending; by Chris D'Lacey. 1st Scholastic ed. Orchard Books 2012 560 p. (hardcover) $18.99
Grades: 6 7 8 9 **Fic**

1. Fantasy 2. Magic -- Fiction 3. Dragons -- Fiction 4. Voyages and travels -- Fiction 5. Quests (Expeditions) -- Fiction
ISBN 0545402166; 9780545402163
LC 2012003120

This book is the seventh installment of Chris D'Lacey's Last Dragon Chronicles series. The story follows "a young boy named Agawin. He's raised by a seer and lives near the peak of Kasgarden where the dragon Galen has gone to shed its dying tear. . . . Evil comes in the forms of Sybyl's like Hilde and Gwilanna, then there's the darkling army led by Voss in search of the fraas (sparks emitted from a dying dragon's tear)." (Children's Literature)

The **fire** eternal; [by] Chris d'Lacey. 1st Scholastic ed.; Orchard Books 2008 506p lib bdg $16.99
Grades: 6 7 8 9 **Fic**

1. Dragons -- Fiction 2. Supernatural -- Fiction 3. Arctic regions -- Fiction
ISBN 978-0-545-05163-7 lib bdg; 0-545-05163-0 lib bdg
LC 2007046493

Sequel to Fire star (2007)
First published 2007 in the United Kingdom

As the weather grows wilder and the ice caps melt, Arctic bears starve, dragons awake, the earth goddess Gaia becomes restless, and Alexa, the daughter of best-selling author David Rain, uses her special abilities in an attempt to save the world from the forces of evil.

Fire star; [by] Chris D'Lacey. 1st Scholastic hardcover ed.; Orchard Books 2007 549p $15.99
Grades: 6 7 8 9 **Fic**

1. Bears -- Fiction 2. Dragons -- Fiction 3. Supernatural -- Fiction 4. Arctic regions -- Fiction
ISBN 978-0-439-90185-7; 978-0-439-84582-3 lib bdg
LC 2006018004

Sequel to Icefire (2006)

David Rain is faced with the most perilous task yet when Gwilanna returns, this time determined to resurrect the dragon Gawain on the ice cap of the Tooth of Ragnar, unless David and her friends can stop her.

"The story, with its involving and thought-provoking plot full of clever little dragons, mystical polar bears, and spiritual and ecological aspects, will appeal to many fantasy lovers." SLJ

Followed by The fire eternal (2008)

The **fire** within. Orchard Books 2005 340p $15.99
Grades: 6 7 8 9 **Fic**

1. Dragons -- Fiction 2. Authorship -- Fiction 3. Supernatural -- Fiction

ISBN 0-439-67244-9

LC 2004-58327

When college student David Rain rents a room in an unusual boardinghouse full of clay dragons, he has no idea that they, along with some lively squirrels, will help jumpstart his writing career.

This "has a satisfying domestic reality, spiced with some very unusual dragons." SLJ

Other titles in this series are:
Icefire (2006)
Fire star (2007)
The fire eternal (2008)
Dark fire (2010)
Fire world (2011)

Fire world. Orchard Books 2011 562p (The last dragon chronicles) $18.99
Grades: 6 7 8 9 **Fic**

1. Fantasy fiction 2. Dragons -- Fiction 3. Supernatural -- Fiction 4. Good and evil -- Fiction

ISBN 978-0-545-28368-7; 0-545-28368-X

LC 2010053114

Sequel to: Dark fire

On the planet Co:per:nica, which is a parallel world to that of Crescent Lane, David is twelve years old and is trying to save a firebird that has been turned to evil by the malevolent Ix.

Icefire; [by] Chris D'Lacey. Orchard Books 2006 421p $14.99
Grades: 6 7 8 9 **Fic**

1. Bears -- Fiction 2. Dragons -- Fiction 3. Supernatural -- Fiction 4. Arctic regions -- Fiction

ISBN 0-439-67245-7

LC 2004058329

Sequel to The fire within (2005)

While researching the existence of dragons for an essay that could win him a trip to the Arctic, Chris opens himself to the possibility that a great, ancient treasure exists there, guarded by bears, and that he has some role in its protection.

"Readers will find action and mysteries aplenty in this fantastic tale, as well as a group of appealing dragons who are tricky, heroic, and often charming." SLJ

Followed by Fire star (2007)

Dakin, Glenn

The **Society** of Unrelenting Vigilance; [illustrations by Greg Swearingen] Egmont 2009 300p il (Candle Man) $15.99; lib bdg $18.99
Grades: 4 5 6 7 **Fic**

1. Adventure fiction 2. Superheroes -- Fiction

ISBN 978-1-60684-015-3; 1-60684-015-0; 978-1-60684-047-4 lib bdg; 1-60684-047-9 lib bdg

LC 2009-14035

Thirteen-year-old Theo, who has lived in seclusion his entire life, discovers he is the descendant of the Candle Man, a Victorian vigilante with the ability to melt criminals with a single touch.

This is a "lighthearted, action-driven adventure. . . . With the help of a cast of appealing characters, the nonstop action rolls to a satisfying conclusion." SLJ

Followed by: The Society of Dread (2010)

Dallas, Sandra

The **quilt** walk; by Sandra Dallas. Sleeping Bear Press 2012 213 p. (hardcover) $15.95
Grades: 3 4 5 6 7 **Fic**

1. Oregon Trail 2. Quilts -- Fiction 3. Frontier and pioneer life 4. Historical fiction 5. Quilting -- Fiction 6. Friendship -- Fiction 7. Wagon trains -- Fiction

ISBN 1585368008; 9781585367993; 9781585368006

LC 2012005863

This children's historical story, by Sandra Dallas, begins in "1863 and Emily Blue Hatchett has been told by her father that, come spring, their family will leave their farm . . . in Quincy, Illinois and travel the Overland Trail to a new home in Golden, Colorado. . . . When Emmy s grandmother comes to say goodbye, she gives Emmy a special gift, something to occupy her time along the trail. The journey by wagon train is long and full of hardships." (Publisher's note)

Damico, Gina

Croak; by Gina Damico. Houghton Mifflin Harcourt 2012 311 p. $8.99
Grades: 7 8 9 10 **Fic**

1. Mystery fiction 2. Soul -- Fiction 3. Death -- Fiction 4. Justice -- Fiction 5. Future life -- Fiction

ISBN 9780547608327

LC 2011017125

This book tells the story of "sixteen-year-old bad girl Lex Bartleby [who] is shipped off to her uncle Mort's farm, supposedly to figure out her anger issues with the help of manual labor. Instead, she learns that "farmer" Mort is a reaper of another kind entirely and that, as mayor of Croak, a small collection of Grim Reapers, he will be teaching Lex the family business. Although she initially takes to ferrying souls into the Afterlife with aplomb, Lex begins to question the roles of Reapers as silent witnesses to the world's injustices, especially when their knowledge of people's deaths would allow them to wreak karmic justice upon the murderers and rapists that otherwise get away with their crimes." (Bulletin of the Center for Children's Books)

Rogue; by Gina Damico. Graphia 2013 336 p. (paperback) $8.99
Grades: 8 9 10 **Fic**

1. Future life -- Fiction 2. Grim Reaper (Symbolic character) -- Fiction 3. Death -- Fiction 4. Humorous stories 5. Ghosts -- Fiction

ISBN 0544108841; 9780544108844

LC 2013004154

This book by Gina Damico follows a "band of surly teenage grim reapers risking everything on their mission to save the Afterlife. Uncle Mort's plan to save the Afterlife by enlisting Junior Grims to help destroy the portals that access it is full of risks, loopholes and secrets—and fiery-tempered, impulsive Lex is the plan's unstable lynchpin." (Kirkus Reviews)

Scorch; Gina Damico. Houghton Mifflin Harcourt 2012 332 p. (paperback) $8.99
Grades: 7 8 9 10 **Fic**

1. Fantasy fiction 2. Death -- Fiction 3. Humorous stories 4.

Future life -- Fiction
ISBN 0547624573; 9780547624570

LC 2012014799

In this novel by Gina Damico "Lex is a full-time teenage grim reaper -- but now has the bizarre ability to Damn souls. . . . [S]he and her friends embark on a wild road trip to DeMyse. Though this sparkling desert oasis is full of luxuries and amusements, it feels like a prison to Lex. Her best chance at escape would be to stop all the senseless violence that she caused—but how can she do that from DeMyse, where the Grims seem mysteriously oblivious to the bloodshed?" (Publisher's note)

Daneshvari, Gitty

Class is not dismissed! [illustrations by Carrie Gifford] Little, Brown and Company 2010 307p il $16.99

Grades: 4 5 6 **Fic**

1. School stories 2. Phobias -- Fiction
ISBN 978-0-316-03328-2; 0-316-03328-6

LC 2010006889

Sequel to: School of Fear (2009)

Thirteen-year-olds Madeleine, Theo, and Lulu, fourteen-year-old Garrison, and ten-year-old new "contestant" Hyacinth, must face their phobias and join forces to learn who is stealing wigs and pageant trophies from the School of Fear.

"Filled with an eclectic, and often eccentric, cast of characters, this sequel uses the wry humor and outrageous situations that characterized the first book and makes for an entertaining read." SLJ

School of Fear; illustrated by Carrie Gifford. Little, Brown Books for Young Readers 2009 339p il $15.99

Grades: 4 5 6 **Fic**

1. School stories 2. Phobias -- Fiction
ISBN 978-0-316-03326-8; 0-316-03326-X

LC 2008051309

Twelve-year-olds Madeleine, Theo, and Lulu, and thirteen-year-old Garrison, are sent to a remote Massachusetts school to overcome their phobias, but tragedy strikes and the quartet must work together—with no adult assistance—to face their fears.

This is "tautly paced, spine-tingling and quite funny." Publ Wkly

Followed by: Class is not dismissed! (2010)

Danziger, Paula

The **cat** ate my gymsuit; [by] Paula Danziger. 30th anniversary edition; G.P. Putnam's Sons 2004 151p $15.99; pa $5.99

Grades: 4 5 6 7 **Fic**

1. School stories 2. Teachers -- Fiction
ISBN 0-399-24307-0; 0-14-240654-6 pa

LC 2004001892

A reissue of the title first published 1974 by Delacorte Press

When the unconventional English teacher who helped her conquer many of her feelings of insecurity is fired, thirteen-year-old Marcy Lewis uses her new found courage to campaign for the teacher's reinstatement.

"Paula Danziger's compassionate and accurate portrayal of a young girl struggling to find her own voice rings as true today as it did 30 years ago. A full cast brings this modern American classic of teenage angst to life with humor and pathos." SLJ

Darrows, Eva

Dead little mean girl; Eva Darrows. Harlequin Books 2017 250 p. (hardcover) $18.99

Grades: 7 8 9 10 **Fic**

1. Stepsisters -- Fiction 3. Teenage girls -- Fiction 4. Death -- Fiction 5. Grief -- Fiction 6. Bullying -- Fiction
ISBN 0373212410; 9780373212415

LC 2017296991

In this book, by Eva Darrows, "a proud geek girl, Emma loves her quiet life on the outskirts. . . . When her nightmare of a new stepsister moves into the bedroom next door, her world is turned upside down. Quinn is a queen bee with a nasty streak who destroys anyone who gets in her way. . . . Emma wants nothing more than to get this girl out of her life, but when Quinn dies suddenly, Emma realizes there was more to her stepsister than anyone ever realized." (Publisher's note)

"Darrows' (The Awesome, 2015) new YA novel is a seriously smart, funny, and empathetic look at how someone's manufactured exterior might be hiding inner turmoil, and ultimately advocates for looking past labels and categories." Booklist

Dasgupta, Sayantani

Game of stars; Sayantani DasGupta ; illustrations by Vivienne To. Scholastic Press 2019 384 p. $17.99

Grades: 4 5 6 7 **Fic**

1. Magic -- Fiction 2. Adventure stories 3. Princesses -- Fiction 4. East Indian Americans -- Fiction 5. Adventure and adventurers -- Fiction 6. East Indian Americans -- Fiction
ISBN 9781338185737

LC 2018035373

In this book in the Kiranmala and the Kingdom Beyond series, by Sayantani DasGupta, illustrated by Vivienne To, "it's been weeks since . . . [twelve-year-old Kiranmala] last heard from her friends in the Kingdom Beyond, the alternate dimension where she was born as an Indian princess. But after a call to action over an interdimensional television station and a visit with some all-seeing birds, Kiran decides that she has to once again return to her homeland." (Publisher's note)

The **serpent's** secret; Sayantani DasGupta. Scholastic Press 2018 368 p. (Kiranmala and the Kingdom Beyond) $17.99

Grades: 4 5 6 7 **Fic**

1. Fantasy 2. Magic -- Fiction 3. Adventure stories 4. Princesses -- Fiction 5. Missing persons -- Fiction 6. East Indian Americans -- Fiction
ISBN 1338185705; 9781338185706

LC 2017044381

In this novel in the Kiranmala and the Kingdom Beyond series, by Sayantani DasGupta, "Kiranmala is just a regular sixth grader living in Parsippany, New Jersey . . . until her parents mysteriously vanish and a drooling rakkhosh demon slams through her kitchen, determined to eat her alive. Turns out there might be some truth to her parents' fantastical stories--like how Kiranmala is a real Indian princess and how she comes from a secret place not of this world." (Publisher's note)

Another title in this series is:
The game of stars (2018)

Dashner, James

The **death** cure. Delacorte Press 2011 325p $17.99; lib bdg $20.99

Grades: 7 8 9 10 **Fic**

1. Science fiction
ISBN 978-0-385-73877-4; 0-385-73877-3; 978-0-385-90746-0 lib bdg; 0-385-90746-X lib bdg

LC 2011022236

Sequel to: The scorch trials (2010)

As the third Trial draws to a close, Thomas and some of his cohorts manage to escape from WICKED, their memories having been restored, only to face new dangers as WICKED claims to be trying to protect the human race from the deadly FLARE virus.

"Dashner again displays his mastery of the action sequence, making readers turn pages even as they become further invested in the well-developed characters. Heart pounding to the very last moment." Kirkus

The **kill** order; James Dashner. Delacorte Press 2012 329 p. $17.99

Grades: 7 8 9 10 11 12 **Fic**

1. Viruses -- Fiction 2. Survival skills -- Fiction 3. Natural disasters -- Fiction 4. Science fiction 5. Survival -- Fiction 6. Virus diseases -- Fiction

ISBN 9780307979117; 9780375990823; 9780385742887; 0385742886

LC 2012016790

In this book by James Dashner "sun flares hit the earth and mankind fell to disease. Mark and Trina were there when it happened, and they survived. But surviving the sun flares was easy compared to what came next. Now a disease of rage and lunacy races across the eastern United States, and there's something suspicious about its origin. Worse yet, it's mutating, and all evidence suggests that it will bring humanity to its knees." (Publisher's note)

★ The **maze** runner. Delacorte Press 2009 375p $16.99; lib bdg $19.99

Grades: 7 8 9 10 11 12 **Fic**

1. Science fiction 2. Amnesia -- Fiction

ISBN 0-385-73794-7; 0-385-90702-8 lib bdg; 978-0-385-73794-4; 978-0-385-90702-6 lib bdg

LC 2009-1345

Sixteen-year-old Thomas wakes up with no memory in the middle of a maze and realizes he must work with the community in which he finds himself if he is to escape.

"With a fast-paced narrative steadily answering the myriad questions that arise and an ever-increasing air of tension, Dashner's suspenseful adventure will keep readers guessing until the very end." Publ Wkly

Other titles in this series are:

The scorch trials (2010)

The death cure (2011)

The **scorch** trials. Delacorte Press 2010 361p $17.99; lib bdg $20.99

Grades: 7 8 9 10 11 12 **Fic**

1. Science fiction 2. Science -- Experiments -- Fiction

ISBN 978-0-385-73875-0; 0-385-73875-7; 978-0-385-90745-3 lib bdg; 0-385-90745-1 lib bdg

Sequel to: The maze runner (2009)

After surviving horrific conditions in the Maze, Thomas is entrapped, along with nineteen other boys, in a scientific experiment designed to observe their responses and gather data believed to be essential for the survival of the human race.

"Taut and bleak, continually intriguing and surprising, this is a solid sequel that keeps both Thomas and readers wondering what is really going on. Hooked readers will hope they won't have to wait long for the answers that have been promised in the next installment." Kirkus

Daud, Somaiya

Mirage; Somaiya Daud. Flatiron Books 2018 311 p. illustrations, map (hardback) $18.99

Grades: 8 9 10 11 12 **Fic**

1. Princesses -- Fiction 2. Kidnapping victims -- Fiction 3. Impostors and imposture -- Fiction

ISBN 9781250126429; 9781250126443; 9781250126436

LC 2018013549

"Amani is a dreamer. She dreams of what life was like before the occupation; . . . she dreams of receiving a sign from Dihya that one day, she, too, will have adventure, and travel beyond her isolated home. But when adventure comes for Amani, it is not what she expects: she is kidnapped by the regime and taken in secret to the royal palace, where she discovers that she is nearly identical to the cruel half-Vathek Princess Maram." (Publisher's note)

Davies, Nicola, 1958-

The **Promise**; Nicola Davies, illustrated by Laura Carlin. Candlewick Press 2014 40 p. $16.99; paperback $8.99

Grades: K 1 2 3 4 **Fic**

1. Girls -- Fiction 2. Life change events -- Fiction 3. Acorns -- Fiction 4. Promises -- Fiction

ISBN 0763666335; 9780763666330; 9780763693039

LC 2013934311

In this children's book by Nicola Davies, illustrated by Laura Carlin, "on a mean street in a mean, broken city, a young girl tries to snatch an old woman's bag. But the frail old woman, holding on with the strength of heroes, says the thief can't have it without giving something in return: the promise. It is the beginning of a journey that will change the thieving girl's life--and a chance to change the world, for good." (Publisher's note)

"A girl, with no name and of no particular age, describes a place as gritty as its people are hard: When I was young, I lived in a city that was mean and hard and ugly. She lives by stealing, and one day, she wrestles with an old woman for her bag, which the lady finally lets go of, with a condition: If you promise to plant them...Bright hues and plenty of greenery enliven the pages and lift the spirits. Lots to look at, think about, and discuss here." Booklist

Davis, Mandy

Superstar; Mandy Davis. HarperCollins 2017 320 p. (hardcover) $16.99

Grades: 4 5 6 7 **Fic**

1. Autistic children 2. Friendship in children -- Fiction 3. Bullying -- Fiction 4. Friendship -- Fiction

ISBN 9780062377791; 9780062377777

LC 2016939551

This book, by Mandy Davis, "follows space-obsessed Lester Musselbaum as he experiences the challenges of his first days of public school: making friends, facing bullies, finding his 'thing,' and accidentally learning of his autism-spectrum diagnosis. . . . A touching peek into the life of a sensitive autism-spectrum boy facing the everydayness of elementary school." (Publisher's note)

"This unsentimental portrait of an endearing and memorable protagonist offers powerful insight into living with autism." Pub Wkly

Davis, Tanita S.

Mare's war. Alfred A. Knopf 2009 341p $16.99; lib bdg $19.99

Grades: 7 8 9 10 **Fic**

1. Alabama -- Fiction 2. Sisters -- Fiction 3. Grandmothers -- Fiction 4. African Americans -- Fiction 5. Automobile travel -- Fiction 6. World War, 1939-1945 -- Fiction 7. United States -- Army -- Women's Army Corps -- Fiction

ISBN 978-0-375-85714-0; 0-375-85714-1; 978-0-375-95714-7 lib bdg; 0-375-95714-6 lib bdg

LC 2008-33744

ALA EMIERT Coretta Scott King Author Award Honor Book (2010)

Teens Octavia and Tali learn about strength, independence, and courage when they are forced to take a car trip with their grandmother, who tells about growing up Black in 1940s Alabama and serving in Europe during World War II as a member of the Women's Army Corps.

"The parallel travel narratives are masterfully managed, with postcards from Octavia and Tali to the folks back home in San Francisco signaling the shift between 'then' and 'now.' Absolutely essential reading." Kirkus

De Fombelle, Timothée, 1973-

The **book** of Pearl; Timothee de Fombelle ; translated by Sarah Ardizzone and Sam Gordon. Candlewick Press 2018 355 p. (hardcover) $17.99

Grades: 7 8 9 10 11 12 **Fic**

1. Fairy tales 2. Memory -- Fiction 3. Teenagers -- Fiction 4. Paris (France) -- History -- 1870-1940 -- Fiction 5. Europe -- History -- 1918-1945 -- Fiction

ISBN 9780763691264; 9780763694081; 0763691267

In this book by Timothée de Fombelle, "Joshua Pearl comes from a world that we no longer believe in -- a world of fairy tale. He knows that his great love waits for him there, but he is stuck in an . . . old-world marshmallow shop in Paris on the eve of World War II. As his memories begin to fade, Joshua seeks out strange objects: tiny fragments of tales that have already been told, trinkets that might possibly help him prove his own story before his love is lost forever." (Publisher's note)

"A luminous, haunting, intriguingly intricate modern fairy tale." Kirkus

Toby alone; translated by Sarah Ardizzone; illustrated by Francois Place. Candlewick Press 2009 384p il $17.99; pa $8.99

Grades: 5 6 7 8 **Fic**

1. Fantasy fiction 2. Trees -- Fiction

ISBN 0-7636-4181-2; 0-7636-4815-9 pa; 978-0-7636-4181-8; 978-0-7636-4815-2 pa

Original French edition 2006

Toby is just one and a half millimeters tall, and he's the most wanted person in his world of the great oak Tree. When Toby's father discovers that the Tree is alive, he realizes that exploiting it could do damage to their world. Refusing to reveal the secret to an enraged community, Toby's parents have been imprisoned. Only Toby has managed to escape, but for how long?

"The impressive debut novel from French playwright de Fombelle deftly weaves mature political commentary, broad humor and some subtle satire into a thoroughly enjoyable adventure." Publ Wkly

Followed by Toby and the secrets of the tree (2010)

Toby and the secrets of the tree; illustrated by Fran¿cois Place; translated by Sarah Ardizzone. Candlewick Press 2010 414p il $16.99

Grades: 5 6 7 8 **Fic**

1. Fantasy fiction 2. Trees -- Fiction

ISBN 978-0-7636-4655-4; 0-7636-4655-5

LC 2009014833

Sequel to: Toby alone (2009)

Thirteen-year-old Toby's tiny world is under greater threat than ever as Leo Blue holds Elisha prisoner while hunting the Grass People and anyone who stands in the way of his devastating plans for the oak Tree in which they all live, but this time Toby is not alone.

"Place's pen-and-ink illustrations are scattered generously throughout and enhance the overall quirkiness. . . . This interesting piece of eco-fantasy provides a satisfying conclusion for those who enjoyed the first book." SLJ

Vango; between sky and earth. Timothee de Fombelle. Candlewick Press 2014 432 p. illustrations hc $17.99

Grades: 9 10 11 12 **Fic**

1. Adventure fiction 2. Clergy -- Fiction 3. Historical fiction 4. Friendship -- Fiction 5. False accusation -- Fiction

ISBN 9780763671969; 0763671967

LC 2013955696

In this book, by Timothée de Fombelle, translated by Sarah Ardizzone, "minutes from joining the priesthood in 1934, Vango, who was found washed ashore on a tiny Italian island as a toddler, must suddenly avoid both arrest and a simultaneous assassination attempt. Establishing his innocence while on the run across Europe requires untangling his mysterious past." (Kirkus Reviews)

"de Fombelle has written a brilliant, wonderfully exciting story of flight and pursuit, filled with colorful characters and head-scratching mystery. As the novel proceeds, the suspense is ratcheted up to breathtaking levels as the boy remains only one step ahead of his relentless pursuers." Booklist

De Goldi, Kate

The **10** p.m. question. Candlewick Press 2010 245p $15.99

Grades: 6 7 8 9 10 **Fic**

1. School stories 2. Worry -- Fiction 3. Agoraphobia -- Fiction 4. Family life -- Fiction 5. New Zealand -- Fiction 6. Eccentrics and eccentricities -- Fiction

ISBN 978-0-7636-4939-5; 0-7636-4939-2

LC 2009-49726

First published 2008 in New Zealand

Twelve-year-old Frankie Parsons has a quirky family, a wonderful best friend, and a head full of worrying questions that he shares with his mother each night, but when free-spirited Sydney arrives at school with questions of her own, Frankie is forced to face the ultimate ten p.m. question.

"De Goldi's novel is an achingly poignant, wryly comic story of early adolescence. . . . Nearly every character . . . is a loving, talented, unforgettable eccentric whose dialogue, much like De Goldi's richly phrased narration, combines heart-stopping tenderness with perfectly timed, deliciously zany humor." Booklist

De la Peña, Matt

The **living**; Matt de la Peña. Delacorte Press 2013 320 p.

Grades: 8 9 10 11 12 **Fic**

1. Cruise ships -- Fiction 2. Natural disasters -- Fiction 3. Survival after airplane accidents, shipwrecks, etc. -- Fiction 4. Diseases -- Fiction 5. Survival -- Fiction 6. Mexican Americans -- Fiction

ISBN 9780375989919; 9780385741200

LC 2012050778

Pura Belpre Author Award (2014)

In this book, by Matt de la Peña, "Shy took [a] summer job to make some money. In a few months on a luxury cruise liner, he'll rake in the tips and be able to help his mom and sister out with the bills. . . . But everything changes when the Big One hits. Shy's only weeks out at sea when an earthquake more massive than ever before recorded hits California, and his life is forever changed. The earthquake is only the first disaster. Suddenly it's a fight to survive for those left living." (Publisher's note)

"Shy Espinoza's summer job on Paradise Cruise Lines is, literally, a disaster. A series of catastrophes befall the cruise and eventually threaten civilization as he knows it; Shy finds himself on a life raft in the Pacific Ocean with a racist "spoiled-ass blond chick." Readers wanting a fast-paced survival story with plenty of action won't mind the over-the-top plot." (Horn Book)

Mexican whiteboy. Delacorte Press 2008 249p $15.99; lib bdg $18.99

Grades: 8 9 10 11 12 **Fic**

1. Cousins -- Fiction 2. California -- Fiction 3. Mexican Americans -- Fiction 4. Racially mixed people -- Fiction

ISBN 978-0-385-73310-6; 0-385-73310-0; 978-0-385-90329-5 lib bdg; 0-385-90329-4 lib bdg

LC 2007-32302

Sixteen-year-old Danny searches for his identity amidst the confusion of being half-Mexican and half-white while spending a summer with his cousin and new friends on the baseball fields and back alleys of San Diego County, California.

"The author juggles his many plotlines well, and the portrayal of Danny's friends and neighborhood is rich and lively." Booklist

We were here. Delacorte Press 2009 357p $17.99; lib bdg $20.99

Grades: 7 8 9 10 11 12 **Fic**

1. Brothers -- Fiction 2. California -- Fiction 3. Friendship -- Fiction 4. Runaway teenagers -- Fiction 5. Juvenile delinquency -- Fiction

ISBN 978-0-385-73667-1; 0-385-73667-3; 978-0-385-90622-7 lib bdg; 0-385-90622-6 lib bdg

LC 2008-44568

Haunted by the event that sentences him to time in a group home, Miguel breaks out with two unlikely companions and together they begin their journey down the California coast hoping to get to Mexico and a new life.

"The contemporary survival adventure will keep readers hooked, as will the tension that builds from the story's secrets." Booklist

De Lint, Charles

The **blue** girl; Charles de Lint. Viking 2004 368p hardcover o.p. pa $7.99

Grades: 7 8 9 10 **Fic**

1. Ghost stories 2. School stories 3. Fairies -- Fiction

ISBN 0-670-05924-2; 0-14-240545-0 pa

LC 2004-19051

New at her high school, Imogene enlists the help of her introverted friend Maxine and the ghost of a boy who haunts the school after receiving warnings through her dreams that soul-eaters are threatening her life

"The book combines the turmoil of high school intertwined with rich, detailed imagery drawn from traditional folklore and complex characters with realistic relationships. . . . This book is not just another ghost story, but a novel infused with the true sense of wonder and magic that is De Lint at his best. It is strongly recommended." Voice Youth Advocates

Deangelis, Camille

The **boy** from tomorrow; Camille DeAngelis. Amberjack Pub. 2018 268 p. (hardcover) $15.99

Grades: 4 5 6 7 **Fic**

1. Psychics -- Fiction 2. Friendship -- Fiction 3. Spiritualism -- Fiction

ISBN 9781944995614; 9781944995621

LC 2017954150

In this book, by Camille DeAngelis, "Josie and Alec both live at 444 Sparrow Street. They sleep in the same room, but they've never laid eyes on each other. . . . The children meet through a hand-painted talking board--Josie in 1915, Alec in 2015--and form a friendship across the century that separates them. But a chain of events leave Josie and her little sister Cass trapped in the house and afraid for their safety, and Alec must find out what's going to happen to them." (Publisher's note)

Deebs, Tracy

Tempest rising. Walker & Co. 2011 344p $16.99

Grades: 8 9 10 11 12 **Fic**

1. War stories 2. Mermaids and mermen -- Fiction

ISBN 978-0-8027-2231-7; 0-8027-2231-8

LC 2010-34339

On her seventeenth birthday, Tempest must decide whether to remain a human and live on land or submit to her mermaid half, like her mother before her, and enter into a long-running war under the sea.

"Tempest is a gutsy, independent heroine with more than enough agency to save herself from danger. . . . For readers wanting a solid, familiar, but slightly different paranormal romance." Booklist

Defelice, Cynthia

Fort; Cynthia DeFelice. Farrar, Straus & Giroux 2015 208 p. (hardback) $16.99; paperback $6.99

Grades: 4 5 6 7 **Fic**

1. Summer -- Fiction 2. Bullies -- Fiction 3. Friendship -- Fiction 4. Bullying -- Fiction 5. Great-aunts -- Fiction 6. Best friends -- Fiction 7. Great-uncles -- Fiction

ISBN 0374324271; 9780374324278; 9781250079732; 9780374324292

LC 2014040167

This book by Cynthia DeFelice "is told as a flashback in the 'What I Did on My Summer Vacation' essay that" narrator Wyatt "has no intention of showing to a teacher." (Booklist) "When older boys tear apart the fort where they have been enjoying a wonderful summer, Wyatt and Augie team up with another bullied kid to exact revenge, with unexpected consequences." (Publisher's note)

"Stuffed full of clever pranks and summertime nostalgia, this is a story of kindness and adventure, and a rare breed in the middle-grade canon that doesn't rely on cheap humor to hold attention. A boisterous and poignant coming-of-age tale." Booklist

★ The **ghost** of Fossil Glen; by Cynthia DeFelice. Farrar, Straus & Giroux 1998 167p (Ghost Mysteries) OP; pa $7.99

Grades: 4 5 6 **Fic**

1. Ghost stories

ISBN 0-374-31787-9; 9780312602130 pa; 9781429930536

LC 97-33230

"Strange events begin when a calm, unknown voice prevents Allie from panicking and falling from a dangerous cliff while fossil hunting. Then, an old journal mysteriously appears in her mailbox. Allie often feels a presence nearby and dreams of a girl falling from the cliff. She then discovers the grave marker of an 11-year-old girl who was missing and presumed dead in 1994. Because of her reputation for telling stories, Allie cannot convince anyone to believe her except her longtime friend and fellow fossil hunter, Dub. Driven to pursue the mystery, Allie finds an old diary that provides her with facts about the girl's death. Foolishly, she reveals what she knows and endangers her own life. . . . Grades four to six." (SLJ)

"Sixth-grader Allie Nichols encounters the ghost of Lucy Stiles and becomes involved with Lucy's unsolved death, eventually finding proof that Lucy was murdered." Horn Book Guide

Other titles in this series are:

The ghost and Mrs. Hobbs (2001)

The ghost of Cutler Creek (2004)

The ghost of Poplar Point (2007)

Defoe, Daniel

Robinson Crusoe; edited with an introduction by Thomas Keymer and notes by Thomas Keymer and James Kelly. New ed.; Oxford University Press 2009 lii, 321p il (Oxford world's classics) pa $7.95

Grades: 8 9 10 11 12 Adult **Fic**

1. Adventure fiction 2. Islands -- Fiction 3. Survival after airplane accidents, shipwrecks, etc. -- Fiction
ISBN 978-0-19-955397-6

LC 2006-26022

First published 1719

"A minutely circumstantial account of the hero's shipwreck and escape to an uninhabited island, and the methodical industry whereby he makes himself a comfortable home. The story is founded on the actual experiences of Alexander Selkirk, who spent four years on the island of Juan Fernandez in the early 18th century." Lenrow. Reader's Guide to Prose Fic

Delaney, Joseph, 1945-

The **ghost** prison; Joseph Delaney. Sourcebooks Fire 2013 112 p. (hc : alk. paper) $12.99; paperback $5.99

Grades: 4 5 6 7 8 **Fic**

1. Horror fiction 2. Prisons -- Fiction 3. Horror stories 4. Ghosts -- Fiction 5. Orphans -- Fiction 6. Supernatural -- Fiction
ISBN 1402293186; 9781402293184; 9781402293207; 9781402293191; 9781492601746

LC 2013017898

This novella is set in the same universe as Joseph Delaney's Last Apprentice series. The story "is narrated by orphan Billy Calder, who is apprehensive about the new job he has landed: helping guard an infamously haunted prison on the night shift. The ghosts and dangers turn out to be all too real, as Billy learns about the prison's bloody history and has a life-altering encounter one night while on the job." (Publishers Weekly)

A **new** darkness; 1 Joseph Delaney. Greenwillow Books, an imprint of HarperCollinsPublishers 2014 352 p. 22 cm (Starblade Chronicles) (hardback) $17.99

Grades: 7 8 9 10 **Fic**

1. Horror fiction 2. Witches -- Fiction 3. Monsters -- Fiction 4. Apprentices -- Fiction 5. Supernatural -- Fiction 6. Horror stories
ISBN 0062334530; 9780062334534

LC 2014011963

"Tom Ward is the Spook, the one person who can defend the county from bloodthirsty creatures of the dark. But he's only seventeen, and his apprenticeship was cut short when his master died in battle. . . . [F] ifteen-year-old . . . Jenny . . . is a seventh daughter of a seventh daughter, and she wants to be Tom's first apprentice. . . . Together, Tom and Jenny will uncover the grave danger heading straight toward the county." (Publisher's note)

"A plethora of action involving ghastly creatures, sword fights, and magic coupled with just enough backstory and description make this novel engaging enough to keep even the most reluctant reader turning pages until the end. Tom's story has a doozy of a cliff-hanger that is sure to bring teens back for more." SLJ

Other titles in this series are:
The dark army (2016)
Spook's dark assassin (2017)

★ **Revenge** of the witch; illustrations by Patrick Arrasmith. Greenwillow Bks. 2005 344p il (The last apprentice) $14.99; lib bdg $15.89; pa $7.99

Grades: 5 6 7 8 **Fic**

1. Witches -- Fiction 2. Supernatural -- Fiction
ISBN 0-06-076618-2; 0-06-076619-0 lib bdg; 0-06-076620-4 pa

LC 2004-54003

Young Tom, the seventh son of a seventh son, starts work as an apprentice for the village spook, whose job is to protect ordinary folk from "ghouls, boggarts, and all manner of wicked beasties"

"Delaney grabs readers by the throat and gives them a good shake in a smartly crafted story. . . . This is a gristly thriller. . . . Yet the twisted horror is amply buffered by an exquisitely normal young hero, matter-of-fact prose, and a workaday normalcy." Booklist

Other titles in this series are:
Curse of the bane (2006)
Night of the soul-stealer (2007)
Attack of the fiend (2008)
Wrath of the Bloodeye (2008)
Clash of the demons (2009)
Rise of the huntress (2010)
Rage of the fallen (2011)
Grimalkin, the witch assassin (2012)
Lure of the dead (2012)
Slither (2013)
I am Alice (2013)
Fury of the seventh son (2014)

Dellinger, Paul

Fuzzy; by Tom Angleberger and Paul Dellinger. Amulet Books 2016 272 p. paperback $8.99; (hardback) $14.95

Grades: 4 5 6 7 **Fic**

1. Robots -- Fiction 2. Schools -- Fiction 3. Secrets -- Fiction 4. Middle schools -- Fiction
ISBN 9781419729683; 9781613120484; 9781419721229

LC 2016012399

In this book by Tom Angleberger and Paul Dellinger "when Max—Maxine Zelaster—befriends her new robot classmate Fuzzy, part of Vanguard One Middle School's new Robot Integration Program, she helps him learn everything he needs to know about surviving middle school—the good, the bad, and the really, really, ugly. Little do they know that surviving seventh grade is going to become a true matter of life and death, because Vanguard has an evil presence at its heart." (Publisher's note)

"The result is a smart, sci-fi page-turner that will grab kids' imagination and appeal to their conscience and sense of humor." Booklist

Delsol, Wendy

Stork. Candlewick Press 2010 357p $15.99; pa $8.99

Grades: 7 8 9 10 **Fic**

1. School stories 2. Minnesota -- Fiction 3. Supernatural -- Fiction
ISBN 978-0-7636-4844-2; 0-7636-4844-2; 978-0-7636-5687-4 pa; 0-7636-5687-9 pa

LC 2009-51357

After her parents' divorce, Katla and her mother move from Los Angeles to Norse Falls, Minnesota, where Kat immediately alienates two boys at her high school and, improbably, discovers a kinship with a mysterious group of elderly women—the Icelandic Stork Society—who "deliver souls."

"This snappy, lighthearted supernatural romance blends Norse mythology and contemporary issues with an easy touch." Booklist

Other titles in this series are:
Frost (2011)
Flock (2012).

Dennard, Susan

Something strange and deadly; Susan Dennard. 1st ed. Harpercollins Childrens Books 2012 388 p. (hardback) $17.99; (paperback) $9.99

Grades: 7 8 9 10 11 12 **Fic**

1. Fairs 2. Ghost stories 3. Zombies -- Fiction 4. Horror stories 5. Dead -- Fiction 6. Magic -- Fiction 7. Brothers and sisters -- Fiction 8. Philadelphia (Pa.) -- History -- 19th century -- Fiction

ISBN 0062083260; 9780062083265; 9780062083272

LC 2011042114

Author Susan Dennard's protagonist Eleanor Fitt "and her dear Mama have just about run out of funds, and she misses [her brother] Elijah terribly [while he is on a] . . . three-year odyssey abroad. So when . . . he's been detained, she is mightily distressed. The next day, the determined teen is off for some help from the Spirit-Hunters. . . . Her can-do attitude finds her at one point systematically disabling a throng of zombies by smashing their kneecaps with her parasol." (Kirkus Reviews)

Other titles in this series are:

A darkness strange and lovely (2013)

Strange and ever after (2014)

Truthwitch; by Susan Dennard. St. Martin's Press 2016 416 p. (The Witchlands) $18.99

Grades: 8 9 10 11 12 **Fic**

1. Fantasy fiction 2. Witches -- Fiction 3. Friendship -- Fiction

ISBN 0765379287; 9780765379283

LC 2015031484

In this book, by Susan Dennard, "Safiya is a Truthwitch, able to discern truth from lie. . . . Iseult, a Threadwitch, can see the invisible ties that bind and entangle the lives around her--but she cannot see the bonds that touch her own heart. Her unlikely friendship with Safi has taken her from life as an outcast into one of of reckless adventure, where she is a cool, wary balance to Safi's hotheaded impulsiveness." (Publisher's note)

"A great choice for fans of fantasy adventure and strong female characters." SLJ

Other titles in this series are:

Windwitch (2017)

Deracine, Anat

Driving by starlight; Anat Deracine. Godwin Books 2018 280 p. (hardcover) $17.99

Grades: 8 9 10 11 12 **Fic**

1. Women -- Fiction 2. Friendship -- Fiction 3. Teenage girls -- Fiction 4. Saudi Arabia -- Fiction 5. Best friends -- Fiction 6. Women -- Saudi Arabia -- Fiction 7. Teenagers -- Saudi Arabia -- Fiction

ISBN 9781250133427; 9781250133434

LC 2017957736

In this novel, by Anat Deracine, "sixteen-year-olds Leena and Mishie are best friends. They delight in small rebellions against the Saudi cultural police--secret Western clothing, forbidden music, flirtations. But Leena wants college, independence--she wants a different life. Though her story is specific to her world . . . , ultimately it's a story about friendship, family, and freedom that transcends cultural differences." (Publisher's note)

"The fast-paced narrative and unexpected twists make for an engaging yet educational novel with a powerful message about the complexities of being a woman in a man's world." Kirkus

Derting, Kimberly

★ The **body** finder. Harper 2009 329p $16.99

Grades: 7 8 9 10 11 12 **Fic**

1. Mystery fiction 2. Dead -- Fiction 3. Supernatural -- Fiction 4. Extrasensory perception -- Fiction

ISBN 978-0-06-177981-7; 0-06-177981-4

LC 2009-39675

"Violet Ambrose can find dead bodies. Their aura of sound, color, or even taste imprints itself on their murderers, and Violet's extrasensory perception picks up on those elements. . . . Derting has written a suspenseful mystery and sensual love story that will captivate readers who enjoy authentic high-school settings, snappy dialogue, sweet romance, and heart-stopping drama." Booklist

Followed by: Desires of the dead (2011)

Desires of the dead. HarperCollins 2011 358p $16.99

Grades: 7 8 9 10 **Fic**

1. School stories 2. Homicide -- Fiction 3. Friendship -- Fiction 4. Supernatural -- Fiction 5. Washington (State) -- Fiction 6. Extrasensory perception -- Fiction 7. United States -- Federal Bureau of Investigation -- Fiction

ISBN 978-0-06-177984-8; 0-06-177984-9

LC 2010017838

Sequel to: The body finder (2010)

Sixteen-year-old Violet Ambrose's ability to find murder victims and their killers draws the attention of the FBI just as her relationship with Jay, her best-friend-turned-boyfriend, heats up.

"The author paces the story beautifully, weaving together several story lines as she inches up to the final, desperate scene. . . . Imaginative, convincing and successful suspense." Kirkus

The **last** echo; Kimberly Derting. Harper 2012 360 p. (hbk.) $17.99

Grades: 7 8 9 10 11 12 **Fic**

1. Romance fiction 2. Parapsychology -- Fiction 3. Serial killers -- Fiction 4. Dead -- Fiction 5. Schools -- Fiction 6. Friendship -- Fiction 7. Best friends -- Fiction 8. High schools -- Fiction 9. Serial murders -- Fiction 10. Psychic ability -- Fiction 11. Washington (State) -- Fiction

ISBN 0062082191; 9780062082190

LC 2011044633

Sequel to: Desires of the dead (2011)

This book, "the third installment of the Body Finder series," begins with protagonist Violet "working for a secret agency that specializes in using paranormal powers to fight crime. . . . She still loves her normal boyfriend Jay, so she worries about the strong physical response she feels whenever she touches Rafe, a member of the team. Meanwhile, Violet doesn't know she's become the target of a terrifying serial killer." (Kirkus Reviews)

"As always, this author writes a gripping tale... Personalities come across quite strongly, as several of the characters tend toward the eccentric." Kirkus

The **pledge**. Margaret K. McElderry Books 2011 323p $16.99

Grades: 7 8 9 10 **Fic**

1. Fantasy fiction 2. Ability -- Fiction 3. Social classes -- Fiction 4. Language and languages -- Fiction

ISBN 978-1-4424-2201-8; 1-4424-2201-7; 978-1-4424-2202-5 e-book

LC 2010053773

In a dystopian kingdom where the classes are separated by the languages they speak, Charlaina 'Charlie' Hart has a secret gift that is revealed when she meets a mysterious young man named Max.

Derting "keeps her story consistently engaging through vivid description and brisk pacing. . . . Great suspense from a prolific new writer with a vibrant imagination." Kirkus

Despain, Bree

The **dark** Divine. Egmont USA 2010 372p $17.99; lib bdg $20.99

Grades: 7 8 9 10 11 **Fic**

1. School stories 2. Minnesota -- Fiction 3. Family life -- Fiction 4. Supernatural -- Fiction 5. Christian life -- Fiction

ISBN 978-1-60684-057-3; 1-60684-057-6; 978-1-60684-065-8 lib bdg; 1-60684-065-7 lib bdg

LC 2009-18680

Grace Divine, almost seventeen, learns a dark secret when her childhood friend—practically a brother—returns, upsetting her pastor-father and the rest of her family, around the time strange things are happening in and near their small Minnesota town.

"Despain raises complex issues of responsibility and forgiveness and offers no easy answers. Atmospheric and compelling." Booklist

Followed by: The lost saint (2010)

Dessen, Sarah

★ **Along** for the ride; a novel. Viking 2009 383p $19.99

Grades: 7 8 9 10 **Fic**

1. Divorce -- Fiction 2. Infants -- Fiction 3. Stepfamilies -- Fiction 4. Dating (Social customs) -- Fiction

ISBN 978-0-670-01194-0; 0-670-01194-0

LC 2009-5661

When Auden impulsively goes to stay with her father, stepmother, and new baby sister the summer before she starts college, all the trauma of her parents' divorce is revived, even as she is making new friends and having new experiences such as learning to ride a bike and dating.

"Dessen explores the dynamics of an extended family headed by two opposing, flawed personalities, revealing their parental failures with wicked precision yet still managing to create real, even sympathetic characters. . . . [This book] provides the interpersonal intricacies fans expect from a Dessen plot." Horn Book

Lock and key; a novel. Viking Children's Books 2008 422p $18.99

Grades: 7 8 9 10 **Fic**

1. Child abuse -- Fiction 2. Family life -- Fiction 3. Abandoned children -- Fiction

ISBN 978-0-670-01088-2; 0-670-01088-X

LC 2007-25370

When she is abandoned by her alcoholic mother, high school senior Ruby winds up living with Cora, the sister she has not seen for ten years, and learns about Cora's new life, what makes a family, how to allow people to help her when she needs it, and that she too has something to offer others.

"The dialogue, especially between Ruby and Cora, is crisp, layered, and natural. The slow unfolding adds to an anticipatory mood. . . . Recommend this one to patient, sophisticated readers." SLJ

The **moon** and more; by Sarah Dessen. Viking 2013 384 p. (hardcover) $19.99

Grades: 7 8 9 10 **Fic**

1. Bildungsromans 2. Dating (Social customs) -- Fiction 3. Father-daughter relationship -- Fiction 4. Beaches -- Fiction 5. Resorts -- Fiction 6. Coming of age -- Fiction 7. Fathers and daughters -- Fiction 8. Family-owned business enterprises -- Fiction 9. Documentary films -- Production and direction -- Fiction

ISBN 0670785601; 9780670785605

LC 2012035720

In this novel, by Sarah Dessen, "Luke is the perfect boyfriend. . . . But now, in the summer before college, Emaline wonders if perfect is good enough. Enter Theo, a super-ambitious outsider. . . . Emaline's . . . father, too, thinks Emaline should have a bigger life. . . . Emaline is attracted to the bright future that Theo and her father promise. But she also clings to the deep roots of her loving mother, stepfather, and sisters." (Publisher's note)

"Dessen's characters behave as deliciously unpredictably as people do in real life, and just as in real life, they sometimes have to make difficult choices with not-so-predictable outcomes... Completely engaging." Kirkus

Saint Anything; a novel. Sarah Dessen. Viking Juvenile 2015 432 p. (hardback) $19.99

Grades: 7 8 9 10 11 12 **Fic**

1. Family -- Fiction 2. Self-acceptance -- Fiction 3. Friendship -- Fiction 4. Family life -- Fiction 5. Family problems -- Fiction 6. Self-perception -- Fiction 7. Brothers and sisters -- Fiction 8. Dating (Social customs) -- Fiction

ISBN 0451474708; 9780451474704

LC 2014039813

In Sara Dessen's novel "Sydney has always felt invisible. She's grown accustomed to her brother, Peyton, being the focus of the family's attention. Now, after a drunk-driving accident that crippled a boy, Peyton's serving some serious jail time, and Sydney is on her own, questioning her place in the family and the world. Then she meets the Chatham family. Drawn into their warm, chaotic circle, Sydney experiences unquestioning acceptance for the first time." (Publisher's note)

"Once again, Dessen demonstrates her tremendous skill in evoking powerful emotions through careful, quiet prose, while delivering a satisfying romance." Pub Wkly

That summer. Orchard Books 1996 198p hardcover o.p. pa $8.99

Grades: 7 8 9 10 **Fic**

1. Sisters -- Fiction 2. Weddings -- Fiction

ISBN 0-531-09538-X; 0-531-08888-X lib bdg; 978-0-14-240172-9 pa; 0-14-240172-2 pa

LC 96-7643

During the summer of her divorced father's remarriage and her sister's wedding, fifteen-year-old Haven comes into her own by letting go of the myths of the past

"Dessen adds a fresh twist to a traditional sister-of-the-bride story with her keenly observant narrative full of witty ironies. Her combination of unforgettable characters and unexpected events generates hilarity as well as warmth." Publ Wkly

The **truth** about forever. Viking 2004 382p $16.99; pa $6.50

Grades: 7 8 9 10 **Fic**

1. Death -- Fiction 2. Catering -- Fiction

ISBN 0-670-03639-0; 0-440-21928-0 pa

LC 2003-28298

The summer following her father's death, Macy plans to work at the library and wait for her brainy boyfriend to return from camp, but instead she goes to work at a catering business where she makes new friends and finally faces her grief.

"All of Dessen's characters . . . are fully and beautifully drawn. Their dialogue is natural and believable, and their care for one another is palpable. . . . Dessen charts Macy's navigation of grief in such an honest way it will touch every reader who meets her. " SLJ

What happened to goodbye. Viking 2011 402p $19.99
Grades: 8 9 10 11 12 **Fic**

1. School stories 2. Divorce -- Fiction
ISBN 978-0-670-01294-7; 0-670-01294-7

LC 2010-41041

"The novel nimbly weaves together familiar story lines of divorce, high-school happiness and angst, and teen-identity struggles with likable, authentic adult and teen characters and intriguing yet credible situations." Booklist

DeStefano, Lauren

A **curious** tale of the in-between; by Lauren DeStefano. Bloomsbury 2015 240 p. paperback $7.99; (hardcover) $16.99
Grades: 4 5 6 7 **Fic**

1. Ghost stories 2. Aunts -- Fiction 3. Orphans -- Fiction 4. Friendship -- Fiction 5. Loss (Psychology) -- Fiction 6. Ghosts -- Fiction 7. Psychic ability -- Fiction
ISBN 9781619636026; 161963600X; 9781619636002

LC 2014035767

In this book, by Lauren DeStefano, "Pram Bellamy is special--she can talk to ghosts. She doesn't have too many friends amongst the living, but that's all right. . . . Then Pram meets Clarence, a boy from school who has also lost a parent and is looking for answers. Together they arrive at the door of the mysterious Lady Savant, who promises to help. But this spiritualist knows the true nature of Pram's power, and what she has planned is more terrifying than any ghost. " (Publisher's note)

"Pram's pregnant mother committed suicide, but the doctors managed to save the baby. Eleven years later, eccentric Pram talks to the dead, and her best friend is ghostly Felix. When she enters the memories of the dead, Pram learns more about her own past, and Felix's, than she bargained for. Fans of Holly Black's Doll Bones may well enjoy this creepy, character-based tale." Horn Book

Dreaming dangerous; by Lauren DeStefano. Bloomsbury 2018 208 p. (hardcover) $16.99
Grades: 4 5 6 7 **Fic**

1. Dreams -- Fiction 2. Orphans -- Fiction 3. Friendship -- Fiction 4. Ability -- Fiction 5. Schools -- Fiction 6. Best friends -- Fiction 7. Supernatural -- Fiction 8. Adventure and adventurers -- Fiction
ISBN 9781681194479

LC 2017034053

In this book by Lauren DeStefano, "tucked deep in the woods and surrounded by a great iron fence lies Brassmere Academy for the Extraordinary, a school for orphans with strange and wonderful gifts. Twelve-year-old Plum has lived there for as long as she can remember. Each night, she ventures into her dreams alongside her three best friends, Vien, Gwendle, and Artem to fight monsters and journey on dangerous quests." (Publisher's note)

Perfect ruin; by Lauren DeStefano and illustrated by Teagan White. Simon and Schuster Books for Young Readers 2013 368 p. (The Internment chronicles) (hardcover : alk. paper) $17.99
Grades: 7 8 9 10 **Fic**

1. Imaginary places 2. Criminal investigation -- Fiction 3. Science fiction 4. Utopias -- Fiction
ISBN 1442480610; 9781442480612

LC 2013014392

Sequel: Burning Kingdoms (2015)

In this book by Lauren DeStefano "Morgan Stockhour knows getting too close to the edge of Internment, the floating city in the clouds where she lives, can lead to madness.Then a murder, the first in a generation, rocks the city. With whispers swirling and fear on the wind, Morgan can no longer stop herself from investigating, especially once she meets Judas. Betrothed to the victim, he is the boy being blamed for the murder, but Morgan is convinced of his innocence." (Publisher's note)

Detorie, Rick

The **accidental** genius of Weasel High. Egmont USA 2011 197p il pa $9.99
Grades: 5 6 7 8 **Fic**

1. Motion pictures -- Fiction
ISBN 1-60684-149-1 pa; 978-1-60684-149-5 pa

LC 2011-02776

Larkin Pace, a film-obsessed high school freshman, chronicles his experiences as he tries to raise money for a new camcorder and get a date with the girl who has been his best friend since third grade. "Grades five to eight." (Bull Cent Child Books)

"Larkin serves as a relatable 'everykid,' and many readers will enjoy spending some time with him." SLJ

Deuker, Carl

★ **Gym** candy. Houghton Mifflin Company 2007 313p $16
Grades: 7 8 9 10 11 12 **Fic**

1. School stories 2. Football -- Fiction 3. Steroids -- Fiction 4. Washington (State) -- Fiction 5. Father-son relationship -- Fiction
ISBN 978-0-618-77713-6; 0-618-77713-X

LC 2007-12749

Groomed by his father to be a star player, football is the only thing that has ever really mattered to Mick Johnson, who works hard for a spot on the varsity team his freshman year, then tries to hold onto his edge by using steroids, despite the consequences to his health and social life.

"Deuker skillfully complements a sobering message with plenty of exciting on-field action and locker-room drama, while depicting Mick's emotional struggles with loneliness and insecurity as sensitively and realistically as his physical ones." Booklist

High heat. Houghton Mifflin 2003 277p $16; pa $6.99
Grades: 7 8 9 10 **Fic**

1. School stories 2. Fathers -- Fiction
ISBN 0-618-31117-3; 0-06-057248-5 pa

LC 2002-15324

When high school sophomore Shane Hunter's father is arrested for money laundering at his Lexus dealership, the star pitcher's life of affluence and private school begins to fall apart

This is "a story that delivers baseball action along with a rich psychological portrait, told through a compelling first-person narration." SLJ

★ **Payback** time. Houghton Mifflin Harcourt 2010 298p $16
Grades: 7 8 9 10 **Fic**

1. School stories 2. Courage -- Fiction 3. Obesity -- Fiction 4. Football -- Fiction 5. Journalists -- Fiction
ISBN 978-0-547-27981-7; 0-547-27981-7

LC 2010-6779

Deuker "really cranks up the suspense in his newest page-turner. . . . The game action alone is riveting . . . but Deuker enriches the tale with several well-tuned subplots and memorable narrator/protagonist." Booklist

Swagger; Carl Deuker. Houghton Mifflin Harcourt 2013 304 p. $17.99

Grades: 7 8 9 10 11 12 **Fic**

1. Basketball -- Fiction 2. Child sexual abuse -- Fiction 3. Sexual abuse -- Fiction

ISBN 0547974590; 9780547974590

LC 2012045062

In this book, by Carl Deuker, "high school senior Jonas moves to Seattle [and] is glad to meet Levi, a nice, soft-spoken guy and fellow basketball player." Then, readers are introduced to "Ryan Hartwell, a charismatic basketball coach and sexual predator. When Levi reluctantly tells Jonas that Hartwell abused him, Jonas has to decide whether he should risk his future career to report the coach." (Publisher's note)

"When his family moves to Seattle, high school basketball star Jonas befriends new neighbor Levi, who plays power forward. Assistant coach Ryan Hartwell appreciates Jonas's fast-breaking style, but something about Hartwell feels wrong. Eventually his misdeeds lead to tragedy, and Jonas must find the courage to do what's right. Basketball fans will love the realistic hardwood action and the story's quick pacing." (Horn Book)

Devlin, Ivy

Low red moon. Bloomsbury Children's Books 2010 244p $16.99

Grades: 7 8 9 10 **Fic**

1. Wolves -- Fiction 2. Homicide -- Fiction 3. Grandmothers -- Fiction 4. Supernatural -- Fiction 5. Forests and forestry -- Fiction

ISBN 978-1-59990-510-5; 1-59990-510-8

LC 2010-03480

Seventeen-year-old Avery can remember nothing to explain her parents' violent death in the woods where they live, but after meeting Ben, a mysterious new neighbor, she begins to believe some of the stories she has heard about creatures of the forest.

This is "an eerie and engrossing paranormal murder mystery. . . . The emotion pouring off the pages should sweep readers into this haunting story." Publ Wkly

DeWoskin, Rachel

Someday we will fly; Rachel DeWoskin. Viking, published by Penguin Group 2019 368 p. (hardback) $17.99

Grades: 7 8 9 10 **Fic**

1. Holocaust, 1939-1945 -- Fiction 2. Immigration and emigration -- Fiction 3. Circus performers -- Fiction 4. Jews -- China -- Shanghai -- Fiction 5. Emigration and immigration -- Fiction 6. Sino-Japanese War, 1937-1945 -- Fiction 7. China -- History -- 1937-1945 -- Fiction 8. Shanghai (China) -- History -- 20th century -- Fiction

ISBN 9780670014965

LC 2018018516

Author Rachel Dewoskin's book is set in 1940 where Lillia, 15, flees Warsaw, Poland with her father "and younger sister, Naomi, to Shanghai, one of the few places that will accept Jews without visas. There they struggle to make a life; they have no money, there is little work. . . . Meanwhile, the conflict grows more intense as the Americans declare war and the Japanese force the Americans in Shanghai into camps. . . . Can they survive, caught in the crossfire?" (Publisher's note)

"DeWoskin captures the crushing destruction of war and occupation, the unfathomable resilience communities can muster through cross-cultural friendships and acts of kindness, andthe power of the performing arts to foster hope in times of struggle and desperation." Pub Wkly

Diamand, Emily

Raiders' ransom. Chicken House/Scholastic 2009 334p map OP; paperback OP

Grades: 4 5 6 7 **Fic**

1. Science fiction 2. Adventure fiction 3. Pirates -- Fiction 4. Kidnapping -- Fiction 5. Great Britain -- Fiction 6. Environmental degradation -- Fiction

ISBN 978-0-545-14297-7; 0-545-14297-0; 9780545142984; 9780545415125

LC 2008-43692

It's the 22nd century and, because of climate change, much of England is underwater. Poor Lilly is out fishing with her trusty sea-cat when greedy raiders pillage the town—and kidnap the prime minister's daughter. Her village blamed, Lilly decides to find the girl.

This is a "captivating story. . . . A well-drawn world, plot twists galore and spunky characters make this one a true page-turner." Kirkus

Folllowed by: Flood and fire (2011)

DiCamillo, Kate, 1934

★ **Because** of Winn-Dixie. Candlewick Press 2000 182p $15.99; pa $6.99

Grades: 4 5 6 7 **Fic**

1. Dogs -- Fiction 2. Florida -- Fiction

ISBN 978-0-7636-0776-0; 0-7636-0776-2; 978-0-7636-4432-1 pa; 0-7636-4432-3 pa

LC 99-34260

A Newbery honor book, 2001

Ten-year-old India Opal Buloni describes her first summer in the town of Naomi, Florida, and all the good things that happen to her because of her big ugly dog Winn-Dixie

"This well-crafted, realistic, and heartwarming story will be read and reread as a new favorite deserving a long-term place on library shelves." SLJ

★ **Flora** and Ulysses; The Illuminated Adventures. by Kate DiCamillo ; illustrated by K. G. Campbell. Candlewick Press 2013 240 p. ill. (reinforced) $17.99; paperback $6.99; paperback OP

Grades: 3 4 5 6 **Fic**

1. Fantasy fiction 2. Adventure fiction 3. Girls -- Fiction 4. Squirrels -- Fiction 5. Superheroes -- Fiction

ISBN 076366040X; 9780763660406; 9780763667245; 9780763687649; 9780763676711

LC 2012947748

Parents' Choice Awards: Gold Medal Fiction (2013)

National Book Awards: Young People's Literature Long List (2013)

Newberry Medal (2014)

In this book by Kate DiCamillo, "bitter about her parents' divorce. Flora Buckman has withdrawn into her favorite comic book The Amazing Incandesto! and memorized the advisories in its ongoing bonus feature, Terrible Things Can Happen to You! She puts those life-saving tips into action when a squirrel is swallowed whole by a neighbor's new vacuum cleaner. . . . Flora resuscitates the squirrel," who now has superpowers. (Publishers Weekly)

★ **Louisiana's** way home; Kate DiCamillo. Candlewick Press 2018 240 p. $16.99

Grades: 4 5 6 7 8 **Fic**

1. Moving -- Fiction 2. Grandmothers -- Fiction 3. Grandparent-grandchild relationship -- Fiction

ISBN 0763694630; 9780763694630

In this book, by Kate DiCamillo, "when Louisiana Elefante's granny wakes her up in the middle of the night to tell her that the day of reckoning has arrived and they have to leave home immediately, Louisiana isn't overly worried. After all, Granny has many middle-of-the-night ideas. But this time, things are different. This time, Granny intends for them never to return." (Publisher's note)

"DiCamillo offers a master class in how to tell and shape a story once all fat has been cut away. Though set in the mid-1970s, there's a fairy-tale quality to this, with heroes, helpers, villains, and one princess looking for a home." (Booklist)

★ The **magician's** elephant; illustrated by Yoko Tanaka. Candlewick Press 2009 201p il $16.99; paperback $6.99; paperback $7.99

Grades: 4 5 6 7 **Fic**

1. Adventure fiction 2. Orphans -- Fiction 3. Siblings -- Fiction 4. Elephants -- Fiction 5. Missing children -- Fiction

ISBN 978-0-7636-4410-9; 0-7636-4410-2; 9780062118943; 9780062118950; 9780763649418; 9780763680886

LC 2009-07359

When ten-year-old orphan Peter Augustus Duchene encounters a fortune teller in the marketplace one day and she tells him that his sister, who is presumed dead, is in fact alive, he embarks on a remarkable series of adventures as he desperately tries to find her.

"The profound and deeply affecting emotions at work in the story are bouyed up by the tale's succinct, lyrical text; gentle touches of humor; and uplifting message." Booklist

★ **Raymie** Nightingale; by Kate DiCamillo. Candlewick Press 2016 272 p. paperback $7.99; hbk $16.99

Grades: 4 5 6 7 8 **Fic**

1. Emotions -- Fiction 2. Female friendship -- Fiction 3. Competition (Psychology) -- Fiction 4. Father-daughter relationship -- Fiction 5. Beauty contests -- Fiction 6. Family problems -- Fiction

ISBN 9780763696917; 9780763681173; 9780763687083; 0763681172

National Book Award Finalist: Young People's Literature (2016)

In this book, by Kate DiCamillo, "Raymie Clarke has come to realize that everything . . . depends on her. . . . If Raymie can win the Little Miss Central Florida Tire competition, then her father, who left town two days ago . . . will see Raymie's picture in the paper and come home. . . . She also has to contend with the wispy, frequently fainting Louisiana Elefante, who has a show-business background, and the fiery, stubborn Beverly Tapinski, who's determined to sabotage the contest." (Publisher's note)

"The limited third-person narration gives Raymie her distinctive voice and spot-on pre-adolescent perspective of a young girl trying to make sense of the world around her. Here DiCamillo returns--triumphantly--to her Winn-Dixie roots." Horn Book

Other titles in this series are:

Louisiana's way home (2018)

Beverly right here (2019)

Dickens, Charles

A **Christmas** carol; [by] Charles Dickens; illustrated by P.J. Lynch. Candlewick Press 2006 156p il $19.99

Grades: 5 6 7 8 **Fic**

1. Ghost stories 2. Christmas -- Fiction 3. Great Britain -- History -- 19th century -- Fiction

ISBN 978-0-7636-3120-8; 0-7636-3120-5

LC 2005058122

A miser learns the true meaning of Christmas when three ghostly visitors review his past and foretell his future.

Lynch's "watercolor-and-gouache illustrations lavishly enhance this handsome edition." SLJ

Dickerson, Melanie

The **merchant's** daughter. Zondervan 2011 284p pa $9.99

Grades: 7 8 9 10 11 12 **Fic**

1. Love -- Fiction 2. Middle Ages -- Fiction 3. Christian life -- Fiction 4. Contract labor -- Fiction 5. Great Britain -- History -- 1154-1399, Plantagenets -- Fiction

ISBN 978-0-31072761-3

LC 2011034338

In 1352 England, seventeen-year-old Annabel, granddaughter of a knight and a would-be nun, eludes a lecherous bailiff but falls in love with Lord Le Wyse, the ferocious and disfigured man to whom her family owes three years of indentured servitude, in this tale loosely based on Beauty and the Beast.

Dickerson "manages a heartfelt romance that will stick with readers, not only for its morality but also for the exploration of a woman's place within fourteenth-century English Christianity." Booklist

Dickinson, Peter

Eva. Delacorte Press 1989 219p hardcover o.p. pa $6.50; pa $7.99

Grades: 7 8 9 10 **Fic**

1. Science fiction 2. Chimpanzees -- Fiction

ISBN 0-385-29702-5; 0-440-20766-5 pa; 9780440207665 pa

LC 88-29435

"Eva wakes up from a deep coma that was the result of a terrible car accident and finds herself drastically altered. The accident leaves her so badly injured that her parents consent to a radical experiment to transplant her brain and memory into the body of a research chimpanzee. With the aid of a computer for communication, Eva slowly adjusts to her new existence while scientists monitor her progress, feelings, and insight into the animal world." Voice Youth Advocates

★ The **ropemaker**. Delacorte Press 2001 375p $15.95; pa $7.95

Grades: 7 8 9 10 **Fic**

1. Fantasy fiction 2. Magic -- Fiction

ISBN 0-385-72921-9; 0-385-73063-2 pa

LC 2001-17422

Michael L. Printz Award honor book, 2002

When the magic that protects their Valley starts to fail, Tilja and her companions journey into the evil Empire to find the ancient magician Faheel, who originally cast those spells

"The suspense does not let up until the very last pages. While on one level this tale is a fantasy, it is also a wonderful coming-of-age story." SLJ

Followed by: Angel Isle

Dinerstein, Eric

What elephants know; Eric Dinerstein. Disney-Hyperion 2016 288 p. illustrations, maps (ebook) $16.99; (hardcover) $16.99

Grades: 4 5 6 7 **Fic**

1. Nepal -- Fiction 2. Jungles -- Fiction 3. Orphans -- Fiction 4. Elephants -- Fiction 5. Jungle animals -- Fiction 6. India -- History -- 20th century -- Fiction 7. Nepal -- History -- 20th century -- Fiction

ISBN 9781484748701; 9781484728543

LC 2015024177

"Abandoned in the jungle of the Nepalese Borderlands, two-year-old Nandu is found living under the protective watch of a pack of wild dogs. From his mysterious beginnings, fate delivers him to the King's elephant stable, where he is raised by unlikely parents-the wise head of the stable, Subba-sahib, and Devi Kali, a fierce and affectionate female elephant." (Publisher's note)

Dionne, Erin

Models don't eat chocolate cookies. Dial Books for Young Readers 2009 243p pa $7.99

Grades: 6 7 8 9 **Fic**

1. Obesity -- Fiction 2. Fashion models -- Fiction

ISBN 978-0-8037-3296-4; 0-8037-3296-1

LC 2008-20612

Overweight thirteen-year-old Celeste begins a campaign to lose weight in order to make sure she does not win the Miss HuskeyPeach modeling challenge, in which her mother and aunt have entered her--against her wishes.

"Wry first-person narrative also provides convincing views of middle-school friendships, family dynamics, and incremental personal growth. . . . A light, well-paced first novel." Booklist

The **total** tragedy of a girl named Hamlet. Dial Books for Young Readers 2010 290p $16.99

Grades: 6 7 8 9 **Fic**

1. School stories 2. Sisters -- Fiction 3. Theater -- Fiction

ISBN 978-0-8037-3298-8; 0-8037-3298-8

"Some sisterly bonding, the sweet flutterings of a first romance, and a creatively contrived comeuppance for the mean girls make this a cheerful read for younger middle-schoolers." Booklist

DiTerlizzi, Tony

The **battle** for WondLa; Tony DiTerlizzi ; with illustrations by the author. 1st edition Simon & Schuster Books for Young Readers 2014 480 p. col. ill., col. map (The search for WondLa) (hardcover) $17.99; paperback $9.99

Grades: 2 3 4 5 **Fic**

1. Fantasy fiction 2. Extraterrestrial beings -- Fiction 3. War -- Fiction 4. Science fiction 5. Human-alien encounters -- Fiction

ISBN 1416983147; 9781416983149; 9781481403887; 9781416983156

LC 2013035219

"All hope for a peaceful coexistence between humankind and aliens seems lost in the third installment of the WondLa trilogy. Eva Nine has gone into hiding for fear of luring the wicked Loroc to her companions. However, news of the city Solas being captured by the human leader, Cadmus Pryde, forces Eva into action once again." (Publisher's note)

"Of particular interest is Eva's development into a young woman of unwavering compassion and courage, even in the face of betrayal, loss, and injury. DiTerlizzi's beautiful illustrations are worth the price of admission, as usual, and they do much to help the reader distinguish among the plethora of strange creatures." Booklist

A **hero** for WondLa; by Tony DiTerlizzi ; with illustrations by the author. Simon & Schuster Books for Young Readers 2012 445 p. (hardcover) $17.99; paperback $8.99

Grades: 5 6 7 8 **Fic**

1. Science fiction 2. Rescue work -- Fiction 3. Life on other planets -- Fiction 4. Identity -- Fiction 5. Human-alien encounters -- Fiction

ISBN 1416983120; 9781416983125; 9781442450844; 9781416983132

LC 2011037031

Author Tony DiTerlizzi tells a science fiction story. "Eva Nine had never seen another human, but after a human boy named Hailey rescues her along with her companions, she couldn't be happier. Eva thinks she has everything she's ever dreamed of, especially when Hailey brings her and her friends to the colony of New Attica, where humans of all shapes and sizes live in apparent peace and harmony. But all is not idyllic in New Attica, and Eva Nine soon realizes that something sinister is going on . . . [that] could mean the end of everything and everyone on planet Orbona." (Publisher's note)

★ The **search** for WondLa; with illustrations by the author. Simon & Schuster Books for Young Readers 2010 477p il $17.99; paperback $12.99

Grades: 5 6 7 8 **Fic**

1. Science fiction 2. Extraterrestrial beings -- Fiction

ISBN 978-1-4169-8310-1; 1-4169-8310-4; 9781416983118 ; 9781442413030

LC 2010-01326

Living in isolation with a robot on what appears to be an alien world populated with bizarre life forms, a twelve-year-old human girl called Eva Nine sets out on a journey to find others like her.

"The abundant illustrations, drawn in a flat, two-tone style, are lush and enhance readers' understanding of this unique universe. . . . DiTerlizzi is pushing the envelope in his latest work, nearly creating a new format that combines a traditional novel with a graphic novel and with the interactivity of the computer. Yet, beneath this impressive package lies a theme readers will easily relate to: the need to belong, to connect, to figure out one's place in the world. The novel's ending is a stunning shocker that will leave kids frantically awaiting the next installment." SLJ

Other titles in this series include:

A Hero for WondLa (2012)

The Battle for WondLa (2014)

Divakaruni, Chitra Banerjee

The **conch** bearer. Roaring Brook Press 2003 265p (Brotherhood of the conch) $16.95; lib bdg $23.90; paperback $8.99

Grades: 5 6 7 8 **Fic**

1. India -- Fiction 2. Magic -- Fiction

ISBN 978-0-7613-1935-1; 0-7613-1935-2; 978-0-7613-2793-6 lib bdg; 0-7613-2793-2 lib bdg; 9780689872426

LC 2003-8578

In India, a healer invites twelve-year-old Anand to join him on a quest to return a magical conch to its safe and rightful home, high in the Himalayan mountains

"Divakaruni keeps her tale fresh and riveting." Publ Wkly

Other titles in this series are:

The mirror of fire and dreaming (2005)

Shadowland (2009)

Dixon, Heather

★ **Entwined**. Greenwillow Books 2011 472p

Grades: 7 8 9 10 **Fic**

1. Fantasy fiction 2. Dance -- Fiction 3. Death -- Fiction 4. Magic -- Fiction 5. Princesses -- Fiction 6. Kings and rulers -- Fiction 7. Father-daughter relationship -- Fiction

ISBN 0-06-200103-5; 978-0-06-200103-0

LC 2010-11686

Confined to their dreary castle while mourning their mother's death, Princess Azalea and her eleven sisters join The Keeper, who is trapped in a magic passageway, in a nightly dance that soon becomes nightmarish.

"The story gracefully explores significant themes of grief and loss, mercy and love. Full of mystery, lush settings, and fully orbed characters, Dixon's debut is both suspenseful and rewarding." Booklist

Doctorow, Cory

★ **Little** brother. Tor Teen 2008 380p

Grades: 8 9 10 11 12 **Fic**

1. Computers -- Fiction 2. Terrorism -- Fiction 3. Civil rights -- Fiction 4. San Francisco (Calif.) -- Fiction 5. United States -- Dept. of Homeland Security -- Fiction

ISBN 0765319853; 9780765319852

LC 2008-1827

After being interrogated for days by the Department of Homeland Security in the aftermath of a terrorist attack on San Francisco, California, 17-year-old Marcus, released into what is now a police state, decides to use his expertise in computer hacking to set things right. "High school." (Horn Book)

"The author manages to explain naturally the necessary technical tools and scientific concepts in this fast-paced and well-written story. . . . The reader is privy to Marcus's gut-wrenching angst, frustration, and terror, thankfully offset by his self-awareness and humorous observations." Voice Youth Advocates

Pirate cinema; Cory Doctorow. 1st ed. Tor Teen 2012 384 p. (hardback) $19.99; (paperback) $9.99; (audiobook) $24.00

Grades: 7 8 9 10 **Fic**

1. Copyright 2. Runaway teenagers -- Fiction 3. Science fiction 4. England -- Fiction 5. Internet -- Fiction 6. Protest movements -- Fiction 7. Motion pictures -- Production and direction -- Fiction

ISBN 0765329085; 9780765329080; 9781429943185; 9780765329097; 9780307879585

LC 2012019871

In this book, author Cory Doctorow tells the story of Trent McCauley, a boy who "has an irrepressible drive to create . . . [films] through illegal downloading, and when he's caught, . . . [he] runs away to London, where he's taken under the wing of streetwise Jem Dodger. . . . He meets 26 and creates the persona Cecil B. DeVil. Pulled by 26 into the politics of copyright and the lobbyist money that purchases laws, Cecil becomes a creative figurehead for reform against escalating laws that aggressively jail kids." (Kirkus Reviews)

Dogar, Sharon

Annexed. Houghton Mifflin Harcourt 2010 333p $17

Grades: 8 9 10 11 12 **Fic**

1. Children 2. Diarists 3. Holocaust victims 4. Netherlands -- Fiction 5. Holocaust, 1933-1945 -- Fiction

ISBN 978-0-547-50195-6; 0-547-50195-1

LC 2010-282410

"On July 13, 1942, 15-year-old Peter van Pels and his parents entered the attic that became their home for two years. Peter is angry that he is hiding and not fighting Nazis. He is also not happy to be sharing cramped living quarters with the Franks, especially know-it-all Anne. In this novel, Dogar 'reimagines' what happened between the families who lived in the secret annex immortalized in Anne Frank's diary. In doing so, she creates a captivating historical novel and fully fleshes out the character of Peter, a boy whom teens will easily relate to." SLJ

Doherty, Berlie

The **girl** who saw lions. Roaring Brook Press 2008 249p $16.95

Grades: 6 7 8 9 **Fic**

1. Adoption -- Fiction 2. Tanzania -- Fiction 3. Great Britain -- Fiction 4. AIDS (Disease) -- Fiction

ISBN 978-1-59643-377-9; 1-59643-377-9

LC 2007-44054

In alternating voices, thirteen-year-old Rosa and her mother are trying to adopt a Tanzanian child in England, while in Tanzania, nine-year-old Abela watches her family die and her uncle illegally sends her to England, in the hopes of selling her.

"Packs in a great deal of information about the AIDS crisis in Africa, female genital mutilation, international adoptions, the foster care system, and the many challenges facing parentless children and the social workers who try to place them. Girls will love this emotionally powerful novel." Voice Youth Advocates

Doktorski, Jennifer Salvato

Famous last words; Jennifer Salvato Doktorski. Henry Holt and Company 2013 288 p. (hardcover) $17.99

Grades: 7 8 9 10 **Fic**

1. Women journalists -- Fiction 2. Internship programs -- Fiction 3. Journalism -- Fiction 4. Newspapers -- Fiction 5. Self-perception -- Fiction 6. Dating (Social customs) -- Fiction

ISBN 0805093672; 9780805093674

LC 2012046312

In this book, "aspiring reporter Sam D'Angelo, 16, is interning at her local New Jersey paper for the summer, stuck writing obituaries with her occasionally annoying, college-age fellow intern AJ. When she's not taking phone calls about dead people, Sam writes humorous imaginary obits (including one for herself); spends time with her grandmother; lusts after the 'incredibly hot' features intern, Tony Roma; and covertly investigates the shady mayor with AJ." (Publishers Weekly)

"Something of a love note to print journalism, the story is nevertheless snappy and contemporary, furthered by Sam's wry, self-deprecating narration and convincingly colloquial dialogue. Cleverly titled, realistically written, and on the whole engaging and sympathetic, this story rings true." Kirkus

Donnelly, Jennifer

Stepsister; Jennifer Donnelly. Scholastic Press 2019 342 p. (hardback) $17.99

Grades: 8 9 10 11 12 **Fic**

1. Stepsisters -- Fiction 2. Self-realization -- Fiction 3. Fate and fatalism -- Fiction 4. Choice (Psychology) -- Fiction 5. Heroes -- Fiction 6. Beauty, Personal -- Fiction 7. Women heroes -- Fiction

ISBN 9781338268461; 9781338268485

LC 2019003322

In this novel, by Jennifer Donnelly, "Isabelle should be blissfully happy - she's about to win the handsome prince. Except Isabelle isn't the beautiful girl who lost the glass slipper and captured the prince's heart. . . . When the prince discovers Isabelle's deception, she's turned away in shame. It's no more than she deserves: she's a plain girl in a world that values beauty; a bold girl in a world that wants her to be pliant." (Publisher's note)

"Printz Honor Book author Donnelly offers up a stunningly focused story that rips into the heart of a familiar fairy tale. The gorgeous prose and the fairy tale themes have obvious appeal, but the real strengths here are the depth of character across the board; the examination of the cost of beauty in a world that reveres it; and Isabelle herself, a shattered but not unredeemable girl with a warrior's heart." Booklist.

These shallow graves; Jennifer Donnelly. Delacorte Press 2015 496 p. (hc) $19.99

Grades: 7 8 9 10 **Fic**

1. Death -- Fiction 2. Gender role -- Fiction 3. Social classes -- Fiction 4. New York (N.Y.) -- History -- Fiction 5. Father-daughter relationship -- Fiction 6. Sex role -- Fiction 7. Fathers and daughters -- Fiction 8. New York (N.Y.) -- History -- 19th century -- Fiction

ISBN 9780385737654

LC 2014047825

In this book, by Jennifer Donnelly, "Jo Montfort . . . [will] graduate from finishing school and be married off to a wealthy bachelor. Which is the last thing she wants. Jo dreams of becoming a writer. . . . Wild aspirations aside, Jo's life seems perfect until tragedy strikes: her father is found dead. Charles Montfort shot himself while cleaning his pistol. One of New York City's wealthiest men . . . Jo knows he was far too smart to clean a loaded gun." (Publisher's note)

"Melodrama and intrigue drive this fast-paced thriller with a Wharton-esque setting and a naïve young protagonist willing to be exposed to the shadier side of life—prostitutes, uncouth men, and abject poverty—on her way to solving a mystery and asserting her right to claim her future for herself. The author keeps the clues coming at a rate that allows readers to be one small step ahead of Jo as the story races to its surprising conclusion. Readers who love costume dramas will relish this one." Kirkus

Donovan, John

I'll get there; it better be worth the trip. John Donovan. 40th anniversary edition; Flux 2010 228p pa $9.95

Grades: 7 8 9 10 11 **Fic**

1. LGBT youth -- Fiction 2. Alcoholism -- Fiction 3. Friendship -- Fiction 4. New York (N.Y.) -- Fiction

ISBN 978-0-7387-2134-7 pa; 0-7387-2134-4 pa

LC 2010014266

First published 1969 by Harper & Row

In this novel, by John Donovan, 13-year-old "Davy Ross . . . move[s] to Manhattan to live with his estranged mother. Between alcohol-infused lectures about her self-sacrifice and awkward visits with his distant father, Davy's only comfort is his beloved dachshund. . . . Things start to look up when he and a boy from school become friends. But when their relationship takes an unexpected turn, Davy struggles to understand what happened and what it might mean." (Publisher's note)

"Donovan's novel is startlingly outspoken and honest in its presentation of a young teen questioning his sexuality. . . . Such is the author's skill that the reader knows this young man's journey of self-discovery will get him to his 'there,' wherever it may be. This welcome fortieth-anniversary edition of a YA classic is an essential purchase for all libraries." Voice Youth Advocates

Dooley, Sarah

Free verse; Sarah Dooley. Penguin Group USA 2016 352 p. (hardback) $16.99; paperback $8.99

Grades: 5 6 7 8 **Fic**

1. Poetry -- Fiction 2. Bereavement -- Fiction 3. Family life -- Fiction

ISBN 9780399165030; 9781101657256; 9780147509154; 0399165037

LC 2015038249

This novel, by Sarah Dooley, is "set in a West Virginia coal-mining town. When her brother dies in a fire, Sasha Harless has no one left. . . . But then Sasha discovers family she didn't know she had. . . . Sasha even makes her first friend at school, and is slowly learning to cope with her brother's death through writing poetry, finding a new way to express herself when spoken words just won't do." (Publisher's note)

"Dooley winningly combines engaging plot twists and rich character development with the introspective and thematic power of poetry: not to be missed." Kirkus

Dorris, Michael

Morning Girl. Hyperion Bks. for Children 1992 74p hardcover o.p. pa $4.99

Grades: 4 5 6 7 **Fic**

1. Taino Indians -- Fiction 2. America -- Exploration -- Fiction

ISBN 0-7868-1358-X pa

LC 92-52989

Twelve year old Morning Girl, a Taino Indian who loves the day, and her younger brother Star Boy, who loves the night, take turns describing their life on a Bahamian island in 1492; in Morning Girl's last narrative, she witnesses the arrival of the first Europeans to her world

"The author uses a lyrical, yet easy-to-follow, style to place these compelling characters in historical context. . . . Dorris does a superb job of showing that family dynamics are complicated, regardless of time and place. . . . A touching glimpse into the humanity that connects us all." Horn Book

Sees Behind Trees. Hyperion Bks. for Children 1996 104p hardcover o.p. pa $4.99

Grades: 4 5 6 7 **Fic**

1. Native Americans -- Fiction 2. Vision disorders -- Fiction

ISBN 0-7868-1357-1 pa

LC 96-15859

"For the partially sighted Walnut, it is impossible to prove his right to a grown-up name by hitting a target with his bow and arrow. With his highly developed senses, however, he demonstrates that he can do something even better: he can see 'what cannot be seen' which earns him the name Sees Behind Trees. . . . Set in sixteenth-century America, this richly imagined and gorgeously written rite-of-passage story has the gravity of legend. Moreover, it has buoyant humor and the immediacy of a compelling story that is peopled with multidimensional characters." Booklist

Dowd, Siobhan

★ **Bog** child. David Fickling Books 2008 321p

Grades: 8 9 10 11 12 **Fic**

1. Mummies -- Fiction 2. Prisoners -- Fiction 3. Terrorism -- Fiction 4. Family life -- Fiction 5. Northern Ireland -- Fiction

ISBN 0-385-75170-2 lib bdg; 978-0-385-75169-8; 0-385-75169-9; 978-0-385-75170-4 lib bdg

LC 2008-2998

This novel is set in Northern Ireland in 1981. 18-year-old Fergus is distracted from his upcoming A-level exams by the discovery of a girl's body in a peat bog, his imprisoned brother's hunger strike, and the stress of being a courier for Sinn Fein. "Grades eight to twelve." (Bull Cent Child Books)

"Dowd raises questions about moral choices within a compelling plot that is full of surprises, powerfully bringing home the impact of political conflict on innocent bystanders." Publ Wkly

★ The **London** Eye mystery. David Fickling Books 2008 322p lib bdg $18.99; pa $7.50; $15.99

Grades: 5 6 7 8 **Fic**

1. Mystery fiction 2. Cousins -- Fiction 3. Siblings -- Fiction 4. London (England) -- Fiction 5. Missing children -- Fiction 6.

Asperger's syndrome -- Fiction
ISBN 0375849769; 9780375949760 lib bdg; 9780385751841 pa; 9780375849763; 0385751842 pa

LC 2007-15119

First published 2007 in the United Kingdom

When Ted and Kat's cousin Salim disappears from the London Eye ferris wheel, the two siblings must work together—Ted with his brain that is "wired differently" and impatient Kat—to try to solve the mystery of what happened to Salim.

"Everything rings true here, the family relationships, the quirky connections of Ted's mental circuitry, and . . . the mystery. . . . A page turner with heft." Booklist

Another title in this series is:
The Guggenheim mystery (2018)

Dowell, Frances O'Roark

★ **Dovey** Coe. Atheneum Bks. for Young Readers 2000 181p $16; pa $5.99

Grades: 5 6 7 8 **Fic**

1. Mountain life -- Fiction 2. North Carolina -- Fiction
ISBN 0-689-83174-9; 0-689-84667-3 pa

LC 99-46870

When accused of murder in her North Carolina mountain town in 1928, Dovey Coe, a stronged-willed twelve-year-old girl, comes to a new understanding of others, including her deaf brother

"Dowell has created a memorable character in Dovey, quick-witted and honest to a fault. . . . This is a delightful book, thoughtful and full of substance." Booklist

Falling in. Atheneum Books for Young Readers 2010 245p il $16.99; paperback $8.99

Grades: 4 5 6 7 **Fic**

1. Fantasy fiction
ISBN 978-1-4169-5032-5; 1-4169-5032-X; 9781416999027; 9781442422056

LC 2009-10412

Middle-schooler Isabelle Bean follows a mouse's squeak into a closet and falls into a parallel universe where the children believe she is the witch they have feared for years, finally come to devour them.

"This perfectly paced story has enough realistic elements to appeal even to nonfantasy readers." Booklist

The **kind** of friends we used to be. Atheneum Books for Young Readers 2009 234p $16.99; paperback $7.99

Grades: 5 6 7 8 **Fic**

1. School stories 2. Friendship -- Fiction
ISBN 978-1-4169-5031-8; 1-4169-5031-1; 978-1416997795; 9781442406162

LC 2008-22245

Sequel to: The secret language of girls (2004)

Twelve-year-olds Kate and Marylin, friends since preschool, draw further apart as Marylin becomes involved in student government and cheerleading, while Kate wants to play guitar and write songs, and both develop unlikely friendships with other girls and boys.

"Dowell gets middle-school dynamics exactly right, and while her empathetic portraits of Kate and Marylin are genuine and heartfelt, even secondary characters are memorable. A realistic and humorous look at the trials and tribulations of growing up and growing independent." SLJ

The **second** life of Abigail Walker; Frances O'Roark Dowell. Atheneum Books for Young Readers 2012 228 p. (hardcover) $16.99; paperback $5.99

Grades: 4 5 6 7 **Fic**

1. Self-confidence -- Fiction 2. Middle schools -- Fiction 3. Friendship -- Fiction 4. Overweight persons -- Fiction 5. Human-animal relationships -- Fiction
ISBN 1442405937; 9781442405936; 9781442405943; 9781442405950

LC 2012010646

This novel, by Frances O'Roark Dowell, follows a youth struggling with popularity. "Seventeen pounds. That's the difference between . . . chubby and slim, between teased and taunting. Abby is fine with her body, . . . so she speaks out against Kristen and her groupies--and becomes officially unpopular. Embracing her new status, Abby heads to an abandoned lot across the street and crosses an unfamiliar stream that leads her to a boy who's as different as they come." (Publisher's note)

Shooting the moon. Atheneum Books for Young Readers 2008 163p $16.99; pa $5.99

Grades: 4 5 6 7 **Fic**

1. Soldiers -- Fiction 2. Family life -- Fiction 3. Vietnam War, 1961-1975 -- Fiction
ISBN 978-1-4169-2690-0; 1-4169-2690-9; 978-1-4169-7986-9 pa; 1-4169-7986-7 pa

LC 2006-100347

Boston Globe-Horn Book Award honor book: Fiction and Poetry (2008)

When her brother is sent to fight in Vietnam, twelve-year-old Jamie begins to reconsider the army world that she has grown up in.

"The clear, well-paced first-person prose is perfectly matched to this novel's spare setting and restrained plot. . . . This [is a] thoughtful and satisfying story. . . . Readers will find beauty in its resolution, and will leave this eloquent heroine reluctantly." SLJ

Ten miles past normal. Atheneum Books for Young Readers 2011 211p $16.99

Grades: 6 7 8 9 10 **Fic**

1. School stories 2. Farm life -- Fiction 3. Bands (Music) -- Fiction 4. North Carolina -- Fiction
ISBN 1-4169-9585-4; 978-1-4169-9585-2

LC 2010-22041

Because living with "modern-hippy" parents on a goat farm means fourteen-year-old Janie Gorman cannot have a normal high school life, she tries joining Jam Band, making friends with Monster, and spending time with elderly former civil rights workers.

"Janie narrates her first year in high school with her sure, smart, sarcastic voice. . . . Dowell gets all the details of ninth grade right." Horn Book

Downer, Ann

Hatching magic. Atheneum Bks. for Young Readers 2003 242p $16.95; pa $5.99

Grades: 4 5 6 7 **Fic**

1. Magic -- Fiction 2. Dragons -- Fiction
ISBN 0-689-83400-4; 0-689-87057-4 pa

LC 00-56570

When a thirteenth-century wizard confronts twenty-first century Boston while seeking his pet dragon, he is followed by a rival wizard and a very unhappy demon, but eleven-year-old Theodora Oglethorpe may hold the secret to setting everything right

"With likable characters, and laced with plenty of humor and adventure, Downer's fantasy will have solid appeal for young genre fans." Booklist

Another title about Theodora is:
The dragon of never-was (2006)

Downham, Jenny

★ **Before** I die. David Fickling Books 2007 326p hardcover o.p. pa $9.99

Grades: 8 9 10 11 12 **Fic**

1. Death -- Fiction 2. Terminally ill -- Fiction

ISBN 978-0-385-75155-1; 978-0-385-75183-4 pa

LC 2007-20284

A terminally ill teenaged girl makes and carries out a list of things to do before she dies.

"Downham holds nothing back in her wrenchingly and exceptionally vibrant story." Publ Wkly

Dowswell, Paul

The **Auslander**. Bloomsbury Children's Books 2011 295p $16.99

Grades: 7 8 9 10 **Fic**

1. Orphans -- Fiction 2. Adoption -- Fiction 3. Insurgency -- Fiction 4. Berlin (Germany) -- Fiction 5. National socialism -- Fiction 6. World War, 1939-1945 -- Fiction 7. Germany -- History -- 1933-1945 -- Fiction

ISBN 1599906333; 9781599906331

LC 2010035626

First published 2009 in the United Kingdom

German soldiers take Peter from a Warsaw orphanage, and soon he is adopted by Professor Kaltenbach, a prominent Nazi, but Peter forms his own ideas about what he sees and hears and decides to take a risk that is most dangerous in 1942 Berlin.

"The characters are rich and nuanced; . . . the action is swift and suspenseful; and the juxtaposition of wartime nobility and wartime cruelty is timeless." Horn Book

Doyle, Arthur Conan, Sir, 1859-1930

The **adventures** and the memoirs of Sherlock Holmes; by Arthur Conan Doyle ; illustrated by Scott McKowen. Sterling Pub. Co. 2004 vi, 569 p.p ill. (hardcover) $9.95

Grades: 7 8 9 10 11 12 Adult **Fic**

1. Mystery fiction 2. Detective and mystery stories, English 3. Private investigators -- England -- Fiction 4. Holmes, Sherlock (Fictitious character) -- Fiction

ISBN 140271453X; 9781402714535

LC 2004016067

This book is a collection of Sir Arthur Conan Doyle's mystery stories featuring detective "Sherlock Holmes, with his unequalled powers of deduction." This edition has illustrations created by Scott McKowen "in scratchboard, an engraving medium which evokes the look of popular art from the period of these stories." (Publisher's note)

Doyle, Catherine

The **storm** keeper's island; by Catherine Doyle. Bloomsbury 2019 304 p. (hardcover) $16.99

Grades: 4 5 6 7 **Fic**

1. Islands -- Fiction 2. Paranormal fiction 3. Grandfathers -- Fiction 4. Ireland -- Fiction 5. Supernatural -- Fiction 6. Brothers and sisters -- Fiction

ISBN 9781681199597

LC 2018024284

In this book in the Storm Keeper's Island series, by Catherine Doyle, "Fionn Boyle comes from a long line of brave seafarers, people with the ocean behind their eyes. But he can't help but fear the open sea. For years, Fionn's mother has told him stories of Arranmore Island, a strange place that seems to haunt her. Fionn has always wondered about this mysterious island, and from the day he arrives he starts noticing things that can't be explained." (Publisher's note)

Doyle, Marissa

Bewitching season. Henry Holt 2008 346p $16.95; pa $8.99

Grades: 7 8 9 10 **Fic**

1. Magic -- Fiction 2. Twins -- Fiction 3. Sisters -- Fiction 4. Missing persons -- Fiction 5. London (England) -- Fiction 6. Great Britain -- History -- 19th century -- Fiction

ISBN 978-0-8050-8251-7; 0-8050-8251-4; 978-0-312-59695-8 pa; 0-312-59695-2 pa

In 1837, as seventeen-year-old twins, Persephone and Penelope, are starting their first London Season they find that their beloved governess, who has taught them everything they know about magic, has disappeared.

"Doyle takes as much care with characters . . . as with story details. This [is a] delightful mélange of genres." Booklist

Other titles in this series are:

Betraying Season (2009)

Courtship and Curses (2012).

Followed by: Betraying season (2009)

Doyle, Roddy, 1958-

A **greyhound** of a girl; Roddy Doyle. Amulet Books 2012 208 p. (hbk.) $16.95

Grades: 7 8 9 10 11 12 **Fic**

1. Dog racing -- Fiction 2. Family life -- Fiction 3. Dublin (Ireland) -- Fiction 4. Women -- Ireland -- Fiction 5. Death -- Fiction 6. Ghosts -- Fiction 7. Ireland -- Fiction 8. Grandmothers -- Fiction 9. Voyages and travels -- Fiction 10. Mothers and daughters -- Fiction

ISBN 9781407129334 Marion Lloyd; 1407129333 Marion Lloyd; 9781419701689 Amulet; 1419701681 Amulet

LC 2011042200

This book tells the story of "Twelve-year-old Mary O'Hara," an Irish girl who "is surrounded by good-humored women . . . her mum at home, her mum's mum, who is dying in Dublin's Sacred Heart Hospital, and her mum's mum's mum, who has just materialized as a ghost on her street. . . . [Roddy] Doyle divides up the novel by character, giving readers first-hand glimpses into the nature of each woman through time." (Kirkus)

Draper, Sharon M.

★ The **Battle** of Jericho. Atheneum Books for Young Readers 2003 297p $16.95; pa $6.99

Grades: 7 8 9 10 **Fic**

1. School stories 2. Clubs -- Fiction 3. Death -- Fiction 4. Cousins -- Fiction

ISBN 0-689-84232-5; 0-689-84233-3 pa

LC 2002-8612

"When Jericho is invited to pledge for the Warriors of Distinction, he thinks his life can't get any better. As the most exclusive club in school, the Warriors give the best parties, go out with the hottest girls, and great grades are a given. When Arielle, one of the finest girls in his class, starts coming on to him once the pledge announcements are made, Jericho is determined to do anything to become a member But as the initiation week becomes progressively harrowing, Jericho is forced to make choices he's not entirely comfortable with." (Publisher's note)

"This title is a compelling read that drives home important lessons about making choices." SLJ

Other titles in this series are:

Just another hero (2009)

November blues (2007)

Blended; Sharon M. Draper. Atheneum 2018 320 p. (hardback) $16.99
Grades: 4 5 6 7 **Fic**

1. Divorce -- Fiction 2. Family life -- Fiction 3. Stepfamilies -- Fiction 4. Ohio -- Fiction 5. Race relations -- Fiction 6. Family life -- Ohio -- Fiction 7. Racially mixed people -- Fiction
ISBN 9781442495005; 9781442495012
LC 2018025777

"Eleven-year-old Isabella's blended family is more divided than ever in this thoughtful story about divorce and racial identity from . . . author . . . Sharon M. Draper. . . . She has to switch lives every week: One week she's Isabella with her dad, his girlfriend Anastasia, and her son Darren. . . . The next week she's Izzy with her mom and her boyfriend John-Mark. . . . Because of this, Isabella has always felt pulled between two worlds." (Publisher's note)

Double Dutch. Atheneum Bks. for Young Readers 2002 183p $16; pa $4.99
Grades: 6 7 8 9 **Fic**

1. Friendship -- Fiction 2. Rope skipping -- Fiction 3. African Americans -- Fiction
ISBN 0-689-84230-9; 0-689-84231-7 pa
LC 00-50247

Three eighth-grade friends, preparing for the International Double Dutch Championship jump rope competition in their home town of Cincinnati, Ohio, cope with Randy's missing father, Delia's inability to read, and Yo Yo's encounter with the class bullies

"Teens will like the high-spirited, authentic dialogue . . . the honest look at tough issues, and the team workout scenes that show how sports can transform young lives." Booklist

Fire from the rock. Dutton Children's Books 2007 229p $16.99
Grades: 6 7 8 9 **Fic**

1. School stories 2. Arkansas -- Fiction 3. Race relations -- Fiction 4. African Americans -- Fiction 5. Central High School (Little Rock, Ark.) -- Fiction
ISBN 978-0-525-47720-4; 0-525-47720-9
LC 2006-102952

In 1957, Sylvia Patterson's life is disrupted by the impending integration of Little Rock's Central High when she is selected to be one of the first black students to attend the previously all white school.

"This historical fiction novel is a must have. It keeps the reader engaged with vivid depictions of a time that most young people can only imagine." Voice Youth Advocates

Just another hero. Atheneum Books for Young Readers 2009 280p $16.99
Grades: 7 8 9 10 **Fic**

1. School stories 2. Violence -- Fiction 3. African Americans -- Fiction
ISBN 978-1-4169-0700-8; 1-4169-0700-9
LC 2008-30961

Sequel to November blues

As Kofi, Arielle, Dana, November, and Jericho face personal challenges during their last year of high school, a misunderstood student brings a gun to class and demands to be taken seriously.

"The author presents a timeless theme in a well-crafted, highly readable story." Voice Youth Advocates

November blues. Atheneum Books for Young Readers 2007 316p $16.99; pa $6.99
Grades: 8 9 10 11 12 **Fic**

1. School stories 2. Pregnancy -- Fiction 3. African Americans -- Fiction
ISBN 978-1-4169-0698-8; 1-4169-0698-3; 978-1-4169-0699-5 pa; 1-4169-0699-1 pa
LC 2006-101343

Sequel to The battle of Jericho (2003)

A teenaged boy's death in a hazing accident has lasting effects on his pregnant girlfriend and his guilt-ridden cousin, who gives up a promising music career to play football during his senior year in high school.

"Urban teens often ask, 'Where are the books about us, Miss?' and with this novel Draper has . . . given them something meaty and meaningful to read." SLJ

Followed by Just another hero (2009)

★ **Out** of my mind. Atheneum 2010 295p $16.99; paperback $9.99
Grades: 5 6 7 8 **Fic**

1. Cerebral palsy -- Fiction
ISBN 978-1-4169-7170-2; 1-4169-7170-X; 9781416971719; 9781416980452
LC 2009-18404

Josette Frank Award for Fiction, 2011

"Fifth-grader Melody has cerebral palsy, a condition that affects her body but not her mind. Although she is unable to walk, talk, or feed or care for herself, she can read, think, and feel. A brilliant person is trapped inside her body, determined to make her mark in the world despite her physical limitations. . . . Told in Melody's voice, this highly readable, compelling novel quickly establishes her determination and intelligence and the almost insurmountable challenges she faces. . . . Uplifting and upsetting." Booklist

★ **Stella** by starlight; Sharon Draper. Atheneum Books for Young Readers 2015 336 p. (hardcover) $16.99; (tradepaper) $8.99
Grades: 4 5 6 7 8 **Fic**

1. Ku Klux Klan 2. Segregation -- Fiction 3. Southern States -- Fiction 4. Prejudices -- Fiction 5. Civil rights -- Fiction 6. African Americans -- Fiction 7. North Carolina -- History -- 20th century -- Fiction
ISBN 1442494972; 9781442494978; 9781442494985; 9781442494992
LC 2014038728

NAACP Image Award Nominee: Outstanding Literary Work- Youth/ Teens (2016)

In this novel by Sharon M. Draper "when the Ku Klux Klan's unwelcome reappearance rattles Stella's segregated southern town, bravery battles prejudice in this Depression-era tour de force. As Stella's community--her world--is upended, she decides to fight fire with fire. And she learns that ashes don't necessarily signify an end." (Publisher's note)

"Coretta Scott King Award winner Draper draws inspiration from her grandmother's journal to tell the absorbing story of a young girl growing up in Depression-era, segregated North Carolina...This is an engrossing historical fiction novel with an amiable and humble heroine who does not recognize her own bravery or the power of her words. She provides inspiration not only to her fellow characters but also to readers who will relate to her and her situation. Storytelling at its finest." SLJ

Duane, Diane

So you want to be a wizard; Diane Duane. HMH Books for Young Readers 2001 400 p. (Young Wizards) (pbk.) $7.99; (hbk.) $14.95

Grades: 6 7 8 9 10 **Fic**

1. Fantasy 2. Bullies -- Fiction 3. Wizards -- Fiction
ISBN 015216250X; 0385293054; 9780152162504; 9780385293051

LC 83005216

Originally published 1983

"Kit, 12, and Nita, 13, turn to magic in desperation as a way to protect themselves from bullies who beat them up regularly. They and Fred, a white mole they called up, jump through a worldgate into an alternate Manhattan where malevolent machines attack them at every turn. Their task is to rescue The Book of Night with Moon, which the evil Starsnuffer has hidden." (Voice of Youth Advocates)

Other titles in this series are:
Deep wizardry (1985)
High wizardry (1990)
A wizard abroad (1997)
The wizard's dilemma (2001)
A wizard alone (2002)
Wizard's holiday (2003)
Wizards at war (2005)
A wizard of Mars (2010)
Games wizards play (2016)

Duble, Kathleen Benner

The **sacrifice**. Margaret K. McElderry Books 2005 211p $15.95

Grades: 6 7 8 9 **Fic**

1. Puritans -- Fiction 2. Witchcraft -- Fiction 3. Massachusetts -- History -- 1600-1775, Colonial period -- Fiction
ISBN 0-689-87650-5

LC 2004-18355

Two sisters, aged ten and twelve, are accused of witchcraft in Andover, Massachusetts, in 1692 and await trial in a miserable prison while their mother desperately searches for some way to obtain their freedom.

"Well written with accessible language, this book will appeal to a wide range of readers." SLJ

Includes bibliographical references

Dubosarsky, Ursula

The **golden** day; by Ursula Dubosarsky. Candlewick 2013 160 p. $15.99

Grades: 7 8 9 10 **Fic**

1. Mystery fiction 2. Friendship -- Fiction 3. Missing persons -- Fiction
ISBN 0763663999; 9780763663995; 9781742374710

LC 2012452201

In this novel by Ursula Dubosarsky "eleven schoolgirls embrace their own chilling history when their teacher abruptly goes missing on a field trip. Who was the mysterious poet they had met in the Garden? What actually happened in the seaside cave that day? And most important — who can they tell about it?" (Publisher's note)

"Spare and well written, this slim novel covers the days following a teacher's disappearance during a class outing. Eleven girls must make their way back to school where they are determined to keep their teacher's rendezvous with the local park's gardener a secret. The book's chilling atmosphere and mature tone are best suited for older readers." (Horn Book)

Duey, Kathleen

Sacred scars. Atheneum Books for Young Readers 2009 554p il (A resurrection of magic) $17.99

Grades: 7 8 9 10 **Fic**

1. School stories 2. Fantasy fiction 3. Magic -- Fiction
ISBN 978-0-689-84095-1; 0-689-84095-0

LC 2008-56044

In alternate chapters, Sadima works to free captive boys forced to copy documents in the caverns of Limori, and Hahp makes a pact with the remaining students of a wizards' academy in hopes that all will survive their training, as both learn valuable lessons about loyalty.

"The text so successfully portrays Hahp's experience in this grueling, cold-blooded wizard 'academy'—isolation, starvation, abuse and constant, unsolvable puzzles—that readers may absorb his strain, confusion and desolation themselves. . . . Absorbing and unwaveringly suspenseful." Kirkus

Dumas, Alexandre

The **three** musketeers; translated by Jacques Le Clercq. Modern Library 1999 xxi, 598 p.p (hardcover) $26.00

Grades: 7 8 9 10 11 12 Adult **Fic**

1. Adventure 2. France -- Gascony 3. France -- 17th century 4. Courts and courtiers -- France 5. France -- History -- 1589-1789, Bourbons -- Fiction
ISBN 0679603328; 9780679603320

Original French edition, 1844

"D'Artagnan arrives in Paris one day in 1625 and manages to be involved in three duels with three musketeers . . . Athos, Porthos and Aramis. They become d'Artagnan's best friends. The account of their adventures from 1625 on develops against the rich historical background of the reign of Louis XIII and the early part of that of Louis XIV, the main plot being furnished by the antagonism between Cardinal de Richelieu and Queen Anne d'Autriche." Haydn. Thesaurus of Book Dig

Dumas, Firoozeh

★ **It** ain't so awful, falafel; by Firoozeh Dumas. Clarion Books/Houghton Mifflin Harcourt 2016 384 p. (hardback) $16.99; paperback $7.99

Grades: 4 5 6 7 **Fic**

1. Moving -- Fiction 2. Iranian Americans -- Fiction 3. Nineteen seventies -- Fiction 4. Immigrants -- United States -- Fiction
ISBN 9780544612310; 0544612310; 9781328740960; 9780544612372

LC 2015034779

In this book, by Firoozeh Dumas, "Zomorod (Cindy) Yousefzadeh is the new kid on the block . . . for the fourth time. California's Newport Beach is her family's latest perch, and she's determined to shuck her brainy loner persona and start afresh with a new Brady Bunch name--Cindy. It's the late 1970s, and fitting in becomes more difficult as Iran makes U.S. headlines with protests, revolution, and finally the taking of American hostages." (Publisher's note)

"On her own journey to maturity, Cindy deftly guides young readers through Iran's complicated realities in this fresh take on the immigrant experience---authentic, funny, and moving from beginning to end." Kirkus

Duncan, Lois, 1934-2016

I know what you did last summer. Little, Brown 1973 199p hardcover o.p. pa $6.50

Grades: 7 8 9 10 11 12 **Fic**

1. Mystery fiction
ISBN 0-440-22844-1 pa

ALA YALSA Margaret A. Edwards Award (1992)

This book "has vivid characterization, good balance, and the boding sense of impending danger that adds excitement to the best mystery stories." Bull Cent Child Books

Killing Mr. Griffin. Dell 1990 223p hardcover o.p. pa $6.50

Grades: 7 8 9 10 Fic

1. School stories 2. Kidnapping -- Fiction

ISBN 0-440-94515-1 pa

First published 1978 by Little, Brown

ALA YALSA Margaret A. Edwards Award (1992)

The author's "skillful plotting builds layers of tension that draws readers into the eye of the conflict. The ending is nicely handled in a manner which provides relief without removing any of the chilling implications." SLJ

Locked in time. Little, Brown 1985 210p hardcover o.p. pa $6.50

Grades: 7 8 9 10 Fic

1. Mystery fiction 2. Louisiana -- Fiction

ISBN 0-316-19555-3; 0-440-94942-4 pa

LC 85-23

This "is the story of a domineering mother, Lisette, and her two teenage children, Gabe and Josie, who have all drunk from the cup of eternal youth. Seventeen-year-old Nore Robbins goes to visit her father, Charles, and her new stepfamily, Lisette, Gabe and Josie, at Lisette's beautiful old estate deep in the Louisiana bayou country. Nore discovers her stepfamily's secret and, in an attempt to expose this knowledge, becomes Lisette's target for death. . . . Grades seven to ten." (SLJ)

"The writing style is smooth, the characters strongly developed, and the plot, which has excellent pace and momentum, is an adroit blending of fantasy and realism." Bull Cent Child Books

Stranger with my face. Little, Brown 1981 250p hardcover o.p. pa $8.95

Grades: 7 8 9 10 Fic

1. Twins -- Fiction 2. Supernatural -- Fiction

ISBN 0-440-98356-8

LC 81-8299

"The ghostly Lia is deliciously evil; the idea of astral projection—Lia's method of travel—is novel; the island setting is vivid; and the relationships among the young people are realistic in the smoothly written supernatural tale." Horn Book

The **third** eye. Little, Brown 1984 220p $12.95 Fic

1. Kidnapping -- Fiction 2. Extrasensory perception -- Fiction

ISBN 0-316-19553-7

LC 83-26777

High school senior Karen, who worries that her psychic powers will make her seem different from other people, is frightened at first when a young policeman asks her to use her gift to help the police locate missing children. "Grades nine to twelve." (SLJ)

Dunkle, Clare B.

The **sky** inside. Atheneum Books for Young Readers 2008 229p $16.99

Grades: 6 7 8 9 Fic

1. Science fiction

ISBN 978-1-41692-422-7; 1-41692-422-1

After the disappearance of his sister, Cassie, and other children who ask questions about their carefully choreographed life in a domed suburb cut off from the outside world, Martin and his intelligent dog investigate.

"Dunkle surrounds her protagonists with an enthralling range of settings, a memorable cast of characters. . . . Fans of the author will . . . recognize her evocative storytelling and intricate plotting." Bull Cent Child Books

Followed by: The walls have eyes (2009)

The **walls** have eyes. Atheneum Books for Young Readers 2009 225p $16.99

Grades: 6 7 8 9 Fic

1. Science fiction 2. Dogs -- Fiction 3. Robots -- Fiction 4. Family life -- Fiction 5. Genetic engineering -- Fiction

ISBN 978-1-41695-379-1; 1-41695-379-5

LC 2008038298

Sequel to: The sky inside (2008)

Having spirited his parents out of their domed suburb, Martin goes to the school for help and finds that his sister, Cassie, and the other Wonder Babies are gone again, but his AllDog, Chip, may hold the means to save them all.

"Throughout, Dunkle creates a vivid sense of imminent danger. . . . The book is recommended for readers who enjoyed the first volume." Booklist

Dunlap, Susanne Emily

The **musician's** daughter; [by] Susanne Dunlap. Bloomsbury 2009 322p $16.99

Grades: 8 9 10 11 12 Fic

1. Composers 2. Mystery fiction 3. Homicide -- Fiction 4. Romanies -- Fiction 5. Vienna (Austria) -- Fiction

ISBN 978-1-59990-332-3; 1-59990-332-6

LC 2008-30307

In eighteenth-century Vienna, Austria, fifteen-year-old Theresa seeks a way to help her mother and brother financially while investigating the murder of her father, a renowned violinist in Haydn's orchestra at the court of Prince Esterhazy, after his body is found near a gypsy camp.

"Dunlap skillfully builds suspense until the final page. . . . Readers will root for courageous Theresa through the exciting intrigue even as they absorb deeper messages about music and art's power to lift souls and inspire change." Booklist

Dunmore, Helen

The **deep**. HarperCollinsPublishers 2009 326p $16.99

Grades: 6 7 8 9 Fic

1. Fantasy fiction 2. Mermaids and mermen -- Fiction

ISBN 978-0-06-081858-6; 0-06-081858-1

Sequel to: The tide knot (2008)

When the ferocious shape-shifting Kraken awakes after thousands of years and threatens the Mer, Sapphire agrees to help them by going with her brother Conor and their friend Faro into the Deep to lull the monster back to sleep.

The author "evokes setting well, and her descriptions of the sea world are lovely. She writes knowledgably about the sperm whale." Voice Youth Advocates

Ingo. HarperCollins Pubs. 2005 328p $16.99; lib bdg $17.89

Grades: 6 7 8 9 **Fic**

1. Great Britain -- Fiction 2. Mermaids and mermen -- Fiction

ISBN 978-0-06-081852-4; 0-06-081852-2; 978-0-06-081853-1 lib bdg; 0-06-081853-0 lib bdg

LC 2005-19079

As they search for their missing father near their Cornwall home, Sapphy and her brother Conor learn about their family's connection to the domains of air and of water.

"Strong character development combines with an engaging plot and magical elements to make this a fine choice for fantasy readers, who will look forward to the next installments in this planned trilogy." SLJ

Other titles about Sapphire are:

The tide knot (2008)

The deep (2009)

Tide knot. HarperCollins Publishers 2008 330p $16.99; $17.89

Grades: 6 7 8 9 **Fic**

1. Great Britain -- Fiction 2. Mermaids and mermen -- Fiction

ISBN 978-0-06-081855-5; 0-06-081855-7; 978-0-06-081856-2 lib bdg; 0-06-081856-5 lib bdg

LC 2007-06991

Sequel to: Ingo (2006)

First published 2006 in the United Kingdom

Two years after the disappearance of their father, Sapphire and Conor, having moved with their mother to the town of St. Pirans, try to make a new life for themselves, but Sapphire, unlike her mother and brother, finds it increasingly difficult to adjust to her new circumstances and is drawn more and more to the undersea world of Ingo.

"Supporting the brightly adventurous plot are believably flawed and conflicted characters." Horn Book

Followed by: The deep (2009)

DuPrau, Jeanne

★ The **city** of Ember. Random House 2003 270p (Books of Ember) $15.95; lib bdg $17.99; pa $6.99

Grades: 5 6 7 8 **Fic**

1. Science fiction

ISBN 0-375-82273-9; 0-375-92274-1 lib bdg; 0-385-73628-2 pa

LC 2002-10239

"The writing and storytelling are agreeably spare and remarkably suspenseful." Horn Book

Other titles in this series are:

The people of Sparks (2004)

The prophet of Yonwood (2006)

The diamond of Darkhold (2008)

The **diamond** of Darkhold. Random House 2008 285p (Books of Ember) $16.99; lib bdg $19.99

Grades: 5 6 7 8 **Fic**

1. Fantasy fiction

ISBN 978-0-375-85571-9; 0-375-85571-8; 978-0-375-95571-6 lib bdg; 0-375-95571-2 lib bdg; 978-0-375-85572-6 pa; 0-375-85572-6 pa

LC 2007-47929

When a roamer trades them an ancient book with only a few pages remaining, Lina and Doon return to Ember to seek the machine the book seems to describe in hopes that it will get their new community, Sparks, through the winter.

"A solid and satisfying conclusion to the 'Ember Saga,' set in a post-disaster future." SLJ

The **people** of Sparks. Random House 2004 338p (Books of Ember) $15.95; lib bdg $17.99

Grades: 5 6 7 8 **Fic**

1. Science fiction

ISBN 0-375-82824-9; 0-375-92824-3 lib bdg

LC 2003-20760

Sequel to The City of Ember

"DuPrau continues the adventures of Lina and Doon, who have led the 400 residents from the underground city of Ember to the unfamiliar world above. The refugees are tentatively welcomed, housed, and fed by the people of Sparks, located near the wasteland left by the long-ago Disaster that destroyed most of civilization. Conflicts arise between the two groups. . . . DuPrau clearly explores themes of nonviolence and when to stand up for oneself. The text smoothly involves new readers and fans of the first story, creating a range of three-dimensional characters." Booklist

The **prophet** of Yonwood. Random House 2006 289p (Books of Ember) $15.95; lib bdg $17.99; pa $6.99

Grades: 5 6 7 8 **Fic**

1. Science fiction

ISBN 0-375-87526-3; 0-375-97526-8 lib bdg; 0-440-42124-1 pa

LC 2005-22423

Prequel to The city of Ember (2003) and The people of Sparks (2004)

While visiting the small town of Yonwood, North Carolina, eleven-year-old Nickie makes some decisions about how to identify both good and evil when she witnesses the townspeople's reactions to the apocalyptic visions of one of their neighbors

"This novel has a great deal of immediacy in light of current world events. It sharply brings home the idea of people blindly following a belief without questioning it." SLJ

Durbin, William

The **broken** blade. Delacorte Press 1997 163p hardcover o.p. pa $5.50

Grades: 5 6 7 8 **Fic**

1. Canada -- Fiction 2. Fur trade -- Fiction

ISBN 0-385-32224-0; 0-440-41184-X

LC 96-22114

When an injury prevents his father from going into northern Canada with fur traders, thirteen-year-old Pierre decides to take his father's place as a voyageur

"This look at the early nineteenth-century Canadian fur trade should appeal to reluctant readers as well as adventure buffs, and it may be a welcome suggestion for middle-school historical fiction reports." Bull Cent Child Books

Durham, Paul

Fork -tongue charmers; Paul Durham ; illustrations by Petur Antonsson. Harper, an imprint of HarperCollinsPublishers 2015 416 p. illustrations, maps (The Luck Uglies) (hardcover) $16.99; paperback $7.99

Grades: 4 5 6 7 8 **Fic**

1. Magic -- Fiction 2. Criminals -- Fiction 3. Fantasy 4. Monsters -- Fiction 5. Secret societies -- Fiction 6. Adventure and adventurers -- Fiction

ISBN 0062271539; 9780062271532; 9780062271549; 9780062271556

LC 2014038648

Sequel to: The Luck Uglies (2014)

In this novel by Paul Durham, illustrated by Petur Antonsson, "Rye O'Chanter was shocked to discover that her father was the leader . . .

of outlaws known as the Luck Uglies. Now she too has been declared a criminal . . . and she must flee to the strange and remote Isle of Pest while her father faces off against . . . the Fork-Tongue Charmers, on the mainland. When the battle moves to the shores of Pest . . . Rye must . . . lead the charge in defending the island." (Publisher's note)

"There is not a single dull moment in this story, which packs in as many clever twists and fully fleshed characters as the first book. And the writing remains a total delight: witty, richly layered, and capable of creating a world as real as this one. A bittersweet ending assures the reader that Rye's adventures are not over yet." Booklist

The **luck** uglies; Paul Durham ; illustrations by Petur Antonsson. Harper, an imprint of HarperCollinsPublishers 2014 400 p. (hardback) $16.99; paperback $6.99
Grades: 4 5 6 7 8 **Fic**

1. Fantasy fiction 2. Secret societies -- Fiction 3. Monsters -- Fiction 4. Adventure and adventurers -- Fiction
ISBN 0062271504; 9780062271501; 9780062271525; 9780062271518

LC 2013047720

In this book, by Paul Durham, "a terrifying encounter has eleven-year-old Rye O'Chanter convinced that the monstrous, supposedly extinct Bog Noblins have returned. Now Rye's only hope is an exiled secret society so notorious its name can't be spoken aloud: the Luck Uglies. As Rye dives into Village Drowning's maze of secrets, rules, and lies, she'll discover the truth behind the village's legends of outlaws and beasts . . . and that it may take a villain to save them from the monsters." (Publisher's note)

"Rye O'Chanter and her friends Quinn and Folly live in Drowning, which is ruled by the tyrannical Earl Longchance, who bans women from reading. When the earl does nothing to protect the villagers from marauding monsters, Drowning's only hope is the Luck Uglies, a notorious outlaw gang--that may or may not exist. Durham's fast-paced narrative and clever characters enhance this humorous and engaging tale." Horn Book

Durrant, S. E.

Running on empty; by S.E. Durrant. Holiday House 2018 201 p. (hardcover) $17.99
Grades: 4 5 6 7 **Fic**

1. Running -- Fiction 2. Grandfathers -- Fiction 3. Family life -- England -- Fiction 4. Death -- Fiction 5. England -- Fiction 6. Responsibility -- Fiction 7. People with disabilities -- Fiction 8. People with mental disabilities -- Fiction
ISBN 9780823438402

LC 2017035204

In this book, by S. E. Durrant, "CJ is a runner--and when he's running, he's fast, free, and flying. It was Grandad who taught him to run, and who did a lot more, besides. Grandad always made sure things were in order around CJ's house, because his parents could not. . . . But now, with Grandad's sudden passing . . . , CJ knows it's up to him to make sure Mum and Dad are okay and to keep the household going." (Publisher's note)

Durst, Sarah Beth

The **girl** who could not dream; by Sarah Beth Durst. Clarion Books, Houghton Mifflin Harcourt 2015 384 p. paperback $7.99; (hardback) OP
Grades: 4 5 6 7 **Fic**

1. Dreams -- Fiction 2. Monsters -- Fiction 3. Family life -- Fiction 4. Adventure and adventurers -- Fiction 5. Families -- Fiction
ISBN 9780544935266; 9780544464995; 0544464974; 9780544464971

LC 2015001324

In this book, by Sarah Beth Durst, "Sophie loves the hidden shop below her parents' bookstore, where dreams are secretly bought and sold. When the dream shop is robbed and her parents go missing, Sophie must unravel the truth to save them. Together with her best friend, a wise-cracking and fanatically loyal monster named Monster, she must decide whom to trust with her family's carefully guarded secrets. Who will help them, and who will betray them?" (Publisher's note)

"Sophie's parents run a secret shop beneath their bookstore selling dreams. One night Sophie, who can't dream, steals one and discovers that she has the dangerous power to bring dream-creatures into the waking world. Sophie's dream-friends Monster and the delightfully arrogant unicorn Glitterhoof keep the story merry with their precocious quips, but the adventure does take some turns through dark and perilous territory." Horn Book

Ice. Margaret K. McElderry Books 2009 308p $16.99
Grades: 7 8 9 10 **Fic**

1. Fairy tales 2. Polar bear -- Fiction 3. Scientists -- Fiction 4. Supernatural -- Fiction 5. Arctic regions -- Fiction
ISBN 978-1-4169-8643-0; 1-4169-8643-X

LC 2009-8618

A modern-day retelling of "East o' the Sun, West o' the Moon" in which eighteen-year-old Cassie learns that her grandmother's fairy tale is true when a Polar Bear King comes to claim her for his bride and she must decide whether to go with him and save her long-lost mother, or continue helping her father with his research

"Told in a descriptive style that perfectly captures the changing settings, Durst's novel is a page-turner that readers who enjoy adventure mixed with fairy-tale romance will find hard to put down." Booklist

Into the Wild. Razorbill 2007 260p $15.99
Grades: 6 7 8 9 **Fic**

1. Fairy tales 2. Magic -- Fiction
ISBN 978-1-59514-156-9; 1-59514-156-1

LC 2007-01942

Having escaped from the Wild and the preordained fairy tale plots it imposes, Rapunzel, along with her daughter Julie Marchen, tries to live a fairly normal life, but when the Wild breaks free and takes over their town, it is Julie who has to prevent everyone from being trapped in the events of a story.

"The novel is a creative romp through the fairy tale genre, highlighting the strength of the female characters whose stories we all know so well." Kliatt

Another title about Julie is:
Out of the wild (2008)

Spark; Sarah Beth Durst. Clarion Books, Houghton Mifflin Harcourt 2019 311 p. (hardback) $17.99
Grades: 4 5 6 7 **Fic**

1. Magic -- Fiction 2. Dragons -- Fiction 3. Mythical animals -- Fiction 4. Fantasy 5. Weather -- Fiction 6. Quietude -- Fiction
ISBN 1328973425; 9781328973429

LC 2018035180

In this book, by Sarah Beth Durst, "storm beasts and their guardians create perfect weather every day, and Mina longs for a storm beast of her own. But when the gentle girl bonds with a lightning beast--a creature of fire and chaos--everyone's certain it's a mistake. Everyone but Mina and the beast himself, Pixit. . . . Mina struggles to master a guardian's skills, and she discovers that her country's weather comes at a devastating cost--a cost powerful people wish to hide." (Publisher's note)

"A reassuring journey of self-discovery that will charm readers of Claire Fayers and Kristin Bailey's middle grade fantasy tales" (School Library Journal)

The **stone** girl's story; Sarah Beth Durst. Clarion Books/ Houghton Mifflin Harcourt 2018 336 p. (hardcover) $16.99
Grades: 4 5 6 7 8 **Fic**

1. Fantasy fiction 2. Storytelling -- Fiction 3. Authorship -- Fiction 4. Stone carvers -- Fiction 5. Adventure and adventurers -- Fiction
ISBN 9781328729453

LC 2017012702

In this book, by Sarah Beth Durst, "Mayka and her stone family were brought to life by the stories etched into their bodies. Now time is eroding these vital marks, and Mayka must find a stonemason to recarve them. But the search is more complex than she had imagined, and Mayka uncovers a scheme endangering all stone creatures. Only someone who casts stories into stone can help--but whom can Mayka trust?" (Publisher's note)

Vessel; Sarah Beth Durst. Margaret K. McElderry Books 2012 424 p. (hardcover) $16.99
Grades: 7 8 9 10 **Fic**

1. Deserts -- Fiction 2. Fantasy fiction 3. Adventure fiction -- Fiction 5. Gods and goddesses -- Fiction 6. Survival -- Fiction 7. Goddesses -- Fiction 8. Fate and fatalism -- Fiction
ISBN 1442423765; 9781442423763; 9781442423787

LC 2011044691

In this book by Sarah Beth Durst, "Liyana has trained all her life to be the vessel for her desert tribe's goddess Bayla. . . . "Bayla never shows up, but the trickster god Korbyn appears in human form and gives Liyana some startling news: the gods have all been imprisoned in false vessels, and he and Liyana must retrieve the various tribes' unsuccessful vessels, figure out where the deities are being held, and rescue them." (Bulletin of the Center for Children's Books)

Eagar, Lindsay

★ **Hour** of the Bees; Lindsay Eagar. Candlewick Press 2016 368 p. (hardcover) $16.99
Grades: 5 6 7 8 **Fic**

1. Magic realism (Literature) 2. Grandparent-grandchild relationship -- Fiction
ISBN 0763679224; 9780763679224

LC 2015954524

In this novel, by Lindsay Eagar, "magic blends with reality in a stunning coming-of-age novel about a girl, a grandfather, wanderlust, and reclaiming your roots. . . . At first, Carol avoids prickly Grandpa Serge. But as the summer wears on and the heat bears down, Carol finds herself . . . fascinated by the crazy stories he tells her. . . . As the thin line between magic and reality starts to blur, Carol must decide for herself what is possible." (Publisher's note)

"Both Carol's journey and Serge's stories seem inherently true, and the juxtaposition of the two results in a moving, atmospheric novel of family, heritage, and fairy tales that are more real than not." Booklsit

Race to the bottom of the sea; Lindsay Eagar. Candlewick Press 2017 423 p. (hardcover) $17.99
Grades: 4 5 6 7 8 **Fic**

1. Grief -- Fiction 2. Pirates -- Fiction 3. Kidnapping -- Fiction 4. Marine biologists -- Fiction 5. Girls -- Fiction 6. Orphans -- Fiction
ISBN 9780763679231; 9780763693923; 0763679232

LC 2017956984

In this book, by Lindsay Eagar, "when her parents, the great marine scientists Dr. and Dr. Quail, are killed in a tragic accident, eleven-year-old Fidelia Quail is racked by grief — and guilt. It was a submarine of Fidelia's invention that her parents were in when they died. . . . But Fidelia is forced out of her mourning when she's kidnapped by Merrick the Monstrous, a pirate whose list of treasons stretches longer than a ribbon eel." (Publisher's note)

"Earnest and exciting, this swashbuckling voyage of self-discovery sparkles even when threatened by the stormiest seas." Booklist

Edwards, Janet

Earth girl; by Janet Edwards. Pyr 2013 350 p. (Earth girl trilogy) hbk $17.95
Grades: 7 8 9 10 **Fic**

1. Science fiction 2. People with disabilities -- Fiction
ISBN 9781616147655; 1616147652

LC 2012044570

In this young adult novel set in the future, Jarra and other Handicapped are discriminated against by the Norms. "Jarra decides to show them that she is just as good as they are and applies to an off-world college conducting an archaeology dig on the abandoned buildings of New York. Reinventing herself as Jarra Military Kid, JMK watches vids and takes combat lessons. . . . Since she grew up on Earth and has been to the New York digs many times, her skills quickly allow her to shine." (School Library Journal)

"The future that Edwards constructs is creative and the dig descriptions are well thought out. . . . The 'person against nature' conflict with unstable dig conditions and solar flares makes a refreshing change." SLJ

★ **Earth** star; Janet Edwards. Pyr, an imprint of Prometheus Books 2014 360 p. (hardback) $17.99
Grades: 7 8 9 10 11 12 **Fic**

1. Children with disabilities -- Abuse of -- Fiction
ISBN 1616148977; 9781616148973

LC 2013040057

In this sequel to Janet Edwards's "Earth Girl," "it's 2789. People portal between planets in seconds, often many times per day--except the Handicapped, like Jarra, whose immune systems can survive only on Earth. . . . She plans to continue studying prehistory by excavating sites of long-dead cities. But before the next dig begins, Jarra and boyfriend Fian are whisked off to a military base and inexplicably sworn in as officers. An unidentified alien sphere is hovering above Africa." (Kirkus Reviews)

"This far-future science-fiction sequel skips tired genre tropes to offer a fresh and thrilling adventure about hazardous archaeological excavation, a mystery in the sky and a potential threat to all of humanity... Nitty-gritty archaeology details are vivid, and easy slang creates color ("Twoing" is dating; "amaz" means amazing). Edwards shows that speculative fiction needn't be dystopic, conspiracy-filled or love-triangled to be riveting and satisfying. Amaz—simply amaz." (Kirkus)

Edwardson, Debby Dahl

★ **My** name is not easy. Marshall Cavendish 2011 248p $17.99; e-book $17.99
Grades: 7 8 9 10 **Fic**

1. School stories 2. Alaska -- Fiction 3. Native Americans -- Fiction
ISBN 978-0-7614-5980-4; 0-7614-5980-4; 978-0-7614-6091-6 e-book

LC 2011002108

National Book Award Finalist: Young People's Literature (2011)

"Edwardson's skillful use of dialogue and her descriptions of rural Alaska as well as boarding-school life invoke a strong sense of empathy and compassion in readers. . . Edwardson is to be applauded for her depth of research and her ability to portray all sides of the equation in a fair and balanced manner while still creating a very enjoyable read." SLJ

Efaw, Amy

Battle dress. HarperCollins Pubs. 2000 291p hardcover o.p. lib bdg $16.89

Grades: 7 8 9 10 **Fic**

1. Military education -- Fiction 2. Women in the armed forces -- Fiction 3. United States Military Academy -- Fiction

ISBN 0-06-028411-0 lib bdg; 0-06-053520-2

LC 99-34516

As a newly arrived freshman at West Point, seventeen-year-old Andi finds herself gaining both confidence and self esteem as she struggles to get through the grueling six weeks of new cadet training known as the Beast

"This book by a West Point graduate is a gripping, hard-to-put-down look at a young woman's struggle to succeed in a traditionally all-male environment." Voice Youth Advocates

Ehrlich, Esther

Nest; by Esther Ehrlich. Wendy Lamb Books, an imprint of Random House Children's Books 2014 336 p. (lib. bdg.) $19.99; (hbk) $16.99

Grades: 4 5 6 7 **Fic**

1. Bird watching -- Fiction 2. Cape Cod (Mass.) -- Fiction 3. Multiple sclerosis -- Fiction 4. Sick -- Fiction 5. Schools -- Fiction 6. Family life -- Fiction

ISBN 0385386087; 9780385386081; 9780385386104; 9780385386074

LC 2013036245

"In 1972 home is a cozy nest on Cape Cod for eleven-year-old Naomi 'Chirp' Orenstein, her older sister, Rachel; her psychiatrist father; and her dancer mother. But then Chirp's mom develops symptoms of a serious disease, and everything changes. Chirp finds comfort in watching her beloved wild birds. She also finds a true friend in Joey, the mysterious boy who lives across the street." (Publisher's note)

"The focus on nature and the outdoors helps set the pace as the seasonal changes quietly indicate the passage of time. Sensitive readers should be aware of the tough issues that it addresses--suicide, depression, and personal loss. However, the story also offers a hopeful message." SLJ

Elfman, Eric

Tesla's attic; by Neal Shusterman and Eric Elfman. Disney-Hyperion Books 2014 256 p. (Accelerati trilogy) $16.99

Grades: 5 6 7 8 **Fic**

1. Houses -- Fiction 2. Tesla, Nikola, 1856-1943 3. Science fiction 4. Inventions -- Fiction 5. Colorado Springs (Colo.) -- Fiction

ISBN 1423148037; 9781423148036

LC 2012039773

This children's novel, by Eric Elfman and Neal Shusterman, is the first book of "The Accelerati Trilogy." "After getting rid of . . . odd antiques in a garage sale, Nick befriends some local kids . . . and they discover that all of the objects have extraordinary properties. What's more, Nick figures out that the attic is a strange magnetic vortex, which attracts all sorts of trouble. It's as if the attic itself has an intelligence . . . and a purpose." (Publisher's note)

"Lively, intelligent prose elevates this story of teenagers versus mad scientists, the third-person point of view offering a stage to various players in their play of galactic consequence." Kirkus

Other titles in this series are:
Edison's alley (2015)
Hawking's hallway (2016)

Elkeles, Simone

How to ruin a summer vacation. Flux 2006 234p pa $9.95

Grades: 7 8 9 10 11 12 **Fic**

1. Jews -- Fiction 2. Israel -- Fiction 3. Family life -- Fiction 4. Father-daughter relationship -- Fiction

ISBN 978-0-7387-0961-1; 0-7387-0961-1

LC 2006-40592

When sixteen-year-old Amy, a spoiled American, goes to Israel for a three-month summer vacation with a father she barely knows, she is not prepared for his Jewish family and the changes they bring about in her life.

"Amy's feisty attitude and penchant for drama keep the reader engaged. With just a touch of spice to the romance, this [is a] fast read." Voice Youth Advocates

Followed by: How to ruin my teenage life (2007)

How to ruin my teenage life. Flux 2007 281p pa $8.95

Grades: 7 8 9 10 11 12 **Fic**

1. Jews -- Fiction 2. Israelis -- Fiction 3. Chicago (Ill.) -- Fiction 4. Father-daughter relationship -- Fiction

ISBN 978-0-7387-0961-1; 0-7387-1019-9

LC 2007005535

Living with her Israeli father in Chicago, seventeen-year-old Amy Nelson-Barak feels like a walking disaster, worried about her "non-boyfriend" in the Israeli army, her mother, new stepfather, and the baby they are expecting, a new boy named Nathan who has moved into her apartment building and goes to her school, and whether or not she really is the selfish snob that Nathan says she is.

"This book has laugh-out-loud moments. . . . Amy's thoughtfulness and depth raise this book above most of the chick-lit genre." Voice Youth Advocates

Other titles in this series are:
How to ruin a summer vacation (2006)
How to ruin your boyfriend's reputation (2009)

How to ruin your boyfriend's reputation. Flux 2009 257p pa $9.95

Grades: 7 8 9 10 11 12 **Fic**

1. Israel -- Fiction 2. Soldiers -- Fiction 3. Military bases -- Fiction

ISBN 978-0-7387-1879-8 pa; 0-7387-1879-3 pa

LC 2009-23853

Sequel to: How to ruin my teenage life (2007)

During the summer between her junior and senior year of high school, spoiled Chicagoan Amy Nelson-Barak volunteers for Israeli military boot camp when she learns that her boyfriend, a commando in the Israeli Defense Force, will be at the same military base

"Readers can't help but get drawn in by Amy's fun way of telling her story, and they learn a lot about Israeli teens' mandatory military service." SLJ

Elliott, Laura

Hamilton and Peggy! a revolutionary friendship. L.M. Elliott. Katherine Tegen Books 2018 436 p. (hardcover) $17.99

Grades: 7 8 9 10 11 12 **Fic**

1. Sisters -- Fiction 2. Friendship -- Fiction 3. United States --

History -- Revolution, 1775-1783 -- Fiction
ISBN 9780062671325; 9780062671301

LC 2017944492

In this novel, author Laura Elliott "successfully navigates the challenge of maintaining historical accuracy while upholding the personalities popularized by the musical ['Hamilton!']. [Peggy] is showcased as a strong protagonist who is confident in the best possible ways. Her memorable story will keep readers interested from start to finish." (Booklist)

Includes bibliographical references (pages 427-436).

Under a war-torn sky; [by] L.M. Elliott. Hyperion Bks. for Children 2001 284p hardcover o.p. pa $5.99

Grades: 7 8 9 10 **Fic**

1. France -- Fiction 2. World War, 1939-1945 -- Fiction
ISBN 0-7868-0755-5; 0-7868-1753-4 pa

LC 2001-16633

After his plane is shot down by Hitler's Luftwaffe, nineteen-year-old Henry Forester of Richmond, Virginia, strives to walk across occupied France, with the help of the French Resistance, in hopes of rejoining his unit

"It's packed with action, intrigue, and suspense, but this novel celebrates acts of kindness and heroism without glorifying war." Booklist

Followed by: A troubled peace (2009)

Elliott, Patricia

The **Pale** Assassin. Holiday House 2009 336p $17.95

Grades: 7 8 9 10 **Fic**

1. Adventure fiction 2. Siblings -- Fiction 3. France -- History -- 1789-1799, Revolution -- Fiction
ISBN 978-0-8234-2250-0; 0-8234-2250-X

LC 2009-7554

In early 1790s Paris, as the Revolution gains momentum, young and sheltered Eugenie de Boncoeur finds it difficult to tell friend from foe as she and the royalist brother she relies on become the focus of "le Fantome," the sinister spymaster with a long-held grudge against their family.

"The best aspect of this excellent work of historical fiction is Eugenie herself. Her gradual coming of age and growing political awareness provides resonant depth to what becomes a highly suspenseful survival tale." Booklist

Followed by: The traitor's smile (2011)

The **traitor's** smile. Holiday House 2011 304p $17.95

Grades: 7 8 9 10 **Fic**

1. Adventure fiction 2. Cousins -- Fiction 3. France -- History -- 1789-1799, Revolution -- Fiction
ISBN 978-0-8234-2361-3; 0-8234-2361-1

Sequel to: The Pale Assassin (2009)

First published 2010 in the United Kingdom

As the French Revolutin rages around her, wealthy and beautiful Eugenie de Boncoeur is no longer safe in her own country. She flees the bloody streeets of Paris for her cousin Hetta's house in England, narrowly excaping the clutches of the evil Pale Assassin, who is determined to force her to marry him.

Ellis, Ann Dee

This is what I did. Little, Brown 2007 157p $16.99

Grades: 6 7 8 9 **Fic**

1. School stories 2. Bullies -- Fiction
ISBN 978-0-316-01363-5; 0-316-01363-3

LC 2006-01388

Bullied because of an incident in his past, eighth-grader Logan is unhappy at his new school and has difficulty relating to others until he meets a quirky girl and a counselor who believe in him.

"Part staccato prose, part transcript, this haunting first novel will grip readers right from the start. . . . A particularly attractive book design incorporates small drawings between each segment of text." Publ Wkly

Ellis, Deborah

My name is Parvana. Groundwood Books/House of Anansi Press 2012 201 p. (hardcover) $16.95

Grades: 5 6 7 8 **Fic**

1. Afghanistan -- Fiction 2. Interrogation -- Fiction 3. Women -- Afghanistan -- Fiction
ISBN 1554982979; 9781554982974

In this novel by Deborah Ellis "15-year-old Parvana is imprisoned and interrogated as a suspected terrorist in Afghanistan. . . . Parvana's captors" read "aloud the words in her notebook to decide if the angry written sentiments of a teenage girl can be evidence of guilt. . . . The interrogation, the words of the notebook and the effective third-person narration combine for a . . . portrait of a girl and her country." (Kirkus Reviews)

No ordinary day. Groundwood Books 2011 160p $16.95; paperback $9.95

Grades: 5 6 7 **Fic**

1. India -- Fiction 2. Leprosy -- Fiction 3. Orphans -- Fiction 4. Poverty -- Fiction 5. Homeless persons -- Fiction
ISBN 978-1-55498-134-2; 1-55498-134-4; 9781554981083

"Valli, about 10, lives in the poverty-stricken town of Jharia, India, where she is a coal picker. When she makes a shocking discovery about her family, she runs away and, after a series of harrowing events, reaches the bustling city of Kolkata. . . . While begging for change one day, she is befriended by a kind doctor who recognizes Valli's symptoms of leprosy. . . . With the help of the doctor and other leprosy patients, Valli gets treatment and education, learns tolerance for people different from herself, and simultaneously realizes her own self-worth. Although many important lessons are presented in this even-paced, clearly written story, it is never heavyhanded or didactic. Valli is a well-developed, realistic, and engaging narrator. . . . An important, inspiring tale." SLJ

Elston, Ashley

The **rules** for disappearing; Ashley Elston. 1st ed. Hyperion 2013 320 p. (reinforced) $16.99

Grades: 7 8 9 10 11 12 **Fic**

1. Witnesses -- Fiction 2. Friendship -- Fiction 3. Dysfunctional families -- Fiction 4. Schools -- Fiction 5. High schools -- Fiction 6. Moving, Household -- Fiction 7. Natchitoches (La.) -- Fiction 8. Family life -- Louisiana -- Fiction
ISBN 1423168976; 9781423168973

LC 2012035122

In this book by Ashley Elston, "seventeen-year-old Meg Jones . . . and her family are in the witness protection program, and they've changed towns six times in less than a year. . . . Meg's mother is an alcoholic, her father is depressed and secretive, and her 11-year-old sister is having trouble coping with all of the change. Fed up, Meg wants out of the program and will do anything to save her family, including digging up what her father did to get them into this mess." (Publishers Weekly)

"The fresh first-person narration serves the story well, providing grounding in reality as events spin out of control. Though the plot may seem a bit far-fetched at times, the realistic setting, believable romance and spunky protagonist will make this one worth the trip for mystery and romance fans." Kirkus

Followed by The rules for breaking (2014)

Emerson, Kevin

Last day on Mars; Kevin Emerson ; [edited by] Jordan Brown. HarperCollins 2017 336 p. (Chronicle of the dark star) (hardcover) $16.99

Grades: 4 5 6 7 8 **Fic**

1. Science fiction 2. Mars (Planet) -- Fiction
ISBN 9780062306715

LC 2016938987

In this book, by Kevin Emerson, "it is Earth year 2213--but, of course there is no Earth anymore. . . . The human race has fled to Mars, . . . Liam Saunders-Chang is one of the last humans left on Mars. The son of two scientists who have been racing against time to create technology vital to humanity's survival, Liam, along with his friend Phoebe, will be on the last starliner to depart before Mars, like Earth before it, is destroyed." (Publisher's note)

Other titles in this series are:
The oceans between stars (2018)
The shores beyond time (2019)

Emond, Stephen

Bright lights, dark nights; Stephen Emond. Roaring Brook Press 2015 384 p. illustrations (hardback) $17.99

Grades: 7 8 9 10 **Fic**

1. Race relations -- Fiction 2. Dating (Social customs) -- Fiction 3. Schools -- Fiction 4. Friendship -- Fiction 5. Best friends -- Fiction 6. High schools -- Fiction 7. Fathers and sons -- Fiction 8. Single-parent families -- Fiction
ISBN 1626722064; 9781626722064

LC 2014047413

In this novel, by Stephen Emond, "Walter Wilcox has never been in love. That is, until he meets Naomi, and sparks, and clever jokes, fly. But when his cop dad is caught in a racial profiling scandal, Walter and Naomi, who is African American, are called out at school, home, and online. Can their bond (and mutual love of the Foo Fighters) keep them together?" (Publisher's note)

"Readers coming to this story for romance may feel shortchanged, as the relationship here is more true-to-life and awkward than swooningly romantic, but that's what sets Emond's book apart. A real slice of contemporary teenage life that's painfully honest about the below-the-surface racism in today's America." Booklist

Happyface. Little, Brown and Co. 2010 307p il $16.99

Grades: 7 8 9 10 **Fic**

1. School stories 2. Diaries -- Fiction 3. Divorce -- Fiction 4. Dating (Social customs) -- Fiction
ISBN 978-0-316-04100-3; 0-316-04100-9

LC 2008-47386

After going through traumatic times, a troubled, socially awkward teenager moves to a new school where he tries to reinvent himself.

"The illustrations range from comics to more fleshed-out drawings. Just like Happyface's writing, they can be whimsical, thoughtful, boyishly sarcastic, off-the-cuff, or achingly beautiful." Publ Wkly

★ **Winter** town; Story and art by Stephen Emond. Little, Brown 2011 336p il $17.99

Grades: 7 8 9 **Fic**

1. Romance fiction 2. Teenagers -- Fiction 3. High school students -- Fiction 4. Cartoons and caricatures -- Fiction 5. Love stories
ISBN 0316133329; 9780316133326

LC 2011012966

Evan and Lucy, childhood best friends who grew apart after years of seeing one another only during Christmas break, begin a romance at age seventeen but his choice to mindlessly follow his father's plans for an Ivy League education rather than becoming the cartoonist he longs to be, and her more destructive choices in the wake of family problems, pull them apart.

This is a "remarkable illustrated work of contemporary fiction. . . . Interspersed throughout are both realistic illustrations and drawings of a comic strip being created by Evan and Lucy; these black-and-white, almost chibi-style panels form an effective parallel with the plot and appeal mightily on their own. Compelling, honest and true—this musing about art and self-discovery, replete with pitch-perfect dialogue, will have wide appeal." Kirkus

Engdahl, Sylvia Louise

★ **Enchantress** from the stars; foreword by Lois Lowry. Firebird 2003 288p pa $6.99

Grades: 7 8 9 10 11 12 **Fic**

1. Science fiction
ISBN 0-14-250037-2

A reissue of the title first published 1970 by Atheneum Pubs.
A Newbery Medal honor book, 1971

When young Elana unexpectedly joins the team leaving the spaceship to study the planet Andrecia, she becomes an integral part of an adventure involving three very different civilizations, each one centered on the third planet from the star in its own solar system

"Emphasis is on the intricate pattern of events rather than on characterization, and readers will find fascinating symbolism—and philosophical parallels to what they may have observed or thought. The book is completely absorbing and should have a wider appeal than much science fiction." Horn Book

Engle, Margarita

★ **Firefly** letters; a suffragette's journey to Cuba. Henry Holt & Co. 2010 151p $16.99

Grades: 7 8 9 10 11 12 **Fic**

1. Authors 2. Novelists 3. Novels in verse 4. Cuba -- Fiction 5. Slavery -- Fiction 6. Sex role -- Fiction
ISBN 978-0-8050-9082-6; 0-8050-9082-7

LC 2009-23445

"This engaging title documents 50-year-old Swedish suffragette and novelist Fredrika Bremer's three-month travels around Cuba in 1851. Based in the home of a wealthy sugar planter, Bremer journeys around the country with her host's teenaged slave Cecilia, who longs for her mother and home in the Congo. Elena, the planter's privileged 12-year-old daughter, begins to accompany them on their trips into the countryside. . . . Using elegant free verse and alternating among each character's point of view, Engle offers powerful glimpses into Cuban life at that time. Along the way, she comments on slavery, the rights of women, and the stark contrast between Cuba's rich and poor." SLJ

★ The **Lightning** Dreamer; Cuba's Greatest Abolitionist. Margarita Engle. Houghton Mifflin Harcourt 2013 192 p. $16.99

Grades: 6 7 8 9 10 **Fic**

1. Historical fiction 2. Novels in verse 3. Authors -- Fiction 4. Feminists -- Fiction 5. Abolitionists -- Fiction 6. Cuba -- History -- 1810-1899 -- Fiction
ISBN 0547807430; 9780547807430

LC 2013003913

Pura Belpre Author Honor Book (2014)

This book is a "work of historical fiction about Cuban poet, author, antislavery activist and feminist Gertrudis Gómez de Avellaneda. Written in free verse, the story tells of how Tula, which was her childhood nickname, grows up in libraries, which she calls 'a safe place to heal/ and dream . . . ,' influenced by the poetry of Jose Maria Heredia." (School Library Journal)

Includes bibliographical references.

★ **Silver** people; voices from the Panama Canal. Margarita Engle. Houghton Mifflin Harcourt 2014 272 p. (hardback) $17.99; paperback $8.99

Grades: 5 6 7 8 **Fic**

1. Panama Canal 2. Novels in verse 3. Rain forests -- Fiction 4. Migrant labor -- Fiction 5. Racism -- Fiction 6. Segregation -- Fiction 7. Panama Canal (Panama) -- History -- Fiction

ISBN 0544109414; 9780544109414; 9780544109223; 9780544668706

LC 2013037485

This children's book, by Margarita Engle, is an "exploration of the construction of the Panama Canal. . . . Mateo, a 14-year-old Cuban lured by promises of wealth, journeys to Panama only to discover the recruiters' lies and a life of harsh labor. However, through his relationships with Anita, an 'herb girl,' Henry, a black Jamaican worker, and Augusto, a Puerto Rican geologist, Mateo is able to find a place in his new land." (Kirkus Reviews)

"In melodic verses, Engle offers the voices of the dark-skinned workers (known as the 'silver people'), whose backbreaking labor helped build the Panama Canal, along with the perspective of a local girl. Interspersed are occasional echoes from flora and fauna as well as cameo appearances by historical figures. Together, they provide an illuminating picture of the project's ecological sacrifices and human costs." Horn Book

Includes bibliographical references

The **wild** book; Margarita Engle. Harcourt Children's Books 2012 133p $16.99; paperback $7.99

Grades: 5 6 7 8 **Fic**

1. Novels in verse 2. Dyslexia -- Fiction 3. Cuba -- History -- 1909-1933 -- Fiction

ISBN 9780547581316; 9780544022751

LC 2011027320

This book tells the story of "Josefa 'Fefa' de la Caridad Uría Peña. . . . Diagnosed with 'word blindness' (a misnomer for dyslexia), Fefa struggles at school. . . . Discounting a doctor's opinion . . . her mother gives her a blank diary: 'Let the words sprout / like seedlings, / then relax and watch / as your wild diary / grows.' . . . Her reading difficulties are heightened when bandits begin roving the countryside, kidnapping local children for ransom." (Kirkus Reviews)

English, Karen

Francie. Farrar, Straus & Giroux 1999 199p hardcover o.p. $17; paperback $8.99

Grades: 5 6 7 8 **Fic**

1. Alabama -- Fiction 2. Race relations -- Fiction 3. African Americans -- Fiction

ISBN 0-374-32456-5; 0-374-42459-4 pa; 9780312373832

LC 98-53047

Coretta Scott King honor book for text, 2000

"The best student in her small, all-black school in preintegration Alabama, 12-year-old Francie hopes for a better life. . . . When Jessie, an older school friend who is without family, is forced on the run by a racist employer, Francie leaves her mother's labeled canned food for him in the woods. Only when the sheriff begins searching their woods . . . does she realize the depth of the danger she may have brought to her family. Francie's smooth-flowing, well-paced narration is gently assisted by just the right touch of the vernacular. Characterization is evenhanded and believable, while place and time envelop readers." SLJ

★ **It** all comes down to this; by Karen English. Clarion Books, Houghton Mifflin Harcourt 2017 355 p. (hardback) $16.99

Grades: 5 6 7 8 **Fic**

1. Family life -- Fiction 2. African American teenagers -- Fiction 3. Riots -- Fiction 4. Race relations -- Fiction 5. African Americans -- Fiction 6. Family life -- California -- Los Angeles -- Fiction 7. Los Angeles (Calif.) -- History -- 20th century -- Fiction

ISBN 9781328695710; 9780544839571

LC 2016028946

Kirkus Prize Finalist: Young Readers' Literature (2017)

In this book, by Karen English, "all twelve-year-old Sophie wants to do is write her book, star in the community play, and hang out with her friend Jennifer. But she's the new black kid in a nearly all-white neighborhood; her beloved sister, Lily, is going away to college soon; and her parents' marriage is rocky. . . . When riots erupt in nearby Watts and a friend is unfairly arrested, Sophie learns that life—and her own place in it—is even more complicated than she'd once thought." (Publisher's note)

"A slice of African-American life seldom explored in stories for young people and a must for readers of middle-grade fiction." Kirkus

Erdrich, Louise, 1954-

★ The **birchbark** house. Hyperion Bks. for Children 1999 244p il hardcover o.p. pa $6.99

Grades: 5 6 7 8 **Fic**

1. Ojibwa Indians -- Fiction

ISBN 0-7868-0300-2; 0-7868-1454-3 pa

LC 98-46366

Omakayas, a seven-year-old Native American girl of the Ojibwa tribe, lives through the joys of summer and the perils of winter on an island in Lake Superior in 1847.

"Erdrich crafts images of tender beauty while weaving Ojibwa words seamlessly into the text. Her gentle spot art throughout complements this first of several projected stories that will 'attempt to retrace [her] own family's history.'" Horn Book Guide

Other titles in this series are:
The game of silence (2005)
The porcupine year (2008)
Chickadee (2012)
Makoons (2016)

★ **Chickadee**; Louise Erdrich. Harper 2012 256p. (trade bdg.) $16.99

Grades: 5 6 7 8 **Fic**

1. Brothers -- Fiction 2. Ojibwe Indians -- Fiction 3. Voyages and travels -- Fiction 4. Kidnapping -- Fiction 5. Family life -- Fiction 6. Métis -- Fiction 7. Ojibwa Indians -- Fiction 8. Great Plains -- History -- 19th century -- Fiction 9. Superior, Lake, Region -- History -- 19th century -- Fiction

ISBN 9780060577902; 9780060577919

LC 2012006565

Sequel to: The porcupine year.

Scott O'Dell Award for Historical Fiction (2013)

This book is the "fourth book of The Birchbark House Series. Omakayas is now a young mother with lively 8-year-old twins named Chickadee and Makoons." Makoons plays a trick on the tribe's bully, resulting in the bully's sons kidnapping Chickadee. He escapes, then "runs into his Uncle Quill driving an ox cart of furs to sell in St. Paul. Quill and

Chickadee travel with fellow traders on the Red River ox cart trail, arriving in Pembina to find Makoons seriously ill." (Kirkus)

★ The **game** of silence; [by] Louise Erdrich. HarperCollins 2004 256p $15.99; lib bdg $16.89; pa $5.99
Grades: 5 6 7 8 **Fic**

1. Ojibwa Indians -- Fiction
ISBN 0-06-029789-1; 0-06-029790-5 lib bdg; 0-06-441029-3 pa
LC 2004-6018

Sequel to: The birchbark house (1999)

Nine-year-old Omakayas, of the Ojibwa tribe, moves west with her family in 1849

"Erdrich's captivating tale of four seasons portrays a deep appreciation of our environment, our history, and our Native American sisters and brothers." SLJ

Followed by: The porcupine year (2008)

Makoons; by Louise Erdrich. Harpercollins Childrens Books 2016 176 p. $16.99
Grades: 5 6 7 8 **Fic**

1. Ojibwe Indians -- Fiction
ISBN 0060577932; 9780060577933; 9780807581391

In this book, author and illustrator Louise Erdrich "continues her award-winning Birchbark House series. . . . Named for the Ojibwe word for little bear, Makoons and his twin, Chickadee, have traveled with their family to the Great Plains of Dakota Territory. There they must learn to become buffalo hunters and once again help their people make a home in a new land. But Makoons has had a vision that foretells great challenges—challenges that his family may not be able to overcome." (Publisher's note)

"Erdrich's simple text and delicate pencil illustrations provide a detailed, honest portrait of Plains life through the antics and experiences of two Ojibwe boys.A warm and welcome addition to the unfolding saga of a 19th-century Ojibwe family." Kirkus

★ The **porcupine** year. HarperCollinsPublishers 2008 193p $15.99; lib bdg $16.89
Grades: 5 6 7 8 **Fic**

1. Family life -- Fiction 2. Ojibwa Indians -- Fiction 3. Voyages and travels -- Fiction
ISBN 978-0-06-029787-9; 0-06-029787-5; 978-0-06-029788-6 lib bdg; 0-06-029788-3 lib bdg
LC 2008000757

Sequel to: The game of silence (2004)

In 1852, forced by the United States government to leave their beloved Island of the Golden Breasted Woodpecker, fourteen-year-old Omokayas and her Ojibwe family travel in search of a new home.

"Based on Erdrich's own family history, this celebration of life will move readers with its mischief, its anger, and its sadness. What is left unspoken is as powerful as the story told." Booklist

Erlingsson, Fridrik

Benjamin Dove. North-South 2007 206p $15.95; pa $7.95
Grades: 6 7 8 9 **Fic**

1. Friendship -- Fiction
ISBN 978-0-7358-2150-7; 0-7358-2150-X; 978-0-7358-2149-1 pa; 0-7358-2149-6 pa

"Benjamin tells the story of the summer her was 12, when free-spirited Roland moved into the neighborhood and changed the lives of Benjamin and his friends Jeff and Manny forever. . . . This is a well-written, attention-grabbing tale of desire for acceptance, conflict between good and evil, and coming-of-age." SLJ

Erskine, Kathryn

The **absolute** value of Mike. Philomel Books 2011 247p $16.99; paperback $7.99
Grades: 5 6 7 8 **Fic**

1. Pennsylvania -- Fiction 2. Business enterprises -- Fiction 3. Father-son relationship -- Fiction 4. Eccentrics and eccentricities -- Fiction
ISBN 978-0-399-25505-2; 0-399-25505-2; 9780142421017
LC 2010-13333

Fourteen-year-old Mike, whose father is a brilliant mathematician but who has no math aptitude himself, spends the summer in rural Pennsylvania with his elderly and eccentric relatives Moo and Poppy, helping the townspeople raise money to adopt a Romanian orphan.

"Erskine weaves together a large but entertaining cast of characters. . . . Despite many laugh-out-loud moments, the heart of the book is essentially serious." Horn Book

★ **Mockingbird**. Philomel Books 2010 235p paperback $7.99
Grades: 4 5 6 **Fic**

1. School stories 2. Siblings -- Fiction 3. Bereavement -- Fiction 4. Asperger's syndrome -- Fiction 5. Father-daughter relationship -- Fiction
ISBN 0-399-25264-9; 978-0-399-25264-8; 9780142417751 ; 9781101149317
LC 2009-06741

National Book Award, 2010

Ten-year-old Caitlin, who has Asperger's Syndrome, struggles to understand emotions, show empathy, and make friends at school, while at home she seeks closure by working on a project with her father. "Age ten and up." (Publisher's note)

Seeing red; by Kathryn Erskine. Scholastic Press 2013 352 p. $16.99
Grades: 5 6 7 8 **Fic**

1. Family -- Fiction 2. Friendship -- Fiction 3. Race relations -- Fiction 4. Grief -- Fiction 5. Bereavement -- Fiction 6. Family life -- Virginia -- Fiction 7. Race relations -- Fiction 8. Virginia -- History -- Fiction 9. Families -- Virginia -- Fiction 10. Virginia -- History -- 20th century -- Fiction
ISBN 0545464404; 9780545464406; 9780545464413; 9780545576451
LC 2013004261

Author Kathryn Erskin presents a "story of family, friendship, and race relations in the South. Red's daddy, his idol, has just died, leaving Red and Mama with some hard decisions and a whole lot of doubt. Should they sell the Porter family business? When Red discovers the injustices that have been happening in Rocky Gap since before he was born, he's faced with unsettling questions about his family's legacy." (Publisher's note)

Eshbaugh, Julie

Ivory and bone; Julie Eshbaugh. HarperTeen 2016 376 p. (hardback) $17.99
Grades: 7 8 9 10 **Fic**

1. Love -- Fiction 2. Families -- Fiction 3. Prehistoric peoples -- Fiction 4. Survival -- Fiction
ISBN 9780062399267; 9780062399274; 9780062399250
LC 2015958594

In this young adult novel, by Julie Eshbaugh, edited by Alexandra Cooper, "hunting, gathering, and keeping his family safe--that's the life seventeen-year-old Kol knows. Then bold, enigmatic Mya arrives from the south with her family, and Kol is captivated. . . . What Kol doesn't know is that underneath Mya's cool disdain is a history wrought with loss that comes to light when another clan arrives. With them is Lo, an enemy from Mya's past who Mya swears has ulterior motives." (Publisher's note)

"Eshbaugh packs her debut with a classic love triangle, feuding clans, a well-drawn prehistoric setting, and a handful of fan fiction elements that will appeal to teens." SLJ

Obsidian and stars; Julie Eshbaugh. HarperTeen 2017 359 p. (Ivory and bone) (hardcover) $17.99

Grades: 7 8 9 10 **Fic**

1. Clans -- Fiction 2. Teenagers -- Fiction 3. Prehistoric peoples -- Fiction

ISBN 9780062399304; 9780062399298; 9780062399281

LC 2016961162

In this book, by Julie Eshbaugh, "after surviving the battle that erupted after Lo and the Bosha clan attacked, now Mya is looking ahead to her future with Kol. . . . But the same night as Kol and Mya's betrothal announcement, Mya's brother Chev reveals his plan to marry their youngest sister, Lees, to his friend Morsk. . . . In an effort to protect her sister, Mya whisks Lees away to a secret island." (Publisher's note)

Eulberg, Elizabeth

Revenge of the Girl With the Great Personality; Elizabeth Eulberg. Scholastic 2013 272 p. (hardcover) $17.99

Grades: 7 8 9 10 **Fic**

1. Sisters -- Fiction 2. Beauty contests -- Fiction

ISBN 9780545476997; 0545476992

"Everybody loves Lexi. She's popular, smart, funny . . . but she's never been one of . . . the pretty ones who get all the attention from guys. And on top of that, her seven-year-old sister, Mackenzie, is a terror in a tiara. . . . Lexi's sick of it. . . . The time has come for Lexi to step out from the sidelines. Girls without great personalities aren't going to know what hit them. Because Lexi's going to play the beauty game." (Publisher's note)

Evans, Lissa

Horten's miraculous mechanisms; magic, mystery & a very strange adventure. by Lissa Evans. Sterling 2012 270 p. hardcover o.p. $14.95

Grades: 3 4 5 6 7 **Fic**

1. Mystery fiction 2. Adventure fiction 3. Inventors -- Fiction 4. Magicians -- Fiction

ISBN 9781402798061

In this book, author Lissa "Evans borrows several classic tropes and themes--magic, riddles, a quest, and even a night at a museum--for the . . . story of 10-year-old Stuart Horten . . . who stumbles into a family mystery when he and his parents move to the small British town of Beeton. There, Stuart discovers that his Great-Uncle Tony Horten, who disappeared years ago without a trace, was both an inventor of mechanical devices and a magician. A chance phone call in a broken phone booth is the first step in a journey that leads Stuart around town, as he unearths his great-uncle's legacy and secrets. Stuart also draws the attention of April, May, and June (the journalistically inclined triplets next door), as well as Beeton residents with more sinister intentions." (Publishers Weekly)

Wed wabbit; Lissa Evans. Scholastic 2018 256 p. $17.99

Grades: 4 5 6 7 **Fic**

1. Rabbits -- Fiction 2. Friendship -- Fiction

ISBN 1338185276; 9781338185270

Carnegie Medal Shortlist (2018)

In this children's book, by Lissa Evans, "your name is Fidge and you're nearly eleven. You've been hurled into a strange world. You have three companions: two are unbelievably weird and the third is your awful cousin, Graham. You have to solve a series of nearly impossible clues. You need to deal with a cruel stuffed animal dictator and three thousand Wimbley Woos (yes, you read that sentence correctly). And the whole situation--the whole, entire thing--is your fault." (Publisher's note)

Evans, Richard Paul

★ The **prisoner** of cell 25; Richard Paul Evans. Mercury Ink/Simon Pulse 2011 326p (Michael Vey) $17.99

Grades: 6 7 8 9 **Fic**

1. Friendship -- Fiction 2. Electricity -- Fiction 3. Superheroes -- Fiction 4. Tourette syndrome -- Fiction

ISBN 978-1-4516-5650-3; 1-4516-5650-5

"To everyone at Meridian High School, Michael Vey is an ordinary fourteen-year-old. In fact, the only thing that seems to set him apart is the fact that he has Tourette's syndrome. But Michael is anything but ordinary. Michael has special powers. Electric powers. Michael thinks he's unique until he discovers that a cheerleader named Taylor also has special powers. With the help of Michael's friend, Ostin, the three of them set out to discover how Michael and Taylor ended up this way, but their investigation brings them to the attention of a powerful group who wants to control the electric children – and through them the world." (Publisher's note)

"Short chapters with intriguing titles, excellent writing, and engaging characters make this action-packed story a compulsively entertaining read. The tale progresses with altering points of view. Michael tells his story in first-person and Taylor's tale is narrated in third-person. . . . Though contemporary and edgy, this book contains no bad language, sex, or gratuitous violence. This is a book Rick Riordan's fans will want to read." Voice Youth Advocates

Other titles in this series are:
Rise of the Elgen (2012)
Battle of the Ampere (2013)
Hunt for Jade Dragon (2014)
Storm of lightning (2015)
Fall of Hades (2016)
The final spark (2017)

Eves, Rosalyn

Blood Rose Rebellion; Rosalyn Eves. Random House Childrens Books 2017 416 p. (Blood rose rebellion) $17.99

Grades: 7 8 9 10 **Fic**

1. Magic -- Fiction 2. Young women -- Fiction 3. Romanies -- Fiction

ISBN 1101935995; 9781101935996

LC 2017011094

In this book in the Blood Rose Rebellion series, by Rosalyn Eves, "sixteen-year-old Anna Arden is barred from society by a defect of blood. . . . She is Barren, unable to perform the simplest spells. . . . But her fate takes another course when, after inadvertently breaking her sister's debutante spell—an important chance for a highborn young woman to show her prowess with magic—Anna finds herself exiled to her family's once powerful but now crumbling native Hungary." (Publisher's note)

"Intrigue, romance, and revolution, with enough unanswered questions that fans will cross fingers for a sequel." Kirkus

Another title in this series is:

Lost Crow Conspiracy (2018)

Fairlie, Emily

The **lost** treasure of Tuckernuck; Emily Fairlie. Katherine Tegen Books 2012 283 p. (hardback) $16.99
Grades: 4 5 6 7 8 **Fic**

1. Mystery fiction 2. Buried treasure -- Fiction 3. Historic buildings -- Fiction 4. Schools -- Fiction
ISBN 0062118900; 9780062118905
LC 2012025279

This book by Emily Fairlie "tells the story of Bud and Laurie's quest to find the infamous Tutweiler Treasure. They're hot (or at least lukewarm) on the trail of clues, but time is running out -- the school board wants to tear down Tuckernuck Hall. Can Bud and Laurie find the treasure before it's lost forever?" (Publisher's note)

The **magician's** bird; a Tuckernuck mystery. Emily Fairlie ; Illustrated by Antonio Javier Caparo. Katherine Tegen Books, an imprint of HarperCollinsPublishers 2013 288 p. (hardcover bdg.) $16.99
Grades: 4 5 6 **Fic**

1. Magicians 2. Treasure hunt (game) -- Fiction 3. Schools -- Fiction 4. Historic buildings -- Fiction 5. Mystery and detective stories
ISBN 0062118935; 9780062118936
LC 2012051738

In this book, by Emily Fairlie, "the mystery Bud and Laurie must solve is much more serious than a treasure hunt—their beloved school founder, Maria Tutweiler, has been accused of murdering Marchetti the Magician! Can Bud and Laurie—with the help of enthusiastic Misti and evil but useful Calliope—prove Maria Tutweiler's innocence? Or will Tuckernuck Hall be closed down for good?" (Publisher's note)

Falkner, Brian

The **project**. Random House 2011 275p $17.99
Grades: 6 7 8 9 10 **Fic**

1. Adventure fiction 2. Time travel -- Fiction 3. National socialism -- Fiction 4. World War, 1939-1945 -- Fiction
ISBN 978-0-375-96945-4; 0-375-96945-4
LC 2010033449

After discovering a terrible secret hidden in the most boring book in the world, Iowa fifteen-year-olds Luke and Tommy find out that members of a secret Nazi organization intend to use this information to rewrite history.

"The wacky unbelievability of this story in no way detracts from its enjoyment. It reads like an action movie, with plenty of chases, explosions, and by-a-hair escapes." SLJ

Falls, Kat

Dark life. Scholastic Press 2010 297p $16.99; pa $6.99; paperback $7.99
Grades: 4 5 6 7 **Fic**

1. Science fiction 2. Ocean -- Fiction
ISBN 978-0-545-17814-3; 0-545-17814-2; 978-0-545-17815-0 pa; 0-545-17815-0 pa; 9780545178150
LC 2009-24907

"Ty has lived subsea his entire life. His family members moved below the water to make a better life for themselves. In this future, the climate changes on Earth have been so drastic that hardly any solid ground exits anymore. . . . This book will appeal to middle grade readers, who will enjoy the novel's mystery and suspense. It is a definite must-read for SF fans." Voice Youth Advocates

Followed by: Rip tide (2011)

Inhuman; Kat Falls. Scholastic Press 2013 384 p. $17.99
Grades: 7 8 9 10 **Fic**

1. Dystopian fiction 2. Apocalyptic fiction 3. Dystopias 4. Science fiction 5. Survival -- Fiction 6. Quarantine -- Fiction 7. Virus diseases -- Fiction 8. Fathers and daughters -- Fiction
ISBN 054537099X; 9780545370998
LC 2013026360

In this dystopian novel by Kat Falls, "the United States east of the Mississippi has been abandoned. Now called the Feral Zone, a reference to the virus that turned millions of people into bloodthirsty savages, the entire area is off-limits. . . . [Protagonist] Lane gets the shock of her life when she learns that someone close to her has crossed into the Feral Zone." (Publisher's note)

"Years ago, the U.S. was bisected by a pandemic (spread by biting) that causes humans to mutate into feral human-animal hybrids. When pampered teenager Lane is blackmailed into the Feral Zone, she joins the search for a cure and discovers the gray area between human and feral. While Lane and her love triangle are bland, the zombie-apocalypse-meets-wereanimals-gone-wild setup captures the imagination." (Horn Book)

Another title in this series is:
Undaunted (2019)

Rip tide. Scholastic Press 2011 320p $16.99
Grades: 4 5 6 7 **Fic**

1. Science fiction 2. Ocean -- Fiction
ISBN 0-545-17843-6; 978-0-545-17843-3
Sequel to: Dark life (2010)

"While preparing to sell the season's seaweed crop, Ty stumbles across an abandoned township, its doors chained shut and its residents murdered. Soon after, the colonists' deal with another township goes bad, and Ty's parents are kidnapped. As Ty and Gemma try to track down those responsible and save their loved ones, they're forced to join up with the notorious Seablite Gang, infiltrate the rough-and-tumble town of Rip Tide, fight for their lives against sea monsters and human predators, and discover who's killing entire townships—and why. . . . There's no shortage of action, intrigue, or daring exploits in this aquatic thriller. Atmospheric and tense, built around an expertly used postapocalyptic meets Wild West setting, this story's a whole lot of fun." Publ Wkly

Fantaskey, Beth

Buzz kill; by Beth Fantaskey. Houghton Mifflin Harcourt 2014 368 p. $17.99
Grades: 8 9 10 11 12 **Fic**

1. Murder -- Fiction 2. High schools -- Fiction 3. Football -- Coaching -- Fiction 4. Mystery and detective stories 5. Coaches (Athletics) -- Fiction 6. Dating (Social customs) -- Fiction
ISBN 0547393105; 9780547393100
LC 2013011423

In this book, by Beth Fantaskey, "when the widely disliked Honeywell Stingers football coach is found murdered, 17-year-old Millie is determined to investigate. She is chasing a lead for the school newspaper--and looking to clear her father, the assistant coach, and prime suspect. . . . Millie joins forces with her mysterious classmate Chase who seems to want to help her even while covering up secrets of his own." (Publisher's note)

"When the head football coach is killed, seventeen-year-old Millie, a school reporter obsessed with Nancy Drew, sets out to learn the truth and clear her assistant-coach father of any suspicion. She gets some unexpected help from dreamy quarterback Chase, who's hiding some secrets.

This entertaining sleuth story is a good choice for teens now graduated from books featuring Millie's literary hero." Horn Book

Jessica's guide to dating on the dark side. Harcourt 2009 354p $17

Grades: 8 9 10 11 12 **Fic**

1. Vampires -- Fiction

ISBN 978-0-15-206384-9; 0-15-206384-6

LC 2007-49002

Seventeen-year-old Jessica, adopted and raised in Pennsylvania, learns that she is descended from a royal line of Romanian vampires and that she is betrothed to a vampire prince, who poses as a foreign exchange student while courting her.

"Fantaskey makes this premise work by playing up its absurdities without laughing at them. . . . The romance sizzles, the plot develops ingeniously and suspensefully, and the satire sings." Publ Wkly

Farber, E. S.

Seagulls don't eat pickles; by Erica Farber ; illustrated by Jason Beene. Chronicle Books 2013 184 p. (Fish Finelli) (alk. paper) $15.99

Grades: 4 5 6 7 **Fic**

1. Pirates -- Fiction 2. Adventure fiction -- Fiction 3. Librarians -- Fiction 4. Historic sites -- Fiction 5. Buried treasure -- Fiction

ISBN 145210820X; 9781452108209

LC 2012027739

This is the first book in E.S. Farber's Fish Finelli series. "Fish Finelli wants nothing more . . . than to fix up his boat with a supercharged Seagull motor and win Whooping Hollow's annual Captain Kidd Classic boat race," but has only saved half the necessary funds. "When local bully Bryce Billings baits Fish into a bet that he and his friends Roger and T.J. can't find Captain Kidd's fabled lost treasure, . . . Fish finds himself knee-deep in a mysterious pirate adventure." (School Library Journal)

Other titles in this series are:

Operation fireball (2014)

Ghosts don't wear glasses (2015)

Farizan, Sara

Here to stay; Sara Farizan. Algonquin Young Readers 2018 272 p. (hardback) $17.95

Grades: 9 10 11 12 **Fic**

1. Basketball -- Fiction 2. Cyberbullying -- Fiction 3. Arab Americans -- Fiction 4. Schools -- Fiction 5. Bullying -- Fiction 6. High schools -- Fiction

ISBN 9781616207007

LC 2018008382

In this book, by Sara Farizan, "what happens when a kid who's flown under the radar for most of high school gets pulled off the bench to make the winning basket in a varsity playoff game? If his name is Bijan Majidi, life is suddenly high fives in the hallways and invitations to exclusive parties--along with an anonymous photo sent by a school cyberbully that makes Bijan look like a terrorist." (Publisher's note)

Farmer, Nancy

★ The **Ear,** the Eye, and the Arm; a novel. Puffin Books 1995 311p pa $6.99

Grades: 6 7 8 9 10 **Fic**

1. Science fiction 2. Zimbabwe -- Fiction

ISBN 978-0-14-131109-8; 0-14-131109-6

LC 95019982

First published 1994 by Orchard Books

A Newbery Medal honor book, 1995

In 2194 in Zimbabwe, General Matsika's three children are kidnapped and put to work in a plastic mine while three mutant detectives use their special powers to search for them

"Throughout the story, it's the thrilling adventure that will grab readers, who will also like the comic, tender characterizations." Booklist

A **girl** named Disaster. Orchard Bks. 1996 309p $19.95; pa $7.99

Grades: 6 7 8 9 **Fic**

1. Adventure fiction 2. Zimbabwe -- Fiction 3. Mozambique -- Fiction 4. Supernatural -- Fiction

ISBN 0-531-09539-8; 0-14-038635-1 pa

LC 96-15141

A Newbery Medal honor book, 1997

While journeying from Mozambique to Zimbabwe to escape an arranged marriage, eleven-year-old Nhamo struggles to escape drowning and starvation and in so doing comes close to the luminous world of the African spirits

"This story is humorous and heartwrenching, complex and multilayered." SLJ

★ The **house** of the scorpion. Atheneum Bks. for Young Readers 2002 380p $17.95; pa $7.99

Grades: 7 8 9 10 **Fic**

1. Science fiction 2. Cloning -- Fiction

ISBN 0-689-85222-3; 0-689-85223-1 pa

LC 2001-56594

Printz Honor Book (2003)

National Book Award: Young People's Literature (2002)

A Newbery Medal honor book, 2003

In a future where humans despise clones, Matt enjoys special status as the young clone of El Patrón, the 142-year-old leader of a corrupt drug empire nestled between Mexico and the United States. "Grades seven to ten." (Bull Cent Child Books)

"This is a powerful, ultimately hopeful, story that builds on today's sociopolitical, ethical, and scientific issues and prognosticates a compelling picture of what the future could bring." Booklist

The **Islands** of the Blessed. Atheneum Books for Young Readers 2009 479p (Sea of Trolls) $18.99

Grades: 5 6 7 8 9 **Fic**

1. Fantasy fiction 2. Norse mythology -- Fiction 3. Druids and Druidism -- Fiction

ISBN 978-1-4169-0737-4; 1-4169-0737-8

LC 2008045415

Sequel to: Land of the Silver Apples (2007)

Two years after their adventures in The Land of the Silver Apples, the apprentice bard Jack and his Viking companion Thorgil confront the malevolent spirit of a vengeful mermaid and begin a quest that casts them among the fin folk of Notland.

This is an "exciting story, which contains a cast of lively, multifaceted characters." Booklist

Includes bibliographical references

The **Land** of the Silver Apples. Atheneum Books for Young Readers 2007 496p il $18.99; pa $9.99

Grades: 5 6 7 8 9 **Fic**

1. Fantasy fiction 2. Vikings -- Fiction 3. Norse mythology -- Fiction 4. Druids and Druidism -- Fiction

ISBN 978-1-4169-0735-0; 1-4169-0735-1; 978-1-4169-0736-7 pa; 1-4169-0736-x pa

LC 2006-31433

Sequel to: The Sea of Trolls (2004)

After escaping from the Sea of Trolls, the apprentice bard Jack plunges into a new series of adventures, traveling underground to Elfland and uncovering the truth about his little sister Lucy.

"Farmer beautifully balances pell-mell action and quieter thematic points. . . . This hearty adventure, as personal as it is epic, will cradle readers in the 'hollow it its hand.'" Booklist

Followed by: The Islands of the Blessed (2009)

★ The **lord** of Opium; Nancy Farmer. Atheneum Books for Young Readers 2013 432 p. (hardcover) $17.99

Grades: 7 8 9 10 **Fic**

1. Fantasy fiction 2. Drug traffic -- Fiction 3. Science fiction 4. Cloning -- Fiction 5. Environmental degradation -- Fiction

ISBN 1442482540; 9781442482548

LC 2012030418

Sequel to: House of the scorpion (2002)

This book is the sequel to Nancy Farmer's "The House of the Scorpion." Here, "Matt was a clone of El Patrón, drug lord of Opium, but with El Patrón dead, Matt is now considered by international law to be fully human and El Patrón's rightful heir. But it's a corrupt land . . . ruled over by drug lords and worked by armies of Illegals turned into 'eejits,' or zombies. Matt wants to bring reform." (Kirkus Reviews)

★ The **Sea** of Trolls. Atheneum Books for Young Readers 2004 459p $17.95; pa $9.99

Grades: 5 6 7 8 9 **Fic**

1. Fantasy fiction 2. Vikings -- Fiction 3. Norse mythology -- Fiction 4. Druids and Druidism -- Fiction

ISBN 0-689-86744-1; 0-689-86746-8 pa

LC 2003-19091

After Jack becomes apprenticed to a Druid bard, he and his little sister Lucy are captured by Viking Berserkers and taken to the home of King Ivar the Boneless and his half-troll queen, leading Jack to undertake a vital quest to Jotunheim, home of the trolls.

"This exciting and original fantasy will capture the hearts and imaginations of readers." SLJ

Includes bibliographical references

Other titles in this series are:

The Land of the Silver Apples (2007)

The Islands of the Blessed (2009)

Farrant, Natasha

After Iris; by Natasha Farrant. Dial Books for Young Readers 2013 272 p. (hardcover) $16.99

Grades: 5 6 7 8 **Fic**

1. Grief -- Fiction 2. Babysitters -- Fiction 3. Twins -- Fiction 4. Diaries -- Fiction 5. Au pairs -- Fiction 6. Brothers and sisters -- Fiction 7. Family life -- England -- London -- Fiction 8. Video recordings -- Production and direction -- Fiction

ISBN 0803739826; 9780803739826

LC 2012039136

In this book, 12-year-old "Bluebell Gadsby's family has been collapsing ever since Blue's twin sister. Iris, died three years ago. Blue's father is working on the other side of the country, and their mother is traveling overseas, which leaves new au pair Zoran in charge. Between Blue's older sister Flora's rebelliousness, her two younger siblings' antics, and the family's pet rats, which live in the garden of their London home, Zoran has his hands full." (Publishers Weekly)

Farrar, Josh

Rules to rock by. Walker Books for Young Readers 2010 244p $16.99

Grades: 4 5 6 7 **Fic**

1. Moving -- Fiction 2. Bullies -- Fiction 3. Rock music -- Fiction 4. Rhode Island -- Fiction 5. Rock musicians -- Fiction

ISBN 978-0-8027-2079-5; 0-8027-2079-X

Annabella Cabrera tries to start a rock band at her new middle school in Providence, Rhode Island, but has trouble when the members of a rival band bully her and she develops a case of writer's block.

"Rock prevails in this spirited, never-say-die story about a girl and her dream. Farrar's first novel hits home about tween life, especially among the creative set, and for anyone who has ever been bullied." SLJ

Farrey, Brian

The **Grimjinx** rebellion; Brian Farrey. HarperCollins 2014 432 p. illustrations (hardcover) $16.99

Grades: 4 5 6 7 **Fic**

1. Fantasy fiction 2. Magic -- Fiction 3. Brothers and sisters -- Fiction 4. Swindlers and swindling -- Fiction 5. Fantasy

ISBN 0062049348; 9780062049346

LC 2013043194

In this book, by Brian Farrey, "Jaxter Grimjinx and his family haven't had much time for thieving. Through no fault of their own, they've been too busy saving the day. But the danger in the Five Provinces is only just beginning. The Palatinate Mages are almost ready to unveil their master plan, and legendary monsters will soon roam the land once more. Then Jaxter's sister, Aubrin, is kidnapped by the Mages." (Publisher's note)

"When mage sentinels carry off Jaxter Grimjinx's little sister Aubrin to be their new augur, the family's quest to get her back leads to the opening elements of a prophecy in which Jaxter will save the Five Provinces from a deadly scourge but die doing so. The twisted but coherent puzzle plot unfolds swiftly, speeded along by irreverent Grimjinx humor." Horn Book

Other titles in the series include:

The Vengekeep Prophecies (2012)

The Shadowhand Covenant (2013)

The **secret** of Dreadwillow Carse; Brian Farrey. Algonquin Young Readers 2016 240 p. $16.95

Grades: 4 5 6 7 8 **Fic**

1. Fairy tales 2. Friendship -- Fiction 3. Princesses -- Fiction 4. Kings and rulers -- Fiction 5. Depression (Psychology) -- Fiction 6. Depression, Mental -- Fiction 7. Kings, queens, rulers, etc. -- Fiction

ISBN 9781616205058

LC 2015031467

In this book, by Brian Farrey, a "princess and a peasant girl embark on a dangerous quest. . . . In the center of the verdant Monarchy lies Dreadwillow Carse, a desolate bog the people of the land do their best to ignore. Little is known about it except an ominous warning: If any monarch enters Dreadwillow Carse, then the Monarchy will fall. Twelve-year-old Princess Jeniah yearns to know what the marsh could conceal that might topple her family's thousand-year reign." (Publisher's note)

"Part fairy tale, part seemingly utopian society with a dark underbelly, this is a gripping, compelling story that will leave readers mulling over the ethical questions raised." Booklist

The **Shadowhand** Covenant; by Brian Farrey and illustrated by Brett Helquist. HarperCollins 2013 384 p. (hardback) $16.99

Grades: 4 5 6 7 8 **Fic**

1. Thieves -- Fiction 2. Conspiracies -- Fiction 3. Secret societies -- Fiction 4. Fantasy

ISBN 0062049313; 9780062049315

LC 2013021825

Sequel to: The Vengekeep prophecies

In this book by Brian Farrey, "trouble is brewing in the Five Provinces. Mysterious magical artifacts have gone missing from the royal vaults. Master thieves from a secret society known as the Shadowhands are disappearing. And without explanation, the High Laird has begun imprisoning the peaceful Sarosan people. Jaxter Grimjinx and his parents receive a summons from the Shadowhands—a summons that they would be foolish to ignore—and Jaxter is thrust into the heart of the conspiracy." (Publisher's note)

The **Vengekeep** prophecies; Brian Farrey ; illustrated by Brett Helquist. Harper 2012 390 p. (hardback) $16.99

Grades: 4 5 6 7 **Fic**

1. Magic -- Fiction 2. Prophecies -- Fiction 3. Swindlers and swindling -- Fiction 4. Fantasy 5. Monsters -- Fiction

ISBN 0062049283; 9780062049285

LC 2012025282

In this book by Brian Farrey, "12-year-old Jaxter Grimjinx is anxious to prove himself at the family business: thievery. Jaxter's first attempt at burglary ends with . . . his family being jailed, but his parents have . . . replaced the prophetic tapestry that predicts the year ahead . . . with one that shows the Grimjinx family as heroes. The family quickly discovers, however, that the fake tapestry is actually enchanted, and every disaster it depicts is coming true." (Publishers Weekly)

Fawcett, Heather

Even the darkest stars; Heather Fawcett. Balzer + Bray 2017 427 p. (hardcover) $17.99

Grades: 8 9 10 11 12 **Fic**

1. Fantasy fiction 2. Magic -- Fiction 3. Mountaineering -- Fiction 4. Imaginary places -- Fiction

ISBN 9780062463388; 9780062463401

LC 2017932797

In this novel by Heather Fawcett, "Kamzin has always dreamed of becoming one of the Emperor's . . . . elite climbers. . . . [Explorer] River Shara, . . . hire[s] Kamzin . . . for his next expedition. The challenges of climbing Raksha are unlike anything Kamzin expected. . . . And as dark secrets are revealed, Kamzin must unravel the truth of their mission and of her companions--while surviving the deadliest climb she has ever faced." (Publisher's note)

"Add in a detailed, well-realized setting, an unsettling villain that lingers just off the page, and buckets of danger to result in an utterly inventive and wholly original debut." Booklist

Followed by: All the wandering light (2018)

Fayers, Claire

The **voyage** to Magical North; Claire Fayers. Henry Holt & Co. 2016 320 p. illustrations (hardback) $16.99; (ebook) $60

Grades: 6 7 8 **Fic**

1. Magic -- Fiction 2. Adventure fiction 3. Pirates -- Fiction 4. Voyages and travels -- Fiction 5. Adventure and adventurers -- Fiction

ISBN 9781627794206; 9781627796583

LC 2015022325

In this book, by Claire Fayers, "Twelve-year-old Brine Seaborne is a girl with a past--if only she could remember what it is. Found alone in a rowboat as a child, clutching a shard of the rare starshell needed for spell-casting, she's spent the past years keeping house for an irritable magician and his obnoxious apprentice, Peter. When Brine and Peter get themselves into a load of trouble and flee, they blunder into the path of the legendary pirate ship the Onion." (Publisher's note)

"A robust debut, well stocked with heroic exploits, monsters, pirates, explosions, magical transformations, and life-changing adventures, and a promising series starter." Kirkus

Another title in this series is:

The journey to Dragon Island (2017)

Federle, Tim

★ **Better** Nate than ever; Tim Federle. Simon & Schuster Books for Young Readers 2013 288 p. (hardcover) $16.99

Grades: 5 6 7 8 **Fic**

1. Theater -- Fiction 2. Musicals -- Fiction 3. Auditions -- Fiction 4. New York (N.Y.) -- Fiction

ISBN 1442446897; 9781442446892; 9781442446908

LC 2011050388

Rainbow List (2014)

Odyssey Honor Recording (2014)

Stonewall Honor Book: Children and Young Adult (2014)

Lambda Literary Awards Finalist (2014)

In author Tim Federle's book, "Nate Foster has big dreams. His whole life, he's wanted to star in a Broadway show. (Heck, he'd settle for seeing a Broadway show.) But how is Nate supposed to make his dreams come true when he's stuck in Jankburg, Pennsylvania . . . ? With Libby's help, Nate plans a daring overnight escape to New York. There's an open casting call for 'E.T.: The Musical,' and Nate knows this could be the difference between small-town blues and big-time stardom." (Publisher's note)

Other titles in this series are:

Five, six, seven, Nate (2014)

Nate expectations (2018)

Five, six, seven, Nate! by Tim Federle. Simon & Schuster Books for Young Readers 2014 304 p. (hardcover) $16.99

Grades: 5 6 7 8 **Fic**

1. Theater 2. Actors -- Fiction 3. Theater -- Fiction 4. Musicals -- Fiction 5. Friendship -- Fiction 6. Best friends -- Fiction 7. New York (N.Y.) -- Fiction 8. Broadway (New York, N.Y.) -- Fiction

ISBN 1442446935; 9781442446939

LC 2012051239

Sequel to: Better Nate than ever

In this book, by Tim Federle, "Nate is off to start rehearsals for 'E.T.: The Broadway Musical.' It's everything he ever practiced his autograph for! But as thrilling as Broadway is, rehearsals are nothing like Nate expects: full of intimidating child stars, cut-throat understudies, and a director who can't even remember Nate's name." (Publisher's note)

"Nate successfully auditioned for Broadway's E.T.: The Musical in Better Nate Than Ever. Of course, he's actually only an understudy's understudy, his chorus part keeps diminishing, and rehearsals are going poorly, but good-humored Nate takes it all in stride. Federle addresses his likable character's burgeoning interest in boys in a laudably straightforward way, making this entertaining backstage pass especially rewarding." (Horn Book)

Nate expectations; Tim Federle. Simon & Schuster Books for Young Readers 2018 249 p. (hardback) $17.99

Grades: 5 6 7 8 **Fic**

1. Musicals -- Fiction 2. Friendship -- Fiction 3. High schools -- Fiction 4. Gays -- Fiction 5. Schools -- Fiction 6. Theater -- Fiction 7. Pennsylvania -- Fiction 8. Famly life -- Pennsylvania

-- Fiction
ISBN 9781481404143; 9781481404129; 9781481404136
LC 2017046573

Sequel to: Fix, six, seven, Nate!

In this book in the Nate series, by Tim Federle, "when the news hits that E.T.: The Musical wasn't nominated for a single Tony Award . . . the show closes, leaving Nate both out of luck and out of a job. And while Nate's cast mates are eager to move on (the boy he understudies already landed a role on a TV show!), Nate knows it's back to square one, also known as Jankburg, Pennsylvania. Where horror (read: high school) awaits." (Publisher's note)

Fehler, Gene

Beanball; by Gene Fehler. Clarion Books 2008 119p $16
Grades: 7 8 9 10 **Fic**

1. School stories 2. Novels in verse 3. Baseball -- Fiction
ISBN 0-618-84348-5; 978-0-618-84348-0
LC 2007013058

Relates, from diverse points of view, events surrounding the critical injury of popular and talented high school athlete, Luke "Wizard" Wallace, when he is hit in the face by a fastball.

This is a "moving baseball novel in free verse. . . . This swift read will appeal to both reluctant readers and baseball players." KLIATT

Feinstein, John

Change up; mystery at the World Series. Alfred A. Knopf 2009 336p $16.99; lib bdg $19.99
Grades: 6 7 8 9 **Fic**

1. Mystery fiction 2. Baseball -- Fiction 3. Journalism -- Fiction
ISBN 978-0-375-85636-5; 0-375-85636-6; 978-0-375-95636-2 lib bdg; 0-375-95636-0 lib bdg

"Stevie Thomas and Susan Carol Anderson are back on the newspaper sports beat, this time at the World Series. . . . It seems that Stevie has hit it big when he interviews Norbert Doyle, a pitcher for the Washington Nationals. . . . As Stevie digs for more material for his story, he finds out there is more to Doyle than he first thought. . . . Readers will appreciate the sports details and real-life characters Feinstein includes throughout the novel. . . . This book is an enjoyable trifecta of sports, mystery and journalism for young readers." Voice Youth Advocates

Cover -up; mystery at the Super Bowl. Alfred A. Knopf 2007 298p $16.99; lib bdg $19.99
Grades: 6 7 8 9 **Fic**

1. Mystery fiction 2. Football -- Fiction 3. Journalists -- Fiction
ISBN 978-0-375-84247-4; 0-375-84247-0; 978-0-375-94247-1 lib bdg; 0-375-94247-5 lib bdg
LC 2007-22015

Fledgling fourteen-year-old sports reporters Susan Carol and Stevie investigate suspicious activities at the Super Bowl after Stevie gets fired from his co-anchor job on a ground-breaking teen sports show.

This "delivers an entertaining mix of mystery, insider detail, . . . and ripped-from-the-headlines subject matter." Booklist

Last shot; a Final Four mystery. Knopf 2005 251p $16.95; lib bdg $18.99
Grades: 6 7 8 9 **Fic**

1. Mystery fiction 2. Basketball -- Fiction 3. Journalists -- Fiction
ISBN 0-375-83168-1; 0-375-93168-6 lib bdg
LC 2004-26535

After winning a basketball reporting contest, eighth graders Stevie and Susan Carol are sent to cover the Final Four tournament, where they discover that a talented player is being blackmailed into throwing the final game.

"The action on the court is vividly described. . . . Mystery fans will find enough suspense in this fast-paced narrative to keep them hooked." SLJ

Other titles in this series are:
Vanishing act (2006)
Cover-up (2007)
Change-up (2009)
Rivalry (2010)

The **rivalry**; mystery at the Army-Navy game. Alfred A. Knopf 2010 266p $16.99; lib bdg $19.99
Grades: 7 8 9 10 **Fic**

1. Mystery fiction 2. Football -- Fiction 3. Journalism -- Fiction
ISBN 978-0-375-86570-1; 0-375-86570-5; 978-0-375-96570-8 lib bdg; 0-375-96570-X lib bdg
LC 2010019614

Eighth-grade sportswriters Stevie and Susan Carol up to solve a mystery at the famous Army-Navy football game.

"Readers looking for a solid sports story tinged with excitement will enjoy this book. The game details are exciting, the suspense builds in the last fifty pages, and there is both a satisfying conclusion." Voice Youth Advocates

Vanishing act. Alfred A. Knopf 2006 279p $16.95; lib bdg $18.99
Grades: 6 7 8 9 **Fic**

1. Mystery fiction 2. Tennis -- Fiction 3. Kidnapping -- Fiction 4. Journalists -- Fiction
ISBN 978-0-375-83592-6; 0-375-83592-X; 978-0-375-93592-3 lib bdg; 0-375-93592-4 lib bdg
LC 2005-35823

Eighth-grade sports reporters Susan Carol and Stevie reunite at the U.S. Open tennis championships where they investigate the mysterious disappearance of a top Russian player.

"Sports fans will be fascinated by the insider's view of the tournament, and even teens ambivalent about sports will connect with the memorable, high-achieving kids and the messages about maintaining integrity versus selling out—in sports and in life." Booklist

Feldman, Ruth Tenzer

Blue thread; Ruth Tenzer Feldman. Ooligan Press 2012 302 p. $12.95
Grades: 7 8 9 10 **Fic**

1. Historical fiction 2. Jewish women -- Fiction 3. Women's rights -- Fiction
ISBN 1932010416; 9781932010411
LC 2011024382

This young adult novel focuses on Miriam, a young Jewish girl in 1912 Portland, Oregon. "While her mother plans their trip to New York City to find her a husband, Miriam gets caught up in the fight for women's suffrage. At first she's nervous about going against her parents' wishes, but curiosity gets the better of her . . . . However, after a mysterious girl named Serakh whisks Miriam back to biblical times, her desire to be a larger part of the movement becomes stronger." (School Library Journal)

Fergus, Maureen

Ortega. Kids Can Press 2010 224p $16.95

Grades: 5 6 7 8 **Fic**

1. Science fiction 2. Gorillas -- Fiction

ISBN 978-1-55453-474-6; 1-55453-474-7

Eleven years ago, an infant lowland gorilla was acquired by a privately funded laboratory. An elite surgical team undertook a series of radical procedures designed to make it physically possible for the infant gorilla to acquire speech.

"The story's excitement and suspense as well as the emotional drama will ensnare readers. This interesting, affecting novel will definitely find an audience." SLJ

Ferraiolo, Jack D.

The **big** splash; by Jack D. Ferraiolo. Amulet Books 2008 277p $15.95

Grades: 4 5 6 7 **Fic**

1. School stories 2. Mystery fiction

ISBN 978-0-8109-7067-0; 0-8109-7067-8

LC 2007-49978

Matt Stevens, an average middle schooler with a glib tongue and a knack for solving crimes, uncovers a mystery while working with "the organization," a mafia-like syndicate run by seventh-grader Vincent "Mr. Biggs" Biggio, specializing in forged hall passes, test-copying rings, black market candy selling, and taking out hits with water guns.

This "novel delivers plenty of laughs, especially in the opening chapters, and fans of private-eye spoofs will enjoy this entertaining read." Booklist

★ **Sidekicks**. Amulet 2011 309p $16.95

Grades: 6 7 8 9 **Fic**

1. Superheroes -- Fiction

ISBN 978-0-8109-9803-2; 0-8109-9803-3

"By all outward appearances, Bright Boy is an average middle-school student, but at night, he becomes the sidekick to superhero Rogue Warrior. . . . Ferraiolo is delightfully unafraid to inject irreverence into the superhero formula, adding plenty of humor to the high-adventure high jinks." Booklist

Ferris, Jean

Much ado about Grubstake. Harcourt 2006 265p $17

Grades: 5 6 7 8 **Fic**

1. Orphans -- Fiction 2. Colorado -- Fiction 3. City and town life -- Fiction 4. Gold mines and mining -- Fiction

ISBN 0-15-205706-4

When two city folks arrive in the depressed mining town of Grubstake, Colorado in 1888, sixteen-year-old orphaned Arley tries to discover why they want to buy the supposedly worthless mines in the area

"Ferris combines adventure, love, and off-the-wall characters in a page-turning story full of good laughs and common sense messages." Voice Youth Advocates

Once upon a Marigold; by Jean Ferris. Harcourt 2002 266 p. $17

Grades: 5 6 7 8 **Fic**

1. Love -- Fiction 2. Princesses -- Fiction 3. Triangles (Interpersonal relations) -- Fiction 4. Fairy tales 5. Princesses/Fiction

ISBN 0152050841; 0152167919; 9780152167912

LC 2002000311

Marigold series

This novel by Jean Ferris focuses on Christian, who did not know "love could be so amazing. He was clueless when he started spying on the royal family. He lives in a cave with a troll for a dad. If his dad had only warned him about all that mind-boggling love stuff, maybe things wouldn't be such a mess. But then, maybe, Princess Marigold would be dead. And now that he's fallen for the princess, it's up to him to untwist an odd love triangle . . . and foil a scheming queen." (Publisher's note)

"This complex, fast-paced plot, a mixture of fantasy, romance, comedy, and coming-of-age novel, succeeds because these characters are compelling, well developed, and sympathetic." SLJ

Followed by: Twice upon a Marigold (2008)

Twice upon a Marigold. Harcourt 2008 297p $17

Grades: 5 6 7 8 **Fic**

1. Fairy tales 2. Princesses -- Fiction 3. Kings and rulers -- Fiction

ISBN 978-0-15-206382-5; 0-15-206382-X

LC 200735761

Sequel to: Once upon a Marigold (2002)

After a quiet, happy year in a small town, Queen Olympia regains her memory and initiates new plots and manipulations, as the residents of Zandelphia and Beaurivage, now ruled by Christian, Marigold, and Swithbert, feel the effects of her bad energy.

"Appealing new characters and fresh plot twists give this sequel a life of its own, though fans of the earlier book will enjoy the continuation of its story line, wry humor, and offbeat sense of fun." Booklist

Fforde, Jasper

★ The **last** Dragonslayer; Jasper Fforde. Hodder & Stoughton 2010 281 p. (The Chronicles of Kazam) $16.99; (hbk.) $16.99

Grades: 7 8 9 10 **Fic**

1. Magic -- Fiction 2. Dragons -- Fiction 3. Employment agencies -- Fiction

ISBN 978-0547738475; 1444707175; 1444707191; 9781444707175; 9781444707199

LC 2010551874

In this book by Jasper Fforde, part of the Chronicles of Kazam series, "magic is fading. . . . Fifteen-year-old foundling Jennifer Strange runs Kazam, an employment agency for magicians -- but it's hard to stay in business when magic is drying up. And then the visions start, predicting the death of the world's last dragon at the hands of an unnamed Dragonslayer. If the visions are true, everything will change for Kazam -- and for Jennifer." (Publisher's note)

Other titles in this series are:

The song of the Quarkbeast (2011)

The eye of Zoltar (2014)

Fink, Mark

The **summer** I got a life. WestSide 2009 196p $15.95

Grades: 7 8 9 **Fic**

1. Romance fiction 2. Love stories 3. Wisconsin -- Fiction 4. People with disabilities -- Fiction

ISBN 978-1-934813-12-6; 1-934813-12-5

"Andy is pumped that his freshman year is over and his vacation is about to begin. Then his dad's promotion changes everything. Instead of Hawaii, Andy is spending two weeks on a farm in Wisconsin with his somewhat odd, but well-meaning, aunt and uncle. Once there, though, he finds that things aren't so bad particularly when he spots 'the most incredible-looking girl he has ever seen.' . . . Andy discovers that an accident at age four has left Laura confined to a wheelchair. . . . This is an engaging novel filled with life lessons, a little romance, humor, sports, and fraternal love." SLJ

Finn, Mary

Belladonna. Candlewick Press 2011 371p $16.99

Grades: 7 8 9 10 **Fic**

1. Artists 2. Painters 3. Horses -- Fiction 4. Great Britain -- History -- 1714-1837 -- Fiction
ISBN 978-0-7636-5106-0; 0-7636-5106-0
LC 2010038707

This book is set "[i]n rural England in 1757, [where] Thomas Rose is on the verge-of becoming a man. Clever, but unable to learn reading and writing . . . Tom meets the enigmatic Hélène, a circus performer who goes by the name of Ling . . .Enchanted with Ling's stories of her life in the circus as much as with the girl herself, Tom commits to helping her find her beloved horse, Belladonna . . . Their search leads them to George Stubbs, known in the village as a horse butcher . . . the teens discover that Stubbs is a painter who is completing an anatomical study of horses that involves dissection of the animals. Stubbs takes Tom on as an apprentice and secures Ling a position in the household of the wealthy family that purchased Belladonna, not knowing that the girl's ultimate goal is to escape with her horse." (School Libr J)

"A touch of intrigue and interesting details about horses, early necropsy, and everyday life add a rich frame to this historical coming-of-age story, unique in both its setting and subject." Booklist

Finneyfrock, Karen

The **sweet** revenge of Celia Door; by Karen Finneyfrock. Viking 2013 272 p. (hardcover) $16.99

Grades: 7 8 9 10 **Fic**

1. School stories 2. Revenge -- Fiction 3. Teenagers -- Fiction 4. Gays -- Fiction 5. Poetry -- Fiction 6. Schools -- Fiction 7. High schools -- Fiction 8. Hershey (Pa.) -- Fiction 9. Family life -- Pennsylvania -- Hershey -- Fiction
ISBN 0670012750; 9780670012756
LC 2011047221

In this teen novel, by Karen Finneyfrock, "Celia Door enters her freshman year . . . with giant boots, dark eyeliner, and a thirst for revenge against Sandy Firestone. . . . But then Celia meets Drake, the cool new kid from New York City who entrusts her with his deepest, darkest secret. When Celia's quest for justice threatens her relationship with Drake, she's forced to decide which is sweeter: revenge or friendship." (Publisher's note)

Fisher, Catherine

The **dark** city. Dial Books for Young Readers 2011 376p (Relic master) $16.99

Grades: 6 7 8 9 **Fic**

1. Fantasy fiction 2. Apprentices -- Fiction
ISBN 978-0-8037-3673-3; 0-8037-3673-8
LC 2010028801

"Relic Master Galen injured both his body and his mind when he dismantled an ancient technological artifact. While his physical injuries have healed, the loss of his psychic gifts has left him reluctantly dependent on his talented young apprentice, Raffi. Together they travel the dangerous road to the ruined Antaran city of Tasceron, where Galen hopes to reclaim his abilities from a shadowy figure known only as the Crow." Booklist

"Well-crafted storytelling provides more than the sum of its parts." Kirkus

Darkwater; by Catherine Fisher. Penguin Group USA 2012 229p (hardcover) $16.99

Grades: 6 7 8 9 10 11 12 **Fic**

1. Sin 2. Teenagers -- Fiction 3. Private schools -- Fiction 4. Soul -- Fiction 5. Twins -- Fiction 6. England -- Fiction 7. Schools -- Fiction 8. Brothers -- Fiction 9. Supernatural -- Fiction 10. Great Britain -- History -- Edward VII, 1901-1910 -- Fiction
ISBN 9780803738188
LC 2011048063

In author Catherine Fisher's book, "Sarah Trevelyan would give anything to regain the power and wealth her family has lost, so she makes a bargain with Azrael, Lord of Darkwater Hall. He gives her one hundred years and the means to accomplish her objective--in exchange for her soul. Fast-forward a hundred years to Tom, a fifteen-year-old boy who dreams of attending Darkwater Hall School but doesn't believe he has the talent. Until he meets a professor named Azrael, who offers him a bargain. Will Sarah be able to stop Tom from making the same mistake she did a century ago?" (Publisher's note)

The **hidden** Coronet. Dial Books for Young Readers 2011 421p (Relic master) $16.99

Grades: 6 7 8 9 **Fic**

1. Fantasy fiction 2. Apprentices -- Fiction
ISBN 978-0-8037-3675-7; 0-8037-3675-4
LC 2010039315

Sequel to: The lost heiress (2011)

Sixteen-year-old Raffi and Master Galen continue to evade the Watch as they seek the Coronet, a potent ancient relic that could be their only hope for defeating the power that is destroying Anara.

"The climactic integration of visionary mysticism and gee-whiz gadgetry, rendered bittersweet by all-too human failures, leads directly to a cliffhanger ending." Kirkus

★ **Incarceron**. Dial Books 2010 442p $17.99

Grades: 7 8 9 10 **Fic**

1. Fantasy fiction 2. Prisoners -- Fiction
ISBN 978-0-8037-3396-1; 0-8037-3396-8
LC 2008-46254

First published 2007 in the United Kingdom

To free herself from an upcoming arranged marriage, Claudia, the daughter of the Warden of Incarceron, a futuristic prison with a mind of its own, decides to help a young prisoner escape.

"Complex and inventive, with numerous and rewarding mysteries, this tale is certain to please." Publ Wkly

Followed by Sapphique (2011)

The **lost** heiress. Dial Books for Young Readers 2011 375p (Relic master) $16.99

Grades: 6 7 8 9 **Fic**

1. Fantasy fiction 2. Apprentices -- Fiction
ISBN 978-0-8037-3674-0; 0-8037-3674-6
LC 2010038156

Sequel to: Dark city (2011)

Even though the city of Tasceron and its emperor have fallen, when Master Galen and his sixteen-year-old apprentice Raffi hear a rumor that the heiress to the throne still lives, they must try to find her and keep her safe.

"Separate plot threads intertwine in a satisfying climax, posing puzzles to keep readers ensnared while providing pleasing narrative momentum to the overall series." Kirkus

Followed by: The hidden coronet (2011)

The **Margrave**. Dial Books for Young Readers 2011 464p (Relic master) $16.99

Grades: 6 7 8 9 **Fic**

1. Fantasy fiction 2. Apprentices -- Fiction
ISBN 978-0-8037-3676-4; 0-8037-3676-2
LC 2010043237

Their quest to find a secret relic with great power leads Master Galen and his sixteen-year-old apprentice Raffi into the Pit of Maar and the deep evil world at the heart of the Watch.

"The conclusion to Fisher's science-fantasy quartet satisfies." Kirkus

The **obsidian** mirror; by Catherine Fisher. Dial Books 2013 384 p. (Chronoptika) (hardcover) $17.99

Grades: 7 8 9 10 11 12 **Fic**

1. Fantasy fiction 2. Science fiction 3. Fathers -- Fiction 4. Time travel -- Fiction 5. Missing persons -- Fiction

ISBN 0803739699; 9780803739697

LC 2012019459

This book is the first in a trilogy from Catherine Fisher. The "mirror of the title, a dangerous gateway to other time periods, is being pursued by not one but three equally unpleasant and obsessive mad scientists. One of them, Oberon Venn, is the master of spooky Wintercombe Abbey. . . . Jake Wilde, Venn's teenage godson and his equal in arrogance, has been expelled from boarding school and shipped off to Wintercombe, where the boy plans to accuse Venn of having murdered Jake's father." (Publishers Weekly)

Other titles in this series are:

The slanted worlds (2013)

The door in the moon (2015)

The speed of darkness (2016)

Sapphique. Dial Books 2011 460p $17.99

Grades: 7 8 9 10 **Fic**

1. Fantasy fiction 2. Computers -- Fiction 3. Prisoners -- Fiction 4. Identity (Psychology) -- Fiction

ISBN 978-0-8037-3397-8; 0-8037-3397-6

LC 2009-31479

Sequel to: Incarceron (2010)

After his escape from the sentient prison, Incarceron, Finn finds that the Realm is not at all what he expected, and he does not know whether he is to be its king, how to free his imprisoned friends, or how to stop Incarceron's quest to be free of its own nature.

"Fisher's superb world-building marks this title, effectively drawing the reader in to a place so rife with secrets even its inhabitants don't entirely understand the depth of its illusions." Bull Cent Child Books

Fitzgerald, Laura Marx

The **gallery**; Laura Marx Fitzgerald. Dial Books for Young Readers 2016 336 p. (hardback) $16.99

Grades: 4 5 6 7 **Fic**

1. Art -- Fiction 2. Mystery fiction 3. Irish Americans -- Fiction 4. New York (N.Y.) -- Fiction 5. Household employees -- Fiction 6. Mystery and detective stories 7. New York (N.Y.) -- History -- 1898-1951 -- Fiction

ISBN 9780525428657

LC 2015029009

In this book, by Laura Marx Fitzgerald, "Martha has no choice but to work as a maid in the New York City mansion of the wealthy Sewell family. But, despite the Gatsby-like parties and trimmings of success, she suspects something might be deeply wrong in the household--specifically with Rose Sewell, the formerly vivacious lady of the house who now refuses to leave her room. The other servants say Rose is crazy, but scrappy, strong-willed Martha thinks there's more to the story." (Publisher's note)

"Fitzgerald balances mystery and history in a feminist narrative that invites readers to find out more." Kirkus

Under the egg; by Laura Marx Fitzgerald. Dial Books for Young Readers 2014 256 p. (hardcover) $16.99

Grades: 4 5 6 7 **Fic**

1. Mystery fiction 2. Art -- Fiction 3. Recluses -- Fiction 4. Friendship -- Fiction 5. Neighborhoods -- Fiction 6. New York (N.Y.) -- Fiction 6. Mystery and detective stories 7. Holocaust, Jewish (1939-1945) -- Fiction 8. Greenwich Village (New York N.Y.) -- Fiction

ISBN 0803740018; 9780803740013

LC 2013017790

In this book, by Laura Marx Fitzgerald, "Theodora Tenpenny spills a bottle of rubbing alcohol on her late grandfather's painting [and] discovers . . . an old Renaissance masterpiece underneath. That's great news for Theo, who's struggling to hang onto her family's . . . townhouse and support her unstable mother. . . . There's just one problem: Theo's grandfather was a security guard at the Metropolitan Museum of Art, and she worries the painting may be stolen." (Publisher's note)

"Theo's household is vividly portrayed, from her grandfather's creative ingenuity to her mother's tenuous hold on reality. Smart and determined, down-to-earth and insightful, Theo makes an engaging narrator as she follows a winding trail of discovery." Booklist

Fitzgerald, Sarah Moore

The **apple** tart of hope; by Sarah Moore Fitzgerald. Holiday House 2016 160 p. (hardcover) $16.95

Grades: 5 6 7 8 **Fic**

1. Hope -- Fiction 2. Friendship -- Fiction 3. Missing children -- Fiction

ISBN 9780823435616

LC 2015022313

In this book, by Sarah Moore Fitzgerald, "fourteen-year-old Oscar Dunleavy is missing, presumed dead. His bike was found at sea, out past the end of the pier, and everyone in town seems to have accepted this as a teenage tragedy. But Oscar's best friend Meg knows he isn't dead. Oscar is an optimistic and kind boy who bakes the world s best apple tarts; he would never kill himself, and Meg is going to prove it." (Publisher's note)

" Fully developed secondary characters—such as Oscar's disabled younger brother and Paloma, who tries to take Meg's place—add richness and depth to this lyrically written tale, which explores themes of manipulation, self-discovery, hope, and love... This touching novel is one to savor." Booklist

Fitzmaurice, Kathryn

Destiny, rewritten; Kathryn Fitzmaurice ; [edited by] Molly O'Neill. Katherine Tegen Books 2013 352 p. (hardcover) $16.99

Grades: 4 5 6 7 **Fic**

1. Father-daughter relationship -- Fiction

ISBN 0061625019; 9780061625015

LC 2012945971

In this novel, sixth-grader Emily, named for the poet Emily Dickinson, is pushed to become a poet by her mother "(she even commemorates the important moments of Emily's life in a first edition of Dickinson's poetry). Emily, however, thrives on predictability and order, and has no feel for poetry." She wants to find "her unknown father. . . . Just as Emily learns his name is hidden in the Dickinson book, it is accidentally taken and Emily sets out to find it." (Publishers Weekly)

A **diamond** in the desert; Kathryn Fitzmaurice. Viking 2012 258 p. (hardcover) $16.99

Grades: 5 6 7 8 **Fic**

1. Baseball -- Fiction 2. Father-son relationship -- Fiction 3. World War, 1939-1945 -- United States -- Fiction 4. Japanese Americans --

Evacuation and relocation, 1942-1945 -- Fiction 5. Guilt -- Fiction 6. Gila River Relocation Center -- Fiction
ISBN 0670012920; 9780670012923
LC 2011012041

In this book, "Tetsu is twelve when he and his mother and sister are relocated by World War II's infamous Executive Order 9066, which justified the internment of Japanese-Americans, to the camp at Gila River. His father, a leader in the Japanese-American community, is detained separately in another location, and Tetsu generally takes his responsibility as the oldest male in the immediate family very seriously. He's particularly solicitous of his younger sister, Kimi, who is . . . traumatized by the lack of privacy in the camp. . . . Kimi . . . wanders out into the desert, where she nearly dies. Guilt-stricken, Tetsu withdraws from baseball and from his friends, until his father arrives at Gila River and rekindles his son's interest in life." (Bulletin of the Center for Children's Books)

Includes bibliographical references (p. 255)

Fixmer, Elizabeth

Saint training. Zonderkidz 2010 239p $14.99
Grades: 5 6 7 8 **Fic**
1. School stories 2. Catholics -- Fiction 3. Family life -- Fiction 4. Christian life -- Fiction
ISBN 978-0-310-72018-8; 0-310-72018-4
LC 2010010831

During the turbulent 1960s, sixth-grader Mary Clare makes a deal with God: she will try to become a saint if He provides for her large, cash-strapped family.

"The politically fervent period of the late 1960s, with its dramatic upheavals in family, gender, social, and religious conventions, comes to life with pathos and humor in this powerful debut." Publ Wkly

Flake, Sharon G.

Bang! Jump at the Sun/Hyperion Books for Children 2005 298p hardcover o.p. pa $7.99
Grades: 8 9 10 11 12 **Fic**
1. Violence -- Fiction 2. Family life -- Fiction 3. African Americans -- Fiction
ISBN 0-7868-1844-1; 0-7868-4955-X pa
LC 2005-47434

A teenage boy must face the harsh realities of inner city life, a disintegrating family, and destructive temptations as he struggles to find his identity as a young man.

"This disturbing, thought-provoking novel will leave readers with plenty of food for thought and should fuel lively discussions." SLJ

Pinned; Sharon G. Flake. Scholastic Press 2012 228 p. $17.99
Grades: 9 10 11 12 **Fic**
1. Schools -- Fiction 2. Friendship -- Fiction 3. Best friends -- Fiction 4. High schools -- Fiction 5. African Americans -- Fiction 6. Learning disabilities -- Fiction 7. People with disabilities -- Fiction
ISBN 0545057183; 9780545057189; 9780545057332
LC 2012009239

This novel by Sharon G. Flake is "about a teen boy and girl, each tackling disabilities. Autumn is outgoing and has lots of friends. Adonis is shy and not so eager to connect with people. But even with their differences, the two have one thing in common--they're each dealing with a handicap. For Autumn, who has a learning disability, reading is a painful struggle that makes it hard to focus in class. . . . Adonis is confined to a wheelchair. But he's a strong reader who loves books." (Publisher's note)

★ The **skin** I'm in. Jump at the Sun 1998 171p $14.95; pa $5.99
Grades: 6 7 8 9 **Fic**
1. School stories 2. Teachers -- Fiction 3. African Americans -- Fiction
ISBN 0-7868-0444-0; 0-7868-1307-5 pa
LC 98-19615

Thirteen-year-old Maleeka, uncomfortable because her skin is extremely dark, meets a new teacher with a birthmark on her face and makes some discoveries about how to love who she is and what she looks like

This "novel is fast-paced and realistic." Horn Book Guide

Unstoppable Octobia May; Sharon G. Flake. Scholastic Press 2014 276 p. (hardcover) $16.99
Grades: 4 5 6 **Fic**
1. Racism -- Fiction 2. Secrecy -- Fiction 3. Friendship -- Fiction 4. African Americans -- Southern States -- Fiction 5. Secrets -- Fiction 7. Boardinghouses -- Fiction
ISBN 9780545609623; 9780545609609; 9780545609616
LC 2014003496

In this novel, by Sharon G. Flake, "Octobia May is [a] girl filled with questions. . . . [She lives in her Aunt's] boarding house that is filled with old folks. . . . When Octobia starts to question the folks in her world, an adventure and a mystery unfold that beg some troubling questions: Who is black and who is 'passing' for white? What happens when a vibrant African American community must face its own racism? And, perhaps most important: Do vampires really exist?" (Publisher's note)

"Flake's novel is not only a mystery but also an examination of racial discrimination in the pre–civil rights era...Flake has done a fine job of integrating her expository material into a reader-satisfying and page-turning mystery." Booklist

Includes bibliographical references

Flanagan, John

The **battle** for Skandia; [by] John Flanagan. 1st American ed.; Philomel Books 2008 294p (Ranger's apprentice) $16.99; pa $7.99
Grades: 5 6 7 8 **Fic**
1. Fantasy fiction
ISBN 978-0-399-24457-5; 0-399-24457-3; 978-0-14-241340-1 pa; 0-14-241340-2 pa
LC 2007023646

Sequel to The icebound land (2007)

After Ranger's apprentice Will battles Temujai warriors to rescue Evanlyn, Will's kingdom of Skandia joins forces with rival kingdom Araluen to defeat a common enemy.

"Even readers drawn to the series for its deftly drawn characters and setting may find themselves caught up in the action." Booklist

The **burning** bridge. Philomel Books 2006 262p (Ranger's apprentice) $16.99
Grades: 5 6 7 8 **Fic**
1. Fantasy fiction
ISBN 0-399-24455-7

Sequel to The ruins of Gorlan (2005)

Will is forced to overcome his fear of Wargals, the foot soldiers of rebel warlord Morgarath, as Araluen's army prepares to battle Morgarath's forces.

"The pace is swift, and action is often at the forefront, but elements of humor and nuances of emotion are apparent as well." Booklist

Followed by The icebound land (2007)

The **emperor** of Nihon-Ja. Philomel Books 2011 438p (Ranger's apprentice) $17.99
Grades: 5 6 7 8 **Fic**

1. Fantasy fiction 2. Kings and rulers -- Fiction
ISBN 978-0-399-25500-7; 0-399-25500-1

LC 2010025784

Sequel to: Halt's peril (2010)

In a faraway land, a young warrior must protect an emperor from an uprising and train an inexperienced army, with assistance from his Ranger friends.

Erak's ransom. Philomel Books 2010 373p (Ranger's apprentice) $17.99
Grades: 5 6 7 8 **Fic**

1. War stories 2. Fantasy fiction 3. Deserts -- Fiction 4. Apprentices -- Fiction
ISBN 978-0-399-25205-1; 0-399-25205-3

LC 2009011665

Sequel to: The siege of Macindaw (2009)

First published 2007 in Australia

On a mission to pay the ransom of a new ally, apprentice Will and his friends find themselves in a desert wasteland awash with enemies.

"Bringing together many favorite characters for a grand adventure, this book delivers both excitement and quiet good times." Booklist

Followed by: The kings of Clonmel (2010)

Halt's peril. Philomel Books 2010 386p (Ranger's apprentice) $17.99
Grades: 5 6 7 8 **Fic**

1. Fantasy fiction 2. Cults -- Fiction
ISBN 978-0-399-25207-5; 0-399-25207-X

Sequel to: The kings of Clonmel (2010)

Tennyson, the false prophet of the Outsider cult, has escaped and Halt is determined to stop him before he crosses the border into Araluen, but Genovesan assassins put Will and Halt's extraordinary archery skills to the test.

"Series fans will enjoy the dialogue and camaraderie as much as the action." Booklist

Followed by: The Emperor of Nihon-Ja (2011)

The **hunters**; John Flanagan. Philomel 2012 403 p. (hardback) $18.99
Grades: 5 6 7 8 **Fic**

1. Fantasy 2. Courage -- Fiction 3. Pirates -- Fiction 4. Friendship -- Fiction 5. Seafaring life -- Fiction 6. Adventure and adventurers -- Fiction
ISBN 0399256210; 9780399256219

LC 2012020986

This book by John Flanagan is part of the Brotherband Chronicles series. "Hal and his brotherband crew are hot on the trail of the pirate Zavac and they have one thing only on their minds: Stopping the bloodthirsty thief before he can do more damage. Of course, they also know Zavac has the Andomal, the priceless Skandian artifact stolen when the brotherband let down their guard. The chase leads down mighty rivers, terrifying rapids, to the lawless fortress of Ragusa." (Publisher's note)

The **icebound** land; [by] John Flanagan. 1st American ed.; Philomel Books 2007 260p (Ranger's apprentice) $16.99
Grades: 5 6 7 8 **Fic**

1. Fantasy fiction
ISBN 978-0-399-24456-8

LC 2006034561

Sequel to The burning bridge (2006)

Chasing the Skandian slave-traders who kidnapped Will and Evanlyn, Ranger Halt and warrior student Horace find themselves in the frozen northern islands, where they battle a ruthless black-clad knight as they attempt to rescue their friends.

"Flanagan's deft character portrayals and well-paced story will engage readers." Booklist

Followed by The battle for Skandia (2008)

The **invaders**; John Flanagan. Philomel Books 2012 429 p. (The Brotherband chronicles) (hardback) $18.99
Grades: 5 6 7 8 **Fic**

1. Adventure fiction 2. Fantasy 3. Courage -- Fiction 4. Pirates -- Fiction 5. Friendship -- Fiction 6. Seafaring life -- Fiction
ISBN 0399256202; 9780399256202

LC 2012000424

This book by John Flanagan is part of the Brotherband Chronicles series. "Hal and the Herons have done the impossible. This group of outsiders has beaten out the strongest, most skilled young warriors in all of Skandia to win the Brotherband competition. But their celebration comes to an abrupt end when the Skandians' most sacred artifact, the Andomal, is stolen--and the Herons are to blame." (Publisher's note)

The **kings** of Clonmel. Philomel Books 2010 358p (Ranger's apprentice) $17.99
Grades: 5 6 7 8 **Fic**

1. War stories 2. Fantasy fiction 3. Cults -- Fiction
ISBN 978-0-399-25206-8; 0-399-25206-1

Sequel to: Erak's ransom (2010)

Hair, Will, and Horace set out for Hiberia, where a quasi-religious group, the Outsiders, is sowing confusion and sedition, and they find that secrets from Halt's past may hold the key to restoring order before the last kingdom is undermined.

"There's wit as well as action here, and the revelation of Halt's backstory adds a new dimension to the saga." Booklist

Followed by: Halt's peril (2010)

★ The **outcasts**. Philomel Books 2011 434p (Brotherband chronicles) $18.99
Grades: 5 6 7 8 **Fic**

1. Fantasy fiction 2. Adventure fiction 3. Friendship -- Fiction
ISBN 978-0-399-25619-6; 0-399-25619-9

Hal, who does not fit into Skandian society, ends up in a brotherband, a group of boys learning the skills that they need to become warriors, with other outcasts, and they compete with other brotherbands in a series of challenges.

"This enjoyable, old-fashioned tale should have easy appeal for Flanagan's many fans, who are already invested in the world he's created." Publ Wkly

Other titles in this series are:
The invaders (2012)
The hunters (2012)
Slaves of Socorro (2014)
Scorpion Mountain (2014)
The ghostfaces (2016)
The caldera (2017)

The **red** fox clan; John Flanagan. Philomel Books 2018 346 p. (hardback) $18.99
Grades: 5 6 7 8 **Fic**

1. Apprentices -- Fiction 2. Fantasy fiction 3. Adventure fiction
ISBN 1524741388; 9781524741389
LC 2018011891

In this book in the Ranger's Apprentice: The Royal Ranger series, by John Flanagan, "after passing her third-year assessment as a ranger's apprentice, Maddie is called home to Castle Araluen. Forced to keep her ranger training a secret, Maddie feels trapped by the monotony of castle life. . . . But there are whisperings of a new threat to the kingdom. The mysterious Red Fox Clan, a group of anarchists . . . , question Princess Cassandra and Madelyn's succession to the throne." (Publisher's note)

The **royal** ranger; John Flanagan. Philomel Books, an imprint of Penguin Group (USA) Inc. 2013 464 p.
Grades: 5 6 7 8 **Fic**

1. Apprentices -- Fiction 2. Fantasy fiction 3. Adventure and adventurers
ISBN 9780399163609
LC 2013015910

In this book, by John Flanagan, "Will Treaty has come a long way from the small boy with dreams of knighthood. Life had other plans for him, and as an apprentice Ranger under Halt, he grew into a legend. . . . The time has come to take on an apprentice of his own, and it's the last person he ever would have expected. Fighting his personal demons, Will has to win the trust and respect of his difficult new companion—a task that at times seems almost impossible." (Publisher's note)

"Taking place at least 16 years after the original 10 volumes of the Ranger's Apprentice series, this sequel sees Will training 15-year-old Maddie, the first girl to become a ranger's apprentice. . . . Maddie emerges as a strong character and could easily develop a following among readers who enjoy Tamora Pierce's books about Alanna, another resourceful, independent-minded heroine." Booklist

Followed by:
The red fox clan (2018)

★ The **ruins** of Gorlan. Philomel Books 2005 249p (Ranger's apprentice) $15.99; pa $7.99
Grades: 5 6 7 8 **Fic**

1. Fantasy fiction
ISBN 0-399-24454-9; 0-14-240663-5 pa

When fifteen-year-old Will is rejected by battleschool, he becomes the reluctant apprentice to the mysterious Ranger Halt, and winds up protecting the kingdom from danger.

"Flanagan concentrates on character, offering readers a young protagonist they will care about and relationships that develop believably over time." Booklist

Other titles in this series are:
The burning bridge (2006)
The icebound land (2007)
The battle for Skandia (2008)
The socerer of the north (2008)
The siege of Macindaw (2009)
Erak's ransom (2010)
The kings of Clonmel (2010)
Halt's peril (2010)
The Emperor of Nihon-Ja (2011)

The **siege** of Macindaw. Philomel Books 2009 293p (Ranger's apprentice) $17.99; pa $7.99
Grades: 5 6 7 8 **Fic**

1. War stories 2. Fantasy fiction
ISBN 978-0-399-25033-0; 0-399-25033-6; 978-0-14-241524-5 pa; 0-14-241524-3 pa
LC 2008032630

Sequel to: The sorcerer of the north (2008)

Now a full-fledged Ranger, Will must rescue his friend Alyss from a rogue knight and uncover vital information needed to ward off a Scotti invasion.

"Series fans will relish the familiar details of warfare and comradeship as well as the surprising fireworks in both war and love." Booklist

Followed by: Erak's Ransom (2010)

The **sorcerer** of the north; [by] John Flanagan. Philomel Books 2008 288p (Ranger's apprentice) $16.99
Grades: 5 6 7 8 **Fic**

1. Fantasy fiction
ISBN 978-0-399-25032-3; 0-399-25032-8
LC 2008-16528

Sequel to: The battle for Skandia (2008)

Now a full-fledged Ranger responsible for a sleepy fief, Will finds a new adventure seeking the traitors who poisoned the king, investigating rumors of sorcery, and trying to rescue his friend Alyss, who is taken hostage.

"Flanagan is to be complimented for creating a fantasy world that relies on character and action rather than magic." Voice Youth Advocates

Fleischman, Paul

Bull Run; woodcuts by David Frampton. HarperCollins Pubs. 1993 104p il pa $4.99
Grades: 6 7 8 9 **Fic**

1. Bull Run, 1st Battle of, 1861 -- Fiction 2. United States -- History -- 1861-1865, Civil War -- Fiction
ISBN 0-06-440588-5 pa
LC 92-14745

"Abandoning the conventions of narrative fiction, Fleischman tells a vivid, many-sided story in this original and moving book. An excellent choice for readers' theater in the classroom or on stage." Booklist

★ **Seedfolks**; illustrations by Judy Pedersen. HarperCollins Pubs. 1997 69p $14.99; lib bdg $15.89; pa $4.99
Grades: 4 5 6 7 **Fic**

1. Gardens -- Fiction 2. City and town life -- Fiction
ISBN 0-06-027471-9; 0-06-027472-7 lib bdg; 0-06-447207-8 pa
LC 96-26696

This "novel is the story of an urban garden started by a child and nurtured by people of all ages and ethnic backgrounds. Each of the thirteen chapters is narrated by a different character, allowing the reader to watch as a community develops out of disconnected lives and previous suspicions." (Horn Book) "Grade four and up." (SLJ)

This "novel tells about an urban garden started by a child and nurtured by people of all ages and ethnic and economic backgrounds. Each of the thirteen chapters is narrated by a different character, allowing the reader to watch as a community develops out of disconnected lives and prior suspicions." Horn Book Guide

Seek. Simon Pulse 2003 167p pa $7.99
Grades: 7 8 9 10 **Fic**

1. Radio -- Fiction 2. Fathers -- Fiction
ISBN 0-689-85402-1
First published 2001 by Front St./Cricket Bks.

"Fleischman has orchestrated a symphony that is both joyful and poignant with this book designed for reader's theatre." Voice Youth Advocates

Fleischman, Sid

The **entertainer** and the dybbuk. Greenwillow Books 2007 180p lib bdg $17.89; pa $6.99; $16.99

Grades: 6 7 8 9 **Fic**

1. Ghost stories 2. Jews -- Fiction 3. Supernatural -- Fiction 4. Ventriloquism -- Fiction 5. Holocaust, 1933-1945 -- Fiction

ISBN 0-06-13444-1; 978-0-06-134446-6 lib bdg; 0-06-134446-X lib bdg; 978-0-06-177140-8 pa; 0-06-177140-6 pa; 978-0-06-134445-9

LC 2007-17267

A struggling American ventriloquist in post-World War II Europe is possessed by the mischievous spirit of a young Jewish boy killed in the Holocaust.

"This exciting and thought-provoking book belongs in every collection." SLJ

The **whipping** boy; illustrations by Peter Sis. Greenwillow Bks. 1986 90p il $16.99; pa $5.99

Grades: 5 6 7 8 **Fic**

1. Adventure fiction 2. Thieves -- Fiction

ISBN 0-688-06216-4; 0-06-052122-8 pa

LC 85-17555

Awarded the Newbery Medal, 1987

"A round tale of adventure and humor, this follows the fortunes of Prince Roland (better known as Prince Brat) and his whipping boy, Jemmy, who has received all the hard knocks for the prince's mischief. . . . There's not a moment's lag in pace, and the stock characters, from Hold-Your-Nose Billy to Betsy's dancing bear Petunia, have enough inventive twists to project a lively air to it all." Bull Cent Child Books

Fleming, David

★ The **Saturday** boy; by David Fleming. Viking Children's 2013 240 p. (hardcover) $16.99

Grades: 5 6 7 8 **Fic**

1. School stories -- Fiction 2. Families of soldiers -- Fiction 3. Bullies -- Fiction 4. Schools -- Fiction 5. Behavior -- Fiction 6. Family life -- Fiction 7. Families of military personnel -- Fiction

ISBN 0670785512; 9780670785513

LC 2012029680

In this book, Derek is the son of "a soldier who flies Apache helicopters and is stationed in Afghanistan for another tour. . . . Derek is a good-hearted kid who just naturally attracts trouble--he doesn't mean to, but he's always in the wrong place at the wrong time and often the victim. He's also impulsive and has a hard time staying focused, which adds to his problems." Then one day, "he sees his dad on the news and his world falls apart." (School Library Journal)

Fletcher, Charlie

Ironhand. Hyperion Books for Children 2008 400p (Stoneheart trilogy) lib bdg $16.99

Grades: 5 6 7 8 **Fic**

1. Fantasy fiction

ISBN 978-1-4231-0177-2 lib bdg; 1-4231-0177-4 lib bdg

LC 2007-42073

Sequel to: Stoneheart (2007)

Having upset the balance between the warring statues of London, twelve-year-old George is confronted with new challenges as he tries to free his captured friends Edie and The Gunner from the formidable Walker and deal with the three strange veins of marble, bronze, and stone that have begun to grow out of his hand.

"Cliff-hanger chapters . . . will leave readers breathless. George's story is particularly vivid." Booklist

Followed by: Silvertongue (2009)

Silvertongue. Hyperion Books for Children 2009 (Stoneheart trilogy) $16.99

Grades: 5 6 7 8 **Fic**

1. Fantasy fiction

ISBN 978-1-4231-0179-6; 1-4231-0179-0

Sequel to: Ironhand (2008)

The battle between the statues and gargoyles of London rages on-and 12-year-old George Chapman and his friend Edie are caught in the middle. With the Walker intent on forcing his evil designs on the city and the world, George realizes that his destiny is inextricably tied to the Walker's destruction.

"George and Edie's action-packed experiences are told in alternate chapters. . . . The book does not stand on its own, but those familiar with the earlier titles will be satisfied." SLJ

Stoneheart. Hyperion Books for Children 2007 450p (Stoneheart trilogy) $16.99; pa $7.99

Grades: 5 6 7 8 **Fic**

1. Fantasy fiction

ISBN 978-1-4231-0175-8; 1-4231-0175-8; 978-1-4231-0176-5 pa; 1-4231-0176-6 pa

LC 2007-01138

When twelve-year-old George accidentally decapitates a stone statue in London, England, he falls into a parallel dimension where he must battle ancient "live" statues and solve a dangerous riddle.

This "is an action-packed fantasy filled with battles, chases, and an intriguing variety of characters." SLJ

Other titles in this series are:

Ironhand (2008)

Silvertongue (2009)

Fletcher, Susan

Ancient, strange, and lovely. Atheneum Books for Young Readers 2010 315p il (The dragon chronicles) $16.99

Grades: 6 7 8 9 **Fic**

1. Fantasy fiction 2. Dragons -- Fiction 3. Poaching -- Fiction

ISBN 978-1-4169-5786-7; 1-4169-5786-3

LC 2009053797

Fourteen-year-old Bryn must try to find a way to save a baby dragon from a dangerous modern world that seems to have no place for something so ancient.

"This book offers a wondrous mix of dystopic science fiction and magical fantasy. . . . Fletcher has done an outstanding job of creating a believable place and space for this story to unfold. The plot flows smoothly and quickly with a lot of action." SLJ

Dragon's milk. Atheneum Pubs. 1989 242p hardcover o.p. pa $5.99

Grades: 7 8 9 10 **Fic**

1. Fantasy fiction 2. Dragons -- Fiction

ISBN 0-689-31579-1; 0-689-71623-0 pa

LC 88-35059

Kaeldra, an outsider adopted by an Elythian family as a baby, possesses the power to understand dragons and uses this power to try to save her younger sister who needs dragon's milk to recover from an illness

"High-fantasy fans will delight in the clash of swords, the flash of magic, the many escape-and-rescue scenes." Booklist

Other titles in this series are:
Flight of the Dragon Kyn (1993)
Sign of the dove (1996)

Flight of the Dragon Kyn. Atheneum Pubs. 1993 213p (Dragon chronicles) hardcover o.p. pa $5.99
Grades: 7 8 9 10 **Fic**

1. Fantasy fiction 2. Dragons -- Fiction
ISBN 0-689-31880-4; 0-689-81515-8 pa
LC 92-44787

Second title in the author's series set in Elythia; a prequel to Dragon's milk

Fifteen-year-old Kara is summoned by King Orrik, who believes she has the power to call down the dragons that have been plundering his realm, and she is caught up in the fierce rivalry between Orrik and his jealous brother Rog

"This is a solid fantasy in a medieval Scandinavian-like setting, and there's plenty of drama, romance, and knavery to keep genre fans happy." Bull Cent Child Books

Journey of the pale bear; Susan Fletcher. Margaret K. McElderry Books 2018 280 p. (hardback) $16.99
Grades: 4 5 6 7 **Fic**

1. Bears -- Fiction 2. Polar bear -- Fiction 3. Voyages and travels -- Fiction 4. Adventure and adventurers -- Fiction 5. Human-animal relationships -- Fiction 6. Great Britain -- History -- Henry III, 1216-1272 -- Fiction
ISBN 9781534420779; 9781534420786
LC 2017049316

Golden Kite Honor Book (2019)

This book, by Susan Fletcher, is about "a runaway boy [who] befriends a polar bear that's being transported from Norway to London. The polar bear is a royal bear, a gift from the King of Norway to the King of England. The first time Arthur encounters the bear, he is shoved in her cage as payback for stealing food. Restless and deadly, the bear terrifies him. Yet, strangely, she doesn't harm him--though she has attacked anyone else who comes near." (Publisher's note)

Sign of the dove. Atheneum Bks. for Young Readers 1996 214p (Dragon chronicles) hardcover o.p. pa $7.99
Grades: 7 8 9 10 **Fic**

1. Fantasy fiction 2. Dragons -- Fiction
ISBN 0-689-80460-1; 1-416-99714-8 pa
LC 95-584

Sequel to: Flight of the Dragon Kyn

As the last of the dragon eggs, laid long ago, begin to hatch, Lyf becomes a reluctant friend who tries to save both the dragon mothers and their newly born children from their enemies

The author "offers a stalwart heroine in a rousing story filled with well-realized dragon lore." Booklist

Walk across the sea. Atheneum Bks. for Young Readers 2001 214p hardcover o.p. pa $4.99
Grades: 5 6 7 8 **Fic**

1. Prejudices -- Fiction 2. Chinese Americans -- Fiction
ISBN 0-689-84133-7; 0-689-85707-1 pa
LC 00-50246

In late nineteenth-century California, when Chinese immigrants are being driven out or even killed for fear they will take jobs from whites, fifteen-year-old Eliza Jane McCully defies the townspeople and her lighthouse-keeper father to help a Chinese boy who has been kind to her

"This is a gripping and complex story, and Fletcher's lyrical depiction of 19th-century life, her exceptionally well-drawn protagonist, and her deft analysis of racial discrimination make the book even more powerful." SLJ

Flinn, Alex

Beastly. HarperTeen 2007 304p $16.99; lib bdg $17.89; pa $8.99
Grades: 6 7 8 9 10 **Fic**

1. Fantasy fiction 2. New York (N.Y.) -- Fiction
ISBN 978-0-06-087416-2; 0-06-087416-3; 978-0-06-087417-9 lib bdg; 0-06-087417-1 lib bdg; 978-0-06-196328-5 pa; 0-06-196328-3 pa
LC 2006-36241

A modern retelling of "Beauty and the Beast" from the point of view of the Beast, a vain Manhattan private school student who is turned into a monster and must find true love before he can return to his human form.

This "is creative enough to make it an engaging read. . . . [This is an] engrossing tale that will have appeal for fans of fantasy and realistic fiction." Voice Youth Advocates

Cloaked. HarperTeen 2011 341p $16.99
Grades: 6 7 8 9 **Fic**

1. Fairy tales 2. Magic -- Fiction 3. Shoes -- Fiction 4. Animals -- Fiction 5. Florida -- Fiction 6. Princesses -- Fiction 7. Missing persons -- Fiction
ISBN 978-0-06-087422-3; 0-06-087422-8
LC 2009-53387

Seventeen-year-old Johnny is approached at his family's struggling shoe repair shop in a Miami, Florida, hotel by Alorian Princess Victoriana, who asks him to find her brother who was turned into a frog.

"A diverting, whimsical romp through fairy-tale tropes." Bull Cent Child Books

A **kiss** in time. HarperTeen 2009 384p $16.99; pa $8.99
Grades: 7 8 9 10 11 12 **Fic**

1. Florida -- Fiction 2. Witches -- Fiction 3. Princesses -- Fiction
ISBN 978-0-06-087419-3; 0-06-087419-8; 978-0-06-087421-6 pa; 0-06-087421-X pa
LC 2008-22582

Sixteen-year-old Princess Talia persuades seventeen-year-old Jack, the modern-day American who kissed her awake after a 300-year sleep, to take her to his Miami home, where she hopes to win his love before the witch who cursed her can spirit her away.

This is a "clever and humorous retelling of 'Sleeping Beauty.' . . . Alternating between the teenagers' distinctive points of view, Flinn skillfully delineates how their upbringings set them apart while drawing parallels between their family conflicts. Fans of happily-ever-after endings will delight in the upbeat resolution." Publ Wkly

Flood, Nancy Bo

★ **Warriors** in the crossfire. Front Street 2010 142p $17.95
Grades: 6 7 8 9 **Fic**

1. World War, 1939-1945 -- Fiction 2. Islands of the Pacific -- Fiction
ISBN 978-1-59078-661-1; 1-59078-661-0

Twelve-year-old Joseph helps his family to survive when the natives of Saipan are caught in the crossfire between Japanese and American soldiers towards the end of World War II.

"Intense and powerful reading that avoids bleakness by celebrating family, culture, and a longing for peace." Booklist

Flores-Gabis, Enrique

★ **90** miles to Havana. Roaring Brook Press 2010 292p $17.99

Grades: 5 6 7 8 **Fic**

1. Cuba -- Fiction 2. Florida -- Fiction 3. Cuban refugees -- Fiction
ISBN 978-1-59643-168-3; 1-59643-168-7

"Drawing on his own experience as a child refugee from Cuba, Flores-Galbis offers a gripping historical novel about children who were evacuated from Cuba to the U.S. during Operation Pedro Pan in 1961. Julian, a young Cuban boy, experiences the violent revolution and watches mobs throw out his family's furniture and move into their home. For his safety, his parents send him to a refugee camp in Miami. . . . This is a seldom-told refugee story that will move readers with the first-person, present-tense rescue narrative, filled with betrayal, kindness, and waiting for what may never come." Booklist

Foley, Jessie Ann

Sorry for your loss; Jessie Ann Foley ; [edited by] Alexandra Cooper. HarperTeen 2019 336 p. (hardcover) $17.99

Grades: 8 9 10 11 12 **Fic**

1. Death -- Fiction 2. Grief -- Fiction 3. Brothers -- Fiction
ISBN 9780062571915

LC 2018968292

In this book, by Jessie Ann Foley, edited by Alexandra Cooper, "painfully average Pup Flanagan is used to flying under the radar. . . . The only person who ever made him think he could be more was his older brother Patrick. But that was before Patrick died suddenly. . . . When Pup excels at a photography assignment he thought he'd bomb, things start to come into focus. . . . [But] the photograph . . . reveals someone else who is still stuck in their own." (Publisher's note)

"Written with Foley's keen ear for family dynamics, this is definitely a strong choice for fans of her work and those new to the author." (School Library Journal)

Foley, Lizzie K.

Remarkable; a novel. by Lizzie K. Foley. Dial Books for Young Readers 2012 325 p. (hardcover) $16.99

Grades: 3 4 5 6 7 **Fic**

1. Fantasy fiction 2. Humorous fiction 3. Ability -- Fiction 4. Community life -- Fiction 5. Humorous stories 6. Pirates -- Fiction 7. Secrets -- Fiction 8. Eccentrics and eccentricities -- Fiction
ISBN 9780803737068

LC 2011021641

This book presents the story of an average girl named Jane Doe who lives in "the town of Remarkable, so named for its abundance of talented citizens, everyone lives up to its reputation. . . . Jane should be just as remarkable. Instead, this average 10-year-old girl is usually overlooked. . . . Mix in a rival town's dispute over jelly, hints of a Loch Ness Monster-like creature and a psychic pizzeria owner who sees the future in her reflective pizza pans. . . . With the help of her quiet Grandpa John, who's also forgotten most of the time, Jane learns to be true to herself and celebrate the ordinary in life." (Kirkus)

Fontes, Justine

Benito runs. Darby Creek 2011 104p (Surviving Southside) lib bdg $27.93; pa $7.99

Grades: 7 8 9 10 **Fic**

1. Fathers -- Fiction 2. Hispanic Americans -- Fiction 3. Post-traumatic stress disorder -- Fiction
ISBN 978-0-7613-6151-0 lib bdg; 0-7613-6151-0; 978-0-7613-6165-7 pa; 0-7613-6165-0 pa

LC 2010023820

"Benito's dad comes home from the war in Iraq. The family has been looking forward to his return, but he now has PTSD and is prone to loud, embarrassing outbursts. Ultimately, Benito leaves the house on an ill-fated bus journey." Voice Youth Advocates

This "well-written [story reinforces] the importance of family, friends, values, and thoughtful decision-making. . . . [An] excellent [purchase, this book] will attract and engage reluctant readers." SLJ

Ford, John C.

The **morgue** and me. Viking 2009 313p $17.99

Grades: 8 9 10 11 12 **Fic**

1. Mystery fiction 2. Homicide -- Fiction 3. Michigan -- Fiction 4. Journalists -- Fiction 5. Criminal investigation -- Fiction
ISBN 978-0-670-01096-7; 0-670-01096-0

LC 2009-1956

Eighteen-year-old Christopher, who plans to be a spy, learns of a murder cover-up through his summer job as a morgue assistant and teams up with Tina, a gorgeous newspaper reporter, to investigate, despite great danger.

"Ford spins a tale that's complex but not confusing, never whitewashing some of the harsher crimes people commit. The result is a story that holds its own as a mainstream mystery as well as a teen novel." Publ Wkly

Ford, Michael

★ The **poisoned** house. Albert Whitman 2011 319p $16.99

Grades: 6 7 8 9 10 **Fic**

1. Ghost stories 2. Supernatural -- Fiction 3. London (England) -- Fiction 4. Household employees -- Fiction 5. Great Britain -- History -- 19th century -- Fiction
ISBN 978-0-8075-6589-6; 0-8075-6589-X

LC 2010048250

As the widowed master of an elegant house in Victorian-era London slips slowly into madness and his tyrannical housekeeper takes on more power, a ghostly presence distracts a teenaged maidservant with clues to a deadly secret.

"This ghost story is light fare, chilling, and suspenseful." SLJ

Z. HarperTeen 2010 276p $16.99; lib bdg $17.89

Grades: 7 8 9 10 **Fic**

1. Science fiction 2. Games -- Fiction 3. Zombies -- Fiction
ISBN 978-0-06-073758-0; 0-06-073758-1; 978-0-06-073759-7 lib bdg; 0-06-073759-X lib bdg

LC 2009-44005

In the year 2032, after a virus that turned people into zombies has been eradicated, Josh is invited to join an underground gaming society, where the gamers hunt zombies and the action is more dangerous than it seems.

"This book is a thriller, and the clever plot and characters will have readers hoping for more." SLJ

Forester, Victoria

★ The **girl** who could fly. Feiwel and Friends 2008 329p $16.95

Grades: 4 5 6 7 **Fic**

1. School stories 2. Science fiction 3. Flight -- Fiction
ISBN 978-0-312-37462-4; 0-312-37462-3

LC 2008-06882

When homeschooled farm girl Piper McCloud reveals her ability to fly, she is quickly taken to a secret government facility to be trained with other exceptional children, but she soon realizes that something is very wrong and begins working with brilliant and wealthy Conrad to escape.

"The story soars, just like Piper, with enough loop-de-loops to keep kids uncertain about what will come next. . . . Best of all are the book's strong, lightly wrapped messages about friendship and authenticity and the difference between doing well and doing good." Booklist

Forman, Gayle

★ **If** I stay; a novel. Dutton Children's Books 2009 201p $16.99

Grades: 7 8 9 10 **Fic**

1. Coma -- Fiction 2. Death -- Fiction 3. Oregon -- Fiction 4. Medical care -- Fiction
ISBN 0-525-42103-3; 978-0-525-42103-0

LC 2008-23938

While in a coma following an automobile accident that killed her parents and younger brother, seventeen-year-old Mia, a gifted cellist, weighs whether to live with her grief or join her family in death.

"Intensely moving, the novel will force readers to take stock of their lives and the people and things that make them worth living." Publ Wkly

Followed by: Where she went (2011)

Where she went. Dutton Books 2011 264p $16.99

Grades: 7 8 9 10 **Fic**

1. Musicians -- Fiction 2. Rock music -- Fiction 3. Violoncellos -- Fiction 4. New York (N.Y.) -- Fiction
ISBN 978-0-525-42294-5; 0-525-42294-3

LC 2010-13474

Forward, Toby

Dragonborn; by Toby Forward. Bloomsbury Childrens 2012 344 p.

Grades: 6 7 8 **Fic**

1. Fantasy fiction 2. Magic -- Fiction 3. Dragons -- Fiction 4. Apprentices -- Fiction 5. Wizards -- Fiction
ISBN 9781599907246

LC 2010051029

This book focuses on "Sam, an unworldly wizard's apprentice whose beloved master dies unexpectedly, leaving the 12-year-old boy half-trained, without clear direction, and fought over by a number of other wizards, not all of whom have his best interests at heart." (Publishers Wkly) "His closest companion has been Starback, a small dragon that has followed him loyally, but when he makes his escape from Flaxfield's little home . . . even Starback deserts him. . . . A dwarfish being called a roffle convinces him that if he wants to continue his magical education, he can do no better than the College. On arrival, Sam finds that the dean is more interested in parlor tricks than in the deep magic that Flaxfield taught him to respect. Moving on, he becomes caught up in a wizards' war that leaves him near death." (School Libr J)

Fireborn; by Toby Forward. Bloomsbury 2013 432 p. (hardback) $16.99

Grades: 6 7 8 **Fic**

1. Fire 2. Magic -- Fiction 3. Fantasy 4. Wizards -- Fiction 5. Apprentices -- Fiction
ISBN 1599908891; 9781599908892

LC 2013012055

In this book, the prequel to Toby Forward's book "Dragonborn," "when greedy wizard Slowin steals both name and power from his apprentice, Bee, the conflagration affects magic everywhere. Meanwhile, twelve-year-old Cabbage's own master, Flaxfield, suddenly loses all his magic, and Cabbage finds that he and a newm friend, Perry the (Hobbit-like) roffle, are the only ones with the ability to amend the situation." (Horn Book Magazine)

Fox, Janet

The **charmed** children of Rookskill Castle; Janet Fox. Viking 2016 400 p. illustrations (hardcover) $16.99

Grades: 5 6 7 8 9 **Fic**

1. Castles -- Fiction 2. Haunted houses -- Fiction 3. World War, 1939-1945 -- Fiction 4. Magic -- Fiction 5. Secrets -- Fiction 6. Detective and mystery stories 7. Brothers and sisters -- Fiction 8. Scotland -- History -- 20th century -- Fiction
ISBN 0451476336; 9780451476333

LC 2015020813

In this novel, by Janet Fox, "the Nazis have begun bombing London. Katherine Bateson's . . . mother decides that Katherine and her siblings should go to the Scottish highlands to escape. Katherine's great-aunt Margaret gives her a farewell gift: Margaret's chatelaine, an ornament worn by women. As the Batesons and other children arrive in Scotland at Lord Gregor's manor . . . Katherine immediately realizes something is amiss." (Publisher's note)

"Fox presents readers with a wonderfully paced, exciting story with enough twists to keep the pages turning." SLJ

Foxlee, Karen

★ The **anatomy** of wings. Alfred A. Knopf 2009 361p $16.99; lib bdg $19.99

Grades: 8 9 10 11 12 **Fic**

1. Sisters -- Fiction 2. Suicide -- Fiction 3. Australia -- Fiction 4. Bereavement -- Fiction 5. Family life -- Fiction
ISBN 978-0-375-85643-3; 0-375-85643-9; 978-0-375-95643-0 lib bdg; 0-375-95643-3 lib bdg

LC 2008-19373

First published 2007 in Australia

After the suicide of her troubled teenage sister, eleven-year-old Jenny struggles to understand what actually happened.

Jenny's "observations are . . . poetic and washed with magic realism. . . . With heart-stopping accuracy and sly symbolism, Foxlee captures the small ways that humans reveal themselves, the mysterious intensity of female adolescence, and the surreal quiet of a grieving house, which slowly and with astonishing resilience fills again with sound and music." Booklist

★ **Ophelia** and the marvelous boy; by Karen Foxlee. Alfred A. Knopf 2014 240 p. $16.99

Grades: 4 5 6 7 8 **Fic**

1. Snow -- Fiction 2. Museums -- Fiction 3. Prisoners -- Fiction 4. Magic -- Fiction 5. Heroes -- Fiction 6. Wizards -- Fiction 7. Kings, queens, rulers, etc. -- Fiction
ISBN 0385753543; 9780385753548; 9780385753555

LC 2013012236

In this book, by Karen Foxlee, "Ophelia Jane Worthington-Whittard . . . and her sister Alice are still grieving for their dead mother when their father takes a job in a strange museum in a city where it always snows. On her very first day in the museum Ophelia discovers a boy locked away in a long forgotten room. He is a prisoner of Her Majesty the Snow Queen. As Ophelia embarks on an incredible journey to rescue the boy everything that she believes will be tested." (Publisher's note)

"Loosely based on Hans Christian Andersen's The Snow Queen, this clever story-within-a-story reads easily yet offers deep lessons about trust, responsibility, and friendship." Booklist

Fraillon, Zana

The **Bone** Sparrow; by Zana Fraillon. Disney-Hyperion 2016 240 p. (hardback) $16.99

Grades: 4 5 6 7 8 **Fic**

1. Refugees -- Fiction 2. Australia -- Fiction 3. Friendship -- Fiction 4. Storytelling -- Fiction

ISBN 9781484781517

LC 2016002391

In this children's book, by Zana Fraillon, "Subhi is a refugee. He was born in an Australian permanent detention center after his mother and sister fled the violence of a distant homeland, and the center is the only world he knows. . . . One night, . . . Subhi sees a scruffy girl . . . named Jimmie, who appears with a notebook written by the mother she lost. Unable to read it herself, Jimmie asks Subhi to unravel her family's love songs and tragedies that are penned there." (Publisher's note)

"Appended with a glimpse at the 'all-too-true reality' of refugee maltreatment, this tale is breathtaking and indispensable." Booklist

Frank, Steven B.

Armstrong & Charlie; written by Steven B. Frank. Houghton Mifflin Harcourt 2017 298 p. (hardcover) $16.99

Grades: 5 6 7 8 **Fic**

1. School stories 2. Jews -- Fiction 3. Friendship -- Fiction 4. Race relations -- Fiction 5. African Americans -- Fiction 6. School integration -- Fiction 7. Los Angeles (Calif.) -- Fiction 8. Schools -- Fiction 9. Best friends -- Fiction 10. Jews -- United States -- Fiction

ISBN 9780544826083

LC 2016014199

In this book, written by Steven B. Frank, "Charlie isn't looking forward to sixth grade. If he starts sixth grade, chances are he'll finish it. And when he does, he'll grow older than the brother he recently lost. Armstrong isn't looking forward to sixth grade, either. . . . When these two land at the same desk, it's the Rules Boy next to the Rebel, a boy who lost a brother elbow-to-elbow with a boy who longs for one." (Publisher's note)

Class action; by Steven B. Frank. Houghton Mifflin Harcourt 2018 272 p. $16.99

Grades: 4 5 6 7 8 **Fic**

1. Legal stories 2. Homework -- Fiction

ISBN 9781328799203

LC 2017014151

In this book, by Steven B. Frank, "NO. MORE. HOMEWORK. That's what sixth grader Sam Warren tells his teacher. . . . Suspended for his protest, Sam decides to fight back. He recruits his elderly neighbor/retired attorney Mr. Kalman to help him file a class action lawsuit on behalf of all students in Los Angeles. Their argument? Homework is unconstitutional. . . . Sam takes his case to federal court. He learns about the justice system, kids' rights, and constitutional law." (Publisher's note)

Frazier, Angie

The **Eternal** Sea. Scholastic Press 2011 362p $17.99

Grades: 8 9 10 11 12 **Fic**

1. Adventure fiction 2. Egypt -- Fiction 3. Supernatural -- Fiction

ISBN 978-0-545-11475-2; 0-545-11475-6

Sequel to: Everlasting (2010)

Realizing that the magic of Umandu, the stone that grants immortality, is not done, seventeen-year-old Camille accompanies Oscar, Ira, and Randall to Egypt, where all their lives are in grave danger.

"Readers who enjoy sea romances won't go wrong." SLJ

Everlasting. Scholastic Press 2010 329p $17.99

Grades: 8 9 10 11 12 **Fic**

1. Adventure fiction 2. Australia -- Fiction 3. Shipwrecks -- Fiction 4. Supernatural -- Fiction 5. Seafaring life -- Fiction 6. Father-daughter relationship -- Fiction

ISBN 978-0-545-11473-8; 0-545-11473-X

LC 2009-20519

In 1855, seventeen-year-old Camille sets out from San Francisco, California, on her last sea voyage before entering a loveless marriage, but when her father's ship is destroyed, she and a friend embark on a cross-Australian quest to find her long-lost mother who holds a map to a magical stone.

"Although this novel takes place in the nineteenth century, many of the themes are relevant for today's teens. The author does a nice job of developing strong and funny characters while keeping the plot moving at a readable pace." Voice Youth Advocates

Followed by: The eternal sea (2011)

The **mastermind** plot; by Angie Frazier. Scholastic Press 2012 231 p. (Suzanna Snow mysteries) (hardcover : alk. paper) $16.99

Grades: 4 5 6 7 **Fic**

1. Mystery fiction 2. Adventure fiction 3. Arson -- Fiction 4. Uncles -- Fiction 5. Schools -- Fiction 6. Grandmothers -- Fiction 7. Mystery and detective stories 8. Family life -- Massachusetts -- Boston -- Fiction 9. Boston (Mass.) -- History -- 20th century -- Fiction

ISBN 0545208645; 9780545208642

LC 2011003770

Sequel to: The midnight tunnel

This children's mystery by Angie Frazier continues the adventures of Suzanna Snow. "She's just arrived in Boston, the city she's wanted to visit for as long as she can remember. . . . Her grandmother and cousin, Will, welcome her warmly, but her famous detective uncle, Bruce Snow, seems anything but pleased. He doesn't want [her] meddling in his current case involving a string of mysterious warehouse fires along the harbor front. But Zanna can't help herself. Is someone setting the fires? Just when she thinks she's on to something, a strange man starts following her. Is he a threat? Zanna needs to solve the case before she has the chance to find out." (Publisher's note)

The **midnight** tunnel; a Suzanna Snow mystery. Scholastic Press 2011 283p $16.99

Grades: 4 5 6 7 **Fic**

1. Mystery fiction 2. Canada -- Fiction 3. Uncles -- Fiction 4. Missing children -- Fiction 5. Hotels and motels -- Fiction

ISBN 978-0-545-20862-8; 0-545-20862-9

LC 2010-26770

In 1905, Suzanna is in training to be a well-mannered hostess at a Loch Harbor, New Brunswick, hotel, but her dream of being a detective gets a boost when a seven-year-old guest goes missing and Suzanna's uncle, a famous detective, comes to solve the case.

"What Zanna lacks in grace and composure, she makes up for in pluck, persistence and cleverness, emerging a likely and likable Edwardian Nancy Drew." Kirkus

Frazier, Sundee Tucker

★ The **other** half of my heart; [by] Sundee T. Frazier. Delacorte Press 2010 296p $16.99

Grades: 5 6 7 8 **Fic**

1. Twins -- Fiction 2. Sisters -- Fiction 3. Prejudices -- Fiction 4. Grandmothers -- Fiction 5. Beauty contests -- Fiction 6. African Americans -- Fiction 7. Racially mixed people -- Fiction

ISBN 978-0-385-73440-0; 0-385-73440-9

LC 2009013209

Twin daughters of interracial parents, eleven-year-olds Keira and Minna have very different skin tones and personalities, but it is not until their African American grandmother enters them in the Miss Black Pearl Pre-Teen competition in North Carolina that red-haired and pale-skinned Minna realizes what life in their small town in the Pacific Northwest has been like for her more outgoing, darker-skinned sister.

"Frazier addresses issues faced by mixed-race children with a grace and humor that keep her from being pedantic. The story is enjoyable in its own right, and will also encourage readers to rethink racial boundries and what it means to be black or white in America." SLJ

Freedman, Paula J.

★ **My** basmati bat mitzvah; by Paula J. Freedman. Harry N. Abrams 2013 256 p. (alk. paper) $16.95

Grades: 4 5 6 **Fic**

1. Bat mitzvah -- Fiction 2. Jewish children -- Fiction 3. Judaism -- Fiction 4. East Indian Americans -- Fiction 5. Jews -- United States -- Fiction

ISBN 1419708066; 9781419708060

LC 2013005791

In this book, by Paula J. Freedman, "during the fall leading up to her bat mitzvah, Tara Feinstein has a lot more than her Torah portion on her mind. Between Hebrew school and study sessions with the rabbi, there doesn't seem to be enough time to hang out with her best friend Ben-O--who might also be her boyfriend--and her other best friend, Rebecca. Amid all this drama, Tara considers how to balance her Indian and Jewish identities and what it means to have a bat mitzvah while questioning her faith." (Publisher's note)

"How could Tara let know-it-all Sheila Rosenberg get away with saying, "You're not even Jewish," when Tara's Indian-born mother converted "way before I was even born"? With her bat mitzvah on the horizon, Tara secretly wonders: "Was I about to become more Jewish, or less Indian?" A light, warm, humorous story about cultural identity, inner harmony, and ordinary middle-school trials and tribulations. Glos." (Horn Book)

Freitas, Donna

★ The **possibilities** of sainthood. Farrar, Straus & Giroux 2008 272p $16.95

Grades: 7 8 9 10 11 12 **Fic**

1. School stories 2. Saints -- Fiction 3. Catholics -- Fiction 4. Family life -- Fiction 5. Rhode Island -- Fiction 6. Italian Americans -- Fiction

ISBN 978-0-374-36087-0; 0-374-36087-1

LC 2007-33298

While regularly petitioning the Vatican to make her the first living saint, fifteen-year-old Antonia Labella prays to assorted patron saints for everything from help with preparing the family's fig trees for a Rhode Island winter to getting her first kiss from the right boy.

"With a satisfying ending, this novel about the realistic struggles of a chaste teen is a great addition to all collections." SLJ

Unplugged; Donna Freitas ; [edited by] Tara Weikum. HarperTeen 2016 448 p. (hardcover) $17.99

Grades: 8 9 10 11 **Fic**

1. Science fiction 2. Dystopian fiction

ISBN 9780062118608

LC 2015956266

In this book, by Donna Freitas, "humanity is split into a dying physical world for the poor and an extravagant virtual world for the wealthy. Years ago, Skylar Cruz crossed over to the App World for a chance at a better life, and her family stayed behind in the Real World. Now Skye is a virtual teenager, surrounded by glamorous apps and expensive downloads—yet she's never felt like she fits in, and all she wants is to see her mother and sister again." (Publisher's note)

"Despite imperfections, one of the more ambitious and thought-provoking entries in a crowded genre." Kirkus

French, Vivian

The **robe** of skulls; [illustrated by] Ross Collins. Candlewick Press 2008 208p il (Tales from the five kingdoms) $14.99; pa $5.99

Grades: 4 5 6 **Fic**

1. Fairy tales 2. Bats -- Fiction 3. Magic -- Fiction 4. Trolls -- Fiction

ISBN 0-7636-3531-6; 0-7636-4364-5 pa; 978-0-7636-3531-2; 978-0-7636-4364-5 pa

LC 2007-38290

The sorceress Lady Lamorna has her heart set on a very expensive new robe, and she will stop at nothing—including kidnapping and black magic—to get the money to pay for it.

"Collins' black-and-white line drawings, dropped haphazardly into the text, perfectly complement the story, offering visual metaphors for the heady narrative mix of melodrama and humor." Bull Cent Child Books

Freymann-Weyr, Garret

My heartbeat. Houghton Mifflin 2002 154p $15

Grades: 7 8 9 10 **Fic**

1. Family life -- Fiction 2. Gay teenagers -- Fiction 3. Bisexual people -- Fiction 4. Siblings -- Fiction

ISBN 0-618-14181-2

LC 2001-47059

Michael L. Printz Award honor book, 2003

As she tries to understand the closeness between her older brother and his best friend, fourteen-year-old Ellen finds her relationship with each of them changing

"This beautiful novel tells a frank, upbeat story of teen bisexual love in all its uncertainty, pain, and joy. . . . The fast, clipped dialogue will sweep teens into the story, as will Ellen's immediate first-person, present-tense narrative." Booklist

Friedman, Aimee

The **year** my sister got lucky. Scholastic 2008 370p $16.99

Grades: 7 8 9 10 **Fic**

1. Moving -- Fiction 2. Sisters -- Fiction 3. Country life -- Fiction 4. New York (State) -- Fiction 5. City and town life -- Fiction

ISBN 978-0-439-92227-2; 0-439-92227-5

LC 2007-16416

When fourteen-year-old Katie and her older sister, Michaela, move from New York City to upstate New York, Katie is horrified by the country lifestyle but is even more shocked when her sister adapts effortlessly, enjoying their new life, unlike Katie.

"Friedman gets the push and pull of the sister bond just right in this delightful, funny, insightful journey." Booklist

Friedman, D. Dina

Escaping into the night. Simon & Schuster for Young Readers 2006 199p $17.99; pa $7.99

Grades: 6 7 8 9 **Fic**

1. Poland -- Fiction 2. Jewish refugees -- Fiction 3. Holocaust, 1933-1945 -- Fiction 4. World War, 1939-1945 -- Fiction

ISBN 978-1-4169-0258-4; 1-4169-0258-9; 978-1-4169-8648-5 pa; 1-4169-86480 pa

"Halina, a Jewish teen, is expelled from her Polish ghetto just before residents are being exterminated or sent to concentration camps. She joins a group of refugees who have banded together in an underground encampment in the Belorussian forests during World War II. . . . This compelling story offers an unusual insight into a different war experience." Voice Youth Advocates

Friedman, Laurie B., 1964-

Can you say catastrophe? by Laurie Friedman. Darby Creek 2013 151 p. (The mostly miserable life of April Sinclair) hardcover $17.95

Grades: 5 6 7 8 **Fic**

1. Summer -- Fiction 2. Family life -- Fiction 3. Dating (Social customs) -- Fiction

ISBN 1467709255; 9781467709255

LC 2012048867

Too good to be true (2014); Truth and kisses (2014); Love or something like it (2015); Not what I expected (2015); Too much drama (2016); A twist of fate (2016); Life, loss, and lemonade (2017)

In this book, by Laurie Friedman, "April Sinclair just wants what any normal thirteen-year-old would want: to disown her parents and obnoxious little sisters; to escape to summer camp ASAP with her two best friends, Billy and Brynn; and to make a good impression on Matt Parker. . . . Unfortunately, Matt witnesses April's utter humiliation at her birthday party. Then Billy kisses her. Just as April is trying to figure things out, her parents cancel her camp plans in lieu of a family RV trip." (Publisher's note)

"By tale's end, it is evident that this humorous, spirited teen is poised to triumph over the challenges of adolescence." Kirkus

Other titles in this series are:

Friend, Catherine

Barn boot blues. Marshall Cavendish 2011 142p $16.99

Grades: 5 6 7 8 **Fic**

1. Moving -- Fiction 2. Farm life -- Fiction 3. Minnesota -- Fiction

ISBN 978-0-7614-5827-2; 0-7614-5827-1

LC 2011001909

When her parents swap urban life in Minneapolis for rural life on a farm 100 miles away, twelve-year-old Taylor feels as if she is living on another planet.

"In this refreshingly compact novel, readers learn interesting, authentic details about everything from spinning wool to collecting eggs to in a kind-of-gross, kind-of-wonderful climax birthing lambs. In Taylor, Friend has created a plucky, lightly sarcastic protagonist whose frustration at her situation is palpable but who never comes off as unlikable or bratty." Horn Book

Friend, Natasha

★ **Bounce**; [by] Natasha Friend. Scholastic Press 2007 188p $16.99

Grades: 6 7 8 9 **Fic**

1. Moving -- Fiction 2. Remarriage -- Fiction 3. Stepfamilies -- Fiction 4. Massachusetts -- Fiction

ISBN 978-0-439-85350-7; 0-439-85350-8

LC 2006038126

Thirteen-year-old Evyn's world is turned upside-down when her father, widowed since she was a toddler, suddenly decides to remarry a woman with six children, move with Ev and her brother from Maine to Boston, and enroll her in private school.

The author "presents, through hip conversations and humor, believable characters and a feel-good story with a satisfying amount of pathos." SLJ

How we roll; by Natasha Friend. Farrar, Straus & Giroux 2018 272 p. (hardcover) $17.99

Grades: 7 8 9 10 11 **Fic**

1. Self-acceptance -- Fiction 2. Dating (Social customs) -- Fiction 3. People with disabilities -- Fiction 4. Amputees -- Fiction 5. Massachusetts -- Fiction 6. Alopecia areata -- Fiction 7. Family life -- Massachusetts -- Fiction

ISBN 9780374305666

LC 2017042313

In this book, by Natasha Friend, "Quinn is a teen who loves her family, skateboarding, basketball, and her friends, but after she's diagnosed with a condition called alopecia which causes her to lose all of her hair, her friends abandon her. Jake was once a star football player, but because of a freak accident--caused by his brother--he loses both of his legs. Quinn and Jake meet and find the confidence to believe in themselves again, and maybe even love." (Publisher's note)

Lush. Scholastic Press 2006 178p $16.99

Grades: 7 8 9 10 **Fic**

1. Fathers -- Fiction 2. Alcoholism -- Fiction

ISBN 0-439-85346-X

LC 2005-031333

Unable to cope with her father's alcoholism, thirteen-year-old Sam corresponds with an older student, sharing her family problems and asking for advice.

"Friend adeptly takes a teen problem and turns it into a believable, sensitive, character-driven story, with realistic dialogue." Booklist

Perfect. Milkweed Editions 2004 172p $16.95; pa $6.95

Grades: 6 7 8 9 **Fic**

1. Bulimia -- Fiction 2. Bereavement -- Fiction

ISBN 1-57131-652-3; 1-57131-651-5 pa

LC 2004-6371

Following the death of her father, thirteen-year-old Isabelle uses bulimia as a way to avoid her mother's and ten-year-old sister's grief, as well as her own.

"Isabelle's grief and anger are movingly and honestly portrayed, and her eventual empathy for her mother is believable and touching." Booklist

Friesen, Jonathan

★ The **last** Martin. Zonderkidz 2011 266p $14.99

Grades: 4 5 6 7 **Fic**

1. Family life -- Fiction

ISBN 978-0-310-72080-5; 0-310-72080-X

LC 2010-48275

Thirteen-year-old Martin Boyle struggles to break a family curse after discovering that he has twelve weeks to live.

"Spiced with plenty of slapstick, the yarn speeds its protagonist through a succession of highs, lows and improbable triumphs on the way to a hilariously melodramatic finish." Kirkus

Friesner, Esther

Nobody's princess; [by] Esther Friesner. Random House 2007 305p hardcover o.p. pa $7.99

Grades: 6 7 8 9 10 **Fic**

1. Adventure fiction 2. Sex role -- Fiction 3. Classical mythology -- Fiction 4. Helen of Troy (Legendary character) -- Fiction

ISBN 978-0-375-87528-1; 0-375-87528-X; 978-0-375-87529-8 pa; 0-375-87529-8 pa

LC 2006-06515

Determined to fend for herself in a world where only men have real freedom, headstrong Helen, who will be called queen of Sparta and Helen of Troy one day, learns to fight, hunt, and ride horses while disguised as a boy, and goes on an adventure throughout the Mediterranean world.

This "is a fascinating portrait. . . . Along the way, Friesner skillfully exposes larger issues of women's rights, human bondage, and individual destiny. It's a rollicking good story." Booklist

Other titles in this series are:
Nobody's prize (2008)
Sphinx's princess (2009)
Sphinx's queen (2010)
Spirit's princess (2012)
Spirit's chosen (2013)
Deception's princess (20140
Deception's pawn (2015).

Nobody's prize. Random House 2008 320p $16.99; lib bdg $19.99

Grades: 6 7 8 9 **Fic**

1. Adventure fiction 2. Sex role -- Fiction 3. Jason (Greek mythology) -- Fiction 4. Helen of Troy (Legendary character) -- Fiction

ISBN 978-0-375-87531-1; 0-375-87531-X; 978-0-375-97531-8 lib bdg; 0-375-97531-4 lib bdg

LC 2007-08395

Sequel to Nobody's princess (2007)

Still longing for adventure, Princess Helen of Sparta maintains her disguise as a boy to join her unsuspecting brothers as part of the crew of the Argo, the ship commanded by Prince Jason in his quest for the Golden Fleece.

"Friesner is an accomplished writer who is able to interweave a contemporary feel for these ancient characters with pieces of history and mythology. She can also be funny. . . . It is possible for readers to begin with this book. . . . But it is surely best enjoyed as part of a series, and libraries with the first book will want to make sure fans get their second helping." Voice Youth Advocates

Sphinx's princess. Random House 2009 370p il map $17.99; lib bdg $20.99

Grades: 8 9 10 11 12 **Fic**

1. Queens 2. Young adult literature 3. Queens -- Fiction 4. Egypt -- History -- Fiction

ISBN 978-0-375-85654-9; 0-375-85654-4; 978-0-375-95654-6 lib bdg; 0-375-95654-9 lib bdg

LC 2009-13719

Although she is a dutiful daughter, Nefertiti's dancing abilities, remarkable beauty, and intelligence garner attention near and far, so much so that her family is summoned to the Egyptian royal court, where Nefertiti becomes a pawn in the power play of her scheming aunt, Queen Tiye.

"Dramatic plot twists, a powerful female subject, and engrossing details of life in ancient Egypt make for lively historical fiction." Booklist

Followed by: Sphinx's queen (2010)

Sphinx's queen. Random House 2010 352p $17.99; lib bdg $29.99

Grades: 8 9 10 11 12 **Fic**

1. Queens -- Fiction 2. Egypt -- History -- Fiction

ISBN 978-0-375-85657-0; 0-375-85657-9; 978-0-375-95657-7 lib bdg; 0-375-95657-3 lib bdg

LC 2010-13769

Sequel to: Sphinx's princess (2009)

Chased after by the prince and his soldiers for a crime she did not commit, Nefertiti finds temporary refuge in the wild hills along the Nile's west bank before returning to the royal court to plead her case to the Pharaoh.

This is written "in fine prose that expresses the questioning of religion that most young people experience as they approach maturity. . . . This deeply moral book tells a good story; or, rather, this good story reveals deeply moral truths." SLJ

Spirit's princess; Esther Friesner. 1st ed. Random House Childrens Books 2012 449 p. (trade) $17.99; (paperback) $10.99; (ebook) $53.97; (lib bdg.) $20.99

Grades: 7 8 9 10 **Fic**

1. Family -- Fiction 2. Father-daughter relationship -- Fiction 3. Children with physical disabilities -- Fiction 4. Magic -- Fiction 5. Shamans -- Fiction 6. Spirits -- Fiction 7. Sex role -- Fiction 8. Japan -- History -- To 645 -- Fiction

ISBN 0375869077; 9780375869075; 9780375873140; 9780375873157; 9780375899904; 9780375969072

LC 2011010468

In the book by Esther Friesner, "Himiko's chieftain father adores her, as do her older brother and her father's wives. Despite their love and affection, none of them takes Himiko seriously when she insists she is a shaman. Himiko herself isn't sure she can achieve her goal; with one leg lame since she was a child, she can't do a shaman's dances. Though the current shaman insists Himiko will be her heir, it can't happen until Himiko is ready to stand up to her father." (Kirkus Reviews)

Followed by Spirit's chosen (2013)

Threads and flames; by Esther Friesner. Viking 2010 390p $17.99

Grades: 6 7 8 9 10 **Fic**

1. Jews -- Fiction 2. Fires -- Fiction 3. Immigrants -- Fiction 4. New York (N.Y.) -- Fiction 5. Polish Americans -- Fiction 6. Triangle Shirtwaist Company, Inc. -- Fiction

ISBN 978-0-670-01245-9; 0-670-01245-9

"Friesner's sparkling prose makes the immigrant experience in New York's Lower East Side come alive. . . . Readers will turn the pages with rapt attention to follow the characters' intrepid, risk-all adventures in building new lives." Booklist

Frost, Helen

The **braid**. Farrar, Straus and Giroux 2006 95p $16

Grades: 7 8 9 10 **Fic**

1. Novels in verse 2. Canada -- Fiction 3. Sisters -- Fiction 4. Scotland -- Fiction 5. Immigrants -- Fiction

ISBN 0-374-30962-0

LC 2005-40148

Two Scottish sisters, living on the western island of Barra in the 1850s, relate, in alternate voices and linked narrative poems, their experiences after their family is forcible evicted and separated with one sister accompanying their parents and younger siblings to Cape Breton, Canada, and the other staying behind with other family on the small island of Mingulay.

"The book will inspire both students and teachers to go back and study how the taut poetic lines manage to contain the powerful feelings." Booklist

★ **Crossing** stones. Farrar, Straus and Giroux 2009 184p $16.99

Grades: 6 7 8 9 10 **Fic**

1. War stories 2. Novels in verse 3. Soldiers -- Fiction 4. Family life -- Fiction 5. Women -- Suffrage -- Fiction 6. World War, 1914-1918 -- Fiction

ISBN 0-374-31653-8; 978-0-374-31653-2

LC 2008-20755

In their own voices, four young people, Muriel, Frank, Emma, and Ollie, tell of their experiences during the first World War, as the boys enlist and are sent overseas, Emma finishes school, and Muriel fights for peace and women's suffrage.

"Beautifully written in formally structured verse. . . . This [is a] beautifully written, gently told story." Voice Youth Advocates

Diamond Willow. Farrar, Straus and Giroux 2008 111p $16

Grades: 5 6 7 8 **Fic**

1. Novels in verse 2. Dogs -- Fiction 3. Alaska -- Fiction 4. Athapascan Indians -- Fiction

ISBN 0-374-31776-3; 978-0-374-31776-8

LC 2006-37438

In a remote area of Alaska, twelve-year-old Willow helps her father with their sleigh dogs when she is not at school, all the while unaware that the animals surrounding her carry the spirits of dead ancestors and friends who care for her. ¿Grades six to nine.¿ (Bull Cent Child Books)

"Willow relates her story in one-page poems, each of which contains a hidden message printed in darker type. . . . Her poems offer pensive imagery and glimpses of character, and strong emotion. This complex and elegant novel will resonate with readers who savor powerful drama and multifaceted characters." SLJ

Hidden. Farrar Straus Giroux 2011 147p $16.99

Grades: 6 7 8 9 10 **Fic**

1. Novels in verse 2. Camps -- Fiction 4. Friendship -- Fiction

ISBN 0-374-38221-2; 978-0-374-38221-6

LC 2010-24854

When Wren Abbott and Darra Monson are eight years old, Darra's father steals a minivan. He doesn't know that Wren is hiding in the back. Years later, in a chance encounter at camp, the girls face each other for the first time.

"This novel in verse stands out through its deliberate use of form to illuminate emotions and cleverly hide secrets in the text." Booklist

★ **Keesha's** house. Frances Foster Bks./Farrar, Straus & Giroux 2003 116p hardcover o.p. pa $8

Grades: 7 8 9 10 **Fic**

1. Home -- Fiction

ISBN 0-374-34064-1; 0-374-40012-1 pa

LC 2002-22698

Michael L. Printz Award honor book, 2004

Seven teens facing such problems as pregnancy, closeted homosexuality, and abuse each describe in poetic forms what caused them to leave home and where they found home again

"Spare, eloquent, and elegantly concise. . . . Public, private, or correctional educators and librarians should put this must-read on their shelves." Voice Youth Advocates

★ **Salt**; by Helen Frost. Farrar, Straus, and Giroux 2013 160 p. (hardcover) $17.99

Grades: 5 6 7 8 **Fic**

1. War stories 2. Native Americans 3. Historical fiction 4. War of 1812 -- Fiction 5. Novels in verse 6. Friendship -- Fiction 7. Miami Indians -- Fiction 8. Trading posts -- Fiction 9. Frontier and pioneer life -- Indiana -- Fiction 10. United States -- History -- War of 1812 -- Fiction 11. Fort Wayne (Ind.) -- History -- 19th century -- Fiction

ISBN 0374363870; 9780374363871

LC 2012029521

This book, by Helen Frost, "set during the War of 1812 . . . is the story of the friendship between Anikwa, a Miami Indian boy, and James, the son of a trader. As both British and American armies advance on the area, other Native American peoples arrive hoping to fight with the British against the Americans. The plan fails, and Anikwa's peaceful people must flee. Will they have to abandon their traditional home, and will the friendship between the boys be sundered?" (Publisher's note)

When my sister started kissing; Helen Frost. Farrar, Straus & Giroux 2017 208 p. (hardback) $16.99; (ebook) $60

Grades: 5 6 7 8 9 **Fic**

1. Sisters -- Fiction 2. Stepmothers -- Fiction 3. Dating (Social customs) -- Fiction 4. Novels in verse 5. Lakes -- Fiction

ISBN 9780374303037; 9780374303044

LC 2016028011

In this novel, by Helen Frost, "Claire and Abi have always loved their summers at the lake house, but this year, everything's different. Dad and Pam, their stepmom, are expecting a new baby, and they've cleared out all of Mom's belongings to make room. And last summer, Abi was looking at boys, but this summer, boys are looking back at her. . . . Claire doesn't want her family to change, but there doesn't seem to be a way of stopping it." (Publisher's note)

Fry, Michael

The **Odd** Squad; Bully Bait. by Michael Fry. Disney Hyperion 2013 224 p. (hardcover) $12.99

Grades: 4 5 6 7 **Fic**

1. Bullies -- Fiction 2. Schools -- Fiction 3. Middle schools -- Fiction 4. Interpersonal relations -- Fiction

ISBN 1423169247; 9781423169246

LC 2012014286

This children's story, by Michael Fry, is part of the "Odd Squad" series. "Nick is the shortest seventh-grader in the history of the world . . . , doesn't fit in . . . , and spends more time inside than outside his locker. . . . When a well-intentioned guidance counselor forces Nick to join the school's lamest club . . . , what starts off as a reluctant band of hopeless oddballs morphs into an effective and empowered team ready to face whatever middle school throws at them." (Publisher's note)

"Cartoonist Fry humorously mines the world of middle school as seen through the eyes of bullied Nick to answer the question: Can three oddballs team together to take down the school bully? ...Abundant cartoon-style illustrations enhance the book's silly yet sensitive portrayal of bullying and unlikely friendships." Kirkus

Other titles in this series are:

Zero Tolerance (2013)

King Karl (2014)

Fukuda, Andrew

The **Prey**; Andrew Fukuda. St Martins Press 2013 336 p. $18.99

Grades: 7 8 9 10 11 12 **Fic**

1. Horror fiction 2. Paranormal fiction 3. Young adult literature 4. Survival skills -- Fiction

ISBN 1250005116; 9781250005113

LC 2013002667

This teen horror thriller, by Andrew Fukuda, is book 2 of the "Hunt" series. "With death only a heartbeat away, Gene and the remaining humans must find a way . . . to escape the hungry predators chasing them through the night. . . . Their escape takes them to a refuge of humans living high in the mountains. Gene and his friends think they're finally safe, but not everything here is as it seems." (Publisher's note)

Funaro, Gregory

Watch hollow; Gregory Funaro, Matthew Griffin. HarperCollins 2019 256 p. (hardback) $16.99

Grades: 4 5 6 7 **Fic**

1. Fantasy fiction 2. Magic -- Fiction 3. Monsters -- Fiction

ISBN 9780062643452

LC 2018952012

In this book, by Gregory Funaro, illustrated by Matthew Griffin, "when Lucy and Oliver Tinker arrive in Watch Hollow, they have no idea that anything is wrong. [Then a] mysterious stranger . . . [ask their father to] fix the clock at Blackford House. . . . And before they can entirely understand the strange world they've stumbled into, Lucy and Oliver must join forces with a host of magical clock animals to defeat the [vicious monster] Garr." (Publisher's note)

"Filled with clever, magical, and instantly likable characters, Funaro's excellent, fast-paced, and twisty mystery—packed with suspense, facts, magic, and an incredible, deeply thought-out world—will leave readers eagerly awaiting the next chapter." (Booklist)

Funke, Cornelia, 1958-

Fearless; Cornelia Funke. Little, Brown Books for Young Readers 2013 432 p. (hardcover) $19.99

Grades: 6 7 8 9 **Fic**

1. Fantasy fiction 2. Brothers -- Fiction 3. Blessing and cursing -- Fiction 4. Fantasy 5. Magic -- Fiction 6. Adventure and adventurers -- Fiction

ISBN 0316056103; 9780316056106

LC 2012028742

This fantasy novel, by Cornelia Funke, translated by Oliver Latsch, is part of the "Mirrorworld" series. "Jacob Reckless has . . . tried everything to shake the Fairy curse that traded his life for his brother's. . . . But . . . they hear of one last possibility . . . : a crossbow that can kill thousands, or heal one, when shot through the heart. But a Goyl treasure hunter is also searching for the prized crossbow." (Publisher's note)

"Adroitly building on layers of European fairy tale, Funke's original, rapid-fire narrative fearlessly transports Jacob and a bevy of ominous, multifaceted fantastical characters through a dark, decaying landscape in which death waits and honor is rare. Provocative, harrowing, engrossing." Kirkus

Inkdeath; [by] Cornelia Funke; translated from the German by Anthea Bell. Scholastic 2008 683p il map $24.99

Grades: 5 6 7 8 **Fic**

1. Fantasy fiction 2. Kidnapping -- Fiction 3. Books and reading -- Fiction

ISBN 978-0-439-86628-6; 0-439-86628-6

LC 2008-19922

Sequel to: Inkspell (2005)

As Bluejay—Mo's fictitious double—tries to keep the Book of Immortality from unraveling, Adderhead kidnaps all the children in the kingdom, asking for Bluejay's surrender or the children will be doomed to slavery in the silver mines.

"The assortment of villains is vivid and frightening. . . . The finale includes a thoroughly engrossing climax." SLJ

★ **Inkheart**; [by] Cornelia Funke; translated from the German by Anthea Bell. Scholastic 2003 534p $19.95; pa $9.99

Grades: 5 6 7 8 **Fic**

1. Fantasy fiction 2. Books and reading -- Fiction

ISBN 0-439-53164-0; 0-439-70910-5 pa

LC 2003-45844

Twelve-year-old Meggie learns that her father, who repairs and binds books for a living, can "read" fictional characters to life when one of those characters abducts them and tries to force him into service.

The author "proves the power of her imagination; readers will be captivated by the chilling and thrilling world she has created here." Publ Wkly

Other titles in this series are:

Inkspell (2005)

Inkdeath (2008)

Inkspell; [by] Cornelia Funke; translated from the German by Anthea Bell. Scholastic 2005 635p il $19.99

Grades: 5 6 7 8 **Fic**

1. Fantasy fiction 2. Books and reading -- Fiction

ISBN 0-439-55400-4

Sequel to: Inkheart (2005)

"This is an involving story that will draw readers smoothly to its conclusion and leave them waiting for the final volume in this projected trilogy." SLJ

Followed by: Inkdeath (2008)

★ **Reckless**; written and illustrated by Cornelia Funke; translated by Oliver Latsch. Little, Brown 2010 394p il $19.99

Grades: 6 7 8 9 **Fic**

1. Fantasy fiction 2. Adventure fiction 3. Magic -- Fiction 4. Brothers -- Fiction

ISBN 978-0-316-05609-0; 0-316-05609-X; 031605609X; 9780316056090

LC 2010006877

Jacob and Will Reckless have looked out for each other ever since their father disappeared, but when Jacob discovers a magical mirror that transports him to a warring world populated by witches, giants, and ogres, he keeps it to himself until Will follows him one day, with dire consequences.

"The fluid, fast-paced narrative exposes Jacob's complex character, his complicated sibling relationship and a densely textured world brimming with vile villains and fairy-tale detritus." Kirkus

Fusco, Kimberly Newton

Beholding Bee; Kimberly Newton Fusco. Alfred A. Knopf 2013 336 p. $16.99

Grades: 5 6 7 8 **Fic**

1. Ghost stories 2. Orphans -- Fiction 3. Carnivals -- Fiction 4. Identity -- Fiction 5. Runaways -- Fiction 6. Self-esteem -- Fiction

7. Disfigured persons -- Fiction
ISBN 0375868364; 9780375868368; 9780375898860; 9780375968365

LC 2012005091

In this book by Kimberly Newton Fusco, "11-year-old orphan Bee travels with a carnival, assisting her guardian at the hot-dog stand and shielding the diamond-shaped birthmark on her face from stares and taunts. . . . When Pauline and her new boyfriend are sent away by the sinister carnival owner . . . Bee runs away. . . . She comes upon an inviting old house and is welcomed by two elderly women only she can see: Mrs. Potter . . . and Mrs. Swift, a prickly suffragette." (School Library Journal)

Chasing Augustus; Kimberly Newton Fusco. Alfred A. Knopf 2017 326 p. (lib. bdg.) $19.99
Grades: 4 5 6 7 8 **Fic**

1. Orphans -- Fiction 2. Friendship -- Fiction 3. Dogs -- Fiction 4. Families -- Fiction 5. Grandfathers -- Fiction 6. Lost articles -- Fiction
ISBN 9780385754026; 0385754027; 9780385754019; 0385754019; 9780385754033

LC 2017297072

In this novel, by Kimberly Newton Fusco, "Rosie's led a charmed life with her loving dad. . . . Her mother abandoned them when Rosie was just a baby, but her dad's all she's ever needed. But now that her father's had a stroke, Rosie lives with her . . . grandfather. And her beloved dog, Gloaty Gus, has just gone missing. Rosie's determined to find him. With the help of a new friend and her own determination, she'll follow the trail anywhere . . . no matter where it leads." (Publisher's note)

The **wonder** of Charlie Anne. Alfred A. Knopf 2010 272p $16.99; lib bdg $19.99
Grades: 5 6 7 8 **Fic**

1. Farm life -- Fiction 2. Friendship -- Fiction 3. Massachusetts -- Fiction 4. Race relations -- Fiction 5. African Americans -- Fiction 6. Great Depression, 1929-1939 -- Fiction
ISBN 978-0-375-86104-8; 0-375-86104-1; 978-0-375-96104-5 lib bdg; 0-375-96104-6 lib bdg

LC 2009-38831

In a 1930s Massachusetts farm town torn by the Depression, racial tension, and other hardships, Charlie Anne and her black next-door neighbor Phoebe form a friendship that begins to transform their community.

"Good humor, kindness and courage triumph in this warm, richly nuanced novel that cheers the heart like a song sweetly sung." Kirkus

Gagnon, Michelle

Don't let go; Michelle Gagnon. Harper, an imprint of HarperCollinsPublishers 2014 352 p. (hardback) $17.99
Grades: 7 8 9 10 11 12 **Fic**

1. Dystopian fiction 2. Experiments -- Fiction 3. Computer hackers -- Fiction 4. Foster home care -- Fiction 5. Abandoned children -- Fiction 6. Adventure and adventurers -- Fiction
ISBN 0062102966; 9780062102966

LC 2014001880

Sequel to: Don't look now

"Noa Torson is out of options. On the run with Peter and the two remaining teens of Persephone's Army, and with quickly failing health, she is up against immeasurable odds. The group is outnumbered, outsmarted, and outrun. But they will not give up. They know they must return to where this all began." (Publisher's note)

Don't Look Now; Michelle Gagnon. Harpercollins Childrens Books 2013 336 p. $17.99
Grades: 7 8 9 10 11 12 **Fic**

1. Computer hackers -- Fiction 2. Abandoned children -- Fiction 3. Experiments -- Fiction 4. Foster home care -- Fiction
ISBN 0062102931; 9780062102935

LC 2013021823

In this book, by Michelle Gagnon, "Noa Torsen is on the run. Having outsmarted the sinister Project Persephone, Noa and her friend Zeke now move stealthily across the country . . . Back in Boston, Peter anxiously follows Noa's movements from his computer, using his hacker skills to feed her the information she needs to stay alive. . . . It will take everything Noa and Peter have to bring down the Project before it gets them first." (Publisher's note)

"Still suffering strange side effects from her stint as a human lab rat at Pike & Dolan, Noa (Don't Turn Around) leads a group of homeless teens bent on sabotaging the corporation. In Boston, her "hacktivist" friend Peter and his ex-girlfriend, Amanda, uncover new evidence that places them all in danger. This tense, suspenseful tech-thriller will engage readers from beginning to end." (Horn Book)

Don't turn around; by Michelle Gagnon. Harper 2012 320 p. (trade bdg.) $17.99
Grades: 7 8 9 10 11 12 **Fic**

1. Dystopian fiction 2. Teenagers -- Fiction 3. Conspiracies -- Fiction 4. Computer hackers -- Fiction 5. Experiments -- Fiction 6. Foster home care -- Fiction 7. Abandoned children -- Fiction
ISBN 0062102907; 9780062102904

LC 2012009691

This book tells the story of "[t]eenage hackers Noa and Peter." Orphan Noa escapes a hospital after waking up from an operation she has no memory of. After having his computer seized when he investigated his father's files, "Peter enlists his hacktivist group /ALLIANCE/ (of which Noa is a member) to" investigate and counterattack. "The attack only serves to dig the teens in deeper when they uncover a frightening conspiracy of human experimentation and corporate malfeasance." (Kirkus Reviews)

Strangelets; by Michelle Gagnon. Soho Teen 2013 1 p. (alk. paper) $17.99
Grades: 8 9 10 11 12 **Fic**

1. Horror fiction 2. Mystery fiction 3. Science fiction 4. Escapes -- Fiction 5. Survival -- Fiction 6. Near-death experiences -- Fiction
ISBN 1616951370; 9781616951375

LC 2012038333

This book by Michelle Gagnon shows the "horror endured by six teens trapped in a hospital-like bunker. They come from every point on the globe: cancer-stricken Sophie from California, petty thief Declan from Ireland, military trainee Anat from Israel, hiker Nico from Switzerland, shy Yosh from Japan, and studious Zain from India." They must figure out why they are there. (Publishers Weekly)

Gaiman, Neil, 1960-

★ **Coraline**; [by] Neil Gaiman; with illustrations by Dave McKean. HarperCollins Pubs. 2002 162p il pa $6.99; $16.99
Grades: 5 6 7 8 **Fic**

1. Horror fiction 2. Supernatural -- Fiction
ISBN 0-380-80734-3 pa; 0-380-97778-8

LC 2002-18937

Looking for excitement, Coraline ventures through a mysterious door into a world that is similar, yet disturbingly different from her own, where she must challenge a gruesome entity in order to save herself, her parents, and the souls of three others

"Gaiman twines his taut tale with a menacing tone and crisp prose fraught with memorable imagery . . . yet keeps the narrative just this side of terrifying." Publ Wkly

★ **Fortunately,** the milk; by Neil Gaiman ; illustrated by Skottie Young. Harper, an imprint of HarperCollinsPublishers 2013 128 p. (hardcover bdgs) $14.99

Grades: 4 5 6 7 **Fic**

1. Humorous stories 2. Fathers -- Fiction 3. Space and time -- Fiction 4. Adventure and adventurers -- Fiction

ISBN 0062224077; 9780062224071

LC 2012050670

This children's picture book by Neil Gaiman is "about a father who has taken an excessively long time to return from the corner store with milk for his children's breakfast." He "is abducted by aliens, made to walk the plank by pirates, and rescued by a stegosaurus in a balloon, among other outrageous escapades." (Publishers Weekly)

★ The **graveyard** book; with illustrations by Dave McKean. HarperCollins 2008 312p il $17.99; lib bdg $18.89

Grades: 5 6 7 8 9 10 **Fic**

1. Death -- Fiction 2. Cemeteries -- Fiction 3. Supernatural -- Fiction

ISBN 0-06-053092-8; 0-06-053093-6 lib bdg; 978-0-06-053092-1; 978-0-06-053093-8 lib bdg

LC 2008-13860

Awarded the Newbery Medal (2009)

Nobody Owens, nicknamed Bod, is a normal boy, except that he has been raised by in a graveyard by ghosts. "Grades five to nine." (Bull Cent Child Books)

"Gaiman writes with charm and humor, and again he has a real winner." Voice Youth Advocates

★ The **Sleeper** and the Spindle; Neil Gaiman ; illustrated by Chris Riddell. Harpercollins Childrens Books 2015 72 p. illustrations $19.99

Grades: 5 6 7 8 9 10 **Fic**

1. Fantasy fiction 2. Sleep -- Fiction 3. Fractured fairy tales

ISBN 0062398245; 9780062398246

LC 2015033123

"Three dwarves discover a realm in which everyone has fallen asleep, and they cross into the next country to warn its queen [Snow White] of the great plague that threatens her people. . . . Traveling to the cursed kingdom, the queen and dwarves encounter threatening zombie sleepers and more." (Publishers Weekly)

"Each page is packed with marvelous details--vines claustrophobically twist everywhere and expressions convey far more emotion than the words let on. Gaiman's narrative about strength, sacrifice, choice, and identity is no simple retelling; he sends readers down one path then deliciously sends the story veering off in an unexpected direction." SLJ

Galante, Cecilia

Willowood. Simon & Schuster 2010 265p $16.99

Grades: 4 5 6 7 **Fic**

1. Geckos -- Fiction 2. Moving -- Fiction 3. Friendship -- Fiction 4. Single parent family -- Fiction

ISBN 978-1-4169-8022-3; 1-4169-8022-9

Eleven-year-old Lily has trouble leaving her best friend behind and moving to the city when her mother changes jobs, but she makes some very unlikely friends that soon become like family members.

"The characters . . . are fully realized individuals. . . . [This book has a] finely tuned plot and poetic language. . . . Children will enjoy the story of Lily's first few months in the big city." SLJ

Gale, Eric Kahn

The **Bully** Book; Eric Kahn Gale. Harpercollins Childrens Books 2012 240 p. $16.99

Grades: 4 5 6 7 8 **Fic**

1. School stories 2. Bullies -- Fiction 3. Friendship -- Fiction 4. Middle schools -- Fiction 5. Diaries -- Fiction

ISBN 0062125117; 9780062125118

LC 2012050677

Originally published in a different format as an ebook by the author

"When the author was eleven, he was bullied. This book is loosely based on incidents that happened to him in sixth grade. Eric Haskins, the new sixth-grade bully target, is searching for answers. And unlike many of us who experienced something awful growing up, he finds them. Though they may not be what he expected." (Publisher's note)

"The juxtaposition of Eric's journal against the Bully Book allows readers to see both the bullies' methodology and Eric's unwitting complicity. . . . A compelling and unusual look at a complex and intractable problem that succeeds admirably as story as well." Kirkus

The **Zoo** at the Edge of the World; by Eric Kahn Gale ; illustrations by Matthew Howley. Balzer + Bray, an imprint of HarperCollinsPublishers 2014 240 p. illustrations (hardback) $16.99

Grades: 4 5 6 7 **Fic**

1. Zoos -- Fiction 2. Stuttering -- Fiction 3. Jungle animals -- Fiction 4. Human-animal communication -- Fiction

ISBN 0062125168; 9780062125163

LC 2014002144

In this book, by Eric Kahn Gale, "Marlin is not slow, or mute; what he is is a stutterer, and that makes it impossible for him to convince people otherwise. What he is also is a Rackham: the youngest son of the world-famous explorer Roland Rackham, who is the owner and proprietor of the Zoo at the Edge of the World, a resort where the well-to-do from all over the world can come to experience the last bit of the wild left in the world at the end of the nineteenth century." (Publisher's note)

"A secondary plot concerning Marlin's relationships with his father and brother is equally nuanced and powerful, making the book a formidable read on two fronts. The romantic setting and striking prose are icing on the cake, creating an intoxicatingly charming book. Beautiful and fully absorbing." Kirkus

Gansworth, Eric

★ **If** I ever get out of here; Eric Gansworth. Arthur A. Levine Books 2013 368 p. (hardcover : alk. paper) $17.99

Grades: 6 7 8 9 **Fic**

1. Identity -- Fiction 2. Friendship -- Fiction 3. Race relations -- Fiction 4. Tuscarora Indians -- Fiction 5. Families of military personnel -- Fiction 6. Tuscarora Nation Reservation (N.Y.) -- Fiction 7. New York (State) -- History -- 20th century -- Fiction 8. Indians of North America -- New York (State) -- Fiction 9. New York (State) -- Ethnic relations

ISBN 0545417309; 9780545417303; 9780545417310

LC 2012030553

American Indian Youth Literature Awards Honor Book: Young Adult (2014)

"Lewis lives in abject poverty on the reservation. . . . He's the only Indian in the class for smart kids. And he's in middle school. Times are tough. When George, a military kid, arrives, the two bond over their mutual appreciation of music. Lewis shares select pieces of his life with George. . . . Forces of nature eventually compel Lewis to face everything: the bully, what he is hiding and his own shame." (Kirkus Reviews)

Gantos, Jack

★ **Dead** end in Norvelt; Jack Gantos. Farrar Straus Giroux 2011 341p. $15.99

Grades: 4 5 6 7 **Fic**

1. Old age -- Fiction 2. Pennsylvania -- Fiction

ISBN 978-0-374-37993-3; 0-374-37993-9

LC 2010054009

Newbery Medal (2012)

Scott O'Dell Historical Fiction Award (2012)

In the historic town of Norvelt, Pennsylvania, twelve-year-old Jack Gantos spends the summer of 1962 grounded for various offenses until he is assigned to help an elderly neighbor with a most unusual chore involving the newly dead, molten wax, twisted promises, Girl Scout cookies, underage driving, lessons from history, typewriting, and countless bloody noses.

This is a "wildly entertaining meld of truth and fiction. . . . Memorable in every way." Publ Wkly

★ **From** Norvelt to nowhere; Jack Gantos. Farrar, Straus and Giroux 2013 288 p. (hardback) $16.99

Grades: 4 5 6 7 **Fic**

1. Old age -- Fiction 2. Friendship -- Fiction 3. Humorous stories 4. Mystery and detective stories 5. Norvelt (Pa.) -- History -- 20th century -- Fiction

ISBN 0374379947; 9780374379940

LC 2013022251

Sequel to: Dead end in Norvelt

National Book Awards: Young People's Literature Long List (2013)

Author Jack Gantos' book "opens deep in the shadow of the Cuban missile crisis. But . . . other kinds of trouble are raining down on young Jack Gantos. . . . After an explosion, a new crime by an old murderer, and the sad passing of the town's founder, twelve-year-old Jack will soon find himself launched on a mission that takes him hundreds of miles away, escorting his slightly mental elderly mentor, Miss Volker, on her relentless pursuit of the oddest of outlaws." (Publisher's note)

★ **Heads** or tails; stories from the sixth grade. Farrar, Straus Giroux 1994 151p il $16; pa $4.95

Grades: 5 6 7 8 **Fic**

1. School stories 2. Diaries -- Fiction 3. Family life -- Fiction

ISBN 0-374-32909-5; 0-374-42923-5 pa

LC 93-43117

"Jack is trying to survive his sixth-grade year, and he narrates, through a series of short-stories-cum-chapters, his difficulties in dodging the obstacles life throws in his path. . . . The writing is zingy and specific, with snappily authentic dialogue and a vivid sense of juvenile experience. . . . Jack and his family have a recognizably thorny relationship. This is a distinctive and lively sequence of everyday-life stories." Bull Cent Child Books

Other titles about Jack are:

Jack adrift (2003)

Jack on the tracks (1999)

Jack's black book (1997)

Jack's new power (1995)

I am not Joey Pigza. Farrar, Straus and Giroux 2007 215p $16

Grades: 5 6 7 8 **Fic**

1. Fathers -- Fiction 2. Restaurants -- Fiction 3. Attention deficit disorder -- Fiction

ISBN 978-0-374-39941-2; 0-374-39941-7

LC 2006-38681

Joey's father returns, calling himself Charles Heinz and apologizing for his past bad behavior, and he swears that once Joey and his mother change their names and help him fix up the old diner he has bought, their lives will change for the better

"The plot doesn't move so much as careen from one over-the-top event to the next, the achievement being that every one of them feels entirely plausible." Publ Wkly

Jack on the tracks; four seasons of fifth grade. Farrar, Straus & Giroux 1999 182p il $16; pa $5.95

Grades: 5 6 7 8 **Fic**

1. School stories 2. Family life -- Fiction 3. Miami (Fla.) -- Fiction

ISBN 0-374-33665-2; 0-374-43717-3 pa

LC 99-27897

Moving with his unbearable sister to Miami, Florida, Jack tries to break some of his bad habits but finds himself irresistibly drawn to things disgusting, gross, and weird

"Jack is a likable and appealing fifth grader. His first-person preadolescent musings and worries are poignant, funny, and real." SLJ

Other titles in this series are:

Heads or tails (1994)

Jack's black book (1997)

Jack's new power (1995)

Jack's black book. Farrar, Straus & Giroux 1997 165p hardcover o.p. pa $7.99

Grades: 5 6 7 8 **Fic**

1. Authorship -- Fiction

ISBN 0-374-33662-8; 0-374-43716-5 pa

LC 96-53107

"Back in Florida, Jack decides that becoming a writer will allow him to turn his worst experiences, and he has many, into money. He flubs his IQ test, nearly flunks wood shop, almost gets a date with a beautiful girl, visits a fortune teller, digs up his dead dog not once but twice, and copes with members of an off-kilter family who constantly remind him of his stupidity. . . . The narrative sparkles with wit and, although exaggerated, rings with the authenticity of adolescent humor, embarrassment, and fascination with the absolutely gross." SLJ

Jack's new power; stories from a Caribbean year. Farrar, Straus & Giroux 1995 214p hardcover o.p. pa $8.99

Grades: 5 6 7 8 **Fic**

1. Barbados -- Fiction 2. Family life -- Fiction

ISBN 0-374-33657-1; 978-0-374-43715-2 pa

LC 94-44442

"Gantos achieves an intriguing balance of the bitter and the sweet in this account; young readers whose lives are similarly mixed will appreciate Jack's narrative." Bull Cent Child Books

Joey Pigza loses control. Farrar, Straus & Giroux 2000 195p $16

Grades: 5 6 7 8 **Fic**

1. Father-son relationship -- Fiction 2. Attention deficit disorder -- Fiction

ISBN 0-374-39989-1

LC 00-20098

A Newbery Medal honor book, 2001

Joey, who is still taking medication to keep him from getting too wired, goes to spend the summer with the hard-drinking father he has never known and tries to help the baseball team he coaches win the championship

"This high-voltage, honest novel mixes humor, pain, fear and courage with deceptive ease." Publ Wkly

★ **Joey** Pigza swallowed the key. Farrar, Straus & Giroux 1998 153p $16.99

Grades: 5 6 7 8 **Fic**

1. School stories 2. Schools -- Fiction 3. Single-parent families -- Fiction 4. Attention deficit disorder -- Fiction 5. Attention-deficit hyperactivity disorder -- Fiction

ISBN 0-374-33664-4

LC 98-24264

To the constant disappointment of his mother and his teachers, Joey has trouble paying attention or controlling his mood swings when his prescription meds wear off and he starts getting worked up and acting wired

This "frenetic narrative pulls at heartstrings and tickles funny bones." SLJ

Other titles about Joey Pigza are:
Joey Pigza loses control (2000)
What would Joey do? (2002)
I am not Joey Pigza (2007)
The key that swallowed Joey Pigza (2014)

★ The **key** that swallowed Joey Pigza; Jack Gantos. Farrar, Straus & Giroux 2014 160 p. (hardback) $16.99

Grades: 4 5 6 7 **Fic**

1. Boys -- Fiction 2. Family life -- Fiction 3. Babies -- Fiction 4. Brothers -- Fiction 5. Single-parent families -- Fiction 6. Attention-deficit hyperactivity disorder -- Fiction

ISBN 0374300836; 9780374300838

LC 2014023370

This book by Jack Gantos is "the fifth and final book in the groundbreaking Joey Pigza series. . . . With his dad MIA in the wake of appearance-altering plastic surgery, Joey must give up school to look after his new baby brother and fill in for his mom, who hospitalizes herself to deal with a bad case of postpartum blues." (Publisher's note)

"Joey's indomitable spirit, grounded in his fierce, tender devotion to baby Carter and expressed through Gantos' inimitable comic tone, shows the fragile adults around him just what it looks like to be the man of the house." Booklist

The **trouble** in me; Jack Gantos. Farrar, Straus & Giroux 2015 224 p. (hardback) $17.99

Grades: 6 7 8 9 10 **Fic**

1. Humorous fiction 2. Moving -- Fiction 3. Florida -- Fiction 4. Friendship -- Fiction 5. Juvenile delinquency -- Fiction 6. Humorous stories 7. Behavior -- Fiction 8. Moving, Household -- Fiction

ISBN 9780374379957

LC 2015013115

This autobiographical novel, by Jack Gantos, "opens with an explosive encounter in which Jack first meets his awesomely rebellious older neighbor, Gary Pagoda, just back from juvie for car theft. Instantly mesmerized, Jack decides he will do whatever it takes to be like Gary. As a follower, Jack is eager to leave his old self behind, and desperate for whatever crazy, hilarious, frightening thing might happen next. But he may not be as ready as he thinks." (Publisher's note)

"Gantos has won a Newbery Medal, Printz Honor, Sibert Honor, and countless hearts. Readers will want to know how he became one of a kind." Booklist

What would Joey do? Farrar, Straus & Giroux 2002 229p $16.99; pa $5.99

Grades: 5 6 7 8 **Fic**

1. Grandmothers -- Fiction 2. Attention deficit disorder -- Fiction

ISBN 0-374-39986-7; 0-06-054403-1 pa

LC 2002-22823

Joey tries to keep his life from degenerating into total chaos when his mother sends him to be home-schooled with a hostile blind girl, his divorced parents cannot stop fighting, and his grandmother is dying of emphysema

"The boy's first-person narration is as frenetically fun as it was in the first two books." SLJ

Garcia, Cristina

★ **I** wanna be your shoebox. Simon & Schuster Books for Children 2008 198p $16.99; pa $6.99

Grades: 4 5 6 7 **Fic**

1. Jews -- Fiction 2. California -- Fiction 3. Family life -- Fiction 4. Grandfathers -- Fiction 5. Cuban Americans -- Fiction 6. Racially mixed people -- Fiction

ISBN 978-1-4169-3928-3; 1-4169-3928-8; 978-1-4169-7904-3 pa; 1-4169-7904-2 pa

Thirteen-year-old, clarinet-playing, Southern California surfer, Yumi Ruiz-Hirsch, comes from a complex family—her father is Jewish-Japanese, her mother is Cuban, and her parents are divorced—and when her grandfather Saul is diagnosed with terminal cancer, Yumi asks him to tell her his life story, which helps her to understand her own history and identity.

"García's . . . exceptional ability to channel a range of voices lights up her first children's novel. . . . The large personalities propel the story and bring tenderness and credibility to a classic message about change." Publ Wkly

Garcia, Kami

Unbreakable; by Kami Garcia. Little Brown & Co 2013 320 p. (international) $18

Grades: 7 8 9 10 **Fic**

1. Paranormal fiction 2. Secret societies -- Fiction 3. Love -- Fiction 4. Demonology -- Fiction 5. Supernatural -- Fiction

ISBN 9780316210171; 031621017X

LC 2012048435

In this young adult paranormal novel, by Kami Garcia, "when Kennedy Waters finds her mother dead, she doesn't realize that paranormal forces are responsible--not until mysterious identical twins Jared and Lukas Lockhart break into her room and destroy a deadly spirit sent to kill her. Kennedy learns that her mother's death was no accident, and now she has to take her place in the Legion of the Black Dove--a secret society whose five members were all murdered on the same night." (Publisher's note)

"Readers are quickly drawn into the action, from the murder at the beginning to the cliff-hanger at the end. It's the horror aspect more than the fast-paced intrigue, however, that is the book's strong point. The Legion members must travel from one terrifying location to another, and Garcia describes these chilling locations with flawless detail." - SLJ reviews

Garden, Nancy

Endgame. Harcourt 2006 287p $17

Grades: 8 9 10 11 12 **Fic**

1. School stories 2. Bullies -- Fiction 3. Violence -- Fiction 4. Family life -- Fiction

ISBN 0-15-205416-2; 978-0-15-205416-8

LC 2005-19486

Fifteen-year-old Gray Wilton, bullied at school and ridiculed by an unfeeling father for preferring drums to hunting, goes on a shooting rampage at his high school.

"This is a hard-hitting and eloquent look at the impact of bullying, and the resulting destruction of lives touched by the violence." SLJ

Gardner, Lyn

★ **Into** the woods; pictures by Mini Grey. David Fickling Books 2007 427p il $16.99; lib bdg $19.99; pa $7.50

Grades: 4 5 6 7 8 **Fic**

1. Fantasy fiction 2. Sisters -- Fiction

ISBN 978-0-385-75115-5; 0-385-75115-X; 978-0-385-75116-2 lib bdg; 0-385-75116-8 lib bdg; 978-0-440-42223-5 pa; 0-440-42223-X pa

LC 2006-24350

Pursued by the sinister Dr. DeWilde and his ravenous wolves, three sisters—Storm, the inheritor of a special musical pipe, the elder Aurora, and the baby Any—flee into the woods and begin a journey filled with danger as they try to find a way to defeat their pursuer and keep him from taking the pipe and control of the entire land. "Grades five to eight." (Bull Cent Child Books)

"Gardner's fast-paced fantasy-adventure cleverly borrows from well-known fairy tales, and astute readers will enjoy identifying the many folkloric references. . . . Grey's appealing black-and-white illustrations add humor and detail to the story." Booklist

Followed by: Out of the woods (2010)

Out of the woods; pictures by Mini Grey. David Fickling Books 2010 348p il $17.99; lib bdg $20.99

Grades: 4 5 6 7 8 **Fic**

1. Fantasy fiction 2. Sisters -- Fiction

ISBN 978-0-385-75154-4; 0-385-75154-0; 978-0-385-75156-8 lib bdg; 0-385-75156-7 lib bdg

Sequel to: Into the woods (2007)

This is a sequel to Into the Woods (2007). The Eden sisters "are being lured into a wicked witch's lair. . . . Belladonna wants Aurora's heart and Storm's all-powerful musical pipe, and she will stop at nothing to get them." (Publisher's note) "Grades five to eight." (Bull Cent Child Books)

"Aurora, Storm, and Any Eden thought their troubles were over when Storm tossed the Pied Piper's powerful, seductive pipe . . . into the sea and defeated the pipe's erstwhile owner, the villainous Dr. DeWilde. . . . But it seems their troubles have only begun. . . . A missing prince, a cowardly lion, a marauding dragon, seven dwarfs, and even the Grimm brothers all make appearances, and while the fractured fairy-tale stew is considerably more haphazard than that of the sisters' first outing, it's a well-conceived and entertaining mash-up nonetheless." Horn Book

Gardner, Sally

The **door** that led to where; Sally Gardner. Delacorte Press 2016 288 p. (ebook) $53.97; (hardcover) $17.99

Grades: 7 8 9 10 **Fic**

1. Time travel -- Fiction 2. London (England) -- Fiction 3. Mystery and detective stories

ISBN 9780399549991; 9780399549977; 9780399549984

LC 2015034396

In this novel, by Sally Gardner, "AJ Flynn has just failed all but one of his major exams. . . . So when he's offered a junior clerk position at a London law firm, he hopes his life is about to change. . . . While on the job, AJ finds an old key labeled with his birth date, and he's determined to find the door it will open. When he does just that, AJ and his group of scrappy friends begin a series of amazing journeys to the past—1830, to be exact." (Publisher's note)

"Gardner's prose, peppered with colorful metaphors and period language, moves the plot along quickly, sketching out a pungent, vivid world in both present and past." Horn Book

I, Coriander; [illustrations by Lydia Corry] Dial Bks. 2005 280p il $16.99

Grades: 6 7 8 9 **Fic**

1. Magic -- Fiction 2. Fairies -- Fiction

ISBN 0-8037-3099-3

LC 2005--06050

In 17th century London, Coriander, a girl who has inherited magic from her mother, must find a way to use this magic in order to save both herself and an inhabitant of the fairy world where her mother was born

"Seamlessly meshing fact and fantasy, the author composes a suspenseful masterpiece that will have audience members gladly suspending their disbelief." Publ Wkly

★ **Maggot** moon; Sally Gardner. Candlewick Press 2013 288 p. (reinforced) $16.99

Grades: 7 8 9 10 11 12 **Fic**

1. Dystopian fiction 2. Alternative histories -- Fiction

ISBN 0763665533; 9780763665531

LC 2012947247

Costa Children's Book Award Winner 2012

Printz Honor Book (2014)

In this dystopian novel, "Standish Treadwell, 15, has lost parents, neighbors, best friend: All disappeared from Zone Seven, a post-war occupied territory, into the hellish clutches of the Motherland. Now a new horror approaches. . . . Standish and [his friend] Hector spin fantasies about the far-off tantalizing consumer culture they glimpsed on television (now banned), but they lack a vision of the future beyond vague dreams of rescue." (Kirkus Reviews)

★ The **red** necklace; a story of the French Revolution. Dial Books 2008 378p $16.99

Grades: 8 9 10 11 12 **Fic**

1. Adventure fiction 2. Romanies -- Fiction 3. France -- History -- 1789-1799, Revolution -- Fiction

ISBN 978-0-8037-3100-4; 0-8037-3100-0

LC 2007-39813

In the late eighteenth-century, Sido, the twelve-year-old daughter of a self-indulgent marquis, and Yann, a fourteen-year-old Gypsy orphan raised to perform in a magic show, face a common enemy at the start of the French Revolution.

"Scores are waiting to be settled on every page; this is a heart-stopper." Booklist

Followed by: The silver blade (2009)

The **Silver** Blade. Dial Books 2009 362p $16.99

Grades: 8 9 10 11 12 **Fic**

1. Adventure fiction 2. Magic -- Fiction 3. France -- History -- 1789-1799, Revolution -- Fiction

ISBN 978-0-8037-3377-0; 0-8037-3377-1

LC 2009-9282

Sequel to: The red necklace (2008)

As the Revolution descends into the ferocious Reign of Terror, Yann, now an extraordinary practioner of magic, uses his skills to confound his enemies and help spirit refugees out of France, but the question of his true identity and the kidnapping of his true love, Sido, expose him to dangers that threaten to destroy him.

"A luscious melodrama, rich in sensuous detail from horrific to sublime, with an iridescent overlay of magic." Kirkus

Gardner, Whitney

You're Welcome, Universe; Whitney Gardner. Alfred A. Knopf 2017 304 p. illustrations library $20.99; paperback $9.99; hardcover $17.99

Grades: 8 9 10 11 12 **Fic**

1. Graffiti -- Fiction 2. Children of gay parents -- Fiction 3. Deaf culture -- Fiction

ISBN 9780399551420; 9780399551444; 9780399551413; 9780399551437; 0399551417

LC 2017286263

Schneider Family Book Award (2018)

"When Julia finds a slur about her best friend scrawled across the back of the Kingston School for the Deaf, she covers it up with a beautiful (albeit illegal) graffiti mural. Her supposed best friend snitches, the principal expels her, and her two mothers set Julia up with a one-way ticket to a 'mainstream' school in the suburbs, where she's treated like an outcast as the only deaf student. . . . Out in the 'burbs, Julia paints anywhere she can, eager to claim some turf of her own. But Julia soon learns that she might not be the only vandal in town." (Publisher's note)

"Gardner brings together Deaf culture, discrimination, sexuality, friendship, body image, trust, betrayal, and even a potential Banksy spotting for this fresh novel, brightened by black-and-white illustrations from Julia's notebooks." Booklist

Garner, Em

Contaminated; by Em Garner. Egmont USA 2013 336 p. (hardcover) $17.99; (ebook) $17.99

Grades: 7 8 9 10 **Fic**

1. Horror fiction 2. Dystopian fiction 3. Science fiction 4. Mothers -- Fiction

ISBN 1606843540; 9781606843543; 9781606843550

LC 2012024472

This book is set two years after "a diet drink with genetically modified ingredients transformed countless Americans into mindlessly violent animals" Now, "the Contaminated are controlled by electronic collars, and the unclaimed are housed in kennels like that in which Velvet Ellis, 17, finds her mother." Velvet and her sister's "shaky hold on normal life is finally upended when Velvet brings their mother home, facing anger and fear from neighbors and eviction from their landlord." (Kirkus Reviews)

Garretson, Dee

Wildfire run. Harper 2010 261p $16.99; pa $6.99

Grades: 5 6 7 8 **Fic**

1. Adventure fiction 2. Fires -- Fiction 3. Presidents -- Fiction 4. Earthquakes -- Fiction 5. Wilderness survival -- Fiction

ISBN 978-0-06-195347-7; 0-06-195347-4; 978-0-06-195350-7 pa; 0-06-195350-4 pa

LC 2009049482

A relaxing retreat to Camp David turns deadly after a faraway earthquake sets off a chain of disastrous events that traps the president's twelve-year-old son, Luke, and his two friends within the compound.

"Along with a breathlessly paced plot, Garretson crafts a preteen protagonist who grows out of being a whiny, moody sort and, with his companions, displays generous measures of courage and ingenuity in rising to the occasion." Booklist

Gavin, Rohan

3 of a kind; Rohan Gavin. Bloomsbury Children's Books 2016 272 p. (Knightley and Son) (hardback) $16.99

Grades: 5 6 7 8 9 **Fic**

1. Las Vegas (Nev.) -- Fiction 2. Adventure fiction -- Fiction 5. Father-son relationship -- Fiction 6. Missing persons -- Fiction 7. Fathers and sons -- Fiction 8. Mystery and detective stories

ISBN 9781619638303

LC 2015037726

In this book by Rohan Gavin, "Darkus Knightley is . . . an extraordinary solver of crimes. . . . Despite trying to leave his detective ways behind to lead a normal teenage life, when his father's loyal housekeeper, Bogna, goes missing, Darkus must return to the family fold and follow the clues to America and the bright lights of Las Vegas. Alongside his father, Alan, and stepsister, Tilly, Darkus must once again face the deadly criminal organisation, the Combination." (Publisher's note)

"There's plenty of mystery, suspense, and humor here, but series fans will mainly enjoy watching the many idiosyncratic characters in action once again." Booklist

Knightley and son; Rohan Gavin. Bloomsbury 2014 320 p. (hardback) $16.99

Grades: 5 6 7 8 9 **Fic**

1. Mystery fiction 2. Organized crime -- Fiction 3. Father-son relationship -- Fiction 4. Conspiracies -- Fiction 5. Fathers and sons -- Fiction 6. Mystery and detective stories

ISBN 1619631539; 9781619631533

LC 2013034316

In this novel by Rohan Gavin, "since 13-year-old Darkus Knightley's parents split, he sees his father, Alan--a detective of obsessive professional dedication--once a week. Darkus' sponge of a brain has absorbed the details of every former case of his father's, which fuel conversation during their visits. The conversations tend to be one-sided, though, as Alan has been comatose for four years. One evening, Alan miraculously wakes from his coma, ready to investigate a series of bizarre crimes." (Kirkus Reviews)

"Set in modern-day London, Gavin's series-opener has an entertaining Holmes-ian influence and enjoyably quirky characters." Horn Book

Other titles in this series are:

K-9 (2015)

3 of a kind (2016)

Gayton, Sam

Hercufleas; by Sam Gayton. Clarion Books 2016 272 p. (hardback) $16.99; (ebook) $16.99

Grades: 4 5 6 7 **Fic**

1. Fleas -- Fiction 2. Humorous fiction 3. Heroes and heroines -- Fiction

ISBN 9780544636200; 9780544635340

LC 2015034636

This novel by Sam Gayton is "a story about family, friendship and loss, and the power of hope and unity. . . . To protect her village from a giant, Greta recruits a champion: Hercufleas! He may be tiny, but this young flea is certain he's destined for greatness. Being a hero is harder than it seems, though, and Hercufleas and Greta face unexpected choices--and consequences--in their desperate attempts to save the village, and each other." (Publisher's note)

"Twists and turns, reversals, and chance meetings prove several times over that hope and determination are the most reliable weapons—and armor—no matter the size or situation of the hero." Kirkus

Gebhart, Ryan

★ **There** will be bears; Ryan Gebhart. First edition Candlewick Press 2014 224 p. $16.99

Grades: 6 7 8 **Fic**

1. Bears -- Fiction 2. Grandfathers -- Fiction 3. Wilderness survival -- Fiction

ISBN 0763665215; 9780763665210

LC 2013946620

In this book, by Ryan Gebhart, "thirteen-year-old Tyson loves hanging out with his . . . Grandpa Gene. . . . So when Grandpa Gene has to move to a nursing home that can manage his kidney disease, Tyson feels like he's losing his only friend. Not only that, but Tyson was counting on Grandpa Gene to take him on his first big hunt. So in defiance of Mom and Dad's strict orders, and despite reports of a . . . man-eating grizzly named Sandy, the two sneak off to the Grand Tetons." (Publisher's note)

"Fully developed characters, complex and realistic relationships (especially between Tyson and Gramps), and Tyson's spot-on narrative voice--which balances faux bravado, risqué humor, and real emotional pain--make this story stand out." Pub Wkly

Gee, Maurice

Gool. Orca Book Publishers 2010 215p (The Salt trilogy) lib bdg $18

Grades: 6 7 8 9 10 **Fic**

1. Fantasy fiction

ISBN 978-1-55469-214-9; 1-55469-214-8

Sequel to: Salt (2009)

Xantee and Lo set out to find the Dog King, Tarl, whose help they will need if they are to have any hope of destroying the gool and ridding the world of its life-sucking force.

"The unexpected twists of this original fantasy adventure keep the pages turning. The fascinating buildup leads to a thrilling climax." Kirkus

Followed by: The Limping Man (2011)

The **Limping** Man. Orca Book Publishers 2011 195p il (The Salt trilogy) lib bdg $18

Grades: 6 7 8 9 10 **Fic**

1. Fantasy fiction

ISBN 978-1-55469-216-3 ib bdg; 1-55469-216-4 lib bdg

LC 2010-413414

Sequel to: Gool (2010)

Hana narrowly escapes Blood Burrow after her mother chooses to swallow poison rather than die in the great witch-burning in People's Square. Deep in the forest she meets Ben, son of Lo, and Hawk, who becomes her silent protector and guide. But even in the forest there is no peace. When they learn of the advancing armies that will wipe out all those who have sought refuge in the wilderness, they realize they have no choice but to return to the city and confront the terrible power of the Limping Man head-on.

★ **Salt**. Orca Book Publishers 2009 252p map (The Salt trilogy) $18; pa $12.95

Grades: 6 7 8 9 10 **Fic**

1. Fantasy fiction 2. Extrasensory perception -- Fiction

ISBN 978-1-55469-209-5; 1-55469-209-1; 978-1-55469-369-6 pa; 1-55469-369-1 pa

"Hari lives in Blood Burrow, a hellacious, rat-infested slum. . . . Pearl is a pampered daughter of Company, her only purpose in life to be married off to cement one of her father's political alliances. When both young people, who share rare psychic gifts, revolt against their fates, they find themselves on a desperate journey across a hostile landscape, with the forces of Company at their heels. . . . A compelling tale of anger and moral development that also powerfully explores the evils of colonialism and racism." Publ Wkly

Other titles in this series are:

Gool (2010)

The Limping Man (2011)

Gemeinhart, Dan

The **honest** truth; Dan Gemeinhart. Scholastic Press 2015 229 p. $16.99

Grades: 5 6 7 8 **Fic**

1. Dogs -- Fiction 2. Cancer -- Fiction 3. Runaway children -- Fiction 4. Human-animal relationship -- Fiction 5. Runaways -- Fiction 6. Friendship -- Fiction 7. Best friends -- Fiction 8. Rainier, Mount (Wash.) -- Fiction

ISBN 0545665736; 9780545665735

LC 2014028474

In this book, by Dan Gemeinhart, "Mark is a normal kid. He's got a dog named Beau and a best friend, Jessie. He likes to take photos and write haiku poems in his notebook. He dreams of climbing a mountain one day. But in one important way, Mark is not like other kids at all. Mark is sick. . . . The kind of sick some people never get better from. So Mark runs away. He leaves home with his camera, his notebook, his dog, and a plan to reach the top of Mount Rainier." (Publisher's note)

Some Kind of Courage; Dan Gemeinhart. Scholastic 2016 240 p. (hardcover) $16.99

Grades: 4 5 6 7 **Fic**

1. Theft -- Fiction 2. Courage -- Fiction 3. Western stories -- Fiction

ISBN 0545665779; 9780545665773

LC 2015047293

In this juvenile western novel, by Dan Gemeinhart, "Joseph Johnson has lost just about everyone he's ever loved. . . . And now, he's lost his pony-fast, fierce, beautiful Sarah. . . . Joseph can sure enough get her back, though. The odds are stacked against him, but he isn't about to give up. He will face down deadly animals, dangerous men, and the fury of nature itself on his quest to be reunited with the only family he has left." (Publisher's note)

"Gemeinhart's riveting tale of grit and grief is equally tragic and triumphant." SLJ

Gensler, Sonia

The **revenant**. Alfred A. Knopf 2011 336p $16.99; lib bdg $19.99

Grades: 7 8 9 10 **Fic**

1. Ghost stories 2. School stories 3. Oklahoma -- Fiction 4. Teachers -- Fiction 5. Cherokee Indians -- Fiction 6. Young adult literature -- Works 7. Cherokee National Female Seminary -- Fiction

ISBN 978-0-375-86701-9; 0-375-86701-5; 978-0-375-96701-6 lib bdg; 0-375-96701-X lib bdg

LC 2010-28701

When seventeen-year-old Willemina Hammond fakes credentials to get a teaching position at a school for Cherokee girls in nineteenth-century Oklahoma, she is haunted by the ghost of a drowned student.

"Gensler makes a solid debut with an eerie and suspenseful work of historical fiction in which everyone is a murder suspect. . . . The layers of detail address the complex social structure of the period, and Gensler's characters and dialogue are believably crafted." Publ Wkly

George, Jean Craighead

My side of the mountain trilogy; written and illustrated by Jean Craighead George. Dutton Children's Books 2000 177, 170, 258p il $24.99

Grades: 5 6 7 8 **Fic**

1. Falcons -- Fiction 2. New York (State) -- Fiction 3. Wilderness survival -- Fiction

ISBN 0-525-46269-4

LC 00-712305

George, Jessica Day

Dragon flight; [by] Jessica Day George. 1st U.S. ed.; Bloomsbury Children's Books 2008 262p $16.95

Grades: 5 6 7 8 **Fic**

1. Fantasy fiction 2. Dragons -- Fiction

ISBN 978-1-59990-110-7; 1-59990-110-2

LC 2007050762

Sequel to: Dragon slippers (2007)

Young seamstress Creel finds herself strategizing with the dragon king Shardas once again when a renegade dragon in a distant country launches a war against their country, bringing an entire army of dragons into the mix.

"Fans of the first book will find the same strengths here: the imaginatively detailed scenes; the thrilling, spell-fueled action; the possibility of romance with a prince; and the appealing, brave heroine." Booklist

Dragon slippers. Bloomsbury Children's Books 2007 324p $16.95; pa $7.99

Grades: 5 6 7 8 **Fic**

1. Fantasy fiction 2. Dragons -- Fiction 3. Orphans -- Fiction

ISBN 978-1-59990-057-5; 1-59990-057-2; 978-1-59990-275-3 pa; 1-59990-275-3 pa

LC 2006-21142

Orphaned after a fever epidemic, Creel befriends a dragon and unknowingly inherits an object that can either save or destroy her kingdom.

"The plot is fast paced with all the right touches of romance and adventure. . . . The characters are wonderfully drawn." Voice Youth Advocates

Followed by: Dragon flight (2008)

Dragon spear; Jessica Day George. Bloomsbury 2009 248 p. $16.99

Grades: 5 6 7 8 **Fic**

1. Fantasy fiction 2. Dragons -- Fiction 3. Fantasy 4. Kings, queens, rulers, etc. -- Fiction

ISBN 1599903695; 9781599903699

LC 2008044414

Sequel to: Dragon flight

In this book, by Jessica Day George, "with peace established between the humans and the dragons, young couple Creel and Luka are planning their wedding. But then the dragon queen, Velika, is kidnapped by a band of rogue dragons in need of a ruler. When Creel and Luka rush to help, they discover that Luka's father has plans to take back the Far Islands from the dragons. Creel's happily ever after just might be postponed . . . again." (Publisher's note)

"As in the previous series titles, George creates richly satisfying fantasy realms, from opulent palaces to forest lairs, while the tender romances, genuine friendships, rapid dialogue, and thrilling adventures will continue to delight readers." Booklist.

Princess of glass. Bloomsbury Children's Books 2010 266p $16.99

Grades: 6 7 8 9 10 **Fic**

1. Fairy tales 2. Princesses -- Fiction

ISBN 978-1-59990-478-8; 1-59990-478-0

Sequel to: Princess of the Midnight Ball (2009)

In the midst of maneuverings to create political alliances through marriage, sixteen-year-old Poppy, one of the infamous twelve dancing princesses, becomes the target of a vengeful witch while Prince Christian tries to save her.

"In a clever reworking of the Cinderella story, George once again proves adept at spinning her own magical tale." Booklist

★ **Princess** of the midnight ball. Bloomsbury Children's Books 2009 280p $16.99

Grades: 6 7 8 9 10 **Fic**

1. Fairy tales

ISBN 978-1-59990-322-4; 1-59990-322-9

LC 2008-30310

A retelling of the tale of twelve princesses who wear out their shoes dancing every night, and of Galen, a former soldier now working in the king's gardens, who follows them in hopes of breaking the curse.

"Fans of fairy-tale retellings . . . will enjoy this story for its magic, humor, and touch of romance." SLJ

Followed by: Princess of glass (2010)

Sun and moon, ice and snow. Bloomsbury 2008 336p $16.95

Grades: 7 8 9 10 11 12 **Fic**

1. Fairy tales 2. Fantasy fiction 3. Folklore -- Norway

ISBN 1-59990-109-9; 978-1-59990-109-1

LC 2007030848

A girl travels east of the sun and west of the moon to free her beloved prince from a magic spell. "Grades seven to twelve." (Bull Cent Child Books)

"George has adapted Norse myths and fairy tales to create this eerily beautiful, often terrifying world. . . . Mystery, adventure, and the supernatural, and a touch of love are woven together to create a vivid, well-crafted, poetic fantasy." Booklist

Gephart, Donna

★ **How** to survive middle school. Delacorte Press 2010 247p $15.99; lib bdg $18.99

Grades: 5 6 7 8 **Fic**

1. School stories 2. Family life -- Fiction

ISBN 978-0-385-73793-7; 0-385-73793-9; 978-0-385-90701-9 lib bdg; 0-385-90701-X lib bdg

LC 2009-21809

When thirteen-year-old David Greenberg's best friend makes the start of middle school even worse than he feared it could be, David becomes friends with Penny, who shares his love of television shows and posts one of their skits on YouTube, making them wildly popular—online, at least.

"Gephart crafts for her likable protagonist an engaging, feel-good transition into adolescence that's well stocked with tears and laughter." Booklist

Lily and Dunkin; Donna Gephart. Delacorte Press 2016 352 p. (hc) $16.99

Grades: 5 6 7 8 **Fic**

1. School stories 2. Florida -- Fiction 3. Friendship -- Fiction 4. Mental illness -- Fiction 5. Middle schools -- Fiction 6. Transgender people -- Fiction 7. Manic-depressive illness -- Fiction

8. Schools -- Fiction
ISBN 9780553536744; 9780553536751

LC 2015017801

In this book, by Donna Gephart, "Lily Jo McGrother, born Timothy McGrother, is a girl. But being a girl is not so easy when you look like a boy. Especially . . . in the eighth grade. Dunkin Dorfman, birth name Norbert Dorfman, is dealing with bipolar disorder and has just moved from the New Jersey town he's called home for the past thirteen years. . . . [H]e is also hiding from a painful secret. . . . One summer morning, Lily Jo McGrother meets Dunkin Dorfman." (Publisher's note)

Olivia Bean, trivia queen; Donna Gephart. Delacorte Press 2012 278 p. $16.99
Grades: 3 4 5 6 7 **Fic**

1. Game shows -- Fiction 2. Children of divorced parents -- Fiction 3. Father-daughter relationship -- Fiction 4. Divorce -- Fiction 5. Fathers -- Fiction 6. Curiosities and wonders -- Fiction 7. Jeopardy (Television program) -- Fiction
ISBN 0385740522; 9780385740524

LC 2011006023

In this book, "Olivia Bean has watched 'Jeopardy!' every evening since she was a little girl, but the nightly tradition just hasn't been the same since her father . . . took off for California two years ago. When the show announces auditions for Kids Week, Olivia is intent on making the cut, not only to compete but, more importantly, to get a plane ticket out to the show's taping in L.A. with the hopes of meeting up with her estranged dad." (Bulletin of the Center for Children's Books).

Gerber, Alyson

Braced; Alyson Gerber. Arthur A. Levine Books, an imprint of Scholastic Inc. 2017 304 p. (ebook) $16.99; (hardcover : alk. paper) $16.99
Grades: 5 6 7 8 **Fic**

1. Scoliosis -- Fiction 2. Massachusetts -- Fiction 3. Andover (Mass.) -- Fiction 4. Orthopedic braces -- Fiction 5. Mothers and daughters -- Fiction 6. Genetic disorders -- Fiction 7. Scoliosis in children -- Fiction 8. Self-consciousness (Sensitivity) -- Fiction 9. Family life -- Massachusetts -- Andover -- Fiction
ISBN 9780545907637; 9780545902144

LC 2016016818

In this novel, by Alyson Gerber, "Rachel Brooks is excited for the new school year. She's finally earned a place as a forward on her soccer team. Her best friends make everything fun. . . . After one last appointment with her scoliosis doctor, this will be her best year yet. Then the doctor delivers some terrible news: The sideways curve in Rachel's spine has gotten worse, and she needs to wear a back brace twenty-three hours a day." (Publisher's note)

Focused; Alyson Gerber. Scholastic 2019 304 p. (hardcover) $16.99
Grades: 4 5 6 7 **Fic**

1. Chess -- Fiction 2. Family life -- Fiction 3. Attention deficit disorder -- Fiction 4. Life skills -- Fiction 5. Parent and child -- Fiction 6. Families -- Fiction 7. Attention-deficit hyperactivity disorder -- Fiction 8. Developmentally disabled children -- Fiction
ISBN 9781338185973

LC 2018044094

In this book, by Alyson Gerber, "Clea can't control her thoughts. She knows she has to do her homework . . . but she gets distracted. . . . When Clea fails one too many tests, her parents take her to be tested, and she finds out that she has ADHD, which means her attention is all over the place instead of where it needs to be. Clea knows life can't continue the way it's been going. . . . [She must] find a way to focus." (Publisher's note)

"An accurate and compassionate picture of growing up with ADHD is the icing on the cake of this well-told novel." (Kirkus Reviews)

Gerhardt, Jake

Me and Miranda Mullaly; by Jake Gerhardt. Viking Childrens Books 2016 256 p. (hardback) $16.99
Grades: 6 7 8 **Fic**

1. School stories 2. Love -- Fiction 3. Humorous fiction 4. Middle schools -- Fiction 5. Schools -- Fiction
ISBN 9780451475404

LC 2015020368

In this book, by Jake Gerhardt, "meet Sam, the comedian; Duke, the intellectual; and Chollie, the athlete. Their fates converge at Penn Valley Middle as each falls desperately for the enigmatic Miranda Mullaly—the girl who smiles like she means it, the girl who makes Christmas truly magic when she sings, the girl who barely realizes her admirers exist!" (Publisher's note)

"While the characters could have been more likable, they are well drawn and the situations are believable and show an understanding of the inner workings of middle school... This is a strong purchase for middle school libraries that will circulate well." SLJ

Gewirtz, Adina Rishe

Zebra forest; Adina Rishe Gewirtz. Candlewick Press 2013 208 p. (reinforced) $15.99
Grades: 5 6 7 8 **Fic**

1. Hostages -- Fiction 2. Siblings -- Fiction
ISBN 0763660418; 9780763660413

LC 2012947251

In this novel, by Adina Rishe Gewirtz, "an escaped fugitive upends everything two siblings think they know about their family, their past, and themselves. . . . A rattling at the back door, an escapee from the prison holding them hostage in their own home, four lives that will never be the same. . . . [The book] portrays an unfolding standoff of truth against family secrets." (Publisher's note)

"Debut author Gewirtz successfully conveys the terror and tedium of being trapped. . . While the situation may frighten some readers, the matter-of-fact way [the protagonists] make the best of difficult circumstances . . . may be comforting to those whose families don't match the ideal. An emotionally honest family story with an ending that's hopeful without being implausibly upbeat." Pub Wkly

Gibbs, Stuart

Belly up. Simon & Schuster Books for Young Readers 2010 294p $15.99; pa $6.99
Grades: 4 5 6 7 **Fic**

1. Mystery fiction 2. Zoos -- Fiction 3. Hippopotamus -- Fiction
ISBN 1-4169-8731-2; 1-4169-8732-0 pa; 978-1-4169-8731-4; 978-1-4169-8732-1 pa

LC 2009-34860

Twelve-year-old Teddy investigates when a popular Texas zoo's star attraction, Henry the hippopotamus, is murdered.

"The characters are well-developed and believable, making this book appealing to reluctant readers and those who enjoy animal stories and mysteries." Libr Media Connect

Big game; Stuart Gibbs. Simon & Schuster Books for Young Readers 2015 342 p. (hardcover) $16.99
Grades: 4 5 6 7 **Fic**

1. Mystery fiction 2. Zoos -- Fiction 3. Poaching -- Fiction 4.

Rhinoceros -- Fiction 5. Endangered species -- Fiction 6. Zoo animals -- Fiction 7. Mystery and detective stories
ISBN 1481423339; 9781481423335; 9781481423342
LC 2014042145

Sequel to: Poached

In this book, by Stuart Gibbs, "When someone takes aim at Rhonda Rhino, FunJungle's pregnant (and endangered) Asian greater one-horned rhinoceros, the zoo steps up security measures in order to protect this rare animal and her baby. But the extra security isn't enough—someone is still getting too close for comfort. Teddy and company start to suspect that whoever is after Rhonda is really after her horn, which is worth a lot of money on the black market." (Publisher's note)

"Monkey business included, this adventure strikes a neat balance between shenanigans and gravitas to inspire young conservationists." Kirkus

The **last** musketeer. Harper 2011 244p $16.99
Grades: 5 6 7 8 **Fic**

1. Cardinals 2. Statesmen 3. Adventure fiction 4. Time travel -- Fiction 5. France -- History -- 1589-1789, Bourbons -- Fiction
ISBN 978-0-06-204838-7; 0-06-204838-4
LC 2011019376

In Paris with his parents to sell family heirlooms, fourteen-year-old Greg Rich suddenly finds himself four hundred years in the past, and is aided by boys who will one day be known as 'The Three Musketeers.'

"From the gripping first sentence . . . the excitement never flags in this newly imagined Musketeer adventure. . . . Using Alexandre Dumas' stories as a jumping-off point, Gibbs mixes fact, fantasy and thrills to create a galloping swashbuckler." Kirkus

Panda -monium; Stuart Gibbs. Simon & Schuster Books for Young Readers 2017 352 p. (FunJungle) (hardcover) $16.99
Grades: 4 5 6 7 **Fic**

1. Zoos -- Fiction 2. Pandas -- Fiction 3. Zoo animals -- Fiction 4. Mystery and detective stories
ISBN 9781481445672; 9781481445689
LC 2016002113

Sequel to: Big game

In this book in the FunJungle series, by Stuart Gibbs, "FunJungle is frenzied, awaiting the arrival of its most thrilling animal yet--Li Ping--a rare and very expensive giant panda that the zoo went to enormous lengths to secure. But when the truck transporting Li Ping shows up, its precious cargo has vanished into thin air. The FBI steps in to investigate, and Teddy is happy to leave the job in their (supposedly) capable hands." (Publisher's note)

Poached; Stuart Gibbs. Simon & Schuster Books for Young Readers 2014 329 pages (hardcover) $15.99
Grades: 4 5 6 7 **Fic**

1. Mystery fiction 2. Zoos -- Fiction 3. Koalas -- Fiction 4. Bullies -- Fiction 5. Texas -- Fiction 6. Zoo animals -- Fiction 7. Mystery and detective stories 8. Family life -- Texas -- Fiction
ISBN 1442467770; 9781442467774
LC 2013000539

In this sequel to "Belly Up," by Stuart Gibbs, "12-year-old trouble-magnet Teddy is still living at FunJungle, a massive zoo and amusement park, with his primatologist mother and wildlife photographer father. . . . When the school bully, Vance, forces Teddy to throw a fake arm into the shark tank . . . [it] has a large-scale snowball effect that positions Teddy as the key suspect in the theft of Kazoo, a koala on loan from Australia." (Kirkus Reviews)

"Gibbs weaves interesting trivia (newborn koalas are jellybean-size) and plenty of humor (a poop-throwing chimp helps ID an industrial spy/saboteur) into his action-packed mystery." Horn Book

Spy camp; Stuart Gibbs. 1st ed. Simon & Schuster Books for Young Readers 2013 336 p. (hardcover) $17.99
Grades: 4 5 6 7 **Fic**

1. Spies -- Fiction 2. Camping -- Fiction 3. Camps -- Fiction 4. Survival -- Fiction
ISBN 1442457538; 9781442457539
LC 2012019416

Sequel to: Spy school

In this story by Stuart Gibbs, "Ben Ripley is a middle-schooler . . . [who] spent the last year training to be a top-level spy and dodging all sorts of associated danger. So now that summer's finally here, Ben's ready to have some fun and relax. Except . . . a spy-in-training's work is never done, and the threats from SPYDER, an enemy spy organization, are as unavoidable as the summer heat. Will Ben be able to keep his cover--and his cool?" (Publisher's note)

"After escaping assassination by the top-secret organization SPYDER, Ben Ripley (Spy School) is looking forward to chilling out this summer. But SPYDER is turning up the heat, insisting that Ben come to work for them. Gorgeous fellow-spy-in-training Erica is ready to help, and her legendary grandfather also appears on the scene. Clever descriptions and plot twists make this a top-notch summer read." Horn Book

★ **Spy** school; Stuart Gibbs. Simon & Schuster Books for Young Readers 2012 290 p. (hardcover) $16.99
Grades: 4 5 6 7 **Fic**

1. School stories 2. Adventure fiction 3. Spies -- Fiction 4. Schools -- Fiction
ISBN 1442421827; 9781442421820; 9781442421844
LC 2011015023

Edgar Nominee: Best Juvenile (2013)

"When a suave, dashing man in a tuxedo shows up at Ben Ripley's house offering him a slot at the CIA's Academy of Espionage, Ben has his bags packed in a heartbeat. . . . Ben realizes he's been selected on the basis of cryptography skills he knows full well he doesn't have; in fact, he is only being used as bait to flush out a mole who threatens to undermine the academy. Ben's . . . determined . . . [to] demonstrate his merits." (Bulletin of the Center for Children's Books)

"Ben is well-defined; he is a math nerd, a geek who has never gotten the girl, but he comes into his own when he is under attack. Similar in many ways to the Alex Rider books for an older audience, this romp is a great choice for reluctant readers of either gender." Booklist

Other titles in this series are:
Spy camp (2013)
Evil spy school (2015)
Spy ski school (2016)
Spy school secret service (2017)

Spy ski school; Stuart Gibbs. Simon & Schuster Books for Young Readers 2016 368 p. (A Spy school novel) (hardcover) $16.99; (ebook) $15.99
Grades: 4 5 6 7 **Fic**

1. Spy stories -- Fiction 2. Spies -- Fiction 3. Schools -- Fiction 4. Friendship -- Fiction 5. Skis and skiing -- Fiction
ISBN 1481445626; 9781481445627; 9781481445634; 9781481445658
LC 2015037993

In this middle grade novel in the Spy School series by Stuart Gibbs, "Ben Ripley is not exactly the best student spy school has ever seen--he keeps flunking Advanced Self Preservation. But outside of class, Ben is pretty great at staying alive. . . . After all . . . [his] unexpected success, the CIA has decided to activate Ben for real. The Mission: Become friends with Jessica Shang, the daughter of a suspected Chinese crime boss, and find out all of her father's secrets." (Publisher's note)

"Readers will be glad they strapped on their boots and went along for the ride." Kirkus

Gibney, Shannon

See no color; Shannon Gibney. Carolrhoda Lab 2015 186 p. $18.99

Grades: 7 8 9 10 **Fic**

1. Adopted children -- Fiction 2. Baseball players -- Fiction 3. Adoption -- Fiction 4. Baseball -- Fiction 5. Identity -- Fiction 6. Family life -- Fiction 7. Self-acceptance -- Fiction 8. African Americans -- Fiction

ISBN 9781467776820; 1467776823

LC 2015001619

"For as long as she can remember, sixteen-year-old Alex Kirtridge has known two things: 1. She has always been Little Kirtridge, a stellar baseball player, just like her father. 2. She's adopted. But now, things are changing: she meets Reggie, the first black guy who's wanted to get to know her; she discovers the letters from her biological father that her adoptive parents have kept from her; and her body starts to grow into a woman's, affecting her game." (Publisher's note)

Gibson, Julia Mary

Copper magic; Julia Mary Gibson. Starscape 2014 336 p. map (hardback) $16.99

Grades: 4 5 6 7 8 **Fic**

1. Magic -- Fiction 2. Historical fiction 3. Great Lakes region -- Fiction 4. Talismans -- Fiction 5. Teenage girls -- Fiction 6. United States -- History -- 20th century -- Fiction

ISBN 0765332116; 9780765332110

LC 2014014660

"The year is 1906, and on the shores of Lake Michigan twelve-year-old Violet Blake unearths an ancient talisman--a copper hand. Violet's touch warms the copper hand and it begins to reveal glimpses of another time." (Publisher's note)

"The summer of 1906 promises to be an exciting one for twelve-year-old Violet Blake: she gets her first job as an assistant for a visiting photographer; she meets a new friend; and best of all, she discovers an ancient copper talisman in the shape of a hand buried near the creek where her mother used to harvest medicinal herbs. . . . The presence of magic is subtle in the story, but in the end, it matters little whether the copper hand has magical power or not. Instead it is Violet's growth from a self-centered child to one who carefully considers the feelings and needs of those around her that give this story weight." VOYA

Gidwitz, Adam, 1982-

The **Grimm** conclusion; by Adam Gidwitz and illustrated by Hugh D'Andrade. Dutton Children's Books 2013 368 p. (hardcover) $16.99

Grades: 4 5 6 **Fic**

1. Fairy tales 2. Horror fiction 3. Humorous stories 4. Brothers and sisters -- Fiction 5. Characters in literature -- Fiction 6. Adventure and adventurers -- Fiction

ISBN 0525426159; 9780525426158

LC 2013021686

In this book by Adam Gidwitz and illustrated by Hugh D'Andrade, "two children venture through forests, flee kingdoms, face ogres and demons and monsters, and, ultimately, find their way home. Oh yes, and they may die. Just once or twice." (Publisher's note) "An omniscient narrator comments throughout, offering warnings, consolation, and explanations." (Horn Book Magazine)

In a glass Grimmly; Adam Gidwitz. Dutton Juvenile 2012 314 p. (hardback) $16.99

Grades: 4 5 6 7 8 **Fic**

1. Horror fiction 2. Paranormal fiction 3. Fractured fairy tales 4. Fairy tales 5. Frogs -- Fiction 6. Humorous stories 7. Cousins -- Fiction 8. Characters in literature -- Fiction 9. Adventure and adventurers -- Fiction

ISBN 0525425810; 9780525425816

LC 2012015515

This book is Adam Gidwitz's second collection of reimagined fairy tales. "The protagonists in this installment are Jack, Jill, and a talking frog, whose adventures begin separately in reworkings of 'The Frog Prince' and 'The Emperor's New Clothes,' before the three join forces in 'Jack and the Bean-stalk.'" (Publishers Weekly)

★ The **Inquisitor's** Tale; Or, The Three Magical Children and Their Holy Dog. Adam Gidwitz, illustrated by Hatem Aly. Penguin 2016 384 p. illustrations $17.99

Grades: 5 6 7 8 9 **Fic**

1. France -- Fiction 2. Fairy tales -- Fiction 3. Adventure fiction -- Fiction 4. Friars -- Fiction 5. Prophets -- Fiction 6. Middle Ages -- Fiction 7. Persecution -- Fiction 8. Jews -- France -- Fiction 9. Adventure and adventurers -- Fiction 10. France -- History -- Louis IX, 1226-1270 -- Fiction

ISBN 9781101612606; 0525426167; 9780525426165

LC 2016024174

Newbery Honor Book (2017)

In this book, by Adam Gidwitz, illustrated by Hatem Aly, it is "1242. On a dark night, travelers from across France cross paths at an inn and begin to tell stories of three children. Their adventures take them on a chase through France: they are taken captive by knights, sit alongside a king, and save the land from a farting dragon. On the run to escape prejudice and persecution and save precious and holy texts from being burned." (Publisher's note)

"A masterpiece of storytelling that is addictive and engrossing." Kirkus

Includes bibliographical references (pages 355-363).

★ A **tale** dark & Grimm. Dutton 2010 256p il

Grades: 5 6 7 8 **Fic**

1. Fairy tales 2. Siblings -- Fiction

ISBN 978-0-525-42334-8; 0-525-42334-6

LC 2009-53289

This book follows Hansel and Gretel as they walk out of their own story and into eight more tales. "Age ten and up." (N Y Times Book Rev)

"An audacious debut that's wicked smart and wicked funny." Publ Wkly

Gier, Kerstin

Emerald green; Kerstin Gier ; translated by Anthea Bell. Henry Holt and Co 2013 464 p. (hardback) $17.99

Grades: 7 8 9 10 **Fic**

1. Romance fiction 2. Time travel -- Fiction 3. Secret societies -- Fiction 4. Love -- Fiction 5. England -- Fiction 6. London (England) -- Fiction 7. Great Britain -- History -- Fiction 8. Family life -- England -- London -- Fiction

ISBN 0805092676; 9780805092677

LC 2013017885

Sequel to: Sapphire blue

In the conclusion to author Kerstin Gier's Ruby Red trilogy, Gwen has "recently learned that she is the Ruby, the final member of the time-traveling Circle of Twelve, and since then nothing has been going right. She suspects the founder of the Circle, Count Saint-German, is up to something nefarious, but nobody will believe her. And she's just learned that her charming time-traveling partner, Gideon, has probably been using her all along." (Publisher's note)

★ **Ruby** red; translated from the German by Anthea Bell. Henry Holt 2011 330p $16.99
Grades: 7 8 9 10 **Fic**
1. Family life -- Fiction 2. Time travel -- Fiction 3. London (England) -- Fiction 4. Secret societies -- Fiction
ISBN 978-0-8050-9252-3; 0-8050-9252-8
LC 2010-49223

Original German edition, 2009

"Sixteen-year-old Gwyneth has known all her life that a time-traveling gene runs in her family: her cousin, Charlotte, has been trained as the carrier since birth. Gwyneth starts to experience time traveling symptoms. When she suddenly finds herself sent to different eras three times within forty-eight hours, she begins to wonder whether her family made a mistake about who was to inherit the gene." (VOYA)

"Adventure, humor, and mystery all have satisfying roles here." Booklist

Other titles in this series are:
Sapphire blue (2012)
Emerald green (2013).

Sapphire blue; Kerstin Gier ; translated from the German by Anthea Bell. Henry Holt 2012 362 p. (hc) $16.99
Grades: 7 8 9 10 **Fic**
1. Fantasy fiction 2. Time travel -- Fiction 3. Secret societies -- Fiction 4. England -- Fiction 5. London (England) -- Fiction 6. Great Britain -- History -- Fiction 7. Family life -- England -- London -- Fiction
ISBN 0805092668; 9780805092660
LC 2011034011

Sequel to: Ruby red

In this young adult fantasy novel, by Kerstin Gier, "16-year-old Gwen continues her time-traveling adventures as the newest member of the Circle of Twelve.... Her life's now controlled by . . . a secret society monitoring time travel.... All 12 time travelers must be introduced into the chronograph so the Circle can be closed, and the Guardians have assigned Gwen and irresistible Gideon de Villiers the task of locating four missing time travelers." (Kirkus Reviews)

Giff, Patricia Reilly, 1935

Eleven. Wendy Lamb Books 2008 164p $15.99; lib bdg $18.99; pa $6.50
Grades: 4 5 6 7 **Fic**
1. Woodwork -- Fiction 2. Friendship -- Fiction 3. Kidnapping -- Fiction 4. Learning disabilities -- Fiction
ISBN 978-0-385-73069-3; 978-0-385-90098-0 lib bdg; 978-0-440-23802-7 pa
LC 2007-12638

When Sam, who can barely read, discovers an old newspaper clipping just before his eleventh birthday, it brings forth memories from his past, and, with the help of a new friend at school and the castle they are building for a school project, his questions are eventually answered.

This is an "exquisitely rendered story of self-discovery." Publ Wkly

Lily's crossing. Delacorte Press 1997 180p $15.95; pa $6.50; $15.95
Grades: 4 5 6 7 **Fic**
1. Friendship -- Fiction 2. World War, 1939-1945 -- Fiction
ISBN 0-385-32142-2; 0-440-41453-9 pa; 9780385321426
LC 96-23021

A Newbery Medal honor book, 1998

"Set during World War II, this . . . story tells of the war's impact on two children, one an American and one a Hungarian refugee. Lily Mollahan, a spirited, sensitive youngster being raised by her grandmother and Poppy, her widower father, has a comfortable routine that includes the family's annual summer migration to Gram's beach house in Rockaway, NY. Lily looks forward to summer's freedom and fishing outings with Poppy. She meets Albert, a Hungarian boy who is staying at a neighbor's house. . . . Eventually the two become good friends. The war interferes directly with Lily's life when Poppy, an engineer, is sent to Europe to help with clean-up operations." (SLJ) "Grades five to eight." (Booklist)

"Gentle elements of danger and suspense . . . keep the plot moving forward, while the delicate balance of characters and setting gently coalesces into an emotional whole that is fully satisfying." Bull Cent Child Books

Maggie's door. Wendy Lamb Bks. 2003 158p pa $6.50
Grades: 5 6 7 8 **Fic**
1. Ireland -- Fiction 2. Immigrants -- Fiction
ISBN 0-385-32658-0; 0-385-90095-3 lib bdg; 0-440-41581-0 pa
LC 2003-2415

Sequel to: Nory Ryan's song (2000)

In the mid-1800s, Nory and her neighbor and friend, Sean, set out separately on a dangerous journey from famine-plagued Ireland, hoping to reach a better life in America

"Giff uses vivid language and precisely detailed observation to convey both experience and emotion." Horn Book

Nory Ryan's song. Delacorte Press 2000 148p hardcover o.p. pa $5.99
Grades: 5 6 7 8 **Fic**
1. Famines -- Fiction 2. Ireland -- Fiction
ISBN 0-385-32141-4; 0-440-41829-1 pa
LC 00-27690

When a terrible blight attacks Ireland's potato crop in 1845, twelve-year-old Nory Ryan's courage and ingenuity help her family and neighbors survive

"Giff brings the landscape and the cultural particulars of the era vividly to life and creates in Nory a heroine to cheer for. A beautiful, heart-wrenching novel that makes a devastating event understandable." Booklist

Another title about Nory is:
Maggie's door (2003)

★ **Pictures** of Hollis Woods. Wendy Lamb Bks. 2002 166p $15.95; pa $6.50
Grades: 5 6 7 8 **Fic**
1. Artists -- Fiction 2. Old age -- Fiction 3. Foster home care -- Fiction
ISBN 0-385-32655-6; 0-440-41578-0 pa
LC 2002-426

A Newbery Medal honor book, 2003

"She was named for the place where she was found as an abandoned baby. Twelve-year-old Hollis Woods has been through many foster homes—and she runs away, every time. In her latest placement, with an artist named Josie, the tightly wound Hollis begins to relax ever so slightly. . . . But Josie is slowly slipping into dementia, and Hollis knows that she'll be taken away from her if Josie is found out. . . . Giff has a sure hand with language, and the narrative is taut and absorbing." Booklist

R my name is Rachel. Wendy Lamb Books 2011 166p $15.99; lib bdg $18.99; e-book $10.99
Grades: 4 5 6 7 **Fic**

1. Moving -- Fiction 2. Siblings -- Fiction 3. Farm life -- Fiction 4. Great Depression, 1929-1939 -- Fiction
ISBN 978-0-375-83889-7; 0-375-83889-9; 978-0-375-93889-4 lib bdg; 0-375-93889-3; 978-0-375-98389-4 e-book
LC 2011004303

Three city siblings, now living on a farm during the Great Depression, must survive on their own when their father takes a construction job miles away.

"Rachel's searing, present-tense narrative exposes her fears, determination, and hopefulness in the face of wrenching challenges. Recurring motifs—color, flowers, and drawings by a neighbor that Rachel discovers in unlikely places—add lyricism to this story of family solidarity." Publ Wkly

Storyteller. Wendy Lamb Books 2010 166p $15.99; lib bdg $18.99
Grades: 5 6 7 8 **Fic**

1. Aunts -- Fiction 2. Family life -- Fiction 3. New York (State) -- Fiction 4. Father-daughter relationship -- Fiction 5. United States -- History -- 1775-1783, Revolution -- Fiction
ISBN 978-0-375-83888-0; 0-375-83888-0; 978-0-375-93888-7 lib bdg; 0-375-93888-5 lib bdg
LC 2009-48130

Forced to spend months at an aunt's house, Elizabeth feel a connection to her ancestor Zee, whose picture hangs on the wall, and who reveals her story of hardships during the Revolutionary War as Elizabeth comes to terms with her own troubles

"As she brings these characters and history alive, Giff again demostrates her own gift for storytelling." Publ Wkly

Water Street. Wendy Lamb Books 2006 164p $15.95; lib bdg $17.99; pa $6.50
Grades: 5 6 7 8 **Fic**

1. Family life -- Fiction 2. Irish Americans -- Fiction 3. Brooklyn (New York, N.Y.) -- Fiction
ISBN 978-0-385-90097-3; 0-385-73068-3; 978-0-385-90097-3 lib bdg; 0-385-90097-X lib bdg; 978-0-440-41921-1 pa; 0-440-41921-2 pa
LC 2006-02024

In the shadow of the construction of the Brooklyn Bridge, eighth-graders and new neighbors Bird Mallon and Thomas Neary make some decisions about what they want to do with their lives.

"Continuing the Irish American immigration story begun in Nory Ryan's Song (2000) and Maggie's Door (2003), [this] novel, set in 1875, is about the next generation. . . . A poignant immigration story of friendship, work, and the meaning of home." Booklist

Winter sky; by Patricia Reilly Giff. Wendy Lamb Books, an imprint of Random House Children's Books 2014 160 p. illustrations (hardback) $15.99
Grades: 4 5 6 7 **Fic**

1. Courage -- Fiction 2. Friendship -- Fiction 3. Family life -- Fiction 4. Fire fighters -- Fiction
ISBN 0375838929; 9780375838927; 9780385371926
LC 2013022399

In this book, by Patricia Reilly Giff, "Siria's dad is a firefighter who doesn't know that someone special watches out for him; each time his daughter hears a siren, she sneaks out of her apartment building to chase his fire truck and make sure he is safe. During one such nightly pursuit, Siria discovers evidence of what she believes to be arson. Who could be purposely setting fires? When clues point to someone close to home, Siria must find the strength to unravel the mystery." (School Library Journal)

"Worried about her firefighter father's safety, every time a siren wails eleven-year-old Siria sneaks out and chases the truck, watching to make sure he escapes harm. Over Christmas break, Siria notices small fires being set all over town and decides to investigate on her own. Unadorned but engaging prose and Giff's well-drawn characters add depth to a simple story about courage and friendship." Horn Book

Giles, Lamar

★ The **last** last-day-of-summer; by Lamar Giles, illustrated by Dapo Adeola. Houghton Mifflin Harcourt 2019 304 p. (hardback) $16.99
Grades: 4 5 6 7 **Fic**

1. Time -- Fiction 2. Adventure fiction 3. Cousins -- Fiction 4. Science fiction 5. Supernatural -- Fiction 6. African Americans -- Fiction 7. Adventure and adventurers -- Fiction
ISBN 9781328460837
LC 2018034805

In this book, by Lamar Giles, illustrated by Dapo Adeola, "Otto and Sheed are the local sleuths in their zany Virginia town, masters of unraveling mischief using their unmatched powers of deduction. And as the summer winds down and the first day of school looms, the boys are craving just a little bit more time for fun, even as they bicker over what kind of fun they want to have. That is, until a mysterious man appears with a camera that literally freezes time." (Publisher's note)

"With total mastery, Giles creates in Logan County an exuberant vortex of weirdness, where the commonplace sits cheek by jowl with the utterly fantastic, and populates it with memorable characters who more than live up to their setting." (Kirkus Reviews)

Overturned; Lamar Giles. Scholastic Press 2017 352 p. $17.99
Grades: 7 8 9 10 11 12 **Fic**

1. Poker -- Fiction 2. Murder -- Fiction 3. Casinos -- Fiction 4. Gambling -- Fiction 5. Las Vegas (Nev.) -- Fiction 6. African Americans -- Fiction 7. Fathers and daughters -- Fiction
ISBN 9780545812504
LC 2016035488

"A fast-paced, compelling mystery and memorable characters and relationships make this selection a first choice for most YA collections." (School Library Journal)

Spin; Lamar Giles. Scholastic Press 2019 400 p. $17.99
Grades: 7 8 9 10 **Fic**

1. Celebrities -- Fiction 2. Grief -- Fiction 3. Friendship -- Fiction 4. Disc jockeys -- Fiction 5. Murder -- Fiction 6. Fans (Persons) -- Fiction 7. African Americans -- Fiction 8. Detective and mystery stories
ISBN 9781338219210
LC 2018044097

In this novel, by Lamar Giles, "when rising star Paris Secord (aka DJ ParSec) is found dead on her turntables, it sends the local music scene reeling. No one is feeling that grief more than her shunned pre-fame best friend, Kya, and ParSec's chief groupie, Fuse. . . . As ParSec Nation takes to social media and the streets in their crusade for justice, Fuse and Kya start digging into Paris's past, stumbling across a deadly secret. With new info comes new motives. " (Publisher's note)

"This is genre fiction at its best: a taut mystery with rich characterization and a strong sense of place." Kirkus

Gill, David Macinnis

★ **Black** hole sun. Greenwillow Books 2010 340p $16.99
Grades: 8 9 10 11 12 **Fic**

1. Science fiction 2. Miners -- Fiction 3. Mars (Planet) -- Fiction
ISBN 0-06-167304-8; 978-0-06-167304-7

LC 2009-23050

"Now that life on Mars has evolved beyond mere survival, humans have increasingly brought their corruption and vices from Earth to the newly inhabited planet. As the story opens, Durango and his crew of teenage bounty hunters are working to liberate the daughter of a wealthy aristocrat from the clutches of a kidnapper. Their next assignment takes them to Mars's South Pole to defend poor miners against the attacks of savage cannibals. . . . High school." (Horn Book)

"Durango is the 16-year-old chief of a team of mercenaries who eke out a living on Mars by earning meager commissions for their dangerous work. Their current job, and the main thrust of this high-energy, action-filled, science-fiction romp, is to protect South Pole miners from the Dræu, a cannibalistic group who are after the miners' treasure. . . . Throughout the novel, the dialogue crackles with expertly delivered sarcastic wit and venom. . . . Readers will have a hard time turning the pages fast enough as the body count rises to the climactic, satisfying ending." Booklist

Invisible sun; by David Macinnis Gill. 1st ed. Greenwillow Books 2012 370 p. (Black Hole Sun Trilogy) (paperback) $9.99; (trade bdg.) $16.99
Grades: 8 9 10 11 **Fic**

1. Science fiction 2. Mars (Planet) -- Fiction 3. Adventure and adventurers -- Fiction
ISBN 9780062073334; 006207332X; 9780062073327

LC 2011002841

Sequel to Black Hole Sun.

This science fiction adventure story, by David Macinnis Gill, is the sequel to "Black Hole Sun," continuing to describe how "Martian freedom fighters Durango and Vienne infiltrate an evil government compound in search of missing data they hope will render the planet safe from future harm. This . . . novel is packed with . . . death-defying escapes, ambushes and . . . shootouts." (Kirkus)

Shadow on the sun; David Macinnis Gill. 1st ed. Greenwillow Books, an imprint of HarperCollins Publishers 2013 432 p. (Black Hole Sun Trilogy) (hardcover) $17.99
Grades: 8 9 10 11 **Fic**

1. Science fiction 2. Mars (Planet) -- Fiction
ISBN 0062073354; 9780062073358

LC 2013008361

This young adult science fiction novel, by David Macinnis Gill, is the sequel to "Invisible Sun." "Ex-Regulators Durango and Vienne are at it again in a race against time on a dangerous Martian landscape. Shocked to have learned that his father heads up the enemy forces who captured him at the end of the previous book, wisecracking teen soldier Durango fights to escape the clutches of his evil dad and to reunite with his ex-assassin sidekick and love interest, Vienne." (Kirkus Reviews)

"This sequel doesn't stand alone, and Gill inserts just enough left turns and red herrings to keep seasoned series readers guessing. . . . A refreshingly nondystopic sci-fi adventure." Kirkus

Gilman, Charles

Professor Gargoyle; Charlie Ward. Quirk Books 2012 175 p. (hardcover) $13.99
Grades: 7 8 9 10 **Fic**

1. Horror fiction 2. School stories 3. Monsters -- Fiction 4. Teachers -- Fiction 5. Middle schools -- Fiction
ISBN 1594745919; 9781594745911

LC 2011946052

"Strange things are happening at Lovecraft Middle School. Rats are leaping from lockers. Students are disappearing. The school library is a labyrinth of secret corridors. And the science teacher is acting very peculiar -- in fact, he just might be a monster-in-disguise. Twelve-year-old Robert Arthur knew that seventh grade was going to be weird, but this is ridiculous!" (Publisher's note)

Gilman, David

Blood sun. Delacorte Press 2011 (Danger zone) $17.99; lib bdg $20.99; e-book $10.00
Grades: 7 8 9 10 11 12 **Fic**

1. Mystery fiction 2. Adventure fiction 3. Rain forests -- Fiction 4. Great Britain -- Fiction 5. Central America -- Fiction 6. Wilderness survival -- Fiction 7. Environmental protection -- Fiction
ISBN 978-0-385-73562-9; 978-0-385-90548-0 lib bdg; 978-0-375-89809-9 e-book

LC 2010005169

Sequel to: Ice claw (2010)

Desperate to uncover the secret of his mother's death, fifteen-year-old Max Gordon, pursued by enemies, travels from the bleakness of Dartmoor to the rainforest of Central America, where the environmental devastation hides a sinister secret.

"Max Gordon is a likable character who faces tough challenges with determination, physical strength and a positive attitude. . . . This is . . . a solid read from start to breathless finish." Kirkus

The **devil's** breath. Delacorte Press 2008 391p (Danger zone) $15.99; lib bdg $18.99
Grades: 7 8 9 10 11 12 **Fic**

1. Adventure fiction 2. Namibia -- Fiction 3. Environmental protection -- Fiction
ISBN 978-0-385-73560-5; 978-0-385-90546-6 lib bdg

LC 2007-46744

When fifteen-year-old Max Gordon's environmentalist-adventurer father goes missing while working in Namibia and Max becomes the target of a would-be assassin at his school in England, he decides he must follow his father to Africa and find him before they both are killed.

"The action is relentless. . . . Gilman has a flair for making the preposterous seem possible." Booklist

Other titles in this series are:
Ice claw (2010)
Blood sun (2011)

Ice claw. Delacorte Press 2010 439p (Danger zone) $15.99; lib bdg $18.99
Grades: 7 8 9 10 11 12 **Fic**

1. Mystery fiction 2. Adventure fiction
ISBN 978-0-385-73561-2; 0-385-73561-8; 978-0-385-90547-3 lib bdg; 0-385-90547-5 lib bdg

LC 2009-13228

Sequel to: The Devil's breath (2008)

High in the French Pyrenees, fifteen-year-old Max Gordon's race to win an extreme sports challenge becomes a race to survive when he is accused of causing the death of a mysterious Basque monk who has predicted a cataclysmic ecological disaster

"The omniscent point of view . . . does a lot for clarity, which is his strong suit—few authors are able to depict action scenes so lucidly. . . . But it's Max's humanity . . . that makes Gilman's research and storytelling come alive." Booklist

Followed by: Blood sun (2011)

Gino, Alex

★ **George**; Alex Gino. Scholastic Press 2015 240 p. (jacketed hardcover) $16.99

Grades: 4 5 6 7 **Fic**

1. School stories 2. Identity (Psychology) 3. Gender role -- Fiction 4. Transgender people -- Fiction

ISBN 0545812542; 9780545812542

LC 2014957885

Lambda Literary Awards: LGBT Children's/Young Adult (2016)

Stonewall Book Award, Children's (2016)

In this novel by Alex Gino, "when people look at George, they think they see a boy. But she knows she's not a boy. She knows she's a girl. Then her teacher announces that their class play is going to be Charlotte's Web. George really, really, REALLY wants to play Charlotte. But the teacher says she can't even try out for the part. With the help of her best friend, Kelly, George comes up with a plan. Not just so she can be Charlotte -- but so everyone can know who she is, once and for all." (Publisher's note)

"George, a fourth-grader who knows she is a girl, despite appearances, begins to tell her secret. The word 'transgender' is used midway through, but far more work is done by the simple choice to tell George's story using third-person narration and the pronouns 'she' and 'her'. . . . A coda to the Charlotte's Web story, in which George presents herself as a girl for the first time, is deeply moving in its simplicity and joy. Warm, funny, and inspiring." Kirkus

Gipson, Frederick Benjamin

Old Yeller; [by] Fred Gipson; drawings by Carl Burger. Harper & Row 1956 158p il $23; pa $5.99

Grades: 6 7 8 9 **Fic**

1. Dogs -- Fiction 2. Texas -- Fiction 3. Frontier and pioneer life -- Fiction

ISBN 0-06-011545-9; 0-06-440382-3 pa

LC 56-8780

A Newbery Medal honor book, 1957

"Travis at fourteen was the man of the family during the hard summer of 1860 when his father drove his herd of cattle from Texas to the Kansas market. It was the summer when an old yellow dog attached himself to the family and won Travis' reluctant friendship. Before the summer was over, Old Yeller proved more than a match for thieving raccoons, fighting bulls, grizzly bears, and mad wolves. This is a skillful tale of a boy's love for a dog as well as a description of a pioneer boyhood and it can't miss with any dog lover." Horn Book

Gläser, Mechthild

The **book** jumper; Mechthild Gläser, translated by Romy Fursland. Henry Holt & Co. 2017 384 p. (hardback) $17.99; (ebook) $60

Grades: 8 9 10 **Fic**

1. Books and reading -- Fiction 2. Characters in literature -- Fiction

ISBN 9781250086662; 9781250086679

LC 2016007363

In this book, by Mechthild Gläser, translated by Romy Fursland, "Amy Lennox . . . and her mother . . . [leave] for Scotland, heading to her mother's childhood home of Lennox House. . . . Amy must read while she resides at Lennox House—but not in the usual way. It turns out that Amy is a book jumper, able to leap into a story and interact with the world inside. As thrilling as Amy's new power is, it also brings danger: someone is stealing from the books she visits." (Publisher's note)

"This offering is the first U.S. title from an award-winning German author and would be a good additional purchase for fans of Cornelia Funke's Inkheart or Kristin Kladstrup'sThe Book of Story Beginnings." SLJ

Glatstein, Jacob

Emil and Karl; by Yankev Glatshteyn; translated by Jeffrey Shandler. Roaring Brook Press 2006 194p $17.95; pa $6.99

Grades: 5 6 7 8 **Fic**

1. Jews -- Fiction 2. Friendship -- Fiction 3. Vienna (Austria) -- Fiction 4. Holocaust, 1933-1945 -- Fiction

ISBN 1-59643-119-9; 0-312-37387-2 pa

LC 2005-26800

Original Yiddish edition 1940

A story about the dilemma faced by two young boys—one Jewish, the other not—when they suddenly find themselves without homes or families in Vienna on the eve of World War II.

"The fast-moving prose is stark and immediate. Glatshteyn was, of course, writing about what was happening to children in his time. . . . The translation, 65 years after the novel's original publication, is nothing short of haunting." Booklist

Gleason, Colleen

The **clockwork** scarab; Colleen Gleason. Chronicle Books 2013 356 p. (Stoker & Holmes) (alk. paper) $17.99

Grades: 7 8 9 10 **Fic**

1. Mystery fiction 2. Historical fiction 3. Scarabs -- Fiction 4. Time travel -- Fiction 5. Secret societies -- Fiction 6. Detective and mystery stories 7. Mystery and detective stories 8. Great Britain -- History -- 1837-1901 -- Fiction 9. London (England) -- History -- 19th century -- Fiction

ISBN 1452110700; 9781452110707

LC 2012036578

This is the first book in Colleen Gleason's Stoker and Holmes series. The "narrative switches between two young women living in 1889 London: observant and cerebral Alvermina Holmes (she goes by Mina . . .), the niece of Sherlock Holmes; and Evaline Stoker, the headstrong (and physically strong) younger sister to Bram, and member of a proud line of vampire hunters." They "investigate the connection between the disappearance of a young woman and several recent murders." (Publishers Weekly)

Other titles in this series are:

The spiritglass charade (2014)

The chess queen enigma (2015)

The carnelian crow (2017)

Gleitzman, Morris

Now; Morris Gleitzman. Henry Holt 2012 184 p. (hc) $16.99

Grades: 7 8 9 10 **Fic**

1. Psychological fiction 2. Family life -- Fiction 3. Grandfathers -- Fiction 4. Holocaust survivors -- Fiction 5. Australia -- Fiction 6. Wildfires -- Fiction 7. Jews -- Australia -- Fiction 8. Separation (Psychology) -- Fiction

ISBN 0805093788; 9780805093780

LC 2011033496

Sequel to: Then

This novel by Morris Gleitzman is "[s]et in the current day, this is the final book in the series that began with Once, continued with Then and is . . . Now. . . . While her physician-parents are working in Africa, eleven-year-old Zelda is living with her grandfather, eighty-year-old Holocaust-survivor Felix Salinger, in Australia . . . He has achieved much in his life and is widely admired in the community. He has mostly buried the painful memories of his childhood . . . when a disaster leads them both to deal with unresolved feelings about the first Zelda, Felix's childhood friend." (Publisher's note)

★ **Once**. Henry Holt and Company 2010 163p $16.99
Grades: 7 8 9 10 **Fic**

1. Jews -- Poland -- Fiction 2. Holocaust, 1933-1945 -- Fiction
ISBN 978-0-8050-9026-0; 0-8050-9026-6
LC 2009-24153

"The horror of the Holocaust is told here through the eyes of a Polish Jewish child, Felix, who loses his innocence as he witnesses Nazi-led roundups, shootings, and deportations. . . . Most moving is the lack of any idealization. . . . Felix escapes, but one and a half million Jewish children did not, and this gripping novel will make readers want to find out more about them." Booklist

Followed by: Then (2011)

Then. Henry Holt 2010 198p $16.99
Grades: 7 8 9 10 **Fic**

1. Poland -- Fiction 2. Orphans -- Fiction 3. Jews -- Poland -- Fiction 4. Holocaust, 1933-1945 -- Fiction 5. World War, 1939-1945 -- Fiction
ISBN 978-0-8050-9027-7; 0-8050-9027-4
LC 2009050774

Sequel to: Once (2010)

In early 1940s Poland, ten-year-old Felix and his friend Zelda escape from a cattle car headed to the Nazi death camps and struggle to survive, first on their own and then with Genia, a farmer with her own reasons for hating Germans.

"There is no triumphant climax, and right up until the shocking end, the story of hidden children will grab readers with its details of the daily tension of rescue and betrayal." Booklist

Glewwe, Eleanor

Sparkers; Eleanor Glewwe. Viking, published by the Penguin Group 2014 336 p. (hardcover) $16.99
Grades: 5 6 7 8 9 **Fic**

1. Fantasy fiction 2. Magic -- Fiction 3. Diseases -- Fiction 4. Social classes -- Fiction 5. Fantasy
ISBN 0451468767; 9780451468765
LC 2013038475

In this book, by Eleanor Glewwe, "Marah Levi is halani--one of the lower class, unable to do magic like members of the elite class, the kasiri. . . . When she impulsively saves a young kasir girl, Sarah, from being hurt in a crowd, the girl invites her home, where she finds a kindred spirit in Sarah's brother Azariah. . . . Together they find the cure for a disease. . . . Their work uncovers a sinister plot, however, putting them in grave danger." (Bulletin of the Center for Children's books)

"An unusual protagonist and a South Asian inspired setting make this a promising fantasy debut." Horn Book

Wildings; Eleanor Glewwe. Viking Childrens Books 2016 336 p. (ebook) $50.97; (hardback) $16.99
Grades: 5 6 7 8 9 **Fic**

1. Fantasy fiction 2. Magic -- Fiction 3. Twins -- Fiction 4. Brothers and sisters -- Fiction 5. Fantasy
ISBN 9780698151253; 9780451468857
LC 2016014413

In this young adult fantasy novel, by Eleanor Glewwe, "Rivka is one of the magical elite and the daughter of an important ambassador. But she harbors a deep secret: She once had a twin brother, Arik. When Arik failed to develop his own magical abilities, the government declared him a wilding, removed him from his home, placed him with non-magical adoptive parents, and forbade him any contact with his birth family. . . . But Rivka refuses to forget her twin brother." (Publisher's note)

"Rivka and her friends are strong-willed, fiercely intelligent, and fearless as they set out to take down the status quo." Pub Wkly

Goelman, Ari

The **path** of names; by Ari Goelman. Arthur A. Levine Books 2013 352 p. (hard cover : alk. paper) $16.99
Grades: 7 8 9 10 **Fic**

1. Ghost stories -- Fiction 3. Mystery fiction -- Fiction 4. Camps -- Fiction 5. Magic -- Fiction 6. Cabala -- Fiction 7. Labyrinths -- Fiction 8. Magic tricks -- Fiction 9. Brothers and sisters -- Fiction 10. Jews -- United States -- Fiction
ISBN 0545474302; 9780545474306; 9780545474313; 9780545540148
LC 2012030554

This book features Dahlia whom "her parents have sent . . . to Camp Arava. . . . When Dahlia first sees two young girls disappear through the cabin wall, she's convinced it's a great magic trick, but soon she realizes that they're actually ghosts. . . . These strange phenomena begin to converge around a mysterious garden maze on the campgrounds, a maze that is rumored to be connected to the disappearance of children and that is ferociously guarded by the skulking camp caretaker." (Bulletin of the Center for Children's Books)

"Thirteen-year-old magic nerd Dahlia loathes her Jewish summer camp until she starts dreaming about a Jewish teen in 1940s New York City who seems to be connected to a pair of ghosts haunting the camp. Readers with an interest in Jewish mysticism will enjoy the book's paranormal elements and tweens will appreciate the realistic relationships among the campers." (Horn Book)

Going, K. L.

The **garden** of Eve. Harcourt 2007 234p $17; pa $6.99
Grades: 4 5 6 7 **Fic**

1. Death -- Fiction 2. Magic -- Fiction 3. Bereavement -- Fiction 4. New York (State) -- Fiction
ISBN 978-0-15-205986-6; 0-15-205986-5; 978-0-15-206614-7 pa; 0-15-206614-4 pa
LC 2007-05074

Eve gave up her belief in stories and magic after her mother's death, but a mysterious seed given to her as an eleventh-birthday gift by someone she has never met takes her and a boy who claims to be a ghost on a strange journey, to where their supposedly cursed town of Beaumont, New York, flourishes.

"Believably and with delicacy, Going paints a suspenseful story suffused with the poignant questions of what it means to be alive, and what might await on the other side." Horn Book

Goldblatt, Mark

Finding the worm; Mark Goldblatt. Random House Inc 2015 352 p. (lib. bdg.) $19.99
Grades: 5 6 7 8 **Fic**

1. School discipline 2. Teenagers -- Fiction 3. Vandalism -- Fiction 4. Friendship -- Fiction 5. Bar mitzvah -- Fiction 6. Conduct of life -- Fiction 7. Jews -- United States -- Fiction 8. Queens (New

York, N.Y.) -- History -- 20th century -- Fiction
ISBN 0385391099; 9780385391085; 9780385391092
LC 2014004052

Sequel to: Twerp

In this novel by Mark Goldblatt "trouble always seems to find thirteen-year-old Julian Twerski. He's been accused of vandalizing a painting. The principal doesn't want to suspend him again, so instead, he asks Julian to write a 200-word essay on good citizenship. Being falsely accused is bad enough, but outside of school, Julian's dealing with even bigger issues. His friend Quentin has been really sick. How can life be fair when the nicest guy in your group has cancer?" (Publishers' note)

"Julian Twerski and the gang from Twerp (Random, 2013) are now in seventh grade, and it seems like they're dealing with an even bigger set of challenges than last year. . . . Goldblatt takes advantage of Julian's newfound love of writing, adding an honest and forthright tone to the boy's journal entries. A wide variety of readers will relate to Julian's questions about fairness, faith, and friendship.." SLJ

Twerp; Mark Goldblatt. Random House Inc 2013 288 p. $16.99

Grades: 6 7 8 **Fic**

1. School stories 2. Diaries -- Fiction 3. Friendship -- Fiction 4. Conduct of life -- Fiction 5. Self-realization -- Fiction 6. Interpersonal relations -- Fiction 7. Queens (New York, N.Y.) -- Fiction 8. Schools -- Fiction 9. Queens (New York, N.Y.) -- History -- 20th century -- Fiction
ISBN 0375971424; 9780375971426
LC 2012005033

In this book, by Mark Goldblatt, "Julian Twerski isn't a bully. He's just made a big mistake. So when he returns to school after a weeklong suspension, his English teacher offers him a deal: if he keeps a journal and writes about the terrible incident that got him and his friends suspended, he can get out of writing a report on Shakespeare. Julian jumps at the chance. And so begins his account of life in sixth grade." (Publisher's note)

Golden, Christopher

The **sea** wolves; by Christopher Golden & Tim Lebbon ; with illustrations by Greg Ruth. Harper 2012 384 p. $16.99

Grades: 7 8 9 10 **Fic**

1. Sea stories 2. Adventure fiction 3. Monsters -- Fiction 4. Pirates -- Fiction 5. Supernatural -- Fiction
ISBN 0061863203; 9780061863202; 9780061863219
LC 2011010031

This young adult fantasy adventure novel by Christopher Golden and Tim Lebbon follows "Jack London . . . a writer who lived his own real-life adventures. But . . . even he couldn't set down [all his adventures] in writing. Terrifying, mysterious, bizarre, and magical. . . . Clinging to life after he is captured in an attack by savage pirates, Jack is unprepared for what he faces at the hands of the crew and their charismatic, murderous captain, Ghost. For these mariners are not mortal men but hungry beasts chasing gold and death across the North Pacific. Jack's only hope lies with Sabine—a sad, sultry captive of Ghost's insatiable hunger. But on these waters, nothing is as it seems, and Sabine may be hiding dangerous secrets of her own." (Publisher's note)

The **wild**; by Christopher Golden & Tim Lebbon; with illustrations by Greg Ruth. Harper 2011 348p il (The secret journeys of Jack London) $15.99; lib bdg $16.89

Grades: 7 8 9 10 **Fic**

1. Authors 2. Novelists 3. Adventure fiction 4. Wolves -- Fiction 5. Short story writers 6. Supernatural -- Fiction 7. Wilderness survival -- Fiction 8. Gold mines and mining -- Fiction 9. Yukon River valley (Yukon and Alaska) -- Fiction
ISBN 978-0-06-186317-2; 0-06-186317-3; 978-0-06-186318-9 lib bdg; 0-06-186318-1 lib bdg
LC 2010-07475

Seventeen-year-old Jack London makes the arduous journey to the Yukon's gold fields in 1893, becoming increasingly uneasy about supernatural forces in the wilderness that seem to have taken a special interest in him.

"Golden and Lebbon write with a gritty assurance that brings the fantasy elements . . . down to earth. . . . Occasional sketches add a bit of cinematic drama." Booklist

Golden, Laura

Every day after; Laura Golden. 1st ed. Delacorte Press 2013 216 p. (ebook) $47.97; (library) $18.99; (hardcover) $15.99

Grades: 5 6 7 **Fic**

1. Historical fiction -- Fiction 2. Great Depression, 1929-1939 -- Fiction 3. Self-reliance -- Fiction 4. Family problems -- Fiction 5. Abandoned children -- Fiction 6. Depressions -- 1929 -- Fiction 7. Alabama -- History -- 1819-1950 -- Fiction
ISBN 0385743262; 9780307983121; 9780375991035; 9780385743266
LC 2012015770

This book, set in 1932 in small-town Alabama, "details the struggles and injustices facing 11-year-old Lizzie Hawkins after her father loses his job and leaves town. Stuck with an overdue mortgage and a mother paralyzed by depression, Lizzie believes she just has to hold it together until her father returns, as she is sure he will." (Publishers Weekly)

Golding, Julia

Cat among the pigeons; a Cat Royal adventure. [by] Julia Golding. 1st ed.; Roaring Brook Press 2008 368p (Cat Royal Quartet) $16.95

Grades: 6 7 8 9 **Fic**

1. Orphans -- Fiction 2. Slavery -- Fiction 3. Theater -- Fiction 4. London (England) -- Fiction 5. Drury Lane Theatre (London, England) -- Fiction 6. Great Britain -- History -- 1714-1837 -- Fiction
ISBN 978-1-5964-3352-6; 1-5964-3352-3
LC 2008020292

Sequel to: The diamond of Drury Lane (2008)

First published 2006 in the United Kingdom

Catherine "Cat" Royal, an orphan who lives at the Drury Lane Theater in 1790s London, rallies her friends to try to save Pedro from the clutches of Mr. Hawkins, a slavemaster who considers Pedro his property.

"Golding weaves a fine historic tale . . . by way of an ensemble of colorful characters, death-defying adventures, witty dialogue and narration, and lively action." Booklist

Followed by: Den of thieves (2009)

Cat o' nine tails; a Cat Royal adventure. Roaring Brook Press 2009 379p map (Cat Royal Quartet) $16.99

Grades: 6 7 8 9 **Fic**

1. Adventure fiction 2. Orphans -- Fiction 3. Seafaring life -- Fiction 4. Voyages and travels -- Fiction
ISBN 978-1-59643-445-5; 1-59643-445-7

First published 2008 in United Kingdom

While staying at the seaside, Catherine "Cat" Royal and her friends are captured and pressed into service in the British Navy and Cat, once again disguised as a boy, travels to the New World with survival her only goal.

"This whirlwind adventure is action-packed." SLJ

Den of thieves; a Cat Royal adventure. Roaring Brook Press 2009 417p map (Cat Royal adventure) $16.95
Grades: 6 7 8 9 **Fic**

1. Spies -- Fiction 2. Orphans -- Fiction 3. France -- History -- 1789-1799, Revolution -- Fiction
ISBN 978-1-59643-444-8; 1-59643-444-9
Sequel to: Cat among the pigeons (2008)

"Series fans will once again be treated to a look at the fiery-tempered redhead, always in trouble, who charms commoners and gentry alike." Booklist

★ The **diamond** of Drury Lane. Roaring Brook Press 2008 424p (Cat Royal Quartet) $16.99; pa $7.99
Grades: 6 7 8 9 **Fic**

1. Orphans -- Fiction 2. Theater -- Fiction 3. London (England) -- Fiction 4. Drury Lane Theatre (London, England) -- Fiction 5. Great Britain -- History -- 1714-1837 -- Fiction
ISBN 978-1-59643-351-9; 1-59643-351-5; 978-0-312-56123-9 pa; 0-312-56123-7 pa

LC 2007-23604

Orphan Catherine "Cat" Royal, living at the Drury Lane Theater in 1790s London, tries to find the "diamond" supposedly hidden in the theater, which unmasks a treasonous political cartoonist, and involves her in the street gangs of Covent Garden and the world of nobility.

This is "a story with as many cliff-hangers as there are chapters. But the real thrills also come from the varied, sharply drawn cast. . . . [Golding] offers a view of London readers can grasp with all their senses." Booklist

Other titles in this series are:
Cat among the pigeons (2008)
Den of thieves (2009)
Cat o' nine tails (2009)

Golding, William

Lord of the flies; introduction by E. M. Forster; with a biographical and critical note by E. L. Epstein; illustrated by Ben Gibson. 50th anniversary ed; Berkley 2003 315p $23.95; pa $13
Grades: 8 9 10 11 12 **Fic**

1. Allegories 2. Boys -- Fiction 3. Survival after airplane accidents, shipwrecks, etc. -- Fiction
ISBN 0-399-52920-9; 0-399-50148-7 pa

LC 2003-54825

First published 1954 in the United Kingdom; first United States edition, 1955, by Coward-McCann

"Stranded on an island, a group of English schoolboys leave innocence behind in a struggle for survival. A political structure modeled after English government is set up and a hierarchy develops, but forces of anarchy and aggression surface. The boys' existence begins to degenerate into a savage one. They are rescued from their microcosmic society to return to an adult, stylized milieu filled with the same psychological tensions and moral voids. Adventure and allegory are brilliantly combined in this novel." Shapiro. Fic for Youth. 3d edition

Golds, Cassandra

The **museum** of Mary Child. Kane Miller 2009 329p $16.99
Grades: 6 7 8 9 10 **Fic**

1. Dolls -- Fiction 2. Museums -- Fiction
ISBN 978-1-935279-13-6; 1-935279-13-0

LC 2009-922719

"Lonely Heloise wants only to be loved, but lives as if jailed in the house of her stern and sometimes cruel godmother. One day Heloise uncovers a beautiful doll, Maria, hidden under the floorboards of her room, and it is love at first sight. Heloise hides Maria from her godmother, whose personal Ten Commandments include forbidding play, 'pretty clothes' and the possession of a doll. . . . Once Maria is discovered, Heloise finds out the horrible truth about the museum that adjoins her godmother's cottage and is thrust down a strange and magical path that reveals how sheltered she has been. . . . Golds's novel is pure fun, filled with mystery and nearly impossible to put down." Publ Wkly

Goldstyn, Jacques

The **eleventh** hour; Written and illustrated by Jacques Goldstyn. Owlkids Books, Inc. 2018 64 p. (hardcover) $18.95
Grades: 5 6 7 8 **Fic**

1. Friendship -- Fiction 2. World War, 1914-1918 -- France -- Fiction
ISBN 9781771473484

LC 2018934227

In this book, by Jacques Goldstyn, "Jim and Jules are childhood friends, born on the same day in the same village. All their lives, Jim has been first — born two minutes before Jules, always faster, always stronger. When the First World War breaks out in Europe, the two young men enlist in the fight. . . . On November 11, 1918, Jim and Jules are sent out to fight one last time. Jim, always first over the top of the trench, is shot and dies at 10:58am." (Publisher's note)

Gonzalez, Christina Diaz, 1969-

Moving target; Christina Diaz Gonzalez. Scholastic Press 2015 248 p. illustrations (ebook) $6.99; (hardcover) $17.99
Grades: 4 5 6 7 8 **Fic**

1. Italy -- Fiction 2. Murder -- Fiction 3. Holy Lance -- Fiction 4. Rome (Italy) -- Fiction 5. Secret societies -- Fiction 6. Americans -- Italy -- Fiction 7. Mystery and detective stories
ISBN 9780545773201; 0545773180; 9780545773188

LC 2014038851

In this middle grade novel by Christina Diaz Gonzalez, "Cassie Arroyo, an American studying in Rome, has her world ripped apart when someone tries to kill her father, an art history professor. . . . [Cassie learns] that she is a member of an ancient bloodline that enables her to use the Spear of Destiny--a legendary object that can alter the future. . . . Cassie must--with the help of some friends--decipher the clues that will lead her to the Spear." (Publisher's note)

"An adventure that will keep readers engaged until the cliffhanger ending and leave them waiting for the next book." Kirkus

★ The **red** umbrella. Alfred A. Knopf 2010 284p $16.99; lib bdg $19.99
Grades: 6 7 8 9 **Fic**

1. Cuba -- Fiction 2. Family life -- Fiction
ISBN 0375861904; 0375961909 lib bdg; 9780375861901; 9780375961908 lib bdg

LC 2009022309

In 1961 after Fidel Castro comes to power in Cuba, fourteen-year-old Lucia and her seven-year-old brother are sent to the United States because her parents fear that the children will be taken away from them as others have been. "Grades five to eight." (Bull Cent Child Books)

"The pain of the revolution for those who disagreed is made clear and pressing, and the text manages to balance between being informative and entertaining. This could prove a helpful tie-in for classroom history lessons or a solid recommendation for fans of quietly engaging historical fiction." Bull Cent Child Books

Gonzalez, Julie

Imaginary enemy. Delacorte Press 2008 241p $15.99; lib bdg $18.99

Grades: 6 7 8 9 10 **Fic**

1. Imaginary playmates -- Fiction

ISBN 978-0-385-73552-0; 0-385-73552-9; 978-0-385-90530-5 lib bdg; 0-385-90530-0 lib bdg

LC 2007-45752

Although her impetuous behavior, smart-mouthed comments, and slacker ways have landed her in trouble over the years, sixteen-year-old Jane has always put the blame on her "imaginary enemy," until a new development forces her to decide whether or not to assume responsibility for her actions.

"Gonzalez has written a witty, realistic novel . . . peppered with funny, authentic dialogue." Booklist

Goobie, Beth

Before wings; a novel. Orca Bk. Pubs. 2001 203p hardcover o.p. pa $8.95

Grades: 7 8 9 10 **Fic**

1. Camps -- Fiction 2. Death -- Fiction

ISBN 1-55143-161-0; 1-55143-163-7 pa

LC 00-105582

"Full of magic realism and beautifully written, this is a story of good triumphing over evil, life triumphing over death, the power of love, friendship, and the hope for an afterlife." Booklist

Goodman, Alison

The **Dark** Days Club; Alison Goodman. Viking 2016 496 p. (hardcover) $18.99

Grades: 8 9 10 11 12 **Fic**

1. Secrets -- Fiction 2. Conspiracies -- Fiction 3. Supernatural -- Fiction 4. London (England) -- Fiction 5. Courts and courtiers -- Fiction 6. Great Britain -- History -- 1714-1837 -- Fiction 7. Great Britain -- History -- 1800-1837 -- Fiction 8. London (England) -- History -- 19th century -- Fiction

ISBN 9780670785476

LC 2015006792

In this book, by Alison Goodman, "Lady Helen Wrexhall is on the eve of her debut presentation at the royal court of George III. Her life should revolve around gowns, dancing, and securing a suitable marriage. Instead, when one of her family's maids disappears, she is drawn into the shadows of Regency London. There, she meets Lord Carlston, one of the few able to stop the perpetrators: a cabal of demons that has infiltrated all levels of society." (Publisher's note)

"Readers willing to embrace the deep, deliberately paced journey will find the pace and tension increasing until the end leaves them eager for the next volume." Kirkus

Another title in this series is:
The Dark Days Pact (2017)

★ **Eon** : Dragoneye reborn. Viking 2009 531p $19.99

Grades: 7 8 9 10 **Fic**

1. Fantasy fiction 2. Magic -- Fiction 3. Dragons -- Fiction 4. Sex role -- Fiction 5. Apprentices -- Fiction

ISBN 978-0-670-06227-0; 0-670-06227-8

LC 2008-33223

Sixteen-year-old Eon hopes to become an apprentice to one of the twelve energy dragons of good fortune and learn to be its main interpreter, but to do so will require much, including keeping secret that she is a girl.

"Entangled politics and fierce battle scenes provide a pulse-quickening pace, while the intriguing characters add interest and depth." Booklist

Followed by: Eona: The last Dragoneye (2011)

Eona : the last Dragoneye. Viking 2011 637p il $19.99

Grades: 7 8 9 10 **Fic**

1. Fantasy fiction 2. Magic -- Fiction 3. Dragons -- Fiction 4. Apprentices -- Fiction

ISBN 978-0-670-06311-6; 0-670-06311-8

LC 2011-02997

Sequel to: Eon: Dragoneye reborn (2009)

Eon has been revealed as Eona, the first female Dragoneye in hundreds of years. Along with fellow rebels Ryko and Lady Dela, she is on the run from High Lord Sethon's army. The renegades are on a quest for the black folio, stolen by the drug-riddled Dillon; they must also find Kygo, the young Pearl Emperor, who needs Eona's power and the black folio if he is to wrest back his throne from the selfstyled "Emperor" Sethon.

"One of those rare and welcome fantasies that complicate black-and-white morality." Kirkus

Singing the Dogstar blues. Viking 2003 261p $16.99

Grades: 7 8 9 10 **Fic**

1. Science fiction 2. Australia -- Fiction

ISBN 0-670-03610-2

LC 2002-12161

First published 1998 in Australia

In a future Australia, the saucy eighteen-year-old daughter of a famous newscaster and a sperm donor teams up with a hermaphrodite from the planet Choria in a time travel adventure that may significantly change both of their lives

"This wildly entertaining novel successfully mixes adventure, humor, mystery, and sf into a fast-paced, thrilling story that will apeal to a wide audience." Booklist

Gordon, Roderick

Closer; [by] Roderick Gordon, Brian Williams. Chicken House 2011 527p $18.99

Grades: 6 7 8 9 **Fic**

1. Adventure fiction 2. Archeology -- Fiction 3. London (England) -- Fiction

ISBN 978-0-545-20115-5; 0-545-20115-2

LC 2010035754

Sequel to: Freefall (2010)

Will Burrows believes he is safe at the very center of the earth, in a world that no one knows exists, but the Styx are close behind and will follow him anywhere, while on the surface, Drake and some unlikely allies unearth some critical secrets.

"There is a lot of action; lively dialogue; diabolical villains and feisty teens; clever catlike companion hunters; things that blow up; torture and mind manipulation; family and friends in danger; and trust and betrayal. . . . This is a great science fiction adventure series for boys, and of course, girls will enjoy it as well." Voice Youth Advocates

Deeper; [by] Roderick Gordon, Brian Williams. Scholastic 2009 643p $18.99

Grades: 6 7 8 9 **Fic**

1. Adventure fiction 2. Archeology -- Fiction 3. London (England)

-- Fiction
ISBN 978-0-439-87178-5; 0-439-87178-6
LC 2008-13703

Sequel to: Tunnels (2008)

As Will Burrows continues to search for his lost archaeologist father in the strange underground world he has discovered, he stumbles across a sinister plot with terrible implications for the world above.

"This page-turner has lots of action and deeds of derring-do for fans of dark, dystopian fantasies." Voice Youth Advocates

Followed by: Freefall (2010)

Freefall; [by] Roderick Gordon, Brian Williams. Chicken House 2010 599p $18.99

Grades: 6 7 8 9 **Fic**

1. Adventure fiction 2. London (England) -- Fiction
ISBN 978-0-545-13877-2; 0-545-13877-9

Sequel to: Deeper (2009)

As fourteen-year-old archaeologist Will and his friends plummet down a subterranean pore, they face deadly creatures and discover a strange fungal shelf, which not only reveals artifacts from ancient civilizations, but clues to a lost land at the end of the Earth.

Tunnels; [by] Roderick Gordon, Brian Williams. Chicken House/Scholastic 2008 480p il $17.99

Grades: 6 7 8 9 **Fic**

1. Adventure fiction 2. London (England) -- Fiction
ISBN 978-0-439-87177-8; 0-439-87177-8
LC 2007-09169

When Will Burrows and his friend Chester embark on a quest to find Will's archaeologist father, who has inexplicably disappeared, they are led to a labyrinthine world underneath London, full of sinister inhabitants with evil intentions toward "Topsoilers" like Will and his father.

This is "compelling. . . . The authors add distinctive, vivid touches to the . . . premise . . . and the murderous, refreshingly competant Styx makes an uncommonly challenging adversary." Booklist

Other titles in this series are:
Deeper (2009)
Freefall (2010)
Closer (2011)

Gosselink, John

The **defense** of Thaddeus A. Ledbetter; a novel. drawings by Jason Rosenstock. Amulet Books 2010 231p il $14.95

Grades: 4 5 6 7 **Fic**

1. School stories
ISBN 978-0-8109-8977-1; 0-8109-8977-8
LC 2009052209

Twelve-year-old Thaddeus A. Ledbetter, who considers it a duty to share his knowledge and talent with others, refutes each of the charges which have sent him to "In-School Suspension" for the remainder of seventh grade.

"This original and entertaining book, with its smarty-pants narrator and case-file format, will draw comparisons to the Wimpy Kid series." Booklist

Goto, Hiromi

★ **Half** World; illustrations by Jillian Tamaki. Viking 2010 221p il $16.99

Grades: 7 8 9 10 **Fic**

1. Fantasy fiction 2. Mother-daughter relationship -- Fiction
ISBN 978-0-670-01220-6; 0-670-01220-3

"Raised in impoverished circumstances by her single mother, overweight 14-year-old Melanie is the target of ridicule at school and leads a lonely, introverted life. Then an evil being named Mr. Glueskin kidnaps her mother, forcing Melanie to travel to Half World, a colorless land that has been sundered from the realms of flesh and spirit, its deceased inhabitants cursed to relive the most traumatic moments of their lives. . . . Goto writes the hellish Half World as miserably surreal yet horrifyingly believable. . . . It's a fast-moving and provocative journey with cosmically high stakes, and one that should readily appeal to fans of dark, nightmarish fantasy." Publ Wkly

Gourlay, Candy

★ **Tall** story. David Fickling Books 2011 295p $16.99; $19.99

Grades: 6 7 8 9 **Fic**

1. Size -- Fiction 2. Giants -- Fiction 3. Siblings -- Fiction 4. Basketball -- Fiction 5. Philippines -- Fiction 6. Culture conflict -- Fiction 7. London (England) -- Fiction
ISBN 0385752172; 0385752180 lib bdg; 978-0-385-75217-6; 9780385752183 lib bdg
LC 2010011891

In this book, "Bernardo, who suffers from gigantism, lives in a world where real life and magic collide. . . . To his younger sister, Andi, born and raised in London, Bernardo is both the brother she has always loved and the freakishly tall boy who is going to draw way too much attention at school. . . . When an earthquake devastates San Andres just after Bernardo leaves, he's sure it's his fault. He believes that he brings destruction and danger wherever he goes, but everyone else thinks that Bernardo brings miracles." (School Library Journal)

"This will capture the hearts and minds of sports lovers—and just about everyone else as well." Booklist

Grabenstein, Chris

Beach party surf monkey; by Chris Grabenstein ; illustrations by Brooke Allen. Random House 2017 320 p. illustrations (Welcome to Wonderland) (hardcover) $13.99

Grades: 4 5 6 7 **Fic**

1. Florida -- Fiction 2. Hotels and motels -- Fiction 3. Motion pictures -- Production and direction -- Fiction
ISBN 9780553536102; 9780553536119; 9780553536133
LC 2016014007

In this book, by Chris Grabenstein, illustrated by Brooke Allen, "there's always something wacky happening when you live in a motel, and P.T. . . . has grown up at the world's wackiest! When word gets out that the hottest teen idols in Hollywood (plus current YouTube sensation Kevin the Monkey!) will be filming their next movie—Beach Party Surf Monkey—right in St. Pete's Beach, Florida, P.T. and his friend Gloria know that the Wonderland would be the perfect location." (Publisher's note)

The **black** heart crypt; a haunted mystery. Random House 2011 328p (Haunted places mystery) $16.99; lib bdg $19.99; e-book $16.99

Grades: 5 6 7 8 **Fic**

1. Ghost stories 2. Mystery fiction 3. Demonology -- Fiction
ISBN 978-0-375-86900-6; 0-375-86900-X; 978-0-375-96900-3 lib bdg; 0-375-96900-4 lib bdg; 978-0-375-89987-4 e-book
LC 2011001939

A 200-year-old ghost inhabits a living ancestor in order to take revenge on eleven-year-old Zack and his family.

"The pace never flags. Through flurries of ultrashort chapters, events spiral to a suspenseful climax, and the mix of corpses and comedy add up to a faintly macabre tone that isn't dispelled even by the end's just deserts and happy outcomes." Kirkus

The **crossroads**. Random House 2008 325p (Haunted places mystery) $16.99; lib bdg $19.99; pa $6.99
Grades: 5 6 7 8 **Fic**

1. Ghost stories 2. Connecticut -- Fiction 3. Stepmothers -- Fiction
ISBN 978-0-375-84697-7; 0-375-84697-2; 978-0-375-94697-4 lib bdg; 0-375-94697-7 lib bdg; 978-0-375-84698-4 pa; 0-375-84698-0 pa

LC 2007024803

When eleven-year-old Zack Jennings moves to Connecticut with his father and new stepmother, they must deal with the ghosts left behind by a terrible accident, as well as another kind of ghost from Zack's past

"An absorbing psychological thriller . . . as well as a rip-roaring ghost story, this switches points of view among humans, trees, and ghosts with astonishing élan." Booklist

Other titles in this series are:
The Hanging Hill (2009)
The smoky corridor (2010)
The Black Heart Crypt (2011)

★ **Escape** from Mr. Lemoncello's library; Chris Grabenstein. 1st ed. Random House Inc. 2013 304 p. (hardcover) $16.99; (library) $19.99
Grades: 5 6 7 **Fic**

1. Contests -- Fiction 2. Games -- Fiction 3. Libraries -- Fiction 4. Books and reading -- Fiction
ISBN 037587089X; 9780375870897; 9780375970894

LC 2012048122

In this book, twelve "seventh-graders win a chance to spend an overnight lock-in previewing their town's new public library," which was "conceived by Luigi Lemoncello, the . . . founder of Mr. Lemoncello's Imagination Factory, which is a source for every kind of game imaginable. During the lock-in the winners . . . are offered a further challenge: 'Find your way out of the library using only what's in the library.' The winner will become spokesperson for the Imagination Factory." (Publishers Weekly)

Another title in this series is:
Mr. Lemoncello's Great Library Race (2017)

The **Hanging** Hill. Random House 2009 322p (Haunted places mystery) $16.99; lib bdg $19.99
Grades: 5 6 7 8 **Fic**

1. Ghost stories 2. Theater -- Fiction 3. Criminals -- Fiction 4. Connecticut -- Fiction 5. Stepmothers -- Fiction
ISBN 978-0-375-84699-1; 0-375-84699-9; 978-0-375-94699-8 lib bdg; 978-0-375-84700-4 pa

LC 2008027274

While working at a summer stock theater, eleven-year-old Zack and his stepmother encounter the ghost of one of Connecticut's most notorious criminals.

"The story line is hauntingly delicious as the fully fleshed-out creepiness comes tempered with humor." SLJ

Home sweet motel; Chris Grabenstein ; illustrated by Brooke Allen. Random House Inc. 2016 304 p. illustrations (Welcome to Wonderland) (ebook) $41.97; (hardcover) $13.99
Grades: 4 5 6 7 **Fic**

1. Mystery and detective stories 2. Hotels, motels, etc. -- Fiction
ISBN 9780553536041; 0553536028; 9780553536027; 9780553536034

LC 2015030808

In this first book in the Welcome to Wonderland series by Chris Grabenstein, illustrated by Brooke Allen, "P. T. Wilkie may be the greatest storyteller alive. But he knows one thing for a fact: the Wonderland Motel is the best place a kid could ever live! . . . There's only one thing the Wonderland doesn't have, though—customers. And if the Wonderland doesn't get them soon, P.T. and his friend Gloria may have to say goodbye to their beloved motel forever." (Publisher's note)

"A funny and promising start to a new series." Kirkus

House of robots; James Patterson and Chris Grabenstein ; illustrated by Juliana Neufeld. Little, Brown & Co. 2014 352 p. illustrations
Grades: 4 5 6 7 8 **Fic**

1. School stories 2. Robots -- Fiction 3. Humorous stories 4. Schools -- Fiction 5. Inventors -- Fiction 6. Family life -- Fiction 7. Middle schools -- Fiction
ISBN 9780316405911

LC 2013041672

In this book by James Patterson and Chris Grabbenstein, "an extraordinary robot signs up for an ordinary fifth grade class. It was never easy for Sammy Hayes-Rodriguez to fit in, so he's dreading the day when his genius mom insists he bring her newest invention to school: a walking, talking robot he calls E--for 'Error.' Sammy's no stranger to robots--his house is full of a colorful cast of them. But this one not only thinks it's Sammy's brother... it's actually even nerdier than Sammy." (Publisher's note)

"A fast-moving plot, lots of jokes, and a host of weird robots will draw readers in." SLJ

Mr. Lemoncello's great library race; Chris Grabenstein. Random House 2017 279 p. (Mr. Lemoncello's Library) (hardcover) $16.99
Grades: 5 6 7 **Fic**

1. Contests -- Fiction 2. Libraries -- Fiction 3. Books and reading -- Fiction 4. Eccentrics and eccentricities -- Fiction
ISBN 9780553536089; 9780553536065; 9780553536072

LC 2015040525

Sequel to: Mr. Lemoncello's Library Olympics

This book, by Chris Grabenstein, is "the third fantastically fun, puzzle-packed MR. LEMONCELLO adventure! . . . Everyone's favorite game maker, Mr. Lemoncello, is testing out his new FABULOUS FACT-FINDING FRENZY game! If Kyle can make it through the first round, he and the other lucky finalists will go on a great race—by bicycle, bookmobile, and even Mr. Lemoncello's corporate banana jet!—to find fascinating facts about famous Americans." (Publisher's note)

"Fans will embrace this new entry, which, like the previous books, features lightning-fast pacing and zany plotlines. Educators will be pleased by the emphasis on careful research and fact-checking." SLJ

Mr. Lemoncello's Library Olympics; Chris Grabenstein. Random House Inc 2016 288 p. (hardcover) $16.99
Grades: 5 6 7 **Fic**

1. Libraries -- Fiction 2. Contests -- Fiction 3. Censorship -- Fiction 4. Books and reading -- Fiction 5. Eccentrics and eccentricities -- Fiction
ISBN 9780553510409; 9780553510416; 055351041X

LC 2015024473

In this children's novel, by Chris Grabenstein, "the world-famous game maker, Luigi Lemoncello . . . has invited teams from all across America to compete in the first ever LIBRARY OLYMPICS. But something suspicious is going on . . . books are missing from Mr. Lemoncello's library. Is someone trying to CENSOR what the kids are reading?! In between figuring out mind-boggling challenges, the kids will have to band together to get to the bottom of this mystery." (Publisher's note)

"This is a successful blend of mystery, adventure, and suspense, with a sizable cast of characters, in a wholly satisfying sequel that easily stands alone." SLJ

The **smoky** corridor. Random House 2010 326p (Haunted places mystery) $16.99; lib bdg $19.99

Grades: 5 6 7 8 **Fic**

1. Ghost stories 2. School stories 3. Zombies -- Fiction 4. Connecticut -- Fiction 5. Family life -- Fiction 6. Stepmothers -- Fiction 7. Buried treasure -- Fiction

ISBN 978-0-375-86511-4; 0-375-86511-X; 978-0-375-96511-1 lib bdg; 0-375-96511-4 lib bdg

LC 2009-50694

With the help of his stepmother, his dog Zipper, and new friend Malik, Zack Jennings faces ghosts and zombies at his new middle school, which is said to house a lost Confederate treasure.

"Grabenstein is a riveting storyteller most kids won't be able to put this book down. Its appeal will be wide, as it is a mystery, a thriller, a ghost story, a school story, an action adventure, and a humorous book." SLJ

Graff, Lisa

★ **Absolutely** almost; Lisa Graff. Philomel Books, an imprint of Penguin Group (USA) 2014 304 p. $16.99

Grades: 4 5 6 7 **Fic**

1. Self-esteem -- Fiction 2. Ability -- Fiction 3. Schools -- Fiction 4. Babysitters -- Fiction 5. Racially mixed people -- Fiction 6. Family life -- New York (State) -- New York -- Fiction

ISBN 0399164057; 9780399164057

LC 2013023620

In this book, by Lisa Graff, "Albie has never been the smartest kid in his class. He has never been the tallest. Or the best at gym. Or the greatest artist. Or the most musical. In fact, Albie has a long list of the things he's not very good at. But then Albie gets a new babysitter, Calista, who helps him figure out all of the things he is good at and how he can take pride in himself." (Publisher's note)

"Ten-year-old New Yorker Albie is a middle-of-the-road (at best) student. He's buoyed by small successes in math club and on spelling tests, and by his new babysitter's low-key approach to confidence-boosting. Albie is a sweet, vulnerable kid who just needs a little extra help and to whom readers may well relate. Short chapters add to the story's accessibility and keep the pace moving." (Horn Book)

★ **Lost** in the sun; Lisa Graff. Philomel Books, an imprint of Penguin Group (USA) 2015 304 p. $16.99

Grades: 4 5 6 7 8 9 **Fic**

1. Guilt -- Fiction 2. Brothers -- Fiction 3. Friendship -- Fiction 4. Remarriage -- Fiction 5. Tricks -- Fiction

ISBN 0399164065; 9780399164064

LC 2014027868

In this book by Lisa Graff, "Trent knows nothing could be worse than the year he had in fifth grade, when a freak accident on Cedar Lake left one kid dead, and Trent with a brain full of terrible thoughts he can't get rid of. Trent's pretty positive the entire disaster was his fault. . . . It isn't until Trent gets caught up in the whirlwind that is Fallon Little--the girl with the mysterious scar across her face--that things begin to change." (Publisher's note)

"Trent Zimmerman is consumed by rage. The universe has been manifestly unfair to him and he doesn't know how to handle it. Seven months ago, he struck a hockey puck at a bad angle, sending it like a missile into the chest of a boy with a previously undiagnosed heart ailment. That boy died and Trent feels responsible...Weighty matters deftly handled with humor and grace will give this book wide appeal." SLJ

A **tangle** of knots; Lisa Graff. Philomel Books 2013 240 p. $16.99

Grades: 3 4 5 6 **Fic**

1. Baking -- Fiction 2. Ability -- Fiction 3. Orphans -- Fiction 4. Identity -- Fiction 5. Poughkeepsie (N.Y.) -- Fiction 6. Family life -- New York -- Fiction

ISBN 0399255176; 9780399255175

LC 2012009573

Parents' Choice: Gold Medal Fiction (2013)

This novel is set "in a slightly magical world where everyone has a Talent. . . . Eleven-year-old Cady is an orphan with a phenomenal Talent for cake baking. . . . And her destiny leads her to a mysterious address that houses a lost luggage emporium, an old recipe, a family of children searching for their own Talents, and a Talent Thief who will alter her life forever. However, these encounters hold the key to Cady's past and how she became an orphan." (Publisher's note)

Followed by: A clatter of jars (2016)

Grant, Holly

The **dastardly** deed; Holly Grant ; illustrated by Josie Portillo. Random House 2015 368 p. illustrations (hardcover library binding) $19.99

Grades: 4 5 6 7 **Fic**

1. Family secrets -- Fiction 2. Adventure fiction -- Fiction 3. Humorous stories 4. Orphans -- Fiction 5. Secrets -- Fiction 6. Kidnapping -- Fiction 7. Princesses -- Fiction

ISBN 9780385370257; 9780385370264

LC 2015009492

In this middle-grade novel, by Holly Grant, illustrated by Josie Portillo, book 2 in "The League of Beastly Dreadfuls" series, "after their narrow escape from a NEFARIOUS kidnapping ring, Anastasia, Ollie, and Quentin (a.k.a. The League of Beastly Dreadfuls!) are looking forward to a relaxing vacation. . . . [But] Anastasia makes the SHOCKING discovery that her family is at the heart of a centuries-old scandal . . . [and] the Dreadfuls have another MYSTERY to solve." (Publisher's note)

"With its strong characterization, especially of the most despicable figures, and Lemony Snicket appeal, this adventure will keep fans hooked and eager for the next installment." Booklist

The **league** of beastly dreadfuls; book 1 Holly Grant. Random House Inc 2015 294 p. illustrations (hardcover library binding) $19.99

Grades: 4 5 6 7 **Fic**

1. Aunts -- Fiction 2. Institutional care 3. Orphans -- Fiction 4. Humorous stories 5. Shadows -- Fiction 6. Kidnapping -- Fiction

ISBN 0385370083; 9780385370073; 9780385370080

LC 2013050800

Other titles in this series: The dastardly deed

In this children's novel by Holly Grant "Anastasia is a completely average almost-eleven-year-old. That is, UNTIL her parents die in a tragic vacuum-cleaner accident. UNTIL she's rescued by two long-lost great-aunties. . . . Anastasia soon begins to suspect that her aunties are not who they say they are. So when she meets . . . two mysterious brothers, the three join together to plot their great escape!" (Publisher's note)

"With just the right mix of humor, magic, maliciousness, and suspense, Grant leaves readers waiting for Anastasia's next adventure." Booklist

Grant, K. M.

Blaze of silver; [by] K. M. Grant. Walker & Co. 2007 261p $16.95

Grades: 6 7 8 9 **Fic**

1. Horses -- Fiction 2. Muslims -- Fiction 3. Knights and knighthood -- Fiction 4. Great Britain -- History -- 1154-1399, Plantagenets -- Fiction

ISBN 978-0-8027-9625-7; 0-8027-9625-7

LC 2006012098

Sequel to Green jasper (2006)

Using principles of their shared Muslim faith to persuade him, an agent of the Old Man of the Mountain convinces Kamil to lead Will and Ellie into a trap, but Kamil repents and seeks a way to save his friends and redeem himself.

"This last volume of The de Granville Trilogy presents an exciting, appropriate end to the story." Voice Youth Advocates

Blood red horse. Walker & Co. 2005 277p $16.95

Grades: 6 7 8 9 **Fic**

1. Horses -- Fiction 2. Crusades -- Fiction 3. Middle Ages -- Fiction

ISBN 0-8027-8960-9

LC 2005-42280

First published 2004 in the United Kingdom

A special horse named Hosanna changes the lives of two English brothers and those around them as they fight with King Richard I against Saladin's armies during the Third Crusades.

This "story . . . transcends boundaries of gender and genre, with something to offer fans of equestrian fare, historical fiction, and battlefield drama alike." Booklist

Other titles in this series are:
Green jasper (2006)
Blaze of silver (2007)

Blue flame; book one of the Perfect Fire trilogy. Walker & Co. 2008 246p (Perfect fire trilogy) $16.99

Grades: 7 8 9 10 **Fic**

1. Middle Ages -- Fiction 2. Knights and knighthood -- Fiction 3. France -- History -- 0-1328 -- Fiction

ISBN 0-8027-9694-X; 978-0-8027-9694-3

LC 2007-51384

This first volume in a projected trilogy is set in southern France (Occitan) in 1242 amidst the struggle between Cathars and Catholics. "Many years have passed since the Occitanian knights killed Richard the Lionheart in a courageous battle to keep the Blue Flame—sparked at the moment of Christ's death—from falling into the wrong hands. Now it is in danger once again, as enemies from the north draw near. . . . Lifelong friends Raimon, son of a Cathar weaver, and Yolanda, daughter of a Catholic Count, are falling in love. But a new religious crusade is about to begin, setting boy against girl, family against family, south against north." (Publisher's note) "Middle school, high school." (Horn Book)

"Characters are as complex as the moral issues they face, and Grant's nuanced, thought-provoking look at the religious conflicts they face will resonate today." Booklist

Other books in this series are Paradise red (2010)
White heat (2009)

Green jasper; [by] K.M. Grant. Walker 2006 249p $16.95

Grades: 6 7 8 9 **Fic**

1. Horses -- Fiction 2. Brothers -- Fiction 3. Knights and knighthood -- Fiction 4. Great Britain -- History -- 1154-1399, Plantagenets -- Fiction

ISBN 0-8027-8073-3; 978-0-8027-8073-7

LC 2005024083

Sequel to Blood red horse (2005)

Having returned to a politically unstable England after the Crusades, brothers Will and Gavin—with the help of the red horse Hosanna—attempt to rescue their friend Ellie who is being held prisoner by an enemy of King Richard I.

"Grant balances simplistic elements with unsentimental explorations of medieval conflicts between romantic love, brotherly loyalty, and political fealty while fully capitalizing on the quintessential appeal of tales heavy on sword fights and hoofbeats." Booklist

Followed by Blaze of silver (2007)

How the hangman lost his heart. Walker & Co. 2007 244p $16.95

Grades: 7 8 9 10 **Fic**

1. Adventure fiction 2. Great Britain -- History -- 1714-1837 -- Fiction

ISBN 978-0-8027-9672-1; 0-8027-9672-9

LC 2006-53182

When her Uncle Frank is executed for treason against England's King George in 1746, and his severed head is mounted on a pike for public viewing, daring Alice tries to reclaim the head for a proper burial, finding an unlikely ally in the softhearted executioner, while incurring the wrath of the royal guard.

"The story is filled with action and interesting characters. . . . This is a rousing read." SLJ

Paradise red; by K.M. Grant. Walker & Co. 2010 279 p. (hardcover) $17.99

Grades: 7 8 9 10 **Fic**

1. Fantasy fiction 2. Romance fiction 3. Albigenses -- Fiction 4. Middle Ages -- Fiction 5. Knights and knighthood -- Fiction 6. France -- History -- Louis IX, 1226-1270 -- Fiction 7. Languedoc (France) -- History -- 13th century -- Fiction 8. Montségur (France) -- History -- 13th century -- Fiction

ISBN 0802796966; 9780802796967

LC 2009054214

This is the final book in K.M. Grant's Perfect Fire trilogy. The novel "concludes the story of Raimon's quest to save the mystical blue flame which is at the heart of his love for the land he grew up in. This runs alongside the complicated story of his relationship with Yolanda who has made a political marriage to one of the enemy." (School Librarian)

White heat. Walker & Co. 2009 260p (Perfect fire trilogy) $16.99

Grades: 7 8 9 10 **Fic**

1. Inquisition -- Fiction 2. Middle Ages -- Fiction 3. Knights and knighthood -- Fiction 4. France -- History -- 0-1328 -- Fiction

ISBN 978-0-8027-9695-0; 0-8027-9695-8

LC 2008-46984

Sequel to: Blue heat (2008)

As the conflict in Languedoc, also called Occitan, intensifies, Raimon, having escaped the pyre, suppresses his longing to find his beloved Yolanda and, together with Parsifal, carries the Blue Flame to the mountains where it serves to rally loyal Occitanians to organize against the formidable French forces set to invade their beloved country.

"With thorough scholarship and an immersion into medieval sights, sounds, and points of view, Grant invites readers on a thrilling trip back in time." Horn Book

Grant, Katy

Hide and seek. Peachtree 2010 230p $15.95

Grades: 5 6 7 8 **Fic**

1. Arizona -- Fiction 2. Divorce -- Fiction 3. Kidnapping -- Fiction 4. Family life -- Fiction 5. Wilderness survival -- Fiction

ISBN 978-1-56145-542-3; 1-56145-542-3

LC 2009040519

In the remote mountains of Arizona where he lives with his mother, stepfather, and two sisters, fourteen-year-old Chase discovers two kidnapped boys and gets caught up in a dangerous adventure when he comes up with a plan to get them to safety.

"Mystery and adventure propel this readable survival story that will hit the spot with Gary Paulsen's fans and may also entice reluctant readers." SLJ

Grant, Michael, 1954-

★ The **call**; Michael Grant. 1st ed. Katherine Tegen Books 2010 243 p. ill. (The Magnificent 12) (hardcover) $16.99

Grades: 4 5 6 **Fic**

1. Fantasy fiction 2. Adventure fiction 3. Fantasy 4. Humorous stories 5. Good and evil -- Fiction 6. Adventure and adventurers -- Fiction

ISBN 0061833665; 9780061833663

LC 2009044815

A seemingly average twelve-year-old learns that he is destined to gather a team of similarly gifted children to try to save the world from a nameless evil, which is threatening to reappear after an absence of three thousand years. "Age ten and up." (Publisher's note)

"The author keeps the story moving at a brisk pace with suspenseful action and laugh-out-loud humor." Kirkus

Followed by: The trap (2011)

Eve & Adam; by Michael Grant and Katherine Applegate. Feiwel and Friends 2012 291p. $17.99

Grades: 7 8 9 10 **Fic**

1. Medical genetics 2. Biomedical engineering 3. Mother-daughter relationship -- Fiction

ISBN 0312583516; 9780312583514

In this book by authors Michael Grant and Katherine Applegate, "a run-in with a streetcar left Evening Spiker's body seriously mangled . . . [H]er widowed mother, Terra, insists on moving her from the hospital to . . . [the] biotech company . . . Spiker Biopharmaceuticals. . . . Eve's healing is strangely swift [and] Terra drops a project . . . in her lap: Design a virtual human being from scratch. With help from her feisty, reckless friend Aislin, Eve takes up the challenge." (Kirkus Reviews)

Fear; a Gone novel. Michael Grant. Katherine Tegen Books 2012 509 p. maps (Gone) (hardcover) $17.99

Grades: 7 8 9 10 **Fic**

1. Fear -- Fiction 2. Supernatural -- Fiction 3. Good and evil -- Fiction 4. Survival -- Fiction 5. Prophecies -- Fiction

ISBN 9780061449178; 9780061449154; 9780062099242; 9780061449161; 0061449156; 0061449164

LC 2011019374

In this book, by Michael Grant, "it's been one year since all the adults disappeared. Gone. Despite the hunger, despite the lies, even despite the plague, the kids of Perdido Beach are determined to survive. Creeping into the tenuous new world they've built, though, is the worst incarnation yet of the enemy known as the Darkness: fear." (Publisher's note)

"Fans can count on more excellent storytelling, multidimensional characters who continue to develop in unexpected ways, and some mighty fine eye-popping moments." VOYA

★ **Gone**. HarperTeen 2008 576p $17.99; lib bdg $18.89; pa $9.99

Grades: 7 8 9 10 **Fic**

1. Supernatural -- Fiction 2. Good and evil -- Fiction

ISBN 978-0-06-144876-8; 978-0-06-144877-5 lib bdg; 978-0-06-144878-2 pa

LC 2007-36734

In a small town on the coast of California, everyone over the age of fourteen suddenly disappears, setting up a battle between the remaining town residents and the students from a local private school, as well as those who have "The Power" and are able to perform supernatural feats and those who do not.

"A tour de force that will leave readers dazed, disturbed, and utterly breathless." Booklist

Other titles in this series are:
Hunger (2009)
Lies (2010)
Plague (2011)
Fear (2012)
Light (2013)
Monster (2017)

Hunger; a Gone novel. HarperTeen 2009 590p $17.99; lib bdg $18.89

Grades: 7 8 9 10 **Fic**

1. Horror fiction 2. Supernatural -- Fiction 3. Good and evil -- Fiction

ISBN 978-0-06-144906-2; 0-06-144906-7; 978-0-06-144907-9 lib bdg; 0-06-144907-5 lib bdg

LC 2008-36465

Sequel to: Gone (2008)

Conditions worsen for the remaining young residents of a small California coastal town isolated by supernatural events when their food supplies dwindle and the Darkness underground awakens.

"Readers will be unable to avoid involuntarily gasping, shuddering, or flinching while reading this suspense-filled story. The tension starts in the first chapter and does not let up until the end." Voice Youth Advocates

Followed by: Lies (2010)

Lies; a Gone novel. Katherine Tegen Books 2010 447p (Gone) $17.99; lib bdg $18.89; pa $9.99

Grades: 7 8 9 10 **Fic**

1. Supernatural -- Fiction 2. Good and evil -- Fiction

ISBN 978-0-06-144909-3; 0-06-144909-1; 978-0-06-144910-9 lib bdg; 0-06-144910-5 lib bdg; 978-0-06-144911-6 pa; 0-06-144911-3 pa

Sequel to: Hunger (2009)

A girl who died now walks among the living; Zil and the Human Crew set fire to Perdido Beach; and amid the flames and smoke, Sam sees the figure of the boy he fears the most: Drake. But Drake is dead. Sam and Caine defeated him along with the Darkness—or so they thought.

"This book retains all the action, unexpected twists, and engaging characters of the previous stories; readers will learn answers to old questions but new questions will proliferate. . . . Fascinating, frightening and absolutely worth an obsessive wait for the next installment, mature teen readers will embrace this thrill ride tempered with a touch of smart social commentary." Voice Youth Advocates

Followed by: Plague (2011)

Monster; Michael Grant. Katherine Tegen Books 2017 420 p. (Gone) (hardcover) $18.99
Grades: 7 8 9 10 **Fic**
1. Science fiction 2. Extraterrestrial beings -- Fiction 3. Survival -- Fiction 4. Virus diseases -- Fiction
ISBN 9780062467867; 0062467840; 9780062467843
LC 2017932879

In this book, by Michael Grant, "it's been four years since a meteor hit Perdido Beach and everyone disappeared. Everyone, except the kids trapped in the FAYZ—an invisible dome that was created by an alien virus. Inside the FAYZ, animals began to mutate and teens developed dangerous powers. The terrifying new world was plagued with hunger, lies, and fear of the unknown." (Publisher's note)

"A bombastic, engaging start to a sequel series full of potential." Kirkus

Another title in this series is:
Villain (2018)

Plague; a Gone novel. Katherine Tegen Books 2011 492p (Gone) $17.99; lib bdg $18.89
Grades: 7 8 9 10 **Fic**
1. Plague -- Fiction 2. Supernatural -- Fiction 3. Good and evil -- Fiction
ISBN 978-0-06-144912-3; 0-06-144912-1; 978-0-06-144913-0 lib bdg; 0-06-144913-X lib bdg
LC 2010021834

Sequel to: Lies (2010)

A deadly, flu-like epidemic and a plague of flesh-eating creatures threaten the lives of the children at Perdido Beach while Sam, Astrid, Caine, and Diana each struggle with doubts and uncertainties.

"Grant's sf-fantasy thrillers continue to be the very definition of page-turner." Booklist

The **trap**. Katherine Tegen Books 2011 294p (The Magnificent 12) $16.99
Grades: 4 5 6 **Fic**
1. Fantasy fiction 2. Adventure fiction 3. Good and evil -- Fiction
ISBN 0-06-183368-1; 978-0-06-183368-7
LC 2010040580

Sequel to: The call (2010)

Mack MacAvoy, an average-seeming twelve-year-old boy who happens to have special powers, travels to China in an effort to assemble an elite team of his peers to help him thwart the evil Pale Queen.

Grant, Vicki

Quid pro quo. Orca 2005 160p $16.95; pa $7.95
Grades: 7 8 9 10 **Fic**
1. Mystery fiction 2. Lawyers -- Fiction 3. Missing persons -- Fiction 4. Mother-son relationship -- Fiction
ISBN 1-55143-394-X; 1-55143-370-2 pa

"Cyril Floyd MacIntyre, 13, is perplexed over the disappearance of his mother, a 28-year-old law-school graduate. . . . Cyril becomes involved in a web of intrigue and deceit searching for her. His discovery of resurfacing shady characters who played a role in Andy's disappearance makes for a suspense-filled, well-plotted legal thriller." SLJ

Followed by: Res judicata (2008)

Res judicata. Orca Book Publishers 2008 172p pa $9.95
Grades: 7 8 9 10 **Fic**
1. Mystery fiction 2. Lawyers -- Fiction 3. Criminals -- Fiction 4. Mother-son relationship -- Fiction
ISBN 978-1-55143940-2; 1-55143940-9

Sequel to: Quid pro quo (2005)

Cyril MacIntyre is on the case again, working for his eccentric mother and giving new meaning to the term "legal aid" in this sequel to Quid Pro Quo.

"The novel features laugh-out-loud bits between mother and son and plenty of hilarious insights from Cyril about life and the law. Students who enjoy quick-witted writing and good mysteries will enjoy how well Vicki Grant cracks the case." Libr Media Connect

Gratz, Alan

Allies; Alan Gratz. Scholastic Press 2019 336 p. $17.99
Grades: 4 5 6 7 **Fic**
1. War stories 2. Soldiers -- Fiction 3. Survival -- Fiction 4. German Americans -- Fiction 5. France -- History -- 20th century -- Fiction 6. Normandy (France) -- History -- 20th century -- Fiction 7. France -- History -- German occupation, 1940-1945 -- Fiction 8. World War, 1939-1945 -- Campaigns -- France -- Normandy -- Fiction 9. World War, 1939-1945 -- Underground movements -- France -- Fiction
ISBN 9781338245721
LC 2019012188

"Welcome to D-Day. Dee, a young U.S. soldier, is on a boat racing toward the French coast. And Dee -- along with his brothers-in-arms -- is terrified. He feels the weight of World War II on his shoulders. But Dee is not alone. Behind enemy lines in France, a girl named Samira works as a spy, trying to sabotage the German army. Meanwhile, paratrooper James leaps from his plane to join a daring midnight raid. And in the thick of battle, Henry, a medic, searches for lives to save." (Publisher's note)

★ The **Brooklyn** nine; a novel in nine innings. Dial Books 2009 299p $16.99
Grades: 5 6 7 8 9 **Fic**
1. Baseball -- Fiction 2. Family life -- Fiction 3. German Americans -- Fiction 4. United States -- History -- Fiction 5. Brooklyn (New York, N.Y.) -- Fiction
ISBN 978-0-8037-3224-7; 0-8037-3224-4
LC 2008-21263

This novel follows the fortunes of a German immigrant family through nine generations, beginning in 1845, as they experience American life and play baseball. "Grades five to nine." (Bull Cent Child Books)

Gratz "builds this novel upon a clever . . . conceit . . . and executes it with polish and precision." Booklist

The **League** of Seven; Alan Gratz ; illustrated by Brett Helquist. Starscape 2014 352 p. map (hardback) $16.99
Grades: 5 6 7 8 **Fic**
1. Steampunk fiction 2. United States -- History -- Fiction 3. Science fiction 4. Monsters -- Fiction 5. Secret societies -- Fiction 6. Adventure and adventurers -- Fiction
ISBN 076533822X; 9780765338228
LC 2014015435

"'The League of Seven' is the first book in [a] steampunk series by the acclaimed author of 'Samurai Shortstop,' Alan Gratz. In an alternate 1875 America electricity is forbidden, Native Americans and Yankees are united, and eldritch evil lurks in the shadows. Young Archie Dent knows there really are monsters in the world. His parents are members of the Septemberist Society, whose job it is to protect humanity from hideous giants called the Mangleborn." (Publisher's note)

"This hybrid of steampunk and alternate American history features a hell-raising girl's school, Atlantis, and three highly likable leads in a yarn rip-roaring from start to finish. . . . Moments of humor and pathos enliven the history and fantasy." Booklist

Prisoner B-3087; by Alan Gratz. Scholastic Press 2013 272 p. (hardcover) $16.99
Grades: 7 8 9 10 **Fic**

1. Biographical fiction 2. Jews -- Poland -- Fiction 3. Holocaust, 1939-1945 -- Fiction 4. Poland -- History -- Fiction 5. Holocaust survivors -- Fiction 6. Jews -- Poland -- Kraków -- Fiction 7. Kraków (Poland) -- History -- Fiction 8. Holocaust survivors -- Poland -- Fiction 9. Holocaust, Jewish (1939-1945) -- Poland -- Fiction

ISBN 054545901X; 9780545459013

LC 2012012460

This novel by Ruth Gruener, Jack Gruener and Alan Gratz tells the story of "a Jewish boy in 1930s Poland, [namely] Yanek [who] is at the mercy of the Nazis who have taken over. . . . And then Yanek himself is taken prisoner. . . . He is forced from one nightmarish concentration camp to another, as World War II rages all around him. . . . Can Yanek make it through the terror without losing his hope, his will--and, most of all, his sense of who he really is inside?" (Publisher's note)

Projekt 1065; A Novel of World War II. Alan Gratz. Scholastic Press 2016 320 p. (hardcover) $16.99; (ebook) $16.99
Grades: 5 6 7 8 **Fic**

1. Spy stories 2. Spies -- Fiction 3. Jet planes -- Fiction 4. Hitler Youth -- Fiction 4. Irish -- Germany -- Fiction 5. Germany -- History -- 1933-1945 -- Fiction 6. World War, 1939-1945 -- Germany -- Fiction 7. Espionage, British -- Germany -- Fiction 8. Berlin (Germany) -- History -- 1918-1945 -- Fiction 9. Jet planes -- Germany -- History -- Fiction

ISBN 9780545880169; 9780545880176

LC 2016016960

In this children's novel by Alan Gratz, "Michael O'Shaunessey, originally from Ireland, now lives in Nazi Germany with his parents. Like the other boys in his school, Michael is a member of the Hitler Youth, but . . . he and his parents are spies. . . . When Michael learns about Projekt 1065, a secret Nazi war mission, things get even more complicated. He must prove his loyalty to the Hitler Youth at all costs -- even if it means risking everything he cares about." (Publisher's note)

"A rare insider's glimpse into the Hitler Youth: animated, well-researched, and thought-provoking." Kirkus

Includes bibliographical references

★ **Refugee**; Alan Gratz. Scholastic Press 2017 338 p. maps (hardback) $16.99
Grades: 5 6 7 8 **Fic**

1. Refugees -- Fiction 2. Immigration and emigration -- Fiction 3. Survival -- Fiction 4. Emigration and immigration -- Fiction

ISBN 9780545880831; 9780545880879

LC 2017017544

In this novel, by Alan Gratz, Josef, Isabel and Mahmoud "go on harrowing journeys in search of refuge. All will face unimaginable dangers -- from drownings to bombings to betrayals. But there is always the hope of tomorrow. And although Josef, Isabel, and Mahmoud are separated by continents and decades, shocking connections will tie their stories together in the end." (Publisher's note)

"Poignant, respectful, and historically accurate while pulsating with emotional turmoil, adventure, and suspense." Kirkus

Samurai shortstop. Dial Books 2006 280p hardcover o.p. pa $7.99
Grades: 7 8 9 10 **Fic**

1. School stories 2. Baseball -- Fiction 3. Tokyo (Japan) -- Fiction 4. Father-son relationship -- Fiction

ISBN 0-8037-3075-6; 978-0-8037-3075-5; 0-14-241099-3 pa

LC 2005-22081

While obtaining a Western education at a prestigious Japanese boarding school in 1890, sixteen-year-old Toyo also receives traditional samurai training which has profound effects on both his baseball game and his relationship with his father. This book features some scenes of graphic violence.

"This is an intense read about a fascinating time and place in world history." Publ Wkly

Graves, Keith

The **orphan** of Awkward Falls. Chronicle Books 2011 337p $16.99
Grades: 4 5 6 7 **Fic**

1. Mystery fiction 2. Orphans -- Fiction 3. Homicide -- Fiction 4. Inventors -- Fiction 5. Mentally ill -- Fiction 6. Science -- Experiments -- Fiction

ISBN 978-0-8118-7814-2; 0-8118-7814-7

LC 2011008008

Josephine Cravitz, the new girl in Awkward Falls, and her neighbor Thaddeus Hibble, a reclusive and orphaned boy inventor, become the targets of a mad cannibal from the local asylum for the criminally insane.

"Graves crafts a quick-moving plot composed of macabre twists. . . . Wordless opening and closing sequences, plus a handful of interior illustrations, both fill in background detail and intensify the overall macabre atmosphere." Kirkus

Gray, Claudia

Defy the stars; Claudia Gray. Little, Brown & Co. 2017 503 p. (hardback) $17.99
Grades: 7 8 9 10 11 12 **Fic**

1. Science fiction 2. Robots -- Fiction 3. Orphans -- Fiction 4. Soldiers -- Fiction 5. Interstellar travel -- Fiction

ISBN 9780316394062; 9780316394031

LC 2016028390

In this novel in the Defy the Stars series, by Claudia Gray, "Noemi and Abel are enemies in an interstellar war, forced by chance to work together as they embark on a daring journey through the stars. Their efforts would end the fighting for good, but they're not without sacrifice. The stakes are even higher than either of them first realized, and the more time they spend together, the more they're forced to question everything they'd been taught was true." (Publisher's note)

"Nuanced philosophical discussions of religion, terrorism, and morality advise and direct the high-stakes action, informing the beautiful, realistic ending. Intelligent and thoughtful, a highly relevant far-off speculative adventure." Kirkus

Another title in this series is:
Defy the worlds (2018)

Defy the worlds; Claudia Gray. Little, Brown & Co. 2018 467 p. (Defy the stars) (hardcover) $17.99
Grades: 7 8 9 10 11 12 **Fic**

1. Robots -- Fiction 2. Soldiers -- Fiction 3. Interplanetary voyages -- Fiction 4. Science fiction 5. Plague -- Fiction 6. Orphans -- Fiction 7. Immortality -- Fiction 8. Interstellar travel -- Fiction

ISBN 9780316394086; 9780316394109

LC 2017034001

Sequel to: Defy the Stars (2017)

In this book in the Defy the Stars series, by Claudia Gray, "an outcast from her home--shunned after a trip through the galaxy with Abel, the most advanced cybernetic man ever created, Noemi Vidal dreams of traveling through the stars one more time. And when a deadly plague arrives on Genesis, Noemi gets her chance. As the only soldier to have ever left the planet, it will be up to her to save its people...if only she wasn't flying straight into a trap." (Publisher's note)

"Romantic and adventurous, this novel contains a plethora of STEM-related content and is a worthy discussion starter for conversations about the ethics of technology." Booklist

A **thousand** pieces of you; Claudia Gray. HarperTeen, an imprint of HarperCollinsPublishers 2014 368 p. (hardcover) $17.99

Grades: 8 9 10 11 **Fic**

1. Science fiction 2. Adventure fiction 3. Murder -- Fiction 4. Family life -- Fiction 5. Space and time -- Fiction 6. Adventure and adventurers -- Fiction

ISBN 0062278967; 9780062278968

LC 2014001894

This book, by Claudia Gray, is "about a girl who must chase her father's killer through multiple dimensions. Marguerite Caine's physicist parents are known for their groundbreaking achievements. Their most astonishing invention, called the Firebird, allows users to jump into multiple universes. . . . But then Marguerite's father is murdered, and the killer--her parent's handsome, enigmatic assistant Paul--escapes into another dimension before the law can touch him." (Publisher's note)

"Readers will appreciate Marguerite's determination to help her parents, even though she is a misfit, the lone artist in a family of scientific geniuses. The secondary players are equally well rounded, and their various incarnations in each dimension make for intriguing character explorations. In resourceful Marguerite's first-person narration, the story moves quickly, and the science is explained enough to make the plot clear, but not so much as to bog things down." Booklist

Gray, Keith

Ostrich boys. Random House 2010 297p $17.99; lib bdg $20.99

Grades: 8 9 10 11 12 **Fic**

1. Death -- Fiction 2. Scotland -- Fiction 3. Friendship -- Fiction 4. Great Britain -- Fiction

ISBN 978-0-375-85843-7; 0-375-85843-1; 978-0-375-95843-4 lib bdg; 0-375-95843-6 lib bdg

LC 2008-21729

After their best friend Ross dies, English teenagers Blake, Kenny, and Sim plan a proper memorial by taking his ashes to Ross, Scotland, an adventure-filled journey that tests their loyalty to each other and forces them to question what friendship means.

"Gray's writing is cheeky, crisp, and realistic. He has created funny, bright characters whom readers cannot help but root for." SLJ

Green, Tim, 1963-

Baseball great. HarperCollinsPublishers 2009 250p $16.99; lib bdg $17.89

Grades: 5 6 7 8 **Fic**

1. School stories 2. Baseball -- Fiction 3. Father-son relationship -- Fiction

ISBN 978-0-06-162686-9; 0-06-162686-4; 978-0-06-162687-6 lib bdg; 0-06-162687-2 lib bdg

LC 2008051778

All twelve-year-old Josh wants to do is play baseball but when his father, a minor league pitcher, signs him up for a youth championship team, Josh finds himself embroiled in a situation with potentially illegal consequences.

"Issues of peer and family pressure are well handled, and the short, punchy chapters and crisp dialogue are likely to hold the attention of young baseball fans." SLJ

Other titles in this series are:
Rivals (2010)
Best of the best (2011)
Home run (2016)

Best of the best; a baseball great novel. Harper 2011 262p $16.99; lib bdg $17.89

Grades: 5 6 7 8 **Fic**

1. Divorce -- Fiction 2. Baseball -- Fiction

ISBN 978-0-06-168622-1; 0-06-168622-0; 978-0-06-168623-8 lib bdg; 0-06-168623-9 lib bdg

LC 2010022976

Sequel to: Rivals (2010)

Determined to play in the Little League World Series, twelve-year-old Josh struggles to concentrate on his game and be the team's leader while also trying to cope with his parents' impending divorce.

"Ethics in sports lifts this above the usual sports saga." Kirkus

The **big** time; a Football genius novel. Harper 2010 277p (Football genius) $16.99; lib bdg $17.89

Grades: 5 6 7 8 **Fic**

1. Football -- Fiction 2. Criminals -- Fiction 3. Atlanta (Ga.) -- Fiction 4. Father-son relationship -- Fiction

ISBN 978-0-06-168619-1; 0-06-168619-0; 978-0-06-168620-7 lib bdg; 0-06-168620-4 lib bdg

LC 2010009398

Twelve-year-old Troy always dreamed of meeting his father, but when the man finally appears his mother's anger, his father's shady business dealings, and Troy's own feelings make the reunion difficult and confusing.

"The story moves along at a brisk clip, the language is straightforward and accessible, and the issues raised are likely to engage readers." SLJ

Deep zone. Harper Collins 2011 265p (Football genius) $15.99

Grades: 5 6 7 8 **Fic**

1. Football -- Fiction

ISBN 978-0-06-201244-9; 0-06-201244-4

Twelve-year-old football stars Troy White and Ty Lewis are eager to face each other in a seven-on-seven tournament being held at the Super Bowl in Miami, unaware that bad choices made by members of their families will put both boys in danger.

"The football insights are the best part, as both professional games and seven-on-seven play are described in satisfying detail." Kirkus

Football champ. HarperCollins Children's Books 2009 280p $16.99; lib bdg $17.89

Grades: 5 6 7 8 **Fic**

1. Football -- Fiction 2. Journalists -- Fiction 3. Atlanta (Ga.) -- Fiction 4. Atlanta Falcons (Football team) -- Fiction.

ISBN 978-0-06-162689-0; 0-06-162689-9; 978-0-06-162690-6 lib bdg; 0-06-162690-2 lib bdg

LC 2008-51775

Sequel to: Football genius (2007)

Twelve-year-old Troy's uncanny gift for predicting football plays proves a powerful secret weapon for the Atlanta Falcons, but a seedy reporter with a vendetta suspects something is going on and sets out to shred the reputations of Troy and star linebacker Seth Halloway.

"The characters are engaging and the game action is exciting. Short cliffhanger chapters make this a good bet for reluctant readers." SLJ

Football genius. HarperCollinsPublishers 2007 244p $16.99; lib bdg $17.89; pa $6.99
Grades: 5 6 7 8 **Fic**

1. Football -- Fiction 2. Atlanta (Ga.) -- Fiction
ISBN 978-0-06-112270-5; 0-06-112270-X; 978-0-06-112272-9 lib bdg; 0-06-112272-6 lib bdg; 978-0-06-112273-6 pa; 0-06-112273-4 pa

LC 2006-29470

Troy, a sixth-grader with an unusual gift for predicting football plays before they occur, attempts to use his ability to help his favorite team, the Atlanta Falcons, but he must first prove himself to the coach and players.

The author "imparts many insider details that football fans will love. Green makes Troy a winning hero, and he ties everything together with a fast-moving plot." Booklist

Other titles in this series are:
Football champ (2009)
The big time (2010)
Deep zone (2011)

Football hero. HarperCollinsPublishers 2008 297p $16.99; lib bdg $17.89; pa $6.99
Grades: 5 6 7 8 **Fic**

1. Mafia -- Fiction 2. Football -- Fiction 3. New Jersey -- Fiction
ISBN 978-0-06-112274-3; 0-06-112274-2; 978-0-06-112275-0 lib bdg; 0-06-112275-0 lib bdg; 978-0-06-112276-7 pa; 0-06-112276-9 pa

LC 2007-24184

When twelve-year-old Ty's brother Thane is recruited out of college to play for the New York Jets, their Uncle Gus uses Ty to get insider information for his gambling ring, landing Ty and Thane in trouble with the Mafia.

"The novel is briskly paced and undemanding, and might be a good bet for sports-minded reluctant readers." SLJ

Force out; Tim Green. 1st ed. Harper 2013 288 p. (hardcover) $16.99
Grades: 4 5 6 **Fic**

1. Baseball -- Fiction 2. Friendship -- Fiction 3. Best friends -- Fiction 4. Conduct of life -- Fiction 5. Competition (Psychology) -- Fiction
ISBN 0062089595; 9780062089595

LC 2012026752

In this juvenile novel, by Tim Green, "Joey and Zach have always been best friends. They're also two of the best baseball players in their league, and shoo-ins for the all-star team at the end of the season. Their dream is to play together on the Center State select team, and they will do anything to help each other get there. . . . Then the unthinkable happens: The boys learn there's only one open spot on the select team." (Publisher's note)

"Though Green is no stylist, he does a better job of avoiding the sports fantasy and sticking to real life than usual. There's plenty of play-by-play for those who want the sports to be the focus, but the interactions off the field are never shortchanged. . . . A slice of life for middle school readers who know that their sport is a microcosm of the larger world." Kirkus

New kid; Tim Green. HarperCollins 2014 320 p. (hardback) $16.99
Grades: 4 5 6 7 8 **Fic**

1. School stories 2. Moving -- Fiction 3. Baseball players -- Fiction 4. Schools -- Fiction 5. Baseball -- Fiction 6. Fathers and sons -- Fiction 7. Moving, Household -- Fiction 8. Interpersonal relations -- Fiction
ISBN 0062208721; 9780062208729

LC 2013032816

In this "baseball novel," by Tim Green, "Tommy's the new kid in town--who now goes by the name Brock--and he's having a hard time fitting in. Thanks to a prank gone wrong, he may be able to settle in on the baseball team. But can he prove himself before he becomes a new kid . . . again?" (Publisher's note)

"A teenage baseball star struggles not only with game-day stress, but also with the ever-present fear that his world is about to end. . . . His dad's job is mysterious and dangerous, and it requires them to stay on the run. Moving abruptly has only gotten harder as Brock gets older, and when he finds a great baseball coach and a good friend—and a potential girlfriend—the thought of leaving it all behind terrifies him even more. Best-selling author and former NFL defensive end Green delivers a riveting book about the complexities of being a teenager caught in unusual circumstances beyond his control. His writing is both compelling and intelligent, and even the implausible scenes—like a visit from a baseball great—still maintain a feel of authenticity. Even readers who aren't sports fans will find plenty of familiar drama and entertainment in this book. Exciting, romantic and thought-provoking, this book scores a home run." Kirkus

Rivals. Harper 2010 261p $16.99
Grades: 5 6 7 8 **Fic**

1. Baseball -- Fiction
ISBN 978-0-06-162692-0; 0-06-162692-9
Sequel to: Baseball great (2009)

"12-year-old Josh LeBlanc has his hands full as he tries to lead his team to victory in the Hall of Fame National Championship Tournament. . . . He uncovers a plot on the part of a former major leaguer to fix the games. . . . Everything is handled with a light, deft touch. . . . Enjoyable, unpretentious escapism for youngsters, especially reluctant readers." SLJ

Followed by: Best of the best (2011)

Greenwald, Lisa

★ **My** life in pink and green. Amulet Books 2010 288 p. (hbk.) $16.95
Grades: 4 5 6 7 **Fic**

1. Cosmetics -- Fiction 2. Environmental protection -- Fiction 3. Mother-daughter relationship -- Fiction
ISBN 0810983524; 0810989840 pa; 9780810983526; 9780810989849

LC 2008025577

When the family's drugstore is failing, seventh-grader Lucy uses her problem solving talents to come up with solution that might resuscitate the business, along with helping the environment.

"Greenwald deftly blends eco-facts and makeup tips, friendship dynamics, and spot-on middle-school politics into a warm, uplifting story." Booklist

Sweet treats, secret crushes. Amulet Books 2010 291p $16.95
Grades: 5 6 7 8 **Fic**

1. Friendship -- Fiction 2. Valentine's Day -- Fiction 3. Apartment houses -- Fiction 4. Brooklyn (New York, N.Y.) -- Fiction
ISBN 978-0-8109-8990-0; 0-8109-8990-5

LC 2009052208

When a snowstorm keeps thirteen-year-old best friends Olivia, Kate, and Georgia inside their Brooklyn, New York, apartment building on Valentine's Day, they connect with their neighbors by distributing homemade fortune cookies and uncover one another's secrets along the way.

"An affectionate, insightful ode to friendship. An enjoyable, sure-to-be popular read." Booklist

Welcome to Dog Beach; Lisa Greenwald. Amulet Books 2014 272 p. (Seagate summers) $15.95

Grades: 5 6 7 8 **Fic**

1. Dogs -- Fiction 2. Summer -- Fiction 3. Beaches -- Fiction 4. Friendship -- Fiction 5. Vacations -- Fiction 6. Dog walking -- Fiction

ISBN 9781419710186; 1419710184

LC 2013023282

"Eleven-year-old Remy loves Seagate, the island where her grandmother had a house and where her family spends every summer vacation. But this year's different. Remy misses her dog, Danish, who recently passed away. The usual Seagate traditions don't feel the same--and neither does her relationship with her two best friends, Micayla and Bennett. . . . Remy takes comfort in the company of Dog Beach." (Publisher's note)

"Greenwald's gentle read is tailor-made for those on the cusp of friendship misunderstandings, burgeoning popularity awareness, awkward crushes, and the wobbly feeling that can come from deviating from comfortable routine." Booklist

Greenwald, Tommy

★ **Charlie** Joe Jackson's guide to not reading. Roaring Brook Press 2011 220p il $14.99

Grades: 4 5 6 7 **Fic**

1. School stories 2. Books and reading -- Fiction

ISBN 978-1-59643-691-6; 1-59643-691-3

LC 2010-24079

Middle schooler Charlie Joe is proud of his success at avoiding reading, but eventually his schemes go too far.

"With its subversive humor and contemporary details drawn straight from kids' worlds, this clever title should attract a wide following." Booklist

Charlie Joe Jackson's guide to summer vacation; by Tommy Greenwald ; illustrated by J. P. Coovert. 1st ed. Roaring Brook Press 2013 231 p. ill. (hardcover) $14.99

Grades: 4 5 6 7 **Fic**

1. Camps -- Fiction 2. Reading -- Fiction 3. Vacations -- Fiction 4. Humorous stories 5. Interpersonal relations -- Fiction

ISBN 159643757X; 9781596437579; 9781596438804

LC 2012034249

In this graphic novel by Tommy Greenwald "Charlie Joe Jackson finds himself in a terrible dream he can't wake up from: Camp Rituhbukkee . . . a place filled with grammar workshops, Read-a-Ramas, and kids who actually like reading. But Charlie Joe is determined to convince the entire camp to hate reading and writing—one genius at a time. Tommy Greenwald's 'Charlie Joe Jackson's Guide to Summer Vacation' is another . . . installment in the life of a reluctant reader." (Publisher's note)

Game changer; Tommy Greenwald. Amulet Books 2018 287 p. (hardback) $16.99

Grades: 6 7 8 9 **Fic**

1. Coma -- Fiction 2. Hazing -- Fiction 3. Football -- Fiction 4. Family problems -- Fiction 5. Sports injuries -- Fiction

ISBN 9781419731433

LC 2017055217

In this book, by Tommy Greenwald, "thirteen-year-old Teddy Youngblood is in a coma fighting for his life after an unspecified football injury at training camp. His family and friends flock to his bedside to support his recovery—and to discuss the events leading up to the tragic accident. Was this an inevitable result of playing a violent sport, or was something more sinister happening on the field that day?" (Publisher's note)

Gregg, Stacy

The **princess** and the foal; Stacy Gregg. Philomel Books, an imprint of Penguin Group (USA) 2014 272 p. illustrations (hardback) $16.99

Grades: 5 6 7 8 **Fic**

1. Horses -- Fiction 2. Princesses -- Fiction 3. Jordan -- Fiction 4. Show jumping -- Fiction 5. Animals -- Infancy -- Fiction

ISBN 0399168877; 9780399168871

LC 2014005307

In this juvenile novel, by Stacy Gregg, "when Queen Alia is killed in a tragic accident, Princess Haya is devastated. Knowing how unhappy she is and how much she loves horses, Haya's father, King Hussein, gives her a special present: a foal of her very own. And this foal changes Princess Haya's world completely." (Publisher's note)

"It's also a refreshingly active story—Haya is riding and leaping and playing outdoors (when she's not grounded) on nearly every page. Empowering and vigorous, this is a story sure to please princess fans, horse fans and, yes, even tomboys." Kirkus

Griffin, Adele

The **Julian** game. G.P. Putnam's Sons 2010 200p $16.99

Grades: 8 9 10 11 12 **Fic**

1. School stories 2. Bullies -- Fiction

ISBN 978-0-399-25460-4; 0-399-25460-9

LC 2010-2281

In an effort to improve her social status, a new scholarship student at an exclusive girls' school uses a fake online profile to help a popular girl get back at her ex-boyfriend, but the consequences are difficult to handle.

This is a "perceptive novel. . . . Canny use of details makes Griffin's characters fully realized and believable. . . . Strong pacing and a sympathetic protagonist ought to keep readers hooked." Publ Wkly

Where I want to be. G.P. Putnam's Sons 2005 150p pa $6.99

Grades: 7 8 9 10 **Fic**

1. Death -- Fiction 2. Sisters -- Fiction 3. Rhode Island -- Fiction 4. Mental illness -- Fiction

ISBN 0-399-23783-6; 0-14-240948-0 pa

LC 2004-1887

National Book Award Finalist: Young People's Literature (2005)

Two teenaged sisters, separated by death but still connected, work through their feelings of loss over the closeness they shared as children that was later destroyed by one's mental illness, and finally make peace with each other

"Thoughtful, unique, and ultimately life-affirming, this is a fascinating take on the literary device of a main character speaking after death." SLJ

Griffin, Paul

Saving Marty; by Paul Griffin. Dial Books for Young Readers 2017 195 p. illustrations (hardcover) $16.99

Grades: 5 6 7 8 **Fic**

1. Pigs -- Fiction 2. Farm life -- Fiction 3. Friendship -- Fiction 4. Pennsylvania -- Fiction 5. Single-parent families -- Fiction 6. Swine -- Fiction 7. Heroes -- Fiction 8. Best friends -- Fiction

ISBN 9780399539091; 0399539077; 9780399539077

LC 2017008131

In this book, by Paul Griffin, "eleven-year-old Lorenzo Ventura knows heroes are rare—like his father, who died in the war, or his friend Paloma Lee, who fearlessly pursues her dream of being a famous musician. Renzo would never describe himself as a hero, but his chance comes when he adopts Marty, a runt piglet. Marty is extraordinary—he thinks he's a dog and acts like one too—and his bond with Renzo is truly one of a kind." (Publisher's note)

"Griffin captures a slice of Americana—the flyover farms of middle America—rarely depicted so sensitively in contemporary middle-grade fiction." Booklist

Griffin, Peni R.

The **ghost** sitter. Dutton Children's Bks. 2001 131p $14.99; pa $5.99

Grades: 4 5 6 7 **Fic**

1. Ghost stories

ISBN 0-525-46676-2; 0-14-230216-3 pa

LC 00-65859

When she realizes that her new house is haunted by the ghost of a ten-year-old girl who used to live there, Charlotte tries to help her find peace

"Griffin's book has several strong appeals: new best friends solving a mystery together, a just-scary-enough ghost girl, and a deathless bond between sisters that provides the book with its resoundingly satisfying conclusion and bang-up last sentence." Horn Book

Grimes, Nikki

★ **Bronx** masquerade. Dial Bks. 2002 167p $16.99; pa $5.99

Grades: 7 8 9 10 **Fic**

1. School stories 2. African Americans -- Fiction 3. Bronx (New York, N.Y.) -- Fiction

ISBN 0-8037-2569-8; 0-14-250189-1 pa

LC 00-31701

While studying the Harlem Renaissance, students at a Bronx high school read aloud poems they've written, revealing their innermost thoughts and fears to their formerly clueless classmates

"Funny and painful, awkward and abstract, the poems talk about race, abuse, parental love, neglect, death, and body image. . . . Readers will enjoy the lively, smart voices that talk bravely about real issues and secret fears. A fantastic choice for readers' theater." Booklist

Dark sons. Jump at the Sun 2005 216p $15.99

Grades: 6 7 8 9 10 **Fic**

1. Novels in verse 2. Stepfamilies -- Fiction 3. Father-son relationship -- Fiction

ISBN 0-7868-1888-3

LC 2004-54208

Alternating poems compare and contrast the conflicted feelings of Ishmael, son of the Biblical patriarch Abraham, and Sam, a teenager in New York City, as they try to come to terms with being abandoned by their fathers and with the love they feel for their younger stepbrothers.

"The simple words eloquently reveal what it's like to miss someone. . . . but even more moving is the struggle to forgive and the affection each boy feels for the baby that displaces him. The elemental connections and the hope . . . will speak to a wide audience." Booklist

A **girl** named Mister. Zondervan 2010 223p $15.99

Grades: 8 9 10 11 **Fic**

1. Saints 2. Novels in verse 3. Pregnancy -- Fiction 4. Christian life -- Fiction 5. African Americans -- Fiction

ISBN 978-0-310-72078-2; 0-310-72078-8

LC 2010-10830

A pregnant teenager finds support and forgiveness from God through a book of poetry presented from the Virgin Mary's perspective.

"Writing in lovely prose with lyrical, forthright language that avoids over-moralizing while driving home the big issues of teen pregnancy, award-winning Nikki Grimes just may help a few young women make different choices. At the same time, she effectively makes the case for parents and schools to continue to educate, educate, educate." Voice Youth Advocates

★ **Jazmin's** notebook. Dial Bks. 1998 102p $15.99

Grades: 6 7 8 9 **Fic**

1. Authorship -- Fiction 2. African Americans -- Fiction 3. Harlem (New York, N.Y.) -- Fiction

ISBN 0-8037-2224-9

LC 97-5850

A Coretta Scott King honor book for text, 1999

Jazmin, an Afro-American fourteen-year-old who lives with her older sister in a small Harlem apartment in the 1960s, finds strength in writing poetry and keeping a record of the events in her sometimes difficult life

"An articulate, admirable heroine, Jazmin leaps over life's hurdles with agility and integrity." Publ Wkly

★ **Planet** middle school; Nikki Grimes. Bloomsbury Childrens 2011 154p $15.99

Grades: 4 5 6 7 **Fic**

1. School stories 2. Novels in verse 3. Basketball -- Fiction 4. Friendship -- Fiction 5. Family life -- Fiction

ISBN 978-1-59990-284-5; 1-59990-284-2

LC 2010050744

In this book, by Nikki Grimes, "for twelve years, Joylin Johnson's life has been just fine. . . . A game of basketball with the boys-especially her friend Jake-was all it took to put a smile on her face. . . . Then suddenly . . . everything changed at once. Her best girl friend is now flirting with her best guy friend. Her clothes seem all wrong. Jake is acting weird, and basketball isn't the same. And worst of all, there is this guy, Santiago." (Publisher's note)

"In freeflowing free-verse poems, multi–awardwinning author and poet Grimes . . . explores the riot of hormones and expected gender roles that can make negotiating the preteen years such a challenge. . . . A work that should help adolescent readers find the courage and humor to grow into the individuals they already are." Kirkus

The **road** to Paris. G. P. Putnam's Sons 2006 153p $15.99; pa $6.99

Grades: 4 5 6 7 **Fic**

1. Siblings -- Fiction 2. Foster home care -- Fiction 3. Racially mixed people -- Fiction

ISBN 0-399-24537-5; 978-0-399-24537-4; 978-0-14-241082-0 pa; 0-14-241082-9 pa

LC 2005-28920

Inconsolable at being separated from her older brother, eight-year-old Paris is apprehensive about her new foster family but just as she learns to trust them, she faces a life-changing decision.

"In clear, short chapters, Grimes tells a beautiful story of family, friendship, and faith from the viewpoint of a child in search of home in a harsh world." Booklist

Grisham, John, 1955-

The **accused**; by John Grisham. 1st ed. Dutton Children's Books 2012 271 p. (hardcover) $16.99

Grades: 4 5 6 7 **Fic**

1. Legal stories 2. Stalking -- Fiction 3. Courts -- Fiction 4. Lawyers -- Fiction 5. Stealing -- Fiction

ISBN 0525425764; 9780525425762

LC 2012013972

In this book by John Grisham, "Theodore Boone is being stalked. His lawyer parents are involved in a high-profile case. On the last day of the trial, Theo discovers that his locker has been broken into. Later that day, one of his bike tires is slashed. . . . The 13-year-old becomes the main suspect after a local store is robbed and computers are found in his locker. With the help of his uncle, Theo uses his investigative skills to determine who is behind these crimes." (School Library Journal)

Theodore Boone: kid lawyer. Dutton Children's Books 2010 263p $16.99

Grades: 4 5 6 7 **Fic**

1. Mystery fiction 2. Lawyers -- Fiction

ISBN 0-525-42384-2; 978-0-525-42384-3

With two attorneys for parents, thirteen-year-old Theodore Boone knows more about the law than most lawyers do. But when a high profile murder trial comes to his small town and Theo gets pulled into it, it's up to this amateur attorney to save the day.

"Grisham serves up a dandy legal adventure that moves along quickly. Without intruding on the story's trajectory, he gives plenty of background about the legal process and explores various ethical questions." Horn Book Guide

Other titles in this series are:
The abduction (2010)
The accused (2012)
The activist (2013)
The fugitive (2015)
The scandal (2016)

Theodore Boone: the abduction. Dutton Children's Books 2011 217p $16.99

Grades: 4 5 6 7 **Fic**

1. Lawyers -- Fiction 2. Kidnapping -- Fiction

ISBN 978-0-525-42557-1; 0-525-42557-8

LC 2011006060

When his best friend disappears from her bedroom in the middle of the night, thirteen-year-old Theo uses his legal knowledge and investigative skills to chase down the truth and save April.

"The book is smoothly written, and there's a mild tutorial on the criminal justice system." Publ Wkly

Grossman, Nancy

A **world** away; Nancy Grossman. Hyperion 2012 394 p. $16.99

Grades: 7 8 9 10 **Fic**

1. Bildungsromans 2. Amish -- Fiction 3. Adolescence -- Fiction 4. Aunts -- Fiction 5. Self-realization -- Fiction

ISBN 1423151534; 9781423151531

LC 2011032890

This book is the story of 16-year-old Eliza, who "feels trapped by the conservative traditions of her Amish community. During her 'rumspringa,' a time when Amish teenagers are allowed to 'step out of the plain world,' she" works as "a nanny . . . . Eliza is thrilled with her new contemporary wardrobe and the modern conveniences available to her, but she didn't anticipate falling in love with a neighbor . . . or discovering secrets that will significantly change her view of her family." (Publishers Weekly)

Groth, Darren

Munro vs. the coyote; Darren Groth. Orca Book Publishers 2017 276 p. (hardcover) $19.95

Grades: 7 8 9 10 11 12 **Fic**

1. Death -- Fiction 2. Teenage boys -- Fiction 3. Brothers and sisters -- Fiction 4. Australia -- Fiction

ISBN 1459814096; 9781459814103; 9781459814097; 9781459814110

LC 2017932501

In this book, by Darren Groth, "since the sudden death of his younger sister, Evie, sixteen-year-old Munro Maddux has been having flashbacks and anger-management issues. . . . And there's a taunting, barking, biting voice he calls 'the Coyote.' Munro . . . intends to move beyond his troubled past. It is there, at an assisted living residence called Fair Go Community Village, that Munro discovers the Coyote can be silenced." (Publisher's note)

"Characters that will steal readers' hearts with their humor and resilience, smooth writing, and a satisfying and hopeful ending make this a book to enjoy both emotionally and critically." Kirkus

Grove, S. E.

The **crimson** skew; S.E. Grove. Viking, an imprint of Penguin Random House LLC 2016 448 p. maps (Mapmakers) (hardback) $17.99

Grades: 6 7 8 9 10 **Fic**

1. Fantasy fiction 2. Magic -- Fiction 3. Fantasy 4. Maps -- Fiction

ISBN 9780670785049

LC 2015036703

In this book, by S.E. Grove, "Sophia Tims is coming home from a foreign Age. . . . But her homecoming is anything but peaceful. Threatening clouds hang over New Orleans harbor. Sinkholes have been opening in Boston. . . . Rogue weirwinds tear up the Baldlands. Worst of all, New Occident is at war, led by a prime minister who . . . has blackmailed Sophia's beloved uncle Shadrack into drawing the battle maps that will lead countless men and boys . . . to their deaths." (Publisher's note)

"Pirates, sea captains, fortunetellers, a dragon, poisonous red fog, former slave traders, and healers populate a story that may introduce young readers to the old-fashioned pleasure of settling into a long, rich, and complicated tale.A triumphant conclusion to a prodigious feat of storytelling." Kirkus

★ The **glass** sentence; S.E. Grove. Viking, an imprint of Penguin Group (USA) 2014 512 p. (Mapmakers) (hardcover) $17.99

Grades: 6 7 8 9 10 **Fic**

1. Historical fiction 2. Kidnapping -- Fiction 3. Fantasy 4. Maps -- Fiction

ISBN 0670785024; 9780670785025

LC 2013025832

In this young adult novel by S. E. Grove, part of The Mapmakers Trilogy, "Shadrack is kidnapped. And Sophia, who has rarely been outside of Boston, is the only one who can search for him. Together with Theo, a refugee from the West, she travels over rough terrain and uncharted ocean, encounters pirates and traders, and relies on a combination of Shadrack's maps, common sense, and her own slantwise powers of observation." (Publisher's note)

"In a world fractured into disparate eras during the Great Disruption, Sophia Tims is entrusted with the Tracing Glass (containing a memory thought to be the cause of the Disruption) when her uncle, the cartographer Shadrack Elli, is kidnapped. An intricate fantasy with a Gilded-Age feel, this solidly constructed quest features maps of all kinds and unusual steampunk-flavored elements." Horn Book

The **golden** specific; S.E. Grove ; maps by Dave A. Stevenson. Viking, an imprint of Penguin Group (USA) LLC 2015 528 p. maps (Mapmakers) (hardcover) $17.99
Grades: 6 7 8 9 10 **Fic**

1. Fantasy 2. Fantasy fiction 3. Maps -- Fiction 4. Missing persons -- Fiction
ISBN 9780670785032

LC 2014034892

"In the second installment of the Mapmakers trilogy, Sophia Tims goes on a journey in search of her parents in a world broken apart by the Great Disruption of 1799. Sophia's parents are missing, and finding them is no simple task in this new world of 'intermingled futures and pasts,' in which the former United States has splintered--into New Occident, Indian Territories, and the Baldlands--Canada is now Prehistoric Snows, and large pockets of the world are simply 'Unknown.'" (Kirkus Reviews)

"Brilliantly imagined and full of wonder." Kirkus

Gurevich, Margaret

Chloe by design; making the cut. by Margaret Gurevich ; illustrated by Brooke Hagel. Capstone Young Readers, a Capstone imprint" 2014 384 p. illustrations (chiefly color) (Chloe by design) (paper over board) $14.95
Grades: 5 6 7 8 9 **Fic**

1. Teenage girls -- Fiction 2. Fashion designers -- Fiction 3. Fashion design -- Fiction 4. Television game shows -- Fiction 5. Competition (Psychology) -- Fiction 6. Reality television programs -- Fiction
ISBN 1623701120; 9781623701123

LC 2013050317

In this novel by Margaret Gurevich "Chloe has always loved everything to do with fashion. And when she finds out a new reality series for aspiring teenage designers is holding auditions in her town, she's desperate to win a spot on the show. Chloe knows this is her chance. But before Chloe can realize her dreams, she has to survive the competition." (Publisher's note)

"Project Runway meets Mean Girls in this fashion-inspired first volume of the Chloe by Design series. Chloe Montgomery has always dreamed of becoming a fashion designer, so when her favorite reality show, Design Diva, offers up a teen version of the show, Chloe knows she has to audition—the show's wild challenges will push her creatively. She gets in, but can she overcome her shy instincts and handle criticism from both the judges and her fashion nemesis?...While the outcome is predictable, Chloe's journey (and the fashions that accompany it) make for an enjoyable, fluffy read. Perfect for readers obsessed with fashion, clothing design, and reality TV." Booklist

Another book about Chloe is:
Balancing act (2015)

Gurtler, Janet

I'm not her. Sourcebooks Fire 2011 288p pa $9.99
Grades: 7 8 9 10 **Fic**

1. Cancer -- Fiction 2. Sisters -- Fiction 3. Identity (Psychology) -- Fiction
ISBN 978-1-4022-5636-3; 1-4022-5636-1

Brainy Tess Smith is the younger sibling of the beautiful, popular, volleyball-scholarship-bound Kristina. When Kristina is diagnosed with bone cancer, it drastically changes both sisters' lives.

"This quick and heartbreaking read realistically shows how one person's illness affects an entire community." SLJ

Gutman, Dan

Abner & me; a baseball card adventure. HarperCollins 2005 166p (Baseball card adventure) $16.99; lib bdg $17.89; pa $5.99
Grades: 4 5 6 7 **Fic**

1. Baseball -- Fiction 2. Gettysburg (Pa.), Battle of, 1863 -- Fiction 3. United States -- History -- 1861-1865, Civil War -- Fiction
ISBN 0-06-053443-5; 0-06-053444-3 lib bdg; 0-06-053445-1 pa

LC 2004-6315

With his ability to travel through time using baseball cards and photographs, thirteen-year-old Joe and his mother go back to 1863 to ask Abner Doubleday whether he invented baseball, but instead find themselves in the middle of the Battle of Gettysburg.

Babe & me; a baseball card adventure. Avon Bks. 2000 161p il (Baseball card adventure) $15.99
Grades: 4 5 6 7 **Fic**

1. Baseball players 2. Baseball -- Fiction
ISBN 0-380-97739-7

LC 99-36778

With their ability to travel through time using vintage baseball cards, Joe and his father have the opportunity to find out whether Babe Ruth really did call his shot when he hit that homerun in the third game of the 1932 World Series against the Chicago Cubs

"Readers will enjoy the action, the rich baseball lore, and the sense of adventure." Booklist

Honus & me; a baseball card adventure. Avon Bks. 1997 140p il (Baseball card adventure) $16.99; pa $5.99
Grades: 4 5 6 7 **Fic**

1. Baseball players 2. Baseball coaches 3. Baseball managers 4. Baseball -- Fiction
ISBN 0-380-97350-2; 0-380-78878-0 pa

LC 96-31439

Joey, who loves baseball but is not very good at it, finds a valuable 1909 Honus Wagner card and travels back in time to meet Honus

"This clever adventure will capture the hearts of anyone who has ever held a baseball bat in his or her hands. Gutman's voice rings true from start to finish." SLJ

Jackie & me; a baseball card adventure. Avon Bks. 1999 145p il (Baseball card adventure) $15.99; pa $5.99
Grades: 4 5 6 7 **Fic**

1. Baseball players 2. Army officers 3. Baseball -- Fiction
ISBN 0-380-97685-4; 0-380-80084-5 pa

LC 98-53347

With his ability to travel through time by using baseball cards, Joe goes back to 1947 to meet Jackie Robinson, turning into a black boy in the process

"Full of action, this title will spark history discussions and be a good choice for book reports and leisure reading." SLJ

Jim & me; a baseball card adventure. HarperCollins Publishers 2008 195p (Baseball card adventure) $15.99; lib bdg $16.89

Grades: 4 5 6 7 **Fic**

1. Decathletes 2. Pentathletes 3. Olympic athletes 4. Baseball -- Fiction

ISBN 978-0-06-059494-7; 978-0-06-059495-4 lib bdg

LC 2007030703

Joe and his longtime enemy, Bobby Fuller, use a vintage baseball card to travel in time, hoping to stop Jim Thorpe from participating in the 1912 Olympics and losing his medals, but instead they watch Thorpe struggle during his first season with the New York Giants.

Mickey & me; a baseball card adventure. HarperCollins Pubs. 2003 152p il (Baseball card adventure) $15.99; pa $5.99

Grades: 4 5 6 7 **Fic**

1. Baseball players 2. Baseball -- Fiction

ISBN 0-06-029247-4; 0-06-029248-2 lib bdg; 0-06-447258-2 pa

LC 2002-5641

When Joe travels back in time to 1944, he meets the Milwaukee Chicks, one of the only all-female professional baseball teams in the history of the game

"Like the other books in the series, this one delivers a fast-moving plot, lots of action, and colorful depictions of famous sports heroes of the past." Booklist

The **million** dollar shot. Hyperion Bks. for Children 1997 114p hardcover o.p. pa $5.99

Grades: 4 5 6 7 **Fic**

1. Contests -- Fiction 2. Basketball -- Fiction

ISBN 0-7868-2275-9; 1-4231-0084-0 pa

LC 97-6461

Eleven-year-old Eddie gets a chance to win a million dollars by sinking a foul shot at the National Basketball Association finals

This "will appeal to both sports readers and general audiences. Gutman's subtle humor, exciting sports action, and excruciating suspense make this title an outstanding choice for reluctant readers." SLJ

Mission unstoppable. Harper 2011 293p (The genius files) $16.99; lib bdg $17.89

Grades: 5 6 7 8 **Fic**

1. Adventure fiction 2. Twins -- Fiction 3. Genius -- Fiction 4. Siblings -- Fiction 5. Family life -- Fiction

ISBN 0-06-182764-9; 0-06-182765-7 lib bdg; 978-0-06-182764-8; 978-0-06-182765-5 lib bdg

LC 2010-09390

On a cross-country vacation with their parents, twins Coke and Pepsi, soon to be thirteen, fend off strange assassins as they try to come to terms with their being part of a top-secret government organization known as The Genius Files.

"Gutman's novel offers a quirky look at Americana that will engage curious minds. . . . Those looking for a fun and suspenseful read . . . will not be disappointed." Booklist

Other titles in this series are:
Never say genius (2012)
You only die twice (2013)
From Texas with love (2014)
License to thrill (2015)

Never say genius. Harper 2012 (Genius files) $16.99; lib bdg $17.89

Grades: 5 6 7 8 **Fic**

1. Adventure fiction 2. Twins -- Fiction 3. Genius -- Fiction 4. Siblings -- Fiction 5. Family life -- Fiction

ISBN 978-0-06-182767-9; 0-0-6182767-3; 978-0-06-182768-6 lib bdg; 0-06-182768-1 lib bdg

LC 2011019363

As their cross-country journey with their parents continues through the midwest, twins Coke and Pepsi, now thirteen, again face strange assassins at such places as the first McDonald's restaurant and Cedar Point amusement park.

"The author brings his confused but resourceful youngsters to an explosive climax and a shocking revelation that guarantees further adventures on the road back to the left coast." Kirkus

Ray & me; a baseball card adventure. HarperCollinsPublishers 2009 173p (Baseball card adventure) $15.99

Grades: 4 5 6 7 **Fic**

1. Baseball players 2. Baseball -- Fiction

ISBN 978-0-06-123481-1; 0-06-123481-8; 978-0-06-123482-8 lib bdg

LC 2008019645

After recovering from being hit in the head during a baseball game, Stosh travels back in time to try to save Ray Chapman, a batter who was killed by a pitch in New York in 1920.

Roberto & me; a baseball card adventure. Harper 2010 180p (Baseball card adventure) $15.99; lib bdg $16.89

Grades: 4 5 6 7 **Fic**

1. Baseball players 2. Baseball -- Fiction

ISBN 978-0-06-123484-2; 0-06-123484-2; 978-0-06-123485-9 lib bdg; 0-06-123485-0 lib bdg

LC 2009014267

Stosh travels back to 1969 to try to prevent the untimely death of Roberto Clemente, a legendary baseball player and humanitarian, but upon his return to the present, he meets his own great-grandson who takes him into the future, and what he finds there is more shocking than anything he has encountered in his travels to the past.

"This series entry is both amusing and informative." Booklist

Satch & me; a baseball card adventure. HarperCollins 2006 175p (Baseball card adventures) $15.99; lib bdg $16.89

Grades: 4 5 6 7 **Fic**

1. Baseball players 2. Baseball -- Fiction

ISBN 978-0-06-059491-6; 0-06-059491-8; 978-0-06-059492-3 lib bdg; 0-06-059492-6 lib bdg

LC 2005005717

With his ability to travel through time using vintage baseball cards, Joe takes Flip with him to find out whether Satchel Paige really was the fastest pitcher ever.

"Enhancing the action-driven story are plenty of well-written baseball scenes, black-and-white photos, and the appearance of Negro League players Josh Gibson, Cool Papa Bell, and Buck ONeil." SLJ

Shoeless Joe & me; a baseball card adventure. HarperCollins Pubs. 2002 163p (Baseball card adventures) hardcover o.p. lib bdg $17.89; pa $5.99

Grades: 4 5 6 7 **Fic**

1. Baseball players 2. Baseball -- Fiction

ISBN 0-06-029253-9; 0-06-029254-7 lib bdg; 0-06-447259-0 pa

LC 2001-24638

Joe Stoshack travels back to 1919, where he meets Shoeless Joe Jackson and tries to prevent the fixing of the World Series in which Jackson was wrongly implicated

"Shoeless Joe is compelling, and Joe's adventures are exciting." Voice Youth Advocates

Other titles in the Baseball card adventures series are:
Abner & me (2005)
Babe & me (2000)
Honus & me (1997)
Jackie & me (1999)
Jim & me (2008)
Mickey & me (2003)
Ray & me (2009)
Roberto & me (2010)
Satch & me (2006)

Haber, Melissa Glenn

Dear Anjali. Aladdin 2010 282p $16.99
Grades: 5 6 7 8 **Fic**

1. Letters -- Fiction 2. Friendship -- Fiction 3. Bereavement -- Fiction

ISBN 978-1-4169-9599-9; 1-4169-9599-4

When her best friend dies at the age of thirteen, Meredith writes letters to her as she tries to endure her grief and other confusing emotions.

"Haber skillfully handles the child's heartache, her loneliness, and the conflicting desires. . . . By placing the story between the keys of Meredith's dad's old typewriter, the author gives the narrative a believable realism. . . . The realistic, not-too-tidy ending brings truth to this novel, underscoring that life is complicated." SLJ

Haddix, Margaret Peterson, 1964-

The **always** war. Simon & Schuster Books for Young Readers 2011 197p $16.99
Grades: 7 8 9 10 **Fic**

1. War stories 2. Science fiction 3. Computers -- Fiction 4. Heroes and heroines -- Fiction 5. Post-traumatic stress disorder -- Fiction

ISBN 978-1-4169-9526-5; 1-4169-9526-9

LC 2010033344

In a war-torn future United States, fifteen-year-old Tessa, her childhood friend Gideon, now a traumatized military hero, and Dek, a streetwise orphan, enter enemy territory and discover the shocking truth about a war that began more than seventy-five years earlier.

"The short chapters with cliff-hanger endings and the action-packed plot make this book and excellent choice for reluctant readers." SLJ

Among the Barons. Simon & Schuster Bks. for Young Readers 2003 182p $17.99; pa $6.99
Grades: 5 6 7 8 **Fic**

1. Science fiction

ISBN 0-689-83906-5; 0-689-83910-3 pa

LC 2002-4534

Sequel to Among the betrayed

This "fourth installment in the series that began with Among the Hidden (1998) focuses on 'shadow child' Luke Garner, a third child in a futuristic society that allows families only two children. Luke, who has gone underground to escape the Population Police, reemerges after 12 years in hiding to assume the identity of Lee Grant. . . . The impersonation goes smoothly until Smits, Grant's younger brother, enters the picture. . . . There is enough background information in the opening chapter to fill in readers new to the series, and series fans of the books won't be disappointed; there's plenty of suspense, and there are lots of thrilling twists and turns." Booklist

Among the betrayed. Simon & Schuster Bks. for Young Readers 2002 156p $17.99; pa $6.99
Grades: 5 6 7 8 **Fic**

1. Science fiction

ISBN 0-689-83905-7; 0-689-83909-X pa

LC 2001-32214

Sequel to Among the imposters

Thirteen-year-old Nina is imprisoned by the Population Police, who give her the option of helping them identify illegal "third-born" children, or facing death

"As a character, Nina is well drawn and believable but it is the agonizing moral decisions that she must make that elevate the book beyond the average tale." SLJ

Among the brave. Simon & Schuster Books for Young Readers 2004 229p $17.99; pa $6.99 **Fic**

1. Science fiction

ISBN 0-689-85794-2; 0-689-85795-0 pa

LC 2003-9602

Sequel to Among the Barons

"Like its predecessors in the Shadow Children series, this novel concerns children hidden from society because their families have exceeded the strictly enforced, two-child limit. Trey struggles to survive during a dangerous political shift, as the most repressive faction of the government seizes power. . . .Haddix writes a compelling story, full of intrigue, danger, and adventure." Booklist

Among the enemy. Simon & Schuster Books for Young Readers 2005 214p (Shadow children) $17.99; pa $6.99
Grades: 5 6 7 8 **Fic**

1. Science fiction

ISBN 0-689-85796-9; 0-689-85797-7 pa

LC 2004-9645

Sequel to: Among the brave

In a society that allows families to have only two children, third child Matthias joins the Population Police to infiltrate their system.

"The brisk, efficient pacing facilitated by occasionally abrupt plot turns is precisely what has cemented Haddix's strong following among both avid and reluctant readers. Series fans and newcomers alike will devour this whole." Booklist

Followed by: Among the free

Among the free; [by] Margaret Peterson Haddix. 1st ed.; Simon & Schuster Books for Young Readers 2006 194p $16.95
Grades: 5 6 7 8 **Fic**

1. Science fiction

ISBN 978-0-689-85798-0; 0-689-85798-5

LC 2005013025

When thirteen-year-old Luke Garner unwittingly sets off a rebellion which sweeps the country and ousts the Population Police from power, he quickly realizes that the new regime is corrupt and he may hold the only key to true freedom.

"This is a light, easy read that delivers what it promises. Fans of the series won't be disappointed." SLJ

★ **Among** the hidden. Simon & Schuster Bks. for Young Readers 1998 153p $16.95; pa $5.99
Grades: 5 6 7 8 **Fic**

1. Science fiction

ISBN 0-689-81700-2; 0-689-82475-0 pa

LC 97-33052

In a future where the Population Police enforce the law limiting a family to only two children, Luke has lived all his twelve years in isolation and fear on his family's farm, until another 'third' convinces him that the government is wrong

"The fully realized setting, honest characters, and fast paced plot combine for a suspenseful tale." ALAN

Other titles in this series are:
Among the Barons (2003)
Among the betrayed (2002)
Among the brave (2004)
Among the enemy (2005)
Among the free (2006)
Among the impostors (2001)

Among the impostors. Simon & Schuster Bks. for Young Readers 2001 172p $17.99; pa $6.99

Grades: 5 6 7 8 **Fic**

1. Science fiction

ISBN 0-689-83904-9; 0-689-83908-1 pa

LC 00-58325

Sequel to: Among the hidden

In a future where the law limits a family to only two children, third-born Luke has been in hiding for the entire twelve years of his life, until he enters boarding school under an assumed name and is forced to face his fears

"Luke's quest for selfhood is convincingly portrayed in an unusually tense plot." Horn Book Guide

Caught; Book 5 Margaret Peterson Haddix. Simon & Schuster Books for Young Readers 2012 343 p. (The Missing) (hardcover : alk. paper) $16.99

Grades: 5 6 7 8 **Fic**

1. Science fiction 2. Time travel -- Fiction 3. Einstein, Albert, 1879-1955 -- Fiction 4. Space and time -- Fiction 5. Serbia -- History -- 1804-1918 -- Fiction 6. Switzerland -- History -- 20th century -- Fiction

ISBN 141698982X; 9781416989820; 9781442422889

LC 2011018654

In this fifth installment of Margaret Peterson Haddix's "Missing" series, "Jonah and Katherine are accustomed to traveling through time, but when learn they next have to return Albert Einstein's daughter to history, they think it's a joke -- they've only heard of his sons. But it turns out that Albert Einstein really did have a daughter, Lieserl, whose 1902 birth and subsequent disappearance was shrouded in mystery." (Publisher's note)

Children of exile; Margaret Peterson Haddix. Simon & Schuster Books for Young Readers 2016 304 p. (ebook) $15.99; (hardcover) $17.99

Grades: 5 6 7 8 9 **Fic**

1. Science fiction 2. Parent-child relationship -- Fiction 3. Parent and child -- Fiction

ISBN 9781442450059; 9781442450035; 9781442450042

LC 2015031239

In this novel by Margaret Peterson Haddix, "Rosi must decide what she's willing to risk to save her family—and maybe even all of humanity. . . . For the past twelve years, adults called 'Freds' have raised Rosi, her younger brother Bobo, and the other children of their town, saying it is too dangerous for them to stay with their parents, but now they are all being sent back. . . . Will Rosi and the other kids be able to adjust to their new reality?" (Publisher's note)

"Haddix gives readers lots to mull over regarding conflict, justice, and prejudice." Pub Wkly

Another title in this series is:
Children of refuge (2017)

Children of refuge; Margaret Peterson Haddix. Simon & Schuster Books for Young Readers 2017 262 p. (Children of exile) (hardcover) $17.99

Grades: 5 6 7 8 9 **Fic**

1. Science fiction 2. Extraterrestrial beings -- Fiction 3. Boarding schools -- Fiction 4. Brothers and sisters -- Fiction

ISBN 9781442450080; 9781442450066; 9781442450080

LC 2016028252

Sequel to: Children of Exile (2016)

In this book in the Children of Exile series, by Margaret Peterson Haddix, "it's been barely a day since Edwy left Fredtown to be with his parents and, already, he is being sent away . . . to boarding school in Refuge City. . . . The boarding school is nothing like the school that he knew. . . . Alone and confused, Edwy seeks out other children brought back from Fredtown and soon discovers that Rosi and the others--still stuck in the Cursed Town--might be in danger." (Publisher's note)

"An excellent dystopian adventure for tweens that avoids graphic violence while bringing up issues of social justice and prejudice." Booklist

Full ride; Margaret Peterson Haddix. Simon & Schuster Books for Young Readers 2013 352 p. (hardcover) $16.99

Grades: 6 7 8 9 10 11 12 **Fic**

1. Scholarships -- Fiction 2. Family secrets -- Fiction 3. Ohio -- Fiction 4. Schools -- Fiction 5. Secrets -- Fiction 6. Criminals -- Fiction 7. High schools -- Fiction 8. Mothers and daughters -- Fiction

ISBN 1442442786; 9781442442788; 9781442442795; 9781442442801

LC 2012038146

In this book, by Margaret Peterson Haddix, "Becca's claim to fame is one she's been hiding from for the past three years: Her father is a notorious embezzler. . . . Three years after the trial and imprisonment that destroyed Becca's life, she and her mother have started over again and are living in a town where no one knows their secret. But as college--and its cost--looms large, Becca begins to wonder how they'll afford it. And how she can apply for financial aid without divulging her secret?" (Publisher's note)

"Her father in prison for embezzlement, fourteen-year-old Becca and her mother flee to an Ohio suburb to hide from the media and start new lives. Years later, a chain of events reveals layers of secrets behind Becca's father's crimes, his victims, and her mother's motivations. Haddix deftly emphasizes relatable issues: moving, losing faith in a parent, and falling out of economic comfort." (Horn Book)

★ **Double** identity. Simon & Schuster Books for Young Readers 2005 218p $15.95

Grades: 5 6 7 8 **Fic**

1. Science fiction 2. Cloning -- Fiction

ISBN 0-689-87374-3

LC 2004-13448

Thirteen-year-old Bethany's parents have always been overprotective, but when they suddenly drop out of sight with no explanation, leaving her with an aunt she never knew existed, Bethany uncovers shocking secrets that make her question everything she thought she knew about herself and her family.

This is a "suspenseful sf novel guaranteed to keep readers riveted." Booklist

★ **Found**. Simon & Schuster Books for Young Readers 2008 314p (The missing) $15.99; pa $6.99

Grades: 5 6 7 8 9 **Fic**

1. Science fiction 2. Adoption -- Fiction

ISBN 978-1-4169-5417-0; 1-4169-5417-1; 978-1-4169-5421-7 pa; 1-4169-5421-X pa

LC 2007-23614

When thirteen-year-olds Jonah and Chip, who are both adopted, learn they were discovered on a plane that appeared out of nowhere, full of babies with no adults on board, they realize that they have uncovered a mystery involving time travel and two opposing forces, each trying to repair the fabric of time.

This is "a tantalizing opener to a new series. . . . Readers will be hard-pressed to wait for the next installment." Publ Wkly

Other titles in this series are:

Sent (2009)
Sabotaged (2010)
Torn (2011)
Caught (2012)
Risked (2013)
Revealed (2014)
Redeemed (2015)

Just Ella. Simon & Schuster Bks. for Young Readers 1999 185p hardcover o.p. pa $5.99

Grades: 7 8 9 10 **Fic**

1. Sex role -- Fiction 2. Princesses -- Fiction

ISBN 0-689-82186-7; 0-689-83128-5 pa

LC 98-8384

In this continuation of the Cinderella story, fifteen-year-old Ella finds that accepting Prince Charming's proposal ensnares her in a suffocating tangle of palace rules and royal etiquette, so she plots to escape

"In lively prose, with well-developed characters, creative plot twists, wit, and drama, Haddix transforms the Cinderella tale into an insightful coming-of-age story." Booklist

Risked; Margaret Peterson Haddix. Simon & Schuster Books for Young Readers 2013 320 p. (The missing) (hardcover : alk. paper) $16.99

Grades: 5 6 7 8 9 **Fic**

1. Time travel -- Fiction 2. Soviet Union -- History -- 1917-1921, Revolution -- Fiction 3. Science fiction 4. Soviet Union -- History -- Revolution, 1917-1921 -- Fiction

ISBN 1416989846; 9781416989844; 9781442426474

LC 2012006770

In this book, by Margaret Peterson Haddix, "When Jonah and Katherine find themselves on a mission to return Alexei and Anastasia Romanov to history and then save them from the Russian Revolution, they are at a loss. Because in their own time, the bones of Alexei and Anastasia have been positively identified through DNA testing. What hope do they have of saving Alexis and Anastasia's lives when the twenty-first century has proof of their deaths?" (Publisher's note)

Sabotaged. Simon & Schuster Books for Young Readers 2010 377p (The missing) $16.99

Grades: 5 6 7 8 9 **Fic**

1. Science fiction 2. Colonists 3. Roanoke Island (N.C.) -- History -- Fiction

ISBN 978-1-4169-5424-8; 1-4169-5424-4

Sequel to: Sent (2009)

Time-travelers Jonah and Katherine are summoned to help another missing child from history, this time Virginia Dare from the Roanoke Colony, but their journey is sabotaged and goes dangerously awry, leaving them in the wrong time period. Includes author's note about the history of Roanoke Colony and Virginia Dare.

Sent. Simon & Schuster Books for Young Readers 2009 313p (The missing) $15.99; pa $6.99

Grades: 5 6 7 8 9 **Fic**

1. Science fiction 2. Kings 3. Time travel -- Fiction 4. Great Britain -- Fiction

ISBN 978-1-4169-5422-4; 1-4169-5422-8; 978-1-4169-5423-1 pa; 1-4169-5423-6 pa

LC 2008-11552

Sequel to: Found (2008)

Jonah, Katherine, Chip, and Alex suddenly find themselves in 1483 at the Tower of London, where they discover that Chip and Alex are Prince Edward V and Richard of Shrewsbury, imprisoned by their uncle, King Richard III, but trying to repair history without knowing what is supposed to happen proves challenging. Author's note includes historical facts about the princes and king

"Haddix conveys quite a bit of real history painlessly to her target audience and even mixes in some physics. . . . Valuable fun for tweens." Kirkus

Followed by: Sabotaged (2010)

The **strangers**; Margaret Peterson Haddix. Katherine Tegen Books, an imprint of HarperCollinsPublishers 2019 416 p. (hardback) $17.99

Grades: 4 5 6 7 8 **Fic**

1. Secrets -- Fiction 2. Family life -- Fiction 3. Supernatural -- Fiction 4. Missing persons -- Fiction 5. Brothers and sisters -- Fiction

ISBN 9780062838377

LC 2018013963

In this book in the Greystone Secrets series, by Margaret Peterson Haddix, illustrated by Anne Lambelet, "the Greystone kids thought they knew. Chess has always been the protector over his younger siblings, Emma loves math, and Finn does what Finn does best--acting silly and being adored. They've been a happy family, just the three of them and their mom. But everything changes when reports of three kidnapped children reach the Greystone kids." (Publisher's note)

"A secret-stacked, thrilling series opener about perception, personal memories, and the idiosyncrasies that form individual identities." (Publishers Weekly)

★ **Under** their skin; Margaret Peterson Haddix. Simon & Schuster Books for Young Readers 2016 320 p. (hardcover) $16.99

Grades: 4 5 6 7 **Fic**

1. Science fiction 2. Twins -- Fiction 3. Robots -- Fiction 4. Secrets -- Fiction 5. Human beings -- Fiction 6. Brothers and sisters -- Fiction 7. Extinction (Biology) -- Fiction

ISBN 9781481417587; 9781481417594

LC 2014036962

This juvenile novel, by Margaret Peterson Haddix, is "the first book in a brand-new thrilling series about twins who are on a quest to discover the secrets being kept by their new family. Nick and Eryn's mom is getting remarried, and the twelve-year-old twins are skeptical when . . . Mom tells them . . . they won't ever have to meet their stepsiblings. . . . So the twins set out on a mission to find out who these kids are—and why they're being kept hidden." (Publisher's note)

"Haddix offers a gripping blend of science fiction, suspense, and mystery, taking middle graders and teens on a fast-paced ride that will interest even the most reluctant reader." SLJ

Another title in this series is:

In over their heads (2017)

★ **Uprising**. Simon & Schuster Books for Young Readers 2007 346p $16.99; pa $7.99

Grades: 6 7 8 9 10 **Fic**

1. Fires -- Fiction 2. Strikes -- Fiction 3. Triangle Shirtwaist Company, Inc. -- Fiction

ISBN 978-1-4169-1171-5; 1-4169-1171-5; 978-1-4169-1172-2 pa; 1-4169-1172-3 pa

LC 2006-34870

In 1927, at the urging of twenty-one-year-old Harriet, Mrs. Livingston reluctantly recalls her experiences at the Triangle Shirtwaist factory, including miserable working conditions that led to a strike, then the fire that took the lives of her two best friends, when Harriet, the boss's daughter, was only five years old. Includes historical notes.

"This deftly crafted historical novel unfolds dramatically with an absorbing story and well-drawn characters who readily evoke empathy and compassion." SLJ

Hagen, George

Gabriel Finley & the Lord of Air and Darkness; George D. Hagen. Schwartz & Wade Books 2017 278 p. (hardcover) $16.99

Grades: 5 6 7 8 **Fic**

1. Fantasy fiction 2. Magic -- Fiction 3. Voyages and travels -- Fiction

ISBN 9780399553479; 9780399553486

LC 2017006772

Sequel to: Gabriel Finley & the Raven's Riddle (2014).

In this book, by George Hagen, "Gabriel Finley. . . .[,] along with . . . [his] raven, Paladin . . . and his three friends, . . . ventures back to the . . . city of Aviopolis to free her [mother] from the rune in which she has been imprisoned. But Aviopolis is home to Corax, the Lord of Air and Darkness, who is also Gabriel's uncle. And before Tabitha Finley is released, Gabriel must answer a riddle...or else be imprisoned for eternity within a rune himself." (Publisher's note)

"To survive will require teamwork, courage, and of course an aptitude for solving riddles. The cast is a largely white one. This series' second installment delivers quirky characters, offbeat humor, an enjoyably convoluted plot, and a distinctive take on urban wildlife—imaginary and real." Kirkus.

★ **Gabriel** Finley and the raven's riddle; George Hagen. Schwartz & Wade Books 2014 384 p. illustrations, maps (lib bdg) $19.99

Grades: 5 6 7 8 **Fic**

1. Fantasy fiction 2. Ravens -- Fiction 3. Magic -- Fiction 4. Missing persons -- Fiction 5. Voyages and travels -- Fiction 6. Adventure and adventurers -- Fiction

ISBN 9780385371049; 0385371047; 9780385371032

LC 2013032533

This fantasy by George Hagen follows the "twelve-year-old Gabriel [trying to] find his missing father, who seems to have vanished without a trace. . . . With the help of Paladin--a young raven with whom he has a magical bond that enables them to become one creature--he flies to the foreboding land of Aviopolis, where he must face a series of difficult challenges and unanswerable riddles that could lead to his . . . or to his death." (Publisher's note)

"Hagen's first children's book, flavored with Norse mythology, is brimful of antic energy and inventive flair, like the best middle-grade fantasies." Kirkus

Another title in this series is:

Gabriel Finley and the lord of air and darkness (2017)

Hahn, Mary Downing

★ The **ghost** of Crutchfield Hall. Clarion Books 2010 153p $17

Grades: 5 6 7 8 **Fic**

1. Ghost stories 2. Cousins -- Fiction 3. Orphans -- Fiction 4. Great Britain -- History -- 19th century -- Fiction

ISBN 978-0-547-38560-0; 0-547-38560-9

In the nineteenth century, ten-year-old Florence Crutchfield leaves a London orphanage to live with her great-uncle, great-aunt, and sickly cousin James, but she soon realizes the home has another resident, who means to do her and James harm.

"A deliciously spine-tingling tale that even the most reluctant readers will enjoy." SLJ

Hear the wind blow. Clarion Bks. 2003 212p $15

Grades: 5 6 7 8 **Fic**

1. Siblings -- Fiction 2. United States -- History -- 1861-1865, Civil War -- Fiction

ISBN 0-618-18190-3

LC 2002-15977

With their mother dead and their home burned, a thirteen-year-old boy and his little sister set out across Virginia in search of relatives during the final days of the Civil War

The author "gives readers an entertaining and thought-provoking combination: a strong adventure inextricably bound to a specific time and place, but one that resonates with universal themes." Horn Book

Mister Death's blue-eyed girls; Mary Downing Hahn. Clarion Books 2012 330 p. $16.99

Grades: 8 9 10 11 12 **Fic**

1. Mystery fiction 2. Historical fiction 3. Homicide -- Fiction 4. Grief -- Fiction 5. Murder -- Fiction 6. Coming of age -- Fiction 7. Baltimore (Md.) -- History -- 20th century -- Fiction

ISBN 0547760620; 9780547760629

LC 2011025950

In this work of historical fiction, "[t]he high-school year is almost over, there's a party in the park and Mister Death will soon be there, rifle in hand. . . . Two girls, Cheryl and Bobbi Jo, never make it to school the next day, their bloody bodies found in the park where they were shot. [Mary Downing] Hahn's . . . story traces the effects of a crime on everyone involved, including Buddy Novak, accused of a crime he didn't commit." (Kirkus Reviews)

One for sorrow; a ghost story. Mary Downing Hahn. Clarion Books, Houghton Mifflin Harcourt 2017 293 p. (hardcover) $16.99

Grades: 5 6 7 8 **Fic**

1. Historical fiction 2. Bullies -- Fiction 3. Ghost stories -- Fiction 4. Horror stories 5. Ghosts -- Fiction 6. Friendship -- Fiction 7. Best friends -- Fiction 8. Influenza Epidemic, 1918-1919 -- Fiction 9. World War, 1914-1918 -- United States -- Fiction

ISBN 9781328699022; 9780544818095

LC 2016010761

In this juvenile novel, by Mary Downing Hahn, "against the ominous backdrop of the influenza epidemic of 1918, Annie, a new girl at school, is claimed as best friend by Elsie, a classmate who is a tattletale, a liar, and a thief. Soon Annie makes other friends and finds herself joining them in teasing and tormenting Elsie. Elsie dies from influenza, but then she returns to reclaim Annie's friendship and punish all the girls who bullied her." (Publisher's note)

"Hahn's story is characteristically steeped in eerie atmosphere, and the novel's blend of historical drama, the supernatural, and the intricacies of adolescent friendship is a gripping combination." Pub Wkly

Promises to the dead. Clarion Bks. 2000 202p hardcover o.p. pa $5.99
Grades: 5 6 7 8 **Fic**
1. Slavery -- Fiction 2. Maryland -- Fiction 3. United States -- History -- 1861-1865, Civil War -- Fiction
ISBN 0-395-96394-X; 0-547-25838-0 pa
LC 99-48525

Twelve-year-old Jesse leaves his home on Maryland's Eastern Shore to help a young runaway slave find a safe haven in the early days of the Civil War

"Hahn skillfully blends the language and customs of the Civil War era with an exciting plot." Voice Youth Advocates

★ **Stepping** on the cracks. Clarion Bks. 1991 216p $16; pa $6.99
Grades: 5 6 7 8 **Fic**
1. World War, 1939-1945 -- Fiction
ISBN 0-395-58507-4; 0-547-07660-6 pa
LC 91-7706

In 1944, while her brother is overseas fighting in World War II, eleven-year-old Margaret gets a new view of the school bully Gordy when she finds him hiding his own brother, an army deserter, and decides to help him

"Well-drawn characters and a satisfying plot. . . . There is plenty of action and page-turning suspense to please those who want a quick read, but there is much to ponder and reflect on as well." SLJ

★ **Wait** till Helen comes; a ghost story. Clarion Bks. 1986 184p $15; pa $5.95; pa $6.99
Grades: 4 5 6 **Fic**
1. Ghost stories 2. Stepchildren -- Fiction
ISBN 0-89919-453-2; 0-547-02864-4 pa; 9780380704422 pa
LC 86-2648

"Molly, the 12-year-old narrator, and her brother Michael dislike their bratty 5-year-old stepsister Heather and resent the family move to an isolated converted church in the country. The adjourning graveyard frightens Molly, but Heather seems drawn to it. Molly discovers that the ghost of a child (Helen) who died in a fire a century ago wants to lure Heather to her doom. Molly determines to save her stepsister. In so doing, she learns that Heather's strange behavior stems from her feelings of guilt at having accidentally caused her mother's death by playing near a stove and starting a fire. Eventually, Molly wrests Heather from Helen's arms as the ghost attempts to drown them. The girls discover the skeletons of Helen's parents, and their burial finally puts to rest Helen's spirit. . . . Grades four to seven." (SLJ)

"Intertwined with the ghost story is the question of Molly's moral imperative to save a child she truly dislikes. Though the emotional turnaround may be a bit quick for some, this still scores as a first-rate thriller." Booklist

Hahn, Rebecca

A **creature** of moonlight; Rebecca Hahn. Houghton Mifflin Harcourt 2014 224 p. $17.99
Grades: 7 8 9 10 11 12 **Fic**
1. Fantasy fiction 2. Dragons -- Fiction 3. Fantasy 4. Magic -- Fiction 5. Flowers -- Fiction 6. Identity -- Fiction 7. Princesses -- Fiction 8. Forests and forestry -- Fiction
ISBN 054410935X; 9780544109353
LC 2013020188

In this novel, by Rebecca Hahn, "as the only heir to the throne, Marni should have been surrounded by wealth and privilege, not living in exile--but now the time has come when she must choose between claiming her birthright as princess of a realm whose king wants her dead, and life with the father she has never known: a wild dragon who is sending his magical woods to capture her." (Publisher's note)

"Marni lives in a shack at the edge of the woods with her Gramps, where she tends flowers, as she's done for most of her life. Yet change is afoot... This book's greatest strength lies in the vivid woodland scenes and the rich detail that describes the mystical pieces of Marni's tale." (School Library Journal)

★ The **shadow** behind the stars; Rebecca Hahn. Atheneum Books for Young Readers 2015 256 p. (hardcover) $17.99
Grades: 7 8 9 10 11 12 **Fic**
1. Oracles -- Fiction 2. Prophecies -- Fiction 3. Greek mythology -- Fiction 4. Fate and fatalism -- Fiction 5. Gods and goddesses -- Fiction 6. Goddesses, Greek -- Fiction 7. Mythology, Greek -- Fiction
ISBN 9781481435710; 9781481435727
LC 2014026428

In this book, by Rebecca Hahn, "Chloe is the youngest. . . . She and her sisters have been on their isolated Greek island for longer than any mortal can remember. . . . So when a beautiful girl named Aglaia shows up on their doorstep, Chloe tries to make sure her sisters don't become attached. But in seeking to protect them, Chloe discovers the dark power of Aglaia's destiny." (Publisher's note)

"Hahn's lovingly crafted characters and the brief, unexpected pops of violence in an otherwise peaceful narrative enhance yet another explication of the tragedy of humankind, making this an obvious choice for mythology fans (plenty of those around) and teen philosophers alike." Booklist

Haines, Kathryn Miller

★ The **girl** is murder. Roaring Brook Press 2011 352p $16.99
Grades: 7 8 9 10 **Fic**
1. Mystery fiction 2. Social classes -- Fiction 3. Missing persons -- Fiction 4. New York (N.Y.) -- Fiction 5. Father-daughter relationship -- Fiction
ISBN 978-1-59643-609-1; 1-59643-609-3
LC 2010-32935

In 1942 New York City, fifteen-year-old Iris grieves for her mother who committed suicide, and secretly helps her father with his detective business since he, having lost a leg at Pearl Harbor, struggles to make ends meet. "Grades six to ten." (Bull Cent Child Books)

This is "a smart offering that gives both mysteries and historical fiction a good name. . . . The mystery is solid, but what makes this such a standout is the cast. . . . The characters, young and old, leap off the pages." Booklist

The **girl** is trouble; Kathryn Miller Haines. Roaring Brook Press 2012 336p. $17.99
Grades: 6 7 8 **Fic**
1. Mystery fiction 2. Historical fiction 3. Women detectives -- Fiction
ISBN 9781596436107
LC 2011031806

This book is set in "the Fall of 1942 and Iris's world is rapidly changing. Her Pop is back from the war with a missing leg, limiting his ability to do the physically grueling part of his detective work. Iris is dying to help, especially when she discovers that one of Pop's cases involves a boy at her school. Now, instead of sitting at home watching Deanna Durbin movies, Iris is sneaking out of the house, double crossing her friends, and dancing at the Savoy till all hours of the night. There's certainly never a dull moment in the private eye business." (Publisher's note)

Halam, Ann

Snakehead. Wendy Lamb Books 2008 289p il map $16.99; lib bdg $19.99

Grades: 6 7 8 9 10 **Fic**

1. Gods and goddesses -- Fiction 2. Classical mythology -- Fiction 3. Medusa (Greek mythology) -- Fiction 4. Perseus (Greek mythology) -- Fiction

ISBN 978-0-375-84108-8; 978-0-375-94108-5 lib bdg

LC 2007-28318

Compelled by his father Zeus to accept the evil king Polydectes's challenge to bring the head of the monstrous Medusa to the Aegean island of Serifos, Perseus, although questioning the gods' interference in human lives, sets out, accompanied by his beloved Andromeda, a princess with her own harsh destiny to fulfill.

"Mythology buffs will appreciate the plethora of classical figures, while periodic references to contemporary culture (e.g., a band of rich, rowdy teens are dubbed the Yacht Club kids) and occasional slang drive the story home for the target audience without sacrificing its heroic dimensions." Publ Wkly

Hale, Marian

The **goodbye** season. Henry Holt and Co. 2009 271p $16.99

Grades: 7 8 9 10 **Fic**

1. Texas -- Fiction 2. Bereavement -- Fiction 3. Family life -- Fiction 4. Household employees -- Fiction 5. Mother-daughter relationship -- Fiction

ISBN 978-0-8050-8855-7; 0-8050-8855-5

LC 2008-50275

In Canton, Texas, seventeen-year-old Mercy's dreams of a different life than her mother's are postponed by harsh circumstances, including the influenza epidemic of 1918-19, which forces her into doing domestic work for a loving, if troubled, family.

This is a "compelling, tautly written novel." SLJ

The **truth** about sparrows. Henry Holt & Co. 2004 260p $16.95; pa $6.99

Grades: 5 6 7 8 **Fic**

1. Moving -- Fiction 2. Friendship -- Fiction 3. Great Depression, 1929-1939 -- Fiction

ISBN 0-8050-7584-4; 0-312-37133-0 pa

LC 2003-56981

Twelve-year-old Sadie promises that she will always be Wilma's best friend when their families leave drought-stricken Missouri in 1933, but once in Texas, Sadie learns that she must try to make a new home—and new friends, too

"Rich with social history, this first novel is informative, enjoyable, and evocative." SLJ

Hale, Shannon

★ **Book** of a thousand days; illustrations by James Noel Smith. Bloomsbury Children's Books 2007 305p il $17.95

Grades: 7 8 9 10 **Fic**

1. Fantasy fiction 2. Romance fiction 3. Love stories

ISBN 978-1-59990-051-3; 1-59990-051-3

LC 2006-36999

Fifteen-year-old Dashti, sworn to obey her sixteen-year-old mistress, the Lady Saren, shares Saren's years of punishment locked in a tower, then brings her safely to the lands of her true love, where both must hide who they are as they work as kitchen maids.

This is a "captivating fantasy filled with romance, magic, and strong female characters." Booklist

Enna burning. Bloomsbury 2004 317p $17.95 **Fic**

1. Fairy tales 2. Princesses -- Fiction

ISBN 1-58234-889-8

LC 2003-65817

Sequel to: Goose Girl (2003)

Enna hopes that her new knowledge of how to wield fire will help protect her good friend Isi — the Princess Anidori — and all of Bayern against their enemies, but the need to burn is uncontrollable and puts Enna and her loved ones in grave danger.

"With a richly detailed setting, eloquent descriptions, a complex plot, a large cast of characters, and romance, this high fantasy will be welcomed both by fans of The Goose Girl and those who have yet to discover it." SLJ

Followed by: Forest born (2009)

Forest born. Bloomsbury USA Children's Books 2009 389p map $17.99

Grades: 6 7 8 9 **Fic**

1. Fairy tales 2. Trees -- Fiction

ISBN 978-1-59990-167-1; 1-59990-167-6

LC 2009-641

Sequel to: Enna burning (2004)

When her beloved forest no longer gives her comfort and her brother Razo invites Rinna to the city to be one of Queen Ani's waiting women, she happily accepts, only to discover her own strength comes from places both expected and unexpected.

"Fans of the earlier titles as well as admirers of the genre will find Rin's journey a compelling read." SLJ

The **Goose** girl. Bloomsbury Children's Books 2003 383p $17.95; pa $8.99

Grades: 6 7 8 9 **Fic**

1. Fairy tales 2. Princesses -- Fiction

ISBN 1-58234-843-X; 1-58234-990-8 pa

LC 2002-28336

On her way to marry a prince she's never met, Princess Anidori is betrayed by her guards and her lady-in-waiting and must become a goose girl to survive until she can reveal her true identity and reclaim the crown that is rightfully hers

"A fine adventure tale full of danger, suspense, surprising twists, and a satisfying conclusion." Booklist

Other titles in this series are:
Enna burning (2004)
River secrets (2006)
Forest born (2009)

Princess Academy; palace of stone. Shannon Hale. Bloomsbury 2012 321 p. (hardcover) $16.99

Grades: 6 7 8 9 **Fic**

1. Schools -- Fiction 2. Sex role -- Fiction 3. Mountains -- Fiction

4. Telepathy -- Fiction 5. Self-confidence -- Fiction
ISBN 1599908735; 9781599908731
LC 2012003875

A Newbery Medal honor book, 2006

While attending a strict academy for potential princesses with the other girls from her mountain village, fourteen-year-old Miri discovers unexpected talents and connections to her homeland.

"Hale weaves an intricate, multilayered story about families, relationships, education, and the place we call home." SLJ

Palace of stone

River secrets. Bloomsbury Children's Books 2006 290p map $17.95

Grades: 6 7 8 9 **Fic**

1. Fairy tales
ISBN 1-58234-901-0; 978-1-58234-901-5
LC 2005-35500

Young Razo travels from Bayern to Tira at war's end as part of a diplomatic corps, but mysterious events in the Tiran capital fuel simmering suspicions and anger, and Razo must spy out who is responsible before it is too late and he becomes trapped in an enemy land.

The author "continues the story begun in Goose Girl (2003) and Enna Burning (2004) in this stirring, stand-alone adventure. . . . Hale's accomplished writing will easily pull readers into her vividly realized world." Booklist

Hall, Teri

Away. Dial Books 2011 234 p. $16.99

Grades: 5 6 7 8 **Fic**

1. Science fiction 2. Resistance to government -- Fiction
ISBN 9780803735026; 0803735022
LC 2011001163

Sequel to: The Line (2010)

After helping heal Malgam, Rachel learns that her father is still living in the devastated territory of Away, captured by members of another clan who are planning to use him to make a deal with the government on the other side of the Line, and she joins the rescue party that must risk much to save him.

"This worthy sequel . . . continues to build a dystopian world rich with suspense and moral choices." Kirkus

The **Line**. Dial Books 2010 219p $16.99

Grades: 5 6 7 8 **Fic**

1. Science fiction
ISBN 978-0-8037-3466-1; 0-8037-3466-2
LC 2009-12301

Rachel thinks that she and her mother are safe working for Ms. Moore at her estate close to The Line, an invisible border of the Unified States, but when Rachel has an opportunity to Cross into the forbidden zone, she is both frightened and intrigued

This "sets readers up for a series about another world that might have come from situations too close to our own." Libr Media Connect

Followed by: Away (2011)

Halpern, Julie

Get well soon. Feiwel & Friends 2007 193p $16.95; pa $8.99

Grades: 7 8 9 10 **Fic**

1. Mental illness -- Fiction 2. Psychiatric hospitals -- Fiction
ISBN 0-312-36795-3; 978-0-312-36795-4; 0-312-58148-3 pa; 978-0-312-58148-0 pa
LC 2006-32358

When her parents confine her to a mental hospital, Anna, an overweight teenage girl who suffers from panic attacks, describes her experiences in a series of letters to a friend.

"Halpern creates a narrative that reflects the changes in Anna with each passing day that includes self-reflection and a good dose of humor." Voice Youth Advocates

Have a nice day; Julie Halpern. Feiwel and Friends 2012 325 p. $16.99

Grades: 7 8 9 10 11 12 **Fic**

1. Mental illness -- Fiction 2. Self-perception -- Fiction 3. Parent-child relationship -- Fiction
ISBN 0312606605; 9780312606602

In author Julie Halpern's book, "Anna Bloom has just come home from a three-week stay in a mental hospital. She feels...okay. It's time to get back to some sort of normal life, whatever that means. She has to go back to school, where teachers and friends are dying to know what happened to her, but are too afraid to ask. And Anna is dying to know what's going on back at the hospital with her crush, Justin, but is too afraid to ask. Meanwhile, Anna's parents are"t getting along, and she wonders if she's the cause of her family's troubles." (Publisher's note)

Halpin, Brendan

Shutout. Farrar, Straus and Giroux 2010 183p $16.99

Grades: 6 7 8 9 **Fic**

1. Soccer -- Fiction 2. Friendship -- Fiction
ISBN 978-0-374-36899-9; 0-374-36899-6
LC 2009-32972

Fourteen-year-old Amanda and her best friend Lena start high school looking forward to playing on the varsity soccer team, but when Lena makes varsity and Amanda only makes junior varsity, their long friendship rapidly changes.

"The dialogue is spot-on, and the characters are fully fleshed out. . . . While there is plenty of soccer action for fans of the sport, the book will also appeal to teens looking for a solid friendship story." SLJ

Hamilton, Kersten

In the forests of the night; Kersten Hamilton. Clarion Books 2011 295 p. $16.99

Grades: 7 8 9 10 **Fic**

1. Fantasy fiction 2. Goblins -- Fiction 3. Zoos -- Fiction 4. Magic -- Fiction 5. Finn MacCool -- Fiction 6. Irish Americans -- Fiction 7. Imaginary creatures -- Fiction 8. People with mental disabilities -- Fiction
ISBN 0547435606; 9780547435602
LC 2011009846

This book is the second in Kersten Hamilton's Goblin Wars series. Here, "Teagan and her friends must cope with the aftermath of escaping from the Dark Man's forces as well as new dangers. As she picks up the pieces of her life, Teagan begins a tentative relationship with goblin hunter Finn and struggles with her newly revealed goblin heritage." (School Library Journal)

"In her second book, high schooler Teagan (who found out in Tyger, Tyger that she's half-goblin) is back safely from Mag Mell. While she, her little brother Aiden, and love interest Finn Mac Cumhaill (Finn MacCool from Irish folklore) regroup at home in Chicago, wicked forces track them. Well-incorporated folklore elements blend nicely with everyday concerns (e.g., Teagan's post-high-school plans; best friend/boyfriend rivalry)." (Horn Book)

Tyger tyger; by Kersten Hamilton. Clarion Books 2010 308p (Goblin wars) $17

Grades: 7 8 9 10 **Fic**

1. Fantasy fiction 2. Magic -- Fiction 3. Goblins -- Fiction 4. Irish Americans -- Fiction 5. Children with mental disabilities -- Fiction

ISBN 978-0-547-33008-2; 0-547-33008-1

LC 2010-01337

Soon after the mysterious and alluring Finn arrives at her family's home, sixteen-year-old Teagan Wylltson and her disabled brother are drawn into the battle Finn's family has fought since the thirteenth century, when Finn MacCumhaill angered the goblin king. "Grades eight to ten." (Bull Cent Child Books)

"Laced with humor, packed with surprises and driven by suspense, the plot grabs readers from the start using the stylistic tactics of the best fantasy writing. Major characters are beautifully drawn, and many of the secondary characters are equally distinct." Kirkus

Followed by: In the forests of the night (2011) and When the Stars Threw Down Their Spears (2013)

When the stars threw down their spears; by Kersten Hamilton. Clarion Books 2013 400 p. (hardback) $16.99

Grades: 7 8 9 10 **Fic**

1. Romance fiction 2. Magic -- Fiction 3. Goblins -- Fiction 4. Zoos -- Fiction 5. Horror & Ghost Stories 6. Finn MacCool -- Fiction 7. Chicago (Ill.) -- Fiction 8. Irish Americans -- Fiction 9. Imaginary creatures -- Fiction 10. People with mental disabilities -- Fiction

ISBN 0547739648; 9780547739649

LC 2012029195

"Magical creatures are tumbling through mysterious portals from Mag Mell, the world-between-worlds, into the streets of Chicago. Meanwhile, the romance between seventeen-year-old Teagan, who is part goblin, and the alluring bad boy Finn Mac Cumhaill is heating up . . . which is awkward, to say the least, considering he is bound by a family curse to fight goblins his entire life." (Publisher's note)

"In this third book, Teagan and her friends deal with the evil creatures seeping out of Mag Mell and into the streets of Chicago. Teagan and Finn work together to fight the darkness while their love continues to grow, even though it's now forbidden. Fans of fast-paced adventures and Irish folklore will find the two components nicely intertwined." (Horn Book)

Hamilton, Virginia

★ The **house** of Dies Drear; illustrated by Eros Keith. Macmillan 1968 246p il hardcover o.p. pa $5.99

Grades: 5 6 7 8 **Fic**

1. Mystery fiction 2. Ohio -- Fiction 3. African Americans -- Fiction

ISBN 0-02-742500-2; 1-4169-1405-6 pa

"The answer to the mystery comes in a startling dramatic dénouement that is pure theater. This is gifted writing; the characterization is unforgettable, the plot imbued with mounting tension." Saturday Rev

Followed by The mystery of Drear House (1987)

★ The **planet** of Junior Brown. Macmillan 1971 210p hardcover o.p. pa $5.99

Grades: 6 7 8 9 **Fic**

1. Friendship -- Fiction 2. African Americans -- Fiction

ISBN 0-689-71721-0; 1-4169-1410-2 pa

A Newbery Medal honor book, 1972

"This is the story of a crucial week in the lives of two black, eighth-grade dropouts who have been spending their time with the school janitor. Each boy is presented as a distinct individual. Jr. is a three-hundred pound musical prodigy as neurotic as his overprotective mother. Buddy has learned to live by his wits in a world of homeless children. Buddy becomes Jr. Brown's protector and says to the other boys, 'We are together because we have to learn to live for each other.'" Read Ladders for Hum Relat. 6th edition

Han, Jenny

It's not summer without you; a summer novel. Simon & Schuster Books for Young Readers 2010 275p $16.99

Grades: 7 8 9 10 **Fic**

1. Summer -- Fiction 2. Beaches -- Fiction 3. Friendship -- Fiction

ISBN 978-1-4169-9555-5; 1-4169-9555-2

LC 2009-42180

Sequel to: The summer I turned pretty (2009)

Teenaged Isobel "Belly" Conklin, whose life revolves around spending the summer at her mother's best friend's beach house, reflects on the tragic events of the past year that changed her life forever

"Han artfully weaves together Belly's and Jeremiah's back stories, recent and long past, to create a solid fabric of relationship and longing. Flashes of humor, realistic (and often salty) dialogue and growing-up moments both painful and authentic create a convincing and poignant read." Publ Wkly

Followed by: We'll always have summer (2011)

Shug; [by] Jenny Han. 1st ed.; Simon & Schuster Books for Young Readers 2006 248p $14.95

Grades: 5 6 7 8 **Fic**

1. School stories 2. Family life -- Fiction

ISBN 978-1-4169-0942-2; 1-4169-0942-7

LC 2005009367

"Tall, freckled, gawky seventh-grader Annemarie Wilcox (whose family calls her Shug) has a beautiful, popular older sister; a gorgeous, alcoholic mother who doesn't fit in their small Georgia town; and a father who's always away on business. She also has a huge crush on Mark, the neighborhood boy who has always been her best friend. . . . Shug's direct, honest narration reveals a wholly believable, endearing, hot-tempered young woman who faces painful truths and survives." Booklist

★ The **summer** I turned pretty. Simon & Schuster Books for Young Readers 2009 276p $16.99

Grades: 7 8 9 10 **Fic**

1. Summer -- Fiction 2. Beaches -- Fiction 3. Vacations -- Fiction 4. Friendship -- Fiction

ISBN 1-4169-6823-7; 978-1-4169-6823-8

LC 2008-27070

Belly spends the summer she turns sixteen at the beach just like every other summer of her life, but this time things are very different.

"Romantic and heartbreakingly real. . . . The novel perfectly blends romance, family drama, and a coming-of-age tale, one that is substantially deeper than most." SLJ

Other titles in this series are:

It's not summer without you (2010)

We'll always have summer (2011)

We'll always have summer; a Summer novel. Simon & Schuster Books for Young Readers 2011 291p $17.99

Grades: 7 8 9 10 **Fic**

1. Romance fiction 2. Love stories 3. Summer -- Fiction 4. Beaches -- Fiction 5. Brothers -- Fiction 6. Vacations -- Fiction

ISBN 978-1-4169-9558-6; 1-4169-9558-7; 978-1-4169-9560-9 eBook

LC 2010046670

Sequel to: It's not summer without you (2010)

The summer after her first year of college, Isobel "Belly" Conklin is faced with a choice between Jeremiah and Conrad Fisher, brothers she has always loved, when Jeremiah proposes marriage and Conrad confesses that he still loves her.

"In Han's conclusion to the trilogy that began with The Summer I Turned Pretty, she both underscores the folly of getting engaged too young and vividly depicts the emotions of a girl on the brink of womanhood." Publ Wkly

Hand, Cynthia

★ **My** Lady Jane; Cynthia Hand, Brodi Ashton, and Jodi Meadows. Harpercollins Childrens Books 2016 512 p. $17.99
Grades: 7 8 9 10 11 **Fic**

1. Kings and rulers -- Fiction 2. Courts and courtiers -- Fiction
ISBN 0062391747; 9780062391742

LC 2015948301

In this novel, by Cynthia Hand, Brodi Ashton, and Jodi Meadows, "at sixteen, Lady Jane Grey is about to be married off to a stranger and caught up in a conspiracy to rob her cousin, King Edward, of his throne. But those trifling problems aren't for Jane to worry about. Jane gets to be Queen of England. Like that could go wrong." (Publisher's note)

"Wonky, offbeat, and happily anachronistic—the references run the gamut from Shakespeare to Monty Python, with plenty of nods to The Princess Bride—this fantasy adventure politely tips its hat to history before joyfully punting it out of the way. An utter delight." Booklist

My plain Jane; Cynthia Hand, Brodi Ashton, Jodi Meadows. HarperTeen, an imprint of HarperCollinsPublishers 2018 xi, 450 p.p (hardcover) $17.99
Grades: 7 8 9 10 11 **Fic**

1. Ghost stories 2. Governesses -- Fiction 3. Supernatural -- Fiction
ISBN 9780062652799; 9780062652775

LC 2018933339

In this novel, by Cynthia Hand, Brodi Ashton and Jodi Meadows, "you may think you know the story. Penniless orphan Jane Eyre begins a new life as a governess at Thornfield Hall, where she meets one dark, brooding Mr. Rochester--and, Reader, she marries him. Or does she? Prepare for an adventure of Gothic proportions in this stand-alone follow-up to 'My Lady Jane.'" (Publisher's note)

"A fun, supernatural mashup of different literary novels that shines on its own merit." Kirkus

Unearthly; [by] Cynthia Hand. HarperTeen 2011 435p $17.99
Grades: 7 8 9 10 **Fic**

1. School stories 2. Angels -- Fiction 3. Moving -- Fiction 4. Wyoming -- Fiction 5. Supernatural -- Fiction
ISBN 978-0-06-199616-0; 0-06-199616-5

LC 2010-17849

Sixteen-year-old Clara Gardner's purpose as an angel-blood begins to manifest itself, forcing her family to pull up stakes and move to Jackson, Wyoming, where she learns that danger and heartbreak come with her powers.

"Hand avoids overt discussion of religion while telling an engaging and romantic tale with a solid backstory. Her characters deal realistically with the uncertainty of being on the cusp of maturity without wrapping themselves in angst." Publ Wkly

Other titles in this series are:
Hallowed (2012)
Boundless (2013)

Handler, Daniel, 1970-

★ **Why** we broke up; art by Maira Kalman. Little, Brown 2012 354p il $19.99
Grades: 8 9 10 11 12 **Fic**

1. Man-woman relationship -- Fiction 2. Breaking up (Interpersonal relations) 3. Letters -- Fiction 5. Dating (Social customs) -- Fiction
ISBN 978-0-316-12725-7

LC 2011009714

Printz Honor Book (2012)

Sixteen-year-old Min Green writes a letter to Ed Slaterton in which she breaks up with him, documenting their relationship and how items in the accompanying box, from bottle caps to a cookbook, foretell the end.

Hannigan, Katherine

True (. . . sort of) Greenwillow Books 2011 360p $16.99; lib bdg $17.89
Grades: 4 5 6 **Fic**

1. School stories 2. Siblings -- Fiction 3. Friendship -- Fiction 4. Family life -- Fiction
ISBN 978-0-06-196873-0; 0-06-196873-0; 978-0-06-196874-7 lib bdg; 0-06-196874-9 lib bdg

For most of her eleven years, Delly has been in trouble without knowing why, until her little brother, R. B., and a strange, silent new friend, Ferris, help her find a way to be good—and happy—again.

"Told in carefully crafted language that begs to be read aloud, the story runs the gamut from laugh-out-loud funny to emotionally wrenching." SLJ

Hansen, Joyce

The **gift** -giver; Joyce Hansen. Clarion Bks. 1980 118p (163 Street trilogy) pa $6.95
Grades: 4 5 6 7 **Fic**

1. School stories 2. Friendship -- Fiction 3. Foster home care -- Fiction 4. African Americans -- Fiction 5. Bronx (New York, N.Y.) -- Fiction
ISBN 0-618-61123-1

LC 80-12969

Doris tells the story of her friendship with Amir, a foster child in her Bronx neighborhood, and how it brings her into closer understanding with her family even though it divides her from her old friends.

This "has well-developed plot threads that are nicely knit, a memorable depiction of a person whose understanding and compassion are gifts to his friends, and a poignantly realistic ending." Bull Cent Child Books

Other titles in this series are:
Yellow Bird and me (1986)
One true friend (2001)

One true friend. Clarion Bks. 2001 154p hardcover o.p. pa $6.95
Grades: 4 5 6 7 **Fic**

1. Friendship -- Fiction 2. Foster home care -- Fiction 3. New York (State) -- Fiction 4. African Americans -- Fiction 5. Bronx (New York, N.Y.) -- Fiction
ISBN 0-395-84983-7; 0-618-60991-1 pa

LC 2001-28483

Fourteen-year-old orphan Amir, living in Syracuse, exchanges letters with his friend Doris, still living in their old Bronx neighborhood, in which they share their lives and give each other advice on friendship, family, foster care, and making decisions

"Both sad and hopeful, this story dramatizes the struggle for survival, the primal pull of family, and the gift of 'one true friend.'" Booklist

Other titles about Amir and Doris are:

The gift-giver (1980)
Yellow Bird and me (1985)

Yellow Bird and me. Clarion Bks. 1985 155p hardcover o.p. pa $6.95

Grades: 4 5 6 7 **Fic**

1. Dyslexia -- Fiction 2. Friendship -- Fiction 3. New York (State) -- Fiction 4. African Americans -- Fiction 5. Bronx (New York, N.Y.) -- Fiction

ISBN 0-89919-335-8; 0-618-61116-9 pa

LC 85-484

"Hansen's familiarity with reading problems and young people is evident in her credible characters and lively dialogue that rings true." SLJ

Hardinge, Frances

★ **Cuckoo** song; Frances Hardinge. Amulet Books 2014 416 p. (hardback) $17.95

Grades: 7 8 9 10 11 12 **Fic**

1. Horror fiction 2. Identity (Psychology) -- Fiction 3. Memory -- Fiction 4. Paranormal fiction 5. Family life -- England -- Fiction 6. Great Britain -- History -- George V, 1910-1936

ISBN 9781419714801; 9780330519731; 0330519735; 1419714805

LC 2014045264

In this suspense novel, by Frances Hardinge, "when Triss wakes up after an accident, she knows that something is very wrong. She is insatiably hungry; her sister seems scared of her and her parents whisper behind closed doors. She looks through her diary to try to remember, but the pages have been ripped out. Soon Triss discovers that what happened to her is more strange and terrible than she could ever have imagined, and that she is quite literally not herself." (Publisher's note)

"Nuanced and intense, this painstakingly created tale mimics the Escher-like constructions of its villainous Architect, fooling the eyes and entangling the emotions of readers willing and able to enter into a world like no other." Kirkus

★ A **face** like glass; by Frances Hardinge. Amulet Books 2017 487 p. (hardcover) $19.95

Grades: 6 7 8 9 10 **Fic**

1. Fantasy fiction 2. Emotions -- Fiction 3. Masks (Facial) -- Fiction 4. Underground areas -- Fiction

ISBN 9781683350781; 1419724843; 9781419724848

LC 2016037692

Originally published 2013 in the U.K.

In this book, by Frances Hardinge, "in the underground city of Caverna, the world's most skilled craftsmen toil in the darkness to create delicacies beyond compare. . . . On the surface, the people of Caverna seem ordinary, except for one thing: their faces are as blank as untouched snow. . . . Into this dark and distrustful world comes Neverfell, a girl with no memory of her past and a face so terrifying to those around her that she must wear a mask at all times. " (Publisher's note)

"Hardinge's characteristically lush and sophisticated language will entrance readers, and she makes wonderful use of her singular setting and wildly eccentric cast to pose haunting questions about reality, artifice, and the things we attempt to conceal." Pub Wkly

★ **Fly** by night. HarperCollinsPublishers 2006 487p hardcover o.p. lib bdg $17.89; pa $7.99

Grades: 5 6 7 8 **Fic**

1. Fantasy fiction

ISBN 978-0-06-087627-2; 0-06-087627-1; 978-0-06-087629-6 lib bdg; 0-06-087629-8 lib bdg; 978-0-06-087630-2 pa; 0-06-087630-1 pa

LC 2005-20598

Mosca Mye and her homicidal goose, Saracen, travel to the city of Mandelion on the heels of smooth-talking con-man, Eponymous Clent.

"Through rich, colorful language and a sure sense of plot and pacing, Hardinge has created a distinctly imaginative world full of engaging characters, robust humor, and true suspense." SLJ

Followed by: Fly trap (2011)

Fly trap; Frances Hardinge. HarperCollins 2011 592 p. hbk $16.99

Grades: 5 6 7 8 **Fic**

1. Fantasy fiction 2. Geese -- Fiction 3. Orphans -- Fiction

ISBN 0060880449; 9780060880446

LC 2010027755

Sequel to: Fly by night (2006)

"Having barely escaped the revolution they had a huge (if accidental) part in causing, sharp-eyed orphan Mosca Mye; her guard goose, Saracen; and their sometimes-loyal companion, the con man Eponymous Clent, must start anew.

All too quickly, they find themselves embroiled in fresh schemes and twisting politics as they are trapped in Toll, an odd town that changes its entire personality as day turns to night. Mosca and her friends attempt to fend off devious new foes, subvert old enemies, prevent the kidnapping of the mayor's daughter, steal the town's Luck, and somehow manage to escape with their lives--and hopefully a little money in their pockets." (Publisher's note)

Crammed with eccentric, Dickensian characters, unexpected plot turns, and numerous very niche gods and goddesses . . . , Hardinge's world is rich enough to fuel two or three fantasy novels. It's a beautifully written tale, by turns humorous and heartbreaking and a sheer pleasure to read. Publ Wkly

★ The **Lie** Tree; Frances Hardinge. Amulet Books 2016 416 p. $17.95

Grades: 7 8 9 10 11 12 **Fic**

1. Murder -- Fiction 2. Secrets -- Fiction 3. Scientists -- Fiction

ISBN 1419718959 ; 9781419718953

LC 2015028326

Originally published in the United Kingdom by Macmillan Children's Books, 2015

Boston Globe-Horn Book Award: Fiction (2016)

In this book, by Frances Hardinge, "Faith Sunderly leads a double life. To most people, she is . . . a proper young lady. . . . But inside, Faith is full of questions and curiosity, and she cannot resist mysteries. . . . She knows that her family moved to the close-knit island of Vane because her famous scientist father was fleeing a reputation-destroying scandal. And she knows, when her father is discovered dead shortly thereafter, that he was murdered." (Publisher's note)

"Smart, feminist, and shadowy, Hardinge's talents are on full display here." SLJ

The **lost** conspiracy. Harper 2009 568p $16.99; lib bdg $17.89

Grades: 6 7 8 9 10 **Fic**

1. Fantasy fiction 2. Sisters -- Fiction

ISBN 978-0-06-088041-5; 0-06-088041-4; 978-0-06-088042-2 lib bdg; 0-06-088042-2 lib bdg

LC 2008-45380

Published in the United Kingdom with title: Gullstruck Island

When a lie is exposed and their tribe turns against them, Hathin must find a way to save her sister Arilou—once considered the tribe's oracle—and herself.

"A deeply imaginative story, with nuanced characters, intricate plotting, and an amazingly original setting. . . . A perfectly pitched, hopeful ending caps off this standout adventure." Booklist

A **skinful** of shadows; Frances Hardinge. Amulet Books 2017 415 p. (hardback) $19.99

Grades: 7 8 9 10 **Fic**

1. Ghost stories 2. Horror fiction 3. Fantasy fiction 4. Girls -- Fiction 5. Families -- Fiction 6. Friendship -- Fiction 7. Family secrets -- Fiction 8. Spirit possession -- Fiction 9. Identity (Psychology) -- Fiction 10. Inheritance and succession -- Fiction 11. Great Britain -- History -- Civil War, 1642-1649 -- Fiction

ISBN 9781419725722; 9781683351061

LC 2017039466

This historical fantasy, by Frances Hardinge, is "set in the early part of the English Civil War. Makepeace is an illegitimate daughter of the aristocratic Fellmotte family, and as such, she shares their unique hereditary gift: the capacity to be possessed by ghosts. Reluctant to accept her appointed destiny as vessel for a coterie of her ancestors, she escapes. As she flees the pursuing Fellmottes across war-torn England, she accumulates a motley crew of her own allies." (Publisher's note)

"Hardinge's writing is stunning, and readers will be taken hostage by its intensity, fascinating developments, and the fierce, compassionate girl leading the charge." Booklist

Hardy, Janice

Blue fire. Balzer + Bray 2010 373p (The Healing Wars) $16.99

Grades: 5 6 7 8 **Fic**

1. War stories 2. Fantasy fiction 3. Orphans -- Fiction 4. Sisters -- Fiction

ISBN 978-0-06-174741-0; 0-06-174741-6

LC 2009053446

Sequel to: The shifter (2009)

While trying to lead the Takers out of Geveg, fifteen-year-old Nya is captured by bounty-hunters and taken to Baseer, where she escapes and soon finds herself helping the Baseeri.

"The climax . . . yields much narrative tension but doesn't resolve the driving issues of the story. For that, readers will have to wait for book three in this thrilling, complex saga." Horn Book

Darkfall. Balzer + Bray 2011 418p (The healing wars) $16.99

Grades: 5 6 7 8 **Fic**

1. Fantasy fiction 2. Orphans -- Fiction 3. Sisters -- Fiction

ISBN 978-0-06-174750-2; 0-06-174750-5

LC 2011001946

With the rebellion in full swing, fifteen year-old Nya's loyaltie are put to the ultimate test,and she is forced to choose between leading an army against the Duke or abandoning her people to save her sister.

"The finale offers suspense, resolution of prior wrongs, the sweetness of first love and a battle-tested heroine who fights with her head and heart." Kirkus

The **shifter**. Balzer + Bray 2009 370p (The Healing Wars) $16.99; pa $7.99

Grades: 5 6 7 8 **Fic**

1. War stories 2. Fantasy fiction 3. Orphans -- Fiction 4. Sisters -- Fiction

ISBN 978-0-06-174704-5; 0-06-174704-1; 978-0-06-174708-3 pa; 0-06-174708-4 pa

LC 2008-47673

Nya is an orphan struggling for survival in a city crippled by war. She is also a Taker—with her touch, she can heal injuries, pulling pain from another person into her own body. But unlike her sister, Tali, and the other Takers who become Healers' League apprentices, Nya's skill is flawed: She can't push that pain into pynvium, the enchanted metal used to store it. All she can do is shift it into another person

"The ethical dilemmas raised . . . provide thoughtful discussion material and also make the story accessible to more than just fantasy readers." Booklist

Other titles in this series are:

Blue fire (2010)

Darkfall (2011)

Hargrave, Kiran Millwood

The **island** at the end of everything; Kiran Millwood Hargrave. Alfred A. Knopf 2018 256 p. (hardback) $16.99

Grades: 4 5 6 7 8 **Fic**

1. Leprosy -- Fiction 2. Friendship -- Fiction 3. Mother-daughter relationship -- Fiction 4. Orphanages -- Fiction 5. Mothers and daughters -- Fiction 6. Philippines -- History -- 20th century -- Fiction 7. Culion Island (Philippines) -- History -- 20th century -- Fiction

ISBN 9780553535327; 9780553535334

LC 2017021578

In this book, by Kiran Millwood Hargrave, "Ami lives on Culion, an island in the Philippines for people who have leprosy. Her mother is among the infected. . . . [T]he arrival of malicious government official Mr. Zamora changes her world forever. Islanders untouched by sickness are forced to leave for a neighboring island, where the children are placed in an orphanage. Banished across the sea, Ami is desperate to return to Culion before her mother's death." (Publisher's note)

"Hargrave tells an incredible story of compassion, love, and daring in this book's pages, and her lyrical writing glides with the grace of a butterfly. An author's note gives the real history of Culion's leper colony and speaks to the complexity of human nature, further enriching Ami's unforgettable story." Booklist

Harlow, Joan Hiatt

The **watcher**; Joan Hiatt Harlow. Margaret K. McElderry Books 2014 290 p. (hardback) $16.99

Grades: 5 6 7 **Fic**

1. Germany -- Fiction 2. Identity -- Fiction 3. Parental kidnapping -- Fiction 4. World War, 1939-1945 -- Fiction 5. Mother-daughter relationship -- Fiction 6. National socialism -- History -- Fiction 7. Nazis -- Fiction 8. Mothers and daughters -- Fiction 9. Germany -- History -- 1933-1945 -- Fiction 10. World War, 1939-1945 -- Germany -- Berlin -- Fiction 11. World War, 1939-1945 -- Underground movements -- Germany -- Fiction

ISBN 1442429119; 9781442429116; 9781442429123

LC 2014030259

"Wendy is kidnapped . . . by her own mother, who is actually a Nazi spy. As a new Berliner - and now a German - Wendy is expected to speak in a language she's never known and support a cause she doesn't believe in. There are allies, though, among the Germans. Allies who have been watching over Wendy since she arrived. And Wendy, along with her new German shepherd puppy, must confront them. If only she can find them." (Publisher's note)

"Harlow knows how to develop a story that will draw students in and keep their attention to the very end. The story combines adventure and suspense, with a heartwarming story of friendship and loyalty. The historical aspect also makes it well-suited to Social Studies classes covering World War II." Lib Med Con

Includes bibliographical references

Harper, Charise Mericle

Alien encounter; Charise Mericle Harper. First edition Christy Ottaviano Books, Henry Holt & Company 2014 208 p. illustrations (Sasquatch and aliens) (hardback) $12.99

Grades: 3 4 5 6 **Fic**

1. Yeti -- Fiction 2. Friendship -- Fiction 3. Family life -- Fiction 4. Extraterrestrial beings -- Fiction 5. Humorous stories 6. Family life -- Northwest, Pacific -- Fiction

ISBN 0805096213; 9780805096217

LC 2013039906

This book, the first in Charise Mericle Harper's "Sasquatch and Aliens" series, "introduces a pair of nine-year-old boys who are propelled into an adventure that may or may not involve otherworldly creatures. Anxiety-prone Morgan first meets new kid Lewis as Lewis is hanging from a tree by his underwear. After Morgan reluctantly rescues Lewis (whose family just bought a creepy motel), a tentative friendship is born." (Publishers Weekly)

"With an authentic, zany splash of fourth-grade humor, perspective, and imagination, this inaugural series title targets boys and will captivate elementary readers. . . . Morgan is a spunky, verbal, resourceful protagonist whose nonstop adventures resonate with self-discovery, family relationships, friendships, and creative problem-solving." SLJ

Harrell, Rob

Troll overboard; by Rob Harrell. Dial Books for Young Readers, an imprint of Penguin Random House, LLC 2016 265 p. illustrations (Life of Zarf) (hardcover) $15.99; (ebook) $23.97

Grades: 4 5 6 7 **Fic**

1. Trolls -- Fiction 2. Humorous stories 3. Adventure and adventurers -- Fiction

ISBN 0803741057; 9780803741058; 9780698145757

LC 2015049505

Sequel to: Troll who cried wolf

In this third book in the Life of Zarf series by Rob Harrell, the troll Zarf "is already at the bottom of the food chain when it comes to popularity at Cotswin Middle School. So when his Gramps shows up at career day, Zarf is sure his cool factor will hit an all-time low. What he doesn't expect is for the super-obnoxious Prince Roquefort to take an interest in Gramps's nautical know-how. Zarf is sure the prince is up to something."(Publisher's note)

"Interspersed with bratty illustrations, this ought to find a sweet spot at the nexus between fans of humor and fans of fractured fantasies." Booklist

Harrington, Janice N.

Catching a storyfish; Janice N. Harrington. WordSong 2016 224 p. $17.95

Grades: 4 5 6 7 **Fic**

1. Moving -- Fiction 2. Listening -- Fiction 3. Friendship -- Fiction 4. Grandfathers -- Fiction

ISBN 1629794295; 9781629794297; 9781629797434

LC 2016936167

In this book, by Janice N. Harrington, "Keet knows the only good thing about moving away from her Alabama home is that she'll live near her beloved grandfather. When Keet starts school, it's even worse than she expected, as the kids tease her about her southern accent. Now Keet, who can 'talk the whiskers off a catfish,' doesn't want to open her mouth. Slowly, though, while fishing with her grandfather, she learns the art of listening." (Publisher's note)

"A gentle-spirited book about a black girl who almost gives up her gift but for love and friendship." Kirkus

Harrington, Karen

Courage for beginners; by Karen Harrington. Little, Brown and Co. 2014 304 p. (hardcover) $17

Grades: 4 5 6 7 8 **Fic**

1. Texas -- Fiction 2. Friendship -- Fiction 3. Schools -- Fiction 4. Agoraphobia -- Fiction 5. Middle schools -- Fiction 6. Family problems -- Fiction

ISBN 031621048X; 9780316210485

LC 2013021596

Sequel to: Sure Signs of Crazy (2013)

"Twelve-year-old Mysti Murphy wishes she were a character in a book. If her life were fictional, she'd magically know how to deal with the fact that her best friend, Anibal Gomez, has abandoned her in favor of being a 'hipster.' She'd be able to take care of everyone when her dad has to spend time in the hospital. And she'd certainly be able to change her family's secret." (Publisher's note)

"Mysti's curatorial narration--as if she were describing paintings or book characters--works on multiple levels, showing off her snark and emphasizing her mother's sheltered influence. Her mother is flawed but sympathetic; she knows her fears are disproportionate, but their debilitating effect is real.With gallows humor and believable small victories, this unusual novel is a window into making friends and facing fears." Kirkus

Mayday; by Karen Harrington. Little, Brown Books for Young Readers 2016 352 p. (hardback) $16.99

Grades: 5 6 7 8 **Fic**

1. Grief -- Fiction 2. Voice -- Fiction 3. Family -- Fiction 4. Aircraft accidents -- Fiction 5. Families -- Fiction

ISBN 0316298018; 9780316298018

LC 2015020622

In this book, by Karen Harrington, "Wayne Kovok lives in a world of After. After his uncle in the army was killed overseas. After Wayne and his mother survived a plane crash while coming back from the funeral. After he lost his voice. Wayne has always used his love of facts to communicate. . . . Without his voice, how will he wow the prettiest girl in school? How will he stand up to his drill-sergeant grandfather? And how will he share his hopes with his deadbeat dad?" (Publisher's note)

"Wayne is an appealing protagonist with a strong voice who develops believably over the difficult months, as do the other characters. A well-done book on all levels." Pub Wkly

Sure signs of crazy; by Karen Harrington. 1st ed. Little Brown & Co 2013 288 p. (hardcover) $17

Grades: 4 5 6 7 8 **Fic**

1. Adolescence -- Fiction 2. Parent-child relationship -- Fiction 3. Texas -- Fiction 4. Coming of age -- Fiction 5. Mental illness -- Fiction 6. Family problems -- Fiction

ISBN 0316210587; 9780316210584

LC 2012030683

Parents' Choice: Silver Medal Fiction (2013)

In this book, "worried that she will grow up to be crazy like her mother or alcoholic like her father, rising seventh-grader Sarah Nelson takes courage from Harper Lee's 'To Kill a Mockingbird,' writing letters to Atticus Finch and discovering her own strengths. . . . She describes the events of the summer she turns 12, gets her period, develops a crush on a neighbor and fellow word lover, and comes to terms with her parents' failings." (Kirkus Reviews)

Harris, Teresa E.

The **perfect** place; Teresa E. Harris. Clarion Books 2014 272 p. (hardcover) $16.99

Grades: 5 6 7 8 **Fic**

1. Aunts -- Fiction 2. Family life -- Fiction 3. African Americans -- Fiction 4. Home -- Fiction 5. Virginia -- Fiction 6. Great-aunts -- Fiction 7. Segregation -- Fiction 8. Moving, Household -- Fiction 9. Family life -- Virginia -- Fiction

ISBN 0547255195; 9780547255194

LC 2013036214

In this book, "12-year-old Treasure is tired of moving from place to place every time her unreliable father leaves the family. At the opening of the novel, Treasure's father is gone and her mother leaves her and her younger sister, Tiffany, with their Great-Aunt Grace in the small town of Black Lake, Virginia. Treasure does not want to be there, and her introduction to her no-nonsense relative only strengthens her resolve to stay detached during her mother's absence." (School Library Journal)

"Two months after 12-year-old Treasure's dad left without further word, her mom decides to search for him, and she takes Treasure and her younger sister to stay with their cantankerous Great-Aunt Grace in Black Lake, Virginia... Readers will find sly humor here as well as the pleasure of seeing justice done on several levels. A satisfying first novel with a realistic but heartening ending." Booklist

Harrison, Michelle

13 curses. Little, Brown 2011 486p (13 Treasures Trilogy) $15.99; pa $6.99

Grades: 5 6 7 8 **Fic**

1. Magic -- Fiction 2. Fairies -- Fiction 3. Orphans -- Fiction 4. Kidnapping -- Fiction

ISBN 978-0-316-04150-8; 0-316-04150-5; 978-0316041492 pa

Sequel to: 13 treasures (2010)

When fairies steal her brother, thirteen-year-old Rowan Fox promises that in exchange for his return she will find the thirteen charms that the fairies have enchanted and hidden in the human world.

"The sure-handed storytelling creates a completely credible setting—by turns violent and tender, sinister and poignant. . . . Contrasts between human emotion and commitment and the cold, often cruel magic and mischief of the fairy realm create terrific tension and afford opportunities for heroism for the young protagonists." Kirkus

13 secrets; Michelle Harrison ; [interior illustrations by Kelly Louise Judd] Little, Brown & Co. 2012 421 p. illustrations (The 13 treasures trilogy) $16.99

Grades: 5 6 7 8 **Fic**

1. Fantasy fiction 2. Fairies -- Fiction 3. Secrets -- Fiction 4. Changelings -- Fiction

ISBN 0316185639; 9780316185639

LC 2011033368

In this book, by Michelle Harrison, with illustrations by Kelly Louise Judd, "happy with life at Elvesden Manor, Rowan is doing her best to put the past behind her. But it's tough to forget the past when fairy messengers won't leave her be, no matter how many magical boundaries are put in place to keep them away. When Tanya arrives to spend the summer at the manor, she notices that Rowan is acting strangely and becomes determined to find out what she's hiding." (Publisher's note)

13 treasures. Little, Brown Books for Young Readers 2010 355p il $15.99

Grades: 5 6 7 8 **Fic**

1. Mystery fiction 2. Fairies -- Fiction 3. Grandmothers -- Fiction 4. Great Britain -- Fiction

ISBN 978-0-316-04148-5; 0-316-04148-3

LC 2008-45511

Bedeviled by evil fairies that only she can see, thirteen-year-old Tanya is sent to stay with her cold and distant grandmother at Elvesden Manor, where she and the caretaker's son solve a disturbing mystery that leads them to the discovery that Tanya's life is in danger.

"Harrison writes with great assuredness, creating a seductive setting and memorable, fully developed characters. . . . It's an excellent choice for fans of the Spiderwick Chronicles and other modern-day fairy tales." Publ Wkly

Followed by: 13 curses (2011)

Harrold, A. F.

The **imaginary**; by A.F. Harrold ; illustrations by Emily Gravett. Bloomsbury 2015 224 p. illustrations (some color) (hardcover) $16.99

Grades: 4 5 6 7 8 **Fic**

1. Friendship -- Fiction 2. Supernatural -- Fiction 3. Adventure and adventurers 4. Imaginary playmates -- Fiction 5. Mother-daughter relationship -- Fiction 6. Best friends -- Fiction 7. Mothers and daughters -- Fiction

ISBN 0802738117; 9780802738110; 9781619636965

LC 2014016677

"Rudger is Amanda Shuffleup's imaginary friend. Nobody else can see Rudger-until the evil Mr. Bunting arrives at Amanda's door. Mr. Bunting hunts imaginaries. Rumor has it that he even eats them. And now he's found Rudger. Soon Rudger is alone, and running for his imaginary life. He needs to find Amanda before Mr. Bunting catches him-and before Amanda forgets him and he fades away to nothing." (Publisher's note)

"This inventive mix of humor and suspense starts with the amusing appearance of Amanda's imaginary friend, Rudger. Their summer of make-believe adventures quickly darkens, though, when Mr. Bunting shows up. He's a grown-up who can not only see "Imaginaries" like Rudger, but also eats them to prolong his own life. . . . A great choice for readers who like fantastic tales with a dose of true scariness." SLJ

Hart, Alison

Gabriel's horses; by Alison Hart. 1st ed.; Peachtree 2007 161p (Racing to freedom) $14.95

Grades: 6 7 8 9 **Fic**

1. Slavery -- Fiction 2. Kentucky -- Fiction 3. Horse racing -- Fiction 4. African Americans -- Fiction 5. United States -- History -- 1861-1865, Civil War -- Fiction

ISBN 978-1-56145-398-6; 1-56145-398-6

LC 2006027697

Other titles in this series are: Gabriel's triumph (2007); Gabriel's journey (2008)

In Kentucky, during the Civil War, the twelve-year-old slave Gabriel, contends with a cruel new horse trainer and skirmishes with Confederate soldiers as he pursues his dream of becoming a jockey.

"The author grounds this fast-paced tale in historical fact by providing a nonfiction epilogue. Readers will find this wonderful blend of history and horses appealing." SLJ

Gabriel's triumph; by Alison Hart. 1st ed.; Peachtree 2007 164p (Racing to freedom) $14.95

Grades: 6 7 8 9 **Fic**

1. Kentucky -- Fiction 2. Horse racing -- Fiction 3. African

Americans -- Fiction 4. United States -- History -- 1861-1865, Civil War -- Fiction
ISBN 978-1-56145-410-5
LC 2007001430

Sequel to: Gabriel's horses (2007)

A thirteen-year-old newly-freed slave faces the challenges of freedom and horse racing as he pursues his dream of becoming a famous jockey in Civil War Kentucky and New York.

"Thrilling horse racing once again frames a stirring Civil War story." Booklist

Hartinger, Brent

Project Sweet Life. HarperTeen 2009 282p $16.99
Grades: 6 7 8 9 **Fic**

1. Friendship -- Fiction 2. Summer employment -- Fiction 3. Washington (State) -- Fiction
ISBN 978-0-06-082411-2; 0-06-082411-5
LC 2008-19644

When their fathers insist that they get summer jobs, three fifteen-year-old friends in Tacoma, Washington, dedicate their summer vacation to fooling their parents into thinking that they are working, which proves to be even harder than having real jobs would have been.

This "will keep readers laughing and engaged." SLJ

Hartley, A. J.

★ **Steeplejack**; A Novel. by A. J. Hartley. St. Martin's Press 2016 336 p. (ebook) $60; $17.99
Grades: 8 9 10 11 12 **Fic**

1. Fantasy fiction 2. Mystery fiction 3. Steampunk fiction
ISBN 9781466891692; 076538342X; 9780765383426

"Seventeen-year-old Anglet Sutonga lives repairing the chimneys, towers, and spires of the city of Bar-Selehm. Dramatically different communities live and work alongside each other. . . . When Ang is supposed to meet her new apprentice Berrit, she finds him dead. That same night, the Beacon, an invaluable historical icon, is stolen." (Publisher's note)

"Hartley's (the Darwen Arkwright series) story is a thought-provoking blend of action and intrigue, with a competent and ethical heroine in Ang and a fully imagined setting whose atmosphere and cultural cues also play important roles. The result is an unforgettable page-turner built on surprises and full of potential." Pub Wkly

Hartman, Rachel

★ **Seraphina**; a novel. by Rachel Hartman. Random House 2012 465 p. (hardcover) $17.99
Grades: 7 8 9 10 11 12 **Fic**

1. Fantasy fiction 2. Dragons -- Fiction 3. Kings and rulers -- Fiction 4. Fantasy 5. Music -- Fiction 6. Secrets -- Fiction 7. Identity -- Fiction 8. Courts and courtiers -- Fiction 9. Self-actualization (Psychology) -- Fiction
ISBN 9780375866562; 9780375896583; 9780375966569; 0375866566
LC 2011003015

William C. Morris Award (2013)

Boston Globe-Horn Book Honor: Fiction (2013).

In this book, "[a]fter 40 years of peace between human and dragon kingdoms, their much-maligned treaty is on the verge of collapse. Tensions are already high with an influx of dragons, reluctantly shifted to human forms, arriving for their ruler Ardmagar Comonot's anniversary. But when Prince Rufus is found murdered in the fashion of dragons--that is, his head has been bitten off--things reach a fever pitch." (Booklist)

Other titles in this series are:
Shadow scale (2015)
Tess of the road (2018)

Shadow scale; Rachel Hartman. Random House Books for Young Readers 2015 596 p. $21.99
Grades: 7 8 9 10 11 12 **Fic**

1. Magic -- Fiction 2. Dragons -- Fiction 3. War stories 4. Fantasy fiction 5. Courts and courtiers -- Fiction
ISBN 0375966579; 9780375866579; 9780375966576
Sequel to: Seraphina (2012)

In this sequel to her novel "Seraphina," author Rachel Hartman "continues the adventures of that book's eponymous half-dragon, who is now assigned with finding and uniting her fellow 'ityasaari' before the full-blooded dragons can resolve their civil war and mobilize to wipe out the southern human kingdoms. But some ityasaari don't want to be found, and one, who has the power to enter and control minds, would rather see them united for her own bitter purpose." (Publishers Weekly)

"From graceful language to high stakes to daring intrigue, this sequel shines with the same originality, invention, and engagement of feeling that captivated readers in Hartman's debut." Horn Book

★ **Tess** of the road; Rachel Hartman. Random House 2018 536 p. (hardcover) $18.99
Grades: 7 8 9 10 11 12 **Fic**

1. Runaway teenagers -- Fiction 2. Courts and courtiers -- Fiction 3. Dragons -- Fiction 4. Sex role -- Fiction
ISBN 9781101931301; 9781101931288; 9781101931295
LC 2016041764

In this book, by Rachel Hartman, edited by Jenna Lettice, "in the medieval kingdom of Goredd, women are expected to be ladies, men are their protectors, and dragons can be whomever they choose. Tess is none of these things. . . . So Tess's family decide the only path for her is a nunnery. But on the day she is to join the nuns, Tess chooses a different path for herself. She cuts her hair, pulls on her boots, and sets out on a journey." (Publisher's note)

"Like Tess' journey, surprising, rewarding, and enlightening, both a fantasy adventure and a meta discourse on consent, shame, and female empowerment." Kirkus

Hartnett, Sonya, 1968-

★ **Butterfly**. Candlewick Press 2010 232p $16.99
Grades: 7 8 9 10 11 12 **Fic**

1. Australia -- Fiction 2. Family life -- Fiction
ISBN 0-7636-4760-8; 978-0-7636-4760-5
LC 2009046549

In 1980s Australia, nearly fourteen-year-old Ariella "Plum" Coyle fears the disapproval of her friends, feels inferior to her older brothers, and hates her awkward, adolescent body but when her glamorous neighbor befriends her, Plum starts to become what she wants to be—until she discovers her neighbor's ulterior motive.

"The deliberate pacing, insight into teen angst, and masterful word choice make this a captivating read to savor." SLJ

★ The **children** of the King; Sonya Hartnett. 1st U.S. edition Penguin Books (Australia) 2012 265 p. ill. $16.99
Grades: 5 6 7 8 **Fic**

1. Historical fiction 2. Friendship -- Fiction 3. World War, 1939-1945 -- Great Britain -- Fiction 4. World War, 1939-1945 -- Evacuation of civilians -- Fiction 5. England -- Fiction 6. World War, 1939-1945 -- Children -- Great Britain -- Fiction 7. World War, 1939-1945 -- Evacuation of civilians -- England -- Fiction
ISBN 0763667358; 9780670076130; 9780763667351
LC 2013414845

This book, by Sonya Hartnett, "takes place in England during World War II. . . . Siblings Cecily and Jeremy, along with their mother Heloise, are sent to the northern countryside to live with Heloise's brother, Peregrine Lockwood, in mysterious Heron Hall. . . . The family winds up taking in May Bright, a 10-year-old refugee from London. The two girls become fast friends and . . . come across two boys in the ruins of a nearby castle." (School Library Journal)

"Twelve-year-old Cecily, her older brother Jeremy, and their mother flee WWII London for the safety of Uncle Peregrine's country manor. Once there, Cecily discovers two boys hiding in some nearby ruins. Hartnett's gift for language deftly conveys both the sublime and the mundane in life. She grounds the book's fantasy elements with a heartfelt examination of the hardships endured by civilians in wartime." Horn Book

What the birds see. Candlewick Press 2003 196p $15.99
Grades: 7 8 9 10 **Fic**

1. Missing children -- Fiction
ISBN 0-7636-2092-0

LC 2002-73717

While the residents of his town concern themselves with the disappearance of three children, a lonely, rejected nine-year-old boy worries that he may inherit his mother's insanity

"Tightly composed and ripe with symbolism, this complex book will offer opportunities for rich discussion." SLJ

Hartry, Nancy

Watching Jimmy. Tundra Books 2009 152p $16.95
Grades: 5 6 7 8 **Fic**

1. Child abuse -- Fiction 2. Brain -- Wounds and injuries -- Fiction
ISBN 0-88776-871-7; 978-0-88776-871-2

This story takes place in Canada in 1958. Eleven-year-old Carolyn walks an emotional tightrope knowing what really happened to her best friend, Jimmy, the day his Uncle Ted chose to teach him a lesson that left Jimmy brain-damaged. But when Uncle Ted threatens his beleaguered family with even more abuse and the loss of their home, Carolyn must find the courage to match wits with him and to speak out, using the truth as her only weapon. "Age nine and up." (Quill Quire)

"Like a steady beat that pulses louder and louder, the story unfolds against a backdrop of postwar social and political concerns and Remembrance Day. Carolyn is a passionate and feisty character, delineated with love and precision, and readers will be drawn to her. A compelling and satisfying novel." SLJ

Harvey, Sarah N.

Death benefits. Orca Book Publishers 2010 212p pa $12.95
Grades: 7 8 9 10 **Fic**

1. Old age -- Fiction 2. Grandfathers -- Fiction
ISBN 978-1-55469-226-2 pa; 1-55469-226-1 pa

Royce is pressed into service as a caregiver for his ninety-five-year-old grandfather and gradually comes to appreciate the cantankerous old man.

"Harvey's writing is energetic, and Royce's snarky narration is sure to keep readers' attention." Publ Wkly

Hashimi, Nadia

One half from the east; Nadia Hashimi. HarperCollins 2016 272 p. (ebook) $15.99; (hardcover) $16.99
Grades: 4 5 6 7 8 **Fic**

1. Bombings -- Fiction 2. Impersonation -- Fiction 3. Gender identity -- Fiction 4. Female friendship -- Fiction 5. Children of parents with disabilities -- Fiction 6. Girls -- Afghanistan -- Social conditions -- Fiction
ISBN 9780062421920; 0062421905; 9780062421906

LC 2016938972

In this middle grade novel by Nadia Hashimi that is set in Afghanistan, "Obayda's family is in need of some good fortune, and her aunt has an idea to bring the family luck—dress Obayda, the youngest of four sisters, as a boy, a bacha posh. . . . Once Obayda meets another bacha posh, everything changes. Their transformation won't last forever, though—unless the two best friends can figure out a way to make it stick and make their newfound freedoms endure." (Publisher's note)

"Well-told through appealing characters, this tale sheds light from a unique cultural perspective on the link between vastly different, rigidly enforced roles for boys and girls and gender-identity issues." Kirkus

The **sky** at our feet; Nadia Hashimi ; [edited by] Rosemary Brosnan. HarperCollins 2018 304 p. (hardcover) $16.99
Grades: 4 5 6 7 **Fic**

1. Afghan Americans -- Fiction 2. Runaway children -- Fiction 3. Mother-son relationship -- Fiction
ISBN 9780062421937

LC 2017942899

In this novel, by Nadia Hashimi, "twelve-year-old Jason D. Riazi is on the run from his New Jersey home after his mother, an undocumented Afghani immigrant, is apprehended by police. Hoping to find his Auntie Seema in New York City, he takes the train to Penn Station, but, fainting from hunger on the platform and suffering a concussion, he lands in the hospital. . . . Befriended by a young female patient, Max, . . . the two escape into the city streets." (School Library Journal)

Haskell, Merrie

Handbook for dragon slayers; Merrie Haskell. 1st ed. HarperCollins 2013 336 p. (hardcover) $16.99
Grades: 6 7 8 **Fic**

1. Fairy tales 2. Dragons -- Fiction 3. Authorship -- Fiction 4. Princesses -- Fiction 5. Books and reading -- Fiction 6. People with disabilities -- Fiction 7. Adventure and adventurers -- Fiction
ISBN 0062008161; 9780062008169

LC 2012022159

Schneider Family Book Awards: Middle School (2014)

In this juvenile fantasy story, by Merrie Haskell, "political upheaval sends Princess Tilda fleeing from her kingdom in the company of two hopeful dragon slayers. The princess never had any interest in chasing dragons. . . . But the princess finds herself making friends with magical horses, facing the Wild Hunt, and pointing a sword at the fire-breathing creatures. While doing things she never imagined, Tilda finds qualities in herself she never knew she possessed." (Publisher's note)

The **princess** curse. Harper 2011 325p $16.99
Grades: 4 5 6 7 **Fic**

1. Fairy tales 2. Magic -- Fiction 3. Princesses -- Fiction
ISBN 978-0-06-200813-8; 0-06-200813-7

LC 2010040424

"Author Haskell has her way with the story of 'The Twelve Dancing Princesses,' incorporating references to other myths and legends and adding many twists of her own, not least of which is making the royals' attempted rescuer a strong-willed, 13-year-old apprentice herbalist, Reveka. . . . When Vasile offers the hand of any of his daughters in marriage to anyone who banishes the curse (or a 'fabulous dowry' if the curse-breaker is female), Reveka is determined to win the reward. . . . With a good sense of humor, an able and empowered protagonist, and a highly original take on this tale, Haskell's story gives readers much to enjoy." Publ Wkly

Hatfield, Ruth

The **Book** of Storms; Ruth Hatfield. Henry Holt & Co 2014 368 p. $16.99

Grades: 5 6 7 8 **Fic**

1. Missing persons 2. Adventure fiction 3. Storms -- Fiction 4. Supernatural -- Fiction 5. Human-animal communication -- Fiction

ISBN 0805099980; 9780805099980

LC 2014029352

In this juvenile novel, by Ruth Hatfield, illustrated by Greg Call, when "Danny O'Neill . . . wakes the morning after a storm to find his house empty, his parents gone, and himself able to hear the thoughts of a dying tree, he has no choice but to set out to find answers. He soon learns that the enigmatic Book of Storms holds the key to what he seeks . . . but unraveling its mysteries won't be easy." (Publisher's note)

"This debut novel is an entertaining fantasy adventure set across a modern European landscape. The book follows 11-year-old Danny O'Neill as he struggles to piece together the seemingly incomprehensible details left behind by a devastating storm. The quest takes him deep within himself where he must find courage that he never knew he possessed...Not only does Hatfield take readers inside the thoughts and minds of all sorts of flora and fauna, but she uses their observable traits to guide their humanistic presence in very believable ways." SLJ

Other titles in this series are:

The color of darkness (2016)

The book of shadows (2017)

Hautman, Pete, 1952-

★ **All** -in. Simon & Schuster Books for Young Readers 2007 181p hardcover o.p. pa $5.99

Grades: 7 8 9 10 **Fic**

1. Poker -- Fiction 2. Gambling -- Fiction 3. Las Vegas (Nev.) -- Fiction

ISBN 978-1-4169-1325-2; 1-4169-1325-4; 978-1-4169-1326-9 pa

LC 2006-23871

Sequel to No limit (2005)

Having won thousands of dollars playing high-stakes poker in Las Vegas, seventeen-year-old Denn Doyle hits a losing streak after falling in love with a young casino card dealer named Cattie Hart.

"Skillfully using the multiple-voice approach, Hautman brings to life the intricacies of poker, crafting a thrilling story of loss, good versus evil, and redemption." Voice Youth Advocates

★ The **big** crunch. Scholastic Press 2011 280p $17.99

Grades: 8 9 10 11 12 **Fic**

1. School stories 2. Dating (Social customs) -- Fiction

ISBN 978-0-545-24075-8; 0-545-24075-1

LC 2010-40011

"Wes Andrews has just ended a suffocating relationship with Izzy. June is new to the school—her sixth in the last four years. Like Wes, she's not looking to get entangled. . . . But in the high-school world of 'users, posers, geeks, skanks, preps, gangstas, macho-morons, punks, burnouts, and so forth,' the two relatively normal, nice kids do find each other . . . eventually. Hautman uses a third-person point of view to weave a humorous and bittersweet tale of romance and the convoluted, uncertain paths that bring two people together. A poignant and quiet tale in which the only special effect is love—refreshing." Kirkus

Blank confession. Simon & Schuster Books for Young Readers 2010 170p $16.99

Grades: 7 8 9 10 **Fic**

1. School stories 2. Bullies -- Fiction 3. Drug traffic -- Fiction

ISBN 978-1-4169-1327-6; 1-4169-1327-0

LC 2009-50169

A new and enigmatic student named Shayne appears at high school one day, befriends the smallest boy in the school, and takes on a notorious drug dealer before turning himself in to the police for killing someone.

"Masterfully written with simple prose, solid dialogue and memorable characters, the tale will grip readers from the start and keep the reading in one big gulp, in the hope of seeing behind Shayne's mask. A sure hit with teen readers." Kirkus

The **Cydonian** pyramid; Pete Hautman. Candlewick Press 2013 368 p. (The Klaatu Diskos) (reinforced) $16.99

Grades: 7 8 9 10 11 12 **Fic**

1. Science fiction 2. Time travel -- Fiction 3. Young adult literature

ISBN 0763654043; 9780763654047

LC 2012942673

This novel, by Pete Hautman, is part of the "Klaatu Diskos" series. "More than half a millennium in the future, in the shadow of the looming Cydonian Pyramid, a pampered girl named Lah Lia has been raised for one purpose: to be sacrificed. . . . But just as she is about to be killed, a strange boy appears from the diskos, providing a cover of chaos that allows her to escape and launching her on a time-spinning journey in which her fate is irreversibly linked to his." (Publisher's note)

Doppelganger; by Pete Hautman and Mary Logue. G.P. Putnams Sons 2008 159p (Bloodwater mysteries) $16.99

Grades: 7 8 9 10 **Fic**

1. Mystery fiction 2. Adoption -- Fiction 3. Korean Americans -- Fiction 4. Missing children -- Fiction

ISBN 978-0-399-24379-0; 0-399-24379-8

LC 2007020421

High school newspaper reporter Roni finds an age-progressed photograph on a missing children's website of a boy that looks just like her sidekick Brian, throwing the pair into an investigation of Brian's past and family heritage.

"Readers will be drawn into this creative tale of espionage. . . . The plot is satisfyingly twisted, and there are plenty of creepy characters." Voice Youth Advocates

★ **Godless**. Simon & Schuster Books for Young Readers 2004 208p $15.95; pa $8.99

Grades: 7 8 9 10 **Fic**

1. Religion -- Fiction

ISBN 0-689-86278-4; 1-4169-0816-1 pa

LC 2003-10468

National Book Award: Young People's Literature (2004)

When sixteen-year-old Jason Bock and his friends create their own religion to worship the town's water tower, what started out as a joke begins to take on a power of its own. "Grades seven to twelve." (Bull Cent Child Books)

"The witty text and provocative subject will make this a supremely enjoyable discussion-starter as well as pleasurable read." Bull Cent Child Books

Hole in the sky. Simon & Schuster Bks. for Young Readers 2001 179p $16; pa $11.95

Grades: 7 8 9 10 **Fic**

1. Science fiction 2. Grand Canyon (Ariz.) -- Fiction

ISBN 0-689-83118-8; 1-4169-6822-9 pa

LC 00-58324

In a future world ravaged by a mutant virus, sixteen-year-old Ceej and three other teenagers seek to save the Grand Canyon from being flooded, while trying to avoid capture by a band of renegade Survivors

"Readers will appreciate the novel's intense action and fascinating premise." Horn Book Guide

How to steal a car. Scholastic Press 2009 170p $16.99
Grades: 7 8 9 10 **Fic**

1. Theft -- Fiction 2. Family life -- Fiction
ISBN 978-0-545-11318-2; 0-545-11318-0

LC 2008-54146

Fifteen-year-old, suburban high school student Kelleigh, who has her learner's permit, recounts how she began stealing cars one summer, for reasons that seem unclear even to her.

"A sharply observed, subversive coming-of-age tale." Kirkus

The **Klaatu** terminus; Pete Hautman. Candlewick Press 2014 368 p. (The Klaatu diskos) $16.99
Grades: 7 8 9 10 11 12 **Fic**

1. Science fiction 2. Dystopian fiction 3. Apocalyptic fiction
ISBN 0763654051; 9780763654054

LC 2013944132

In this series finale, Pete Hautman "weaves several diverging time streams into one . . . masterwork. . . . In a far distant future, Tucker Feye and . . . Lia find themselves atop a crumbling pyramid in an abandoned city. In present-day Hopewell, Tucker's uncle Kosh faces armed resistance . . . as he attempts to help a terrorized woman named Emma. . . . And on a train platform in 1997, a seventeen-year-old Kosh is given an instruction that will change his life." (Publisher's note)

"Pulling together elaborate strands of the first two books, this conclusion rewards readers with a surprising yet cogent and satisfying chronicle across time." Horn Book

The **obsidian** blade. Candlewick Press 2012 308p $16.99
Grades: 7 8 9 10 **Fic**

1. Uncles -- Fiction 2. Religion -- Fiction 3. Supernatural -- Fiction 4. Space and time -- Fiction 5. Missing persons -- Fiction
ISBN 978-0-7636-5403-0

LC 2011018617

After thirteen-year-old Tucker Feye's parents disappear, he suspects that the strange disks of shimmering air that he keeps seeing are somehow involved, and when he steps inside of one he is whisked on a time-twisting journey trailed by a shadowy sect of priests and haunted by ghostlike figures.

Road tripped; Pete Hautman. Simon & Schuster Books for Young Readers 2019 330 p. (hardcover) $18.99
Grades: 8 9 10 11 12 **Fic**

1. Automobile travel -- Fiction 2. Interpersonal relations -- Fiction 3. Runaways -- Fiction 4. Coming of age -- Fiction 5. Mississippi River Region -- Fiction
ISBN 9781534405905; 9781534405912

LC 2018030155

This book, by Pete Hautman, is a "captivating story about loss, love, and changing your ways. . . . Steven Gerald Gabel—a.k.a. Stiggy—needs to get out of Minnesota. . . . . Armed with his mom's credit card and a tourist map of Great River Road, Stiggy sets off in his dad's car. The only problem is, life on his own isn't exactly what he expected and, soon enough, he finds himself at a crossroads: keep running from his demons, or let them hitch a ride back home with him." (Publisher's note)

"True-to-life conversations, a keen sense of Midwestern topography, and sharply detailed supporting characters round out this superb road trip novel. By turns introspective and humorous."

Skullduggery; by Pete Hautman and Mary Logue. Putnam 2007 186p (Bloodwater mysteries) $16.99
Grades: 7 8 9 10 **Fic**

1. Mystery fiction
ISBN 978-0-399-24378-3; 0-399-24378-X

LC 2006020576

During a field trip in the local woods, Roni and Brian find the local archaeology professor, Andrew Dart, knocked unconscious in a cave, which leads them to investigate a land development scheme.

"Written with wit and style, the story shows empathy for the main characters' foibles and respect for their unconventional and sometimes fractious working relationship." Booklist

Slider; Pete Hautman. Candlewick Press 2017 278 p. (hardcover) $16.99
Grades: 4 5 6 7 8 **Fic**

1. Food -- Fiction 2. Brothers -- Fiction 3. Contests -- Fiction 4. Autism -- Fiction 5. Competitive eating -- Fiction
ISBN 9780763690700; 9780763697655; 0763690708

In this book, by Pete Hautman, "David can eat an entire sixteen-inch pepperoni pizza in four minutes and thirty-six seconds. Not bad. But he knows he can do better. In fact, he'll have to do better: he's going to compete in the Super Pigorino Bowl, the world's greatest pizza-eating contest, and he has to win it, because he borrowed his mom's credit card and accidentally spent $2,000 on it. So he really needs that prize money. Like, yesterday." (Publisher's note)

"This novel is laugh-out-loud funny and genuinely sweet. . . . ultimately a meaningful book with insight into having a sibling with special needs and the general ups and downs that come with being a teenager." SLJ

Snatched; [by] Pete Hautman and Mary Logue. Putnam 2006 200p (Bloodwater mysteries) $15.99
Grades: 7 8 9 10 **Fic**

1. Mystery fiction 2. Kidnapping -- Fiction
ISBN 0-399-24377-1

LC 2005-28558

Too curious for her own good, Roni, crime reporter for her high school newspaper, teams up with Brian, freshman science geek, to investigate the beating and kidnapping of a classmate.

"Give this solid marks for plotting and characterization, as well as for suspense." Booklist

Other titles in this series are:
Skullduggery (2007)
Doppelganger (2008)

Sweetblood. Simon & Schuster Bks. for Young Readers 2003 180p $16.95; pa $6.99
Grades: 7 8 9 10 **Fic**

1. Diabetes -- Fiction
ISBN 0-689-85048-4; 0-689-87324-7 pa

LC 2002-11179

"Hautman does an outstanding job of making Lucy's theory and her struggle to accept herself credible. . . . Lucy's clever, self-deprecating voice is endlessly original." Booklist

Hawkins, Aaron R.

The **year** money grew on trees; written and illustrated by Aaron R. Hawkins. Houghton Mifflin 2010 293p il $16

Grades: 5 6 7 8 **Fic**

1. Apples -- Fiction 2. Cousins -- Fiction 3. Siblings -- Fiction 4. Farm life -- Fiction 5. New Mexico -- Fiction 6. Money-making projects for children -- Fiction

ISBN 978-0-547-27977-0; 0-547-27977-9

In early 1980s New Mexico, thirteen-year-old Jackson Jones recruits his cousins and sisters to help tend an elderly neighbor's neglected apple orchard for the chance to make big money and, perhaps, to own the orchard.

"Hawkins's children's book debut is rich with details that feel drawn from memory, . . . and Jackson's narration sparkles. His hard work, setbacks, and motivations make this a highly relatable adventure in entrepreneurship." Publ Wkly

Haydu, Corey Ann

Eventown; Corey Ann Haydu. Katherine Tegen Books, an imprint of HarperCollinsPublishers 2019 336 p. (hardback) $16.99

Grades: 5 6 7 **Fic**

1. Twins -- Fiction 2. Memory -- Fiction 3. Sisters -- Fiction 4. Conformity -- Fiction 5. Family life -- Fiction 6. Moving, Household -- Fiction 7. City and town life -- Fiction

ISBN 9780062689801

LC 2018013964

In this book, by Corey Ann Haydu, "the world tilted for Elodee this year, and now it's impossible for her to be the same as she was before. . . . Not when she and her twin sister, Naomi, seem to be drifting apart. So when Elodee's mom gets a new job in Eventown, moving seems like it might just fix everything. Indeed, life in Eventown is comforting and exciting all at once. . . . [U]ntil Elodee realizes that there are only three ice cream flavors in Eventown. Ever." (Publisher's note)

"Although not as dark as The Giver, the narrative will evoke comparisons about the nature of perfection and the importance of memories" (Kirkus Reviews).

The **someday** suitcase; by Corey Ann Haydu. Katherine Tegen Books 2017 304 p. (hardcover) $16.99

Grades: 5 6 7 8 **Fic**

1. Sick -- Fiction 2. Magic -- Fiction 3. Best friends -- Fiction

ISBN 9780062352750

LC 2016949691

In this book, by Corey Ann Haydu, "Clover and Danny are the kind of best friends who make each other even better. . . . But when Danny comes down with a mysterious illness that won't go away, the doctors can't figure out what's wrong with him. So Clover decides to take matters into her own hands. . . . Will science be able to save Danny, or is this the one time when magic can overcome the unthinkable?" (Publisher's note)

Hayles, Marsha

Breathing room; Marsha Hayles. Henry Holt and Co. 2012 244 p. (hc) $17.99

Grades: 5 6 7 8 **Fic**

1. Bildungsromans 2. Historical fiction 3. Teenagers -- Fiction 4. Tuberculosis -- Fiction 5. Sick -- Fiction 6. Hospitals -- Fiction 7. Coming of age -- Fiction 8. Minnesota -- History -- 20th century -- Fiction

ISBN 0805089616; 9780805089615

LC 2011034055

Author Marsha Hayles' book is "set in 1940 at a sanitarium in Loon Lake, Minn. . . . Thirteen-year-old Evvy Hoffmeister has tuberculosis and feels abandoned by her family when she's sent to the sanitarium to be cured. The cold nurses, strict rules, mind-numbing routines, and endless bed rest are dispiriting for Evvy and her roommates: kind Beverly, glamorous Pearl, and defensive Dena. . . . Nonetheless, the girls find strength in each other and discover creative ways to bring cheer." (Publishers Weekly)

Headley, Justina Chen

North of beautiful. Little, Brown 2009 373p $16.99

Grades: 7 8 9 10 11 12 **Fic**

1. Aesthetics -- Fiction

ISBN 978-0-316-02505-8; 0-316-02505-4

LC 2008-09260

Headley's "finely crafted novel traces a teen's uncharted quest to find beauty. Two things block Terra's happiness: a port-wine stain on her face and her verbally abusive father. . . . A car accident brings her together with Jacob, an Asian-born adoptee with unconventional ideas. . . . The author confidently addresses very large, slippery questions about the meaning of art, travel, love and of course, beauty." Publ Wkly

Healey, Karen

The **shattering**. Little, Brown 2011 311p $17.99

Grades: 7 8 9 10 **Fic**

1. Mystery fiction 2. Suicide -- Fiction 3. Homicide -- Fiction 4. New Zealand -- Fiction 5. Supernatural -- Fiction

ISBN 978-0-316-12572-7; 0-316-12572-5

LC 2010047996

When a rash of suicides disturbs Summerton, an oddly perfect tourist town on the west coast of New Zealand, the younger siblings of the dead boys become suspicious and begin an investigation that reveals dark secrets and puts them in grave danger.

"Juggling multiple viewpoints, Healey skillfully keeps her characters on an emotional roller-coaster even as they deal with physical threats. The climax delivers a gut punch that only underscores the sensitivity of the subject matter (without lessening the thrill at all)." Publ Wkly

When we wake; Karen Healey. Little, Brown Books for Young Readers 2013 304 p. (hardcover) $17.99

Grades: 7 8 9 10 11 12 **Fic**

1. Science fiction 2. Dystopian fiction 3. Science Fiction 4. Australia -- Fiction

ISBN 031620076X; 9780316200769

LC 2012028739

"Sixteen-year-old Tegan is just like every other girl living in 2027--But on what should have been the best day of Tegan's life, she dies--and wakes up a hundred years in the future, locked in a government facility with no idea what happened. . . . But the future isn't all she hoped it would be, and when . . . secrets come to light, Tegan must make a choice: Does she keep her head down and survive, or fight for a better future?" (Publisher's note)

While we run; by Karen Healey. Little Brown & Co 2014 336 p. (hardcover) $18

Grades: 7 8 9 10 11 12 **Fic**

1. Cryonics 2. Science fiction 3. Cryonics -- Fiction 4. Australia -- Fiction

ISBN 031623382X; 9780316233828

LC 2013022281

Sequel to: When we wake

In this science fiction novel by Karen Healey, "Abdi Taalib thought he was moving to Australia for a music scholarship. But after meeting the beautiful and brazen Tegan Oglietti, his world was turned upside down. Tegan's no ordinary girl--she died in 2027, only to be frozen and brought back to life in Abdi's time, 100 years later." (Publisher's note)

"In When We Wake, Tegan and Abdi revealed the government's plan to populate a new planet with cryogenically frozen slaves. Abdi begins narrating six months after their capture by the government. Like its predecessor, Run succeeds simply as a sci-fi thriller, but it's elevated by its social commentary, emphasizing the importance of fighting for justice in a world that has little of it." Horn Book

Healy, Christopher

The **Hero's** Guide to Being an Outlaw; Christopher Healy, illustrated by Todd Harris. Harpercollins Childrens Books 2014 528 p. illustrations (The Hero's guide ; book 3) $16.99

Grades: 4 5 6 7 **Fic**

1. Fantasy fiction 2. Princes -- Fiction

ISBN 006211848X; 9780062118486

LC 2014018251

"The League of Princes returns in the hilariously epic conclusion to the hit series that began with Christopher Healy's 'The Hero's Guide to Saving Your Kingdom.' . . . Posters plastered across the thirteen kingdoms are saying that Briar Rose has been murdered--and the four Princes Charming are the prime suspects. Now they're on the run in a desperate attempt to clear their names." (Publisher's note)

"Throughout the heroes' and heroines' travels, the antiprince conspiracy is revealed in each kingdom--it's directly related to loose ends from The Hero's Guide to Storming the Castle (2013). Side characters make comedic final appearances, and a surprise villain team-up provides closure to the trilogy. Part screwball comedy, part sly wit and all fun." Kirkus

The **hero's** guide to saving your kingdom; written by Christopher Healy ; with drawings by Todd Harris. Walden Pond Press 2012 438 p. ill., map $16.99

Grades: 4 5 6 7 **Fic**

1. Princes -- Fiction 2. Fairy tales -- Fiction 3. Heroes and heroines -- Fiction 4. Fairy tales 5. Humorous stories 6. Witches -- Fiction

ISBN 0062117432; 9780062117434

LC 2011053347

In this book, "four Princes . . . must team up on a . . . quest to save their kingdoms. . . . Cinderella wants adventure more than sheltered Prince Frederic does. Prince Gustav's pride is still badly damaged from having needed Rapunzel's teary-eyed rescue. Through Sleeping Beauty, Prince Liam learns kissing someone out of enchanted sleep doesn't guarantee compatibility. . . . Although she loves wacky Prince Duncan, Snow White needs some solitude." (Kirkus Reviews)

The **hero's** guide to storming the castle; by Christopher Healy ; with drawings by Todd Harris. Walden Pond Press, an imprint of HarperCollinsPublishers 2013 496 p. (Hero's Guide) (hardcover) $16.99

Grades: 4 5 6 7 **Fic**

1. Fractured fairy tales 2. Humorous fiction -- Fiction 3. Fairy tales 4. Humorous stories 5. Heroes -- Fiction 6. Princes -- Fiction 7. Characters in literature -- Fiction

ISBN 0062118455; 9780062118455

LC 2012050668

Sequel to: The hero's guide to saving your kingdom

In this humorous, middle-grade fantasy story, by Christopher Healy, illustrated by Todd Harris, "the charming princes from the fairy tales of Cinderella, Rapunzel, Snow White, and Briar Rose, saved the countryside from an evil witch in 'The Hero's Guide to Saving Your Kingdom.' And now, they have to save the day again, by keeping a magical object from falling into the hands of power-mad warlords who would use it for evil." (Publisher's note)

Hearn, Julie

Hazel; a novel. Atheneum Books for Young Readers 2009 389p $17.99

Grades: 8 9 10 11 **Fic**

1. Slavery -- Fiction 2. Social classes -- Fiction 3. Caribbean region -- Fiction 4. London (England) -- Fiction 5. Racially mixed people -- Fiction

ISBN 978-1-4169-2504-0; 1-4169-2504-X

LC 2008-53961

Thirteen-year-old Hazel leaves her comfortable, if somewhat unconventional, London home in 1913 after her father has a breakdown, and goes to live in the Caribbean on her grandparents' sugar plantation where she discovers some shocking family secrets.

"Hearn's characters vividly reveal class distinctions and racial prejudices prevalent in 1913." Voice Youth Advocates

★ **Ivy**; a novel. Atheneum Books for Young Readers 2008 355p $17.99; pa $9.99

Grades: 8 9 10 11 12 **Fic**

1. Artists -- Fiction 3. Criminals -- Fiction 2. Drug abuse -- Fiction 3. London (England) -- Fiction 4. Great Britain -- History -- 19th century -- Fiction

ISBN 978-1-4169-2506-4; 1-4169-2506-6; 978-1-4169-2507-1 pa; 1-4169-2507-4 pa

LC 2007-045463

In mid-nineteenth-century London, young, mistreated, and destitute Ivy, whose main asset is her beautiful red hair, comes to the attention of an aspiring painter of the pre-Raphaelite school of artists who, with the connivance of Ivy's unsavory family, is determined to make her his model and muse.

"Quirky characters, darkly humorous situations, and quick action make this enjoyable historical fiction." SLJ

The **minister's** daughter. Atheneum Books for Young Readers 2005 263p hardcover o.p. pa $7.99

Grades: 7 8 9 10 **Fic**

1. Young adult literature 2. Witchcraft -- Fiction 3. Supernatural -- Fiction 4. Salem (Mass.) -- Fiction 5. Great Britain -- History -- 1642-1660, Civil War and Commonwealth -- Fiction

ISBN 0-689-87690-4; 0-689-87691-2 pa

LC 2004-18324

In 1645 in England, the daughters of the town minister successfully accuse a local healer and her granddaughter of witchcraft to conceal an out-of-wedlock pregnancy, but years later during the 1692 Salem trials their lie has unexpected repercussions.

"With its thought-provoking perceptions about human nature, magic and persecution, this tale will surely cast a spell over readers." Publ Wkly

Heath, Jack

The **Lab**. Scholastic Press 2008 311p $17.99

Grades: 7 8 9 10 **Fic**

1. Science fiction 2. Adventure fiction 3. Spies -- Fiction 4. Genetic engineering -- Fiction

ISBN 978-0-545-06860-4; 0-545-06860-6

"A gritty dystopic world exists under the iron rule of the mega-corporation Chao-Sonic, with only a few vigilante groups around to act as resistance. Six of Hearts is easily the best agent on one such group, the Deck, and he is fiercely dedicated to justice, using his extensive genetic modifications to his advantage. . . . The compelling and memorable protagonist stands out even against the intricately described and disturbing city whose vividness makes the place's questionable fate a suspenseful issue in its own right." Bull Cent Child Books

Followed by: Remote control (2010)

Money run; by Jack Heath. 1st American ed. Scholastic Press 2013 245 p. (hardcover) $17.99

Grades: 8 9 10 **Fic**

1. Crime -- Fiction 2. Adventure fiction 3. Stealing -- Fiction 4. Assassins -- Fiction 5. Theft -- Fiction 6. Thieves -- Fiction 7. Robbers and outlaws -- Fiction

ISBN 0545512662; 9780545512664

LC 2013004005

In this book, "Ashley and Benjamin are two teen partners in crime--real crime, as in major heists--who rely on their youth to avoid suspicion. . . . Their prey today happens to be a billionaire businessman who has sponsored an essay contest with a prize of $10,000 (Ash has won with an essay ghostwritten by Benjamin), but that's peanuts compared to the $2 million they hope to loot." (Kirkus Reviews)

Remote control. Scholastic Press 2010 326p $17.99

Grades: 7 8 9 10 **Fic**

1. Science fiction 2. Adventure fiction 3. Spies -- Fiction 4. Genetic engineering -- Fiction

ISBN 978-0-545-07591-6; 0-545-07591-2

Sequel to: The Lab (2008)

First published 2007 in Australia

Agent Six of Hearts, 16-year-old superhuman, is on a mission. His brother Kyntak has been kidnapped. A strange and sinister new figure is rising in power. Six is suspected of being a double agent. The Deck has been put into lockdown by the Queen of Spades. A mysterious girl has appeared who acts as Six's guardian angel. Who can he trust?

"The technothriller begun in The Lab (2008) takes several intriguing twists . . . on its way to a satisfying, if temporary, resolution." Booklist

Heathfield, Lisa

Seed; Lisa Heathfield. Running Press Teens 2015 336 p. (hbk.) $16.95

Grades: 7 8 9 10 **Fic**

1. Hi-Lo books 2. Cults -- Fiction 3. Teenage girls -- Fiction 4. Communal living -- Fiction

ISBN 9780762456345

LC 2014949872

In this young adult novel, by Lisa Heathfield, "Seed is at the center of 15-year-old Pearl's life: it is the isolated family of which she is part . . . and . . . the remote patch of land . . . where she sows and gathers crops. . . . She does not often leave because . . . Seed is pure and leaving risks contact with poisoned Outsiders who may taint Pearl's spiritual core. . . . But when three Outsiders unexpectedly join the family, . . . Pearl's entire reality is challenged." (School Library Journal)

"Well-developed secondary characters and Heathfield's willingness to do serious damage to central ones make this novel a powerful read." Pub Wkly

Heffernan, John

Hotaka; John Heffernan. Allen & Unwin 2017 216 p. (Through my eyes: Natural disaster zones) (paperback) $12.99

Grades: 4 5 6 7 **Fic**

1. Death -- Fiction 2. Friendship -- Fiction 3. Natural disasters -- Fiction 4. Tsunamis -- Japan -- Fiction 5. Grief -- Fiction 6. Tohoku Earthquake and Tsunami, Japan, 2011 -- Fiction

ISBN 9781760113766; 9781925576382; 176011376X

In this book in the Through My Eyes series, by John Heffernan, "when the tsunami strikes . . . Omori-wan, the effects are . . . devastating. Three years later, . . . [as] Hotaka sets about convincing local performers to appear at the town's upcoming Memorial Concert, he . . . [was] haunted by memories of best friend, Takeshi, who perished . . . in the tsunami. . . . As the town and its people struggle to rebuild their lives, can Hotaka piece together what happened that day." (Publisher's note)

"In this riveting historical fiction novel, Heffernan offers insight into the devastating tsunami that occurred in Japan in March 2011 and forever altered the people of the coastal town Omori-Wan." SLJ

Hegamin, Tonya

Pemba's song; a ghost story. [by] Tonya Hegamin & Marilyn Nelson. Scholastic Press 2008 109p $16.99

Grades: 7 8 9 10 **Fic**

1. Moving -- Fiction 2. Slavery -- Fiction 3. Connecticut -- Fiction 4. Parapsychology -- Fiction 5. African Americans -- Fiction

ISBN 978-0-545-02076-3; 0-545-02076-X

LC 2007051044

As fifteen-year-old Pemba adjusts to leaving her Brooklyn, New York, home for small-town Connecticut, a Black history researcher helps her understand the paranormal experiences drawing her into the life of a mulatto girl who was once a slave in her house.

"Written in shifting voices and styles, this vivid, collaborative novella tells a supernatural story of a young girl's connection with history." Booklist

Heider, Mary Winn

The **mortification** of Fovea Munson; by Mary Winn Heider, illustrated by Chi Birmingham. Disney-Hyperion 2018 336 p. (hardcover) $16.99

Grades: 4 5 6 7 **Fic**

1. Dead -- Fiction 2. Head -- Fiction 3. Friendship -- Fiction 4. Supernatural -- Fiction 5. Chicago (Ill.) -- Fiction 6. Medical laboratories -- Fiction 7. Family life -- Illinois -- Chicago -- Fiction

ISBN 148478054X; 9781484780541

LC 2017025226

In this book, by Mary Winn Heider, illustrated by Chi Birmingham, "Fovea Munson is nobody's Igor. True, her parents own a cadaver lab where they perform surgeries on dead bodies. . . . And sure, Fovea's stuck working at the lab now that her summer camp plans have fallen through. But she is by no means Dr. Frankenstein's snuffling assistant! That is, until three disembodied heads, left to thaw in the wet lab, start talking. To her. Out loud." (Publisher's note)

Helgerson, Joseph

Horns & wrinkles. Houghton Mifflin 2006 357p il $16; pa $4.95

Grades: 4 5 6 7 **Fic**

1. Magic -- Fiction 2. Trolls -- Fiction 3. Bullies -- Fiction 4. Mississippi River -- Fiction

ISBN 0-618-61679-9; 0-618-98178-0 pa

LC 2005025448

Along a magic-saturated stretch of the Mississippi River near Blue Wing, Minnesota, twelve-year-old Claire and her bullying cousin Duke are drawn into an adventure involving Bodacious Deepthink the Great Rock Troll, a helpful fairy, and a group of trolls searching for their fathers.

"Tongue-in-cheek humor brings a delightful zing to the playfully inventive storytelling and fast-paced plot. Enchanting sketches foreshadow each chapter, adding to the wonder." SLJ

Hemingway, Edith Morris

Road to Tater Hill; [by] Edith M. Hemingway. Delacorte Press 2009 213p map $16.99; lib bdg $19.99

Grades: 5 6 7 8 **Fic**

1. Friendship -- Fiction 2. Bereavement -- Fiction 3. Grandparents -- Fiction 4. Mountain life -- Fiction 5. North Carolina -- Fiction 6. Depression (Psychology) -- Fiction

ISBN 978-0-385-73677-0; 0-385-73677-0; 978-0-385-90627-2 lib bdg; 0-385-90627-7 lib bdg

LC 2008-24906

At her grandparents' North Carolina mountain home during the summer of 1963, eleven-year-old Annie Winters, grief-stricken by the death of her newborn sister and isolated by her mother's deepening depression, finds comfort in holding an oblong stone 'rock baby' and in the friendship of a neighbor boy and a reclusive mountain woman with a devastating secret

"Drawing on the author's childhood roots, the heart of this first novel is the sense of place, described in simple lyrical words. . . . True to Annie's viewpoint, the particulars tell a universal drama of childhood grief, complete in all its sadness, anger, loneliness, and healing." Booklist

Hemphill, Helen

The **adventurous** deeds of Deadwood Jones. Front Street 2008 228p $16.95

Grades: 5 6 7 8 **Fic**

1. Cousins -- Fiction 2. Cowhands -- Fiction 3. West (U.S.) -- Fiction 4. Race relations -- Fiction 5. African Americans -- Fiction

ISBN 978-1-59078-637-6; 1-59078-637-8

LC 2008005422

Thirteen-year-old Prometheus Jones and his eleven-year-old cousin Omer flee Tennessee and join a cattle drive that will eventually take them to Texas, where Prometheus hopes his father lives, and they find adventure and face challenges as African Americans in a land still recovering from the Civil War.

"Prometheus is an always sympathetic and engaging character, and the dangers and misadventures he encounters . . . make for compelling reading." Booklist

Hemphill, Michael

Stonewall Hinkleman and the Battle of Bull Run; [by] Michael Hemphill and Sam Riddleburger. Dial Books for Young Readers 2009 168p $16.99

Grades: 4 5 6 **Fic**

1. Time travel -- Fiction 2. Bull Run, 1st Battle of, 1861 -- Fiction 3. United States -- History -- 1861-1865, Civil War -- Fiction

ISBN 978-0-8037-3179-0; 0-8037-3179-5

LC 2008-15795

While participating in a reenactment of the Battle of Bull Run, twelve-year-old Stonewall Hinkleman is transported back to the actual Civil War battle by means of a magic bugle.

This is a "well-paced time-travel novel. . . . Stonewall is a likable character whose attitude changes for the better in the story. . . . A good choice for historical fiction fans." SLJ

Hemphill, Stephanie

Hideous love; the story of the girl who wrote Frankenstein. Stephanie Hemphill. Balzer + Bray, an imprint of HarperCollinsPublishers 2013 320 p. (hardcover bdg.) $17.99

Grades: 9 10 11 12 **Fic**

1. Novels in verse 2. Historical fiction 3. Love -- Fiction 4. Authorship -- Fiction

ISBN 0061853313; 9780061853319

LC 2013000237

This book is a fictionalized verse biography of author Mary Shelley. Stephanie Hemphill "explores the particular challenges facing a gifted female artist who allies herself with a renowned male poet. Central to the plot is the parentage of Mary Wollstonecraft Godwin Shelley, daughter of Mary Wollstonecraft, the pioneering feminist philosopher who died days after Mary was born, and William Godwin, a radical political philosopher who espoused free love for all but his daughters." (Kirkus Reviews)

Sisters of glass; Stephanie Hemphill. Alfred A. Knopf 2012 150 p. $16.99

Grades: 7 8 9 10 **Fic**

1. Novels in verse 2. Romance fiction 3. Historical fiction 4. Love stories 5. Families -- Fiction 6. Family life -- Fiction 7. Venice (Italy) -- Fiction 8. Glass blowing and working -- Fiction

ISBN 0375861092; 0375961097; 9780375861093; 9780375961090

LC 2011277551

This book presents "[a] . . . tale of destiny, fidelity, and true love" set in "fourteenth-century Murano, Italy (of glassmaking renown) and . . . told through verse. . . . Maria is disdainful of her training to be a society woman and yearns instead to spend her time with her art or in the family's furnaces with Luca, an employee whose skill with glass is the marvel that leads Maria, who once aspired to be a glassblower, to fall in love with him." (Booklist)

★ **Wicked** girls; a novel of the Salem witch trials. Balzer + Bray 2010 408p il $17.99; lib bdg $17.89

Grades: 7 8 9 10 11 12 **Fic**

1. Novels in verse 2. Trials -- Fiction 3. Witchcraft -- Fiction 4. Salem (Mass.) -- Fiction

ISBN 0-06-185328-3; 0-06-185329-1 lib bdg; 978-0-06-185328-9; 978-0-06-185329-6 lib bdg

LC 2010-9593

This is "a fictionalized account of the Salem witch trials told from the perspectives of three of the real young women living in Salem in 1692. Ann Putnam Jr. plays the queen bee. When her father suggests that a spate of illnesses within the village is the result of witchcraft, Ann . . . puts in motion a chain of events that will change the lives of the people around her forever. Mercy Lewis, the beautiful servant in Ann's house, inspires adulation in some and envy in others. With a troubled past, she seizes her only chance at safety. Margaret Walcott, Ann's cousin, is desperately in love and consumed with fiery jealousy. She is torn between staying loyal to her friends and pursuing the life she dreams of with her betrothed." (Publisher's note)

"Hemphill's raw, intimate poetry probes behind the abstract facts and creates characters that pulse with complex emotion." Booklist

Includes bibliographical references

Henderson, Jason

The **Triumph** of Death; Jason Henderson. HarperTeen 2012 310 p.

Grades: 8 9 10 11 12 **Fic**

1. Vampires -- Fiction 2. Occult fiction -- Fiction 3. Adventure fiction 4. Horror stories 5. Witches -- Fiction 6. Supernatural -- Fiction

ISBN 9780061951039

LC 2012004297

This young adult paranormal adventure, by Jason Henderson, is book three of the "Alex Van Helsing" series. "There is a famous painting in Madrid that holds the key to an apocalypse only Alex Van Helsing can stop . . . [and] a newly risen vampire queen threatens the fate of the world. . . . Teaming up with a motorcycle-riding witch, Alex jets between Switzerland, the UK, and Spain in a frantic race to prevent the queen from . . . [plunging] the world into darkness." (Publisher's note)

★ **Vampire** rising. HarperTeen 2010 249p (Alex Van Helsing) $16.99

Grades: 6 7 8 9 10 **Fic**

1. Horror fiction 2. School stories 3. Vampires -- Fiction 45. Switzerland -- Fiction 5. Supernatural -- Fiction

ISBN 978-0-06-195099-5; 0-06-195099-8

LC 2009-39663

At a boarding school in Switzerland, fourteen-year-old Alex Van Helsing learns that vampires are real, that he has a natural ability to sense them, and that an agency called the Polidorium has been helping his family fight them since 1821.

"Henderson references Mary Shelley's Frankenstein to weave a great story line full of action, suspense, and adventure. The satisfying story captivates readers with a modern-day spin of James Bond meets Dracula." SLJ

Another title about Alex Van Helsing is:
Voice of the undead (2011)

Voice of the undead. HarperTeen 2011 297p (Alex Van Helsing) $16.99

Grades: 6 7 8 9 10 **Fic**

1. Horror fiction 2. School stories 3. Vampires -- Fiction 4. Switzerland -- Fiction 5. Supernatural -- Fiction

ISBN 978-0-06-195101-5; 0-06-195101-3

LC 2010045554

Sequel to: Vampire rising (2010)

After a fire damages his boarding school in Switzerland, fourteen-year-old Alex and his friends move to the girls' school across the lake, where supernatural happenings are disturbing the peace, and in the meantime, more Van Helsing family secrets are revealed.

"Henderson continues to spin a James Bond-type of action adventure story with a supernatural twist. It's an entertaining read that is full of suspense and intrigue." SLJ

Heneghan, James

Payback. Groundwood/House of Anansi Press 2007 184p $16.95; pa $8.95

Grades: 6 7 8 9 **Fic**

1. Guilt -- Fiction 2. Bullies -- Fiction 3. Suicide -- Fiction 4. Immigrants -- Fiction 5. Irish -- Canada -- Fiction

ISBN 0-88899-701-9; 978-0-88899-701-2; 978-0-88899-704-3 pa; 0-88899-704-3 pa

"After his eighth-grade classmate Benny commits suicide, Charley blames himself. . . . Why did he do nothing when he saw the bullies torment Benny and call him 'fag'? Was it because, as a new Irish immigrant in Vancouver, Charley himself was threatened and bullied? . . . The drama of guilt, sorrow, and redemption is honest and heartfelt, told in Charley's spare, fast, first-person narrative." Booklist

Safe house. Orca Book Publishers 2006 151p pa $7.95

Grades: 6 7 8 9 **Fic**

1. Belfast (Northern Ireland) -- Fiction

ISBN 1-55143-640-X pa; 978-1-55143-640-1 pa

"Readers will be drawn by the fast action and the breathless escape adventure, but they'll also respond to the politics of war in Belfast." Booklist

Henkes, Kevin

★ **Olive's** ocean. Greenwillow Bks. 2003 217p $15.99; pa $6.99

Grades: 5 6 7 8 **Fic**

1. Family life -- Fiction 2. Grandmothers -- Fiction

ISBN 0-06-053543-1; 0-06-053545-8 pa

LC 2002-29782

A Newbery Medal honor book, 2004

On a summer visit to her grandmother's cottage by the ocean, twelve-year-old Martha gains perspective on the death of a classmate, on her relationship with her grandmother, on her feelings for an older boy, and on her plans to be a writer.

"Rich characterizations move this compelling novel to its satisfying and emotionally authentic conclusion." SLJ

Protecting Marie. Greenwillow Bks. 1995 195p $18.99; pa $5.99

Grades: 5 6 7 8 **Fic**

1. Dogs -- Fiction 2. Father-daughter relationship -- Fiction

ISBN 0-688-13958-2; 0-06-053545-8 pa

LC 94-16387

Relates twelve-year-old Fanny's love-hate relationship with her father, a temperamental artist, who has given Fanny a new dog

"The characters ring heartbreakingly true in this quiet, wise story; they are complex and difficult—like all of us—and worthy of our attention." Horn Book

Henry, Katie

★ **Heretics** Anonymous; Katie Henry. Katherine Tegen Books, an imprint of HarperCollinsPublishers 2018 336 p. (hardcover) $17.99

Grades: 8 9 10 11 12 **Fic**

1. Conduct of life -- Fiction 2. Family problems -- Fiction 3. Self-help groups -- Fiction 4. Faith -- Fiction 5. Schools -- Fiction 6. Catholic schools -- Fiction

ISBN 9780062698872

LC 2017034682

In this book, by Katie Henry, "when Michael walks through the doors of Catholic school, things can't get much worse. His dad has just made the family move again, and Michael needs a friend. When a girl challenges their teacher in class, Michael thinks he might have found one, and a fellow atheist at that. Only this girl, Lucy, isn't just Catholic . . . she wants to be a priest. Lucy introduces Michael to other St. Clare's outcasts, and he officially joins Heretics Anonymous." (Publisher's note)

"The story adeptly asks readers to question what they believe and why, without being preachy, judgmental, or dismissive. Humor interlaced with more serious ideas make for an interesting and enjoyable read." (School Library Journal)

Henry, O.

The **gift** of the Magi; illustrations by P.J. Lynch. Candlewick Press 2008 un il $15.99

Grades: 5 6 7 8 **Fic**

1. Gifts -- Fiction 2. Christmas -- Fiction

ISBN 978-0-7636-3530-5; 0-7636-3530-8

LC 2007052028

A husband and wife sacrifice treasured possessions in order to buy each other Christmas presents.

The story "enjoys a gentle new interpretation through watercolor illustrations in worn grays and warm brown tones. . . . Lynch's illustrations of wintry landscapes and the protagonists' animated faces add an accessible level of storytelling to the sophisticated prose." Horn Book Guide

Hensley, Joy N.

Rites of passage; Joy N. Hensley. First edition HarperTeen 2014 416 p. (hardback) $17.99

Grades: 7 8 9 10 **Fic**

1. School stories 2. Bullies -- Fiction 3. Secret societies -- Fiction 4. Schools -- Fiction 5. Bullying -- Fiction 6. Sex role -- Fiction 7. Military training -- Fiction 8. Blue Ridge Mountains -- Fiction

ISBN 0062295195; 9780062295194

LC 2014010022

In this novel by Joy N. Hensley, "sixteen-year-old Sam McKenna discovers that becoming one of the first girls to attend a revered military academy means living with a target on her back. As Sam struggles to prove herself, she learns that a decades-old secret society is alive and active . . . and determined to force her out." (Publisher's note)

"The narrative flows along terrifically as Sam courageously battles to make it even while the forces against her increase. The characters stand out as individual and real; readers will cheer Sam on throughout. Absolutely compelling." Kirkus

Henson, Heather

Dream of Night. Atheneum 2010 218p $15.99

Grades: 6 7 8 9 **Fic**

1. Horses -- Fiction 2. Child abuse -- Fiction 3. Foster home care -- Fiction

ISBN 978-1-4169-4899-5; 1-4169-4899-6

"Once Dream of Night was a champion racehorse, but by the time Jess DiLima gets him he's nearly dead from starvation and pneumonia, and his thin hide is covered in scars. Twelve-year-old Shiloh is scarred, too, both from physical abuse and from the emotional withering of years in foster care. . . . [Henson's] novel, like her characters, shimmers with anger and hope. She doesn't pull her punches—the scenes and flashbacks of abuse are realistically graphic—but she also never lets the details overwhelm the narrative, always offering the possibility of redemption." Kirkus

Herbach, Geoff

I'm with stupid; Geoff Herbach. Sourcebooks Fire 2013 320 p. (tp : alk. paper) $9.99

Grades: 7 8 9 10 **Fic**

1. Suicide -- Fiction 2. Football players -- Fiction 3. Father-son relationship -- Fiction 4. Anxiety -- Fiction 5. Schools -- Fiction 6. Athletes -- Fiction 7. Identity -- Fiction 8. Wisconsin -- Fiction 9. High schools -- Fiction

ISBN 1402277911; 9781402277917

LC 2012042814

Sequel to: Stupid fast

This book explores a "Wisconsin football phenom's high-school years. The pressure is truly on as Felton, a senior, has to cope with the stresses of college recruitment. When his girlfriend, Aleah, breaks off their long-distance romance, and the brother of the bullied freshman he mentors kills himself, Felton violently unravels. Identifying with Shakespeare's Hamlet, Felton struggles with his own royal role as sports hero and his father's legacy as angry suicide." (Booklist)

Nothing special; Geoff Herbach. Sourcebooks Inc. 2012 290 p. (paperback) $9.99; (ebook) $9.99

Grades: 6 7 8 9 10 **Fic**

1. Friendship -- Fiction 2. Dysfunctional families -- Fiction 3. Teenagers -- Conduct of life -- Fiction

ISBN 1402265077; 9781402265075; 9781402265099

In this book, author Geoff Herbach tells the story of Felton, a football and track star who deals with his girlfriend Aleah abroad in Germany and "the possibility that his younger brother Andrew could be falling apart. Andrew has convinced their mother to let him go to band camp, but Felton discovers that Andrew, usually the sane member of the family, has in fact run away to Florida. An impromptu road trip with erstwhile best friend Gus turns up surprising reasons for Andrew's escape." (Kirkus Reviews)

Stupid fast. Sourcebooks 2011 311p pa $9.99

Grades: 6 7 8 9 10 **Fic**

1. Boys -- Fiction 2. Football -- Fiction

ISBN 978-1-4022-5630-1; 1-4022-5630-2

"Herbach is at his peak limning the confusion and frustration of a young man who no longer recognizes his own body, and Felton's self-deprecating take on his newly awarded A-list status is funny and compelling." Bull Cent Child Books

Herlong, M. H.

The **great** wide sea; [by] M. H. Herlong. Viking Children's Books 2008 283p pa $6.99; $16.99

Grades: 7 8 9 10 **Fic**

1. Sailing -- Fiction 2. Brothers -- Fiction 3. Bereavement -- Fiction 4. Father-son relationship -- Fiction 5. Survival after airplane accidents, shipwrecks, etc. -- Fiction

ISBN 0-14-241670-3 pa; 0-670-06330-4; 978-0-14-241670-9 pa; 978-0-670-06330-7

LC 2008-08384

Still mourning the death of their mother, three brothers go with their father on an extended sailing trip off the Florida Keys and have an adventure at sea. "Grades six to ten." (Bull Cent Child Books)

"Herlong makes the most of the three boys' characters, each exceptionally well developed here, to make this as much a novel of brotherhood as a sea story." Bull Cent Child Books

Hernández, Carlos

★ **Sal** and Gabi break the universe; Carlos Hernandez. Disney-Hyperion 2019 400 p. $16.99

Grades: 4 5 6 7 8 **Fic**

1. Grief -- Fiction 2. Universe -- Fiction 3. Science fiction 4. Cuban Americans -- Fiction

ISBN 9781368022828

LC 2018021081

In this book, by Carlos Hernandez, "[Gabi] is determined to prove that somehow, Sal planted a raw chicken in Yasmany's locker, even though nobody saw him do it and the bloody poultry has since mysteriously disappeared. . . . When Gabi learns that he's capable of conjuring things much bigger than a chicken . . . and she takes it all in stride, Sal knows that she is someone he can work with . . . [but] their manipulation of time and space could put the entire universe at risk." (Publisher's note)

"Artfully balancing comical antics with a meaningful exploration of grief, Hernandez fills his fast-paced novel with an intriguing blend of sf, folklore, and Cuban culture and populates it with delightfully well-rounded, clever, and exceptionally kind characters, all in a lively, distinctive voice." Booklist

Herrera, Robin

Hope is a ferris wheel; Robin Herrera. Amulet Books 2014 272 p. (alk. paper) $16.95

Grades: 4 5 6 7 **Fic**

1. Clubs -- Fiction 2. Moving -- Fiction 3. Poetry -- Fiction 4. Trailer parks -- Fiction 5. Trailer camps -- Fiction

ISBN 1419710397; 9781419710391

LC 2013026392

In this book, by Robin Herrera, "ten-year-old Star Mackie lives in a trailer park with her flaky mom and her melancholy older sister. . . . Moving to a new town has made it difficult for Star to make friends, when her classmates tease her because of where she lives and because of her layered blue hair. But when Star starts a poetry club, she develops a love of Emily Dickinson and . . . learns some important lessons about herself and comes to terms with her hopes for the future." (Publisher's note)

"Herrera has created a delightful narrator with a memorable voice and surrounded her with a unique supporting cast." Booklist

Herrick, Amy

The **Time** Fetch; a novel. Amy Herrick. Algonquin Young Readers 2013 320 p. $16.95

Grades: 5 6 7 8 **Fic**

1. Time travel -- Fiction 2. Science fiction -- Fiction 3. Space and time -- Fiction 4. Adventure and adventurers -- Fiction

ISBN 1616202203; 9781616202200

LC 2013008612

In this book, "when eighth-grader Edward picks up what he thinks is a rock for science class, he accidentally disturbs a Time Fetch, little knowing it's full of time-eating foragers. Soon, he and three classmates—athletic Danton, painfully shy Brigit, and abrasive Feenix—are pulled into a quest to prevent the out-of-control foragers from destroying everything." (Publishers Weekly)

Hesse, Karen

Brooklyn Bridge; a novel. Feiwel and Friends 2008 229p il map $17.95

Grades: 5 6 7 8 9 10 **Fic**

1. Immigrants -- Fiction 2. Family life -- Fiction 3. Social classes -- Fiction 4. Homeless persons -- Fiction 5. Russian Americans -- Fiction 6. Brooklyn (New York, N.Y.) -- Fiction

ISBN 978-0-312-37886-8; 0-312-37886-6

LC 2008-05624

In 1903 Brooklyn, fourteen-year-old Joseph Michtom's life changes for the worse when his parents, Russian immigrants, invent the teddy bear and turn their apartment into a factory, while nearby the glitter of Coney Island contrasts with the dismal lives of children dwelling under the Brooklyn Bridge.

Hesse "applies her gift for narrative voice to this memorable story. . . . The novel explodes with dark drama before its eerie but moving resolution." Publ Wkly

★ **Letters** from Rifka. Holt & Co. 1992 148p $16.95; pa $6.99

Grades: 5 6 7 8 **Fic**

1. Jews -- Fiction 2. Letters -- Fiction 3. Immigrants -- Fiction

ISBN 0-8050-1964-2; 0-312-53561-9 pa

LC 91-48007

In letters to her cousin, Rifka, a young Jewish girl, chronicles her family's flight from Russia in 1919 and her own experiences when she must be left in Belgium for a while when the others emigrate to America

"Based on the true story of the author's great-aunt, the moving account of a brave young girl's story brings to life the day-to-day trials and horrors experienced by many immigrants as well as the resourcefulness and strength they found within themselves." Horn Book

★ **Out** of the dust. Scholastic 1997 227p $16.95; pa $6.99

Grades: 5 6 7 8 **Fic**

1. Novels in verse 2. Oklahoma -- Fiction 3. Farm life -- Fiction 4. Dust storms -- Fiction 5. Great Depression, 1929-1939 -- Fiction

ISBN 0-590-36080-9; 0-590-37125-8 pa

LC 96-40344

Awarded the Newbery Medal, 1998

"Hesse's writing transcends the gloom and transforms it into a powerfully compelling tale of a girl with enormous strength, courage, and love. The entire novel is written in very readable blank verse." Booklist

Safekeeping; Karen Hesse. Feiwel and Friends 2012 294 p. ill., map $17.99

Grades: 7 8 9 10 11 12 **Fic**

1. Alternative histories 2. Revolutions -- Fiction 3. Voyages and travels -- Fiction

ISBN 1250011345; 9781250011343

LC 2012288414

In this book, a "group of rebels called the American People's Party has taken control" in the U.S. "Radley, an American teenager returning home from doing volunteer work in Haiti, finds her parents gone and her Vermont home abandoned. Not knowing whom to trust or where she'll be safe, she sets out on foot to Canada, befriending a reticent girl along the way. The two form a tentative friendship and manage to cross into Canada." (Publishers Weekly)

Witness. Scholastic Press 2001 161p $16.95; pa $5.99

Grades: 6 7 8 9 **Fic**

1. Novels in verse 2. Vermont -- Fiction 3. Prejudices -- Fiction 4. Ku Klux Klan -- Fiction

ISBN 0-439-27199-1; 0-439-27200-9 pa

LC 00-54139

A series of poems express the views of eleven people in a small Vermont town, including a young black girl and a young Jewish girl, during the early 1920s when the Ku Klux Klan is trying to infiltrate the town

"The story is divided into five acts, and would lend itself beautifully to performance. The plot unfolds smoothly, and the author creates multidimensional characters." SLJ

Hesse, Monica

★ The **war** outside; Monica Hesse. Little, Brown & Co. 2018 336 p. (hardcover) $17.99

Grades: 8 9 10 11 12 **Fic**

1. Friendship -- Fiction 2. World War, 1939-1945 -- United States -- Fiction 3. Japanese Americans -- Evacuation and relocation, 1942-1945 -- Fiction 4. Crystal City Internment Camp (Crystal City, Tex.) -- Fiction 5. German Americans -- Evacuation and relocation, 1941-1948 -- Fiction

ISBN 9780316316699

LC 2018005733

In this book, by Monica Hesse, "it's 1944, and World War II is raging across Europe and the Pacific. . . . Haruko and Margot meet at the high school in Crystal City, a 'family internment camp' for those accused of colluding with the enemy. . . . With everything around them falling apart, Margot and Haruko find solace in their growing, secret friendship. But in a prison the government has deemed full of spies, can they trust anyone--even each other?" (Publisher's note)

"Interned in a Texas camp during World War II, Japanese-American Haruko and German-American Margot watch their families fall apart and are driven to depend on each other, even if they should not." (Kirkus Reviews)

Hesser, Terry Spencer

Kissing doorknobs. Delacorte Press 1998 149p hardcover o.p. pa $6.50

Grades: 7 8 9 10 **Fic**

1. Obsessive-compulsive disorder -- Fiction

ISBN 0-385-32329-8; 0-440-41314-1 pa

LC 97-26937

Fourteen-year-old Tara describes how her increasingly strange compulsions begin to take over her life and affect her relationships with her family and friends

"An honest, fresh, and multilayered story to which readers will instantly relate. . . . The prose is forthright, economical, and peppered with wry humor." SLJ

Hiaasen, Carl

★ **Flush**. Knopf 2005 263p $16.95; lib bdg $18.99; pa $8.99

Grades: 5 6 7 8 **Fic**

1. Florida -- Fiction 2. Boats and boating -- Fiction 3. Environmental protection -- Fiction

ISBN 0-375-82182-1; 0-375-92182-6 lib bdg; 0-375-84185-7 pa

LC 2005-05259

With their father jailed for sinking a river boat, Noah Underwood and his younger sister, Abbey, must gather evidence that the owner of this floating casino is emptying his bilge tanks into the protected waters around their Florida Keys home

"This quick-reading, fun, family adventure harkens back to the Hardy Boys in its simplicity and quirky characters." SLJ

★ **Hoot**. Knopf 2002 292p $15.95; pa $8.95

Grades: 5 6 7 8 **Fic**

1. Owls -- Fiction 2. Florida -- Fiction 3. Environmental protection -- Fiction

ISBN 0-375-82181-3; 0-375-82916-4 pa

LC 2002-25478

A Newbery Medal honor book, 2003

Roy, who is new to his small Florida community, becomes involved in another boy's attempt to save a colony of burrowing owls from a proposed construction site. "Grades six to nine." (Bull Cent Child Books)

"The story is full of offbeat humor, buffoonish yet charming supporting characters, and genuinely touching scenes of children enjoying the wildness of nature." Booklist

★ **Scat**. Knopf 2009 371p $16.99; pa $8.99; lib bdg $19.99

Grades: 5 6 7 8 **Fic**

1. Florida -- Fiction 2. Teachers -- Fiction 3. Missing persons -- Fiction 4. Wildlife conservation -- Fiction

ISBN 0-375-83486-9; 0-375-83487-7 pa; 0-375-93486-3 lib bdg; 978-0-375-83486-8; 978-0-375-83487-5 pa; 978-0-375-93486-5 lib bdg

LC 2008-28266

Nick and his friend Marta investigate when a mysterious fire starts near a Florida wildlife preserve and biology teacher Mrs. Starch goes missing. "Grades six to nine." (Bull Cent Child Books)

"Once again, Hiaasen has written an edge-of-the-seat eco-thriller. . . . From the first sentence, readers will be hooked. . . . This well-written and smoothly plotted story, with fully realized characters, will certainly appeal to mystery lovers." SLJ

Skink --no surrender; Carl Hiaasen. Alfred A. Knopf 2014 288 p. (hardback) $18.99

Grades: 8 9 10 11 12 **Fic**

1. Mystery fiction 2. Missing persons -- Fiction 3. Florida -- Fiction 4. Missing children -- Fiction 5. Wilderness areas -- Fiction 6. Mystery and detective stories

ISBN 0375870512; 9780375870514; 9780375970511

LC 2014006036

"Classic Malley--to avoid being shipped off to boarding school, she takes off with some guy she met online. Poor Richard--he knows his cousin's in trouble before she does. Wild Skink--he's a ragged, one-eyed ex-governor of Florida, and enough of a renegade to think he can track Malley down. With Richard riding shotgun, the unlikely pair scour the state, undaunted by blinding storms, crazed pigs, flying bullets, and giant gators." (Publisher's note)

Hicks, Deron R.

The **secrets** of Shakespeare's grave; by Deron R. Hicks ; [illustrated by Mark Edward Geyer] Houghton Mifflin Harcourt 2012 273 p. (hardcover) $16.99

Grades: 4 5 6 **Fic**

1. Mystery fiction 2. Shakespeare, William, 1564-1616 -- Fiction 3. Cousins -- Fiction 4. Mystery and detective stories 5. Brothers and sisters -- Fiction 6. Adventure and adventurers -- Fiction

ISBN 0547840349; 9780547840345

LC 2012014801

In this book by Deron R. Hicks "Twelve-year-old Colophon Letterford has a serious mystery on her hands. Will she discover the link between her family's literary legacy and Shakespeare's tomb before it's too late? Antique paintings, secret passages, locked mausoleums, a four-hundred-year-old treasure, and a cast of quirky (and some ignoble) characters all add up to a . . . journey through literary time and space in real-world locales from Mont St. Michel to Stratford-Upon-Avon to Central Park!" (Publisher's note)

Higgins, F. E.

★ The **Black** Book of Secrets. Feiwel and Friends 2007 273p (Tales from the sinister city) $14.95

Grades: 4 5 6 7 **Fic**

1. Apprentices -- Fiction 2. Pawnbrokers -- Fiction

ISBN 978-0-312-36844-9; 0-312-36844-5

LC 2007-32559

When Ludlow Fitch runs away from his thieving parents in the City, he meets up with the mysterious Joe Zabbidou, who calls himself a secret pawnbroker, and who takes Ludlow as an apprentice to record the confessions of the townspeople of Pagus Parvus, where resentments are many and trust is scarce.

This is "an intriguing blend of adventure and historical fiction spiced with a light touch of the fantastic." Voice Youth Advocates

Other titles in this series are:
The bone magician (2008)
The eyeball collector (2009)
The lunatic's curse (2011)

The **Eyeball** Collector. Feiwel & Friends 2009 251p $14.99

Grades: 7 8 9 10 **Fic**

1. Horror fiction 2. Mystery fiction

ISBN 978-0-312-56681-4; 0-312-56681-6

"In what the author dubs a 'polyquel' that partially bridges her Black Book of Secrets (2007) and its prequel Bone Magician (2008), Higgins sends a suddenly penniless young orphan from the filthy streets of Urbs Umida's South Side to an extravagantly rococo estate house in search of vengeance for his family's ruin. . . . Readers with a taste for lurid prose, macabre twists, riddles, exotic poisons, high-society caricatures, murderous schemes and scenes of stomach-churning degeneracy will find some or all of these in every chapter, and though the author trots in multiple characters and references from previous episodes, this one stands sturdily on its own." Kirkus

The **lunatic's** curse. Feiwel and Friends 2011 336p $15.99

Grades: 6 7 8 9 **Fic**

1. Horror fiction

ISBN 978-0-312-56682-1; 0-312-56682-4

"The prosperous town of Oppum Oppidulum, the deep and cold adjacent Lake Beluarum and the Asylum for the Peculiar and Bizarre that sits on an island in said lake all hold horrifying secrets. Young Rex discovers this when his father is confined to the Asylum after suddenly going mad and eating his own hand—to the open glee of Rex's sinister new stepmother Acantha Grammaticus. . . . Strewing her narrative with dark hints, obscure clues, assorted lunatics and, in particular, both macabre cuisine and a panoply of noxious or tantalizingly evocative odors, the author contrives a highly atmospheric experience. Readers with strong stomachs and a taste for melodramatic narratives . . . will devour this yarn with relish." Kirkus

Higgins, Jack

Death run; by Jack Higgins with Justin Richards. G.P. Putnam's Sons 2008 253p $16.99

Grades: 6 7 8 9 **Fic**

1. Adventure fiction 2. Spies -- Fiction 3. Twins -- Fiction 4. Fathers -- Fiction 5. Organized crime -- Fiction

ISBN 978-0-399-25081-1; 0-399-25081-6

LC 2007-42830

Sequel to: Sure fire (2007)

First published 2007 in the United Kingdom

A mafia banker with access to a large number of criminal accounts is willing to give evidence in exchange for help retiring from the mob, but when spy John Chase assists him, he puts his fifteen-year-old twins, Rich and Jade, in the line of fire.

This is an "enjoyable romp." Booklist

Followed by: Sharp shot (2010)

First strike; [by] Jack Higgins with Justin Richards. G. P. Putnam's Sons 2010 224p $16.99

Grades: 6 7 8 9 **Fic**

1. Adventure fiction 2. Spies -- Fiction 3. Twins -- Fiction 4. Fathers -- Fiction 5. Siblings -- Fiction 6. Terrorism -- Fiction

ISBN 978-0-399-25240-2; 0-399-25240-1

Sequel to: Sharp shot (2009)

First published 2009 in the United Kingdom

British twins Rich and Jade are once again thrown into danger as they try to help their spy father, John Chance, save the President of the United States from a radical group holding the White House hostage and attempting to steal the nation's nuclear launch codes.

"Fans of the twins' exploits will enjoy this thrill ride." Booklist

Sharp shot; [by] Jack Higgins with Justin Richards. G.P. Putnam's Sons 2009 xxi, 214p $16.99

Grades: 6 7 8 9 **Fic**

1. Adventure fiction 2. Spies -- Fiction 3. Twins -- Fiction 4. Fathers -- Fiction 5. Siblings -- Fiction 6. Terrorism -- Fiction 7. Middle East -- Fiction

ISBN 978-0-399-25239-6; 0-399-25239-8

LC 2008052886

Sequel to: Death run (2008)

British twins Rich and Jade Chance are back for a third adventure with their spy father as they try to save the Middle East and the President of the United States from a terrorist government coup.

"Higgins and Richards have crafted another page-turner punctuated with gunfire and highlighted by heroism and explosions." Booklist

Followed by: First strike (2010)

★ **Sure** fire; [by] Jack Higgins with Justin Richards. G.P. Putnam's Sons 2007 237p $16.99

Grades: 6 7 8 9 **Fic**

1. Adventure fiction 2. Spies -- Fiction 3. Twins -- Fiction 4. Fathers -- Fiction

ISBN 978-0-399-24784-2; 0-399-24784-X

LC 2007008144

First published 2006 in the United Kingdom

Resentful of having to go and live with their estranged father after the death of their mother, fifteen-year-old twins, Rich and Jade, soon find they have more complicated problems when their father is kidnapped and their attempts to rescue him involve them in a dangerous international plot to control the world's oil.

This is a "standout YA spy novel. . . . Each chapter ends with a cliff-hanger, maintaining the high level of suspense." Publ Wkly

Other titles in this series are:

Death run (2008)

Sharp shot (2009)

First strike (2010)

Higgins, Joanna

Waiting for the queen; Joanna Higgins. Milkweed Editions 2013 256 p. (alk. paper) $16.95

Grades: 6 7 8 9 10 **Fic**

1. Historical fiction 2. Immigrants -- United States -- Fiction 3. Shakers -- Fiction 4. Slavery -- Fiction 5. Friendship -- Fiction 6. Social classes -- Fiction 7. Pennsylvania -- History -- 1775-1865 -- Fiction 8. Frontier and pioneer life -- Pennsylvania -- Fiction 9. France -- History -- Revolution, 1789-1799 -- Fiction

ISBN 1571317007; 9781571317001

LC 2012042167

In this book, "Eugenie, 15 and haunted by the horrors [of the French Revolution] they've escaped, arrives unprepared for the harshly primitive conditions they find [in America], and she's annoyed by her unrealistic mother's matchmaking with an unpleasant young noble. In alternating chapters, her story is contrasted with that of Quaker Hannah, who . . . has been hired to help the French out for a year but whose faith keeps her from the subservience the noblemen demand." (Kirkus Reviews)

Higgins, M. G.

Bi -Normal; M. G. Higgins. Saddleback Pub 2013 191 p. (paperback) $9.95

Grades: 7 8 9 10 11 12 **Fic**

1. School stories 2. Gay teenagers -- Fiction

ISBN 1622500040; 9781622500048

In this book, "a teen football player with a girlfriend discovers he has feelings for another boy. When Brett first notices his attraction to Zach, a boy who sits next to him in art class, he wants to push it away Brett and his friends are the kind of guys who ogle girls' bodies and pick on boys they perceive as gay. As his feelings intensify, however, Brett is torn between acting on his attraction and acting out of his denial." (Kirkus Reviews)

Higgins, Simon

Moonshadow; rise of the ninja. Little Brown & Co. 2010 325p il $15.99

Grades: 4 5 6 7 **Fic**

1. Japan -- Fiction 2. Ninja -- Fiction 3. Spies -- Fiction 4. Secret societies -- Fiction

ISBN 978-0-316-05531-4; 0-316-05531-X

First published 2008 in Australia with title: Moonshadow: eye of the beast

It's the dawn of an age of peace in medieval Japan. But a power-hungry warlord is plotting to plunge the national into a deadly civil war. Enter Moonshadow, the newest agent for the Grey Light Order, a secret brotherhood of ninja spy warriors. Can Moonshadow defeat the evil warlord or will his first mission be his last?

"The swordplay is fast and furious, and Japanese terms and places are integrated in a manner that reluctant readers will find accessible. This adventure is part spy novel, part magic, and all fun." SLJ

Followed by: The nightmare ninja (2011)

The **nightmare** ninja. Little, Brown 2011 368p (Moonshadow) $15.99

Grades: 4 5 6 7 **Fic**

1. Japan -- Fiction 2. Ninja -- Fiction 3. Orphans -- Fiction 4. Supernatural -- Fiction

ISBN 978-0-316-05533-8; 0-316-05533-6

LC 2010043177

Sequel to: Moonshadow: rise of the ninja (2010)

Battling a power-hungry warlord in medieval Japan, teenaged Moonshadow, an orphaned ninja in the shogun's secret service with the ability to see through the eyes of animals, encounters a weaponless assassin who enters the mind of his victims during their sleep.

"Higgins effectively uses this work to set the stage for a compelling third installment." Kirkus

Hill, C. J.

Erasing time; C. J. Hill. Katherine Tegen Books 2012 361 p. $17.99

Grades: 8 9 10 11 **Fic**

1. Secrecy -- Fiction 2. Future life -- Fiction 3. Resistance to government -- Fiction 4. Science fiction 5. Twins -- Fiction 6. Sisters -- Fiction 7. Time travel -- Fiction

ISBN 0062123920; 9780062123923

LC 2011044624

"When twins Sheridan and Taylor wake up 400 years in the future, they find a changed world: domed cities, no animals, and a language that's so different, it barely sounds like English. And the worst news: They can't go back home. The twenty-fifth-century government transported the girls to their city hoping to find a famous scientist to help perfect a devastating new weapon. The same government has implanted tracking devices in the citizens, limiting and examining everything they do. Taylor and Sheridan have to find a way out of the city before the government discovers their secrets."

(Publisher's note)

Followed by Echo in time (2013)

Slayers. Feiwel and Friends 2011 373p $16.99

Grades: 7 8 9 10 11 12 **Fic**

1. Fantasy fiction 2. Camps -- Fiction 3. Ability -- Fiction 4. Dragons -- Fiction 5. Supernatural -- Fiction

ISBN 978-0-312-61414-0; 0-312-61414-4

LC 2011023559

At a rustic summer camp, sixteen-year-old Tori, a senator's daughter, learns that she is descended from medieval dragon slayers, that dragons still exist, and that she is expected to hone her special abilities to join her fellow campers in battling the beasts and the man who controls them.

"The dragon mythos has a good dollop of modern science, and Hill offers cunning peeks into the minds of characters on all sides of the power struggle. . . . The character development, plotting, and ethical quandries make this more than a worthy equal to the works of Rick Riordan or Christopher Paolini." Booklist

Other titles in this series are:

Friends and Traitors (2013)

Playing with Fire (2016)

Hilmo, Tess

Skies like these; Tess Hilmo. Margaret Ferguson Books, Farrar Straus Giroux 2014 240 p. (hardback) $16.99

Grades: 4 5 6 7 **Fic**

1. Western stories 2. Friendship -- Fiction 3. Aunts -- Fiction 4. Wyoming -- Fiction 5. Eccentrics and eccentricities -- Fiction

ISBN 0374369984; 9780374369989

LC 2013033675

"Twelve-year-old Jade's perfect summers have always been spent reading and watching TV reruns, so she's not happy when her parents send her off to Wyoming to her aunt's house. She meets a boy who calls himself Roy Parker--just like the real name of the legendary rebel cowboy Butch Cassidy. . . . Jade wants to be a good friend, but she's not so sure about Roy's schemes." (Publisher's note)

"In Hilmo's second middle-grade novel, a 12-year-old city girl spends a month in Wyoming and finds big skies, a boy who idolizes Butch Cassidy, and her own sense of adventure. . . . But rest assured, if there's a sequel, their future big plans will likely center around climbing Grand Teton rather than robbing banks." Booklist

★ **With** a name like Love. Margaret Ferguson Books/Farrar Straus Giroux 2011 249p $16.99

Grades: 5 6 7 8 **Fic**

1. Mystery fiction 2. Arkansas -- Fiction 3. Country life -- Fiction 4. Christian life -- Fiction 5. Conduct of life -- Fiction

ISBN 978-0-374-38465-4; 0-374-38465-7

LC 2010036314

Thirteen-year-old Olivene Love gets tangled up in a murder mystery when her itinerant preaching family arrives in the small town of Binder, Arkansas in 1957.

"Hilmo creates a family, town and a mystery that readers won't soon forget." Kirkus

Hilton, Marilyn

Full cicada moon; by Marilyn Hilton. Dial Books, an imprint of Penguin Group (USA) Inc. 2015 400 p. (hardcover) $17.99

Grades: 4 5 6 7 **Fic**

1. Novels in verse 2. Vermont -- Fiction 3. Astronauts -- Fiction 4. Gender role -- Fiction 5. Racially mixed people -- Fiction 6. Sex role -- Fiction

ISBN 0525428755; 9780525428756

LC 2014044894

This book, by Marilyn Hilton, is a "novel-in-verse about fitting in. . . . It's 1969, and the Apollo 11 mission is getting ready to go to the moon. But for half-black, half-Japanese Mimi, moving to a predominantly white Vermont town is enough to make her feel alien. . . . She struggles to fit in with her classmates. . . . And even though teachers and neighbors balk at her mixed-race family and her refusals to conform, Mimi¿s dreams of becoming an astronaut never fade." (Publisher's note)

"Mimi Yoshiko Oliver and her family just moved from Berkeley, California, to Hillsborough, Vermont, where she immediately encounters barrier after barrier to overcome. Mimi's goal is to become an astronaut; however, it's 1969, a time when young girls are encouraged to become mothers, secretaries, teachers, or nurses. . . . Mimi's voice as narrator is clear and focused: she must figure out who she is, instead of answering the question, "What are you?" Out of respect for her parents, the decisions she makes pull from both halves to make a whole. Perfect for readers who straddle societies, feel they don't fit in, or need that confirmation of self-celebration." Booklist

Hinton, S. E.

★ The **outsiders**. Viking 1967 188p $17.99; pa $9.99
Grades: 7 8 9 10 **Fic**

1. Social classes -- Fiction 2. Juvenile delinquency -- Fiction
ISBN 0-670-53257-6; 0-14-038572-X pa
ALA YALSA Margaret A. Edwards Award (1988)

"This remarkable novel by a seventeen-year-old girl gives a moving, credible view of the outsiders from the inside—their loyalty to each other, their sensitivity under tough crusts, their understanding of self and society." Horn Book

Hinwood, Christine

The **returning**. Dial Books 2011 302p map $17.99
Grades: 6 7 8 9 10 **Fic**

1. War stories 2. Villages -- Fiction
ISBN 978-0-8037-3528-6; 0-8037-3528-6
LC 2010-08398
First published 2009 in Australia with title: Bloodflower
Printz Honor Book (2012)

When the twelve-year war between the Uplanders and Downlanders is over and Cam returns home to his village, questions dog him, from how he lost an arm to why he was the only one of his fellow soldiers to survive, such that he must leave until his own suspicions are resolved.

"Themes of rebuilding and redemption are powerful, but it is in the small, acutely observed details of debut author Hinwood's world that her story truly shines." Publ Wkly

Hirahara, Naomi

1001 cranes. Delacorte Press 2008 230p $15.99; lib bdg $18.99; pa $6.50
Grades: 5 6 7 8 **Fic**

1. Family life -- Fiction 2. Grandparents -- Fiction 3. Japanese Americans -- Fiction
ISBN 978-0-385-73556-8; 0-385-73556-1; 978-0-385-90541-1 lib bdg; 0-385-90541-6 lib bdg; 978-0-440-42234-1 pa; 0-440-42234-5 pa
LC 2007-27655

With her parents on the verge of separating, Angela, a twelve-year-old Japanese American girl, spends the summer in Los Angeles with her grandparents, where she folds paper cranes into wedding displays, becomes involved with a young skateboarder, and learns how complicated relationships can be.

Angela's "colorful, bold voice captures the excitement of her first love as well as the anxiety of not understanding the many secrets of the adults around her. By experiencing her family's support, by learning about her Japanese heritage, and by acknowledging the various ways that love is expressed, Angela emerges into a strong, caring person." SLJ

Hiranandani, Veera

★ The **night** diary; Veera Hiranandani. Dial Books for Young Readers 2018 272 p. (hardcover) $16.99
Grades: 5 6 7 8 **Fic**

1. Hindus -- Fiction 2. Diaries -- Fiction 3. Muslims -- Fiction 4. Refugees -- Fiction 5. Family life -- India -- Fiction 6. India -- History -- Partition, 1947 -- Fiction
ISBN 9780735228511
LC 2017012579
Newbery Honor Book (2019)

In this book, by Veera Hiranandani, "it's 1947, and India, newly independent of British rule, has been separated into two countries: Pakistan and India. . . . Half-Muslim, half-Hindu twelve-year-old Nisha doesn't know where she belongs, or what her country is anymore. When Papa decides it's too dangerous to stay in what is now Pakistan, Nisha and her family become refugees and embark first by train but later on foot to reach her new home." (Publisher's note)

"Hiranandani's prose shines in both emotion and simple, rich description, especially with regards to Nisha's developing love of cooking. This new passion ties her to the beloved Muslim cook her family left behind, and becomes a way for Nisha to connect to her complicated family, fractured past, and homeland--old and new. A clear, compelling, and deeply felt historical novel." Booklist

★ The **whole** story of half a girl. Delacorte Press 2012 $16.99; lib bdg $19.99
Grades: 4 5 6 7 **Fic**

1. School stories 2. East Indian Americans -- Fiction 3. Racially mixed people -- Fiction 4. Depression (Psychology) -- Fiction
ISBN 978-0-385-74128-6; 0-385-74128-6; 978-0-375-98995-7 lib bdg; 0-375-98995-1 lib bdg; 978-0-375-98441-9 ebook
LC 2011026178

In this book, "[w]hen Sonia's father loses his job at the end of her fifth-grade year, it means she can't return to her beloved private school and instead must navigate the rocky waters of public school for the first time. Up until this point, eleven-year-old Sonia has never thought that much about her identity as the daughter of an Indian father and a Jewish-American mother, but she is suddenly faced with questions that she can't always answer about her race, her ethnicity, and her core values. She . . . begins two friendships: with Kate, a very perky, popular girl who encourages Sonia to try out for cheerleading but seems very keen on transforming her into something she isn't, and with Alisha, who, like Sonia, aspires to be a writer." (Bulletin of the Center for Children's Books).

"Sonia's struggles are painfully realistic. . . True to life, her problems do not wrap up neatly, but Sonia's growth is deeply rewarding in this thoughtful and beautifully wrought novel." Publ Wkly

Hirano, Cathy

Moribito; Guardian of the Spirit. [by] Nahoko Uehashi; translated by Cathy Hirano; illustrated by Yuko Shimizu. Arthur A. Levine Books 2008 248p il hardcover o.p. O.P.
Grades: 6 7 8 9 **Fic**

1. Fantasy fiction 2. Japan -- Fiction 3. Martial arts -- Fiction
ISBN 978-0-5450-0542-5; 0-5450-0542-6

The wandering warrior Balsa is hired to protect Prince Chagum from both a mysterious monster and the prince's father, the Mikado.

"This book is first in a series of ten that have garnered literary and popular success in Japan. . . . Balsa and Chagum's story is brought to America with a strong translation. . . . Readers who are fans of action manga, especially with strong female characters, will enjoy the ninja-like fighting scenes. . . . The exciting premise, combined with an attractive cover, should insure that this title will circulate well." Voice Youth Advocates

Followed by: Moribito II: Guardian of the Darkness (2009)

Hirsch, Jeff

The **39** clues: Breakaway; unstoppable: breakaway. Jeff Hirsch. Scholastic 2014 192 p. (The 39 clues: unstoppable) (paper over board) $12.99

Grades: 4 5 6 7 **Fic**

1. Betrayal 2. Adventure stories 3. Brothers and sisters -- Fiction
ISBN 0545521424; 9780545521420

LC 2013942298

In this 39 Clues series book by Jeff Hirsch, "Dan and Amy are facing their greatest threat yet, an enemy who has found a way to use the source of the Cahill family power against them. To stop him, Dan and Amy must set out on a desperate mission that will take them from one of the world's hottest regions all the way to the frozen blast of the Arctic Circle. But with the enemy closing in, Dan finds himself facing the one terror he never imagined--being betrayed by his own sister." (Publisher's note)

The **eleventh** plague. Scholastic Press 2011 278p $17.99

Grades: 7 8 9 10 **Fic**

1. Science fiction
ISBN 978-0-545-29014-2; 0-545-29014-7

LC 2010048966

The Darkest Path (2013; Black River Falls (2016)

Twenty years after the start of the war that caused the Collapse, fifteen-year-old Stephen, his father, and grandfather travel post-Collapse America scavenging, but when his grandfather dies and his father decides to risk everything to save the lives of two strangers, Stephen's life is turned upside down.

This "novel is an impressive story with strong characters. . . . Hirsch delivers a tight, well-crafted story." Publ Wkly

Hitchcock, Bonnie-Sue

The **smell** of other people's houses; Bonnie-Sue Hitchcock. Wendy Lamb Books 2016 240 p. (trade) $17.99

Grades: 7 8 9 10 **Fic**

1. Alaska -- Fiction 2. Teenagers -- Fiction 3. Friendship -- Fiction 4. Alaska -- History -- 20th century -- Fiction
ISBN 9780553497786; 9780553497793; 9780553497816

LC 2015011309

Morris Finalist (2017)

"Alaska, 1970. . . . Ruth has a secret that she can't hide forever. Dora wonders if she can ever truly escape where she comes from, even when good luck strikes. Alyce is trying to reconcile her desire to dance, with the life she's always known on her family's fishing boat. Hank and his brothers decide it's safer to run away than to stay home—until one of them ends up in terrible danger." (Publisher's note)

"Less a narrative and more a series of portraits, this is an exquisitely drawn, deeply heartfelt look at a time and place not often addressed. Hitchcock's measured prose casts a gorgeous, almost otherworldly feel over the text, resulting in a quietly lovely look at the various sides of human nature and growing up in a difficult world." Booklist

Hitchcock, Shannon

The **ballad** of Jessie Pearl; Shannon Hitchcock. 1st ed. Namelos llc 2012 131 p. ill. (hardcover) $18.95

Grades: 5 6 7 8 **Fic**

1. Romance fiction 2. Historical fiction 3. Tuberculosis -- Fiction
ISBN 160898141X; 9781608981410; 9781608981427

LC 2012936706

In this novel, by Shannon Hitchcock, "it's 1922, and Jessie has big plans for her future, but that's before tuberculosis strikes. Though she has no talent for cooking, cleaning, or nursing, Jessie puts her dreams on hold to help her family. She falls in love for the first time ever, and suddenly what she wants is not so simple anymore." (Publisher's note)

Hobbs, Valerie

★ The **last** best days of summer. Frances Foster Books 2010 197p $16.99

Grades: 5 6 7 8 **Fic**

1. Artists -- Fiction 2. Old age -- Fiction 3. Popularity -- Fiction 4. Grandmothers -- Fiction 5. Down syndrome -- Fiction
ISBN 978-0-374-34670-6; 0-374-34670-4

LC 2008-47145

During a summer visit, twelve-year-old Lucy must come to terms with both her grandmother's failing memory and how her mentally-challenged neighbor will impact her popularity when both enter the same middle school in the fall.

"The story's finely tuned realism is refreshing, particularly in Lucy's yearning for social acceptance and in the fully drawn and wholly memorable characters." Booklist

Hobbs, Will

Beardance. Atheneum Pubs. 1993 197p il pa $5.99

Grades: 7 8 9 10 **Fic**

1. Bears -- Fiction 2. Ute Indians -- Fiction
ISBN 0-689-31867-7; 0-689-87072-8 pa

LC 92-44874

Sequel to Bearstone

While accompanying an elderly rancher on a trip into the San Juan Mountains, Cloyd, a Ute Indian boy, tries to help two orphaned grizzly cubs survive the winter and, at the same time, completes his spirit mission.

"The story offers plenty of action and memorable characters, and the descriptions of Ute rituals and legends, the setting, and Cloyd's first experiences with spirit dreams are particularly well done." Horn Book Guide

★ **Bearstone**. Atheneum Pubs. 1989 154p hardcover o.p. pa $4.99

Grades: 7 8 9 10 **Fic**

1. Ute Indians -- Fiction
ISBN 0-689-87071-X pa

LC 89-6641

"The growth and maturity that Cloyd acquires as the summer progresses is juxtaposed poetically against the majestic Colorado landscape. Hobbs has creatively blended myth and reality as Cloyd forges a new identity for himself." Voice Youth Advocates

Followed by Beardance (1993)

Crossing the wire. HarperCollins 2006 216p $15.99; lib bdg $16.89; pa $5.99

Grades: 5 6 7 8 **Fic**

1. Mexicans -- Fiction 2. Illegal aliens -- Fiction
ISBN 978-0-06-074138-9; 0-06-074138-4; 978-0-06-074139-6 lib bdg; 0-06-074139-2 lib bdg; 978-0-06-074140-2 pa; 0-06-074140-6 pa

LC 2005-19697

Fifteen-year-old Victor Flores journeys north in a desperate attempt to cross the Arizona border and find work in the United States to support his family in central Mexico.

This is "an exciting story in a vital contemporary setting." Voice Youth Advocates

Downriver. Atheneum Pubs. 1991 204p hardcover o.p. pa $6.99

Grades: 7 8 9 10 **Fic**

1. White-water canoeing -- Fiction

ISBN 0-689-31690-9; 0-440-22673-2 pa

LC 90-1044

Fifteen-year-old Jessie and the other rebellious teenage members of a wilderness survival school team abandon their adult leader, hijack his boats, and try to run the dangerous white water at the bottom of the Grand Canyon

"The book is exquisitely plotted, with nail-biting suspense and excitement." SLJ

Ghost canoe. Morrow Junior Bks. 1997 195p $16.99

Grades: 5 6 7 8 **Fic**

1. Adventure fiction 2. Buried treasure -- Fiction 3. Pacific Northwest -- Fiction

ISBN 0-688-14193-5

LC 96-34417

Fourteen-year-old Nathan, fishing with the Makah in the Pacific Northwest, finds himself holding a vital clue when a mysterious stranger comes to town looking for Spanish treasure

"Hobbs blends together a number of elements to create an exciting adventure set in 1874. . . . A winning tale that artfully combines history, nature, and suspense." SLJ

Go big or go home. HarperCollinsPublishers 2008 185p $15.99; lib bdg $16.89; pa $5.99

Grades: 6 7 8 9 **Fic**

1. Science fiction 2. Cousins -- Fiction 3. Meteorites -- Fiction 4. South Dakota -- Fiction

ISBN 0-06-074141-4; 0-06-074142-2 lib bdg; 0-06-074143-0 pa; 978-0-06-074141-9; 978-0-06-074142-6 lib bdg; 978-0-06-074143-3 pa

LC 2006100440

Fourteen-year-old Brady and his cousin Quinn love extreme sports, but nothing could prepare them for the aftermath of Brady's close encounter with a meteorite after it crashes into his Black Hills, South Dakota, bedroom.

"The sense of place is powerful, with bits of lore about the region making the reader feel immersed in the story and its setting, and the characterizations are especially strong." Voice Youth Advocates

★ **Jason's** gold. Morrow Junior Bks. 1999 221p $16.99; pa $5.99

Grades: 5 6 7 8 **Fic**

1. Orphans -- Fiction 2. Voyages and travels -- Fiction 3. Klondike River Valley (Yukon) -- Gold discoveries -- Fiction

ISBN 0-688-15093-4; 0-380-72914-8 pa

LC 99-17973

When news of the discovery of gold in Canada's Yukon Territory in 1897 reaches fifteen-year-old Jason, he embarks on a 10,000-mile journey to strike it rich

"The successful presentation of a fascinating era, coupled with plenty of action, makes this a good historical fiction choice." SLJ

Followed by Down the Yukon (2001)

Leaving Protection. HarperCollins 2004 178p il map $15.99; pa $5.99

Grades: 7 8 9 10 **Fic**

1. Alaska -- Fiction 2. Fishing -- Fiction 3. Buried treasure -- Fiction

ISBN 0-688-17475-2; 0-380-73312-9 pa

LC 2003-15545

Sixteen-year-old Robbie Daniels, happy to get a job aboard a troller fishing for king salmon off southeastern Alaska, finds himself in danger when he discovers that his mysterious captain is searching for long-buried Russian plaques that lay claim to Alaska and the Northwest

This "nautical thriller brims with detail about the fishing life and weaves in historical facts as well. . . . Robbie's doubts build to a climactic finale involving a dramatic and fateful storm at sea, grippingly rendered. Fans of maritime tales will relish the atmosphere and the bursts of action." Publ Wkly

Never say die; by Will Hobbs. HarperCollins Children's Books 2012 224 p. (trade bdg.) $16.99

Grades: 4 5 6 7 **Fic**

1. Canada -- Fiction 2. Wilderness survival -- Fiction 3. Adventure fiction -- Fiction 4. Bears -- Fiction 5. Caribou -- Fiction 6. Eskimos -- Fiction 7. Brothers -- Fiction 8. Inuit -- Canada -- Fiction 9. Photojournalism -- Fiction 10. Aklavik (N.W.T.) -- Fiction 11. Climatic changes -- Fiction 12. Adventure and adventurers -- Fiction

ISBN 006170878X; 9780061708787; 9780061708794

LC 2011053289

This juvenile adventure novel, by Will Hobbs, is set "in Canada's Arctic, [where] Nick Thrasher is an accomplished Inuit hunter at fifteen. . . . Ryan Powers . . . invites Nick to come along and help him find the caribou. Barely down the river, disaster strikes. . . . With nothing but the clothes on his back and the knife on his hip, Nick is up against it in a world of wolves, caribou, and grizzlies. All the while, the monstrous grolar bear stalks the land." (Publisher's note)

Take me to the river. HarperCollins 2011 184p $15.99; lib bdg $16.89

Grades: 5 6 7 8 **Fic**

1. Texas -- Fiction 2. Cousins -- Fiction 3. Canoes and canoeing -- Fiction

ISBN 978-0-06-074144-0; 0-06-074144-9; 978-0-06-074145-7 lib bdg; 0-06-074145-7 lib bdg

LC 2010003147

When North Carolina fourteen-year-old Dylan Sands joins his fifteen-year-old cousin Rio in running the Rio Grande River, they face a tropical storm and a fugitive kidnapper.

"The story unfolds in a disarming manner. The pace is quick, and the challenges are relentless, but the writing is so grounded in physical details and emotional realism that every turn of events seems convincing within the context of the story." Booklist

Wild Man Island. HarperCollins Pubs. 2002 184p $15.99; lib bdg $16.89; pa $5.99

Grades: 6 7 8 9 **Fic**

1. Alaska -- Fiction 2. Wilderness survival -- Fiction

ISBN 0-688-17473-6; 0-06-029810-3 lib bdg; 0-380-73310-2 pa

LC 2001-39818

After fourteen-year-old Andy slips away from his kayaking group to visit the wilderness site of his archaeologist father's death, a storm strands him on Admiralty Island, Alaska, where he manages to survive, encounters unexpected animal and human inhabitants, and looks for traces of the earliest prehistoric immigrants to America

"A well-paced adventure, this novel combines survival saga, mystery, and archaeological expedition." Voice Youth Advocates

Hocking, Amanda

Wake; Amanda Hocking. St. Martin's Griffin 2012 309 p. (hardback) $17.99

Grades: 7 8 9 10 **Fic**

1. Fantasy fiction 2. Paranormal fiction 3. Sirens (Mythology) -- Fiction 4. Love -- Fiction 5. Sisters -- Fiction 6. Supernatural -- Fiction 7. Seaside resorts -- Fiction

ISBN 1250008123; 9781250008121; 9781429956581

LC 2012014630

This is the first in Amanda Hocking's Watersong series. Here, "Gemma Fisher is happy—she's a star on the swim team, her family is loving and supportive, and the crush-worthy boy next door returns her interest. The only downside: three gorgeous but creepy new girls who have her in their sights." These girls ultimately turn out to be Sirens who trick Gemma into drinking potion that turns her into a Siren as well. (Publishers Weekly)

Followed by Lullaby (2012) and Tidal (2013)

Hodge, Rosamund

Cruel Beauty; Rosamund Hodge. Balzer + Bray, an imprint of HarperCollinsPublishers 2014 352 p. (hardcover) $17.99

Grades: 8 9 10 11 12 **Fic**

1. Romance fiction 2. Imaginary places 3. Magic -- Fiction 4. Fantasy

ISBN 0062224735; 9780062224736

LC 2013015418

In this book, by Rosamund Hodge, "betrothed to the evil ruler of her kingdom, Nyx has always known her fate was to marry him, kill him, and free her people from his tyranny. On her seventeenth birthday, when she moves into his castle high on the kingdom's mountaintop, nothing is as she expected. Nyx knows she must save her homeland at all costs, yet she can't resist the pull of her sworn enemy--who's gotten in her way by stealing her heart." (Publisher's note)

"Hodge's story infuses elements of Greek mythology and classic fairy tales. The plot moves quickly, and the characters are well formed; their transgressions make them interesting and authentic. The complex relationship between Nyx and Ignifex is especially engaging. An entertaining read for teens who enjoy romantic fantasy.—" (School Library Journal)

Hodkin, Michelle

The **unbecoming** of Mara Dyer. Simon & Schuster 2011 456p $16.99

Grades: 7 8 9 10 11 12 **Fic**

1. School stories 2. Florida -- Fiction 3. Family life -- Fiction 4. Supernatural -- Fiction 5. Post-traumatic stress disorder -- Fiction

ISBN 978-1-4424-2176-9; 1-4424-2176-2

LC 2010050862

Seventeen-year-old Mara cannot remember the accident that took the lives of three of her friends but, after moving from Rhode Island to Florida, finding love with Noah, and more deaths, she realizes uncovering something buried in her memory might save her family and her future.

"The characters are real and wonderful, and the supernatural story is riveting." SLJ

Other titles in this series are:

The evolution of Mara Dyer (2012)

The retribution of Mara Dyer (2014)

Hof, Marjolijn

Mother number zero. Groundwood Books 2011 179p $16.95

Grades: 4 5 6 7 **Fic**

1. Adoption -- Fiction 2. Siblings -- Fiction 3. Family life -- Fiction 4. Netherlands -- Fiction

ISBN 978-1-55498-078-9; 1-55498-078-X

Fay "and his older sister An Bing Wa were both adopted; she was an abandoned baby in China, and he was born to a mother traumatized in the Bosnian conflict. A new girl in the neighborhood, Maud, takes a keen interest in Fay's story and urges him to find his birth mother. . . . Hof . . . writes Fay's narration with a calm, matter-of-fact voice that possesses a literalness and simplicity in keeping with his youth. . . . The story nonetheless treats the characters with quiet percipience. . . . Younger fans of domestic novels who like a tale with more gravitas if not reading difficulty will appreciate this thoughtful family story." Bull Cent Child Books

Hoffman, Mary

★ The **falconer's** knot; a story of friars, flirtation and foul play. Bloomsbury Children's Books 2007 297p $16.95

Grades: 7 8 9 10 **Fic**

1. Renaissance -- Fiction 2. Religious life -- Fiction 3. Italy -- History -- 0-1559 -- Fiction

ISBN 978-1-59990-056-8; 1-59990-056-4

LC 2006-16365

Silvano and Chiara, teens sent to live in a friary and a nunnery in Renaissance Italy, are drawn to one another and dream of a future together, but when murders are committed in the friary, they must discover who is behind the crimes before they can realize their love.

"Hoffman creates utterly engaging characters and vivid settings, and she skillfully turns up the suspense, wrapping her varied plot threads into a satisfying whole." Booklist

Hoffman, Nina Kiriki

A **stir** of bones. Viking 2003 211p $15.99

Grades: 7 8 9 10 **Fic**

1. Ghost stories 2. Wife abuse -- Fiction

ISBN 0-670-03551-3

LC 2003-5029

Prequel to the author's adult novels, A red heart of memories (1999) and Past the size of dreaming (2000)

Fourteen-year-old Susan Blackstrom "begins the painful process of breaking away from her abusive father, with help from allies both human and supernatural. A chance encounter with three classmates leads Susan to an abandoned house that . . . harbors an uncommonly substantial ghost named Nathan. . . . Richly endowed with complex relationships, a strange and subtle brand of magic, evocative language, and suspenseful storytelling, this will draw readers into a world less safe and simple than it seems at first glance." Booklist

Holczer, Tracy

Everything else in the universe; Tracy Holczer. G.P. Putnam's Sons Books for Young Readers 2018 272 p. (hardback) $16.99

Grades: 4 5 6 7 8 **Fic**

1. Amputees -- Fiction 2. Friendship -- Fiction 3. Family life -- Fiction 4. Italian Americans -- Fiction 5. Vietnam War, 1961-1975 -- United States -- Fiction

ISBN 9780399163944; 9780698173859

LC 2017057236

In this book, by Tracy Holczer, "[Lucy's dad was] sent to Vietnam to serve as an Army doctor, Lucy and her mother are forced to move to San

Jose, California, to be near their relatives--the Rossis--people known for their superstitions and all around quirky ways. Lucy can't wait for life to go back to normal, so she's over the moon when she learns her father is coming home early. It doesn't even matter that he's coming back 'different.'" (Publisher's note)

The **secret** hum of a daisy; Tracy Holczer. G.P. Putnam's Sons, an imprint of Penguin Group (USA) 2014 320 p. (hardback) $16.99

Grades: 5 6 7 8 **Fic**

1. Home -- Fiction 2. Death -- Fiction 3. Moving -- Fiction 4. Grandmothers -- Fiction 5. Treasure hunt (Game) -- Fiction 6. Moving, Household -- Fiction

ISBN 039916393X; 9780399163937

LC 2013039962

In this book, by Tracy Holczer, "twelve-year-old Grace and her mother . . . [travel] from place to place like gypsies. But Grace wants to finally have a home all their own. Just when she thinks she's found it her mother says it's time to move again. Grace summons the courage to tell her mother how she really feels and will always regret that her last words to her were angry ones. After her mother's sudden death, Grace is forced to live with a grandmother she's never met." (Publisher's note)

"Grace is a multifaceted, relatable protagonist: she's pensive, stubborn, lonely, and caring--much like Grandma, which is why they are able to help heal each other's grief. Their relationship evolves in an honest and tender way in this heartfelt debut about loss and love." Horn Book

Holder, Nancy

Crusade; by Nancy Holder and Debbie Viguie. Simon Pulse 2010 470p $16.99

Grades: 7 8 9 10 11 **Fic**

1. Horror fiction 2. Sisters -- Fiction 3. Vampires -- Fiction 4. Supernatural -- Fiction

ISBN 978-1-4169-9802-0; 1-4169-9802-0

LC 2010-9094

An international team of six teenaged vampire hunters, trained in Salamanca, Spain, goes to New Orleans seeking to rescue team-member Jenn's younger sister as the vampires escalate their efforts to take over the Earth.

"The cinematic writing and apocalyptic scenario should find a ready audience." Publ Wkly

Other titles in this series are:
Damned (2011)
Vanquished (2012)

Holland, Elise

The **thorn** queen; a novel. Elise Holland. SparkPress 2018 256 p. (pbk) $16.95

Grades: 5 6 7 8 **Fic**

1. Fantasy fiction 2. Magic -- Fiction 3. Witchcraft -- Fiction

ISBN 9781943006793; 9781943006809

LC 2018937853

In this novel, by Elise Holland, "welcome to Glendoch! Hidden to most, this glacial world once crackled with alchemy. Now it waits for war--divided and bound by strict rules. So when twelve-year-old Meylyne falls from a tree onto Glendoch's sickly prince, she must flee or face imprisonment in the Shadow-Cellars. The only way she may return home is with a cure for the prince's peculiar disease." (Publisher's note)

Holland, Sara

Everless; Sara Holland. HarperTeen 2018 364 p. (hardcover) $17.99

Grades: 8 9 10 11 12 **Fic**

1. Fantasy fiction 2. Time -- fiction 3. Social classes -- fiction 4. Weddings -- fiction

ISBN 9780062653659; 9780062653680

LC 2017942898

In this book, by Sara Holland, "in the kingdom of Sempera, time is currency. . . . The rich aristocracy, like the Gerlings, tax the poor to the hilt, extending their own lives by centuries. No one resents the Gerlings more than Jules Ember. A decade ago, she and her father were servants at Everless. . . . until a fateful accident forced them to flee. . . . When Jules discovers that her father is dying, she knows that she must return to Everless." (Publisher's note)

"Holland's debut is set in an intricate and immersive fantasy world, a world she skillfully builds through layers of flashbacks and memories." Booklist

Other titles in this series are:
Evermore (2018)

Hollingsworth, Alyssa

The **eleventh** trade; Alyssa Hollingsworth. Roaring Brook Press 2018 288 p. (hardback) $16.99

Grades: 4 5 6 7 **Fic**

1. Friendship -- Fiction 2. Family life -- Fiction

ISBN 9781250155771; 9781250155764

LC 2018936543

In this novel, by Alyssa Hollingsworth, "when . . . Sami's grandfather's most-prized possession--a traditional Afghan instrument called a rebab--is stolen, Sami resolves to get it back. He finds it at a music store, but it costs $700, and Sami doesn't have even one penny. What he does have is a keychain that has caught the eye of his classmate. If he trades the keychain for something more valuable, could he keep trading until he has $700? Sami is about to find out." (Publisher's note)

Holm, Jennifer L.

★ **Boston** Jane: an adventure. HarperCollins Pubs. 2001 273p hardcover o.p. pa $6.99

Grades: 6 7 8 9 **Fic**

1. Chinook Indians -- Fiction 2. Washington (State) -- Fiction 3. Frontier and pioneer life -- Fiction

ISBN 0-06-028738-1; 0-06-028739-X; 0-06-440849-3 pa

LC 2001-16753

Schooled in the lessons of etiquette for young ladies of 1854, Miss Jane Peck of Philadelphia finds little use for manners during her long sea voyage to the Pacific Northwest and while living among the American traders and Chinook Indians of Washington Territory

"Strong characterizations, meticulous attention to historical details . . . and a perceptive understanding of human nature make this a first-rate story not to be missed." Booklist

Other titles about Boston Jane are:
Boston Jane: the claim (2004)
Boston Jane: wilderness days (2002)

Boston Jane: the claim. HarperCollins Pub. 2004 230p hardcover o.p. pa $7.99 **Fic**

1. Chinook Indians -- Fiction 2. Washington (State) -- Fiction 3. Frontier and pioneer life -- Fiction

ISBN 0-06-029045-5; 0-06-029046-3 lib bdg; 0-375-86206-4 pa

LC 2003-9556

Sequel to Boston Jane: wilderness days

The arrival from Philadelphia of her spiteful nemesis Sally Biddle and the return of her corrupt ex-fiance Richard Baldt spell trouble for seventeen-year-old Miss Jane Peck, who has survived on her own in

Shoalwater Bay, a community of white settlers and Chinook Indians in 1850s Washington Territory.

"The story is fast paced and lively, and Holm successfully campaigns for diversity and feminism without making her plot seem like a thinly disguised message." Voice Youth Advocates

Boston Jane: wilderness days. HarperCollins Pubs. 2002 242p hardcover o.p. pa $7.99
Grades: 6 7 8 9 **Fic**

1. Washington (State) -- Fiction 2. Frontier and pioneer life -- Fiction

ISBN 0-06-029043-9; 0-06-029044-7 lib bdg; 0-375-86205-6 pa
LC 2002-1473

Sequel to: Boston Jane: an adventure

Far from her native Philadelphia, Miss Jane Peck continues to prove that she's more than an etiquette-schooled graduate of Miss Hepplewhite's Young Ladies Academy as she braves the untamed wilderness of Washington Territory in the mid 1850s

"Holm once again delivers an action-packed story with a strong female protagonist." SLJ

Followed by: Boston Jane: the claim

The **fourteenth** goldfish; Jennifer L. Holm. Random House Inc 2014 208 p. (hardcover) $16.99; (library binding) $19.99
Grades: 4 5 6 7 **Fic**

1. Scientists -- Fiction 2. Grandfathers -- Fiction 3. Aging -- Fiction 4. Family life -- Fiction

ISBN 0375870644; 9780375870644; 9780375970641
LC 2013035052

"Eleven-year-old Ellie has never liked change. She misses fifth grade. She misses her old best friend. She even misses her dearly departed goldfish. Then one day a strange boy shows up. He's bossy. He's cranky. And weirdly enough . . . he looks a lot like Ellie's grandfather, a scientist who's always been slightly obsessed with immortality." (Publisher's note)

"With humor and heart, Holm has crafted a story about life, family, and finding one's passion that will appeal to readers willing to imagine the possible." SLJ

Includes bibliographical references

Followed by The third mushroom (2018)

★ **Middle** school is worse than meatloaf; a year told through stuff. by Jennifer L. Holm; pictures by Elicia Castaldi. Atheneum Books for Young Readers 2007 un il $12.99
Grades: 5 6 7 8 **Fic**

1. School stories 2. Family life -- Fiction

ISBN 0-689-85281-9

"Ginny Davis begins seventh grade with a list of items to accomplish. This list, along with lots of other 'stuff'—including diary entries, refrigerator notes, cards from Grandpa, and IM screen messages—convey a year full of ups and downs. Digitally rendered collage illustrations realistically depict the various means of communication, and the story flows easily from one colorful page to the next. . . . The story combines honesty and humor to create a believable and appealing voice." SLJ

★ **Our** only May Amelia. HarperCollins Pubs. 1999 253p il hardcover o.p. pa $5.99
Grades: 5 6 7 8 **Fic**

1. Family life -- Fiction 2. Finnish Americans -- Fiction 3. Washington (State) -- Fiction 4. Frontier and pioneer life -- Fiction

ISBN 0-06-027822-6; 0-06-440856-6 pa
LC 98-47504

A Newbery Medal honor book, 2000

As the only girl in a Finnish American family of seven brothers, May Amelia Jackson resents being expected to act like a lady while growing up in Washington State in 1899

"The voice of the colloquial first-person narrative rings true and provides a vivid picture of frontier and pioneer life. . . . An afterword discusses Holm's research into her own family's history and that of other Finnish immigrants." Horn Book Guide

Followed by: The trouble with May Amelia (2011)

★ **Penny** from heaven. Random House 2006 274p il $15.95; lib bdg $17.99; pa $6.99
Grades: 5 6 7 8 **Fic**

1. New Jersey -- Fiction 2. Family life -- Fiction 3. Italian Americans -- Fiction

ISBN 0-375-83687-X; 0-375-93687-4 lib bdg; 0-375-83689-6 pa
LC 2005-13896

A Newbery Medal honor book, 2007

As she turns twelve during the summer of 1953, Penny gains new insights into herself and her family while also learning a secret about her father's death.

"Holm impressively wraps pathos with comedy in this coming-of-age story, populated by a cast of vivid characters." Booklist

The **third** mushroom; Jennifer L. Holm. Random House Children's Books 2018 217 p. (hardback) $16.99
Grades: 4 5 6 7 **Fic**

1. Aging -- Fiction 2. Schools -- Fiction 3. Friendship -- Fiction 4. Scientists -- Fiction 5. Grandfathers -- Fiction 6. Middle schools -- Fiction

ISBN 9781524719821; 9781524719814; 9781524719807
LC 2017043070

Sequel to: The Fourteenth Goldfish

In this book, by Jennifer L. Holm, "Ellie's grandpa Melvin is a world-renowned scientist . . . in the body of a fourteen-year-old boy. . . . Grandpa may not exactly fit in at middle school, but he certainly keeps things interesting. When he and Ellie team up for the county science fair, no one realizes just how groundbreaking their experiment will be. The formula for eternal youth may be within their reach! And when Ellie's cat . . . gets sick, the stakes become even higher." (Publisher's note)

The **trouble** with May Amelia; illustrated by Adam Gustavson. Atheneum Books for Young Readers 2011 204p il $15.99
Grades: 5 6 7 8 **Fic**

1. Sex role -- Fiction 2. Siblings -- Fiction 3. Finnish Americans -- Fiction 4. Washington (State) -- Fiction 5. Frontier and pioneer life -- Fiction

ISBN 1-4169-1373-4; 978-1-4169-1373-3
LC 2010042092

Sequel to: Our only May Amelia (1999)

Living with seven brothers and her father, who thinks girls are useless, a thirteen-year-old Finnish American farm girl is determined to prove her worth when a enterprising gentleman tries to purchase their cash-strapped family settlement in Washington State in 1900.

"Holm gets her heroine just right. Narrating events in dryly witty, plainspoken first-person, this indomitable teen draws readers in with her account, through which her world comes alive." Kirkus

Holmes, Sara Lewis

Operation Yes. Arthur A. Levine Books 2009 234p $16.99

Grades: 5 6 7 8 **Fic**

1. School stories 2. Acting -- Fiction 3. Cousins -- Fiction 4. Teachers -- Fiction 5. Military bases -- Fiction
ISBN 978-0-545-10795-2; 0-545-10795-4; 978-0-545-10796-9 pa; 0-545-10796-2 pa

LC 2008053732

In her first ever teaching job, Miss Loupe uses improvisational acting exercises with her sixth-grade students at an Air Force base school, and when she experiences a family tragedy, her previously skeptical class members use what they have learned to help her, her brother, and other wounded soldiers

"Quick, funny, sad, full of heart, and irresistibly absorbing." Booklist

Holt, K. A.

Knockout; by K. A. Holt. Chronicle Books LLC 2018 288 p. (alk. paper) $16.99

Grades: 5 6 7 8 9 **Fic**

1. Boxing stories 2. Novels in verse 3. Boxing -- Fiction 4. Divorce -- Fiction 5. Brothers -- Fiction 6. Fathers and sons -- Fiction 7. Mothers and sons -- Fiction 8. Self-actualization (Psychology) -- Fiction 9. Prematurely born children -- fiction 10. Children of divorced parents -- fiction
ISBN 1452163588; 9781452163581

LC 2017042925

In this book, by K. A. Holt, "as a baby, . . . [Levi] had a serious disease that caused him respiratory issues. He's fine now, but his mom and . . . brother still think of him as damaged. . . . So when his dad . . . suggests he take up boxing, he falls in love with the sport. And when he finds out about a school with a killer boxing team and a free-study curriculum, it feels like he's found a ticket to a new Levi. But how can he tell his mom about boxing?" (Publisher's note)

Holt, Kimberly Willis

★ The **water** seeker. Henry Holt 2010 309p $16.99

Grades: 4 5 6 7 **Fic**

1. Father-son relationship -- Fiction 2. Frontier and pioneer life -- Fiction 3. Overland journeys to the Pacific -- Fiction
ISBN 978-0-8050-8020-9; 0-8050-8020-1

LC 2009-24149

Traces the hard life, filled with losses, adversity, and adventure, of Amos, son of a trapper and dowser, from 1833 when his mother dies giving birth to him until 1859, when he himself has grown up and has a son of his own.

"Drawing on such diverse themes as Manifest Destiny, personal identity and cross-cultural relationships, the author has crafted a satisfying all-ages story that hosts a dazzling array of richly realized secondary characters . . . and flows as effortlessly as the Platte River." Kirkus

★ **When** Zachary Beaver came to town. Holt & Co. 1999 227p $17.99

Grades: 5 6 7 8 **Fic**

1. Texas -- Fiction 2. Obesity -- Fiction 3. Friendship -- Fiction
ISBN 0-8050-6116-9

LC 99-27998

During the summer of 1971 in a small Texas town, thirteen-year-old Toby and his best friend Cal meet the star of a sideshow act, 600-pound Zachary, the fattest boy in the world

"Holt writes with a subtle sense of humor and sensitivity, and reading her work is a delightful experience." Voice Youth Advocates

Holyoke, Polly

The **Neptune** Project; Polly Holyoke. 1st ed. Disney-Hyperion Books 2013 352 p. (reinforced) $16.99

Grades: 4 5 6 7 **Fic**

1. Science fiction 2. Ocean -- Fiction 3. Genetic engineering -- Fiction 4. Survival -- Fiction 5. Undersea colonies -- Fiction 6. Environmental degradation -- Fiction
ISBN 1423157567; 9781423157564

LC 2013000353

In this novel, by Polly Holyoke, "Nere . . . is one of a group of kids who . . . have been genetically altered to survive in the ocean. . . . In order to reach the safe haven of the Neptune colony, Nere and her fellow mutates must swim through hundreds of miles of dangerous waters, relying only on their wits, dolphins, and each other to evade terrifying undersea creatures and a government that will stop at nothing to capture the Neptune kids." (Publisher's note)

Followed by The Neptune Challenge (2015)

Hoobler, Dorothy

The **demon** in the teahouse; [by] Dorothy and Thomas Hoobler. Philomel Bks. 2001 181p $17.99

Grades: 6 7 8 9 **Fic**

1. Mystery fiction 2. Japan -- Fiction
ISBN 0-399-23499-3

LC 00-50184

In eighteenth-century Japan, fourteen-year-old Seikei, a merchant's son in training to be a samurai, helps his patron investigate a series of murders and arson in the capital city of Edo, each of which is associated in some way with a popular geisha

"Details of Shogun-era Japan are seamlessly woven into a gripping story." Horn Book Guide

★ The **ghost** in the Tokaido Inn; [by] Dorothy and Thomas Hoobler. Philomel Bks. 1999 214p $17.99; pa $6.99

Grades: 6 7 8 9 **Fic**

1. Mystery fiction 2. Japan -- Fiction
ISBN 0-399-23330-X; 0-698-11879-0 pa

LC 98-14089

While attempting to solve the mystery of a stolen jewel, Seikei, a merchant's son who longs to be a samurai, joins a group of kabuki actors in eighteenth-century Japan

"Precise characterization, suspenseful plot twists, and a pace defined by swift and sometimes violent action make this a lively period thriller." Bull Cent Child Books

Other titles about Seikei are:
The demon in the teahouse (2001)
In darkess, death (2004)
The sword that cut the burning grass (2005)
A samurai never fears death (2007)
Seven paths to death (2008)

Seven paths to death; a samurai mystery. [by] Dorothy and Thomas Hoobler. Philomel Books 2008 192p $14.99

Grades: 6 7 8 9 **Fic**

1. Mystery fiction 2. Maps -- Fiction 3. Japan -- Fiction 4. Samurai -- Fiction 5. Tattooing -- Fiction
ISBN 978-0-399-24610-4; 0-399-24610-X

LC 2007042092

Samurai Seikei and Judge Ooka, his foster-father, seek seven men who have seven maps on their backs in order to locate a cache of dangerous weapons before they fall into the wrong hands.

"This is a successful historical mystery, chockablock with adventure . . . and cultural details." Booklist

The **sword** that cut the burning grass; a samurai mystery. [by] Dorothy & Thomas Hoobler. Sleuth/Philomel 2005 211p $10.99

Grades: 6 7 8 9 **Fic**

1. Mystery fiction 2. Japan -- Fiction

ISBN 0-399-24272-4

In his latest adventure in eighteenth-century Japan, fourteen-year-old samurai apprentice Seikei, with the help of a servant girl and an imperious old man, sets out to rescue the young Emperor Yasuhito from his kidnappers.

"There's plenty of rousing action to propel the story forward, and, as always, Seikei makes a thoughtful hero." Booklist

Hood, Susan

Lifeboat 12; Susan Hood. Simon & Schuster Books for Young Readers 2018 336 p. (hardcover : alk. paper) $17.99

Grades: 4 5 6 7 **Fic**

1. Novels in verse 2. Survival -- Fiction 3. Lifeboats -- Fiction 4. Ocean liners -- Fiction 5. Ocean travel -- Fiction 6. World War, 1939-1945 -- Children -- Fiction 7. World War, 1939-1945 -- Evacuation of civilians -- Great Britain -- Fiction

ISBN 9781481468831; 9781481468848

LC 2017034872

"It's 1940, the beginning of the Blitz, and 13-year-old Kenneth Sparks is selected to go to Canada as part of a program to send British children to the safety of the U.K.'s overseas dominions. When his ship is torpedoed, Kenneth, five other boys from the program, and about 40 adults make it aboard Lifeboat 12, one of the only lifeboats remaining after the evening's gale-force winds. Together, they must survive the North Atlantic in a boat with limited supplies." (School Library Journal)

Hooper, Mary

Fallen Grace. Bloomsbury 2011 309p $16.99

Grades: 7 8 9 10 **Fic**

1. People with mental disabilities -- Fiction 2. Orphans -- Fiction 3. Poverty -- Fiction 4. Sisters -- Fiction 5. London (England) -- Fiction 6. Swindlers and swindling -- Fiction 7. Funeral rites and ceremonies -- Fiction 8. Great Britain -- History -- 19th century -- Fiction

ISBN 978-1-59990-564-8; 1-59990-564-7

LC 2010-25498

In Victorian London, impoverished fifteen-year-old orphan Grace takes care of her older but mentally unfit sister Lily, and after enduring many harsh and painful experiences, the two become the victims of a fraud perpetrated by the wealthy owners of several funeral businesses.

Hooper "packs her brisk Dickensian fable with colorful characters and suspenseful, satisfying plot twists. The sobering realities of child poverty and exploitation are vividly conveyed, along with fascinating details of the Victorian funeral trade." Kirkus

Includes bibliographical references

Hoover, P. J.

Tut; My Epic Battle to Save the World. P.J. Hoover. St. Martin's Press 2017 336 p. (ebook) $40; $16.99

Grades: 5 6 7 8 **Fic**

1. Tutankhamen, King of Egypt

ISBN 0765390825; 9781466814752; 9780765390820

LC 2017006334

In this book, by P.J. Hoover, "Meet Tut! He used to rule Egypt. Now he's stuck in middle school. Having defeated his evil uncle and the Cult of Set, who tried to send him to the afterlife, the perpetually fourteen-year-old King Tut is looking forward to a relaxing summer vacation. But then Tut discovers that his brother Gilgamesh has been captured by the Egyptian god Apep, Lord of Chaos. Gil helped to vanquish Apep thousands of years ago, and now Apep is back for vengeance." (Publisher's note)

"A sequel that doesn't disappoint; purchase where there are fans of the first book, or buy the series for readers looking for history and adventure." SLJ

Hopkins, Ellen

Rumble; Ellen Hopkins. Margaret K. McElderry Books 2014 560 p. (hardcover) $19.99

Grades: 8 9 10 11 12 **Fic**

1. Novels in verse 2. Grief -- Fiction 3. Suicide -- Fiction 4. Schools -- Fiction 5. High schools -- Fiction 6. Family problems -- Fiction

ISBN 1442482842; 9781442482845

LC 2013037681

In this young adult verse novel by Ellen Hopkins, "Matthew Turner doesn't have faith in anything. Not in family--his is a shambles after his younger brother was bullied into suicide. Not in so-called friends who turn their backs when things get tough. Not in some all-powerful creator who lets too much bad stuff happen. . . . No matter what his girlfriend Hayden says about faith and forgiveness, there's no way Matt's letting go of blame." (Publisher's note)

"Matt is a wonderfully faceted character that readers will alternately sympathize with and dislike. His actions are directly related to his emotional turmoil, and teens will understand his pain and admire his intellect, even while shaking their heads over his actions.." SLJ

Hopkinson, Deborah

A **bandit's** tale; the muddled misadventures of a pickpocket. Deborah Hopkinson. Alfred A. Knopf 2016 304 p. illustrations (hardcover) $16.99

Grades: 4 5 6 7 8 **Fic**

1. Thieves -- Fiction 2. New York (N.Y.) -- History -- Fiction 3. Immigrants -- United States -- Fiction 4. Immigrants -- Fiction 5. Child abuse -- Fiction 6. Child labor -- Fiction 7. Conduct of life -- Fiction 8. Animals -- Treatment -- Fiction 9. Italians -- New York (State) -- New York -- Fiction 10. New York (N.Y.) -- History -- 19th century -- Fiction

ISBN 9780385754996; 9780385755009; 038575499X

LC 2015004491

In this book, by Deborah Hopkinson, "eleven-year-old Rocco is an Italian immigrant who finds himself alone in New York City after he's sold to a padrone by his poverty-stricken parents. While working as a street musician, he meets the boys of the infamous Bandits' Roost, who teach him the art of pickpocketing. Rocco embraces his new life of crime . . . But when he meets Meddlin' Mary, a strong-hearted Irish girl . . . , things begin to change." (Publisher's note)

"Rocco's conversational voice resounds with humor, compassion, and an inspiring energy for change. A dynamic historical novel ideal for both classroom studies and pleasure reading." Kirkus

The **Great** Trouble; a mystery of London, the blue death, and a boy called Eel. by Deborah Hopkinson. Alfred A. Knopf 2013 256 p. (hard cover) $16.99

Grades: 4 5 6 7 8 **Fic**

1. Orphans -- Fiction 2. London (England) -- Fiction 3. Cholera

-- Fiction 4. Epidemics -- Fiction 5. London (England) -- History -- 19th century -- Fiction 6. Great Britain -- History -- Victoria, 1837-1901 -- Fiction

ISBN 0375848185; 9780375848186; 9780375948183

LC 2012032799

Author Deborah Hopkinson's book, "equal parts medical mystery, historical novel, and survival story about the 1854 London cholera outbreak, . . . introduces Eel, a boy trying to make ends meet on Broad Street. When he visits one of his regular employers, he learns the man has fallen ill. Eel enlists the help of Dr. Snow, and together they work to solve the mystery of what exactly is causing the spread of cholera and how they can prevent it." (Booklist)

Includes bibliographical references (p. 245-247)

Into the firestorm; a novel of San Francisco, 1906. Alfred A. Knopf 2006 200p hardcover o.p. pa $5.99

Grades: 5 6 7 8 **Fic**

1. Orphans -- Fiction 2. Earthquakes -- Fiction 3. San Francisco (Calif.) -- Fiction

ISBN 0-375-83652-7; 0-440-42129-2 pa

LC 2005-37189

Days after arriving in San Francisco from Texas, eleven-year-old orphan Nicholas Dray tries to help his new neighbors survive the 1906 San Francisco earthquake and the subsequent fires.

"The terror of the 1906 disaster is brought powerfully alive in this fast-paced tale. . . . Nick is a thoroughly developed protagonist, as are the supporting characters." SLJ

Includes bibliographical references

Hopkinson, Nalo

The **Chaos**; Nalo Hopkinson. Margaret K. McElderry Books 2012 241p. (hardcover) $16.99

Grades: 7 8 9 10 11 12 **Fic**

1. Science fiction 2. Toronto (Ont.) -- Fiction 3. Siblings -- fiction 4. Racially mixed people -- Fiction 5. Supernatural -- fiction 6 Canada -- Fiction 7. Identity -- Fiction 8. Supernatural -- Fiction 9. Brothers and sisters -- Fiction 10. Family life -- Canada -- Fiction 11. Interpersonal relations -- Fiction

ISBN 1416954880; 9781416954880; 9781442409552

LC 2011018154

In this young adult science fiction novel, "Scotch's womanly build and mixed heritage (white Jamaican dad, black American mom) made her the target of small-town school bullies. Since moving to Toronto, she's found friends and status. . . . When a giant bubble appears at an open-mic event, Scotch dares her brother, Rich, to touch it. He disappears, a volcano rises from Lake Ontario and chaos ripples across city and world, transforming reality in ways bizarre." (Kirkus Reviews)

Horowitz, Anthony

★ The **complete** Horowitz horror; by Anthony Horowitz. Puffin Books 2008 432 p. $7.99

Grades: 7 8 9 10 **Fic**

1. Horror fiction

ISBN 0142411620; 9780142411629

This book presents Anthony Horowitz's "horror collections, now in one volume! Welcome to a world where everything seems normal. At least, at first. But the sinister and truly terrifying lurk just beneath the surface. . . . This wicked collection of eighteen macabre tales combining both Horowitz Horror and More Horowitz Horror will send shivers up your spine." (Publisher's note)

Evil star; book two of the Gatekeepers. Scholastic Press 2006 318p (Gatekeepers) $17.99

Grades: 6 7 8 9 **Fic**

1. Peru -- Fiction 2. Incas -- Fiction

ISBN 0-439-67996-6

Sequel to Raven's gate

Having locked the Raven's gate, fourteen-year-old Matt travels to Peru where he meets the second of the five gatekeepers and works with him to try to stop the opening of a second gate somehow related to the Nazca Lines.

"Though this is the second installment in this series, new readers will catch on quickly. . . . The plot turns and emotional relationships will more than satisfy thrill seekers." SLJ

Followed by Nightrise

The **Falcon's** Malteser; a Diamond brothers mystery. [by] Anthony Horowitz. 1st American ed; Philomel Books 2004 191p $16.99

Grades: 5 6 7 8 **Fic**

1. Mystery fiction

ISBN 0-399-24153-1

LC 2004-48322

After his older brother, a fledgling private detective, agrees to safeguard a package for a dwarf who does not live long, thirteen-year-old Nick scampers to solve the mystery while also trying to stay one step ahead of an assortment of thugs.

"The Diamond Brothers stories are invariably funny and full of excitement. Mystery readers with a sense of humor will enjoy [this tale]." Voice Youth Advocates

The **Greek** who stole Christmas; a Diamond Brothers mystery. [by] Anthony Horowitz. Puffin Books 2008 105p pa $6.99

Grades: 5 6 7 8 **Fic**

1. Mystery fiction

ISBN 978-0-14-240375-4 pa; 0-14-240375-X pa

LC 2008025944

Fourteen-year-old Nick and his brother, an ineffectual private detective, try to prevent the threatened murder of an international pop star in London at Christmas time.

"The witty banter between the characters keeps this short novel moving at breakneck speed." SLJ

Necropolis. Levithan/Scholastic Press 2009 389p (Gatekeepers) $17.99

Grades: 6 7 8 9 **Fic**

1. Supernatural -- Fiction 2. Hong Kong (China) -- Fiction

ISBN 978-0-439-68003-5; 0-439-68003-4

LC 2008-44892

Sequel to: Nightrise (2007)

To stop the evil corporation Nightrise from unleashing its devastating power around the globe, fifteen-year-old Matt and three other Gatekeepers travel to Hong Kong to find Scarlet, the final Gatekeeper, whose fate is inextricably joined to their own.

"There are many action-filled sequences and Scarlett is an interesting new addition to the cast of characters. . . . Fans of the series will naturally want to read it and prepare themselves for the final great battle." Voice Youth Advocates

Never say die; Anthony Horowitz. Philomel Books 2017 349 p. (Alex Rider) (hardback) $17.99

Grades: 5 6 7 8 Fic

1. Spies -- Fiction 2. Adventure fiction 3. Terrorism -- Fiction 4. Teenage boys -- Fiction 5. Great Britain. MI6 -- Fiction

ISBN 9781524739317; 9781524739300

LC 2017010203

In this book in the Alex Rider series, by Anthony Horowitz, "Alex relocates to San Francisco as he slowly recovers from the tragic death of his best friend and caregiver, Jack Starbright, at the hands of terrorists working for SCORPIA. . . . But then, out of the blue, he receives a cryptic email, . . . enough to make Alex believe that Jack may be alive. Armed with this shred of hope, Alex boards a flight bound for Egypt and embarks on a dubious quest to track Jack." (Publisher's note)

"Having given his hyperpopular series something of a breather, Horowitz now sets it back on track with a fresh caper that roars along to a (naturally) explosive climax and tidy resolution." Booklist

Nightrise; book three of the Gatekeepers. [by] Anthony Horowitz. Scholastic Press 2007 365p (Gatekeepers) $17.99

Grades: 6 7 8 9 Fic

1. Twins -- Fiction 2. Nevada -- Fiction 3. Brothers -- Fiction 4. Telepathy -- Fiction 5. Supernatural -- Fiction

ISBN 978-0-439-68001-1; 0-439-68001-8

LC 2006035882

Sequel to Evil star

As fourteen-year-old telepathic twins struggle to escape the clutches of the Nightrise Corporation, one of them travels through dreams to a time when the evil Old Ones ruled and learns the role that he, his brother, and three other Gatekeepers must play to keep the world safe from the Old Ones' return.

"There's no lack of plot or action in this breathless fantasy thriller." Kliatt

Public enemy number two; a Diamond brothers mystery. Philomel Books 2004 190p $16.99; pa $5.99

Grades: 5 6 7 8 Fic

1. Mystery fiction

ISBN 0-399-24154-X; 0-14-240218-4 pa

LC 2004-10418

When thirteen-year-old Nick is framed for a jewel robbery, he and his brother, the bumbling detective Tim Diamond, attempt to clear his name by capturing the master criminal known as the Fence.

"Horowitz has a knack for puns and humor, and he successfully combines it with a nonstop action mystery that has everything from hydraulically controlled buses to secret caverns. A readable and exciting adventure." SLJ

Other titles in the Diamond Brothers Mystery series are:

The falcon's Maltester (2004)

South by southeast (2005)

Three of Diamonds (2005)

The Greek who stole Christmas (2008)

Raven's gate; book one of the Gatekeepers. [by] Anthony Horowitz. 1st ed; Scholastic Press 2005 254p (Gatekeepers) $17.95

Grades: 6 7 8 9 Fic

1. Witchcraft -- Fiction 2. Supernatural -- Fiction 3. Great Britain -- Fiction

ISBN 0-439-67995-8

LC 2004-21512

Sent to live in a foster home in a remote Yorkshire village, Matt, a troubled fourteen-year-old English boy, uncovers an evil plot involving witchcraft and the site of an ancient stone circle.

"The creepy activities and the overall atmosphere of fear are well defined, and once the action starts, it doesn't let up. . . . This powerful struggle between good and evil is a real page-turner." SLJ

Other titles in the Gatekeepers series are:

Evil star (2006)

Nightrise (2007)

Necropolis (2009)

South by southeast; a Diamond brothers mystery. [by] Anthony Horowitz. Philomel Bks. 2005 148p $16.99; pa $5.99

Grades: 5 6 7 8 Fic

1. Mystery fiction

ISBN 0-399-24155-8; 0-14-240374-1 pa

LC 2005043169

First published 1997 in the United Kingdom

Fourteen-year-old Nick and his bumbling detective brother Tim Diamond investigate a mystery involving international spies and assassins.

"Horowitz has created another well-written, well-paced spy melodrama." SLJ

★ **Stormbreaker**. Philomel Books 2001 192p (An Alex Rider adventure) $17.99; pa $7.99

Grades: 5 6 7 8 Fic

1. Adventure fiction 2. Spies -- Fiction 3. Orphans -- Fiction 4. Terrorism -- Fiction 5. Great Britain -- Fiction

ISBN 0-399-23620-1; 0-14-240611-2 pa

LC 00-63683

First published 2000 in the United Kingdom

After the death of the uncle who had been his guardian, fourteen-year-old Alex Rider is coerced to continue his uncle's dangerous work for Britain's intelligence agency, MI6

"Horowitz thoughtfully balances Alex's super-spy finesse with typical teen insecurities to create a likable hero living a fantasy come true. An entertaining, nicely layered novel." Booklist

Other titles about Alex Rider are:

Point blank (2002)

Skeleton key (2003)

Eagle strike (2004)

Scorpia (2005)

Ark angel (2006)

Snakehead (2007)

Crocodile tears (2009)

Scorpia rising (2011)

Russian roulette (2013)

Never say die (2017)

Three of diamonds; three Diamonds Brothers mysteries. [by] Anthony Horowitz. Philomel Books 2005 214p $16.99

Grades: 5 6 7 8 Fic

1. Mystery fiction

ISBN 0-399-24157-4

LC 2005276176

A collection of three Diamond Brothers mysteries in which Tim and Nick bungle their way through a search for a missing philanthropist, find themselves in a Parisian prison, and are stranded on a Scottish island with a murderer.

"Nick is a realistic character with a voice that is sarcastic and fresh, while Tim's lack of intelligence makes even the most dangerous situations laughable. Plenty of plays on words add to the humor." SLJ

Horvath, Polly

The **canning** season. Farrar, Straus & Giroux 2003 195p $16; pa $6.95

Grades: 6 7 8 9 **Fic**

1. Aunts -- Fiction

ISBN 0-374-39956-5; 0-374-41042-9 pa

LC 2002-66296

National Book Award: Young People's Literature (2003)

Thirteen-year-old Ratchet spends a summer in Maine with her eccentric great-aunts Tilly and Penpen, hearing strange stories from the past and encountering a variety of unusual and colorful characters

"Offbeat, slapstick humor is mitigated by poignancy in Horvath's distinctive rollicking style. There is occasional use of strong language, and the family stories are woven with death, often gruesomely described. . . . Readers are in for a wise and wacky ride when they open this novel." SLJ

Everything on a waffle. Farrar, Straus & Giroux 2001 149p hardcover o.p. $16

Grades: 4 5 6 7 **Fic**

1. Uncles -- Fiction 2. British Columbia -- Fiction

ISBN 0-374-32236-8; 0-374-42208-7 pa

LC 00-35399

Boston Globe-Horn Book Award Honor: Fiction (2001)

Eleven-year-old Primrose living in a small fishing village in British Columbia recounts her experiences and all that she learns about human nature and the unpredictability of life in the months after her parents are lost at sea

"The story is full of subtle humor and wisdom, presented through the eyes of a uniquely appealing young protagonist." SLJ

★ **My** one hundred adventures. Schwartz & Wade Books 2008 260p $16.99; lib bdg $19.99; pa $7.99

Grades: 4 5 6 7 **Fic**

1. Summer -- Fiction 2. Beaches -- Fiction 3. Siblings -- Fiction 4. Babysitters -- Fiction 5. Single parent family -- Fiction

ISBN 978-0-375-84582-6; 0-375-84582-8; 978-0-375-95582-2 lib bdg; 0-375-95582-8 lib bdg; 978-0-375-85526-9 pa; 0-375-85526-2 pa

LC 2008-02243

Twelve-year-old Jane, who lives at the beach in a run-down old house with her mother, two brothers, and sister, has an eventful summer accompanying her pastor on bible deliveries, meeting former boyfriends of her mother's, and being coerced into babysitting for a family of ill-mannered children.

With writing as foamy as waves, as gritty as sand, or as deep as the sea, this book may startle readers with the freedom given the heroine. . . . Unconventionality is Horvath's stock and trade, but here the high quirkiness quotient rests easily against Jane's inner story with its honest, childlike core. Booklist

Followed by: Northward to the Moon (2010)

The **night** garden; Polly Horvath. Margaret Ferguson Books/Farrar, Straus & Giroux 2017 304 p.

Grades: 4 5 6 7 8 **Fic**

1. Canada -- Fiction 2. Wishes -- Fiction 3. Adoption -- Fiction 4. British Columbia -- Fiction 5. World War, 1939-1945 -- Fiction

ISBN 9780374304522

LC 2016043678

This book, by Polly Horvath, is "about a garden that grants wishes. It is World War II, and Franny and her parents, Sina and Old Tom, enjoy a quiet life on a farm on Vancouver Island. Franny writes, Sina sculpts, and Old Tom tends to their many gardens—including the ancient, mysterious night garden. Their peaceful life is interrupted when their neighbor, Crying Alice, begs Sina to watch her children while she goes to visit her husband at the military base." (Publisher's note)

Northward to the moon. Schwartz & Wade Books 2010 244p $17.99; lib bdg $20.99

Grades: 4 5 6 7 **Fic**

1. Canada -- Fiction 2. Nevada -- Fiction 3. Ranch life -- Fiction 4. Family life -- Fiction 5. Grandmothers -- Fiction 6. Massachusetts -- Fiction 7. Automobile travel -- Fiction

ISBN 978-0-375-86110-9; 0-375-86110-6; 978-0-375-96110-6 lib bdg; 0-375-96110-0 lib bdg

LC 2009-10133

Sequel to: My one hundred adventures (2008)

When her stepfather loses his job in Saskatchewan, Jane and the rest of the family set off on a car trip, ending up in Nevada after improbably being given a bag full of possibly stolen money.

"Many characters here are distinct, wonderfully idiosyncratic individuals, and Horvath's fine-tuned observations are conveyed with subtlety and precision." Booklist

One year in Coal Harbor; Polly Horvath. Schwartz & Wade Books 2012 216 p. (hardcover) $16.99

Grades: 5 6 7 **Fic**

1. Cookbooks -- Fiction 2. Friendship -- Fiction 3. British Columbia -- Fiction 4. Self-reliance -- Fiction 5. Family problems -- Fiction 6. Foster home care -- Fiction 7. Interpersonal relations -- Fiction 8. Eccentrics and eccentricities -- Fiction

ISBN 0375869700; 9780375869709; 9780375969706

LC 2011023591

In this book by Polly Horvath, "Primrose Squab . . . chronicl[es] the latest goings-on in her British Columbian fishing village. Now 12 and happily reunited with her parents, Primrose has set her sights on compiling a cookbook. . . . When Ked, a foster child, arrives in town, Primrose gains an accomplice in her culinary efforts and an ally in opposing a local logging operation. More importantly, she hopes she has found a true best friend." (Publishers Weekly)

The **vacation**; [by] Polly Horvath. 1st ed; Farrar, Straus & Giroux 2005 197p $16

Grades: 5 6 7 8 **Fic**

1. Aunts -- Fiction 2. Vacations -- Fiction 3. Family life -- Fiction 4. Automobile travel -- Fiction

ISBN 0-374-38070-8

LC 2004-57667

When his parents go to Africa to work as missionaries, twelve-year-old Henry's eccentric aunts, Pigg and Mag, take him on a cross-country car trip, allowing him to gain insight into his family and himself.

"Horvath spins another delightfully offbeat yarn, complete with her signature cast of eccentric characters, wacky situations, poignant moments, and snappy dialogue." SLJ

Hosler, Jay

Last of the sandwalkers; written and illustrated by Jay Hosler. First Second 2015 312 p. illustrations (paperback) $16.99

Grades: 5 6 7 8 9 10 **Fic**

1. Graphic novels 2. Science fiction 3. Adventure fiction 4. Beetles -- Fiction 5. Scientific expeditions -- Fiction

ISBN 162672024X; 9781626720244

LC 2014045542

This book, by Jay Hosler, is about a "civilization of beetles. In this bug's paradise, beetles write books, run restaurants, and even do scientific research. But not too much scientific research is allowed by the powerful elders, who guard a terrible secret about the world outside. . . . Lucy is not one to quietly cooperate, however. This tiny field scientist defies the law of her safe but authoritarian home and leads a team of researchers out into the desert." (Publisher's note)

"Hosler's cartooning is no less meticulous than his writing and similarly retains a sense of animated energy and humor, engaging readers with characters that are far from human, but filled with humanity." Booklist

Includes bibliographical references

House, Silas

Eli the Good. Candlewick Press 2009 295p $16.99

Grades: 5 6 7 8 **Fic**

1. Aunts -- Fiction 2. Veterans -- Fiction 3. Friendship -- Fiction 4. Family life -- Fiction 5. Post-traumatic stress disorder -- Fiction

ISBN 978-0-7636-4341-6; 0-7636-4341-6

LC 2009004589

In the summer of 1976, ten-year-old Eli Book's excitement over Bicentennial celebrations is tempered by his father's flashbacks to the Vietnam War and other family problems, as well as concern about his tough but troubled best friend, Edie.

"House writes beautifully, with a gentle tone. He lays out Eli's world in exquisite detail. . . . The story flows along as steadily as a stream. . . . Eli is good company and children will enjoy accompanying him on his journey." SLJ

Houston, Julian

New boy. Houghton Mifflin Co. 2005 282p $16

Grades: 8 9 10 11 12 **Fic**

1. School stories 2. Prejudices -- Fiction 3. African Americans -- Fiction

ISBN 0-618-43253-1

LC 2004-27207

"As the first black student in an elite Connecticut boarding school in the late 1950s, Rob Garrett, 16, knows he is making history. . . . When his friends in the South plan a sit-in against segregation, he knows he must be part of it. . . . The honest first-person narrative makes stirring drama. . . . This brings up much for discussion about then and now." Booklist

Houtman, Jacqueline

The **reinvention** of Edison Thomas. Front Street 2010 189p $17.95

Grades: 6 7 8 9 **Fic**

1. School stories 2. Friendship -- Fiction 3. Inventions -- Fiction

ISBN 978-1-59078-708-3; 1-59078-708-0

Middle school student Eddy Thomas loves science and inventing, but has trouble with people. Finally he meets some friends who appreciate his abilities and respect his unique view of the world.

"A perceptive look at a complicated mind, the novel is steeped in the world of science (binomial nomenclature appears throughout), and the quirky humor and authentic characters should have wide appeal." Publ Wkly

Houts, Michelle

The **Beef** Princess of Practical County. Delacorte Press 2009 226p $16.99; lib bdg $19.99

Grades: 6 7 8 9 **Fic**

1. Cattle -- Fiction 2. Indiana -- Fiction 3. Farm life -- Fiction

ISBN 978-0-385-73584-1; 978-0-385-90568-8 lib bdg

LC 2008-34712

Twelve-year-old Libby, the daughter of an Indiana cattle farmer, raises two calves in hopes of winning the annual steer competition at the county fair, but fails to follow her father's warning about developing a bond with animals that are destined to be sold at auction.

"Houts paints an idyllic yet authentic picture of farm life as she takes Libby and her family through the ups and downs of cattle raising and fair showing with sly humor and a flair for description and characterization." Booklist

Howard, J. J.

That time I joined the circus; J.J. Howard. Point 2013 272 p. (hardcover) $17.99

Grades: 7 8 9 10 **Fic**

1. Circus -- Fiction 2. Absent mothers -- Fiction 3. Florida -- Fiction 4. Friendship -- Fiction 5. Best friends -- Fiction 6. New York (N.Y.) -- Fiction 7. Mothers and daughters -- Fiction 8. Single-parent families -- Fiction

ISBN 0545433819; 9780545433815

LC 2012016715

In this novel, 17-year-old Lexi lives with her father Gavin, a musician in New York City. Her "long-absent mother . . . has apparently joined the circus. When Gavin dies unexpectedly, leaving his daughter penniless, her only option is to track down her mother in Florida. Failing to find her, Lexi gratefully accepts work with the Circus Europa." (Publishers Weekly)

Howe, James, 1946-

Addie on the inside; James Howe. Atheneum Books for Young Readers 2011 206 p. $16.99

Grades: 5 6 7 8 **Fic**

1. School stories 2. Novels in verse 3. Self-acceptance -- Fiction 4. Interpersonal relations -- Fiction 5. Grandmothers -- Fiction 6. Identity (Psychology) -- Fiction

ISBN 141691384X; 9781416913849

LC 2010024497

This book, by James Howe, "follows 13-year-old Addie's struggles to define herself according to her own terms. Through her poems, Addie reflects on her life and life in general: her first boyfriend, what it means to be accepted and her endeavors to promote equality. Addie is at her most fragile when she examines her relationship with her boyfriend and the cruel behavior of her former best friend. Her forthright observations address serious topics with a maturity beyond her age." (Kirkus Reviews)

"Howe's artfully crafted lines show Addie's intelligence and wit, and his imagery evokes the aura of sadness surrounding 'this purgatory of/ the middle school years/ when so many things/ that never mattered before/ and will never matter again/ matter.' Readers will empathize with Addie's anguish and admire her courage to keep fighting." Publ Wkly

Also known as Elvis; James Howe. Atheneum Books for Young Readers 2014 288 p. (Misfits) (hardcover) $16.99

Grades: 5 6 7 8 9 **Fic**

1. Friendship -- Fiction 2. Family life -- Fiction 3. Summer employment -- Fiction 4. Single-parent families -- Fiction 5. Fathers and sons -- Fiction 6. Mothers and sons -- Fiction

ISBN 1442445106; 9781442445109; 9781442445116

LC 2013015974

In this book, by James Howe, "Skeezie Tookis, also known as Elvis, isn't looking forward to this summer in Paintbrush Falls. While his best friends Bobby, Joe, and Addie are off on exciting adventures, he's stuck at home, taking care of his sisters and working five days a week to help out his mom. True, he gets to hang out at the Candy Kitchen with the awesome HellomynameisSteffi, but he also has to contend with Kevin Hennessey's never-ending bullying." (Publisher's note)

"As an adult, Skeezie reflects on the summer when his absent father returned home seeking reconciliation. As Skeezie tries to hold his fragile family life together, he explores his own emotions toward his parents and sisters, and is surprised by the bonds he feels. A satisfying conclusion to the Misfit books, with glimpses into adulthood for each member of the Gang of Five." Horn Book

★ The **misfits**; James Howe. Atheneum Books for Young Readers 2001 274 p. $17.99

Grades: 5 6 7 8 **Fic**

1. School stories 2. Bullies -- Fiction 3. Elections -- Fiction 4. Friendship -- Fiction 5. Teasing

ISBN 0689839553; 9780689839559

LC 0066390

This book, by James Howe, is "about junior high school politics and nasty name calling. . . . Bobby Goodspeed [is] an overweight seventh grader who belongs to the Gang of Five, which (ironically) is made up of four not five kids who consider themselves misfits. The student council elections are coming up, and [the Gang of Five] decide to run on the 'No-Name Party,' which promises to bring an end to all name calling in the school." (School Library Journal)

This is a "timely, sensitive, laugh-out-loud must-read for all middle school students and teachers." Voice Youth Advocates

★ **Totally** Joe; James Howe. Atheneum Books for Young Readers 2005 189 p. $17.99

Grades: 5 6 7 8 9 **Fic**

1. School stories 2. Friendship -- Fiction 3. LGBT youth -- Fiction 4. Adolescence -- Fiction

ISBN 068983957X; 9780689839573

LC 2004022242

In this book, by James Howe, "Joe's teacher asks his seventh-grade class to write an alphabiography throughout the year, presenting themselves and their lives in entries from A to Z. Joe's essays begin and end with friends, from Addie, a long-time pal and confidant, to Zachary, a new student who, like Joe, has a unique approach to life. . . . Joe demonstrates that he truly is a one-of-a-kind kid, mostly comfortable with himself but still struggling with common adolescent issues." (School Library Journal)

"Joe, one of the characters in The Misfits (2001), has his say, in a voice uniquely his own. Twelve-year-old Joe knows he is gay. He played with Barbies as a young child, prefers cooking to sports, and has a crush on a male classmate...Joe himself often comes off as a cross between Niles Crane and Harvey Fierstein. But he also reacts like a kid, and readers in his situation will wish for the love and support he receives from friends and family, as well as the happy life he so clearly envisions." Booklist

Howe, Katherine

Conversion; Katherine Howe. G. P. Putnam's Sons 2014 432 p. (hardback) $18.99

Grades: 7 8 9 10 11 12 **Fic**

1. School stories 2. Salem witch trials 3. Schools -- Fiction 4. Epidemics -- Fiction 5. Friendship -- Fiction 6. Massachusetts -- Fiction 7. Preparatory schools -- Fiction

ISBN 0399167773; 9780399167775

LC 2014000397

In this young adult novel by Katherine Howe, "It's senior year at St. Joan's Academy, and school is a pressure cooker. College applications, the battle for valedictorian, deciphering boys' texts: Through it all, Colleen Rowley and her friends are expected to keep it together. Until they can't. . . . Only Colleen--who's been reading 'The Crucible' for extra credit--comes to realize what nobody else has: Danvers was once Salem Village." (Publisher's note)

"St. Joan's Academy in Danvers, Massachusetts, a well-to-do private girl's school for the best and brightest, is usually only home to hysteria of the college-admissions kind. But when Clara starts convulsing in class, a media frenzy fixates on the St. Joan's mystery disease...A simmering blend of relatable high-school drama with a persistent pinprick of unearthliness in the background." Booklist

Howe, Peter

Waggit's tale; drawings by Omar Rayyan. HarperCollinsPublishers 2008 288p il $16.99; lib bdg $17.89; pa $6.99

Grades: 5 6 7 **Fic**

1. Dogs -- Fiction

ISBN 978-0-06-124261-8; 0-06-124261-6; 978-0-06-124262-5 lib bdg; 0-06-124262-4 lib bdg; 978-0-06-124263-2 pa; 0-06-124263-2 pa

LC 2007020878

When Waggit is abandoned by his owner as a puppy, he meets a pack of wild dogs who become his friends and teach him to survive in the city park, but when he has a chance to go home with a kind woman who wants to adopt him, he takes it

"The novel celebrates the wild freedom of the feral dog pack, while also emphasizing the many hazards of urban life for homeless companion animals." Voice Youth Advocates

Other titles in this series are:

Waggit again (2009)

Waggit forever (2009)

Howland, Leila

The **forget** -me-not summer; Leila Howland. First edition Harpercollins 2015 352 p. illustrations (hardcover) $16.99

Grades: 4 5 6 7 **Fic**

1. Summer -- fiction 2. Vacations -- fiction 3. Sisters -- Fiction 4. Great aunts -- Fiction 5. Cape Cod (Mass.) -- Fiction 6. Actors and actresses -- Fiction 7. Interpersonal relations -- Fiction

ISBN 0062318691; 9780062318695

LC 2014027413

"Though Marigold, Zinnia, and Lily Silver couldn't be more different, they're all excited about their various plans for summer vacation. But any expectation of summer fun comes crashing down when the sisters' parents send them to Cape Cod to visit their aunt Sunny. Small-town life is not what these L.A. girls had in mind. They must adjust, however, to things like sharing a room and living without a TV." (Publisher's note)

"An old-fashioned story well-told, with engaging characters--a beach read for preteens that is as comfortable as the old tennis shoes worn on the Massachusetts shore." Kirkus

Hrdlitschka, Shelley

Allegra; by Shelley Hrdlitschka. Orca Book Publishers 2013 280 p. (paperback) $12.95; (ebook) $12.99; (ebook) $12.99

Grades: 7 8 9 10 **Fic**

1. School stories 2. Teacher-student relationship -- Fiction 3.

Performing arts high schools -- fiction
ISBN 1459801970; 9781459801974; 9781459801998; 9781459801981

LC 2012952952

In this book, Allegra, daughter of two musicians, is thrilled to be at Deer Lake School for the Fine and Performing Arts. She "has her sights set on becoming a professional dancer. However, her excitement is dimmed by the school's requirement that she take a music-theory class. Despite her initial reluctance, Allegra soon begins to enjoy the class due to the charisma of its young and attractive teacher," Mr. Rocchelli. Is their relationship too close? (School Library Journal)

★ **Sister** wife. Orca 2008 269p pa $12.95
Grades: 8 9 10 11 12 **Fic**

1. Polygamy -- Fiction
ISBN 978-1-55143-927-3; 1-55143-927-1

In a remote polygamist community, Celeste struggles to accept her destiny while longing to be free to live her life her way.

"This compelling story combines with authentic characters to pique the interest of a wide array of teens and get them talking about faith and free will." Voice Youth Advocates

Hughes, Dean

★ **Four** -Four-Two; Dean Hughes. Atheneum Books for Young Readers 2016 272 p. illustrations (hardback) $17.99
Grades: 7 8 9 10 **Fic**

1. Soldiers -- Fiction 2. World War, 1939-1945 -- Fiction 3. United States. Army. Regimental Combat Team, 442nd -- Fiction 4. Prejudices -- Fiction 5. Japanese Americans -- Evacuation and relocation, 1942-1945 -- Fiction
ISBN 9781481462525; 9781481462532

LC 2015043700

In this novel, by Dean Hughes, "Yuki Nakahara is an American. But it's the start of World War II, and America doesn't see it that way. . . . But Yuki . . . [is] going to prove it by enlisting in the army to fight for the Allies. When Yuki and his friend Shig ship out, they aren't prepared for the experiences they'll encounter as members of the 'Four-Four-Two,' a segregated regiment made up entirely of Japanese-American soldiers." (Publisher's note)

"Nuanced and riveting in equal parts." Kirkus

Includes bibliographical references

Missing in action. Atheneum Books for Young Readers 2010 228p $16.99; pa $6.99
Grades: 6 7 8 9 **Fic**

1. Utah -- Fiction 2. Baseball -- Fiction 3. Prejudices -- Fiction 4. Family life -- Fiction 5. Grandparents -- Fiction 6. World War, 1939-1945 -- Fiction 7. Racially mixed people -- Fiction 8. Japanese Americans -- Evacuation and relocation, 1942-1945 -- Fiction
ISBN 978-1-4169-1502-7; 1-4169-1502-8; 978-1-4424-1248-4 pa; 1-4424-1248-8 pa

LC 2009-11276

While his father is missing in action in the Pacific during World War II, twelve-year-old Jay moves with his mother to small-town Utah, where he sees prejudice from both sides, as a part-Navajo himself and through an unlikely friendship with Japanese American Ken from the nearby internment camp.

"Jay's pain and eventual resolution will touch readers in this sure-to-be-popular work of historical fiction." Booklist

Search and destroy. Atheneum Books for Young Readers 2006 216p $16.95
Grades: 7 8 9 10 **Fic**

1. Vietnam War, 1961-1975 -- Fiction
ISBN 0-689-87023-X

LC 2005-11255

Recent high school graduate Rick Ward, undecided about his future and eager to escape his unhappy home life, joins the army and experiences the horrors of the war in Vietnam.

"This is a compelling, insightful story about the emotional, physical, and psychological scars that wars leave upon soldiers." Booklist

Soldier boys. Atheneum Bks. for Young Readers 2001 162p $16.95; pa $5.99
Grades: 7 8 9 10 **Fic**

1. Soldiers -- Fiction 2. World War, 1939-1945 -- Fiction 3. Ardennes, Battle of the, 1944-1945 -- Fiction
ISBN 0-689-81748-7; 0-689-86021-8 pa

LC 00-46920

"This World War II novel tells the parallel stories of two young soldiers fighting on opposite sides of the conflict—a paratrooper from Utah and a Hitler Youth who joins the German army. Spence and Dieter's paths cross briefly on a snow-covered Belgian hill in a scene both compassionate and tragic. Hughes tells their tales in assured prose that's harrowing without being exploitive." Horn Book Guide

Hughes, Gregory

Unhooking the moon; by Gregory Hughes. Quercus 2010 374 p. (hardcover) $16.95
Grades: 6 7 8 **Fic**

1. Orphans -- fiction 2. Voyages and travels -- fiction 3. United States -- fiction
ISBN 1623650208; 9781623650209

LC 2010478376

In this book, orphans Bob and Marie Claire (aka Rat) travel from Winnipeg to New York City in search of their drug dealer uncle. "For lack of a better plan, they wander Manhattan and the Bronx asking passersby if they know him. This strategy leads to encounters with a host of colorful city types, notably a pair of softhearted con men and a lonely rising rap star." (Kirkus Reviews)

Hughes, Mark Peter

A **crack** in the sky. Delacorte Press 2010 405p il $16.99; lib bdg $19.99
Grades: 5 6 7 8 **Fic**

1. Science fiction
ISBN 978-0-385-73708-1; 0-385-73708-4; 978-0-385-90645-6 lib bdg; 0-385-90645-5 lib bdg

LC 2009-43532

In a post-apocalyptic world, thirteen-year-old Eli, part of the most powerful family in the world, keeps noticing problems with the operations of his domed city but his family denies them, while in the surrounding desert, the Outsiders struggle to survive while awaiting a prophesied savior.

"Hughes keeps his protagonist an individual, and in fact an amiable, scrappy one with whom readers will identify." Bull Cent Child Books

Hughes, Pat Raccio

Five 4ths of July; by Pat Raccio Hughes. Viking 2011 278p $16.99
Grades: 7 8 9 10 **Fic**

1. Adventure fiction 2. Connecticut -- Fiction 3. United States

-- History -- 1775-1783, Revolution -- Fiction
ISBN 978-0-670-01207-7; 0-670-01207-6

LC 2010-49521

On July 4th, 1777, fourteen-year-old Jake Mallory and his friends are celebrating their new nation's independence, but over the next four years Jake finds himself in increasingly adventurous circumstances as he battles British forces, barely survives captivity on a prison ship, and finally returns home to Connecticut, war-torn and weary, but hopeful for America's future.

This is a "straightforward and well-conceived novel. . . . A fine addition to collections on the war and an eye-opening look at the horrors of British prison ships." Kirkus

Hughes, Shirley, 1927-

★ **Hero** on a bicycle; Shirley Hughes. Candlewick Press 2013 224 p. $15.99

Grades: 5 6 7 **Fic**

1. Historical fiction 2. World War, 1939-1945 -- Fiction
ISBN 076366037X; 9780763660376

LC 2012943650

This book is set in Italy during World War II. "The narrative focuses on a city under German occupation, events being perceived principally through the eyes of three members of the Crivelli family: teenager Paolo, his older sister Constanza and Rosemary, their English-born mother. . . . When an opportunity arises for Paolo, Constanza and Rosemary to lend their practical support to the Partisan cause Paolo, in particular, seizes it enthusiastically." (School Librarian)

Hulme, John

★ The **glitch** in sleep; [by] John Hulme and Michael Wexler; illustrations by Gideon Kendall. Bloomsbury Children's Books 2007 277p il (The Seems) $16.95; pa $7.99

Grades: 4 5 6 7 **Fic**

1. Science fiction 2. Sleep -- Fiction
ISBN 978-1-59990-129-9; 1-59990-129-3; 978-1-59990-298-2 pa; 1-59990-298-2 pa

LC 2007-2598

When twelve-year-old Becker Drane is recruited by The Seems, a parallel universe that runs everything in The World, he must fix a disastrous glitch in the Department of Sleep that threatens everyone's ability to ever fall asleep again

"The story is upbeat and full of humor. . . . Dynamic full-page illustrations appear throughout." SLJ

Another title in this series is:
The split second (2008)

The **lost** train of thought; by John Hulme and Michael Wexler ; illustrated by Gideon Kendall. 1st U.S. ed. Bloomsbury 2009 289 p. ill. (alk. paper) $16.99

Grades: 5 6 7 8 **Fic**

1. Fantasy fiction -- fiction 2. Voyages and travels -- fiction 3. Technology -- Fiction 4. Space and time -- Fiction 5. Thought and thinking -- Fiction
ISBN 1599901315; 9781599901312

LC 2009002145

This is the third book in John Hulme's Seems series. Here, "Becker Drane's coolest job in The World—as a Fixer in The Seems—is in jeopardy. So when a trainload of Thought goes missing, Becker reluctantly agrees to join a veteran team of Fixers on a mission in The Middle of Nowhere. Turns out getting the train back on track is just a temporary Fix, and Becker's real mission just might end his Fixing days forever." (Publisher's note)

The **split** second; by John Hulme and Michael Wexler; illustrations by Gideon Kendall. 1st U.S. ed.; Bloomsbury Children's Books 2008 301p il (The Seems) $16.99

Grades: 5 6 7 8 **Fic**

1. Science fiction 2. Terrorism -- Fiction
ISBN 978-1-599-90130-5; 1-599-90130-7

LC 2008012241

Sequel to: The glitch in sleep (2007)

Now thirteen-years-old and still a Fixer in the parallel universe called the Seems, Becker Drane is called upon to repair the damage caused by an enormous bomb planted in the Department of Time, an act of terrorism perpetrated by the evil members of the Tide, a group that is trying to destroy the World.

"This sequel continues to develop a truly ingenious setting while proving every bit as much of a nail-biter as the first." Booklist

Hunt, Lynda Mullaly

One for the Murphys; Lynda Mullaly Hunt. Nancy Paulsen Books 2012 224 p. (hardback) $16.99

Grades: 5 6 7 8 **Fic**

1. Girls -- fiction 2. Family -- fiction 3. Foster children -- fiction 4. Connecticut -- Fiction 5. Stepfathers -- Fiction 6. Family problems -- Fiction 7. Foster home care -- Fiction 8. Mothers and daughters -- Fiction 9. Family life -- Connecticut -- Fiction
ISBN 0399256156; 9780399256158

LC 2011046708

This book by Lynda Mullaly Hunt follows "eighth-grader Carley Connors [as she] learns about a different kind of family life, first resisting and then resisting having to leave the loving, loyal Murphys. . . . She's torn between her love for her mother and her memory of the fight that sent her to the hospital, when her mother caught and held her for her stepfather. Slowly won over at home . . . Carley also finds a friend at school in the prickly, Wicked-obsessed Toni." (Kirkus Reviews)

Hunter, Erin

★ **Broken** pride; Vol. 1 Erin Hunter. HarperCollins 2017 319 p. illustrations, map (Bravelands) (hardcover) $16.99

Grades: 5 6 7 8 **Fic**

1. Lions -- Fiction 2. Africa -- Fiction 3. Animals -- Fiction 4. Baboons -- Fiction 5. Elephants -- Fiction
ISBN 9780062642059; 9780062642028; 9780062642035

LC 2016963712

This book, by Erin Hunter, is an "action-packed animal fantasy. . . . For generations, the animals of the African plains have followed a single rule: only kill to survive. But when an unthinkable act of betrayal shatters the peace, the fragile balance between predators and prey will rest in the paws of three unlikely heroes." (Publisher's note)

"Deep characters, a complex plot, rich mythology, and a stunning setting all come together to prove once again that the Hunter collective are master storytellers." Kirkus

Other titles in this series are:
Code of honor (2018)
Blood and bone (2018)

Code of the clans; illustrated by Wayne McLoughlin. HarperCollinsPublishers 2009 156p il (Warriors) $16.99; lib bdg $17.89

Grades: 6 7 8 9 **Fic**

1. Fantasy fiction 2. Cats -- Fiction

ISBN 978-0-06-166009-2; 0-06-166009-4; 978-0-06-166010-8 lib bdg; 0-06-166010-8 lib bdg

LC 2008045061

Explores the fifteen rules that govern the daily life of a warrior cat.

A **dangerous** path; [by] Erin Hunter. 1st ed; HarperCollins 2004 (Warriors) $16.99; lib bdg $17.89; pa $6.99

Grades: 6 7 8 9 **Fic**

1. Fantasy fiction 2. Cats -- Fiction

ISBN 0-06-000006-6; 0-06-052564-9 lib bdg; 0-06-052565-7 pa

LC 2003-13962

Sequel to Rising storm (2004)

Tigerclaw is back and more dangerous than ever as the new leader of ShadowClan, but he is not the most terrifying enemy Fireheart must face as a new force sweeps through the woods.

"With compelling intrigue and fast-paced actions, this is one of the most exciting books in the series." Booklist

Followed by The darkest hour (2004)

The **darkest** hour; [by] Erin Hunter. 1st ed; HarperCollins 2004 315p (Warriors) $16.99; lib bdg $17.89; pa $6.99

Grades: 6 7 8 9 **Fic**

1. Fantasy fiction 2. Cats -- Fiction

ISBN 0-06-000007-4; 0-06-052584-3 lib bdg; 0-06-052585-1 pa

LC 2003-22493

Sequel to A dangerous path (2004)

ThunderClan's darkest hour is upon them and Fireheart, the warrior cat, must protect his clan from a threat unlike any the forest has ever seen, as the time comes for prophecies to unfold and heroes to rise.

Dawn; [by] Erin Hunter. 1st ed.; HarperCollins 2005 335p (Warriors: the new prophecy) $15.99; lib bdg $17.89; pa $6.99

Grades: 6 7 8 9 **Fic**

1. Fantasy fiction 2. Cats -- Fiction

ISBN 978-0-06-074455-7; 0-06-074455-3; 978-0-06-074456-4 lib bdg; 0-06-074456-1 lib bdg; 978-0-06-074457-1 pa; 0-06-074457-X pa

LC 2005009175

Sequel to Moonrise (2005)

The questing cats return to a forest devastated by the Twolegs, where they must find a way to convince their Clans to leave in search of a new home, even though they have no idea where they are going.

"Fans will relish this eminently satisfying episode." Booklist

Followed by Starlight (2006)

Fire and ice; [by] Erin Hunter. 1st ed; HarperCollins 2003 317p (Warriors) $15.99; lib bdg $16.89

Grades: 6 7 8 9 **Fic**

ISBN 0-06-000003-1; 0-06-052556-8 lib bdg

LC 2002-14415

Sequel to In the wild (2003)

Fireheart, a full-fledged warrior cat, must confront questions of loyalty and identity as he faces the possibility of betrayal from within his own forest clan.

"Characters remain true to their feline natures, adding to the plausibility of events in this tension-filled story." Booklist

Followed by Forest of secrets (2003)

Forest of secrets; [by] Erin Hunter. 1st ed; HarperCollins 2003 312p (Warriors) $16.99; lib bdg $17.89; pa $6.99

Grades: 6 7 8 9 **Fic**

1. Fantasy fiction 2. Cats -- Fiction

ISBN 0-06-000004-X; 0-06-052560-6 lib bdg; 0-06-052561-4 pa

LC 2003-445

Sequel to Fire and ice (2003)

The warrior cat Fireheart's determination to uncover the truth about another warrior's death leads him deep into danger, and reveals secrets that test the strength of clan loyalties.

"This exciting book is not for the faint of heart as it is often violent. . . . Fans of the series will lap it up." SLJ

Followed by Rising storm (2004)

★ **Into** the wild. HarperCollins Pubs. 2003 272p il map (Warriors) $15.99; lib bdg $16.89; pa $5.99

Grades: 6 7 8 9 **Fic**

1. Fantasy fiction 2. Cats -- Fiction

ISBN 0-06-000002-3; 0-06-052548-7 lib bdg; 0-06-052550-9 pa

For generations, four clans of wild cats have shared the forest. When their warrior code is threatened by mysterious deaths, a house cat named Rusty may turn out to be the bravest warrior of all.

"The author has created an intriguing world with an intricate structure and mythology, and an engaging young hero." SLJ

Other titles in the Warriors series are:

Code of the clans (2009)
A dangerous path (2004)
The darkest hour (2004)
Fire and ice (2003)
Forest of secrets (2003)
Rising storm (2004)

Rising storm; [by] Erin Hunter. 1st ed; HarperCollins 2004 315p (Warriors) $16.99; lib bdg $17.89; pa $6.99

Grades: 6 7 8 9 **Fic**

1. Fantasy fiction 2. Cats -- Fiction

ISBN 0-06-000005-8; 0-06-052562-2 lib bdg; 0-06-052563-0 pa

LC 2003-6982

Sequel to Forest of secrets (2003)

Fireheart, the warrior cat, faces many challenges in his new role of ThunderClan deputy as his apprentice, Cloudpaw, resists following the warrior code, Bluestar weakens, and Tigerclaw continues to haunt the forest seeking revenge.

"Hunter once again tells a good, suspenseful adventure story that urges readers onward." Booklist

Followed by A dangerous path (2004)

The **sight**; [by] Erin Hunter. HarperCollins Pub. 2007 363p (Warriors: power of three) $16.99; lib bdg $17.89

Grades: 6 7 8 9 **Fic**

1. Fantasy fiction 2. Cats -- Fiction

ISBN 978-0-06-089201-2; 0-06-089201-3; 978-0-06-089203-6 lib bdg; 0-06-089203-X lib bdg

LC 2007-11860

In a troubled time for the Clans, three young cats, grandchildren of the legendary Firestar, begin their training as warriors and, in the course of many adventures, discover their true destiny.

"Plenty of action and solid characterizations make this an enticing choice for fans of the long-running enterprise." Booklist

Other titles in this series are:

Dark river (2008)
Outcast (2008)
Eclipse (2008)
Long shadows (2009)
Sunrise (2009)

Huntley, Amy

The **everafter**. Balzer + Bray 2009 144p $16.99; lib bdg $17.89; pa $8.99

Grades: 7 8 9 10 **Fic**

1. Dead -- Fiction 2. Death -- Fiction 3. Friendship -- Fiction 4. Lost and found possessions -- Fiction

ISBN 978-0-06-177679-3; 0-06-177679-3; 978-0-06-177680-9 lib bdg; 0-06-177680-7 lib bdg; 978-0-06-177681-6 pa; 0-06-177681-5 pa

LC 2008-46149

ALA YALSA Morris Award Finalist, 2010

Madison Stanton doesn't know where she is or how she got there. But she does know this—she is dead. And alone in a vast, dark space. The only company Maddy has in this place are luminescent objects that turn out to be all the things she lost while she was alive. And soon she discovers that, with these artifacts, she can re-experience—and even—change moments from her life.

"This fresh take on a teen's journey of self-exploration is a compelling and highly enjoyable tale. Huntley expertly combines a coming-of-age story with a supernatural mystery that keeps readers engrossed until the climactic ending. This touching story will appeal to those looking for a ghost story, romance, or family drama." SLJ

Hurley, Tonya

★ **Ghostgirl**. Little, Brown 2008 328p $17.99

Grades: 7 8 9 10 **Fic**

1. Ghost stories 2. School stories 3. Death -- Fiction 4. Popularity -- Fiction

ISBN 978-0-316-11357-1; 0-316-11357-3

LC 2007-31541

After dying, high school senior Charlotte Usher is as invisible to nearly everyone as she always felt, but despite what she learns in a sort of alternative high school for dead teens, she clings to life while seeking a way to go to the Fall Ball with the boy of her dreams.

"Hurley combines afterlife antics, gothic gore, and high school hell to produce an original, hilarious satire. . . . Tim Burton and Edgar Allan Poe devotees will die for this fantastic, phantasmal read." SLJ

Other titles in this series are:

Ghostgirl: Homecoming (2009)

Ghostgirl: Lovesick (2010)

Hurwitz, Gregg, 1973-

The **rains**; by Gregg Hurwitz. SDC Publications 2016 352 p. (ebook) $60; (hardcover) $17.99

Grades: 8 9 10 11 **Fic**

1. Paranormal fiction 2. Zombies -- Fiction 3. Brothers -- Fiction

ISBN 9781466888517; 9780765382672; 0765382679

LC 2016041559

In this novel, by Gregg Hurwitz, "in one terrifying night, the peaceful community of Creek's Cause turns into a war zone. No one under the age of eighteen is safe. Chance Rain and his older brother, Patrick, have already fended off multiple attacks from infected adults by the time they arrive at the school where other young survivors are hiding." (Publisher's note)

"This zombie-esque sci-fi novel will feed the needs of readers looking for a fast-paced, adrenaline-pumping story with elements of horror. " Kirkus

Hurwitz, Michele Weber

The **summer** I saved the world-- in 65 days; by Michele Weber Hurwitz. Wendy Lamb Books, an imprint of Random House Children's Books 2014 272 p. (trade) $16.99

Grades: 5 6 7 8 **Fic**

1. Summer -- Fiction 2. Neighbors -- Fiction 3. Family life -- Fiction 4. Helping behavior -- Fiction 5. Illinois -- Fiction 6. Friendship -- Fiction 7. Helpfulness -- Fiction 8. Conduct of life -- Fiction 9. Family life -- Illinois -- Fiction

ISBN 0385371063; 9780385371063; 9780385371070; 9780385371094

LC 2013016843

In this book, by Michele Weber Hurwitz, "thirteen-year-old Nina Ross is feeling kind of lost. . . . This summer, Nina decides to change things. She hatches a plan. There are sixty-five days of summer. Every day, she'll anonymously do one small but remarkable good thing for someone in her neighborhood, and find out: does doing good actually make a difference? Along the way, she discovers that her neighborhood, and her family, are full of surprises and secrets." (Publisher's note)

"Insightful writing, realistic dialogue infused with humor, and a sweet romantic element add depth to the story." Booklist

Hyde, Catherine Ryan

The **year** of my miraculous reappearance. Alfred A. Knopf 2007 228p $15.99; lib bdg $18.99

Grades: 7 8 9 10 **Fic**

1. Siblings -- Fiction 2. Alcoholism -- Fiction 3. Down syndrome -- Fiction

ISBN 978-0-375-83257-4; 978-0-375-93257-1 lib bdg; 0-375-83257-2; 0-375-93257-7 lib bdg

LC 2006-29194

Thirteen-year-old Cynnie has had to deal with her mother's alcoholism and stream of boyfriends all her life, but when her grandparents take custody of her brother, Bill, who has Down Syndrome, Cynnie becomes self-destructive and winds up in court-mandated Alcoholics Anonymous meetings.

"Cynnie's love for and devotion to Bill are wholly believable, as are her attempts to snare a stable adult presence in her life. Secondary characters are multidimensional and well drawn." Booklist

Hyman, Fracaswell

Mango delight; Fracaswell Hyman. Sterling Children's Books 2017 219 p. (hardcover) $14.95

Grades: 4 5 6 7 8 **Fic**

1. Popularity -- fiction 2. Female friendship -- fiction 3. Girls -- fiction 4. Friendship -- fiction 5. Middle school students -- fiction

ISBN 1454923326; 9781454923329

In this story, by Fracaswell Hyman, illustrated by Frank Morrison, "what happens when your BFF becomes your EFF . . . EX-Friend-Forever? When seventh-grader Mango Delight Fuller accidentally breaks her BFF Brooklyn's new cell phone, her life falls apart. . . . Soon Mango finds herself forced to make tough choices about the kind of friend she wants to have . . . and, just as important, the kind of friend she wants to be." (Publisher's note)

"A short and sweet story that will encourage deeper conversations around shame, honesty, and courage." Kirkus

Ibbitson, John

The **Landing**; a novel. KCP Fiction 2008 160p $17.95; pa $7.95

Grades: 7 8 9 10 **Fic**

1. Canada -- Fiction 2. Uncles -- Fiction 3. Violinists -- Fiction

ISBN 978-1-55453-234-6; 1-55453-234-5; 978-1-55453-238-4 pa; 1-55453-238-8 pa

Ben thinks he will always be stuck at Cook's Landing, barely making ends meet like his uncle. But when he meets a wealthy widow from

New York City, he sees himself there too. When she hires him to play his violin, he realizes his gift could unlock the possibilities of the world. Then, during a stormy night on Lake Muskoka, everything changes.

"With lovely prose, Ibbitson brings to life the rugged beauty and the devastating poverty of the Lake Muskoka region. His characters are as strong and remote as their surroundings." Voice Youth Advocates

Ibbotson, Eva

★ The **dragonfly** pool; illustrated by Kevin Hawkes. Dutton Children's Books 2008 377p il $17.99; pa $7.99

Grades: 5 6 7 8 **Fic**

1. School stories 2. World War, 1939-1945 -- Fiction

ISBN 978-0-525-42064-4; 0-525-42064-9; 978-0-14-241486-6 pa; 0-14-241486-7 pa

"Ibbotson's trademark eccentric characters and strongly contrasted principles of right and wrong brighten and broaden this uplifting tale." Booklist

★ The **Ogre** of Oglefort; [illustrations by Lisa K. Weber] Dutton Children's Books 2011 246p il $16.99

Grades: 4 5 6 **Fic**

1. Fairy tales 2. Magic -- Fiction 3. Orphans -- Fiction 4. Princesses -- Fiction

ISBN 978-0-525-42382-9; 0-525-42382-6

LC 2010038137

When the Hag of Dribble, an orphan boy, and a troll called Ulf are sent to rescue a princess from an ogre, it turns out to be far from the routine magical mission they expect.

"Magical creatures abound in this effervescent fairy tale that effectively merges classic tropes with modern sensibilities." Bull Cent Child Books

★ The **star** of Kazan; illustrated by Kevin Hawkes. Dutton 2004 405p il $16.99; pa $7.99

Grades: 5 6 7 8 **Fic**

1. Mystery fiction 2. Germany -- Fiction 3. Vienna (Austria) -- Fiction

ISBN 0-525-47347-5; 0-14-240582-5 pa

LC 2004-45455

After twelve-year-old Annika, a foundling living in late nineteenth-century Vienna, inherits a trunk of costume jewelry, a woman claiming to be her aristocratic mother arrives and takes her to live in a strangely decrepit mansion in Germany

"This is a rich saga . . . full of stalwart friends, sly villains, a brave heroine, and good triumphing over evil. . . . An intensely satisfying read." SLJ

Ingold, Jeanette

Hitch. Harcourt, Inc 2005 272p $17

Grades: 7 8 9 10 **Fic**

1. Montana -- Fiction 2. Great Depression, 1929-1939 -- Fiction 3. Civilian Conservation Corps (U.S.) -- Fiction

ISBN 0-15-204747-6

LC 2004-19447

To help his family during the Depression and avoid becoming a drunk like his father, Moss Trawnley joins the Civilian Conservation Corps, helps build a new camp near Monroe, Montana, and leads the other men in making the camp a success.

This is "a credible, involving story. . . . Both [the author's] writing style and her 1930s setting feels totally true to the time." Booklist

Irving, Washington

The **Legend** of Sleepy Hollow; illustrated by Gris Grimly. Atheneum Books for Young Readers 2007 un il $16.99

Grades: 4 5 6 **Fic**

1. Ghost stories 2. New York (State) -- Fiction

ISBN 1-4169-0625-8; 978-1-4169-0625-4

LC 2005-27502

A superstitious schoolmaster, in love with a wealthy farmer's daughter, has a terrifying encounter with a headless horseman.

"The tale, . . . slightly condensed but with language and ambiguities intact, is reimagined here with humor, vigor, [and] clarity. . . . Irving's language is challenging . . . but Grimly's numerous Halloween-hued panel and spot illustrations . . . parse it into comprehensible tidbits. The comically amplified emotions and warm yellow and orange tones balance the horror aspects of the text." Horn Book

Isbell, Tom

The **Prey**; Tom Isbell. Harperteen 2015 416 p. $17.99

Grades: 7 8 9 10 **Fic**

1. Science fiction 2. Dystopian fiction 3. Twins -- Fiction 4. Orphans -- Fiction 5. Survival -- Fiction

ISBN 0062216015; 9780062216014

Sequel: The Capture (2015)

In this young adult science fiction novel, by Tom Isbell, "orphaned teens, soon to be hunted for sport, must flee their resettlement camps in their fight for survival and a better life. For in the Republic of the True America, it's always hunting season. . . . As unlikely Book and fearless Hope lead their quest for freedom, these teens must find the best in themselves to fight the worst in their enemies." (Publisher's note)

"An electromagnetic pulse followed by radiation—they called it Omega, the end—destroyed civilization as it once existed. The survivors established the Republic of the True America. But the future still looks like a dead end for Book and Hope, two teens who find themselves in the camps that purport to be orphanages...Careful readers will appreciate the irony and subtle, deeper meanings in character and location names as Isbell shapes his own vision of a dark world..." Booklist

Iserles, Inbali

The **Taken**; by Inbali Iserles. Scholastic Press 2015 272 p. illustrations, map (Foxcraft) $16.99

Grades: 4 5 6 7 **Fic**

1. Fantasy fiction 2. Foxes -- Fiction 3. Magic -- Fiction

ISBN 0545690811; 9780545690812

In this book, by Inbali Iserles, "Isla and her brother are two young foxes living just outside the lands of the furless -- humans. The life of a fox is filled with dangers, but Isla has begun to learn mysterious skills meant to help her survive. Then the unthinkable happens. Returning to her den, Isla finds it set ablaze and surrounded by strange foxes, and her family is nowhere in sight. Forced to flee, she escapes into the cold, gray world of the furless." (Publisher's note)

"Vivid details, intriguing characters, and a riveting plot are smoothly executed in this exciting new series from one of the authors who write under the pseudonym of Erin Hunter. Beautifully rendered and magical." Kirkus

Iturbe, Antonio

★ The **librarian** of Auschwitz; by Antonio Iturbe ; translated by Lilit Thwaites. Henry Holt & Co. 2017 423 p. illustrations (hardcover) $19.99

Grades: 7 8 9 10 11 12 **Fic**

1. Jews -- Germany -- Fiction 2. Books and reading -- Fiction 3. Concentration camps -- Fiction 4. Holocaust, 1939-1945 -- Fiction

5. Germany -- History -- 1933-1945 -- Fiction 6. Auschwitz (Poland: Concentration camp) -- Fiction 7. Jews -- Germany -- History -- 1933-1945 -- Fiction 8. Holocaust, Jewish (1939-1945) -- Germany -- Fiction
ISBN 9781627796187; 9781627796194

LC 2017007363

In this book, by Antonio Iturbe, translated by Lilit Thwaites, "[14]-year-old Dita is one of the many imprisoned by the Nazis at Auschwitz. Taken, along with her mother and father, from the Terezín ghetto in Prague, Dita is adjusting to the constant terror that is life in the camp. When Jewish leader Freddy Hirsch asks Dita to take charge of the [8] . . . volumes the prisoners have managed to sneak past the guards, she agrees. And so Dita becomes the librarian of Auschwitz." (Publisher's note)

"Despite being a fictional retelling of a true story, this novel is one that could easily be recommended or taught alongside Elie Wiesel's Night and The Diary of Anne Frank and a text that, once read, will never be forgotten." SLJ

Includes bibliographical references.

Jackson, Alison

Rainmaker. Boyds Mills Press 2005 192p $16.95
Grades: 5 6 7 8 **Fic**

1. Florida -- Fiction 2. Droughts -- Fiction 3. Great Depression, 1929-1939 -- Fiction
ISBN 1-59078-309-3

"For 13-year-old Pidge Martin, the summer of 1939 brings changes and challenges. Her town, Frostfree, Florida, faces its longest drought in 40 years, and if it doesn't rain soon, area families . . . may lose their farms. A miracle is in order, and Pidge's father hopes a rainmaker can provide one. . . . Pidge is a well-characterized, sympathetic protagonist that readers will connect with." Booklist

Jackson, Tiffany D.

★ **Let** me hear a rhyme; Tiffany D. Jackson. Katherine Tegen Books 2019 384 p. (hardcover) $17.99
Grades: 8 9 10 11 12 **Fic**

1. Fraud -- Fiction 2. Teenagers -- Fiction 3. Rap musicians -- Fiction
ISBN 9780062840325

LC 2018968472

This novel, by Tiffany D. Jackson, is about "three Brooklyn teens who plot to turn their murdered friend into a major rap star by pretending he's still alive. . . . Quadir and Jarrell are [not] . . . letting their best friend Steph's music lie forgotten under his bed after he's murdered. . . . With the help of Steph's younger sister Jasmine, they come up with a plan to promote Steph's music under a new rap name: the Architect. Soon, everyone wants a piece of him." (Publisher's note)

"After a Brooklyn teen is murdered, his sister and best friends set out to launch his rap career." (Kirlus Reviews)

★ **Monday's** not coming; Tiffany D. Jackson. Katherine Tegen Books 2018 435 p. (hardcover) $17.99
Grades: 8 9 10 11 12 **Fic**

1. Friendship -- Fiction 2. Missing persons -- Fiction 3. High school students -- Fiction
ISBN 9780062422699; 9780062422675

LC 2018933268

Coretta Scott King/John Steptoe New Talent Author Award (2019)

In this book, by Tiffany D. Jackson, "Monday Charles is missing, and only Claudia seems to notice. Claudia and Monday have always been inseparable--more sisters than friends. So when Monday doesn't turn up for the first day of school, Claudia's worried. When she doesn't show for the second day, or second week, Claudia knows that something is wrong." (Publisher's note)

"This is a powerful and emotional novel that is gripping and heartbreaking and hits upon serious topics." Booklist

Jacobson, Andrew

Circle of heroes; Adam Jay Epstein & Andrew Jacobson. Harper 2012 327 p. (The familiars) (trade bdg.) $16.99
Grades: 4 5 6 **Fic**

1. Fantasy 2. Magic -- Fiction 3. Animals -- Fiction 4. Wizards -- Fiction 5. Zombies -- Fiction
ISBN 0061961140; 9780061961144

LC 2012005740

"Aldwyn, a street-smart alley cat, pretended he had telekinetic powers so young wizard Jack would chose him as a familiar. Aldwyn then learned that he and two other familiars—Skylar the blue jay and Gilbert the tree frog—were destined to undertake a perilous quest to defeat Paksahara, an evil hare who'd been familiar to the queen. In Circle of Heroes, the third book of The Familiars series for middle-grade readers, Paksahara and her undead animal army control the Shifting Fortress. Aldwyn and his friends have to recapture it to return magic to the queendom of Vastia." (Publisher's Note)

"In this third installment, cat Aldwyn, frog Gilbert, and blue jay Skylar, the prophesied familiars, embark on a quest to unite seven magical animal descendants before the evil hare Paksahara and her Dead Army of zombie animals forever rid the world of human magic. Rollicking adventure and playful humor add whimsy to this series' theme of fulfilling destiny." Horn Book

Jacobson, Jennifer Richard, 1958-

Paper things; Jennifer Richard Jacobson. Candlewick Press 2015 384 p. $16.99
Grades: 5 6 7 8 **Fic**

1. Maine -- Fiction 2. Orphans -- Fiction 3. Siblings -- Fiction 4. Middle schools -- Fiction 5. Homeless persons -- Fiction 6. Promises -- Fiction 7. Gifted girls -- Fiction
ISBN 0763663239; 9780763663230

LC 2014944677

In this book, by Jennifer Richard Jacobson, "when Ari's mother died four years ago, she had two final wishes: that Ari and her older brother, Gage, would stay together always, and that Ari would go to Carter, the middle school for gifted students. So when nineteen-year-old Gage decides he can no longer live with their bossy guardian, Janna, Ari knows she has to go with him. But it's been two months, and Gage still hasn't found them an apartment." (Publisher's note)

"Before her death four years earlier, Ari and Gage's mother had urged them to "stay together always." Now it has been two months since nineteen-year-old Gage and eleven-year-old Ari left their overbearing guardian's home to strike out on their own, and the challenges of finding a permanent job and stable living situation have frayed Gage's confidence... In this poignant view of one child's experience with homelessness, Jacobson deftly shows how easily it can happen, an insidious downward spiral with heart-wrenching consequences." Horn Book

★ **Small** as an elephant; [by] Jennifer Richard Jacobson. Candlewick Press 2011 275p $15.99
Grades: 5 6 7 8 **Fic**

1. Adventure fiction 2. New England -- Fiction 3. Abandoned children -- Fiction 4. Mother-son relationship -- Fiction
ISBN 0-7636-4155-3; 978-0-7636-4155-9

LC 2010039175

When his mother disappears from an Acadia National Park campground, Jack tries to make his way back home to Boston, with only a small toy elephant for company. "Intermediate, middle school." (Horn Book)

"Jacobson masterfully puts readers into Jack's mind—he loves and understands his mother, but sometimes his judgments are not always good, and readers understand. . . . Jack's journey to a new kind of family is inspiring and never sappy." Kirkus

Jacques, Brian

The **angel's** command; a tale from the castaways of the Flying Dutchman. illustrated by David Elliot. Philomel Bks. 2003 374p il $23.99; pa $7.99

Grades: 6 7 8 9 **Fic**

1. Adventure fiction 2. Dogs -- Fiction 3. Orphans -- Fiction 4. Pirates -- Fiction

ISBN 0-399-23999-5; 0-14-240285-0 pa

LC 2002-75279

Sequel to Castaways of the Flying (2002)

Ben and Ned, a boy and dog gifted with eternal youth and the ability to communicate with one another nonverbally, encounter pirates on the high seas and rescue a kidnapped prince from a band of gypsy thieves

"Jacques spins a rousing yarn that fairly bursts at the seams with exciting escapades, exotic locations, poems, shanties, treachery and derring-do." Publ Wkly

Castaways of the Flying Dutchman; illustrated by Ian Schoenherr. Philomel Bks. 2001 327p il $22.95; pa $7.99

Grades: 6 7 8 9 **Fic**

1. Adventure fiction 2. Dogs -- Fiction 3. Angels -- Fiction 4. Orphans -- Fiction

ISBN 0-399-23601-5; 0-14-250118-2 pa

LC 00-59822

In 1620, a boy and his dog are rescued from the doomed ship, Flying Dutchman, by an angel who guides them in travelling the world, eternally helping those in great need

"The swashbuckling language brims with color and melodrama; the villains are dastardly and stupid; and buried treasure, mysterious clues, and luscious culinary descriptions . . . keep the pages turning." Booklist

Other titles in this series are:

The angel's command (2003)

Voyage of slaves (2006)

Mariel of Redwall; illustrated by Gary Chalk. Philomel Bks. 1992 387p il $24.99; pa $7.99

Grades: 5 6 7 8 9 **Fic**

1. Fantasy fiction 2. Mice -- Fiction 3. Animals -- Fiction

ISBN 978-0-399-22144-6; 0-399-22144-1; 978-0-441-00694-6 pa; 0-441-00694-9 pa

LC 91-17157

"Jacques' characters are fully developed and true to their natures; his dialectal dialog resounds with wit; the plot is filled with action, drama, and larger-than-life violence; and good conquers all. A satisfying tale with wide appeal that extends beyond its intended audience." Booklist

Martin the Warrior; illustrated by Gary Chalk. Philomel Bks. 1994 376p il pa $8.99

Grades: 5 6 7 8 9 **Fic**

1. Fantasy fiction 2. Mice -- Fiction 3. Animals -- Fiction

ISBN 0-399-22670-2; 978-0-14-240055-5 pa; 0-14-240055-6 pa

LC 93-26434

Captured and enslaved by the corsair stoat Badrang, young mouse warrior Martin vows to end the evil beast's plundering and killing

"Studded with vibrant and distinct animal characters, Jacques's classically inspired . . . plot-weaving achieves virtuosity as moments of sensitivity shake his fierce heroes off their warrior paths." Publ Wkly

Mattimeo; illustrated by Gary Chalk. Philomel Bks. 1990 446p il hardcover o.p. pa $8.99

Grades: 5 6 7 8 9 **Fic**

1. Mice -- Fiction 2. Animals -- Fiction

ISBN 0-399-21741-X; 978-0-14-230240-8 pa; 0-14-230240-6 pa

LC 89-37005

Mattimeo, the son of the warrior mouse Matthias, learns to take up the sword and joins the other animal inhabitants of Redwall Abbey in resisting Slagar the fox and his band of marauders

This is "truly thrilling. . . . Jacques's realistically drawn characters are full of personality. . . . The fierceness with which the Redwallers fight back to save their young lends the story credibility within the realm of the animal kingdom, while at the same time taking wonderful liberties with the imagination." Publ Wkly

Mossflower; illustrated by Gary Chalk. Philomel Bks. 1988 431p il $24.99; pa $8.99

Grades: 5 6 7 8 9 **Fic**

1. Fantasy fiction 2. Mice -- Fiction 3. Animals -- Fiction

ISBN 978-0-399-21549-0; 0-399-21549-2; 978-0-14-230238-5 pa; 0-14-230238-4 pa

LC 88-17921

Martin the warrior mouse and Gonff the mousethief set out to find the missing ruler of Mossflower, while the other animal inhabitants of the woodland prepare to rebel against the evil wildcat who has seized power

"The writing is smooth and swift-paced." SLJ

Pearls of Lutra; illustrated by Allan Curless. Philomel Bks. 1997 408p il $23.99; pa $7.99

Grades: 5 6 7 8 9 **Fic**

1. Fantasy fiction 2. Animals -- Fiction

ISBN 978-0-399-22946-6; 0-399-22946-9; 978-0-441-00508-6 pa; 0-441-00508-X pa

LC 96-18444

Tansy, a young hedgehog living at Redwall Abbey, attempts to solve the riddle of the missing pearls while at the same time the evil marten, Mad Eyes, desires them for himself

★ **Redwall**; illustrated by Gary Chalk. 20th anniversary ed.; Philomel 2007 351p il $23.99; pa $7.99

Grades: 5 6 7 8 9 **Fic**

1. Fantasy fiction 2. Mice -- Fiction 3. Animals -- Fiction

ISBN 978-0-399-24794-1; 0-399-24794-7; 978-0-441-00548-2 pa; 0-441-00548-9 pa

First published 1986

"Thoroughly engrossing, this novel captivates despite its length. . . . The theme will linger long after the story is finished." Booklist

Other titles in this series are:

The Bellmaker (1995)

Doomwyte (2008)

Eulalia! (2007)

High Rhulain (2005)

The legend of Luke (2000)

Loamhedge (2003)

The long patrol (1998)

Lord Brocktree (2000)

Mariel of Redwall (1992)

Marlfox (1998)

Martin the Warrior (1994)
Mattimeo (1990)
Mossflower (1998)
The outcast of Redwall (1996)
Pearls of Lutra (1997)
Rakkety Tam (2004)
The Rogue Crew (2011)
Sable Quean (2009)
Salamandastron (1993)
Taggerung (2001)
Triss (2002)

Salamandastron; illustrated by Gary Chalk. Philomel Bks. 1993 391p il $24.99; pa $8.99
Grades: 5 6 7 8 9 **Fic**

1. Fantasy fiction 2. Animals -- Fiction
ISBN 978-0-399-21992-4; 0-399-21992-7; 978-0-14-250152-8 pa; 0-14-250152-2 pa

LC 91-46423

Urthstripe the Strong, a wise old badger, leads the animals of the great fortress of Salamandastron and Redwall Abbey against the weasel Ferahgo the Assassin and his corps of vermin

"The reader feels included in the Abbey's history as it is being written, and Jacques encourages that empathy by creating animal characters that respond to extraordinary circumstances with compellingly human-like humility and strength. Chalk's black-and-white illustrations above each chapter number are small marvels of nuance and personality." Publ Wkly

Jaden, Denise

Losing Faith. Simon Pulse 2010 381p pa $9.99
Grades: 7 8 9 10 11 12 **Fic**

1. School stories 2. Cults -- Fiction 3. Death -- Fiction 4. Sisters -- Fiction 5. Bereavement -- Fiction 6. Christian life -- Fiction
ISBN 978-1-4169-9609-5; 1-4169-9609-5

LC 2010-7296

Brie tries to cope with her grief over her older sister Faith's sudden death by trying to learn more about the religious "home group" Faith secretly joined and never talked about with Brie or her parents.

"With pitch-perfect portrayals of high school social life and a nuanced view into a variety of Christian experiences of faith, this first novel gives readers much to think about." SLJ

James, Helen Foster

Paper son; Lee's journey to America. written by Helen Foster James and Virginia Shin-Mui Loh ; illustrated by Wilson Ong. Sleeping Bear Press 2013 32 p. ill. (reinforced) $16.99
Grades: 5 6 7 8 **Fic**

1. Historical fiction -- fiction 2. Immigrants -- United States -- fiction 3. Orphans -- Fiction 4. Immigrants -- Fiction 5. Chinese Americans -- Fiction 6. Emigration and immigration -- Fiction 7. Angel Island Immigration Station (Calif.) -- Fiction 8. Angel Island (Calif.) -- History -- 20th century -- Fiction
ISBN 1585368334; 9781585368334

LC 2012033691

This historical novel, by Helen Foster James, Virginia Shin-Mui Loh, and illustrated by Wilson Ong, is part of the "Tales of Young Americans" series. "In 1926, 12-year-old Fu Lee['s] . . . parents . . . spent all of their money buying a 'paper son slot' for Lee to go to America. Being a 'paper son' means pretending to be the son of a family already in America. . . . But first he must pass the test at Angel Island Immigration Station in San Francisco." (Publisher's note)

Jansen, Hanna

Over a thousand hills I walk with you; translated from the German by Elizabeth D. Crawford. Carolrhoda Books 2006 342p $16.95
Grades: 7 8 9 10 **Fic**

1. Rwanda -- Fiction
ISBN 1-57505-927-4; 978-1-57505-927-3

LC 2005-21123

Original German edition, 2002

"Eight-year-old Jeanne was the only one of her family to survive the 1994 Rwanda genocide. Then a German family adopted her, and her adoptive mother now tells Jeanne's story in a compelling fictionalized biography that stays true to the traumatized child's bewildered viewpoint." Booklist

Jaramillo, Ann

La linea. Roaring Brook Press 2006 131p o.p.; pa $7.99
Grades: 5 6 7 8 **Fic**

1. Mexicans -- Fiction 2. Siblings -- Fiction 3. Immigrants -- Fiction
ISBN 9781250111234; 9780312373542; 1-59643-154-7; 0-312-37354-6 pa

LC 2005-20133

When fifteen-year-old Miguel's time finally comes to leave his poor Mexican village, cross the border illegally, and join his parents in California, his younger sister's determination to join him soon imperils them both.

"A gripping contemporary survival adventure, this spare first novel is also a heart-wrenching family story of courage, betrayal, and love." Booklist

Jeffrey, Mark

Max Quick: the pocket and the pendant. Harper 2011 294p $15.99
Grades: 4 5 6 7 **Fic**

1. Science fiction 2. Time -- Fiction 3. Voyages and travels -- Fiction 4. Identity (Psychology) -- Fiction
ISBN 978-0-06-198892-9; 0-06-198892-8

LC 2010-42663

First released 2005 as a podcast audiobook

Young Max, a troubled boy with a mysterious past, joins two other youths unaffected when the rest of the world was frozen in time on a journey across America—and time itself—seeking the source of the "Time-stop."

"This fast-paced adventure . . . will keep readers turning pages." SLJ

Jenkins, A. M.

Night road. HarperTeen 2008 362p $16.99; lib bdg $17.89; pa $8.99
Grades: 8 9 10 11 12 **Fic**

1. Horror fiction 2. Vampires -- Fiction 3. Automobile travel -- Fiction
ISBN 978-0-06-054604-5; 0-06-054604-2; 978-0-06-054605-2 lib bdg; 0-06-054605-0 lib bdg; 978-0-06-054606-9 pa; 0-06-054606-9 pa

LC 2007-31703

Battling his own memories and fears, Cole, an extraordinarily conscientious vampire, and Sandor, a more impulsive acquaintance, spend a few months on the road, trying to train a young man who recently joined their ranks.

"The real strength of the novel lies in the noirish atmosphere, accessible prose, and crisp, sharp dialogue." Horn Book

Repossessed. HarperTeen 2007 218p $15.99
Grades: 7 8 9 10 **Fic**
1. School stories 2. Devil -- Fiction 3. Demoniac possession -- Fiction
ISBN 978-0-06-083568-2; 0-06-083568-0
LC 2007-09142
Michael L. Printz Award honor book, 2008
A fallen angel, tired of being unappreciated while doing his pointless, demeaning job, leaves Hell, enters the body of a seventeen-year-old boy, and tries to experience the full range of human feelings before being caught and punished, while the boy's family and friends puzzle over his changed behavior.
"Funny and clever. . . . It's a quick, quirky and entertaining read, with some meaty ideas in it, too." Kliatt

Jennings, Patrick
Odd, weird, and little; Patrick Jennings. Egmont USA 2014 160 p. (hardcover) $15.99
Grades: 4 5 6 7 **Fic**
1. Owls -- fiction 2. Bullies -- Fiction 3. Schools -- Fiction 4. Friendship -- Fiction 5. Middle schools -- Fiction 6. Eccentrics and eccentricities -- Fiction
ISBN 1606843745; 9781606843741
LC 2013018248
In this book, by Patrick Jennings, "Woodrow and his classmates are surprised at the old-fashioned clothing and the tiny, delicate appearance of Toulouse, a newly arrived student from Canada. . . . Woodrow risks regaining his place as top [bullying] victim as he decides to befriend and protect Toulouse. . . . Readers also learn about the psychology behind bullying and about self-empowerment." (Kirkus Reviews)

Jeter, Derek, 1974-
The **contract**; Derek Jeter ; with Paul Mantell. Jeter Publishing, Simon & Schuster Books for Young Readers 2014 176 p. (hardcover) $16.99
Grades: 5 6 7 **Fic**
1. Sports -- Fiction 2. Baseball -- Fiction 3. Goal (Psychology) -- Fiction 4. Teamwork (Sports) -- Fiction
ISBN 1481423126; 9781481423120
LC 2014004045
This book, by baseball player Derek Jeter, "is a middle grade baseball novel. . . . As a young boy, Derek Jeter dreams of being the shortstop for the New York Yankees. He even imagines himself in the World Series. So when Derek is chosen for the Little League Tigers, he hopes to play shortstop. But on the day of the assignments, Derek Starts at second base. Still, he tries his best while he wishes and dreams of that shortstop spot." (Publisher's note)
"A boy named Derek Jeter chases his dreams of playing in the Major Leagues. The author's note states the story is "based on some of my experiences growing up and playing baseball," and the book's "theme" is: "Set Your Goals High." Third-grade Derek (the character) is remarkably--and unrealistically--self-possessed and self-aware, but fans will get a kick out of this kid-version of their hero." Horn Book

Jimenez, Francisco
★ **Breaking** through. Houghton Mifflin 2001 195p il $15; pa $6.95
Grades: 7 8 9 10 11 12 **Fic**
1. California -- Fiction 2. Migrant labor -- Fiction 3. Mexican Americans -- Fiction
ISBN 0-618-01173-0; 0-618-34248-6 pa
LC 2001-16941
Sequel to: The circuit (1997)
Having come from Mexico to California ten years ago, fourteen-year-old Francisco is still working in the fields but fighting to improve his life and complete his education
"For all its recounting of deprivation, this is a hopeful book, told with rectitude and dignity." Horn Book

★ The **circuit** : stories from the life of a migrant child. Houghton Mifflin 1999
Grades: 7 8 9 10 11 12 **Fic**
1. California -- Fiction 2. Family life -- Fiction 3. Migrant labor -- Fiction 4. Mexican Americans -- Fiction
ISBN 978-0-395-97902-0
First published 1997 by University of New Mexico Press
The story "begins in Mexico when the author is very young and his parents inform him that they are going on a very long trip to 'El Norte.' What follows is a series of stories of the family's unending migration from one farm to another as they search for the next harvesting job. Each story is told from the point of view of the author as a young child. The simple and direct narrative stays true to this perspective. . . . Lifting the story up from the mundane, Jiménez deftly portrays the strong bonds of love that hold this family together." Publ Wkly
Followed by: Breaking through (2001)

★ **Reaching** out. Houghton Mifflin 2008 196p $16; pa $6.99
Grades: 7 8 9 10 11 12 **Fic**
1. California -- Fiction 2. Mexican Americans -- Fiction 3. Father-son relationship -- Fiction
ISBN 978-0-618-03851-0; 0-618-03851-5; 978-0-547-25030-4 pa; 0-547-25030-4 pa
Sequel to: Breaking through (2001)
A Pura Belpre Author Award honor book, 2009
"Papa's raging depression intensifies young Jiménez's personal guilt and conflict in the 1960s. . . . He is the first in his Mexican American migrant family to attend college in California. . . . Like his other fictionalized autobiographies, The Circuit (1997) and Breaking Through (2001), this sequel tells Jiménez's personal story in self-contained chapters that join together in a stirring narrative. . . . The spare episodes will draw readers with the quiet daily detail of work, anger, sorrow, and hope." Booklist

Jinks, Catherine
★ **Evil** genius. Harcourt 2007 486p $17
Grades: 7 8 9 10 **Fic**
1. School stories 2. Crime -- Fiction 3. Genius -- Fiction 4. Australia -- Fiction 5. Good and evil -- Fiction
ISBN 978-0-15-205988-0; 0-15-205988-1
LC 2006-14476
First published 2005 in Australia
Child prodigy Cadel Piggot, an antisocial computer hacker, discovers his true identity when he enrolls as a first-year student at an advanced crime academy.
"Cadel's turnabout is convincingly hampered by his difficulty recognizing appropriate outlets for rage, and Jinks' whiplash-inducing suspense writing will gratify fans of Anthony Horowitz's high-tech spy scenarios." Booklist
Other titles about Cadel Piggot are:
Genius squad (2008)

Genius wars (2010)

Genius squad. Harcourt 2008 436p $17
Grades: 7 8 9 10 **Fic**

1. Crime -- Fiction 2. Genius -- Fiction 3. Australia -- Fiction 4. Good and evil -- Fiction
ISBN 978-0-15-205985-9; 0-15-205985-7

After the Axis Institute is blown up, fifteen-year-old Cadell Piggot is unhappily stuck in foster care with constant police surveillance to protect him from the evil Prosper English until he gets an offer to join a mysterious group called Genius Squad.

"Readers who loved Evil Genius will find this sequel as gripping, devilish and wonderfully dark as its predecessor." Publ Wkly

The **genius** wars. Harcourt 2010 378p $17
Grades: 7 8 9 10 **Fic**

1. Science fiction 2. Crime -- Fiction 3. Genius -- Fiction 4. Australia -- Fiction 5. Good and evil -- Fiction
ISBN 978-0-15-206619-2; 0-15-206619-5

LC 2009-49979

Fifteen-year-old genius Cadel Piggot Greenaus sets aside his new, crime-free life when his best friend Sonja is attacked, and he crosses oceans and continents trying to track down his nemesis Prosper English, breaking whatever rules he must.

"The climax is taut, absorbing and tantalizingly ambiguous." Kirkus

★ **How** to catch a bogle; by Catherine Jinks ; illustrated by Sarah Watts. Harcourt Children's Books 2013 320 p. ill. (hardcover) $16.99
Grades: 5 6 7 8 **Fic**

1. Fantasy fiction 2. Alternative histories 3. Orphans -- Fiction 4. Monsters -- Fiction 5. Apprentices -- Fiction 6. Supernatural -- Fiction 7. London (England) -- History -- 19th century -- Fiction 8. Great Britain -- History -- Victoria, 1837-1901 -- Fiction
ISBN 0544087089; 9780544087088

LC 2012045936

This is the first in a historical fantasy trilogy from Catherine Jinks. Here, "child-eating bogles infest Victorian London, providing work aplenty for 'Go-Devil Man' Alfred Bunce and his intrepid young apprentice, Birdie." Birdie is kidnapped by "would-be warlock Roswell Morton, out to capture one of the monsters for his own evil uses." She also must deal with the unwanted "attentions of Miss Edith Eames," who wants "to see Birdie cleaned up and educated in the social graces." (Kirkus Reviews)

The **last** bogler; Catherine Jinks ; illustrated by Sarah Watts. Houghton Mifflin Harcourt 2016 336 p. illustrations, map (hardback) $16.99
Grades: 5 6 7 8 **Fic**

1. Monsters -- Juenile fiction 2. Great Britain -- History -- Victoria, 1837-1901 -- Fiction 3. Orphans -- Fiction 4. Monsters -- Fiction 5. Apprentices -- Fiction 6. Supernatural -- Fiction 7. London (England) -- History -- 19th century -- Fiction
ISBN 9780544086968

LC 2015002204

In this juvenile fantasy adventure novel, by Catherine Jinks, illustrated by Sarah Watts, "in Victorian London . . . , bogle hunter Alfred Bunce needs all the help he can get. So Ned Roach becomes a bogler's apprentice, luring child-eating monsters from their lairs just like his friends Jem and Birdie. . . . Yet . . . in London . . . as the machine age emerges, the very existence of bogles is questioned, and the future of bogling is in jeopardy." (Publisher's note)

"A highly satisfying conclusion to this wonderfully crafted fantasy series." SLJ

A **plague** of bogles; Catherine Jinks ; illustrated by Sarah Watts. Houghton Mifflin Harcourt 2014 336 p. illustrations, map $16.99
Grades: 5 6 7 8 **Fic**

1. Monsters -- Fiction 2. Great Britain -- History -- Victoria, 1837-1901 -- Fiction 3. Orphans -- Fiction 4. Apprentices -- Fiction 5. London (England) -- History -- 19th century -- Fiction
ISBN 054408747X; 9780544087477

LC 2013042823

Sequel to: How to catch a bogle

In this book by Catherine Jinks "Jem Barbary spent most of his early life picking pockets for a wily old crook named Sarah Pickles--until she betrayed him. Now Jem wants revenge, but first he needs a new job. Luckily Alfred the bogler, the man who kills the child-eating monsters that hide in the shadows of Victorian London, needs a new apprentice." (Publisher's note)

Jobling, Curtis

The **rise** of the wolf. Viking Childrens Books 2011 412p (Wereworld) $16.99
Grades: 4 5 6 7 **Fic**

1. Fantasy fiction 2. Adventure fiction 3. Werewolves -- Fiction
ISBN 978-0-670-01330-2; 0-670-01330-7

LC 2010049517

When a vicious beast invades his father's farm and sixteen-year-old Drew suddenly transforms into a werewolf, he runs away from his family, seeking refuge in the most out of the way parts of Lyssia, only to be captured by Lord Bergan's men and forced to battle numerous werecreatures while trying to prove that he is not the enemy.

"Jobling's characterizations are solid, his world-building is complex and fascinating, and the combat scenes are suitably exciting. The book's themes are familiar—lost prince in exile, voyage of self-discovery, young heroes rebelling against injustice and evil—but Jobling uses them to tell a thoroughly enjoyable adventure that makes particularly inventive use of its shapeshifter elements and mythology." Publ Wkly

Jocelyn, Marthe

How it happened in Peach Hill. Wendy Lamb Books 2007 232p $15.99; lib bdg $18.99
Grades: 6 7 8 9 **Fic**

1. Clairvoyance -- Fiction 2. New York (State) -- Fiction 3. Swindlers and swindling -- Fiction 4. Mother-daughter relationship -- Fiction
ISBN 978-0-375-83701-2; 0-375-93701-9; 978-0-375-93701-9 lib bdg; 0-375-93701-3 lib bdg

LC 2006-26688

When fifteen-year-old Annie Grey and her "clairvoyant" mother arrive in Peach Hill, New York, in 1924, each finds a reason for wanting to finally settle down, but to reach their goals they will have to do some serious lying and Annie will have to stand up for herself.

"The blend of coming-of-age, adventure, and intrigue, framed by details of small-town life and a classic con, will appeal to fans of spunky female characters and readers of historical fiction alike." Booklist

★ **Would** you. Wendy Lamb Books 2008 165p $15.99; lib bdg $18.99; pa $6.50
Grades: 8 9 10 11 12 **Fic**

1. Coma -- Fiction 2. Sisters -- Fiction 3. Family life -- Fiction 4.

Medical care -- Fiction 5. Traffic accidents -- Fiction
ISBN 978-0-375-83703-6; 0-375-83703-5; 978-0-375-93703-3 lib bdg; 0-375-93703-X lib bdg; 978-0-375-83704-3 pa; 0-375-83704-3 pa

LC 2007-18913

When her beloved sister, Claire, steps in front of a car and winds up in a coma, Nat's anticipated summer of working, hanging around with friends, and seeing Claire off to college is transformed into a nightmare of doctors, hospitals, and well-meaning neighbors.

"Jocelyn captures a teen's thoughts and reactions in a time of incredible anguish without making her overly dramatic. Readers will fly through the pages of this book, crying, laughing, and crying some more." SLJ

John, Antony

Five flavors of dumb. Dial Books 2010 337p $16.99
Grades: 7 8 9 10 Fic

1. Deaf -- Fiction 2. Rock musicians -- Fiction 3. Seattle (Wash.) -- Fiction
ISBN 978-0-8037-3433-3; 0-8037-3433-6

LC 2009-44449

Eighteen-year-old Piper is profoundly hearing impaired and resents her parent's decision raid her college fund to get cochlear implants for her baby sister. She becomes the manager for her classmates' popular rock band, called Dumb, giving her the chance to prove her capabilities to her parents and others, if only she can get the band members to get along.

"Readers interested in any of the narrative strands . . . will find a solid, satisfyingly complex story here." Bull Cent Child Books

John, Jory

The **terrible** two; by Mac Barnett & Jory John ; illustrated by Kevin Cornell. Harry N. Abrams 2015 224 p. illustrations (The terrible two) (hardback) $13.95
Grades: 4 5 6 7 8 Fic

1. School stories 2. Humorous stories 3. Tricks -- Fiction 4. Schools -- Fiction 5. Practical jokes -- Fiction 6. Moving, Household -- Fiction
ISBN 1419714910; 9781419714917

LC 2014027503

"Miles Murphy is not happy to be moving. In his old school, everyone knew him as the town's best prankster, but Miles quickly discovers that Yawnee Valley already has a prankster, and a great one. If Miles is going to take the title from this mystery kid, he is going to have to raise his game. It's prankster against prankster in an epic war of trickery, until the two finally decide to join forces and pull off the biggest prank ever seen." (Publisher's note)

"Cornell's (The Chicken Squad) b&w cartoons layer on the laughs, especially when portraying the megalomaniacal Principal Barkin, and Barnett and John's deadpan writing lets Yawnee Valley's absurdity shine." Pub Wkly

The **terrible** two get worse; Mac Barnett, Jory John ; illustrated by Kevin Cornell. Amulet Books 2016 224 p. illustrations (hardback) $13.95
Grades: 4 5 6 7 8 Fic

1. Humorous fiction 2. Friendship -- Fiction 3. Practical jokes -- Fiction˙ 4. School superintendants and principals -- Fiction 5. Tricks -- Fiction 6. Schools -- Fiction
ISBN 9781419716805

LC 2015011114

Sequel to: The terrible two

In this book, by Mac Barnett and Jory John, illustrated by Kevin Cornell, "On their own, pranksters Miles and Niles were pretty devious. Now that they've formed a pranking duo, they're terrible! But their powers will be tested when their favorite nemesis, Principal Barkin, is replaced by his stern and cunning father, Former Principal Barkin. Now Miles and Niles will do just about anything to get their old antagonist back --including pranking alongside him." (Publisher's note)

"This humorous sequel makes for engaging, fast-paced reading that again highlights the meaning of friendship, and animated, amusing cartoon illustrations enhance and extend the story." Booklist

Johnson, Angela, 1961-

★ A **certain** October; Angela Johnson. Simon & Schuster Books For Young Readers 2012 176 p. (hardback) $16.99
Grades: 7 8 9 10 11 12 Fic

1. Bildungsromans 2. Death -- Fiction 3. Guilt -- Fiction 4. Teenagers -- Fiction 5. Autism -- Fiction 6. Friendship -- Fiction 7. High schools -- Fiction
ISBN 9781442417267; 9780689865053; 9780689870651

LC 2012001595

In this book, "when a terrible accident occurs, Scotty feels responsible for the loss of someone she hardly knew, and the world goes wrong. She cannot tell what is a dream and what is real. Her friends are having a hard time getting through to her and her family is preoccupied with their own trauma. But the prospect of a boy, a dance, and the possibility that everything can fall back into place soon help Scotty realize that she is capable of adding her own flavor to life." (Publisher's note)

★ A **cool** moonlight. Dial Bks. 2003 133p hardcover o.p. pa $6.99
Grades: 4 5 6 Fic

1. Skin -- Diseases -- Fiction
ISBN 0-8037-2846-8; 0-14-240284-2 pa

LC 2002-31521

Nine-year-old Lila, born with xeroderma pigmentosum, a skin disease that make her sensitive to sunlight, makes secret plans to feel the sun's rays on her tenth birthday

"The book's real magic resides in the spell cast by Johnson's spare, lucid, lyrical prose. Using simple words and vivid sensory images, she creates Lila's inner world as a place of quiet intensity." Booklist

★ The **first** part last. Simon & Schuster Bks. for Young Readers 2003 131p $15.95
Grades: 7 8 9 10 Fic

1. Infants -- Fiction 2. Teenage fathers -- Fiction 3. African Americans -- Fiction
ISBN 0-689-84922-2

LC 2002-36512

Prequel to Heaven (1998)
Michael L. Printz Award, 2004

Bobby's carefree teenage life changes forever when he becomes a father and must care for his adored baby daughter.

"Brief, poetic, and absolutely riveting." SLJ
Followed by: Sweet hereafter (2010)

★ **Heaven**. Simon & Schuster Bks. for Young Readers 1998 138p $16.95; pa $7.99
Grades: 6 7 8 9 Fic

1. Adoption -- Fiction 2. African Americans -- Fiction
ISBN 0-689-82229-4; 1-4424-0342-X pa

LC 98-3291

Coretta Scott King Award for text, 1999

Fourteen-year-old Marley's seemingly perfect life in the small town of Heaven is disrupted when she discovers that her father and mother are not her real parents

"In spare, often poetic prose . . . Johnson relates Marley's insightful quest into what makes a family." SLJ

★ **Sweet,** hereafter; Angela Johnson. 1st ed. Simon and Schuster Books for Young Readers 2010 118 p. (paperback) $7.99; (hardcover) $16.99

Grades: 7 8 9 10 **Fic**

1. Iraq War, 2003-2011 2. African Americans -- Fiction 3. Iraq War, 2003-2011 -- Fiction

ISBN 0689873859; 9780689873867; 9780689873850; 0689873867

LC 2009027618

"Grades seven to ten." (Bull Cent Child Books)

"Johnson concludes the trilogy that began with Heaven (1998) and The First Part Last (2003). . . . Johnson's stripped-down, poetic prose is filled with shattering emotional truths about war's incalculable devastation, love's mysteries, and the bewildering, necessary search for happiness." Booklist

"With heartfelt empathy, we share in Shoogy's personal loss and her need for a new direction. Characters from the two other titles reappear, and we get a glimpse of how their lives are moving forward. This book belongs in all junior and senior high school collections, especially those who already own the first two titles. . . . Johnson now has one more well-woven character development novel to her name." Libr Media Connect

★ **Toning** the sweep. Orchard Bks. 1993 103p hardcover o.p. pa $5.99

Grades: 6 7 8 9 **Fic**

1. Death -- Fiction 2. Family life -- Fiction 3. Grandmothers -- Fiction 4. African Americans -- Fiction

ISBN 0-531-05476-4; 0-531-08626-7 lib bdg; 978-0-590-48142-7 pa; 0-590-48142-8 pa

LC 92-34062

Coretta Scott King Award (Author) (1994)

Margaret A. Edwards Award (2018)

On a visit to her grandmother Ola, who is dying of cancer in her house in the desert, fourteen-year-old Emmie hears many stories about the past and her family history and comes to a better understanding of relatives both dead and living

"Full of subtle nuance, the novel is overlaid with meaning about the connections of family and the power of friendship." SLJ

Johnson, J. J.

★ The **theory** of everything; by J.J. Johnson Peachtree Publishers 2012 334 p. ill. (hardcover) $16.95

Grades: 7 8 9 10 **Fic**

1. Bereavement -- Fiction 2. Interpersonal relations -- Fiction 3. Grief -- Fiction 4. Friendship -- Fiction 5. Best friends -- Fiction 6. New York (State) -- Fiction 7. Loss (Psychology) -- Fiction 8. Family life -- New York (State) -- Fiction

ISBN 1561456233; 9781561456239

LC 2011020973

In this novel, by J. J. Johnson, "ever since Sarah Jones's best friend Jamie died in a freak accident, life has felt sort of . . . random. Sarah has always followed the rules. . . . Now what? . . . In a last ditch effort to pull it together, Sarah ends up working for Roy, a local eccentric who owns a Christmas tree farm, and who might also be trying to understand the rules, patterns, and connections in life." (Publisher's note)

Johnson, Jaleigh

The **door** to the lost; Jaleigh Johnson. Delacorte Press 2018 304 p. (hc) $16.99

Grades: 5 6 7 8 **Fic**

1. Fantasy fiction 2. Magic -- fiction

ISBN 9781101933169; 9781101933183

LC 2017038305

In this book, by Jaleigh Johnson, "there was no warning the day magic died in Talhaven. It happened with a giant explosion and the arrival of a skyship full of children, all with magic running through their veins and no memory of home. Rook and Drift are two of those children, and ever since that day, they've been on the run, magical refugees in a world that doesn't trust magic. Because magic doesn't die right away--it decays, twists, and poisons all that it touches." (Publisher's note)

★ The **mark** of the dragonfly; Jaleigh Johnson. First edition Delacorte Press 2014 400 p. map (glb) $19.99; (hc) $16.99

Grades: 5 6 7 8 **Fic**

1. Magic -- fiction 2. Adventure and adventurers -- fiction 3. Fantasy

ISBN 0385376456; 9780385376457; 9780385376150

LC 2013019716

This book, by Jaleigh Johnson, is an "adventure story about a mysterious girl and a fearless boy, set in a magical world. . . . Piper has never seen the Mark of the Dragonfly until she finds the girl amid the wreckage of a caravan in the Meteor Fields. The girl doesn't remember a thing about her life, but the intricate tattoo on her arm is proof that she's from the Dragonfly Territories and that she's protected by the king. Which means a reward for Piper if she can get the girl home." (Publisher's note)

"Heart, brains and courage find a home in a steampunk fantasy worthy of a nod from Baum. . . . A well-imagined world of veritable adventure." Kirkus

Other titles in this series are:

The secrets of Solace (2016)

The quest to the Uncharted Lands (2017)

Johnson, Maureen

13 little blue envelopes. HarperCollins Publishers 2005 317p $15.99; pa $8.99

Grades: 8 9 10 11 12 **Fic**

1. Aunts -- Fiction 2. Europe -- Fiction 3. Voyages and travels -- Fiction

ISBN 0-06-054141-5; 0-06-054143-1 pa

LC 2005-02658

When seventeen-year-old Ginny receives a packet of mysterious envelopes from her favorite aunt, she leaves New Jersey to criss-cross Europe on a sort of scavenger hunt that transforms her life.

"Equal parts poignant, funny and inspiring, this tale is sure to spark wanderlust." Publ Wkly

Followed by: The last little blue envelope (2011)

The **last** little blue envelope. HarperTeen 2011 282p $16.99

Grades: 8 9 10 11 12 **Fic**

1. Aunts -- Fiction 2. Europe -- Fiction 3. Artists -- Fiction 4. Letters -- Fiction 5. Voyages and travels -- Fiction 6. Swindlers and swindling -- Fiction

ISBN 978-0-06-197679-7; 0-06-197679-2

LC 2010033580

"Ginny's narrative, told in an intelligent, third-person voice, establishes her firmly as a sympathetic, often hilarious everygirl, whose efforts to understand herself and who she'd like to be are fraught with moments both romantic and heartbreaking. Johnson's skill in creating secondary characters that are unusual, realistically flawed and utterly believable is again on display here. . . . This is an appealingly smart and honest read that fans of the first will find deeply satisfying." Kirkus

The **madness** underneath; Maureen Johnson. G. P. Putnam's Sons 2013 304 p. (Shades of London) (hardback) $17.99

Grades: 6 7 8 9 10 **Fic**

1. Ghost stories 2. Mystery fiction 3. Paranormal fiction 4. Ghosts -- Fiction 5. Murder -- Fiction 6. England -- Fiction 7. Schools -- Fiction 8. Boarding schools -- Fiction 9. London (England) -- Fiction

ISBN 039925661X; 9780399256615

LC 2012026755

This paranormal mystery novel, by Maureen Johnson, is book two of "The Shades of London Trilogy." "After her near-fatal run-in with the Jack the Ripper copycat, Rory Devereaux . . . [has] become a human terminus, with the power to eliminate ghosts on contact. . . . The Ripper may be gone, but now there is a string of new inexplicable deaths threatening London. Rory has evidence that the deaths are no coincidence. Something much more sinister is going on." (Publisher's note)

The **name** of the star. G. P. Putnam's Sons 2011 384p $16.99

Grades: 6 7 8 9 10 **Fic**

1. Ghost stories 2. School stories 3. Homicide -- Fiction 4. Witnesses -- Fiction 5. London (England) -- Fiction

ISBN 978-0-399-25660-8; 0-399-25660-1; 9780399256608; 0399256601

LC 2011009003

"Johnson's trademark sense of humor serves to counterbalance some grisly murders in this page-turner, which opens her Shades of London series. . . . As one mutilated body after another turns up, Johnson . . . amplifies the story's mysteries with smart use of and subtle commentary on modern media shenanigans and London's infamously extensive surveillance network. . . . Readers looking for nonstop fun, action, and a little gore have come to the right place." Publ Wkly

Scarlett fever. Point/Scholastic 2010 336p $16.99

Grades: 7 8 9 10 **Fic**

1. School stories 2. Actors -- Fiction 3. Family life -- Fiction 4. New York (N.Y.) -- Fiction 5. Hotels and motels -- Fiction 6. Dating (Social customs) -- Fiction

ISBN 978-0-439-89928-4; 0-439-89928-1

Sequel to: Suite Scarlett (2008)

Fifteen-year-old Scarlett, who is beginning to get over her breakup with Eric, stays busy as assistant to her theatrical-agent friend who is not only promoting Scarlett's brother Spencer, but also a new client whose bad-boy brother has transferred to Scarlett's school.

"While the novel may be enjoyed for the light if slightly madcap romance that it is, it is notable for its attention to social class and to the Martins' struggles with money." SLJ

The **shadow** cabinet; Maureen Johnson. G. P. Putnam's Sons, an imprint of Penguin Group (USA) 2015 384 p. (Shades of London) (hardback) $17.99

Grades: 6 7 8 9 10 **Fic**

1. Ghost stories 2. London (England) -- Fiction 3. Ghosts -- Fiction 4. Murder -- Fiction 5. England -- Fiction 6. Schools -- Fiction 7. Boarding schools -- Fiction

ISBN 0399256628; 9780399256622

LC 2014031153

"Time is running out as Rory fights to find her friends and the ghost squad struggles to stop Jane from unleashing her spectral nightmare on the entire city. In the process, they'll discover the existence of an organization that underpins London itself . . . and Rory will learn that someone she trusts has been keeping a tremendous secret." (Publisher's note)

"The plot . . . is among Johnson's finest and incorporates creepy bits of backstory, fascinating historical asides, and truly ghoulish side characters--take, for example, a lumpen cemetery ghost that is 'just a glob of people pieces mixed together.'" Booklist

Suite Scarlett. Scholastic Point 2008 353p $16.99

Grades: 6 7 8 9 10 **Fic**

1. Authorship -- Fiction 2. Family life -- Fiction 3. New York (N.Y.) -- Fiction 4. Hotels and motels -- Fiction

ISBN 978-0-439-89927-7; 0-439-89927-3

LC 2007-041903

Fifteen-year-old Scarlett Marvin is stuck in New York City for the summer working at her quirky family's historic hotel, but her brother's attractive new friend and a seasonal guest who offers her an intriguing and challenging writing project improve her outlook.

"Utterly winning, madcap Manhattan farce, crafted with a winking, urbane narrative and tight, wry dialogue." Booklist

Another title about Scarlett is:
Scarlett fever (2010)

Truly devious; a mystery. Maureen Johnson ; [edited by] Katherine Tegen. Katherine Tegen Books 2018 432 p. (hardcover) $17.99

Grades: 8 9 10 11 12 **Fic**

1. Mystery fiction 2. Private schools -- Fiction 3. Cold cases (Criminal investigation) -- Fiction

ISBN 9780062338051

LC 2017951264

"Stevie Bell is a dyed-in-the-wool true-crime buff. And what better place to deepen her understanding than at Ellingham Academy, the Vermont private school founded in the 1930s by wealthy eccentric Albert Ellingham? Partly because the custom courses of study are tailored to students' passion—writing, engineering, film, math—but also because the school was the scene of a notorious crime not long after it opened: Albert Ellingham's wife and daughter were kidnapped, ostensibly for ransom, and a student was killed. His wife's body was found eventually, but his daughter, Alice, never was. Stevie plans to solve the case. But when a classmate is killed, everything changes." (School Library Journal)

Johnson "deftly twists two mysteries together--Stevie's investigation is interspersed with case files and recollections from the Ellington kidnapping--and the result is a suspenseful, attention-grabbing mystery with no clear solution. Invested readers, never fear—this is just the first in a series." Booklist

Another title in this series is:
The vanishing stair (2019)

The **vanishing** stair; Maureen Johnson. Katherine Tegen Books 2019 384 p. illustrations (Truly devious) (hardback) $17.99

Grades: 8 9 10 11 12 **Fic**

1. Mystery fiction 2. Private schools -- Fiction 3. Cold cases (Criminal investigation) -- Fiction

ISBN 9780062338082

LC 2018959001

"The Truly Devious case--an unsolved kidnapping and triple murder that rocked Ellingham Academy in 1936--has consumed Stevie for years. It's the very reason she came to the academy. But then her classmate was murdered, and her parents quickly pull her out of school." (Publisher's note)

"In this second trilogy installment, Johnson gives and she takes away: a few major mysteries are satisfying solved, but other long-standing riddles remain tantalizingly indecipherable, and several new ones come into play by the enigmatic end." Booklist

Johnson, Terry Lynn

Ice dogs; by Terry Lynn Johnson. Houghton Mifflin, Houghton Mifflin Harcourt 2013 288 p. $16.99

Grades: 5 6 7 8 9 **Fic**

1. Wilderness survival -- Fiction 2. Sled dog racing -- fiction 3. Dogs -- Fiction 4. Alaska -- Fiction 5. Survival -- Fiction 6. Sled dogs -- Fiction 7. Dogsledding -- Fiction 8. Wilderness areas -- Fiction

ISBN 0547899262; 9780547899268

LC 2012045061

In this book, by Terry Lynn Johnson, "Victoria Secord, a fourteen-year-old Alaskan dogsled racer, loses her way on a routine outing with her dogs. With food gone and temperatures dropping, her survival and that of her dogs and the mysterious boy she meets in the woods is entirely up to her." (Publisher's note)

Johnson, Varian

The **great** Greene heist; by Varian Johnson. Arthur A. Levine Books 2014 240 p. (hardcover) $16.99

Grades: 5 6 7 8 **Fic**

1. School stories 2. Schools -- Fiction 3. Elections -- Fiction 4. Friendship -- Fiction 5. Best friends -- Fiction 6. Middle schools -- Fiction 7. Practical jokes -- Fiction

ISBN 0545525527; 9780545525534; 0545525535; 9780545525527

LC 2013029145

"Jackson Greene has reformed. No, really he has. He was once the best con artist at Maplewood Middle School, and everyone still talks about his Blitz at the Fitz.... But after Principal Kelsey caught him in his office, Jackson swore off scheming for good. Then Keith Sinclair--loser of the Blitz--announces he's running for school president, against Jackson's former almost-girlfriend Gaby de la Cruz." (Publisher's note)

"This fast-paced caper reads like Ocean's 11 for the middle-school set, and that's no coincidence: Johnson (Saving Maddie, 2010) openly credits the film as inspiration, and he has pretty much pulled it off, right down to the dizzying plot twists, incredulous access to the latest tech, and unflappable swagger. " Booklist

★ The **Parker** inheritance; Varian Johnson. Arthur A. Levine Books 2018 331 p. (hardback) $16.99

Grades: 4 5 6 7 **Fic**

1. Mystery fiction 2. African American girls -- fiction 3. Friendship -- Fiction 4. Grandmothers -- Fiction 5. South Carolina -- Fiction 6. Buried treasure -- Fiction 7. African Americans -- Fiction 8. Detective and mystery stories 9. Mothers and daughters -- Fiction 10. Treasure troves -- fiction

ISBN 9780545952798; 9780545952781; 9780545946179

LC 2017042551

Boston Globe–Horn Book Honor Book: Fiction and Poetry (2018)

Coretta Scott King (Author) Honor Book (2019)

In this novel, by Varian Johnson, "when Candice finds a letter in an old attic in Lambert, South Carolina, she isn't sure she should read it. It's addressed to her grandmother, who left the town in shame. But the letter describes a young woman. An injustice that happened decades ago. A mystery enfolding the letter-writer. And the fortune that awaits the person who solves the puzzle. So with the help of Brandon Jones . . . , she begins to decipher the clues." (Publisher's note)

"A dazzling and emotional read that deals with serious topics such as bullying, racism, and divorce." Booklist

To catch a cheat; A Jackson Greene Novel. by Varian Johnson. Arthur A. Levine Books, an imprint of Scholastic Inc. 2016 256 p. (hardcover : alk. paper) $16.99

Grades: 5 6 7 8 **Fic**

1. School stories 2. Extortion -- Fiction 3. Friendship -- Fiction 4. African Americans -- Fiction 5. Cheating (Education) -- Fiction 6. Schools -- Fiction 7. Cheating -- Fiction 8. Best friends -- Fiction 9. Middle schools -- Fiction

ISBN 9780545722391; 9780545722407

LC 2015025232

Sequel to: The Great Greene Heist

In this book, by Varian Johnson, "Jackson Greene . . . is officially retired from conning, so Principal Kelsey is (mostly) off his back. His friends have great new projects of their own. . . . Then Jackson receives a link to a faked security video that seems to show him and the rest of Gang Greene flooding the school gym. The jerks behind the video threaten to pass it to the principal -- unless Jackson steals an advance copy of the school's toughest exam." (Publisher's note)

"Fast-paced antics, clever writing, and a diverse cast of characters give this ample broad appeal." Booklist

Johnson-Shelton, Nils

The **Invisible** Tower. HarperCollins 2011 335p (Otherworld chronicles) $16.99

Grades: 4 5 6 7 **Fic**

1. Adventure fiction 2. Kings

ISBN 978-0-06-207086-9; 0-06-207086-X

LC 2011022928

A twelve-year-old boy learns that he is actually King Arthur brought back to life in the twenty-first century—and that the fate of the universe rests in his hands.

"This new take on the Arthurian legends, told in third-person, pits wisecracking contemporary teens with their contemporary banter. . . . against all manner of obstacles. . . . It's always high-spirited and fun. Gives new life to Arthurian legends and may just send readers back to more traditional tellings." Kirkus

The **seven** swords; Nils Johnson-Shelton. HarperCollins 2013 368 p. (Otherworld chronicles) (hardback) $16.99

Grades: 4 5 6 7 **Fic**

1. Arthurian romances -- Adaptations 2. Fantasy fiction -- fiction 3. Adventure and adventurers -- Fiction

ISBN 0062070940; 9780062070944

LC 2012019088

This juvenile adventure fantasy, by Nils Johnson-Shelton, second in the "Otherworld Chronicles," follows "Artie Kingfisher, the new King Arthur. On a quest to recover seven magical swords of the Dark Ages, Artie and Kay gather 'New Knights of the Round Table' and try to unite two worlds. Standing in their way is Lordess Morgaine. . . . Artie and his band travel from Ohio via crossover points between worlds in search of swords in Sweden, France and Japan." (Kirkus Reviews)

Johnston, E. K.

Prairie fire; E.K. Johnston. Carolrhoda Books 2015 304 p. (trade hard cover : alk. paper) $18.99

Grades: 7 8 9 10 11 12 **Fic**

1. Dragons -- Fiction 2. Friendship -- Fiction 3. Fame -- Fiction 4. High schools -- Fiction 5. Bards and bardism -- Fiction 6. Family life -- Canada -- Fiction 7. Adventure and adventurers -- Fiction
ISBN 146773909X; 9781467739092; 9781467761819; 9781467776790; 9781467776806; 9781467776813

LC 2014008995

Sequel to: The story of Owen

In this young adult novel by E. K. Johnston, the sequel to "The Story of Owen," "Every dragon slayer owes the Oil Watch a period of service, and young Owen was no exception. What made him different was that he did not enlist alone. His two closest friends stood with him shoulder to shoulder. . . . But the arc of history is long and hardened by dragon fire. Try as they might, Owen and his friends could not twist it to their will." (Publisher's note)

"A fantasy YA novel that steers clear of love triangles, teen angst, and a tidy ending is hard to come by; Prairie Fire and its prequel are must-haves." SLJ

The **story** of Owen; dragon slayer of Trondheim. E. K. Johnston. Carolrhoda Lab 2014 305 p. (hardcover) $17.95

Grades: 7 8 9 10 11 12 **Fic**

1. Adventure fiction 2. Canada -- Fiction 3. Dragons -- Fiction 4. Family life -- Fiction 5. Fame -- Fiction 6. Schools -- Fiction 7. High schools -- Fiction 8. Bards and bardism -- Fiction 9. Family life -- Canada -- Fiction 10. Adventure and adventurers -- Fiction
ISBN 9781467710664; 1467710660

LC 2013020492

William C. Morris Finalist (2015)

In this book, author E. K. Johnston, "envisions an Earth nearly identical to our own, with one key difference: dragons. . . . After 16-year-old Siobhan McQuaid agrees to become the bard for dragon-slayer-in-training Owen Thorskard, who has moved with his famous dragon-slaying family to her small Ontario town, she winds up at the.center of a grassroots effort to understand an odd spike in dragon numbers." (Publishers Weekly)

"Humor, pathos and wry social commentary unite in a cleverly drawn, marvelously diverse world. Refreshingly, the focus is on the pair as friends and partners, not on potential romance." Kirkus

Johnston, Julie, 1941-

Little red lies; by Julie Johnston. Tundra Books 2013 352 p. (hardcover) $19.95

Grades: 7 8 9 **Fic**

1. Family life -- Fiction 2. College and school drama 3. Teenage girls -- Fiction
ISBN 1770493131; 9781770493131; 9781770493148

LC 2012947608

In this book by Julie Johnston "the war is over, but for thirteen-year-old Rachel, the battle has just begun. Putting childhood behind her, she knows what she wants--to prove she has acting talent worthy of the school drama club, and what she doesn't want--to romantically fall for someone completely inappropriate. Ultimately, she finds a way to come to terms with life as it reaches an end and life as it begins." (Publisher's note)

Johnston, Tony

Any small goodness; a novel of the barrio. illustrations by Raúl Colón. Blue Sky Press (NY) 2001 128p il $16.95; pa $4.99

Grades: 4 5 6 7 **Fic**

1. Mexican Americans -- Fiction 2. Los Angeles (Calif.) -- Fiction
ISBN 0-439-18936-5; 0-439-23384-4 pa

LC 99-59877

Arturo and his family and friends share all kinds of experiences living in the barrio of East Los Angeles—reclaiming their names, playing basketball, championing the school librarian, and even starting their own gang

"The characters are likable and warm. . . . The message is positive and the episodes, while occasionally serious, are more often humorous and gratifying." SLJ

Beast rider; a boy's journey beyond the border. Tony Johnston and María Elena Fontanot de Rhoads. Amulet Books 2019 192 p. (hardback) $17.99

Grades: 6 7 8 9 **Fic**

1. Violence -- Fiction 2. Voyages and travels -- Fiction 3. Mexico -- Immigration and emigration -- Fiction 4. Mexico -- Fiction 5. Emigration and immigration -- Fiction
ISBN 9781419733635

LC 2018038535

In this novel, by Tony Johnston and María Elena Fontanot de Rhoads, "[12]-year-old Manuel leaves his small town in Mexico to join his older brother in Los Angeles. To cross the US border, he must become a 'beast rider'--someone who hops on a train. The first time he tries, he is stopped by the Mexican police. . . . When he finally arrives in LA and is reunited with his brother, he is elated. But the longer he's there, the more he realizes that something isn't right." (Publisher's note)

"Told directly and effectively, this story gives readers an opportunity to be present for one young man's harrowing journey as an immigrant to the U.S." (School Library Journal)

Jones, Diana Wynne

★ **Enchanted** glass. Greenwillow Books 2010 292p $16.99

Grades: 6 7 8 9 **Fic**

1. Magic -- Fiction 2. Orphans -- Fiction 3. Villages -- Fiction 4. Great Britain -- Fiction
ISBN 978-0-06-186684-5; 0-06-186684-9

LC 2009006195

After his grandfather dies, Andrew Hope inherits a house and surrounding land in an English village, but things become very complicated when young orphan Aidan shows up and suddenly a host of variously magical townsfolk and interlopers start intruding on their lives.

"Jones hits all the bases, combining fluid storytelling, sly humor, and exquisitely drawn characters." Booklist

★ **Howl's** moving castle. Greenwillow Books 1986 212p hardcover o.p. pa $6.99

Grades: 5 6 7 8 **Fic**

1. Fantasy fiction
ISBN 0-06-147878-4 pa; 0-688-06233-4; 978-0-06-147878-9 pa

LC 85-21981

Sophie "resigns herself to making a living as a hatter and helping her younger sisters prepare to make their fortunes. But adventure seeks her out in the shop where she sits alone dreaming over her hats. The wicked Witch of the Waste, angered by 'competition' in the area, turns her into an old woman, so she seeks refuge inside the strange moving castle of the wizard Howl. Howl, advertised by his apprentice as an eater of souls, lives a mad, frantic life trying to escape the curse the witch has placed on him, find the perfect girl of his dreams and end the contract he and his fire demon have entered. Sophie, against her best instincts and at first unaware of her own powers, falls in love. . . . Grade six and up." (SLJ)

"Satisfyingly, Sophie meets a fate far exceeding her dreary expectations. This novel is an exciting, multi-faceted puzzle, peopled with vibrant, captivating characters. A generous sprinkling of humor adds potency to this skillful author's spell." Voice Youth Advocates

Followed by: House of many ways (2008)

The **islands** of Chaldea; by Diana Wynne Jones ; completed by Ursula Jones. Greenwillow Books, an imprint of HarperCollinsPublishers 2013 368 p. (trade ed.) $17.99

Grades: 4 5 6 7 8 **Fic**

1. Cats -- Fiction 2. Fantasy fiction 3. Aunts -- Fiction 4. Magic -- Fiction 5. Self-confidence -- Fiction 6. Voyages and travels -- Fiction

ISBN 0062295071; 9780062295071

LC 2013036422

In this book, by Diana Wynne Jones and Ursula Jones, "Aileen comes from a long line of magic makers, and her Aunt Beck is the most powerful magician on Skarr. But even though she is old enough, Aileen's magic has yet to reveal itself. When Aileen is sent over the sea on a mission for the King, she worries that she'll be useless and in the way. A powerful (but mostly invisible) cat changes all of that—and with every obstacle Aileen faces, she becomes stronger and more confident and her magic blooms." (Publisher's note)

"Diana Wynne Jones's humor, insight, and brisk, inventive style shine in this posthumously published novel. Aileen is embarrassed when she fails her Wise Woman initiation. She discovers her own "very vigorous" powers on a quest with her Wise Aunt Beck, a prince, and his attendant through the islands of Chaldea. Jones's imaginative vigor is unabated in this last, picaresque novel." Horn Book

Jones, Kelly

Murder, magic, and what we wore; Kelly Jones. Alfred A. Knopf 2017 293 p. (hardcover) $17.99

Grades: 7 8 9 10 11 12 **Fic**

1. Spy stories 2. Magic -- Fiction 3. Spies -- Fiction 4. Magic -- fiction 5. Murder -- fiction 6. Dressmaking -- fiction 7. Great Britain -- History -- 1800-1837 -- fiction 8. London (England) -- History -- 1800-1950 -- fiction

ISBN 055353520X; 9780553535228; 9780553535204

LC 2017297170

In this book, by Kelly Jones, "Annis Whitworth has just learned that her father is dead and all his money is missing. . . . [So] she decides to become a spy . . . [and] crafts a new double life for herself. . . . [Annis] will appear to live a quiet life . . . with her aunt, and Annis-in-disguise as Madame Martine, glamour artist. . . . That way she can earn a living, maintain her social standing, and . . . follow the coded clues her father left behind and unmask his killer." (Publisher's note)

"A cross between Jane Austen dramas and Harriet the Spy, this delightful strong female-led title mixes historical fiction and spy mystery with a touch of magic to produce a story filled with adventure. " SLJ

Jones, Kimberly K.

Sand dollar summer. Margaret K. McElderry Books 2006 206p $15.95; pa $5.99

Grades: 5 6 7 8 **Fic**

1. Maine -- Fiction 2. Islands -- Fiction 3. Family life -- Fiction

ISBN 978-1-4169-0362-8; 1-4169-0362-3; 978-1-4169-5834-5 pa; 1-4169-5834-7 pa

LC 2005012740

When twelve-year-old Lise spends the summer on an island in Maine with her self-reliant mother and bright—but oddly mute—younger brother, her formerly safe world is complicated by an aged Indian neighbor, her mother's childhood friend, and a hurricane.

"The drama in [the] smart, tough, first-person narrative is understated; the spaces between the words are as eloquent as what is said. . . . The family story . . . is exquisitely told." Booklist

Jones, Marcia Thornton

Woodford Brave; Marcia Thornton Jones; illustrated by Kevin Whipple. Calkins Creek 2015 200 p. illustrations $16.95

Grades: 2 3 4 5 6 **Fic**

1. Friendship -- Fiction 2. World War, 1939-1945 -- Children -- Fiction

ISBN 1629793051; 9781629793054

In this children's book by Marcia Thornton Jones, illustrated by Kevin Whipple, "while his father is off fighting in World War II, eleven-year-old Cory and his friends spend the summer building go-carts, drawing comics, playing baseball . . . and tracking down Nazi spies. Right and wrong are more complicated than in Cory's beloved comics, and he and his friends soon learn that the world isn't as black and white as they thought. In an age when friendships are deep and complex, Cory makes mistakes and hurtful decisions." (Publisher's note)

"Jones, best known for her contributions to the Bailey School Kids series, has written a moving period piece that explores heroism and the ghosts we all live with." Booklist

Includes bibliographical references (pages 190-192).

Jones, Patrick

★ **Bridge**; Patrick Jones. Darby Creek 2014 92 p. (The alternative) $7.95

Grades: 6 7 8 9 10 11 12 **Fic**

1. School stories 2. Family life -- Fiction 3. High schools -- Fiction 4. Hispanic Americans -- Fiction 5. Unauthorized immigrants -- Fiction 6. Work -- Fiction 7. Schools -- Fiction 8. Illegal aliens -- Fiction 9. Spanish language -- Fiction

ISBN 1467744824; 9781467739030; 9781467744829

LC 2013041390

"José can't keep up. As the only English speaker in a family of undocumented immigrants, he handles everything from taking family members to the doctor to bargaining with the landlord. Plus he works two jobs. With all this responsibility, he's missing a lot of school. . . . José knows he has to turn things around if he wants to graduate from Rondo Alternative High School. Can he raise his grades enough to have a shot at college and a better life?" (Publisher's note)

"The author's effective use of flashbacks and crisp portraits of positive adult characters add further emotional depth to this emotional glimpse at the high-pressure difficulties facing children in immigrant families. References to O'Brien's book will likely spark the interest of readers in that title as well." PW Reviews

Jones, Rob Lloyd

Wild boy and the black terror; Rob Lloyd Jones. Candlewick Press 2015 336 p. illustrations, map $16.99

Grades: 5 6 7 8 **Fic**

1. Serial killers -- Fiction 2. Circus performers -- Fiction 3. Great Britain -- History -- Victoria, 1837-1901 -- Fiction 4. Murderers--England--London 5. Detective and mystery stories

ISBN 0763662534; 9780763662530

LC 2014945722

This novel by Rob Lloyd Jones is set in "London, 1842. Wild Boy, master detective and former freak-show performer, and Clarissa, circus acrobat and troublemaker, are the secret last hope of a city beset by horror. A poisoner stalks the streets, leaving victims mad with terror--and then dead. Can the Black Terror be traced to a demon called Malphas? Can Wild Boy and Clarissa uncover a cure in time to save the queen and the city?" (Publisher's note)

"Adventure, conspiracy and adrenaline intermingle with dark deeds, devil worship and blood diamonds in this sequel to Wild Boy (2013). . . . The queen and the Gentlemen need them to unearth the cause of a mysterious sickness that blackens veins and sends victims into a stupor of madness before tragic death. . . . Can the duo save all of London from a hellbent killer? Diamonds are a Wild Boy's worst enemy in this steampunk romp not intended for the faint—or black—of heart." Kirkus

Jones, Traci L.

★ **Silhouetted** by the blue. Farrar, Straus & Giroux 2011 200p $16.99

Grades: 5 6 7 8 **Fic**

1. School stories 2. Theater -- Fiction 3. Bereavement -- Fiction 4. African Americans -- Fiction 5. Depression (Psychology) -- Fiction

ISBN 978-0-374-36914-9; 0-374-36914-3

LC 2010008419

After the death of her mother in an automobile accident, seventh-grader Serena, who has gotten the lead in her middle school play, is left to handle the day-to-day challenges of caring for herself and her younger brother when their father cannot pull himself out of his depression.

"Jones has written another winner with this beautiful, haunting tale rich in story and characterization." Booklist

Standing against the wind; 1st ed.; Farrar, Straus and Giroux 2006 184p $16

Grades: 6 7 8 9 **Fic**

1. School stories 2. African Americans -- Fiction 3. City and town life -- Fiction

ISBN 978-0-374-37174-6; 0-374-37174-1

LC 2005-51226

As she tries to escape her poor Chicago neighborhood by winning a scholarship to a prestigious boarding school, shy and studious eighth-grader Patrice discovers that she has more options in life than she previously realized.

"Handled without obscenity, the lively street talk will draw readers to the gripping story of a contemporary kid who works to make her dreams come true." Booklist

Jordan, Rosa

The **goatnappers**; [by] Rosa Jordan. 1st ed.; Peachtree 2007 209p $14.95

Grades: 5 6 7 8 **Fic**

1. School stories 2. Goats -- Fiction 3. Florida -- Fiction 4. Family life -- Fiction

ISBN 978-1-56145-400-6; 1-56145-400-1

LC 2006030173

Sequel to: Lost Goat Lane (2004)

Justin's place as the first high school freshman in twenty years to make the varsity baseball team is at risk when his math grade plummets while he is trying to cope with the abuse of a young billy goat he sold and a visit from his estranged father to Lost Goat Lane.

"Justin's family is beautifully drawn. . . . The animal cruelty issues will draw readers, and so will the friendships across race, gender, and age that show the meaning of community." Booklist

Followed by: The last wild place (2008)

Lost Goat Lane. Peachtree Publisher 2004 197p $14.95

Grades: 5 6 7 8 **Fic**

1. Goats -- Fiction 2. Florida -- Fiction 3. Race relations -- Fiction 4. African Americans -- Fiction

ISBN 1-56145-325-0

LC 2004-5343

Two families—one white, one black—living near one another in rural Florida overcome their suspicions of each other and find ways to work together, with the help of their children and a few goats

"The fully realized characters and the warmth of the story make up for the small sermons. A tender, satisfying offering." SLJ

Other titles in this series are:

The goatnappers (2007)

The last wild place (2008)

Joseph, Lynn

The **color** of my words. HarperCollins Pubs. 2000 138p hardcover o.p. pa $5.99

Grades: 5 6 7 8 **Fic**

1. Siblings -- Fiction 2. Family life -- Fiction 3. Dominican Republic -- Fiction

ISBN 0-06-028232-0; 0-06-447204-3 pa

LC 00-22440

When life gets difficult for Ana Rosa, a twelve-year-old would-be writer living in a small village in the Dominican Republic, she can depend on her older brother to make her feel better—until the life-changing events on her thirteenth birthday

"A finely crafted novel, lovely and lyrical." SLJ

Flowers in the sky; by Lynn Joseph. HarperTeen 2013 240 p. (hardcover) $17.99

Grades: 8 9 10 11 12 **Fic**

1. Bildungsromans 2. New York (N.Y.) -- Fiction 3. Brothers and sisters -- Fiction 4. Love -- Fiction 5. Immigrants -- Fiction 6. Coming of age -- Fiction 7. Dominican Republic -- Fiction 8. Dominican Americans -- Fiction

ISBN 0060297948; 9780060297947

LC 2012038122

In this novel, by Lynn Joseph, "fifteen-year-old Nina Perez . . . must leave her . . . lush island home in Samana, Dominican Republic, when she's sent . . . to live with her brother, Darrio, in New York, to seek out a better life. . . . But then she meets . . . [a] tall, green-eyed boy . . . , who just might help her learn to see beauty in spite of tragedy." (Publisher's note)

Joyce, Graham, 1954-

The **exchange**. Viking 2008 241p $16.99

Grades: 7 8 9 10 **Fic**

1. Tattooing -- Fiction 2. Supernatural -- Fiction 3. Single parent family -- Fiction 4. Dating (Social customs) -- Fiction

ISBN 978-0-670-06207-2; 0-670-06207-3

LC 2007-32160

Cursed by the elderly recluse whose home she and a friend were creeping through late one night, fourteen-year-old Caz soon finds her life disintegrating and realizes she must find a way of lifting the curse—or at least understanding its power.

"Joyce has crafted a bizarre, magically realistic tale. . . . It's a wild ride with subtly moralistic undertones and a surprisingly happy ending that will stay with readers." Booklist

Juby, Susan

★ The **fashion** committee; a novel of art, crime and applied design. Susan Juby. Viking 2017 305 p. illustrations (hardcover) $18.99

Grades: 7 8 9 10 **Fic**

1. Fashion -- Fiction 2. Friendship -- Fiction 3. Competition (Psychology) -- Fiction

ISBN 9780451468789; 9780698151055; 0451468783

LC 2017014294

In this book, by Susan Juby, "Charlie Dean is a style-obsessed girl who eats, sleeps, and breathes fashion. John Thomas-Smith is a boy who forges metal sculptures in his garage and couldn't care less about clothes. Both are gunning for a scholarship to the private art high school that could make all their dreams come true. Whoever wins the fashion competition will win the scholarship--and only one can win." (Publisher's note)

"Juby's thoughtful bildungsroman excels in showcasing and normalizing those on society's fringe—whether it be in her bold portrayal of differing socio-economic class issues or subtle examination of gender identity." Kirkus

Getting the girl; a guide to private investigation, surveillance, and cookery. [by] S. Juby. HarperTeen 2008 341p $16.99; lib bdg $17.89; pa $8.99

Grades: 6 7 8 9 10 **Fic**

1. School stories 2. Mystery fiction 3. Popularity -- Fiction 4. British Columbia -- Fiction

ISBN 978-0-06-076525-5; 0-06-076525-9; 978-0-06-076527-9 lib bdg; 0-06-076527-5 lib bdg; 978-0-06-076528-6 pa; 0-06-076528-3 pa

LC 2008-00788

Ninth-grader Sherman Mack investigates the "Defilers," a secret group at his British Columbia high school that marks certain female students as pariahs, at first because he is trying to protect the girl he has a crush on, but later as a matter of principle.

Juby "applies her signature brand of humor to a detective novel. . . . [This offers a] strong and memorable female cast. . . . Here's hoping that Juby delivers on the promise of sequels." Horn Book

Jung, Mike

Geeks, girls, and secret identities; by Mike Jung ; with illustrations by Mike Maihack. Arthur A. Levine Books 2012 307 p. (hardcover : alk. paper) $16.99

Grades: 3 4 5 6 7 **Fic**

1. Boys' clubs 2. Secrecy -- Fiction 3. Friendship -- fiction 4. Science fiction 5. Clubs -- Fiction 6. Humorous stories 7. Robots -- Fiction 8. Schools -- Fiction 9. Superheroes -- Fiction 10. Middle schools -- Fiction

ISBN 0545335485; 9780545335485; 9780545335492; 9780545392518

LC 2011042548

In author Mike Jung's book, "Vincent Wu is Captain Stupendous's No. 1 Fan, but even he has to admit that Captain Stupendous has been a little off lately. During Professor Mayhem's latest attack, Captain Stupendous barely made it out alive, although he did manage to save Vincent from a giant monster robot. It's Vincent's dream come true . . . until he finds out Captain Stupendous's secret identity: It's Polly Winnicott-Lee, the girl Vincent happens to have a crush on." (Publisher's note)

Kade, J. V.

Bot Wars; by J.V. Kade. Dial Books for Young Readers 2013 368 p. (hardcover) $16.99

Grades: 5 6 7 8 **Fic**

1. Science fiction 2. Apocalyptic fiction 3. Father-son relationship -- Fiction 4. War -- Fiction 5. Robots -- Fiction 6. Fathers -- Fiction 7. Missing persons -- Fiction

ISBN 0803738609; 9780803738607

LC 2012017682

This book is set in the future, where the "Robot Wars [have] left the U.S. in shambles, divided between Bot Territory and the United Districts. Even though the wars ended months ago, 12-year-old Trout St. Kroix is still waiting for his soldier father to come home. When Trout makes one last desperate attempt to bring attention to his father's plight, he discovers the surprising truth about where his father is and what he's been up to." (Publishers Weekly)

Kadohata, Cynthia

Cracker! the best dog in Vietnam. Atheneum Books for Young Readers 2007 312p $16.99; pa $7.99

Grades: 5 6 7 8 **Fic**

1. Dogs -- Fiction 2. Vietnam War, 1961-1975 -- Fiction

ISBN 978-1-4169-0637-7; 1-4169-0637-1; 978-1-4169-0638-4 pa; 1-4169-0638-X pa

LC 2006-22022

The author "tells a stirring, realistic story of America's war in Vietnam, using the alternating viewpoints of an army dog named Cracker and her 17-year-old handler, Rick Hanski. . . . The heartfelt tale explores the close bond of the scout-dog team." Booklist

Half a world away; Cynthia Kadohata. Atheneum Books for Young Readers 2014 240 p. hbk $16.99

Grades: 5 6 7 8 **Fic**

1. Adoptees -- Fiction 2. Adoption -- Fiction 3. Love -- Fiction 4. Abandoned children -- Fiction 5. Emotional problems -- Fiction

ISBN 1442412755; 9781442412750

LC 2013031627

In this middle grade book by Cynthia Kadohata, "eleven-year-old Jaden is adopted, and he knows he's an 'epic fail.' That's why his family is traveling to Kazakhstan to adopt a new baby--to replace him, he's sure. . . . But when they get to Kazakhstan, it turns out the infant they've travelled for has already been adopted, and literally within minutes are faced with having to choose from six other babies." (Publisher's note)

"Twelve-year-old Jaden, adopted from Romania and suffering from attachment disorder, travels to Kazakhstan with his parents, who have decided to adopt a second child. As his parents struggle to bond with an emotionally unresponsive infant, Jaden bonds with disabled toddler Dimash--a breakthrough for Jaden. This story about a troubled adoptee and the equally troubling issues of international adoption is compelling and involving." Horn Book

★ **Kira** -Kira. Atheneum Bks. for Young Readers 2004 244p $15.95; pa $6.99

Grades: 5 6 7 8 **Fic**

1. Death -- Fiction 2. Georgia -- Fiction 3. Sisters -- Fiction 4. Japanese Americans -- Fiction

ISBN 0-689-85639-3; 0-689-85640-7 pa

Awarded the Newbery Medal, 2005

Chronicles the close friendship between two Japanese-American sisters growing up in rural Georgia during the late 1950s and early 1960s, and the despair when one sister becomes terminally ill.

"This beautifully written story tells of a girl struggling to find her own way in a family torn by illness and horrendous work conditions. . . . All of the characters are believable and well developed." SLJ

★ A **million** shades of gray. Atheneum Books for Young Readers 2010 216p $16.99
Grades: 5 6 7 8 **Fic**

1. Vietnam -- Fiction 2. Elephants -- Fiction 3. Wilderness survival -- Fiction

ISBN 1-4169-1883-3; 978-1-4169-1883-7

LC 2009-33307

In 1975 after American troops pull out of Vietnam, a thirteen-year-old boy and his beloved elephant escape into the jungle when the Viet Cong attack his village. "Grades five to eight." (Bull Cent Child Books)

"Kadohata delves deep into the soul of her protagonist while making a faraway place and stark consequences of war seem very near." Publ Wkly

★ **Outside** beauty. Atheneum Books for Young Readers 2008 265p $16.99; pa $8.99
Grades: 5 6 7 8 **Fic**

1. Sisters -- Fiction 2. Japanese Americans -- Fiction 3. Father-daughter relationship -- Fiction 4. Mother-daughter relationship -- Fiction

ISBN 978-0-689-86575-6; 0-689-86575-9; 978-1-4169-9818-1 pa; 1-4169-9818-7 pa

LC 2007-39711

Thirteen-year-old Shelby and her three sisters must go to live with their respective fathers while their mother, who has trained them to rely on their looks, recovers from a car accident that scarred her face

Kadohata's "gifts for creating and containing drama and for careful definition of character prove as powerful as ever in this wise, tender and compelling novel." Publ Wkly

★ The **thing** about luck; Cynthia Kadohata ; illustrated by Julia Kuo. 1st ed. Atheneum Books for Young Readers 2013 288 p. (hardcover) $16.99
Grades: 5 6 7 8 **Fic**

1. Luck -- Fiction 2. Japanese Americans -- Fiction 3. Brothers and sisters -- Fiction 4. Kansas -- Fiction 5. Grandparents -- Fiction 6. Farm life -- Kansas -- Fiction

ISBN 1416918825; 9781416918820; 9781442474673

LC 2012021287

National Book Award Winner (2013)

Parents' Choice: Silver Medal Fiction (2013)

Asian/Pacific American Awards for Literature: Children's Literature Winner (2014)

In this novel, by Newbery Medalist Cynthia Kadohata, "Summer knows that kouun means 'good luck' in Japanese, and this year her family has none of it. Just when she thinks nothing else can possibly go wrong, an emergency whisks her parents away to Japan--right before harvest season. Summer and her little brother, Jaz, are left in the care of their grandparents, who come out of retirement in order to harvest wheat and help pay the bills." (Publisher's note)

"Kadohata expertly captures the uncertainties of the tween years as Summer navigates the balance of childlike concerns with the onset of increasingly grown-up responsibilities." (SLJ)

Weedflower. Atheneum Books for Young Readers 2006 260p $16.95; pa $5.99
Grades: 5 6 7 8 **Fic**

1. Arizona -- Fiction 2. World War, 1939-1945 -- Fiction 3. Japanese Americans -- Evacuation and relocation, 1942-1945 -- Fiction

ISBN 0-689-86574-0; 1-4169-7566-7 pa

LC 2004-24912

After twelve-year-old Sumiko and her Japanese-American family are relocated from their flower farm in southern California to an internment camp on a Mojave Indian reservation in Arizona, she helps her family and neighbors, becomes friends with a local Indian boy, and tries to hold on to her dream of owning a flower shop.

Sumiko "is a sympathetic heroine, surrounded by well-crafted, fascinating people. The concise yet lyrical prose conveys her story in a compelling narrative." SLJ

Kagawa, Julie

The **Eternity** Cure; Julie Kagawa. Harlequin Books 2013 448 p. (hardcover) $16.99
Grades: 7 8 9 10 11 12 **Fic**

1. Science fiction 2. Vampires -- Fiction 3. Epidemics -- Fiction

ISBN 0373210698; 9780373210695

This vampire novel, by Julie Kagawa, is part of the "Blood of Eden" series. "Allie will follow the call of blood to save her creator, Kanin, from the psychotic vampire Sarren. But when the trail leads to Allie's birthplace in New Covington, what Allie finds there will change the world forever. . . . There's a new plague on the rise, a strain of the Red Lung virus that wiped out most of humanity generations ago--and this strain is deadly to humans and vampires alike." (Publisher's note)

The **forever** song; by Julie Kagawa. Harlequin Books 2014 416 p. (Blood of Eden) $16.99
Grades: 7 8 9 10 11 12 **Fic**

1. Vampires -- Fiction 2. Revenge 3. Horror tales 4. Fantasy fiction

ISBN 0373211120; 9780373211128

In this novel, by Julie Kagawa, "Allie will embrace her cold vampire side to hunt down and end Sarren, the psychopathic vampire who murdered Zeke. But the trail is bloody and long, and Sarren has left many surprises for Allie and her companions--her creator, Kanin, and her blood brother, Jackal. The trail is leading straight to the one place they must protect at any cost--the last vampire-free zone on Earth, Eden. And Sarren has one final, brutal shock in store for Allie." (Publisher's note)

The **immortal** rules; a legend begins. Julie Kagawa. Harlequin Teen 2012 504 p. (Blood of Eden) (hardcover) $18.99
Grades: 7 8 9 10 11 12 **Fic**

1. Romance fiction 2. Diseases -- Fiction 3. Vampires -- Fiction

ISBN 0373210515; 9780373210510

LC 2011279454

In this book, "[r]abids, vicious hybrid creatures born of the plague, prowl the land beyond the walled vampire cities. . . . When Allie is savagely attacked by a rabid, . . . a mysterious vampire offers her the choice of a human death or 'life' as a vampire. . . . Allie's determination to remain more human than monster is put to the test, particularly when she joins a band of humans on a desperate journey to safety on the island of Eden. Particularly when she falls in love." (Kirkus)

"Kagawa wraps excellent writing and skillful plotting around a well-developed concept and engaging characters, resulting in a fresh and imaginative thrill-ride that deserves a wide audience." Pub Wkly

Talon; by Julie Kagawa. Harlequin Books Teen 2014 464 p. $17.99
Grades: 8 9 10 11 **Fic**

1. Fantasy fiction 2. Dragons -- Fiction 3. Brothers and sisters -- Fiction 4. Shapeshifting

ISBN 0373211392; 9780373211395

In this book, by Julie Kagawa, "dragons were hunted to near extinction by the Order of St. George, a legendary society of dragon slayers.

Hiding in human form and growing their numbers in secret, the dragons of Talon have become strong and cunning. . . . Ember and Dante Hill are the only sister and brother known to dragonkind. Trained to infiltrate society, Ember wants to live the teen experience and enjoy a summer of freedom before taking her destined place in Talon." (Publisher's note)

"Young love, sibling rivalry, rogue dragons, and plots for world domination create an intriguing mix in this new series." Horn Book

Kang, Hildi

Chengli and the Silk Road caravan. Tanglewood 2011 178p $14.95

Grades: 5 6 7 8 **Fic**

1. China -- Fiction 2. Fathers -- Fiction 3. Princesses -- Fiction 4. Trade routes -- Fiction

ISBN 978-1-933718-54-5; 1-933718-54-4

LC 2010047359

Called to follow the wind and search for information about his father who disappeared many years ago, thirteen-year-old Chengli, carrying a piece of jade with strange writing that had belonged to his father, joins a caravan charged with giving safe passage to the Emperor's daughter as it navigates the constant dangers of the Silk Road in 630 A.D.

"This fast-paced adventure is filled with friendship, historical detail, changing scenery, and action. It will appeal to a wide range of readers." SLJ

Katcher, Brian

Deacon Locke went to prom; Brian Katcher. Katherine Tegen Books 2017 389 p. (hardcover) $17.99

Grades: 7 8 9 10 **Fic**

1. Proms -- Fiction 2. Grandmothers -- Fiction 3. Grandparent and child -- Fiction 4. Social media -- fiction 5. Grandparent and child -- fiction

ISBN 9780062422545; 9780062422521

LC 2016957990

In this novel, by Brian Katcher, edited by Claudia Gabel, "with graduation looming, shy and unusually tall Deacon doesn't think he can get up the nerve to ask anyone to the dance. Especially given all the theatrics. It isn't until Deacon confides in his witty and outgoing best friend Jean that he realizes could be a great person to take. . . . But when Deacon meets Soraya . . . he fears he has totally squandered his chances of having a prom he'll never forget." (Publisher's note)

The **improbable** theory of Ana and Zak; Brian Katcher. Katherine Tegen Books, an imprint of HarperCollinsPublishers 2015 336 p. (hardcover) $17.99

Grades: 7 8 9 10 11 12 **Fic**

1. Love -- Fiction 2. Teenagers -- Fiction 3. Brothers and sisters -- Fiction 4. High school students -- Fiction 5. Genius -- Fiction 6. Schools -- Fiction 7. Contests -- Fiction 8. Seattle (Wash.) -- fiction 9. Science fiction -- Congresses -- Fiction

ISBN 0062272772; 9780062272775

LC 2014030718

This book, by Brian Katcher, is a "he said/she said romance about two teens discovering themselves. . . . When Ana Watson's brother ditches a high school trip to run wild at Washingcon, type-A Ana knows that she must find him. . . . In her desperation, she's forced to enlist the last person she'd ever want to spend time with¿slacker Zak Duquette¿to help find her brother before morning comes." (Publisher's note)

"Type-A Ana and relaxed geek Zak take turns narrating as they spend a night searching for Ana's younger brother at a comic-book convention. The he said/she said romance has been done before, of course, but the unconventional setting, quirky convention-goers, and many over-the-top hijinks (e.g., multiple fights, a sci-fi-themed gay wedding, inadvertent drug-running) give this one a unique twist." Horn Book

Playing with matches. Delacorte Press 2008 294p $15.99; lib bdg $18.99

Grades: 8 9 10 11 12 **Fic**

1. School stories 2. Missouri -- Fiction 3. Burns and scalds -- Fiction 4. Dating (Social customs) -- Fiction

ISBN 978-0-385-73544-5; 0-385-73544-8; 978-0-385-90525-1 lib bdg; 0-385-90525-4 lib bdg

LC 2007-27654

While trying to find a girl who will date him, Missouri high school junior Leon Sanders befriends a lonely, disfigured female classmate.

"This is a strong debut novel with a cast of quirky, multidimensional characters struggling with issues of acceptance, sexuality, identity, and self-worth." SLJ

Katsoulis, Gregory Scott

Access restricted; by Gregory Scott Katsoulis. Harlequin Teen 2018 480 p. (Word$) (hbk.) $18.99

Grades: 7 8 9 10 11 12 **Fic**

1. Debt -- Fiction 2. Silence -- Fiction 3. Freedom of expression -- Fiction

ISBN 1335016252; 9781335016256

"On the day she went silent, Speth never meant for anyone to follow her lead--or to start a rebellion of Silents. But after taking down the tyrant Silas Rog and freeing the city from his grasp, everyone is looking to Speth for answers she doesn't have. All she wants is to find her parents, who are shackled to a lifetime of servitude in exchange for a debt they can never repay." (Publisher's note)

All rights reserved; Gregory Scott Katsoulis. Harlequin Teen 2017 392 p. map (Word$) (hardcover) $18.99

Grades: 7 8 9 10 11 12 **Fic**

1. Debt -- Fiction 2. Families -- Fiction 3. Copyright -- fiction 4. Dystopias -- fiction 5. Teenage girls -- fiction 6. Manners and customs -- fiction

ISBN 9780373212446; 9781488015472; 0373212445

In this book in the Word$ series, by Gregory Scott Katsoulis, "Speth Jime is anxious to deliver her Last Day speech and celebrate her transition into adulthood. The moment she turns fifteen, Speth must pay for every word she speaks . . . and even every gesture of affection. . . . But when Speth's friend Beecher commits suicide . . . , she can't express her shock and dismay without breaking her Last Day contract and sending her family into Collection." (Publisher's note)

"A fresh and detailed dystopian tale that will capture and make demands upon the attention of its readers, as the genre should, with a conclusion that sets readers up for the sequel." Kirkus

Another title in this series is:

Access restricted (2018)

Keating, Jess

How to outrun a crocodile when your shoes are untied; by Jess Keating. Sourcebooks Jabberwocky 2014 288 p. (My Life Is A Zoo) (trade pbk) $7.99

Grades: 5 6 7 8 **Fic**

1. Zoos -- Fiction 2. Middle schools -- Fiction 3. Twins -- Fiction 4. Popularity -- Fiction 5. Family life -- Fiction

ISBN 1572339470; 9781402297557

LC 2014006806

In this middle grades book by Jess Keating, "Ana Wright's social life is now officially on the endangered list: she lives in a zoo (umm, elephant droppings!?), her best friend lives on the other side of the world, and the Sneerers are making junior high miserable. All Ana wants is to fade into the background." (Publisher's note)

"Humor, poignancy and fascinating zoological facts infuse the narrative with a warm conversational tone that welcomes readers into the drama that is middle school." Kirkus

Other titles in this series are:

How to outswim a shark without a snorkel (2015)

How to outfox your friends when you don't have a clue (2015)

Kehret, Peg

Abduction! Dutton Children's Books 2004 215p $16.99; pa $6.99

Grades: 5 6 7 8 **Fic**

1. Kidnapping -- Fiction

ISBN 0-525-47294-0; 0-14-240617-1 pa

LC 2003-63531

Thirteen-year-old Bonnie has a feeling of foreboding on the very day that her six-year-old brother Matt and their dog Pookie are abducted, and she becomes involved in a major search effort as well as a frightening adventure

"This novel has enough suspense to keep children interested, and it will also appeal to reluctant readers." SLJ

The **ghost's** grave. Dutton Children's Books 2005 210p $16.99; pa $5.99

Grades: 5 6 7 8 **Fic**

1. Ghost stories 2. Coal miners -- Fiction 3. Washington (State) -- Fiction

ISBN 0-525-46162-0; 0-14-240819-0 pa

LC 2004022064

Apprehensive about spending the summer in Washington State with his Aunt Ethel when his parents get an overseas job, twelve-year-old Josh soon finds adventure when he meets the ghost of a coal miner.

"This fast-paced and engaging book should be a hit with fans of ghost stories. Josh is a rich character to whom readers can relate." SLJ

Keith, Harold

★ **Rifles** for Watie. Crowell 1957 332p $16.89; pa $5.99

Grades: 6 7 8 9 **Fic**

1. Generals 2. Indian leaders 3. United States -- History -- 1861-1865, Civil War -- Fiction

ISBN 0-690-04907-2; 0-06-447030-X pa

Awarded the Newbery Medal, 1958

"An exceptionally well-written story of the Civil War as it was fought in the western states." Bull Cent Child Books

Keller, Julia

Back home. Egmont USA 2009 194p $15.99; lib bdg $18.99

Grades: 6 7 8 9 **Fic**

1. Fathers -- Fiction 2. Soldiers -- Fiction 3. Family life -- Fiction 4. Iraq War, 2003-2011 -- Fiction 5. Brain -- Wounds and injuries -- Fiction

ISBN 978-1-60684-005-4; 1-60684-005-3; 978-1-60684-048-1 lib bdg; 1-60684-048-7 lib bdg

LC 2009-15877

Thirteen-year-old Rachel Browning understands that her father will be different after being injured in the Iraq War, but no one is prepared for the impact that his traumatic brain injury and other wounds have on the entire family

"No one who reads this heartbreaking book will ever forget it. With integrity, authenticity, and immediacy, Keller has captured the extraordinary complexity and challenge of unexpected change and, to her everlasting credit, unsparingly shares the whole truth of it with her readers." Booklist

Keller, Tae

The **science** of breakable things; Tae Keller. Random House 2018 304 p. (hardcover) $16.99

Grades: 4 5 6 7 **Fic**

1. Domestic fiction 2. Depression (Psychology) -- fiction 3. Schools -- Fiction 4. Friendship -- Fiction 5. Middle schools -- Fiction 6. Family problems -- Fiction 7. Depression, Mental -- Fiction 8. Racially mixed people -- Fiction 9. Science -- Methodology -- Fiction

ISBN 9781524715663; 9781524715670

LC 2016057633

In this novel, by Tae Keller, "How do you grow a miracle? For the record, this is not the question Mr. Neely is looking for when he says everyone in class must answer an important question using the scientific process. But Natalie's botanist mother is suffering from depression, so this is The Question that's important to Natalie. When Mr. Neely suggests that she enter an egg drop competition, Natalie has hope. . . . Natalie has a secret plan for the prize money." (Publisher's note)

Kelley, Jane

The **girl** behind the glass; [by] Jane Kelley. Random House 2011 183p $16.99; lib bdg $19.99; e-book $16.99

Grades: 4 5 6 7 **Fic**

1. Ghost stories 2. Twins -- Fiction 3. Moving -- Fiction 4. Sisters -- Fiction 5. Family life -- Fiction

ISBN 978-0-375-86220-5; 0-375-86220-X; 978-0-375-96220-2 lib bdg; 0-375-96220-4 lib bdg; 978-0-375-88996-7 e-book

LC 2010-43568

Moving from Brooklyn to a rental house in the country strains the relationship between eleven-year-old identical twins Hannah and Anna Zimmer, a situation made worse by the ghost of a girl who is trapped in the house because of problems with her own sister eighty years before.

"Both chilling and lyrical. . . . The tensions within the Zimmer family are especially well-observed, and Kelley . . . conveys an impressive amount of emotion with few words. The ethereal tone and steady parceling out of warning, clues, and bits of information . . . maintain the novel's intrigue and will keep readers invested in the unfolding mystery." Publ Wkly

Kelly, Erin Entrada

Blackbird fly; by Erin Entrada Kelly. Greenwillow Books, an imprint of HarperCollinsPublishers 2015 304 p. (hardback) $16.99

Grades: 4 5 6 7 8 **Fic**

1. School stories 2. Music -- Fiction 3. Bullies -- Fiction 4. Guitar -- Fiction 5. Middle schools -- Fiction 6. Filipino Americans -- Fiction

ISBN 0062238612; 9780062238610

LC 2014029444

"Apple has always felt a little different from her classmates. . . . It becomes unbearable in middle school, when the boys . . . in Apple's class put her name on the Dog Log, the list of the most unpopular girls in school. When Apple's friends turn on her and everything about her life starts to seem weird and embarrassing, Apple turns to music." (Publisher's note)

"Debut author Kelly skillfully weaves together the story of misfit Apple, her love of music, and a budding romance with a new boy at school, while never losing focus on the central issue of what it is like to be the 'other. . .'" Booklist

★ **Hello** universe; Erin Entrada Kelly, illustrated by Isabel Roxas. Greenwillow Books, an imprint of HarperCollins Publishers 2017 320 p. illustrations (hardback) $16.99; (ebook) $15.99

Grades: 4 5 6 7 **Fic**

1. Bullies -- Fiction 2. Sisters -- Fiction 3. Friendship -- Fiction 4. Psychic ability -- Fiction 5. Hearing impaired -- Fiction 6. Missing children -- Fiction 7. Bullying -- Fiction

ISBN 9780062414151; 9780062414175

LC 2016022723

Newbery Medal (2018)

This book, by Erin Entrada Kelly, illustrated by Isabel Roxas, "is a funny and poignant neighborhood story about unexpected friendships. Told from four intertwining points of view—two boys and two girls—the novel celebrates bravery, being different, and finding your inner bayani (hero)." (Publisher's note)

"An original and resonant exploration of interconnectedness and friendship." Kirkus

You go first; Erin Entrada Kelly. Greenwillow Books 2018 304 p. (hardback) $16.99

Grades: 4 5 6 7 **Fic**

1. Bullies -- Fiction 2. Friendship -- Fiction 3. Family life -- Fiction 4. Divorce -- Fiction 5. Schools -- Fiction 6. Bullying -- Fiction 7. Middle schools -- Fiction 8. Scrabble (Game) -- Fiction 9. Heart -- Surgery -- Fiction

ISBN 9780062414182

LC 2017047338

In this book, by Erin Entrada Kelly, "twelve-year-old Charlotte Lockard and eleven-year-old Ben Boxer are separated by more than a thousand miles. On the surface, their lives seem vastly different . . . . Charlotte wants to be a geologist and keeps a rock collection in her room. Ben is obsessed with Harry Potter, presidential history, and recycling. But the two have more in common than they think. They're both highly gifted." (Publisher's note)

Kelly, Jacqueline

The **curious** world of Calpurnia Tate; Jacqueline Kelly. Henry Holt & Co. 2015 320 p. (hardcover) $16.99

Grades: 4 5 6 **Fic**

1. Girls -- fiction 2. Gender role -- fiction 3. Sex role -- Fiction 4. Veterinarians -- Fiction 5. Family life -- Texas -- Fiction 6. Texas -- History -- 1846-1950 -- Fiction

ISBN 9780805097443; 0805097449

LC 2015000920

Sequel to: The evolution of Calpurnia Tate

In this children's story, by Jacqueline Kelly, "thirteen-year-old Callie Vee returns in this . . . sequel to . . . 'The Evolution of Calpurnia Tate.' . . . Callie's thirst for scientific discovery remains strong, as does her parents' disregard for any[thing but] . . . debutante balls and marrying a well-respected gentleman. In between recording questions and observations in her journal, Callie and brother Travis attempt to make pets of an armadillo, a blue jay, and a coyote mix, to mostly disastrous results." (School Library Journal)

"Recommended for fans of the original novel and strong readers who enjoy character-driven narratives." SLJ

★ The **evolution** of Calpurnia Tate. Henry Holt and Co. 2009 340p $16.99

Grades: 4 5 6 7 **Fic**

1. Texas -- Fiction 2. Nature -- Fiction 3. Family life -- Fiction 4. Naturalists -- Fiction 5. Grandfathers -- Fiction

ISBN 0-8050-8841-5; 978-0-8050-8841-0

LC 2008-40595

A Newbery Medal honor book (2010)

In central Texas in 1899, eleven-year-old Callie Vee Tate is instructed to be a lady by her mother, learns about love from the older three of her six brothers, and studies the natural world with her grandfather. "Grades five to eight." (Bull Cent Child Books)

"Callie is a charming, inquisitive protagonist; a joyous, bright, and thoughtful creation. . . . Several scenes . . . mix gentle humor and pathos to great effect." SLJ

Kenneally, Miranda

Racing Savannah; Miranda Kenneally. Sourcebooks Fire 2013 304 p. (tp : alk. paper) $9.99

Grades: 8 9 10 11 12 **Fic**

1. Horsemanship -- Fiction 3. Love -- Fiction 4. Horses -- Fiction 5. Tennessee -- Fiction

ISBN 1402284764; 9781402284762

LC 2013023322

In this book, by Miranda Kenneally, "Savannah has always been much more comfortable around horses than boys. Especially boys like Jack Goodwin. . . . She knows the rules: no mixing between the staff and the Goodwin family. But Jack has no such boundaries. With her dream of becoming a jockey, Savannah isn't exactly one to follow the rules either." (Publisher's note)

"Kenneally (Stealing Parker, 2012) again looks at sports through a female lens, this time tackling male-dominated horse racing, in this fourth Hundred Oaks novel. Savannah, her widowed horse-trainer father, and her father's pregnant girlfriend move to Tennessee's Cedar Hill, a farm that trains horses for races including the Kentucky Derby... The author's knack for weaving forbidden romance, breezy dialogue, and details of this lesser-known sports venue places it in the winner's circle for reluctant readers and chick-lit fans." (Booklist)

Kennedy, James

The **Order** of Odd-Fish; [by] James Kennedy. Delacorte Press 2008 403p $15.99; lib bdg $18.99

Grades: 6 7 8 9 **Fic**

1. Adventure fiction 2. Aunts -- Fiction

ISBN 978-0-385-73543-8; 0-385-73543-X; 978-0-385-90524-4 lib bdg; 0-385-90524-6 lib bdg

LC 2008-00711

Thirteen-year-old Jo suddenly finds her humdrum life turned upside down when Colonel Anatoly Kordakov shows up at her aunt's party and announces he has come to protect her.

"This clever, creative story will keep readers engaged and laughing." Libr Media Connect

Kent, Rose

Kimchi & calamari. HarperCollinsPublishers 2007 220p $15.99; lib bdg $16.89

Grades: 4 5 6 7 **Fic**

1. Adoption -- Fiction 2. Korean Americans -- Fiction 3. Italian Americans -- Fiction

ISBN 978-0-06-083769-3; 0-06-083769-1; 978-0-06-083770-9 lib bdg; 0-06-083770-5 lib bdg

LC 2006-20041

"Fourteen-year-old Korean adoptee Joseph Calderaro is stumped when his social studies teacher assigns an ancestry essay. . . . Kent's debut novel humorously captures the feelings of a young teen who thoroughly enjoys his Italian-American family but still wonders about his birth parents." Booklist

Kent, Trilby

★ **Medina** Hill. Tundra Books 2009 172p $19.95
Grades: 6 7 8 9 **Fic**

1. Great Britain -- Fiction
ISBN 978-0-88776-888-0; 0-88776-888-1

This is a "highly original debut." Booklist

"In the grimy London of 1935, eleven-year-old Dominic Walker has lost his voice. His mother is sick and his father's unemployed. Rescue comes in the form of his Uncle Roo, who arrives to take him and his young sister, Marlo, to Cornwall." Publisher's note

Stones for my father. Tundra Books 2011 170p $19.95
Grades: 6 7 8 9 **Fic**

1. Afrikaners -- Fiction 2. South Africa -- Fiction 3. South African War, 1899-1902 -- Fiction
ISBN 978-1-77049-252-3; 1-77049-252-6

"This meticulously researched novel about a white Afrikaner girl caught up in the Boer War at the turn of the 19th century brings to light a hitherto overlooked aspect of South African history. Corlie Roux is living with her harsh mother and younger brothers on an isolated farm in what was the South African Republic (now Mpumalanga). As the war reaches their farm, they flee, but are captured and interned in a concentration camp. . . . Kent tackles the challenge of depicting the complex relationships between Afrikaner colonists and English imperialists, and also the relationships of both these groups to the indigenous Africans." SLJ

Kephart, Beth

★ **Going** over; Beth Kephart. Chronicle Books 2014 262 p. map (alk. paper) $17.99
Grades: 8 9 10 11 12 **Fic**

1. Love -- Fiction 2. Family life -- Fiction 3. Family life -- Germany -- Fiction 4. Germany -- History -- 1945-1990 -- Fiction 5. Berlin Wall, Berlin, Germany, 1961-1989 -- Fiction 6. Berlin (Germany) -- History -- 1945-1989 -- Fiction
ISBN 1452124574; 9781452124575

LC 2012046894

In this book, by Beth Kephart, "Ada lives among the rebels, punkers, and immigrants of Kreuzberg in West Berlin. Stefan lives in East Berlin, in a faceless apartment bunker of Friedrichshain. Bound by love and separated by circumstance, their only chance for a life together lies in a high-risk escape. But will Stefan find the courage to leap? Or will forces beyond his control stand in his way?" (Publisher's note)

"In a present-tense narration alternating between Ada's first-person and Stefan's second-person, the young lovers on opposite sides of the Berlin Wall in 1983 plan for Stefan's escape to the West. Kephart works romantic chemistry into a danger-packed plot with moving results in this captivating glimpse into an underrepresented era that will appeal to older readers with a taste for literary historical fiction." Horn Book

The **heart** is not a size. HarperTeen 2010 244p $16.99
Grades: 7 8 9 10 **Fic**

1. Mexico -- Fiction 2. Poverty -- Fiction 3. Friendship -- Fiction 4. Volunteer work -- Fiction
ISBN 978-0-06-147048-6; 0-06-147048-1

LC 2008-55721

Fifteen-year-old Georgia learns a great deal about herself and her troubled best friend Riley when they become part of a group of suburban Pennsylvania teenagers that go to Anapra, a squatters village in the border town of Juarez, Mexico, to undertake a community construction project.

"Kephart's prose is typically poetic. She pens a faster-paced novel that explores teens' inner selves. . . . The writing is vivid, enabling readers to visualize Anapra's desolation and hope." Voice Youth Advocates

House of Dance. HarperTeen 2008 263p $16.99; lib bdg $17.89; pa $10.99
Grades: 7 8 9 10 **Fic**

1. Death -- Fiction 2. Cancer -- Fiction 3. Dancers -- Fiction 4. Grandfathers -- Fiction 5. Mother-daughter relationship -- Fiction
ISBN 978-0-06-142928-6; 0-06-142928-7; 978-0-06-142929-3 lib bdg; 0-06-142929-5 lib bdg; 978-0-06-142930-9 pa; 0-06-142930-9 pa

LC 2007-26011

During one of her daily visits across town to visit her dying grandfather, fifteen-year-old Rosie discovers a dance studio that helps her find a way to bring her family members together.

This is "distinguished more by its sharp, eloquent prose than by its plot. . . . Poetically expressed memories and moving dialogue both anchor and amplify the characters' emotions." Publ Wkly

This is the story of you; Beth Kephart. Chronicle Books Llc 2016 264 p. $17.99
Grades: 7 8 9 10 11 12 **Fic**

1. Islands -- Fiction 2. Hurricanes -- Fiction 3. New Jersey -- Fiction 4. Survival skills -- Fiction 5. Survival -- Fiction
ISBN 9781452142845

LC 2015003765

In this book, by Beth Kephart, "on Haven, a six-mile long, half-mile-wide stretch of barrier island, Mira Banul and her Year-Rounder friends have proudly risen to every challenge. But then a superstorm defies all predictions and devastates the island, upending all logic and stranding Mira's mother and brother on the mainland. Nothing will ever be the same." (Publisher's note)

"At once an exploration of the unrelenting power of nature and a reminder of the one thing in the world that is irreplaceable: family." Booklist

Undercover. HarperTeen 2007 278p $16.99; lib bdg $17.89; pa $8.99
Grades: 8 9 10 11 12 **Fic**

1. School stories 2. Poetry -- Fiction 3. Family life -- Fiction
ISBN 978-0-06-123893-2; 0-06-123893-7; 978-0-06-123894-9 lib bdg; 0-06-123894-5 lib bdg; 978-0-06-123895-6 pa; 0-06-123895-3 pa

LC 2007-2981

High school sophomore Elisa is used to observing while going unnoticed except when classmates ask her to write love notes for them, but a teacher's recognition of her talent, a "client's" desire for her friendship, a love of ice skating, and her parent's marital problems draw her out of herself.

"Kephart tells a moving story. . . . Readers will fall easily into the compelling premise and Elisa's memorable, graceful voice." Booklist

Keplinger, Kody

Run; Kody Keplinger. Scholastic Press 2016 295 p. (hbk.) $17.99; (ebook) $17.99
Grades: 7 8 9 10 11 12 **Fic**

1. Secrets -- Fiction 2. Friendship -- Fiction 3. Runaway teenagers

-- Fiction 4. Blind -- Fiction 5. Runaways -- Fiction 6. Best friends -- Fiction 7. Fugitives from justice -- Fiction 8. People with disabilities -- Fiction

ISBN 054583113X; 9780545831130; 9780545831154

LC 2015048824

In this book, by Kody Keplinger, "Bo Dickinson is a girl with a wild reputation, a deadbeat dad, and a mama who's not exactly sober most of the time. . . . Agnes Atwood has never gone on a date, never even stayed out past ten, and never broken any of her parents' overbearing rules. . . . Despite everything, Bo and Agnes become best friends. And it's the sort of friendship that runs truer and deeper than anything else." (Publisher's note)

"A good unlikely friendship story with compelling characters and a nuanced portrait of disability and small-town life." SLJ

That's not what happened; Kody Keplinger. Scholastic Press 2018 336 p. $18.99

Grades: 7 8 9 10 11 12 **Fic**

1. Bullies -- fiction 2. Schools -- Fiction 3. Secrets -- Fiction 4. Bullying -- Fiction 8. High schools -- Fiction 5. School shootings -- Fiction 6. Secrecy -- fiction 7. Rural schools -- fiction 8. Massacre survivors -- fiction 9. Truthfulness and falsehood -- fiction

ISBN 9781338186529

LC 2017060501

In this novel, by Kody Keplinger, "it's been three years since the Virgil County High School Massacre. Three years since my best friend, Sarah, was killed in a bathroom stall during the mass shooting. Everyone knows Sarah's story--that she died proclaiming her faith. But it's not true. I know because I was with her when she died. . . . But I'm not the only survivor with a story to tell about what did--and didn't--happen that day." (Publisher's note)

Kerr, M. E.

Gentlehands. Harper & Row 1978 183p hardcover o.p. pa $5.99

Grades: 7 8 9 10 **Fic**

1. Criminals -- Fiction 2. Grandfathers -- Fiction 3. Social classes -- Fiction

ISBN 978-0-06-447067-4 pa; 0-06-447067-9 pa

LC 77-11860

ALA YALSA Margaret A. Edwards Award (1993)

"Buddy Boyle falls for Skye and her affluent, breezy way of life. Finding his own parents not 'cultured' enough for this new relationship, Buddy turns to his grandfather, whose love of opera and other refinements make him more suitable to make Skye's acquaintance. A shocking surprise awaits Buddy when Mr. DeLucca, pursuer of an infamous Nazi, finally identifies his quarry." Shapiro. Fic for youth. 3rd edition

If I love you, am I trapped forever? Marshall Cavendish 2008 178p $16.99

Grades: 8 9 10 11 12 **Fic**

1. School stories 2. Newspapers -- Fiction 3. New York (N.Y.) -- Fiction 4. Dating (Social customs) -- Fiction 5. Father-son relationship -- Fiction

ISBN 978-0-7614-5545-5

LC 2007051768

A reissue of the title first published 1973 by Harper & Row

Alan, a popular senior high school student, faces painful changes after a new student, Duncan "Doomed" Stein, comes to town and starts an influential underground newspaper.

"Extremely humorous at times, the story is also occasionally touched with sadness and poignancy." Horn Book Guide

Kerz, Anna

Better than weird. Orca Book Publishers 2011 218p pa $9.95

Grades: 4 5 6 7 **Fic**

1. School stories 2. Autism -- Fiction 3. Bullies -- Fiction 4. Father-son relationship -- Fiction

ISBN 978-1-55469-362-7 pa; 1-55469-362-4 pa

When Aaron's long-absent father returns, Aaron must cope with bullying at school, his grandmother's illness and his father's pregnant new wife.

"Yet another in a long line of recent books about kids with autism, Kerz's effort nevertheless shines. . . . A heartwarming read for fans of realistic fiction." Booklist

The **gnome's** eye. Orca Book Publishers 2010 210p pa $12.95

Grades: 4 5 6 7 **Fic**

1. Fear -- Fiction 2. Canada -- Fiction 3. Immigrants -- Fiction

ISBN 978-1-55469-195-1 pa; 1-55469-195-8 pa

When Theresa and her family immigrate to Canada after World War II, she confronts her many fears with the help of a talisman given to her by a friend in Austria.

"Both laughter and genuine concern will be evident through Theresa's imaginative storytelling and descriptive narrative." SLJ

Key, Watt

Alabama moon. Farrar, Straus & Giroux 2006 294p $16; pa $6.99

Grades: 5 6 7 8 **Fic**

1. Alabama -- Fiction 2. Orphans -- Fiction 3. Wilderness survival -- Fiction

ISBN 0-374-30184-0; 0-312-38428-9 pa

LC 2005-40165

After the death of his father, ten-year-old Moon leaves their forest shelter home and is sent to an Alabama institution, becoming entangled in the outside world he has never known and making good friends, a relentless enemy, and finally a new life

"The book is well written with a flowing style, plenty of dialogue, and lots of action. The characters are well drawn and three-dimensional." SLJ

Followed by: Dirt road home (2010)

Dirt road home. Farrar Straus Giroux 2010 211p $16.99

Grades: 5 6 7 8 **Fic**

1. Gangs -- Fiction 2. Alabama -- Fiction 3. Violence -- Fiction 4. Reformatories -- Fiction 5. Father-son relationship -- Fiction

ISBN 978-0-374-30863-6; 0-374-30863-2

LC 2010-11319

Sequel to: Alabama moon (2006)

At Hellenweiler, a reformatory for second-offenders, fourteen-year-old Hal Mitchell will soon be free if he can avoid the gang violence of his fellow inmates, but the real enemy may lie elsewhere.

"With authentic characters and a candid first-person narrative, Key's story offers a disturbing appraisal of life in a juvenile facility, and a riveting battle for justice." Publ Wkly

★ **Fourmile**; Watt Key. Farrar Straus Giroux 2012 227 p, (hardcover) $16.99

Grades: 5 6 **Fic**

1. Child abuse -- Fiction 2. Father-son relationship -- Fiction 3. Mother-son relationship -- Fiction 4. Alabama -- Fiction 5.

Violence -- Fiction 6. Loss (Psychology) -- Fiction
ISBN 0374350957; 9780374324414; 9780374350956
LC 2012003220

In the book by Watt Key, "[m]iddle schooler Foster and his mother have been barely getting by since his father's death a year ago. . . . Mother has begun a relationship with dangerous, unpleasant Dax, a man she seems powerless to keep from abusing both Foster and his dog, Joe. Then Gary shows up, hiking along the rural road. . . . Foster, desperate to find some steady ground in his life, connects to Gary immediately." (Kirkus Reviews)

Keyser, Amber J.

★ **Pointe,** claw; by Amber J. Keyser. Carolrhoda Lab 2017 278 p. (hardcover) $18.99

Grades: 8 9 10 11 12 **Fic**

1. Diseases -- Fiction 2. Friendship -- Fiction 3. Ballet dancers -- Fiction 4. Zoonoses -- Fiction 5. Best friends -- Fiction 6. Ballet dancing -- Fiction
ISBN 9781512408959; 9781467775915
LC 2016006114

In this novel, by Amber J. Keyser, "Jessie Vale dances in an elite ballet program. She has to be perfect to land a spot with the professional company. When Jessie is cast in an animalistic avant-garde production, her careful composure cracks wide open. . . . Meanwhile, her friend Dawn McCormick's world is full of holes. She wakes in strange places, bruised, battered, and unable to speak. The doctors are out of ideas." (Publisher's note)

"Keyser's writing shimmers with raw emotion and empathy, and her finale, much like in dance, is poetic, bittersweet, and life affirming." Pub Wkly

Khan, Hena

★ **Amina's** voice; Hena Khan. Salaam Reads / Simon & Schuster Books for Young Readers 2017 208 p. (hardcover) $16.99

Grades: 4 5 6 7 8 **Fic**

1. Muslims -- Fiction 2. Friendship -- Fiction 3. Pakistani Americans -- Fiction
ISBN 9781481492065; 9781481492072
LC 2016024621

In this middle grade novel by Hena Khan, "A Pakistani-American Muslim girl struggles to stay true to her family's vibrant culture while simultaneously blending in at school after tragedy strikes her community. . . . Amina has never been comfortable in the spotlight. She is happy just hanging out with her best friend, Soojin. Except now that she's in middle school everything feels different." (Publisher's note)

"A universal story of self-acceptance and the acceptance of others." School Library Journal.

Khan, Rukhsana

Wanting Mor. Groundwood/House of Anansi Books 2009 190p $17.95

Grades: 6 7 8 9 **Fic**

1. Sex role -- Fiction 2. Afghanistan -- Fiction 3. Bereavement -- Fiction 4. Birth defects -- Fiction
ISBN 0-88899-858-9; 978-0-88899-858-3; 978-0-88899-862-0 pa

Jameela and her family live in a poor, war-torn village in Afghanistan. Even with her cleft lip and lack of educational opportunities, Jameela feels relatively secure, sustained by her Muslim faith and the love of her mother, Mor. But when Mor dies, Jameela's father impulsively decides to start a new life in Kabul.

"This compelling story is based on real incidents. Jameela's matter-of-fact, first person narrative will awaken young readers to life and conditions in Afghanistan." Booklist

Khorram, Adib

★ **Darius** the Great is not okay; Adib Khorram. Dial Books 2018 320 p. (hardback) $17.99

Grades: 7 8 9 10 11 12 **Fic**

1. Friendship -- Fiction 2. Grandparents -- Fiction 3. Depression (Psychology) -- Fiction 4. Iran -- Fiction 5. Depression, Mental -- Fiction
ISBN 9780525552963; 9780525552987
LC 2018009825

William C. Morris Award (2019)
Asian/Pacific American Award for Young Adult Literature (2019)

"Darius has never really fit in at home, and he's sure things are going to be the same in Iran. His clinical depression doesn't exactly help matters. . . . Then Darius meets Sohrab, the boy next door, and everything changes. Soon, they're spending their days together. . . . Sohrab calls him Darioush--the original Persian version of his name--and Darius has never felt more like himself than he does now that he's Darioush to Sohrab." (Publisher's note)

"Darius is a well-crafted, awkward but endearing character, and his cross-cultural story will inspire reflection about identity and belonging." SLJ

Khoury, Jessica

Origin; Jessica Khoury. Razorbill 2012 393 p. (hardcover) $17.99

Grades: 6 7 8 **Fic**

1. Science fiction 2. Immortality -- Fiction 3. Science -- Experiments -- Fiction 4. Rain forests -- Fiction 5. Indigenous peoples -- Fiction 6. Amazon River Region -- Fiction
ISBN 1595145958; 9781595145956
LC 2012014447

In this young adult novel by Jessica Khoury "Pia has grown up in a secret laboratory hidden deep in the Amazon rainforest. She was raised by a team of scientists who have created her to be the start of a new immortal race. But on the night of her seventeenth birthday . . . and sneaks outside the compound for the first time in her life . . . Pia meets Eio, a boy from a nearby village. Together, they embark on a race against time to discover the truth about Pia's origin." (Author's note)

Kidd, Ronald

Night on Fire; Ronald Kidd. Albert Whitman & Co 2015 288 p. $16.99

Grades: 4 5 6 7 8 **Fic**

1. Racism -- Fiction 2. Segregation -- Fiction 3. Civil rights -- Fiction
ISBN 0807570249; 9780807570241
LC 2015025153

In this novel by Ronald Kidd "thirteen-year-old Billie Simms doesn't think her hometown of Anniston, Alabama, should be segregated, but few . . . share her opinion. So when Billie learns that the Freedom Riders, a group of peace activists . . . will be traveling through Anniston on their way to Montgomery, she thinks that maybe change is finally coming. But what starts as a series of angry grumbles soon turns to brutality as Anniston residents show just how deep their racism runs." (Publisher's note)

"Beautifully written and earnestly delivered, the novel rolls to an inexorable, stunning conclusion readers won't soon forget." Kirkus

The **year** of the bomb. Simon & Schuster Books for Young Readers 2009 202p $15.99

Grades: 6 7 8 9 **Fic**

1. Fear -- Fiction 2. Cold war -- Fiction 3. California -- Fiction 4. Blacklisting of entertainers -- Fiction 5. Motion pictures -- Production and direction -- Fiction

ISBN 978-1-4169-5892-5; 1-4169-5892-4

LC 2008023646

In 1955 California, as "Invasion of the Body Snatchers" is filmed in their hometown, thirteen-year-old Arnie discovers a real enemy when he and three friends go against a young government agent determined to find communists at a neaby university or on the movie set.

"The book is vividly imbued with historical detail; parallels between the Red Scare witch hunters and the movie's body-invading aliens are particularly effective." Horn Book Guide

Kiely, Brendan

Tradition; Brendan Kiely. Margaret K. McElderry Books 2018 339 p. (hardcover) $18.99

Grades: 7 8 9 10 11 12 **Fic**

1. Rape -- Fiction 2. Sexism -- Fiction 3. Teenagers -- Sexual behavior -- Fiction 4. Wealth -- Fiction 5. Schools -- Fiction 6. High schools -- Fiction 7. Conduct of life -- Fiction 8. Preparatory schools -- Fiction

ISBN 1481480340; 9781481480345; 9781481480352; 9781481480369

LC 2017026455

This book, by Brendan Kiely, "explores the insidious nature of tradition at [Fullbrook Academy,] a prestigious boarding school. . . . When Jamie and Jules meet, they recognize in each other a similar instinct for survival. . . As Jules and Jamie's lives intertwine, and the pressures to play by the rules and remain silent about the school's secrets intensify, they see Fullbrook for what it really is. That tradition, a word Fullbrook hides behind, can be ugly, even violent." (Publisher's note)

"A thoughtfully crafted argument for feminism and allyship." Kirkus

Kilworth, Garry

Attica. Little, Brown 2009 334p pa $11.95

Grades: 5 6 7 8 **Fic**

1. Fantasy fiction 2. Stepfamilies -- Fiction

ISBN 978-1-904233-56-5 pa; 1-904233-56-2 pa

"The children have distinct personalities and react to Attica in realistic ways, finding their own strengths in this exhilarating, unpredictable environment. This book is a rare find." Booklist

Kimmel, Elizabeth Cody

The **reinvention** of Moxie Roosevelt. Dial Books for Young Readers 2010 256p $16.99

Grades: 4 5 6 7 **Fic**

1. School stories

ISBN 978-0-8037-3303-9; 0-8037-3303-8

LC 2009-37939

On her first day of boarding school, a thirteen-year-old girl who feels boring and invisible decides to change her personality to match her unusual name.

"Kimmel's sharply observed novel reflects a keen understanding of the agony of self-definition that is adolescence. Readers will cheer for Moxie as she charts her path toward self-acceptance." Kirkus

Kinard, Kami

The **Boy** Project; notes and observations of Kara McAllister. Scholastic Press 2012 $12.99

Grades: 6 7 8 9 **Fic**

1. School stories 2. Science projects -- Fiction 3. Dating (Social customs) -- Fiction

ISBN 978-0-545-34515-6; 0-545-34515-4

LC 2011008332

Eighth-grader Kara McAllister chronicles her efforts when she tries to use the scientific method to transform her social blunders into romantic victories.

"This middle-school drama is hip to the moment, with breakup texting, kissing and popularity tug of wars. . . . Kara's irrepressible spirit, clever wit and introspection save this story from vapidity." Kirkus

Kincaid, S. J.

The **diabolic**; S. J. Kincaid. Simon & Schuster Books for Young Readers 2016 407 p. (Diabolic trilogy) (hardback) $17.99

Grades: 8 9 10 11 12 **Fic**

1. Science fiction 2. Bodyguards -- Fiction 3. Courts and courtiers -- Fiction

ISBN 9781481472692; 9781481472678

LC 2016003698

In this book, by S. J. Kincaid, "Nemesis is a Diabolic, a humanoid teenager created to protect a galactic senator's daughter, Sidonia. . . . When the power-mad Emperor learns Sidonia's father is participating in a rebellion, he summons Sidonia to the Galactic court. She is to serve as a hostage. Now, there is only one way for Nemesis to protect Sidonia. She must become her. Nemesis travels to the court disguised as Sidonia." (Publisher's note)

"Kincaid has crafted incredible characters who readers can relate to and care for even if they range from privileged, bratty children to creations designed to kill. The imagery used in establishing these protagonists and the complex setting will thrill the YA audience." SLJ

The **empress**; S.J. Kincaid. Simon & Schuster BFYR 2017 378 p. (Diabolic trilogy) (hardback) $17.99

Grades: 8 9 10 11 12 **Fic**

1. Kings and rulers -- Fiction 2. Courts and courtiers -- Fiction 3. Emperors -- Fiction 4. Empresses -- Fiction 5. Identity (Psychology) -- Fiction 6. Human beings -- Genetic engineering -- Moral and ethical aspects -- Fiction

ISBN 1534409920; 9781534409927; 9781534409941

LC 2017023825

In this book in The Diabolic series, by S. J. Kincaid, "it's a new day in the Empire. Tyrus has ascended to the throne with Nemesis by his side and now they can find a new way forward. . . . One where creatures like Nemesis will be given worth and recognition, where science and information can be shared with everyone and not just the elite. But having power isn't the same thing as keeping it, and change isn't always welcome." (Publisher's note)

"Kincaid deftly juggles high-octane action with emotionally devastating punches, and readers will riot for the next installment." Kirkus

Kindl, Patrice

Keeping the castle; a tale of romance, riches, and real estate. by Patrice Kindl. Viking Childrens Books 2012 261 p. $16.99; (hardcover) $16.99

Grades: 7 8 9 10 11 **Fic**

1. Regency novels 2. Romance fiction 3. Marriage -- Fiction 4. Castles -- Fiction 5. Courtship -- Fiction 6. Social classes -- Fiction 7. Great Britain -- History -- 1789-1820 -- Fiction 8. England --

Social life and customs -- 19th century -- Fiction
ISBN 0670014389; 9780670014385

LC 2011033185

In this book, "[s]eventeen-year-old Althea Crawley is . . . on a quest to marry rich so that she may secure the family's only inheritance, a dilapidated castle on the edge of the North Sea. . . . Marriage prospects in tiny Lesser Hoo are slim, to say the least, until dashing and wealthy Lord Boring arrives on the scene. Matters are further complicated by a revolving cast of potential suitors, including Lord Boring's cousin, Mr. Fredericks." (Booklist)

A **school** for brides; a story of maidens, mystery, and matrimony. by Patrice Kindl. Viking, an imprint of Penguin Group (USA) LLC 2015 272 p. (hardcover) $17.99

Grades: 7 8 9 10 **Fic**

1. School stories 2. Marriage -- Fiction 3. Great Britain -- History -- 1714-1837 -- Fiction 4. Schools -- Fiction 5. Courtship -- Fiction 6. Boarding schools -- Fiction 7. Mystery and detective stories 8. Great Britain -- History -- 1789-1820 -- Fiction 9. England -- Social life and customs -- 19th century -- Fiction
ISBN 9780670786084

LC 2014028087

Sequel to: Keeping the castle

In this companion novel to "Keeping the Castle," also written by Patrice Kindl, "[t]he Winthrop Hopkins Female Academy of Lesser Hoo, Yorkshire, has one goal: to train its students in the feminine arts with an eye toward getting them married off. This year, there are five girls of marriageable age. There's only one problem: the school is in the middle of nowhere, and there are no men." (Publisher's note)

"This affectionate homage to the genre delivers what's missing: a witty, intelligent plot whose characters—complex, conniving, hypocritical, and hilarious—seek happiness within an ordered world. This airy soufflé of a tale, garnished with quirky charm, is an unmitigated delight from start to finish." Kirkus

King, Caro

Seven sorcerers; Caro King. Aladdin 2011 324 p. (hbk.) $15.99

Grades: 5 6 7 8 **Fic**

1. Fantasy 2. Missing children -- Fiction 3. Brothers and sisters -- Fiction 4. Adventure and adventurers -- Fiction
ISBN 1442420421; 9781442420427

LC 2011001432

Sequel: Shadow spell

First published 2009 in the United Kingdom

"Nineveh 'Nin' Redstone is 11 years old and resolutely ordinary. Her four-year-old brother is nothing but a nuisance until the awful Wednesday when she wakes up and he's gone. Worse, no one but Nin remembers he exists. It's left to her to reclaim him from Skerridge (a bogeyman) and the Terrible House of Strood." (Publishers Weekly)

A "complex, intelligent fantasy that is at turns funny and terrifying." Booklist

King, Emily R.

The **hundredth** queen; Emily R. King. Skyscape 2017 287 p. (Hundredth queen series) (paperback) $9.99

Grades: 7 8 9 10 **Fic**

1. Bildungsromans 2. Fantasy fiction 3. Orphans -- Fiction 4. Imaginary places -- Fiction 5. Survival -- fiction 6. Young women -- fiction 7. Quests (Expeditions) -- fiction
ISBN 9781503943650; 1503943658

In this book in the Hundredth Queen Series, by Emily R. King, "an orphan girl blossoms into a warrior, summoning courage and confidence in her fearless quest to upend tradition, overthrow an empire, and reclaim her life as her own. . . . Eighteen-year-old Kalinda is destined for nothing more than a life of seclusion and prayer. . . . But a visit from the tyrant Rajah Tarek disrupts Kalinda's life." (Publisher's note)

"Strong characterization, deep worldbuilding, page-turning action scenes and intrigue, as well as social commentary, make this book stand out." Kirkus

Kinney, Jeff

★ **Diary** of a wimpy kid: Greg Heffley's journal. Amulet Books 2007 217p pa $14.95

Grades: 5 6 7 8 **Fic**

1. School stories 2. Friendship -- Fiction
ISBN 978-0-8109-9313-6 pa; 0-8109-9313-9 pa

LC 2006-31847

Greg records his sixth grade experiences in a middle school where he and his best friend, Rowley, undersized weaklings amid boys who need to shave twice daily, hope just to survive, but when Rowley grows more popular, Greg must take drastic measures to save their friendship

"Kinney's background as a cartoonist is apparent in this hybrid book that falls somewhere between traditional prose and graphic novel. . . . The pace moves quickly. The first of three installments, it is an excellent choice for reluctant readers, but more experienced readers will also find much to enjoy and relate to." SLJ

Other titles in this series are:
Rodrick rules (2008)
The last straw (2009)
Dog days (2009)
The ugly truth (2010)
Cabin fever (2011)
The third wheel (2012)
Hard luck (2013)
The long haul (2014)
Old school (2015)
Double down (2016)
The getaway (2017)
The meltdown (2018)

Diary of a wimpy kid; the getaway. by Jeff Kinney. Amulet Books 2017 217 p. illustrations (Diary of a wimpy kid) (hardcover) $13.95

Grades: 5 6 7 8 **Fic**

1. Humorous fiction 2. Diaries -- Fiction 3. Vacations -- Fiction 4. Family life -- Fiction
ISBN 9781683351115; 9781419725456; 1419725459

LC 2017036062

In this children's book, by Jeff Kinney, "Greg and his family are getting out of town. With the cold weather and the stress of the approaching holiday season, the Heffleys decide to escape to a tropical island resort for some much-needed rest and relaxation. A few days in paradise should do wonders for Greg and his frazzled family. But the Heffleys soon discover that paradise isn't everything it's cracked up to be." (Publisher's note)

"Highly entertaining and relatable, Kinney proves he's still got it after all these years." Booklist

Diary of a wimpy kid: dog days. Amulet Books 2009 224p

Grades: 5 6 7 8 **Fic**

1. Summer -- Fiction 2. Vacations -- Fiction
ISBN 0810983915; 9780810983915

LC 2009024953

In the of middle-schooler Greg Heffley, he records his attempts to spend his summer vacation sensibly indoors playing video games and watching television, despite his mother's other ideas.

"Kinney's gift for telling, pitch-perfect details in both his writing and art remains." Publ Wkly

Diary of an awesome friendly kid; Rowley Jefferson's journal. by Jeff Kinney. Amulet Books 2019 224 p. (hardback) $13.99

Grades: 5 6 7 8 **Fic**

1. Humorous stories 2. Diaries -- Fiction 3. Biography -- Fiction 4. Authorship -- Fiction 5. Friendship -- Fiction 6. Best friends -- Fiction

ISBN 9781419740275

LC 2019006267

In this graphic novel, by Jeff Kinney, "Rowley's best friend Greg Heffley has been chronicling his middle-school years in thirteen Diary of a Wimpy Kid journals . . . and counting. But it's finally time for readers to hear directly from Rowley in a journal of his own. In Diary of an Awesome Friendly Kid, Rowley writes about his experiences and agrees to play the role of biographer for Greg along the way." (Publisher's note)

"Kinney has mastered this format, and fans of the beloved series will be delighted by this fresh perspective. This is certainly one of the biggest books to come out this year. Kinney's fans already know all about it, so plan accordingly." (Booklist)

The **meltdown**; by Jeff Kinney. Amulet Books 2018 217 p. (hardback) $13.95

Grades: 5 6 7 8 **Fic**

1. Humorous fiction 2. Snow -- Fiction 3. Humorous stories 4. Winter -- Fiction 5. Diaries -- Fiction 6. Friendship -- Fiction 7. Best friends -- Fiction

ISBN 1419727435; 9781419727436

LC 2018038582

In this book in the Diary of a Wimpy Kid, by Jeff Kinney, "when snow shuts down Greg Heffley's middle school, his neighborhood transforms into a wintry battlefield. Rival groups fight over territory, build massive snow forts, and stage epic snowball fights. . . . It's a fight for survival as Greg and [his best friend] Rowley navigate alliances, betrayals, and warring gangs in a neighborhood meltdown. When the snow clears, will Greg and Rowley emerge as heroes?" (Publisher's note)

Kinsey-Warnock, Natalie

True colors; by Natalie Kinsey-Warnock. Alfred A. Knopf Books for Young Readers 2012 242 p. (hard cover) $15.99

Grades: 4 5 6 7 **Fic**

1. Absent mothers -- Fiction 2. Orphans -- fiction 3. Abandoned children -- Fiction 4. Identity -- Fiction 5. Foundlings -- Fiction 6. Farm life -- Vermont -- Fiction 7. People with mental disabilities -- Fiction 8. Vermont -- History -- 20th century -- Fiction

ISBN 0375860991; 9780375854538; 9780375860997; 9780375897061; 9780375960994

LC 2011037863

This book by Natalie Kinsey-Warnock "tells the story of one girl's journey to find the mother she never had, set against the period backdrop of a small farming town in 1950s Vermont. For her entire life, 10-year-old Blue has never known her mother. . . . Over the course of one summer, she resolves to finally find out who she is. . . . Her search leads her down a road of self-discovery that will change her life forever." (Publisher's note)

Kipling, Rudyard, 1865-1936

★ The **jungle** book; by Rudyard Kipling; illustrated by Robert R. Ingpen. Sterling Children's Books 2012 192 p. ill. (hardcover) $19.95

Grades: 4 5 6 7 **Fic**

1. Picture books for children 2. Fantasy fiction -- fiction

ISBN 1402782845; 9781402782848

This book is an illustrated version of Rudyard Kipling's 1894 children's story collection "The Jungle Book." Illustrations by Robert Ingpen accompany the stories "of the boy Mowgli, rescued and raised by tigers in the heart of the jungle. The tales feature such . . . creatures such as Bagheera, the graceful black panther; Baloo, the kindly brown bear; and Kaa, the snake with the hypnotic stare." The stories 'Rikki-Tikki-Tavi,' 'The White Seal,' and 'Toomai of the Elephants'" are included, too. (Publisher's note)

Kirby, Jessi

Golden; Jessi Kirby. 1st ed. Simon & Schuster Books for Young Readers 2013 288 p. (hardcover) $16.99

Grades: 7 8 9 10 11 12 **Fic**

1. Mystery fiction 2. Romance fiction 3. Diaries -- Fiction 4. Love -- Fiction 5. Choice -- Fiction 6. Family problems -- Fiction 7. Mothers and daughters -- Fiction

ISBN 1442452161; 9781442452169; 9781442452183; 9781442452251

LC 2012042216

In this novel, by Jessi Kirby, "seventeen-year-old Parker Frost has never taken the road less traveled. . . . Julianna Farnetti and Shane Cruz are remembered as the golden couple of Summit Lakes High . . . but Julianna's journal tells . . . . the secrets that were swept away with her the night that Shane's jeep plunged into an icy river. . . . Reading Julianna's journal gives Parker . . . reasons to question what really happened the night of the accident." (Publisher's note)

"Kirby's . . . third novel is inspirational and contemplative in its mood and tone. Multifaceted characters and dashes of mystery and romance come together in a successful mediation on the value of taking an active role in one's life." Pub Wkly

Kirby, Matthew J.

★ The **clockwork** three. Scholastic Press 2010 391p $17.99

Grades: 5 6 7 8 **Fic**

1. Fantasy fiction 2. Friendship -- Fiction 3. Clocks and watches -- Fiction

ISBN 978-0-545-20337-1; 0-545-20337-6

LC 2009-37879

As mysterious circumstances bring Giuseppe, Frederick, and Hannah together, their lives soon interlock like the turning gears in a clock and they realize that each one holds a key to solving the others' mysteries

This is a "riveting historical fantasy. . . . Kirby has assembled all the ingredients for a rousing adventure, which he delivers with rich, transporting prose." Publ Wkly

Icefall. Scholastic Press 2011 325p $17.99

Grades: 5 6 7 8 **Fic**

1. Fantasy fiction 2. Ice -- Fiction 3. Winter -- Fiction 4. Storytelling -- Fiction

ISBN 978-0-545-27424-1; 0-545-27424-9

LC 2011000890

"Kirby turns in a claustrophobic, thought-provoking coming-of-age adventure that shows a young woman growing into her own, while demonstrating the power of myth and legend. Kirby's attention to detail and stark descriptions make this an effective mood piece." Publ Wkly

★ A **taste** for monsters; Matthew J. Kirby. Scholastic Press 2016 352 p. (ebook) $18.99; $18.99
Grades: 7 8 9 10 **Fic**

1. Ghost stories 2. Jack the Ripper murders, London, England, 1888 -- fiction 3. Murder -- Fiction 4. Serial murderers -- Fiction 5. Neurofibromatosis -- Fiction 6. Disfigured persons -- Fiction 7. London (England) -- History -- 19th century -- Fiction 8. Great Britain -- History -- Victoria, 1837-1901 -- Fiction 9. Murder -- Investigation -- England -- London -- History -- 19th century -- fiction

ISBN 9780545817943; 9780545817844

LC 2015048826

This novel by Matthew J. Kirby is set in London in 1888, "Jack the Ripper is terrorizing the people of the city. Evelyn, a young woman disfigured by her dangerous work in a matchstick factory . . . [becomes] maid to [Joseph] the Elephant Man in London Hospital, [in whom] . . . she finds a gentle kindred. . . . When the murders begin, however, Joseph and Evelyn are haunted nightly by the ghosts of the Ripper's dead, setting Evelyn on a path to facing her fears." (Publisher's note)

"A lovely, suspenseful, lyrical, imperfect paranormal mystery." Kirkus

Kisner, Adrienne

Dear Rachel Maddow; a novel. Adrienne Kisner. Feiwel & Friends 2018 272 p. (hardcover) $17.99
Grades: 7 8 9 10 11 **Fic**

1. E-mail -- Fiction 2. Drug abuse -- Fiction 3. Dating (Social customs) -- Fiction

ISBN 9781250146014; 9781250146021

LC 2017956981

In this book, by Adrienne Kisner, "Brynn Haper's life has one steadying force--Rachel Maddow. She watches her daily, and after writing to Rachel for a school project . . . Brynn starts drafting e-mails to Rachel but never sending them. . . . Then Brynn is confronted with a moral dilemma. One student representative will be allowed to have a voice among the administration in the selection of a new school superintendent. . . . Brynn feels all students deserve a voice." (Publisher's note)

Kittle, Katrina

Reasons to be happy. Sourcebooks Jabberwocky 2011 281p pa $7.99
Grades: 7 8 9 10 **Fic**

1. School stories 2. Ghana -- Fiction 3. Bulimia -- Fiction 4. Popularity -- Fiction 5. Bereavement -- Fiction 6. Personal appearance -- Fiction

ISBN 978-1-4022-6020-9; 1-4022-6020-2

LC 2011020276

Eighth-grader Hannah Carlisle feels unattractive compared to her movie star parents and cliquish Beverly Hills classmates, and when her mother's cancer worsens and her father starts drinking heavily, Hannah's grief and anger turn into bulimia, which only her aunt, a documentary filmmaker, understands.

"Hannah's believability as a character as well as the realistic, painful depiction of bulimia make this a standout." Booklist

Kittredge, Caitlin

The **Iron** Thorn. Delacorte Press 2011 493p (Iron Codex) $17.99; lib bdg $20.99
Grades: 7 8 9 10 **Fic**

1. Fantasy fiction

ISBN 0-385-73829-3; 0-385-90720-6 lib bdg; 978-0-385-73829-3; 978-0-385-90720-0 lib bdg

LC 2010-00972

In an alternate 1950s, mechanically gifted fifteen-year-old Aoife Grayson, whose family has a history of going mad at sixteen, must leave the totalitarian city of Lovecraft and venture into the world of magic to solve the mystery of her brother's disappearance and the mysteries surrounding her father and the Land of Thorn.

"Steampunk fans will delight in this first title in the sure-to-be-popular Iron Codex series. . . . There's plenty of tame but satisfying romance, too, and plot twists galore. Aoife is a caustic-tongued, feisty, and independent young woman, with plenty of nerve and courage." Booklist

Other titles in this series are:
The Nightmare Garden (2012)
The Mirrored Shard (2013)

Kizer, Amber

A **matter** of days; Amber Kizer. 1st ed. Delacorte Press 2013 288 p. (ebook) $50.97; (hardcover) $16.99; (library) $19.99
Grades: 7 8 9 10 **Fic**

1. Apocalyptic fiction -- fiction 3. Voyages and travels -- fiction 4. Science fiction 5. Survival -- Fiction 6. Epidemics -- Fiction 7. Virus diseases -- Fiction 8. Brothers and sisters -- Fiction

ISBN 0385908040; 9780375898259; 9780385739733; 9780385908047

LC 2012012200

In this book, "Nadia and Rabbit's military doctor uncle, Bean, visited them and insisted on injecting them with a vaccine for a 'new bug.' Not long afterward, the disease XRD TB . . . starts ravaging the world, and 16-year-old Nadia and 11-year-old Rabbit are the only survivors in their entire town. With the assorted survival gear their uncle ordered for them, they attempt to make their way from their Seattle suburb to their grandfather in West Virginia." (Publishers Weekly)

"This post-apocalyptic tale is particularly frightening as it doesn't take place in some distant, imagined future. A solid, realistically imagined survival tale with a strong female protagonist." Kirkus

Kladstrup, Kristin

Garden princess; Kristin Kladstrup. Candlewick Press 2013 272 p. $15.99
Grades: 6 7 8 **Fic**

1. Occult fiction -- fiction 2. Fantasy fiction -- fiction

ISBN 0763656852; 9780763656850

LC 2012943642

This book features a garden where "every flower in it is always in bloom, but Princess Adela, a gardening expert and enthusiast, is sure that can't be true. When the princess's friend Garth receives a mysterious invitation to Hortensia's garden party, Adela arranges to accompany him. . . . Wandering among flowers she knows shouldn't be in bloom, Adela learns the frightening secret of Hortensia's magic garden and finds herself in terrible danger." (School Library Journal)

Klages, Ellen

The **green** glass sea. Viking 2006 321p $16.99; pa $7.99
Grades: 5 6 7 8 **Fic**

1. New Mexico -- Fiction 2. Scientists -- Fiction 3. Atomic bomb -- Fiction 4. World War, 1939-1945 -- Fiction

ISBN 0-670-06134-4; 0-14-241149-3 pa

It is 1943, and 11-year-old Dewey Kerrigan is traveling west on a train to live with her scientist father—but no one will tell her exactly where he is. When she reaches Los Alamos, New Mexico, she learns why: he's working on a top secret government program.

"Many readers will know as little about the true nature of the project as the girls do, so the gradual revelation of facts is especially effective, while those who already know about Los Alamos's historical significance will experience the story in a different, but equally powerful, way." SLJ

Followed by: White sands, red menace (2008)

Out of left field; Ellen Klages. Viking 2018 320 p. (hardback) $16.99

Grades: 4 5 6 7 **Fic**

1. Baseball -- Fiction 2. Gender role -- fiction 3. Sex role -- Fiction 4. Women's rights -- Fiction 5. Little League baseball -- Fiction 6. Single-parent families -- Fiction 7. All-American Girls Professional Baseball League -- Fiction 8. San Francisco (Calif.) -- History -- 20th century -- Fiction

ISBN 0425288595; 9780425288597

LC 2018009872

In this book, by Ellen Klages, in 1957, "inspired by what . . . [Katy Gordon is] learning about civil rights in school, she sets out to prove that she's not the only girl who plays baseball. With the help of friendly librarians and some tenacious research skills, Katy discovers the forgotten history of female ball players. Why does no one know about them? Where are they now? And how can one ten-year-old change people's minds about what girls can do?" (Publisher's note)

"The narrative, though rich in details, never gets bogged down. This title also includes substantial back matter, such as a list of female ballplayers, an author's note, a glossary of baseball terms, and further recommended reading. Klages gives Katy a strong voice and helps spotlight the history of marginalized women in sports history. Featuring powerful female characters, this is historical fiction that doesn't drag for a second. A fine purchase." SLJ

White sands, red menace. Viking 2008 337p $16.99

Grades: 5 6 7 8 **Fic**

1. Cold war -- Fiction 2. New Mexico -- Fiction 3. Scientists -- Fiction 4. Atomic bomb -- Fiction

ISBN 978-0-670-06235-5; 0-670-06235-9

Sequel to: The green glass sea (2006)

"The groundbreaking science is part of daily life for the smart techno-teens, and the adult characters are as compelling as the kids. . . . Along with . . . global issues, Klages' compelling story explores personal relationships and what it means to be a family." Booklist

Klass, David

Firestorm. Frances Foster Books 2006 289p (The Caretaker trilogy) $17

Grades: 8 9 10 11 12 **Fic**

1. Science fiction

ISBN 0-374-32307-0

LC 2005-52112

After learning that he has been sent from the future for a special purpose, eighteen-year-old Jack receives help from an unusual dog and a shape-shifting female fighter.

"The sobering events and tone are leavened with engaging humor, and the characters are multidimensional. The relentless pace, coupled with issues of ecology, time travel, self-identity, and sexual awakening, makes for a thrilling and memorable read." SLJ

Other books in the Caretaker Trilogy are:
Whirlwind (2008)
Timelock (2009)

Second impact; David Klass and Perri Klass. Frances Foster Books 2013 288 p. (hardback) $16.99

Grades: 8 9 10 11 12 **Fic**

1. School stories 2. Brain -- Wounds and injuries -- Fiction 3. Blogs -- Fiction 4. Schools -- Fiction 5. Football -- Fiction 6. High schools -- Fiction 7. Conduct of life -- Fiction 8. Sports injuries -- Fiction

ISBN 0374379963; 9780374379964

LC 2012040873

In this book, "Carla Jenson, sports reporter for her school paper, convinces Jerry Downing, star quarterback and excellent writer, to blog about the team's season—a novel idea with unexpected repercussions." This is especially true once Carla latches onto the topic of "sports-related concussions even though she is opposed by Jerry and practically everyone else in the school and town as the controversy escalates." (Kirkus Reviews)

★ **Stuck** on Earth. Farrar Straus & Giroux 2010 227p $16.99

Grades: 4 5 6 7 **Fic**

1. Science fiction 2. Bullies -- Fiction 3. Extraterrestrial beings -- Fiction

ISBN 978-0-374-39951-1; 0-374-39951-4

LC 2008--48133

On a secret mission to evaluate whether the human race should be annihilated, a space alien inhabits the body of a bullied fourteen-year-old boy.

"Klass's . . . thoughtful, often wrenching book offers plenty to think about, from what's really going on in Tom's head to questions about human responsibility to the planet and each other. It takes 'alienation' to a whole new level." Publ Wkly

Timelock. Farrar, Straus and Giroux 2009 246p (The Caretaker trilogy) $17.99

Grades: 8 9 10 11 12 **Fic**

1. Science fiction 2. Ecology -- Fiction 3. Time travel -- Fiction

ISBN 978-0-374-32309-7; 0-374-32309-7

LC 2008-23280

Sequel to: Whirlwind (2008)

Jack discovers that the only way to protect the Earth from ecological disaster at the hands of the Dark Army is to lock time, and he must choose between staying in the present or returning to the future world from which he came.

"Every bit as fast paced, thrilling, and similar to a gripping computer game as its predecessors, this final volume in the trilogy will keep readers absorbed while presenting them with a valuable warning about the need for environmental awareness." SLJ

Whirlwind; [by] David Klass. 1st ed.; Farrar Straus Giroux 2008 295p (The Caretaker trilogy) $17.95; pa $8.99

Grades: 8 9 10 11 12 **Fic**

1. Science fiction

ISBN 978-0-374-32308-0; 0-374-32308-9; 978-0-312-38429-6 pa; 0-312-38429-7 pa

LC 2007014160

Sequel to: Firestorm (2006)

Jack finds himself embroiled in another dangerous adventure when, after a six-month absence, he returns to the Hudson River town where he grew up to find his girlfriend PJ only to discover that she is missing and everyone believes him to be responsible for her disappearance and the death of his family.

"The fast-paced, gripping plot is an excellent vehicle for presenting a significant environmental message to an audience that might not hear it otherwise." SLJ

Followed by: Timelock (2009)

Klass, Sheila Solomon

★ **Soldier's** secret; the story of Deborah Sampson. Henry Holt 2009 215p $17.95

Grades: 6 7 8 9 10 **Fic**

1. Soldiers 2. Memoirists 3. Soldiers -- Fiction 4. United States -- History -- 1775-1783, Revolution -- Fiction

ISBN 978-0-8050-8200-5; 0-8050-8200-X

LC 2008-36783

During the Revolutionary War, a young woman named Deborah Sampson disguises herself as a man in order to serve in the Continental Army.

In this novel, Sampson "is strong, brave, and witty. . . . Klass doesn't shy away from the horrors of battle; she also is blunt regarding details young readers will wonder about, like how Sampson dealt with bathing, urination, and menstruation. . . . Sampson's romantic yearnings for a fellow soldier . . . is given just the right notes or restraint and realism." Booklist

Klavan, Andrew

MindWar; a novel. Andrew Klavan. Thomas Nelson, Inc. 2014 352 p. (The MindWar Trilogy) (hardback) $15.99

Grades: 7 8 9 10 **Fic**

1. Teenagers -- Fiction 2. Video games -- Fiction 3. Virtual reality -- Fiction 4. Video gamers -- Fiction 5. Undercover operations -- Fiction 6. Cyberterrorism -- Prevention -- Fiction

ISBN 1401688926; 9781401688929

LC 2013050887

In this novel by Andrew Klaven "high school football star Rick Dial . . . immerses himself in video games after a car accident leaves his legs painfully useless. The teen is recruited to fight real life baddies. . . a virtual reality world created by Kurodar, a terrorist out to destroy the free world. He must fight for his life, because what happens to you in this virtual world affects your body in real life." (School Library Journal)

"Edgar Award–winning Klavan's well-orchestrated fantasy thriller features brisk but compelling character development, a touch of wry humor, Christian sensitivity that doesn't proselytize, and an imaginative mix of gaming action with real-life stakes. With just the right cliff-hanger ending, this trilogy opener shows promise." Booklist

Other titles in this series are:

Hostage Run (2015)

Game Over (2016)

Klein, Lisa M.

Cate of the Lost Colony; by Lisa Klein. Bloomsbury 2010 329p $16.99

Grades: 8 9 10 11 12 **Fic**

1. Poets 2. Queens 3. Authors 4. Explorers 5. Historians 6. Courtiers 7. Travel writers 8. Orphans -- Fiction 9. Lumbee Indians -- Fiction 10. Roanoke Island (N.C.) -- History -- Fiction 11. Great Britain -- History -- 1485-1603, Tudors -- Fiction

ISBN 978-1-59990-507-5; 1-59990-507-8

LC 2010-8299

When her dalliance with Sir Walter Ralegh is discovered by Queen Elizabeth in 1587, lady-in-waiting Catherine Archer is banished to the struggling colony of Roanoke, where she and the other English settlers must rely on a Croatoan Indian for their survival. Includes author's note on the mystery surrounding the Lost Colony.

"This robust, convincing portrait of the Elizabethan world with complex, rounded characters wraps an intriguingly plausible solution to the 'lost colony' mystery inside a compelling love story of subtle thematic depth." Kirkus

Includes bibliographical references

Klise, Kate

★ **Grounded**. Feiwel and Friends 2010 196p $16.99

Grades: 4 5 6 7 **Fic**

1. Death -- Fiction 2. Missouri -- Fiction 3. Bereavement -- Fiction 4. Swindlers and swindling -- Fiction

ISBN 978-0-312-57039-2; 0-312-57039-2

LC 2010013008

After her father, brother, and sister are killed in a plane crash, twelve-year-old Daralynn's life in tiny Digginsville, Missouri, proceeds as her mother turns angry and embittered, her grandmother becomes senile, and her flamboyant aunt continues to run the Summer Sunset Retirement Home for Distinguished Gentlemen, while being courted by the owner of the town's new crematorium.

"Dark humor melds with genuine pathos in Klise's moving novel. . . . This quiet story illuminates and celebrates the human need for connection beyond the grave." Booklist

Homesick; Kate Klise. 1st ed. Feiwel and Friends 2012 192 p. (hardcover) $16.99

Grades: 4 5 6 7 8 **Fic**

1. Divorce -- Fiction 2. Family life -- Fiction

ISBN 1250008425; 9781250008428

In this book by Kate Klise, "Benny's parents are splitting up. . . . Benny's dad has always liked clutter, but now, he begins hoarding everything. . . . As his house grows more cluttered and his father grows more distant, Benny tries to sort out whether he can change anything at all. Meanwhile, a local teacher enters their quiet Missouri town in America's Most Charming Small Town contest, and the pressure is on to clean up the area, especially Benny's ramshackle of a house." (Publisher's note)

Letters from camp; illustrated by M. Sarah Klise. Avon Bks. 1999 178p il hardcover o.p. pa $5.99

Grades: 4 5 6 7 **Fic**

1. Camps -- Fiction 2. Letters -- Fiction 3. Siblings -- Fiction

ISBN 0-380-97539-4; 0-380-79348-2 pa

LC 98-52315

Sent to Camp Happy Harmony to learn how to get along with each other, pairs of brothers and sisters chronicle in letters home how they come to suspect the intentions of the singing family running the camp

This is a "delightfully wacky story. . . . The humor is very gentle and tongue-in-cheek. . . . An entirely satisfying camp adventure." Booklist

Regarding the bathrooms; a privy to the past. illustrated by M. Sarah Klise. Harcourt 2006 140p il $15

Grades: 4 5 6 7 **Fic**

1. School stories

ISBN 978-0-15-205164-8; 0-15-205164-3

LC 2005016813

In this novel told through letters, newspaper articles, and police reports, a middle school principal's bathroom renovation project leads to the discovery of stolen Roman antiquities.

"Puns abound, and there are a few bathroom jokes, though nothing really crass enough to compromise an entertaining novel that celebrates community and history." Booklist

Regarding the bees; a lesson, in letters, on honey, dating, and other sticky subjects. [by] Kate Klise; illustrated by M. Sarah Klise. Harcourt 2007 122p $15

Grades: 4 5 6 7 **Fic**

1. School stories

ISBN 978-0-15-205711-4

LC 2006017716

While corresponding with their globetrotting substitute teacher, the seventh graders at Geyser Creek Middle School nervously prepare for an important standardized test, navigate the tricky waters of first crushes, and try to bring their bee mascot to a local spelling competition.

"Fans of the series will appreciate this installment, reluctant readers will be drawn to the format, and more advanced readers will appreciate the wordplay and puns sprinkled throughout." SLJ

Regarding the fountain; illustrations by M. Sarah Klise. Avon Bks. 1998 138p $16.99; pa $5.99

Grades: 4 5 6 7 **Fic**

1. School stories

ISBN 0-380-97538-6; 978-0-380-97538-9; 0-380-79347-4 pa; 978-0-380-79347-1 pa

LC 97-18205

When the principal asks a fifth-grader to write a letter regarding the purchase of a new drinking fountain for Geyser Creek Middle School, he finds that all sorts of chaos results

"Fresh, funny, and a delight to read." SLJ

Regarding the sink; where, oh where, did Waters go? illustrated by M. Sarah Klise. Harcourt 2004 127p il $15

Grades: 4 5 6 7 **Fic**

1. School stories

ISBN 0-15-205019-1

LC 2003-26560

A series of letters reveals the selection of the famous fountain designer, Florence Waters, to design a new sink for the Geyser Creek Middle School cafeteria, her subsequent disappearance, and the efforts of a class of sixth-graders to find her

"Piecing the story and clues together is satisfying. Introduce this book to savvy readers who are ready for the jump to a clever, unconventional reading experience." SLJ

Other titles in this series are:

Regarding the bathrooms (2006)

Regarding the bees (2007)

Regarding the fountain (1998)

Regarding the trees (2005)

Regarding the trees; a splintered saga rooted in secrets. illustrated by M. Sarah Klise. Harcourt 2005 143p il $15

Grades: 4 5 6 7 **Fic**

1. School stories 2. Trees -- Fiction

ISBN 0-15-205163-5

In this story told primarily through letters, Principal Russ wants the Geyser Creek Middle School trees to be trimmed before his administrative evaluation, but the project is interrupted by a town gender war, dueling chefs, student tree protests, and a surprise wedding.

Kluger, Jeffrey

Freedom stone. Philomel Books 2011 316p $16.99

Grades: 4 5 6 **Fic**

1. Magic -- Fiction 2. Slavery -- Fiction 3. African Americans -- Fiction 4. United States -- History -- 1861-1865, Civil War -- Fiction

ISBN 978-0-399-25214-3; 0-399-25214-2

LC 2010-06028

With the help of a magical stone from Africa, a thirteen-year-old slave travels to the battle of Vicksburg to clear her father's name and free her family from bondage.

Kluger "adeptly mixes drama, fantasy, romance, and history, while creating characters so determined to survive that readers can't help being drawn into their plights. In a climax that breaks with reality but that will keep readers hungry to learn the outcome, Kluger proves his storytelling prowess." Publ Wkly

Kluger, Steve

★ **My** most excellent year; a novel of love, Mary Poppins, & Fenway Park. Dial Books 2008 403p $16.99; pa $8.99

Grades: 8 9 10 11 12 **Fic**

1. Friendship -- Fiction 2. Boston (Mass.) -- Fiction

ISBN 978-0-8037-3227-8; 0-8037-3227-9; 978-0-14-241343-2 pa; 0-14-2413437 pa

LC 2007-26651

"Three bright and funny Brookline, MA, eleventh graders look back on their most excellent year—ninth grade—for a school report. Told in alternating chapters by each of them, this enchanting, life-affirming coming-of-age story unfolds through instant messages, emails, memos, diary entries, and letters. . . . This is a rich and humorous novel for older readers." SLJ

Knowles, Jo

See you at Harry's; Jo Knowles. 1st ed. Candlewick Press 2012 310 p. $16.99

Grades: 6 7 8 9 10 11 **Fic**

1. Siblings -- Fiction 2. LGBT youth -- Fiction 3. Bereavement -- Fiction 4. Restaurants -- Fiction 5. Gay teenagers -- Fiction 6. Family -- fiction 7. Grief -- Fiction 8. Family life -- Fiction 9. Family problems -- Fiction 10. Brothers and sisters -- Fiction

ISBN 9780763654078

LC 2011018619

In this children's novel, "seventh grader Fern . . . relates the . . . tragedies of her family. Her high-school-freshman older brother Holden has come to the place in his life where he's acknowledged that he's gay. . . . Fern offers him support and love. . . . And then there's 3-year-old Charlie, always messy, often annoying, but deeply loved. Fern's busy, distracted parents leave all of the kids wanting for more attention--until a tragic accident tears the family apart." (Kirkus Reviews)

Knox, Elizabeth

Dreamhunter; book one of the Dreamhunter duet. Farrar, Straus & Giroux 2006 365p (Dreamhunter duet) $19; pa $8.99

Grades: 7 8 9 10 **Fic**

1. Fantasy fiction 2. Dreams -- Fiction

ISBN 0-374-31853-0; 0-312-53571-6 pa

LC 2005-46366

First published 2005 in the United Kingdom

In a world where select people can enter "The Place" and find dreams of every kind to share with others for a fee, a fifteen-year-old girl is training to be a dreamhunter when her father disappears, leaving her to carry on his mysterious mission. "Grades nine to twelve." (Bull Cent Child Books)

This first of a two-book series is "a highly original exploration of the idea of a collective unconscious, mixed with imagery from the raising of Lazarus and with the brave, dark qualities of the psyche of an adolescent female." Horn Book Guide

Followed by Dreamquake (2007)

Dreamquake; book two of the Dreamhunter duet. Farrar, Straus & Giroux 2007 449p map (Dreamhunter duet) $19

Grades: 7 8 9 10 **Fic**

1. Fantasy fiction 2. Dreams -- Fiction

ISBN 978-0-374-31854-3; 0-374-31854-9

LC 2006-48109

Sequel to Dreamhunter

Michael L. Printz Award honor book, 2008

Aided by her family and her creation, Nown, Laura investigates the powerful Regulatory Body's involvement in mysterious disappearances and activities and learns, in the process, the true nature of the Place in which dreams are found.

The author's "haunting, invigorating storytelling will leave readers eager to return to its puzzles—and to reap its rewards." Booklist

Mortal fire; by Elizabeth Knox. 1st ed. Frances Foster Books 2013 448 p. (hardcover) $17.99

Grades: 7 8 9 10 11 **Fic**

1. Fantasy fiction 2. Paranormal fiction 3. Magic -- Fiction 3. Identity -- Fiction 4. Stepbrothers -- Fiction 5. Islands of the Pacific -- Fiction

ISBN 0374388296; 9780374388294

LC 2012040872

This novel, set in a fictional area of New Zealand, stars Canny, a "16-year-old Ma'eu, taciturn, antisocial, and exceptionally gifted in math." She has what she calls "Extra," an "ethereal script that Canny alone can see, attached to plants, buildings, or nothing at all." When she and friends "come upon a valley dense with the Extra, Canny realizes that there is more to her visions than her own oddness—there are people, the Zarenes, whose existence is interwoven with this magical language." (Publishers Weekly)

Knudsen, Michelle

The **dragon** of Trelian. Candlewick Press 2009 407p $16.99

Grades: 4 5 6 7 **Fic**

1. Fantasy fiction 2. Magic -- Fiction 3. Dragons -- Fiction 4. Princesses -- Fiction

ISBN 978-0-7636-3455-1; 0-7636-3455-7

LC 2008025378

A mage's apprentice, a princess, and a dragon combine their strength and magic to bring down a traitor and restore peace to the kingdom of Trelian.

"Knudsen does a fantastic job of creating sympathetic and realistic characters that really drive the story. The tale is adventurous and exciting with many twists and turns along the way." SLJ

Followed by: The princess of Trelian (2012)

The **princess** of Trelian; Michelle Knudsen. Candlewick Press 2012 437 p. (reinforced) $16.99

Grades: 4 5 6 7 **Fic**

1. Fantasy 2. Magic -- Fiction 3. Dragons -- Fiction 4. Princesses -- Fiction

ISBN 0763650625; 9780763650629

LC 2011047174

Sequel to: The dragon of Trelian (2009)

In this juvenile fantasy novel, by Michelle Knudsen, a "sequel to 'The Dragon of Trelian,' . . . Princess Meg is now heir to the throne, but her subjects are uneasy about her . . . dragon, and it only becomes worse when a neighboring king accuses the dragon of ravaging the countryside. . . . Meanwhile, Meg's best friend Calen has earned his mage's mark, but a mysterious, magical attack occurs. . . . [T]he deposed villain from the previous book is behind all the mischief." (Horn Book Magazine)

Knutsson, Catherine

Shadows cast by stars; Catherine Knutsson. 1st ed. Atheneum Books for Young Readers 2012 456 p. (hardcover) $17.99; (paperback) $9.99

Grades: 7 8 9 10 **Fic**

1. Blood 2. Science fiction 3. Plague -- Fiction 4. Young adult literature 5. Native Americans -- Fiction 6. Twins -- Fiction 7. Spirits -- Fiction 8. Family life -- Fiction 9. Brothers and sisters -- Fiction

ISBN 1442401915; 9781442401914; 9781442401938; 9781442401921

LC 2011038419

Author Catherine Knutsson tells the story of Native American Cassandra Mercredi. The "sixteen-year-old . . . [may] be immune to Plague, but that doesn't mean she's safe--government forces are searching for those of aboriginal heritage to harvest their blood. When a search threatens Cassandra and her family, they flee to the Island: a mysterious and idyllic territory protected by the Band, a group of guerilla warriors--and by an enigmatic energy barrier that keeps outsiders out and the spirit world in." (Publisher's note)

Koertge, Ronald

Now playing; Stoner & Spaz II. [by] Ron Koertge. Candlewick Press 2011 208p $16.99

Grades: 8 9 10 11 12 **Fic**

1. School stories 2. Drug abuse -- Fiction 3. Cerebral palsy -- Fiction 4. Self-acceptance -- Fiction 5. Dating (Social customs) -- Fiction

ISBN 978-0-7636-5081-0; 0-7636-5081-1

LC 2010040151

Sequel to: Stoner & Spaz (2002)

High schooler Ben Bancroft, a budding filmmaker with cerebral palsy, struggles to understand his relationship with drug-addict Colleen while he explores a new friendship with A.J., who shares his obsession with movies and makes a good impression on Ben's grandmother.

"Koertge writes sharp dialogue and vivid scenes." Publ Wkly

Shakespeare bats cleanup; [by] Ron Koertge. Candlewick Press 2003 116p hardcover o.p. pa $5.99

Grades: 6 7 8 9 **Fic**

1. Poetry -- Fiction

ISBN 0-7636-2116-1; 0-7636-2939-1 pa

LC 2002-31171

When a fourteen-year-old baseball player catches mononucleosis, he discovers that keeping a journal and experimenting with poetry not only helps fill the time, it also helps him deal with life, love, and loss

"Koertge does an excellent job of creating the authentic voice of a teenage boy exclusively through poems. The poems are funny, touching, and always energetic." Booklist

Shakespeare makes the playoffs; [by] Ron Koertge. Candlewick Press 2010 170p lib bdg $15.99; pa $5.99

Grades: 6 7 8 9 Fic

1. Novels in verse 2. Poetry -- Fiction 3. Baseball -- Fiction
ISBN 978-0-7636-4435-2 lib bdg; 0-7636-4435-8 lib bdg; 978-0-7636-5852-6 pa

LC 2009-14519

Sequel to: Shakespeare bats cleanup (2003)

Fourteen-year-old Kevin Boland, poet and first baseman, is torn between his cute girlfriend Mira and Amy, who is funny, plays Chopin on the piano, and is also a poet.

"The well-crafted poetry is firmly rooted in the experiences of regular teens and addresses subjects that range from breakups to baseball. . . . Appealing and accessible." Booklist

Stoner & Spaz; [by] Ron Koertge. Candlewick Press 2002 169p hardcover o.p. pa $6.99

Grades: 8 9 10 11 12 Fic

1. School stories 2. Cerebral palsy -- Fiction
ISBN 0-7636-1608-7; 0-7636-2150-1 pa

LC 2001-43050

A troubled youth with cerebral palsy struggles toward self-acceptance with the help of a drug-addicted young woman

"Funny, touching, and surprising, it is a hopeful yet realistic view of things as they are and as they could be." Booklist

Followed by: Now Playing: Stoner & Spaz II (2011)

★ **Strays**; [by] Ron Koertge. Candlewick Press 2007 167p $16.99

Grades: 7 8 9 10 11 12 Fic

1. Orphans -- Fiction 2. Foster home care -- Fiction
ISBN 978-0-7636-2705-8; 0-7636-2705-4

LC 2007-24096

After his parents are killed in a car accident, high school senior Sam wonders whether he will ever feel again or if he will remain numbed by grief.

"Though Koertge never soft pedals the horrors faced by some foster children, this thoughtful novel about the lost and abandoned is a hopeful one." Booklist

Koja, Kathe

Buddha boy. Speak 2004 117p pa $5.99

Grades: 7 8 9 10 Fic

1. School stories 2. Artists -- Fiction 3. Buddhism -- Fiction 4. Conduct of life -- Fiction
ISBN 0-14-240209-5

LC 2004041669

First published 2003 by Farrar, Straus & Giroux

Justin spends time with Jinsen, the unusual and artistic new student whom the school bullies torment and call Buddha Boy, and ends up making choices that impact Jinsen, himself, and the entire school.

"A compelling introduction to Buddhism and a credible portrait of how true friendship brings out the best in people." Publ Wkly

Headlong. Farrar, Straus and Giroux 2008 195p $16.95

Grades: 8 9 10 11 12 Fic

1. School stories 2. Orphans -- Fiction 3. Social classes -- Fiction
ISBN 978-0-374-32912-9; 0-374-32912-5

LC 2007-23612

High school sophomore Lily opens herself to new possibilities when, despite warnings, she becomes friends with 'ghetto girl' Hazel, a new student at the private Vaughn School which Lily, following in her elitist mother's footsteps, has attended since preschool.

"Class, identity and friendship are the intersecting subjects of this intelligent novel. . . . [The author] relays this story with her usual insight and, through her lightning-fast characterizations, an ability to project multiple perspectives simultaneously." Publ Wkly

Kissing the bee. Farrar, Straus and Giroux 2007 121p $16

Grades: 8 9 10 11 12 Fic

1. School stories 2. Romance fiction 3. Love stories 4. Bees -- Fiction 5. Friendship -- Fiction
ISBN 978-0-374-39938-2; 0-374-39938-7

LC 2006-37378

While working on a bee project for her advanced biology class, quiet high school senior Dana reflects on her relationship with gorgeous best friend Avra and Avra's boyfriend Emil, whom Dana secretly loves.

The "understated, tightly focused language evokes vivid scenes and heady emotions." Publ Wkly

Konigsberg, Bill

★ **Honestly** Ben; Bill Konigsberg. Arthur A. Levine Books, an imprint of Scholastic Inc. 2017 326 p. (hardcover : alk. paper) $17.99

Grades: 7 8 9 10 11 12 Fic

1. Gay teenagers -- Fiction 2. Identity (Psychology) -- Fiction 3. Schools -- Fiction 4. Massachusetts -- Fiction 5. Sexual orientation -- Fiction 6. Preparatory schools -- Fiction 7. Homosexuality -- fiction 8. Fathers and sons -- fiction
ISBN 9780545858267; 9780545858311

LC 2016008865

In this book, by Bill Konigsberg, "Ben Carver is back to normal. He's working steadily in his classes at the Natick School. He just got elected captain of the baseball team. He's even won a full scholarship to college, if he can keep up his grades. All that foolishness with Rafe Goldberg the past semester is in the past." (Publisher's note)

"Packed with literary references, pranks, heady conversations, humor, honesty, and tribulation, this is one that will be remembered. A fresh, insightful, inspiring take on what it means to come out." Kirkus

★ **Openly** straight; Bill Konigsberg. Arthur A. Levine Books 2013 336 p. (hard cover : alk. paper) $17.99

Grades: 8 9 10 11 Fic

1. School stories 2. Gay teenagers -- Fiction 3. Identity -- Fiction 4. Massachusetts -- Fiction 5. Preparatory schools -- Fiction
ISBN 0545509890; 9780545509893; 9780545509909

LC 2012030552

Lambda Literary Awards Finalist (2014)

In this book, "Coloradan Rafe Goldberg has always been the token gay kid. He's been out since eighth grade. His parents and community are totally supportive. . . . On the outside, Rafe seems fine, but on the inside, he's looking for change, which comes with the opportunity to reinvent himself at the prestigious Natick Academy in Massachusetts. There for his junior year, Rafe cloaks his gayness in order to be just like one of the other guys." All is well until he falls for a straight friend. (Kirkus Reviews)

"Rafe is sick of being the poster child for all things gay at his uber-liberal Colorado high school, so when he gets into a Massachusetts boarding school for his junior year, he decides to reboot himself as "openly straight." Konigsberg slyly demonstrates how thoroughly assumptions of straightness are embedded in everyday interactions. For a thought-provoking take on the coming-out story, look no further." (Horn Book)

Konigsburg, E. L.

The **mysterious** edge of the heroic world. Atheneum Books for Young Readers 2007 244p $16.99; pa $5.99

Grades: 5 6 7 8 **Fic**

1. Florida -- Fiction 2. Friendship -- Fiction 3. Art museums -- Fiction

ISBN 978-1-4169-4972-5; 1-4169-4972-0; 978-1-4169-5353-1 pa; 1-4169-5353-1 pa

"This humorous, poignant, tragic, and mysterious story has intertwining plots that peel away like the layers of an onion." SLJ

The **outcasts** of 19 Schuyler Place. Atheneum Bks. for Young Readers 2004 296p $16.95

Grades: 5 6 7 8 **Fic**

1. Social action -- Fiction

ISBN 0-689-86636-4

LC 2003-8067

A prequel to Silent to the bone

Upon leaving an oppressive summer camp, twelve-year-old Margaret Rose Kane spearheads a campaign to preserve three unique towers her grand uncles have been building in their back yard for over forty years

"The plot is well paced and has excellent foreshadowing. Konigsburg's characters are particularly well motivated. . . . Funny and thought-provoking by turns, this is Konigsburg at her masterful best." SLJ

Silent to the bone. Atheneum Bks. for Young Readers 2000 261p hardcover o.p. pa $5.99

Grades: 7 8 9 10 **Fic**

1. Mystery fiction 2. Siblings -- Fiction 3. Babysitters -- Fiction

ISBN 0-689-83601-5; 0-689-83602-3 pa

LC 00-20043

When he is wrongly accused of gravely injuring his baby half-sister, thirteen-year-old Branwell loses his power of speech and only his friend Connor is able to reach him and uncover the truth about what really happened

"A compelling mystery that is also a moving story of family, friendship, and seduction." Booklist

★ The **view** from Saturday. Atheneum Bks. for Young Readers 1996 163p $16.95; pa $5.99

Grades: 4 5 6 7 **Fic**

1. School stories 2. Friendship -- Fiction 3. People with physical disabilities -- Fiction

ISBN 0-689-80993-X; 0-689-81721-5 pa

LC 95-52624

Awarded the Newbery Medal, 1997

Four students, with their own individual stories, develop a special bond and attract the attention of their teacher, a paraplegic, who choses them to represent their sixth-grade class in the Academic Bowl competition

"Glowing with humor and dusted with magic. . . . Wrought with deep compassion and a keen sense of balance." Publ Wkly

Korman, Gordon

★ The **Juvie** three. Hyperion 2008 249p lib bdg $15.99

Grades: 7 8 9 10 **Fic**

1. Friendship -- Fiction 2. Juvenile delinquency -- Fiction

ISBN 978-1-4231-0158-1; 1-4231-0158-8

LC 2008-19087

Gecko, Arjay, and Terence, all in trouble with the law, must find a way to keep their halfway house open in order to stay out of juvenile detention.

"Korman keeps lots of balls in the air as he handles each boy's distinct voice and character—as well as the increasingly absurd situation—with humor and flashes of sadness." Booklist

★ **Schooled**. Hyperion Books for Children 2007 208p $15.99

Grades: 6 7 8 9 **Fic**

1. School stories 2. Hippies -- Fiction

ISBN 0-7868-5692-0

Homeschooled by his hippie grandmother, Capricorn (Cap) Anderson has never watched television, tasted a pizza, or even heard of a wedgie. But when his grandmother lands in the hospital, Cap is forced to move in with a guidance counselor and attend the local middle school.

"This rewarding novel features an engaging main character and some memorable moments of comedy, tenderness, and reflection." Booklist

★ **Son** of the mob. Hyperion Bks. for Children 2002 262p hardcover o.p. pa $7.99

Grades: 7 8 9 10 **Fic**

1. Mafia -- Fiction

ISBN 0-7868-0769-5; 0-7868-1593-0 pa

LC 2002-68672

Seventeen-year-old Vince's life is constantly complicated by the fact that he is the son of a powerful Mafia boss, a relationship that threatens to destroy his romance with the daughter of an FBI agent

"The fast-paced, tightly focused story addresses the problems of being an honest kid in a family of outlaws—and loving them anyway. Korman doesn't ignore the seamier side of mob life, but even when the subject matter gets violent . . . he keeps things light by relating his tale in the first-person voice of a humorously sarcastic yet law-abiding wise guy." Horn Book

Another title about Vince is:

Son of the mob: Hollywood hustle (2004)

Swindle; Gordan Korman. Scholastic Press 2008 252p (Swindle)

Grades: 4 5 6 **Fic**

1. Baseball cards -- Fiction 2. Swindlers and swindling -- Fiction

ISBN 0-439-90344-0; 0-439-90345-9 pa; 978-0-439-90344-8; 978-0-439-90345-5 pa

LC 2007-17225

After unscrupulous collector S. Wendell Palomino cons him out of a valuable baseball card, sixth-grader Griffin Bing puts together a band of misfits to break into Palomino's store and steal the card back, planning to use the money to finance his father's failing invention, the SmartPick fruit picker. "Grades four to six." (Bull Cent Child Books)

"The plot is the main attraction, and its clever intricacies—silly, deceptively predictable, and seasoned with the occasional unexpected twist—do not disappoint." Booklist

Other titles in this series are:

Zoobreak (2009)
Framed (2010)
Showoff (2012)
Hideout (2013)
Jackpot (2014)
Unleashed (2015)
Jingle (2016)

Ungifted; Gordon Korman. Balzer + Bray 2012 280 p. $16.99

Grades: 4 5 6 **Fic**

1. School stories 2. Humorous fiction -- fiction 3. Robots -- Fiction 4. Schools -- Fiction 5. Behavior -- Fiction 6. Robotics -- Fiction 7. Middle schools -- Fiction 8. Gifted children -- Fiction

ISBN 006174266X; 9780061742668

LC 2012008408

In this children's book, "hyperactive, heedless Donovan Curtis whacks a school statue of Atlas with a stick, which sends the huge metal globe on Atlas's shoulders rolling into the gym during a basketball game, which lands Donovan in the superintendent's office, where his name is mistakenly entered by the irate administrator onto a list of candidates for the district's middle-school gifted program." The plot includes "Donovan's shallow yet indispensable contribution to his team's robotics competition." (Bulletin of the Center for Children's Books)

Followed by Supergifted (2018)

Zoobreak. Scholastic Press 2009 230p $16.99; pa $6.99

Grades: 3 4 5 6 **Fic**

1. Adventure fiction 2. Zoos -- Fiction 3. Theft -- Fiction 4. Long Island (N.Y.) -- Fiction 5. Lost and found possessions -- Fiction

ISBN 978-0-545-12499-7; 0-545-12499-9; 978-0-545-12500-0 pa; 0-545-12500-6 pa

LC 2009015456

Sequel to: Swindle (2008)

After a class trip to a floating zoo where animals are mistreated and Savannah's missing pet monkey is found in a cage, Long Island sixth-grader Griffin Bing and his band of misfits plan a rescue.

"Both children and adults will find the story fast moving and enjoyable. The often-unpredictable plot is interesting, full of humor, and good fun." Voice Youth Advocates

Kositsky, Lynne

The **thought** of high windows. Kids Can Press 2004 175p hardcover o.p. pa $6.95

Grades: 7 8 9 10 **Fic**

1. Jews -- Fiction 2. Holocaust, 1933-1945 -- Fiction

ISBN 1-55337-621-8; 1-55337-622-6 pa

"Esther describes her life as one of a group of Jewish children taken from Germany to France by the Red Cross during World War II. The novel begins when she is 15 and living in a French castle; her childhood in Berlin is described through flashbacks. . . . Based on true events, this is an immediate, painfully honest story." SLJ

Kostick, Conor

Edda. Viking 2011 440p il

Grades: 7 8 9 10 **Fic**

1. War stories 2. Science fiction 3. Video games -- Fiction

ISBN 0-670-01218-1; 978-0-670-01218-3

LC 2011003000

Sequel to: Saga (2008)

In the virtual world of Edda, ruler Scanthax decides he wants to invade another virtual world, embroiling the universes of Edda, Saga, and Epic in war, with only three teenagers to try to restore peace.

"Humans, electronic beings and servers are separated by light years and metaphysics, but Kostick's action-filled series conclusion is immediate and relevant." Kirkus

★ **Epic**. Viking 2007 364p $17.99

Grades: 7 8 9 10 **Fic**

1. Fantasy fiction 2. Video games -- Fiction

ISBN 0-670-06179-4; 978-0-670-06179-2

LC 2006-19958

On New Earth, a world based on a video role-playing game, fourteen-year-old Erik pursuades his friends to aid him in some unusual gambits in order to save his father from exile and safeguard the futures of each of their families.

"There is intrigue and mystery throughout this captivating page-turner. Veins of moral and ethical social situations and decisions provide some great opportunities for discussion. Well written and engaging." SLJ

Other titles in this series are:
Edda (2011)
Saga (2008)

Saga. Viking 2008 367p $18.99

Grades: 7 8 9 10 **Fic**

1. Fantasy fiction 2. Video games -- Fiction

ISBN 978-0-6700-6280-5; 0-6700-6280-4

LC 2007-32175

Sequel to Epic (2007)

On Saga, a world based on a video role-playing game, fifteen-year-old Ghost lives to break rules, but the Dark Queen who controls Saga plans to enslave its people and those of New Earth, and Ghost and her airboarding friends, along with Erik and his friends from Epic, try to stop her.

"The plot and pacing are near perfect in this tale of a world cramped by fear and tradition. . . . Compulsively readable and palpable (the descriptions of airboarding are a near-physical experience), it will appeal to SF fans across the board." Voice Youth Advocates

Kottaras, E. Katherine

The **best** possible answer; E. Katherine Kottaras. St. Martin's Griffin 2016 272 p. (hardcover) $18.99

Grades: 8 9 10 11 **Fic**

1. Perfection -- fiction 2. Teenage girls -- fiction

ISBN 9781250072818

LC 2016014556

In this novel, by E. Katherine Kottaras, "super-achiever Viviana Rabinovich-Lowe has never had room to be anything less than perfect. But her quest for perfection is derailed when her boyfriend leaks secret pictures of her to the entire school—pictures no one was ever meant to see. Making matters worse, her parents might be getting divorced and now her perfect family is falling apart. For the first time, Vivi feels like a complete and utter failure." (Publisher's note)

"A sensitive novel about accepting imperfection." Kirkus

Kraus, Daniel

The **death** and life of Zebulon Finch; Volume one At the edge of empire. as prepared by the esteemed fictionist, Daniel Kraus. Simon & Schuster Books for Young Readers 2015 656 p. (hardcover : alk. paper) $18.99

Grades: 9 10 11 12 **Fic**

1. Death -- Fiction 2. Murder -- Fiction 3. Dead -- Fiction

ISBN 9781481411394; 9781481411400

LC 2014039293

In this book, by Daniel Kraus, "Zebulon Finch is gunned down by the shores of Lake Michigan. But after mere minutes in the void, he is mysteriously resurrected. His second life will be nothing like his first. Zebulon's new existence begins as a sideshow attraction in a traveling medicine show. From there he will be poked and prodded by a scientist obsessed with mastering the secrets of death." (Publisher's note)

"A hefty volume for fans of historical fiction with an undead twist." SLJ

Followed by:
Empire decayed (2016)

Krieg, Jim

★ **Griff** Carver, hallway patrol. Razorbill 2010 224p $15.99

Grades: 4 5 6 7 **Fic**

1. School stories 2. Counterfeits and counterfeiting -- Fiction
ISBN 978-1-59514-276-4; 1-59514-276-2

LC 2009-32553

Legendary Griff Carver joins the Rampart Middle School Hallway Patrol and, with the help of his friend Tommy, Griff solves the case of counterfeit hall passes.

"With comically over-the-top cop lingo . . . Griff and Tommy tell their stories through incident reports and interviews, adding drama and humor to the most mundane aspects of school. . . . Krieg will keep readers chuckling through the hilarious but action-packed showdown." Publ Wkly

Krishnaswami, Uma

★ The **grand** plan to fix everything; [illustrations by Abigail Halpin] Atheneum Books for Young Readers 2011 224p il $16.99

Grades: 4 5 6 7 **Fic**

1. India -- Fiction 2. Actors -- Fiction 3. Moving -- Fiction 4. Friendship -- Fiction 5. East Indian Americans -- Fiction
ISBN 978-1-4169-9589-0; 1-4169-9589-7

LC 2010035145

Eleven-year-old Dini loves movies, and so when she learns that her family is moving to India for two years, her devastation over leaving her best friend in Maryland is tempered by the possibility of meeting her favorite actress, Dolly Singh.

"An out-of-the-ordinary setting, a distinctive middle-grade character with an unusual passion, and the pace of a lively Bollywood 'fillum' make this novel a delight." Publ Wkly

Step up to the plate, Maria Singh; by Uma Krishnaswami. Tu Books, an imprint of Lee & Low Books 2017 276 p. (hardback) $16.95

Grades: 4 5 6 7 8 **Fic**

1. Softball -- fiction 2. East Indian Americans -- fiction 3. Racially mixed people -- fiction 4. World War, 1939-1945 -- fiction
ISBN 9781600602610

LC 2016055988

In this book, by Uma Krishnaswami, "Maria Singh longs to play softball in the first-ever girls' team forming in Yuba City, California. . . . Meanwhile, Maria's parents--Papi from India and Mama from Mexico--can no longer protect their children from prejudice and from the discriminatory laws. . . . When the family is on the brink of losing their farm, Maria must decide if she has what it takes to step up and find her voice in an unfair world." (Publisher's note)

"Filled with heart, this tale brings to life outspoken and determined Maria, her love for baseball, and her multicultural community and their challenges and triumphs." Kirkus

Kristoff, Jay

★ **Aurora** rising; Amie Kaufman and Jay Kristoff. Alfred A. Knopf 2019 480 p. illustrations (The Andromeda cycle) (hardcover) $18.99

Grades: 8 9 10 11 12 **Fic**

1. Science fiction 2. Space flight -- Fiction 3. Human-alien encounters -- Fiction 4. Adventure and adventurers -- Fiction
ISBN 9781524720964; 9781524720971

LC 2018026944

"The year is 2380, and the graduating cadets of Aurora Academy are being assigned their first missions. Star pupil Tyler Jones is ready to recruit the squad of his dreams, but . . . [he is] stuck with the dregs nobody else in the academy would touch . . . . And Ty's squad isn't even his biggest problem--that'd be Aurora Jie-Lin O'Malley, the girl he's just rescued from interdimensional space." (Publisher's note)

"Rotating perspectives and never-flagging energy propel this narrative forward, which, if it weren't compelling enough on its own, is given illustrious life by its ragtag, always-at-odds cast." Booklist

Dev1at3; Deviate. Jay Kristoff. Alfred A. Knopf 2019 422 p. $18.99

Grades: 7 8 9 10 11 12 **Fic**

1. Science fiction 2. Robots -- Fiction 3. Androids -- Fiction
ISBN 1524713961; 9781524713966

In this book in the LIFEL1K3 series, by Jay Kristoff, "in the wake of a climactic battle in the ruined city of Babel, . . . Eve is torn between the memories of the girl she was, and the synthetic she's discovered herself to be. Together with her lifelike 'siblings,' Eve sets out to find the real Ana Monrova, whose DNA is the key to building an army of lifelikes. Meanwhile, Eve's best friend, Lemon, is coming to terms with a power that she has long denied." (Publisher's note)

"The worldbuilding, from lingo to Brotherhood mythology, develops alongside action sequences as the story builds to an exciting cliffhanger. Solid and fresh, especially for the second installment in a trilogy." --Kirkus

Lifel1k3, Knopf, 2018

Gemina; Amie Kaufman & Jay Kristoff ; journal illustrations by Marie Lu. Knopf Books for Young Readers 2016 672 p. illustrations (hardcover) $19.99

Grades: 8 9 10 11 12 **Fic**

1. Science fiction 2. Space stations -- Fiction 3. Interplanetary voyages -- Fiction 4. Artificial intelligence -- Fiction
ISBN 9780553499155; 9780553499162

LC 2015037131

Sequel to: Illuminae (2015)

This second book in the Illuminae Files series by Amie Kaufman and Jay Kristoff "describes the experience of Hanna, who lives aboard the Heimdall. . . . Her world unravels when agents attempt to seize control of the space station. . . . Hanna finds an unlikely ally in Nik, an unsavory gang member who deals 'dust' in the space station, as they attempt to defend the Heimdall, save the Hypatia, contain vicious alien creatures, and fix a rip in the space-time continuum." (School Library Journal)

"An action-packed thrill ride and stellar head trip." Kirkus

★ **Illuminae**; Amie Kaufman ; Jay Kristoff. Alfred A. Knopf 2015 608 p. illustrations (hardcover) $18.99

Grades: 8 9 10 11 12 **Fic**

1. Science fiction 2. Interplanetary voyages -- Fiction 3. Plague -- Fiction 4. Artificial intelligence -- Fiction
ISBN 9780553499117; 9780553499124; 9780553499148

LC 2014017908

In this young adult novel, by Amie Kaufman and Jay Kristoff, "the year is 2575, and two rival megacorporations are at war over a planet that's little more than an ice-covered speck at the edge of the universe. Too bad nobody thought to warn the people living on it. With enemy fire raining down on them, Kady and Ezra--who are barely even talking to each other--are forced to fight their way onto one of the evacuating fleet, with an enemy warship in hot pursuit." (Publisher's note)

Other titles in this series are:
Gemina (2016)

Obsidio (2018)

Lifel1k3; Jay Kristoff. Random House Childrens Books 2018 416 p. $18.99

Grades: 7 8 9 10 11 12 **Fic**

1. Robots -- Fiction 2. Androids -- Fiction

ISBN 1524713929; 9781524713928

In this book in the Lifelike series, by Jay Kristoff, "Eve isn't looking for secrets--she's too busy looking over her shoulder. The robot gladiator she's just spent six months building has been reduced to a smoking wreck, and the only thing keeping her Grandpa from the grave was the fistful of credits she just lost to the bookies. To top it off, she's discovered she can destroy electronics with the power of her mind, and the puritanical Brotherhood are building a coffin her size." (Goodreads)

Other titles in this series are:

Dev1at3 (2019)

Obsidio; Amie Kaufman & Jay Kristoff ; with journal illustrations by Marie Lu. Alfred A. Knopf 2018 624 p. (hardcover) $19.99

Grades: 8 9 10 11 12 **Fic**

1. Science fiction 2. Interplanetary voyages -- Fiction 3. Artificial intelligence -- Fiction

ISBN 9780553499193; 9780553499209

LC 2017020645

In this book in the Illuminae Files series, by Amie Kaufman and Jay Kristoff, illustrated by Marie Lu, "Kady, Ezra, Hanna, and Nik narrowly escaped with their lives from the attacks on Heimdall station and now find themselves crammed with 2,000 refugees on the container ship, Mao. With the jump station destroyed and their resources scarce, the only option is to return to Kerenza." (Publisher's note)

Kuehn, Stephanie

Complicit; Stephanie Kuehn. St. Martin's Griffin 2014 256 p. illustrations (hardback) $19.99

Grades: 8 9 10 11 12 **Fic**

1. Orphans -- Fiction 2. Mental illness -- Fiction 3. Private schools -- Fiction 4. Brothers and sisters -- Fiction 5. Amnesia -- Fiction 6. Schools -- Fiction

ISBN 1250044596; 9781250044594

LC 2014008117

"Cate is out of juvie. For her little brother, 17-year-old Jamie, that's bad. It's been two years since Cate horribly injured a rival by setting a barn on fire.This was the last in a long series of tempestuous, violent acts Cate committed since she and Jamie were adopted following the murder of their mother. With Cate locked up, Jamie is almost a whole being. . . . But Cate's return brings everything flooding back." (Booklist)

"...every page shows a firm, surprising choice, whether you like it or not. Cate, naturally, is the main event, the alternatingly irrational, gentle, explosive, and enigmatic center of this fast, black whirlpool of a novel." (Booklist)

Kuhlman, Evan

The **last** invisible boy; written by Evan Kuhlman; illustrated by J. P. Coovert. Atheneum Books for Young Readers 2008 233p il $16.99; pa $5.99

Grades: 4 5 6 7 **Fic**

1. School stories 2. Ohio -- Fiction 3. Bereavement -- Fiction 4. Family life -- Fiction 5. Father-son relationship -- Fiction

ISBN 978-1-4169-5797-3; 1-4169-5797-9; 978-1-4169-6089-8 pa; 1-4169-6089-9 pa

LC 2007-40258

In the wake of his father's sudden death, twelve-year-old Finn feels he is becoming invisible as his hair and skin become whiter by the day, and so he writes and illustrates a book to try to understand what is happening and to hold on to himself and his father

"Vivid details . . . add depth to the characterizations and grow in meaning as the story progresses. . . . Finn's distinct narrative voice, and the sweet precision with which the story unfolds, give this title a touching resonance." Booklist

Kuhn, Sarah

I love you so Mochi; Sarah Kuhn. Scholastic 2019 320 p. $17.99

Grades: 8 9 10 11 12 **Fic**

1. Japan -- Fiction 2. Teenagers -- Fiction 3. Mothers and daughters -- Fiction

ISBN 1338302884; 9781338302882

In this book, by Sarah Kuhn, "Kimi Nakamura . . . [is] obsessed with transforming everyday ephemera into Kimi Originals. . . . But her mother disapproves . . . [so when] Kimi's estranged grandparents, invit[e] her to Kyoto . . . she seizes the opportunity to get away from the disaster of her life. . . . And what begins as a trip to escape her problems quickly becomes a way for Kimi to learn more about the mother she left behind, and to figure out where her own heart lies." (Publisher's note)

"Kuhn ... has brought together travel, fashion, food, romance, and family to create an incredibly sweet and heartwarming coming of age romantic comedy. weaving in Japanese vocabulary and slang, she also subtly addresses racism and differences between Japanese and Japanese -American cultures." (Kirkus)

Kurti, Richard

Monkey wars; Richard Kurti. Delacorte Press 2015 416 p. (hardcover) $17.99

Grades: 7 8 9 10 11 12 **Fic**

1. Monkeys -- Fiction 2. Human-animal relationships -- Fiction 3. War -- Fiction 4. Langurs -- Fiction 5. Rhesus monkey -- Fiction

ISBN 0385744412; 9780375991653; 9780385744416

LC 2014038203

In this novel by Richard Kurti, "when rhesus monkeys are brutally massacred on the dusty streets of Kolkata by a troop of power-hungry langur monkeys, Mico, a privileged langur, becomes entangled in the secrets at the heart of his troop's leadership. He feels compelled to help the few surviving rhesus, especially Papina, a young female he befriends, even though doing so goes against everything he's been taught." (Publisher's note)

"This book will be useful in discussions about apathy versus taking a stand, the domination of one culture over another through time, ethnic cleansing, relocation, boundaries, and genocide." VOYA

Kurtz, Chris

The **adventures** of a South Pole pig; a novel of snow and courage. Chris Kurtz ; illustrations by Jennifer Black Reinhardt. Harcourt Children's Books, Houghton Mifflin Harcourt 2013 288 p. $16.99

Grades: 4 5 6 7 **Fic**

1. Sled dog racing -- fiction 2. Dogs -- Fiction 3. Pigs -- Fiction 4. Sled dogs -- Fiction 5. Antarctica -- Fiction 6. Dogsledding -- Fiction 7. Adventure and adventurers -- Fiction

ISBN 0547634552; 9780547634555

LC 2012027226

In this children's story, by Chris Kurtz, illustrated by Jennifer Black Reinhardt, "the day Flora spots a team of sled dogs is the day she sets her heart on becoming a sled pig. Before she knows it, she's on board a ship to Antarctica for the most exhilarating--and dangerous--adventure of her life." (Publisher's note)

L'Engle, Madeleine

A **swiftly** tilting planet. Farrar, Straus & Giroux 1978 278p $18; pa $6.99

Grades: 5 6 7 8 9 10 Fic

1. Fantasy fiction

ISBN 978-0-374-37362-7; 0-374-37362-0; 978-0-312-36856-2 pa; 0-312-36856-9 pa

LC 78-9648

Sequel to: A wind in the door (1973)

ALA YALSA Margaret A. Edwards Award (1998)

The youngest of the Murry children must travel through time and space in a battle against an evil dictator who would destroy the entire universe

A **wind** in the door. Farrar, Straus & Giroux 1973 211p $17.99; pa $6.99

Grades: 5 6 7 8 9 10 Fic

1. Fantasy fiction

ISBN 0-374-38443-6; 0-312-36854-2 pa

LC 73-751176

Sequel to: A wrinkle in time (1962)

"L'Engle mixes classical theology, contemporary family life, and futuristic science fiction to make a completely convincing tale that should put under its spell both readers familiar with the Murrys and those meeting them for the first time." N Y Times Book Rev

Followed by: A swiftly tilting planet (1978)

★ A **wrinkle** in time. Farrar, Straus & Giroux 1962 211p $17; pa $7.99

Grades: 5 6 7 8 9 10 Fic

1. Fantasy fiction

ISBN 0-374-38613-7; 0-312-36754-6 pa

Awarded The Newbery Medal, 1963

ALA YALSA Margaret A. Edwards Award (1998)

This book "makes unusual demands on the imagination and consequently gives great rewards." Horn Book

Other titles in this series are:

A wind in the door (1973)

A swiftly tilting planet (1978)

Many waters (1986)

An acceptable time (1989)

La Fevers, R. L.

Theodosia and the eyes of Horus; [illustrated by Yoko Tanaka] Houghton Mifflin Harcourt 2010 375p il $16

Grades: 4 5 6 7 Fic

1. Adventure fiction 2. Magic -- Fiction 3. Museums -- Fiction 4. Family life -- Fiction 5. London (England) -- Fiction

ISBN 978-0-547-22592-0; 0-547-22592-X

Eleven-year-old Theodosia's ability to detect black magic raises her suspicions about a magician known as the Great Awi Bubu, while Henry, home for the spring holidays, discovers an artifact at the Museum of Legends and Antiquities that is coveted by every black-cloaked occultist in London.

"Once again, supernaturally talented Theodosia navigates around her etiquette-obsessed grandmother and absentminded parents in a suspenseful, satisfying fantasy that's filled with the specifics of magical ritual sure to delight readers." Booklist

Theodosia and the last pharaoh; illustrated by Yoko Tanaka. Houghton Mifflin Harcourt 2011 394p il $16.99

Grades: 4 5 6 7 Fic

1. Adventure fiction 2. Egypt -- Fiction 3. Magic -- Fiction 4. Museums -- Fiction 5. Family life -- Fiction

ISBN 978-0-547-39018-5; 0-547-39018-1

LC 2010032224

When eleven-year-old Theodosia and her cat, Isis, travel to Egypt to return the Orb of Ra and the Emerald Tablet, she hopes to learn more about her origins but finds, instead, the Serpents of Chaos and a precious treasure that suddenly appears and disappears.

"Tanaka's drawings nicely extend the action." Booklist

Theodosia and the Staff of Osiris; [by] R.L. LaFevers; illustrated by Yoko Tanaka. Houghton Mifflin Co. 2008 387p il $16

Grades: 4 5 6 7 Fic

1. Adventure fiction 2. Magic -- Fiction 3. Mummies -- Fiction 4. Museums -- Fiction 5. Family life -- Fiction 6. London (England) -- Fiction

ISBN 978-0-618-92764-7; 0-618-92764-6

LC 2008007277

When mummies go missing all over London, eleven-year-old Theodosia puts aside her fight against the Serpents of Chaos to save her father, who is suspected in the thefts, all the while avoiding a string of new governesses.

"Clever and exciting just like the previous book, this also features a layered relationship between Theodosia and her grandmother." Booklist

La Valley, Josanne

The **Vine** basket; by Josanne La Valley. Clarion Books 2013 252 p. (hardcover) $16.99

Grades: 4 5 6 7 8 Fic

1. China -- Fiction 2. Farm life -- Fiction 3. Basket making -- Fiction 4. Ethnic relations -- Fiction 5. Farm life -- China -- Fiction 6. Fathers and daughters -- Fiction 7. Uighur (Turkic people) -- Fiction

ISBN 0547848013; 9780547848013

LC 2012021007

Asian/Pacific American Awards for Literature: Children's Literature Honor (2014)

In this novel, by Josanne La Valley, "things aren't looking good for fourteen-year-old Mehrigul. She yearns to be in school, but she's needed on the family farm. . . . Her only hope is an American woman who buys one of her decorative vine baskets for a staggering sum and says she will return in three weeks for more. Mehrigul must brave terrible storms, torn-up hands from working the fields, and her father's scorn to get the baskets done." (Publisher's note)

"The vivid and authentic sense of place, custom, and politics serves as an effective vehicle for the skillfully characterized, emotionally charged story. . . . The realistic and satisfying resolution will resonate with readers . . . An absorbing read and an excellent choice for expanding global understanding." SLJ

Laban, Elizabeth

The **Tragedy** Paper; Elizabeth LaBan. Alfred A. Knopf 2013 320 p. $17.99

Grades: 7 8 9 10 11 12 Fic

1. School stories 2. Romance fiction 3. Albinos and albinism -- Fiction 4. Schools -- Fiction 5. High schools -- Fiction 6. Boarding schools -- Fiction 7. Dating (Social customs) -- Fiction 8.

Interpersonal relations -- Fiction
ISBN 0375870407; 9780375870408; 9780375970405; 9780375989124

LC 2012011294

This novel by Elizabeth Laban "follows the story of Tim Macbeth, a seventeen-year-old albino and a recent transfer to the prestigious Irving School. . . . He finds himself falling for the quintessential 'It' girl, Vanessa Sheller. . . . Vanessa is into him, too, but she can kiss her social status goodbye if anyone ever finds out. Tim and Vanessa begin a clandestine romance, but looming over them is the Tragedy Paper, Irving's version of a senior year thesis." (Publisher's note)

Lacey, Josh

Island of Thieves; Josh Lacey. Houghton Mifflin 2012 228 p.

Grades: 4 5 6 7 8 **Fic**

1. Peru -- Fiction 2. Adventure fiction 3. Uncles -- Fiction 4. Pirates -- Fiction 5. Buried treasure -- Fiction 6. Islands -- Fiction 7. Mystery and detective stories 8. Adventure and adventurers -- Fiction
ISBN 0547763271; 9780547763279

LC 2011033893

In this children's novel, a boy takes part in "swashbuckling adventures in faraway places, freed from the strictures of parents, school, siblings and caregivers. . . . Tom nearly ruins his parents' vacation by accidentally burning down the shed in his backyard. . . . Harvey welcomes Tom . . . but as soon as Tom's parents leave, he starts packing for Peru. . . . When he tells Tom it's because he has an opportunity to hunt for pirate treasure, Tom blackmails his uncle into taking him along." (Kirkus)

LaFaye, A.

Stella stands alone; [by] A. LaFaye. Simon & Schuster Books for Young Readers 2008 245p map $16.99

Grades: 7 8 9 10 **Fic**

1. Orphans -- Fiction 2. African Americans -- Fiction 3. Swindlers and swindling -- Fiction 4. Reconstruction (1865-1876) -- Fiction
ISBN 978-1-4169-1164-7; 1-4169-1164-2

LC 2007-38725

Fourteen-year-old Stella, orphaned just after the Civil War, fights to keep her family's plantation and fulfill her father's desire to turn land over to the people who have worked on it for generations, but first she must find her father's hidden deed and will.

"Readers will be drawn along by Stella's refusal to act helpless and sweet and her discovery of strength and kindness in unexpected places. The sadness and anger, and the wrenching legacy of slavery are present throughout." Booklist

Water steps. Milkweed Editions 2009 175p $16.95; pa $6.95

Grades: 4 5 6 7 **Fic**

1. Water -- Fiction 2. Phobias -- Fiction 3. Irish Americans -- Fiction
ISBN 978-1-57131-687-5; 1-57131-687-6; 978-1-57131-686-8 pa; 1-57131-686-8 pa

LC 2008011684

Eleven-year-old Kyna, terrified of water since her family drowned in a storm that nearly took her life as well, works to overcome her phobia when her adoptive parents, Irish immigrants with a mysterious past, rent a cabin on Lake Champlain for the summer.

"The language is almost poetic with its use of sensory detail, alliteration, and precise word choices. A satisfying story of overcoming one's fears and discovering secrets." SLJ

LaFleur, Suzanne

Beautiful blue world; Suzanne LaFleur. Wendy Lamb Books 2016 224 p. illustrations (hardback) $16.99

Grades: 5 6 7 8 **Fic**

1. Child soldiers -- fiction 2. Children and war -- fiction 3. Female friendship -- fiction 4. War -- Fiction 5. Survival -- Fiction 6. Best friends -- Fiction
ISBN 9780307980328; 9780375990892; 9780385743006

LC 2015046201

In this children's book by Suzanne LaFleur, "Sofarende is at war. For twelve-year-old Mathilde, it means food shortages, feuding neighbors, and bombings. Even so, as long as she and her best friend, Megs, are together, they'll be all right. But the army is recruiting children, and paying families well for their service. If Megs takes the test, Mathilde knows she will pass. Megs hopes the army is the way to save her family. Mathilde fears it might separate them forever." (Publisher's note)

"Deeply emotional, compelling, and brilliant." Kirkus

Another title in this series is:
Threads of blue (2017)

Threads of blue; Suzanne LaFleur. Wendy Lamb Books 2017 203 p. map (hardcover) $16.99

Grades: 5 6 7 8 **Fic**

1. Refugees -- Fiction 2. Friendship -- Fiction 3. War -- Fiction 4. Espionage -- Fiction
ISBN 9781101939994; 9781101940013; 9781101940006; 9781101940020

LC 2016048219

Sequel to: Beautiful blue world (2016)

In this book, by Suzanne LaFleur, "a war took Mathilde away from her family when she was chosen to serve her country, Sofarende, with other children working on a secret military project. . . . In this . . . sequel . . . , Mathilde must make her way through a new stage of the war. Haunted by the bold choice she made on the night she chose her country's future over her own well-being, she clings to the promise Megs made long ago: 'Whatever happens, I'll be with you.'" (Publisher's note)

"Beautifully written in first-person narrative, LaFleur has crafted a tale about the ravages of war and survival, starring an unforgettable heroine." SLJ

LaFleur, Suzanne M.

★ **Love,** Aubrey. Wendy Lamb Books 2009 262p $15.99; lib bdg $18.99

Grades: 5 6 7 8 **Fic**

1. School stories 2. Letters -- Fiction 3. Vermont -- Fiction 4. Friendship -- Fiction 5. Bereavement -- Fiction 6. Grandmothers -- Fiction 7. Abandoned children -- Fiction 8. Depression (Psychology) -- Fiction
ISBN 978-0-385-73774-6; 0-385-73774-2; 978-0-385-90686-9 lib bdg; 0-385-90686-2 lib bdg

LC 2008-31742

While living with her Gram in Vermont, eleven-year-old Aubrey writes letters as a way of dealing with losing her father and sister in a car accident, and then being abandoned by her grief-stricken mother.

Aubrey's "detailed progression from denial to acceptance makes her both brave and credible in this honest and realistic portrayal of grief." Kirkus

Lai, Thanhha

★ **Inside** out and back again. Harper 2011 262p $15.99

Grades: 4 5 6 7 **Fic**

1. Novels in verse 2. Alabama -- Fiction 3. Vietnam -- Fiction 4.

Immigrants -- Fiction 5. Vietnamese Americans -- Fiction
ISBN 978-0-06-196278-3; 0-06-196278-3

LC 2010007855

National Book Award: Young People's Literature (2011)

"For all the ten years of her life, Hà has only known Saigon: the thrills of its markets, the joy of its traditions, and the warmth of her friends close by. But now the Vietnam War has reached her home. Hà and her family are forced to flee as Saigon falls, and they board a ship headed toward hope. In America, Hà discovers the foreign world of Alabama: the coldness of its strangers, the dullness of its food . . . and the strength of her very own family." (Publisher's note)

"Based on Lai's personal experience, this first novel captures a child-refugee's struggle with rare honesty. Written in accessible, short free-verse poems." Booklist

Lai, Thanhha, 1965-

★ **Listen,** Slowly; Thanhha Lai. Harpercollins Childrens Books 2015 272 p. illustration $16.99

Grades: 4 5 6 7 8 **Fic**

1. Culture 2. Family -- Fiction 3. Vietnam -- Fiction 4. Families -- Fiction 5. Grandmothers -- Fiction 6. Vietnam War, 1961-1975 -- Missing in action -- Fiction
ISBN 0062229184; 9780062229182

"A California girl born and raised, Mai . . . has to travel to Vietnam with her grandmother, who is going back to find out what really happened to her husband during the Vietnam War. Mai's parents think this trip will be a great opportunity for their out-of-touch daughter to learn more about her culture. But to Mai, those are their roots, not her own. To survive her trip, Mai must find a balance between her two completely different worlds." (Publisher's note)

"Gracefully written and enriched by apposite figures of speech, Listen, Slowly is a superb, sometimes humorous, always thought-provoking coming-of-age story." Booklist

Lairamore, Dawn

Ivy and the meanstalk. Holiday House 2011 227p $16.95

Grades: 4 5 6 7 **Fic**

1. Fairy tales 2. Giants -- Fiction 3. Dragons -- Fiction 4. Princesses -- Fiction
ISBN 978-0-8234-2392-7; 0-8234-2392-1

LC 2010048627

Sequel to: Ivy's ever after (2010)

Fourteen-year-old Princess Ivy wants nothing more than to have a little fun in the company of her dragon friend, Elridge, but unless she can recover the magical harp snatched by a thieving youth named Jack long ago, her entire kingdom will suffer an unspeakable fate.

This is "delightful and humorous. . . . Lairamore's well-developed characters are excellent riffs on fairy-tale traditions. . . . Various settings are depicted in rich detail while never detracting from the narrative. The plot is filled with action-packed scenes." SLJ

★ **Ivy's** ever after. Holiday House 2010 311p $16.95

Grades: 4 5 6 7 **Fic**

1. Fairy tales 2. Dragons -- Fiction 3. Princesses -- Fiction
ISBN 978-0-8234-2261-6; 0-8234-2261-5

LC 2009-43288

Fourteen-year-old Ivy, a most unroyal princess, befriends Elridge, the dragon sent to keep her in a tower, and together they set out on a perilous quest to find Ivy's fairy godmother, who may be able to save both from their dire fates.

"Ivy is an engaging alternative to the standard damsel-in-distress figure, and with a lushly vivid setting, witty dialogue, and lots of adventure, this well-plotted first novel will appeal to fans of Vivian Vande Velde's A Hidden Magic (1985) and A Well-Timed Enchantment (1990)." Booklist

Followed by: Ivy and the meanstalk (2011)

Laird, Elizabeth

The **betrayal** of Maggie Blair. Houghton Mifflin 2011 423p il $16.99

Grades: 7 8 9 10 **Fic**

1. Uncles -- Fiction 2. Witchcraft -- Fiction 3. Scotland -- History -- 17th century -- Fiction
ISBN 978-0-547-34126-2; 0-547-34126-1

LC 2010-25120

In seventeenth-century Scotland, sixteen-year-old Maggie Blair is sentenced to be hanged as a witch but escapes to the home of her uncle, placing him and his family in great danger as she risks her life to save them all from the King's men.

"Laird seamlessly weaves a fairly comprehensive history lesson into an engaging, lively story." Bull Cent Child Books

Lancaster, Mike A.

The **future** we left behind; Mike A. Lancaster. Egmont USA 2012 367 p. (hardback) $16.99

Grades: 7 8 9 10 **Fic**

1. Science fiction 2. Cults -- Fiction 3. England -- Fiction 4. Computer programs -- Fiction 5. Family life -- England -- Fiction 6. Technological innovations -- Fiction
ISBN 1606844105; 9781606844106; 9781606844113

LC 2012003794

Sequel to: Human.4

This sequel to "Human.4" is set in the future. Here, "Peter is the son of the man who saved the world by inventing robot bees. Destined by his wealthy genius father for a future in science, Peter rebels against both by enrolling in a literature class and befriending Alpha, a girl in a wacky religious cult. Alpha is a Strakerite, following the ancient tapes of Kyle Straker. Kyle and his girlfriend Lilly believed humans are regularly upgraded by aliens. Skeptical at first, Peter is soon convinced." (Kirkus)

★ **Human.4**. Egmont USA 2011 231p $16.99

Grades: 7 8 9 10 **Fic**

1. Science fiction 2. Computers -- Fiction 3. Family life -- Fiction 4. Great Britain -- Fiction
ISBN 978-1-6068-4099-3; 1-6068-4099-1

LC 2010030313

Twenty-first century fourteen-year-old Kyle was hypnotized when humanity was upgraded to 1.0 and he, incompatible with the new technology, exposes its terrifying impact in a tape-recording found by the superhumans of the future.

"Lancaster fashions a fast-paced, upsetting little thriller punctuated by ominous editorial notes that translate Kyle's details for the futuristic audience." Booklist

Landman, Tanya

★ **Hell** and high water; Tanya Landman. Candlewick Press 2017 312 p. (hardcover) $17.99

Grades: 7 8 9 10 **Fic**

1. Racially mixed people -- Fiction 2. Offenses against the person -- Fiction 3. Historical fiction 4. Detective and mystery stories
ISBN 0763688754; 9780763688752; 9780763693824

LC 2017942652

This book, by Tanya Landman, is "set in 18th-century England. Fifteen-year-old Caleb Chappell is a mixed-race boy whose life is shrouded in mystery. . . . His white father--a talented puppeteer--is the son of a disgraced earl but never discusses his past. When his father is falsely convicted of theft, Caleb is forced to seek protection from a hitherto-unknown paternal aunt. . . . [Until] Caleb receives a shock when a body bearing his father's signet ring washes up on the shore." (Kirkus Reviews)

"Murder and mystery abound in this engrossing and atmospheric tale set in 18th-century England." Kirkus

Landon, Kristen

The **limit**. Aladdin 2010 291p $15.99

Grades: 6 7 8 9 **Fic**

1. Science fiction

ISBN 978-1-4424-0271-3; 1-4424-0271-7

LC 2010-12707

When his family exceeds its legal debt limit, thirteen-year-old Matt is sent to the Federal Debt Rehabilitation Agency workhouse, where he discovers illicit activities are being carried out using the children who have been placed there.

"From the first sentence . . . Landon captures readers' attention and keeps it. This first-person, part realistic fiction, part fantasy should appeal to readers looking for high-action adventure." Booklist

Landy, Derek

The **Faceless** Ones. Bowen Press 2009 422p (Skullduggery Pleasant) $16.99

Grades: 4 5 6 7 **Fic**

1. Fantasy fiction 2. Magic -- Fiction

ISBN 978-0-06-124091-1; 0-06-124091-5

LC 2008051714

Sequel to: Playing with fire (2008)

Fourteen-year-old Valkyrie and the skeleton mage, Skulduggery Pleasant, try to foil a plot set in motion fifty years before to find and open the gate that will allow the Faceless Ones to return to this reality.

"A gifted storyteller, the author will hook readers on the first page and leave them on the last as wrung out as he leaves his teenage protagonist—who pays a high price indeed for killing a god or two. Rattling good fun." Kirkus

Playing with fire; by Derek Landy. HarperCollins Pub. 2008 389p $16.99; pa $7.99

Grades: 4 5 6 7 **Fic**

1. Fantasy fiction 2. Magic -- Fiction

ISBN 978-0-06-124088-1; 0-06-124088-5; 978-0-06-124090-4 pa; 0-06-124090-7 pa

Sequel to: Skulduggery Pleasant (2007)

Skulduggery Pleasant, the living-dead wizard-detective, and his apprentice, Valkyrie Cain (once known as twelve-year-old Stephanie Edgley), try to prevent Baron Vengeous from bringing the monster Grotesquery to life and to save the world from the Faceless Ones.

The "style is cinematic, and the action nonstop. Skullduggery's subtle humorous asides . . . lighten the mood, and magical details, such as Valkyrie's ability to throw fireballs, add to the fun." Booklist

Followed by: The faceless ones (2009)

★ **Skulduggery** Pleasant. HarperCollinsPublishers 2007 392p $17.99; lib bdg $18.89; pa $7.99

Grades: 4 5 6 7 **Fic**

1. Fantasy fiction 2. Magic -- Fiction

ISBN 978-0-06-123115-5; 0-06-123115-0; 978-0-06-123116-2 lib bdg; 0-06-123116-9 lib bdg; 978-0-06-123117-9 pa; 0-06-123117-7 pa

LC 2006-29403

When twelve-year-old Stephanie inherits her weird uncle's estate, she must join forces with Skulduggery Pleasant, a skeleton mage, to save the world from the Faceless Ones

This "is a rich fantasy that is as engaging in its creative protagonists and villains as it is in the lightning-paced plot and sharp humor." Bulletin Cent Child Books

Other titles in this series are:

Playing with fire (2008)

The faceless ones (2009)

Lane, Andrew

Black ice; Andrew Lane. Farrar Straus Giroux 2013 288 p. (Sherlock Holmes. The legend begins) (hardcover) $17.99

Grades: 5 6 7 8 **Fic**

1. Murder -- Fiction 2. Mystery and detective stories 3. Moscow (Russia) -- History -- 19th century -- Fiction 4. Russia -- History -- Alexander II, 1855-1881 -- Fiction 5. Great Britain -- History -- Victoria, 1837-1901 -- Fiction

ISBN 0374387699; 9780374387693

LC 2012004996

This novel, by Andrew Lane, is the third book of the "Sherlock Holmes: The Legend Begins" series. "When Sherlock and Amyus Crowe, his American tutor, visit Sherlock's brother, Mycroft, in London, all they are expecting is lunch and some polite conversation. What they find shocks both of them to the core: a locked room, a dead body, and Mycroft holding a knife. . . . Threatened with the gallows, Mycroft needs Sherlock to save him." (Publisher's note)

Rebel fire; Andrew Lane. Farrar Straus Giroux 2012 343 p. (Sherlock Holmes. The legend begins) $16.99

Grades: 5 6 7 8 **Fic**

1. Mystery fiction 2. Mystery and detective stories 3. Great Britain -- History -- Victoria, 1837-1901 -- Fiction

ISBN 0374387680; 9780374387686

LC 2011000124

This novel, by Andrew Lane, is part of the "Sherlock Holmes: The Legend Begins" series. "Fourteen-year-old Sherlock Holmes knows that Amyus Crowe, his mysterious American tutor, has some dark secrets. But he didn't expect to find John Wilkes Booth, the notorious assassin, apparently alive and well in England--and Crowe somehow mixed up in it. . . . And so begins an adventure that will take Sherlock across the Atlantic, to the center of a deadly web." (Publisher's note)

Includes bibliographical references

Lange, Erin Jade

Butter; Erin Jade Lange. Bloomsbury 2012 296 p. (hardback) $16.99

Grades: 8 9 10 11 12 **Fic**

1. Eating habits 2. Suicide -- Fiction 3. Teenagers -- Fiction 4. Obesity -- Fiction 5. Eating disorders -- Fiction

ISBN 1599907801; 9781599907802

LC 2011045509

In author Erin Jade Lange's book, a "lonely obese boy everyone calls 'Butter' is about to make history. He is going to eat himself to death-live on the Internet-and everyone is invited to watch. When he first makes the announcement online to his classmates, Butter expects pity, insults, and possibly sheer indifference. What he gets are morbid cheerleaders rallying around his deadly plan. Yet as their dark encouragement grows, it begins to feel a lot like popularity . . . But what happens when Butter reaches his suicide deadline?" (Publisher's note)

Langrish, Katherine

★ The **shadow** hunt. Harper 2010 322p $16.99
Grades: 6 7 8 9 **Fic**

1. Fantasy fiction
ISBN 978-0-06-111676-6; 0-06-111676-9

LC 2009-930446

First published 2009 in the United Kingdom

"Thirteen-year-old Wolf is running away from the abbey where he was raised when he unexpectedly meets renowned knight Sir Hugo. Together, they capture a mysterious elf-child and return to Hugo's castle, where Wolf will be allowed to stay—if he gets the elf-child to speak. . . . In this medieval fantasy, Langrish . . . provides a vividly rendered, engrossing tale. Epic themes—good and evil, faith and doubt, sin and redemption—are made personal and poignant through the losses and longings of the notably well-drawn, dimensional main characters." Booklist

Larbalestier, Justine

How to ditch your fairy. Bloomsbury 2008 307p $16.99
Grades: 6 7 8 9 10 **Fic**

1. Magic -- Fiction 2. Fairies -- Fiction
ISBN 978-1-59990-301-9; 1-59990-301-6

LC 2008-02408

In a world in which everyone has a personal fairy who tends to one aspect of daily life, fourteen-year-old Charlie decides she does not want hers—a parking fairy—and embarks on a series of misadventures designed to rid herself of the invisible sprite and replace it with a better one, like her friend Rochelle's shopping fairy.

"Charlie is totally likable, smart, and sarcastic, a perfectly self-involved, insecure teen. At its core, this is a typical coming-of-age story, but the addition of the fairies, the slightly alternative setting, and the made-up slang make it much more." SLJ

Magic lessons. Razorbill 2006 275p $16.99; pa $7.99
Grades: 8 9 10 11 12 **Fic**

1. Magic -- Fiction 2. Australia -- Fiction 3. Space and time -- Fiction 4. New York (N.Y.) -- Fiction
ISBN 1-59514-054-9; 1-59514-124-3 pa

LC 2005-23870

Sequel to Magic or madness (2005)

When fifteen-year-old Reason is pulled through the magical door connecting New York City with the Sydney, Australia, home of her grandmother, she encounters an impossibly ancient man who seems to have some purpose in mind for her.

"Larbalestier creates complex relationships among her characters, and their realistic flaws, combined with the sense of danger throughout, make this a good choice for even reluctant readers." SLJ

Followed by Magic's child (2007)

Magic or madness. Razorbill 2005 288p $16.99; pa $7.99
Grades: 8 9 10 11 12 **Fic**

1. Magic -- Fiction 2. Australia -- Fiction 3. Grandmothers -- Fiction 4. Space and time -- Fiction 5. New York (N.Y.) -- Fiction
ISBN 1-59514-022-0; 1-59514-124-3 pa

LC 2004-18263

From the Sydney, Australia home of a grandmother she believes is a witch, fifteen-year-old Reason Cansino is magically transported to New York City, where she discovers that friends and foes can be hard to distinguish

"Readers looking for layered, understated fantasy will follow the looping paths of Larbalestier's fine writing . . . with gratitude and awe." Booklist

Other titles about Reason Cansino are:
Magic lessons (2006)
Magic's child (2007)

Team Human; Justine Larbalestier and Sarah Rees Brennan. HarperTeen 2012 344 p. (tr. bdg.) $17.99
Grades: 8 9 10 11 12 **Fic**

1. School stories 2. Romance fiction 3. Vampires -- Fiction 4. Female friendship -- Fiction 5. Maine -- Fiction 6. Schools -- Fiction 7. High schools -- Fiction
ISBN 0062089641; 9780062089649

LC 2011026149

In this book, "[h]igh school senior Mel Duan is not impressed when a 150-year old vampire (who looks like a teenager and talks like a 19th-century poet) enrolls in her school. Sure, New Whitby, Maine, is known for its large vampire population, but the vamps and humans keep to their own. Mel finds Francis merely annoying until her best friend Cathy falls for him and decides to become a vampire herself, at which point Mel shifts into full-blown protective mode." (Publishers Weekly)

Larson, Kirby

Audacity Jones; Kirby Larson. Scholastic Press 2016 224 p. (jacketed hardcover) $16.99
Grades: 4 5 6 7 **Fic**

1. Adventure fiction 2. Kidnapping -- fiction 3. Orphans -- Fiction 4. Conspiracies -- Fiction 5. Adventure and adventurers -- Fiction 6. Washington (D.C.) -- fiction 7. Washington (D.C.) -- History -- 20th century -- Fiction
ISBN 0545840562; 9780545840569

LC 2015015919

In this children's novel by Kirby Larson "Audacity Jones is an eleven-year-old orphan who aches for adventure, a challenge to break up the monotony of her life at Miss Maisie's School for Wayward Girls. So when the mysterious Commodore Crutchfield visits the school and whisks Audie off to Washington, DC, she knows she's in for the journey of a lifetime. But soon, it becomes clear that the Commodore has unsavory plans for Audie -- plans that involve the president of the United States and a sinister kidnapping plot." (Publisher's note)

"Larson's entertaining narration shifts attention among multiple characters amid the unfolding mystery of what, exactly, the Commodore is planning. First in a series, Larson's thriller deftly mixes humor, heart-pounding moments, and a strongly evoked historical setting—it's truly a story with something for everyone." Pub Wkly

Dash; Kirby Larson. Scholastic Press 2014 256 p. (hardcover) $16.99
Grades: 4 5 6 7 **Fic**

1. Dogs -- Fiction 2. World War, 1939-1945 -- Fiction 3. Japanese American children -- Fiction 4. Puyallup Assembly Center (Puyallup, Wash.) -- Fiction 5. Japanese Americans -- Evacuation and relocation, 1942-1945 -- Fiction
ISBN 0545416353; 9780545416351

LC 2013042525

"Although Mitsi Kashino and her family are swept up in the wave of anti-Japanese sentiment following the attack on Pearl Harbor, Mitsi never expects to lose her home--or her beloved dog, Dash. But, as World War II rages and people of Japanese descent are forced into incarceration camps, Mitsi is separated from Dash, her classmates, and life as she knows it." (Publisher's note)

"Spot-on dialogue, careful cultural details and the inclusion of specific historical characters such as artist Eddie Sato make this an educational read as well as a heartwarming one. An author's note adds further authenticity.This emotionally satisfying and thought-provoking book will have readers pulling for Mitsi and Dash." Kirkus

Duke; Kirby Larson. Scholastic Press 2013 240 p. (jacketed hardcover) $16.99

Grades: 4 5 6 7 **Fic**

1. Dogs -- Fiction 2. Dogs -- War use -- Fiction 3. German shepherd dog -- Fiction 4. Human-animal relationships -- Fiction 5. United States -- History -- 1933-1945 -- Fiction 6. World War, 1939-1945 -- United States -- Fiction

ISBN 054541637X; 9780545416375

LC 2012046636

In this World War II story by Kirby Larson, "when fifth-grader Hobie Hanson's father leaves his fishing boat in Seattle to pilot a B-24 in Europe, he tells Hobie 'to step up and do what needs to be done.' Whether it is buying war bonds, collecting rubber or simply making due with less, Hobie is giving all he can to the war effort. But when he begins to feel the pressure to lend his beloved German shepherd, Duke, to the Army, Hobie realizes he still has more to give." (Kirkus Reviews)

Hattie Big Sky. Delacorte Press 2006 289p hardcover o.p. pa $6.99

Grades: 6 7 8 9 10 **Fic**

1. Montana -- Fiction 2. Orphans -- Fiction 3. World War, 1914-1918 -- Fiction 4. Frontier and pioneer life -- Fiction

ISBN 0-385-73313-5; 0-385-73595-2 pa

LC 2005-35039

A Newbery Medal honor book, 2007

After inheriting her uncle's homesteading claim in Montana, sixteen-year-old-orphan Hattie Brooks travels from Iowa in 1917 to make a home for herself, befriends a German-American family and encounters some unexptected problems related to the war in Europe. "Grades six to nine." (Bull Cent Child Books)

This is "a richly textured novel full of memorable characters." Booklist

Hattie ever after; Kirby Larson. Delacorte Press 2013 240 p. (hc) $16.99

Grades: 6 7 8 9 10 **Fic**

1. Historical fiction 2. Orphans -- Fiction 3. Reporters and reporting -- Fiction 4. Self-reliance -- Fiction 5. San Francisco (Calif.) -- History -- 20th century -- Fiction

ISBN 0385737467; 9780307979681; 9780385737463; 9780385906685

LC 2012007068

Sequel to: Hattie Big Sky

In this novel, by Newbury Honor award-winning author Kirby Larson, "after leaving Uncle Chester's homestead claim, orphan Hattie Brooks throws a lasso around a new dream, even bigger than the Montana sky. She wants to be a reporter . . . , go to Grand Places, and do Grand Things, like Hattie's hero Nellie Bly. Another girl might be stymied by this, but . . . nothing can squash her desire to write for a big city newspaper." (Publisher's note)

Includes bibliographical references

Liberty; Kirby Larson. Scholastic Press 2016 221 p. (ebook) $16.99; $16.99

Grades: 4 5 6 7 **Fic**

1. Dogs -- Fiction 2. Friendship -- Fiction 3. Race relations -- Fiction 4. African Americans -- Fiction 5. New Orleans (La.) -- Fiction 6. World War, 1939-1945 -- Fiction 7. Poliomyelitis -- Fiction 8. Prisoners of war -- Fiction 9. People with disabilities -- Fiction 10. African American girls -- fiction 11. Interracial friendship -- fiction 12. Children with disabilities -- fiction 13. Family life -- Louisiana -- New Orleans -- Fiction 14. Prisoners of war -- United States -- fiction 15. New Orleans (La.) -- History -- 20th century -- Fiction

ISBN 9780545840736; 0545840716; 9780545840712

LC 2015048827

In this book, by Kirby Larson, "Fish has a knack for inventing. His annoying neighbor, Olympia, has a knack for messing things up. But when his latest invention leads Fish to Liberty, a beautiful stray dog who needs a home, he and Olympia work together to rescue her. However, a friendship that crosses racial lines is not the norm in 1940s New Orleans." (Publisher's note)

"Larson once again creates an engaging story that is rich in historical details. She purposefully captures both the fear and the hope in a world torn by war as well as the simple love of a boy for his dog. Practically perfect." Kirkus

Larson, M. A.

Pennyroyal Academy; M. A. Larson. G. P. Putnam's Sons, an imprint of Penguin Group (USA) 2014 304 p. maps (hardback) $16.99

Grades: 5 6 7 8 **Fic**

1. Princesses -- Fiction 2. Knights and knighthood -- Fiction 3. Fantasy 4. Dragons -- Fiction 5. Schools -- Fiction 6. Witches -- Fiction 7. Military education -- Fiction 8. Adventure and adventurers -- Fiction

ISBN 0399163247; 9780399163241

LC 2014014516

In this novel by M.A. Larson, "a girl from the forest arrives in a bustling kingdom with no name and no idea why she is there, only to find herself at the center of a world at war. She enlists at Pennyroyal Academy, where princesses and knights are trained to battle the two great menaces of the day: witches and dragons. As Evie learns what it truly means to be a princess, she realizes surprising things about herself and her family." (Publisher's note)

"Forget the notion of traditional princesses. At Pennyroyal Academy, princesses are trained to fight witches and save kingdoms, and, yes, knights learn to slay dragons...the focus and detailed character development is on the young women, their hopes and dreams (sometimes dreadfully scary), their real fears, and their disappointments in themselves, their friends, and the adults around them. Since the book ends with some of the princesses and knights selected to return for another school year, Larson has left the door open for a welcome second year at Pennyroyal with Evie and her friends." Booklist

Larwood, Kieran

Freaks; Kieran Larwood. Chicken House/Scholastic 2013 256 p. $16.99

Grades: 5 6 7 8 **Fic**

1. Mystery fiction 2. Circus performers -- Fiction 3. Freak shows -- Fiction 4. Mystery and detective stories 5. Abnormalities, Human -- Fiction 6. London (England) -- History -- 19th century -- Fiction 7. Great Britain -- History -- Victoria, 1837-1901 -- Fiction

ISBN 0545474248; 9780545474245; 9780545474252

LC 2012002639

In this book, 10-year-old "Sheba, better known as the Wolfgirl for her layer of fur and ability to sprout fangs and claws, is an orphan who ends up as part of Plumpscuttle's Peculiars, a freak show that also stars a teenage ninja, a trash-talking monkey boy, a romance-writing strongman, and a woman who talks to rats. This gang of unlikely heroes gets caught up in a mystery involving missing street urchins, steampunk monstrosities, and a fiendish set of villains." (Publishers Weekly)

Laskas, Gretchen Moran

The **miner's** daughter. Simon & Schuster Books for Young Readers 2007 250p $15.99
Grades: 8 9 10 11 12 **Fic**

1. Family life -- Fiction 2. West Virginia -- Fiction 3. Coal mines and mining -- Fiction 4. Great Depression, 1929-1939 -- Fiction
ISBN 978-1-4169-1262-0; 1-4169-1262-2
LC 2006-00684

Sixteen-year-old Willa, living in a Depression-era West Virginia mining town, works hard to help her family, experiences love and friendship, and finds an outlet for her writing when her family becomes part of the Arthurdale, West Virginia, community supported by Eleanor Roosevelt.

"Richly drawn characters and plot make this an excellent novel that explores the struggles endured by many in America in the 1930s." SLJ

Laskin, Pamela L.

Ronit & Jamil; Pamela L. Laskin. Katherine Tegen Books 2017 183 p. (hardcover) $17.99
Grades: 7 8 9 10 11 12 **Fic**

1. Romance fiction 2. Teenagers -- Fiction 3. Gaza -- fiction 4. Israel -- fiction 5. Families -- fiction 6. Israelis -- fiction 7. Palestinian Arabs -- fiction 8. Arab-Israeli conflict -- fiction 9. Conflict of generations -- fiction 10. Man-woman relationships -- fiction
ISBN 9780062458551; 9780062458544
LC 2016949687

This book, by Pamela L. Laskin, presents "accessible verse and universal questions about crossing cultural lines [that] make for a quick and powerful read. An obvious choice to pair with Romeo and Juliet in a literature class, this can also open discussion about the Israeli/Palestinian conflict and about bridging cultural boundaries." (School Library Journal)

"At once romantic and revealing, an important window into contemporary conditions in the Middle East." Kirkus

Lasky, Kathryn

★ **Ashes**. Viking 2010 318p $16.99
Grades: 6 7 8 9 10 11 12 **Fic**

1. Germany -- Fiction 2. National socialism -- Fiction
ISBN 978-0-670-01157-5; 0-670-01157-6
LC 2009-33127

In 1932 Berlin, thirteen-year-old Gaby Schramm witnesses the beginning of Hitler's rise to power, as soldiers become ubiquitous, her beloved literature teacher starts wearing a jewelled swastika pin, and the family's dear friend, Albert Einstein, leaves the country while Gaby's parents secretly bury his books and papers in their small yard.

"Gaby's questioning but assertive nature helps form a compelling, readable portrait of pre-WWII Germany." Publ Wkly

The **escape**; Kathryn Lasky. Scholastic Press 2014 240 p. illustrations (Horses of the dawn) (hardcover) $16.99
Grades: 4 5 6 7 8 **Fic**

1. Horses -- Fiction 2. Mother-daughter relationship -- Fiction 3. Responsibility -- Fiction 4. North America -- History -- Fiction
ISBN 9780545397162; 0545397162
LC 2013037215

This book "reimagines the history of the reintroduction of horses to North America by Spanish conquistadors through the eyes of the horses they brought with them. Estrella, a plucky foal unexpectedly born on board a Spanish ship bound for the New World, is strong, brave, and wise beyond her years. She, along with three others, survives being tossed overboard into shark-infested waters by swimming to the Yucatan Peninsula. Thus begins her quest to find the land of the sweet grass only she can smell." (Booklist)

"Lasky successfully fuses fantasy and fact as she gives her equine characters credible emotional depth and underscores the tensions and disparity between Old and New World sensibilities." Pub Wkly

Other titles in this series are:
Star rise (2015)
Wild blood (2016)

Frost wolf. Scholastic Press 2011 238p il (Wolves of the Beyond) $16.99
Grades: 5 6 7 8 **Fic**

1. Fantasy fiction 2. Wolves -- Fiction
ISBN 978-0-545-09316-3; 0-545-09316-3
LC 2011028151

When a terrible danger threatens the wolves of the Beyond, outsider Faolan must take a leadership role and inspire the pack to stand together.

Hawksmaid; the untold story of Robin Hood and Maid Marian. Harper 2010 292p $16.99
Grades: 5 6 7 8 **Fic**

1. Falconry -- Fiction 2. Robin Hood (Legendary character) -- Fiction 3. Maid Marian (Legendary character) -- Fiction 4. Great Britain -- History -- 1154-1399, Plantagenets -- Fiction
ISBN 978-0-06-000071-4; 0-06-000071-6

In twelfth-century England, Matty grows up to be a master falconer, able to communicate with the devoted birds who later help her and Fynn, also known as Robin Hood, to foil Prince John's plot to steal the crown.

"Lasky nicely weaves details of 12th-century life into this suspenseful adventure whose fantasy ending may surprise but will certainly please readers." SLJ

Lone wolf. Scholastic Press 2010 219p il map (Wolves of the Beyond) $16.99
Grades: 5 6 7 8 **Fic**

1. Fantasy fiction 2. Wolves -- Fiction
ISBN 978-0-545-09310-1; 0-545-09310-4
LC 2009-17007

Abandoned by his pack, a baby wolf with a mysterious mark on his deformed paw survives and embarks on a journey that will change the world of the wolves of the Beyond.

"Lasky merges anthropomorphic fantasy with realistic details about wolves and bears to produce an almost plausible emotional narrative, complete with dialogue and personalities. . . . The author builds a captivating world of forest, snow and volcanoes populated by intelligent animals and weaves a compelling story sure to bring readers back for the second installment." Kirkus

Other titles in this series are:
Shadow wolf (2010)
Watch wolf (2011)
Frost worlf (2011)

Shadow wolf. Scholastic Press 2010 260p (Wolves of the Beyond) $16.99
Grades: 5 6 7 8 **Fic**

1. Fantasy fiction 2. Wolves -- Fiction
ISBN 978-0-545-09312-5; 0-545-09312-0
LC 2010015227

Sequel to: Lone wolf (2010)

After earning the right to return to the wolf pack that abandoned him, the exiled Faolan joins the clan as a lowly "gnaw wolf," but his goal of rising in the pack order is threatened when a jealous rival frames him for an unspeakable crime.

This is a "tightly plotted, lyrical tale. . . . Lasky blends her powerful skill in establishing a setting with Faolan's lilting poetry and song." SLJ

Watch wolf. Scholastic Press 2011 230p il (Wolves of the beyond) $16.99

Grades: 5 6 7 8 **Fic**

1. Fantasy fiction 2. Wolves -- Fiction

ISBN 978-0-545-09314-9; 0-545-09314-7

LC 2010049786

Faolan, poised to take his place as a member of the revered Wolves of the Watch, may be the only one who can stop Dunbar MacHeath and his clan from provoking a war between the Watch and the bears.

Latham, Irene

Leaving Gee's Bend. G.P. Putnam's Sons 2010 230p $16.99

Grades: 5 6 7 8 **Fic**

1. Quilts -- Fiction 2. Alabama -- Fiction 3. African Americans -- Fiction

ISBN 978-0-399-25179-5; 0-399-25179-0

LC 2009-08732

Ludelphia Bennett, a determined, ten-year-old African American girl in 1932 Gee's Bend, Alabama, leaves home in an effort to find medical help for her sick mother, and she recounts her ensuing adventures in a quilt she is making.

"Ludelphia's voice is authentic and memorable, and Latham captures the tension of her dangerous journey and the racism she encounters." Booklist

Lauren, Ruth

Prisoner of ice and snow; by Ruth Lauren. Bloomsbury 2017 288 p. (hardback) $16.99

Grades: 4 5 6 7 **Fic**

1. Fantasy 2. Prisons -- Fiction 3. Sisters -- Fiction

ISBN 9781681191317

LC 2016025579

In this middle grade novel, by Ruth Lauren, "when thirteen-year-old Valor is sent to jail, she couldn't be happier. Demidova's prison for criminal children is exactly where she wants to be. Valor's twin sister, Sasha, is serving a life sentence for stealing from the royal family, and Valor is going to help her escape. . . . If Valor's plan is to succeed, she'll need to make some unlikely allies. And if the plan fails, she and Sasha could end up with fates worse than prison." (Publisher's note)

"Anyone who likes adventure, survival stories, folktales, or novels with strong female protagonists will not be able to put this down." SLJ

Another title in this series is:

Seeker of the crown (2018)

Laurie, Victoria

Forever, again; Victoria Laurie. Hyperion 2016 368 p. (ebook) $17.99; (hardback) $17.99

Grades: 7 8 9 10 **Fic**

1. Mystery fiction 2. Romance fiction 3. Reincarnation -- Fiction 4. Love -- Fiction 5. Mystery and detective stories

ISBN 9781484700440; 1484700090; 9781484700099

LC 2015045683

In this novel, by Victoria Laurie, "Lily Bennett is less than thrilled to be the new kid as she starts her junior year in high school. But soon after classes begin, she meets . . . Cole Drepeau, with whom she forms an immediate and intimate bond. As Cole and Lily grow closer, Lily learns about the murder that divided the town more than thirty years before. . . . Lily feels inexplicably linked to Amber, and she can't help but think that there's more to [her tragic story]." (Publisher's note)

"With plot twist after plot twist, the book never dulls, and readers will be totally entertained page after page." VOYA

Law, Ingrid

★ **Savvy**. Dial Books for Young Readers 2008 342p $16.99

Grades: 4 5 6 7 **Fic**

1. Magic -- Fiction 2. Family life -- Fiction 3. Voyages and travels -- Fiction

ISBN 978-0-8037-3306-0; 0-8037-3306-2

LC 2007-39814

Boston Globe-Horn Book Award honor book: Fiction and Poetry (2008)

A Newbery Medal honor book, 2009

Recounts the adventures of Mississippi (Mibs) Beaumont, whose thirteenth birthday has revealed her "savvy"—a magical power unique to each member of her family—just as her father is injured in a terrible accident.

"Short chapters and cliffhangers keep the pace quick, while the mix of traditional language and vernacular helps the story feel both fresh and timeless. . . . [This is] a vibrant and cinematic novel that readers are going to love." Publ Wkly

Other titles in this series are:

Scrumble (2010)

Switch (2015)

★ **Scumble.** Dial Books for Young Readers 2010 400p il $16.99

Grades: 4 5 6 7 **Fic**

1. Magic -- Fiction 2. Wyoming -- Fiction 3. Ranch life -- Fiction

ISBN 978-0-8037-3307-7; 0-8037-3307-0

LC 2010-02444

Mibs's cousin Ledge is disappointed to discover that his "savvy"—the magical power unique to each member of their family—is to make things fall apart, which endangers his uncle Autry's ranch and reveals the family secret to future reporter Sarah.

This provides a "satisfying plot, delightful characters, alliterative language, and rich imagery." Booklist

Switch; by Ingrid Law. Dial Books for Young Readers 2015 368 p. (hardback) $16.99

Grades: 4 5 6 7 **Fic**

1. Magic -- Fiction 2. Family -- Fiction 3. Grandmothers -- Fiction 4. Alzheimer's disease -- Fiction 5. Families -- Fiction

ISBN 0803738625; 9780803738621

LC 2015006965

In this book, by Ingrid Law, "Gypsy Beaumont has always been a whirly-twirly free spirit, so as her thirteenth birthday approaches, she hopes to get a magical ability that will let her fly, or dance up to the stars. Instead, she wakes up on her birthday with blurry vision. . . . But when Momma and Poppa announce that her very un-magical, downright mean Grandma Pat has Alzheimer's and is going to move in with them, Gypsy's savvy . . . suddenly becomes its opposite." (Publisher's note)

"Law tenderly handles the challenges of having a grandparent with Alzheimer's, highlighting the power of familial love. Though no explanation for the switch is given, readers will be caught up in this snowy, magical adventure and the characters' efforts to balance their true, sparkly selves with growing up." Booklist

The "second sequel" to Savvy.

Lawrence, Caroline

★ The **case** of the deadly desperados; Caroline Lawrence. G.P. Putnam's Sons 2011 279 p. (Western mysteries) $16.99
Grades: 4 5 6 7 8 **Fic**

1. Mystery fiction 2. Western stories 3. Orphans -- Fiction 4. Racially mixed people -- Fiction 5. Disguise -- Fiction 6. Mystery and detective stories 7. Nevada -- History -- 19th century -- Fiction
ISBN 9780399256332

LC 2011013305

In this book, Caroline "Lawrence shifts her sleuthing . . . [to] Virginia City, Montana in the 1860s. . . . Whittlin' Walt . . . has just scalped and slain the foster parents of twelve-year-old P. K. (Pinky) Pinkerton, . . . who holds a coveted deed to an entire region of silver mines. Pinky hightails it to Virginia City . . . to register his claim, . . . [then] to Chicago, where he wants to join the detective whom he believes to be his father." (Bulletin of the Center for Children's Books)

★ **P.K.** Pinkerton and the petrified man; Caroline Lawrence. G.P. Putnam's Sons 2013 320 p. (hardcover) $16.99
Grades: 4 5 6 7 8 **Fic**

1. Mystery fiction 2. Western stories 3. Orphans -- Fiction 4. Disguise -- Fiction 5. Mystery and detective stories 6. Racially mixed people -- Fiction 7. Nevada -- History -- 19th century -- Fiction
ISBN 0399256342; 9780399256349

LC 2012026737

This western mystery adventure novel, by Caroline Lawrence, is "starring Master-of-Disguise, P.K. Pinkerton. After vanquishing three notorious Desperados, twelve-year-old P.K. Pinkerton opens a private-eye business in Virginia City. P.K.'s skills are quickly put to the test: When a maid named Martha witnesses a murder, she hires the young detective to track the killer before he finds her too." (Publisher's note)

★ **P.K.** Pinkerton and the pistol-packing widows; Caroline Lawrence. G.P. Putnam's Sons, an imprint of Penguin Group (USA) Inc. 2014 304 p. maps (hardcover) $16.99
Grades: 4 5 6 7 8 **Fic**

1. Mystery fiction 2. Nevada -- Fiction 3. Disguise -- Fiction 4. Detectives -- Fiction 5. Orphans -- Fiction 6. Mystery and detective stories 7. Racially mixed people -- Fiction 8. Nevada -- History -- 19th century -- Fiction
ISBN 0399256350; 9780399256356

LC 2013000211

In this book, by Caroline Lawrence, "P.K. Pinkerton's detective agency is thriving in Virginia City--until the evening P.K. is abruptly stuffed into a turnip sack and tossed into the back of a wagon! Surfacing in Chinatown, P.K. is forced into taking a job trailing the abductor's fiancé in Carson City. Danger lurks at every turn. P.K. must battle quicksand, escape the despicable former Deputy Marshall, Jack Williams, and save Poker Face Jace from certain death." (Publisher's note)

"The young detective's dryly hilarious first-person accounts keep the story at a gallop. No disguise can mask P.K. Pinkerton's stout heart and steely resolve in Lawrence's third (and mighty fine) Wild West adventure." Kirkus

Lawrence, Iain

The **buccaneers**. Delacorte Press 2001 244p hardcover o.p. pa $6.50
Grades: 5 6 7 8 **Fic**

1. Adventure fiction 2. Pirates -- Fiction 3. Seafaring life -- Fiction
ISBN 0-385-32736-6; 0-440-41671-X pa

LC 00-60281

Sequel to: The smugglers (1999)

In the eighteenth century sixteen-year-old John Spencer sails from England in his schooner, the Dragon, to the Caribbean, where he and the crew encounter pirates, fierce storms, fever, and a strange man who some fear may be cursed.

"This high-seas tale set in the 19th century offers plenty of full-blooded salty characters, cunning dialogue, surprises around every corner and a classic battle between good and evil. The author's firsthand knowledge of sailing and skill at building suspense will keep readers riveted from first page to last." Publ Wkly

★ The **giant** -slayer. Delacorte Press 2009 292p $16.99
Grades: 5 6 7 8 **Fic**

1. Imagination -- Fiction 2. Medical care -- Fiction 3. Storytelling -- Fiction 4. Poliomyelitis -- Fiction 5. Father-daughter relationship -- Fiction
ISBN 978-0-385-73376-2; 0-385-73376-3

LC 2008-35409

When her eight-year-old neighbor is stricken with polio in 1955, eleven-year-old Laurie discovers that there is power in her imagination as she weaves a story during her visits with him and other patients confined to iron lung machines.

This is "compelling. . . . This effectively shows how children face life-changing challenges with incredible determination." Booklist

The **seance**. Delacorte Press 2008 262p il $15.99; lib bdg $18.99; pa $6.99
Grades: 4 5 6 7 **Fic**

1. Magicians 2. Mystery fiction 3. Nonfiction writers 4. Magicians -- Fiction 5. Spiritualism -- Fiction
ISBN 978-0-385-73375-5; 0-385-73375-5; 978-0-385-90392-9 lib bdg; 0-385-90392-8 lib bdg; 978-0-440-23970-3 pa; 0-440-23970-2 pa

LC 2007-27994

In 1926, magician Harry Houdini arrives in the city to perform magic and to expose fradulent mediums but thirteen-year-old Scooter King, who works for his mother making her seances seem real, needs Houdini's help to solve a murder.

"Mystery lovers will get a kick out of this rollicking whodunit featuring swashbuckling soothsayers, outlandish séances, magic tricks and more." Publ Wkly

The **smugglers**. Delacorte Press 1999 183p $15.95; pa $6.50
Grades: 5 6 7 8 **Fic**

1. Adventure fiction 2. Smuggling -- Fiction 3. Great Britain -- History -- 1714-1837 -- Fiction
ISBN 0-385-32663-7; 0-440-41596-9 pa

LC 98-41582

Sequel to: The wreckers (1998)

As the nineteenth century begins, sixteen-year-old John Spencer sets out to sail his father's schooner, The Dragon, from Kent to London and becomes involved in smuggling and danger

"The book's nonstop action, fast-paced plot, and picturesque characters make for a real page-turner." SLJ

Followed by: The buccaneers (2001)

★ The **wreckers**. Delacorte Press 1998 196p hardcover o.p. pa $5.99
Grades: 5 6 7 8 **Fic**

1. Adventure fiction 2. Shipwrecks -- Fiction 3. Great Britain --

History -- 1714-1837 -- Fiction
ISBN 0-385-32535-5; 0-440-41545-4 pa
LC 97-31625

"In 1799 fourteen-year-old John Spencer survives a shipwreck on the coast of Cornwall. To his horror, he soon learns that the villagers are not rescuers, but pirates who lure ships ashore in order to plunder their cargoes. . . . Lawrence creates an edge-of-the-chair survival/mystery story. Fast-moving, mesmerizing." Horn Book Guide

Other titles in this series are:
The smugglers (1999)
The buccaneers (2001)

Lawson, Jessica

Nooks & crannies; by Jessica Lawson (Author) ; Natalie Andrewson (Illustrator) First edition Simon & Schuster Books for Young Readers 2015 336 p. illustrations (hardcover) $16.99
Grades: 3 4 5 6 7 **Fic**

1. Identity -- Fiction 2. Mystery and detective stories 3. Aristocracy (Social class) -- Fiction 4. Inheritance and succession -- Fiction 5. Great Britain -- History -- Edward VII, 1901-1910 -- Fiction
ISBN 1481419218; 9781481419215; 9781481419222
LC 2014023223

In this children's mystery story, by Jessica Lawson and illustrated by Natalie Andrewson, "Tabitha Crum . . . receives one of six invitations to the country estate of wealthy Countess Camilla DeMoss. . . . Then the children beginning disappearing, one by one. So Tabitha takes a cue from her favorite detective novels and, with [her pet mouse] Pemberley by her side, attempts to solve the case and rescue the other children." (Publisher's note)

"Lawson offers a compelling puzzle, vividly drawn characters, and a clever and capable young detective, who bravely sniffs out clues before the final secrets are revealed--with everyone together in the parlor, naturally." Booklist

Le Guin, Ursula K.

The **farthest** shore. Pocket Books 2004 259p $15
Grades: 6 7 8 9 **Fic**

1. Fantasy fiction
ISBN 978-1-416-50964-6; 1-416-50964-X
Sequel to: The Tombs of Atuan
First published 1972 by Atheneum Pubs.

This book continues "the story of Ged and introduces a new hero, Arren, the young prince who travels with the Archmage Ged on his last perilous mission. The writing has, as the concept has, a majestic intricacy; to appreciate it the reader must enjoy ornate language, the grave discussion of life and death and love, and courage, and the tongue-rolling exotic names of a legendary land." Bull Cent Child Books

Gifts. Harcourt 2004 274p $17; $17; pa $7.95
Grades: 7 8 9 10 **Fic**

1. Fantasy fiction
ISBN 9780152051235; 0-15-205123-6; 0-15-205124-4 pa
LC 2003-21449

"Brantors, or chiefs, of the various clans of the Uplands have powers passed down through generations, powers to call animals to the hunt, start fires, cast a wasting disease, or undo the very essence of a life or thing. The clans live isolated from the inhabitants of the Lowland cities in an uneasy truce, where each people's ambitions are kept at bay by fear of the other's vengeance. Two Upland teenagers, Gry and Orrec, have grown from childhood friendship into romance and also into a repudiation of their hereditary powers. . . . Rejecting traditions that bind them to roles unwanted and undesired, Gry and Orrec decide to leave their homes and seek a freer if less privileged life in the Lowlands. . . . Grades seven to twelve." (Bull Cent Child Books)

"Although intriguing as a coming-of-age allegory, Orrec's story is also rich in . . . earthy magic and intelligent plot twists." Booklist

Powers. Harcourt 2007 502p map $17; pa $7.99
Grades: 7 8 9 10 **Fic**

1. Fantasy fiction
ISBN 978-0-15-205770-1; 0-15-205770-6; 978-0-15-206674-1 pa; 0-15-206674-8 pa
LC 2006-13549

Sequel to Voices (2006)

When young Gavir's sister is brutally killed, he escapes from slavery and sets out to explore the world and his own psychic abilities.

"Le Guin uses her own prodigious power as a writer to craft lyrical, precise sentences, evoking a palpable sense of place and believable characters." SLJ

Tehanu. Pocket Books 2004 281p (Earthsea cycle) $18.99
Grades: 6 7 8 9 **Fic**

1. Fantasy fiction
ISBN 978-1-416-50963-9; 1-416-50963-1
Sequel to: The farthest shore
First published 1990 by Atheneum

A young prince joins forces with a master wizard on a journey to discover a cause and remedy for the loss of magic in Earthsea.

"Sharply defined characterizations give rich resonance to Tehanu 's themes of aging, feminism and child abuse as well as its emotional chords of grief and loss. Tehanu is a heartbreaking farewell to a world that is passing, and is full of tantalizing hints of the new world to come." Publ Wkly

The **Tombs** of Atuan. Pocket Books 2004 179p $15.95
Grades: 6 7 8 9 **Fic**

1. Fantasy fiction
ISBN 978-1-416-50962-2; 1-416-50962-3
Sequel to: A wizard of Earthsea
First published 1971 by Atheneum Pubs.

"The author has created a successful high fantasy which may be read on a number of levels." Horn Book

Followed by: The farthest shore

Voices. Harcourt 2006 341p $17
Grades: 7 8 9 10 **Fic**

1. Fantasy fiction
ISBN 978-015-205678-0; 0-15-205678-5
LC 2005020753

Sequel to Gifts (2004)

Young Memer takes on a pivotal role in freeing her war-torn homeland from its oppressive captors.

"While her prose is simple and unadorned, Le Guin's superior narrative voice and storytelling power make even small moments ring with truth, and often with beauty." SLJ

Followed by Powers (2007)

★ A **wizard** of Earthsea; [by] Ursula K. Le Guin; illustrated by Ruth Robbins. Bantam trade pbk. ed.; Bantam Books 2004 182p il pa $15
Grades: 6 7 8 9 **Fic**

1. Fantasy fiction 2. Science fiction 3. Magic -- Fiction
ISBN 0-553-38304-3; 978-0-553-38304-1
LC 2004558962

A reissue of the title first published 1968 by Parnassus Press

ALA YALSA Margaret A. Edwards Award (2004)

A "powerful fantasy-allegory. Though set as prose, the rhythms of the langaugc are truly and consistently poetical." Read Ladders for Hum Relat. 5th edition

Other titles in this series are:
The Tombs of Atuan (1971)
The farthest shore (1972)
Tehanu (1990)

Leal, Ann Haywood

Also known as Harper. Henry Holt 2009 246p $16.95

Grades: 4 5 6 7 **Fic**

1. Poets -- Fiction 2. Siblings -- Fiction 3. Single parent family -- Fiction 4. People with disabilities -- Fiction

ISBN 978-0-8050-8881-6; 0-8050-8881-4

LC 2008-36940

Writing poetry helps fifth-grader Harper Lee Morgan cope with her father's absence, being evicted, and having to skip school to care for her brother while their mother works, and things look even brighter after she befriends a mute girl and a kindly disabled woman.

"The characters are memorable as are the descriptive passages. . . . Most touching are Harper's pithy poems that expose the raw emotions of a bright but disadvantaged girl. This book is rich with discussion opportunity for middle school students." Voice Youth Advocates

A **finders** -keepers place. Henry Holt 2010 259p $16.99

Grades: 5 6 7 **Fic**

1. School stories 2. Sisters -- Fiction 3. Mental illness -- Fiction 4. Missing persons -- Fiction 5. Single parent family -- Fiction 6. Manic-depressive illness -- Fiction

ISBN 978-0-8050-8882-3; 0-8050-8882-2

LC 2009-50771

As their mother's manic-depression grows worse, eleven-year-old Esther and her sister Ruth visit various churches hoping to find their father, a preacher named Ezekiel who left them seven years before in 1966.

"Leal excels in pithy characterization, mainly through spot-on dialogue, yielding sympathetic characters, a gripping plot, and no shortage of heartbreaking moments." Publ Wkly

Lean, Sarah

★ A **dog** called Homeless; Sarah Lean. Katherine Tegen Books 2012 202 p. (trade bdg) $16.99

Grades: 3 4 5 6 7 **Fic**

1. Dogs -- Fiction 2. Blind -- Fiction 3. Grief -- Fiction 4. Hearing impaired -- Fiction 5. Selective mutism -- Fiction 6. Single-parent families -- Fiction 7. People with disabilities -- Fiction

ISBN 0062122207; 9780062122209

LC 2011044628

Schneider Family Book Award (2013)

In this book by Sarah Lean, "a girl grieving for her dead mother gives up talking when she becomes convinced that what she says doesn't matter. . . . Cally begins to see her mother . . . dressed in a red raincoat and sometimes accompanied by a very large dog. . . . Cally also meets Mrs. Cooper, a neighbor in their new apartment building who lovingly cares for her blind, nearly deaf 11-year-old son, Sam." (Kirkus Reviews)

Leavitt, Lindsey

Going vintage; by Lindsey Leavitt. 1st U.S. ed. Bloomsbury 2013 320 p. (hardcover) $16.99

Grades: 7 8 9 10 **Fic**

1. School stories 2. Sisters -- Fiction 3. Dating (Social customs) -- Fiction 4. Lists -- Fiction 5. Schools -- Fiction 6. California -- Fiction 7. High schools -- Fiction 8. Family life -- California -- Fiction

ISBN 1599907879; 9781599907871

LC 2012023269

In this book, "after discovering her boyfriend has a serious online relationship with another girl, Mallory very publicly dumps him on his social media site. She complicates the situation by deciding to try to fulfill a to-do list her grandmother crafted at the beginning of her junior year of high school in 1962, a time Mallory thinks must have been much simpler than today. . . . She's aided by her loyal younger sister, Ginnie, and the growing affection of her ex's cousin, charming Oliver." (Kirkus)

Sean Griswold's head. Bloomsbury 2011 276p $16.99

Grades: 7 8 9 10 **Fic**

1. School stories 2. Family life -- Fiction 3. Pennsylvania -- Fiction 4. Multiple sclerosis -- Fiction

ISBN 978-1-59990-498-6; 1-59990-498-5

LC 2010-06949

"Leavitt capably handles the issues of chronic illness with sensitivity, making this an insightful, humorous, and ultimately uplifting family drama." Bull Cent Child Books

Leavitt, Martine

★ **Calvin**; Martine Leavitt. Farrar Straus Giroux 2015 192 p. (hardback) $17.99

Grades: 7 8 9 10 11 12 **Fic**

1. Teenagers -- Fiction 2. Schizophrenia -- Fiction 3. Hallucinations and illusions 4. Schools -- Fiction 5. High schools -- Fiction 6. Mental illness -- Fiction 7. Characters in literature -- Fiction

ISBN 0374380732; 9780374380731

LC 2015002574

In Martine Leavitt's novel "Calvin has always known his fate is linked to the comic book character from Calvin & Hobbes. He was born on the day the last strip was published. As a child Calvin played with the toy Hobbes. But now Calvin is a teenager who has been diagnosed with schizophrenia, Hobbes is back--as a delusion--and Calvin can't control him. Calvin decides that if he can convince Bill Watterson to draw one final comic strip, showing a normal teenaged Calvin, he will be cured." (Publisher's note)

"Funny, intellectual, and entertaining, it's a sensitive yet irreverent adventure about a serious subject." Pub Wkly

My book of life by Angel; Martine Leavitt. Farrar, Straus and Giroux Books for Young Readers 2012 252 p. $17.99; (hardback) $17.99; (ebook) $12.95

Grades: 8 9 10 11 **Fic**

1. Novels in verse 2. Runaway teenagers -- Fiction 3. Juvenile prostitution -- Fiction 4. Runaways -- Fiction 5. Drug abuse -- Fiction 6. Prostitution -- Fiction 7. Vancouver (B.C.) -- Fiction

ISBN 0374351236; 9780374351236; 9781554983179

LC 2011044563

This "novel in verse tells the story of 16-year-old Angel, who has been working as a prostitute in Vancouver. . . . After Angel's friend Serena disappears, Angel decides to give up" the drugs her pimp Call feeds her "and try to return home. Angel's withdrawal is severe . . . but it's nothing compared to the pain she feels when Call brings home an 11-year-old girl, Melli, to follow in Angel's footsteps. Angel is determined to keep Melli safe, even while other women continue to disappear." (Publishers Weekly)

Lecesne, James

★ **Absolute** brightness. HarperTeen 2008 472p $17.99; lib bdg $18.89

Grades: 7 8 9 10 **Fic**

1. Cousins -- Fiction 2. New Jersey -- Fiction 3. Good and evil -- Fiction

ISBN 0-06-125627-7; 0-06-125628-5 lib bdg; 978-0-06-125627-1; 978-0-06-125628-8 lib bdg

LC 2007-02988

ALA YALSA Morris Award Finalist, 2009

In the beach town of Neptune, New Jersey, Phoebe's life is changed irrevocably when her gay cousin moves into her house and soon goes missing.

"This thoughtful novel is beautifully written; its themes are haunting, and in spite of the central tragedy, it's often laugh-out-loud funny." Kliatt

Leck, James

★ The **adventures** of Jack Lime; written by James Leck. Kids Can Press 2010 126p $16.95; pa $8.95

Grades: 5 6 7 8 **Fic**

1. Mystery fiction 2. Narcolepsy -- Fiction

ISBN 978-1-55453-364-0; 1-55453-364-3; 978-1-55453-365-7 pa; 1-55453-365-1 pa

"Jack Lime is the guy you come to if you've got a problem. . . . He'll find out what needs finding out. . . . This slim volume contains three cases. In the first, Jack susses out the whereabouts of a missing bike. In the second, he shakes down a hamster-napping and blackmail scheme. And in the final, he recounts his first case on the job. . . . All the touchstones that make for great noir are translated for kids. . . . The lingo that makes hard-boiled reading so much fun is here, but never schticky, and Leck knows that a great hero needs a debilitating flaw: for Jack, it's his narcolepsy." Booklist

Lee, Harper

★ **To** kill a mockingbird; Harper Lee. 50th anniversary ed; Harper 2010 323p $25.00

Grades: 8 9 10 11 12 Adult **Fic**

1. Alabama -- Fiction 2. Race relations -- Fiction

ISBN 9780061743528

"Scout, as Jean Louise is called, is a precocious child. She relates her impressions of the time when her lawyer father, Atticus Finch, is defending a black man accused of raping a white woman in a small Alabama town during the 1930's. Atticus's courageous act brings the violence and injustice that exists in their world sharply into focus as it intrudes into the lighthearted life that Scout and her brother Jem have enjoyed until that time." Shapiro. Fic for Youth. 3d edition

Lee, Mackenzi

★ The **gentleman's** guide to vice and virtue; Mackenzi Lee. Katherine Tegen Books 2017 513 p. (hardcover) $18.99

Grades: 7 8 9 10 11 12 **Fic**

1. Europe -- Fiction 2. Travel -- Fiction 3. Gay men -- Fiction 4. Hedonism -- fiction 5. Bisexual teenagers -- fiction 6. Young bisexual men -- fiction 7. Grand tours (Education) -- fiction 8. Europe -- History -- 18th century -- fiction 9. Self-actualization (Psychology) in adolescence -- fiction

ISBN 9780062382825; 9780062382801

LC 2016949692

Stonewall Book Award Honor Book: Children's & Young Adult Literature (2018)

In this book, by Mackenzi Lee, "a young bisexual British lord embarks on an unforgettable Grand Tour of Europe with his best friend. . . . Henry 'Monty' Montague doesn't care that his roguish passions are far from suitable for the gentleman he was born to be. . . . So Monty vows to make this yearlong escapade one last hedonistic hurrah and flirt with Percy from Paris to Rome. But . . . one of Monty's reckless decisions turns their trip abroad into a harrowing manhunt." (Publisher's note)

"Austen, Wilde, and Indiana Jones converge in this deliciously anachronistic bonbon." Kirkus

Followed by: The Lady's Guide to Petticoats and Piracy

Lee, Stacey

Outrun the moon; Stacey Lee. G. P. Putnam's Sons 2016 400 p. (hardback) $17.99

Grades: 7 8 9 10 **Fic**

1. Earthquakes -- Fiction 2. Private schools -- Fiction 3. Chinese Americans -- Fiction

ISBN 9780399175411

LC 2015032478

"San Francisco, 1906: Fifteen-year-old Mercy Wong is determined to [gain] . . . an education at St. Clare's School for Girls. . . . Mercy gains admittance through a mix of cunning and a little bribery, only to discover that getting in was the easiest part. . . . On April 18, a historic earthquake rocks San Francisco, destroying Mercy's home and school. Now she's forced to wait with her classmates for their families in a temporary park encampment." (Publisher's note)

Lee, Tanith

Piratica; being a daring tale of a singular girl's adventure upon the high seas. presented most handsomely by the notorious Tanith Lee. Dutton Children's Books 2004 288p $17.99

Grades: 6 7 8 9 **Fic**

1. Adventure fiction 2. Pirates -- Fiction 3. Sex role -- Fiction

ISBN 0-525-47324-6

First published 2003 in the United Kingdom

A bump on the head restores Art's memories of her mother and the exciting life they led, so the sixteen-year-old leaves Angels Academy for Young Maidens, seeks out the pirates who were her family before her mother's death, and leads them back to adventure on the high seas.

"Piratica is a refreshing, tongue-in-cheek, tangled tale that will entice readers who crave adventure and fantasy." SLJ

Followed by Piratica II: return to Parrot Island (2006)

Piratica II: return to Parrot Island; being the return of a most intrepid heroine to sea and secrets. Dutton Children's Books 2006 320p $17.99

Grades: 6 7 8 9 **Fic**

1. Adventure fiction 2. Pirates -- Fiction 3. Sex role -- Fiction

ISBN 0-525-47769-1

Sequel to Piratica (2004)

Art Blastside is bored with life ashore, so she jumps at the chance to return to sea.

"Lee's writing is complex, and she uses her skill to craft subtle pundit humor and lush description." Voice Youth Advocates

Lee, Ying S.

The **body** at the tower. Candlewick Press 2010 337p (The Agency) $16.99

Grades: 8 9 10 11 12 **Fic**

1. Mystery fiction 2. Orphans -- Fiction 3. Great Britain -- History -- 19th century -- Fiction

ISBN 978-0-7636-4968-5; 0-7636-4968-6

Sequel to: A spy in the house (2010)

"Mary Quinn returns in another case for the Agency, a covert all-female detective agency in Victorian London. A man has recently fallen out of the soon-to-be-completed clock tower of the Houses of Parliament. Mary disguises herself as an errand boy and attempts to infiltrate the work site to discover potential suspects. . . . This second book is much stronger than the first, both in terms of character development and the central mystery." SLJ

Followed by: The traitor in the tunnel (2012)

A **spy** in the house. Candlewick Press 2010 335p (The Agency) $16.99

Grades: 8 9 10 11 12 **Fic**

1. Mystery fiction 2. Orphans -- Fiction 3. Household employees -- Fiction 4. Swindlers and swindling -- Fiction 5. Great Britain -- History -- 19th century -- Fiction

ISBN 978-0-7636-4067-5; 0-7636-4067-0

LC 2009-32736

Rescued from the gallows in 1850s London, young orphan and thief Mary Quinn is offered a place at Miss Scrimshaw's Academy for Girls where she is trained to be part of an all-female investigative unit called The Agency and, at age seventeen, she infiltrates a rich merchant's home in hopes of tracing his missing cargo ships.

"Lee fills the story with classic elements of Victorian mystery and melodrama. Class differences, love gone awry, racial discrimination, London's growing pains in the 1850s, and the status of women in society are all addressed. Historical details are woven seamlessly into the plot, and descriptive writing allows readers to be part of each scene." SLJ

Other titles in this series are:

The body at the tower (2010)

The traitor in the tunnel (2012)

Lee, Yoon Ha

Dragon Pearl; by Yoon Ha Lee. Disney-Hyperion 2019 320 p. (alk. paper) $16.99

Grades: 4 5 6 7 **Fic**

1. Siblings -- fiction 2. Science fiction 3. Magic -- Fiction 4. Space flight -- Fiction 5. Brothers and sisters -- Fiction 6. Adventure and adventurers -- Fiction

ISBN 9781368013352

LC 2018005367

"Rick Riordan Presents Yoon Ha Lee's space opera about thirteen-year-old Min, who comes from a long line of fox spirits. . . . To keep the family safe, Min's mother insists that none of them use any fox-magic. . . . They must appear human at all times. . . . When word arrives that [her brother] Jun is suspected of leaving his post to go in search of the Dragon Pearl, Min knows that something is wrong. . . . She decides to run away to find him and clear his name." (Publisher's note)

Leeds, Constance

The **unfortunate** son; by Constance Leeds. Viking Childrens Books 2012 302 p. (hardcover) $16.99

Grades: 4 5 6 7 **Fic**

1. Bildungsromans 2. Historical fiction 3. Pirates -- Fiction 4. Kidnapping -- Fiction 5. Luck -- Fiction 6. Fishing -- Fiction 7. Slavery -- Fiction 8. Identity -- Fiction 9. Abnormalities, Human -- Fiction 10. Africa -- History -- To 1498 -- Fiction 11. France -- History -- 15th century -- Fiction

ISBN 0670013986; 9780670013982

LC 2011027530

This book is the story of Luc, whose "father hates him, seemingly without reason, so" the boy runs away "to apprentice with a local fisherman. . . . Living with the fisherman's family he grows close to their ward, the beautiful Beatrice, and things seem to be looking up . . . until he's kidnapped by pirates and sold to a Tunisian in North Africa. While Luc receives an education from his learned master, Beatrice" attempts to unravel Luc's past. (Kirkus Reviews)

Legrand, Claire

Some kind of happiness; Claire Legrand. Simon & Schuster Books for Young Readers 2016 384 p. (hardback) $16.99

Grades: 4 5 6 7 **Fic**

1. Fantasy fiction 2. Cousins -- Fiction 3. Secrets -- Fiction 4. Family life -- Fiction 5. Forests and forestry -- Fiction

ISBN 9781442466012

LC 2015033782

In this book, by Claire Legrand, "Finley Hart doesn't want to talk about . . . when life feels overwhelming, and it's hard to keep her head up. . . . Finley's only retreat is the Everwood, a forest kingdom that exists in the pages of her notebook. Until she discovers the endless woods behind her grandparents' house and realizes the Everwood is real. . . .With the help of her cousins, Finley sets out on a mission to save the dying Everwood and uncover its secrets." (Publisher's note)

"A quiet magic is at work in Legrand's novel, in which she adeptly interweaves Fin's imaginative writing with the real-life narrative, underpinning all with an appeal to honesty and self-acceptance. This beautiful and reflective tale carries echoes of Katherine Patterson's The Bridge to Terabithia (1977) and will resonate with thoughtful readers who enjoy pondering life's bigger questions." Booklist

Lennon, Tom

When love comes to town; Tom Lennon. Albert Whitman 2013 304 p. (reinforced) $15.99

Grades: 8 9 10 11 12 **Fic**

1. Historical fiction 2. Gay teenagers -- Fiction 3. Gays -- Fiction 4. Ireland -- Fiction 5. Coming out (Sexual orientation) -- Fiction

ISBN 0807589160; 9780807589168

LC 2012020160

In this novel, by Tom Lennon, "the year is 1990, and in his hometown of Dublin, Ireland, Neil Byrne plays rugby, keeps up with the in-crowd at his school, and is just a regular guy. A guy who's gay. It's a secret he keeps from the wider world as he explores the city at night and struggles to figure out how to reveal his real self--and to whom." (Publisher's note)

Leno, Katrina

The **lost** & found; Katrina Leno. HarperTeen, an imprint of HarperCollinsPublishers 2016 352 p.

Grades: 7 8 9 10 11 **Fic**

1. Automobile travel -- Fiction 2. Loss (Psychology) -- Fiction 3. Brothers and sisters -- Fiction 4. Post-traumatic stress disorder -- Fiction

ISBN 9780062231208

LC 2015038550

"Forging a friendship through an online support group, Frannie and Louis, teens whose losses are tied to mysterious disappearances, search for answers during a road trip to Austin, where they find magical things that the other has lost." (Publisher's note)

"This is a beautiful exploration of loss in many forms and the emotional toll it can take on those who are affected. . . . An emotional journey that's well worth the ride." SLJ

Leonard, Julia Platt

Cold case. Aladdin 2011 281p $15.99

Grades: 6 7 8 9 **Fic**

1. Mystery fiction 2. Spies -- Fiction 3. Brothers -- Fiction 4. Homicide -- Fiction 5. Family life -- Fiction 6. Restaurants -- Fiction 7. Santa Fe (N.M.) -- Fiction
ISBN 978-1-4424-2009-0; 1-4424-2009-X

LC 2010041854

When thirteen-year-old Oz Keillor finds a dead body in his family's Santa Fe, New Mexico, restaurant, he is determined to solve the mystery in which his older brother is implicated, but which also involves their long-dead father, who was accused of being a spy.

"The well-plotted double mystery is propped up by a few choice details about restaurant life, some sly red herrings, and a cast of nicely rounded characters." Booklist

Leonard, M. G.

Beetle boy; by M.G. Leonard. Chicken House/Scholastic 2016 270 p. (hbk.) $16.99

Grades: 4 5 6 7 8 **Fic**

1. Father-son relationship -- fiction 2. Uncles -- Fiction 3. Beetles -- Fiction 4. Friendship -- Fiction 5. Best friends -- Fiction 6. Missing persons -- Fiction 7. Fathers and sons -- Fiction 8. Insects -- fiction 9. Mystery and detective stories
ISBN 054585346X; 9780545853460

LC 2015028492

In this juvenile novel, by by M. G. Leonard, "Darkus Cuttle's dad mysteriously goes missing . . . so Darkus moves in with his eccentric Uncle Max and next door to . . . two lunatic cousins with an enormous beetle infestation. Darkus soon discovers that the beetles are anything but ordinary. . . . It's up to Darkus and his friends to save the beetles. But they're up against an even more terrifying villain -- mad scientist of fashion, haute couture villainess Lucretia Cutter." (Publisher's note)

"Overall, a charming and (at times) affecting romp through beetle land." Kirkus

Other titles in this series are:
Revenge of the beetle queen (2018)
Battle of the beetles (2019)

Lerangis, Peter

The **colossus** rises; Peter Lerangis. Harper 2013 348 p. (Seven wonders) (hardcover bdg.) $17.99; (pbk.) $6.99

Grades: 4 5 6 7 8 9 **Fic**

1. Fantasy fiction -- fiction 2. Science fiction 3. Ability -- Fiction 4. Friendship -- Fiction 5. Adventure and adventurers -- Fiction 6. Atlantis (Legendary place) -- Fiction 7. FICTION -- Interactive Adventures 8. FICTION -- Legends, Myths, Fables -- General
ISBN 0062070401; 006207041X; 9780062070401; 9780062070418

LC 2012025334

This children's fantasy story, by Peter Lerangis, illustrated by Torstein Norstrand and Mike Reagan, is the first of the "Seven Wonders" series. "13-year-old Jack McKinley will die unless he can locate the magic Loculi containing the ancient powers of Atlantis. . . . The problem is that . . . Atlantis was . . . divided into seven containers and hidden in the Seven Wonders of the Ancient World. Finding the powers will not only save Jack's life, but also give him superpowers." (Kirkus Reviews)

Teens Jack, Marco, Aly, and Cass begin a quest to find seven pieces of Atlantis' power that were hidden long ago and that will, if returned to Atlantis, save them from certain death due to the genetic abnormality that also gives them superior abilities.

Lost in babylon; by Peter Lerangis and translated by Torstein Norstrand. HarperCollins 2013 384 p. (Seven wonders) (hardcover bdg.) $17.99

Grades: 4 5 6 7 8 9 **Fic**

1. Occult fiction -- fiction 2. Adventure fiction -- fiction 3. Seven Wonders of the World -- Fiction
ISBN 0062070436; 9780062070432

LC 2013942765

This book, by Peter Lerangis, "chronicles Jack McKinley and his friends as they carry on their mission to save their lives—and the world—by locating seven magic orbs called Loculi, which are hidden in the Seven Wonders of the Ancient World. After defeating the Colossus of Rhodes and capturing the first of the Loculi, their friend Marco has disappeared. With no leads, no clues, and no one else to turn to, the kids have no choice but to trust Professor Bhegad and the Karai Institute again as they head off to Babylon." (Publisher's note)

Tomb of shadows; Peter Lerangis, Torstein Norstrand ; [edited by] David Linker. HarperCollins 2014 352 p. (Seven wonders) (hardcover) $17.99

Grades: 4 5 6 7 8 9 **Fic**

1. Fantasy fiction 2. Seven Wonders of the World -- Fiction 3. Adventure stories 4. Betrayal -- Fiction
ISBN 0062070460; 9780062070463

LC 2014931071

This middle grades fantasy novel by Peter Lerangis, illustrated by Torstein Norstrand, part of the Seven Wonders series, "chronicles the adventures of Jack McKinley and his friends in a life-or-death race to the Mausoleum at Halicarnassus. In the rubble of this Wonder of the Ancient World, they have to face down their own demons and engage in an epic battle with foes long gone." (Publisher's note)

"—Jack, Ally, and Cass continue their quest to save the world—even as their friend Marco joins the enemy's side. Epic battles and fast-moving chapters will keep fans of this "Percy Jackson"-like series engaged." SLJ

Other titles in the series include:
The Colossus Rises (2013)
Lost in Bablyon (2013)

Les Becquets, Diane

Season of ice. Bloomsbury U.S.A. Children's Books 2008 281p $16.95

Grades: 8 9 10 11 12 **Fic**

1. Lakes -- Fiction 2. Maine -- Fiction 3. Stepfamilies -- Fiction 4. Missing persons -- Fiction 5. Father-daughter relationship -- Fiction
ISBN 978-1-59990-063-6; 1-59990-063-7

LC 2007-30845

When seventeen-year-old Genesis Sommer's father disappears on Moosehead Lake near their small-town Maine home in mid-November, she must cope with the pressure of keeping her family together, even while rumors about the event plague her.

This is "a heartbreaking story from the very beginning, but Les Becquets turns it into something well beyond a mere tearjerker. . . . It's a tender story of a tough, smart, loving girl who finds that she can rise to the challenge of what she's lost because of what she's gained. Readers will understand her and admire her, and find her difficult indeed to forget." Bull Cent Child Books

Lester, Alison

Quicksand pony. Houghton Mifflin 1998 136p $15

Grades: 5 6 7 8 **Fic**

1. Horses -- Fiction 2. Australia -- Fiction
ISBN 0-395-93749-3

LC 98-6930

First published 1997 in Australia

After her pony Bella, trapped in quicksand, is rescued by a mysterious unseen person, ten-year-old Biddy follows the trail into the Australian bush and discovers the solution to a disappearance that happened years ago

"A multilayered story of survival, love, mystery, and family relationships." SLJ

Lester, Joan Steinau

★ **Black,** white, other. Zondervan 2011 222p $15.99
Grades: 7 8 9 10 **Fic**

1. Divorce -- Fiction 2. Slavery -- Fiction 3. California -- Fiction 4. Family life -- Fiction 5. Grandmothers -- Fiction 6. Race relations -- Fiction 7. Racially mixed people -- Fiction
ISBN 978-0-310-72763-7; 0-310-72763-4
LC 2011015208

Twenty miles from Oakland, California, where fires have led to racial tension, multi-racial fifteen-year-old Nina faces the bigotry of longtime friends, her parents' divorce, and her brother's misbehavior, while learning of her great-great grandmother Sarah's escape from slavery.

"Lester . . . conjures a credible plot and complications; divorce is a fact of life and racially mixed heritage is conspicuously becoming one. The simple contrapuntal narrative of Sarah Armstrong's escaping slavery distinguishes the book emotionally and psychologically, raising it above other issue-oriented YA novels. Lester writes with social sensitivity and an ear for teen language and concerns. This is engaging treatment of a challenging subject that comes with little precedent." Publ Wkly

Includes bibliographical references

Lester, Julius

Day of tears; a novel in dialogue. Hyperion 2005 177p hardcover o.p. pa $7.99
Grades: 7 8 9 10 **Fic**

1. Slavery -- Fiction 2. African Americans -- Fiction
ISBN 0-7868-0490-4; 1-42310-409-9 pa
Coretta Scott King Award for text

Emma has taken care of the Butler children since Sarah and Frances's mother, Fanny, left. Emma wants to raise the girls to have good hearts, as a rift over slavery has ripped the Butler household apart. Now, to pay off debts, Pierce Butler wants to cash in his slave "assets", possibly including Emma.

"The horror of the auction and its aftermath is unforgettable. . . . The racism is virulent (there's widespread use of the n-word). The personal voices make this a stirring text for group discussion." Booklist

★ **Guardian**. Amistad/HarperTeen 2008 129p $16.99; lib bdg $17.89
Grades: 7 8 9 10 **Fic**

1. Lynching -- Fiction 2. Race relations -- Fiction 3. Southern States -- Fiction 4. African Americans -- Fiction
ISBN 978-0-06-155890-0; 0-06-155890-7; 978-0-06-155891-7 lib bdg; 0-06-155891-5 lib bdg
LC 2008-14251

In a rural southern town in 1946, a white man and his son witness the lynching of an innocent black man. Includes historical note on lynching.

"The author's understated, haunting prose is as compelling as it is dark; . . . [the story] leaves a deep impression." Publ Wkly

Includes bibliographical references

Time's memory. Farrar, Straus & Giroux 2006 230p $17
Grades: 8 9 10 11 12 **Fic**

1. Slavery -- Fiction 2. African Americans -- Fiction
ISBN 0-374-37178-4; 978-0-374-37178-4
LC 2005-47716

Ekundayo, a Dogon spirit brought to America from Africa, inhabits the body of a young African American slave on a Virginia plantation, where he experiences loss, sorrow, and reconciliation in the months preceding the Civil War.

"More than a picture of slavery through the eyes of those enslaved or their captors, Lester's narrative evokes spiritual images of Mali's Dogon people." SLJ

Levenseller, Tricia

Daughter of the pirate king; Tricia Levenseller. Feiwel & Friends 2017 320 p. (hardback) $17.99
Grades: 8 9 10 11 **Fic**

1. Love -- Fiction 2. Pirates -- Fiction 3. Princesses -- Fiction
ISBN 9781250095961; 9781250095978
LC 2016009251

"Sent on a mission to retrieve an ancient hidden map--the key to a legendary treasure trove--seventeen-year-old pirate captain Alosa deliberately allows herself to be captured by her enemies, giving her the perfect opportunity to search their ship. More than a match for the ruthless pirate crew, Alosa has only one thing standing between her and the map: her captor, the unexpectedly clever and unfairly attractive first mate Riden." (Publisher's note)

"Resourceful and confident, Alosa swaggers through the pages with style and panache, and her supporting cast is just as delightful." Pub Wkly

Followed by Daughter of the siren queen (2018)

Levine, Gail Carson

Ella enchanted. HarperCollins Pubs. 1997 232p $16.99; lib bdg $17.89; pa $6.50
Grades: 5 6 7 8 **Fic**

1. Fantasy fiction 2. Fairy tales
ISBN 0-06-027510-3; 0-06-027511-1 lib bdg; 0-06-440705-5 pa
LC 96-30734

A Newbery Medal honor book, 1998

"Ella is blessed by a fairy at birth with the gift of obedience. But the blessing is a horror for Ella, who must literally do what everyone tells her, from sweeping the floor to giving up a beloved heirloom necklace. After her mother dies, and her covetous, caustic father leaves on a trading trip, Ella's world is turned upside down. She battles both ogres and wicked stepsisters, makes friends and loses them, and must deny her love for her prince, Charmont, to save his life and his realm. In making this ultimate sacrifice, she breaks the curse." (Booklist)

"As finely designed as a tapestry, Ella's story both neatly incorporates elements of the original tale and mightily expands them." Booklist

Ever. HarperCollinsPublishers 2008 256p $16.99; lib bdg $17.89; pa $6.99
Grades: 5 6 7 8 **Fic**

1. Winds -- Fiction 2. Immortality -- Fiction 3. Fate and fatalism -- Fiction 4. Gods and goddesses -- Fiction
ISBN 978-0-06-122962-6; 0-06-122962-8; 978-0-06-122963-3 lib bdg; 0-06-122963-6 lib bdg; 978-0-06-122964-0 pa; 0-06-122964-4 pa
LC 2007-32289

Fourteen-year-old Kezi and Olus, Akkan god of the winds, fall in love and together try to change her fate—to be sacrificed to a Hyte god because of a rash promise her father made—through a series of quests that might make her immortal.

"Levine conducts a riveting journey, offering passion and profound pondering along the way." Publ Wkly

Fairest. HarperCollins 2006 326p $16.99

Grades: 6 7 8 9 **Fic**

1. Fairy tales 2. Singing -- Fiction
ISBN 978-0-06-073408-4; 0-06-073408-6

LC 2006-00337

In a land where beauty and singing are valued above all else, Aza eventually comes to reconcile her unconventional appearance and her magical voice, and learns to accept herself for who she truly is.

"The plot is fast-paced, and Aza's growth and maturity are well crafted and believable." SLJ

★ A **tale** of Two Castles. Harper 2011 328p $16.99; lib bdg $17.89

Grades: 4 5 6 **Fic**

1. Fantasy fiction 2. Mystery fiction 3. Dragons -- Fiction 4. Apprentices -- Fiction 5. Kings and rulers -- Fiction
ISBN 978-0-06-122965-7; 0-06-122965-2; 978-0-06-122966-4 lib bdg; 0-06-122966-0 lib bdg

LC 2010027756

"Hoping to apprentice as an actor, Elodie travels from her rural home to the city of Two Castles. . . . When she's robbed and then rejected as an actor, she apprentices herself to crafty dragon Meenore as a detective. Shape-shifting Count Jonty Um, a kindly ogre, is their first client. . . . But who is to be trusted and who isn't? . . . Intermediate, middle school." (Horn Book)

"Readers are certain to be pulled, like Elodie herself, right into the midst of the rich and swirling life of Two Castles." SLJ

Levine, Kristin

★ The **best** bad luck I ever had. Putnam 2009 266p $16.99

Grades: 6 7 8 9 **Fic**

1. Alabama -- Fiction 2. Friendship -- Fiction 3. Prejudices -- Fiction 4. Family life -- Fiction 5. Country life -- Fiction 6. Race relations -- Fiction
ISBN 978-0-399-25090-3; 0-399-25090-5

LC 2008-11570

In Moundville, Alabama, in 1917, twelve-year-old Dit hopes the new postmaster will have a son his age, but instead he meets Emma, who is black, and their friendship challenges accepted ways of thinking and leads them to save the life of a condemned man.

"Tension builds just below the surface of this energetic, seamlessly narrated . . . novel. . . . Levine handles the setting with grace and nuance." Publ Wkly

★ The **lions** of Little Rock; Kristin Levine. G. P. Putnam's Sons 2012 298p.

Grades: 5 6 7 8 **Fic**

1. School stories 2. African Americans -- Fiction 3. School integration -- Fiction 4. Friendship -- Fiction 5. Bashfulness -- Fiction 6. Middle schools -- Fiction 7. Race relations -- Fiction 8. Family life -- Arkansas -- Fiction 9. Little Rock (Ark.) -- History -- 20th century -- Fiction
ISBN 9780399256448

LC 2011031835

This book presents a "portrait of 1958 Little Rock, Ark., the tumultuous year when the governor refused integration by closing local high schools. The story is told through the . . . voice of painfully quiet 12-year-old Marlee Nisbett, who makes a rare friend in Liz, a new student at her middle school. Liz instills some much-needed confidence in Marlee, but when it's revealed that Liz is 'passing' as a white student, Liz must leave school abruptly, putting their friendship to the test. The girls meet in secret, and Marlee joins an antisegregationist organization, both actions inviting serious risk amid escalating racist threats." (Publishers Weekly)

The **paper** cowboy; Kristin Levine. Putnam Juvenile 2014 352 p. illustrations (hardback) $16.99

Grades: 5 6 7 8 **Fic**

1. Family -- Fiction 2. Neighbors -- Fiction 3. Conduct of life -- Fiction 4. Newspaper carriers -- Fiction 5. Communism -- Fiction 6. Neighborliness -- Fiction 7. Family problems -- Fiction 8. Illinois -- History -- 20th century -- Fiction
ISBN 039916328X; 9780399163289

LC 2014004421

In this book, by Kristin Levine, "Tommy is . . . a bully. He's always playing cruel jokes on classmates or stealing from the store. But Tommy has a reason: life at home is tough. His abusive mother isn't well; in fact, she may be mentally ill, and his sister, Mary Lou, is in the hospital badly burned from doing a chore it was really Tommy's turn to do. To make amends, Tommy takes over Mary Lou's paper route." (Publisher's note)

"Twelve-year-old Tommy wants to be a cowboy. That's not so easy, though, in 1950s Downers Grove, Illinois. After he plays a prank that ends up costing the local grocery store owner his business, a remorseful Tommy goes about becoming a different kind of cowboy--one "who stands up for others." Themes of bullying, community, and growing up in a dysfunctional family are explored sensitively." Horn Book

Levithan, David

Invisibility; Andrea Cremer and David Levithan. Philomel Books 2013 320 p. (hardcover) $18.99

Grades: 7 8 9 10 11 12 **Fic**

1. Love -- Fiction 2. Invisibility -- Fiction 3. Magic -- Fiction 4. Charms -- Fiction 5. Friendship -- Fiction 6. Family problems -- Fiction 7. New York (N.Y.) -- Fiction
ISBN 0399257608; 9780399257605

LC 2012024514

This book by Andrea Cremer and David Levithan chronicles the "romance between a boy cursed with invisibility and the one girl who can see him. . . . Stephen is used to invisibility. He was born that way. . . . Elizabeth sometimes wishes for invisibility. . . . To Stephen's amazement, she can see him. And to Elizabeth's amazement, she wants him to be able to see her--all of her. But as the two become closer, an invisible world gets in their way." (Publisher's note)

"Though it begins as a stumbling, near–coming-out story (for Stephen), the novel deftly switches gears to a fast-paced supernatural thriller that will surely leave readers wanting more." Kirkus

Two boys kissing; by David Levithan. Alfred A. Knopf 2013 208 p. (hardcover library binding) $19.99

Grades: 8 9 10 11 12 **Fic**

1. School stories 2. LGBT youth -- Fiction 3. Gay teenagers -- Fiction 4. Gays -- Fiction 5. Love -- Fiction 6. Social change -- Fiction
ISBN 0307931900; 0375971122; 9780307931900; 9780307931917; 9780375971129

LC 2012047089

Lambda Literary Award: LGBT Children's/YA (2014)
Stonewall Honor Book: Children and Young Adult (2014)

In this book, students Craig and Henry are trying to set a world record for the longest kiss They "are no longer dating, throwing an element of uncertainty into an act that's romantic, political, and personal. Neil and Peter have been dating for a year and are beginning to wonder what's next. Avery, 'born a boy that the rest of the world saw as a girl,' and Ryan are caught up in the dizzying excitement of meeting someone new. And Cooper is rapidly losing himself into a digital oblivion." (Publishers Weekly)

"Craig and Harry attempt to break the world record for longest kiss, which, in turn, affects the lives of the people around them. Narrated by a ghostly chorus of past generations of gay men who died of AIDS, Levithan's latest novel weaves together an informed (sometimes melodramatic) perspective on the past with the present-day stories of seven boys constructing their own sexual identities." (Horn Book)

Levitin, Sonia

★ **Strange** relations. Alfred A. Knopf 2007 298p hardcover o.p. pa $6.50

Grades: 7 8 9 10 **Fic**

1. Jews -- Fiction 2. Hawaii -- Fiction 3. Cousins -- Fiction 4. Religion -- Fiction

ISBN 978-0-375-83751-7; 0-375-83751-5; 978-0-440-23963-5 pa; 0-440-23963-X pa

LC 2006-33275

Fifteen-year-old Marne is excited to be able to spend her summer vacation in Hawaii, not realizing the change in her lifestyle it would bring staying with her aunt, seven cousins, and uncle who is a Chasidic rabbi.

"It's rare to find such well-developed characters, empathetic and sensitive religious treatment, and carefully crafted plotlines in one novel." SLJ

Levy, Dana Alison

The **family** Fletcher takes Rock Island; Dana Alison Levy. Delacorte Press 2016 272 p. (hc) $16.99

Grades: 4 5 6 7 **Fic**

1. Humorous fiction 2. Summer -- Fiction 3. Neighbors -- Fiction 4. Family life -- Fiction 5. Lighthouses -- Fiction 6. Humorous stories 7. Gay fathers -- Fiction

ISBN 9780553521306; 9780553521313

LC 2015014134

In this book, by Dana Alison Levy, the "Fletchers are back on Rock Island, home of all their best summer memories. But from their first day on vacation, it's clear that this year, things have changed. . . . Over the course of the summer, the Fletchers will learn that sometimes, even in a place where time stands still, the wildest, weirdest, and most wonderful surprises await." (Publisher's note)

"There is constant action and delightful humor, but there are also realistic present-day problems and happy solutions. An old-fashioned summer adventure set in a very modern world, this lively family tale will leave readers impatient for more." Kirkus

★ **It** wasn't me; Dana Alison Levy. Random House Childrens Books 2018 336 p. $16.99

Grades: 4 5 6 7 8 **Fic**

1. School stories 2. Vandalism -- Fiction 3. Friendship -- Fiction

ISBN 1524766437; 9781524766436

In this book, by Dana Alison Levy, "when Theo's photography project is . . . vandalized at school there are five suspected students who all say 'it wasn't me.' Theo just wants to forget about . . . [it] but his favorite teacher is determined to get to the bottom of it and has the six of them come into school over vacation to talk. . . . The six students . . . think of it as detention. . . . That is until they realize they might get along after all, despite their differences." (Publisher's note)

"Six seventh-graders in small-town Massachusetts reluctantly spend school vacation week participating in a restorative-practice justice circle in hopes of identifying a vandal." (Kirkus Reviews)

The **misadventures** of the family Fletcher; Dana Levy. Delacorte Press 2014 272 p. (glb) $18.99

Grades: 4 5 6 7 **Fic**

1. Interracial adoption 2. Children of gay parents -- Fiction 3. Humorous stories 4. Schools -- Fiction 5. Adoption -- Fiction 6. Brothers -- Fiction 7. Neighbors -- Fiction 8. Family life -- Fiction

ISBN 0385376545; 9780385376525; 9780385376549

LC 2013026320

In this middle grades book by Dana Alison Levy, "With four brothers, a dog, a cat, school projects, soccer matches, and a grumpy neighbor, the Fletchers are your typical American family . . . with two dads, and siblings who are adopted kids from various ethnic backgrounds. While 12-year-old Sam ponders . . . trying out for the school play . . . , 10-year-old Jax negotiates changing friendships and a veteran project that involves talking to the unfriendly Vietnam vet next door." (School Library Journal)

"Four adopted (and racially diverse) brothers and two dads star in this Penderwicks-esque chronicle of a year in their lives. Focusing each chapter on one boy while still keeping the whole family in the picture, Levy provides a compelling, compassionate, and frequently hilarious look at their daily concerns. Readers will want to be part of (or at least friends with) this delightful family." Horn Book

This would make a good story someday; Dana Alison Levy. Delacorte Press 2017 320 p. (hardback) $16.99

Grades: 4 5 6 7 8 **Fic**

1. Authorship -- Fiction 2. Family life -- Fiction 3. Gay parents -- Fiction 4. Lesbian mothers -- Fiction 5. Railroad travel -- Fiction

ISBN 9781101938171; 9781101938188

LC 2016032310

In this book, by Dana Alison Levy, "Sara Johnston-Fischer loves her family, of course. But that doesn't mean she's thrilled when her summer plans are upended for a surprise cross-country train trip with her two moms, Mimi and Carol; her younger sister, Ladybug; her older sister, Laurel; and Laurel's poncho-wearing activist boyfriend, Root. And to make matters worse, one of her moms is writing a tell-all book about the trip." (Publisher's note)

Lewis, C. S.

The **horse** and his boy; illustrated by Pauline Baynes. HarperCollins 1994 224p il (The chronicles of Narnia) lib bdg $17; pa $6.99

Grades: 4 5 6 7 **Fic**

1. Fantasy fiction

ISBN 0-06-023489-X lib bdg; 0-06-447106-3 pa

LC 93014300

Sequel to: The silver chair

A reissue of the title first published 1954

A boy and a talking horse share an adventurous and dangerous journey to Narnia to warn of invading barbarians.

Followed by: The magician's nephew

The **last** battle; illustrated by Pauline Baynes. HarperCollins 1994 211p il (The chronicles of Narnia) pa $6.99

Grades: 4 5 6 7 **Fic**

1. Fantasy fiction

ISBN 0-06-023494-6 lib bdg; 0-06-447108-X pa

LC 93014302

Sequel to: The magician's nephew

A reissue of the title first published 1956

When evil comes to Narnia, Jill and Eustace help fight the great last battle and Aslan leads his people to a glorious new paradise.

★ The **lion,** the witch, and the wardrobe; illustrated by Pauline Baynes. HarperCollins Pubs. 1994 189p il (The chronicles of Narnia) $17.99; lib bdg $18.89; pa $7.99
Grades: 4 5 6 7 **Fic**

1. Fantasy fiction
ISBN 0-06-023481-4; 0-06-023482-2 lib bdg; 0-06-440499-4 pa
LC 93-8889

A reissue of the title first published 1950 by Macmillan

Four English schoolchildren find their way through the back of a wardrobe into the magic land of Narnia and assist Aslan, the golden lion, to triumph over the White Witch, who has cursed the land with eternal winter

This begins "the 'Narnia' stories, outstanding modern fairy tales with an underlying theme of good overcoming evil." Child Books Too Good to Miss

Other titles in this series are:
Prince Caspian (1951)
The voyage of the Dawn Treader (1952)
The silver chair (1953)
The horse and his boy (1954)
The magician's nephew (1956)
The last battle (1956)

The **magician's** nephew; illustrated by Pauline Baynes. HarperCollins 1994 202p il (The chronicles of Narnia) lib bdg $18.89; pa $7.99
Grades: 4 5 6 7 **Fic**

1. Fantasy fiction
ISBN 0-06-023498-9 lib bdg; 0-06-440505-2 pa
LC 93014301

Sequel to: The horse and his boy
A reissue of the title first published 1956

When Digory and Polly try to return the wicked witch Jadis to her own world, the magic gets mixed up and they all land in Narnia where they witness Aslan blessing the animals with human speech.

Followed by: The last battle

Prince Caspian; the return to Narnia. illustrated by Pauline Baynes. HarperCollins 1994 223p il (The chronicles of Narnia) lib bdg $18.89; pa $6.99
Grades: 4 5 6 7 **Fic**

1. Fantasy fiction
ISBN 0-06-023484-9 lib bdg; 0-06-447105-5 pa
LC 93011514

Sequel to: The lion, the witch, and the wardrobe
A reissue of the title first published 1951

Four children help Prince Caspian and his army of Talking Beasts to free Narnia from evil.

Followed by: The voyage of the Dawn Treader

The **silver** chair; illustrated by Pauline Baynes. HarperCollins 1994 243p il (The chronicles of Narnia) lib bdg $18.89; pa $6.99
Grades: 4 5 6 7 **Fic**

1. Fantasy fiction
ISBN 0-06-023496-2 lib bdg; 0-06-447109-8 pa
LC 93014299

Sequel to: The voyage of the Dawn Treader
A reissue of the title first published 1953

Two English children undergo hair-raising adventures as they go on a search and rescue mission for the missing Prince Rilian, who is held captive in the underground kingdom of the Emerald Witch.

Followed by: The horse and his boy

The **voyage** of the Dawn Treader; illustrated by Pauline Baynes. HarperCollins 1994 248p il (The chronicles of Narnia) lib bdg $17.99; pa $6.99
Grades: 4 5 6 7 **Fic**

1. Fantasy fiction
ISBN 0-06-023487-3 lib bdg; 0-06-447107-1 pa
LC 93011515

Sequel to: Prince Caspian
A reissue of the title first published 1952

Lucy and Edmund, accompanied by their peevish cousin Eustace, sail to the land of Narnia where Eustace is temporarily transformed into a green dragon because of his selfish behavior and skepticism.

Followed by: The silver chair

Lewis, Gill

Gorilla dawn; Gill Lewis, illustrated by Susan Meyer. Atheneum Books for Young Readers 2017 432 p. illustrations (ebook) $15.99; (hardcover) $16.99
Grades: 5 6 7 8 9 **Fic**

1. Africa -- Fiction 2. Gorillas -- Fiction 3. Rain forests -- Fiction 4. Congo (Republic) -- Fiction
ISBN 9781481486590; 1481486578; 9781481486576; 9781481486583
LC 2016041998

In this book, by Gill Lewis, illustrated by Susan Meyer, "deep in the heart of the Congo, a baby gorilla is captured by a group of rebel soldiers. Imara and Bobo are also prisoners in the rebels' camp. When they learn that the gorilla will be sold into captivity, they swear to return it to the wild before it's too late. . . . Will the bond between the gorilla and the children give them the courage they need to escape?" (Publisher's note)

"A riveting survival adventure with an important message." Kirkus

Moon bear; Gill Lewis ; illustrated by Alessandro Gottardo. Atheneum Books for Young Readers 2015 384 p. illustrations (hardcover) $16.99
Grades: 4 5 6 7 8 **Fic**

1. Laos -- Fiction 2. Bears -- Fiction 3. Asiatic black bear -- Fiction 4. Animals -- Treatment -- Fiction
ISBN 1481400940; 9781481400947; 9781481400954
LC 2013049285

In this book, by Gill Lewis, "[t]welve-year-old Tam, on a dare, ventures into a moon bear den in the mountains of Northern Laos. His goal is to steal the cub and sell it, making a fortune for his family. But the mother bear's unexpected return upends Tam's plan, and he barely escapes with his life. And then his life implodes anyway. . . . Tam is forced to work hundreds of miles away in the city, at a moon bear farm where bile from bear gall bladders is used for medicine." (Publisher's note)

"Through Tam's selfless quest to get the bear back to the wild, and his protection of the cub at the expense of his own well-being, readers witness the depths of his bravery, compassion, and strong moral compass." Pub Wkly

One white dolphin; Gill Lewis ; illustrated by Raquel Aparicio. Atheneum Books for Young Readers 2012 p. cm. (hardback) $15.99
Grades: 5 6 7 **Fic**

1. Ecology -- Fiction 2. England -- Fiction 3. Dolphins -- Fiction

4. Seashore -- Fiction 5. Marine ecology -- Fiction 6. Wildlife rescue -- Fiction 7. Environmental protection -- Fiction
ISBN 9781442414471; 9781442414501
LC 2012009182

In this book, "a boy with cerebral palsy and an injured albino dolphin calf help Kara Wood come to terms with her mother's death and the sale of the family's boat, Moana. Kara's mother vanished a year ago on a dolphin-saving trip to the South Pacific. With debts mounting, her father plans to sell the sailboat they built. . . . The temporary protection of the reef near their British coastal home is about to expire." (Kirkus Reviews)

★ **Wild** wings; illustrated by Yuta Onoda. Atheneum Books for Young Readers 2011 287p il $15.99
Grades: 4 5 6 7 **Fic**
1. Gambia -- Fiction 2. Ospreys -- Fiction 3. Scotland -- Fiction 4. Farm life -- Fiction 5. Friendship -- Fiction
ISBN 1-4424-1445-6; 978-1-4424-1445-7
LC 2010-49228

Callum becomes friends with Iona, a practically feral classmate who has discovered an osprey, thought to be gone from Scotland, on Callum's family farm, and they eventually share the secret with others, including Jeneba who encounters the same bird at her home in Gambia.

This is a "rich, moving tale. . . . The suspenseful story line is surrounded with precise details. . . . Short chapters, some with cliffhanging endings, will read-aloud well. . . . A powerfully memorable story." Kirkus

Lewis, Stewart

The **secret** ingredient; Stewart Lewis. Delacorte Press 2013 256 p. (hc) $17.99
Grades: 7 8 9 10 **Fic**
1. Cooking -- Fiction 2. Mothers -- Fiction 3. Interpersonal relations -- Fiction 4. Self-realization -- Fiction 5. Los Angeles (Calif.) -- Fiction
ISBN 0385743319; 9780375991066; 9780385743310
LC 2012027203

This novel by Stewart Lewis is a "journey of family, food, romance, and self-discovery as Olivia, a teen chef living in L.A., finds a vintage cookbook and begins a search for her birthmother that will change her life forever. A new job leads Olivia to a gorgeous, mysterious boy named Theo. And as Olivia cooks the recipes from a vintage cookbook she stumbles upon, she begins to wonder if the mother she's never known might be the secret ingredient she's been lacking." (Publisher's note)

"Adopted by two dads, Olivia begins to sense a void in her life. Serendipitously, Olivia finds her supposedly "nameless" birth mother but quickly realizes that maybe the secret ingredient to a fulfilled life is appreciating what one already has. Lewis's mature protagonist adapts remarkably well to her nontraditional life in this story that limns themes of adolescence, adoption, illness, and financial instability." (Horn Book)

Lieberman, Leanne

Lauren Yanofsky hates the Holocaust; Leanne Lieberman. Orca Book Publishers 2013 240 p. (paperback) $12.95; (ebook) $12.99
Grades: 7 8 9 10 **Fic**
1. Hi-Lo books 2. Jews -- Fiction 3. Holocaust, 1939-1945 -- Fiction
ISBN 1459801091; 9781459801097; 9781459801103 pdf; 9781459801110
LC 2012952950

In this novel, by Leanne Lieberman, "Lauren Yanofsky doesn't want to be Jewish anymore. Her father, a noted Holocaust historian, keeps giving her Holocaust memoirs to read, and her mother doesn't understand why Lauren hates the idea of Jewish youth camps and family vacations to Holocaust memorials. But when Lauren sees some of her friends . . . playing Nazi war games, she is faced with a terrible choice: betray her friends or betray her heritage." (Publisher's note)

"Lieberman . . . smoothly weaves humor and knowledge about Judaism through Lauren's story. Lauren's narration is contemplative and from the heart, and readers should relate to her attempts to identify her beliefs and tackle life's big questions." Pub Wkly

Off pointe; Leanne Lieberman. Orca Book Publishers 2015 128 p. (Orca limelights) (pbk.) $9.95
Grades: 6 7 8 9 **Fic**
1. Hi-Lo books 2. Ballet -- Fiction 3. Dancers -- Fiction 4. Friendship -- Fiction 5. Camps -- Fiction 6. Ballet dancers -- Fiction
ISBN 1459802802; 9781459802803; 9781459802810; 9781459802827
LC 2014935396

In this novel by Leanne Lieberman "Meg's summer ballet program is canceled and her ballet teacher suggests she attend Camp Dance to learn new dance styles. At camp, Meg struggles to learn contemporary dance. A girl named Logan, who is jealous of Meg's ballet technique and her friendship with Nio . . . makes Meg's life even more difficult. When Meg, Nio and Logan have to work together to create a piece for the final show, arguments threaten to ruin their dance. " (Publisher's note)

Lieurance, Suzanne

The **locket**; surviving the Triangle Shirtwaist fire. [by] Suzanne Lieurance. Enslow Publishers 2008 160p il (Historical fiction adventures) lib bdg $27.93
Grades: 4 5 6 7 **Fic**
1. Sisters -- Fiction 2. Factories -- Fiction 3. Immigrants -- Fiction 4. Jews -- United States -- Fiction 5. Triangle Shirtwaist Company, Inc. -- Fiction
ISBN 978-0-7660-2928-6 lib bdg; 0-7660-2928-X lib bdg
LC 2007-5281

After Galena, an eleven-year-old Russian immigrant, survives a terrible fire at the non-unionized Triangle Shirtwaist factory while her older sister and many others do not, she begins fighting for improved working conditions in New York City factories.

"Woven together in perfect compatibility, the historical background and fictional plot give readers a clear insight into Jewish immigrants and . . . unfair labor practices, and there is excellent foreshadowing of the fire." SLJ

Includes bibliographical references

Lin, Grace, 1974-

★ **Starry** River of the Sky; by Grace Lin. Little, Brown 2012 288 p. col. ill. $17.99
Grades: 3 4 5 6 **Fic**
1. Fairy tales 2. Moon -- Fiction 3. Villages -- Fiction 4. Storytelling -- Fiction
ISBN 0316125954; 9780316125956
LC 2012012651

In this novel by Grace Lin, "the moon is missing from the remote Village of Clear Sky, but only a young boy named Rendi seems to notice! Rendi has run away from home and is now working as a chore boy at the village inn. He can't help but notice the village's peculiar inhabitants and their problems . . . but one day, a mysterious lady arrives at the Inn with the gift of storytelling, and slowly transforms the villagers and Rendi himself." (Publisher's note)

Includes bibliographical references.

★ **When** the sea turned to silver; Grace Lin. Little, Brown Books for Young Readers 2016 384 p. color illustrations (ebook) $57; (hardback) $18.99

Grades: 4 5 6 7 **Fic**

1. Adventure fiction 2. Kidnapping -- Fiction 3. Grandmothers -- Fiction 4. Storytelling -- Fiction 5. China -- History -- Fiction 6. Fairy tales 7. Storytellers -- Fiction 8. Adventure and adventurers -- Fiction

ISBN 9780316396387; 9780316125925

LC 2015041876

National Book Award Finalist: Young People's Literature (2016)

In this book, by Grace Lin, "Pinmei's gentle, loving grandmother always has the most exciting tales for her granddaughter and the other villagers. However, the peace is shattered one night when soldiers of the Emperor arrive and kidnap the storyteller. Everyone knows that the Emperor wants something called the Luminous Stone That Lights the Night. Determined to have her grandmother returned, Pinmei embarks on a journey to find the Luminous Stone alongside her friend Yishan." (Publisher's note)

"A stunning addition to a deservedly beloved set of novels" SLJ

Includes bibliographical references

★ **Where** the mountain meets the moon. Little, Brown and Co. 2009 278p il $16.99

Grades: 4 5 6 7 **Fic**

1. Fairy tales 2. Moon -- Fiction 3. Dragons -- Fiction

ISBN 978-0-316-11427-1; 0-316-11427-8

LC 2008-32818

A Newbery Medal honor book, 2010

Minli, an adventurous girl from a poor village, buys a magical goldfish, and then joins a dragon who cannot fly on a quest to find the Old Man of the Moon in hopes of bringing life to Fruitless Mountain and freshness to Jade River

"With beautiful language, Lin creates a strong, memorable heroine and a mystical land. . . . Children will embrace this accessible, timeless story about the evil of greed and the joy of gratitude." Booklist

Lindelauf, Benny, 1964-

★ **Nine** Open Arms; Benny Lindelauf ; translated from the Dutch by John Nieuwenhuizen ; jacket and interior art by Dasha Tolstikova. Enchanted Lion 2014 264 p. illustrations, map $16.95

Grades: 5 6 7 8 9 **Fic**

1. Dutch literature 2. Historical fiction 3. Family life -- Fiction

ISBN 1592701469; 9781592701469

LC 2014014977

Mildred L. Batchelder Honor Book (2015)

"A ghost story, a fantasy, a historical novel, and literary fiction all wrapped into one, this highly awarded novel for young readers begins with the Boon family's move to an isolated, dilapidated house. Is it the site of a haunting tragedy, as one of the daughters believes, or an end to all their worries, as their father hopes?" (Publisher's note)

"Every element of the tale has a purpose, and in the end, the multiple layers of past and present separate and come together in surprising, often discomfiting twists and turns.A challenging and entirely unique Dutch import." Kirkus

Followed by:

Fing's war (2019)

Lipsyte, Robert

★ The **contender**. Harper & Row 1967 182p hardcover o.p. pa $5.99

Grades: 7 8 9 10 **Fic**

1. Boxing -- Fiction 2. African Americans -- Fiction 3. Harlem (New York, N.Y.) -- Fiction

ISBN 0-06-447039-3

ALA YALSA Margaret A. Edwards Award (2001)

"After a street fight in which he is the chief target, Alfred wanders into a gym in his neighborhood. He decides not only to improve his physical condition but also to become a boxer. Because of this interest Alfred's life is completely changed. He assumes a more positive outlook on his immediate future, even within the confines of a black ghetto." Shapiro. Fic for Youth. 3d edition

Followed by The brave (1991) and The chief (1993)

The **twinning** project; by Robert Lipsyte. Clarion Books 2012 269 p. (hardback) $16.99

Grades: 4 5 6 7 **Fic**

1. Science fiction 2. Twins -- Fiction 3. Parallel universes -- Fiction 4. Schools -- Fiction 5. Middle schools -- Fiction 6. Space and time -- Fiction

ISBN 0547645716; 9780547645711

LC 2011050252

This book by Robert Lipsyte follows protagonist Tom, who has been "expelled from school after school for fighting bullies. . . . The boy's only comfort comes from talking through his problems with his imaginary twin, Eddie, a jock who lives on a version of Earth 50 years behind Tom's. . . . When the boys' 'grandfather' on both Earths reveals that the twin planets were created by alien scientists, the boys switch places to fight for the survival of both Earths." (Publishers Weekly)

Lisle, Holly

★ The **Ruby** Key. Orchard Books 2008 361p (Moon & sun) $16.99; pa $7.99

Grades: 5 6 7 8 **Fic**

1. Fantasy fiction 2. Siblings -- Fiction

ISBN 978-0-545-00012-3; 0-545-00012-2; 978-0-545-00013-0 pa; 0-545-00013-0 pa

LC 2007-30217

In a world where an uneasy peace binds Humans and Nightlings, fourteen-year-old Genna and her twelve-year-old brother Dan learn of their uncle's plot to gain immortality in exchange for human lives, and the two strike their own bargain with the Nightling lord, which sets them on a dangerous journey along the Moonroads in search of a key.

"Lisle's fertile imagination provides the nightworlds with monsters . . . but it is her clever plotting in this . . . fantasy, leading up to a thrilling finish . . . That will bewitch her audience." Horn Book

Followed by: The silver door (2009)

The **silver** door. Orchard Books 2009 366p (Moon & sun) $17.99

Grades: 5 6 7 8 **Fic**

1. War stories 2. Fantasy fiction

ISBN 978-0-545-00014-7; 0-545-00014-9

LC 2008-40153

When Genna is chosen as the Sunrider of prophecy, her destiny is to unite the magic of the sun and the moon for the good of both Nightlings and humans.

"This second book of the Moon & Sun series has jarring stop-start feel, but the complexities of the interlaced human and nightling societies continue to unfold in fascinating way, creating a multi-hued, fully realized world for readers to explore." Horn Book

Lisle, Janet Taylor

Quicksand Pond; Janet Taylor Lisle. Atheneum Books for Young Readers 2017 256 p. illustrations, map (hardcover) $16.99

Grades: 5 6 7 8 **Fic**

1. Ponds -- Fiction 2. Homicide -- Fiction 3. Friendship -- Fiction 4. Murder -- Fiction

ISBN 9781481472227; 9781481472234

LC 2016009707

In this book, author Janet Taylor Lisle "crafts a stirring story that raises crucial questions about the assumptions we make, the distances we keep, and the vulnerable voices we often fail to hear. As Lisle details Terri's determination to cease a vicious cycle, Henrietta's resolve to remedy an unjust past, and Jessie's aching ambivalence between the cautionary advice of others and her own hard-won revelations, readers are sure to listen." (Booklist)

"A strong purchase for fans of layered, realistic mysteries and drama." School Library Journal.

Little, Kimberley Griffiths

★ **Circle** of secrets. Scholastic Press 2011 326p $17.99

Grades: 5 6 7 8 **Fic**

1. Ghost stories 2. Guilt -- Fiction 3. Louisiana -- Fiction 4. Mother-daughter relationship -- Fiction

ISBN 978-0-545-16561-7; 0-545-16561-X

LC 2011000889

A year after her mother has deserted the family, eleven-year-old Shelby goes to stay with her, deep in the Louisiana bayou, where they both confront old hurts and regrets.

"The gently spooky ghost angle is handled nicely with some religious overtones. A very dramatic climax leads to a sweet, satisfying ending with some surprising twists and with reconciliation occurring for several characters." Kirkus

The **healing** spell. Scholastic Press 2010 354p $17.99

Grades: 5 6 7 8 **Fic**

1. Coma -- Fiction 2. Guilt -- Fiction 3. Mother-daughter relationship -- Fiction

ISBN 978-0-545-16559-4; 0-545-16559-8

LC 2009-28016

Twelve-year-old Livie is living with a secret and it's crushing her. She knows she is responsible for her mother's coma, but she can't tell anyone. It's up to her to find a way to wake her momma up.

"Little explores the extremes of childhood guilt and its consequences in this harsh yet well-crafted story about fully drawn people. The bayou, with its rich culture, is an atmospheric character that overlays the story with mystery and dread." Booklist

The **time** of the fireflies; Kimberley Griffiths Little. Scholastic Press 2014 368 p. (jacketed hardcover) $18.99

Grades: 5 6 7 8 **Fic**

1. Mystery fiction 2. Family secrets -- Fiction 3. Secrets -- Fiction 4. Fireflies -- Fiction 5. Louisiana -- Fiction 6. Family life -- Fiction 7. Time travel -- Fiction 8. Family problems -- Fiction

ISBN 0545165636; 9780545165631

LC 2013027396

In this middle grades book by Kimberley Griffiths Little, "When Larissa Renaud starts receiving eerie phone calls on a disconnected old phone in her family's antique shop, she knows she's in for a strange summer. A series of clues leads her to the muddy river banks. . . . It soon becomes clear that it is up to Larissa to prevent history from repeating itself and a fatal tragedy from striking the people she loves." (Publisher's note)

"Twelve-year-old Larissa's parents own Bayou Bridge Antiques, which features a wall of old phones. When one of the phones begins ringing, Larissa hesitantly picks it up. The female voice on the other end begs Larissa to find the fireflies. . . . [F]ans of Mary Downing Hahn's books will appreciate the spooky porcelain dolls and family curse." Booklist

Littlefield, Sophie

Infected; Sophie Littlefield. First edition Delacorte Press 2015 256 p. (hc : alk. paper) $17.99

Grades: 7 8 9 10 **Fic**

1. Conspiracies -- Fiction 2. Family secrets -- Fiction 3. National security -- United States 4. Spies -- Fiction 5. Survival -- Fiction 6. Dating (Social customs) -- Fiction

ISBN 0385741065; 9780375989834; 9780385741064

LC 2013046923

"Carina's senior year is spiraling downward. Fast. Both her mother and her uncle, the only two family members she's ever known, are dead. Their deaths were accidents, unfortunate results of the highly confidential research they performed for a national security organization. The people Carina loved kept dangerous secrets. Secrets that make her question the life she's been living up to now." (Publisher's note)

"Nail-biting action with a scientifically and technologically involved plotline gives this novel an edge, and, moreover, the character development is surprisingly rich given the fast pace of the narrative. The weight of the themes also keeps the story from reading like a movie script. Red herrings keep the reader guessing until the end." Booklist

Littman, Sarah

Backlash; Sarah Darer Littman. First edition Scholastic Press 2015 325 p. $17.99

Grades: 7 8 9 **Fic**

1. Bullies -- Fiction 2. Sisters -- Fiction 3. Suicide -- Fiction 4. Neighbors -- Fiction 5. Friendship -- Fiction 6. Family life -- Fiction 7. Cyberbullying -- Fiction 8. Bullying -- Fiction 9. Families -- fiction 10. Suicidal behavior -- fiction

ISBN 0545651263; 9780545651264; 9780545651271; 9780545755023

LC 2014020226

In this book, by Sarah Darer Littman, "Lara just got told off on Facebook. She thought that Christian liked her, that he was finally going to ask her to his school's homecoming dance. It's been a long time since Lara's felt this bad, this depressed. . . . Bree used to be BBFs with overweight, depressed Lara in middle school, but constantly listening to Lara's problems got to be too much. Bree's secretly glad that Christian's pointed out Lara's flaws to the world." (Publisher's note)

"The depression and bullying are handled realistically without sugarcoating, and fortunately, consequences are applied. An excellent choice for any antibullying campaign." Booklist

Life, after; [by] Sarah Darer Littman. Scholastic Press 2010 281p $17.99

Grades: 7 8 9 10 11 12 **Fic**

1. Argentina -- Fiction 2. Terrorism -- Fiction 3. Immigrants -- Fiction

ISBN 978-0-545-15144-3; 0-545-15144-9

After a terrorist attack kills Dani's aunt and unborn cousin, life in Argentina—private school, a boyfriend, a loving family—crumbles quickly. In order to escape a country that is sinking under their feet, Dani and her family move to the United States.

The author "weaves sensitively articulated themes . . . and credible teen banter into an emotionally complex tale." Booklist

Llewellyn, Sam

Darksolstice. Orchard Books 2010 365p map (Lyonesse) $17.99

Grades: 5 6 7 8 **Fic**

1. Fantasy fiction 2. Kings

ISBN 978-0-439-93471-8; 0-439-93471-0

LC 2009006283

Sequel to: The well between the worlds (2009)

While Idris Limpet, Rightful King of the Land of Lyonesse, is making the treacherous journey to the distant land of Aegypt to rescue his dear friend and sister, Morgan, he meets a company of friends who shall become his Knights of the Round Table and lead armies to battle the evil regent, Fisheagle.

The **well** between the worlds. Orchard Books 2009 339p (Lyonesse) $17.99

Grades: 5 6 7 8 **Fic**

1. Fantasy fiction 2. Kings

ISBN 978-0-439-93469-5; 0-439-93469-9

LC 2008-20075

Eleven-year-old Idris Limpet, living with his family in the once noble but now evil and corrupt island country of Lyonesse, finds his life taking a dramatic turn when, after a near-drowning incident, he is accused of being allied to the feared sea monsters and is rescued from a death sentence by a mysterious and fearsome stranger.

"Seldom does one find a new fantasy that is so richly textured, so original in concept, and with such a wonderfully interesting story. . . . Fantasy lovers will be impatient to find out where their paths take them." Voice Youth Advocates

Followed by: Darksolstice (2010)

Lloyd Jones, Rob

Wild boy; Rob Lloyd Jones. Candlewick Press 2013 304 p. $16.99

Grades: 5 6 7 8 **Fic**

1. Mystery fiction 2. Steampunk fiction

ISBN 0763662526; 9780763662523

LC 2013931467

In this book, "Wild Boy's head-to-toe fur has garnered him scorn and abuse from commoners, but his extraordinary intellectual gifts eventually win him a future with a powerful, elite group called the Gentlemen. . . . When Wild Boy is about to be hanged by the unseemly circus crew for a murder he did not commit, teen acrobat Clarissa helps him escape. Together, they follow clues through sewers and back alleys, learning about an extraordinary electrical device linked to the murder." (Kirkus Reviews)

Lloyd, Alison

Year of the tiger. Holiday House 2010 194p $16.95

Grades: 5 6 7 8 **Fic**

1. Adventure fiction 2. China -- Fiction 3. Archery -- Fiction 4. Social classes -- Fiction

ISBN 978-0-8234-2277-7; 0-8234-2277-1

LC 2009033651

First published 2008 in Australia

In ancient China, Hu and Ren forge an unlikely alliance in an effort to become expert archers and, ultimately, to save their city from invading barbarians.

"Brimming with details of daily life in the Han Dynasty, this fast-paced story alternates in the third person between Hu and Ren." Kirkus

Lloyd, Natalie

★ A **snicker** of magic; by Natalie Lloyd. Scholastic Press 2014 320 p. hbk $16.99

Grades: 4 5 6 7 **Fic**

1. Magic -- Fiction 2. Curses -- Fiction 3. Tennessee -- Fiction 4. Friendship -- Fiction 5. Family life -- Fiction 6. Mothers and daughters -- Fiction

ISBN 9780545552707; 0545552702

LC 2013027779

"Midnight Gulch used to be a magical place, a town where people could sing up thunderstorms and dance up sunflowers. But that was long ago, before a curse drove the magic away. Twelve-year-old Felicity knows all about things like that; her nomadic mother is cursed with a wandering heart. . . . But when she arrives in Midnight Gulch, Felicity thinks her luck's about to change." (Publisher's note)

"The unusual language, showing a tinge of Tennessee mountain dialect, spins a web around the story that touches on helping others, budding friendships, and strength of family." Booklist

Lloyd, Saci

★ The **carbon** diaries 2015. Holiday House 2009 330p il map $17.95

Grades: 8 9 10 11 12 **Fic**

1. Science fiction 2. Family life -- Fiction 3. Great Britain -- Fiction 4. Conservation of natural resources -- Fiction

ISBN 0-8234-2190-2; 978-0-8234-2190-9

LC 2008-19712

First published 2008 in the United Kingdom

In 2015, when England becomes the first nation to introduce carbon dioxide rationing in a drastic bid to combat climate change, sixteen-year-old Laura documents the first year of rationing. "Grades nine to twelve." (Bull Cent Child Books)

"Deeply compulsive and urgently compulsory reading." Booklist

Includes bibliographical references

Followed by The carbon diaries 2017 (2010)

The **carbon** diaries 2017. Holiday House 2010 326p il map $17.95

Grades: 8 9 10 11 12 **Fic**

1. Science fiction 2. College students -- Fiction 3. London (England) -- Fiction 4. Conservation of natural resources -- Fiction

ISBN 978-0-8234-2260-9; 0-8234-2260-7

Sequel to: The carbon diaries 2015 (2009)

First published 2009 in the United Kingdom

Two years after England introduces carbon dioxide rationing to combat climatic change, eighteen-year-old Laura chronicles her first year at a London university as natural disasters and political upheaval disrupt her studies.

"The friction of living life in times of radical upheaval remains potent, sobering, and awfully exciting." Booklist

Lloyd-Jones, Emily

Illusive; Emily Lloyd-Jones. Little, Brown & Co. 2014 416 p. (hardcover) $18

Grades: 7 8 9 10 11 12 **Fic**

1. Science fiction 2. Dystopian fiction 3. Vaccines -- Fiction 4. Superheroes -- Fiction 5. Organized crime -- Fiction 6. Robbers

and outlaws -- Fiction 7. Adventure and adventurers -- Fiction
ISBN 0316254568; 9780316254564

LC 2013025295

Sequel: Deceptive (2015)

In this young adult science fiction novel by Emily Lloyd-Jones, "When the MK virus swept across the planet, a vaccine was created to stop the epidemic, but it came with some unexpected side effects. A small percentage of the population developed superhero-like powers. Seventeen-year-old Ciere Giba has the handy ability to change her appearance at will. She's what's known as an illusionist...She's also a thief." (Publisher's note)

"Ciere, a teenage career criminal with the ability to create illusions, lives in a dystopian future where a vaccine gone wrong created a feared minority of people with superpowers. Her latest job pulls her and her Dickensian gang of misfit allies into a power struggle involving the future of the vaccine. Innovative world-building and a scrappy protagonist strengthen this high-stakes caper." Horn Book

Lo, Malinda

A **line** in the dark; by Malinda Lo. Dutton Books 2017 281 p. (hardcover) $17.99

Grades: 8 9 10 11 **Fic**

1. Lesbians -- Fiction 2. Friendship -- Fiction 3. Dating (Social customs) -- Fiction 4. Murder -- Fiction 5. Best friends -- Fiction 6. Massachusetts -- Fiction 7. Social classes -- Fiction 8. Chinese Americans -- Fiction
ISBN 9780735227422; 9780735227446

LC 2017003862

In this book, by Malinda Lo, "Jess Wong is Angie Redmond's best friend. And that's the most important thing. . . . But when Angie . . . fall[s] for Margot Adams, a girl from the nearby boarding school, Jess can see it coming a mile away. . . . As Angie drags Jess further into Margot's circle, Jess discovers . . . [that s]ecrets and cruelty lie just beneath the . . . world of wealth and privilege, and . . . Jess knows [that] Angie won't be able to handle the consequences." (Publisher's note)

"In this unusually structured murder mystery, Lo (Inheritance) explores the knotty jealousies, romantic longings, and class disparities among students at a pair of Massachusetts high schools." Pub Wkly

Lockhart, E.

★ The **disreputable** history of Frankie Landau-Banks. Hyperion 2008 352p $16.99; pa $8.99

Grades: 7 8 9 10 11 12 **Fic**

1. School stories
ISBN 0-7868-3818-3; 0-7868-3819-1 pa; 978-0-7868-3818-9; 978-0-7868-3819-6 pa

Michael L. Printz Award honor book, 2009

National Book Award Finalist: Young People's Literature (2008)

"Frankie Landau-Banks at age 14: Debate Club. Her father's 'bunny rabbit.' A mildly geeky girl attending a highly competitive boarding school. Frankie Landau-Banks at age 15: A knockout figure. A sharp tongue. A chip on her shoulder. And a gorgeous new senior boyfriend: . . . Matthew Livingston. Frankie Landau-Banks. No longer the kind of girl to take 'no' for an answer. Especially when 'no' means she's excluded from her boyfriend's all-male secret society. . . . Not when she knows she's smarter than any of them. When she knows Matthew's lying to her. . . . Frankie Banks at age 16: Possibly a criminal mastermind. This is the story of how she got that way." (Publisher's note) "Grades nine to twelve." (Bull Cent Child Books)

"On her return to Alabaster Prep . . . [Frankie] attracts the attention of gorgeous Matthew . . . [who] is a member of the Loyal Order of the Basset Hounds, an all-male Alabaster secret society. . . . Frankie engineers her own guerilla membership by assuming a false online identity. . . . Lockhart creates a unique, indelible character. . . . Teens will be galvanized." Booklist

★ **Dramarama**. Hyperion 2007 311p $15.99

Grades: 7 8 9 10 11 12 **Fic**

1. School stories 2. Actors -- Fiction 3. Friendship -- Fiction
ISBN 0-7868-3815-9; 978-0-7868-3815-8

LC 2006-49599

Spending their summer at Wildewood Academy, an elite boarding school for the performing arts, tests the bond between best friends Sadye and Demi.

"Teens will identify strongly with both the heartbreak and the humor in this authentic portrayal of friendships maturing and decaying." SLJ

★ **Genuine** fraud; E. Lockhart. Delacorte Press 2017 272 p. (trade hardcover) $18.99

Grades: 7 8 9 10 11 12 **Fic**

1. Deception -- Fiction 2. Psychological fiction 3. Best friends -- Fiction
ISBN 9781471406638; 9780375991844; 9780385744775; 9781524770679

LC 2017009709

In this book, by E. Lockhart, "Jule West Williams is 18, white, and an orphan, all of which she has in common with her best friend, heiress Imogen Sokoloff--or does she? Jule, an impulsive, complicated protagonist like no other, tells her story as though she were living in an adventure movie. . . . She's proud of her strength and fighting ability, her talents for disguises and imitating accents." (Kirkus Reviews)

"This quietly unsettling, cinematic novel is deliciously suspenseful, and while it's slim, it packs a real punch." (Booklist)

★ **We** were liars; E. Lockhart. Delacorte Press 2014 240 p. (hardback) $17.99

Grades: 7 8 9 10 11 12 **Fic**

1. Summer -- Fiction 2. Wealth -- Fiction 3. Family life -- fiction 4. Love -- Fiction 5. Amnesia -- Fiction 6. Families -- Fiction 7. Friendship -- Fiction
ISBN 038574126X; 9780375989940; 9780385741262

LC 2013042127

In this book, by E. Lockhart, "Cadence Sinclair Eastman is the oldest grandchild of a preeminent family. The Sinclairs have . . . a private island off the coast of Massachusetts called Beechwood. Harris, the family patriarch, has three daughters: Bess, Carrie, and Penny, who is Cadence's mother. And then there is the next generation, 'the Liars': Cadence, Johnny, . . . Mirren, . . . and outsider Gat, an Indian boy and the nephew of Carrie's boyfriend." (Booklist)

"Cadence Sinclair Easton comes from an old-money family, headed by a patriarch who owns a private island off of Cape Cod. Each summer, the extended family gathers at the various houses on the island, and Cadence, her cousins Johnny and Mirren, and friend Gat (the four "Liars"), have been inseparable since age eight....The story, while lightly touching on issues of class and race, more fully focuses on dysfunctional family drama, a heart-wrenching romance between Cadence and Gat, and, ultimately, the suspense of what happened during that fateful summer. The ending is a stunner that will haunt readers for a long time to come." (School Library Journal)

Lockwood, Vicki

The **magnificent** Lizzie Brown and the mysterious phantom; by Vicki Lockwood ; illustrated by Stephanie Hans. Stone Arch Books, a Capstone imprint 2014 200 p. (The magnificent Lizzie Brown) (paper over board) $10.95

Grades: 5 6 7 8 **Fic**

1. Mystery fiction 2. Circus -- Fiction 3. Criminals -- Fiction 4. Psychic ability -- Fiction 5. Mystery and detective stories

ISBN 1623700698; 9781434279408; 9781434279422; 9781623700690

LC 2013050830

Sequel to: The Magnificent Lizzie Brown and the Devil's Hound (2014)

In this juvenile novel, by Vicki Lockwood, illustrated by Stephanie Hans, "a mysterious Phantom is terrorizing London, and when Lizzie realizes she has a talent that will let her stop the crimes before they happen she and her new circus friends feel compelled to intervene. But when one of their own is blamed for the crimes instead, their investigation takes a turn for the worse." (Publisher's note)

"In Victorian London, a twelve-year-old escapes grinding poverty and an abusive father by joining a traveling circus and finding first work, then acceptance and love, and finally a vocation: she becomes the circus fortuneteller. Despite plot contrivances and conversational anachronisms, Lizzie is an appealing heroine and these first two series entries are satisfying." Horn Book

Loftin, Nikki

Nightingale's nest; Nikki Loftin. Razorbill 2014 256 p. 22 cm (hardcover) $16.99

Grades: 4 5 6 7 **Fic**

1. Boys -- Fiction 2. Friendship -- Fiction 3. Birds -- Fiction 4. Magic -- Fiction 5. Singing -- Fiction 6. Family problems -- Fiction 7. Foster home care -- Fiction 8. Dysfunctional families -- fiction

ISBN 159514546X; 9781595145468

LC 2013047556

"Twelve-year-old John Fischer Jr. . . . is spending his summer helping his father with his tree removal business, clearing brush for Mr. King, the wealthy owner of a chain of Texas dollar stores, when he hears a beautiful song that transfixes him. Inspired by a Hans Christian Andersen story, 'Nightingale's Nest' is a . . . novel about a boy with the weight of the world on his shoulders and a girl with the gift of healing in her voice." (Publisher's note)

"John narrates his story in fluid, lyrical prose, Loftin blending the raw realism of a boy who makes the wrong choice with the fairy-tale magic of a girl with a nightingale voice. Unusual, finely crafted story of loss, betrayal and healing." Kirkus

Wish girl; Nikki Loftin. Razorbill 2015 256 p. (hardcover) $16.99

Grades: 4 5 6 7 **Fic**

1. Friendship -- Fiction 2. Cancer patients -- Fiction 3. Runaway children -- Fiction 4. Texas -- Fiction 5. Cancer -- Fiction 6. Best friends -- Fiction 7. Individuality -- Fiction 8. Family problems -- Fiction 9. Family life -- Texas -- Fiction

ISBN 1595146865; 9781595146861

LC 2014031004

In this children's novel by Nikki Loftin, "when his family moves to the Texas Hill Country, . . . Peter finds a tranquil, natural valley where he can, at last, hear himself think. There, he meets a girl his age: Annie Blythe . . . a 'Make-A-Wish Girl.' And in two weeks she will begin a dangerous treatment to try and stop her cancer from spreading. Annie and Peter hatch a plan to escape into the valley. But the pair soon discovers that the valley--and life--may have other plans for them." (Publisher's note)

"This thoughtful entry into realistic fiction for young teens explores family dysfunction and discord, the depression and emotional issues that plague young people trying to find their way, the importance of mentors, the unfortunate effects of bullying, and last but not least, cancer's impact on children and their families." VOYA

Companion to:
Nightingale's Nest (2014)

Loizeaux, William

★ **Clarence** Cochran, a human boy; pictures by Anne Wilsdorf. Farrar, Straus and Giroux 2009 152p il $16

Grades: 4 5 6 **Fic**

1. Toleration -- Fiction 2. Cockroaches -- Fiction 3. Environmental protection -- Fiction

ISBN 978-0-374-31323-4; 0-374-31323-7

LC 2007-35358

With the threat of extermination looming, a cockroach who has been transformed into a tiny human learns to communicate with his human hosts, leading to an agreement both sides can live with, and a friendship between Clarence and ten-year-old Mimi, a human environmentalist.

"There's a serious message here about environmentalism and the power of words, and the action and suspense make this a good read-aloud or classroom-discussion choice." SLJ

London, Alex

Black wings beating; Alex London. Farrar, Straus & Giroux 2018 432 p. (hardcover) $17.99

Grades: 8 9 10 11 12 **Fic**

1. Fantasy fiction 2. Twins -- Fiction 3. Falconry -- Fiction 4. Fantasy 5. Brothers and sisters -- Fiction

ISBN 9780374306823

LC 2018001439

In this book in the Skybound Saga, by Alex London, "the people of Uztar have long looked to the sky with hope and wonder. Nothing in their world is more revered than the birds of prey and no one more honored than the falconers who call them to their fists. Brysen strives to be a great falconer--while his twin sister, Kylee, rejects her ancient gifts for the sport. . . . Together the twins must journey into the treacherous mountains to trap the Ghost Eagle." (Publisher's note)

Guardian; Alex London. Philomel Books, an imprint of Penguin Group (USA) Inc. 2014 352 p. $17.99

Grades: 7 8 9 **Fic**

1. Science fiction 2. Dystopian fiction 3. Epidemics -- Fiction 4. Social classes -- Fiction 5. Gays -- Fiction

ISBN 0399165762; 9780399165764

LC 2013025938

Sequel to: Proxy

"It's a grave new world when the revolution a reluctant hero inspired could mean the death of everyone he tried to save, including himself. In this sequel to Proxy (2013), radical groups form in the wake of the Jubilee. The Reconciliation staunchly endorses tech-free purity, while Machinists demand a renaissance of the networks. Reluctant 16-year-old hero Syd is paraded as a political puppet, labeled a savior by supporters and marked a target by the opposition. His importance as a mascot for the Reconciliation necessitates a bodyguard, 17-year-old Liam. Liam is strong (he has a killer metal hand), silent (too shy for vocal eloquence) and will do anything to remain near Syd for reasons other than professional integrity. Amid political upheaval, an illness begins to spread, rendering victims' blue blood black and diminishing their mental faculties. Syd has been a hesitant political figure but knows he is the only hope for ending the illness." (Kirkus)

"Nonstop action and breakneck pace characterize this exceptional thriller. London provides his audience with an intricate plot, enriched by fine world-building and believable characters. The ample backstory will enable readers to enjoy Guardian without having read Proxy, although most will want to read these in sequence. This thought-provoking and breathtaking novel belongs in all collections serving young adults." VOYA

Proxy; Alex London. Philomel 2013 379 p. $17.99
Grades: 7 8 9 10 **Fic**

1. Science fiction 2. Dystopian fiction 3. Gays -- Fiction 4. Social classes -- Fiction
ISBN 0399257764; 9780399257766

LC 2012039704

In this book, "Knox is a 'patron,' a privileged and wealthy citizen of Mountain City. His only concerns are hacking, scoring with girls, and causing trouble while angering his bigwig dad. His proxy, a person who is contractually obligated to serve out Knox's punishments, is a gay teen. In exchange for working as a proxy, Syd is able to pay off his debts. When Knox accidentally kills a girl, 16 years at the Old Sterling Work Colony is too great a punishment for Syd to bear, so he escapes." (School Library Journal)

London, Jack

★ The **call** of the wild; pictures by Wendell Minor. Atheneum Books for Young Readers 1999 112p il $24; pa $4.95
Grades: 5 6 7 8 9 10 11 12 Adult **Fic**

1. Dogs -- Fiction 2. Alaska -- Fiction 3. Yukon River valley (Yukon and Alaska) -- Fiction
ISBN 0-689-81836-X; 1-4165-0019-7 pa

LC 97-45019

First published 1903 by Macmillan

"Buck, half-St. Bernard, half-Scottish sheepdog, is stolen from his comfortable home in California and pressed into service as a sledge dog in the Klondike. At first he is abused by both man and dog, but he learns to fight ruthlessly. He becomes lead dog on a sledge team, after bettering Spitz, the vicious old leader, in a brutal fight to the death. In John Thornton, he finally finds a master whom he can respect and love. When Thornton is killed by Indians, Buck breaks away to the wilds and becomes the leader of a wolf pack, returning each year to the site of Thornton's death." Reader's Ency. 4th edition

Long, Hayley

Sophie someone; Hayley Long. Candlewick Press 2017 258 p. $16.99
Grades: 6 7 8 9 **Fic**

1. Domestic fiction 2. Teenagers -- Fiction 3. Family secrets -- Fiction
ISBN 0763689955; 9780763689957

LC 2017933643

In this novel, by Hayley Long, "Sophie and her circle of family and friends are sympathetic and appealing in all their flawed humanity. Her peculiar way of speech soon reads as clearly as plain English and perfectly mirrors her internal turmoil as she navigates her parents' shift from just mambo and don to people with a past she never imagined--which, to some extent, is a transformation every young person will understand." (Kirkus Reviews)

Long, Ruth Frances

The **treachery** of beautiful things; by Ruth Frances Long. Dial Books 2012 363 p. (hardcover) $17.99
Grades: 7 8 9 10 11 12 **Fic**

1. Fantasy fiction 2. Fairies -- Fiction 3. Forests and forestry -- Fiction 4. Love -- Fiction 5. Kings, queens, rulers, etc. -- Fiction
ISBN 0803735804; 9780803735804

LC 2011027165

In this book by Ruth Long, "the trees swallowed her brother whole, and Jenny was there to see it. Now seventeen, she revisits the woods where Tom was taken. . . . She's lured into the trees, where she finds strange and dangerous creatures. . . . Among them is Jack, mercurial and magnetic, with secrets of his own. Determined to find her brother, with or without Jack's help, Jenny struggles to navigate a faerie world where stunning beauty masks some of the most treacherous evils." (Publisher's note)

Lopez, Diana

Ask my mood ring how I feel; by Diana Lopez. 1st ed. Little, Brown and Co. 2013 324 p. (hardcover) $17
Grades: 4 5 6 7 **Fic**

1. Breast cancer -- fiction 2. Children of cancer patients -- fiction 3. Cancer -- Fiction 4. Promises -- Fiction 5. Friendship -- Fiction 6. Fund-raising -- Fiction 7. Christian life -- Fiction 8. Hispanic Americans -- Fiction 9. San Antonio (Tex.) -- Fiction 10. Family life -- Texas -- Fiction
ISBN 0316209961; 9780316209960

LC 2012029856

In this book, Chia's "mother is diagnosed with breast cancer, which spurs . . . changes throughout their family. . . . After visiting the Basilica of Our Lady of San Juan del Valle in southern Texas, Chia dedicates herself to a promesa, vowing to secure 500 sponsors for a Walk for the Cure in exchange (she hopes) for her mother's recovery." (Publishers Weekly)

Confetti girl. Little, Brown and Company 2009 198p $15.99
Grades: 4 5 6 7 **Fic**

1. School stories 2. Texas -- Fiction 3. Friendship -- Fiction 4. Bereavement -- Fiction 5. Mexican Americans -- Fiction 6. Father-daughter relationship -- Fiction
ISBN 978-0-316-02955-1; 0-316-02955-6

LC 2008032819

After the death of her mother, Texas sixth-grader Lina's grades and mood drop as she watches her father lose himself more and more in books, while her best friend uses Lina as an excuse to secretly meet her boyfriend.

"Lopez effectively portrays the Texas setting and the characters' Latino heritage. . . . This . . . novel puts at its center a likable girl facing realistic problems on her own terms." Booklist

Lord, Cynthia

Half a chance; Cynthia Lord. Scholastic Press 2014 224 p. (hc) $16.99
Grades: 4 5 6 7 **Fic**

1. Photography -- Fiction 2. Father-daughter relationship -- Fiction 3. Friendship -- Fiction 4. New Hampshire -- Fiction
ISBN 0545035333; 9780545035330

LC 2013013431

"When Lucy's family moves to an old house on a lake, Lucy tries to see her new home through her camera's lens, as her father has taught her--he's a famous photographer, away on a shoot. . . . When she discovers that he's judging a photo contest, Lucy decides to enter anonymously. She wants to find out if her eye for photography is really special--or only good enough." (Publisher's note)

"The story is moving, and readers will find themselves caught up in sensitive Lucy's honest and thoughtful narration." Horn Book

★ **Touch** blue. Scholastic Press 2010 186p $16.99
Grades: 4 5 6 7 **Fic**

1. Maine -- Fiction 2. Islands -- Fiction 3. Foster home care

-- Fiction
ISBN 0-545-03531-7; 978-0-545-03531-6
LC 2009042306

When the state of Maine threatens to shut down their island's one-room schoolhouse, 11-year-old Tess and her family take in foster child Aaron in order to increase the school's population. "Intermediate." (Horn Book)

"Aaron's relationship with his foster family . . . develops believably. The tight-knit community and lobster-catching details make for a warm, colorful environment. This is a feel-good story." Booklist

Lord, Emery

When we collided; by Emery Lord. Bloomsbury 2016 352 p. (hardback) $17.99

Grades: 8 9 10 11 12 **Fic**

1. Love -- Fiction 2. Family -- Fiction 3. Mental illness -- Fiction 4. Depression (Psychology) -- Fiction 5. Family problems -- Fiction
ISBN 1619638452; 9781619638457
LC 2015011933

Schneider Family Book Award: Teen (2017)

In this book, by Emery Lord, "seventeen year-old Jonah Daniels has lived in Verona Cove, California, his whole life, and only one thing has ever changed: his father used to be alive, and now he is not. With a mother lost in a deep bout of depression, Jonah and his five siblings struggle to keep up their home and the restaurant their dad left behind. But at the start of summer, a second change rolls in: Vivi Alexander, the new girl in town." (Publisher's note)

As much about the fragility of the human experience as it is about mental illness, this offers a refreshing perspective on a spectrum of mental health disorders. This love story veers away from tragedy, instead firmly entrenching itself in hope and possibility." Booklist

Lottridge, Celia Barker

The **listening** tree. Fitzhenry & Whiteside 2011 172p $11.95

Grades: 4 5 6 7 **Fic**

1. Canada -- Fiction 2. Courage -- Fiction 3. Great Depression, 1929-1939 -- Fiction
ISBN 978-1-55455-052-4; 1-55455-052-1

It's 1935, and Ellen and her mother must leave their dried-up Saskatchewan farm to board with Aunt Gladys in Toronto. Intimidated by her new surroundings, Ellen chooses to hide in the branches of the large leafy tree outside her window and watch the neighbourhood children playing, rather than joining in their games. But when Ellen overhears a plan to evict the family-next-door from their home, she must overcome her fears and help her neighbours.

"Lottridge provides a wealth of well-developed, believable characters, especially Ellen. The story is a deftly-written, heartbreaking, and heartwarming tale of friendship and the perseverance to withstand hardships. This is a great book to introduce young readers to the impact of the Great Depression." Voice Youth Advocates

Love, D. Anne

Semiprecious. Margaret K. McElderry Books 2006 293p $16.95; pa $6.99

Grades: 5 6 7 8 **Fic**

1. Oklahoma -- Fiction 2. Family life -- Fiction
ISBN 978-0-689-85638-9; 0-689-85638-5; 978-0-689-87389-8 pa; 0-689-87389-1 pa
LC 2005-14906

Uprooted and living with an aunt in 1960s Oklahoma, thirteen-year-old Garnet and her older sister Opal brave their mother's desertion and their father's recovery from an accident, learning that "the best home of all is the one you make inside yourself"

"An involving novel of hurt, healing, and adjustment." Booklist

Lovejoy, Sharon

Running out of night; Sharon Lovejoy. Delacorte Press 2014 304 p. (hc) $16.99

Grades: 5 6 7 **Fic**

1. Friendship -- Fiction 2. Fugitive slaves -- Fiction 3. Runaways -- Fiction 4. Race relations -- Fiction 5. African Americans -- Fiction
ISBN 0385744099; 9780375991479; 9780385744096
LC 2013026375

In this novel by Sharon Lovejoy "when Zenobia, a fugitive slave, creeps onto the porch of an 1858 Virginia home, the white girl inside schemes to prevent her abusive father from spotting the escapee. Denied a name and mistreated by her motherless family, the girl quickly concludes that her circumstances look little better than plucky Zenobia's and the two resolve to flee together." (School Library Journal)

"In 1858, twelve-year-old Girl, white, lower-class, and abused, flees her Virginia home and travels toward Quaker Waterford with runaway slaves. As she befriends the slaves, first-person narrator Girl (renamed Lark) astutely differentiates between her own subjugation and that of black slaves. Unfortunately, several characters' near-miraculous recoveries from escape-related injuries undermine an otherwise head-on look at multiple forms of enslavement. Websites. Bib., glos." Horn Book

Lowry, Lois

Anastasia at your service; decorations by Diane DeGroat. Houghton Mifflin 1982 149p il pa $5.50

Grades: 4 5 6 **Fic**

1. Friendship -- Fiction 2. Household employees -- Fiction
ISBN 0-395-32865-9; 0-440-40290-5 pa
LC 82009231

Twelve-year-old Anastasia has a series of disastrous experiences when, expecting to get a job as a lady's companion, she is hired instead to be a maid.

★ **Anastasia** Krupnik. Houghton Mifflin 1979 113p $17; pa $5.99

Grades: 4 5 6 **Fic**

1. Family life -- Fiction
ISBN 0-395-28629-8; 0-440-40852-0 pa

Anastasia's 10th year has some good things like falling in love and really getting to know her grandmother and some bad things like finding out about an impending baby brother

"Anastasia's father and mother—an English professor and an artist—are among the most humorous, sensible, and understanding parents to be found in . . . children's fiction, and Anastasia herself is an amusing and engaging heroine." Horn Book

Other titles about Anastasia Krupnik are:
Anastasia again! (1981)
Anastasia at your service (1982)
Anastasia, ask your analyst (1984)
Anastasia on her own (1985)
Anastasia has the answers (1986)
Anastasia's chosen career (1987)
Anastasia at this address (1991)
Anastasia, absolutely (1995)

Gathering blue. Houghton Mifflin 2000 215p $16; pa $8.95

Grades: 5 6 7 8 **Fic**

1. Science fiction

ISBN 0-618-05581-9; 0-385-73256-2 pa

LC 00-24359

Lame and suddenly orphaned, Kira is mysteriously removed from her squalid village to live in the palatial Council Edifice, where she is expected to use her gifts as a weaver to do the bidding of the all-powerful Guardians

"Lowry has once again created a fully realized world full of drama, suspense, and even humor." SLJ

★ The **giver**; Lois Lowry. Houghton Mifflin Harcourt 1993 180 p

Grades: 5 6 7 8 9 10 **Fic**

1. Science fiction

ISBN 0395645662; 0440237688; 9780547995663

Awarded the Newbery Medal, 1994

Given his lifetime assignment at the Ceremony of Twelve, Jonas becomes the receiver of memories shared by only one other in his community and discovers the terrible truth about the society in which he lives.

"A riveting, chilling story that inspires a new appreciation for diversity, love, and even pain. Truly memorable." SLJ

★ **Number** the stars; Lois Lowry. 25th Anniversary Edition Houghton Mifflin Harcourt 2014 137 p. $17.99

Grades: 4 5 6 7 **Fic**

1. Jews -- Fiction 2. Denmark -- Fiction 3. Friendship -- Fiction 4. World War, 1939-1945 -- Fiction

ISBN 0544340000; 9780544340008

LC 8837134

First published 1989

Newbery Medal (1990)

Written by Lois Lowry, "as the German troops begin their campaign to 'relocate' all the Jews of Denmark, Annemarie Johansen's family takes in Annemarie's best friend, Ellen Rosen, and conceals her as part of the family. Through the eyes of ten-year-old Annemarie, we watch as the Danish Resistance smuggles almost the entire Jewish population of Denmark, nearly seven thousand people, across the sea to Sweden." (Publisher's note)

"The appendix details the historical incidents upon which Lowry bases her plot. . . . The whole work is seamless, compelling, and memorable." Horn Book

★ **Son**; by Lois Lowry. Houghton Mifflin 2012 393 p. $17.99

Grades: 6 7 8 9 10 11 12 **Fic**

1. Science fiction 2. Dystopian fiction 3. Amnesia -- Fiction 4. Mothers -- Fiction 5. Secrecy -- Fiction 6. Identity -- Fiction 7. Mother-child relationship -- Fiction 8. Separation (Psychology) -- Fiction

ISBN 0547887205; 9780547887203

LC 2012014034

Author Lois Lowry tells the story of "14-year-old Claire, [who] has no contact with her baby Gabe until she surreptitiously bonds with him in the community Nurturing Center. . . . After living for years with Alys, a childless healer, Claire's memory returns. Intent on finding Gabe, she . . . encounters the sinister Trademaster and exchanges her youth for his help in finding her child, now living in the same village as middle-aged Jonas and his wife Kira. Elderly and failing, Claire reveals her identity to Gabe, who must use his unique talent to save the village." (Kirkus Reviews)

Lu, Marie

Batman; Nightwalker. Marie Lu. Random House 2018 252 p. (DC icons) (lib. bdg.) $21.99

Grades: 7 8 9 10 **Fic**

1. Mystery fiction 2. Teenagers -- fiction 3. Batman (Fictional character) --fiction 4. Community service (Punishment) -- fiction

ISBN 9780399549779; 9780399549786; 9780399549793

LC 2017021544

In this book, in the DC Icons Series, by Marie Lu, "the Nightwalkers are terrorizing Gotham City. . . . The city's elites are being taken out one by one. . . . Meanwhile, Bruce is about to become eighteen and inherit his family's fortune. . . .But on the way home from his birthday party, he makes an impulsive choice and is sentenced to community service at Arkham Asylum, . . . [a] prison that holds . . . nefarious criminals." (Publisher's note)

"A fast-paced story line, action-packed fight sequences, and hi-tech gadgetry expected from any Batman story make this a fun read with wide appeal." SLJ

★ **Champion**; a Legend novel. Marie Lu. G.P. Putnam's Sons, an imprint of Penguin Group (USA) 2013 384 p. (hardback) $18.99

Grades: 8 9 10 11 12 **Fic**

1. Love -- Fiction 2. Dystopian fiction 3. Plague -- Fiction 4. Science fiction

ISBN 0399256776; 9780399256776

LC 2013028221

In this novel, by Marie Lu, "June and Day have sacrificed so much for the people of the Republic—and each other—and now their country is on the brink of a new existence. June is back in the good graces of the Republic, working within the government's elite circles as Princeps Elect while Day has been assigned a high level military position. But neither could have predicted the circumstances that will reunite them once again." (Publisher's note)

"Having been diagnosed with a terminal illness, Day (Legend; Prodigy) takes care of his brother, Eden, victim of the Republic's experiments in biological warfare. International diplomacy raises the stakes in this final volume of the trilogy, but readers will likely care more about whether Day and June (the Republic's prodigy) can repair their passionate romance. Lu's storytelling is compulsively readable." (Horn Book)

★ **Legend**. G. P. Putnam's Sons 2011 305p $17.99

Grades: 8 9 10 11 12 **Fic**

1. War stories 2. Science fiction 3. Plague -- Fiction 4. Siblings -- Fiction 5. Soldiers -- Fiction 6. Criminals -- Fiction 7. Resistance to government -- Fiction

ISBN 978-0-399-25675-2; 0-399-25675-X

LC 2011002003

"The characters are likable, the plot moves at a good pace, and the adventure is solid." SLJ

★ **Prodigy**; a Legend novel. Marie Lu. G. P. Putnam's Sons 2012 384 p. (Legend) $17.99

Grades: 8 9 10 11 12 **Fic**

1. Science fiction 2. Dystopian fiction 3. Fugitives from justice -- Fiction 4. Resistance to government -- Fiction 5. War -- Fiction 6. Soldiers -- Fiction 7. Criminals -- Fiction 8. Assassination -- Fiction

ISBN 0399256768; 9780399256769

LC 2012003773

This young adult science fiction adventure novel, by Marie Lu, is the sequel to her novel "Legend." "Injured and on the run, it has been seven days since June and Day barely escaped Los Angeles and the Republic with their lives. Day is believed dead. . . . June is now the Republic's most wanted traitor. Desperate for help, they turn to the Patriots--a vigilante rebel group sworn to bring down the Republic. But can they trust them?" (Publisher's note)

"This is a well-molded mixture of intrigue, romance, and action, where things can change with almost any turn of the page, and frequently do." Booklist

★ **Warcross**; Marie Lu. Putnam Publishing Group 2017 368 p. $18.99; ebook $56.97

Grades: 8 9 10 11 12 **Fic**

1. Internet games -- Fiction 2. Computer hackers -- Fiction

ISBN 0399547967; 9780399547966; 9780399547980

LC 2017016555

In this book, by Marie Lu, "teenage hacker Emika Chen works as a bounty hunter, tracking down Warcross players who bet on the game illegally. But the bounty-hunting world is a competitive one, and survival has not been easy. To make some quick cash, Emika takes a risk and hacks into the opening game of the international Warcross Championships--only to accidentally glitch herself into the action and become an overnight sensation." (Publisher's note)

"Readers will move effortlessly through Lu's fantastic writing, and they will enjoy getting to know this international cast of characters. The author adeptly weaves together exciting video games scenes, virtual reality, and romance." (SLJ)

Another title in this series is:

Wildcard (2018)

Wildcard; Marie Lu. G.P. Putnam's Sons 2018 352 p. (Warcross) (hardback) $18.99

Grades: 8 9 10 11 12 **Fic**

1. Internet games -- Fiction 2. Computer crimes -- Fiction 3. Computer hackers -- Fiction 4. Spies -- Fiction 5. Bounty hunters -- Fiction

ISBN 9780399547997

LC 2018011748

"Emika Chen barely made it out of the Warcross Championships alive. Now that she knows the truth behind Hideo's new NeuroLink algorithm, she can no longer trust the one person she's always looked up to. . . . Determined to put a stop to Hideo's grim plans, Emika and the Phoenix Riders band together, only to find a new threat lurking on the neon-lit streets of Tokyo." (Publisher's note)

"The plotting is exquisite, with tiny details connecting back to the first book, big twists that never feel forced, and emotional power drawn from character growth." Kirkus

The **Young** Elites; Marie Lu. Putnam Publishing Group 2014 368 p. map (hardback) $18.99

Grades: 8 9 10 11 12 **Fic**

1. Fantasy fiction 2. Supernatural -- Fiction 3. Secret societies -- Fiction 4. Ability -- Fiction 5. Adventure and adventurers -- Fiction

ISBN 0399167838; 9780399167836

LC 2014025732

In this fantasy novel, by Marie Lu, "Adelina Amouteru is a survivor of the blood fever. . . . But some of the fever's survivors are rumored to possess . . . mysterious and powerful gifts, and though their identities remain secret, they have come to be called the Young Elites. . . . Teren Santoro . . . , as Leader of the Inquisition Axis, it is his job to seek out the Young Elites. . . . Enzo Valenciano is a member of . . . [a] secret sect of Young Elites [that] seeks out others like them before the Inquisition Axis can." (Publisher's note)

"In a gorgeously constructed world that somewhat resembles Renaissance Italy but with its own pantheon, geography and fauna, the multiethnic and multisexual Young Elites offer a cinematically perfect ensemble of gorgeous-but-unusual illusionists, animal speakers, fire summoners and wind callers. A must for fans of Kristin Cashore's Fire (2009) and other totally immersive fantasies." Kirkus

Lubar, David

★ **Character,** driven; David Lubar. Tor Teen 2016 304 p. (hardback) $17.99

Grades: 8 9 10 11 12 **Fic**

1. Teenagers -- Fiction 2. High school students -- Fiction 3. Sex -- Fiction 4. Fathers and sons -- Fiction

ISBN 9780765316332; 0765316331

LC 2015032626

In this novel, by David Lubar, "with only one year left of high school, seventeen-year-old Cliff Sparks is desperate to find a girlfriend. But he's never had much luck with girls. At the same time, Cliff has to figure out what to do with the rest of his life, since he's pretty sure his unemployed father plans to kick him out of the house the minute he turns eighteen. Time is running out. Cliff is at the edge, on the verge, dangling--and holding on for dear life." (Publisher's note)

Includes bibliographical references and index

True talents. Tom Doherty Associates 2007 315p $17.95; pa $5.99

Grades: 6 7 8 9 **Fic**

1. Friendship -- Fiction 2. Kidnapping -- Fiction 3. Extrasensory perception -- Fiction

ISBN 978-0-7653-0977-8; 0-7653-0977-7; 978-0-7653-4856-2 pa; 0-7653-4856-X pa

LC 2006-39763

Sequel to: Hidden talents

Over a year after fourteen-year-old Eddie "Trash" Thalmeyer and his friends from Edgeview Alternative School find out about their psychic abilities, Trash is kidnapped and Torchie, Cheater, Lucky, Flinch, and Martin must join forces to rescue their friend, discovering their true talents in the process.

This is "a gripping page-turner, with a flawlessly structured plot and compelling, struggling characters who never let each other down." Voice Youth Advocates

Lucier, Makiia

A **death** -struck year; Makiia Lucier. Houghton Mifflin Harcourt 2014 288 p. (hardback) $17.99

Grades: 9 10 11 12 **Fic**

1. Nurses -- Fiction 2. Epidemics -- Fiction 3. Influenza -- Fiction 4. Portland (Or.) -- Fiction 5. Influenza Epidemic, 1918-1919 -- Fiction 6. Portland (Or.) -- History -- 20th century -- Fiction 7. Influenza Epidemic, 1918-1919 -- Oregon -- Portland -- Fiction

ISBN 0544164504; 9780544164505

LC 2013037482

In this novel, by Makiia Lucier, "the Spanish influenza is devastating . . . Pacific Northwest. Schools, churches, and theaters are shut down. The entire city [of Portland, Oregon] is thrust into survival mode--and into a panic. Seventeen-year-old Cleo is told to stay put in her quarantined boarding school, but when the Red Cross pleads for volunteers, she cannot ignore the call for help." (Publisher's note)

"A teen girl struggles to survive the Spanish influenza pandemic of 1918...Readers will be swept up in the story as Cleo builds friendships and manages to find hope amid disease and death. A notable debut." (Kirkus)

Includes bibliographical references

Isle of blood and stone; Makiia Lucier. Houghton Mifflin Harcourt 2018 390 p. (hardcover) $17.99

Grades: 7 8 9 10 11 12 **Fic**

1. Secrets -- Fiction 2. Kings and rulers -- Fiction 3. Missing children -- Fiction 4. Maps -- Fiction 5. Secrecy -- Fiction 6. Cartographers -- Fiction 7. Missing persons -- Fiction 8. Voyages and travels -- Fiction

ISBN 9780544968578; 9780544968608

LC 2017015656

In this book, by Makiia Lucier, "eighteen years ago two princes of the island kingdom of St. John del Mar were kidnapped and murdered. . . . Everyone knows the story, but for Elias, Mercedes, and Ulises, the aftermath of that tragic day is deeply personal. . . . Now, the three friends just want to move on with their lives. But when two maps surface . . . , troubling questions arise." (Publisher's note)

"A romantic maritime epic and a charming tribute to mapmakers, calligraphers, and explorers." Kirkus

Other titles in this series are:

Song of the abyss (2019)

Luddy, Karon

★ **Spelldown**. Simon & Schuster Books for Young Readers 2007 211p $15.99; pa $5.99

Grades: 5 6 7 8 **Fic**

1. School stories 2. Spelling bees -- Fiction 3. South Carolina -- Fiction

ISBN 1-4169-1610-5; 978-1-4169-1610-9; 1-4169-5452-X pa; 978-1-4169-5452-1 pa

LC 2006-21956

In 1969, the town of Red Clover, South Carolina, led by an enthusiastic new Latin teacher, supports thirteen-year-old Karlene as she wins her school spelling bee and strives to qualify for the National Bee, despite family problems and a growing desire for romance.

"This heartrending and funny debut novel deftly evokes place, time and character." Publ Wkly

Lundin, Britta

Ship it; Britta Lundin. Freeform Books 2018 384 p. illustrations (hardcover) $17.99

Grades: 7 8 9 10 11 12 **Fic**

1. Fan fiction 2. Popularity -- Fiction 3. Blogs -- Fiction 4. Homosexuality -- Fiction 5. Actors and actresses -- Fiction 6. Television -- Production and direction -- Fiction

ISBN 9781368003131

LC 2017034202

"Claire, a teen fan fiction author, is beyond thrilled when the stars of her favorite TV show, Demon Heart, come to nearby Boise, ID, for a convention. But when she asks Forrest, the show's star, about the possibility that his character is gay, he calls her 'crazy,' and she leaves the room in tears. In an effort to repair this publicity nightmare, the show sends Claire on the rest of the convention tour, where she goes to increasingly desperate lengths to make her "ship" a reality. The book alternates between Forrest and Claire's perspectives, as Forrest confronts some internalized homophobia and Claire begins to explore her own queer identity." (School Library Journal)

Luper, Eric

Bug boy. Farrar, Straus and Giroux 2009 248p $16.99

Grades: 7 8 9 10 **Fic**

1. Gambling -- Fiction 2. Horse racing -- Fiction 3. New York (State) -- Fiction 4. Father-son relationship -- Fiction 5. Swindlers and swindling -- Fiction

ISBN 978-0-374-31000-4; 0-374-31000-9

LC 2008-26730

In 1934 Saratoga, New York, just as fifteen-year-old Jack Walsh finally realizes his dream of becoming a jockey, complications arise in the form of a female bookie, an unexpected visit from his father, and a man who wants him to "fix" a race.

"This well-written, engaging story effectively captures the desperate times of the Depression and the hard-edged world of horse racing." SLJ

Lupica, Mike

The **batboy**. Philomel Books 2010 247p $17.99

Grades: 5 6 7 8 **Fic**

1. Baseball -- Fiction 2. Detroit (Mich.) -- Fiction 3. Mother-son relationship -- Fiction 4. Detroit Tigers (Baseball team) -- Fiction

ISBN 978-0-399-25000-2; 0-399-25000-X

LC 2009015067

Even though his mother feels baseball ruined her marriage to his father, she allows fourteen-year-old Brian to become a bat boy for the Detroit Tigers, who have just drafted his favorite player back onto the team.

Lupica gives "his readers a behind-the-scenes look at major league sports. In this novel, he adds genuine insights into family dynamics and the emotional state of his hero." Booklist

The **big** field. Philomel Books 2008 243p $17.99

Grades: 5 6 7 8 **Fic**

1. Baseball -- Fiction 2. Father-son relationship -- Fiction

ISBN 978-0-399-24625-8; 0-399-24625-8

LC 2007-23647

When fourteen-year-old baseball player Hutch feels threatened by the arrival of a new teammate named Darryl, he tries to work through his insecurities about both Darryl and his remote and silent father, who was once a great ballplayer too.

"Writing in typically fluid prose and laying in a strong supporting lineup, Lupica strikes the right balance between personal issues and game action." Booklist

Fantasy league; Mike Lupica. Philomel, an imprint of Penguin Group (USA) 2014 304 p. (hardback) $17.99

Grades: 5 6 7 8 **Fic**

1. Football -- Fiction 2. Football teams -- Fiction 3. Fantasy football -- Fiction

ISBN 0399256075; 9780399256073

LC 2014007442

In this book, by Mike Lupica, "12-year-old Charlie is a fantasy football guru. He may be just a bench warmer for his school's football team, but when it comes to knowing and loving the game, he's first-string. He even becomes a celebrity when his podcast gets noticed by a sports radio host, who plays Charlie's fantasy picks for all of Los Angeles to hear. Soon Charlie befriends the elderly owner of the L.A. Bulldogs . . . and convinces him to take a chance on an aging quarterback." (Publisher's note)

"Usually a football book is about whether or not the kid makes the team and the problems that follow. So it's refreshing that those issues are only a part of 12-year-old Charlie Gains' story. See, Charlie is known as the Brain, because he is a football stats genius. He understands which players should be playing where and why. . . . There's a lot of football here: pro and fantasy teams and Charlie's own Pop Warner career. Veteran sportswriter Lupica handles it all very well. However, it's the heart and depth he adds to the story depicting Charlie's relationships with a sterling cast of characters that make this unique. This Moneyball story with kids is on the money." Booklist

Heat. Philomel Books 2006 220p $16.99

Grades: 5 6 7 8 **Fic**

1. Cubans -- Fiction 2. Orphans -- Fiction 3. Baseball -- Fiction 4. Illegal aliens -- Fiction

ISBN 0-14-240757-7 pa; 0-399-24301-1

LC 2005013521

Pitching prodigy Michael Arroyo is on the run from social services after being banned from playing Little League baseball because rival coaches doubt he is only twelve years old and he has no parents to offer them proof. "Grades five to eight." (Bull Cent Child Books)

"The dialogue crackles, and the rich cast of supporting characters' . . . nearly steals the show. Topnotch entertainment." Booklist

Heavy hitters; Mike Lupica. Scholastic 2014 219 p. hbk $16.99

Grades: 3 4 5 6 7 **Fic**

1. Baseball -- Fiction 2. Children of divorced parents -- Fiction 3. Fear -- Fiction 4. Friendship -- Fiction 5. Baseball players -- Fiction 6. Dysfunctional families -- Fiction

ISBN 0545381843; 9780545381840

LC 2014430128

In this middle grade book by Mike Lupica, part of the Game Changers series, "Ben and his friends, the Core Four Plus One, are so excited to play in their town's All-Star Baseball league. But in the first game of the season Ben gets hit by a pitch. It's never happened to him before and it shakes him up. . . . Ben discovers that Justin's parents are getting a divorce and Justin is thinking about quitting the team." (Publisher's note)

"Charismatic Ben McBain joins his favorite sidekicks . . . for another sports season, this time All-Star baseball. Conflict comes quickly when Ben slumps after being hit by a pitch and Justin struggles with his parent's divorce. By trying to help one another, the friends also help themselves. Lupica's captivating play-by-play details pull the reader into the games, right alongside these sports-loving characters." Horn Book

Other titles in this series are:

Game changers (2012)

Play makers (2013)

Hero. Philomel Books 2010 289p $17.99

Grades: 6 7 8 9 **Fic**

1. Adventure fiction 2. Death -- Fiction 3. Politics -- Fiction 4. Family life -- Fiction 5. Superheroes -- Fiction 6. New York (N.Y.) -- Fiction 7. Father-son relationship -- Fiction

ISBN 978-0-399-25283-9; 0-399-25283-5

LC 2010-01772

Fourteen-year-old Zach learns he has the same special abilities as his father, who was the President's globe-trotting troubleshooter until "the Bads" killed him, and now Zach must decide whether to use his powers in the same way at the risk of his own life.

"Lupica effectively unfolds this high-adventure story." Booklist

Miracle on 49th Street. Philomel Books 2006 246p $17.99; pa $7.99

Grades: 5 6 7 8 **Fic**

1. Basketball -- Fiction 2. Boston (Mass.) -- Fiction 3. Father-daughter relationship -- Fiction

ISBN 0-399-24488-3; 0-14-240942-1 pa

LC 2005-32648

After her mother's death, twelve-year-old Molly learns that her father is a basketball star for the Boston Celtics.

"Lupica creates intriguing, complex characters . . . and he paces his story well, with enough twists and cliff-hangers to keep the pages turning." SLJ

No slam dunk; Mike Lupica. Philomel Books 2018 240 p. (hardback) $17.99

Grades: 5 6 7 8 **Fic**

1. Veterans -- Fiction 2. Basketball -- Fiction 3. Post-traumatic stress disorder -- Fiction 4. Fathers -- Fiction

ISBN 9780525514855

LC 2018006767

In this book, by Mike Lupica, "Wes' father always told him that there was only one ball in basketball. . . . So at every practice and game, Wes tries his best to be a good basketball player and, above all, a good teammate. As the season kicks off, Wes finds that not everyone on his team has the same idea. . . . If Wes is to lead the Hawks to the playoffs, he'll need to find new ways to dish out an assist--even if it means his most important one comes off the court." (Publisher's note)

The **only** game; Mike Lupica. Simon & Schuster Books for Young Readers 2015 320 p. (hardcover) $16.99

Grades: 4 5 6 7 **Fic**

1. Baseball -- Fiction 2. Brothers -- Fiction 3. Friendship -- Fiction 4. Grief -- Fiction 5. Bullies -- Fiction

ISBN 1481409956; 9781481409957; 9781481409964

LC 2014015989

"Jack Callahan is the star of his baseball team and sixth grade is supposed to be his year. That is, until he up and quits. Jack's brother has passed away, and though [everyone] thinks baseball is just the thing he needs to move on, Jack feels it's anything but. Time spent with . . . new friends unlocks something within Jack, and with their help . . . Jack discovers sometimes it's more than just the love of the game that keeps us moving." (Publisher's note)

"Although the story is sports related, this is more than a baseball book and will appeal to a wide variety of readers. A must-buy." SLJ

Play Makers; Mike Lupica. Scholastic 2013 224 p. (hardcover) $16.99

Grades: 3 4 5 6 7 **Fic**

1. School stories 2. Basketball -- Fiction 3. Competition (Psychology) -- Fiction

ISBN 0545381835; 9780545381833

This novel, by Mike Lupica, is the book 2 of the "Game Changers" series. "Ben McBain and his crew must now prepare for basketball season. . . . But there is a new kid in town, Chase Braggs, a point guard like Ben who seems to be better, stronger, and faster. . . . Ben's rivalry with Chase seems to take the fun out of playing ball with his best friends. Will Ben be able to pull it together for his team and for himself?" (Publisher's note)

Summer ball; [by] Mike Lupica. Philomel Books 2007 244p $17.99

Grades: 6 7 8 9 **Fic**

1. Camps -- Fiction 2. Basketball -- Fiction

ISBN 978-0-399-24487-2

LC 2006021781

Sequel to Travel team (2004)

Thirteen-year-old Danny must prove himself all over again for a disapproving coach and against new rivals at a summer basketball camp.

"Lupica breathes life into both characters and story. Danny is . . . sympathetic and engaging. He is surrounded by a cast of supporting characters who add humor and whose interactions ring true." SLJ

Lurie, April

The **latent** powers of Dylan Fontaine. Delacorte Press 2008 208p $15.99; lib bdg $18.99

Grades: 8 9 10 11 12 **Fic**

1. Family life -- Fiction 2. New York (N.Y.) -- Fiction

ISBN 978-0-385-73125-6; 978-0-385-90153-6 lib bdg

LC 2007-32313

Fifteen-year-old Dylan's friend Angie is making a film about him while he is busy trying to keep his older brother from getting caught with drugs, to deal with his mother having left the family, and to figure out how to get Angie to think of him as more than just a friend.

"This is a story about guys, primarily . . . brothers; fathers and sons; lonely young men who are feeling somewhat lost. Any reader will care for each one of them. Lurie does a wonderful job of making them real." KLIATT

Ly, Many

Roots and wings; [by] Many Ly. Delacorte Press 2008 262p $15.99; lib bdg $18.99

Grades: 6 7 8 9 10 **Fic**

1. Buddhism -- Fiction 2. Cambodian Americans -- Fiction

ISBN 978-0-385-73500-1; 978-0-385-90494-0 lib bdg; 0-385-73500-6; 0-385-90494-0 lib bdg

LC 2008-00474

While in St. Petersburg, Florida, to give her grandmother a Cambodian funeral, fourteen-year-old Grace, who was raised in Pennsylvania, finally gets some answers about the father she never met, her mother's and grandmother's youth, and her Asian-American heritage.

"The book is beautifully written . . . [and] the author allows family secrets to unfold carefully and explores them with sincerity." SLJ

Lyga, Barry

Archvillain. Scholastic Press 2010 180p $16.99

Grades: 4 5 6 7 **Fic**

1. Science fiction 2. Superheroes -- Fiction 3. Good and evil -- Fiction 4. Extraterrestrial beings -- Fiction

ISBN 978-0-545-19649-9; 0-545-19649-3

LC 2010-05291

Twelve-year-old Kyle Camden develops greater mental agility and superpowers during a plasma storm that also brings Mighty Mike, an alien, to the town of Bouring, but while each does what he thinks is best, Kyle is labeled a villain and Mike a hero.

"Comic book fans in particular will appreciate this clever origin story, first in a new series. . . . Lyga . . . laces his story with ample humor. . . . Readers will find plenty to ponder." Publ Wkly

Other titles in this series are:

The Mad Mask (2012)

Yesterday Again (2013)

★ The **astonishing** adventures of Fanboy & Goth Girl. Houghton Mifflin 2006 311p $16.95

Grades: 8 9 10 11 12 **Fic**

1. School stories 2. Friendship -- Fiction 3. Cartoons and caricatures -- Fiction

ISBN 0-618-72392-7

LC 2005-33259

A fifteen-year-old "geek" who keeps a list of the high school jocks and others who torment him, and pours his energy into creating a great graphic novel, encounters Kyra, Goth Girl, who helps change his outlook on almost everything, including himself.

"This engaging first novel has good characterization with genuine voices. . . . The book is compulsively readable." Voice Youth Advocates

Followed by: Goth Girl rising (2009)

Goth girl rising. Houghton Mifflin Harcourt 2009 390p $17

Grades: 8 9 10 11 12 **Fic**

1. School stories 2. Psychotherapy -- Fiction

ISBN 978-0-547-07664-5; 0-547-07664-9

Sequel to: The astonishing adventures of Fanboy and Goth Girl (2006)

"After six months in a mental hospital, Kyra, the newly shaven-headed heroine of The Astonishing Adventures of Fan Boy and Goth Girl (2006), has only one plan: to exact embarrassing revenge on sweet, loyal Fan Boy for not contacting her while she was away. . . . Goth teens and fans of the first novel will be drawn into the darkness that is her life." Kirkus

Hero -type. Houghton Mifflin Co. 2008 295p $16

Grades: 7 8 9 10 **Fic**

1. School stories 2. Maryland -- Fiction 3. Patriotism -- Fiction 4. Heroes and heroines -- Fiction

ISBN 978-0-547-07663-8; 0-547-07663-0

LC 2008-7276

Feeling awkward and ugly is only one reason sixteen-year-old Kevin is uncomfortable with the publicity surrounding his act of accidental heroism, but when a reporter photographs him apparently being unpatriotic, he steps into the limelight to encourage people to think about what the symbols of freedom really mean.

"Leavened by much humor . . . this neatly plotted look at what real patriotism and heroism mean will get readers thinking." KLIATT

The **mad** mask; by Barry Lyga. Scholastic Press 2012 226 p. (Archvillain) $6.99

Grades: 5 6 7 8 **Fic**

1. Science fiction 2. Robots -- Fiction 3. Superheroes -- Fiction 4. Good and evil -- Fiction 5. Extraterrestrial beings -- Fiction

ISBN 0545196531; 9780545196512; 9780545196536

LC 2011001085

This is the second book in Barry Lyga's Archvillain series. "Endowed with extraordinary strength and brainpower by a mysterious 'space plasma,' sixth-grader Kyle (aka the Azure Avenger) . . . is working on a new device to expose [his rival Mighty Mike] when he is contacted by yet another would-be archvillain. Calling himself the Mad Mask, the newcomer . . . needs Kyle's help to finish his Ultitron robot and promises assistance against Mighty Mike in return." (School Library Journal)

Lynch, Chris, 1962-

Angry young man. Simon & Schuster BFYR 2011 167p $16.99

Grades: 7 8 9 10 **Fic**

1. Brothers -- Fiction 2. Conduct of life -- Fiction 3. Single parent family -- Fiction 4. Mother-son relationship -- Fiction

ISBN 0-689-84790-4; 978-0-689-84790-5

LC 2009-52832

Eighteen-year-old Robert tries to help his half-brother Xan, a seventeen-year-old misfit, to make better choices as he becomes increasingly attracted to a variety of protesters, anarchists, and the like.

"For those who wonder about the roots of homegrown terror and extremism, . . . Lynch pushes the spotlight from the individual to society in a story that can be brutal and ugly, yet isn't devoid of hope." Publ Wkly

★ **Hothouse**. HarperTeen 2010 198p $16.99

Grades: 8 9 10 11 12 **Fic**

1. Death -- Fiction 2. Friendship -- Fiction 3. Bereavement -- Fiction 4. Fire fighters -- Fiction 5. Father-son relationship -- Fiction

ISBN 978-0-06-167379-5; 0-06-167379-X

LC 2010-3145

Teens D.J. and Russell, life-long friends and neighbors, had drifted apart but when their firefighter fathers are both killed, they try to help one another come to terms with the tragedy and its aftermath.

"Lynch fully commits to the first-person voice, giving into Russ' second-by-second conflicts and contradictions. The author also has a strong grasp of the garrulous slaps and punches that make up many male relationships. Russ' friendships are so real they hurt. The story hurts, too, but that's how it should be." Booklist

I pledge allegiance. Scholastic Press 2011 183p (Vietnam) $16.99

Grades: 8 9 10 11 12 **Fic**

1. Sailors -- Fiction 2. Vietnam War, 1961-1975 -- Fiction

ISBN 978-0-545-27029-8; 0-545-27029-4

Four best friends serving in the Vietnam War make a pledge to one another that they will do all they can to return home safely together.

"This compelling novel, the first in a series, follows Morris, who joins the navy. . . . Lynch puts his readers in the center of intense conflict. . . . Readers will likely seek out future volumes in the series, each of which will focus on another of the four friends and his war experiences." Booklist

Sharpshooter (2012), Free-Fire Zone (2012), Casualties of War (2013), Walking Wounded (2014)

★ **Inexcusable**. Atheneum Books for Young Readers 2005 165p $16.95; pa $6.99

Grades: 8 9 10 11 12 **Fic**

1. School stories 2. Rape -- Fiction 3. Football -- Fiction

ISBN 0-689-84789-0; 1-416-93972-5 pa

LC 2004-30874

National Book Award Finalist: Young People's Literature (2005)

High school senior and football player Keir sets out to enjoy himself on graduation night, but when he attempts to comfort a friend whose date has left her stranded, things go terribly wrong. "Grades nine to twelve." (Bull Cent Child Books)

"This finely crafted and thought-provoking page-turner carefully conveys that it is simply inexcusable to whitewash wrongs, and that those responsible should (and hopefully will) pay the price." SLJ

Irreversible (2016)

Pieces; Chris Lynch. Simon & Schuster Books for Young Readers 2013 176 p. (hardcover) $16.99

Grades: 7 8 9 10 11 12 **Fic**

1. Brothers -- Fiction 2. Bereavement -- Fiction 3. Donation of organs, tissues, etc. -- Fiction 4. Death -- Fiction 5. Grief -- Fiction 7. Interpersonal relations -- Fiction

ISBN 1416927034; 9781416927037; 9781442453111

LC 2011042049

In this book, "a year after his 20-year-old brother Duane died in a diving accident, 18-year-old Eric still can't seem to move forward. In an attempt to keep the 'nothingness that is filling the Duane space' from taking hold, he reaches out to three of the donors who received his brother's 'pieces.' After meeting shy, redheaded Phil, brassy Barry and sweet single mom Melinda, Eric finds himself constantly asking the questions, 'Who are these people? Who are they, to me? Who am I, to them?'" (Kirkus Reviews)

Lyon, Annabel

All -season Edie. Orca Book Publishers 2008 179p pa $8.95

Grades: 5 6 7 8 **Fic**

1. Canada -- Fiction 2. Family life -- Fiction 3. Grandfathers -- Fiction

ISBN 978-1-55143-713-2 pa; 1-55143-713-9 pa

"Wry, fast, and funny. . . . Set in a Vancouver suburb . . . [this book] gets the preteen voice perfectly." Booklist

Lyons, Mary E.

Letters from a slave boy; the story of Joseph Jacobs. Atheneum Books for Young Readers 2007 197p il map $15.99; pa $5.99

Grades: 6 7 8 9 **Fic**

1. Slaves 2. Letters -- Fiction 3. Slavery -- Fiction 4. African Americans -- Fiction

ISBN 978-0-689-87867-1; 0-689-87867-2; 978-0-689-87868-8 pa; 0-689-87868-0 pa

LC 2006-01277

Companion volume to Letters from a Slave Girl (1992)

A fictionalized look at the life of Joseph Jacobs, son of a slave, told in the form of letters that he might have written during his life in pre-Civil War North Carolina, on a whaling expedition, in New York, New England, and finally in California during the Gold Rush.

"The 'letters' are short and the pace is quick. The dialect and spelling give authenticity without making the text difficult to read and understand. . . . This title stands on its own, but children who appreciated the forthright perspective of the first book will want to read this one as well." SLJ

★ **Letters** from a slave girl; the story of Harriet Jacobs. Scribner 1992 146p il hardcover o.p. pa $5.99; pa $5.99

Grades: 6 7 8 9 **Fic**

1. Slaves 2. Authors 3. Domestics 4. Memoirists 5. Letters -- Fiction 6. Slavery -- Fiction 7. African Americans -- Fiction

ISBN 0-684-19446-5; 1-4169-3637-8 pa; 9781416936374 pa

LC 91-45778

This is a fictionalized version of the life of Harriet Jacobs, told in the form of letters that she might have written during her slavery in North Carolina and as she prepared for escape to the North in 1842. Glossary. Bibliography. "Age twelve and up." (Horn Book)

This "is historical fiction at its best. . . . Mary Lyons has remained faithful to Jacobs's actual autobiography throughout her readable, compelling novel. . . . Her observations of the horrors of slavery are concise and lucid. The letters are written in dialect, based on Jacobs's own writing and on other slave narrations of the period." Horn Book

Maas, Sarah J., 1986-

Catwoman; soulstealer. Sarah J. Maas. Random House 2018 384 p. (hardback) $18.99

Grades: 7 8 9 10 **Fic**

1. Criminals -- Fiction 2. Friendship -- Fiction

ISBN 9780399549694; 9780399549700

LC 2017051966

In this book in the DC Icons Series, by Sarah J. Maas, "two years after escaping Gotham City's slums, Selina Kyle returns as the mysterious and wealthy Holly Vanderhees. She quickly discovers that with Batman off on a vital mission, Gotham City looks ripe for the taking. . . . Selina is playing a desperate game of cat and mouse, forming unexpected friendships and entangling herself with Batwing by night and her devilishly handsome neighbor Luke Fox by day." (Publisher's note)

Maberry, Jonathan

The **orphan** army; Jonathan Maberry. Simon & Schuster Books for Young Readers 2015 400 p. (The Nightsiders) (hardcover) $16.99

Grades: 5 6 7 8 **Fic**

1. Science fiction 2. Monsters -- Fiction 3. Heroes and heroines -- Fiction 4. Magic -- Fiction 5. Supernatural -- Fiction 6. Extraterrestrial beings -- Fiction

ISBN 1481415751; 9781481415750

LC 2014014576

In this juvenile novel, by Jonathan Maberry, part of "The Nightsiders" series, set "in a slightly futuristic world, where ruthless insectlike monsters are exterminating humans and the Earth itself, Milo discovers secrets that change the tides of war in a serious way. The Nightsiders are a group of mystical beasts leading the fight to defend Earth and its inhabitants from the maleficent Bugs." (School Library Journal)

"Maberry's prowess in fiction as well as comic books is evident in his well-crafted story, which balances over-the-top battle scenes with the quiet moments between characters that give substance to what could be a heartless thriller. This first book in an explosive new series is the perfect mix of science fiction and magic." Kirkus

Rot & ruin. Simon & Schuster Books for Young Readers 2010 458p (Benny Imura books) $17.99

Grades: 9 10 11 12 **Fic**

1. Horror fiction 2. Zombies -- Fiction 3. Brothers -- Fiction

ISBN 1-4424-0232-6; 978-1-4424-0232-4

LC 2009-46041

In a post-apocalyptic world where fences and border patrols guard the few people left from the zombies that have overtaken civilization, fifteen-year-old Benny Imura is finally convinced that he must follow in his older brother's footsteps and become a bounty hunter.

"In turns mythic and down-to-earth, this intense novel combines adventure and philosophy to tell a truly memorable zombie story." Publ Wkly

Other titles in this series are:
Dust & decay (2011)
Flesh & bone (2012)
Fire & ash (2013)
Bits & pieces (2015)

Vault of shadows; Jonathan Maberry. Simon & Schuster Books for Young Readers 2016 464 p. (Nightsiders) (hardback) $16.99

Grades: 5 6 7 8 **Fic**

1. Science fiction 2. Magic -- Fiction 3. Monsters -- Fiction 4. Supernatural -- Fiction 5. Heroes and heroines -- Fiction 6. Extraterrestrial beings -- Fiction

ISBN 9781481415781; 9781481415798; 9781481415804

LC 2015027662

In this book, by Jonathan Maberry, "after joining forces with the magical Nightsiders and surviving a trip to the enemy Bugs' Hive ship, Milo Silk still has a lot to fear. The Huntsman has pledged a revenge worse than death on Milo, a group of nefarious fairies are bent on taking back Earth, and zombie-like holo-men are trapping humans for the Bugs to take. Even more unsettling is that the Witch of the World has disappeared and a mysterious boy is haunting Milo's dreams in her stead." (Publisher's note)

"With dramatic, humorous, and occasionally dark, edgy touches, this offers another engrossing blend of action-adventure, dystopian elements, magic, and retro sci-fi with some classic lit allusions, and its appealing, diversely drawn cast together face dangers and dilemmas with courage and ingenuity while trying to save Earth and beyond from obliteration." Booklist

Mac, Carrie

★ **10** things I can see from here; Carrie Mac. Alfred A. Knopf 2017 312 p. (lib. bdg.) $20.99

Grades: 7 8 9 10 11 12 **Fic**

1. Anxiety -- Fiction 2. Lesbian teenagers -- Fiction 3. Love -- Fiction 4. Lesbians -- Fiction 5. Anxiety disorders -- Fiction 6. Fathers and daughters -- Fiction

ISBN 9780399556258; 9780399556258; 9780399556272; 9780399556265

LC 2015046690

In this young adult novel, by Carrie Mac, "Maeve has . . . been struggling with severe anxiety for a long time, and as much as she wishes it was something she could just talk herself out of, it's not. . . . But Maeve finds brief moments of calm . . . with Salix, a local girl who doesn't seem to worry about anything. Between her dad's wavering sobriety . . . and her bumbling courtship with Salix, this summer brings more catastrophes than even Maeve could have foreseen." (Publisher's note)

"With Maeve, Mac delivers a character who's heartwarmingly real and sympathetic, and her story provides a much needed mirror for anxious queer girls everywhere." Kirkus

Ten things I can see from here

MacColl, Michaela

Promise the night. Chronicle Books 2011 $16.99

Grades: 6 7 8 9 **Fic**

1. Air pilots 2. Memoirists 3. Horse trainers 4. Kenya -- Fiction 5. Women air pilots -- Fiction

ISBN 978-0-8118-7625-4; 0-8118-7625-X

LC 2011010938

This novel explores the early life of Beryl Markham, who grew up on a farm in Kenya, and became the first person to fly solo across the Atlantic from east to west.

"MacColl vividly portrays her headstrong protagonist . . . with fierce, exuberant spirit." Booklist

Rory's promise; Michaela MacColl, Rosemary Nichols. Calkins Creek 2014 288 p. (Hidden Histories) $16.95

Grades: 5 6 7 8 **Fic**

1. Orphans -- Fiction 2. Interracial adoption 3. Sisters -- Fiction 4. Orphanages -- Fiction 5. Orphan trains -- Fiction 6. New York (N.Y.) -- Fiction 7. New York Foundling Hospital -- Fiction

ISBN 1620916231; 9781620916230

LC 2014935295

In this novel by Michaela MacColl and Rosemary Nichols "Rory and her little sister, Violet are . . . together in the Catholic Foundling Hospital in New York City. But in 1904 the hospital begins to send orphans to the Arizona Territory to be adopted by devout Catholic families. Too old to be adopted, Rory is desperate to find a way to accompany Violet. Rory soon discovers that the families the Sisters have chosen for the white orphans are actually Mexican immigrant families." (Publisher's note)

"Outspoken twelve-year-old Rory, who lives in NYC's Catholic Foundling Hospital in 1904, vows to protect her sister, Violet. When Violet is placed with a family in racially divided Arizona Territory, Rory sneaks aboard the train headed west. Despite some lackluster dialogue and underdeveloped characters, Rory is a feisty and compelling protagonist in an action-packed story based on historical events." Horn Book

MacCullough, Carolyn

Always a witch. Clarion Books 2011 276p $16.99

Grades: 8 9 10 11 12 **Fic**

1. Witches -- Fiction 2. Time travel -- Fiction 3. Good and evil -- Fiction 4. New York (N.Y.) -- Fiction

ISBN 978-0-547-22485-5; 0-547-22485-0

LC 2011008148

Sequel to: Once a witch (2009)

Haunted by her grandmother's prophecy that she will soon be forced to make a terrible decision, witch Tamsin Greene risks everything to travel back in time to 1887 New York to confront the enemy that wants to destroy her family.

This is "an enjoyable magical adventure." Kirkus

★ **Once** a witch. Clarion Books 2009 292p $16

Grades: 8 9 10 11 12 **Fic**

1. Sisters -- Fiction 2. Witches -- Fiction 3. Time travel -- Fiction 4. Good and evil -- Fiction 5. New York (N.Y.) -- Fiction

ISBN 978-0-547-22399-5; 0-547-22399-4

LC 2008-49234

Born into a family of witches, seventeen-year-old Tamsin is raised believing that she alone lacks a magical "Talent," but when her beautiful and powerful sister is taken by an age-old rival of the family in an attempt to change the balance of power, Tamsin discovers her true destiny.

"The book will appeal to teen readers who enjoy stories with romance, magic, or time travel, along with hardcore fantasy aficionados, and it is appropriate for all young adult collections." Voice Youth Advocates

Followed by: Always a witch (2011)

Macdonald, Maryann, 1947-

Odette's secrets; by Maryann Macdonald. Bloomsbury 2013 240 p. (hardback) $16.99

Grades: 6 7 8 9 **Fic**

1. Novels in verse 2. Hidden children (Holocaust) -- fiction 3. France -- History -- 1940-1945, German occupation -- Fiction 4. Identity -- Fiction 5. Jews -- France -- Fiction 6. Holocaust, Jewish (1939-1945) -- Fiction 7. World War, 1939-1945 -- France -- Fiction 8. France -- History -- German occupation, 1940-1945 -- Fiction

ISBN 159990750X; 9781599907505

LC 2012015549

This biographical story-in-verse, by Maryann Macdonald, takes place in Nazi-occupied France. "Odette is a young Jewish girl living in Paris during a dangerous time. . . . After Odette's father enlists in the French army and her mother joins the Resistance, Odette is sent to the countryside until it is safe to return. On the surface, she leads the life of a regular girl . . . but inside, she is burning with secrets about the life she left behind and her true identity." (Publisher's note)

MacFarlane, John

Stormstruck! John Macfarlane. Holiday House 2015 160 p. map (hardcover) $16.95

Grades: 4 5 6 7 **Fic**

1. Dogs -- Fiction 2. Children and death 3. Survival after airplane accidents, shipwrecks, etc. -- fiction 4. Sea stories 5. Storms -- Fiction 6. Survival -- Fiction 7. Labrador retriever -- Fiction 8. Islands of the Atlantic -- Fiction 9. Adventure and adventurers -- Fiction

ISBN 0823433943; 9780823433940

LC 2014046751

In this children's novel by John MacFarlane "when twelve-year-old Sam overhears his parents talking about their elderly and infirm Labrador retriever, Pogo, he's convinced they plan to have the dog put down. To save Pogo, Sam sets sail with the dog in a fourteen foot boat for an island off the coast of Maine. The elements conspire against them as they move from one danger to another. As he battles nature's fury, Sam is finally able to come to terms with . . . his brother's death in Afghanistan." (Publisher's note)

"A gripping adventure with weighty themes that will enthrall middle grade readers." SLJ

MacHale, D. J.

Black water. Simon & Schuster Books for Young Readers 2007 427p (Pendragon) $16.99; pa $8.99

Grades: 7 8 9 10 **Fic**

1. Fantasy fiction 2. Adventure fiction 3. Space and time -- Fiction

ISBN 978-1-4169-5779-9; 1-4169-5779-0; 978-0-689-86911-2 pa; 0-689-86911-8 pa

LC 2008274260

When a mysterious plague threatens to wipe out the inhabitants of Eelong, fifteen-year-old Bobby Pendragon must decide whether to risk getting the antidote and, thereby, endangering himself, his friends, and the future of every other being in Halla.

The **lost** city of Faar. Aladdin 2003 385p (Pendragon) $17.99; pa $8.95

Grades: 7 8 9 10 **Fic**

1. Fantasy fiction 2. Adventure fiction 3. Uncles -- Fiction

ISBN 978-1-4169-3626-8; 1-4169-3626-2; 978-0-7434-3732-5 pa; 0-7434-3732-2 pa

LC 2002108580

Bobby finds himself in the territory of Cloral, a world entirely covered by water, which is nearing a huge disaster. He learns that it is up to him to help rid the area of marauders and locate the legendary lost land of Faar, which may hold the key to Cloral's survival.

"The ideas are clever and the descriptions inviting and easy to picture. . . . The teenaged protagonists enlist readers' sympathy and involvement and the nonstop plot developments keep the many pages turning and readers wanting more." SLJ

The **merchant** of death. Aladdin 2002 375p (Pendragon) $17.99; pa $8.99

Grades: 7 8 9 10 **Fic**

1. Fantasy fiction 2. Adventure fiction

ISBN 978-1-4169-3625-1; 1-4169-3625-4; 978-0-7434-3731-8 pa; 0-7434-3731-4 pa

LC 2002101645

Bobby Pendragon is a seemingly normal fourteen-year-old boy. He has a family, a home, and even Marley, his beloved dog. But there is something very special about Bobby. He is going to save the world. . . . Before he can object, he is swept off to an alternate dimension known as Denduron, a territory inhabited by strange beings, ruled by a magical tyrant, and plagued by dangerous revolution.

Other titles in this series are:

The lost city of Faar (2003)
The never war (2003)
The reality bug (2003)
Black water (2004)
The rivers of Zadaa (2005)
Quillan games (2006)
The pilgrims of Rayne (2007)
Raven rise (2008)
The soldiers of Halla (2009).

The **never** war. Simon & Schuster Books for Young Readers 2007 336p (Pendragon) $16.99; pa $8.99

Grades: 7 8 9 10 Fic

1. Fantasy fiction 2. Adventure fiction 3. New York (N.Y.) -- Fiction

ISBN 978-1-4169-3627-5; 1-4169-3627-0; 978-0-7434-3733-2 pa; 0-7434-3733-0 pa

LC 2007276621

Fifteen-year-old Bobby Pendragon and Spader, the Traveler from Cloral, flume to 1937 New York City and try to uncover the evil Saint Dane's newest plot.

This book has "a fast pace, suspenseful plotting, and cliffhanger chapter endings that will make it popular." SLJ

The **Quillan** games. Aladdin 2006 486p (Pendragon) $16.99; pa $8.99

Grades: 7 8 9 10 Fic

1. Fantasy fiction 2. Adventure fiction 3. Diaries -- Fiction

ISBN 978-1-4169-1423-5; 1-4169-1423-4; 978-0-689-86913-6 pa; 0-689-86913-4 pa

LC 2005029902

With more questions than answers about Saint Dane, Bobby travels to the territory of Quillan and is forced to play games where only the winner survives.

The **reality** bug. Aladdin 2003 375p (Pendragon) $17.99; pa $8.99

Grades: 7 8 9 10 Fic

1. Fantasy fiction 2. Diaries -- Fiction 3. Demonology -- Fiction 4. Space and time -- Fiction 5. Virtual reality -- Fiction

ISBN 978-1-4169-3628-2; 1-4169-3628-9; 978-0-7434-3734-9 pa; 0-7434-3734-9 pa

LC 2003105075

In his ongoing battle to save Earth and its parallel worlds from the demon Saint Dane, fifteen-year-old Bobby Pendragon travels to Veelox, a world whose inhabitants have abandoned their real lives in favor of virtual reality.

The **Rivers** of Zadaa. Aladdin 2005 405p (Pendragon) $16.99; pa $8.99

Grades: 7 8 9 10 Fic

1. Fantasy fiction 2. Adventure fiction 3. Droughts -- Fiction

ISBN 978-1-4169-0710-7; 1-4169-0710-6; 978-0-689-86912-9 pa; 0-689-86912-6 pa

Taking advantage of a severe drought and the longstanding distrust between two tribes, the demonic Saint Dane attempts to take over Loor's home planet of Zadaa, opposed once again by the teenaged Pendragon and other Travelers.

This is a "fast-moving, rip-roaring . . . story. . . . The action never stops for long, and [this book] is sure to hold the interest of fans of the series." SLJ

The **soldiers** of Halla. Aladdin 2009 594p (Pendragon) $17.99

Grades: 7 8 9 10 Fic

1. Fantasy fiction 2. Adventure fiction 3. Diaries -- Fiction 4. Space and time -- Fiction 5. Fate and fatalism -- Fiction

ISBN 978-1-4169-1420-4; 1-4169-1420-X

LC 2008-53573

Each of the Travelers returns home to learn the truth about their origins before being reunited for a final, ineveitable confrontation with Saint Dane, whose efforts to control Halla are destroying its very foundations.

SYLO; by D.J. MacHale. Penguin Group USA 2013 416 p. (SYLO chronicles) (hardcover) $17.99

Grades: 5 6 7 8 9 Fic

1. Dystopian fiction 3. Adventure fiction

ISBN 1595146652; 9781595146656

This is the first book in a proposed trilogy from D.J. MacHale. Here, Tucker Pierce has a small but satisfying life on a small island. But when the island is quarantined by the U.S. Navy, things start to fall apart. . . . People start dying. The girl he wants to get to know a whole lot better, Tori, is captured along with Tucker and imprisoned behind barbed wire." They must escape to the mainland and try to figure out what this SYLO organization that is imprisoning them is. (Kirkus Reviews)

Other titles in the series include:

Storm (2014)

Strike (2014).

Mack, Tracy

The **fall** of the Amazing Zalindas; casebook no. 1. by Tracy Mack and Michael Citrin; illustrations by Greg Ruth. Orchard Books 2006 259p il (Sherlock Holmes and the Baker Street irregulars) $16.99; pa $6.99

Grades: 4 5 6 7 Fic

1. Mystery fiction 2. Circus -- Fiction 3. Great Britain -- Fiction

ISBN 0-439-82836-8; 0-545-06939-4 pa

LC 2005-34000

The ragamuffin boys known as the Baker Street Irregulars help Sherlock Holmes solve the mysterious deaths of a family of circus tightrope walkers.

"Colorful, well-defined characters . . . and plenty of historical detail, Cockney slang . . . and Sherlockian references bring Victorian England to life. Vintage-style design elements and evocative black-and-white illustrations further the effect." Booklist

The **mystery** of the conjured man; [by] Tracy Mack & Michael Citrin; [illustrations by Greg Ruth] Orchard Books 2009 il (Sherlock Holmes and the Baker Street Irregulars) hardcover o.p.

Grades: 4 5 6 Fic

1. Mystery fiction 2. Spiritualism -- Fiction 3. Great Britain -- Fiction 4. Swindlers and swindling -- Fiction

ISBN 978-0-439-83667-8 pa

LC 2006035701

The ragtag group of orphan boys known as the Baker Street Irregulars faces shady characters and seemingly real ghosts when they assist the famous detective, Sherlock Holmes, in investigating the mysterious death of Greta Berlinger during a seance.

"A great addition to an entertaining series." SLJ

Mack, W. C.

Athlete vs. mathlete; by W.C. Mack. Bloomsbury. Distributed to the trade by Macmillan 2013 208 p. (hardback) $16.99

Grades: 5 6 7 Fic

1. Sibling rivalry -- fiction 2. Twins -- Fiction 3. Schools -- Fiction 4. Brothers -- Fiction 5. Basketball -- Fiction 6. Competition (Psychology) -- Fiction

ISBN 1599909154; 9781599908588; 9781599909158

LC 2012014146

This book "introduces athletic seventh-grader Owen and his klutzy, academic-minded fraternal twin, Russell. The boys are content with their respective roles until the new school basketball coach, impressed by Russell's height, invites him to try out for the team. No one is more shocked than Russell when he makes the cut, along with Owen, but his victory precipitates a flurry of conflicts for both boys." The story is "told from the boys' alternating points of view." (Publishers Weekly)

Mackel, Kathy

★ **Boost**. Dial Books 2008 248p $16.99; pa $7.99

Grades: 6 7 8 9 **Fic**

1. Steroids -- Fiction 2. Basketball -- Fiction

ISBN 978-0-8037-3240-7; 0-8037-3240-6; 978-0-14-241539-9 pa; 0-14-241539-1 pa

LC 2007-49441

Thirteen-year-old Savvy's dreams of starting for her elite basketball team are in danger when she is accused of taking steroids

"Mackel has turned a tough subject in the world of teen competitive sports into a highly readable blend of intense action, interfamily relationships, and intrigue." SLJ

Mackey, Heather

Dreamwood; Heather Mackey. G.P. Putnam's Sons 2014 336 p. (hardback) $16.99

Grades: 4 5 6 7 8 **Fic**

1. Supernatural -- Fiction 2. Missing persons -- Fiction 3. Runaway children -- Fiction 4. Forests and forestry -- Fiction 5. Adventure and adventurers -- Fiction 6. Northwest, Pacific -- History -- 19th century -- Fiction

ISBN 0399250670; 9780399250675

LC 2013039402

In this book, by Heather Mackey, "Lucy Darrington has no choice but to run away from boarding school. Her father, an expert on the supernatural, has been away for too long while doing research in Saarthe, a remote territory in the Pacific Northwest populated by towering redwoods, timber barons, and the Lupine people. But upon arriving, she learns her father is missing: Rumor has it he's gone in search of dreamwood, a rare tree with magical properties." (Publisher's note)

"Dialogue and perilous situations nudge the story along at a steady clip, with the second half a breathless page turner. Dreamwood will please character-focused readers." SLJ

Mackey, Weezie Kerr

Throwing like a girl; [by] Weezie Kerr Mackey. Marshall Cavendish 2007 271p $16.99

Grades: 6 7 8 9 **Fic**

1. School stories 2. Texas -- Fiction 3. Softball -- Fiction 4. Family life -- Fiction

ISBN 978-0-7614-5342-0

LC 2006030233

After moving from Chicago to Dallas in the spring of her sophomore year, fifteen-year-old Ella finds that joining the softball team at her private school not only helps her make friends, it also provides unexpected opportunities to learn and grow.

"Readers will be delighted with how well the athletics and the girly stuff work in tandem." Booklist

Mackler, Carolyn

The **earth,** my butt, and other big, round things. Candlewick Press 2003 246p $15.99; pa $8.99

Grades: 7 8 9 10 **Fic**

1. School stories 2. Obesity -- Fiction 3. Family life -- Fiction 4. New York (N.Y.) -- Fiction

ISBN 0-7636-1958-2; 0-7636-2091-2 pa

LC 2002-73921

Sequel is: The Universe is Expanding and So Am I (2018).

Michael L. Printz Award honor book, 2004

Feeling like she does not fit in with the other members of her family, who are all thin, brilliant, and good-looking, fifteen-year-old Virginia tries to deal with her self-image, her first physical relationship, and her disillusionment with some of the people closest to her

"The e-mails [Virginia] exchanges . . . and the lists she makes (e.g., 'The Fat Girl Code of Conduct') add both realism and insight to her character. The heroine's transformation into someone who finds her own style and speaks her own mind is believable—and worthy of applause." Publ Wkly

★ The **future** of us; [by] Jay Asher and Carolyn Mackler. Razorbill 2011 356p $18.99

Grades: 8 9 10 11 12 **Fic**

1. School stories 2. Computers -- Fiction 3. Supernatural -- Fiction

ISBN 978-1-59514-491-1; 1-59514-491-9

In this book by Jay Asher and Carolyn Mackler, "it's 1996, before Facebook's been invented. Yet Emma's first computer leads her to her Facebook page from fifteen years in the future. She tells only her friend and would-be boyfriend Josh, and they contemplate their futures with concern. Can their current actions change who they become?" (Voice of Youth Advocates)

"It's 1996, and Emma Nelson has just received her first computer. . . . When Emma powers up the computer, she discovers her own Facebook page (even though Facebook doesn't exist yet) and herself in an unhappy marriage—15 years in the future. Alternating chapters from Josh and Emma over the course of five days propel this riveting read, as Emma discovers she can alter her future by adjusting her present actions and intentions." Booklist

MacLachlan, Patricia, 1938-

Kindred souls; Patricia MacLachlan. HarperCollins 2012 119 p. (trade bdg.) $16.99

Grades: 4 5 6 **Fic**

1. Bereavement -- Fiction 2. Family life -- Fiction 3. Family farms -- Fiction 4. Grandfathers -- Fiction 5. Houses -- Remodeling -- Fiction 6. Dogs -- Fiction 7. Old age -- Fiction 8. Prairies -- Fiction 9. Farm life -- Fiction 10. Sod houses -- Fiction

ISBN 9780060522971; 9780060522988

LC 2011016617

This book follows narrator Jake and his 88-year-old grandfather Billy, the eponymous kindred souls of the story's title. The pair "live on a farm that their family has owned for generations; in fact, Billy was born in a sod house he remembers fondly, the ruins of which still exist on the property." To comfort their dying grandfather, "Jake and his siblings undertake a remarkably ambitious project: They rebuild the sod house; Billy moves into it, and he eventually passes away there." The "first-person account of a boy coping with his grandfather's death . . . portrays . . . the opportunity to grieve for a loved one even while he is still alive." (Kirkus)

Maddox, Jake

Free throw; by Jake Maddox; illustrated by Sean Tiffany; text by Anastasia Suen. Stone Arch Books 2007 65p il lib bdg $22.60; pa $5.95

Grades: 4 5 6 7 **Fic**

1. Basketball -- Fiction

ISBN 978-1-59889-060-0 lib bdg; 1-59889-060-3 lib bdg; 978-1-59889-238-3 pa; 1-59889-238-X pa

LC 2006006076

Since Derek is now the tallest player on his basketball team, the coach decides to have him play center but Jason, the former center, has little confidence in Derek and will not pass him the ball.

"The clear descriptions, realistic dialogue, abundant action, and touches of humor will appeal to younger children, as well as to middle school or older readers who are working to bolster their skills. They will appreciate the large font and the comic-book-style drawings that illuminate the [text]." SLJ

Maetani, Valynne E.

Ink & ashes; Valynne E. Maetani. Tu Books, an imprint of Lee & Low Books, Inc. 2015 368 p. (hardback) $19.95
Grades: 7 8 9 10 **Fic**

1. Mystery fiction 2. Organized crime -- Fiction 3. Japanese Americans -- Fiction 4. Love -- Fiction 5. Fathers -- Fiction
ISBN 9781620142110
LC 2015006632

In this mystery novel by Valynne E. Maetani, "Claire Takata has never known much about her father. . . . But on the anniversary of his death, she finds a letter from her deceased father to her stepfather. . . . Struggling to understand why her parents kept this surprising history hidden, Claire combs through anything that might give her information about her father . . . until she discovers that he was a member of the yakuza, a Japanese organized crime syndicate." (Publisher's note)

"Maetani's fast-paced debut will appeal to readers who like their intrigue with a generous helping of romance." Booklist

Mafi, Tahereh

Furthermore; by Tahereh Mafi. Dutton Children's Books, an imprint of Penguin Random House 2016 416 p. illustrations (hardback) $17.99
Grades: 4 5 6 7 8 **Fic**

1. Fantasy fiction 2. Magic -- Fiction 3. Adventure fiction 4. Missing persons -- Fiction
ISBN 9781101994764
LC 2015044898

In this book, by Tahereh Mafi, "there are only three things that matter to twelve-year-old Alice Alexis Queensmeadow: Mother, who wouldn't miss her; magic and color, which seem to elude her; and Father, who always loved her. The day Father disappears from Ferenwood he takes nothing but a ruler with him. But it's been almost three years since then, and Alice is determined to find him." (Publisher's note)

"While Oliver and Alice start off at odds, their friendship, forged in adversity, is the best part of a fast-paced, funny, and richly imaginative story that embraces and celebrates individuality." Pub Wkly

★ **Shatter** me; Tahereh Mafi. HarperTeen 2011 338 p $17.99
Grades: 8 9 10 11 12 **Fic**

1. Romance fiction 2. Science fiction 3. Love stories 4. Ability -- Fiction 5. Soldiers -- Fiction
ISBN 9780062085481
LC 2011019370

"Juliette knows that she is a monster; her touch is fatal. She has been living in a cell in a mental institution for 264 days, all alone. When a boy is brought in as her cell mate, his arrival sparks an explosion of events that changes her life as well as the world. Shatter Me takes place in a future time in which a lack of resources has so frightened the citizens that they have handed over all of their basic rights to a totalitarian government. The regime has plans for Juliette, but she finds the strength to resist the powers that be and joins in a rebel movement, becoming the central figure that everyone is fighting to possess." (School Library Journal)

Other titles in this series are:
Unravel me (2013)
Ignite me (2014)
Restore me (2018)
Defy me (2019)

★ A **very** large expanse of sea; Tahereh Mafi. HarperTeen 2018 320 p. (hardback) $18.99
Grades: 8 9 10 11 12 **Fic**

1. Romance fiction 2. Muslims -- Fiction 3. Prejudices -- Fiction
ISBN 9780062866561
LC 2018945999

In this book, by Tahereh Mafi, "it's 2002, a year after 9/11. It's an extremely turbulent time politically, but especially so for someone like Shirin, a sixteen-year-old Muslim girl who's tired of being stereotyped. . . . So she's built up protective walls and refuses to let anyone close enough to hurt her. . . . But then she meets Ocean James. He's the first person . . . who really seems to want to get to know . . . [her.]" (Publisher's note)

"Shirin and Ocean's interactions are palpable, and the discussions and exploration of what it means to be a Muslim in politically charged America will resonate with many teens and will be enlightening for some." School Lib Jnl

Whichwood; by Tahereh Mafi. Dutton Children's Books Young Readers/Penguin Random House LLC 2017 360 p. (hardcover) $17.99
Grades: 4 5 6 7 8 **Fic**

1. Dead -- Fiction 2. Magic -- Fiction 3. Friendship -- Fiction 4. Dead -- fiction 5. Magic -- fiction 6. Friendship -- fiction
ISBN 9781101994818; 9781101994795
LC 2017020411

Sequel to: Furthermore (2016)

In this book, by Tahereh Mafi, "Laylee can barely remember the happier times before her . . . mother died. Before her father . . . lost his wits . . . and she was left as the sole remaining mordeshoor . . . of Whichwood, destined to . . . scrubbing the skins and souls of the dead in preparation for the afterlife. . . . But soon, a pair of familiar strangers appear, and Laylee's world is turned upside down as she rediscovers color, magic, and the healing power of friendship." (Publisher's note)

"Memorable new characters experience the restorative power of friendship in this darkly fascinating, somewhat ghoulish sequel to Furthermore." Kirkus

Magoon, Kekla

Camo girl. Aladdin 2010 218p $16.99
Grades: 5 6 7 8 **Fic**

1. Friendship -- Fiction 2. Prejudices -- Fiction 3. Racially mixed people -- Fiction
ISBN 978-1-4169-7804-6; 1-4169-7804-6

A novel about a biracial girl living in the suburbs of Las Vegas examines the friendships that grow out of, and despite, her race.

"Magoon . . . offers a sensitive and articulate portrayal of a pair of middle-school outsiders. . . . This poetic and nuanced story addresses the courage it takes to truly know and support someone, as well as the difficult choices that come with growing up." Publ Wkly

Fire in the streets; by Kekla Magoon. 1st Aladdin hardcover ed. Aladdin 2012 336 p. $15.99
Grades: 7 8 9 10 **Fic**

1. Historical fiction 2. Black nationalism -- Fiction 3. African Americans -- Civil rights -- Fiction 4. Racism -- Fiction 5. African Americans -- Fiction 6. Black Panther Party -- Fiction 7. Brothers and sisters -- Fiction 8. Civil rights movements -- Fiction 9. United States -- History -- 20th century -- Fiction 10. Chicago (Ill.) --

History -- 20th century -- Fiction
ISBN 1442422300; 9781442422308

LC 2011039129

Sequel to: The rock and the river

This historical novel by Kekla Magoon, is set "in the sweltering Chicago summer of 1968. [Maxie] is a Black Panther--or at least she wants to be one. . . . At fourteen, she's allowed to help out in the office, but she certainly can't help patrol the streets. Then Maxie realizes that there is a traitor in their midst, and if she can figure out who it is, it may be her ticket to becoming a real Panther. But when she learns the truth, the knowledge threatens to destroy her world." (Publisher's note)

★ The **rock** and the river. Aladdin 2009 290p $15.99
Grades: 7 8 9 10 **Fic**

1. Brothers -- Fiction 2. Chicago (Ill.) -- Fiction 3. African Americans -- Fiction 4. Black Panther Party -- Fiction
ISBN 1-4169-7582-9; 978-1-4169-7582-3

LC 2008-29170

ALA EMIERT Coretta Scott King John Steptoe New Talent Award (2010)

In 1968 Chicago, fourteen-year-old Sam Childs is caught in a conflict between his father's nonviolent approach to seeking civil rights for African Americans and his older brother, who has joined the Black Panther Party. "Grades seven to ten." (Bull Cent Child Books)

This "novel will make readers feel what it was like to be young, black, and militant 40 years ago, including the seething fury and desperation over the daily discrimination that drove the oppressed to fight back." Booklist

★ The **season** of Styx Malone; Kekla Magoon. Wendy Lamb Books 2018 304 p. (trade) $16.99
Grades: 4 5 6 7 **Fic**

1. Secrecy -- fiction 2. Brothers -- fiction 3. Friendship -- fiction 4. Indiana -- Fiction 5. Foster children -- Fiction 6. African Americans -- Fiction 7. Family life -- Indiana -- Fiction 8. Adventure and adventurers -- Fiction
ISBN 9781524715953; 9781524715960; 9781524715984

LC 2017050786

Coretta Scott King (Author) Honor Book (2019)

In this book, by Kekla Magoon, brothers "Caleb and Bobby Gene meet new neighbor Styx Malone. Styx is sixteen and oozes cool. . . . Styx promises Caleb and Bobby Gene that together, they can pull off the Great Escalator Trade--exchanging one small thing for something better until they achieve their wildest dream. But as the trades get bigger, ... [i]t becomes clear that Styx has secrets--secrets so big they could ruin everything." (Publisher's note)

"A summertime romp filled with trouble-making, camaraderie, and substance. A solid purchase, especially for collections where realism circulates well." (School Library Journal)

Magras, Diane

The **mad** wolf's daughter; Diane Magras. Kathy Dawson Books 2018 288 p. hardback $16.99
Grades: 4 5 6 7 **Fic**

1. Adventure fiction 2. Family life -- Fiction 3. Heroes and heroines -- Fiction 4. War -- Fiction 5. Heroes -- Fiction 6. Middle Ages -- Fiction 7. Knights and knighthood -- Fiction 8. Family life -- Scotland -- Fiction 9. Adventure and adventures -- Fiction 10. Scotland -- History -- 1057-1603 -- Fiction
ISBN 9780735229280; 9780735229266

LC 2017040115

In this book, by Diane Magras, "Drest is a likable and headstrong character, and the composite of various regions in Scotland will appeal to tweens who appreciate atmospheric woodsy settings. Readers will learn, along with Drest, about feudal village life, contemporaneous attitudes toward gender, and the relationship between truth and legend. . . . Drest's embrace of unlikely friendships and a new code of honor are well done." (School Library Journal)

Maguire, Gregory, 1954-

★ **Egg** & spoon; a novel by Gregory Maguire. Candlewick Press 2014 475 p. hbk $17.99
Grades: 7 8 9 10 11 12 **Fic**

1. Poor -- Fiction 2. Girls -- Fiction 3. Russia -- Fiction 4. Monks 5. Princes 6. Mistaken identity 7. Baba Yaga (Legendary Character)
ISBN 0763672203; 9780763672201

LC 2014931834

Boston Globe-Horn Book Honor: Fiction (2015)

In this young adult novel by Gregory Maguire, "Elena Rudina lives in the impoverished Russian countryside. Her father has been dead for years. . . . Her mother is dying, slowly, in their tiny cabin. And there is no food. But then a train arrives in the village, a train carrying untold wealth, a cornucopia of food, and a noble family destined to visit the Tsar in Saint Petersburg." (Publisher's note)

"With one brother conscripted into the Tsar's army and another bound to serve a local landowner, Elena is left alone to care for her widowed and ailing mother in early 20th-century Russia. When an elegant train bearing a noble her age rolls through their barren village, Elena and her counterpart, Cat, accidentally swap places. . . . The author weaves a lyrical tale full of magic and promise, yet checkered with the desperation of poverty and the treacherous prospect of a world gone completely awry. Egg and Spoon is a beautiful reminder that fairy tales are at their best when they illuminate the precarious balance between lighthearted childhood and the darkness and danger of adulthood." SLJ

Maldonado, Torrey

Secret Saturdays. G.P. Putnam's Sons 2010 195p $16.99
Grades: 6 7 8 9 **Fic**

1. School stories 2. African Americans -- Fiction 3. Single parent family -- Fiction 4. Racially mixed people -- Fiction 5. Brooklyn (New York, N.Y.) -- Fiction
ISBN 978-0-399-25158-0; 0-399-25158-8

LC 2009-10361

Twelve-year-old boys living in a rough part of New York confront questions about what it means to be a friend, a father, and a man.

"Maldonado convincingly portrays roughneck playgrounds where boys are expected to be 'hard' and . . . Justin's narration resonates with the authenticity of a preteen doing his best in an urban landscape that has taught him all he knows. . . . The book remains a moving portrayal of the hope to be found through honest relationships." Publ Wkly

Tight; Torrey Maldonado. Nancy Paulsen Books 2018 192 p. (hardback) $16.99
Grades: 4 5 6 7 **Fic**

1. Friendship -- Fiction 2. Conduct of life -- Fiction 3. African Americans -- Fiction 4. Inner cities -- Fiction 5. Brooklyn (New York, N.Y.) -- Fiction 6. Family life -- Brooklyn (New York, N.Y.) -- Fiction
ISBN 9781524740559

LC 2018007927

In this book, by Torrey Maldonado, "Bryan knows what's tight for him--reading comics, drawing superheroes, and hanging out with no drama. But drama is every day where he's from. . . . And now Bryan's friend Mike pressures him with ideas of fun that are crazy risky. . . . But Bryan never really feels right acting so wrong, and drama really isn't him. So which way will he go, especially when his dad tells him it's better to be hard and feared than liked?" (Publisher's note)

Malley, Gemma

The **Declaration**. Bloomsbury 2007 300p $16.95

Grades: 7 8 9 10 **Fic**

1. Science fiction 2. Immortality -- Fiction 3. Great Britain -- Fiction

ISBN 978-1-59990-119-0; 1-59990-119-6

LC 2006-102138

In 2140 England, where drugs enable people to live forever and children are illegal, teenaged Anna, an obedient "Surplus" training to become a house servant, discovers that her birth parents are trying to find her.

This is "gripping. . . . The indoctrinated teen's awakening to massive injustice makes compulsive reading." Booklist

Other titles in this series are:

The legacy (2011)

The resistance (2008)

The **resistance**. Bloomsbury Children's Books 2008 323p $16.99

Grades: 7 8 9 10 **Fic**

1. Science fiction 2. Immortality -- Fiction 3. Great Britain -- Fiction

ISBN 978-1-59990-302-6

LC 2008-10310

Sequel to The declaration (2007)

In a future England where young people, or "Surpluses," are heavily regulated and everyone takes a drug called Longevity, a member of the Underground infiltrates the Pincent Pharma manufacturing plant, and uncovers horrific acts being committed in an attempt to create eternal youth.

"The novel is well written and will be enjoyed by readers who liked the first book." Voice Youth Advocates

Followed by: The legacy (2011)

Mann, J. Albert

What every girl should know; Margaret Sanger's journey : a novel. by J. Albert Mann. Atheneum 2019 240 p. (hardcover : alk. paper) $18.99

Grades: 7 8 9 10 11 12 **Fic**

1. Biographical fiction 2. Family life -- Fiction 3. Gender role -- Fiction 4. Schools -- Fiction 5. Sex role -- Fiction 6. Family life -- New York (State) -- Fiction 7. New York (State) -- History -- 19th century -- Fiction

ISBN 9781534419322; 9781534419339

LC 2018017991

In this novel, by J. Albert Mann, "Margaret was determined to get out. She didn't want to clean the dirty dishes and soiled diapers that piled up day in and day out in her large family's small home. She didn't want to disappoint her ailing mother, who cared tirelessly for an ever-growing number of children despite her incessant cough. And Margaret certainly didn't want to be labeled a girl of 'promise,' destined to become either a teacher or a mother." (Publisher's note)

"An important, readable novel about Sanger, who changed the fate of millions of women through access to contraception." (Kirkus Reviews)

Includes bibliographical references

Mantchev, Lisa

Eyes like stars. Feiwel and Friends 2009 356p $16.99

Grades: 8 9 10 11 12 **Fic**

1. Magic -- Fiction 2. Actors -- Fiction 3. Orphans -- Fiction 4. Theater -- Fiction 5. Books and reading -- Fiction

ISBN 978-0-312-38096-0; 0-312-38096-8

LC 2008-15317

Thirteen-year-old Bertie strives to save Theater Illuminata, the only home she has ever known, but is hindered by the Players who magically live on there, especially Ariel, who is willing to destroy the Book at the center of the magic in order to escape into the outside world.

"The story contains enough mystery and mayhem to keep readers engaged, even as they analyze." Voice Youth Advocates

Other titles in this series include:

Perchance to dream (2010)

So silver bright (2011)

Perchance to dream. Feiwel and Friends 2010 337p $16.99; pa $9.99

Grades: 8 9 10 11 12 **Fic**

1. Magic -- Fiction 2. Fairies -- Fiction 3. Orphans -- Fiction 4. Theater -- Fiction

ISBN 978-0-312-38097-7; 0-312-38097-6; 978-0-312-67510-3 pa; 0-312-67510-0 pa

Sequel to Eyes like stars (2009)

Bertie, who is blessed with word magic, and her fairy sidekicks seek to save Nate, who has been kidnapped by the Sea Witch, but Bertie is torn between Nate and Ariel, an air spirit who loves Bertie enough to die for her.

"The pace is fast and furious . . . but it's Mantchev's fresh, intelligent style that delights most. . . . This fantastical romp—an absolute must for theater buffs—might stand alone, but it'd be a pity not to start with the first." Kirkus

Followed by So silver bright (2011)

So silver bright. Feiwel and Friends 2011 356p $16.99; ebook $9.99

Grades: 8 9 10 11 12 **Fic**

1. Magic -- Fiction 2. Actors -- Fiction 3. Fairies -- Fiction 4. Theater -- Fiction 5. Books and reading -- Fiction

ISBN 978-0-312-38098-4; 978-1-4299-9540-5 ebook

LC 2011023907

Bertie thinks that to complete her quest to have a true family she need only reunite her father, the Scrimshander, with her mother, Ophelia, but complications arise and she is torn between her responsibilities and the dream of flying free, just as she is torn between Nate and Ariel.

Manzano, Sonia

★ The **revolution** of Evelyn Serrano; Sonia Manzano. Scholastic 2012 205 p. $17.99

Grades: 6 7 8 9 10 **Fic**

1. Historical fiction 2. Puerto Ricans -- Fiction 3. Identity -- Fiction 4. Grandmothers -- Fiction 5. Protest movements -- Fiction 6. Grandparent and child -- fiction 7. Identity (Psychology) -- fiction 8. Puerto Rican families -- fiction 9. Family life -- New York (State) -- Harlem -- Fiction 10. New York (N.Y.) -- History -- 20th century -- Fiction 11. Puerto Ricans -- New York (State) -- New York -- Fiction 12. East Harlem (New York, N.Y.) -- History -- 20th century -- Fiction

ISBN 0545325056; 9780545325059; 9780545325066

LC 2012009240

Pura Belpré Author Honor Book (2013)

This novel, by Sonia Manzano, is set "in New York's El Barrio in 1969. . . . The Young Lords, a Puerto Rican activist group, dump garbage in the street and set it on fire, igniting a powerful protest. When Abuela steps in to take charge, Evelyn is thrust into the action. . . . Evelyn learns important truths about her Latino heritage and the history makers who shaped a nation." (Publisher's note)

Includes bibliographical references

Marchetta, Melina

★ **Finnikin** of the rock. Candlewick Press 2010 399p map $18.99

Grades: 8 9 10 11 12 **Fic**

1. Fantasy fiction

ISBN 0-7636-4361-0; 978-0-7636-4361-4

LC 2009-28046

In this fantasy novel, "Finnikin was only a child during the five days of the unspeakable, when the royal family of Lumatere were brutally murdered, and an imposter seized the throne. . . . Finnikin, now on the cusp of manhood, is compelled to join forces with an arrogant and enigmatic young novice named Evanjalin, who claims that her dark dreams will lead the exiles to a surviving royal child and a way to pierce the cursed barrier and regain the land of Lumatere." (Publisher's note)

"The skillful world building includes just enough detail to create a vivid sense of place, and Marchetta maintains suspense with unexpected story arcs. It is the achingly real characters, though, and the relationships that emerge through the captivating dialogue that drive the story. Filled with questions about the impact of exile and the human need to belong, this standout fantasy quickly reveals that its real magic lies in its accomplished writing." Booklist

★ **Froi** of the exiles. Candlewick 2012 608 p.

Grades: 8 9 10 11 12 **Fic**

1. Exiles 2. War stories 3. Fantasy fiction

ISBN 9780763647599

In this fantasy book, "Froi, a former street thief who has started a new life in Lumatere, is sent to Charyn in disguise to assassinate its king, but his worldview is shaken by revelations about his own unknown past. Tensions between the two kingdoms ratchet up, and Froi's loyalties are tested as he becomes entrenched in the chaotic political situation in Charyn and is drawn to its unpredictable princess, Quintana, who has been horribly abused in an attempt to break Charyn's curse." (Publishers Weekly)

★ **Quintana** of Charyn; Melina Marchetta. Candlewick Press 2013 528 p. (Lumatere chronicles) $18.99

Grades: 8 9 10 11 12 **Fic**

1. War stories 2. Fantasy fiction

ISBN 0763658359; 9780763658359

LC 2012955120

This is the conclusion of Melina Marchetta's trilogy which began with "Finnikin of the Rock." Here, "the kingdoms of Lumatere and Charyn attempt to bridge past atrocities through a new generation of leaders. Although tragedies arise, unity and healing are core themes, compared to the horrors of the previous books. As the title suggests, Quintana--the rightful ruler of Charyn, hidden following the uprising in the kingdom in Froi of the Exiles--is at the center of this final book." (Publishers Weekly)

Marcus, Kimberly

Exposed. Random House 2011 260p $16.99; lib bdg $19.99

Grades: 8 9 10 **Fic**

1. School stories 2. Novels in verse 3. Rape -- Fiction 4. Guilt -- Fiction 5. Friendship -- Fiction 6. Photography -- Fiction

ISBN 0-375-86693-0; 0-375-96693-5 lib bdg; 978-0-375-86693-7; 978-0-375-89724-5 e-book; 978-0-375-96693-4 lib bdg

LC 2009-51545

High school senior Liz, a gifted photographer, can no longer see things clearly after her best friend accuses Liz's older brother of a terrible crime.

"The narrative largely zooms in on Liz's pain and her struggle to ground herself in her photography and gain admission to art school as events swirl around her. As a result of tethering the narrative to Liz's perspective, the ongoing discussion of Kate's rape and ensuing trial are not heavyhanded or gratuitous. In Liz, Marcus has created a sympathetic lead. A worthy addition to any collection." SLJ

Margolis, Leslie

Girl's best friend. Bloomsbury USA Childrens Books 2010 261p $14.99

Grades: 4 5 6 7 **Fic**

1. School stories 2. Mystery fiction 3. Dogs -- Fiction 4. Twins -- Fiction 5. Siblings -- Fiction 6. Family life -- Fiction 7. Brooklyn (New York, N.Y.) -- Fiction

ISBN 978-1-59990-525-9; 1-59990-525-6

LC 2010000562

In Brooklyn, New York, twelve-year-old dog-walker Maggie, aided by her twin brother Finn and best friend Lucy, investigates someone she believes is stealing pets.

"Characters are well-developed, typical preteens. Readers will easily identify with these seventh graders, and they will love the eccentric landlady who adds a bit of humor. Mystery fans will enjoy this lighthearted whodunit." SLJ

Marillier, Juliet

★ **Cybele's** secret. Alfred A. Knopf 2008 432p $17.99; lib bdg $20.99

Grades: 7 8 9 10 **Fic**

1. Magic -- Fiction 2. Turkey -- Fiction 3. Sisters -- Fiction 4. Supernatural -- Fiction

ISBN 978-0-375-83365-6; 0-375-83365-X; 978-0-375-93365-3 lib bdg; 0-375-93365-4 lib bdg

LC 2008-4758

Scholarly eighteen-year-old Paula and her merchant father journey from Transylvania to Istanbul to buy an ancient pagan artifact rumored to be charmed, but others, including a handsome Portuguese pirate and an envoy from the magical Wildwood, want to acquire the item, as well.

This is a "honeyed draught of a [novel]. . . . Marillier embroiders Ottoman Empire cultural details into every fold and drape of her story." Booklist

Raven flight; a Shadowfell novel. Juliet Marillier. Alfred A. Knopf 2013 416 p.

Grades: 7 8 9 10 **Fic**

1. Fantasy fiction 2. Paranormal fiction 3. Magic -- Fiction 4. Orphans -- Fiction 5. Insurgency -- Fiction 6. Voyages and travels -- Fiction

ISBN 9780375869556; 9780375969553

LC 2012039483

This is the second volume of Juliet Marillier's Shadowfell series. Here, "Neryn's time among the rebels has left her stronger and healthier but no closer to grasping her power and becoming a true Caller. When a potential ally sets a time limit for rebelling against tyrannical King Keldec, Neryn can no longer hide and sets off to find the Hag of the Isles and the Lord of the North." (Kirkus Reviews)

Shadowfell; Juliet Marillier. Alfred A. Knopf 2012 410 p. map (trade) $16.99
Grades: 7 8 9 10 11 12 **Fic**

1. Fantasy fiction 2. Magic -- Fiction 3. Adventure fiction 4. Orphans -- Fiction 5. Insurgency -- Fiction 6. Voyages and travels -- Fiction

ISBN 0375869549; 9780375869549; 9780375969546; 9780375983665

LC 2011041050

Originally published: Sydney, N.S.W. : Pan Macmillan, 2012.

In this novel by Juliet Marillier "Fifteen-year-old Neryn is alone in the land of Alban, where the oppressive king has ordered anyone with magical strengths captured and brought before him. Eager to hide her own canny skill--a uniquely powerful ability to communicate with the fairy-like Good Folk--Neryn sets out for the legendary Shadowfell, a home and training ground for a secret rebel group determined to overthrow the evil King Keldec." (Publisher's note)

Wildwood dancing. Knopf 2007 416p $16.99; lib bdg $18.99
Grades: 7 8 9 10 **Fic**

1. Magic -- Fiction 2. Sisters -- Fiction 3. Supernatural -- Fiction

ISBN 0-375-83364-1; 0-375-93364-6 lib bdg

LC 2006-16075

Five sisters who live with their merchant father in Transylvania use a hidden portal in their home to cross over into a magical world, the Wildwood.

This is told "with a striking sense of place, magical elements, beautifully portrayed characters, strong heroines, and an emotional core that touches the heart." Voice Youth Advocates

Followed by: Cybele's secret (2008)

Marr, Melissa

Darkest mercy. Harper 2011 327p $16.99; lib bdg $17.89
Grades: 8 9 10 11 12 **Fic**

1. Fantasy fiction 2. Fairies -- Fiction

ISBN 978-0-06-165925-6; 0-06-165925-8; 978-0-06-165926-3 lib bdg; 0-06-165926-6 lib bdg

LC 2010-33584

Sequel to: Radiant shadows (2010)

The political and romantic tensions that began when Aislin became Summer Queen threaten to boil over as the Faerie Courts brace against the threat of all-out war.

Fragile eternity. Bowen Press 2009 389p $16.99; lib bdg $17.89
Grades: 8 9 10 11 12 **Fic**

1. Fantasy fiction 2. Fairies -- Fiction

ISBN 978-0-06-121471-4; 0-06-121471-X; 978-0-06-121472-1 lib bdg; 0-06-121472-8 lib bdg

LC 2008-34420

Sequel to: Ink exchange (2008)

Aislinn and Seth struggle with the unforeseen consequences of Aislinn's transformation from mortal girl to faery queen as the world teeters on the brink of cataclysmic violence.

Followed by: Radiant shadows (2010)

Ink exchange. HarperTeen 2008 325p il lib bdg $17.89; $16.99
Grades: 8 9 10 11 12 **Fic**

1. Fantasy fiction 2. Fairies -- Fiction 3. Tattooing -- Fiction 4. Kings and rulers -- Fiction

ISBN 978-0-06-121469-1 lib bdg; 0-06-121469-8 lib bdg; 978-0-06-121468-4; 0-06-121468-X

LC 2007-40106

Sequel to: Wicked lovely (2007)

Seventeen-year-old Leslie wants a tattoo as a way of reclaiming control of herself and her body, but the eerie image she selects pulls her into the dangerous Dark Court of the faeries, where she draws on inner strength to make a horrible choice.

"Readers will be drawn in by Marr's darkly poetic imagery and language, her vivid portrayal of the art of tattooing, and her shadowy love triangle. This is indeed a delicious, smoky delight." Bull Cent Child Books

Followed by Fragile eternity (2009)

Loki's wolves; by K.L. Armstrong and M.A. Marr. 1st ed. Little, Brown and Co. 2013 368 p. ill. (The Blackwell pages) (hardcover) $16.99
Grades: 4 5 6 7 8 **Fic**

1. Norse mythology -- Fiction 2. Gods -- Fiction 4. Monsters -- Fiction 5. Supernatural -- Fiction 6. Shapeshifting -- Fiction 7. Adventure and adventurers -- Fiction

ISBN 031620496X; 9780316204965

LC 2012029851

This juvenile fantasy novel, by K. L. Armstrong and M. A. Marr, is the first book in the "Blackwell Pages" series. "Matt hears the words, but he can't believe them. He's Thor's representative? Destined to fight trolls, monstrous wolves and giant serpents . . . or the world ends? He's only thirteen. . . . But now Ragnarok is coming, and it's up to the champions to fight in the place of the long-dead gods." (Publisher's note)

"It is so methodically constructed that readers will welcome the action Ragnarök will offer. . . . Norse mythology brought to life with engaging contemporary characters and future volumes that promise explosive action; ideal for Percy Jackson fans who want to branch out." Kirkus

Odin's ravens; K.L. Armstrong ; M.A. Marr. First edition Little, Brown and Co. 2014 352 p. illustrations (The Blackwell pages) (hardcover) $17
Grades: 4 5 6 7 8 **Fic**

1. Adventure fiction 2. Supernatural -- Fiction 3. Norse mythology -- Fiction 4. Gods and goddesses -- Fiction 5. Gods -- Fiction 6. Monsters -- Fiction 7. Valhalla -- Fiction 8. Shapeshifting -- Fiction

ISBN 0316204986; 9780316204989

LC 2013018519

In this sequel to "Loki's Wolves," by K.L. Armstrong and M.A. Marr, "when thirteen-year-old Matt Thorsen, a modern day descendant of the Norse god Thor, was chosen to represent Thor in an epic battle to prevent the apocalypse he thought he knew how things would play out. Gather the descendants standing in for gods like Loki and Odin, defeat a giant serpent, and save the world. No problem, right?" (Publisher's note)

"This sequel stands by itself, as essential details of the first are neatly woven throughout. Intense action, well-crafted scenes and humor-laced dialogue add up to a sure winner. Just enough black-and-white illustrations add a visual dimension to the vivid text." Kirkus

Radiant shadows. HarperCollins 2010 340p $16.99; lib bdg $17.89

Grades: 8 9 10 11 12 Fic

1. Fantasy fiction 2. Fairies -- Fiction

ISBN 978-0-06-165922-5; 0-06-165922-3; 978-0-06-165923-2 lib bdg; 0-06-165923-1 lib bdg

LC 2009-53458

Sequel to: Fragile eternity (2009)

Ani, a half-mortal driven by her hungers, and Devlin, faery assassin and brother to the High Queen, have reason to fear one another even as they are drawn together to save all of Faerie.

"This is a worthy addition to a fine series. Readers who have enjoyed the early books will find this a satisfying read." SLJ

Followed by: Darkest mercy (2011)

Wicked lovely. HarperTeen 2007 328p il $16.99; lib bdg $17.89

Grades: 8 9 10 11 12 Fic

1. Fantasy fiction 2. Fairies -- Fiction 3. Kings and rulers -- Fiction

ISBN 978-0-06-121465-3; 0-06-121465-5; 978-0-06-121466-0 lib bdg; 0-06-121466-3 lib bdg

LC 2007-09143

Seventeen-year-old Aislinn, who has the rare ability to see faeries, is drawn against her will into a centuries-old battle between the Summer King and the Winter Queen, and the survival of her life, her love, and summer all hang in the balance.

"This story explores the themes of love, commitment, and what it really means to give of oneself for the greater good to save everyone else. It is the unusual combination of past legends and modern-day life that gives a unique twist to this 'fairy' tale." SLJ

Other titles in this series are:

Darkest mercy (2011)

Fragile eternity (2009)

Ink exchange (2008)

Radiant shadows (2010)

Marsden, John, 1950-

★ **Tomorrow,** when the war began. Houghton Mifflin 1995 286p (Tomorrow) pa $9.99

Grades: 7 8 9 10 Fic

1. War stories 2. Australia -- Fiction

ISBN 9780439829106; 0395706734

LC 94-29299

First published 1993 in Australia

"Australian teenager Ellie and six of her friends return from a winter break camping trip to find their homes burned or deserted, their families imprisoned, and their country occupied by a foreign military force in league with a band of disaffected Australians. As their shock wears off, the seven decide they must stick together if they are to survive. After a life-threatening skirmish with the occupiers, the teens retreat to their isolated campsite in the bush country and make plans to fight a guerilla war against the invaders." (School Library Journal)

"The novel is a riveting adventure through which Marsden explores the capacity for evil and the necessity of working together to oppose it." Horn Book

Other titles in the series are:

The Dead of Night (1994)

A Killing Frost (1995)

Darkness, Be My Friend (1996)

Burning for Revenge (2000)

The Night is For Hunting (1998)

The Other Side of Dawn (1999).

Marsh, Katherine

Nowhere boy; Katherine Marsh. Roaring Brook Press 2018 368 p. (hardcover) $16.99

Grades: 5 6 7 8 9 Fic

1. Orphans -- Fiction 2. Friendship -- Fiction 3. Teenage boys -- Fiction

ISBN 9781250307576; 9781250307583

LC 2018935592

In this book, by Katherine Marsh, "newly arrived in Brussels, Belgium, [14-year-old] Ahmed fled a life of uncertainty and suffering in Aleppo, Syria, only to lose his father on the perilous journey to the shores of Europe. . . . Then he meets Max, a [13]-year-old American boy from Washington, D.C. . . . Max is struggling at his new school and just can't seem to do anything right. But with one startling discovery, Max and Ahmed's lives collide and a friendship begins to grow." (Publisher's note)

Marshall, Kate

I am still alive; Kate Alice Marshall. Penguin Group USA 2018 336 p. $17.99

Grades: 8 9 10 11 Fic

1. Revenge -- Fiction 2. Survival skills -- Fiction 3. Father-daughter relationship -- Fiction

ISBN 0425290980; 9780425290989

In this book, by Kate Alice Marshall, "Jess hadn't seen her survivalist, off-the-grid dad in over a decade. But after a car crash killed her mother and left her injured, she was forced to move to his cabin in the remote Canadian wilderness. Just as Jess was beginning to get to know him, a secret from his past paid them a visit, leaving her father dead and Jess stranded. . . . Jess will survive. She has to. She knows who killed her father…and she wants revenge." (Publisher's note)

Martin, Ann M., 1955-

Better to wish; Ann M. Martin. 1st ed. Scholastic 2013 240 p. (Family tree) (hardcover) $16.99

Grades: 3 4 5 6 7 Fic

1. Discrimination -- fiction 2. Historical fiction -- fiction 3. Depressions -- 1929 -- Fiction 4. Family life -- Maine -- Fiction 5. Families -- Maine -- fiction 6. Maine -- History -- 20th century -- Fiction

ISBN 0545359422; 9780545359429

LC 2012047940

This is the first book in Ann M. Martin's Family Tree series. "Growing up in Maine, eight-year-old Abby Nichols is the oldest daughter of an ambitious carpenter eager to realize the American Dream. But his prejudices are strong, too: he won't let Abby associate with her Irish Catholic neighbor, Orrin. . . . As Abby's father gains success, she enjoys more privileges, . . . but the family's newfound prosperity doesn't ease her outrage over her father's mistreatment of the less fortunate." (Publishers Weekly)

A **corner** of the universe. Scholastic Press 2002 189p $15.95; pa $5.99

Grades: 5 6 7 8 Fic

1. Uncles -- Fiction 2. Friendship -- Fiction 3. People with mental disabilities -- Fiction

ISBN 0-439-38880-5; 0-439-38881-3 pa

LC 2001-57611

A Newbery Medal honor book, 2003

The summer that Hattie turns twelve, she meets the childlike uncle she never knew and becomes friends with a girl who works at the carnival that comes to Hattie's small town

"Martin delivers wonderfully real characters and an engrossing plot through the viewpoint of a girl who tries so earnestly to connect with those around her." SLJ

Everything for a dog. Feiwel and Friends 2009 211p $16.99

Grades: 5 6 7 8 **Fic**

1. Dogs -- Fiction 2. Loneliness -- Fiction 3. Bereavement -- Fiction

ISBN 978-0-312-38651-1; 0-312-38651-6

LC 2008-34747

In parallel stories, Bone, an orphaned dog, finds and loses a series of homes, Molly, a family pet, helps Charlie through the grief and other after-effects of his brother's death, and lonely Henry pleads for a dog of his own

"This is a sensitive, gentle read that surrounds its occasional heartbreak with plenty of hope and warm feelings." Booklist

★ **Rain** Reign; Ann M. Martin. Feiwel & Friends 2014 240 p. $16.99

Grades: 4 5 6 7 **Fic**

1. Dogs -- Fiction 2. English language -- Homonyms 3. Lost items -- Fiction 4. Asperger's syndrome -- Fiction

ISBN 0312643004; 9780312643003

Schneider Family Book Award (Ages 11 - 13) (2015)

In this middle grades novel by Ann M. Martin, "Rose Howard is obsessed with homonyms. She's thrilled that her own name is a homonym, and she purposely gave her dog Rain a name with two homonyms (Reign, Rein), which, according to Rose's rules of homonyms, is very special. . . . When a storm hits their rural town, rivers overflow, the roads are flooded, and Rain goes missing. . . . Now Rose has to find her dog, even if it means leaving her routines and safe places to search." (Publisher's note)

"Rose, a fifth-grader who has been diagnosed with Asperger syndrome, is often teased at school about her obsession with homonyms and her steadfast conviction that everyone should follow the rules at all times. Rose lives with her harsh, troubled father, but it's Uncle Weldon who cares for her in the ways that matter most. Still, her father did give her Rain, a stray dog that comforts and protects Rose. After Rain is lost in a storm and recovered, Rose learns that her dog has an identification microchip...Rose is driven by the unwavering belief that she must follow the rules, find Rain's former owners, and give the dog back to them... Readers will be moved by the raw portrayal of Rose's difficult home life, her separation from other kids at school, and her loss of the dog that has loved her and provided a buffer from painful experiences. A strong story told in a nuanced, highly accessible way." (Booklist)

Martin, Darragh

The **Keeper**; Darragh Martin. Little Island 2013 280 p. $15.99

Grades: 7 8 9 10 **Fic**

1. Fantasy fiction 2. Magic -- Fiction 3. Orphans -- Fiction 4. Kidnapping -- Fiction 5. Books and reading -- Fiction 6. Brothers and sisters -- Fiction

ISBN 1908195843; 9781908195845

LC 2014407173

In this book, by Darragh Martin, "Oisín is not sure he wants to be Keeper of the Book of Magic, but when his little sister Sorcha is kidnapped by the Morrígan, a raven-goddess with a heart as dark as her feathers, he has to learn how to use the Book for good. Soon Oisín has a long journey ahead of him with only Stephen, his annoying older brother, and Antimony, a headstrong orphan with her own quest, to help him." (Publisher's note)

"Fans of Percy Jackson and Harry Potter will enjoy this fast-paced high fantasy adventure that adds a refreshing twist to Celtic myths and legends." SLJ

Martin, Laura

The **ark** plan; Laura Martin ; illustrated by Eric Deschamps ; [edited by] Tara Weikum. HarperCollins 2016 368 p. illustrations, map (Edge of extinction) (hardcover) $16.99

Grades: 4 5 6 7 8 **Fic**

1. Dinosaurs -- fiction 2. Friendship -- fiction 3. Adventure fiction -- fiction

ISBN 9780062416223

LC 2015946556

This book in the Edge of Extinction series, by Laura Martin, illustrated by Eric Deschamps, and edited by Tara Weikum, is a "clever take on Michael Crichton's Jurassic Park, [with] the tale . . . reimagined on a worldwide scale. Nonstop action, marauding dinosaurs, and kids on the run: What's not to like? This is a great buy for the sci-fi adventure-loving crowd." (School Library Journal)

Another title in this series is:

Code name flood (2017)

Martin, Maggie Ann

To be honest; Maggie Ann Martin. Swoon Reads 2018 304 p. (hardcover) $16.99

Grades: 8 9 10 11 12 **Fic**

1. Body image -- Fiction 2. Interpersonal relations -- Fiction 3. Mother-daughter relationship -- Fiction

ISBN 1250183154; 9781250183156; 9781250184740

LC 2017957589

In this book, by Maggie Ann Martin, "Savannah is dreading being home alone with her overbearing mother after her big sister . . . goes off to college. . . . And then she meets George, the cute new kid at school who has insecurities of his own. As Savvy and George grow closer, they help each other discover how to live in the moment and enjoy the here and now before it disappears." (Publisher's note)

Martinez, Claudia Guadalupe

Pig Park; by Claudia Guadalupe Martinez. First edition Cinco Puntos Press 2014 248 p. illustrations (hardback) $15.95

Grades: 8 9 10 11 **Fic**

1. Ghost towns 2. Community life 3. Building -- Fiction 4. Neighborhoods -- Fiction 5. Hispanic Americans -- Fiction 6. Bakers and bakeries -- Fiction 7. Family life -- Illinois -- Chicago -- Fiction

ISBN 1935955764; 9781935955764; 9781935955771

LC 2013040645

In this novel by Claudia Guadalupe Martinez "Masi Burciaga hauls bricks to help build a giant pyramid in her neighborhood park. Her neighborhood is becoming more of a ghost town each day since the lard company moved away. As a last resort, the neighborhood grown-ups enlist all the remaining able-bodied boys and girls into this scheme in hopes of luring visitors. But something's not right about the entrepreneur behind it all." (Publisher's note)

"Martinez uses nicely specific physical details to relate Masi's experiences, and the moments in the bakery seem particularly authentic and are suffused with love.The warm, diverse community setting and the realistic family interactions help overcome the somewhat jumbled plotlines." Kirkus

The **smell** of old lady perfume. Cinco Puntos Press 2008 249p il $15.95

Grades: 5 6 7 8 **Fic**

1. School stories 2. Death -- Fiction 3. Grandmothers -- Fiction 4. Hispanic Americans -- Fiction

ISBN 978-1-9336-9318-7; 1-9336-9318-5

LC 2007-38296

When sixth-grader Chela Gonzalez's father has a stroke and her grandmother moves in to help take care of the family, her world is turned upside down.

"Short, well-crafted chapters offer perceptive glimpses into life on the border, the dynamics of middle-grade girls, and a family in turmoil." Horn Book Guide

Martinez, Jessica

★ **Virtuosity**. Simon Pulse 2011 294p $16.99

Grades: 8 9 10 11 12 **Fic**

1. Musicians -- Fiction 2. Drug abuse -- Fiction 3. Violinists -- Fiction 4. Chicago (Ill.) -- Fiction 5. Mother-daughter relationship -- Fiction

ISBN 978-1-4424-2052-6; 1-4424-2052-9

LC 2010042513

This is a "riveting novel. . . . The portrayal of Carmen's world . . . is unique and convincing. . . . Even readers without much interest in music will enjoy this exceptional novel." SLJ

Mass, Wendy

★ **Every** soul a star; a novel. Little, Brown and Co. 2008 322p $15.99; pa $6.99

Grades: 5 6 7 8 **Fic**

1. Friendship -- Fiction 2. Solar eclipses -- Fiction

ISBN 978-0-316-00256-1; 0-316-00256-9; 978-0-316-00257-8 pa; 0-316-00257-7 pa

LC 2008009259

Ally, Bree, and Jack meet at the one place the Great Eclipse can be seen in totality, each carrying the burden of different personal problems, which become dim when compared to the task they embark upon and the friendship they find.

Mass "combines astronomy and storytelling for a well-balanced look at friendships and the role they play in shaping identity. . . . Information about solar eclipses and astronomy is carefully woven into the plot to build drama and will almost certainly intrigue readers." Publ Wkly

Includes bibliographical references

Heaven looks a lot like the mall; a novel. Little, Brown 2007 251p $16.99

Grades: 8 9 10 11 12 **Fic**

1. School stories 2. Coma -- Fiction 3. Shopping centers and malls -- Fiction

ISBN 978-0-316-05851-3; 0-316-05851-3

LC 2007-12333

When high school junior Tessa Reynolds falls into a coma after getting hit in the head during gym class, she experiences heaven as the mall where her parents work, and she revisits key events from her life, causing her to reevaluate herself and how she wants to live.

"Tessa's journey and authentic voice is one that readers will appreciate. . . . Funny, thought-provoking, and at times heartbreaking, this story will entertain and inspire readers." SLJ

Jeremy Fink and the meaning of life. Little, Brown 2006 289p $15.99; pa $6.99

Grades: 5 6 7 8 **Fic**

1. Conduct of life -- Fiction 2. Father-son relationship -- Fiction

ISBN 978-0-316-05829-2; 0-316-05829-7; 978-0-316-05849-0 pa; 0-316-05849-1 pa

LC 2005037291

Just before his thirteenth birthday, Jeremy Fink receives a keyless locked box—set aside by his father before his death five years earlier—that purportedly contains the meaning of life.

"Mass fashions an adventure in which both journey and destination are worth the trip." Horn Book

A **mango** -shaped space; a novel. Little, Brown 2003 220p $16.95

Grades: 5 6 7 8 **Fic**

1. School stories 2. Synesthesia -- Fiction

ISBN 0-316-52388-7

LC 2002-72989

Afraid that she is crazy, thirteen-year-old Mia, who sees a special color with every letter, number, and sound, keeps this a secret until she becomes overwhelmed by school, changing relationships, and the loss of something important to her

"Mass skillfully conveys Mia's emotions, and readers will be intrigued with this fictional depiction of an actual, and fascinating, condition." Horn Book Guide

Pi in the sky; Wendy Mass. 1st ed. Little, Brown and Co. 2013 256 p. (hardcover) $17

Grades: 3 4 5 6 7 **Fic**

1. Creation -- Fiction 2. Science fiction 3. Earth -- Fiction 4. Universe -- Fiction

ISBN 0316089168; 9780316089166

LC 2012030638

In this humorous children's novel, by Wendy Mass, "Joss is the seventh son of the Supreme Overlord of the Universe, and all he gets to do is deliver pies. . . . But when Earth suddenly disappears, Joss is tasked with the not-so-simple job of bringing it back. With the help of an outspoken girl from Earth named Annika, Joss embarks on the adventure of a lifetime and learns that the universe is an even stranger place than he'd imagined." (Publisher's note)

Matas, Carol

After the war. Simon & Schuster Bks. for Young Readers 1996 116p map hardcover o.p. pa $4.99

Grades: 7 8 9 10 **Fic**

1. Jews -- Fiction 2. Holocaust, 1933-1945 -- Fiction

ISBN 0-689-80350-8; 0-689-80722-8

LC 95-43613

After being released from Buchenwald at the end of World War II, fifteen-year-old Ruth risks her life to lead a group of children across Europe to Palestine

"Rich in texture and simple in its honesty, this story resonates with feeling." Voice Youth Advocates

Followed by The garden

Matson, Morgan

Since you've been gone; Morgan Matson. Simon & Schuster Books for Young Readers 2014 464 p. (hardback) $17.99

Grades: 7 8 9 10 **Fic**

1. Friendship -- Fiction 2. Family life -- Fiction 3. Self-reliance -- Fiction 4. Dating (Social customs) -- Fiction 5. Connecticut -- Fiction 6. Best friends -- Fiction 7. Family life -- Connecticut

-- Fiction

ISBN 1442435003; 9781442435001; 9781442435018

LC 2013041617

In this book, by Morgan Matson, "Emily is about to take some risks and have the most unexpected summer ever. . . . Before Sloane, Emily didn't go to parties, she barely talked to guys, and she didn't do anything crazy. Enter Sloane, social tornado and the best kind of best friend—someone who yanks you out of your shell. But right before what should have been an epic summer, Sloane just...disappears. . . . There's just a random to-do list with thirteen bizarre tasks that Emily would never try." (Publisher's note)

"Emily feels lost when her best friend, Sloane, disappears without explanation. But Sloane left Emily a daunting to-do list (with items like 'kiss a stranger'), and Emily bravely takes on each task, finding new friends, confidence, and a crush along the way. A perfectly awkward protagonist; well-rounded, quirky supporting characters; and spot-on dialogue make this novel of self-discovery stand out." Horn Book

Matti, Truus

★ **Departure** time; translated from the Dutch by Nancy Forest-Flier. Namelos 2010 214p $18.95; pa $9.95

Grades: 5 6 7 8 **Fic**

1. Memory -- Fiction 2. Father-daughter relationship -- Fiction

ISBN 978-1-60898-087-1; 1-60898-087-1; 978-1-60898-009-3 pa; 1-60898-009-X pa

Original Dutch edition 2009

"A 10-year-old girl is lost in a surrealistic landscape—a red-earth desert threatened by an approaching storm. Nothing looks familiar. She can't remember how she got to this place. Alternating with this classic bad-dream setting, which is narrated in the third person, is a first-person, furious tirade by a girl who feels abandoned by her father and neglected by her mother. Readers will be intrigued by the way Matti interweaves these stories and tantalizes with the possible connections between them. . . . Remarkable and arresting and wholly original, this novel lingers in the mind long after the last page has been read." SLJ

★ **Mister** Orange; Truus Matti ; translated from the Dutch by Laura Watkinson. Enchanted Lion Books 2013 156 p. (hardcover) $16.95

Grades: 5 6 7 8 **Fic**

1. Historical fiction 2. Friendship -- Fiction 3. Child-adult relationship -- Fiction 4. Artists -- Fiction 5. World War, 1939-1945 -- Fiction 6. New York (N.Y.) -- History -- 1898-1951 -- Fiction 7. Family life -- New York (State) -- New York -- Fiction

ISBN 159270123X; 9781592701230

LC 2012051313

Mildred L. Batchelder Award (2014)

This children's story, by Truus Matti, translated by Laura Watkinson, is set in Manhattan in "1943. . . . Linus Muller works at the family grocery store in the east 70s. . . . One of his customers . . . arranges to have a crate of oranges delivered every other week. Over the course of these deliveries, an intimacy develops between Linus and . . . Mister Orange. In the peacefulness of Mister Orange's spare kitchen, they discuss the war, the future, freedom and imagination." (Publisher's note)

Mazer, Harry

A **boy** at war; a novel of Pearl Harbor. Simon & Schuster Bks. for Young Readers 2001 104p il hardcover o.p. pa $4.99

Grades: 7 8 9 10 **Fic**

1. Pearl Harbor (Oahu, Hawaii), Attack on, 1941 -- Fiction

ISBN 0-689-84161-2; 0-689-84160-4 pa

LC 00-49687

While fishing with his friends off Honolulu on December 7, 1941, teenaged Adam is caught in the midst of the Japanese attack and through the chaos of the subsequent days tries to find his father, a naval officer who was serving on the U.S.S. Arizona when the bombs fell

"Mazer's graphic, sensory descriptions give the narrative immediacy, putting readers alongside Adam, watching with him as 'pieces of the ship and pieces of men rained down around him.' . . . This is a thought-provoking, sobering account of the human costs of war." Horn Book Guide

Other titles in this series are:

A boy no more (2004)

Heroes don't run (2005)

A **boy** no more. Simon & Schuster Books for Young Readers 2004 136p hardcover o.p. pa $5.99

Grades: 7 8 9 10 **Fic**

1. California -- Fiction 2. World War, 1939-1945 -- Fiction

ISBN 0-689-85533-8; 978-1-4169-1404-4 pa; 1-4169-1404-8 pa

LC 2003-21130

Sequel to: A boy at war

After his father is killed in the attack on Pearl Harbor, Adam, his mother, and sister are evacuated from Hawaii to California, where he must deal with his feelings about the war, Japanese internment camps, his father, and his own identity.

"A satisfying coming-of-age story in a well-documented historical setting." Booklist

Heroes don't run; a novel of the Pacific War. Aladdin 2005 113p hardcover o.p. pa $5.99

Grades: 7 8 9 10 **Fic**

1. World War, 1939-1945 -- Fiction

ISBN 0-689-85534-6; 978-1-4169-3394-6 pa; 1-4169-3394-8 pa

LC 2004-10935

Sequel to: A boy no more

To honor his father who died during the Japanese invasion of Pearl Harbor, seventeen-year-old Adam Pelko eagerly enlists in the Marines in 1944, survives boot camp, and faces combat on the tiny island of Okinawa.

"The clear first-person narrative is terse and gripping, graphic about the slaughter and heartfelt about the loss." Booklist

★ The **last** mission. Dell 1981 188p pa $5.99

Grades: 7 8 9 10 **Fic**

1. Jews -- Fiction 2. Prisoners of war -- Fiction 3. World War, 1939-1945 -- Fiction

ISBN 0-440-94797-9

First published 1979 by Delacorte Press

In 1944 a 15-year-old Jewish boy tells his family he will travel in the West but instead, enlists in the United States Air Corps and is subsequently taken prisoner by the Germans.

"Told in a rapid journalistic style, occasionally peppered with barrack-room vulgarities, the story is a vivid and moving account of a boy's experience during World War II as well as a skillful, convincing portrayal of his misgivings as a Jew on enemy soil and of his ability to size up—in mature human fashion—the misery around him." Horn Book

Somebody, please tell me who I am; Harry Mazer and Peter Lerangis. 1st ed; Simon & Schuster Books for Young Readers 2012 148p. $15.99

Grades: 6 7 8 9 10 11 12 **Fic**

1. Family -- Fiction 2. Amnesia -- Fiction 3. Veterans -- Fiction
ISBN 9781416938958 (hardcover)

LC 2011006010

Schneider Family Book Award (2013)

In this book, "[i]n May, Ben tells his family and friends he's joining the army after graduation; in June, he goes off to basic training; in July, he's deployed to Iraq; in September, . . . [he] return[s] stateside with a traumatic brain injury. His girlfriend, his best friend, and his family, all sick with grief and worry, come together to support Ben as he struggles to recover and communicate." (Bulletin of the Center for Children's Books)

Mazer, Norma Fox

The **missing** girl. HarperTeen 2008 288p $16.99; lib bdg $17.89

Grades: 7 8 9 10 **Fic**

1. Sisters -- Fiction 2. Kidnapping -- Fiction 3. New York (State) -- Fiction 5. Child sexual abuse -- Fiction
ISBN 978-0-06-623776-3; 978-0-06-623777-0 lib bdg

LC 2007-09136

In Mallory, New York, as five sisters, aged eleven to seventeen, deal with assorted problems, conflicts, fears, and yearnings, a mysterious middle-aged man watches them, fascinated, deciding which one he likes the best.

"Fans of . . . classic tales of high-tension peril will appreciate the way this successfully plays on their deepest fears." Bull Cent Child Books

McAnulty, Stacy

The **miscalculations** of Lightning Girl; Stacy McAnulty. Random House 2018 304 p. (hardcover) $16.99

Grades: 4 5 6 7 8 **Fic**

1. Middle schools -- Fiction 2. Interpersonal relations -- Fiction 3. Savants (Savant syndrome) -- Fiction 4. Schools -- Fiction 5. Obsessive-compulsive disorder -- Fiction
ISBN 9781524767570; 9781524767587; 9781524767600

LC 2017021152

In this book, by Stacy McAnulty, "Lucy Callahan was struck by lightning. She doesn't remember it, but it changed her life forever. The zap gave her genius-level math skills, and ever since, Lucy has been homeschooled. Now, at 12 years old, she's technically ready for college. She just has to pass 1 more test--middle school! Lucy's grandma insists: Go to middle school for 1 year. Make 1 friend. Join 1 activity. And read 1 book (that's not a math textbook!)" (Publisher's note)

"McAnulty captures the drama and trauma of middle school with well-rounded and believable characters and a convincing and appealing story. The math focus (for instance, McAnulty nicely weaves information about pi and Fibonacci numbers) adds a useful STEM component as well." Booklist

McCaffrey, Anne

Dragon's fire; [by] Anne McCaffrey, Todd McCaffrey. 1st ed.; Del Rey/Ballantine Books 2006 366p $24.95

Grades: 7 8 9 10 11 12 **Fic**

1. Fantasy fiction 2. Dragons -- Fiction
ISBN 0-345-48028-7

LC 2006040236

"The deadly Thread has not fallen on Pern for nearly 200 turns, but it is due to in another 18, and the firestone needed by the dragons to breathe fire and fight Thread is in short supply. . . . A number of well-limned major characters move the plot forward with the long series' expected momentum, and as usual, the interactions between humans, dragons, fire lizards, and whers put the richly detailed story on a par with the rest of the Pern canon." Booklist

Dragonflight; volume 1 of The Dragonriders of Pern. Ballantine Bks. 1978 337p il (Dragonriders of Pern) hardcover o.p. pa $12.95

Grades: 8 9 10 11 12 Adult **Fic**

1. Fantasy fiction 2. Science fiction 3. Dragons -- Fiction
ISBN 0-345-27749-X; 0-345-48426-6 pa

LC 78-16707

First published 1968 in paperback. Based on two award winning stories entitled: Weyr search and Dragonrider. Many titles co-written by Todd McCaffrey

ALA YALSA Margaret A. Edwards Award (1999)

The planet Pern, originally colonized from Earth but long out of contact with it, has been periodically threatened by the deadly silver Threads which fall from the wandering Red Star. To combat them a life form on the planet was developed into winged, fire-breathing dragons. Humans with a high degree of empathy and telepathic power are needed to train and preserve these creatures. As the story begins, Pern has fallen into decay, the threat of the Red Star has been forgotten, the Dragonriders and dragons are reduced in number and in disrepute, and the evil Lord Fax has begun conquering neighboring holds.

Fantasy titles set on Pern include:
All the Weyrs of Pern (1991)
The chronicles of Pern: first fall (1993)
Dragon Harper (2007)
Dragon's fire (2006)
Dragon's kin (2003)
Dragon's time (2011)
Dragondrums (1979)
Dragonquest (1971)
Dragonsdawn (1988)
Dragonseye (1997)
Dragonsinger (1977)
Dragonsong (1976)
The masterharper of Pern (1998)
Morets: Dragonlady of Pern (1983)
Nerilka's story (1986)
The Renegades of Pern (1989)
The skies of Pern (2001)
White dragon (1978)

McCahan, Erin

The **lake** effect; by Erin McCahan. Dial Books, an imprint of Penguin Random House LLC 2017 391 p. (hardback) $17.99

Grades: 7 8 9 10 11 12 **Fic**

1. Bildungsromans 2. Romance fiction 3. Old age -- Fiction 4. Michigan, Lake -- Fiction 5. Family problems -- Fiction 6. Serbian Americans -- Fiction 7. Summer employment -- Fiction 8. Dating (Social customs) -- Fiction
ISBN 9781101625989; 9780803740525

LC 2016047984

In this coming-of-age novel, by Erin McCahan, "it's the summer after senior year, and Briggs Henry is out the door. He's leaving behind his ex-girlfriend and his parents' money troubles for Lake Michigan and its miles of sandy beaches, working a summer job as a personal assistant, and living in a gorgeous Victorian on the shore. . . . [But when] he gets there . . . his eighty-four-year-old boss tells him to put on a suit for her funeral." (Publisher's note)

"Observant, sarcastic, compelling, and very funny, narrator Briggs is entirely convincing and—ably abetted by an abundance of diverse characters—never less than good company." Kirkus

Love and other foreign words; by Erin McCahan. Dial Books, an imprint of Penguin Group (USA) Inc. 2014 336 p. (hardcover) $17.99

Grades: 8 9 10 11 12 Fic

1. Love -- Fiction 2. Romance fiction 3. Sisters -- Fiction 4. Friendship -- Fiction 5. Interpersonal relations -- Fiction 6. Best friends -- Fiction 7. Interpersonal communication -- Fiction

ISBN 0803740514; 9780803740518

LC 2013027095

In this book, by Erin McCahan, "[s]ixteen-year-old Josie lives her life in translation. She speaks High School, College, Friends, Boyfriends, Break-ups, and even the language of Beautiful Girls. But none of these is her native tongue--the only people who speak that are her best friend Stu and her sister Kate. So when Kate gets engaged to an epically insufferable guy, how can Josie see it as anything but the mistake of a lifetime?" (Publisher's note)

"Josie doesn't like change. So when her sister Kate announces she's going to marry Geoff, Josie immediately tries everything to alienate him. But she also becomes curious about the nature of love and, with the help of her friends and family, tries to understand it. The highlight of this effectively drawn, often funny novel is its smart, precocious, and irrepressibly inquisitive protagonist." Horn Book

Mccall, Guadalupe Garcia

All the stars denied; by Guadalupe García McCall. Tu Books, an imprint of Lee & Low Books Inc. 2018 336 p. (hardback) $19.95

Grades: 6 7 8 9 10 Fic

1. Race relations -- Fiction 2. Mexican Americans -- Fiction 3. Depressions -- 1929 -- Fiction 4. Deportation -- Fiction 5. Family life -- Texas -- Fiction 6. Texas -- History -- 20th century -- Fiction

ISBN 9781620142813; 9781620142837

LC 2017058034

In this book, by Guadalupe García McCall, "when Estrella organizes a protest against the treatment of tejanos in their town of Monteseco, Texas, her whole family becomes a target of repatriation efforts to send Mexicans back to Mexico whether they were ever Mexican citizens or not. Dumped across the border and separated from half her family, Estrella must figure out a way to survive and care for her mother and baby brother." (Publisher's note)

Shame the Stars; by Guadalupe Garcia McCall. Lee & Low Books 2016 320 p. illustrations $19.95

Grades: 6 7 8 9 Fic

1. Texas -- Fiction 2. Historical fiction

ISBN 1620142783; 9781620142783

LC 2016031436

In this book, by Guadalupe Garcia McCall, "eighteen-year-old Joaquin del Toro's future looks bright. With his older brother in the priesthood, he s set to inherit his family s Texas ranch. He s in love with Dulcena and she s in love with him. But it s 1915, and trouble has been brewing along the US-Mexico border. On one side, the Mexican Revolution is taking hold; on the other, Texas Rangers fight Tejano insurgents, and ordinary citizens are caught in the middle." (Publisher's note)

"Pura Belpré winner McCall delivers an ambitious, sardonically relevant historical novel—a must-read, complex twist on a political Shakespearean tragedy." Kirkus

Includes bibliographical references.

★ **Under** the mesquite. Lee & Low Books 2011 224p $17.95

Grades: 7 8 9 10 11 12 Fic

1. Texas -- Fiction 2. Cancer -- Fiction 3. Family life -- Fiction 4. Mexican Americans -- Fiction

ISBN 978-1-60060-429-4; 1-60060-429-3; 978-1-60060-875-9 ebook

LC 2010052567

"With poignant imagery and well-placed Spanish, the author effectively captures the complex lives of teenagers in many Latino and/or immigrant families." Kirkus

McCarthy, Andrew

Just fly away; Andrew McCarthy. Algonquin Young Readers 2017 260 p. (hardcover) $17.95

Grades: 7 8 9 10 11 12 Fic

1. Family secrets -- fiction 3. Father-daughter relationship -- fiction 4. Secrecy -- fiction 5. Families -- fiction 6. Brothers and sisters -- fiction

ISBN 9781616207113; 9781616206291

LC 2016038077

In this novel, by Andrew McCarthy, "when 15-year-old Lucy Willows discovers that her father has a child from a brief affair, . . . she begins to question everything she thinks she knows about her home and her life. . . . Lucy grows more and more isolated from her friends, her family, and even her boyfriend, Simon. . . . When Lucy escapes to Maine, the home of her mysteriously estranged grandfather, she finally begins to get to the bottom of her family's secrets and lies." (Publisher's note)

"This is a moving coming-of-age story for young adults who enjoy calm, character-driven reading." VOYA

McCaughrean, Geraldine

The **glorious** adventures of the Sunshine Queen. Harper 2011 325p $16.99

Grades: 5 6 7 8 Fic

1. Adventure fiction 2. Theater -- Fiction 3. Missouri River -- Fiction

ISBN 978-0-06-200806-0; 0-06-200806-4

LC 2010021958

Sequel to: Stop the train! (2003)

When a diphtheria outbreak forces twelve-year-old Cissy to leave her Oklahoma hometown in the 1890s, she and her two classmates embark on a wild adventure down the Missouri River with a team of traveling actors who are living on a dilapidated paddle steamer.

"McCaughrean invests her characters with humanity and shows a farcical sense for dialogue, while her arch narrative voice, includes the theatrical and clever turns of phrase." Booklist

The **white** darkness. HarperTempest 2007 384p hardcover o.p. pa $8.99

Grades: 8 9 10 11 12 Fic

1. Antarctica -- Fiction 2. Wilderness survival -- Fiction

ISBN 978-0-06-089035-3; 0-06-089035-5; 978-0-06-089037-7 pa; 0-06-089037-1 pa

LC 2006-02503

First published 2005 in the United Kingdom

Michael L. Printz Award, 2008

Taken to Antarctica by the man she thinks of as her uncle for what she believes to be a vacation, Symone—a troubled fourteen year old—discovers that he is dangerously obsessed with seeking Symme's Hole, an opening that supposedly leads into the center of a hollow Earth.

"McCaughrean's lyrical language actively engages the senses, plunging readers into a captivating landscape that challenges the boundaries of reality." Booklist

McClintock, Norah

Out of tune; Norah McClintock. Orca Book Publishers 2017 222 p. (Riley Donovan mystery) (paperback) $10.95

Grades: 7 8 9 10 **Fic**

1. Mystery fiction 2. High school students -- Fiction 3. Murder -- Investigation -- Fiction 4. Musicians -- fiction

ISBN 9781459814677; 9781459814660; 9781459814653

LC 2017933015

In this book, by Norah McClintock, "when Alicia, a talented violinist at Riley Donovan's high school, is found bludgeoned to death in a field on the outskirts of town, suspicion immediately falls on Carrie, the teen's musical rival. But Riley isn't convinced of Carrie's guilt, and even though her police-officer aunt tells her to stay out of it, Riley goes searching for the truth. Did Carrie really kill Alicia in a fit of jealous rage, or is there another explanation for Alicia's death?" (Publisher's note)

"The plot is complex and tightly woven, the reveal is both surprising and satisfying, the violence is prominent but tastefully presented, and Riley continues to be a strong and relatable protagonist with good moral fiber." Booklist

She said/she saw. Orca Book Publishers 2011 211p pa $12.95

Grades: 7 8 9 10 **Fic**

1. Homicide -- Fiction 2. Witnesses -- Fiction 3. Criminal investigation -- Fiction

ISBN 1-55469-335-7 pa; 978-1-55469-335-1 pa

When Tegan's two best friends are gunned down in front of her, nobody believes her that she didn't see who did it and doesn't know why.

"The brisk pace, solid character development and inventive structuring make for fast, page-turning reading, and at all wraps up with an unpredictable plot twist and ending. Mysterious and haunting, packed with hard truths about adolescence." Kirkus

Taken. Orca Book Publishers 2009 166p pa $12.95

Grades: 7 8 9 10 **Fic**

1. Kidnapping -- Fiction 2. Wilderness survival -- Fiction

ISBN 978-1-55469-152-4; 1-55469-152-4

"After two girls from a nearby town go missing everyone goes on high alert, suspecting a serial killer, and while walking home, Stephanie is grabbed from behind and injected with a drug that knocks her out. She awakens hours later to find herself tied up in an abandoned cabin deep in a densely wooded area. . . . Her harrowing journey back to safety propels this plot-driven, fast-paced tale forward. . . . Told in the first person, this suspenseful survival story is sure to have strong appeal." Kirkus

Trial by fire; Norah McClintock. Orca Book Pub 2016 231 p. (Riley Donovan mystery) (paperback) $10.95

Grades: 7 8 9 10 **Fic**

1. Mystery fiction 2. Arson -- fiction 3. Prejudices -- fiction 4. Immigrants -- fiction

ISBN 9781459809383; 9781459809376; 9781459809369; 145980936X

LC 2015946343

In this novel in the Riley Donovan series, by Norah McClintock, "Riley Donovan is the new kid in a small town where her aunt . . . [is] a detective on the town's police force. Riley is home alone when a neighbor's barn catches on fire; . . . she calls 9-1-1 and then tries to save him. . . . Riley finds herself the target of vandalism and violence. . . . Riley . . . uncovers the depth of the town's prejudice and corruption, and figures out who is targeting Mr. Goran--and why." (Publisher's note)

"The mystery is compelling, the ending surprising, the protagonist plucky, and the language appealing for reluctant and avid readers alike, while the small-town race issues ground it as a discussion piece." Booklist

Other titles in this series are:
From above (2016)
Out of tune (2017)

McCormick, Patricia, 1956-

Cut. Front St. 2000 168p $16.95

Grades: 7 8 9 10 **Fic**

1. Family problems 2. Self-mutilation 3. Emotional problems 4. Psychiatric hospitals 5. Self-mutilation -- Fiction 6. Psychiatric hospitals -- Fiction

ISBN 1-88691-061-8

LC 00-34840

While confined to a mental hospital, thirteen-year-old Callie slowly comes to understand some of the reasons behind her self-mutilation, and gradually starts to get better. "Age twelve and up." (N Y Times Book Rev)

"Realistic, sensitive, and heartfelt." Voice Youth Advocates

Purple Heart. Balzer + Bray 2009 198p $16.99; lib bdg $17.89; pa $8.99

Grades: 7 8 9 10 **Fic**

1. Iraq War, 2003-2011 2. Memory -- Fiction 3. Soldiers -- Fiction 4. Hospitals -- Fiction 5. Iraq War, 2003-2011 -- Fiction 6. Brain -- Wounds and injuries -- Fiction

ISBN 978-0-06-173090-0; 0-06-173090-4; 978-0-06-173091-7 lib bdg; 0-06-173091-2 lib bdg; 978-0-06-173092-4 pa; 0-06-173092-0 pa

LC 2009-1757

While recuperating in a Baghdad hospital from a traumatic brain injury sustained during the Iraq War, eighteen-year-old soldier Matt Duffy struggles to recall what happened to him and how it relates to his ten-year-old friend, Ali.

"Strong characters heighten the drama. . . . McCormick raises moral questions without judgment and will have readers examining not only this conflict but the nature of heroism and war." Publ Wkly

McCoy, Chris

The **prom** goer's interstellar excursion; by Chris McCoy. Alfred A. Knopf 2015 304 p. $17.99

Grades: 8 9 10 11 12 **Fic**

1. Science fiction 2. Adventure fiction 3. Interplanetary voyages -- Fiction 4. Dating (Social customs) -- Fiction 5. Extraterrestrial beings -- Fiction 6. Humorous stories 7. Bands (Music) -- Fiction 8. Alien abduction -- Fiction

ISBN 9780375855993; 9780375955990

LC 2013045875

In this book, by Chris McCoy, "Bennett pulls off something he never imagined possible: his dream girl, Sophie, agrees to be his date [to the prom]. Moments afterward, however, he watches Sophie get abducted by aliens in the middle of the New Mexico desert. Faced with a dateless prom (and likely kidnapping charges), Bennett does the only thing he can think of: he catches a ride into outer space with a band of extraterrestrial musicians to bring her back." (Publisher's note)

"Readers will root for Bennett to get the girl and even for crusty band member Skark to accomplish his dream of becoming better than the one billionth and sixteenth band in the universe. The book's ending is a nicely placed, realistic surprise. Witty and action-packed, the plot boldly glazes over science-fiction details in favor of well-wrought characters." SLJ

McCoy, Mary

I, Claudia; Mary McCoy. Carolrhoda Lab 2018 418 p. (hardback) $18.99

Grades: 8 9 10 11 12 **Fic**

1. School stories 2. Student government -- Fiction 3. High school students -- Fiction 4. Schools -- Fiction 5. High schools -- Fiction 6. Conduct of life -- Fiction 7. Los Angeles (Calif.) -- Fiction 8. People with disabilities -- Fiction 9. Family life -- California -- Los Angeles -- Fiction

ISBN 9781512448467

LC 2017038714

Printz Honor Book (2019)

In this book, by Mary McCoy, "teen historian Claudia McCarthy . . . [become] in charge of Imperial Day Academy. . . . Suddenly, Claudia is wielding power over her fellow students that she never expected to have and isn't sure she wants. Claudia vows to use her power to help the school. But there are forces aligned against her. . . . As Claudia struggles to be a force for good in the universe, she wrestles with the question: does power inevitably corrupt?" (Publisher's note)

McCrite, K. D.

In front of God and everybody. Thomas Nelson 2011 298p (Confessions of April Grace) pa $9.99

Grades: 4 5 6 7 **Fic**

1. Arkansas -- Fiction 2. Farm life -- Fiction 3. Christian life -- Fiction 4. Swindlers and swindling -- Fiction

ISBN 978-1-4003-1722-6; 1-4003-1722-3

LC 2011005583

In the summer of 1986, eleven-year-old April Grace, who lives on a rural Arkansas farm with her family, across a field from her grandmother, has her sense of Christian charity tested when a snooty couple from San Francisco moves into a dilapidated house down the road and her grandmother takes up with a loud, obnoxious, and suspicious-acting Texan.

"With keen eyes and good humor, April Grace notes the quirks, presumptions, and motivations of family and neighbors; she has plenty of fodder—the characters' personalities are dialed up to 11." Publ Wkly

McDonald, Abby

The **anti** -prom. Candlewick Press 2011 280p $16.99

Grades: 8 9 10 11 **Fic**

1. School stories

ISBN 978-0-7636-4956-2; 0-7636-4956-2

LC 2010-39170

On prom night, Bliss, Jolene, and Meg, students from the same high school who barely know one another, band together to get revenge against Bliss's boyfriend and her best friend, whom she caught together in the limousine they rented.

"McDonald instills more intelligence than you'd expect from such a plot while not skimping on the simple pleasures, either." Booklist

McDonald, Janet

Harlem Hustle. Frances Foster Books 2006 182p $16

Grades: 8 9 10 11 **Fic**

1. Rap music -- Fiction 2. African Americans -- Fiction 3. Harlem (New York, N.Y.) -- Fiction

ISBN 978-0-374-37184-5; 0-374-37184-9

LC 2005-52108

Eric "Hustle" Samson, a smart and streetwise seventeen-year-old dropout from Harlem, aspires to rap stardom, a dream he naively believes is about to come true.

"The author nails the hip-hop lingo and the street slang, and her characters strike just the right attitude. . . . Young adults will love this book." SLJ

McDunn, Gillian

Caterpillar summer; by Gillian McDunn. Bloomsbury 2019 304 p. (hardcover) $16.99

Grades: 4 5 6 7 8 **Fic**

1. Family life -- Fiction 2. Grandparents -- Fiction 3. Brothers and sisters -- Fiction 4. Islands -- Fiction 5. North Carolina -- Fiction 6. Responsibility -- Fiction 7. Family problems -- Fiction 8. Single-parent families -- Fiction 9. Family life -- North Carolina -- Fiction

ISBN 9781681197432

LC 2018010841

In this book, by Gillian McDunn, "Cat has been the glue holding her family together. But even the strongest glue sometimes struggles to hold. When a summer trip doesn't go according to plan, Cat and Chicken end up spending three weeks with grandparents they never knew. . . . Cat has the opportunity to be a kid again, and the journey she takes shows that even the most broken . . . relationships can be healed if people take the time to walk in one another's shoes." (Publisher's note)

"An engrossing, heartwarming, beautifully written debut about building and rebuilding family ties." Kirkus

McElligott, Matthew

Benjamin Franklinstein lives! [by] Matthew McElligott & Larry Tuxbury; illustrated by Matthew McElligott. G. P. Putnam's Sons 2010 121p il $12.99

Grades: 4 5 6 7 **Fic**

1. Authors 2. Diplomats 3. Inventors 4. Statesmen 5. Scientists 6. Science fiction 7. Writers on science 8. Zombies -- Fiction 9. Members of Congress

ISBN 978-0-399-25229-7; 0-399-25229-0

While working on a science fair project, a Philadelphia school boy discovers both a secret laboratory in his basement and Benjamin Franklin, who comes to life after receiving a jolt of electricity.

"It's a light fun read, and McElligott's many diagrams, graphs, and drawings are a nice addition." Booklist

Followed by: Benjamin Franklinstein meets the fright brothers (2011)

Benjamin Franklinstein meets the Fright brothers; by Matthew McElligott and Larry Tuxbury; [illustrated by Matthew McElligott] G. P. Putnam's Sons 2011 147p il $16.99

Grades: 4 5 6 7 **Fic**

1. Authors 2. Diplomats 3. Inventors 4. Statesmen 5. Scientists 6. Writers on science 7. Members of Congress 8. Scientists -- Fiction 9. Secret societies -- Fiction

ISBN 978-0-399-25480-2; 0-399-25480-3

LC 2010040431

Sequel to: Benjamin Franklinstein lives! (2010)

Victor and his friends, aided by Benjamin Franklin, uncover an evil scheme involving giant bats and two mysterious brothers, and learn more about the secretive Modern Order of Prometheus.

"Enhanced by frequent charts, diagrams, lists and other visual aids, a spirit of rational (if often reckless) scientific inquiry pervades the tale, as Ben and his allies translate coded messages, analyze evidence, get a lesson in meteorology and conduct experiments using both real and science-fictional gear on the way to a literally electrifying climax. . . . The authors have way too much fun taking the opener's premise and evil conspiracy to the next level. Readers will too." Kirkus

McEntire, Myra

Hourglass. Egmont USA 2011 390p $17.99

Grades: 7 8 9 10 **Fic**

1. Science fiction 2. Orphans -- Fiction 2. Homicide -- Fiction 3. Siblings -- Fiction 4. Parapsychology -- Fiction 5. Space and time -- Fiction

ISBN 1-60684-144-0; 978-1-60684-144-0

LC 2010-43618

Seventeen-year-old Emerson uses her power to manipulate time to help Michael, a consultant hired by her brother, to prevent a murder that happened six months ago. "Grades seven to ten." (Bull Cent Child Books)

"Em is an entertainingly cheeky narrator and appealingly resilient heroine. . . . McEntire deftly juggles plot, characters and dialogue; her portrait of grief is particularly poignant." Kirkus

McGarry, Katie

Only a breath apart; Katie McGarry. Tor Teen 2019 368 p. (hardcover) $17.99

Grades: 8 9 10 11 12 **Fic**

1. Love -- Fiction 2. Friendship -- Fiction 3. Farms -- Fiction 4. Best friends -- Fiction 5. Family problems -- Fiction

ISBN 9781250193858

LC 2018044554

In this novel, by Katie McGarry, "the only curse Jesse Lachlin believes in is his grandmother's will: in order to inherit his family farm he must win the approval of his childhood best friend, the girl he froze out his freshman year. A fortuneteller tells Scarlett she's psychic, but what is real is Scarlett's father's controlling attitude and the dark secrets at home. She may be able to escape, but only if she can rely on the one boy who broke her heart." (Publisher's note)

"The novel manages to tackle domestic violence in a way that never feels clichéd, and the romance is sure to win over even the most cynical reader." Booklist

McGraw, Eloise Jarvis

The **moorchild**; [by] Eloise McGraw. Margaret K. McElderry Bks. 1996 241p $17; pa $5.99

Grades: 4 5 6 7 **Fic**

1. Fantasy fiction 2. Fairies -- Fiction

ISBN 0-689-80654-X; 1-4169-2768-9 pa

LC 95-34107

A Newbery Medal honor book, 1997

"Incorporating some classic fantasy motifs and icons, McGraw . . . conjures up an appreciably familiar world that, as evidence of her storytelling power, still strikes an original chord." Publ Wkly

McGuigan, Mary Ann

Morning in a different place. Front Street 2009 195p $17.95

Grades: 7 8 9 10 **Fic**

1. Friendship -- Fiction 2. Race relations -- Fiction 3. African Americans -- Fiction 4. Bronx (New York, N.Y.) -- Fiction

ISBN 978-1-59078-551-5; 1-59078-551-7

LC 2007-17547

In 1963 in the Bronx, New York, eighth-graders Fiona and Yolanda help one another face hard decisions at home despite family and social opposition to their interracial friendship, but Fiona is on her own when popular classmates start paying attention to her and give her a glimpse of both a different way of life and a new kind of hatefulness.

This book is "never didactic. McGuigan's writing is spare and low-key, and her metaphors are acute." Booklist

McIntosh, Will, 1962-

Watchdog; Will McIntosh. Delacorte Press 2017 192 p. (hc) $16.99

Grades: 4 5 6 7 8 **Fic**

1. Robots -- Fiction 2. Orphans -- Fiction 3. Criminals -- Fiction 4. Brothers and sisters -- Fiction 5. Science fiction 6. Twins -- Fiction 7. Autism -- Fiction 8. Homeless persons -- Fiction

ISBN 9781524713843; 9781524713867

LC 2016049554

In this book, by Will McIntosh, "twins Vick and Tara have built an incredible machine--a loyal robotic watchdog named Daisy. But, when local crime boss Ms. Alba schemes to add Daisy to her robot army, Vick and Tara must go to great lengths to protect their prized pet. Because Daisy is more than just any robot--she's their constant protector, and together the three make a great team." (Publisher's note)

McKay, Hilary

★ **Binny** for short; by Hilary McKay and illustrated by Micah Player. Margaret K. McElderry Books 2013 291 p. (hardcover) $16.99

Grades: 4 5 6 7 **Fic**

1. Aunts -- Fiction 2. Family -- fiction 3. Ghosts -- literature 4. Family life -- Fiction 5. Loss (Psychology) -- Fiction 6. Moving, Household -- Fiction

ISBN 1442482753; 9781442482753

LC 2013000053

In this book, by Hilary McKay and illustrated by Micah Player, "Aunty Violet has died, and left Binny and her family an old house in a seaside town. Binny is faced with a new crush, a new frenemy, and a ghost. It seems Aunty Violet may not have completely departed. [For Binny] it's odd being haunted by her aunt, but there is also the warmth of a busy and loving mother, a musical older sister, and a hilarious little brother, who is busy with his experiments." (Publisher's note)

Other titles in this series are:

Binny in secret (2015)

Binny bewitched (2017)

Caddy ever after; 1st ed.; Margaret K. McElderry Books 2006 218p $15.95

Grades: 5 6 7 8 **Fic**

1. Weddings -- Fiction 2. Family life -- Fiction 3. Great Britain -- Fiction

ISBN 1-4169-0930-3

LC 2005-31449

Sequel to Permanent Rose (2005)

The four eccentric Casson siblings each contribute written accounts of the events—which include a Valentine's Day dance, the appearance of a sinister balloon, and the breakdown of a car—that lead to Caddy's wedding day.

"The depth of the story is conveyed in the dynamic of this family that is at times both touching and hilarious." SLJ

Followed by Forever Rose (2008)

Forever Rose. Margaret K. McElderry Books 2008 304p $16.99

Grades: 5 6 7 8 **Fic**

1. Christmas -- Fiction 2. Family life -- Fiction 3. Great Britain -- Fiction

ISBN 978-1-4169-5486-6; 1-4169-5486-4

LC 2007-15273

Sequel to Caddy ever after (2006)

As Christmas approaches, eleven-year-old Rose, the youngest member of the eccentric Casson family, discovers that life is filled with both catastrophic problems and wonderful surprises.

"Those who know the characters will rejoice in this final sly, celebratory view of a messy, imperfect, and fiercely loving family." Booklist

Indigo's star; [by] Hilary McKay. Margaret K. McElderry Books 2004 272p $15.95

Grades: 5 6 7 8 **Fic**

1. Family life -- Fiction 2. Great Britain -- Fiction

ISBN 0-689-86563-5

LC 2003-9941

Sequel to Saffy's angel (2002)

First published 2003 in the United Kingdom

Spurred on by his youngest sister, Rose, twelve-year-old Indigo sticks up for himself and an American boy who has replaced him as the primary target of the school bullies.

This offers "sly humor, deft characterization, and brisk pacing. . . . Readers will love revisiting the chaotic but loving Casson household." SLJ

Followed by Permanent Rose (2005)

Love to everyone; Hilary McKay. Margaret K. McElderry Books 2018 336 p. (hardback) $17.99

Grades: 5 6 7 8 9 **Fic**

1. Family problems -- Fiction 2. World War, 1914-1918 -- Fiction 3. Great Britain -- History -- Edward VII, 1901-1910 -- Fiction 4. Family life -- England -- Fiction 5. Great Britain -- History -- George V, 1910-1936 -- Fiction

ISBN 9781534427105; 9781534427112

LC 2017047702

In this book, by Hilary McKay, "Clarry Penrose finds the good in everyone. . . . Her grandparents, who care for her in the summers, assume that she'll play nicely and do what she's told. . . . But Clarry longs for a life of her own. She wants to dive off cliffs and go swimming with her brother Peter and cousin Rupert. . . . Then Rupert is declared missing, and Clarry is devastated. Now she must take a momentous step into the wide world." (Publisher's note)

Includes bibliographical references

Permanent Rose. Margaret K. McElderry Books 2005 234p $16.99

Grades: 5 6 7 8 **Fic**

1. Friendship -- Fiction 2. Family life -- Fiction 3. Great Britain -- Fiction

ISBN 1-4169-0372-0; 978-1-4169-0372-7

LC 2004-25891

Sequel to Indigo's star (2004)

While trying to reconnect with her friend Tom, who has returned to the United States without leaving a forwarding address, eight-year-old Rose inadvertently discovers the identity of her adopted sister Saffy's father.

The "narration is engaging and energetic. . . . The rainbow of experiences and the quick-moving plot will enthrall listeners." SLJ

Followed by Caddy ever after (2006)

★ **Saffy's** angel. Margaret K. McElderry Bks. 2002 152p $16; pa $4.99

Grades: 5 6 7 8 **Fic**

1. Adoption -- Fiction 2. Family life -- Fiction 3. Great Britain -- Fiction

ISBN 0-689-84933-8; 0-689-84934-6 pa

LC 2001-44110

First published 2001 in the United Kingdom

Boston Globe-Horn Book Award Honor: Fiction (2002)

After learning that she was adopted, thirteen-year-old Saffron's relationship with her eccentric, artistic family changes, until they help her go back to Italy where she was born to find a special momento of her past

"Like the Casson household itself, the plot is a chaotic whirl that careens off in several directions simultaneously. But McKay always skillfully draws each clearly defined character back into the story with witty, well-edited details; rapid dialogue; and fine pacing." Booklist

Other titles in this series are:

Indigo's star (2004)

Permanent Rose (2005)

Caddy ever after (2006)

Forever Rose (2008)

McKay, Sharon E.

Enemy territory; Sharon McKay. Annick Press 2012 184 p. $21.95

Grades: 6 7 8 9 10 11 12 **Fic**

1. Toleration -- Fiction 2. Friendship -- Fiction 3. Israel-Arab conflicts -- Fiction

ISBN 1554514312; 9781554514311

In author Sharon E. McKay's book, "Sam, an Israeli teen whose leg may have to be amputated, and Yusuf, a Palestinian teen who has lost his left eye, find themselves uneasy roommates in a Jerusalem hospital. One night, the boys decide to slip away while the nurses aren't looking and go on an adventure to the Old City. . . . They band together to find their way home and to defend themselves against unfriendly locals, arrest by the military police, and an encounter with a deadly desert snake." (Publisher's note)

Thunder over Kandahar; photographs by Rafal Gerszak. Annick Press 2010 260p il $21.95; pa $12.95

Grades: 7 8 9 10 11 12 **Fic**

1. Afghanistan -- Fiction 2. Afghan War, 2001- -- Fiction

ISBN 978-1-55451-267-6; 1-55451-267-0; 978-1-55451-266-9 pa; 1-55451-266-2 pa

"When her British and American-educated parents' return to Afghanistan is cut short by a terrible attack, 14-year-old Yasmine is sent to Kandahar for safety. Instead, the driver abandons her and her friend Tamanna along the way, and they must travel on their own through Taliban-controlled mountains. . . . In spite of unrelenting violence, along with grinding poverty, restrictive customs, and the horrors of war, what shines through this sad narrative is the love Afghans have for their country. . . . [The author] traveled to Afghanistan and provides numerous credits for this gripping tale." SLJ

McKenzie, Paige

The **awakening** of Sunshine girl; Paige McKenzie with Alyssa Sheinmel ; story by Nick Hagen & Alyssa Sheinmel ; based on the web series created by Nick Hagen ; illustrations by Paige McKenzie. Weinstein Books 2016 296 p. illustrations (Haunting of Sunshine girl) (hardcover) $16

Grades: 7 8 9 **Fic**

1. Ghosts -- fiction 2. Supernatural -- fiction 3. Teenage girls -- fiction 4. Mexico -- fiction

ISBN 9781602863125; 9781602865822; 9781602862746; 1602862745

LC 2015431358

In this novel in the Haunting of Sunshine Girl series, by Paige McKenzie and Alyssa Sheinmel, "Sunshine's Luiseach powers are now fully awakened for months now Sunshine has felt spirits everywhere heard voices felt emotions intense and sometimes overwhelming. . . . Hoping to get her powers under control and hoping for answers to her never ending questions she agrees to undergo training with her Luiseach mentor even though she still hopes to give up her powers someday." (Publisher's note)

The **Haunting** of Sunshine Girl; Book one Paige McKenzie with Alyssa Sheinmel ; story by Nick Hagen & Alyssa Sheinmel based on the web series created by Nick Hagen. Weinstein Books 2015 296 p. (Haunting of Sunshine Girl) (hardcover) $16

Grades: 7 8 9 **Fic**

1. Girls -- Fiction 2. Haunted houses -- Fiction 3. Adopted children -- Fiction 4. Washington (State) -- Fiction 5. Mothers and daughters -- Fiction

ISBN 9781602862722; 1602862729

In this book in The Haunting of Sunshine Girl Series, by Paige McKenzie and Alyssa Sheinmel, "after her sixteenth birthday, Sunshine Griffith and her mother Kat move from sunny Austin, Texas, to the . . . town of Ridgemont, Washington. . . . But from the moment they arrive, Sunshine feels her world darken with an eeriness she cannot place. And even if Kat doesn't recognize it, Sunshine knows that something about their new house is just . . . creepy." (Publisher's note)

"Sunshine's adventure is filled with bumps in the night and shadowy figures, alluding to a larger mystery and larger world that has plenty to offer imaginative readers who grew up on Goosebumps and the like. Suspenseful, exciting and endlessly entertaining." Kirkus

Other titles in this series are:

The Awakening of Sunshine Girl (2016)

The Sacrifice of Sunshine Girl (2017)

McKernan, Victoria

Shackleton's stowaway. Knopf 2005 336p $15.95; lib bdg $17.99

Grades: 7 8 9 10 **Fic**

1. Explorers 2. Adventure fiction 3. Endurance (Ship) -- Fiction 4. Survival after airplane accidents, shipwrecks, etc. -- Fiction

ISBN 0-375-82691-2; 0-375-92691-7 lib bdg

LC 2004-10313

A fictionalized account of the adventures of eighteen-year-old Perce Blackborow, who stowed away for the 1914 Shackleton Antarctic expedition and, after their ship Endurance was crushed by ice, endured many hardships, including the loss of the toes of his left foot to frostbite, during the nearly two-year return journey across sea and ice

"This book provides historical information for history and geography classes who are interested in exploration, the Antarctic, and early history of great sea voyages." Libr Media Connect

McKinlay, Meg

Below; Meg McKinlay. Candlewick Press 2013 224 p. (reinforced) $15.99

Grades: 4 5 6 7 **Fic**

1. Reservoirs -- Fiction 2. Extinct cities -- Fiction

ISBN 0763661260; 9780763661267

LC 2012943652

In this book by Meg McKinlay, "Cassie was . . . the first baby born in the Australian town of New Lower Grange, which was established after the intentional flooding of the previous town to accommodate a dam. . . . [S]he feels the pull of the forbidden lake above Old Lower Grange. There, she is joined by Liam, a classmate whose life was altered in a tragic accident, and together they search for the truth about the town's past as its centenary celebration approaches." (Publishers Weekly)

"Although the author does a masterful job of making sure all the pieces fit at the end, the central mystery is hard to buy. This is mitigated by a reasonably suspenseful climax, an earned family solidarity message and the lesson: that to find the truth, one must delve below the surface. A quietly intriguing meditation on history and truth." Kirkus

McKinley, Robin

★ **Beauty**; a retelling of the story of Beauty & the beast. Harper & Row 1978 247p $15.99; pa $5.99

Grades: 7 8 9 10 **Fic**

1. Fairy tales

ISBN 0-06-024149-7; 0-06-440477-3 pa

LC 77-25636

"McKinley's version of this folktale is embellished with rich descriptions and settings and detailed characterizations. The author has not modernized the story but varied the traditional version to attract modern readers. The values of love, honor, and beauty are placed in a magical setting that will please the reader of fantasy." Shapiro. Fic for Youth. 3d edition

★ The **blue** sword. Greenwillow Bks. 1982 272p $17.99; pa $6.99

Grades: 7 8 9 10 **Fic**

1. Fantasy fiction

ISBN 0-688-00938-7; 0-441-06880-4 pa

LC 82-2895

A Newbery Medal honor book, 1983

Harry, bored with her sheltered life in the remote orange-growing colony of Daria, discovers magic in herself when she is kidnapped by a native king with mysterious powers.

"This is a zesty, romantic, heroic fantasy with an appealing stalwart heroine, a finely realixed mythical kingdom, and a grounding in reality." Booklist

Chalice. G.P. Putnam's Sons 2008 263p $18.99

Grades: 7 8 9 10 11 12 **Fic**

1. Fantasy fiction 2. Bees -- Fiction

ISBN 978-0-399-24676-0; 0-399-24676-2

LC 2008-704

A beekeeper by trade, Mirasol's life changes completely when she is named the new Chalice, the most important advisor to the new Master, a former priest of fire.

"The fantasy realm is evoked in thorough and telling detail. . . . A lavish and lasting treat." Publ Wkly

★ The **hero** and the crown. Greenwillow Bks. 1985 246p lib bdg $16.99

Grades: 6 7 8 9 Fic
1. Fantasy fiction
ISBN 0-688-02593-5
LC 84-4074

Awarded the Newbery Medal, 1985

The author "has in this suspenseful prequel . . . created an utterly engrossing fantasy, replete with a fairly mature romantic subplot as well as adventure." N Y Times Book Rev

Pegasus. G.P. Putnam's Sons 2010 404p $18.99
Grades: 8 9 10 11 12 Fic
1. Fantasy fiction 2. Magic -- Fiction 3. Princesses -- Fiction 4. Pegasus (Greek mythology) -- Fiction
ISBN 0-399-24677-0; 978-0-399-24677-7
LC 2010-2279

Because of a thousand-year-old alliance between humans and pegasi, Princess Sylvi is ceremonially bound to Ebon, her own pegasus, on her twelfth birthday, but the closeness of their bond becomes a threat to the status quo and possibly to the safety of their two nations.

"McKinley's storytelling is to be savored. She lavishes page after page upon rituals and ceremonies, basks in the awe of her intricately constructed world, and displays a masterful sense of pegasi physicality and mannerisms." Booklist

Rose daughter. Greenwillow Bks. 1997 306p pa $7.99
Grades: 7 8 9 10 Fic
1. Fairy tales
ISBN 0-688-15439-5; 0-441-00583-7 pa
LC 96-48783

Compared to Beauty, this "is fuller bodied, with richer characterizations and a more mystical, darker edge. . . . There is more background on the Beast in this version . . . and Beauty's choice at the end, a departure from that in Beauty, is just so right. Readers will be enchanted, in the best sense of the word." Booklist

McKissack, Pat, 1944-2017

A **friendship** for today. Scholastic Press 2007 172p $16.99
Grades: 4 5 6 7 Fic
1. Divorce -- Fiction 2. Missouri -- Fiction 3. Friendship -- Fiction 4. Race relations -- Fiction 5. African Americans -- Fiction 6. School integration -- Fiction
ISBN 978-0-439-66098-3
LC 2006-29293

In 1954, when desegregation comes to Kirkland, Missouri, ten-year-old Rosemary faces many changes and challenges at school and at home as her parents separate.

"A real, at times raw tale about a winning and insightful young heroine during a bittersweet era." Publ Wkly

★ **Nzingha,** warrior queen of Matamba; by Patricia McKissack. Scholastic 2000 136p (Royal diaries) hardcover o.p. O.P.
Grades: 5 6 7 8 Fic
1. Queens 2. Angola -- Fiction 3. Princesses -- Fiction 4. Slave trade -- Fiction
ISBN 0-439-11210-9
LC 00-24216

Presents the diary of thirteen-year-old Nzingha, a sixteenth-century West African princess who loves to hunt and hopes to lead her kingdom one day against the invasion of the Portuguese slave traders

"The diary format will appeal to readers and the author's use of time lines, seasons, and actual place names makes the story believable and interesting." SLJ

McLemore, Anna-Marie

Blanca & Roja; Anna-Marie McLemore. Feiwel and Friends 2018 384 p. (hardcover) $17.99
Grades: 8 9 10 11 Fic
1. Swans -- Fiction 2. Sisters -- Fiction 3. Blessing and cursing -- Fiction
ISBN 9781250162700; 9781250162717
LC 2018936436

In this book, by Anna-Marie McLemore, "the del Cisne girls [Blanca and Roja] have never just been sisters; they're also rivals. . . . They know that, because of a generations-old spell, . . . [that] one day, the swans will pull them into a dangerous game that will leave one of them a girl, and trap the other in the body of a swan. But when two local boys become drawn into the game, the swans' spell intertwines with the strange and unpredictable magic lacing the woods." (Publisher's note)

McMann, Lisa

Cryer's Cross. Simon Pulse 2011 232p $16.99
Grades: 7 8 9 10 Fic
1. Mystery fiction 2. Montana -- Fiction 3. Supernatural -- Fiction 4. Missing persons -- Fiction 5. Obsessive-compulsive disorder -- Fiction
ISBN 978-1-4169-9481-7; 1-4169-9481-5; 978-1-4169-9483-1 ebook
LC 2010-15410

"Kendall is a unique character, and the details of her OCD compulsions are well drawn. Haunting passages from another world, which provide just enough detail to intrigue and disturb readers, are intertwined with Kendall's story. Part mystery, part ghost story, and part romance, this book has enough to satisfy a variety of readers." Booklist

Fade. Simon Pulse 2009 248p $15.99
Grades: 8 9 10 11 Fic
1. School stories 2. Rape -- Fiction 3. Dreams -- Fiction
ISBN 978-1-4169-5358-6; 1-4169-5358-2
LC 2008-15201

Sequel to: Wake (2008)

Using her ability to tap into other people's dreams, eighteen-year-old Janie investigates an alleged sex ring at her high school that involves teachers using the date rape drug on students.

"A great blend of mystery, romance, and supernatural elements, and featuring a strong but vulnerable female protagonist." Booklist

Followed by: Gone (2010)

Gone. Simon Pulse 2010 214p $16.99
Grades: 8 9 10 11 Fic
1. Dreams -- Fiction 2. Alcoholism -- Fiction 3. Father-daughter relationship -- Fiction
ISBN 978-1-4169-7918-0; 1-4169-7918-2
Sequel to: Fade (2009)

McMann "wraps up the trilogy that began with Wake (2008) and Fade (2009). . . . Janie . . . learns that the father she never knew has been living in an isolated house not far from her and now lies in a hospital bed. By entering his unconscious, she also learns that he is a dream catcher too, while a search through his home reveals that he has avoided the debilitating blindness and gnarled hands of Janie's dream-catching mentor, Miss Stubin, but has sacrificed love in the process. . . . A fitting completion to this popular series." Kirkus

Wake. Simon Pulse 2008 210p $15.99; pa $8.99
Grades: 7 8 9 10 **Fic**

1. School stories 2. Dreams -- Fiction
ISBN 978-1-4169-5357-9; 1-4169-5357-4; 978-1-4169-7447-5 pa; 1-4169-7447-4 pa

LC 2007036267

Ever since she was eight years old, high school student Janie Hannagan has been uncontrollably drawn into other people's dreams, but it is not until she befriends an elderly nursing home patient and becomes involved with an enigmatic fellow-student that she discovers her true power.

"A fast pace, a great mix of teen angst and supernatural experiences, and an eerie, attention-grabbing cover will make this a hit." Booklist

Other titles in this series are:
Fade (2009)
Gone (2010)

McMullan, Margaret

★ **How** I found the Strong; a Civil War story. Houghton Mifflin 2004 136p $15
Grades: 5 6 7 8 **Fic**

1. Slavery -- Fiction 2. Mississippi -- Fiction 3. United States -- History -- 1861-1865, Civil War -- Fiction
ISBN 0-618-35008-X

LC 2003-12294

Frank Russell, known as Shanks, wishes he could have gone with his father and brother to fight for Mississippi and the Confederacy, but his experiences with the war and his changing relationship with the family slave, Buck, change his thinking.

"The crisply written narrative is full of regional speech and detail, creating a vivid portrait." Voice Youth Advocates

★ **Sources** of light. Houghton Mifflin 2010 233p $15
Grades: 6 7 8 9 **Fic**

1. Mississippi -- Fiction 2. Photography -- Fiction 3. Race relations -- Fiction 4. African Americans -- Civil rights -- Fiction
ISBN 978-0-547-07659-1; 0-547-07659-2

LC 2009-49708

"When 14-year-old Samantha Thomas moves to Jackson, Miss., in 1962, following her father's death in Vietnam, she learns about love and hate all in the same year. Her mother meets Perry Walker, a photographer who teaches Sam about taking photographs and seeing the world in new ways, but what she begins seeing and pondering is the racial situation in Jackson—lunch-counter sit-ins, voter-registration protests and the violent reprisals of many in the white community, including the father of the boy she begins to like. . . . This offers a superb portrait of a place and time and a memorable character trying to make sense of a world both ugly and beautiful." Kirkus

★ **When** I crossed No-Bob. Houghton Mifflin Company 2007 209p $16
Grades: 5 6 7 8 **Fic**

1. Farm life -- Fiction 2. Mississippi -- Fiction 3. Race relations -- Fiction 4. Abandoned children -- Fiction 5. Reconstruction (1865-1876) -- Fiction
ISBN 978-0-618-71715-6; 0-618-71715-3

LC 2007-12753

Ten years after the Civil War's end, twelve-year-old Addy, abandoned by her parents, is taken from the horrid town of No-Bob by schoolteacher Frank Russell and his bride, but when her father returns to claim her she must find another way to leave her O'Donnell past behind.

"The simple prose can be pure poetry. . . . Readers will be drawn by the history close-up and by the elemental moral choice." Booklist

McMullen, Beth

Mrs. Smith's Spy School for Girls; by Beth McMullen. Aladdin 2017 295 p. (hardback) $16.99
Grades: 4 5 6 7 8 **Fic**

1. Private schools -- fiction 2. Spies -- Fiction 3. Schools -- Fiction 4. Boarding schools -- Fiction 5. Adventure and adventurers -- Fiction
ISBN 9781481490221; 9781481490207; 9781481490214

LC 2016042030

In this juvenile novel, by Beth McMullen, "after a botched escape plan from her boarding school, Abigail is stunned to discover the school is actually a cover for an elite spy ring called The Center, along with being training grounds for future spies. . . . Along with a former nemesis and charming boy from her grade, Abigail goes through a crash course in Spy Training 101, often with hilarious—and sometimes painful—results." (Publisher's note)

"Abigail's entertaining narration tempers suspense with levity, and readers will have a blast accompanying her through sticky situations." Booklist

Another title in this series is:
Power Play (2018)

McNab, Andy

Avenger; [by] Andy McNab and Robert Rigby. 1st American ed.; G. P. Putnam's Sons 2007 263p $16.99
Grades: 7 8 9 10 **Fic**

1. Spies -- Fiction 2. Orphans -- Fiction 3. Terrorism -- Fiction 4. Grandfathers -- Fiction 5. Great Britain -- Fiction
ISBN 978-0-399-24685-2; 0-399-24685-1

LC 2007008153

Sequel to Payback (2006)

Seventeen-year-old Danny, his grandfather, Fergus, who is an ex-SAS explosives expert, and friend Elena set out to stop the evil computer hacker who is sending teenaged suicide bombers to their deaths around the world.

"Scary, slick suspense, with no false steps in the plotting. . . . Realistic details about undercover work are on every page." Kliatt

Meltdown; [by] Andy McNab and Robert Rigby. G.P. Putnam's Sons 2008 248p $16.99
Grades: 7 8 9 10 **Fic**

1. Spies -- Fiction 2. Orphans -- Fiction 3. Terrorism -- Fiction 4. Grandfathers -- Fiction 5. Great Britain. -- Army. -- Special Air Service -- Fiction.
ISBN 978-0-399-24686-9; 0-399-24686-X

LC 2007-22674

Eighteen-year-old Danny Watts and his grandfather Fergus, an ex-SAS explosives expert, travel to England, Spain, and Germany, in a life-or-death race to save the population from the spread of a lethal new drug that has been unleashed by terrorists.

"This compelling, fast-paced, plot-driven dose of espionage and intrigue features a bit of appropriately gruesome violence thrown in for good measure." Voice Youth Advocates

Payback; [by] Andy McNab and Robert Rigby. G. P. Putnam's Sons 2006 263p $16.99
Grades: 7 8 9 10 **Fic**

1. Spies -- Fiction 2. Orphans -- Fiction 3. Grandfathers -- Fiction 4. Great Britain -- Fiction
ISBN 0-399-24465-4

LC 2005032657

Sequel to Traitor (2005)

As teenage suicide bombers terrorize England, seventeen-year-old Danny tries to help his grandfather, an ex-SAS explosives expert falsely accused of being a traitorous spy by the government's intelligence agencies.

"Teens will . . . enjoy the fast-paced, action-laden plot and the wealth of details about tricks of the spy trade." Booklist

Followed by Avenger (2007)

Traitor; [by] Andy McNab and Robert Rigby. G.P. Putnam's Sons 2005 265p $15.99

Grades: 7 8 9 10 **Fic**

1. Spies -- Fiction 2. Orphans -- Fiction 3. Grandfathers -- Fiction 4. Great Britain -- Fiction

ISBN 0-399-24464-6

LC 2005-6701

"Orphaned Londoner Danny Watts wants nothing to do with his estranged grandfather, a traitor who went MIA years ago, until the British military offers Danny a proposition: find his grandfather and he'll receive a scholarship. . . . With help from his best friend, Elena, he sets off to find his relative and the truth. . . . The well-crafted language includes a few coarse phrases. . . . With its brisk plot and unpredictable characters, this story of intrigue rises above many standard adventure stories." Booklist

Other titles in this series are:

Payback (2006)

Avenger (2007)

Meltdown (2008)

McNally, Janet

The **looking** glass; Janet McNally. HarperTeen 2018 336 p. (hardback) $17.99

Grades: 7 8 9 10 **Fic**

1. Ballet -- Fiction 2. Sisters -- Fiction 3. Supernatural -- Fiction 4. Runaways -- Fiction 5. Ballet dancing -- Fiction

ISBN 9780062436276

LC 2017034545

In this book, by Janet McNally, "GIRLS IN TROUBLE. That's what Sylvie Blake's older sister Julia renamed their favorite fairy tale book, way back when they were just girls themselves. Now Julia has disappeared--and no one knows for sure if she wants to be away, or if she's the one in trouble. Then a copy of their old storybook arrives with a mysterious list inside, and Sylvie begins to see signs of her sister, and their favorite fairy tales, everywhere she goes." (Publisher's note)

McNamee, Eoin

City of Time; Eoin McNamee; illustrated by Jon Goodell. Wendy Lamb Books 2008 324p il (Navigator trilogy) hardcover o.p. O.P.; lib bdg O.P.

Grades: 6 7 8 9 **Fic**

1. Fantasy fiction 2. Time -- Fiction

ISBN 978-0-375-83912-2; 0-375-83912-7; 978-0-375-93912-9 lib bdg; 0-375-93912-1 lib bdg

LC 2007-37131

Sequel to: The navigator (2007)

When he receives the cryptic message that "time is running out," Owen, known as "The Navigator," summons Cati and Dr. Diamond and together they journey to the City of Time in order to discover what has gone wrong.

"Pacing and story details are excellent with just the right amount of suspense and withheld information to keep readers wanting more." SLJ

Followed by: The Frost Child (2009)

The **Frost** Child. Wendy Lamb Books 2009 343p (Navigator trilogy) $15.99; lib bdg $18.99

Grades: 6 7 8 9 **Fic**

1. Fantasy fiction 2. Time -- Fiction

ISBN 978-0-385-73563-6; 978-0-385-90551-0 lib bdg; 978-0-440-42246-4 pa

LC 2008036220

Sequel to: City of Time (2008)

Owen the Navigator is once again called on to marshall the Resistors and beat back the enemy Harsh in their attempt to take over time.

"The author's skillful use of fantasy tropes produces interesting juxtapositions that place traditional elements in unexpected settings with unique, eccentric characters. The ending will please fans: The climax is breathtaking." Kirkus

The **Navigator**. Wendy Lamb Books 2007 342p il (Navigator trilogy) hardcover o.p. O.P.; pa O.P.

Grades: 6 7 8 9 **Fic**

1. Fantasy fiction 2. Time -- Fiction

ISBN 978-0-375-83910-8; 0-375-83910-0; 978-0-385-73554-4 pa; 0-385-73554-5 pa

LC 2006-26691

Owen has always been different, and not only because his father committed suicide, but he is not prepared for the knowledge that he has a mission to help the Wakeful—the custodians of time—to stop the Harsh from reversing the flow of time.

McNamee "shows a deft hand in writing for children. Excellent world-building, a thrilling and propulsive plot, internal consistency and a multitude of child heroes guarantee a following for this exciting fantasy." Kirkus

Other titles in this series are:

City of Time (2008)

The Frost Child (2009)

McNeal, Tom

★ **Far** far away; by Tom McNeal. 1st ed. Alfred A. Knopf Books for Young Readers 2013 371 p. (hardcover) $17.99; (ebook) $53.97; (library) $20.99

Grades: 7 8 9 10 **Fic**

1. Fantasy fiction 2. Paranormal fiction 3. Ghosts -- Fiction 4. Friendship -- Fiction 5. Supernatural -- Fiction 6. Missing persons -- Fiction

ISBN 0375849726; 9780375849725; 9780375896989; 9780375949722

LC 2012020603

Parents' Choice: Gold Medal Fiction (2013)

National Book Awards: Young People's Literature Finalist (2013)

This book "is narrated by the ghost of Jacob Grimm . . . , unhappily caught in the Zwischenraum (a plane of existence between life and death). For now, he is the nearly constant companion of Jeremy Johnson," who hears voices. This ability "has made him an object of derision for many in his little town, though—thrillingly—not to the electrifyingly vibrant Ginger Boultinghouse, who is more than happy to lure Jeremy into more trouble than he's ever encountered." (School Library Journal)

McNeil, Gretchen

I'm not your manic pixie dream girl; Gretchen McNeil. Balzer + Bray 2016 352 p. (ebook) $16.99; (hardback) $17.99

Grades: 8 9 10 11 **Fic**

1. Bullies -- fiction 2. Revenge -- fiction 3. Romance fiction -- fiction 4. High school students -- fiction 5. Love -- Fiction 6.

Dating (Social customs) -- Fiction
ISBN 9780062409133; 9780062409119

LC 2016013283

In this novel, by Gretchen McNeil, "Beatrice Maria Estrella Giovannini has life all figured out. She's starting senior year at the top of her class, she's a shoo-in for a scholarship to M.I.T., and she's got a new boyfriend. . . The only problem: . . . Bea and her best friends Spencer and Gabe have been the targets of horrific bullying. So Bea uses her math skills to come up with The Formula, a 100% mathematically guaranteed path to social happiness in high school." (Publisher's note)

"The love rhombus crafted here is a tad predictable, but the excitement's in the execution: the author's strong characterizations and smart humor put this above most similar titles." Kirkus

McQuerry, Maureen Doyle

The **Peculiars**; a novel. Maureen Doyle McQuerry. Amulet Books 2012 359 p. (hardback) $16.95

Grades: 7 8 9 10 11 12 **Fic**

1. Fantasy fiction 2. Voyages and travels -- Fiction 3. Father-daughter relationship -- Fiction 4. Goblins -- Fiction 5. Identity -- Fiction 6. Abnormalities, Human -- Fiction 7. Adventure and adventurers -- Fiction
ISBN 1419701789; 9781419701788

LC 2012000844

This is the story of Lena Mattacascar, who at age 18 "travel[s] to Scree, an uncharted wilderness of 'indigenous folks' and deported convicts," sitting on the train with young librarian "Jimson Quiggley," with "marshal Thomas Saltre" watching them. "Lena cannot stop thinking about her mysterious father" or the possibility that she's part Peculiar (goblin). "Scree is the place where Lena's questions might be answered, but arriving there just multiplies them." (Publishers Weekly)

McStay, Moriah

Everything that makes you; Moriah McStay. First edition Katherine Tegen Books, an imprint of HarperCollins Children's Books 2015 346 p. 22 cm (hardcover) $17.99

Grades: 8 9 10 11 **Fic**

1. Accidents -- Fiction 2. Family life -- Fiction 3. Self-confidence -- Fiction 4. Interpersonal relations -- Fiction 5. Disfigured persons -- Fiction
ISBN 0062295489; 9780062295484

LC 2014005864

In this book, by Moriah McStay, "Fiona Doyle's face was horribly scarred as a child. She writes about her frustrations and dreams in notebooks, penning song lyrics. But she'd never be brave enough to sing those songs in public. Fi Doyle . . . [is] the best lacrosse player in the state and can't be distracted by her friend who wants to be more than that. But then her luck on the field goes south. Alternating chapters between Fiona and Fi tell two stories about the same girl." (Publisher's note)

"Entertaining and intellectually stimulating, the novel invites discussion about how much of a person's life is determined by events and whether some tendencies are inborn." Publishers Weekly

Meaker, Marijane, 1927-

Night kites. Harper & Row 1986 216p hardcover o.p. pa $5.99

Grades: 7 8 9 10 **Fic**

1. Brothers -- Fiction 2. Homosexuality -- Fiction 3. AIDS (Disease) -- Fiction
ISBN 0-06-023253-6; 0-06-447035-0

LC 85-45386

ALA YALSA Margaret A. Edwards Award (1993)

"Pete and his methods of coping with his disease and its effects on himself, his friends, his family, and ultimately, his community, are sensitively and non-sentimentally drawn, and seem to be portrayed accurately. This is sure to be a popular title, and will be a natural for booktalks." Voice Youth Advocates

Medina, Meg

★ **Merci** Suarez changes gears; Meg Medina. Candlewick Press 2018 368 p. (hbk.) $16.99

Grades: 4 5 6 7 8 **Fic**

1. Girls -- fiction 2. Middle schools -- fiction 3. Grandparent-grandchild relationship -- fiction
ISBN 076369049X; 9780763690496
Newbery Medal (2019)
Kirkus Prize Finalist: Young Readers' Literature (2018)

In this novel, by Meg Medina, "Merci Suarez knew that sixth grade would be different, but she had no idea just how different. For starters, Merci has never been like the other kids at her private school in Florida, because she and her older brother, Roli, are scholarship students. They don't have a big house or a fancy boat, and they have to do extra community service to make up for their free tuition." (Publisher's note)

"Medina writes with sincerity and humor to convey the experience of growing up in a close-knit family that tends to mingle too much in everyone's business while unfailingly and dedicatedly supporting and helping one another." Horn Book

Meehl, Brian

★ **Suck** it up. Delacorte Press 2008 323p $15.99; pa $8.99

Grades: 8 9 10 11 **Fic**

1. Vampires -- Fiction
ISBN 978-0-385-73300-7; 0-385-73300-3; 978-0-440-42091-0 pa; 0-440-42091-1 pa

LC 2007-27995

After graduating from the International Vampire League, a scrawny, teenaged vampire named Morning is given the chance to fulfill his childhood dream of becoming a superhero when he embarks on a League mission to become the first vampire to reveal his identity to humans and to demonstrate how peacefully-evolved, blood-substitute-drinking vampires can use their powers to help humanity.

This "an original and light variation on the current trend in brooding teen vampire protagonists. . . . Puns abound in this lengthy, complicated romp. . . . Teens will find it delightful." Booklist

Meloy, Colin

Under Wildwood; Colin Meloy ; illustrated by Carson Ellis. Balzer + Bray 2012 559 p. (hardback) $17.99

Grades: 5 6 7 8 **Fic**

1. Fantasy fiction 2. Adventure fiction 3. Animals -- Fiction 4. Portland (Or.) -- Fiction
ISBN 006202471X; 9780062024718

LC 2012019040

Sequel to: Wildwood

This children's picture book is a sequel to "Wildwood." Here, bookish "Prue and bandit-in-training Curtis team up once again to fight a nefarious governess and evil science teacher in this fast-paced fantasy set in Oregon. . . . In this strange land, it can be difficult to tell friend from foe, making for deliciously suspenseful adventures with a rat named Septimus and a circus bear with hooks instead of paws." (Children's Literature)

★ **Wildwood**; illustrations by Carson Ellis. Balzer + Bray 2011 541p il $16.99

Grades: 5 6 7 8 **Fic**

1. Fantasy fiction 2. Animals -- Fiction 3. Siblings -- Fiction 4. Portland (Or.) -- Fiction 5. Missing persons -- Fiction

ISBN 978-0-06-202468-8; 0-06-202468-X

LC 2011010072

When her baby brother is kidnapped by crows, seventh-grader Prue McKeel ventures into the forbidden Impassable Wilderness—a dangerous and magical forest in the middle of Portland, Oregon—and soon finds herself involved in a war among the various inhabitants.

"Illustrations by Ellis . . . bring forest and inhabitants to gently whimsical life. A satisfying blend of fantasy, adventure story, eco-fable and political satire with broad appeal." Kirkus

Wildwood imperium; Colin Meloy ; illustrations by Carson Ellis. Balzer + Bray 2014 592 p. ill (some col.), maps (Wildwood chronicles) (hardcover) $17.99

Grades: 5 6 7 8 **Fic**

1. Fairy tales 2. Fantasy fiction 3. Orphans -- Fiction 4. Friendship -- Fiction

ISBN 0062024744; 9780062024749

LC 2013953784

This fairy tale, by Colin Meloy, is the third book in the fantasy "Wildwood" series. "A young girl's midnight séance awakens a long-slumbering malevolent spirit. . . . A band of runaway orphans allies with an underground collective of saboteurs and plans a daring rescue of their friends, imprisoned in . . . an industrial wasteland. . . . Two old friends draw closer to their goal of bringing together a pair of exiled toy makers in order to reanimate a mechanical boy prince." (Publisher's note)

"Dramatic shifts in tone and mood--by turns politically astute and subversively witty, elegiac, droll and philosophical--are par for the course, while narrative style ranges from intimate to intergalactically distant." Kirkus

Meloy, Maile

★ The **apothecary**. G. P. Putnam's Sons 2011 353p $16.99

Grades: 6 7 8 9 **Fic**

1. Adventure fiction 2. Alchemy -- Fiction 3. Cold war -- Fiction 4. Great Britain -- Fiction 5. London (England) -- Fiction

ISBN 978-0-399-25627-1; 0-399-25627-X

LC 2010045003

"With evocative, confident prose and equally atmospheric spot art from Schoenherr, adult author Meloy's first book for young readers is an auspicious one." Publ Wkly

The **apprentices**; by Maile Meloy ; illustrated by Ian Schoenherr. G.P. Putnam's Sons, an imprint of Penguin Group (USA) Inc. 2013 432 p. (hardcover) $16.99

Grades: 6 7 8 9 **Fic**

1. Magic -- Fiction 2. Alchemy -- Fiction 3. Voyages and travels -- Fiction 4. Adventure and adventurers -- Fiction 5. Southeast Asia -- History -- 1945- -- Fiction

ISBN 9780399162459

LC 2012048715

"Janie, now 16, is alone at an elite American boarding school, unaware of the whereabouts of her first boyfriend, Benjamin, and his apothecary father. After she is wrongly expelled, she realizes she is the victim of a nefarious scheme, which again poses a threat to world peace. The . . . plot spans the globe as the heroes find their way back to each other." (Publishers Weekly)

Menon, Sandhya

★ **From** Twinkle, with love; Sandhya Menon. Simon Pulse 2018 330 p. (hardback) $18.99

Grades: 7 8 9 10 11 **Fic**

1. Twins -- Fiction 2. East Indian Americans -- Fiction 3. Dating (Social customs) -- Fiction 4. Letters 5. Brothers -- Fiction 6. Producers and directors -- Fiction

ISBN 9781481495424; 9781481495400

LC 2017048138

In this book, by Sandhya Menon, aspiring filmmaker and wallflower Twinkle Mehra has stories she wants to tell. . . . So when fellow film geek Sahil Roy approaches her to direct a movie for the . . . Summer Festival, Twinkle is all over it. . . . When mystery man 'N' begins emailing her, Twinkle is sure it's Neil, [Sahil's twin brother] finally ready to begin their happily-ever-after. The only . . . problem is that, . . . she's fallen madly in love with . . . Sahil." (Publisher's note)

"This is an often laugh-out-loud funny journey through the tribulations of high school that's tempered by Twinkle's very real feelings of isolation . . . A charming addition to the rom-com canon." Booklist

There's something about sweetie; by Sandhya Menon. Simon Pulse 2019 378 p. (hardback) $18.99

Grades: 7 8 9 10 **Fic**

1. Romance fiction 2. East Indian Americans -- Fiction 3. Dating (Social customs) -- Fiction 4. Schools -- Fiction 5. Family life -- Fiction 6. High schools -- Fiction 7. Overweight persons -- Fiction

ISBN 9781534416789

LC 2019004082

In this novel, by Sandhya Meno, "Ashish Patel didn't know love could be so sucky. After being dumped by his ex-girlfriend, his mojo goes AWOL. Even worse, his parents are annoyingly, smugly confident they could find him a better match. So, in a moment of weakness, Ash challenges them to set him up. The Patels insist that Ashish date an Indian-American girl--under contract." (Publisher's note)

"This companion book to her successful debut, When Dimple Met Rishi (2017), hits all the right notes and delivers a joyful relationship that discards society's dictates about appearance in favor of loving the whole person. Give this to readers who love a good rom-com with a message." --Booklist 03/2019

When Dimple met Rishi; Sandhya Menon. Simon Pulse 2017 380 p. (hardcover) $17.99

Grades: 7 8 9 10 **Fic**

1. Arranged marriage -- Fiction 2. East Indian Americans -- Fiction 3. Family life -- Fiction 4. Dating (Social customs) -- Fiction

ISBN 9781481478687; 9781481478700

LC 2016023129

This novel, by Sandhya Menon, is "about two Indian-American teens whose parents conspire to arrange their marriage. Dimple Shah . . . [is] more than ready for a break from her family, from Mamma's inexplicable obsession with her finding the 'Ideal Indian Husband.' . . . Rishi Patel is a hopeless romantic. So when his parents tell him that his future wife will be attending the same summer program as him--wherein he'll have to woo her--he's totally on board." (Publisher's note)

"The strength of the story comes from its blending of Indian culture and values into a modern-day romance that scores of readers can enjoy. This novel touches on issues of identity while remaining light and fun." SLJ

Merrill, Jean

★ The **pushcart** war; by Jean Merrill; with illustrations by Ronni Solbert. Bantam Doubleday Dell Books for Young Readers 1987 222p il pa $6.50

Grades: 5 6 7 8 **Fic**

1. Trucks -- Fiction 2. New York (N.Y.) -- Fiction

ISBN 0-440-47147-8

A reissue of the title first published 1964 by W. R. Scott

The outbreak of a war between truck drivers and pushcart peddlers brings the mounting problems of traffic to the attention of both the city of New York and the world.

"A book that is both humorous and downright funny. . . . Such a lively book will need little introducing." Horn Book

Messner, Kate

The **brilliant** fall of Gianna Z. Walker 2009 198p $16.99

Grades: 5 6 7 8 **Fic**

1. Trees -- Fiction 2. Old age -- Fiction 3. Running -- Fiction 4. Vermont -- Fiction 5. Grandmothers -- Fiction

ISBN 978-0-8027-9842-8; 0-8027-9842-X

Gianna has less than one week to complete her leaf project if she wants to compete in the upcoming cross-country sectionals, but issues like procrastination, disorganization—and her grandmother's declining health—seem destined to keep her from finishing.

"Youngsters will find much to relate to in this likable protagonist's struggle to balance family and academic commitments. . . . Plot twists keep readers engaged, and Messner's warm and humorous tone will capture even reluctant readers." SLJ

The **seventh** wish; by Kate Messner. Bloomsbury 2016 240 p. (hardback) $16.99

Grades: 4 5 6 7 **Fic**

1. Magic -- Fiction 2. Wishes -- Fiction 3. Family life -- Fiction 4. Schools -- Fiction

ISBN 9781619633773; 9781619633766

LC 2015036430

In this book, by Kate Messner, "Charlie feels like she's always coming in last. From her Mom's new job to her sister's life away at college, everything else always seems to be more important than Charlie's upcoming dance competition or science project. Unsure of how to get her family's attention, Charlie comes across the surprise of her life one day while ice-fishing . . . in the form of a floppy, scaly fish offering to grant her a wish in exchange for its freedom." (Publisher's note)

"Hopeful, empathetic, and unusually enlightening." Kirkus

Meyer, Carolyn

Beware, Princess Elizabeth. Harcourt 2001 214p (Young royals) hardcover o.p. pa $5.95

Grades: 7 8 9 10 **Fic**

1. Queens 2. Great Britain -- History -- 1485-1603, Tudors -- Fiction

ISBN 0-15-202659-2; 0-15-204556-2 pa

LC 00-11700

After the death of her father, King Henry VIII, in 1547, thirteen-year-old Elizabeth must endure the political intrigues and dangers of the reigns of her half-brother Edward and her half-sister Mary before finally becoming Queen of England eleven years later

"The story moves along swiftly with hints of romance, life-and-death plots, and snippets of everyday life." Book Rep

Cleopatra confesses. Simon & Schuster Books for Young Readers 2011 289p $16.99

Grades: 6 7 8 9 **Fic**

1. Queens -- Fiction 2. Princesses -- Fiction 3. Egypt -- History -- Fiction

ISBN 978-1-4169-8727-7; 1-4169-8727-4

LC 2010025989

Princess Cleopatra, the third (and favorite) daughter of King Ptolemy XII, comes of age in ancient Egypt, accumulating power and discovering love.

Meyer's "lush, detail-rich prose ably evokes Cleopatra's life as a young princess, beginning at age 10 and continuing on until she turns 22. . . . Narrating with the poise and confidence of a born leader, this Cleopatra should win readers over." Publ Wkly

Includes bibliographical references

Duchessina; a novel of Catherine de' Medici. Harcourt 2007 261p (Young royals) $17

Grades: 7 8 9 10 **Fic**

1. Queens 2. Regents 3. Italy -- Fiction 4. Orphans -- Fiction

ISBN 978-0-15-205588-2; 0-15-205588-6

LC 2006028876

While her tyrannical family is out of favor in Italy, young Catherine de Medici is raised in convents, then in 1533, when she is fourteen, her uncle, Pope Clement VII, arranges for her marriage to prince Henri of France, who is destined to become king.

"With meticulous historical detail, sensitive characterizations, and Catherine's strong narration, Meyer's memorable story of a fascinating young woman who relies on her intelligence, rather than her beauty, will hit home with many teens." Booklist

Meyer, Kai

The **glass** word; [by] Kai Meyer; translated by Elizabeth D. Crawford. 1st U.S. ed.; Margaret K. McElderry Books 2008 282p (Dark reflections) hardcover o.p. O.P.

Grades: 5 6 7 8 **Fic**

1. Fantasy fiction 2. Magic -- Fiction 3. Orphans -- Fiction 4. Mythical animals -- Fiction

ISBN 978-0-689-87791-9; 0-689-87791-9

LC 2006033185

Sequel to: The stone light (2007)

While Merle, Junipa, and the great flying stone lion accompany an Egyptian high priest to the fortress of the powerful sphinx, Serafin and Eft voyage deep beneath the ocean to ask the help of a sea witch in freeing Venice from the Pharoah and his mummy warriors.

"As in the other volumes in this dark, complex fantasy series, not everything is what it seems and not everyone can be trusted. Magic and mysteries abound, along with unusual characters." KLIATT

The **stone** light; [by] Kai Meyer; translated by Elizabeth D. Crawford. 1st U.S. ed.; Margaret K. McElderry Books 2007 350p (Dark reflections) hardcover o.p. O.P.

Grades: 5 6 7 8 **Fic**

1. Fantasy fiction 2. Orphans -- Fiction

ISBN 978-0-689-87789-6; 0-689-87789-7

LC 2006002252

Sequel to The water mirror (2005)

Original German edition 2002

While Merle and the Flowing Queen travel to Hell to enlist Lord Light's help in Venice's fight against the invading Egyptian army, Serafin joins a resistance group that is led by an ancient sphinx.

"The landscapes and creatures the characters encounter are jaw dropping, and readers of the first adventure will certainly want to go along for the ride." Booklist

Followed by The glass word (2008)

The **water** mirror; translated by Elizabeth D. Crawford. Margaret K. McElderry Books 2005 250p (Dark reflections) hardcover o.p. O.P.
Grades: 5 6 7 8 **Fic**

1. Fantasy fiction 2. Orphans -- Fiction 3. Mermaids and mermen -- Fiction
ISBN 0-689-87787-0
LC 2005-11943

Original German edition 2001

In Venice two teenaged orphans, apprenticed to a maker of magic mirrors, begin to realize that their fates are tied to the magical protector of the city known as the Flowing Queen and to the ruler of Hell, respectively.

An "inventive and original fantasy . . . A powerful mix of political intrigue, adventure, and magic." SLJ

Other titles in this series are:
The stone light (2007)
The glass word (2008)

Meyer, L. A.

★ **Bloody** Jack; being an account of the curious adventures of Mary Jacky Faber, ship's boy. Harcourt 2002 278p hardcover o.p. pa $6.95
Grades: 7 8 9 10 **Fic**

1. Adventure fiction 2. Orphans -- Fiction 3. Pirates -- Fiction 4. Sex role -- Fiction 5. Seafaring life -- Fiction
ISBN 0-15-216731-5; 0-15-205085-X pa
LC 2002-759

Reduced to begging and thievery in the streets of 18th-century London, a thirteen-year-old orphan disguises herself as a boy and connives her way onto a British warship set for high sea adventure in search of pirates

"From shooting a pirate in battle to foiling a shipmate's sexual attack to surviving when stranded alone on a Caribbean island, the action in Jacky's tale will entertain readers with a taste for adventure." Booklist

Other titles in this series are:
Curse of the blue tattoo (2004)
In the belly of The Bloodhound (2006)
The mark of the golden dragon (2011)
Mississippi Jack (2007)
My bonny light horseman (2008)
Rapture of the deep (2009)
Under the Jolly Roger (2005)
The wake of the Lorelei Lee (2010)

In the belly of The Bloodhound; being an account of a particularly peculiar adventure in the life of Jacky Faber. [by] L. A. Meyer. 1st ed.; Harcourt 2006 515p $17
Grades: 7 8 9 10 **Fic**

1. Orphans -- Fiction 2. Kidnapping -- Fiction 3. Seafaring life -- Fiction
ISBN 978-0-15-205557-8; 0-15-205557-6
LC 2005033562

Sequel to: Under the Jolly Roger

Jacky Faber and her classmates at the Lawson Peabody School for Young Girls in Boston are kidnapped while on a school outing and transported in the hold of a slave ship bound for the slave markets of North Africa.

"This plot-driven novel . . . is one more fabulous adventure for Jacky and friends and a thoroughly delightful story." Voice Youth Advocates

Followed by: Mississippi Jack

The **mark** of the golden dragon; being an account of the further adventures of Jacky Faber, jewel of the East, vexation of the West, and pearl of the South China Sea. Harcourt 2011 378p $16.99
Grades: 7 8 9 10 **Fic**

1. Thieves -- Fiction 2. Indonesia -- Fiction 3. Seafaring life -- Fiction 4. London (England) -- Fiction
ISBN 978-0-547-51764-3; 0-547-51764-5
LC 2011009598

In 1807, having survived a typhoon in the East Indies, Jacky Faber makes her way to London to seek a pardon for herself and her betrothed, Jaimy Fletcher, who, posing as a highwayman, is trying to avenge her supposed death.

"The writing style is simple yet entertaining. The multiple viewpoints, including the thoughts of various characters, add interest to the story. Meyer also adds a little spice without being explicit, although a few words could be offensive to younger readers, so this selection is better suited to young adults, but all in all it is a very enjoyable read." Voice Youth Advocates

Mississippi Jack; being an account of the further waterborne adventures of Jacky Faber, midshipman, fine lady, and the Lily of the West. [by] L.A. Meyer. 1st ed.; Harcourt 2007 611p $17; pa $7.99
Grades: 7 8 9 10 **Fic**

1. Orphans -- Fiction 2. Mississippi River -- Fiction 3. Voyages and travels -- Fiction
ISBN 978-0-15-206003-9; 978-0-15-206632-1 pa
LC 2006034709

Sequel to: In the belly of The Bloodhound (2006)

In 1806, the exploits of Jacky Faber continue as she heads west to avoid capture by the British and discovers adventure aboard a keelboat on the mighty Mississippi River.

"The descriptions of the new frontier, river life, and the social climate of early nineteenth-century America seem right on. Jacky continues to amaze readers with her clever plots, narrow escapes, and the uncanny ability to outwit thieves and bureaucrats, make money, and have some fun." Voice Youth Advocates

My bonny light horseman; being an account of the further adventures of Jacky Faber, in love and war. Harcourt 2008 436p $17
Grades: 7 8 9 10 **Fic**

1. Adventure fiction 2. Spies -- Fiction 3. Orphans -- Fiction 4. France -- History -- 1799-1815 -- Fiction
ISBN 978-0-15-206187-6; 0-15-206187-8
LC 2007049582

Sequel to: Mississippi Jack (2007)

While trying to run a respectable shipping business in 1806, teenaged Jacky Faber finds herself in France, spying for the British Crown in order to save her friends.

"Jacky's wit and lots of action make it an engaging read." Voice Youth Advocates

Followed by: Rapture of the deep (2009)

Rapture of the deep; being an account of the further adventures of Jacky Faber, soldier, sailor, mermaid, spy. Harcourt 2009 454p $17
Grades: 7 8 9 10 **Fic**

1. Adventure fiction 2. Spies -- Fiction 3. Orphans -- Fiction 4.

Kidnapping -- Fiction 5. Seafaring life -- Fiction 6. Buried treasure -- Fiction 7. Caribbean region -- Fiction
ISBN 978-0-15-206501-0; 0-15-206501-6
LC 2009-19494

Sequel to: My bonny light horseman (2008)

In 1806, star-crossed lovers Jacky Faber and Jaimy Fletcher are kidnapped by British Naval Intelligence and forced to embark on yet another daring mission—this time to search for sunken Spanish gold off the Florida coast.

"Meyer weaves details of nineteenth-century history, lore, and ballads into a fast-paced and often amusing swashbuckler." Booklist

Followed by: The wake of the Lorelei Lee (2010)

Under the Jolly Roger; being an account of the further nautical adventures of Jacky Faber. Harcourt 2005 518p $17
Grades: 7 8 9 10 **Fic**

1. Orphans -- Fiction 2. Pirates -- Fiction 3. Sex role -- Fiction 4. Seafaring life -- Fiction
ISBN 0-15-205345-X
LC 2004-22463

Sequel to: Curse of the blue tattoo

In 1804, fifteen-year-old Jacky Faber heads back to sea where she gains control of a British warship and eventually becomes a privateer.

"Readers will root for resilient Jacky and her memorable friends as she cannily makes the best of even the least-promising situations. A swashbuckling saga with a decidedly unconventional heroine." Booklist

Followed by: In the belly of The Bloodhound

Viva Jacquelina! being an account of the further adventures of Jacky Faber, over the hills and far away. written by L.A. Meyer. Harcourt 2012 p. cm. $16.99
Grades: 7 8 9 10 **Fic**

1. Spain -- History -- Fiction 2. Historical fiction -- fiction 3. Spies -- Fiction 4. Sex role -- Fiction 5. Seafaring life -- Fiction 6. Adventure and adventurers -- Fiction 7. Europe -- History -- 1789-1815 -- Fiction 8. Great Britain -- History -- George III, 1760-1820 -- Fiction
ISBN 9780547763507
LC 2011041931

This young adult adventure novel, by L. A. Meyer, continues the "Bloody Jack Adventures" series. "Once again under the thumb of British Intelligence, Jacky is sent to Spain to spy for the Crown during the early days of the nineteenth-century Peninsular War. She finds herself in the company of guerilla freedom fighters, poses for the famous artist Goya, runs with the bulls, is kidnapped by the Spanish Inquisition, and travels with a caravan of gypsies." (Publisher's note)

The **wake** of the Lorelei Lee; being an account of the adventures of Jacky Faber on her way to Botany Bay. Harcourt 2010 554p $17
Grades: 7 8 9 10 **Fic**

1. Sea stories 2. Orphans -- Fiction 3. Sex role -- Fiction 4. Australia -- Fiction 5. Prisoners -- Fiction 6. Seafaring life -- Fiction
ISBN 978-0-547-32768-6; 0-547-32768-4
LC 2010-8686

Sequel to: Rapture of the deep (2009)

Now rich, Jacky Faber has purchased the Lorelei Lee to carry passengers across the Atlantic, and believing she has been absolved of past sins against the Crown, she docks in London, where she is arrested and sentenced to life in the newly formed penal colony in Australia.

"L. A. Meyer's writing style is easy to read and entertaining. The story moves along at a brisk pace, with new turns in the plot keeping the reader's attention throughout." Voice Youth Advocates

Meyer, Marissa, 1984-

★ **Cinder**; Marissa Meyer. Feiwel & Friends 2012 320 p. $17.99
Grades: 7 8 9 10 11 12 **Fic**

1. Fairy tales 2. Science fiction 3. Robots -- Fiction
ISBN 9780312641894
LC 2011036123

In this book, "as plague ravages the overcrowded Earth, observed by a ruthless lunar people, Cinder, a gifted mechanic and cyborg, becomes involved with handsome Prince Kai and must uncover secrets about her past in order to protect the world in this futuristic take on the Cinderella story." (Publisher's note)

Followed by: Scarlet (2013)

★ **Cress**; Marissa Meyer. Feiwel & Friends 2014 560 p. $18.99
Grades: 7 8 9 10 11 12 **Fic**

1. Fugitives from justice -- Fiction 2. Human-alien encounters -- Fiction
ISBN 0312642970; 9780312642976

In this book by Marissa Meyer, third in her Lunar Chronicles series, "Cinder and Captain Thorne are fugitives on the run, now with Scarlet and Wolf in tow. Together, they're plotting to overthrow Queen Levana and prevent her army from invading Earth. Their best hope lies with Cress, a girl trapped on a satellite since childhood. When a daring rescue of Cress goes awry, the group is splintered. Meanwhile, Queen Levana will let nothing prevent her marriage to Emperor Kai." (Publisher's note)

"—Cress is locked away in a floating satellite. She dreams of visiting Earth, the planet she has been forced to spy on, and meeting Carswell Thorne, the handsome ship captain who teamed up with Cinder in Scarlet (Feiwel & Friends, 2013)....Cress fills in more historical details about Earth and Luna's relationship—most of which will be of no surprise to the reader—and Cinder's rebirth as a cyborg. Fans of Scarlet and Wolf may be disappointed that their relationship takes a backseat to the newly introduced pairing. As always, Meyer excels at interweaving new characters that extend beyond the archetypes of their fairy tale into the main story. Readers will eagerly await the final installment of this highly appealing and well-constructed series." (School Library Journal)

Heartless; Marissa Meyer. Feiwel & Friends 2016 464 p. (hardback) $19.99; (ebook) $60
Grades: 7 8 9 10 **Fic**

1. Fantasy fiction 2. Love -- Fiction 3. Fantasy 4. Characters in literature -- Fiction
ISBN 1250044650; 9781250044655; 9781250080271
LC 2015021393

In this book, by Marissa Meyer, "Catherine may be one of the most desired girls in Wonderland, and a favorite of the unmarried King of Hearts, but her interests lie elsewhere. A talented baker, all she wants is to open a shop with her best friend. But according to her mother, such a goal is unthinkable for the young woman who could be the next queen. Then Cath meets Jest, the handsome and mysterious court joker." (Publisher's note)

"If you only read one fractured fairy tale this year, make it Heartless. A must-have title." SLJ

Renegades; Marissa Meyer. Feiwel & Friends 2017 556 p. (Renegades) (hardcover) $19.99

Grades: 8 9 10 11 12 Fic

1. Science fiction 2. Superheroes -- Fiction 3. Heroes -- Fiction 4. Good and evil -- Fiction 5. Revenge -- fiction 6. Supervillains -- fiction 7. Interpersonal relations -- fiction

ISBN 1250044669; 9781250044662; 9781250164070

LC 2017902456

In this novel, by Marissa Meyer, "the Renegades are a syndicate of prodigies . . . who emerged from the ruins of a crumbled society and established peace and order where chaos reigned. . . . Nova has a reason to hate the Renegades, and she is on a mission for vengeance. As she gets closer to her target, she meets Adrian, a Renegade boy who believes in justice--and in Nova. But Nova's allegiance is to the villains who have the power to end them both." (Publisher's note)

"Fans of Marissa Meyer and teens who enjoy a deep storyline will be more than satisfied with all the clever details, plot twists, and thought-provoking dilemmas that fill the pages of this first book in a new series." VOYA

Other titles in this series are:
Archenemies (2018)

★ **Scarlet**; Marissa Meyer. Feiwel and Friends 2013 464 p. $17.99

Grades: 7 8 9 10 11 12 Fic

1. Science fiction 2. Fractured fairy tales 3. Cyborgs -- Fiction 4. Missing persons -- Fiction 5. Extraterrestrial beings -- Fiction

ISBN 0312642962; 9780312642969

LC 2012034060

This novel, by Marissa Meyer, is the second book of the "Lunar Chronicles" series. "Cinder, the cyborg mechanic, . . . [is] trying to break out of prison. . . . [Meanwhile,] Scarlet Benoit's grandmother is missing. . . . When Scarlet encounters Wolf, a street fighter who may have information . . . , she is loath to trust this stranger. . . . As Scarlet and Wolf unravel one mystery, they encounter another when they meet Cinder." (Publisher's note)

Meyer, Stephenie

Breaking dawn; [by] Stephenie Meyer. Little, Brown 2008 756p $22.99

Grades: 8 9 10 11 12 Fic

1. Marriage -- Fiction 2. Vampires -- Fiction 3. Werewolves -- Fiction

ISBN 978-0-316-06792-8; 0-316-06792-X

Sequel to: Eclipse (2007)

Although eighteen-year-old Bella joins the dark but seductive world of the immortals by marrying Edward the vampire, her connection to the powerful werewolf Jacob remains unsevered.

"For those who find it hard to say farewell to Bella and company, take heart: it may not be goodbye." Booklist

Eclipse. Little, Brown 2007 629p $18.99

Grades: 8 9 10 11 12 Fic

1. School stories 2. Vampires -- Fiction 3. Werewolves -- Fiction 4. Washington (State) -- Fiction

ISBN 978-0-316-16020-9; 0-316-16020-2

LC 2007-12325

Sequel to: New moon (2006)

Bella must choose between her friendship with Jacob, a werewolf, and her relationship with Edward, a vampire, but when Seattle is ravaged by a mysterious string of killings, the three of them need to decide whether their personal lives are more important than the well-being of an entire city.

"Meyer knows what her fans want: thrills, chills, and a lot of romance, and she delivers on all counts." SLJ

New moon. Little, Brown and Co. 2006 563p $17.99

Grades: 8 9 10 11 12 Fic

1. School stories 2. Vampires -- Fiction 3. Washington (State) -- Fiction

ISBN 978-0-316-16019-3; 0-316-16019-9

LC 2006012309

Sequel to Twilight (2005)

When the Cullens, including her beloved Edward, leave Forks rather than risk revealing that they are vampires, it is almost too much for eighteen-year-old Bella to bear, but she finds solace in her friend Jacob until he is drawn into a "cult" and changes in terrible ways.

"Vampire aficionados will voraciously consume this mighty tome in one sitting, then flip back and read it once more. It maintains a brisk pace and near-genius balance of breathtaking romance and action." Voice Youth Advocates

Followed by Eclipse (2007)

★ **Twilight**. Little, Brown and Co. 2005 498p $17.99; pa $8.99

Grades: 8 9 10 11 12 Fic

1. School stories 2. Vampires -- Fiction 3. Washington (State) -- Fiction

ISBN 0-316-16017-2; 0-316-01584-9 pa

LC 2004-24730

When seventeen-year-old Bella leaves Phoenix to live with her father in Forks, Washington, she meets an exquisitely handsome boy at school for whom she feels an overwhelming attraction and who she comes to realize is not wholly human.

"Realistic, subtle, succinct, and easy to follow, . . . [this book] will have readers dying to sink their teeth into it." SLJ

Other titles in this series are:
Breaking dawn (2008)
Eclipse (2007)
New moon (2006)

Meyer, Susan

Black radishes; [by] Susan Lynn Meyer. Delacorte Press 2010 228p map $16.99; lib bdg $19.99

Grades: 5 6 7 8 Fic

1. France -- Fiction 2. Jews -- France -- Fiction 3. Paris (France) -- Fiction 4. Holocaust, 1933-1945 -- Fiction

ISBN 978-0-385-73881-1; 0-385-73881-1; 978-0-385-90748-4 lib bdg; 0-385-90748-6 lib bdg

LC 2009-47613

"Set in France during World War II, this historical novel follows eleven-year-old Gustave as his family escapes Paris for safer quarters in the small, provincial town of Saint-Georges. . . . Not long after Gustave's family arrives in Saint-Georges, the Nazis invade and occupy Paris and establish a demarcation line between occupied northern France and unoccupied Vichy France in the south. . . . The episodic narrative offers abundant detail, and the wartime dangers, especially Gustave's father's illicit travel between occupied and unoccupied zones, adds considerable suspense. Gustave's growth over the course of the novel is both realistic and relatable, making this an appealing topical entry for the upper elementary/middle school set." Bull Cent Child Books

Another title in this series is:
Skating with the Statue of Liberty (2016)

Michael, Jan

★ **City** boy. Clarion Books 2009 186p $16

Grades: 5 6 7 8 **Fic**

1. Malawi -- Fiction 2. Orphans -- Fiction 3. Country life -- Fiction
ISBN 978-0-547-22310-0; 0-547-22310-2

LC 2008-37418

First published in the United Kingdom with title: Leaving home

In the southern African country of Malawi, after the AIDS-related deaths of both of his parents, a boy leaves his affluent life in the city to live in a rural village, sharing a one-roomed hut with his aunt, his cousins, and other orphans.

"This is a powerful portrait of poverty and hardship, evenly balanced with shades of hope. Michael's simple prose subtly layers detail, building full-bodied descriptions of landscapes and characters, leaving no room for shortcuts. . . . A stoic tale of surviving life's uncertainties." Kirkus

Milan, Maura

Ignite the stars; by Maura Milan. Albert Whitman & Co. 2018 400 p. (hardcover) $17.99

Grades: 7 8 9 10 **Fic**

1. Science fiction 2. Loyalty -- Fiction 3. Criminals -- Fiction
ISBN 9780807536254

LC 2017061615

In this book, by Maura Milan, "everyone in the universe fears him. But no one realizes that notorious outlaw Ia Cōcha is a seventeen-year-old girl. A criminal mastermind . . . , Ia has spent her life terrorizing the Olympus Commonwealth, the imperialist nation that destroyed her home. When the Commonwealth captures her and her true identity is exposed, they see Ia . . . as an opportunity: by forcing her to serve them, they will prove that no one is beyond their control." (Publisher's note)

Milford, Kate

Bluecrowne; a Greenglass House story. Kate Milford ; with illustrations by Nicole Wong. Clarion Books, Houghton Mifflin Harcourt 2018 272 p. (hardback) $17.99

Grades: 5 6 7 8 **Fic**

1. Siblings -- Fiction 2. Criminals -- Fiction 3. Stepmothers -- Fiction 4. Fireworks -- Fiction 5. Supernatural -- Fiction 6. Chinese Americans -- Fiction 7. Robbers and outlaws -- Fiction 8. Brothers and sisters -- Fiction
ISBN 9781328466884

LC 2018006963

In this book, in the Greenglass House series, by Kate Milford, illustrated by Nicole Wong, "Lucy Bluecrowne is beginning a new life ashore with her stepmother and half brother, though she's certain the only place she'll ever belong is with her father on a ship. . . . But then two nefarious strangers identify her little brother as the pyrotechnical prodigy they need to enact an evil plan, and it will take all Lucy's fighting instincts to keep her family together." (Publisher's note)

★ The **Boneshaker**; [illustrations by Andrea Offermann] Clarion Books 2010 372p il $17

Grades: 5 6 7 8 9 **Fic**

1. Young adult literature 2. Bicycles -- Fiction 3. Missouri -- Fiction 4. Demonology -- Fiction 5. Supernatural -- Fiction
ISBN 978-0-547-24187-6; 0-547-24187-9

LC 2009-45350

When Jake Limberleg brings his traveling medicine show to a small Missouri town in 1913, thirteen-year-old Natalie senses that something is wrong and, after investigating, learns that her love of automata and other machines make her the only one who can set things right.

"Natalie is a well-drawn protagonist with sturdy supporting characters around her. The tension built into the solidly constructed plot is complemented by themes that explore the literal and metaphorical role of crossroads and that thin line between good and evil." Kirkus

The **Broken** Lands; by Kate Milford ; with illustrations by Andrea Offermann. Clarion Books 2012 455 p. ill. (hardback) $16.99

Grades: 5 6 7 8 9 10 **Fic**

1. Bridges -- Fiction 2. Supernatural -- Fiction 3. New York (N.Y.) -- Fiction 4. Orphans -- Fiction 5. Demonology -- Fiction 6. Good and evil -- Fiction 7. New York (N.Y.) -- History -- 1865-1898 -- Fiction 8. Coney Island (New York, N.Y.) -- History -- 19th century -- Fiction
ISBN 0547739664; 9780547739663

LC 2011049466

This book, a prequel to "Kate Milford's 'The Boneshaker,' [is] set in . . . nineteenth-century Coney Island and New York City. Few crossroads compare to the one being formed by the Brooklyn Bridge and the East River, and as the bridge's construction progresses, forces of unimaginable evil seek to bend that power to their advantage. . . . Can the teenagers Sam, a card sharp, and Jin, a fireworks expert, stop them before it's too late?" (Publisher's note)

Ghosts of Greenglass House; Kate Milford ; with illustrations by Jaime Zollars. Clarion Books, Houghton Mifflin Harcourt 2017 456 p. illustrations (hardcover) $17.99

Grades: 5 6 7 8 **Fic**

1. Smuggling -- Fiction 2. Ghosts -- fiction 3. Hotels and motels -- fiction 4. Adoption -- fiction 5. Identity (Psychology) -- fiction 6. Identity (Philosophical concept) -- fiction
ISBN 9781328828927; 9780544991460

LC 2016049761

In this book, by Kate Milford, "thirteen-year-old Milo is, once again, spending the winter holidays stuck in [the Greenglass House,] a house full of strange guests who are not what they seem. There are fresh clues to uncover as friends old and new join in his search for a mysterious map and a famous smuggler's lost haul." (Publisher's note)

"A brainy, satisfying assemblage of puzzles with an immensely likable protagonist." Kirkus

Greenglass House; by Kate Milford ; with illustrations by Jaime Zollars. Clarion Books, Houghton Mifflin Harcourt 2014 384 p. (hardback) $17.99

Grades: 5 6 7 8 **Fic**

1. Mystery fiction 2. Hotels and motels -- Fiction 3. Magic -- Fiction 4. Adoption -- Fiction 5. Mystery and detective stories
ISBN 0544052706; 9780544052703

LC 2013036212

National Book Award Long List: Young People's Literature (2014)
Edgar Award: Best Juvenile (2015)

In this middle grade book by Kate Milford, illustrated by Jaime Zollars, "it's wintertime at Greenglass House. The creaky smuggler's inn is always quiet during this season, and twelve-year-old Milo, the innkeepers' adopted son, plans to spend his holidays relaxing. . . . As objects go missing and tempers flare, Milo and Meddy, the cook's daughter, must decipher clues and untangle the web of deepening mysteries to discover the truth about Greenglass House--and themselves." (Publisher's note)

The **Left** -Handed Fate; Kate Milford ; illustrated by Eliza Wheeler. Henry Holt & Co. 2016 384 p. illustrations (hardback) $16.99

Grades: 5 6 7 8 **Fic**

1. Sea stories 2. Magic -- Fiction 3. War of 1812 -- Fiction 4.

United States -- History -- War of 1812 -- Fiction
ISBN 9780805098006

LC 2015033437

In this book, by Kate Milford, illustrated by Eliza Wheeler, "Lucy Bluecrowne and Maxwell Ault are on a mission: find the three pieces of a strange and arcane engine they believe can stop the endless war raging between their home country of England and Napoleon Bonaparte's France. During the search, however, their ship, the famous privateer the Left-Handed Fate, is taken by the Americans, who have just declared war on England, too." (Publisher's note)

"Rich and strange of place and premise; suspenseful and thought-provoking." Kirkus

Miller, Jessica

Elizabeth and Zenobia; Jessica Miller ; illustrated by Yelena Bryksenkova. Amulet Books 2017 208 p. illustrations (hardcover with jacket : alk. paper) $16.99

Grades: 4 5 6 7 8 **Fic**

1. Friendship -- Fiction 2. Imagination -- Fiction
ISBN 9781419727245

LC 2017009964

In this book, by Jessica Miller, illustrated by Yelena Bryksenkova, "abandoned by her mother and neglected by her scientist father, . . . Elizabeth Murmur has only her fearless friend, Zenobia. . . . When Elizabeth's father takes them to live in his family home, . . . Zenobia becomes obsessed with finding a ghost . . . and forces Elizabeth to hold séances. . . . Elizabeth . . . learns that . . . [h]er father's younger sister disappeared from the grounds without a trace." (Publisher's note)

"Miller's painstaking crafting of language and attention to atmospheric detail create a clever story where nothing is as it seems. Drawings reminiscent of Gorey and references to gloomy classic poetry add beguiling texture. Eerie and dazzling—a perfect book for a dark and stormy afternoon or a favorite graveyard reading spot." Kirkus.

Miller, Kirsten

All you desire; can you trust your heart? Razorbill 2011 423p hardcover o.p. O.P.

Grades: 6 7 8 9 10 **Fic**

1. Romance fiction 2. Love stories 3. Reincarnation -- Fiction 4. New York (N.Y.) -- Fiction 5. Fate and fatalism -- Fiction
ISBN 978-1-59514-323-5; 1-59514-323-8

Haven Moore and Iain Morrow have been living a blissful life in Rome, an ocean way from the Ouroboros Society and its diabolical leader. But paradise is not to last. The mysterious disappearance of Haven's best friend, Beau, sends the pair running back to New York, where they encounter the Horae, an underground group of women who have spent centuries scheming to destroy Adam Rosier.

"A multi-layered mystery with (mostly) rounded characters." Kirkus

★ The **eternal** ones. Razorbill 2010 411p hardcover o.p. O.P.

Grades: 6 7 8 9 10 **Fic**

1. Romance fiction 2. Love stories 3. Faith -- Fiction 4. Tennessee -- Fiction 5. Reincarnation -- Fiction 6. New York (N.Y.) -- Fiction 7. Fate and fatalism -- Fiction
ISBN 978-1-59514-308-2; 1-59514-308-4

LC 2010-22775

Seventeen-year-old Haven Moore leaves East Tennessee to attend the Fashion Institute of Technology in New York City, where she meets playboy Iain Morrow, whose fate may be tied to hers through a series of past lives.

"Miller's writing elevates the supernatural romance well beyond typical fare, and Haven's mix of naïveté and determination makes her a solid, credible heroine." Publ Wkly

Followed by: All you desire (2011)

Kiki Strike; the darkness dwellers. by Kirsten Miller. Bloomsbury 2013 416 p. (hardback) $17.99

Grades: 5 6 7 8 **Fic**

1. Girls -- Fiction 2. Adventure fiction 3. Teenagers -- Fiction 4. Crime -- Fiction 5. France -- Fiction 6. Identity -- Fiction 7. Paris (France) -- Fiction 8. New York (N.Y.) -- Fiction
ISBN 1599907364; 9781599907369

LC 2012023303

This teen adventure novel, by Kirsten Miller, is part of the "Kiki Strike" series. "First they ventured deep under New York to save the city itself. Then things got personal as the Irregulars ventured into a haunted mansion in Chinatown to uncover an evil twin. Now, . . . this . . . group of delinquent geniuses jump feet first into a[n] . . . international pursuit, going underground in Paris to pursue a pair of treacherous royals who have killed Kiki's parents." (Publisher's note)

★ **Kiki** Strike: inside the shadow city; [by] Kirsten Miller. Bloomsbury Children's Books 2006 387p $16.95

Grades: 5 6 7 8 **Fic**

1. Mystery fiction 2. New York (N.Y.) -- Fiction
ISBN 978-1-58234-960-2; 1-58234-960-6

LC 2005030945

Life becomes more interesting for Ananka Fishbein when, at the age of twelve, she discovers an underground room in the park across from her New York City apartment and meets a mysterious girl called Kiki Strike who claims that she, too, wants to explore the subterranean world

"If a 12-year-old can be a hardboiled detective, Ananka Fishbein is one. Her narration is fresh and funny, and the author's unadorned, economical, yet descriptive style carries her character through with verve." SLJ

Another title about Kiki Strike is:
Kiki Strike: The empress's tomb (2007)

Kiki Strike: the Empress's tomb. Bloomsbury Children's Books 2007 369p $16.95

Grades: 5 6 7 8 **Fic**

1. Mystery fiction 2. New York (N.Y.) -- Fiction
ISBN 978-1-59990-047-6; 1-59990-047-5

LC 2007012000

Companion volume to Kiki Strike: inside the shadow city (2006)

Fourteen-year-olds Ananka Fishbein, Kiki Strike, and the other Irregulars encounter a Chinese mummy, a ghost, trained squirrels, and old enemies as they try to stop an art forgery ring and safeguard the secret streets hidden beneath New York City.

"A must-have for libraries where the first book is popular and a recommended purchase for collections that could use a good ghost/spy/action/mystery/story." SLJ

Miller, Michael

Shadow run; AdriAnne Strickland & Michael Miller. Delacorte Press 2017 390 p. (hardback) $17.99

Grades: 7 8 9 10 11 12 **Fic**

1. Science fiction 2. Adventure fiction 3. Princes -- Fiction 4. Families -- Fiction
ISBN 9780399552533; 9780399552557; 9780399552540

LC 2015044876

In this novel, by Michael Miller and AdriAnne Strickland, "Nev has just joined the crew of the starship Kaitan Heritage as the cargo loader. His captain, Qole, is the youngest-ever person to command her own ship, but she brooks no argument from her crew of orphans, fugitives, and con men. . . . As for Nev, he's a prince, in hiding on the ship. He believes Qole holds the key to changing galactic civilization, and . . . [he'll] get her to his home planet by any means necessary." (Publisher's note)

"The world-building is excellent, with a convincingly unique source of cosmic energy that has the potential for extraordinary power. The writing is accomplished; the plot, though familiar, has good twists; and the pace is appropriately fast." SLJ

Miller, Sarah

The **lost** crown. Atheneum Books for Young Readers 2011 412p $17.99

Grades: 8 9 10 11 12 **Fic**

1. Emperors 2. Sisters -- Fiction 3. Kings and rulers -- Fiction 4. World War, 1914-1918 -- Fiction 5. Russia -- History -- 1905, Revolution -- Fiction

ISBN 978-1-4169-8340-8; 1-4169-8340-6

LC 2010037001

In alternating chapters, Grand Duchesses Olga, Tatiana, Maria, and Anastasia tell how their privileged lives as the daughters of the tsar in early twentieth-century Russia are transformed by world war and revolution.

"Each Grand Duchess comes across as a unique personality. . . . Like the best historical novels, this allows modern-day teens to see themselves in very different people." Booklist

★ **Miss** Spitfire; reaching Helen Keller. Atheneum Books for Young Readers 2007 208p $16.99

Grades: 7 8 9 10 11 **Fic**

1. Deaf -- Fiction 2. Blind -- Fiction 3. Teachers -- Fiction

ISBN 978-1-4169-2542-2; 1-4169-2542-2

LC 2006014738

At age twenty-one, partially-blind, lonely but spirited Annie Sullivan travels from Massachusetts to Alabama to try and teach six-year-old Helen Keller, deaf and blind since age two, self-discipline and communication skills. Includes historical notes and timeline.

"This excellent novel is compelling reading even for those familiar with the Keller/Sullivan experience." SLJ

Includes bibliographical references

Mills, Emma, 1989-

Famous in a small town; Emma Mills. Henry Holt & Co. BYR 2019 320 p. (hardcover) $17.99

Grades: 7 8 9 10 11 **Fic**

1. Friendship -- Fiction 2. Fund raising -- Fiction 3. High school students -- Fiction

ISBN 9781250179630; 9781250179647

LC 2018945021

In this book, by Emma Mills, "for Sophie, small town life has never felt small. With her four best friends . . . she can weather any storm. But when Sophie's beloved Acadia High School marching band is selected to march in the upcoming Rose Parade, it's her job to get them all the way to LA. Her plan? To persuade country singer Megan Pleasant, their Midwestern town's only claim to fame, to come back to Acadia to headline a fundraising festival." (Publisher's note)

"A comfortable, readable tale of deep friendship, small towns, and big love in all its guises" (Booklist).

First & then; Emma Mills. Henry Holt & Co. 2015 272 p. (hardcover) $17.99

Grades: 8 9 10 11 12 **Fic**

1. School stories 2. Dating (Social customs) -- Fiction 3. Cousins -- Fiction 4. Florida -- Fiction 5. Schools -- Fiction 6. High schools -- Fiction 7. Family life -- Florida -- Fiction 8. Football players -- fiction 9. Families -- Florida -- fiction 10. High schools -- Florida -- fiction

ISBN 9781627792356

LC 2014043456

In this novel, by Emma Mills, "Devon Tennyson . . . [is] happy watching Friday night games from the bleachers, silently crushing on best friend Cas, and blissfully ignoring the future after high school. . . . [Until] Devon's cousin Foster, an unrepentant social outlier with a surprising talent for football, and the obnoxiously superior and maddeningly attractive star running back, Ezra, [arrive] . . . first into her P.E. class and then into every other aspect of her life." (Publisher's note)

"With sporadic references to Jane Austen's famous characters and wickedly inventive language, Mills closely observes the social milieu of an American high school obsessed with our favorite sport and makes readers care what happens." Kirkus

This adventure ends; Emma Mills. Henry Holt & Co. 2016 320 p. (ebook) $60; (hardback) $17.99

Grades: 8 9 10 11 **Fic**

1. School stories 2. Florida -- Fiction 3. Friendship -- Fiction 4. Dating (Social customs) -- Fiction 5. Schools -- Fiction 6. High schools -- Fiction 7. Moving, Household -- Fiction

ISBN 9781627799362; 9781627799355

LC 2016001536

In this novel, by Emma Mills, "Sloane isn't expecting to fall in with a group of friends when she moves from New York to Florida—especially not a group of friends so intense, so in love, so all-consuming. Yet that's exactly what happens. Sloane becomes closest to Vera, a social-media star who lights up any room, and Gabe, Vera's twin brother and the most serious person Sloane's ever met." (Publisher's note)

"Mild in every way but language, this tale of privileged teens offers a fairly satisfying glimpse of an almost alternate universe in which mundane life can be ignored." Kirkus

Mills, Geraldine

Gold; Geraldine Mills. Little Island 2017 241 p. map (paperback) $11.99

Grades: 4 5 6 7 8 **Fic**

1. Science fiction 2. Dystopian fiction 3. Twins -- fiction 4. Treasure 5. Adventure stories

ISBN 9781910411551; 1910411558; 9781910411698

In this book, by Geraldine Mills, "Esper and Starn are twin boys who live in a grim world that has been almost laid waste by massive volcanic explosions. . . . When the boys discover an . . . old manuscript, . . . which tells of gold on one of the forbidden islands the people can see from the coastline, they determine to go on a gold-hunt. They manage to construct a glider that takes them far from their home territory, and so begins a whole new adventure for the boys." (Publisher's note)

"Strong world-building and thought-provoking themes make this ideal for tweens looking for dystopian tales." SLJ

Mills, Wendy

All we have left; by Wendy Mills. Bloomsbury 2016 368 p. (hardback) $17.99; (ebook) $42

Grades: 8 9 10 11 12 **Fic**

1. Romance fiction -- fiction 2. Love -- Fiction 3. Muslims --

Fiction 4. Conduct of life -- Fiction 5. Interpersonal relations -- Fiction 6. September 11 Terrorist Attacks, 2001 -- Fiction
ISBN 9781619633438; 9781619633445
LC 2015037717

This coming-of-age story by Wendy Mills "traces the lives of two girls whose worlds intersect on September 11, 2001. Chapters alternate between the present-day story of Jesse, whose brother died on that fateful day, and . . . of Muslim teen Alia's experience inside one of the beleaguered Twin Towers. . . . Jesse's journey to discover why Travis was at the Twin Towers . . . eventually leads her to a search for Alia, the girl Travis was with when the planes hit." (School Library Journal)

"This outstanding, touching look at a national tragedy promotes healing and understanding and belongs in every library." SLJ

Miranda, Megan

Soulprint; by Megan Miranda. Bloomsbury/Walker 2015 368 p. (hardcover) $17.99
Grades: 7 8 9 10 **Fic**

1. Science fiction 2. Reincarnation -- Fiction 3. Fugitives from justice -- Fiction 4. Soul -- Fiction 5. Guilt -- Fiction 6. Prisoners -- Fiction 7. Conduct of life -- Fiction
ISBN 0802737749; 9780802737748
LC 2014009921

This novel by Megan Miranda is set "in a future where reincarnation can be scientifically tracked. . . .17-year-old half-Hispanic Alina Chase has spent her life isolated, allegedly for her own protection. She carries within her the soul of a charismatic and destructive whistleblower turned blackmailer, June Calahan. Broken out of confinement by a daring trio barely older than she is, Alina finds she still cannot escape June's shadow." (Publishers Weekly)

"A unique spin on recent dystopian reads featuring genetic heritability . . . [Soulprint] will fascinate teens already enthralled with questions about what they might do with their lives. A surprising new sf thriller with just enough of a touch of romance." Booklist

Miyabe, Miyuki, 1960-

Brave story; Miyuki Miyabe ; translated by Alexander O. Smith. Haikasoru/Viz Media, LLC 2009 816 p. illustrations, color map (pbk.) $16.99
Grades: 6 7 8 9 **Fic**

1. Japanese fiction
ISBN 1421527731; 9781421527734
LC 2009027395

Batchelder Award (2010)

In this book, Miyuki Miyabe, translated by Alexander O. Smith, "young Wataru Mitani's life is a mess. His father has abandoned him, and his mother has been hospitalized after a suicide attempt. Desperately he searches for some way to change his life--a way to alter his fate. To achieve his goal, he must navigate the magical world of Vision, a land filled with creatures both fierce and friendly. And to complicate matters, he must outwit a merciless rival from the real world." (Publisher's note)

Miéville, China, 1972-

★ **Railsea**; China Mieville. Del Rey/Ballantine Books 2012 424 p. ill. (hbk. : alk. paper) $18.00
Grades: 7 8 9 10 **Fic**

1. Adventure fiction 2. Steampunk fiction 3. Railroads -- Fiction 4. Imaginary places -- Fiction
ISBN 0345524527; 9780345524522; 9780345524546
LC 2012009516

This book presents "a steampunk spin on 'Moby-Dick' . . . . Instead of chasing whales on the sea, the crew of the diesel train Medes hunt moldywarpes—enormous, man-eating, molelike creatures who are only one of the countless menacing species who burrow in the perilous earth beneath a tangled ocean of train tracks. And it is one moldywarpe in particular, the great Mocker-Jack, that Captain Naphi is after—it's trendy for any captain worth her iron to have such a defining obsession, and she is fully aware that they hunt metaphor in beast form. Aboard for the grand adventure is your hero, young Sham (don't call him Ishmael)." (Booklist)

★ **Un** Lun Dun. Ballantine Books 2007 432p il hardcover o.p. pa $9
Grades: 5 6 7 8 9 **Fic**

1. Fantasy fiction
ISBN 0-345-45844-3 pa; 0-345-49516-0; 978-0-345-45844-5 pa; 978-0-345-49516-7
LC 2007-296921

When 12-year-old Zanna and her friend Deeba find a secret entrance leading out of London and into the strange city of Un Lun Dun, it appears that an ancient prophesy is coming true at last

"Miéville's fantastical city is vivid and splendidly crafted. . . . The story is exceptional and the action moves along at a quick pace." SLJ

Mlynowski, Sarah

Don't even think about it; Sarah Mlynowski. Delacorte Press 2014 336 p. (hc : alk. paper) $17.99
Grades: 7 8 9 10 **Fic**

1. Telepathy -- Fiction 2. Extrasensory perception -- Fiction 3. Schools -- Fiction 4. High schools -- Fiction 5. New York (N.Y.) -- Fiction 6. TriBeCa (New York, N.Y.) -- Fiction
ISBN 0385737386; 9780385737388; 9780385906623
LC 2012050777

This book, by Sarah Mlynowski, follows three girls who "used to be average New York City high school sophomores" but develop "telepathic powers." The girls use their powers to find about "romance, secrets, [and] scandals" involving their friends, boyfriends and students at their high school. (Publisher's note)

"When a group of Manhattan 10th graders inadvertently receives telepathic abilities from tainted flu shots, things rapidly get chaotic (and noisy). Finding out too much information dramatically upends family relationships, friendships, and romances. . . . Filled with heartbreak, hilarity, and some brutal truths, Mlynowski's novel will leave readers thinking about the gaps between our private and public selves and the lies we tell others and ourselves." Pub Wkly

Do not even think about it

Gimme a call. Delacorte Press 2010 301p $17.99; lib bdg $20.99
Grades: 7 8 9 10 **Fic**

1. School stories 2. Time travel -- Fiction
ISBN 978-0-385-73588-9; 0-385-73588-X; 978-0-385-90574-9 lib bdg; 0-385-90574-2 lib bdg
LC 2009-20020

"When Devi's high-school sweetheart breaks up with her right before their senior prom, she is devastated. Not only is she dateless but she is also friendless and relegated to a mediocre college because she has concentrated on her boyfriend instead of academics. . . . In a fresh twist on time travel, she contacts her freshman self via cell phone and proceeds to change their future. Of course, one small change leads to others, and both girls begin to wonder about the wisdom of this collaboration. Mlynowski has given herself a complicated, challenging story, and she is particularly effective in conveying the differences in maturity and perspective between a freshman and a senior." Booklist

Ten things we did (and probably shouldn't have) HarperTeen 2011 357p $16.99; ebook $9.99

Grades: 7 8 9 10 **Fic**

1. Friendship -- Fiction 2. Connecticut -- Fiction

ISBN 978-0-06-170124-5; 0-06-170124-6; 978-0-06-208461-3 ebook; 0-06-208461-5 ebook

LC 2010-45556

Sixteen-year-old April, a high school junior, and her friend Vi, a senior, get a crash course in reality as the list of things they should not do becomes a list of things they did while living parent-free in Westport, Connecticut, for the semester.

"With wit, energy, and an uncanny understanding of teenage logic, Mlynowski . . . weighs the pros and cons of independence in this modern cautionary tale. . . . Mlynowski avoids sermonizing, offering 10 madcap and remarkably tense escapades that will have readers laughing, cringing, and guessing how April will get out of the next pickle." Publ Wkly

Mobley, Jeannie

★ **Katerina's** wish; Jeannie Mobley. Margaret K. McElderry Books 2012 256 p. (hardcover) $15.99

Grades: 4 5 6 7 **Fic**

1. Wishes -- Fiction 2. Historical fiction 3. Immigrants -- Fiction 4. Czech Americans -- Fiction 5. Coal mines and mining -- Fiction 6. Family life -- Colorado -- Fiction 7. Colorado -- History -- 1876-1950 -- Fiction

ISBN 1442433434; 9781442433434; 9781442433458

LC 2011044392

In this young adult novel, Katerina and her family have immigrated from Bohemia and "settled in a coal mining camp, [where] they are still buried in work and trapped by debt. Then Trina sees a fish that reminds her of a fairy tale about a magic carp; soon after, her two younger sisters' frivolous wishes are granted. Initially skeptical, Trina eventually makes her wish: for a farm that will make her family happy." (Publishers Weekly)

Moderow, Hannah

Lily's mountain; written by Hannah Moderow. Houghton Mifflin Harcourt 2017 182 p. (hardcover) $16.99

Grades: 4 5 6 7 **Fic**

1. Sisters -- Fiction 2. Mountaineering -- Fiction 3. Father-daughter relationship -- Fiction 4. Alaska -- fiction 5. Families -- Alaska -- fiction 8. Fathers and daughters -- fiction 9. Denali, Mount (Alaska) -- fiction

ISBN 9781328829030; 9780544978003

LC 2016037231

In this novel, by Hannah Moderow, "Lily refuses to believe what everyone else accepts to be true: that her father has died while climbing Denali, the highest mountain in North America. Lily has grown up hiking in the Alaskan wilderness with her dad. He's an expert climber. There's no way he would let something like this happen. So instead of grieving, Lily decides to rescue him. Her plan takes her to Denali and on a journey that tests her physically and emotionally." (Publisher's note)

"There is strong character development, and readers will be inspired by Lily's and Sophie's ambition, perseverance, and self-determination." SLJ

Molope, Kagiso Lesego

This book betrays my brother; Kagiso Lesego Molope. Mawenzi House Publishers Ltd. 2018 192 p. $15

Grades: 8 9 10 11 12 **Fic**

1. Rape -- Fiction 2. Siblings -- Fiction 3. Teenage girls -- Fiction

ISBN 1988449294; 9781988449296

In this novel, by Kagiso Lesego Molope, "all her life, Naledi has been in awe of Basi, her charming and outgoing older brother. They've shared their childhood, with its jokes and secrets, the alliances and stories about the community. Having reached thirteen, she is preparing to go to the school dance. Then she sees Basi commit an act that violates everything she believes about him. How will she live her life now?" (Publisher's note)

Monaghan, Annabel

A **girl** named Digit; by Annabel Monaghan. Houghton Mifflin Harcourt 2012 187 p. $16.99; $16.99

Grades: 7 8 9 **Fic**

1. School stories 2. Terrorism -- Fiction 3. Cryptography -- Fiction 4. Kidnapping -- Fiction 5. Interpersonal relations -- Fiction 6. Adventure and adventurers -- Fiction

ISBN 054766852X; 9780547668529; 9780544022485

LC 2011012239

In this book, "saddled with the nickname Digit, Farrah resolved to fit in once she reached high school by hiding her math skills. Then Farrah stumbles upon an eco-terrorist organization after their suicide bomb attack on JFK Airport, and the terrorists want her dead. . . . Farrah's FBI protector, the cute, young rookie agent John Bennett, . . . works with Farrah to uncover a blackmail scheme involving the attack's bomber." (Kirkus Reviews)

Mone, Gregory

Fish. Scholastic Press 2010 241p $16.99

Grades: 4 5 6 7 **Fic**

1. Adventure fiction 2. Ciphers -- Fiction 3. Pirates -- Fiction 4. Buried treasure -- Fiction

ISBN 978-0-545-11632-9; 0-545-11632-5

Eleven-year-old Fish, seeking a way to help his family financially, becomes a reluctant cabin boy on a pirate ship, where he soon makes friends—and enemies—and is asked to help decipher clues that might lead to a legendary treasure.

"Mone seamlessly integrates factual information into his tale of friendship, loyalty, and exploration. . . . Fish makes a splashing good addition to adventure fiction." SLJ

Monir, Alexandra

The **girl** in the picture; Alexandra Monir. Delacorte Press 2016 272 p. (hc) $17.99

Grades: 7 8 9 10 **Fic**

1. Mystery fiction 2. Murder -- Fiction 3. Secrets -- Fiction 4. High schools -- Fiction 5. Schools -- Fiction 6. Disfigured persons -- Fiction

ISBN 9780375991370; 9780385743907; 9780385372527

LC 2015042550

In this book, by Alexandra Monir, "Nicole Morgan has been labeled many things—the geeky music girl, the shy sidekick of Miss Popularity, and the girl with the scar. . . . After heartthrob Chace Porter is found dead . . . , the police search for the girl snuggled up next to him in a picture discovered among his personal effects. A girl no one knew was even close to him—and whose best friend, Lana Rivera, was his girlfriend. Nicole is . . . the primary suspect in his murder." (Publisher's note)

"Teens will enjoy the cleverly crafted ride of this whodunit." SLJ

Monninger, Joseph

Whippoorwill; by Joseph Monninger. Houghton Mifflin Harcourt 2015 288 p. (hardback) $17.99

Grades: 7 8 9 10 **Fic**

1. Dogs -- Fiction 2. Neighbors -- Fiction 3. Single-parent families

-- Fiction 4. Dating (Social customs) -- Fiction 5. Father-daughter relationship -- Fiction 6. Neighborhoods -- Fiction 7. Dogs -- Training -- Fiction 8. Labrador retriever -- Fiction 9. Animals -- Treatment -- Fiction

ISBN 9780544531239

LC 2014046833

In this young adult novel, by Joseph Monninger, "Sixteen-year-old Clair Taylor has neighbors who are what locals call whippoorwills, the kind of people who fill their yards with rusty junk. Clair tries to ignore her surroundings, choosing instead to dream of a future beyond her rural New Hampshire town. But, when a black dog named Wally is chained up to a pole next door, Clair can't look the other way." (Publisher's note)

"Monninger revitalizes the boy-and-his-dog trope in this sweet novel." SLJ

Moon, Sarah

Sparrow; Sarah Moon. Arthur A. Levine Books, an imprint of Scholastic Inc. 2017 264 p. (hardcover : alk. paper) $18.99

Grades: 7 8 9 10 11 **Fic**

1. Suicide -- Fiction 2. Psychotherapy -- Fiction 3. African American teenage girls -- Fiction 4. Grief -- Fiction 5. Librarians -- Fiction 6. African Americans -- Fiction 9. Mothers and daughters -- Fiction 10. Brooklyn (New York, N.Y.) -- Fiction 12. School librarians -- fiction

ISBN 1338032585; 9781338032581; 9781338032598

LC 2017017322

In this book, by Sarah Moon, "Sparrow has always had a difficult time making friends. . . . And that's made school a lonely experience for her. . . . But when the one teacher who really understood her -- Mrs. Wexler, the school librarian, . . . is killed in a freak car accident, Sparrow's world unravels. . . . With the help of an insightful therapist, Sparrow finally reveals the truth of her inner life. And it's here that she discovers an outlet in rock & roll music." (Publisher's note)

"An elegantly told and important novel about learning to cope, live, and be happy with depression and anxiety." Booklist

Moore, David Barclay

★ The **stars** beneath our feet; David Barclay Moore. Alfred a Knopf 2017 304 p. hardcover $16.99

Grades: 5 6 7 8 **Fic**

1. Bildungsromans 2. Death -- Fiction 3. African Americans -- Fiction

ISBN 1524701246; 9781524701260; 9781524701253; 9781524701246

Coretta Scott King/John Steptoe New Talent Author Award (2018)

In this book, by David Barclay Moore, "it's Christmas Eve in Harlem, but twelve-year-old Lolly Rachpaul and his mom aren't celebrating. They're still reeling from his older brother's death in a gang-related shooting just a few months earlier. Then Lolly's mother's girlfriend brings him a gift . . . : two enormous bags filled with Legos. . . . Now, faced with a pile of building blocks and no instructions, Lolly must find his own way forward." (Publisher's note)

"Moore imbues his first novel with a strong voice and includes a diverse cast." Booklist

Moore, Perry

Hero. Hyperion 2007 428p $16.99

Grades: 7 8 9 10 11 12 **Fic**

1. Science fiction 2. LGBT youth -- Fiction 3. Gay teenagers -- Fiction 4. Superheroes -- Fiction 5. Father-son relationship -- Fiction

ISBN 978-1-4231-0195-6; 1-4231-0195-2

Thom Creed, the gay son of a disowned superhero, finds that he, too, has special powers and is asked to join the very League that rejected his father, and it is there that Thom finds other misfits whom he can finally trust.

"The combination of mystery, fantasy, thriller, and romance create a delightful and compelling read." Voice Youth Advocates

Moore, Peter

Red moon rising. Hyperion 2011 328p $16.99

Grades: 7 8 9 10 **Fic**

1. Vampires -- Fiction 2. Werewolves -- Fiction

ISBN 978-1-4231-1665-3; 1-4231-1665-8

LC 2009-40375

In a world where vampires dominate and werewolves are despised, a teenaged half-vampire discovers his recessive werewolf genes are developing with the approaching full moon.

"The details are imaginative and believable, as are the social interactions at school and in Danny's home." Booklist

V is for villain; Peter Moore. Hyperion 2014 336 p. $17.99

Grades: 7 8 9 10 **Fic**

1. Adventure fiction 2. Ability -- Fiction 3. Brothers -- Fiction 4. Superheroes -- Fiction 5. Good and evil -- Fiction

ISBN 1423157494; 9781423157496

LC 2013026304

"When Brad makes friends who are more into political action than weight lifting, he's happy to join a new crew-especially since it means spending more time with Layla, a girl who may or may not have a totally illegal, totally secret super-power. And with her help, Brad begins to hone a dangerous new power of his own." (Publisher's note)

"Well-crafted characters, moral nuance, and a tale with nice, believable twists make this a great addition to the teen-superhero genre." Kirkus

Moranville, Sharelle Byars

27 magic words; Sharelle Byars Moranville. Holiday House 2016 199 p. (hardcover) $16.95; (ebook) $16.95

Grades: 5 6 7 8 **Fic**

1. Children and death -- fiction 2. Truthfulness and falsehood -- fiction 3. Grief -- Fiction 4. Self-perception -- Fiction

ISBN 0823436578; 9780823436576; 9780823437061

LC 2015049142

In this children's novel about facing the future, by Sharelle Byars Moranville, "although Kobi's parents sailed into a storm at sea five years ago, she knows they are alive. If she says Avanti she can see them. Now that her life is being turned upside down again, she will need the magic words her mother left behind more than ever. . . . [But] she must confront not only the untruths she has told others but the stories she has made herself believe." (Publisher's note)

"Distinctive, well-drawn characters drive the plot and provide their own magical contributions to Kobi's widening world. Both tragic and uplifting, this winsome tale perfectly depicts some of the many aspects of magic." Kirkus

Moreno, Nina

Don't date Rosa Santos; by Nina Moreno. Hyperion 2019 336 p. (hardcover) $17.99

Grades: 8 9 10 11 **Fic**

1. Family life -- Fiction 2. Cuban Americans -- Fiction 3. Blessing and cursing -- Fiction 4. Love -- Fiction 5. Magic -- Fiction 6. Ocean -- Fiction 7. Florida -- Fiction 8. Family life -- Florida

-- Fiction
ISBN 9781368039703; 9781368040860

LC 2018030125

In this novel, by Nina Moreno, "Rosa Santos is cursed by the sea-at least, that's what they say. Dating her is bad news, especially if you're a boy with a boat. But Rosa feels more caught than cursed. Caught between cultures and choices. Between her abuela . . . and her mother. . . . As her college decision looms, Rosa collides-literally-with Alex Aquino, the mysterious boy with tattoos of the ocean whose family owns the marina." (Publisher's note)

"Full of complex family relationships, a diverse community, and plenty of swoonworthy moments, fans of rom-coms won't be able to put this one down." (Kirkus)

Morgan, Page

The **beautiful** and the cursed; by Page Morgan. 1st ed. Delacorte Press 2013 352 p. (library) $21.99; (hardcover) $18.99

Grades: 7 8 9 10 11 12 **Fic**

1. Romance fiction 2. Gargoyles -- Fiction 3. Brothers and sisters -- Fiction 4. Sisters -- Fiction 5. Supernatural -- Fiction 6. Paris (France) -- History -- 1870-1940 -- Fiction 7. France -- History -- Third Republic, 1870-1940 -- Fiction

ISBN 0385743114; 9780375990953; 9780385743112

LC 2012022378

In this book by Page Morgan, "Ingrid, her sister Gabby, and their mom arrive at the abandoned abbey that they plan to turn into an art gallery. Grayson, Ingrid's twin brother, had procured the place and was supposed to meet them there. Grayson, however, does not show up and the girls are surprised to learn that he has actually been missing for several days. . . . [Ingrid] and Gabby . . .discover a world of living gargoyles that can transform into humans." (Children's Literature)

Other titles in the series are:
The Lovely and the Lost (2014)
The Wondrous and the Wicked (2015)

Moriarty, Jaclyn

★ A **corner** of white; Jaclyn Moriarty. Arthur A. Levine Books 2013 384 p. (Colors of Madeleine trilogy) (hardcover) $17.99

Grades: 7 8 9 10 11 12 **Fic**

1. Fantasy fiction 2. Epistolary fiction 3. Color -- Fiction 4. Magic -- Fiction 5. England -- Fiction 6. Princesses -- Fiction 7. Missing persons -- Fiction 8. Cambridge (England) -- Fiction 9. Interpersonal relations -- Fiction

ISBN 0545397367; 9780545397360

LC 2012016582

Boston Globe-Horn Book Honor: Fiction (2013).

This opening volume of a fantasy series from Jaclyn Moriarty focuses on 14-year-old Madeleine, who "lives in Cambridge, England, with her zany mother in uncertain circumstances, having run away from their fabulously privileged international existence. Meanwhile, Elliot lives in Bonfire, The Farms, Cello, a parallel reality. . . . Through a crack between their worlds, they begin exchanging letters." (Kirkus Reviews)

"Australian writer Moriarty's marvelously original fantasy is quirky and clever... [she] captures the proud iconoclasm of many homeschoolers and does not shy away from tenderness and poignancy." BookList

★ The **cracks** in the kingdom; Jaclyn Moriarty. Arthur A. Levine Books, an imprint of Scholastic Inc. 2014 480 p. (The colors of Madeleine) (hardcover : alk. paper) $18.99

Grades: 7 8 9 10 11 12 **Fic**

1. Fantasy fiction 2. Princesses -- Fiction 3. Missing persons -- Fiction 4. Color -- Fiction 5. Magic -- Fiction 6. England -- Fiction 7. Cambridge (England) -- Fiction 8. Interpersonal relations -- Fiction

ISBN 0545397383; 9780545397384; 9780545397391

LC 2013022827

In this book, by Jaclyn Moriarty, "Princess Ko's been bluffing about the mysterious absence of her father. . . . If she can't get him back in a matter of weeks, the consequence may be a devastating war. So under the guise of a publicity stunt she gathers a group of teens - each with a special ability - from across the kingdom to crack the unsolvable case of the missing royals of Cello." (Publisher's note)

"In this lively follow-up to A Corner of White (Scholastic, 2013), Moriarty chronicles the ever-intertwining lives of Cambridge resident Madeline Tully and her secret correspondent Elliot Baranski, a quick-witted farm boy from the Kingdom of Cello...The RYA's work around Cello expands an already complex and intricately drawn world. Readers will be clamoring for the next title after the thrilling yet satisfying conclusion.—" (School Library Journal)

Feeling sorry for Celia; Jaclyn Moriarty. 1st U.S. ed; St. Martin's Griffin 2002 276 p. $15.99

Grades: 7 8 9 10 11 12 **Fic**

1. Epistolary fiction 2. Teenage girls -- Fiction 3. Australia -- Fiction

ISBN 0312287364; 9780312287368

LC 00045969

In this epistolary novel, by Jaclyn Moriarty, "life is pretty complicated for Elizabeth Clarry. Her best friend Celia keeps disappearing, her absent father suddenly reappears, and her communication with her mother consists entirely of wacky notes left on the fridge. On top of everything else, because her English teacher wants to rekindle the 'Joy of the Envelope,' a Complete and Utter Stranger knows more about Elizabeth than anyone else." (Publisher's note)

"Moriarty poignantly captures the trials of adolescent friendships and the bittersweet evolution of the teenage subconscious." Booklist

Other Ashby/Brookfield books are:
The Year of Secret Assignments (2004)
The Murder of Bindy MacKenzie (2006)
The Ghosts of Ashbury High (2010)

The **ghosts** of Ashbury High. Arthur A. Levine Books 2010 480p $18.99

Grades: 8 9 10 11 12 **Fic**

1. School stories 2. Australia -- Fiction

ISBN 978-0-545-06972-4; 0-545-06972-6

LC 2009-32651

Student essays, scholarship committee members' notes, and other writings reveal interactions between a group of modern-day students at an exclusive New South Wales high school and their strange connection to a young Irishman transported to Australia in the early 1800s.

"The off-the-rails zaniness . . . is . . . satisfying, and in between all the irreverence, Moriarty slips in plenty of sharp-eyed, poignant observations." SLJ

The **murder** of Bindy Mackenzie. Arthur A. Levine Books 2006 494p $16.99

Grades: 8 9 10 11 12 **Fic**

1. School stories 2. Australia -- Fiction

ISBN 0-439-74051-7; 0-439-74052-5 pa

LC 2006-07562

Class brain Bindy Mackenzie has alienated her entire high school but when she realizes someone is trying to kill her, she has to make friends in order to get help.

"The truths about family, school, and social pressures and Bindy's unforgettable, earnest, hilariously high-strung voice . . . will capture and hold readers." Booklist

The **year** of secret assignments. Arthur A. Levine Books 2004 340p $16.95; pa $7.99

Grades: 8 9 10 11 12 **Fic**

1. School stories 2. Australia -- Fiction 3. Friendship -- Fiction

ISBN 0-439-49881-3; 0-439-49882-1 pa

LC 2003-14278

Three female students from Ashbury High write to three male students from rival Brookfield High as part of a pen pal program, leading to romance, humiliation, revenge plots, and war between the schools

"There are a few coarse moments—a reference to a blow job and some caustic outbursts. . . . This is an unusual novel with an exhilarating pace, irrepressible characters, and a screwball humor that will easily attract teens." Booklist

Other titles set at Ashbury High are:

The ghosts of Ashbury High (2010)

The murder of Bindy Mackenzie (2006)

Morpurgo, Michael

The **amazing** story of Adolphus Tips; [by] Michael Morpurgo. Scholastic Press 2006 140p hardcover o.p. O.P.

Grades: 4 5 6 7 **Fic**

1. Cats -- Fiction 2. Grandmothers -- Fiction 3. World War, 1939-1945 -- Fiction

ISBN 0-439-79661-X

LC 2005049038

When Boowie reads the diary that his grandmother sends him, he learns of her childhood in World War II England when American and British soldiers practiced for D-Day's invasion in the area of her home, and about her beloved cat, Adolphus Tips, and the cat's namesake

"The personal story of anger and love is as gripping as the war drama, and Morpurgo includes a fascinating note about the invasion rehearsal and why its history is seldom told." Booklist

An **elephant** in the garden. Feiwel and Friends 2011 199p $16.99

Grades: 6 7 8 9 **Fic**

1. Zoos -- Fiction 2. Germany -- Fiction 3. Elephants -- Fiction 4. World War, 1939-1945 -- Fiction

ISBN 978-0-312-59369-8; 0-312-59369-4

Lizzie and Karl's mother is a zoo keeper; the family has become attached to an orphaned elephant named Marlene, who will be destroyed as a precautionary measure so she and the other animals don't run wild should the zoo be hit by bombs. The family persuades the zoo director to let Marlene stay in their garden instead. When the city is bombed, the family flees with thousands of others, but how can they walk the same route when they have an elephant in tow, and keep themselves safe?

"This well-paced, heartwarming narrative by a master storyteller will appeal to readers on several levels—as a tale of adventure and suspense, as a commentary on human trauma and animal welfare during war, as a perspective on the hardships facing the German people in the final months of World War II, and as a tribute to the rich memories and experiences of an older generation." SLJ

Half a man; Michael Morpurgo, illustrated by Gemma O'Callaghan. Candlewick Press 2015 64 p. $16.99

Grades: 7 8 9 10 **Fic**

1. Grandfathers -- Fiction 2. World War, 1939-1945 -- Fiction 3. Veterans -- Fiction 4. Grandparent and child -- Fiction

ISBN 0763677477; 9780763677473

LC 2014939339

In this book, "author Michael Morpurgo evokes the post-war Britain of his childhood. . . . From a young age, Michael was both fascinated by and afraid of his grandfather. Grandpa's ship was torpedoed during the Second World War, leaving him with terrible burns. . . . As he grows older, Michael stays with his grandfather during the summer holidays and learns the story behind Grandpa's injuries, finally getting to know the real man behind the solemn figure from his childhood." (Publisher's note)

"With our returning wounded warriors of today, this is a timely and superb addition to all collections and not to be missed." SLJ

★ **Kensuke's** kingdom. Scholastic Press 2003 164p hardcover o.p. pa $5.99

Grades: 4 5 6 7 **Fic**

1. Survival after airplane accidents, shipwrecks, etc. -- Fiction

ISBN 0-439-38202-5; 0-439-59181-3 pa

LC 2002-9078

First published 1999 in the United Kingdom

When Michael is swept off his family's yacht, he washes up on a desert island, where he struggles to survive—until he finds he is not alone

This is "highly readable. . . . The end is bittersweet but believable, and the epilogue is a sad commentary on the long-lasting effects of war." Booklist

Listen to the Moon; by Michael Morpurgo. Feiwel & Friends 2015 352 p. $16.99

Grades: 5 6 7 8 9 **Fic**

1. England -- Fiction 2. Girls -- fiction 3. World War, 1914-1918 -- fiction 4. Father-son relationship -- fiction

ISBN 1250042046; 9781250042040

"In May 1915 a fisherman and his son, Alfie, from the Scilly Isles west of Great Britain, find a little girl near death on a deserted island, take her home, and care for her. She does not speak but clings to a teddy bear and a blanket with a German name sewn on it. Naming her Lucy Lost, Alfie and his parents and a kindly and wise doctor nurture her with love, music from a gramophone, and drawing material. Months go by, and still no one can uncover any details about her life. But World War I is raging, the British harbor fierce anti-German sentiments, and when news of the name on her blanket spreads, the family is shunned." (Kirkus)

"A framing device, built around the research of Lucy's future grandson, allows Morpurgo to shift among multiple narrators as he unspools the mystery of where she came from. Along the way, Morpurgo offers powerful descriptions of shipwreck, mass drowning, and devastation, as well as healing and growth." Pub Wkly

The **Mozart** question; [by] Michael Morpurgo; illustrated by Michael Foreman. Candlewick Press 2008 66p il hardcover o.p. O.P.

Grades: 4 5 6 7 **Fic**

1. Violinists -- Fiction 2. Venice (Italy) -- Fiction 3. Holocaust, 1933-1945 -- Fiction

ISBN 978-0-7636-3552-7; 0-7636-3552-9

A young journalist goes to Venice, Italy, to interview a famous violinist, who tells the story of his parents' incarceration by the Nazis, and explains why they can no longer listen to the music of Mozart.

"Morpurgo breathes life into this touching tale, which is conveyed with compassion and honesty. Foreman's watercolors enrich the narrative." SLJ

Private Peaceful. Scholastic Press 2004 202p $16.95; pa $5.99
Grades: 7 8 9 10 **Fic**

1. Great Britain -- Fiction 2. World War, 1914-1918 -- Fiction
ISBN 0-439-63648-5; 0-439-63653-1 pa

LC 2003-65347

First published 2003 in the United Kingdom

When Thomas Peaceful's older brother is forced to join the British Army, Thomas decides to sign up as well, although he is only fourteen years old, to prove himself to his country, his family, his childhood love, Molly, and himself

"In this World War I story, the terse and beautiful narrative of a young English soldier is as compelling about the world left behind as about the horrific daily details of trench warfare. . . . Suspense builds right to the end, which is shocking, honest, and unforgettable." Booklist

War horse; by Michael Morpurgo. Scholastic 2007 165p $16.99
Grades: 5 6 7 8 **Fic**

1. Horses -- Fiction 2. World War, 1914-1918 -- Fiction
ISBN 978-0-439-79663-7; 0-439-79663-6

LC 2006044368

First published 1982 in the United Kingdom

Joey the horse recalls his experiences growing up on an English farm, his struggle for survival as a cavalry horse during World War I, and his reunion with his beloved master

"At times deeply affecting, the story balances the horror with moments of respite and care." Horn Book Guide

Morris, Gerald

The **ballad** of Sir Dinadan. Houghton Mifflin 2003 245p (The squire's tales) $16; pa $6.99
Grades: 6 7 8 9 **Fic**

1. Minstrels -- Fiction 2. Knights and knighthood -- Fiction 3. Great Britain -- History -- 0-1066 -- Fiction
ISBN 0-618-19099-6; 0-618-54894-7 pa

LC 2002-10818

Sequel to: The savage damsel and the dwarf (2000)

Though he would rather pursue his talent as a musician, eighteen-year-old Dinadan is forced to follow his older brother Tristram's path and become a knight. Set at the time of King Arthur

"Written in accessible prose and laced with occasional magic, the novel moves at a quick pace and showcases a continually maturing hero." Horn Book

Followed by: The princess, the crone, and the dung-cart knight (2004)

The **legend** of the king. Houghton Mifflin Books for Children 2010 295p (The squire's tales) $16
Grades: 6 7 8 9 **Fic**

1. Knights and knighthood -- Fiction 2. Great Britain -- History -- 0-1066 -- Fiction
ISBN 978-0-547-14420-7; 0-547-14420-2

Sequel to: The squire's quest (2009)

Terence and his fellow Knights of the Round Table must come together in a last stand to save Camelot.

"Morris pulls off a spectacular conclusion to his humane and witty Squire's Tales series." Kirkus

The **lioness** & her knight. Houghton Mifflin 2005 343p (The squire's tales) $16; pa $6.99
Grades: 6 7 8 9 **Fic**

1. Knights and knighthood -- Fiction 2. Great Britain -- History -- 0-1066 -- Fiction
ISBN 0-618-50772-8; 0-547-01485-6 pa

LC 2004-15782

Sequel to: The princess, the crone, and the dung-cart knight (2004)

Headstrong sixteen-year-old Lady Luneta and her distant cousin, Sir Ywain, travel to Camelot and beyond finding more adventure than they hoped for until, with the help of a fool, Luneta discovers what she really wants from life.

"Adventure, magic, love, and knights of the realm collide in this delightfully witty tale." SLJ

Parsifal's page. Houghton Mifflin 2001 232p $16
Grades: 6 7 8 9 **Fic**

1. Kings 2. Knights and knighthood -- Fiction 3. Perceval (Legendary character) -- Fiction
ISBN 0-618-05509-6

LC 00-31894

In medieval England, eleven-year-old Piers' dream comes true when he becomes page to Parsifal, a peasant whose quest for knighthood reveals important secrets about both of their families

"Filled with action and laced with humor, the entertaining story proceeds at a rollicking pace." Horn Book Guide

The **princess,** the crone, and the dung-cart knight. Houghton Mifflin 2004 310p $17; pa $6.95
Grades: 6 7 8 9 **Fic**

1. Knights and knighthood -- Fiction 2. Lancelot (Legendary character) -- Fiction 3. Great Britain -- History -- 0-1066 -- Fiction
ISBN 0-618-37823-5; 0-618-73748-0 pa

LC 2003-12296

Sequel to The ballad of Sir Dinadan

Determined to find the knight responsible for the terrible deaths of her mother and the Jewish peddler who had given them a home, thirteen-year-old Sarah is helped in her quest by a strange old woman, a magical sword, a young faery, and an unkempt knight with little armor and no horse.

"The novel is driven by a keen sense of justice and lightened by droll wit. A terrific cast of characters energizes the story, which plays out against a colorful, well-developed historical background." Booklist

The **quest** of the Fair Unknown. Houghton Mifflin 2006 264p (The squire's tales) $16 Grades: 6 7 8 9 **Fic**

1. Knights and knighthood -- Fiction 2. Gawain (Legendary character) -- Fiction 3. Galahad (Legendary character) -- Fiction 4. Great Britain -- History -- 0-1066 -- Fiction
ISBN 978-0-618-63152-0; 0-618-63152-6

LC 2005034850

Sequel to: The lioness & her knight (2005)

Having grown up in an isolated forest, Beaufils sets off for Camelot to find his father and winds up undertaking quests with Sirs Gawain and Galahad, visiting various hermits, and traveling to the fairy world.

Morris' "language is sly and charming and funny; his characters embody both the tale and the gentle lessons he imparts." Booklist

Followed by: The squire's quest (2009)

The **savage** damsel and the dwarf. Houghton Mifflin 2000 213p (The squire's tales) $16; pa $6.99

Grades: 6 7 8 9 **Fic**

1. Knights and knighthood -- Fiction 2. Gareth (Legendary character) -- Fiction

ISBN 0-395-97126-8; 0-547-01437-6 pa

LC 99-16457

Sequel to: The squire, his knight, and his lady (1999)

Lynet, a feisty young woman, journeys to King Arthur's court in order to find a champion to rescue her beautiful older sister, and she is joined in her quest by a clever dwarf and a bold kitchen knave, neither of whom are not what they seem

"The whimsical narrative features wry dialogue and memorable characterizations." Horn Book Guide

Followed by: Parsifal's page (2001)

The **squire's** quest. Houghton Mifflin Harcourt 2009 275p (The squire's tales) $15

Grades: 6 7 8 9 **Fic**

1. Fairies -- Fiction 2. Middle Ages -- Fiction 3. Knights and knighthood -- Fiction 4. Great Britain -- History -- 0-1066 -- Fiction

ISBN 978-0-547-14424-5; 0-547-14424-5

LC 2008045903

Terence worries about the lengthy absence of his faery friends as he travels to Greece to aid the Emperor Alexander and attempts to thwart a nefarious plot by Mordred to assume the throne held by King Arthur.

"Morris misses no opportunity to poke fun at knightly traditions and the more ridiculous conventions of courtly love, but there is also a serious undertone here, foreshadowing events to come later in the Arthurian cycle. . . . Morris's treatment of the Byzantine Empire is also fresh and interesting." SLJ

★ The **squire's** tale. Houghton Mifflin 1998 212p (The squire's tales) $15; pa $5.50

Grades: 6 7 8 9 **Fic**

1. Knights and knighthood -- Fiction 2. Gawain (Legendary character) -- Fiction 3. Great Britain -- History -- 0-1066 -- Fiction

ISBN 0-395-86959-5; 0-440-22823-9 pa

LC 97-12447

In medieval England, fourteen-year-old Terence finds his tranquil existence suddenly changed when he becomes the squire of the young Gawain of Orkney and accompanies him on a long quest, proving Gawain's worth as a knight and revealing an important secret about his own true identity

"Well-drawn characters, excellent, snappy dialogue, detailed descriptions of medieval life, and a dry wit put a new spin on this engaging tale of the characters and events of King Arthur's time." Booklist

Other titles in this series are:

The squire, his knight, & his lady (1999)

The savage damsel and the dwarf (2000)

Parsifal's page (2001)

The ballad of Sir Dinadan (2003)

The princess, the crone, and the dung-cart knight (2004)

The lionness & her knight (2005)

The quest of the Fair Unknown (2006)

The squire's quest (2009)

The legend of the king (2010)

The **squire,** his knight, and his lady. Houghton Mifflin 1999 232p (The squire's tales) $16; pa $6.99

Grades: 6 7 8 9 **Fic**

1. Knights and knighthood -- Fiction 2. Gawain (Legendary character) -- Fiction 3. Great Britain -- History -- 0-1066 -- Fiction

ISBN 0-395-91211-3; 0-547-01438-4 pa

LC 98-28718

Sequel to: The squire's tale (1998)

After several years at King Arthur's court, Terence, as Sir Gawain's squire and friend, accompanies him on a perilous quest that tests all their skills and whose successful completion could mean certain death for Gawain

"Laced with magic, humor, and chivalry, this reworking of Sir Gawain and the Green Knight, in which Gawain learns humility and Terence discovers his true place in the world, provides an engaging introduction to the original tale." Horn Book

Followed by: The savage damsel and the dwarf (2000)

Morris, Paula

Ruined; a novel. Point 2009 309p $16.99

Grades: 6 7 8 9 10 **Fic**

1. Ghost stories 2. New Orleans (La.) -- Fiction

ISBN 978-0-545-04215-4; 0-545-04215-1

Set in New Orleans, this is "the story of 15-year-old Rebecca Brown, a proud New Yorker sent to live with a family friend while her father travels overseas. Ostracized as an outsider, Rebecca struggles to fit in and cope with her new surroundings. When she befriends Lisette, a ghost who has haunted the cemetery ever since her mysterious death 155 years earlier, Rebecca is drawn into an eerie story of betrayal, loss, old curses and family secrets. . . . This moody tale thoroughly embraces the rich history, occult lore and complex issues of race, ethnicity, class and culture that have defined New Orleans for centuries." Publ Wkly

Morrison, Laurie

Up for air; Laurie Morrison. Amulet Books 2019 282 p. (hardback) $16.99

Grades: 5 6 7 8 **Fic**

1. Swimming -- Fiction 2. Friendship -- Fiction 3. Conduct of life -- Fiction 4. Learning disabilities -- Fiction

ISBN 9781419733666

LC 2018034292

In this novel, by Laurie Morrison, "an awesome swimmer with a frustrating learning disability struggles in the roiling waters of adolescence . . . Readers will root for [Annabelle] as she ricochets between ebullience and despair, empathy and hurt, confidence and doubt, pride and self-loathing--we've been there, too, or soon will be. Captures the turmoil of adolescence with wisdom and humor in near-pointillist detail." (Kirkus Reviews)

"Captures the turmoil of adolescence with wisdom and humor in near-pointillist detail." --Kirkus 03/2019

Morrison, Megan

Disenchanted; the trials of Cinderella. Megan Morrison. Arthur A. Levine Books, an imprint of Scholastic Inc. 2016 416 p. illustrations, maps (Tyme) (hardcover : alk. paper) $17.99; (ebook) $17.99

Grades: 5 6 7 8 **Fic**

1. Fairy tales 2. Magic -- Fiction 3. Princes -- Fiction 4. Blessing and cursing -- Fiction 5. Interpersonal relations -- Fiction 6. Characters in literature -- Fiction 7. Cinderella (Legendary character) -- fiction

ISBN 054564271X; 9780545642712; 9780545642736

LC 2016008854

In this middle grade novel in the Tyme series by Megan Morrison, "Ella Coach has one wish: revolution. Her mother died working in a sweatshop, and Ella wants every laborer in the Blue Kingdom to receive fairer treatment. . . . Prince Dash Charming has one wish: evolution. . . . Serge can grant any wish -- and has. . . . This is a story about three people who want something better and who together find the faith to change their worlds." (Publisher's note)

"Morrison's magical descriptions illuminate more of the wide magical world that she's created in Tyme. Engrossing and delightful reading—a can't-miss choice for middle-graders." Booklist

Grounded; the tale of Rapunzel. Megan Morrison. Arthur A. Levine Books, an imprint of Scholastic Inc. 2015 384 p. (Tyme) (alk. paper) $17.99

Grades: 5 6 7 8 **Fic**

1. Fractured fairy tales 2. Thieves -- fiction 3. Fairy tales 4. Magic -- Fiction 5. Fairies -- Fiction 6. Witches -- Fiction 7. Robbers and outlaws -- Fiction 8. Characters in literature -- Fiction 9. Adventure and adventurers -- Fiction

ISBN 0545638267; 9780545638265; 9780545642699; 9780545642705; 9780545754682

LC 2014027138

This story by Megan Morrison, is a retelling of the Rapunzel legend. "In all of Tyme, . . . no one is as lucky as Rapunzel. . . . And she knows this because Witch tells her so--her beloved Witch. . . . [Then] Rapunzel descends to the ground for the first time, and finds a world filled with more peril than Witch promised . . . and more beauty, wonder, and adventure than she could have dreamed." (Publisher's note)

Other titles in this series are:
Disenchanted (2016)
Transformed (2019)

Morton-Shaw, Christine

The **riddles** of Epsilon. Katherine Tegen Books 2005 375p $16.99; lib bdg $17.89

Grades: 7 8 9 10 **Fic**

1. Supernatural -- Fiction 2. Great Britain -- Fiction

ISBN 0-06-072819-1; 0-06-072820-5 lib bdg

LC 2004-14641

After moving with her parents to a remote English island, fourteen-year-old Jess attempts to dispel an ancient curse by solving a series of riddles, aided by Epsilon, a supernatural being.

Moses, Shelia P.

Joseph. Margaret K. McElderry Books 2008 174p $16.99

Grades: 7 8 9 10 **Fic**

1. Drug abuse -- Fiction 2. African Americans -- Fiction 3. Mother-son relationship -- Fiction

ISBN 978-1-4169-1752-6; 1-4169-1752-7; 1-4169-9442-4 pa

Fourteen-year-old Joseph tries to avoid trouble and keep in touch with his father, who is serving in Iraq, as he and his alcoholic, drug-addicted mother move from one homeless shelter to another.

"Moses creates a compelling character in Joseph. His struggle to survive his current situation intact is fascinating to read. . . . Negative influences such as drug dealers and users are described in a clear, cold light. Education and hard work are praised for their positive influences. Middle school and junior high teens will enjoy this story." Voice Youth Advocates

Followed by: Joseph's grace (2010)

The **legend** of Buddy Bush. Margaret K. McElderry Books 2004 216p $15.95

Grades: 6 7 8 9 **Fic**

1. North Carolina -- Fiction 2. Race relations -- Fiction 3. African Americans -- Fiction

ISBN 0-689-85839-6

LC 2003-8024

National Book Award Finalist: Young People's Literature (2004)

In 1947, twelve-year-old Pattie Mae is sustained by her dreams of escaping Rich Square, North Carolina, and moving to Harlem when her Uncle Buddy is arrested for attempted rape of a white woman and her grandfather is diagnosed with a terminal brain tumor.

"Patti Mae's first-person voice, steeped in the inflections of the South, rings true, and her observations richly evoke a time, place, and a resilient African American community." Booklist

Another title about Buddy Bush is:
The return of Buddy Bush (2005)

The **return** of Buddy Bush. Simon & Schuster 2006 143p il $15.95

Grades: 6 7 8 9 **Fic**

1. Family life -- Fiction 2. North Carolina -- Fiction 3. Race relations -- Fiction 4. African Americans -- Fiction

ISBN 0-689-87431-6

Sequel to: The legend of Buddy Bush

Pattie Mae goes to Harlem to visit her sister after the death of her beloved grandfather. She hopes to soak up the Northern lifestyle and is on a secret mission to find her Uncle Buddy, who is hiding out after being falsely accused of rape in their North Carolina hometown.

"Pattie Mae's voice is fresh and colloquial, and her spunky narration will speak to readers." SLJ

Mosier, Paul

Train I ride; Paul Mosier ; [edited by] Karen Chaplin. HarperCollins 2017 192 p. (ebook) $15.99; (hardcover) $16.99

Grades: 6 7 8 9 10 **Fic**

1. Railroad travel -- Fiction

ISBN 9780062455758; 9780062455734

LC 2016935895

In this book, by Paul Mosier, "Rydr is on a train heading east, leaving California, where her gramma can't take care of her anymore, and traveling to Chicago, to live with an unknown relative. She brings with her a backpack, memories both happy and sad, and a box, containing something very important. As Rydr meets her fellow passengers and learns their stories, her own story begins to emerge." (Publisher's note)

"A harrowing, moving, immersive, and ultimately uplifting debut novel." Kirkus

Mosley, Walter

47. Little, Brown 2005 232p $16.99

Grades: 7 8 9 10 **Fic**

1. Magic -- Fiction 2. Slavery -- Fiction 3. African Americans -- Fiction

ISBN 0-316-11035-3

LC 2004-12500

Number 47, a fourteen-year-old slave boy growing up under the watchful eye of a brutal master in 1832, meets the mysterious Tall John, who introduces him to a magical science and also teaches him the meaning of freedom.

"Time travel, shape-shifting, and intergalactic conflict add unusual, provocative elements to this story. And yet, well-drawn characters; lively dialogue filled with gritty, regional dialect; vivid descriptions; and poignant reflections ground it in harsh reality." SLJ

Moulton, Courtney Allison

Angelfire; 1st ed. Katherine Tegen Books 2011 453 p. (trade bdg.) $17.99

Grades: 7 8 9 10 **Fic**

1. Horror fiction 2. Souls -- Fiction 3. Angels -- Fiction 4. Monsters -- Fiction 5. Reincarnation -- Fiction

ISBN 9780062002327; 9780062002341

LC 2010012821

A seventeen-year-old girl discovers that she has the reincarnated soul of an ancient warrior destined to battle the reapers --creatures who devour humans and send their souls to Hell. --Grades nine to twelve. -- (Bull Cent Child Books)

"The author has introduced a dark and compelling world of action and intrigue, albeit with enough 'normal' drama and humor sprinkled throughout to lighten it. . . . Older junior and senior high school readers will find themselves engrossed in the story until its powerful conclusion—then anxiously awaiting the second installment." Voice Youth Advocates

Mukherjee, Sonya

Gemini; Sonya Mukherjee. Simon & Schuster Books for Young Readers 2016 326 p. paperback $10.99; hardcover $17.99

Grades: 8 9 10 11 12 **Fic**

1. Bildungsromans 2. Sisters -- Fiction 3. Conjoined twins -- Fiction

ISBN 9781481456784; 9781481456791; 1481456776; 9781481456777

LC 2015019774

In this novel by Sonya Mukherjee, "conjoined twins Clara and Hailey have lived in the same small town their entire lives . . . but there are cracks in their quiet existence. . . . Clara wants to stay close to home, avoid all attention, and study the night sky. Hailey wants to travel the world, learn from great artists, and dance with mysterious boys. . . . Each twin must untangle her dreams from her sister's and figure out what it means to be her own person." (Publisher's note)

"Even for sisters, Clara and Hailey are close. They have to be--they're conjoined twins attached at the spine. . . . [T]his debut is a well-researched and particularly heartfelt account of a rare medical condition and the people it affects. Though they share a body, Clara and Hailey are two very different people with different dreams, and their fight for a normal life will resonate with many." Booklist

Mull, Brandon

Rogue Knight; by Brandon Mull. Aladdin 2014 480 p. (Five kingdoms) (hardback) $17.99

Grades: 4 5 6 7 **Fic**

1. Fantasy fiction 2. Knights and knighthood -- Fiction 3. Adventure and adventurers -- Fiction

ISBN 1442497033; 9781442497030; 9781442497047

LC 2014025800

Sequel to: Sky Raiders (2014)

In this novel, by Brandon Mull, book two of the "Five Kingdoms" series, "young Cole enters the second of five kingdoms in the otherworldly Outskirts, is exposed to a second culture and a second flavor of magic, and battles a second monster made of stolen magic as he continues the search for his fellow earthly kidnappees." (Kirkus Reviews)

"Cole is a relatable and brave Everykid hero, and his friends bring different perspectives to this ongoing tale. Mull's latest series continues to be excellent, and it should easily find a home among fans of middle-grade fantasy stories." Booklist

Sky Raiders; by Brandon Mull. Aladdin 2014 432 p. (Five kingdoms) (hardback) $16.99

Grades: 4 5 6 7 **Fic**

1. Fantasy fiction 2. Adventure fiction

ISBN 1442497009; 9781442497009

LC 2013032734

"Cole Randolph was just trying to have a fun time with his friends on Halloween (and maybe get to know Jenna Hunt a little better). But when a spooky haunted house turns out to be a portal to something much creepier, Cole finds himself on an adventure on a whole different level." (Publisher's note)

"Although Mull packs quite a bit into this initial installment, he skillfully mixes the capricious logic of dreams with high stakes and constant danger. The intriguing premise, strong world-building, and numerous twists make this a real page-turner." Pub Wkly

Other titles in this series are:

Rogue Night (2014)

Crystal Keepers (2015)

Death Weaver (2016)

Spirit animals; 1 wild born. Brandon Mull. Scholastic Press 2013 224 p. (Spirit animals) $12.99

Grades: 4 5 6 7 **Fic**

1. Spirits -- Fiction 2. Children and animals 3. Magic -- fiction

ISBN 0545522439; 9780545522434

LC 2013932302

This book, by Brandon Mull, is set in "the world of Erdas, where every child who comes of age must discover if they have a spirit animal, a rare bond between human and beast that bestows great powers to both. A dark force has risen from distant and long-forgotten lands, and has begun an onslaught that will ravage the world. Now the fate of Erdas has fallen on the shoulders of four young strangers." (Publisher's note)

Other titles in this series are:

Hunted (2013)

Blood Ties (2014)

Fire and Ice (2014)

Against the Tide (2014)

Rise and Fall (2014)

The Evertree (2015)

★ A **world** without heroes. Aladdin 2011 454p (Beyonders) $19.99

Grades: 4 5 6 7 **Fic**

1. Fantasy fiction 2. Magic -- Fiction 3. Space and time -- Fiction 4. Heroes and heroines -- Fiction

ISBN 978-1-4169-9792-4; 1-4169-9792-X

LC 2010-23437

Fourteen-year-old Jason Walker is transported to a strange world called Lyrian, where he joins Rachel, who was also drawn there from our world, and a few rebels, to piece together the Word that can destroy the malicious wizard emperor, Surroth.

"Mull moves his story at a brisk pace, preventing the tragedies from overwhelming the adventure, while offering ample action and feisty dialogue to keep fantasy lovers entertained." Publ Wkly

Mulligan, Andy

★ **Trash**. David Fickling Books 2010 232p $16.99; lib bdg $19.99

Grades: 6 7 8 9 **Fic**

1. Mystery fiction 2. Poverty -- Fiction 3. Political corruption

-- Fiction 4. Refuse and refuse disposal -- Fiction
ISBN 978-0-385-75214-5; 0-385-75214-8; 978-0-385-75215-2 lib bdg; 0-385-75215-6 lib bdg

LC 2010-15940

Fourteen-year-olds Raphael and Gardo team up with a younger boy, Rat, to figure out the mysteries surrounding a bag Raphael finds during their daily life of sorting through trash in a third-world country's dump.

"While on the surface the book reads like a fast-paced adventure title, it also makes a larger statement about the horrors of poverty and injustice in the world. . . . Trash is a compelling read." SLJ

Munday, Evan

Connect the Scotts; the Dead Kid Detective Agency. Evan Munday. ECW Press 2018 336 p. $9.95

Grades: 5 6 7 8 9 **Fic**

1. Death -- fiction 2. Spirits -- fiction 3. Secret societies -- fiction
ISBN 1770413332; 9781770413337

In this book in the Dead Kid Detective Agency series, by Evan Munday, "while investigating the cause of the long-dead Tabetha Scott's death way back in the 1860s, October and the Dead Kids discover that Sticksville, Ontario, served as an endpoint for the Underground Railroad, the secret network by which enslaved people escaped to free states and Canada. But October Schwartz finds herself with more detective work than she can handle." (Publisher's note)

Murdock, Catherine Gilbert

★ The **book** of boy; Catherine Gilbert Murdock, illustrated by Ian Schoenherr. Greenwillow Books 2018 288 p. (hardback) $16.99

Grades: 4 5 6 7 8 **Fic**

1. Relics -- Fiction 2. Friendship -- Fiction 3. People with disabilities -- Fiction 4. Pilgrims and pilgrimages -- Fiction
ISBN 9780062686206

LC 2017043536

Newbery Honor Book (2019)

"Boy has always been relegated to the outskirts of his small village. With a large hump on his back, a mysterious past, and a tendency to talk to animals, he is often mocked by others in his town--until the arrival of a shadowy pilgrim named Secondus. Impressed with Boy's climbing and jumping abilities, Secondus engages Boy as his servant, pulling him into an action-packed and suspensful expedition across Europe to gather the seven precious relics of Saint Peter. Boy quickly realizes this journey is not an innocent one. They are stealing the relics and accumulating dangerous enemies in the process. But Boy is determined to see this pilgrimage through until the end--for what if St. Peter can make Boy's hump go away?." (Publisher's note)

Murdock "evokes the bleak, plague-decimated villages of Europe, provides details of the seamy yet powerful trade in relics, and limns a world in which every aspect of life is steeped in religious belief. . . . The story is beautifully served by its presentation--generous page design, thick deckle-edged paper, and gorgeous woodcut-style illustrations that head each chapter." Horn Book

★ **Dairy** Queen; a novel. Houghton Mifflin 2006 275p $16

Grades: 7 8 9 10 **Fic**

1. Football -- Fiction 2. Farm life -- Fiction
ISBN 0-618-68307-0

LC 2005-19077

After spending her summer running the family farm and training the quarterback for her school's rival football team, sixteen-year-old D.J. decides to go out for the sport herself, not anticipating the reactions of those around her.

"D. J.'s voice is funny, frank, and intelligent, and her story is not easily pigeonholed." Voice Youth Advocates

Other titles about D.J. Schwenk are:
Front and center (2009)
The off season (2007)

Front and center. Houghton Mifflin 2009 256p (The dairy queen trilogy) $16

Grades: 7 8 9 10 **Fic**

1. Farm life -- Fiction 2. Basketball -- Fiction
ISBN 978-0-618-95982-2; 0-618-95982-3

LC 2009-24167

Sequel to: The off season (2007)

"In the third and final book . . . about farm girl, linebacker, and basketball star D.J. Schwenk, the self-aggrandizing heroine must decide her future: is she up to playing basketball for the Big Ten schools that are starting to recruit her, or should she choose a smaller college, where the game is less brutal but also less challenging? . . . D.J.'s voice is intimate and compelling, her story both universal and unique, familiar and eye-opening." Horn Book

The **off** season. Houghton Mifflin 2007 277p $16

Grades: 7 8 9 10 **Fic**

1. Football -- Fiction 2. Farm life -- Fiction
ISBN 978-0-618-68695-7; 0-618-68695-9

LC 2006029278

Sequel to: Dairy Queen (2006)

High school junior D.J. staggers under the weight of caring for her badly injured brother, her responsibilities on the dairy farm, a changing relationship with her friend Brian, and her own athletic aspirations.

This "depicts a believably maturing D.J., a young woman whose character shines through even as she struggles to find her voice. Readers will root for her at every tragicomic turn." SLJ

Followed by: Front and center (2009)

★ **Princess** Ben; being a wholly truthful account of her various discoveries and misadventures, recounted to the best of her recollection, in four parts. written by Catherine Gilbert Murdock. Houghton Mifflin 2008 344p $16; pa $8.99

Grades: 7 8 9 10 **Fic**

1. Fairy tales 2. Magic -- Fiction 3. Princesses -- Fiction 4. Courts and courtiers -- Fiction
ISBN 978-0-618-95971-6; 0-618-95971-8; 978-0-547-22325-4 pa; 0-547-22325-0 pa

LC 2007-34300

A girl is transformed, through instruction in life at court, determination, and magic, from sullen, pudgy, graceless Ben into Crown Princess Benevolence, a fit ruler of the kindgom of Montagne as it faces war with neighboring Drachensbett.

"Murdock's prose sweeps the reader up and never falters, blending a formal syntax and vocabulary with an intimate tone that bonds the reader with Ben." Horn Book

Murphy, Julie

★ **Ramona** Blue; Julie Murphy. Balzer + Bray 2017 408 p. (hardcover) $17.99

Grades: 8 9 10 11 **Fic**

1. Bildungsromans 2. Lesbians -- Fiction 3. Sexual orientation -- fiction 4. Interpersonal relations -- fiction
ISBN 9780062418371; 9780062418357

LC 2016950250

In this young adult novel, by Julie Murphy, "Ramona was only five years old when Hurricane Katrina changed her life forever. Since then, it's been Ramona and her family against the world. Standing over six feet tall with unmistakable blue hair, Ramona is sure of three things: she likes girls, she's fiercely devoted to her family, and she knows she's destined for something bigger than the trailer she calls home in Eulogy, Mississippi." (Publisher's note)

"An exquisite, thoughtful exploration of the ties that bind and the fluidity of relationships, sexuality, and life." Kirkus

Mussi, Sarah

★ The **door** of no return. Margaret K. McElderry Books 2008 394p $17.99; pa $8.99

Grades: 8 9 10 11 12 **Fic**

1. Adventure fiction 2. Ghana -- Fiction 3. Blacks -- Fiction 4. Homicide -- Fiction 5. Great Britain -- Fiction 6. Buried treasure -- Fiction

ISBN 978-1-4169-1550-8; 1-4169-1550-8; 978-1-4169-6825-2 pa; 1-4169-6825-3 pa

LC 2007-18670

Sixteen-year-old Zac never believed his grandfather's tales about their enslaved ancestors being descended from an African king, but when his grandfather is murdered and the villains come after Zac, he sets out for Ghana to find King Baktu's long-lost treasure before the murderers do.

"This exciting narrative takes place in England and Africa; in jungles, dark caves, and on the sea. . . . Overall, this is a complex, masterful story for confident readers." SLJ

Myers, Walter Dean, 1937-2014

★ **Darius** & Twig; Walter Dean Myers. 1st ed. Harper, an imprint of HarperCollinsPublishers 2013 208 p. (hardcover) $17.99

Grades: 8 9 10 11 12 **Fic**

1. Friendship -- Fiction 2. Harlem (New York, N.Y.) -- Fiction 3. Running -- Fiction 4. Authorship -- Fiction 5. Best friends -- Fiction 6. New York (N.Y.) -- Fiction 7. African Americans -- Fiction 8. Dominican Americans -- Fiction

ISBN 0061728233; 9780061728235; 9780061728242

LC 2012050678

Coretta Scott King Honor Book: Author (2014)

In this book by Walter Dean Myers, "Harlem teenager Darius, a writer, wants to get out of his neighborhood and make it to college, but his grades aren't good enough. He's hoping that if he can get a story published, he might nab a college scholarship. His best friend Twig is a track star, and sees athletics as his escape. Both are skeptical of the hype they are fed about how hard work pays off, and they face obstacles ranging from school bullies . . . to indifferent educators." (Publishers Weekly)

"This encouraging text may inspire teens who feel trapped by their surroundings...Told in Darius's voice, the prose is poetic but concise. This would be a worthwhile addition to any middle or high school media center or public library shelf and would make a valuable book for discussion in a middle school classroom.—" VOYA

Dope sick. HarperTeen/Amistad 2009 186p $16.99; lib bdg $17.89

Grades: 8 9 10 11 12 **Fic**

1. Drug abuse -- Fiction 2. Supernatural -- Fiction 3. African Americans -- Fiction 4. Harlem (New York, N.Y.) -- Fiction

ISBN 978-0-06-121477-6; 0-06-121477-9; 978-0-06-121478-3 lib bdg; 0-06-121478-7 lib bdg

LC 2008-10568

Seeing no way out of his difficult life in Harlem, seventeen-year-old Jeremy "Lil J" Dance flees into a house after a drug deal goes awry and meets a weird man who shows different turning points in Lil J's life when he could have made better choices.

"Myers uses street-style lingo to cover Lil J's sorry history of drug use, jail time, irresponsible fatherhood and his own childhood grief. A didn't-see-that-coming ending wraps up the story on a note of well-earned hope and will leave readers with plenty to think about." Publ Wkly

★ **Fallen** angels; Walter Dean Myers. Scholastic Paperbacks 2008 336 p. hardcover o.p. (pbk.) $7.99

Grades: 8 9 10 11 12 **Fic**

1. Vietnam War, 1961-1975 -- Fiction 2. African American soldiers -- Fiction

ISBN 9780545055765; 0545055768

First published 1988

ALA YALSA Margaret A. Edwards Award (1994)

"Black, seventeen, perceptive and sensitive, Richie (the narrator) has enlisted and been sent to Vietnam; in telling the story of his year of active service, Richie is candid about the horror of killing and the fear of being killed, the fear and bravery and confusion and tragedy of the war." Bull Cent Child Books

"Except for occasional outbursts, the narration is remarkably direct and understated; and the dialogue, with morbid humor sometimes adding comic relief, is steeped in natural vulgarity, without which verisimilitude would be unthinkable. In fact, the foul talk, which serves as the story's linguistic setting, is not nearly as obscene as the events." Horn Book

Game. HarperTeen 2008 218p $16.99; lib bdg $17.89

Grades: 8 9 10 11 12 **Fic**

1. School stories 2. Basketball -- Fiction 3. Czech Americans -- Fiction 4. African Americans -- Fiction 5. Harlem (New York, N.Y.) -- Fiction

ISBN 978-0-06-058294-4; 978-0-06-058295-1 lib bdg

LC 2007-18370

If Harlem high school senior Drew Lawson is going to realize his dream of playing college, then professional, basketball, he will have to improve at being coached and being a team player, especially after a new—white—student threatens to take the scouts' attention away from him.

"Basketball fans will love the long passages of detailed court action. . . . The authentic thoughts of a strong, likable, African American teen whose anxieties, sharp insights, and belief in his own abilities will captivate readers of all backgrounds." Booklist

★ **Hoops**; a novel. Delacorte Press 1981 183p hardcover o.p. pa $5.99

Grades: 7 8 9 10 **Fic**

1. Basketball -- Fiction 2. African Americans -- Fiction 3. Harlem (New York, N.Y.) -- Fiction

ISBN 0-440-93884-8 pa

LC 81-65497

ALA YALSA Margaret A. Edwards Award (1994)

"This story offers the reader some fast, descriptive basketball action, a love story between Lonnie and girlfriend Mary-Ann, peer friendship problems, and gangster intrigues. Most importantly, however, it portrays the growth of a trusting and deeply caring father-son relationship between [the coach] Cal and [fatherless] Lonnie." Voice Youth Advocates

Followed by The outside shot (1988)

Invasion! Walter Dean Myers. Scholastic Press 2013 224 p. $17.99

Grades: 7 8 9 10 **Fic**

1. Friendship -- fiction 2. Normandy (France), Attack on, 1944 -- fiction 3. War -- Fiction 4. Soldiers -- Fiction 5. African American soldiers -- Fiction 6. France -- History -- 20th century -- Fiction 7. Normandy (France) -- History -- 20th century -- Fiction 8. Segregation -- United States -- History -- 20th century -- Fiction 9. World War, 1939-1945 -- Campaigns -- France -- Normandy -- Fiction 10. World War, 1939-1945 -- Participation, African American -- fiction 11. United States -- Armed Forces -- African Americans -- History -- 20th century -- fiction

ISBN 0545384281; 9780545384285; 9780545384292; 9780545576598

LC 2013005595

In this book by Walter Dean Myers, "old friends Josiah 'Woody' Wedgewood and Marcus Perry see each other in England prior to the invasion of Normandy. Woody is with the 29th Infantry, and Marcus, who's black, is with the Transportation Corps, the segregation of their Virginia hometown following them right into wartime. Their friendship frames the story, as the two occasionally encounter each other in the horrific days ahead." (Kirkus Reviews)

"Myers eloquently conveys how exhausting war is physically and emotionally. . . . [T]his novel can be hard to read, but it is also hard to put down." SLJ

Kick; [by] Walter Dean Myers and Ross Workman. HarperTeen 2011 197p $16.99; lib bdg $17.89

Grades: 7 8 9 10 **Fic**

1. Police -- Fiction 2. Soccer -- Fiction 3. Mentoring -- Fiction 4. New Jersey -- Fiction 56. Family life -- Fiction 6. Criminal investigation -- Fiction

ISBN 978-0-06-200489-5; 0-06-200489-1; 978-0-06-200490-1 lib bdg; 0-06-200490-5 lib bdg

LC 2010-18441

Told in their separate voices, thirteen-year-old soccer star Kevin and police sergeant Brown, who knew his father, try to keep Kevin out of juvenile hall after he is arrested on very serious charges.

"Workman is a genuine talent, writing short, declarative sentences that move that narrative forward with assurance and a page-turning tempo. Myers, of course, is a master. . . . The respective voices and characters play off each other as successfully as a high-stakes soccer match." Booklist

Lockdown. Amistad 2010 247p $16.99; lib bdg $17.89

Grades: 8 9 10 11 12 **Fic**

1. Old age -- Fiction 2. Friendship -- Fiction 3. African Americans -- Fiction 4. Juvenile delinquency -- Fiction

ISBN 978-0-06-121480-6; 0-06-121480-9; 978-0-06-121481-3 lib bdg; 0-06-121481-7 lib bdg

LC 2009-7287

Coretta Scott King Author Award honor book, 2011

Teenage Reese, serving time at a juvenile detention facility, gets a lesson in making it through hard times from an unlikely friend with a harrowing past.

"Reese's first-person narration rings with authenticity. . . . Myers' storytelling skills ensure that the messages he offers are never heavy-handed." Booklist

★ **Monster**; illustrations by Christopher Myers. HarperCollins Pubs. 1999 281p il $14.95; lib bdg $14.89; pa $8.99

Grades: 7 8 9 10 **Fic**

1. Trials -- Fiction 2. African Americans -- Fiction

ISBN 0-06-028077-8; 0-06-028078-6 lib bdg; 0-06-440731-4 pa

LC 98-40958

Michael L. Printz Award, 2000

While on trial as an accomplice to a murder, sixteen-year-old Steve Harmon records his experiences in prison and in the courtroom in the form of a film script as he tries to come to terms with the course his life has taken.

"Balancing courtroom drama and a sordid jailhouse setting with flashbacks to the crime, Myers adeptly allows each character to speak for him or herself, leaving readers to judge for themselves the truthfulness of the defendants, witnesses, lawyers, and, most compellingly, Steve himself." Horn Book Guide

Scorpions. Harper & Row 1988 216p $16.99; lib bdg $16.89; pa $5.99

Grades: 6 7 8 9 **Fic**

1. African Americans -- Fiction 2. Juvenile delinquency -- Fiction 3. Harlem (New York, N.Y.) -- Fiction

ISBN 0-06-024364-3; 0-06-024365-1 lib bdg; 0-06-447066-0 pa

LC 85-45815

A Newbery Medal honor book, 1989

Set in Harlem, this "story presents a brutally honest picture of the tragic influence of gang membership and pressures on a young black adolescent. Jamal Hicks, age twelve, reluctantly follows the orders of his older brother, now serving time in prison for robbery, and takes his place as leader of the Scorpions. When Jamal's leadership is challenged, disaster follows and Jamal learns some tragic lessons about friendship and owning a gun." Child Book Rev Serv

★ **Slam!** Scholastic Press 1996 266p hardcover o.p. pa $5.99

Grades: 7 8 9 10 **Fic**

1. School stories 2. Basketball -- Fiction 3. African Americans -- Fiction

ISBN 0-590-48667-5; 0-590-48668-3 pa

LC 95-46647

Coretta Scott King Award for text

Seventeen-year-old "Slam" Harris is counting on his noteworthy basketball talents to get him out of the inner city and give him a chance to succeed in life, but his coach sees things differently

Myers "descriptions of Slam on the court . . . use crisp details, not flowery language, to achieve their muscular poetry, and Myers is equally vivid in relating the torment Slam feels as he stares at a page of indecipherable algebra formulas. . . . [This is an] admirably realistic coming-of-age novel." Booklist

Street love. Amistad/Harper Tempest 2006 134p $15.99; lib bdg $16.89

Grades: 8 9 10 11 12 **Fic**

1. Novels in verse 2. African Americans -- Fiction 3. Harlem (New York, N.Y.) -- Fiction

ISBN 978-0-06-028079-6; 0-06-028079-4; 978-0-06-028080-2 lib bdg; 0-06-028080-8 lib bdg

LC 2006-02457

This story told in free verse is set against a background of street gangs and poverty in Harlem in which seventeen-year-old African American Damien takes a bold step to ensure that he and his new love will not be separated.

"The realistic drama on the street and at home tells a gripping story." Booklist

★ **Sunrise** over Fallujah. Scholastic Press 2008 290p $17.99
Grades: 8 9 10 11 12 **Fic**
1. African Americans -- Fiction 2. Iraq War, 2003-2011 -- Fiction
ISBN 978-0-439-91624-0; 0-439-91624-0
LC 2007-25444

"Instead of heading to college as his father wishes, Robin leaves Harlem and joins the army to stand up for his country after 9/11. While stationed in Iraq with a war looming that he hopes will be averted, he begins writing letters home to his parents and to his Uncle Richie. . . . Myers brilliantly freeze-frames the opening months of the current Iraq War by realistically capturing its pivotal moments in 2003 and creating a vivid setting. Memorable characters share instances of wry levity that balance the story without deflecting its serious tone." SLJ

Myklusch, Matt

Jack Blank and the Imagine Nation. Aladdin 2010 480p $16.99
Grades: 4 5 6 7 **Fic**
1. Fantasy fiction 2. Science fiction 3. Orphans -- Fiction 4. Superheroes -- Fiction
ISBN 978-1-4169-9561-6; 1-4169-9561-7

Twelve-year-old Jack, freed from a dismal orphanage, makes his way to the elusive and impossible Imagine Nation, where a mentor saves him from dissection and trains him to use his superpower, despite the virus he carries that makes him a threat.

This creates "a richly imagined world with strong appeal to fans of comics. The island is populated by a fun cast of heroes and villains. . . . Brisk narration captures the superhero world with a mixture of fast-paced action, wry humor, and occasional heartfelt speeches about courage and friendship." SLJ

Followed by: Jack Blank and the secret war (2011)

The **secret** war. Aladdin 2011 529p $16.99
Grades: 4 5 6 7 **Fic**
1. Fantasy fiction 2. Orphans -- Fiction 3. Viruses -- Fiction 4. Superheroes -- Fiction
ISBN 978-1-4169-9564-7; 1-4169-9564-1
LC 2010041779

Sequel to: Jack Blank and the Imagine Nation (2010)

Twelve-year-old Jack may be the Imagine Nation's only hope of fending off a new Rustov attack, with the help of his fellow superheroes-in-training, but the virus he carries, and Jonas's suspicions, provide new complications.

Myracle, Lauren

Luv ya bunches. Amulet Books 2009 335p $15.95
Grades: 4 5 6 **Fic**
1. School stories 2. Friendship -- Fiction
ISBN 978-0-8109-4211-0; 0-8109-4211-9
LC 2009012585

Four friends—each named after a flower—navigate the ups and downs of fifth grade. Told through text messages, blog posts, screenplay, and straight narrative

Myracle "displays a shining awareness of and sensitivity to the highly textured society of tween girls. . . . This is a fun, challenging, and gently edifying story." Booklist

Another title about these characters is:
Violet in bloom (2010)

Peace, love, and baby ducks. Dutton Children's Books 2009 292p $16.99; pa $8.99
Grades: 8 9 10 11 12 **Fic**
1. Sisters -- Fiction 2. Atlanta (Ga.) -- Fiction
ISBN 978-0-525-47743-3; 0-525-47743-8; 978-0-14-241527-6 pa; 0-14-241527-8 pa
LC 2008-34221

Fifteen-year-old Carly's summer volunteer experience makes her feel more real than her life of privilege in Atlanta ever did, but her younger sister starts high school pretending to be what she is not, and both find their relationships suffering.

"Myracle empathetically explores issues of socioeconomic class, sibling rivalry, and parental influence in a story that is deeper and more nuanced than the title and cutesy cover." Booklist

Violet in bloom; a flower power book. Amulet Books 2010 366p $15.95
Grades: 4 5 6 **Fic**
1. School stories 2. Food -- Fiction 3. California -- Fiction 4. Friendship -- Fiction
ISBN 978-0-8109-8983-2; 0-8109-8983-2
LC 2010-24319

Fifth-graders Katie-Rose, Violet, Milla, and Yasaman seem to have little in common except their flower-related names, but they nurture their new friendship through a social-networking site and a campaign to have healthier snacks served at school.

This is "a realistic, easy-to-relate-to riot of pre-adolescent exuberance. A triumph." Kirkus

Na, An

Wait for me. Putnam 2006 169p hardcover o.p. pa $7.99
Grades: 8 9 10 11 12 **Fic**
1. Deaf -- Fiction 2. Sisters -- Fiction 3. Korean Americans -- Fiction 4. Mother-daughter relationship -- Fiction
ISBN 0-399-24275-9; 0-14-240918-9 pa
LC 2005-30931

As her senior year in high school approaches, Mina yearns to find her own path in life but working at the family business, taking care of her little sister, and dealing with her mother's impossible expectations are as stifling as the southern California heat, until she falls in love with a man who offers a way out.

"This is a well-crafted tale, sensitively told. . . . The mother-daughter conflict will resonate with teens of any culture who have wrestled parents for the right to choose their own paths." Bull Cent Child Books

Naidoo, Beverley

Journey to Jo'burg; a South African story. illustrations by Eric Velasquez. Lippincott 1986 80p il hardcover o.p. paperback $6.99
Grades: 5 6 7 8 **Fic**
1. South Africa -- Race relations -- Fiction
ISBN 9780062881793 paperback; 0-06-440237-1
LC 85-45508

"This touching novel graphically depicts the plight of Africans living in the horror of South Africa. Thirteen-year-old Maledi and her 9-year-old brother leave their small village, take the perilous journey to the city, and encounter, firsthand, the painful struggle for justice, freedom, and dignity in the 'City of Gold.' A provocative story with a message readers will long remember." Soc Educ

Followed by Chain of fire (1990)

The **other** side of truth. HarperCollins Pubs. 2001 252p hardcover o.p. pa $5.99

Grades: 5 6 7 8 **Fic**

1. Nigeria -- Fiction 2. Africans -- Fiction 3. Refugees -- Fiction 4. London (England) -- Fiction

ISBN 0-06-029628-3; 0-06-441002-1 pa

LC 00-54112

First published 2000 in the United Kingdom

Smuggled out of Nigeria after their mother's murder, Sade and her younger brother are abandoned in London when their uncle fails to meet them at the airport and they are fearful of their new surroundings and of what may have happened to their journalist father back in Nigeria

"Part survival adventure, part docudrama, the narrative stays true to Sade's viewpoint. . . . This powerful novel brings the news images very close." Booklist

Followed by Web of lies (2006)

Namioka, Lensey

An **ocean** apart, a world away. Delacorte Press 2002 197p hardcover o.p. pa $5.50

Grades: 5 6 7 8 **Fic**

1. Chinese -- United States -- Fiction

ISBN 0-385-73002-0; 0-440-22973-1 pa

LC 2002-73550

Despite the odds facing her decision to become a doctor in 1920's Nanking, China, teenaged Yanyan leaves her family to study at Cornell University where, along with hard work, she finds prejudice and loneliness as well as friendship and a new sense of accomplishment

"Without heavy messages, Namioka explores what it means to be independent." Booklist

Nanji, Shenaaz

Ghost boys; by Jewell Parker Rhodes. Little, Brown & Co. 2018 224 p. (hardcover) $16.99

Grades: 4 5 6 7 8 **Fic**

1. Racism -- Fiction 2. Police shootings -- Fiction 3. Death -- Fiction 4. Chicago (Ill.) -- Fiction 5. African Americans -- Fiction 6. Family life -- Illinois -- Chicago -- Fiction

ISBN 0316262285; 9780316262286

LC 2017019240

In this book, by Jewell Parker Rhodes, "twelve-year-old Jerome is shot by a police officer who mistakes his toy gun for a real threat. As a ghost, he observes the devastation that's been unleashed on his family and community. . . . Soon Jerome meets another ghost: Emmett Till. . . . Emmett helps Jerome process what has happened, on a journey towards recognizing how historical racism may have led to the events that ended his life." (Publisher's note)

Napoli, Donna Jo

★ **Beast**. Atheneum Bks. for Young Readers 2000 260p hardcover o.p. pa $8

Grades: 7 8 9 10 **Fic**

1. Fairy tales 2. Iran -- Fiction

ISBN 0-689-83589-2; 0-689-87005-1 pa

LC 99-89923

"The reader is immersed in the imagery and spirituality of ancient Persia. . . . Although Napoli uses Farsi (Persian) and Arabic words in the text (there is a glossary), this only adds to the texture and richness of her remarkable piece of writing." Book Rep

Bound. Atheneum Books for Young Readers 2004 186p hardcover o.p. pa $5.99

Grades: 8 9 10 11 12 **Fic**

1. China -- Fiction 2. Sex role -- Fiction

ISBN 0-689-86175-3; 0-689-86178-8 pa

LC 2004-365

In a novel based on Chinese Cinderella tales, fourteen-year-old step-child Xing-Xing endures a life of neglect and servitude, as her step-mother cruelly mutilates her own child's feet so that she alone might marry well

The author "fleshes out and enriches the story with well-rounded characters and with accurate information about a specific time and place in Chinese history; the result is a dramatic and masterful retelling." SLJ

★ **Hush**; an Irish princess' tale. Atheneum Books for Young Readers 2007 308p $16.99

Grades: 8 9 10 11 12 **Fic**

1. Young adult literature 2. Ireland -- Fiction 3. Slavery -- Fiction 4. Princesses -- Fiction 5. Middle Ages -- Fiction

ISBN 978-0-689-86176-5; 0-689-86176-1

LC 2007-2676

Fifteen-year-old Melkorka, an Irish princess, is kidnapped by Russian slave traders and not only learns how to survive but to challenge some of the brutality of her captors, who are fascinated by her apparent muteness and the possibility that she is enchanted.

This is a "powerful survival story. . . . Napoli does not shy from detailing practices that will make readers wince . . . and the Russian crew repeatedly gang-rapes an older captive. . . . The tension over Mel's hopes for escape paces this story like a thriller." Publ Wkly

The **smile**. Dutton Children's Books 2008 260p $17.99

Grades: 7 8 9 10 **Fic**

1. Painters 2. Scientists 3. Artists -- Fiction 4. Writers on science 5. Renaissance -- Fiction 6. Italy -- History -- 0-1559 -- Fiction

ISBN 978-0-525-47999-4; 0-525-47999-6

LC 2007-48522

In Renaissance Italy, Elisabetta longs for romance, and when Leonardo da Vinci introduces her to Guiliano de Medici, whose family rules Florence but is about to be deposed, she has no inkling of the romance—and sorrow—that will ensue.

"Napoli skillfully draws readers into the vibrant settings . . . with tangible, sensory details that enliven the novel's intriguing references to history and art. Elisabetta's strength and individuality . . . will captivate readers." Booklist

Stones in water. Dutton Children's Bks. 1997 209p hardcover o.p. pa $5.99

Grades: 5 6 7 8 **Fic**

1. World War, 1939-1945 -- Fiction

ISBN 0-525-45842-5; 0-14-130600-9 pa

LC 97-14253

After being taken by German soldiers from a local movie theater along with other Italian boys including his Jewish friend, Roberto is forced to work in Germany, escapes into the Ukrainian winter, before desperately trying to make his way back home to Venice

This is a "gripping, meticulously researched story (loosely based on the life of an actual survivor)." Publ Wkly

Followed by:

Fire in the hills (2006)

The **wager**. Henry Holt 2010 262p il $16.99

Grades: 8 9 10 11 12 **Fic**

1. Fairy tales 2. Devil -- Fiction 3. Sicily (Italy) -- Fiction

ISBN 978-0-8050-8781-9; 0-8050-8781-8

LC 2009-23436

Having lost everything in a tidal wave in 1169 Sicily, nineteen-year-old Don Giovanni makes a simple-sounding wager with a stranger he recognizes as the devil but, while desperate enough to surrender his pride and good looks for three years, he is not willing to give up his soul.

"Evocative of Hermann Hesse's Siddhartha, this marvelous story is well told, and the rich, sophisticated language will grip skilled readers." SLJ

Naylor, Phyllis Reynolds

Faith, hope, and Ivy June. Delacorte Press 2009 280p $16.99; lib bdg $19.99

Grades: 5 6 7 8 **Fic**

1. School stories 2. Kentucky -- Fiction 3. Appalachian region -- Fiction

ISBN 978-0-385-73615-2; 0-385-73615-0; 978-0-385-90588-6 lib bdg; 0-385-90588-2 lib bdg

LC 2008-19625

During a student exchange program, seventh-graders Ivy June and Catherine share their lives, homes, and communities, and find that although their lifestyles are total opposites they have a lot in common.

"This finely crafted novel . . . depicts a deep friendship growing slowly through understanding. As both girls wait out tragedies at the book's end, they cling to hope—and each other—in a thoroughly real and unaffected way. Naylor depicts Appalachia with sympathetic realism." Kirkus

Shiloh. Atheneum Pubs. 1991 144p $16.95; pa $6.99

Grades: 4 5 6 **Fic**

1. Dogs -- Fiction 2. West Virginia -- Fiction

ISBN 0-689-31614-3; 0-689-83582-5 pa

LC 90-603

Awarded the Newbery Medal, 1992

When he finds a lost beagle in the hills behind his West Virginia home, Marty tries to hide it from his family and the dog's real owner, a mean-spirited man known to shoot deer out of season and to mistreat his dogs

"A credible plot and characters, a well-drawn setting, and nicely paced narration combine in a story that leaves the reader feeling good." Horn Book

Other titles about Shiloh are:
Shiloh season (1996)
Saving Shiloh (1997)
A Shiloh Christmas (2015)

Nazemian, Abdi

Like a love story; Abdi Nazemian. Harpercollins Childrens Books 2019 432 p. $17.99

Grades: 8 9 10 11 12 **Fic**

ISBN 0062839365; 9780062839367

1. Teenagers -- Fiction 2. Friendship -- Fiction 3. Gay teenagers -- Fiction

In this book, by Abdi Nazemian, "it's 1989 in New York City, and for three teens, the world is changing. Reza knows he's gay. . . . Judy is an aspiring fashion designer who worships her uncle Stephen, a gay man with AIDS. . . . Judy has never imagined finding romance...until she falls for Reza. . . . Art is Judy's best friend, their school's only out and proud teen. . . . As Reza and Art grow closer, Reza struggles to find a way out of his deception . . . [of] Judy." (Publisher's note)

"This is a beautifully written exploration of first love's fragility in the face of a world full of hate and fear. But just as compelling is its look into a friendship that isn't shattered by a betrayal; instead, its cracks are revealed as two friends grow into the people they're meant to be." (Booklist)

Nelson, Marilyn, 1946-

American ace; Marilyn Nelson. Dial Books 2016 128 p. illustrations (hardcover) $17.99

Grades: 8 9 10 11 12 **Fic**

1. Fathers -- Fiction 2. Family secrets -- Fiction 3. Novels in verse 4. Identity -- Fiction 5. Family life -- Fiction 6. Fathers and sons -- Fiction 7. Racially mixed people -- Fiction 8. United States. Army Air Forces. Bombardment Group, 477th -- Fiction

ISBN 9780803733053; 0803733054

LC 2015000851

In this novel, by Marilyn Nelson, "Connor's grandmother leaves his dad a letter when she dies, and the letter's confession shakes their tight-knit Italian-American family: The man who raised Dad is not his birth father. But the only clues to this birth father's identity are a class ring and a pair of pilot's wings. And so Connor takes it upon himself to investigate. What Connor discovers will lead him and his father to a new, richer understanding of race, identity, and each other." (Publisher's note)

"The author's meticulous verse is the perfect vehicle to convey the devastating fragility of racial and familial identity in an America where interracial love is still divided through the problem of the color line. Readers will join Nelson's protagonist in quietly hoping for that healing, too." Kirkus

Nelson, Theresa

Ruby electric; a novel. Atheneum Bks. for Young Readers 2003 264p hardcover o.p. pa $5.99

Grades: 5 6 7 8 **Fic**

1. Fathers -- Fiction 2. Siblings -- Fiction 3. Authorship -- Fiction 4. California -- Fiction

ISBN 0-689-83852-2; 0-689-87146-5 pa

LC 2002-8034

Twelve-year-old Ruby Miller, movie buff and aspiring screen writer, tries to resolve the mysteries surrounding her little brother's stuffed woolly mammoth and their father's five year absence

"Ruby's voice is electric, and she is an unforgettable character with courage, a cause, and imagination." Booklist

Nelson, Vaunda Micheaux

No crystal stair; a documentary novel of the life and work of Lewis Michaux, Harlem bookseller. by Vaunda Micheaux Nelson ; art work by R. Gregory Christie. Carolrhoda Lab 2012 188p. ill.

Grades: 6 7 8 9 10 11 12 **Fic**

1. Harlem (New York, N.Y.) 2. African American authors 3. Booksellers and bookselling 4. African Americans -- Books and reading -- fiction 5. Bookstores -- New York (State) -- New York -- fiction

ISBN 9780761361695

LC 2011021251

Coretta Scott King Author Honor Book (2013)

This "biographical novel presents the life and work of a man whose Harlem bookstore became an intellectual, literary haven for African Americans from 1939 until 1975. [The book proceeds t]hrough alternating voices of actual family members, acquaintances, journalists, and the subject himself, [Lewis] Michaux. . . . Influenced by the nationalism of Marcus Garvey and the intellect of Frederick Douglass, he believed that black people needed to educate themselves . . . [and h]e opened the National Memorial African Bookstore. . . . He accumulated works by black writers and talked to customers and passersby about cultural awareness and self-improvement. His bookstore attracted Harlem residents; civil-rights activists, including Malcolm X and Muhammad Ali; and political attention." (School Libr J)

Nemeth, Sally

The **heights,** the depths, and everything in between. Alfred A. Knopf 2006 263p hardcover o.p. lib bdg $17.99; pa $6.99

Grades: 5 6 7 8 **Fic**

1. Size -- Fiction 2. Dwarfism -- Fiction 3. Friendship -- Fiction
ISBN 0-375-83458-3; 0-375-93458-8 lib bdg; 0-553-49499-6 pa
LC 2005-33273

In 1977, best friends Lucy Small, a seventh grader from Wilmington, Delaware, who is five feet ten inches tall, and Jake Little, a dwarf, try unsuccessfully to go unnoticed during their first year of junior high school

"Playwright Nemeth has a real gift for capturing teen dialogue and emotions. . . . Readers will relate to this satisfying tale." Booklist

Neri, G.

Ghetto cowboy; [by] G. Neri; illustrated by Jesse Joshua Watson. Candlewick Press 2011 218p il $15.99

Grades: 4 5 6 7 **Fic**

1. Horses -- Fiction 2. Moving -- Fiction 3. African Americans -- Fiction 4. City and town life -- Fiction 5. Philadelphia (Pa.) -- Fiction 6. Father-son relationship -- Fiction
ISBN 978-0-7636-4922-7; 0-7636-4922-8
LC 2010007565

Twelve-year-old Cole's behavior causes his mother to drive him from Detroit to Philadelphia to live with a father he has never known, but who soon has Cole involved with a group of African-American "cowboys" who rescue horses and use them to steer youths away from drugs and gangs.

"This well-written book is based on a true story of urban cowboys in Philadelphia and New York. Cole's spot-on emotional insight is conveyed through believable dialogue. . . . Watson's illustrations punctuate the intriguing aspects of the story and make the novel more appealing." SLJ

Nesbet, Anne

Cloud and Wallfish; Anne Nesbet. Candlewick Press 2016 400 p. (ebook) $16.99; $16.99

Grades: 5 6 7 8 **Fic**

1. Family secrets -- Fiction 2. Berlin Wall (1961-1989) -- Fiction
ISBN 9780763691806; 9780763688035
LC 2016946908

In this book, by Anne Nesbet, "Noah Keller has a pretty normal life, until one wild afternoon when his parents pick him up from school and head straight for the airport, telling him on the ride that his name isn't really Noah. . . . As Noah—now 'Jonah Brown'—and his parents head behind the Iron Curtain into East Berlin, the rules and secrets begin to pile up so quickly that he can hardly keep track of the questions bubbling up inside him." (Publisher's note)

"Noah's friendship with his neighbor Claudia is genuinely touching, and some truly tense scenes unfold as secrets are revealed and readers witness events leading to the fall of the Berlin Wall." Booklist

Ness, Patrick

★ **And** the ocean was our sky; Patrick Ness ; illustrated by Rovina Cai. HarperTeen 2018 160 p. illustrations (some color) (hardback) $19.99

Grades: 7 8 9 10 11 12 **Fic**

1. Ships -- Fiction 2. Whales -- Fiction 3. Human-animal relationships -- Fiction
ISBN 9780062860729
LC 2018938254

This book, by Patrick Ness, illustrated by Rovina Cia, "asks harrowing questions about power, loyalty, obsession, and the monsters we make of others. With harpoons strapped to their backs, the proud whales of Bathsheba's pod live for the hunt, fighting in the ongoing war against the world of men. When they attack a ship bobbing on the surface of the Abyss, they expect to find easy prey. Instead, they find the trail of a myth, a monster, perhaps the devil himself." (Publisher's note)

Ness "mines Moby-Dick for incidents and motifs, pitting men against whales in a futuristic alternate world. . . . The story, though far shorter than its progenitor, conjures similar allegorical weight by pairing the narrative's rolling cadences with powerful, shadowy illustrations featuring looming whales, an upside-down ship in full sail, and swarms of red-eyed sharks, all amid dense swirls of water and blood." Kirkus

The **Ask** and the Answer; a novel. Candlewick Press 2009 519p (Chaos walking) $18.99

Grades: 8 9 10 11 12 **Fic**

1. Science fiction 2. Telepathy -- Fiction 3. Space colonies -- Fiction 4. Social problems -- Fiction
ISBN 978-0-7636-4490-1; 0-7636-4490-0
LC 2009-7329

Sequel to: The knife of never letting go (2008)

Alternate chapters follow teenagers Todd and Viola, who become separated as the Mayor's oppressive new regime takes power in New Prentisstown, a space colony where residents can hear each other's thoughts.

"Provocative questions about gender bias, racism, the meaning of war and the price of peace are thoughtfully threaded throughout a breathless, often violent plot peopled with heartbreakingly real characters." Kirkus

Followed by: Monsters of men (2010)

★ The **knife** of never letting go. Candlewick Press 2008 479p (Chaos walking) $18.99

Grades: 8 9 10 11 12 **Fic**

1. Boys -- Fiction 2. Science fiction 3. Dystopian fiction 4. Psychics -- Fiction 5. Young adult literature 6. Telepathy -- Fiction 7. Space colonies -- Fiction
ISBN 978-0-7636-3931-0; 0-7636-3931-1
LC 2007-52334

Pursued by power-hungry Prentiss and mad minister Aaron, young Todd and Viola set out across New World searching for answers about his colony's true past and seeking a way to warn the ship bringing hopeful settlers from Old World.

"This troubling, unforgettable opener to the Chaos Walking trilogy is a penetrating look at the ways in which we reveal ourselves to one another, and what it takes to be a man in a society gone horribly wrong." Booklist

★ A **monster** calls; a novel. inspired by an idea from Siobhan Dowd; illustrations by Jim Kay. Candlewick Press 2011 204p il $15.99

Grades: 6 7 8 9 10 **Fic**

1. School stories 2. Cancer -- Fiction 3. Monsters -- Fiction 45. Great Britain -- Fiction 5. Loss (Psychology) -- Fiction 6. Mother-son relationship -- Fiction
ISBN 978-0-7636-5559-4; 0-7636-5559-7
LC 2010040741

"Conor O'Malley is struggling with his mother's illness and terrorized by nightmares which seem to come to life. The monster who visits him tells Conor three allegorical stories, each time instructing Conor that he will have to tell his own truth in the fourth and final story. Conor's daily life and "truth" are even more haunting than the monster." (Library Media Connection)

This is a "profoundly moving, expertly crafted tale of unaccountable loss. . . . A singular masterpiece, exceptionally well-served by Kay's atmospheric and ominous illustrations." Publ Wkly

Monsters of men. Candlewick Press 2010 603p (Chaos walking) $18.99; pa $9.99
Grades: 8 9 10 11 12 **Fic**
1. War stories 2. Science fiction 3. Young adult literature 4. Telepathy -- Fiction 5. Space colonies -- Fiction 6. Social problems -- Fiction
ISBN 978-0-7636-4751-3; 0-7636-4751-9; 978-0-7636-5665-2 pa; 0-7636-5665-8 pa
Sequel to: The Ask and the Answer (2009)

As a world-ending war surges to life around them, Todd and Viola face monstrous decisions, questioning all they have ever known as they try to step back from the darkness and find the best way to achieve peace.

"The Chaos Walking trilogy comes to a powerful conclusion in this grueling but triumphant tale." Publ Wkly

Neumeier, Rachel

The **keeper** of the mist; Rachel Neumeier. Alfred A. Knopf 2016 400 p. (lib. bdg.) $20.99
Grades: 7 8 9 10 11 12 **Fic**
1. Fantasy fiction 2. Magic -- Fiction 3. Kings and rulers -- Fiction
ISBN 9780553509281; 9780553509298
LC 2015000547

In this book, by Rachel Neumeier, "Keri has been struggling to run her family bakery since her mother passed away. Now the father she barely knew—the Lord of Nimmira—has died, and ancient magic has decreed that she will take his place as the new Lady. The position has never been so dangerous: the mists that hide Nimmira from its vicious, land-hungry neighbors have failed, and Keri's people are visible to strangers for the first time since the mists were put in place generations ago." (Publisher's note)

"This is a beautifully written story that emphasizes intelligence and diplomacy. Recommend to fans of Patricia Wrede and Tamora Pierce, as well as lovers of traditional fantasy." SLJ

★ The **white** road of the moon; Rachel Neumeier. Alfred A. Knopf 2017 376 p. map (hardcover) $17.99
Grades: 7 8 9 10 11 12 **Fic**
1. Ghost stories 2. Aunts -- Fiction 3. Runaway teenagers -- Fiction 4. Psychic ability -- fiction
ISBN 0553509322; 9780553509342; 9780553509328
LC 2017288569

In this novel, by Rachel Neumeier, "imagine you live with your aunt, who hates you so much she's going to sell you into a dreadful apprenticeship. Imagine you run away before that can happen. Imagine that you can see ghosts--and talk with the dead. People like you are feared, even shunned. Now imagine . . . the first people you encounter after your escape are a mysterious stranger and a ghost boy, who seem to need you desperately." (Publisher's note)

"A richly rewarding stand-alone story evoking far more color than its titular tint might suggest." Kirkus

Nicholls, Sally

Season of secrets. Arthur A. Levine Books 2011 225p $16.99
Grades: 4 5 6 **Fic**
1. Sisters -- Fiction 2. Bereavement -- Fiction 3. Family life -- Fiction 4. Great Britain -- Fiction
ISBN 978-0-545-21825-2; 0-545-21825-X
LC 2010017070

Sent by their father to live in the country with their grandparents after the sudden death of their mother, Molly's older sister Hannah expresses her grief in a raging rebellion while imaginative Molly finds herself increasingly distracted by visions, that seemingly only she can see, of a strange hunt in the nearby forest.

"Written in gently flowing prose, the plot appropriately transitions from autumn into summer as Molly emerges from grief to acceptance and hope. A poignant story of healing tinged with mystery." Kirkus

★ **Ways** to live forever; [by] Sally Nicholls. Arthur A. Levine Books 2008 212p il $16.99
Grades: 4 5 6 7 **Fic**
1. Death -- Fiction 2. Leukemia -- Fiction 3. Authorship -- Fiction 4. Family life -- Fiction
ISBN 978-0-545-06948-9; 0-545-06948-3
LC 2007047341

Eleven-year-old Sam McQueen, who has leukemia, writes a book during the last three months of his life, in which he tells about what he would like to accomplish, how he feels, and things that have happened to him.

This "skirts easy sentiment to confront the hard questions head-on, intelligently and realistically and with an enormous range of feeling." Publ Wkly

Nicholson, William

Seeker. Harcourt 2006 413p (Noble warriors) $17; pa $7.95
Grades: 7 8 9 10 **Fic**
1. Fantasy fiction
ISBN 978-0-15-205768-8; 0-15-205768-4; 978-0-15-205866-1 pa; 0-15-205866-4 pa
LC 2005-17171

"The classic coming-of-age tale is combined with a rich setting of cold villains, strange powers, and disturbing warriors." Voice Youth Advocates

Other titles in this series are:
Jango (2007)
Noman (2008)

Nielsen, Jennifer A.

The **false** prince; by Jennifer A. Nielsen. Scholastic Press 2012 342 p. (The ascendance trilogy) hbk $17.99
Grades: 4 5 6 7 8 **Fic**
1. Fantasy fiction 2. Adventure fiction 3. Impersonation -- Fiction 4. Orphans -- Fiction 5. Princes -- Fiction 6. Secrets -- Fiction 7. Courts and courtiers -- Fiction
ISBN 9780545284134
LC 2011006692

This fantasy book depicts the adventures of Sage, a "brazen 15-year-old orphan living in the imaginary kingdom of Carthya [who] becomes embroiled in a treasonous power-play to install a false prince on the vacant throne." He is selected with three other boys from the orphanage by Bevin Connor to compete to impersonate the missing Prince Jaron and act as Connor's pawn on the throne. "Sage's disdain, defiance and reckless arrogance mark him for failure, but his boldness, instinct and innate decency indicate there's more than meets the eye. Could Sage become Prince Jaron?" Jennifer A. Nielsen's story features "ruthless ambition, fierce action and plotting . . . and lots of sword play and hidden passages." (Kirkus)

The **runaway** king; Jennifer A. Nielsen. Scholastic Press 2013 352 p. (The ascendance trilogy) (hardcover) $17.99
Grades: 4 5 6 7 8 **Fic**

1. Fantasy fiction -- fiction 2. Princesses -- Fiction 3. Conspiracies -- Fiction 4. Courts and courtiers -- Fiction 5. Kings, queens, rulers, etc. -- Fiction
ISBN 0545284155; 9780545284158
LC 2012035290

"Just weeks after Jaron has taken the throne, an assassination attempt forces him into a deadly situation. Rumors of a coming war are winding their way between the castle walls, and Jaron feels the pressure quietly mounting within Carthya. Soon, it becomes clear that deserting the kingdom may be his only hope of saving it." (Publisher's note)

The **shadow** throne; Jennifer A. Nielsen. First edition Scholastic Press 2014 336 p. (Ascendance trilogy) (hardcover) $17.99
Grades: 4 5 6 7 8 **Fic**

1. Kings and rulers 2. Adventure fiction 3. Battles -- Fiction 4. Adventure stories 5. Rescues -- Fiction
ISBN 9780545284172; 0545284171
LC 2013021841

This book, by Jennifer A. Nielsen, is the "finale of the Ascendance Trilogy. . . . Jaron learns than King Vargan of Avenia and allies from Gelyn and Mendenwal have invaded Carthya and captured Jaron's friend Imogen. Determined to save Imogen, Jaron attempts a rescue and fails, leaving him a prisoner and Imogen presumed dead. As he tries to cope with Imogen's death, captive Jaron discovers how much he loved her." (Kirkus Reviews)

"There's enough adventure, mystery, and romance in this concluding volume to please a variety of genre readers." Horn Book

Nielsen, Susin

No fixed address; Susin Nielsen. Wendy Lamb Books, an imprint of Random House Children's Books 2018 288 p. (trade) $16.99
Grades: 6 7 8 9 **Fic**

1. Friendship -- Fiction 2. Homeless persons -- Fiction 3. Mothers and sons -- Fiction 4. Faith -- Fiction 5. Canada -- Fiction 6. Game shows -- Fiction
ISBN 9781524768348; 9781524768355; 9781524768379
LC 2017040581

In this book, by Susin Nielsen, "Felix Knutsson has a knack for trivia. His favorite game show is Who What Where When. . . . Felix's mom, Astrid, is loving but can't seem to hold on to a job. So when they get evicted from their latest shabby apartment, they have to move into a van. Astrid swears him to secrecy. . . . [Then,] Felix gets a chance to audition for a junior edition of Who What Where When, and he's determined to earn a spot on the show." (Publisher's note)

Optimists die first; Susin Nielsen. Wendy Lamb Books 2017 228 p. (lib. bdg.) $20.99
Grades: 7 8 9 10 11 12 **Fic**

1. Fear -- Fiction 2. Romance fiction 3. High school students -- Fiction 4. Friendship -- Fiction 5. Art therapy -- Fiction 6. Sisters -- Death -- Fiction 7. Love in adolescence -- Fiction 8. Emotional problems of teenagers -- Fiction
ISBN 9780553496901; 9780553496918; 9780553496932; 9780553496925
LC 2016014407

In this book, by Susin Nielsen, "sixteen-year-old Petula de Wilde is anything but wild. A former crafting fiend with a happy life, Petula shut herself off from the world after a family tragedy. She sees danger in all the ordinary things. . . . She knows: life is out to get you. The worst part of her week is her comically lame mandatory art therapy class with a small group of fellow misfits. Then a new boy, Jacob, appears at school and in her therapy group." (Publisher's note)

"Heartbreaking and hopeful, this is a solid choice for readers looking for a book to make them cry and laugh at the same time." Booklist

The **reluctant** journal of Henry K. Larsen; Susin Nielsen. Tundra Books of Northern New York 2012 243 p. (hardcover) $17.95
Grades: 7 8 9 10 11 12 **Fic**

1. Bullies 2. Grief -- fiction 3. Diaries -- fiction
ISBN 1770493727; 9781770493728
LC 2011938782

In this novel, by Susin Nielsen, "thirteen-year-old Henry's happy life abruptly ends when his older brother kills the boy who bullied him in school and then takes his own life. Henry refers to this tragedy as 'IT.' He moves to a new city . . . for a fresh start. To help him cope with IT, Henry's therapist recommends he keep a journal. Henry hates the suggestion but soon finds himself recording his thoughts and feelings constantly, even updating it multiple times per day." (Kirkus Reviews)

Word nerd. Tundra Books 2008 248p $18.95; pa $12.95
Grades: 5 6 7 8 **Fic**

1. Friendship -- Fiction 2. Scrabble (Game) -- Fiction 3. Mother-son relationship -- Fiction
ISBN 0-88776-875-X; 0-88776-990-X pa; 978-0-88776-875-0; 978-0-88776-990-0 pa

Twelve-year old Ambrose is "home-schooled. Alone in the evenings when [his mother] Irene goes to work, Ambrose pesters Cosmo, the twenty-five-year-old son of the Greek landlords who live upstairs. Cosmo has just been released from jail for breaking and entering to support a drug habit. Quite by accident, Ambrose discovers that they share a love of Scrabble and coerces Cosmo into taking him to the West Side Scrabble Club, where Cosmo falls for Amanda, the club director. . . . Cosmo, Amanda, and Ambrose soon form an unlikely alliance and, for the first time in his life, Ambrose blossoms." (Publisher's note) "Grades six to nine." (Bull Cent Child Books)

"Twelve-year-old Ambrose Bukowski and his widowed, overprotective mother . . . move frequently. When he almost dies after he bites into a peanut that bullies put in his sandwich, just to see if he is really allergic, Irene . . . decides to homeschool him. . . . Ambrose gets to know 25-year-old-Cosmo, recently released from jail and the son of the Bukowskis' . . . landlords. . . . Ambrose . . . talks Cosmo into taking him to a Scrabble Club. . . . This is a tender, often funny story with some really interesting characters. It will appeal to word nerds, but even more to anyone who has ever longed for acceptance or had to fight unreasonable parental restrictions." SLJ

Nimmo, Jenny

Midnight for Charlie Bone. Orchard Bks. 2003 401p (Children of the Red King) $12.99
Grades: 5 6 7 8 **Fic**

1. School stories 2. Magic -- Fiction 3. Great Britain -- Fiction
ISBN 978-0-439-47429-0; 0-439-47429-9
LC 2002-30738

First published 2002 in the United Kingdom

Charlie Bone's life with his widowed mother and two grandmothers undergoes a dramatic change when he discovers that he can hear people in photographs talking.

"This marvelous fantasy is able to stand on its own despite inevitable comparisons to the students of Hogwarts." Voice Youth Advocates

Other titles in this series are:
Charlie Bone and the time twister (2003)
Charlie Bone and the invisible boy (2004)
Charlie Bone and the castle of mirrors (2005)
Charlie Bone and the hidden king (2006)
Charlie Bone and the beast (2007)
Charlie Bone and the shadow (2008)
Charlie Bone and the Red Knight (2010)

Nix, Garth

★ **Abhorsen**. HarperCollins Pubs. 2003 358p $17.99; lib bdg $18.89; pa $7.99
Grades: 7 8 9 10 **Fic**
1. Fantasy fiction
ISBN 0-06-027825-0; 0-06-027826-9 lib bdg; 0-06-052873-7 pa
LC 2002-3151

Sequel to Lirael, daughter of Clayr

Abhorsen-In-Waiting Lirael and Prince Sameth, a Wallmaker, must confront and bind the evil spirit Oranis before it can destroy all life

"The tension throughout the story is palatable, and despite a solid, satisfying conclusion, Nix leaves himself a bit of room to revisit his intricately designed universe." Booklist

★ **Clariel**; the lost Abhorsen. Garth Nix. HarperCollins 2014 400 p. maps (hardcover) $18.99
Grades: 7 8 9 10 **Fic**
1. Fantasy fiction 2. Young adult literature 3. Magic -- Fiction
ISBN 006156155X; 9780061561559
LC 2013047958

In this fantasy novel by Garth Nix, part of the Old Kingdom series, "Clariel is the daughter of one of the most notable families in the Old Kingdom, with blood relations to the Abhorsen and, most important, to the King. She dreams of living a simple life but discovers this is hard to achieve when a dangerous Free Magic creature is loose in the city, her parents want to marry her off to a killer, and there is a plot brewing against the old and withdrawn King Orrikan." (Publisher's note)

"Nix's intricate world building reveals more Old Kingdom history and its ever-shifting alliance between the political and magical. Themes of freedom and destiny underpin Clariel's harrowing, bittersweet story, and readers will delight in the telling." Booklist

Frogkisser! Garth Nix. Scholastic Press 2017 372 p. (hardcover) $18.99
Grades: 8 9 10 **Fic**
1. Dogs -- Fiction 2. Magic -- Fiction 3. Sisters -- Fiction 4. Wizards -- Fiction 5. Princesses -- Fiction
ISBN 9781338052107; 9781338052084
LC 2016026559

Kirkus: Best Books (2016)

In this book, by Garth Nix, "poor Princess Anya. Forced to live with her evil stepmother's new husband, her evil stepstepfather. Plagued with an unfortunate ability to break curses with a magic-assisted kiss. And forced to go on the run when her stepstepfather decides to make the kingdom entirely his own. Aided by a loyal talking dog . . . and some extraordinarily mischievous wizards, Anya sets off on a Quest that, if she plays it right, will ultimately free her land." (Publisher's note)

"Well-developed characters, an unfailing sense of humor, and polished prose make Nix's uproarious adventure a pleasure to read." Pub Wkly

★ **Goldenhand**; Garth Nix. Katherine Tegen Books 2016 368 p. maps (Old Kingdom) (hardcover) $19.99; (ebook) $18.99
Grades: 7 8 9 10 **Fic**
1. Magic -- Fiction 2. Adventure fiction 3. Fantasy and magic
ISBN 9780061561580; 9780062216786
LC 2016935936

In this book, in the Old Kingdom series by Garth Nix, "Lirael lost one of her hands in the binding of Orannis, but now she has a new hand, one of gilded steel and Charter Magic. . . . Lirael returns to her . . . home, the Clayr's Glacier, where she was once a Second Assistant Librarian. There, a young woman from the distant North brings her a message from her long-dead mother. . . . It is a warning about the Witch with No Face. But who is the Witch, and what is she planning?" (Publisher's note)

"A masterfully spun tale well worth the yearslong wait." Kirkus

★ **Lirael,** daughter of the Clayr. HarperCollins Pubs. 2001 487p $17.99; lib bdg $18.89; pa $7.99
Grades: 7 8 9 10 **Fic**
1. Fantasy fiction
ISBN 0-06-027823-4; 0-06-027824-2 lib bdg; 0-06-000542-4 pa
LC 00-59707

Sequel to Sabriel

"Sound world-building, swift plotting, and superb characterization, including some of the strongest animal characters in recent fantasy, make this sequel must reading for those who have read the first volume and a brisk, involving experience for those who have not." Voice Youth Advocates

Mister Monday; Keys to the kingdom, book one. Scholastic 2003 361p (Keys to the kingdom) $15.99; pa $5.99
Grades: 6 7 8 9 **Fic**
1. Fantasy fiction
ISBN 0-439-70370-0; 0-439-55123-4 pa
LC 2004-540574

Arthur Penhaligon is supposed to die at a young age, but is saved by a key that is shaped like the minute hand of a clock. The key causes bizarre creatures to come from another realm, bringing with them a plague. A man named Mister Monday will stop at nothing to get the key back. Arthur goes to a mysterious house that only he can see, so that he can learn the truth about himself and the key

"The first in a seven part series for middle graders is every bit as exciting and suspenseful as the author's previous young adult novels." SLJ

Other titles in the Keys to the Kingdom series are:
Grim Tuesday (2004)
Drowned Wednesday (2005)
Sir Thursday (2006)
Lady Friday (2007)
Superior Saturday (2008)
Lord Sunday (2010)

★ **Sabriel**. HarperCollins Pubs. 1996 292p hardcover o.p. pa $7.99
Grades: 7 8 9 10 **Fic**
1. Fantasy fiction
ISBN 0-06-027322-4; 0-06-447183-7 pa
LC 96-1295

First published 1995 in Australia

Sabriel, daughter of the necromancer Abhorsen, must journey into the mysterious and magical Old Kingdom to rescue her father from the Land of the Dead.

"The final battle is gripping, and the bloody cost of combat is forcefully presented. The story is remarkable for the level of originality of the fantastic elements . . . and for the subtle presentation, which leaves readers to explore for themselves the complex structure and significance of the magic elements." Horn Book

Other titles in this series are:
Lirael, daughter of the Clayr (2001)
Abhorsen (2003)
Across the wall (2005)
Clariel (2014)
To hold the bridge (2015)
Goldenhand (2016)

To Hold the Bridge; by Garth Nix. Harpercollins Childrens Books 2015 416 p. $17.99
Grades: 6 7 8 9 10 11 12 Fic
1. Spirits -- Fiction 2. Vampires -- Fiction 3. Detectives -- Fiction 4. Short stories -- Collections 5. Fantasy fiction
ISBN 0062292528; 9780062292520

This book, by Garth Nix, "offers nineteen short stories from every genre of literature including science fiction, paranormal, realistic fiction, mystery, and adventure. Whether writing about vampires, detectives, ancient spirits, or odd jobs, Garth Nix's ability to pull his readers into new worlds is extraordinary." (Publisher's note)

"This anthology's titular novella is a suspenseful prequel to The Old Kingdom Chronicles. Eighteen other tales are organized by theme, with a satisfying variety of genres and tones. Some pay homage to famous speculative fiction (Hellboy; John Carter of Mars), others are companion pieces to Nix's own work; the majority stand alone. Nix's superb worldbuilding and tight plotting are evident here." Horn Book

Nolan, Han

★ **Crazy**. Harcourt 2010 348p $17
Grades: 7 8 9 10 Fic
1. School stories 2. Friendship -- Fiction 3. Bereavement -- Fiction 4. Mental illness -- Fiction 5. Father-son relationship -- Fiction
ISBN 978-0-15-205109-9; 0-15-205109-0
LC 2009-49969

Fifteen-year-old loner Jason struggles to hide father's declining mental condition after his mother's death, but when his father disappears he must confide in the other members of a therapy group he has been forced to join at school.

"Nolan leavens this haunting but hopeful story with spot-on humor and a well-developed cast of characters." Booklist

A **summer** of Kings. Harcourt 2006 334p $17
Grades: 6 7 8 9 Fic
1. Black Muslims -- Fiction 2. Race relations -- Fiction 3. African Americans -- Fiction
ISBN 0-15-205108-2
LC 2005-19487

Over the course of the summer of 1963, fourteen-year-old Esther Young discovers the passion within her when eighteen-year-old King-Roy Johnson, accused of murdering a white man in Alabama, comes to live with her family.

"Infused with rhetoric that is as meaningful today as it was two generations ago, this young teen's account of a life-changing summer not only opens a window to history, but also displays Nolan's brilliant gift for crafting profoundly appealing protagonists." SLJ

Nolen, Jerdine

Eliza's freedom road; an Underground Railroad diary. Simon & Schuster Books for Young Readers 2011 139p il map $14.99
Grades: 4 5 6 7 Fic
1. Diaries -- Fiction 2. Slavery -- Fiction 3. African Americans -- Fiction 4. Underground railroad -- Fiction
ISBN 1-4169-5814-2; 978-1-4169-5814-7
LC 2010-20931

A twelve-year-old slave girl begins writing in a journal where she documents her journey via the Underground Railroad from Alexandria, Virginia, to freedom in St. Catharines, Canada.

"Nolen reveals some of the traumas and tragedies of slavery but keeps her focus on those things that allow Eliza the power to escape: literacy, her mother's legacy, a bit of luck and a great deal of courage." Kirkus

Includes bibliographical references

North, Phoebe

Starglass; by Phoebe North. 1st ed. Simon & Schuster Books for Young Readers 2013 448 p. (hardcover) $17.99
Grades: 7 8 9 10 Fic
1. Jews -- Fiction 2. Underground movements -- Fiction 3. Interplanetary voyages -- Fiction 4. Science fiction 5. Insurgency -- Fiction 6. Fathers and daughters -- Fiction
ISBN 1442459530; 9781442459533; 9781442459557
LC 2012021171

In this book by Phoebe North, "[o]n a generation ship that left Earth 500 years ago, a teenager grapples with disillusionment and emotional isolation as her society nears the planet it intends to land on. Terra lives with her harsh, alcoholic father and awaits her adult job assignment . . . from the strict ruling Council." She "discovers a secret rebellion aboard the Asherah." (Kirkus Reviews)

Northrop, Michael

Polaris; Michael Northrop. Scholastic Press 2017 278 p. (hardcover) $16.99
Grades: 4 5 6 7 8 Fic
1. Sea stories 2. Ships -- Fiction 3. Seafaring life -- Fiction
ISBN 9780545297172; 9781338163995; 9780545297165
LC 2016059059

In this book, by Michael Northrop, the "sailing ship Polaris is on a mission to explore new lands, and its crew is eager to bring their discoveries back home. But when half the landing party fails to return from the Amazon jungle, the tensions lead to a bloody mutiny. The remaining adults abandon ship, leaving behind a cabin boy, a botanist's assistant, and a handful of deckhands -- none of them older than twelve." (Publisher's note)

"This fast-moving adventure-survival novel with a science-fiction focus . . . will appeal to reluctant readers who like thrills and chills." Booklist

Nye, Naomi Shihab

★ **Habibi**. Simon & Schuster Bks. for Young Readers 1997 259p $16; pa $5.99
Grades: 7 8 9 10 Fic
1. Jerusalem -- Fiction 3. Jewish-Arab relations -- Fiction
ISBN 0-689-80149-1; 0-689-82523-4 pa
LC 97-10943

When fourteen-year-old Liyanne Abboud, her younger brother, and her parents move from St. Louis to a new home between Jerusalem and the Palestinian village where her father was born, they face many changes and must deal with the tensions between Jews and Palestinians

"Poetically imaged and leavened with humor, the story renders layered and complex history understandable through character and incident." SLJ

Nylund, Eric S.

The **Resisters**; [by] Eric Nylund. Random House 2011 210p $16.99; lib bdg $19.99

Grades: 5 6 7 8 **Fic**

1. Science fiction 2. Brainwashing -- Fiction 3. Extraterrestrial beings -- Fiction

ISBN 978-0-375-86856-6; 0-375-86856-9; 978-0-375-96856-3 lib bdg; 0-375-96856-3 lib bdg

LC 2010-19230

When twelve-year-olds Madison and Felix kidnap him, Ethan learns that the Earth has been taken over by aliens and that all the adults in the world are under mind control.

"Ethan, Felix, and Madison are multidimensional characters with authentic emotions and realistic attitudes and motives. This book mixes considerable background exposition with fast-moving action. While the immediate plot issues are resolved, there are plenty of threads left dangling. Middle school boys will enjoy the high-tech battle action and will look forward to the next installment." SLJ

O'Brien, Annemarie

Lara's gift; by Annemarie O'Brien. Alfred A. Knopf 2013 176 p. (hardcover) $16.99; (ebook) $50.97; (library binding) 19.99

Grades: 5 6 7 8 9 **Fic**

1. Young adult literature 2. Historical fiction -- fiction 3. Dogs -- Breeding -- Juvenile literature 4. Dogs -- Fiction 5. Borzoi -- Fiction 6. Visions -- Fiction 7. Sex role -- Fiction 8. Family life -- Russia -- Fiction 9. Fathers and daughters -- Fiction 10. Russia -- History -- 1904-1914 -- Fiction

ISBN 0307931749; 9780307931740; 9780307975485; 9780375971051

LC 2012034070

In this book, on "a remote estate in 1910s Russia, Lara must prove herself capable of following in her father's footsteps as the head of a prestigious borzoi breeding kennel. There are so many things between her and the realization of her dream. That she is female is the biggest obstacle, but she must also hide the fact that she has visions of future occurrences that involve the dogs and the dangerous wolves that populate the estate." (Kirkus Reviews)

O'Brien, Caragh M.

Birthmarked. Roaring Brook Press 2010 362p map $16.99

Grades: 6 7 8 9 10 **Fic**

1. Science fiction 2. Young adult literature 3. Midwives -- Fiction 4. Genetic engineering -- Fiction

ISBN 978-1-59643-569-8; 1-59643-569-0

LC 2010-281716

In a future world baked dry by the sun and divided into those who live inside the wall and those who live outside it, sixteen-year-old midwife Gaia Stone is forced into a difficult choice when her parents are arrested and taken into the city.

"Readers who enjoy adventures with a strong heroine standing up to authority against the odds will enjoy this compelling tale." SLJ

O'Brien, Robert C.

Mrs. Frisby and the rats of NIMH; [by] Robert C. O'Brien; illustrated by Zena Bernstein. Atheneum Books for Young Readers 2006 233p il $18; pa $6.99

Grades: 4 5 6 7 **Fic**

1. Mice -- Fiction 2. Rats -- Fiction

ISBN 978-0-689-20651-1; 0-689-20651-8; 978-0-689-71068-1 pa; 0-689-71068-2 pa

A reissue of the title first published 1971

Awarded the Newbery Medal, 1972

Having no one to help her with her problems, a widowed mouse visits the rats whose former imprisonment in a laboratory made them wise and long lived.

"The story is fresh and ingenious, the style witty, and the plot both hilarious and convincing." Saturday Rev

Z for Zachariah. Atheneum Pubs. 1975 246p hardcover o.p. pa $7.99

Grades: 7 8 9 10 **Fic**

1. Science fiction

ISBN 0-689-30442-0; 1-416-93921-0 pa

Seemingly the only person left alive after a nuclear war, a sixteen-year-old girl is relieved to see a man arrive into her valley until she realizes that he is a tyrant and she must somehow escape.

"The journal form is used by O'Brien very effectively, with no lack of drama and contrast, and the pace and suspense of the story are adroitly maintained until the dramatic and surprising ending." Bull Cent Child Books

O'Connor, Barbara

★ **How** to steal a dog; a novel. Farrar, Straus & Giroux 2007 170p pa $6.99; $16

Grades: 4 5 6 **Fic**

1. Dogs -- Fiction 2. Siblings -- Fiction 3. Homeless persons -- Fiction

ISBN 0-312-56112-1 pa; 0-374-33497-8; 978-0-312-56112-3 pa; 978-0-374-33497-0

LC 2005-40166

Living in the family car in their small North Carolina town, Georgina persuades her younger brother to help her in an elaborate scheme to get money by stealing a dog and then claiming the reward that the owners are bound to offer

This is told "in stripped-down, unsentimental prose. . . . The myriad effects of homelessness and the realistic picture of a moral quandry will surely generate discussion." Booklist

O'Connor, Sheila

Sparrow Road. G. P. Putnam's Sons 2011 247p $16.99

Grades: 5 6 7 8 **Fic**

1. Artists -- Fiction

ISBN 978-0-399-25458-1; 0-399-25458-7

LC 2010-28290

Twelve-year-old Raine spends the summer at a mysterious artists colony and discovers a secret about her past.

This is a "beautifully written novel. . . . Readers finding themselves in this quiet world will find plenty of space to imagine and dream for themselves." Kirkus

O'Dell, Scott

★ **Island** of the Blue Dolphins; illustrated by Ted Lewin. 50th anniversary ed.; Houghton Mifflin Books for Children 2010 177p il $22

Grades: 5 6 7 8 **Fic**

1. Native Americans -- Fiction 2. Wilderness survival -- Fiction 3. San Nicolas Island (Calif.) -- Fiction

ISBN 978-0-547-42483-5; 0-547-42483-3

A reissue of the newly illustrated edition published 1990; first published 1960

Awarded the Newbery Medal, 1961

Left alone on a beautiful but isolated island off the coast of California, a young Indian girl spends eighteen years, not only merely surviving through her enormous courage and self-reliance, but also finding a measure of happiness in her solitary life.

The edition illustrated by Ted Lewin "features twelve full-page, full-color watercolors in purple and blue hues that are appropriate to the island setting. This handsome gift-edition version includes a new introduction by Lois Lowry to commemorate the book's fiftieth anniversary." Horn Book Guide

Sing down the moon. Houghton Mifflin 1970 137p hardcover o.p. pa $6.99

Grades: 5 6 7 8 **Fic**

1. Navajo Indians -- Fiction

ISBN 0-395-10919-1; 978-0-547-40632-9 pa; 0-547-40632-0 pa

A Newbery Medal honor book, 1971

"There is a poetic sonority of style, a sense of identification, and a note of indomitable courage and stoicism that is touching and impressive." Saturday Rev

Streams to the river, river to the sea; a novel of Sacagawea. Houghton Mifflin 1986 191p hardcover o.p. pa $6.99

Grades: 5 6 7 8 **Fic**

1. Interpreters 2. Guides (Persons) 3. Native Americans -- Fiction 4. Lewis and Clark Expedition (1804-1806) -- Fiction

ISBN 0-395-40430-4; 0-618-96642-0 pa

LC 86-936

"An informative and involving choice for American history students and pioneer-adventure readers." Bull Cent Child Books

O'Neal, Eilis

The **false** princess. Egmont USA 2010 319p $16.99

Grades: 6 7 8 9 **Fic**

1. Magic -- Fiction 2. Princesses -- Fiction 3. Witchcraft -- Fiction 4. Conspiracies -- Fiction 5. Identity (Psychology) -- Fiction

ISBN 978-1-60684-079-5; 1-60684-079-7

LC 2009040903

This is a "compelling fantasy, which is filled with magic, political drama, and romance." Publ Wkly

O'Reilly, Jane

The **notations** of Cooper Cameron; Jane O'Reilly. Carolrhoda Books 2017 312 p. (hardcover : alk. paper) $17.99

Grades: 5 6 7 8 **Fic**

1. Family problems -- Fiction 2. Anxiety -- fiction 3. Compulsive behavior -- Fiction 4. Lakes -- fiction 5. Vacation homes -- fiction

ISBN 9781512467604; 9781512404159

LC 2016042763

In this children's novel, by Jane O'Reilly, "eleven-year-old Cooper Cameron likes things to be in order. . . . He invented . . . rituals after the death of his beloved grandfather to protect others he loves from terrible harm. But when Cooper's strange behavior drives a wedge between his parents, . . . his mother's only solution is to take Cooper and Caddie to the family cabin for the summer. . . . [There] Cooper vows to cure himself and bring his damaged family back together." (Publisher's note)

"The novel provides a heartfelt portrayal of one boy's experience with obsessive-compulsive disorder. Cooper is helped by a cast of supporting characters, who shine almost as brightly as he does." SLJ

O'Rourke, Erica

Torn. Kensington 2011 310p pa $9.95

Grades: 7 8 9 10 **Fic**

1. Magic -- Fiction 2. Homicide -- Fiction 3. Friendship -- Fiction

ISBN 978-0-7582-6703-0; 0-7582-6703-7

Mo Fitzgerald knows about secrets. But when she witnesses her best friend's murder, she discovers Verity was hiding things she never could have guessed. To find the answers she needs and the vengeance she craves, Mo will have to enter a world of raw magic and shifting alliances. And she'll have to choose between two very different, equally dangerous guys.

"O'Rourke's heroine is refreshing: determined, spunky, and unpredictable. . . . Torn should . . . satisfy readers with an insatiable thirst for well-written, fast-paced fantasy and leave them eager for the next installment in the series." SLJ

Other titles in this series are:

Tangled (2012)

Bound (2012)

O'Sullivan, Joanne

★ **Between** Two Skies; by Joanne O'Sullivan. Candlewick Press 2017 267 p. (hardcover) $16.99

Grades: 7 8 9 10 11 12 **Fic**

1. Fishing -- Fiction 2. Teenage girls -- Fiction 3. Hurricane Katrina, 2005 -- Fiction

ISBN 9780763690342; 9780763693862; 0763690341

LC 2017935665

In this book, by Joanne O'Sullivan, "Bayou Perdu, . . . Louisiana, is home to sixteen-year-old Evangeline Riley. She has her best friends; . . . her wise, beloved Mamere; and back-to-back titles in the under-sixteen fishing rodeo. But, dearest to her heart, she has the peace that only comes when she takes her skiff out to where there is nothing but sky and air and water and wings. It's a small life, but it is Evangeline's. And then the storm comes, and everything changes." (Publisher's note)

"Told in a strong, purposeful voice filled with controlled emotion and hope, the impact of Katrina on families is as compelling as Evangeline's drive to regain her sense of self and belonging." Booklist

Oakes, Cory Putman

Dinosaur boy; Cory Putman Oakes. Sourcebooks Jabberwocky 2015 224 p. illustrations (alk. paper) $12.99

Grades: 4 5 6 7 **Fic**

1. Bullies -- fiction 2. School superintendants and principals -- Fiction 3. Rescues -- Fiction 4. Schools -- Fiction 5. Bullying -- Fiction 6. Dinosaurs -- Fiction 7. Stegosaurus -- Fiction 8. Extraterrestrial beings -- Fiction

ISBN 1492605379; 9781492605379

LC 2014030138

In this children's book by Cory Putnam Oakes about a boy with dinosaur genes, "despite the Principal's Zero Tolerance Policy, Sawyer becomes a bully magnet, befriended only by Elliot aka 'Gigantor' and the weird new girl. When the bullies start disappearing, Sawyer is relieved-until he discovers a secret about the principal that's more shocking than Dino DNA. The bullies are in for a galactically horrible fate...and it's up to Sawyer and his friends to rescue them." (Publisher's note)

"A fun mix of school drama, science fiction, and humor, the story explores the daily hassles of living as part dinosaur, along with the real pain of bullying. First in a planned series, it should find a wide audience." Booklist

Oakes, Stephanie

The **arsonist**; Stephanie Oakes. Dial Books 2017 493 p. (hardcover) $17.99

Grades: 7 8 9 **Fic**

1. Epilepsy -- Fiction 2. Identity (Psychology) -- Fiction 3. People with disabilities -- Fiction 4. Mother-daughter relationship -- Fiction 5. Kuwaiti Americans -- Fiction 6. Germany (East) -- History -- 20th century -- Fiction 7. Identity (Philosophical concept) -- fiction

ISBN 9781101633724; 9780803740716

LC 2016032499

In this novel, by Stephanie Oakes, Molly Mavity and Pepper Al-Yusef are dealing with their own personal tragedies "when Molly gets a package leading her to Pepper, they're tasked with solving a decades-old mystery: find out who killed Ava [Dreyman], back in 1989. Using Ava's diary for clues, Molly and Pepper realize there's more to her life--and death--than meets the eye. Someone is lying to them. And someone out there is guiding them along, desperate for answers." (Publisher's note)

"Packed with dynamic characters, thoughtful writing, and a decades-spanning mystery, this will appeal to readers looking for something off the beaten path." Booklist

Oates, Joyce Carol

Big Mouth & Ugly Girl. HarperCollins Pubs. 2002 265p hardcover o.p. pa $7.99

Grades: 7 8 9 10 **Fic**

1. School stories 2. Friendship -- Fiction

ISBN 0-06-623756-4; 0-06-447347-3 pa

LC 2001-24601

When sixteen-year-old Matt is falsely accused of threatening to blow up his high school and his friends turn against him, an unlikely classmate comes to his aid.

"Readers will be propelled through these pages by an intense curiosity to learn how events will play out. Oates has written a fast-moving, timely, compelling story." SLJ

Obstfeld, Raymond

Stealing the game; Kareem Abdul-Jabbar and Raymond Obstfeld. Disney-Hyperion Books 2015 304 p. (Streetball crew) hc $16.99

Grades: 4 5 6 7 **Fic**

1. Brothers -- Fiction 2. Basketball -- Fiction 3. Schools -- Fiction 4. Middle schools -- Fiction 5. African Americans -- Fiction 6. Mystery and detective stories 7. Robbers and outlaws -- Fiction 8. Criminal investigation -- Fiction

ISBN 9781423178712; 1423178718

LC 2013046413

In this book, part of the Streetball Crew series by Kareem Abdul-Jabbar, "Jax asks Chris to recruit his best middle school teammates for a pick-up basketball game. Chris doesn't think much of it until the wrong team wins and Jax goes ballistic. It turns out that Jax bet on the game, hoping to earn enough money to repay a debt. While Chris tries to walk a thin tightrope between helping his brother and staying out of trouble, his friend Theo [tries] to learn what Jax has been up to." (Publisher's note)

"The shifting structure of the story and a clever series of blind alleys keep readers on tenterhooks. A deft, understated sports thriller with a solid moral compass." Kirkus

Odhiambo, Eucabeth

Auma's long run; by Eucabeth Odhiambo. Carolrhoda Books 2017 298 p. (hardcover) $17.99

Grades: 5 6 7 8 9 **Fic**

1. Running -- Fiction 2. AIDS (Disease) -- Fiction 3. Blacks -- Kenya -- Fiction 4. Kenya -- History -- 20th century -- Fiction

ISBN 9781512467574; 9781512448528; 9781512427844

LC 2016041225

In this book, by Eucabeth Odhiambo, "in her small Kenyan village, [Auma is] . . . a track star. . . . A track scholarship could allow her to attend high school and maybe even become a doctor. But a . . . new sickness called AIDS is ravaging the village. . . . Soon more people are getting sick even dying. . . . Should she stay to support her . . . family or leave to pursue her own future? . . . [B]ut leaving might be the only way to find the answers to . . . this new disease." (Publisher's note)

"The novel spans two years, and Odhiambo smoothly weaves in medical details throughout, along with the evolving understanding of AIDS. A hard-hitting story of a resilient and intelligent girl who bravely confronts a devastating health crisis." Pub Wkly

Oh, Ellen

Spirit hunters; Ellen Oh. HarperCollins 2017 276 p. (hardcover) $16.99

Grades: 4 5 6 7 **Fic**

1. Ghosts -- fiction 2. Brothers and sisters -- fiction 3. Memory -- fiction 4. Detective and mystery stories 5. Haunted houses -- fiction 6. Spirit possession -- fiction

ISBN 9780062430106; 9780062430083

LC 2016961854

This book in the Spirit Hunters series, by Ellen Oh, edited by Alyson Day, is "about Harper Raine, the new seventh grader in town who must face down the dangerous ghosts haunting her younger brother. A riveting ghost story and captivating adventure, this tale will have you guessing at every turn!" (Publisher's note)

"Even more impressive than the shiver factor is the way the author skillfully uses the compelling premise to present a strong, consistent message of not rejecting what you don't understand—a most welcome message." Booklist

Okorafor, Nnedi, 1974-

Akata warrior; Nnedi Okorafor. Viking 2017 477 p. (hardback) $18.99

Grades: 6 7 8 9 10 **Fic**

1. Magic -- Fiction 2. Nigeria -- Fiction 3. Supernatural -- Fiction 4. Secret societies -- Fiction 5. Blacks -- Nigeria -- Fiction 6. Albinos and albinism -- Fiction

ISBN 067078561X; 9780670785612; 9781101598986

LC 2016055398

Sequel to: Akata witch (2011)

In this book, by Nnedi Okorafor, "a year ago, Sunny Nwazue, an American-born girl Nigerian girl, was inducted into the secret Leopard Society. As she began to develop her magical powers, Sunny learned that she had been chosen to lead a dangerous mission to avert an apocalypse, brought about by the terrifying masquerade, Ekwensu. Now, stronger, feistier, and a bit older, Sunny is studying with her mentor Sugar Cream and struggling to unlock the secrets in her strange Nsibidi book." (Publisher's note)

"Okorafor's novel will ensnare readers and keep them turning pages until the very end to see if and how Sunny fulfills the tremendous destiny that awaits her." Booklist

Akata witch; Nnedi Okorafor. Viking 2011 349p $16.99

Grades: 6 7 8 9 10 **Fic**

1. Fantasy fiction 2. Nigeria -- Fiction 3. Witchcraft -- Fiction 4. Albinos and albinism -- Fiction

ISBN 978-0-670-01196-4; 0-670-01196-7

In this book, by Nnedi Okorafor, "twelve-year-old Sunny lives in Nigeria, but she was born American. Her features are African, but she's albino. She's a terrific athlete, but can't go out into the sun to play soccer. There seems to be no place where she fits in. And then she discovers something amazing--she is a 'free agent' with latent magical power. Soon she's part of a quartet of magic students, studying the visible and invisible, learning to change reality." (Publisher's note)

"Although 12-year-old Sunny is Nigerian, she was born in America, and her Nigerian classmates see her as an outsider. Worse, she's an albino, an obvious target for bullies and suspected of being a ghost or a witch. Things change, however, when she has a vision of impending nuclear war. Then her classmate Orlu and his friend Chichi turn out to be Leopard People—witches—and insist that she is, too. . . . This tale is filled with marvels and is sure to appeal to teens whose interest in fantasy goes beyond dwarves and fairies." Publ Wkly

Followed by Akata Warrior (2017)

The **shadow** speaker; [by] Nnedi Okorafor-Mbachu. Jump at the Sun/Hyperion Books for Children 2007 336p hardcover o.p. pa $8.99

Grades: 7 8 9 10 **Fic**

1. Fantasy fiction 2. Science fiction 3. West Africa -- Fiction 4. Sahara Desert -- Fiction

ISBN 978-1-4231-0033-1; 1-4231-0033-6; 978-1-4231-0036-2 pa; 1-4231-0036-0 pa

LC 2007-13313

In West Africa in 2070, after fifteen-year-old "shadow speaker" Ejii witnesses her father's beheading, she embarks on a dangerous journey across the Sahara to find Jaa, her father's killer, and upon finding her, she also discovers a greater purpose to her life and to the mystical powers she possesses.

"Okorafor-Mbachu does an excellent job of combining both science fiction and fantasy elements into this novel. . . . The action moves along at a quick pace and will keep most readers on their toes and wanting more at the end of the novel." Voice Youth Advocates

Older, Daniel José

Dactyl Hill Squad; by Daniel José Older. Arthur A. Levine Books/Scholastic Inc. 2018 272 p. (hardcover) $16.99

Grades: 4 5 6 7 **Fic**

1. Dinosaurs -- fiction 2. Alternative histories -- fiction 3. Riots -- Fiction 4. Adventure stories 5. Orphans -- Fiction 6. Race relations -- Fiction 7. African Americans -- Fiction 8. Race riots -- fiction 9. Brothers and sisters -- Fiction 10. Brothers and sisters -- fiction 11. New York (N.Y.) -- Race relations -- fiction 12. New York (N.Y.) -- History -- Civil War, 1861-1865 -- Fiction

ISBN 9781338268812; 9781338268829

LC 2018016850

In this book in the Dactyl Hill Squad series, by Daniel José Older, "it's 1863 and dinosaurs roam . . . New York as the Civil War rages between raptor-mounted armies down South. Magdalys Roca and her friends from the Colored Orphan Asylum are on a field trip when the Draft Riots break out, and . . . their fellow orphans are kidnapped by an evil magistrate, Richard Riker. . . . Together with the Vigilance Committee, they . . . plot to take down Riker." (Publisher's note)

Includes bibliographical references

Other titles in this series are:

Freedom fire (2019)

Freedom fire; Daniel José Older. Arthur A. Levine Books, an imprint of Scholastic Inc. 2019 304 p. (Dactyl Hill Squad) (hardcover : alk. paper) $16.99

Grades: 4 5 6 7 **Fic**

1. Adventure stories 2. Dinosaurs -- Fiction 3. African Americans -- Fiction 4. Alternative histories (Fiction) 5. African Americans -- fiction 6. Human-animal communication -- Fiction 7. United States -- History -- Civil War, 1861-1865 -- Fiction

ISBN 1338268848; 1338268856; 9781338268843; 9781338268850

LC 2019004549

In this book in the Dactyl Hill Squad series, by Daniel José Older, "the squad links up with the dino-mounted troops of the Louisiana Native Guard, an all-black regiment in the Union Army fighting to free their people. . . . Magdalys's burgeoning powers might be the Union's last hope. But she doesn't want to abandon the search for her brother. And she might not be the only one with a mysterious connection to dinosaurs." (Publisher's note)

"The Dactyl Hill Squad, led by Magdalys Roca, is on the move, heading south to find her soldier brother, who is missing in action during the American Civil War in this alternate history adventure yarn ... older has middle-graders' number with this Dino-charged series. Stampedes are likely!" (Booklist)

Includes bibliographical references

Oliver, Lauren

★ **Liesl** & Po; illustrated by Kei Acedera. Harper 2011 307p il $16.99

Grades: 4 5 6 7 **Fic**

1. Ghost stories 2. Fantasy fiction 3. Magic -- Fiction 4. Bereavement -- Fiction

ISBN 978-0-06-201451-1; 0-06-201451-X

Liesl lives in a tiny attic bedroom, locked away by her cruel stepmother. Her only friends are the shadows and the mice—until one night a ghost appears from the darkness. It is Po, who comes from the Other Side. That same night, an alchemist's apprentice, Will, accidentally bungles an important delivery. He switches a box containing the most powerful magic in the world with one containing something decidedly less remarkable.

This is a "charming, insightful fantasy. . . . This original fairy tale, told by a wise and humorous omniscient narrator and peopled with broadly drawn but instantly recognizable characters, avoids sentimentality to show the magic of accepting loss without letting go and finding joy in the lives left behind." Booklist

The **spindlers**; Lauren Oliver ; illustrated by Iacopo Bruno. 1st ed. Harper 2012 246 p. ill. (hardcover) $16.99

Grades: 4 5 6 **Fic**

1. Monsters -- fiction 2. Fantasy 3. Soul -- Fiction 4. Brothers and sisters -- Fiction

ISBN 0061978086; 9780061978081

LC 2012009698

This children's fantasy novel, by Lauren Oliver, is about a young girl who travels to a fantasy realm to rescue her younger brother from monsters. "When Liza's brother, Patrick, changes overnight, Liza knows exactly what has happened: The spindlers have gotten to him and stolen his soul. . . . To rescue Patrick, Liza must go Below, armed with little more than her wits and a broom. There, she uncovers a vast world populated with . . . terrible dangers." (Publisher's note)

Oppel, Kenneth

Airborn. Eos 2004 355p $16.99; lib bdg $17.89

Grades: 7 8 9 10 **Fic**

1. Fantasy 2. Pirates 3. Airships 4. Fantasy fiction 5. Airships -- Fiction 6. Imaginary creatures

ISBN 0-06-053180-0; 0-06-053181-9 lib bdg

LC 2003-15642

Michael L. Printz Award honor book, 2005

Matt, a young cabin boy aboard an airship, and Kate, a wealthy young girl traveling with her chaperone, team up to search for the existence of mysterious winged creatures reportedly living hundreds of feet above the Earth's surface.

"This rousing adventure has something for everyone: appealing and enterprising characters, nasty villains, and a little romance." SLJ

"Other titles in this series are:
Skybreaker (2005)
Starclimber (2009)

★ The **Boundless**; Kenneth Oppel. First edition Simon & Schuster Books for Young Readers 2014 332 p. illustrations (hardcover : alk. paper) $16.99
Grades: 4 5 6 7 8 **Fic**

1. Adventure fiction 2. Circus -- Fiction 3. Railroads -- Fiction 4. Canada -- History -- 1867-1914 -- Fiction
ISBN 144247288X; 9781442472884; 9781442472891
LC 2013009879

In this book, by Kenneth Oppel, "The Boundless . . . is on its maiden voyage across the country, and first-class passenger Will Everett is about to embark on the adventure of his life! When Will ends up in possession of the key to a train car containing priceless treasures, he becomes the target of sinister figures from his past. In order to survive, Will must join a traveling circus, enlisting the aid of Mr. Dorian, the ringmaster and leader of the troupe." (Publisher's note)

"Will's father is driving the Boundless, the longest train ever, on her maiden voyage. After a series of adventures (involving a sasquatch and a murder), Will finds himself stranded in the caboose, where, with the help of a cute tightrope walker, he dodges a nefarious villain. The third-person present-tense narrative creates suspense as the well-drawn characters travel through an alternate-universe Canadian wilderness." (Horn Book)

Half brother. Scholastic Press 2010 375p $17.99
Grades: 7 8 9 10 **Fic**

1. Canada -- Fiction 2. Research -- Fiction 3. Chimpanzees -- Fiction 4. Family life -- Fiction
ISBN 978-0-545-22925-8; 0-545-22925-1
LC 2010-2696

In 1973, when a renowned Canadian behavioral psychologist pursues his latest research project—an experiment to determine whether chimpanzees can acquire advanced language skills—he brings home a baby chimp named Zan and asks his thirteen-year-old son to treat Zan like a little brother.

"Oppel has taken a fascinating subject and molded it into a topnotch read. Deftly integrating family dynamics, animal-rights issues, and the painful lessons of growing up, Half Brother draws readers in from the beginning and doesn't let go." SLJ

★ The **nest**; by Kenneth Oppel ; illustrated by Jon Klassen. Simon & Schuster Books for Young Readers 2015 256 p. illustrations (hardcover) $16.99
Grades: 4 5 6 7 **Fic**

1. Wasps -- Fiction 2. Brothers -- fiction 3. Babies -- Fiction 4. Supernatural -- Fiction 5. Horror stories -- Fiction
ISBN 148143232X; 9781481432320; 9781481432337
LC 2014038101

In this juvenile novel, by Kenneth Oppel, "Steve, an older brother struggling with anxiety and his family's distress after his newborn brother, Theodore, is diagnosed with a rare congenital disorder. After a curious gray and white wasp from the hive above their house stings Steve, he develops the ability to speak to the hive's queen, who promises to replace the ailing baby with a new one." (Publishers Weekly)

"Klassen's eerie, atmospheric illustrations, all shadowy corners and half-concealed shapes, contribute to the spooky mood. With subtle, spine-chilling horror at its heart, this tale of triumph over monsters--both outside and in--is outstanding."

Silverwing. Simon & Schuster Bks. for Young Readers 1997 217p hardcover o.p. pa $6.99
Grades: 5 6 7 8 **Fic**

1. Bats -- Fiction
ISBN 0-689-81529-8; 1-4169-4998-4 pa
LC 97-10977

When a newborn bat named Shade but sometimes called "Runt" becomes separated from his colony during migration, he grows in ways that prepare him for even greater journeys

"Oppel's bats are fully developed characters who, if not quite cuddly, will certainly earn readers' sympathy and respect. In Silverwing the author has created an intriguing microcosm of rival species, factions, and religions." Horn Book

Other titles in this series are:
Sunwing (2000)
Firewing (2003)
Darkwing (2007)

★ **This** dark endeavor; the apprenticeship of Victor Frankenstein. Simon & Schuster Books for Young Readers 2011 298p $17.99
Grades: 7 8 9 10 **Fic**

1. Horror fiction 2. Twins -- Fiction 3. Alchemy -- Fiction 4. Brothers -- Fiction
ISBN 1-4424-0315-2; 1-4424-0317-9 ebook; 978-1-4424-0315-4; 978-1-4424-0317-8 ebook
LC 2011016974

When his twin brother falls ill in the family's chateau in the independent republic of Geneva in the eighteenth century, sixteen-year-old Victor Frankenstein embarks on a dangerous and uncertain quest to create the forbidden Elixir of Life described in an ancient text in the family's secret Biblioteka Obscura.

"Written in a readable approximation of early 19th-century style, Oppel's . . . tale is melodramatic, exciting, disquieting, and intentionally over the top." Publ Wkly

Followed by:
Such wicked intent (2012)

Orenstein, Denise Gosliner

The **secret** twin. Katherine Tegen Books 2007 385p $16.99; lib bdg $17.89
Grades: 7 8 9 10 **Fic**

1. Twins -- Fiction 2. Orphans -- Fiction 3. Siamese twins -- Fiction
ISBN 978-0-06-078564-2; 0-06-078564-0; 978-0-06-078565-9 lib bdg; 0-06-078565-9 lib bdg
LC 2006-03876

Born a conjoined twin, thirteen-year-old Noah bears the secret guilt of being the only survivor, and now finds himself in the care of a stranger with a secret of her own.

"This spellbinding story will entangle readers at the first sentence. . . . Orenstein's writing is magic—every word and phrase precisely chosen." Booklist

Orlev, Uri

Run, boy, run; a novel. translated from the Hebrew by Hillel Halkin. Houghton Mifflin 2003 186p $15

Grades: 7 8 9 10 Fic

1. Jews -- Poland -- Fiction 2. Holocaust, 1933-1945 -- Fiction
ISBN 0-618-16465-0

LC 2003-1550

Original Hebrew edition, 2001

Based on the true story of a nine-year-old boy who escapes the Warsaw Ghetto and must survive throughout the war in the Nazi-occupied Polish countryside

"The story is totally engrossing as it vividly describes the hardships faced by so many youngsters during the war. Orlev has . . . successfully used historical fiction to illustrate the Holocaust experience." SLJ

Ormsbee, K. E.

The **house** in Poplar Wood; by K.E. Ormsbee. Chronicle Books 2018 344 p. (alk. paper) $16.99

Grades: 5 6 7 8 Fic

1. Murder -- Investigation -- fiction 2. Death -- Fiction 3. Twins -- Fiction 4. Paranormal fiction 5. Brothers -- Fiction 6. Supernatural -- Fiction 7. Mystery and detective stories
ISBN 9781452149868

LC 2017058843

In this book, by K. E. Ormsbee, "for as long as the Vickery twins can remember, Lee and his mother have served Memory, while Felix and his father assist Death. This is the Agreement. But one Halloween, Gretchen Whipple smashes her way into their lives. Her bargain is simple: If the twins help her solve the murder of local girl Essie Hasting, she'll help them break the Agreement." (Publisher's note)

Orr, Wendy

Dragonfly song; Wendy Orr. Pajama Press 2017 393 p. illustrations, map $17.95

Grades: 5 6 7 8 Fic

1. Fantasy fiction 2. Bulls -- fiction 3. Mythology -- fiction 4. Bronze age -- Greece -- fiction 5. Civilization, Classical -- fiction 6. Human-animal communication -- fiction
ISBN 1772780375; 9781772780376

In this book, by Wendy Orr, "the girl has had many selves in her short life. The first she remembers is Aissa, the daughter of Mama and Dada. . . . Then the Bull King's raiders came, and Mama said, 'Don't make a sound till I come back.' And when the villagers found her she was silent as stone, because Mama never come back again. So the villagers cursed her as bad luck and made her No-Name, lowest of the servants to the Lady, the island's priestess." (Publisher's note)

"[Wendy] Orr tells her tale in both narrative poetry and prose for an effect that is both fanciful and urgent, drawing a rich fantasy landscape filled with people and creatures worthy of knowing. . . . As mesmerizing as a mermaid's kiss, the story dances with emotion, fire, and promise."--Kirkus Reviews

Swallow's dance; Wendy Orr. Pajama Press 2018 274 p. (hardback) $17.95

Grades: 5 6 7 8 Fic

1. Nobility -- fiction 2. Bronze Age -- fiction 3. Natural disasters -- fiction
ISBN 9781772780628

In this book, by Wendy Orr, "Leira is about to start her initiation as a priestess when . . . a violent earthquake leaves her home - and her family - in pieces. . . . With her family, Leira flees across the sea to Crete, expecting sanctuary. But a volcanic eruption throws the entire world into darkness. After the resulting tsunami, society descends into chaos. . . . With her injured mother, . . . Leira must find the strength and resourcefulness within herself to find safety." (Publisher's note)

Orwell, George, 1903-1950

Animal farm; a fairy story. with a foreword to the Centennial edition by Ann Patchett; with a preface by Russell Baker; introduction by C.M. Woodhouse. Centennial ed.; Harcourt Brace 2003 xxix, 97p $14

Grades: 7 8 9 10 11 12 Adult Fic

1. Animals -- Fiction 2. Totalitarianism -- Fiction
ISBN 978-0-45228-424-1; 0-45228-424-4

First published 1945 in the United Kingdom; first United States edition 1946

Orwell's 1945 fable about the power struggles among animals on a farm parallels the situation in Russia at the time as Orwell saw it; the characters include the ruthless pig Stalin, his idealistic Trotsky-like adversary, and the simple, kindly horse who represents the common man.

Oshiro, Mark

Anger is a gift; a novel. Mark Oshiro. St. Martin's Press 2018 464 p. $17.99

Grades: 8 9 10 11 12 Fic

1. Anger -- Fiction 2. Anxiety -- Fiction 3. Teenagers -- Fiction
ISBN 1250167027; 9781250167026

Schneider Family Book Award: Teens (2019)

In this book by Mark Oshiro, "Moss [Jeffries] . . . and his friends are subject to the lack of funds and crumbling infrastructure at West Oakland High, as well as constant intimidation by the resource officer stationed in their halls. That was even before the new regulations--it seems sometimes that the students are treated more like criminals. Something will have to change--but who will listen to a group of teens?" (Publisher's note)

"Oshiro deftly captures the simmering rage that ultimately transforms Moss from a quiet teenager to a committed activist against a brutal, menacing system." Pub Wkly

Ostlere, Cathy

Karma; a novel in verse. Razorbill 2011 517p map $18.99

Grades: 7 8 9 10 11 12 Fic

1. Novels in verse 2. India -- Fiction 3. Violence -- Fiction 4. Culture conflict -- Fiction
ISBN 978-1-59514-338-9; 1-59514-338-6

"The novel's pace and tension will compel readers to read at a gallop, but then stop again and again to turn a finely crafted phrase, whether to appreciate the richness of the language and imagery or to reconsider the layers beneath a thought. This is a book in which readers will consider the roots and realities of destiny and chance. Karma is a spectacular, sophisticated tale that will stick with readers long after they're done considering its last lines." SLJ

Ostow, Micol

So punk rock (and other ways to disappoint your mother) a novel. with art by David Ostow. Flux 2009 246p il pa $9.95

Grades: 8 9 10 11 12 Fic

1. School stories 2. New Jersey -- Fiction 3. Rock music -- Fiction 4. Bands (Music) -- Fiction 5. Jews -- United States -- Fiction
ISBN 978-0-7387-1471-4; 0-7387-1471-2

LC 2009-8216

Four suburban New Jersey students from the Leo R. Gittleman Jewish Day School form a rock band that becomes inexplicably popular, creating exhiliration, friction, confrontation, and soul-searching among its members.

The "comic-strip-style illustrations are true show-stoppers. . . . A rollicking, witty, and ultra-contemporary book that drums on the funny bone and reverberates through the heart." Booklist

Oz, Amos, 1939-2018

Suddenly in the depths of the forest; translated from the Hebrew by Sondra Silverston. Harcourt 2011 134p $15.99

Grades: 4 5 6 7 **Fic**

1. Fables 2. Animals -- Fiction

ISBN 978-0-547-55153-1; 0-547-55153-3

LC 2011-08664

In a gray and gloomy village, all of the animals—from dogs and cats to fish and snails—disappeared years before. No one talks about it and no one knows why, though everyone agrees that the village has been cursed. But when two children see a fish—a tiny one and just for a second—they become determined to unravel the mystery of where the animals have gone.

"In this swiftly moving fable . . . Oz creates palpable tension with a repetitive, almost hypnotic rhythm and lyrical language that twists a discussion-provoking morality tale into something much more enchanting." Booklist

Palacio, R. J., 1963-

★ **Wonder**; by R.J. Palacio. Alfred A. Knopf 2012 315 p. (hardcover) $15.99

Grades: 3 4 5 6 **Fic**

1. Middle schools 2. Interpersonal relations 3. Birth defects -- Fiction 4. Schools -- Fiction 5. Middle schools -- Fiction 6. Self-acceptance -- Fiction 7. Abnormalities, Human -- Fiction

ISBN 9780375869020; 9780375899881; 9780375969027

LC 2011027133

In this book, "[a]fter being homeschooled for years, Auggie Pullman is about to start fifth grade, but he's worried: How will he fit into middle-school life when he looks so different from everyone else? Auggie has had 27 surgeries to correct facial anomalies he was born with, but he still has a face that has earned him such cruel nicknames as Freak, Freddy Krueger, Gross-out and Lizard face. . . . Palacio divides the novel into eight parts, interspersing Auggie's first-person narrative with the voices of family members and classmates, . . . expanding the story beyond Auggie's viewpoint and demonstrating that Auggie's arrival at school doesn't test only him, it affects everyone in the community." (Kirkus)

Panteleakos, Nicole

Planet earth is blue; Nicole Panteleakos. Wendy Lamb Books, an imprint of Random House Children's Books 2019 240 p. (trade) $16.99

Grades: 4 5 6 7 **Fic**

1. Autism -- Fiction 2. Sisters -- Fiction 3. Space vehicles -- Fiction 4. Foster children -- Fiction 5. Schools -- Fiction 6. Middle schools -- Fiction 7. Space shuttles -- Accidents -- Fiction 8. Challenger (Spacecraft) -- Accidents -- Fiction

ISBN 9780525646570; 9780525646587; 9780525646600

LC 2018022142

In this novel, by Nicole Panteleakos, "twelve-year-old Nova is eagerly awaiting the launch of the space shuttle Challenger--it's the first time a teacher is going into space, and kids across America will watch the event on live TV in their classrooms. Nova and her big sister, Bridget, share a love of astronomy and the space program. They planned to watch the launch together. But Bridget has disappeared, and Nova is in a new foster home." (Publisher's note)

"In Panteleakos' debut, a nonverbal, autistic astronomy enthusiast counts down to the space shuttle challenger's launch—and her runaway sister's return—in January 1986." (Kirkus Reviews)

Paolini, Christopher

★ **Eragon**; Christopher Paolini. Knopf Books for Young Readers 2005 509p (Inheritance) (hbk.) $18.95; (library binding) $20.99; (pbk.) $6.99; (pbk.) $11.99

Grades: 7 8 9 10 **Fic**

1. Fantasy fiction 2. Dragons -- Fiction

ISBN 0375826688; 0375826696; 0375926682; 044023848X; 9780375826696

LC 2003047481

First published 2002 in different form by Paolini International

In Alagaesia, a fifteen-year-old boy of unknown lineage called Eragon finds a mysterious stone that weaves his life into an intricate tapestry of destiny, magic, and power, peopled with dragons, elves, and monsters.

"This unusual, powerful tale . . . is the first book in the planned Inheritance trilogy. . . . The telling remains constantly fresh and fluid, and [the author] has done a fine job of creating an appealing and convincing relationship between the youth and the dragon." Booklist

Other titles in this series are:

Eldest (2005)

Brisingr (2008)

Inheritance (2011)

Papademetriou, Lisa

Homeroom diaries; by James Patterson and Lisa Papademetriou ; illustrated by Keino. First Edition Little, Brown and Co. 2014 272 p. illustrations (hardcover) $18

Grades: 7 8 9 10 **Fic**

1. School stories 2. Teenage girls -- Fiction 3. Diaries -- Fiction 4. Friendship -- Fiction 5. High schools -- Fiction 6. Foster home care -- Fiction 7. Interpersonal relations -- Fiction

ISBN 0316207624; 9780316207621

LC 2013016061

In this young adult novel by James Patterson and Lisa Papademetriou, illustrated by Keino, "Margaret 'Cuckoo' Clarke recently had a brief stay in a mental institution following an emotional breakdown, but she's turning over a new leaf with her 'Operation Happiness.' She's determined to beat down the bad vibes of the Haters, the Terror Teachers, and all of the trials and tribulations of high school by writing and drawing in her diary." (Publisher's note)

"Despite the fact that serious issues (a negligent mother, an attempted sexual assault, and an incident of cyberbullying) are at play, the lighthearted tone adds levity to the work. The novel is fully illustrated with humorous artwork that contributes to the story in a meaningful way. Fans of the popular "diary fiction" genre (as well as those simply looking for an approachable and quick read) will find much to enjoy here." SLJ

Paquette, Ammi-Joan

Nowhere girl. Walker & Co. 2011 246p $16.99

Grades: 6 7 8 9 **Fic**

1. Fathers -- Fiction 2. Thailand -- Fiction 3. Voyages and travels -- Fiction

ISBN 978-0-8027-2297-3; 0-8027-2297-0

LC 2010049591

Fair-skinned and blond-haired, thirteen-year-old Luchi was born in a Thai prison where her American mother was being held and she has never had any other home, but when her mother dies Luchi sets out into the world to search for the family and home she has always dreamed of.

"The classic quest story gets expanded here with contemporary details in spare lyrical prose that intensify the perilous, archetypal journey.

. . . The realistic specifics . . . make the story of betrayal and kindness immediate and universal." Booklist

Paratore, Coleen

The **wedding** planner's daughter; [by] Coleen Murtagh Paratore. Simon & Schuster Books for Young Readers 2005 200p $15.95; pa $5.99

Grades: 5 6 7 8 **Fic**

1. Weddings -- Fiction 2. Mother-daughter relationship -- Fiction

ISBN 0-689-87340-9; 1-4169-1854-X pa

LC 2004-14502

Willa, a romantic girl who wants a father, tries to find a husband for her mother, Cape Cod's most popular wedding planner.

"This book is as sweet a confection as the cherry cordials its 12-year-old protagonist is so fond of eating. . . . The girl's letter to her mother . . . provides emotional heft to what has up to that point been just a pleasant story." SLJ

Other titles about Willa are:

The cupid chronicles (2007)

Willa by heart (2008)

Forget me not (2009)

Park, Barbara

The **graduation** of Jake Moon. Atheneum Bks. for Young Readers 2000 115p $15; pa $4.99

Grades: 4 5 6 7 **Fic**

1. Grandfathers -- Fiction 2. Alzheimer's disease -- Fiction

ISBN 0-689-83912-X; 0-689-83985-5 pa

LC 99-87475

Fourteen-year-old Jake recalls how he has spent the last four years of his life watching his grandfather descend slowly but surely into the horrors of Alzheimer's disease

"Jake is a well-rounded and believable character surrounded by colorful and equally realistic supporting characters. . . . This novel . . . is written in an accessible style that will appeal to a wide audience." SLJ

Park, Linda Sue

Beast of stone; Linda Sue Park, illustrated by Jim Madsen ; edited by Rosemary Brosnan. HaprerCollins 2018 368 p. (hardcover) $16.99

Grades: 4 5 6 7 **Fic**

1. Fantasy fiction 2. Adventure fiction 3. Forest animals -- fiction

ISBN 9780062327444

LC 2017954099

In this book in the Wing & Claw series, by Linda Sue Park, illustrated by Jim Madsen, edited by Rosemary Brosnan, Raffa Santana, a gifted apothecary, "failed to free the animals that the heartless Chancellor captured and turned against the people of Obsidia. . . . Now Raffa and his . . . allies are preparing to confront the Chancellor's armies in battle. Great beasts, small animals, and humans alike will be joining the fight, and Raffa's heart yearns to prevent injuries." (Publisher's note)

"The thoughtful, suspenseful third-person narration focuses on the resolution of Raffa's long quest for the moral imperative driving his life and profession. Black-and-white illustrations feature animal characters and key venues. A satisfying, moving, smashing finale with a very relevant message."

Cavern of secrets; Linda Sue Park, James Madsen ; [edited by] Abby Ranger. HarperCollins 2017 320 p. illustrations (Wing & claw) (ebook) $15.99; (hardcover) $16.99

Grades: 4 5 6 7 **Fic**

1. Magic -- fiction 2. Adventure fiction -- fiction

ISBN 9780062327437; 0062327410; 9780062327413

LC 2016935902

In this book, by Linda Sue Park, illustrated by James Madsen, "Raffa Santana has spent all winter hiding in the harsh wilderness of the Sudden Mountains, and now it's time to return home. Home, where his parents will help him fight back against the vile Chancellor who has captured and altered the wild creatures of the Forest of Wonders. Home, where Raffa's beloved companion, Echo the bat, will recover from his mysterious sickness." (Publisher's note)

"The nail-biting adventure, relevant moral dilemmas, and complex characters will leave readers eager for the final installment." Kirkus

Click; [by] Linda Sue Park [et al.] Arthur A. Levine Books 2007 217p $16.99

Grades: 7 8 9 10 **Fic**

1. Adventure fiction 2. Young adult literature 3. Photojournalism -- Fiction

ISBN 0-439-41138-6; 978-0-439-41138-7

LC 2006-100069

"Ten distinguished authors each write a chapter of this intriguing novel of mystery and family, which examines the lives touched by a photojournalist George Keane, aka Gee. . . . The authors' distinctive styles remain evident; although readers expecting a more straightforward or linear story may find the leaps through time and place challenging, the thematic currents help the chapters gel into a cohesive whole." Publ Wkly

Forest of wonders; Linda Sue Park ; Jim Madsen (illustrator) Harpercollins Childrens Books 2016 352 p. illustrations, map (Wing & Claw) (hardcover) $16.99

Grades: 4 5 6 7 **Fic**

1. Forest animals -- fiction 2. Fantasy fiction -- fiction

ISBN 9780062327383; 0062327380

LC 2015940700

In this juvenile fantasy adventure novel, by Linda Sue Park and illustrated Jim Madsen, part one of the "Wing and Claw" trilogy, "after discovering a vine with powerful properties in the protected Forest of Wonders, 12-year-old Raffa journeys to Obsidia's capital, where he uncovers a sinister government plan to use botanicals to endanger and enslave animals." (Kirkus Reviews)

"With its engaging hero, talking animals, arcane magic, moral issues, and unresolved plot, this first of a proposed trilogy promises more exciting forest wonders." Kirkus

Other titles in this series are:

Cavern of secrets (2017)

Beast of stone (2018)

Keeping score. Clarion Books 2008 202p map $16; pa $6.99

Grades: 4 5 6 7 **Fic**

1. Baseball -- Fiction 2. Family life -- Fiction 3. Brooklyn (New York, N.Y.) -- Fiction

ISBN 978-0-618-92799-9; 0-618-92799-9; 978-0-547-24897-4 pa; 0-547-24897-0 pa

LC 2007-46522

"Maggie's perspective is authentically childlike and engaging, and her relations with her family and friends ring true. . . . This finely crafted novel should resonate with a wide audience of readers." SLJ

★ A **long** walk to water; based on a true story. Clarion Books 2010 121p map $16
Grades: 6 7 8 9 10 **Fic**

1. Refugees 2. Relief workers 3. Water -- Fiction 4. Africans -- Fiction 5. Refugees -- Fiction 6. Sudan -- History -- Civil War, 1983-2005 -- Fiction

ISBN 0-547-25127-0; 978-0-547-25127-1

LC 2009-48857

When the Sudanese civil war reaches his village in 1985, eleven-year-old Salva becomes separated from his family and must walk with other Dinka tribe members through southern Sudan, Ethiopia, and Kenya in search of safe haven. Based on the life of Salva Dut, who, after emigrating to America in 1996, began a project to dig water wells in Sudan.

This is a "spare, immediate account. . . . Young readers will be stunned by the triumphant climax of the former refugee who makes a difference." Booklist

Project Mulberry; a novel. Clarion 2005 225p $16; pa $6.99
Grades: 5 6 7 8 **Fic**

1. Korean Americans -- Fiction

ISBN 0-618-47786-1; 0-440-42163-2 pa

LC 2004-18159

While working on a project for an afterschool club, Julia, a Korean American girl, and her friend Patrick learn not just about silkworms, but also about tolerance, prejudice, friendship, patience, and more. Between the chapters are short dialogues between the author and main character about the writing of the book

"The unforgettable family and friendship story, the quiet, almost unspoken racism, and the excitement of the science make this a great cross-curriculum title." Booklist

★ A **single** shard. Clarion Bks. 2001 152p $15; pa $6.99
Grades: 5 6 7 8 **Fic**

1. Korea -- Fiction 2. Pottery -- Fiction

ISBN 0-395-97827-0; 0-440-41851-8 pa

LC 00-43102

Awarded the Newbery Medal, 2002

Tree-ear, a thirteen-year-old orphan in medieval Korea, lives under a bridge in a potters' village, and longs to learn how to throw the delicate celadon ceramics himself

"This quiet, but involving, story draws readers into a very different time and place. . . . A well-crafted novel with an unusual setting." Booklist

Storm warning. Scholastic 2010 190p (The 39 clues) $12.99
Grades: 4 5 6 7 **Fic**

1. Ciphers -- Fiction

ISBN 978-0-545-06049-3; 0-545-06049-4

Sequel to: The emperor's code by Gordon Korman (2010)

Amy and Dan hit the high seas as they follow the trail of some infamous ancestors to track down a long lost treasure. However, the real prize isn't hidden in a chest. It's the discovery of the Madrigals' most dangerous secret and, even more shockingly, the true identity of the mysterious man in black.

Followed by: Into the gauntlet by Margaret Peterson Haddix (2010)

Trust no one; Linda Sue Park. 1st ed. Scholastic Press 2013 190 p. (reinforced) $12.99
Grades: 4 5 6 7 **Fic**

1. Spy stories -- fiction 2. Mystery fiction -- fiction

ISBN 0545298431; 9780545298438

LC 2012939109

This is the fifth installment of Linda Sue Park's Cahills vs. Vespers series. Here, "Amy and Dan discover that one of their friends is a spy for the Vespers, a group of evil agents who kidnapped seven of their family members. But which friend is it? The shocking secrets continue when the Cahill siblings finally figure out the Vespers' real plan, and it's much worse than they originally thought." (Owl Magazine)

When my name was Keoko. Clarion Bks. 2002 199p $16; pa $6.99
Grades: 5 6 7 8 **Fic**

1. Korea -- Fiction 2. World War, 1939-1945 -- Fiction

ISBN 0-618-13335-6; 0-440-41944-1 pa

LC 2001-32487

With national pride and occasional fear, a brother and sister face the increasingly oppressive occupation of Korea by Japan during World War II, which threatens to suppress Korean culture entirely

"Park is a masterful prose stylist, and her characters are developed beautifully. She excels at making traditional Korean culture accessible to Western readers." Voice Youth Advocates

Includes bibliographical references

Parker, Robert B.

Chasing the bear; a young Spenser novel. Philomel Books 2009 169p $14.99
Grades: 7 8 9 10 **Fic**

1. Bullies -- Fiction 2. Friendship -- Fiction 3. Kidnapping -- Fiction 4. Child abuse -- Fiction

ISBN 978-0-399-24776-7; 0-399-24776-9

LC 2008-52725

Spenser reflects back to when he was fourteen-years-old and how he helped his best friend Jeannie when she was abducted by her abusive father.

"A clean, sharp jab of a read." Booklist

Parkinson, Siobhan

Blue like Friday. Roaring Brook Press 2008 160p $16.95
Grades: 4 5 6 7 **Fic**

1. Ireland -- Fiction 2. Family life -- Fiction 3. Synesthesia -- Fiction 4. Missing persons -- Fiction

ISBN 978-1-59643-340-3; 1-59643-340-X

When Olivia helps her quirky friend Hal, whose synesthesia causes him to experience everything in colors, with a prank intended to get rid of Hal's potential stepfather, there are unexpected consequences, including the disappearance of Hal's mother.

"Parkinson creates a warm, moving story of real families facing real problems. . . . The economy of her prose is admirable; all the characters are well drawn." Booklist

Parry, Rosanne

Last of the name; Rosanne Parry. Carolrhoda Books 2019 335 p. (hardback) $17.99
Grades: 4 5 6 7 8 **Fic**

1. Immigrants -- Fiction 2. Brothers and sisters -- Fiction 3. United States -- History -- 1861-1865, Civil War -- Fiction 4. Irish Americans -- Fiction 5. New York (N.Y.) -- History -- 1775-1865 -- Fiction 6. United States -- History -- Civil War, 1861-1865 --

Fiction
ISBN 9781541542358; 9781541541597
LC 2018015861

In this book, by Rosanne Parry, "twelve-year-old Danny O'Carolan and his sister, Kathleen, arrive in New York City in 1863. Kathleen refuses to be parted from her only remaining relative, so she finds a job in domestic service for herself and her younger...sister. Danny reluctantly pretends to be a girl to avoid being sent to the children's workhouse or recruited as a drummer boy for the Union army." (Publisher's note)

"Middle grade readers with an interest in historical fiction will enjoy this selection. Parry is successful at detailing the Irish immigrant experience in America. She retains a youthful perspective on the important, relevant topics of immigration and acceptance." SLJ.

Second fiddle. Random House 2011 233p map $16.99; lib bdg $19.99
Grades: 5 6 7 8 **Fic**

1. Music -- Fiction 2. France -- Fiction 3. Germany -- Fiction 4. Soldiers -- Fiction 5. Paris (France) -- Fiction 6. Berlin (Germany) -- Fiction
ISBN 978-0-375-86196-3; 0-375-86196-3; 978-0-375-96196-0 lib bdg; 0-375-96196-8 lib bdg; 978-0-375-89350-6 e-book
LC 2009-33324

Six months after the fall of the Berlin Wall, three eighth-grade girls living on an American military base with their families in Berlin try to save a Russian soldier, who has been beaten and left for dead, by smuggling him to Paris, where they are going to perform in a music competition.

"This reads like first-class historical fiction; Parry . . . vividly conjures the political tensions of the period, the challenges of life as an army brat, and the redemptive power of music." Publ Wkly

Partridge, Elizabeth

Dogtag summer. Bloomsbury Books for Young Readers 2011 226p $16.99
Grades: 4 5 6 7 **Fic**

1. Hippies -- Fiction 2. Adoption -- Fiction 3. California -- Fiction 4. Family life -- Fiction 5. Vietnamese Americans -- Fiction 6. Racially mixed people -- Fiction 7. Vietnam War, 1961-1975 -- Fiction
ISBN 978-1-59990-183-1; 1-59990-183-8
LC 2010-25515

In the summer of 1980 before she starts junior high school in Santa Rosa, California, Tracy, who was adopted from Vietnam when she was six years old, finds an old ammo box with a dog tag and picture that bring up painful memories for both her Vietnam-veteran father and her.

"This gripping yet tender coming-of-age story reveals multiple nuanced perspectives of the Vietnam War and its aftermath. . . . Powerful historical fiction." Publ Wkly

Pastis, Stephan

Timmy failure : now look what you've done; Now Look What You've Done. Stephan Pastis. Candlewick Press 2014 288 p. illustrations $14.99
Grades: 4 5 6 7 **Fic**

1. Detectives -- Fiction 2. Polar bear -- Fiction 3. Problem solving -- Fiction 4. Self-confidence -- Fiction 5. Globes 6. Schools 7. Contests 8. Humorous stories 9. Detective and mystery stories
ISBN 0763660515; 9780763660512
LC 2013944145

In this book, by Stephan Pastis, "the too-smart-for-his-own-good kid detective is back for a second zany installment, along with his 1500-pound polar/bear business partner, Total. Timmy has big dreams for his crime-solving empire, fueled by his complete self-confidence, delusions of grandeur, and his assured win in a competition to find a stolen globe worth $500. But first, shenanigans are afoot and must be thwarted." (School Library Journal)

"Great-aunt Coriander and her own wacky aspirations add a new layer to the winning combination of sardonically humorous text and pen-and-ink cartoons that has won Timmy many fans." Horn Book

Timmy failure; we meet again. Stephan Pastis. Candlewick Press 2014 272 p. illustrations $14.99
Grades: 4 5 6 7 **Fic**

1. Boys -- Fiction 2. Polar bears -- Fiction 3. Private investigators -- Fiction
ISBN 0763673757; 9780763673758
LC 2014933979

This illustrated children's book, by Stephan Pastis, the third in the "Timmy Failure" series, continues to follow "Timmy Failure. And his detective agency is on the verge of global domination. Global riches. Global fame. And yet the gods keep throwing him curveballs: for starters, academic probation. The coveted Miracle Report is the key to everything, including a good grade." (Publisher's note)

"Timmy, while still taking refuge in the fantasy world of his polar bear and the detective agency, has noticeably grown over the series. In particular, his behavior toward overly affectionate Molly reveals an empathetic side of Timmy, as he observes how her father constantly belittles her. At times laugh-out-loud funny, then disarmingly sweet, Timmy's brand of failure continues to succeed with style." Booklist

Paterson, Katherine

Bread and roses, too. Clarion Books 2006 275p $16; pa $6.99
Grades: 5 6 7 8 **Fic**

1. Strikes -- Fiction 2. Immigrants -- Fiction 3. Lawrence (Mass.) -- Fiction 4. United States -- History -- 1898-1919 -- Fiction
ISBN 978-0-618-65479-6; 0-618-65479-8; 978-0-547-07651-5 pa; 0-547-07651-7 pa
LC 2005-31702

Jake and Rosa, two children, form an unlikely friendship as they try to survive and understand the 1912 Bread and Roses strike of mill workers in Lawrence, Massachusetts.

"Paterson has skillfully woven true events and real historical figures into the fictional story and created vivid settings, clearly drawn characters, and a strong sense of the hardship and injustice faced by the mostly immigrant mill workers." SLJ

★ **Bridge** to Terabithia; illustrated by Donna Diamond. Crowell 1977 128p il $15.99; lib bdg $16.89; pa $5.99
Grades: 4 5 6 7 **Fic**

1. Death -- Fiction 2. Virginia -- Fiction 3. Friendship -- Fiction
ISBN 0-690-01359-0; 0-690-04635-9 lib bdg; 0-06-440184-7 pa
LC 77-2221

Awarded the Newbery Medal, 1978

The life of Jess, a ten-year-old boy in rural Virginia expands when he becomes friends with a newcomer who subsequently meets an untimely death trying to reach their hideaway, Terabithia, during a storm

"Jess and his family are magnificently characterized; the book abounds in descriptive vignettes, humorous sidelights on the clash of cultures, and realistic depictions of rural school life." Horn Book

The **day** of the pelican. Clarion Books 2009 145p $16
Grades: 6 7 8 9 **Fic**

1. Muslims -- Fiction 2. Refugees -- Fiction 3. Albanians -- Fiction

4. Kosovo (Serbia) -- Fiction
ISBN 978-0-547-18188-2; 0-547-18188-4
LC 2009-14998

In 1998 when the Kosovo hostilities escalate, thirteen-year-old Meli's life as an ethnic Albanian, changes forever after her brother escapes his Serbian captors and the entire family flees from one refugee camp to another until they are able to immigrate to America.

"Paterson offers a realistic and provocative account of these refugees' plight, balanced by the hope of new beginnings and the resilience of the human spirit." Publ Wkly

★ The **great** Gilly Hopkins. Crowell 1978 148p $15.99; lib bdg $16.89; pa $5.99
Grades: 5 6 7 8 **Fic**
1. Foster home care -- Fiction
ISBN 0-690-03837-2; 0-690-03838-0 lib bdg; 0-06-440201-0 pa
LC 77-27075

A Newbery Medal honor book, 1979

"A well-structured story, [this] has vitality of writing style, natural dialogue, deep insight in characterization, and a keen sense of the fluid dynamics in human relationships." Bull Cent Child Books

★ **Jacob** have I loved. Crowell 1980 216p $15.99; lib bdg $17.89; pa $6.99
Grades: 5 6 7 8 **Fic**
1. Twins -- Fiction 2. Sisters -- Fiction 3. Chesapeake Bay (Md. and Va.) -- Fiction
ISBN 0-690-04078-4; 0-690-04079-2 lib bdg; 0-06-440368-8 pa
LC 80-668

Awarded the Newbery Medal, 1981

Filled with resentment over the attention showered upon her twin sister, and awaiting the day she can leave her town behind, young Louise meets a wise old sea captain and begins learning how to let go of her anger.

"Each incident and feeling in the life of her young protagonist rings true because the younger voice is so alive and direct. This is a book full of humor and compassion and sharpness." Bull Cent Child Books

Lyddie. Lodestar Bks. 1991 182p $17.99; pa $6.99
Grades: 5 6 7 8 9 **Fic**
1. Factories -- Fiction 2. Massachusetts -- Fiction 3. United States -- History -- 1815-1861 -- Fiction
ISBN 0-525-67338-5; 0-14-240254-0 pa
LC 90-42944

Impoverished Vermont farm girl Lyddie Worthen is determined to gain her independence by becoming a factory worker in Lowell, Massachusetts, in the 1840s

"Not only does the book contain a riveting plot, engaging characters, and a splendid setting, but the language—graceful, evocative, and rhythmic—incorporates the rural speech patterns of Lyddie's folk, the simple Quaker expressions of the farm neighbors, and the lilt of fellow mill girl Bridget's Irish brogue. . . . A superb story of grit, determination, and personal growth." Horn Book

Preacher's boy. Clarion Bks. 1999 168p $15; pa $4.95
Grades: 5 6 7 8 **Fic**
1. Vermont -- Fiction 2. Family life -- Fiction 3. Christian life -- Fiction
ISBN 0-395-83897-5; 0-06-447233-7 pa
LC 98-50083

In 1899, ten-year-old Robbie, son of a preacher in a small Vermont town, gets himself into all kinds of trouble when he decides to give up being Christian in order to make the most of his life before the end of the world

"With warmth, humor, and her powerful yet plain style, Paterson draws empathetic and memorable characters." SLJ

Patrick, Cat

Forgotten; a novel. Little, Brown 2011 288p $17.99
Grades: 7 8 9 10 11 **Fic**
1. School stories 2. Memory -- Fiction 3. Family life -- Fiction 4. Dating (Social customs) -- Fiction
ISBN 978-0-316-09461-0; 0-316-09461-7
LC 2010-43032

Sixteen-year-old London Lane forgets everything each night and must use notes to struggle through the day, even to recall her wonderful boyfriend, but she "remembers" future events and as her "flashforwards" become more disturbing she realizes she must learn more about the past lest it destroy her future.

"Patrick raises philosophical issues of real interest. . . . Thoughtful readers will enjoy the mind games, romance readers will enjoy the relationship dynamics, and all readers will find themselves inexorably pulled into a logical yet surprising and compelling finish." Booklist

The **Originals**; Cat Patrick. 1st ed. Little, Brown and Co. 2013 304 p. (hardcover) $18
Grades: 8 9 10 11 12 **Fic**
1. Sisters -- Fiction 2. Dating (Social customs) -- Fiction 5. Cloning -- Fiction 6. Individuality -- Fiction 7. Single-parent families -- Fiction
ISBN 0316219436; 9780316219433
LC 2012029853

In this novel, by Cat Patrick, "17-year-olds Lizzie, Ella, and Betsey Best grew up as identical triplets . . . until they discovered a shocking family secret. They're actually closer than sisters, they're clones . . . , hiding from a government agency that would expose them. . . . Then Lizzie meets Sean Kelly. . . . As their relationship develops, Lizzie realizes that she's not a carbon copy of her sisters; she's an individual with unique dreams and desires." (Publisher's note)

Revived; by Cat Patrick. 1st ed. Little, Brown & Co. 2012 336 p. (hardcover) $17.99; (paperback) $8.99
Grades: 7 8 9 10 11 12 **Fic**
1. Drugs -- Testing 2. Secrecy -- Fiction 3. Science -- Experiments -- Fiction 4. Death -- Fiction 5. Drugs -- Fiction 6. Schools -- Fiction 7. High schools -- Fiction 8. Moving, Household -- Fiction
ISBN 0316094625; 9780316094627; 9780316094634
LC 2011026950

This book, by Cat Patrick, follows Daisy, who since the age of five has been "part of a top-secret clinical trial for a drug called Revive that can bring the deceased back to life. . . . Daisy uncovers some secrets within the program: a mysterious extra case file, a new test batch of Revive, some unexplained car crashes, and the erratic behavior of the mysterious man at the top, nicknamed God." (Bulletin of the Center for Children's Books)

Patron, Susan

Behind the masks; the diary of Angeline Reddy. Susan Patron. Scholastic 2012 293 p. ill., map (paper-over-board) $12.99
Grades: 5 6 7 8 **Fic**
1. Mystery fiction 2. Diaries -- Fiction 3. Thieves -- Fiction 4. Gold mines and mining -- Fiction 5. Frontier and pioneer life -- California -- Fiction 6. Lawyers -- Fiction 7. Robbers and outlaws

-- Fiction 8. California -- History -- 19th century -- Fiction
ISBN 9780545304375

LC 2011023826

"[T]his Dear America series title [is] set in Bodie, California, in 1880. Fourteen-year-old diarist and would-be dramatist Angeline Reddy does not believe her father, criminal lawyer Patrick Reddy, has been murdered. Convinced his disappearance is purposeful, Angie investigates his 'demise' and tries to bring him back to their rough-and-tumble mining community. Assisted by friends, a dashing young Wells Fargo clerk, and the members of a local theater troupe, . . . Angie offers a revealing look at frontier life "especially preoccupations with thespian entertainments, racial and social prejudices, and vigilante justice."(Booklist)

Patt, Beverly

★ **Best** friends forever; a World War II scrapbook. with illustrations by Shula Klinger. Marshall Cavendish 2010 92p il $17.99; paperback $9.99

Grades: 5 6 7 8 **Fic**

1. Friendship -- Fiction 2. Washington (State) -- Fiction 3. World War, 1939-1945 -- Fiction 4. Puyallup Assembly Center (Wash.) -- Fiction 5. Japanese Americans -- Evacuation and relocation, 1942-1945 -- Fiction

ISBN 978-0-7614-5577-6; 0-7614-5577-9; 9781477810453; 9780761458692

LC 2008-20875

Fourteen-year-old Louise keeps a scrapbook detailing the events in her life after her best friend, Dottie, a Japanese-American girl, and her family are sent to a relocation camp during World War II.

"If the drama of the girls separation isn't enough, a romantic subplot and the antics of Dottie's goofy dog (living with Louise in her absence) will surely keep young readers interested. This heartwarming tale of steadfast friendship makes a wonderful access point for learning more about World War II and Japanese internment." SLJ

Includes bibliographical references

Patten, E. J.

Return to Exile; illustrated by John Rocco. Simon & Schuster 2011 512p (The Hunter chronicles) $16.99

Grades: 5 6 7 8 **Fic**

1. Fantasy fiction 2. Uncles -- Fiction 3. Monsters -- Fiction
ISBN 978-1-4424-2032-8; 1-4424-2032-4; 978-1-4169-8259-3 e-book

LC 2010053480

"Sky's twelfth birthday is a mix. His mother's delicious homemade goulash cannot overshadow the disappearance of his beloved uncle, Phineas, or the family's return to the small town of Exile. Sky has grown up reading about the Hunters of Legend, but he never dreamed that they were real until monsters appear in Exile and make Sky their target. . . . Patten's first novel excels at world building and pacing; the monsters . . . are fully formed and vividly drawn. . . . Interspersed with humor to keep an otherwise dark story from becoming overbearing, the balance is just right." Booklist

Patterson, James, 1947-

Maximum Ride: the angel experiment. Little, Brown 2005 422p (Maximum Ride) $16.99

Grades: 7 8 9 10 **Fic**

1. Science fiction 2. Genetic engineering -- Fiction
ISBN 0-316-15556-X

LC 2004-18623

After the mutant Erasers abduct the youngest member of their group, the "bird kids," who are the result of genetic experimentation, take off in pursuit and find themselves struggling to understand their own origins and purpose.

"Smart-mouthed sympathetic characters and copious butt-kicking make this fast read pure escapist pleasure." Horn Book Guide

Other titles in this series are:
School's out ¿ forever (2006)
Saving the world and other extreme sports (2007)
Final warning (2008)
Max (2009)
Fang (2010)
Angel (2011)

★ **Middle** school, the worst years of my life; [by] James Patterson and Chris Tebbetts; illustrated by Laura Park. Little, Brown 2011 281p il $15.99

Grades: 4 5 6 7 **Fic**

1. School stories 2. Bereavement -- Fiction 3. Family life -- Fiction

ISBN 0-316-10187-7; 978-0-316-10187-5

LC 2010022852

When Rafe Kane enters middle school, he teams up with his best friend, "Leo the Silent," to create a game to make school more fun by trying to break every rule in the school's code of conduct.

"The book's ultrashort chapters, dynamic artwork, and message that 'normal is boring' should go a long way toward assuring kids who don't fit the mold that there's a place for them, too." Publ Wkly

Pattou, Edith

East. Harcourt 2003 498p hardcover o.p. pa $8.95

Grades: 7 8 9 10 **Fic**

1. Fairy tales 2. Bears -- Fiction
ISBN 0-15-204563-5; 0-15-205221-6 pa

LC 2003-2338

A young woman journeys to a distant castle on the back of a great white bear who is the victim of a cruel enchantment

"Readers with a taste for fantasy and folklore will embrace Pattou's . . . lushly rendered retelling of 'East of the Sun and West of the Moon'." Publ Wkly

Followed by West (2018)

Paulsen, Gary, 1939-

Brian's hunt. Wendy Lamb Books 2003 103p $14.95; pa $5.99

Grades: 6 7 8 9 **Fic**

1. Dogs -- Fiction 2. Bears -- Fiction 3. Hunting -- Fiction
ISBN 0-385-74647-4; 0-385-90882-2 lib bdg; 0-553-49415-5 pa

LC 2003-19477

Companion volume to Hatchet, The river, Brian's return, and Brian's winter

Two years after having survived a plane crash into the Canadian wilderness, a sixteen-year-old returns to the wild to befriend a wounded dog and hunt a rogue bear.

"Paulsen's latest will satisfy his many fans." Booklist

Brian's return. Delacorte Press 1999 117p $15.95; pa $6.50

Grades: 6 7 8 9 **Fic**

1. Wilderness survival -- Fiction
ISBN 0-385-32500-2; 0-440-41379-6 pa

LC 98-24278

Companion volume to Hatchet and Brian's Winter

After having survived alone in the wilderness, Brian finds that he can no longer live in the city but must return to the place where he really belongs

"This work is bold, confident and persuasive, its transcendental themes powerfully seductive." Publ Wkly

Brian's winter. Delacorte Press 1996 133p $15.95; pa $6.95

Grades: 6 7 8 9 **Fic**

1. Winter -- Fiction 2. Survival after airplane accidents, shipwrecks, etc. -- Fiction

ISBN 0-385-32198-8; 0-440-22719-4 pa

LC 95-41337

Instead of being rescued from a plane crash, as in the author's book Hatchet, this story portrays what would have happened to Brian had he been forced to survive a winter in the wilderness with only his survival pack and hatchet

"The same formula that worked before is successful here: the driving pace of the narration, the breathtaking descriptions of nature, and the boy who triumphs on the merits of efficient problem solving. The author's ability to cast a spell, mesmerize his audience, and provide a clinic in winter survival is reason enough to buy this novel." SLJ

Dogsong. Atheneum Books for Young Readers 2000 177p $17.99; pa $6.99

Grades: 6 7 8 9 **Fic**

1. Inuit -- Fiction 2. Arctic regions -- Fiction 3. Sled dog racing -- Fiction

ISBN 0-689-83960-X; 1-416-93962-8 pa

A reissue of the title first published 1985 by Bradbury Press

A Newbery Medal honor book, 1986

A fourteen-year-old Eskimo boy who feels assailed by the modernity of his life takes a 1400-mile journey by dog sled across ice, tunda, and mountains seeking his own "song" of himself

The author's "mystical tone and blunt prose style are well suited to the spare landscape of his story, and his depictions of Russell's icebound existence add both authenticity and color to a slick rendition of the vision-quest plot, which incorporates human tragedy as well as promise." Booklist

★ **Harris** and me; a summer remembered. Harcourt Brace & Co. 1993 157p $16

Grades: 5 6 7 8 **Fic**

1. Cousins -- Fiction 2. Farm life -- Fiction

ISBN 0-15-292877-4

LC 93-19788

Sent to live with relatives on their farm because of his unhappy home life, an eleven-year-old city boy meets his distant cousin Harris and is given an introduction to a whole new world

"Readers will experience hearts as large as farmers' appetites, humor as broad as the country landscape and adventures as wild as boyhood imaginations. All this adds up to a hearty helping of old-fashioned, rip-roaring entertainment." Publ Wkly

★ **Hatchet**; [by] Gary Paulsen; illustrated by Drew Willis. 20th anniversary ed.; Simon & Schuster Books for Young Readers 2007 188p il $19.99; pa $6.99

Grades: 6 7 8 9 **Fic**

1. Divorce -- Fiction 2. Survival after airplane accidents, shipwrecks, etc. -- Fiction

ISBN 978-1-416-92508-8; 1-416-92508-2; 978-1-416-93647-3 pa; 1-416-93647-5 pa

A reissue of the title first published 1987 by Bradbury Press

A Newbery Medal honor book, 1988

After a plane crash, thirteen-year-old Brian spends fifty-four days in the wilderness, learning to survive initially with only the aid of a hatchet given him by his mother, and learning also to survive his parents' divorce

"Paulsen's knowledge of our national wilderness is obvious and beautifully shared." Voice Youth Advocates

Other titles in this series are:

The river (1991)

Brian's winter (1996)

Brian's return (1999)

Brian's hunt (2003)

Liar, liar; the theory, practice, and destructive properties of deception. Wendy Lamb Books 2011 120p $12.99; lib bdg $15.99

Grades: 4 5 6 **Fic**

1. School stories 2. Family life -- Fiction 3. Truthfulness and falsehood -- Fiction 4. Children's literature -- Works -- Grades two through six

ISBN 0-385-74001-8; 0-385-90817-2 lib bdg; 978-0-385-74001-2; 978-0-385-90817-7 lib bdg

LC 2010-28356

Fourteen-year-old Kevin is very good at lying and doing so makes life easier, until he finds himself in big trouble with his friends, family, and teachers. "Ages eight to twelve." (Publisher's note)

"Kevin's grappling with family troubles adds . . . emotional dimension to Paulsen's novel." Publ Wkly

Other titles about Kevin are:

Flat broke (2011)

Crush (2012)

Vote (2013)

Family ties (2014)

Notes from the dog. Wendy Lamb Books 2009 133p $15.99; lib bdg $18.99

Grades: 5 6 7 8 **Fic**

1. Cancer -- Fiction 2. Gardening -- Fiction 3. Children's literature -- Works -- Grades two through six

ISBN 0-385-73845-5; 0-385-90730-3 lib bdg; 978-0-385-73845-3; 978-0-385-90730-9 lib bdg

LC 2009-13300

When Johanna shows up at the beginning of summer to house-sit next door to Finn, he has no idea of the profound effect she will have on his life by the time summer vacation is over.

"The plot is straightforward, but Paulsen's thoughtful characters are compelling and their interactions realistic. This emotional, coming-of-age journey about taking responsibilty for one's own happiness and making personal connections will not disappoint." Publ Wkly

Nightjohn. Delacorte Press 1993 92p $15.95; pa $5.99

Grades: 7 8 9 10 **Fic**

1. Reading -- Fiction 2. Slavery -- Fiction 3. African Americans -- Fiction

ISBN 0-385-30838-8; 0-440-21936-1 pa

LC 92-1222

Twelve-year-old Sarny's brutal life as a slave becomes even more dangerous when a newly arrived slave offers to teach her how to read

"Paulsen is at his best here: the writing is stark and bareboned, without stylistic pretensions of any kind. The narrator's voice is strong and true, the violence real but stylized with an almost mythic tone. . . . The simplicity of the text will make the book ideal for older reluctant readers who can handle violence but can't or won't handle fancy writing in long books. Best of all, the metaphor of reading as an act of freedom speaks for itself through striking action unembroidered by didactic messages." Bull Cent Child Books

Soldier's heart; a novel of the Civil War. Delacorte Press 1998 106p $15.95; pa $5.99
Grades: 7 8 9 10 **Fic**
1. Young adult literature 2. Post-traumatic stress disorder -- Fiction 3. United States -- History -- 1861-1865, Civil War -- Fiction
ISBN 0-385-32498-7; 0-440-22838-7 pa
LC 98-10038
"This compelling and realistic depiction of war is based on a true story. . . . Paulsen's writing is crisp and fast-paced, and this soldier's story will haunt readers long after they finish reading the novel." Book Rep

The **Transall** saga. Delacorte Press 1998 248p pa $6.50
Grades: 5 6 7 8 **Fic**
1. Science fiction
ISBN 0-440-21976-0 pa
LC 97-40773
While backpacking in the desert, thirteen-year-old Mark falls into a tube of blue light and is transported into a more primitive world, where he must use his knowledge and skills to survive
"A riveting tale of adventure and action." Voice Youth Advocates

The **winter** room. Orchard Bks. 1989 103p $16.95; pa $5.99
Grades: 5 6 7 8 **Fic**
1. Farm life -- Fiction 2. Minnesota -- Fiction
ISBN 0-531-05839-5; 0-545-08534-9 pa
LC 89-42541
A Newbery Medal honor book, 1990
A young boy growing up on a northern Minnesota farm describes the scenes around him and recounts his old Norwegian uncle's tales of an almost mythological logging past
"While this seems at first to be a collection of anecdotes organized around the progression of the farm calendar, Paulsen subtly builds a conflict that becomes apparent in the last brief chapters, forceful and well-prepared. . . . Lyrical and only occasionally sentimental, the prose is clean, clear, and deceptively simple." Bull Cent Child Books

Woods runner. Wendy Lamb Books 2010 164p $15.99; lib bdg $18.99
Grades: 6 7 8 9 **Fic**
1. Spies -- Fiction 2. Soldiers -- Fiction 3. Kidnapping -- Fiction 4. Pennsylvania -- Fiction 5. Native Americans -- Fiction 6. Frontier and pioneer life -- Fiction 7. United States -- History -- 1775-1783, Revolution -- Fiction
ISBN 978-0-385-73884-2; 0-385-73884-6; 978-0-385-90751-4 lib bdg; 0-385-90751-6 lib bdg
LC 2009-27397
From his 1776 Pennsylvania homestead, thirteen-year-old Samuel, who is a highly-skilled woodsman, sets out toward New York City to rescue his parents from the band of British soldiers and Indians who kidnapped them after slaughtering most of their community. Includes historical notes.
"Paulsen fortifies this illuminating and gripping story with interspersed historical sections that offer details about frontier life and the war (such as technology, alliances, and other period information), helping place Sam's struggles in context." Publ Wkly

Pausewang, Gudrun

Dark hours; translated by John Brownjohn. Annick Press 2006 208p $21.95
Grades: 6 7 8 9 **Fic**
1. Germany -- Fiction 2. Refugees -- Fiction 3. World War, 1939-1945 -- Fiction
ISBN 1-55451-042-2
"Well written with suspense and powerful sentiments, this story will spark discussion." SLJ

Traitor; translated from the German by Rachel Ward. Carolrhoda Books 2006 220p hardcover o.p. pa $9.95
Grades: 7 8 9 10 **Fic**
1. Germany -- Fiction 2. Prisoners of war -- Fiction 3. World War, 1939-1945 -- Fiction
ISBN 0-8225-6195-6; 0-7613-6571-0 pa
LC 2005-33379
During the closing months of World War II, a fifteen-year-old German girl must decide whether or not to help an escaped Russian prisoner of war, despite the serious consequences if she does so.
"Pausewang presents an exciting and thought-provoking novel." SLJ

Paver, Michelle

Wolf brother. HarperCollins 2005 295p (Chronicles of ancient darkness) $16.99; lib bdg $17.89; pa $6.99
Grades: 5 6 7 8 **Fic**
1. Bears -- Fiction 2. Wolves -- Fiction 3. Demoniac possession -- Fiction 4. Prehistoric peoples -- Fiction
ISBN 0-06-072825-6; 0-06-072826-4 lib bdg; 0-06-072827-2 pa
LC 2004-8857
First published 2004 in the United Kingdom
6,000 years in the past, twelve-year-old Tarak and his guide, a wolf cub, set out on a dangerous journey to fulfill an oath the boy made to his dying father—to travel to the Mountain of the World Spirit seeking a way to destroy a demon-possessed bear that threatens all the clans
"Paver's depth of research into the spiritual world of primitive peoples makes this impressive British import, slated to be the first in a six-book series, intriguing and believable." SLJ
Other titles in this series are:
Spirit walker (2006)
Soul eater (2007)
Outcast (2008)
Oath breaker (2009)
Ghost hunter (2010)

Peacock, Carol Antoinette

Red thread sisters; by Carol Antoinette Peacock. Viking 2012 236 p. (hardcover) $15.99
Grades: 4 5 6 7 8 **Fic**
1. Adoptees -- Fiction 2. Friendship -- Fiction 3. Chinese Americans -- Fiction 4. Adoption -- Fiction 5. Family life -- Fiction 6. Interracial adoption -- Fiction 7. Intercountry adoption -- Fiction
ISBN 0670013862; 9780670013869
LC 2012019511
This novel, by Carol Antoinette Peacock, offers a "story of friendship, family, and love. Wen has spent the first eleven years of her life at an orphanage in rural China . . . [with] her best friend, Shu Ling. When Wen is adopted by an American couple, she struggles . . . knowing that Shu Ling remains back at the orphanage, alone. Wen knows that her best friend deserves a family and a future, too. But finding a home for Shu Ling isn't easy, and time is running out." (Publisher's note)

Peacock, Shane

★ **Eye** of the crow. Tundra Books 2007 264p (The boy Sherlock Holmes) $24.99; pa $9.95

Grades: 6 7 8 9 10 **Fic**

1. Mystery fiction 2. Great Britain -- History -- 19th century -- Fiction

ISBN 978-0-88776-850-7; 0-88776-850-4; 978-0-88776-919-1 pa; 0-88776-919-5 pa

"A young woman is brutally murdered in a dark back street of Whitechapel; a young Arab is discovered with the bloody murder weapon; and a thirteen-year-old Sherlock Holmes, who was seen speaking with the alleged killer as he was hauled into jail, is suspected to be his accomplice. . . . Although imaginative reconstruction of Holmes childhood has been the subject of literary and cinematic endeavors, Peacock's take ranks among the most successful." Bull Cent Child Books

Other titles in this series are:
Death in the air (2008)
The dragon turn (2011)
The secret fiend (2010)
Vanishing girl (2009)

Pearsall, Shelley

All of the above; a novel. illustrations by Javaka Steptoe. Little, Brown 2006 234p il hardcover o.p. pa $5.99

Grades: 5 6 7 8 **Fic**

1. School stories 2. City and town life -- Fiction

ISBN 0-316-11524-X; 978-0-316-11524-7; 978-0-316-11526-1 pa; 0-316-11526-6 pa

LC 2005-33109

Five urban middle school students, their teacher, and other community members relate how a school project to build the world's largest tetrahedron affects the lives of everyone involved.

"Pearsall's novel, based on a real event in 2002—is a delightful story about the power of a vision and the importance of a goal. The authentic voices of the students and the well-intentioned, supportive adults surrounding them illustrate all that is good about schools, family, friendship, and community." Booklist

All shook up; [by] Shelley Pearsall. Alfred A. Knopf 2008 261p il $15.99; lib bdg $18.99

Grades: 6 7 8 9 **Fic**

1. Chicago (Ill.) -- Fiction 2. Father-son relationship -- Fiction

ISBN 978-0-375-83698-5; 0-375-83698-5; 978-0-375-93698-2 lib bdg; 0-375-93698-X lib bdg

LC 2007-22931

When thirteen-year-old Josh goes to stay with his father in Chicago for a few months, he discovers—to his horror—that his dad has become an Elvis impersonator.

"This affecting story of a typical, clever middle-school boy dealing with divorce and the new families that sometimes replace the old is also a very funny tale told by a terrifically engaging young narrator." Voice Youth Advocates

Jump into the sky; Shelley Pearsall. Alfred A. Knopf 2012 344 p. (hbk.) $16.99

Grades: 4 5 6 7 **Fic**

1. Historical fiction 2. Father-son relationship -- Fiction 3. World War, 1939-1945 -- Children -- Fiction 4. World War, 1939-1945 -- African Americans -- Fiction 5. Prejudices -- Fiction 6. Segregation -- Fiction 7. Fathers and sons -- Fiction 8. African Americans -- Fiction 9. United States -- History -- World War, 1939-1945 -- Fiction 10. United States. Army. Parachute Infantry Battalion, 555th -- Fiction

ISBN 0375836993; 0375895485; 0375936998; 0440421403; 9780375836992; 9780375895487; 9780375936999; 9780440421405

LC 2011024935

This novel by Shelley Pearsall presents a "tale of the 555th Parachute Infantry Battalion, little known all-black paratroopers serving during WWII. . . . Her tale of 13-year-old Levi Battle's struggle to find his place in the world during World War II . . . [is the] story of a displaced boy hungry to connect with the war-hero father who is more legend than parent. . . . Levi is [sent to] his father at a base in North Carolina. . . . [and] is plunged into the racist South." (Kirkus Reviews)

★ The **seventh** most important thing; Shelley Pearsall. Knopf Books for Young Readers 2015 288 p. illustrations (hardback) $16.99

Grades: 5 6 7 8 **Fic**

1. Artists -- Fiction 2. Punishment -- Fiction 3. African Americans -- Fiction 4. Juvenile delinquency -- Fiction 5. Folk art -- Fiction 6. Community service (Punishment) -- Fiction 7. Hampton, James, 1909-1964 -- fiction

ISBN 0553497286; 9780553497281; 9780553497298

LC 2014047761

This book, by Shelley Pearsall, is a "story of anger and art, loss and redemption. . . . It was a bitterly cold day when Arthur T. Owens grabbed a brick and hurled it at the trash picker. Arthur had his reasons, and the brick hit the Junk Man in the arm, not the head. But none of that matters to the judge - he is ready to send Arthur to juvie for the foreseeable future. Amazingly, it's the Junk Man himself who offers an alternative: 120 hours of community service . . . working for him." (Publisher's note)

"A middle school student learns the meaning of redemption in this excellent coming-of-age story. For the rest of the country, it was the year President Kennedy was assassinated. For Arthur Owens, it would always be the year his Dad died." SLJ

Pearson, Mary E.

The **adoration** of Jenna Fox; [by] Mary E. Pearson. Henry Holt and Co. 2008 272p $16.95; pa $8.99

Grades: 7 8 9 10 11 12 **Fic**

1. Science fiction 2. Bioethics -- Fiction

ISBN 978-0-8050-7668-4; 0-8050-7668-9; 978-0-312-59441-1 pa; 0-312-59441-0 pa

LC 2007-27314

In the not-too-distant future, when biotechnological advances have made synthetic bodies and brains possible but illegal, a seventeen-year-old girl, recovering from a serious accident and suffering from memory lapses, learns a startling secret about her existence.

"The science . . . and the science fiction are fascinating, but what will hold readers most are the moral issues of betrayal, loyalty, sacrifice, and survival." Booklist

Other titles in this series are:
The Fox inheritance (2011)
Fox forever (2013)

Dance of thieves; Mary E. Pearson. Henry Holt & Co. 2018 512 p. (hardcover) $18.99

Grades: 8 9 10 11 12 **Fic**

1. Romance fiction 2. Thieves -- Fiction 3. Criminals -- Fiction

ISBN 9781250159014; 9781250159021

LC 2017957735

In this book, by Mary E. Pearson "a formidable outlaw family that claims to be the first among nations. A son destined to lead, thrust suddenly into power. Three fierce young women of the Rahtan, the queen's premier guard. A legendary street thief leading a mission. . . . When outlaw leader meets reformed thief, a cat-and-mouse game of false moves ensues, bringing them intimately together in a battle that may cost them their lives--and their hearts." (Publisher's note)

Other titles in this series are:

Vow of thieves (2019)

Peck, Richard 1934-2018

Are you in the house alone? Viking 1976 156p pa $5.99

Grades: 8 9 10 11 12 **Fic**

1. Rape -- Fiction

ISBN 0-14-130693-9 pa

LC 76-28810

ALA YALSA Margaret A. Edwards Award (1990)

"Gail is frightened by the obscene telephone calls she receives and the notes that are left on her school locker. It is after she has been raped by a classmate while she is babysitting that she begins to understand the real meaning of fear. Although she is a victim, she is doubted by her family, friends, and the police. Most unendurable is the fact that she is forced frequently to cross the path of her attacker, the son of a prominent member of the community." Shapiro. Fic for Youth. 2d edition

★ The **best** man; Richard Peck. Penguin Group USA 2017 256 p. (pbk.) $8.99; (hbk.) $16.99

Grades: 4 5 6 7 **Fic**

1. School stories 2. Weddings -- Fiction 3. Family life -- Fiction 4. Gays -- Fiction 5. Schools -- Fiction 6. Role models -- Fiction

ISBN 0803738390; 9780147515797; 9780803738393; 0147515793

LC 2015049803

In this book, by Richard Peck, "Archer Magill has spent a lively five years of grade school with one eye out in search of grown-up role models. Three of the best are his grandpa, the great architect; his dad, the great vintage car customizer; and his uncle Paul, who is just plain great. These are the three he wants to be. Along the way he finds a fourth—Mr. McLeod, a teacher. In fact, the first male teacher in the history of the school." (Publisher's note)

"It's an indelible portrait of what it looks like to grow up in an age of viral videos and media frenzies, undergirded by the same powerful sense of family that characterizes so much of Peck's work." Pub Wkly

Fair weather; a novel. Dial Bks. 2001 130p il $16.99; pa $5.99

Grades: 5 6 7 8 **Fic**

1. Actors 2. Singers 3. Scouts 4. Hunters 5. Circus executives 6. Circus performers 7. Family life -- Fiction 8. Chicago (Ill.) -- Fiction

ISBN 0-8037-2516-7; 0-14-250034-8 pa

LC 00-55561

In 1893, thirteen-year-old Rosie and members of her family travel from their Illinois farm to Chicago to visit Aunt Euterpe and attend the World's Columbian Exposition which, along with an encounter with Buffalo Bill and Lillian Russell, turns out to be a life-changing experience for everyone

"Peck's unforgettable characters, cunning dialogue and fast-paced action will keep readers in stitches." Publ Wkly

Here lies the librarian. Dial Books 2006 145p $16.99; pa $6.99

Grades: 4 5 6 **Fic**

1. Indiana -- Fiction 2. Librarians -- Fiction 3. Automobiles -- Fiction 4. Country life -- Fiction

ISBN 0-8037-3080-2; 0-14-240908-1 pa

LC 2005-20279

Fourteen-year-old Eleanor "Peewee" McGrath, a tomboy and automobile enthusiast, discovers new possibilities for her future after the 1914 arrival in her small Indiana town of four young librarians.

"Another gem from Peck, with his signature combination of quirky characters, poignancy, and outrageous farce." SLJ

★ A **long** way from Chicago; a novel in stories. Dial Bks. for Young Readers 1998 148p pa $5.99; $15.99

Grades: 5 6 7 8 **Fic**

1. Illinois -- Fiction 2. Grandmothers -- Fiction 3. Depressions -- 1929 -- Fiction 4. Country life -- Illinois -- Fiction 5. Great Depression, 1929-1939 -- Fiction

ISBN 0-14-240110-2 pa; 0-8037-2290-7

LC 98-10953

A Newbery Medal honor book, 1999

Joe recounts his annual summer trips to rural Illinois with his sister during the Great Depression to visit their larger-than-life grandmother

"The novel reveals a strong sense of place, a depth of characterization, and a rich sense of humor." Horn Book

Followed by: A year down yonder (2000)

★ **On** the wings of heroes. Dial Books 2007 148p $16.99; pa $6.99

Grades: 4 5 6 7 **Fic**

1. Illinois -- Fiction 2. World War, 1939-1945 -- Fiction

ISBN 0-8037-3081-0; 0-14-241204-X pa

LC 2006011906

A boy in Illinois remembers the homefront years of World War II, especially his two heroes, his brother in the Air Force and his father, who fought in the previous war.

"Peck's masterful, detail-rich prose describes wartime in the United States. . . . Peck's characters are memorable. . . . This book is an absolute delight." SLJ

The **river** between us. Dial Bks. 2003 164p $16.99; pa $6.99

Grades: 7 8 9 10 **Fic**

1. Race relations -- Fiction 2. Racially mixed people -- Fiction 3. United States -- History -- 1861-1865, Civil War -- Fiction

ISBN 0-8037-2735-6; 0-14-240310-5 pa

LC 2002-34815

National Book Award Finalist: Young People's Literature (2003)

During the early days of the Civil War, the Pruitt family takes in two mysterious young ladies who have fled New Orleans to come north to Illinois

"The harsh realities of war are brutally related in a complex, always surprising plot that resonates on mutiple levels." Horn Book Guide

★ A **season** of gifts. Dial Books for Young Readers 2009 156p $16.99

Grades: 5 6 7 8 **Fic**

1. Moving -- Fiction 2. Illinois -- Fiction

ISBN 978-0-8037-3082-3; 0-8037-3082-9

LC 2008-48050

Relates the surprising gifts bestowed on twelve-year-old Bob Barnhart and his family, who have recently moved to a small Illinois town in 1958, by their larger-than-life neighbor, Mrs. Dowdel.

"The type of down-home humor and vibrant characterizations Peck fans have come to adore re-emerge in full as Peck resurrects Mrs.

Dowdel, the irrepressible, self-sufficient grandmother featured in A Year Down Yonder and A Long Way from Chicago." Publ Wkly

The **teacher's** funeral; a comedy in three parts. Dial Books 2004 190p $16.99; pa $6.99

Grades: 5 6 7 8 **Fic**

1. Indiana -- Fiction 2. Teachers -- Fiction 3. Country life -- Fiction

ISBN 0-8037-2736-4; 0-14-240507-8 pa

LC 2004-4361

In rural Indiana in 1904, fifteen-year-old Russell's dream of quitting school and joining a wheat threshing crew is disrupted when his older sister takes over the teaching at his one-room schoolhouse after mean, old Myrt Arbuckle "hauls off and dies."

"The dry wit and unpretentious tone make the story's events comical, its characters memorable, and its conclusion unexpectedly moving." Booklist

★ A **year** down yonder. Dial Bks. for Young Readers 2000 130p $16.99; pa $5.99

Grades: 5 6 7 8 **Fic**

1. Grandmothers -- Fiction 2. Great Depression, 1929-1939 -- Fiction

ISBN 0-8037-2518-3; 0-14-230070-5 pa

LC 99-43159

Awarded the Newbery Medal, 2001

"Peck has created a delightful, insightful tale that resounds with a storyteller's wit, humor, and vivid description." SLJ

Peck, Robert Newton

A **day** no pigs would die. Knopf 1973 150p $25; pa $5.50

Grades: 6 7 8 9 **Fic**

1. Pigs -- Fiction 2. Shakers -- Fiction 3. Vermont -- Fiction 4. Farm life -- Fiction 5. Family life -- Fiction 6. Father-son relationship -- Fiction

ISBN 0-394-48235-2; 0-679-85306-5 pa

"Rob lives a rigorous life on a Shaker farm in Vermont in the 1920s. Since farm life is earthy, this book is filled with Yankee humor and explicit descriptions of animals mating. A painful incident that involves the slaughter of Rob's beloved pet pig is instrumental in urging him toward adulthood. The death of his father completes the process of his accepting responsibility." Shapiro. Fic for Youth. 3d edition

Peet, Mal, 1947-2015

Mysterious traveler; Mal Peet, Elspeth Graham, illustrated by P. J. Lynch. Candlewick Press 2013 48 p. $15.99

Grades: 3 4 5 **Fic**

1. Sahara Desert -- Fiction 2. Picture books for children

ISBN 0763662321; 9780763662325

LC 2012947823

This children's picture book was "inspired by the guides who navigate the Sahara in Mali." An old man named Issa rescues a baby wearing a valuable necklace and "raises the infant as his granddaughter, relying more and more on young Mariama once his eyesight begins to fail. . . . After a trio of arrogant visitors rejects Issa's guidance, he and Mariama rescue them just as a potentially deadly sandstorm swirls up." One of the boys turns out to be Mariama's brother. (School Library Journal)

★ **Tamar**. Candlewick Press 2007 424p $17.99

Grades: 8 9 10 11 12 **Fic**

1. Netherlands -- Fiction 2. Grandfathers -- Fiction 3. World War, 1939-1945 -- Fiction

ISBN 978-0-7636-3488-9; 0-7636-3488-3

LC 2006-51837

In 1995, 15-year-old Tamar inherits a box containing a series of coded messages from his late grandfather. The messages show Tamar the life that his grandfather lived during World War II the life of an Allied undercover operative in Nazi-occupied Holland.

"Peet's plot is tightly constructed, and striking, descriptive language, full of metaphor, grounds the story." Booklist

Pellegrino, Marge

Journey of dreams. Frances Lincoln Children's Books 2009 250p map $15.95

Grades: 6 7 8 9 **Fic**

1. Refugees -- Fiction 2. Guatemala -- Fiction

ISBN 978-1-84780-061-9; 1-84780-061-0

"This novel will captivate both Latin American survivors of civil war and their peers. Outstanding." Kirkus

Includes glossary

Pennington, Kate

Brief candle; [by] Kate Pennington. Hodder Children's 2004 262p

Grades: 6 7 8 9 **Fic**

1. Poets 2. Authors 3. Novelists 4. Great Britain -- Fiction

ISBN 9780340873700

"Along with losing herself in romantic poetry, 14-year-old Emily Bronte loves to wander the wild landscape around her father's parsonage. . . . Her two passions thrillingly collide when she encounters a distraught young man, whose courtship of a girl outside his station has left him jobless and desperate. . . . Pennington's homage offers the most to teens familiar with Bronte's Wuthering Heights. . . . But even readers without much previous knowledge about the book's underpinnings . . . will enjoy the universally accessible view of an ill-fated love and the dreamy restless teen who acts on its behalf." SLJ

Pennypacker, Sara, 1951-

★ **Pax**; Sara Pennypacker; iillustrated by Jon Klassen. Balzer + Bray 2016 288 p. illustrations (hardback) $16.99

Grades: 4 5 6 7 **Fic**

1. Foxes -- fiction 2. Human-animal relationships -- Fiction 3. Foxes as pets -- Fiction

ISBN 9780062377012; 0062377019

LC 2015015400

This children's novel, by Sara Pennypacker and illustrated by Jon Klassen, is "about the powerful relationship between a boy and his fox. Pax and Peter have been inseparable ever since Peter rescued him as a kit. But one day . . . Peter's dad enlists in the military and makes him return the fox to the wild. At his grandfather's house, three hundred miles away from home, Peter . . . strikes out on his own despite the encroaching war, spurred by love, loyalty, and grief, to be reunited with his fox." (Publisher's note)

"Every moment in the graceful, fluid narrative is believable. Klassen's cover art has a sense of contained, powerful stillness. (Interior illustrations not seen.) Moving and poetic." Kirkus

★ The **summer** of the gypsy moths; Sara Pennypacker. Balzer + Bray 2012 275 p. (tr. bdg.) $15.99

Grades: 4 5 6 **Fic**

1. Siblings -- fiction 2. Family life -- fiction 3. Foster children -- fiction 4. Death -- Fiction 5. Secrets -- Fiction 6. Great aunts -- Fiction 7. Cape Cod (Mass.) -- Fiction 8. Loss (Psychology)

-- Fiction
ISBN 0061964204; 9780061964206

LC 2011026095

This middle reader story by Sara Pennypacker follows "Stella[, who] loves living with Great-aunt Louise in her big old house near the water on Cape Cod . . . since her mom is . . . unreliable. So while Mom 'finds herself,' Stella fantasizes that someday she'll come back to the Cape and settle down. The only obstacle to her plan? Angel, the foster kid Louise has taken in. . . . [T]he girls hardly speak to each other. But when tragedy unexpectedly strikes, Stella and Angel are forced to rely on each other to survive." (Publisher's note)

Perera, Anna

★ **Guantanamo** boy. Albert Whitman 2011 339p $17.99
Grades: 7 8 9 10 11 12 **Fic**

1. Cousins -- Fiction 2. Muslims -- Fiction 3. Torture -- Fiction 4. Prisoners -- Fiction 5. Prejudices -- Fiction 6. Guantanamo Bay Naval Base (Cuba) -- Detention Camp -- Fiction
ISBN 978-0-8075-3077-1; 0-8075-3077-8

LC 2010048016

"Readers will feel every ounce of Khalid's terror, frustration, and helplessness in this disturbing look at a sad, ongoing chapter in contemporary history." Publ Wkly

Perez, Ashley Hope

What can(t) wait. Carolrhoda 2011 234p $17.95
Grades: 7 8 9 10 **Fic**

1. Family life -- Fiction 2. Mexican Americans -- Fiction
ISBN 978-0-7613-6155-8; 0-7613-6155-3

LC 2010-28175

"Pérez fills a hole in YA lit by giving Marisa an authentic voice that smoothly blends Spanish phrases into dialogue and captures the pressures of both Latina life and being caught between two cultures." Kirkus

Perez, Marlene

Dead is a battlefield; Marlene Perez. Graphia 2012 227 p.
Grades: 7 8 9 10 **Fic**

1. Zombies -- Fiction 2. Perfumes -- Fiction 3. Supernatural -- Fiction 4. Female friendship -- Fiction 5. High school students -- Fiction 6. Schools -- Fiction 7. High schools -- Fiction 8. Interpersonal relations -- Fiction
ISBN 0547607342; 9780547607344

LC 2011031489

In this young adult novel, a "high-school freshman learns that she's one of a group of women who fight evil beasties in her supernatural town of Nightshade, Calif. In this sixth installment of the "Dead Is . . ." series, Jessica discovers to her dismay that she's a "virago," a woman warrior destined to fight paranormal baddies. Jessica worries, too, about her very best friend in the whole world, Eva, who's been acting strangely since she discovered a new perfume. . . . Jessica also finds herself attracted to Dominic . . . while she's juggling dates with Connor. . . . Meanwhile, Eva joins the groupies hanging around creepy Edgar and becomes ever more hostile toward Jessica, even trying to bite her. It seems that Edgar's perfume turns girls into zombies. Now Jessica has to find a cure and drive Edgar out of town." (Kirkus)

Dead is a killer tune; Marlene Perez. Graphia 2012 204 p. (paperback) $7.99
Grades: 8 9 10 11 12 **Fic**

1. Accidents -- Fiction 2. Bands (Music) -- Fiction 3. Mystery fiction -- fiction 4. Music -- Fiction 5. Schools -- Fiction 6. High schools -- Fiction 7. Supernatural -- Fiction 8. Interpersonal relations -- Fiction
ISBN 0547608349; 9780547608341

LC 2012014798

Author Marlene Perez tells the story of a Battle of the Bands competition. "Jessica's romance with Dominic hasn't exactly progressed smoothly . . . Dominic's band, Side Effects May Vary, finds competition in an out-of-town act followed by a large entourage of obsessed fans--Hamlin, fronted by Brett Piper. When the most competitive bands start losing members to recklessness and bizarre accidents, Jessica must not only get to the bottom of the mystery, but also step into the spotlight as a musician herself." (Kirkus)

Dead is just a dream; by Marlene Perez. Houghton Mifflin Harcourt 2013 164 p. (Dead is) (hardback) $16.99
Grades: 8 9 10 **Fic**

1. Fantasy fiction 2. Clowns -- Fiction 3. Homicide -- Fiction 4. Murder -- Fiction 5. Schools -- Fiction 6. Nightmares -- Fiction 7. High schools -- Fiction 8. Supernatural -- Fiction 9. Psychic ability -- Fiction 10. Interpersonal relations -- Fiction
ISBN 0544102622; 9780544102620

LC 2013003883

In this book, by Marlene Perez "Jessica and her virago friends are . . .in the midst of four murders, all seemingly connected to creepy paintings being installed in the homes of Nightshade's most influential citizens. Just when the girls think they've solved the mystery, a bloody clown begins to stalk Jessica, confounding their original suspicions. Jessica and Dominic's status as a happy couple is also threatened when Dominic announces he will be touring with his band during part of their senior year." (Booklist)

"Jessica and her virago friends are back in this latest Dead Is series entry. This time they're in the midst of four murders, all seemingly connected to creepy paintings being installed in the homes of Nightshade's most influential citizens. Just when the girls think they've solved the mystery, a bloody clown begins to stalk Jessica, confounding their original suspicions...Girl drama, sweet romance, and murder - —what more could young teens want in a breezy read?" Booklist

Dead is the new black. Harcourt 2008 190p pa $7.95
Grades: 7 8 9 10 **Fic**

1. School stories 2. Cheerleading -- Fiction 3. Supernatural -- Fiction 4. Extrasensory perception -- Fiction
ISBN 978-0-15-206408-2; 0-15-206408-7

LC 2007027677

While dealing with her first boyfriend and suddenly being pressed into service as a substitute cheerleader, seventeen-year-old Daisy Giordano, daughter and sister of psychics but herself a 'normal', attempts to help her mother discover who is behind a series of bizarre attacks on teenage girls in their little town of Nightshade, California.

"This is the witty and humorous first installment in a series; it provides romance, mystery, friendship, adventure, and the supernatural all rolled up in a fast-paced, plot-twisting story." SLJ

Other titles in this series are:
Dead is a state of mind (2009)
Dead is so last year (2009)
Dead is just a rumor (2010)
Dead is not an option (2011)
Dead is a battlefield (2012)
Dead is a killer tune (2012)
Dead is just a dream (2013)

Perkins, Lynne Rae

All alone in the universe. Greenwillow Bks. 1999 140p il hardcover o.p. pa $5.99

Grades: 5 6 7 8 **Fic**

1. Friendship -- Fiction

ISBN 0-688-16881-7; 0-380-73302-1 pa

LC 98-50093

Debbie is dismayed when her best friend Maureen starts spending time with ordinary, boring Glenna

"A poignant story written with sensitivity and tenderness." SLJ

As easy as falling off the face of the earth. Greenwillow Books 2010 352p il $16.99

Grades: 8 9 10 11 12 **Fic**

1. Adventure fiction 2. Chance -- Fiction 3. Accidents -- Fiction

ISBN 978-0-06-187090-3; 0-06-187090-0

LC 2009-42524

A teenaged boy encounters one comedic calamity after another when his train strands him in the middle of nowhere, and everything comes down to luck.

"The real pleasure is Perkins' relentlessly entertaining writing. . . . Wallowing in the wry humor, small but potent truths, and cheerful implausibility is an absolute delight." Booklist

Criss cross. Greenwillow Books 2005 337p $16.99; lib bdg $17.89; pa $6.99

Grades: 6 7 8 9 **Fic**

1. Nineteen sixties -- Fiction 2. Identity (Psychology) -- fiction

ISBN 0-06-009272-6; 0-06-009273-4 lib bdg; 0-06-009274-2 pa

LC 2004-54023

Awarded the Newbery Medal, 2006

Teenagers in a small town in the 1960s experience new thoughts and feelings, question their identities, connect, and disconnect as they search for the meaning of life and love. "Grades five to eight." (Bull Cent Child Books)

"Debbie . . . and Hector . . . narrate most of the novel. Both are 14 years old. Hector is a fabulous character with a wry humor and an appealing sense of self-awareness. . . . The descriptive, measured writing includes poems, prose, haiku, and question-and-answer formats. There is a great deal of humor in this gentle story." SLJ

Perkins, Mitali

★ **Bamboo** people. Charlesbridge 2010 272p $16.95

Grades: 5 6 7 8 **Fic**

1. Myanmar -- Fiction 2. Wilderness survival -- Fiction

ISBN 978-1-58089-328-2; 1-58089-328-7

LC 2009005495

Two Burmese boys, one a Karenni refugee and the other the son of an imprisoned Burmese doctor, meet in the jungle and in order to survive they must learn to trust each other.

"Perkins seamlessly blends cultural, political, religious, and philosophical context into her story, which is distinguished by humor, astute insights into human nature, and memorable characters." Publ Wkly

Secret keeper. Delacorte Press 2009 225p $16.99; lib bdg $19.99

Grades: 7 8 9 10 **Fic**

1. India -- Fiction 2. Sisters -- Fiction 3. Family life -- Fiction

ISBN 978-0-385-73340-3; 0-385-73340-2; 978-0-385-90356-1 lib bdg; 0-385-90356-1 lib bdg

LC 2008-21475

In 1974 when her father leaves New Delhi, India, to seek a job in New York, Ashi, a tomboy at the advanced age of sixteen, feels thwarted in the home of her extended family in Calcutta where she, her mother, and sister must stay, and when her father dies before he can send for them, they must remain with their relatives and observe the old-fashioned traditions that Ashi hates.

"The plot is full of surprising secrets rooted in the characters' conflicts and deep connections with each other. The two sisters and their mutual sacrifices are both heartbreaking and hopeful." Booklist

Tiger boy; Mitali Perkins ; illustrated by Jamie Hogan. Charlesbridge 2015 144 p. (reinforced for library use) $14.95

Grades: 3 4 5 6 **Fic**

1. Tigers -- Fiction 2. Bangladesh -- Fiction 3. Family life -- Fiction 4. Animal rescue -- Fiction 5. Wildlife rescue -- Fiction 6. Family life -- Bangladesh -- Fiction 7. Sundarbans (Bangladesh and India) -- Fiction

ISBN 158089660X; 9781580896603; 9781607345435; 9781607346647

LC 2013049028

"When a tiger cub goes missing from the reserve, Neel is determined to find her before the greedy Gupta gets his hands on her to kill her and sell her body parts on the black market. Neel's parents, however, are counting on him to study hard and win a prestigious scholarship to study in Kolkata. Neel doesn't want to leave his family or his island home and he struggles with his familial duty." (Publisher's note)

Perkins, Stephanie

Anna and the French kiss. Dutton 2010 372p $16.99

Grades: 7 8 9 10 **Fic**

1. School stories 2. France -- Fiction 3. Foreign study -- Fiction 4. Paris (France) -- Fiction

ISBN 978-0-525-42327-0; 0-525-42327-3

LC 2009-53290

"Perkin's debut surpasses the usual chick-lit fare with smart dialogue, fresh characters and plenty of tingly interactions, all set amid pastries, parks and walks along the Seine in arguably the most romantic city in the world." Kirkus

Perl, Erica S.

The **capybara** conspiracy; A Novel in Three Acts. Erica S. Perl. Alfred A. Knopf Books for Young Readers 2016 192 p. (ebook) $50.97; (hardback) $16.99

Grades: 5 6 7 8 **Fic**

1. Humorous fiction 2. Friendship -- fiction 3. School life -- fiction 4. Mascots -- Fiction 5. Schools -- Fiction 6. Theater -- Fiction 11. Capybara -- Fiction 7. Middle schools -- Fiction

ISBN 9780399551734; 0399551719; 9780399551710; 9780399551727

LC 2015047497

In this children's book by Erica S. Perl, "seventh-grade playwright Olive Henry is frustrated by her middle school's lack of appreciation for anything but sports. . . . So Olive and her best friend, Reynaldo, hatch a plan to kidnap the school's capybara mascot, planning to return it, heroically, just in time for the school's pep rally and claim a reward . . . and, hopefully, some overdue respect for the school's non-athletes." (Publisher's note)

"Staged over three acts, Perl's novel zips along thanks to all the back-and-forth dialogue, and is well suited to be performed. An unexpected ending and comprehensive notes on how to stage the play round out an amusing tale." Pub Wkly

Peterfreund, Diana

Omega City; by Diana Peterfreund. Harpercollins Childrens Books 2015 336 p. $16.99

Grades: 4 5 6 7 **Fic**

1. Adventure fiction 2. Cold war -- Fiction 3. Scientists -- Fiction 4. Conspiracies -- Fiction

ISBN 0062310852; 9780062310859

LC 2014952614

In this middle grades book, by Diana Peterfreund, "Gillian Seagret doesn't listen to people who say her father's a crackpot. His conspiracy theories about the lost technology of Cold War-era rocket scientist Dr. Aloysius Underberg may have cost him his job and forced them to move to the middle of nowhere, but Gillian knows he's right and plans to prove it. . . . Gillian sets off on a journey into the ruins of Omega City, a vast doomsday bunker deep inside the earth." (Publisher's note)

Other titles in this series are:

The forbidden fortress (2017)

Infinity base (2018)

Peters, Julie Anne

Define normal; a novel. Little, Brown 2000 196p $14.95; pa $5.95

Grades: 7 8 9 10 **Fic**

1. School stories 2. Friendship -- Fiction

ISBN 0-316-70631-0; 0-316-73489-6 pa

LC 99-42774

When she agrees to meet with Jasmine as a peer counselor at their middle school, Antonia never dreams that this girl with the black lipstick and pierced eyebrow will end up helping her deal with the serious problems she faces at home and become a good friend

"Readers who are looking for believable characters and a good story about friendship, being different, and growing wiser will appreciate Define 'Normal'" Voice Youth Advocates

Petrucha, Stefan

Teen, Inc. [by] Stefan Petrucha. Walker 2007 244p $16.95

Grades: 8 9 10 11 12 **Fic**

1. Orphans -- Fiction 3. Pollution -- Fiction 4. Business ethics -- Fiction

ISBN 978-0-8027-9650-9; 0-8027-9650-8

LC 2007-2368

Fourteen-year-old Jaiden has been raised by NECorp. since his parents were killed when he was a baby, so when he discovers that the corporation has been lying about producing illegal levels of mercury emissions, he and his two friends decide to try to do something about it.

"Witty and provocative without being preachy, this novel has both daring characters and a heady plot." Booklist

Petruck, Rebecca

Boy bites bug; Rebecca Petruck. Amulet Books 2018 272 p. (hardcover with jacket) $16.99

Grades: 4 5 6 7 **Fic**

1. Racism -- Fiction 2. Insects -- Fiction 3. Best friends -- Fiction 4. Schools -- Fiction 5. Friendship -- Fiction 6. Middle schools -- Fiction 7. Hispanic Americans -- Fiction

ISBN 9781419721410

LC 2017032176

In this book, by Rebecca Petruck, "Will didn't plan to eat a stinkbug. But when his friend Darryl called new kid Eloy Herrera a racial slur, Will did it as a diversion. Now Will is Bug Boy, and everyone is cracking up inventing insect meals for him . . . Turns out eating bugs for food is a real thing, called entomophagy. Deciding that means he can use a class project to feed everyone grasshoppers, Will bargains for Eloy's help in exchange for helping him with wrestling." (Publisher's note)

Steering toward normal; Rebecca Petruck. Amulet Books 2014 336 p. illustrations (hardback) $16.95

Grades: 5 6 7 8 **Fic**

1. Brothers -- Fiction 2. Ranch life -- Fiction 3. Sibling rivalry -- Fiction

ISBN 1419707329; 9781419707322

LC 2013045512

In this book, by Rebecca Petruck, "eighth grade is set to be a good year for Diggy Lawson. He's chosen a great calf to compete at the Minnesota State Fair, he'll see a lot of July, the girl he secretly likes at 4-H, and he and his dad Pop have big plans for April Fool's Day. But everything changes when classmate Wayne Graf's mother dies, which brings to light the secret that Pop is Wayne's father, too. Suddenly, Diggy has a half brother, who moves in and messes up his life." (Publisher's note)

"Diggy Lawson has high hopes for eighth grade, including plans to win Grand Champion at the State Fair with his calf, Joker. Then it's revealed that Diggy's classmate Wayne is actually his half-brother, upending Diggy's family and their community. Petruck handles her characters with a balanced mix of humor and heart, allowing them to emerge as real boys with complicated emotions." Horn Book

Pfeffer, Susan Beth

Life as we knew it. Harcourt 2006 337p $17

Grades: 7 8 9 10 **Fic**

1. Science fiction 2. Family life -- Fiction 3. Natural disasters -- Fiction

ISBN 0-15-205826-5; 978-0-15-205826-5

LC 2005-36321

Through journal entries sixteen-year-old Miranda describes her family's struggle to survive after a meteor hits the moon, causing worldwide tsunamis, earthquakes, and volcanic eruptions.

"Each page is filled with events both wearying and terrifying and infused with honest emotions. Pfeffer brings cataclysmic tragedy very close." Booklist

Other titles in this series are:

The dead & gone (2008)

This world we live in (2010)

Philbin, Joanna

The **daughters**. Little, Brown 2010 275p il $16.99

Grades: 6 7 8 9 **Fic**

1. School stories 2. Fame -- Fiction 3. Wealth -- Fiction 4. Friendship -- Fiction 5. New York (N.Y.) -- Fiction

ISBN 978-0-316-04900-9; 0-316-04900-X

In New York City, three fourteen-year-old best friends who are all daughters of celebrities watch out for each other as they try to strike a balance between ordinary high school events, such as finding a date for the homecoming dance, and family functions like walking the red carpet with their famous parents.

This is a "fun, quick read. . . . Readers will be intrigued by the well-drawn characters and their growth over the course of several months." SLJ

Other titles in this series are:

The daughters break the rules (2010)

The daughters take the stage (2011)

Philbrick, Rodman, 1951-

The **mostly** true adventures of Homer P. Figg; [by] Rodman Philbrick. Blue Sky Press 2009 224p $16.99

Grades: 5 6 7 8 **Fic**

1. Adventure fiction 2. Orphans -- Fiction 3. Brothers -- Fiction 4.

United States -- History -- 1861-1865, Civil War -- Fiction
ISBN 978-0-439-66818-7; 0-439-66818-2

LC 2008-16925

A Newbery Medal honor book, 2010

Twelve-year-old Homer, a poor but clever orphan, has extraordinary adventures after running away from his evil uncle to rescue his brother, who has been sold into service in the Civil War

"The book wouldn't be nearly as much fun without Homer's tall tales, but there are serious moments, too, and the horror of war and injustice of slavery ring clearly above the din of playful exaggerations." Publ Wkly

Zane and the hurricane; a story of Katrina. Rodman Philbrick. The Blue Sky Press, an imprint of Scholastic Inc. 2014 181 p. maps (hardback) $16.99

Grades: 5 6 7 8 **Fic**

1. Rescue work -- Fiction 2. Hurricane Katrina, 2005 -- Fiction 3. Survival -- Fiction 4. African Americans -- Fiction 5. New Orleans (La.) -- Fiction 6. Racially mixed people -- Fiction
ISBN 0545342384; 9780545342384

LC 2013025489

In this children's novel, by Rodman Philbrick, "Zane Dupree is a charismatic 12-year-old boy of mixed race visiting a relative in New Orleans when Hurricane Katrina hits. Unexpectedly separated from all family, Zane and his dog experience the terror of Katrina's wind, rain, and horrific flooding. Facing death, they are rescued from an attic air vent by a kind, elderly musician and a scrappy young girl." (Publisher's note)

"Careful attention to detail in representations of the storm, the city and local dialect give this tale a realistic feel. Zane's perspective as an outsider allows Philbrick to weave in social commentary on race, class, greed and morality, offering rich fodder for reflection and discussion." Kirkus

Pierce, Tamora

Alanna : the first adventure; Tamora Pierce. Atheneum Pubs. 1983 241p $12.95

Grades: 7 8 9 10 **Fic**

1. Fantasy fiction 2. Gender role -- Fiction 3. Knights and knighthood -- Fiction
ISBN 0-689-30994-5

LC 83-2595

"Neither Alanna nor her twin brother Thom were happy with their father's decision to send Alanna to a convent and Thom to court. The two decide to switch places and Alanna posing as 'Alan' becomes a page at court while Tom goes to the convent to learn sorcery. Alanna finds life as a page hard, particularly as she is lighter and smaller than the other pages, but she struggles hard to overcome these disadvantages. She makes many friends at court, including . . . Prince Jonathan whose life she saves using her magical gift of healing." (Voice Youth Advocates)

Other titles in this series are:
In the hand of the goddess
The woman who rides like a man
Lioness rampant

Bloodhound. Random House 2009 551p il (Beka Cooper) $18.99; lib bdg $21.99; pa $10.99

Grades: 7 8 9 10 **Fic**

1. Fantasy fiction 2. Police -- Fiction 3. Counterfeits and counterfeiting -- Fiction
ISBN 978-0-375-81469-3; 0-375-81469-8; 978-0-375-91469-0 lib bdg; 0-375-91469-2 lib bdg; 978-0-375-83817-0 pa; 0-375-83817-1 pa

LC 2008025838

Sequel to Terrier (2006)

Having been promoted from "Puppy" to "Dog," Beka, now a full-fledged member of the Provost's Guard, and her former partner head to a neighboring port city to investigate a case of counterfeit coins.

"Quirky, endearing characters save the story." Booklist

Followed by Mastiff (2011)

Briar's book. Scholastic Press 1999 258p (Circle of magic) hardcover o.p. pa $6.99

Grades: 6 7 8 9 **Fic**

1. Fantasy fiction 2. Magic -- Fiction
ISBN 0-590-55359-3; 0-590-55411-5 pa

LC 98-26148

Sequel to: Daja's book

Briar, a young mage-in-training, and his teacher Rosethorn must use their magic to fight a deadly plague that is ravaging Summersea

"This fast-paced, imaginative fantasy could be read and enjoyed on its own, but it works better as part of the quartet, which covers the span of a year and begins with Sandry's Book." SLJ

Daja's book. Scholastic Press 1998 234p (Circle of magic) hardcover o.p. pa $6.99

Grades: 6 7 8 9 **Fic**

1. Fantasy fiction 2. Magic -- Fiction
ISBN 0-590-55358-5; 0-590-55410-7 pa

LC 97-44825

Sequel to: Tris's book

While at Gold Ridge castle to the north of Winding Circle, Daja and the three other mages-in-training who have become her friends develop their unique magical talents as they try to prevent a devastating forest fire from consuming everything in its path

"The fantasy elements of the series as a whole are satisfyingly well imagined, as are the main characters, and readers who have not read the first two novels will understand what is going on." SLJ

Followed by: Briar's book

★ **First** test. Random House 1999 216p (Protector of the small) hardcover o.p. pa $5.99

Grades: 6 7 8 9 **Fic**

1. Fantasy fiction
ISBN 0-679-88914-0; 0-679-98914-5 lib bdg; 0-679-88917-5 pa

LC 98-30903

First title in the Protector of the small series. Ten-year-old Keladry of Mindalen, daughter of nobles, serves as a page but must prove herself to the males around her if she is ever to fulfill her dream of becoming a knight

"Pierce spins a whopping good yarn, her plot balanced on a solid base of action and characterization." Bull Cent Child Books

Other titles in this series are:
Page (2001)
Squire (2002)
Lady knight (2002)

Lady knight. Random House 2002 429p (Protector of the small) hardcover o.p. pa $7.50

Grades: 6 7 8 9 **Fic**

1. Fantasy fiction

ISBN 0-375-81465-5; 0-375-91465-X lib bdg; 0-375-81471-X pa

LC 2002-69862

Sequel to: Squire

"Kel's world is completely realized in quick, precise detail." Booklist

Mastiff. Random House 2011 593p (Beka Cooper) $18.99; lib bdg $21.99; e-book $10.99

Grades: 7 8 9 10 **Fic**

1. Fantasy fiction 2. Police -- Fiction 3. Kidnapping -- Fiction 4. Kings and rulers -- Fiction

ISBN 978-0-375-81470-9; 978-0-375-91470-6 lib bdg; 978-0-375-89328-5 e-book

LC 2011024152

Sequel to Bloodhound (2009)

Beka, having just lost her fiance in a slaver's raid, is able to distract herself by going with her team on an important hunt at the queen's request, unaware that the throne of Tortall depends on their success.

"This novel provides both crackerjack storytelling and an endearingly complex protagonist." Kirkus

★ **Melting** stones. Scholastic Press 2008 312p $17.99

Grades: 8 9 10 11 12 **Fic**

1. Fantasy fiction 2. Magic -- Fiction

ISBN 978-0-545-05264-1; 0-545-05264-5

LC 2007045036

Residents of the island of Starns send for help from Winding Circle temple, and when prickly green mage Rosethorn and young stone mage trainee Evvy respond, Evvy finds that the problem is with a long-dormant volcano and tries to use her talents to avert the looming destruction.

This "is a riveting story that has many inventive and exciting plot twists and turns. . . . The story features excellent character development." SLJ

Page. Random House 2000 257p (Protector of the small) hardcover o.p. pa $6.99

Grades: 6 7 8 9 **Fic**

1. Fantasy fiction

ISBN 0-679-88915-9; 0-679-98915-3 lib bdg; 0-679-88918-3 pa

LC 99-89894

Sequel to: First test

In the second title of series, Keladry of Mindelan continues her training to become a squire with the aid of a new maid, the support of her friends, interference from some other pages, and some serious, even dangerous opposition

"The plot is engaging and Kel's character growth continues." SLJ

Followed by: Squire

★ **Sandry's** book. Scholastic Press 1997 252p (Circle of magic) hardcover o.p. pa $6.99

Grades: 6 7 8 9 **Fic**

1. Fantasy fiction 2. Magic -- Fiction

ISBN 0-590-55356-9; 0-590-55408-5 pa

LC 95-39540

Four young misfits find themselves living in a strictly disciplined temple community where they become friends while also learning to do crafts and to use their powers, especially magic

"Pierce has created an excellent new world where magic is a science and utterly believable and populated it with a cast of well-developed characters." Booklist

Other available titles in this series are:

Tris's book (1998)

Daja's book (1998)

Briar's book (1999)

Squire. Random House 2001 399p (Protector of the small) hardcover o.p. pa $6.99

Grades: 6 7 8 9 **Fic**

1. Fantasy fiction

ISBN 0-679-88916-7; 0-679-98916-1 lib bdg; 0-679-88919-1 pa

LC 2001-19280

Sequel to: Page

The third title in the series. After becoming a squire to Lord Raoul, commander of the King's Own, Kel of Mindelan, must face a terrifying test in the Chamber of the Ordeal before she can be a knight

"The novel expertly juxtaposes outward action and introspection, as Kel matures in both her knightly skills and personal outlook." Horn Book Guide

Followed by: Lady knight

★ **Terrier**. Random House 2006 581p il map (Beka Cooper) hardcover o.p. pa $9.99

Grades: 7 8 9 10 **Fic**

1. Fantasy fiction 2. Magic -- Fiction 3. Police -- Fiction

ISBN 0-375-81468-X; 0-375-83816-3 pa; 978-0-375-81468-6; 978-0-375-83816-3 pa

LC 2006-14834

When sixteen-year-old Beka becomes "Puppy" to a pair of "Dogs," as the Provost's Guards are called, she uses her police training, natural abilities, and a touch of magic to help them solve the case of a murdered baby in Tortall's Lower City. "Grades seven to ten." (Bull Cent Child Books)

"Pierce deftly handles the novel's journal structure, and her clear homage to the police-procedural genre applies a welcome twist to the girl-legend-in-the-making story line." Booklist

Other titles featuring Beka Cooper are:

Bloodhound (2009)

Mastiff (2011)

★ **Trickster's** choice. Random House 2003 422p $17.95; pa $8.95

Grades: 7 8 9 10 **Fic**

1. Fantasy fiction

ISBN 0-375-81466-3; 0-375-82879-6 pa

LC 2003-5202

Alianne must call forth her mother Alanna's courage and her father's wit in order to survive on the Copper Isles in a royal court rife with political intrigue and murderous conspiracy

"This series opener is packed with Pierce's alluring mix of fantasy, adventure, romance, and humor, making the book an essential purchase for school and public libraries." Voice Youth Advocates

Another title in this series is:

Trickster's queen (2004)

Tris's book. Scholastic Press 1998 251p (Circle of magic) hardcover o.p. pa $7.99

Grades: 6 7 8 9 **Fic**

1. Fantasy fiction 2. Magic -- Fiction
ISBN 0-590-55357-7; 0-590-55409-3 pa

LC 97-8521

Sequel to: Sandry's book

With the defenses of Winding Circle Temple seriously weakened by an earthquake, Tris and her fellow mages-in-training try to join their different magic powers to protect the Winding Circle community from a pirate attack

"Pierce has created another gripping adventure that's sure to please her many fans." SLJ

Followed by: Daja's book

★ **Wild** magic; Tamora Pierce. Simon & Schuster 2015 344 p map (The immortals) hardcover $19.99; paperback $11.99

Grades: 6 7 8 9 10 **Fic**

1. Fantasy -- fiction 2. Human-animal communication -- fiction
ISBN 9781481440233; 9781481440226

LC 2014043620

Originally published 1992

"Thirteen-year-old Daine has always had a special connection with animals, but only when she's forced to leave home does she realize it's more than a knack--it's magic. With this wild magic, not only can Daine speak to animals, but she can also make them obey her. Daine takes a job handling horses for the Queen's Riders, where she meets the master mage Numair and becomes his student. Under Numair's guidance, Daine explores the scope of her magic. But she encounters other beings, too, who are not so gentle. These terrifying creatures, called Immortals, have been imprisoned in the Divine Realms for the past four hundred years--but now someone has broken the barrier. And it's up to Daine and her friends to defend their world from an Immortal attack." (Publisher's note)

Other titles in this series are:
Wolf-speaker
Emperor mage
The realms of the gods

★ The **will** of the empress. Scholastic Press 2005 550p $17.99; pa $8.99

Grades: 8 9 10 11 12 **Fic**

1. Fantasy fiction 2. Young adult literature
ISBN 0-439-44171-4; 0-439-44172-2 pa

LC 2005-02874

On visit to Namorn to visit her vast landholdings and her devious cousin, Empress Berenene, eighteen-year-old Sandry must rely on her childhood friends and fellow mages, Daja, Tris, and Briar, despite the distance that has grown between them

"This novel begins two years after the Circle of Magic and The Circle Opens series. . . . Readers will enjoy being reacquainted with these older but still very well-developed characters." SLJ

Pierpoint, Eric

The **last** ride of Caleb O'Toole; Eric Pierpoint. Sourcebooks Jabberwocky 2013 304 p. (tp : alk. paper) $7.99

Grades: 4 5 6 7 **Fic**

1. Historical fiction -- fiction 2. Orphans -- Fiction 3. Wagon trains -- Fiction 4. Bozeman Trail -- Fiction 5. Coming of age -- Fiction 6. Brothers and sisters -- Fiction 7. Adventure and adventurers -- Fiction 8. Oregon National Historic Trail -- Fiction 9. West (U.S.) -- History -- 1860-1890 -- Fiction
ISBN 1402281714; 9781402281716

LC 2013011800

In this book, it's "1877 in Great Bend, Kan., and cholera has panicked citizens and killed scores, including Caleb O'Toole's father. The story opens as 12-year-old Caleb races through town to find one of his sisters while his mother lies dying of the disease and a mob threatens to burn down their house. Caleb then witnesses a murder, and the O'Toole children escape amid an explosive gunfight, after agreeing to . . . take the Oregon Trail to their aunt's ranch in Montana Territory." (Publishers Weekly)

The **secret** mission of William Tuck; Eric Pierpoint. Sourcebooks Jabberwocky 2015 312 p. (13 : alk. paper) $7.99

Grades: 4 5 6 7 8 **Fic**

1. Spies -- Fiction 2. United States -- History -- 1775-1783, Revolution -- Fiction
ISBN 1402281749; 9781402281747

LC 2015009887

In Eric Pierpont's novel "the whispered words of a dying soldier, and a mysterious watch, give William all the ammunition he needs; a secret message for the leader of the rebel army. Rebecca disguises herself as a boy, and she and William join the American troops. They embark on an epic journey that pulls them into a secret network of spies, pits them against dangerous gunmen, and leads them on a quest to find General George Washington himself." (Publisher's note)

"Richly detailed and exhilarating." Kirkus

Pierson, D. C., 1984-

The **boy** who couldn't sleep and never had to; a novel. DC Pierson. Vintage Books 2010 226 p. ill. $14.95

Grades: 11 12 Adult **Fic**

1. Science fiction 2. Teenagers -- Fiction 3. Friendship -- Fiction 4. Sleep disorders -- Fiction 5. Sleep -- Fiction 6. Schools -- Fiction 7. High schools -- Fiction 8. Cartoons and comics -- Fiction
ISBN 9780307474612

LC 2009021984

Alex Award (2011)

In this book, the recipient of a 2010 ALA Alex Award, "[w]hen [high-school student] Darren Bennett meets [classmate] Eric Lederer, there's an instant connection. They share a love of drawing, the bottom rung on the cruel high school social ladder and a pathological fear of girls. Then Eric reveals a secret: He doesn't sleep. Ever. When word leaks out about Eric's condition, he and Darren find themselves on the run. Is it the government trying to tap into Eric's mind, or something far darker? It could be that not sleeping is only part of what Eric's capable of, and the truth is both better and worse than they could ever imagine." (Publisher's note)

Pignat, Caroline

Wild geese. Red Deer Press 2010 335p pa $12.95

Grades: 7 8 9 10 **Fic**

1. Irish -- Fiction 2. Canada -- Fiction 3. Immigrants -- Fiction 4. Seafaring life -- Fiction
ISBN 978-0-88995-432-8 pa; 0-88995-432-1 pa

Sequel to: Greener grass (2009)

"Kit, pursued as a criminal, has safely made it on board an immigrant 'coffin' ship bound for Canada, disguised as a boy and accompanied by Mick, her best friend. Along the way, with historically gritty authenticity, she encounters a lethal fever, near-starvation conditions and terrifying storms. . . . When she finally reaches Canada, there is more disease and separation." Kirkus

Pike, Aprilynne

Earthbound. Penguin Group USA 2013 352 p. $17.99
Grades: 7 8 9 10 **Fic**

1. Science fiction 2. Paranormal fiction
ISBN 1595146504; 9781595146502

This is the first book in a series from Aprilynne Pike. Here, plane crash survivor Tavia "is in rehab and finishing her senior year online. She has time to look at the world with attentive eyes, and what she sees is often unnerving: glowing triangles on the historic houses of Portsmouth, N.H., or pedestrians who flicker. She tries to attribute these visions to the brain injury she sustained in the crash, but she can't dismiss the stalker with a blond ponytail so easily." (Publishers Weekly)

"The characters are well developed and the narrative is easy to follow... Pike does take a while to get to the heart of the matter, but overall the story is compelling. Readers of supernatural romances will be clamoring." SLJ

★ **Glitter**; Aprilynne Pike. Random House Inc 2016 384 p. illustrations (hardback) $17.99
Grades: 8 9 10 11 **Fic**

1. Drug dealers -- Fiction 2. Courts and courtiers -- Fiction 3. Versailles (France) -- 18th century -- Fiction 4. Science fiction 5. Adventure and adventurers -- Fiction
ISBN 9781101933701; 9781101933718

LC 2015039116

In this novel by Aprilynne Pike, it's the twenty-first century, but at the palace of Versailles everyone "acts like it's the eighteenth century. . . . When Danica witnesses an act of murder by the young king, her mother makes a cruel power play . . . blackmailing the king into making Dani his queen. . . . She has six months to escape her . . . destiny. . . . Her ticket out? Glitter. A drug so powerful that a tiny pinch . . . can make the wearer hopelessly addicted." (Publisher's note)

"Poufy gowns and corsets in a futuristic setting make for an interesting spin on a perennially popular genre." Kirkus

Wings. HarperTeen 2009 294p $16.99; lib bdg $17.89; pa $8.99
Grades: 7 8 9 10 **Fic**

1. Fantasy fiction 2. Plants -- Fiction 3. Trolls -- Fiction 4. Fairies -- Fiction
ISBN 978-0-06-166803-6; 0-06-166803-6; 978-0-06-166804-3 lib bdg; 0-06-166804-4 lib bdg; 978-0-06-166805-0 pa; 0-06-166805-2 pa

LC 2008-24653

When a plant blooms out of fifteen-year-old Laurel's back, it leads her to discover the fact that she is a faerie and that she has a crucial role to play in keeping the world safe from the encroaching enemy trolls.

"Replete with budding romance, teen heroics, a good smattering of evil individuals, and an ending that serves up a ready sequel, this novel nonetheless provides an unusual approach to middle level fantasy through its startlingly creative premise that faeries are of the plant world and not the animal world. . . . Both male and female fantasy readers will enjoy this fast-paced action fantasy." Voice Youth Advocates

Other titles in this series are:
Illusions (2011)
Spells (2010)

Pileggi, Leah

Prisoner 88; Leah Pileggi. Charlesbridge 2013 142 p. (reinforced for library use) $16.95
Grades: 4 5 6 7 8 **Fic**

1. Prisons -- Idaho Territory -- Fiction 2. Prisoners -- Idaho Territory -- Fiction 3. Idaho Territory -- History -- 19th century -- Fiction
ISBN 1580895603; 9781580895606; 9781607345343; 9781607346111

LC 2012024443

In this book, by Leah Pileggi, "ten-year-old Jake Evans has just received a five-year sentence for manslaughter. . . . The warden and guards are at a bit of a loss on how to treat so young a convict, and . . . Jake's life improves considerably in the aftermath of his conviction." But "there are hardened criminals who would like to take Jake down just for the grim pleasure of it, and Jake is drawn into the turmoil of an jailbreak attempt." (Bulletin of the Center for Children's Literature)

Pincus, Greg

The **14** fibs of Gregory K; Greg Pincus. Arthur A. Levine Books 2013 240 p. (hardcover : alk. paper) $17.99
Grades: 4 5 6 7 **Fic**

1. Honesty -- Fiction 2. Schools -- Fiction 3. Mathematics -- Fiction 4. Middle schools -- Fiction 5. Creative writing -- Fiction 6. Fathers and sons -- Fiction 7. Brothers and sisters -- Fiction 8. Middle-born children -- Fiction 9. Truthfulness and falsehood -- fiction
ISBN 0439912997; 9780439912990; 9780439913003

LC 2012044117

In this book, by Greg Pincus, "Gregory K is the middle child in a family of mathematical geniuses. But if he claimed to love math? Well, he'd be fibbing. What he really wants most is to go to Author Camp. But to get his parents' permission he's going to have to pass his math class, which has a probability of 0. THAT much he can understand!" (Publisher's note)

Another title in this series is:
The homework strike (2017)

Pinkney, Andrea Davis

★ **Bird** in a box; illustrations by Sean Qualls. Little, Brown Books for Young Readers 2011 278p il $16.99
Grades: 4 5 6 7 **Fic**

1. Boxing -- Fiction 2. African Americans -- Fiction 3. Radio broadcasting -- Fiction 4. Harlem (New York, N.Y.) -- Fiction 5. Great Depression, 1929-1939 -- Fiction
ISBN 978-0-316-07403-2; 0-316-07403-9

LC 2010-22851

In 1936, three children meet at the Mercy Home for Negro Orphans in New York State, and while not all three are orphans, they are all dealing with grief and loss which together, along with the help of a sympathetic staff member and the boxing matches of Joe Louis, they manage to overcome.

"Pinkney weaves quite a bit of 1930s history into her story and succeeds admirably in showing how Louis came to represent so much more than his sport. Her detailed notes make this an accessible and inspiring piece of historical fiction that belongs in most collections." SLJ

★ The **red** pencil; a novel told in poems, pictures, and possibilities. by Andrea Davis Pinkney ; illustrated by Shane Evans. First edition Little, Brown & Co. 2014 336 p. illustrations, map (hardcover) $17
Grades: 4 5 6 7 **Fic**

1. Sudan -- Fiction 2. Refugees -- Fiction 3. Novels in verse 4. Blacks -- Sudan -- Fiction
ISBN 9780316247801; 0316247804

LC 2013044753

Amelia Bloomer Project (2014)

"Amira is twelve. . . . Maybe old enough to go to school in Nyala--Amira's one true dream. But life in her peaceful Sudanese village is shattered when the Janjaweed arrive. . . . After she loses nearly everything, Amira needs . . . to make the long journey . . . to safety at a refugee camp. Her days are tough at the camp, until the gift of a simple red pencil opens her mind." (Publisher's note)

"Amira's thoughts and drawings are vividly brought to life through Pinkney's lyrical verse and Evans's lucid line illustrations, which infuse the narrative with emotional intensity." SLJ

With the might of angels; the diary of Dawnie Rae Johnson. Scholastic 2011 324p il map (Dear America) $12.99
Grades: 5 6 7 8 **Fic**

1. School stories 2. Diaries -- Fiction 3. Virginia -- Fiction 4. Family life -- Fiction 5. Race relations -- Fiction 6. African Americans -- Fiction 7. School integration -- Fiction
ISBN 0-545-29705-2; 978-0-545-29705-9
LC 2011001363

In 1955 Hadley, Virginia, twelve-year-old Dawnie Rae Johnson, a tomboy who excels at baseball and at her studies, becomes the first African American student to attend the all-white Prettyman Coburn school, turning her world upside down. Includes historical notes about the period.

"Dawnie's journal is realistic, encompassing thoughts and emotions one would expect of someone so stressed. . . . The author seamlessly incorporates historical events into the child's journal. The end matter contains age-appropriate photographs, a time line, and brief biographical sketches of the people mentioned. A first purchase." SLJ

Pinkwater, Daniel Manus, 1941-

Bushman lives! written by Daniel Pinkwater ; illustrated by Calef Brown. Houghton Mifflin Harcourt 2012 247 p. $16.99
Grades: 5 6 7 8 **Fic**

1. Gorillas -- Fiction 2. Teenagers -- Fiction 3. Friendship -- Fiction 4. Humorous stories 5. Artists -- Fiction 6. Coming of age -- Fiction 7. Adventure and adventurers -- Fiction 8. Chicago (Ill.) -- History -- 20th century -- Fiction
ISBN 0547385390; 9780547385396
LC 2011048211

In author Daniel Pinkwater's book, "Harold Knishke has no idea he wants to be an artist until the guy in the army cap in Bughouse Square just asks him. Almost immediately Harold is taking drawing classes from a taxidermist and acquires a studio of his own in a building so mysterious he can't tell a soul about it . . . He also has a best friend who is convinced that Bushman, the 427-pound gorilla who once lived in the Lincoln Park Zoo and is now stuffed and on display in the Field Museum of Natural History, is still alive." (Kirkus)

The **Neddiad**; how Neddie took the train, went to Hollywood, and saved civilization. by Daniel Pinkwater; illustrations by Calef Brown. Houghton Mifflin 2007 307p il $16
Grades: 5 6 7 8 **Fic**

1. Turtles -- Fiction 2. Los Angeles (Calif.) -- Fiction
ISBN 978-0-618-59444-3; 0-618-59444-2
LC 2006033944

Followed by: The Yggyssey (2009)

When shoelace heir Neddie Wentworthstein and his family take the train from Chicago to Los Angeles in the 1940s, he winds up in possession of a valuable Indian turtle artifact whose owner is supposed to be able to prevent the impending destruction of the world, but he is not sure exactly how.

"A bright and breezy adventure with a smart and funny narrator. . . . [This is a] goofy and lovingly nostalgic historical fantasy." SLJ

Pinter, Jason

Zeke Bartholomew, superspy. Sourcebooks Jabberwocky 2011 256p pa $7.99
Grades: 4 5 6 7 **Fic**

1. Adventure fiction 2. Spies -- Fiction
ISBN 978-1-4022-5755-1; 1-4022-5755-4

Zeke Bartholomew has always dreamed of being a spy. But when a case of mistaken identity goes horribly wrong, he's thrust into a world of real-life espionage beyond his wildest dreams. Soon this 7th grade nobody finds himself hunted by the lava-powered behemoth Ragnarok, aided by a mysterious butt-kicking girl who goes only by the codename 'Sparrow.'

"Zeke's first-person narration and ample one-liners provide plenty of laughs in a novel that combines espionage, wild sci-fi, and a satiric take on the ever-growing kids-save-the-world subgenre." Booklist

Pitcher, Annabel

Silence is goldfish; a novel. by Annabel Pitcher. Little, Brown & Co. 2016 352 p. (hardback) $17.99
Grades: 7 8 9 10 **Fic**

1. Selective mutism -- Fiction 2. Identity (Psychology) -- Fiction 3. England -- Fiction 4. Fathers -- Fiction 5. Identity -- Fiction 6. Manchester (England) -- Ficition
ISBN 9780316370752
LC 2015024312

In this young adult novel, by Annabel Pitcher, "fifteen-year-old Tess doesn't mean to become mute. At first, she's just too shocked to speak. . . . Reeling from her family's betrayal, Tess sets out to discover the identity of her real father. . . . Tess continues to investigate, uncovering a secret that could ruin multiple lives. It all may be too much for Tess to handle, but how can she ask for help when she's forgotten how to use her voice?" (Publisher's note)

"Tess, fifteen, is an offbeat English introvert with a highly involved dad. After she discovers his startling blog post recounting her own birth ('It wasn't my daughter. It was...some sperm donor's'), her anger emboldens her to stand up against Dad's expectations. Her rebellion of choice is silence, but her narrative voice speaks loudly--Tess is a witty and appealing protagonist." Horn Book

Pixley, Marcella

★ **Freak**. Farrar, Straus and Giroux 2007 131p $16
Grades: 6 7 8 9 10 **Fic**

1. School stories 2. Bullies -- Fiction
ISBN 0-374-32453-0; 978-0-374-32453-7
LC 2006-50683

Twelve-year-old Miriam, poetic, smart, and quirky, is considered a freak by the popular girls at her middle school, and she eventually explodes in response to their bullying, revealing an inner strength she did not know she had.

"The story's conflicts are exceptionally riveting and believable." Booklist

Pla, Sally J.

★ **Stanley** will probably be fine; Sally J. Pla, illustrated by Steve Wolfhard. Harpercollins Childrens Books 2018 288 p. $16.99
Grades: 4 5 6 7 **Fic**

1. Anxiety -- fiction 2. Courage -- fiction 3. Self-esteem -- fiction
ISBN 0062445790; 9780062445797

In this book, by Sally J. Pla, "nobody knows comics trivia like Stanley [Fortinbras] knows comics trivia. It's what he takes comfort in when the world around him gets to be too much. And after he faints during a safety assembly, Stanley takes his love of comics up a level by inventing his own imaginary superhero, named John Lockdown, to help him through." (Publisher's note)

Platt, Chris

Astra. Peachtree 2010 144p $15.95

Grades: 5 6 7 8 **Fic**

1. Horses -- Fiction 2. Father-daughter relationship -- Fiction
ISBN 978-1-56145-541-6; 1-56145-541-5

LC 2010001654

Forbidden to ride after her mother's death in a riding accident, thirteen-year-old Lily nurses her mother's beloved horse, Astra, back to health, hoping that someday Astra will win the Tevis Cup endurance race

"Filled with information about endurance racing as well as a cast of interesting supporting characters, including the dishy new boy in town, this novel is a quick and enjoyable read." SLJ

Plozza, Shivaun

Tin heart; a novel. Shivaun Plozza. Flatiron Books 2019 336 p. (hardcover) $18.99

Grades: 8 9 10 11 12 **Fic**

1. Dating (Social customs) -- Fiction 2. Heart -- Transplantation -- Fiction 3. Eccentrics and eccentricities -- Fiction 4. Identity -- Fiction 5. Family life -- Fiction
ISBN 9781250312761

LC 2018037890

In this novel, by Shivaun Plozza, "when Marlowe gets a heart transplant and a second chance at life, all she wants to do is to thank her donor's family. Maybe then she can move on.... But with a little brother who dresses like every day is Halloween, a vegan warrior for a mother, and an all-out war with the hot butcher's apprentice next door, Marlowe's life is already pretty complicated. And her second chance is about to take an unexpected turn..." (Publisher's note)

"Funny and direct, this book by Plozza . . . is capable of balancing heartbreak, first love, mortality, and the absurd." Pub Wkly

Poblocki, Dan

The **haunting** of Gabriel Ashe; Dan Poblocki. Scholastic Press 2013 288 p. (hardcover) $16.99

Grades: 6 7 8 **Fic**

1. School stories -- fiction 2. Horror tales 3. Monsters -- Fiction 4. Friendship -- Fiction 5. Imagination -- Fiction
ISBN 0545402700; 9780545402705

LC 2013004009

In this book, after "a fire destroys his home, Gabe and his family move into his grandmother's mansion in a small Massachusetts town. Gabe quickly befriends his neighbor, Seth Hopper, and the two play a dark fantasy game in the woods between their houses." Worried about his status at school, Gabe is concerned when he realizes Seth might be the class dork. Increasingly dark pranks begin to occur. (Kirkus Reviews)

Polak, Monique

What world is left. Orca Book Pub. 2008 215p pa $12.95

Grades: 7 8 9 10 11 12 **Fic**

1. Jews -- Netherlands -- Fiction 2. Holocaust, 1933-1945 -- Fiction 3. World War, 1939-1945 -- Netherlands -- Fiction 4. Netherlands -- History -- 1940-1945, German occupation -- Fiction
ISBN 978-1-5514-3847-4; 1-5514-3847-X

"Growing up in a secular Jewish home in Holland, Anneke cares little about Judaism, so she has no faith to lose when, in 1943, her family is deported to Theresienstadt, the Nazi concentration camp. . . . Based on the experiences of the author's mother . . . this novel is narrated in Anneke's first-person, present-tense voice. The details are unforgettable. . . . An important addition to the Holocaust curriculum." Booklist

Polisner, Gae

The **pull** of gravity. Frances Foster Books 2011 202p $16.99

Grades: 6 7 8 9 **Fic**

1. Death -- Fiction 2. Bereavement -- Fiction 3. Family life -- Fiction 4. Father-son relationship -- Fiction
ISBN 978-0-374-37193-7; 0-374-37193-8

LC 2010-21749

When their friend Scooter dies of a rare disease, teenagers Nick Gardner and Jaycee Amato set out on a secret journey to find the father who abandoned "The Scoot" when he was an infant, and give him a signed first edition of "Of Mice and Men."

"Polisner's first novel begins with a bang and ends with another . . . . There is a great deal to enjoy throughout, and literary kids will surely enjoy a subplot involving John Steinbeck." Booklist

Pollen, Samuel

★ The **year** I didn't eat; Samuel Pollen. Yellow Jacket 2019 400 p. (hardcover) $17.99

Grades: 6 7 8 9 **Fic**

1. Diaries -- Fiction 2. Teenage boys -- Fiction 3. Anorexia nervosa -- Fiction
ISBN 9781499808087

LC 2018950079

In this novel, by Samuel Pollen, "fourteen-year-old Max doesn't like to eat, and the only one he can confess his true feelings to is Ana--also known as his eating disorder, anorexia. In a journal that his therapist makes him keep, he tells Ana his unfiltered thoughts and fears while also keeping track of his food intake. . . . As Max's eating disorder intensifies, his family unit fractures." (Publisher's note)

"Max is a thoughtful, appealing narrator to whom readers will relate, and his story brings attention to an illness most commonly associated with girls and older teens or adults." Booklist

Polonsky, Ami

★ **Gracefully** Grayson; Ami Polonsky. Hyperion 2014 256 p. $16.99

Grades: 6 7 8 9 **Fic**

1. School stories 2. Transgender teenagers 3. Teacher-student relationship -- Fiction 4. Orphans -- Fiction 5. Theater -- Fiction 6. Family life -- Fiction 7. Middle schools -- Fiction 8. Self-acceptance -- Fiction 9. Transgender people -- Fiction
ISBN 1423185277; 9781423185277

LC 2014010155

In this novel by Ami Polonsky "Grayson Sender has been holding onto a secret for what seems like forever: 'he' is a girl on the inside, stuck in the wrong gender's body. The weight of this secret is crushing, but sharing it would mean facing ridicule, scorn, rejection, or worse. Despite the risks, Grayson's true self itches to break free. Will new strength from an unexpected friendship and a caring teacher's wisdom be enough to help Grayson?" (Publisher's note)

"Sixth grader Grayson daydreams about being a girl, despite being seen by everyone as male. Grayson keeps people at a distance until Amelia moves to town. After landing the (female) lead in a play, Grayson fights for the right to present her truest self to others--both on and off stage. Polonsky captures her protagonist's loneliness, then courage, in an immediate and intimate narrative." Horn Book

Threads; Ami Polonsky. Disney-Hyperion 2016 256 p. $16.99
Grades: 4 5 6 7 **Fic**
1. Factories -- Fiction 2. Child labor -- Fiction 3. Human trafficking -- Fiction 4. China -- Social conditions -- Fiction
ISBN 9781484746905
LC 2015043621

In this book, by Ami Polonsky, "the day twelve-year-old Clara finds a desperate note in a purse in Bellman's department store, she is still reeling from the death of her adopted sister, Lola. By that day, thirteen-year-old Yuming has lost hope that the note she stashed in the purse will ever be found. She may be stuck sewing in the pale pink factory outside of Beijing forever. Clara grows more and more convinced that she was meant to find Yuming's note." (Publisher's note)

"Based on a true incident, this is an engaging offering for readers who seek to broaden their global perspective. Especially good for teachers to use as a spark for classroom conversation." SLJ

Ponti, James

★ **Framed!** by James Ponti. Aladdin 2016 304 p. (hardback) $17.99
Grades: 5 6 7 8 **Fic**
1. Humorous fiction 2. Art thefts -- Fiction 3. Friendship -- Fiction 4. Washington (D.C.) -- Fiction 5. Mystery and detective stories 6. United States. Federal Bureau of Investigation -- Fiction
ISBN 9781481436304
LC 2015045506

"Florian [Bates] is twelve years old and has just moved to Washington. He's learning his way around using TOAST, which stands for the Theory of All Small Things. It's a technique he invented to solve life's little mysteries. . . . But when he teaches it to his new friend Margaret, they uncover a mystery . . . , and it involves the National Gallery, the FBI, and a notorious crime syndicate known as EEL." (Publisher's note)

Other titles in this series are:
Vanished! (2017)
Trapped! (2018)

★ **Trapped!** a framed! novel. by James Ponti. Aladdin 2018 384 p. (hardback) $17.99
Grades: 5 6 7 8 **Fic**
1. Spies -- Fiction 2. Friendship -- Fiction 3. Washington (D.C.) -- Fiction 4. Mystery and detective stories 5. Library of Congress -- Fiction 6. United States. Federal Bureau of Investigation -- Fiction
ISBN 9781534408913; 9781534408920
LC 2018005076

In this novel in the Framed! series, by James Ponti, "middle school is hard. Solving cases for the FBI is even harder. Doing both at the same time, well that's just crazy. But that doesn't stop Florian Bates! Along with his best friend . . . , Margaret, Florian's making the case that kids can do anything. When Florian and Margaret's FBI supervisor, Marcus Rivers, is accused of a crime, it's up to this mystery-solving duo to jump into action and clear his name." (Publisher's note)

★ **Vanished!** by James Ponti. Aladdin 2017 384 p. (alk. paper) $16.99
Grades: 5 6 7 8 **Fic**
1. Schools -- Fiction 2. Practical jokes -- Fiction 3. Washington (D.C.) -- Fiction 4. Mystery and detective stories 5. Preparatory schools -- Fiction 6. United States. Federal Bureau of Investigation -- Fiction
ISBN 9781481436335
LC 2016041962

Edgar Award: Best Juvenile (2018)

In this Framed! mystery novel, by James Ponti, "after helping the FBI solve an art theft at the National Gallery and uncovering a DC spy ring, Florian's finding life at Alice Deal Middle School a little boring. But that's all about to change! His FBI handler, Marcus, has a job for him! . . . It's middle school pranks . . . [that] are happening at a prestigious private school attended by the President's daughter who may--or may not--be involved." (Publisher's note)

Porter, Tracey

★ **Billy** Creekmore. Joanna Cotler Books 2007 305p $16.99; lib bdg $17.89; pa $6.99
Grades: 5 6 7 8 **Fic**
1. Circus -- Fiction 2. Orphanages -- Fiction 3. West Virginia -- Fiction 4. Coal mines and mining -- Fiction
ISBN 978-0-06-077570-4; 0-06-0-77570-X; 978-0-06-077571-1 lib bdg; 0-06-077571-8 lib bdg; 978-0-06-077572-8 pa; 0-06-077572-6 pa
LC 2007-00001

In 1905, ten-year-old Billy is taken from an orphanage to live with an aunt and uncle he never knew he had, and he enjoys his first taste of family life until his work in a coal mine and involvement with a union brings trouble, then he joins a circus in hopes of finding his father.

"Porter's writing is strong, and the story, told in Billy's steadfast yet child-true voice, makes the shocking history about the lives of children at the turn of the last century come alive for today's readers." Booklist

Potter, Ellen

★ **Slob**. Philomel Books 2009 199p $16.99
Grades: 5 6 7 8 **Fic**
1. Obesity -- Fiction 2. Orphans -- Fiction 3. Siblings -- Fiction 4. Inventions -- Fiction 5. Bereavement -- Fiction 6. New York (N.Y.) -- Fiction
ISBN 978-0-399-24705-7; 0-399-24705-X
LC 2008-40476

Picked on, overweight genius Owen tries to invent a television that can see the past to find out what happened the day his parents were killed.

"An intriguingly offbeat mystery, . . . at turns humorous, suspenseful and poignant." Kirkus

Powell, Laura

The **game** of triumphs. Alfred A. Knopf 2011 269p $16.99; lib bdg $19.99; ebook $10.99
Grades: 7 8 9 10 **Fic**
1. Games -- Fiction 2. Tarot -- Fiction 3. Supernatural -- Fiction 4. Space and time -- Fiction 5. London (England) -- Fiction
ISBN 978-0-375-86587-9; 0-375-86587-X; 978-0-375-96587-6 lib bdg; 0-375-96587-4 lib bdg; 978-0-375-89774-0 ebook
LC 2010021813

Fifteen-year-old Cat and three other London teens are drawn into a dangerous game in which Tarot cards open doorways into a different dimension and while there is everything to win, losing can be fatal.

"Original and engrossing." Kirkus

Followed by:
The master of misrule (2012)

Powell, Randy

Swiss mist. Farrar, Straus & Giroux 2008 210p $16.95
Grades: 6 7 8 9 10 **Fic**
1. Divorce -- Fiction 2. Washington (State) -- Fiction
ISBN 978-0-374-37356-6; 0-374-37356-6
LC 2007-27680

Follows Milo from fifth grade, when his mother and philosopher father get divorced, through tenth grade, when his mother has married a wealthy businessman and Milo is still a bit of a loner, looking for the meaning of life.

"This book is rewardingly remarkable for the characters and bits of truth that Milo never stops pursuing, even as he learns that truth is not what matters most." SLJ

Powell, William Campbell

Expiration day; William Campbell Powell. Tor Teen 2014 336 p. (hardback) $17.99

Grades: 8 9 10 11 12 **Fic**

1. Bildungsromans 2. Science fiction 3. Robots -- Fiction 4. Diaries -- Fiction 5. England -- Fiction 6. Coming of age -- Fiction

ISBN 0765338289; 9780765338280

LC 2013025453

In this book, by William Campbell Powell, "it is the year 2049, and humanity is on the brink of extinction. . . . Tania Deeley has always been told that she's a rarity: a human child in a world where most children are sophisticated androids manufactured by Oxted Corporation. . . . Though she has always been aware of the existence of teknoids, it is not until her first day at The Lady Maud High School for Girls that Tania realizes that her best friend, Siân, may be one." (Publisher's note)

"In this coming-of-age diary, a girl navigates life in a dystopic near-future. By the year 2049, the world has become a rather unfriendly place for humans and robots alike. England is divided into color-coded zones, parts of the African continent are shadowed in mystery, and very few humans are still able to procreate....The author pays homage to the genre's giants while combining realistic characters (both human and android) and detailed worldbuilding with an unpredictably optimistic conclusion. In the end, the thoughtful balance of narrative and description and the well-paced plot are marred only by a mildly distracting subplot that unreels in interstitial "Intervals." An auspicious debut. " (Kirkus)

Powers, J. L.

This thing called the future; a novel. Cinco Puntos 2011 213p $16.95

Grades: 8 9 10 11 12 **Fic**

1. Sick -- Fiction 2. South Africa -- Fiction 3. Mother-daughter relationship -- Fiction

ISBN 978-1-933693-95-8; 1-933693-95-9

Powers "composes a compelling, often harrowing portrait of a struggling country, where old beliefs and rituals still have power, but can't erase the problems of the present. Readers will be fully invested in Khosi's efforts to secure a better future." Publ Wkly

Pratchett, Terry, 1948-2015

★ The **amazing** Maurice and his educated rodents. HarperCollins Pubs. 2001 241p hardcover o.p. pa $6.99

Grades: 7 8 9 10 **Fic**

1. Fantasy fiction 2. Cats -- Fiction 3. Rats -- Fiction

ISBN 0-06-001233-1; 0-06-001235-8 pa

LC 2001-42411

A talking cat, intelligent rats, and a strange boy cooperate in a Pied Piper scam until they try to con the wrong town and are confronted by a deadly evil rat king

"In this laugh-out-loud fantasy, his first 'Discworld' novel for younger readers, Pratchett rethinks a classic story and comes up with a winner." SLJ

Other titles in the series are:

The Wee Free Men (2003)

A Hat Full of Sky (2004)

Wintersmith (2006)

I Shall Wear Midnight (2010)

The Shepherd's Crown (2015)

★ **Dodger**; by Terry Pratchett. HarperCollins 2012 360 p. (hardback) $17.99

Grades: 7 8 9 10 **Fic**

1. Lifesaving 2. Romance fiction -- fiction 4. Historical fiction -- fiction 5. Love -- Fiction 6. Humorous stories 7. Conduct of life -- Fiction 8. Adventure and adventurers -- Fiction 9. Todd, Sweeney (Legendary character) -- Fiction 10. London (England) -- History -- 19th century -- Fiction 11. Great Britain -- History -- Victoria, 1837-1901 -- Fiction

ISBN 0062009494; 9780062009494; 9780062009500

LC 2012022155

Michael L. Printz Honor Book (2013)

Author Terry Pratchett presents a story of historical fiction. "Dodger is a guttersnipe and a tosher . . . [and] a petty criminal but also (generally) one of the good guys. One night he rescues a beautiful young woman and finds himself hobnobbing quite literally with the likes of Charlie Dickens . . . and Ben Disraeli . . . And when he attempts to smarten himself up to impress the damsel in distress, he unexpectedly comes face to face with . . . Sweeney Todd." (Kirkus)

★ **I** shall wear midnight. Harper 2010 355p $16.99

Grades: 7 8 9 10 **Fic**

1. Ghost stories 2. Fantasy fiction 3. Young adult literature 4. Fairies -- Fiction 5. Witches -- Fiction

ISBN 978-0-06-143304-7; 0-06-143304-7

LC 2010-24442

Sequel to: Wintersmith (2006)

Fifteen-year-old Tiffany Aching, the witch of the Chalk, seeks her place amid a troublesome populace and tries to control the ill-behaved, six-inch-high Wee Free Men who follow her as she faces an ancient evil that agitates against witches.

"The final adventure in Pratchett's Tiffany Aching series brings this subset of Discworld novels to a moving and highly satisfactory conclusion." Publ Wkly

★ **Nation**. HarperCollins 2008 367p $16.99; lib bdg $17.89; pa $8.99

Grades: 7 8 9 10 11 12 **Fic**

1. Islands -- Fiction 3. Tsunamis -- Fiction 4. Survival after airplane accidents, shipwrecks, etc. -- Fiction

ISBN 978-0-06-143301-6; 0-06-143301-2; 978-0-06-143302-3 lib bdg; 0-06-143302-0 lib bdg; 978-0-06-143303-0 pa; 0-06-143303-9 pa

LC 2008-20211

Printz Honor Book (2009)

After a devastating tsunami destroys all that they have ever known, Mau, an island boy, and Daphne, an aristocratic English girl, together with a small band of refugees, set about rebuilding their community and all the things that are important in their lives.

"Quirky wit and broad vision make this a fascinating survival story on many levels." Booklist

Only you can save mankind. HarperCollins 2005 207p hardcover o.p. lib bdg $16.89; pa $6.99

Grades: 5 6 7 8 **Fic**

1. War stories 2. Computer games -- Fiction

ISBN 0-06-054185-7; 0-06-054186-5 lib bdg; 0-06-054187-3 pa

First published 1992 in the United Kingdom

Twelve-year-old Johnny endures tensions between his parents, watches television coverage of the Gulf War, and plays a computer game called Only You Can Save Mankind, in which he is increasingly drawn into the reality of the alien ScreeWee

This is "a wild ride, full of Pratchett's trademark humor; digs at primitive, low-resolution games . . . ; and some not-so-subtle philosophy about war and peace." Booklist

Other titles in this trilogy are:
Johnny and the dead (2006)
Johnny and the bomb (2006)

★ The **Wee** Free Men. HarperCollins Pubs. 2003 263p hardcover o.p. pa $9.99
Grades: 7 8 9 10 **Fic**

1. Fantasy fiction 2. Witches -- Fiction
ISBN 0-06-001236-6; 0-06-201217-7 pa

LC 2002-15396

A young witch-to-be named Tiffany teams up with the Wee Free Men, a clan of six-inch-high blue men, to rescue her baby brother and ward off a sinister invasion from Fairyland. "Grades six to ten." (Bull Cent Child Books)

"Pratchett invites readers into his well-established realm of Discworld where action, magic, and characters are firmly rooted in literary reality. Humor ripples throughout, making tense, dangerous moments stand out in stark contrast." Bull Cent Child Books

Other titles about Tiffany are:
A hat full of sky (2004)
Wintersmith (2006)
I shall wear midnight (2010)
The Shepherd's crown (2015)

Preller, James

Better off undead; by James Preller. Feiwel & Friends 2017 288 p. (hardcover) $16.99
Grades: 4 5 6 7 **Fic**

1. Mystery fiction 2. Zombies -- Fiction 3. Middle schools -- Fiction 4. Bees -- Fiction 5. Schools -- Fiction 6. Mystery and detective stories 7. Environmental protection -- Fiction 8. Adventure and adventurers -- Fiction
ISBN 9781250066480

LC 2016058773

In this book, by James Preller, "Adrian Lazarus has met with a curious fate. He's returned from the dead . . . . But it's not . . . being a zombie that makes Adrian feel different. He notices the world has changed. . . . The holographic advertisements in the night sky assure people that all is well. Adrian and his friends--a beekeeping boy, a mysterious new girl, and a seventh-grade sleuth--aren't so sure." (Publisher's note)

Bystander. Feiwel and Friends 2009 226p $16.99
Grades: 5 6 7 8 **Fic**

1. School stories 2. Moving -- Fiction 3. Bullies -- Fiction 4. Divorce -- Fiction 5. Family life -- Fiction 6. Long Island (N.Y.) -- Fiction
ISBN 0312379064; 9780312379063

LC 2008-28554

Thirteen-year-old Eric discovers there are consequences to not standing by and watching as the bully at his new school hurts people, but although school officials are aware of the problem, Eric may be the one with a solution.

"Although there are no pat answers, the message (that a bystander is hardly better than an instigator) is clear, and Preller's well-shaped characters, strong writing, and realistic treatment of middle-school life deliver it cleanly." Booklist

The **courage** test; James Preller. Feiwel & Friends 2016 224 p. (hardcover) $16.99
Grades: 4 5 6 7 **Fic**

1. Father-son relationship -- Fiction 2. Lewis and Clark Expedition (1804-1806)
ISBN 9781250093912; 9781250093929; 9781250093936

LC 2016937798

In this book, by James Preller, "Will has no choice. His father drags him along on a wilderness adventure in the footsteps of legendary explorers Lewis and Clark--whether he likes it or not. All the while, Will senses that something about this trip isn't quite right. Along the journey, Will meets fascinating strangers and experiences new thrills, including mountain cliffs, whitewater rapids, and a heart-hammering bear encounter." (Publisher's note)

"Additionally, not only does the author slip cogent historical facts and insights into his simply told narrative without disturbing its flow, he offers more detail, plus sources of information, in an afterword." Booklist

Six innings; a game in the life. Feiwel and Friends 2008 147p $16.95
Grades: 4 5 6 7 **Fic**

1. Cancer -- Fiction 2. Baseball -- Fiction
ISBN 978-0-312-36763-3; 0-312-36763-5

LC 2007-32846

Earl Grubb's Pool Supplies plays Northeast Gas & Electric in the Little League championship game, while Sam, who has cancer and is in a wheelchair, has to call the play-by-play instead of participating in the game.

"The outcome is predictable but the journey is nailbitingly tense. Kids will be nodding in agreement at the truths laid bare." Publ Wkly

Preus, Margi

Enchantment Lake; a Northwoods mystery. by Margi Preus. University of Minnesota Press 2015 200 p. (hardback) $16.95
Grades: 6 7 8 9 10 **Fic**

1. Mystery fiction 2. Aunts -- Fiction 3. Lakes -- Fiction 4. Minnesota -- Fiction 5. Great-aunts -- Fiction 6. Buried treasure -- Fiction 7. Mystery and detective stories 8. Swindlers and swindling -- Fiction
ISBN 0816683026; 9780816683024

LC 2014042651

In this book, by Margi Preus, a "call from her great aunts Astrid and Jeannette sends seventeen-year-old Francie far from her new home in New York into a tangle of mysteries. Ditching an audition in a Manhattan theater, Francie travels to . . . the shores of Enchantment Lake in the woods of northern Minnesota, [where] something ominous is afoot, and as Francie begins to investigate, the mysteries multiply." (Publisher's note)

Preus "offers intriguing characters, suspenseful moments, and a love interest--plenty to keep readers involved." Booklist

★ **Heart** of a samurai; based on the true story of Nakahama Manjiro. Abrams/Amulet 2010 301p il $15.95
Grades: 7 8 9 10 11 12 **Fic**

1. Interpreters 2. Japanese -- United States -- Fiction 3. Survival after airplane accidents, shipwrecks, etc. -- Fiction
ISBN 978-0-8109-8981-8; 0-8109-8981-6

LC 2009-51634

A Newbery Medal honor book, 2011

In 1841, rescued by an American whaler after a terrible shipwreck leaves him and his four companions castaways on a remote island, fourteen-year-old Manjiro, who dreams of becoming a samurai, learns new laws and customs as he becomes the first Japanese person to set foot in the United States.

The author "mixes fact with fiction in a tale that is at once adventurous, heartwarming, sprawling, and nerve-racking in its depictions of early anti-Asian sentiment. She succeeds in making readers feel every bit as 'other' as Manjiro, while showing America at its best and worst through his eyes." Publ Wkly

Includes bibliographical references

Shadow on the mountain; a novel inspired by the true adventures of a wartime spy. by Margi Preus. Amulet Books 2012 286 p. (alk. paper) $16.95

Grades: 6 7 8 9 **Fic**

1. Adventure fiction -- fiction 2. Historical fiction -- fiction 3. World War, 1939-1945 -- fiction 4. Spies -- Fiction 5. Norway -- History -- German occupation, 1940-1945 -- Fiction 6. World War, 1939-1945 -- Underground movements -- Norway -- Fiction

ISBN 1419704249; 9781419704246

LC 2012015623

This juvenile historical fiction novel, by Margi Preus, "recounts the adventures of a 14-year-old Norwegian boy named Espen during World War II. After Nazi Germany invades and occupies Norway, Espen and his friends are swept up in the Norwegian resistance movement. Espen gets his start by delivering illegal newspapers, then graduates to the role of courier and finally becomes a spy, dodging the Gestapo along the way." (Publisher's note)

Includes bibliographical references.

West of the moon; Margi Preus. Amulet Books 2014 224 p. (alk. paper) $16.95

Grades: 5 6 7 8 **Fic**

1. Norway -- Fiction 2. Folklore -- Norway 3. Human trafficking -- Fiction 4. United States -- Immigration and emigration -- Fiction 5. Norway -- History -- 19th century -- Fiction

ISBN 1419708961; 9781419708961

LC 2013023250

Author Margi Preus "weaves original fiction with myth and folktale to tell the story of Astri, a young Norwegian girl desperate to join her father in America. After being separated from her sister and sold to a cruel goat farmer, Astri makes a daring escape. She quickly retrieves her little sister, and, armed with a troll treasure, a book of spells and curses, and a possibly magic hairbrush, they set off for America." (Publisher's note)

"In the Scandinavian fairy tale 'East of the Sun and West of the Moon,' a young girl is taken from her home to a magnificent castle by a great bear, whom she discovers is really a prince. . . . Preus (Heart of a Samurai, 2010) interweaves the mesmerizing tale of Astri's treacherous and harrowing mid-nineteenth-century immigration to America with bewitching tales of magic. A fascinating author's note only adds to the wonder." Booklist

Includes bibliographical references

Price, Lissa

Enders; by Lissa Price. Delacorte Press 2014 288 p. (hc : alk. paper) $17.99

Grades: 7 8 9 10 **Fic**

1. Brainwashing 2. Teenagers -- Fiction 3. Science -- Experiments -- Fiction 5. Science fiction

ISBN 0385742495; 9780375990618; 9780385742498

LC 2013011679

Sequel to: Starters

In this book by Lissa Price, the conclusion to her Starters series, "someone is after Starters like Callie and Michael--teens with chips in their brains. They want to experiment on anyone left over from Prime Destinations--Starters who can be controlled and manipulated. With the body bank destroyed, Callie no longer has to rent herself out to creepy Enders. But Enders can still get inside her mind and make her do things she doesn't want to do." (Publisher's note)

"Some glossed-over twists stretch believability, though the threat (and villain's secret plan), smaller-scale than in Starters, is personal in a creepy way. Metals can be controlled remotely, and Callie's modified chip keeps her awake and aware, leading to a delightfully disturbing climax. It's not as intense as Starters, but it offers some answers and a solid conclusion that will repay readers." (Kirkus)

Starters; Lissa Price. Delacorte Press 2012 336 p. (paperback) $9.99; (ebook) $53.97; (glb) $20.99; (hardcover) $17.99

Grades: 7 8 9 10 **Fic**

1. Science fiction 2. Orphans -- Fiction 3. Intergenerational relations -- Fiction 4. Brothers and sisters -- Fiction

ISBN 9780385742481; 0385742371; 9780307975232; 9780375990601; 9780385742375

LC 2011040820

In this book, "[w]hen a deadly virus wipes out the entire population of the U.S. save the elderly and the young, . . . the result is a dysfunctional society polarized between young 'Starters' and the increasingly long-lived 'Enders.' Children who are unclaimed by surviving relatives are institutionalized, and many -- like Callie and her little brother, Tyler -- learn to fend for themselves in virtual hiding from the law to escape that fate." (Bulletin of the Center for Children's Books)

Priest, Cherie

I Am Princess X; Cherie Priest ; with comic art by Kali Ciesemier. Scholastic Inc. 2015 240 p. $18.99

Grades: 7 8 9 10 11 12 **Fic**

1. Female friendship -- Fiction 2. Comic books, strips, etc. -- Fiction 3. Webcomics -- Fiction 4. Best friends -- Fiction 5. Missing children -- Fiction

ISBN 0545620856; 9780545620857

LC 2015003694

In this novel, by Cherie Priest, with comic art by Kali Ciesemier, "two best friends created a princess together . . . and their heroine, Princess X, slayed all the dragons and scaled all the mountains their imaginations could conjure. Once upon a few years later, . . . Libby passed away, and Princess X died with her. Once upon a now: May is sixteen and lonely, wandering the streets of Seattle, when she sees a sticker slapped in a corner window. Princess X?" (Publisher's note)

"May and Libby created Princess X on the day they met in fifth grade. That was before Libby and her mother died in a car crash. Now May is 16 and looking at another long, lonely summer in Seattle when she spots a Princess X sticker on the corner of a store window. Suddenly she starts seeing Princess X everywhere, including in a webcomic at IAmPrincessX.com, where the princess story is eerily similar to Libby's. . . . An excellent book with loads of cross-genre and cross-format appeal." SLJ

Prineas, Sarah

Lost; illustrated by Antonio Javier Caparo. HarperCollinsPublishers 2009 385p il (The magic thief) $16.99; lib bdg $17.89

Grades: 4 5 6 7 **Fic**

1. Fantasy fiction 2. Magic -- Fiction 3. Apprentices -- Fiction
ISBN 978-0-06-137589-7; 0-06-137589-6; 978-0-06-137591-0 lib bdg; 0-06-137591-8 lib bdg
LC 2008022595

Sequel to: The magic thief (2008)

Young wizard's apprentice Connwaer travels to the city of Desh to find the source of the malevolent shadowmen who are plaguing Wellmet City.

"Strong female characters populate Conn's world, opening the series to girls as well as boys. Short chapters with plenty of suspense make it a good choice for reluctant readers." Voice Youth Advocates

Followed by: Found (2010)

★ The **magic** thief; illustrations by Antonio Javier Caparo. HarperCollins Pubs. 2008 419p il map

Grades: 4 5 6 7 **Fic**

1. Fantasy fiction 2. Magic -- Fiction 3. Thieves -- Fiction 4. Apprentices -- Fiction
ISBN 0-06-137587-X; 0-06-137588-8 lib bdg; 0-06-137590-X pa; 978-0-06-137587-3; 978-0-06-137588-0 lib bdg; 978-0-06-137590-3 pa
LC 2007031704

Conn is a young thief who is drawn into a life of adventure after picking the pocket of the wizard Nevery Flinglas. Finglas has returned from exile to try to reverse the decline of magic in Wellmet City. "Grades five to nine." (Bull Cent Child Books)

"Conn is a thief but, through desire and inevitability, becomes a wizard . . . This evolution begins when Conn picks the pocket of the wizard Nevery. . . . What works wonderfully well here is the boy's irresistable voice." Booklist

Other titles in this series are:
Lost (2009)
Found (2010)

Proimos, James, 1958-

12 things to do before you crash and burn. Roaring Brook Press 2011 121p $14.99

Grades: 7 8 9 10 **Fic**

1. Uncles -- Fiction 2. Bereavement -- Fiction 3. Baltimore (Md.) -- Fiction 4. Father-son relationship -- Fiction
ISBN 978-1-59643-595-7; 1-59643-595-X
LC 2010043935

Sixteen-year-old James 'Hercules' Martino completes twelve tasks while spending two weeks in Baltimore with his Uncle Anthony, and gains insights into himself, his uncle, and his recently deceased father, a self-help author and daytime talk show host who was beloved by the public but a terrible father.

"Proimos fully inhabits the mind and voice of his hero, whose almost mythic journey offers moments hilarious, heartbreaking, and triumphant." Publ Wkly

Pryor, Bonnie

The **iron** dragon; the courageous story of Lee Chin. Enslow Publishers 2010 160p (Historical fiction adventures) lib bdg $27.93; pa $14.95

Grades: 4 5 6 **Fic**

1. Railroads -- Fiction 2. California -- Fiction 3. Immigrants -- Fiction 4. Chinese Americans -- Fiction
ISBN 978-0-7660-3389-4 lib bdg; 0-7660-3389-9 lib bdg; 978-1-59845-215-0 pa; 1-59845-215-0 pa
LC 2009017930

In the mid-nineteenth century, teenager Lee Chin and his father leave China for California to work on the transcontinental railroad, where Lee defies his father's wishes and saves money to free his younger sister from slavery in China, then brings her to join him in beginning a new life in America. Includes historical note about the Chinese who helped build the transcontinental railroad

"Lee Chin's tale is compellingly told. . . . Historical information is accurate and honest about the period depicted." SLJ

Pullman, Philip, 1946-

The **amber** spyglass; His Dark Materials book III. [appendix illustrations by Ian Beck] Deluxe ed.; Alfred A. Knopf 2007 518p il $22.99; lib bdg $25.99

Grades: 7 8 9 10 11 12 **Fic**

1. Fantasy fiction
ISBN 978-0-375-84673-1; 978-0-375-94673-8 lib bdg
LC 2006-48865

Sequel to: The subtle knife
First published 2000

Third volume in His Dark Materials trilogy "starts where The Subtle Knife . . . left off. Lyra has been hidden away by her mother, and Will is determined to find her. Meanwhile, Lord Asriel is preparing to fight the forces of the Church's Consistorial Court, as well as the God-like Authority's Lieutenant, Metatron, who hungers for ultimate power over all worlds. At the heart of this discord is Dust, the mysterious substance that is linked irrevocably to consciousness; it is streaming away at an increasing rate, causing havoc in its wake. It is Lyra and Will's destiny to determine the outcome of this situation." SLJ

★ The **golden** compass; his dark materials book I. [appendix illustrations by Ian Beck] Deluxe 10th anniversary ed.; Alfred A. Knopf 2006 399p il $22.95

Grades: 7 8 9 10 11 12 **Fic**

1. Fantasy fiction
ISBN 978-0-375-83830-9; 0-375-83830-9
LC 2005-32556

First published 1995 in the United Kingdom with title: Northern lights

This first title in a fantasy trilogy "introduces the characters and sets up the basic conflict, namely, a race to unlock the mystery of a newly discovered type of charged particles simply called 'dust' that may be a bridge to an alternate universe. The action follows 11-year-old protagonist Lyra Belacqua from her home at Oxford University to the frozen wastes of the North on a quest to save dozens of kidnapped children from the evil 'Gobblers,' who are using them as part of a sinister experiment involving dust." Libr J [review of 1996 edition]

Other titles in the His dark materials series are:
The amber spyglass (2000)
The subtle knife (1997)

★ **La** Belle Sauvage; Philip Pullman. Alfred A. Knopf 2017 449 p. color illustration (Book of dust) (hbk.) $22.99

Grades: 8 9 10 11 12 **Fic**

1. Spies -- Fiction 2. England -- Fiction 3. Friendship -- Fiction 4. Familiars (Spirits) -- fiction 5. Belacqua, Lyra (Fictitious character) -- fiction
ISBN 9780375815300; 0375815309; 9780553510737
LC 2017478729

In this novel in the Book of Dust series, by Philip Pullman, "Malcolm Polstead is the kind of boy who notices everything but is not much noticed himself. . . . He finds a secret message inquiring about a dangerous substance called Dust--and the spy it was intended for finds him. . . . He sees suspicious characters everywhere. . . . All are asking about . . . a girl--just a baby--named Lyra. . . . And Malcolm will brave any danger . . . to bring her safely through the storm." (Publisher's note)

"Magisterial storytelling will sweep readers along; the cast is as vividly drawn as ever; and big themes running beneath the surface invite profound responses and reflection." Kirkus

★ **Once** upon a time in the North; illustrated by John Lawrence. Knopf 2008 95p il $12.99
Grades: 7 8 9 10 11 12 **Fic**

1. Fantasy fiction
ISBN 978-0-375-84510-9; 0-375-84510-0

LC 2007-43993

Prequel to: The golden compass

In a time before Lyra Silvertongue was born, the tough American balloonist Lee Scoresby and the great armoured bear Iorek Byrnison meet when Lee and his hare daemon Hester crash-land their trading balloon onto a port in the far Arctic North and find themselves right in the middle of a political powder keg.

"The precise narrative prose is spiced up with Lee's flights of 'oratorical flamboyancy,' and the sardonic banter between Lee and his daemon Hester is as amusing as ever. [Illustrated with] engraved spot illustrations and 'reproduced' documents." Horn Book

The **subtle** knife; His Dark Materials book II. [appendix illustrations by Ian Beck] Deluxe 10th anniversary ed.; Alfred A. Knopf 2007 326p il $22.99; lib bdg $25.99
Grades: 7 8 9 10 11 12 **Fic**

1. Fantasy fiction
ISBN 978-0-375-84672-4; 978-0-375-94672-1 lib bdg

LC 2006-48866

Sequel to: The golden compass
First published 1997

In the second volume of His dark materials trilogy the boundaries between worlds begin to dissolve. Lyra and her daemon help Will Parry in his search for his father and for a powerful, magical knife.

"More than fulfilling the promise of The Golden Compass, this second volume in the His Dark Materials trilogy starts off at a heart-thumping pace and never slows down." Publ Wkly

Followed by: The amber spyglass

Two crafty criminals! and how they were captured by the daring detectives of the New Cut Gang ; including Thunderbolt's Waxwork & the gas-fitters' ball. Philip Pullman. Alfred A. Knopf 2012 281 p. (hardback) $16.99
Grades: 5 6 7 8 **Fic**

1. Crime -- Fiction 2. Gangs -- Fiction 3. Humorous fiction 4. Humorous stories 5. Mystery and detective stories 6. Adventure and adventurers -- Fiction 7. London (England) -- History -- 19th century -- Fiction 8. Great Britain -- History -- Victoria, 1837-1901 -- Fiction
ISBN 9780375870293; 9780375970290; 9780375988684

LC 2011042391

This children's book by Philip Pullman was published in 1994 as two novellas: "Thunderbolt's Waxwork" and "The Gas-Fitters' Ball," which are set in "1894 London . . . [and] star . . . the intrepid boy and girl detectives of the New Cut Gang. . . . Thunderbolt Dobney sees his own father hauled off to jail for what he thinks must be 'coining.' . . . [H]e and the New Cut Gang expose the real criminal. . . . In 'The Gas-Fitters' Ball,' . . . the Gas-Fitters' Hall is burgled." (Kirkus Reviews)

Pyron, Bobbie

The **dogs** of winter; by Bobbie Pyron. Arthur A. Levine Books 2012 312 p. (hardcover : alk. paper) $16.99
Grades: 5 6 7 8 **Fic**

1. Wild dogs -- Fiction 2. Abandoned children -- Fiction 3. Wilderness survival -- Fiction 4. Dogs -- Fiction 5. Gangs -- Fiction 6. Moscow (Russia) -- Fiction 7. Street children -- Fiction 8. Homeless persons -- Fiction 9. Russia (Federation) -- Fiction 10. Human-animal relationships -- Fiction
ISBN 0545399300; 9780545399302; 9780545399319; 9780545469852

LC 2011051519

In this book by Bobbie Pyron "Ivan's mother disappears, [and] he's abandoned on the streets of Moscow, with little chance to make it through the harsh winter. But help comes in an unexpected form: Ivan is adopted by a pack of dogs, and the dogs quickly become more than just his street companions: They become his family. Soon Ivan, who used to love reading fairytales, is practically living in one." But "when help is finally offered to him, will he be able to accept it?" (Publisher's note)

Lucky strike; Bobbie Pyron. Arthur A. Levine Books, an imprint of Scholastic Inc. 2015 262 p. hbk $16.99
Grades: 4 5 6 7 **Fic**

1. Luck -- Fiction 2. Florida -- Fiction 3. Lightning -- Fiction 4. Grandparent-grandchild relationship -- Fiction 5. Grandparent and child -- Fiction 6. Franklin County (Fla.) -- Fiction
ISBN 9780545592178; 0545592178; 0545592186; 9780545592185

LC 2014013764

In this book, by Bobbie Pyron, "Nate Harlow has never had a lucky day in his life. . . . His best friend, Genesis Beam (aka Gen), believes in science and logic, and she doesn't think for one second that there's such a thing as luck, good or bad. But only an extremely unlucky person could be struck by lightning on his birthday... and that person is Nate Harlow. By some miracle, though, Nate survives, and the strike seems to have changed his luck." (Publisher's note)

"The quirkiness of the characters and the town never goes too far, and there is an overall cozy feeling to the book. Genesis's dad is the preacher at The Church of the One True Redeemer and Everlasting Light, but she is a scientist through and through, which adds complexity to the text, including musings on destiny, fate, probability, and weather." SLJ

Pérez, Celia C.

The **first** rule of punk; by Celia C. Perez. Viking 2017 336 p. illustrations (hardback) $16.99
Grades: 3 4 5 6 **Fic**

1. Friendship -- fiction 2. Individuality -- fiction
ISBN 9780425290415; 9780425290408

LC 2017010474

Pura Belpré Author Honor Book (2018)
Boston Globe–Horn Book Honor Book: Fiction and Poetry (2018)

In this book, by Celia C. Pérez, "on Day One, twelve-year-old Malú . . . inadvertently upsets Posada Middle School's queen bee, violates the school's dress code with her punk rock look, and disappoints her college-professor mom in the process. . . . Malú loves rock music, skateboarding, zines, and Soyrizo. . . And when she assembles a group of like-minded misfits at school and starts a band, Malú finally begins to feel at home. She'll do anything to preserve this." (Publisher's note)

"With tenderness and humor, Pérez explores the joys and challenges of being biracial. Readers will connect with Malu, a strong protagonist who leaps off the page and whose zine-inspired artistry boldly illustrates how she deals with life." (SLJ)

Qamar, Amjed

Beneath my mother's feet. Atheneum Books for Young Readers 2008 198p $16.99

Grades: 7 8 9 10 **Fic**

1. Poverty -- Fiction 2. Pakistan -- Fiction 3. Sex role -- Fiction 4. Household employees -- Fiction

ISBN 978-1-4169-4728-8; 1-4169-4728-0

LC 2007-19001

When her father is injured, fourteen-year-old Nazia is pulled away from school, her friends, and her preparations for an arranged marriage, to help her mother clean houses in a wealthy part of Karachi, Pakistan, where she finally rebels against the destiny that is planned for her.

This novel "provides a fascinating glimpse into a world remarkably distant from that of most American teens, and would be an excellent suggestion for readers who want to know about how other young people live." SLJ

Quick, Matthew

Sorta like a rockstar; a novel. Little, Brown 2010 355p $16.99; pa $8.99

Grades: 7 8 9 10 11 **Fic**

1. School stories 2. Homeless persons -- Fiction 3. Depression (Psychology) -- Fiction

ISBN 978-0-316-04352-6; 0-316-04352-4; 978-0-316-04353-3 pa; 0-316-04353-2 pa

LC 2008-46746

Although seventeen-year-old Amber Appleton is homeless, living in a school bus with her unfit mother, she is a relentless optimist who visits the elderly at a nursing home, teaches English to Korean Catholic women with the use of rhythm and blues music, and befriends a solitary Vietnam veteran and his dog, but eventually she experiences one burden more than she can bear and slips into a deep depression.

"This book is the answer to all those angst-ridden and painfully grim novels in the shortcut lingo of short attention-span theater. Hugely enjoyable." SLJ

Quigley, Dawn

Apple in the middle; Dawn Quigley. North Dakota State University Press 2018 264 p. (hardcover : alk. paper) $25.95

Grades: 6 7 8 9 10 **Fic**

1. Stepfamilies -- Fiction 2. Teenage girls -- Fiction 3. Native Americans -- Fiction

ISBN 9781946163073

LC 2018941180

In this book in the Contemporary Voice of Indigenous Peoples, by Dawn Quigley, "Apple Starkington turned her back on her Native American heritage the moment she was called a racial slur for someone of white and Indian descent, not that she really even knew how to be an Indian in the first place. Too bad the white world doesn't accept her either. And so begins her quirky habits to gain acceptance." (Publisher's note)

Quintero, Sofia

Efrain's secret. Alfred A. Knopf 2010 265p $16.99; lib bdg $19.99

Grades: 8 9 10 11 12 **Fic**

1. School stories 2. Violence -- Fiction 3. Drug traffic -- Fiction 4. Hispanic Americans -- Fiction 5. Bronx (New York, N.Y.) -- Fiction

ISBN 978-0-375-84706-6; 0-375-84706-5; 978-0-375-94706-3 lib bdg; 0-375-94706-X lib bdg

LC 2009-8493

Ambitious high school senior and honor student Efrain Rodriguez makes some questionable choices in pursuit of his dream to escape the South Bronx and attend an Ivy League college.

"Quintero imbues her characters with unexpected grace and charm. . . . Mostly, though, it is Quintero's effortless grasp of teen slang that gives her first-person story its heart." Booklist

Railsback, Lisa

Noonie's masterpiece; art by Sarajo Frieden. Chronicle Books 2010 208p il $18.99

Grades: 4 5 6 7 **Fic**

1. School stories 2. Artists -- Fiction 3. Family life -- Fiction 4. Father-daughter relationship -- Fiction 5. Eccentrics and eccentricities -- Fiction

ISBN 978-0-8118-6654-5; 0-8118-6654-8

LC 2008-26831

Upon learning that her deceased mother, an artist, went through a "Purple Period," ten-year-old Noonie decides to do the same, hoping that this will bring her archaeologist father home to see her win a school art contest and that the aunt, uncle, and cousin she lives with will come to understand her just a little.

"Noonie may be an unreliable and even unlikable narrator at times, but her pain and vulnerability are as evident as her belief in herself as an artist, and by the end of the story, she'll have readers in her corner. The ink-and-watercolor illustrations, appearing throughout the book, have a 1960s-retro look." Booklist

Ramée, Lisa Moore

★ A **good** kind of trouble; Lisa Moore Ramée. Harpercollins Childrens Books 2019 368 p. $16.99

Grades: 4 5 6 7 8 **Fic**

1. Racism -- Fiction 2. Friendship -- Fiction 3. African American teenage girls -- Fiction

ISBN 0062836684; 9780062836687

In this book, by Lisa Moore Ramée, "all [12-year-old Shayla] wants to do is to follow the rules. . . . But in junior high, it's like all the rules have changed. Now she's suddenly questioning who her best friends are and some people at school are saying she's not black enough. . . . Shay's sister, Hana, is involved in Black Lives Matter, but Shay doesn't think that's for her. After experiencing a powerful protest, though, Shay decides some rules are worth breaking." (Publisher's note)

"This is a solid story for middle-schoolers dealing with issues such as friendship across racial lines, being strong girls, #BLM, #MeToo, civil rights, diversity, and justice." (Booklist)

Randall, Thomas

Dreams of the dead. Bloomsbury Children's Books 2009 276p (The waking) pa $8.99

Grades: 8 9 10 11 12 **Fic**

1. School stories 2. Death -- Fiction 3. Japan -- Fiction 4. Supernatural -- Fiction

ISBN 978-1-59990-250-0; 1-59990-250-8

LC 2008-30844

After her mother dies, sixteen-year-old Kara and her father move to Japan, where he teaches and she attends school, but she is haunted by a series of frightening nightmares and deaths that might be revenge—or something worse

"The story has suspense, mystery, and horror. It will be a great hit with fans of manga, anime, or Japanese culture." SLJ

Followed by: Spirits of the Noh (2011)

Spirits of the Noh. Bloomsbury U.S.A. Children's Books 2010 264p (The waking) $8.99
Grades: 8 9 10 11 12 **Fic**
1. Horror fiction 2. School stories 3. Japan -- Fiction 4. Monsters -- Fiction 5. Supernatural -- Fiction
ISBN 978-1-59990-251-7; 1-59990-251-6
LC 2009018251

Sequel to: Dreams of the dead (2009)

Just as Kara and her friends at the Monju-no-Chie school in Japan are beginning to get over the horrifying deaths of two students, another monster emerges to terrorize the school.

"Using all the usual horror elements, Randall constructs a fine teen chiller complete with mean-girl drama, a dash of romance and the angst of teens who believe that adults do not understand them." Kirkus

Raskin, Ellen

★ The **Westing** game. Dutton Children's Books 2003 182p $16.99; pa $5.99
Grades: 5 6 7 8 **Fic**
1. Mystery fiction
ISBN 0-525-47137-5; 0-14-240120-X pa
LC 2004-268658

First published 1978

Awarded the Newbery Medal, 1979

"The rules of the game make eight pairs of the players; each oddly matched couple is given a ten thousand dollar check and a set of clues. The result is a fascinating medley of word games, disguises, multiple aliases and subterfuges—in a demanding but rewarding book." Horn Book

Rawlings, Marjorie Kinnan

The **yearling**; with pictures by N. C. Wyeth. Scribner 1985 400p il hardcover o.p. pa $5.95
Grades: 5 6 7 8 **Fic**
1. Deer -- Fiction 2. Florida -- Fiction
ISBN 0-684-18461-3; 0-02-044931-3 pa
LC 85-40301

Reissue of the title first published 1938; awarded Pulitzer Prize, 1939

"With its excellent descriptions of Florida scrub landscapes, its skillful use of native vernacular, its tender relation between Jody and his pet fawn, The Yearling is a simply written, picturesque story of boyhood." Time

Rawls, Wilson

Where the red fern grows; the story of two dogs and a boy. Bantam Bks. 1996 212p $16.95; pa $5.99
Grades: 4 5 6 7 **Fic**
1. Dogs -- Fiction 2. Ozark Mountains -- Fiction
ISBN 0-385-32330-1; 0-440-41267-6 pa
First published 1961 by Doubleday

"Looking back more than 50 years to his boyhood in the Ozarks, the narrator, recalls how he achieved his heart's desire in the ownership of two redbone hounds, how he taught them all the tricks of hunting, and how they won the championship coon hunt before Old Dan was killed by a mountain lion and Little Ann died of grief. Although some readers may find this novel hackneyed and entirely too sentimental, others will enjoy the fine coonhunting episodes and appreciate the author's feelings for nature." Booklist

Ray, Delia

Singing hands. Clarion Books 2006 248p il $16
Grades: 4 5 6 7 **Fic**
1. Deaf -- Fiction 2. Clergy -- Fiction 3. Alabama -- Fiction 4. Family life -- Fiction
ISBN 0-618-65762-2
LC 2005-22972

In the late 1940s, twelve-year-old Gussie, a minister's daughter, learns the definition of integrity while helping with a celebration at the Alabama School for the Deaf—her punishment for misdeeds against her deaf parents and their boarders.

"While the portrayal of a signing household is natural and convincing, the focus is on Gussie's rebellion and growth, the real heart of the story." Horn Book Guide

Reedy, Trent

Words in the dust. Arthur A. Levine Books 2011 266p $17.99
Grades: 5 6 7 8 **Fic**
1. Literacy -- Fiction 2. Sex role -- Fiction 3. Afghanistan -- Fiction 4. Birth defects -- Fiction
ISBN 0-545-26125-2; 978-0-545-26125-8
LC 2010-26160

Zulaikha, a thirteen-year-old girl in Afghanistan, faces a series of frightening but exhilarating changes in her life as she defies her father and secretly meets with an old woman who teaches her to read, her older sister gets married, and American troops offer her surgery to fix her disfiguring cleft lip.

"The evolution of key relationships presents a nuanced look at family dynamics and Afghan culture. Though unsentimental and fraught with tragedy, Reedy's narrative offers hope and will go a long way toward helping readers understand the people behind the headlines." Publ Wkly

Reeve, Philip

★ **Fever** Crumb. Scholastic Press 2010 325p $17.99
Grades: 6 7 8 9 10 **Fic**
1. Science fiction 2. Orphans -- Fiction 3. Sex role -- Fiction 4. London (England) -- Fiction
ISBN 978-0-545-20719-5; 0-545-20719-3
LC 2009-15457

Prequel to: The Hungry City Chronicles series

Foundling Fever Crumb has been raised as an engineer although females in the future London, England, are not believed capable of rational thought, but at age fourteen she leaves her sheltered world and begins to learn startling truths about her past while facing danger in the present.

"Reeve's captivating flights of imagination play as vital a role in the story as his endearing heroine, hiss-worthy villains, and nifty array of supporting characters." Booklist

Followed by A web of air (2011)

★ **Here** lies Arthur. Scholastic Press 2008 339p $16.99
Grades: 7 8 9 10 **Fic**
1. Kings 2. Magic -- Fiction 3. Great Britain -- History -- 0-1066 -- Fiction
ISBN 978-0-545-09334-7; 0-545-09334-1
LC 2008-05787

When her village is attacked and burned, Gwyna seeks protection from the bard Myrddin, who uses Gwyna in his plan to transform young Arthur into the heroic King Arthur.

"Powerfully inventive. . . . Events rush headlong toward the inevitable ending, but Gwyna's observations illuminate them in a new way." Booklist

No such thing as dragons. Scholastic Press 2010 186p $16.99

Grades: 4 5 6 7 **Fic**

1. Fantasy fiction 2. Dragons -- Fiction
ISBN 978-0-545-22224-2; 0-545-22224-9

A young, mute boy who is apprenticed to a dragon-slayer suspects that the winged beasts do not exist, until he—and his master—learn the truth.

"This is certainly different from anything that Reeve has done previously, but is still shot through with his trademark imagination and feel for action. It will be eagerly devoured by young readers." SLJ

Scrivener's moon; the third book in the Fever Crumb series. Philip Reeve. Scholastic Press 2012 341 p. (Fever Crumb series) (hardcover) $17.99

Grades: 6 7 8 9 10 **Fic**

1. Steampunk fiction 2. Technology -- Fiction 3. Science fiction 4. England -- Fiction 5. Identity -- Fiction 6. London (England) -- Fiction 7. Dystopias -- fiction 8. Mutation (Biology) -- Fiction 9. Identity (Psychology) -- fiction
ISBN 0545222184; 9780545222181

LC 2012008124

This young adult steampunk adventure novel, by Philip Reeve, is the conclusion to the "Fever Crumb" trilogy. "The Scriven people are brilliant, mad--and dead. All except one, whose monstrous creation is nearly complete--a giant city on wheels. New London terrifies the rest of the world, and an army of mammoth-riders gathers to fight it. Meanwhile, young Fever Crumb begins a hunt for Ancient technology in the icy strongholds of the north." (Publisher's note)

A **Web** of Air. Scholastic Press 2011 293p $17.99

Grades: 6 7 8 9 10 **Fic**

1. Science fiction 2. Flight -- Fiction 3. Orphans -- Fiction
ISBN 0-545-22216-8; 978-0-545-22216-7

LC 2010043341

Sequel to: Fever Crumb (2010)

Two years ago, Fever Crumb escaped the wartorn city of London in a traveling theater. Now, she arrives in the extraordinary city of Mayda, where buildings ascend the cliffs on funicular rails, and a mysterious recluse is building a machine that can fly.

"It's clear that Reeve . . . is building toward an epic, and his remarkable storytelling gifts, coupled with a trenchant understanding of human nature, make these projected volumes worth the wait." Horn Book

Reger, Rob

Emily the Strange: dark times. Harper 2010 226p il $16.99

Grades: 7 8 9 10 **Fic**

1. Adventure fiction 2. Aunts -- Fiction 3. Family -- Fiction 4. Time travel -- Fiction 5. Supernatural -- Fiction
ISBN 978-0-06-145235-2; 0-06-145235-1

LC 2009032256

Traveling in her homemade TimeOut Machine, Emily journeys to the eighteenth century to uncover the truth behind a Strange family rumor.

"Entertaining and thought-provoking, Emily's adventures maintain the series' popularity and present an interesting choice for a mother/daughter reading group." Voice Youth Advocates

Emily the Strange: stranger and stranger. Harper 2010 263p $16.99

Grades: 7 8 9 10 **Fic**

1. Moving -- Fiction 2. Supernatural -- Fiction
ISBN 978-0-06-145232-1; 0-06-145232-7

LC 2009007289

After moving to a new town with her mother, Emily the Strange finds her troubles multiplying when she accidentally duplicates herself.

"Emily's second journal, a sequel to The Lost Days (HarperCollins, 2009), is a dark delight, filled with all kinds of Strangeness. . . . Fans of the first book and newcomers alike will thoroughly enjoy the zaniness and clamor for more." SLJ

Reichs, Brendan

Chrysalis; Brendan Reichs. G.P. Putnam's Sons Books for Young Readers 2019 403 p. (Project Nemesis) (hardback) $18.99

Grades: 8 9 10 11 12 **Fic**

1. Suspense fiction 2. Survival skills -- Fiction 3. Science fiction 4. Survival -- Fiction 5. Cooperativeness -- Fiction
ISBN 0525517057; 9780525517054

LC 2018051632

In this book in the Project Nemesis series, by Brendan Reichs, "the 64 members of Fire Lake's sophomore class have managed to survive the first two phases of the Program--and each other. Now, they alone have emerged into the dawn of a new era on Earth, into a Fire Lake valley that's full of otherworldly dangers and challenges. Although staying alive in this broken world should force Min, Noah, Tack, and the others to form new alliances, old feuds die hard." (Publisher's note)

Genesis; Brendan Reichs. G. P. Putnam's Sons 2018 499 p. (hardback) $18.99

Grades: 8 9 10 11 12 **Fic**

1. Science fiction 2. Conspiracies -- Fiction 3. Survival -- Fiction
ISBN 9780399544965; 9780399544972; 9780399544989

LC 2017028972

In this book in the Project Nemesis series, by Brendan Reichs, "Noah Livingston knows he is destined to survive. The 64 members of Fire Lake's sophomore class are trapped in a place where morals have no meaning and zero rules apply. But Noah's deaths have trained him-hardened him-to lead the strongest into the future ... whatever that may be. And at any cost. Min Wilder knows that survival alone isn't enough." (Publisher's note)

"Nemesis was a page-turner, and Genesis has plenty of fevered action and startling surprises, especially as the book nears its conclusion. ...Fans of the first book will certainly want to read this and look forward to the trilogy's conclusion." Booklist.

Reinhardt, Dana

How to build a house; a novel. Wendy Lamb Books 2008 227p $15.99; lib bdg $18.99

Grades: 8 9 10 11 12 **Fic**

1. Divorce -- Fiction 2. Building -- Fiction 3. Tennessee -- Fiction 4. Stepfamilies -- Fiction 5. Volunteer work -- Fiction
ISBN 978-0-375-84453-9; 0-375-84453-8; 978-0-375-94454-3 lib bdg; 0-375-94454-0 lib bdg

LC 2007-33403

Seventeen-year-old Harper Evans hopes to escape the effects of her father's divorce on her family and friendships by volunteering her summer to build a house in a small Tennessee town devastated by a tornado.

"This meticulously crafted book illustrates how both homes and relationships can be resurrected through hard work, hope and teamwork." Publ Wkly

The **summer** I learned to fly. Wendy Lamb Books 2011 216p $15.99; lib bdg $18.99; e-book $15.99

Grades: 5 6 7 8 **Fic**

1. Rats -- Fiction 2. California -- Fiction 3. Family life -- Fiction

4. Retail trade -- Fiction 5. Single parent family -- Fiction
ISBN 978-0-385-73954-2; 0-385-73954-0; 978-0-385-90792-7 lib bdg; 0-385-90792-3 lib bdg; 978-0-375-89787-0 e-book; 0-375-89787-9 e-book

LC 2010029412

Thirteen-year-old Drew starts the summer of 1986 helping in her mother's cheese shop and dreaming about co-worker Nick, but when her widowed mother begins dating, Drew's father's book of lists, her pet rat, and Emmett, a boy on a quest, help her cope.

"This quiet novel invites readers to share in its heroine's deepest yearnings, changing moods, and difficult realizations." Publ Wkly

★ The **things** a brother knows. Wendy Lamb Books 2010 245p $16.99

Grades: 7 8 9 10 11 12 **Fic**

1. Brothers -- Fiction 2. Soldiers -- Fiction 3. Family life -- Fiction 4. Boston (Mass.) -- Fiction 5. Jews -- United States -- Fiction
ISBN 978-0-375-84455-3; 0-375-84455-4; 0-375-94455-9 lib bdg

Although they have never gotten along well, seventeen-year-old Levi follows his older brother Boaz, an ex-Marine, on a walking trip from Boston to Washington, D.C. in hopes of learning why Boaz is completely withdrawn.

"Reinhardt's poignant story of a soldier coping with survivor's guilt and trauma, and his Israeli American family's struggle to understand and help, is timely and honest." Booklist

Respicio, Mae

The **house** that Lou built; Mae Respicio. Wendy Lamb Books 2018 240 p. (trade) $16.99

Grades: 4 5 6 7 8 **Fic**

1. Home -- Fiction 2. Moving -- Fiction 3. Family life -- Fiction 4. Building -- Fiction 5. California -- Fiction 6. Coming of age -- Fiction 7. Moving, Household -- Fiction 8. Filipino Americans -- Fiction 9. Family life -- California -- Fiction
ISBN 9781524717940; 9781524717957; 9781524717971

LC 2017022047

Asian/Pacific American Award for Children's Literature: Honor Book (2019)

This book, by Mae Respicio, is "a coming-of-age story that explores culture and family, forgiveness and friendship, and what makes a true home. . . . Lou Bulosan-Nelson . . . [is] going to build her own 'tiny house' . . . where she can escape her crazy but lovable extended Filipino family. . . . She plans to build the house on land she inherited from her dad, who died before she was born. But then she finds out that the land may not be hers for much longer." (Publisher's note)

Revis, Beth

Give the dark my love; Beth Revis. Razorbill 2018 351 p. (hardback) $17.99

Grades: 9 10 11 12 **Fic**

1. Magic -- Fiction 2. Plague -- Fiction 3. Alchemy -- Fiction 4. Fantasy -- Fiction
ISBN 9781595147172

LC 2018013398

In this book, by Beth Revis, "Nedra Brysstain leaves her home . . . to attend the prestigious Yugen Academy with only one goal in mind: master the trade of medicinal alchemy. . . . Greggori 'Grey' Astor . . . notices [that Nedra] is especially invested in her studies. And that's for a good reason: a deadly plague . . . [is] making its way toward the cities. With her family's life . . . on the line, Nedra is determined to find a cure for the plague." (Publisher's note)

Rex, Adam

Champions of breakfast; Adam Rex. Balzer + Bray 2014 368 p. (The cold cereal saga) (hardcover bdg. : alk. paper) $16.99

Grades: 4 5 6 7 **Fic**

1. Imaginary places 2. Magic -- Fiction 3. Fairies -- Fiction 4. Cereals, Prepared -- Fiction 5. Adventure and adventurers -- Fiction
ISBN 0062060082; 9780062060082

LC 2013021387

In this book by Adam Rex, part of the Cold Cereal Saga series, "time is quickly running out before Nimue, who has been working with the corrupt Goodco Cereal Company, finds another portal and uses it to bring the mythical dragon Saxbriton into our world--and launch the terrible fairy invasion. In the end, it's up to Scott and his companions to save the fate of two worlds." (Publisher's note)

"Scott, Polly, Emily, and Erno, together with a large supporting cast, rescue the miniaturized Queen of England and quell a fairy invasion by killing the dragon Saxbriton and healing the rift between the worlds. The superabundance of characters is hard to keep track of, but for readers following the Arthurian-reimagining trilogy, action, magic, and humor combine for a whiz-bang conclusion." (Horn Book)

Cold cereal. Balzer + Bray 2012 421p il $16.99

Grades: 4 5 6 7 **Fic**

1. Adventure fiction 2. Food -- Fiction 3. Magic -- Fiction 4. Twins -- Fiction 5. Siblings -- Fiction
ISBN 978-0-06-206002-0; 0-06-206002-3

LC 2011019538

A boy who may be part changeling, twins involved in a bizarre secret experiment, and a clurichaun in a red tracksuit try to save the world from an evil cereal company whose ultimate goal is world domination.

"The author tucks in portrait illustrations and hilariously odd TV-commercial storyboards, along with a hooded Secret Society, figures from Arthurian legend, magical spells and potions, a certain amount of violence, many wonderful throwaway lines. . . . All in all, it's a mad scramble that culminates in the revelation of a dastardly plot that will require sequels to foil." Kirkus

Smek for president! Adam Rex. Disney-Hyperion Books 2014 272 p. illustrations (hardback) $16.99

Grades: 5 6 7 8 **Fic**

1. Science fiction 2. Humorous fiction 3. Human-alien encounters -- Fiction 4. Extraterrestrial beings -- Fiction 5. Interplanetary voyages -- Fiction 6. Adventure and adventurers -- Fiction
ISBN 1484709519; 9781484709511

LC 2014010764

Sequel to: The True Meaning of Smekday (2007)

In this book, by Adam Rex, "Tip and J.Lo are back for another hilarious intergalactic adventure. . . . After Tip and J.Lo banished the Gorg from Earth in a scheme involving the cloning of many, many cats, the pair is notorious--but not for their heroics. Instead, human Dan Landry has taken credit for conquering the Gorg, and the Boov blame J.Lo for ruining their colonization of the planet." (Publisher's note)

"Rex packs his sequel with loads of action and a steady spotlight on friendship; plus, he adds witty send-ups of political elections, time travel, and even sports rules (again using cartoon panels to good effect). And his humor is, as it was in Smekday, laugh-out-loud funny." Horn Book

The **true** meaning of Smekday. Hyperion Books for Children 2007 423p il $16.99; pa $6.99

Grades: 5 6 7 8 **Fic**

1. Science fiction 2. End of the world -- Fiction 3. Extraterrestrial

beings -- Fiction
ISBN 0-7868-4900-2; 978-0-7868-4900-0; 0-7868-4901-0 pa; 978-0-7868-4901-7 pa

When her mother is abducted by aliens on Christmas Eve (or "Smekday" Eve since the Boov invasion), 11 year-old Tip hops in the family car and heads south to find her and meets an alien Boov mechanic who agrees to help her and save the planet from disaster.

"Incorporating dozens of his weird and wonderful illustrations and fruitfully manipulating the narrative structure, Rex skewers any number of subjects." Publ Wkly

Unlucky charms; Adam Rex. Balzer + Bray 2013 400 p. (The cold cereal saga) (hardback) $16.99
Grades: 4 5 6 7 **Fic**

1. Fantasy fiction -- fiction 2. Humorous fiction -- fiction 3. Magic -- Fiction 4. Twins -- Fiction 5. Cereals, Prepared -- Fiction 6. Brothers and sisters -- Fiction 7. Adventure and adventurers -- Fiction
ISBN 0062060058; 9780062060051
LC 2012026714

This humorous juvenile fantasy book, by Adam Rex, is part of the "Cold Cereal Saga." "In this hectic middle volume, [Adam] Rex's notably diverse crew of human, part-human and nonhuman allies splits up in hopes of scotching the schemes of the sorceress Nimue, who is out to create a worldwide army of mind-controlled 'sugar zombies' through magically enhanced breakfast cereal." (Kirkus Reviews)

Reynolds, Jason, 1983-

★ **Boy** in the black suit; Jason Reynolds. Atheneum Books for Young Readers 2015 272 p. (hardcover) $17.99
Grades: 7 8 9 10 **Fic**

1. Grief -- Fiction 2. African Americans -- Fiction 3. Undertakers and undertaking -- Fiction 4. Funeral homes -- Fiction 5. Brooklyn (New York, N.Y.) -- Fiction 6. Funeral rites and ceremonies -- Fiction 7. Family life -- New York (State) -- Brooklyn -- Fiction
ISBN 1442459506; 9781442459502; 9781442459519
LC 2014001493

Coretta Scott King Author Award, Honor Book (2016)

In this teen novel, by Jason Reynolds, "with his mother newly dead, a job in a funeral home somehow becomes the perfect way for Matthew to deal with his crushing grief. Initially skeptical, he plans to use his early-release senior year program to work at a fried-chicken joint that's staffed by an entrancing girl with whom he eventually develops a . . . relationship. But the funerals intrigue him and then become deeply satisfying; Matthew finds solace in seeing others experiencing his pain." (Kirkus Reviews)

"High-school senior Matt has a job at Mr. Ray's funeral home, but he's also in mourning, for his mother who died and his long-on-the-wagon father who's returned to drink. While all this sounds like heavy problem-novel territory, it isn't. Reynolds writes about urban African American kids in a warm and empathetic way that the late Walter Dean Myers would have applauded." Horn Book

★ **Ghost**; Jason Reynolds. Atheneum Books For Young Readers 2016 181 p. (hardback) $16.99; (ebook) $15.99
Grades: 4 5 6 7 **Fic**

1. Running -- Fiction 2. Track athletics -- Fiction 3. Self-realization -- Fiction 4. Track and field -- Fiction 5. Coaches (Athletics) -- Fiction
ISBN 1481450158; 9781481450157; 9781481450164; 9781481450171
LC 2016029678

National Book Award Finalist: Young People's Literature (2016)

In this book, by Jason Reynolds, "Ghost wants to be the fastest sprinter on his elite middle school track team, but his past is slowing him down. . . . If he can stay on track, literally and figuratively, he could be the best sprinter in the city. But Ghost has been running for the wrong reasons—it all starting with running away from his father. . . . Since then, Ghost has been the one causing problems—and running away from them—until he meets Coach." (Publisher's note)

"Reynolds has created a wonderfully dynamic character in Ghost; his first-person narrative is one with which young readers will readily identify." Horn Book

Other titles in this series are:
Patina (2017)
Sunny (2018)

★ **Long** way down; Jason Reynolds. Atheneum 2017 320 p. (hardback) $17.99
Grades: 6 7 8 9 10 11 12 **Fic**

1. Novels in verse 2. Murder -- Fiction 3. Revenge -- Fiction 4. Brothers -- Fiction 5. Conduct of life -- Fiction 6. Ghosts -- Fiction
ISBN 1481438255; 9781481438254; 9781481438261
LC 2017001395

Newbery Honor Book (2018)
Coretta Scott King Author Award Honor Book (2018)
LA Times Book Prize: Young Adult Literature (2017)
Printz Honor Book (2018)

This book, by Jason Reynolds, "takes place in sixty potent seconds--the time it takes a kid to decide whether or not he's going to murder the guy who killed his brother. . . . Revenge. That's where Will's now heading, with that gun shoved in the back waistband of his jeans, the gun that was his brother's gun. He gets on the elevator, seventh floor, stoked. He knows who he's after. Or does he?" (Publisher's note)

"Teens are left with an unresolved ending that goes beyond the simple question of whether Will will seek revenge. Told in verse, this title is fabulistic in its simplicity and begs to be discussed." SLJ

Lu; Jason Reynolds. Atheneum 2018 224 p. (hardback) $16.99
Grades: 5 6 7 8 **Fic**

1. Pregnancy -- Fiction 2. Family life -- Fiction 3. Conduct of life -- Fiction 4. Track and field -- Fiction 5. African Americans -- Fiction 6. Albinos and albinism -- Fiction
ISBN 9781481450249; 9781481450256
LC 2018025798

In this book in the Track series, by Jason Reynolds, "Lu was born to be cocaptain of the Defenders. Well, actually, he was born albino, but that's got nothing to do with being a track star. . . . Lu knows he can lead Ghost, Patina, Sunny, and the team to victory at the championships, but it might not be as easy as it seems. Suddenly, there are hurdles in Lu's way . . . and Lu needs to figure out, fast, what winning the gold really means." (Publisher's note)

Miles Morales; Spider-Man. Jason Reynolds. Marvel Press 2017 272 p. (hardcover) $17.99
Grades: 7 8 9 10 11 12 **Fic**

1. Superheroes -- Fiction
ISBN 9781484787489
LC 2017000504

In this book by Jason Reynolds, "Miles Morales is just your average teenager. Dinner every Sunday with his parents, chilling out playing old-school video games with his best friend, Ganke, crushing on brainy, beautiful poet Alicia. He's even got a scholarship spot at the prestigious Brooklyn Visions Academy. Oh yeah, and he's Spider Man. . . . When a misunderstanding leads to his suspension from school, Miles begins to question his abilities. After all, his dad and uncle were Brooklyn jackboys with criminal records. Maybe kids like Miles aren't meant to be superheroes. Maybe Miles should take his dad's advice and focus on saving himself." (Publisher's note)

"Reynolds builds on a comic book plot and neatly ties in Miles' Marvel Universe background, but he focuses more on his 16-year-old protagonist's struggle with self-doubt in a vividly rendered urban setting stocked with engaging supporting characters." Booklist

★ **Patina**; Jason Reynolds. Atheneum Books for Young Readers 2017 233 p. (Track) (hardcover) $16.99
Grades: 4 5 6 7 **Fic**

1. Running -- Fiction 2. Adoption -- Fiction 3. Mothers and daughters -- Fiction 4. Diabetes -- fiction 5. Families -- fiction 6. Track and field -- fiction 7. African Americans -- fiction 8. Stress (Physiology) -- fiction
ISBN 9781481450201; 9781481450188; 9781481450195
LC 2017018004

In this book, by Jason Reynolds, "Patina, or Patty, runs like a flash. She runs for many reasons--to escape the taunts from the kids at the fancy-schmancy new school she's been sent to since she and her little sister had to stop living with their mom. She runs from the reason WHY she's not able to live with her 'real' mom any more: her mom has The Sugar, and Patty is terrified that the disease that took her mom's legs will one day take her away forever." (Publisher's note)

"The second entry in the four-book Track series, this serves as a complete, complex, and sparkling stand-alone novel." Booklist

★ **Sunny**; Jason Reynolds. Atheneum Books for Young Readers 2018 159 p. (hardback) $16.99
Grades: 4 5 6 7 8 **Fic**

1. Self-esteem -- Fiction 2. Family problems -- Fiction 3. Father-son relationship -- Fiction 4. Diaries -- Fiction 5. Home schooling -- Fiction 6. Track and field -- Fiction 7. Fathers and sons -- Fiction
ISBN 9781481450218; 9781481450225
LC 2017061137

In this book in the Track series, by Jason Reynolds, "Sunny is just that--sunny. . . . [He] is the chillest dude on the Defenders team. But Sunny's life hasn't always been sun beamy-bright. . . . His mother died giving birth to him, and based on how Sunny's dad treats him . . . it's no wonder Sunny thinks he's to blame. It seems the only thing Sunny can do right in his dad's eyes is win first place ribbons running the mile, just like his mom did." (Publisher's note)

"On the surface, African-American Sunny appears to have a wealthy, comfortable life that his less-fortunate teammates on the Defenders cannot help but envy. Privilege, however, cannot hide pain, and Sunny feels smothered by guilt over his mother's death immediately after his birth and crushed beneath the weight of his father's expectations for him to become the marathon runner that his beloved mother no longer can be." (Kirkus)

Rhodes, Jewell Parker

★ **Ninth** Ward. Little, Brown 2010 217p $15.99
Grades: 5 6 7 8 **Fic**

1. New Orleans (La.) -- Fiction 2. Extrasensory perception -- Fiction 3. Hurricane Katrina, 2005 -- Fiction
ISBN 978-0-316-04307-6; 0-316-04307-9
LC 2009-34423

Coretta Scott King Author Award honor book, 2011

In New Orleans' Ninth Ward, twelve-year-old Lanesha, who can see spirits, and her adopted grandmother have no choice but to stay and weather the storm as Hurricane Katrina bears down upon them.

"The dynamics of the diverse community enrich the survival story, and the contemporary struggle of one brave child humanizes the historic tragedy." Booklist

Sugar; Jewell Parker Rhodes. 1st ed. Little, Brown and Co. 2013 288 p. (hardcover) $16.99
Grades: 3 4 5 6 7 8 **Fic**

1. Historical fiction -- fiction 2. Race relations -- Fiction 3. African Americans -- Fiction 4. Chinese Americans -- Fiction 5. Plantation life -- Louisiana -- Fiction 6. Louisiana -- History -- 1865-1950 -- Fiction 7. Reconstruction (U.S. history, 1865-1877) -- Fiction
ISBN 0316043052; 9780316043052
LC 2012026218

In this historical novel, by Jewell Parker Rhodes, "ten-year-old Sugar lives on the River Road sugar plantation along the banks of the Mississippi. Slavery is over, but laboring in the fields all day doesn't make her feel very free. . . . Here's another tale of a strong, spirited young girl who rises beyond her circumstances and inspires others to work toward a brighter future." (Publisher's note)

"Sugar's clipped narration is personable and engaging, strongly evoking the novel's historical setting and myriad racial tensions, making them accessible and meaningful to beginning readers." Pub Wkly

Towers falling; Jewell Parker Rhodes. Little, Brown & Co. 2016 240 p. (hardcover) $16.99
Grades: 4 5 6 7 **Fic**

1. Racism -- fiction 2. Schools -- Fiction 3. Friendship -- Fiction 4. Family problems -- Fiction 5. Homeless persons -- Fiction 6. September 11 Terrorist Attacks, 2001 -- Fiction
ISBN 9780316262224
LC 2015021096

In this children's book, by Jewell Parker Rhodes, "when her fifth-grade teacher hints that a series of lessons about home and community will culminate with one big answer about two tall towers once visible outside their classroom window, Dèja can't help but feel confused. She sets off on a journey of discovery, with new friends Ben and Sabeen by her side." (Publisher's note)

Ribay, Randy

★ **Patron** saints of nothing; Randy Ribay. Kokila 2019 352 p. (hardback) $17.99
Grades: 8 9 10 11 12 **Fic**

1. Murder -- Fiction 2. Cousins -- Fiction 3. Philippines -- Fiction 4. Drug traffic -- Fiction 5. Family life -- Philippines -- Fiction
ISBN 9780525554912; 9780525554936
LC 2018044009

In this book, by Randy Ribay, "Jay Reguero plans to spend the last semester of his senior year playing video games before heading to the University of Michigan in the fall. But when he discovers that his Filipino cousin Jun was murdered as part of President Duterte's war on drugs, and no one in the family wants to talk about what happened, Jay travels to the Philippines to find out the real story." (Publisher's note)

"By deftly weaving key details into Jay's quest for the truth, Ribay provides a much-needed window for young people of the West to better understand the Filipino history of colonization, occupation, and revolution." (Booklist)

Includes bibliographical references

Richards, Jame

★ **Three** rivers rising; a novel of the Johnstown flood. Alfred A. Knopf 2010 293p $16.99; lib bdg $19.99

Grades: 6 7 8 9 10 **Fic**

1. Novels in verse 2. Floods -- Fiction 4. Pennsylvania -- Fiction 5. Social classes -- Fiction

ISBN 978-0-375-85885-7; 0-375-85885-7; 978-0-375-95885-4 lib bdg; 0-375-95885-1 lib bdg

LC 2009-4251

Sixteen-year-old Celestia is a wealthy member of the South Fork Fishing and Hunting Club, where she meets and falls in love with Peter, a hired hand who lives in the valley below, and by the time of the torrential rains that lead to the disastrous Johnstown flood of 1889, she has been disowned by her family and is staying with him in Johnstown. Includes an author's note and historical timeline.

This is a "striking novel in verse. . . . Richards builds strong characters with few words and artfully interweaves the lives of these independent thinkers." Publ Wkly

Includes bibliographical references

Richter, Conrad

The **light** in the forest. Everyman's Library 2005 176p $14.95; pa $6.50

Grades: 7 8 9 10 **Fic**

1. Delaware Indians -- Fiction 3. Frontier and pioneer life -- Fiction

ISBN 1-4000-4426-X; 1-4000-7788-5 pa

First published 1953 by Knopf

"A boy stolen in early childhood and brought up by the Delawares is at fifteen suddenly returned to the family he has forgotten. He resents his loss of independence, hates the brutality of the white man's civilization, and longs only for a return to the Indians whom he remembers as peace-loving and kind. His return to the Delawares does not, however, bring him peace; rather, he must make a bitter choice between helping his indian brothers kill agroup of unsuspecting white men or helping the white men escape. This is both vivid re-creation of outdoor life and a provocative study in conflicting loyalties." Horn Book

Riggs, Ransom, 1979-

Hollow city; by Ransom Riggs. Quirk Books 2014 399 p. (Novel of Miss Peregrine's Peculiar Children) $17.99

Grades: 6 7 8 9 10 **Fic**

1. Supernatural -- Fiction 2. London (England) -- Fiction 3. Escapes -- Fiction 4. Orphanages -- fiction

ISBN 1594746125; 9781594746123

"Having escaped Miss Peregrine's island by the skin of their teeth, Jacob and his new friends must journey to London, the peculiar capital of the world. Along the way, they encounter new allies, a menagerie of peculiar animals, and other unexpected surprises." (Publisher's note)

"Like the first volume, this one is generously illustrated with peculiar period photographs that capture and enhance the eerie mood and mode." Booklist

Library of souls; Ransom Riggs. Quirk Books 2015 458 p. illustrations, portraits (hardcover) $18.99

Grades: 6 7 8 9 10 **Fic**

1. Paranormal fiction 2. Rescue work -- Fiction

ISBN 9781594747588; 159474758X

LC 2015939051

"Time is running out for the Peculiar Children. With a dangerous madman on the loose and their beloved Miss Peregrine still in danger, Jacob Portman and Emma Bloom are forced to stage the most daring of rescue missions. They'll travel through a war-torn landscape, meet new allies, and face greater dangers than ever." (Publisher's Note)

A **map** of days; a novel. Ransom Riggs. Dutton Books 2018 496 p. (hardback) $22.99

Grades: 6 7 8 9 10 **Fic**

1. Grandfathers -- Fiction 2. Supernatural -- Fiction 3. Voyages and travels -- Fiction

ISBN 9780735232143

LC 2018031547

In this book in the Miss Peregrine's Peculiar Children series, by Ransom Riggs, "having defeated the monstrous threat that nearly destroyed the peculiar world, Jacob Portman is back . . . in Florida. Except now Miss Peregrine, Emma, and their peculiar friends are with him, and doing their best to blend in. But carefree days of beach visits and normalling lessons are soon interrupted by a discovery--a subterranean bunker that belonged to Jacob's grandfather, Abe." (Publisher's note)

Miss Peregrine's home for peculiar children. Quirk Books 2011 352p il (Miss Peregrine's Peculiar Children) $17.99

Grades: 6 7 8 9 10 **Fic**

1. Ghost stories 2. Wales -- Fiction

ISBN 978-1-59474-476-1; 1-59474-476-9

"When Jacob's grandfather, Abe, a WWII veteran, is savagely murdered, Jacob has a nervous breakdown, in part because he believes that his grandfather was killed by a monster that only they could see. On his psychiatrist's advice, Jacob and his father travel from their home in Florida to Cairnholm Island off the coast of Wales, which, during the war, housed Miss Peregrine's Home for Peculiar Children. . . . Nearly 50 unsettling vintage photographs appear throughout, forming the framework of this dark but empowering tale, as Riggs creates supernatural backstories and identities for those pictured in them. . . . It's an enjoyable, eccentric read, distinguished by well-developed characters, a believable Welsh setting, and some very creepy monsters." Publ Wkly

Other titles in this series are:

Hollow City (2014)

Library of Souls (2015)

A Map of Days (2018)

Tales of the Peculiar; by Ransom Riggs, illustrated by Andrew Davidson. Penguin Group USA 2016 192 p. illustrations $24.99

Grades: 7 8 9 10 **Fic**

1. Fantasy fiction 2. Short stories -- Collections

ISBN 0399538534; 9780399538537

LC 2016031018

This book, by Ransom Riggs, illustrated by Andrew Davidson, is "a companion to the New York Times bestselling Miss Peregrine's Home for Peculiar Children. . . . Riggs now invites you to share his secrets of peculiar history, with a collection of original stories in this deluxe volume of Tales of the Peculiar, as collected and annotated by Millard Nullings, ward of Miss Peregrine and scholar of all things peculiar." (Publisher's note)

"Elegantly detailed engravings from Davidson open each story, setting the tone for the tale that follows." Pub Wkly

Riley, James

Secret origins; by James Riley. Aladdin 2017 372 p. (Story Thieves) (hardcover) $17.99

Grades: 5 6 7 8 **Fic**

1. Magic -- Fiction 2. Books and reading -- Fiction 3. Superheroes -- Fiction 4. Characters in literature -- Fiction 5. Adventure and adventurers -- Fiction 6. Comic books, strips, etc. -- Fiction

ISBN 1481461257; 9781481461252

LC 2016025387

In this juvenile novel, by James Riley, "[l]ife is boring when you live in the real world, instead of starring in your own book series. Owen knows that better than anyone, what with the real world's homework and chores. But everything changes the day Owen sees the impossible happen: his classmate Bethany climb out of a book in the library. It turns out Bethany's half-fictional and has been searching every book she can find for her missing father, a fictional character." (Publisher's note)

"A literary hall of mirrors, with plenty of thrills and laughs to keep 'nonfictionals' in the game" Kirkus

Other titles in this series are:

The stolen chapters (2016)

Secret origins (2017)

Rinaldi, Ann

The **redheaded** princess. HarperCollinsPublishers 2008 214p $15.99; lib bdg $16.89

Grades: 6 7 8 9 **Fic**

1. Queens 2. Great Britain -- History -- 1485-1603, Tudors -- Fiction

ISBN 978-0-06-073374-2; 0-06-073374-8; 978-0-06-073375-9 lib bdg; 0-06-073375-6 lib bdg

LC 2007-18577

In 1542, nine-year-old Lady Elizabeth lives on an estate near London, striving to get back into the good graces of her father, King Henry VIII, and as the years pass she faces his death and those of other close relatives until she finds herself next in line to ascend the throne of England in 1558.

"The rich scene-setting and believable, appealing heroine will satisfy Rinaldi's many fans." Booklist

Riordan, Rick, 1964-

The **battle** of the Labyrinth. Hyperion Books for Children 2008 361p (Percy Jackson & the Olympians) lib bdg $17.99; pa $7.99

Grades: 5 6 7 8 9 **Fic**

1. Classical mythology -- Fiction

ISBN 978-1-4231-0146-8 lib bdg; 1-4231-0146-4 lib bdg; 978-1-4231-0149-9 pa; 1-4231-0149-9 pa

LC 2007-42957

Sequel to: The Titan's curse (2007)

When demonic cheerleaders invade his high school, Percy Jackson hurries to Camp Half Blood, from whence he and his demigod friends set out on a quest through the Labyrinth, while the war between the Olympians and the evil Titan lord Kronos draws near.

"The wit, rousing swordplay and breakneck pace will once again keep kids hooked." Publ Wkly

Followed by: The last Olympian (2009)

The **blood** of Olympus; Rick Riordan. 1st edition Disney-Hyperion Books 2014 528 p. (The heroes of Olympus) (hardback) $19.99

Grades: 5 6 7 8 **Fic**

1. Adventure fiction 2. Classical mythology -- Fiction 3. Mythology, Greek -- Fiction 4. Mythology, Roman -- Fiction 5. Gaia (Greek deity) -- Fiction

ISBN 1423146735; 9781423146735

LC 2014017392

In this novel by Rick Riordan, book 5 of the "The Heroes of Olympus" series, "though the Greek and Roman crewmembers of the Argo II have made progress in their many quests, they still seem no closer to defeating the earth mother, Gaea. Her giants have risen . . . and they're stronger than ever. They must be stopped before the Feast of Spes, when Gaea plans to have two demigods sacrificed in Athens." (Publisher's note)

"Readers looking forward to the battle scenes will find plenty here, but the young heroes also rely on their wits as they dupe, charm, and negotiate their way through a series of encounters with gods, goddesses, and mythological creatures." Booklist

The **hidden** oracle; Rick Riordan. Disney-Hyperion 2016 376 p. (Trials of Apollo) (hardback) $19.99

Grades: 5 6 7 8 **Fic**

1. Greek mythology -- Fiction 2. Gods and goddesses -- Fiction 3. Gods, Greek -- Fiction 4. Mythology, Greek -- Fiction

ISBN 9781484732748

LC 2015045235

In this book, by Rick Riordan, "after angering his father Zeus, the god Apollo is cast down from Olympus. Weak and disoriented, he lands in New York City as a regular teenage boy. Now, without his godly powers, the four-thousand-year-old deity must learn to survive in the modern world until he can somehow find a way to regain Zeus's favor. But Apollo has many enemies-gods, monsters, and mortals who would love to see the former Olympian permanently destroyed." (Publisher's note)

"A clash of mythic intrigues and centuries of pop culture to thrill die-hard and new fans alike." Kirkus

The **house** of Hades; Rick Riordan. Disney-Hyperion 2013 597 p. (Heroes of Olympus) (hardback) $19.99

Grades: 5 6 7 8 **Fic**

1. Hell -- Fiction 2. Gods and goddesses -- Fiction 3. Classical mythology -- Fiction 4. Camps -- Fiction 5. Giants -- Fiction 6. Mythology, Greek -- Fiction 7. Mythology, Roman -- Fiction 8. Gaia (Greek deity) -- Fiction 9. Hera (Greek deity) -- Fiction

ISBN 1423146727; 9781423146728

LC 2013015946

In this book, by Rick Riordan, "Annabeth and Percy tumble into a pit leading straight to the Underworld. The other five demigods have to put aside their grief and follow Percy's instructions to find the mortal side of the Doors of Death. If they can fight their way through the Gaea's forces, and Percy and Annabeth can survive the House of Hades, then the Seven will be able to seal the Doors from both sides and prevent the giants from raising Gaea." (Publisher's note)

"In this fourth in Riordan's series pitting Roman and Greek demigods against an awakening goddess Gaea, Percy and Annabeth trek through Tartarus to escape through the Doors of Death, while their friends fight their way to the Doors' mortal side to rescue them. The wisecracking teens reveal emotional depths while overcoming monsters and personal obstacles in this high velocity continuation of the gripping franchise." Horn Book

The **last** Olympian. Hyperion Books for Children 2009 381p map (Percy Jackson & the Olympians) $17.99

Grades: 5 6 7 8 9 **Fic**

1. Classical mythology -- Fiction

ISBN 978-1-4231-0147-5; 1-4231-0147-5

Sequel to: The battle of the Labyrinth (2008)

All year the half-bloods have been preparing for battle against the Titans. Now it's up to Percy Jackson and an army of young demi-gods to stop the Lord of Time.

"Riordan masterfully orchestrates the huge cast of characters and manages a coherent, powerful tale at once exciting, philosophical and tear-jerking." Kirkus

★ The **lightning** thief. Miramax Books/Hyperion Books for Children 2005 377p (Percy Jackson & the Olympians) pa $7.99

Grades: 5 6 7 8 9 **Fic**

1. Classical mythology -- Fiction

ISBN 0-7868-5629-7; 1-4231-3494-X pa; 978-0-6417-2344-5; 978-1-4231-3494-7 pa

LC 2005-299400

Twelve-year-old Percy Jackson learns he is a demigod, the son of a mortal woman and Poseidon, god of the sea. His mother sends him to a summer camp for demigods where he and his new friends set out on a quest to prevent a war between the gods.

"Riordan's fast-paced adventure is fresh, dangerous, and funny." Booklist

The **lost** hero. Disney/Hyperion Books 2010 553p $18.99

Grades: 5 6 7 8 **Fic**

1. Camps -- Fiction 2. Monsters -- Fiction 3. Classical mythology -- Fiction

ISBN 978-1-4231-1339-3; 1-4231-1339-X

LC 2010015469

"Completely in control of pacing and tone, . . . [Riordan] . . . balances a faultless comic banter against deeper notes that reveal the characters' vulnerabilities." Horn Book

Magnus Chase and the Gods of Asgard: The Hammer of Thor; Rick Riordan. Disney-Hyperion 2016 468 p. (Magnus Chase and the gods of Asgard) $19.99

Grades: 5 6 7 8 9 **Fic**

1. Gender identity -- Fiction 2. Lost and found possessions -- Fiction 3. Mythology, Norse -- Fiction 4. Thor (Norse deity) -- Fiction 5. Adventure and adventurers -- Fiction

ISBN 9781423160922

LC 2016025920

Stonewall Book Award, Youth (2017)

In this book, by Rick Riordan, "Thor's hammer is missing again. The thunder god has a disturbing habit of misplacing his weapon--the mightiest force in the Nine Worlds. But this time the hammer isn't just lost, it has fallen into enemy hands. If Magnus Chase and his friends can't retrieve the hammer quickly, the mortal worlds will be defenseless against an onslaught of giants." (Publisher's note)

"An entertaining sequel that will whet fans' appetites for the next installment." Kirkus

The **maze** of bones. Scholastic 2008 220p il (The 39 clues) $12.99

Grades: 4 5 6 7 **Fic**

1. Family -- Fiction 2. Ciphers -- Fiction

ISBN 978-0-545-06039-4; 0-545-06039-7

At the reading of their grandmother's will, Dan and Amy Cahill are given the choice of receiving a million dollars or uncovering the 39 clues hidden around the world that will lead to the source of the family's power, but by taking on the clues, they end up in a dangerous race against their own family members.

"Adeptly incorporating a genuine kids' perspective, the narrative unfolds like a boulder rolling downhill and keeps readers glued to the pages. . . . The book dazzles with suspense, plot twists, and snappy humor." SLJ

Other titles in this series are:

One false note by Gordon Korman (2008)
The sword thief by Peter Lerangis (2009)
The black circle by Patrick Carman (2009)
Beyond the grave by Jude Watson (2009)
In too deep by Jude Watson (2010)
The viper's nest by Peter Lerangis (2010)
The emperor's code by Gordon Korman (2010)
Storm warning by Linda Sue Park (2010)
Into the gauntlet by Margaret Peterson Haddix (2010)

Percy Jackson's Greek Gods; Rick Riordan ; illustrated by John Rocco. Disney-Hyperion 2014 336 p. color illustrations (hardback) $24.99

Grades: 5 6 7 8 **Fic**

1. Greek mythology 2. Gods and goddesses -- Fiction 3. Gods, Greek -- Fiction

ISBN 1423183649; 9781423183648

LC 2013034612

"Riordan takes the classic guide to Greek myths and makes it his own, with an introduction and narration by beloved character Percy Jackson. With 19 chapters, this oversize hardcover includes a variety of stories, from the early tales of Gaea and the Titans to individual tales of gods readers encounter in the 'Percy Jackson' series. . ., such as Ares, Apollo, and Dionysus." (School Library Journal)

"Combining the sarcasm and wit of Percy Jackson with the original Greek myths is a great way to hook tweens and teens on the stories without boring them. The beautiful illustrations by John Rocco enhance each story without taking away from the action and drama." VOYA

Includes bibliographical references and index

★ The **Red** Pyramid; Rick Riordan. Hyperion 2010 516 p. (Kane chronicles) (hardback) $17.99

Grades: 4 5 6 7 **Fic**

1. Fantasy fiction 2. Brothers and sisters -- Fiction 3. Egypt -- Fiction 4. Siblings -- Fiction 5. Secret societies -- Fiction 6. Gods and goddesses -- Fiction 7. Voyages and travels -- Fiction

ISBN 1423113381; 9781423113386

LC 2010549563

This is the first installment of the Kane chronicles. "Since their mother's death, Carter and Sadie have become near strangers. While Sadie has lived with her grandparents in London, her brother has traveled the world with their father, the brilliant Egyptologist, Dr. Julius Kane. . . . [Dr. Kane] unleashes the Egyptian god Set, who banished him to oblivion and forces the children to flee for their lives." (Publisher's note)

"The first-person narrative shifts between Carter and Sadie, giving the novel an intriguing dual perspective made more complex by their biracial heritage and the tension between the siblings. . . . This fantasy adventure delivers . . . young protagonists with previously unsuspected magical powers, a riveting story marked by headlong adventure, a complex background rooted in ancient mythology, and wry, witty twenty-first-century narration." Booklist

The **Sea** of Monsters. Miramax Books/Hyperion Books for Children 2006 279p (Percy Jackson & the Olympians) $17.95; pa $7.99

Grades: 5 6 7 8 9 **Fic**

1. Classical mythology -- Fiction

ISBN 978-0-7868-5686-2; 0-7868-5686-6; 978-1-4231-0334-9 pa; 1-4231-0334-3 pa

LC 2006280771

Sequel to: The lightning thief (2005)

Demigod Percy Jackson and his friends must journey into the Sea of Monsters to save their camp. But first Percy will discover a secret that makes him wonder whether being claimed as Poseidon's son is an honor or a cruel joke

"Adventure follows chaotic adventure at a rapid pace, and readers with even a passing acquaintance with the Odyssey will enjoy this fresh use of familiar stories." SLJ

Followed by: The Titan's curse (2007)

The **Serpent's** Shadow; Rick Riordan. Disney/Hyperion Books 2012 viii, 406 p.p (hardcover) $19.99

Grades: 4 5 6 7 **Fic**

1. Supernatural -- Fiction 2. Magic -- Fiction 3. Mythology, Egyptian -- Fiction 4. Voyages and travels -- Fiction 5. Brothers and sisters -- Fiction 6. Adventure and adventurers -- Fiction

ISBN 1423140575; 9781423140573

LC 2012454979

This book by Rick Riordan is the third installment of the Kane Chronicles series. "Despite their best efforts, Carter and Sadie Kane can't seem to keep Apophis, the chaos snake, down. Now Apophis is threatening to plunge the world into eternal darkness, and the Kanes are faced with the impossible task of having to destroy him once and for all." (Publisher's note)

The **Ship** of the Dead; Rick Riordan. Disney-Hyperion 2017 421 p. (hardback) $19.99

Grades: 5 6 7 8 **Fic**

1. Loki (Norse deity) -- fiction 2. Ships -- Fiction 3. Mythology, Norse -- Fiction 4. Adventure and adventurers -- Fiction

ISBN 9781484758601; 9781368024440; 9781423160939

LC 2017029354

In this book in the Magnus Chase and the Gods of Asgard series, by Rick Riordan, "Magnus Chase . . . is . . . one of Odin's chosen warriors. As the son of Frey, . . . Magnus isn't naturally inclined to fighting. But he has strong and steadfast friends . . . and together they have achieved brave deeds.. . . Now Magnus faces his most dangerous trial yet. His cousin . . . recruits her boyfriend, Percy Jackson, to give Magnus some pointers, but will his training be enough?" (Publisher's note)

The **son** of Neptune. Disney/Hyperion Books 2011 521p (The heroes of Olympus) $19.99

Grades: 5 6 7 8 **Fic**

1. Camps -- Fiction 2. Monsters -- Fiction 3. Prophecies -- Fiction 4. Classical mythology -- Fiction

ISBN 978-1-4231-4059-7; 1-4231-4059-1

LC 2011017658

Demigod Percy Jackson, still with no memory, and his new friends from Camp Jupiter, Hazel and Frank, go on a quest to free Death, but their bigger task is to unite the Greek and Roman camps so that the Prophecy of Seven can be fulfilled.

The **sword** of summer; Rick Riordan. Disney-Hyperion 2015 512 p. (Magnus Chase and the gods of Asgard) $19.99

Grades: 5 6 7 8 **Fic**

1. Fantasy fiction -- fiction 2. Mythology, Norse -- Fiction

ISBN 1423160916; 9781423160915

LC 2015018467

In this juvenile novel, by Rick Riordan, "Magnus Chase has always been a troubled kid. Since his mother's mysterious death, he's lived alone on the streets of Boston, surviving by his wits. . . . One day, he's tracked down by an uncle he barely knows-a man his mother claimed was dangerous. Uncle Randolph tells him an impossible secret: Magnus is the son of a Norse god. The Viking myths are true. The gods of Asgard are preparing for war." (Publisher's note)

"There's appeal for new readers, but Percy Jackson fans will also undoubtedly snap this up, and there's even some overlap: Magnus' cousin is Annabeth Chase." Booklist

Other titles in this series are:

The hammer of Thor (2016)

The ship of the dead (2017)

The **throne** of fire; Rick Riordan. Disney/Hyperion Books 2011 (Kane chronicles) $18.99

Grades: 4 5 6 7 **Fic**

ISBN 978-1-4231-4056-6; 1-4231-4056-7; 1423140567; 9781423140566

Sequel to: The red pyramid (2010)

Carter and Sadie, offspring of the brilliant Egyptologist Dr. Julius Kane, embark on a worldwide search for the Book of Ra, but the House of Life and the gods of chaos are determined to stop them.

"Lit by flashes of humor, this fantasy adventure is an engaging addition to the Kane Chronicles series." Booklist

The **Titan's** curse. Miramax Books/Hyperion Books for Children 2007 312p (Percy Jackson & the Olympians) $17.95

Grades: 5 6 7 8 9 **Fic**

1. Classical mythology -- Fiction

ISBN 1423101456; 1423101480 pa; 9781423101451

LC 2006-35731

Sequel to The Sea of Monsters (2006)

When the goddess Artemis disappears while hunting a rare, ancient monster, a group of her followers joins Percy and his friends in an attempt to find and rescue her before the winter solstice, when her influence is needed to sway the Olympian Council regarding the war with the Titans.

"Intricate prophecies and relationships are neatly braided into the adventurous plot." SLJ

Followed by The battle of the Layrinth (2008)

Vespers rising; [by] Rick Riordan, Peter Lerangis, Gordon Korman, Jude Watson. Scholastic 2011 238p (The 39 clues) $12.99

Grades: 4 5 6 7 **Fic**

1. Ciphers -- Fiction

ISBN 978-0-545-29059-3; 0-545-32606-0

Fourteen-year-old Amy Cahill and her younger brother Dan thought they could return to their regular lives when they found the 39 clues. But the Vespers, powerful enemies, will stop at nothing to get the clues. And with the Vespers rising, the world is in jeopardy.

Ritter, John H.

The **boy** who saved baseball. Philomel Books 2003 216p $17.99; pa $6.99

Grades: 5 6 7 8 **Fic**

1. Baseball -- Fiction

ISBN 0-399-23622-8; 0-14-240286-9 pa

LC 2002-15792

A prequel to this title is: The desperado who stole baseball (2009)

The fate of a small California town rests on the outcome of one baseball game, and Tom Gallagher hopes to lead his team to victory with the secrets of the now disgraced player, Dante Del Gato

"This tale is peppered with both optimism and dilemmas; it has plenty of play-by-play action, lots of humor, and a triumphant ending." SLJ

Ritter, William

The **dire** king; William Ritter. Algonquin Young Readers 2017 344 p. (Jackaby series) (hardcover) $17.95

Grades: 7 8 9 10 **Fic**

1. Magic -- Fiction 2. New England -- Fiction 3. Supernatural -- Fiction 4. Zombies -- Fiction 5. Private investigators -- Fiction 6. Animals, Mythical -- fiction 7. New England -- Social life and customs -- 19th century -- Fiction

ISBN 9781616207625; 9781616206703

LC 2017002941

In this book, by William Ritter, "the fate of the world is in the hands of detective of the supernatural R. F. Jackaby and his . . . assistant, Abigail Rook. An evil king is turning ancient tensions into modern strife, using a blend of magic and technology to push Earth and the Otherworld into a mortal competition. Jackaby and Abigail are caught in the middle as they continue to solve the daily mysteries of New Fiddleham, New England." (Publisher's note)

"A humorous, energetic, action-packed, and magical conclusion." Kirkus

Jackaby; R. William Ritter. First edition Algonquin Young Readers 2014 304 p. (alk. paper) $16.95

Grades: 7 8 9 10 11 12 **Fic**

1. Mystery fiction 2. Historical fiction 3. Supernatural -- Fiction 4. Murder -- Fiction 5. Serial killers -- Fiction 6. Mystery and detective stories 7. Imaginary creatures -- Fiction 8. New England -- History -- 19th century -- Fiction

ISBN 1616203536; 9781616203535

LC 2014014706

"Newly arrived in New Fiddleham, New England, 1892 . . . Abigail Rook meets R. F. Jackaby, an investigator of the unexplained with . . . the ability to see supernatural beings. Abigail has a gift for noticing ordinary but important details, which makes her perfect for the position of Jackaby's assistant. On her first day, Abigail finds herself in the midst of a thrilling case: A serial killer is on the loose." (Publisher's note)

Other titles in this series are:
Beastly bones (2015)
Ghostly echoes (2016)
The dire king (2017)

Rivers, Karen

Finding Ruby Starling; by Karen Rivers. Arthur A. Levine Books, an imprint of Scholastic Inc. 2014 288 p. (hardcover) $17.99

Grades: 5 6 7 8 **Fic**

1. Twins -- Fiction 2. Adoption -- Fiction 3. Blogs -- Fiction 4. Email -- Fiction 5. Sisters -- Fiction 6. Mothers and daughters -- Fiction

ISBN 0545534798; 9780545534796

LC 2014002269

In this middle grade book by Karen Rivers, "when Ruby Starling gets a message from a Ruth Quayle proclaiming them to be long-lost twin sisters, she doesn't know what to do with it. . . . Ruth is an extroverted American girl. Ruby is a shy English one. As they investigate the truth of their birth and the circumstances of their separation, they also share lives full of friends, family, and possible romances." (Publisher's note)

"In this epistolary, dual-narrator story, Ruth, an American twelve-year-old, e-finds her identical twin, Ruby, in England. As with any novel in letters (in this case emails, handwritten notes, and the occasional Tumblr posting), voice is everything, and Ruth and Ruby have distinctive, convincing, and entertaining writing styles. Subplots abound, including the backstory of two complicated families. Hectic, highly textured, and good-natured without being soppy." Horn Book

The **girl** in the well is me; Karen Rivers. Algonquin Young Readers 2016 224 p. $16.95

Grades: 5 6 7 8 9 **Fic**

1. Girls -- fiction 2. Popularity -- fiction 3. Imagination -- fiction 4. Fear -- Fiction 5. Bullying -- Fiction 6. Self-perception -- Fiction

ISBN 1616205695; 9781616205690

LC 2015023956

In this children's novel, by Karen Rivers, "longing to be one of the popular girls in her new town, Kammie Summers has fallen into a well during a (fake) initiation into their club. Now Kammie's trapped in the dark. As hours pass, Kammie's real-life predicament mixes with memories of the best and worst moments of her life so far, including the awful reasons her family moved to this new town in the first place." (Publisher's note)

"A different sort of bullying book, with the spotlight never leaving the victim, it should strike a chord with its tween audience." Booklist

Love, Ish; Karen Rivers. Algonquin Young Readers 2017 279 p. $16.95

Grades: 6 7 8 9 **Fic**

1. Cancer -- Fiction 2. Ambition -- Fiction 3. Friendship -- Fiction 4. Best friends -- Fiction 5. Mars (Planet) -- Fiction 6. Brain -- Tumors -- Fiction

ISBN 9781616205706

LC 2016038086

In this novel, by Karen Rivers, "Ish, who is determined to be among the first settlers on Mars, goes on a different and unexpected journey after she is diagnosed with a malignant brain tumor. She's prone to long stream-of-consciousness monologues anyway, but after discovery of the tumor that she imagines as a sort of Brussels sprout and starting on chemotherapy and radiation treatments, many of her dreams (and nightmares) focus on her imagined life in a Mars colony." (Kirkus Reviews)

Roat, Sharon Huss

How to Disappear; by Sharon Huss Roat. HarperTeen 2017 377 p. (hardcover) $17.99

Grades: 7 8 9 10 11 12 **Fic**

1. Girls -- Fiction 2. Emotions -- Fiction 3. Friendship -- Fiction 4. Popularity -- Fiction 5. Introverts -- fiction 6. Social media -- fiction 7. High school girls -- fiction

ISBN 0062291750; 9780062291752; 9780062291776

In this book, by Sharon Huss Roat, "Vicky Decker's social anxiety has helped her to master the art of hiding in plain sight, appearing only to her best friend, Jenna. But when Jenna moves away, Vicky's isolation becomes unbearable. So she decides to invent a social life by Photoshopping herself into other people's photos and posting them on Instagram under the screen name Vicurious." (Publisher's note)

"This is a witty, hard-to-put-down novel that's appropriate for younger teens. However, the lack of grittiness won't deter older teens, who will be carried along by familiar lingo and references to social networks and celebrities." SLJ

Robinet, Harriette Gillem

Walking to the bus-rider blues. Atheneum Bks. for Young Readers 2000 146p hardcover o.p. pa $4.99

Grades: 5 6 7 8 **Fic**

1. Race relations -- Fiction 2. African Americans -- Fiction
ISBN 0-689-83191-9; 0-689-83886-7 pa

LC 99-29054

Twelve-year-old Alfa Merryfield, his older sister, and their grandmother struggle for rent money, food, and their dignity as they participate in the Montgomery, Alabama bus boycott in the summer of 1956

"Ingredients of mystery, suspense, and humor enhance and personalize this well-constructed story that offers insight into a troubled era." SLJ

Robinson, Gary

Little Brother of War; Gary Robinson. 7th Generation 2013 120 p. (pbk.) $9.95

Grades: 6 7 8 **Fic**

1. Brothers -- Fiction 2. Ball games -- Fiction 3. Mississippi -- Fiction 4. Individuality -- Fiction 5. Choctaw Indians -- Fiction 6. Family life -- Mississippi -- Fiction 7. Indians of North America -- Mississippi -- Fiction
ISBN 1939053021; 9781939053022

LC 2013013182

This book by Gary Robinson is part of the "PathFinders series about Native American teens, written by Native authors. Randy is pressured to pursue high school sports, like his father and recently deceased war-hero brother before him. But the 16-year-old discovers that he loves--and has a talent for--Choctaw stickball or toli, an ancient game similar to lacrosse that isn't a school sport and that his father thinks is a relic." (Publishers Weekly)

Rodgers, Mary

Freaky Friday. Harper & Row 1972 145p hardcover o.p. pa $5.99

Grades: 4 5 6 7 **Fic**

1. Mother-daughter relationship -- Fiction
ISBN 0-06-025048-8; 0-06-025049-6 lib bdg; 0-06-057010-5 pa

"A fresh, imaginative, and entertaining story." Bull Cent Child Books

Rodkey, Geoff

Stuck in the stone age; Geoff Rodkey ; illustrated by Hatem Aly ; Vince Boberski. St. Martin's Press 2018 304 p. $13.99

Grades: 3 4 5 **Fic**

1. Stone Age -- fiction 2. Scientists -- fiction 3. Time travel -- fiction
ISBN 1635650895; 9781635650891

"Tom Edison . . . is a hopeful janitor who dreams of becoming a scientist--and Dr. Morice is a shy scientist who dreams of making friends. When an accident at the lab sends them back in time to the stone age, Tom and Dr. Morice must work together to face down cavemen, saber-tooth tigers, and other B.C. hazards, with only one problem." (Publisher's note)

The **Tapper** twins go to war (with each other) Geoff Rodkey. Little, Brown & Co. 2015 240 p. illustrations (Tapper twins) (hardcover) $13.99

Grades: 4 5 6 7 **Fic**

1. School stories 2. Twins -- Fiction 3. New York (N.Y.) -- Fiction 4. Practical jokes -- Fiction 5. Brothers and sisters -- Fiction 6. Schools -- Fiction 7. Oral history -- Fiction 8. Internet games -- Fiction 9. Family life -- New York (State) -- New York -- Fiction
ISBN 0316297798; 9780316297790

LC 2014015918

This book, by Geoff Rodkey, is a "comedy featuring twelve-year-old fraternal twins, Claudia and Reese, who couldn't be more different... except in their determination to come out on top in a vicious prank war! But when the competition escalates into an all-out battle that's fought from the cafeteria of their New York City private school all the way to the fictional universe of an online video game, the twins have to decide if their efforts to destroy each other are worth the price." (Publisher's note)

"Through oral-history interviews, text messages, e-mails, chat-room comments, photographs, and margin notes, Claudia documents the history of the Tapper twins' war. . . . Thanks to the inclusion of various points of view, Claudia's reasonably balanced narrative offers plenty of humorous insight, and occasional doodles and photos keep it peppy." Booklist

Other titles in this series are:
The Tapper twins tear up New York (2015)
The Tapper twins run for president (2016)

We're not from here; Geoff Rodkey. Random House Childrens Books 2019 256 p. $16.99

Grades: 4 5 6 7 8 **Fic**

1. Outer space -- Fiction 2. Human-alien encounters -- Fiction 3. Extraterrestrial beings -- Fiction
ISBN 1524773042; 9781524773045

In this novel, by Geoff Rodkey, "the first time I heard about Planet Choom, we'd been on Mars for almost a year. But life on the Mars station was grim, and since Earth was no longer an option (we may have blown it up), it was time to find a new home. That's how we ended up on Choom with the Zhuri. They're very smart. They also look like giant mosquitoes. But that's not why it's so hard to live here. . . . The Zhuri don't like us." (Publisher's note)

"A quirky sci-fi adventure with a surprising layer of political irony." (Kirkus Reviews)

Roe, Robin

★ A **list** of cages; Robin Roe. Hyperion 2017 320 p. $17.99; (ebook) $17.99

Grades: 8 9 10 11 **Fic**

1. Friendship -- Fiction 2. Child abuse -- Fiction
ISBN 9781484763803; 9781484781098

LC 2015045422

In this novel, by Robin Roe, "when Adam Blake lands the best elective ever in his senior year, serving as an aide to the school psychologist, he thinks he's got it made. Sure, it means a lot of sitting around, which isn't easy for a guy with ADHD. . . . Then the doctor asks him to track down the troubled freshman who keeps dodging her, and Adam discovers that the boy is Julian--the foster brother he hasn't seen in five years." (Publisher's note)

"A triumphant story about the power of friendship and of truly being seen." Kirkus

Rogerson, Margaret

An **enchantment** of ravens; Margaret Rogerson. Margaret K. McElderry Books 2017 300 p. (hardback) $17.99

Grades: 7 8 9 10 **Fic**

1. Fantasy fiction 2. Fairies -- Fiction 3. Princes -- Fiction 4. Painters -- Fiction
ISBN 9781481497596; 9781481497589

LC 2017297177

In this novel, by Margaret Rogerson, "Isobel is a prodigy portrait artist with a dangerous set of clients: the sinister fair folk, immortal creatures who cannot bake bread, weave cloth, or put a pen to paper without crumbling to dust. . . . But when she receives her first royal patron--Rook, the autumn prince--she makes a terrible mistake. She paints mortal sorrow in his eyes--a weakness that could cost him his life." (Publisher's note)

"Rogerson ably builds this fantasy world through canny details and contemporary dialogue, allowing for an enjoyable read by fantasy and non-fantasy readers alike. She also craftily depicts the power imbalance between Isobel and Rook, offering a refreshing dynamic in which Isobel often comes out on top." SLJ.

Rose, Caroline Starr

★ **May** B. a novel-in-verse. Schwartz & Wade Books 2012 $15.99; lib bdg $18.99

Grades: 4 5 6 7 **Fic**

1. Novels in verse 2. Kansas -- Fiction 3. Frontier and pioneer life -- Fiction

ISBN 978-1-58246-393-3; 1-58246-393-X; 978-1-58246-412-1 lib bdg; 1-58246-412-X lib bdg

LC 2010033222

When a failed wheat crop nearly bankrupts the Betterly family, Pa pulls twelve-year-old May from school and hires her out to a couple new to the Kansas frontier.

"If May is a brave, stubborn fighter, the short, free-verse lines are one-two punches in this Laura Ingalls Wilder-inspired ode to the human spirit." Kirkus

Rosen, Michael J.

Sailing the unknown; around the world with Captain Cook. written by Michael J. Rosen ; illustrated by Maria Cristina Pritelli. Creative Editions 2012 37 p. $17.99

Grades: 3 4 5 6 7 **Fic**

1. Sea stories 2. Explorers -- Fiction 3. Voyages around the world -- Fiction 4. Diaries -- Fiction

ISBN 1568462166; 9781568462165

LC 2011040840

This children's book, by Michael J. Rosen, illustrated by Maria Cristina Pritelli, tells the story of "an 11-year-old sailor named Nicholas, . . . [who in 1768] took to the seas with British explorer James Cook on a 3-year expedition of discovery, venturing into an uncharted world filled with strange lands, mysterious peoples, and peculiar creatures." (Publisher's note)

The **tale** of rescue; Michael J. Rosen, Stan Fellows. Candlewick Press 2015 112 p. color illustrations $14.99

Grades: 4 5 6 7 8 **Fic**

1. Blizzards -- fiction 2. Rescue work -- fiction

ISBN 0763671673; 9780763671679

LC 2014949722

In this children's story, by Michael J. Rosen, illustrated by Stan Fellows, "when a blizzard traps a family outside in a whiteout, a cattle dog devises a stunning rescue. . . . They are panicked, exhausted, freezing, and stranded in waist-deep drifts. From off in the distance, the cattle dog has heard their faint, snow-drowned cries. Her inexhaustible attention turns to saving them." (Publisher's note)

"Lavishly illustrated in full-page watercolors, the book is visually beautiful and will appeal to adults looking for a feel-good dog story to share with a child." Booklist

Rosen, Renee

★ **Every** crooked pot. St. Martin's Griffin 2007 227p pa $8.95

Grades: 7 8 9 10 **Fic**

1. Birth defects -- Fiction 3. Father-daughter relationship -- Fiction

ISBN 978-0-312-36543-1; 0-312-36543-8

LC 2007-10457

"Rosen looks back at the life of Nina Goldman, whose growing up is tied to two pillars: a port-wine stain around her eye and her inimitable father, Artie. The birthmark, she hates; her father, she loves. Both shape her in ways that merit Rosen's minute investigation. . . . There's real power in the writing." Booklist

Rosenberg, Madelyn

This is just a test; by Madelyn Rosenberg and Wendy Wan-Long Shang. Scholastic Press 2017 243 p. illustrations (hardcover) $17.99

Grades: 4 5 6 7 8 **Fic**

1. Bildungsromans 2. Humorous fiction 3. Ethnicity -- Fiction 4. Friendship -- Fiction 5. Family life -- Fiction 6. Grandmothers -- Fiction 7. Chinese Americans -- Fiction 8. Jews -- United States -- Fiction 9. United States -- History -- 1945- -- Fiction 10. United States -- History -- 1945- -- fiction 11. United States -- Social life and customs -- 20th century -- Fiction

ISBN 9781338037746; 9781338037722

LC 2016037804

In this novel, by Madelyn Rosenberg and Wendy Wan Long Shang, "David Da-Wei Horowitz has a lot on his plate. Preparing for his upcoming bar mitzvah would be enough work even if it didn't involve trying to please his Jewish and Chinese grandmothers, who argue about everything. But David just wants everyone to be happy. That includes his friend Scott, who is determined to win their upcoming trivia tournament but doesn't like their teammate--and David's best friend--Hector." (Publisher's note)

"An appealing historical novel, even for readers resistant to the genre." Booklist

Rosoff, Meg, 1956-

★ **There** is no dog; Meg Rosoff. G. P. Putnam's Sons 2011 243p. $17.99

Grades: 7 8 9 **Fic**

1. God -- Fiction 2. Romance fiction 3. Man-woman relationship -- Fiction

ISBN 9780399257643

LC 2011020651

This book "looks at the world's natural disasters, injustices, and chaos and presents a[n] . . . explanation: God is a horny teenage boy. According to this . . . account, God, aka 'Bob,' was given Earth by his mother, who won the planet in a poker game. Bob showed flashes of brilliance during Creation, but he feels little responsibility for the planet. When he falls head-over-heels in lust with a beautiful zoo employee, Lucy, Bob's passion and growing anger toward those who would keep them apart is manifested through wildly fluctuating weather and rampant flooding." (Publishers Weekly)

Ross, Elizabeth

Belle epoque; Elizabeth Ross. Delacorte Press 2013 336 p. (ebook) $53.97; (library) $20.99; (hardcover) $17.99

Grades: 7 8 9 10 11 12 **Fic**

1. Romance fiction 2. Historical fiction 3. Female friendship -- Fiction 4. Runaways -- Fiction 5. Social classes -- Fiction 6. Conduct of life -- Fiction 7. Beauty, Personal -- Fiction 8. Interpersonal relations -- Fiction 9. Paris (France) -- History -- 1870-1940 -- Fiction 10. France -- History -- Third Republic, 1870-

1940 -- Fiction
ISBN 0375990054; 9780375985270; 9780375990052; 9780385741460

LC 2012034694

William C. Morris Honor Book (2014)

In this book, "sixteen-year-old runaway Maude Pichon is ugly—so much so that she lands a job as a 'repoussoir,' an unattractive girl paid to be seen with a lovelier girl to make her appear even more beautiful by comparison . . . . Maude is humiliated by the idea, but her poverty leaves her few options." Then "chance sends a dashing composer Maude's way, and a countess hires her to befriend her independent-minded daughter, Isabelle." (Publishers Weekly)

"Ross models her plot on an 1866 story by Zola, "Les Repoussoirs," expanding its focus to highlight Maude's plight and using that to illuminate the chasm that existed between the wealthy and the poor... A refreshingly relevant and inspiring historical venture." Kirkus

Ross, Joel

The **Fog** diver; Joel Ross. HarperCollins 2015 336 p. (hardback) $16.99

Grades: 4 5 6 7 **Fic**

1. Aeronautics -- fiction 2. Science fiction 3. Orphans -- Fiction 4. Survival -- Fiction 5. Recycling (Waste) -- Fiction 6. Adventure and adventurers -- Fiction 7. Environmental degradation -- Fiction
ISBN 0062352938; 9780062352934

LC 2014034154

In this juvenile novel, by Joel Ross, "living in the sky is the new reality and a few determined slum kids just might become heroes. . . . Thirteen-year-old Chess and his friends Hazel, Bea, and Swedish sail their rickety air raft over the deadly Fog, scavenging the ruins for anything they can sell to survive. But now survival isn't enough. They must risk everything to get to the miraculous city of Port Oro, the only place where their beloved Mrs. E can be cured of fogsickness." (Publisher's note)

"[A] fresh approach, convincingly delivered, with overtones reminiscent of Dickens...the only thing missing is a sequel, which readers will hope won't be far behind." Kirkus

Another title in this series is:
The Lost Compass (2016)

Rossetti, Rinsai

The **girl** with borrowed wings; by Rinsai Rossetti. Dial Books 2012 300 p. (hardcover) $17.99

Grades: 7 8 9 10 11 12 **Fic**

1. Cats -- Fiction 2. Voyages and travels -- Fiction 3. Father-daughter relationship -- Fiction 4. Love -- Fiction 5. Flying -- Fiction 6. Deserts -- Fiction 7. Shapeshifting -- Fiction
ISBN 0803735669; 9780803735668

LC 2011027164

This is Rinsai Rossetti's debut, a coming-of-age novel. Of "Thai descent, 17-year-old Frenenqer Paje has grown up" with "her coldly overbearing father . . . . [S]he disobeys her father by rescuing a mistreated cat" who "is actually a shape-shifting 'Free person' named Sangris . . . . By night, he flies Frenenqer around the world to places both real and magical, slowly chipping away at the defenses she has built up to withstand her father's callous cruelty." (Publishers Weekly)

Rossi, Veronica

Under the never sky; Veronica Rossi. HarperCollins 2012 376 p. (hardback) $17.99

Grades: 6 7 8 9 10 11 12 **Fic**

1. Science fiction 2. Apocalyptic fiction 3. Cannibalism -- Fiction 4. Man-woman relationship -- Fiction
ISBN 9780062072030

LC 2011044631

This book tells the story of "Aria [who] knows her chances of surviving in the outer wasteland--known as The Death Shop--are slim. . . . Then Aria meets an Outsider named Perry. He's wild--a savage--and her only hope of staying alive. A hunter for his tribe in a merciless landscape, Perry views Aria as sheltered and fragile--everything he would expect from a Dweller. . . . Opposites in nearly every way, Aria and Perry must accept each other to survive." (Publisher's note)

Rowling, J. K.

Harry Potter and the Chamber of Secrets; by J.K. Rowling; illustrations by Mary Grandpré. Arthur A. Levine Bks. 1999 341p il $22.99; pa $8.99

Grades: 4 5 6 7 8 9 10 **Fic**

1. Fantasy fiction 2. Witches -- Fiction
ISBN 0-439-06486-4; 0-439-06487-2 pa

LC 98-46370

Sequel to Harry Potter and the Sorcerer's Stone

When the Chamber of Secrets is opened again at the Hogswart School for Witchcraft and Wizardry, second-year student Harry Potter finds himself in danger from a dark power that has once more been released on the school

Followed by Harry Potter and the prisoner of Azkaban

Harry Potter and the deathly hallows; illustrations by Mary Grandpré. Arthur A. Levine Books 2007 759p il $34.99; pa $14.99

Grades: 4 5 6 7 8 9 10 **Fic**

1. Fantasy fiction 2. Witches -- Fiction
ISBN 978-0-545-01022-1; 0-545-01022-5; 978-0-545-13970-0 pa; 0-545-13970-8 pa

Sequel to: Harry Potter and the Half-blood Prince (2005)

This book is the final installment of J. K. Rowling's Harry Potter series. "With the Dark Lord in control of the Ministry of Magic, the trio uses their combined wizardly talents to stay hidden as they follow [Albus] Dumbledore's assignment to destroy the dangerous horcruxes. Finding those fragmented pieces of their enemy's soul lead the friends to angry arguments, near fatal encounters and, occasionally, humorous episodes." (School Library Journal)

Harry Potter and the Goblet of Fire; illustrations by Mary Grandpré. Arthur A. Levine Bks. 2000 734p il $29.99; pa $9.99

Grades: 4 5 6 7 8 9 10 **Fic**

1. Fantasy fiction 2. Witches -- Fiction
ISBN 0-439-13959-7; 0-439-13960-0 pa

LC 00-131084

Sequel to Harry Potter and the prisoner of Azkaban

Harry Potter, a fourth-year student at Hogwarts School of Witchcraft and Wizardry, longs to escape his hateful relatives, the Dursleys, and live as a normal fourteen-year-old wizard, but what Harry does not yet realize is that he is not a normal wizard, and in his case, different can be deadly.

Followed by Harry Potter and the Order of the Phoenix

Harry Potter and the Half-blood Prince; illustrations by Mary Grandpré. Arthur A. Levine 2005 652p il $29.99; pa $9.99

Grades: 4 5 6 7 8 9 10 **Fic**

1. Fantasy fiction 2. Witches -- Fiction

ISBN 0-439-78454-9; 0-439-78596-0 pa

Sequel to Harry Potter and the Half-blood Prince

Sixth-year Hogwarts student Harry Potter gains valuable insights into the boy Voldemort once was, even as his own world is transformed by maturing friendships, schoolwork assistance from an unexpected source, and devastating losses.

Followed by Harry Potter and the Deathly Hallows

Harry Potter and the Order of the Phoenix; illustrations by Mary Grandpre. Levine Bks. 2003 870p il $29.99; pa $9.99

Grades: 4 5 6 7 8 9 10 **Fic**

1. Fantasy fiction 2. Witches -- Fiction

ISBN 0-439-35806-X; 0-439-35807-8 pa

LC 2003-102525

Sequel to Harry Potter and the Goblet of Fire

When the government of the magic world and authorities at Hogwarts School of Witchcraft and Wizardry refuse to believe in the growing threat of a freshly revived Lord Voldemort, fifteen-year-old Harry Potter finds support from his loyal friends in facing the evil wizard and other new terrors

Followed by Harry Potter and the Half-blood Prince

Harry Potter and the prisoner of Azkaban; illustrations by Mary Grandpré. Arthur A. Levine Bks. 1999 435p il $22.99; pa $8.99

Grades: 4 5 6 7 8 9 10 **Fic**

1. Fantasy fiction 2. Witches -- Fiction

ISBN 0-439-13635-0; 0-439-13636-9 pa

LC 99-23982

Sequel to Harry Potter and the Chamber of Secrets

During his third year at Hogwarts School for Witchcraft and Wizardry, Harry Potter must confront the devious and dangerous wizard responsible for his parents' deaths

Followed by Harry Potter and the Goblet of Fire

★ **Harry** Potter and the Sorcerer's Stone; illustrations by Mary Grandpré. Arthur A. Levine Bks. 1998 309p il $22.99; pa $8.99

Grades: 4 5 6 7 8 9 10 **Fic**

1. Fantasy fiction 2. Young adult literature 3. Witches -- Fiction

ISBN 0-590-35340-3; 0-590-35342-X pa

LC 97-39059

First published 1997 in the United Kingdom with title: Harry Potter and the Philosopher's Stone

Rescued from the outrageous neglect of his aunt and uncle, a young boy with a great destiny proves his worth while attending Hogwarts School for Witchcraft and Wizardry.

This "is a brilliantly imagined and beautifully written fantasy." Booklist

Other titles in this series are:

Harry Potter and the Chamber of Secrets (1999)
Harry Potter and the Prisoner of Azkaban (1999)
Harry Potter and Goblet of Fire (2000)
Harry Potter and the Order of the Phoenix (2003)
Harry Potter and the Half-Blood Prince (2005)
Harry Potter and the Deathly Hallows (2007)

Roy, Carter

The **blood** guard; Carter Roy. Two Lions 2014 288 p. (trade pbk. : alk. paper) $17.99

Grades: 5 6 7 8 **Fic**

1. Fantasy fiction 2. Adventure and adventurers 3. Survival skills -- Fiction 4. Secret societies -- Fiction 5. Adventure stories 6. Kidnapping -- Fiction

ISBN 1477847251; 9781477847251

LC 2013958330

In this book, by Carter Roy, "when thirteen-year-old Ronan Truelove's . . . mom snatches him from school, then sets off on a high speed car chase, Ronan is shocked. His . . . dad has been kidnapped? And the kidnappers are after him, too? His mom, he quickly learns, is . . . a member of an ancient order of knights, the Blood Guard, a sword-wielding secret society sworn to protect the Pure—thirty-six noble souls whose safety is crucial if the world as we know it is to survive." (Publisher's note)

"As Ronan embarks on a hero's journey, familiar tropes of righting wrongs and self-discovery persist but nevertheless remain entertaining as mystery, mysticism, and action abound." Horn Book

Other titles in this series are:

The glass gauntlet (2015)
The blazing bridge (2017)

Roy, Jennifer

★ **Mindblind**; [by] Jennifer Roy. Marshall Cavendish 2010 248p il $15.99

Grades: 7 8 9 10 11 **Fic**

1. Genius -- Fiction 2. Bands (Music) -- Fiction 3. Asperger's syndrome -- Fiction

ISBN 0-7614-5716-X; 978-0-7614-5716-9

LC 2010-6966

Fourteen-year-old Nathaniel Clark, who has Asperger's Syndrome, tries to prove that he is a genius by writing songs for his rock band, so that he can become a member of the prestigious Aldus Institute, the premier organization for the profoundly gifted.

"Mature readers will empathize with Nathaniel as his friends, Jessa and Cooper, do. This book is for teens who appreciate a story about self-discovery, dreams, and friendship." Voice Youth Advocates

★ **Yellow** star; by Jennifer Roy. Marshall Cavendish 2006 227p $16.95

Grades: 5 6 7 8 **Fic**

1. Jews -- Fiction 2. Poland -- Fiction 3. Holocaust, 1933-1945 -- Fiction

ISBN 0-7614-5277-X; 978-0-7614-5277-5

LC 2005-50788

Boston Globe-Horn Book Honor: Fiction and Poetry (2006)

From 1939, when Syvia is four and a half years old, to 1945 when she has just turned ten, a Jewish girl and her family struggle to survive in Poland's Lodz ghetto during the Nazi occupation.

"In a thoughtful, vividly descriptive, almost poetic prose, Roy retells the true story of her Aunt Syvia's experiences. . . . This book is a standout in the genre of Holocaust literature." SLJ

Rubens, Michael

Sons of the 613; Mike Rubens. Clarion Books 2012 305 p. (hardcover) $16.99

Grades: 7 8 9 10 **Fic**

1. Brothers -- Fiction 2. Bar mitzvah -- Fiction 3. Masculinity -- Fiction 4. Schools -- Fiction 5. Minnesota -- Fiction 6. Coming of age -- Fiction 7. Junior high schools -- Fiction 8. Jews -- United States -- Fiction 9. Family life -- Minnesota -- Fiction

ISBN 0547612168; 9780547612164

LC 2011044352

In this book by Michael Rubens, "Isaac's parents have abandoned him for a trip to Italy in the final days before his bar mitzvah. And even worse, his hotheaded older brother, Josh, has been left in charge. . . . When Josh declares that there is more to becoming a man than memorization, the mad 'quest' begins for Isaac. . . . But when Isaac begins to fall for Josh's girlfriend, Leslie, the challenges escalate from bad to worse." (Publisher's note)

Ruby, Laura

The **clockwork** ghost; Laura Ruby. Harpercollins Childrens Books 2019 464 p. $17.99

Grades: 5 6 7 8 **Fic**

1. Twins -- fiction 2. Puzzles -- fiction 3. Buried treasure -- fiction
ISBN 0062306960; 9780062306968

In this book in the York series, by Laura Ruby, "it was only a few weeks ago that the Biedermann twins, Tess and Theo, along with their friend Jaime Cruz, followed the secrets of the Morningstarrs' cipher further than anyone had in its century-and a-half history. . . . But the Old York Cipher still isn't solved. . . . [I]f Tess, Theo, and Jaime want to discover what lies at the end of the puzzle . . . , they will need to press on." (Publisher's note)

"Ruby takes a classic puzzle mystery and compellingly draws it out, both in the time the puzzles take and by giving the characters room to contemplate their feelings." (Booklist)

The **shadow** cipher; by Laura Ruby ; illustrated by Dave Stevenson. Walden Pond Press 2017 496 p. map (York) $17.99

Grades: 5 6 7 8 9 **Fic**

1. Mystery fiction 2. Twins -- fiction 3. Puzzles -- fiction
ISBN 0062306936; 9780062306937

In this book in the York series, by Laura Ruby, illustrated by Dave Stevenson, "it was 1798 when the Morningstarr twins arrived in New York with a vision for a magnificent city. . . . Fifty-seven years later, the enigmatic architects disappeared, leaving behind for the people of New York the Old York Cipher--a puzzle laid into the shining city they constructed, at the end of which was promised a treasure beyond all imagining." (Publisher's note)

Other titles in this series are:
The clockwork ghost (2019)

Ruiz Zafón, Carlos, 1964-

Marina; Carlos Ruiz Zafon ; translated by Lucia Graves. Little, Brown & Co. 2014 336 p. (hardcover) $19

Grades: 8 9 10 11 12 **Fic**

1. Suspense fiction 2. Barcelona (Spain) -- Fiction 3. Love -- Fiction 4. Supernatural -- Fiction 5. Mystery and detective stories 6. Spain -- History -- 20th century -- Fiction
ISBN 0316044717; 9780316044714

LC 2013016666

In this novel by Carlos Ruiz Zafón, "15-year-old Oscar Drai suddenly vanishes from his boarding school in the old quarter of Barcelona. For seven days and nights no one knows his whereabouts. . . . His story begins in the heart of old Barcelona when he meets Marina and her father German Blau, a portrait painter." (Publisher's note)

"Set in Barcelona, Spain from late 1979 to May 1980, this gothic novel centers around 15-year-old boarding school student Oscar Drai. Instead of studying during his free time, the teen explores the city, and one day ends up in an area that seems deserted. Drawn in by music coming from an old dilapidated house, Oscar is given a scare by the owner, an eccentric and haunted German artist...With elements of romance, mystery, and horror, none of them overwhelming the other, this complex volume that hints at Mary Shelley's Frankenstein manages to weave together three separate stories for a cohesive and eerie result." SLJ

The **Midnight** Palace; translated by Lucia Graves. Little, Brown 2011 298p $17.99

Grades: 7 8 9 10 **Fic**

1. India -- Fiction 2. Twins -- Fiction 3. Orphans -- Fiction 4. Siblings -- Fiction 5. Demonology -- Fiction 6. Calcutta (India) -- Fiction 7. Secret societies -- Fiction
ISBN 978-0-316-04473-8; 0-316-04473-3

LC 2010-43131

Original Spanish edition 1994

When a mysterious threat reenters the lives of twins Ben and Sheere, separated as babies and reunited as teenagers in 1930s Calcutta, the siblings must confront an unspeakable terror, with the help of their secret society of fellow orphans.

"The sense of dread and mystery that pervades the story, and the themes of lost innocence and sacrifice keep readers turning the pages." SLJ

★ The **Prince** of Mist; translated by Lucia Graves. Little, Brown 2010 320p $17.99

Grades: 6 7 8 9 10 **Fic**

1. Dead -- Fiction 2. Magic -- Fiction 3. Siblings -- Fiction 5. Shipwrecks -- Fiction 4. Supernatural -- Fiction 5. Europe -- History -- 1918-1945 -- Fiction
ISBN 978-0-316-04477-6; 0-316-04477-6

LC 2009-51256

In 1943, in a seaside town where their family has gone to be safe from war, thirteen-year-old Max Carver and sister, fifteen-year-old Alicia, with new friend Roland, face off against an evil magician who is striving to complete a bargain made before he died.

"Zafon is a master storyteller. From the first page, the reader is drawn into the mystery and suspense that the young people encounter when they move into the Fleischmann house. . . . This book can be read and enjoyed by every level of reader." Voice Youth Advocates

Rundell, Katherine

★ **Cartwheeling** in thunderstorms; Katherine Rundell. Simon & Schuster Books for Young Readers 2014 256 p. (hardcover) $16.99

Grades: 4 5 6 7 8 **Fic**

1. School stories 2. Bullies -- Fiction 3. Orphans -- Fiction 4. Boarding schools -- Fiction 5. Interpersonal relations -- Fiction 6. Zimbabweans -- England -- London -- Fiction
ISBN 1442490616; 9781442490611; 9781442490635

LC 2013021053

Boston Globe-Horn Book Award: Fiction (2015)

In this middle grade novel by Katherine Rundell, illustrated by Melissa Castrillón, "Wilhelmina Silver's world is golden. Living half-wild on an African farm with her horse, her monkey, and her best friend, every day is beautiful. But when her home is sold and Will is sent away to boarding school in England, the world becomes impossibly difficult. Lions and hyenas are nothing compared to packs of vicious schoolgirls." (Publisher's note)

"Wilhelmina, daughter of William Silver, white foreman of the Two Tree Hill Farm in Zimbabwe, leads a 'wildcat' life. Her idyll ends abruptly and tragically with her father's death from malaria, after which she's shipped off to boarding school in England. Rundell's finely drawn etchings of the people in Will's sphere and rich descriptions of African colonial farm life sprawl across the pages." Horn Book

Rooftoppers; by Katherine Rundell and illustrated by Terry Fan. Simon & Schuster Books for Young Readers 2013 288 p. (hardcover) $16.99

Grades: 4 5 6 7 **Fic**

1. Orphans -- Fiction 2. Mother-daughter relationship -- Fiction 3. Roofs -- Fiction 4. France -- Fiction 5. Paris (France) -- Fiction 6. Missing persons -- Fiction 7. Homeless persons -- Fiction 8. Guardian and ward -- Fiction

ISBN 1442490586; 9781442490581

LC 2012049469

In this book, by Katherine Rundell, "everyone thinks that Sophie is an orphan. . . . Her guardian tells her it is almost impossible that her mother is still alive. . . . When the Welfare Agency writes to her guardian, threatening to send Sophie to an orphanage, she takes matters into her own hands and flees to Paris to look for her mother. . . . She meets Matteo and his network of rooftoppers--urchins who live in the hidden spaces above the city. Together they scour the city in a search for Sophie's mother." (Publisher's note)

The **wolf** wilder; Katherine Rundell. Simon & Schuster Books for Young Readers 2015 231 p. (hardcover) $16.99

Grades: 4 5 6 7 8 **Fic**

1. Wolves -- Fiction 2. Human-animal relationship -- Fiction 3. Mother-daughter relationship -- Fiction 4. Mothers and daughters -- Fiction 5. Russia -- History -- Nicholas II, 1894-1917 -- Fiction

ISBN 1481419420; 9781481419420; 9781481419437

LC 2014048206

In this novel, by Katherine Rundell, "Feo's . . . mother trains domesticated wolves to be able to fend for themselves in the snowy wilderness of Russia, and Feo is following in her footsteps to become a wolf wilder. . . . But not everyone is enamored with the wolves, or with the fact that Feo and her mother are turning them wild. And when her mother is taken captive, Feo must travel through the cold, harsh woods to save her--and learn from her wolves how to survive." (Publisher's note)

"Her spirited, half-wild nature shines brightly on the page, even as her vulnerabilities endear her to readers' hearts. It is a wonderful thing to see Feo's quest inspire a nation to stand up and fight, and readers will cheer her on every step of the way." Booklist

Runyon, Brent

Surface tension; a novel in four summers. Alfred A. Knopf 2009 197p $16.99; lib bdg $19.99

Grades: 8 9 10 11 **Fic**

1. Vacations -- Fiction 2. Family life -- Fiction 3. New York (State) -- Fiction

ISBN 978-0-375-84446-1; 0-375-84446-5; 978-0-375-94446-8 lib bdg; 0-375-94446-X lib bdg

LC 2008-9193

During the summer vacations of his thirteenth through his sixteenth year at the family's lake cottage, Luke realizes that although some things stay the same over the years that many more change.

"With sensitivity and candor, Runyon reveals how life changes us all and how these unavoidable changes can be full of both turmoil and wonder." Kirkus

Rupp, Rebecca

After Eli; Rebecca Rupp. 1st ed. Candlewick 2012 245 p. (hardcover) $15.99; (ebook) $15.99

Grades: 4 5 6 7 8 **Fic**

1. Bildungsromans 2. Family -- Fiction 3. Brothers -- Fiction 4. Bereavement -- Fiction 5. Death -- Fiction 6. Books and reading -- Fiction 7. Interpersonal relations -- Fiction

ISBN 0763658103; 9780763658106; 9780763661946

LC 2011048344

In this book, "Daniel, a wry and thoughtful narrator, looks back on the summer when he was 14, three years after his older brother, Eli, died in Iraq at age 22." Daniel's "memories of larger-than-life Eli and his lingering anger about his death" are interwoven with "Daniel's day-to-day challenges, including his dysfunctional family . . . ; his frustrations with his . . . friends; his attraction to Isabelle, a . . . newcomer to town; and his nascent friendship with school outcast Walter." (Publishers Weekly)

Octavia Boone's big questions about life, the universe, and everything. Candlewick Press 2010 185p $15.99

Grades: 5 6 7 8 **Fic**

1. School stories 2. Vermont -- Fiction 3. Religion -- Fiction 4. Family life -- Fiction 5. Christian life -- Fiction

ISBN 978-0-7636-4491-8; 0-7636-4491-9

LC 2009-47408

Seventh-grader Octavia puzzles over life's biggest questions when her mother seems to find the answers in a conservative Christian church, while her artist father believes the writings of Henry David Thoreau hold the key.

"This hopeful novel highlights the resilience of children and the courage of those who seek truth in a complicated world." Publ Wkly

Russell, Chris

Songs about a girl; Chris Russell. Flatiron Books 2017 362 p. (paperback) $10.99

Grades: 7 8 9 10 **Fic**

1. Fame -- Fiction 2. Photography -- Fiction 3. Bands (Music) -- Fiction 4. Bullying -- Fiction 5. Popular music -- Fiction 6. Single-parent families -- Fiction

ISBN 1250095166; 9781250095169; 9781250095152

LC 2017003061

In this book, by Chris Russell, "when former classmate Olly Samson . . . ask[ed Charlie Bloom] . . . to take backstage pictures of his new band, she takes him up on it. . . . But Olly's band, Fire&Lights, isn't playing ordinary gigs. They're stars on the rise . . . . As the boys' rivalry threatens to tear the band apart, Charlie stumbles on a secret about the band--and herself--hidden within the lyrics of their new #1 single." (Publisher's note)

Russell, Rachel Renée

Locker hero; Rachel Renée Russell ; with Nikki Russell and Erin Russell. Aladdin 2016 320 p. illustrations (The misadventures of Max Crumbly) $13.99

Grades: 3 4 5 6 **Fic**

1. Teenage boys -- Fiction 2. Middle schools -- Fiction 3. Bullies -- fiction

ISBN 1481460013; 9781481460019

"Max Crumbly is about to face the scariest place he's ever been: South Ridge Middle School. There's a lot that's great about his new school, but there's also one big problem--Doug, the school bully whose hobby is stuffing Max in his locker. . . . But that doesn't mean Max won't do his best to be the hero his school needs!" (Publisher's note)

Other titles in this series are:
Middle school mayhem (2017)
Masters of mischief (2019)

Tales from a not-so-fabulous life; Rachel Renee Russell. 1st Aladdin ed.; Aladdin 2009 282 p. illustrations (Dork diaries) $13.99

Grades: 4 5 6 7 **Fic**

1. Artists -- Fiction 2. Diaries -- Fiction 3. Schools -- Fiction 4. Friendship -- Fiction 5. Popularity -- Fiction

ISBN 9781416986553; 1416980067; 9781416980063

LC 2008048567

In this book in the Dork Diaries series, by Rachel Renee Russell, "Nikki confesses all in her first diary ever: her epic battle with her mom for an iPhone, meeting her new soon-to-be BFFs Chloe and Zoey, falling for adorably sweet crush Brandon, dealing with her zany little sister Brianna's antics--and the immediate clashes with mean girl Mackenzie, who becomes Nikki's rival in a schoolwide art competition." (Publisher's note)

"Nikki's journey of self-discovery will appeal to preadolescent readers struggling to find their places in the world." Kirkus

Other titles in this series are:

Tales from a not-so-friendly frenemy (2016)

Tales from a not-so-secret crush (2017)

Rutkoski, Marie

The **Cabinet** of Wonders; [by] Marie Rutkoski. Farrar Straus Giroux 2008 258p (The Kronos Chronicles) $16.95; pa $6.99

Grades: 5 6 7 8 **Fic**

1. Fantasy fiction 2. Romanies -- Fiction

ISBN 978-0-374-31026-4; 0-374-31026-2; 978-0-312-60239-0 pa; 0-312-60239-1 pa

LC 2007037702

Twelve-year-old Petra, accompanied by her magical tin spider, goes to Prague hoping to retrieve the enchanted eyes the Prince of Bohemia took from her father, and is aided in her quest by a Roma boy and his sister.

"Add this heady mix of history and enchantment to the season's list of astonishingly accomplished first novels. . . . Infusions of folklore (and Rutkowski's embellishments of them) don't slow the fast plot but more deeply entrance readers." Publ Wkly

Other titles in this series are:

The Celestial Globe (2009)

The Jewel of the Kalderash (2011)

The **Celestial** Globe. Farrar Straus Giroux 2010 296p (The Kronos Chronicles) $16.99

Grades: 5 6 7 8 **Fic**

1. Fantasy fiction 2. Magic -- Fiction 3. Princes -- Fiction

ISBN 978-0-374-31027-1; 0-374-31027-0

LC 2008-35599

Sequel to: The Cabinet of Wonders (2008)

Thirteen-year-old Petra, her tin spider Astrophil, and their Roma friends Neel and Tomik are surprised by revelations about Dee, Kit, and Petra's father as they face Prince Rodolfo of Bohemia, who will do anything to possess a powerful object, the Celestial Globe

"This stellar sequel to The Cabinet of Wonders surpasses its predecessor by navigating the intelligent fantasy adventure outside 16th-century Bohemia and deepening the scope of its magic. . . . Strong characters and fast-paced plotting let this compelling installment stand independently, but the ending will leave readers eager for the next." Publ Wkly

The **Jewel** of the Kalderash. Farrar Straus Giroux 2011 320p (The Kronos Chronicles) $16.99

Grades: 5 6 7 8 **Fic**

1. Fantasy fiction 2. Magic -- Fiction 3. Kings and rulers -- Fiction

ISBN 978-0-374-33678-3; 0-374-33678-4

LC 2010037716

Fourteen-year-old Petra, her tin spider Astrophil, and their friends become entangled in the competition for the Roma crown, then set out for Prague in hopes of finally finding a cure for Petra's father.

"Short, action-packed chapters lead to a climax of heroic courage, violent horror and tragic sacrifice, and an epilogue perfectly admixes restrained melancholy and tender hope. Thrilling, heartrending and unexpectedly sweet; Petra's adventures could not have had a more satisfying conclusion." Kirkus

The **winner's** crime; Marie Rutkoski. First edition Farrar Straus & Giroux 2015 416 p. (The winner's trilogy) (hardback) $17.99

Grades: 7 8 9 10 11 12 **Fic**

1. Fantasy fiction 2. Romance fiction 3. Secrets -- Fiction 4. Weddings -- Fiction 5. Love -- Fiction 6. Fantasy -- Fiction

ISBN 0374384703; 9780374384708

LC 2014025185

"Lady Kestrel has successfully bargained for limited independence for the Herrani people, but only at the price of her own freedom. Now betrothed to the feckless Imperial heir, she risks even more as a spy, while managing to convince everyone--most particularly Arin, once her slave, then her captor, now governor of Herran--of her ruthless devotion to tyrannical Valorian dominion." (Kirkus Reviews)

"A rich and complex story of political intrigue, missed opportunities, and thwarted trust fill the pages of this sequel to The Winner's Curse (2014). Rutkoski's world is splendid in its cruelty and beauty, with characters that continue to claim our hearts." Booklist

The **winner's** curse; Marie Rutkoski. Farrar Straus & Giroux 2014 368 p. (The winner's trilogy) (hardcover) $17.99

Grades: 7 8 9 10 11 12 **Fic**

1. Love -- Fiction 2. Slavery -- Fiction 3. Imperialism -- Fiction

ISBN 0374384673; 9780374384678

LC 2013000312

In this book, by Marie Rutkoski, "winning what you want may cost you everything you love. As a general's daughter in a vast empire that revels in war and enslaves those it conquers, seventeen-year-old Kestrel has two choices: she can join the military or get married. But Kestrel has other intentions. One day, she is startled to find a kindred spirit in a young slave up for auction. Arin's eyes seem to defy everything and everyone. Following her instinct, Kestrel buys him." (Publisher's note)

"Full-bodied characters explore issues of loyalty, class, and values (for example, arts versus military strengths), without sacrificing any of the relationship-related tension that is a hallmark of this kind of story." (Booklist)

Other titles in this series are:

The winner's crime (2015)

The winner's kiss (2016)

The **winner's** kiss; by Marie Rutkoski. Farrar, Straus & Giroux 2016 484 p. (Winner's trilogy) (hardback) $17.99

Grades: 7 8 9 10 11 12 **Fic**

1. Fantasy fiction 2. Love -- Fiction 3. War -- Fiction

ISBN 9780374384746; 9780374384739

LC 2015037277

In this book in the Winner's Trilogy, by Marie Rutkoski, "war has begun. Arin is in the thick of it with untrustworthy new allies and the empire as his enemy. Though he has convinced himself that he no longer loves Kestrel, Arin hasn't forgotten her. . . . In the frozen north, Kestrel is a prisoner in a brutal work camp. As she searches desperately for a way to escape, she wishes Arin could know what she sacrificed for him." (Publisher's note)

Ryan, Carrie

City of thirst; Carrie Ryan and John Parke Davis; illustrated by Todd Harris. Little, Brown & Co. 2015 400 p. illustrations (hardback) $17

Grades: 4 5 6 7 **Fic**

1. Magic -- fiction 2. Pirates -- fiction 3. Friendship -- fiction 4. Fantasy 5. Maps -- Fiction 6. Magic -- Fiction 7. Pirates -- Fiction 8. Friendship -- Fiction 9. Adventure and adventurers -- Fiction

ISBN 0316240842; 9780316240840

LC 2015008673

In this children's book by Carrie Ryan and John Parke Davis "when the magical waters of the Pirate Stream begin flooding Marrill's world, the only way to stop the destruction is to return to the Stream and find the source of the mysterious Iron Tide. Reunited with her best friend Fin . . . Marrill, her disbelieving babysitter, and the Enterprising Kraken crew must make the treacherous trek to the . . . world of Monerva and uncover the secrets of its long-lost wish machine." (Publisher's note)

The **map** to everywhere; by Carrie Ryan & John Parke Davis. Little, Brown & Co. 2014 448 p. illustrations (The map to everywhere) (hardcover) $17

Grades: 4 5 6 7 **Fic**

1. Maps -- Fiction 2. Magic -- Fiction 3. Wizards -- Fiction 4. Stealing -- Fiction 5. Adventure and adventurers -- Fiction

ISBN 031624077X; 9780316240772

LC 2013044752

In this juvenile novel, by Carrie Ryan and John Parke Davis, "to Master Thief Fin, an orphan from the murky pirate world of the Khaznot Quay, the Map is the key to finding his mother. To suburban schoolgirl Marrill, it's her only way home after getting stranded on the Pirate Stream, the magical waterway that connects every world in creation. With the help of a bumbling wizard and his crew, they must scour the many worlds of the Pirate Stream to gather the pieces of the Map to Everywhere." (Publisher's note)

"Multifaceted characters, high stakes, imaginative magic, and hints of hidden twists and complexities to come add up to a memorable start to a projected four-volume voyage." Kirkus

Ryan, Pam Muñoz

★ The **dreamer**; drawings by Peter Sís. Scholastic Press 2010 372p il $17.99

Grades: 4 5 6 7 **Fic**

1. Authors 2. Diplomats 3. Novelists 4. Nobel laureates for peace 5. Nobel laureates for literature 6. Father-son relationship -- Fiction

ISBN 978-0-439-26970-4; 0-439-26970-9

Boston Globe-Horn Book Award honor book: Fiction (2010)

Neftali finds beauty and wonder everywhere. He loves to collect treasures, daydream, and write—pastimes his authoritarian father thinks are for fools. Against all odds, Neftali prevails against his father's cruelty and his own crippling shyness to become one of the most widely read poets in the world, Pablo Neruda.

"Ryan loads the narrative with vivid sensory details. And although it isn't poetry, it eloquently evokes the sensation of experiencing the world as someone who savors the rhythms of words and gets lost in the intricate surprises of nature. The neat squares of Sis' meticulously stippled illustrations, richly symbolic in their own right, complement and deepen the lyrical quality of the book." Booklist

★ **Echo**; by Pam Muñoz Ryan. Scholastic Press 2015 585 p. $19.99

Grades: 4 5 6 7 8 **Fic**

1. Music -- Fiction 2. Fate and fatalism -- Fiction 3. Harmonica -- Fiction 4. Family life -- Fiction 5. Germany -- History -- Fiction 6. California -- History -- Fiction 7. Pennsylvania -- History -- Fiction

ISBN 0439874025; 9780439874021

LC 2014021482

Odyssey Honor Recording (2016)

Kirkus Prize: Young Readers' Literature (2015)

Newbery Honor Book (2016)

In this novel by Pam Muñoz Ryan, "lost and alone in a forbidden forest, Otto meets three mysterious sisters and suddenly finds himself entwined in a puzzling quest involving a prophecy, a promise, and a harmonica. Decades later, Friedrich in Germany, Mike in Pennsylvania, and Ivy in California each, in turn, become interwoven when the very same harmonica lands in their lives." (Publisher's note)

"The harmonica and the love of music serve as the unifying threads for these tales of young people who save the lives and spirits of their families and neighbors, each in a time marked by bigotry and violence. It's an ambitious device, but Ryan's storytelling prowess and vivid voice lead readers expertly through a hefty tome illuminated by layers of history, adventure, and the seemingly magical but ultimately very human spirit of music." Horn Book

★ **Esperanza** rising. Scholastic Press 2000 262p $15.95; pa $4.99

Grades: 5 6 7 8 **Fic**

1. California -- Fiction 2. Mexican Americans -- Fiction 3. Agricultural laborers -- Fiction

ISBN 0-439-12041-1; 0-439-12042-X pa

LC 00-24186

Esperanza and her mother are forced to leave their life of wealth and privilege in Mexico to go work in the labor camps of Southern California, where they must adapt to the harsh circumstances facing Mexican farm workers on the eve of the Great Depression

"Ryan writes movingly in clear, poetic language that children will sink into, and the [book] offers excellent opportunities for discussion and curriculum support." Booklist

Rylant, Cynthia

★ A **fine** white dust. Simon & Schuster 2000 106p $25; pa $4.99

Grades: 5 6 7 8 **Fic**

1. Religion -- Fiction 2. Friendship -- Fiction 3. Family life -- Fiction

ISBN 978-0-689-84087-6; 0-689-84087-X; 978-1-4169-2769-3 pa; 1-4169-2769-7 pa

A reissue of the title first published 1986 by Bradbury Press

A Newbery Medal honor book, 1987

The visit of the traveling Preacher Man to his small North Carolina town gives new impetus to thirteen-year-old Peter's struggle to reconcile his own deeply felt religious belief with the beliefs and non-beliefs of his family and friends

"Blending humor and intense emotion with a poetic use of language, Cynthia Rylant has created a taut, finely drawn portrait of a boy's growth from seeking for belief, through seduction and betrayal, to a spiritual acceptance and a readiness 'for something whole.'" Horn Book

★ **God** got a dog; Cynthia Rylant ; illustrated by Marla Frazee. 1st Beach Lane Books ed. Beach Lane Books 2013 48 p. ill. (hardcover) $17.99

Grades: 5 6 7 8 **Fic**

1. God -- Poetry 2. Picture books for children 3. Femininity of God -- Poetry 4. God -- Fiction 5. Novels in verse

ISBN 1442465182; 9781442465183

LC 2013005577

This book is an illustrated collection of poetry from Cynthia Rylant. A major theme is the multiplicity of God, which Maria Frazee's illustrations expand on, "depicting Him or Her as a black, tattooed nail artist; a middle-aged white woman eating by herself; a little dark-skinned boy on roller skates . . . ; a bearded, dark-skinned dude playing poker with Gabriel; a homeless black woman. An illustration appears opposite each poem." (Kirkus Reviews)

★ **Missing** May. Orchard Bks. 1992 89p hardcover o.p. pa $5.99

Grades: 5 6 7 8 **Fic**

1. Death -- Fiction 2. West Virginia -- Fiction

ISBN 0-531-05996-0; 0-439-61383-3 pa

LC 91-23303

Awarded the Newbery Medal, 1993

After the death of the beloved aunt who has raised her, twelve-year-old Summer and her uncle Ob leave their West Virginia trailer in search of the strength to go on living

"There is much to ponder here, from the meaning of life and death to the power of love. That it all succeeds is a tribute to a fine writer who brings to the task a natural grace of language, an earthly sense of humor, and a well-grounded sense of the spiritual." SLJ

Sachar, Louis

★ The **cardturner**; a novel about a king, a queen, and a joker. Delacorte Press 2010 336p $17.99; lib bdg $20.99

Grades: 8 9 10 11 12 **Fic**

1. Uncles -- Fiction 2. Family life -- Fiction 3. Bridge (Game) -- Fiction

ISBN 978-0-385-73662-6; 0-385-73662-2; 978-0-385-90619-7 lib bdg; 0-385-90619-6 lib bdg

LC 2009-27585

"Alton gets roped into serving as a card turner for his great-uncle, Lester Trapp, a bridge whizz who recently lost his eyesight. . . . To Alton's surprise, he becomes enamored of the game and begins to bond with his crusty uncle. . . . With dry, understated humor, Alton makes the intricacies of bridge accessible, while his relationships with and observations about family members and friends . . . form a portrait of a reflective teenager whose life is infinitely enriched by connections he never expected to make." Publ Wkly

★ **Holes**; [by] Louis Sachar. 10th anniversary ed.; Farrar, Straus and Giroux 2008 265p $18

Grades: 5 6 7 8 **Fic**

1. Friendship -- Fiction 2. Buried treasure -- Fiction 3. Homeless persons -- Fiction 4. Juvenile delinquency -- Fiction

ISBN 978-0-374-33266-2; 0-374-33266-5

LC 2007045430

A reissue of the title first published 1998. Includes additional information about the author and his Newbery acceptance speech

National Book Award: Young People's Literature (1998)

As further evidence of his family's bad fortune which they attribute to a curse on a distant relative, Stanley Yelnats is sent to a hellish correctional camp in the Texas desert where he finds his first real friend, a treasure, and a new sense of himself

"This delightfully clever story is well-crafted and thought-provoking, with a bit of a folklore thrown in for good measure." Voice Youth Advocates

Small steps; [by] Louis Sachar. Delacorte Press 2006 257p $16.95; lib bdg $19.99

Grades: 5 6 7 8 **Fic**

1. Cerebral palsy -- Fiction 2. African Americans -- Fiction 3. Juvenile delinquency -- Fiction

ISBN 0-385-73314-3; 0-385-90333-2 lib bdg

LC 2005-09102

Sequel to Holes

Three years after being released from Camp Green Lake, Armpit is trying hard to keep his life on track, but when his old pal X-Ray shows up with a tempting plan to make some easy money scalping concert tickets, Armpit reluctantly goes along.

This "is a story of redemption, of the triumph of the human spirit, of self-sacrifice, and of doing the right thing. Sachar is a master storyteller who creates memorable characters." SLJ

Saeed, Aisha

Amal unbound; Aisha Saeed. Nancy Paulsen Books 2018 240 p. (hardback : alk. paper) $17.99

Grades: 4 5 6 7 8 **Fic**

1. Pakistan -- Fiction 2. Family life -- Fiction 3. Contract labor -- Fiction 4. Courage -- Fiction 5. Conduct of life -- Fiction 6. Indentured servants -- Fiction 7. Family life -- Pakistan -- Fiction

ISBN 9780399544682

LC 2017038160

In this middle-grade novel, by Aisha Saeed, "life is quiet and ordinary in Amal's Pakistani village, but she had no complaints, and besides, she's busy pursuing her dream of becoming a teacher one day. . . . Then the unimaginable happens--after an accidental run-in with the son of her village's corrupt landlord, Amal must work as his family's servant to pay off her own family's debt." (Publisher's note)

Saenz, Benjamin Alire

★ **He** forgot to say good-bye. Simon & Schuster 2008 321p $16.99

Grades: 8 9 10 11 **Fic**

1. Drug abuse -- Fiction 2. Mexican Americans -- Fiction

ISBN 978-1-4169-4963-3; 1-4169-4963-1

LC 2007-21959

Two teenaged boys with very different lives find that they share a common bond—fathers they have never met who left when they were small boys—and in spite of their differences, they become close when they each need someone who understands.

"The affirming and hopeful ending is well-earned for the characters and a great payoff for the reader. . . . Characters are well-developed and complex. . . . Overall it is a strong novel with broad teenage appeal." Voice Youth Advocates

Sage, Angie

Magyk; Septimus Heap, book one. illustrations by Mark Zug. Katherine Tegen Books 2005 576p il $16.99; lib bdg $17.89; pa $7.99

Grades: 5 6 7 8 **Fic**

1. Fantasy fiction 2. Magic -- Fiction

ISBN 0-06-057731-2; 0-06-057732-0 lib bdg; 0-06-057733-9 pa

LC 2003-28185

After learning that she is the Princess, Jenna is whisked from her home and carried toward safety by the Extraordinary Wizard, those she always believed were her father and brother, and a young guard known only as Boy 412, pursued by agents of those who killed her mother ten years earlier.

"Youngsters will lose themselves happily in Sage's fluent, charismatic storytelling, which enfolds supportive allies and horrific enemies, abundant quirky details, and poignant moments of self-discovery." Booklist

Other titles in this series are:
Flyte (2006)
Physik (2007)
Queste (2008)
Syren (2009)
Darke (2011)

Pathfinder; Angie Sage ; illustrations by Mark Zug. Katherine Tegen Books, an imprint of HarperCollinsPublishers 2014 480 p. (Septimus Heap : TodHunter moon) (hardback) $17.99
Grades: 5 6 7 Fic

1. Imaginary places 2. Magic -- Fiction 3. Fantasy 4. Wizards -- Fiction 5. Kidnapping -- Fiction
ISBN 0062272454; 9780062272454
LC 2013051281

This novel by Angie Sage "tells the story of Alice TodHunter Moon, a young PathFinder who leaves her seaside village in search of her friend Ferdie. Rumor has it that Ferdie has been taken by mysterious creatures called Garmin under orders from the malevolent Lady." (Publisher's note)

"After Tod's father and village are kidnapped, she must learn PathFinder Magyk and team up with Septimus to save them. Fans of the Septimus Heap books will enjoy seeing the old characters in this spinoff series, but the sheer number of cameos bogs down the plot; new secondary characters are flat, but Tod has a clear, relatable voice." Horn Book

Another title in this series is:
Sandrider (2015)

SandRider; Angie Sage ; illustrations by Mark Zug. Katherine Tegen Books, an imprint of HarperCollinsPublishers 2015 480 p. illustrations (TodHunter Moon) (hardback) $17.99
Grades: 5 6 7 Fic

1. Magic -- Fiction 2. Adventure fiction 3. Friendship -- Fiction 4. Fantasy 5. Wizards -- Fiction 6. Apprentices -- Fiction 7. Imaginary creatures -- Fiction
ISBN 0062272489; 9780062272485
LC 2015005851

This novel by Angie Sage and illustrated by Mark Zug "taking place seven years after the events of the original Septimus Heap series, TodHunter Moon tells the story of Alice TodHunter Moon, a young PathFinder who comes to the Castle with a Magyk all her own. In this second book, Tod sets out for the Desert of the Singing Sands to retrieve the Egg of the Orm--a journey that will test not only her Magykal and PathFinding skills but her friendships, too." (Publisher's note)

"This exciting and accessible adventure tale rests solidly on Sage's appreciable skills as a story spinner and is supported by Zug's chapter-opening illustrations (final art not seen). Another great read-aloud choice for the young set and a delight for all ages." Booklist

Sequel to "Pathfider"

StarChaser; Angie Sage ; illustrations by Mark Zug. Katherine Tegen Books, an imprint of HarperCollinsPublishers 2016 496 p. illustrations (TodHunter Moon) (hardback) $17.99; (ebook) $16.99
Grades: 5 6 7 Fic

1. Magic -- fiction 2. Wizards -- fiction 3. Apprentices -- fiction 4. Fantasy fiction -- fiction
ISBN 0062272519; 9780062272515; 9780062272539
LC 2016019328

In this third book in the World of Septimus Heap series by Angie Sage, illustrated by Mark Zug, "Tod must find a replacement Egg of the Orm before the Castle—and all its Magyk—disappears forever. . . . Almost one year ago, Alice TodHunter Moon left her PathFinder village to become Apprentice to ExtraOrdinary Wizard Septimus Heap. Now in faraway lands, the Castle is in peril. . . . Can she save the Castle while evading the fate that befell her mother?" (Publisher's note)

"Pencil drawings sprinkled throughout enhance the narrative and substantiate the book's setting in an alternative, medieval-ish, largely white world. A delightful ending to a Magykal ride." Kirkus

Saint-Exupery, Antoine de

The **little** prince; written and illustrated by Antoine de Saint-Exupery; translated from the French by Richard Howard. Harcourt 2000 83p il $18; pa $12
Grades: 4 5 6 7 8 9 10 11 12 Adult Fic

1. Fantasy fiction 2. Princes -- Fiction 3. Air pilots -- Fiction 4. Extraterrestrial beings -- Fiction
ISBN 0-15-202398-4; 0-15-601219-7 pa
LC 99-50439

A new translation of the title first published 1943 by Reynal & Hitchcock

"This many-dimensional fable of an airplane pilot who has crashed in the desert is for readers of all ages. The pilot comes upon the little prince soon after the crash. The prince tells of his adventures on different planets and on Earth as he attempts to learn about the universe in order to live peacefully on his own small planet. A spiritual quality enhances the seemingly simple observations of the little prince." Shapiro. Fic for Youth. 3d edition

Salazar, Aida

The **moon** within; Aida Salazar. Arthur A. Levine Books, an imprint of Scholastic Inc. 2019 240 p. (hardcover : alk. paper) $17.99
Grades: 4 5 6 7 8 Fic

1. Novels in verse 2. Friendship -- Fiction 3. Best friends -- Fiction 4. Transgender people -- Fiction 5. Mothers and daughters -- Fiction 6. Racially mixed people -- Fiction 7. Life change events -- fiction 8. Transgender children -- fiction 9. Racially mixed children -- fiction 10. Racially mixed families -- fiction 11. Puberty -- Rites and ceremonies -- fiction 12. Menstrual cycle -- Rites and ceremonies -- fiction
ISBN 1338283375; 1338283383; 9781338283372; 9781338283389
LC 2018017565

In this children's book, by Aida Salazar, "Celi Rivera's life swirls with questions. About her changing body. Her first attraction to a boy. And her best friend's exploration of what it means to be genderfluid. But most of all, her mother's insistence she have a moon ceremony when her first period arrives. It's an ancestral Mexican ritual that Mima and her community have reclaimed, but Celi promises she will NOT be participating." (Publisher's note)

"An excellent addition for upper middle grade and middle school readers, especially for maturing tweens in the midst of puberty." (School Library Journal)

Saldaña, René

Dancing with the devil and other tales from beyond; = Bailando con el diablo y otros cuentos del más allá. by = por René Saldaña, Jr. ; Spanish translation by = traducción al español de Gabriela Baeza Ventura. Piñata Books 2012 81 p. (alk. paper) $9.95

Grades: 5 6 7 8 9 **Fic**

1. Short stories 2. Mexican Americans -- Fiction 3. Mexican Americans -- fiction 4. Spanish language materials -- Bilingual 5. Children's stories, American -- Translations into Spanish

ISBN 1558857443; 9781558857445

LC 2012008729

Author Rene Saldaña Jr. presents a book of short stories. "Lauro and Miguel run for their lives--with La Llorona's cold breath on their necks-- after being caught smoking cigarettes down by the river. There's Felipe, who's so determined to win back the Peñitas Grand Master Marble Champion title that he's willing to make a deal for a shooter with a supernatural edge. And when Louie's leg swells up after he cuts his toe playing with a knife, he can't help but wonder if his mom's warning could be true." (Publisher's note)

Salisbury, Graham

★ **Eyes** of the emperor. Wendy Lamb Books 2005 228p hardcover o.p. pa $6.99

Grades: 7 8 9 10 **Fic**

1. Japanese Americans -- Fiction 2. World War, 1939-1945 -- Fiction

ISBN 0-385-72971-5; 0-440-22956-1 pa

LC 2004-15142

Following orders from the United States Army, several young Japanese American men train K-9 units to hunt Asians during World War II.

"Based on the experiences of 26 Hawaiian-Americans of Japanese ancestry, this novel tells an uncomfortable story. Yet it tells of belief in honor, respect, and love of country." Libr Media Connect

Hunt for the bamboo rat; by Graham Salisbury. Wendy Lamb Books, an imprint of Random House Children's Books 2014 336 p. illustration (hardback) $16.99

Grades: 6 7 8 9 10 **Fic**

1. Spy stories 2. Japanese Americans -- Fiction 3. World War, 1939-1945 -- Fiction 4. Spies -- Fiction 5. Survival -- Fiction 6. Prisoners of war -- Fiction 7. World War, 1939-1945 -- Philippines -- Fiction 8. Philippines -- History -- Japanese occupation, 1942-1945 -- Fiction

ISBN 0375842667; 9780375842665; 9780375940705

LC 2014005743

This book by Graham Salisbury is set "in August 1941. . . . Seventeen-year-old Zenji Watanabe . . . is Nisei, speaks perfect English and Japanese, and is recruited by the U.S. Army as a special undercover intelligence agent working in Manila, code name: Bamboo Rat. It's a dangerous assignment to be in the Philippines on the eve of Japanese invasion and imminent American involvement. He's American, but looks Japanese, and soon finds himself caught in the middle." (Horn Book Magazine)

"Written in short, rapid-fire paragraphs that move the plot along at a brisk pace, the story will leave readers spellbound. A gripping saga of wartime survival. (maps, author's note, glossary, resources)" Kirkus

Lord of the deep. Delacorte Press 2001 182p hardcover o.p. pa $7.99

Grades: 5 6 7 8 **Fic**

1. Hawaii -- Fiction 2. Fishing -- Fiction 3. Stepfathers -- Fiction

ISBN 0-385-72918-9; 0-440-22911-1 pa

LC 00-60280

Boston Globe-Horn Book Award: Fiction (2002)

Working for Bill, his stepfather, on a charter fishing boat in Hawaii teaches thirteen-year-old Mikey about fishing, and about taking risks, making sacrifices, and facing some of life's difficult choices

"With its vivid Hawaiian setting, this fine novel is a natural for book-discussion groups that enjoy pondering moral ambiguity. Its action-packed scenes will also lure in reluctant readers." SLJ

★ **Night** of the howling dogs; a novel. Wendy Lamb Books 2007 191p $16.99; lib bdg $19.99; pa $6.50

Grades: 5 6 7 8 **Fic**

1. Hawaii -- Fiction 2. Camping -- Fiction 3. Tsunamis -- Fiction 4. Earthquakes -- Fiction 5. Boy Scouts of America -- Fiction 6. Survival after airplane accidents, shipwrecks, etc. -- Fiction

ISBN 978-0-385-73122-5; 978-0-385-90146-8 lib bdg; 978-0-440-23839-3 pa

LC 2007-07054

In 1975, eleven Boy Scouts, their leaders, and some new friends camping at Halape, Hawaii, find their survival skills put to the test when a massive earthquake strikes, followed by a tsunami.

This is a "vivid adventure. . . . Salisbury weaves Hawaiian legend into the modern-day narrative to create a haunting, unusual novel." Booklist

Samphire, Patrick

Secrets of the dragon tomb; Patrick Samphire. Henry Holt & Co. 2016 336 p. (hardcover) $16.99

Grades: 4 5 6 7 **Fic**

1. Adventure fiction 2. Mars -- Fiction 3. Science fiction 4. Kidnapping -- Fiction 5. Family life -- Fiction 6. Eccentrics and eccentricities -- Fiction

ISBN 9780805099065

LC 2015004517

In this juvenile novel, by Patrick Samphire, "twelve-year-old Edward Sullivan wishes his life on 19th-century British Mars were more like the adventures he reads about in his Thrilling Martian Tales magazine. . . . But before he knows it, he is tangled up in a madcap adventure. . . . It seems that Edward's father's latest invention, the water abacus, is thought to be the key to perhaps one of the last of the great dragon tombs of Mars." (School Library Journal)

"Abundant humor, intricate worldbuilding details, and precisely timed slapstick and mayhem mesh as neatly as the gears and levers of the water abacus, producing a gorgeously articulated clockwork of a novel." Pub Wkly

Sanchez, Alex

Bait. Simon & Schuster Books for Young Readers 2009 239p $16.99

Grades: 7 8 9 10 **Fic**

1. Stepfathers -- Fiction 2. Mexican Americans -- Fiction 3. Child sexual abuse -- Fiction

ISBN 978-1-4169-3772-2; 1-4169-3772-2

LC 2008-38815

Diego keeps getting into trouble because of his explosive temper until he finally finds a probation officer who helps him get to the root of his anger so that he can stop running from his past.

"This groundbreaking novel brings to life an appealing young man who is neither totally a victim nor a victimizer, one who struggles to handle conflicts that derail many young lives. . . . High interest and accessible, this coming-of-age story belongs in every collection." SLJ

Sanderson, Brandon, 1975-

Alcatraz versus the evil Librarians. Scholastic Press 2007 308p $16.99; pa $6.99

Grades: 4 5 6 7 **Fic**

1. Fantasy fiction 2. Librarians -- Fiction 3. Grandfathers -- Fiction
ISBN 0-439-92550-9; 978-0-439-92550-1; 0-439-92552-5 pa; 978-0-439-92552-5 pa

LC 2006-38378

On his thirteenth birthday, foster child Alcatraz Smedry receives a bag of sand which is immediately stolen by the evil Librarians who are trying to take over the world. Soon, Alcatraz is introduced to his grandfather and his own special talent, and told that he must use it to save civilization.

"Readers whose sense of humor runs toward the subversive will be instantly captivated. . . . This nutty novel isn't for everyone, but it's also sure to win passionate fans." Publ Wkly

Other titles about Alcatraz are:
Alcatraz versus the scrivener's bones (2008)
Alcatraz versus the Knights of Crystallia (2009)
Alcatraz versus the shattered lens (2010)

The **dark** talent; Alcatraz vs. the evil librarians. Brandon Sanderson, illustrated by Hayley Lazo. Starscape, a Tom Doherty Associates Book 2016 300 p. illustrations (Alcatraz vs. the evil librarians) $16.99

Grades: 4 5 6 7 **Fic**

1. Librarians -- Fiction 2. Imaginary places -- Fiction 3. Heroes and heroines -- Fiction 4. Fantasy 5. Humorous stories
ISBN 0765381400; 9780765381408

LC 2016288328

In this novel in the Alcatraz Versus the Evil Librarians series, by Brandon Sanderson, illustrated by Hayley Lazo, "Alcatraz Smedry has . . . defeated the army of Evil Librarians and saved the kingdom of Mokia. Too bad he managed to break the Smedry Talents. . . . Even worse, his father is trying to enact a scheme that could ruin the world, and his friend, Bastille, is in a coma. To revive her, Alcatraz must infiltrate the Highbrary . . . the seat of Evil Librarian power." (Publisher's note)

"As in previous volumes, the narrative is rife with bizarre situations, thrilling seat-of-the-pants action, and metafictional musings; the ending will set readers back on their heels." Horn Book

The **Rithmatist**; Brandon Sanderson. Tor Teen 2013 384 p. ill. (hardcover) $17.99

Grades: 7 8 9 10 **Fic**

1. Fantasy fiction 2. Magic -- Fiction
ISBN 0765320320; 9780765320322

LC 2012043417

In this young adult fantasy novel, by Brandon Sanderson, "Joel wants to be a Rithmatist. Chosen by the Master in a mysterious inception ceremony, Rithmatists have the power to infuse life into two-dimensional figures known as Chalklings. Rithmatists are humanity's only defense against the Wild Chalklings--merciless creatures that leave mangled corpses in their wake. Having nearly overrun the territory of Nebrask, the Wild Chalklings now threaten all of the American Isles." (Publisher's note)

Skyward; Brandon Sanderson. Delacorte Press 2018 528 p. (hardback) $19.99

Grades: 7 8 9 10 **Fic**

1. War stories 2. Air pilots -- Fiction 3. Extraterrestrial beings -- Fiction 4. War -- Fiction 5. Science fiction 6. Survival -- Fiction
ISBN 9780399555770; 9780399555787

LC 2018026175

In this book, by Brandon Sanderson, "Spensa's world has been under attack for decades. Now pilots are the heroes of what's left of the human race, and becoming one has always been Spensa's dream. Since she was a little girl, she has imagined soaring skyward and proving her bravery. But her fate is intertwined with her father's--a pilot himself who was killed years ago when he abruptly deserted his team, leaving Spensa's chances of attending flight school at slim to none." (Publisher's note)

Sands, Kevin

★ The **blackthorn** key; by Kevin Sands. Aladdin 2015 384 p. (hardcover) $17.99

Grades: 4 5 6 7 8 **Fic**

1. Friendship -- Fiction 2. Apprentices -- Fiction 3. Supernatural -- Fiction 4. London (England) -- Fiction 5. Secret societies -- Fiction 6. Great Britain -- History -- 1660-1688, Restoration -- Fiction 7. Pharmacists -- Fiction 8. London -- History -- 17th century -- Fiction 9. Great Britain -- History -- Charles II, 1660-1685 -- Fiction
ISBN 1481446517; 9781481446518

LC 2014048032

Sequel: Mark of the Plague (2016)

This book, by Kevin Sands, presents a "tale of alchemy and dark secrets set during the late-17th-century reign of King Charles II. Fourteen-year-old orphan Christopher Rowe is lucky to be apprenticed to a kindly apothecary, Master Benedict Blackthorn. But someone--the Cult of the Archangel, it is rumored--is murdering London's apothecaries, believing that members of the Apothecary's Guild are concealing a dangerous secret." (Publishers Weekly)

"This stunning and smart mystery is made even better by well-researched historical detail, intriguing characters, and genuinely funny moments." Kirkus

Sangster, Caitlin

Last star burning; by Caitlin Sangster. Simon Pulse 2017 396 p. (hardback) $18.99

Grades: 7 8 9 10 11 12 **Fic**

1. Adventure fiction 2. Runaway teenagers -- Fiction 3. Fugitives from justice -- Fiction 4. Survival -- Fiction 5. Epidemics -- Fiction
ISBN 9781481486132; 9781481486156

LC 2016046285

In this novel, by Caitlin Sangster, "when the government blames Sev for a horrific bombing, she must escape the city or face the chopping block. . . . Sev's only hope of survival lies with the most unlikely person--Howl, the chairman's son. Though he promises to lead her to safety, Howl has secrets, and Sev can't help but wonder if he knows more about her past . . . than he lets on." (Publisher's note)

"Brimming with rich detail in an Asian-inflected alternative world that's lightly touched with Maoist terminology and concepts and helmed by achingly real characters, Sevvy's story is thrilling to get lost in. . . . Incredibly immersive and tightly plotted." Kirkus

Other titles in this series are:
Shatters the sun (2018)

Sattar, Arshia

Ramayana; an illustrated retelling. by Arshia Sattar, illustrated by Sonali Zohra. Restless Books 2018 192 p. $19.99

Grades: 5 6 7 8 9 **Fic**

1. Hindu mythology -- fiction 2. Rama (Hindu deity) -- fiction 3. Sita (Hindu deity) -- fiction

ISBN 9781632061775

LC 2017944635

In this retelling of the Indian epic Ramayana, by Arshia Sattar, illustrated by Sonali Zohra, "Rama is a brave young prince who is forced into exile. His brother Lakshmana and his wife, . . . princess Sita, loyally follow him into the depths of the mysterious forest. . . . Ravana, the ten-headed demon king . . . kidnaps Sita. . . . To rescue her, Rama enlists the help of hundreds of thousands of magical monkeys and bears to fight the demon army and win her back." (Publisher's note)

Saunders, Kate

The **curse** of the chocolate phoenix; a companion to The Whizz Pop Chocolate Shop. Kate Saunders. Delacorte Press 2015 272 p. (hc) $16.99

Grades: 5 6 7 8 **Fic**

1. Cats -- Fiction 2. Magic -- Fiction 3. Twins -- Fiction 4. England -- Fiction 5. Witches -- Fiction 6. Time travel -- Fiction 7. London (England) -- Fiction 8. Brothers and sisters -- Fiction 9. Adventure and adventurers -- Fiction

ISBN 9780375991837; 9780385744720

LC 2014022137

In this juvenile novel, by Kate Saunders, sequel to "The Whizz Pop Chocolate Shop," "Oz and Lily have a top-secret mission. Alba the witch has gotten her hands on a magical chocolate phoenix and is plotting to use it for some serious evil. With the help of an army of rats and an unreliable talking cat, the children must pursue her not only across London but through time itself." (Publisher's note)

"Saunders weaves the supernatural with the ordinary with ease." Booklist

The **Whizz** Pop Chocolate Shop; Kate Saunders. 1st ed. Delacorte Press 2013 293 p. (hardcover) $16.99

Grades: 5 6 7 8 **Fic**

1. Chocolate -- Fiction 2. Fantasy fiction -- fiction 3. Cats -- Fiction 4. Magic -- Fiction 5. Twins -- Fiction 6. England -- Fiction 7. Immortality -- Fiction 8. London (England) -- Fiction 9. Brothers and sisters -- Fiction 10. Adventure and adventurers -- Fiction

ISBN 0385743017; 9780385743013

LC 2011053081

In this children's story, by Kate Saunders, "the family of eleven-year-old twins Oz and Lily have inherited [a house], together with the mysterious shop downstairs. Long ago, the shop's famous chocolate-makers . . . were clever sorcerers. Now evil villains are hunting for the secret of their greatest recipe. . . . This magic chocolate [has] the ability to destroy the world. . . . It's up to them to stop the villains and keep the magical chocolate recipe out of harm's way." (Publisher's note)

Savit, Gavriel

Anna and the Swallow Man; Gavriel Savit. Alfred A. Knopf 2016 240 p. illustrations $17.99

Grades: 8 9 10 11 12 **Fic**

1. Poland -- Fiction 2. Survival skills -- Fiction 3. World War, 1939-1945 -- Fiction 4. Survival -- Fiction 5. World War, 1939-1945 -- Poland -- Fiction 6. Poland -- History -- Occupation, 1939-1945 -- Fiction

ISBN 9780553513349; 9780553522068

LC 2014034472

This novel, by Gavriel Savit, is "set in Poland during the Second World War. . . . Anna Łania is just seven years old when the Germans take her father, a linguistics professor, during their purge of intellectuals in Poland. She's alone. And then Anna meets the Swallow Man. He is a mystery, strange and tall, a skilled deceiver with more than a little magic up his sleeve. And when the soldiers in the streets look at him, they see what he wants them to see." (Publisher's note)

"Full of sophisticated questions and advanced vocabulary, Savit's debut occasionally feels like an adult novel, but young readers with the patience for his gauzy pacing and oblique plot turns will be rewarded by a moving, thought-provoking story about coming-of-age in the midst of trauma." Booklist

Scanlon, Liz Garton

The **great** good summer; Liz Garton Scanlon. Beach Lane Books 2015 224 p. (hardcover) $16.99

Grades: 4 5 6 7 **Fic**

1. Summer -- fiction 2. Runaway children -- fiction 3. Runaways -- Fiction 4. Bus travel -- Fiction 5. Friendship -- Fiction 6. Christian life -- Fiction 7. Mothers and daughters -- Fiction

ISBN 1481411470; 9781481411479; 9781481411486

LC 2014014988

In this children's story, by Liz Garton Scanlon, "Ivy and Paul are both having a crummy summer. . . . Ivy's mama hasn't been herself since the spring, when wildfires destroyed everything. . . . Meanwhile, Paul is sad because NASA's space shuttle program is being shut down and now he will never be able to become an astronaut. . . . The two become an unlikely pair when they hatch a plan to find Mama and say goodbye to the space shuttle." (School Library Journal)

"Equal parts peculiar and poignant, Ivy's story will have readers giggling as they root for her to find everything she's looking for." Kirkus

Schlitz, Laura Amy

★ The **hired** girl; Laura Amy Schlitz. Candlewick Press 2015 400 p. $17.99

Grades: 7 8 9 10 **Fic**

1. Diaries -- Fiction 2. Young women -- Fiction 3. Household employees -- Fiction

ISBN 9780763678180

LC 2014955411

Boston Globe-Horn Book Fiction Honor Book (2016)

In this book, by Laura Amy Schlitz, "Joan Skraggs . . . yearns for real life and true love. But what hope is there for adventure, beauty, or art on a hardscrabble farm in Pennsylvania where the work never ends? Over the summer of 1911, Joan pours her heart out into her diary as she seeks a new, better life for herself—because maybe, just maybe, a hired girl cleaning and cooking for six dollars a week can become what a farm girl could only dream of—a woman with a future." (Publisher's note)

"A wonderful look into the life of strong girl who learns that she needs the love of others to truly grow up." SLJ

★ **Splendors** and glooms; Laura Amy Schlitz. Candlewick 2012 384 p. (reinforced trade ed.) $17.99

Grades: 4 5 6 7 **Fic**

1. Mystery fiction 2. Orphans -- Fiction 3. Kidnapping -- Fiction 4. Puppets and puppet plays -- Fiction 5. Witches -- Fiction 6. Blessing and cursing -- Fiction 7. London (England) -- History -- 19th century -- Fiction 8. Great Britain -- History -- Victoria, 1837-1901 -- Fiction

ISBN 0763653802; 9780763653804

LC 2011048366

John Newbery Honor Book (2013)

In this book by Laura Amy Schlitz "Clara Wintermute . . . invites . . . the master puppeteer, Gaspare Grisini, . . . to entertain at her birthday party. . . . When Clara vanishes that night, suspicion of kidnapping falls upon the puppeteer and, by association, Lizzie Rose and Parsefall. As they seek to puzzle out Clara's whereabouts, Lizzie and Parse uncover Grisini's criminal past." (Publisher's note)

Schmatz, Pat

★ **Bluefish**. Candlewick Press 2011 226p $15.99

Grades: 7 8 9 10 **Fic**

1. School stories 2. Literacy -- Fiction 3. Teachers -- Fiction
ISBN 978-0-7636-5334-7; 0-7636-5334-9

LC 2010044815

"Travis is missing his old home in the country, and he's missing his old hound, Rosco. Now there's just the cramped place he shares with his well-meaning but alcoholic grandpa, a new school, and the dreaded routine of passing when he's called on to read out loud. But that's before Travis meets Mr. McQueen, who doesn't take "pass" for an answer--a rare teacher whose savvy persistence has Travis slowly unlocking a book on the natural world. And it's before Travis is noticed by Velveeta, a girl whose wry banter and colorful scarves belie some hard secrets of her own." (Publisher's Note)

"A cast of richly developed characters peoples this work of contemporary fiction, told in the third person from Travis' point of view, with first-person vignettes from Velveeta's perspective peppered throughout. . . . A story rife with unusual honesty and hope." Kirkus

Schmidt, Gary D.

★ **Lizzie** Bright and the Buckminster boy. Clarion Books 2004 219p $15; pa $6.99

Grades: 7 8 9 10 **Fic**

1. Maine -- Fiction 2. Race relations -- Fiction
ISBN 0-618-43929-3; 0-553-49495-3 pa

LC 2003-20967

A Newbery Medal honor book, 2005

In 1911, Turner Buckminster hates his new home of Phippsburg, Maine, but things improve when he meets Lizzie Bright Griffin, a girl from a poor, nearby island community founded by former slaves that the town fathers—and Turner's—want to change into a tourist spot

"Although the story is hauntingly sad, there is much humor, too. Schmidt's writing is infused with feeling and rich in imagery. With fully developed, memorable characters and a fascinating, little-known piece of history, this novel will leave a powerful impression on readers." SLJ

★ **Okay** for now. Clarion Books 2011 360p il $16.99

Grades: 4 5 6 7 **Fic**

1. Moving -- Fiction 2. New York (State) -- Fiction 3. City and town life -- Fiction
ISBN 978-0-547-15260-8; 0-547-15260-4

LC 2010942981

National Book Award Finalist: Young People's Literature (2011)

"It's 1968. The Vietnam War and Apollo 11 are in the background, and . . . Doug Swieteck starts a new life in tiny Marysville, N.Y. . . . He may have moved away, but his cruel father and abusive brothers are still with him. . . . This is Schmidt's best novel yet—darker than The Wednesday Wars and written with more restraint, but with the same expert attention to voice, character and big ideas." Kirkus

★ **Orbiting** Jupiter; Gary D. Schmidt. Clarion Books, Houghton Mifflin Harcourt 2015 192 p. (hardback) $17.99

Grades: 6 7 8 9 **Fic**

1. Teenage fathers -- Fiction 2. Foster home care -- Fiction 3. Friendship -- Fiction 4. Child abuse -- Fiction 5. Emotional problems -- Fiction
ISBN 9780544462229

LC 2015001338

This young adult novel, by Gary D. Schmidt, tells the "story of Joseph, 14, who joins his family as a foster child. Damaged in prison, Joseph wants nothing more than to find his baby daughter, Jupiter, whom he has never seen. When Joseph has begun to believe he'll have a future, he is confronted by demons from his past that force a tragic sacrifice." (Publisher's note)

"The matter-of-fact narrative voice ensures that the tragic plot never overwhelms this wrenching tale of growth and loss." SLJ

★ **Pay** attention, Carter Jones; Gary Schmidt. Clarion Books, Houghton Mifflin Harcourt 2019 224 p. (hardback) $16.99

Grades: 4 5 6 **Fic**

1. Family life -- Fiction 2. Middle schools -- Fiction 3. Conduct of life -- Fiction 4. Butlers -- Fiction 5. Schools -- Fiction
ISBN 9780544790858

LC 2018033909

In this book, by Gary Schmidt, "Carter Jones opens the front door one morning to find an English butler on his doorstep. . . . Mr. Bowles-Fitzpatrick reforms the household with his wit . . . and commitment to decorum. As Carter deals with his father's deployment, Mr. Bowles-Fitzpatrick also takes on the role of emotional caretaker and support for Carter. Together, they play cricket and learn that the rules of the game are also the rules for a healthy and happy life." (School Library Journal)

"A rich and nuanced middle grade novel that will appeal to readers who feel a little on the outskirts." (School Library Journal)

★ **Trouble**. Clarion Books 2008 297p $16

Grades: 6 7 8 9 10 **Fic**

1. Death -- Fiction 2. Prejudices -- Fiction 3. Family life -- Fiction 4. Traffic accidents -- Fiction 5. Cambodian Americans -- Fiction
ISBN 978-0-618-92766-1; 0-618-92766-2

LC 2007-40104

Fourteen-year-old Henry, wishing to honor his brother Franklin's dying wish, sets out to hike Maine's Mount Katahdin with his best friend and dog, but fate adds another companion—the Cambodian refugee accused of fatally injuring Franklin—and reveals troubles that predate the accident.

"Schmidt creates a rich and credible world peopled with fully developed characters who have a lot of complex reckoning to do. . . . [The author's prose] is flawless, and Henry's odyssey of growth and understanding is pitch-perfect and deeply satisfying." Bull Cent Child Books

★ The **Wednesday** wars. Clarion Books 2007 264p pa $6.99; $16

Grades: 5 6 7 8 **Fic**

1. Poets 2. Authors 3. Dramatists 4. School stories
ISBN 054723760X; 0618724834; 9780547237602; 9780618724833

LC 2006-23660

A Newbery Medal honor book, 2008

During the 1967 school year, on Wednesday afternoons when all his classmates go to either Catechism or Hebrew school, seventh-grader Holling Hoodhound stays in Mrs. Baker's classroom where they read the plays of William Shakespeare and Holling learns something of value about the world he lives in. "Grades five to seven." (Bull Cent Child Books)

"The serious issues are leavened with ample humor, and the supporting cast . . . is fully dimensional. Best of all is the hero." Publ Wkly

Schmitt, Adam P.

Speechless; Adam P. Schmitt. Candlewick Press 2018 293 p. $16.99

Grades: 5 6 7 8 **Fic**

1. Teenage boys -- Fiction 2. Family secrets -- Fiction 3. Funeral rites and ceremonies -- Fiction 4. Cousins -- Fiction 5. Eulogies -- Fiction 6. Families -- Fiction 7. Speech anxiety -- Fiction 8. Public speaking -- Fiction 9. Boys -- Conduct of life -- Fiction

ISBN 1536200921; 9781536200928

LC 2018960057

In this book, by Adam Schmitt, "Jimmy has just learned from his mother that he has to say a few words at the funeral [of his cousin] the next day. . . . [Jimmy] draws on humor, heartfelt concern, and a good deal of angst while racking his brain . . . for a decent and meaningful memory to share. But it's not until faced with a microphone that the realization finally hits him: it's not the words that are spoken that matter the most, but those that are truly heard." (Publisher's note)

Schrefer, Eliot

★ **Endangered**; Eliot Schrefer. Scholastic Press 2012 264 p. (reinforced) $17.99

Grades: 7 8 9 10 11 12 **Fic**

1. Animal sanctuaries -- Fiction 2. Wildlife conservation -- Fiction 3. Congo (Democratic Republic) -- Fiction 4. Apes -- Fiction 5. Bonobo -- Fiction 6. Divorce -- Fiction 7. Wildlife rescue -- Fiction 8. Racially mixed people -- Fiction 9. Blacks -- Congo (Democratic Republic) -- Fiction 10. Children of divorced parents -- fiction 11. Animal rescue -- Congo (Democratic Republic) -- fiction

ISBN 0545165768; 9780545165761

LC 2012030877

National Book Award Finalist: Young People's Literature (2012)

This book by Eliot Schrefer was a 2012 National Book Award Finalist for Young People's Literature. "When one girl has to follow her mother to her sanctuary for bonobos, she's not thrilled to be there. It's her mother's passion, and she'd rather have nothing to do with it. But when revolution breaks out and their sanctuary is attacked, she must rescue the bonobos and hide in the jungle. Together, they will fight to keep safe, to eat, and to survive." (Publisher's note)

Gogi's gambit; Eliot Schrefer. Katherine Tegen Books 2019 352 p. (hardback) $16.99

Grades: 4 5 6 7 **Fic**

1. Fantasy 2. Magic -- Fiction 3. Monkeys -- Fiction 4. Rain forests -- Fiction 5. Rain forest animals -- Fiction

ISBN 9780062491114

LC 2018013965

In this book in The Lost Rainforest series, by Eliot Schrefer, "Caldera always existed in harmony between the creatures who walk by day and those who walk by night--until an ancient evil awakened. . . . Gogi, a shadowwalker monkey still learning to wield his fire powers, embarks on a quest with his friends . . . for a powerful object that can harness the magic of the eclipse to defeat the Ant Queen." (Publisher's note)

The **lost** rainforest; Mez's magic. by Eliot Schrefer, illustrated by Emilia Dziubak. Harpercollins Childrens Books 2018 368 p. $16.99

Grades: 4 5 6 7 **Fic**

1. Fantasy fiction 2. Magic -- fiction 3. Rain forests -- fiction

ISBN 0062491075; 9780062491077

In this book in the Lost Rainforest series, by Eliot Schrefer, illustrated by Emilia Dziubak, "Caldera . . . [is] divided into those animals who walk by night and those who walk by day. Nightwalker panthers, like young Mez and her . . . sister, have always feared daywalkers. . . . Until the eclipse. Now Mez has discovered that she can . . . enter the daylight world. . . . [B]ut she must rush to discover it after a mysterious stranger['s] warning. . . of a reawakened evil." (Publisher's note)

★ **Threatened**; Eliot Schrefer. Scholastic Press 2014 288 p. map (jacketed hardcover) $17.99

Grades: 7 8 9 10 11 12 **Fic**

1. Orphans -- Fiction 2. Chimpanzees -- Fiction 3. Animal rescue -- Fiction 4. Gabon -- Fiction 5. Adventure stories 6. Wildlife rescue -- Fiction 7. Orphans -- Gabon -- Fiction

ISBN 0545551439; 9780545551434

LC 2013018599

National Book Award Shortlist: Young People's Literature (2014)

In this juvenile story, by Eliot Schrefer, "Luc and Prof head into the rough, dangerous jungle in order to study the elusive chimpanzees. There, Luc finally finds a new family--and must act when that family comes under attack. . . . [It] is the story of a boy fleeing his present, a man fleeing his past, and a trio of chimpanzees who are struggling not to flee at all." (Publisher's note)

Schreiber, Joe

Game over, Pete Watson; by Joe Schreiber. Houghton Mifflin Harcourt 2014 224 p. (hardback) $16.99

Grades: 4 5 6 7 **Fic**

1. Humorous fiction 2. Spies -- Fiction 3. Video games -- Fiction 4. Father-son relationship -- Fiction

ISBN 0544157567; 9780544157569

LC 2013024335

In this book, by Joe Schreiber, "after he sells a vintage console of his dad's to the neighborhood exterminator, [Pete's] dad gets kidnapped before his eyes. Pete discovers that his father is a CIA agent and is now trapped in the gaming system, which also doubles as a database for government secrets. Aided by his geeky ex-best friend Wesley and Wesley's attractive older sister, Pete must stop the supervillain . . . by going into the game himself." (Bulletin of the Center for Children's Books)

"With rapid-fire plot twists, slapstick comedy, and interactive illustrations complete with an 'eight-bit' Pete animated through the page turns, this light read champions video-game history and skills." Horn Book

Schröder, Monika

The **dog** in the wood. Front Street 2009 163p $17.95

Grades: 6 7 8 9 **Fic**

1. Russians -- Fiction 2. Family life -- Fiction 3. Political prisoners -- Fiction 4. World War, 1939-1945 -- Fiction 5. Germany -- History -- 1933-1945 -- Fiction

ISBN 978-1-59078-701-4; 1-59078-701-3

LC 2009-04970

As World War II draws to an end, Russian soldiers occupy Schwartz, Germany, bringing both friendship and hardship to the family of ten-year-old Fritz, whose grandfather was a Nazi sympathizer, eventually forcing them to leave their farm, then arresting Fritz's mother and her hired hand.

"The action in this important addition of WWII literature will grab readers, and Schröder's story is an excellent, authentic portrait of children in war." Booklist

My brother's shadow. Farrar Straus Giroux 2011 217p $16.99

Grades: 6 7 8 9 10 **Fic**

1. Germany -- Fiction 2. Journalism -- Fiction 3. Family life --

Fiction 4. Political activists -- Fiction 5. World War, 1914-1918 -- Fiction
ISBN 978-0-374-35122-9; 0-374-35122-8
LC 2010033107

In 1918 Berlin, Germany, sixteen-year-old Moritz struggles to do what is right on his newspaper job, in his relationship with his mother and sister who are outspoken socialists, and with his brother, who returns from the war physically and emotionally scarred.

"In this nuanced and realistic work of historical fiction, Schröder . . . immerses readers in her setting with meticulous details and dynamic characters that contribute to a palpable sense of tension." Publ Wkly

Saraswati's way. Farrar Straus Giroux 2010 233p $15.99
Grades: 5 6 7 8 **Fic**
1. India -- Fiction 2. Education -- Fiction 3. Mathematics -- Fiction
ISBN 978-0-374-36411-3; 0-374-36411-7
LC 2009-37286

Leaving his village in rural India to find a better education, mathematically gifted, twelve-year-old Akash ends up at the New Delhi train station, where he relies on Saraswati, the Hindu goddess of knowledge, to guide him as he negotiates life on the street, resists the temptations of easy money, and learns whom he can trust.

"With skillfully integrated cultural details . . . and a fully realized child's story, Schröder presents a view, sobering and inspiring, of remarkably resilient young people surviving poverty without losing themselves." Booklist

Schroeder, Lisa

Chasing Brooklyn. Simon Pulse 2010 412p $15.99
Grades: 7 8 9 10 **Fic**
1. Novels in verse 2. Dreams -- Fiction 4. Bereavement -- Fiction
ISBN 978-1-4169-9168-7; 1-4169-9168-9
LC 2009-19442

As teenagers Brooklyn and Nico work to help each other recover from the deaths of Brooklyn's boyfriend—Nico's brother Lucca—and their friend Gabe, the two begin to rediscover their passion for life, and a newly blossoming passion for one another.

"Chasing Brooklyn is told in a verse format that enables the author to cut right to the emotional quick. The short sentences and minimal dialogue keep the focus on the pain and fear of the two main characters. . . . While the wrenching impact will leave readers raw, the ultimately hopeful ending is comforting. A quick read, but one with substance." SLJ

My secret guide to Paris; by Lisa Schroeder. First edition Scholastic Press 2015 216 p. $16.99
Grades: 4 5 6 **Fic**
1. Bereavement -- Fiction 2. Family life -- Fiction 3. Grandmothers -- Fiction 4. Paris (France) -- Fiction 5. Grandparent-grandchild relationship -- Fiction 6. Grief -- Fiction 7. France -- Fiction 8. Mothers and daughters -- Fiction 19. Family life -- France -- Paris -- Fiction
ISBN 9780545708081; 0545708087
LC 2014017073

In this book, by Lisa Schroeder, "Nora loves everything about Paris. . . . Of course, she's never actually been there -- she's only visited through her Grandma Sylvia's stories. And just when they've finally planned a trip together, Grandma Sylvia is suddenly gone. . . . She misses her grandmother terribly, but she still wants to see the city they both loved. So when Nora finds letters and a Paris treasure map among her Grandma Sylvia's things, she dares to dream again." (Publisher's note)

"The bittersweet circumstances of the Paris trip are offset by strong elements of wish fulfillment, including gowns and a fancy fashion show. This is a sweet, reassuring contemporary read about handling grief and reconnecting with family." Booklist

Another title in this series is:
Sealed with a secret (2016)

Schulz, Heidi

Hook's revenge; by Heidi Schulz ; illustrations by John Hendrix. Disney-Hyperion Books 2014 304 p. $16.99
Grades: 4 5 6 7 **Fic**
1. Fictional characters 2. Pirates -- Fiction 3. Revenge -- Fiction 4. Fathers and daughters -- Fiction 5. Characters in literature -- Fiction
ISBN 1423198670; 9781423198673
LC 2013045281

In this book, by Heidi Schulz, illustrated by John Hendrix, "[t]welve-year-old Jocelyn dreams of becoming every bit as daring as her infamous father, Captain James Hook. Her grandfather, on the other hand, intends to see her starched and pressed into a fine society lady. When she's sent to Miss Eliza Crumb-Biddlecomb's Finishing School for Young Ladies, Jocelyn's hopes of following in her father's fearsome footsteps are lost in a heap of dance lessons, white gloves, and way too much pink." (Publisher's note)

"A delightfully curmudgeonly narrator sets the tone for this fast-paced and witty reimagining of Barrie's Neverland. This time readers see the pirates, mermaids, cannibals, fairies, and Lost Boys through the eyes of thirteen-year-old Jocelyn, Captain Hook's unapologetically energetic daughter, who gleefully escapes finishing school and the horrors of corsets to join Smee in hunting down the infamous crocodile that finished off her father." Horn Book

The **pirate** code; by Heidi Schulz ; with illustrations by John Hendrix. Disney-Hyperion 2015 339 p. illustrations (Other titles in this series: Hook's revenge (2014)) (hardback) $16.99
Grades: 5 6 7 8 **Fic**
1. Kidnapping -- fiction 2. Pirates -- Fiction 3. Buried treasure -- Fiction 4. Characters in literature -- Fiction
ISBN 1484717171; 9781484717172
LC 2014049766

In this children's book by Heidi Schulz, illustrated by John Hendrix, "fresh off a fearsome encounter with the Neverland crocodile, Jocelyn Hook decides the most practical plan is to hunt down her father's famous fortune. The map proves to be a bit harder to crack . . . and she's convinced that . . . Peter Pan might be the only one with the answers. He doesn't really feel like helping her, so Jocelyn . . . kidnaps his mother." (Publisher's note)

"An imaginative adventure filled with humor and heart." Kirkus

Schwab, Victoria

City of ghosts; Victoria Schwab. Scholastic Press 2018 285 p. $17.99
Grades: 4 5 6 7 8 **Fic**
1. Ghost stories 2. Ghosts -- Fiction 3. Paranormal fiction 4. Psychics -- Fiction 5. Scotland -- Fiction 6. Best friends -- Fiction 7. Haunted places -- Fiction 8. Parapsychology -- Fiction 9. Edinburgh (Scotland) -- Fiction 10. Ghost television programs -- fiction
ISBN 1338111000; 9781338111002
LC 2018033242

In this book, by Victoria Schwab, "ever since Cass almost drowned . . . , she can pull back the Veil that separates the living from the dead. . . . When Cass's parents start hosting a TV show about the world's most haunted places, the family heads off to Edinburgh, Scotland. Here, graveyards, castles, and secret passageways teem with restless phantoms. And when Cass meets a girl who shares her 'gift,' she realizes how much she still has to learn about the Veil--and herself." (Publisher's note)

"This atmospheric ghost story from Schwab (the Monsters of Verity duology) chills and charms while challenging readers to face their fears. Courageous, quick-witted Cassidy inspires, her relationship with Jacob is tender, and the thrilling conclusion is sure to gratify." Pub Wkly

Other titles in this series are:
Tunnel of bones (2019)

The **Near** Witch. Hyperion Books 2011 282p $16.99
Grades: 7 8 9 10 **Fic**
1. Witches -- Fiction 3. Villages -- Fiction 4. Supernatural -- Fiction
ISBN 978-1-4231-3787-0; 1-4231-3787-6
LC 2010036289

Sixteen-year-old Lexi, who lives on an enchanted moor at the edge of the village of Near, must solve the mystery when, the day after a mysterious boy appears in town, children start disappearing.

"Part fairy tale, part legend with a little romance, this well-written mystery will capture the attention of teens." SLJ

Schwabach, Karen

The **storm** before Atlanta. Random House 2010 307p $16.99; lib bdg $19.99
Grades: 5 6 7 8 **Fic**
1. Freedom -- Fiction 2. Slavery -- Fiction 3. Soldiers -- Fiction 4. Runaway children -- Fiction 5. United States -- History -- 1861-1865, Civil War -- Fiction
ISBN 978-0-375-85866-6; 0-375-85866-0; 978-0-375-95866-3 lib bdg; 0-375-95866-5 lib bdg
LC 2010014514

In 1863 northwestern Georgia, an unlikely alliance forms between ten-year-old New York drummer boy Jeremy, fourteen-year-old Confederate Charlie, and runaway slave Dulcie as they learn truths about the Civil War, slavery, and freedom.

"Richly detailed and well paced, the story provides both well-developed characters and plenty of suspense and gore. For those who like to know the facts behind historical fiction, the author provides historical notes and selected sources. An appealing Civil War title for readers with strong stomachs." Kirkus

Schwartz, Ellen

Stealing home. Tundra Books 2006 217p pa $8.95
Grades: 5 6 7 8 **Fic**
1. Jews -- Fiction 2. Orphans -- Fiction 3. Family life -- Fiction 4. Racially mixed people -- Fiction
ISBN 978-0-88776-765-4 pa; 0-88776-765-6 pa

"Joey, an orphaned, mixed-race 10-year-old isn't the only one who has to make adjustments after he's taken in by Jewish relatives he never knew he had. Wondering why his mother never told him about her side of the family, Joey moves to Brooklyn—to find a warm welcome from Aunt Frieda, an instant ally in baseball-loving cousin Bobbie, and a decidedly cold shoulder from his grandfather. . . . Keenly felt internal conflicts, lightened by some sparky banter, put this more than a cut above the average." Booklist

Scott, Elaine

Secrets of the Cirque Medrano. Charlesbridge 2008 216p lib bdg $15.95
Grades: 4 5 6 7 **Fic**
1. Artists 2. Painters 3. Circus -- Fiction 4. Orphans -- Fiction 5. Restaurants -- Fiction 6. Paris (France) -- Fiction
ISBN 978-1-57091-712-7 lib bdg; 1-57091-712-4 lib bdg
LC 2007-2329

In the Paris village of Montmartre in 1904, fourteen-year-old Brigitte works long hours in her aunt's cafe, where she serves such regular customers as the young artist Pablo Picasso, encounters Russian revolutionaries, and longs to attend the exciting circus nearby. Includes author's note on the Picasso painting "Family of Saltimbanques"

This "places an interesting historical moment within the grasp of middle-schoolers." Kirkus

Scott, Michael

★ The **alchemyst**. Delacorte Press 2007 375p (The secrets of the immortal Nicholas Flammel) $16.99; lib bdg $19.99
Grades: 7 8 9 10 **Fic**
1. Magicians 2. Mathematicians 3. Alchemists 4. Astrologers 5. Biographers 6. Magic -- Fiction 7. Twins -- Fiction 8. Alchemy -- Fiction 9. Writers on science 10. Siblings -- Fiction 11. San Francisco (Calif.) -- Fiction
ISBN 978-0-385-73357-1; 0-385-73357-7; 978-0-385-90372-1 lib bdg; 0-385-90372-3 lib bdg
LC 2006-24417

While working at pleasant but mundane summer jobs in San Francisco, fifteen-year-old twins, Sophie and Josh, suddenly find themselves caught up in the deadly, centuries-old struggle between rival alchemists, Nicholas Flamel and John Dee, over the possession of an ancient and powerful book holding the secret formulas for alchemy and everlasting life.

"Scott uses a gigantic canvas for this riveting fantasy. . . . A fabulous read." SLJ

Other titles in this series are:
The magician (2008)
The sorceress (2009)
The necromancer (2010)
The warlock (2011)
The Enchantress (2012)

The **enchantress**; Michael Scott. Delacorte Press 2012 517 p. $18.99
Grades: 7 8 9 10 **Fic**
1. Atlantis -- Fiction 2. Monsters -- Fiction 3. Time travel -- Fiction 4. Flamel, Nicolas, d. 1418 -- Fiction 5. Magic -- Fiction 6. Twins -- Fiction 7. Alchemists -- Fiction 8. Supernatural -- Fiction 9. Brothers and sisters -- Fiction
ISBN 0385735359; 9780385735353
LC 2012006497

In this book, the final installment of the "Secrets of the Immortal Nicholas Flamel" series, "Nicholas Flamel and his beloved wife, Perenelle, are making a final stand to save San Francisco from an attack of monsters large and small, launched from Alcatraz Island by Quetzalcoatl. Twins Josh (Gold) and Sophie (Silver) are being staged to take power from Aten and become rulers of an overthrown Danu Talis 10,000 years earlier." (Booklist)

"[Scott] fully fleshes out his main characters in their final roles, realistically and sometimes surprisingly melding their lives, their deaths, and their futures. This is a powerful and tidy conclusion to [the] series." Booklist

The **magician**. Delacorte Press 2008 455p (The secrets of the immortal Nicholas Flamel) $16.99; lib bdg $19.99

Grades: 7 8 9 10 **Fic**

1. Authors 2. Magicians 3. Statesmen 4. Dramatists 5. Mathematicians 6. Alchemists 7. Astrologers 8. Biographers 9. Magic -- Fiction 10. Twins -- Fiction 11. Alchemy -- Fiction 12. Writers on science 13. Siblings -- Fiction 14. Writers on politics 15. Paris (France) -- Fiction 16. Political and social philosophers

ISBN 978-0-385-73358-8; 0-385-73358-5; 978-0-385-90373-8 lib bdg; 0-385-90373-1 lib bdg

LC 2007-51598

Sequel to: The alchemyst (2007)

Fifteen-year-old twins Sophie and Josh Newman continue their magical training in Paris with Nicholas Flamel, Scatty, and the Comte de Sant Germaine, pursued by Doctor Dee and the immortal Niccolo Machiavelli.

"Although the novel is essentially plot driven, the book's characters are well developed and engaging. The addition of historical figures in the story . . . add an appealing intrigue to the book. Teens who like fast-paced fantasies with lots of action . . . are sure to enjoy this new addition to the genre." Voice Youth Advocates

Followed by: The sorceress (2009)

The **necromancer**. Delacorte Press 2010 403p (The secrets of the immortal Nicholas Flamel) $18.99; lib bdg $21.99

Grades: 7 8 9 10 **Fic**

1. Magic -- Fiction 2. Twins -- Fiction 3. Siblings -- Fiction 4. Supernatural -- Fiction 5. Great Britain -- Fiction 6. London (England) -- Fiction

ISBN 978-0-385-73531-5; 0-385-73531-6; 978-0-385-90516-9 lib bdg; 0-385-90516-5 lib bdg

LC 2010003372

Sequel to: The sorceress (2009)

Back in London, fifteen-year-old twins Sophie and Josh Newman must determine whom they can and cannot trust as they search for both Scatty and an immortal who can teach Josh the magic of fire, while Doctor Dee and Machiavelli continue to seek power.

The **sorceress**. Delacorte Press 2009 502p (The secrets of the immortal Nicholas Flamel) $17.99; lib bdg $20.99

Grades: 7 8 9 10 **Fic**

1. Authors 2. Magicians 3. Statesmen 4. Dramatists 5. Mathematicians 6. Alchemists 7. Astrologers 8. Biographers 9. Magic -- Fiction 10. Twins -- Fiction 11. Alchemy -- Fiction 12. Writers on science 13. Siblings -- Fiction 14. Writers on politics 15. Supernatural -- Fiction 16. Great Britain -- Fiction 17. Political and social philosophers 18. Alcatraz Island (Calif.) -- Fiction

ISBN 978-0-385-73529-2; 0-385-73529-4; 978-0-385-90515-2 lib bdg; 0-385-90515-7 lib bdg

LC 2009000493

Sequel to: The magician (2008)

While armies of the Shadowrealms gather and Machiavelli goes to Alcatraz to kill Perenelle Flamel, fifteen-year-old twins Sophie and Josh Newman accompany the Alchemist to England to seek Gilgamesh.

"Master yarnspinner that he is, Scott expertly cranks up the suspense while keeping his now-large cast in quick motion. . . . Ending in a welter of revelations, reunions and unresolved plotlines, this page-turner promises plenty of action to come." Kirkus

Followed by: The necromancer (2010)

The **warlock**. Delacorte Press 2011 385p (The secrets of the immortal Nicholas Flamel) $18.99; lib bdg $21.99

Grades: 7 8 9 10 **Fic**

1. Authors 2. Magicians 3. Statesmen 4. Dramatists 5. Mathematicians 6. Alchemists 7. Astrologers 8. Biographers 9. Twins -- Fiction 10. Alchemy -- Fiction 11. Writers on science 12. Siblings -- Fiction 13. Writers on politics 14. Supernatural -- Fiction 15. Political and social philosophers 16. San Francisco (Calif.) -- Fiction

ISBN 978-0-385-73533-9; 0-385-73533-2; 978-0-385-90517-6 lib bdg; 0-385-90517-3 lib bdg; 978-0-375-89954-6 e-book

LC 2011005716

Fifteen-year-old Josh has chosen to side neither with his twin sister Sophie nor with the Alchemyst, Nicholas Flamel, but rather to fight alongside Dr. John Dee and the mysterious Virginia Dare, while the immortal Machiavelli and Billy the Kid follow the Elders' plans to set loose the monsters of Alcatraz on San Francisco and trigger the end of the humani race.

Scrimger, Richard

Viminy Crowe's comic book; Marthe Jocelyn, Richard Scrimger. Tundra Books of Northern New York 2014 317 p. illustrations (hardcover) $17.99

Grades: 4 5 6 7 **Fic**

1. Adventure fiction 2. Comic books, strips, etc. 3. Steampunk fiction 4. Caricatures and cartoons -- Fiction. 5. Congresses and conventions -- Fiction

ISBN 1770494790; 9781770494794; 9781770494800

LC 2013943886

"Is there a personality conflict? Oh, yes. Addy wants to go home; Wylder wants to stay and explore the world of Viminy Crowe's comic book. Do things go wrong? You bet they do, from the very start, when Addy loses her pet rat, Catnip, and almost gets shot by a Red Rider. All the while the actual comic book story is going on around them." (Publisher's note)

"A bathroom portal at ComicFest launches two kids, Wylder Wallace and Addy Crowe, into the pages of a comic book. Suspense builds as the kids' presence affects the story, their adventures shown (in interspersed comic panels) in Davila's clear, humorous illustrations. It's a clever concept that's well executed by Jocelyn and Scrimger." Horn Book

Sedgwick, Marcus

★ **Midwinterblood**; Marcus Sedgwick. Roaring Brook Press 2013 272 p. (hardcover) $17.99

Grades: 7 8 9 10 11 12 **Fic**

1. Reincarnation -- Fiction 2. Romance fiction -- fiction 3. Love -- Fiction 4. Islands -- Fiction 5. Scandinavia -- Fiction

ISBN 1596438002; 9781596438002

LC 2012013302

Printz Award Winner (2014)

Author Marcus Sedgwick presents seven stories about "an archaeologist who unearths a mysterious artifact, an airman who finds himself far from home, a painter, a ghost, a vampire, and a Viking." The stories "take place on the remote Scandinavian island of Blessed where a curiously powerful plant that resembles a dragon grows. . . . What secrets lurk beneath the surface of this idyllic countryside? And what might be powerful enough to break the cycle of midwinterblood?" (Publisher's note)

★ **Revolver**. Roaring Brook Press 2010 204p $16.99

Grades: 7 8 9 10 **Fic**

1. Death -- Fiction 2. Siblings -- Fiction 3. Arctic regions -- Fiction 4. Alaska -- Gold discoveries -- Fiction

ISBN 978-1-59643-592-6; 1-59643-592-5

First published 2009 in the United Kingdom

A Michael L. Printz honor book, 2011

In an isolated cabin, fourteen-year-old Sig is alone with a corpse: his father, who has fallen through the ice and frozen to death only hours earlier. Then comes a stranger claiming that Sig's father owes him a share of a horde of stolen gold. Sig's only protection is a loaded Colt revolver hidden in the cabin's storeroom.

"Tight plotting and a wealth of moral concerns—good versus evil; faith, love, and hope; the presence of God; survival in a bleak landscape; trusting the lessons parents teach—make this a memorable tale." Horn Book

★ **She** is not invisible; Marcus Sedgwick. Roaring Brook Press 2014 224 p. (hardback) $16.99

Grades: 7 8 9 10 11 12 **Fic**

1. Blind -- Fiction 2. Missing persons -- Fiction 3. Brothers and sisters -- Fiction 4. Fathers -- Fiction 5. Mystery and detective stories 6. People with disabilities -- Fiction

ISBN 1596438010; 9781596438019

LC 2013029561

In this book, by Marcus Sedgwick, "Laureth Peak's father has taught her to look for recurring events, patterns, and numbers - a skill at which she's remarkably talented. Her secret: She is blind. But when her father goes missing, Laureth and her 7-year-old brother Benjamin are thrust into a mystery that takes them to New York City where surviving will take all her skill at spotting the amazing, shocking, and sometimes dangerous connections in a world full of darkness." (Publisher's note)

"Laureth is sixteen, smart, self-doubting, and blind. She is also desperate to find her missing famous writer father -- desperate enough to boost her mother's credit card to buy two plane tickets from London to New York City, forge travel documents, and "abduct" her beloved seven-year-old brother in order to disguise her blindness... Laureth herself is worth the journey. The tricks she uses to negotiate in a sighted world.. her determination to fight the tendency of sighted people to treat blind people as stupid or deaf or, most insidiously, invisible -- all are presented matter-of-factly and sympathetically. Readers will applaud Laureth's believable evolution into a more confident -- and definitely more visible -- young woman." (Horn Book)

★ **White** crow. Roaring Brook Press 2011 234p $15.99

Grades: 8 9 10 11 12 **Fic**

1. Horror fiction 2. Villages -- Fiction 3. Friendship -- Fiction 4. Good and evil -- Fiction 5. Great Britain -- Fiction

ISBN 978-1-59643-594-0; 1-59643-594-1

LC 2010034053

"Sixteen-year-old Rebecca moves with her father from London to a small, seaside village, where she befriends another motherless girl and they spend the summer together exploring the village's sinister history." (Publisher's Note)

"Showing his customary skill with a gothic setting and morally troubled characters, Sedgwick keeps readers guessing to the very end." Publ Wkly

Selfors, Suzanne

Smells like dog. Little, Brown 2010 360p $15.99

Grades: 4 5 6 7 **Fic**

1. Dogs -- Fiction 2. Uncles -- Fiction 3. Buried treasure -- Fiction

ISBN 978-0-316-04398-4; 0-316-04398-2

When farm boy Homer Pudding's explorer-uncle dies and leaves him a droopy dog with a mysterious coin hidden on its collar, it leads him to The City, where they meet Madame La Directeur, the conniving head of the Natural History Museum, who is trying to steal the coin and take Homer's place in a secret society of adventurers.

"Full of fantasy, fun, and humorous dialogue, this will attract dog lovers, mystery enthusiasts, adventure addicts, and reluctant readers. A thoroughly enjoyable read." Voice Youth Advocates

Another title about Homer Pudding is:

Smells like treasure (2011)

Smells like treasure. Little, Brown and Company 2011 407p $15.99

Grades: 4 5 6 7 **Fic**

1. Mystery fiction 2. Adventure fiction 3. Dogs -- Fiction 4. Buried treasure -- Fiction 5. Secret societies -- Fiction

ISBN 978-0-316-04399-1; 0-316-04399-0

LC 2010041541

Sequel to: Smells like dog (2010)

Farm boy Homer faces another challenger for his uncle's spot in the society of Legends, Objects, Secrets, and Treasures but Dog's hidden ability to smell treasure guides the duo as clues lead them to fantastic mansions and hidden islands.

"The author weaves in enough details of the earlier book to refesh readers' memories in this droll, satisfying sequel. The suspense of the challenge . . . will keep readers turning the pages. . . . There was plenty of rip-roaring fun here." Kirkus

The **sweetest** spell; Suzanne Selfors. Walker & Co. 2012 404 p. (hardback) $16.99

Grades: 7 8 9 10 11 12 **Fic**

1. Fantasy fiction 2. Romance fiction 3. People with physical disabilities -- Fiction 4. Magic -- Fiction 5. Chocolate -- Fiction 6. Prejudices -- Fiction

ISBN 0802723764; 9780802723765

LC 2011034591

This book follows "Emmeline . . . an outcast among her people, the Kell. When the king enslaves the men and her village is destroyed in a flood, Emmeline is taken in by Owen Oak and his family. She discovers that she can churn butter into chocolate -- a food that's been lost for years in the land of Anglund. Romance blossoms, but the two are separated when the girl is kidnapped for her magical abilities." (School Library Journal)

"Selfors's story line initially comes across as chaotic, but the pacing is strong, and the elements of her tale fall into place in a logical and entirely satisfying manner. An exhilarating, romantic, and frequently funny story of self-discovery." Pub Wkly

Selzer, Adam

How to get suspended and influence people; a novel. Delacorte Press 2007 183p $15.99; lib bdg $18.99

Grades: 6 7 8 9 **Fic**

1. School stories 2. Censorship -- Fiction 3. Motion pictures -- Fiction

ISBN 978-0-385-73369-4; 978-0-385-90384-4 lib bdg

LC 2006-20438

Gifted eighth-grader Leon Harris becomes an instant celebrity when the film he makes for a class project sends him to in-school suspension.

"This funny, fast-paced novel is filled with characters who epitomize the middle school experience, and it presents a lesson or two about free speech as well." SLJ

Another title about Leon is:

Pirates of the retail wasteland (2008)

Selznick, Brian

★ The **invention** of Hugo Cabret; a novel in words and pictures. Scholastic Press 2007 533p il $22.95

Grades: 4 5 6 7 **Fic**

1. Robots -- Fiction 2. Orphans -- Fiction 3. Motion picture

directors 4. Paris (France) -- Fiction 5. Motion pictures -- Fiction
ISBN 0-439-81378-6

LC 2006-07119

Caldecott Medal (2008)

National Book Award Finalist: Young People's Literature (2007)

When twelve-year-old Hugo, an orphan living and repairing clocks within the walls of a Paris train station in 1931, meets a mysterious toy-seller and his goddaughter, his undercover life and his biggest secret are jeopardized.

"With characteristic intelligence, exquisite images, and a breathtaking design, Selznick shatters conventions related to the art of bookmaking." SLJ

★ The **Marvels**; Brian Selznick. Scholastic Press 2015 640 p. illustrations (hard cover : alk. paper) $32.99

Grades: 5 6 7 8 **Fic**

1. Theater -- Fiction 2. Actors -- fiction 3. Actresses -- fiction 4. Family life -- fiction 5. London (England) -- fiction 6. Adventure stories 7. Theater -- England -- London -- fiction
ISBN 0545448689; 9780545448680

LC 2015023161

In this book, author Brian Selznick presents "[t]wo seemingly unrelated stories -- one in words, the other in pictures. . . . The illustrated story begins in 1766 with Billy Marvel, the lone survivor of a shipwreck, and charts the adventures of his family of actors over five generations. The prose story opens in 1990 and follows Joseph, who has run away from school to an estranged uncle's puzzling house in London, where he, along with the reader, must piece together many mysteries." (Publisher's note)

"This brilliant journey through time in words and pictures is also a story of a theatrical family and their fortunes. This heavy tome opens to tell of one family, the Marvels, from 1766 to 1900 as their connection to the Royal Theatre in London begins and perhaps ends. In the first half of the book, all of this complex history is vividly conveyed through illustrations, with minor hints from playbills, cards, and letters that appear as part of the art. . . . Complex, entertaining, and full of gorgeous art and writing, this is a powerhouse of a book." SLJ

★ **Wonderstruck**; a novel in words and pictures. Scholastic Press 2011 637p il $29.99

Grades: 4 5 6 7 **Fic**

1. Deaf -- Fiction 2. Museums -- Fiction 3. New York (N.Y.) -- Fiction 4. Runaway children -- Fiction 5. American Museum of Natural History -- Fiction
ISBN 978-0-545-02789-2; 0-545-02789-6

LC 2011009113

"Readers know that the two stories will converge, but Selznick keeps them guessing, cutting back and forth with expert precision. . . . Both stories are equally immersive and impeccably paced. . . . Visually stunning, completely compelling." Kirkus

Sepetys, Ruta

★ **Between** shades of gray; Ruta Sepetys. Philomel Books 2011 344p map $17.99

Grades: 8 9 10 11 12 **Fic**

1. Lithuania -- Fiction 2. Soviet Union -- Fiction
ISBN 978-0-399-25412-3; 0-399-25412-9

LC 2009-50092

In this novel by Ruta Sepetys, "Fifteen-year-old Lina is a Lithuanian girl living an ordinary life--until Soviet officers invade her home and tear her family apart. Separated from her father and forced onto a crowded train, Lina, her mother, and her young brother make their way to a Siberian work camp, where they are forced to fight for their lives." (Publisher's note)

"A harrowing page-turner, made all the more so for its basis in historical fact, the novel illuminates the persecution suffered by Stalin's victims (20 million were killed), while presenting memorable characters who retain their will to survive even after more than a decade in exile." Publ Wkly

★ **Salt** to the sea; a novel. Ruta Sepetys. Philomel Books 2016 400 p. maps $18.99

Grades: 8 9 10 11 12 **Fic**

1. Prussia 2. Refugees -- Fiction 3. World War, 1939-1945 -- Fiction
ISBN 0399160302; 9780399160301

LC 2015009057

In this novel, by Ruta Sepetys, "World War II is drawing to a close in East Prussia and thousands of refugees are on a desperate trek toward freedom, many with something to hide. Among them are Joana, Emilia, and Florian, whose paths converge en route to the ship that promises salvation, the Wilhelm Gustloff. Forced by circumstance to unite, the three find their strength, courage, and trust in each other tested with each step closer to safety." (Publisher's note)

Sepetys "describes an almost unknown maritime disaster whose nearly 9,000 casualties dwarfed those of both the Titanic and the Lusitania. Told alternately from the perspective of each of the main characters, the novel also highlights the struggle and sacrifices that ordinary people--children--were forced to make. At once beautiful and heart-wrenching, this title will remind readers that there are far more casualties of war than are recorded in history books." LJ

Shang, Wendy Wan-Long

★ The **way** home looks now; Wendy Wan-Long Shang. Scholastic Press 2015 272 p. $16.99

Grades: 4 5 6 7 8 **Fic**

1. Grief -- Fiction 2. Baseball -- Fiction 3. Pittsburgh (Pa.) -- Fiction 4. Chinese Americans -- Fiction 5. Traffic accidents -- Fiction 6. Bereavement 7. Baseball stories 8. Traffic accidents 9. Little League baseball -- Fiction 10. Chinese American families -- Pennsylvania -- Pittsburgh
ISBN 0545609569; 9780545609562

LC 2014028707

This book is a "story of family and loss, healing and friendship, and the great American pastime, baseball. Twelve-year-old Peter Lee and his family are baseball lovers, who bond over back lot games and talk of the Pittsburgh Pirates. But when tragedy strikes, the family flies apart and baseball no longer seems to matter. Is that true? Peter wonders if just maybe the game they love can pull them together and bring them back." (Publisher's note)

"The first-person narration is smooth and believable. This is a fine story of family, loss, growing up and learning to play baseball, raised to a higher level by gracefully incorporated themes of feminism and kindness." Kirkus

Sharenow, Robert

★ The **Berlin** Boxing Club. HarperTeen 2011 404p il $17.99

Grades: 7 8 9 10 **Fic**

1. Boxers (Persons) 2. Boxing -- Fiction 3. Family life -- Fiction 4. Jews -- Germany -- Fiction 5. Berlin (Germany) -- Fiction 6. National socialism -- Fiction 7. Holocaust, 1933-1945 -- Fiction 8. Germany -- History -- 1933-1945 -- Fiction
ISBN 978-0-06-157968-4; 0-06-157968-8

LC 2010024446

"Readers will be drawn by the sports detail and by the close-up narrative of the daily oppression." Booklist

Shaw, Susan

★ **Safe**. Dutton Books 2007 168p $16.99

Grades: 7 8 9 10 **Fic**

1. Rape -- Fiction 2. Mothers -- Fiction

ISBN 978-0-525-47829-4; 0-525-47829-9

LC 2006-36428

When thirteen-year-old Tracy, whose mother died when she was three years old, is raped and beaten on the last day of school, all her feelings of security disappear and she does not know how to cope with the fear and dread that engulf her.

This is an "extraordinarily tender novel. . . . Intimate, first-person narrative honestly expresses Tracy's full range of emotions." Publ Wkly

Tunnel vision. Margaret K. McElderry Books 2011 272p $16.99

Grades: 5 6 7 8 **Fic**

1. Crime -- Fiction 2. Homicide -- Fiction 3. Witnesses -- Fiction 4. Organized crime -- Fiction

ISBN 978-1-4424-0839-5; 1-4424-0839-1

LC 2010036306

After witnessing her mother's murder, sixteen-year-old high school student Liza Wellington and her father go into the witness protection program.

"The author creates a completely believable character in Liza, who often reverts to childlike emotions only to learn the hard way that cold reality takes precedence over even dearly held wishes. Kudos for the unexpected double ending, both illusory and realistic, giving readers a choice." Kirkus

Shepherd, Gail

The **true** history of Lyndie B. Hawkins; Gail Shepherd. Kathy Dawson Books 2019 304 p. (hardcover) $16.99

Grades: 4 5 6 7 **Fic**

1. Secrets -- Fiction 2. Veterans -- Fiction 3. Grandparents -- Fiction 4. Foster children -- Fiction 5. Family life -- Tennessee -- Fiction 6. Tennessee -- History -- 20th century -- Fiction

ISBN 9780525428459

LC 2018009940

In this novel, by Gail Shepherd, "Lyndie B. Hawkins loves history, research, and getting to the truth no matter what. But when it comes to her family, her knowledge is full of holes. . . . Determined to mold recalcitrant Lyndie into a nice Southern girl even if it kills her, her fusspot grandmother starts with lesson number one: Family=Loyalty=keeping quiet about family secrets. Especially when it comes to Lyndie's daddy." (Publisher's note)

"Noteworthy for its strong narrative voice and dramatic character development, including well-drawn secondary figures, this book depicts both the troubling and uplifting vicissitudes of family and camaraderie with unflinching honesty and humor." Pub Wkly

Sheth, Kashmira

Blue jasmine; [by] Kashmira Sheth. Hyperion Books for Children 2004 186p $15.99; pa $5.99

Grades: 5 6 7 8 **Fic**

1. India -- Fiction 2. Immigrants -- Fiction 3. East Indians -- Fiction

ISBN 0-7868-1855-7; 0-7868-5565-7 pa

LC 2003-50818

When twelve-year-old Seema moves to Iowa City with her parents and younger sister, she leaves friends and family behind in her native India but gradually begins to feel at home in her new country

"Seema's story, which articulates the ache for distant home and family, will resonate with fellow immigrants and enlighten their classmates." Booklist

Boys without names. Balzer & Bray 2010 316p $15.99

Grades: 4 5 6 7 **Fic**

1. India -- Fiction 2. Slavery -- Fiction 3. Child labor -- Fiction 4. Missing persons -- Fiction

ISBN 978-0-06-185760-7; 0-06-185760-2

LC 2009-11747

Eleven-year-old Gopal and his family leave their rural Indian village for life with his uncle in Mumbai, but when they arrive his father goes missing and Gopal ends up locked in a sweatshop from which there is no escape.

"Readers quickly come to care for this clever, perceptive boy who tries hard to do the right thing. . . . The author includes more about child labor at the end of this well-told survival story with a social conscience." SLJ

★ **Keeping** corner. Hyperion 2007 281p hardcover o.p. pa $5.99

Grades: 7 8 9 10 11 12 **Fic**

1. India -- Fiction 2. Widows -- Fiction 3. Women's rights -- Fiction

ISBN 978-0-7868-3859-2; 0-7868-3859-0; 978-0-7868-3860-8 pa; 0-7868-3860-4 pa

LC 2007-15314

In India in the 1940s, twelve-year-old Leela's happy, spoiled childhood ends when her husband since age nine, whom she barely knows, dies, leaving her a widow whose only hope of happiness could come from Mahatma Ghandi's social and political reforms.

Sheth "sets up a thrilling premise in which politics become achingly personal." Booklist

Shevah, Emma

★ **Dara** Palmer's major drama; Emma Shevah. Sourcebooks Jabberwocky 2016 288 p. illustrations (alk. paper) $16.99

Grades: 4 5 6 7 **Fic**

1. Acting -- Fiction 2. Adoption -- Fiction 3. Prejudices -- Fiction 4. Self-confidence -- Fiction 5. Cambodians -- Great Britain -- Fiction

ISBN 9781492631385

LC 2015031876

In this book, by Emma Shevah, "Dara Palmer longs for stardom-but when she isn't cast in her middle school's production of The Sound of Music, she get suspicious. It can't be because she's not the best. She was born to be a famous movie star. It must because she's adopted from Cambodia and doesn't look like a typical fraulein. . . . So irrepressible Dara comes up with a genius plan to shake up the school: write a play about her own life. Then she'll have to be the star." (Publisher's note)

"Crawford-White's charming doodle illustrations along the margins reflects Dara's inner monologues throughout the book.This funny, charismatic heroine will capture her readers' hearts." Kirkus

Shimko, Bonnie

The **private** thoughts of Amelia E. Rye. Farrar, Straus Giroux 2010 234p $16.99

Grades: 5 6 7 8 **Fic**

1. Friendship -- Fiction 2. New York (State) -- Fiction 3. Mother-daughter relationship -- Fiction

ISBN 978-0-374-36131-0; 0-374-36131-2

LC 2008048092

Growing up in a small town in upstate New York during the 1960s, 13-year-old Amelia E. Ryel, unwanted by her mother, searches for love and acceptance.

"The book is peopled with believable, multilayered characters. . . . Shimko's . . . story is original, and Amelia's distinctive voice and likable nature will have readers rooting for her in times of trouble and cheering her ultimate good fortune." Publ Wkly

Shinn, Sharon

★ **Gateway**. Viking 2009 280p $17.99

Grades: 6 7 8 9 10 **Fic**

1. Space and time -- Fiction 3. Chinese Americans -- Fiction

ISBN 978-0-670-01178-0; 0-670-01178-9

LC 2009-14002

While passing through the Arch in St. Louis, Missouri, a Chinese American teenager is transported to a parallel world where she is given a dangerous assignment.

The author's "fantasy finds the right balance between adventure and romance, while illuminating how seductive evil can be and that sometimes the best weapon one can possess is a skeptical mind." Publ Wkly

Shoemaker, Tim

Back before dark; Timothy Shoemaker. Zondervan 2013 384 p. (hardcover) $14.99

Grades: 7 8 9 10 **Fic**

1. Friendship -- Fiction 2. Kidnapping -- Fiction 3. Best friends -- Fiction 4. Christian life -- Fiction 5. Conduct of life -- Fiction 6. Mystery and detective stories

ISBN 0310734991; 9780310734994

LC 2012049855

"The kids find themselves in the wrong place at the wrong time. It's every kid's worst nightmare, when a ride through the park gets Gordy abducted. Their powers of observation are put to the test like never before, as they fight the clock to find their friend. In the dark, things are never what they seem." (Publisher's Note)

"In this sequel to Code of Silence, Gordy is kidnapped and his friends Hiro, Cooper, and Lunk decide to take his rescue into their own hands. While the suspense is vitiated by an excess of description and a slow pace, Shoemaker raises interesting questions about law and morality as the friends find themselves resorting to dubious means to catch the criminal." Horn Book

Shofner, Corabel

Almost paradise; Corabel Shofner. Farrar, Straus & Giroux 2017 296 p. (hardback) $16.99

Grades: 5 6 7 **Fic**

1. Nuns -- Fiction 2. Aunts -- Fiction 3. Cancer -- Fiction 4. Prisoners -- Fiction 5. Single-parent families -- Fiction 6. Mother-daughter relationship -- Fiction 7. Mothers and daughters -- Fiction

ISBN 9780374303792; 9780374303785

LC 2016038518

In this novel, by Corabel Shofner, "twelve-year-old Ruby Clyde Henderson's life changes the day her mother's boyfriend holds up a convenience store, and her mother is wrongly jailed for assisting with the crime. Ruby and her pet pig, Bunny, find their way to her estranged Aunt Eleanor's home. Aunt Eleanor is an ornery nun who lives in the midst of a peach orchard on Paradise Ranch. With a little patience, she and Ruby begin to get along, but Eleanor has secrets of her own." (Publisher's note)

"Shofner has taken all the established, important elements of a good middle-grade novel, given them a brisk shake, and served them up to readers in way that both entertains and enlightens." Booklist

Shreve, Susan

The **lovely** shoes; [by] Susan Shreve. Arthur A. Levine Books 2011 252p $16.99

Grades: 6 7 8 9 **Fic**

1. Shoemakers 2. School stories 3. Shoe designers 3. Shoes -- Fiction 4. Birth defects -- Fiction 5. Florence (Italy) -- Fiction 6. Mother-daughter relationship -- Fiction

ISBN 978-0-439-68049-3; 0-439-68049-2

LC 2010027937

In 1950s Ohio, ninth-grader Franny feels isolated and self-conscious at high school because of her deformed leg and feet, but her irrepressibly high-spirited mother is determined to find shoes for Franny to wear at the school dances.

"Celebrating the rewards of determination and a positive attitude, this atmospheric novel credibly depicts Franny's internal growth and changing attitude. The contrast between smalltown Ohio and splendorous Florence provides an intriguing framework for the book's classic themes." Publ Wkly

Shulman, Mark

★ **Scrawl**. Roaring Brook Press 2010 234p $16.99

Grades: 6 7 8 9 10 **Fic**

1. School stories 2. Bullies -- Fiction 3. Diaries -- Fiction 4. Poverty -- Fiction 5. Self-perception -- Fiction

ISBN 978-1-59643-417-2; 1-59643-417-1

LC 2010-10521

When eighth-grade school bully Tod and his friends get caught committing a crime on school property, his penalty—staying after school and writing in a journal under the eye of the school guidance counsellor—reveals aspects of himself that he prefers to keep hidden.

"Blackmail, cliques, and a sense of hopelessness from both students and teachers sets up an unexpected ending that will leave readers with a new appreciation for how difficult high school can be. With the potential to occupy the rarified air of titles like S.E. Hinton's The Outsiders and Chris Crutcher's Staying Fat for Sarah Byrnes . . ., Scrawl paints the stereotypical school bully in a different, poignant light." Voice Youth Advocates

Shulman, Polly

★ The **Grimm** Legacy. G. P. Putnam's Sons 2010 325p $16.99

Grades: 5 6 7 8 **Fic**

1. Fantasy fiction 2. Magic -- Fiction 3. Libraries -- Fiction 4. New York (N.Y.) -- Fiction

ISBN 0-399-25096-4; 978-0-399-25096-5

LC 2009028919

New York high school student Elizabeth gets an after-school job as a page at the "New-York Circulating Material Repository," and when she gains coveted access to its Grimm Collection of magical objects, she and the other pages are drawn into a series of frightening adventures involving mythical creatures and stolen goods.

"This modern fantasy has intrigue, adventure, and romance, and the magical aspects of the tale are both clever and intricately woven. . . . Shulman's prose is fast paced, filled with humor, and peopled with characters who are either true to life or delightfully bizarre." SLJ

The **Poe** Estate; by Polly Shulman. Nancy Paulsen Books, an imprint of Penguin Group (USA) 2015 272 p. $16.99
Grades: 5 6 7 8 **Fic**

1. Ghost stories 2. Family -- Fiction 3. Supernatural -- Fiction 4. Haunted houses -- Fiction 5. Buried treasure -- Fiction 6. Books and reading -- Fiction 7. Ghosts -- Fiction 8. Families -- Fiction
ISBN 9780399166143

LC 2014042105

In this book, by Polly Shulman, "Sukie's been lonely since the death of her big sister, Kitty—but Kitty's ghost is still with her. At first that was comforting, but now Kitty's terrifying anyone who gets too close. Things get even weirder when Sukie moves into her family's ancestral home, and an older, less familiar ghost challenges her to find a treasure." (Publisher's note)

"Shulman's novel stands alone and is all the richer for readers who know the backstory of the Grimm Collection, and the treasures kept in the Repository." SLJ

The **Wells** Bequest; by Polly Shulman. Nancy Paulsen Books, an imprint of Penguin Group (USA) Inc. 2013 272 p. (hardcover) $16.99
Grades: 5 6 7 8 **Fic**

1. Fantasy fiction -- fiction 2. Science fiction 3. Time travel -- Fiction
ISBN 0399256466; 9780399256462

LC 2012036571

This book is a companion to Polly Shulman's "The Grimm Legacy." Here, New York Circulating Material Repository page "Leo notices an object materializing on the floor. The glittering, football-sized machine has 'gears and rods and knobs and a little saddle' —and two miniscule humans, one of whom is himself." He discovers that he and his fellow page Jaya must travel in time to prevent another page from misusing Nikola Tesla's death ray. (Kirkus Reviews)

Shurtliff, Liesl

Rump; the true story of Rumpelstiltskin. Liesl Shurtliff. 1st ed. Alfred A. Knopf 2013 272 p. (hardcover) $16.99
Grades: 3 4 5 6 7 **Fic**

1. Fractured fairy tales 2. Fairy tales 3. Gold -- Fiction 4. Humorous stories 5. Magic -- Fiction 6. Names, Personal -- Fiction
ISBN 0307977935; 9780307977939 trade; 9780307977946; 9780307977953; 9780307977960

LC 2012005093

In this fractured fairy tale, by Liesl Shurtliff, "12-year-old [Rumpelstiltskin] . . . finds an old spinning wheel, . . . [and] discovers he has a gift for spinning straw into gold. His best friend, Red Riding Hood, warns him that magic is dangerous, and she's right. With each thread he spins, he weaves himself deeper into a curse. To break the spell, Rump must go on a perilous quest, fighting off pixies, trolls, poison apples, and a wickedly foolish queen." (Publisher's note)

"Debut author Shurtliff upends the traditional characterization of this fairy tale's antihero, recasting Rumpelstiltskin as a sympathetic and tragically doomed protagonist. . . . [T]he picaresque-style narrative gives the maligned character a refreshingly plainspoken voice, while honoring the original story's hauntingly strange events." Pub Wkly

Shusterman, Neal

★ **Antsy** does time. Dutton Children's Books 2008 247p $16.99
Grades: 7 8 9 10 **Fic**

1. School stories 2. Death -- Fiction 3. Brooklyn (New York, N.Y.) -- Fiction
ISBN 978-0-525-47825-6; 0-525-47825-6

LC 2008-00459

Sequel to: The Schwa was here (2004)

Fourteen-year-old Anthony "Antsy" Bonano learns about life, death, and a lot more when he tries to help a friend with a terminal illness feel hopeful about the future.

"Featuring a terrific supporting cast led by Antsy's wise, acerbic mother, an expert blend of comedy and near tragedy, and the wry observations of a narrator . . . this will keep tween readers hooked from start to finish." Booklist

Dry; Neal Shusterman and Jarrod Shusterman. Simon & Schuster Books for Young Readers 2018 400 p. (hardback) $18.99
Grades: 7 8 9 10 11 12 **Fic**

1. Droughts -- Fiction 2. Siblings -- Fiction 3. Conduct of life -- Fiction 4. Survival -- Fiction 5. California -- Fiction 6. Brothers and sisters -- Fiction
ISBN 9781481481960; 9781481481977

LC 2018008928

In this book, by Neal Shusterman and Jarrod Shusterman, "the drought--or the Tap-Out . . . --has been going on for a while now. . . . Until the taps run dry. Suddenly, Alyssa's quiet suburban street spirals into a warzone of desperation; neighbors and families turned against each other on the hunt for water. And when her parents don't return and her life--and the life of her brother--is threatened, Alyssa has to make impossible choices if she's going to survive." (Publisher's note)

Everlost. Simon & Schuster Books for Young Readers 2006 313p (The Skinjacker trilogy) $16.95; pa $8.99
Grades: 8 9 10 11 12 **Fic**

1. Death -- Fiction 2. Future life -- Fiction 3. Traffic accidents -- Fiction
ISBN 978-0-689-87237-2; 0-689-87237-2; 978-1-4169-9749-8 pa; 1-4169-9749-0 pa

LC 2005-32244

When Nick and Allie are killed in a car crash, they end up in Everlost, or limbo for lost souls, where although Nick is satisfied, Allie will stop at nothing—even skinjacking—to break free.

"Shusterman has reimagined what happens after death and questions power and the meaning of charity. While all this is going on, he has also managed to write a rip-roaring adventure complete with monsters, blimps, and high-diving horses." SLJ

Other titles in this series are:
Everfound (2011)
Everwild (2009)

The **Schwa** was here; [by] Neal Shusterman. 1st ed; Dutton Children's Books 2004 228p $15.99
Grades: 7 8 9 10 **Fic**

1. Friendship -- Fiction 2. Brooklyn (New York, N.Y.) -- Fiction
ISBN 0-525-47182-0

LC 2004-45072

Boston Globe-Horn Book Award: Fiction (2005)

A Brooklyn eighth-grader nicknamed Antsy befriends the Schwa, an "invisible-ish" boy who is tired of blending into his surroundings and going unnoticed by nearly everyone.

"Antsy is one funny narrator. . . . Shusterman has created yet another very readable and refreshingly different story." Voice Youth Advocates

Followed by: Antsy does time (2008)

Scythe; Neal Shusterman. Simon & Schuster Books for Young Readers 2016 448 p. (hardcover) $18.99
Grades: 8 9 10 11 12 **Fic**

1. Science fiction 2. Death -- Fiction 3. Murder -- Fiction
ISBN 1442472421; 144247243X; 9781442472426; 9781442472433

LC 2016006502

Printz Honor Book (2017)

This book, by Neal Shusterman, takes place in "a world with no hunger, no disease, no war, no misery: humanity has conquered all those things, and has even conquered death. Now Scythes are the only ones who can end life--and they are commanded to do so, in order to keep the size of the population under control. Citra and Rowan are chosen to apprentice to a scythe--a role that neither wants." (Publisher's note)

"Elegant and elegiac, brooding but imbued with gallows humor, Shusterman's dark tale thrusts realistic, likable teens into a surreal situation and raises deep philosophic questions." Kirkus

Ship out of luck; a companion to The Schwa was here. Neal Shusterman. Dutton Books, an imprint of Penguin Group (USA) Inc. 2013 256 p. (hardcover : alk. paper) $16.99
Grades: 6 7 8 **Fic**

1. Smuggling -- Fiction 2. Cruise ships -- Fiction 3. Caribbean Area -- Fiction 4. Adventure and adventurers -- Fiction
ISBN 0525422269; 9780525422266

LC 2013000031

In this book, "Old Man Crawley, a filthy-rich irascible codger with a soft spot for his blind, 16-year-old granddaughter, Lexie, is about to turn 80. To celebrate, he invites--commands, really--Antsy and his family to join him and Lexie for a week aboard the incredibly fabulous cruise ship Plethora of the Deep." During the trip, Antsy meets and tries to help "Tilde, who claims she's a stowaway and smuggler of illegal immigrants." (Kirkus Reviews)

★ **Thunderhead**; Neal Shusterman. Simon & Schuster Books for Young Readers 2018 512 p. (hardcover) $18.99
Grades: 8 9 10 11 12 **Fic**

1. Science fiction 2. Death -- Fiction 3. Murder -- Fiction
ISBN 9781442472457; 9781442472464

LC 2017040210

In this book in the Arc of a Scythe series, by Neal Shusterman, "a year has passed since Rowan had gone off grid. Since then, he has become an urban legend. . . . As Scythe Anastasia, Citra gleans with compassion and openly challenges the ideals of the 'new order.' But when her life is threatened and her methods questioned, it becomes clear that not everyone is open to the change. Will the Thunderhead intervene? Or will it simply watch as this perfect world begins to unravel?" (Publisher's note)

Silberberg, Alan

★ **Milo**; sticky notes and brain freeze. written and illustrated by Alan Silberberg. Aladdin 2010 275p il $15.99
Grades: 5 6 7 8 **Fic**

1. Death -- Fiction 2. Mothers -- Fiction 3. Friendship -- Fiction 4. Bereavement -- Fiction
ISBN 978-1-4169-9430-5; 1-4169-9430-0

LC 2010012708

"This is more than just another funny story about a middle school misfit who is the new kid in the neighborhood. While Milo does struggle with all the normal tween anxieties and self-consciousness about his family, there is more. Silberberg details the daily events with Wimpy Kid-like drawings and quick-witted humor that will keep the pages turning. Milo's new friendships with classmates Marshall and Hillary and elderly neighbor Sylvia Poole allow readers to glimpse at the deeper truth–Milo's mother's death–as it emerges between laugh lines. Silberberg takes on a tough topic and always stays true to the age of the character through dialogue and artwork while maintaining that wisecracking, 12-year-old humor." SLJ

Silvey, Craig

★ **Jasper** Jones; a novel. Alfred A. Knopf 2011 312p $16.99
Grades: 6 7 8 9 10 **Fic**

1. Mystery fiction 2. Homicide -- Fiction 3. Australia -- Fiction 4. Family life -- Fiction
ISBN 0-375-86666-3; 0-375-96666-8 lib bdg; 978-0-375-86666-1; 978-0-375-96666-8 lib bdg

LC 2010-9364

Printz Honor Book (2012)

In small-town Australia, teens Jasper and Charlie form an unlikely friendship when one asks the other to help him cover up a murder until they can prove who is responsible.

"Silvey infuses his prose with a musician's sensibility—Charlie's pounding heart is echoed in the terse staccato sentences of the opening scenes, alternating with legato phrases laden with meaning. The author's keen ear for dialogue is evident in the humorous verbal sparring between Charlie and Jeffrey, typical of smart 13-year-old boys. . . . A richly rewarding exploration of truth and lies by a masterful storyteller." Kirkus

Simner, Janni Lee

Bones of Faerie. Random House 2009 247p $16.99; lib bdg $19.99
Grades: 7 8 9 10 **Fic**

1. Fantasy fiction 2. Magic -- Fiction 3. Fairies -- Fiction
ISBN 978-0-375-84563-5; 978-0-375-94563-2 lib bdg

LC 2008-2022

Fifteen-year-old Liza travels through war-ravaged territory, accompanied by two companions, in a struggle to bridge the faerie and human worlds and to bring back her mother while learning of her own powers and that magic can be controlled.

This is a "compelling developed, highly vulnerable trio whose resolute defiance against the status quo will resonate with readers long after specific details of the story may be forgotten." Bull Cent Child Books

Other titles in this series are:
Faerie winter (2011)
Faerie after (2013)

Faerie after; Janni Lee Simner. Random House Inc. 2013 272 p. (ebook) $50.97; (hardcover) $16.99; (library) $19.99
Grades: 7 8 9 10 **Fic**

1. Fantasy fiction 2. Fairies -- Fiction 3. Paranormal fiction 4. Magic -- Fiction 5. Coming of age -- Fiction
ISBN 0375870695; 9780307974556; 9780375870699; 9780375970696

LC 2012006430

Sequel to: Faerie winter

This is the third book in Janni Lee's Bones of Faerie trilogy. "Relative peace has descended upon Liza's town, where she practices her summoner magic and waits for her half-faerie baby sister to be born. But the forest is showing new dangers, though subtle ones," particularly a strange dust. "Liza's quest to find out what's wrong reveals fresh disasters." (Kirkus)

Faerie winter. Random House Children's Books 2011 270p $16.99; lib bdg $19.99

Grades: 7 8 9 10 **Fic**

1. Magic -- Fiction 2. Fairies -- Fiction 3. Mother-daughter relationship -- Fiction

ISBN 978-0-375-86671-5; 0-375-86671-X; 978-0-375-96671-2 lib bdg; 0-375-96671-4 lib bdg

LC 2010014250

Sequel to: Bones of Faerie (2009)

Unable to get answers from her mother, sixteen-year-old Liza learns from Karin that while her own actions may have doomed the fairy and human worlds, she may be able to save them with more training, if the Faerie Queen can first be stopped.

"Simner tells a more streamlined story this time around and keeps up the dark atmospherics of her high-appeal blend of unsettling speculative-fiction scenarios." Booklist

Simon, Francesca

The **monstrous** child; Francesca Simon, with illuminations by Olivia Lomenech Gill. Faber & Faber 2017 286 p. illustrations (paperback) $11.95

Grades: 7 8 9 10 **Fic**

1. Dead -- Fiction 2. Hell -- Fiction 3. Fantasy -- fiction 4. Mythology, Norse -- literature

ISBN 9780571330270; 0571330274

This book, by Francesca Simon is "a stunning, operatic, epic drama, like no other. Meet Hel, an ordinary teenager--and goddess of the Underworld. Why is life so unfair? Hel tries to make the best of it, creating gleaming halls in her dark kingdom and welcoming the dead who she is forced to host for eternity. Until eternity itself is threatened." (Publisher's note)

"Readers may enjoy Hel's flippant insolence . . . while others may find the quirky presentation of Norse mythology a good companion to Rick Riordan's Magnus Chase and the Gods of Asgard series." Booklist

Simon, T. R.

Zora and me; the cursed ground. T. R. Simon. Candlewick Press 2018 272 p. $16.99

Grades: 5 6 7 8 **Fic**

1. African American girls -- fiction 2. Racism -- United States -- fiction 3. United States -- Race relations -- fiction

ISBN 0763643017; 9780763643010

In this book, by T. R. Simon, "when Zora Neale Hurston and her best friend, Carrie Brown, discover that the town mute can speak after all, they think they've uncovered a big secret. But Mr. Polk's silence is just one piece of a larger puzzle that stretches back half a century to the tragic story of an enslaved girl named Lucia. . . . Lucia's struggle for freedom resonates through the years, threatening the future of America's first incorporated black township." (Publisher's note)

Sitomer, Alan Lawrence

The **downside** of being up; Alan Sitomer. G.P. Putnam's Sons 2011 215p $16.99

Grades: 6 7 8 9 **Fic**

1. School stories 2. Puberty -- Fiction 3. Family life -- Fiction

ISBN 978-0-399-25498-7; 0-399-25498-6

LC 2010044203

In this book, by Alan Sitomer, "thirteen-year-old Bobby Connor is a normal adolescent boy--at least he hopes he is--just trying to survive middle school. But it seems he's being foiled at every turn, and even his own body is conspiring against him. And when his math teacher is seriously injured from the shock and fright of witnessing just how out of control Bobby's changing adolescent body is getting, he starts to worry he's anything but normal." (Publisher's note)

"It is impossible to dislike this pun-filled tale. . . . This fiction provides some long-needed realism, served up by a narrator who knows what he is talking about." Booklist

The **secret** story of Sonia Rodriguez. Jump at the Sun/Hyperion Books For Children 2008 312p lib bdg $17.99

Grades: 7 8 9 10 **Fic**

1. Family life -- Fiction 2. Mexican Americans -- Fiction

ISBN 978-1-4231-1072-9; 1-4231-1072-2

LC 2007-45265

Tenth-grader Sonia reveals secrets about her life and her Hispanic family as she studies hard to become the first Rodriguez to finish high school.

"Sonia's immediate voice will hold teens with its mix of anger, sorrow, tenderness, and humor." Booklist

Skelton, Matthew

Endymion Spring. Delacorte Press 2006 392p il $17.95; lib bdg $19.99; pa $9.99

Grades: 5 6 7 8 **Fic**

1. Inventors 2. Printers 3. Magic -- Fiction 4. Great Britain -- Fiction 5. Books and reading -- Fiction

ISBN 0-385-73380-1; 0-385-90397-9 lib bdg; 0-385-73456-5 pa

LC 2006-46259

Having reluctantly accompanied his academic mother and pesky younger sister to Oxford, twelve-year-old Blake Winters is at loose ends until he stumbles across an ancient and magical book, secretly brought to England in 1453 by Gutenberg's mute apprentice to save it from evil forces, and which now draws Blake into a dangerous and life-threatening quest

"This book is certain to reach an audience looking for a page-turner, and it just might motivate readers to explore the . . . facts behind the fiction." SLJ

Skrypuch, Marsha Forchuk, 1954-

Making bombs for Hitler; Marsha Forchuk Skrypuch. Scholastic Press 2017 240 p. (ebook) $17.99; $17.99

Grades: 5 6 7 8 **Fic**

1. Child labor -- Fiction 2. World War, 1939-1945 -- Fiction 3. Germany -- History -- 1933-1945 -- Fiction 4. Ukrainians -- Germany -- Fiction 5. Slave labor -- Germany -- fiction 6. Children -- Nazi persecution -- fiction 7. World War, 1939-1945 -- Deportations from Ukraine -- fiction

ISBN 9780545931922; 0545931916; 9780545931915

LC 2016026561

In this book, by Marsha Forchuk Skrypuch, "Lida thought she was safe. Her neighbors wearing the yellow star were all taken away, but Lida is not Jewish. She will be fine, won't she? . . . Lida's parents are ripped away from her and she is separated from her beloved sister, Larissa. The Nazis take Lida to a brutal work camp, where she and other Ukrainian children are forced into backbreaking labor." (Publisher's note)

"A well-told story of persistence, lost innocence, survival, and hope." Kirkus

Sleator, William

The **duplicate**. Dutton 1988 154p hardcover o.p. pa $5.99

Grades: 7 8 9 10 **Fic**
1. Science fiction
ISBN 0-14-130431-6
LC 87-30562

Sixteen-year-old David, finding a strange machine that creates replicas of living organisms, duplicates himself and suffers the horrible consequences when the duplicate turns against him

"There are some points in the story when the roles of the clones (referred to as Duplicates A and B) become congested to the detriment of the book's pace, but fantasy fans will doubtless find the concept fresh enough and eerie enough to compensate for this, and Sleator is, as always, economical in casting and structuring his story." Bull Cent Child Books

★ **Interstellar** pig. Dutton 1984 197p hardcover o.p. pa $6.99
Grades: 5 6 7 8 **Fic**
1. Science fiction
ISBN 0-14-037595-3 pa
LC 84-4132

Barney's boring seaside vacation suddenly becomes more interesting when the cottage next door is occupied by three exotic neighbors who are addicted to a game they call "Interstellar Pig."

The author "draws the reader in with intimations of danger and horror, but the climactic battle is more slapstick than horrific, and the victor's prize could scarcely be more ironic. Problematic as straight science fiction but great fun as a spoof on human-alien contact." Booklist

Another title about Barney is:
Parasite Pig (2002)

Singularity. Dutton 1985 170p hardcover o.p. pa $5.99
Grades: 7 8 9 10 **Fic**
1. Science fiction 2. Twins -- Fiction
ISBN 0-525-44161-1; 0-14-037598-8 pa
LC 84-26075

Sixteen-year-old twins Harry and Barry stumble across a gateway to another universe, where a distortion in time and space causes a dramatic change in their competitive relationship

"The book has a title with a fine double entendre and is an unusual, suspenseful yarn told by a master storyteller." Horn Book

Sloan, Holly Goldberg

★ **Counting** by 7s; by Holly Goldberg Sloan. Dial Books for Young Readers 2012 384 p. (hardcover) $16.99
Grades: 4 5 6 7 **Fic**
1. Genius -- Fiction 2. Orphans -- Fiction 3. Alienation (Social psychology) -- Fiction 4. Schools -- Fiction 5. Gardening -- Fiction 6. High schools -- Fiction 7. Eccentrics and eccentricities -- Fiction
ISBN 0803738552; 9780803738553
LC 2012004994

This book follows "Willow Chance . . . an extremely precocious and analytical 12-year-old 'genius'. . . . Despite Willow's social difficulties, she makes an impression on everyone around her--whether it's Dell Duke, a lonely and ineffectual school district counselor, or Jairo Hernandez, the taxi driver Willow hires to drive her to her meetings with Dell. After Willow's parents die in a car crash, her new friend Mai Nguyen persuades her mother to take Willow in." (Publishers Weekly)

★ **I'll** be there. Little, Brown 2011 392p $17.99
Grades: 7 8 9 10 **Fic**
1. Brothers -- Fiction 2. Family life -- Fiction 3. Mental illness -- Fiction 4. Father-son relationship -- Fiction
ISBN 978-0-316-12279-5; 0-316-12279-3
LC 2010-42994

"Protecting his mute younger brother from their unstable father and the factors that force them to continuously move and prevent their school attendance, Sam finds everything changing when he meets Emily, who tempts them to consider a normal life. A first novel." (Publisher's Note)

"This riveting story will keep readers interested and guessing until the end." SLJ

Short; Holly Goldberg Sloan. Dial Books for Young Readers 2017 304 p. $16.99
Grades: 4 5 6 7 8 **Fic**
1. Size -- Fiction 2. Theater -- Fiction 3. Self-acceptance -- Fiction
ISBN 9780399186219
LC 2016013964

In this book, by Holly Goldberg Sloan, "Julia is very short for her age, but by the end of the summer run of The Wizard of Oz, she'll realize how big she is inside, where it counts. She hasn't ever thought of herself as a performer, but when the wonderful director of Oz casts her as a Munchkin, she begins to see herself in a new way. Julia becomes friendly with the poised and wise Olive--one of the adults with dwarfism who've joined the production's motley crew of Munchkins." (Publisher's note)

"Her self-acceptance is inspiring, and the joy she experiences in her foray into theater is irresistible." Booklist

Smiley, Jane

Gee Whiz; Jane Smiley ; with illustrations by Elaine Clayton. Alfred A. Knopf 2013 272 p. (The horses of Oak Valley Ranch) (library binding) $19.99
Grades: 4 5 6 7 **Fic**
1. Ranch life -- Fiction 2. Christian life -- Fiction 3. Horses -- Training -- Fiction 4. Ranch life -- California -- Fiction 5. Family life -- California -- Fiction 6. California -- History -- 1950- -- Fiction
ISBN 0375969691; 9780375869693; 9780375969690; 9780375985331
LC 2012024370

In this book, by Jane Smiley, "Gee Whiz is a striking horse, and only part of that is because of his size. . . . When Abby is confronted with an onslaught of reminders of just how little of the world she has seen, she finds herself connecting with Gee Whiz's calm and curious nature, and his desire to know more." (Publisher's note)

★ The **Georges** and the Jewels; with illustrations by Elaine Clayton. Alfred A. Knopf 2009 232p il $16.99; lib bdg $19.99
Grades: 4 5 6 7 **Fic**
1. Horses -- Fiction 2. California -- Fiction 3. Ranch life -- Fiction 4. Christian life -- Fiction
ISBN 978-0-375-86227-4; 0-375-86227-7; 978-0-375-96227-1 lib bdg; 0-375-96227-1 lib bdg
LC 2009-06241

Seventh-grader Abby Lovitt grows up on her family's California horse ranch in the 1960s, learning to train the horses her father sells and trying to reconcile her strict religious upbringing with her own ideas about life.

"As might be expected from the skilled hands of Smiley . . . there are synchronous storylines . . . [and] many will find it difficult to say goodbye to Abby, Jack and especially to Ornery George." Publ Wkly

Other titles in this series are:
A good horse (2010)

True blue (2011)

A **good** horse; with illustrations by Elaine Clayton. Alfred A. Knopf 2010 246p il $16.99; lib bdg $19.99

Grades: 4 5 6 7 **Fic**

1. Horses -- Fiction 2. California -- Fiction 3. Ranch life -- Fiction 4. Family life -- Fiction 5. Christian life -- Fiction 6. Swindlers and swindling -- Fiction

ISBN 0-375-86229-3; 0-375-96228-X lib bdg; 978-0-375-86229-8; 978-0-375-96228-8 lib bdg

LC 2009051264

Sequel to: The Georges and the Jewels (2009)

On her family's California horse ranch in the 1960s, eighth-grader Abby Lovitt tries to rely on her Christian faith as she faces the possibility of giving up her beloved colt, Jack.

This "is Smiley at her finest—detailed, nuanced, absorbing." Kirkus

Followed by: True Blue (2011)

Pie in the Sky; Book Four of the Horses of Oak Valley Ranch. Jane Smiley ; with illustrations by Elaine Clayton. Alfred A. Knopf Books for Young Readers 2012 257 p. (hardback) $16.99

Grades: 4 5 6 7 **Fic**

1. Horsemanship -- Fiction 2. Schools -- Fiction 3. High schools -- Fiction 4. Christian life -- Fiction 5. Horses -- Training -- Fiction 6. Ranch life -- California -- Fiction 7. Family life -- California -- Fiction

ISBN 0375869689; 9780375869686; 9780375969683; 9780375985324

LC 2011044104

In this book, by Jane Smiley, "Abby Lovitt doesn't realize how unprepared she is when she takes her beloved horse, True Blue, to a clinic led by the most famous equestrian anyone knows. The biggest surprise, though, is that Sophia . . . stops riding. Who will ride her horse? Abby's dad seems to think it will be Abby. Pie in the Sky is the most expensive horse Abby has ever ridden. But he is proud and irritable, and he takes Abby's attention away from the continuing mystery that is True Blue." (Publisher's note)

True Blue; with illustrations by Elaine Clayton. Alfred A. Knopf 2011 297p il $16.99; lib bdg $19.99

Grades: 4 5 6 7 **Fic**

1. Horses -- Fiction 2. California -- Fiction 3. Ranch life -- Fiction 4. Family life -- Fiction 5. Christian life -- Fiction

ISBN 978-0-375-86231-1; 0-375-86231-5; 978-0-375-96229-5 lib bdg; 0-375-96229-8 lib bdg

LC 2010035975

In 1960s California, eighth-grader Abby Lovitt has trouble with True Blue, the newest horse on her family's ranch, a beautiful dappled gray who is so often spooked, Abby wonders if he is haunted by the ghost of his deceased former owner.

"Readers who have been with this story from the beginning will enjoy watching narrator Abby continue to grow; newcomers will want to go back and start at the beginning with The Georges and the Jewels (2009)." Kirkus

Smith, Alexander Gordon

Death sentence. Farrar Straus Giroux 2011 272p (Escape from Furnace) $15.99

Grades: 7 8 9 10 **Fic**

1. Horror fiction 2. Science fiction 3. Prisoners -- Fiction

ISBN 978-0-374-32494-0; 0-374-32494-8

LC 2010010938

After his failed attempt to escape from Furnace Penitentiary, Alex struggles to survive the bloodstained laboratories beneath where monsters are manufactured, with a death sentence—or worse—hanging over his head.

"Smith strikes the ideal balance between action and introspection. Readers will feel genuine sympathy for antihero Alex." Kirkus

Lockdown. Farrar, Straus and Giroux 2009 273p (Escape from Furnace) $14.99

Grades: 7 8 9 10 **Fic**

1. Science fiction 2. Escapes -- Fiction 3. Prisoners -- Fiction

ISBN 978-0-374-32491-9; 0-374-32491-3

LC 2008-43439

When fourteen-year-old Alex is framed for murder, he becomes an inmate in the Furnace Penitentiary, where brutal inmates and sadistic guards reign, boys who disappear in the middle of the night sometimes return weirdly altered, and escape might just be possible.

"Once a plot is hatched, readers will be turning pages without pause, and the cliffhanger ending will have them anticipating the next installment. Most appealing is Smith's flowing writing style, filled with kid-speak, colorful adjectives, and amusing analogies." SLJ

Other titles in this series are:

Death sentence (2011)

Solitary (2010)

Solitary. Farrar Straus Giroux 2010 232p (Escape from Furnace) $14.99

Grades: 7 8 9 10 **Fic**

1. Horror fiction 2. Science fiction 3. Prisoners -- Fiction

ISBN 978-0-374-32492-6; 0-374-32492-1

LC 2009-30843

Sequel to: Lockdown (2009)

Imprisoned for a murder he did not commit, fourteen-year-old Alex Sawyer thinks that he has escaped the hellish Furnace Penitentiary, but instead he winds up in solitary confinement, where new horrors await him.

"The author knows what keeps his readers locked to the page and delivers it soundly." Kirkus

Followed by: Death sentence (2011)

Smith, Hope Anita

★ **Keeping** the night watch; with illustrations by E.B. Lewis. Henry Holt 2008 73p il $18.95

Grades: 4 5 6 7 **Fic**

1. Novels in verse 2. Fathers -- Fiction 3. Family life -- Fiction 4. African Americans -- Fiction

ISBN 978-0-8050-7202-0; 0-8050-7202-0

LC 2007-12372

Sequel to: The way a door closes (2003)

Coretta Scott King honor book for text, 2009

A thirteen-year-old African American boy chronicles what happens to his family when his father, who temporarily left, returns home and they all must deal with their feelings of anger, hope, abandonment, and fear.

"The words are simple . . . and the beautiful watercolor pictures of the African American family have the same quiet intensity as pictures in the first book. . . . Although mainly in free verse, there's also a sonnet." Booklist

The **way** a door closes; [by] Hope Anita Smith; with illustrations by Shane W. Evans. Holt & Co. 2003 52p il $18.95
Grades: 4 5 6 7 **Fic**

1. Novels in verse 2. Fathers -- Fiction 3. Family life -- Fiction 4. African Americans -- Fiction
ISBN 0-8050-6477-X

LC 2002-67884

In this novel in verse "readers are drawn into the thoughts and feelings of a 13-year-old African American as he tries to understand and cope with a parent's departure from the family. . . . In carefully chosen, straightforward language, Smith conveys the boy's roller-coaster emotions with pinpoint accuracy. The results are poems that are heartbreaking, angry, and tender. Done in warm shades of mostly brown, blue, and gold, Evans's color spot and full-page paintings have a realistic, slightly sculptural appearance and are a perfect complement to the poems." SLJ

Followed by: Keeping the night watch (2008)

Smith, Icy

Half spoon of rice; a survival story of the Cambodian genocide. written by Icy Smith; illustrated by Sopaul Nhem. East West Discovery Press 2010 42p il
Grades: 5 6 7 8 **Fic**

1. Cambodia -- Fiction 2. Genocide -- Fiction
ISBN 0-9821675-8-X; 978-0-9821675-8-8

LC 2009002973

Nine-year-old Nat and his family are forced from their home on April 17, 1975, marched for many days, separated from each other, and forced to work in the rice fields, where Nat concentrates on survival. Includes historical notes and photographs documenting the Cambodian genocide

"Bold, impressionistic oil paintings, mainly full page but some full spreads, speak volumes, and archival photographs are appended. This powerful child's eye view of war is harsh and realistic—like its subject—though accessible and thought-provoking." SLJ

Smith, Jennifer E.

The **comeback** season. Simon & Schuster Books for Young Readers 2008 246p $15.99
Grades: 6 7 8 9 10 **Fic**

1. Baseball -- Fiction 2. Bereavement -- Fiction 3. Family life -- Fiction 4. Chicago (Ill.) -- Fiction 5. Father-daughter relationship -- Fiction
ISBN 978-1-4169-3847-7; 1-4169-3847-8

LC 2007-17067

High school freshman Ryan Walsh, a Chicago Cubs fan, meets Nick when they both skip school on opening day, and their blossoming relationship becomes difficult for Ryan when she discovers that Nick is seriously ill and she again feels the pain of losing her father five years earlier.

"Smith deftly twines strands of grief, romance, baseball, family, and friendships lost and regained into this tale. . . . The present-tense narrative has an immediacy that will engage readers and the supporting cast is unusually vivid." Booklist

The **geography** of you and me; Jennifer E. Smith. Little, Brown & Co. 2014 352 p. (hardcover) $18
Grades: 7 8 9 10 11 12 **Fic**

1. Love -- Fiction 2. Social classes -- Fiction 3. Voyages and travels -- Fiction 4. Electric power failures -- Fiction 5. New York (N.Y.) -- Fiction
ISBN 0316254770; 9780316254779

LC 2013022845

In this book, by Jennifer E. Smith, "Lucy lives on the 24th floor. Owen lives in the basement. It's fitting, then, that they meet in the middle–stuck between two floors of a New York City apartment building, on an elevator rendered useless by a citywide blackout. After they're rescued, Lucy and Owen spend the night wandering the darkened streets. . . . But once the power is back, so is reality. Lucy soon moves abroad with her parents, while Owen heads out west with his father." (Publisher's note)

"Owen and Lucy meet during a citywide blackout in New York and spend a memorable (chaste) night together. Soon afterward, Lucy's parents take her to Europe, and Owen and his dad move to San Francisco, but even on opposite sides of the world, they think about each other. Smith's fans will recognize the alternating narration; reflective, deliberate writing style; and serendipitous coincidences." Horn Book

Smith, Lindsay

Sekret; Lindsay Smith. Roaring Brook Press 2014 345 p. (hardback) $17.99
Grades: 8 9 10 11 12 **Fic**

1. Spies -- Fiction 2. Psychics -- Fiction 3. Soviet Union -- Fiction 4. Russia -- History -- 1917-1991, Soviet Union -- Fiction 5. KGB -- Fiction 6. Psychic ability -- Fiction 7. Soviet Union -- History -- 1953-1985 -- Fiction
ISBN 1596438924; 9781596438927

LC 2013027913

Sequel: Skandal (2015)

In this book, by Lindsay Smith, "Yulia's father always taught her to hide her thoughts and control her emotions to survive the harsh realities of Soviet Russia. But when she's captured by the KGB and forced to work as a psychic spy with a mission to undermine the U.S. space program, she's thrust into a world of suspicion, deceit, and horrifying power." (Publisher's note)

"We the Living meets Genius Squad, this novel follows the misfortunes of Yulia, one of a group of psychic teens pressed into the service of the 1960s KGB. The concept is ambitious and the heroine fiery, but there is a surfeit of plot elements (including a hokey love triangle) and the writing is frequently turgid." Horn Book

Smith, Roland C., 1951-

Chupacabra; Roland Smith. Scholastic Press 2013 336 p. illustrations $16.99
Grades: 5 6 7 8 **Fic**

1. Cryptozoology 2. Kidnapping -- Fiction 3. Mythical animals -- Fiction 4. Father-daughter relationship -- Fiction 5. Chupacabras -- Fiction 6. Missing persons -- Fiction 7. Adventure and adventurers -- Fiction
ISBN 0545178177; 9780545178174

LC 2013404665

This book, part of the Cryptid Hunters series, by Roland Smith, "reunites Marty and his unusual uncle, cryptozoologist Travis Wolfe, as they search the world for Wolfe's daughter, Grace. Grace has been kidnapped by her grandfather, the ruthless and dangerous Noah Blackwood. . . . Now, with word that the mysterious creature known as Chupacabra has been sighted again, Wolfe is torn between his obsession with finding cryptids and his desperate need to rescue his daughter." (Publisher's note)

"Plunging readers in where Tentacles (Scholastic, 2009) left off, this fast-paced novel opens right after Grace discovers that her twin brother, Marty, is in fact her cousin, and that her father's unscrupulous enemy, Noah Blackwood, is actually her grandfather...Though this sequel suffers in comparison to the previous books in the series, Smith adeptly adds enough new characters, dangers, and cool science to reel in reluctant readers and keep them turning pages long after their lights should have been turned off.—" SLJ

Other titles in the series include:

Cryptid Hunters (2005)
Mutation (2014)
Tentacles (2009)

Cryptid hunters. Hyperion Books for Children 2005 348p $15.99; pa $5.99

Grades: 5 6 7 8 **Fic**

1. Adventure fiction 2. Twins -- Fiction 3. Congo (Republic) -- Fiction

ISBN 0-7868-5161-9; 0-7868-5162-7 pa

Twins, Grace and Marty, along with a mysterious uncle, are dropped into the middle of the Congolese jungle in search of their missing photojournalist parents.

"The action is nonstop in this well-paced jungle adventure, and Smith adds a deeper layer in scenes of Marty and Grace discovering truths about their complicated family relationships." Booklist

Followed by: Tentacles (2009)

The **edge**; by Roland Smith. Houghton Mifflin Harcourt 2015 240 p. $17.99

Grades: 6 7 8 9 10 **Fic**

1. Snow leopard -- Fiction 2. Mountaineering -- Fiction 3. Wilderness survival -- Fiction 4. Leopard -- Fiction 5. Survival -- Fiction 6. Hindu Kush Mountains (Afghanistan and Pakistan) -- Fiction

ISBN 9780544341227

LC 2014044086

Sequel to: Peak

"The International Peace Ascent is the brainchild of billionaire Sebastian Plank: Recruit a global team of young climbers and film an inspiring, world-uniting documentary. The adventure begins when fifteen-year-old Peak Marcello and his mountaineer mother are helicoptered to . . . the Hindu Kush Mountains on the Afghanistan-Pakistan border. When the camp is attacked and his mother taken, Peak has no choice but to track down the perpetrators." (Publisher's note)

Elephant run. Hyperion Books for Children 2007 318p $15.99

Grades: 6 7 8 9 10 11 12 **Fic**

1. Myanmar -- Fiction 2. Elephants -- Fiction 3. Prisoners of war -- Fiction 4. World War, 1939-1945 -- Fiction

ISBN 978-1-4231-0402-5; 1-4231-0402-1

LC 2007-13310

Nick endures servitude, beatings, and more after his British father's plantation in Burma is invaded by the Japanese in 1941.

"The Burmese setting and the role of elephants in the lumbering industry are exceptionally well integrated into this wartime adventure tale." Bull Cent Child Books

Eruption; Roland Smith. Scholastic Press 2012 156 p. (Storm runners.)

Grades: 5 6 7 8 **Fic**

1. Circus -- Fiction 2. Rescue work -- Fiction 3. Volcanoes -- Mexico -- Fiction 4. Earthquakes -- Mexico -- Fiction 5. Father-son relationship -- Fiction 6. Mexico -- Fiction 7. Survival -- Fiction 8. Volcanoes -- Fiction 9. Earthquakes -- Fiction 10. Storm chasers -- Fiction 11. Circus animals -- Fiction

ISBN 0545081742; 9780545081740

LC 2011042743

In the third "installment in the 'Storm Runners' series, Chase and his father are off to Mexico to find the missing Rossi Family Circus. . . . [T]hey end up near a rumbling volcano. [Roland] Smith . . . gives the survival story an extra dose of octane with some escaped wild animals—in this case, a tiger that nearly devours Chase." (Booklist) ". . . [A]ll contact has been lost with the Rossi Brothers' Circus, on tour near Mexico City, in the wake of a major earthquake. This sends a crew headed by catastrophe experts Chase and his father John to the rescue. . . . [They find themselves on] Popocatepetl's shaking, landslide ridden slopes amid clouds of ash to discover human corpses, dead elephants and big cats, desperados, trapped refugees, dozens of badly injured villagers and . . . an escaped tiger." (Kirkus)

I, Q.: book one, Independence Hall. Sleeping Bear Press 2008 302p pa $8.95

Grades: 5 6 7 8 **Fic**

1. Adventure fiction 2. Spies -- Fiction 3. Terrorism -- Fiction

ISBN 978-1-58536-325-4 pa; 1-58536-325-1 pa

In Philadelphia, Angela realizes she's being followed, and Q soon learns the secret about Angela's real mother, a former Secret Service agent

"Adventure, suspense, humor, fascinating characters, and plot twists galore will draw middle-graders to this series starter." Booklist

Other titles in this series are:
The White House (2010)
Kitty Hawk (2012)
The Alamo (2013)
The Windy City (2014)
Alcatraz (2014)

I. Q.: book two, The White House. Sleeping Bear Press 2010 pa $8.95

Grades: 5 6 7 8 **Fic**

1. Spies -- Fiction 2. Siblings -- Fiction 3. Terrorism -- Fiction 4. Remarriage -- Fiction 5. Washington (D.C.) -- Fiction 6. Philadelphia (Pa.) -- Fiction 7. White House (Washington, D.C.) -- Fiction

ISBN 978-1-58536-456-5; 1-58536-456-8

LC 2011378292

Q (Quest) and Angela make it to the White House in Washington, D.C. to find that it is even harder to determine who are the 'good' and 'bad' guys than ever before.

"This spellbinding James Bond genre espionage novel for the middle school set will leave readers breathlessly waiting for the next installment." Voice Youth Advocates

Mutation; Roland Smith. Scholastic Press 2014 352 p. (Cryptid hunters) (hardback) $16.99

Grades: 5 6 7 8 **Fic**

1. Brazil -- Fiction 2. Missing persons -- Fiction 3. Jungles -- Fiction 4. Animals, Mythical -- Fiction 5. Adventure and adventurers -- Fiction

ISBN 0545081807; 9780545081801; 9780545081818

LC 2014017169

In this book by Roland Smith "Marty and his best friend, Luther, have managed to rescue Marty's cousin Grace from the clutches of the nefarious pseudo-naturalist Noah Blackwood, but . . . Marty's parents have been missing in Brazil for months. With time running out, Marty and the Cryptos Island crew race off for Brazil -- where they discover that Noah Blackwood has twisted the natural order of things beyond their wildest, most terrifying dreams." (Publisher's note)

"Marty, Grace, and friends make their way to Brazil to continue their twofold quest: find Marty's missing parents and stop the evil Noah Blackwood from continuing his unethical genetic experiments. Action, adventure, and high-tech gadgetry all combine into an exciting but over-the-top story. Stunning revelations and other dramatic turns provide additional impetus to keep readers turning the pages." Horn Book

★ **Peak**. Harcourt 2007 246p $17
Grades: 7 8 9 10 **Fic**
1. Mountaineering -- Fiction 3. Father-son relationship -- Fiction 4. Mount Everest (China and Nepal) -- Fiction
ISBN 978-0-15-202417-8
LC 2006024325

After fourteen-year-old Peak Marcello is arrested for scaling a New York City skyscraper, he is sent to live with his long-lost father, who wants him to be the youngest person to reach the Everest summit.

"This is a thrilling, multifaceted adventure story. Smith includes plenty of mountaineering facts told in vivid detail. . . . But he also explores other issues, such as the selfishness that nearly always accompanies the intensely single-minded." Booklist

Storm runners. Scholastic Press 2011 143p $16.99
Grades: 5 6 7 8 **Fic**
1. Florida -- Fiction 2. Hurricanes -- Fiction 3. Father-son relationship -- Fiction
ISBN 978-0-545-08175-7; 0-545-08175-0
LC 2010-32720

Twelve-year-old Chase Masters travels the country with his father, a "storm runner," but he is tested in ways he never could have imagined when he and a new friend are caught in a hurricane near St. Petersburg, Florida.

"This is an exciting, quick read. . . . Readers will feel engaged with Chase and his friends in their struggles to survive." SLJ

Followed by: The surge (2011)

The **surge**. Scholastic Press 2011 133p il (Storm runners) $16.99
Grades: 5 6 7 8 **Fic**
1. Circus -- Fiction 2. Storms -- Fiction 3. Florida -- Fiction 4. Hurricanes -- Fiction
ISBN 978-0-545-08179-5; 0-545-08179-3
LC 2011017358

After barely surviving a terrifying hurricane, Chase and his friends Nicole and Rashawn have made it to the safety of Nicole's family farm, which is also the winter home of the Rossi Brothers Circus, where flood waters are rising and dangerous circus animals are on the loose.

"A high-velocity page-turner." Kirkus

Smith, Ronald L.

★ **Hoodoo**; by Ronald L. Smith. Houghton Mifflin Harcourt 2015 224 p. (hardback) $16.99
Grades: 4 5 6 7 **Fic**
1. Magic -- Fiction 2. Alabama -- Fiction 3. Demonology -- Fiction 4. African Americans -- Fiction 5. Family life -- Alabama -- Fiction 6. Country life -- Alabama -- Fiction 7. Alabama -- History -- 20th century -- Fiction
ISBN 0544445252; 9780544445253
LC 2014046838

Coretta Scott King/John Steptoe New Talent Author Award (2016)

In this novel by Ronald L. Smith "twelve-year-old Hoodoo Hatcher was born into a family with a rich tradition of practicing folk magic: hoodoo, as most people call it. But even though his name is Hoodoo, he can't seem to cast a simple spell. When a mysterious man called the Stranger comes to town, Hoodoo starts dreaming of the dead rising from their graves. The entire town is at risk from the Stranger's black magic, and only Hoodoo can defeat him. He'll just need to learn how to conjure first." (Publisher's note)

"Folks in the insular 1930s African American community of Sardis, Alabama, believe in God and in folk magick, or hoodoo. Twelve-year-old Hoodoo Hatcher's father tried to cheat death by transporting part of his soul into Hoodoo. To free him, Hoodoo must destroy the evil Stranger. This creepy Southern Gothic ghost story is steeped in time and place; Hoodoo's folksy asides relieve tension." Horn Book

Smith, Sarah

The **other** side of dark. Atheneum Books for Young Readers 2010 312p $16.99
Grades: 6 7 8 9 10 **Fic**
1. Ghost stories 2. Orphans -- Fiction 4. Supernatural -- Fiction 5. Boston (Mass.) -- Fiction 6. Race relations -- Fiction 7. African Americans -- Fiction
ISBN 978-1-4424-0280-5; 1-4424-0280-6
LC 2010-14690

Since losing both of her parents, fifteen-year-old Katie can see and talk to ghosts, which makes her a loner until fellow student Law sees her drawing of a historic house and together they seek a treasure rumored to be hidden there by illegal slave-traders.

The author "weaves complicated racial issues into a romantic, mysterious novel." Booklist

Smith, Sherri L.

★ **Flygirl**. G.P. Putnam's Sons 2009 275p $16.99
Grades: 7 8 9 10 **Fic**
1. Air pilots -- Fiction 2. Women air pilots -- Fiction 3. African Americans -- Fiction 4. World War, 1939-1945 -- Fiction
ISBN 978-0-399-24709-5; 0-399-24709-2
LC 2008-25407

During World War II, a light-skinned African American girl "passes" for white in order to join the Women Airforce Service Pilots.

"The details about navigation are exciting, but tougher than any flight maneuver are Ida Mae's loneliness, shame, and fear that she will be thrown out of the the military, feelings that culminate in an unforgettable climax." Booklist

Smy, Pam

Thornhill; Pam Smy. First American edition Roaring Brook Press 2017 544 p. ill. (hardcover) $19.99
Grades: 5 6 7 8 9 **Fic**
1. Ghost stories 2. Orphanages -- Fiction 3. Conduct of life -- Fiction 4. Selective mutism -- Fiction 5. Ghosts -- Fiction 6. Puppets -- Fiction 7. Bullying -- Fiction
ISBN 162672654X; 9781626726543
LC 2017001991

In this book, by Pam Smy, "parallel stories set in different times, one told in prose and one in pictures, converge as a girl unravels the mystery of the abandoned Thornhill Institute next door. 1982: Mary is a lonely orphan at the Thornhill Institute For Children. . . . 2017: Ella has just moved. . . . From her room on the top floor of her new home, she has a perfect view of the dilapidated, abandoned Thornhill Institute across the way." (Publisher's note)

"Dual stories set decades apart unfold together in this hybrid novel told in diary entries and eerie grayscale illustrations." Booklist

Snicket, Lemony, 1970-

File under: 13 suspicious incidents; by Lemony Snicket ; art by Seth. Little Brown & Co 2014 259 p. (All the wrong questions) (hardback) $12
Grades: 4 5 6 7 **Fic**
1. Humorous fiction 3. Apprentices -- Fiction 4. City and town life

-- Fiction 5. Mystery and detective stories
ISBN 0316284033; 9780316284035

LC 2013037873

This book, by Lemony Snicket, presents "thirteen mini-mysteries. Paintings have been falling off of walls, a loud and loyal dog has gone missing, a specter has been seen walking the pier at midnight--strange things are happening all over the town of Stain'd-By-The-Sea. . . . Join the investigation and tackle the mysteries alongside Snicket, then turn to the back of the book to see the solution revealed." (Publisher's note)

"Kid-detective Lemony Snicket treats us to thirteen short mysteries (missing newt, ghostly appearance, series of break-ins) in which he leaves readers poised just before the reveal, with a chance to solve the mystery themselves before they flip to the back of the book. (It's Encyclopedia Brown for Snicket-Hipsters.) The actual puzzles are dandy, and the format is ideal for the author's comic avalanche." Horn Book

Other titles in the series include:
Who Could That be at This Hour
When Did You See Her Last
Shouldn't You Be in School

Shouldn't you be in school? Lemony Snicket. Little, Brown & Co. 2014 325 p. illustrations (some color) (All the wrong questions) (hardcover) $16

Grades: 4 5 6 7 **Fic**

1. School stories 2. Arson -- Fiction 3. Humorous stories 4. Apprentices -- Fiction 5. Detective and mystery stories 6. Arson investigation -- Fiction
ISBN 0316123064; 9780316123068; 9780316225045; 9780316279703; 9780316409681

LC 2014933203

In this children's book by Lemony Snicket "Lemony Snicket must work together with his incompetent chaperone to figure out who is burning down all of the buildings in the quaint town of Stain'd-by-the-Sea. Snicket is part of a special program, the V.F.D., and spends his days sleuthing with his chaperone, Theodora, in an attempt to catch the elusive and mysterious Hangfire, who is supposedly to blame for all of the mysterious happenings." (School Library Journal)

"In his third adventure, twelve-year-old Lemony Snicket, apprentice investigator, tackles a series of arsons in the economically depressed and highly mysterious town of Stain'd-by-the-Sea. Readers already hooked by this series will be pleased to check in with heroic librarian Qwerty, investigative journalist Moxie Mallahan, and the bickering Officers Mitchum and their bullying son, Stewart...As to the actual story, clues of the gray-matter sort (such as anagrams) combine with escapes, attacks, cliffhangers, and looming bad guys, keeping the whole crazy plot buoyant. Just." Horn Book

When did you see her last? Lemony Snicket ; illustrated by Seth. Little Brown & Co 2013 288 p. (All the wrong questions) (hardcover) $16

Grades: 4 5 6 7 **Fic**

1. Missing persons -- fiction 2. Mystery fiction -- fiction
ISBN 0316123056; 9780316123051; 9780316251952

LC 2012955921

Parents' Choice: Silver Medal Fiction (2013)

In this book, author Lemony Snicket "has a new case to solve when he and his chaperone are hired to find a missing girl. Is the girl a runaway? Or was she kidnapped? Was she seen last at the grocery store? Or could she have stopped at the diner? Is it really any of your business? These are All The Wrong Questions." (Publisher's note)

"A further adventure for the young private eye Lemony Snicket involves the disappearance of a brilliant young chemist, the only hope for rejuvenation of the town of Stain'd-by-the-Sea. In the course of Snicket's investigation he reconnects with characters from "Who Could That Be at This Hour?". This tongue-in-cheek adventure is peppered with references to classic children's books." (Horn Book)

★ **Who** could that be at this hour? by Lemony Snicket ; art by Seth. Little, Brown 2012 272 p. $15.99

Grades: 4 5 6 7 **Fic**

1. Bildungsromans 2. Mystery fiction 3. Humorous fiction 4. Statues -- Fiction 5. Stealing -- Fiction 6. Apprentices -- Fiction
ISBN 0316123080; 9780316123082

LC 2012012657

This children's adventure mystery, by Lemony Snicket, begins in "Stain'd-by-the-Sea, the mostly deserted town where 12-year-old Lemony Snicket takes his first case as apprentice to chaperone S. Theodora Markson. They have been hired by Mrs. Murphy Sallis to retrieve a vastly valuable statue of the local legend, the Bombinating Beast. . . . With the help and/or hindrance of girls Moxie and Ellington, can Snicket keep his promises and come close to solving a mystery?" (Kirkus Reviews)

Other titles in this series are:
When did you see her last? (2013)
Shouldn't you be in school? (2014)
Why is this night different from all the other nights? (2015)

Sniegoski, Tom

Quest for the spark; book one. written by Tom Sniegoski; illustrated by Jeff Smith; color by Steve Hamaker. Graphix 2011 218p il (Bone) $22.99; pa $10.99

Grades: 4 5 6 7 **Fic**

1. Fantasy fiction 2. Adventure fiction 3. Magic -- Fiction 4. Dreams -- Fiction 5. Heroes and heroines -- Fiction
ISBN 978-0-545-14101-7; 0-545-14101-X; 978-0-545-14102-4 pa; 0-545-14102-8 pa

LC 2010017002

Twelve-year-old Tom Elm, his raccoon friend Roderick, Percival, Abbey, and Barclay Bone, warrior-priest Randolf, and forest-woman Lorimar join in a quest to find the pieces of the Spark that can save Dreaming—and the Waking World—from a Darkness created by the Nacht.

"At long last . . . we return to the Valley that was the setting for Smith's comics-landscape-changing Bone, though this adventure takes place in prose rather than panels. . . . As long as fans are not expecting a repeat of the old magic and not too disappointed that there isn't nearly enough of Smith's always excellent full-color, full-page artwork helping out, it looks as if they're in for a cheery jaunt back through a beloved world." Booklist

Quest for the Spark; Book 2 written by Tom Sniegoski ; illustrated by Jeff Smith ; color by Steve Hamaker. Graphix 2012 234 p. (hardcover : alk. paper) $22.99

Grades: 4 5 6 7 **Fic**

1. Fantasy fiction 2. Magic -- Fiction 3. Dreams -- Fiction 4. Dragons -- Fiction 5. Humorous stories 6. Heroes -- Fiction 7. Adventure and adventurers -- Fiction
ISBN 9780545141031; 9780545141048

LC 2011020281

This book is set in the world of illustrator Jeff Smith's "Bone" graphic novels. Here, author Tom Sniegoski tells the story of "Tom, a Valley turnip farmer" who "receives a vision that the peaceful otherworld of the Dreaming is under attack. The evil Nacht, a renegade Dragon, seeks to control the dreamland, and through it, the Waking World as well. A mysterious forest woman tells Tom that he has been chosen to lead a quest to find the scattered pieces of the Spark--the light of creation that can drive back the dark power. When his family falls under the Nacht's corrupted sleep spell, Tom realizes that he has no choice and sets out with his best friend, a talking raccoon." (School Libr J)

Snow, Alan

Here be monsters! an adventure involving magic, trolls, and other creatures. written and illustrated by Alan Snow. Atheneum Books for Young Readers 2006 529p il (The Ratbridge chronicles) $17.95; pa $8.99

Grades: 4 5 6 7 **Fic**

1. Fantasy fiction 2. Monsters -- Fiction

ISBN 978-0-689-87047-7; 0-689-87047-7; 978-0-689-87048-4 pa; 0-689-87048-5 pa

LC 2005-24438

While gathering food to bring to his grandfather, young Arthur becomes trapped in the city of Ratbridge, where he and some new friends try to stop a plot to shrink the monsters of Arthur's home, the Underworld, for a nefarious purpose

"Helpful in creating the settings and bringing the more fantastic characters to life, the illustrations, which are often amusing, also make the book accessible to younger children who like lengthy books. Snow's inventive fantasy . . . combines stout hearts, terrible troubles, and inspired lunacy." Booklist

Followed by:

Worse things happen at sea! (2013)

Somper, Justin

Black heart. Little, Brown 2009 504p (Vampirates) $15.99

Grades: 6 7 8 9 **Fic**

1. Adventure fiction 2. Twins -- Fiction 3. Pirates -- Fiction 4. Vampires -- Fiction

ISBN 978-0-316-02087-9; 0-316-02087-7

Sequel to: Blood Captain (2008)

When a high-profile pirate is slain, the Pirate Federation takes decisive action and begins training up a ship of dedicated vampire hunters led by Captain Cheng Li and pirate prodigy Connor Tempest. Meanwhile, Connor's twin sister Grace enjoys a bittersweet reunion with their mother and learns some important and shocking news that will leave the twins facing a very uncertain future.

"This is a fast-paced adventure story with a few surprises along the way." SLJ

Blood Captain; 1st U.S. ed.; Little, Brown and Co. 2008 569p (Vampirates) $15.99

Grades: 6 7 8 9 **Fic**

1. Adventure fiction 2. Twins -- Fiction 3. Pirates -- Fiction 4. Vampires -- Fiction

ISBN 978-0-316-02085-5; 0-316-02085-0

LC 2007031538

Sequel to: Tide of terror (2007)

First published 2007 in the United Kingdom

While Connor faces trouble in the form of an obnoxious new crewmate, Grace, his twin sister, seeks out a vampirate guru who might be able to heal their dear friend Lorcan's blindness.

"The haunting characters, both new and from earlier books, are again well rounded and believable, each described with care and an attention to detail that should allow new readers to follow the story." Voice Youth Advocates

Followed by: Black heart (2009)

Demons of the ocean. Little, Brown 2006 330p (Vampirates) $15.99

Grades: 6 7 8 9 **Fic**

1. Adventure fiction 2. Twins -- Fiction 3. Pirates -- Fiction 4. Vampires -- Fiction

ISBN 0-316-01373-0

When twins Connor and Grace's ship is wrecked in a storm and Connor is rescued by pirates, he believes that Grace has been taken aboard the mythical Vampirate's ship, and he is determined to find her.

"This winning fantasy features both pirates and vampires with adventure, bloodcurling action, and sinister characters." Voice Youth Advocates

Other titles in this series are:

Tide of terror (2007)

Blood Captain (2008)

Black heart (2009)

Empire of night (2010)

Empire of night. Little, Brown 2010 490p il (Vampirates) $15.99

Grades: 6 7 8 9 **Fic**

1. Twins -- Fiction 2. Pirates -- Fiction 3. Siblings -- Fiction 4. Vampires -- Fiction 5. Seafaring life -- Fiction

ISBN 978-0-316-03322-0; 0-316-03322-7

LC 2010019251

Evil Sidorio continues to expand his empire across the oceans, but as he faces growing opposition from both the Pirate Federation and the vampirate realm, twins Grace and Connor Tempest are caught in the conflict.

"Readers looking for suspense and gore won't be disappointed; those wanting character development will find some satisfaction too." Horn Book Guide

Tide of terror. Little, Brown 2007 459p (Vampirates)

Grades: 6 7 8 9 **Fic**

1. Pirates -- Fiction 2. Vampires -- Fiction

ISBN 9780316013741

Sequel to: Demons of the ocean (2006)

Fourteen-year-old orphaned twins Grace and Connor are aboard the pirate ship Diablo when an attack goes wrong and one of Connor's friends is killed. Hoping to keep her brother safe, Grace discovers the elite Pirate Academy, a place where Connor could learn about the pirate way without risking his life.

Sones, Sonya

Stop pretending; what happened when my big sister went crazy. HarperCollins Pubs. 1999 149p lib bdg $14.89; pa $6.99

Grades: 6 7 8 9 **Fic**

1. Sisters -- Fiction 2. Mental illness -- Fiction

ISBN 0-06-028386-6 lib bdg; 0-06-446218-8 pa

LC 99-11473

"Based on the journals Sones wrote at the age of 13 when her 19-year-old sister was hospitalized due to manic depression, the simply crafted but deeply felt poems reflect her thoughts, fears, hopes, and dreams during that troubling time." SLJ

★ **What** my girlfriend doesn't know. Simon & Schuster Books for Young Readers 2007 291p $16.99

Grades: 7 8 9 10 **Fic**

1. School stories 2. Artists -- Fiction 3. Boston (Mass.) -- Fiction 4. Dating (Social customs) -- Fiction

ISBN 978-0-689-87602-8; 0-689-87602-5

LC 2006-14682

Sequel to What my mother doesn't know (2001)

Fourteen-year-old Robin Murphy is so unpopular at high school that his name is slang for "loser," and so when he begins dating the beautiful and popular Sophie her reputation plummets, but he finds acceptance as a student in a drawing class at Harvard.

"Robin's believable voice is distinctive, and Sones uses her spare words (and a few drawings) to expert effect." Booklist

What my mother doesn't know. Simon & Schuster Bks. for Young Readers 2001 259p hardcover o.p. pa $7.99

Grades: 7 8 9 10 **Fic**

1. Novels in verse 2. Dating (Social customs) -- Fiction
ISBN 0-689-84114-0; 0-689-85553-2 pa

LC 00-52634

This is "a fast, funny, touching book. . . . The very short, sometimes rhythmic lines make each page fly. Sophie's voice is colloquial and intimate." Booklist

Followed by What my girlfriend doesn't know (2007)

Sonnenblick, Jordan

★ **After** ever after. Scholastic Press 2010 260p $16.99

Grades: 5 6 7 8 **Fic**

1. School stories 2. Cancer -- Fiction 3. Friendship -- Fiction 4. Family life -- Fiction
ISBN 978-0-439-83706-4; 0-439-83706-5

Jeffery's cancer is in remission but the chemotherapy and radiation treatments have left him with concentration problems, and he worries about school work, his friends, his family, and a girl who likes him

"Sonnenblick imbues Jeffrey with a smooth, likable, and unaffected voice. . . . As hilarious as it is tragic, and as honest as it is hopeful . . . [this book is] irresistable reading." Booklist

Drums, girls, & dangerous pie. Scholastic Press 2005 273p $16.99

Grades: 5 6 7 8 **Fic**

1. Brothers -- Fiction 2. Leukemia -- Fiction
ISBN 0-439-75519-0

LC 2004-62563

First published 2004 by Turning Tide Press

When his younger brother is diagnosed with leukemia, thirteen-year-old Steven tries to deal with his complicated emotions, his school life, and his desire to support his family.

"A story that could have morphed into melodrama is saved by reality, rawness, and the wit Sonnenblick infuses into Steven's first-person voice." Booklist

Followed by: After ever after (2010)

Falling over sideways; Jordan Sonnenblick. Scholastic Press 2016 272 p.

Grades: 7 8 9 10 **Fic**

1. Stroke -- Fiction 2. Family life -- Fiction 3. Children of parents with disabilities -- Fiction 4. Schools -- Fiction 5. Brothers and sisters -- Fiction 6. Fathers and daughters -- Fiction 7. Mothers and daughters -- Fiction 8. Cerebrovascular disease -- Fiction
ISBN 9780545863247

LC 2016022926

"The butt of jokes in her school and at home, awkward Claire is forced to confront more serious aspects of her life in the wake of her father's medical emergency, which challenges Claire to bring laughter back into the lives of those she loves." (Publisher's note)

"In Claire, Sonnenblick crafts a convincing, lightly sardonic narrator, and her bittersweet and hopeful story will likely stay with readers for some time." Horn Book

★ **Notes** from the midnight driver. Scholastic Press 2006 265p $16.99

Grades: 8 9 10 11 12 **Fic**

1. Old age -- Fiction 2. Musicians -- Fiction 3. Friendship -- Fiction
ISBN 0-439-75779-7

LC 2005-27972

After being assigned to perform community service at a nursing home, sixteen-year-old Alex befriends a cantankerous old man who has some lessons to impart about jazz guitar playing, love, and forgiveness.

The author "deftly infiltrates the teenage mind to produce a first-person narrative riddled with enough hapless confusion, mulish equivocation, and beleaguered deadpan humor to have readers nodding with recognition, sighing with sympathy, and gasping with laughter—often on the same page." Horn Book

★ **Zen** and the art of faking it. Scholastic Press 2007 264p $16.99; pa $7.99

Grades: 5 6 7 8 **Fic**

1. School stories 2. Pennsylvania -- Fiction 3. Zen Buddhism -- Fiction 4. Asian Americans -- Fiction
ISBN 978-0-439-83707-1; 0-439-83707-3; 978-0-439-83709-5 pa; 0-439-83709-X pa

LC 2006-28841

When thirteen-year-old San Lee moves to a new town and school for the umpteenth time, he is looking for a way to stand out when his knowledge of Zen Buddhism, gained in his previous school, provides the answer—and the need to quickly become a convincing Zen master.

The author gives readers "plenty to laugh at. . . . Mixed with more serious scenes, . . . lighter moments take a basic message about the importance of honesty and forgiveness and treat it with panache." Publ Wkly

Sonnichsen, A. L.

Red butterfly; A. L. Sonnichsen, illustrated by Amy June Bates. Simon & Schuster Books for Young Readers 2015 392 p. hardcover $16.99

Grades: 4 5 6 7 **Fic**

1. Novels in verse 2. China -- Fiction 3. Adoption -- Fiction 4. Families -- Fiction 5. Foundlings -- Fiction 6. Abnormalities, Human -- Fiction 7. Intercountry adoption -- Fiction
ISBN 1481411098; 9781481411097

LC 2013050300

In this book by A. L. Sonnichsen, "Kara never met her birth mother. Abandoned as an infant, she was taken in by an American woman living in China. Now eleven, Kara spends most of her time in their apartment, wondering why she and Mama cannot leave the city of Tianjin and go live with Daddy in Montana. Mama tells Kara to be content with what she has. . . but what if Kara secretly wants more?" (Publisher's note)

"Sympathetic readers will appreciate that Kara learns to build trust with those who demonstrate their compassion in constructive attempts to right some of the wrongs of her difficult beginnings." Booklist

Sorosiak, Carlie

Wild blue wonder; Carlie Sorosiak. HarperTeen, an imprint of Harpercollins Publishers 2018 346 p. $17.99

Grades: 7 8 9 10 11 **Fic**

1. Grief -- Fiction 2. Friendship -- Fiction 3. Family life -- Fiction
ISBN 0062563998; 9780062563996

In this book, by Carlie Sorosiak, "last June, the summer camp Quinn's family owns in Winship, Maine, was still a magical place. . . . [It was where] Quinn fell in love with her best friend, Dylan. Then the accident happened. Now it's winter, the magic has drained from Quinn's life. . . . But the new boy in town, Alexander, doesn't see her as the monster she believes herself to be. . . . [S]he begins to understand the truth about love, loss, and monsters--real and imagined." (Publisher's note)

Sovern, Megan Jean

★ The **meaning** of Maggie; by Megan Jean Sovern. Chronicle Books 2014 224 p. (alk. paper) $16.99

Grades: 4 5 6 7 **Fic**

1. Family life -- Fiction 2. Middle schools -- Fiction 3. Multiple sclerosis -- Fiction 4. Father-daughter relationship -- Fiction 5. Fathers and daughters -- Fiction

ISBN 1452110212; 9781452110219

LC 2013029644

In this book, by Megan Jean Sovern, "Maggie Mayfield has decided to write a memoir of the past year of her life. And what a banner year it's been! During this period she's Student of the Month on a regular basis, an official shareholder of Coca-Cola stock, and defending Science Fair champion. Most importantly, though, this is the year Maggie has to pull up her bootstraps (the family motto) and finally learn why her cool-dude dad is in a wheelchair, no matter how scary that is." (Publisher's note)

"Maggie's self-realizations come quickly, but her distinct voice, with a snarky superiority that often masks her true vulnerability, creates a character who's not easy to love but tough to forget." Horn Book

Speare, Elizabeth George, 1908-1994

Calico Captive; illustrated by W. T. Mars. Sandpiper 2001 274p ill. (pbk.) $6.95

Grades: 6 7 8 **Fic**

1. Historical fiction 2. Prisoners -- Fiction 3. Native Americans -- Fiction 4. United States -- History -- 1755-1763, French and Indian War -- Fiction

ISBN 9780618150762

LC 57009017

In this book, set "[i]n the year 1754, the stillness of Charlestown, New Hampshire, is shattered by the terrifying cries of an Indian raid. Young Miriam Willard . . . finds herself . . . a captive on a forest trail, caught up in the ebb and flow of the French and Indian War. It is a harrowing march north. . . . At the end of the trail waits a life of hard work and, perhaps, even a life of slavery. . . . Miriam and her companions finally reach Montreal, a city of shifting loyalties filled with the intrigue of war, and here, by a sudden twist of fortune, Miriam meets the prominent Du Quesne family, who introduce her to a life she has never imagined. Based on an actual narrative diary published in 1807, . . . [the book] reenacts a . . . facet of history." (Publisher's note)

★ The **witch** of Blackbird Pond. Houghton Mifflin 1958 249p $17

Grades: 6 7 8 9 **Fic**

1. Young adult literature 2. Puritans -- Fiction 3. Witchcraft -- Fiction 4. Connecticut -- History -- 1600-1775, Colonial period -- Fiction

ISBN 0-395-07114-3

LC 58-11063

Awarded the Newbery Medal, 1959

"Headstrong and undisciplined, Barbados-bred Kit Tyler is an embarrassment to her Puritan relatives, and her sincere attempts to aid a reputed witch soon bring her to trial as a suspect." Child Books Too Good to Miss

Spinelli, Jerry, 1941

★ **Crash**. Knopf 1996 162p hardcover o.p. pa $6.99; lib bdg $17.99

Grades: 5 6 7 8 **Fic**

1. Football -- Fiction 2. Friendship -- Fiction 3. Grandfathers -- Fiction

ISBN 0440238579; 0679879579; 0679979573

LC 95030942

"Crash is a star football player. He torments Penn, a classmate who is everything Crash is not—friendly, small, and a pacifist. When his beloved grandfather comes to live with his family and suffers a debilitating stroke, Crash begins to see value in many of the things he has scorned." Horn Book Guide

Hokey Pokey; by Jerry Spinelli. Alfred A. Knopf Books for Young Readers 2013 304 p. (hard cover) $15.99

Grades: 5 6 7 8 **Fic**

1. Bildungsromans 2. Fantasy fiction 3. Imaginary places 4. Play -- Fiction 5. Growth -- Fiction

ISBN 0375831983; 9780307975706; 9780375831980; 9780375832017; 9780375931987

LC 2012004177

In this book, Jerry Spinelli "creates a surreal landscape." There are no adults in "Hokey Pokey, where boys and girls dine on flavored ice and spend their days watching cartoons, playing cowboy games, and using their bicycles as trusty steeds. Jack's bike, Scramjet, is . . . stolen by his archenemy, Jubilee. This marks the first of a series of unsettling events that give Jack, a boy on the brink of adolescence, the eerie impression that 'things have shifted.'" (Publishers Weekly)

Jake and Lily; Jerry Spinelli. 1st ed. Balzer + Bray 2012 335 p. (hardback) $15.99

Grades: 3 4 5 6 7 **Fic**

1. Twins -- Fiction 2. Bullies -- Fiction 3. Children's stories 4. Friendship -- Fiction 5. Individuality -- Fiction 6. Brothers and sisters -- Fiction

ISBN 9780060281359; 9780060281366

LC 2011053362

This book offers a "story about a pair of twins growing apart. For almost as long as they can remember, Jake and Lily have shared a 'special sense,' which they call 'goombla.' . . . Lily tries to find out who she is without her brother, but it's hard work, and most of her attempts are unsuccessful. . . . Though the twins eventually rediscover their 'goombla,' . . . [author Jerry] Spinelli doesn't suggest that the two will go back to being the people they once were." (Publishers Weekly)

Love, Stargirl; [by] Jerry Spinelli. Alfred A. Knopf 2007 274p $16.99; lib bdg $19.99

Grades: 7 8 9 10 **Fic**

1. Letters -- Fiction 2. Pennsylvania -- Fiction

ISBN 978-0-375-81375-7; 978-0-375-91375-4 lib bdg

LC 2007002308

Still moping months after being dumped by her Arizona boyfriend Leo, fifteen-year-old Stargirl, a home-schooled free spirit, writes "the world's longest letter" to Leo, describing her new life in Pennsylvania.

"Fans of Stargirl will be charmed by this satisfying sequel." Kliatt

★ **Maniac** Magee; a novel. Little, Brown 1990 184p $16.99; pa $6.99

Grades: 5 6 7 8 **Fic**

1. Orphans -- Fiction 2. Race relations -- Fiction 3. Homeless

persons -- Fiction
ISBN 0-316-80722-2; 0-316-80906-3 pa
LC 89-27144

Awarded the Newbery Medal, 1991

"Orphaned at three, Jeffery Lionel Magee, after eight unhappy years with relatives, one day takes off running. A year later, he ends up 200 miles away in Two Mills, a highly segregated community. Part tall tale and part contemporary realistic fiction, this unusual novel magically weaves timely issues of homelessness, racial prejudice, and illiteracy into an energetic story that bursts with creativity, enthusiasm, and hope for the future. In short, it's a celebration of life." Booklist

Smiles to go. Joanna Cotler Books 2008 248p $16.99; lib bdg $17.89; pa $6.99

Grades: 6 7 8 9 10 **Fic**

1. School stories 2. Siblings -- Fiction 3. Friendship -- Fiction 4. Family life -- Fiction
ISBN 978-0-06-028133-5; 0-06-028133-2; 978-0-06-028134-2 lib bdg; 0-06-028134-0 lib bdg; 978-0-06-447197-8 pa; 0-06-447197-7 pa
LC 2007-29563

Will Tuppence's life has always been ruled by science and common sense but in ninth grade, shaken up by the discovery that protons decay, he begins to see the entire world differently and gains new perspective on his relationships with his little sister and two closest friends.

"What makes a Spinelli novel isn't plotting so much as character, dialogue, voice and humor. The Spinelli touch remains true in this funny and thoroughly enjoyable read." Publ Wkly

★ **Stargirl**. Knopf 2000 186p pa $8.95; $15.95; lib bdg $17.99

Grades: 7 8 9 10 **Fic**

1. School stories 2. Arizona 3. Schools 4. Popularity 5. High schools 6. Individuality 7. Arizona -- Fiction 8. Eccentrics and eccentricities
ISBN 0-375-82233-X pa; 0-679-88637-0; 0-679-98637-5 lib bdg
LC 99-87944

In this story about the perils of popularity, the courage of nonconformity, and the thrill of first love, an eccentric student named Stargirl changes Mica High School forever

"As always respectful of his audience, Spinelli poses searching questions about loyalty to one's friends and oneself and leaves readers to form their own answers." Publ Wkly

Another title about Stargirl is:
Love, Stargirl (2007)

★ **Wringer**. HarperCollins Pubs. 1997 228p $16.99; lib bdg $16.89; pa $6.50

Grades: 4 5 6 7 **Fic**

1. Courage -- Fiction 2. Pigeons -- Fiction 3. Violence -- Fiction
ISBN 0-06-024913-7; 0-06-024914-5 lib bdg; 0-06-440578-8 pa
LC 96-37897

A Newbery Medal honor book, 1998

"Palmer LaRue is running out of birthdays. For as long as he can remember, he's dreaded the day he turns ten -- the day he'll take his place beside all the other ten-year-old boys in town, the day he'll be a wringer. But Palmer doesn't want to be a wringer...Palmer can't stop himself from being a wringer just like he can't stop himself from growing one year older, just like he can't stand up to a whole town -- right?" (Publisher's note)

"During the annual pigeon shoot, it is a town tradition for 10-year-old boys to break the necks of wounded birds. In this riveting story told with verve and suspense, Palmer rebels." SLJ

Spratt, R. A.

Friday Barnes, girl detective; by R.A. Spratt ; illustrations by Phil Gosier. Roaring Brook Press 2016 272 p. illustrations (Friday Barnes) (hardback) $13.99

Grades: 4 5 6 7 **Fic**

1. School stories 2. Genius -- Fiction 3. Private schools -- Fiction 4. Boarding schools -- Fiction 5. Mystery and detective stories
ISBN 9781626722972
LC 2015005923

In this book, by R. A. Spratt, illustrated by Phil Gosier, "When Friday Barnes, girl genius, solves a bank robbery, she uses the reward money to send herself to Highcrest Academy, the most exclusive boarding school in the country—and discovers it's a hotbed of crime! Soon she's investigating everything from disappearing homework to the terrifying Yeti haunting the school swamp. But the biggest mystery yet is Ian Wainscott." (Publisher's note)

"Delightful, highly logical, and well-informed fun." Kirkus

Other titles in this series are:
Under suspicion (2016)
Big trouble (2017)
No rules (2017)

Springer, Nancy

The **case** of the bizarre bouquets; an Enola Holmes mystery. [by] Nancy Springer. Philomel Books 2008 170p $14.99

Grades: 5 6 7 8 **Fic**

1. Mystery fiction 2. Missing persons -- Fiction 3. London (England) -- Fiction
ISBN 978-0-399-24518-3; 0-399-24518-9
LC 2007020435

Fourteen-year-old Enola Holmes, disguised as a beautiful woman, finds clues in floral bouquets as she searches for the missing Doctor Watson, a companion of her famous older brother, Sherlock.

"Springer's descriptions of late-19th-century England are vivid, the mystery is intriguing, and Enola's cleverness and capability will appeal to readers who like their heroines both sprightly and savvy." SLJ

The **case** of the cryptic crinoline; an Enola Holmes mystery. Philomel Books 2009 160p $14.99

Grades: 5 6 7 8 **Fic**

1. Nurses 2. Mystery fiction 3. Nonfiction writers 4. Great Britain -- Fiction 5. Missing persons -- Fiction 6. London (England) -- Fiction
ISBN 978-0-399-24781-1; 0-399-24781-5
LC 2008040475

In late nineteenth-century London, fourteen-year-old Enola Holmes, much younger sister of detective Sherlock Holmes, turns to Florence Nightingale for help when her investigation into the disappearance of a Crimean War widow grows cold.

"From the riveting prologue to the satisfying conclusion, readers are hurled headlong into Enola Holmes's latest case." SLJ

The **case** of the gypsy good-bye; an Enola Holmes mystery. Philomel Books 2010 166p

Grades: 5 6 7 8 **Fic**

1. Mystery fiction 2. Missing persons -- Fiction
ISBN 0399252363; 9780399252365

This is the concluding volume in the Enola Holmes mystery series. "As Enola searches for the missing Lady Blanchefleur del Campo, she discovers that her brother Sherlock is just as diligently searching for Enola herself. . . . He is in possession of a . . . message from their long-lost mother that only Enola can decipher. Sherlock, along with their brother Mycroft, must follow Enola into the reeking tunnels of London's dark underbelly as they solve a triple mystery: What has happened to their mother? And to Lady Blanchefleur? And what does either have to do with Mycroft, who holds Enola's future in his hands?" (Publisher's note) "Intermediate, middle school." (Horn Book)

"The series that features Enola Holmes, the (much) younger sister of Sherlock, continues to be flat-out among the best mysteries being written for young people today. Not only are the mysteries sharp attention holders but the conclusions are well thought out, with i's dotted and t's crossed in true Holmesian fashion." Booklist

The **case** of the left-handed lady; an Enola Holmes mystery. [by] Nancy Springer. Philomel Books 2007 234p $12.95

Grades: 5 6 7 8 **Fic**

1. Mystery fiction 2. Kidnapping -- Fiction 3. London (England) -- Fiction

ISBN 978-0-399-24517-6

LC 2006008261

Pursued by her much older brother, famed detective Sherlock Holmes, fourteen-year-old Enola, disguised and using false names, attempts to solve the kidnapping of a baronet's sixteen-year-old daughter in nineteenth-century London.

"Enola is beautifully drawn, as are the sights and sounds of late-nineteenth-century London." Booklist

★ The **case** of the missing marquess; an Enola Holmes mystery. Philomel Books 2006 216p pa $6.99; $10.99

Grades: 5 6 7 8 **Fic**

1. Mystery fiction 2. Missing persons -- Fiction 3. London (England) -- Fiction

ISBN 0-14-240933-2 pa; 0-399-24304-6

Enola Holmes, much younger sister of detective Sherlock Holmes, must travel to London in disguise to unravel the disappearance of her missing mother. "Grades four to eight." (Bull Cent Child Books)

"Enola's loneliness, intelligence, sense of humor, and sheer pluck make her an extremely appealing heroine." SLJ

Other titles about Enola Holmes are:

The case of the left-handed lady (2007)

The case of the bizarre bouquets (2008)

The case of the peculiar pink fan (2008)

The case of the cryptic crinoline (2009)

The case of the gypsy good-bye (2010)

The **case** of the peculiar pink fan; an Enola Holmes mystery. [by] Nancy Springer. Philomel Books 2008 183p $14.99

Grades: 5 6 7 8 **Fic**

1. Mystery fiction 2. London (England) -- Fiction 3. Lost and found possessions -- Fiction

ISBN 978-0-399-24780-4; 0-399-24780-7

LC 2008006933

While fourteen-year-old Enola Holmes endeavors to save her friend Lady Cecily Alistair from an unwelcome arranged marriage, she meets with some assistance from her older brother, Sherlock, and interference by the eldest, Mycroft.

"This features a strong mystery, intriguing family relationships, and the continuing thread of a daughter and mother lost to each other. . . . A rousing read with plenty of terrific Victorian detail." Booklist

Lionclaw; a tale of Rowan Hood. Philomel Bks. 2002 122p $16.99

Grades: 4 5 6 7 **Fic**

1. Adventure fiction 2. Middle Ages -- Fiction 3. Robin Hood (Legendary character) -- Fiction

ISBN 0-399-23716-X

LC 2001-45929

Sequel to: Rowan Hood, outlaw girl of Sherwood Forest (2001)

Young Lionel, minstrel in the outlaw band of Rowan Hood, daughter of Robin, tries to find his courage when she is abducted from Sherwood Forest

"Springer excels at keeping the action and adventure in high gear, and she creates strong characters with clear motivations." Booklist

Followed by: Outlaw princess of Sherwood (2003)

Rowan Hood returns; the final chapter. Philomel Bks. 2005 169p il $16.99

Grades: 4 5 6 7 **Fic**

1. Adventure fiction 2. Middle Ages -- Fiction 3. Robin Hood (Legendary character) -- Fiction

ISBN 0-399-24206-6

When she finds out who murdered her mother, Celandine, Rowan Hood returns to her former home to seek revenge.

★ **Rowan** Hood, outlaw girl of Sherwood Forest. Philomel Bks. 2001 170p hardcover o.p. pa $5.99

Grades: 4 5 6 7 **Fic**

1. Adventure fiction 2. Middle Ages -- Fiction 3. Robin Hood (Legendary character) -- Fiction

ISBN 0-399-23368-7; 0-698-11972-X pa

LC 00-63694

In her quest to connect with Robin Hood, the father she has never met, thirteen-year-old Rosemary disguises herself as a boy, befriends a half-wolf, half-dog, a runaway princess, and an overgrown boy whose singing is hypnotic, and makes peace with her elfin heritage

"This tale is a charmer, filled with exciting action, plenty of humor, engaging characters, and a nice fantasy twist." Booklist

Other titles about Rowan Hood are:

Lionclaw (2002)

Outlaw princess of Sherwood (2003)

Wild boy (2004)

Rowan Hood returns (2005)

Wild boy, a tale of Rowan Hood. Philomel Books 2004 115p hardcover o.p. pa $5.99

Grades: 4 5 6 7 **Fic**

1. Adventure fiction 2. Middle Ages -- Fiction 3. Robin Hood (Legendary character) -- Fiction

ISBN 0-399-24015-2; 978-0-14-240395-2 pa; 0-14-240395-4 pa

LC 2003-19146

Sequel to: Outlaw princess of Sherwood (2003)

Determined to avenge the death of his swineherd father at the hands of the Sheriff of Nottingham, Rook finally gets his chance when the Sheriff's son is captured by Robin Hood.

This includes "plenty of merrie-olde-England atmosphere and action." Booklist

Followed by: Rowan Hood returns (2005)

Springstubb, Tricia

Every single second; Tricia Springstuff; [edited by] Donna Bray. Balzer + Bray 2016 368 p. illustrations, map (hardback) $16.99

Grades: 4 5 6 7 8 **Fic**

1. Death -- Fiction 2. Family -- Fiction 3. Accidents -- Fiction 4.

Friendship -- Fiction
ISBN 9780062366283

LC 2015958372

This book, by Tricia Springstuff, is "about the effects of an accidental shooting on family, friendship, and community. . . . Twelve-year-old Nella Sabatini's life is changing too soon, too fast. Her best friend, Clem, doesn't seem concerned. . . . The only person who might understand how Nella feels is Angela, but the two of them have gone from being 'secret sisters' to not talking at all. Then Angela's idolized big brother makes a terrible, fatal mistake." (Publisher's note)

"The narrative structure of then and now, with short chapters devoted to the musings of a statue, sometimes intrudes upon the story, but this is rich in complex issues that include caring for the elderly, the problems of friendship, and the role of God in everyday life. Lots of plates here, but Springstubb keeps them spinning to a satisfying end." Booklist

St. Antoine, Sara, 1966-

Three bird summer; Sara St. Antoine. Candlewick Press 2014 256 p. $16.99

Grades: 5 6 7 **Fic**

1. Mystery fiction 2. Lakes -- Fiction 3. Summer -- Fiction 4. Neighbors -- Fiction 5. Grandmothers -- Fiction 6. Vacations -- Fiction 7. Summer resorts -- Fiction

ISBN 0763665649; 9780763665647

LC 2013946623

In this book, by Sara St. Antoine, "[f]or as long as he can remember, Adam and his parents have spent their summers at his grandmother's rustic cabin on Three Bird Lake. But this year will be different. There will be no rowdy cousins running around tormenting Adam. There will be no Uncle John or Aunt Jean. And there'll be no Dad to fight with Mom. This year, the lake will belong just to Adam. But then Adam meets Alice, the girl next door, who seems to want to become friends." (Publisher's note)

"St. Antoine's setting is remarkably palpable and lyrically described: pine trees are 'spindly giants in pointy hats.' And her characters are well realized, with Grandma both strong-willed and fragile and loner Adam experiencing true friendship." Horn Book

St. Crow, Lili

Betrayals; a strange angels novel. Razorbill 2009 296p pa $9.99

Grades: 8 9 10 11 12 **Fic**

1. Orphans -- Fiction 2. Vampires -- Fiction 3. Werewolves -- Fiction 4. Supernatural -- Fiction 5. Extrasensory perception -- Fiction

ISBN 978-1-59514-252-8; 1-59514-252-5

LC 2009021856

Sequel to: Strange Angels (2009)

For her own protection, sixteen-year-old Dru is taken to a secret training facility that feels more like a prison, but she faces great danger there and learns that a traitor who was involved in her mother's death now wants Dru dead.

Followed by: Jealousy (2010)

Defiance; a strange angels novel. Razorbill 2011 259p pa $9.99

Grades: 8 9 10 11 12 **Fic**

1. Orphans -- Fiction 2. Vampires -- Fiction 3. Werewolves -- Fiction 4. Supernatural -- Fiction 5. Extrasensory perception -- Fiction

ISBN 978-1-59514-392-1; 1-59514-392-0

LC 2010054253

Sequel to: Jealousy (2010)

When sixteen-year-old Dru's worst fears come true and Sergej kidnaps her best friend Graves, she embarks on a suicidal rescue mission in which she will test Christophe's training and try to defeat her mother's betrayer, Anna, for good.

Jealousy; a strange angels novel. Razorbill 2010 316p pa $9.99

Grades: 8 9 10 11 12 **Fic**

1. Orphans -- Fiction 2. Vampires -- Fiction 3. Werewolves -- Fiction 4. Supernatural -- Fiction 5. Extrasensory perception -- Fiction

ISBN 978-1-59514-290-0; 1-59514-290-8

Sequel to: Betrayals (2009)

Dru's best friend, Graves, and her strange and handsome savior, Christophe, are ready to help her take on the ultimate evil. But will their battle for Dru's heart get in the way of her survival?

Followed by: Defiance (2011)

Strange angels. Razorbill 2009 293p pa $9.99

Grades: 8 9 10 11 12 **Fic**

1. Orphans -- Fiction 2. Vampires -- Fiction 3. Werewolves -- Fiction 4. Supernatural -- Fiction 5. Extrasensory perception -- Fiction

ISBN 978-1-59514-251-1; 1-59514-251-7

LC 2008-39720

Sixteen-year-old Dru's psychic abilities helped her father battle zombies and other creatures of the "Real World," but now she must rely on herself, a "werwulf"-bitten friend, and a half-human vampire hunter to learn who murdered her parents, and why.

"The book grabs readers by the throat, sets hearts beating loudly and never lets go." Kirkus

Other titles in this series are:

Betrayals (2009)

Defiance (2011)

Jealousy (2010)

St. John, Lauren

Dolphin song; [by] Lauren St. John. Dial Books for Young Readers 2008 346p $16.99; pa $6.99

Grades: 4 5 6 7 **Fic**

1. Orphans -- Fiction 2. Dolphins -- Fiction 3. South Africa -- Fiction 4. Wildlife conservation -- Fiction

ISBN 978-0-8037-3214-8; 0-8037-3214-7; 978-0-14-241375-3 pa; 0-14-241375-5 pa

LC 2007-29248

Sequel to: The white giraffe (2007)

A second prophesy, this time involving dolphins, comes true for eleven-year-old Martine, an orphaned South African girl who has mystical powers over animals, when she embarks on a school trip to study marine life off the coast of Mozambique.

"This is an action-packed story with a strong environmental message and an admirable heroine." SLJ

Followed by: The last leopard (2009)

The **elephant's** tale. Dial Books for Young Readers 2010 221p (Legend of the animal healer) $16.99

Grades: 4 5 6 7 **Fic**

1. Orphans -- Fiction 2. Elephants -- Fiction 3. South Africa -- Fiction

ISBN 978-0-8037-3291-9; 0-8037-3291-0

A fourth prophecy, this time involving elephants, comes true for eleven-year-old Martine, an orphaned South African girl with mystical healing powers over animals, when she and her grandmother are faced with losing the Sawubona Game Reserve forever.

"This is a fast-paced mystery with an underlying conservation theme. Tween readers will be absorbed by the adventure, the animals, and the African setting." SLJ

The **last** leopard; [by] Lauren St. John. Dial Books for Young Readers/Walden Media 2009 197p $16.99; pa $6.99
Grades: 4 5 6 7 **Fic**

1. Animals -- Fiction 2. Orphans -- Fiction 3. Leopards -- Fiction 4. Zimbabwe -- Fiction 5. Wildlife conservation -- Fiction
ISBN 978-0-8037-3342-8; 0-8037-3342-9; 978-0-14-241515-3 pa; 0-14-241515-4 pa

LC 2008010003

Sequel to: Dolphin song (2008)

A third prophecy, this time involving a leopard, comes true for eleven-year-old Martine, an orphaned South African girl who has mystical healing powers over animals, when she travels with her grandmother and best friend Ben to Zimbabwe.

"This uncomplicated adventure offers plenty of narrow squeaks and strong animal-conservation message while being shot through with threads of mysticism." Booklist

The **white** giraffe; illustrated by David Dean. Dial Books for Young Readers 2007 180p il $16.99; pa $6.99
Grades: 4 5 6 7 **Fic**

1. Orphans -- Fiction 2. Giraffes -- Fiction 3. South Africa -- Fiction 4. Mythical animals -- Fiction
ISBN 978-0-8037-3211-7; 0-8037-3211-2; 978-0-14-241152-0 pa; 0-14-241152-3 pa

LC 2006-21323

After a fire kills her parents, eleven-year-old Martine must leave England to live with her grandmother on a wildlife game reserve in South Africa, where she befriends a mythical white giraffe

"The story is captivating and well spun." SLJ

Other titles in this series are:
Dolphin song (2008)
Last leopard (2009)
The elephant's tale (2010)

Standiford, Natalie

The **secret** tree; Natalie Standiford. Scholastic Press 2012 245 p. $16.99
Grades: 4 5 6 7 **Fic**

1. Bildungsromans 2. Mystery fiction 3. Friendship -- fiction
ISBN 0545334799; 9780545334792

This coming of age story combines "[m]iddle-school dynamics, pesky sibling relations, a rumored haunted house, . . . and a mystery. . . . When 10-year-old Minty discovers a hollow tree in the woods . . . [and] find[s] a secret written on a scrap of paper stashed inside, it sets the stage for a . . . mystery. . . . [W]hile Minty tries to figure out what's going on, she . . . befriend[s] an apparently parentless kid, Raymond, who seems to live in an abandoned spec house." (Kirkus)

Switched at birthday; Natalie Standiford. Scholastic Press 2014 240 p. (jacketed hardcover) $16.99
Grades: 4 5 6 7 **Fic**

1. Change -- Fiction 2. Birthdays -- Fiction 3. Friendship -- Fiction 4. Identity (Psychology) -- Fiction 5. Magic -- Fiction 6. Schools -- Fiction 7. Identity -- Fiction 8. Middle schools -- Fiction 9. Change (Psychology) -- Fiction
ISBN 0545346509; 9780545346504

LC 2013018598

In this book, by Natalie Standiford, "Lavender and Scarlet are nothing alike. . . . There's only one thing Lavender and Scarlet know for sure they have in common: the same birthday. . . . They've never swapped presents. But this year, because of two wishes that turned all too true, they are about to swap something much bigger than presents. Because the morning after their birthdays, Lavender is going to wake up in Scarlet's body . . . and Scarlet is going to make up in Lavender's." (Publisher's note)

"While the body switch is not a new idea, Standiford uses it effectively in this engaging story. Though swiftly drawn, even the minor characters are convincing, and the two leads are memorable in their separate ways." Booklist

Stanley, Diane

★ **Bella** at midnight; illustrated by Bagram Ibatoulline. HarperCollins Pubs. 2006 278p il $15.99; lib bdg $16.89; pa $6.99
Grades: 5 6 7 8 **Fic**

1. Fairy tales 2. Knights and knighthood -- Fiction
ISBN 978-0-06-077573-5; 0-06-077573-4; 978-0-06-077574-2 lib bdg; 0-06-077574-2 lib bdg; 978-0-06-077575-9 pa; 0-06-077575-0 pa

LC 2005-05906

Raised by peasants, Bella discovers that she is actually the daughter of a knight and finds herself caught up in a terrible plot that will change her life and the kingdom forever

"What raises this above other recreated fairy tales is the quality of the writing, dotted with jeweled description and anchored by the strong values—loyalty, truth, honor." Booklist

The **cup** and the crown; Diane Stanley. Harper 2012 344 p. (hardback) $16.99
Grades: 5 6 7 8 **Fic**

1. Fantasy fiction 2. Magic -- Fiction 3. Identity -- Fiction 4. Clairvoyance -- Fiction 5. Drinking cups -- Fiction 6. Kings, queens, rulers, etc. -- Fiction
ISBN 0061963216; 9780061963216

LC 2012025280

In this fantasy novel by Diane Stanley "Molly has visions of a beautiful goblet: one of her grandfather's loving cups, which he filled with magic that bound people together. So it hardly surprises Molly when handsome King Alaric asks her to find a loving cup to help him win the heart of the beautiful Princess of Cortova. As Molly and her friends Winifred and Tobias journey far beyond the safe borders of Westria, a mysterious raven appears to guide their quest." (Publisher's note)

The **mysterious** matter of I.M. Fine. HarperCollins Pubs. 2001 201p hardcover o.p. pa $5.99
Grades: 4 5 6 7 **Fic**

1. Mystery fiction 2. Magic -- Fiction 3. Books and reading -- Fiction
ISBN 0-688-17546-5; 0-380-73327-7 pa

LC 00-54040

Noticing that a popular series of horror novels is having a bizarre effect on the behavior of its readers, Franny and Beamer set out to find the mysterious author

"The solidly constructed mystery, well-rounded characters, and playful jab at wildly successful horror writers go down a treat." Horn Book Guide

Another title about Franny and her friends is:

The mysterious case of the Allbright Academy (2008)

★ The **princess** of Cortova; Diane Stanley. Harper, an imprint of HarperCollinsPublishers 2013 320 p. (hardback) $16.99

Grades: 5 6 7 8 **Fic**

1. Betrothal -- fiction 2. Occult fiction -- fiction 3. Alternative histories -- fiction 4. Fantasy 5. Magic -- Fiction 6. Princesses -- Fiction 7. Clairvoyance -- Fiction 8. Courts and courtiers -- Fiction 9. Kings, queens, rulers, etc. -- Fiction

ISBN 0062047302; 9780062047304; 9780062047311

LC 2013021824

Sequel to: The cup and the crown

This book is the final one in Diane Stanley's trilogy about prescient Molly and her friends. Here, Molly and "young Kind Alaric and . . . Tobias journey from Westria to the Kingdom of Cortova in search of an alliance that will include Alaric's betrothal to Princess Elizabetta. To complicate matters, however, Alaric's cousin, the foxy Reynard, King of Austlind, has arrived with a similar goal. Who will win the hand of the fair Elizabetta?" (Booklist)

★ The **silver** bowl. Harper 2011 307p $16.99

Grades: 5 6 7 8 **Fic**

1. Fantasy fiction 2. Clairvoyance -- Fiction

ISBN 978-0-06-157543-3; 0-06-157543-7

"Molly is a young scullery maid in the castle of King Edmund, and like her mother before her, she sees visions and hears voices that offer glimpses of the future. But is this a blessing or a curse?. . . . The girl's choice of silence . . . is challenged when she learns that a rumored curse on the royal family is true and only by sharing her visions might they be saved. Combining carefully chosen details of setting with a richly realized fantasy premise, Stanley succeeds in creating a believable world large enough to accommodate not only menace and evil but also loyalty, enduring friendship, and love." Booklist

Staples, Suzanne Fisher

Haveli. Knopf 1993 259p pa $6.50

Grades: 8 9 10 11 12 **Fic**

1. Pakistan -- Fiction 2. Sex role -- Fiction

ISBN 0-679-84157-1; 0-679-86569-1 pa

LC 92-29054

Sequel to: Shabanu, daughter of the wind

Having relented to the ways of her people in Pakistan and married the rich older man to whom she was pledged against her will, Shabanu is now the victim of his family's blood feud and the malice of his other wives.

"Staples brews a potent mix here: the issue of a woman's role in a traditional society, page-turning intrigue, tough women characters, and a fluidity of writing that blends it all together." Booklist

Followed by: The house of djinn

The **house** of djinn. Farrar, Straus and Giroux 2008 207p $16.95

Grades: 8 9 10 11 12 **Fic**

1. Pakistan -- Fiction 2. Sex role -- Fiction 3. Family life -- Fiction

ISBN 978-0-374-39936-8; 0-374-39936-0

LC 2007-05093

Sequel to: Haveli

An unexpected death brings Shabanu's daughter, Mumtaz, and nephew, Jameel, both aged fifteen, to the forefront of an attempt to modernize Pakistan, but the teens must both sacrifice their own dreams if they are to meet family and tribal expectations.

"As atmospheric and suspenseful as its predecessors, Shabanu and Haveli, this evocative novel transports readers to an intriguing corner of the universe to provide an insightful look at modern Middle Eastern culture." Publ Wkly

Shabanu; daughter of the wind. Knopf 1989 240p hardcover o.p. pa $6.50

Grades: 8 9 10 11 12 **Fic**

1. Pakistan -- Fiction 2. Sex role -- Fiction

ISBN 0-394-84815-2; 0-440-23856-0 pa

LC 89-2714

A Newbery Medal honor book, 1990

When eleven-year-old Shabanu, the daughter of a nomad in the Cholistan Desert of present-day Pakistan, is pledged in marriage to an older man whose money will bring prestige to the family, she must either accept the decision, as is the custom, or risk the consequences of defying her father's wishes

"Interspersing native words throughout adds realism, but may trip up readers, who must be patient enough to find meaning through context. This use of language is, however, an important element in helping Staples paint an evocative picture of life in the desert that includes references to the hard facts of reality." Booklist

Other titles in this series are:

Haveli (1993)

The house of djinn (2008)

Under the Persimmon tree. Farrar, Straus & Giroux 2005 275p $17

Grades: 7 8 9 10 **Fic**

1. Pakistan -- Fiction 2. Afghanistan -- Fiction

ISBN 0-374-38025-2

During the 2001 Afghan War, the lives of Najmal, a young refugee from Kunduz, Afghanistan, and Nusrat, an American teacher who has converted to Islam, intersect at a school in Peshawar, Pakistan. "Grades four to six." (MultiCult Rev)

"Staples weaves a lot of history and politics into her story. . . . But . . . it's the personal story . . . that compels as it takes readers beyond the modern stereotypes of Muslims as fundamentalist fanatics. There are no sweet reunions, but there's hope in heartbreaking scenes of kindness and courage." Booklist

Stark-Mcginnis, Sandy

Extraordinary birds; by Sandy Stark-McGinnis. Bloomsbury 2019 224 p. (hardcover) $16.99

Grades: 4 5 6 7 **Fic**

1. Birds -- Fiction 2. Orphans -- Fiction 3. Wildlife rescue -- Fiction 4. Foster home care -- Fiction

ISBN 9781547601004

LC 2018045422

"This heartbreaking but ultimately redemptive middle grade novel shows the beauty of accepting one's true self and finding a place to belong." (ForeWord)

Starmer, Aaron

The **only** ones. Delacorte Press 2011 321p $17.99; lib bdg $20.99; e-book $17.99

Grades: 4 5 6 7 **Fic**

1. Supernatural -- Fiction

ISBN 978-0-385-74043-2; 0-385-74043-3; 978-0-385-90839-9 lib bdg; 0-385-90839-3 lib bdg; 978-0-375-89919-5 e-book

LC 2010040383

After setting off from the island where he has been leading a solitary existence, thirteen-year-old Martin discovers a village with other children who have been living similarly without any adults, since the grown-ups have all been spirited away.

"Both literary and engaging, this is the kind of book readers will want to return to for new discoveries." Kirkus

The **Riverman**; Aaron Starmer. Farrar Straus Giroux 2014 320 p. (hardback) $15.99

Grades: 5 6 7 8 9 **Fic**

1. Fantasy fiction 2. Imaginary places 3. Friendship -- Fiction 4. Missing children -- Fiction 5. Fantasy 6. Space and time

ISBN 0374363099; 9780374363093

LC 2013027900

In this book, by Aaron Starmer, "Fiona Loomis shows up at Alistair's door asking him to pen her biography and begins to tell him of a strange land she's visited called Aquavania. . . . Fiona warns Alistair that the Riverman is stealing the souls of children and that she is next. Alistair, drawn into Fiona's story, wants to protect her—if only he can discover the full truth." (Booklist)

Other titles in this series are:

The whisper (2015)

The storyteller (2016)

The **storyteller**; Aaron Starmer. Farrar, Straus & Giroux 2016 336 p. (Riverman trilogy) (hardcover) $16.99

Grades: 5 6 7 8 9 **Fic**

1. Fantasy fiction 2. Storytelling -- Fiction 3. Diaries -- Fiction 4. Friendship -- Fiction 5. Family life -- Fiction 6. Missing children -- Fiction 7. Brothers and sisters -- Fiction

ISBN 9780374363130

LC 2015004696

In this novel, by Aaron Starmer, part 3 of "The RIverman" trilogy, "as the one witness to a shooting, [Alistair] has been shocked into silence. But . . . who shot Kyle Dwyer? Where is Charlie Dwyer? What does this all have to do with the disappearance of Fiona Loomis? . . . As Alistair makes strange confessions to his sister, Keri becomes inspired. She tells stories, tales that may reveal hidden truths, fiction that may cause real things to happen." (Publisher's note)

"In a subsection of publishing where trilogies often seem formulaic or forced, this refreshing take challenges traditionally reiterated narrative devices by never dealing in absolutes and not tying things off into neat bows. Fans of fantasy and realistic fiction alike will find something to love about this book, in which narrative ambiguity has never been so well leveraged." SLJ

The **whisper**; Aaron Starmer. Farrar, Straus & Giroux 2015 361 p. (The Riverman trilogy) (hardback) $16.99

Grades: 5 6 7 8 **Fic**

1. Imaginary places 2. Shipwrecks -- Fiction 3. Imagination -- Fiction 4. Fantasy 5. Friendship -- Fiction

ISBN 0374363110; 9780374363116

LC 2014013168

In this children's novel by Aaron Starmer "twelve-year-old Alistair Cleary has washed up on shore. But where? It seems to be Aquavania, the magical realm where children create entire worlds from their imagination. There's something wrong, though. The creators have disappeared and the worlds are falling apart. All Alistair wants is to find his friend Fiona Loomis and go home. To find Fiona, Alistair must travel from world to world. And he must face countless monsters, including the soul-stealing stalker that some people call the Riverman." (Publisher's note)

"A riveting, imaginative, disconcerting, inscrutable, unresolved sequel, guaranteed to leave readers anxious for the finale." Kirkus

Stead, Rebecca

First light. Wendy Lamb Books 2007 328p $15.99; pa $6.99

Grades: 5 6 7 8 **Fic**

1. Greenland -- Fiction 2. Supernatural -- Fiction 3. Greenhouse effect -- Fiction

ISBN 978-0-375-84017-3; 0-375-84017-6; 0-375-94017-0 lib bdg; 978-0-440-42222-8 pa; 0-440-42222-1 pa

LC 2006-39733

This "novel is an exciting, engaging mix of science fiction, mystery, and adventure. . . . Peter and Thea are fully developed main characters." SLJ

★ **Goodbye** stranger; Rebecca Stead. Wendy Lamb Books, an imprint of Random House Children's Books 2015 304 p. (trade) $16.99

Grades: 5 6 7 8 9 **Fic**

1. Friendship -- Fiction 2. Family life -- Fiction 3. Middle schools -- Fiction 4. New York (N.Y.) -- Fiction 5. Schools -- Fiction 6. Best friends -- Fiction

ISBN 0385743173; 9780307980861; 9780375990984; 9780385743174

LC 2014037289

Boston Globe Horn Book Fiction Honor Book (2016)

In this book, by Rebecca Stead, "Bridge is an accident survivor who's wondering why she's still alive. Emily has new curves and an almost-boyfriend who wants a certain kind of picture. Tabitha sees through everybody's games--or so she tells the world. The three girls are best friends with one rule: No fighting. Can it get them through seventh grade?" (Publisher's note)

"Ah, seventh grade! A year when your friends transform inexplicably, your own body and emotions perplex you, and the world seems fraught with questions, and the most confusing ones of all concern the nature of love. Stead focuses on Bridge Barsamian, her best girlfriends, and her newest friend Sherm—a boy who is definitely not her boyfriend (probably). . . . An immensely satisfying addition for Stead's many fans." SLJ

Liar & spy; by Rebecca Stead. Wendy Lamb Books 2012 180 p. (hardback) $15.99

Grades: 4 5 6 7 8 **Fic**

1. Spy stories 2. Boys -- Fiction 3. Neighbors -- Fiction 4. Friendship -- Fiction 5. Spies -- Fiction 6. Schools -- Fiction 7. Middle schools -- Fiction 8. Apartment houses -- Fiction 9. Brooklyn (New York, N.Y.) -- Fiction 10. Family life -- New York (State) -- New York -- Fiction

ISBN 0385737432; 9780375899539; 9780385737432; 9780385906654

LC 2011042674

In this book, protagonist "Georges has a lot going on. Dad was laid off so Mom has started working extra shifts at the hospital, and they had to sell their house in Brooklyn and move into an apartment. One good thing about the new building is Safer, an unusual boy who lives on the top floor. He's determined to teach Georges how to be a spy. Their main case: spy on the mysterious Mr. X in the apartment above Georges. As Georges and Safer go deeper into their Mr. X plan, the line between games, lies, and reality begin to blur." (Barnes and Noble)

★ **When** you reach me. Wendy Lamb Books 2009 199p $15.99; lib bdg $18.99
Grades: 5 6 7 8 **Fic**

1. Space and time -- Fiction 2. New York (N.Y.) -- Fiction
ISBN 0-385-73742-4; 0-385-90664-1 lib bdg; 978-0-385-73742-5; 978-0-385-90664-7 lib bdg
LC 2008-24998

Awarded the Newbery Medal, 2010

As her mother prepares to be a contestant on the 1980s television game show, The 20,000 Pyramid, a twelve-year-old New York City girl tries to make sense of a series of mysterious notes received from an anonymous source. "Ages nine to fourteen." (Publisher's note)

"The '70s New York setting is an honest reverberation of the era; the mental gymnastics required of readers are invigorating; and the characters . . . are honest bits of humanity." Booklist

Steer, Dugald

The **dragon** diary; [by] Dugald A. Steer; illustrated by Douglas Carrel. Candlewick Press 2009 248p il (Dragonology chronicles) $16.99
Grades: 5 6 7 8 **Fic**

1. Fantasy fiction 2. Dragons -- Fiction 3. Siblings -- Fiction
ISBN 978-0-7636-3425-4; 0-7636-3425-5
LC 2009005795

Apprentice dragonologists Daniel and Beatrice Cook's mentor is called away at a crucial time, leaving the brother and sister alone to search for an ancient diary that could cure some gravely ill dragons

"This fast-paced fantasy features sibling rivalry, multitudes of dragons, and mid-air heroics." Horn Book Guide

Other titles in this series are:
The dragon's eye (2006)
The dragon's apprentice (2011)
The dragon prophecy (2012)

Steinbeck, John

The **pearl**; John Steinbeck centennial ed; Penguin Books 2002 87p pa $11
Grades: 7 8 9 10 **Fic**

1. Mexico -- Fiction 2. Poverty -- Fiction
ISBN 0-14-200069-8
LC 2001-56113

First published 1947

"Kino, a poor pearl-fisher, lives a happy albeit spartan life with his wife and their child. When he finds a magnificent pearl, the Pearl of the World, he is besieged by dishonest pearl merchants and envious neighbors. Even a greedy doctor ties his professional treatment of their baby when it is bitten by a scorpion to the possible acquisition of the pearl. After a series of disasters, Kino throws the pearl away since it has brought him only unhappiness." Shapiro. Fic for Youth. 3d edition

The **red** pony. Viking 1993 100p pa $9
Grades: 4 5 6 7 8 **Fic**

1. Horses -- Fiction 2. California -- Fiction 3. Ranch life -- Fiction
ISBN 0-670-59184-X; 0-14-017736-1 pa
LC 86-1610

First published 1937

"Jody Tiflin, ten years old, begins to grow up in these four vignettes describing his life on a farm in California. He takes responsibility for his red pony and suffers when it dies. An old man arouses Jody's curiosity about what is beyond the mountains, and he anxiously awaits the birth of a colt. His grandfather's tales are a source of interest and wonder for Jody." Shapiro. Fic for Youth. 3d edition

Stephens, John

The **black** reckoning; John Stephens. Alfred A. Knopf 2015 432 p. (Books of beginning) (hardback) $17.99
Grades: 4 5 6 7 **Fic**

1. Magic -- Fiction 2. Identity -- Fiction 3. Monsters -- Fiction 4. Prophecies -- Fiction 5. Space and time -- Fiction 6. Brothers and sisters -- Fiction 7. Books and reading -- Fiction
ISBN 0375868720; 9780375868726; 9780375968723
LC 2014023538

In this novel, by John Stephens, part of the Books of Beginning series, "the adventures of siblings Kate, Michael, and Emma come to a stunning conclusion when they must find the last Book of Beginning--the Book of Death--before the Dire Magnus does, for when all three books are united, their combined power will be unstoppable." (Publisher's note)

"Heartbreaking sacrifices, joyous reunions, and poignant partings round out this rousing old-school fantasy adventure." Horn Book

Other titles in the trilogy are:
The Emerald Atlas (2011)
The Fire Chronicle (2012)

★ The **emerald** atlas. Alfred A. Knopf 2011 417p (The books of beginning) $17.99; lib bdg $20.99
Grades: 4 5 6 **Fic**

1. Magic -- Fiction 2. Monsters -- Fiction 3. Siblings -- Fiction 4. Prophecies -- Fiction 5. Space and time -- Fiction 6. Books and reading -- Fiction
ISBN 978-0-375-86870-2; 0-375-86870-4; 978-0-375-96870-9 lib bdg; 0-375-96870-9 lib bdg
LC 2010029100

Kate, Michael, and Emma have passed from one orphanage to another in the ten years since their parents disappeared to protect them, but now they learn that they have special powers, a prophesied quest to find a magical book, and a fearsome enemy.

"This fast-paced, fully imagined fantasy is by turns frightening and funny, and the siblings are well-crafted and empathetic heroes. Highly enjoyable, it should find many readers." Publ Wkly

★ The **fire** chronicle; John Stephens. Alfred A. Knopf 2012 437 p. (hardback) $17.99
Grades: 4 5 6 **Fic**

1. Fantasy fiction 2. Adventure fiction 3. Time travel -- fiction 4. Magic -- Fiction 5. Identity -- Fiction 6. Monsters -- Fiction 7. Prophecies -- Fiction 8. Space and time -- Fiction 9. Books and reading -- Fiction 10. Brothers and sisters -- Fiction 11. New York (N.Y.) -- History -- 1898-1951 -- Fiction
ISBN 0375868712; 9780375868719; 9780375899560; 9780375968716
LC 2012016139

In this novel by John Stephens, part of the Books of Beginning series, "Kate, Michael, and Emma long to continue the hunt for their missing parents. . . . A frantic chase sends Kate a hundred years into the past, to a perilous, enchanted New York City. . . . Meanwhile, Michael and Emma have set off to find the second of the Books of Beginning. A series of clues leads them into a hidden world where they must brave harsh polar storms, track down an ancient order of warriors, and confront terrible monsters." (Publisher's note)

Stevens, Robin

First class murder; Robin Stevens. Simon & Schuster Books for Young Readers 2017 320 p. (Wells & Wong mystery) (hardcover) $16.99

Grades: 4 5 6 7 **Fic**

1. Mystery fiction 2. Murder -- Fiction 3. Friendship -- Fiction 4. Railroad travel -- Fiction 5. Europe -- History -- 1918-1945 -- Fiction 6. Chinese -- Europe -- Fiction 7. Mystery and detective stories 8. Orient Express (Express train) -- Fiction

ISBN 9781481422185; 9781481422192

LC 2015050408

In this book, by Robin Stevens, "Hazel Wong and Daisy Wells are taking a vacation across Europe on world-famous passenger train, the Orient Express—and it's clear that each of their fellow first-class travelers has something to hide. Even more intriguing: There's rumor of a spy in their midst. Then, during dinner, a bloodcurdling scream comes from inside one of the cabins. When the door is broken down, a passenger is found murdered—her stunning ruby necklace gone." (Publisher's note)

Murder is bad manners; Robin Stevens. Simon & Schuster Books for Young Readers 2015 320 p. (Wells & Wong mysteries) (hardcover) $16.99

Grades: 4 5 6 7 **Fic**

1. School stories 2. Mystery fiction 3. Murder -- Fiction 4. Friendship -- Fiction 5. Boarding schools -- Fiction 6. Chinese -- England -- Fiction 7. Mystery and detective stories

ISBN 148142212X; 9781481422123; 9781481422130

LC 2014003939

"Daisy Wells and Hazel Wong are best friends at Deepdean School for Girls, and they both have a penchant for solving mysteries. . . . [T] hey form their own (secret!) detective agency. The only problem? They have nothing to investigate. But that changes once Hazel discovers the body of their science teacher, Miss Bell--and the body subsequently disappears." (Publisher's note)

"Here's a mystery import, set in the 1930s, that does justice to its British roots. Hazel Wong has come from Hong Kong to attend Deepdean boarding school. An outcast until she is accepted by upper-crust Daisy Wells, Hazel is happy to be half of a two-girl detective agency. . . . Hazel makes a good narrator, and while the mystery plods a bit and has too many teachers--though a cast list helps--not every reader will guess the ending. Nancy Drew, meet Wells and Wong." Booklist

Other titles in this series are:

Poison is not polite (2016)

First class murder (2017)

Poison is not polite; Robin Stevens. Simon & Schuster Books for Young Readers 2016 336 p. (A Wells & Wong mystery) (hardback) $16.99; (paperback) $7.99

Grades: 4 5 6 7 **Fic**

1. Parties -- fiction 2. Murder -- Fiction 3. Friendship -- Fiction 4. Chinese -- England -- Fiction 5. Mystery and detective stories 6. Great Britain -- History -- George V, 1910-1936 -- Fiction

ISBN 1481422162; 9781481422154; 9781481422161

LC 2015015300

In this juvenile novel, by Robin Stevens, part of the "Wells & Wong Mystery" series, "schoolgirl detectives Daisy Wells and Hazel Wong are at Daisy's home . . . for the holidays. Daisy's glamorous mother is throwing a tea party for Daisy's birthday, and the whole family is invited. . . . But . . . when one of their guests falls seriously and mysteriously ill--and everything points to poison . . . , it's up to Daisy and Hazel to find out what's really going on." (Publisher's note)

"A first-rate whodunit, reminiscent of a game of Clue and terrific preparation for the works of Agatha Christie." Kirkus

Stevenson, Robert Louis

Kidnapped; [by] Robert Louis Stevenson; with an introduction by Sid Hite. F. Watts 2007 213p (Scholastic classics) $25.50

Grades: 7 8 9 10 11 12 Adult **Fic**

1. Adventure fiction 2. Scotland -- Fiction 3. Kidnapping -- Fiction

ISBN 978-0-531-16990-2; 0-531-16990-1

LC 2006006816

First published 1886

A sixteen-year-old orphan is kidnapped by his villainous uncle, but later escapes and becomes involved in the struggle of the Scottish highlanders against English rule.

Treasure Island; Robert Louis Stevenson ; illustrated by John Lawrence. 1st U.S. ed. Candlewick Press 2009 269 p. col. ill. (reinforced) $24.99

Grades: 5 6 7 8 9 10 11 12 Adult **Fic**

1. Adventure fiction 2. Pirates -- Fiction 3. Buried treasure -- Fiction

ISBN 0763644455; 9780763644451

LC 2009007338

First published in 1883.

While going through the possessions of a deceased guest who owed them money, the mistress of the inn and her son find a treasure map that leads them to a notorious pirate's fortune

"Lawrence evokes the essence of classic adventure stories with his vinyl-cut illustrations, as thick black shapes are tempered by muted tones of blue, gold and green. . . . Readers will feel they've discovered a true relic with this edition." Publ Wkly

Stevermer, Caroline

Magic below stairs. Dial Books for Young Readers 2010 199p $16.99

Grades: 4 5 6 7 **Fic**

1. Magic -- Fiction 2. Orphans -- Fiction 3. Household employees -- Fiction 4. Great Britain -- History -- 19th century -- Fiction

ISBN 978-0-8037-3467-8; 0-8037-3467-0

LC 2009-25100

Ten-year-old Frederick, who is surreptitiously watched over by a household elf, is plucked from a London orphanage to be a servant to a wealthy wizard, and eventually his uncanny abilities lead him to become the wizard's apprentice.

"A well-developed fictional world and the many concrete details of belowstairs life make the magical events in this engaging chapter book more believable." Booklist

Stewart, Martin

Riverkeep; Martin Stewart. Viking, an imprint of Penguin Random House LLC 2016 416 p. map (hardcover) $17.99

Grades: 6 7 8 9 10 **Fic**

1. Fantasy fiction 2. Rivers -- Fiction 3. Sea monsters -- Fiction 4. Father-son relationship -- Fiction 5. Fantasy

ISBN 9781101998298

LC 2015028442

In this novel by Martin Stewart, "Wulliam's father, the current Riverkeep, is proud of this work. Wull dreads it. . . . Then the unthinkable happens. While recovering a drowned man, Wull's father is pulled under—and when he emerges, he is no longer himself. A dark spirit possesses him, devouring him from the inside. . . . When he hears that a cure for his father lurks in the belly of a great sea-dwelling beast known as the mormorach, he embarks on an epic journey." (Publisher's note)

"Filled with wild adventure and hilarious dialogue (Tillinghast has a particularly saucy mouth), this vivid, engrossing fantasy will delight readers, even those who occasionally find the dialect tricky to navigate." Pub Wkly

Stewart, Paul

The **curse** of the night wolf; [by] Paul Stewart and Chris Riddell; illustrated by Chris Riddell. David Fickling Books 2008 204p il (Barnaby Grimes) $15.99; lib bdg $18.99

Grades: 4 5 6 7 **Fic**

1. Mystery fiction 2. Physicians -- Fiction 3. Werewolves -- Fiction 4. London (England) -- Fiction 5. Great Britain -- History -- 19th century -- Fiction

ISBN 978-0-385-75125-4; 0-385-75125-7; 978-0-385-75126-1 lib bdg; 0-385-75126-5 lib bdg

LC 2008-01697

Soon after Victorian messenger Barnaby Grimes is attacked by a huge beast while crossing London's rooftops, he becomes entangled in a mystery involving patent medicine, impoverished patients, and very expensive furs.

"Moody, highly detailed pen-and-ink drawings provide ornamentation throughout, lending a classic Victorian feel to help punctuate the drama. . . . Possessing an easy confidence and quick wit . . . Barnaby is an appealing character." Booklist

Other titles in this series are:
Return of the emerald skull (2009)
Legion of the Dead (2010)

Legion of the Dead; [by] Paul Stewart & Chris Riddell; illustrated by Chris Riddell. David Fickling Books 2010 224p il (Barnaby Grimes) $16.99; lib bdg $19.99

Grades: 4 5 6 7 **Fic**

1. Mystery fiction 2. Dead -- Fiction 3. Supernatural -- Fiction 4. Great Britain -- History -- 19th century -- Fiction

ISBN 978-0-385-75131-5; 0-385-75131-1; 978-0-385-75132-2 lib bdg; 0-385-75132-X lib bdg

First published 2008 in the United Kingdom

"The funeral of a master criminal bring a dozen squabbling gangs together for a moment of peace, but when Barnaby shortcuts through the graveyard and sees a body rise from the earth, a terrifying mystery is born. Stewart ramps up the ick factor in his decadent descriptions of rotting corpses, and Riddell matches note for note in devilishly detailed ink drawings. Barnaby's pervading good cheer and chim-chiminey rooftop skittering again make for entertaining reading." Booklist

Phantom of Blood Alley; [by] Paul Stewart & Chris Riddell; illustrated by Chris Riddell. David Fickling Books 2010 201p il (Barnaby Grimes) $16.99

Grades: 4 5 6 7 **Fic**

1. Mystery fiction 2. Photography -- Fiction 3. Supernatural -- Fiction 4. Great Britain -- History -- 19th century -- Fiction

ISBN 978-0-385-75134-6; 0-385-75134-6

First published 2009 in the United Kingdom

Barnaby finds himself in the fiercely competitive world of early photography, where the rewards are immense but so are the risks. After an experiment goes disastrously wrong, Barnaby is on the trail of a mad chemist with a talent for disappearing into thin air.

Return of the emerald skull; [by] Paul Stewart & Chris Riddell; illustrated by Chris Riddell. 1st American ed.; David Fickling Books 2009 202p il (Barnaby Grimes) $15.99; lib bdg $18.99

Grades: 4 5 6 7 **Fic**

1. School stories 2. Mystery fiction 3. Supernatural -- Fiction 4. London (England) -- Fiction 5. Great Britain -- History -- 19th century -- Fiction

ISBN 978-0-385-75128-5; 0-385-75128-1; 978-0-385-75129-2 lib bdg; 0-385-75129-X lib bdg

LC 2008046227

Weird and evil events at a London boarding school provide messenger Barnaby Grimes an opportunity to test his budding knowledge of the ancient Chinese art of yinchido, in which one focuses on silences and empty spaces.

"Riddell's full-page ink drawings and small silhouettes add great visual appeal. . . . This will please readers with a taste for blookthirsty adventures and a tolerance for unlikely story lines." Booklist

Stewart, Trenton Lee

The **extraordinary** education of Nicholas Benedict; by Trenton Lee Stewart ; illustrated by Diana Sudyka. Little, Brown & Co. 2012 470 p. (pbk.) $9.99; (hbk.) $18.99

Grades: 4 5 6 7 8 **Fic**

1. Bullies -- Fiction 2. Orphans -- Fiction 3. Friendship -- Fiction 4. Narcolepsy -- Fiction 5. Orphanages -- Fiction 6. Genius -- Fiction 7. Mystery and detective stories 8. Adventure and adventurers -- Fiction

ISBN 9780316176200; 9780316176194

LC 2011031690

In this book, by Trenton Lee Stewart, "nine-year-old Nicholas Benedict has more problems than most children his age, . . . he has narcolepsy, a condition that gives him terrible nightmares and makes him fall asleep at the worst possible moments. Now he's sent to a new orphanage, where he encounters vicious bullies, selfish adults, strange circumstances -- and a mystery that could change his life forever. Luckily, he has one important thing in his favor: He's a genius." (Publisher's note)

★ The **mysterious** Benedict Society; illustrated by Carson Ellis. Little, Brown 2007 485p il $16.99; pa $6.99

Grades: 5 6 7 8 **Fic**

1. Science fiction 2. Adventure fiction

ISBN 978-0-316-05777-6; 0-316-05777-0; 978-0-316-00395-7 pa; 0-316-00395-6 pa

LC 2006-09925

After passing a series of mind-bending tests, four children are selected for a secret mission that requires them to go undercover at the Learning Institute for the Very Enlightened, where the only rule is that there are no rules

"Stewart's unusual characters, threatening villains, and dramatic plot twists will grab and hold readers' attention." SLJ

Other titles about the Benedict Society are:
The mysterious Benedict Society and the perilous journey (2008)
The mysterious Benedict Society and the prisoner's dilemma (2009)
The extraordinary education of Nicholas Benedict (2012)
The mysterious Benedict Society and the riddle of ages (2019)

The **mysterious** Benedict Society and the perilous journey; by Trenton Lee Stewart; illustrated by Carson Ellis. Little, Brown and Co. 2008 440p il $16.99

Grades: 5 6 7 8 **Fic**

1. Science fiction 2. Adventure fiction

ISBN 978-0-316-05780-6; 0-316-05780-0

LC 2007031540

Sequel to: The mysterious Benedict Society (2007)

Reynie, Kate, Sticky, and Constance, all graduates of the Learning Institute for the Very Enlightened and members of the Benedict Society, embark on a scavenger hunt that turns into a desperate search for the missing Mr. Benedict.

"This is pure adventure—lots of racing, scheming, fighting." Booklist

The **mysterious** Benedict Society and the prisoner's dilemma; written by Trenton Lee Stewart; illustrations by Diana Sudyka. Little, Brown and Company 2009 391p il $16.99
Grades: 5 6 7 8 **Fic**

1. School stories 2. Science fiction 3. Adventure fiction 4. Friendship -- Fiction

ISBN 978-0-316-04552-0; 0-316-04552-7

LC 2009-25459

When an unexplained blackout engulfs Stonetown, Benedict Society members Reynie, Kate, Sticky, and Constance follow clues on an adventure that threatens to separate them from their families, friends, and even one another.

"The children's well-delineated characters are believable as those of young prodigies, the narrative puzzles mesh with thumping good action scenes, and the good-versus-evil plot balances the warmth of family connections with the excitement of deathly peril." Horn Book

The **secret** keepers; Trenton Lee Stewart ; illustrated by Diana Sudyka. Little, Brown & Co. 2016 512 p. illustrations (ebook) $57; (hardcover) $18.99
Grades: 3 4 5 6 **Fic**

1. Magic -- Fiction 2. Adventure fiction 3. Secrets -- Fiction 4. Invisibility -- Fiction 5. Clocks and watches -- Fiction 6. Adventure and adventurers -- Fiction

ISBN 9780316319126; 9780316389556

LC 2016006406

In this book, by Trenton Lee Stewart, illustrated by Diana Sudyka, "when Reuben discovers an extraordinary antique watch, he soon learns it has a secret power and his life takes an intriguing turn. At first he is thrilled with his new treasure, but as one secret leads to another, Reuben finds himself torn between his innately honest nature and the lure to be a hero. Now he is on a dangerous adventure . . . as he races to solve the mystery before it is too late." (Publisher's note)

"This epic story filled with adventure and twists and turns is certain to keep readers' interest from beginning to end." SLJ

Stiefvater, Maggie

★ The **dream** thieves; Maggie Stiefvater. Scholastic 2013 416 p. (Raven cycle) (jacketed hardcover) $18.99
Grades: 8 9 10 11 12 **Fic**

1. Fantasy fiction 2. Paranormal fiction 3. Magic -- Fiction 4. Dreams -- Fiction 5. Secrets -- Fiction 6. Occultism -- Fiction 7. Magic -- fiction 8. Dreams -- fiction 9. Family secrets -- fiction

ISBN 0545424941; 9780545424943

LC 2013018731

This is the second book in Maggie Stiefvater's Raven Cycle series. Here, after "the transformative events at Cabeswater . . . , the context in which Gansey, Blue, Adam, Ronan, and Noah operate is further altered by the arrival of the Gray Man, a self-described hit man. . . . The Gray Man brings with him the machinations of larger, previously unknown forces as he takes orders from a voice on the phone to hunt the Greywaren, the identity of which is revealed early on." (Publishers Weekly)

"In this darker second book (The Raven Boys), Gansey, Blue, and the search for Glendower take a backseat to the exploration of Ronan's and Adam's tortured personalities. Stiefvater's descriptive prose reveals a complicated plot, multiple viewpoints, and detailed backstories. Many mysteries remain, but the cliffhanger ending makes it clear that Glendower will resurface as the main focus of book three." (Horn Book)

Hunted; Maggie Stiefvater. Scholastic Inc. 2014 192 p. map (Spirit animals) (paper-over-board) $12.99
Grades: 4 5 6 7 **Fic**

1. Fantasy fiction 2. Wolves -- Fiction 3. Human-animal relationship -- Fiction

ISBN 0545522447; 9780545522441; 9780545522564; 9780545599726

LC 2013947126

This fantasy novel by Maggie Stiefvater, part of the Spirit Animals series, describes how its "four young heroes have barely had time to come together as a team, and their own spirit animal bonds are still greatly untested. But now they face a brutal confrontation against an enemy who will break any rule to defeat them." (Publisher's note)

"Stiefvater blends Mull's brilliant world building with her talent of writing memorable villains." Booklist

★ The **raven** boys; Maggie Stiefvater. Scholastic Press 2012 409 p. (Raven Cycle) (hardcover) $18.99
Grades: 8 9 10 11 12 **Fic**

1. Magic -- Fiction 2. Supernatural -- Fiction 3. Private schools -- Fiction 4. Paranormal fiction 5. Occultism -- Fiction 6. Clairvoyance -- Fiction

ISBN 0545424925; 9780545424929

LC 2012030880

"16-year-old Blue Sargent, daughter of a small-town psychic, has lived her whole life under a prophecy: If she kisses her true love, he will die. . . . She sees a vision of a dying Raven boy named Gansey. The Raven Boys--students at Aglionby, a nearby prep school, so-called because of the ravens on their school crest--soon encounter Blue in person." (Kirkus Reviews)

Other titles in the Raven Cycle are:
The dream thieves (2013)
Blue lily, lily blue (2014)
The raven king (2016)

★ The **Raven** King; by Maggie Stiefvater. Scholastic Inc. 2016 400 p. (Raven Cycle) $18.99
Grades: 8 9 10 11 12 **Fic**

1. Bildungsromans 2. Love -- Fiction 3. Magic -- Fiction 4. Teenagers -- Fiction

ISBN 0545424984; 9780545424981

"This [final] installment finds the world of the Raven Boys (Gansey, Ronan, Adam, and Noah) and their best friend Blue in considerable and dangerous disarray. As strange, increasingly sinister things begin happening in Henrietta and the magic forest of Cabeswater, the search for sleeping king Owen Glendower becomes more imperative, as it becomes apparent that something wicked this way comes." (Booklist)

"Stiefvater excels at building an intricately layered narrative with twisting, unpredictable turns, and her ability to introduce new, complex characters and storylines while also tying up previous loose ends is remarkable." VOYA

★ The **Scorpio** Races. Scholastic Press 2011 409p $17.99
Grades: 8 9 10 11 12 **Fic**

1. Fantasy fiction 2. Romance fiction 3. Love stories 4. Horses -- Fiction 5. Racing -- Fiction 6. Orphans -- Fiction

ISBN 978-0-545-22490-1; 0-545-22490-X

LC 2011015775

Printz Honor Book (2012)

"Stiefvater's narration is as much about atmospherics as it is about event, and the water horses are the environment in which Sean and Puck move, allies and rivals to the end. It's not a feel-good story—dread, loss, and hard choices are the islanders' lot. As a study of courage and loyalty tested, however, it is an utterly compelling read." Publ Wkly

Stohl, Margaret

Black Widow; forever red. by Margaret Stohl. Marvel 2015 416 p. $17.99

Grades: 7 8 9 10 11 12 **Fic**

1. Assassins -- Fiction 2. Superheroes -- Fiction 3. Secret societies -- Fiction 4. Avengers (Fictional characters) 5. Adventure stories

ISBN 9781484726433; 148472643X

LC 2015020692

This is a prose novel about the Marvel character. "Natasha Romanoff is one of the world's most lethal assassins. . . . Natasha was given the title of Black Widow by Ivan Somodorov, her brutal teacher at the Red Room, Moscow's infamous academy for operatives. Ava Orlova is just trying to fit in as an average Brooklyn teenager. . . . The daughter of a missing Russian quantum physicist, Ava was once subjected to a series of ruthless military experiments-until she was rescued by Black Widow." (Publisher's note)

"Great fight sequences, plenty of action, twists in the plot, and characters motivated by strong emotions will keep readers engaged and entertained." SLJ

Stokes, Paula

Girl against the universe; Paula Stokes ; [edited by] Karen Chaplin. HarperTeen 2016 400 p. (hardcover) $17.99

Grades: 8 9 10 11 **Fic**

1. Luck -- fiction 2. Fortune -- fiction 3. Teenagers -- fiction 4. Tennis players -- fiction 5. Romance fiction -- fiction

ISBN 9780062379962

LC 2015961051

In this novel by Paula Stokes, "no matter how many charms she buys off the internet or good luck rituals she performs each morning, horrible things happen when Maguire is around. Like that time her brother, father, and uncle were all killed in a car crash--and Maguire walked away with barely a scratch. But then on her way out of her therapist's office, she meets Jordy, an aspiring tennis star, who wants to help Maguire break her unlucky streak." (Publisher's note)

"Stokes' engaging prose and sympathetic characters serve up great lessons in acceptance for teens dealing with trauma." Kirkus

Stone, Phoebe

Deep down popular; a novel. by Phoebe Stone. Arthur A. Levine Books 2008 280p $16.99; pa $4.99

Grades: 4 5 6 7 **Fic**

1. School stories 2. Virginia -- Fiction 3. Friendship -- Fiction 4. Family life -- Fiction 5. Country life -- Fiction

ISBN 978-0-439-80245-1; 0-439-80245-8; 978-0-439-80244-4 pa; 0-439-80244-X pa

LC 2007017198

In a small Virginia town, sixth-grader Jessie Lou Ferguson has a crush on the hugely popular Conrad Parker Smith, and when he suddenly develops a medical problem and the teacher asks Jessie Lou to help him, they become friends, to her surprise

"Jessie Lou tells her tale with the strong, rough-edged purity of a young poet, which she is; equally strong are the story's underpinnings, longing and laughter, and a willingness to believe in something despite the facts." Booklist

★ The **Romeo** and Juliet code. Arthur A. Levine Books 2011 300p $16.99

Grades: 4 5 6 7 **Fic**

1. Maine -- Fiction 2. Ciphers -- Fiction 3. Family life -- Fiction 4. World War, 1939-1945 -- United States -- Fiction 5. World War, 1939-1945 -- Evacuation of civilians -- Fiction

ISBN 978-0-545-21511-4; 0-545-21511-0

LC 2010-30005

During World War II, eleven-year-old Felicity is sent from London to Bottlebay, Maine, to live with her grandmother, aunt, uncle, and a reclusive boy who helps her decode mysterious letters that contain the truth about her missing parents.

Felicity "is endearingly portrayed, and the back story, so gradually revealed, provides a peek into the depths of the souls of some of the adults. The pacing is deliberately slow, yet Felicity's growing awareness of how she can help heal the troubled adults makes this an eminently satisfying read." Kirkus

Romeo blue; by Phoebe Stone. 1st ed. Arthur A. Levine Books 2013 352 p. (hardcover) $16.99

Grades: 4 5 6 7 **Fic**

1. Espionage -- Fiction 2. World War, 1939-1945 -- Children -- Fiction 3. World War, 1939-1945 -- Evacuation of civilians -- Fiction 4. Identity -- Fiction 5. Foster children -- Fiction 6. Family life -- Maine -- Fiction 7. World War, 1939-1945 -- Maine -- Fiction 8. Maine -- History -- 20th century -- Fiction 9. Foster children -- Maine -- fiction 10. World War, 1939-1945 -- Evacuation of civilians -- Great Britain -- Fiction

ISBN 0545443601; 9780545443609

LC 2012038060

Parents' Choice: Silver Medal Fiction (2013)

"In this sequel to the WWII historical mystery 'The Romeo and Juliet Code,' . . . twelve-year old . . . Flissy now knows her Uncle Gideon is actually her biological father. . . . And she knows her whole family are some kind of spies, but she does not know . . . if they are still alive. And she has no idea why the creepy neighbor, Mr. Fitzwilliam, has invited her and adopted cousin Derek for tea, how he seems to know about her parents' secret activities." (Children's Literature)

Stone, Tamara Ireland

Time between us; Tamara Ireland Stone. Hyperion 2012 384 p. (hardcover) $17.99

Grades: 7 8 9 10 **Fic**

1. Romance fiction 2. Time travel -- Fiction 3. Love -- Fiction 4. Schools -- Fiction 5. Illinois -- Fiction 6. High schools -- Fiction 7. Space and time -- Fiction 8. Family life -- Illinois -- Fiction

ISBN 142315956X; 9781423159568

LC 2011053368

This book by Tamara Ireland Stone follows "Anna and Bennett," a couple who "were never supposed to meet: she lives in 1995 Chicago and he lives in 2012 San Francisco. But Bennett's unique ability to travel through time and space brings him into Anna's life, and with him, a new world of adventure and possibility. As their relationship deepens, they face the reality that time might knock Bennett back where he belongs." (Publisher's note)

Followed by:

Time after time (2013)

Stork, Francisco X.

Disappeared; Francisco X. Stork. Arthur A. Levine Books, an imprint of Scholastic Inc. 2017 326 p. (hardcover : alk. paper) $17.99

Grades: 7 8 9 10 **Fic**

1. Kidnapping -- Fiction 2. Brothers and sisters -- Fiction 3. Mexico -- Fiction 4. Reporters and reporting -- Fiction 5. Ciudad Juárez (Mexico) -- Fiction 6. Crime -- Mexico -- Ciudad Juárez -- fiction 7. Kidnapping -- Mexico -- Ciudad Juárez -- fiction 8. Brothers and sisters -- Mexico -- Ciudad Juárez -- fiction 9. Reporters and reporting -- Mexico -- Ciudad Juárez -- fiction 10. Women -- Violence against -- Mexico -- Ciudad Juárez -- fiction

ISBN 9780545945844; 9780545944472

LC 2017017320

In this book, by Francisco X. Stork, "Sara Zapata's best friend disappeared, kidnapped by the web of criminals who terrorize Juarez. . . . Emiliano Zapata fell in love with Perla Rubi, who will never be his so long as he's poor. . . . In the next four days, Sara and Emiliano will each face impossible choices. . . . But when the web closes in on Sara, only one path remains for the siblings: the way across the desert to the United States." (Publisher's note)

"Stork (The Memory of Light) crafts a narrative that is both riveting and eye-opening. Part thriller, part sociological study, the novel sheds light on poverty, corruption, and greed while bringing readers intimately close to the plight of those who illegally cross borders with the hope of a brighter future." Pub Wkly

★ The **last** summer of the death warriors. Arthur A. Levine Books 2010 344p $17.99

Grades: 8 9 10 11 12 **Fic**

1. Death -- Fiction 2. Orphans -- Fiction 3. New Mexico -- Fiction 4. Mexican Americans -- Fiction

ISBN 978-0-545-15133-7; 0-545-15133-3

LC 2009-19853

"This novel, in the way of the best literary fiction, is an invitation to careful reading that rewards serious analysis and discussion. Thoughtful readers will be delighted by both the challenge and Stork's respect for their abilities." Booklist

★ **Marcelo** in the real world. Arthur A. Levine Books 2009 312p $17.99

Grades: 8 9 10 11 12 **Fic**

1. Autism -- Fiction 2. Asperger's syndrome -- Fiction

ISBN 0-545-05474-5; 978-0-545-05474-4

LC 2008-14729

ALA Schneider Family Book Award Honor Book (2010)

This book features "Marcelo Sandoval [who] is a 17-year-old looking forward to his senior year in high school. Living with something akin to Asperger's syndrome, Marcelo has spent his life learning step by step how to do things that many people learn intuitively. . . . Marcelo's father makes a deal with him: if he will spend the summer working at his father's law firm and successfully follow the rules of the real world, he can choose where he will spend his senior year." (Christian Century)

"Stork introduces ethical dilemmas, the possibility of love, and other 'real world' conflicts, all the while preserving the integrity of his characterizations and intensifying the novel's psychological and emotional stakes." Publ Wkly

Strange, Lucy

★ **Our** castle by the sea; Lucy Strange. Scholastic 2019 336 p. $17.99

Grades: 5 6 7 8 **Fic**

1. Lighthouses -- Fiction 2. World War, 1939-1945 -- Great Britain -- Fiction

ISBN 1338353853; 9781338353853

In this book, by Lucy Strange, "growing up in a lighthouse, 11-year-old Pet's world has been one of storms, secret tunnels, and stories about sea monsters. But now the country is at war and the clifftops are a terrifying battleground. Pet will need to muster all her bravery to uncover why her family is being torn apart." (Publisher's note)

"A standout historical novel with a memorable protagonist, strongly sketched setting, and a compelling, twisty plot." (Publishers Weekly)

The **secret** of Nightingale Wood; Lucy Strange. Chicken House 2017 288 p. (hardback) $16.99

Grades: 4 5 6 7 **Fic**

1. Historical fiction 2. Grief -- fiction 3. Imagination -- fiction 4. Family secrets -- fiction 5. Mental illness -- fiction 6. Books and reading -- fiction

ISBN 9781338312850; 9781338157475; 9781338157499

LC 2018295898

In this book, by Lucy Strange, "Mama is ill. Father has taken a job abroad. Nanny Jane is too busy to pay any attention to Henrietta and the things she sees . . . in the shadows of their new home, Hope House. All alone, with only stories for company, Henry discovers that Hope House is full of strange secrets. . . . One night she ventures into the darkness of Nightingale Wood. What she finds there will change her whole world..." (Publisher's note)

"An evocative, beautifully written, mesmerizing debut tale with lush fairy-tale themes and a poignant exploration of mental illness—enthralling." Kirkus

Strasser, Todd

Boot camp. Simon & Schuster Books for Young Readers 2007 238p hardcover o.p. pa $6.99

Grades: 8 9 10 11 12 **Fic**

1. Torture -- Fiction 2. Juvenile delinquency -- Fiction

ISBN 978-1-4169-0848-7; 1-4169-0848-X; 978-1-4169-5942-7 pa; 1-4169-5942-4 pa

LC 2006-13634

After ignoring several warnings to stop dating his former teacher, Garrett is sent to Lake Harmony, a boot camp that uses brutal methods to train students to obey their parents.

"The ending is both realistic and disturbing. . . . Writing in the teen's mature and perceptive voice, Strasser creates characters who will provoke strong reactions from readers. . . . [This is a] fast-paced and revealing story." SLJ

Fallout; Todd Strasser. Candlewick Press 2013 272 p. $16.99

Grades: 5 6 7 8 **Fic**

ISBN 0763655341; 9780763655341

LC 2012955123

1. Cuban Missile Crisis, 1962 -- Fiction 2. Fallout shelters -- Fiction

This book is an alternate history novel by Todd Strasser. "In the summer of 1962, the possibility of nuclear war is all anyone talks about. But Scott's dad is the only one in the neighborhood who actually prepares for the worst. . . . . When the unthinkable happens," their neighbors "force their way into the shelter. . . . With not enough room, not enough food, and not enough air, life inside the shelter is filthy, physically draining, and emotionally fraught." (Publisher's note)

No place; Todd Strasser. Simon & Schuster Books for Young Readers 2014 272 p. (hardcover) $17.99

Grades: 7 8 9 10 **Fic**

1. Homelessness 2. Homeless persons -- Fiction 3. Poverty -- Fiction

ISBN 144245721X; 9781442457218

LC 2012043701

In this novel, by Todd Strasser, "It seems like Dan has it all. . . . Then his family loses their home. Forced to move into the town's Tent City, Dan feels his world shifting. . . . As Dan struggles to adjust to his new life, he gets involved with the people who are fighting for better conditions and services for the residents of Tent City. But someone wants Tent City gone, and will stop at nothing until it's destroyed." (Publisher's note)

Price of duty; Todd Strasser. Simon & Shuster Books for Young Readers 2018 192 p. (hardcover) $17.99

Grades: 8 9 10 11 **Fic**

1. Duty -- Fiction 2. Soldiers -- Fiction 3. Post-traumatic stress disorder -- Fiction 4. War -- Fiction 5. Heroes -- Fiction 6. Family life -- Fiction 7. Dating (Social customs) -- Fiction

ISBN 148149709X; 1481497103; 9781481497091; 9781481497107

LC 2017025647

In this novel, by Todd Strasser, "Jake Liddell is a war hero. The military is considering awarding him a Silver Star, a huge honor for any soldier--especially for the son of a military family. Only Jake's questioning everything his family brought him up to believe. Now at home, recovering from his physical wounds, the memories of what he experienced 'over there' haunt him." (Publisher's note)

Stratton, Allan

Chanda's secrets. Annick Press 2004 193p $19.95; pa $8.95

Grades: 7 8 9 10 **Fic**

1. Africa -- Fiction 2. AIDS (Disease) -- Fiction

ISBN 1-55037-835-X; 1-55037-834-1 pa

Michael L. Printz Award honor book, 2005

"The details of sub-Saharan African life are convincing and smoothly woven into this moving story of poverty and courage, but the real insight for readers will be the appalling treatment of the AIDS victims. Strong language and frank description are appropriate to the subject matter." SLJ

Another title about Chanda is:
Chanda's war (2007)

Chanda's wars; with an afterword by Roméo Dallaire. HarperCollinsPublishers 2008 384p $17.99; lib bdg $18.89; pa $8.99

Grades: 8 9 10 11 12 **Fic**

1. War stories 2. Africa -- Fiction 3. Orphans -- Fiction 4. Kidnapping -- Fiction

ISBN 978-0-06-087262-5; 0-06-087262-4; 978-0-06-087264-9 lib bdg; 0-06-087264-0 lib bdg; 978-0-06-087265-6 pa; 0-06-087265-9 pa

LC 2007-10829

Sequel to: Chanda's secrets (2004)

Chanda Kabelo, a teenaged African girl, must save her younger siblings after they are kidnapped and forced to serve as child soldiers in General Mandiki's rebel army.

"The characters are drawn without sentimentality, and the story is a moving portrayal of betrayal and love. The army's brutality and the traumas of the child soldiers are graphic and disturbing." Booklist

Strohmeyer, Sarah

Smart girls get what they want; by Sarah Strohmeyer. 1st ed. Harpercollins Childrens Books 2012 348 p. (tr. bdg.) $17.99; (paperback) $9.99

Grades: 7 8 9 10 11 12 **Fic**

1. Female friendship -- Fiction 2. Grading and marking (Education) 3. High school students -- Fiction 4. Schools -- Fiction 5. Friendship -- Fiction 6. Best friends -- Fiction 7. High schools -- Fiction 8. Interpersonal relations -- Fiction

ISBN 0061953407; 9780061953408; 9780061953415

LC 2011026094

Author Sarah Strohmeyer tells the story of Gigi, Neerja, and Bea, three friends who "stumble upon . . . [Neerja's sister] Parad's signatureless yearbook, making them think that maybe studying isn't everything. . . . When Gigi is accused of cheating on the AP Chemistry midterm along with Mike, a Man Clan wannabe who calls her 'Einstein,' the girls launch into action. Gigi finds herself running for student rep against Will, the new guy from California. . . . Neerja tries out for the lead in Romeo and Juliet and Bea convinces Gigi to join the ski team with her." (Kirkus Reviews)

Strong, Karen

Just south of home; Karen Strong. Simon & Schuster Books for Young Readers 2019 320 p. (hardcover : alk. paper) $17.99

Grades: 4 5 6 7 **Fic**

1. Ghost stories 2. Cousins -- fiction 3. Ghosts -- Fiction 4. Georgia -- Fiction 5. Supernatural -- Fiction 6. African Americans -- Fiction 7. Family life -- Georgia -- Fiction

ISBN 9781534419384; 9781534419391

LC 2018030146

In this book, by Karen Strong, "twelve-year-old Sarah is finally in charge. At last, she can spend her summer months reading her favorite science books and bossing around her younger brother. . . But when their cousin, Janie arrives for a visit, Sarah's plans are completely squashed. Janie has a knack for getting into trouble and asks Sarah to take her to Creek Church: a landmark of their small town that she heard was haunted. It's also off-limits." (Publisher's note)

"Twelve-year-old aspiring astrobiologist Sarah Greene digs into a dark history to help heal her family, both those present and from the past A stirring southern middle-grade book that burns brighter than fireworks on the Fourth." (Kirkus)

Stroud, Jonathan

★ The **Amulet** of Samarkand. Hyperion Bks. for Children 2003 462p (Bartimaeus trilogy) $17.95; pa $7.99

Grades: 7 8 9 10 **Fic**

1. Fantasy fiction

ISBN 0-7868-1859-X; 0-7868-5255-0 pa

LC 2003-49904

Nathaniel, a magician's apprentice, summons up the djinni Bartimaeus and instructs him to steal the Amulet of Samarkand from the powerful magician Simon Lovelace.

"There is plenty of action, mystery, and humor to keep readers turning the pages. This title, the first in a trilogy, is a must for fantasy fans." SLJ

Other titles in this series are:
The golem's eye (2004)
Ptolemy's gate (2006)

The **creeping** shadow; Jonathan Stroud ; illustrations by Kate Adams. Disney-Hyperion 2016 445 p. illustrations (Lockwood & Co.) (hardback) $16.99

Grades: 4 5 6 7 **Fic**

1. Paranormal fiction -- fiction 2. Ghosts -- Fiction 3. England -- Fiction 4. Supernatural -- Fiction 5. Psychic ability -- Fiction

6. London (England) -- Fiction 7. Mystery and detective stories
ISBN 9781484709672

LC 2016014383

Lucy has become "a freelance operative. . . . One day she is pleasantly surprised by a visit from Lockwood, who tells her . . . [that] Penelope Fittes, the leader of the giant Fittes Agency, wants them--and only them--to locate and remove the Source for the legendary Brixton Cannibal. They succeed in their very dangerous task, but tensions remain high between Lucy and the other agents." (Publisher's note)

"Stroud's scene setting and storytelling are second to none, but it's his ability to create credible, idiosyncratic characters and relationships that makes avid fans of the Lockwood & Co. series." Booklist

The **empty** grave; Jonathan Stroud, illustrations by Kate Adams. Disney-Hyperion 2017 448 p. (hardcover) $16.99
Grades: 4 5 6 7 **Fic**

1. Psychics -- Fiction 2. Supernatural -- Fiction 3. Ghosts -- Fiction 4. England -- Fiction 5. Psychic ability -- Fiction 6. London (England) -- Fiction 7. Mystery and detective stories
ISBN 9781484778722

LC 2017029086

In this book in the Lockwood & Co. series, by Jonathan Stroud, with illustrations by Kate Adams, "five months after the events in 'The Creeping Shadow,' we join Lockwood, Lucy, George, Holly, and their associate Quill Kipps on a perilous night mission: they have broken into the booby-trapped Fittes Mausoleum, where the body of the legendary psychic heroine Marissa Fittes lies. Or does it?" (Publisher's note)

The **golem's** eye. Hyperion Books for Children 2004 562p (Bartimaeus trilogy) $17.95; pa $7.99
Grades: 7 8 9 10 **Fic**

1. Fantasy fiction
ISBN 0-7868-1860-3; 0-7868-3654-7 pa
Sequel to The amulet of Samarkand (2003)

In their continuing adventures, magician's apprentice Nathaniel, now fourteen years old, and the djinni Bartimaeus travel to Prague to locate the source of a golem's power before it destroys London.

"The characters are well developed and the action never lets up. A must-purchase for all fantasy collections." SLJ

Followed by Ptolemy's gate (2006)

Heroes of the valley. Hyperion Books for Children 2009 483p $17.99
Grades: 7 8 9 10 **Fic**

1. Adventure fiction 2. Middle Ages -- Fiction
ISBN 978-1-4231-0966-2; 1-4231-0966-X

"Twelve Houses control sections of a valley. Halli Sveinsson—at 15, the youngest child of the rulers of the House of Svein—goes against tradition when he sets out to avenge the death of his murdered uncle, and his actions result in warfare among Houses for the first time in generations. . . . Smart, funny dialogue and prose, revealing passages about the exploits of the hero Svein, bouts of action and a touch of romance briskly move the story along." Publ Wkly

The **hollow** boy; Jonathan Stroud. Disney-Hyperion 2015 385 p. (Lockwood & Co.) (hardback) $16.99
Grades: 4 5 6 7 **Fic**

1. Paranormal fiction 2. Ghosts -- Fiction 3. England -- Fiction 4. Supernatural -- Fiction 5. London (England) -- Fiction 6. Mystery and detective stories
ISBN 9781484709689

LC 2015015076

In this juvenile novel, by Jonathan Stroud, part of the "Lockwood & Co." series, "as a massive outbreak of supernatural Visitors baffles Scotland Yard and causes protests throughout London, Lockwood & Co. continue to demonstrate their effectiveness in exterminating spirits. Anthony Lockwood is dashing, George insightful, and Lucy dynamic, while the skull in the jar utters sardonic advice from the sidelines." (Publisher's note)

"As always, the descriptions of the hauntings are genuinely frightening, especially that of a spindly, humanoid creature that crawls on all fours and whispers Lucy's name." SLJ

Ptolemy's gate. Hyperion Books For Children 2006 501p (Bartimaeus trilogy) $17.95; pa $8.99
Grades: 7 8 9 10 **Fic**

1. Fantasy fiction
ISBN 0-7868-1861-1; 978-0-7868-1861-7; 0-7868-3868-X pa; 978-0-7868-3868-4 pa

LC 2005-52655

Sequel to The golem's eye (2004)

Dangerous adventures continue for the djinni Bartimaeus and his master, seventeen-year-old Nathaniel, a powerful magician who is serving as England's minister of information.

This "is an exciting and eminently satisfying conclusion to the trilogy. . . . literate, entertaining, and exciting." SLJ

★ The **ring** of Solomon; a Bartimaeus novel. Disney/Hyperion Books 2010 398p $17.99
Grades: 7 8 9 10 **Fic**

1. Fantasy fiction 2. Kings 3. Magic -- Fiction 4. Jerusalem -- Fiction 5. Witchcraft -- Fiction
ISBN 978-1-4231-2372-9; 1-4231-2372-7

LC 2010015468

Wise-cracking djinni Bartimaeus finds himself at the court of King Solomon with an unpleasant master, a sinister servant, and King Solomon's magic ring.

"In this exciting prequel set in ancient Israel, Stroud presents an early adventure of his sharp-tongued djinn, Bartimaeus. . . . This is a superior fantasy that should have fans racing back to those books." Publ Wkly

★ The **screaming** staircase; by Jonathan Stroud. Disney-Hyperion 2013 400 p. (Lockwood & Co.) hbk $16.99
Grades: 4 5 6 7 **Fic**

1. Adventure fiction 2. Ghosts -- Fiction 3. England -- Fiction 4. Supernatural -- Fiction 5. Haunted houses -- Fiction 6. Psychic ability -- Fiction 7. London (England) -- Fiction
ISBN 1423164911; 9781423164913

LC 2013000352

This is the first book in Jonathan Stroud's Lockwood & Co. series. Lucy Carlyle has joined the Lockwood & Co. firm to help with England's ghost problem. "As its third member, she teams with glib, ambitious Anthony Lockwood and slovenly-but-capable scholar George Cubbins to entrap malign spirits for hire. The work is fraught with peril, not only because a ghost's merest touch is generally fatal, but also, as it turns out, as none of the three is particularly good at careful planning." (Kirkus Reviews)

Other titles in this series are:
The whispering skull (2014)
The hollow boy (2015)
The creeping shadow (2016)
The empty grave (2017)

The **whispering** skull; by Jonathan Stroud. Disney-Hyperion 2014 448 p. illustrations (Lockwood & Co.) (hardback) $17.99

Grades: 4 5 6 7 **Fic**

1. Mystery fiction 2. Paranormal fiction 3. Ghosts -- Fiction 4. England -- Fiction 5. Supernatural -- Fiction 6. Psychic ability -- Fiction 7. London (England) -- Fiction 8. Mystery and detective stories

ISBN 142316492X; 9781423164920

LC 2014014683

This novel, by Jonathan Stroud, is book 2 in the "Lockwood & Co." supernatural mystery series. "In the six months since Anthony, Lucy, and George survived a night in the most haunted house in England, Lockwood & Co. hasn't made much progress. . . . A new client, Mr. Saunders, hires Lockwood & Co. to be present at the excavation of Edmund Bickerstaff. . . . Saunders needs the coffin sealed with silver to prevent any supernatural trouble. All goes well-until George's curiosity attracts a horrible phantom." (Publisher's note)

"Stroud writes with a fine ear for dialogue, a wry sense of humor, and a knack for describing haunted places. Creating tension that ebbs and flows, he slowly builds the dramatic narrative to a resounding crescendo, and he makes the quieter scenes that follow just as compelling." Booklist

Stuber, Barbara

★ **Crossing** the tracks. Margarert K. McElderry Books 2010 258p $16.99

Grades: 6 7 8 9 **Fic**

1. Missouri -- Fiction 3. Household employees -- Fiction 4. Father-daughter relationship -- Fiction

ISBN 978-1-4169-9703-0; 1-4169-9703-2

LC 2009-42672

Morris Finalist (2011)

In Missouri in 1926, fifteen-year-old Iris Baldwin discovers what family truly means when her father hires her out for the summer as a companion to a country doctor's invalid mother.

"Thought-provoking and tenderhearted, Iris's story is one of a mature young woman who faces life with courage and common sense. . . . This thoughtful novel offers strong character development and an engaging protagonist." SLJ

Sturtevant, Katherine

The **brothers** story. Farrar, Straus and Giroux 2009 271p $16.99

Grades: 7 8 9 10 11 **Fic**

1. Twins -- Fiction 2. Brothers -- Fiction 3. Apprentices -- Fiction 4. Great Britain -- Fiction 5. Mentally handicapped children -- Fiction

ISBN 978-0-374-30992-3; 0-374-30992-2

LC 2008-35513

In the late seventeenth century, fifteen-year-old Kit, driven to desperation by the starvation of one brother and mistreatment of his own simpleminded twin, realizes his dream of becoming an apprentice in London but feels drawn by duty to return home to Essex.

"Readers will quickly empathize with Kit; his conflicted feelings toward his brother, a mixture of great tenderness and shame, are sensitively drawn. He experiences the beginnings of his sexual awakening in scenes that are occasionally ribald but never gratuitous. Sturtevant invokes the cacophony of noises, smells, and sights of London, along with the sorrows and kindnesses found in daily life." SLJ

Sugiura, Misa

It's not like it's a secret; Misa Sugiura. HarperTeen 2017 394 p. (hardcover) $17.99

Grades: 7 8 9 10 11 **Fic**

1. Bildungsromans 2. Romance fiction 3. Lesbians -- Fiction 4. Adultery -- fiction 5. California -- fiction 6. Teenage girls -- fiction 7. Lesbian teenagers -- fiction 8. Japanese Americans -- fiction 9. Fathers and daughters -- fiction

ISBN 9780062473431; 9780062473417

LC 2016961849

"Sixteen-year-old Sana Kiyohara has too many secrets. Some are small, like how it bothers her when her friends don't invite her to parties. Some are big, like the fact that her father may be having an affair. And then there's the one that she can barely even admit to herself—the one about how she might have a crush on her best friend. When Sana and her family move to California, she begins to wonder if it's finally time for some honesty, especially after she meets Jamie Ramirez. Jamie is beautiful and smart and unlike anyone Sana's ever known." (Publisher's note)

"Well-paced, brimming with drama, and utterly vital." Kirkus

Includes bibliographical references (pages 389-390).

Sullivan, Laura L.

Guardian of the Green Hill; [illustrations by David Wyatt] Henry Holt and Company 2011 293p il $16.99

Grades: 5 6 7 8 **Fic**

1. Fantasy fiction 2. Fairies -- Fiction 3. Siblings -- Fiction 4. Supernatural -- Fiction 5. Great Britain -- Fiction

ISBN 978-0-8050-8985-1; 0-8050-8985-3

LC 2010029231

Sequel to: Under the Green Hill (2010)

After the Midsummer War ends, Meg Morgan faces a madman in the battle for control of the last bastion of fairies in England, aided by her siblings Rowan, Silly, and James, and American neighbors Dickie Rhys, and Finn Fachan.

"Sullivan's writing has a timelessness that contrasts nicely with Meg's distinctly modern ideas and weaves a compelling story that will pull readers along." SLJ

Sullivan, Mary

Dear Blue Sky; Mary Sullivan. Nancy Paulsen Books 2012 248 p. (hardcover) $16.99

Grades: 4 5 6 7 **Fic**

1. Children and war 2. Siblings -- Fiction 3. War -- Fiction 4. Pen pals -- Fiction 5. Family life -- Fiction 6. Down syndrome -- Fiction 7. Iraq War, 2003-2011 -- Fiction 8. Brothers and sisters -- Fiction

ISBN 0399256849; 9780399256844

LC 2011046952

In the book by Mary Sullivan, "Cassie's whole world changes when her beloved older brother, Sef, goes to war in Iraq . . . While her parents are preoccupied, her best friend, Sonia, inexplicably stops talking to her; her older sister, Van, tests out risky behaviors; and her developmentally delayed younger brother, Jack, becomes altogether silent. When a seventh-grade social-studies project leads her to a blog called Blue Sky, written by an Iraqi girl of similar age, Cassie starts to see the war from a different perspective." (Kirkus)

Sullivan, Tara

Golden boy; Tara Sullivan. G.P. Putnam's Sons, an imprint of Penguin Group (USA) Inc. 2013 368 p. (hardcover) $16.99

Grades: 7 8 9 10 11 12 **Fic**

1. Voyages and travels -- Fiction 2. Albinos and albinism -- Fiction

3. Survival -- Fiction 4. Tanzania -- Fiction 5. Human rights -- Fiction 7. Human skin color -- Fiction
ISBN 0399161120; 9780399161124
LC 2012043310

In this book, an albino boy named Habo does not fit in with his Tanzanian family, who shun him. "Only Habo's sister, Asu, protects and nurtures him. Poverty forces the family from their rural home near Arusha to Mwanza, hundreds of miles away, to stay with relatives. After their bus fare runs out, they hitch a ride across the Serengeti with an ivory poacher who sees opportunity in Habo. Forced to flee for his life, the boy eventually becomes an apprentice to Kweli, a wise, blind carver." (Kirkus)

Summers, Courtney

This is not a test; Courtney Summers. St. Martin's Griffin 2012 336 p. $9.99; (pbk.) $9.99
Grades: 7 8 9 10 11 12 **Fic**

1. Adventure fiction 2. Zombies -- Fiction 3. Child abuse -- Fiction 4. Horror stories 5. Schools -- Fiction 6. Survival -- Fiction 7. High schools -- Fiction 8. Family problems -- Fiction
ISBN 0312656742; 9780312656744; 9781250011817
LC 2012004633

In this book, "six teens who barely know or like each other seek refuge in their high school while the undead hordes lurk outside. . . . The end of the world unfolds through the eyes of high school junior Sloane Price, who has been contemplating suicide since her older sister ran away six months earlier, leaving Sloane with their physically abusive father. But these worries are pushed aside as Sloane tries to keep her fellow students alive." (Publishers Weekly)

Supplee, Suzanne

Somebody everybody listens to. Dutton 2010 245p $16.99
Grades: 7 8 9 10 11 12 **Fic**

1. Singers -- Fiction 2. Country music -- Fiction 3. Nashville (Tenn.) -- Fiction
ISBN 978-0-525-42242-6; 0-525-42242-0
LC 2009-25089

Retta Lee Jones is blessed with a beautiful voice and has big dreams of leaving her tiny Tennessee hometown. With a beaten down car, a pocketful of hard-earned waitressing money, and stars in her eyes, Retta sets out to make it big in Nashville.

"While a must read for country music lovers, . . . [this book] will appeal to a wide audience, especially those who long to pursue a dream against the odds." Publ Wkly

Sutton, Kelsey

Some quiet place; by Kelsey Sutton. 1st ed. Flux 2013 336 p. (paperback) $9.99
Grades: 7 8 9 10 **Fic**

1. Occult fiction -- fiction 2. Fear -- Fiction 3. Schools -- Fiction 4. Emotions -- Fiction 5. Wisconsin -- Fiction 6. High schools -- Fiction 7. Supernatural -- Fiction 8. Family problems -- Fiction 9. Farm life -- Wisconsin -- Fiction
ISBN 0738736430; 9780738736433
LC 2013005021

In this book, "Elizabeth Caldwell's best friend is dying of cancer, one of the cutest boys in school loves her, and her alcoholic father beats her—but Elizabeth doesn't care about any of it. Her only meaningful interactions are with the Emotions, immortal personifications of the feelings she can't experience. With them, she does not have to pretend, as she must when she tries to muster believable social responses." The book explores the reasons behind Elizabeth's coldness. (Publishers Weekly)

"Haunting, chilling and achingly romantic, Sutton's debut novel for teens will keep readers up until the wee hours, unable to tear themselves away from this strange and beautifully crafted story. Elizabeth Caldwell can't feel emotions, yet she sees them everywhere, human in appearance, standing alongside their "summons."...Chills and goose bumps of the very best kind accompany this haunting, memorable achievement." (Kirkus)

Svingen, Arne

The **Ballad** of a Broken Nose; by Arne Svingen, translated by Kari Dickson. Simon & Schuster 2016 224 p. $16.99
Grades: 5 6 7 **Fic**

1. Opera -- Fiction 2. Bullies -- fiction 3. Friendship -- fiction
ISBN 1481415425; 9781481415422
Batchelder Honor Book (2017)

In this book, by Arne Svingen, translated by Kari Dickson, "Bart is an eternal optimist. At thirteen years old, he's had a hard life. But Bart knows that things won't get any better if you have a negative attitude. His mother has pushed him into boxing lessons so that Bart can protect himself, but Bart already has defense mechanisms: he is relentlessly positive and he loves opera." (Publisher's note)

"An absorbing, well-paced story with a heartening conclusion." Booklist

Sweeney, Diana

The **minnow**; Diana Sweeney. Text Publishing Co. 2015 263 p. $9.95
Grades: 8 9 10 11 12 **Fic**

1. Grief -- Fiction 2. Teenage mothers -- Fiction 3. Loss (Psychology) -- Fiction 4. Teenage pregnancy -- Fiction 5. Bildungsromans 6. Coming of age -- Fiction
ISBN 192218201X; 9781922182012
LC 2015376822

In this book, by Diana Sweeney, "Tom survived a devastating flood that claimed the lives of her sister and parents. Now she lives with Bill in his old shed by the lake. But it's time to move out--Tom is pregnant. . . . In her longing for what is lost, Tom talks to fish: Oscar the carp in the pet shop, little Sarah catfish who might be her sister, an unhelpful turtle in a tank at the maternity ward. And the Minnow." (Publisher's note)

"Readers who can accept the ambiguous chronology and Tom's glib ability to communicate beyond worlds will be rewarded: the universe into which Minnow is born and will undoubtedly thrive is engaging and extraordinary. A promising and welcome debut." Booklist

Swift, Jonathan

Gulliver's travels; illustrated by Scott McKowen. Sterling Pub. Co. 2007 293p il (Sterling unabridged classics) $9.95
Grades: 7 8 9 10 11 12 Adult **Fic**

1. Fantasy fiction 2. Voyages and travels -- Fiction
ISBN 978-1-4027-4339-9; 1-4027-4339-4
LC 2007003974

First published 1726

"In the account of his four wonder-countries Swift satirizes contemporary manners and morals, art and politics-in fact the whole social scheme-from four different points of view. The huge Brobdingnagians reduce man to his natural insignificance, the little people of Lilliput parody Europe and its petty broils, in Laputa philosophers are ridiculed, and finally all Swift's hatred and contempt find their satisfaction in degrading humanity to a bestial condition." Baker. Guide to the Best Fic

Sáenz, Benjamin Alire, 1954-

★ The **inexplicable** logic of my life; by Benjamin Alire Sáenz. Clarion Books, Houghton Mifflin Harcourt 2017 445 p. (hardcover) $17.99

Grades: 8 9 10 11 12 **Fic**

1. Families -- Fiction 2. Identity -- Fiction 3. Mexican Americans -- Fiction 4. Death -- Fiction 5. Adoption -- Fiction 6. Friendship -- Fiction 7. High school students -- Fiction 8. Children of gay parents -- Fiction

ISBN 9780544586505; 9780544583528

LC 2016001079

In this young adult novel by Benjamin Alire Saenz, "Sal used to know his place with his adoptive gay father, their loving Mexican American family, and his best friend, Samantha. But it's senior year, and suddenly Sal is throwing punches, questioning everything, and realizing he no longer knows himself. If Sal's not who he thought he was, who is he?" (Publisher's note)

"The themes of love, social responsibility, death, and redemption are expertly intertwined with well-developed characters and a compelling story line. This complex, sensitive, and profoundly moving book is beautifully written and will stay with readers." SLJ

Tak, Bibi Dumon

Soldier bear; written by Bibi Dumon Tak; illustrated by Philip Hopman; translated by Laura Watkinson. Eerdmans Books for Young Readers 2011 145p il $13

Grades: 4 5 6 7 **Fic**

1. Iran -- Fiction 2. Bears -- Fiction 3. Italy -- Fiction 4. Poland -- Fiction 5. Soldiers -- Fiction 6. World War, 1939-1945 -- Fiction

ISBN 978-0-8028-5375-2; 0-8028-5375-7

LC 2011013963

Original Dutch edition 2008

An orphaned Syrian brown bear cub is adopted by Polish soldiers during World War II and serves for five years as their mischievous mascot in Iran and Italy. Based on a true story.

"This is smoothly translated and engagingly illustrated with sketches and helpful maps. Funny, fresh and heartwarming." Kirkus

Talley, Robin

Our own private universe; Robin Talley. Harlequin Teen 2017 376 p. (hardcover) $18.99

Grades: 7 8 9 10 11 12 **Fic**

1. Romance fiction 2. Lesbians -- Fiction 3. High school students -- Fiction 4. Teenagers -- fiction 5. Church group work -- fiction 6. Bisexual teenagers -- fiction 7. Americans -- Mexico -- fiction 8. Bisexual high school students -- fiction

ISBN 9781488015274; 9780373211982; 0373211988

LC 2017296952

In this book, by Robin Talley, "Aki Simon has a theory, and it's mostly about sex. . . . Aki already knows she's bisexual--even if, until now, it's mostly been in the hypothetical sense. . . . Her best friend, Lori, is the only person who knows she likes girls, too. Aki's theory is that she's got only one shot at living an interesting life--and that means she's got to stop sitting around and thinking so much. It's time for her to actually do something. Or at least try." (Publisher's note)

"An important and heartfelt contribution to contemporary teen lit about queer women: hopeful, realistic, and romantic, Talley's newest is sure to satisfy." Kirkus

Pulp; Robin Talley. Harlequin Books 2018 416 p. $18.99

Grades: 8 9 10 11 12 **Fic**

1. Lesbians -- Fiction 2. Lesbianism -- Fiction 3. Lesbian teenagers -- Fiction

ISBN 1335012907; 9781335012906

"In this novel told in dual narratives, 'New York Times' bestselling author Robin Talley weaves together the lives of two young women connected across generations through the power of words. A stunning story of bravery, love, how far we've come and how much farther we have to go." (Publisher's note)

"Two Washington, D.C., lesbian teens, 62 years apart, each discover classic lesbian pulp fiction—late midcentury paperbacks depicting a shadowy world of forbidden love." (Kirkus)

Tamaki, Mariko

Lumberjanes : unicorn power! Mariko Tamaki ; illustrated by Brooke Allen. Amulet Books 2017 239 p. color illustrations (Lumberjanes) (hardback) $14.99

Grades: 3 4 5 6 7 8 **Fic**

1. Fantasy fiction 2. Adventure fiction

ISBN 9781419727252

LC 2017028472

In this book in the Lumberjanes series, by Mariko Tamaki, illustrated by Brooke Allen, "when challenge-loving April leads the girls on a hike up the TALLEST mountain they've ever seen, things don't go quite as planned. For one, they didn't expect to trespass into the lands of the ancient Cloud People, and did anyone happen to read those ominous signs some unknown person posted at the bottom of the mountain? Also, unicorns." (Publisher's note)

"The primary focus, however, is on the rollicking adventure and the power of friendship, and Lumberjanes fans will be satisfied on that front. Occasionally, the cartoonish action and pace of the story, which was so successful in the comics, doesn't quite land in narrative form, but that's a fairly minor quibble unlikely to bother readers eager for anything and everything Lumberjanes." Booklist

Other titles in this series are:

The moon is up (2018)

Saving Montgomery Sole; by Mariko Tamaki. Roaring Brook Press 2016 240 p. (hardback) $17.99

Grades: 7 8 9 10 **Fic**

1. Clubs -- fiction 2. Friendship -- fiction 3. Family life -- fiction 4. Self-perception -- fiction 5. California -- Fiction 6. Lesbian mothers -- Fiction

ISBN 9781626722712; 1626722714

LC 2015004007

In this book, by Mariko Tamaki, "Montgomery Sole is a square peg in a small town, forced to go to a school full of jocks and girls who don't even know what irony is. It would all be impossible if it weren't for her best friends, Thomas and Naoki. The three are also the only members of Jefferson High's Mystery Club, dedicated to exploring the weird and unexplained, from ESP and astrology to superpowers and mysterious objects." (Publisher's note)

"Montgomery's slow confrontation with reality creates a realistic, satisfying arc, and Tamaki's economical storytelling results in dimensional characters whose struggles feel viscerally real." Pub Wkly

Tan, Shaun

Cicada; Shaun Tan. Arthur A. Levine Books, an imprint of Scholastic Inc. 2019 32 p. (hardcover : alk. paper) $19.99

Grades: 6 7 8 9 **Fic**

1. Cicadas -- Fiction 2. Discrimination -- Fiction 3. Conduct of life -- Fiction

ISBN 9781338298390

LC 2018018042

This book, by Shaun Tan, "tells the story of a hardworking little cicada who is completely unappreciated for what he does. But in the end, just when you think he's given up, he makes a transformation into something ineffably beautiful. A metaphor for growing up? A bit of inspiration for the unappreciated striver in all of us? Yes, yes, and more." (Publisher's note)

Tanner, Lian

City of lies. Delacorte Press 2011 278 p. (The Keeper's trilogy) lib bdg $20.99; $17.99
Grades: 5 6 7 8 **Fic**
1. Fantasy fiction 2. Adventure fiction 3. Thieves -- Fiction 4. Kidnapping -- Fiction
ISBN 0385739060; 0385907699 lib bdg; 9780385907699 lib bdg; 9780385739061
LC 2010048579
Sequel to: Museum of thieves (2010)
Twelve-year-old Goldie, impulsive and bold, relies on her skills as a liar and a thief to try to rescue her captured friends from the child-stealers running rampant in the City of Spoke.

Ice Breaker; Lian Tanner. Feiwel & Friends 2015 304 p. $16.99
Grades: 5 6 7 8 **Fic**
1. Secrets -- Fiction 2. Ocean travel -- Fiction 3. Tribes -- fiction 4. Ships -- Fiction 5. Outcasts -- Fiction
ISBN 1250052165; 9781250052162
First published 2013 in Australia
In Lian Tanner's novel "Petrel is an outcast on the ancient ship . . . that has been following the same course for 300 years. In that time, the ship's crew has . . . broken into three warring tribes. A mysterious boy is discovered barely alive on an iceberg, and brought onto the ship. The tribes don't trust strangers, so Petrel hides the boy. What she doesn't know is that the ship guards a secret - a secret the boy has been sent to destroy." (Publisher's note)
Other titles in this series are:
Sunker's Deep (2016)
Battlesong (2017)

Museum of thieves. Delacorte Press 2010 312p (The Keepers Trilogy) $16.99; lib bdg $19.99
Grades: 5 6 7 8 **Fic**
1. Fantasy fiction 2. Adventure fiction 3. Museums -- Fiction 4. Thieves -- Fiction
ISBN 978-0-385-73905-4; 0-385-73905-2; 978-0-385-90768-2 lib bdg; 0-385-90768-0 lib bdg
LC 2009053655
Goldie, an impulsive and bold twelve-year-old, escapes the oppressive city of Jewel, where children are required to wear guardchains for their protection, and finds refuge in the extraordinary Museum of Dunt, an ever-shifting world where she discovers a useful talent for thievery and mysterious secrets that threaten her city and everyone she loves.
"Readers will be quickly caught up in the highly dramatic chases, the intriguing museum that shifts layout at will, and the nifty otherworld elements. There's depth beneath that, though. . . . [The book] may set young readers thinking about their own world's choices." Bull Cent Child Books
Other titles in this series are:
City of lies (2011)
Path of beasts (2012)

Tanquary, Kathryn

The **night** parade; Kathryn Tanquary. Sourcebooks Jabberwocky 2016 332 p. (alk. paper) $16.99
Grades: 5 6 7 8 **Fic**
1. Japan -- Fiction 2. Curses -- Fiction 3. Grandmothers -- Fiction 4. Supernatural -- Fiction 5. Blessing and cursing -- Fiction
ISBN 1492623245; 9781492623243
LC 2015022869
In this book, by Kathryn Tanquary, "The last thing Saki Yamamoto wants to do for her summer vacation is trade in exciting Tokyo for the antiquated rituals . . . of her grandmother's village. Preparing for the Obon ceremony is boring. Then the local kids [dare] Saki [to disrespect] her family's ancestral shrine. . . . But as Saki rings the sacred bell, the darkness shifts. A death curse has been invoked...and Saki has three nights to undo it." (Publisher's note)
"Vivid details and realistic situations ensure accessibility, and subtle teaching moments are wrapped in wide-eyed enchantment." Pub Wkly

Tarshis, Lauren

Emma -Jean Lazarus fell in love. Dial Books for Young Readers 2009 169p $16.99; pa $6.99
Grades: 5 6 7 **Fic**
1. School stories 2. Friendship -- Fiction
ISBN 978-0-8037-3321-3; 0-8037-3321-6; 978-0-14-241568-9 pa; 0-14-241568-5 pa
Sequel to: Emma-Jean Lazarus fell out of a tree (2007)
Seventh-grader Emma-Jean Lazarus uses her logical, scientific mind to navigate the mysteries of the upcoming Spring Fling, her friend Colleen's secret admirer, and other love-related dilemmas
"Tarshis deftly weaves in important details from the previous book . . . providing those new to Emma-Jean some necessary back story. . . . Fans will appreciate the continuity and relish the reappearance of familiar characters, especially Ms Wright, the lovable school janitor, and the rest of Emma Jean's true blue friends. The story ends on a happy note with the possibility of more adventures to come." Kirkus

★ **Emma** -Jean Lazarus fell out of a tree. Dial Books for Young Readers 2007 199p $16.99
Grades: 5 6 7 **Fic**
1. School stories 2. Friendship -- Fiction
ISBN 978-0-8037-3164-6; 0-8037-3164-7
LC 2006-18428
A quirky and utterly logical seventh-grade girl named Emma-Jean Lazarus discovers some interesting results when she gets involved in the messy everyday problems of her peers.
"Readers will be fascinated by Emma-Jean's emotionless observations and her adult-level vocabulary. Tarshis pulls off a balancing act, showing the child's detachment yet making her a sympathetic character. Exceptionally fleshed-out secondary characters add warmth to the story." SLJ
Followed by: Emma-Jean Lazarus fell in love (2009)

I survived the Battle of Gettysburg, 1863; Lauren Tarshis. Scholastic 2013 89 p. (paperback) $4.99
Grades: 3 4 5 6 **Fic**
1. Fugitive slaves -- fiction 2. Gettysburg (Pa.), Battle of, 1863 -- fiction
ISBN 0545459362; 9780545459365
This children's book, by Lauren Tarshis, is book 7 in the "I Survived" series. "It's 1863, and Thomas and his little sister, Birdie, have fled the farm where they were born and raised as slaves. . . . They soon cross paths with a Union soldier . . . , marching with the army. But then

orders come through: The men are called to battle in Pennsylvania. Thomas has made it so far . . . but does he have what it takes to survive Gettysburg?" (Publisher's note)

Tashjian, Janet

gospel The gospel according to Larry. Holt & Co. 2001 227p il $16.95; pa $5.99

Grades: 7 8 9 10 **Fic**

1. Web sites -- Fiction

ISBN 0-8050-6378-1; 0-440-23792-0 pa

LC 2001-24568

Seventeen-year-old Josh, a loner-philosopher who wants to make a difference in the world, tries to maintain his secret identity as the author of a web site that is receiving national attention

"Tashjian fabricates a cleverly constructed scenario and expertly carries it out to the bittersweet end." Horn Book Guide

Other titles about Larry are:

Vote for Larry (2004)

Larry and the meaning of life (2008)

Larry and the meaning of life. Henry Holt and Co. 2008 211p $16.95

Grades: 7 8 9 10 **Fic**

1. Authors 2. Naturalists 3. Essayists 4. Pacifists 5. Writers on nature 6. Nonfiction writers 7. Massachusetts -- Fiction 8. Political activists -- Fiction 9. Identity (Psychology) -- Fiction

ISBN 978-0-8050-7735-3; 0-8050-7735-9

LC 2007-46936

Larry (otherwise known as Josh) is in the doldrums, but after meeting a spiritual guru at Walden Pond who convinces him to join his study group, he starts to question his grasp of reality.

★ **My** life as a book; with cartoons by Jake Tashjian. Henry Holt 2010 211p il $16.99; pa $6.99

Grades: 4 5 6 7 **Fic**

1. Summer -- Fiction 2. Animals -- Fiction 3. Family life -- Fiction 4. Books and reading -- Fiction 5. Young adult literature -- Works 6. Children's literature -- Works -- Grades two through six

ISBN 978-0-8050-8903-5; 0-8050-8903-9; 978-0-312-67289-8 pa; 0-312-67289-6 pa

LC 2009-18909

Dubbed a "reluctant reader" by his teacher, twelve-year-old Derek spends summer vacation learning important lessons even though he does not complete his summer reading list.

"The protagonist is by turns likable and irritating, but always interesting. He is sure to engage fans of Jeff Kinney's 'Diary of a Wimpy Kid' books . . . as well as those looking for a spunky, contemporary boy with a mystery to solve. Reluctant readers will appreciate the book's large print and quick-paced story." SLJ

"Another title about Derek is:

My life as a stuntboy (2011)

My life as a cartoonist; Janet Tashjian ; with cartoons by Jake Tashjian. Henry Holt and Company 2013 272 p. illustrations (hardcover) $13.99

Grades: 4 5 6 7 **Fic**

1. School stories 2. People with disabilities -- Fiction 3. Schools -- Fiction 4. Cartoonists -- Fiction 5. Wheelchairs -- Fiction

ISBN 0805096094; 9780805096095

LC 2012046201

In this book, by Janet Tashjian, "[t]here's a new kid in Derek Fallon's class. His name is Umberto and he uses a wheelchair. Derek's family is still fostering Frank the monkey, and Derek thinks it would be great to train Frank to assist Umberto. But Derek quickly realizes that Umberto is definitely not looking for any help. Derek soon becomes the butt of Umberto's jokes. On top of that, Umberto starts stealing Derek's cartoon ideas and claiming them as his own." (Publisher's note)

"Cartoonist Derek grapples with a perplexing association between disability and bullying in this stand-alone sequel to My Life as a Book (2010) and My Life as a Stuntboy (2011). . . . This entertaining read leaves some provoking questions unanswered--usefully." Kirkus

Companion titles include:

My Life as a Book (2010)

My Life as a Stuntboy (2011)

My Life as a Joke (2014)

My Life as a Gamer (2015)

My life as a joke; Janet Tashjian ; with cartoons by Jake Tashjian. Henry Holt and Company 2014 252 p. illustrations (hardback) $13.99

Grades: 4 5 6 7 **Fic**

1. School stories 2. Middle schools -- Fiction 3. Friendship -- Fiction 4. Maturation (Psychology) -- Fiction

ISBN 080509850X; 9780805098501

LC 2013046395

In this middle grade book by Janet Tashjian, illustrated by Jake Tashjian, "Derek Fallon discovers all the angst that comes with being twelve--he just wants to feel grown up, but life gets in the way with a series of mishaps that make him look like a baby. . . . Why isn't being in middle school as great as Derek imagined?" (Publisher's note)

"In his fourth appearance, twelve-year-old Derek resolves to appear more mature, but he's constantly a laughingstock. . . . Fans will enjoy the fast plot, Derek's supportive friends, and cartoon marginalia representing Derek's ever-expanding collection of vocabulary words." Horn Book

My life as a stuntboy; with cartoons by Jake Tashjian. Henry Holt and Company 2011 256p il $13.99

Grades: 4 5 6 7 **Fic**

1. School stories 2. Monkeys -- Fiction 3. Stunt flying -- Fiction 4. Motion pictures -- Fiction

ISBN 978-0-8050-8904-2; 0-8050-8904-7

LC 2010029884

Twelve-year-old Derek Fallon has the opportunity of a lifetime--to perform stunts in a movie featuring a popular twelve-year-old star—but complications arise involving his best friend, a capuchin monkey, and Derek's chronic inability to concentrate on schoolwork.

"The generous margins are filled with Derek's often quite clever stick-figure cartoons illustrating vocabulary words such as 'flabbergasted' and 'camouflage'—all rendered by the author's teenage son. Another fun, emotionally resonant read for the Wimpy Kid set and beyond." Kirkus

Vote for Larry. Henry Holt and Co 2004 224p $16.95

Grades: 7 8 9 10 **Fic**

1. Politics -- Fiction 2. Elections -- Fiction

ISBN 0-8050-7201-2

LC 2003-56578

Sequel to: The gospel according to Larry (2005)

Not yet eighteen years old, Josh, a.k.a. Larry, comes out of hiding and returns to public life, this time to run for President as an advocate for issues of concern to youth and to encourage voter turnout.

"A solid and timely work that will make readers laugh, but more important, will make them think." Voice Youth Advocates

Followed by: Larry and the meanin of life (2008)

Taylor, Chloe

Ready to wear; Chloe Taylor. 1st ed. Simon Spotlight 2013 176 p. (Sew Zoey) (paperback) $5.99; (hardcover) $15.99

Grades: 3 4 5 6 7 **Fic**

1. Fashion -- literature 2. Middle schools -- fiction 3. School stories -- fiction

ISBN 1442479345; 9781442479333; 9781442479340

LC 2013935204

In this children's novel, by Chloe Taylor, illustrated by Nancy Zhang, "fashion-loving Zoey Webber gets the best news ever: Her middle school is getting rid of uniforms! . . . Zoey has sketchbooks full of fashion designs, but nothing to wear! So with a little help from her best friends Kate and Priti, she learns to make her own clothes. She even begins to post her fashion design sketches online in a blog. That's how the Sew Zoey blog begins, and soon it becomes much more." (Publisher's note)

Other titles in this series are:
On Pins and Needles
Lights, Camera, Fashion!
Stitches and Stones
Cute as a Button
A Tangled Thread
Knot Too Shabby!
Swatch Out!
A Change of Lace
Bursting at the Seams
Clothes Minded
Dressed to Frill
Sewing in Circles
Cut from the Same Cloth

Taylor, Greg

Killer Pizza. Feiwel and Friends 2009 346p $16.99

Grades: 6 7 8 9 **Fic**

1. Horror fiction 2. Monsters -- Fiction

ISBN 978-0-312-37379-5; 0-312-37379-1

LC 2008028543

While working as summer employees in a local pizza parlor, three teenagers are recruited by an underground organization of monster hunters.

"Toby is an easygoing and relatable young adult, and young teens will enjoy the fun, slightly scary read." Voice Youth Advocates

Followed by: Killer pizza: the slice (2011)

Killer Pizza: the slice. Feiwel and Friends 2011 341p $16.99

Grades: 6 7 8 9 **Fic**

1. Horror fiction 2. Adventure fiction 3. Monsters -- Fiction

ISBN 978-0-312-58088-9; 0-312-58088-6

LC 2010048928

Sequel to: Killer pizza (2009)

Having passed the tests to become Monster Combat Officers, teens Toby, Annabel, and Strobe are sent on a secret mission to deliver to the Monster Protection Program a beautiful fourteen-year-old monster who wants to defect, regardless of the considerable dangers this poses.

Taylor, Laini

Blackbringer. G. P. Putnam's Sons 2007 437p (Faeries of Dreamdark) $17.99

Grades: 6 7 8 9 **Fic**

1. Fantasy fiction 2. Magic -- Fiction 3. Fairies -- Fiction

ISBN 978-0-399-24630-2; 0-399-24630-4

LC 2006026540

Magpie Windwitch, faerie, devil hunter, and granddaughter of the West Wind, must defeat an ancient evil creature, the Blackbringer, who has escaped from his bottle and threatens to unmake all of creation.

"Taylor drives the story forward by slowly teasing the reader with twists and turns in the plot. . . . Teen readers will identify with this faerie's humanness." Voice Youth Advocates

★ **Daughter** of smoke and bone. Little, Brown 2011 418p $18.99

Grades: 8 9 10 11 12 **Fic**

1. Fantasy fiction 2. Romance fiction 3. Paranormal fiction 4. School stories 5. Angels -- Fiction 6. Artists -- Fiction 7. Supernatural -- Fiction 9. Classical mythology -- Fiction

ISBN 978-0-316-13402-6; 0-316-13402-3; 9780316196192

LC 2010045802

Seventeen-year-old Karou, a lovely, enigmatic art student in a Prague boarding school, carries a sketchbook of hideous, frightening monsters—the chimaerae who form the only family she has ever known.

Taylor "again weaves a masterful mix of reality and fantasy with cross-genre appeal. Exquisitely written and beautifully paced." Publ Wkly

★ **Days** of blood & starlight; Laini Taylor. 1st ed. Little, Brown Books for Young Readers 2012 528 p. maps (Daughter of smoke and bone trilogy) (hardcover) $18.99

Grades: 9 10 11 12 **Fic**

1. Occult fiction -- fiction 3. Fantasy fiction -- fiction 4. Angels -- Fiction 5. Demonology -- Fiction 6. Supernatural -- Fiction 7. Czech Republic -- Fiction 8. Mythology, Greek -- Fiction 9. Prague (Czech Republic) -- Fiction 10. Chimera (Greek mythology) -- Fiction

ISBN 0316133973; 9780316133975

LC 2012028752

Sequel to: Daughter of smoke and bone

In this fantasy sequel to "Daughter of Smoke and Bone," "Karou . . . has taken up the resurrection work . . . under the direction of the dangerous chimaera leader, Thiago. . . . The angel army is menacing the countryside in an attempt to kill the remaining chimaera, so she is designing and resurrecting stronger, more effective winged warriors to protect her people." (Bulletin of the Center for Children's Books)

Dreams of gods & monsters; by Laini Taylor. Little, Brown and Co. 2014 624 p. (hardback) $19

Grades: 8 9 10 11 12 **Fic**

1. Angels -- Fiction 2. Supernatural -- Fiction 3. Good and evil -- Fiction 4. Greek mythology -- Fiction 5. Fantasy 6. Demonology -- Fiction 7. Mythology, Greek -- Fiction 8. Chimera (Greek mythology) -- Fiction

ISBN 0316134074; 9780316134071

LC 2014003645

"In Taylor's third and final installment in her Daughter of Smoke and Bone trilogy, Karou and Akiva's dream of peace and a life together comes tantalizingly close, only to be repeatedly thwarted by their peoples' separate and conflicting histories, both mystical and real. Joined by angels and chimaera, Karou and Akiva lead their armies and fight side by side to prevent the apocalypse by banishing Jael, captain of the Dominion of Seraphim, from the earth he is determined to destroy." (Booklist)

Taylor, Mildred D.

The **friendship**; pictures by Max Ginsburg. Dial Bks. for Young Readers 1987 53p il $15.99; pa $4.99
Grades: 4 5 6 7 **Fic**

1. Mississippi -- Fiction 2. Race relations -- Fiction 3. African Americans -- Fiction
ISBN 0-8037-0417-8; 0-14-038964-4 pa
LC 86-29309

Coretta Scott King Award for text

This "story about race relations in rural Mississippi during the Depression focuses on an incident between an old Black man, Mr. Tom Bee, and a white storekeeper, Mr. John Wallace. Indebted to Tom for saving his life as a young man, John had promised they would always be friends. But now, years later, John insists that Tom call him 'Mister' and shoots the old man for defiantly—and publicly—calling him by his first name. Narrator Cassie Logan and her brothers . . . are verbally abused by Wallace's villainous sons before witnessing the encounter." Bull Cent Child Books

★ The **gold** Cadillac; pictures by Michael Hays. Dial Bks. for Young Readers 1987 43p il $16.99; pa $4.99
Grades: 4 5 6 7 **Fic**

1. Prejudices -- Fiction 2. Race relations -- Fiction 3. African Americans -- Fiction
ISBN 0-8037-0342-2; 0-14-038963-6 pa
LC 86-11526

"Full-page sepia paintings effectively portray the characters, setting, and mood of the story events as Hays ably demonstrates his understanding of the social and emotional environments which existed for blacks during this period." SLJ

★ The **land**. Phyllis Fogelman Bks. 2001 375p $17.99; pa $6.99
Grades: 7 8 9 10 **Fic**

1. Race relations -- Fiction 2. African Americans -- Fiction 3. Racially mixed people -- Fiction
ISBN 0-8037-1950-7; 0-14-250146-8 pa
LC 00-39329

Prequel to Roll of Thunder, Hear My Cry
Coretta Scott King Award for text

After the Civil War Paul-Edward Logan, the son of a white father and a black mother, finds himself caught between the two worlds of colored folks and white folks as he pursues his dream of owning land of his own.

"Taylor masterfully uses harsh historical realities to frame a powerful coming-of-age story that stands on its own merits." Horn Book Guide

★ **Let** the circle be unbroken. Dial Bks. for Young Readers 1981 394p $17.99; pa $7.99
Grades: 4 5 6 7 **Fic**

1. Mississippi -- Fiction 2. African Americans -- Fiction 3. Great Depression, 1929-1939 -- Fiction
ISBN 0-8037-4748-9; 0-14-034892-1 pa
LC 81-65854

Sequel to: Roll of thunder, hear my cry

The author "provides her readers with a literal sense of witnessing important American history. . . . Moreover, [she] never neglects the details of her volatile 9-year-old heroine's interior life. The daydreams, the jealousy, the incredible ardor of that age come alive." N Y Times Book Rev

★ The **road** to Memphis; by Mildred Taylor. Dial Bks. 1989 290p pa $6.99; $18.99
Grades: 4 5 6 7 **Fic**

1. Mississippi -- Fiction 2. Race relations -- Fiction 3. African Americans -- Fiction
ISBN 0-14-036077-8 pa; 0-8037-0340-6
LC 88-33654

Coretta Scott King Award for text

This is a sequel to Let the Circle Be Unbroken (BRD 1982). "The time is 1941, with the U.S. on the verge of war; Cassie {Logan} . . . is sure that nothing will stop her from college and career. When her friend Moe is humiliated and ridiculed by local bigots, he loses control and attacks three men with a crowbar. Cassie and her brothers and friends (including one white friend, Jeremy Simms) help Moe escape. . . . Grades seven to twelve." (Booklist)

"Taylor's continued smooth, easy language provides readability for all ages, with a focus on universal human pride, worthy values, and individual responsibility. This action-packed drama is highly recommended." Voice Youth Advocates

★ **Roll** of thunder, hear my cry; Mildred D. Taylor ; introduction by Jacqueline Woodson ; illustration by Kadir Nelson. 40th anniversary edition Dial Books for Young Readers 2016 276 p illustrations hardcover $19.99; paperback $7.99
Grades: 4 5 6 7 8 9 **Fic**

1. Mississippi -- Fiction 2. African Americans -- Fiction 3. Racism -- Fiction
ISBN 110199388X; 9781101993880; 0140384510; 9780140384512
LC 2015026310

First published 1976
Newbery Medal (1977)

"Why is the land so important to Cassie's family? It takes the events of one turbulent year--the year of the night riders and the burnings, the year a white girl humiliates Cassie in public simply because she is black--to show Cassie that having a place of their own is the Logan family's lifeblood. It is the land that gives the Logans their courage and pride, for no matter how others may degrade them, the Logans possess soemthing no one can take away." (Publisher's note)

The **well**; David's story. Dial Bks. for Young Readers 1995 92p hardcover o.p. pa $5.99
Grades: 4 5 6 7 **Fic**

1. Mississippi -- Fiction 2. Race relations -- Fiction 3. African Americans -- Fiction
ISBN 0-8037-1802-0; 0-14-038642-4 pa
LC 94-25360

This story "delivers an emotional wallop in a concentrated span of time and action. . . . This story reverberates in the heart long after the final paragraph is read." Horn Book

Taylor, S. S.

The **Expeditioners** and the Treasure of Drowned Man's Canyon; by S. S. Taylor; illustrated by Katherine Roy. Pgw 2012 320 p. $22
Grades: 5 6 7 8 **Fic**

1. Adventure fiction 2. Maps -- fiction 3. Exploration -- fiction
ISBN 1938073061; 9781938073069

In this book by S. S. Taylor, illustrated by Katherine Roy, "computers have failed, electricity is extinct, and the race to discover new lands is underway! Brilliant explorer Alexander West has just died under mysterious circumstances, but not before smuggling half of a strange map to his intrepid children--Kit the brain, M.K. the tinkerer, and Zander the brave. Why are so many government agents trying to steal the half-map? (And where is the other half?)" (Publisher's note)

Taylor, Theodore

★ The **cay**. Delacorte Press 1987 137p $16.95; pa $5.50
Grades: 5 6 7 8 **Fic**

1. Blind -- Fiction 2. Race relations -- Fiction 3. Caribbean region -- Fiction 4. Survival after airplane accidents, shipwrecks, etc. -- Fiction

ISBN 0-385-07906-0; 0-440-22912-X pa

A reissue of the title first published 1969

When the freighter on which they are traveling is torpedoed by a German submarine during World War II, Phillip, an adolescent white boy blinded by a blow on the head, and Timothy, an old black man, are stranded on a tiny Caribbean island where the boy acquires a new kind of vision, courage, and love from his old companion

"Starkly dramatic, believable and compelling." Saturday Rev

Followed by: Timothy of the cay

★ **Timothy** of the cay. Harcourt Brace & Co. 1993 161p hardcover o.p. pa $5.95
Grades: 5 6 7 8 **Fic**

1. Blind -- Fiction 2. Race relations -- Fiction 3. Caribbean region -- Fiction 4. Survival after airplane accidents, shipwrecks, etc. -- Fiction

ISBN 0-15-288358-4; 0-15-206320-X pa

LC 93-7898

Sequel to: The cay

Having survived being blinded and shipwrecked on a tiny Caribbean island with the old black man Timothy, twelve-year-old white Phillip is rescued and hopes to regain his sight with an operation. Alternate chapters follow the life of Timothy from his days as a young cabin boy

"Somewhat more thoughtful than its well-loved antecedent, this boldly drawn novel is no less commanding." Publ Wkly

Teague, David

★ **Saving** Lucas Biggs; by Marisa de los Santos and David Teague. Harper, an imprint of HarperCollinsPublishers 2014 288 p. (hardback) $16.99
Grades: 5 6 7 8 **Fic**

1. Girls -- Fiction 2. Time travel -- Fiction 3. Detective and mystery stories

ISBN 0062274627; 9780062274625

LC 2013043189

This "time-travel story from husband-and-wife team Marisa de los Santos and David Teague follows one girl's race to change the past in order to save her father's future. Thirteen-year-old Margaret knows her father is innocent, but that doesn't stop the cruel Judge Biggs from sentencing him to death. Margaret is determined to save her dad, even if it means using her family's secret--and forbidden--ability to time travel." (Publisher's note)

"The authors weave a tale of justice and family bonds with threads of historical fiction accented with the fantastical physics of time travel. The heroine begins to realize that the very stuff that makes people who they are--that combination of all their life experiences—can sometimes shift the very fabric of history. At least that's what Margaret is hoping, because the only way to save her father is to first save corrupt Lucas Biggs from himself." SLJ

Teague, Mark

★ The **doom** machine; a novel. Blue Sky Press 2009 376p $17.99
Grades: 4 5 6 7 **Fic**

1. Science fiction 2. Space and time -- Fiction 3. Extraterrestrial beings -- Fiction

ISBN 978-0-545-15142-9; 0-545-15142-2

LC 2009-14262

When a spaceship lands in the small town of Vern Hollow in 1956, juvenile delinquent Jack Creedle and prim, studious Isadora Shumway form an unexpected alliance as they try to keep a group of extraterrestrials from stealing eccentric Uncle Bud's space travel machine.

"This book is filled with humor and dramatic figurative language that makes the setting completely approachable. It is a great fit for science fiction, humor, and adventure genre fans." Voice Youth Advocates

Teller, Janne

★ **Nothing**; translated from the Danish by Martin Aitken. Atheneum Books for Young Readers 2010 227p $16.99
Grades: 7 8 9 10 11 12 **Fic**

1. School stories 2. Meaning (Philosophy) -- Fiction

ISBN 978-1-4169-8579-2; 1-4169-8579-4

LC 2009-19784

Michael J. Printz honor book, 2011

When thirteen-year-old Pierre Anthon leaves school to sit in a plum tree and train for becoming part of nothing, his seventh grade classmates set out on a desperate quest for the meaning of life.

"Indelible, elusive, and timeless, this uncompromising novel has all the marks of a classic." Booklist

Temblador, Alex

Secrets of the Casa Rosada; by Alex Temblador. Pinata Books, an imprint of Arte Publico Press 2018 160 p. (alk. paper) $12.95
Grades: 8 9 10 11 12 **Fic**

1. Healers -- Fiction 2. Grandmothers -- Fiction 3. Mexican Americans -- Fiction 4. Secrets -- Fiction 5. Blessing and cursing -- Fiction 6. Family life -- Texas -- Fiction 7. Texas -- History -- 20th century -- Fiction

ISBN 1558858709; 9781558858701

LC 2018029355

This novel, by Alex Temblador, presents "a magical story about a girl who awakens to her potential when her vagabond mother abandons her at her grandmother's home in Laredo, Texas. Kept in the dark her entire life, 16-year-old Martha discovers that everything she thinks she knows about herself is a lie. . . . As Martha endeavors to learn the language of her long-lost family, she discovers that her grandmother is a curandera with healing powers." (Kirkus Reviews)

Terry, Teri

Fractured; Teri Terry. Nancy Paulsen Books 2013 336 p. (Slated trilogy) $17.99
Grades: 7 8 9 10 **Fic**

1. Dystopian fiction 2. Memory -- Fiction 3. Science fiction 4. England -- Fiction 5. Schools -- Fiction 6. Identity -- Fiction 7. Terrorism -- Fiction 8. High schools -- Fiction

ISBN 0399161732; 9780399161735

LC 2012044317

Author Teri Terry presents the "second installment of the Slated trilogy . . . set in a future where violent teens have their memory erased as an alternative to jail. Kyla has been Slated--her personality wiped blank, her memories lost to her forever. Or so she thought. When a mysterious man from her past comes back into her life and wants her help, she thinks she's on her way to finding the truth." (Publisher's note)

"Kyla's memories, wiped by the government in Slated, are slowly returning; she's been found by an anti-government group that claims she's a member and wants her to complete one last mission. Kyla's struggles to uncover her identity and think through the consequences of her actions are realistic and add an emotional backbone to this fast-paced middle volume of the trilogy." (Horn Book)

Slated; Teri Terry. Nancy Paulsen Books 2013 346 p. (hardcover) $17.99

Grades: 7 8 9 10 **Fic**

1. Science fiction 2. Memory -- Fiction 3. Identity -- Fiction 4. Schools -- Fiction 5. High schools -- Fiction 6. Family life -- England -- Fiction

ISBN 0399161724; 9780399161728

LC 2012020873

In this novel, by Teri Terry, "Kyla has been Slated--her memory and personality erased as punishment for committing a crime she can't remember. The government has taught her how to walk and talk again, given her a new identity and a new family, and told her to be grateful for this second chance that she doesn't deserve. It's also her last chance--because they'll be watching to make sure she plays by their rules." (Publisher's note)

Other titles in this series are:

Fractured (2013)

Shattered (2014)

Testa, Dom

The **Cassini** code. Tor Teen 2010 283p (Galahad) pa $8.99

Grades: 7 8 9 10 11 12 **Fic**

1. Science fiction 2. Interplanetary voyages -- Fiction

ISBN 978-0-7653-6079-3; 0-7653-6079-9

First published 2008 by Profound Impact Group with title: Galahad 3

"The teen crew members of the starship Galahad find themselves navigating the treacherous asteroid field known as the Kuiper Belt with only their onboard computer, Roc, to guide them. Simultaneously, one crew member needs an emergency operation, while a boy named Merit begins leading a mutinous movement known as R.T.E. (Return to Earth). As before, Testa relies on interpersonal dynamics more than action, but his pacing has never been finer, making this the most satisfying entry yet." Booklist

Cosmic storm. Tor Teen 2011 267p (Galahad) $16.99

Grades: 7 8 9 10 **Fic**

1. Science fiction 2. Interplanetary voyages -- Fiction

ISBN 978-0-7653-2111-4; 0-7653-2111-4

LC 2011021556

One year into their mission, as the teenaged crew of the Galahad is faced with waves of radiation that threaten the survival of their ship, Council leader Triana disappears and the crew must decide how to deal with assaults from both the outside and within their ranks.

Testa's "got his act down so well that it remains highly pleasurable." Booklist

The **dark** zone; a Galahad book. Tor 2011 284p (Galahad) $16.99

Grades: 7 8 9 10 **Fic**

1. Science fiction 2. Interplanetary voyages -- Fiction

ISBN 978-0-7653-2110-7; 0-7653-2110-6

LC 2010052388

After navigating safely through the minefield of the Kuiper Belt, the teenaged crew of Galahad, led by Triana, decides to push forward through a group of incredibly fast and maneuverable organisms, setting off a cataclysmic series of events.

"Testa's teens remain refreshingly grounded, perceptive, and intelligent." Booklist

The **web** of Titan. Tor Teen 2010 255p (Galahad) pa $8.99

Grades: 7 8 9 10 **Fic**

1. Science fiction 2. Interplanetary voyages -- Fiction

ISBN 978-0-7653-6078-6; 0-7653-6078-0

Sequel to: The comet's curse (2009)

First published 2006 by Profound Impact Group

As the spaceship Galahad passes Titan, one of Saturn's moons, the teenage crew discovers a strange pod orbiting the moon, and when they investigate they face a crippling illness that is affecting the crew.

Followed by: The Cassini code (2010)

Tharp, Tim

Knights of the hill country. Alfred A. Knopf 2006 233p hardcover o.p. pa $6.99

Grades: 8 9 10 11 12 **Fic**

1. School stories 2. Football -- Fiction 3. Oklahoma -- Fiction

ISBN 978-0-375-83653-4; 0-375-83653-5; 978-0-553-49513-3 pa; 0-553-49513-5 pa

LC 2005-33279

In his senior year, high school star linebacker Hampton Greene finally begins to think for himself and discovers that he might be interested in more than just football.

"Taut scenes on the football field and the dilemmas about choosing what feels right over what's expected are all made memorable by Hamp's unforgettable, colloquial voice." Booklist

Thomas, Rhiannon

Long may she reign; Rhiannon Thomas. HarperTeen 2017 422 p. (hardcover) $17.99

Grades: 7 8 9 10 11 12 **Fic**

1. Queens -- Fiction 2. Courts and courtiers -- Fiction 3. Poisons and poisoning -- Fiction 4. Fathers and daughters -- fiction 5. Murder -- Investigation -- fiction

ISBN 9780062418708; 9780062418685

LC 2016952956

In this novel, by Rhiannon Thomas, "Freya was never meant to be queen. Twenty-third in line to the throne, she never dreamed of a life in the palace, and would much rather research in her laboratory than participate in the intrigues of the court. However, when an extravagant banquet turns deadly and the king and those closest to him are poisoned, Freya suddenly finds herself on the throne." (Publisher's note)

"A clever, absorbing mystery of court intrigue, intense friendships, and newfound courage." Booklist

Thompson, Holly

The **language** inside; Holly Thompson. 1st ed. Delacorte Press 2013 528 p. (hardcover) $17.99

Grades: 7 8 9 10 11 12 **Fic**

1. Novels in verse 2. Moving -- Fiction 3. Interpersonal relations -- Fiction 4. Japan -- Fiction 5. Cancer -- Fiction 6. Tsunamis -- Fiction 7. Massachusetts -- Fiction 8. Moving, Household --

Fiction 9. Family life -- Massachusetts -- Fiction
ISBN 0385739796; 9780375898358; 9780385739795; 9780385908078

LC 2012030596

In this novel in verse, by Holly Thompson, "Emma's family moves to a town outside Lowell, Massachusetts, to stay with Emma's grandmother while her mom undergoes treatment. Emma feels out of place in the United States. She begins to have migraines, and longs to be back in Japan. At her grandmother's urging, she volunteers in a long-term care center to help Zena, a patient with locked-in syndrome, write down her poems." (Publisher's note)

Includes bibliographical references (p. 520).

Orchards; Holly Thompson; illustrations by Grady McFerrin. Delacorte Press 2011 327p il $17.99; lib bdg $20.99

Grades: 7 8 9 10 **Fic**

1. Novels in verse 2. Japan -- Fiction 3. Suicide -- Fiction 4. Bereavement -- Fiction 5. Family life -- Fiction 6. Racially mixed people -- Fiction

ISBN 978-0-385-73977-1; 0-385-73977-X; 978-0-385-90806-1 lib bdg; 0-385-90806-7 lib bdg

LC 2010-23724

"After a classmate commits suicide, Kana, a half-Japanese, half-Jewish American eighth grader, is sent to her maternal grandmother's farm in rural Japan for personal reflection. Kana tells her story in poignantly straightforward verse directed at the deceased classmate as she struggles with blame and regret, wondering if she and her friends are responsible because they took part in ostracizing the girl. She struggles, too, with her biracial, bicultural identity, feeling isolated in her new surroundings." (School Library Journal)

"Kanako's urgent teen voice, written in rapid free verse and illustrated with occasional black-and-white sketches, will hold readers with its nonreverential family story." Booklist

Thompson, J. E.

The **girl** from Felony Bay; John Thompson. Walden Pond Press, an imprint of HarperCollinsPublishers 2013 384 p. (hardcover bdg.) $16.99

Grades: 4 5 6 7 **Fic**

1. Theft -- fiction 2. Mystery fiction -- fiction 3. Coma -- Fiction 4. Fathers -- Fiction 5. Families -- Fiction 6. Charleston (S.C.) -- Fiction 7. Mystery and detective stories

ISBN 0062104462; 9780062104465

LC 2012025338

In this book, 12-year-old Abbey Force's "father has suffered an accident and now lies in the hospital in a coma. Meanwhile, he has been accused of stealing from a client named Miss Lydia Jenkins, and his law firm . . . has sold the Force family home, Reward Plantation, in order to repay her." Abbey makes friends with the new owners' daughter Bee and the girls "stumble upon a mystery--someone is digging holes at Felony Bay, perhaps in search of buried treasure." (Kirkus Reviews)

Thompson, Kate

The **new** policeman. Greenwillow Books 2007 442p hardcover o.p. pa $8.99

Grades: 7 8 9 10 **Fic**

1. Fantasy fiction 2. Music -- Fiction 3. Fairies -- Fiction 4. Ireland -- Fiction 5. Space and time -- Fiction

ISBN 978-0-06-117427-8; 0-06-117427-0; 978-0-06-117429-2 pa; 0-06-117429-7 pa

LC 2006-8246

First published 2005 in the United Kingdom

Irish teenager JJ Liddy discovers that time is leaking from his world into Tir na nOg, the land of the fairies, and when he attempts to stop the leak he finds out a lot about his family history, the music that he loves, and a crime his great-grandfather may or may not have committed.

"Mesmerizing and captivating, this book is guaranteed to charm fantasy fans." Voice Youth Advocates

Other titles in this series are:
The last of the High Kings (2008)
The white horse trick (2010)

The **white** horse trick. Greenwillow Books 2010 405p

Grades: 7 8 9 10 **Fic**

1. Fantasy fiction 2. Fairies -- Fiction 3. Ireland -- Fiction 4. Refugees -- Fiction 5. Family life -- Fiction

ISBN 0-06-200416-6; 0-06-200417-4 lib bdg; 978-0-06-200416-1; 978-0-06-200417-8 lib bdg

LC 2010-10287

Sequel to: The last of the High Kings (2008)

First published 2009 in the United Kingdom

This is the "final volume of a trilogy that began with The New Policeman [2007] and continued with The Last of the High Kings [2008]. Former protagonist J.J. Liddy, now an old man, has retired to the fairy world, but his sons, Aidan and Donal, are wreaking havoc in the human realm. They have become warlords in a world ravaged beyond repair by global warming. . . . Middle school, high school." (Horn Book)

The author "offers readers a taste of genre-bending that is both challenging and successful." Booklist

Thor, Annika

Deep sea; Annika Thor ; translated from the Swedish by Linda Schenck. First American edition Delacorte Press 2015 240 p. (hc) $17.99

Grades: 7 8 9 10 11 12 **Fic**

1. Jews -- Fiction 2. Sweden -- Fiction 3. Sisters -- Fiction 4. Refugees -- Fiction 5. Friendship -- Fiction 6. World War, 1939-1945 -- Refugees -- Fiction 7. Schools -- Fiction 8. Jews -- Sweden -- Fiction 9. Sweden -- History -- Gustav V, 1907-1950 -- Fiction

ISBN 0385743858; 9780375991325; 9780385743853

LC 2014005586

Sequel to The Lily Pond

Originally published 1998 in Sweden

In this book, by Annika Thor, "Stephie and her younger sister, Nellie, escaped the Nazis in Vienna and fled to an island in Sweden, where they were taken in by different families. . . . Nellie wants to be adopted by her foster family. Stephie, on the other hand, can't stop thinking about her parents, who are in a Nazi camp in Austria." (Publisher's note)

"This novel about coming of age during a complicated, tragic time in history is both delicate and poignant, as when Stephie and Nellie sit on the dock, remembering a lullaby their mother sang. Thor's novel capably demonstrates the loneliness, powerlessness, and prejudice Stephie faces, as well as her growing inner strength." Pub Wkly

A **faraway** island; translated from the Swedish by Linda Schenck. Delacorte Press 2009 247p map $16.99; lib bdg $19.99

Grades: 4 5 6 7 **Fic**

1. Jews -- Fiction 2. Sweden -- Fiction 3. Islands -- Fiction 4. Sisters -- Fiction 5. Refugees -- Fiction 6. World War, 1939-1945 -- Fiction

ISBN 978-0-385-73617-6; 0-385-73617-7; 978-0-385-90590-9 lib bdg; 0-385-90590-4 lib bdg

LC 2009-15420

ALA ALSC Batchelder Award (2010)

In 1939 Sweden, two Jewish sisters wait for their parents to flee the Nazis in Austria, but while eight-year-old Nellie settles in quickly, twelve-year-old Stephie feels stranded at the end of the world, with a foster mother who is as cold and unforgiving as the island on which they live.

"Children will readily empathize with Stephie's courage. Both sisters are well-drawn, likable characters. This is the first of four books Thor has written about the two girls." SLJ

Followed by: The lily pond (2011)

Followed by The Lily Pond

The **lily** pond; translated from the Swedish by Linda Schenck. Delacorte Press 2011 217p $16.99; lib bdg $19.99

Grades: 4 5 6 7 **Fic**

1. School stories 2. Sweden -- Fiction 3. Refugees -- Fiction 4. Friendship -- Fiction 5. Jews -- Sweden -- Fiction 6. World War, 1939-1945 -- Fiction

ISBN 978-0-385-74039-5; 0-385-74039-5; 978-0-385-90838-2 lib bdg; 0-385-90838-5 lib bdg; 978-0-375-89914-0 e-book

LC 2010053548

"A year after Stephie Steiner and her younger sister, Nellie, left Nazi-occupied Vienna, Stephie has finally adapted to life on the rugged Swedish island where she now lives. But more change awaits Stephie: her foster parents have allowed her to enroll in school on the mainland, in Goteberg. Stephie is eager to go. Not only will she be pursuing her studies, she'll be living in a cultured city again—under the same roof as Sven, the son of the lodgers who rented her foster parents' cottage for the summer." (Publisher's note)

Followed by: Deep Sea

Thornburgh, Blair

★ **Ordinary** girls; Blair Thornburgh ; [edited by] Alexandra Cooper. HarperTeen 2019 368 p. (hardcover) $17.99

Grades: 7 8 9 10 11 12 **Fic**

1. Sisters -- Fiction 2. Families -- Fiction

ISBN 9780062447814

LC 2019932653

"Thornburgh offers a story that's as witty, intelligent, and perceptive as its narrator. A rewarding novel that revolves around change, reflection, and, yes, sisterhood."

Thorne, Jack, 1978-

Harry Potter and the cursed child parts one and two; the official script book of the original west end production. J.K. Rowling, John Tiffany, Jack Thorne. Arthur A. Levine Books 2016 327 p. (ebook) $44.97; (jacketed hardcover : alk. paper) $29.99

Grades: 4 5 6 7 8 9 10 **Fic**

1. Magic -- Drama 2. Time travel -- Drama 3. Good and evil -- Drama

ISBN 9781781107041; 1338099132; 9781338099133

LC 2016944764

This play by J. K. Rowling, John Tiffany, and Jack Thorne, "is the eighth story in the Harry Potter series and the first official Harry Potter story to be presented on stage..... While Harry grapples with a past that refuses to stay where it belongs, his youngest son Albus must struggle with the weight of a family legacy he never wanted. As past and present fuse ominously, both father and son learn the uncomfortable truth: sometimes, darkness comes from unexpected places." (Publisher's note)

"Series fans can breathe easy knowing this play has been respectfully and lovingly wrought. Tensions thrum, spells fly, and Slytherins finally have their day in the sun—but at center stage, as always in the Potterverse, is the overriding importance of love and friendship, especially in the face of danger." Booklist

Tingle, Tim

Danny Blackgoat, Navajo prisoner; Tim Tingle. 7th Generation 2013 160 p. (pbk.) $9.95

Grades: 6 7 8 **Fic**

1. Navajo Indians -- Fiction 2. Bullies -- Fiction 3. Prisoners -- Fiction 4. Conduct of life -- Fiction 5. Navajo Long Walk, 1863-1867 -- Fiction 6. Indians of North America -- Texas -- Fiction 7. Fort Davis National Historic Site (Tex.) -- Fiction

ISBN 193905303X; 9781939053039

LC 2013013183

American Indian Youth Literature Awards Honor Book: Middle School (2014)

In this book, "Danny Blackgoat is a teenager in Navajo country when soldiers burn down his home, kill his sheep and capture his family. During the Long Walk of 1864, Danny is labeled a troublemaker. . . . Refusing to accept captivity, he is sent to Fort Davis, Texas, a Civil War prisoner outpost. There . . . he meets Jim Davis. Jim teaches Danny how to hold his anger and . . . aids Danny in a daring and dangerous escape." (Publisher's note)

How I became a ghost; a Choctaw trail of tears story. by Tim Tingle. RoadRunner Press 2013 160 p. (The how I became a ghost series) (hardcover : alk. paper) $18.95

Grades: 4 5 6 7 **Fic**

1. Ghost stories 2. Choctaw Indians -- Fiction

ISBN 1937054535; 9781937054533; 9781937054540; 9781937054557

LC 2013935579

American Indian Youth Literature Award Winner (2014)

In this book, "a 10-year-old Choctaw boy recounts the beginnings of the forced resettlement of his people from their Mississippi-area homelands in 1830. . . . Even as the Choctaw prepare to leave their homes, Isaac begins to have unsettling visions. . . [The] visions begin to come true, as some are burned to death by the Nahullos and others perish due to smallpox-infested blankets. . . . But the Choctaw barrier between life and death is a fluid one, and ghosts follow Isaac, providing reassurance." (Kirkus Reviews)

Stone River crossing; Tim Tingle. Lee & Low Books Inc. 2019 320 p. $20.95

Grades: 5 6 7 8 **Fic**

1. Slavery -- fiction 2. Friendship -- fiction 3. Choctaw Indians -- fiction

ISBN 1620148234; 9781620148235

"Choctaw storyteller Tim Tingle offers a novel that reminds readers that the strongest bridge between cultures is friendship. . . . Martha Tom knows better than to cross the Bok Chitto River to pick blackberries. The Bok Chitto is the only border between her town in the Choctaw Nation and the slave-owning plantation in Mississippi territory. . . . But crossing the river brings a surprise friendship with Lil Mo, a boy who is enslaved on the other side." (Publisher's note)

"Richly descriptive and leavened with humor, Tingle's complex novel offers valuable insights into rarely told history." (Publishers Weekly)

When a ghost talks, listen; a Choctaw trail of tears story. Tim Tingle. RoadRunner Press 2017 188 p. (hardcover : alk. paper) $18.95

Grades: 7 8 9 10 **Fic**

1. Time travel -- Fiction 2. Choctaw Indians -- Fiction 3. Native

Americans -- Relocation -- Fiction
ISBN 9781937054519; 9781937054656

LC 2017952749

In this book in the How I Became a Ghost series, by Tim Tingle, ten-year-old Isaac's "family continues the long walk to Indian Territory . . . [while] Isaac . . . now a ghost, meets the famed Choctaw Chief and U.S. Army General Pushmataha. . . . [Then] Isaac and his three Choctaw comrades learn they can now also time travel. . . . Isaac and friends head back in . . . [1824] Washington,D.C. . . to bear witness for the Choctaw chief who has come to the nation's capital." (Publisher's note)

Toksvig, Sandi

★ **Hitler's** canary. Roaring Brook Press 2007 191p $16.95
Grades: 5 6 7 8 **Fic**

1. Jews -- Fiction 2. Denmark -- Fiction 3. World War, 1939-1945 -- Fiction
ISBN 978-1-59643-247-5; 1-59643-247-0

LC 2006-16607

Ten-year-old Bamse and his Jewish friend Anton participate in the Danish Resistance during World War II.

"Though . . . suspenseful episodes will thrill readers, it is Bamse's growing courage and deepening understanding that drive the story." Booklist

Tolan, Stephanie S.

★ **Surviving** the Applewhites. HarperCollins Pubs. 2002 216p $15.99; lib bdg $17.89; pa $5.99
Grades: 5 6 7 8 **Fic**

1. Theater -- Fiction 2. Family life -- Fiction 3. Eccentrics and eccentricities -- Fiction
ISBN 0-06-623602-9; 0-06-623603-7 lib bdg; 0-06-441044-7 pa

LC 2002-1474

A Newbery Medal honor book, 2003

Jake, a budding juvenile delinquent, is sent for home schooling to the arty and eccentric Applewhite family's Creative Academy, where he discovers talents and interests he never knew he had

This is a "thoroughly enjoyable book with humor, well-drawn characters, and a super cover." Voice Youth Advocates

Tolkien, J. R. R. (John Ronald Reuel), 1892-1973

★ The **hobbit,** or, There and back again. Houghton Mifflin 2001 330p il $18; pa $10
Grades: 5 6 7 8 9 10 11 12 Adult **Fic**

1. Fantasy fiction
ISBN 0-618-16221-6; 0-618-26030-7 pa

LC 2001276594

A reissue of the title first published 1938

"Bilbo Baggins is a hobbit who enjoys a comfortable, unambitious life, rarely traveling any farther than his pantry or cellar. But his contentment is disturbed when the wizard Gandalf and a company of dwarves arrive on his doorstep one day to whisk him away on an adventure. They have launched a plot to raid the treasure hoard guarded by Smaug the Magnificent, a large and very dangerous dragon. Bilbo reluctantly joins their quest, unaware that on his journey to the Lonely Mountain he will encounter both a magic ring and a frightening creature known as Gollum." (Publisher's note)

"This fantasy features the adventures of hobbit Bilbo Baggins, who joins a band of dwarves led by Gandalf the Wizard. Together they seek to recover the stolen treasure that is hidden in Lonely Mountain and guarded by Smaug the Dragon. This book precedes the Lord of the Rings trilogy." Shapiro. Fic for Youth. 3d edition

Followed by: The lord of the rings trilogy: The fellowship of the ring; The two towers; The return of the king

★ The **lord** of the rings; 50th Anniversary ed; Houghton Mifflin 2004 xxv, 1157p il map slip case $100
Grades: 7 8 9 10 11 12 Adult **Fic**

1. Fantasy fiction
ISBN 0-618-51765-0

LC 2004-275215

First published 1954 in the United Kingdom

"This is a tale of imaginary gnomelike creatures who battle against evil. Led by Frodo, the hobbits embark on a journey to prevent a magic ring from falling into the grasp of the powers of darkness. The forces of good succeed in their fight against the Dark Lord of evil, and Frodo and Sam bring the Ring to Mount Doom, where it is destroyed." Shapiro. Fic for Youth. 3d edition

Tooke, Wes

King of the mound; my summer with Satchel Paige. Simon & Schuster Books for Young Readers 2012 155p $15.99
Grades: 4 5 6 **Fic**

1. Baseball players 2. People with disabilities -- Fiction 3. Baseball -- Fiction 4. Poliomyelitis -- Fiction 5. African Americans -- Fiction 6. Father-son relationship -- Fiction
ISBN 978-1-4424-3346-5; 1-4424-3346-9

LC 2011012740

Twelve-year-old Nick loves baseball so after a year in the hospital fighting polio and with a brace on one leg, Nick takes a job with the minor league team for which his father is catcher and gets to see the great pitcher, Satchel Paige, play during the 1935 season. Includes historical notes.

"Tooke sticks closely to historical records, with the addition of a few extra Paige exploits and aphorisms, and . . . the fictional overlay offers a comfortably predictable 'hard work brings just rewards' arc. Nourishing fare for Matt Christopher graduates." Kirkus

Towell, Katy

Skary childrin and the carousel of sorrow. Alfred A. Knopf 2011 265p $16.99; lib bdg $19.99; ebook $16.99
Grades: 4 5 6 7 **Fic**

1. Ghost stories 2. School stories 3. Supernatural -- Fiction
ISBN 978-0-375-86859-7; 0-375-86859-3; 978-0-375-96860-0 lib bdg; 0-375-96860-1 lib bdg; 978-0-375-89931-7 e-book; 0-375-89931-6 e-book

LC 2010-38830

In Widowsbury, an isolated village where people believe "known is good, new is bad," three outcasts from the girls' school join forces with a home-schooled boy to uncover and combat the evil that is making people disappear.

"Towell tucks violent tempests, maggoty slime, hideous transformations, nightmares, sudden terrors and like atmosphere-building elements into a rousingly melodramatic literary debut." Kirkus

Townley, Rod

The **blue** shoe; a tale of thievery, villainy, sorcery, and shoes. by Roderick Townley; illustrated by Mary GrandPré. Alfred A. Knopf 2009 254p il $16.99; lib bdg $19.99
Grades: 4 5 6 7 **Fic**

1. Fables 2. Fairy tales
ISBN 978-0-375-85600-6; 0-375-85600-5; 978-0-375-95600-3 lib bdg; 0-375-95600-X lib bdg

LC 2008-43851

A mysterious stranger commissions a single, valuable shoe from a humble cobbler, changing the cobbler's life and the life of his young apprentice forever.

This is a "fun, whimsical fairy tale. . . . The good-versus-evil plotline, dynamic cast of characters, . . . light romance between Hap and Sophia, and copious amounts of magic and intrigue will be a hit with a wide range of readers." Booklist

Townsend, Jessica

The **trials** of Morrigan Crow; Jessica Townsend ; illustrated by Jim Madsen. Little, Brown & Co. 2017 xiii, 465 p.p (Nevermoor) (hardcover) $17.99

Grades: 4 5 6 7 8 **Fic**

1. Fantasy fiction 2. Magic -- fiction 3. Contests -- fiction 4. Imaginary places -- fiction 5. Blessing and cursing -- fiction
ISBN 9780316508902; 9780316439954; 9780316508889
LC 2017003436

In this book in the Nevermoor series, by Jessica Townsend, "Morrigan Crow is cursed. Having been born on Eventide, the unluckiest day for any child to be born, she's blamed for all local misfortunes, . . . and, worst of all, the curse means that Morrigan is doomed to die . . . on her eleventh birthday. But as Morrigan awaits her fate, . . . Jupiter North appears [and] . . . whisks her away into the safety of a secret, magical city called Nevermoor." (Publisher's note)

"Whimsical worldbuilding, humorous dialogue, and colorful supporting characters complement an adventurous, magic-filled plot that champions bravery, self-confidence, and hope." Pub Wkly

Another title in this series is:
Wundersmith (2018)

Tracy, Kristen

The **reinvention** of Bessica Lefter. Delacorte Press 2011 305p $15.99

Grades: 4 5 6 7 **Fic**

1. School stories 2. Idaho -- Fiction 3. Friendship -- Fiction
ISBN 978-0-385-90634-0; 0-385-90634-X
LC 2010-04844

Eleven-year-old Bessica's plans to begin North Teton Middle School as a new person begin to fall apart even before school begins.

Tracy "offers a positive and comforting message about learning to make adjustments, ending the book on a happy note, with Bessica finding her niche as school mascot." Publ Wkly

Followed by Bessica Lefter bites back (2012)

Trafton, Jennifer

★ The **rise** and fall of Mount Majestic; illustrations by Brett Helquist. Dial Books for Young Readers 2010 338p il $16.99

Grades: 4 5 6 7 **Fic**

1. Fairy tales 2. Adventure fiction 3. Giants -- Fiction
ISBN 978-0-8037-3375-6; 0-8037-3375-5
LC 2009-51659

Ten-year-old Persimmony Smudge, who longs for heroic adventures, overhears a secret that thrusts her into the middle of a dangerous mission that could destroy the island on which she lives.

"Trafton imbues her tale with a delightful sense of fun and fascinating, well-rounded characters-playful wordsmithing and flowing dialogue make this an excellent choice for bedtime read-aloud." Publ Wkly

Trevayne, Emma

The **accidental** afterlife of Thomas Marsden; by Emma Trevayne. Simon & Schuster Books for Young Readers 2015 256 p. (hardcovers) $16.99

Grades: 5 6 7 8 **Fic**

1. Magic -- Fiction 2. Fairies -- Fiction 3. Identity -- Fiction 4. Grave robbing -- Fiction 5. Spiritualists -- Fiction 6. London (England) -- Fiction 7. Great Britain -- History -- 19th century -- Fiction 8. Changelings -- Fiction 9. London (England) -- History -- 19th century -- Fiction 10. Great Britain -- History -- Victoria, 1837-1901 -- Fiction
ISBN 144249882X; 9781442498822; 9781442498846
LC 2014032574

In this book, by Emma Trevayne, "[g]rave robbing is a messy business. . . . And for Thomas Marsden, on what was previously an unremarkable spring night in London, it becomes a very spooky business. For lying in an unmarked grave and half covered with dirt is a boy the spitting image of Thomas himself. This is only the first clue that . . . lead[s] Thomas into a strange world of spiritualists, death, and faery folk." (Publisher's note)

"Full of hidden messages, midnight graveyard escapades, unlikely friendships, magic, and deceit, it's an engaging tale of one boy's efforts to find himself and his way back home." Pub Wkly

Trigiani, Adriana

Viola in reel life. HarperTeen 2009 282p $16.99

Grades: 7 8 9 10 **Fic**

1. Ghost stories 2. School stories 3. Indiana -- Fiction 4. Video recording -- Fiction 5. Dating (Social customs) -- Fiction
ISBN 978-0-06-145102-7; 0-06-145102-9
LC 2009-14269

When fourteen-year-old Viola is sent from her beloved Brooklyn to boarding school in Indiana for ninth grade, she overcomes her initial reservations as she makes friends with her roommates, goes on a real date, and uses the unsettling ghost she keeps seeing as the subject of a short film—her first.

This "is a sweet, character-driven story. Viola is very real, as are her feelings, hopes, desires, and dreams." SLJ

Followed by: Viola in the spotlight (2011)

Viola in the spotlight. HarperTeen 2011 283p $16.99

Grades: 7 8 9 10 **Fic**

1. Theater -- Fiction 2. Family life -- Fiction 3. Dating (Social customs) -- Fiction 4. Brooklyn (New York, N.Y.) -- Fiction
ISBN 978-0-06-145105-8; 0-06-145105-3
LC 2010045553

Sequel to: Viola in reel life (2009)

Back home in Brooklyn, fifteen-year-old Viola has big summer plans but with one best friend going to camp and the other not only working but experiencing her first crush, Viola is glad to be overworked as an unpaid lighting intern when her grandmother's play goes to Broadway.

"An equally enjoyable follow-up to Viola in Reel Life." Booklist

Tripp, Ben

The **accidental** highwayman; being the tale of Kit Bristol, his horse Midnight, a mysterious princess, and sundry magical persons besides. Ben Tripp. Tor Teen 2014 304 p. illustrations (hardback) $17.99

Grades: 7 8 9 10 **Fic**

1. Magic -- Fiction 2. Adventure fiction 3. Fairies -- Fiction 4. Princesses -- Fiction 5. Great Britain -- Fiction 6. Fate and fatalism -- Fiction 7. Robbers and outlaws -- Fiction 8. Adventure

and adventurers -- Fiction 9. Great Britain -- History -- George III, 1760-1820 -- Fiction
ISBN 0765335492; 9780765335494
LC 2014033724

In this book, by Ben Tripp, "Christopher 'Kit' Bristol is the unwitting servant of notorious highwayman Whistling Jack. One dark night, Kit finds his master bleeding from a mortal wound, dons the man's riding cloak to seek help, and changes the course of his life forever. Mistaken for Whistling Jack and on the run from redcoats, . . . Kit takes up his master's quest to rescue a rebellious fairy princess from an arranged marriage to King George III of England." (Publisher's note)

"Readers will root for star-crossed lovers, Kit and Morgana, and delight in their 'opposites attract' romance, drawn onward by a rollicking plot . . . Fantasy readers, especially fans of Cathrynne Valente's work, will enjoy the author's elegant turns of phrase. A first purchase for all fantasy collections." SLJ

Trueit, Trudi

The **falcon's** feather; Trudi Trueit. National Geographic Kids 2019 207 p. (library binding) $26.90
Grades: 4 5 6 7 **Fic**
1. Adventure fiction 2. Explorers -- Fiction 3. Private schools -- Fiction 4. Schools -- Fiction 5. Boarding schools -- Fiction 6. Mystery and detective stories
ISBN 9781426333064; 9781426333057; 9781426333040
LC 2018036048

In this book in the Explorer Academy series, by Trudi Trueit, "Cruz, Sailor, and Emmett, along with their new ally Bryndis, embark on their first globe-trotting mission aboard the ship Orion. Cruz jumps right back into school and starts using the latest technology in submersible underwater dives, but is soon reminded of the dangers of exploration when his equipment fails and he almost drowns. Determined to keep his eyes on the prize, Cruz sneaks away to try to find answers." (Publisher's note)

Trueman, Terry

Cruise control; 1st ed; HarperTempest 2004 149p $15.99; lib bdg $16.89; pa $8.99
Grades: 7 8 9 10 **Fic**
1. Brothers -- Fiction 2. Basketball -- Fiction 3. Cerebral palsy -- Fiction 4. Father-son relationship -- Fiction
ISBN 0-06-623960-5; 0-06-623961-3 lib bdg; 0-06-447377-5 pa
LC 2003-19822

A talented basketball player struggles to deal with the helplessness and anger that come with having a brother rendered completely dysfunctional by severe cerebral palsy and a father who deserted the family.

"This powerful tale is extremely well written and will give readers an understanding of what it's like to have a challenged sibling." SLJ

Life happens next; a novel. Terry Trueman. HarperTeen 2012 132 p. (trade bdg.) $17.99
Grades: 7 8 9 10 **Fic**
1. Romance fiction 2. Down syndrome -- Fiction 3. Cerebral palsy -- Fiction 4. Dogs -- Fiction 5. Communication -- Fiction 6. Seattle (Wash.) -- Fiction 7. Special education -- Fiction 8. People with disabilities -- Fiction 9. Family life -- Washington (State) -- Seattle -- Fiction
ISBN 0062028030; 9780062028037; 9780062028051
LC 2011044627

Sequel to: Stuck in neutral

This book is the sequel to author Terry Trueman's "Stuck in Neutral." Here, Shawn McDaniel, who has cerebral palsy, "fantasizes about his sister's best friend, Ally, and what it would be like if he ever got up the courage to tell her how he felt about her." He is also dealing with "Debi, [who] moves in with them. . . . Debi has Down's syndrome and is often disruptive, but . . . she becomes the first person to connect with Shawn on more than a surface level." (Voice of Youth Advocates)

Stuck in neutral. HarperCollins Pubs. 2000 114p $14.95; lib bdg $16.89; pa $6.99
Grades: 7 8 9 10 **Fic**
1. Euthanasia -- Fiction 2. Cerebral palsy -- Fiction 3. Father-son relationship -- Fiction
ISBN 0-06-028519-2; 0-06-028518-4 lib bdg; 0-06-447213-2 pa
LC 99-37098

Michael L. Printz Award honor book, 2001

"Shawn McDaniel thinks his father is considering killing him. Of course, no one knows that Shawn is able to think at all because the 14-year-old, who has cerebral palsy, can't speak, interact, or control his movements and bodily functions. But Shawn is also a genius; he remembers everything that he hears and is even able to read." (Publisher's note)

"Trueman has created a compelling novel that poses questions about ability and existence while fostering sympathy for people with severe physical limitations." Bull Cent Child Books

Tubb, Kristin O'Donnell

★ **Selling** hope. Feiwel and Friends 2010 215p $16.99
Grades: 6 7 8 **Fic**
1. Comets -- Fiction 2. Mothers -- Fiction 3. Magic tricks -- Fiction 4. Single parent family -- Fiction
ISBN 978-0-312-61122-4; 0-312-61122-6
LC 2010-12571

In 1910, just before the earth passes through the tail of Halley's Comet, thirteen-year-old Hope McDaniels, whose father is a magician in a traveling vaudeville show, tries to earn enough money to quit the circuit by selling "anti-comet pills," with the help of fellow-performer Buster Keaton.

"Tubb deftly ingrains a thoughtful ethical question into the story . . . but never overdoes it in this bouncy tale populated by a terrific cast of characters." Booklist

Tucholke, April Genevieve

The **boneless** mercies; April Genevieve Tucholke. Farrar, Straus & Giroux 2018 339 p. (hardback) $18.99
Grades: 7 8 9 10 11 12 **Fic**
1. Monsters -- Fiction 2. Euthanasia -- Fiction 3. Mercenary soldiers -- Fiction 4. Fantasy 5. Mercenary troops -- Fiction 6. Mythology, Norse -- Fiction
ISBN 9780374307066; 9781250211507; 9780374307080
LC 2018003350

In this novel, by April Genevieve Tucholke, "Frey, Ovie, Juniper, and Runa are the Boneless Mercies--girls hired to kill quickly, quietly, and mercifully. But Frey is weary of the death trade and . . . dreams of a bigger life. When she hears of an unstoppable monster ravaging a nearby town, Frey decides this is the Mercies' one chance out. The fame and fortune of bringing down such a beast would ensure a new future for all the Mercies." (Publisher's note)

Tucker, Laura

★ **All** the greys on Greene Street; Laura Tucker ; illustrations by Kelly Murphy. Viking Childrens Books 2019 320 p. illustrations $17.99
Grades: 5 6 7 8 **Fic**
1. Historical fiction 2. Disappeared persons 3. Art -- fiction 4. Art -- fiction. 5. Artists -- New York (State) -- New York -- fiction
ISBN 045147953X; 9780451479532

"SoHo, 1981. Twelve-year-old Olympia is an artist. . . . Her dad and his business partner Apollo bring antique paintings back to life, while her mother makes intricate sculptures. . . . [Then] Ollie's dad disappears . . . leaving her only a cryptic note and instructions to destroy it. Her mom has gone to bed, and she's not getting up. . . . And someone keeps calling, looking for a missing piece of art." (Publisher's note)

"Tucker skillfully balances themes of mental illness, friendship, and creativity under tough circumstances in her memorable debut. The vibrant, eccentric characters are authentic, the early-1980s SoHo setting is clearly wrought (rich with descriptive details such as fad diets and artist-in-residence lofts), and the Konigsburg-tinged art mystery satisfies." Pub WKly

Turnage, Sheila

★ The **ghosts** of Tupelo Landing; by Sheila Turnage. Kathy Dawson Books 2014 368 p. (hardcover) $16.99

Grades: 5 6 7 8 **Fic**

1. Ghost stories 2. Hotels and motels 3. City and town life -- Fiction 4. Ghosts -- Fiction 5. Hotels -- Fiction 6. Identity -- Fiction 7. Foundlings -- Fiction 8. Haunted places -- Fiction 9. North Carolina -- Fiction 10. Mystery and detective stories 11. Community life -- North Carolina -- Fiction

ISBN 0803736711; 9780803736719

LC 2013019376

In this book, by Sheila Turnage, "when Miss Lana makes an Accidental Bid at the Tupelo auction and winds up the mortified owner of an old inn, she doesn't realize there's a ghost in the fine print. Naturally, Desperado Detective Agency (aka Mo and Dale) opens a paranormal division to solve the mystery of the ghost's identity. But Mo and Dale start to realize . . . [p]eople can also be haunted by their own past." (Publisher's note)

The **law** of finders keepers; Sheila Turnage. Kathy Dawson Books 2018 368 p. (hardback) $16.99

Grades: 5 6 7 8 **Fic**

1. Pirates -- Fiction 2. Community life -- Fiction 3. Buried treasure -- Fiction 4. Identity -- Fiction 5. Foundlings -- Fiction 6. North Carolina -- Fiction 7. Mystery and detective stories 8. Community life -- North Carolina -- Fiction

ISBN 9780803739628

LC 2018009941

In this book in the Mo & Dale Mysteries series, by Sheila Turnage, "pirate fever sweeps through the town after an opportunistic treasure hunter shows up looking to lay claim to Blackbeard's lost gold buried somewhere in Tupelo Landing. When the (probably) world-famous Desperado Detectives--Mo and Dale and Harm--are hired by Mayor Little's mother to find the pirate loot for her, and the high-stakes race for riches is on!" (Publisher's note)

The **odds** of getting even; by Sheila Turnage. Kathy Dawson Books, an imprint of Penguin Group (USA) Inc. 2015 352 p. illustration (hardback) $16.99

Grades: 5 6 7 8 **Fic**

1. Crime -- Fiction 2. Fathers -- Fiction 3. North Carolina -- Fiction 4. Mystery and detective stories 5. Community life -- North Carolina -- Fiction

ISBN 9780803739611

LC 2015008293

In this book, by Sheila Turnage, "Mo and Dale, aka Desperado Detectives, head to court as star witnesses against Dale's daddy--confessed kidnapper Macon Johnson. Dale's nerves are jangled, but Mo, who doesn't mind getting even with Mr. Macon for hurting her loved ones, looks forward to a slam dunk conviction--if everything goes as expected." (Publisher's note)

"The author gracefully weaves a laundry list of characters with a plot that has a lot of moving pieces, and she does it with charm and humor, hitting the sweet spot for young readers searching for more-complex tales but not ready to leave the silly behind." Kirkus

★ **Three** times lucky; by Sheila Turnage. Dial Books for Young Readers 2012 256 p. (hardcover) $16.99

Grades: 5 6 7 8 **Fic**

1. Absent mothers -- Fiction 2. Adopted children -- Fiction 3. Abandoned children -- Fiction 4. Murder -- Fiction 5. Identity -- Fiction 6. Foundlings -- Fiction 7. Restaurants -- Fiction 8. North Carolina -- Fiction 9. Mystery and detective stories 10. Community life -- North Carolina -- Fiction

ISBN 0803736703; 9780803736702

LC 2011035027

Newbery Honor Book (2013)

This is the story of Mo LoBeau, who washed downstream as an infant 11 years ago and who has since been in the care of the Colonel, "a stranger who can't remember anything about his own past," and "Miss Lana, owner of the Tupelo Cafe. Mo . . . loves the Colonel and Lana, but" wonders about her origins. She "send[s] messages in bottles to her 'Upstream Mother.'" Also featured are "an out-of-town detective, a dead body . . . , a long-forgotten bank robbery, and a kidnapping." (Publishers Weekly)

Other titles in this series are:

The ghosts of Tupelo Landing (2014)

The odds of getting even (2015)

The law of finders keepers (2018)

Turner, Megan Whalen

A **conspiracy** of kings. Greenwillow Books 2010 316p $16.99; lib bdg $17.89

Grades: 7 8 9 10 **Fic**

1. Adventure fiction 2. Princes -- Fiction 3. Kidnapping -- Fiction 4. Kings and rulers -- Fiction

ISBN 978-0-06-187093-4; 0-06-187093-5; 978-0-06-187094-1 lib bdg; 0-06-187094-3 lib bdg

LC 2009-23052

Boston Globe-Horn Book Honor: Fiction (2010)

Kidnapped and sold into slavery, Sophos, an unwilling prince, tries to save his country from being destroyed by rebellion and exploited by the conniving Mede empire.

"Given the complexity of Turner's plot, readers should reread the first three books before beginning this one, which derives its power from the intricate construction of Turner's imagined world, a realm in which her founding mythology is as impressive as her descriptions of the land itself. . . . Strong evidence emerges that the story doesn't end here, and fans will savor this while they wait for more." Publ Wkly

The **King** of Attolia. Greenwillow Books 2006 387p lib bdg $17.89; paperback 9.99; $16.99

Grades: 7 8 9 10 **Fic**

1. Adventure fiction

ISBN 0-06-083578-8 lib bdg; 9780062642981; 0-06-083577-X

LC 2005-40303

Eugenides, still known as a Thief of Eddis, faces palace intrigue and assassins as he strives to prove himself both to the people of Attolia and to his new bride, their queen.

"Fans who've been waiting . . . for the sequel to The Queen of Attolia (2000) and The Thief (1996. . .) can finally rejoice. . . . To appreciate the amazingly charismatic and beguiling character of Eugenides fully, its best to read the titles in order." SLJ

The **Queen** of Attolia. Greenwillow Bks. 2000 279p pa $9.99
Grades: 6 7 8 9 **Fic**

1. Adventure fiction 2. Thieves -- Fiction
ISBN 0-688-17423-X; 0-06-084182-6 pa; 9780062642974 pa
LC 99-26916

"In this intense, intelligent sequel to The Thief . . . , war breaks out among three Balkanesque countries, engendering a series of crafty maneuvers and terrifying, high-stakes gambles. The uneasy balance between mountainous Eddis and larger neighbors Attolia and Sounis tips when Eugenides, the Queen of Eddis's official Thief, is captured by the ruthless young Queen of Attolia, and has his right hand struck off. Reprisals escalate, until Eddis is attacked on two sides and, ominously, troop ships from the huge Mede Empire approach. Turner creates a complex web of intrigue, hidden motives, feints, and counterfeints." (Kirkus)

"The intense read is thoroughly involving and wholly satisfying on all fronts." Horn Book

★ **Thick** as thieves; Megan Whalen Turner. Greenwillow Books, an imprint of HarperCollins Publishers 2017 336 p. maps (Queen's thief) (hardcover) $17.99
Grades: 7 8 9 10 11 12 **Fic**

1. Fantasy 2. Slavery -- Fiction 3. Secretaries -- Fiction 4. Adventure and adventurers -- Fiction 5. Kings, queens, rulers, etc. -- Fiction
ISBN 0062568248; 9780062568243
LC 2016047028

In this book in the Queen's Thief series, by Megan Whalen Turner, "Kamet, a secretary and slave to his Mede master, has the ambition and the means to become one of the most powerful people in the Empire. But with a whispered warning the future he envisioned is wrenched away, and he is forced onto a very different path. Set in the world of the Queen's Thief, this epic adventure sees an ordinary hero take on an extraordinary mission." (Publisher's note)

"This series fifth can stand alone without reading the rest of the books. . . . This invites an older audience, but . . . offer[s] more teen appeal than the political drama of earlier Queen's Thief novels." Kirkus.

★ The **thief**. Greenwillow Bks. 1996 219p $17.99; pa $6.99; 9.99
Grades: 7 8 9 10 **Fic**

1. Adventure fiction 2. Thieves -- Fiction
ISBN 0-688-14627-9; 0-06-082497-2 pa; 9780062642967
LC 95-41040

A Newbery Medal honor book, 1997

"A tantalizing, suspenseful, exceptionally clever novel. . . . The author's characterization of Gen is simply superb." Horn Book

Other titles in this series are:
The Queen of Attolia (2000)
The King of Attolia (2006)
A conspiracy of kings (2010)
Thick as thieves (2017)

Turrisi, Kim

Just a normal Tuesday; Kim Turrisi. Kids Can Press 2017 252 p. (hardcover) $17.95
Grades: 7 8 9 10 **Fic**

1. Death -- Fiction 2. Grief -- Fiction 3. Teenagers -- Suicide -- Fiction
ISBN 9781771387934; 9781771388634; 1771387939

In this book, by Kim Turrisi, "what begins as just a normal Tuesday becomes a day that will shatter sixteen-year-old Kai's life forever. All it takes is a letter. . . . from Kai's older sister, Jen. . . . Jen has committed suicide. . . . Kai is heartbroken and furious, and soon she's caught in a vicious downward spiral. . . . That's when her parents shock her: they're sending her to the Tree House, a summer camp for grieving teens." (Publisher's note)

"A nuanced tale about grief in the aftermath of suicide." SLJ

Turtschaninoff, Maria

★ **Maresi**; Maria Turtschaninoff; translated by A. A. Prime. Harry N Abrams Inc 2017 256 p. illustrations (The Red Abbey chronicles) (hardcover) $17.95; (ebook) $15.54
Grades: 8 9 10 11 **Fic**

1. Fantasy fiction 2. Abbeys -- Fiction
ISBN 1419722697; 9781419722691; 9781613129746
LC 2016054460

In this book in the Red Abbey Chronicles series, by Maria Turtschaninoff, "the Red Abbey [is] a haven from abuse and oppression. Maresi, a thirteen-year-old novice there, arrived in the hunger winter and now lives a happy life in the Abbey. . . . Into this idyllic existence comes Jai, a girl with a dark past. . . . Soon the dangers of the outside world follow Jai into the sacred space of the Abbey, and Maresi can no longer hide in books and words but must become one who acts." (Publisher's note)

"Utterly satisfying and completely different from standard YA fantasy, this Finnish import seems primed to win over American readers." Booklist

Another title in this series is:
Naondel (2018)

Naondel; by Maria Turtschaninoff ; translated by A.A. Prime. Amulet Books 2018 375 p. (Red Abbey chronicles) (hardback : alk. paper) $18.99
Grades: 8 9 10 11 **Fic**

1. Fantasy fiction 2. Escapes -- Fiction 3. Abused women -- Fiction 4. Sex crimes -- fiction
ISBN 9781683351412; 9781419725555
LC 2017011854

This book in The Red Abbey Chronicles series, by Maria Turtschaninoff, translated by A.A. Prime, "tells the story of the First Sisters--the founders of the female utopia the Red Abbey. Imprisoned in a harem by a dangerous man with a dark magic that grants him power over life and death, the First Sisters must overcome their mistrust of one another in order to escape. But they can only do so at a great cost, both for those who leave and for those left behind." (Publisher's note)

"This is not an easy story, with its perpetual backdrop of sexual violence, but in the foreground is a fierce, slow-burning exposition of female courage and resilience." Horn Book

Twain, Mark, 1835-1910

The **prince** and the pauper; introduction by Christopher Paul Curtis. Modern Library 2003 211p (The Modern Library classics) pa $8.95
Grades: 5 6 7 8 9 10 11 12 Adult **Fic**

1. Kings 2. Great Britain -- History -- 1485-1603, Tudors -- Fiction
ISBN 0-375-76112-8
LC 2002-26302

First published 1881

"Edward VI of England and a little pauper change places a few days before Henry VIII's death. The prince wanders in rags, while Tom Canty suffers the horrors of princedom. At the last moment, the mistake is rectified." Reader's Ency. 4th edition

Uchida, Yoshiko

★ A **jar** of dreams. Atheneum Pubs. 1981 131p hardcover o.p. pa $4.99

Grades: 5 6 7 8 **Fic**

1. California -- Fiction 2. Prejudices -- Fiction 3. Family life -- Fiction 4. Japanese Americans -- Fiction

ISBN 0-689-50210-9; 0-689-71672-9 pa

LC 81-3480

"Rinko in her guilelessness is genuine and refreshing, and her worries and concerns seem wholly natural, honest, and convincing." Horn Book

Other titles about Rinko Tsujimura and her family are:

The best bad thing (1983)

The happiest ending (1985)

★ **Journey** to Topaz; a story of the Japanese-American evacuation. illustrated by Donald Carrick. Heyday Books 2005 149p il pa $9.95

Grades: 5 6 7 8 **Fic**

1. World War, 1939-1945 -- Fiction 2. Japanese Americans -- Evacuation and relocation, 1942-1945 -- Fiction

ISBN 978-1-890771-91-1 pa; 1-890771-91-0 pa

LC 2004-16537

First published 1971 by Scribner

After the Pearl Harbor attack an eleven-year-old Japanese-American girl and her family are forced to go to an aliens camp in Utah

Followed by: Journey home (1978)

Uehashi, Nahoko

Moribito II; Guardian of the Darkness. by Nahoko Uehashi; translated by Cathy Hirano; illustrated by Yuko Shimizu. Arthur A. Levine Books 2009 245p il hardcover o.p. O.P.

Grades: 6 7 8 9 **Fic**

1. Fantasy fiction 2. Young adult literature

ISBN 978-0-545-10295-7; 0-545-10295-2

LC 2008-37444

Sequel to: Moribito: Guardian of the Spirit (2008)

ALA ALSC Batchelder Award Honor Book (2010)

The wandering female bodyguard Balsa returns to her native country of Kanbal, where she uncovers a conspiracy to frame her mentor and herself.

"Once again, Uehashi immerses readers in the culture, traditions, mythology–even diet–of the populace, creating a full, captivating world. . . . This growing series has something for everyone." Publ Wkly

Umminger, Alison

★ **American** Girls; A Novel. Alison Umminger. St. Martin's Press 2016 304 p. $17.99

Grades: 8 9 10 11 **Fic**

1. Stepsisters -- Fiction 2. Self-realization -- Fiction 3. Runaway teenagers -- Fiction 4. Los Angeles (Calif.) -- Fiction 5. Motion picture industry -- Fiction

ISBN 1250075009; 9781250075000; 9781250075024

In this novel by Alison Umminger, "Anna is a fifteen-year-old girl . . . [who] 'borrows' her stepmom's credit card and runs away to Los Angeles, where her half-sister takes her in. But LA isn't quite the glamorous escape Anna had imagined. As Anna spends her days on TV and movie sets, she engrosses herself in a project researching the murderous Manson girls—and . . . begins to notice the parallels between herself and the lost girls of LA, and of America, past and present." (Publisher's note)

"An insightful, original take on the coming-of-age story, this novel plumbs the depths of American culture to arrive at a poignant emotional truth." Kirkus

Unsworth, Tania

The **one** safe place; a novel. by Tania Unsworth. Algonquin Young Readers 2014 304 p. $15.95

Grades: 6 7 8 9 10 **Fic**

1. Dystopian fiction 2. Orphans -- Fiction 3. Survival skills -- Fiction 2. Abandoned children -- Fiction 3. Science fiction 4. Survival -- Fiction

ISBN 1616203293; 9781616203290

LC 2013043145

This book, by Tania Unsworth, is a "near-future dystopia. . . . Devin doesn't remember life before the world got hot; he has grown up farming the scorched earth with his grandfather in their remote valley. When his grandfather dies, Devin heads for the city. Once there, among the stark glass buildings, he finds scores of children, just like him, living alone on the streets. They tell him rumors of a place for abandoned children, . . . but only the luckiest get there." (Publisher's note)

"Orphaned twelve-year-old Devin is invited to live at the paradisaical Home for Childhood, but something terrifying is happening to the children there. Devin's synesthesia, which makes him interesting to the Home's sinister Administrator, may provide the key to their escape. Set in a world of post climate change desperation, Unsworth's story thoughtfully explores the theme of adults' nostalgia for childhood." Horn Book

Urban, Linda

★ The **center** of everything; by Linda Urban. Houghton Mifflin Harcourt 2013 208 p. $15.99

Grades: 4 5 6 7 **Fic**

1. Wishes -- fiction 2. Bereavement -- fiction

ISBN 0547763484; 9780547763484

LC 2012954515

In this book, "months after her grandmother's death, 12-year-old Ruby Pepperdine composes a winning essay honoring her New Hampshire town's namesake" and will get to read it to the community. But she's more concerned that "she didn't listen to her grandmother's final words before she died. Ruby thinks that maybe if she wishes hard enough, 'everything will be back to how it is supposed to be,' but making a wish the right way is a tricky business." (Publishers Weekly)

Ursu, Anne

★ **Breadcrumbs**; drawings by Erin McGuire. Walden Pond Press 2011 313p il $16.99

Grades: 4 5 6 7 **Fic**

1. Fairy tales 2. Magic -- Fiction 3. Friendship -- Fiction

ISBN 978-0-06-201505-1; 0-06-201505-2

LC 2010045666

"Fifth-grader Hazel embarks on a memorable journey into the Minnesota woods to find her best friend Jack, who vanishes after a shard of glass pierces his eye. . . . Hazel enters the woods to find 'an entirely different place,' populated by creatures from the pages of Hans Christian Andersen. . . . [This is a] multi-layered, artfully crafted, transforming testament to the power of friendship." Kirkus

Vail, Rachel

Lucky. HarperTeen 2008 233p $16.99; lib bdg $17.89

Grades: 7 8 9 10 **Fic**

1. School stories 2. Wealth -- Fiction 3. Friendship -- Fiction
ISBN 978-0-06-089043-8; 978-0-06-089044-5 lib bdg

As Phoebe and her clique of privileged girlfriends get ready to graduate from eighth grade, a financial scandal threatens her family's security—as well as Phoebe's social status—but ultimately it teaches her the real meaning of friendship.

"Vail's insightful characterizations of teen girls and their shifting loyalties is right on target." Booklist

Other titles in this series are:
Gorgeous (2009)
Brilliant (2010)

Unfriended; Rachel Vail. Viking, published by Penguin Group 2014 288 p. (hardback) $16.99

Grades: 6 7 8 9 **Fic**

1. Social media 2. Middle schools -- Fiction 3. Schools -- Fiction 4. Friendship -- Fiction 5. Popularity -- Fiction 6. Social media -- Fiction
ISBN 0670013072; 9780670013074

LC 2014006247

In this young adult novel by Rachel Vail, "when Truly is invited to sit at the Popular Table with the group she has dreamed of joining, she can hardly believe her luck. Everyone seems so nice, so kind to one another. But all is not as it seems with her new friends, and soon she's caught in a maelstrom of lies, misunderstandings, accusations and counter-accusations, all happening very publicly in the relentless, hyperconnected social media world from which there is no escape." (Publisher's note)

"The points of view allow the reader to be drawn into the teens' motivations and illustrate the importance of clear communication, the dangers of online bullying, and the universal struggles teens face. Mean girls, misunderstood girls, awkward boys, friendship, popularity, social misfits, all play into this book that epitomizes the roller coaster that is middle school." Lib Med Con

Well, that was awkward; Rachel Vail. Viking 2017 320 p. (hardcover) $16.99

Grades: 5 6 7 8 **Fic**

1. Friendship -- Fiction 2. Triangles (Interpersonal relations) -- Fiction
ISBN 9780670013081

LC 2016020347

In his book, by Rachel Vail, "Gracie has never felt like this before. . . . And the reason is standing right there in front of her, all tall and weirdly good-looking: A.J. But it turns out A.J. likes not Gracie but Gracie's beautiful best friend, Sienna. Obviously Gracie is happy for Sienna. . . . She helps Sienna compose the best texts, responding to A.J.'s surprisingly funny and appealing texts. . . . Because Gracie is fine. . . . She's had lots of practice being the sidekick, second-best." (Publisher's note)

"Hilarious and heartfelt." Kirkus

Valente, Catherynne M.

The **boy** who lost Fairyland; Catherynne M. Valente ; illustrated by Ana Juan. Feiwel & Friends 2015 240 p. (Fairyland) (hardback) $16.99

Grades: 5 6 7 8 **Fic**

1. Fantasy fiction 2. Trolls -- Fiction 3. Fantasy 4. Changelings -- Fiction
ISBN 1250023491; 9781250023490; 9781250073327

LC 2014042417

In this novel, by Catherynne M. Valente, illustrated by Ana Juan, "when a young troll named Hawthorn is stolen from Fairyland by the Golden Wind, he becomes a changeling--a human boy--in the strange city of Chicago. . . . Left with a human family, Hawthorn struggles with his troll nature and his changeling fate. But when he turns twelve, he stumbles upon a way back home, to a Fairyland much changed from the one he remembers." (Publisher's note)

"In this fourth book in the fantastical series, a young troll named Hawthorn is stolen away by the Golden Wind and brought to live in Chicago as a changeling. When he turns 12, he finds a way back to Fairyland, a place now much changed from the magical realm he left...While readers unfamiliar with the series can certainly jump in with this novel, most will want to start at the beginning. A phenomenal fantasy series worthy of a spot in every library collection." SLJ

Other titles in this series are:
The Girl who Soared Over Fairyland and Cut the Moon in Two (2013)
The Girl who Circumnavigated Fairyland in a Ship of her Own Making (2011)
The Girl who Fell Beneath Fairyland and Led the Revels There (2012)

★ The **girl** who circumnavigated Fairyland in a ship of her own making; [by] Catherynne M. Valente; with illustrations by Ana Juan. Feiwel and Friends 2011 247p il $16.99

Grades: 4 5 6 7 8 **Fic**

1. Fantasy fiction
ISBN 978-0-312-64961-6; 0-312-64961-4

LC 2010050895

"The book's appeal is crystal clear from the outset: this is a kind of The Wonderful Wizard of Oz by way of Alice's Adventures in Wonderland, made vivid by Juan's Tenniel-inflected illustrations. . . . Those who thrill to lovingly wrought tales of fantasy and adventure . . . will be enchanted." Publ Wkly

Other titles in this series are:
The girl who fell beneath Fairyland and led the revels there (2012)
The girl who soared over Fairyland and cut the moon in two (2013)
The boy who lost Fairyland (2015)
The girl who raced fairyland all the way home (2016)

The **girl** who fell beneath Fairyland and led the revels there; by Catherynne M. Valente ; with illustrations by Ana Juan. Feiwel and Friends 2012 258 p. $16.99

Grades: 4 5 6 7 8 **Fic**

1. Fantasy fiction 2. Magic -- fiction 3. Fairies -- fiction
ISBN 0312649622; 9780312649623

In this book by Catherynne M. Valente, illustrated by Ana Juan, "September has longed to return to Fairyland after her first adventure there. And when she finally does, she learns that its inhabitants have been losing their shadows--and their magic--to the world of Fairyland Below. This underworld has a new ruler: Halloween, the Hollow Queen, who is September's shadow. And Halloween does not want to give Fairyland's shadows back." (Publisher's note)

The **Girl** Who Soared over Fairyland and Cut the Moon in Two; by Catherynne M. Valente ; illustrated by Ana Juan. Feiwel & Friends 2013 256 p. $16.99

Grades: 4 5 6 7 8 **Fic**

1. Moon -- fiction 2. Fairies -- fiction 3. Female friendship -- fiction
ISBN 1250023505; 9781250023506

In this book, by Catherynne M. Valente, September is "tasked with delivering a package to the moon, which has begun to shudder and shake with moonquakes because a . . . yeti is trying to break it to pieces. September and her friends traverse the moon, meet their fates, encounter older and younger versions of themselves, and wonder what, exactly, makes them who they are--all while trying to find the speedy yeti and stop him from his destructive plans." (Booklist)

"In this third volume, following The Girl Who Fell Beneath Fairyland and Led the Revels There, September returns to Fairyland and finds herself on a mission to stop a vengeful yeti from destroying his Fairy abusers--and everyone else on the moon. September is now wiser and sadder, and longs for autonomy; likewise, Fairyland and its inhabitants have become darker and more adult." (Horn Book)

The **Glass** Town Game; Catherynne M. Valente ; illustrated by Rebecca Green. Margaret K. McElderry Books 2017 535 p. illustrations (hardcover) $17.99

Grades: 4 5 6 7 8 **Fic**

1. Fantasy fiction 2. Sisters -- Fiction 3. Imaginary places -- Fiction 4. Games -- fiction 5. Imagination -- fiction 6. Haworth (England) -- fiction 7. Brothers and sisters -- fiction

ISBN 9781481476980; 1481476963; 9781481476966

In this novel, by Catherynne M. Valente, illustrated by Rebecca Green, "Charlotte and Emily must enter a fantasy world that they invented in order to rescue their siblings. . . . Charlotte, Branwell, Emily, and Anne Brontë have invented a game called Glass Town, where their toy soldiers fight Napoleon and no one dies. . . . But . . . something incredible happens: the train whisks them all away to a real Glass Town, and the children trade the moors for a wonderland all their own." (Publisher's note)

"A lovely, fanciful piece of middle-grade fiction about the worlds we make, and the lives they can take on." Booklist

Valentine, Jenny

★ **Me,** the missing, and the dead. HarperTeen 2008 201p paper $8.99

Grades: 8 9 10 11 **Fic**

1. Death -- Fiction 2. Fathers -- Fiction 3. Missing persons -- Fiction 4. London (England) -- Fiction 5. Single parent family -- Fiction

ISBN 978-0-06-085068-5; 0-06-085068-X; 978-0-06-085069-2 lib bdg; 0-06-085069-8 lib bdg; 9780060850708

LC 2007-14476

First published 2007 in the United Kingdom with title: Finding Violet Park

ALA YALSA Morris Award finalist, 2009

When a series of chance events leaves him in possession of an urn with ashes, sixteen-year-old Londoner Lucas Swain becomes convinced that its occupant, Violet Park, is communicating with him, initiating a voyage of self-discovery that forces him to finally confront the events surrounding his father's sudden disappearance.

"Part mystery, part magical realism, part story of personal growth, and in large part simply about a funny teenager making light of his and his family's pain, this short novel is engaging from start to finish." SLJ

Van de Ruit, John

Spud. Razorbill 2007 331p hardcover o.p. pa $16.99

Grades: 6 7 8 9 10 **Fic**

1. School stories 2. South Africa -- Fiction

ISBN 978-1-59514-170-5; 0-14-302484-1; 978-1-59514-187-3 pa; 1-59514-187-1 pa; 9781595141873

LC 2007-6065

In 1990, thirteen-year-old John "Spud" Milton, a prepubescent choirboy, keeps a diary of his first year at an elite, boys-only boarding school in South Africa.

"This raucous autobiographical novel about a scholarship boy in an elite boys' boarding school in 1990 is mainly farce but also part coming-of-age tale." Booklist

Followed by Spud¿the madness continues... (2008)

Van Draanen, Wendelin

The **running** dream. Alfred A. Knopf 2011 336p $16.99; lib bdg $19.99

Grades: 7 8 9 10 11 12 **Fic**

1. School stories 2. Running -- Fiction 3. Amputees -- Fiction 4. People with Disabilities -- Fiction

ISBN 978-0-375-86667-8; 0-375-86667-1; 978-0-375-96667-5 lib bdg; 0-375-96667-6 lib bdg

LC 2010-07072

"It's a classic problem novel in a lot of ways. . . . Overall, though, this is a tremendously upbeat book. . . . Van Draanen's extensive research into both running and amputees pays dividends." Booklist

★ **Sammy** Keyes and the hotel thief. Knopf 1998 163p il hardcover o.p. pa $6.50; reinforced $16.99; paperback $7.99

Grades: 4 5 6 7 **Fic**

1. Mystery fiction

ISBN 978-0-679-88839-0; 0-679-89264-8 pa; 9781435277687; 9780679892649; 9780375890444

LC 97-40776

Thirteen-year-old Sammy's penchant for speaking her mind gets her in trouble when she involves herself in the investigation of a robbery at the "seedy" hotel across the street from the seniors' building where she is living with her grandmother

"This is a breezy novel with vivid characters." Bull Cent Child Books

Other titles about Sammy Keyes are:
Sammy Keyes and the skeleton man (1998)
Sammy Keyes and the Sisters of Mercy (1999)
Sammy Keyes and the runaway elf (1999)
Sammy Keyes and the curse of Moustache Mary (2000)
Sammy Keyes and the Hollywood mummy (2001)
Sammy Keyes and the search for Snake Eyes (2002)
Sammy Keyes and the art of deception (2003)
Sammy Keyes and the psycho Kitty Queen (2004)
Sammy Keyes and the dead giveaway (2005)
Sammy Keyes and the wild things (2007)
Sammy Keyes and the cold hard cash (2008)
Sammy Keyes and the wedding crasher (2010)
Sammy Keyes and the night of skulls (2011)
Sammy Keyes and the power of Justice Jack (2012)
Sammy Keyes and the showdown in Sin City (2013)
Sammy Keyes and the killer cruise (2013)
Sammy Keyes and the kiss goodbye (2014)

Van Eekhout, Greg

The **boy** at the end of the world. Bloomsbury Children's Books 2011 212p $16.99

Grades: 4 5 6 7 **Fic**

1. Science fiction 2. Robots -- Fiction

ISBN 978-1-59990-524-2; 1-59990-524-8

LC 2010035741

Born half-grown in a world that is being destroyed, Fisher has instinctive knowledge of many things, including that he must avoid the robot that knows his name.

"A pleaser for readers who prefer their sf livened up with unpredictable elements and emotional complexity." Booklist

Van Etten, David

All that glitters. Alfred A. Knopf 2008 295p (Likely story) $15.99; lib bdg $18.99

Grades: 7 8 9 10 **Fic**

1. Television -- Fiction 2. Hollywood (Calif.) -- Fiction 3. Mother-daughter relationship -- Fiction

ISBN 978-0-375-84678-6; 0-375-84678-6; 978-0-375-94678-3 lib bdg; 0-375-94678-0 lib bdg

LC 2007050903

Sequel to: Likely story (2008)

Now that her soap opera is in production and everyone has ideas on how it can be improved, sixteen-year-old Mallory struggles to maintain control of her original plot and characters as the broadcast premier draws near.

"With more twists, turns, and intrigue than a daytime soap, this novel is great fun." SLJ

Followed by: Red carpet riot (2009)

Van Leeuwen, Jean

Lucy was there-- Phyllis Fogelman Bks. 2002 165p $16.99

Grades: 4 5 6 7 **Fic**

1. Dogs -- Fiction 2. Death -- Fiction 3. Friendship -- Fiction

ISBN 0-8037-2738-0

LC 2001-33974

With the help of new friends and a very special dog, Morgan begins to come to terms with the loss of her mother and five-year-old brother, who boarded a plane and never came back. "Grades five to seven." (Bull Cent Child Books)

"Morgan's anguish is palpable but never overwrought, and the short chapters, appealing heroine, and well-told story leavened with humor give this solid . . . appeal." Booklist

Van Rijckeghem, Jean-Claude

A **sword** in her hand; by Jean-Claude Van Rijckeghem and Pat Van Beirs; translated by John Nieuwenhuizen. Annick 2011 276p $21.95

Grades: 5 6 7 8 **Fic**

1. Plague -- Fiction 2. Princesses -- Fiction 3. Middle Ages -- Fiction 4. Father-daughter relationship -- Fiction

ISBN 978-1-55451-291-1; 1-55451-291-3

The Count of Flanders flies in a rage when his newborn child is not the expected male heir but a girl. Marguerite growing up under the disapproving eye of her heartless father learns to survive in the violent male world of the Middle Ages. Will she be able to resist the combined presure of politics, power and a foreign prince?

"The deft characterization of Marguerite and the sumptuous details woven throughout this captivating novel will engage readers." SLJ

Van Vleet, Carmella

Eliza Bing is (not) a big, fat quitter; by Carmella Van Vleet ; illustrated by Karen Donnelly. Holiday House 2014 165 p. (hardcover) $16.95

Grades: 3 4 5 6 7 **Fic**

1. Family life -- Fiction 2. Tae kwon do -- Fiction 3. Attention deficit disorder -- Fiction 4. Martial arts -- Fiction 5. Determination (Personality trait) -- Fiction 6. Attention-deficit hyperactivity disorder -- Fiction

ISBN 082342944X; 9780823429448

LC 2013015279

This novel, written by Carmella Van Vleet and illustrated by Karen Donnelly, is "about determination and the rewards of hard work[.] A preteen girl struggling with ADHD must stick with a summer taekwondo class to prove that she s dedicated enough to pursue her true passion: cake decorating." (Publisher's note)

"Fast moving and humorous with chapter titles such as 'Sticky Note to Self: Wear White Underwear on Wednesdays and Saturdays,' feisty Eliza will have readers, especially those with ADHD, rooting for her." SLJ

Another title in this series is:
Eliza Bing is not a star (2018)

Vance, Alexander

The **Heartbreak** Messenger. Feiwel & Friends 2013 288 p. $16.99

Grades: 6 7 8 **Fic**

1. School stories -- fiction 2. Dating (Social customs) -- fiction

ISBN 1250029694; 9781250029690

In this book by Alexander Vance, after "seventh-grader Quentin accepts $20 to deliver a breakup message for a friend's older brother, a new business is born: he becomes the 'Heartbreak Messenger,' hired to perform breakups for the weak-willed. Quentin believes his single mother, an auto mechanic, is struggling to pay their bills, so there's an altruistic side to his entrepreneurship, but he also enjoys the power the job gives him. Problems arise." (Publishers Weekly)

Vande Velde, Vivian

Heir apparent. Harcourt 2002 315p $17; pa $6.95

Grades: 6 7 8 9 **Fic**

1. Science fiction 2. Virtual reality -- Fiction

ISBN 0-15-204560-0; 0-15-205125-2 pa

LC 2002-2441

While playing a total immersion virtual reality game of kings and intrigue, fourteen-year-old Giannine learns that demonstrators have damaged the equipment to which she is connected, and she must win the game quickly or be damaged herself

"This adventure includes a cast of intriguing characters and personalities. The feisty heroine has a funny, sarcastic sense of humor and succeeds because of her ingenuity and determination." SLJ

Frogged; Vivian Vande Velde. Houghton Mifflin Harcourt 2013 208 p. $16.99

Grades: 5 6 7 8 **Fic**

1. Fantasy fiction 2. Fractured fairy tales 3. Fairy tales 4. Frogs -- Fiction 5. Humorous stories 6. Princesses -- Fiction 7. Self-perception -- Fiction

ISBN 054794215X; 9780547942155

LC 2013003905

In this alternate version of "The Frog Prince," "Princess Imogene, who is 12 and 'gawky,' is tired of falling short in her family's eyes. The real trouble begins when a . . . frog, who tells Imogene he's a prince beset by a witch's spell, tricks her into kissing him. He returns to his human form, but she is transformed into a frog as a result; worse, he was just the lowly son of a wagon maker. Too kind to use that sort of deceit on someone else, Imogene searches for another solution." (Publishers Weekly)

Vanderpool, Clare

★ **Moon** over Manifest. Delacorte Press 2010 351p $16.99; lib bdg $19.99

Grades: 5 6 7 8 **Fic**

1. Kansas -- Fiction 2. Fathers -- Fiction 3. Great Depression, 1929-1939 -- Fiction

ISBN 978-0-385-73883-5; 0-385-73883-8; 978-0-385-90750-7 lib bdg; 0-385-90750-8 lib bdg

LC 2009-40042

Awarded the Newbery Medal, 2011

Twelve-year-old Abilene Tucker is the daughter of a drifter who, in the summer of 1936, sends her to stay with an old friend in Manifest, Kansas, where he grew up, and where she hopes to find out some things about his past.

"The absolute necessity of story as a way to redemption and healing past wounds is at the heart of this beautiful debut, and readers will cherish every word up to the heartbreaking yet hopeful and deeply gratifying ending." Kirkus

Vanhee, Jason

Engines of the broken world; Jason Vanhee. Henry Holt and Company 2013 272 p. (hardcover) $16.99

Grades: 8 9 10 11 12 **Fic**

1. Supernatural -- Fiction 2. Brothers and sisters -- Fiction 3. Science fiction

ISBN 0805096299; 9780805096293

LC 2013026768

In this book, by Jason Vanhee, "Merciful Truth and her brother, Gospel, have just pulled their dead mother into the kitchen and stowed her under the table. It was a long illness, and they wanted to bury her--they did--but it's far too cold outside, and they know they won't be able to dig into the frozen ground. The Minister who lives with them, who preaches through his animal form, doesn't make them feel any better about what they've done." (Publisher's note)

"Unlike most action-packed dystopias, the story's slower pace . . . allows readers to feel the fog encroaching on Merciful and Gospel's rustic home, and hear every scratch of their dead mother's awkward movements upon the cellar stairs." Booklist

Vaughn, Carrie

Steel. HarperTeen 2011 294p $16.99; lib bdg $17.89

Grades: 7 8 9 10 **Fic**

1. Fencing -- Fiction 3. Pirates -- Fiction 4. Time travel -- Fiction 5. Caribbean region -- Fiction

ISBN 978-0-06-154791-1; 0-06-154791-3; 978-0-06-195648-5 lib bdg; 0-06-195648-1 lib bdg

LC 2010012631

When Jill, a competitive high school fencer, goes with her family on vacation to the Bahamas, she is magically transported to an early-eighteenth-century pirate ship in the middle of the ocean.

This is "thoroughly enjoyable. . . . Through her assertive, appealing protagonist and a satisfying plot that sheds light on lesser-known aspects of pirate life, Vaughn introduces readers to an intriguing sport with an ancient pedigree." Kirkus

Vaught, Susan

Freaks like us; by Susan Vaught. Bloomsbury 2012 240 p. (hardcover) $16.99

Grades: 7 8 9 10 11 12 **Fic**

1. Friendship -- Fiction 2. Schizophrenia -- Fiction 3. Mental illness -- Fiction 4. Missing persons -- Fiction 5. Love -- Fiction 6. Missing children -- Fiction 7. Mystery and detective stories

ISBN 1599908727; 9781599908724

LC 2012004227

This is the story of Jason, whose selectively mute friend Sunshine has "vanished, and Jason, whose schizophrenia has shaped his life, is a suspect in her disappearance. Seniors Jason, Drip and Sunshine have ridden the short bus and gone through school labeled SED--that's 'Severely Emotionally Disturbed.' Bullying at the hands of kids with behavioral disabilities goes unreported and unpunished, but the trio's alliance made life bearable in their catchall special ed program . . . . As the FBI investigates, Jason's always-shaky world threatens to come apart. Not taking "fuzzy pills" keeps his brain sharp, but the voices plaguing him grow louder. Jason carries Sunshine's secrets--should he break his promise not to tell?" (Kirkus)

Me and Sam-Sam handle the apocalypse; Susan Vaught. Simon & Schuster Books for Young Readers 2019 320 p. (hardcover) $17.99

Grades: 4 5 6 7 **Fic**

1. Tornadoes -- Fiction 2. Theft -- fiction 3. Dogs -- Fiction 4. Autism -- Fiction 5. Bullying -- Fiction 6. Stealing -- Fiction 7. Family life -- Fiction 8. Pomeranian dog -- Fiction 9. Mystery and detective stories

ISBN 9781534425019

LC 2018039713

In this book, by Susan Vaught, "when the cops show up at Jesse's house and arrest her dad, she figures out in a hurry that he's the #1 suspect in the missing library fund money case. With the help of her (first and only) friend Springer, she rounds up suspects (leading to a nasty confrontation with three notorious school bullies) and asks a lot of questions. But she can't shake the feeling that she isn't exactly cut out for being a crime-solving hero." (Publisher's note)

In a memorable week for Jesse, a devastating tornado comes to her small Kentucky town, she's faced with the traumatic sight of her dad in handcuffs after a large amount of money disappears from his desk at school, and confrontations with a trio of relentless bullies escalate ... Edgar-winning Vaught, a neuropsychologist, has both personal and professional experience to draw on in crafting a narrator who is admirably smart and resilient despite an 'itchy' brain and a compulsion to count things." (Booklist)

Things too huge to fix by saying sorry; Susan Vaught. Simon & Schuster Books for Young Readers 2016 352 p. (ebook) $15.99; (hardcover) $16.99

Grades: 5 6 7 8 **Fic**

1. Vendetta -- Fiction 2. Mississippi -- Fiction 3. Civil rights -- Fiction 4. Grandmothers -- Fiction 5. Race relations -- Fiction 6. Alzheimer's disease -- Fiction 7. Families -- Fiction 8. Oxford (Miss.) -- Fiction 9. Civil rights movements -- Fiction 10. Oxford (Miss.) -- History -- 20th century -- Fiction

ISBN 9781481422819; 1481422790; 9781481422796

LC 2015025579

In this book, by Susan Vaught, "a mysterious note takes Dani Beans into the secrets of Ole Miss and its dark past. . . . Lately, Grandma Beans doesn't make a lot of sense. But when she tells Dani to find a secret key and envelope that she's hidden, Dani can't ignore her. So she investigates, with the help of her friend, Indri, and her not-friend, Mac." (Publisher's note)

"Combining middle-school mystery and civil rights history with reflections on dying, friendship, and the ethics of writing another's story from a racially different perspective, this novel is ambitious, thought provoking, and very readable." Booklist

Includes bibliographical references.

Vawter, Vince

Copyboy; by Vince Vawter ; illustrated by Alessia Trunfio. Capstone Editions 2018 240 p. (hardcover) $15.95

Grades: 7 8 9 10 **Fic**

1. Self-esteem -- Fiction 2. Automobile travel -- Fiction 3. Interpersonal relations -- Fiction 4. Stuttering -- Fiction 5. Newspaper employees -- Fiction 6. Family life -- Tennessee --

Fiction 7. Memphis (Tenn.) -- History -- 20th century -- Fiction
ISBN 9781630791056

LC 2018001840

Sequel to: Paperboy

In this book, by Vince Vawter, illustrated by Alessia Trunfio, "Victor Vollmer isn't a paperboy anymore. He's a copyboy now, but his duties at the newspaper get interrupted by a last request from Mr. Spiro, the old man who became Victor's mentor and helped him take on his stutter. . . . Victor takes off on a journey that sends him hundreds of miles from home--toward the teeth of a gathering storm." (Publisher's note)

★ **Paperboy**; Vince Vawter. 1st ed. Delacorte Press 2013 240 p. (library) $19.99; (hardcover) $16.99

Grades: 5 6 7 8 **Fic**

1. Stuttering -- Fiction 2. Race relations -- Fiction 3. Newspaper carriers -- Fiction 4. Self-esteem -- Fiction 5. Interpersonal relations -- Fiction 6. Family life -- Tennessee -- Fiction 7. Memphis (Tenn.) -- History -- 20th century -- Fiction
ISBN 0385742444; 9780307975058; 9780375990588; 9780385742443

LC 2012030546

Newbery Honor Book (2014)

In this book by Vince Vawter, "[a]fter an overthrown baseball busts his best friend's lip, 11-year-old Victor Vollmer takes over the boy's paper route. This is a particularly daunting task for the able-armed Victor, as he has a prominent stutter that embarrasses him. . . .Through the paper route he meets a number of people, gains a much-needed sense of self and community, and has a life-threatening showdown with a local cart man." (School Library Journal)

"Carefully crafted language, authenticity of setting and quirky characters that ring fully true all combine to make this a worthwhile read. Although Little Man's stutter holds up dialogue, that annoyance also powerfully reflects its stultifying impact on his life. An engaging and heartfelt presentation that never whitewashes the difficult time and situation as Little Man comes of age." Kirkus

Followed by Copyboy (2018)

Venkatraman, Padma

The **bridge** home; Padma Venkatraman. Nancy Paulsen Books 2019 208 p. (hardback) $16.99

Grades: 5 6 7 8 **Fic**

1. Siblings -- Fiction 2. Homeless persons -- Fiction 3. Runaway children -- Fiction 4. India -- Fiction 5. Runaways -- Fiction 6. Chennai (India) -- Fiction
ISBN 9781524738112; 9781524738129

LC 2018035686

In this novel, by Padma Venkatraman, "life is harsh in Chennai's teeming streets, so when runaway sisters Viji and Rukku arrive, their prospects look grim. . . . Fortunately, the girls find shelter . . . on an abandoned bridge. With two homeless boys, Muthi and Arul, the group forms a family of sorts. . . . But when illness strikes, Viji must decide whether to risk seeking help from strangers or to keep holding on to their fragile, hard-fought freedom." (Publisher's note)

"An unforgettable tale of families lost, found, and moving ahead without leaving those they love behind." (School Library Journal)

★ **Climbing** the stairs. G.P. Putnam's Sons 2008 247p $16.99

Grades: 6 7 8 9 10 **Fic**

1. Prejudices -- Fiction 2. Family life -- Fiction 3. Brain -- Wounds and injuries -- Fiction 4. India -- History -- 1765-1947, British occupation -- Fiction
ISBN 978-0-399-24746-0; 0-399-24746-7

LC 2007-21757

In India, in 1941, when her father becomes brain-damaged in a nonviolent protest march, fifteen-year-old Vidya and her family are forced to move in with her father's extended family and become accustomed to a totally different way of life.

"Venkatraman paints an intricate and convincing backdrop of a conservative Brahmin home in a time of change. . . . The striking cover art . . . will draw readers to this vividly told story." Booklist

★ A **time** to dance; Padma Venkatraman. Nancy Paulsen Books, an imprint of Penguin Group (USA) Inc. 2014 320 p. $17.99

Grades: 8 9 10 11 12 **Fic**

1. Novels in verse 2. Dance -- Fiction 3. India -- Fiction 4. Amputees -- Fiction 5. People with disabilities -- Fiction
ISBN 0399257101; 9780399257100

LC 2013024244

Author Padma Venkatraman's "story of a young girl's struggle to regain her passion and find a new peace is told lyrically through verse that captures the beauty and mystery of India and the ancient bharatanatyam dance form. . . .Veda, a classical dance prodigy in India, lives and breathes dance - so when an accident leaves her a below-knee amputee, her dreams are shattered. . . . But Veda refuses to let her disability rob her of her dreams, and she starts all over again." (Publisher's note)

"This free-verse novel set in contemporary India stars Veda, a teenage Bharatanatyam dancer. After a tragic accident, one of Veda's legs must be amputated below the knee. Veda tries a series of customized prosthetic legs, determined to return to dancing as soon as possible. Brief lines, powerful images, and motifs of sound communicate Veda's struggle to accept her changed body." Horn Book

Verne, Jules, 1828-1905

★ **20,000** leagues under the sea; illustrated by the Dillons; translated by Anthony Bonner. Books of Wonder 2000 394p il $21.95

Grades: 5 6 7 8 9 10 11 12 Adult **Fic**

1. Science fiction 2. Submarines -- Fiction
ISBN 0-688-10535-1

LC 00-24336

Original French edition, 1870

Retells the adventures of a French professor and his two companions as they sail above and below the world's oceans as prisoners on the fabulous electric submarine of the deranged Captain Nemo

Vernick, Audrey

Two Naomis; by Olugbemisola Rhuday-Perkovich and Audrey Vernick. Harpercollins Childrens Books 2016 208 p. $16.99; (ebook) $15.99

Grades: 4 5 6 7 **Fic**

1. Stepfamilies -- Fiction 2. Personal names -- Fiction 3. Children of divorced parents -- Fiction
ISBN 0062414259; 9780062414250; 9780062414274

This book, by Olugbemisola Rhuday-Perkovich and Audrey Vernick, is the "story of two girls, both named Naomi, whose divorced parents begin to date. . . . Other than their first names, Naomi Marie and Naomi Edith are sure they have nothing in common, and they wouldn't mind keeping it that way. . . . When Naomi Marie's mom and Naomi Edith's dad get serious about dating, each girl tries to cling to the life she knows and loves." (Publisher's note)

"A smart, endearing story about two girls who are blending families, growing up, and building a friendship." Kirkus

★ **Water** balloon. Clarion Books 2011 312p $16.99
Grades: 4 5 6 7 **Fic**

1. Dogs -- Fiction 2. Divorce -- Fiction 3. Friendship -- Fiction 4. Babysitters -- Fiction 5. Father-daughter relationship -- Fiction
ISBN 978-0-547-59554-2; 0-547-59554-9

LC 2011009847

With her best friends pulling away from her, her newly-separated parents deciding she should spend the summer at her father's new home, and a babysitting job she does not want, Marley's life is already as precarious as an overfull water balloon when a cute boy enters the picture.

"The book moves along at a pace that will keep tweens interested, and the dialogue among the characters feels real. Marley's relationships with her friends and family are complex, and even the most reluctant readers will relate to her and the choices that she makes." SLJ

Vernick, Shirley Reva

The **blood** lie; a novel. Cinco Puntos Press 2011 141p $15.95
Grades: 5 6 7 8 **Fic**

1. Love -- Fiction 2. Prejudices -- Fiction 3. Antisemitism -- Fiction 4. New York (State) -- Fiction 5. Jews -- United States -- Fiction
ISBN 978-1-933693-84-2; 1-933693-84-3

LC 2011011429

"Based on an actual incident in Massena in 1928, the slim novel effectively mines layers of ignorance, fear, intolerance and manipulation, and it connects the incident to Henry Ford's anti-Semitic writing and to the lynching of Jewish businessman Leo Frank in 1915." Kirkus

Vernon, Ursula

Castle Hangnail; by Ursula Vernon. Dial Books for Young Readers, an imprint of Penguin Group (USA) Inc. 2015 384 p. (hardback) $16.99
Grades: 5 6 7 8 9 **Fic**

1. Humorous fiction 2. Magic -- Fiction 3. Witches -- Fiction 4. Haunted houses -- Fiction 5. Humorous stories
ISBN 0803741294; 9780803741294

LC 2014017106

In this book, by Ursula Vernon, "Molly shows up on Castle Hangnail's doorstep to fill the vacancy for a wicked witch [and] the castle's minions are understandably dubious. After all, she is twelve years old, barely five feet tall, and quite polite. . . . But the castle desperately needs a master or else the Board of Magic will decommission it, leaving all the minions without the home they love." (Publisher's note)

"Creatively drawn characters--from a Minotaur cook to a donkey-dragon to clockwork bees--enjoy mutual respect and will sacrifice whatever is needed to safeguard the castle and its master. The illustrations add whimsy to this delightful tale." Booklist

Vigilante, Danette

Saving Baby Doe; Danette Vigilante. G.P. Putnam's Sons, an imprint of Penguin Group (USA) Inc. 2014 240 p. (hardback) $16.99
Grades: 5 6 7 8 **Fic**

1. Orphans -- Fiction 2. Friendship -- Fiction 3. Family life -- Fiction 4. Single-parent families -- Fiction 5. Neighbors -- Fiction 6. Foundlings -- Fiction 7. Best friends -- Fiction 8. Conduct of life -- Fiction 9. Hispanic Americans -- Fiction
ISBN 039925160X; 9780399251603

LC 2013022728

In this book, by Danette Vigilante, "a cry in a building-site portable toilet leads thirteen-year-old Lionel and his friend Anisa to the discovery of an abandoned newborn baby. . . . Lionel, himself abandoned by his father, fears that Baby Doe will be hurt by a similar loss, so he schemes to bring her home with him. Realizing baby supplies cost money, a rare commodity around his house, he reluctantly agrees to take on some work for a local drug dealer." (Bulletin of the Center for Children's Books)

"Thirteen-year-old Lionel Perez and his friend Anisa Torres stumble across a newborn baby. Despite his mother's efforts to tie up his time with piano lessons, Lionel gets mixed up with a drug dealer in the hopes of earning enough money to take care of the baby himself. Vigilante's finely tuned depiction of Lionel's Red Hook, Brooklyn, neighborhood is believable and engaging." Horn Book

Vivat, Booki

Frazzled; Everyday Disasters and Impending Doom. Booki Vivat. HarperCollins 2016 240 p. illustrations (hardcover) $12.99
Grades: 4 5 6 7 **Fic**

1. Girls -- fiction 2. School children -- fiction 3. Child psychology -- fiction
ISBN 9780062398796

LC 2016936039

In this children's book by Booki Vivat, "Abbie is in crisis—and not just because she's starting middle school or because she's stuck in a family that doesn't quite get her or because everyone seems to have a Thing except her. . . . Frazzled dives right into the mind of this hilariously neurotic middle school girl as she tries to figure out who she is and where she belongs." (Publisher's note)

"Abbie's phobias and worries are charmingly depicted in this heavily illustrated hybrid novel. The humorous, doodlelike artwork makes her struggles entertaining and relatable." SLJ

Other titles in this series are:
Ordinary mishaps and inevitable catastrophes (2017)
Minor incidents and absolute uncertainties (2019)

Vivian, Siobhan

The **list**; Siobhan Vivian. Scholastic 2012 333 p. (hardcover : alk. paper) $17.99
Grades: 7 8 9 10 11 12 **Fic**

1. Female friendship 2. Self-perception -- Fiction 3. Personal appearance -- Fiction 4. High school students -- Fiction 5. Identity (Psychology) -- Fiction 6. Friendship -- Fiction 7. Self-esteem -- Fiction 8. High schools -- Fiction
ISBN 0545169178; 9780545169172

LC 2012004248

This young adult novel presents an "exploration of physical appearance and the status it confers. . . . Every year during homecoming week, a list is posted anonymously at Mount Washington High naming the prettiest and ugliest girls in each class. . . . The list confers instant status, transforming formerly homeschooled sophomore Lauren from geeky to hot while consigning her counterpart . . . Candace, to pariah. But what the label mainly confers is anxiety. Prettiest junior Bridget despairs that she'll ever be thin enough to merit her title. . . . Jennifer, four-time 'ugliest' winner, tries to relish the notoriety. . . . Whether clued in or clueless to the intricate social complexities, boyfriends reinforce the status quo, while moms carry scars of their own past physical insecurities." (Kirkus)

Vlahos, Len

★ **Life** in a fishbowl; by Len Vlahos. Bloomsbury 2017 336 p. (hardback) $17.99

Grades: 7 8 9 10 **Fic**

1. Terminally ill -- Fiction 2. Brain -- Tumors -- Fiction 3. Family problems -- Fiction 4. Reality television programs -- Fiction 5. Cancer -- Fiction

ISBN 9781681190358

LC 2016022364

In this book, by Len Vlahos, "when Jackie discovers that her father has been diagnosed with a terminal brain tumor, her whole world starts to crumble. . . . In a desperate act to secure his family's future, Jackie's father . . . puts his life up for auction on eBay. . . . Jackie can do nothing but watch and wait, . . . no one can predict how the auction will finally end, or any of the very public fallout that ensues. Life as Jackie knows it is about to change forever." (Publisher's note)

"From page one, it's evident that the ending will not be a happy one, but numerous laugh-out-loud moments and beautifully drawn characters make for a powerful journey that will leave a lasting imprint on readers." Pub Wkly

Voelkel, J.

The **end** of the world club; [by] J&P Voelkel. Egmont USA 2011 384p (The Jaguar stones) $16.99

Grades: 4 5 6 7 **Fic**

1. Adventure fiction 2. Mayas -- Fiction 3. Supernatural -- Fiction 4. Central America -- Fiction

ISBN 978-1-60684-072-6; 1-60684-072-X

LC 2010036641

Sequel to: Middleworld (2007)

With the end of the Mayan calendar fast approaching, fourteen-year-old Max Murphy and his friend Lola, the Maya girl who saved his life in the perilous jungle, race against time to outwit the twelve villainous Lords of Death, following the trail of the conquistadors into a forgotten land steeped in legend and superstition.

"The authors use Maya mythology and terms and add interesting facts about Spain and Spanish culture. This is a fast-paced book, and the action starts right away." SLJ

Voigt, Cynthia

★ **Dicey's** song. Atheneum Pubs. 1982 196p $17.95; pa $6.99

Grades: 5 6 7 8 **Fic**

1. Siblings -- Fiction 2. Grandmothers -- Fiction

ISBN 0-689-30944-9; 0-689-86362-4 pa

LC 82-3882

Sequel to Homecoming

Awarded the Newbery Medal, 1983

"The vividness of Dicey is striking; Voigt has plumbed and probed her character inside out to fashion a memorable protagonist." Booklist

★ **Homecoming**. Atheneum Pubs. 1981 312p $18.95; pa $6.99

Grades: 6 7 8 9 **Fic**

1. Siblings -- Fiction 2. Abandoned children -- Fiction

ISBN 0-689-30833-7; 0-689-86361-6 pa

LC 80-36723

ALA YALSA Margaret A. Edwards Award (1995)

"The characterizations of the children are original and intriguing, and there are a number of interesting minor characters encountered in their travels." SLJ

Other books about the Tillermans are:

Dicey's Song
A Solitary Blue
The Runner
Come a Stranger
Sons from Afar
Seventeen Against the Dealer

★ **Izzy,** willy-nilly; Rev. format ed.; Atheneum Books for Young Readers 2005 327p $17.95; pa $6.99

Grades: 7 8 9 10 **Fic**

1. Amputees -- Fiction 2. Friendship -- Fiction 3. Drunk driving -- Fiction

ISBN 978-1-4169-0340-6; 1-4169-0340-2; 978-1-4169-0339-0 pa; 1-4169-0339-9 pa

LC 2005299062

A reissue of the title first published 1986

ALA YALSA Margaret A. Edwards Award (1995)

A car accident causes fifteen-year-old Izzy to lose one leg and face the need to start building a new life as an amputee.

"Voigt shows unusual insight into the workings of a 15-year-old girl's mind. . . . Just as Voigt's perceptive empathy brings Izzy to life, other characterizations are memorable, whether of Izzy's shallow former friends or of her egocentric 10-year-old sister." Pub Wkly [review of 1986 edition]

Mister Max; the book of kings. Newbery Medalist Cynthia Voigt ; illustrated by Iacopo Bruno. Alfred A. Knopf 2015 352 p. illustrations (trade) $16.99

Grades: 5 6 7 8 **Fic**

1. Adventure fiction 2. Parents -- Fiction 3. Self-reliance -- Fiction 4. Missing persons -- Fiction 5. Problem solving -- Fiction 6. Adventure and adventurers -- Fiction

ISBN 0307976874; 9780307976871; 9780375971259

LC 2014017699

Sequel to: Mister Max : the book of secrets

In this book, by Cynthia Voigt, illustrated by Iacopo Bruno, Mister Max "sets off to rescue his missing parents! . . . He's solved case after case for other people in his business as 'solutioneer.' And he's puzzled out the coded messages sent by his father. He doesn't know exactly what's happened, but he knows his parents are in danger--and it's up to Max to save them." (Publisher's note)

★ A **solitary** blue. Atheneum Pubs. 1983 189p hardcover o.p. pa $6.99

Grades: 7 8 9 10 **Fic**

1. Divorce -- Fiction 2. Parent-child relationship -- Fiction

ISBN 0689310080; 0689863608; 9781442450622

LC 83-6007

A Newbery honor book, 1984

"Jefferson Greene, a minor character from Dicey's Song {BRD 1983}, is the subject of the new novel. Beginning when Jeff was seven years old and ending when he was in high school, the book overlaps and goes beyond the earlier one. . . . {This novel} explores the relationships among Jeff, his mother Melody, and his father 'the Professor.' After Melody walked out on the family to pursue a long line of unrealistic causes, the Professor and his young son went on as if nothing had changed. Their . . . coexistence continued until Jeff at the age of eleven received an unexpected invitation to spend the summer with his mother and her family in South Carolina. . . . Age twelve and up." (Horn Book)

"This is the most mature and sophisticated of Voigt's novels. . . . Beautifully knit . . . compelling and intelligent." Bull Cent Child Books

Volponi, Paul

Black and white. Viking 2005 185p $15.99; pa $6.99

Grades: 7 8 9 10 **Fic**

1. Basketball -- Fiction 2. Race relations -- Fiction 3. African Americans -- Fiction

ISBN 0-670-06006-2; 0-14-240692-9 pa

LC 2004-24543

Two star high school basketball players, one black and one white, experience the justice system differently after committing a crime together and getting caught.

"These complex characters share a mutual respect and struggle with issues of loyalty, honesty, and courage. Social conflicts, basketball fervor, and tough personal choices make this title a gripping story." SLJ

Hurricane song; a novel of New Orleans. Viking Childrens Books 2008 144p $15.99

Grades: 7 8 9 10 11 12 **Fic**

1. Young adult literature 2. Jazz music -- Fiction 3. New Orleans (La.) -- Fiction 4. Father-son relationship -- Fiction 5. Hurricane Katrina, 2005 -- Fiction

ISBN 978-0-670-06160-0; 0-670-06160-3

LC 2007-38215

Twelve-year-old Miles Shaw goes to live with his father, a jazz musician, in New Orleans, and together they survive the horrors of Hurricane Katrina in the Superdome, learning about each other and growing closer through their painful experiences.

"A brilliant blend of reality and fiction, this novel hits every chord just right." Voice Youth Advocates

Wagner, Hilary

Nightshade City; [illustrations by Omar Rayyan] Holiday House 2010 262p il $17.95

Grades: 5 6 7 8 **Fic**

1. Fantasy fiction 2. Rats -- Fiction

ISBN 978-0-8234-2285-2; 0-8234-2285-2

LC 2010-02474

Eleven years after the cruel Killdeer took over the Catacombs far beneath the human's Trillium City, Juniper Belancourt, assisted by Vincent and Victor Nightshade, leads a maverick band of rats to escape and establish their own city.

"The themes of love, loss and loyalty resonate through the novel, and the moments of darkness and violence are ultimately overpowered by hope and redemption. A good story well-told." Kirkus

Other titles in this series are:

The white assassin (2011)

Lords of Trillium (2014)

Walden, Mark

H.I.V.E; The Higher Institute of Villainous Education. Simon & Schuster Books for Young Readers 2007 309p $15.99; pa $6.99

Grades: 5 6 7 8 **Fic**

1. Criminals -- Fiction

ISBN 1-4169-3571-1; 978-1-4169-3571-1; 978-1-4169-3572-8 pa; 1-4169-3572-X pa

LC 2007-16205

"H.I.V.E. is operated on a volcanic island in a distant ocean by G.L.O.V.E., a shadowy organization of worldwide wickedness. And, as 13-year-old master of mischief Otto Malpense soon discovers, here the slickest of young tricksters, thieves, and hackers have been brought against their will to be trained as the next generation of supervillains. . . . [This] novel is a real page-turner; those who love superhero stories will eat it up." SLJ

Other titles about H.I.V.E. are:

The Overlord protocol (2008)

Escape velocity (2011)

Dreadnought (2011)

Wallace, Kali

City of islands; Kali Wallace. Katherine Tegen Books 2018 336 p. (hardcover) $16.99

Grades: 5 6 7 8 **Fic**

1. Magic -- fiction 2. Ocean -- fiction 3. Orphans -- fiction

ISBN 9780062499813

LC 2018933267

This book, by Kali Wallace, is "about an archipelago of magical islands and one girl's dangerous discovery on the ocean floor. . . . In a foggy archipelago called the City of Islands, twelve-year-old Mara has always been fascinated by the magic that drifts on the air as songs. But as a servant for the powerful Lady of the Tides, Mara must earn her keep by searching for magical treasures deep in the murky ocean." (Publisher's note)

Wallace, Rich

One good punch. Alfred A. Knopf 2007 114p $15.99

Grades: 7 8 9 10 11 12 **Fic**

1. School stories 2. Journalism -- Fiction 3. Pennsylvania -- Fiction 4. Track athletics -- Fiction

ISBN 978-0-375-81352-8; 0-375-81352-7

LC 2006-33270

Eighteen-year-old Michael Kerrigan, writer of obituaries for the Scranton Observer and captain of the track team, is ready for the most important season of his life—until the police find four joints in his school locker, and he is faced with a choice that could change everything.

"This novel's success is in creating a multidimensional male character in a format that will appeal to all readers. The moral dilemma . . . makes this novel ripe for ethical discussions." Voice Youth Advocates

Perpetual check. Alfred A. Knopf 2009 112p $15.99; lib bdg $18.99

Grades: 8 9 10 11 **Fic**

1. Chess -- Fiction 2. Brothers -- Fiction 3. Father-son relationship -- Fiction

ISBN 978-0-375-84058-6; 0-375-84058-3; 978-0-375-94058-3 lib bdg; 0-375-94058-8 lib bdg

LC 2008-04159

Brothers Zeke and Randy participate in an important chess tournament, playing against each other while also trying to deal with their father's intensely competitive tendencies.

"Wallace cleverly positions Randy and Zeke for a win-win conclusion in this satisfying, engaging, and deceptively simple story." SLJ

War and watermelon. Viking 2011 184p $15.99

Grades: 6 7 8 9 **Fic**

1. School stories 2. Brothers -- Fiction 3. Football -- Fiction 4. New Jersey -- Fiction 5. Family life -- Fiction 6. Vietnam War, 1961-1975 -- Fiction 7. Father-son relationship -- Fiction 8. United States -- History -- Fiction

ISBN 978-0-670-01152-0; 0-670-01152-5

LC 2010-41043

As the summer of 1969 turns to fall in their New Jersey town, twelve-year-old Brody plays football in his first year at junior high while his older brother's protest of the war in Vietnam causes tension with their father.

"Sixties culture and events . . . are well integrated into the story, and humorous vignettes . . . help lighten the mood." Booklist

Wrestling Sturbridge. Knopf 1996 135p hardcover o.p. pa $4.99

Grades: 7 8 9 10 **Fic**

1. Wrestling -- Fiction 2. Friendship -- Fiction

ISBN 0-679-87803-3; 0-679-88555-2 pa

LC 95-20468

"The wresting scenes are thrilling. . . . Like Ben, whose voice is so strong and clear here, Wallace weighs his words carefully, making every one count in this excellent, understated first novel." Booklist

Wallenfels, Stephen

POD. Namelos 2009 212p $18.95; pa $9.95

Grades: 7 8 9 10 **Fic**

1. Science fiction 2. Extraterrestrial beings -- Fiction

ISBN 978-1-60898-011-6; 1-60898-011-1; 978-1-60898-010-9 pa; 1-60898-010-3 pa

LC 2008-29721

As alien spacecrafts fill the sky and zap up any human being who dares to go outside, fifteen-year-old Josh and twelve-year-old Megs, living in different cities, describe what could be their last days on Earth.

"The dire circumstances don't negate the humor, the hormones, or the humanity found in the young narrators. This is solid, straightforward sci-fi." Booklist

Waller, Sharon Biggs

A **mad,** wicked folly; Sharon Biggs Waller. Viking, published by the Penguin Group 2014 448 p. map (hardback) $17.99

Grades: 8 9 10 11 12 **Fic**

1. Love -- Fiction 2. Gender role -- Fiction 3. London (England) -- Fiction 4. Great Britain -- History -- Edward VII, 1901-1910 -- Fiction 5. Artists -- Fiction 7. Sex role -- Fiction 6. London (England) -- History -- 20th century -- Fiction

ISBN 0670014680; 9780670014682

LC 2013029858

This book, by Sharon Biggs Waller, is "about a young English woman who is talented, beautiful, passionate, and wealthy. Despite these advantages, Victoria Darling struggles with the harsh limitations imposed upon women prior to and during the Edwardian era of 1901-1910, which curtail her attempts to attend art school. While Victoria does not initially associate with the Suffragette Movement, she ultimately discovers that her fate is intertwined with the cause." (School Library Journal)

"Victoria's dream of becoming an artist leads her naively into scandals, tempts her into a convenient marriage, and drives her to join the Women's Social and Political Union. Persistence eventually triumphs, and friendships, love, and art lessons are her rewards. Sound historical research provides the backbone for this warm novel about the development of women's opportunities in Edwardian London." Horn Book

Includes bibliographical references

Walrath, Dana

★ **Like** water on stone; Dana Walrath. Delacorte Press 2014 368 p. (hc) $16.99

Grades: 8 9 10 11 12 **Fic**

1. Orphans -- Fiction 2. Armenian massacres, 1915-1923 -- Fiction 3. Turkey -- History -- Ottoman Empire, 1288-1918 -- Fiction 4. Novels in verse 5. Genocide -- Fiction 6. Armenians -- Turkey -- Fiction 7. Brothers and sisters -- Fiction

ISBN 0385743971; 9780375991424; 9780385743976

LC 2013026323

"Shahen Donabedian dreams of going to New York. Sosi, his twin sister, never wants to leave her home, especially now that she is in love. But when the Ottoman pashas set in motion their plans to eliminate all Armenians, neither twin has a choice. They flee into the mountains . . . [b]ut the children are not alone. An eagle watches over them as they run at night and hide each day, making their way across mountain ridges and rivers red with blood." (Publisher's note)

"This beautiful, yet at times brutally vivid, historical verse novel will bring this horrifying, tragic period to life for astute, mature readers.... A cast of characters, and author note with historical background are thoughtfully included." SLJ

Walsh, Pat

★ The **Crowfield** curse. Chicken House 2010 326p il $16.99

Grades: 5 6 7 8 **Fic**

1. Magic -- Fiction 2. Orphans -- Fiction 3. Monasteries -- Fiction 4. Great Britain -- History -- 1154-1399, Plantagenets -- Fiction

ISBN 0-545-22922-7; 978-0-545-22922-7

LC 2009-51483

In 1347, when fourteen-year-old orphan William Paynel, an impoverished servant at Crowfield Abbey, goes into the forest to gather wood and finds a magical creature caught in a trap, he discovers he has the ability to see fays and becomes embroiled in a strange mystery involving Old Magic, a bitter feud, and ancient secrets.

"This suspenseful and spooky story will thrill readers. . . . With fascinating attention to detail and an edgy battle between evil and good, Walsh sweeps readers almost effortlessly into another time and place." SLJ

Followed by:

The Crowfield demon (2012)

Walter, Jon

My name is not Friday; by Jon Walter. David Fickling Books/Scholastic Inc. 2016 384 p. (hardcover) $18.99

Grades: 7 8 9 10 **Fic**

1. Orphans -- Fiction 2. Brothers -- Fiction 3. Slavery -- Fiction 4. African Americans -- Fiction 5. United States -- History -- Civil War, 1861-1865 -- Fiction

ISBN 9780545855228

LC 2015035464

In this novel, by Jon Walter, "well-mannered Samuel and his mischievous younger brother Joshua are free black boys living in an orphanage during the end of the Civil War. Samuel takes the blame for Joshua's latest prank, and the consequence is worse than he could ever imagine. He's taken from the orphanage to the South, given a new name -- Friday -- and sold into slavery." (Publisher's note)

"While readers on the young end of the age range and those unfamiliar with religious concepts may find the opening chapters somewhat confusing, Samuel's endearing, immersive narration makes the novel a fascinating and unforgettable account of a brutal and shameful chapter in America's history. A heartbreaking story about family, justice, and the resilience of the human spirit." Kirkus

Walters, Eric

The **money** pit mystery. Fitzhenry & Whiteside 2011 289p pa $9.95

Grades: 4 5 6 7 **Fic**

1. Mystery fiction 2. Islands -- Fiction 3. Family life -- Fiction 4.

Buried treasure -- Fiction
ISBN 978-1-55455-123-1; 1-55455-123-4

"Sam's grandfather and mother had a fight years ago, and now Sam, his sister, and their mother are visiting him for the first time in years. When they arrive on tiny Oak Island, they are shocked to discover how rundown the man's once-immaculate house has become. To make matters worse, he isn't even there. When Sam, Beth, and their friend, Buzz, do some exploring, they are surprised by some security guards at the town's 'money pit.' Some folks believe that Captain Kidd buried treasure here. . . . This is a well-thought-out mystery with lots of suspense and a fully realized picture of a struggling family." SLJ

Walton, Julia

Words on bathroom walls; Julia Walton. Random House 2017 294 p. (hardback) $17.99

Grades: 7 8 9 10 11 12 **Fic**

1. Schizophrenia -- Fiction 2. Mental illness -- Fiction 3. Dating (Social customs) -- Fiction 4. Secrecy -- fiction 5. Hallucinations and illusions -- fiction 6. Schizophrenia in adolescence -- fiction
ISBN 9780399550904; 9780399550881; 9780399550898
LC 2016017419

In this book, by Julia Walton, "Adam has just been diagnosed with schizophrenia. He sees and hears people who aren't there. . . . Still, there's hope. As Adam starts fresh at a new school, he begins a drug trial that helps him ignore his visions. . . . When he meets Maya, a fiercely intelligent girl, he desperately wants to be the great guy that she thinks he is. But then the . . . drug begins to fail, and Adam will do anything to keep Maya from discovering his secret." (Publisher's note)

"First-time author Walton creates a psychologically tense story with sympathetic characters while dispelling myths about a much-feared condition." Pub Wkly

Wang, Corrie

The **takedown**; Corrie Wang. Freeform 2017 369 p. (hardcover) $17.99

Grades: 7 8 9 10 **Fic**

1. Schools -- Fiction 2. Popularity -- Fiction 3. High schools -- Fiction 4. Social media -- Fiction 5. Cyberbullying -- Fiction 6. Racially mixed people -- Fiction 7. Brooklyn (New York, N.Y.) -- Fiction
ISBN 9781484757420; 1484757424
LC 2016028339

In this novel, by Corrie Wang, "a week before college applications are due, a video of Kyla 'doing it' with her crush-worthy English teacher is uploaded to her school's website. It instantly goes viral, but here's the thing: it's not Kyla in the video. With time running out, Kyla delves into a world of hackers, haters and creepy stalkers in an attempt to do the impossible-take something off the internet-all while dealing with the fallout from her own karmic footprint." (Publisher's note)

"A thought-provoking, entertaining read, Wang's debut illustrates a future that is easily conceivable." Kirkus

Ward, David

Beneath the mask; [by] David Ward. Amulet Books 2008 243p il (The grassland trilogy) $15.95

Grades: 7 8 9 10 **Fic**

1. Science fiction 2. Slavery -- Fiction
ISBN 978-0-8109-7074-8; 0-8109-7074-0
Sequel to: Escape the mask (2008)

After tasting freedom, the former slaves are soon back under the control of the menacing Spears, and this time Corki and Pippa are separated as Corki, in training to be a Spear, seeks a way to work within the system to gain freedom for himself and his friends.

This "is an excellent continuation of a trilogy fraught with daring escapes, dangerous situations, and genuine characters." Voice Youth Advocates

Followed by: Beyond the mask (2010)

Ward, Rachel

The **Chaos**. Chicken House 2011 339p $17.99

Grades: 8 9 10 11 12 **Fic**

1. Science fiction 2. Death -- Fiction 3. Orphans -- Fiction 4. London (England) -- Fiction 5. Blacks -- Great Britain -- Fiction 6. Extrasensory perception -- Fiction
ISBN 978-0-545-24269-1; 0-545-24269-X
Sequel to: Numbers (2010)

When rising flood waters force him and his grandmother to evacuate their coastal home and return to London, sixteen-year-old Adam, who has inherited his mother's curse of being able to see the day that someone will die when he looks into their eyes, becomes disturbed when he begins to see January 1, 2027, a date six months into the future, in nearly everyone around him.

"In this sequel to Numbers a fascinating premise is again worked out through gripping episodes and a lightly handled metaphysical dilemma." Horn Book

★ **Numbers**. Chicken House/Scholastic 2010 325p $17.99

Grades: 8 9 10 11 12 **Fic**

1. Science fiction 2. Death -- Fiction 3. Runaway teenagers -- Fiction 4. Blacks -- Great Britain -- Fiction 5. Extrasensory perception -- Fiction
ISBN 978-0-545-14299-1; 0-545-14299-7
LC 2008-55440

"Ward's debut novel is gritty, bold, and utterly unique. Jem's isolation and pain, hidden beneath a veneer of toughness, are palpable, and the ending is a real shocker." SLJ

Other titles in this series are:
The chaos (2011)
Infinity (2012)

Wardlaw, Lee

101 ways to bug your teacher; Lee Wardlaw. Dial Books 2004 246p hardcover o.p. pa $6.99

Grades: 4 5 6 7 **Fic**

1. School stories
ISBN 0-8037-2658-9; 0-14-240331-1 pa
LC 2003-20068

Steve "Sneeze" Wyatt attempts to thwart his parents' plan to have him skip eighth grade, but he has bigger problems when his friends disapprove of his new list and Mrs. "Fierce" Pierce threatens to keep him from the Invention Convention.

"In spite of the title, the characters show respect for their teachers and parents, and for one another. A delightful read." SLJ

Warga, Jasmine

★ **Other** words for home; Jasmine Warga. Balzer + Bray 2019 352 p. (hardcover) $16.99

Grades: 5 6 7 8 9 **Fic**

1. Refugees -- Fiction 2. Immigration and emigration -- Fiction
ISBN 9780062747808
LC 2018961861

In this book, by Jasmine Warga, "Jude never thought she'd be leaving her beloved older brother and father behind, all the way across the ocean in Syria. But when things in her hometown start becoming volatile, Jude and her mother are sent to live in Cincinnati with relatives. . . .

The American movies that Jude has always loved haven't quite prepared her for starting school in the US--and her new label of 'Middle Eastern,' an identity she's never known before." (Publisher's note)

"Highly recommended for all libraries, this title will easily find a home next to books like Refugee by Alan Gratz and Inside Out and Back Again by Thanhha Lai." (Publishers Weekly)

Warman, Janice

The **world** beneath; one South African boy's struggle to be free. Janice Warman. Candlewick Press 2015 176 p. (ebook) $16.99; (hbk.) $16.99

Grades: 8 9 10 11 **Fic**

1. Bildungsromans 2. Historical fiction 3. South Africa -- Race relations -- Fiction

ISBN 9780763680572; 9780763678562; 0763678562

LC 2015931429

This novel, by Janice Warman, is set in "South Africa, 1976. Joshua lives with his mother in the maid's room, in the backyard of their wealthy white employers' house in the city by the sea. He doesn't quite understand the events going on around him. But when he rescues a stranger and riots begin to sweep the country, Joshua has to face the world beneath—the world deep inside him—to make heartbreaking choices that will change his life forever." (Publisher's note)

"A good complement to nonfiction about apartheid South Africa, a little-explored place and period in children's literature." Kirkus

Wasserman, Robin

The **book** of blood and shadow; by Robin Wasserman. Alfred A. Knopf 2012 352p. (trade hardcover) $17.99

Grades: 7 8 9 **Fic**

1. Mystery fiction 2. Suspense fiction 3. Homicide -- Fiction 4. Prague (Czech Republic) -- Fiction 5. Murder -- Fiction 7. Conspiracies -- Fiction 6. Supernatural -- Fiction 7. Czech Republic -- Fiction 8. Secret societies -- Fiction 9. Mystery and detective stories

ISBN 9780375868764; 9780375872778; 9780375899614; 9780375968761

LC 2011003920

In this book, "Nora . . . help[s] an eccentric professor translate a sixteenth-century book by a notable alchemist (and the letters left by his daughter, Elizabeth), . . . spending more time with her best friend, Chris, and his roommate, Max, who are also working on the project. Just as quickly as Nora becomes invested in Elizabeth's life, Max transforms from a slightly creepy tagalong to a sweet, solicitous boyfriend. Then Chris is brutally murdered, his girlfriend Adriane is left without memory of the night, and Max (the main suspect in the crime) disappears. . . . Nora . . . continu[es] her translation of the secrets encrypted in Elizabeth's . . . communications and uncovering conspiracies . . . in which she herself is . . . a key figure." (Bulletin of the Center for Children's Books)

Watkins, Steve

Great Falls; Steve Watkins. Candlewick Press 2016 256 p. $17.99

Grades: 8 9 10 11 **Fic**

1. Brothers -- Fiction 2. Veterans -- Fiction 3. Post-traumatic stress disorder -- Fiction

ISBN 076367155X; 9780763671556

"Shane has always worshiped his big brother, Jeremy. But three tours in Iraq and Afghanistan have taken their toll, and the easy-go-lucky brother Shane knew has been replaced by a surly drunk. When Jeremy . . . offers to take him to the family cabin overnight, Shane goes along. But as the camping trip turns into a days-long canoe trip . . . Shane realizes he . . . has no idea how to persuade Jeremy to return home and get the help he needs." (Publisher's note)

"Watkins (Juvie) delivers a powerful, emotionally raw tale, heartbreaking in its portrayal of damaged veterans, the price some pay to serve, and the toll it takes on their friends and family. It's also a raw coming-of-age journey for Shane as he struggles with his own feelings, especially toward 'the Colonel,' the brothers' emotionally abusive, micromanaging, ex-military stepfather." Pub Wkly

Watkins, Yoko Kawashima

★ **So** far from the bamboo grove. Lothrop, Lee & Shepard Bks. 1986 183p map hardcover o.p. pa $5.99

Grades: 6 7 8 9 **Fic**

1. Japan -- Fiction 2. Korea -- Fiction 3. World War, 1939-1945 -- Fiction

ISBN 0-688-13115-8 pa

LC 85-15939

A fictionalized autobiography in which eight-year-old Yoko escapes from Korea to Japan with her mother and sister at the end of World War II

"An admirably told and absorbing novel." Horn Book

Followed by: My brother, my sister and I

Watson, Jude

The **39** clues; unstoppable: nowhere to run. Jude Watson. Scholastic 2013 272 p. (The 39 clues: unstoppable) (paper over board) $12.99

Grades: 4 5 6 7 **Fic**

1. Supernatural -- fiction 2. Brothers and sisters -- fiction 3. Adventure and adventurers -- fiction

ISBN 9780545521376; 0545521378

LC 2013934701

In this book, by Jude Watson, "the Cahill family has a secret. For five hundred years, they have guarded the 39 Clues – thirty-nine ingredients in a serum that transforms whomever takes it into the most powerful person on earth. . . . Certain Cahills have always made it their mission to keep the serum safe. . . . Thirteen-year-old Dan Cahill and his older sister, Amy, are the latest guardians of the Clues. They think they've done everything right, but a tiny mistake leads to catastrophe." (Publisher's note)

"Six months after sixteen-year-old Amy and thirteen-year-old Dan defeated the Vespers, the Cahill siblings set out on another quest to stop the serum their family has protected for centuries from wreaking havoc on the world. This first entry in a new spinoff series is formulaic, but the suspense and high stakes that 39 Clues fans love are front and center." (Horn Book)

Beyond the grave. Scholastic 2009 190p (The 39 clues) $12.99

Grades: 4 5 6 7 **Fic**

1. Ciphers -- Fiction 2. Orphans -- Fiction 3. Siblings -- Fiction

ISBN 978-0-545-06044-8; 0-545-06044-3

Sequel to: The sword thief by Peter Lerangis (2009)

A clue sends Amy and Dan jetting off to find out just what's behind the fierce rivalry between the Tomas and Ekaterina branches of the Cahill family. Was a Clue stolen from the Tomas branch? Where is it now? And most important, can Amy and Dan get their hands on it before their rivals do?

"Like the previous books, historical information is woven into the fast-paced adventure." SLJ

Followed by: The black circle by Patrick Carman (2009)

Loot; how to steal a fortune. Jude Watson. Scholastic Press 2014 272 p. (alk. paper) $16.99

Grades: 4 5 6 7 **Fic**

1. Twins -- Fiction 2. Adventure fiction 3. Jewelry -- Fiction 4. Orphans -- Fiction 5. Robbers and outlaws -- Fiction 6. Brothers and sisters -- Fiction 7. Adventure and adventurers -- Fiction

ISBN 0545468027; 9780545468022

LC 2014001218

"When master jewel thief Alfie McQuinn dies, his stashed set of clues and cryptic last words to March, his 12-year-old son and apprentice, mark the beginning of a race against time. The first clue leads March to discover his twin sister, Jules, a traveling circus acrobat. Tossed into a group home, they meet Darius, a juvenile delinquent with a soft spot for Izzy, a code-cracking hacker." (Booklist)

"Pitch-perfect characters, from scheming criminals to a twisted former cop to the twins' father, move in and out of the narrative, but it's the four young teens that drive the tale forward with enviable schemes and ingenious plans.Taut, engrossing and unstoppable." Kirkus

Watson, Renée, 1978-

★ **Piecing** me together; Renée Watson. Bloomsbury 2017 264 p. (hardcover) $17.99

Grades: 7 8 9 10 11 12 **Fic**

1. School stories 2. Mentoring -- Fiction 3. African Americans -- Fiction 4. Schools -- Fiction 5. High schools -- Fiction

ISBN 9781681191065; 9781681191058

LC 2016023127

Newbery Honor Book (2018)

Coretta Scott King Author Award (2018)

In this book, by Renée Watson, "Jade believes she must get out of her poor neighborhood if she's ever going to succeed. Her mother tells her to take advantage of every opportunity that comes her way. . . . She accepted . . . an invitation to join . . . a mentorship program for 'at-risk' girls. Except really, it's for black girls. From 'bad' neighborhoods. And just because Maxine, her college-graduate mentor, is black doesn't mean she understands Jade." (Publisher's note)

"A timely, nuanced, and unforgettable story about the power of art, community, and friendship." Kirkus

Watch us rise; by Renée Watson and Ellen Hagan. Bloomsbury 2019 368 p. (hardback) $18.99

Grades: 7 8 9 10 11 12 **Fic**

1. Feminist fiction 2. Best friends -- Fiction 3. Women's rights -- Fiction 4. Clubs -- Fiction 5. Schools -- Fiction 6. Friendship -- Fiction 7. High schools -- Fiction 8. New York (N.Y.) -- Fiction

ISBN 9781547600083

LC 2018045153

In this novel, by Renee Watson and Ellen Hagan, "Jasmine and Chelsea are best friends on a mission--they're sick of the way women are treated even at their progressive NYC high school, so they decide to start a Women's Rights Club. They post their work online--poems, essays, videos of Chelsea performing her poetry, and Jasmine's response to the racial microaggressions she experiences--and soon they go viral. But with such positive support, the club is also targeted by trolls." (Publisher's note)

"Told from the viewpoints of Chelsea and Jasmine, this thought-provoking novel explores ideas of body-shaming, racial stereotypes, and gender inequality." (School Library Journal)

Weatherford, Carole Boston

★ **Becoming** Billie Holiday; art by Floyd Cooper. Wordsong 2008 116p il $19.95

Grades: 7 8 9 10 **Fic**

1. Singers 2. Blues musicians 3. Novels in verse 4. Singers -- Fiction 5. Jazz music -- Fiction 6. African Americans -- Fiction

ISBN 978-1-59078-507-2; 1-59078-507-X

LC 2007-51214

Coretta Scott King honor book for text, 2009

Jazz vocalist Billie Holiday looks back on her early years in this fictional memoir written in verse.

"This captivating title places readers solidly into Holiday's world, and is suitable for independent reading as well as a variety of classroom uses." SLJ

Includes bibliographical references

Weaver, Will

Saturday night dirt. Farrar, Straus and Giroux 2008 163p $14.95; pa $7.99

Grades: 8 9 10 11 **Fic**

1. Minnesota -- Fiction 2. Automobile racing -- Fiction

ISBN 978-0-374-35060-4; 0-374-35060-4; 978-0-312-56131-4 pa; 0-312-56131-8 pa

LC 2007-6988

In a small town in northern Minnesota, the much-anticipated Saturday night dirt-track race at the old-fashioned, barely viable, Headwaters Speedway becomes, in many ways, an important life-changing event for all the participants on and off the track.

"Weaver presents compelling character studies. . . . Young racing fans . . . will find much that rings true here." Booklist

Other titles in this series are Checkered flag cheater (2010)

Super stock rookie (2009)

Webber, Katherine

The **heartbeats** of Wing Jones; Katherine Webber. Delacorte Press 2017 328 p. (hc) $17.99

Grades: 7 8 9 10 11 12 **Fic**

1. Traffic accidents -- Fiction 2. Emotional problems -- Fiction 3. Brothers and sisters -- Fiction 4. Running -- fiction 5. Coma -- Patients -- fiction 6. Racially mixed people -- fiction 7. Emotional problems of teenagers -- fiction

ISBN 9780399555022; 9780399555046; 9780399555039

LC 2016005580

In this novel, by Katherine Webber, "Wing Jones, like everyone else in her town, has worshipped her older brother for as long as she can remember. . . . Marcus is everything his sister is not. Until . . . Marcus, drunk at the wheel after a party, kills two people and barely survives himself. With Marcus now in a coma, Wing is crushed, confused, and angry. She is tormented at school for Marcus's mistake, haunted at home by her mother and grandmothers' grief." (Publisher's note)

"Written in Wing's believable first-person voice, the novel conveys the teen's perspective of the changing world around her as the plot moves quickly along. Recommend this to fans of Jandy Nelson's and Stephanie Perkins's books." SLJ

Weber, David

★ A **beautiful** friendship. Baen Books 2011 361p $18.99

Grades: 6 7 8 9 **Fic**

1. Science fiction 2. Animals -- Fiction 3. Space colonies -- Fiction

ISBN 978-1-4516-3747-2; 1-4516-3747-0

LC 2011015815

Twelve-year-old Stephanie Harrington, a genetically-enhanced girl on the pioneer planet of Sphinx, bonds with a treecat, a telepathic and fully sentient animal, putting her in danger from highly placed enemies who want to ensure that the planet remains entirely in human hands.

"The environmenatal messages, human-animal friendship, humor, action, and inventive techology will make this series starter an easy hit with teen sf readers." Booklist

Other titles in this series are:
Fire season (2012)
Treecat wars (2013)

Wedekind, Annie

A **horse** of her own; by Annie Wedekind. Feiwel and Friends 2008 275p $16.95; pa $7.99

Grades: 5 6 7 8 **Fic**

1. Camps -- Fiction 2. Horses -- Fiction 3. Kentucky -- Fiction 4. Horsemanship -- Fiction

ISBN 978-0-312-36927-9; 0-312-36927-1; 978-0-312-58146-6 pa; 0-312-58146-7 pa

LC 2007032769

At summer camp Jane feels like an outsider among the cliquish rich girls who board their horses at Sunny Acres farm, and when the horse she has been riding is sold to another camper, she feels even worse until her teacher asks her to help train a beautiful but skittish new horse, and the experience brings out the best in her.

"Tenacious and thoughtful, Jane is an appealing protagonist who gradually recognizes that being accepted no longer matters to her. The plot . . . has enough twists, including a hint of romance, to sustain readers' interest." SLJ

Weeks, Sarah

Jumping the scratch; a novel. Laura Geringer Books 2006 167p il $15.99; pa $5.99

Grades: 5 6 7 8 **Fic**

1. Aunts -- Fiction 2. Memory -- Fiction 3. Child sexual abuse -- Fiction

ISBN 978-0-06-054109-5; 0-06-054109-1; 978-0-06-054110-1 pa; 0-06-054111-3 pa

LC 2005-17776

After moving with his mother to a trailer park to care for an injured aunt, eleven-year-old Jamie Reardon struggles to cope with a deeply buried secret

"Weeks alludes to sexual abuse, but with a broad brush and no graphic details. . . . Weeks perfectly captures not only the guilt, shame, and pain of the abused boy but also the tenor of a fifth-grade classroom from the point of view of a new student who is friendless, targeted, and belittled by an insensitive teacher. Touches of humor ameliorate the pain and poignancy." SLJ

Pie. Scholastic Press 2011 183p $16.99

Grades: 4 5 6 7 **Fic**

1. Cats -- Fiction 2. Pies -- Fiction 3. Aunts -- Fiction

ISBN 978-0-545-27011-3; 0-545-27011-1

In the 1950s in the small town of Ipswitch, PA, Polly Portman dies and leaves the recipe for her prize-winning piecrust to her cat Lardo, in the care of her niece Alice, but then the cat is kidnapped and the bakery is trashed.

"Weeks deftly leavens moments of hilarity with the process of grieving in this sweet coming-of-age story in which Alice learns from Aunt Polly to follow her heart and to open it as well. Readers will close the book with a satisfied sigh and may seek out an adult to help them bake a pie. Recipes included." SLJ

Wees, Alyssa

The **waking** forest; Alyssa Wees. Delacorte Press 2019 304 p. (hc) $17.99

Grades: 8 9 10 11 12 **Fic**

1. Magic -- Fiction 2. Sisters -- Fiction 3. Witches -- Fiction 4. Foxes -- Fiction 5. Wishes -- Fiction

ISBN 9780525581161; 9780525581178

LC 2018022935

In this book, by Alyssa Wees, "the waking forest has secrets. . . . [W]hen . . . [Rhea] reaches out to touch it, the forest vanishes. She's desperate to know more--until she finds a peculiar boy who offers to reveal its secrets. If she plays a game. To the Witch, the forest is her home. . . . One night, a mysterious visitor arrives and asks her what she wishes for, but the Witch sends him away. And then the uninvited guest returns." (Publisher's note)

"Dreams and stories—their power to escape reality and to restore it—are in the bones of this masterfully wo ven fantasy debut. And at its heart? The power of revolution in the face of coldly violent injustice." (Kirkus Reviews)

Wegelius, Jakob

★ The **murderer's** ape; Jakob Wegelius ; translated from the Swedish by Peter Graves. Delacorte Press 2017 624 p. illustrations, color maps (ebook) $53.97; (hardback) $17.99

Grades: 7 8 9 10 **Fic**

1. Gorilla -- Fiction 2. Friendship -- Fiction 3. Mystery and detective stories 4. Adventure and adventurers -- Fiction 8. Human-animal relationships -- Fiction

ISBN 9781101931776; 9781101931752; 9781101931769

LC 2016010508

Mildred L. Batchelder Award (2018)

This novel, by Jakob Wegelius, translated by Peter Graves, is a "quirky mystery featuring a gorilla named Sally Jones. . . . While carrying what they think is a crate of tiles, Sally Jones and the Chief are attacked by robbers, and [their] ship is sunk. Things go from bad to worse when the Chief is shortly thereafter arrested for the murder of the man who hired them to transport the cargo. . . . Jones forges a new life but is determined to prove the Chief's innocence." (School Library Journal)

"While the sheer length and thoughtful pace of Sally Jones' journey might discourage some, those who persevere will have a richly imagined and thoroughly unique adventure in store." Booklist

Weil, Cynthia

I'm glad I did; Cynthia Weil. Soho Teen 2015 272 p. (hardback) $18.99

Grades: 8 9 10 11 12 **Fic**

1. Nineteen sixties 2. Rock music -- Fiction 3. Songwriters and songwriting 4. Love -- Fiction 5. Secrets -- Fiction 6. Composers -- Fiction 7. Popular music -- Fiction

ISBN 161695356X; 9781616953560

LC 2014025047

In this novel by Cynthia Weil "it's the summer of 1963 and JJ Green is a born songwriter . . . [and] she takes an internship at the Brill Building, the epicenter of a new sound called rock and roll. She even finds herself a writing partner in Luke Silver, a boy . . . who seems to connect instantly with her music. Best of all, they'll be cutting their first demo with legendary singer Dulcie Brown. But Dulcie's past is a tangle of secrets." (Publisher's note)

"Grammy-winning songwriter Weil makes an impressive YA debut with this period novel set against the rapidly changing music industry of the early 1960s. . . [s]howing both the bright and the dark sides of the music business, Weil crafts an enticing tale of a sheltered teenager's induction into a world where ambitions and morals are repeatedly tested." PW

Wein, Elizabeth

★ **Black** dove, white raven; Elizabeth Wein. Disney-Hyperion 2015 368 p. (hardback) $17.99
Grades: 8 9 10 11 12 **Fic**

1. Adoption -- Fiction 2. Air pilots -- Fiction 3. Race relations -- Fiction 4. Brothers and sisters -- Fiction 5. Italo-Ethiopian War, 1935-1936 -- Fiction 6. Americans -- Ethiopia -- Fiction 7. Adventure and adventurers -- Fiction 8. Ethiopia -- History -- 1889-1974 -- Fiction
ISBN 142318310X; 9781423183105
LC 2014044446

In this book, by Elizabeth Wein, "Emilia and Teo's lives changed in a fiery, terrifying instant when a bird strike brought down the plane their stunt pilot mothers were flying. Teo's mother died immediately, but Em's survived, determined to raise Teo according to his late mother's wishes. . . . But in 1930s America, a white woman raising a black adoptive son alongside a white daughter is too often seen as a threat." (Publisher's note)

"The intellectual, psychological, and emotional substance of this story is formidable, and Wein makes it all approachable and engaging." Horn Book

★ The **pearl** thief; by Elizabeth Wein. Hyperion 2017 325 p. map (hardcover) $18.99
Grades: 8 9 10 11 **Fic**

1. Friendship -- Fiction 2. Prejudices -- Fiction 3. Mystery and detective stories 4. Scotland -- History -- 20th century -- Fiction 5. Scottish Travellers (Nomadic people) -- Fiction
ISBN 9781484719510; 1484717163; 9781484717165
LC 2016041527

Prequel to: Code name Verity (2012)

In this novel, by Elizabeth Wein, "fifteen-year-old Julia Beaufort-Stuart. . . . begins to realize that her injury might not have been an accident. One of her family's employees . . . disappeared on the . . . day she landed in the hospital. . . . She befriends Euan McEwen, . . . [a] Scottish Traveller. . . . As Julie grows closer to this family, she witnesses . . . some of the prejudices they've grown used to . . . and finds herself exploring . . . new experiences. . . ." (Publisher's note)

"A finely crafted book that brings one girl's coming-of-age story to life, especially poignant for those who already know her fate." Booklist

Includes bibliographical references.

Weissman, Elissa Brent

The **short** seller; Elissa Brent Weissman. 1st ed. Atheneum Books for Young Readers 2013 256 p. (hardcover) $15.99
Grades: 3 4 5 6 **Fic**

1. Girls -- Fiction 2. Stocks -- Fiction 3. Friendship -- Fiction 4. Best friends -- Fiction 5. Mononucleosis -- Fiction 6. Electronic trading of securities -- Fiction
ISBN 1442452552; 9781442452558
LC 2012018632

In this middle-grade novel, by Elissa Brent Weissman, "a twelve-year-old takes on the stock market. . . . It all starts when seventh grader Lindy Sachs is granted $100 and access to her father's online trading account. . . . With trading talent and access to her parents' savings, the opportunity to make some real dough is too tempting to pass up. In fact, given how well Lindy's stocks are doing, it would be a disservice to not invest it all. . . . Right?" (Publisher's note)

Welch, Sheila Kelly

Waiting to forget. Namelos 2011 170p $18.95
Grades: 5 6 7 8 **Fic**

1. Siblings -- Fiction 2. Foster home care -- Fiction
ISBN 978-1-60898-114-4; 1-60898-114-2

T.J. and his sister, Angela, learn how to move forward and be happy while in foster care.

"T.J.'s authentic voice and the multilayered presentation of his memories, shifting between the waiting room and his past, make for a poignant, realistic tale of child-survivors." Kirkus

Welford, Ross

Time traveling with a hamster; Ross Welford. Schwartz & Wade Books 2016 432 p. (ebook) $50.97; (hardcover) $16.99
Grades: 5 6 7 8 **Fic**

1. Death -- Fiction 2. Hamsters -- Fiction 3. Time travel -- Fiction 4. Fathers and sons -- Fiction
ISBN 9780399551512; 0399551492; 9780399551505; 9780399551499
LC 2015036913

In this children's novel by Ross Welford, "on his twelfth birthday, Al Chaudhury receives a letter from his dead father . . . [that] outlines a mission: travel back to 1984 and prevent the go-kart accident that will eventually take his father's life. But as Al soon discovers, whizzing back thirty years requires not only imagination and courage, but also lying to your mom, stealing a moped, and . . . keeping your pet hamster safe." (Publisher's note)

"Welford addresses all the complications of time travel, including the impossibility of being in two places at the same time and the threat of obliterating one's present self. Nods to classic time travel stories will delight some readers; those merely looking for a page-turning adventure will find that and more." Kirkus

Wells, Ken

Rascal; a dog and his boy. illustrations by Christian Slade. Alfred A. Knopf 2010 201p il $16.99; lib bdg $19.99
Grades: 4 5 6 7 **Fic**

1. Dogs -- Fiction 2. Louisiana -- Fiction
ISBN 978-0-375-86652-4; 0-375-86652-3; 978-0-375-96652-1 lib bdg; 0-375-96652-8 lib bdg
LC 2009-37606

Rascal may be the happiest beagle ever to live. He used to live on Voclain's Farm, but now he lives with his very own boy, Meely. Together they explore the Louisiana bayou. But when Meely gets stuck on a rotting bridge deep in the bayou, it's up to Rascal to save his boy from danger.

"This is a cracking good animal story of classic pedigree. . . . Characterizations of both humans and animals are sharp and distinct. . . . [The] narration sings with the same lively Cajun-flavored spice as the dialogue, and it's an easy dialect to get the hang of." Bull Cent Child Books

Wells, Robison E.

Variant. HarperTeen 2011 376p $17.99
Grades: 7 8 9 10 **Fic**

1. School stories 2. Science fiction
ISBN 978-0-06-202608-8; 0-06-202608-9
LC 2010042661

After years in foster homes, seventeen-year-old Benson Fisher applies to New Mexico's Maxfield Academy in hopes of securing a brighter future, but instead he finds that the school is a prison and no one is what he or she seems.

"Hard to put down from the very first page, this fast-paced novel with Stepford overtones answers only some of the questions it poses, holding some of the most tantalizing open for the next installment in a series that is anything but ordinary." Kirkus

Another title in this series is:
Feedback (2012)

Wells, Rosemary

My Havana; [by] Rosemary Wells with Secundino Fernandez; illustrated by Peter Ferguson. Candlewick Press 2010 65p il $17.99

Grades: 4 5 6 7 **Fic**

1. Architects 2. Cuba -- Fiction 3. Dictators -- Fiction 4. Family life -- Fiction

ISBN 0-7636-4305-X; 978-0-7636-4305-8

LC 2009-12053

This novel relates events in the childhood of architect Secundino Fernandez, who left Havana, Cuba, with his parents, first to spend a year in Spain, and later to move to New York City. "Grades four to seven." (Bull Cent Child Books)

"Wells has chosen anecdotes wisely, and Ferguson's illustrations are atmospheric, capturing Dino's childlike enthusiasm and longing." Kirkus

Red moon at Sharpsburg. Viking 2007 236p $16.99; pa $7.99

Grades: 6 7 8 9 10 **Fic**

1. United States -- History -- 1861-1865, Civil War -- Fiction

ISBN 0-670-03638-2; 978-0-670-03638-7; 0-14-241205-8 pa; 978-0-14-241205-3 pa

As the Civil War breaks out, India, a young Southern girl, summons her sharp intelligence and the courage she didn't know she had to survive the war that threatens to destroy her family, her Virginia home and the only life she has ever known.

"This powerful novel is unflinching in its depiction of war and the devastation it causes, yet shows the resilience and hope that can follow such a tragedy. India is a memorable, thoroughly believable character." SLJ

Welsh, M. L.

★ **Mistress** of the Storm; a Verity Gallant tale. David Fickling Books 2011 318p $16.99; lib bdg $19.99

Grades: 5 6 7 8 **Fic**

1. Fantasy fiction 2. Sailing -- Fiction 3. Witches -- Fiction 4. Friendship -- Fiction 5. Family life -- Fiction 6. Books and reading -- Fiction

ISBN 978-0-385-75244-2; 0-385-75244-X; 978-0-385-75245-9 lib bdg; 0-385-75245-8 lib bdg

LC 2010018721

First published in the United Kingdom

After a stranger gives an ancient book to unpopular, twelve-year-old Verity Gallant, she and her new-found friends, Henry and Martha, uncover secrets stirring in the harbor town of Wellow and use them to face a powerful, vengeful witch.

"Welsh's prose is lovely, her characters are well-drawn, and the atmosphere of the town is palpable. In creating a place in the world where a story read aloud can become true, Welsh offers a benediction of sorts to readers, that 'every child who is alone or out of place will find the friends they need, and the love they deserve.'" Publ Wkly

Wendig, Chuck

Under the Empyrean Sky. Amazon Childrens Pub 2013 368 p. $17.99

Grades: 7 8 9 10 **Fic**

1. Science fiction 2. Apocalyptic fiction 3. Young adult literature

ISBN 1477817204; 9781477817209

In this first book in Chuck Wendig's Heartland Trilogy, "the haves hover above ruined Earth in luxurious flotillas and the have-nots toil below in the Heartland, [are] told whom to marry and what to grow. . . . When Cael and his friends discover a trail of precious, prohibited vegetables growing deep in the corn, they stumble on a secret that may save them—or get them killed." (Kirkus Reviews)

Other titles in this series are:
Blightborn (2014)
The Harvest (2015)

Werlin, Nancy

Double helix. Dial Books 2004 252p hardcover o.p. pa $6.99

Grades: 7 8 9 10 **Fic**

1. Science fiction 2. Bioethics -- Fiction 3. Genetic engineering -- Fiction

ISBN 0-8037-2606-6; 0-14-240327-X pa

LC 2003-12269

Eighteen-year-old Eli discovers a shocking secret about his life and his family while working for a Nobel Prize–winning scientist whose specialty is genetic engineering.

"Werlin clearly and dramatically raises fundamental bioethical issues for teens to ponder. She also creates a riveting story with sharply etched characters and complex relationships that will stick with readers long after the book is closed." SLJ

Impossible; a novel. Dial Books 2008 376p $17.99

Grades: 7 8 9 10 **Fic**

1. Magic -- Fiction 3. Pregnancy -- Fiction 4. Teenage mothers -- Fiction

ISBN 978-0-8037-3002-1; 0-8037-3002-0

LC 2008-06633

When seventeen-year-old Lucy discovers her family is under an ancient curse by an evil Elfin Knight, she realizes to break the curse she must perform three impossible tasks before her daughter is born in order to save them both.

"Werlin earns high marks for the tale's graceful interplay between wild magic and contemporary reality." Booklist

Other titles in this series are:
Unthinkable (2013)
Extraordinary (2010)

The **rules** of survival. Dial Books 2006 259p $16.99

Grades: 8 9 10 11 12 **Fic**

1. Siblings -- Fiction 2. Child abuse -- Fiction

ISBN 0-8037-3001-2

LC 2006-1675

Seventeen-year-old Matthew recounts his attempts, starting at a young age, to free himself and his sisters from the grip of their emotionally and physically abusive mother.

The author "tackles the topic of child abuse with grace and insight. . . . Teens will empathize with these siblings and the secrets they keep in this psychological horror story." SLJ

West, Jacqueline

The **collectors**; Jacqueline West. Greenwillow Books 2018 376 p. (hardback) $16.99

Grades: 4 5 6 7 **Fic**

1. Magic -- Fiction 2. Wishes -- Fiction 3. Hearing impaired -- Fiction 4. Collectors and collecting -- Fiction 5. People with disabilities -- Fiction

ISBN 9780062691699

LC 2018027798

Schneider Family Book Award Honor Book: Middle Grades (2019)

"Van has always been an outsider. Most people don't notice him. But he notices them. And he notices the small trinkets they drop, or lose, or throw away--that's why his collection is full of treasures. Then one day, Van notices a girl stealing pennies from a fountain, and everything changes. He follows the girl, Pebble, and uncovers an underground world full of wishes and the people who collect them." (Publisher's note)

West, Kasie

Pivot point; Kasie West. HarperTeen 2013 352 p. (hardback) $17.99

Grades: 7 8 9 10 **Fic**

1. Romance fiction 2. Divorce -- Fiction 3. Paranormal fiction 4. Love -- Fiction 5. Schools -- Fiction 6. High schools -- Fiction 7. Choice (Psychology) -- Fiction

ISBN 0062117378; 9780062117373

LC 2012019089

This book tells the story of Addie Coleman, who has the ability to see into the future and choose between the better of two options. "She is a Searcher living in the Compound, the southern Texas home of the most gifted individuals in the county. When her parents decide to divorce, with her mother staying in the Compound, and her father opting to live in the normal world, she decides to use her ability to help her chose with whom to live." (Booklist)

Followed by Split second (2014)

Westerfeld, Scott

Behemoth; written by Scott Westerfeld; illustrated by Keith Thompson. Simon Pulse 2010 485p il

Grades: 7 8 9 10 **Fic**

1. War stories 2. Science fiction 3. Princes -- Fiction 4. Mythical animals -- Fiction 5. Genetic engineering -- Fiction

ISBN 1-4169-7175-0; 978-1-4169-7175-7

LC 2010-9755

Sequel to: Leviathan (2009)

Continues the story of Austrian Prince Alek who, in an alternate 1914 Europe, eludes the Germans by traveling in the Leviathan to Constantinople, where he faces a whole new kind of genetically-engineered warships.

"This exciting and inventive tale of military conflict and wildly reimagined history should captivate a wide range of readers. Thompson's evocative and detailed spot art (as well as the luridly gorgeous endpapers) only sweetens the deal." Publ Wkly

Followed by: Goliath (2011)

Extras. Simon Pulse 2011 399p $17.99; pa $9.99

Grades: 7 8 9 10 **Fic**

1. Science fiction

ISBN 978-1-4424-3007-5; 978-1-4424-1978-0 pa

Sequel to Specials (2006)

First published 2007

Aya is "an 'extra' (face rank stuck in the mid-400,000s) in a city run on a 'reputation economy.' If Aya can win fame as a 'kicker,' reporting with her trusty hovercam on a story that captures the city's imagination, her face rank will soar. . . . Westerfeld shows he has a finger on the pulse of our reputation economy, alchemizing the cult of celebrity, advertising's constant competition for consumer attention." Horn Book

Goliath; written by Scott Westerfeld; illustrated by Keith Thompson. Simon Pulse 2011 543p il $19.99

Grades: 7 8 9 10 **Fic**

1. War stories 2. Science fiction 3. Princes -- Fiction 4. Mythical animals -- Fiction 5. Genetic engineering -- Fiction

ISBN 978-1-4169-7177-1; 1-4169-7177-7

LC 2011015892

Sequel to: Behemoth (2010)

Alek and Deryn encounter obstacles on the last leg of their round-the-world quest to end World War I, reclaim Alek's throne as prince of Austria, and finally fall in love.

"The alternative-history steampunk extravaganza that began with Leviathan (2009) ends with this third volume, and it does not disappoint. Westerfeld propels the story to a satisfying close. . . . Once again, Thompson's evocative art enlivens the narrative." Booklist

★ **Leviathan**; written by Scott Westerfeld; illustrated by Keith Thompson. Simon Pulse 2009 440p il map $19.99; pa $9.99

Grades: 7 8 9 10 **Fic**

1. War stories 2. Science fiction 3. Princes -- Fiction 5. Mythical animals -- Fiction 6. Genetic engineering -- Fiction

ISBN 978-1-4169-7173-3; 1-4169-7173-4; 978-1-4169-7174-0 pa; 1-4169-7174-2 pa

LC 2009-881

In this novel, by Scott Westerfeld, "it is the cusp of World War I. The Austro-Hungarians and Germans have their Clankers, steam-driven iron machines loaded with guns and ammunition. The British Darwinists employ genetically fabricated animals as their weaponry. Their Leviathan is a whale airship, and the most masterful beast in the British fleet. Aleksandar Ferdinand, a Clanker, and Deryn Sharp, a Darwinist, are on opposite sides of the war. But their paths cross in the most unexpected way." (Publisher's note)

"The protagonists' stories are equally gripping and keep the story moving, and Thompson's detail-rich panels bring Westerfeld's unusual creations to life." Publ Wkly

Other titles in this series are:

Behemoth (2010)

Goliath (2011)

★ **Pretties**. Simon Pulse 2011 348p $17.99; pa $9.99

Grades: 7 8 9 10 **Fic**

1. Science fiction

ISBN 978-1-4169-3639-8; 978-1-4424-1980-3 pa

Sequel to Uglies

First published 2005

Tally's transformation to perfect and popular including her totally hot boyfriend is everything she always wanted. But beneath the fun and freedom something is wrong and now Tally has to fight for her life because what she knows has put her in danger with the authorities.

"Riveting and compulsively readable, this action-packed sequel does not disappoint." Booklist

Followed by Specials

So yesterday; a novel. Razorbill 2004 225p $16.99; pa $7.99

Grades: 7 8 9 10 **Fic**

1. Mystery fiction 2. Missing persons -- Fiction 4. New York (N.Y.) -- Fiction

ISBN 1-59514-000-X; 1-59514-032-8 pa

LC 2004-2302

Hunter Braque, a New York City teenager who is paid by corporations to spot what is "cool," combines his analytical skills with girlfriend Jen's creative talents to find a missing person and thwart a conspiracy directed at the heart of consumer culture

"This hip, fascinating thriller aggressively questions consumer culture. . . . Teens will inhale this wholly entertaining, thought-provoking look at a system fueled by their purchasing power. " Booklist

Specials. Simon Pulse 2011 350p $17.99; pa $9.99
Grades: 7 8 9 10 **Fic**

1. Science fiction 2. Young adult literature
ISBN 978-1-4424-3008-2; 978-1-4424-1979-7 pa
Sequel to Pretties
First published 2006

Tally has been transformed from a repellent ugly to supermodel pretty. Now she's a super-amped fighting machine. Her mission is to keep the uglies down and the pretties stupid. But Tally's never been good at playing by the rules.

"Readers who enjoyed Uglies and Pretties . . . will not want to miss Specials. . . . Westerfeld's themes include vanity, environmental conservation, Utopian idealism, fascism, violence, and love." SLJ

Followed by Extras

★ **Uglies**; Scott Westerfeld. Simon Pulse 2011 406 p. (paperback) $9.99; (hardcover) $17.99
Grades: 7 8 9 10 **Fic**

1. Science fiction 2. Friendship -- Fiction 3. Beauty, Personal -- Fiction
ISBN 9781442419810; 9781416936381
LC 2011534116

Originally published 2005

"Fifteen-year-old Tally's eerily harmonious, postapocalyptic society gives extreme makeovers to teens on their sixteenth birthdays. . . . When a top-secret agency threatens to leave Tally ugly forever unless she spies on runaway teens, she agrees to infiltrate the Smoke, a shadowy colony of refugees from the 'tyranny of physical perfection.'" Booklist

Other titles in this series are:
Pretties (2005)
Specials (2006)
Extras (2007)

Weston, Carol

Speed of life; Carol Weston. Sourcebooks Jabberwocky 2017 329 p. (alk. paper) $16.99
Grades: 7 8 9 10 **Fic**

1. Advice columns 2. Grief -- Fiction 3. New York (N.Y.) -- Fiction 4. Advice columnists -- Fiction 5. Spanish Americans -- Fiction
ISBN 1492654493; 9781492654490
LC 2016051104

In this book, by Carol Weston, "Sofia lost her mother eight months ago, and her friends were 100% there for her. Now it's a new year and they're ready for Sofia to move on. Problem is, Sofia can't bounce back, can't recharge like a cellphone. She decides to write Dear Kate, an advice columnist for Fifteen Magazine, and is surprised to receive a fast reply. Soon the two are exchanging emails, and Sofia opens up and spills all." (Publisher's note)

Weston, Robert Paul

Zorgamazoo. Razorbill 2008 281p il $15.99
Grades: 4 5 6 7 **Fic**

1. Novels in verse 2. Adventure fiction 3. Imagination -- Fiction
ISBN 978-1-59514-199-6; 1-59514-199-5
LC 2007-51682

Imaginative and adventurous Katrina eludes her maniacal guardian to help Morty, a member of a vanishing breed of zorgles, with his quest to uncover the fate of the fabled zorgles of Zorgmazoo as well as of other creatures that seem to have disappeared from the earth.

"This book is a natural descendant to the works of Dr. Seuss and Roald Dahl." Booklist

Westrick, A. B.

Brotherhood; Anne Westrick. Viking Juvenile 2013 368 p. (hardback) $17.99
Grades: 5 6 7 8 9 **Fic**

1. Historical fiction 2. Ku Klux Klan -- Fiction 3. Prejudices -- Fiction 4. Race relations -- Fiction 5. Family life -- Virginia -- Fiction 6. Reconstruction (U.S. history, 1865-1877) -- Fiction 7. Richmond (Va.) -- History -- 19th century -- Fiction
ISBN 0670014397; 9780670014392
LC 2013008272

In this historical novel, 14-year-old Shad Weaver's "life is full of secrets. Desperate to learn to read, he begins attending a school for African-Americans. . . . He is very careful not to be seen, especially by any members of the other secret group to which he belongs, the Klan. Shad is deeply ambivalent about the brotherhood, appreciating it for the camaraderie it fosters but becoming increasingly uncomfortable with the violence it perpetuates." He must make a stand when his teacher is murdered. (Kirkus Reviews)

Weyr, Garret

The **language** of spells; Garret Weyr ; illustrated by Katie Harnett. Chronicle Books 2018 299 p. (alk. paper) $16.99
Grades: 4 5 6 7 **Fic**

1. Magic -- Fiction 2. Austria -- Fiction 3. Dragons -- Fiction 4. Vienna (Austria) -- Fiction 5. Mystery and detective stories 6. Adventure and adventurers -- Fiction
ISBN 9781452159584
LC 2017027778

In this book, by Garret Weyr, illustrated by Katie Harnett, "Grisha is a dragon in a world that's forgotten how to see him. Maggie is a unusual child who thinks she's perfectly ordinary. They're an unlikely duo--but magic, like friendship, is funny. Sometimes it chooses those who might not look so likely. And magic has chosen Grisha and Maggie to solve the darkest mystery in Vienna." (Publisher's note)

Weyr builds the fascinating story slowly, and her writing will appeal to children who enjoy the magisterial, fairy-tale quality. Its underlying focus—on things of importance that are hidden away when they disturb others—has contemporary resonance. --Booklist

Whelan, Gloria

Chu Ju's house. HarperCollins 2004 227p $15.99; lib bdg $16.89
Grades: 5 6 7 8 **Fic**

1. China -- Fiction 2. Sex role -- Fiction 3. Runaway teenagers -- Fiction
ISBN 0-06-050724-1; 0-06-050725-X lib bdg
LC 2003-6979

In order to save her baby sister, fourteen-year-old Chu Ju leaves her rural home in modern China and earns food and shelter by working on a sampan, tending silk worms, and planting rice seedlings, while wondering if she will ever see her family again.

"Whelan tells a compelling adventure story, filled with rich cultural detail, about a smart, likable teenage girl who overcomes society's gender restrictions." Booklist

Goodbye, Vietnam. Knopf 1992 135p hardcover o.p. pa $5.50

Grades: 4 5 6 7 Fic

1. Refugees -- Fiction 2. Vietnamese -- Fiction
ISBN 0-679-82376-X; 0-679-92263-6 pa

LC 91-3660

Thirteen-year-old Mai and her family embark on a dangerous sea voyage from Vietnam to Hong Kong to escape the unpredictable and often brutal Vietnamese government

"While the book has the suspense and appeal of any good escape story, Whelan is neither melodramatic nor sentimental, and the sometimes horrific details of the scary voyage are plain but understated." Bull Cent Child Books

★ **Homeless** bird. HarperCollins Pubs. 2000 216p hardcover o.p. pa $5.99

Grades: 6 7 8 9 10 Fic

1. India -- Fiction 2. Women -- India -- Fiction
ISBN 0-06-028454-4; 0-06-440819-1 pa

LC 99-33241

When thirteen-year-old Koly enters into an ill-fated arranged marriage, she must either suffer a destiny dictated by India's tradition or find the courage to oppose it.

"This beautifully told, inspiring story takes readers on a fascinating journey through modern India and the universal intricacies of a young woman's heart." Booklist

Small acts of amazing courage. Simon & Schuster Books for Young Readers 2011 217p $15.99

Grades: 6 7 8 9 10 Fic

1. Aunts -- Fiction 2. Bereavement -- Fiction 3. Great Britain -- Fiction 4. London (England) -- Fiction 5. India -- History -- 1765-1947, British occupation -- Fiction
ISBN 978-1-4424-0931-6; 1-4424-0931-2

LC 2010-13164

In 1919, independent-minded fifteen-year-old Rosalind lives in India with her English parents, and when they fear she has fallen in with some rebellious types who believe in Indian self-government, she is sent "home" to London, where she has never been before and where her older brother died, to stay with her two aunts.

"Whelan balances the facts with distinctive, sometimes comical characterizations and vibrant, original sensory descriptions. . . . Whelan's vibrant, episodic story explores the tension between doing what's right, rather than what's expected, and the infinite complexities of colonialism." Booklist

White, Andrea

Surviving Antarctica; reality TV 2083. HarperCollins Publishers 2005 327p hardcover o.p. pa $6.99

Grades: 7 8 9 10 Fic

1. Science fiction 2. Antarctica -- Fiction
ISBN 0-06-055454-1; 0-06-055456-8 pa

LC 2004-6249

In the year 2083, five fourteen-year-olds who were deprived by chance of the opportunity to continue their educations reenact Scott's 1910-1913 expedition to the South Pole as contestants on a reality television show, secretly aided by a Department of Entertainment employee

"A real page-turner, this novel will give readers pause as they ponder the ethics of teens risking their lives in adult-contrived situations for the entertainment of the masses." Booklist

Window boy. Bright Sky Press 2008 255p $17.95

Grades: 6 7 8 9 Fic

1. Statesmen 2. Historians 3. School stories 4. Prime ministers 5. Memoirists 6. Cabinet members 7. Members of Parliament 8. Cerebral palsy -- Fiction 9. Imaginary playmates -- Fiction 10. Nobel laureates for literature
ISBN 978-1-933979-14-4; 1-933979-14-3

LC 2008-492

After his mother finally convinces the principal of Greenfield Junior High to admit him, twelve-year-old Sam arrives for his first day of school, along with his imaginary friend Winston Churchill, who encourages him to persevere with his cerebral palsy.

"Strong character development is combined with an accurate representation of the lack of educational opportunities for those who were physically and mentally disabled pre-IDEA." SLJ

White, Ellen Emerson

White House autumn. Feiwel and Friends 2008 236p pa $9.99

Grades: 7 8 9 10 Fic

1. School stories 2. Politics -- Fiction 3. Presidents -- Fiction 4. Family life -- Fiction 5. Washington (D.C.) -- Fiction
ISBN 0-312-37489-5; 978-0-312-37489-1

LC 2008-6883

First published 1985

Seventeen-year-old Meg's surging emotions after her mother, the United States President, is shot, threaten her relationship with boyfriend Josh and best friend Beth, but she strives to maintain control to help her father and younger brothers.

"Apart from its novelistic merits, the book prompts thought on the burdens of public office, the need for character in the elect and their families." Publ Wkly

White, J. A.

Nightbooks; J. A. White ; [edited by] Katherine Tegen. Katherine Tegen Books 2018 304 p. (hardcover) $16.99

Grades: 4 5 6 7 8 Fic

1. Witches -- fiction 2. Storytelling -- fiction
ISBN 9780062560087

LC 2017954128

In this book, by J. A. White, "a boy is imprisoned by a witch and must tell her a new scary story each night to stay alive. . . . Alex's . . . tales are the only thing keeping the witch Natacha happy, but soon he'll run out of pages to read from and be trapped forever. He's loved scary stories . . . and he knows most don't have a happily ever after. Now that Alex is trapped in a true . . . tale, he's desperate for a different ending--and a way out of this twisted place." (Publisher's note)

The **Thickety**; a path begins. J.A. White. Katherine Tegen Books, an imprint of HarperCollinsPublishers 2014 496 p. (hardcover bdg.) $16.99

Grades: 5 6 7 8 Fic

1. Fantasy fiction 2. Magic -- Fiction 3. Witches -- Fiction
ISBN 0062257242; 9780062257246

LC 2013021509

This book, by J.A. White, "is the thrilling start of a new middle-grade fantasy series about a girl, a mysterious forest, and a book of untold magical powers. Kara and her brother, Taff, are shunned by their village because their mother was a witch. The villagers believe nothing is more evil than magic, except for what lurks in the nearby Thickety. But when Kara enters the forbidden forest, she discovers a strange book, a grimoire that might have belonged to her mother." (Publisher's note)

"When Kara was just a child, she was accused of witchcraft and forced to watch her mother executed for the same crime. Ever after, she and her family have lived in their isolated theocratic community as pariahs...White's persistent dark imagery, along with Offermann's eerie silhouette spot illustrations, adds to the overall dark atmosphere." Booklist

Other books in this series are:

The Whispering Trees (2015)

Well of Witches (2016)

The Last Spell (2017)

White, Ruth

★ **Belle** Prater's boy. Farrar, Straus & Giroux 1996 196p $17

Grades: 5 6 7 8 **Fic**

1. Cousins -- Fiction 2. Virginia -- Fiction 3. Appalachian region -- Fiction

ISBN 0-374-30668-0

LC 94-43625

A Newbery Medal honor book, 1997

"Gypsy and her cousin Woodrow become close friends after Woodrow's mother disappears. Both sixth-graders feel deserted by their parents—Gypsy discovers that her father committed suicide—and need to define themselves apart from these tragedies. White's prose evokes the coal mining region of Virginia and the emotional quality of her characters' transformations." Horn Book Guide

Another title about Belle Prater is:

The search for Belle Prater (2005)

The **treasure** of Way Down Deep; Ruth White. Margaret Ferguson Books 2013 176 p. (hardcover) $16.99

Grades: 5 6 7 8 **Fic**

1. Halloween -- Fiction 2. Buried treasure -- Fiction 3. Dogs -- Fiction 4. Orphans -- Fiction 5. Foundlings -- Fiction 6. Boardinghouses -- Fiction 7. Community life -- West Virginia -- Fiction 8. West Virginia -- History -- 1951- -- Fiction

ISBN 0374380678; 9780374377472; 9780374380670

LC 2012021665

Sequel to: Way Down Deep

Parents' Choice: Silver Medal Fiction (2013)

In this book by Ruth White, "Ruby loves her life, but things start turning when her pet goat dies and Miss Arbutus feels an ill wind blowing into town. Then the local mines start closing, and everyone in Way Down Deep feels the pinch. Can Ruby help save the town? Will the special button Rita gave her as a gift be part of the solution? And can the town come together when a treasure appears?" (Booklist)

Way Down Deep. Farrar, Straus and Giroux 2007 197p $16

Grades: 5 6 7 8 **Fic**

1. Orphans -- Fiction 2. West Virginia -- Fiction

ISBN 0-374-38251-4; 978-0-374-38251-3

LC 2006-46324

In the West Virginia town of Way Down Deep in the 1950s, a foundling called Ruby June is happily living with Miss Arbutus at the local boarding house when suddenly, after the arrival of a family of outsiders, the mystery of Ruby's past begins to unravel.

This is "a story as tender as a breeze and as sharp as a tack. . . . At the heart of the story are profound questions that readers will enjoy puzzling out." Booklist

Followed by: The treasure of the way down deep (2013)

White, T. H.

★ The **once** and future king. Putnam 1958 677p $25.95

Grades: 8 9 10 11 12 Adult **Fic**

1. Fantasy fiction 2. Kings 3. Knights and knighthood -- Fiction 4. Great Britain -- History -- 0-1066 -- Fiction

ISBN 0-399-10597-2

LC 58-10760

"White's contemporary retelling of Malory's Le Morte d'Arthur is both romantic and exciting." Shapiro. Fic for Youth. 3d edition

Whitley, David

The **children** of the lost. Roaring Brook Press 2011 357p $16.99

Grades: 7 8 9 10 **Fic**

1. Fantasy fiction

ISBN 978-1-59643-614-5; 1-59643-614-X

LC 2010-28112

Sequel to: Midnight charter (2009)

Banished from Agora, the ancient city-state where absolutely everything must be bartered, Mark and Lily are happy to find the apparently perfect land of Giseth except that the inhabitants seem fearful, something strange lurks in the surrounding forest, and a mysterious woman keeps appearing in their dreams urging them to find the children of the lost.

This "explores tantalizing new territory and solidifies the Agora Trilogy as one of the more literary ambitious and complex fantasies going." Booklist

Whitman, Emily

Wildwing. Greenwillow Books 2010 359p $16.99

Grades: 7 8 9 10 **Fic**

1. Falcons -- Fiction 2. Time travel -- Fiction 3. Social classes -- Fiction 4. Great Britain -- History -- 1066-1154, Norman period -- Fiction

ISBN 978-0-06-172452-7; 0-06-172452-1

LC 2009-44189

In 1913 London, fifteen-year-old Addy is a lowly servant, but when she gets inside an elevator car in her employer's study, she is suddenly transported to a castle in 1240 and discovers that she is mistaken for the lord's intended bride.

"Whitman populates both of her worlds with vivid, believable characters. . . . This historical novel with a time-travel twist of sci-fi will find an avid readership." SLJ

Whittemore, Jo

Odd girl in. Simon & Schuster 2011 234p pa $6.99

Grades: 4 5 6 **Fic**

1. School stories 2. Siblings -- Fiction

ISBN 978-1-4424-1284-2; 1-4424-1284-4

"Spunky 12-year-old Alex doesn't really want friends or a social life. . . . She hates girly giggling parties and doesn't see any other girls in her middle school that she'd want to have as a friend, so she just concentrates on following in the footsteps of her prankster older twin brothers. . . . Alex's absent mother provides an element of drama in this otherwise witty, laugh-out-loud romp. Whittemore handles not only the comedy but deftly portrays Alex's and her brothers' advancement into a more mature state of mind. It should keep middle-schoolers laughing from start to finish." Kirkus

Wiechman, Kathy Cannon

Like a river; a civil war novel. Kathy Cannon Wiechman. Calkins Creek 2015 336 p. illustrations $17.95

Grades: 5 6 7 8 **Fic**

1. Historical fiction 2. United States -- History -- 1861-1865, Civil War -- Fiction

ISBN 1629792098; 9781629792095

LC 2014945289

In this novel, by Kathy Cannon Wiechman, "Leander and Polly are two teenage Union soldiers who carry deep, dangerous secrets. Leander is underage when he enlists and Polly follows her father into war disguised as his son. . . . Polly mourns the death of her father, endures Andersonville Prison, and narrowly escapes the Sultana steamboat disaster. As the lives of these . . . soldiers intersect, each . . . learns about the importance of loyalty, family, and love." (Publisher's note)

"Three years have passed since the beginning of the Civil War, when two underage teens, West Virginian Paul Settles and Ohioan Leander Jordan, both with secrets to guard, enlist in the Union Army. Their paths cross in a military hospital, where their mysteries begin to unravel, but the plot takes them in separate directions...A truly excellent first purchase for all fans of historical fiction who enjoy a hint of romance." SLJ

Includes bibliographical references (pages 335-336).

Wiggins, Bethany

Stung; Bethany Wiggins. Walker & Company 2013 304 p. (hardcover) $17.99

Grades: 7 8 9 10 11 12 **Fic**

1. Science fiction 2. Epidemics -- Fiction 3. Survival -- Fiction

ISBN 0802734189; 9780802734181

LC 2012027183

In this novel, by Bethany Wiggins, "a worldwide pandemic occurred and the government tried to bio-engineer a cure. Only the solution was deadlier than the original problem-the vaccination turned people into ferocious, deadly beasts who were branded as a warning to un-vaccinated survivors. Key people needed to rebuild society are protected from disease and beasts inside a fortress-like wall. But Fiona has awakened branded, alone-and on the wrong side of the wall." (Publisher's note)

"Wiggins. . . muses on the dangers of science and medicine and deftly maps out the chain of events that has led to catastrophe, creating a violent world vastly different from ours but still recognizable. With a stirring conclusion and space for a sequel, it's an altogether captivating story." Kirkus

Followed by: Cured (2014)

Wiles, Deborah

★ The **Aurora** County All-Stars. Harcourt 2007 242p il $16; pa $5.99

Grades: 4 5 6 **Fic**

1. Death -- Fiction 2. Baseball -- Fiction 3. Mississippi -- Fiction 4. Race relations -- Fiction

ISBN 978-0-15-206068-8; 0-15-206068-5; 978-0-15-206626-0 pa; 0-15-206626-8 pa

LC 2006-102551

In a small Mississippi town, after the death of the old man to whom twelve-year-old star pitcher House Jackson has been secretly reading for a year, House uncovers secrets about the man and the history of baseball in Aurora County.

"Quotations from Walt Whitman's poetry, baseball players and Aurora County news dispatches pepper the story and add color. . . . A home run for Wiles." Publ Wkly

★ **Countdown**. Scholastic 2010 377p il (The sixties trilogy) $17.99

Grades: 5 6 7 8 **Fic**

1. Cold war -- Fiction 2. Family life -- Fiction 3. Cuban Missile Crisis, 1962 -- Fiction

ISBN 978-0-545-10605-4; 0-545-10605-2

It's 1962, and it seems everyone is living in fear. Twelve-year-old Franny Chapman lives with her family in Washington, DC, during the days surrounding the Cuban Missile Crisis. Amidst the pervasive threat of nuclear war, Franny must face the tension between herself and her younger brother, figure out where she fits in with her family, and look beyond outward appearances.

"Wiles skillfully keeps many balls in the air, giving readers a story that appeals across the decades as well as offering enticing paths into the history." Booklist

Other titles in this series are:

Revolution (2014)

Anthem (2019)

★ **Revolution**; Deborah Wiles. First edition Scholastic 2014 495 p. illustrations, map (The sixties trilogy) $19.99

Grades: 5 6 7 8 **Fic**

1. Family life -- Fiction 2. Nineteen sixties -- Fiction 3. United States -- History -- Fiction 4. African Americans -- Civil rights -- Fiction

ISBN 0545106079; 9780545106078

LC 2014935954

National Book Award Shortlist: Young People's Literature (2014)

In this book, by Deborah Wiles, "it's 1964, and Sunny's town is being invaded. Or at least that's what the adults of Greenwood, Mississippi are saying. All Sunny knows is that people from up north are coming to help people register to vote. They're calling it Freedom Summer. Meanwhile, Sunny can't help but feel like her house is being invaded, too. She has a new stepmother, a new brother, and a new sister crowding her life, giving her little room to breathe." (Publisher's note)

"Wiles does an excellent job of entwining the two plot strands and seamlessly integrating her exhaustive research, which is detailed at the book's conclusion. . . . As in Countdown, the outstanding period artwork, photographs, snippets of sayings, and songs interspersed throughout bring a troubled time close." Booklist

Wilhelm, Doug

The **revealers**. Farrar, Straus & Giroux 2003 207p $16

Grades: 4 5 6 7 **Fic**

1. School stories 2. Internet -- Fiction 3. Friendship -- Fiction

ISBN 0-374-36255-6

LC 2002-35321

Tired of being bullied and picked on, three seventh-grade outcasts join forces and, using scientific methods and the power of the Internet, begin to create a new atmosphere at Parkland Middle School. "Grades five to nine." (Bull Cent Child Books)

"Briskly plotted, the novel shows how bringing the stories to light transforms stereotypes into real people and provides a vehicle for others to become involved. . . . The novel is effective and will fascinate even reluctant readers." SLJ

Wilkinson, Lili

Pink. HarperTeen 2011 310p $16.99

Grades: 7 8 9 10 11 12 **Fic**

1. School stories 2. LGBT youth -- Fiction 2. Theater -- Fiction 3. Australia -- Fiction 4. Identity (Psychology) -- Fiction

ISBN 978-0-06-192653-2; 0-06-192653-1

LC 2010-9389

Sixteen-year-old Ava does not know who she is or where she belongs, but when she tries out a new personality—and sexual orientation—at a different school, her edgy girlfriend, potential boyfriend, and others are hurt by her lack of honesty.

"The novel is in turn laugh-out-loud funny, endearing, and heartbreaking as Ava repeatedly steps into teenage social land mines—with unexpected results. Because Wilkinson doesn't rely on stereotypes, the characters are well-developed, and interactions between them feel genuine." Voice Youth Advocates

Willey, Margaret

Beetle Boy; by Margaret Willey. Carolrhoda Lab 2014 208 p. hbk $17.95

Grades: 8 9 10 11 **Fic**

1. Child authors -- Fiction 2. Father-son relationship -- Fiction 3. Family problems -- Fiction 4. Emotional problems -- Fiction 5. Dating (Social customs) -- Fiction

ISBN 1467726397; 9781467726399

LC 2013036853

"When he was seven, Charlie Porter never intended to become the world's youngest published author. . . . But Charlie's story not only made his father stop crying. It made him start planning. The story became a book, and then it became school events and book festivals, and a beetle costume, and a catchphrase--'I was born to write!' . . . Beetle Boy is a novel of a broken family, the long shadow of neglect, and the light of small kindnesses." (Publisher's note)

"Willey takes readers along on Charlie's painful journey back to physical and emotional health via a meandering timeline of flashbacks, dreams and wrenching conversations, skillfully weaving together the bits and pieces of his life. Innovative use of type brings an immediacy to Charlie's struggles as he slowly looks the truth--and his brother--squarely in the face." Kirkus

Williams, Alicia D.

Genesis begins again; Alicia D. Williams. Atheneum 2019 384 p. (hardback) $17.99

Grades: 5 6 7 8 **Fic**

1. Prejudices -- Fiction 2. Self-esteem -- Fiction 3. African Americans -- Fiction 4. Family problems -- Fiction 5. Human skin color -- Fiction 6. Moving, Household -- Fiction

ISBN 9781481465809; 9781481465816

LC 2018030079

In this novel, by Alicia D. Williams, "there are ninety-six things Genesis hates about herself. She knows the exact number because she keeps a list. Like #95: Because her skin is so dark, people call her charcoal and eggplant--even her own family. And #61: Because her family is always being put out of their house, belongings laid out on the sidewalk for the world to see. When your dad is a gambling addict and loses the rent money every month, eviction is a regular occurrence." (Publisher's note)

"With its relatable and sympathetic protagonist, complex setting, and exceptional emotional range, this title is easy to recommend" (Publishers Weekly).

Williams, Carol Lynch

The **chosen** one. St. Martin's Griffin 2009 213p $16.95

Grades: 7 8 9 10 **Fic**

1. Cults -- Fiction 2. Polygamy -- Fiction 3. Family life -- Fiction

ISBN 978-0-312-55511-5; 0-312-55511-3

LC 2009-4800

In a polygamous cult in the desert, Kyra, not yet fourteen, sees being chosen to be the seventh wife of her uncle as just punishment for having read books and kissed a boy, in violation of Prophet Childs' teachings, and is torn between facing her fate and running away from all that she knows and loves.

"This book is a highly emotional, terrifying read. It is not measured or objective. Physical abuse, fear, and even murder are constants. It is a girl-in-peril story, and as such, it is impossible to put down and holds tremendous teen appeal." Voice Youth Advocates

Williams, Ismee

Water in May; Ismee Williams. Amulet Books 2017 309 p. (hardback) $17.99

Grades: 7 8 9 10 11 12 **Fic**

1. Pregnancy -- Fiction 2. Family problems -- Fiction 3. Dominican Americans -- Fiction 4. Friendship -- Fiction 5. Heart -- Abnormalities -- Fiction

ISBN 9781419725395; 9781683351344

LC 2017008518

In this book, by Ismee Williams, "fifteen-year-old Mari Pujols believes that the baby she's carrying will finally mean she'll have a family member who will love her deeply and won't ever leave her--not like her mama, . . . or her papi, . . . or her abuela. . . . But when doctors discover a potentially fatal heart defect in the fetus, Mari faces choices she never could have imagined." (Publisher's note)

"Debut author Williams creates an unforgettable young character who will make readers reconsider their assumptions about teen moms, in particular Latina teen moms." Kirkus

Williams, Kathryn

Pizza, love, and other stuff that made me famous; Kathryn Williams. Henry Holt 2012 231 p. (hc) $16.99

Grades: 7 8 9 10 **Fic**

1. Cooking -- Fiction 2. Reality television programs -- Fiction 3. Restaurants -- Fiction 4. Interpersonal relations -- Fiction 5. Competition (Psychology) -- Fiction 6. Television -- Production and direction -- Fiction

ISBN 0805092854; 9780805092851

LC 2011034053

"Sixteen-year-old Sophie Nicolaides was practically raised in the kitchen of her family's Italian-Greek restaurant, Taverna Ristorante. When her best friend, Alex, tries to persuade her to audition for a new reality show, 'Teen Test Kitchen,' Sophie is reluctant. But the prize includes a full scholarship to one of America's finest culinary schools and a summer in Napa, California, not to mention fame. Once on set, Sophie immediately finds herself in the thick of the drama -- including a secret burn book, cutthroat celebrity judges, and a very cute French chef." (Publisher's note)

Williams, Michael

Diamond boy; Michael Williams. First edition Little, Brown & Co. 2014 400 p. maps (hardcover) $18

Grades: 7 8 9 10 **Fic**

1. Blacks -- Fiction 2. Zimbabwe -- Fiction 3. Survival skills -- Fiction 4. Mines and mineral resources -- Fiction 5. Survival -- Fiction 6. Blacks -- Zimbabwe -- Fiction 7. Shona (African people) -- Fiction 8. Diamond mines and mining -- Fiction

ISBN 0316320692; 9780316320672; 9780316320696

LC 2013042071

"Patson Moyo's life is perfectly ordinary. . . . His father, a teacher, is often a little dreamy but a wonderful storyteller. . . . Patson never would have guessed that his smart, university-graduate father . . . can barely make ends meet, due to government corruption and the massive devaluation of the Zimbabwean dollar. Egged on by Patson's stepmother, Sylvia, the Moyos decide to improve their situation by traveling to Marage." (School Library Journal)

"Written in diary format, the story brings the reader into the mind and soul of a young refugee suffering in a hell created by the greed and violence of powerful adults. More than simply a good read, Diamond Boy is a multilayered, teachable novel with a variety of approaches and is highly recommended for middle and high school collections." VOYA

Williams-Garcia, Rita

★ **Gone** Crazy in Alabama; by Rita Williams-Garcia. Harpercollins Childrens Books 2015 304 p. $16.99

Grades: 4 5 6 7 8 **Fic**

1. Sisters -- Fiction 2. Family secrets -- Fiction 3. African American children -- Fiction 4. Mothers -- Fiction

ISBN 0062215876; 9780062215871

Coretta Scott King Author Award (2016)

This novel by Rita Williams-Garcia "tells the story of the Gaither sisters, who are about to learn what it's like to be fish out of water as they travel from the streets of Brooklyn to the rural South for the summer of a lifetime. . . . As Delphine hears about her family history, she uncovers the surprising truth that's been keeping the sisters apart. But when tragedy strikes, Delphine discovers that the bonds of family run deeper than she ever knew possible." (Publisher's note)

"This well-crafted depiction of a close-knit community in rural Alabama works beautifully, with language that captures its humor, sorrow and resilience. Rich in all areas, Delphine and her sisters' third outing will fully satisfy the many fans of their first two." Kirkus

★ **Jumped**. HarperTeen 2009 169p $16.99; lib bdg $17.89

Grades: 8 9 10 11 12 **Fic**

1. School stories 2. Bullies -- Fiction

ISBN 978-0-06-076091-5; 0-06-076091-5; 978-0-06-076092-2 lib bdg; 0-06-076092-3 lib bdg

LC 2008-22381

National Book Award Finalist: Young People's Literature (2009)

The lives of Leticia, Dominique, and Trina are irrevocably intertwined through the course of one day in an urban high school after Leticia overhears Dominique's plans to beat up Trina and must decide whether or not to get involved.

"In alternating chapters narrated by Leticia, Trina, and Dominique, Williams-Garcia has given her characters strong, individual voices that ring true to teenage speech, and she lets them make their choices without judgment or moralizing." SLJ

★ **Like** sisters on the homefront. Lodestar Bks. 1995 165p hardcover o.p. pa $5.99

Grades: 7 8 9 10 **Fic**

1. Family life -- Fiction 2. Teenage mothers -- Fiction 3. African Americans -- Fiction

ISBN 0-525-67465-9; 0-14-038561-4 pa

LC 95-3690

"Beautifully written, the text captures the cadence and rhythm of New York street talk and the dilemma of being poor, black, and uneducated. This is a gritty, realistic, well-told story." SLJ

★ **One** crazy summer. Amistad 2010 218p $15.99; lib bdg $16.89

Grades: 4 5 6 7 8 **Fic**

1. Poets -- Fiction 2. Mothers -- Fiction 3. Sisters -- Fiction 4. Black Panther Party -- Fiction. 5. African Americans -- Civil rights -- Fiction

ISBN 978-0-06-076088-5; 0-06-076088-5; 978-0-06-076089-2 lib bdg; 0-06-076089-3 lib bdg

LC 2009-09293

Coretta Scott King Author Award, 2011

National Book Award Finalist: Young People's Literature (2010)

A Newbery Medal honor book, 2011

In the summer of 1968, after travelling from Brooklyn to Oakland, California, to spend a month with the mother they barely know, eleven-year-old Delphine and her two younger sisters arrive to a cold welcome as they discover that their mother, a dedicated poet and printer, is resentful of the intrusion of their visit and wants them to attend a nearby Black Panther summer camp.

"Delphine's growing awareness of injustice on a personal and universal level is smoothly woven into the story in poetic language that will stimulate and move readers." Publ Wkly

Other titles in this series are:

P.S. be eleven (2013)

Gone crazy in Alabama (2015)

★ **P.S.** Be Eleven; Rita Williams-Garcia. Harpercollins Childrens Books 2013 288 p. $16.99

Grades: 4 5 6 7 8 **Fic**

1. Historical fiction -- fiction 2. African American children -- fiction

ISBN 0061938629; 9780061938627

Coretta Scott King Author Award (2014)

This book is a follow-up to Rita Williams-Garcia's Newbery Honor-winning "One Crazy Summer." Here, "Delphine and her sisters return to Brooklyn from visiting their estranged mother, Cecile, a poet . . . . Change and conflict have the Gaither household in upheaval: Pa has a new girlfriend, Uncle Darnell returns from Vietnam a damaged young man, and the sixth-grade teacher Delphine hoped to get has been replaced by a man from Zambia." (Publishers Weekly)

"Soars as a finely drawn portrait of a family in flux and as a memorable slice of a specific time in our nation's history." Booklist

Williamson, Victoria

The **fox** girl and the white gazelle; Victoria Williamson. Kelpies 2018 243 p. (paperback) $9.95

Grades: 5 6 7 8 9 **Fic**

1. Refugees -- Fiction 2. Friendship -- Fiction

ISBN 9781782504900; 9781782504917

LC 2018194355

In this book, by Victoria Williamson, "twelve-year-old refugee Reema is struggling to find her place in a new country. . . . Her Glasgwegian neighbor Caylin is lonely and lashing out. When they discover an injured fox and her cubs hiding on their estate, the girls form a wary friendship. . . . As Reema and Caylin learn to believe again, in themselves, . . . they find friendship, freedom and the discovery that home isn't a place, it's the people you love." (Publisher's note)

Wilson, Diane Lee

★ **Firehorse**. Margaret K. McElderry Books 2006 325p $16.95

Grades: 7 8 9 10 **Fic**

1. Arson -- Fiction 3. Horses -- Fiction 4. Sex role -- Fiction 5. Family life -- Fiction 6. Boston (Mass.) -- Fiction 7. Veterinary medicine -- Fiction

ISBN 1-4169-1551-6; 978-1-4169-1551-5

LC 2005-30785

Spirited fifteen-year-old horse lover Rachel Selby determines to become a veterinarian, despite the opposition of her rigid father, her proper mother, and the norms of Boston in 1872, while that city faces a serial arsonist and an epidemic spreading through its firehorse population.

"Wilson paces the story well, with tension building. . . . The novel's finest achievement, though, is the convincing depiction of family dynamics in an era when men ruled the household and and women, who had few opportunities, folded their dreams and put them away with the linens they embroidered." Booklist

Wilson, John

Written in blood. Orca Book Publishers 2010 157p (Desert legends trilogy) pa $12.95

Grades: 6 7 8 9 **Fic**

1. Fathers -- Fiction 2. West (U.S.) -- Fiction 3. Voyages and travels -- Fiction 4. Frontier and pioneer life -- Fiction

ISBN 978-1-55469-270-5 pa; 1-55469-270-9 pa

A young man's search for the father who abandoned him takes him through the wilds of the Arizona territory and northern Mexico during the 1870's and brings him in contact with an assortment of intriguing characters.

"Told in a terse, present-tense narrative, James' adventures will thrill all fans of traditional pulp-style oaters." Booklist

Other titles in this series are:

Ghost moon (2011)

Victorio's war (2012)

Wilson, Kip

White Rose; by Kip Wilson. Houghton Mifflin Harcourt 2019 358 p. (hardcover) $17.99

Grades: 7 8 9 10 11 12 **Fic**

1. World War, 1939-1945 -- Fiction 2. Germany -- History -- 1933-1945 -- Fiction 3. Novels in verse 4. White Rose (German resistance group) -- Fiction

ISBN 9781328594433

LC 2018026607

"Sophie Scholl, her brother, and his fellow soldiers formed the White Rose, a group that wrote and distributed anonymous letters criticizing the Nazi regime and calling for action from their fellow German citizens. The following year, Sophie and her brother were arrested for treason and interrogated for information about their collaborators. This debut novel [by Kip Wilson] . . . highlights their brave stand against fascism in Nazi Germany." (Publisher's note)

"Real events made deeply personal in an intense, bone-chilling reading experience." --Kirkus 02/19

Includes bibliographical references

Wilson, N. D.

★ The **dragon's** tooth; [by] N. D. Wilson. Random House 2011 485p (Ashtown burials) $16.99; lib bdg $19.99; e-book $16.99

Grades: 5 6 7 8 **Fic**

1. Fantasy fiction 2. Magic -- Fiction 3. Siblings -- Fiction 4. Secret societies -- Fiction

ISBN 978-0-375-86439-1; 0-375-86439-3; 978-0-375-96439-8 lib bdg; 0-375-96439-8 lib bdg; 978-0-375-89572-2 e-book

LC 2009038651

"This fast-paced fantasy quickly draws readers in to its alternate reality. . . . Allusions to mythology and complex character development . . . make Wilson's first in a proposed series a gem." Booklist

Winerip, Michael

Adam Canfield of the Slash. Candlewick Press 2005 326p $15.99; pa $6.99

Grades: 5 6 7 8 **Fic**

1. School stories 2. Journalism -- Fiction

ISBN 0-7636-2340-7; 0-7636-2794-1 pa

While serving as co-editors of their school newspaper, middle-schoolers Adam and Jennifer uncover fraud and corruption in their school and in the city's government.

"This is a deceptively fun read that somehow manages to present kids with some of the most subtle social and ethical questions currently shaping their futures." SLJ

Other titles about Adam Canfield are:

Adam Canfield, watch you back! (2007)

Adam Canfield, the last reporter (2009)

Winfrey, Kerry

Things Jolie needs to do before she bites it; Kerry Winfrey. Feiwel and Friends 2018 288 p. (hardcover) $17.99

Grades: 8 9 10 11 **Fic**

1. Teeth -- Fiction 2. Teenagers -- Fiction 3. Self-acceptance -- Fiction

ISBN 9781250119544; 9781250119551

LC 2017957509

In this novel, by Kerry Winfrey, "[Jolie] has mandibular prognathism, which is the medical term for underbite. Chewing is a pain, headaches are a common occurrence, and she's never been kissed. She's months out from having a procedure to correct her underbite, and she cannot wait to be fixed. . . . She and her best friends, Evelyn and Derek, decide to make a 'Things Jolie Needs to Do Before She Bites It' [list]. . . . But since when did everything ever go exactly to plan?" (Publisher's note)

Winget, Dianna Dorisi

A **million** ways home; Dianna Dorisi Winget. Scholastic Press 2014 272 p. $16.99

Grades: 4 5 6 7 **Fic**

1. Dogs -- Fiction 2. Witnesses -- Fiction 3. Friendship -- Fiction 4. Grandmothers -- Fiction 5. Washington (State) -- Fiction 6. German shepherd dog -- Fiction 7. Spokane County (Wash.) -- Fiction 8. Witnesses -- Protection -- Fiction

ISBN 0545667062; 9780545667067; 9780545667074

LC 2014005037

"Poppy's life has been turned upside down after her grandma (and guardian) had a stroke and ended up in the hospital. . . . [W]hen she witnesses an armed robbery, 'back to normal' slips even further out of her reach. To keep Poppy safe, the budget-strapped police devise an unusual 'witness protection program,' wherein Poppy will stay with Detective Brannigan's mother." (Publisher's note)

"Readers will cheer on this sassy, relatable, pre-teen as they get to know her. Most of her trials are beyond Poppy's years and certainly out of her control. Even reluctant readers will enjoy the journey Poppy takes to find a new, perhaps unexpected, version of family, friendship, and home." Lib Med Con

Winston, Sherri

President of the whole sixth grade; girl code. Sherri Winston. Little, Brown & Co. 2018 262 p. (hardcover) $16.99

Grades: 4 5 6 7 **Fic**

1. Schools -- Fiction 2. Journalism -- Fiction 3. Cheerleading -- Fiction 4. Middle schools -- Fiction 5. Social classes -- Fiction 6. African Americans -- Fiction 7. Computer programming -- Fiction 8. Stereotypes (Social psychology) -- Fiction

ISBN 0316505285; 9780316505284

LC 2017037191

In this book in the President Series, by Sherri Winston, "when budding middle school journalist Brianna Justice learns that Yavonka Steele, rising star of the nightly news broadcast, is looking to mentor a student as part of a program at her school, she's thrilled! That is until she's paired instead with a 'boring' reporter from the community news desk." (Publisher's note)

Girl code

Winters, Ben H.

The **secret** life of Ms. Finkleman. Harper 2010 247p $16.99

Grades: 4 5 6 7 **Fic**

1. School stories 2. Teachers -- Fiction 3. Musicians -- Fiction 4. Rock music -- Fiction

ISBN 978-0-06-196541-8; 0-06-196541-3

LC 2010-04601

Spurred by a special project from her social studies teacher, seventh-grader Bethesda Fielding uncovers the secret identity of her music teacher, which leads to a most unusual concert performance and a tutoring assignment.

"Liberally laced with humor and featuring an upbeat heroine, unexpected friendship and rock-music trivia, this witty middle-school drama offers a lighthearted lesson in the importance of getting the facts straight." Kirkus

Another title about Bethesda Fielding is:

The mystery of missing everything (2011)

Winters, Cat

★ **In** the shadow of blackbirds; Cat Winters. Amulet Books 2013 400 p. $16.95

Grades: 8 9 10 11 12 **Fic**

1. Historical fiction 2. Paranormal fiction 3. Ghosts -- Fiction 4. Spiritualism -- Fiction 5. World War, 1914-1918 -- Fiction 6. Influenza Epidemic, 1918-1919 -- Fiction 7. San Diego (Calif.) -- History -- 20th century -- Fiction

ISBN 141970530X; 9781419705304

LC 2012039262

William C. Morris Honor Book (2014)

In this book, sixteen-year-old Mary Shelley Black lives in 1918. "With WWI raging on and Mary's father on trial for treason, she goes to live with her Aunt Eva in San Diego, Calif. . . . Grieving for her childhood beau Stephen, who died while fighting overseas with the Army, Mary goes outside during a thunderstorm and is struck dead by lightning—for a few minutes. When Mary comes to, she discovers she can communicate with the dead, including Stephen." (Publishers Weekly)

"Winters strikes just the right balance between history and ghost story . . . . Vintage photographs contribute to the authenticity of the atmospheric and nicely paced storytelling." Kirkus

Odd & true; by Cat Winters. Amulet Books 2017 358 p. (hardcover) $17.99

Grades: 8 9 10 11 12 **Fic**

1. Historical fiction 2. Sisters -- Fiction 3. Monsters -- Fiction 4. Poliomyelitis -- Fiction 5. Missing persons -- Fiction 6. People with disabilities -- fiction

ISBN 9781419723100; 9781683351443

LC 2017009966

In this book, by Cat Winters, "Trudchen grew up hearing Odette's stories of their monster-slaying mother and a magician's curse. But now that Tru's older, she's starting to wonder if her older sister's tales were just comforting lies, especially because there's nothing fantastic about her own life—permanently disabled and in constant pain from childhood polio. In 1909, after a two-year absence, Od reappears with a suitcase supposedly full of weapons and a promise to rescue Tru." (Publisher's note)

"Winters has woven an intricate and innovative pattern of structure, genre, and history that cannot fail to capture readers' imaginations." Kirkus

Winthrop, Elizabeth

Counting on Grace. Wendy Lamb Books 2006 232p $15.95; lib bdg $17.99; pa $6.99

Grades: 5 6 7 8 **Fic**

1. Photographers 2. Vermont -- Fiction 3. Factories -- Fiction 4. Child labor -- Fiction 5. Photographers -- Fiction

ISBN 0-385-74644-X; 0-385-90878-4 lib bdg; 0-553-48783-3 pa

It's 1910 in Pownal, Vermont. At 12 Grace and her best friend Arthur must go to work in the mill, helping their mothers work the looms. Together Grace and Arthur write a secret letter to the Child Labor Board about underage children working in the mill. A few weeks later, Lewis Hine, a famous reformer, arrives undercover to gather evidence. Grace meets him and appears in some of his photographs. "Grades five to eight." (Bull Cent Child Books)

"Much information on early photography and the workings of the textile mills is conveyed, and history and fiction are woven seamlessly together in this beautifully written novel." SLJ

Wiseman, Eva

Puppet; a novel. Tundra Books 2009 243p $17.95

Grades: 7 8 9 10 11 12 **Fic**

1. Prejudices -- Fiction 2. Jews -- Hungary -- Fiction

ISBN 0-88776-828-8; 978-0-88776-828-6

"The year is 1882. A young servant girl named Esther disappears from a small Hungarian village. Several Jewish men from the village of Tisza Eszvar face the 'blood libel'—the centuries-old calumny that Jews murder Christian children for their blood. A fourteen-year-old Jewish boy named Morris Scharf becomes the star witness of corrupt authorities who coerce him into testifying against his fellow Jews, including his own father, at the trial. This . . . fictionalized account of one of the last blood libel trials in Europe is told through the eyes of Julie, a friend of the murdered Esther, and a servant at the jail where Morris is imprisoned." (Publisher's note) "Age eleven and up." (Quill Quire)

"Times are hard in Julie Vamosi's Hungarian village in the late nineteenth-century, and the townspeople . . . blame the Jews. After Julie's best friend, Esther, . . . disappears, the rumor spreads that the Jews cut her throat and drained her blood to drink with their Passover matzos. . . . Based on the records of a trial in 1883, this searing novel dramatizes virulent anti-Semitism from the viewpoint of a Christian child. . . . The climax is electrifying." Booklist

Wisler, G. Clifton

Red Cap. Lodestar Bks. 1991 160p hardcover o.p. pa $5.99

Grades: 4 5 6 7 **Fic**

1. Andersonville Prison -- Fiction 2. United States -- History -- 1861-1865, Civil War -- Fiction

ISBN 0-14-036936-8 pa

LC 90-21944

A young Yankee drummer boy displays great courage when he's captured and sent to Andersonville Prison

The author "presents a well-researched view of the war. He effectively interweaves the known facts of Powell's life with first-person accounts of other soldiers and prisoners to create an exciting story." SLJ

Wittlinger, Ellen

Hard love. Simon & Schuster Bks. for Young Readers 1999 224p hardcover o.p. pa $8.99

Grades: 7 8 9 10 **Fic**

1. Divorce -- Fiction 2. Identity -- Fiction 3. Lesbians -- Fiction 4.

Authorship -- Fiction 5. Underground press publications -- Fiction
ISBN 0-689-82134-4; 0-689-84154-X pa

LC 98-6668

Michael L. Printz Award honor book, 2000

"John is a high school junior whose difficult family life has left him feeling lost and confused. He discovers the world of 'zines,' homemade magazines written and published by people like himself. Soon John meets another zine writer, Marisol, a self-proclaimed 'Puerto Rican Cuban Yankee Cambridge, Massachusetts, rich spoiled lesbian private-school gifted-and-talented writer virgin looking for love.' These mismatched teens discover that they are kindred spirits, and a close friendship develops. Unfortunately, John finds himself falling for Marisol, who cannot return his love. . . . Grade eight and up." (SLJ)

"John, cynical yet vulnerable, thinks he's immune to emotion until he meets bright, brittle Marisol, the author of his favorite zine. He falls in love, but Marisol, a lesbian, just wants to be friends. A love story of a different sort—funny, poignant, and thoughtful." Booklist

Followed by: Love & lies: Marisol's story (2008)

Parrotfish. Simon & Schuster Books for Young Readers 2007 294p $16.99

Grades: 7 8 9 10 **Fic**

1. School stories 2. Transgender people -- Fiction 3. Family life -- Fiction

ISBN 978-1-4169-1622-2; 1-4169-1622-9

LC 2006-9689

Grady, a transgendered high school student, yearns for acceptance by his classmates and family as he struggles to adjust to his new identity as a male.

"The author demonstrates well the complexity faced by transgendered people and makes the teen's frustration with having to fit into a category fully apparent." Publ Wkly

Wolf, Allan

New found land; Lewis and Clark's voyage of discovery: a novel. Candlewick Press 2004 500p map $18.99

Grades: 7 8 9 10 **Fic**

1. Lewis and Clark Expedition (1804-1806) -- Fiction

ISBN 0-7636-2113-7

LC 2003-65254

The letters and thoughts of Thomas Jefferson, members of the Corps of Discovery, their guide Sacagawea, and Captain Lewis's Newfoundland dog, all tell of the historic exploratory expedition to seek a water route to the Pacific Ocean.

"This is an extraordinary, engrossing book that would appeal most to serious readers, but it should definitely be added to any collection." SLJ

Includes glossary and bibliographical references

The **watch** that ends the night; voices from the Titanic. Candlewick Press 2011 466p $21.99

Grades: 7 8 9 10 **Fic**

1. Novels in verse 2. Shipwrecks -- Fiction 3. Titanic (Steamship) -- Fiction

ISBN 978-0-7636-3703-3

LC 2010040150

"Millionaire John Jacob Astor hopes to bring home his pregnant teen bride with a minimum of media scandal. A beautiful Lebanese refugee, on her way to family in Florida, discovers the first stirrings of love. And an ancient iceberg glides south, anticipating its fateful encounter. The voices in this remarkable re-creation of the Titanic disaster span classes and stations, from Margaret ('the unsinkable Molly') Brown to the captain who went down with his ship; from the lookout and wireless men to a young boy in search of dragons and a gambler in search of marks." (Publisher's note)

"A lyrical, monumental work of fact and imagination that reads like an oral history revved up by the drama of the event." Kirkus

Who killed Christopher Goodman? based on a true crime. Allan Wolf. Candlewick Press 2017 288 p. $16.99

Grades: 8 9 10 11 12 **Fic**

1. Violence -- Fiction 2. Teenagers -- Fiction 3. Murder -- Investigation -- Fiction

ISBN 0763656135; 9780763656133

This book, by Allan Wolf, "examines the circumstances of one boy's inexplicable murder and the fateful summer leading up to it. Everybody likes Chris Goodman. . . . He wears those funny bell-bottoms and he really likes the word ennui and he shakes your hand when he meets you, but he's also the kind of guy who's always up for a good time. . . . Everybody likes Chris Goodman, which makes it especially shocking when he's murdered." (Publisher's note)

Wolff, Virginia Euwer

★ **Make** lemonade. Holt & Co. 1993 200p $17.95; pa $7.95

Grades: 8 9 10 11 12 **Fic**

1. Novels in verse 2. Poverty -- Fiction 3. Babysitters -- Fiction 4. Teenage mothers -- Fiction

ISBN 978-0-8050-2228-5; 0-8050-2228-7; 978-0-8050-8070-4 pa; 0-8050-8070-8 pa

LC 92-41182

"Fourteen-year-old LaVaughn accepts the job of babysitting Jolly's two small children but quickly realizes that the young woman, a seventeen-year-old single mother, needs as much help and nurturing as her two neglected children. The four become something akin to a temporary family, and through their relationship each makes progress toward a better life. Sixty-six brief chapters, with words arranged on the page like poetry, perfectly echo the patterns of teenage speech." Horn Book Guide

Other titles in this trilogy are:
This full house (2009)
True believer (2001)

The **Mozart** season. Holt & Co. 1991 249p hardcover o.p. pa $6.99

Grades: 6 7 8 9 **Fic**

1. Violinists -- Fiction

ISBN 0-8050-1571-X; 0-312-36745-7 pa

LC 90-23635

Allegra spends her twelfth summer practicing a Mozart concerto for a violin competition and finding many significant connections in her world

"With a clear, fresh voice that never falters, Wolff gives readers a delightful heroine, a fully realized setting, and a slowly building tension that reaches a stunning climax." SLJ

Wolitzer, Meg

To night owl from dogfish; by Holly Goldberg Sloan & Meg Wolitzer. Dial Books for Young Readers & Dutton Children's Books 2019 304 p. (hardcover) $17.99

Grades: 4 5 6 7 **Fic**

1. Children of gay parents -- Fiction 2. Dating (Social customs) -- Fiction 3. Father-daughter relationship -- Fiction 4. Camps -- Fiction 5. Friendship -- Fiction 6. Gay fathers -- Fiction 7. Fathers and daughters -- Fiction 8. Text messages (Cell phone systems)

-- Fiction
ISBN 9780525553236; 9780525553250

LC 2018015400

In this novel, by Holly Goldberg Sloan and Meg Wolitzer, "Avery Bloom, who's bookish, intense, and afraid of many things, . . . lives in New York City. Bett Devlin, who's fearless, outgoing, and loves all animals . . . , lives in California. What they have in common is that they are both twelve years old, and are both being raised by single, gay dads. When their dads fall in love, Bett and Avery are sent, against their will, to the same sleepaway camp." (Publisher's note)

"The Parent Trap gets a modern makeover in this entertaining and endearing middle-grade novel about two 12-year-old girls, one camp, and a summer that will bond them for a lifetime." (Kirkus Reviews)

Wolk, Lauren

★ **Beyond** the bright sea; Lauren Wolk. Dutton Children's Books 2017 283 p. (hardcover) $16.99

Grades: 5 6 7 8 **Fic**

1. Islands -- Fiction 2. Orphans -- Fiction 3. Massachusetts -- Fiction 4. Families -- Massachusetts -- fiction 5. Massachusetts -- History -- 20th century -- fiction
ISBN 9781101994856; 9781101994863

LC 2016056541

In this book, by Lauren Wolk, "twelve-year-old Crow has lived her entire life on a tiny, isolated piece of the starkly beautiful Elizabeth Islands in Massachusetts. Abandoned and set adrift in a small boat when she was just hours old, Crow's only companions are Osh, the man who rescued and raised her, and Miss Maggie, their fierce and affectionate neighbor across the sandbar." (Publisher's note)

"This is a tear-jerking yet ultimately uplifting tale of establishing one's place in the world and realizing that sometimes your family is the one you make, not the one you are born into." SLJ

★ **Wolf** Hollow; a novel. by Lauren Wolk. Dutton Children's Books, an imprint of Penguin Random House LLC 2016 304 p. (hardback) $16.99

Grades: 4 5 6 7 8 **Fic**

1. Bullies -- Fiction 2. Veterans -- Fiction 3. Pennsylvania -- Fiction 4. Conduct of life -- Fiction 5. Homeless persons -- Fiction 6. Bullying -- Fiction 7. Family life -- Pennsylvania -- Fiction 8. Pennsylvania -- History -- 20th century -- Fiction
ISBN 9781101994825; 1101994827

LC 2015038506

Newbery Honor Book (2017)

In this book, by Lauren Wolk, "Annabelle has lived a mostly quiet, steady life in her small Pennsylvania town. Until the day new student Betty Glengarry walks into her class. Betty quickly reveals herself to be cruel and manipulative, and while her bullying seems isolated at first, things quickly escalate, and reclusive World War I veteran Toby becomes a target of her attacks. While others have always seen Toby's strangeness, Annabelle knows only kindness." (Publisher's note)

"Wolk is relentless in her message: lies and secrets, even for the most noble of reasons, have unintended consequences, as Annabelle's poignant dilemma reminds us long after the last page is turned.' Booklist

Wood, Fiona

Cloudwish; by Fiona Wood. Little, Brown & Co. 2016 320 p. (ebook) $54; (hc) $17.99

Grades: 7 8 9 10 **Fic**

1. Magic -- Fiction 2. Wishes -- Fiction 3. Australia -- Fiction 4. Dating (Social customs) -- Fiction 5. Vietnamese -- Australia -- Fiction 6. Dating (Social life and customs) -- Fiction 7. Vietnamese -- Australia -- fiction
ISBN 9780316242134; 9780316242127

LC 2015036989

In this novel by Fiona Wood, "Vân Uoc tries to stick to her reality--keeping a low profile as a scholarship student at her prestigious Melbourne private school, managing her mother's PTSD from a traumatic emigration from Vietnam, and admiring Billy from afar. Until she makes a wish that inexplicably (possibly magically) comes true. Billy actually notices her. . . . . [But] Vân Uoc can't help but wonder why Billy has suddenly fallen for her." (Publisher's note)

" It's an inspiring story with a sympathetic heroine, who will especially appeal to those who feel pressured to follow paths they don't want to travel." Pub Wkly

Wood, Maggie L.

Captured. Lobster Press 2011 284p (The Divided Realms) $12.95

Grades: 6 7 8 9 **Fic**

1. Fantasy fiction
ISBN 978-1-77080-071-7 pa; 1-77080-071-9 pa

"Willow was brought up believing she was just a normal girl with a grandmother that had a penchant for telling fantastic stories about another realm where she was a princess and magic and fairies were everyday occurrences. . . . Or, at least that is what Willow thought until the day her Nana died and she was transported to the home she never knew to save a family she never knew she had. . . . Wood's characters must think outside the game to save their world. Sometimes it takes an outsider to see things that those on the inside cannot. This is a wonderful book—well written and likely to fly off the shelves while fantasy is still the hot genre." Voice Youth Advocates

Followed by: The darkening (2011)

Wood, Maryrose

Nightshade; based on a concept by the Duchess of Northumberland. Balzer + Bray 2011 (The poison diaries) $17.99

Grades: 8 9 10 **Fic**

1. Plants -- Fiction 2. Medical care -- Fiction 3. Supernatural -- Fiction 4. Poisons and poisoning -- Fiction 5. Father-daughter relationship -- Fiction 6. Great Britain -- History -- 1714-1837 -- Fiction
ISBN 978-0-06-180242-3; 0-06-180242-5

LC 2011024911

In late eighteenth-century Northumberland, England, sixteen-year-old Jessamine Luxton is so desperate to find Weed, who her father says deserted her when she was at death's door, that she asks for help from the evil Oleander.

"Promising Weed's continued pursuit (and, hopefully, reviving the intriguing issue of Mr. Luxton's poisoning), part three's sure to levy as much page-turning enthrallment as its predecessors." Kirkus

Wooding, Chris

★ **Malice**; illustrated by Dan Chernett. Scholastic Press 2009 377p il $14.99; pa $8.99

Grades: 6 7 8 9 10 **Fic**

1. Horror fiction 2. Comic books, strips, etc. -- Fiction
ISBN 978-0-545-16043-8; 0-545-16043-X; 978-0-545-16044-5 pa; 0-545-16044-8 pa

Everyone's heard the rumors. Call on Tall Jake and he'll take you to Malice, a world that exists inside a horrifying comic book. A place most kids never leave. Seth and Kady think it's all a silly myth. But then their friend disappears.

"This nail-biter will keep readers glued to the story until the very last page is turned. . . . Seth and Kady are strong and exciting characters." SLJ

Followed by: Havoc (2010)

Silver; Chris Wooding. Scholastic Press 2014 320 p. (hc) $17.99

Grades: 7 8 9 10 11 12 **Fic**

1. Horror fiction 2. School stories 3. Schools -- Fiction 4. Survival -- Fiction 5. Boarding schools -- Fiction 6. Communicable diseases -- Fiction

ISBN 0545603927; 9780545603928

LC 2013014037

In this young adult science fiction horror novel, by Chris Wooding, "without warning, a horrifying infection will spread across the school grounds [of Mortingham Boarding Academy], and a group of students with little in common will find themselves barricaded in a classroom, fighting for their lives. Some will live. Some will die. And then it will get even worse." (Publisher's note)

"When strange insects assault a remote boarding school in England, the kids try to save the day in this tense page-turner...Skillfully managed subplots keep the pages flying. It looks like the end of the world is nigh.... It's just all kinds of white-knuckle fun." (Kirkus)

Woodruff, Elvira

Dear Austin; letters from the Underground Railroad. illustrated by Nancy Carpenter. Knopf 1998 137p il $16; lib bdg $17.99; pa $5.50

Grades: 4 5 6 **Fic**

1. Slavery -- Fiction 2. Pennsylvania -- Fiction 3. African Americans -- Fiction 4. Underground railroad -- Fiction

ISBN 0-679-88594-3; 0-679-98594-8 lib bdg; 0-375-80356-4 pa

LC 98-5314

Sequel to Dear Levi (1994)

In 1853, in letters to his older brother, eleven-year-old Levi describes his adventures in the Pennsylvania countryside with his black friend Jupiter and his experiences with the Underground Railroad

"The smoothly written text is fast paced." Horn Book Guide

Fearless. Scholastic Press 2008 224p il $16.99; pa $6.99

Grades: 5 6 7 8 **Fic**

1. Artists 2. Engravers 3. Inventors 4. Architects 5. Adventure fiction 6. Orphans -- Fiction 7. Lighthouses -- Fiction 8. Great Britain -- History -- 1603-1714, Stuarts -- Fiction

ISBN 978-0-439-67703-5; 0-439-67703-3; 978-0-439-67704-2 pa; 0-439-67704-1 pa

LC 2006-10137

In late seventeenth-century England, eleven-year-old Digory, forced to leave his hometown after his father is lost at sea, becomes an apprentice to the architect Henry Winstanley, who built a lighthouse on the treacherous Eddystone Reef—the very rocks that sank Digory's grandfather's ship years before.

"This fascinating, well-written story is closely based on the life of the real Henry Winstanley. . . . The characters are finely drawn and the action is nonstop." SLJ

George Washington's spy; a time travel adventure. Scholastic Press 2010 229p $16.99

Grades: 4 5 6 **Fic**

1. Authors 2. Diplomats 3. Inventors 4. Statesmen 5. Scientists 6. Writers on science 7. Members of Congress 8. Time travel -- Fiction 9. Boston (Mass.) -- Fiction 10. United States -- History -- 1775-1783, Revolution -- Fiction

ISBN 978-0-545-10487-6; 0-545-10487-4

LC 2009032700

Sequel to: George Washington's socks (1991)

Ten-year-old Matt and six other children travel to 1776 Boston, living out American history as they meet Benjamin Franklin, learn about colonial medicine, and become part of a rebel spy ring

"Woodruff does an excellent job of conveying the complexities of war. . . . This is a great introduction to the Revolutionary period. . . . The story is fast paced, exciting, and informative." SLJ

Woods, Brenda

My name is Sally Little Song. G.P. Putnam's Sons 2006 182p $15.99; pa $5.99

Grades: 4 5 6 7 **Fic**

1. Florida -- Fiction 2. Georgia -- Fiction 3. Slavery -- Fiction 4. Seminole Indians -- Fiction 5. African Americans -- Fiction

ISBN 0-399-24312-7; 0-14-240943-X pa

LC 2005-32651

When their owner plans to sell one of them in 1802, twelve-year-old Sally and her family run away from their Georgia plantation to look for both freedom from slavery and a home in Florida with the Seminole Indians.

"Based on historical accounts, this novel provides readers with an alternative view of the realities of slavery—an escape to the South rather than North. . . . This accessible tale will prove a rich resource for study and discussion." SLJ

Woodson, Jacqueline

★ **After** Tupac and D Foster. G.P. Putnam's Sons 2008 153p $15.99

Grades: 7 8 9 10 **Fic**

1. Poets 2. Actors 2. Rap musicians 3. Friendship -- Fiction 4. African Americans -- Fiction 5. Queens (New York, N.Y.) -- Fiction

ISBN 978-0-399-24654-8

LC 2007-23725

A Newbery honor book, 2009

In the New York City borough of Queens in 1996, three girls bond over their shared love of Tupac Shakur's music, as together they try to make sense of the unpredictable world in which they live.

"The subtlety and depth with which the author conveys the girls' relationships lend this novel exceptional vividness and staying power." Publ Wkly

Feathers. G.P. Putnam's Sons 2007 118p $15.99; pa $6.99

Grades: 4 5 6 7 **Fic**

1. Religion -- Fiction 2. Race relations -- Fiction 3. African Americans -- Fiction

ISBN 978-0-399-23989-2; 0-399-23989-8; 978-0-14-241198-8 pa; 0-14-241198-1 pa

LC 2006-24713

A Newbery Medal honor book, 2008

When a new, white student nicknamed "The Jesus Boy" joins her sixth grade class in the winter of 1971, Frannie's growing friendship with him makes her start to see some things in a new light.

"Woodson creates in Frannie a strong protagonist who thinks for herself and recognizes the value and meaning of family. The story ends with hope and thoughtfulness while speaking to those adolescents who struggle with race, faith, and prejudice." SLJ

★ **From** the notebooks of Melanin Sun. G.P. Putnam's Sons 2010 126p $17.99; pa $7.99

Grades: 7 8 9 10 **Fic**

1. Lesbians -- Fiction 2. African Americans -- Fiction 3. Mother-son relationship -- Fiction 4. Brooklyn (New York, N.Y.) -- Fiction
ISBN 978-0-399-25280-8; 0-399-25280-0; 978-0-14-241641-9 pa; 0-14-241641-X pa

LC 2009011314

A reissue of the title first published 1995 by Blue Sky Press

A Coretta Scott King honor book, 1996

Almost-fourteen-year-old Melanin Sun's comfortable, quiet life is shattered when his mother reveals she has fallen in love with a woman

"Offering no easy answers, Woodson teaches the reader that love can lead to acceptance of all manner of differences." Publ Wkly

★ **Harbor** me; Jacqueline Woodson. Nancy Paulsen Books 2018 192 p. (hardback) $17.99

Grades: 5 6 7 8 **Fic**

1. Friendship -- Fiction 2. African Americans -- Fiction 3. Dysfunctional families -- Fiction 4. Schools -- Fiction 5. Family problems -- Fiction 6. Hispanic Americans -- Fiction
ISBN 9780399252525; 9780525515135

LC 2018019373

Kirkus Prize Finalist: Young Readers' Literature (2018)

"Jacqueline Woodson's first middle-grade novel since National Book Award winner 'Brown Girl Dreaming' celebrates the healing that can occur when a group of students share their stories. It all starts when six kids have to meet for a weekly chat--by themselves, with no adults to listen in. There, in the room they soon dub the ARTT Room (short for 'A Room to Talk'), they discover it's safe to talk about what's bothering them." (Publisher's note)

"Woodson tells stories torn from headlines but personalizes them with poetry and memories, blunting their trauma with understanding and love. Haley's history weaves in and out, drawing readers close. These children become each other's safe harbors, and Woodson brilliantly shows readers how to find the connections we all need." Booklist

★ **If** you come softly. Putnam 1998 181p $15.99; pa $5.99

Grades: 7 8 9 10 **Fic**

1. Race relations -- Fiction 2. New York (N.Y.) -- Fiction 3. African Americans -- Fiction
ISBN 0-399-23112-9; 0-698-11862-6 pa

LC 97-32212

ALA YALSA Margaret A. Edwards Award (2006)

After meeting at their private school in New York, fifteen-year-old Jeremiah, who is black and whose parents are separated, and Ellie, who is white and whose mother has twice abandoned her, fall in love and then try to cope with people's reactions

"The gentle and melancholy tone of this book makes it ideal for thoughtful readers and fans of romance." Voice Youth Advocates

Another title about Jeremiah is:
Behind you (2004)

Lena; by Jacqueline Woodson. 1st G.P. Putnam's Sons ed.; G. P. Putnam's Sons 2006 135p $17.99

Grades: 6 7 8 9 **Fic**

1. Sisters -- Fiction 2. Runaway teenagers -- Fiction
ISBN 0-399-24469-7

LC 2005032666

Sequel to: I hadn't meant to tell you this (1994)

A reissue of the title first published 1999 by Delacorte Press

ALA YALSA Margaret A. Edwards Award (2006)

Thirteen-year-old Lena and her younger sister Dion mourn the death of their mother as they hitchhike from Ohio to Kentucky while running away from their abusive father.

"Soulful, wise and sometimes wrenching, this taut story never loses its grip on the reader." Publ Wkly

★ **Locomotion**. Putnam 2003 100p $17.99; pa $5.99

Grades: 4 5 6 7 **Fic**

1. Novels in verse 2. Foster home care -- Fiction 3. African Americans -- Fiction
ISBN 978-0-399-23115-5; 0-399-23115-3; 978-0-14-241552-8 pa; 0-14-241552-9 pa

LC 2002-69779

Boston Globe-Horn Book Award Honor: Fiction (2003)

National Book Award Finalist: Young People's Literature (2003)

In a series of poems, eleven-year-old Lonnie writes about his life, after the death of his parents, separated from his younger sister, living in a foster home, and finding his poetic voice at school

"In a masterful use of voice, Woodson allows Lonnie's poems to tell a complex story of loss and grief and to create a gritty, urban environment. Despite the spare text, Lonnie's foster mother and the other minor characters are three-dimensional, making the boy's world a convincingly real one." SLJ

★ **Peace,** Locomotion. G.P. Putnam's Sons 2009 134p $15.99; pa $7.99

Grades: 4 5 6 7 **Fic**

1. Letters -- Fiction 2. Orphans -- Fiction 3. Siblings -- Fiction 4. Foster home care -- Fiction 5. African Americans -- Fiction
ISBN 978-0-399-24655-5; 0-399-24655-X; 978-0-14-241512-2 pa; 0-14-241512-X pa

LC 2008-18583

Through letters to his little sister, who is living in a different foster home, sixth-grader Lonnie, also known as "Locomotion," keeps a record of their lives while they are apart, describing his own foster family, including his foster brother who returns home after losing a leg in the Iraq War

"Woodson creates a full-bodied character in kind, sensitive Lonnie. Readers will understand his quest for peace, and appreciate the hard work he does to find it." Publ Wkly

Wrede, Patricia C., 1953-

Calling on dragons. Harcourt Brace 1993 244p (The Enchanted Forest Chronicles) hardcover o.p. pa $6.99

Grades: 5 6 7 8 **Fic**

1. Fairy tales 2. Magic -- Fiction 3. Dragons -- Fiction
ISBN 0-15-200950-7; 0-15-204692-5 pa

LC 92-35469

Sequel to: Searching for dragons (1991)

Queen Cimorene turns to her friends Morwen, Telemain, and Kazul for help when troublesome wizards make their way back into the Enchanted Forest and begin to soak up its magic

"Wrede's strengths are numerous: sparkling dialogue, amusingly fractured fairy-tale conventions, solid characterization, plenty of action, and truly terrific chapter headings." SLJ

Followed by: Talking to dragons (1993)

Dealing with dragons. Harcourt Brace Jovanovich 1990 212p (The Enchanted Forest Chronicles) hardcover o.p. pa $6.99

Grades: 5 6 7 8 **Fic**

1. Fairy tales 2. Magic -- Fiction 3. Dragons -- Fiction

ISBN 0-15-222900-0; 0-15-204566-X pa

LC 89-24599

Bored with traditional palace life, a princess goes off to live with a group of dragons and soon becomes involved with fighting against some disreputable wizards who want to steal away the dragons' kingdom

"A decidedly diverting novel with plenty of action and many slightly skewed fairy-tale conventions that add to the laugh-out-loud reading pleasure and give the story a wide appeal." Booklist

Other titles in this series are:
Searching for dragons (1991)
Calling on dragons (1993)
Talking to dragons (1993)

The **Far** West; Patricia C. Wrede. Scholastic Press 2012 378 p. $17.99

Grades: 7 8 9 10 11 12 **Fic**

1. Steampunk fiction 2. Fantasy 3. Magic -- Fiction 4. Twins -- Fiction 5. Friendship -- Fiction

ISBN 0545033446; 9780545033442

LC 2012288790

This young adult speampunk novel, by Patricia C. Wrede, concludes the "Frontier Magic" trilogy. "Eff is an unlucky thirteenth child . . . but also the seventh daughter in her family. Her twin brother, Lan, is a powerful double seventh son. Her life at the edge of the Great Barrier Spell is different from anyone else's that she knows. . . . With Lan, William, Professor Torgeson, Wash, and Professor Ochiba, Eff finds that nothing on the wild frontier is as they expected." (Publisher's note)

Searching for dragons. Harcourt Brace 1991 242p (The Enchanted forest chronicles) hardcover o.p. pa $6.99

Grades: 5 6 7 8 **Fic**

1. Fairy tales 2. Magic -- Fiction 3. Dragons -- Fiction

ISBN 0-15-200898-5; 0-15-204565-1 pa

LC 91-8305

Sequel to: Dealing with dragons (1990)

With the aid of King Mandanbar, Princess Cimorene rescues the dragon Kazul and saves the Enchanted Forest from a band of wicked wizards

"Wrede's tongue-in-cheek humor balances well with sweet adolescent discovery, and the result is another winning chapter in a delightful tale." SLJ

Followed by:Calling on dragons (1993)

Sorcery and Cecelia, or, The enchanted chocolate pot; being the correspondence of two young ladies of quality regarding various magical scandals in London and the country. [by] Patricia C. Wrede and Caroline Stevermer. Harcourt 2003 316p $17; pa $6.95

Grades: 7 8 9 10 **Fic**

1. Cousins -- Fiction 2. Supernatural -- Fiction 3. Great Britain -- Fiction

ISBN 0-15-204615-1; 0-15-205300-X pa

LC 2002-38706

In 1817 in England, two young cousins, Cecilia living in the country and Kate in London, write letters to keep each other informed of their exploits, which take a sinister turn when they find themselves confronted by evil wizards

"This is a fun story that quickly draws in the reader." Voice Youth Advocates

Other titles about Kate and Cecilia are:
The grand tour (2004)
The mislaid magician (2006)

Talking to dragons. Harcourt Brace & Co. 1993 255p (The Enchanted Forest chronicles) hardcover o.p. pa $6.99

Grades: 5 6 7 8 **Fic**

1. Fairy tales 2. Magic -- Fiction 3. Dragons -- Fiction

ISBN 0-15-284247-0; 0-15-204691-7 pa

LC 92-40719

Sequel to: Calling on dragons (1993)

A revised version of the title first published 1985 in paperback

Queen Cimorene sends her sixteen-year-old son Daystar into the Enchanted Forest with the only weapon that can combat an evil wizard's magic in an effort to restore the balance of power in the kingdom

This "grand adventure is both suspenseful and hilarious." Booklist

The **thirteenth** child. Scholastic Press 2009 344p (Frontier magic) $16.99

Grades: 7 8 9 10 11 12 **Fic**

1. School stories 2. Fantasy fiction 2. Magic -- Fiction 3. Twins -- Fiction 4. Frontier and pioneer life -- Fiction

ISBN 978-0-545-03342-8; 0-545-03342-X

LC 2008-34048

Eighteen-year-old Eff must finally get over believing she is bad luck and accept that her special training in Aphrikan magic, and being the twin of the seventh son of a seventh son, give her extraordinary power to combat magical creatures that threaten settlements on the western frontier.

Wrede "creates a rich world where steam dragons seem as normal as bears, and a sympathetic character in Eff." Publ Wkly

Followed by Across the Great Barrier (2011)

Wright, Randall

★ The **Cheshire** Cheese cat; a Dickens of a tale. [by] Carmen Agra Deedy & Randall Wright; drawings by Barry Moser. Peachtree Publishers 2011 228p il $16.95; paperback $8.95

Grades: 5 6 7 8 **Fic**

1. Cats -- Fiction 2. Mice -- Fiction 3. London (England) -- Fiction 4. Great Britain -- History -- 19th century -- Fiction

ISBN 978-1-56145-595-9; 1-56145-595-4; 9781561458103

LC 2010052275

"The vagaries of tavern life in 19th-century London come alive in this delightful tale. . . . The fast-moving plot is a masterwork of intricate detail that will keep readers enthralled, and the characters are well-rounded and believable. Language is a highlight of the novel; words both elegant and colorful fill the pages. . . . Combined with Moser's precise pencil sketches of personality-filled characters, the book is a success in every way." SLJ

Wulffson, Don L.

Soldier X. Viking 2001 226p $15.99; pa $6.99

Grades: 7 8 9 10 **Fic**

1. Russia -- Fiction 2. World War, 1939-1945 -- Fiction

ISBN 0-670-88863-X; 0-14-250073-9 pa

LC 99-49418

In 1943 sixteen-year-old Erik experiences the horrors of war when he is drafted into the German army and sent to fight on the Russian front

"Erik's first-person narrative records battlefield sequences with an unflinching—and occasionally numbing—brutality, in a story notable for its unusual perspective." Horn Book Guide

Wunder, Wendy

★ The **museum** of intangible things; Wendy Wunder. Razorbill 2014 304 p. (hardback) $17.99

Grades: 8 9 10 11 12 **Fic**

1. Mental illness -- Fiction 2. Female friendship -- Fiction 3. Runaway teenagers -- Fiction 4. Manic-depressive illness -- Fiction 5. Runaways -- Fiction 6. Friendship -- Fiction 7. Best friends -- Fiction 8. Automobile travel -- Fiction

ISBN 1595145141; 9781595145147

LC 2013030169

In this book, by Wendy Wunder, "Hannah and Zoe haven't had much in their lives, but they've always had each other. So when Zoe tells Hannah she needs to get out of their down-and-out New Jersey town, they . . . head west. . . . As they chase storms and make new friends, Zoe tells Hannah she wants more for her. She wants her to live bigger, dream grander, aim higher. And so Zoe begins teaching Hannah all about life's intangible things." (Publisher's note)

"As Hannah and best friend Zoe (diagnosed bipolar) embark on a cross-country road trip, Zoe gives Hannah "intangible lessons" (e.g., Hannah learns insouciance when they overnight in an IKEA). When Zoe's irrationality gets scary, Hannah learns betrayal and, later, forgiveness. With each lesson, Hannah becomes more confident, building her own distinct identity. Meanwhile, Zoe is a complex character--intelligent, loyal, and funny." Horn Book

Yancey, Richard

The **extraordinary** adventures of Alfred Kropp; by Rick Yancey. Bloomsbury Pub. 2005 339p $16.95; pa $7.95

Grades: 7 8 9 10 **Fic**

1. Adventure fiction 2. Kings 3. Orphans -- Fiction

ISBN 1-58234-693-3; 1-59990-044-0 pa

LC 2005-13044

Through a series of dangerous and violent misadventures, teenage loser Alfred Kropp rescues King Arthur's legendary sword Excalibur from the forces of evil.

"True to its action-adventure genre, the story is lighthearted, entertaining, occasionally half-witted, but by and large fun." SLJ

Other titles about Alfred Kropp are:

Alfred Kropp: the seal of Solomon (2007)

Alfred Kropp: the thirteenth skull (2008)

Yee, F. C.

★ The **epic** crush of Genie Lo; a novel by F.C. Yee. Amulet Books 2017 310 p. ebook $15.54; (hardback : alk. paper) $18.99

Grades: 7 8 9 10 **Fic**

1. California -- Fiction 2. Supernatural -- Fiction 3. High school students -- Fiction 4. Oakland (Calif.)

ISBN 9781683351221 ; 9781419725487

LC 2017018271

In this book, by F.C. Yee, "the struggle to get into a top-tier college consumes sixteen-year-old Genie's every waking thought. But when she discovers she's a celestial spirit who's powerful enough to bash through the gates of heaven with her fists, her perfectionist existence is shattered. Enter Quentin, a transfer student from China whose tone-deaf assertiveness beguiles Genie to the brink of madness." (Publisher's note)

"Hard-driving, hyperachieving Chinese-American sophomore Genie Lo may have to put her take-no-prisoners rush to the Ivy Leagues aside so she can save the world, or at least the local region of California currently under attack by Chinese demons. . . . Loads of action, a touch of comedy, a bit of well-controlled lust, and even some serious discussion of Eastern philosophy should leave readers eager for a return performance." Bulletin of the Center for Children's Books

Yee, Lisa

Millicent Min, girl genius. Arthur A. Levine Books 2003 248p $16.95; pa $4.99

Grades: 5 6 7 **Fic**

1. School stories 2. Gifted children -- Fiction 3. Chinese Americans -- Fiction

ISBN 0-439-42519-0; 0-439-42520-4 pa

LC 2003-3747

"At the tender age of eleven, Millicent Min has completed her junior year of high school. Summer school is Millie's idea of fun, so she is excited that her parents are allowing her to take a college poetry course. . . . The tension between Millie's formal, overly intellectual way of expressing herself and her emotional immaturity makes her a very funny narrator. . . . Readers considerably older than Millicent's eleven years will enjoy this strong debut novel." Voice Youth Advocates

Other titles about Millicent Min and her friends are:

Stanford Wong flunks big-time (2005)

So totally Emily Ebers (2007)

Warp speed. Arthur A. Levine Books 2011 310p $16.99

Grades: 5 6 7 8 **Fic**

1. School stories 2. Bullies -- Fiction 3. California -- Fiction 4. Popularity -- Fiction 5. Family life -- Fiction

ISBN 978-0-545-12276-4; 0-545-12276-7

LC 2010-24228

"Entering 7th grade is no big deal for Marley Sandelski: Same old boring classes, same old boring life. The only thing he has to look forward to is the upcoming Star Trek convention. But when he inadvertently draws the attention of Digger Ronster, the biggest bully in school, his life has officially moved from boring to far too dramatic . . . from invisible to center stage." (Publisher's note)

"Yee's combination of humor and sympathy works a charm here, giving Marley a life of his own and a chance at success in this solid addition to her prismatic look at middle school." Kirkus

Yelchin, Eugene, 1956-

★ The **assassination** of Brangwain Spurge; by M.T. Anderson and Eugene Yelchin. Candlewick Press 2018 544 p. illustrations (hbk.) $24.99

Grades: 5 6 7 8 9 **Fic**

1. Fantasy fiction 2. Elves -- Fiction 3. Goblins -- Fiction

ISBN 0763698229; 9780763698225

National Book Award Finalist: Young People's Literature (2018)

In this book, by M.T. Anderson and Eugene Yelchin, "elfin historian Brangwain Spurge is on a mission: survive being catapulted across the mountains into goblin territory, deliver a . . . peace offering to their . . . dark lord, and spy on the goblin kingdom. . . . [Brangwain and] goblin archivist Werfel . . . should be the best of friends, but a series of . . . . . [incidents] throws . . . [them] into the middle of an international crisis . . . and war for their nations." (Publisher's note)

"Together, Anderson and Yelchin craft something that feels impossible, a successfully unorthodox epistolary, pictorial, and prose narrative that interrogates the cultural ramifications of unchallenged viewpoints and the government violence they abet even as it recounts the comedic blunderings of a spy mission gone wrong." Kirkus

★ **Breaking** Stalin's nose; written and illustrated by Eugene Yelchin. Henry Holt and Company 2011 140p il $15.99

Grades: 4 5 6 7 **Fic**

1. Communism -- Fiction 2. Soviet Union -- Fiction 3. Father-son relationship -- Fiction

ISBN 0-8050-9216-1; 978-0-8050-9216-5

LC 2011005792

In the Stalinist era of the Soviet Union, ten-year-old Sasha idolizes his father, a devoted Communist, but when police take his father away and leave Sasha homeless, he is forced to examine his own perceptions, values, and beliefs.

"Readers will quickly pick up on the dichotomy between Sasha's ardent beliefs and the reality of life under Stalinism, and be glad for his ultimate disillusion, even as they worry for his future. An author's note concisely presents the chilling historical background and personal connection that underlie the story." Publ Wkly

The **haunting** of Falcon House; written and illustrated by Eugene Yelchin. Henry Holt & Co. 2016 320 p. illustrations (hardcover) $15.99

Grades: 4 5 6 7 8 **Fic**

1. Aunts -- Fiction 2. Orphans -- Fiction 3. Haunted houses -- Fiction

ISBN 9780805098457

LC 2015049783

In this book, by Eugene Yelchin, "when twelve-year-old Prince Lev Lvov goes to live with his aunt at Falcon House, he takes his rightful place as heir to the Lvov family estate. Prince Lev dreams of becoming a hero of Russia like his great ancestors. But he'll discover that dark secrets haunt this house. Prince Lev is the only one who can set them free-will he be the hero his family needs?" (Publisher's note)

"This is a haunting tale at its very best." Booklist

Spy runner; Eugene Yelchin (author and illus) Henry Holt & Co. BYR 2019 352 p. (hardcover) $17.99

Grades: 5 6 7 8 9 **Fic**

1. Boys -- fiction 2. Spies -- fiction 3. Family secrets -- fiction

ISBN 9781250120816; 9781250120823

LC 2018945030

"An illustrated middle grade novel [by Eugene Yelchin] set in the 1950s in which 12-year-old Jake gets caught in Red Scare paranoia when his mother takes in a peculiar lodger who may or may not be a Russian spy." (Goodreads)

"Well-plotted and -paced, Yelchin's thriller will be a favorite among readers who have an interest in history and intrigue." (Publishers Weekly)

Yep, Laurence

A **dragon's** guide to the care and feeding of humans; Laurence Yep & Joanne Ryder ; Illustrations by Mary GrandPré. Crown Books for Young Readers 2015 160 p. illustrations (hc) $15.99

Grades: 4 5 6 7 **Fic**

1. Pets -- Fiction 2. Dragons -- Fiction 3. Magic -- Fiction 4. Artists -- Fiction 5. Friendship -- Fiction 6. Imaginary creatures -- Fiction

ISBN 0385392281; 9780385392280; 9780385392297

LC 2014017803

In this novel by Laurence Yep and Joanne Ryder, "crusty dragon Miss Drake has a new pet human, precocious Winnie. Oddly enough, Winnie seems to think Miss Drake is her pet. . . . Unknown to most . . . , the City by the Bay is home to many . . . fantastic creatures. . . . And Winnie wants to draw every new creature she encounters. . . . But Winnie's sketchbook is not what it seems. Somehow, her sketchlings have been set loose on the city streets!" (Publisher's note)

"With a black-and-white spot illustration opening most chapters, an engaging narrator, and a consistently fluid writing style, this title makes a fine dragon choice for readers not yet ready for more weighty fantasy novels." SLJ

City of fire. Tom Doherty Associates 2009 320p $15.99

Grades: 5 6 7 8 **Fic**

1. Fantasy fiction 2. Magic -- Fiction 3. Hawaii -- Fiction 4. Dragons -- Fiction

ISBN 978-0-7653-1924-1; 0-7653-1924-1

LC 2009016737

Twelve-year-old Scirye and her companions travel to Houlani, a new Hawaiian island created by magic, where they enlist the help of volcano goddess Pele in an attempt to stop an evil dragon and a mysterious man from altering the universe.

"Readers will be on tenterhooks awaiting the next episode of this exhilarating chase." Booklist

Followed by: City of ice (2011)

★ **Dragon's** gate; Golden Mountain chronicles: 1867. HarperCollins Pubs. 1993 273p $16.99; pa $6.99

Grades: 6 7 8 9 **Fic**

1. Railroads -- Fiction 2. Chinese -- United States -- Fiction

ISBN 0-06-022971-3; 0-06-440489-7 pa

LC 92-43649

Sequel to The serpent's children (1984) and Mountain light (1985)

A Newbery Medal honor book, 1994

When he accidentally kills a Manchu, a fifteen-year-old Chinese boy is sent to America to join his father, an uncle, and other Chinese working to build a tunnel for the transcontinental railroad through the Sierra Nevada mountains in 1867

"Yep has succeeded in realizing the primary characters and the irrepressibly dramatic story. . . . The carefully researched details will move students to thought and discussion." Bull Cent Child Books

★ **Dragonwings**; Golden Mountain chronicles: 1903. Harper & Row 1975 248p lib bdg $16.89; pa $6.99

Grades: 6 7 8 9 **Fic**

1. Chinese Americans -- Fiction 2. San Francisco (Calif.) -- Fiction

ISBN 0-06-026738-0 lib bdg; 0-06-440085-9 pa

A Newbery Medal honor book, 1976

"In 1903 Moon Shadow, eight years old, leaves China for the 'Land of the Golden Mountains,' San Francisco, to be with his father, Windrider, a father he has never seen. There, beset by the trials experienced by most foreigners in America, Moonrider shares his father's dream—to fly. This dream enables Windrider to endure the mockery of the other Chinese, the poverty he suffers in this hostile place—the land of the white demons—and his loneliness for his wife and his own country." Shapiro. Fic for Youth. 3d edition

Hiroshima; a novella. Scholastic 1995 56p hardcover o.p. pa $4.99

Grades: 4 5 6 7 **Fic**

1. Hiroshima (Japan) -- Bombardment, 1945 -- Fiction

ISBN 0-590-20832-2; 0-590-20833-0 pa

LC 94-18195

Through a "present-tense narration that moves back and forth between the experiences of a 12-year-old girl and the men on the Enola Gay, Yep's novella tells the events of the day the first atomic bomb was dropped and its aftermath. Sachi survives but is badly burned; her sister dies and her soldier father is killed in action. For three years the girl spends most of her time indoors, as newcomers to the city fear the scarred survivors. Then she travels to America for plastic surgery, which enables her to take part in her society again. She returns to Japan, hoping to help other victims. Yep ends with two chapters on the destructive potential of nuclear warfare and on some of the efforts being made toward disarmament." (SLJ) Bibliography. "Grades four to seven." (Booklist)

"This moving and detailed narrative chronicles the dropping of the atomic bomb on Hiroshima and its effects on its citizens, especially on twelve-year-old Sachi. Based on true accounts, this book describes the horrors and sadness as well as the courage and hope that result from war." Soc Educ

★ The **star** maker. Harper 2010 100p $15.99; lib bdg $16.89

Grades: 5 6 7 8 **Fic**

1. Uncles -- Fiction 2. Family life -- Fiction 3. Chinese New Year -- Fiction 4. Chinese Americans -- Fiction 5. San Francisco (Calif.) -- Fiction

ISBN 978-0-06-025315-8; 0-06-025315-0; 978-0-06-025316-5 lib bdg; 0-06-025316-9 lib bdg

LC 2010-07856

With the help of his popular Uncle Chester, a young Chinese American boy tries hard to fulfill a promise to have firecrackers for everyone on the Chinese New Year in 1954. Includes an afterword with information about the Chinese customs portrayed in the story.

"Yep skillfully portrays the significance and emotional nature of common childhood dramas, from fears of going back on one's word to worries of losing a favorite uncle to a new girlfriend. . . . Yep has crafted other memorable characters, including Chinatown itself, which sparkle with energy and camaraderie." Publ Wkly

Includes bibliographical references

Yhard, Jo Ann

The **fossil** hunter of Sydney Mines. Nimbus Pub. 2010 169p il pa $10.95

Grades: 4 5 6 7 **Fic**

1. Mystery fiction 2. Fossils -- Fiction

ISBN 978-1-55109-760-2; 1-55109-760-5

"When a mining company wants to strip mine, Grace's father disagrees due to the damage it would do to the area's irreplaceable fossils. Grace and her father lead the protests, but the protests stop once her father disappears and is presumed dead in an accident. . . . Yhard excels at providing enough information to allow the reader to follow the clues and solve the crime. Nothing is too far-fetched nor too obvious as the suspense builds to a satisfying resolution." Libr Media Connect

Yolen, Jane

B.U.G. (Big Ugly Guy) by Jane Yolen and Adam Stemple. Dutton Children's Books 2013 344 p.

Grades: 4 5 6 7 8 **Fic**

1. Golem -- Fiction 2. Magic -- Fiction 3. Bullies -- Fiction 4. Friendship -- Fiction 5. Bands (Music) -- Fiction 6. Klezmer music -- Fiction 7. Jews -- United States -- Fiction

ISBN 9780525422389

LC 2012018217

A constant target for bullies, Sammy Greenburg is glad to make friends with a boy named Skink, who even agrees to "start up a Klezmer fusion garage band after Sammy introduces Skink to the unique combination of jazz and Jewish folk music. When the bullies beat up Skink, however, Sammy decides enough is enough, and, using a formula he finds in his rabbi's study, he creates a golem to take vengeance on his enemies—and fill the missing drummer spot in his new band." (Bulletin of the Center for Children's Books)

★ **Briar** Rose. Doherty Assocs. 1992 190p (Fairy tale series) hardcover o.p. pa $10.99

Grades: 8 9 10 11 12 Adult **Fic**

1. Fantasy fiction 2. Grandmothers -- Fiction 3. Jews -- Poland -- Fiction 4. Holocaust, 1933-1945 -- Fiction

ISBN 0-312-85135-9; 9780765382948 pa

LC 92-25456

"Yolen takes the story of Briar Rose (commonly known as Sleeping Beauty) and links it to the Holocaust. . . . Rebecca Berlin, a young woman who has grown up hearing her grandmother Gemma tell an unusual and frightening version of the Sleeping Beauty legend, realizes when Gemma dies that the fairy tale offers one of the very few clues she has to her grandmother's past. . . . By interpolating Gemma's vivid and imaginative story into the larger narrative, Yolen has created an engrossing novel." Publ Wkly

Curse of the Thirteenth Fey; the True Tale of Sleeping Beauty. Jane Yolen. Philomel Books 2012 290 p. $16.99

Grades: 6 7 8 9 10 **Fic**

1. Curses -- Fiction 2. Princesses -- fiction 3. Fairy tales 4. Elves -- Fiction 5. Magic -- Fiction 6. Fairies -- Fiction 7. Prophecies -- Fiction 8. Family life -- Fiction

ISBN 0399256644; 9780399256646

LC 2011038847

In author Jane Yolen's book, "Gorse is the thirteenth . . . in a family of fairies tied to the evil king's land and made to do his bidding. . . . When accident-prone Gorse falls ill just as the family is bid to bless the new princess . . . [she] races to the castle with the last piece of magic the family has left. . . . But that is when accident, mayhem, and magic combine to drive Gorse's story into the unthinkable, threatening the baby, the kingdom, and all." (Publisher's note)

Dragon's blood. Harcourt 2004 303p (Pit dragon chronicles) pa $6.95

Grades: 6 7 8 9 **Fic**

1. Fantasy fiction 2. Dragons -- Fiction

ISBN 0-15-205126-0

LC 2003-56661

A reissue of the title first published 1982 by Delacorte Press

Jakkin, a bond boy who works as a Keeper in a dragon nursery on the planet Austar IV, secretly trains a fighting pit dragon of his own in hopes of winning his freedom

"An original and engrossing fantasy." Horn Book

Other titles in this series are:

Heart's blood (2004)

Sending of dragons (2004)

Dragon's heart (2009)

Mapping the bones; Jane Yolen. Philomel Books 2018 432 p. $17.99

Grades: 6 7 8 9 **Fic**

1. Twins -- Fiction 2. Concentration camps -- Fiction 3. Holocaust, 1939-1945 -- Fiction 4. Jews -- Poland -- Fiction 5. Brothers and sisters -- Fiction 6. Concentration camps -- Poland -- Fiction 7. Holocaust, Jewish (1939-1945) -- Fiction 8. Poland -- History -- 1918-1945 -- Fiction

ISBN 9780399257780

LC 2016059474

Golden Kite Award (2019)

This book, by Jane Yolen, "follows twins as they travel from the Lodz ghetto, to the partisans in the forest, to a horrific concentration camp where they lose everything but each other. It's 1942 in Poland, and the world is coming to pieces. At least that's how it seems to Chaim and Gittel, twins whose lives feel like a fairy tale torn apart. . . . But in all darkness there is light, and the twins find it through Chaim's poetry and the love they have for each other." (Publisher's note)

"Using the framework of the Hansel and Gretel story, Yolen does a superb job of dramatizing the horrors of WWII and the Holocaust, bringing vivid fear and suspense to her captivating story. It makes for altogether memorable and essential reading." Booklist

Pay the piper; [by] Jane Yolen and Adam Stemple. Tor/Starscape 2005 175p $16.95

Grades: 6 7 8 9 **Fic**

1. Fantasy fiction 2. Rock music -- Fiction

ISBN 0-7653-1158-5

When Callie interviews the band, Brass Rat, for her school newspaper, her feelings are ambivalent, but when all the children of Northampton begin to disappear on Halloween, she knows where the dangerous search must begin.

The authors "have produced a rollicking good riff on the Pied Piper. . . . The authors keep the action moving. . . . An entertaining as well as meaty read." Booklist

The **queen's** own fool; a novel of Mary Queen of Scots. [by] Jane Yolen and Robert J. Harris. Philomel Bks. 2000 390p pa $7.99

Grades: 7 8 9 10 **Fic**

1. Queens 2. Scotland -- Fiction

ISBN 0-399-23380-6; 0-698-11918-5 pa

LC 99-55070

When twelve-year-old Nicola leaves Troupe Brufort and serves as the fool for Mary, Queen of Scots, she experiences the political and religious upheavals in both France and Scotland

"The authors have woven fiction and historical fact into a seamless tapestry." Horn Book Guide

Yoon, Nicola, 1972-

★ The **Sun** Is Also a Star; by Nicola Yoon. Random House Childrens Books 2016 384 p. $21.99

Grades: 8 9 10 11 12 **Fic**

1. Teenagers -- Fiction 2. Immigrants -- Fiction 3. Korean Americans -- Fiction 4. Jamaican Americans -- Fiction

ISBN 0553496689; 0553496697; 9780553496680; 9780553496697

Printz Honor Book (2017)

Coretta Scott King/John Steptoe New Talent Author Award (2017)

National Book Award Finalist: Young People's Literature (2016)

In this book, by Nicola Yoon, "it is Natasha's last day in New York City, where she has lived for 10 years. Her family, living as undocumented immigrants in a small Brooklyn apartment, are being deported to Jamaica after her father's arrest for drunk driving. Natasha is scouring the city for a chance to stay in the United States legally. She wants the normal teen existence of her peers." (Publisher's note)

"With appeal to cynics and romantics alike, this profound exploration of life and love tempers harsh realities with the beauty of hope in a way that is both deeply moving and satisfying." Kirkus

Young, Karen Romano

Doodlebug; a novel in doodles. Feiwel and Friends 2010 un il $14.99

Grades: 4 5 6 7 **Fic**

1. School stories 2. Moving -- Fiction 3. California -- Fiction 4. Family life -- Fiction 5. Racially mixed people -- Fiction

ISBN 978-0-312-56156-7; 0-312-56156-3

Doreen Bussey, aka Dodo, takes the nickname Doodlebug when her family moves from Los Angeles to San Francisco and she records her experiences in a notebook with words, scribbles, and drawings.

This offers "an engaging, originial heroine, a satisfying story and lots of great pictures. . . . Some details, like the fact that the family is interracial, are shown but not stated, rewarding careful examination of the artwork. . . . Charming and thoughtful." Kirkus

Hundred percent; by Karen Romano Young. Chronicle Books 2016 256 p. (alk. paper) $16.99

Grades: 5 6 7 **Fic**

1. Girls -- fiction 2. Emotions in children -- fiction 3. Schools -- Fiction 4. Nicknames -- Fiction 5. Friendship -- Fiction 6. Family life -- Fiction 7. Best friends -- Fiction 8. Families -- fiction 9. Sixth grade (Education) -- fiction

ISBN 9781452138909

LC 2015047481

In this children's book by Karen Romano Young, "Christine Gouda faces change at every turn, starting with her own nickname—Tink—which just doesn't fit anymore. Readers will relate to this strong female protagonist whose voice rings with profound authenticity and absolute novelty, and her year's cringingly painful trials in normalcy—uncomfortable Halloween costumes, premature sleepover parties, crushed crushes, and changing friendships." (Publisher's note)

"Romano's characters jump off the page in a thoughtful and realistic look at what it means to be on the precipice of adolescence." Pub Wkly

Young, Moira

Blood red road. Margaret K. McElderry Books 2011 512p (Dustlands trilogy) $17.99

Grades: 6 7 8 9 10 **Fic**

1. Science fiction 2. Twins -- Fiction 3. Orphans -- Fiction 4. Siblings -- Fiction 5. Kidnapping -- Fiction

ISBN 978-1-4424-2998-7; 1-4424-2998-4

LC 2011-03423

"When 18-year-old Saba's father is killed and her twin brother, Lugh, is kidnapped, she sets out to rescue him, along with their younger sister, Emmi, and Saba's intelligent raven, Nero. Their travels across the desert wasteland bring them to a violent city in which Saba is forced to fight for her life in an arena. When she escapes with the help of a group of women warriors, she and her new allies (including a handsome and infuriating male warrior named Jack) try to prevent Lugh from being sacrificed." (Publishers Weekly)

"Readers will . . . be riveted by the book's fast-paced mix of action and romance. It's a natural for Hunger Games fans." Publ Wkly

Yovanoff, Brenna

The **replacement**; Brenna Yovanoff. Razorbill 2010 343p $17.99

Grades: 9 10 11 12 **Fic**

1. Fantasy fiction 2. Death -- Fiction 3. Siblings -- Fiction 4. Supernatural -- Fiction 5. Missing children -- Fiction

ISBN 978-1-59514-337-2; 1-59514-337-8

LC 2010-36066

Sixteen-year-old Mackie Doyle knows that he replaced a human child when he was just an infant, and when a friend's sister disappears he goes against his family's and town's deliberate denial of the problem to confront the beings that dwell under the town, tampering with human lives.

"Yovanoff's spare but haunting prose creates an atmosphere shrouded in gloom and secrecy so that readers, like Mackie, must attempt to make sense of a situation ruled by chaos and fear. The ethical complications of the town's deal with the creatures of Mayhem are clearly presented but never overwrought, while Mackie's problematic relationship to the townspeople as both an outsider and a savior is poignantly explored." Bull Cent Child Books

Zahler, Diane

The **thirteenth** princess. Harper 2009 243p

Grades: 4 5 6 7 **Fic**

1. Fairy tales 2. Magic -- Fiction 3. Sisters -- Fiction 4. Princesses -- Fiction 5. Household employees -- Fiction 6. Father-daughter relationship -- Fiction 7. Folklore -- Germany -- literature

ISBN 0-06-182498-4; 0-06-182499-2 lib bdg; 978-0-06-182498-2; 978-0-06-182499-9 lib bdg

LC 2009-14575

Zita, cast aside by her father and raised as a kitchen maid, learns when she is nearly twelve that she is a princess and that her twelve sisters love her, and so when she discovers they are victims of an evil enchantment, she desperately tries to save them. Inspired by the Grimm fairy tale, "The twelve dancing princesses."

Zahler "deftly and thoughtfully embellishes the tale's classic elements. . . . Zahler takes a light story and gives it gratifying depth, rounding out the characters and their motivations without betraying the source material and wrapping it all together in a graceful and cohesive romantic drama." Publ Wkly

A **true** princess. Harper 2011 182p $15.99

Grades: 4 5 6 **Fic**

1. Fairy tales 2. Friendship -- Fiction 3. Princesses -- Fiction 4. Voyages and travels -- Fiction

ISBN 978-0-06-182501-9; 0-06-182501-8

LC 2010017846

Twelve-year-old Lilia goes north to seek the family she has never known, accompanied by her friends Kai and Karina and their dog Ove, on an adventure fraught with peril, especially when they become lost in Bitra Forest, the Elf King's domain. Inspired by the Hans Christian Andersen tale, The princess and the pea.

"Readers who enjoyed . . . Zahler's The Thirteenth Princess . . . will also relish this tale." SLJ

Zail, Suzy

Playing for the commandant; Suzy Zail. Candlewick Press 2014 256 p. $16.99

Grades: 7 8 9 10 11 12 **Fic**

1. Pianists -- Fiction 2. Holocaust, 1939-1945 -- Fiction 3. War stories 4. Historical fiction 6. Concentration camp inmates - Fiction

ISBN 0763664030; 9780763664039

LC 2013955694

In this young adult novel by Suzy Zail, "Before, Hanna was going to be a famous concert pianist. She was going to wear her yellow dress to a dance. And she was going to dance with a boy. But then the Nazis came. Now it is up to Hanna to do all she can to keep her mother and sister alive, even if that means playing piano for the commandant and his guests." (Publisher's note)

"Zail's story is as gut-wrenching as any Holocaust tale . . . The haunting, matter-of-fact tone of Hanna's story will likely resonate with teens learning about the Holocaust." Booklist

Zarr, Sara

★ **How** to save a life; Sara Zarr. Little, Brown 2011 341 p. $17.99

Grades: 6 7 8 9 10 11 12 **Fic**

1. Adoption -- Fiction 2. Bereavement -- Fiction 3. Mother-daughter relationship -- Fiction 4. Colorado -- Fiction 5. Pregnancy -- Fiction 6. Family life -- Fiction

ISBN 9780316036061

LC 2010045832

Told from their own viewpoints, seventeen-year-old Jill, in grief over the loss of her father, and Mandy, nearly nineteen, are thrown together when Jill's mother agrees to adopt Mandy's unborn child but nothing turns out as they had anticipated.

The **Lucy** variations; by Sara Zarr. 1st ed. Little, Brown and Co. 2013 320 p. (hardcover) $17.99

Grades: 7 8 9 10 11 12 **Fic**

1. Pianists -- Fiction 2. Brothers and sisters -- Fiction 3. Ability -- Fiction 4. San Francisco (Calif.) -- Fiction 5. Family life -- California -- Fiction 6. Self-actualization (Psychology) -- Fiction

ISBN 031620501X; 9780316205016

LC 2012029852

In this novel, by Sara Zarr, "Lucy Beck-Moreau once had a promising future as a concert pianist. . . . Now, at sixteen, it's over. A death, and a betrayal, led her to walk away. That leaves her talented ten-year-old brother, Gus, to shoulder the full weight of the Beck-Moreau family expectations. Then Gus gets a new piano teacher who is young, kind, and interested in helping Lucy rekindle her love of piano--on her own terms." (Publisher's note)

"The third-person narration focuses entirely on Lucy but allows readers enough distance to help them understand her behavior in ways Lucy cannot. Occasional flashbacks fill out the back story. The combination of sympathetic main character and unusual social and cultural world makes this satisfying coming-of-age story stand out." Kirkus

★ **Once** was lost. Little, Brown 2009 217p $16.99

Grades: 7 8 9 10 **Fic**

1. Clergy -- Fiction 2. Alcoholism -- Fiction 3. Kidnapping -- Fiction 4. Christian life -- Fiction

ISBN 978-0-316-03604-7; 0-316-03604-8

LC 2009-25187

As the tragedy of a missing girl unfolds in her small town, fifteen-year-old Samara, who feels emotionally abandoned by her parents, begins to question her faith.

"This multilayered exploration of the intersection of the spiritual life and imperfect people features suspense and packs an emotional wallop." SLJ

Roomies; Sara Zarr and Tara Altebrando. Little, Brown and Company 2014 288 p. $18

Grades: 9 10 11 12 **Fic**

1. Roommates -- Fiction 2. Teenage girls -- Fiction 3. Email -- Fiction 4. Friendship -- Fiction 5. Dating (Social customs) -- Fiction 6. Family life -- California -- Fiction 7. Family life -- New Jersey -- Fiction

ISBN 0316217492; 9780316217491

LC 2012048431

In this book, by Sara Zarr and Tara Altebrando, "Elizabeth receives her freshman-year roommate assignment at the beginning of summer [and] she shoots off an email to coordinate the basics. She can't wait to escape her New Jersey beach town, and her mom, and start life over in California. The first note to Lauren in San Francisco comes as a surprise; she had requested a single. . . . Soon the girls are emailing back and forth, sharing secrets even though they've never met." (Publisher's note)

"Jersey girl Elizabeth (EB) and San Franciscan Lauren, soon to be college roommates, correspond throughout the summer; chapters with alternating perspectives unwrap each girl's backstory, personality, and coming-to-terms with changes looming on the horizon. The premise will have mass appeal with teens who fantasize about their post-high-school futures, and the authors succeed in presenting two distinct and relatable narrative voices." (Horn Book)

Sweethearts. Little, Brown and Co. 2008 217p $16.99
Grades: 8 9 10 11 12 **Fic**

1. School stories 2. Romance fiction 3. Love stories 4. Utah -- Fiction 5. Weight loss -- Fiction

ISBN 978-0-316-01455-7; 0-316-01455-9

LC 2007-41099

After losing her soul mate, Cameron, when they were nine, Jennifer, now seventeen, transformed herself from the unpopular fat girl into the beautiful and popular Jenna, but Cameron's unexpected return dredges up memories that cause both social and emotional turmoil.

"Zarr's writing is remarkable. . . . She conveys great delicacy of feeling and shades of meaning, and the realistic, moving ending will inspire excellent discussion." Booklist

Zenatti, Valerie

A **bottle** in the Gaza Sea; translated by Adriana Hunter. Bloomsbury Children's Books 2008 149p il $16.95
Grades: 7 8 9 10 11 12 **Fic**

1. Israel -- Fiction 2. Letters -- Fiction 3. Israel-Arab conflicts -- Fiction

ISBN 978-1-59990-200-5; 1-59990-200-1

LC 2007-42361

Original French edition, 2005

Seventeen-year-old Tal Levine of Jerusalem, despondent over the ongoing Arab-Israeli conflict, puts her hopes for peace in a bottle and asks her brother, a military nurse in the Gaza Strip, to toss it into the sea, leading ultimately to friendship and understanding between her and an 'enemy.'

"Zenatti uses short, riveting chapters, . . . to pack a punch with readers reluctant to voracious. The overall effect is one of a haunting relationship that will help teens understand both sides of the Israeli-Palestinian conflict." Kirkus

Zephaniah, Benjamin

Face. Bloomsbury Pub. 2002 207p $15.95; pa $6.95
Grades: 7 8 9 10 **Fic**

1. Great Britain -- Fiction 2. Burns and scalds -- Fiction

ISBN 1-58234-774-3; 1-58234-921-5 pa

LC 2002-22758

First published 1999 in the United Kingdom

"This book will not only be enjoyed by teen readers for its entertaining story, but also for its statement about prejudice." Voice Youth Advocates

Zettel, Sarah

Bad luck girl; Sarah Zettel. Random House Inc 2014 368 p. (The American fairy trilogy) (hardcover) $17.99
Grades: 7 8 9 10 **Fic**

1. Magic -- Fiction 2. Fairies -- Fiction 3. Chicago (Ill.) -- Fiction 4. Racially mixed people -- Fiction 5. Chicago (Ill.) -- History -- 20th century -- Fiction

ISBN 0375869409; 9780375869402; 9780375969409

LC 2013013855

Other titles in this series are: Dust girl (2012); Golden girl (2013)

In this book, by Sarah Zettel, "after rescuing her parents from the Seelie king at Hearst Castle, Callie is caught up in the war between the fairies of the Midnight Throne and the Sunlit Kingdoms. By accident, she discovers that fairies aren't the only magical creatures in the world. There's also Halfers, misfits that are half fairy and half other - laced with strange magic and big-city attitude. As the war heats up, Callie's world falls apart." (Publisher's note)

"Half-fairy, half-human Callie (Golden Girl; Dust Girl) has reunited with her family, thus starting a war between the two fairy kingdoms. Fleeing Los Angeles for Chicago, Callie realizes that to end the war she must stand and fight. Zettel brings the street life, locales, and culture of jazz-age Chicago into the imagery of her fantasy, packing the story with incident and adventure." Horn Book

Palace of Spies; being a true, accurate, and complete account of the scandalous and wholly remarkable adventures of Margaret Preston Fitzroy... by Sarah Zettel. Harcourt, Houghton Mifflin Harcourt 2013 368 p. (Palace of spies) $16.99
Grades: 8 9 10 **Fic**

1. Spies -- Fiction 2. London (England) -- Fiction 3. Great Britain -- History -- 1714-1837 -- Fiction 4. Love -- Fiction 5. Orphans -- Fiction 6. Courts and courtiers -- Fiction 7. London (England) -- History -- 18th century -- Fiction 8. Great Britain -- History -- George I, 1714-1727 -- Fiction

ISBN 0544074114; 9780544074118

LC 2012046366

In author Sarah Zettel's book, "sixteen-year-old Peggy is a well-bred orphan who is coerced into posing as a lady in waiting at the palace of King George I. Life is grand, until Peggy starts to suspect that the girl she's impersonating might have been murdered. Unless Peggy can discover the truth, she might be doomed to the same terrible fate. But in a court of shadows and intrigue, anyone could be a spy--perhaps even the handsome young artist with whom Peggy is falling in love." (Publisher's note)

"In eighteenth-century London, destitute orphan Peggy Fitzroy agrees to impersonate the recently deceased spy Lady Francesca as maid of honor to Princess Caroline. With a war of succession, jilted love, and religious turmoil in the mix, Peggy must navigate intrigue and shady liaisons to uncover the truth behind her predecessor's death. The feisty narrator and lush period details will garner fans for this new series." (Horn Book)

Other titles in this series are:
Dangerous Deceptions (2014)
The Assasin's Masque (2016)

Zevin, Gabrielle

★ **Memoirs** of a teenage amnesiac. Farrar, Straus and Giroux 2007 271p $17; pa $8.99; eboook $40.00
Grades: 7 8 9 10 **Fic**

1. School stories 2. Amnesia -- Fiction 3. Friendship -- Fiction

ISBN 978-0-374-34946-2; 0-374-34946-0; 978-0-312-56128-4 pa; 0-312-56128-8 pa; 9781429956291

LC 2006-35287

After a nasty fall, Naomi realizes that she has no memory of the last four years and finds herself reassessing every aspect of her life.

This is a "sensitive, joyful novel. . . . Pulled by the the heart-bruising love story, readers will pause to contemplate irresistible questions." Booklist

Zhang, Kat, 1991-

Once we were; the second book in the Hybrid chronicles. Kat Zhang. HarperTeen 2014 340 p. $17.99
Grades: 8 9 10 11 12 **Fic**

1. Science fiction 2. Sisters -- Fiction 3. Identity (Psychology) --

Fiction 4. Resistance to government -- Fiction 5. Identity -- Fiction 6. Government, Resistance to -- Fiction
ISBN 0062114905; 9780062114907; 9780062114914
LC 2013032811

In this sequel to "What's Left of Me," by Kat Zhang, "Eva and Addie struggle to share their body as they clash over romance and join the fight for hybrid freedom. . . . Addie and Eva escaped imprisonment at a horrific psychiatric hospital. Now they should be safe, living among an underground hybrid movement. But safety is starting to feel constricting. Faced with the possibility of being in hiding forever, the girls are eager to help bring about change—now." (Publisher's note)

"Zhang has a unique challenge: she must give each character two distinct personalities, which she skillfully manages. While this book lacks some of the freshness of What's Left of Me (HarperCollins, 2012), simply by virtue of being a sequel, the lovely, atmospheric storytelling is still very much present. Zhang has envisioned a complex, unique world and deftly brings it to life." (School Library Journal)

Zindel, Paul

★ The **Pigman**; a novel. Harper & Row 1968 182p hardcover o.p.

Grades: 7 8 9 10 **Fic**

1. Secrets -- Fiction 2. Friendship -- Fiction
ISBN 9781480642102
ALA YALSA Margaret A. Edwards Award (2002)

"John Conlan and Lorraine Jensen, high school sophomores, are both troubled young people who have problems at home. They become friendly with an elderly widower, Mr. Pignati, who welcomes them into his home and shares with them his simple pleasures, including his collection of ceramic pigs, of which he is proud. When the Pigman, as the young people call him, goes to the hospital after a heart attack, they take advantage of his house for a party that becomes destructive. The consequences are tragic and propel the two young friends into more responsible behavior." Shapiro. Fic for Youth. 3d edition

Another title about the Pigman is:
The Pigman's legacy (1980)

Zink, Michelle

Prophecy of the sisters. Little, Brown 2009 343p $17.99

Grades: 7 8 9 10 **Fic**

1. Twins -- Fiction 2. Sisters -- Fiction 3. Supernatural -- Fiction 4. Good and evil -- Fiction
ISBN 978-0-316-02742-7; 0-316-02742-1
LC 2008-45290

In late nineteenth-century New York state, wealthy sixteen-year-old twin sisters Lia and Alice Milthorpe find that they are on opposite sides of an ancient prophecy that has destroyed their parents and seeks to do even more harm.

"This arresting story takes readers to other planes of existence." Booklist

Other titles in this series are:
Guardian of the gate (2010)
Circle of fire (2011)

Zinn, Bridget

Poison; by Bridget Zinn. 1st ed. Disney/Hyperion Books 2013 276 p. (hardcover) $16.99

Grades: 7 8 9 10 11 12 **Fic**

1. Occult fiction -- fiction 3. Fantasy 4. Magic -- Fiction 5. Heroes -- Fiction 6. Princesses -- Fiction 7. Impersonation -- Fiction 8. Fugitives from justice -- Fiction
ISBN 1423139933; 9781423139935
LC 2012008693

In this novel, sixteen-year-old "Kyra is on the run. She may be one of the Kingdom of Mohr's most highly skilled potions masters, but she has also just tried—and failed—to poison Princess Ariana. And Kyra is determined to finish her mission even if it means killing her best friend. . . . In order to save her kingdom from a nefarious plot, Kyra will have to come to terms with all the gifts she possesses." (School Library Journal)

Zoboi, Ibi

Pride; Ibi Zoboi. Balzer + Bray 2018 289 p. (hardback) $17.99

Grades: 8 9 10 11 12 **Fic**

1. Bildungsromans 2. Love -- Fiction 3. Racism -- Fiction
ISBN 9780062564047; 9780062564054

"Zuri Benitez has pride. Brooklyn pride, family pride, and pride in her Afro-Latino roots. But pride might not be enough to save her rapidly gentrifying neighborhood from becoming unrecognizable. . . . In a timely update of Jane Austen's 'Pride and Prejudice,' . . . Zoboi skillfully balances cultural identity, class, and gentrification against the heady magic of first love in her vibrant reimagining of this beloved classic." (Publisher's note)

Zuckerman, Linda

A **taste** for rabbit. Arthur A. Levine Books 2007 310p $16.99

Grades: 7 8 9 10 **Fic**

1. Foxes -- Fiction 2. Animals -- Fiction 3. Rabbits -- Fiction 4. Resistance to government -- Fiction
ISBN 0-439-86977-3; 978-0-439-86977-5
LC 2007-7787

Quentin, a rabbit who lives in a walled compound run by a militaristic government, must join forces with Harry, a fox, to stop the sinister disappearances of outspoken and rebellious rabbit citizens.

"The blend of adventure, mystery and morality in this heroic tale of honor and friendship will appeal to middle-school fantasy fans." Publ Wkly

Zusak, Markus, 1975-

★ The **book** thief. Knopf 2006 552p il $16.95; lib bdg $18.99

Grades: 8 9 10 11 12 **Fic**

1. Death -- Fiction 2. Jews -- Germany -- Fiction 3. Books and reading -- Fiction 4. Holocaust, 1933-1945 -- Fiction 5. World War, 1939-1945 -- Fiction
ISBN 0-375-83100-2; 0-375-93100-7 lib bdg
LC 2005-08942

Michael L. Printz Award honor book, 2007

Trying to make sense of the horrors of World War II, Death relates the story of Liesel—a young German girl whose book-stealing and storytelling talents help sustain her family and the Jewish man they are hiding, as well as their neighbors.

"This hefty volume is an achievement—a challenging book in both length and subject, and best suited to sophisticated older readers." Publ Wkly

S C STORY COLLECTIONS

13; thirteen stories that capture the agony and ecstasy of being thirteen. edited by James Howe. Atheneum Books for Young Readers 2003 278p $16.95; pa $7.99
Grades: 4 5 6 7 S C
1. Short stories
ISBN 0-689-82863-2; 1-416-92684-4 pa

"The stories are a mixture of humor, pathos, and poignancy, and most are based on personal experiences. . . . Howe has chosen excellent authors for this volume and they have written oh-so-true stories about that wonderful, terrible first year of being a teenager. " SLJ

Alexander, Lloyd

★ The **foundling** and other tales of Prydain; rev & expanded ed; Holt & Co. 1999 98p hardcover o.p. pa $5.99
Grades: 5 6 7 8 S C
1. Short stories 2. Fantasy fiction
ISBN 0-8050-6130-4; 0-8050-8053-8 pa
LC 98-42807

First published 1973; this revised and expanded edition includes two additional stories Coll and his white pig and The truthful harp, first published separately 1965 and 1967 respectively

Eight short stories dealing with events that preceded the birth of Taran, the Assistant Pig-Keeper and key figure in the author's five works on the Kingdom of Prydain which began with The book of three

"The stories are written with vivid grace and humor." Chicago. Children's Book Center [review of 1973 edition]

Almond, David, 1951-

Half a creature from the sea; A Life in Stories. David Almond ; illustrated by Eleanor Taylor. Candlewick Press 2015 222 p. illustrations $16.99
Grades: 7 8 9 10 S C
1. Short stories -- Collections 2. England -- Fiction
ISBN 0763678775; 9780763678777
LC 2015931431

In this book, author David Almond "presents a beautiful collection of short fiction, interwoven with pieces that illuminate the inspiration behind the stories. May Malone is said to have a monster in her house, but what Norman finds there may just be the angel he needs. Joe Quinn's house is noisy with poltergeists, or could it be Davie's raging causing the disturbance? Fragile Annie learns the truth about herself in a photograph taken by a traveling man near the sea." (Publisher's note)

"Taylor's illustrations help add depth, as do the interstitial author's notes offering glimpses into each story's autobiographical roots and other inspirations. Likely to appeal to aspiring writers and fans of The Tightrope Walkers." Horn Book

America street; a multicultural anthology of stories. edited by Anne Mazer and Brice Particelli. Revised edition Persea Books 2019 224 p. (pbk) $13.95
Grades: 7 8 9 10 11 12 Adult S C
1. Anthologies 2. Children's stories 3. American short stories 4. Short stories 5. Children's stories, American
ISBN 9780892554911; 0892554916
LC 2018045202

This book, edited by Anne Mazer and Brice Particelli, "was the very first collection of stories about young people growing up in our diverse society. It has informed and inspired hundreds of thousands of readers. Now this influential and much-loved anthology is expanded and updated for a new generation. Twenty stories, twelve new and eight returning favorites, focus on life issues, from the personal to the political." (Publisher's note)

"A lyrical, poignant collection of voices that reflect the racial and ethnic diversity of modern America." Kirkus

Amnesty International

Free? : stories about human rights; [edited by] Amnesty International. Candlewick Press 2010 202p il $17.99; pa $8.99
Grades: 7 8 9 10 S C
1. Short stories 2. Freedom -- Fiction 3. Human rights -- Fiction
ISBN 978-0-7636-4703-2; 0-7636-4703-9; 978-0-7636-4926-5 pa; 0-7636-4926-0 pa
LC 2009-14720

An anthology of fourteen stories by young adult authors from around the world, on such themes as asylum, law, education, and faith, compiled in honor of the sixtieth anniversary of the Universal Declaration of Human Rights.

"Margaret Mahy writes about class with wit and intensity, as does Jamila Gavin, who sets the class war in India, where a young girl's family throws her out for resisting an arranged marriage. . . . David Almond explores school power plays in a story about a boy who says no to a popular bully. Hurricane Katrina is Rita Williams-Garcia's setting. Two contemporary Palestinian stories compare the current occupation with Native American experiences of oppression. . . . Sure to spark discussion and perhaps participation in Amnesty International." Booklist

Appelt, Kathi

Kissing Tennessee and other stories from the Stardust Dance. Harcourt 2000 118p hardcover o.p. pa $5.95
Grades: 6 7 8 9 S C
1. Short stories 2. School stories
ISBN 0-15-202249-X; 0-15-205127-9 pa
LC 99-50505

Graduating eighth graders relate their stories of love and heartbreak that have brought them to Dogwood Junior High's magical Stardust Dance.

"This collection will spark conversation in contemporary literature discussions, will quietly unsettle readers, and will elevate the quality of short-story collections." SLJ

Asimov, Isaac

I, robot; Bantam hardcover ed.; Bantam Books 2004 224p (Robot series) $24; pa $7.99
Grades: 7 8 9 10 11 12 Adult S C
1. Short stories 2. Science fiction 3. Robots -- Fiction
ISBN 0-553-80370-0; 0-553-29438-5 pa
LC 2003-69139

First published 1950 by Gnome Press

"These loosely connected stories cover the career of Dr. Susan Calvin and United States Robots, the industry that she heads, from the time of the public's early distrust of these robots to its later dependency on them. This collection is an important introduction to a theme often found in science fiction: the encroachment of technology on our lives." Shapiro. Fic for Youth. 3d edition

Aspin, Diana

Ordinary miracles. Red Deer Press 2003 168p (Northern Lights young novels) pa $7.95
Grades: 7 8 9 10 S C
1. Short stories 2. Canada -- Fiction
ISBN 0-88995-277-9

A collection of 13 short stories concerning life in a small Canadian community, covering such topics as an old man's memories of abandonment by his mother and his abusive life as an orphan, a teen's struggle with his sexuality, and issues such as alcoholism, death, adultery, and poverty.

This is "a riveting collection. . . . The author has created a work that leaves readers awash with feelings of empathy for each young protagonist." SLJ

Avi, 1937-

★ The **Most** Important Thing; Stories About Sons, Fathers, and Grandfathers. by Avi. Candlewick Press 2016 224 p. $16.99

Grades: 5 6 7 8 **S C**

1. Short stories -- Collections 2. Father-son relationship -- Fiction

ISBN 0763681113; 9780763681111

LC 2015941423

This book, by Avi, "presents seven short stories exploring the vital ties between fathers and sons. Luke sees the ghost of his father but can't figure out what Dad wants him to do. Paul takes a camping trip with the grandfather he's just met and discovers what lies behind the man's erratic behavior. Ryan has some surprising questions when he interviews his prospective stepfather for the job." (Publisher's note)

"Avi's deft incorporation of humor, heartache, and the occasional touch of the supernatural will draw readers in as they ponder how family ties bind in both positive and negative ways." Pub Wkly

Strange happenings; five tales of transformation. Harcourt 2006 147p $15; pa $5.95

Grades: 5 6 7 8 **S C**

1. Short stories 2. Supernatural -- Fiction

ISBN 0-15-205790-0; 0-15-206461-3 pa

LC 2004-29579

"In this short story collection, Avi offers five fantastical tales, set in both contemporary and fairy-tale lands, that explore the notion of transformation. . . . The pieces are vividly imagined and shot through with a captivating, edgy spookiness, which, along with their brevity and some droll, crackling dialogue, makes them great choices for sharing aloud in class or as inspiration in creative-writing units." Booklist

What do fish have to do with anything? and other stories; illustrated by Tracy Mitchell. Candlewick Press 1997 202p il hardcover o.p. pa $6.99

Grades: 4 5 6 7 **S C**

1. Short stories

ISBN 0-7636-0329-5; 0-7636-2319-9 pa

LC 97-1354

"While Avi's endings are not tidy, they are effective: each story brings its protagonist beyond childhood self-absorption to the realization that one is an integral part of a bigger picture." Horn Book

Bachmann, Stefan

The **Cabinet** of Curiosities; 36 Tales Brief & Sinister. by Stefan Bachmann, Katherine Catmull, Claire Legrand and Emma Trevayne; illustrated by Alexander Jansson. Harpercollins Childrens Books 2014 496 p. illustrations $16.99

Grades: 3 4 5 6 7 **S C**

1. Short stories 2. Horror fiction 3. Mystery fiction

ISBN 0062331051; 9780062331052

LC 2013362532

This book, by Stefan Bachmann, Katherine Catmull, Claire Legrand and Emma Trevayne, is "a collection of thirty-six forty eerie, mysterious, intriguing, and very short stories. . . . The book features an introduction and commentary by the authors and black-and-white illustrations throughout." (Publisher's note)

"Many of these are moral tales in which nasty children or adults die horribly; others, though, feature perfectly nice people who meet similarly gruesome ends. Readers who enjoy their Halloween chills all year round will find this anthology a delight." Pub Wkly

Baseball crazy: ten short stories that cover all the bases; edited by Nancy E. Mercado. Dial Books for Young Readers 2008 191p $16.99; pa $6.99

Grades: 4 5 6 7 **S C**

1. Short stories 2. Baseball -- Fiction

ISBN 978-0-8037-3162-2; 0-8037-3162-0; 978-0-14-241371-5 pa; 0-14-241371-2 pa

LC 2007-26649

"There's no shortage of great writing in this collection of 10 stories. Baseball unifies the entries, but there the similarities end. . . . Readers will be drawn in by the masterful storytelling." Publ Wkly

The **beastly** bride; tales of the animal people. edited by Ellen Datlow & Terri Windling; introduction by Terri Windling; selected decorations by Charles Vess. Viking 2010 500p $19.99

Grades: 8 9 10 11 12 **S C**

1. Short stories 2. Supernatural -- Fiction

ISBN 978-0-670-01145-2; 0-670-01145-2

LC 2009-14317

A collection of stories and poems relating to animal transfiguration legends from around the world, retold and reimagined by various authors. Includes brief biographies, authors' notes, and suggestions for further reading

"The majority of these beastly tales make for fun, thoughtful, occasionally gripping, reading." Voice Youth Advocates

Book Wish Foundation

★ **What** you wish for; foreword by Mia Farrow. G.P. Putnam's Sons 2011 252p $17.99

Grades: 6 7 8 9 **S C**

ISBN 978-0-399-25454-3; 0-399-25454-4

LC 2011003215

A collection of stories and poems with the theme of wishes.

This is a "moving anthology. . . . There isn't a weak story in the book, but, of course, a few are standouts. . . . Here's a wish: that this collection might find the widest readership possible." Booklist

Campoy, F. Isabel, 1946-

Yes! we are Latinos; by Alma Flor Ada and F. Isabel Campoy ; illustrated by David Diaz. Charlesbridge 2013 96 p. ill. (reinforced) $18.95

Grades: 7 8 9 10 **S C**

1. Hispanic Americans -- Poetry 2. American poetry -- Latino authors 3. Short stories 4. Immigrants -- Fiction 5. Immigrants -- United States 6. Latin Americans -- United States 7. Emigration and immigration -- Fiction 8. Latin Americans -- Cultural assimilation 9. Latin Americans -- United States -- Fiction

ISBN 158089383X; 9781580893831

LC 2012027214

In this book, the authors "shape fictional portraits of 13 young people living in the U.S., who have diverse experiences and backgrounds but share a Latino heritage. The first-person narrative poems range from reflective to free-spirited, methodical to free-association. . . . Informative nonfictional interludes . . . address relevant subjects, including immigration, the challenges migrant workers face, and Cuba-U.S. history." (Publishers Weekly)

Includes bibliographical references and index

★ The **chronicles** of Harris Burdick; 14 amazing authors tell the tales. Houghton Mifflin Harcourt 2011 un il $24.99
Grades: 5 6 7 8 9 **S C**
1. Short stories
ISBN 978-0-547-54810-4; 0-547-54810-9; 0547548109; 9780547548104
LC 2011006564

"Van Allsburg's The Mysteries of Harris Burdick, published in 1984, paired foreboding sentences with cryptic, highly detailed charcoal-pencil illustrations. With mostly stimulating, sometimes conventional results, seasoned authors (and Van Allsburg himself) play the game children have for decades, incorporating the sentences and visual cues into new stories . . . that expand on the original's enigmas. The liveliest entries pick up on Van Allsburg's haunting ambiguity: Jon Scieszka ends with a cliffhanger, Gregory Maguire weaves a complex tale of magic, and M.T. Anderson concocts a chilling Halloween offering. For a lake-side picture of two children, Sherman Alexie writes a sinister narrative about exasperating twins who pretend to have a third sibling, until their creepy prank backfires. . . . This star-studded exercise in creative writing tests the wits of favorite authors and shows readers how even the big shots hone their craft." Publ Wkly

Cleavage; breakaway fiction for real girls. edited by Deb Loughead & Jocelyn Shipley. Sumach Press 2008 186p il pa $12.95
Grades: 8 9 10 11 12 **S C**
1. Short stories 2. Mother-daughter relationship -- Fiction
ISBN 978-1-894549-76-9; 1-894549-76-7

"Alternately edgy, charming, funny, and sweet, these 15 stories address issues confronting adolescents. Integral to each selection is the complicated relationship between the girls and their mothers. . . . The selections touch on the multiple meanings of the word 'cleavage,' and together form an aptly named collection of stories about body image and mothers and daughters coming together and growing apart. A fresh, honest, and entertaining anthology." SLJ

Compestine, Ying Chang

★ A **banquet** for hungry ghosts; a collection of deliciously frightening tales. illustrated by Coleman Polhemus. Henry Holt and Co. 2009 180p il $16.99
Grades: 6 7 8 9 10 **S C**
1. Ghost stories 2. Short stories 3. China -- Fiction
ISBN 978-0-8050-8208-1; 0-8050-8208-5
LC 2008-50273

Presents and eight-course banquet of ghost stories centering around Chinese cooking and culture. Each story is followed by a recipe and historical notes

"The stories are laced with beautiful (as well as lurid) images and chilling illustrations of the ghosts and their victims. Like the ghosts themselves, Compestine's memorable stories should prove difficult to shake." Publ Wkly

Cornered; 14 stories of bullying and defiance. [edited by] Rhoda Belleza. Running Press Teens 2012 383 p. $9.95
Grades: 7 8 9 10 11 12 **S C**
1. Short stories 2. School stories 3. Bullies -- Fiction
ISBN 9780762444281
LC 2011943133

This book is a "bully-themed anthology" of stories that focus "not only on teens who are targets of bullying, but also those who perpetrate it—and many . . . do both. Bullying [in the stories] takes many forms, including a teacher ridiculing students, a viral racist email and hazing on a soccer team. The contributors largely delve into bullies' behavior without resting on cliché . . . Most contributors also . . . observe that family dynamics can have as much impact as those at school." (Kirkus)

Crutcher, Chris

★ **Athletic** shorts; six short stories. Greenwillow Bks. 1991 154p $17.99; pa $6.99
Grades: 7 8 9 10 **S C**
1. Short stories 2. Sports -- Fiction
ISBN 0-688-10816-4; 0-06-050783-7 pa
LC 91-4418

ALA YALSA Margaret A. Edwards Award (2000)

A collection of short stories about high school sports

"The author seamlessly blends humor with more serious elements. . . These Athletic Shorts will speak to YAs, touch them deeply, and introduce them to characters they'll want to know better." SLJ

Dahl, Roald

Skin and other stories. Viking 2000 212p $15.99; pa $8.99
Grades: 7 8 9 10 **S C**
1. Short stories
ISBN 0-670-89184-3; 0-14-131034-0 pa
LC 99-58600

A collection of 13 of the author's short stories written for adults. "Full of irony and unexpected twists, they smack of the master's touch—every word carefully chosen, characters fully fleshed out in only a few pages, the sense of place immediate." Booklist

Del Negro, Janice

★ **Passion** and poison; tales of shape-shifters, ghosts, and spirited women. Marshall Cavendish 2007 64p il $16.99
Grades: 5 6 7 8 **S C**
1. Ghost stories 2. Short stories 3. Supernatural -- Fiction
ISBN 978-0-7614-5361-1; 0-7614-5361-X
LC 2007-07237

"Including both original tales and retellings, this collection of seven stories . . . features diverse female protagonists facing challenges and perils—from human bullies to ghosts. More eerie than scary, the tales of bravery, revenge, grief, and redemption share a gothic sensibility. . . . The black-and-white illustrations . . . evoke bygone times." Booklist

Delacre, Lulu

★ **Salsa** stories; stories and linocuts by Lulu Delacre. Scholastic Press 2000 105p il hardcover o.p. $16.99
Grades: 4 5 6 **S C**
1. Short stories 2. Family life -- Fiction 3. Latin America -- Fiction
ISBN 0-590-63118-7; 0-590-63121-7 pa
LC 99-25534

A collection of stories within the story of a family celebration where the guests relate their memories of growing up in various Latin American countries. Also contains recipes

"Kids will respond to both the warmth and the anxiety of the family life described in the vivid writing, and in Delacre's nicely composed linocuts." Booklist

Us, in progress; short stories about young Latinos. Lulu Delacre. HarperCollins 2017 xi, 242 p.p illustrations (hardcover) $16.99

Grades: 4 5 6 7 8 **S C**

1. Short stories 2. Children -- United States 3. Latin Americans -- Fiction

ISBN 9780062392145; 9780062392169

LC 2016949990

This short story collection, by Lulu Delacre, "is a groundbreaking look at the diverse Latinos who live in the United States. In this book, you will meet many young Latinos . . . , from a young girl whose day at her father's burrito truck surprises her to two sisters working together to change the older sister's immigration status, and more." (Publisher's note)

"Delacre's collection challenges existing misconceptions by giving readers an intimate and varied look into what it is like to be young and Latino in the United States today." Horn Book

Includes bibliographical references.

Destination unexpected: short stories; collected by Donald R. Gallo. Candlewick Press 2003 240p hardcover o.p. pa $8.99

Grades: 7 8 9 10 **S C**

1. Short stories

ISBN 0-7636-1764-4; 0-7636-3119-1 pa

LC 2002-71599

This collection "features teen protagonists experiencing a transforming experience while on some kind of journey. . . . . Whether humorous or serious, the stories are consistently well written and engaging." Booklist

Does this book make me look fat? edited by Marissa Walsh. Clarion Books 2008 215p $16

Grades: 7 8 9 10 11 12 **S C**

1. Short stories 2. Obesity -- Fiction 3. Eating disorders -- Fiction

ISBN 978-0-547-01496-8; 0-547-01496-1

LC 2008-25070

"This star-studded collection tackles a popular topic—body image—with humor, sensitivity, and creativity. . . . [It includes] Megan McCafferty's story narrated by a pair of skinny jeans. Other highlights are Matt de la Peña's wrenching story of a young man coming to terms with his sister's devastating eating disorder, and Sarra Manning's feisty protagonist, who helps a co-worker find her own style and later faces her own body issues." Booklist

Don't cramp my style; stories about that time of the month. edited by Lisa Rowe Fraustino. Simon & Schuster for Young Readers 2004 295p $15.95

Grades: 7 8 9 10 **S C**

1. Short stories 2. Menstruation -- Fiction

ISBN 0-689-85882-5

A collection of eleven stories concerning menstruation.

"This highly recommended collection . . . encompasses an impressive variety of times, cultures, attitudes, and moods. . . . The writing . . . is consistently excellent." Voice Youth Advocates

Ellis, Deborah

Lunch with Lenin and other stories. Fitzhenry & Whiteside 2008 169p pa $14.95

Grades: 7 8 9 10 11 12 **S C**

1. Short stories 2. Drug abuse -- Fiction

ISBN 978-1-55455-105-7; 1-55455-105-6

A collection of short stories that explore the lives of teenagers affected directly or indirectly by drugs.

"The relatively short stories read quickly, offering neither judgment nor solutions but rather the opportunity for compassion and understanding. . . . The collection's quality . . . is high enough to justify placing this book in every library." Voice Youth Advocates

Enthralled; paranormal diversions. edited by Melissa Marr and Kelley Armstrong. HarperCollins 2011 452p $17.99; pa $9.99

Grades: 7 8 9 10 **S C**

1. Short stories 2. Supernatural -- Fiction 3. Voyages and travels -- Fiction

ISBN 978-0-06-201579-2; 0-06-201579-6; 978-0-06-201578-5 pa; 0-06-201578-8 pa

LC 2011019393

A collection of sixteen original short stories by writers of paranormal tales, featuring journeys made by teens and magical beings.

"These short stories are loosely connected by a very openly interpreted journey motif. Psychics, genies, angels and gargoyles join fairies and vampires to terrorize and romance their fellow characters. The diversity in authors allows for the sometimes-neglected horror implied in paranormal stories to be spotlighted. . . . This collection is ideal as a sampler tray for paranormal readers looking to pick up new authors to follow or to further explore the fictional worlds they already know." Kirkus

Estevis, Anne

Down Garrapata road; by Anne Estevis. Arte Piñata Books 2003 119p pa $12.95

Grades: 7 8 9 10 **S C**

1. Short stories 2. Texas -- Fiction 3. Mexican Americans -- Fiction

ISBN 1-55885-397-9

LC 2003-49837

A collection of short stories set in a small Mexican-American community in southern Texas during the 1940s and 1950s, revealing the traditions, love, and social concerns of the families living there.

"Sly, gentle, and written in lively, simple language, these are stories that will draw readers into the particulars of a culture while capturing universal family dramas." Booklist

★ **Every** man for himself; ten short stories about being a guy. edited by Nancy E. Mercado. Dial Books 2005 154p il hardcover o.p. pa $6.99

Grades: 7 8 9 10 **S C**

1. Short stories 2. Boys -- Fiction

ISBN 0-8037-2896-4; 0-14-240813-1 pa

LC 2004-24069

"This collection provides a refreshing look at the values, decisions, and friendships that ultimately shape a boy into a man. The stories themselves are diverse, ranging from humorous to serious." SLJ

Fear: 13 stories of suspense and horror; [selected by and with an] introduction by R.L. Stine. Dutton 2010 306p $16.99; pa $7.99

Grades: 7 8 9 10 S C

1. Short stories 2. Horror fiction

ISBN 978-0-525-42168-9; 0-525-42168-8; 978-0-14-241774-4 pa; 0-14-241774-2 pa

LC 2009-53284

"Thirteen highly suspenseful short stories. . . . [Stine] enlists some of the best in the business, such as Meg Cabot and F. Paul Wilson, Walter Sorrells and James Rollins, who offer plenty of heart-throbbing supernatural horror, crime suspense, shockers and sometimes a mixture of all three. . . . Fast-paced, shuddery-scary fun." Kirkus

Firebirds; an anthology of original fantasy and science fiction. edited by Sharyn November. Firebird Press 2003 420p il $19.99

Grades: 7 8 9 10 11 12 S C

1. Short stories 2. Fantasy fiction 3. Science fiction

ISBN 0-14-250142-5

"Teens will find much to savor and celebrate in this dazzling collection of 16 short stories by some of the best fantasy writers around." SLJ

Firebirds soaring; an anthology of original speculative fiction. [edited by Sharyn November; illustrated by Mike Dringenberg] Firebird 2009 574p il $19.99

Grades: 7 8 9 10 11 12 S C

1. Short stories 2. Fantasy fiction 3. Science fiction

ISBN 978-0-14-240552-9; 0-14-240552-3

LC 2008-29516

This anthology "contains 19 short stories by some of the top writers in this genre. . . . The selections vary in length, with some short stories, some novellas. Each work is introduced by an evocative illustration that beautifully sets the scene for the written work. The variety of styles and themes and a gathering together of so many talented writers in one work offer readers a banquet for the imagination. For fans of the genre, this is a must read." SLJ

Flake, Sharon G.

★ **Who** am I without him? short stories about girls and the boys in their lives. Jump at the Sun/Hyperion Books for Children 2004 168p $15.99; pa $7.99

Grades: 7 8 9 10 S C

1. Short stories 2. African Americans -- Fiction

ISBN 0-7868-0693-1; 1-4231-0383-1 pa

Ten short stories about African American teenage girls and their relationships with boys.

"Addressing issues and situations that many girls face in today's often complex society, this book is provocative and thought-provoking." SLJ

Flanagan, John

The **lost** stories. Philomel 2011 422p (Ranger's apprentice) $17.99

Grades: 5 6 7 8 S C

1. Short stories 2. Fantasy fiction

ISBN 978-0-399-25618-9; 0-399-25618-0

This is "a collection of nine stories showing events not recorded in the books [of the Ranger's Apprentice series] and following the familiar characters during certain unrecorded times. In the framework story, set in 1896, an archaeologist discovers the fabled lost stories of the medieval Kingdom of Araluen. . . . Inspired by questions from readers, these short stories retain the adventure and the camaraderis of the novels." Booklist

Fleischman, Paul

Graven images; three stories. by Paul Fleischman; illustrations by Bagram Ibatoulline. Candlewick Press 2006 116p il $16.99; pa $5.99

Grades: 5 6 7 8 S C

1. Short stories 2. Supernatural -- Fiction

ISBN 0-7636-2775-5; 0-7636-2984-7 pa

LC 2005054283

A newly illustrated edition with a new afterword of the title first published 1982 by Harper & Row

A Newbery Medal honor book, 1983

A collection of three stories about a child who reads the lips of those who whisper secrets into a statue's ear; a daydreaming shoemaker's apprentice who must find ways to make the girl he loves notice him; and a stone carver who creates a statue of a ghost.

"Readers will be delighted with the return to print of [this title] with haunting new acrylic gouache illustrations . . . evoking the spinetingling aspects of this trio of tales. . . . Via a new afterword, the author explains the stories' inspiration and describes this book's significance early in his career." Publ Wkly

Fleming, Candace, 1962-

On the day I died; stories from the grave. Candace Fleming. Schwartz & Wade Books 2012 199 p. $16.99

Grades: 6 7 8 9 S C

1. Short stories 2. Horror fiction 3. Teenagers -- Fiction 4. Ghosts -- Fiction 5. Illinois -- Fiction 6. Cemeteries -- Fiction

ISBN 0375867813; 9780375867811; 9780375967818

LC 2011018661

This book is a collection of nine "tales told by dead teens." Author Candace Fleming "draws inspiration from several . . . horror shorts, monster movies and actual locales and incidents. . . . Ghostly young people regale [the narrator] with the ghastly circumstances of their demises. These range from being sucked into a magical mirror to being partially eaten by a mutant rubber ducky, from being brained by a falling stone gargoyle at an abandoned asylum to drowning in a car driven by a demonic hood ornament." (Kirkus Reviews)

★ **Flying** lessons & other stories; edited by Ellen Oh. Crown Books for Young Readers 2017 240 p. (hardback) $16.99

Grades: 4 5 6 7 S C

1. Children's stories 2. Short stories -- Collections

ISBN 9781101934616; 9781101934593; 9781101934609; 9781101934623

LC 2016016160

This anthology, edited by Ellen Oh, "celebrates the uniqueness and universality in all of us. In a partnership with We Need Diverse Books, industry giants Kwame Alexander, Soman Chainani, Matt de la Peña, Tim Federle, Grace Lin, Meg Medina, Walter Dean Myers, Tim Tingle, and Jacqueline Woodson join newcomer Kelly J. Baptist in a story collection that is as humorous as it is heartfelt." (Publisher's note)

"A natural for middle school classrooms and libraries, this strong collection should find eager readers." Kirkus

Full house; 10 stories about poker. edited by Pete Hautman. G. P. Putnam's Sons 2007 161p $17.99

Grades: 7 8 9 10 **S C**

1. Short stories 2. Poker -- Fiction

ISBN 978-0-399-24528-2

LC 2007-14116

This is a "compilation of stories about teenage encounters with poker. The characters find themselves in high-stakes situations: playing with the Devil, competing in a scholarship game, fighting to defeat a deadbeat stepdad, and staying one step ahead of an Internet poker company. . . . The stories vary from the eerily realistic to amusingly farfetched. In all cases, teen poker players will recognize themselves and their opponents in this diverse collection." SLJ

Funny girl; funniest. stories. ever. edited by Betsy Bird. Penguin Group USA 2017 240 p. illustrations $16.99

Grades: 4 5 6 7 8 **S C**

1. Humorous fiction 2. American fiction -- Women authors

ISBN 0451477316; 9780451477316

This book, edited by Betsy Bird, "is a collection of uproarious stories, rollicking comics, rib-tickling wit, and more, from 25 of today's funniest female writers for kids. . . . With clever contributions from award-winning and bestselling authors including Cece Bell, Sophie Blackall, . . . and Raina Telgemeier, this anthology of funny girls will make you laugh until you cry. Or cry until you laugh. Or maybe you won't cry at all. Either way, you'll definitely laugh." (Publisher's note)

"Hilarious and heartfelt, this won't only appeal to funny girls and boys, it'll inspire them." Booklist.

Gaiman, Neil

★ **M** is for magic; illustrations by Teddy Kristiansen. HarperCollins Pub. 2007 260p il $16.99; lib bdg $17.89; pa $6.99

Grades: 7 8 9 10 **S C**

1. Short stories 2. Magic -- Fiction

ISBN 978-0-06-118642-4; 0-06-118642-2; 978-0-06-118645-5 lib bdg; 0-06-118645-7 lib bdg; 978-0-06-118647-9 pa; 0-06-118647-3 pa

LC 2007-14472

Gaiman "has selected nine of his short stories and a poem and added a segment from an upcoming children's title for this volume. . . . This well-chosen collection is sure to create a new generation of Gaiman fans who will not need to understand all the allusions to enjoy the stories." Booklist

Gallo, Donald R.

★ **Owning** it; stories about teens with disabilities. edited by Donald R. Gallo. Candlewick Press 2008 215p pbk. $6.99

Grades: 7 8 9 10 **S C**

1. Short stories 2. Diseases -- Fiction 3. People with disabilities -- Fiction

ISBN 9780763646615

LC 2007-24963

This anthology presents ten stories of teenagers facing the challenges of school, parents, boyfriends and girlfriends, in addition to the additional complications that come with having a physical or psychological disability. "Grades seven to ten." (Bull Cent Child Books)

"Each of the stories is strong and will resonate with teens dealing with everything from drinking problems, migraines, Tourette's Syndrome, and even cancer." Libr Media Connect

Geektastic; stories from the nerd herd. edited by Holly Black and Cecil Castellucci. Little Brown & Co. 2009 403p il $16.99

Grades: 7 8 9 10 **S C**

1. Short stories

ISBN 978-0-316-00809-9; 0-316-00809-5

LC 2009-455709

A collection of twenty-nine short stories about geeks.

"Although not all geekdoms are covered, topics include cosplay (dressing as characters), cons (conventions), SF television and movies, RPGs (roleplaying games), fantasy books, baton-twirling, astronomy, Rocky Horror, quiz bowl, and dinosaurs. Geek-themed comics by Hope Larson and Bryan Lee O'Malley separate the stories. . . . Although readers need not necessarily be geeks to appreciate this well-written collection, it will help. Buy for all the geeks in your library—including the librarian." Voice Youth Advocates

Give me shelter; stories about children who seek asylum. edited by Tony Bradman. Frances Lincoln 2007 220p $16.95

Grades: 5 6 7 8 **S C**

1. Short stories 2. Refugees -- Fiction

ISBN 978-1-84507-522-4; 1-84507-522-6

This is a "moving collection of 11 powerful narratives, quite different in their particulars but astonishingly similar in their sense of loss and loneliness. . . . While most of the stories focus on current asylum-seekers in Britain, one looks back to a Vietnamese child's trip to Australia, and another is set in an unnamed Eastern European country." SLJ

Gothic! ten original dark tales. edited by Deborah Noyes. Candlewick Press 2004 241p hardcover o.p. pa $7.99

Grades: 7 8 9 10 **S C**

1. Short stories 2. Horror fiction

ISBN 0-7636-2243-5; 0-7636-2737-2 pa

LC 2004-45188 This "collection features short stories by noted young adult authors such as M. T. Anderson, Caitlín R. Kiernan, Garth Nix, Celia Rees, Janni Lee Simner, and Barry Yourgrau. . . . These varied tales take place in the distant past and in the high-tech present. Some are humorous while others have surprising twists or are reminiscent of classic fairy tales full of malevolent characters, but all share a love of the surreal or supernatural. . . . A sophisticated, thought-provoking, and gripping read." SLJ

★ The **Great** War; an anthology of stories inspired by objects from the first World War. illustrated by Jim Kay. Candlewick Press 2014 304 p. illustrations

Grades: 3 4 5 6 7 8 **S C**

1. World War, 1914-1918 2. War stories 3. Historical fiction

ISBN 9780763675547

LC 2013955699

In this book, illustrated by Jim Kay, "eleven internationally acclaimed writers draw on personal objects to bring the First World War to life. . . . Each author was invited to choose an object that had a connection to the war . . . and use it as the inspiration for an original short story." (Publisher's note)

"Each of the 11 original short stories in this superlative collection about WWI has been inspired by an object evoking the conflict. Thus, the catalyst for contributor Almond is a soldier's writing case; for Timothée de Fombelle, it's a Victoria Cross; for Adèle Geras, a wartime butter dish; for John Boyne, a recruitment poster; and so forth...Haunting black-and-white illustrations by Kate Greenaway Medal–winning illustrator Kay reinforce the stories' somber mood and cumulative power. This book is both beautifully designed and beautifully written." Booklist

Guys Read Terrifying Tales; edited by Jon Scieszka. Harpercollins Childrens Books 2015 288 p. illustrations
Grades: 4 5 6 7 8 **S C**
1. Anthologies 2. Ghost stories 3. Horror fiction 4. Short stories
ISBN 0062385585; 9780062385581

In this anthology, part of the Guys Read series edited by Jon Scieszka, "[e]leven masters of suspense--Kelly Barnhill, Michael Buckley, Adam Gidwitz, Adele Griffin and Lisa Brown, Claire Legrand, Nikki Loftin, Daniel José Older, Dav Pilkey, R.L. Stine, and Rita Williams-Garcia--have come together to bring you a bone-chilling collection of original ghost stories with illustrations by Gris Grimly." (Publisher's note)

"The stories are well-chosen and, unlike too many collections, consistently terrific, every story indeed scary and full of surprises. Strong leads serve many stories well, pulling readers in, perhaps against their own apprehensions." Kirkus

★ **Guys** read: funny business; edited and with an introduction by Jon Scieszka; stories by Mac Barnett [et al.]; with illustrations by Adam Rex. Walden Pond Press 2010 268p il $16.99; pa $5.99
Grades: 4 5 6 7 **S C**
1. Short stories 2. Humorous fiction 3. Boys -- Fiction
ISBN 978-0-06-196374-2; 0-06-196374-7; 978-0-06-196373-5 pa; 0-06-196373-9 pa
LC 2010-08122

A collection of humorous stories featuring a teenaged mummy, a homicidal turkey, and the world's largest pool of chocolate milk.

"A must-have collection for the boys in your library—and while you're at it, get a copy for the girls too!" Booklist

★ **Guys** read: thriller. Walden Pond Press 2011 viii, 272p $16.99; pa $6.99
Grades: 5 6 7 8 **S C**
1. Short stories 2. Adventure fiction
ISBN 978-0-06-196376-6; 0-06-196376-3; 978-0-06-196375-9 pa; 0-06-196375-5 pa

"Scieszka has gathered 10 thrilling stories from stellar writers. There are ghost stories, a deeply touching tale of a wish-granting machine and one about monsters that live in storm drains. . . . This anthology is brimming with choice stuff for guys who appreciate the uncanny, the uncouth and the unput-down-able." Kirkus

★ **Half**-minute horrors; edited by Susan Rich. HarperCollinsPublishers 2009 141p il $12.99
Grades: 5 6 7 8 **S C**
1. Short stories 2. Horror fiction
ISBN 978-0-06-183379-3; 0-06-183379-7
LC 2009-18293

An anthology of very short, scary stories by an assortment of authors and illustrators including Chris Raschka, Joyce Carol Oates, Neil Gaiman, Jack Gantos, and Lane Smith.

"This collection of more than 70 chilling snippets is ideal for campfires and car trips. The stories—some a couple sentences, some a few pages—range from darkly humorous . . . to outright creepy. . . . These are inherently quick reads, but with enough plot and detail to encourage further imagining." Publ Wkly

Holt, Kimberly Willis

Part of me; stories of a Louisiana family. 1st ed.; H. Holt 2006 208p $16.95
Grades: 7 8 9 10 **S C**
1. Short stories 2. Louisiana -- Fiction 3. Family life -- Fiction
ISBN 0-8050-6360-9; 978-0-8050-6360-8
LC 2005-29676

Ten stories trace the connections between four generations of one Louisiana family from 1939 when a young girl leaves school to help support her family to 2006 when an eighty-year-old woman embarks on a book tour. "Grades five to seven." (Bull Cent Child Books)

"Holt once again excels at creating character and an evocative sense of place." SLJ

Hungry hearts; 13 tales of food & love. edited by Elsie Chapman and Caroline Tung Richmond. Simon Pulse 2019 368 p. (jacketed hardcover) $18.99
Grades: 8 9 10 11 12 **Fic**
1. Short stories 2. Food -- Fiction 3. Love -- Fiction 4. Romance fiction 5. Short stories, American
ISBN 9781534421851
LC 2018041522

This book, edited by Elsie Chapman and Caroline Tung Richmond, is "a collection of interconnected short stories that explore the intersection of family, culture, and food in the lives of thirteen teens. . . . A shy teenager attempts to express how she really feels through the confections she makes at her family's pasteleria. A tourist from Montenegro desperately seeks a magic soup dumpling that could cure his fear of death." (Publisher's note)

"A brilliant multicultural collection that reminds readers that stories about food are rarely just about the food alone." (Kirkus)

Johnson, Hal

Fearsome Creatures of the Lumberwoods; 20 Chilling Tales from the Wilderness. by Hal Johnson, illustrated by Tom Mead. Workman Pub Co. 2015 176 p. illustrations $14.95
Grades: 5 6 7 8 **S C**
1. Short stories 2. Horror fiction -- Fiction 3. Mythical animals -- Fiction
ISBN 0761184619; 9780761184614

This children's horror story collection, by Hal Johnson, illustrated by Tom Mead, offers "twenty bone-chilling tales about the most dangerous fantastical beasts in American folklore. Meet the Snoligoster, who feeds on the shadows of its victims. The Hodag, like a spiny-backed bull-horned rhinoceros. The Hoop Snake, which can chase prey at speeds of up to 60 miles per hour and then, with one sting of its tail, cause it to turn purple, swell up, and die." (Publisher's note)

"Look out for what's lurking around every corner. The book is told from the perspective of a cryptozoologist who focuses on the lumberwoods of North America and who recounts many painful and horrifying incidents he witnessed during his years of seeking the most bizarre creatures. . . . A captivating collection for fans of Alvin Schwartz's Scary Tales to Tell in the Dark, this is also ideal for those looking for something fresh, creative, and deliciously creepy. VERDICT Outstanding faux-lore creature tales that will blow away middle school readers." SLJ

Kiss me deadly; 13 tales of paranormal love. edited by Trisha Telep. RP Teens 2010 430p pa $9.95
Grades: 7 8 9 10 **S C**
1. Short stories 2. Romance fiction 3. Love stories 4. Supernatural -- Fiction
ISBN 978-0-7624-3949-2; 0-7624-3949-1
LC 2010-926067

A collection of short stories combining dark seduction and modern romance presents a variety of tales featuring the romantic lives of humans and werewolves, ghosts, fallen angels, zombies, and shape-shifters.

The stories "have varying lengths and tones, representing an impressive range of writing styles; it is likely that any fantasy reader will find at least one memorable story that speaks directly to his or her preferences." Bull Cent Child Books

Le Guin, Ursula K.

Tales from Earthsea. Ace Books 2002 314p (The Earthsea cycle) rpt $16.99; pa $13.95

Grades: 11 12 Adult **S C**

1. Short stories 2. Fantasy fiction

ISBN 9780547851402 rpt; 0-441-00932-8

LC 2001-56673

"Inhabited by people no better or worse than ourselves, Earthsea is dominated by the practice of magic as precise as any science and as unpredictable in its social consequences. Since it is based entirely on language, Earthsea's magic serves as a metaphor for the writer's own sorcery. Yet despite Le Guin's strong bias toward the didactic there is no hint of by-the-numbers allegory here." N Y Times Book Rev

Lester, Julius

Long journey home: stories from black history. Dial Press (NY) 1972 147p hardcover o.p. pa $5.99

Grades: 6 7 8 9 **S C**

1. Short stories 2. African Americans -- Fiction

ISBN 0-14-038981-4 pa

"In a foreword, Julius Lester explains that he has chosen minor figures because the mass of people were the 'movers of history' while the great figures are their symbols. . . . The selections are diversified in their settings and alike in their sharply-etched effectiveness." Bull Cent Child Books

★ **Life** on Mars: tales from the new frontier; an original science fiction anthology. edited by Jonathan Strahan. Viking 2011 333p $19.99

Grades: 7 8 9 10 **S C**

1. Short stories 2. Science fiction 3. Mars (Planet) -- Fiction

ISBN 978-0-670-01216-9; 0-670-01216-5

LC 2011-02998

"In this strong anthology, Strahan . . . collects stories by some of the most talented writers in science fiction. Ranging from the first Mars landing to the far future, they often make use of the most recent scientific data about the Red Planet. . . . Invoking some of the great authors of Martian tales, from Burroughs and Bradbury to Heinlein and Kim Stanley Robinson . . . , this anthology is sure to appeal to any teens who yearn to explore Earth's nearest neighbor." Publ Wkly

Love is hell; [by] Melissa Marr . . . [et al.] HarperTeen 2008 263p $16.99; pa $9.99

Grades: 7 8 9 10 **S C**

1. Short stories 2. Romance fiction 3. Love stories 4. Supernatural -- Fiction

ISBN 978-0-06-144305-3; 0-06-144305-0; 978-0-06-144304-6 pa; 0-06-144304-2 pa

LC 2007-49574

"Supernatural romance is the well-chosen theme of five original stories by as many authors. . . . There's enough variety to round out the central theme, and consistently supple storytelling will lure readers through all five entries." Publ Wkly

Lucky dog; twelve tales of rescued dogs. [by Kirby Larson, Tui T. Sutherland, Ellen Miles, Leslie Margolis, Teddy Slater, Michael Northrop, Randi Barrow, Jane B. Mason & Sarah Hines Stephens, C. Alexander London, Marlane Kennedy, Elizabeth Cody Kimmel, Allan Woodrow] Scholastic Press 2013 192 p. $15.99

Grades: 4 5 6 7 **S C**

1. Short stories 2. Dogs -- Fiction 3. Dog rescue -- Fiction 4. Dog adoption -- Fiction

ISBN 0545554519; 9780545554510

LC 2013011309

This book is a collection of dog stories for children by authors such as Kirby Larson, Tui T. Sutherland, and Ellen Miles. "You'll meet Foxtrot, a feisty Pomeranian who can't bear the thought of leaving her best friend. And Beatrice, whose bark is definitely worse than her bite. And then there's Pumpkin, one of the 101 Chihuahuas who turn life at the center upside down." (Publisher's note)

"A dozen dog-crazy authors, 12 stories of rescued dogs, and one busy animal shelter make up this collection of short stories sure to bring out the dog lover in anyone. The stories are varied in plot, narrative style, and tone, but they all end with a dog finding its one true owner." Booklist

Marston, Elsa

Santa Claus in Baghdad and other stories about teens in the Arab world. Indiana University Press 2008 198p pa $15.95

Grades: 6 7 8 9 10 **S C**

1. Short stories 2. Middle East -- Fiction 3. Arab countries -- Fiction

ISBN 978-0-253-22004-2; 0-253-22004-1

LC 2007-50768

A collection of eight stories, most previously published in other anthologies, about what it is like to grow up in the Middle East today.

"Marston, who has lived and visited the countries of which she writes, offers a realistic portrait of the Middle East that mixes possiblity and bleakness in equal measure." Voice Youth Advocates

McKinley, Robin

The **door** in the hedge. Greenwillow Bks. 1981 216p hardcover o.p. pa $6.99

Grades: 7 8 9 10 **S C**

1. Fairy tales 2. Short stories

ISBN 0-688-00312-5; 0-698-11960-6 pa

LC 80-21903

"These tales are well-written and enjoyable to read. It is too bad they lack illustrations." Child Book Rev Serv

★ **Fire** : tales of elemental spirits; [by] Robin McKinley and Peter Dickinson. G. P. Putnam's Sons 2009 297p $19.99

Grades: 7 8 9 10 **S C**

1. Short stories 2. Fire -- Fiction 3. Mythical animals -- Fiction

ISBN 978-0-399-25289-1; 0-399-25289-4

LC 2009-4730

"The settings of these five tales range from ancient to modern, but they are all united by encounters with magical creatures with an affinity for fire. . . . This collection of beautifully crafted tales will find a warm welcome from fans of either author, as well as from fantasy readers in general." SLJ

Water : tales of elemental spirits; [by] Robin McKinley, Peter Dickinson. Putnam 2002 266p $18.99; pa $6.99

Grades: 7 8 9 10 **S C**

1. Short stories 2. Fantasy fiction 3. Mermaids and mermen -- Fiction

ISBN 0-399-23796-8; 0-14-240244-3 pa

LC 2001-41642

"The masterfully written stories all feature distinct, richly detailed casts and settings . . . and focus as strongly on action as on character. There's plenty here to excite, enthrall, and move even the pickiest readers." SLJ

McKissack, Pat, 1944-2017

★ The **dark** -thirty; Southern tales of the supernatural. illustrated by Brian Pinkney. Knopf 1992 122p il $18.95; lib bdg $20.99; pa $6.50

Grades: 4 5 6 7 **S C**

1. Ghost stories 2. Short stories 3. African Americans -- Fiction

ISBN 0-679-81863-4; 0-679-91853-9 lib bdg; 0-679-89006-8 pa

LC 92-3021

Coretta Scott King Award for text, 1993; A Newbery honor book, 1993

A collection of ghost stories with African American themes, designed to be told during the Dark Thirty—the half hour before sunset—when ghosts seem all too believable

"Strong characterizations are superbly drawn in a few words. The atmosphere of each selection is skillfully developed and sustained to the very end. Pinkney's stark scratchboard illustrations evoke an eerie mood, which heightens the suspense of each tale." SLJ

★ **Porch** lies; tales of slicksters, tricksters, and other wily characters. [by] Patricia C. McKissack; illustrated by André Carrilho. Schwartz & Wade Books 2006 146p il $18.95; lib bdg $22.99

Grades: 4 5 6 7 **S C**

1. Short stories 2. African Americans -- Fiction

ISBN 0-375-83619-5; 0-375-93619-X lib bdg

LC 2005-22048

The "original tales in this uproarious collection draw on African American oral tradition and blend history and legend with sly humor, creepy horror, villainous characters, and wild farce. McKissack based the stories on those she heard as a child while sitting on her grandparents' porch. . . . Carrilho's full-page illustrations—part cartoon, part portrait in silhouette—combine realistic characters with scary monsters." Booklist

★ **Moccasin** thunder; American Indians stories for today. edited by Lori Marie Carlson. HarperCollins 2005 156p $15.99

Grades: 7 8 9 10 **S C**

1. Short stories 2. Native Americans -- Fiction

ISBN 0-06-623957-5

LC 2004-22186

Presents ten short stories about contemporary Native American teens by members of tribes of the United States and Canada, including Louise Erdrich and Joseph Bruchac.

"This distinguished anthology offers powerful, beautifully written stories that are thoughtful and important for teens to hear." SLJ

Monstrous affections; an anthology of beastly tales. edited by Kelly Link & Gavin J. Grant. Candlewick Press 2014 480 p. $22.99

Grades: 8 9 10 11 12 **S C**

1. Fantasy fiction 2. Short stories -- Collections 3. Monsters -- Fiction

ISBN 0763664731; 9780763664732

LC 2013953536

This speculative fiction collection, edited by Kelly Link and Gavin J. Grant, presents "a world where humans live side by side with monsters, from vampires both nostalgic and bumbling to an eight-legged alien who makes tea. Here you'll find mercurial forms that burrow into warm fat, spectral boy toys, a Maori force of nature, a landform that claims lives, and an architect of hell on earth." (Publisher's note)

The editors "present an engrossing, morally complex anthology of 15 stories centered on the seemingly antagonistic concepts of monsters and love. Throughout, troubled protagonists meet genuine monsters--some traditional, like vampires, others much less so. Almost invariably, it's understood that other people in the protagonists' lives are far worse than the monsters." Pub Wkly

My true love gave to me; twelve holiday stories. edited and with a story by Stephanie Perkins. St. Martin's Griffin 2014 336 p. (hardback) $18.99

Grades: 7 8 9 10 11 12 **S C**

1. Romance fiction 2. Holidays -- Fiction 3. Christmas -- Fiction 4. Love stories, American 5. Short stories, American

ISBN 1250059305; 9781250059307

LC 2014030943

This book presents "twelve tales of holiday romance by notable YA authors. . . . Rainbow Rowell's opening 'Midnights' provides snapshots of Noel and Mags' relationship on each New Year's Eve of their high school years. . . . David Levithan provides an alternative to the collection's otherwise predominant heteronormativity with his portrayal of two boys finding warmth and solace on Christmas Eve in their romance even as their family foundations are shaken." (Bulletin of the Center for Children's Books)

Myers, Walter Dean, 1937-2014

145th Street; short stories. Delacorte Press 2000 151p hardcover o.p. pa $5.50

Grades: 7 8 9 10 **S C**

1. Short stories 2. African Americans -- Fiction 3. Harlem (New York, N.Y.) -- Fiction

ISBN 0-385-32137-6; 0-440-22916-2 pa

LC 99-36097

Boston Globe-Horn Book Award Honor: Fiction (2000)

"These ten powerful stories create a vivid mosaic of life in the Harlem neighborhood of 145th Street. Memorable characters range from outgoing Big Joe, who decides to stage his own funeral party in Big Joe's funeral, to book-loving Monkeyman, who outsmarts the Tigros gang. . . . Beautifully told, Myers's stories offer an enticing collection for teens." Voice Youth Advocates

★ **What** they found; love on 145th street. Wendy Lamb Books 2007 243p $15.99; lib bdg $18.99

Grades: 8 9 10 11 12 **S C**

1. Short stories 2. Family life -- Fiction 3. African Americans -- Fiction 4. Harlem (New York, N.Y.) -- Fiction

ISBN 978-0-385-32138-9; 0-385-32138-4; 978-0-375-93709-5 lib bdg; 0-375-93709-9 lib bdg

LC 2007-7057

Companion volume to 145th street (2000)

Fifteen interrelated stories explore different aspects of love, such as a dying father's determination to help start a family business—a beauty salon—and the relationship of two teens who plan to remain celibate until they marry.

"Rich in both character and setting, these urban tales combine heartbreak and hope into a vivid tableau of a community. A priority purchase for all libraries, especially those in urban settings." SLJ

Na, An

No such thing as the real world; a short story collection. [by] An Na [et al.]; introduction by Jill Santopolo; [compiled by Laura Geringer and Jill Santopolo] HarperTeen 2009 246p $16.99

Grades: 8 9 10 S C

1. Short stories

ISBN 978-0-06-147058-5; 0-06-147058-9

LC 2008-22583

Six young adult authors present short stories featuring teens who have to face the "real world" for the first time.

"This unique collection will challenge students' intellect and have them questioning their own decision-making skills. A fine balance is straddled between sophisticated prose and authentic teen voices, uninhibited and peppered with profanity." SLJ

Naidoo, Beverley

Out of bounds: seven stories of conflict and hope. HarperCollins Pubs. 2003 175p $16.99; pa $5.99

Grades: 5 6 7 8 S C

1. Short stories 2. South Africa -- Race relations -- Fiction

ISBN 0-06-050799-3; 0-06-050801-9 pa

LC 2002-68901

First published 2001 in the United Kingdom

Seven stories, spanning the time period from 1948 to 2000, chronicle the experiences of young people from different races and ethnic groups as they try to cope with the restrictions placed on their lives by South Africa's apartheid laws

"Naidoo's book reveals our humanity and inhumanity with starkness and precision. . . . She honors her country's past, present, and future with these brave tales." Horn Book

Nayeri, Daniel

★ **Straw** house, Wood house, Brick house, Blow. Candlewick Press 2011 404p $19.99

Grades: 8 9 10 11 12 S C

1. Short stories 2. Mystery fiction 3. Romance fiction 4. Science fiction 5. Love stories 6. West (U.S.) -- Fiction

ISBN 9780763655266; 0763655260

LC 2011013675

A collection of four novellas in different genres, including a western about a farmer who grows living toys and a rancher who grows half-living people; a science fiction story of the near-future in which the world is as easy to manipulate as the Internet; a crime story in which every wish comes true and only the Imaginary Crimes Unit can stop them; and a comedic love story in which Death describes himself as a charismatic hero.

"Four stylistically brilliant novellas offer readers a range of exquisite reading experiences in this collection." Bull Cent Child Books

Nix, Garth

★ **Across** the wall; a tale of the Abhorsen and other stories. Eos 2005 305p hardcover o.p. pa $7.99

Grades: 7 8 9 10 S C

1. Short stories 2. Fantasy fiction

ISBN 0-06-074713-7; 0-06-074715-3 pa

In Nicholas Sayre and the creature of case, the opening novella, "Nick encounters a bloodsucking Free Magic monster during a visit to Ancelstierre's top-secret intelligence agency. The story teasingly refers to British mysteries and spy fiction, parodic elements that will appeal most to Nix's adult fans. Even less-experienced readers, though, will enjoy getting to know Nick on his own terms. . . . The remaining 11 stories . . . include selections clearly intended for middle-graders as well as more sophisticated offerings containing frank references to sex and violence spattered with 'blood and brains and urine.' Buy this with the understanding that the packaging will attract the full spectrum of Nix's fans but that the younger ones may get more than they bargained for." Booklist

Noyes, Deborah

★ The **ghosts** of Kerfol. Candlewick Press 2008 163p $16.99

Grades: 8 9 10 11 12 S C

1. Ghost stories 2. Short stories 3. Supernatural -- Fiction

ISBN 978-0-7636-3000-3; 0-7636-3000-4

LC 2007-51884

Over the centuries, the inhabitants of author Edith Wharton's fictional mansion, Kerfol, are haunted by the ghosts of dead dogs, fractured relationships, and the taste of bitter revenge.

This collection includes "five wonderfully chilling short stories." Publ Wkly

Nye, Naomi Shihab, 1952-

★ **There** is no long distance now; very short stories. Greenwillow Books 2011 201p $17.99

Grades: 7 8 9 10 11 12 S C

1. Short stories

ISBN 0-06-201965-1; 978-0-06-201965-3

LC 2010025559

"Very short stories offer glimpses into the everyday lives of young people. . . . As she does in her poetry, Nye achieves a perfect marriage of theme and structure in stories that reflect the moments, glimpses and epiphones of growing up." Kirkus

Once upon a cuento; edited by Lyn Miller-Lachman. Curbstone Press 2003 243p pa $15.95

Grades: 9 10 11 12 S C

1. Short stories 2. Hispanic Americans -- Fiction

ISBN 1-88068-499-3

LC 2003-14667

"Writing quality is consisently high throughout. . . . This book . . . succeeds admirably in proving, through literature, that there is no single 'Latino experience.'" Voice Youth Advocates

Other worlds; edited by Jon Scieszka, illustrated by Greg Ruth. Walden Pond Press 2013 352 p. (Guys read) (hardback) $16.99

Grades: 4 5 6 7 8 S C

1. Short stories 2. Science fiction 3. Fantasy fiction

ISBN 0061963801; 9780061963797; 9780061963803

LC 2013021863

This book, edited by Jon Scieszka, is the fourth Guys Read collection of science fiction short stories. It "is anchored by Ray Bradbury's 1946 'Frost and Fire,' about colonists stranded for generations on a planet so harsh that the average life span is less than two weeks." Other topics include "unsuccessful alien invasions of Earth to Tom Angleberger's tale of smart clothes in rebellion, an eerie ghost story from Kenneth Oppel and . . . a 'girl in armor' episode from Shannon Hale." (Kirkus Reviews)

"Though most of the tales here are entertaining and 'mind-expandingly fun,' Shusterman's and Bradbury's especially stand out as intriguing, suspenseful, and thought-provoking." Horn Book

Patrick, Denise Lewis

A **matter** of souls; Denise Lewis Patrick. Carolrhoda Lab 2014 186 p. (trade hard cover : alk. paper) $16.95

Grades: 7 8 9 10 11 12 S C

1. American short stories 2. Race relations -- Fiction 3. Southern States -- Fiction 4. African Americans -- History 5. Southern States -- History -- Fiction 6. African Americans -- Southern States -- Fiction

ISBN 0761392807; 9780761392804

LC 2013017597

This collection of short stories, by Denise Lewis Patrick, "considers the souls of black men and women across centuries and continents. In each, she takes the measure of their dignity, describes their dreams, and catalogs their fears. Brutality, beauty, laughter, rage, and love all take their turns in each story, but the final impression is of indomitable, luminous, and connected souls." (Publisher's note)

"Eight short stories with long memory cut to the quick—all the more as they could be true. Patrick's tales from the distant and not-so-distant past shed fresh light on interracial and intraracial conflicts that shape and often distort the realities of African-Americans. . . . The plots and characters change from one story to the next, but each one artfully tells a poignant truth without flinching. Shocking, informative and powerful, this volume offers spectacular literary snapshots of black history and culture." Kirkus

Paulsen, Gary

Paintings from the cave; three novellas. Wendy Lamb Books 2011 161p $15.99; lib bdg $18.99

Grades: 4 5 6 7 S C

1. Short stories 2. Art -- Fiction 3. Dogs -- Fiction 4. Violence -- Fiction 5. Homeless persons -- Fiction

ISBN 978-0-385-74684-7; 978-0-385-90921-1 lib bdg; 978-0-375-89743-6 e-book

LC 2011016287

"These novellas portray an unflinching look at children who have endured neglectful and abusive homes and are surviving on their own. The atmospheric first tale, 'Man of the Iron Heads,' is narrated by Jake, a boy of about 11, who hides from the local gang until he finds the courage to outsmart its violent leader. 'Jo-Jo the Dog-Faced Girl' presents a lonely girl with three adopted dogs who finds acceptance in befriending a girl with leukemia. Finally, 'Erik's Rules' celebrates the power of art and is told by Jamie, the younger of two homeless brothers, whose unstable existence changes after a chance encounter with a friendly volunteer at the animal shelter. By incorporating the solace found in dogs, art, libraries, and new friends into these tales of heartache and redemption, Paulsen provides his readers with hope of a better life." SLJ

Peck, Richard

Past perfect, present tense: new and collected stories. Dial Bks. 2004 177p hardcover o.p. pa $6.99

Grades: 7 8 9 10 11 12 S C

1. Short stories

ISBN 0-8037-2998-7; 0-14-240537-X pa

LC 2003-10904

A collection of short stories, including two previously unpublished ones, that deal with the way things could be.

"The stories perfectly highlight Peck's range and expertise at characterization. Almost every one is a superb read-aloud. . . . This superior collection is a must for every library." SLJ

★ **Pick**-up game; a full day of full court. edited by Marc Aronson & Charles R. Smith Jr. Candlewick Press 2011 170p il $15.99; pbk. $6.99

Grades: 7 8 9 10 S C

1. Short stories 2. Basketball -- Fiction 3. New York (N.Y.) -- Fiction

ISBN 0-7636-4562-1; 978-0-7636-4562-5; 9780763660680

A series of short stories by such authors as Walter Dean Myers, Rita Williams-Garcia, and Joseph Bruchac, interspersed with poems and photographs, provides different perspectives on a game of streetball played one steamy July day at the West 4th Street court in New York City known as The Cage.

"This anthology squeaks out a win. . . . Sharp-elbow action alternates with an almost spiritual grace." Booklist

Poe, Edgar Allan

Edgar Allan Poe's tales of death and dementia; illustrated by Gris Grimly. Atheneum Books for Young Readers 2009 136p il $18.99

Grades: 7 8 9 10 S C

1. Short stories 2. Horror fiction

ISBN 978-1-4169-5025-7; 1-4169-5025-7

LC 2009003056

"Four of Poe's morbid short stories are adapted for teens in this heavily illustrated presentation: 'The Tell-Tale Heart,' 'The System of Dr. Tarr and Professor Fether,' 'The Oblong Box,' and 'The Facts in the Case of M. Valdemar.' Grimly intersperses his horror-infused ink-and-watercolor cartoon art throughout Poe's putrid prose. The effect is an offering that bridges graphic and traditional print formats. Great for readers who adore the gothic and the gruesome." SLJ

Edgar Allan Poe's tales of mystery and madness; illustrated by Gris Grimley. Atheneum Books for Young Readers 2004 135p il $17.95

Grades: 8 9 10 11 12 S C

1. Short stories 2. Horror fiction

ISBN 0-689-84837-4

LC 2003-10565

"With high-production values and gothic sensibilities thoroughly reflected in both text and art, this is an essential purchase for libraries. Adults can use it to lead young people to some great literature; readers will pluck it off the shelves themselves for creepy, entertaining fun." Booklist

The **radical** element; 12 stories of daredevils, debutantes, and other dauntless girls. edited by Jessica Spotswood. Candlewick Press 2018 320 p. (hardcover) $17.99

Grades: 7 8 9 10 S C

1. Girls -- Fiction 2. Women -- Fiction 3. American short stories

ISBN 9780763694258; 0763694258

LC 2018936969

In this anthology, edited by Jessica Spotswood, "twelve of the most talented writers working in young adult literature today tell the stories of girls of all colors and creeds standing up for themselves and their beliefs--whether that means secretly learning Hebrew in early Savannah, using the family magic to pass as white in 1920s Hollywood, or singing in a feminist punk band in 1980s Boston. And they're asking you to join them." (Publisher's note)

The **restless** dead; ten original stories of the supernatural. edited by Deborah Noyes. Candlewick Press 2007 253p pbk. $7.99; $16.99

Grades: 8 9 10 11 12 **S C**

1. Short stories 2. Horror fiction 3. Supernatural -- Fiction

ISBN 9780763636715; 0-7636-2906-5; 978-0-7636-2906-9

LC 2007-22114

This is a companion volume to Gothic!: Ten Original Dark Tales. This is a collection of ten stories by Kelly Link, Chris Wooding, Annette Curtis Klause, Marcus Sedgwick, Herbie Brennan, Deobrah Noyes, Libba Bray, M.A. Anderson, Holly Black, and Nancy Etchemendy. "Grades seven to nine." (Bull Cent Child Books)

This is a "collection of terrifying stories from some of the most well-known authors writing for teens, including M. T. Anderson, Holly Black, Libby Bray, and Annette Curtis Klause. From vampires to vindictive ghosts, this diverse anthology has it all, and then some." Booklist

Rice, David

Crazy loco; stories about growing up Chicano in southern Texas. Dial Books for Young Readers 2001 135p hardcover o.p. pa $6.99

Grades: 7 8 9 10 11 12 **S C**

1. Short stories 2. Texas -- Fiction 3. Mexican Americans -- Fiction

ISBN 0-8037-2598-1; 0-14-250056-9 pa

LC 00-59042

A collection of nine stories about Mexican American kids growing up in the Rio Grande Valley of southern Texas.

"Two great strengths of these stories are the pitch-perfect sense for the speech and thought patterns of teens and the vivid depiction of the daily lives of Mexican-Americans in Texas's Rio Grande Valley." SLJ

Rowling, J. K.

The **tales** of Beedle the Bard; translated from the ancient runes by Hermione Granger; commentary by Albus Dumbledore; introduction, notes, and illustrations by J.K. Rowling. Arthur A. Levine 2008 111p il $12.99

Grades: 5 6 7 8 9 10 11 12 **S C**

1. Fairy tales 2. Short stories 3. Magic -- Fiction

ISBN 978-0-545-12828-5; 0-545-12828-5

A collection of tales from the world of Harry Potter.

"The introduction is captivating . . . [and] the tales themselves are entertaining. . . . Rowling is at the top of her game as a superb storyteller, providing her legions of fans with an enchanting collection of wizard folklore." Voice Youth Advocates

San Souci, Robert

★ **Dare** to be scared; thirteen stories to chill and thrill. illustrations by David Ouimet. Cricket Bks. 2003 159p il $15.95

Grades: 4 5 6 7 **S C**

1. Short stories 2. Horror fiction

ISBN 0-8126-2688-5

LC 2002-152827

"With crisp, straightforward delivery and some intriguing endings, these 13 tales are great fun for young readers who like to be spooked." Booklist

Haunted houses; [by] Robert D. San Souci; illustrated by Kelly Murphy and Antoine Revoy. Henry Holt 2010 276p il (Are you scared yet?) $16.99

Grades: 4 5 6 7 **S C**

1. Ghost stories 2. Short stories 3. Horror fiction

ISBN 978-0-8050-8750-5; 0-8050-8750-8

LC 2009-50763

"These 10 spooky stories include a classic Halloween scare: visitors get their admission fee of $25 back if they make it to the top floor of a haunted house—but can they? In another, the primary occupant of a dollhouse is a ghost of a child who needs help moving from one consciousness to another. . . . The stories are well paced and satisfyingly startling. . . . This book won't stay on the shelves for long. Murphy and Revoy's black-and-white illustrations heighten the fright factor, making San Souci's collection even more riveting." SLJ

Shards and Ashes; edited by Melissa Marr and Kelley Armstrong ; with additional stories by Veronica Roth, Kami Garcia, Margaret Stohl and more. Harpercollins Childrens Books 2013 x, 369 p.p (ebook) $7.99; (hardcover) $17.99

Grades: 7 8 9 10 **S C**

1. Science fiction 2. Dystopian fiction 3. Apocalyptic fiction

ISBN 9780062098474; 0062098462; 9780062098467

This book, edited by Melissa Marr and Kelley Armstrong, offers nine science fiction short stories. "The world is gone, destroyed by human, ecological, or supernatural causes. Survivors dodge chemical warfare and cruel gods; they travel the reaches of space and inhabit underground caverns. Their enemies are disease, corrupt corporations, and one another; their resources are few and their courage is tested." (Publisher's note)

Shattered: stories of children and war; edited by Jennifer Armstrong. Knopf 2002 166p hardcover o.p. pa $6.50

Grades: 7 8 9 10 **S C**

1. War stories 2. Short stories

ISBN 0-375-81112-5; 0-440-23765-3 pa

LC 2001-18609

"These selections will make teens cry, will make them angry, but most of all they will make them think." SLJ

★ Shelf life: stories by the book; edited by Gary Paulsen. Simon & Schuster Bks. for Young Readers 2003 173p $16.95

Grades: 5 6 7 8 **S C**

1. Short stories 2. Books and reading -- Fiction

ISBN 0-689-84180-9

LC 2002-66901

Ten short stories in which the lives of young people in different circumstances are changed by their encounters with books

"Covering almost every genre of fiction, including mystery, SF, fantasy and realism, these well-crafted stories by familiar authors offer sharply drawn characterizations and intriguing premises." Publ Wkly

Shusterman, Neal

Darkness creeping; twenty twisted tales. Puffin Books 2007 291p pa $7.99

Grades: 5 6 7 8 **S C**

1. Short stories 2. Horror fiction

ISBN 0-14-240721-6

"The author takes a walk on the dark side in this collection of spooky stories, some old, some new, all delightfully creepy. He knows his audience, providing enough horrific touches to appeal to the most challenging readers—those hard-to-reach middle school boys. Each story is introduced with a brief statement describing where he got the idea." Voice Youth Advocates

★ Sideshow; ten original tales of freaks, illusionists, and other matters odd and magical. edited by Deborah Noyes. Candlewick Press 2009 199p il $16.99
Grades: 7 8 9 10 S C
1. Short stories
ISBN 978-0-7636-3752-1; 0-7636-3752-1
LC 2008-37420

"This is a masterpiece of 10 short stories by world-class authors. Contributors include David Almond, Annette Curtis Klause, and Vivian Vande Velde. . . . Not all of the stories are traditional prose; several are graphic renditions, including Matt Phelan's masterfully drawn 'Jargo!' . . . Suspending disbelief, readers of this fantastic anthology may start investing in psychics and sleeping with the light on." SLJ

Sleator, William

★ **Oddballs**; stories. Dutton Children's Bks. 1993 134p hardcover o.p. pa $5.99
Grades: 6 7 8 9 10 S C
1. Short stories 2. Friendship -- Fiction 3. Family life -- Fiction
ISBN 0-525-45057-2; 0-14-037438-8 pa
LC 92-27666

A collection of stories based on experiences from the author's youth and peopled with an unusual assortment of family and friends.

"Fresh, funny, and slightly gross, the quasi-autobiographical glimpses will grab the reader's attention." Horn Book Guide

Soto, Gary

★ **Baseball** in April, and other stories; 10th anniversary ed; Harcourt Brace Jovanovich 2000 111p $16; pa $6
Grades: 5 6 7 8 S C
1. Short stories 2. California -- Fiction 3. Mexican Americans -- Fiction
ISBN 0-15-202573-1; 0-15-202567-7 pa
A reissue of the title first published 1990

A collection of eleven short stories focusing on the everyday adventures of Hispanic young people growing up in Fresno, California

Each story "gets at the heart of some aspect of growing up. The insecurities, the embarrassments, the triumphs, the inequities of it all are chronicled with wit and charm. Soto's characters ring true and his knowledge of, and affection for, their shared Mexican-American heritage is obvious and infectious." Voice Youth Advocates

★ **Help** wanted; stories. by Gary Soto. Harcourt 2005 216p $17; pa $6.95
Grades: 6 7 8 9 S C
1. Short stories 2. California -- Fiction 3. Mexican Americans -- Fiction
ISBN 0-15-205201-1; 978-0-15-205663-6 pa
LC 2004-7510

"The stories are sometimes funny, often poignant, and occasionally provocative." Booklist

Hey 13! Holiday House 2011 197p $16.95
Grades: 6 7 8 9 S C
1. Short stories
ISBN 978-0-8234-2395-8; 0-8234-2395-6
LC 2011007709

A collection of thirteen short stories about the ups and downs of being thirteen years old.

"The author's skill and the short story format are both well utilized. . . . This title offers both comfort and fun for tween readers." Booklist

Local news. Harcourt Brace Jovanovich 1993 148p hardcover o.p. pa $5.95
Grades: 5 6 7 8 S C
1. Short stories 2. California -- Fiction 3. Mexican Americans -- Fiction
ISBN 0-15-248117-6; 0-15-204695-X pa
LC 92-37905

A collection of thirteen short stories about the everyday lives of Mexican American young people in California's Central Valley

"These stories resonate with integrity, verve, and compassion." Horn Book

Spinelli, Jerry

The **library** card. Scholastic 1997 148p pa $4.99
Grades: 4 5 6 7 S C
1. Short stories 2. Books and reading -- Fiction
ISBN 0-590-38633-6
LC 96-18412

"A library card is the magical object common to each of these four stories in which a budding street thug, a television addict, a homeless orphan, and a lonely girl are all transformed by the power and the possibilities that await them within the walls of the public library. Spinelli's characters . . . are unusual and memorable; his writing both humorous and convincing." Horn Book Guide

The **sports** pages; edited and with an introduction by Jon Scieszka ; stories by Dustin Brown, ... [et al.] ; with illustrations by Dan Santat. Walden Pond Press 2012 245 p ill (Guys read) (paberback bdg.) $6.99; (hardcover bdg.) $16.99
Grades: 4 5 6 7 8 S C
1. Short stories 2. Sports -- Fiction
ISBN 9780061963773; 9780061963780
LC 2012012716

This book, edited and with an introduction by Jon Scieszka, "offers a smorgasbord of sportswriting--fiction and nonfiction--to appeal to every sports enthusiast. From baseball to football, ice hockey to track and mixed martial arts, there is plenty here for sports-minded readers to like, with lively action, humor and even a dose of mysticism in the form of magical grapefruit and a witch doctor." (Kirkus Reviews)

"In the third volume of his Guys Read series (the first focused on humor, and the second on thrillers), editor Scieszka turns his attention to sports, serving up 10 stories. . . . In his introduction, Scieszka wisely notes that good stories and good games are alike: Both reveal character and truths bigger than the game or the story." Booklist

Starry-eyed; 16 stories that steal the spotlight. edited by Ted Michael and Josh Pultz. Running Press Teens 2013 400 p. $9.95
Grades: 7 8 9 10 11 12 S C
1. Performing arts 2. Actors -- Fiction 3. Singers -- Fiction
ISBN 0762449497; 9780762449491
LC 2013940578

Editors Ted Michael and Josh Pultz present a "collection of fictional short stories [that] highlight the struggles, hopes, failures, and triumphs of young aspiring singers, dancers, actors, actresses, and performers. While these characters may feel out of place during their everyday lives, they are able to find a home onstage and in rehearsals. Woven throughout the anthology are personal anecdotes from several of today's most celebrated performers of stage, screen, and television." (Publisher's note)

★ **Steampunk!** an anthology of fantastically rich and strange stories. edited by Kelly Link and Gavin J. Grant. Candlewick Press 2011 432p pbk. $12.99
Grades: 8 9 10 11 12 **S C**
1. Short stories 2. Fantasy fiction
ISBN 0763657972; 9780763657970
LC 2010040742

In this collection of short stories edited by Kelly Link and Gavin J. Grant "fourteen [authors] of speculative fiction, including two graphic storytellers, embrace the [steampunk] genre's established themes and refashion them in surprising ways and settings as diverse as Appalachia, ancient Rome, future Australia, and alternate California." (Publisher's note)

"Veteran editors Link and Grant serve up a delicious mix of original stories from 14 skilled writers and artists. . . . Chockful of gear-driven automatons, looming dirigibles, and wildly implausible time machines, these often baroque, intensely anachronistic tales should please steampunks of all ages." Publ Wkly

★ **Talking** leaves; contemporary native American short stories. introduced and edited by Craig Lesley; associate editor, Katheryn Stavrakis. Dell 1991 xxvi, 385p pa $16.95
Grades: 8 9 10 11 12 Adult **S C**
1. Short stories 2. Native Americans -- Fiction
ISBN 0-385-31272-5
LC 92-139334

This anthology includes contributions by such authors as Louise Erdrich, Diane Glancy, Michael Dorris, N. Scott Momaday, Paula Gunn Allen, and Mary Tallmountain

"All these stories have a strong sense of person and place and engagingly inform of the Native American condition." Libr J

Tan, Shaun

★ **Lost** & found; 3 by Shaun Tan. Arthur A. Levine Books 2011 un il $21.99
Grades: 5 6 7 8 **S C**
1. Short stories
ISBN 978-0-545-22924-1; 0-545-22924-3
LC 2010030936

This book comprises three previously published stories by the Australian author-illustrator "In 'The Red Tree,' a young girl moves listlessly through her day with a sense of dreadful ennui that escalates with each page turn . . . until finally finding some hope at the end. In 'The Lost Thing,' a young boy discovers a most peculiar object and dutifully tries to find a proper home for it. . . . Finally, 'The Rabbits' (with a text by John Marsden) is a colonization fable, as rabbits invade and populate a new land, overwhelming the native animal population and severely altering the landscape. . . . Intermediate, middle school." (Horn Book)

"'The Red Tree' follows a solitary girl through a single, not very good day, exploring her feelings as they shift from disappointment and confusion to alienation and despair. The spare, lyrical text provides an anchor for Tan's large, moody, beautiful paintings. 'The Lost Thing' is a more upbeat tale of a boy who discovers an unusual object and then must decide what to do with it. Freedom and imagination are the themes in this story, and here the art includes fascinating and sometimes humorous bits of technical drawings. The prose of John Marsden's 'The Rabbits,' an allegory about imperialism, is so simple and melodic that it verges on poetry. The artist emphasizes the invasive foreignness of the rabbits by dressing them in baroque uniforms, drawing mystifying, gigantic machines and buildings for them to build and deploy in their inexorable drive to dominate." SLJ

★ **Tales** from the inner city; Shaun Tan. Arthur A. Levine Books, an imprint of Scholastic Inc. 2018 224 p. (hardcover : alk. paper) $24.99
Grades: 7 8 9 10 11 12 **Fic**
1. Animal behavior -- Fiction 2. City and town life -- Fiction 3. Human-animal relationships -- Fiction 4. Short stories 5. Urban animals -- Fiction 6. Animals -- Habits and behavior -- Fiction
ISBN 9781338298406
LC 2018017790

This book, by Shaun Tan, "is a collection of incredibly original stories, rich with feeling, strangely moving, almost numinous. And when the reader comes to the artwork, it's like walking into an amazing room, and then throwing open a curtain to see a brilliant scene that makes you understand and appreciate everything you've encountered in a deeper way." (Publisher's note)

"In contrast to the neighborhood settings of Tales from Outer Suburbia (2009), this collection of 25 illustrated poems and stories explores the dynamics between animals and humans amid breathtakingly imaginative scenes in skyscrapers and gutters." (Kirkus Reviews)

★ **Tales** from outer suburbia. Arthur A. Levine Books 2009 92p il $19.99
Grades: 7 8 9 10 **S C**
1. Short stories 2. Suburban life -- Fiction 3. Short stories -- By individual authors
ISBN 0-545-05587-3; 978-0-545-05587-1
LC 2008-13784

This is a collection of fifteen illustrated stories set in the Australian suburbs. "Grades five to ten." (Bull Cent Child Books)

"The term 'suburbia' may conjure visions of vast and generic sameness, but in his hypnotic collection of 15 short stories and meditations, Tan does for the sprawling landscape what he did for the metropolis in The Arrival . . . . Ideas and imagery both beautiful and disturbing will linger." Publ Wkly

Taylor, Laini

★ **Lips** touch; three times. illustrations by Jim Di Bartolo. Arthur A. Levine Books 2009 265p il $17.99
Grades: 8 9 10 11 12 **S C**
1. Short stories 2. Kissing -- Fiction 3. Supernatural -- Fiction
ISBN 978-0-545-05585-7; 0-545-05585-7
LC 2009-5458

National Book Award Finalist: Young People's Literature (2009)

These three stories about kissing feature elements of the supernatural. "Grades nine to twelve." (Bull Cent Child Books)

"Taylor offers a powerful trio of tales, each founded upon the consequences of a kiss. . . . Contemporary Kizzy, who so yearns to be a normal, popular teenager that she forgets the rules of her Old Country upbringing and is seduced by a goblin in disguise; Anamique, living in British colonial India, silenced forever due to a spell cast upon her at birth; and Esmé, who at 14 discovers she is host to another—nonhuman—being. . . . Each is, in vividly distinctive fashion, a mesmerizing love story that comes to a satisfying but never predictable conclusion. Di Bartolo's illustrations provide tantalizing visual preludes to each tale." Publ Wkly

★ A **thousand** beginnings and endings; 15 retellings of Asian myths and legends. edited by Ellen Oh and Elsie Chapman. Greenwillow Books 2018 328 p. (hardback) $17.99
Grades: 6 7 8 9 10 11 12 **S C**
1. Folklore 2. Anthologies 3. Short stories 4. Tales -- Asia --

fiction 5. Mythology, Asian -- fiction
ISBN 9780062671158; 9780062671172; 0062671154
LC 2018020967

This collection, edited by Ellen Oh and Elsie Chapman, presents short stories about "star-crossed lovers, meddling immortals, feigned identities, battles of wits, and dire warnings. . . . Fifteen bestselling and acclaimed authors reimagine the folklore and mythology of East and South Asia in . . . stories that are by turns enchanting, heartbreaking, romantic, and passionate." (Publisher's note)

"A marvelous anthology of retold Asian myths and legends tying the traditional and modern together and accessible to all teens of all backgrounds." Kirkus

Tomo; friendship through fiction : an anthology of Japan teen stories. edited by Holly Thompson ; cover and part-title illustrations by John Shelley. Stone Bridge Press 2012 383 p. (pbk.) $14.95
Grades: 7 8 9 10 **S C**
1. Japan -- Fiction 2. Short stories -- Collections 3. Teenagers -- fiction 4. Friendship -- fiction 5. Short stories 6. Children's stories, Japanese
ISBN 1611720060; 9781611720068
LC 2011051530

This book of short stories, edited by Holly Thompson, is an "anthology of authors with direct or indirect Japanese 'heritage or experience.' The 36 tales (all but six of which are new) were gathered as contributions to the relief effort for victims of the 2011 earthquake and tsunami." The various entries focus on stories about Japanese and half-Japanese teenagers in a variety of genres, including historical fiction, contemporary teenage drama, and fantasy. Stories are indexed by plot themes, including friendship, ghosts, super-powers, and family relationships. (Kirkus)

★ **Troll's** eye view; a book of villainous tales. Viking 2009 200p $16.99; pa $7.99
Grades: 5 6 7 8 **S C**
1. Fairy tales 2. Short stories
ISBN 978-0-670-06141-9; 0-670-06141-7; 978-0-14-241673-0 pa; 0-14-241673-8 pa

Everyone thinks they know the real story behind the villains in fairy tales—evil, no two ways about it. But the villains themselves beg to differ. In this anthology for younger readers, you'll hear from the Giant's wife (from Jack and the Beanstalk), Rumpelstiltskin, the oldest of the Twelve Dancing Princesses, and more.

"A mixed bag of funny, quirky, and downright creepy entries. . . . The collection is largely accessible and very enjoyable." Booklist

★ **Unbroken**; 13 stories starring disabled teens. edited by Marieke Nijkamp. Farrar, Straus & Giroux 2018 320 p. (hardcover) $17.99
Grades: 8 9 10 11 12 **S C**
1. Love -- Fiction 2. Friendship -- Fiction 3. People with disabilities -- Fiction 4. Short stories 5. Children's stories, American
ISBN 9780374306502
LC 2018003352

"This anthology, [by Marieke Nijkamp,] explores disability in fictional tales told from the viewpoint of disabled characters, written by disabled creators. With stories in various genres about first loves, friendship, war, travel, and more, 'Unbroken' will offer today's teen readers a glimpse into the lives of disabled people in the past, present, and future." (Publisher's note)

"The stories feature wide variety and high quality, but most important, none of the teens at the center of the stories are defined by their disabilities. Teens disappointed by the lack of nuanced depictions of disability in YA fiction will cheer for these compassionate, engaging, and masterfully written stories." Booklist

Under my hat; tales from the cauldron. edited by Jonathan Strahan. Random House 2012 415 p. (trade) $16.99
Grades: 5 6 7 8 **S C**
1. Short stories 2. Witches -- Fiction
ISBN 0375868305; 9780375868047; 9780375868306; 9780375898815; 9780375968303
LC 2011031253

This book presents "eighteen short tales about witches. . . . Garth Nix's 'A Handful of Ashes' features a library and librarian. Delia Sherman's 'The Witch in the Woods' . . . [features] deer and bear shapeshifters and no small darkness. . . . Jane Yolen makes Hans Christian Andersen's life a tale itself." (Kirkus Reviews)

Under the weather; stories about climate change. edited by Tony Bradman. Frances Lincoln Children's 2009 215p pbk. $8.99; $16.95
Grades: 5 6 7 8 **S C**
1. Short stories 2. Greenhouse effect -- Fiction
ISBN 9781845079444; 1-84507-930-2; 978-1-84507-930-7

"Eight stories by a variety of authors attempt to make the facts about climate change and its global ramifications relevant to today's children. The majority of the selections are about youngsters enacting change and working toward solutions in tangible ways. For example, 'How to Build the Perfect Sandcastle' is about a Philippino boy who works to rebuild the coral reefs, which are dying due to the rise in ocean temperature. . . . Overall . . . this is a worthwhile effort that will appeal to children wanting to make a difference in their world as well as to teachers trying to make the scientific reality of climate change real to their students." SLJ

Unnatural creatures; stories. Neil Gaiman ; [edited by] Rosemary Brosnan. 1st ed. HarperCollins 2013 480 p. ill. (hardcover) $17.99
Grades: 8 9 10 11 12 **S C**
1. Short stories 2. Fantasy fiction 3. Monsters -- Fiction
ISBN 0062236296; 9780062236296; 9780062236302
LC 2013933032

This fantasy-horror short story collection, compiled by Neil Gaiman and edited by Maria Dahvana Headley, "is a collection of short stories about the fantastical things that exist only in our minds. . . . The sixteen stories . . . range from the whimsical to the terrifying. The magical creatures range from werewolves to sunbirds to beings never before classified. E. Nesbit, Diana Wynne Jones, Gahan Wilson, and other literary luminaries contribute to the anthology." (Publisher's note)

Vande Velde, Vivian

All Hallows' Eve; 13 stories. Harcourt 2006 225p $17
Grades: 7 8 9 10 **S C**
1. Short stories 2. Halloween -- Fiction 3. Supernatural -- Fiction
ISBN 978-0-15-205576-9; 0-15-205576-2
LC 2006-05439

Presents thirteen tales of Halloween horrors, including ghosts, vampires, and pranks gone awry.

"This mistress of the macabre draws readers in with her familiar conversational tone and easily recognizable situations . . . before skillfully shifting the narratives in unsettling, sometimes terrifying, directions. . . . Vande Velde's narrative tricks are a treat." Horn Book

★ **Being** dead; stories. Harcourt 2001 203p hardcover o.p. pa $6.95
Grades: 7 8 9 10 **S C**
1. Short stories 2. Horror fiction 3. Supernatural -- Fiction
ISBN 0-15-216320-4; 0-15-204912-6 pa
LC 00-12996

"Often humorous and sometimes evoking sympathy, this anthology will be enjoyed by lovers of mild horror as well as by those who like clever short stories." Voice Youth Advocates

Cloaked in red. Marshall Cavendish Children 2010 127p $15.99
Grades: 7 8 9 10 **S C**
1. Fairy tales 2. Short stories
ISBN 0-7614-5793-3; 978-0-7614-5793-0
LC 2009-51753

This book presents eight variations on the traditional tale of Little Red Riding Hood. "Grades five to eight." (Bull Cent Child Books)

The stories "blend wry contemporary commentary with fractured-fairy-tale elements, horror, and a subtle bit of sensuality. . . . The wacky tales can easily be used to inspire teens to make up versions of their own." Booklist

Voices in first person; reflections on Latino identity. [edited by Lori Marie Carlson] Atheneum Books for Young Readers 2008 96p il $16.99
Grades: 6 7 8 9 10 11 12 **S C**
1. Short stories 2. American literature -- Hispanic American authors -- Collections
ISBN 978-1-4169-0635-3; 1-4169-0635-5
LC 2006-34161

A collection of brief fictional pieces about the experiences of Latinos in the United States, by such writers as Sandra Cisneros, Gary Soto, Oscar Hijuelos, and others.

"Carlson has drawn from both established and new writers, focusing on finding Latino voices that speak to contemporary readers. . . . This collection sparkles more than its predecessors because of its dynamic design, featuring black-and-white photographs and line illustrations incorporated with the text in a collage-like magazine layout." SLJ

★ **Welcome** to Bordertown; new stories and poems of the Borderlands. edited by Holly Black and Ellen Kushner; introduction by Terri Windling. Random House 2011 517p $19.99; lib bdg $22.99; e-book $19.99
Grades: 7 8 9 10 **S C**
1. Short stories 2. Fantasy fiction 3. Poetry -- Collections 4. Supernatural -- Fiction
ISBN 978-0-375-86705-7; 0-375-86705-8; 978-0-375-96705-4 lib bdg; 0-375-96705-2 lib bdg; 978-0-375-89745-0 e-book
LC 2010-35558

This collection of short stories and poems focuses on Bordertown, "a city on the border between our human world and the elfin realm. Runaway teens come from both sides of the border to find adventure, to find themselves. Elves play in rock bands and race down the street on spell-powered motorbikes. Human kids recreate themselves in the squats and clubs and artists' studios of Soho." (Publisher's note)

"This is punk-rock, DIY fantasy, full of harsh reality and incandescent magic . . . Many of the stories echo with loss and discomfort; standouts include 'Crossings' by Janni Lee Simner, a chilling look at the difference between dreams and reality, and 'A Tangle of Green Men,' Charles De Lint's heartbreaking examination of love, loss and life. Poems and songs (from Patricia A. McKillip, Neil Gaiman and Jane Yolen, among others) balance the fiction. . . . A masterful anthology." Kirkus

You don't have a clue; Latino mystery stories for teens. [edited by Sarah Cortez] Pinata Books 2011 310p pa $16.95
Grades: 6 7 8 9 10 **S C**
1. Short stories 2. Hispanic Americans -- Fiction
ISBN 1-55885-692-7; 978-1-55885-692-9
LC 2011-00117

These short stories are "set in schools and communities from New York City to Venice Beach, California." (Publisher's note) "Grades seven to ten." (Bull Cent Child Books)

AUTHOR, TITLE, AND SUBJECT INDEX

This index to the books in the Classified Collection includes author, title, and subject entries; added entries for publishers' series, illustrators, joint authors, and editors of works entered under title; and name and subject cross-references; all arranged in one alphabet.

The number or symbol in boldface type at the end of each entry refers to the Dewey Decimal Classification or to the Fiction (Fic) or Story Collection (S C) section where the main entry for the book will be found. Works classed in 92 will be found under the headings for the biographies' subject.

ART, RENAISSANCE -- ITALY
Spence, D. Michelangelo **709.2**
ART, VIKING
Allan, T. Exploring the life, myth, and art of the Vikings **948**
Artemis Fowl. Colfer, E. **Fic**
Artemis Fowl: the graphic novel. Colfer, E. **741.5**
ARTHRITIS
See also Diseases
ARTHROPODA
Young, K. R. Bug science **595.7**
Arthur
About
Morris, G. The squire's quest **Fic**
Arthur Conan Doyle. Pascal, J. B. **823**
Arthur, Alex
Shell **594**
Arthur, King
About
Johnson-Shelton, N. The Invisible Tower **Fic**
Johnson-Shelton, N. The seven swords **Fic**
Llewellyn, S. Darksolstice **Fic**
Llewellyn, S. The well between the worlds **Fic**
Morris, G. Parsifal's page **Fic**
Pyle, H. The story of King Arthur and his knights **398.2**
Pyle, H. The story of the Grail and the passing of Arthur **398.2**
Reeve, P. Here lies Arthur **Fic**
White, T. H. The once and future king **Fic**
Yancey, R. The extraordinary adventures of Alfred Kropp **Fic**
ARTHURIAN ROMANCES
Morpurgo, M. Sir Gawain and the Green Knight **398.2**
Pyle, H. The story of King Arthur and his knights **398.2**
Pyle, H. The story of Sir Launcelot and his companions **398.2**
Pyle, H. The story of the champions of the Round Table **398.2**
Pyle, H. The story of the Grail and the passing of Arthur **398.2**
Tennyson, A. T. The Lady of Shalott **821**
ARTHURIAN ROMANCES -- ADAPTATIONS
Johnson-Shelton, N. The seven swords **Fic**
The **Articles** of Confederation. Feinberg, B. S. **342**
ARTICULATION (EDUCATION)
See also Education -- Curricula; Schools -- Administration
Artificial eyes. Sheen, B. **617.7**
ARTIFICIAL FOODS
See also Food; Synthetic products
ARTIFICIAL HEART
See also Artificial organs; Heart
ARTIFICIAL INSEMINATION
See also Reproduction
Artificial intelligence. Henderson, H. **006.3**
ARTIFICIAL INTELLIGENCE
Artificial intelligence **629.8**
Henderson, H. Alan Turing **92**
Henderson, H. Artificial intelligence **006.3**
Artificial intelligence. **629.8**
ARTIFICIAL INTELLIGENCE -- FICTION
Kristoff, J. Gemina **Fic**
Kristoff, J. Obsidio **Fic**
ARTIFICIAL LIMBS
Woog, A. The bionic hand **617**
ARTIFICIAL ORGANS
See also Surgery
ARTIFICIAL SATELLITES
Larson, K. W. International Space Station **629.442**
Miller, R. Satellites **629.44**
Young, K. R. Space junk **629.4**
ARTIFICIAL SATELLITES
See also Astronautics
ARTISANS
Giblin, J. The many rides of Paul Revere **92**
Weber, E. N. R. Rattlesnake Mesa **92**
ARTIST COUPLES -- MEXICO -- BIOGRAPHY
Reef, C. Frida & Diego **920**
Artist to artist. **741.6**
ARTISTIC ANATOMY
See also Anatomy; Art; Drawing; Nude in art
ARTISTIC PHOTOGRAPHY
See also Art; Photography
ARTISTIC PHOTOGRAPHY
Meyerowitz, J. Seeing things **770**
Photographic **741.5**
ARTISTS -- BIOGRAPHY
Reef, C. Frida & Diego **920**
ARTISTS -- FICTION
Pearsall, S. The seventh most important thing **Fic**
Say, A. Silent days, silent dreams **92**
ARTISTS
Heine, F. Impressionism **759.054**
ARTISTS -- NEW YORK (STATE) -- NEW YORK -- FICTION
All the greys on Greene Street **Fic**
ARTISTS -- POETRY
Lewis, J. P. Self-portrait with seven fingers **811**
Spires, E. I heard God talking to me **811**
ARTISTS -- TURKEY -- BIOGRAPHY -- COMIC BOOKS, STRIPS, ETC
Samanci, Ö. Dare to disappoint **92**
ARTISTS -- UNITED STATES
Finger, B. 13 American artists children should know **709**
Greenberg, J. Runaway girl: the artist Louise Bourgeois **92**
High riders, saints and death cars **709.2**
Reich, S. Painting the wild frontier: the art and adventures of George Catlin **92**
Rubin, S. G. Andy Warhol **92**
Rubin, S. G. Edward Hopper **92**
Rubin, S. G. Whaam!: the art & life of Roy Lichtenstein **92**
Rubin, S. G. Wideness and wonder: the life and art of Georgia O'Keeffe **92**
Sherman, P. John James Audubon **92**
Waldman, N. Out of the shadows **92**
Willett, E. Andy Warhol **92**
ARTISTS -- UNITED STATES -- BIOGRAPHY
Rubin, S. G. Everybody paints! **920**
Rubin, S. G. Maya Lin **92**
ARTISTS' MATERIALS

B

F

Chabon, M. Summerland **Fic**
Chee, T. The Reader **Fic**
Chee, T. The speaker **Fic**
Chee, T. The storyteller **Fic**
Chilton, A. S. The goblin's puzzle **Fic**
Chima, C. W. The Demon King **Fic**
Chima, C. W. The warrior heir **Fic**
Clare, C. Clockwork angel **Fic**
Clark, H. What we found in the sofa (and how it saved the world) **Fic**
Cluess, J. A shadow bright and burning **Fic**
Coakley, L. Witchlanders **Fic**
Colfer, E. Artemis Fowl **Fic**
Collins, S. Gregor the Overlander **Fic**
Columbus, C. House of secrets **Fic**
Condie, A. B. Matched **Fic**
Constable, K. The singer of all songs **Fic**
Cooper, S. The dark is rising **Fic**
Cooper, S. Greenwitch **Fic**
Cooper, S. The grey king **Fic**
Cooper, S. Over sea, under stone **Fic**
Cooper, S. Silver on the tree **Fic**
Coville, B. The skull of truth **Fic**
Cypess, L. Death sworn **Fic**
Cypess, L. Mistwood **Fic**
Cyprus, N. Sisters of Glass **Fic**
Damico, G. Scorch **Fic**
Dasgupta, S. The serpent's secret **Fic**
De Fombelle, T. Toby and the secrets of the tree **Fic**
Dennard, S. Truthwitch **Fic**
Derting, K. The pledge **Fic**
Dickinson, P. The ropemaker **Fic**
Dixon, H. Entwined **Fic**
D'Lacey, C. Dark fire **Fic**
D'Lacey, C. The fire ascending **Fic**
D'Lacey, C. Fire world **Fic**
Dowell, F. O. Falling in **Fic**
Duane, D. So you want to be a wizard **Fic**
Duey, K. Sacred scars **Fic**
Dunmore, H. The deep **Fic**
DuPrau, J. The diamond of Darkhold **Fic**
DuPrau, J. The people of Sparks **Fic**
Durham, P. The luck uglies **Fic**
Durst, S. B. The stone girl's story **Fic**
Durst, S. B. Vessel **Fic**
Farmer, N. The Islands of the Blessed **Fic**
Farmer, N. The Land of the Silver Apples **Fic**
Farmer, N. The lord of Opium **Fic**
Farmer, N. The Sea of Trolls **Fic**
Farrey, B. The Grimjinx rebellion **Fic**
Fawcett, H. Even the darkest stars **Fic**
Firebirds **S**
Firebirds soaring **S**
Fisher, C. The dark city **Fic**
Fisher, C. The hidden Coronet **Fic**
Fisher, C. Incarceron **Fic**
Fisher, C. The lost heiress **Fic**
Fisher, C. The Margrave **Fic**
Fisher, C. The obsidian mirror **Fic**
Fisher, C. Sapphique **Fic**
Flanagan, J. The battle for Skandia **Fic**
Flanagan, J. The burning bridge **Fic**
Flanagan, J. The emperor of Nihon-Ja **Fic**
Flanagan, J. Erak's ransom **Fic**
Flanagan, J. Halt's peril **Fic**
Flanagan, J. The icebound land **Fic**
Flanagan, J. The kings of Clonmel **Fic**
Flanagan, J. The lost stories **S**
Flanagan, J. The outcasts **Fic**
Flanagan, J. The red fox clan **Fic**
Flanagan, J. The royal ranger **Fic**
Flanagan, J. The ruins of Gorlan **Fic**
Flanagan, J. The siege of Macindaw **Fic**
Flanagan, J. The sorcerer of the north **Fic**
Fletcher, C. Ironhand **Fic**
Fletcher, C. Silvertongue **Fic**
Fletcher, C. Stoneheart **Fic**
Fletcher, S. Ancient, strange, and lovely **Fic**
Fletcher, S. Dragon's milk **Fic**
Fletcher, S. Flight of the Dragon Kyn **Fic**
Fletcher, S. Sign of the dove **Fic**
Flinn, A. Beastly **Fic**
Flora and Ulysses **Fic**
Foley, L. K. Remarkable **Fic**
Forest of wonders **Fic**
Forward, T. Dragonborn **FIC**
Funaro, G. Watch hollow **Fic**
Funke, C. C. Inkdeath **Fic**
Funke, C. C. Inkheart **Fic**
Funke, C. C. Inkspell **Fic**
Funke, C. Fearless **Fic**
Funke, C. Reckless **Fic**
Gabriel Finley and the raven's riddle **Fic**
Gaiman, N. The Sleeper and the Spindle **Fic**
Gardner, L. Into the woods **Fic**
Gardner, L. Out of the woods **Fic**
Gee, M. Gool **Fic**
Gee, M. The Limping Man **Fic**
Gee, M. Salt **Fic**
George, J. D. Dragon flight **Fic**
George, J. D. Dragon slippers **Fic**
George, J. D. Dragon spear **Fic**
George, J. D. Sun and moon, ice and snow **Fic**
The girl who fell beneath Fairyland and led the revels there **Fic**
The Glass Town Game **Fic**
Glewwe, E. Sparkers **Fic**
Glewwe, E. Wildings **Fic**
Goodman, A. Eon: Dragoneye reborn **Fic**
Goodman, A. Eona: the last Dragoneye **Fic**
Goto, H. Half World **Fic**
Grant, K. M. Paradise red **Fic**
Grant, M. The call **Fic**
Grant, M. The trap **Fic**
Grove, S. E. The crimson skew **Fic**

GREETING CARDS
Turnbull, S. Cards and gifts 745.594

I

J

K

L

M

P

Grimes, N. Planet middle school **Fic**
Hale, S. Princess Academy **Fic**
Han, J. Shug **Fic**
Hand, C. Unearthly **Fic**
Hannigan, K. True (. . . sort of) **Fic**
Hansen, J. The gift-giver **Fic**
Hautman, P. Blank confession **Fic**
Hautman, P. The big crunch **Fic**
Henderson, J. Vampire rising **Fic**
Henderson, J. Voice of the undead **Fic**
Hensley, J. N. Rites of passage **Fic**
Higgins, M. G. Bi-Normal **Fic**
Hiranandani, V. The whole story of half a girl **Fic**
Hodkin, M. The unbecoming of Mara Dyer **Fic**
Holm, J. L. Middle school is worse than meatloaf **Fic**
Holmes, S. L. Operation Yes **Fic**
Homeroom diaries **Fic**
Houston, J. New boy **Fic**
Houtman, J. The reinvention of Edison Thomas **Fic**
Howe, J. Addie on the inside **Fic**
Howe, J. The misfits **Fic**
Howe, J. Totally Joe **Fic**
Howe, K. Conversion **Fic**
Hrdlitschka, S. Allegra **Fic**
Hurley, T. Ghostgirl **Fic**
Ibbotson, E. The dragonfly pool **Fic**
Jaden, D. Losing Faith **Fic**
Jenkins, A. M. Repossessed **Fic**
Jinks, C. Evil genius **Fic**
Johnson, C. G. The breakaways **741.5**
Johnson, M. Scarlett fever **Fic**
Johnson, M. The name of the star **Fic**
Johnson, V. The great Greene heist **Fic**
Johnson, V. To catch a cheat **Fic**
Jones, P. Bridge **Fic**
Jones, T. L. Silhouetted by the blue **Fic**
Jones, T. L. Standing against the wind **Fic**
Jordan, R. The goatnappers **Fic**
Juby, S. Getting the girl **Fic**
Katcher, B. Playing with matches **Fic**
Kelly, E. E. Blackbird fly **Fic**
Kephart, B. Undercover **Fic**
Kerr, M. E. If I love you, am I trapped forever? **Fic**
Kerz, A. Better than weird **Fic**
Kimmel, E. C. The reinvention of Moxie Roosevelt **Fic**
Kinard, K. The Boy Project **Fic**
Kindl, P. A school for brides **Fic**
Kinney, J. Diary of a wimpy kid **Fic**
Kinney, J. Diary of a wimpy kid: Greg Heffley's journal **Fic**
Kittle, K. Reasons to be happy **Fic**
Klass, D. Second impact **Fic**
Klise, K. Regarding the bathrooms **Fic**
Klise, K. Regarding the bees **Fic**
Klise, K. Regarding the fountain **Fic**
Klise, K. Regarding the sink **Fic**
Klise, K. Regarding the trees **Fic**
Koertge, R. Now playing **Fic**
Koertge, R. Stoner & Spaz **Fic**
Koja, K. Buddha boy **Fic**
Koja, K. Headlong **Fic**
Koja, K. Kissing the bee **Fic**
Konigsberg, B. Openly straight **Fic**
Konigsburg, E. L. The view from Saturday **Fic**
Korman, G. Schooled **Fic**
Korman, G. Ungifted **Fic**
Krieg, J. Griff Carver, hallway patrol **Fic**
Kuhlman, E. The last invisible boy **Fic**
Laban, E. The Tragedy Paper **Fic**
LaFleur, S. M. Love, Aubrey **Fic**
Larbalestier, J. Team Human **Fic**
Larson, M. A. Pennyroyal Academy **Fic**
Leal, A. H. A finders-keepers place **Fic**
Leavitt, L. Going vintage **Fic**
Leavitt, L. Sean Griswold's head **Fic**
Levine, K. The lions of Little Rock **Fic**
Levithan, D. Two boys kissing **Fic**
Levy, D. A. It wasn't me **Fic**
Lockhart, E. Dramarama **Fic**
Lockhart, E. The disreputable history of Frankie Landau-Banks **Fic**
Lopez, D. Confetti girl **Fic**
Luddy, K. Spelldown **Fic**
Lupica, M. Play Makers **Fic**
Lyga, B. Goth girl rising **Fic**
Lyga, B. Hero-type **Fic**
Lyga, B. The astonishing adventures of Fanboy & Goth Girl **Fic**
Lynch, C. Inexcusable **Fic**
A monster calls **Fic**
The magician's bird **Fic**
Mackey, W. K. Throwing like a girl **Fic**
Mackler, C. The earth, my butt, and other big, round things **Fic**
Mackler, C. The future of us **Fic**
Maldonado, T. Secret Saturdays **Fic**
Marcus, K. Exposed **Fic**
Margolis, L. Girl's best friend **Fic**
Martinez, C. G. The smell of old lady perfume **Fic**
Mass, W. A mango-shaped space **Fic**
Mass, W. Heaven looks a lot like the mall **Fic**
McCoy, M. I, Claudia **Fic**
McDonald, A. The anti-prom **Fic**
McMann, L. Fade **Fic**
McMann, L. Wake **Fic**
McMullen, B. Mrs. Smith's Spy School for Girls **Fic**
Meyer, S. Eclipse **Fic**
Meyer, S. New moon **Fic**
Meyer, S. Twilight **Fic**
Middle school, the worst years of my life **Fic**
Mills, E. First & then **Fic**
Mills, E. This adventure ends **Fic**
Mlynowski, S. Gimme a call **Fic**
Monaghan, A. A girl named Digit **Fic**
Moriarty, J. The ghosts of Ashbury High **Fic**
Moriarty, J. The murder of Bindy Mackenzie **Fic**

SOCIAL WELFARE *See* Charities; Public welfare; Social problems; Social work

SOCIAL WELFARE LEADERS
Caravantes, P. Waging peace **92**
Delano, M. F. Helen's eyes **92**
Fradin, J. B. Jane Addams **92**
Hamen, S. E. Clara Barton **92**
Keller, H. The story of my life **92**
Krensky, S. Clara Barton **92**
Lawlor, L. Helen Keller: rebellious spirit **92**
Slavicek, L. C. Jane Addams **361.9**
Sullivan, G. Helen Keller **92**

SOCIALISM
See also Collectivism; Economics; Political science

SOCIALIST LEADERS
Bausum, A. Muckrakers **070.4**

SOCIALITES -- FICTION
Axelrod, A. Your friend in fashion, Abby Shapiro **Fic**

SOCIALIZATION
Tym, K. School survival **371.8**

SOCIETY OF FRIENDS
Kanefield, T. The extraordinary Suzy Wright **92**

The **Society** of Unrelenting Vigilance. Dakin, G. **Fic**

SOCIOECONOMICS
See also Economics; Sociology

SOCIOLOGISTS
Bolden, T. W.E.B. Du Bois **92**
Whiting, J. W.E.B. Du Bois **92**

SOCIOLOGY, URBAN *See* Urban sociology

SOCKS
See also Clothing and dress

Socrates. Jun Lim **183**

Socrates

About

Jun Lim Socrates **183**

SOD HOUSES -- FICTION
MacLachlan, P. Kindred souls **Fic**

Sodium. O'Daly, A. **546**

SODIUM
O'Daly, A. Sodium **546**

SOFT TOY MAKING
See also Sewing; Toy making

Softball. Gitlin, M. **796.357**

SOFTBALL
See also Ball games; Baseball; Sports

SOFTBALL
Gitlin, M. Softball **796.357**
Gola, M. Winning softball for girls **796.357**

SOFTBALL -- FICTION
Krishnaswami, U. Step up to the plate, Maria Singh **Fic**
Mackey, W. K. Throwing like a girl **Fic**

The **softer** side of hip-hop. Haskins-Bookser, L. **811**

SOFTWARE ENGINEERS
Freese, S. M. Craigslist **381**
Gitlin, M. eBay **338.7**

Soil. Hirsch, R. E. **631.4**

SOIL CONSERVATION
See also Conservation of natural resources; Environmental protection

SOIL ECOLOGY
Hirsch, R. E. Soil **631.4**
Miller, S. S. Secret lives of soil creatures **591.7**

SOIL ECOLOGY
See also Ecology; Soils

SOIL FERTILITY *See* Soils

SOIL GEOMORPHOLOGY
Hirsch, R. E. Soil **631.4**

SOIL MECHANICS
See also Mechanics; Structural engineering

SOIL MICROBIOLOGY
See also Microbiology; Sanitary engineering

SOILS
See also Agriculture; Economic geology

SOILS
Hirsch, R. E. Soil **631.4**
You wouldn't want to live without dirt **631.4**

Sojourner Truth. Horn, G. M. **92**

Solar cell and renewable energy experiments. Sobey, E. **333.79**

SOLAR ECLIPSES
See also Astronomy

SOLAR ECLIPSES -- FICTION
Mass, W. Every soul a star **Fic**

SOLAR ENERGY
Bearce, S. How to harness solar power for your home **621.47**
Bright, S. Examining solar energy **621.47**
Walker, N. Harnessing power from the sun **621.47**

SOLAR ENERGY
See also Energy resources; Renewable energy resources; Solar radiation; Sun

SOLAR ENGINES
See also Engines; Solar energy

SOLAR HEATING
See also Heating; Solar energy

SOLAR PHYSICS *See* Sun

SOLAR POWER *See* Solar energy

SOLAR RADIATION
See also Meteorology; Space environment

SOLAR SYSTEM
Carson, M. K. Exploring the solar system **523.2**
Tourville, A. D. Exploring the solar system **523.2**

SOLAR SYSTEM
See also Astronomy; Stars

SOLAR SYSTEM -- ATLASES
Trefil, J. Space atlas **520**

SOLDER AND SOLDERING
Nelson, D. E. Soldering **671.5**

SOLDER AND SOLDERING *See* Soldering

Soldering. Nelson, D. E. **671.5**

SOLDERING
See also Metals; Metalwork

Soldier bear. Tak, B. D. **Fic**

Soldier boys. Hughes, D. **Fic**

Soldier X. Wulffson, D. L. **Fic**

Soldier's courage: the story of Stephen Crane. Lukes, B. L. **813**

T

V

Hopkinson, D. Dive! **940.54**
Nelson, P. Left for dead **940.54**
WORLD WAR, 1939-1945 -- NAVAL OPERATIONS, GERMAN
Mullenbach, C. Torpedoed! **940.54**
WORLD WAR, 1939-1945 -- NETHERLANDS -- FICTION
Polak, M. What world is left **Fic**
WORLD WAR, 1939-1945 -- NETHERLANDS -- PERSONAL NARRATIVES
Prins, M. Hidden like Anne Frank **940.53**
WORLD WAR, 1939-1945 -- OCCUPIED TERRITORIES
Samuels, C. Life under occupation **940.53**
WORLD WAR, 1939-1945 -- OCCUPIED TERRITORIES
See also Military occupation; World War, 1939-1945 -- Territorial questions
WORLD WAR, 1939-1945 -- PACIFIC AREA
Samuels, C. Life under occupation **940.53**
WORLD WAR, 1939-1945 -- PARTICIPATION, AFRICAN AMERICAN
Farrell, M. C. Standing up against hate **940.54**
WORLD WAR, 1939-1945 -- PARTICIPATION, AFRICAN AMERICAN -- FICTION
Myers, W. D. Invasion! **Fic**
WORLD WAR, 1939-1945 -- PARTICIPATION, AFRICAN AMERICAN -- JUVENILE POETRY
Weatherford, C. B. You can fly **811**
WORLD WAR, 1939-1945 -- PARTICIPATION, FEMALE
Farrell, M. C. Standing up against hate **940.54**
Pearson, P. O. Fly girls **940.54**
WORLD WAR, 1939-1945 -- PERSONAL NARRATIVES
Allen, T. B. Remember Pearl Harbor **940.54**
Altman, L. J. Hidden teens, hidden lives **940.53**
Byers, A. Trapped--youth in the Nazi ghettos **940.53**
Layson, A. H. Lost childhood **92**
Opdyke, I. G. In my hands **940.53**
WORLD WAR, 1939-1945 -- PERSONAL NARRATIVES
See also Autobiographies; Biography
WORLD WAR, 1939-1945 -- PERSONAL NARRATIVES, AMERICAN
McMullan, J. Leaving China **92**
WORLD WAR, 1939-1945 -- PHILIPPINES -- FICTION
Salisbury, G. Hunt for the bamboo rat **Fic**
WORLD WAR, 1939-1945 -- POETRY
See also Historical poetry; War poetry
WORLD WAR, 1939-1945 -- POLAND -- FICTION
Savit, G. Anna and the Swallow Man **Fic**
WORLD WAR, 1939-1945 -- POLAND -- WARSAW
Mazzeo, T. J. Irena's children **92**
WORLD WAR, 1939-1945 -- PRISONERS AND PRISONS
Farrell, M. C. Pure grit **940.54**
WORLD WAR, 1939-1945 -- PRISONERS AND PRISONS
See also Concentration camps; Prisoners of war; Prisons
WORLD WAR, 1939-1945 -- PRISONERS AND PRISONS, GERMAN
Deem, J. M. The prisoners of Breendonk **940.53**
WORLD WAR, 1939-1945 -- PRISONERS AND PRISONS, JAPANESE
Farrell, M. C. Pure grit **940.54**
WORLD WAR, 1939-1945 -- PROPAGANDA
Samuels, C. Propaganda **940.54**
WORLD WAR, 1939-1945 -- PROTEST MOVEMENTS
See also Protest movements
WORLD WAR, 1939-1945 -- REFUGEES
Hodge, D. Rescuing the children **940.53**
WORLD WAR, 1939-1945 -- REFUGEES
See also Political refugees
WORLD WAR, 1939-1945 -- REFUGEES -- FICTION
Deep sea **Fic**
WORLD WAR, 1939-1945 -- RESISTANCE MOVEMENTS
See World War, 1939-1945 -- Underground movements
WORLD WAR, 1939-1945 -- SECRET SERVICE
Code name Pauline **940.54**
WORLD WAR, 1939-1945 -- SECRET SERVICE -- GREAT BRITAIN
Code name Pauline **940.54**
Sheinkin, S. Bomb **623.4**
WORLD WAR, 1939-1945 -- SECRET SERVICE -- SOVIET UNION
Sheinkin, S. Bomb **623.4**
WORLD WAR, 1939-1945 -- SOCIAL ASPECTS
Samuels, C. Home front **940.53**
WORLD WAR, 1939-1945 -- SUBMARINE OPERATIONS
See World War, 1939-1945 -- Naval operations -- Submarine
WORLD WAR, 1939-1945 -- THEATER AND THE WAR
See also Theater
WORLD WAR, 1939-1945 -- TREATIES
See also Treaties
WORLD WAR, 1939-1945 -- UNDERGROUND MOVEMENTS
Freedman, R. We will not be silent **943**
Hendrix, J. The faithful spy **92**
Hoose, P. M. The boys who challenged Hitler **940.53**
Hopkinson, D. Courage & defiance: stories of spies, saboteurs, and survivors in World War II Denmark **940.53**
The plot to kill Hitler **92**
WORLD WAR, 1939-1945 -- UNDERGROUND MOVEMENTS -- DENMARK
Hoose, P. M. The boys who challenged Hitler **940.53**
Hopkinson, D. Courage & defiance: stories of spies, saboteurs, and survivors in World War II Denmark **940.53**
WORLD WAR, 1939-1945 -- UNDERGROUND MOVEMENTS -- FRANCE
Code name Pauline **940.54**
WORLD WAR, 1939-1945 -- UNDERGROUND MOVEMENTS -- FRANCE -- FICTION
Gratz, A. Allies **Fic**
WORLD WAR, 1939-1945 -- UNDERGROUND MOVEMENTS -- FRANCE -- FICTION
Elliott, L. Under a war-torn sky **Fic**
Gratz, A. Allies **Fic**
WORLD WAR, 1939-1945 -- UNDERGROUND MOVEMENTS -- GERMANY -- FICTION
Harlow, J. H. The watcher **Fic**

X

Z